VideoHound's
GOLDEN
MOVIE
RETRIEVER

Also Available from Visible Ink Press

VideoHound's GOLDEN MOVIE RETRIEVER

Martin Connors and Jim Craddock, Editors

VISIBLE INK PRESS

DETROIT • LONDON

Credits

EDITOR/PUBLISHER:
MARTIN CONNORS

EDITOR:
JIM CRADDOCK

SENIOR EDITOR:
CAROL SCHWARTZ

CONTRIBUTORS:
MICHELLE BANKS
DEAN DAUPHINAIS
BETH A. FHANER
JULIA FURTAW
JUDY GALENS
JEFFREY HERMANN
BRAD MORGAN
TERRI SCHELL
DEVRA M. SLADICS

WITH ADDITIONAL CONTRIBUTIONS BY:
MARTIN CRADDOCK
LYNNE KONSTANTIN
HILARY WEBER

PLUS A SPECIAL APPEARANCE BY:
JIM OLENSKI

AND INTRODUCING:
HEATHER MACK
MATT NOWINSKI

CASTING:
CHRISTA BRELIN

RESEARCH:
CHRISTINE TOMASSINI

SPECIAL COMPUTER F/X:
WAYNE FONG

TITLES AND OPTICALS:
MICHAEL BOYD, ATLIS PUBLISHING SERVICES, INC.

ART DIRECTION:
CYNTHIA BALDWIN

SET DECORATION:
MICHELLE DIMERCURIO

FRONTMATTER TECHNICIAN:
MARCO DI VITA, GRAPHIX GROUP

ILLUSTRATOR:
STEPHEN DUERR

KEY GRIPS:
MARY BETH TRIMPER
DOROTHY MAKI
EVI SEOUD
DEBORAH MILLIKEN
WENDY BLURTON

ASSISTANT TO MR. HOUND:
JANE P. CONNORS

KOPYKAT:
BILL DEMINK

MARKETING:
KIM MARICH
BETSY ROVEGNO
LAURI TAYLOR

HYPE:
MARILOU CARLIN

CRANE OPERATOR:
MARK FLEEMAN

CATERER:
DAN SKAGGS

TRANSPORTATION:
STEVE HOPKINS

ELECTRICIAN:
STEVE STRAW

LOCATION MANAGER:
DON STURTZ

SOUND EDITORS
JEANNIE DUNHAM
CHRISTINE FOYE

CHOREOGRAPHER:
TED WEDEL

CINEMATOGRAPHY:
ROBERT AHLERS

SOUND:
NICOLE FORTIER

COSTUMES:
MICHAEL GORLEY

FILM EDITORS
LINDA ZIEGLER WILSON
TRISHA COSTELLO

COMPOSER:
BILL HOAR

SONGS SELECTED BY:
KEN HILL

WINE STEWART:
ROGER MOSS

IN MEMORIUM:
JERRY STROUD

A Cunning Canine Production®

Contents

Introduction

The American Film Institute's list of The 100 Best Movies of All Time (American Division) started more than a little water cooler conversation among "the people who care about movies." These people wondered about all the films that were overlooked on the final list of 100 (from an original list of 400 nominated films), criticized the inclusion of some movies that were on the list, and even doubted the merits of having created a top 100. Never one to buck a trend, ignore a bad idea, stand up for what we believe in, or avoid a fray when we can add to the confusion, VideoHound simply wants to jump on the bandwagon before the circus leaves town. While we are adverse to presenting a best film list, since that would require deep thought approximating extra work and open the barn door to criticism of all kinds, we thought, why not be bold and run a list of the staff's favorite movies? Everything from *Caddyshack* to *Lawrence of Arabia*. Viva la diversity!

So the staff (including Carol Schwartz, Jim Olenski, Michelle Banks, Jeff Hermann, Chris Tomassini, Beth Fhaner, Jim Craddock, Mike Mayo, Julia Furtaw, and Marty Connors), wrote their favorite movies down. These lists have been merged into one giant, meandering, alphabetic (A-Y) list, in an effort to protect the exact identities of all involved. These are the movies we own, the ones we view again and again, the ones that, if we're flipping channels on the cable and see them, we watch till the end. The ones we keep telling our friends (and each other) "You have to see this movie!" The movies that shaped our expectations of cinema (and in some cases those seem quite minimal). The films we bring up for conversation on first and last dates. The movies we turn to after a bad day, or to sweeten a good one. The objects of our intense affection or obsession. Here then, without further delay, are VideoHound's Top 290 (or so): Our Favorite Movies of the Millenium.

Ace in the Hole (AKA The Big Carnival)
Adam's Rib
The Adventures of Robin Hood
The African Queen
After Hours
Airplane
Alien
All About Eve
All That Jazz
American Graffiti
Angel Heart
Animal House
Anne of Avonlea
Anne of Green Gables
Annie Hall

The Apartment
Apocalypse Now
Apollo 13
Au Revoir Les Enfants
Bachelor Party
The Bad News Bears
Beauty and the Beast (1946)
Ben-Hur
The Best Years of Our Lives
Better Off Dead
Big Night
The Big Red One
The Big Sleep
The Birds
Blade Runner

Blazing Saddles
Blue Velvet
The Blues Brothers
Bonnie & Clyde
Breakfast at Tiffany's
Brewster McCloud
The Bride of Frankenstein
The Bridge on the River Kwai
Bringing Up Baby (1938)
Bull Durham
Butch Cassidy and the Sundance Kid
Caddyshack
Captain Blood
Casablanca
Catch-22
Chinatown
A Christmas Story
Citizen Kane
City Lights
A Clockwork Orange
Close Encounters of the Third Kind
    (Director's Cut)
Comfort and Joy
The Conversation
Cool Hand Luke
Crimes & Misdemeanors
Crossing Delancey
Das Boot
Dawn of the Dead
Dazed and Confused
Dead Alive
Dead Man Walking
Dead Men Don't Wear Plaid
Dead Poets Society
The Deer Hunter
Desperate Hours (1955)
Die Hard
Dirty Harry
Dr. Strangelove
Doctor Zhivago
Double Indemnity
Duck Soup
Dumbo
Easy Rider
Eating Raoul

Eddie Murphy: Raw
Eight Men Out
The English Patient
E.T.: The Extra-Terrestrial
Excalibur
The Exorcist
Fargo
Fantasia
Farewell My Concubine
Fast Times at Ridgemont High
The Fearless Vampire Killers
Ferris Bueller's Day Off
Field of Dreams
Fletch
Forrest Gump
The 400 Blows
Freaks
Frankenstein (1931)
The French Connection
From Here to Eternity (1953)
The General
Gettysburg
Giant
Glory
The Godfather I and II
The Gold Rush
Goldfinger
Gone with the Wind
Goodfellas
The Graduate
The Grapes of Wrath
Grease
The Great Escape
Gremlins I and II
The Hairdresser's Husband
Halloween
Hard-Boiled
Harold and Maude
Hear My Song
Henry V (1989)
High Noon
History of the World: Part 1
Howard's End
The Howling
Immortal Beloved

In a Lonely Place
In the Name of the Father
Indiana Jones and the Last Crusade
Indiana Jones and the Temple of Doom
Indochine
Inherit the Wind
Invasion of the Body Snatchers (1956)
It Happened One Night
It's a Wonderful Life
Jaws
John Carpenter's The Thing
Johnny Dangerously
The Joy Luck Club
The Killer
The King and I
King Kong (1933)
L.A. Confidential
The Lady Vanishes (1938)
The Last Detail
The Last Emperor
Last of the Mohicans (1992)
Laura
Lawrence of Arabia
Lethal Weapon
The Lion King
The Little Mermaid
Living in Oblivion
Local Hero
The Long Riders
Looking for Mr. Goodbar
Love and Death
The Magnificent Ambersons
Magnum Force
The Maltese Falcon
A Man for All Seasons (1966)
The Manchurian Candidate
Manhattan
M*A*S*H
Matewan
McCabe & Mrs. Miller
Mediterraneo
Medium Cool
Midnight Cowboy
Miller's Crossing
Miracle Mile

Mr. Smith Goes to Washington
Modern Times
The Money Pit
Monty Python and the Holy Grail
Monty Python's The Meaning of Life
The Muppet Movie
The Music Man
Mutiny on the Bounty (1935)
My Beautiful Launderette
Nashville
Network
A Night at the Opera
Night of the Hunter
Night of the Living Dead
No Surrender
Nobody's Fool (1994)
North by Northwest
Notorious
The Nutty Professor (1996)
On the Waterfront
Once Upon a Time in America
One Flew Over the Cuckoo's Nest
The Outlaw Josey Wales
Papillon
Passage to Marseilles
P.C.U.
Persuasion (1995)
The Philadelphia Story
Pink Flamingos
The Pink Panther
A Place in the Sun
Planes, Trains, & Automobiles
Platoon
Polyester
The Postman (aka Il Postino)
Priest
The Princess Bride
The Professional
Psycho
Pulp Fiction
The Quiet Man
Raging Bull
Raiders of the Lost Ark
Raising Arizona
Ran

The Rapture
Reality Bites
Rear Window
Rebel Without a Cause
Red Kiss
Red River
Reservoir Dogs
Richard Pryor Live
The Right Stuff
Rio Bravo
Risky Business (1983)
The Road Warrior
The Roaring Twenties
Rocky
Rosencrantz & Guildenstern Are Dead
The Sandlot
Santa Sangre
Schindler's List
The Searchers
Seven
Shag: The Movie
Shane
The Shawshank Redemption
The Silence of the Lambs
Silverado
Singin' in the Rain
Sixteen Candles
Sleepless in Seattle
The Snapper
Snow White and the Seven Dwarfs
Some Like It Hot
The Sound of Music
Stagecoach
Stalag 17
Star Wars
State of Grace
The Sting
Stranger than Paradise
A Streetcar Named Desire
Strictly Ballroom
Stripes
Sullivan's Travels
Sunset Boulevard
Superman 2

The Sure Thing
Sweet Smell of Success
Swimming with Sharks
Swingers
The Tall Guy
Tapeheads
Taxi Driver
The Terminator
The Thin Blue Line
Things Change
The Third Man
The 39 Steps (1935)
This Is Spinal Tap
Throne of Blood
The Tingler
To Kill a Mockingbird
Tootsie
Touch of Evil
Trading Places
Treasure of the Sierra Madre
Trois Couleurs: Rouge
The Trouble with Harry
Truly, Madly, Deeply
2001: A Space Odyssey
Unforgiven
The Usual Suspects
Vertigo
We're No Angels (1955)
West Side Story
When Harry Met Sally...
White Heat
The Wild Bunch
Willy Wonka & the Chocolate Factory
Wings of Desire
The Wizard of Oz
A Woman Under the Influence
Women on the Verge of a Nervous
    Breakdown
Working Girl
Yankee Doodle Dandy
The Year of Living Dangerously
The Yearling
Young Frankenstein

So there you have it. The Top 290 or so Favorite VideoHound Films of All Time and This Millenium. As a public service, you may want to give this list to your local video emporium and ask them to make sure these films are in stock, because there's sure to be a run on them shortly.

Speaking of favorites, some of our favorite actors have died recently: Robert Mitchum, Jimmy Stewart, Frank Sinatra, William Hickey, Burgess Meredith, and J.T. Walsh. Hickey, Meredith, and Walsh were consummate character actors, stealing scenes small and large from more prominent thespians and enlivening every movie in which they appeared. Sinatra's Hollywood career reached a new level of critical appreciation after his death, proving again that every act needs a good close. One of the great Japanese actors, Toshiro Mifune, died on Christmas Eve in 1997. In the U.S., Mifune was best known for *Rashomon, The Seven Samurai,* and other work with director Akira Kurosawa, becoming the Japanese equivalent of John Wayne. Another fellow who worked the macho ethic with distinction was director Sam Fuller, whose *The Big Red One* is one of VideoHound's favorites.

New faces also took center stage: Leonardo DiCaprio's star, smouldering since *Romeo and Juliet*, ignited once again with *Titanic*, a plus for viewers since he can still act if necessary. Ben Affleck and Matt Damon, with a handful of acting credits between them, shared an Oscar for screenwriting *Good Will Hunting*, while Christina Ricci grew up nicely and became this year's Parker Posey, appearing in a high percentage of all independent movies made. To catch up on the movie making of these and thousands of other actors and directors, check out the videographies in the cast and director indexes, conveniently located in the back of the book.

Using VideoHound

Alphabetization

Titles are arranged on a word-by-word basis, including articles and prepositions. Leading articles (<u>A</u>, <u>An</u>, <u>The</u>) are ignored in English-language titles. The equivalent foreign articles are not ignored, however: *The Abyss* appears under "A" while *Les Miserables* appears under "L." **Other points to keep in mind:**

- Acronyms appear alphabetically as if regular words. For example *C.H.U.D.* is alphabetized as "Chud"; *M*A*S*H* as "Mash."

- Common abbreviations in titles file as if they are spelled out, so *St. Elmo's Fire* will be found under "Saint Elmo's Fire" and *Mr. Holland's Opus* will be alphabetized as "Mister Holland's Opus."

- Proper Names in titles are alphabetized beginning with the individual's first name; for instance, *Monty Python's The Meaning of Life* is under "M;" *Eddie Murphy: Raw* under "E."

- Titles with numbers *(2001: A Space Odyssey)* are alphabetized as if the number was spelled out under the appropriate letter, in this case "Two Thousand One." When numeric titles gather in close proximity to each other *(2000 Year Old Man, 2001, 2069: A Sex Odyssey)*, the titles will be arranged in a low *(2000)* to high *(2069)* numeric sequence.

Indexes

Alternate Title Index A number of videos, particularly older or B-type releases, may have variant titles. Alternate titles are listed alphabetically and refer the reader to the title under which the entry is listed. The alternate titles are also noted within the review.

Category Index Subject categories ranging from the orthodox to slightly eccentric permit you to video sleuth from broad type to significant themes to signature scenes. The mix, arranged alphabetically by category, includes hundreds of traditional film genres and sub-genres as well as a feast of *VideoHound* exclusives. Integrated into the index are cross references, while preceding the index is a list of definitions. **A tipped triangle indicates a movie rated three bones or above.**

Kibbles and Series Index Not your everyday categories, Kibbles span the literary side of movie-making (adapted from a play, Books to Film: Hemingway) as well as pointing out key producers and special effects masters. Yearly box-office winners (that are now on video) since 1939 are listed, along with classic movies, four-bone delights, trash films, modern Shakespeare, Disney fare, and of course, bottom of the barrel **Woof!** features, some of which are terrible enough to provide an amusing evening.

The index formerly known as Series, now combined with the Kibbles, provides listings of major movie series, ranging from James Bond to National Lampoon to Indiana Jones. Recurring cinematic collaborations and partnerships of note are also listed, including Hope & Crosby, Abbott & Costello, De Niro & Scorsese, and Rafelson & Nicholson. A complete list of the categories precedes the index. **As in the Category Index, tipped triangles indicate quality views.**

Awards Index The Awards Index lists almost 7,000 films honored by 20 national and international award bodies, representing some 90 categories of competition. Nomination information is now included. This information is also contained in the review following the credits. **Only features available on video and reviewed in the main section are listed in this index; movies not yet released on video are not covered.**

As award-winning and nominated films find their way to video, they will be added to the review section and covered in this index. Awards listed include the American Academy Awards; Australia Film Institute; British Academy of Film and Television Arts; Cannes Film Festival; French Cesar; Canadian Genie; Golden Globe; Directors Guild of America; Independent Spirit; Montreal Film Festival; and the MTV Awards.

Foreign Film Index Here the *Hound* classifies movies by the country/countries of record in which the feature was financed (but not necessarily where they were filmed). Since the producers of a specific film may hail from more than one country, some videos will be listed under more than one country. **The foreign codes also appear in the review immediately following the color or black and white designation. A**

tipped triangle following the title indicates a three bone or above endeavor.

Cast/Director Indexes The Cast Index provides full videographies for all actors and actresses listed in *VideoHound* with more than one movie on their resume. The Director Index lists the works of any director who has made it to video and to *VideoHound*. Although listed in a first name, last name sequence, the names are alphabetized by last name. Film titles, complete with initial year of release, are arranged in chronological order, starting with their most recent.

Writer Index Scriptwriters and script doctors are listed with their vital works. Names are arranged alphabetically by last name. Works are arranged chronologically.

Cinematographer Index Directors of photography are listed alphabetically by last name, along with their work, which is arranged chronologically. Cinematography is often a starting point for feature directors.

Composer Index Videographies of movie music composers, arrangers, lyricists, and so on are listed. Arranged alphabetically by last name.

Digital Formats Index. Laserdisc (not technically digital but included here for convenience), CD-I, and the new DVD format are included. This index will now focus on non-videotape alternatives for home viewing, concentrating on current (as well as any future) digital-based technologies. Movies are listed alphabetically after each format subheading.

Distributor Guide Each video review has at least one and as many as three distributor codes. In the reviews, these are located at the bottom of the review. The full address and phone, toll-free, and fax numbers of the 340 distributors listed can be found in the Distributor Guide. For added convenience and less confusion, the distributors are split into wholesale and retail subheads. In some cases the distributors did not indicate which market they served. These distributors are listed in a straight alphabetical sort at the beginning of the index. **Caution: a small number of distributors adhere to a nomadic life-style that includes frequent address changes. A tiny minority on the list in any given year will also go out of business. An extra caution: Studio distributors do not sell to the general public, they generally act as wholesalers, selling only to retail outlets.** Up to three distributors are listed in order to give you more choice. A Distributor List, preceding the Guide, provides an alphabetical list of the distributor codes which will refer the reader to the proper distributor.

In the main section, those reviews with the code **OM** are on moratorium (distributed at one time, though not currently). Since a title enjoying such status was once distributed, it may well linger on your local video store shelf. When the distributor is not known, the code **NO** appears. For new releases to the theater that have not yet made it to video (but likely will in the coming year), the code **NYR** (not yet released) appears.

Web Site Guide Lists Internet web sites for popular actors, actresses, and directors, studio movie sites, general entertainment information, filmmaker resources, as well as sites for gossip and trivia. Actor and movie sites list the URLs after the main citation. The more popular the personality, the more URLs. Sites with more generalized information contain text after the URL to help you decide if they are worth a visit.

Sample Review

Each *VideoHound* review contains up to 19 items, ranging from title to the review to awards received to the distributor code. The information in these reviews is designed to help you choose a video you'll like, increase your enjoyment of a movie as you watch (especially by answering that nagging question of "What else have I seen that guy in?"), and increase your knowledge of movie trivia.

1 Lost Goob Summer **2** ✐ **3** *Robin & Julie's Excellent Adventure* **4** 1995 **5** (NC-17) **6** Robin and Julie devise a wacky money-making scheme to sell lemonade with the help of con man Friendly Freddie. When lemonade gets switched with rat poison, hilarity ensues. Weak script, weak direction, weak lemonade, but fine performances by Robin and Julie. Look for cameo by Ford. **7** *CW:* Some violence and language. **8** ♪ Bottoms Up; Rats!; One More for the Road. **9&10** 64m/C **11 VHS, DVD.** **12** *GB* **13** Robin Dillon, Julie Thompson, Harrison Ford; **14** *D:* Alan Smithee; **15** *W:* Robin Dillon, Julie Thompson; **16** *C:* Barry Markowitz; **17** *M:* Daniel Lanois. **18** Academy Awards '96: Best Adapted Screenplay; Independent Spirit Awards '97: Best First Feature; Writers Guild of America '96: Best Adapted Screenplay; Nominations: Academy Awards '96: Best Actress (Dillon); Screen Actors Guild Award '96: Best Actress (Thompson), Cast. **19** *TOU*

1.	Title
2.	One-to-four bone rating (or Woof!)
3.	Alternate Title
4.	Year released
5.	MPAA Rating
6.	Description/Review
7.	Content Warning
8.	Songs
9.	Length (in minutes)
10.	Black & White (B) or Color (C)
11.	Format (VHS, Beta, LV-Laserdisc, DVD, CD-I, 8mm, letterboxed, closed captioned)
12.	Country produced in
13.	Cast (V: indicates voiceovers; also includes cameos)
14.	Director
15.	Writer(s)
16.	Cinematographer(s)
17.	Composer(s)/Lyricist(s)
18.	Awards and Nominations
19.	Distributor Code

The movie in the sample entry does not really exist, as far as we know. A reader sent it in, it amused us, we used it.

Mail Order
Video Sources

Some of the movies reviewed in this book may be difficult to find using conventional devices such as the neighborhood video rental chain. Many independent and mail-order video outlets specialize in rare or hard-to-find movies. We have included a small list of such outlets to assist you in your search.

Thomas Video
122 S. Main
Clawson, MI 48017
(248) 280-2833
Fax: (248) 280-4463
E-mail: tomvid@mich.com

Video Vision
Attn: Chris Hendlin
4603 Bloomington Ave.
Minneapolis, MN 55407
(612) 728-0000

Luminous Film & Video
PO Box 1047, Dept. AC
Medford, NY 11763
(516) 289-1644
LFVW@aol.com

House of Monsters
2038 N. Clark St., No. 348
Chicago, Il 60614
Fax: (312) 929-7205

Video Vault
323 S. Washington
Alexandria, VA 22314
(800) VAULT66

Kim's Video
350 Bleeker St.
New York, NY 10014
(800) 617-KIMS (inside U.S.)

(212) 675-8996 (outside U.S.)
Fax: (212) 675-8996
E-mail: info@kimsvideo.com
http://www.kimsvideo.com

A Million and One World-Wide Videos
PO Box 349
Orchard Hill, GA 30266
(800) 849-7309; (770) 227-7309
Fax: (800) 849-0873; (770) 227-0873
E-mail: barbara@wwvideo.com
http://www.wwvideos.com

Video Oyster
145 W. 12th St.
New York, NY 10011
(212) 989-3300
Fax: (212) 989-3533
E-mail: video@VideoOyster.com

China West Video
PO Box 291655, Dept. 8
Los Angeles, CA 90029

Facets Video
1517 Fullerton Ave.
Chicago, IL 60614
(800) 331-6197

Movies Unlimited
3015 Darnell Rd.
Philadelphia, PA 19154
(800) 4-MOVIES

The **Alternate Titles Index** provides variant and foreign titles for movies with more than one name. Titles are listed in alphabetical order, followed by a cross-reference to the appropriate entry in the main video review section. If you don't find a movie you're looking for in the main section, this is the best place to look next.

Az en XX. Szazadom *See* My Twentieth Century (1990)

Azucar Amarga *See* Bitter Sugar (1996)

Baba Yaga *See* Kiss Me, Kill Me (1969)

Baba Yaga—Devil Witch *See* Kiss Me, Kill Me (1969)

Babe, the Gallant Pig *See* Babe (1995)

Babes Ahoy *See* Going Overboard (1989)

Babes in Toyland *See* March of the Wooden Soldiers (1934)

Baby Blood *See* The Evil Within (1994)

Baby Cart 2 *See* Baby Cart at the River Styx (1972)

The Baby Vanishes *See* Broadway Limited (1941)

Bachelor Girl Apartment *See* Any Wednesday (1966)

Bachelor Knight *See* The Bachelor and the Bobby-Soxer (1947)

Backwoods Massacre *See* Midnight (1981)

Bad Boyz *See* Valley Girl (1983)

Bad Girl *See* Teenage Bad Girl (1959)

Bad Girls *See* Delinquent School Girls (1984)

Bad Girls *See* Whore 2 (1994)

Bad Man of Harlem *See* Harlem on the Prairie (1938)

Bad Seed *See* Mauvaise Graine (1933)

Badkonake Sefid *See* The White Balloon (1995)

The Bailiff *See* Sansho the Bailiff (1954)

Baisers Voles *See* Stolen Kisses (1968)

The Bait *See* L'Appat (1994)

The Baited Trap *See* The Trap (1959)

Bakushu *See* Early Summer (1951)

The Banana Monster *See* Schlock (1973)

Bande a Part *See* Band of Outsiders (1964)

The Bandit *See* Crossfire (1967)

Banditi a Orgosolo *See* Bandits of Orgosolo (1961)

Bang Bang *See* Bang Bang Kid (1967)

Bangiku *See* Late Chrysanthemums (1954)

The Bank Detective *See* The Bank Dick (1940)

Banner in the Sky *See* Third Man on the Mountain (1959)

The Bar Sinister *See* It's a Dog's Life (1955)

Barbados Quest *See* Murder on Approval (1956)

Barbarella, Queen of the Galaxy *See* Barbarella (1968)

The Barbarians and Co. *See* The Barbarians (1987)

The Barbaric Beast of Boggy Creek, Part II *See* Boggy Creek II (1983)

Bargain Basement *See* Department Store (1935)

Baron Blood *See* Torture Chamber of Baron Blood (1972)

Batman: The Animated Movie *See* Batman: Mask of the Phantasm (1993)

Batmen of Africa *See* Darkest Africa (1936)

Battle Beyond the Stars *See* The Green Slime (1968)

The Battle for Anzio *See* Anzio (1968)

Battle of the Astros *See* Godzilla vs. Monster Zero (1968)

The Battle of the Mareth Line *See* Battleforce (1978)

The Battle of the River Plate *See* Pursuit of the Graf Spee (1957)

Battle Stripe *See* The Men (1950)

Battletruck *See* Warlords of the 21st Century (1982)

The Battling Bellhop *See* Kid Galahad (1937)

Battling Hoofer *See* Something to Sing About (1936)

Bawang Bie Ji *See* Farewell My Concubine (1993)

Bay of Blood *See* Twitch of the Death Nerve (1971)

The Bay of Saint Michel *See* Pattern for Plunder (1962)

Bayou *See* Poor White Trash (1957)

Be Beautiful but Shut Up *See* Just Another Pretty Face (1958)

Be My Valentine, Or Else... *See* Hospital Massacre (1981)

Be Roringen *See* The Touch (1971)

The Beans of Egypt, Maine *See* Forbidden Choices (1994)

The Bear Hunt *See* Bare Hunt (1963)

The Beast Must Die *See* Black Werewolf (1975)

The Beast of War *See* The Beast (1988)

Beasts *See* Twilight People (1972)

Beatlemania *See* Beatlemania! The Movie (1981)

Beatsville *See* The Rebel Set (1959)

Beaumarchais L'Insolent *See* Beaumarchais the Scoundrel (1996)

Beautiful But Dangerous *See* She Couldn't Say No (1952)

Beautiful But Deadly *See* The Don Is Dead (1973)

A Beautiful Place to Kill *See* Paranoia (1969)

Beethoven's Great Love *See* Beethoven (1936)

Beggars' Opera *See* The Threepenny Opera (1931)

The Beginners *See* The First Time (1969)

The Beginners Three *See* The First Time (1969)

Behind Enemy Lines *See* The P.O.W. Escape (1986)

Behind Locked Doors *See* Human Gorilla (1948)

Behind the Blue *See* L'Enfant d'Eau (1995)

Behind the Iron Mask *See* The Fifth Musketeer (1979)

Believe Me *See* Hollow Reed (1995)

Bells *See* Murder by Phone (1982)

The Beloved *See* Restless (1972)

Berry Gordy's The Last Dragon *See* The Last Dragon (1985)

The Best Way to Walk *See* The Best Way (1976)

Bethune, The Making of a Hero *See* Dr. Bethune (1990)

Betrayal *See* Trahir (1993)

Between Us *See* Entre-Nous (1983)

Beware! The Blob *See* Son of Blob (1972)

Bewitching Scatterbrain *See* Ravishing Idiot (1964)

The Beyond *See* Seven Doors of Death (1982)

Beyond Bedlam *See* Nightscare (1993)

Beyond Justice *See* Guardian Angel (1994)

Beyond Obsession *See* Beyond the Door (1975)

Beyond the Fog *See* Tower of Evil (1972)

Beyond the Living *See* Hospital of Terror (1975)

Beyond the Living Dead *See* The Hanging Woman (1972)

Beyond the Rising Moon *See* Star Quest (1989)

Bez Konca *See* No End (1984)

Bez Znieczulenia *See* Without Anesthesia (1978)

The Big Bankroll *See* The King of the Roaring '20s: The Story of Arnold Rothstein (1961)

The Big Boss *See* Fists of Fury (1973)

The Big Day *See* Jour de Fete (1948)

Big Deal at Dodge City *See* A Big Hand for the Little Lady (1966)

Big Duel in the North *See* Godzilla vs. the Sea Monster (1966)

Big Enough and Old Enough *See* Savages from Hell (1968)

The Big Heart *See* Miracle on 34th Street (1947)

The Big Lobby *See* Rosebud Beach Hotel (1985)

The Big One: The Great Los Angeles Earthquake *See* The Great Los Angeles Earthquake (1991)

The Big Payoff *See* Win, Place, or Steal (1972)

The Big Search *See* East of Kilimanjaro (1957)

Big Time Operators *See* The Smallest Show on Earth (1957)

The Biggest Fight on Earth *See* Ghidrah the Three Headed Monster (1965)

Biggles: Adventures in Time *See* Biggles (1985)

Bijo to Ekitainigen *See* H-Man (1959)

Bikini Genie *See* Wildest Dreams (1990)

Billy the Kid's Fighting Pals *See* Trigger Men (1941)

Billy the Kid's Law and Order *See* Law and Order (1942)

Bio-Force I *See* Mutant Species (1995)

Birds of a Feather *See* The Birdcage (1995)

Birds of Prey *See* Beaks: The Movie (1987)

Birthmark *See* The Omen (1976)

Birumano Tategoto *See* The Burmese Harp (1956)

The Bitch *See* La Chienne (1931)

Bittere Ernte *See* Angry Harvest (1985)

Black Angels *See* Black Bikers from Hell (1970)

Black Arrow Strikes *See* Black Arrow (1948)

The Black Book *See* Reign of Terror (1949)

The Black Bounty Killer *See* Boss (1974)

The Black Buccaneer *See* The Black Pirate (1926)

Black Christmas *See* Black Sabbath (1964)

Black Eliminator *See* Kill Factor (1978)

Black Evil *See* Black Vampire (1973)

Black Flowers for the Bride *See* Something for Everyone (1970)

Black Frankenstein *See* Blackenstein (1973)

Black Gauntlet *See* Black Starlet (1974)

Black Jack *See* Captain Blackjack (1951)

Black Love, White Love *See* Sweet Love, Bitter (1967)

Black Out: The Moment of Terror *See* Black Vampire (1973)

Black Rage *See* Sunshine Run (1979)

Black Rider *See* Joshua (1976)

Black Rose of Harlem *See* Machine Gun Blues (1995)

Brutti, Sporchi, e Cattivi See Down & Dirty (1976)

Buck Rogers See Destination Saturn (1939)

Buckaroo Banzai See The Adventures of Buckaroo Banzai Across the Eighth Dimension (1984)

Bud Abbott and Lou Costello In Hollywood See Abbott and Costello in Hollywood (1945)

Budbringeren See Junk Mail (1997)

Budding Love See L'Amour en Herbe (1977)

The Buddy Factor See Swimming with Sharks (1994)

The Bug See Bug (1975)

Build a Fort Set It on Fire See Basquiat (1996)

Build My Gallows High See Out of the Past (1947)

A Bullet from God See God's Gun (1975)

Bullfighter See Torero (1956)

Bump in the Night See The Final Terror (1983)

The Bunny Caper See Games Girls Play (1975)

The Burden of Proof See Scott Turow's The Burden of Proof (1992)

Buried on Sunday See Northern Extremes (1993)

Burn Hollywood, Burn See An Alan Smithee Film: Burn, Hollywood, Burn (1997)

Burn Out See Journey into Fear (1974)

Burn, Witch, Burn See Mark of the Devil (1969)

Burning Cross See The Klansman (1974)

Burning Hearts See Kolberg (1945)

The Burning Man See Dangerous Summer (1982)

Bushwhacked See French Twist (1995)

The Butcher See Le Boucher (1969)

The Butcher See Psycho from Texas (1983)

Butcher Baker (Nightmare Maker) See Night Warning (1982)

The Butterfly Revolution See Summer Camp Nightmare (1986)

Bvongiorno, Elefante See Pardon My Trunk (1952)

By Hook or By Crook See I Dood It (1943)

By Rocket to the Moon See Woman in the Moon (1929)

Caballos Salvajes See Wild Horses (1995)

Cabiria See Nights of Cabiria (1957)

Caccia Ai Violenti See One Step to Hell (1968)

Caccia alla Volpe See After the Fox (1966)

Cactus Jack See The Villain (1979)

Cafe of the Seven Sinners See Seven Sinners (1940)

The Cage See My Sister, My Love (1978)

Caged Females See Caged Heat (1974)

Caged Heart See L'Addition (1985)

Cain's Way See Cain's Cutthroats (1971)

Calhoun See Nightstick (1987)

The California Dolls See ...All the Marbles (1981)

California Holiday See Spinout (1966)

California Hot Wax See The Bikini Car Wash Company (1990)

California in 1878 See Fighting Thru (1930)

California Man See Encino Man (1992)

The Californian See The Gentleman from California (1937)

Call Harry Crown See 99 & 44/100 Dead (1974)

Call It Love See She's So Lovely (1997)

Call It Murder See Midnight (1934)

Call of the Savage See Savage Fury (1000)

The Call of the Wild: Dog of the Yukon See Jack London's The Call of the Wild (1997)

Call the Cops See Find the Lady (1975)

The Calling See Murder by Phone (1982)

Calling Northside 777 See Call Northside 777 (1948)

Campanadas a Medianoche See Chimes at Midnight (1967)

Camper John See Gentle Savage (1973)

Campsite Massacre See The Final Terror (1983)

A Candle for the Devil See It Happened at Nightmare Inn (1970)

Canicule See Dog Day (1983)

Cannibal Orgy, or the Maddest Story Ever Told See Spider Baby (1964)

Cannibals in the City See Invasion of the Flesh Hunters (1982)

Cannibals in the Streets See Invasion of the Flesh Hunters (1982)

Capitaine Conan See Captain Conan (1996)

Capitaine Morgan See Morgan the Pirate (1960)

Capitalismo Salvaje See Savage Capitalism (1993)

Captain Mephisto and the Transformation Machine See Manhunt of Mystery Island (1945)

Captain Midnight See On the Air Live with Captain Midnight (1979)

Captain Yankee See Jungle Raiders (1985)

Captive See Sex and the Other Man (1995)

Captive Women 3: Sweet Sugar See Sweet Sugar (1972)

Caravans West See Wagon Wheels (1934)

The Card See The Promoter (1952)

Cardigan's Last Case See State's Attorney (1931)

Care of the Spitfire Grill See The Spitfire Grill (1995)

Carlo Collodi's Pinocchio See The Adventures of Pinocchio (1996)

Carnage See Twitch of the Death Nerve (1971)

Carne per Frankenstein See Andy Warhol's Frankenstein (1974)

Carne Tremula See Live Flesh (1997)

Carnival of Fools See Death Wish Club (1983)

Carnival of Thieves See Caper of the Golden Bulls (1967)

Carquake See Cannonball (1976)

Carry On Follow That Camel See Follow That Camel (1967)

The Cars That Eat People See The Cars That Ate Paris (1974)

Cartagine in Fiamme See Carthage in Flames (1960)

Cartes sur Table See Attack of the Robots (1966)

Carthage en Flammes See Carthage in Flames (1960)

The Case of Jonathan Drew See The Lodger (1926)

The Case of the Hillside Stranglers See The Hillside Strangler (1989)

Case of the Missing Switchboard Operator See The Love Affair, or The Case of the Missing Switchboard Operator (1967)

Cash See If I Were Rich (1933)

Cassanova and Co. See Sex on the Run (1978)

Castle in the Sky See Yidl Mitn Fidl (1036)

Castle of Doom See Vampyr (1931)

Castle of Terror See Castle of Blood (1964)

Castle of Terror See The Virgin of Nuremberg (1965)

The Castle of the Spider's Web See Throne of Blood (1957)

Castle of the Walking Dead See The Torture Chamber of Dr. Sadism (1969)

The Cat See Le Chat (1975)

C.A.T. Squad See Stalking Danger (1986)

C.A.T. Squad: Python Wolf See Python Wolf (1988)

Catacombs See Curse 4: The Ultimate Sacrifice (1990)

Catastrophe 1999 See Last Days of Planet Earth (1974)

Catchfire See Backtrack (1989)

Catherine Cook's The Dwelling Place See The Dwelling Place (199?)

Catherine Cookson's The Girl See The Girl (1996)

Catherine Cookson's The Moth See The Moth (1996)

Catherine Cookson's The Rag Nymph See The Rag Nymph (1996)

Catherine Cookson's The Tide of Life See The Tide of Life (1996)

Catholic Boys See Heaven Help Us (1985)

Cathy Tippel See Keetje Tippel (1975)

Cats See Night of a Thousand Cats (1972)

Cauchemares See Cathy's Curse (1977)

Cavalleria Commandos See Cavalry Command (1963)

The Cave Dwellers See One Million B.C. (1940)

Cave Man See One Million B.C. (1940)

Cavegirl See Cave Girl (1985)

C.C. & Company See Chrome Hearts (1970)

Cell Block Girls See Women's Prison Escape (19??)

Cemetery Girls See The Vampire Hookers (1978)

Cemetery Girls See The Velvet Vampire (1971)

Cento Dollari D'Odio See Uncle Tom's Cabin (1969)

Ceremonia Sangrienta See The Legend of Blood Castle (1972)

A Certain Mr. Scratch See The Devil & Daniel Webster (1941)

Cet Obscur Objet Du Desir See That Obscure Object of Desire (1977)

Chacun Cherche Son Chat See When the Cat's Away (1996)

Chaingang Girls See Sweet Sugar (1972)

The Challenge See It Takes a Thief (1959)

Chamber of Fear See The Fear Chamber (1968)

Chamber of Tortures See Torture Chamber of Baron Blood (1972)

Champ d'Honneur See Field of Honor (1987)

Champion Charlie See The Champion/His New Job (1915)

Changes See Danielle Steel's Changes (1991)

Chaos-Kaos See Kaos (1985)

Charlie's Ghost Story See Charlie's Ghost: The Secret of Coronado (1994)

Charterhouse at Parma See La Chartreuse de Parme (1948)

Creeps See Night of the Creeps (1986)

Cria Cuervos See Cria (1976)

The Cricket See La Cicada (1983)

Crime Boss See New Mafia Boss (1972)

Crime et Chatiment See Crime and Punishment (1935)

Crimes in the Wax Museum See Nightmare in Wax (1969)

Crimes, Inc. See Gangs, Inc. (1941)

The Crimes of Dr. Mabuse See Testament of Dr. Mabuse (1962)

The Criminal See The Concrete Jungle (1982)

The Crimson Altar See The Crimson Cult (1968)

Crimson Executioner See The Bloody Pit of Horror (1965)

The Crimson Ghost See Cyclotrode "X" (1946)

Cronica de un Nino Solo See Chronicle of a Boy Alone (1964)

Crooks in Clover See Penthouse (1933)

Crossed Swords See The Prince and the Pauper (1978)

Crossing the Line See The Big Man: Crossing the Line (1991)

The Crown Caper See The Thomas Crown Affair (1968)

Cruel Swamp See Swamp Women (1955)

The Cry See Il Grido (1957)

Crying Out Loud See Cotton Queen (1937)

Crypt of Dark Secrets See Mardi Gras Massacre (1978)

Crypt of the Blind Dead See Tombs of the Blind Dead (1972)

C.S. Lewis Through the Shadowlands See Shadowlands (1985)

Csillagosok, Katonak See The Red and the White (1968)

Cuba Crossing See The Mercenaries (1980)

Cuban Rebel Girls See Assault of the Rebel Girls (1959)

Cult of the Dead See The Snake People (1968)

Cupid in the Rough See Aggie Appleby, Maker of Men (1933)

Curley and His Gang in the Haunted Mansion See Who Killed Doc Robbin? (1948)

Curse of Dark Shadows See Night of Dark Shadows (1971)

The Curse of Demon Mountain See Shadow of Chikara (1977)

The Curse of Dracula See Return of Dracula (1958)

The Curse of Green Eyes See Cave of the Living Dead (1965)

Curse of Melissa See The Touch of Satan (1970)

Curse of the Blood-Ghouls See The Slaughter of the Vampires (1962)

Curse of the Crimson Altar See The Crimson Cult (1968)

The Curse of the Dragon See Bruce Lee: Curse of the Dragon (1993)

Curse of the Living Dead See Kill, Baby, Kill (1966)

Curse of the Mushroom People See Attack of the Mushroom People (1963)

Curses of the Ghouls See The Slaughter of the Vampires (1962)

Cutter and Bone See Cutter's Way (1981)

Cybele See Sundays & Cybele (1962)

Cyber-Chic See Robo-Chic (1989)

Cyberjack See Virtual Assassin (1995)

Cyborg Cop 2 See Cyborg Soldier (1994)

Czlowiek z Zelaza See Man of Iron (1981)

Da Bancarella a Bancarotta See Peddlin' in Society (1947)

Daddy See Danielle Steel's "Daddy" (1991)

Daddy's Deadly Darling See Pigs (1973)

Dad's Week Off See National Lampoon's Dad's Week Off (1997)

Dagboek Van Een Oude Dwaas See Diary of a Mad Old Man (1988)

Dagora See Dagora, the Space Monster (1965)

Dai Koesu Yongkari See Yongkari Monster of the Deep (1967)

Daibosatsu Toge See Sword of Doom (1967)

Daikaiju Baran See Varan the Unbelievable (1961)

Daikaiju Gamera See Gamera, the Invincible (1966)

Daikyoju Gappa See Gappa the Trifibian Monster (1967)

Dalle Ardenne All'Inferno See Dirty Heroes (1971)

Dance of the Dwarfs See Jungle Heat (1984)

Dance of the Vampires See The Fearless Vampire Killers (1967)

Danger Rides the Range See Three Texas Steers (1939)

Dangerous Charter See Creeping Terror (1964)

Dangerous Female See The Maltese Falcon (1931)

A Dangerous Friend See The Todd Killings (1971)

Dangerous Kiss See True Crime (1995)

Dangerous Love Affairs See Dangerous Liaisons (1960)

Danielle Steel's Fine Things See Fine Things (1990)

Danny Travis See The Last Word (1980)

Dans la Ville Blanche See In the White City (1983)

Dans les Griffes du Maniaque See The Diabolical Dr. Z (1965)

Danza Macabra See Castle of Blood (1964)

Daoma Zei See The Horse Thief (1987)

Dark Angel See I Come in Peace (1990)

The Dark Avenger See The Warriors (1955)

Dark Empire See Dark City (1997)

Dark Eyes See Demon Rage (1982)

Dark Eyes of London See Dead Eyes of London (1961)

Dark Eyes of London See The Human Monster (1939)

Dark Prince: Intimate Tales of Marquis de Sade See Marquis de Sade (1997)

Dark Sands See Jericho (1938)

Dark World See Dark City (1997)

Darkness in Tallinn See City Unplugged (1995)

D'Artagnan See The Three Musketeers (1916)

Das Bildness des Dorian Gray See Dorian Gray (1970)

Das Blaue Licht See The Blue Light (1932)

Das Cabinet des Dr. Caligari See The Cabinet of Dr. Caligari (1919)

Das Phantom von Soho See The Phantom of Soho (1964)

Das Schlangenei See The Serpent's Egg (1978)

Das Schloss See The Castle (1968)

Das Ungeheuer von London City See The Monster of London City (1964)

Das Versprechen See The Promise (1994)

Das Zweite Erwachen der Christa Klages See The Second Awakening of Christa Klages (1978)

Dashiell Hammett's The Dain Curse See The Dain Curse (1978)

The Daughter of Frankenstein See Lady Frankenstein (1972)

Daughters of Dracula See Vampyres (1974)

David Lynch's Hotel Room See Hotel Room (1993)

Day of the Woman See I Spit on Your Grave (1977)

The Day the Hot Line Got Hot See The Hot Line (1969)

The Day the Screaming Stopped See The Comeback (1977)

The Day They Gave the Babies Away See All Mine to Give (1956)

A Day to Remember See Two Bits (1996)

Daybreak See Le Jour Se Leve (1939)

De Aanslag See The Assault (1986)

De Eso No Se Habla See I Don't Want to Talk About It (1994)

De la Part des Copains See Cold Sweat (1974)

De Sable et de Sang See Sand and Blood (1987)

De Stilte Rond Christine M See Question of Silence (1983)

De Wisselwachter See The Pointsman (1986)

Dead Aim See Born in America (1990)

Dead Drop See Chain Reaction (1996)

Dead Kids See Strange Behavior (1981)

Dead Man's Walk See Larry McMurtry's Dead Man's Walk (1996)

Dead of Night See Deathdream (1972)

Dead on Course See Wings of Danger (1952)

Dead or Alive See A Minute to Pray, a Second to Die (1967)

Dead or Alive See The Tracker (1988)

Dead People See Messiah of Evil (1974)

Dead Tired See Grosse Fatigue (1994)

Deadlocked: Escape from Zone 14 See Deadlock 2 (1994)

Deadly Companion See The Double Negative (1980)

Deadly Desire See Maybe I'll Be Home in the Spring (1970)

Deadly Desires See Home for the Holidays (1972)

Deadly Encounter See The Meal (1975)

Deadly Harvest See Children of the Corn 4: The Gathering (1996)

Deadly Is the Female See Gun Crazy (1949)

The Deadly Rays from Mars See Flash Gordon: Mars Attacks the World (1938)

Deadly Rivals See Rivals (1972)

The Deadly Spawn See Return of the Aliens: The Deadly Spawn (1983)

Deadly Sting See Evil Spawn (1987)

The Deadly Three See Enter the Dragon (1973)

The Deadly Tower See Sniper (1975)

Deadly Treasure of the Piranha See Killer Fish (1979)

Dear Diary See Caro Diario (1993)

Die Toten Augen von London See Dead Eyes of London (1961)

Die Unsichtbaren Krallen des Dr. Mabuse See The Invisible Dr. Mabuse (1962)

Die Verlorene Ehre Der Katharina Blum See The Lost Honor of Katharina Blum (1975)

Die Xue Shuang Xiong See The Killer (1990)

Die Zwolfte Stunde See Nosferatu (1922)

Dio Mio, Come Sono Caduta in Basso See Till Marriage Do Us Part (1974)

A Dirty Knight's Work See Choice of Weapons (1976)

Dirty Mary See A Very Curious Girl (1969)

Disaster at Valdez See Dead Ahead: The Exxon Valdez Disaster (1992)

Disciple of Dracula See Dracula, Prince of Darkness (1966)

Disco Godfather See Avenging Disco Godfather (1976)

The Discreet See La Discrete (1990)

Disney's Blank Check See Blank Check (1993)

Dispara See Outrage (1993)

Disparen a Matar See Shoot to Kill (1990)

Distant Cousins See Desperate Motives (1992)

Dites-Lui Que Je L'Aime See This Sweet Sickness (1977)

Divertimento See La Belle Noiseuse (1990)

Divine Obsession See Dangerous Obsession (1988)

Divorzio All'Italiana See Divorce—Italian Style (1962)

Djavulens Oga See The Devil's Eye (1960)

Do You Want to Dance with Me? See Voulez-Vous Danser Avec Moi? (1959)

The Dock Brief See Trial & Error (1962)

Docteur M. See Club Extinction (1989)

Docteur Popaul See High Heels (1972)

Dr. Black and Mr. White See Dr. Black, Mr. Hyde (1976)

Doctor Blood Bath See Horror Hospital (1973)

The Doctor from Seven Dials See Corridors of Blood (1958)

Doctor Gore See The Body Shop (1972)

Dr. Jekyll y el Hombre Lobo See Dr. Jekyll and the Wolfman (1971)

Dr. Jekyll's Dungeon of Darkness See Dr. Tarr's Torture Dungeon (1975)

Dr. Maniac See The Man Who Lived Again (1936)

Doctor Maniac See House of the Living Dead (1973)

Doctor of Doom See Wrestling Women vs. the Aztec Ape (1962)

Dr. Terror's Gallery of Horrors See Alien Massacre (1967)

Doctors Wear Scarlet See The Bloodsuckers (1970)

A Dog, a Mouse, and a Sputnik See Sputnik (1961)

Dog Soldiers See Who'll Stop the Rain? (1978)

Doin' It See The First Time (1969)

Doin' It See First Time (1982)

Doing Life See Truth or Die (1986)

Doing Time See Porridge (1991)

Doktor Mabuse der Spieler See Dr. Mabuse, Parts 1 & 2 (1922)

Dolwyn See The Last Days of Dolwyn (1949)

Dom Za Vesanje See Time of the Gypsies (1990)

The Domino Killings See The Domino Principle (1977)

Don Juan See Private Life of Don Juan (1934)

Don Juan, Mi Querido Fantasma See Don Juan, My Love (1990)

Dona Flor e Seus Dois Maridos See Dona Flor and Her Two Husbands (1978)

Dona Herlinda y Su Hijo See Dona Herlinda & Her Son (1986)

Donato and Daughter See Dead to Rights (1993)

The Don's Analyst See National Lampoon's The Don's Analyst (1997)

Don't Fence Me In See Western Double Feature 4: Rogers & Evans (194?)

Don't Look Now, We've Been Shot At See La Grande Vadrouille (1966)

The Doomsday Machine See Escape from Planet Earth (1967)

The Door with Seven Locks See Chamber of Horrors (1940)

Doppelganger See Journey to the Far Side of the Sun (1969)

The Double See Kagemusha (1980)

Double Down See Stacy's Knights (1983)

Double Hit See The Arab Conspiracy (1976)

Double Possession See Black Vampire (1973)

Double Trouble See No Deposit, No Return (1976)

Douce Violence See Sweet Ecstasy (1962)

Down Went McGinty See The Great McGinty (1940)

Dracula See Bram Stoker's Dracula (1992)

Dracula See The Horror of Dracula (1958)

Dracula 71 See Count Dracula (1971)

Dracula Cerca Sangue di Vergine e...Mori de Sete See Andy Warhol's Dracula (1974)

Dracula Contra Frankenstein See Dracula vs. Frankenstein (1971)

Dracula in the Castle of Blood See Web of the Spider (1970)

Dracula Is Dead and Well and Living in London See The Satanic Rites of Dracula (1973)

Dracula Pere et Fils See Dracula & Son (1976)

Dracula Saga See The Saga of the Draculas (1972)

Dracula: The Bloodline Continues... See The Saga of the Draculas (1972)

Dracula: The Love Story See To Die For (1989)

Dracula, the Terror of the Living Dead See The Hanging Woman (1972)

Dracula Today See Dracula A.D. 1972 (1972)

Dracula vs. Frankenstein See The Screaming Dead (1972)

Dracula Vuole Vivere: Cerca Sangue de Vergina See Andy Warhol's Dracula (1974)

Dracula's Castle See Blood of Dracula's Castle (1969)

Dracula's Dog See Zoltan...Hound of Dracula (1978)

Dracula's Virgin Lovers See Dracula's Great Love (1972)

Dragon Chow See Drachenfutter (1987)

Dragon Lady See G.I. Executioner (1971)

Dragonfly See One Summer Love (1976)

Dragon's Food See Drachenfutter (1987)

Draws See American Tickler (1976)

The Dreaded Persuasion See The Narcotics Story (1958)

Dream Slayer See Blood Song (1982)

Dreams See Akira Kurosawa's Dreams (1990)

Dreamworld See Covergirl (1983)

Dripping Deep Red See Deep Red: Hatchet Murders (1975)

Drivers to Hell See Wild Ones on Wheels (1962)

Drole de Drama See Bizarre Bizarre (1939)

The Drum See Drums (1938)

Du Rififi Chez les Hommes See Rififi (1954)

Duck, You Sucker See A Fistful of Dynamite (1972)

The Duckweed Story See Drifting Weeds (1959)

Due Notti Con Cleopatra See Two Nights with Cleopatra (1954)

Due Occhi Diabolici See Two Evil Eyes (1990)

Duel of the Gargantuas See War of the Gargantuas (1970)

Duel of the Space Monsters See Frankenstein Meets the Space Monster (1965)

Duello Nel Texas See Gun Fight at Red Sands (1963)

Dumb Dicks See Detective School Dropouts (1985)

Dumbo Drop See Operation Dumbo Drop (1995)

D'Une Femme a L'Autre See A Business Affair (1993)

Dungeons and Dragons See Mazes and Monsters (1982)

Duvar See The Wall (1983)

Dynamite Women See The Great Texas Dynamite Chase (1976)

Dyrygent See The Conductor (1980)

Each Man For Himself See The Ruthless Four (1970)

Each One For Himself See The Ruthless Four (1970)

The Eagle with Two Heads See The Eagle Has Two Heads (1948)

Earth Defense Forces See The Mysterians (1958)

The Earth Will Tremble See La Terra Trema (1948)

East of Shanghai See Rich and Strange (1932)

East of the Bowery See Follow the Leader (1944)

East of the Rising Sun See Malaya (1949)

Easy Go See Free and Easy (1930)

Eaten Alive See Emerald Jungle (1980)

Eaten Alive by Cannibals See Emerald Jungle (1980)

Eating Pattern See Tales from a Parallel Universe: Eating Pattern (1997)

Ebirah, Terror of the Deep See Godzilla vs. the Sea Monster (1966)

Eboli See Christ Stopped at Eboli (1979)

Edgar Allan Poe's Conqueror Worm See The Conqueror Worm (1968)

Edgar Allen Poe's House of Usher See The House of Usher (1988)

Edgar Allen Poe's The Oblong Box See The Oblong Box (1969)

The Edge of Hell See Rock 'n' Roll Nightmare (1985)

Edipo Re See Oedipus Rex (1967)

Edwards & Hunt: The First American Road Trip See Almost Heroes (1997)

Ein Mann wie Eva *See* A Man Like Eva (1983)

Ein Toter Hing im Netz *See* Horrors of Spider Island (1959)

Eine Liebe in Deutschland *See* A Love in Germany (1984)

Einer Frisst den Anderen *See* Dog Eat Dog (1964)

Ekstase *See* Ecstasy (1933)

El Ataque de los Muertos Sin Ojos *See* Return of the Evil Dead (1975)

El Ataud Del Coffin *See* The Vampire's Coffin (1958)

El Ataud Del Vampiro *See* The Vampire's Coffin (1958)

El Buque Maldito *See* Horror of the Zombies (1974)

El Cazador de la Muerte *See* Deathstalker (1983)

El Cobra *See* The Cobra (1968)

El Coleccionista de Cadaveres *See* Cauldron of Blood (1967)

El Dedo En El Gatillo *See* Finger on the Trigger (1965)

El Diablo se Lleva a los Muertos *See* Lisa and the Devil (1975)

El Espiritu de la Colmena *See* Spirit of the Beehive (1973)

El Grito de la Muerte *See* The Living Coffin (1958)

El la Nave Va *See* And the Ship Sails On (1983)

El Lado Oscuro del Corazon *See* The Dark Side of the Heart (1992)

El Lago de los Muertos Vivientes *See* Zombie Lake (1980)

El Lazarillo de Tormes *See* Lazarillo (1959)

El Mariachi 2 *See* Desperado (1995)

El Mas Fabulosi Golpe del Far West *See* The Boldest Job in the West (1971)

El Patrullero *See* Highway Patrolman (1991)

El Rapto de las Sabinas *See* The Rape of the Sabines (1961)

El Retorno de la Walpurgis *See* Curse of the Devil (1973)

El Retorno del Hombre-Lobo *See* The Craving (1980)

El Returno de la Drequessa Dracula *See* Devil's Wedding Night (1973)

El Robot Humano *See* The Robot vs. the Aztec Mummy (1959)

El Rublo de las dos Caras *See* The Hot Line (1969)

El Sonido de la Muerte *See* Sound of Horror (1964)

El Tesoro del Amazones *See* The Treasure of the Amazon (1984)

El Verano de la Senora Forbes *See* The Summer of Miss Forbes (1988)

Electric Boogaloo "Breakin' 2" *See* Breakin' 2: Electric Boogaloo (1984)

The Electric Man *See* Man Made Monster (1941)

The Electric Monster *See* The Electronic Monster (1957)

Elena et les Hommes *See* Elena and Her Men (1956)

Elevator to the Gallows *See* Frantic (1958)

The 11th Commandment *See* Body Count (1987)

Elisa, My Life *See* Elisa, Vida Mia (1977)

Elisa, My Love *See* Elisa, Vida Mia (1977)

Ella *See* Monkey Shines (1988)

Emergency Landing *See* Robot Pilot (1941)

Emil Und Die Detektive *See* Emil and the Detectives (1964)

Emma Mae *See* Black Sister's Revenge (1976)

The Emperor of Peru *See* The Odyssey of the Pacific (1982)

Empire of Passion *See* In the Realm of Passion (1980)

The Empress Yang Kwei Fei *See* Princess Yang Kwei Fei (1955)

En Compagnie d'Antonin Artaud *See* My Life and Times with Antonin Artaud (1993)

En Effeuillant la Marguerite *See* Mademoiselle Striptease (1957)

En Enda Natt *See* Only One Night (1942)

En Kvinnas Ansikte *See* A Woman's Face (1938)

En Lekiton i Karlek *See* Lesson in Love (1954)

End of the Rainbow *See* Northwest Outpost (1947)

End of the World *See* Panic in the Year Zero! (1962)

End of the World (in Our Usual Bed in a Night Full of Rain) *See* A Night Full of Rain (1978)

Enemies of the Public *See* Public Enemy (1931)

Enemy from Space *See* Quatermass 2 (1957)

Enemy Round-Up *See* Hillbilly Blitzkrieg (1942)

The Engagement *See* Fiances (1963)

The Enigma of Kaspar Hauser *See* Every Man for Himself & God Against All (1975)

Enormous Changes at the Last Minute *See* Enormous Changes (1983)

Enormous Changes at the Last Minute *See* Trumps (1983)

Ensayo de un Crimen *See* The Criminal Life of Archibaldo de la Cruz (1955)

Entebbe: Operation Thunderbolt *See* Operation Thunderbolt (1977)

Entity Force *See* One Dark Night (1982)

Entre Tinieblas *See* Dark Habits (1984)

Episoda Del Mare *See* La Terra Trema (1948)

Ercole al Centro Della Terra *See* Hercules in the Haunted World (1964)

Ercole Alla Conquista di Atlantide *See* Hercules and the Captive Women (1963)

Ercole Contro Molock *See* Conquest of Mycene (1963)

Ercole e la Regina di Lidia *See* Hercules Unchained (1959)

Erik the Conqueror *See* The Invaders (1963)

Ernest Hemingway's the Killers *See* The Killers (1964)

Erotikill *See* The Loves of Irina (198?)

Erzebeth *See* Daughters of Darkness (1971)

Escapade *See* Utopia (1951)

Escape from the Dark *See* The Littlest Horse Thieves (1976)

Escape If You Can *See* St. Benny the Dip (1951)

The Escape of Megagodzilla *See* Terror of Mechagodzilla (1978)

Escape Route *See* I'll Get You (1953)

Escape to Freedom *See* Judgment in Berlin (1988)

Escapement *See* The Electronic Monster (1957)

The Escort *See* L'Escorte (1996)

Escort Girl *See* Half Moon Street (1986)

The Escorts *See* La Scorta (1994)

Espiritismo *See* Spiritism (1961)

Et Dieu Crea la Femme *See* And God Created Woman (1957)

Et Mourir de Plaisir *See* Blood and Roses (1961)

Etat de Siege *See* State of Siege (1973)

Etz Hadomim Tafus *See* Under the Domim Tree (1995)

European Vacation *See* National Lampoon's European Vacation (1985)

Every Day's a Holiday *See* Seaside Swingers (1965)

Every Home Should Have One *See* Think Dirty (1970)

Every Man For Himself *See* The Ruthless Four (1970)

Every Woman's Man *See* The Prizefighter and the Lady (1933)

Everybody's Cheering *See* Take Me Out to the Ball Game (1949)

Evil Angels *See* A Cry in the Dark (1988)

Evil Dead 3 *See* Army of Darkness (1992)

Evil Eden *See* Death in the Garden (1956)

Evil in the Swamp *See* All the Kind Strangers (1974)

The Evils of Dorian Gray *See* Dorian Gray (1970)

Ewiger Walzer *See* The Eternal Waltz (1954)

Except For Me and Thee *See* Friendly Persuasion (1956)

Expedition Moon *See* Rocketship X-M (1950)

Exploring the Kinsey Report *See* One Plus One (1961)

Expose *See* The House on Straw Hill (1976)

Exquisite Tenderness *See* The Surgeon (1994)

Extase *See* Ecstasy (1933)

Extenuating Circumstances *See* Circonstances Attenuantes (1936)

Extreme Close-Up *See* Sex Through a Window (1972)

An Eye for an Eye *See* Psychopath (1973)

An Eye for an Eye *See* Talion (1966)

Eyes of Hell *See* The Mask (1961)

Eyes without a Face *See* The Horror Chamber of Dr. Faustus (1959)

Eyewitness *See* Sudden Terror (1970)

Fabula de la Bella Palomera *See* The Fable of the Beautiful Pigeon Fancier (1988)

The Fabulous Baron Munchausen *See* The Original Fabulous Adventures of Baron Munchausen (1961)

Face of a Stranger *See* The Promise (1979)

Face the Music *See* Black Glove (1954)

The Faceless Monsters *See* Nightmare Castle (1965)

Fair Trade *See* Skeleton Coast (1989)

Fairytales *See* Fairy Tales (1976)

Fakebook *See* American Blue Note (1989)

Falcon's Gold *See* Robbers of the Sacred Mountain (1983)

Fall Break *See* The Mutilator (1985)

The Fall Guy *See* What's Up Front (1963)

The Fall of the House of Usher *See* The House of Usher (1988)

The Fall of the House of Usher *See* La Chute de la Maison Usher (1928)

Falltime *See* Fall Time (1994)

False Face *See* Scalpel (1976)

False Faces *See* Let 'Em Have It (1935)

Falstaff *See* Chimes at Midnight (1967)

Fanatic *See* Die! Die! My Darling! (1965)

The Fanatic *See* The Last Horror Film (1982)

Fanfan the Tulip *See* Fanfan la Tulipe (1951)

Fangelse *See* Devil's Wanton (1949)

Fanny by Gaslight *See* Man of Evil (1948)

Fanny Och Alexander *See* Fanny and Alexander (1983)

Fan's Video *See* Otaku no Video (1991)

The Fantastic Disappearing Man *See* Return of Dracula (1958)

The Far Country *See* Nevil Shute's The Far Country (1985)

Farewell, Friend *See* Honor Among Thieves (1968)

Farewell, My Love *See* Murder, My Sweet (1944)

Farinelli Il Castrato *See* Farinelli (1994)

Farinelli the Castrato *See* Farinelli (1994)

The Farm *See* The Curse (1987)

Farm Girl *See* The Farmer's Other Daughter (1965)

Farm of the Year *See* Miles from Home (1988)

Fashions *See* Fashions of 1934 (1934)

Fast Fortune *See* 11 Harrowhouse (1974)

Fatal Assassin *See* African Rage (1978)

Fatal Woman *See* Femme Fatale (1990)

The Father *See* Baba (1973)

Father & Son: Dangerous Relations *See* Dangerous Relations (1993)

Father Brown *See* The Detective (1954)

Father Damien: The Leper Priest *See* Damien: The Leper Priest (1980)

Father Goose *See* Fly Away Home (1996)

The Father Kino Story *See* Mission to Glory (1980)

Father Master *See* Padre Padrone (1977)

Father, Son and the Mistress *See* For Richer, For Poorer (1992)

Faustrecht der Freiheit *See* Fox and His Friends (1975)

The FBI Murders *See* In the Line of Duty: The FBI Murders (1988)

Fear *See* Night Creature (1979)

The Fear *See* Gates of Hell (1983)

Fear Eats the Soul *See* Ali: Fear Eats the Soul (1974)

Fear in the City of the Living Dead *See* Gates of Hell (1983)

Fear in the Night *See* Dynasty of Fear (1972)

Fearless Little Soldier *See* Fanfan la Tulipe (1951)

Feast of Flesh *See* Blood Feast (1963)

Federico Fellini's 8 1/2 *See* 8 1/2 (1963)

Federico Fellini's Intervista *See* Intervista (1987)

Feel the Heat *See* Catch the Heat (1987)

Female *See* The Violent Years (1956)

The Female Butcher *See* The Legend of Blood Castle (1972)

Female Fiend *See* Theatre of Death (1967)

Feng Yue *See* Temptress Moon (1996)

Fengriffen *See* And Now the Screaming Starts (1973)

A Few Days in the Life of I.I. Oblomov *See* Oblomov (1981)

The Fiend with the Atomic Brain *See* Blood of Ghastly Horror (1972)

The Fiend with the Electronic Brain *See* Blood of Ghastly Horror (1972)

Fiendish Ghouls *See* Mania (1960)

Fierce *See* Fighting Mad (1977)

The Fifth Chair *See* It's in the Bag (1945)

The Fighting Phantom *See* The Mysterious Rider (1933)

The Fighting Pimpernel *See* The Elusive Pimpernel (1950)

The Fighting Seventh *See* Little Big Horn (1951)

Film d'Amore et d'Anarchia *See* Love and Anarchy (1973)

Filofax *See* Taking Care of Business (1990)

The Final Crash *See* Steelyard Blues (1973)

Finally, Sunday *See* Confidentially Yours (1983)

Fine and Dandy *See* The West Point Story (1950)

Fire Festival *See* Himatsuri (1985)

Fire in Eden *See* Tusks (1989)

Fire on the Mountain *See* Volcano: Fire on the Mountain (1997)

The First and the Last *See* 21 Days (1937)

The First Great Train Robbery *See* The Great Train Robbery (1979)

The First Hello *See* High Country (1981)

The First of the Few *See* Spitfire (1942)

The First Rebel *See* Allegheny Uprising (1939)

First Strike *See* Jackie Chan's First Strike (1996)

The First Time *See* The Fighter (1952)

First Woman Into Space *See* Space Monster (1964)

A Fist Full of Chopsticks *See* They Call Me Bruce? (1982)

Fist of Fury *See* Chinese Connection (1973)

Fist Right of Freedom *See* Fox and His Friends (1975)

Five Angles on Murder *See* The Woman in Question (1950)

Five Bloody Days to Tombstone *See* Gun Riders (1969)

Five Bloody Graves *See* Gun Riders (1969)

The Five Day Lover *See* Time Out for Love (1961)

Five Days *See* Paid to Kill (1954)

Five Minutes to Live *See* Door to Door Maniac (1961)

Five Women Around Utamaro *See* Utamaro and His Five Women (1946)

Fixing the Shadow *See* Beyond the Law (1992)

The Flame of Torment *See* Enjo (1958)

Flanagan *See* Walls of Glass (1985)

Flash Gordon's Trip to Mars *See* Flash Gordon: Mars Attacks the World (1938)

Flatbed Annie *See* Flatbed Annie and Sweetiepie: Lady Truckers (1979)

The Flesh and the Fiends *See* Mania (1960)

The Flesh Creatures *See* Horror of the Blood Monsters (1970)

Flesh Creatures of the Red Planet *See* Horror of the Blood Monsters (1970)

Flesh for Frankenstein *See* Andy Warhol's Frankenstein (1974)

The Flight *See* The Taking of Flight 847: The Uli Derickson Story (1988)

Flight from Fear *See* Justice (1955)

Flight of the Dove *See* The Spy Within (1994)

The Flight of the White Stallions *See* The Miracle of the White Stallions (1963)

Flipper and the Pirates *See* Flipper's New Adventure (1964)

Floating Weeds *See* Drifting Weeds (1959)

Flood *See* Hard Rain (1997)

Flying Aces *See* The Flying Deuces (1939)

Flying Wild *See* Fly Away Home (1996)

Fog *See* A Study in Terror (1966)

Folies Bourgeoises *See* Twist (1976)

The Folks at Red Wolf Inn *See* Terror at Red Wolf Inn (1972)

Follow That Bird *See* Sesame Street Presents: Follow That Bird (1985)

Follow the Hunter *See* Fangs of the Wild (1954)

Follow Your Dreams *See* Independence Day (1983)

Fontane Effi Briest *See* Effi Briest (1974)

For a Few Bullets More *See* Any Gun Can Play (1967)

For Better or For Worse *See* Honeymoon Academy (1990)

For Love or Money *See* If I Were Rich (1933)

For Men Only *See* Tall Lie (1953)

For We Too Do Not Forgive *See* Death Is Called Engelchen (1963)

Forbidden Alliance *See* The Barretts of Wimpole Street (1934)

Forbidden Love *See* Freaks (1932)

Forbidden Paradise *See* Hurricane (1979)

Forbidden Passions *See* The Sensuous Teenager (1970)

Forbidden Son *See* Bulldance (1988)

The Forbin Project *See* Colossus: The Forbin Project (1970)

Forbrydelsens Element *See* The Element of Crime (1984)

Ford Fairlane *See* The Adventures of Ford Fairlane (1990)

The Forest Primeval *See* The Final Terror (1983)

Forgotten Prisoners: The Amnesty Files *See* Forgotten Prisoners (1990)

The Forsyte Saga *See* That Forsyte Woman (1950)

Fortune in Diamonds *See* The Adventurers (1951)

47 Samurai *See* 47 Ronin, Part 1 (1942)

Forward March *See* Doughboys (1930)

The Four Just Men *See* The Secret Four (1940)

A Fourth for Marriage *See* What's Up Front (1963)

4...3...2...1...Morte *See* Mission Stardust (1968)

F.P. 1 Antwortet Nicht *See* F.P. 1 Doesn't Answer (1933)

Fra Diavolo *See* The Devil's Brother (1933)

Frameup *See* Jon Jost's Frameup (1993)

Francis *See* Francis the Talking Mule (1949)

Frankenstein *See* Andy Warhol's Frankenstein (1974)

Frankenstein *See* Mary Shelley's Frankenstein (1994)

Frankenstein '88 *See* The Vindicator (1985)

The Goddess *See* Devi (1960)

God's Gift *See* Wend Kuuni (1982)

Godzilla Fights the Giant Moth *See* Godzilla vs. Mothra (1964)

Godzilla Versus the Bionic Monster *See* Godzilla vs. the Cosmic Monster (1974)

Godzilla vs. Gigan *See* Godzilla on Monster Island (1972)

Godzilla vs. Hedora *See* Godzilla vs. the Smog Monster (1972)

Godzilla vs. Mechagodzilla *See* Godzilla vs. the Cosmic Monster (1974)

Godzilla vs. the Giant Moth *See* Godzilla vs. Mothra (1964)

Godzilla vs. the Thing *See* Godzilla vs. Mothra (1964)

Godzilla's Counter Attack *See* Godzilla Raids Again (1959)

Going Ape *See* Where's Poppa? (1970)

Going West in America *See* Switchback (1997)

Gojira *See* Godzilla, King of the Monsters (1956)

Gojira no Musuko *See* Son of Godzilla (1966)

Gojira Tai Hedora *See* Godzilla vs. the Smog Monster (1972)

Gojira Tai Megaro *See* Godzilla vs. Megalon (1976)

Gojira Tai Meka-Gojira *See* Godzilla vs. the Cosmic Monster (1974)

Goke, Body Snatcher from Hell *See* Body Snatcher from Hell (1969)

Goke the Vampire *See* Body Snatcher from Hell (1969)

Gokiburi *See* Twilight of the Cockroaches (1990)

Gold Coast *See* Elmore Leonard's Gold Coast (1997)

Golden Hands of Kurigal *See* Federal Agents vs. Underworld, Inc. (1949)

The Golden Heist *See* Inside Out (1975)

The Golden Hour *See* Pot O' Gold (1941)

Golden Ivory *See* White Huntress (1957)

Golden Marie *See* Casque d'Or (1952)

The Golden Trail *See* Riders of the Whistling Skull (1937)

Golden Virgin *See* The Story of Esther Costello (1957)

Goldy 3 *See* The Magic of the Golden Bear: Goldy 3 (1994)

Goliat Contra Los Gigantes *See* Goliath Against the Giants (1963)

Goliath and the Giants *See* Goliath Against the Giants (1963)

Goliath and the Golden City *See* Samson and the 7 Miracles of the World (1962)

Goliath Contro I Giganti *See* Goliath Against the Giants (1963)

Gomar the Human Gorilla *See* Night of the Bloody Apes (1968)

The Good Girls *See* Les Bonnes Femmes (1960)

Good Luck, Miss Wyckoff *See* The Shaming (1971)

A Good Marriage *See* Le Beau Mariage (1982)

Good Morning Babilonia *See* Good Morning, Babylon (1987)

Good to Go *See* Short Fuse (1988)

Goodbye Bruce Lee: His Last Game of Death *See* Game of Death (1979)

Goodbye, Children *See* Au Revoir Les Enfants (1987)

Goodbye Gemini *See* Twinsanity (1970)

Goodbye to the Hill *See* Paddy (1970)

Gordon il Pirata Nero *See* The Black Pirate (1926)

Gorilla *See* Nabonga (1944)

Gosta Berling's Saga *See* The Atonement of Gosta Berling (1924)

Gotter der Pest *See* Gods of the Plague (1969)

Grace Under Pressure *See* Something to Talk About (1995)

The Grail *See* Lancelot of the Lake (1974)

Gran Amore del Conde Dracula *See* Dracula's Great Love (1972)

The Grand Highway *See* Le Grand Chemin (1987)

The Grand Maneuvers *See* Les Grandes Manoeuvres (1955)

The Grass is Singing *See* Killing Heat (1984)

The Grasshopper *See* The Passing of Evil (1970)

Grave Desires *See* Brides of the Beast (1968)

Grave Robbers from Outer Space *See* Plan 9 from Outer Space (1956)

Graveyard Tramps *See* Invasion of the Bee Girls (1973)

The Great Adventure *See* The Adventurers (1951)

Great American Bugs Bunny-Road Runner Chase *See* The Bugs Bunny/Road Runner Movie (1979)

The Great Balloon Adventure *See* Olly Olly Oxen Free (1978)

The Great Day *See* A Special Day (1977)

Great Friends *See* Grandes Amigos (197?)

The Great Georgia Bank Hoax *See* Great Bank Hoax (1978)

The Great Lester Boggs *See* Hootch Country Boys (1975)

The Great Manhunt *See* The Doolins of Oklahoma (1949)

Great Moments in Aviation *See* Shades of Fear (1993)

Great Monster Yongkari *See* Yongkari Monster of the Deep (1967)

The Great Schnozzle *See* Palooka (1934)

The Great Spy Mission *See* Operation Crossbow (1965)

The Great Wall is a Great Wall *See* A Great Wall (1986)

The Greatest Battle *See* Battleforce (1978)

The Greatest Battle on Earth *See* Ghidrah the Three Headed Monster (1965)

The Greatest Love *See* Europa '51 (1952)

The Greeks Had a Word for Them *See* Three Broadway Girls (1932)

The Green Carnation *See* The Trials of Oscar Wilde (1960)

Green Monkey *See* Blue Monkey (1987)

The Green Ray *See* Summer (1986)

The Greenhouse *See* The Green House (1996)

Greta the Mad Butcher *See* Ilsa, the Wicked Warden (1978)

Grey Matter *See* Mind Warp (1972)

Greystoke 2: Tarzan and Jane *See* Tarzan and the Lost City (1998)

Gridlock *See* Great American Traffic Jam (1980)

Grijpstra and de Gier *See* Fatal Error (1983)

Grimm Brothers' Snow White *See* Snow White: A Tale of Terror (1997)

Grine Felder *See* Green Fields (1937)

Gringo *See* Gun Fight at Red Sands (1963)

The Grip of the Strangler *See* The Haunted Strangler (1958)

The Grip of the Vampire *See* Curse of the Undead (1959)

Gritos en la Noche *See* The Awful Dr. Orloff (1962)

The Groove Room *See* A Man with a Maid (1973)

The Grotesque *See* Grave Indiscretions (1996)

Gruner Felder *See* Green Fields (1937)

Gruppo di Famiglia in un Interno *See* Conversation Piece (1975)

Guardian of the Wilderness *See* Mountain Man (1977)

Guilty Assignment *See* Big Town (1947)

Gun Man from Bodie *See* Gunman from Bodie (1941)

Gun Moll *See* Get Rita (1975)

Gun Moll *See* Jigsaw (1949)

Guney's The Wall *See* The Wall (1983)

Gunpoint *See* At Gunpoint (1955)

Guns in the Afternoon *See* Ride the High Country (1962)

Guns, Sin and Bathtub Gin *See* Lady in Red (1979)

Gwendoline *See* The Perils of Gwendoline (1984)

Gycklarnas Afton *See* Sawdust & Tinsel (1953)

Haakon Haakonsen *See* Shipwrecked (1990)

Hab Og Karlighed *See* Twist & Shout (1984)

Habricha el Hashemesh *See* Escape to the Sun (1972)

Hadaka No Shima *See* The Island (1961)

Hail to the Chief *See* Hail (1973)

Half Slave, Half Free 2 *See* Charlotte Forten's Mission: Experiment in Freedom (1985)

Hallelujah, I'm a Tramp *See* Hallelujah, I'm a Bum (1933)

Halloween: The Origin of Michael Myers *See* Halloween 6: The Curse of Michael Myers (1995)

Hallucination Generation *See* Hallucination (1967)

Ham Ham *See* Jamon, Jamon (1993)

Ha'Matarah Tiran *See* Sinai Commandos (1968)

The Hammond Mystery *See* The Undying Monster (1942)

Hana-Bi *See* Fireworks (1997)

Hand of Night *See* Beast of Morocco (1966)

Handgun *See* Deep in the Heart (1983)

Handle With Care *See* Citizens Band (1977)

Hands of a Killer *See* Planets Against Us (1961)

Hands of a Stranger *See* The Hands of Orlac (1960)

The Hands of Orlac *See* Mad Love (1935)

Hands of the Strangler *See* The Hands of Orlac (1960)

Hands Off the Loot *See* Grisbi (1953)

Handsome Serge *See* Le Beau Serge (1958)

The Hangover *See* The Female Jungle (1956)

Hans Christian Andersen's Thumbelina *See* Thumbelina (1994)

Happiness *See* Le Bonheur (1965)

Happiness *See* Le Bonheur Est Dans le Pre (1995)

Happiness Is In the Fields *See* Le Bonheur Est Dans le Pre (1995)

Happy Go Lucky *See* Hallelujah, I'm a Bum (1933)

Happy Mother's Day, Love, George *See* Run, Stranger, Run (1973)

The Happy New Year Caper *See* Happy New Year (1974)

Happy Times *See* The Inspector General (1949)

Hard Driver *See* The Last American Hero (1973)

Hard Stick *See* A Real American Hero (1978)

Hard to Die *See* Crime Story (1993)

The Hardcore Life *See* Hardcore (1979)

Harem Holiday *See* Harum Scarum (1965)

Harlem Hot Shot *See* The Black King (1932)

Harlequin *See* Dark Forces (1983)

Harold Robbins' The Betsy *See* The Betsy (1978)

Harp of Burma *See* The Burmese Harp (1956)

Harrison Bergeron *See* Kurt Vonnegut's Harrison Bergeron (1995)

Harry Black *See* Harry Black and the Tiger (1958)

Harry Tracy—Desperado *See* Harry Tracy (1983)

Harry's Machine *See* Hollywood Harry (1986)

Hasta Clerto Punto *See* Up to a Certain Point (1983)

The Hatchet Murders *See* Deep Red: Hatchet Murders (1975)

Hatred *See* Hate (1995)

The Haunted *See* Curse of the Demon (1957)

The Haunted and the Hunted *See* Dementia 13 (1963)

The Haunting of Hamilton High *See* Hello Mary Lou: Prom Night 2 (1987)

The Haunting of Julia *See* Full Circle (1977)

Haus Der Tausend Freuden *See* The House of 1000 Dolls (1967)

Haut Bas Fragile *See* Up/Down/Fragile (1995)

Haxan *See* Witchcraft through the Ages (1922)

He Lived to Kill *See* Night of Terror (1933)

He Loved an Actress *See* Mad About Money (1937)

He or She *See* Glen or Glenda: Confessions of Ed Wood (1953)

He, She or It *See* The Doll (1962)

Head On *See* Fatal Attraction (1980)

Head Over Heels *See* Chilly Scenes of Winter (1979)

The Head That Wouldn't Die *See* The Brain that Wouldn't Die (1963)

A Heart in Winter *See* Un Coeur en Hiver (1993)

The Heart of New York *See* Hallelujah, I'm a Bum (1933)

Heartbeat *See* Danielle Steel's Heartbeat (1993)

Heartbeat *See* Le Schpountz (1938)

Heartbreak Motel *See* Poor Pretty Eddie (1973)

Hearts and Minds *See* Master Touch (1974)

Heartstone *See* Demonstone (1989)

Heavenly Pursuits *See* The Gospel According to Vic (1987)

Hector Servadac's Ark *See* On the Comet (1968)

Hei Ma *See* A Mongolian Tale (1994)

The Heir to Genghis Khan *See* Storm over Asia (1928)

The Heist *See* Dollars (1971)

Heidorado *See* Helldorado (1946)

Hell Bent for Glory *See* Lafayette Escadrille (1958)

Hell Fire *See* They (1977)

Hell in Normandy *See* Special Forces (1968)

Hell of the Living Dead *See* Night of the Zombies (1983)

Hell to Macao *See* The Corrupt Ones (1967)

Hellborn *See* The Sinister Urge (1960)

Hellcamp *See* Opposing Force (1987)

Hellfire *See* Primal Scream (1987)

Hellfire on Ice, Part 2: Escape from Hell *See* Escape from Hell (1989)

Hello Elephant *See* Pardon My Trunk (1952)

Hellraiser 2 *See* Hellbound: Hellraiser 2 (1988)

Her Mad Night *See* Held for Murder (1932)

Hercules and the Conquest of Atlantis *See* Hercules and the Captive Women (1963)

Hercules and the Haunted Women *See* Hercules and the Captive Women (1963)

Hercules and the Hydra *See* The Loves of Hercules (1960)

Hercules Goes Bananas *See* Hercules in New York (1970)

Hercules: The Movie *See* Hercules in New York (1970)

Here Come the Tigers *See* Manny's Orphans (1978)

Here Is a Man *See* The Devil & Daniel Webster (1941)

Here Lies Love *See* The Second Woman (1951)

Here We Go Again *See* Pride of the Bowery (1941)

The Hero of Pine Ridge *See* Yodelin' Kid From Pine Ridge (1937)

Heroes Die Hard *See* Mr. Kingstreet's War (1971)

Herzbube *See* King, Queen, Knave (1972)

The Heterosexuals *See* Les Biches (1968)

Hets *See* Torment (1944)

Hex *See* The Shrieking (1973)

Hexen bis aufs Blut Gequaelt *See* Mark of the Devil (1969)

H.G. Wells' New Invisible Man *See* The New Invisible Man (1958)

Hidden Face *See* Jail Bait (1954)

The Hidden Room of 1,000 Horrors *See* The Tell-Tale Heart (1962)

Hidden Vision *See* Night Eyes (1990)

Hide and Shriek *See* American Gothic (1988)

Hifazaat *See* In Custody (1994)

High Rolling *See* High Rolling in a Hot Corvette (1977)

The Highest Bidder *See* Woman Hunt (1972)

Highlander 2: Renegade Version *See* Highlander 2: The Quickening (1991)

Highlander 3: The Magician *See* Highlander: The Final Dimension (1994)

Highlander 3: The Sorcerer *See* Highlander: The Final Dimension (1994)

Highway Hell *See* Honky Tonk Girl (1937)

Highway to Hell *See* Running Hot (1983)

Him *See* Only You (1994)

The Hindu *See* Sabaka (1955)

His Other Woman *See* Desk Set (1957)

Histoires Extraordinaires *See* Spirits of the Dead (1968)

Hitler's Gold *See* Inside Out (1975)

Hitman *See* American Commandos (1984)

HMS Defiant *See* Damn the Defiant (1962)

Hol Volt, Hol Nem Volt *See* A Hungarian Fairy Tale (1987)

Holiday *See* Jour de Fete (1948)

Hollow Point *See* The Wild Pair (1987)

Hollow Triumph *See* The Scar (1948)

Hollyweird *See* Flicks (1985)

Hollywood Cowboy *See* Hearts of the West (1975)

Hollywood Hoodlum *See* Hollywood Mystery (1934)

The Hollywood Strangler *See* Don't Answer the Phone (1980)

Hollywood Stunt Man *See* Movie Stuntmen (1953)

Hollywood Thrillmakers *See* Movie Stuntmen (1953)

Holocaust 2000 *See* The Chosen (1977)

Holy Terror *See* Alice Sweet Alice (1976)

Hombre Mirando Al Sudeste *See* Man Facing Southeast (1986)

Home Fires Burning *See* The Turning (1992)

Home Front *See* Morgan Stewart's Coming Home (1987)

Home in Oklahoma *See* Big Show (1937)

Home is Where the Heart Is *See* Square Dance (1987)

Home on the Range *See* Western Double Feature 2: Wayne & Hale (198?)

Homecoming Night *See* Night of the Creeps (1986)

L'Homme du Minnesota *See* Minnesota Clay (1965)

The Honest Courtesan *See* Dangerous Beauty (1998)

Honeymoon in Bali *See* My Love For Yours (1939)

Honeymoon of Fear *See* Dynasty of Fear (1972)

The Honeymooners: The Lost Episodes *See* Honeymooners Hidden Episodes, Vol. 1 (1953)

Hongfen *See* Blush (1995)

The Honorary Consul *See* Beyond the Limit (1983)

Honour Among Thieves *See* Grisbi (1953)

Hoodlum Girls *See* Youth Aflame (1959)

Hoods *See* Hoodlum (1996)

The Hooker Cult Murders *See* The Pyx (1973)

Hopalong Cassidy Enters *See* Hopalong Cassidy (1935)

The Hopeless Ones *See* The Round Up (1966)

A Hora Da Estrela *See* The Hour of the Star (1985)

The Horrible House on the Hill *See* Devil Times Five (1974)

The Horrible Mill Women *See* Mill of the Stone Women (1960)

Horror Castle *See* The Virgin of Nuremberg (1965)

Horror Convention *See* Nightmare in Blood (1975)

Horror Creatures of the Prehistoric Planet *See* Horror of the Blood Monsters (1970)

Horror High See Twisted Brain (1974)

Horror Hotel Massacre See Eaten Alive (1976)

Horror In the Midnight Sun See Invasion of the Animal People (1962)

Horror Maniacs See The Greed of William Hart (1948)

Horror of the Stone Women See Mill of the Stone Women (1960)

Horror on Snape Island See Tower of Evil (1972)

Horse, My Horse See The Horse (1982)

A Horse Named Comanche See Tonka (1958)

Horsie See Queen for a Day (1951)

Hostage See Savage Attraction (1983)

Hostage: Dallas See Getting Even (1986)

Hostage: The Christine Maresch Story See Savage Attraction (1983)

Hot and Cold See Weekend at Bernie's (1989)

Hot Car Girl See Hot Rod Girl (1956)

Hot Lead See Run of the Arrow (1956)

The Hot One See Corvette Summer (1978)

Hot Seat See The Chair (1987)

Hot Spot See I Wake Up Screaming (1941)

Hot Sweat See Keetje Tippel (1975)

Hotel Sorrento See Sorrento Beach (1995)

The Houghland Murder Case See Murder by Television (1935)

The Hounds of Zaroff See The Most Dangerous Game (1932)

Hour of Glory See The Small Back Room (1949)

The Hour of the Pig See The Advocate (1993)

House 3 See The Horror Show (1989)

House by the Lake See Death Weekend (1976)

House in Nightmare Park See Night of the Laughing Dead (1975)

House of Crazies See Asylum (1972)

House of Doom See The Black Cat (1934)

House of Evil See Dance of Death (1968)

House of Evil See The House on Sorority Row (1983)

The House of Exorcism See Lisa and the Devil (1975)

House of Fear See Fearmaker (1989)

House of Fright See Black Sunday (1960)

House of Fright See The Two Faces of Dr. Jekyll (1960)

House of Insane Women See Exorcism's Daughter (1974)

House of Mortal Sin See The Confessional (1975)

House of Mystery See Night Monster (1942)

House of Pleasure See Le Plaisir (1952)

House of Terror See Face of the Screaming Werewolf (1959)

House of Terror See The Hanging Woman (1972)

House of the Damned See Spectre (1996)

House of the Dark Stairway See A Blade in the Dark (1983)

House of Usher See The Fall of the House of Usher (1960)

The House Where Death Lives See Delusion (1984)

The House Where Hell Froze Over See Keep My Grave Open (1980)

House Without Windows See Seven Alone (1975)

How Is It Going? See Comment Ca Va? (1976)

How Long Can You Fall? See Till Marriage Do Us Part (1974)

How to Be a Player See Def Jam's How to Be a Player (1997)

How to Irritate People See John Cleese on How to Irritate People (1968)

How to Steal a Diamond in Four Easy Lessons See The Hot Rock (1970)

How to Steal a Million Dollars and Live Happily Ever After See How to Steal a Million (1966)

Howard Beach: Making the Case for Murder See Skin (1989)

Howard Stern's Private Parts See Private Parts (1996)

Howling 2: Stirba—Werewolf Bitch See Howling 2: Your Sister Is a Werewolf (1985)

Howling 7 See The Howling: New Moon Rising (1995)

H.P. Lovecraft's The Unnamable Returns See The Unnamable 2: The Statement of Randolph Carter (1992)

Hsi Yen See The Wedding Banquet (1993)

Huang Jia Zhan Shi See Royal Warriors (1986)

Huang Tudi See Yellow Earth (1989)

Huggers See Crazy Moon (1987)

The Human Beast See La Bete Humaine (1938)

The Human Tornado See Dolemite 2: Human Tornado (1976)

Hunchback See The Hunchback of Notre Dame (1982)

Hungry Pets See Please Don't Eat My Mother (1972)

Hungry Wives See Season of the Witch (1973)

Hunt to Kill See The White Buffalo (1977)

The Hunted See Touch Me Not (1974)

Hunter of the Apocalypse See The Last Hunter (1980)

Hunters Are For Killing See Hard Frame (1970)

Huozhe See To Live (1994)

Hurricane See Hurricane Streets (1996)

Hustler Squad See The Doll Squad (1973)

I Accuse See J'Accuse (1937)

I Am a Fugitive From the Chain Gang See I Am a Fugitive from a Chain Gang (1932)

I Bambini Ci Guardano See The Children Are Watching Us (1944)

I Became a Criminal See They Made Me a Criminal (1939)

I Call First See Who's That Knocking at My Door? (1968)

I Can Make You Love Me: The Stalking of Laura Black See Stalking Laura (1993)

I Changed My Sex See Glen or Glenda: Confessions of Ed Wood (1953)

I Cinque Della Vendetta See Five Giants from Texas (1966)

I Coltelli Del Vendicatore See Viking Massacre (1965)

I Compagni See The Organizer (1964)

I Corpi Presentano Tracce Di Violenza Carnale See Torso (1973)

I Crossed the Line See The Black Klansman (1966)

I Fidanzati See Fiances (1963)

I Giorni Dell'Inferno See Days of Hell (1984)

I Hate Your Guts See Shame (1961)

I Have a New Master See Passion for Life (1948)

I Have Lived See After Midnight (1933)

I Have No Mouth But I Must Scream See And Now the Screaming Starts (1973)

I Led Two Lives See Glen or Glenda: Confessions of Ed Wood (1953)

I Love a Man in Uniform See A Man in Uniform (1993)

I Love to Kill See Impulse (1974)

I Married Too Young See Married Too Young (1962)

I Nuovi Barbari See Warriors of the Wasteland (1983)

I Pianeti Contro di Noi See Planets Against Us (1961)

I Skiachtra See The Enchantress (1985)

I Tre Volti della Paura See Black Sabbath (1964)

I, Vampiri See The Devil's Commandment (1956)

I Want Her Dead See W (1974)

I Was a Teenage Boy See Something Special (1986)

I Was a Teenage Teenager See Clueless (1995)

I Worship His Shadow See Tales from a Parallel Universe: I Worship His Shadow (1997)

I You She He See Je Tu Il Elle (1974)

Ich und Er See Me and Him (1989)

Ich Will Doch Nur, Dass Ihr Mich Liebt See I Only Want You to Love Me (1976)

Ici et Ailleurs See Here and Elsewhere (197?)

Identikit See Driver's Seat (1973)

Idi i Smotri See Come and See (1985)

The Idiot See L'Idiot (1946)

Ieri, Oggi E Domani See Yesterday, Today and Tomorrow (1964)

If He Hollers, Let Him Go See Dead Right (1968)

If You Can't Say It, Just See It See Whore (1991)

If You Feel Like Singing See Summer Stock (1950)

Ike: The War Years See Ike (1979)

Il Bidone See The Swindle (1955)

Il Buco See Night Watch (1972)

Il Castello de Morti Vivi See Castle of the Living Dead (1964)

Il Cobra See The Cobra (1968)

Il Conformist See The Conformist (1971)

Il Conte Dracula See Count Dracula (1971)

Il Cristo Proibito See The Forbidden Christ (1950)

Il Crudeli See Hellbenders (1967)

Il Deserto Rosso See The Red Desert (1964)

Il Diario di una Cameriera See Diary of a Chambermaid (1964)

Il Diavolo e i Morti See Lisa and the Devil (1975)

Il Diavolo in Corpo See Devil in the Flesh (1987)

Il Dio Chiamato a Dorian See Dorian Gray (1970)

Il Disprezzo See Contempt (1964)

Il Figlio del Capitano Blood See Son of Captain Blood (1962)

Il Fiume del Grande Caimano See The Great Alligator (1981)

Il Gatto Nero See The Black Cat (1981)

Il Generale Della-Rovere See Generale Della Rovere (1960)

Il Giardino Del Finzi-Contini *See* The Garden of the Finzi-Continis (1971)

Il Gigante Di Metropolis *See* The Giant of Metropolis (1961)

Il Giorno e L'Ora *See* The Day and the Hour (1963)

Il Gladiatore Di Roma *See* Gladiator of Rome (1963)

Il Gladiatore Invincible *See* The Invincible Gladiator (1963)

Il Ladro Di Bagdad *See* Thief of Baghdad (1961)

Il Ladro di Bambini *See* The Stolen Children (1992)

Il Lago di Satana *See* The She-Beast (1965)

Il Mio Nome e Nessuno *See* My Name Is Nobody (1974)

Il Mondo Di Yor *See* Yor, the Hunter from the Future (1983)

Il Montagna di Dio Cannibale *See* Slave of the Cannibal God (1979)

Il Mostre *See* The Monster (1996)

Il Mulino Delle Donne di Pietra *See* Mill of the Stone Women (1960)

Il Natale Che Quasi Non Fu *See* The Christmas That Almost Wasn't (1966)

Il Pianeta Degli Uomini Spenti *See* Battle of the Worlds (1961)

Il Portiere de Notte *See* The Night Porter (1974)

Il Postino *See* The Postman (1994)

Il Processo *See* The Trial (1963)

Il Re Dei Criminali *See* Superargo (1967)

Il Rosso Segmo della Follia *See* Hatchet for the Honeymoon (1970)

Il Sicario *See* The Hit Man (1961)

Il Sigillo de Pechino *See* The Corrupt Ones (1967)

Il Terror Dei Barateri *See* Goliath and the Barbarians (1960)

Il Tigre *See* Tiger and the Pussycat (1967)

Il Treno *See* The Train (1965)

Il Vangelo Secondo Matteo *See* The Gospel According to St. Matthew (1964)

III Met By Moonlight *See* Night Ambush (1957)

Illicit Interlude *See* Summer Interlude (1950)

Illuminacja *See* Illumination (1973)

Illumination *See* Fairytale: A True Story (1997)

Ilsa, the Absolute Power *See* Ilsa, the Wicked Warden (1978)

Ilya Mourometz *See* Sword & the Dragon (1956)

Im Stahlnetz Des Dr. Mabuse *See* The Return of Dr. Mabuse (1961)

Immediate Disaster *See* The Stranger from Venus (1954)

The Important Story of Alcoholism *See* One Too Many (1951)

Impossible Object *See* The Story of a Love Story (1973)

In a Year with 13 Moons *See* In a Year of 13 Moons (1978)

In Bed with Madonna *See* Truth or Dare (1991)

In Einem Jahr Mit 13 Monden *See* In a Year of 13 Moons (1978)

In Fashion *See* A la Mode (1994)

In Love *See* Falling in Love Again (1980)

In Old Oklahoma *See* War of the Wildcats (1943)

In Pursuit of Honor *See* G.I. Jane (1997)

In the Bleak Midwinter *See* A Midwinter's Tale (1995)

In the Devil's Garden *See* Assault (1970)

In the Grip of the Spider *See* Web of the Spider (1970)

In the Line of Duty *See* Royal Warriors (1986)

In the Line of Duty: Manhunt in the Dakotas *See* Midnight Murders (1991)

In the Line of Duty: Siege at Marion *See* Children of Fury (1994)

In the Woods *See* Rashomon (1951)

In Weiter Ferne, So Nah! *See* Faraway, So Close! (1993)

Incense for the Damned *See* The Bloodsuckers (1970)

Incident at Victoria Falls *See* Sherlock Holmes and the Incident at Victoria Falls (1991)

The Incredible Invasion *See* The Sinister Invasion (1968)

The Incredible Praying Mantis *See* The Deadly Mantis (1957)

The Incredible Torture Show *See* Bloodsucking Freaks (1975)

The Incredibly Strange Creatures *See* Incredibly Strange Creatures Who Stopped Living and Became Mixed-Up Zombies (1963)

An Indian in the City *See* Little Indian, Big City (1995)

Indian Love Call *See* Rose Marie (1936)

Indian Summer *See* Alive and Kicking (1996)

Indiscretion *See* Christmas in Connecticut (1945)

Indiscretion *See* Dangerous Beauty (1998)

Indiscretion *See* Indiscretion of an American Wife (1954)

The Infernal Idol *See* Craze (1974)

Infested *See* Ticks (1993)

The Infra Superman *See* Infra-Man (1976)

Inn of the Frightened People *See* Revenge (1971)

Innocence is Bliss *See* Miss Grant Takes Richmond (1949)

The Innocent and the Damned *See* Girls' Town (1959)

The Insect *See* The Insect Woman (1963)

Inseminoid *See* Horror Planet (1980)

L'Insoumis *See* Fight for Us (1989)

Interlude *See* Intermezzo (1936)

Intermezzo: A Love Story *See* Intermezzo (1939)

Intruder *See* Intruso (1993)

The Intruder *See* Shame (1961)

The Invader *See* Old Spanish Custom (1936)

The Invaders *See* The Forty-Ninth Parallel (1941)

Invasion Earth 2150 A.D. *See* Daleks—Invasion Earth 2150 A.D. (1966)

Invasion Force *See* Hangar 18 (1980)

Invasion from Inner Earth *See* They (1977)

Invasion of Planet X *See* Godzilla vs. Monster Zero (1968)

Invasion of the Astro-Monsters *See* Godzilla vs. Monster Zero (1968)

Invasion of the Astros *See* Godzilla vs. Monster Zero (1968)

Invasion of the Flying Saucers *See* Earth vs. the Flying Saucers (1956)

Invasion of the Zombies *See* Horror of Party Beach (1964)

An Investigation of Murder *See* The Laughing Policeman (1974)

The Invisible Horror *See* The Invisible Dr. Mabuse (1962)

The Invisible Killer *See* Curse of the Undead (1959)

Io Speriamo Che Me La Cavo *See* Ciao, Professore! (1993)

The Iron Hand *See* Chinese Connection (1973)

The Iron Kiss *See* Naked Kiss (1964)

Irving Berlin's Alexander's Ragtime Band *See* Alexander's Ragtime Band (1938)

Irving Berlin's Second Fiddle *See* Second Fiddle (1939)

Island of Monte Cristo *See* Sword of Venus (1953)

Island of Shame *See* The Young One (1961)

Island of the Burning Damned *See* Island of the Burning Doomed (1967)

Island of the Fishmen *See* Screamers (1980)

Island of the Living Dead *See* Zombie (1980)

Island of the Living Horror *See* Brides of the Beast (1968)

Isle of Lost Women *See* 99 Women (1969)

Isle of the Living Dead *See* The Snake People (1968)

Isle of the Snake People *See* The Snake People (1968)

Isn't Life A Bitch? *See* La Chienne (1931)

Istanbul, Keep Your Eyes Open *See* Istanbul (1990)

It Comes Up Murder *See* The Honey Pot (1967)

It Fell from the Sky *See* Alien Dead (1979)

It Happened at Lakewood Manor *See* Ants (1977)

It Happened in Paris *See* The Lady in Question (1940)

It Happened One Summer *See* State Fair (1945)

It Hurts Only When I Laugh *See* Only When I Laugh (1981)

It Lives By Night *See* The Bat People (1974)

It Only Take Five Minutes *See* Five Minutes to Love (1963)

It Runs in the Family *See* My Summer Story (1994)

It Stalked the Ocean Floor *See* Monster from the Ocean Floor (1954)

It! The Vampire From Beyond Space *See* It! The Terror from Beyond Space (1958)

It Won't Rub Off, Baby *See* Sweet Love, Bitter (1967)

The Italian Connection *See* Hired to Kill (1973)

The Italian Connection *See* Manhunt (1973)

It's Hot in Hell *See* Un Singe en Hiver (1962)

It's Hot in Paradise *See* Horrors of Spider Island (1959)

It's My Life *See* My Life to Live (1962)

It's Only Money *See* Double Dynamite (1951)

Ivan's Childhood *See* My Name Is Ivan (1962)

Jack London's Klondike Fever *See* Klondike Fever (1979)

Jackals *See* American Justice (1986)

Jackie Chan's Police Force *See* Police Story (1985)

Jackie Chan's Police Story *See* Police Story (1985)

Jack's Wife *See* Season of the Witch (1973)

Jacqueline Susann's Once is Not Enough *See* Once Is Not Enough (1975)

Jacquot de Nantes *See* Jacquot (1991)

Jag, en Kvinna *See* I, A Woman (1966)

J'ai Pas Sommeil *See* I Can't Sleep (1993)

Jail Birds *See* Pardon Us (1931)

Jailbirds' Vacation *See* Les Grandes Gueules (1965)

James A. Michener's Texas *See* Texas (1994)

James Clavell's Shogun *See* Shogun (1980)

Jana Aranya *See* The Middleman (1976)

Jane Austen's Emma *See* Emma (1997)

The Janitor *See* Eyewitness (1981)

Japan Sinks *See* Tidal Wave (1975)

Jatszani Kell *See* Lily in Love (1985)

Jaws 3-D *See* Jaws 3 (1983)

Jayne Mansfield: A Symbol of the '50s *See* The Jayne Mansfield Story (1980)

J.C. *See* Iron Horsemen (1971)

Je Vous Salue Marie *See* Hail Mary (1985)

Jealousy *See* L'Enfer (1993)

Jean de Florette 2 *See* Manon of the Spring (1987)

Jeder fur Sich und Gott Gegen Alle *See* Every Man for Himself & God Against All (1975)

Jekyll's Inferno *See* The Two Faces of Dr. Jekyll (1960)

Jennie *See* Portrait of Jennie (1948)

Jennifer (The Snake Goddess) *See* Jennifer (1978)

Jenseits der Stille *See* Beyond Silence (1996)

The Jester *See* Der Purimshpiler (1937)

Jesus de Montreal *See* Jesus of Montreal (1989)

Jette un Sort *See* Rough Magic (1995)

Jeu de Massacre *See* The Killing Game (1967)

Jew Suss *See* Power (1934)

The Jewish Jester *See* Der Purimshpiler (1937)

The Jezebels *See* Switchblade Sisters (1975)

Jigokumen *See* Gate of Hell (1954)

Jim Buck *See* Portrait of a Hitman (1977)

Job Lazadasa *See* The Revolt of Job (1984)

Joe Palooka *See* Palooka (1934)

John Carpenter Presents Body Bags *See* Body Bags (1993)

John Carpenter's Escape from L.A. *See* Escape from L.A. (1996)

John Le Carre's A Perfect Spy *See* A Perfect Spy (1988)

John Travis, Solar Survivor *See* Omega Cop (1990)

Johnnie Mae Gibson: FBI *See* Johnnie Gibson F.B.I. (1987)

Johnny Vagabond *See* Johnny Come Lately (1943)

Johnny Zombie *See* My Boyfriend's Back (1993)

A Joke of Destiny *See* A Joke of Destiny, Lying in Wait Around the Corner Like a Bandit (1984)

Joker's Wild *See* Body Trouble (1992)

Jonas—Qui Aura 25 Ans en l'An 2000 *See* Jonah Who Will Be 25 in the Year 2000 (1976)

Joseph Conrad's Nostromo *See* Nostromo (1996)

Joseph Conrad's The Secret Agent *See* The Secret Agent (1996)

Joseph Sold by His Brothers *See* Joseph & His Brethren (1960)

Joshua Tree *See* Woman Undone (1995)

Journey into Autumn *See* Dreams (1955)

Journey of the Hyena *See* Touki Bouki (1973)

Joyous Laughter *See* Passionate Thief (1960)

J.R. *See* Who's That Knocking at My Door? (1968)

Jude the Obscure *See* Jude (1996)

A Judgement in Stone *See* The Housekeeper (1986)

A Judgment in Stone *See* La Ceremonie (1995)

Jules et Jim *See* Jules and Jim (1962)

Jules Verne's Rocket to the Moon *See* Those Fantastic Flying Fools (1967)

Julie Darling *See* Daughter of Death (1982)

July Pork Bellies *See* For Pete's Sake (1974)

Jumbo *See* Billy Rose's Jumbo (1962)

Jungfrauenmaschine *See* Virgin Machine (1988)

Jungfrukallan *See* The Virgin Spring (1959)

The Jungle Book *See* Rudyard Kipling's The Jungle Book (1994)

Jungle Book 2 *See* Rudyard Kipling's the Second Jungle Book: Mowgli and Baloo (1997)

Jungle Gold *See* Perils of the Darkest Jungle (1944)

Jungle Woman *See* Nabonga (1944)

Juninatten *See* June Night (1940)

Jurassic Park 2 *See* The Lost World: Jurassic Park 2 (1997)

Jury Duty *See* The Great American Sex Scandal (1994)

Just Another Day at the Races *See* Win, Place, or Steal (1972)

Just Ask for Diamond *See* Diamond's Edge (1988)

Just in Time *See* Only You (1994)

Justice Rides Again *See* Destry Rides Again (1939)

Jutai *See* Traffic Jam (1991)

Kaiju Daisenso *See* Godzilla vs. Monster Zero (1968)

Kaiju Soshingeki *See* Destroy All Monsters (1968)

Kaitei Daisenso *See* Terror Beneath the Sea (1966)

Kakushi Toride No San Akunin *See* The Hidden Fortress (1958)

Kaleidoscope *See* Danielle Steel's Kaleidoscope (1990)

Kamakazi *See* Attack Squadron (197?)

Karakter *See* Character (1997)

Karamazov *See* The Brothers Karamazov (1958)

Karate Cop *See* Slaughter in San Francisco (1981)

Katie's Passion *See* Keetje Tippel (1975)

Kavkazsky Plennik *See* Prisoner of the Mountains (1996)

Kayitz Shel Aviya *See* The Summer of Aviya (1988)

The Kent Chronicles *See* The Bastard (1978)

Kettle Creek *See* Mountain Justice (1930)

The Key *See* Odd Obsession (1960)

Key West Crossing *See* The Mercenaries (1980)

KGOD *See* Pray TV (1980)

Khaneh-Je Doost Kojast? *See* Where Is My Friend's House? (1987)

Kickboxer 5 *See* Redemption: Kickboxer 5 (1995)

Kid Auto Races at Venice *See* Kid's Auto Race/Mabel's Married Life (1915)

The Kidnap of Mary Lou *See* Almost Human (1979)

Kilian's Chronicle *See* The Magic Stone (1995)

Kill Castro *See* The Mercenaries (1980)

Killbots *See* Chopping Mall (1986)

Killer *See* Bulletproof Heart (1995)

Killer Bait *See* Too Late for Tears (1949)

Killer Bats *See* The Devil Bat (1941)

The Killer Behind the Mask *See* Savage Weekend (1980)

Killer Grizzly *See* Grizzly (1976)

Killer of Killers *See* The Mechanic (1972)

The Killer Whale *See* Orca (1977)

Killer With a Label *See* One Too Many (1951)

The Killers *See* Pigs (1973)

Killers of the Wild *See* Children of the Wild (1937)

The Killing Box *See* The Ghost Brigade (1993)

Kilronan *See* Hush (1998)

Kimono No Kiroku *See* I Live in Fear (1955)

Kin Folk *See* All the Lovin' Kinfolk (1989)

Kinfolk *See* All the Lovin' Kinfolk (1989)

King Cobra *See* Jaws of Satan (1981)

King Gun *See* The Gatling Gun (1972)

King Kong Tai Godzilla *See* King Kong vs. Godzilla (1963)

King of Africa *See* One Step to Hell (1968)

The King of Criminals *See* Superargo (1967)

King of the Jungleland *See* Darkest Africa (1936)

Kings Ransom *See* Devastator (1985)

Kisenga, Man of Africa *See* Men of Two Worlds (1946)

A Kiss from Eddie *See* The Arousers (1970)

Kiss My Butterfly *See* I Love You, Alice B. Toklas! (1968)

Kiss of Evil *See* Kiss of the Vampire (1962)

Kjaerlighetens Kjotere *See* Zero Degrees Kelvin (1995)

KKK *See* The Klansman (1974)

The Knack...and How to Get It *See* The Knack (1965)

Knives of the Avenger *See* Viking Massacre (1965)

The Knock-Out Cop *See* Flatfoot (1978)

Ko Zaprem Oci *See* When I Close My Eyes (1993)

Koks I Kulissen *See* Ladies on the Rocks (1983)

Komissar *See* Commissar (1968)

Koneko Monogatari *See* The Adventures of Milo & Otis (1989)

Konjiki Yasha *See* Golden Demon (1953)

Kootenai Brown *See* Showdown at Williams Creek (1991)

Kopek and Broom *See* Find the Lady (1975)

Koroshi no Rakuin *See* Branded to Kill (1967)

Krasnaya Palatka *See* Red Tent (1969)

Krokodillen in Amsterdam *See* Crocodiles in Amsterdam (1989)

La Vie Devant Soi *See* Madame Rosa (1977)

La Vie est Rien d'Autre *See* Life and Nothing But (1989)

La Vie Est Une Longue Fleuve Tranquille *See* Life Is a Long Quiet River (1988)

La Vie Privee *See* A Very Private Affair (1962)

La Vie Revee des Anges *See* The Dreamed Life of Angels (1998)

La Vie Sexuelle des Belges *See* The Sexual Life of the Belgians (1994)

La Vieille qui Marchait dans la Mer *See* The Old Lady Who Walked in the Sea (1991)

La Vita e Bella *See* Life is Beautiful (1997)

Laberinto de Pasiones *See* Labyrinth of Passion (1982)

Labyrinth *See* A Reflection of Fear (1972)

Ladies of the Park *See* The Ladies of the Bois de Bologne (1944)

Ladri di Biciclette *See* The Bicycle Thief (1948)

Ladri di Saponette *See* The Icicle Thief (1989)

The Lady and the Outlaw *See* Billy Two Hats (1974)

Lady Beware *See* 13th Guest (1932)

The Lady Dances *See* The Merry Widow (1934)

The Lady Dracula *See* Lemora, Lady Dracula (1973)

Lady Hamilton *See* That Hamilton Woman (1941)

Lady in the Fog *See* Scotland Yard Inspector (1952)

Lady Jane Grey *See* Nine Days a Queen (1936)

The Lady Killers *See* The Ladykillers (1955)

Lady of Deceit *See* Born to Kill (1947)

Lady of the Shadows *See* The Terror (1963)

Ladykiller *See* Lady Killer (1997)

Laererinden *See* All Things Fair (1995)

L'Aigle a Deux Tetes *See* The Eagle Has Two Heads (1948)

The Lake of the Living Dead *See* Zombie Lake (1980)

L'Albero Degli Zoccoli *See* The Tree of Wooden Clogs (1978)

L'Amant *See* The Lover (1992)

L'Amant de Lady Chatterley *See* Lady Chatterley's Lover (1955)

The Lament of the Path *See* Pather Panchali (1954)

L'Amour en Fuite *See* Love on the Run (1978)

The Lamp *See* The Outing (1987)

Lancelot and Guinevere *See* Sword of Lancelot (1963)

Lancelot du Lac *See* Lancelot of the Lake (1974)

Landru *See* Bluebeard (1963)

The Lane Frost Story *See* 8 Seconds (1994)

L'Anee Derniere a Marienbad *See* Last Year at Marienbad (1961)

The Langoliers *See* Stephen King's The Langoliers (1995)

Larceny Lane *See* Blonde Crazy (1931)

Large as Life *See* Larger Than Life (1996)

Larsen, Wolf of the Seven Seas *See* The Legend of the Sea Wolf (1958)

Las Cartas de Alou *See* Letters from Alou (1990)

Las Luchadoras Contra La Momia *See* Wrestling Women vs. the Aztec Mummy (1959)

Las Vegas Strip War *See* The Vegas Strip Wars (1984)

Lashou Shentan *See* Hard-Boiled (1992)

Lasky ,Jedne Plavovlasky *See* Loves of a Blonde (1965)

L'Associe *See* The Associate (1979)

The Last Adventure *See* Les Aventuriers (1977)

The Last Adventurers *See* Down to the Sea in Ships (1922)

The Last Battle *See* Le Dernier Combat (1984)

Last Chance For a Born Loser *See* Stateline Motel (1975)

The Last Days of John Dillinger *See* Dillinger (1991)

The Last Days of Man on Earth *See* The Final Programme (1973)

The Last Days of Sodom and Gomorrah *See* Sodom and Gomorrah (1962)

The Last Elephant *See* Ivory Hunters (1990)

The Last Frontier *See* Savage Wilderness (1955)

The Last Great Treasure *See* Mother Lode (1982)

Last House on the Left, Part 2 *See* Twitch of the Death Nerve (1971)

Last Message From Saigon *See* Operation C.I.A. (1965)

Last of the Cowboys *See* Great Smokey Roadblock (1976)

The Last Outpost *See* Cavalry Charge (1951)

The Last Page *See* Man Bait (1952)

Last Rites *See* Dracula's Last Rites (1979)

The Last Victim *See* Forced Entry (1975)

The Last Warrior *See* The Final Executioner (1983)

The Last Will of Dr. Mabuse *See* Crimes of Dr. Mabuse (1932)

The Last Will of Dr. Mabuse *See* Testament of Dr. Mabuse (1962)

The Late Edwina Black *See* The Obsessed (1951)

Latin Love *See* Greek Street (1930)

Latin Quarter *See* Frenzy (1946)

Laughterhouse *See* Singleton's Pluck (1984)

The Law *See* Tilai (1990)

The Law *See* Where the Hot Wind Blows (1959)

Law Breakers *See* Les Assassins de L'Ordre (1971)

Lawnmower Man 2: Jobe's War *See* Lawnmower Man 2: Beyond Cyberspace (1995)

The Lay of the Land *See* The Student Affair (1997)

Lazy Bones *See* Hallelujah, I'm a Bum (1933)

Le Blonde de Pekin *See* The Peking Blond (1968)

Le Caporal Epingle *See* The Elusive Corporal (1962)

Le Carrosse D'Or *See* The Golden Coach (1952)

Le Cerveau *See* The Brain (1969)

Le Charme Discret de la Bourgeoisie *See* The Discreet Charm of the Bourgeoisie (1972)

Le Chateau de Ma Mere *See* My Mother's Castle (1991)

Le Cheval D'Orgeuil *See* The Horse of Pride (1980)

Le Ciel et le Boue *See* The Sky Above, the Mud Below (1961)

Le Confessionnal *See* The Confessional (1995)

Le Corniauds *See* The Sucker (1965)

Le Cri du Hibou *See* The Cry of the Owl (1992)

Le Crime de Monsieur Lange *See* The Crime of Monsieur Lange (1936)

Le Danger Vient de l'Escape *See* The Day the Sky Exploded (1957)

Le Declin De L'Empire Americain *See* The Decline of the American Empire (1986)

Le Dejeuner sur l'Herbe *See* Picnic on the Grass (1959)

Le Dernier Metro *See* The Last Metro (1980)

Le Desert des Tartares *See* The Desert of the Tartars (1976)

Le Diable au Corps *See* Devil in the Flesh (1946)

Le Diable, Probablement *See* The Devil, Probably (1977)

Le Distrait *See* The Daydreamer (1975)

Le Docteur Petiot *See* Dr. Petiot (1990)

Le Fantome de la Liberte *See* Phantom of Liberty (1974)

Le Feu Follet *See* The Fire Within (1964)

Le Fils du Requin *See* The Son of the Shark (1993)

Le Fils Prefere *See* The Favorite Son (1994)

Le Fruit Defendu *See* Forbidden Fruit (1952)

Le Gai Savoir *See* The Joy of Knowledge (1965)

Le Geant de la Vallee Das Rois *See* Son of Samson (1962)

Le Gentleman d'Epsom *See* Duke of the Derby (1962)

Le Graal *See* Lancelot of the Lake (1974)

Le Grand Bleu *See* The Big Blue (1988)

Le Grand Blond avec une Chassure Noire *See* The Tall Blond Man with One Black Shoe (1972)

Le Grand Meaulnes *See* The Wanderer (1967)

Le Huitieme Jour *See* The Eighth Day (1995)

Le Hussard sur le Toit *See* The Horseman on the Roof (1995)

Le Jardin des Plantes *See* The Green House (1996)

Le Jour et L'Heure *See* The Day and the Hour (1963)

Le Journal du Seducteur *See* Diary of a Seducer (1995)

Le Journal d'un Cure de Campagne *See* Diary of a Country Priest (1950)

Le Journal d'une Femme de Chambre *See* Diary of a Chambermaid (1964)

Le Juge et L'assassin *See* The Judge and the Assassin (1975)

Le Locataire *See* The Tenant (1976)

Le Maitre de Musique *See* The Music Teacher (1988)

Le Mepris *See* Contempt (1964)

Le Meraviglie Di Aladino *See* The Wonders of Aladdin (1961)

Le Mur *See* The Wall (1983)

Le Mura di Malapaga *See* The Walls of Malapaga (1949)

Le Neveu de Beethoven *See* Beethoven's Nephew (1988)

Le Notti de Cabiria *See* Nights of Cabiria (1957)

Le Pays Bleu *See* Blue Country (1977)

Le Peau Douce *See* The Soft Skin (1964)

Le Petit Monde de Don Camillo *See* Little World of Don Camillo (1951)

Le Plus Vieux Metier du Monde *See* Oldest Profession (1967)

Le Proces *See* The Trial (1963)

Le Rayon Vert *See* Summer (1986)

Le Regle du Jeu *See* The Rules of the Game (1939)

Le Retour de Martin Guerre *See* The Return of Martin Guerre (1983)

Le Retour du Grand Blond *See* Return of the Tall Blond Man With One Black Shoe (1974)

Le Roi de Coeur *See* The King of Hearts (1966)

Le Rouble a Deux Faces *See* The Hot Line (1969)

Le Rouge aux Levres *See* Daughters of Darkness (1971)

Le Rouge et le Noir *See* The Red and the Black (1957)

Le Salaire de la Peur *See* Wages of Fear (1955)

Le Sang d'un Poete *See* The Blood of a Poet (1930)

le Sant de l'Ange *See* Cobra (1971)

Le Sauvage *See* Lovers Like Us (1975)

Le Teur Invisible *See* Curse of the Undead (1959)

Le Tournoi dans la Cite *See* Tournament (1929)

Le Train *See* The Train (1965)

Le Trio Infernal *See* The Infernal Trio (1974)

Le Trou *See* Night Watch (1972)

Le Vieil Homme Et L'Enfant *See* The Two of Us (1968)

Le Voleur De Bagdad *See* Thief of Baghdad (1961)

Leader of the Pack *See* Unholy Rollers (1972)

Lebenszeichen *See* Signs of Life (1968)

L'eclisse *See* The Eclipse (1966)

L'Ecole Buissonniere *See* Passion for Life (1948)

Legacy of Blood *See* Blood Legacy (1973)

The Legacy of Maggie Walsh *See* The Legacy (1979)

The Legend *See* James Dean (1976)

Legend in Leotards *See* Return of Captain Invincible (1983)

Legend of Cougar Canyon *See* The Secret of Navajo Cave (1976)

The Legend of Gosta Berling *See* The Atonement of Gosta Berling (1924)

The Legend of Machine Gun Kelly *See* Melvin Purvis: G-Man (1974)

Legend of the Bayou *See* Eaten Alive (1976)

Legend of the Seven Golden Vampires *See* The 7 Brothers Meet Dracula (1973)

Legend of Witch Hollow *See* The Witchmaker (1969)

Legenda Del Rudio Malese *See* Jungle Raiders (1985)

Legenda Suramskoi Kreposti *See* The Legend of Suram Fortress (1985)

The Legendary Curse of Lemora *See* Lemora, Lady Dracula (1973)

Legion of the Damned *See* Battle of the Commandos (1971)

Lemora: A Child's Tale of the Supernatural *See* Lemora, Lady Dracula (1973)

Len Deighton's Bullet to Beijing *See* Bullet to Beijing (1995)

L'Enfant Sauvage *See* The Wild Child (1970)

Leo Tolstoy's Anna Karenina *See* Leo Tolstoy's Anna Karenina (1996)

Leon *See* The Professional (1994)

Leona Helmsley: The Queen of Mean *See* The Queen of Mean (1990)

Lepa Sela, Lepo Gore *See* Pretty Village, Pretty Flame (1996)

Lepassager de la Pluie *See* Rider on the Rain (1970)

L'Eredita Ferramonti *See* The Inheritance (1976)

Les Amities Particulieres *See* This Special Friendship (1967)

Les Bas Fonds *See* The Lower Depths (1936)

Les Belles de Nuit *See* Beauties of the Night (1952)

Les Choses De La Vie *See* The Things of Life (1970)

Les Corrompus *See* The Corrupt Ones (1967)

Les Cousins *See* The Cousins (1959)

Les Dames du Bois de Bologne *See* The Ladies of the Bois de Bologne (1944)

Les Demons *See* The Demons (1974)

Les Deux Anglaises et le Continent *See* Two English Girls (1972)

Les Deux Rivales *See* Time of Indifference (1964)

Les Diabolique *See* Diabolique (1955)

Les Dimanches de Ville d'Arvay *See* Sundays & Cybele (1962)

Les Enfants du Paradise *See* Children of Paradise (1944)

Les Enfants Gates *See* Spoiled Children (1977)

Les Felins *See* Joy House (1964)

Les Feluettes *See* Lilies (1996)

Les Gaspards *See* The Holes (1972)

Les Grandes Gueules *See* Jailbird's Vacation (1965)

Les Grandes Personnes *See* Time Out for Love (1961)

Les Griffes du Vampire *See* Curse of the Undead (1959)

Les Innocents aux Mains Sales *See* Dirty Hands (1976)

Les Jeux Interdits *See* Forbidden Games (1952)

Les Liaisons Dangereuses *See* Dangerous Liaisons (1960)

Les Liens de Sang *See* Blood Relatives (1977)

Les Louves *See* Letters to an Unknown Lover (1984)

Les Mille Et Une Nuits *See* The Wonders of Aladdin (1961)

Les Mille et Une Recettes du Cuisinier Amoureux *See* A Chef in Love (1996)

Les Mongols *See* The Mongols (1960)

Les Noces de Papier *See* A Paper Wedding (1989)

Les Nuits De La Pleine *See* Full Moon in Paris (1984)

Les Orgueilleux *See* The Proud Ones (1953)

Les Parapluies De Cherbourg *See* Umbrellas of Cherbourg (1964)

Les Parents Terribles *See* The Storm Within (1948)

Les Quartre Cents Coups *See* The 400 Blows (1959)

Les Rendez-vous de Paris *See* Rendezvous in Paris (1995)

Les Ripoux *See* My New Partner (1984)

Les Roseaux Sauvages *See* Wild Reeds (1994)

Les Routes du Sud *See* Roads to the South (1978)

Les Silences du Palais *See* The Silences of the Palace (1994)

Les Somnambules *See* Mon Oncle D'Amerique (1980)

Les Vacances de Monsieur Hulot *See* Mr. Hulot's Holiday (1953)

Les Valseuses *See* Going Places (1974)

Les Visiteurs *See* The Visitors (1995)

Les Yeux Noirs *See* Dark Eyes (1987)

Les Yeux sans Visage *See* The Horror Chamber of Dr. Faustus (1959)

Lesbian Twins *See* The Virgin Witch (1970)

L'Ete Meurtrier *See* One Deadly Summer (1983)

L'Ete Prochain *See* Next Summer (1984)

L'Eternel Retour *See* Eternal Return (1943)

Lethal *See* The KGB: The Secret War (1986)

A Letter to Mama *See* A Brivele der Mamen (1938)

A Letter to Mother *See* A Brivele der Mamen (1938)

Letyat Zhuravit *See* The Cranes Are Flying (1957)

L'Evangile Selon Saint-Matthieu *See* The Gospel According to St. Matthew (1964)

L'Histoire d'Adele H. *See* Story of Adele H. (1975)

L'Homme de Rio *See* That Man from Rio (1964)

L'Homme Qui Aimait les Femmes *See* The Man Who Loved Women (1977)

L'Hypothese du Tableau Vole *See* The Hypothesis of the Stolen Painting (1978)

Liar *See* Deceiver (1997)

Libido *See* The Sensuous Teenager (1970)

Licensed to Kill *See* Second Best Secret Agent in the Whole Wide World (1965)

The Lie Detector *See* Le Polygraphe (1996)

The Life and Adventures of Nicholas Nickleby *See* Nicholas Nickleby (1946)

The Life and Loves of Beethoven *See* Beethoven (1936)

Life at Stake *See* The Key Man (1957)

Life in the Food Chain *See* Age Isn't Everything (1991)

Life is Rosy *See* La Vie est Belle (1987)

Life of Brian *See* Monty Python's Life of Brian (1979)

The Life of Jack London *See* Jack London (1944)

Lifesavers *See* Mixed Nuts (1994)

The Light Fantastic *See* Love Is Better Than Ever (1952)

Lights of Variety *See* Variety Lights (1951)

Like a Crow on a June Bug *See* Sixteen (1972)

Like Father, Like Son *See* The Executioner (1978)

Lila *See* Mantis in Lace (1968)

Lilacs in the Spring *See* Let's Make Up (1955)

L'Inafferrabile Invincible *See* Mr. Superinvisible (1973)

Lincoln *See* Gore Vidal's Lincoln (1988)

L'Innocente *See* The Innocent (1976)

The Lion's Den *See* La Boca del Lobo (1989)

Lisa e il Diavolo *See* Lisa and the Devil (1975)

L'Isola Degli Uomini Pesce *See* Screamers (1980)

The Little Martyr See The Children Are Watching Us (1944)

The Little Mermaid See La Petite Sirene (1980)

Little Mother See Mamele (1938)

Little Pal See Healer (1936)

Little Panda See The Amazing Panda Adventure (1995)

The Little Sister See The Tender Age (1984)

Live a Little, Steal a Lot See Murph the Surf (1975)

Live Bait See L'Appat (1994)

Live to Love See The Devil's Hand (1961)

The Liver Eaters See Spider Baby (1964)

Ljubarni Slucaj See The Love Affair, or The Case of the Missing Switchboard Operator (1967)

Lo Chiamavano Trinita See They Call Me Trinity (1972)

Lo Que Vendra See Times to Come (1981)

Lo Sbarco di Anzio See Anzio (1968)

Lo Scatenato See Catch as Catch Can (1968)

Lo Sceicco Bianco See The White Sheik (1952)

Lo Spettro See The Ghost (1963)

Lo Strano Vizio della Signora Ward See Blade of the Ripper (1970)

Lo Strano Vizio Della Signora Wardh See The Next Victim (1971)

Lo Zio Indegno See The Sleazy Uncle (1989)

Loaded Weapon 1 See National Lampoon's Loaded Weapon 1 (1993)

Lock Your Doors See The Ape Man (1943)

The Lodger: A Case of London Fog See The Lodger (1926)

L'Oeuvre au Noir See The Abyss (1989)

The Lone Troubador See Two-Gun Troubador (1937)

Lone Wolf and Cub: Baby Cart at the River Styx See Baby Cart at the River Styx (1972)

Lone Wolf and Cub: Sword of Vengeance See Baby Cart 1: Lend a Child...Lend an Arm (1972)

The Lonely Hearts Killers See Honeymoon Killers (1970)

Lonely Man See Gun Riders (1969)

The Lonely Wife See Charulata (1964)

The Lonely Woman See Voyage in Italy (1953)

The Loner See Ruckus (1981)

The Long Arm See The Third Key (1957)

The Long, Dark Night See The Pack (1977)

Long John Silver Returns to Treasure Island See Long John Silver (1953)

The Long Ride See Brady's Escape (1984)

The Long Shot See African Rage (1978)

Long Time, Nothing New See No Looking Back (1998)

Look Down and Die See Steel (1980)

The Look of Ulysses See Ulysses' Gaze (1995)

Loonies On Broadway See Zombies on Broadway (1944)

Loose Joints See Flicks (1985)

Looters See Trespass (1992)

L'Opera De Quat'Sous See The Threepenny Opera (1931)

Lorca See The Disappearance of Garcia Lorca (1996)

Lorca and the Outlaws See Starship (1987)

Lord Mountbatten: The Last Viceroy See Mountbatten: The Last Viceroy (1986)

Lords of Treason See Secret Honor (1985)

L'Oro Di Napoli See The Gold of Naples (1954)

L'Orribile Segreto Del Dr. Hichcock See The Horrible Dr. Hichcock (1962)

Los Ambiciosos See Fever Mounts at El Pao (1959)

Los Demonios See The Demons (1974)

Los Despiadados See Hellbenders (1967)

Los Ojos Azules de la Muneca Rota See House of Psychotic Women (1973)

Los Santos Inocentes See The Holy Innocents (1984)

Loser Take All See Strike It Rich (1990)

The Lost Glory of Troy See The Avenger (1962)

The Lost Illusion See The Fallen Idol (1949)

Lost in Time See Waxwork 2: Lost in Time (1991)

Lost Island of Kioga See Hawk of the Wilderness (1938)

Lost Planet Airmen See King of the Rocketmen (1949)

Lost Women See Mesa of Lost Women (1952)

Lost Women of Zarpa See Mesa of Lost Women (1952)

The Loudest Whisper See The Children's Hour (1961)

Louis L'Amour's Conagher See Conagher (1991)

Louis L'Amour's "The Shadow Riders" See The Shadow Riders (1982)

Louis 19, le Roi des Ondes See King of the Airwaves (1994)

Love and Death in Saigon See A Better Tommorow, Part 3 (1989)

Love and Hate: The Story of Colin and Joanne Thatcher See Love and Hate: A Marriage Made in Hell (1990)

Love and the Midnight Auto Supply See Midnight Auto Supply (1978)

The Love Cage See Joy House (1964)

Love Eternal See Eternal Return (1943)

The Love Factor See Alien Women (1969)

Love in Las Vegas See Viva Las Vegas (1963)

Love is Blind See Love at First Sight (1976)

Love Lessons See All Things Fair (1995)

The Love Maniac See Blood of Ghastly Horror (1972)

Love, the Magician See El Amor Brujo (1986)

Love Trap See Curse of the Black Widow (1977)

Love You to Death See Deadly Illusion (1987)

Lover of the Great Bear See Smugglers (1975)

Lover, Wife See Wifemistress (1979)

Lovers from Beyond the Tomb See Nightmare Castle (1965)

Lovers Must Learn See Rome Adventure (1962)

The Lovers of Montparnasse See Modigliani (1958)

Loves of a Scoundrel See Death of a Scoundrel (1956)

The Loves of Isadora See Isadora (1968)

Loving Moments See Bleak Moments (1971)

The Loyal 47 Ronin See 47 Ronin, Part 1 (1942)

L'Ucello dalle Plume di Cristallo See The Bird with the Crystal Plumage (1970)

Luci Del Varieta See Variety Lights (1951)

The Lucifer Project See Barracuda (1978)

Lucky Boots See Gun Play (1936)

Lucky Break See Paperback Romance (1996)

Lucky 13 See Running Hot (1983)

Lucky to Be a Woman See What a Woman! (1956)

The Lullaby See The Sin of Madelon Claudet (1931)

L'Ultimo Uomo Della Terra See The Last Man on Earth (1964)

Lunch on the Grass See Picnic on the Grass (1959)

Lunch Wagon Girls See Lunch Wagon (1981)

L'Une Chante, L'Autre Pas See One Sings, the Other Doesn't (1977)

L'Uomo Dalle Due Ombre See Cold Sweat (1974)

L'Uomo di Rio See That Man from Rio (1964)

Lust for Evil See Purple Noon (1960)

Lust och Fagring Stor See All Things Fair (1995)

Lust of the Vampires See The Devil's Commandment (1956)

Lycanthropus See Werewolf in a Girl's Dormitory (1961)

M. Hire See Monsieur Hire (1989)

Ma and Pa Kettle Go to Paris See Ma and Pa Kettle on Vacation (1953)

Ma Nuit Chez Maud See My Night at Maud's (1969)

Ma Vie Sexuelle...Comment Je Me Suis Dispute See My Sex Life...Or How I Got Into an Argument (1996)

Maboroshi no Hikari See Maborosi (1995)

Macabra See Demonoid, Messenger of Death (1981)

Macabre Serenade See Dance of Death (1968)

Maccheroni See Macaroni (1985)

Maciste Alla Corte Del Gran Khan See Samson and the 7 Miracles of the World (1962)

Maciste at the Court of the Great Khan See Samson and the 7 Miracles of the World (1962)

Maciste la Regina di Samar See Hercules Against the Moon Men (1964)

Maciste, L'Eroe Piu Grande Del Mondo See Goliath and the Sins of Babylon (1964)

Maciste Nella Terra dei Ciclopi See Atlas in the Land of the Cyclops (1961)

Mad Dog See Mad Dog Morgan (1976)

Mad Dog Time See Trigger Happy (1996)

Mad Dogs and Englishmen See Shameless (1994)

The Mad Hatter See Breakfast in Hollywood (1946)

Mad Jake See Blood Salvage (1990)

Mad Magazine's Up the Academy See Up the Academy (1980)

Mad Trapper of the Yukon See Challenge To Be Free (1976)

Mad Wednesday See The Sin of Harold Diddlebock (1947)

Madagascar Landing See Alfred Hitchcock's Aventure Malgache (1944)

Madame De See The Earrings of Madame De... (1954)

Madame Frankenstein See Lady Frankenstein (1972)

Mademoiselle France See Reunion in France (1942)

Madmen of Mandoras See They Saved Hitler's Brain (1964)

Madonna Truth or Dare *See* Truth or Dare (1991)

Mafia Junction *See* Super Bitch (1989)

The Mafu Cage *See* My Sister, My Love (1978)

The Magic Hour *See* Twilight (1998)

The Magnificent One *See* Le Magnifique (1976)

The Magnificent Seven *See* Seven Samurai (1954)

The Magnificent Showman *See* Circus World (1964)

Mahanagar *See* The Big City (1963)

Making It *See* Going Places (1974)

Mako: The Jaws of Death *See* Jaws of Death (1976)

Malenka, the Vampire *See* Fangs of the Living Dead (1968)

Malenkaya Vera *See* Little Vera (1988)

Malice in Wonderland *See* The Rumor Mill (1986)

Malizia *See* Malicious (1974)

Man and His Mate *See* One Million B.C. (1940)

A Man Betrayed *See* Wheel of Fortune (1941)

Man-Eater *See* Shark! (1968)

The Man From C.O.T.T.O.N., Purlie Victorious *See* Gone Are the Days (1963)

Man from Music Mountain *See* Texas Legionnaires (1943)

The Man From Nevada *See* The Nevadan (1950)

Man in a Cocked Hat *See* Carlton Browne of the F.O. (1959)

A Man in Mommy's Bed *See* With Six You Get Eggroll (1968)

The Man in Possession *See* Personal Property (1937)

Man in the Middle *See* 48 Hours to Live (1960)

Man Looking Southeast *See* Man Facing Southeast (1986)

Man of Bronze *See* Jim Thorpe: All American (1951)

Man of the Frontier *See* Red River Valley (1936)

Man of the Hour *See* Colonel Effingham's Raid (1945)

Man on the Move *See* Jigsaw (1971)

The Man Who Changed His Mind *See* The Man Who Lived Again (1936)

The Man Who Watched Trains Go By *See* Paris Express (1953)

The Man With The Deadly Lens *See* Wrong Is Right (1982)

The Man with the Green Carnation *See* The Trials of Oscar Wilde (1960)

The Man with the Synthetic Brain *See* Blood of Ghastly Horror (1972)

The Man With the X-Ray Eyes *See* X: The Man with X-Ray Eyes (1963)

The Man with the Yellow Eyes *See* Planets Against Us (1961)

The Man with Thirty Sons *See* The Magnificent Yankee (1950)

Manen Pa Taket *See* The Man on the Roof (1976)

Mangiati Vivi dai Cannibali *See* Emerald Jungle (1980)

Manhattan Project: The Deadly Game *See* The Manhattan Project (1986)

Manhunt in the Dakotas *See* Midnight Murders (1991)

Manhunt: The Search for the Night Stalker *See* The Hunt for the Night Stalker (1991)

The Maniacs Are Loose *See* The Thrill Killers (1965)

Manifesto *See* A Night of Love (1987)

Mannen fran Mallorca *See* Man from Mallorca (1984)

Manon des Sources *See* Manon of the Spring (1987)

The Manster—Half Man, Half Monster *See* The Manster (1959)

Manuela's Loves *See* Le Jupon Rouge (1987)

Marcelino *See* The Miracle of Marcelino (1955)

Marcelino, Pan y Vino *See* The Miracle of Marcelino (1955)

Marching Along *See* Stars and Stripes Forever (1952)

Margaret Bourke-White *See* Double Exposure: The Story of Margaret Bourke-White (1989)

Maria di Mi Corazon *See* Mary, My Dearest (1983)

Maria Marten *See* Murder in the Old Red Barn (1936)

Marie Walewska *See* Conquest (1937)

Marijuana the Devil's Weed *See* Wild Weed (1949)

Marijuana: The Devil's Weed *See* Marihuana (1936)

Marilyn *See* Roadhouse Girl (1953)

Marine Issue *See* Instant Justice (1986)

Mario Puzo's The Last Don *See* The Last Don (1997)

Marius et Jeannette: Un Conte de L'Estaque *See* Marius and Jeannette (1997)

Mark of Terror *See* Drums of Jeopardy (1931)

Mark of the Avenger *See* The Mysterious Rider (1938)

Mark of the Beast *See* Curse of the Undead (1959)

Mark of the Claw *See* Dick Tracy's Dilemma (1947)

Mark of the Vampire *See* The Vampire (1957)

Mark of the West *See* Curse of the Undead (1959)

Mark Twain *See* The Adventures of Mark Twain (1985)

Married in Haste *See* Consolation Marriage (1931)

Mars Invades Puerto Rico *See* Frankenstein Meets the Space Monster (1965)

The Marseille Contract *See* The Destructors (1974)

Marshal of Heldorado *See* Blazing Guns (1950)

Martin Lawrence You So Crazy *See* You So Crazy (1994)

Marusa No Onna *See* A Taxing Woman (1987)

Marusa No Onna II *See* A Taxing Woman's Return (1988)

The Marvelous Visit *See* La Merveilleuse Visite (1974)

The Marx Brothers at the Circus *See* At the Circus (1939)

Mascskajatek *See* Cat's Play (1974)

Masculin Feminin *See* Masculine Feminine (1966)

Mask of Dust *See* Race for Life (1955)

Mask of Fury *See* First Yank into Tokyo (1945)

Massacre at Fort Holman *See* A Reason to Live, a Reason to Die (1973)

Massacre Hill *See* Eureka Stockade (1949)

Massacre Mafia Style *See* The Executioner (1978)

The Master *See* Master Ninja (1978)

Master of Evil *See* The Demon Lover (1977)

Master of Lassie *See* The Hills of Home (1948)

Matango *See* Attack of the Mushroom People (1963)

Matar al Abuelito *See* Killing Grandpa (1991)

Mater Dolorosa *See* The Torture of Silence (1917)

The Mating of the Sabine Women *See* The Rape of the Sabines (1961)

Matka Joanna Od Aniolow *See* Mother Joan of the Angels (1960)

Matt Riker *See* Mutant Hunt (1987)

A Matter of Life and Death *See* Stairway to Heaven (1946)

Mauri *See* Big Mo (1973)

Mausoleum *See* One Dark Night (1982)

Max, My Love *See* Max, Mon Amour (1986)

Mayerling to Sarajevo *See* De Mayerling a Sarajevo (1940)

The Mayfair Bank Caper *See* The Big Scam (1979)

Mazel Tov Ou le Mariage *See* Marry Me, Marry Me (1969)

McKlusky *See* White Lightning (1973)

The McMasters...Tougher Than the West Itself *See* The McMasters (1970)

Meachorei Hasoragim *See* Beyond the Walls (1984)

Mecaniques Celestes *See* Celestial Clockwork (1994)

The Medicine Hat Stallion *See* Peter Lundy and the Medicine Hat Stallion (1977)

The Medieval Dead *See* Army of Darkness (1992)

Meet Miss Marple *See* Murder She Said (1962)

Meet Ruth Stoops *See* Citizen Ruth (1996)

Meet the Applegates *See* The Applegates (1989)

Meet Whiplash Willie *See* The Fortune Cookie (1966)

The Meetings of Anna *See* Les Rendez-vous D'Anna (1978)

A Meia-Noite Levarei Sua Alma *See* At Midnight, I'll Take Your Soul (1963)

Mekagojira No Gyakushu *See* Terror of Mechagodzilla (1978)

Melanie Rose *See* High Stakes (1989)

Melody of Youth *See* They Shall Have Music (1939)

Men in Tights *See* Robin Hood: Men in Tights (1993)

Men of Steel *See* Steel (1980)

Men with Guns *See* Hombres Armados (1997)

The Mercenaries *See* Dark of the Sun (1968)

Mery per Sempre *See* Forever Mary (1989)

The Message *See* Mohammed: Messenger of God (1977)

Messer Im Kopf *See* Knife in the Head (1978)

Metempsycose *See* Tomb of Torture (1965)

Metisse *See* Cafe au Lait (1994)

Meurtre en 45 Tours See Murder at 45 R.P.M. (1965)

Mi Familia See My Family (1994)

Mia Eoniotita Ke Mia Mera See Eternity and a Day (1997)

MIB See Men in Black (1997)

Mickey Spillane's Margin for Murder See Margin for Murder (1981)

Microscopia See Fantastic Voyage (1966)

Midnight at Madame Tussaud's See Midnight at the Wax Museum (1936)

Midnight Heat See Sunset Heat (1992)

The Mighty Ducks 2 See D2: The Mighty Ducks (1994)

The Mighty Peking Man See Goliathon (1979)

The Mighty Thunder See Tundra (1936)

The Mighty Ursus See Ursus in the Valley of the Lions (1962)

Mignonne See Your Turn Darling (1963)

Mikan No Taikyoku See The Go-Masters (1982)

Mike Leigh's Naked See Naked (1993)

Mikres Aphrodites See Young Aphrodites (1963)

Milagro en Roma See Miracle in Rome (1988)

Milczaca Gwiazda See First Spaceship on Venus (1960)

Mile a Minute Love See Roaring Speedboats (1937)

Milou en Mai See May Fools (1990)

Milou in May See May Fools (1990)

Minaccia d'Amore See Dial Help (1988)

Mind Games See The Agency (1981)

Mind Ripper See Wes Craven Presents Mind Ripper (1995)

Mindwarp: An Infinity of Terror See Galaxy of Terror (1981)

The Miracle of Fatima See Miracle of Our Lady of Fatima (1952)

Miracle of Life See Our Daily Bread (1934)

Miracolo a Milano See Miracle in Milan (1951)

Mirage See Maborosi (1995)

Miss Europe See Prix de Beaute (1930)

Miss Muette See The Diabolical Dr. Z (1965)

Miss Shumway See Rough Magic (1995)

Mrs. Parker and the Round Table See Mrs. Parker and the Vicious Circle (1994)

Mr. Ashton was Indiscreet See The Senator was Indiscreet (1947)

Mr. Bug Goes to Town See Hoppity Goes to Town (1941)

Mr. Celebrity See Turf Boy (1942)

Mr. Forbush and the Penguins See Cry of the Penguins (1971)

Mr. Fox of Venice See The Honey Pot (1967)

Mr. Invisible See Mr. Superinvisible (1973)

Mr. Quilp See The Old Curiosity Shop (1975)

Mr. Sebastian See Sebastian (1968)

Mr. 247 See A Modern Affair (1994)

Mister V See Pimpernel Smith (1942)

Mr. Wrong See Dark of the Night (1985)

Misterios del Ultratumba See Black Pit of Dr. M (1947)

Mit Eva Fing Die Sunde An See The Bellboy and the Playgirls (1962)

Mitt Liv Som Hund See My Life As a Dog (1985)

The Model Killer See The Hollywood Strangler Meets the Skid Row Slasher (1979)

Model Massacre See Color Me Blood Red (1964)

A Modern Bluebeard See Boom in the Moon (1946)

A Modern Hero See Knute Rockne: All American (1940)

Modigliani of Montparnasse See Modigliani (1958)

Mogliamante See Wifemistress (1979)

The Mogul See Ratings Game (1984)

Molly Louvain See The Strange Love of Molly Louvain (1932)

Mondo Pazzo See Mondo Cane 2 (1964)

A Monkey in Winter See Un Singe en Hiver (1962)

Monkey Shines: An Experiment in Fear See Monkey Shines (1988)

Monsieur Hulot's Holiday See Mr. Hulot's Holiday (1953)

Monsoon See Isle of Forgotten Sins (1943)

Monster See Humanoids from the Deep (1980)

The Monster Baran See Varan the Unbelievable (1961)

Monster from a Prehistoric Planet See Gappa the Trifibian Monster (1967)

Monster in the Surf See The Beach Girls and the Monster (1965)

Monster Maker See Monster from the Ocean Floor (1954)

Monster of Monsters See Ghidrah the Three Headed Monster (1965)

Monster of Terror See Die, Monster, Die! (1965)

Monster of the Island See Island Monster (1953)

The Monster Show See Freaks (1932)

The Monster Walked See The Monster Walks (1932)

The Monster with Green Eyes See Planets Against Us (1961)

Monster Yongkari See Yongkari Monster of the Deep (1967)

Monster Zero See Godzilla vs. Monster Zero (1968)

The Monsters Are Loose See The Thrill Killers (1965)

Monsters From the Moon See Robot Monster (1953)

Monsters from the Unknown Planet See Terror of Mechagodzilla (1978)

Monsters of the Night See Navy vs. the Night Monsters (1966)

Monstrosity See The Atomic Brain (1964)

Montana Justice See Man from Montana (1941)

Monte Carlo or Bust See Those Daring Young Men in Their Jaunty Jalopies (1969)

Montenegro—Or Pigs and Pearls See Montenegro (1981)

Montparnasse 19 See Modigliani (1958)

Morgan: A Suitable Case for Treatment See Morgan! (1966)

Morgan il Pirata See Morgan the Pirate (1960)

Morgen Grauen See Time Troopers (1989)

Moriras en Chafarinas See Zafarinas (1994)

The Mormon Peril See Trapped by the Mormons (1922)

Morning Terror See Time Troopers (1989)

Mortal Sins See Dangerous Obsession (1988)

Morte a Venezia See Death in Venice (1971)

The Moscow Chronicle See Final Assignment (1980)

Moscow Distrusts Tears See Moscow Does Not Believe in Tears (1980)

Moscow Nights See I Stand Condemned (1936)

Moskwa Sljesam Nje Jerit See Moscow Does Not Believe in Tears (1980)

The Most Desired Man See Maybe ... Maybe Not (1994)

Mosura Tai Goira See Godzilla vs. Mothra (1964)

Motel See Pink Motel (1982)

Motel Vacancy See Talking Walls (1985)

Mother Goose A Go-Go See The Unkissed Bride (1966)

Mother Riley Meets the Vampire See My Son, the Vampire (1952)

Mothra vs. Godzilla See Godzilla vs. Mothra (1964)

Mountain of Cannibal Gods See Slave of the Cannibal God (1979)

Movie Struck See Pick a Star (1937)

The Moving Target See Harper (1966)

Mowgli and Baloo: Jungle Book 2 See Rudyard Kipling's the Second Jungle Book: Mowgli and Baloo (1997)

Mr. Scarface See Big Boss (1977)

Much Ado about Murder See Theatre of Blood (1973)

Mud See The Stick-Up (1977)

Muhomatsu no Issho See Rikisha-Man (1958)

Mujeres al Borde de un Ataque de Nervios See Women on the Verge of a Nervous Breakdown (1988)

The Mummy See Bram Stoker's The Mummy (1997)

Mumsy, Nanny, Sonny, and Girly See Girly (1970)

Munkbrogreven See The Count of the Old Town (1934)

Murder by Mail See Schizoid (1980)

Murder by Proxy See Blackout (1954)

The Murder in Thorton Square See Gaslight (1944)

Murder, Inc. See The Enforcer (1951)

Murder on Diamond Row See The Squeaker (1937)

Murder One See Death Sentence (1974)

The Murderer Dmitri Karamazov See The Brothers Karamazov (1958)

Muriel, Or the Time of Return See Muriel (1963)

Muriel, Ou le Temps d'Un Retour See Muriel (1963)

The Murri Affair See La Grande Bourgeoise (1974)

Music in Darkness See Night Is My Future (1947)

The Music Room See Jalsaghar (1958)

Mussolini: The Decline and Fall of Il Duce See Mussolini & I (1985)

Mutant See Forbidden World (1982)

The Mutation See The Freakmaker (1973)

Mutations See The Freakmaker (1973)

The Mutilator See The Dark (1979)

The Mutineers See Pirate Ship (1949)

Mutter Kusters Fahrt Zum Himmel See Mother Kusters Goes to Heaven (1976)

The Nights of Dracula *See* Count Dracula (1971)

Nijushi No Hitomi *See* Twenty-Four Eyes (1954)

9/30/55 *See* September 30, 1955 (1977)

1990 I Guerrieri del Bronx *See* 1990: The Bronx Warriors (1983)

1999—Nen No Natsu Yasumi *See* Summer Vacation: 1999 (1988)

Ningen No Joken *See* The Human Condition: Road to Eternity (1959)

Ninja Dragons *See* Magic Kid (1992)

Nippon Chiubotsu *See* Tidal Wave (1975)

Nippon Konchuki *See* The Insect Woman (1963)

No Fear *See* Fear (1996)

No Greater Love *See* The Human Condition: Road to Eternity (1959)

No Hambra mas Penas ni Olvido *See* Funny, Dirty Little War (1983)

No Knife *See* The Frisco Kid (1979)

No Man's Land *See* No Man's Range (1935)

No Place Like Homicide *See* What a Carve-Up! (1962)

The No-Tell Hotel *See* Rosebud Beach Hotel (1985)

No Worries *See* Clueless (1995)

Nobi *See* Fires on the Plain (1959)

Noce In Galilee *See* A Wedding in Galilee (1987)

Nocturna, Granddaughter of Dracula *See* Nocturna (1979)

Norman Rockwell's Breaking Home Ties *See* Breaking Home Ties (1987)

North Sea Hijack *See* ffolkes (1980)

The Northfield Cemetery Massacre *See* Northville Cemetery Massacre (1976)

Northwest Frontier *See* Flame Over India (1960)

Nosferatu, A Symphony of Horror *See* Nosferatu (1922)

Nosferatu, A Symphony of Terror *See* Nosferatu (1922)

Nosferatu, Eine Symphonie des Grauens *See* Nosferatu (1922)

Nosferatu, the Vampire *See* Nosferatu (1922)

Nostradamus No Daiyogen *See* Last Days of Planet Earth (1974)

Not Against the Flesh *See* Vampyr (1931)

Not Me *See* Sous Sol (1996)

Not Quite Jerusalem *See* Not Quite Paradise (1986)

Not Wanted *See* Streets of Sin (1949)

Nothing in Order *See* All Screwed Up (1974)

Nothing to Lose *See* Death in Brunswick (1990)

Notre Dame de Paris *See* The Hunchback of Notre Dame (1957)

Novecento *See* 1900 (1976)

Nowhere to Hide *See* Fatal Chase (1977)

Noz w Wodzie *See* Knife in the Water (1962)

Nuclear Run *See* Chain Reaction (1980)

Nuclear Terror *See* Golden Rendezvous (1977)

Nude in His Pocket *See* Girl in His Pocket (1957)

Nuit et Jour *See* Night and Day (1991)

Nuiyan, Seisap *See* Summer Snow (1994)

Number Two *See* Numero Deux (1975)

Numbered Days *See* Cycle Psycho (1972)

Nuovo Cinema Paradiso *See* Cinema Paradiso (1988)

Nurse Sherri *See* Hospital of Terror (1978)

The Nutcracker *See* George Balanchine's The Nutcracker (1993)

Nybyggarna *See* The New Land (1973)

Nyoka and the Lost Secrets of Hippocrates *See* Nyoka and the Tigermen (1942)

O Estranho Mundo de Ze do Caixao *See* Strange World of Coffin Joe (1968)

Oasis of the Zombies *See* Bloodsucking Nazi Zombies (1982)

Obch Od Na Korze *See* The Shop on Main Street (1965)

Obecna Skola *See* The Elementary School (1991)

Oblivion 2 *See* Backlash: Oblivion 2 (1995)

Obsession *See* The Hidden Room (1949)

Occhi Senza Volto *See* The Horror Chamber of Dr. Faustus (1959)

Ochoa *See* 8-A (1992)

Oci Ciornie *See* Dark Eyes (1987)

October *See* Ten Days That Shook the World (1927)

The Odd Couple 2 *See* Neil Simon's The Odd Couple 2 (1998)

Odio le Bionde *See* I Hate Blondes (1983)

Of a Thousand Delights *See* Sandra of a Thousand Delights (1965)

Of Death, of Love *See* Cemetery Man (1995)

Office Party *See* Hostile Takeover (1988)

The Official History *See* The Official Story (1985)

The Official Version *See* The Official Story (1985)

Oh, Charlie *See* Hold That Ghost (1941)

Oh Woe is Me *See* Helas pour Moi (1994)

Okasan *See* Mother (1952)

The Old and the New *See* The General Line (1929)

The Old Corral *See* Song of the Gringo (1936)

Old Friends *See* As Good As It Gets (1997)

Old Greatheart *See* Way Back Home (1932)

Old Heidelberg *See* The Student Prince in Old Heidelberg (1927)

Old Man *See* William Faulkner's Old Man (1997)

The Old Man and the Boy *See* The Two of Us (1968)

Old Mother Riley Meets the Vampire *See* My Son, the Vampire (1952)

Old Shatterhand *See* Apaches Last Battle (1964)

Olelkezo Tekintetek *See* Another Way (1982)

Omar Mukhtar *See* Lion of the Desert (1981)

The Omen 3 *See* The Final Conflict (1981)

On Connait la Chanson *See* Same Old Song (1997)

On Dangerous Ground *See* Jack Higgins' On Dangerous Ground (1995)

On the Great White Trail *See* Renfrew on the Great White Trail (1938)

On the Road Again *See* Honeysuckle Rose (1980)

Once Upon a Texas Train *See* Texas Guns (1990)

Once Upon a Time There Was a Country *See* Underground (1995)

One Born Every Minute *See* Flim-Flam Man (1967)

One Cup of Coffee *See* Pastime (1991)

One For All *See* The President's Mystery (1936)

One for Sorrow, Two for Joy *See* Signs of Life (1989)

One Horse Town *See* Small Town Girl (1953)

One Hundred Percent Pure *See* The Girl from Missouri (1934)

One-Man Mutiny *See* The Court Martial of Billy Mitchell (1955)

One Plus One *See* Sympathy for the Devil (1970)

One Way Out *See* Crazed Cop (1988)

Onkel Toms Hutte *See* Uncle Tom's Cabin (1969)

Only the French Can! *See* French Can-Can (1955)

Onna Ga Kaidan O Agaru Toki *See* When a Woman Ascends the Stairs (1960)

Oopsie Poopsie *See* Get Rita (1975)

Opera *See* Terror at the Opera (1988)

Operacione Paura *See* Kill, Baby, Kill (1966)

Operation Cicero *See* Five Fingers (1952)

Operation Kid Brother *See* Secret Agent 00 (1967)

Operation Overthrow *See* Power Play (1981)

Operation Serpent *See* Fer-De-Lance (1974)

Operation Snafu *See* On the Fiddle (1961)

Operation Undercover *See* Report to the Commissioner (1974)

Operation Warhead *See* On the Fiddle (1961)

Operazione Goldman *See* Lightning Bolt (1967)

Opium Connection *See* The Poppy Is Also a Flower (1966)

The Oracle *See* The Horse's Mouth (1958)

Orazi e Curiazi *See* Duel of Champions (1961)

Orca—Killer Whale *See* Orca (1977)

Order of Death *See* Corrupt (1984)

Orfeu Negro *See* Black Orpheus (1958)

Orgasmo *See* Paranoia (1969)

Orgy of the Dead *See* The Hanging Woman (1972)

Orkobefogadas *See* Adoption (1975)

Orloff Against the Invisible Man *See* The Invisible Dead (1970)

Orphee *See* Orpheus (1949)

Oru Kaiju Daishingeki *See* Godzilla's Revenge (1969)

Osenny Marafon *See* Autumn Marathon (1979)

Other People's Business *See* Way Back Home (1932)

The Other Side of Paradise *See* Foxtrot (1976)

Otto E Mezzo *See* 8 1/2 (1963)

Our Daily Bread *See* City Girl (1930)

Our Girl Friday *See* The Adventures of Sadie (1955)

Ourselves Alone *See* River of Unrest (1937)

Out of Rosenheim *See* Bagdad Cafe (1988)

Out of the Darkness *See* Night Creature (1979)

Out of the Darkness *See* Teenage Caveman (1958)

Out of the Night *See* Strange Illusion (1945)

Out of the Shadow *See* Murder on the Campus (1952)

Out on Probation *See* Daddy-O (1959)

Outback Vampires *See* The Wicked (1989)

The Outcast *See* Man in the Saddle (1951)

The Outcry *See* Il Grido (1957)

Outer Reach *See* Spaced Out (1980)

Outlaw Gun *See* A Minute to Pray, a Second to Die (1967)

Outomlionnye Solntsem *See* Burnt by the Sun (1994)

Outside In *See* Red, White & Busted (1975)

The Outsider *See* Fatal Error (1983)

The Outsider *See* The Guinea Pig (1948)

Outsider in Amsterdam *See* Fatal Error (1983)

The Outsiders *See* Band of Outsiders (1964)

Over Her Dead Body *See* Enid Is Sleeping (1990)

The Pace That Kills *See* Cocaine Fiends (1936)

The Pale Horse *See* Agatha Christie's The Pale Horse (1996)

Palomino *See* Danielle Steel's Palomino (1991)

Pamela Principle 2 *See* Seduce Me: Pamela Principle 2 (1994)

Pan Jin Lian Zhi Qian Shi Jin Sheng *See* The Reincarnation of Golden Lotus (1989)

Pane e Cioccolata *See* Bread and Chocolate (1974)

Panga *See* Curse 3: Blood Sacrifice (1990)

Panic *See* Panique (1947)

Panic at Lakewood Manor *See* Ants (1977)

Panic in the Trans-Siberian Train *See* Horror Express (1972)

Panic on the Trans-Siberian Express *See* Horror Express (1972)

Panico en el Transiberiano *See* Horror Express (1972)

Panny z Wilka *See* Maids of Wilko (1979)

Paoda Shuang Deng *See* Red Firecracker, Green Firecracker (1993)

Paper Bullets *See* Gangs, Inc. (1941)

The Parasite Murders *See* They Came from Within (1975)

Pardon Me, Your Teeth Are in My Neck *See* The Fearless Vampire Killers (1967)

Paris Brule-t-il? *See* Is Paris Burning? (1966)

Paris Does Strange Things *See* Elena and Her Men (1956)

Paris is Ours *See* Paris Belongs to Us (1960)

Paris Nous Appartient *See* Paris Belongs to Us (1960)

Paris Qui Dort *See* The Crazy Ray (1922)

Paris vu Par *See* Six in Paris (1968)

Park Plaza *See* Norman Conquest (1953)

Paroxismus *See* Venus in Furs (1970)

Parts: The Clonus Horror *See* The Clonus Horror (1979)

The Party *See* Can't Hardly Wait (1998)

Party Girls *See* Party Incorporated (1989)

Pasazerka *See* Passenger (1961)

Pasqualino Settebellezze *See* Seven Beauties (1976)

Pasqualino: Seven Beauties *See* Seven Beauties (1976)

Passages from "Finnegans Wake" *See* Finnegan's Wake (1963)

Passages from James Joyce's "Finnegans Wake" *See* Finnegan's Wake (1963)

The Passerby *See* La Passante (1983)

The Passion Flower Hotel *See* Boarding School (1983)

Passion Play *See* Love Letters (1983)

Passione d'Amore *See* Passion of Love (1982)

Passions *See* The Passing of Evil (1970)

Passport to Shame *See* Room 43 (1958)

The Patsy *See* L'Addition (1985)

Patterns of Power *See* Patterns (1956)

Patton: A Salute to a Rebel *See* Patton (1970)

Patton—Lust for Glory *See* Patton (1970)

Paul Bowles: Halbmond *See* Halfmoon (1995)

Pauline a la Plage *See* Pauline at the Beach (1983)

Paura Nella Citta Dei Morti Viventi *See* Gates of Hell (1983)

P.D. James: A Mind to Murder *See* A Mind to Murder (1996)

P.D. James' Devices & Desires *See* Devices and Desires (1991)

The Peace Game *See* The Gladiators (1970)

Peacemaker *See* The Ambassador (1984)

Peau D'Ane *See* Dos Cruces en Danger Pass (1971)

Peau d'Ane *See* Donkey Skin (1970)

The Peking Medallion *See* The Corrupt Ones (1967)

Penn of Pennsylvania *See* The Courageous Mr. Penn (1941)

Pensionat Oskar *See* Like It Never Was Before (1995)

People Toys *See* Devil Times Five (1974)

People's Enemy *See* Prison Train (1938)

Pepi, Luci, Bom y Otras Chicas del Monton *See* Pepi, Luci, Bom and Other Girls on the Heap (1980)

Percy's Progress *See* It's Not the Size That Counts (1974)

Peril en la Demeure *See* Peril (1985)

Perils from Planet Mongo *See* Flash Gordon: Rocketship (1936)

The Perils of Gwendoline in the Land of the Yik-Yak *See* The Perils of Gwendoline (1984)

Perils of Nyoka *See* Nyoka and the Tigermen (1942)

Persecution *See* The Graveyard (1974)

Persecution and Assassination of Jean-Paul Marat as Performed by the Inmates of the Asylum of Charenton Under the Direction of the Marquis De Sade *See* Marat/Sade (1966)

Perseus the Invincible *See* Medusa Against the Son of Hercules (1962)

Peter Rabbit and Tales of Beatrix Potter *See* Tales of Beatrix Potter (1971)

Petersen *See* Jock Petersen (1974)

Petroleum Girls *See* Legend of Frenchie King (1971)

Phantom Fiend *See* The Return of Dr. Mabuse (1961)

The Phantom of Terror *See* The Bird with the Crystal Plumage (1970)

Phantom of the Air *See* The Phantom Broadcast (1933)

Phantom of the Plains *See* Western Double Feature 7: Wild Bill & Crabbe (1945)

The Phantom Ship *See* The Mystery of the Mary Celeste (1937)

Phar Lap: Heart of a Nation *See* Phar Lap (1984)

Phenomena *See* Creepers (1985)

Philo Vance Returns *See* Infamous Crimes (1947)

Phoebe *See* Zelly & Me (1988)

The Phoenix *See* War of the Wizards (1981)

Pickup on 101 *See* Where the Eagle Flies (1972)

Pigsty *See* Porcile (1969)

Pilgrimage to Rome *See* L'Anne Sainte (1978)

Pillow of Death *See* Dead Man's Eyes/Pillow of Death (1944)

The Pilot *See* Danger in the Skies (1979)

Pinball Pick-Up *See* Pick-Up Summer (1979)

Pinball Summer *See* Pick-Up Summer (1979)

Pinocchio *See* The Adventures of Pinocchio (1996)

Pioneers *See* Pioneer Woman (1973)

Pippi Langstrump Pa de Sju Haven *See* Pippi in the South Seas (1974)

Piranha 2: Flying Killers *See* Piranha 2: The Spawning (1982)

Pirate's Fiancee *See* A Very Curious Girl (1969)

Pirate's Harbor *See* Haunted Harbor (1944)

The Pizza Connection *See* The Sicilian Connection (1985)

The Plains of Heaven *See* Panic Station (1982)

Planet of Horrors *See* Galaxy of Terror (1981)

Planet of Love *See* Galaxies Are Colliding (1992)

Planet of the Lifeless Men *See* Battle of the Worlds (1961)

The Plants Are Watching *See* The Kirlian Witness (1978)

Players *See* The Club (1981)

Playgirl Gang *See* Switchblade Sisters (1975)

The Playgirls and the Bellboy *See* The Bellboy and the Playgirls (1962)

Playing for Keeps *See* Lily in Love (1985)

Playtime *See* Love Play (1960)

Please! Mr. Balzac *See* Mademoiselle Striptease (1957)

Plein Soleil *See* Purple Noon (1960)

Plein Sud *See* Heat of Desire (1984)

Pluck of the Irish *See* Great Guy (1936)

Po Dezju *See* Before the Rain (1994)

Pocomania *See* The Devil's Daughter (1939)

Poe's Tales of Terror *See* Tales of Terror (1962)

Poisoned by Love: The Kern County Murders *See* Murder So Sweet (1993)

Pokayaniye *See* Repentance (1987)

Police Assassins *See* Royal Warriors (1986)

Police Connection *See* The Mad Bomber (1972)

Police Force *See* Police Story (1985)

Police Story 3: Supercop *See* Supercop (1992)

Police Story 4 *See* Jackie Chan's First Strike (1996)

Poncomania *See* The Devil's Daughter (1939)

Pony Express *See* Peter Lundy and the Medicine Hat Stallion (1977)

Pookie *See* The Sterile Cuckoo (1969)

Poopsie *See* Get Rita (1975)

Poor Albert and Little Annie *See* I Dismember Mama (1974)

The Poor Outlaws *See* The Round Up (1966)

The Pope Must Die *See* The Pope Must Diet (1991)

Popiol i Diament *See* Ashes and Diamonds (1958)

Poppies Are Also Flowers *See* The Poppy Is Also a Flower (1966)

Porte Aperte *See* Open Doors (1989)

Portrait of a Woman, Nude *See* Nudo di Donna (1983)

Portrait of Alison *See* Postmark for Danger (1956)

Portrait of Maria *See* Maria Candelaria (1946)

Portraits of Innocence *See* Portraits of a Killer (1995)

Potemkin *See* The Battleship Potemkin (1925)

Potop *See* The Deluge (1973)

Practice Makes Perfect *See* Le Cavaleur (1978)

Prairie Outlaws *See* Wild West (1946)

Prairie Rustlers *See* Western Double Feature 7: Wild Bill & Crabbe (1945)

Pratidwandi *See* The Adversary (1971)

Pre *See* Without Limits (1997)

Precious *See* Citizen Ruth (1996)

Pred dozhdot *See* Before the Rain (1994)

The Prehistoric Sound *See* Sound of Horror (1964)

Prehistoric World *See* Teenage Caveman (1958)

Prenom: Carmen *See* First Name: Carmen (1983)

Preparez Vous Mouchoirs *See* Get Out Your Handkerchiefs (1978)

Preppies *See* Making the Grade (1984)

The President's Women *See* Foreplay (1975)

Pret-a-Porter *See* Ready to Wear (1994)

Pride of Kentucky *See* The Story of Seabiscuit (1949)

Prince of Jutland *See* Royal Deceit (1994)

Priority Red One *See* Delta Force Commando 2 (1990)

Prison *See* Devil's Wanton (1949)

The Prisoner *See* Cold Room (1984)

Prisoner of the Caucasus *See* Prisoner of the Mountains (1996)

The Private Life of Paul Joseph Goebbels *See* Enemy of Women (1944)

The Private Lives of Elizabeth and Essex *See* Elizabeth, the Queen (1968)

Private Snuffy Smith *See* Snuffy Smith, Yard Bird (1942)

The Private Wore Skirts *See* Never Wave at a WAC (1952)

Profession: Reporter *See* The Passenger (1975)

The Profile of Terror *See* The Sadist (1963)

Profumo di Donna *See* The Scent of a Woman (1975)

Profundo Rosso *See* Deep Red: Hatchet Murders (1975)

Project Shadowchaser 2 *See* Night Siege Project: Shadowchaser 2 (1994)

Prom Night 2 *See* Hello Mary Lou: Prom Night 2 (1987)

The Promise *See* La Promesse (1996)

Promise Her Anything *See* Promises! Promises! (1963)

The Promise of Red Lips *See* Daughters of Darkness (1971)

The Promised Land *See* Legal Deceit (1995)

Prophecies of Nostradamus *See* Last Days of Planet Earth (1974)

A Proposito Luciano *See* Lucky Luciano (1974)

Prorva *See* Moscow Parade (1992)

The Protectors, Book One *See* Angel of H.E.A.T. (1982)

Proud, Damned, and Dead *See* The Proud and the Damned (1972)

Prova d'Orchestra *See* Orchestra Rehearsal (1978)

Przesluchanie *See* The Interrogation (1982)

Psycho a Go Go! *See* Blood of Ghastly Horror (1972)

Psycho-Circus *See* Circus of Fear (1967)

Psycho Killers *See* Mania (1960)

Psycho Puppet *See* Delirium (1977)

Psycho Sex Fiend *See* The House that Vanished (1973)

Psycho Sisters *See* The Sibling (1972)

Psychotic *See* Driver's Seat (1973)

Ptang, Yang, Kipperbang *See* Kipperbang (1982)

Public Be Damned *See* The World Gone Mad (1933)

The Public Be Hanged *See* The World Gone Mad (1933)

Puo Una Morta Rivivere Per Amore? *See* Venus in Furs (1970)

The Pupil *See* L'Eleve (1995)

The Purim Player *See* Der Purimshpiler (1937)

Purple Death from Outer Space *See* Flash Gordon Conquers the Universe (1940)

The Purple Riders *See* Purple Vigilantes (1938)

Pursuit *See* Apache Blood (1975)

Putyovka V Zhizn *See* The Road to Life (1931)

Q Planes *See* Clouds Over Europe (1939)

Q: The Winged Serpent *See* Q (The Winged Serpent) (1982)

Qiuyue *See* Autumn Moon (1992)

Quai des Orfevres *See* Jenny Lamour (1947)

Qualcosa di Biondo *See* Aurora (1984)

Quando De Donne Avevando La Coda *See* When Women Had Tails (1970)

Que He Hecho Yo Para Merecer Estol? *See* What Have I Done to Deserve This? (1985)

Que La Bete Meure *See* This Man Must Die (1970)

Queen of Blood *See* Planet of Blood (1966)

Queen of Broadway *See* Kid Dynamite (1943)

Queen of the Cannibals *See* Doctor Butcher M.D. (1980)

Queen of the Gorillas *See* The Bride & the Beast (1958)

The Queen's Husband *See* The Royal Bed (1931)

Quei Temerari Sulle Loro Pazze, Scatenate, Scalcinate Carriole *See* Those Daring Young Men in Their Jaunty Jalopies (1969)

Quella Villa Accanto Al Cimitero *See* The House by the Cemetery (1983)

Quelqu' Un Derriere la Porte *See* Someone Behind the Door (1971)

Quemimada! *See* Burn! (1970)

The Quest *See* The Longest Drive (1976)

Qui Ju Da Guansi *See* The Story of Qui Ju (1991)

Quien Sabe? *See* A Bullet for the General (1968)

A Quiet Little Neighborhood, A Perfect Little Murder *See* A Perfect Little Murder (1990)

A Quiet Place to Kill *See* Paranoia (1969)

Quoi De Neuf, Pussycat? *See* What's New Pussycat? (1965)

Race for the Yankee Zephyr *See* Treasure of the Yankee Zephyr (1983)

Racket Girls *See* Pin Down Girls (1951)

The Radical *See* Katherine (1975)

Radio Ranch *See* The Phantom Empire (1935)

Radon *See* Rodan (1956)

Radon the Flying Monster *See* Rodan (1956)

Rafferty and the Highway Hustlers *See* Rafferty & the Gold Dust Twins (1975)

Rage *See* Rabid (1977)

Rage of the Buccaneers *See* The Black Pirate (1926)

Ragewar *See* Dungeonmaster (1983)

Ragged Angels *See* They Shall Have Music (1939)

The Raging Moon *See* Long Ago Tomorrow (1971)

Raging Waters *See* The Green Promise (1949)

Ragno Gelido *See* Dial Help (1988)

Rags to Riches *See* Callie and Son (1981)

Raiders of the Doomed Kingdom *See* After the Fall of Saigon (1988)

Rainbow on the River *See* It Happened in New Orleans (1936)

The Rainmaker *See* John Grisham's The Rainmaker (1997)

Raise Ravens *See* Cria (1976)

Ramblin' Man *See* The Concrete Cowboys (1979)

Ramrodders *See* The Ramrodder (1969)

The Ranger, the Cook and a Hole in the Sky *See* Hole in the Sky (1995)

Ransom *See* Maniac (1977)

Rape of Innocence *See* Dupont Lajoie (1974)

The Rape of Richard Beck *See* Broken Badge (1985)

Rape Squad *See* Act of Vengeance (1974)

Rasputin: The Mad Monk *See* Rasputin and the Empress (1933)

The Rats *See* Deadly Eyes (1982)

The Raven *See* Le Corbeau (1943)

Re-Animator 2 *See* Bride of Re-Animator (1989)

RE: Lucky Luciano *See* Lucky Luciano (1974)

The Reader *See* La Lectrice (1988)

The Rebel *See* The Bushwackers (1952)

Rebel of the Road *See* Hot Rod (1979)

Rebel with a Cause *See* The Loneliness of the Long Distance Runner (1962)

Rebellion *See* Samurai Rebellion (1967)

Rece do Gory *See* Hands Up (1981)

Record of a Living Being *See* I Live in Fear (1955)

Red *See* Trois Couleurs: Rouge (1994)

Red Dragon *See* Code Name Alpha (1967)

Red Dragon *See* Manhunter (1986)

The Red Hangman *See* The Bloody Pit of Horror (1965)

The Red Head *See* Poil de Carotte (1931)

Red Hot Tires *See* Racing Luck (1935)

Red Hot Wheels *See* To Please a Lady (1950)

Red-Light District *See* Street of Shame (1956)

The Red Lips *See* Daughters of Darkness (1971)

Red Nightmare *See* The Commies Are Coming, the Commies Are Coming (1957)

Red on Red *See* Scarred (1984)

The Red Sign of Madness *See* Hatchet for the Honeymoon (1970)

The Red Tide *See* Blood Tide (1982)

The Redeemer *See* Class Reunion Massacre (1977)

Redheads *See* Desperate Prey (1994)

Redneck County *See* Hootch Country Boys (1975)

Redneck County *See* Poor Pretty Eddie (1973)

Reed, Mexico Insurgente *See* Reed: Insurgent Mexico (1973)

Reflections on a Crime *See* Reflections in the Dark (1994)

The Refugee *See* Three Faces West (1940)

Rehearsal for a Crime *See* The Criminal Life of Archibaldo de la Cruz (1955)

Rejuvenatrix *See* The Rejuvenator (1988)

Rekopis Znaleziony W Saragossie *See* The Saragossa Manuscript (1965)

Religious Racketeers *See* Mystic Circle Murder (1939)

The Remarkable Mr. Kipps *See* Kipps (1941)

Remembrance of Love *See* Holocaust Survivors...Remembrance of Love (1983)

Remorques *See* Stormy Waters (1941)

Renegade Girls *See* Caged Heat (1974)

Renfrew of the Royal Mounted on the Great White Trail *See* Renfrew on the Great White Trail (1938)

Reprieved *See* Sing Sing Nights (1935)

Requiem fur Dominic *See* Requiem for Dominic (1991)

The Rescue *See* Let's Get Harry (1987)

The Resurrection Syndicate *See* Nothing But the Night (1972)

Retaliator *See* Programmed to Kill (1986)

Retik, the Moon Menace *See* Radar Men from the Moon (1952)

Return from the Past *See* Alien Massacre (1967)

The Return of Captain America *See* Captain America (1944)

The Return of Maxwell Smart *See* The Nude Bomb (1980)

The Return of Mr. H. *See* They Saved Hitler's Brain (1964)

Return of the Blind Dead *See* Return of the Evil Dead (1975)

The Return of the Duchess Dracula *See* Devil's Wedding Night (1973)

The Return of the Giant Monsters *See* Gamera vs. Gaos (1967)

Return of the Living Dead *See* Messiah of Evil (1974)

Return of the Magnificent Seven *See* Return of the Seven (1966)

Return of the Texas Chainsaw Massacre *See* The Texas Chainsaw Massacre 4: The Next Generation (1995)

Return of the Wolfman *See* The Craving (1980)

Return of the Zombies *See* The Hanging Woman (1972)

Reunion *See* Reunion in France (1942)

Revenge *See* Blood Feud (1979)

Revenge of Dracula *See* Dracula, Prince of Darkness (1966)

The Revenge of Dracula *See* Dracula vs. Frankenstein (1971)

The Revenge of Milady *See* The Four Musketeers (1975)

The Revenge of the Blood Beast *See* The She-Beast (1965)

Revenge of the Dead *See* Night of the Ghouls (1959)

Revenge of the Innocents *See* South Bronx Heroes (1985)

Revenge of the Living Dead *See* Children Shouldn't Play with Dead Things (1972)

Revenge of the Screaming Dead *See* Messiah of Evil (1974)

Revenge of the Vampire *See* Black Sunday (1960)

Revenge of the Zombie *See* Kiss Daddy Goodbye (1981)

Revenge Squad *See* Hit & Run (1982)

Rhodes of Africa *See* Rhodes (1936)

Rhosyn A Rhith *See* Coming Up Roses (1987)

Rhythm on the Ranch *See* Rootin' Tootin' Rhythm (1938)

Rice, Beans and Ketchup *See* Manhattan Merenque! (1995)

Rich, Young, and Deadly *See* Platinum High School (1960)

Riches and Romance *See* Amazing Adventure (1937)

The Richest Man in the World: The Story of Aristotle Onassis *See* Onassis (1988)

Richie *See* The Death of Richie (1976)

Rickshaw Man *See* Rikisha-Man (1958)

Ride a Dark Horse *See* Man & Boy (1971)

Riders *See* Guerilla Brigade (1939)

Riffraff *See* Riff Raff (1935)

The Right Man *See* Her First Romance (1940)

Riot *See* Riot in the Streets (1996)

Ripped Off *See* Counter Punch (1971)

Risate de Gioia *See* Passionate Thief (1960)

The Rise of Catherine the Great *See* Catherine the Great (1934)

The Rise of Helga *See* Susan Lenox: Her Fall and Rise (1931)

Rising to Fame *See* Susan Lenox: Her Fall and Rise (1931)

Riso Amaro *See* Bitter Rice (1949)

Riten *See* The Rite (1969)

Rites of Summer *See* White Water Summer (1987)

The Ritual *See* The Rite (1969)

Ritual Dos Sadicos *See* Awakenings of the Beast (1968)

Ritual of the Maniacs *See* Awakenings of the Beast (1968)

The Road *See* La Strada (1954)

Road to Avonlea *See* Tales from Avonlea, Vol. 1: The Journey Begins (1990)

The Road to Frisco *See* They Drive by Night (1940)

Roaring Timber *See* Come and Get It (1936)

Rob Roy *See* Rob Roy—The Highland Rogue (1953)

Robert A. Heinlein's The Puppet Masters *See* The Puppet Masters (1994)

Robinson Crusoeland *See* Utopia (1951)

Rocco E I Suoi Fratelli *See* Rocco and His Brothers (1960)

Rocco et Ses Freres *See* Rocco and His Brothers (1960)

Rock and Roll Wrestling Women Vs. the Aztec Mummy *See* Wrestling Women vs. the Aztec Mummy (1959)

Rocket Man *See* RocketMan (1997)

Rocket to the Moon *See* Cat Women of the Moon (1953)

Rocky Mountain Mystery *See* The Fighting Westerner (1935)

Rodgers & Hammerstein's Cinderella *See* Cinderella (1997)

Roger Corman Presents: Black Scorpion *See* Black Scorpion (1995)

Roger Corman Presents Burial of the Rats *See* Burial of the Rats (1995)

Roger Corman Presents: House of the Damned *See* Spectre (1996)

Roger Corman Presents: Humanoids from the Deep *See* Humanoids from the Deep (1996)

Roger Corman Presents Last Exit to Earth *See* Last Exit to Earth (1996)

Roger Corman Presents Subliminal Seduction *See* The Corporation (1996)

Roger Corman Presents: Suspect Device *See* Suspect Device (1995)

Roger Corman Presents: The Alien Within *See* Unknown Origin (1995)

Roger Corman Presents: Vampirella *See* Vampirella (1996)

Roger Corman's Frankenstein Unbound *See* Frankenstein Unbound (1990)

Roma *See* Fellini's Roma (1972)

Roma, Citta Aperta *See* Open City (1945)

Romance and Riches *See* Amazing Adventure (1937)

Romance da Empregada *See* The Story of Fausta (1988)

Romauld et Juliet *See* Mama, There's a Man in Your Bed (1989)

Rome, Open City *See* Open City (1945)

Romeo and Juliet *See* William Shakespeare's Romeo and Juliet (1996)

Romeo in Pyjamas *See* Parlor, Bedroom and Bath (1931)

Romeo, Julia a Tma *See* Sweet Light in a Dark Room (1960)

Romeo, Juliet and Darkness *See* Sweet Light in a Dark Room (1960)

Rommel—Desert Fox *See* The Desert Fox (1951)

Rona Jaffe's Mazes and Monsters *See* Mazes and Monsters (1982)

The Rook *See* Something for Everyone (1970)

Rookies *See* Buck Privates (1941)

Rookies Come Home *See* Buck Privates Come Home (1947)

The Rose and the Sword *See* Flesh and Blood (1985)

Roseanna's Grave *See* For Roseanna (1996)

Rosemary's Killer *See* The Prowler (1981)

The Rotten Apple *See* Five Minutes to Love (1963)

Rouge Baiser *See* Red Kiss (1985)

Rough Company *See* The Violent Men (1955)

Rough Treatment *See* Without Anesthesia (1978)

Roxanne: The Prize Pulitzer *See* The Prize Pulitzer (1989)

Ruby Cairo See Deception (1992)

Rudyard Kipling's Jungle Book See The Jungle Book (1942)

Rue Cases Negres See Sugar Cane Alley (1983)

Rules of Obsession See A Passion to Kill (1994)

Rumpo Kid See Carry On Cowboy (1966)

Run, Simon, Run See Savage Run (1970)

The Runaways See South Bronx Heroes (1985)

Russicum See Third Solution (1989)

Rustler's Roundup See Rustler's Hideout (1944)

The Rutles See All You Need Is Cash (1978)

The Saboteur See Morituri (1965)

Saboteur: Code Name Morituri See Morituri (1965)

The Sabre and the Arrow See Last of the Comanches (1952)

The Sabre Tooth Tiger See Deep Red: Hatchet Murders (1975)

Sabrina Fair See Sabrina (1954)

Sacco e Vanzetti See Sacco & Vanzetti (1971)

Sadko See The Magic Voyage of Sinbad (1952)

The Saga of Dracula See The Saga of the Draculas (1972)

The Saga of Gosta Berling See The Atonement of Gosta Berling (1924)

The Saga of the Road See Pather Panchali (1954)

Saikaku Ichidai Onna See Life of Oharu (1952)

St. George and the Dragon See The Magic Sword (1962)

St. George and the Seven Curses See The Magic Sword (1962)

St. Martin's Lane See Sidewalks of London (1938)

Sakima and the Masked Marvel See The Masked Marvel (1943)

The Salamander See La Salamandre (1971)

Salem's Ghost See Witchcraft 8: Salem's Ghost (1995)

Salerno Beachhead See A Walk in the Sun (1946)

The Salute of the Jugger See The Blood of Heroes (1989)

Salvation! Have You Said Your Prayers Today? See Salvation! (1987)

Sam Cooper's Gold See The Ruthless Four (1970)

Sam Marlowe, Private Eye See The Man with Bogart's Face (1980)

The Samurai See Le Samourai (1967)

San Fernando See San Fernando Valley (1944)

San Michele Aveva un Gallo See St. Michael Had a Rooster (1972)

Sanda Tai Gailah See War of the Gargantuas (1970)

Sandakan House 8 See Sandakan No. 8 (1974)

Sandkings See The Outer Limits: Sandkings (1995)

The Sandpit Generals See Defiant (1970)

Sandra See Sandra of a Thousand Delights (1965)

Sans Toit Ni Loi See Vagabond (1985)

Sansho Dayu See Sansho the Bailiff (1954)

Santa Claus Defeats the Aliens See Santa Claus Conquers the Martians (1964)

Santo en el Museo de Cera See Samson in the Wax Museum (1963)

Santo in the Wax Museum See Samson in the Wax Museum (1963)

Sarajevo See De Mayerling a Sarajevo (1940)

Satan See Mark of the Devil (1969)

Satanic Mechanic See Perfect Killer (1977)

Satan's Bloody Freaks See Dracula vs. Frankenstein (1971)

Satan's Claw See The Blood on Satan's Claw (1971)

Satan's Daughters See Vampyres (1974)

Satan's Dog See Play Dead (1981)

Satan's Mistress See Demon Rage (1982)

Satan's Satellites See Zombies of the Stratosphere (1952)

Satan's Skin See The Blood on Satan's Claw (1971)

Satan's Supper See Cataclysm (1981)

Satansbraten See Satan's Brew (1976)

Satellite of Blood See First Man into Space (1959)

Satin Vengeance See Naked Vengeance (1985)

Saturday Island See Island of Desire (1952)

Satyricon See Fellini Satyricon (1969)

Saul e David See Saul and David (1968)

The Savage See Lovers Like Us (1975)

Savage Abduction See Cycle Psycho (1972)

Savage Apocalypse See Invasion of the Flesh Hunters (1982)

Savage Beasts See The Wild Beasts (1985)

Savage Nights See Les Nuits Fauves (1992)

The Savage State See L'Etat Sauvage (1978)

Sayat Nova See The Color of Pomegranates (1969)

Scaramouche See Loves & Times of Scaramouche (1976)

Scared Stiff See Treasure of Fear (1945)

The Scaremaker See Girls Night Out (1983)

Scarface: The Shame of a Nation See Scarface (1931)

Scarlet Buccaneer See Swashbuckler (1976)

The Scarlet Buccaneer See Swashbuckler (1984)

Scary Movie See Scream (1996)

Schatten der Engel See Shadow of Angels (1976)

Scherben See Shattered (1921)

Schlafes Bruder See Brother of Sleep (1995)

Schloss Vogelod See The Haunted Castle (1921)

The School That Ate My Brain See Zombie High (1987)

Schwestern Oder die Balance des Glucks See Sisters, Or the Balance of Happiness (1979)

The Scotland Yard Mystery See The Living Dead (1936)

Scoundrel in White See High Heels (1972)

Scream See The Night God Screamed (198?)

Scream Again See Scream 2 (1997)

Scream and Die See The House that Vanished (1973)

Scream Free! See Free Grass (1969)

Screamer See Scream and Scream Again (1970)

Screwface See Marked for Death (1990)

Scrooge See A Christmas Carol (1951)

Scum of the Earth See Poor White Trash 2 (1975)

Search for the Mother Lode See Mother Lode (1982)

Searchers of the Voodoo Mountain See Warriors of the Apocalypse (1985)

Season of Dreams See Stacking (1987)

Seated At His Right See Black Jesus (1968)

Second Chances See Probation (1932)

The Second Coming See Messiah of Evil (1974)

The Second Jungle Book: Mowgli and Baloo See Rudyard Kipling's the Second Jungle Book: Mowgli and Baloo (1997)

Seconds to Live See Viva Knievel (1977)

The Secret Cinema See Paul Bartel's The Secret Cinema (1969)

Secret File: Hollywood See Secret File of Hollywood (1962)

Secret Honor: A Political Myth See Secret Honor (1985)

Secret Honor: The Last Testament of Richard M. Nixon See Secret Honor (1985)

The Secret of Dr. Mabuse See The Thousand Eyes of Dr. Mabuse (1960)

The Secret of Dorian Gray See Dorian Gray (1970)

Secret Paper WB1 See Geheimakte WB1 (1942)

The Secret Stranger See Rough Riding Rangers (1935)

Secret Weapon See Sherlock Holmes and the Secret Weapon (1942)

Secrets of the Red Bedroom See Secret Weapons (1985)

Seddok, l'Erede di Satana See Atom Age Vampire (1961)

Sedotta e Abbandonata See Seduced and Abandoned (1964)

The Seducer's Diary See Diary of a Seducer (1995)

The Seductress See The Teacher (1974)

Seduta Alla Sua Destra See Black Jesus (1968)

Seed of Terror See Grave of the Vampire (1972)

The Seekers See Land of Fury (1955)

Seishun Zanoku Monogatari See The Cruel Story of Youth (1960)

Sengoku Gunto-Den See Saga of the Vagabond (1959)

Senior Trip See National Lampoon's Senior Trip (1995)

Sensations See Sensations of 1945 (1944)

Sensuous Vampires See The Vampire Hookers (1978)

Separate Beds See The Wheeler Dealers (1963)

Sept Fois Femme See Woman Times Seven (1967)

Sergeant Steiner See Breakthrough (1978)

The Serpent See Night Flight from Moscow (1973)

Seryozha See A Summer to Remember (1961)

Sette Volte Donna See Woman Times Seven (1967)

Se7en See Seven (1995)

Seven Bad Men See Rage at Dawn (1955)

Seven Different Ways See Quick, Let's Get Married (1971)

Seven Graves for Rogan See Time to Die (1983)

Seven Sisters See The House on Sorority Row (1983)

Seven Waves Away See Abandon Ship (1957)

Sex Crime of the Century *See* Last House on the Left (1972)

The Sex of the Stars *See* Le Sexe des Etoiles (1993)

Sex Play *See* Games Girls Play (1975)

The Sex Racketeers *See* Man of Violence (1971)

Shadow of the Werewolf *See* The Werewolf vs. the Vampire Woman (1970)

The Shadow Versus the Thousand Eyes of Dr. Mabuse *See* The Thousand Eyes of Dr. Mabuse (1960)

The Shadow Warrior *See* Kagemusha (1980)

Shadows in an Empty Room *See* Strange Shadows in an Empty Room (1976)

Shadows of Our Ancestors *See* Shadows of Forgotten Ancestors (1964)

Shadows of Our Forgotten Ancestors *See* Shadows of Forgotten Ancestors (1964)

Shadows of the Peacock *See* Echoes of Paradise (1986)

Shakespeare's Sister *See* The Proposition (1997)

Shalimar *See* Deadly Thief (1978)

Shame of the Sabine Women *See* The Rape of the Sabines (1961)

Shanghai Express *See* The Millionaire's Express (1986)

Shark Reef *See* She Gods of Shark Reef (1956)

Shatter *See* Call Him Mr. Shatter (1974)

Shatterhand *See* Apaches Last Battle (1964)

She Demons of the Swamp *See* Attack of the Giant Leeches (1959)

She Devil *See* Drums O'Voodoo (1934)

She Drives Me Crazy *See* Friends, Lovers & Lunatics (1989)

She Got What She Asked For *See* Yesterday, Today and Tomorrow (1964)

She Knew No Other Way *See* Last Resort (1986)

She Monster of the Night *See* Frankenstein's Daughter (1958)

She Shoulda Said No *See* Wild Weed (1949)

She Was a Hippy Vampire *See* The Wild World of Batwoman (1966)

Sheba *See* The Graveyard (1974)

She'll Be Sweet *See* Magee and the Lady (1978)

Shenanigans *See* Great Bank Hoax (1978)

Sheriff of Wichita *See* Western Double Feature 4: Rogers & Evans (194?)

Sherlock Holmes *See* The Adventures of Sherlock Holmes (1939)

Sherlock Holmes and the Prince of Crime *See* Hands of a Murderer (1990)

Sherlock Holmes and the Scarlet Claw *See* Scarlet Claw (1944)

Sherlock Holmes and the Spider Woman *See* Spider Woman (1944)

Sherlock Holmes and the Woman in Green *See* The Woman in Green (1945)

Sherlock Holmes Grosster Fall *See* A Study in Terror (1966)

Sherlock Holmes in The Hound of London *See* The Hound of London (1993)

Sherlock Holmes Und Das Halsband des Todes *See* Sherlock Holmes and the Deadly Necklace (1962)

She's De Lovely *See* She's So Lovely (1997)

Shichinin No Samurai *See* Seven Samurai (1954)

Shinju Ten No Amijima *See* Double Suicide (1969)

The Ship was Loaded *See* Carry On Admiral (1957)

Shivers *See* They Came from Within (1975)

Shizuka Naru Ketto *See* A Quiet Duel (1949)

Shock *See* Beyond the Door 2 (1979)

Shock (Transfer Suspense Hypnos) *See* Beyond the Door 2 (1979)

Shocked *See* Mesmerized (1984)

Shockwave *See* The Arrival (1996)

Shogun Island *See* Raw Force (1981)

Shoot the Pianist *See* Shoot the Piano Player (1962)

The Shooter *See* Hidden Assassin (1994)

The Shop on High Street *See* The Shop on Main Street (1965)

Shuban *See* Scandal (1950)

Shut Up and Dance *See* Dance With Me (1998)

The Shuttered Room *See* Blood Island (1968)

Sidney Sheldon's Windmills of the Gods *See* Windmills of the Gods (1988)

Siegfried's Death *See* Siegfried (1924)

Siegfrieds Tod *See* Siegfried (1924)

Signe Charlotte *See* Sincerely Charlotte (1986)

Significant Other *See* When a Man Loves a Woman (1994)

The Silence of the Sea *See* La Silence de la Mer (1947)

Silencio de Neto *See* The Silence of Neto (1994)

A Silent Duel *See* A Quiet Duel (1949)

The Silent Flute *See* Circle of Iron (1978)

Silent Night, Evil Night *See* Black Christmas (1975)

Silken Skin *See* The Soft Skin (1964)

Silver Blaze *See* Murder at the Baskervilles (1937)

The Silver Brumby *See* The Silver Stallion: King of the Wild Brumbies (1993)

Silver Devil *See* Wild Horse (1931)

The Sin *See* The Shaming (1971)

Sinai Commandos: The Story of the Six Day War *See* Sinai Commandos (1968)

The Singing Musketeer *See* The Three Musketeers (1939)

Sinister House *See* Who Killed Doc Robbin? (1948)

Sista Dansen *See* The Last Dance (1993)

The Sister of Satan *See* The She-Beast (1965)

Sisters *See* Some Girls (1988)

Sitting Bull's History Lesson *See* Buffalo Bill & the Indians (1976)

The Sixth of June *See* D-Day, the Sixth of June (1956)

Sizzle Beach U.S.A. *See* Malibu Hot Summer (1974)

Skate! *See* Blades of Courage (1988)

Ski Lift to Death *See* Snowblind (1978)

Skipper *See* The Todd Killings (1971)

Skyggen af Emma *See* Emma's Shadow (1988)

The Slammer *See* Short Eyes (1979)

The Slasher *See* Cosh Boy (1961)

Slasher in the House *See* Home Sweet Home (1980)

The Slaughterers *See* Invasion of the Flesh Hunters (1982)

Slave Girls *See* Prehistoric Women (1950)

Slaves of the Invisible Monster *See* The Invisible Monster (1950)

Slay It Again, Sam *See* Codename: Foxfire (1985)

Slip Slide Adventures *See* Water Babies (1979)

Small Town Massacre *See* Strange Behavior (1981)

Smart Alec *See* Movie Maker (1986)

Smokey and the Bandit Ride Again *See* Smokey and the Bandit, Part 2 (1980)

Smorgasbord *See* Cracking Up (1983)

Smultron-Stallet *See* Wild Strawberries (1957)

Snake Eyes *See* Dangerous Game (1993)

Snow White and the Three Clowns *See* Snow White and the Three Stooges (1961)

Snow White in the Black Forest *See* Snow White: A Tale of Terror (1997)

Snuffy Smith *See* Snuffy Smith, Yard Bird (1942)

So Evil, My Sister *See* The Sibling (1972)

So Sweet, So Perverse *See* Kiss Me, Kill Me (1969)

Social Suicide *See* Pre-Madonnas: Rebels Without a Clue (1995)

Sodome et Gomorrhe *See* Sodom and Gomorrah (1962)

Soldier Duroc *See* Soldat Duroc...Ca Va Etre Ta Fete! (196?)

Soldier in Skirts *See* Triple Echo (1977)

The Soldier Who Declared Peace *See* Tribes (1970)

The Soldiers *See* Les Carabiniers (1963)

Solomon Northrup's Odyssey *See* Half Slave, Half Free (1985)

Sombra, the Spider Woman *See* The Black Widow (1947)

Some Like It Cool *See* Sex on the Run (1978)

Someone is Killing the Great Chefs of Europe *See* Who Is Killing the Great Chefs of Europe? (1978)

Someone's Killing the World's Greatest Models *See* She's Dressed to Kill (1979)

Something Fishy *See* Pas Tres Catholique (1993)

Something is Out There *See* Day of the Animals (1977)

Something Like the Truth *See* The Offence (1973)

Something to Hide *See* Shattered (1972)

Something Waits in the Dark *See* Screamers (1980)

Somewhere in France *See* The Foreman Went to France (1942)

Sommarlek *See* Summer Interlude (1950)

Sommarnattens Leende *See* Smiles of a Summer Night (1955)

Son of Darkness: To Die For 2 *See* To Die For 2: Son of Darkness (1991)

Son of My Life *See* Hijazo de Mi Vidaza (197?)

The Song of the Road *See* Pather Panchali (1954)

Song of the Sierra *See* Springtime in the Sierras (1947)

Sons and Warriors *See* Some Mother's Son (1996)

Sons of the Legion *See* Sons of the Desert (1933)

Sons of the Musketeers *See* At Sword's Point (1951)

Sophie's Place *See* Crooks & Coronets (1969)

Sotto gli Occhi dell'Assassino *See* Unsane (1982)

Soul *See* Earth (1930)

Sound From a Million Years Ago *See* Sound of Horror (1964)

Sound of Fury *See* Try and Get Me (1950)

Soup to Nuts *See* Waitress (1981)

Sous le Soleil de Satan *See* Under Satan's Sun (1987)

Sous les Toits de Paris *See* Under the Roofs of Paris (1929)

South of Panama *See* Panama Menace (1941)

South Sea Woman *See* Pearl of the South Pacific (1955)

Southwest to Sonora *See* The Appaloosa (1966)

Space 2074 *See* Star Quest (1989)

The Space Amoeba *See* Yog, Monster from Space (1971)

Space Avenger *See* Alien Space Avenger (1991)

Space Invasion from Lapland *See* Invasion of the Animal People (1962)

Space Invasion of Lapland *See* Invasion of the Animal People (1962)

Space Men *See* Assignment Outer Space (1961)

Space Men Appear in Tokyo *See* Warning from Space (1956)

Space Mission of the Lost Planet *See* Horror of the Blood Monsters (1970)

Space Monster Dagora *See* Dagora, the Space Monster (1965)

Space Mutants *See* Planet of the Vampires (1965)

Space Soldiers *See* Flash Gordon: Rocketship (1936)

Space Travellers *See* Marooned (1969)

Spaceship to the Unknown *See* Flash Gordon: Rocketship (1936)

Spara Forte, Piu Forte...Non Capisco *See* Shoot Loud, Louder, I Don't Understand! (1966)

Spawn *See* Todd McFarlane's Spawn (1997)

The Specter of Freedom *See* Phantom of Liberty (1974)

Speed Brent Wins *See* Breed of the Border (1933)

The Spell of Amy Nugent *See* Spellbound (1941)

Spell of the Hypnotist *See* Fright (1956)

Spettri *See* Specters (1987)

The Spider *See* Earth vs. the Spider (1958)

Spider Baby, or the Maddest Story Ever Told *See* Spider Baby (1964)

Spider-Man *See* The Amazing Spider-Man (1977)

Spies-A-Go-Go *See* Nasty Rabbit (1964)

Spies, Lies, and Alibis *See* Code Name: Chaos (1990)

Spinal Tap *See* This Is Spinal Tap (1984)

Spione *See* Spies (1928)

Spirit of Tattoo *See* Irezumi (1983)

Spirit of the Dead *See* The Asphyx (1972)

Spirit of the People *See* Abe Lincoln in Illinois (1940)

The Spiritualist *See* The Amazing Mr. X (1948)

Spivs *See* I Vitelloni (1953)

The Split *See* The Manster (1959)

The Spooky Movie Show *See* The Mask (1961)

Spoorloos *See* The Vanishing (1988)

Spot *See* Dog Pound Shuffle (1975)

Spotswood *See* The Efficiency Expert (1992)

Spymaker *See* Spymaker: The Secret Life of Ian Fleming (1990)

Squadron of Doom *See* Ace Drummond (1936)

Stacey and Her Gangbusters *See* Stacey (1973)

Stakeout 2 *See* Another Stakeout (1993)

The Stand *See* Stephen King's Stand (1994)

Stand and Deliver *See* Bowery Blitzkrieg (1941)

Stand Easy *See* Goon Movie (1953)

Stanno Tutti Bene *See* Everybody's Fine (1990)

Star *See* Danielle Steel's Star (1993)

Star Child *See* Space Raiders (1983)

The Star Man *See* The Star Maker (1995)

Stardust *See* Mad About Money (1937)

Starflight: the Plane that Couldn't Land *See* Starflight One (1983)

Starknight *See* Star Knight (1985)

Starlight Slaughter *See* Eaten Alive (1976)

The Statutory Affair *See* Lola (1969)

Stella Star *See* Star Crash (1978)

Stepfather *See* Beau Pere (1981)

Stephen King's Cat's Eye *See* Cat's Eye (1985)

Stephen King's Graveyard Shift *See* Graveyard Shift (1990)

Stephen King's Silver Bullet *See* Silver Bullet (1985)

Stephen King's Sleepwalkers *See* Sleepwalkers (1992)

Still Smokin' *See* Cheech and Chong: Still Smokin' (1983)

Stolen Hearts *See* Two If by Sea (1995)

Storia de Ragazzi e di Ragazze *See* The Story of Boys & Girls (1991)

Stormy Crossing *See* Black Tide (1958)

Story of a Marriage *See* On Valentine's Day (1986)

The Story of an Artist's Studio Secrets *See* Artist's Studio Secrets (1964)

The Story of Gosta Berling *See* The Atonement of Gosta Berling (1924)

The Story of Joseph and His Brethren *See* Joseph & His Brethren (1960)

The Story of Robin Hood *See* The Story of Robin Hood & His Merrie Men (1952)

A Story of the Cruelties of Youth *See* The Cruel Story of Youth (1960)

The Story Without A Name *See* Without Warning (1952)

Straight Jacket *See* Dark Sanity (1982)

Straight on Till Morning *See* Dressed for Death (1974)

Strange Adventure *See* Wayne Murder Case (1938)

The Strange Adventure of David Gray *See* Vampyr (1931)

The Strange Case of Madeleine *See* Madeleine (1950)

Strange Confession *See* Calling Dr. Death/ Strange Confession (1943)

Strange Deception *See* The Accused (1948)

Strange Incident *See* The Ox-Bow Incident (1943)

Strange Interval *See* Strange Interlude (1932)

Strange Journey *See* Fantastic Voyage (1966)

The Strange Ones *See* Les Enfants Terrible (1950)

Strange Skirts *See* When Ladies Meet (1941)

The Strange World of Planet X *See* The Cosmic Monsters (1958)

The Stranger *See* Shame (1961)

A Stranger Came Home *See* Unholy Four (1954)

Stranger in Our House *See* Summer of Fear (1978)

Stranger in the House *See* Black Christmas (1975)

A Stranger Walked In *See* Love from a Stranger (1947)

Strangers *See* Voyage in Italy (1953)

Strangler's Morgue *See* The Crimes of Stephen Hawke (1936)

Stray Dogs *See* U-Turn (1997)

Street Gang *See* Vigilante (1983)

Street Kill *See* Death Scream (1975)

Street Legal *See* The Last of the Finest (1990)

Street Love *See* Scarred (1984)

Street of Shadows *See* The Shadow Man (1953)

Street of Sorrow *See* Joyless Street (1925)

Streets of Laredo *See* Larry McMurtry's Streets of Laredo (1995)

Streets of New York *See* The Abe Lincoln of Ninth Avenue (1939)

Strictly Confidential *See* Broadway Bill (1934)

Strictly for Pleasure *See* The Perfect Furlough (1959)

Striking Back *See* Search and Destroy (1981)

Strip Poker *See* The Big Switch (1970)

Striptease Lady *See* Lady of Burlesque (1943)

Struktura Krysztalu *See* The Structure of Crystals (1969)

The Stu Erwin Show *See* The Trouble with Father (1950)

Student Body *See* Getting In (1994)

Subida Al Cielo *See* Mexican Bus Ride (1951)

Subliminal Seduction *See* The Corporation (1996)

The Submersion of Japan *See* Tidal Wave (1975)

Subspecies 2 *See* Bloodstone: Subspecies 2 (1992)

Subspecies 3 *See* Bloodlust: Subspecies 3 (1993)

Succubus *See* The Devil's Nightmare (1971)

Such Men are Dangerous *See* The Racers (1955)

Suicide Run *See* Too Late the Hero (1970)

Suicide Squadron *See* Dangerous Moonlight (1941)

A Suitable Case for Treatment *See* Morgan! (1966)

The Sullivans *See* The Fighting Sullivans (1942)

Sult *See* Hunger (1966)

Summer Camp *See* A Pig's Tale (1994)

Summer Madness *See* Summertime (1955)

Summer Manoeuvres *See* Les Grandes Manoeuvres (1955)

Summer of Innocence *See* Big Wednesday (1978)

The Three Faces of Fear *See* Black Sabbath (1964)

The Three Faces of Terror *See* Black Sabbath (1964)

Three For the Money *See* Win, Place, or Steal (1972)

Three Ninjas: Showdown at Mega Mountain *See* Three Ninjas: High Noon at Mega Mountain (1997)

Three Rascals in the Hidden Fortress *See* The Hidden Fortress (1958)

Three Steps to the Gallows *See* White Fire (1953)

The Three Stooges Go Around the World in a Daze *See* Around the World in a Daze (1963)

The Threepenny Opera *See* Mack the Knife (1989)

Through the Looking Glass *See* The Velvet Vampire (1971)

Thunder *See* Thunder Warrior (1985)

Thunder Mountain *See* Shadow of Chikara (1977)

Thunder on the Trail *See* Thundering Trail (1951)

Thursday the 12th *See* Pandemonium (1982)

Tianguo Niezi *See* The Day the Sun Turned Cold (1994)

Tidal Wave *See* Portrait of Jennie (1948)

The Tiger *See* Tiger Warsaw (1987)

Tiger in the Sky *See* The McConnell Story (1955)

Tiger of Bengal *See* Journey to the Lost City (1958)

The Tiger Woman *See* Perils of the Darkest Jungle (1944)

Tigers Don't Cry *See* African Rage (1978)

Tight Little Island *See* Whiskey Galore (1948)

'Til Christmas *See* Breathing Room (1996)

Til Dawn Do Us Part *See* Dressed for Death (1974)

Till Death Us Do Part *See* The Blood Spattered Bride (1972)

Tim Burton's The Nightmare Before Christmas *See* The Nightmare Before Christmas (1993)

Timber Tramps *See* The Big Push (1975)

Time Flyers *See* The Blue Yonder (1986)

A Time For Caring *See* Generation (1969)

The Time of Return *See* Muriel (1963)

Time of the Beast *See* Mutator (1990)

Time Raiders *See* Warriors of the Apocalypse (1985)

Time Trap *See* The Time Travelers (1964)

Time Warp Terror *See* Bloody New Year (1987)

Timeslip *See* The Atomic Man (1956)

Timewarp *See* Day Time Ended (1980)

Tini Zabutykh Predkiv *See* Shadows of Forgotten Ancestors (1964)

Tintorera *See* Tintorera...Tiger Shark (1978)

Tintorera...Bloody Waters *See* Tintorera...Tiger Shark (1978)

Tirez sur le Pianiste *See* Shoot the Piano Player (1962)

Titan Find *See* Creature (1985)

To Be a Man *See* Cry of Battle (1963)

To Catch a Spy *See* Catch Me a Spy (1971)

To Die For *See* Heaven's a Drag (1994)

To Elvis, With Love *See* Touched by Love (1980)

To Have and to Hold *See* When a Man Loves a Woman (1994)

To Live *See* Ikiru (1952)

To Love a Vampire *See* Lust for a Vampire (1971)

To Vlemma Tou Odyssea *See* Ulysses' Gaze (1995)

Today We Live *See* The Day and the Hour (1963)

A Toi De Faire *See* Your Turn Darling (1963)

Tokyo Nagaremono *See* Tokyo Drifter (1966)

Tomb of the Cat *See* Tomb of Ligeia (1964)

Tomb of the Living Dead *See* Mad Doctor of Blood Island (1969)

The Tommyknockers *See* Stephen King's The Tommyknockers (1993)

The Tomorrow Man *See* 984: Prisoner of the Future (1984)

Ton Kero Ton Hellinon *See* When the Greeks (1981)

Tong Nien Wang Shi *See* A Time to Live and a Time to Die (1985)

Too Many Chefs *See* Who Is Killing the Great Chefs of Europe? (1978)

Topio Stin Omichli *See* Landscape in the Mist (1988)

Torment *See* L'Enfer (1993)

Torture Chamber *See* The Fear Chamber (1968)

Torture Zone *See* The Fear Chamber (1968)

Toto the Hero *See* Toto le Heros (1991)

The Touch of Melissa *See* The Touch of Satan (1970)

Touchez Pas Au Grisbi *See* Grisbi (1953)

Tower of Terror *See* Assault (1970)

Tower of Terror *See* Hard to Die (1990)

A Town Called Bastard *See* A Town Called Hell (1972)

The Town That Cried Terror *See* Maniac (1977)

T.R. Sloane *See* Death Ray 2000 (1981)

Trackers *See* Space Rage (1986)

Trail of the Royal Mounted *See* Mystery Trooper (1932)

Train of Terror *See* Terror Train (1980)

Train 2419 *See* The Return of Casey Jones (1934)

Traitement de Choc *See* Shock Treatment (1981)

Trancers *See* Future Cop (1976)

Transport Z Raje *See* Transport from Paradise (1965)

The Transvestite *See* Glen or Glenda: Confessions of Ed Wood (1953)

Tras el Cristal *See* In a Glass Cage (1986)

Trauma *See* Dario Argento's Trauma (1993)

Trauma *See* The House on Straw Hill (1976)

Travels with Anita *See* Lovers and Liars (1981)

Treasure of the Living Dead *See* Bloodsucking Nazi Zombies (1982)

Tredowata *See* Leper (1976)

The Tree of Hands *See* Innocent Victim (1990)

Tree of Liberty *See* The Howards of Virginia (1940)

Trial by Combat *See* Choice of Weapons (1976)

Trick of the Eye *See* Primal Secrets (1994)

Trigger, Jr. *See* Western Double Feature 6: Rogers & Trigger (1950)

A Trip with Anita *See* Lovers and Liars (1981)

Triple Trouble *See* Kentucky Kernels (1934)

Tristan and Isolde *See* Lovespell (1979)

Triumph des Willens *See* Triumph of the Will (1934)

Trois Hommes et un Couffin *See* Three Men and a Cradle (1985)

Trois Vies et une Seule Mort *See* Three Lives and Only One Death (1996)

The Trollenberg Terror *See* The Crawling Eye (1958)

Tromba *See* Tromba, the Tiger Man (1952)

Trop Belle Pour Toi *See* Too Beautiful for You (1988)

Trop Jolie pour Etre Honette *See* Too Pretty to Be Honest (1972)

Tropicana *See* The Heat's On (1943)

Trottie True *See* The Gay Lady (1949)

Trouble at 16 *See* Platinum High School (1960)

Trouble Chaser *See* Li'l Abner (1940)

The Trout *See* La Truite (1983)

Truman Capote's A Christmas Memory *See* ABC Stage 67: Truman Capote's A Christmas Memory (1966)

Truman Capote's The Glass House *See* The Glass House (1972)

Try and Find It *See* Hi Diddle Diddle (1943)

Tsarskaya Nevesta *See* The Tsar's Bride (1966)

Tsubaki Sanjuro *See* Sanjuro (1962)

Tsvet Granata *See* The Color of Pomegranates (1969)

Tudor Rose *See* Nine Days a Queen (1936)

Tueur de Chicago *See* Scarface Mob (1962)

Tulitkkutehtaan Tytto *See* The Match Factory Girl (1990)

The Tunnel *See* Transatlantic Tunnel (1935)

Turkey Shoot *See* Escape 2000 (1981)

Turn Your Pony Around *See* Mortal Danger (1994)

Turtle Beach *See* The Killing Beach (1992)

Twelve Miles Out *See* The Second Woman (1951)

Twenty-One Days Together *See* 21 Days (1937)

Twice Bitten *See* The Vampire Hookers (1978)

Twilight of the Dead *See* Gates of Hell (1983)

Twinkle, Twinkle, Killer Kane *See* The Ninth Configuration (1979)

Twinky *See* Lola (1969)

Twins of Dracula *See* Twins of Evil (1971)

Twisted *See* Medusa (1974)

The Twisted Road *See* They Live by Night (1949)

2 Cries in the Night *See* Funeral Home (1982)

Two Guys Talkin' About Girls *See* At First Sight (1995)

Two Minds for Murder *See* Someone Behind the Door (1971)

2002: The Rape of Eden *See* Bounty Hunter 2002 (1994)

Two Weeks in September *See* A Coeur Joie (1967)

Tystnaden *See* The Silence (1963)

U-Boat 29 *See* Spy in Black (1939)

U-238 and the Witch Doctor *See* Jungle Drums of Africa (1953)

Viaggio in Italia *See* Voyage in Italy (1953)

The Vicious Circle *See* Woman in Brown (1948)

Victims of the Beyond *See* Sucker Money (1934)

Vincent, Francois, Paul et les Autres *See* Vincent, Francois, Paul and the Others (1976)

Vindicator *See* Wheels of Fire (1984)

Violated *See* Party Girls for Sale (1954)

Violence et Passion *See* Conversation Piece (1975)

Violent Journey *See* The Fool Killer (1965)

Violent Midnight *See* Psychomania (1963)

Violent Rage *See* Fearmaker (1989)

Violent Streets *See* Thief (1981)

Violette Noziere *See* Violette (1978)

Virgin Hunters *See* Test Tube Teens from the Year 2000 (1993)

The Virgin Vampires *See* Twins of Evil (1971)

The Virtuous Tramps *See* The Devil's Brother (1933)

Virus *See* Invasion of the Flesh Hunters (1982)

Viskingar Och Rop *See* Cries and Whispers (1972)

Vita Privata *See* A Very Private Affair (1962)

Vitelloni *See* I Vitelloni (1953)

Vivement Dimanche! *See* Confidentially Yours (1983)

Viviamo Oggi *See* The Day and the Hour (1963)

Vivre Sa Vie *See* My Life to Live (1962)

Vogues *See* Vogues of 1938 (1937)

Voodoo Blood Bath *See* I Eat Your Skin (1964)

Vortex *See* Day Time Ended (1980)

Voyage Beyond the Sun *See* Space Monster (1964)

Voyage to a Prehistoric Planet *See* Voyage to the Prehistoric Planet (1965)

Voyage to Italy *See* Voyage in Italy (1953)

Vrazda Po Cesky *See* Murder Czech Style (1966)

Vredens Dag *See* Day of Wrath (1943)

Vulcan, Son of Jupiter *See* Vulcan God of Fire (1962)

Vzlomschik *See* Burglar (1987)

Wages of Fear *See* Sorcerer (1977)

Waiting Women *See* Secrets of Women (1952)

The Waking Hour *See* The Velvet Vampire (1971)

Waldo Warren: Private Dick Without a Brain *See* Maximum Thrust (1988)

The Wandering Kid *See* Urotsukidoj 1: Legend of the Overfiend (1993)

Wannseekonferenz *See* The Wannsee Conference (1984)

Want a Ride, Little Girl? *See* Impulse (1974)

Wanted Women *See* Jessi's Girls (1975)

The Wanton Contessa *See* Senso (1954)

War Between the Planets *See* Planet on the Prowl (1965)

War Games *See* Suppose They Gave a War and Nobody Came? (1970)

The War of the Monsters *See* Gamera vs. Barugon (1966)

War of the Planets *See* Cosmos: War of the Planets (1980)

War Shock *See* Battle Shock (1956)

Ward 13 *See* Hospital Massacre (1981)

Warlock *See* Skullduggery (1979)

The Warm-Blooded Spy *See* Ravishing Idiot (1964)

Warnung Vor Einer Helligen Nutte *See* Beware of a Holy Whore (1970)

The Warrior of Waverly Street *See* Star Kid (1997)

Warrior's Rest *See* Le Repos du Guerrier (1962)

Warum Lauft Herr R Amok? *See* Why Does Herr R. Run Amok? (1969)

Washington, B.C. *See* Hail (1973)

Watch That Man *See* The Man Who Knew Too Little (1997)

Water Child *See* L'Enfant d'Eau (1995)

Water Cyborgs *See* Terror Beneath the Sea (1966)

The Watts Monster *See* Dr. Black, Mr. Hyde (1976)

The Way Ahead *See* Immortal Battalion (1944)

The Way of Life *See* They Call It Sin (1932)

Ways of Love *See* The Miracle (1948)

We Will All Meet in Paradise *See* Pardon Mon Affaire, Too! (1977)

Wedding Bells *See* Royal Wedding (1951)

Wedding Breakfast *See* The Catered Affair (1956)

Wednesday's Child *See* Family Life (1971)

Weekend Babysitter *See* Weekend with the Babysitter (1970)

Welcome Home Brother Charles *See* Soul Vengeance (1975)

Welcome to Jericho *See* Last Man Standing (1996)

Welcome to Oblivion *See* Ultra Warrior (1992)

The Well-Made Marriage *See* Le Beau Mariage (1982)

Wendy Cracked a Walnut *See* ...Almost (1990)

We're in the Army Now *See* Pack Up Your Troubles (1932)

The Werewolf and the Yeti *See* Night of the Howling Beast (1975)

Wes Craven Presents Wishmaster *See* Wishmaster (1997)

What? *See* Diary of Forbidden Dreams (1973)

What a Chassis! *See* Belle Americaine (1961)

What a Drag *See* Pedale Douce (1996)

What a Man *See* Never Give a Sucker an Even Break (1941)

What Changed Charley Farthing *See* Bananas Boat (1978)

What Lola Wants *See* Damn Yankees (1958)

What the Swedish Butler Saw *See* A Man with a Maid (1975)

The Wheelchair *See* El Cochecito (1960)

Wheels of Terror *See* The Misfit Brigade (1987)

When Knighthood Was in Flower *See* The Sword & the Rose (1953)

When Michael Calls *See* Shattered Silence (1971)

When the Girls Meet the Boys *See* Girl Crazy (1943)

When Youth Conspires *See* Old Swimmin' Hole (1940)

Where is the Friend's Home? *See* Where Is My Friend's House? (1987)

Where the Hell's the Gold? *See* Dynamite and Gold (1988)

Where the River Bends *See* Bend of the River (1952)

While Plucking the Daisy *See* Mademoiselle Striptease (1957)

The Whipping Boy *See* Prince Brat and the Whipping Boy (1995)

White *See* Trois Couleurs: Blanc (1994)

White Paws *See* Pattes Blanches (1949)

White Trash on Moonshine Mountain *See* Moonshine Mountain (1964)

A White White Boy *See* The Mirror (1975)

Who? *See* Roboman (1975)

Who Dares Wins *See* The Final Option (1982)

Who Fears the Devil *See* The Legend of Hillbilly John (1973)

Who Is Killing the Stuntman *See* Stunts (1977)

Who Murdered Joy Morgan? *See* Killjoy (1981)

Who Shot Patakango? *See* Who Shot Pat? (1992)

Whoever Slew Auntie Roo? *See* Who Slew Auntie Roo? (1971)

Why Not? *See* Eijanaika (1981)

Wide-Eyed and Legless *See* The Wedding Gift (1993)

The Widow and the Gigolo *See* Roman Spring of Mrs. Stone (1961)

Wild Beds *See* Tigers in Lipstick (1980)

Wild Drifters *See* Cockfighter (1974)

Wild Flower *See* Fiorile (1993)

Wild Flower *See* Flor Silvestre (1958)

Wild for Kicks *See* Beat Girl (1960)

Wild Geese *See* Mistress (1953)

Wild Horse Mesa *See* When the West Was Young (1932)

Wild Horses of Fire *See* Shadows of Forgotten Ancestors (1964)

Wild Oats *See* The Errors of Youth (1978)

The Wild Pack *See* Defiant (1970)

The Wild Side *See* Suburbia (1983)

Wild Youth *See* Naked Youth (1959)

Wildcat *See* Great Scout & Cathouse Thursday (1976)

Wilderness Family, Part 2 *See* Further Adventures of the Wilderness Family, Part 2 (1977)

Willy Milly *See* Something Special (1986)

Wilt *See* The Misadventures of Mr. Wilt (1990)

The Wind Bloweth Where it Listeth *See* A Man Escaped (1957)

A Window in London *See* Lady in Distress (1939)

A Window to the Sky *See* The Other Side of the Mountain (1975)

The Wingless Bird *See* Catherine Cookson's The Wingless Bird (1997)

Wings of Apache *See* Fire Birds (1990)

Winter Rates *See* Out of Season (1975)

The Wistful Widow *See* The Wistful Widow of Wagon Gap (1947)

The Witch *See* Superstition (1982)

Witch Doctor *See* Men of Two Worlds (1946)

Witchcraft *See* Witchery (1988)

The Witches of Salem *See* The Crucible (1957)

Witchfinder General *See* The Conqueror Worm (1968)

Witchkill *See* The Witchmaker (1969)

Witch's Curse *See* Maciste in Hell (1960)

With Words and Music *See* The Girl Said No (1937)

Wit's End *See* G.I. Executioner (1971)

The Wizard of Mars *See* Horrors of the Red Planet (1964)

Wo Die Grunen Ameisen Traumen *See* Where the Green Ants Dream (1984)

Wo Do I Gotta Kill? *See* Me and the Mob (1994)

Wolf Larsen *See* The Legend of Sea Wolf (1975)

Wolf Larsen *See* The Legend of the Sea Wolf (1958)

Woman Alone *See* Sabotage (1936)

A Woman Destroyed *See* Smash-Up: The Story of a Woman (1947)

Woman, Forty *See* Summer Snow (1994)

The Woman in His House *See* The Animal Kingdom (1932)

Woman of Antwerp *See* Dedee d'Anvers (1949)

Woman of Dolwyn *See* The Last Days of Dolwyn (1949)

Woman of Osaka *See* Osaka Elegy (1936)

Woman of Summer *See* The Stripper (1963)

Woman of the Dunes *See* Woman in the Dunes (1964)

A Woman Scorned: The Betty Broderick Story *See* Till Murder Do Us Part (1992)

A Woman's Devotion *See* Battle Shock (1956)

A Woman's Revenge *See* La Vengeance d'une Femme (1989)

Women in Cages *See* The Big Doll House (1971)

Women in Prison *See* Ladies They Talk About (1933)

Women of Nazi Germany *See* Hitler (1962)

Women without Names *See* Women in Prison (1949)

Women's Penitentiary 1 *See* The Big Doll House (1971)

Women's Penitentiary 2 *See* The Big Bird Cage (1972)

Women's Penitentiary 4 *See* Caged Women (1984)

Wonder Women *See* The Deadly and the Beautiful (1973)

The Word *See* Ordet (1955)

The World and His Wife *See* State of the Union (1948)

The World of Yor *See* Yor, the Hunter from the Future (1983)

The Worlds of Gulliver *See* The Three Worlds of Gulliver (1959)

Worthy Deceivers *See* Big Bluff (1955)

The Wounded Man *See* L'Homme Blesse (1983)

Wrong Bet *See* Lionheart (1990)

The Wrong Kind of Girl *See* Bus Stop (1956)

Wuthering Heights *See* Emily Bronte's Wuthering Heights (1992)

Wuya Yu Maque *See* Crows and Sparrows (1949)

X *See* X: The Man with X-Ray Eyes (1963)

X-Ray *See* Hospital Massacre (1981)

Xich Lo *See* Cyclo (1995)

Xiyan *See* The Wedding Banquet (1993)

Xochimilco *See* Maria Candelaria (1946)

The XYZ Murders *See* Crimewave (1985)

...Y No Se Lo Trago La Tierra *See* ... And the Earth Did Not Swallow Him (1994)

Yangtse Incident *See* Battle Hell (1956)

A Yank In London *See* I Live in Grosvenor Square (1946)

A Yankee in King Arthur's Court *See* A Connecticut Yankee in King Arthur's Court (1949)

The Year of the Jellyfish *See* L'Annee des Meduses (1986)

Yellow Faced Tiger *See* Slaughter in San Francisco (1981)

Yellow Hair and the Pecos Kid *See* Yellow Hair & the Fortress of Gold (1984)

Yiddle with a Fiddle *See* Yidl Mitn Fidl (1936)

Ying Xiong Wei Lei *See* Heroes Shed No Tears (1986)

Yingxiong Bense *See* A Better Tomorrow (1986)

Yo, la Peor de Todas *See* I, the Worst of All (1990)

Yokihi *See* Princess Yang Kwei Fei (1955)

Yosei Gorasu *See* Gorath (1964)

You Better Watch Out *See* Terror in Toyland (1985)

You Can't Steal Love *See* Murph the Surf (1975)

You Don't Need Pajamas at Rosie's *See* The First Time (1969)

The Young and the Damned *See* Los Olvidados (1950)

The Young and the Immortal *See* The Sinister Urge (1960)

The Young and the Passionate *See* I Vitelloni (1953)

Young Commandos *See* Delta Force 3: The Killing Game (1991)

The Young Cycle Girls *See* Cycle Vixens (1979)

Young Dracula *See* Andy Warhol's Dracula (1974)

Young Dracula *See* Son of Dracula (1943)

Young Hearts *See* Promised Land (1988)

Young Hellions *See* High School Confidential (1958)

Young Invaders *See* Darby's Rangers (1958)

Young L.A. Nurses 1 *See* Private Duty Nurses (1971)

Young L.A. Nurses 2 *See* Night Call Nurses (1972)

The Young Ladies of Wilko *See* Maids of Wilko (1979)

Young Scarface *See* Brighton Rock (1947)

The Youngest Spy *See* My Name Is Ivan (1962)

Your Past is Showing *See* The Naked Truth (1958)

Your Red Wagon *See* They Live by Night (1949)

Your Witness *See* Eye Witness (1949)

Youth Takes a Hand *See* Behind Prison Walls (1943)

Yukinojo Henge *See* An Actor's Revenge (1963)

Zabudnite na Mozarta *See* Forget Mozart (1985)

Zamri Oumi Voskresni *See* Freeze-Die-Come to Life (1990)

Zato Ichi To Yojimbo *See* Zatoichi vs. Yojimbo (1970)

Zatoichi Meets Yojimbo *See* Zatoichi vs. Yojimbo (1970)

Zayn Vaybs Lubovnik *See* His Wife's Lover (1931)

Zazie in the Subway *See* Zazie dans le Metro (1961)

Zazie in the Underground *See* Zazie dans le Metro (1961)

Zee & Co. *See* X, Y & Zee (1972)

Zeisters *See* Fat Guy Goes Nutzoid (1986)

Zemlya *See* Earth (1930)

Zendegi Va Digar Hich ... *See* Life and Nothing More ... (1992)

Zerkalo *See* The Mirror (1975)

Zero de Conduit *See* Zero for Conduct (1933)

Zero Kelvin *See* Zero Degrees Kelvin (1995)

Zeta One *See* Alien Women (1969)

Zeta One *See* The Love Factor (1969)

Ziemia Obiecana *See* Land of Promise (1974)

Zire Darakhtan Zeyton *See* Through the Olive Trees (1994)

Zombi 2 *See* Zombie (1980)

Zombie *See* Dawn of the Dead (1978)

Zombie *See* I Eat Your Skin (1964)

Zombie Creeping Flesh *See* Night of the Zombies (1983)

Zombie Flesh-Eaters *See* Zombie (1980)

Zombie ja Kummitusjuna *See* Zombie and the Ghost Train (1991)

Zombies *See* Dawn of the Dead (1978)

Zombies *See* I Eat Your Skin (1964)

Zormba *See* Zorba the Greek (1964)

Zorro *See* The Mask of Zorro (1998)

Z.P.G. *See* Zero Population Growth (1972)

Zuckerbaby *See* Sugarbaby (1985)

Zycie Rodzinne *See* Family Life (1971)

A la Mode 🎬🎬½ *In Fashion* **1994 (R)** It's Paris in the '60s as shy 17-year-old orphan Fausto (Higelin) is apprenticed to fatherly Jewish tailor Mietek (Yanne). But Fausto is transfixed by lovely mechanic Tonie (Darel) and decides what he really wants (besides the girl) is to design women's fashions. Very frothy coming-of-age tale, anchored by Yanne's veteran charm. Based on the novel "Fausto" by Richard Morgieve. French with subtitles.*CW:* Some language and nudity. **89m/C VHS, LV.** *FR* Ken Higelin, Jean Yanne, Florence Darel, Francois Hautesserre; *D:* Remy Duchemin; *W:* Remy Duchemin, Richard Morgieve; *M:* Denis Barbier. *MAX*

A Nos Amours 🎬🎬🎬 **1984 (R)** Craving the attention she is denied at home, a young French girl searches for love and affection from numerous boyfriends in hopes of eradicating her unhappy home. Occasional lapses in quality and slow pacing hamper an otherwise excellent effort. The characterization of the girl Suzanne is especially memorable. In French with English subtitles. **99m/C VHS, Beta, LV.** *FR* Sandrine Bonnaire, Dominique Besnehard, Maurice Pialat, Evelyne Ker; *D:* Maurice Pialat. *COL*

A Nous la Liberte 🎬🎬🎬🎬 **1931** Two tramps encounter industrialization and automation, making one into a wealthy leader, the other into a nature-loving iconoclast. A poignant, fantastical masterpiece by Clair, made before he migrated to Hollywood. Though the view of automation may be dated, it influenced such films as Chaplin's "Modern Times." In French with English subtitles. **87m/B VHS, Beta, 8mm.** *FR* Henri Marchand, Raymond Cordy, Rolla France, Paul Olivier, Jacques Shelly, Andre Michaud; *D:* Rene Clair; *W:* Rene Clair; *C:* Georges Perinal. Nominations: Academy Awards '32: Best Interior Decoration. *NOS, MRV, VYY*

Aaron Loves Angela 🎬🎬 **1975 (R)** Puerto Rican girl falls in love with a black teen amidst the harsh realities of the Harlem ghetto. "Romeo and Juliet" meets "West Side Story" in a cliched comedy drama. **99m/C VHS, Beta.** Kevin Hooks, Irene Cara, Moses Gunn, Robert Hooks, Jose Feliciano; *D:* Gordon Parks Jr.; *M:* Jose Feliciano. *COL*

Abandon Ship 🎬🎬½ *Seven Waves Away* **1957** A luxury liner hits a derelict mine and sinks within minutes, leaving 27 survivors clinging to one tiny lifeboat. Ship's officer Alex Holmes (Power) knows that the amount of food and water they have is limited, the waters are shark-infested, and the injured stand little chance, so he must decide who will survive. **97m/B VHS.** *GB* Tyrone Power, Mai Zetterling, Lloyd Nolan, Stephen Boyd, Moira Lister, James Hayter, Marie Lohr, Gordon Jackson, Finlay Currie, John Stratton, Victor Maddern, Eddie Byrne, Noel Willman, Ralph Michael, David Langton, Ferdinand "Ferdy" Mayne, Austin Trevor, Moultrie Kelsall, Jill Melford; *D:* Richard Sale; *W:* Richard Sale; *C:* Wilkie Cooper; *M:* Arthur Bliss. *COL*

Abbott and Costello Go to Mars 🎬½ **1953** Poor parody of sci-fi films finds the frantic duo aboard a rocket ship and accidentally heading off into outer space. They don't land on Mars, but Venus, which is populated by lots of pretty women and no men. Even this duo looks good to the ladies. Cheapie production and uninspired buffoonery. **77m/B VHS, Closed Caption.** Bud Abbott, Lou Costello, Mari Blanchard, Robert Paige, Martha Hyer, Horace McMahon, Jack Kruschen, Anita Ekberg; *D:* Charles Lamont; *W:* John Grant, D.D. Beauchamp. *USH*

Abbott and Costello in Hollywood 🎬🎬 *Bud Abbott and Lou Costello In Hollywood* **1945** Bud and Lou appear as a barber and porter of a high class tonsorial parlor in Hollywood. A rather sarcastic look at backstage Hollywood, Abbott & Costello style. Ball makes a guest appearance. **111m/B VHS, Beta.** Bud Abbott, Lou Costello, Frances Rafferty, Warner Anderson, Lucille Ball; *D:* Sylvan Simon; *M:* George Bassman. *MGM, CCB*

Abbott and Costello in the Foreign Legion 🎬🎬½ **1950** Fight promoters Jonesy and Max trail their runaway fighter to Algiers where they're tricked into joining the French Foreign Legion. They have to cope with a sadistic sergeant, a sexy spy, and still find their man. Most amusement comes from Lou's wild desert mirages. **80m/B VHS, Closed Caption.** Bud Abbott, Lou Costello, Walter Slezak, Patricia Medina, Douglass Dumbrille, Leon Belasco, Marc Lawrence, Tor Johnson; *D:* Charles Lamont; *W:* John Grant, Martin Ragaway, Leonard Stern. *USH*

Abbott and Costello Meet Captain Kidd 🎬🎬 **1952** With pirates led by Captain Kidd on their trail, Abbott and Costello follow a treasure map. Bland A&C swashbuckler spoof with a disinterested Laughton impersonating the Kidd. One of the duo's few color films. **70m/C VHS, Beta, LV.** Bud Abbott, Lou Costello, Charles Laughton, Hillary Brooke, Fran Warren, Bill Shirley, Leif Erickson; *D:* Charles Lamont. *NOS*

Abbott and Costello Meet Dr. Jekyll and Mr. Hyde 🎬🎬 **1952** Abbott and Costello take on evil Dr. Jekyll, who has transformed himself into Mr. Hyde, and is terrorizing London. A lame attempt at recapturing the success of "Abbott and Costello Meet Frankenstein." **77m/B VHS.** Bud Abbott, Lou Costello, Boris Karloff, Craig Stevens, Helen Westcott, Reginald Denny, John Dierkes; *D:* Charles Lamont; *W:* John Grant, Leo Loeb; *C:* George Robinson. *USH*

Abbott and Costello Meet Frankenstein 🎬🎬🎬 *Abbott and Costello Meet the Ghosts* **1948** Big-budget A&C classic is one of their best efforts and was rewarded handsomely at the boxoffice. Two unsuspecting baggage clerks deliver a crate containing the last but not quite dead remains of Dracula and Dr. Frankenstein's monster to a wax museum. The fiends are revived, wreaking havoc with the clerks. Chaney makes a special appearance to warn the boys that trouble looms. Last film to use the Universal creature pioneered by Karloff in 1931. **83m/B VHS, Beta, LV.** Bud Abbott, Lou Costello, Lon Chaney Jr., Bela Lugosi, Glenn Strange, Lenore Aubert, Jane Randolph; *D:* Charles T. Barton; *W:* John Grant, Robert Lees, Frederic Rinaldo; *C:* Charles Van Enger; *V:* Vincent Price. *USH*

Abbott and Costello Meet the Invisible Man 🎬🎬🎬 1951 Abbott and Costello play newly graduated detectives who take on the murder case of a boxer (Franz) accused of killing his manager. Using a serum that makes people invisible, the boxer helps Costello in a prizefight that will frame the real killers, who killed the manager because the boxer refused to throw a fight. Great special effects and hilarious gags make this one of the best from the crazy duo. **82m/B VHS.** Bud Abbott, Lou Costello, Nancy Guild, Adele Jergens, Sheldon Leonard, William Frawley, Gavin Muir, Arthur Franz; **D:** Charles Lamont; **W:** Frederic Rinaldo, John Grant, Robert Lees; **C:** George Robinson. *USH*

Abbott and Costello Meet the Keystone Kops 🎬🎬½ 1954 It's 1912 and the boys are bilked into buying a fake movie studio by a clever con man. When they find out they've been tricked, the duo head to Hollywood to track him down and find out the crook is trying to cheat Sennett's film company. Sennett himself trained A&C and the new Keystone Kops in recreations of his silent screen routines. Good final chase sequence but the earlier work is tired. **79m/B VHS, Closed Caption.** Bud Abbott, Lou Costello, Fred Clark, Lynn Bari, Mack Sennett, Maxie "Slapsie" Rosenbloom, Frank Wilcox, Harold Goodwin; **D:** Charles Lamont; **W:** John Grant; **M:** Henry Mancini. *USH*

Abbott and Costello Meet the Killer, Boris Karloff 🎬🎬 1949 Unremarkable Abbott and Costello murder mystery. Karloff plays a psychic who tries to frame Lou for murder. Pleasant enough but not one of their best. **84m/B VHS, Beta, LV, Closed Caption.** Bud Abbott, Lou Costello, Boris Karloff, Lenore Aubert, Gar Moore, Donna Martell, Alan Mowbray, James Flavin, Roland Winters; **D:** Charles T. Barton; **W:** John Grant, Hugh Wedlock Jr., Howard Snyder. *USH*

Abbott and Costello Meet the Mummy 🎬🎬½ 1955 Okay comedy from the duo has them stranded in Egypt with a valuable medallion which will lead to secret treasure and the mummy who guards the tomb. The last of the films the twosome made for Universal. **90m/B VHS.** Bud Abbott, Lou Costello, Marie Windsor, Michael Ansara, Dan Seymour, Kurt Katch, Richard Deacon, Mel Welles, Edwin Parker; **D:** Charles Lamont; **W:** John Grant; **C:** George Robinson. *USH, FCT*

ABC Stage 67: Truman Capote's A Christmas Memory *Truman Capote's A Christmas Memory; A Christmas Memory* 1966 A television drama special narrated by Capote about his remembered childhood experience of baking dozens of fruitcakes for friends at Christmas with his elderly distant cousin, Miss Sook Faulk (Page). She is quiet, lovely, and true in this sensitive portrait of why we give and what we have to be thankful for. Adapted from a Capote short story by Capote and Eleanor Perry. **51m/B VHS.** Geraldine Page, Donnie Melvin; **D:** Frank Perry; **W:** Truman Capote. *MOV, VYY*

ABC's of Love & Sex, Australia Style 🎬 1986 An Australian-made sex-education parody. **87m/C VHS, Beta.** *AU* Brigittia Almsrom, Rettima Borer, Ian Broadbent.

Abducted 🎬½ 1986 (PG) A woman jogger is abducted by a crazed mountain man in the Canadian Rockies. Weird and unbelievably tedious film is nevertheless highlighted by some spectacular wilderness footage of the Vancouver area, a travelogue bonus for those in the mood. **87m/C VHS, Beta.** *CA* Dan Haggerty, Roberta Weiss, Lawrence King Phillips; **D:** Boon Collins.

Abducted 2: The Reunion 🎬½ 1994 (R) Three girlfriends decide to go camping for their reunion trip. Oops—psycho mountain man alert! *CW:* Language; brief nudity; violence. **91m/C VHS.** Dan Haggerty, Jan-Michael Vincent, Donna Jason, Raquel Bianca, Debbie Rochon, Lawrence King; **D:** Boon Collins; **W:** Boon Collins; **C:** Danny Nowak. *AVI*

Abduction 🎬½ 1975 (R) Exploitative account of the Patty Hearst kidnapping, loosely adapted from the Harrison James novel written before the kidnapping. A young woman from a wealthy capitalist family is kidnapped by black radicals and held for an unusual ransom. Oh, and she tangles with lesbians, too. **100m/C VHS, Beta.** Judith-Marie Bergan, David Pendleton, Gregory Rozakis, Leif Erickson, Dorothy Malone, Lawrence Tierney; **D:** Joseph Zito.

The Abduction of Allison Tate 🎬½ 1992 (R) Rich developer takes land belonging to a group of Native Americans. Three young tribe members retaliate by kidnapping the developer's daughter. But when their plans go awry and one of the trio is killed, Allison finds herself sympathizing more with them than with her father's ambitions. *CW:* Language and one sex scene. **95m/C VHS.** Leslie Hope, Bernie White; **D:** Paul Leder. *NO*

The Abduction of Kari Swenson 🎬½ 1987 An account of the true-life (it really happened) kidnapping of Olympic biathalon hopeful Swensen by a pair of mischievous Montana mountain men with matrimony in mind. The movie details the abduction of Swenson by the scruffy father and son duo and the massive manhunt. As the put-upon Kari, Pollan exceeds script expectations in this made-for-television exercise in stress avoidance. **100m/C VHS.** Joe Don Baker, M. Emmet Walsh, Ronny Cox, Michael Bowen, Geoffrey Blake, Dorothy Fielding, Tracy Pollan; **D:** Stephen Gyllenhaal. *THV*

Abduction of St. Anne 🎬🎬 1975 An almost interesting made-for-television mystical thriller about a detective and a bishop trying to track down a gangster's daughter, who may have nifty supernatural healing powers the Church would be very interested in having documented. **78m/C VHS, Beta.** Robert Wagner, E.G. Marshall, William Windom, Lloyd Nolan; **D:** Harry Falk; **M:** George Duning. *WOV, GKK*

The Abductors 🎬 1972 (R) Caffaro's super-agent takes on international white slavery, a worthy target for any exploitation effort. While the novelty is a tough and intelligent on-screen heroine, sufficient sleaze and violence bring it all down to the proper level of swampland video. Sequel to the never-to-be-forgotten "Ginger." **90m/C VHS, Beta.** Cheri Caffaro, William Grannell, Richard Smedley, Patrick Wright, Jennifer Brooks; **D:** Don Schain. *MON*

Abdulla the Great 🎬🎬 *Abdullah's Harem* 1956 A dissolute Middle Eastern monarch falls for a model, who spurns him for an army officer. While distracted by these royal shenanigans, the king is blissfully unaware of his subjects' disaffection—until they revolt. Dares to lampoon Egypt's dead King Farouk, going against conventional Hollywood wisdom ("Farouk in film is boxoffice poison"). **89m/C VHS, Beta.** *GB* Gregory Ratoff, Kay Kendall, Sydney Chaplin; **D:** Gregory Ratoff. *VYY*

Abe Lincoln in Illinois 🎬🎬🎬🎬 *Spirit of the People* 1940 Massey considered this not only his finest film but a part he was "born to play." Correct on both counts, this Hollywood biography follows Lincoln from his log cabin days to his departure for the White House. The Lincoln-Douglass debate scene and Massey's post-presidential election farewell to the citizens of Illinois are nothing short of brilliant. Written by Sherwood from his Pulitzer-Prize winning play. Contrasted with the well-known "Young Mr. Lincoln" (Henry Fonda), its relative anonymity is perplexing. **110m/B VHS, Beta.** Raymond Massey, Gene Lockhart, Ruth Gordon, Mary Howard, Dorothy Tree, Harvey Stephens, Minor Watson, Alan Baxter, Howard da Silva, Maurice Murphy, Clem Bevans, Herbert Rudley; **D:** John Cromwell; **W:** Robert Sherwood; **C:** James Wong Howe. Nominations: Academy Awards '40: Best Actor (Massey), Best Black and White Cinematography. *TTC*

The Abe Lincoln of Ninth Avenue 🎬🎬½ *Streets of New York* 1939 All-American tale of a poor young man making good in New York. His role model is Abraham Lincoln. Cooper is exceptional, supported by effective performances by the rest of the cast. **68m/B VHS, Beta, 8mm.** Jackie Cooper, Martin Spelling, Marjorie Reynolds, Dick Purcell, George Cleveland, George Irving; **D:** William Nigh. *VYY*

Abigail's Party 🎬🎬 1977 Steadman plays the hostess for a very ill-fated dinner party, especially when she realizes her husband has just died on her new carpet. Made for British television. **105m/C VHS.** *GB* Alison Steadman; **D:** Mike Leigh. *WBF, BTV*

Abilene Town 🎬🎬🎬 1946 In a post-Civil War Kansas town far from the freeway, Scott is the tough marshal trying to calm the conflict between cattlemen and homesteaders. He also finds time to participate in a romantic triangle with dance hall vixen Dvorak and heart-of-gold Fleming. Snappy pace keeps it interesting. Based on a novel by Ernest Haycox. **90m/B VHS, Beta.** Randolph Scott, Ann Dvorak, Edgar Buchanan, Rhonda Fleming, Lloyd Bridges; **D:** Edwin L. Marin. *MRV, NOS, BAR*

The Abominable Dr. Phibes 🎬🎬🎬 1971 (PG) After being disfigured in a freak car accident that killed his wife, an evil genius decides that the members of a surgical team let his wife die and shall each perish by a different biblical plague. High camp with the veteran cast in top form. **90m/C VHS, Beta, LV.** *GB* Vincent Price, Joseph Cotten, Hugh Griffith, Terry-Thomas, Virginia North, Susan Travers, Alex Scott, Caroline Munro, Peter Gilmore, Aubrey Woods, John Laurie; **D:** Robert Fuest; **W:** William Goldstein, James Whiton; **C:** Norman Warwick. *ORI*

The Abomination 🎬 1988 (R) After a 5,000-year-old creature possesses him during a nightmare, a boy goes on an eye-gouging frenzy. Only the audience gets hurt. **100m/C VHS, Beta.** Van Connery, Victoria Chaney, Gaye Bottoms, Suzy Meyer, Jude Johnson, Blue Thompson, Scott Davis; **D:** Max Raven. *DMP*

About Last Night... 🎬🎬🎬 1986 (R) Semi-realistic comedy-drama which explores the ups and downs of one couple's relationship. Mostly good performances, especially Perkins and Belushi as friends of the young lovers. Based on David Mamet's play "Sexual Perversity in Chicago," but considerably softened so that more people would buy tickets at the boxoffice, the film acts as a historical view of contemporary mating rituals before the onset of the AIDS crisis. **113m/C VHS, Beta, LV.** Rob Lowe, Demi Moore, Elizabeth Perkins, James Belushi, George DiCenzo, Robin Thomas, Michael Alldredge; **D:** Edward Zwick; **W:** Tim Kazurinsky, Denise DeClue; **M:** Miles Goodman. *COL*

Above and Beyond 🎬🎬🎬 1953 Good performance by Taylor as Col. Paul Tibbets, the man who piloted the Enola Gay, which dropped the atomic bomb on Hiroshima. Focuses on the secrecy of the mission and the strain this puts on Tibbets' marriage. Exciting action sequences of the mission itself. **122m/B VHS.** Robert Taylor, Eleanor Parker, James Whitmore, Larry Keating, Larry Gates, Robert Burton, Jim Backus; **D:** Melvin Frank, Norman Panama; **W:** Melvin Frank, Norman Panama, Beirne Lay Jr. Nominations: Academy Awards '53: Best Story, Best Original Dramatic/Comedy Score. *MGM*

Above Suspicion 🎬🎬🎬 1943 MacMurray and Crawford are American honeymooners (poor Fred!) asked to assist an international intelligence organization. They engage the Nazis in a tense battle of wits. Well-made and engaging. **91m/B VHS.** Joan Crawford, Fred MacMurray, Conrad Veidt, Basil Rathbone, Reginald Owen; **D:** Richard Thorpe. *MGM*

Above Suspicion 🎬🎬 1995 (R) Dempsey Cain (Reeve) seems to be the perfect cop, as well as a loving husband and father and a mentor to his younger brother. But when Cain is paralyzed by a drug dealer's bullet, he begins to notice just

how close his wife (Cattrall) and brother (Kerr) are. There's adultery, there's murder, and there's the cop who just may be a cold-blooded killer. Unnervingly, Reeve plays a paraplegic in the last movie he made before his own paralyzing riding accident. Made for cable. **CW:** Strong sex scenes, language and violence. **92m/C VHS.** Christopher Reeve, Kim Cattrall, Joe Mantegna, Edward Kerr; **D:** Steven Schachter. *HBO*

Above the Law 🦴🦴 **1988 (R)** In his debut, Seagal does his wooden best to portray a tough Chicago police detective planning an enormous drug bust of one of the biggest felons in the state. Unfortunately, the FBI has ordered him to back off and find another bust. The reasons are almost as complex as Seagal's character, and like most details of the flick, stupid. However, people don't watch these movies for the acting or the plot, but for the fight scenes, which are well-choreographed and violent. Watch it with someone you love. **99m/C VHS, Beta, LV, 8mm, Closed Caption.** Steven Seagal, Pam Grier, Henry Silva, Sharon Stone, Ron Dean, Daniel Faraldo, Chelcie Ross, Thalmus Rasulala, Michael Rooker; **D:** Andrew Davis; **W:** Andrew Davis, Steven Pressfield; **C:** Robert Steadman. *WAR, TLF*

Above the Rim 🦴🦴½ **1994 (R)** Vulgar, violent hoopster drama about a fiercely competitive inner-city playground game. Kyle-Lee Watson (Martin), a self-involved high school star raised by a saintly single mom (Pinkins), is torn between the lure of the streets and his college recruiting chances. His odds aren't made any easier by homeboy hustler Birdie (Shakur), who wants to improve his chances of making money on the local games by making sure Watson plays for his team. Energetic b-ball sequences, strong performances lose impact amid formulaic melodrama and the usual obscenities. Debut for director Pollack. **CW:** Pervasive strong language and violence. **97m/C VHS, LV, Closed Caption.** Duane Martin, Tupac Shakur, Leon, Marlon Wayans, Tonya Pinkins, Bernie Mac; **D:** Jeff Pollack; **W:** Jeff Pollack, Barry Michael Cooper; **M:** Marcus Miller. Nominations: MTV Movie Awards '95: Best Song ("Regulate"). *NLC*

Above Us the Waves 🦴🦴🦴 **1956** During WWII, the British navy immobilizes a huge German battleship off the coast of Norway. Effectively dramatizes the British naval preparations for what seemed a suicidal mission: using midget submarines to plant underwater explosives on the hull of the German vessel and detonating them before the Germans could detect the danger. **92m/C VHS.** *GB* John Mills, John Gregson, Donald Sinden, James Robertson Justice, Michael Medwin, James Kenney, O.E. Hasse, Thomas Heathcote, Lee Patterson, Theodore Bikel, Lyndon Brook, Anthony Newley; **D:** Ralph Thomas. *REP*

Abraham 🦴🦴½ **1994** Made for cable Biblical epic chronicling the Old Testament story of humble shepherd Abraham (Harris), who's commanded by God to lead his family into the promised land of Canaan. Among his family's many trials will be God's command that Abraham sacrifice his son Isaac as a test of faith and obedience. Filmed on location in Morocco with a commanding performance by Harris that somewhat redeems the film's dullness. **?m/C VHS.** Richard Harris, Barbara Hershey, Maximilian Schell, Vittorio Gassman, Caroline Rosi, Gottfried John, Kevin McNally; **D:** Joseph Sargent. *TTC*

Abraham Lincoln 🦴🦴½ **1930** Griffith's first talking movie takes Abraham Lincoln from his birth through his assassination. This restored version includes the original slavery sequences which were believed to be lost, but obviously were not. Musical score included. **97m/B VHS, Beta, LV.** Walter Huston, Una Merkel, Kay Hammond, E. Alyn Warren, Hobart Bosworth, Fred Warren, Henry B. Walthall, Russell Simpson; **D:** D.W. Griffith; **C:** Karl Struss. *NOS, MRV, CCB*

Abraxas: Guardian of the Universe 🦴½ **1990 (R)** Good space cop versus bad space cop with an ecological twist. Good-guy Abraxas (Ventura) has the task of stopping planets from destroying their environments and fighting senseless wars. His ex-partner Secundas (Ole-Thorsen) has his own mission, seeking an anti-life power which could destroy the universe. They decide to fight it out, using Earth as the battleground. Also available in an edited PG-13 version. **90m/C VHS.** Jesse Ventura, Sven Ole-Thorsen; **Cameos:** James Belushi.

Abroad with Two Yanks 🦴🦴 **1944** Two Marine buddies on furlough exhibit slapstick tendencies while competing for the same girl. Along the way a big chase ensues with the two soldiers in drag. Typical wartime shenanigans likely to incite only weak chuckling or inspired snoozing. **81m/B VHS, Beta.** William Bendix, Dennis O'Keefe, Helen Walker, John Loder, George Cleveland, Janet Lambert, James Flavin, Arthur Hunnicutt; **D:** Allan Dwan. *ART*

Absence of Malice 🦴🦴½ **1981 (PG)** High-minded story about the harm that the news media can inflict. Field is the earnest reporter who, after being fed some facts by an unscrupulous federal investigator, writes a story implicating Newman in a murder he didn't commit. Field hides behind journalistic confidentiality privilege to put off the outraged Newman, who loses a friend to suicide during the debacle. Interesting performances by Field and Newman. **116m/C VHS, Beta, LV, DVD.** Paul Newman, Sally Field, Bob Balaban, Melinda Dillon, Luther Adler, Barry Primus, Josef Sommer, John Harkins, Don Hood, Wilford Brimley; **D:** Sydney Pollack; **W:** Kurt Luedtke; **C:** Owen Roizman; **M:** Dave Grusin. Nominations: Academy Awards '81: Best Actor (Newman), Best Original Screenplay, Best Supporting Actress (Dillon). *COL*

The Absent-Minded Professor 🦴🦴🦴½ **1961** Classic dumb Disney fantasy of the era. A professor accidentally invents an anti-gravity substance called flubber, causing inanimate objects and people to become airborne. Great sequence of the losing school basketball team taking advantage of flubber during a game. MacMurray is convincing as the absent-minded genius in this newly colored version. Followed by "Son of Flubber." **97m/C VHS.** Fred MacMurray, Nancy Olson, Keenan Wynn, Tommy Kirk, Leon Ames, Ed Wynn; **D:** Robert Stevenson; **C:** Edward Colman; **M:** George Bruns. Nominations: Academy Awards '61: Best Art Direction/Set Decoration (B & W), Best Black and White Cinematography. *DIS, BTV*

Absent Without Leave 🦴🦴½ **1995** Ed (McLachlan) marries his pregnant girlfriend Daisy (Hobbs) in 1942 before joining the army. When Daisy miscarries, Ed pledges to take her home even though it means leaving the army without permission. As the newlyweds travel across the New Zealand countryside, they struggle with the new demands of their relationship. **104m/C VHS.** *NZ* Craig McLachlan, Katrina Hobbs; **D:** John Laing. *LEO*

Absolute Beginners 🦴🦴 **1986 (PG)** Fervently stylish camp musical exploring the lives of British teenagers in the 1950s never quite gets untracked, although MTV video moments fill out a spare plot line. Based on a novel by Colin MacInnes. ♫Absolute Beginners; That's Motivation; Volare; Killer Blow; Have You Ever Been Blue?; Quiet Life; Having It All; Selling Out; Va Va Voom. **107m/C VHS, Beta, LV.** *GB* David Bowie, Ray Davies, Mandy Rice-Davies, James Fox, Eddie O'Connell, Patsy Kensit, Anita Morris, Sade Adu, Sandie Shaw; **D:** Julien Temple; **W:** Richard Burridge, Don MacPherson. *NO*

Absolute Power 🦴🦴½ **1997 (R)** Eastwood is "In the Line of Fire," (against the very agents he previously glorified) as an expert thief being pursued by rogue Secret Service men in this fast-paced thriller. While looting a Washington official's place, Luther (Eastwood) inadvertently witnesses a murder committed by none other than U.S. President Richmond (Hackman) and his goons. Immediately, a cover-up is organized

by his unbalanced chief-of-staff (Davis) and Luther becomes the prime suspect. Harris gives his usual solid performance as the homicide detective. Eastwood's simple directorial style keeps up the suspense and propels the film steadily forward, alongside a generally solid plot that gets a bit improbable near the end. Based on the novel by David Baldacci. **CW:** Violence, sexuality, and language. **120m/C VHS, LV, Closed Caption, DVD.** Clint Eastwood, Gene Hackman, Ed Harris, Laura Linney, Judy Davis, Scott Glenn, Dennis Haysbert, E.G. Marshall, Melora Hardin; **D:** Clint Eastwood; **W:** William Goldman; **C:** Jack N. Green; **M:** Lennie Niehaus. *WAR*

Absolutely Fabulous: The Last Shout 🦴🦴½ **1996** The first TV movie from the British comedy series finds Edina (Saunders) selling her fashion PR business after a near-death experience and doing some soul-searching—Ab-Fab style, which involves shopping, travel, and champagne. Naturally, Patsy (Lumley) goes along for the ride. The duo's favorite designer Christian LaCroix even has a cameo. **90m/C VHS.** *GB* Jennifer Saunders, Joanna Lumley; **Cameos:** Marianne Faithfull. *PGV, VIF*

Absolution 🦴🦴 **1981 (R)** Two English boys trapped in a Catholic boarding school conspire to drive a tyrannical priest over the edge of sanity. As a result, bad things (including murder) occur. Burton is interesting in sadistic character study. Not released in the U.S. until 1988 following Burton's death, maybe due to something written in the will. **105m/C VHS, Beta, LV.** *GB* Richard Burton, Dominic Guard, Dai Bradley, Andrew Keir, Billy Connolly, Willoughby Gray; **D:** Anthony Page. *SIM, TWE, FCT*

Abuse 🦴🦴 **1982** Fourteen-year-old Tommy (Sbarge) is the victim of child abuse. After a beating causes convulsions, his parents rush him to a New York hospital where the intern on duty phones his student filmmaker friend Larry (Ryder), who's doing a documentary on child abuse as his master thesis. When Tommy learns that Larry is also gay, he agrees to discuss his problems but their continuing contact leads the duo to fall in love and Larry to worry about exploiting Tommy's affections. Interspersed with their story are interviews and photos of child abuse victims and their abusers. Not necessarily for the squeamish. **93m/B VHS.** Richard Ryder, Raphael Sbarge; **D:** Arthur J. Bressan Jr.; **W:** Arthur J. Bressan Jr.; **C:** Douglas Dickinson; **M:** Shawn Phillips. *CCN*

The Abyss 🦴🦴🦴 *L'Oeuvre au Noir* **1989 (PG-13)** Underwater sci-fi adventure about a team of oil-drilling divers pressed into service by the navy to locate and disarm an inoperative nuclear submarine. A high-tech thriller with fab footage underwater and pulsating score. The laserdisc version contains 27 extra minutes of footage. **140m/C VHS, Beta, LV, Letterbox, Closed Caption.** Ed Harris, Mary Elizabeth Mastrantonio, Todd Graff, Michael Biehn, John Bedford Lloyd, J.C. Quinn, Leo Burmester, Kidd Brewer Jr., Kimberly Scott, Adam Nelson, George Robert Kirk, Chris Elliott, Jimmie Ray Weeks; **D:** James Cameron; **W:** James Cameron; **C:** Mikael Salomon; **M:** Alan Silvestri. Academy Awards '89: Best Visual Effects; Nominations: Academy Awards '89: Best Art Direction/Set Decoration, Best Cinematography, Best Sound. *FXV*

Accatone! 🦴🦴🦴 **1961** Accatone (Citti), a failure as a pimp, tries his luck as a thief. Hailed as a return to Italian neo-realism, this is a gritty, despairing, and dark look at the lives of the street people of Rome. Pasolini's first outing, adapted by the director from his novel, "A Violent Life." Pasolini served as mentor to Bernardo Bertolucci, listed in the credits as an assistant director. **116m/B VHS.** *IT* Franco Citti, Franca Pasut, Roberto Scaringelli, Adele Cambria, Paolo Guidi, Silvana Corsini; **D:** Pier Paolo Pasolini; **C:** Tonino Delli Colli. *WBF*

Acceptable Risks 🦴½ **1986 (R)** Toxic disaster strikes when a plant manager is ordered to cut costs and sacrifice safety at the Citichem plant. Predictable plot stars Dennehy as the plant manager who risks all and fights politicians to reinstate the safety standards. Meanwhile, Tyson is the city manager who tries to warn the town of a possible chemical accident that could have devastating effects on the community. Made for television drama that shamelessly preys on audience fears. 97m/C VHS, Beta, Closed Caption. Brian Dennehy, Cicely Tyson, Kenneth McMillan, Christine Ebersole, Beah Richards, Richard Gilliland; D: Rick Wallace.

Access Code 🎬 1984 Government agents attempt to uncover a private organization that has gained control of nuclear weapons for the purpose of world domination. A ragged patchwork of disconnected scenes meant to test the virtue of patience. 90m/C VHS, Beta. Martin Landau, Michael Ansara, MacDonald Carey; D: Mark Sobel.

Accident 🎬🎬½ 1967 A tangled web of guilt, remorse, humor and thwarted sexuality is unravelled against the background of the English countryside in this complex story of an Oxford love triangle. An inside view of English repression at the university level adapted for the screen by Pinter from the novel by Nicholas Mosley. Longwinded but occasionally engrossing character study with interesting performances. 100m/C VHS, Beta. GB Dirk Bogarde, Michael York, Stanley Baker, Jacqueline Sassard, Delphine Seyrig, Alexander Knox, Vivien Merchant, Freddie Jones, Harold Pinter; D: Joseph Losey; W: Harold Pinter. Cannes Film Festival '67: Grand Jury Prize. NO

Accident 🎬½ 1983 Skate for your life. A hockey game turns into a nightmare when the roof over the arena collapses under the weight of too much ice and snow. One of the few hockey disaster films. 104m/C VHS, Beta. Terence Kelly, Fiona Reid, Frank Perry; D: Donald Britain. TWE

Accidental Meeting 🎬🎬½ 1993 (R) A female version of "Strangers on a Train." Two women meet because of an auto accident and wind up talking about their lives. The main topic is man trouble and both "jokingly" plot to murder each other's man. Only, one woman does the deed and the other soon finds herself on the murderess' hit list. 91m/C VHS, Beta, Closed Caption. Linda Gray, Linda Purl, Leigh McCloskey, David Hayward, Ernie Lively, Kent McCord; D: Michael Zinberg; W: Pete Best, Christopher Horner. PAR

The Accidental Tourist 🎬🎬🎬½ 1988 (PG) A bittersweet and subtle story, adapted faithfully from Anne Tyler's novel, of an introverted, grieving man who learns to love again after meeting an unconventional woman. After his son's death and subsequent separation from wife Turner, Macon Leary (Hurt) avoids emotional confrontation, burying himself in routines with the aid of his obsessive-compulsive siblings. Kooky dog-trainer Muriel Pritchett (an exuberant Davis) wins his attention, but not without struggle. Hurt effectively uses small gestures to describe Macon's emotional journey, while Davis grabs hearts with her open performance. Outstanding supporting cast. 121m/C VHS, Beta, LV, 8mm, Letterbox, Closed Caption. William Hurt, Geena Davis, Kathleen Turner, Ed Begley Jr., David Ogden Stiers, Bill Pullman, Amy Wright; D: Lawrence Kasdan; W: Lawrence Kasdan; C: John Bailey; M: John Williams. Academy Awards '88: Best Supporting Actress (Davis); New York Film Critics Awards '88: Best Film; Nominations: Academy Awards '88: Best Adapted Screenplay, Best Picture, Best Original Score. WAR, BTV

Accidents 🎬½ 1989 (R) A scientist discovers that his invention has been stolen and is going to be used to cause worldwide havoc. He becomes concerned and spends the remainder of the movie trying to relieve himself of anxiety. 90m/C VHS, Beta. Edward Albert, Leigh Taylor-Young, Jon Cypher; D: Gideon Amir. TWE

The Accompanist 🎬🎬½ 1993 (PG) Centers around a Parisian diva Irene's (Safonova) relationship with her talented pianist Sophie (Romane Bohringer), amidst the clamor of WWII Europe. Sophie impresses Irene with her musical abilities, and takes on additional work as her housekeeper. Meanwhile, Charles (Richard Bohringer), Irene's husband, schmoozes with the

Nazis to line his own pockets while she helps the war effort by having an affair with a member of the resistance (Labarthe). Unfortunately, Sophie starts to resent living in Irene's shadow. Adapted from the novel by Nina Berberouva. The Bohringers are father and daughter. French with subtitles. 111m/C VHS. FR Elena Safonova, Romane Bohringer, Richard Bohringer, Samuel Labarthe, Nelly Borgeaud, Julien Rassam; D: Claude Miller; W: Claude Miller, Luc Beraud; M: Alain Jomy. COL

Accomplice 🎬½ 1946 Plodding whodunit with Arlen as a shy, bookish private eye hired by his old flame to locate her missing husband. His investigations uncover several murders and long after the viewers have put 2 + 2 together, the P.I. smells a rat. The missing husband was a ruse to divert him from the real scam-a bank heist. Painfully low-level excitement. 66m/B VHS. Richard Arlen, Veda Ann Borg, Tom Dugan, Francis Ford; D: Walter Colmes. NOS

Accused 🎬🎬½ 1936 Married dancers Fairbanks and Del Rio are working in a Parisian revue when the show's sultry leading lady (Desmond) makes a pass at Fairbanks. Though he's turned her down, through a series of misunderstandings Del Rio believes the worst and the two women get into a vicious argument. When the star is found dead guess who gets the blame? Del Rio is lovely, Desmond is spiteful, and Fairbanks serves as a fine object of two women's affections. 83m/B VHS. GB Douglas Fairbanks Jr., Dolores Del Rio, Florence Desmond, Basil Sydney, Athole Stewart, Esme Percy, Googie Withers, Cecil Humphreys; D: Thornton Freeland. HCV

The Accused 🎬🎬½ Strange Deception 1948 Young is cast against character in this story of a college professor who is assaulted by one of her students and kills him in self-defense. A courtroom drama ensues, where Young is defended by the dead man's guardian. Film noir with nice ensemble performance. 101m/B VHS, Beta. Loretta Young, Robert Cummings, Wendell Corey, Sam Jaffe, Douglas Dick, Sara Allgood, Ann Doran; D: William Dieterle; C: Milton Krasner. PAR

The Accused 🎬🎬🎬 1988 (R) Provocative treatment of a true story involving a young woman gang raped in a bar while onlookers cheer. McGillis is the assistant district attorney who takes on the case and must contend with the victim's questionable past and a powerful lawyer hired by a wealthy defendant's parents. As the victim with a past, Foster gives an Oscar-winning performance that won raves for its strength and complexity. 110m/C VHS, Beta, LV, 8mm, Closed Caption. Jodie Foster, Kelly McGillis, Bernie Coulson, Leo Rossi, Ann Hearn, Carmen Argenziano, Steve Antin, Tom O'Brien, Peter Van Norden, Woody Brown; D: Jonathan Kaplan; W: Tom Topor; C: Ralf Bode; M: Brad Fiedel. Academy Awards '88: Best Actress (Foster); Golden Globe Awards '89: Best Actress—Drama (Foster); National Board of Review Awards '88: Best Actress (Foster). PAR, FCT, BTV

Ace Crawford, Private Eye 🎬🎬 19?? Bumbling private eye struggles with confusing murder and somehow manages to solve the case. 71m/C VHS. Tim Conway, Billy Barty, Bill Henderson. MCG

Ace Drummond 🎬🎬 Squadron of Doom 1936 The complete 13-chapter serial about a murder organization that tries to stop several countries from forming a worldwide clipper ship air service and government troubleshooter Ace Drummond who's out to stop them. 260m/B VHS, Beta. John "Dusty" King, Jean Rogers, Noah Beery Jr.; D: Ford Beebe. GPV, HHT, VCN

Ace High 🎬½ 1968 Spaghetti western about a ruthless outlaw named Cat Stevens trying to save himself from the noose. Patterned after the famous Sergio Leone-Clint Eastwood westerns, with less of a budget and more of camp tendencies. 120m/C VHS, Beta. IT Eli Wallach, Terence Hill, Bud Spencer, Brock Peters, Kevin McCarthy; D: Giuseppe Colizzi. PAR, FCT

Ace of Aces 🎬🎬 1933 An American sculptor is reviled, particularly by his girlfriend, when he does not join fellows in enlisting in what becomes WWI. Out to prove he's not lacking testosterone, he becomes a pilot in France, but is embittered by his experiences. Dated but well-acted war melodrama. 77m/B VHS, Beta. Richard Dix, Elizabeth Allan, Theodore Newton, Ralph Bellamy, Joseph Sawyer, Frank Conroy, William Cagney; D: J. Walter Ruben; M: Max Steiner. TTC

Ace of Hearts 🎬 1985 A seedy story about a rich guy in the South Pacific who pays heavily to have himself killed. 90m/C VHS, Beta. Mickey Rooney, Chris Robinson, Pilar Velasquez. VCD

Ace Ventura: Pet Detective 🎬🎬 1993 (PG-13) Shamelessly silly comedy casts human cartoon Carrey, he of the rubber limbs and spasmodic facial muscles, as Ace, the guy who'll find missing pets, big or small. When the Miami Dolphins' mascot Snowflake is kidnapped, he abandons his search for an albino pigeon to save the lost dolphin just in time for the Super Bowl. This is brain candy, running full throttle with juvenile humor, some charm, and the hyper-energetic Carrey, not to mention Young as the police chief with a secret. Critically trashed boxoffice smash catapulted Carrey into nearly instant stardom after seven seasons as the geeky white guy on "In Living Color." CW: Off-color humor and some nudity. 87m/C VHS, LV, 8mm, Closed Caption. Jim Carrey, Dan Marino, Courteney Cox, Sean Young, Tone Loc; D: Tom Shadyac; W: Jim Carrey, Tom Shadyac, Jack Bernstein; M: Ira Newborn. Blockbuster Entertainment Awards '95: Male Newcomer, Video (Carrey), Comedy Actor, Video (Carrey); Nominations: MTV Movie Awards '94: Best Comedic Performance (Carrey). WAR

Ace Ventura: When Nature Calls 🎬🎬 Ace Ventura Goes to Africa 1995 (PG-13) Ace is back on the case as the pet dick (Carrey) ventures to Africa to restore peace among rival tribes by finding an albino bat that's M.I.A. Plot is secondary, however, to multi-million dollar man Carrey's outrageous brand of physical comedy combined with his unique ability to deliver junior high level lines with pseudo-suave savoir-faire. Contains only a handful of outstanding gags, the best with Ace and a mechanical rhino. Mainly for Carrey aficionados (of which there are many) and original "Ace" fans—the low-brow humor runs a bit thin by the end. CW: Crude humor. 94m/C VHS, LV, Closed Caption. Jim Carrey, Ian McNeice, Simon Callow, Maynard Eziashi, Bob Gunton, Sophie Okonedo, Tommy Davidson; D: Steve Oedekerk; W: Steve Oedekerk; C: Donald E. Thorin; M: Robert Folk. MTV Movie Awards '96: Best Male Performance (Carrey), Best Comedic Performance (Carrey); Blockbuster Entertainment Awards '96: Comedy Actor, Theatrical (Carrey); Nominations: MTV Movie Awards '96: Best Kiss (Jim Carrey/Sophie Okonedo). WAR

Aces and Eights 🎬🎬½ 1936 Gambler McCoy catches a fellow cardsharp cheating and the marshal runs the varmint out of town. When the cheater is murdered, the lawman suspects McCoy, who sets out to prove his innocence. Title refers to the "death hand" held by Wild Bill Hickok, killed while playing poker. Film opens with a shot of Hickok and a speech about gambler's luck. 62m/B VHS. Tim McCoy, Jimmy Aubrey, Luana Walters, Wheeler Oakman, Earle Hodgins, Frank Glennon, Rex Lease, Charles Stevens, Joseph Girard, John Merton; D: Sam Newfield. NOS, DVT, RXM

Aces: Iron Eagle 3 🎬🎬 1992 (R) Colonel "Chappy" Sinclair once again in this air adventure. He's been keeping busy flying in air shows when he stumbles across the nefarious activities of a Peruvian drug baron working out of a remote village. Sinclair recruits a team of maverick air circus pilots and they "borrow" a fleet of WWII vintage aircraft to raid the village, coming up against a fellow Air Force officer who turns out to be another villain. Lots of action and a stalwart cast. CW: War violence. 98m/C VHS, LV, Closed Caption. Louis Gossett Jr., Rachel McLish, Paul Freeman,

Horst Buchholz, Christopher Cazenove, Sonny Chiba, Fred Dalton Thompson, Mitchell Ryan, Robert Estes, I F Freeman; **D:** John Glen. COL

Aces Wild 🎞️½ 1937 Another poker title. Outlaws menace an honest newspaper until the lawmen show up and send them on their way. **62m/B VHS, Beta, LV.** Harry Carey Sr., Gertrude Messinger, Edward Cassidy, Roger Williams; **D:** Harry Fraser. NO

The Acid Eaters 🎞️ 1967 Straight-laced desk jockeys spend their weekends exploring the realm of the senses. Includes nudity. **62m/C VHS.** Buck Kartalian, Pat Barringer; **D:** B. Ron Elliott; **W:** B. Ron Elliott, Carl Monson; **M:** Billy Allen. SMW, TPV

Acla's Descent into Floristella 🎞️🎞️ Acla 1987 Twelve-year-old Acla (Cusimano) is sold by his father to work underground in the sulfur mines for eight years. Repeatedly beaten by his owner, Acla runs away, but there are dire consequences for him and his family. Set in 1930s Sicily. Italian with subtitles. **86m/C VHS.** IT Francesco Cusimano, Tony Sperandeo; **D:** Aurelio Grimaldi; **W:** Aurelio Grimaldi; **C:** Maurizio Calvesi; **M:** Dario Lucantoni. FCT

Acorn People 🎞️🎞️ 1982 An unemployed teacher takes a summer job at a camp for handicapped children and learns sensitivity. Made-for-television weeper adapted by Tewkesbury from the book by Ron Jones. **97m/C VHS, Beta.** Ted Bessell, Cloris Leachman, LeVar Burton, Dolph Sweet, Cheryl Anderson; **D:** Joan Tewkesbury. TLF

Acqua e Sapone 🎞️½ 1983 (PG) A young innocent model goes to Rome under the watchful eyes of an appointed priest-chaperon, but finds love, fun and other sinful things. Sudsy/romantic comedy. **100m/C VHS, Beta.** IT Carlo Verdone, Natasha Hovey, Florinda Bolkan, Elena Bolkan; **D:** Carlo Verdone. NO

Across 110th Street 🎞️🎞️ 1972 (R) Gritty, violent cop thriller in the blaxploitation genre. Both the Mafia and the cops hunt down three black hoods who, in a display of extremely bad judgment, knocked over a mob-controlled bank while disguised as police. Lots of bullets create buckets of blood. Filmed on location in Harlem. **102m/C VHS, Beta.** Anthony Quinn, Yaphet Kotto, Anthony (Tony) Franciosa, Paul Benjamin, Ed Bernard, Antonio Fargas, Tim O'Connor, Lewis Gilbert, Richard Ward; **D:** Barry Shear; **W:** Luther Davis; **C:** Jack Priestley. MGM, FOX

Across the Bridge 🎞️🎞️½ 1957 A man on the run from Scotland Yard for stealing a fortune flees to Mexico, in the process killing a man and assuming his identity. An ironic twist and his love for a dog seal his final destiny. Steiger's psychological study as the fugitive is compelling. Based on a novel by Graham Greene. **103m/B VHS, Beta.** GB Rod Steiger, David Knight, Marla Landi, Noel Willman, Bernard Lee; **D:** Ken Annakin; **M:** James Bernard. BFA

Across the Great Divide 🎞️🎞️½ 1976 (G) Two orphans must cross the rugged snow-covered Rocky Mountains in 1876 in order to claim their inheritance—a 400-acre plot of land in Salem, Oregon. Pleasant coming-of-age tale with majestic scenery. **102m/C VHS, Beta.** Robert F. Logan, George Flower, Heather Rattray, Mark Hall; **D:** Stewart Raffill; **W:** Stewart Raffill; **M:** Angelo Badalamenti. VTR

Across the Moon 🎞️🎞️ 1994 (R) A road trip to the desert takes Carmen and Kathy away from their incarcerated boyfriends but into troubles with cowboys and prospectors. **CW:** Strong language; some sexuality. **88m/C VHS.** Elizabeth Pena, Christina Applegate, Tony Fields, Peter Berg, James Remar, Michael McKean, Burgess Meredith, Jack Nance; **D:** Lisa Gottlieb; **C:** Andrzej Sekula; **M:** Christopher Tyng, Exene Cervenka.

Across the Pacific 🎞️🎞️🎞️½ 1942 Classic Bogie/Huston vehicle made on the heels of "The Maltese Falcon." Bogie is an American Army officer booted out of the service on false charges of treason. When no other military will accept him, he sails to China (via the Panama Canal) to offer his services to Chiang Kai-Shek. On board, he meets a variety of seedy characters who plan to blow up the canal. Huston again capitalizes on the counterpoint between the rotundly acerbic Greenstreet, who plays a spy, and stiff-lipped Bogart, who's wooing Astor. Great Bogie moments and fine direction make this an adventure classic. When he departed for the service just prior to filming the final scenes, Huston turned over direction to Vincent Sherman. Also available colorized. **97m/B VHS.** Humphrey Bogart, Mary Astor, Sydney Greenstreet, Charles Halton, Victor Sen Yung, Roland Got, Keye Luke, Richard Loo; **D:** John Huston. MGM, FCT

Across the Plains 🎞️½ 1939 Predictable oater about two brothers who are raised separately after their parents are murdered by outlaws. One is brought up by Indians, the other by the outlaws responsible for wiping out the folks, who tell the boy that Indians did in his ma and pa. Eventually the brothers meet and fight. Odds favor the good one winning, aided by Indian pals. **59m/B VHS, Beta.** Jack Randall, Frank Yaconelli, Joyce Bryant, Hal Price, Dennis Moore, Glenn Strange, Bud Osborne; **D:** Spencer Gordon Bennet. NOS, GPV, DVT

Across the Tracks 🎞️🎞️ 1989 (PG-13) Two brothers, Billy (Schroder), a juvie-home rebel, and Joe (Pitt), a straight-A jock, are at odds when the black sheep is pressured into selling drugs. In an attempt to save his brother from a life of crime, saintly Joe convinces Billy to join him on the school track team, and the brothers are forced to face off in a big meet. Fairly realistic good guy/bad guy who's really a good guy teen drama. **101m/C VHS.** Rick Schroder, Brad Pitt, Carrie Snodgress; **D:** Sandy Tung; **W:** Sandy Tung; **C:** Michael Delahoussaye; **M:** Joel Goldsmith. MPI

Across the Wide Missouri 🎞️🎞️½ 1951 Pioneer epic stars Gable as a rugged fur trapper who marries an Indian woman (Marques) so he can trap beaver pelts on her people's rich land. On the journey to the Indian territory however, the trapper truly falls in love with his bride. Superior historical drama is marred slightly by the use of narration (provided by Howard Keel). Look for lively performances from Menjou as a French tippler and Naish as the quirky Indian Chief. Beautiful scenery filmed in the spectacular Rocky Mountains. **78m/C VHS.** Clark Gable, Ricardo Montalban, John Hodiak, Adolphe Menjou, Maria Elena Marques, J. Carrol Naish, Jack Holt, Alan Napier; **D:** William A. Wellman; **C:** William Mellor. MGM, CCB

The Act 🎞️🎞️ Bless 'Em All 1982 (R) A muddled satire about political double dealing and union corruption further muddled by a twangy musical score manufactured by folksy Sebastian. **90m/C VHS, Beta.** Jill St. John, Eddie Albert, Pat Hingle, Robert Ginty, Sarah Langenfeld, Nicolas Surovy; **D:** Sig Shore; **M:** John Sebastian. VES

Act of Aggression 🎞️🎞️ 1973 (R) When a Parisian man finds his wife and daughter murdered at a summer resort, he takes the law into his own hands, with predictable results. **100m/C VHS, Beta.** FR Jean-Louis Trintignant, Catherine Deneuve, Claude Brasseur. FCT

Act of Passion: The Lost Honor of Kathryn Beck 🎞️🎞️½ 1983 A woman meets a man at a party and has the proverbial one-night stand. Her privacy is shattered when she discovers that he's a terrorist under surveillance by the police and press. Strong performances by Thomas and Kristofferson help turn this into an interesting American television remake of the German "Lost Honor of Katharina Blum," based loosely on a novel by Heinrich Boll. **100m/C VHS, Beta.** Marlo Thomas, Kris Kristofferson, George Dzundza, Jon DeVries; **D:** Simon Langton. THV

Act of Piracy 🎞️½ 1989 (R) A bankrupt contractor reunites with his estranged wife to track down the brutal terrorists who have kidnapped their son. **105m/C VHS, Beta, LV.** Ray Sharkey, Gary Busey. WAR

Act of Vengeance 🎞️🎞️ Rape Squad 1974 (R) A group of women band together to hunt down and exact revenge on the man who raped them. Exploitative action-filled thriller. **90m/C VHS, Beta.** Jo Ann Harris, Peter Brown, Jennifer Lee, Lisa Moore, Connie Strickland, Pat Estrin; **D:** Bob Kelljan. NO

Act of Vengeance 🎞️🎞️½ 1986 Drama about Jock Yablonski, a United Mine Workers official who challenged the president, Tony Boyle. Made for cable, based on fact, showing the events that led up to the murder of Yablonski and his family. Intriguing story lacking cinematic drive. **97m/C VHS, Beta, Closed Caption.** Charles Bronson, Ellen Burstyn, Wilford Brimley, Hoyt Axton, Robert Schenkan, Ellen Barkin, Keanu Reeves; **D:** John MacKenzie; **W:** Scott Spencer. NO

Acting on Impulse 🎞️🎞️ 1993 (R) Impulsive, troublemaking movie star (Fiorentino) becomes a murder suspect when her producer is killed. This doesn't slow her down. She checks into a hotel with a major party attitude and manages to seduce a conservative businessman (Howell) and his junior exec (Allen) into helping her forget her troubles. And then the businessman's fiance turns up dead. Any connection? Made for cable television. **94m/C VHS.** Linda Fiorentino, C. Thomas Howell, Nancy Allen, Adam Ant, Judith Hoag, Patrick Bauchau, Isaac Hayes, Paul Bartel, Donny Most, Miles O'Keeffe, Dick Sargent, Charles Lane, Mary Woronov, Zelda Rubinstein, Nicholas Sadler, Peter Lupus, Kim McGuire, Cassandra Peterson, Brinke Stevens, Michael Talbot, Robert Alan Golub, Cliff Dorfman, Craig Shoemaker, Scott Thompson Stevens; **D:** Sam Irvin; **W:** Mark Pittman, Alan Moskowitz; **C:** Dean Lent; **M:** Daniel Licht.

Action for Slander 🎞️🎞️½ 1938 A British army officer sporting the typical stiff upper lip is accused of cheating during a card game, and the slander mars his reputation until the case is taken to court. Dryly earnest and honest in its depiction of class differences in pre-war England. Based on a novel by Mary Borden. **84m/B VHS, Beta, 8mm.** GB Clive Brook, Ann Todd, Margaretta Scott, Ronald Squire, Francis L. Sullivan, Felix Aylmer, Googie Withers; **D:** Tim Whelan. VYY

Action in Arabia 🎞️🎞️ 1944 A newsman uncovers a Nazi plot to turn the Arabs against the Allies while investigating a colleague's murder in Damascus. The desert teems with spies, double agents, and sheiks as suave Sanders goes about his investigative business. Quintessential wartime B-movie. **75m/B VHS, Beta.** George Sanders, Virginia Bruce, Lenore Aubert, Gene Lockhart, Robert Armstrong, H.B. Warner, Alan Napier, Michael Ansara; **D:** Leonide Moguy. TTC

Action in the North Atlantic 🎞️🎞️ 1943 Massey and Bogart are the captain and first mate of a Merchant Marine vessel running the lone supply route to the Soviet Union. Eventually they wind up locking horns with a Nazi U-boat. Plenty of action and strenuous flag waving in this propagandorama. Gordon fans won't want to miss her as Massey's wife. Also available colorized. **126m/B VHS.** Humphrey Bogart, Raymond Massey, Alan Hale, Julie Bishop, Ruth Gordon, Sam Levene, Dane Clark; **D:** Lloyd Bacon. Nominations: Academy Awards '43: Best Story. MGM, FCT

Action Jackson 🎞️🎞️ 1988 (R) Power-hungry auto tycoon Nelson tries to frame rebellious black police sergeant Weathers for murder. Being a graduate of Harvard and a tough guy, the cop doesn't go for it. Nelson eats up the screen as the heavy with no redeeming qualities, while Weathers is tongue-in-cheek as the resourceful good guy who keeps running afoul of the law in spite of his best efforts. Lots of action, violence, and a few sexy women help cover the plot's lack of common sense. **96m/C VHS, Beta, LV, Closed Caption.** Carl Weathers, Vanity, Craig T. Nelson, Sharon Stone; **D:** Craig R. Baxley; **W:** Robert Reneau; **M:** Herbie Hancock, Michael Kamen. ORI, WAR

Action U.S.A. *√*½ **1989** A young woman witnesses the murder of her boyfriend by gangsters, who then pursue her to make sure she will never tell what she saw. Throughout Texas she rambles with the mob sniffing at her heels, grateful for the opportunity to participate in numerous stunts and car crashes. **90m/C VHS, Beta.** Barri Murphy, Greg Cummins, William Knight, William Smith, Cameron Mitchell; **D:** John Stewart; **W:** David Reskin; **C:** Thomas Callaway. *IMP*

Actor: The Paul Muni Story *√√* **1978** Musical biography of Paul Muni, from his beginnings as a traveling actor in Hungary to his New York theatre and movie career. **105m/C VHS, Beta.** Herschel Bernardi, Georgia Brown, Harold Gould. *ART*

Actors and Sin *√√*½ **1952** Two-part film casting a critical eye toward actors and Hollywood. "Actor's Blood" is the melodramatic story of Shakespearean actor Robinson and his unhappy actress daughter. She commits suicide and he sets out to prove it was murder. Heavy going. Lighter and more entertaining is "Woman of Sin," which relates a Hollywood satire involving a theatrical agent and his newest client, a precocious nine-year-old. **82m/B VHS, LV.** Edward G. Robinson, Eddie Albert, Marsha Hunt, Alan Reed, Dan O'Herlihy, Tracey Roberts, Rudolph Anders, Paul Guilfoyle, Alice Key, Douglas Evans, Rick Roman, Jenny Hecht, Jody Gilbert, John Crawford; **D:** Lee Garmes, Ben Hecht; **W:** Ben Hecht; **C:** Lee Garmes; **M:** George Antheil. *COL*

An Actor's Revenge *√√*½ *Yukinojo Henge* **1963** In the early 19th century, a female impersonator in a Kabuki troupe takes revenge on the three men who killed his parents. Fascinating study of opposites—male/female, stage/life, love/hate. In Japanese with English subtitles. **110m/C VHS.** *JP* Kazuo Hasegawa, Fujiko Yamamoto, Ayako Wakao, Ganjiro Nakamura; **D:** Kon Ichikawa; **W:** Teinosuke Kinugasa, Daisuke Ito, Natto Wada; **M:** Yashushi Akutagawa. *NYF, ING*

Adam *√√√*½ **1983** Television docu-drama based on a tragic, true story. John and Reve Williams (Travanti and Williams) desperately search for their six-year-old son abducted during an outing. During their long search and struggle, they lobby Congress for use of the FBI's crime computer. Eventually their efforts led to the creation of the Missing Children's Bureau. Sensitive, compelling performances by Travanti and Williams as the agonized, courageous parents. **100m/C VHS, Beta, Closed Caption.** Daniel J. Travanti, JoBeth Williams, Martha Scott, Richard Masur, Paul Regina, Mason Adams; **D:** Michael Tuchner. *NO*

Adam at 6 a.m. *√√* **1970 (PG)** Douglas is a young college professor who decides to spend a summer laboring in Missouri, where life, he thinks, is simpler. Of course, he learns that life in the boonies has its own set of problems, but unfortunately it takes him the entire movie before he catches the drift. **100m/C VHS, Beta.** Michael Douglas, Lee Purcell, Joe Don Baker, Charles Aidman, Marge Redmond, Louise Latham, Grayson Hall, Dana Elcar, Meg Foster, Richard Derr, Anne Gwynne; **D:** Robert Scheerer. *FOX*

Adam Had Four Sons *√√*½ **1941** Satisfying character study involving the typical turn-of-the-century family nearly consumed by love, jealousy, and hatred. In the early part of the century, a goodly governess (Bergman in her second U.S. film) watches sympathetically over four sons of an American businessman after their mother dies. Economic necessity separates Bergman from the family for several years. Upon her return, she tangles with scheming bride-to-be Hayward, a bad girl intent on dividing and conquering the family before walking down the aisle with one of the sons. Based on a novel by Charles Bonner. **81m/B VHS, Beta.** Ingrid Bergman, Warner Baxter, Susan Hayward, Fay Wray, Richard Denning, June Lockhart, Robert Shaw; **D:** Gregory Ratoff. *COL*

Adam's Rib *√√√√* **1950** Classic war between the sexes cast Tracy and Hepburn as married attorneys on opposite sides of the courtroom in the trial of blonde bombshell Holliday, charged with attempted murder of the lover of her philandering husband. The battle in the courtroom soon takes its toll at home as the couple is increasingly unable to leave their work at the office. Sharp, snappy dialogue by Gordon and Kanin with superb direction by Cukor. Perhaps the best of the nine movies pairing Tracy and Hepburn. Also available colorized. **101m/B VHS, Beta, LV.** Spencer Tracy, Katharine Hepburn, Judy Holliday, Tom Ewell, David Wayne, Jean Hagen, Hope Emerson, Polly Moran, Marvin Kaplan, Paula Raymond, Tommy Noonan; **D:** George Cukor; **W:** Garson Kanin, Ruth Gordon; **M:** Miklos Rozsa. National Film Registry '92;; Nominations: Academy Awards '50: Best Story & Screenplay. *MGM, HMV*

The Addams Family 1964 The positively ooky family, based on the characters created by cartoonist Charles Addams, appear in the original, uncut television episodes. Two episodes per tape. This volume includes "The Addams Family Goes to School" and "Morticia and the Psychiatrist." **50m/B VHS.** John Astin, Carolyn Jones, Jackie Coogan, Ted Cassidy, Blossom Rock, Ken Weatherwax, Lisa Loring, Felix Silla. *WOV, MOV*

The Addams Family *√√* **1991 (PG-13)** Everybody's favorite family of ghouls hits the big screen, but something is lost in the translation. An imposter claiming to be long-lost Uncle Fester (Lloyd), who says he was in the Bermuda Triangle for 25 years, shows up at the Addams' home to complete a dastardly deed—raid the family's immense fortune. Although Fester's plan is foiled, a series of plot twists highlight the ghoulish family's eccentricities. Darkly humorous but eventually disappointing: Julia, Huston, and Ricci are great in their roles and the sets look good, but the plot is thin. Much closer to the original comic strip by Charles Addams than the popular TV show ever was. **102m/C VHS, Beta, LV, Letterbox, Closed Caption.** Anjelica Huston, Raul Julia, Christopher Lloyd, Dan Hedaya, Elizabeth Wilson, Judith Malina, Carel Struycken, Dana Ivey, Paul Benedict, Christina Ricci, Jimmy Workman, Christopher Hart, John Franklin; **Cameos:** Marc Shaiman; **D:** Barry Sonnenfeld; **W:** Caroline Thompson, Larry Thompson; **C:** Owen Roizman; **M:** Marc Shaiman. Golden Raspberry Awards '91: Worst Song ("Addams Groove"); Nominations: Academy Awards '91: Best Costume Design. *PAR*

Addams Family Values *√√*½ **1993 (PG-13)** The creepy Addams' are back, but this time they leave the dark confines of the mansion to meet the "real" world. New baby Pubert causes homicidal jealousy in sibs Wednesday and Pugsley, causing Mom and Dad to hire a gold-digging, serial-killing nanny (Cusack) with designs on Uncle Fester to watch over the tot. A step above its predecessor, chock full of black humor, sub-plots, and one-liners. Cusack fits right in with an outrageously over the top performance and Ricci nearly steals the show again as the deadpan Wednesday. **CW:** Macabre humor. **93m/C VHS, Beta, LV, Letterbox, Closed Caption.** Anjelica Huston, Raul Julia, Christopher Lloyd, Joan Cusack, Carol Kane, Christina Ricci, Jimmy Workman, Kaitlyn Hooper, Kristen Hooper, Carel Struycken, David Krumholtz, Christopher Hart, Dana Ivey, Peter MacNicol, Christine Baranski, Mercedes McNab; **D:** Barry Sonnenfeld; **W:** Paul Rudnick; **M:** Marc Shaiman. Golden Raspberry Awards '93: Worst Song ("WHOOMP! There It Is"); Nominations: Academy Awards '93: Best Art Direction/Set Decoration; Golden Globe Awards '94: Best Actress—Musical/Comedy (Huston). *PAR*

Addicted to Love *√√*½ **1996 (R)** Warning: Do not rent this movie with your significant other if you're thinking about breaking up with them. After they're both dumped, mild-mannered Sam (Broderick) and wild woman Maggie (Ryan) discover they have a lot in common. First of all, their exes Linda (Preston) and Anton (Karyo) are dating each other. Secondly, they're both stalkers! Yep! A romantic comedy about stalking. Sam wants nothing more than to reclaim Linda as his own. Maggie wants nothing less than Anton's head on a plate. Interesting comedy wavers between dark and light moments, aided by the rather murky sets and lighting. Directorial debut for Dunne, who makes his father eat a bug in one scene. **CW:** Sexual content. **100m/C VHS.** Meg Ryan, Matthew Broderick, Kelly Preston, Maureen Stapleton, Remak Ramsay, Nesbitt Blaisdell, Dominick Dunne; **D:** Griffin Dunne; **W:** Robert Gordon; **C:** Andrew Dunn; **M:** Rachel Portman. *WAR*

The Addiction *√√*½ **1995 (R)** Ph.D. candidate Kathleen Conklin (Taylor, in a haunting performance) gets bitten by more than the philosophy bug while attending university in Manhattan. When attacked by a female vampire (Sciorra), Kathleen quickly becomes driven by a ferocious blood need, beginning with an attack that parallels drug addiction when she stabs a derelict with a hypodermic needle and injects his blood into her own veins. Bitingly pretentious, themes experiment with the philosophy of Kirkegaard, Nietzsche, and Sartre, and exploitative glimpses of the Holocaust and the My Lai massacre attempt to connect Kathleen's struggle to resist evil to historical atrocities. **CW:** Contains scenes of bloody vampire assaults. **82m/B VHS.** Lili Taylor, Christopher Walken, Annabella Sciorra, Edie Falco, Paul Calderone, Fredro Star, Kathryn Erbe, Michael Imperioli; **D:** Abel Ferrara; **W:** Nicholas St. John; **M:** Joe Delia. Nominations: Independent Spirit Awards '96: Best Actress (Taylor), Best Film. *PGV*

Address Unknown *√√*½ **1996 (PG)** A ten-year-old letter and a priceless stamp provide a teenager with clues to dad's mysterious death. **92m/C VHS.** Kyle Howard, Johna Stewart, Patrick Renna, Corbin Allred, Michel Flynn; **D:** Shawn Levy. *WAR*

Adios Amigo *√√* **1975 (PG)** Offbeat western comedy has ad-libbing Pryor hustling as a perennially inept con man. Script and direction (both provided by Williamson) are not up to Pryor's level, although excessive violence and vulgarity are avoided in a boring attempt to provide good clean family fare. **87m/C VHS, LV.** Fred Williamson, Richard Pryor, Thalmus Rasulala, James Brown, Robert Philip, Mike Henry; **D:** Fred Williamson; **W:** Fred Williamson. *SIM, THV*

Adios Gringo *√*½ **1965** Routine oater in which a young rancher is swindled in a cattle deal and forced to kill in self defense. **?m/C VHS.** Montgomery Wood, Evelyn Stewart. *SNC*

Adios, Hombre *√* **1968** An innocent man who was imprisoned for murder escapes from prison and seeks revenge. You'll be saying adios as well. **90m/C VHS, Beta.** *IT* Craig Hill, Giulia Rubini; **D:** Mario Caiano. *UNI*

The Adjuster *√√*½ **1991 (R)** Critics either loved or hated this strange film. Insurance adjuster Noah Render's clients look to him for all sorts of comfort, so much so that his own identity becomes a blurred reflection of their tragedies. Wife Hera is a film censor who secretly tapes the pornographic videos she watches at work. Their carefully organized lives are invaded by Bubba and Mimi, a wealthy couple who pass themselves off as filmmakers who want to use the Render house as a movie set. They are instead looking to involve the Renders in their latest and most elaborate erotic fantasy. Lots of symbolism, but little substance. **CW:** Language and sensuality. **102m/C VHS.** **CA** Elias Koteas, Arsinee Khanjian, Maury Chaykin, Gabrielle Rose, David Hemblen, Jennifer Dale, Don McKellar, Raoul Trujillo; **D:** Atom Egoyan; **W:** Atom Egoyan; **C:** Paul Sarossy; **M:** Mychael Danna. Toronto-City Award '91: Best Canadian Feature Film. *ORI*

The Admiral Was a Lady *√√* **1950** Four ex-GIs try to get by in life without going to work. Hendrix walks into their lives as a winning ex-Wave gifted with a knack for repartee who is disgusted by their collective lack of ambition. Nevertheless, she is pursued by the zany quartet with predictable results. **87m/B VHS, Beta.** Edmond O'Brien, Wanda Hendrix, Rudy Vallee, Steve Brodie; **D:** Albert Rogell. *NOS, VHE, DVT*

Adomas Nori Buti Zmogumi 🐾🐾 *Adam Wants to Be a Man* 1959 Soviet Lithuanian feature in its original form, with dialogue in Lithuanian. A young worker scrapes together money for a ticket to Buenos Aires, but the money is stolen by the manager of the travel office. 90m/B **VHS.** *RU LI* **D:** V. Zhalakyavichus. *IHF*

Adoption 🐾🐾🐾 *Orkobefogadas* 1975 The third of Meszaros's trilogy, involving a middle-aged Hungarian woman who longs for a child and instead forms a deep friendship with a 19-year-old orphan. In Hungarian with English subtitles. 89m/B **VHS, Beta.** *HU* Kati Berek, Laszlo Szabo, Gyongyver Vigh, Dr. Arpad Perlaky; **D:** Marta Meszaros; **W:** Marta Meszaros, Gyula Hernadi; **C:** Lajos Koltai; **M:** Gyorgy Kovacs. Berlin International Film Festival '75: Golden Berlin Bear. *KIV*

The Adorable Cheat 🐾🐾 1928 A low-budget, late-silent melodrama about a young woman who tries to get involved in the family business, despite her father's refusal of her help. Once in the business, she finds love. 76m/B **VHS, Beta, 8mm.** Lila Lee, Cornelius Keefe, Burr McIntosh; **D:** Burton King. *GPV, VYY*

Adorable Julia 🐾🐾 1962 When an actress takes on a lover many years younger than herself, the laughs begin to fly in this sex comedy based on W. Somerset Maugham's novel. 97m/C **VHS.** *FR* Lilli Palmer, Charles Boyer; **D:** Alfred Weidenmann. *FCT, VEC*

Adrenalin: Fear the Rush 🐾 1996 (R) Dull future thriller in the deadly virus category. In 2007, a plague in Eastern Europe causes those that survive to turn into cannabalistic killers. The U.S. has started quarantine camps, one of which is in Boston, and two cops (Henstridge and Lambert) must track down an infected killer who's escaped. Not worth your time. **CW:** Gruesome violence and gore, strong language. 77m/C **VHS, LV, Closed Caption.** Christopher Lambert, Natasha Henstridge, Norbert Weisser, Craig Davis, Elizabeth Barondes, Xavier DeClie; **D:** Albert Pyun; **W:** Albert Pyun; **C:** George Mooradian; **M:** Tony Riparetti. *TOU*

Adrift 🐾🐾½ 1993 Yet another couple-in-terror-from-psychos-on-the-high-seas flick. Katie and Guy Nast (Jackson and Welsh) are on an anniversary sailing adventure intended to shore up their shaky marriage. They discover a boat adrift with two survivors (Greenwood and Rowan) who have a suspicious story but they help them nonetheless. Big mistake. Made for television. 92m/C **VHS, Closed Caption.** Kate Jackson, Kenneth Welsh, Bruce Greenwood, Kelly Rowan; **D:** Christian Duguay. *WOV*

The Adultress 🐾 1977 (R) When a husband and wife cannot satisfy their desire to have a family, they hire a young man to help them in this dumb made-for-television melodrama. 85m/C **VHS, Beta.** Tyne Daly, Eric (Hans Gudegast) Braeden, Gregory Morton; **D:** Norbert Meisel. *NO*

Adventure 🐾🐾 1945 Gable's first postwar film has him as a roughneck sailor romancing a shy and reserved librarian (Garson). Dull and disappointing—both stars deserve better. However, there is a touching scene of Gable with newborn child that might be of interest to some. Based on the novel by Clyde Brion Davis. 130m/B **VHS.** Clark Gable, Greer Garson, Joan Blondell, Thomas Mitchell, Tom Tully, John Qualen, Richard Haydn, Lina Romay; **D:** Victor Fleming; **W:** Vincent Lawrence, Frederick Hazlitt Brennan; **C:** Joseph Ruttenberg. *MGM*

Adventure Island 🐾½ 1947 En route to Australia, a small ship stops at a remote island for supplies. The crew is greeted by a crazed, tyrannical leader who makes their lives difficult. Dull low-budget remake of 1937's "Ebb Tide." 66m/C **VHS, Beta.** Rory Calhoun, Rhonda Fleming, Paul Kelly, John Abbott; **D:** Sam Newfield. *SNC*

Adventure of the Action Hunters 🐾 1987 (PG) A dying sailor leaves a tourist couple a message leading to a treasure, and they vie for it along with gangsters, mercenaries and other unsavory types. 81m/C **VHS, Beta.**

Ronald Hunter, Sean Murphy, Joe Cimino; **D:** Lee Bonner. *NO*

The Adventurer 🐾🐾½ 1917 An escaped convict saves two wealthy women from death. They mistake him for a gallant sportsman and bring him home. Early Chaplin silent with music track. 20m/B **VHS, Beta.** Charlie Chaplin, Charles Halton; **D:** Charlie Chaplin. *CAB*

The Adventurers 🐾🐾 *Fortune in Diamonds; The Great Adventure* 1951 At the turn of the century, two Boers and an English officer set out to recover stolen jewels hidden in the jungles of South Africa. On the way, greed and anger take their toll a la "The Treasure of Sierra Madre," only on a less convincing scale. 82m/B **VHS, Beta.** *GB* Dennis Price, Jack Hawkins, Siobhan McKenna, Peter Hammond, Bernard Lee; **D:** David MacDonald. *NOS*

The Adventurers woof! 1970 (R) Sleazy Harold Robbins novel retains its trashy aura on film. Unfortunately, this turkey is also long and boring. Set in South America, it tells the tale of a rich playboy who uses and destroys everyone who crosses his path. His vileness results from having seen his mother murdered by outlaws, but his obsession is to avenge his father's murder. Blood, gore, revolutions, and exploitive sex follow him everywhere. Watch and be amazed at the big-name stars who signed on for this one. 171m/C **VHS, Closed Caption.** Candice Bergen, Olivia de Havilland, Bekim Fehmiu, Charles Aznavour, Alan Badel, Ernest Borgnine, Leigh Taylor-Young, Fernando Rey, Thommy Berggren, John Ireland, Sydney Tafler, Rossano Brazzi, Anna Moffo, Christian Roberts, Yorgo Voyagis, Angela Scoular, Yolande Donlan, Ferdinand "Ferdy" Mayne, Jaclyn Smith, Peter Graves, Roberta Haynes; **D:** Lewis Gilbert. *PAR*

Adventures Beyond Belief 🐾 *Neat and Tidy* 1987 An irreverent motorcyclist is chased across Europe for a murder he didn't commit. Firmly within the boundaries of belief. 95m/C **VHS, Beta.** Elke Sommer, Jill Whitlow, Graham Stark, Stella Stevens, Larry Storch, Thick Wilson, Skyler Cole, Edie Adams, John Astin; **D:** Marcus Thompson. *NO*

Adventures in Babysitting 🐾🐾½ 1987 (PG-13) Pleasant comedy has its moments when a babysitter and her charges leave peaceful suburbia for downtown Chicago to rescue a friend in trouble. After a flat tire strands them on the freeway, trouble takes on a new meaning. Shue is charming as the hapless sitter, unexpectedly dateless, who finds herself doing a lot more than just watching the kids. Ludicrous at times, but still fun to watch. 102m/C **VHS, Beta, LV, 8mm, Closed Caption.** Elisabeth Shue, Keith Coogan, Maia Brewton, Anthony Rapp, Calvin Levels, Vincent D'Onofrio, Penelope Ann Miller, George Newbern, John Ford Noonan, Lolita Davidovich, Albert Collins; **D:** Chris Columbus; **W:** David Simkins; **M:** Michael Kamen. *TOU*

Adventures in Dinosaur City 🐾🐾 1992 (PG) Expect to see lots of movies riding on the coattails of the dino mania sweeping the land. Some will be good, others will not. "Adventures" falls into the latter category. Modern-day pre-teen siblings are transported back in time to the stone age. There they meet their favorite TV characters (they're dinosaurs) and help them solve prehistoric crimes. Family film may amuse kids, but adults should stick to "Jurassic Park." 88m/C **VHS, LV, Closed Caption.** Omri Katz, Shawn Hoffman, Tiffanie Poston, Pete Koch, Megan Hughes, Tony Doyle, Mimi Maynard; **D:** Brett Thompson; **W:** Willie Baronet, Lisa Morton; **M:** Fredric Teetsel. *REP*

Adventures in Spying 🐾🐾 1992 (PG-13) Brian McNichols is just trying to enjoy his summer vacation when he discovers that a notorious drug lord is living in his neighborhood. After realizing there is a $50,000 reward for his capture, he enlists the help of his friend (Schoelen) to get the man's picture for the police. Action-packed film is geared towards the junior high set, but relies too heavily on coincidence and other plot connivances to compete with espionage flicks directed at an older market. 92m/C **VHS, Closed Caption.** Jill

Schoelen, Bernie Coulson, Seymour Cassel, G. Gordon Liddy, Michael Emil; **D:** Hil Covington; **W:** Hil Covington; **M:** James Stemple. *NLC*

The Adventures of a Gnome Named Gnorm 🐾🐾½ *A Gnome Named Gnorm* 1993 (PG) Silly cop caper finds LAPD detective Casey (Hall) stuck with a very strange new partner—a bark-wearing gnome named Gnorm. The two team up to go after a diamond smuggling ring. The special-effects creature may hold the kiddies interest. 86m/C **VHS.** Anthony Michael Hall, Jerry Orbach, Claudia Christian; **D:** Stan Winston. *PGV*

Adventures of a Private Eye 🐾 1987 A self-mocking British detective farce about an inept private eye who takes his time tracking down a beautiful girl's blackmailer, bedding down with all the women he meets along the way. 96m/C **VHS, Beta.** *GB* Christopher Neil, Suzy Kendall, Irene Handl; **D:** Stanley Long.

Adventures of a Taxi Driver woof! 1976 Cabbie finds sex, crime, sex, adventure and sex on the road in this off-duty comedy. 89m/C **VHS, Beta.** *GB* Barry Evans, Judy Geeson, Adrienne Posta, Diana Dors, Liz Fraser; **D:** Stanley Long.

The Adventures of Baron Munchausen 🐾🐾🐾½ 1989 (PG) From the director of "Time Bandits," "Brazil," and "The Fisher King" comes an ambitious, imaginative, chaotic, and under-appreciated marvel based on the tall (and often confused) tales of the Baron. Munchausen encounters the King of the Moon, Venus, and other odd and fascinating characters during what might be described as an circular narrative in which flashbacks dovetail into the present and place is never quite what it seems. Wonderful special effects and visually stunning sets occasionally dwarf the actors and prove what Gilliam can do with a big budget. 126m/C **VHS, Beta, LV, 8mm, Closed Caption, DVD.** John Neville, Eric Idle, Sarah Polley, Valentina Cortese, Oliver Reed, Uma Thurman, Sting, Jonathan Pryce, Bill Paterson, Peter Jeffrey, Alison Steadman, Charles McKeown, Dennis Winston, Jack Purvis; **Cameos:** Robin Williams; **D:** Terry Gilliam; **W:** Terry Gilliam; **C:** Giuseppe Rotunno; **M:** Michael Kamen. Nominations: Academy Awards '89: Best Art Direction/Set Decoration, Best Costume Design, Best Makeup. *COL, CRC*

The Adventures of Buckaroo Banzai Across the Eighth Dimension 🐾🐾🐾 *Buckaroo Banzai* 1984 (PG) A man of many talents, Buckaroo Banzai (Weller) travels through the eighth dimension in a jet-propelled Ford Fiesta to battle Planet 10 aliens led by the evil Lithgow. Buckaroo incorporates his vast knowledge of medicine, science, music, racing, and foreign relations to his advantage. Offbeat and often humorous cult sci-fi trip. 100m/C **VHS, Beta, LV, Closed Caption.** Peter Weller, Ellen Barkin, Jeff Goldblum, Christopher Lloyd, John Lithgow, Lewis Smith, Rosalind Cash, Robert Ito, Pepe Serna, Vincent Schiavelli, Dan Hedaya, Yakov Smirnoff, Jamie Lee Curtis; **D:** W.D. Richter; **C:** Fred W. Koenekamp; **M:** Michael Boddicker. *VES, ART*

The Adventures of Bullwhip Griffin 🐾🐾½ 1966 A rowdy, family-oriented comedy-adventure set during the California Gold Rush. Light Disney farce catches Russell at the tail end of his teenage star days. Pleshette and McDowall embark upon an ocean trip from Boston to San Francisco to find her brother, Russell, who's out west digging for gold. Assorted comedic adventures take place. 110m/C **VHS, Beta.** Roddy McDowall, Suzanne Pleshette, Karl Malden, Harry Guardino, Kurt Russell; **D:** James Neilson; **C:** Edward Colman; **M:** George Bruns. *DIS*

Adventures of Captain Fabian 🐾½ 1951 When the captain of the "China Sea" learns that a beautiful woman has been falsely imprisoned, he comes to her rescue. Not one of Flynn's better swashbucklers, with typically low-quality Republic production. 100m/B **VHS, Beta.** Errol Flynn, Vincent Price, Agnes Moorehead, Micheline Presle; **D:** William Marshall. *NO*

The Adventures of Captain Marvel 🐾🐾½ 1941 A 12-episode cliff-hanging serial based on the comic book character. Details the adventures of klutzy Billy Batson, who transforms into superhero Captain Marvel by speaking the magic word, "Shazam!" 240m/B VHS, LV. Tom Tyler, Frank "Junior" Coghlan, Louise Currie; **D:** William Witney. VCN, REP, MLB

Adventures of Don Juan 🐾🐾🐾½ The New Adventures of Don Juan 1949 Flynn's last spectacular epic features elegant costuming and loads of action. Don Juan saves Queen Margaret from her evil first minister. He then swashbuckles his way across Spain and England in an effort to win her heart. Grand, large-scale fun and adventure with Flynn at his self-mocking best. Special laserdisc edition includes the original trailer. 111m/C VHS, Beta, LV. Errol Flynn, Viveca Lindfors, Robert Douglas, Romney Brent, Alan Hale, Raymond Burr, Aubrey Mather, Ann Rutherford; **D:** Vincent Sherman; **M:** Max Steiner. Academy Awards '49: Best Costume Design (Color); Nominations: Academy Awards '49: Best Art Direction/Set Decoration (Color). MGM, MLB

Adventures of Eliza Fraser 🐾½ 1976 A young shipwrecked couple move from bawdy pleasures to cannibalism after being captured by aborigines. 114m/C VHS, Beta, LV. Susannah York, Trevor Howard, Leon Lissek, Abigail, Noel Ferrier, Carole Skinner; **D:** Tim Burstall.

The Adventures of Ford Fairlane woof! Ford Fairlane 1990 (R) The Diceman plays an unusual detective specializing in rock 'n' roll cases. When a heavy metal singer dies on stage, he takes the case in his own inimitable fashion, pursuing buxom gals, sleazy record executives, and even his ex-wife. Not surprisingly, many of his stand-up bits are worked into the movie. Clay, the ever-so-controversial comic in his first (and likely last) starring role haplessly sneers his way through this rock 'n' roll dud of a comedy thriller. A quick effort to cash in on Clay's fading star. Forget about it. 101m/C VHS, Beta, LV, Letterbox, Closed Caption. Andrew Dice Clay, Wayne Newton, Priscilla Presley, Morris Day, Lauren Holly, Maddie Corman, Gilbert Gottfried, David Patrick Kelly, Brandon Call, Robert Englund, Ed O'Neill, Sheila E, Kari Wuhrer, Tone Loc; **D:** Renny Harlin; **W:** David Arnott, Daniel Waters, James Cappe. Golden Raspberry Awards '90: Worst Picture, Worst Actor (Clay), Worst Screenplay. FXL

The Adventures of Frank and Jesse James 1948 The bad brothers of the Wild West are trying to make good for rip-offs committed in their names, so they're hoping to hit pay-dirt with a silver mine. A 13-episode serial on two cassettes. 180m/B VHS. Steve Darrell, Clayton Moore, Noel Neill, Stanley Andrews; **D:** Yakima Canutt. REP, MOV

The Adventures of Frontier Fremont 🐾🐾 1975 A rough and tumble story of a man who leaves the city, grows a beard, and makes the wilderness his home (and the animals his friends). Mountain life, that's the life for me. Almost indistinguishable from Haggerty's "Grizzly Adams," with the usual redeeming panoramic shots of majestic mountains. 95m/C VHS, Beta. Dan Haggerty, Denver Pyle; **D:** Richard Friedenberg. NO

The Adventures of Gallant Bess 🐾🐾 1948 The time-honored story of a rodeo man torn between his girl and his talented horse (the Bess of the title). 73m/C VHS. Cameron Mitchell, Audrey Long, Fuzzy Knight, James Millican; **D:** Lew (Louis Friedlander) Landers. HEG

The Adventures of Hairbreadth Harry 192? Three short spoofs of the early melodramas cranked out by the movie industry. Includes "Sawdust Baby," "Fearless Harry," and "Rudolph's Revenge." 65m/B VHS, Beta. Billy West. GPV

The Adventures of Huck Finn 🐾🐾🐾 1993 (PG) Decent Disney attempt at adapting an American favorite by Mark Twain. Mischievious Huck and runaway slave Jim travel down the muddy Mississippi, working on life and friendship and getting into all sorts of adventures in the pre-Civil War era. Fast-paced and amusing with good performances by Wood (in the title role) and Broadway trained Vance (as Jim). Racial epithets and minstrel show dialect have been eliminated in this version. Some material, including Jim's close call with a lynch mob and Huck's drunken, brutal father may be too strong for immature children. 108m/C VHS, Beta, LV, Letterbox, Closed Caption. Elijah Wood, Courtney B. Vance, Robbie Coltrane, Jason Robards Jr., Ron Perlman, Dana Ivey, Anne Heche, James Gammon, Paxton Whitehead, Tom Aldredge, Curtis Armstrong, Mary Louise Wilson, Frances Conroy; **D:** Stephen Sommers; **W:** Stephen Sommers; **C:** Janusz Kaminski; **M:** Bill Conti. DIS, BTV

The Adventures of Huckleberry Finn 🐾🐾🐾 1939 Mark Twain's classic story about a boy who runs away and travels down the Mississippi on a raft, accompanied by a runaway slave, is done over in MGM-style. Rooney is understated as Huck (quite a feat), while the production occasionally floats aimlessly down the Mississippi. An entertaining follow-up to "The Adventures of Tom Sawyer." 89m/B VHS, Beta. Mickey Rooney, Lynne Carver, Rex Ingram, William Frawley, Walter Connolly; **D:** Richard Thorpe. MGM, HMV

The Adventures of Huckleberry Finn 🐾🐾½ 1960 A lively adaptation of the Twain saga in which Huck and runaway slave Jim raft down the Mississippi in search of freedom and adventure. Miscasting of Hodges as Huck hampers the proceedings, but Randall shines as the treacherous King. Strong supporting cast includes Keaton as a lion-tamer and boxing champ Moore as Jim. 107m/C VHS, Beta. Tony Randall, Eddie Hodges, Archie Moore, Patty McCormack, Neville Brand, Mickey Shaughnessy, Judy Canova, Andy Devine, Sherry Jackson, Buster Keaton, Finlay Currie, Josephine Hutchinson, Parley Baer, John Carradine, Royal Dano, Sterling Holloway, Harry Dean Stanton; **D:** Michael Curtiz. MGM, FCT

The Adventures of Huckleberry Finn 🐾🐾 1978 The classic adventure by Mark Twain of an orphan boy and a runaway slave done again as a TV movie and starring "F-Troop" regulars Tucker and Storch. Lacks the production values of earlier versions. 100m/C VHS, Beta. Forrest Tucker, Larry Storch, Kurt Ida, Mike Mazurki, Brock Peters; **D:** Jack B. Hively. NO

The Adventures of Huckleberry Finn 🐾🐾½ 1985 An adaptation of the Mark Twain story about the adventures encountered by Huckleberry Finn and a runaway slave as they travel down the Mississippi River. Top-notch cast makes this an entertaining version. Originally made for television in a much longer version for PBS's "American Playhouse." 121m/C VHS, Beta. Sada Thompson, Lillian Gish, Richard Kiley, Jim Dale, Barnard Hughes, Patrick Day, Frederic Forrest, Geraldine Page, Butterfly McQueen, Samm-Art Williams; **D:** Peter H. Hunt. USH, MON

The Adventures of Ichabod and Mr. Toad 🐾🐾🐾½ 1949 Disney's wonderfully animated versions of Kenneth Grahame's "The Wind in the Willows" and "The Legend of Sleepy Hollow" by Washington Irving. Rathbone narrates the story of Mr. Toad, who suffers from arrogance and eventually must defend himself in court after being charged with driving a stolen vehicle (Disney did take liberties with the story). Crosby provides all the voices for "Ichabod," which features one of the all-time great animated sequences—Ichabod riding in a frenzy through the forest while being pursued by the headless horseman. A treat for all ages. 68m/C VHS, LV. **D:** Clyde Geronimi, James Nelson Algar; **V:** Jack Kinney, Bing Crosby. DIS

Adventures of Kit Carson 1951 Television western, which ran from 1951-55, set in the 1880s about the famed frontiersman who kept the peace with the help of Mexican sidekick El Toro. Two episodes per tape. 50m/C VHS, Beta. Bill Williams, John Hamilton, Don Diamond. MOV, MVC

The Adventures of Marco Polo 🐾🐾½ 1938 Lavish Hollywood production based on the exploits of 13th-century Venetian explorer Marco Polo (Cooper). He becomes the first white man to record his visit to the Eastern court of Kublai Khan, where he falls for a beautiful princess also desired by the evil Rathbone. Lots of action, though its hard to picture the laconic Cooper in the title role. 100m/B VHS. Gary Cooper, Sigrid Gurie, Basil Rathbone, Ernest Truex, George Barbier, Binnie Barnes, Alan Hale, H.B. Warner; **D:** Archie Mayo; **W:** Robert Sherwood; **M:** Hugo Friedhofer. FCT

The Adventures of Mark Twain 🐾🐾🐾 1944 March stars as Mark Twain, the nom de plume of Samuel Clemens, the beloved humorist and writer. His travels and adventures along the Mississippi and on to the California gold rush would later result in the books and stories which would make him so well-known. March attains a quiet nobility as he goes from young man to old sage, along with Smith, who plays Olivia, Twain's beloved wife. 130m/B VHS, Beta. Fredric March, Alexis Smith, Donald Crisp, Alan Hale, Sir C. Aubrey Smith, John Carradine, William Henry, Robert Barrat, Walter Hampden, Percy Kilbride; **D:** Irving Rapper; **W:** Alan LeMay, Harry Chandlee; **M:** Max Steiner. Nominations: Academy Awards '44: Best Interior Decoration, Best Special Effects, Best Original Dramatic/Comedy Score. MGM, FCT, BTV

The Adventures of Mark Twain 🐾🐾🐾 Mark Twain 1985 (G) A clay-animated fantasy based on, and radically departing from, the life and work of Mark Twain. Story begins with Twain flying into outer space in a blimp with stowaways Huck Finn, Tom Sawyer and Becky Thatcher and takes off from there. Above average entertainment for kids and their folks. 86m/C VHS, Beta, LV. **D:** Will Vinton; **W:** Susan Shadburne; **V:** James Whitmore, Chris Ritchie, Gary Krug, Michele Mariana. BAR

The Adventures of Milo & Otis 🐾🐾🐾 Koneko Monogatari; The Adventures of Chatran 1989 (G) Delightful Japanese children's film about a farm-dwelling dog and cat and their odyssey after the cat is accidentally swept away on a river. Notable since no humans appear in the film. A record-breaking success in its homeland. Well received by U.S. children. Narrated by Dudley Moore. 89m/C VHS, Beta, LV, Closed Caption. JP **D:** Masanori Hata; **W:** Mark Saltzman; **M:** Michael Boddicker. COL, RDG, HMV

The Adventures of Nellie Bly 🐾 1981 Made for television "Classics Illustrated" story of Nellie Bly, a strong-willed female reporter doing her best to expose wrongdoings in the late 19th century. A decent performance by Purl is overshadowed by the general lack of direction. 100m/C VHS, Beta. Linda Purl, Gene Barry, John Randolph, Raymond Buktenica, J.D. Cannon, Elayne Heilveil, Cliff Osmond; **D:** Henning Schellerup. NO

The Adventures of Ozzie & Harriet 195? Each volume in this 12-set series contains four episodes of the Nelsons' hit TV show from 1953-64. Vol. 1 features 17-year-old Mary Tyler Moore doing the commercials. Vol. 2 features Mamie Van Doren as the housemother of Ricky's fraternity (some housemother!). The program was the prototype of family sitcoms. Original commercials included. Tapes are available for purchase individually. 56m/B VHS. Ozzie Nelson, Harriet Hilliard Nelson, Ricky Nelson, David Nelson; **D:** Ozzie Nelson. MOV

The Adventures of Picasso 🐾🐾 1980 A Swedish satire on the life of Picasso, dubbed in English. Don't look for art or facts here, or, for that matter, many laughs. 88m/C VHS, Beta. SW Gosta Ekman, Lena Nyman, Hans Alfredson, Margareta Krook, Bernard Cribbins, Wilfrid Brambell; **D:** Tage Danielsson. NO

The Adventures of Pinocchio 🐾🐾½ Pinocchio; Carlo Collodi's Pinocchio 1996 (G) Live-action version of Carlo Collodi's story about woodcarver Gepetto (Landau) who carves himself a puppet son (Thomas) who longs to be a real boy. Story differs from the Disney cartoon version in that it's a little darker and the cat, the fox, and the cricket have larger roles. Jim Henson's Creature Shop provided the animatronic magic to bring Pinocchio to life. His head alone was jammed with wiring and 18 tiny motors to give the "boy" a full range of facial expressions. It took as many as five puppeteers at a time to animate the character. So lifelike was the puppet that some of the crew actually spoke to it as they did the human actors. **88m/C VHS, LV, Closed Caption.** Martin Landau, Jonathan Taylor Thomas, Rob Schneider, Bebe Neuwirth, Udo Kier; **D:** Steven Barron; **W:** Steven Barron, Tom Benedek, Sherry Mills; **C:** Juan Ruiz-Anchia; **M:** Rachel Portman. *NLC*

The Adventures of Priscilla, Queen of the Desert 🎬🎬🎬 1994 (R)
Quirky down-under musical-comedy follows two drag queens and a transsexual across the Australian Outback on their way to a gig in a small resort town. They make the drive in a pink bus nicknamed Priscilla. Along the way they encounter, and perform for, the usual unusual assortment of local characters. Scenes depicting homophobic natives play out as expected. Finest moments occur on the bus or onstage (all hail ABBA). Strong performances, especially by usually macho Stamp as the widowed Bernadette, rise above the cliches in what is basically a bitchy, cross-dressing road movie, celebrating drag as art and the nonconformity of its heroes. Costumes (by Lizzy Gardner and Tim Chappel) are a lark, the photography's surreal, and the soundtrack fittingly campy. **CW:** Language and sex-related situations. **102m/C VHS, LV.** *AU* Terence Stamp, Hugo Weaving, Guy Pearce, Bill Hunter, Sarah Chadwick, Mark Holmes, Julia Cortez; **D:** Stephan Elliott; **W:** Stephan Elliott; **C:** Brian J. Breheny; **M:** Guy Gross. Academy Awards '94: Best Costume Design; Australian Film Institute '94: Best Costume Design; Nominations: Australian Film Institute '94: Best Actor (Stamp), Best Actor (Weaving), Best Cinematography, Best Director (Elliott), Best Film, Best Original Screenplay; Golden Globe Awards '95: Best Actor—Musical/Comedy (Stamp), Best Film—Musical/Comedy; Writers Guild of America '94: Best Original Screenplay. *PGV*

Adventures of Red Ryder 🎬🎬 1940
The thrills of the rugged West are presented in this 12-episode serial. Based on the then-famous comic strip character. **240m/B VHS, Beta.** Donald (Don "Red") Barry, Noah Beery Sr.; **D:** William Witney. *MLB*

The Adventures of Rex & Rinty 🎬🎬 1935
An adventure serial in 12 chapters, featuring Rin-Tin-Tin, Jr. **156m/B VHS, Beta.** Kane Richmond, Harry Woods, Smiley Burnette; **D:** Ford Beebe, B. Reeves Eason. *NOS, VCN, DVT*

The Adventures of Rin Tin Tin 🎬🎬½ 1947
Chronicles the adventures of that crime-fighting dog, Rin-Tin-Tin. **65m/B VHS.** Robert (Bobby) Blake. *CCB*

The Adventures of Robin Hood 🎬🎬🎬🎬 1938
Rollicking Technicolor tale of the legendary outlaw, regarded as the swashbuckler standard-bearer. The justice-minded Saxon knight battles the Normans, outwits evil Prince John, and gallantly romances Maid Marian. Grand castle sets and lush forest photography display ample evidence of the huge (in 1938) budget of $2 million plus. Just entering his prime, Flynn enthusiastically performed most of his own stunts, including intricate sword play and advanced tree and wall climbing. His Robin brims with charm and bravura, the enthusiastic protector of poor Saxons everywhere and the undeclared king of Sherwood forest. The rest of the cast likewise attacks with zest: de Havilland, a cold but eventually sympathetic Maid Marian; Rains' dastardly Prince John (the predecessor to Alan Rickman's over-the-top spin as the Sheriff in Costner's remake); and Rathbone's conniving Sir Guy to Robin's band of very merry men. Based on various Robin Hood legends as well as Sir Walter Scott's "Ivanhoe" and the opera "Robin Hood" by De Koven-Smith. Also available in letterbox format. **102m/C VHS, Beta, LV, Letterbox, Closed Caption.** Errol Flynn, Olivia de Havilland, Basil Rathbone, Alan Hale, Una O'Connor, Claude Rains, Patric Knowles, Eugene Pallette, Herbert Mundin, Melville Cooper, Ian Hunter, Montagu Love; **D:** Michael Curtiz; **W:** Norman Reilly Raine, Seton I. Miller; **M:** Erich Wolfgang Korngold. Academy Awards '38: Best Film Editing, Best Interior Decoration, Best Original Score, National Film Registry '95;; Nominations: Academy Awards '38: Best Picture. *MGM, FOX, CRC*

The Adventures of Robin Hood 1955
Filmed on location in England and starring Greene as the legendary outlaw/hero, with Pleasance as the evil Prince John. Two episodes per tape. Volume 1 features "The Highlander" and "Tables Turned." Additional episodes are available. **60m/C VHS, Beta.** Richard Greene, Donald Pleasence. *MVC, MOV*

The Adventures of Rusty 🎬🎬½ 1945
Forties family film series begins with this classic boy-meets-dog story. Danny's dog dies in an accident and his widowed father has just remarried so the kid's feeling pretty bad. Then he meets neglected German Shepherd Rusty, a former police dog with an undeservedly bad rep. Naturally, boy and dog bond and even capture a couple of escaped convicts (and Danny learns to love his stepmom too). **67m/B VHS.** Ted Donaldson, Margaret Lindsay, Conrad Nagel, Gloria Holden; **D:** Paul Burnford; **W:** Aubrey Wisberg. *COL*

The Adventures of Sadie 🎬🎬½ *Our Girl Friday* 1955
Collins is stranded on a desert island with three men, two of whom continuously chase her around. Naturally, she falls for the guy who ignores her. Obvious sex comedy which plays on Collins' scantily clad physical assets. Based on the novel "The Cautious Amorist" by Norman Lindsay. **87m/C VHS.** *GB* Joan Collins, George Cole, Kenneth More, Robertson Hare, Hermione Gingold, Walter Fitzgerald; **D:** Noel Langley; **W:** Noel Langley. *NO*

The Adventures of Sherlock Holmes 🎬🎬½ *Sherlock Holmes* 1939
The immortal Sherlock Holmes and his assistant Dr. Watson conflict with Scotland Yard as they both race to stop arch-criminal Professor Moriarty. The Yard is put to shame as Holmes, a mere amateur sleuth, uses his brilliant deductive reasoning to save the damsel in distress and to stop Moriarty from stealing the Crown Jewels. Second in the series. **83m/B VHS, Beta, Closed Caption.** Basil Rathbone, Nigel Bruce, Ida Lupino, George Zucco, E.E. Clive, Mary Gordon; **D:** Alfred Werker; **W:** Edwin Blum; **C:** Leon Shamroy. *FOX*

The Adventures of Sherlock Holmes: Hound of the Baskervilles 1989
Holmes tackles the mysterious and long-lived curse of the Baskervilles. Made for British television. Fine acting, detailed production. A pleasure. **120m/C VHS.** *GB* Jeremy Brett, Edward Hardwicke. *MPI*

The Adventures of Sherlock Holmes' Smarter Brother 🎬🎬🎬 1978 (PG)
The unknown brother of the famous Sherlock Holmes takes on some of his brother's more disposable excess cases and makes some hilarious moves. Moments of engaging farce borrowed from the Mel Brooks school of parody (and parts of the Brooks ensemble as well). **91m/C VHS, Beta.** Gene Wilder, Madeline Kahn, Marty Feldman, Dom DeLuise, Leo McKern, Roy Kinnear, John Le Mesurier, Douglas Wilmer, Thorley Walters; **D:** Gene Wilder; **W:** Gene Wilder. *FOX*

Adventures of Smilin' Jack 1943
WWII flying ace Smilin' Jack Martin comes to life in this action-packed serial. Character from the Zack Mosley comic strip about air force fighting over China. **90m/B VHS, Beta.** Tom Brown, Sidney Toler; **D:** Ray Taylor. *SNC, NOS, VAN*

The Adventures of Tartu 🎬🎬½ *Tartu* 1943
A British secret agent, sent to blow up a Nazi poison gas factory in Czechoslovakia, poses as a Romanian. One of Donat's lesser films, in the style of "The 39 Steps." **103m/C VHS, Beta.** *GB* Robert Donat, Valerie Hobson, Glynis Johns; **D:** Harold Bucquet. *HHT, TIM, VEC*

The Adventures of Tarzan 🎬🎬 1921
The screen's first Tarzan in an exciting jungle thriller. Silent. **153m/B VHS, Beta.** Elmo Lincoln. *VYY, GVV*

The Adventures of the Flying Cadets 🎬½ 1944
Early aerial war adventure serial in 13 complete chapters. **169m/B VHS, Beta.** Johnny Downs, Regis Toomey; **D:** Ray Taylor, Lewis D. Collins. *VYY, VCN, NOS*

The Adventures of the Masked Phantom 🎬½ 1938
The adventures of the Masked Phantom. **56m/B VHS, Beta.** Monte Rawlins, Betty Burgess, Larry Mason, Sonny Lamont, Jack Ingram; **D:** Charles Abbott. *NOS, VYY, RXM*

The Adventures of the Wilderness Family 🎬🎬 1976 (G)
The story of a modern-day pioneer family who becomes bored with the troubles of city life and heads for life in the wilderness. There, they find trouble in paradise. Family-oriented adventure offering pleasant scenery. Followed by "The Wilderness Family, Part 2." **100m/C VHS, Beta, LV.** Robert F. Logan, Susan Damante Shaw; **D:** Stewart Raffill; **W:** Stewart Raffill. *VTR*

The Adventures of Tom Sawyer 🎬🎬🎬 1938
The vintage Hollywood adaptation of the Mark Twain classic, with art direction by William Cameron Menzies. Not a major effort from the Selznick studio, but quite detailed and the best Tom so far. **91m/C VHS, Beta, LV.** Tommy Kelly, Walter Brennan, Victor Jory, May Robson, Victor Kilian, Jackie Moran, Donald Meek, Ann Gillis, Marcia Mae Jones, Clara Blandick, Margaret Hamilton; **D:** Norman Taurog; **C:** James Wong Howe; **M:** Max Steiner. Nominations: Academy Awards '38: Best Interior Decoration. *FOX, FCT, MLB*

The Adventures of Tom Sawyer 🎬🎬½ 1973
Tom Sawyer is a mischievous Missouri boy who gets into all kinds of trouble in this white-washed, made for TV adaptation of the Mark Twain classic. **76m/C VHS, Beta.** Jane Wyatt, Buddy Ebsen, Vic Morrow, John McGiver, Josh Albee, Jeff Tyler. *USH*

The Adventurous Knights woof! 1935
An athlete learns he is the heir to a Transylvanian throne. **60m/B VHS, Beta, LV.** David Sharpe, Mary Kornman, Mickey Daniels, Gertrude Messinger; **D:** Edward Roberts. *NO*

The Adversary 🎬🎬½ *Pratidwandi* 1971
A young man must quit college because of his father's death. He struggles to find employment in Calcutta but his hardships are magnified by the impersonal society. In Bengali with English subtitles. **110m/C VHS.** *IN* **D:** Satyajit Ray; **W:** Satyajit Ray. *FCT*

Advise and Consent 🎬🎬🎬 1962
An interesting political melodrama with a fascinating cast, based upon Allen Drury's novel. The President chooses a candidate for the Secretary of State position which divides the Senate and causes the suicide of a senator. Controversial in its time, though somewhat turgid today. Laughton's last film. **139m/B VHS, Beta.** Don Murray, Charles Laughton, Henry Fonda, Walter Pidgeon, Lew Ayres, Burgess Meredith, Gene Tierney, Franchot Tone, Paul Ford, George Grizzard, Betty White, Peter Lawford, Edward Andrews; **D:** Otto Preminger; **W:** Wendell Mayes; **C:** Sam Leavitt. National Board of Review Awards '62: Best Supporting Actor (Meredith). *WAR, KAR, VTR*

The Advocate 🎬🎬🎬 *The Hour of the Pig* 1993 (R)
Bizarre black comedy about 15th-century Paris lawyer Richard Courtois (Firth) who decides to ply his trade in the country, only to find things stranger than he can imagine. His first case turns out to be defending a pig that's accused of murdering a child. And the pig is owned by beautiful gypsy Samira (Annabi), so the idealistic lawyer can fall in love (or lust). There's religion and superstition, there's power struggles, there's ignorance versus knowledge—things sound very modern indeed. **CW:** Strong sexuality; nudity; vio-

lence; profanity. **102m/C VHS, LV, Closed Caption.** *GB* Colin Firth, Amina Annabi, Nicol Williamson, Ian Holm, Lysette Anthony, Donald Pleasence, Michael Gough, Harriet Walter, Jim Carter; **D:** Leslie Megahey; **W:** Leslie Megahey. **MAX, TOU**

Aelita: Queen of Mars 🎬🎬 *Aelita: The Revolt of the Robots* **1924** Though the title has blockbuster potential, "Aelita" is a little-known silent Soviet sci-fi flick destined to remain little known. After building a rocket to fly to Mars, a Russian engineer finds it's no Martian holiday on the fourth planet from the sun, with the Martians in the midst of a revolution. Silent, with a piano score. **113m/B VHS, LV.** *RU* Yulia Solntseva, Nikolai Batalov, Igor Illinski, Nikolai Tseretelli, Vera Orlova, Pavel Poi, Konstantin Eggert, Yuri Zavadski, Valentina Kuindzi, N. Tretyakova; **D:** Yakov Protazanov; **C:** Yuri Zhelyabuzhsky, Emil Schoenemann. **KIV, FCT, SNC**

The Affair 🎬🎬🎬 **1973** Songwriter/polio victim Wood falls in love for the first time with attorney Wagner. Delicate situation handled well by a fine cast in this television movie. **74m/C VHS, Beta.** Natalie Wood, Robert Wagner, Bruce Davison, Kent Smith, Frances Reid, Pat Harrington; **D:** Gilbert Cates. **NO**

The Affair 🎬🎬½ **1995 (R)** It's 1944 in a small English town, where a troop of black American soldiers are billeted prior to the D-Day invasion. Travis (Vance) falls for the married Maggie (Fox)—whose husband, Edward (Hinds), is supposed to be away at sea—and they begin an affair. Unfortunately, Edward arrives home unexpectedly and accuses Travis of raping his wife. If Maggie denies the accusation, she'll lose her home and family but if she confirms it, Travis, according to Army law, will be condemned to death. Made for cable TV.**CW:** Strong sexuality, some language and drug use. **105m/C VHS.** *GB* Courtney B. Vance, Kerry Fox, Ciaran Hinds, Beatie Edney, Leland Gantt, Bill Nunn, Ned Beatty; **D:** Paul Seed; **W:** Pablo F. Fenjves, Bryan Goluboff; **C:** Ivan Strasburg; **M:** Christopher Gunning. **HBO**

An Affair in Mind 🎬🎬 **1989** British television movie about a professional writer who falls in love with a beautiful woman who tries to convince him to assist her in murdering her husband. **88m/C VHS, Beta, Closed Caption.** *GB* Amanda Donohoe, Stephen Dillon, Matthew Marsh, Kean-Laurent Cochot; **D:** Michael Baker. **FOX**

Affair in Trinidad 🎬🎬 **1952** Fun in the tropics as nightclub singer Hayworth enlists the help of brother-in-law Ford to find her husband's murderer. The trail leads to international thieves and espionage in a romantic thriller that reunites the stars of "Gilda." Hayworth sings (with Jo Ann Greer's voice) "I've Been Kissed Before." **98m/B VHS, LV.** Rita Hayworth, Glenn Ford, Alexander Scourby, Torin Thatcher, Valerie Bettis, Steve Geray; **D:** Vincent Sherman. Nominations: Academy Awards '52: Best Costume Design (B & W). **COL, CCB**

The Affair of the Pink Pearl 🎬½ **1984** The husband-and-wife private investigation team of Tommy and Tuppence must find within 24 hours the culprit who stole a valuable pink pearl. Based on the Agatha Christie series of short stories. Made for British television. **60m/C VHS, Beta.** *GB* James Warwick, Francesca Annis. **TPV**

An Affair to Remember 🎬🎬½ **1957** McCarey remakes his own "Love Affair," with less success. Nightclub singer Kerr and wealthy bachelor Grant discover love on an ocean liner and agree to meet six months later on top of the Empire State Building to see if their feelings are the same. Not as good as the original, but a winner of a fairy tale just the same. Notable for causing many viewers to sob uncontrollably. "Affair" was gathering dust on store shelves until "Sleepless in Seattle" used it as a plot device and rentals skyrocketed. In 1994 real life couple Warren Beatty and Annette Bening attempted a third "Love Affair" remake. **115m/C VHS, Beta, LV, Letterbox, Closed Caption.** Cary Grant, Deborah Kerr, Richard Denning, Cathleen Nesbitt, Neva Patterson, Robert Q. Lewis, Fortunio Bonanova, Matt Moore, Nora Marlowe, Sarah Sel-

by; **D:** Leo McCarey; **W:** Leo McCarey, Delmer Daves, Donald Ogden Stewart; **C:** Milton Krasner; **M:** Hugo Friedhofer. Nominations: Academy Awards '57: Best Cinematography, Best Costume Design, Best Song ("An Affair to Remember"), Best Score. **FOX**

The Affairs of Annabel 🎬🎬½ **1938** The first of the popular series of Annabel pictures Lucy made in the late 1930s. Appealing adolescent is zoomed to movie stardom by her press agent's stunts. A behind-the-scenes satire on Hollywood, stars, and agents. **68m/B VHS, Beta.** Lucille Ball, Jack Oakie, Ruth Donnelly, Fritz Feld, Bradley Page; **D:** Ben Stoloff. **CCB, IME, MLB**

The Affairs of Dobie Gillis 🎬🎬½ **1953** Light musical-comedy about a group of college kids and their carefree antics. Complete with big-band tunes, dance numbers, and plenty of collegiate shenanigans. This '50s classic inspired a hit TV series, "The Many Loves of Dobie Gillis." 🎵I'm Through with Love; All I Do Is Dream of You; You Can't Do Wrong Doing Right; Those Endearing Young Charms. **72m/B VHS.** Debbie Reynolds, Bobby Van, Barbara Ruick, Bob Fosse, Lurene Tuttle, Hans Conried, Charles Lane; **D:** Don Weis; **W:** Max Shulman; **C:** William Mellor. **MGM**

Afraid of the Dark 🎬🎬 **1992 (R)** Convoluted psycho-thriller from a child's point of view. Young Lucas is fearful for his blind mother. It seems a vicious slasher has been attacking blind women and Lucas' father, a policeman, has yet to apprehend the criminal. But...Lucas it seems has a problem with reality. With his fantasies and realities mixed, all the people in his life also play entirely different roles. Characters are so detached and unreal that a viewer is prevented from a clear understanding of anything that may, or may not, be going on. Directorial debut of Peploe.**CW:** Violence and one scene of sensuality. **91m/C VHS, LV, Closed Caption.** *FR GB* Ben Keyworth, James Fox, Fanny Ardant, Paul McGann, Clare Holman, Robert Stephens; **D:** Mark Peploe; **W:** Mark Peploe; **C:** Bruno de Keyzer. **COL, NLC**

Africa Screams 🎬🎬½ **1949** Abbott and Costello go on an African safari in possession of a secret map. Unheralded independent A&C film is actually quite good in the stupid vein, with lots of jungle slapstick, generally good production values, and a supporting cast of familiar comedy faces. **79m/B VHS, Beta, LV.** Lou Costello, Bud Abbott, Shemp Howard, Hillary Brooke, Joe Besser, Clyde Beatty; **D:** Charles T. Barton. **KAR, MRV, CNG**

Africa Texas Style 🎬🎬 **1967** An East African rancher hires an American cowboy and his Navajo sidekick to help run his wild game ranch. Decent family adventure which served as the pilot for the short-lived TV series "Cowboy in Africa." Features lots of wildlife footage and a cameo appearance by Hayley Mills. **109m/C VHS.** Hugh O'Brian, John Mills, Nigel Green, Tom Nardini; **Cameos:** Hayley Mills; **D:** Andrew Marton; **M:** Malcolm Arnold. **REP**

An African Dream 🎬½ **1990 (PG)** A period tale about a black man and a white woman fighting against repression in South Africa. **94m/C VHS, Beta, LV.** Kitty Aldridge, John Kani, Dominic Jephcott, John Carson, Richard Haines, Joy Stewart Spence; **D:** John Smallcombe. **IME, FCT**

African Journey **1989** A moving, cross-cultural drama of friendship. A young black American goes to Africa for the summer to be with his divorced father who is working in the diamond mines. There he meets a young black African like himself; they overcome cultural clashes and learn respect for one another. Beautiful scenery, filmed in Africa. Part of the "Wonderworks" series. **174m/C VHS, Closed Caption.** Jason Blicker, Pedzisai Sithole. **HMV, BTV, FCT**

The African Queen 🎬🎬🎬🎬 **1951** After Bible-thumping spinster Hepburn's missionary brother is killed in WWI Africa, hard-drinking, dissolute steamer captain Bogart offers her safe passage. Not satisfied with sanctuary, she persuades

him to destroy a German gunboat blocking the British advance. The two spend most of their time battling aquatic obstacles and each other, rather than the Germans. Time alone on a African river turns mistrust and aversion to love, a transition effectively counterpointed by the continuing suspense of their daring mission. Classic war of the sexes script adapted from C.S. Forester's novel makes wonderful use of natural dialogue and humor. Shot on location in Africa. **105m/C VHS, Beta, LV.** *GB* Humphrey Bogart, Katharine Hepburn, Robert Morley, Theodore Bikel, Peter Bull, Walter Gotell, Peter Swanwick, Richard Marner; **D:** John Huston; **W:** John Huston, James Agee; **C:** Jack Cardiff. Academy Awards '51: Best Actor (Bogart), National Film Registry '94;; Nominations: Academy Awards '51: Best Actress (Hepburn), Best Director (Huston), Best Screenplay. **FOX, FCT, TLF**

African Rage 🎬🎬 *Tigers Don't Cry; The Long Shot; Target of an Assassin; Fatal Assassin* **1978** Little known release about an aging male nurse (yes, Quinn) who discovers he's dying of an incurable disease. With nothing left to lose, he plans the kidnapping of an African leader, hoping that the ransom will support his family. Meanwhile, another man is plotting the same leader's death. Decent performances help move along the improbable plot. **90m/C VHS, Beta.** *SA* Anthony Quinn, John Phillip Law, Simon Sabela, Ken Gampu, Marius Weyers, Sandra Prinsloo; **D:** Peter Collinson. **MPI**

Afrita Hanen 🎬🎬🎬 **1947** A rare Egyptian fantasy starring the famous Mid-Eastern actor, Farrid El Atrache. In Arabic with titles. **97m/B VHS, Beta.** Farrid El Atrache. **FCT**

After Dark, My Sweet 🎬🎬🎬 **1990 (R)** A troubled young man in search of a little truth ends up entangled in a kidnapping scheme. Muddled direction is overcome by above average performances and gritty realism. Based on the novel by Jim Thompson. **114m/C VHS, LV, Closed Caption.** Jason Patric, Rachel Ward, Bruce Dern, George Dickerson, James Cotton, Corey Carrier, Rocky Giordani; **D:** James Foley; **W:** Robert Redlin, James Foley; **M:** Maurice Jarre. **ART**

After Darkness 🎬 **1985** Slow-moving psycho-suspenser about a man obsessed with trying to remedy his twin brother's schizophrenia. **104m/C VHS, Beta.** *SI GB* John Hurt, Julian Sands, Victoria Abril, Pamela Salem; **D:** Dominique Othenin-Girard. **CEL**

After Hours 🎬🎬🎬½ **1985 (R)** An absurd, edgy black comedy that's filled with novel twists and turns and often more disturbing than funny. An isolated uptown New York yuppie (Dunne) takes a late night stroll downtown and meets a sexy woman in an all-night coffee shop. From there he wanders through a series of threatening and surreal misadventures, leading to his pursuit by a vigilante mob stirred by ice cream dealer O'Hara. Something like "Blue Velvet" with more Catholicism and farce. Or similar to "Something Wild" without the high school reunion. Great cameos from the large supporting cast, including Cheech and Chong as burglars. A dark view of a small hell-hole in the Big Apple. **97m/C VHS, Beta, LV, Letterbox, Closed Caption.** Griffin Dunne, Rosanna Arquette, John Heard, Teri Garr, Catherine O'Hara, Verna Bloom, Linda Fiorentino, Dick Miller, Bronson Pinchot, Will Patton, Rockets Redglare; **Cameos:** Richard "Cheech" Marin, Thomas Chong, Martin Scorsese; **D:** Martin Scorsese; **C:** Michael Ballhaus; **M:** Howard Shore. Cannes Film Festival '86: Best Director (Scorsese); Independent Spirit Awards '86: Best Director (Scorsese), Best Film. **WAR**

After Julius 🎬🎬 **1978** Twenty years after Julius Grace's death, his memory still hovers over his wife's and daughters' lives. British soap opera moves with glacier-like speed. Adapted from the book by Elizabeth Jane Howard. **150m/C VHS.** *GB* Faith Brook, John Carson, Cyd Hayman; **D:** John Glenister. **NO**

After Midnight 🎬 *I Have Lived* **1933** An aspiring playwright tries to get his work produced, only to meet with dead ends. Eventually, he hooks up with a talented young actress with whom he finds romance and success. **69m/B VHS, Beta, Closed**

Caption. Alan Dinehart, Anita Page, Allen Vincent, Gertrude Astor; **D:** Richard Thorpe. *SNC*

After Midnight 🐾🐾 1989 (R)
Suspended in a central story about an unorthodox professor who preys upon the deepest fears of his students, a trio of terror tales come to life. From the writers of "The Fly II" and "Nightmare on Elm Street 4." Some chills, few thrills. **90m/C VHS, Beta, Closed Caption.** Marg Helgenberger, Marc McClure, Alan Rosenberg, Pamela Segall, Nadine Van Der Velde, Ramy Zada, Jillian McWhirter, Billy Ray Sharkey, Judie Aronson, Tracy Wells, Ed Monaghan, Monique Salcido, Penelope Sudrow; **D:** Jim Wheat, Ken Wheat; **W:** Jim Wheat, Ken Wheat. *MGM*

After Pilkington 🐾🐾 1988
British television thriller about an uptight Oxford professor who runs into his bewitching childhood sweetheart after many years. She persuades him to help search for a missing archaeologist. **100m/C VHS, Beta, Closed Caption.** *GB* Bob Peck, Miranda Richardson, Barry Foster; **D:** Christopher Morahan. *FOX*

After the Fall of New York woof!
1985 (R) Dim-witted post-apocalyptic tale set in New York after the fall of the "Big Bomb." A man, driven to search for the last normal woman, has reason to believe she is frozen alive and kept in the heart of the city. His mission: locate her, thaw her, engage in extremely limited foreplay with her, and repopulate the planet. A poorly dubbed dating allegory. **95m/C VHS, Beta.** *IT FR* Michael Sopkiw, Valentine Monnier, Anna Kanakis, Roman Geer, Edmund Purdom, George Eastman; **D:** Martin Dolman. *VES, ART*

After the Fall of Saigon 🐾 Raiders of the Doomed Kingdom 1988
Soldiers in Vietnam go on a killing rampage. Dubbed; country of origin isn't known. **100m/C VHS, Beta.** Danny Aswatep, Peter Ramwa, Rayak Ramnate, Krao Spartacus. *NO*

After the Fox 🐾🐾 Caccia alla Volpe 1966
Sellers is a con artist posing as a film director to carry out a bizarre plan to steal gold from Rome. Features occasional backhand slaps at Hollywood, with Mature turning in a memorable performance as the has-been actor starring in Sellers' movie. Though the screenplay was co-written by Neil Simon, the laughs are marginal. **103m/C VHS, Beta.** *GB IT* Peter Sellers, Victor Mature, Martin Balsam, Britt Ekland; **D:** Vittorio De Sica; **W:** Neil Simon; **M:** Burt Bacharach. *MGM, FOX*

After the Promise 🐾🐾 1987
During the Depression, a poor carpenter tries to regain custody of his four sons following the death of his wife. Maudlin television melodrama based on a true story. **100m/C VHS.** Mark Harmon, Diana Scarwid, Rosemary Dunsmore, Donnelly Rhodes, Mark Hildreth, Trey Ames, Richard Billingsley; **D:** David Greene; **M:** Ralph Burns. *VTR*

After the Rehearsal 🐾🐾🐾 1984 (R)
Two actresses, one young, the other at the end of her career, challenge their director with love and abuse. Each questions his right to use them on stage and off. A thoughtful discussion of the meaning and reason for art originally made for Swedish television. Swedish with English subtitles. **72m/C VHS, Beta.** *SW* Erland Josephson, Ingrid Thulin, Lena Olin; **D:** Ingmar Bergman; **W:** Ingmar Bergman; **C:** Sven Nykvist. *COL*

After the Revolution 🐾🐾 1990
A struggling novelist decides to write his next book from the viewpoint of his cat. In Hungarian with English subtitles. **82m/C VHS.** *HU* Andras Szirtes. *FCT*

After the Shock 🐾🐾 1990 (PG)
Documentary-like dramatization of the San Francisco-Oakland earthquake of October, 1989 and, of course, its aftermath. Incorporates actual footage of the disaster. Made for cable. **92m/C VHS, Beta, Closed Caption.** Yaphet Kotto, Rue McClanahan, Jack Scalia, Scott Valentine; **D:** Gary Sherman; **W:** Gary Sherman. *PAR*

After the Thin Man 🐾🐾🐾 1936
Second in a series of six "Thin Man" films, this one finds Nick, Nora and Asta, the lovable terrier, seeking out a murderer from Nora's own blue-blooded rel-

atives. Fast-paced mystery with a witty script and the popular Powell/Loy charm. Sequel to "The Thin Man," followed by "Another Thin Man." **113m/B VHS, Beta.** William Powell, Myrna Loy, James Stewart, Elissa Landi, Joseph Calleia, Jessie Ralph, Alan Marshal; **D:** Woodbridge S. Van Dyke. **Nominations:** Academy Awards '36: Best Screenplay. *MGM*

Afterburn 🐾🐾🐾 1992 (R)
When Ted, her Air Force pilot husband, is killed in a crash of his F-16 fighter, Janet Harduvel learns the official explanation is pilot error. Convinced that something was wrong with his plane, Janet sets out to investigate, and eventually sue, military contractor General Dynamics. Dern turns in a great performance as the tough widow determined to clear her husband's name. Based on a true story; made for cable television.**CW:** Language. **103m/C VHS, LV, Closed Caption.** Laura Dern, Robert Loggia, Vincent Spano, Michael Rooker, Andy Romano; **D:** Robert Markowitz; **W:** Elizabeth Chandler. *HBO, FCT*

Afterglow 🐾🐾 1997 (R)
Romantic quadrangle skates by on the performances of its two veterans. Lucky Mann (Nolte) is experiencing marital boredom with his longtime wife Phyllis (the ever-beautiful Christie), a former B-movie actress. Meanwhile twentysomething Marianne Byron (Boyle), who is desperate to have a baby, is sexually frustrated by her workaholic hubby, Jeffrey (Miller). Repairman Lucky happens to come along to work on the Bryon's apartment and Marianne decides to throw herself at him. Then Jeffrey meets the sophisticated Phyllis and soon both couples have uncoupled and re-formed.**CW:** Sexuality and some language. **113m/C VHS, Closed Caption.** Nick Nolte, Julie Christie, Lara Flynn Boyle, Jonny Lee Miller; **D:** Alan Rudolph; **W:** Alan Rudolph; **C:** Toyomichi Kurita; **M:** Mark Isham. Independent Spirit Awards '98: Best Actress (Christie); New York Film Critics Awards '97: Best Actress (Christie); National Society of Film Critics Awards '97: Best Actress (Christie); Nominations: Academy Awards '97: Best Actress (Christie). *COL*

Aftermath 🐾½ 1985
Three astronauts return to Earth and are shocked to discover that the planet has been ravaged by a nuclear war. Quickly they make new plans. **96m/C VHS, Beta.** Steve Barkett, Larry Latham, Lynne Margulies, Sid Haig, Forrest J. Ackerman; **D:** Ted V. Mikels.

Aftershock 🐾½ 1988 (R)
A beautiful alien and a mysterious stranger battle the Earth's repressive, evil government. **90m/C VHS, Beta.** Jay Roberts Jr., Elizabeth Kaitan, Chris Mitchum, Richard Lynch, John Saxon, Russ Tamblyn, Michael Berryman, Chris De Rose, Chuck Jeffreys; **D:** Frank Harris.

Afterward 🐾 1985
Made-for-British-television horror story about a family that moves into a supposedly haunted house with deadly results. **60m/C VHS, Beta.** *GB* Michael J. Shannon, Kay Harper, John Grillo.

Against a Crooked Sky 🐾🐾 1975 (G)
A young boy sets out with an elderly trapper to find his sister, who was captured by the Indians. Similiar story to "The Searchers," but no masterpiece. **89m/C VHS, Beta.** Richard Boone, Stewart Peterson, Clint Ritchie, Geoffrey Land, Jewel Blanch; **D:** Earl Bellamy. *ART, VES*

Against All Flags 🐾🐾🐾 1952
An enjoyable Flynn swashbuckler about a British soldier slashing his way through the Spanish fleet at the turn of the 18th century. Though the story has been told before, tight direction and good performances win out. O'Hara is a tarty eyeful as a hot-tempered pirate moll. **81m/C VHS, Beta, LV.** Errol Flynn, Maureen O'Hara, Anthony Quinn, Mildred Natwick; **D:** George Sherman. *BAR, USH*

Against All Odds 🐾🐾½ 1984 (R)
An interesting love triangle evolves when an ex-football player, played by Bridges, travels to Mexico to find his good friend's girlfriend. Contains complicated plot, numerous double crosses, sensual love scenes, and a chase scene along Sunset Boulevard. As the good friend sans conscience, Woods stars. A remake of 1947's "Out of the

Past." **122m/C VHS, Beta, LV, 8mm, Letterbox, Closed Caption.** Jeff Bridges, Rachel Ward, James Woods, Alex Karras, Jane Greer, Richard Widmark, Dorian Harewood, Swoosie Kurtz, Bill McKinney, Saul Rubinek; **D:** Taylor Hackford; **C:** Donald E. Thorin; **M:** Michel Colombier, Larry Carlton. Nominations: Academy Awards '84: Best Song ("Against All Odds (Take a Look at Me Now)"). *COL*

Against the Drunken Cat Paws 🐾 1975
A blind young martial arts student seeks to regain his sight and avenge the death of her father. **94m/C VHS, Beta.** Chia Ling, Ou-Yang Ksiek. *UNI*

Against the Wall 🐾🐾🐾 1994
Compelling and tense dramatization of the 1971 Attica, New York prison uprising in which 10 guards were held hostage and state troopers and the National Guard killed 29 prisoners before regaining control. Partially fictionalized version of the story told from the viewpoints of a young prison guard (MacLachlan) and a politicized prisoner (Jackson). Filmed at a prison in Clarksville, Tennessee. Made for cable television. **115m/C VHS, LV.** Kyle MacLachlan, Samuel L. Jackson, Clarence Williams III, Frederic Forrest, Harry Dean Stanton, Tom Bower, Philip Bosco, Anne Heche, David Ackroyd; **D:** John Frankenheimer; **W:** Ron Hutchinson; **M:** Gary Chang. *HBO*

Against the Wind 🐾🐾½ 1948
A motley crew is trained for a mission into Nazi Germany to blow up records and rescue a prisoner. The first half of the film focuses on the group's training, but despite its intensity they win only a pyrrhic victory. A well-done production with solid performances from the cast. **96m/B VHS.** Robert Beatty, Jack Warner, Simone Signoret, Gordon Jackson, Paul Dupuis, Peter Illing; **D:** Charles Crichton. *NOS, VEC*

Against the Wind 🐾🐾 Contra el Viento 1990
Juan (Banderas) takes refuge in a remote area of Andalusia in an effort to get away from a mutually obsessive love. But his exile is in vain when his lover appears—his sister (Suarez). Spanish with subtitles. **117m/C VHS.** *SP* Antonio Banderas, Emma Suarez; **D:** Paco Perinan. *CVC, FCT*

Agatha 🐾🐾½ 1979 (PG)
A speculative period drama about Agatha Christie's still unexplained disappearance in 1926, and a fictional American reporter's efforts to find her. Beautiful but lackluster mystery. Unfortunately, Hoffman and Redgrave generate few sparks. **98m/C VHS, Beta.** Dustin Hoffman, Vanessa Redgrave, Timothy Dalton, Helen Morse, Tony Britton, Timothy West, Celia Gregory; **D:** Michael Apted. Nominations: Academy Awards '79: Best Costume Design. *WAR*

Agatha Christie's Miss Marple 198?
Elderly, proper Jane Marple hardly seems the sort to get involved in murder and mayhem but her prim exterior hides a razor-sharp mind and intuitive understanding of criminal behavior. Two boxed collections. **65m/C VHS.** *GB* Joan Hickson. *VCO, AEH, NEW*

Agatha Christie's The Pale Horse 🐾🐾½ The Pale Horse 1996
When writer Mark Easterbrook is accused of murdering a priest, the only clue to clearing himself is a mysterious list of names. Now he has to figure out the connection between the names if he expects to clear himself. **100m/C VHS.** *GB* Michael Byrne, Ruth Madoc, Leslie Phillips, Jean Marsh; **D:** Charles Beeson. *AEH*

Age Isn't Everything 🐾 Life in the Food Chain 1991 (R)
An appalling clumsy comedy about a recent college graduate who abruptly becomes an old man while retaining his youthful exterior. He looks the same, but walks slowly and talks with a thick Yiddish accent, get it? The cast just marks time until an inexplicable ending.**CW:** Language. **91m/C VHS.** Jonathan Silverman, Robert Prosky, Rita Moreno, Paul Sorvino, Rita Karin, Robert Cicchini, Brian Williams, Dee Hoty; **Cameos:** Dr. Joyce Brothers, Bella Abzug; **W:** Douglas Katz. *VES*

The Age of Innocence 🐾🐾🐾 1993 (PG)
Magnificently lavish adaptation of Edith Wharton's novel of passion thwarted by convention is visually stunning, but don't expect action since these people kill with a word or gesture.

Lead performances are strong though perhaps miscast, with Ryder an exception. Outwardly docile and conventional, she nevertheless holds on to her husband with steely manipulation. Woodward's narration of Wharton's observations helps sort out what goes on behind the proper facades. Although slow, see this one for the beautiful period authenticity, thanks to Scorsese, who obviously labored over the small details. He shows up as a photographer; his parents appear in a scene on a train. **138m/C VHS, LV, 8mm, Letterbox, Closed Caption.** Daniel Day-Lewis, Michelle Pfeiffer, Winona Ryder, Richard E. Grant, Alec McCowen, Miriam Margolyes, Sian Phillips, Geraldine Chaplin, Stuart Wilson, Mary Beth Hurt, Michael Gough, Alexis Smith, Jonathan Pryce, Robert Sean Leonard; *Cameos:* Martin Scorsese; *D:* Martin Scorsese; *W:* Jay Cocks, Martin Scorsese; *C:* Michael Ballhaus; *M:* Elmer Bernstein. Academy Awards '93: Best Costume Design; British Academy Awards '93: Best Supporting Actress (Margolyes); Golden Globe Awards '94: Best Supporting Actress (Ryder); National Board of Review Awards '93: Best Director (Scorsese), Best Supporting Actress (Ryder); Nominations: Academy Awards '93: Best Adapted Screenplay, Best Art Direction/Set Decoration, Best Supporting Actress (Ryder), Best Original Score; British Academy Awards '94: Best Supporting Actress (Ryder); Directors Guild of America Awards '93: Best Director (Scorsese); Golden Globe Awards '94: Best Actress—Drama (Pfeiffer), Best Director (Scorsese), Best Film—Drama. *COL*

Age Old Friends 🎬🎬🎬½ 1989 Crusty
octogenarian Cronyn must choose. His daughter (played by real-life offspring Tandy) wants him to move out of a retirement home and into her house. But he's struggling to keep neighbor and increasingly senile friend Gardenia from slipping into "zombieland." An emotional treat with two fine actors deploying dignity and wit in the battle against old age. Originally adapted for HBO from the Broadway play, "A Month of Sundays" by Bob Larbey. **89m/C VHS, Beta, Closed Caption.** Vincent Gardenia, Hume Cronyn, Tandy Cronyn, Esther Rolle, Michelle Scarabelli; *D:* Allen Kroeker. *HBO*

The Agency 🎬🎬 *Mind Games* 1981 (R) An
advertising agency attempts to manipulate public behavior and opinion through the use of subliminal advertising. A good premise is bogged down by a dull script and plodding performances by all concerned. Based on a Paul Gottlieb novel. **94m/C VHS, Beta.** *CA* Robert Mitchum, Lee Majors, Valerie Perrine, Saul Rubinek, Alexandra Stewart; *D:* George Kaczender; *M:* Lewis Furey. *VES, MTX, VTR*

Agent on Ice 🎬🎬 1986 (R) Hockey team is
stalked by lawyers. No, wait. An ex-CIA agent is stalked for cover-up purposes by the agency and the mob. One slippery fellow. **96m/C VHS, Beta.** Tom Ormeny, Clifford David, Louis Pastore, Matt Craven; *D:* Clark Worswick. *VTR*

Aggie Appleby, Maker of Men 🎬½
Cupid in the Rough 1933 A wimpy society boy transforms himself into a tough guy, all for the love of a dame. Based on a play by Joseph O. Kesselring. Very slight comedy. **73m/B VHS.** Charles Farrell, Wynne Gibson, William Gargan, ZaSu Pitts; *D:* Mark Sandrich; *M:* Max Steiner. *FCT*

Agnes of God 🎬🎬 1985 (PG-13) Stage to
screen translation of John Pielmeier's play loses something in the translation. Coarse chain-smoking psychiatrist Fonda is sent to a convent to investigate whether young nun Tilly is fit to stand trial. Seems that the nun may have given birth to and then strangled her baby, although she denies ever having sexual relations and knows nothing about an infant. Naive Tilly is frightened by probing Fonda, while worldly mother-superior Bancroft is distrusting. Melodramatic stew of Catholicism, religious fervor, and science features generally good performances, although Fonda often seems to be acting (maybe it's the cigarettes). **99m/C VHS, Beta, LV, Closed Caption.** Jane Fonda, Anne Bancroft, Meg Tilly, Anne Pitoniak, Winston Rekert, Gratien Gelinas; *D:* Norman Jewison; *W:* John Pielmeier; *C:* Sven Nykvist; *M:* Georges Delerue. Golden Globe Awards '86: Best Supporting Actress (Tilly); Nominations: Academy Awards '85:

Best Actress (Bancroft), Best Supporting Actress (Tilly), Best Original Score. *COL*

The Agony and the Ecstasy 🎬🎬½
1965 Big-budget (for 1965 anyway at $12 million) adaptation of the Irving Stone book recounts the conflict between Michelangelo and Pope Julius II after His Holiness directs the artist to paint the Sistine Chapel. Follow the tortured artist through his unpredictable creative process and the hours (it seems literal due to movie length) of painting flat on his back. Heston exudes quiet strength in his sincere interpretation of the genius artist, while Harrison has a fling as the Pope. Slow script is not up to the generally good performances. Disappointing at the boxoffice, but worth a look on the small screen for the sets alone. **136m/C VHS, Beta, LV, Letterbox.** Charlton Heston, Rex Harrison, Harry Andrews, Diane Cilento, Alberto Lupo, Adolfo Celi; *D:* Carol Reed; *W:* Philip Dunne; *C:* Leon Shamroy; *M:* Jerry Goldsmith, Alex North. National Board of Review Awards '65: Best Supporting Actor (Andrews); Nominations: Academy Awards '65: Best Art Direction/Set Decoration (Color), Best Color Cinematography, Best Costume Design (Color), Best Sound, Best Original Score. *FOX, IGP*

Agony of Love 1966 An unhappy home-
maker rents a nearby apartment to live out her wildest fantasies and bring some excitement into her otherwise dull life. **?m/C VHS.** *SMW, TPV*

Aguirre, the Wrath of God 🎬🎬🎬½
1972 Herzog at his best, combining brilliant poetic images and an intense narrative dealing with power, irony, and death. Spanish conquistadors in 1590 search for the mythical city of gold in Peru. Instead, they descend into the hell of the jungle. Kinski is fabulous as Aguirre, succumbing to insanity while leading a continually diminishing crew in this compelling, extraordinary drama shot in the jungles of South America. Both English- and German-language versions available. **94m/C VHS.** *GE* Klaus Kinski, Ruy Guerra, Del Negro, Helena Rojo, Cecilia Rivera, Peter Berling, Danny Ades; *D:* Werner Herzog; *W:* Werner Herzog. National Society of Film Critics Awards '77: Best Cinematography. *NYF*

Ah, Wilderness! 🎬🎬🎬½ 1935 Delightful
tale of a teen boy coming of age in small town America. Watch for the hilarious high school graduation scene. Based on the play by Eugene O'Neill. Remade in 1948 as "Summer Holiday," a musical with Mickey Rooney in the lead. **101m/B VHS.** Wallace Beery, Lionel Barrymore, Aline MacMahon, Eric Linden, Cecilia Parker, Spring Byington, Mickey Rooney, Charley Grapewin, Frank Albertson; *D:* Clarence Brown; *C:* Clyde De Vinna. *MGM, BTV*

Ain't No Way Back 🎬 1989 Two hun-
ters stumble upon a feudin' bunch of moonshiners and must leave their city ways behind if they plan to survive. **90m/C VHS, Beta.** *NO*

Air America 🎬🎬 1990 (R) It's the Vietnam
War and the CIA is operating a secret drug smuggling operation in Southeast Asia to finance the effort. Flyboys Gibson and Downey drop opium and glib lines all over Laos. Big-budget Gibson vehicle with sufficient action but lacking much of a story, which was adapted from a book by Christopher Robbins. **113m/C VHS, Beta, LV, Closed Caption.** Mel Gibson, Robert Downey Jr., Marshall Bell, Nancy Travis, David Marshall Grant, Tim Thomerson, Lane Smith; *D:* Roger Spottiswoode; *W:* Richard Rush; *C:* Roger Deakins. *ART, IME*

Air Bud 🎬🎬½ 1997 (PG) Buddy's a basket-
ball-playing golden retriever (no relation) who befriends lonely misfit Josh (Zegers) and teaches him the nuances of the layup, fade-away J, and pick-and-roll. It's good to see dog athletes getting to stretch beyond the usual frisbee and stick-fetching roles. Teaming animals (especially canines) with kids usually adds up to success. This one's no exception, especially for the grade school crowd. **92m/C VHS, Closed Caption, DVD.** Kevin Zegers, Michael Jeter, Bill Cobbs, Cynthia Stevenson; *D:* Charles Martin Smith; *W:* Paul Tamasy, Aaron Mendelsohn; *C:* Mike Southon; *M:* Brahm Wenger. *DIS*

Air Force 🎬🎬🎬½ 1943 One of the finest of
the WWII movies, Hawks' exciting classic has worn well through the years, in spite of the Japanese propaganda. It follows the hazardous exploits of a Boeing B-17 bomber crew who fight over Pearl Harbor, Manila, and the Coral Sea. Extremely realistic dogfight sequences and powerful, introspective real guy interfacing by the ensemble cast are masterfully combined by Hawks. **124m/B VHS, Closed Caption.** John Garfield, John Ridgely, Gig Young, Arthur Kennedy, Charles Drake, Harry Carey Sr., George Tobias; *D:* Howard Hawks; *C:* James Wong Howe. Academy Awards '43: Best Film Editing; Nominations: Academy Awards '43: Best Black and White Cinematography, Best Original Screenplay. *FOX*

Air Force One 🎬🎬🎬 *AFO* 1997 (R) Ford
stars as U.S. President James Marshall, who is not only tough on crime but tough, period. His policy is to not negotiate with terrorists. Then Air Force One, with him, the First Lady and their daughter aboard is hijacked by Russian nationalists, led by ice cold Ivan (Oldman). Close is first woman Veep, Kathryn Bennett, stuck in D.C. coping with the situation. Ford is in fine form as the President who's forced to kick some Commie butt to save the day. Director Petersen ("In The Line of Fire") is becoming a master of building tension in confined places and puts his strong cast to good use. Nail-biting suspense and breath-taking action sequences cap off tour-de-force adventure. **124m/C VHS, LV, Closed Caption.** Harrison Ford, Gary Oldman, Glenn Close, Dean Stockwell, William H. Macy, Wendy Crewson, Xander Berkeley, Paul Guilfoyle, Liesl Matthews, Bill Smitrovich, Elya Baskin, David Vadim, Tom Everett, Philip Baker Hall, Spencer Garrett, Donna Bullock; *Cameos:* Juergen Prochnow; *D:* Wolfgang Petersen; *W:* Andrew Marlowe; *C:* Michael Ballhaus; *M:* Jerry Goldsmith. Nominations: Academy Awards '97: Best Film Editing, Best Sound; MTV Movie Awards '98: Best Villain (Oldman), Best Fight (Harrison Ford/Gary Oldman). *COL*

Air Hawk 🎬 1984 Australian made for TV
release details the adventures of an outback pilot involved with stolen diamonds. **90m/C VHS, Beta.** *AU* Eric Oldfield, Louise Howitt, Ellie MacLure, David Robson, David Baker; *D:* David Baker. *VCD*

Air Raid Wardens 🎬🎬 1943 Laurel &
Hardy play a couple of small-town failures who become the local air raid wardens during WWII. They even manage to make a mess of this but redeem themselves when they overhear a spy plot and save the town's munitions factory from a German spy ring. A so-so effort from the comic duo. **67m/B VHS.** Stan Laurel, Oliver Hardy, Edgar Kennedy, Jacqueline White, Stephen McNally, Russell Hicks, Howard Freeman, Donald Meek, Henry O'Neill; *D:* Edward Sedgwick. *MGM*

The Air Up There 🎬🎬 1994 (PG) Assis-
tant basketball coach Jimmy Dolan (Bacon) heads to the African village of Winabi to recruit talented (and tall) Saleh (Maina) to play b-ball in the U.S. But Saleh is next in line to be the tribe's king and doesn't want to leave. Stupid American in foreign country learning from the natives story is lighthearted, but relies heavily on formula—and borders on the stereotypical, though climatic game is a lot of fun. **108m/C VHS, LV, Closed Caption.** Kevin Bacon, Charles Gitona Maina, Sean McCann, Dennis Patrick; *D:* Paul Michael Glaser; *W:* Max Apple; *C:* Elliot Davis; *M:* David Newman. *HPH*

Airborne 🎬½ 1993 (PG) Cool California rol-
lerblade dude gets transplanted to Cincinnati for a school year, and has to prove himself when those good ol' midwestern boys come after him. Nothing short of a skate vehicle appealing largely, if not solely, to the high school contingent. **91m/C VHS, Beta, LV, Closed Caption.** Shane McDermott, Seth Green, Brittney Powell, Edie McClurg; *D:* Rob Bowman; *W:* Bill Apablasa; *M:* Stewart Copeland. *WAR*

Airheads 🎬🎬½ 1994 (PG-13) "Wayne's
World" meets "Dog Day Afternoon." Silly farce has three metal heads (Buscemi, Fraser, Sandler) holding a radio station hostage in order to get their demo tape played. Events snowball and they

receive instant fame. Cast and crew rich with sub-
versive comedic talents, including Sandler and
Farley from "Saturday Night Live." Soundtrack
authenticity supplied by White Zombie and The
Galatic Cowboys. **81m/C VHS, LV, Closed Caption.**
Brendan Fraser, Steve Buscemi, Adam Sandler, Chris Far-
ley, Michael McKean, Judd Nelson, Joe Mantegna, Michael
Richards, Ernie Hudson, Amy Locane, Nina Siemaszko,
John Melendez; **D:** Michael Lehmann; **W:** Rich Wilkes; **M:**
Carter Burwell. **FXV**

Airplane! 🐾🐾🐾½ **1980 (PG)** Classic lampoon of disaster flicks is stupid but funny and
launched a bevy wanna-be spoofs. A former pilot
who's lost both his girl (she's the attendant) and
his nerve takes over the controls of a jet when the
crew is hit with food poisoning. The passengers
become increasingly crazed and ground support
more surreal as our hero struggles to land the
plane. Clever, fast-paced, and very funny parody
mangles every Hollywood cliche within reach. The
gags are so furiously paced that when one bombs
it's hardly noticeable. Launched Nielsen's second
career as a comic actor. And it ain't over till it's
over: don't miss the amusing final credits. Followed by "Airplane 2: The Sequel." **88m/C VHS,
Beta, LV, 8mm.** Robert Hays, Julie Hagerty, Lloyd Bridges,
Peter Graves, Robert Stack, Kareem Abdul-Jabbar, Leslie
Nielsen; **Cameos:** Ethel Merman, Barba-
ra Billingsley; **D:** Jerry Zucker, Jim Abrahams, David Zucker; **W:** Jerry Zucker, Jim Abrahams, David Zucker; **C:** Joseph Biroc; **M:** Elmer Bernstein. Writers Guild of America
'80: Best Adapted Screenplay. **PAR**

Airplane 2: The Sequel 🐾🐾 **1982 (PG)**
Not a Zucker, Abrahams and Zucker effort, and
sorely missing their slapstick and script finesse.
The first passenger space shuttle has taken off for
the moon and there's a mad bomber on board.
Given the number of stars mugging, it's more of a
loveboat in space than a fitting sequel to "Airplane." Nonetheless, some funny laughs and
gags. **84m/C VHS, Beta, LV.** Robert Hays, Julie Hagerty,
Lloyd Bridges, Raymond Burr, Peter Graves, William Shatner, Sonny Bono, Chuck Connors, Chad Everett, Stephen
Stucker, Rip Torn, Ken Finkleman, Sandahl Bergman; **D:**
Ken Finkleman; **C:** Joseph Biroc; **M:** Elmer Bernstein. **PAR**

Airport 🐾🐾🐾 **1970 (G)** Old-fashioned disaster thriller built around an all-star cast, fairly moronic script, and an unavoidable accident during
the flight of a passenger airliner. A boxoffice hit
that paved the way for many lesser disaster flicks
(including its many sequels) detailing the reactions of the passengers and crew as they cope
with impending doom. Considered to be best
of the "Airport" series; adapted from the Arthur
Hailey novel. **137m/C VHS, Beta, LV.** Dean Martin, Burt
Lancaster, Jean Seberg, Jacqueline Bisset, George Kennedy, Helen Hayes, Van Heflin, Maureen Stapleton, Barry Nelson, Lloyd Nolan; **D:** George Seaton; **W:** George Seaton; **C:**
Ernest Laszlo. Academy Awards '70: Best Supporting Actress (Hayes); Golden Globe Awards '71: Best Supporting
Actress (Stapleton); Nominations: Academy Awards '70:
Best Adapted Screenplay, Best Art Direction/Set Decora-
tion, Best Cinematography, Best Costume Design, Best
Film Editing, Best Picture, Best Sound, Best Supporting Actress (Stapleton), Best Original Score. **USH, BTV**

Airport '75 🐾🐾 **1975 (PG)** After a mid-air
collision, a jumbo 747 is left pilotless. Airline attendant Black must fly da plane. She does her
cross-eyed best in this absurd sequel to "Airport"
built around a lesser "all-star cast." Safe on the
ground, Heston tries to talk the airline hostess/pi-
lot into landing, while the impatient Kennedy continues to grouse as leader of the foam-ready
ground crew. A slick, insincere attempt to find box
office magic again (which unfortunately worked,
leading to two more sequels). **107m/C VHS, Beta.**
Charlton Heston, Karen Black, George Kennedy, Gloria
Swanson, Helen Reddy, Sid Caesar, Efrem Zimbalist Jr.,
Susan Clark, Dana Andrews, Linda Blair, Myrna Loy; **D:**
Jack Smight. **GKK**

Airport '77 🐾🐾 **1977 (PG)** Billionaire Stewart fills his converted passenger jet with priceless
art and sets off to Palm Beach for a museum
opening, joined by an uninvited gang of hijackers.

Twist to this in-flight disaster is that the bad time
in the air occurs underwater, a novel (and some
might say, desperate) twist to the old panic in the
plane we're all gonna die formula. With a cast of
familiar faces, some of them stars and some of
them just familiar faces, this is yet another sequel
to "Airport" and another boxoffice success, leading to the last of the tired series in 1979. **114m/C
VHS, Beta, LV.** Jack Lemmon, James Stewart, Lee Grant,
Brenda Vaccaro, Joseph Cotten, Olivia de Havilland, Darren
McGavin, Christopher Lee, George Kennedy, Kathleen
Quinlan; **D:** Jack Smight. Nominations: Academy Awards
'77: Best Art Direction/Set Decoration, Best Costume Design. **USH**

Akermania, Vol. 1 🐾🐾🐾 **1992** This
compilation of director Akerman's shorter works
includes "I'm Hungry, I'm Cold," the story of two
Belgian girls on the loose in Paris, and "Saute Ma
Ville," Akerman's first film. Both are in French with
English subtitles. Also included is "Hotel Monter-
ey," a silent experimental film. **89m/C VHS.** **FR** Maria
De Medeiros, Pascale Salkin, Chantal Akerman; **D:** Chantal
Akerman. **WAC**

Akira 🐾🐾 **1989** Secret government experiments on children with ESP go awry, resulting in
an cataclysmic explosion on Tokyo. The city in
turn builds itself up into a Megalopolis and the
experiments continue. Animated; in Japanese
with English subtitles or dubbed. **124m/C VHS, LV.**
JP D: Katsuhiro Otomo, Sheldon Renan; **W:** Katsuhiro Otomo, Izo Hashimoto; **C:** Katsuji Misawa. **STP, CRC**

Akira Kurosawa's Dreams 🐾🐾½
Dreams **1990 (PG)** An anthological lesson regarding
the simultaneous loss of humanity and nature that
threatens us all from the renowned Japanese director. Although the startling and memorable imagery is still present, Kurosawa's lessons are
strangely trite and consequently lack the power
that is normally associated with his work. Watch
for Scorsese as Van Gogh. With English subtitles.
120m/C VHS, LV, Letterbox. **JP** Akira Terao, Mitsuko
Baisho, Meiko Harada, Chishu Ryu, Hisashi Igawa, Mitsu-
nori Isaki, Toshihiko Nakano, Yoshitaka Zushi, Toshie Negi-
shi, Martin Scorsese; **D:** Akira Kurosawa; **W:** Akira Kurosawa; **M:** Shinichiro Ikebe. **WAR, FCT**

Al Capone 🐾🐾🐾 **1959** Film noir character
study of one of the most colorful gangsters of the
Roaring '20s. Sort of an underworld "How to Succeed in Business." Steiger chews scenes and bullets as they fly by, providing the performance of
his career. Plenty of gangland violence and mayhem and splendid cinematography keep the fast-
paced period piece sailing. **104m/C VHS, Beta.** Rod
Steiger, Fay Spain, Murvyn Vye, Nehemiah Persoff, Martin
Balsam, James Gregory, Joe De Santis; **D:** Richard Wilson.
FOX, FCT

Alabama's Ghost 🐾½ **1972 (PG)** Musician steals a dead master magician's secrets, incurring the wrath of the paranormal underworld.
Far from the best of the "blaxploitation" films of
the '70s. **96m/C VHS, Beta.** Christopher Brooks, E. Kerrigan Prescott; **D:** Fredric Hobbs. **ART**

Aladdin 🐾 *Superfantagenio* **1986 (PG)** A comedic Italian modernization of the Aladdin fable. **97m/C
VHS, Beta, Closed Caption.** **IT** Bud Spencer, Luca Venan-
tini, Janet Agren, Julian Voloshin, Umberto Raho; **D:** Bruno
Corbucci.

Aladdin 🐾🐾🐾½ **1992 (G)** Boy meets princess, loses her, finds her, wins her from evil vizier
and nasty parrot. Superb animation triumphs over
average songs and storyline by capitalizing on
Williams' talent for ad-lib with lightning speed genie changes, lots of celebrity spoofs, and even a
few pokes at Disney itself. Adults will enjoy the
1,001 impersonations while kids will get a kick out
of the big blue genie and the songs, three of
which are the late Ashman's legacy. Kane and
Salonga are responsible for the singing voices of
Aladdin and Jasmine; Gottfried is a riot as the
obnoxious parrot sidekick. Be forewarned: small
children may be frightened by some of the scarier
sequences. ♫A Whole New World; Prince Ali;

Friend Like Me; One Jump Ahead; Arabian
Nights. **90m/C VHS, Beta, LV, Closed Caption.** **D:** Ron
Clements, John Musker; **W:** Ron Clements, John Musker,
Ted Elliot, Terry Rossio; **M:** Alan Menken, Howard Ashman,
Tim Rice; **V:** Robin Williams, Scott Weinger, Linda Larkin,
Jonathan Freeman, Frank Welker, Gilbert Gottfried, Doug-
las Seale, Brad Kane, Lea Salonga. Academy Awards '92:
Best Song ("A Whole New World"), Best Original Score;
Golden Globe Awards '93: Best Song ("A Whole New
World"), Best Score; MTV Movie Awards '93: Best Comedic
Performance (Williams); Nominations: Academy Awards
'92: Best Song ("Friend Like Me"), Best Sound, Best Sound
Effects Editing. **DIS, BTV**

**Aladdin and His Wonderful
Lamp** 🐾🐾½ **1984** The story of Aladdin, a
young man who finds a magical oil lamp when he
is trapped in a tiny cave. From the "Faerie Tale
Theatre" series and director of "Beetlejuice" and
"Batman" Tim Burton. **60m/C VHS, Beta, Closed
Caption.** Valerie Bertinelli, Robert Carradine, Leonard Ni-
moy, James Earl Jones; **D:** Tim Burton. **KUI, FOX, FCT**

Aladdin and the King of Thieves
1996 Second-direct-to-video saga (following "The
Return of Jafar") once again features Williams as
the voice of the genie (after settling a dispute with
Disney). On the eve of Aladdin's marriage to Jasmine, thieves try to steal a magic talisman, sending Aladdin on a mission to find the thieves—and
his father. Disney had such terrific success
with"Return" that it was inevitable they would try
again. **82m/C VHS, Closed Caption. D:** Ted Stones; **W:**
Mark McCorkle, Robert Schooley; **M:** Mark Watters; **V:** Robin Williams, Scott Weinger, Jerry Orbach, John Rhys-Davies, Gilbert Gottfried, Linda Larkin, CCH Pounder, Frank
Welker. **DIS**

Alakazam the Great! **1961** Japanese animated film about an arrogant monkey who is sent
on a mission to learn about life. **84m/C VHS. D:** Lee
Kresel; **M:** Les Baxter; **V:** Frankie Avalon, Dodie Stevens,
Jonathan Winters, Arnold Stang, Sterling Holloway. **CNG**

The Alamo 🐾🐾🐾 **1960** Old-fashioned patriotic battle epic recounts the real events of the
1836 fight for independence in Texas. The usual
band of diverse and contentious personalities, including Wayne as a coonskin-capped Davy
Crockett, defend a small fort against a very big
Mexican raiding party outside of San Antonio. Before meeting mythic death, they fight with each
other, learn the meaning of life, and ultimately
come to respect each other. Just to make it more
entertaining, Avalon sings. Big-budget production
features an impeccable musical score by Tiomkin
and an impressive 7,000 extras for the Mexican
army alone. Wayne reportedly received directorial
assistance from John Ford, particularly during the
big massacre finale. **161m/C VHS, Beta, LV,
Letterbox, Closed Caption.** John Wayne, Richard Widmark, Laurence Harvey, Frankie Avalon, Richard Boone,
Carlos Arruza, Chill Wills, Veda Ann Borg; **D:** John Wayne;
C: William Clothier; **M:** Dimitri Tiomkin. Academy Awards
'60: Best Sound; Golden Globe Awards '61: Best Score;
Nominations: Academy Awards '60: Best Color Cinematography, Best Film Editing, Best Picture, Best Song ("The
Green Leaves of Summer"), Best Supporting Actor (Wills),
Best Original Dramatic/Comedy Score. **MGM, FOX, TLF**

Alamo Bay 🐾🐾½ **1985** A slow-moving but
sincere tale of contemporary racism. An angry
Vietnam veteran and his red-neck buddies feel
threatened by Vietnamese refugees who want to
go into the fishing business. Set in Texas, filled
with Texas-sized characters, and based on a true
Texas story, as interpreted by the French Malle.
99m/C VHS, Beta, LV, Closed Caption. Ed Harris, Ho
Nguyen, Amy Madigan, Donald Moffat, Cynthia Carle, Tru-
en V. Tran, Rudy Young; **D:** Louis Malle; **W:** Alice Arlen; **M:**
Ry Cooder. **COL**

**The Alamo: Thirteen Days to
Glory** 🐾🐾 **1987** The legendary Davy Crockett
(Keith), Colonel William Travis (Baldwin), and Jim
Bowie (Arness) overcome personal differences to
unite against the Mexican Army, vowing to hold
down the fort or die. It takes a true Texan to fully
appreciate the merits of this rather pedestrian re-

telling of a familiar story, but the battle scenes are pretty heady (although they lose some of their froth on the small screen). If nothing else, the ever-versatile Julia is worth seeing as Santa Anna in this made-for-TV rendering of J. Lon Tinkle's "Thirteen Days to Glory." You may not want to remember the Alamo this way. **180m/C VHS, Beta, Closed Caption.** James Arness, Lorne Greene, Alec Baldwin, Brian Keith, Raul Julia; **D:** Peter Werner; **M:** Peter Bernstein.

Alamut Ambush 🎥 **1986** A federal agent is stalked by assassins, and decides to hunt them in return. Sequel to "Cold War Killer." **94m/C VHS, Beta.** *GB* Terence Stamp, Michael Culver; **D:** Ken Grieve. **NO**

Alan & Naomi 🎥🎥½ **1992 (PG)** In 1944, 14-year-old Alan Silverman is more concerned with his Brooklyn stickball team than the war raging across Europe. This changes when his upstairs neighbor offers refuge to a French-Jewish mother and her young daughter and he is asked to befriend the girl. Naomi witnessed the brutal death of her father by the Nazis and retreated into a world of her own. Together the two build a sweet, if unlikely, friendship. Fine performances save this average coming of age tale. Based on the novel by Myron Levoy. **95m/C VHS, LV.** Lukas Haas, Vanessa Zaoui, Michael Gross, Amy Aquino, Kevin Connolly, Zohra Lampert; **D:** Sterling Van Wagenen; **W:** Jordan Horowitz; **M:** Dick Hyman. **COL**

An Alan Smithee Film: Burn, Hollywood, Burn 🎥½ *Burn Hollywood, Burn* **1997 (R)** Follows a British director (Idle), whose given name is Alan Smithee, as he kidnaps the reels of his own picture when he realizes he hates the movie but can't remove his name from it since the Directors Guild of America's official pseudonym for disputed films is "Alan Smithee." O'Neal stars as the boorish producer who drives Smithee to the desperate act. This extended in-joke ran into its own problem when director Arthur Hiller, in what seemed like a publicity stunt, repudiated the version producer/writer Eszterhas recut and had his own name removed from the film, thus making "An Alan Smithee Film" one of the more than 30 Alan Smithee films in as many years. The tedious mockumentary style is relentless in narrating the story to the audience, who is never allowed to just watch what happens. Only interest is the parade of star cameos, including Stallone, Goldberg, and Chan (as themselves), along with writer Eszterhas in a scene with the director who declined credit for the film, Hiller. **CW:** Strong language and some sexual humor. **86m/C VHS.** Eric Idle, Ryan O'Neal, Coolio, Richard Jeni, Sandra Bernhard, Cherie Lunghi, Harvey Weinstein, M.C. Lyte, Stephen Tobolowsky, Chuck D, Leslie Stefanson, Gavin Polone, Marcello Thedford, Nicole Nagel; **Cameos:** Joe Eszterhas, Sylvester Stallone, Whoopi Goldberg, Jackie Chan, Larry King, Billy Bob Thornton, Dominick Dunne, Robert Evans, Shane Black; **D:** Arthur Hiller; **W:** Joe Eszterhas; **C:** Reynaldo Villalobos; **M:** Gary G-Wiz. **TOU**

Alaska 🎥🎥½ **1996 (PG)** Fourteen-year-old Vincent Barnes (Kartheiser) and his 12-year-old sister Jessie (Birch) try to rescue their bush pilot father Jake (Benedict) whose plane has crashed in the wilderness. They also rescue an orphaned polar bear cub from an evil poacher (Heston) that manages to help them out along the way. See this flick if only to enjoy the lush backdrop of Alaska and British Columbia and, of course, the absolutely adorable polar cub. Director Fraser C. Heston directs dad Charlton, appropriate payback for landing him the role as the infant Moses in "The Ten Commandments." **109m/C VHS, LV, Closed Caption.** Thora Birch, Vincent Kartheiser, Dirk Benedict, Charlton Heston; **D:** Fraser Heston; **W:** Andy Burg, Carol Fuchs; **C:** Tony Westman. **COL**

The Alaska Wilderness Adventure 🎥🎥 **1978** The tale of a family struggling for survival in the Arctic wilderness. Baby, it's cold out there. **90m/C VHS, Beta.** **NO**

Alberto Express 🎥🎥½ **1992** Black comedy explores the debts children owe their parents—literally. Alberto's family has a peculiar tradition. It seems that now he's married and about to become a father, he's expected to pay back every cent spent on his own upbringing. Cash poor (and panicky) Alberto hops a train from Paris to Rome and frantically tries to raise the necessary cash by preying, in a series of increasingly bizarre ways, on his fellow passengers before he faces his father once again. In French and Italian with English subtitles. **90m/C VHS.** *FR* Sergio Castellito, Nino Manfredi, Marie Trintignant, Jeanne Moreau, Michel Aumont, Dominique Pinon, Marco Messeri, Eugenia Marruzzo; **D:** Arthur Joffe; **W:** Arthur Joffe. **FXL**

Albino woof! **1976 (R)** Albino chief leads African terrorists to murder white settlers, one of whom is an ex-policeman's fiancee. So the ex-cop pursues the bad guys, who are fairly easy to identify (just look for the big group hanging with the albino). Danning, Lee, and Howard only briefly show faces and collect checks. **85m/C VHS, Beta.** Christopher Lee, Trevor Howard, Sybil Danning, Horst Frank, James Faulkner; **D:** Jurgen Goslar.

Albino Alligator 🎥🎥 **1996 (R)** Three small-time crooks bungle a robbery and inadvertently run down a federal officer in Academy Award-winning actor Spacey's directorial debut. The trio, consisting of leader Dova (Dillon), brains Milo (Sinise) and brawn Law (Fichtner) hole up in a seedy bar and grab the occupants as hostages. The police soon surround the dive, and the crooks begin arguing among themselves and with brash barmaid Janet (Dunaway) about their chances and means for escape. All, however, is not as it seems. The claustrophobic setting seems more suitable for the stage than the screen, and the plot twists don't bend very far from predictable. Screenwriter Forte is the son of 60s teen idol Fabian. **CW:** Strong violence and language. **94m/C VHS, LV, Closed Caption.** Matt Dillon, Gary Sinise, Faye Dunaway, William Fichtner, Joe Mantegna, Viggo Mortensen, John Spencer, Skeet Ulrich, M. Emmet Walsh; **D:** Kevin Spacey; **W:** Christian Forte; **C:** Mark Plummer; **M:** Michael Brook. Nominations: Golden Raspberry Awards '97: Worst Supporting Actress (Dunaway). **TOU**

The Alchemist woof! **1981 (R)** See humans transformed into murderous zombies! A bewitched man seeks revenge upon the evil magician who placed a curse on him, causing him to live like an animal. Painfully routine, with a few chills along the way. Amonte is an alias for Charles Band. Filmed in 1981 and released four years later. **86m/C VHS, Beta.** Robert Ginty, Lucinda Dooling, John Sanderford, Viola Kate Stimpson, Bob Glaudini; **D:** James Amonte; **W:** Alan J. Adler; **M:** Richard Band. **VES, ART**

Alex 🎥🎥½ **1992** Inspirational story about 15-year-old New Zealand swimmer Alex Archer (Jackson), who is working towards a spot at the 1960 Rome Olympics. But her goal is threatened by an accident and a new rival and Alex struggles to overcome her obstacles with the help of her boyfriend Andy (Picker). Based on the novel by Tessa Duder. **92m/C VHS, LV.** *AU* Lauren Jackson, Chris Haywood, Josh Picker, Catherine Godbold, Elizabeth Hawthorne; **D:** Megan Simpson. **ORI**

Alex in Wonderland 🎥🎥½ **1970 (R)** A semi-autobiographical and satirical look at Hollywood from the standpoint of a young director who's trying to follow up his recent hit (in real life, "Bob & Carol & Ted & Alice") with a picture of some integrity that will keep the mass audience away. The confused plot provides obvious parallels to Fellini (who appears in a cameo) and some sharp, often bitter insights into the Hollywood of the early '60s. Strong performances by Sutherland and Burstyn compensate somewhat for the patience-trying self-indulgent arty whining of the script. **109m/C VHS, Beta.** Donald Sutherland, Ellen Burstyn, Jeanne Moreau, Paul Mazursky; **Cameos:** Federico Fellini; **D:** Paul Mazursky; **W:** Larry Tucker, Paul Mazursky. **MGM, FCT**

Alexander Nevsky 🎥🎥🎥½ **1938** A story of the invasion of Russia in 1241 by the Teutonic Knights of Germany and the defense of the region by good old Prince Nevsky. Eisenstein's first completed project in nearly ten years, it was widely regarded as an artistic disappointment upon release and as pro-war propaganda for the looming conflict with the Nazis. Fabulous Prokofiev score illuminates the classic battle scenes, which used thousands of Russian army regulars. Russian with subtitles. **110m/B VHS, LV.** *RU* Nikolai Cherkassov, N.P. Okholopkov, Al Abrikossov; **D:** Sergei Eisenstein; **M:** Sergei Prokofiev. **BMG, MRV, NOS**

Alexander the Great 🎥🎥½ **1955** A lavish epic about the legendary Greek conqueror of the fourth century B.C., which provides Burton a rare chance at an adventure role. Here we find Alexander is the product of a dysfunctional royal family who hopes to create an idealized world modeled after Greek culture to make up for the love he lacks from daddy. This he does by conquering everything before dying at the age of 33. The great cast helps to overcome the sluggish pacing of the spectacle, while numerous battle scenes featuring loads of spears and arrows are staged effectively. **135m/C VHS, Beta, LV, Letterbox.** Richard Burton, Fredric March, Claire Bloom, Harry Andrews, Peter Cushing, Danielle Darrieux, Helmut Dantine; **D:** Robert Rossen; **C:** Robert Krasker. **MGM, FCT**

Alexander: The Other Side of Dawn 🎥🎥 **1977** Tired made-for-television sequel to the television movie "Dawn: Portrait of a Teenage Runaway." A young man turns to prostitution to support himself on the street of Los Angeles. **100m/C VHS.** Leigh McCloskey, Eve Plumb, Earl Holliman, Juliet Mills, Jean Hagen, Lonny Chapman; **D:** John Erman. **MOV**

Alexander's Ragtime Band 🎥🎥🎥 *Irving Berlin's Alexander's Ragtime Band* **1938** Energetic musical that spans 1915 to 1938 and has Power and Ameche battling for Faye's affections. Power is a society nabob who takes up ragtime. He puts together a band, naming the group after a piece of music (hence the title), and finds a singer (Faye). Ameche is a struggling composer who brings a Broadway producer to listen to their performance. Faye gets an offer to star in a show and becomes an overnight success. Over the years the trio win and lose success, marry and divorce, and finally end up happy. Corny but charming. ♫Alexander's Ragtime Band; All Alone; Blue Skies; Easter Parade; Everybody's Doin' It; Everybody Step; For Your Country and My Country; Heat Wave; I Can Always Find a Little Sunshine at the YMCA. **105m/B VHS.** Tyrone Power, Alice Faye, Don Ameche, Ethel Merman, Jack Haley, Jean Hersholt, Helen Westley, John Carradine, Paul Hurst, Joe King, Ruth Terry; **D:** Henry King; **W:** Kathryn Scola, Lamar Trotti; **M:** Irving Berlin. Academy Awards '38: Best Score; Nominations: Academy Awards '38: Best Film Editing, Best Interior Decoration, Best Picture, Best Song ("Now It Can Be Told"), Best Story. **FXV**

Alfie 🎥🎥🎥 **1966 (PG)** What's it all about, Alfie? Caine, in his first starring role, plays the British playboy out of control in mod London. Alfie is a despicable, unscrupulous and vile sort of guy who uses woman after woman to fulfill his basic needs and then casts them aside until...tragedy strikes. Though this box office hit was seen as a sophisticated take on current sexual mores upon release, it now seems a dated but engaging comedy, notable chiefly for its performances. From the play by Bill Naughton. The title song "Alfie," sung by Dionne Warwick, was a top ten hit. **113m/C VHS, Beta.** *GB* Michael Caine, Shelley Winters, Millicent Martin, Vivien Merchant, Julia Asher; **D:** Lewis Gilbert. Cannes Film Festival '67: Grand Jury Prize; Golden Globe Awards '67: Best Foreign Film; National Board of Review Awards '66: Best Supporting Actress (Merchant); National Society of Film Critics Awards '66: Best Actor (Caine); Nominations: Academy Awards '66: Best Actor (Caine), Best Adapted Screenplay, Best Picture, Best Song ("Alfie"), Best Supporting Actress (Merchant). **PAR**

Alfred Hitchcock's Aventure Malgache *Madagascar Landing; Alfred Hitchcock's Bon Voyage & Aventure Malgache* **1944** Hitchcock worked with the Moliere Players on this propaganda piece about the French Resistance. He based this story on the experiences of the actor Clarousse. Working for the Resistance in occupied Madagascar, Clarousse is betrayed and sent to prison by the Vichy government. Rescued by the British he returns to resume his work. In French with English subtitles. **31m/B VHS.** *D:* Alfred Hitchcock. *MIL*

Alfred Hitchcock's Bon Voyage *Alfred Hitchcock's Bon Voyage & Aventure Malgache* **1944** One of director Hitchcock's short propaganda pieces filmed as a tribute to the French Resistance. In London an RAF pilot is interrogated by the Free French about his escape from France. He was aided by a Polish agent who was actually working for the Gestapo to learn about the Resistance's movements. Flashbacks show the pilot's adventures from the spy's point-of-view. In French with English subtitles. **26m/B VHS.** John Blythe; *D:* Alfred Hitchcock. *MIL*

Alfredo, Alfredo ���� 1972 (R) Hoffman plays a mild-mannered bank clerk who regrets marrying a sexy woman. Lightweight domestic comedy. In Italian with English subtitles (Hoffman's voice was dubbed). **97m/C VHS, Closed Caption.** *IT* Dustin Hoffman, Stefania Sandrelli, Carla Gravina, Clara Colosimo, Daniela Patella, Dulio Del Prete; *D:* Pietro Germi. *PAR*

Algiers ������ 1938 Nearly a scene-for-scene Americanized remake of the 1937 French "Pepe Le Moko" about a beautiful rich girl (Lamarr) who meets and falls in love with a notorious thief (Boyer, then a leading sex symbol). Pursued by French police and hiding in the underworld-controlled Casbah, Boyer meets up with Lamarr in a tragically fated romance done in the best tradition of Hollywood. Boyer provides a measured performance as Le Moko, while Lamarr is appropriately sultry in her American film debut (which made her a star). Later remade as the semi-musical "Casbah." **96m/B VHS, Beta.** Charles Boyer, Hedy Lamarr, Sigrid Gurie, Gene Lockhart, Joseph Calleia, Alan Hale; *D:* John Cromwell; *C:* James Wong Howe. Nominations: Academy Awards '38: Best Actor (Boyer), Best Cinematography, Best Interior Decoration, Best Supporting Actor (Lockhart). *CNG, MRV, NOS*

Ali Baba and the Forty Thieves ����½ 1943 Ali Baba and his gang of thieves do battle against Hulagu Khan, leader of the Mongols, to save Baghdad and its citizens from ruin and death. **87m/C VHS, Closed Caption.** Jon Hall, Turhan Bey, Maria Montez, Andy Devine, Kurt Katch, Frank Puglia, Fortunio Bonanova, Moroni Olsen, Scotty Beckett; *D:* Arthur Lubin; *W:* Edmund Hartmann; *C:* William Howard Greene. *USH, FCT*

Ali Baba and the 40 Thieves ������ *Ali Baba et les Quarante Voleurs* 1954 French adaptation of the popular novel "A Thousand and One Nights." Servant boy Ali Baba discovers the magic cave holding the stolen treasure of Abdul and his 40 thieves. Shot on location in Morocco. Also available dubbed. **92m/C VHS.** *FR* Samia Gamal, Dieter Borsche, Henri Vilbert; *D:* Jacques Becker; *W:* Jacques Becker. *FRA, FCT*

Ali: Fear Eats the Soul ������ *Fear Eats the Soul* 1974 A widow cleaning woman in her 60s has a love affair with a Moroccan man 30 years her junior. To no one's surprise, both encounter racism and moral hypocrisy in West Germany. Serious melodrama from Fassbinder, who wrote it and appears as the squirmy son-in-law. In German with English subtitles. **68m/C VHS.** *GE* Brigitte Mira, El Hedi Ben Salem, Irm Hermann; *D:* Rainer Werner Fassbinder. *NYF, FCT*

Alias Billy the Kid ���� 1946 Western adventure with Carson posing as a famous outlaw to find out who's behind the scam involving the Denton City cattle trade. **54m/B VHS, Closed Caption.** Sunset Carson. *REP*

Alias Jesse James ���� 1959 (PG) Insurance agent Milford Farnsworth (Hope) is an eastern tenderfoot who holds a policy on Jesse James (Corey). So he heads west to make certain the outlaw doesn't get killed. Only Jesse sets Milford up as himself, hoping to collect on his own policy. Fleming's the local beauty. A number of western stars have cameos, coming to Hope's rescue. **92m/C VHS, Closed Caption.** Bob Hope, Rhonda Fleming, Wendell Corey, Jim Davis, Gloria Talbott, William Wright, Mary Young, Joseph Vitale; *Cameos:* Hugh O'Brian, Ward Bond, James Arness, Roy Rogers, Fess Parker, Gail Davis, James Garner, Gene Autry, Jay Silverheels, Bing Crosby, Gary Cooper; *D:* Norman Z. McLeod; *W:* William Bowers, D.D. Beauchamp; *C:* Lionel Lindon. *MGM*

Alias John Law �� 1935 The Good Guy fights for oil rights against the bad guys. Confused program western with an especially convoluted plot. **54m/B VHS, Beta.** Bob Steele; *D:* Robert North Bradbury. *NO*

Alias John Preston ��½ 1956 Yet another one of those pseudo-psychological to sleep perchance to dream movies. Lee plays a man haunted by dreams in which he's a murderer, and soon starts to question whether his dreams might not imitate life. It's been done before, it's been done since, and it's been done better. **66m/B VHS.** *GB* Betta St. John, Alexander Knox, Christopher Lee, Sandra Dorne, Patrick Holt, Betty Ann Davies, John Longden, Bill Fraser, John Stuart; *D:* David MacDonald. *SNC*

Alias, La Gringa ���� 1991 Follows the adventures of La Gringa, a likeable criminal capable of escaping from any Peruvian jail. After being aided in his latest escape by a political prisoner, La Gringa decides to return in disguise to pay back the favor. But the prison is rocked by rioting and La Gringa finds himself in a situation out of his control. Spanish with subtitles. **100m/C VHS.** *D:* Alberto Durant. *FCT*

Alice ���� 1986 A twist on the "Alice in Wonderland" tale. Alice witnesses an attempted murder, faints, and awakens in a weird, yet strangely familiar environment. Adapted from the stage production. **80m/C VHS, Beta.** Sophie Barjae, Susannah York, Jean-Pierre Cassel, Paul Nicholas. *ORI, WAR*

Alice ������½ 1988 An acclaimed surreal version of Lewis Carroll's already surreal "Alice in Wonderland," with the emphasis on Carroll's obsessiveness. Utilizing animated puppets and a live actor for Alice, Czech director Svankmajer injects grotesque images and black comedy into Wonderland. Not for the kids. **84m/C VHS.** *GB* Kristina Kohoutova; *D:* Jan Svankmajer. *ICA, TPV*

Alice ������ 1990 (PG-13) Farrow is "Alice," a woman plagued with doubts about her lifestyle, her religion, and her happiness. Her perfect children, husband, and apartment don't prevent her backaches, and she turns to an Oriental "herbalist" for aid. She finds his methods unusual and the results of the treatments surprising. Lightweight fairytale of Yuppiedom gone awry. Fine performances, but superficial and pointed story that may leave the viewer looking for more. (Perhaps that's Allen's point.) Farewell performance from character actor Luke, unbilled cameo from Judith Ivey, and first time out for Dylan O'Sullivan Farrow, adopted daughter of Allen and Farrow, as Kate. **106m/C VHS, Beta, LV, Closed Caption.** Mia Farrow, William Hurt, Joe Mantegna, Keye Luke, Alec Baldwin, Cybill Shepherd, Blythe Danner, Gwen Verdon, Bernadette Peters, Judy Davis, Patrick O'Neal, Julie Kavner, Caroline Aaron, Holland Taylor, Robin Bartlett, David Spielberg, Bob Balaban, Dylan O'Sullivan Farrow, Elle Macpherson; *D:* Woody Allen; *W:* Woody Allen; *C:* Carlo DiPalma. National Board of Review Awards '90: Best Actress (Farrow); Nominations: Academy Awards '90: Best Original Screenplay. *ORI, FCT*

Alice Adams ����½ 1935 Based on the classic Booth Tarkington novel about a poor girl from a small Midwestern town who falls in love with a man from the upper level of society. She tries desperately to fit in and nearly alienates her family and friends. The sets may be dated, but the insight on human behavior is timeless. **99m/B VHS, Beta, LV.** Katharine Hepburn, Fred MacMurray, Evelyn Venable, Hattie McDaniel, Fred Stone; *D:* George Stevens; *M:* Max Steiner. Nominations: Academy Awards '35: Best Actress (Hepburn), Best Picture. *CCB, NOS, TTC*

Alice Doesn't Live Here Anymore ����½ 1974 (PG) Scorsese marries road opera with pseudo-feminist semi-realistic melodrama and produces uneven but interesting results. When Alice's husband dies suddenly, leaving her with their 11-year-old son, she leaves for California, but finds herself stranded in Phoenix, down to her last few bucks. There she lands a job as a waitress in a diner where she meets kindly rancher Kristofferson. Notable for its female point of view, it was also the basis for the once-popular TV show "Alice." Burstyn and Ladd lend key performances, while Kristofferson is typically wooden. **105m/C VHS, Beta, LV, Letterbox.** Ellen Burstyn, Kris Kristofferson, Diane Ladd, Jodie Foster, Harvey Keitel, Vic Tayback, Billy Green Bush; *D:* Martin Scorsese; *W:* Robert Getchell. Academy Awards '74: Best Actress (Burstyn); British Academy Awards '75: Best Actress (Burstyn), Best Film, Best Screenplay, Best Supporting Actress (Ladd); Nominations: Academy Awards '74: Best Original Screenplay, Best Supporting Actress (Ladd). *WAR, FCT, BTV*

Alice in the Cities ������½ 1974 American and German culture are compared and contrasted in this early Wenders road work about a German journalist in the USA on assignment who suddenly finds himself custodian to a worldly nine-year-old girl abandoned by her mother. Together they return to Germany and search for the girl's grandmother. Along the way they learn about each other, many with distinctive and graceful Wenders moments. **110m/B VHS, Beta.** Ruediger Vogler, Yella Rottlaender, Elisabeth Kreuzer, Edda Kochi; *D:* Wim Wenders; *W:* Wim Wenders. *FCT, GLV, TPV*

Alice in Wonderland ����½ 1950 Another version of the Lewis Carroll classic which combines the usage of Lou Bunin's puppets and live action to tell the story. Released independently to cash in on the success of the Disney version. Takes a more adult approach to the story and is worth viewing on its own merits. **83m/C VHS, Beta.** *FR* Carol Marsh, Stephen Murray, Pamela Brown, Felix Aylmer, Ernest Milton; *D:* Dallas Bower. *MON*

Alice in Wonderland ������ 1951 (G) Classic Disney dream version of Lewis Carroll's famous children's story about a girl who falls down a rabbit hole into a magical world populated by strange creatures. Beautifully animated with some startling images, but served with a strange dispassion warmed by a fine batch of songs. Wynn's Mad Hatter and Holloway's Cheshire Cat are among the treats in store. ♫Alice in Wonderland; I'm Late; A Very Merry Un-Birthday. **75m/C VHS, Beta, LV, Closed Caption.** *D:* Hamilton Luske, Wilfred Jackson, Clyde Geronimi; *V:* Kathryn Beaumont, Ed Wynn, Sterling Holloway, Jerry Colonna. Nominations: Academy Awards '51: Scoring of a Musical. *DIS, FCT, KUI*

Alice in Wonderland ����½ 1982 Musical version of the Lewis Carroll's classic tale performed by the Children's Theatre Company and School. **81m/C VHS, Beta.** Annie Enneking, Solveig Olsen, Wendy Lehr, Jason McLean, Gary Briggle, Elizabeth Fink. *USH*

Alice Sweet Alice ��½ *Holy Terror; Communion* 1976 (R) Mediocre, gory who-killed-her, best remembered as the debut of Shields (in a small role). **112m/C VHS, Beta.** Linda Miller, Paula Sheppard, Mildred Clinton, Niles McMaster, Jane Lowry, Rudolph Willrich, Brooke Shields; *D:* Alfred Sole; *W:* Alfred Sole, Rosemary Ritvo; *C:* John Friberg, Chuck Hall. *VTR, BTV, HHT*

Alice Through the Looking Glass

1966 Based on Lewis Carroll's classic adventure. Follows the further adventures of young Alice. After a chess piece comes to life, it convinces Alice that excitement and adventure lie through the looking glass. **72m/C VHS, Beta.** Judi Rolin, Ricardo Montalban, Nanette Fabray, Robert Coote, Agnes Moorehead, Jack Palance, Jimmy Durante, Tom Smothers, Roy Castle, Richard Denning; **D:** Alan Handley. *KAR*

Alice to Nowhere 🎬🎬

1986 Concerns a running argument in the Outback over a fortune in gems unknowingly carried by a young woman. Made for Australian television and based on a novel by Evan Green. **210m/C VHS, Beta.** *AU* Rosie Jones, Steve Jacobs, John Waters, Ruth Cracknell; **D:** John Power. *PAR*

Alice's Adventures in Wonderland

1972 Musical adaptation of Lewis Carroll's timeless fantasy of a young girl who meets new friends when she falls into a rabbit hole. **96m/C VHS, Beta.** *GB* Fiona Fullerton, Michael Crawford, Ralph Richardson, Flora Robson, Peter Sellers, Robert Helpmann, Dudley Moore, Michael Jayston, Spike Milligan, Michael Hordern; **D:** William Sterling; **W:** William Sterling; **C:** Geoffrey Unsworth; **M:** John Barry. *VES*

Alice's Restaurant 🎬🎬½ 1969 (PG)

Based on the popular and funny 20-minute Arlo Guthrie song "Alice's Restaurant Massacre" about a Flower Child during the Last Big War who gets hassled for littering, man. Step back in time and study the issues of the hippie era, including avoiding the draft, dropping out of college, and dealing with the local pigs. Sort of a modern movie in the cinematic ambling genre, in that nothing really happens. **111m/C VHS, Beta.** Arlo Guthrie, James Broderick, Pat Quinn, Geoff Outlaw; **D:** Arthur Penn. Nominations: Academy Awards '69: Best Director (Penn). *MVD, MGM*

Alien 🎬🎬🎬½ 1979 (R)

Terse direction, stunning sets and special effects, and a well-seasoned cast save this from being another "Slimy monster from Outerspace" story. Instead it's a grisly rollercoaster of suspense and fear (and a huge boxoffice hit). Intergalactic freighter's crew is invaded by an unstoppable carnivorous alien intent on picking off the crew one by one. While the cast mostly bitches and banters while awaiting the horror of their imminent departure, Weaver is exceptional as Ripley, a self-reliant survivor who goes toe to toe with the Big Ugly. Futuristic, in the belly of the beast visual design creates a vivid sense of claustrophobic doom enhanced further by the ominous score. Oscar-winning special effects include the classic baby alien busting out of the crew guy's chest routine, a rib-splitting ten on the gore meter. Successfully followed by "Aliens" and "Alien 3." **116m/C VHS, Beta, LV.** Tom Skerritt, Sigourney Weaver, Veronica Cartwright, Yaphet Kotto, Harry Dean Stanton, Ian Holm, John Hurt; **D:** Ridley Scott; **W:** Dan O'Bannon; **C:** Derek Vanlint; **M:** Jerry Goldsmith. Academy Awards '79: Best Visual Effects; Nominations: Academy Awards '79: Best Art Direction/Set Decoration. *FOX*

Alien 3 🎬🎬 1992 (R)

Picks up where "Aliens" left off as Ripley crash lands on Fiorina 161, a planet that serves as a penal colony for 25 celibate but horny men who smell bad. Ripley is forced to shave her head because of the planet's lice problem, and she sets out to survive on the cold, unfriendly planet until a rescue ship can come for her. Fending off sexual advances from the men, Ripley soon discovers she wasn't the only survivor of the crash—the alien survived too and has somehow implanted her with an alien of her own. Dark and disturbing, filled with religious allegories, and a universe removed from the two earlier Aliens. Intended as the final installment of the series. *CW:* Language and monster violence. **135m/C VHS, LV, Letterbox, Closed Caption.** Sigourney Weaver, Charles S. Dutton, Charles Dance, Paul McGann, Brian Glover, Ralph Brown, Danny Webb, Christopher John Fields, Holt McCallany, Lance Henriksen; **D:** David Fincher; **M:** Elliot Goldenthal. Nominations: Academy Awards '92: Best Visual Effects. *FXV*

The Alien Agenda: Out of the Darkness

woof! **1996** Cheesy sci-fi with a narrator who ruminates about mysterious aliens who enjoy tormenting humans and can travel through time (and send humans back and forth). You won't care. **80m/C VHS.** Sasha Graham, Scooter McCrae, Mick McCleery; **D:** Kevin J. Lindenmuth, Mick McCleery; **W:** Kevin J. Lindenmuth, Mick McCleery. *TPV*

Alien Chaser 🎬🎬 1996 (R)

Alien android Zagarino, who crashed in the African desert 5000 years ago, returns to life thanks to the unwitting aid of archeologists Jensen and MacDonald. They literally hold the key to stopping his destruction of mankind. **95m/C VHS, LV.** Frank Zagarino, Todd Jensen, Jennifer MacDonald; **D:** Mark Roper; **W:** B.J. Nelson; **C:** Rod Stewart; **M:** Robert O. Ragland. *APX*

Alien Contamination

woof! *Contamination* **1981 (R)** Tale of two astronauts who return to Earth from an expedition on Mars carrying some deadly bacterial eggs. Controlled by a Martian intent on conquering the world, the eggs squirt a gloppy juice that makes people explode on contact (a special effect). A cheap and sloppy attempt to cash in on the success of "Alien." Dubbed. **90m/C VHS, Beta.** *IT* Ian McCulloch, Louise Monroe, Martin Mase, Samuel Rauch, Lisa Hahn; **D:** Lewis (Luigi Cozzi) Coates; **W:** Lewis (Luigi Cozzi) Coates. *NO*

Alien Dead 🎬

It Fell from the Sky **1979 (R)** The teenage victims of a bizarre meteor crash reincarnate as flesh-eating ghouls anxious for a new supply of human food in this extremely low-budget sleep inducer. **75m/C VHS, Beta.** Buster Crabbe, Linda Lewis, Ray Roberts, Mike Bonavia; **D:** Fred Olen Ray; **W:** Fred Olen Ray.

The Alien Factor 🎬½ 1978 (PG)

Another low-budget crazed critter from outerspace dispatch, this one featuring multiple aliens, one of whom is good, who have the misfortune of crash landing near Baltimore. The grotesque extraterrestrials jolt a small town out of its sleepy state by wreaking havoc (except for the good one, of course). Decent special effects. **82m/C VHS, Beta.** Don Leifert, Tom Griffith, Mary Mertens, Dick Dyszel; **D:** Donald M. Dohler. *NO*

Alien from L.A.

woof! **1987 (PG)** Awesomely inept comedy about a California girl who unwittingly stumbles onto the famed continent of Atlantis and can't find a yogurt stand. Weakly plotted and acted and filmed. Like, really. **88m/C VHS, Beta, LV.** Kathy Ireland, Thom Mathews, Don Michael Paul, Linda Kerridge, William R. Moses, Richard Haines; **D:** Albert Pyun; **W:** Albert Pyun, Debra Ricci, Regina Davis; **C:** Tom Fraser.

Alien Intruder 🎬🎬 1993 (R)

What happens when an evil demon appears before the soldiers of the future in the guise of a beautiful woman? Futuristic trash B-movie emerges from the depths. *CW:* Language, violence, and strong sexuality. **90m/C VHS, LV, Closed Caption.** Billy Dee Williams, Tracy Scoggins, Maxwell Caulfield; **D:** Ricardo Jacques Gale. *PMH*

Alien Massacre

woof! *Dr. Terror's Gallery of Horrors; Return from the Past; The Blood Suckers; Gallery of Horror* **1967** One of the worst films of all time—five short horror stories about zombies and vampires. Goes by many names—stinks in all of them. **90m/C VHS, Beta.** Lon Chaney Jr., John Carradine, Rochelle Hudson, Roger Gentry, Mitch Evans; **D:** David L. Hewitt. *MRV*

Alien Nation 🎬🎬½ 1988 (R)

A few hundred thousand alien workers land accidentally on Earth and slowly become part of its society, although widely discriminated against. One of the "newcomers" teams with a surly and bigoted human cop to solve a racially motivated murder. An inconsistent and occasionally transparent script looks at race conflicts and includes some humorous parallels with contemporary American life. Basis for the television series. Producer Hurd was also the force behind "The Terminator" and "Aliens." **89m/C VHS, Beta, LV, Closed Caption.** James Caan, Mandy Patinkin, Terence Stamp, Kevyn Major Ho-

ward, Peter Jason, Jeff Kober, Leslie Bevins; **D:** Graham Baker; **W:** Rockne S. O'Bannon; **M:** Curt Sobel. *FOX*

Alien Nation: Dark Horizon 🎬🎬½

1994 (PG) The alien Newcomers have successfully adapted to life on Earth but face continuing dangers when a human-supremacy group develops a virus to wipe them out and an alien infiltrator is plotting to return them to slavery on Tencton. Naturally, it's up to detectives Sykes and Francisco to save the day. Based on the TV series. **90m/C VHS, Closed Caption.** Gary Graham, Eric Pierpont, Scott Patterson, Terri Treas, Michelle Scarabelli, Lee Bryant, Sean Six, Lauren Woodland, Ron Fassler, Jeff Marcus; **D:** Kenneth Johnson; **W:** Diane Frolov, Andrew Schneider; **M:** David Kurtz. *FXV*

Alien Predators

woof! **1980 (R)** Three friends encounter a malevolent alien in this dull reworking of the plot of "The Andromeda Strain" with laughable special effects tossed in for those outwitted by the script. **92m/C VHS, Beta.** Dennis Christopher, Martin Hewitt, Lynn-Holly Johnson, Luis Prendes; **D:** Deran Sarafian. *VTR*

Alien Prey 🎬½ 1983 (R)

Two lesbians are making love when they are unexpectedly devoured by a hungry and indiscreet alien. No safe sex there. Graphic sex, violence, and cannibalism abound. Interesting twist to the old eat 'em and leave 'em genre. **85m/C VHS, Beta.** Barry Stokes, Sally Faulkner; **D:** Norman J. Warren. *NO*

Alien Private Eye 🎬🎬

Alien P.I **1987** An extraterrestrial detective searches Los Angeles for a missing magic disk while investigating an intergalactic crime ring. **90m/C VHS.** Nikki Fastinetti; **D:** Nik Rubenfeld. *NO*

Alien: Resurrection 🎬🎬🎬 1997 (R)

Despite her fiery end in the last film, Ripley is brought back, through cloning, by a team of scientist anxious to get their hands on the alien embryo that invaded her. A more buffed and equally strange Ripley (Weaver) results as some of her DNA gets mixed with her alien friend. Injecting new life into the franchise, director Jeunet creates a freaky and macabre journey as the aliens get loose on board the mysterious space craft Auriga and create messy havoc for new alien appetizers including Call (Ryder), who has a personal agenda of her own with Ripley. Ryder may be somewhat out of place, but the humor and energy from the supporting cast, along with the film's dank look raises this one from the bowels of formulaic action/horror. Includes some decent scares with a tense underwater sequence. *CW:* Strong sci-fi violence and gore, some grotesque images and language. **108m/C VHS, LV, Letterbox, Closed Caption.** Sigourney Weaver, Winona Ryder, Ron Perlman, Dominique Pinon, Michael Wincott, Kim Flowers, Leland Orser, Brad Dourif, Dan Hedaya, J.E. Freeman, Raymond Cruz; **D:** Jean-Pierre Jeunet; **W:** Joss Whedon; **C:** Darius Khondji; **M:** John Frizzell. *FXV*

Alien Seed 🎬 1989

Aliens kidnap a woman and impregnate her. Estrada is the government scientist hot on her trail. (How far could a woman carrying alien offspring wander?) **88m/C VHS.** Erik Estrada, Heidi Paine, Steven Blade; **D:** Bob James.

Alien Space Avenger 🎬½

Space Avenger **1991** A spaceship piloted by four alien convicts crash lands in New York City. Stalked by an intergalactic bounty hunter whose job is to kill them, the aliens attack and hide inside human bodies to avoid discovery. It's a race against time as the preservation of the human race depends on the avenger's ability to seek and destroy the alien invaders. Bland ripoff of "Aliens" is reminiscent of old-time "B" sci-fi flicks, with more gore and violence. Shot with the old 3-strip Technicolor method. **88m/C VHS.** Robert Prichard, Mike McClerie, Charity Staley, Gina Mastrogiacomo, Kick Fairbanks Fogg, Angela Nicholas, Marty Roberts, James Gillis; **D:** Richard W. Haines; **W:** Richard W. Haines, Linwood Sawyer; **M:** Richard Fiocca.

Alien Terminator ✱ 1995 (R) Scientists experimenting with DNA find themselves creating an organism capable of instant regeneration that also likes to nosh on living flesh. To make matters worse, the scientists are trapped in their lab complex, which happens to be located five miles below Los Alamos. 95m/C VHS. Maria Ford, Kevin Alber, Rodger Halstead, Cassandra Leigh, Emile Levisetti; **D:** Dave Payne. NHO

Alien Warrior woof! 1985 (R) An extraterrestrial fights a street pimp to save a crime-ridden Earth neighborhood. Low-brain rip-off of Superman. 92m/C VHS, Beta. Brett Clark, Pamela Saunders; **D:** Edward Hunt. VES, ART

Alien Women ✱ Zeta One; The Love Factor 1969 (R) A soft-core British science fiction yarn about scantily clad alien babes and the special agent who's trying to uncover their secret. It's all very sketchy, silly and campy, though pleasantly cast with plenty of lovely British actresses. 86m/C VHS, Beta. **GB** James Robertson Justice, Charles Hawtrey, Robin Hawdon, Anna Gael, Brigitte Skay, Dawn Addams, Valerie Leon, Yutte Stensgaard, Wendy Lingham, Rita Webb, Caroline Hawkins; **D:** Michael Cort. SNC

Alienator ✱ 1989 (R) In the improbable future, an unstoppable android killer is sent after an intergalactic villain. An intentional "Terminator" rip-off. 93m/C VHS, Beta, LV. Jan-Michael Vincent, John Phillip Law, Ross Hagen, Dyana Ortelli, Dawn Wildsmith, P.J. Soles, Teagan Clive, Robert Clarke, Leo Gordon, Robert Quarry, Fox Harris, Hoke Howell, Jay Richardson; **D:** Fred Olen Ray.

Aliens ✱✱✱½ 1986 (R) The bitch is back, some 50 years later. Popular sequel to "Alien" amounts to non-stop, ravaging combat in space. Contact with a colony on another planet has mysteriously stopped. Fresh from deep space sleep, Ripley and a slew of pulsar-equipped Marines return to confront the mother alien at her nest, which is also inhabited by a whole bunch of the nasty critters spewing for a fight. Something's gotta give, and the Oscar-winning special effects are especially inventive (and messy) in the alien demise department. Dimension (acting biz talk) is given to our heroine Ripley, as she discovers maternal instincts lurking within her space suit while looking after a young girl, the lone survivor of the colony. Tension-filled gore blaster. Followed by "Aliens 3." **CW:** Language and monster violence. 138m/C VHS, Beta, LV, Letterbox, Closed Caption. Sigourney Weaver, Michael Biehn, Lance Henriksen, Bill Paxton, Paul Reiser, Carrie Henn, Jenette Goldstein; **D:** James Cameron; **W:** James Cameron, Walter Hill; **M:** James Horner. Academy Awards '86: Best Sound Effects Editing, Best Visual Effects; Nominations: Academy Awards '86: Best Actress (Weaver), Best Art Direction/Set Decoration, Best Film Editing, Best Sound, Best Original Score. FOX

Aliens Are Coming ✱½ 1980 A spaceship crash lands on Earth, and its devious denizens begin invading human bodies. TV movie that's a dull echo of "Invasion of the Body Snatchers." 100m/C VHS, Beta. Tom Mason, Melinda Fee, Max Gail, Eric (Hans Gudegast) Braeden, Matthew Laborteaux; **D:** Harvey Hart; **M:** William Goldstein. WOV, GKK

Aliens from Spaceship Earth ✱½ 1977 Are strange, celestial forces invading our universe? If they are, is man prepared to defend his planet against threatening aliens of unknown strength? Lame docudrama featuring the Hurdy Gurdy man himself, Donovan. 107m/C VHS, Beta. Donovan, Lynda Day George; **D:** Don Como. GEM

Alison's Birthday ✱✱ 1979 A teenage girl learns that some of her family and friends are Satan worshipers at a terrifying birthday party. Meanwhile, the ghost of her dad hovers about, asking for more lines. 99m/C VHS, Beta. **AU** Joanne Samuel, Lou Brown, Bunny Brooke; **D:** Ian Coughlan. NO

Alive ✱✱½ 1993 (R) Recounts the true-life survival story of a group of Uruguayan rugby players in 1972. After their plane crashes in the remote, snowy Andes (in a spectacular sequence) they're forced to turn to cannibalism during a 10-week struggle to stay alive. Marshall doesn't focus on the gruesome idea, choosing instead to focus on all aspects of their desperate quest for survival. The special effects are stunning, but other parts of the film are never fully realized, including the final scene. Based on the nonfiction book by Piers Paul Read. **CW:** Psychological intensity. 127m/C VHS, Beta, LV, Letterbox, Closed Caption. Ethan Hawke, Vincent Spano, Josh Hamilton, Bruce Ramsay, John Haymes Newton, David Kriegel, Kevin Breznahan, Sam Behrens, Illeana Douglas, Jack Noseworthy, Christian Meoli, Jake Carpenter; **Cameos:** John Malkovich; **D:** Frank Marshall; **W:** John Patrick Shanley; **C:** Peter James; **M:** James Newton Howard. TOU

Alive and Kicking ✱✱½ Indian Summer 1996 (R) Tonio (Flemyng) is a handsome, vain ballet dancer with AIDS, who hides his emotions beneath a witty facade and his work. At a club he meets the older, equally driven Jack (Sher), an AIDS counselor, who pursues him. Though they become lovers, Tonio's obsession with his latest (and last) dance role causes a rift between them. Subplot between Tonio and lesbian dancer Millie (Parish) is self-conscious and Tonio's theatrics can become annoying but both Flemyng and Sher do their best in somewhat one-note roles. **CW:** Some strong sexuality, and for nudity and language. 100m/C VHS. **GB** Jason Flemyng, Anthony Sher, Dorothy Tutin, Anthony Higgins, Diane Parish; **D:** Nancy Meckler; **W:** Martin Sherman; **C:** Chris Seager; **M:** Peter Salem. NYR

Alive: 20 Years Later 1993 With the release of the big-screen fictional version comes this follow-up documentary with the survivors of the 1972 mountain plane crash telling their own story. 51m/C VHS, Beta, LV, Closed Caption. **D:** Jill Fullerton-Smith. TOU

All About Eve ✱✱✱✱ 1950 One of the wittiest (and most cynical) flicks of all time follows aspiring young actress Baxter as she ingratiates herself with a prominent group of theatre people so she can become a Broadway star without the usual years of work. The not-so-innocent babe becomes secretary to aging star Davis and ruthlessly uses everyone in her climb to the top, much to Davis' initial disbelief and eventual displeasure. Satirical, darkly funny view of the theatre world features exceptional work by Davis, Sanders, and Ritter. Based on "The Wisdom of Eve" by Mary Orr. Later staged as the musical "Applause." 138m/B VHS, Beta, LV. Bette Davis, Anne Baxter, George Sanders, Celeste Holm, Gary Merrill, Thelma Ritter, Marilyn Monroe, Hugh Marlowe, Gregory Ratoff, Eddie Fisher; **D:** Joseph L. Mankiewicz; **W:** Joseph L. Mankiewicz; **C:** Milton Krasner. Academy Awards '50: Best Costume Design (B & W), Best Director (Mankiewicz), Best Picture, Best Screenplay, Best Sound, Best Supporting Actor (Sanders); British Academy Awards '50: Best Film; Cannes Film Festival '51: Best Actress (Davis), Grand Jury Prize; Directors Guild of America Awards '50: Best Director (Mankiewicz); Golden Globe Awards '51: Best Screenplay, National Film Registry '90;; New York Film Critics Awards '50: Best Actress (Davis), Best Director (Mankiewicz), Best Film; Nominations: Academy Awards '50: Best Actress (Baxter), Best Actress (Davis), Best Art Direction/Set Decoration (B & W), Best Black and White Cinematography, Best Supporting Actress (Holm, Ritter), Best Original Dramatic/Comedy Score. FOX, BTV, HMV

All-American Murder ✱✱ 1991 (R) A rebellious young man is enrolled in a typical, all-American college for one last shot at mainstream life. Things start out okay, as he meets an attractive young coed. Hours later, he finds himself accused of her grisly murder. The youth is then given 24 hours to prove his innocence by a canny homicide detective. Average performances highlight this film, which isn't able to rise above the mediocre. **CW:** Language, violence, and sexual scenes. 94m/C VHS, Beta, LV, Closed Caption. Christopher Walken, Charlie Schlatter, Josie Bissett, Joanna Cassidy, Richard Kind, Woody Watson, J.C. Quinn, Amy Davis; **D:** Anson Williams; **W:** Barry Sandler.

All Creatures Great and Small ✱✱✱ 1974 Taken from James Herriot's best selling novels, this is a delightful, quiet drama of a veterinarian's apprentice in rural England. Fine performance by Hopkins. Followed by "All Things Bright and Beautiful" and a popular British television series. 92m/C VHS, Beta, Closed Caption. **GB** Simon Ward, Anthony Hopkins, Lisa Harrow, Brian Stirner, Freddie Jones, T.P. McKenna; **D:** Claude Whatham. RDG, FOX, HMV

All Dogs Go to Heaven ✱✱ 1989 (G) Somewhat heavy-handed animated musical (Reynolds sings) about a gangster dog who is killed by his partner in business. On the way to Heaven, he discovers how to get back to Earth to seek his revenge. When he returns to Earth, he is taken in by a little girl and learns about something he missed in life the first time around: Love. Expertly animated, but the plot may not keep the grown-ups engrossed, and the kids may notice its lack of charm. 85m/C VHS, Beta, LV, 8mm, Closed Caption. **D:** Don Bluth; **W:** Don Bluth, David A. Weiss; **M:** Ralph Burns; **V:** Burt Reynolds, Judith Barsi, Dom DeLuise, Vic Tayback, Charles Nelson Reilly, Melba Moore, Candy Devine, Loni Anderson. MGM, RDG

All Dogs Go to Heaven 2 ✱✱½ 1995 (G) Animated musical finds lovable scamp Charlie (Sheen) the dog discovering that the afterlife is not all it's cracked up to be and pining for dysfunction aplenty back on earth. He gets his chance when Gabriel's Horn is stolen and Charlie is assigned to retrieve it. Charlie teams up again with old buddy Itchy (Deluise) as the two come down from Dog Heaven to stop the villainous Carface (Borgnine) and demonic cat Red (Hearn). Along the way, Charlie falls in love with sexy Irish Setter Sasha (Easton), and finds a chance for redemption by helping a little boy in trouble. Animation not outstanding, but should keep the attention of small children. 82m/C VHS, LV, Closed Caption. **D:** Paul Sabella, Larry Leker; **W:** Arne Olsen, Kelly Ward, Mark Young; **M:** Mark Watters, Barry Mann, Cynthia Weil; **V:** Charlie Sheen, Sheena Easton, Ernest Borgnine, Dom DeLuise, George Hearn, Bebe Neuwirth, Hamilton Camp, Wallace Shawn, Bobby DiCicco, Adam Wylie. MGM

All Fall Down ✱✱½ 1962 A young man (de Wilde) idolizes his callous older brother (Beatty) until a tragedy forces him to grow up. Saint plays the older woman taken in by the brothers' family, who is seduced and abandoned. When she finds herself pregnant and alone, she commits suicide causing the younger brother, who loved her from afar, to vow to kill his older sibling. A well-acted melodrama. Also available colorized. 111m/B VHS. Eva Marie Saint, Brandon de Wilde, Warren Beatty, Karl Malden, Angela Lansbury, Constance Ford, Barbara Baxley; **D:** John Frankenheimer; **W:** William Inge; **C:** Lionel Lindon; **M:** Alex North. MGM

All God's Children ✱✱½ 1980 Made for television drama about the controversial forced busing issue and two families who must face it. Top-notch cast is occasionally mislead by meandering script attempting to stay true to a sensitive issue. 100m/C VHS, Beta. Richard Widmark, Ned Beatty, Ossie Davis, Ruby Dee, Mariclare Costello, George Spell, Trish Van Devere, Ken Swofford; **D:** Jerry Thorpe; **M:** Billy Goldenberg. NO

All I Desire ✱✱½ 1953 Estranged wife and mother (Stanwyck) returns to her hometown after fleeing years ago to pursue a stage career. She desires a new beginning with her family, but finds things have changed in her absence. The story examines the will of a strong woman and small town values. Director Sirk disagreed with the happy ending demanded by producers, but the drama is still noteworthy. 80m/B VHS, Closed Caption. Barbara Stanwyck, Richard Carlson, Lyle Bettger, Maureen O'Sullivan; **D:** Douglas Sirk; **W:** James Gunn, Robert Blees, Carl Guthrie, Gina Kaus; **M:** Joseph Gershenson. USH

All I Want for Christmas ♂♂ 1991

(G) Low-budget, sappy holiday tale of a young girl (Birch) who wants to reunite her divorced parents. Determined to fulfill her Christmas wish, Hallie seeks out the Santa Claus at Macy's department store to tell him the one thing she truly wants for Christmas. Birch is charming as are Bacall as her grandmother and Nielsen as Santa but the story is too squishy and bland to be believable. **92m/C VHS, LV.** Thora Birch, Leslie Nielsen, Lauren Bacall, Jamey Sheridan, Harley Jane Kozak, Ethan Randall, Kevin Nealon, Andrea Martin; **D:** Ron Lieberman; **W:** Richard Kramer, Thom Eberhardt, Neal Israel, Gail Parent; **C:** Robbie Greenberg; **M:** Bruce Broughton. **PAR**

All in a Night's Work ♂♂½ 1961

The founder of a one-man publishing empire is found dead with a smile on his face. His nephew inherits the business and finds himself caught in a series of big and small business misunderstandings. He's also falling in love with the woman he suspects was responsible for his uncle's grin. Nicely paced sex and business comedy with warm performances. **94m/C VHS, Beta.** Dean Martin, Shirley MacLaine, Cliff Robertson, Charlie Ruggles; **D:** Joseph Anthony; **W:** Sidney Sheldon; **M:** Andre Previn. **FOX**

All Mine to Give ♂♂½ The Day They Gave

the Babies Away 1956 Sad saga of a Scottish family of eight who braved frontier hardships, epidemics, and death in the Wisconsin wilderness more than a century ago. Midway through, mom and dad die, leaving the oldest child struggling to keep the family together. A strange, though often effective, combination of pioneer adventures and tearjerking moments that avoids becoming hopelessly soapy due to fine performances. Unless you're pretty weathered, you'll need some hankies. Based on the reminiscences of Dale and Katherine Eunson as detailed in a "Cosmopolitan" magazine article. **102m/C VHS, Beta.** Glynis Johns, Cameron Mitchell, Rex Thompson, Patty McCormack, Ernest Truex, Hope Emerson, Alan Hale Jr., Royal Dano, Reta Shaw, Rita Johnson, Ellen Corby, Jon Provost; **D:** Allen Reisner; **M:** Max Steiner. **NO**

All My Good Countrymen ♂♂½ All

Good Citizens 1968 A lyrical, funny film about the eccentric denizens of a small Moravian village soon after the socialization of Czechoslovakia in 1948. Completed during the Soviet invasion of 1968 and immediately banned. In Czech with English subtitles. **115m/C VHS, Beta.** **CZ** Vladimir Mensik, Radoslav Brzobohaty, Pavel Pavlovsky; **D:** Vojtech Jasny. Cannes Film Festival '69: Best Director (Jasny). **FCT**

All My Sons ♂♂♂ 1948

Joe Keller (Robinson) is a small-town manufacturer enjoying the profits he made from his WWII contracts. But his family is pulled apart by guilt and shame when son Chris (Lancaster) discovers his father sold defective parts to the military that resulted in loss of life and then covered up the crime. Excellent performances; adapted from the play by Arthur Miller. **94m/B VHS.** Edward G. Robinson, Burt Lancaster, Mady Christians, Louisa Horton, Howard Duff, Frank Conroy, Arlene Francis, Harry (Henry) Morgan; **D:** Irving Reis; **W:** Chester Erskine; **C:** Russell Metty; **M:** Leith Horton. **USH**

All My Sons ♂♂♂ 1986

A wealthy family is distraught when their eldest son is listed as missing-in-action during WWII. They must cope with guilt, as well as grief, because the father's business reaped profits from the war. Adapted for television from the acclaimed Arthur Miller play. **122m/C VHS, Beta.** James Whitmore, Aidan Quinn, Joan Allen, Michael Learned; **D:** John Power. **USH**

All Night Long ♂♂♂ 1981

(R) Offbeat middle-age crisis comedy about a burned-out and recently demoted drugstore executive in L.A. who leaves his wife, takes up with his fourth cousin by marriage, and begins a humorous rebellion, becoming an extremely freelance inventor while joining the drifters, weirdos and thieves of the night. An obscure, sometimes uneven little gem with Hackman in top form and an appealing supporting performance by Streisand. Highlighted by

delightful malapropisms and sataric inversion of the usual cliches. **100m/C VHS, Beta.** Gene Hackman, Barbra Streisand, Diane Ladd, Dennis Quaid, Kevin Dobson, William Daniels; **D:** Jean-Claude Tramont; **W:** W.D. Richter; **M:** Ira Newborn. **GKK**

All Night Long/Smile Please 1924

Two classic comedies by the most overlooked of the great silent clowns, both produced by slapstick progenitor Mack Sennett. **66m/B VHS, Beta.** Harry Langdon, Natalie Kingston, Jack Cooper, Alberta Vaughn. **VYY**

All of Me ♂♂½ 1984

(PG) A wealthy woman (Tomlin) dies and her guru accidentally transfers her soul to the right side of her lawyer's body, a modern version of existential hell. Lawyer Martin indulges in some funny slapstick as he discovers that his late client is waging an internal war for control of his body. Flat and cliched at times, but redeemed by the inspired clowning of Martin and witty Martin/Tomlin repartee. Based on the novel "Me Too" by Ed Davis. **93m/C VHS, Beta, LV.** Steve Martin, Lily Tomlin, Victoria Tennant, Madolyn Smith, Richard Libertini, Dana Elcar, Selma Diamond; **D:** Carl Reiner; **W:** Phil Alden Robinson. New York Film Critics Awards '84: Best Actor (Martin); National Society of Film Critics Awards '84: Best Actor (Martin). **FCT**

All Over Me ♂♂♂ 1996

(R) Teen angst/coming of age set in New York's Hell's Kitchen. Ungainly wannabe-guitarist, 15-year-old Claudia-AKA-Claude (Folland), is best friends with flirty blonde Ellen (Subkoff). But their relationship changes when Ellen begins dating the macho older Mark (Hauser) and is soon into sex and drugs, while Claude's sexual quandries lead her to a lesbian bar and an interest in singer Lucy (Hailey). Good performances but a moody and somewhat awkward first feature from Sichel, whose sister wrote the screenplay. **CW:** Sexuality and drug use involving teen girls, and for strong language. **90m/C VHS.** Alison Folland, Tara Subkoff, Cole Hauser, Wilson Cruz, Leisha Hailey, Pat Briggs, Ann Dowd; **D:** Alex Sichel; **W:** Sylvia Sichel; **C:** Joe DeSalvo; **M:** Miki Navazio. Nominations: Independent Spirit Awards '98: Best Actress (Folland). **NLC**

All Over Town ♂♂½ 1937

Two vaudevillians with a trained seal find themselves involved in a murder when they are kidnapped by a gang of thugs. A lesser Olsen and Johnson comedy with scattered funny moments. **52m/B VHS, Beta.** Ole Olsen, Chic Johnson, Mary Howard, Franklin Pangborn, James Finlayson; **D:** James W. Horne; **W:** Jack Townley, Jerome Chodorov. **NOS, MRV, VYY**

All Quiet on the Western

Front ♂♂♂♂ 1930

Extraordinary and realistic anti-war epic based on the novel by Erich Maria Remarque. Seven patriotic German youths go together from school to the battlefields of WWI. They experience the horrors of war first-hand, stuck in the trenches and facing gradual extermination. Centers on experiences of one of the young men, Paul Baumer, who changes from enthusiastic war endorser to battle-weary veteran in an emotionally exact performance by Ayres. Boasts a gigantic budget (for the time) of $1.25 million, and features more than 2,000 extras swarming about battlefields set up on ranchland in California. Relentless anti-war message is emotionally draining and startling with both graphic shots and haunting visual poetry. Extremely controversial in the U.S. and Germany upon release, the original version was 140 minutes long (some versions are available with restored footage) and featured ZaSu Pitts as Ayres mother (later reshot with Mercer replacing her). Remarque, who had fought and been wounded on the Western Front, was eventually forced to leave Germany for the U.S. due to the film's ongoing controversy. **103m/B VHS, Beta, LV.** Lew Ayres, Louis Wolheim, John Wray, Slim Summerville, Russell Gleason, Raymond Griffith, Ben Alexander, Beryl Mercer; **D:** Lewis Milestone. Academy Awards '30: Best Director (Milestone), Best Picture, National Film Registry '90;; Nominations:

Academy Awards '30: Best Cinematography, Best Writing.**USH, FCT, GLV**

All Quiet on the Western

Front ♂♂½ 1979

A big-budget television remake of the 1930 masterpiece starring John Boy. Sensitive German youth Thomas plunges excitedly into WWI and discovers its terror and degradation. Nowhere near the original's quality. **150m/C VHS, Beta, LV.** Richard Thomas, Ernest Borgnine, Donald Pleasence, Patricia Neal; **D:** Delbert Mann. **FOX, FCT**

All Screwed Up ♂♂♂ All in Place; Nothing

in Order 1974 A group of young immigrants come to Milan and try to adjust to city life; they soon find that everything is in its place, but nothing is in order. Wertmuller in a lighter vein than usual. **104m/C VHS, Beta.** **IT** Luigi Diberti, Lina Polito; **D:** Lina Wertmuller; **W:** Lina Wertmuller. **FOX**

All That Heaven Allows ♂♂♂ 1955

Attractive, wealthy middleaged widow Cary Scott (Wyman) falls for her 15-years-younger gardener, Ron Kirby (Hudson), and becomes the target of small-minded gossips and her disapproving family. Ron's no gigolo or fortune-hunter but societal pressure still gets to Cary and she breaks things off. But loneliness makes her realize what she's missing and she decides to make things up with Ron and forget her critics. Hopeful Sirk romance that still takes some jabs at conformity. **89m/B VHS.** Jane Wyman, Rock Hudson, Conrad Nagel, Agnes Moorehead, Virginia Grey, Gloria Talbott, William Reynolds; **D:** Douglas Sirk; **W:** Peggy Fenwick; **C:** Russell Metty; **M:** Frank Skinner, Joseph Gershenson. National Film Registry '95. **USH**

All That Jazz ♂♂♂½ 1979

(R) Fosse's autobiographical portrait with Scheider fully occupying his best role as the obsessed, pill-popping, chain-smoking choreographer/director dancing simultaneously with love and death. But even while dying, he creates some great dancing. Vivid and imaginative with exact editing, and an eerie footnote to Fosse's similar death almost ten years later. Egocentric and self-indulgent for sure, but that's entertainment. ♫ On Broadway; Everything Old is New Again; After You've Gone; There'll be Some Changes Made; Some of These Days; Bye Bye Love. **120m/C VHS, Beta, LV, Letterbox, Closed Caption.** Roy Scheider, Jessica Lange, Ann Reinking, Leland Palmer, Cliff Gorman, Ben Vereen, Erzebet Foldi, John Lithgow, Wallace Shawn, Sandahl Bergman, Nicole Fosse, Keith Gordon, Ben Masters, Theresa Merritt; **D:** Bob Fosse; **C:** Giuseppe Rotunno; **M:** Ralph Burns. Academy Awards '79: Best Art Direction/Set Decoration, Best Costume Design, Best Film Editing, Original Song Score and/or Adaptation; Cannes Film Festival '80: Best Film; Nominations: Academy Awards '79: Best Actor (Scheider), Best Cinematography, Best Director (Fosse), Best Original Screenplay, Best Picture. **FOX, OM**

All the Brothers Were

Valiant ♂♂½ 1953

Brothers Taylor and Granger are New England whaling captains but Granger decides to treasure hunt instead. He finds a priceless cache of black pearls on an island but angers the locals who regard the gems as sacred. When Taylor rescues him, Granger promptly turns his brother's crew into mutineers in order to return to the island and retrieve his prize. Lots of brawling and there's an incidental love story with Blyth desired by both men (she's married Taylor and just happens to be aboard). Last role for Stone. Based on the novel by Ben Ames Williams. **101m/C VHS.** Robert Taylor, Stewart Granger, Ann Blyth, Betta St. John, Keenan Wynn, James Whitmore, Kurt Kasznar, Lewis Stone, Robert Burton, Peter Whitney, John Lupton, Billie Dove; **D:** Richard Thorpe; **W:** Harry Brown; **M:** Miklos Rozsa. Nominations: Academy Awards '53: Best Color Cinematography. **MGM**

All the Kind Strangers ♂♂ Evil in the

Swamp 1974 Traveling photographer Keach picks up a young hitchhiker and takes him to the boy's home. He discovers six other children there who want him as a father, his alternative being death. He and "Mother" Eggar plot their escape from the dangerous orphans. Made-for-television thriller short on suspense. **72m/C VHS, Beta, Closed Caption.** Stacy Keach, Hobby Benson, John Savage, Samantha Eggar; **D:** Burt Kennedy. FOX

All the King's Men 🏆🏆🏆🏆 1949 Grim and graphic classic set in the Depression follows the rise of a Louisiana farm-boy from angry and honest political hopeful to powerful but corrupt governor. Loosely based on the life (and death) of Huey Long and told by a newsman who's followed his career (Ireland). Willy Stark (Crawford, in his break-through role) is the politician who, while appearing to improve the state, rules dictatorially, betraying friends and constituents and proving once again that power corrupts. In her first major role, McCambridge delivers a powerful performance as the cunning political aide. Potent morality play based on the Robert Penn Warren book. **109m/B VHS, Beta, LV.** Broderick Crawford, Mercedes McCambridge, John Ireland, Joanne Dru, John Derek, Anne Seymour, Shepperd Strudwick; **D:** Robert Rossen; **W:** Robert Rossen; **C:** Burnett Guffey. Academy Awards '49: Best Actor (Crawford), Best Picture, Best Supporting Actress (McCambridge); Golden Globe Awards '50: Best Actor—Drama (Crawford), Best Director (Rossen), Best Film—Drama, Best Supporting Actress (McCambridge); New York Film Critics Awards '49: Best Actor (Crawford), Best Film; Nominations: Academy Awards '49: Best Director (Rossen), Best Film Editing, Best Screenplay, Best Supporting Actor (Ireland). COL, BTV

All the Lovin' Kinfolk 🏆 Kin Folk; Kinfolk; The Closest of Kin 1989 (R) Two recent Hillbilly High graduates decide to take on the big city, but find themselves in dire situations. For those with time to kill. **80m/C VHS.** Mady Maguire, Jay Scott, Anne Ryan, John Denis, Donna Young; **D:** John Hayes. NO

...All the Marbles 🏆🏆 The California Dolls 1981 (R) A manager of two beautiful lady wrestlers has dreams of going to the top. Aldrich's last film, and an atypical one, with awkward pacing and a thin veil of sex exploitation. Falk provides needed grace and humor as the seedy manager, with Young contributing his usual competent bit as a hustling promoter dabbling in criminal activity. One of the few tag-team women wrestling pictures, it builds to a rousing finale match in the "Rocky" tradition, although the shift in tone and mounting cliches effectively body slam the intent. **113m/C VHS, Beta, LV.** Peter Falk, Burt Young, Richard Jaeckel, Vicki Frederick; **D:** Robert Aldrich; **C:** Joseph Biroc. MGM, OM

All the President's Men 🏆🏆🏆½ 1976 (PG) True story of the Watergate break-in that led to the political scandal of the decade, based on the best-selling book by Washington Post reporters Bob Woodward and Carl Bernstein. Intriguing, terse thriller is a nail-biter even though the ending is no secret. Expertly paced by Pakula with standout performances by Hoffman and Redford as the reporters who slowly uncover and connect the seemingly isolated facts that ultimately lead to criminal indictments of the Nixon Administration. Deep Throat Holbrook and Robards as executive editor Ben Bradlee lend authenticity to the endeavor, a realistic portrayal of the stop and go of journalistic investigations. **135m/C VHS, Beta, LV, Letterbox.** Robert Redford, Dustin Hoffman, Jason Robards Jr., Martin Balsam, Jane Alexander, Hal Holbrook, F. Murray Abraham, Stephen Collins, Lindsay Crouse; **D:** Alan J. Pakula; **W:** William Goldman; **C:** Gordon Willis; **M:** David Shire. Academy Awards '76: Best Adapted Screenplay, Best Art Direction/Set Decoration, Best Sound, Best Supporting Actor (Robards); National Board of Review Awards '76: Best Director (Pakula), Best Supporting Actor (Robards); New York Film Critics Awards '76: Best Director (Pakula), Best Film, Best Supporting Actor (Robards); National Society of Film Critics Awards '76: Best Film, Best Supporting Actor (Robards); Writers Guild of America '76: Best Adapted Screenplay; Nominations: Academy Awards '76: Best Director (Pakula), Best Film Editing, Best Picture, Best Supporting Actress (Alexander). WAR, BTV

All the Right Moves 🏆🏆½ 1983 (R) Cruise is high school football hero hoping for a scholarship so he can vacate pronto the dying Pennsylvania mill town where he grew up. At least he thinks that's what he wants to do. Further mixing up his own mixed feelings are his pushy, ambitious coach (Nelson, doing what he does best), his understanding dad (Cioffi) and supportive girlfriend (Thompson, in a notable early role). Strong performances push the relatively cliched melodrama into field goal range. Cinematographer Chapman's directorial debut. **90m/C VHS, Beta, LV, Closed Caption.** Tom Cruise, Lea Thompson, Craig T. Nelson, Christopher Penn, Charles Cioffi; **D:** Michael Chapman; **W:** Michael Kane; **C:** Jan De Bont. FOX

All the Rivers Run 1984 First made-for-cable miniseries. A young Australian girl spends her inheritance on a river boat and becomes the first female river captain in Australian history. Directed by George Miller of "Man from Snowy River" fame. Four parts. **400m/C VHS.** AU Sigrid Thornton, John Waters, Diane Craig, Charles Tingwell, Gus Mercurio; **D:** George Miller, Pino Amenta; **C:** David Connell. HBO

All the Vermeers in New York 🏆🏆🏆½ 1991 A stressed-out Wall Street broker flees to the soothing recesses of the Metropolitan Museum's Vermeer Room. There he meets a beautiful, manipulative French actress dreaming of success in Manhattan. Amidst the opulent art world of New York, the two pursue their relationship to an ultimately tragic end. Jost offers an inside look at the collision of commerce and art and the corrupt underside of New York in this elegant contemporary film. **87m/C VHS, LV, Letterbox.** Emmanuelle Chaulet, Stephen Lack, Grace Phillips, Katherine Bean, Laurel Lee Kiefer, Gracie Mansion, Gordon Joseph Weiss, Roger Ruffin; **D:** Jon Jost; **W:** Jon Jost. WAC

All the Way, Boys 🏆½ 1973 (PG) Two inept adventurers crash-land a plane in the Andes in the hope of discovering slapstick, but find none. "Trinity" cast up to no good. **105m/C VHS, Beta.** IT Terence Hill, Bud Spencer, Cyril Cusack, Michel Antoine; **D:** Giuseppe Colizzi.

All the Young Men 🏆🏆🏆 1960 Fairly powerful men-uniting-in-battle story with an interesting cast, highlighted by Poitier in an early role. A tiny marine squadron overrun by the Chinese in the Korean War attempts to resist the numerous attackers. In their spare time, the men confront racial prejudice when a black man (guess who) takes command. **86m/B VHS, Beta.** Alan Ladd, Sidney Poitier, James Darren, Glenn Corbett, Mort Sahl; **D:** Hall Bartlett; **W:** Hall Bartlett; **C:** Daniel F. Fapp. COL

All Things Fair 🏆🏆½ Lust och Fägring Stor; Love Lessons; Laererinden 1995 Coming of age story set in neutral Sweden in 1943. Fifteen-year-old Stig (Widerberg, the director's son) has just arrived in Malmo to begin classes at his all-male school—a situation filled with sexual curiosity and repression. Stig is attracted to his beautiful teacher Viola (Lagercrantz), whose marriage to alcoholic traveling salesman Frank (von Bromssen) is less than ideal, and the duo begin an affair. Frank not only seems not to care but befriends his wife's youthful lover, although the situation is ripe for tragedy. Excellent performances, sensual air, though somewhat lacking in logical narrative. Swedish with subtitles. **128m/C VHS.** DK SW Johan Widerberg, Marika Lagercrantz, Tomas von Bromssen, Bjorn Kjellman, Charles A. Palmer; **D:** Bo Widerberg; **W:** Bo Widerberg; **C:** Morten Bruus. Nominations: Academy Awards '95: Best Foreign Language Film. NYR

All This and Heaven Too 🏆🏆🏆 1940 When a governess arrives at a Parisian aristocrat's home in the 1840s, she causes jealous tension between the husband and his wife. The wife is soon found murdered. Based on Rachel Field's best-seller. **141m/B VHS, Beta.** Charles Boyer, Bette Davis, Barbara O'Neil, Virginia Weidler, Jeffrey Lynn, Helen Westley, Henry Daniell, Harry Davenport; **D:** Anatole Litvak; **M:** Max Steiner. Nominations: Academy Awards '40: Best

Black and White Cinematography, Best Picture, Best Supporting Actress (O'Neil). MGM

All Through the Night 🏆🏆🏆 1942 A very funny spy spoof as well as a thrilling crime story with Bogart playing a gambler who takes on a Nazi spy ring. Features memorable double-talk and a great auction scene that inspired the one with Cary Grant in "North by Northwest." Suspense builds throughout the film as Lorre appears in a sinister role as Pepi and Veidt gives a fine performance as the spymaster. **107m/B VHS, Closed Caption.** Humphrey Bogart, Conrad Veidt, Karen Verne, Jane Darwell, Frank McHugh, Peter Lorre, Judith Anderson, William Demarest, Jackie Gleason, Phil Silvers, Barton MacLane, Martin Kosleck; **D:** Vincent Sherman. MGM

All Tied Up 🏆🏆½ 1992 (R) Ladies man Brian (Galligan) thinks he's found true love with Linda (Hatcher) but that doesn't mean he's stopped seeing other women. And when Linda finds out, she breaks it off. So Brian goes over to her house to work things out and gets tied up—literally—by Linda and her girlfriends. Talk about teaching a guy a lesson. **90m/C VHS.** Zach Galligan, Teri Hatcher, Tracy Griffith, Lara Harris; **D:** John Mark Robinson; **W:** Robert Madero, I. Markie Lane; **M:** Bernardo Bonazzi. COL

All You Need Is Cash 🏆🏆🏆 The Rutles 1978 "The Rutles" star in this parody of The Beatles' legend, from the early days of the "Pre-Fab Four" in Liverpool to their worldwide success. A marvelous pseudo-documentary, originally shown on NBC-TV and with various SNL alumni, which captures the development of the Beatles and '60s rock with devastating effect. Served as the inspiration for "This Is Spinal Tap." **70m/C VHS, Beta, LV.** Eric Idle, Neil Innes, Ricky Fataar, Dan Aykroyd, Gilda Radner, John Belushi, George Harrison, Paul Simon, Mick Jagger, John Halsey; **D:** Eric Idle, Gary Weis. MVD, MLT

Allan Quatermain and the Lost City of Gold 🏆½ 1986 (PG) While trying to find his brother, Quatermain discovers a lost African civilization, in this weak adaptation of an H. Rider Haggard adventure. An ostensible sequel to the equally shallow "King Solomon's Mines." **100m/C VHS, Beta, Closed Caption.** Richard Chamberlain, Sharon Stone, James Earl Jones; **D:** Gary Nelson; **W:** Gene Quintano, Lee Reynolds; **C:** Frederick Elmes. FHE, VTR

Allegheny Uprising 🏆🏆½ The First Rebel 1939 Set in 1759, the story of a frontiersman who clashes with a British military commander in order to stop the sale of firearms to Indians. The stars of "Stagecoach" are back on board in this lesser effort. Also available colorized. **81m/B VHS, Beta, LV, Closed Caption.** John Wayne, Claire Trevor, George Sanders, Brian Donlevy, Chill Wills, Moroni Olsen; **D:** William A. Seiter. CCB, TTC

Allegro Non Troppo 🏆🏆🏆 1976 (PG) An energetic and bold collection of animated skits set to classical music in this Italian version of Disney's "Fantasia." Watch for the evolution of life set to Ravel's Bolero, or better yet, watch the whole darn movie. Features Nichetti (often referred to as the Italian Woody Allen, particularly by people in Italy) in the non-animated segments, who went on to write, direct, and star (he may have sold concessions in the lobby as well) in "The Icicle Thief." **75m/C VHS, LV.** IT Maurizio Nichetti; **D:** Bruno Bozzetto. BMG, IME, BTV

Alley Cat 🏆 1984 (R) Woman uses martial arts to fight back against a street gang that attacked her. **82m/C VHS, Beta.** Karin Mani, Robert Torti, Brit Helfer, Michael Wayne, Jon Greene; **D:** Edward Victor. VES, ART

The Alley Cats 🏆🏆 1965 Leslie, a part of Berlin's swinging '60s set, is being ignored by fiance Logan in favor of his affair with her friend Agnes. So Leslie decides to retaliate by having an affair with a painter, Christian, but since Leslie just can't stand to be alone, when Christian is called away on business, she succumbs to the charms of socialite Irena. **83m/B VHS.** Anna Arthur, Sabrina Koch, Karen Field, Chaz Hickman, Harold Baerow, Uta Levka; **D:** Radley Metzger; **W:** Radley Metzger. *FRF*

Alligator 🎬🎬🎬 **1980 (R)** Dumped down a toilet 12 long years ago, lonely alligator Ramon resides in the city sewers, quietly eating and sleeping. In addition to feasting on the occasional stray human, Ramon devours the animal remains of a chemical plant's experiment involving growth hormones and eventually begins to swell at an enormous rate. Nothing seems to satisfy Ramon's ever-widening appetite: not all the people or all the buildings in the whole town, but he keeps trying, much to the regret of the guilt-ridden cop and lovely scientist who get to know each other while trying to nab the gator. Mediocre special effects are only a distraction in this witty eco-monster take. **94m/C VHS, Beta.** Robert Forster, Robin Riker, Jack Carter, Henry Silva, Dean Jagger, Michael V. Gazzo, Perry Lang, Bart Braverman, Angel Tompkins, Sue Lyon; **D:** Lewis Teague; **W:** John Sayles, Frank Ray Perilli. *ART*

Alligator 2: The Mutation 🎬🎬 **1990 (PG-13)** Not a sequel to 1980's surprisingly good "Alligator," but a bland rehash with a decent cast. Once again a toxic alligator grows to enormous size and menaces a community. A Donald-Trump-like villain and pro wrestlers (!) bring this up to date, but it's all on the level of a TV disaster movie; even the PG-13 rating is a bit too harsh. **92m/C VHS, LV.** Steve Railsback, Dee Wallace Stone, Joseph Bologna, Woody Brown, Bill Daily, Brock Peters, Richard Lynch, Holly Gagnier; **D:** Jon Hess; **W:** Curt Allen; **C:** Joseph Mangine. *COL, NLC*

Alligator Alley 🎬 **1972** When two young divers witness a major drug deal, they become entangled in a web of danger they never expected. **92m/C VHS, Beta.** Steve Alaimo, John Davis Chandler, Willie Pastrano, Jeremy Slate, Cece Stone; **D:** William Grefe.

Alligator Eyes 🎬🎬½ **1990 (R)** Stranger wearing trouble like a cheap perfume enters the midst of a vacationing trio of New Yorkers. Their vulnerabilities are exposed by a young hitchhiker sporting a slinky polka dot ensemble and way cool sunglasses who insinuates herself into their vacation plans (not to mention their private lives), before the three realize she's blind and full of manipulative and vindictive tricks, thanks to the usual brutal childhood. Psycho-sexo-logical thriller has some fine performances and a promising beginning, before fizzling into celluloid cotton candy. **101m/C VHS.** Annabelle Larsen, Roger Kabler, Mary McLain, Allen McCullough, John MacKay; **D:** John Feldman; **W:** John Feldman; **M:** Sheila Silver.

The Allnighter 🎬 **1987 (PG-13)** A college coed searches through the hypersexed beach-party milieu of her senior year for Mr. Right. Bangle Hoffs is directed by her mom, to no avail. **95m/C VHS, Beta.** Susanna Hoffs, John Terlesky, Joan Cusack, Michael Ontkean; **D:** Tamar Simon Hoffs; **M:** Charles Bernstein. *USH*

Allonsanfan 🎬🎬🎬½ **1973** Early Taviani, in which a disillusioned Jacobin aristocrat in 1816, after Napoleon has fallen, struggles with his revolutionary ideals and his accustomed lifestyle. Exciting score. In Italian with English subtitles. **115m/C VHS, Beta.** *IT* Marcello Mastroianni, Laura Betti, Renato de Carmine, Lea Massari, Mimsy Farmer, Claudio Cassinelli, Bruno Cirino; **D:** Paolo Taviani, Vittorio Taviani; **W:** Paolo Taviani, Vittorio Taviani; **C:** Giuseppe Ruzzolini; **M:** Ennio Morricone. *FCT, WBF*

All's Fair 🎬 **1989** Silly and predictable comedy about executives who take on their spouses at weekend war games. An unfortunate waste of a good cast. **89m/C VHS, Beta, LV, Closed Caption.** George Segal, Sally Kellerman, Robert Carradine, Jennifer Edwards, Jane Kaczmarek, John Kapelos, Lou Ferrigno; **D:** Rocky Lane; **C:** Peter Collister.

Almanac of Fall 🎬🎬 **19??** Set in a claustrophic apartment, where the occupants reveal all their deepest hositilies, fears, and obsessions. In Hungarian with English subtitles. **119m/C VHS.** *HU* Hedi Temessy, Erika Bodnar, Miklos B. Szekely, Pal Hetenyi, Janos Dersi; **D:** Bela Tarr; **W:** Bela Tarr. *FCT*

...Almost 🎬🎬 *Wendy Cracked a Walnut* **1990 (PG)** Arquette plays a curiously giddy bookworm with a vivid imagination. When her husband disappears on their anniversary, the man of her dreams shows up to sweep her off her feet. Is he real or is he simply another daydream? Almost a good time. **87m/C VHS, LV.** *AU* Rosanna Arquette, Bruce Spence; **D:** Michael Pattinson. *NO*

Almost an Angel 🎬½ **1990 (PG)** Another in a recent spat of angels and ghosts assigned back to earth by the head office. A life-long criminal (Hogan) commits a heroic act and finds himself a probationary angel returned to earth to gain permanent angel status. He befriends a wheelchair-bound man, falls in love with the guy's sister, and helps her out at a center for potential juvenile delinquents. Melodramatic and hokey in places, relying too much on Hogan's crocodilian charisma. **98m/C VHS, LV, Closed Caption.** Paul Hogan, Linda Kozlowski, Elias Koteas, Doreen Lang, Charlton Heston; **D:** John Cornell; **W:** Paul Hogan; **C:** Russell Boyd. *PAR*

Almost Angels 🎬🎬 **1962** Two boys romp in Austria as members of the Vienna Boys Choir. Lesser sentimental Disney effort that stars the actual members of the Choir; not much of a draw for today's Nintendo-jaded young viewers. **85m/C VHS, Beta.** Vincent Winter, Peter Weck, Hans Holt; **D:** Steve Previn. *DIS*

Almost Blue 🎬½ **1993 (R)** A gigantic, slow-moving, movie cliche. Madsen is a sulky, hard-living sax player going off the deep end because of his wife's death. Walden is the good woman who comes along to save him from himself. Tenor saxman Ernie Watts doubles for Madsen. Do yourself a favor—skip the movie and listen to some good jazz instead. **98m/C VHS, LV.** Michael Madsen, Lynette Walden, Garrett Morris, Gale Mayron, Yaphet Kotto; **D:** Keoni Waxman. *ART*

Almost Dead 🎬🎬½ **1994** Psychiatrist Katherine Roshak's (Doherty) mother committed suicide four years ago and suddenly her corpse is appearing to Katherine. When she visits Mom's grave, Katherine finds an empty coffin. So she teams up with a skeptical cop (Mandylor) to figure out what's going on. Lots of loose ends. Based on the novel "Resurrection" by William Valtos. **92m/C VHS.** Shannen Doherty, Costas Mandylor, John Diehl, William R. Moses; **D:** Ruben Preuss; **W:** Miguel Tejada-Flores; **C:** Zoran Hochstatter. *MNC*

Almost Heroes 🎬½ *Edwards & Hunt: The First American Road Trip* **1997 (PG-13)** Farley's last screen appearance teams him with Perry as explorers Edwards and Hunt, who are racing Lewis and Clark to the Pacific Ocean in 1804. Edwards (Perry) is a glory-seeking fop who's totally out of his league, Hunt (Farley) is a slovenly, clumsy tracker with a soft spot for toilet (or would that be outhouse?) humor. Along with a team of misfits and losers, the duo wreaks havoc on the American frontier. Perry and Farley show some flashes of comic chemistry, but their left to fend for themselves by a script that's lost in the wilderness, sadly relying too much on Farley's patented self-destructive schtick.*CW:* Crude humor and nudity. **87m/C VHS.** Chris Farley, Matthew Perry, Eugene Levy, Bokeem Woodbine, Lisa B, Kevin Dunn, Hamilton Camp; **D:** Christopher Guest; **W:** Tom Wolfe, Mark Nutter, Boyd Hale; **C:** Adam Kimmel, Kenneth Macmillan; **M:** C.J. Vanston; **P:** Harry Shearer. *NYR*

Almost Human woof! *The Kidnap of Mary Lou* **1979 (R)** An Italian Mafia gorefest about a second-class don who kidnaps a businessman's daughter, and then has trouble trying to collect a ransom. For aficionados of Italian Mafia gorefests only (check your weapons at the door). **90m/C VHS,**

Beta. *IT* Henry Silva, Tomas Milian, Laura Belli; **D:** Umberto Lenzi; **M:** Ennio Morricone.

Almost Partners **1987** Grandpa's ashes are in trouble. His urn and remains have been stolen. Fortunately, his teenage granddaughter and a detective are on the case. From the PBS "Wonderworks" television series. **58m/C VHS, Closed Caption.** Paul Sorvino, Royana Black, Mary Wickes; **D:** Alan Kingsberg. *HMV, FCT*

An Almost Perfect Affair 🎬🎬 **1979 (PG)** Taxing romantic comedy about an ambitious independent American filmmaker who, after finishing a movie about an executed murderer, travels to the Cannes festival and proceeds to fall in love or lust with the wife of an Italian producer. Numerous inside jokes and capable performances nearly overcome script lethargy. **92m/C VHS, Beta.** Keith Carradine, Monica Vitti, Raf Vallone, Christian de Sica, Dick Anthony Williams; **D:** Michael Ritchie; **W:** Walter Bernstein; **M:** Georges Delerue. *PAR*

Almost Pregnant 🎬🎬½ **1991 (R)** Linda Anderson (Roberts) desperately wants a baby, but her husband, Charlie (Conaway) is unable to get her pregnant. Dead set against artificial insemination, Linda decides to take a lover. Charlie doesn't want to lose her, so he goes along with her idea. Linda falls in love with the new guy; discovers he's had a vasectomy and takes yet another lover while continuing to see the other two guys. Hilarious complications abound in her outrageous quest for a baby. An unrated version containing explicit scenes is also available.*CW:* Sexual dialogue and sexual content. **90m/C VHS, LV, Closed Caption.** Tanya Roberts, Jeff Conaway, Joan Severance, Dom DeLuise; **D:** Michael DeLuise; **W:** Fred Stroppel. *COL*

Almost Royal Family 🎬 **1984** All kinds of problems arise when a family inherits an island on the St. Lawrence River embargoed by the United States and Canada. **52m/C VHS, Beta.** Sarah Jessica Parker, John Femia. *WAR*

Almost You 🎬🎬 **1985 (R)** Normal marital conflicts and uncertainties grow exponentially when a wealthy New York City 30-something couple hires a lovely young nurse to help care for the wife after a car accident. An unsentimental marital comedy with a good cast that still misses. **91m/C VHS, Beta, Closed Caption.** Brooke Adams, Griffin Dunne, Karen Young, Marty Watt, Christine Estabrook, Josh Mostel, Laura Dean, Dana Delany, Miguel Pinero, Joe Silver, Suzzy Roche, Spalding Gray; **D:** Adam Brooks; **M:** Jonathan Elias. *FOX*

Aloha, Bobby and Rose 🎬🎬½ **1974 (PG)** A mechanic and his girlfriend in L.A. become accidentally involved in a potential robbery and murder and go on the run for Mexico, of course. Semi-satisfying drama in the surf, with fine location photography. **90m/C VHS, Beta.** Paul LeMat, Dianne Hull, Robert Carradine, Tim McIntire, Edward James Olmos, Leigh French; **D:** Floyd Mutrux.

Aloha Summer 🎬🎬 **1988 (PG)** Six surfing teenagers of various ethnic backgrounds learn of love and life in 1959 Hawaii while riding the big wave of impending adulthood, with a splash of Kung Fu thrown in for good measure. Sensitive and bland. **97m/C VHS, Beta, LV.** Chris Makepeace, Lorie Griffin, Don Michael Paul, Sho Kosugi, Yuji Okumoto, Tia Carrere; **D:** Tommy Lee Wallace; **W:** Robert Benedetto. *WAR, ORI*

Alone Against Rome 🎬½ **1962** A muscle-bound warrior takes on the forces of Rome to avenge himself against a scornful woman. **100m/B VHS, Beta.** *IT* Lang Jeffries, Rossana Podesta, Phillippe LeRoy; **D:** Herbert Wise. *SNC*

Alone in the Dark 🎬🎬 **1982 (R)** Slash and dash horror attempt featuring four escaped patients from a mental hospital who decide that they must kill their doctor because they don't like him. Conveniently, a city-wide blackout provides the opportunity, as the good doctor defends home and family against the aging stars intent on chewing up as much scenery as possible. **92m/C VHS,**

Beta. Jack Palance, Donald Pleasence, Martin Landau, Dwight Schultz; *D:* Jack Sholder. *NLC, COL*

Alone in the Neon Jungle 🐾🐾 1987 A glamorous big-city police captain is assigned to clean up the most corrupt precinct in town. Pleshette is untypically cast but still manages to make her role believable in a serviceable TV cop drama with more dialogue than action. 90m/C VHS. Suzanne Pleshette, Danny Aiello, Georg Stanford Brown, Frank Converse, Joe Morton; *D:* Georg Stanford Brown. *NLC*

Alone in the T-Shirt Zone 🐾 1986 A maniacal T-shirt designer lands in a mental institution. 81m/C VHS, Beta. Michael Barrack, Taylor Gilbert, Bill Barron.

Alone in the Woods 🐾🐾 1995 (PG) Ten-year-old Justin mistakenly gets into the wrong van while on his way to his family's annual mountain vacation. Turns out the duo in the van are would-be kidnappers after Chelsea Stuart, the daughter of a toy magnate and now Justin must escape and rescue Chelsea. 81m/C VHS. Brady Bluhm, Chick Vennera, Matthias Hues, Laraine Newman, Daniel McVicar, John Putch. *NHO*

Along Came Jones 🐾🐾🐾 1945 Cowboy Cooper, who can't handle a gun and is saddled with grumpy sidekick Demarest, is the victim of mistaken identity as both the good guys and the bad guys pursue him thinking he is a vicious killer. Young is the woman who rides to his defense. Offbeat and charming western parody based on a novel by Alan le May. 93m/B VHS, Beta. Gary Cooper, Loretta Young, Dan Duryea, William Demarest; *D:* Stuart Heisler; *W:* Nunnally Johnson; *C:* Milton Krasner. *MGM, FCT*

Along the Great Divide 🐾🐾 1951 A U.S. marshal and his deputy battle pursuing vigilantes and the untamed frontier to bring a falsely accused murderer to trial (and of course, find the real bad guy). Douglas' first western has the usual horse opera cliches supported by excellent cinematography. 88m/B VHS, Beta. Kirk Douglas, John Agar, Walter Brennan, Virginia Mayo; *D:* Raoul Walsh. *WAR, TLF*

Along the Sundown Trail 🐾½ 1942 Standard western escapades as cowboy G-men round up the villains. 59m/B VHS, Beta. William Boyd, Art Davis, Lee Powell, Julie Duncan, Kermit Maynard, Charles "Blackie" King; *D:* Sam Newfield. *GPV, VCN*

Alpha Beta 🐾🐾½ 1973 A stage production set to film studying the break-up of a marriage, where all the husband and wife have in common is the children. Finney and Roberts efficiently carry the load. 70m/C VHS, Beta. Albert Finney, Rachel Roberts; *D:* Anthony Page. *NO*

The Alpha Incident 🐾½ 1976 (PG) Timeworn doomsday drama about an alien organism with the potential to destroy all living things. Government works hard to cover up. 86m/C VHS, Beta. Ralph Meeker, Stafford Morgan, John Goff, Carol Irene Newell, John Alderman; *D:* Bill Rebane.

Alphabet City 🐾🐾 1984 (R) A drug kingpin who runs New York's Lower East Side has decided to turn over a new leaf, but first he must survive his last night as a criminal while figuring out a way to pay off his large debts. Very stylish and moody, but light on content and plot. 85m/C VHS, Beta. Vincent Spano, Michael Winslow, Kate Vernon, Jami Gertz, Zohra Lampert, Raymond Serra, Kenny Marino, Daniel Jordano, Miguel Pinero; *D:* Amos Poe; *W:* Amos Poe. *FOX*

The Alphabet Murders 🐾🐾 *ABC Murders* 1965 Picture this: Randall playing Agatha Christie's famous Belgian sleuth, Hercule Poirot, and Rutherford—in a cameo—as Miss Marple. As if that wouldn't be enough to make Dame Agatha roll over in her grave, there's plenty of cloying wisecracking and slapsticking throughout. An adaptation of "The ABC Murders" in which Poirot stalks a literate killer who snuffs out his victims in alphabetical order. Hardly a must-see, unless you're hellbent on viewing the entire Randall

opus. 90m/B VHS, Beta. Tony Randall, Anita Ekberg, Robert Morley, Maurice Denham, Guy Rolfe, Sheila Allen; *Cameos:* Margaret Rutherford; *D:* Frank Tashlin. *MGM, FCT*

Alphaville 🐾🐾🐾 *Alphaville, a Strange Case of Lemmy Caution; Alphaville, Une Etrange Aventure de Lemmy Caution* 1965 Engaging and inimitable Godard attempt at science fiction mystery. P.I. Lemmy Caution searches for a scientist in a city (Paris as you've never seen it before) run by robots and overseen by a dictator. The futuristic techno-conformist society must be upended so that Caution may save the scientist as well as nonconformists everywhere. In French with subtitles. 100m/B VHS, Beta. *FR* Eddie Constantine, Anna Karina, Akim Tamiroff; *D:* Jean-Luc Godard; *W:* Jean-Luc Godard. Berlin International Film Festival '65: Golden Berlin Bear. *HMV, SNC, MRV*

Alpine Fire 🐾🐾½ 1989 (R) Coming of age story about an adolescent girl and her deaf-mute brother living an isolated life in the Swiss Alps. When life on the mountain overwhelms them, they turn to each other for love. Sharply observed with a naturalistic style, elevating the proceedings above mere voyeurism. 119m/C VHS, Beta. *SI* Thomas Knock, Johanna Lier, Dorothea Moritz, Rolf Illig; *D:* Fredi M. Murer. *VES, ART*

Alsino and the Condor 🐾🐾🐾 1982 (R) An acclaimed Nicaraguan drama about a young boy, caught in war-torn Nicaragua between the Somoza government and the Sandinista rebels, who dreams of flying above the human strife. In Spanish with English subtitles. 89m/C VHS, Beta, LV. *NI* Dean Stockwell, Alan Esquivel; *D:* Miguel Littin. Nominations: Academy Awards '82: Best Foreign Language Film. *FCT, TPV*

Altered States 🐾🐾🐾 1980 (R) Obsessed with the task of discovering the inner man, Hurt's ambitious researcher ignores his family while consuming hallucinogenic drugs and floating in an immersion tank. He gets too deep inside, slipping way back through the evolutionary order and becoming a menace in the process. Confusing script based upon Chayefsky's (alias Sidney Aaron) confusing novel is supported by great special effects and the usual self-indulgent and provocative Russell direction. Chayefsky eventually washed his hands of the project after artistic differences with the producers. Others who departed from the film include initial director William Penn and special effects genius John Dykstra (relieved ably by Bran Ferren). Hurt's a solemn hoot in his first starring role. 103m/C VHS, Beta, LV. William Hurt, Blair Brown, Bob Balaban, Charles Haid, Dori Brenner, Drew Barrymore, Miguel Godreau, John Larroquette; *D:* Ken Russell; *W:* Paddy Chayefsky; *C:* Jordan Cronenweth. Nominations: Academy Awards '80: Best Sound, Best Original Score. *WAR*

Alternative 🐾🐾 1976 A female magazine editor finds herself unmarried and quite pregnant. She is caught in a tug-of-war between the baby's father and her current lover. Dated liberated woman and career snoozer. 90m/C VHS, Beta. Wendy Hughes, Peter Adams, Mary Mackie, Carla Hoogeveen, Tony Bonner. *NO*

Alvarez Kelly 🐾🐾½ 1966 Offbeat western with Holden as the Mexican-Irish Kelly who has just sold a herd of cattle to the North during the Civil War. Confederate officer Widmark kidnaps Holden in an effort to have the cattle redirected to the South. Aided by the traditional women in the midst of men intent on double-crossing each other, a fierce hatred develops between the two, erupting into violence. Sleepy performance by Holden is countered by an intensive Widmark. Based on a true Civil War incident, the script occasionally wanders far afield with the cattle, who cleverly heighten the excitement by stampeding. 109m/C VHS, Beta. William Holden, Richard Widmark, Janice Rule, Patrick O'Neal, Harry Carey Jr.; *D:* Edward Dmytryk. *COL, GKK*

Alvin Purple 🐾½ 1070 (N) Pedestrian comedy about a Mr. Purple, an ordinary Aussie who sells waterbeds and for some reason constantly being pursued by throngs of sexually insatiable women. Fortunately, he too enjoys sex, even though complications abound. Sexual situations, double entendres, and a script that aims for cleverness (but rarely attains it) somehow made the lust romp a hit in its native Australia, while worldwide it helped establish a market for Down Under cinema. Shot in Melbourne, and followed by "Alvin Rides Again." 97m/C VHS, Beta, LV. *AU* Graeme Blundell, George Whaley, Ellie MacLure, Jacki Weaver; *D:* Tim Burstall; *W:* Alan Finney, Alan Hopgood, Tim Burstall.

Alvin Rides Again 🐾🐾 1974 The sexually insatiable Alvin Purple is asked to impersonate an American gangster who was accidentally killed. Another Aussie sex farce from the original writers, who conspire to create a decent sequel to "Alvin Purple," with much of the same cast and crew. 89m/C VHS, Beta. *AU* Graeme Blundell, Alan Finney, Brionny Behets, Frank Thring Jr., Jeff Ashby, Robin Copping; *D:* David Bilcock; *W:* Tim Burstall, Alan Finney, Alan Hopgood.

Always 🐾🐾🐾 1985 (R) Jaglom fictionally documents his own divorce and reconciliation with Patrice Townsend: set in the director's home and starring his friends and family, the film provides comic insight into the dynamics of married/about-to-be-married/and used-to-be-married relationships. Set at a Fourth of July barbecue, this bittersweet romantic comedy is a veritable feast for Jaglom fans, but not everyone will find the director's free-form narrative to their taste. 105m/C VHS, Beta, LV, Closed Caption. Henry Jaglom, Patrice Townsend, Bob Rafelson, Melissa Leo, Andre Gregory, Michael Emil, Joanna Frank, Alan Rachins, Jonathan Kaufer; *D:* Henry Jaglom; *W:* Henry Jaglom; *C:* Hanania Baer. *VES, ART*

Always 🐾🐾½ 1989 (PG) A hotshot pilot (Dreyfuss) meets a fiery end and finds that his spirit is destined to become a guardian angel to the greenhorn fire-fighting flyboy (Johnson) who steals his girl's heart. Warm remake of "A Guy Named Joe," one of Spielberg's favorite movies. Sparks between Dreyfuss and Hunter eventually ignite, but Goodman delivers the most heat. Hepburn makes an appearance as the angel who guides Dreyfuss. An old-fashioned tree-burner romance that includes actual footage of the 1988 Yellowstone fire. 123m/C VHS, Beta, LV, Letterbox, Closed Caption. Holly Hunter, Richard Dreyfuss, John Goodman, Audrey Hepburn, Brad Johnson, Marg Helgenberger, Keith David, Roberts Blossom; *D:* Steven Spielberg; *W:* Jerry Belson; *C:* Mikael Salomon; *M:* John Williams. *USH, FCT*

Amadeus 🐾🐾🐾½ 1984 (PG) Entertaining adaptation by Shaffer of his play about the intense rivalry between 18th century composers Antonio Salieri and Wolfgang Amadeus Mozart. Abraham's Salieri is a man who desires greatness but is tortured by envy and sorrow. His worst attacks of angst occur when he comes into contact with Hulce's Mozart, an immature, boorish genius who, despite his gifts, remains unaffected and delighted by the beauty he creates while irking the hell out of everyone around him. Terrific period piece filmed on location in Prague; excellent musical score, beautiful sets, nifty billowy costumes, and realistic American accents for the 18th century Europeans. ♫Concert No. 27 for Pianoforte and Orchestra in B Flat Major; Ave Verum Corpus; A Quintet For Strings in E Flat; A Concerto for Clarinet and Orchestra in A Major; Number 39 in E Flat Major; Number 40 in G Minor; Number 41 in C Major. 158m/C VHS, Beta, LV. F. Murray Abraham, Tom Hulce, Elizabeth Berridge, Simon Callow, Roy Dotrice, Christine Ebersole, Jeffrey Jones, Kenny Baker, Cynthia Nixon, Vincent Schiavelli; *D:* Milos Forman; *W:* Peter Shaffer. Academy Awards '84: Best Actor (Abraham), Best Adapted Screenplay, Best Art Direction/Set Decoration, Best Costume Design, Best Director (Forman), Best Makeup, Best Picture, Best Sound; Cesar Awards '85: Best

Foreign Film; Directors Guild of America Awards '84: Best Director (Forman); Golden Globe Awards '85: Best Actor—Drama (Abraham), Best Director (Forman), Best Film—Drama, Best Screenplay; Los Angeles Film Critics Association Awards '84: Best Director (Forman), Best Film, Best Screenplay; Nominations: Academy Awards '84: Best Actor (Hulce), Best Cinematography, Best Film Editing; Los Angeles Film Critics Association Awards '84: Best Actor (Abraham), Best Director (Forman), Best Screenplay. *REP, GLV, BTV*

Amanda and the Alien 🎬½ 1995 (R)
Dumb cable TV saga finds flaky Californian Amanda (Eggert) taking care of a sex-starved, shape-changing extraterrestrial (Meneses) while a couple of feds hunt him down. Based on a story by Robert Silverberg.**CW:** Sexuality and language. **94m/C VHS, Closed Caption.** Alex Meneses, Nicole Eggert, Michael Dorn, Stacy Keach, Michael C. Bendetti; **D:** Jon Kroll; **W:** Jon Kroll. *REP*

Amarcord 🎬🎬🎬½ 1974 (R)
Semi-autobiographical Fellini fantasy which takes place in the village of Rimini, his birthplace. Focusing on the young Zanin's impressions of his town's colorful slices of life, Fellini takes aim at fascism, family life, and religion in 1930s Italy. Visually ripe, delivering a generous, occasionally uneven mix of satire, burlesque, drama, and tragicomedic lyricism. Considered by people in the know as one of Fellini's best films and the topic of meaningful discussions among art film students everywhere. **124m/C VHS, DVD.** IT Magali Noel, Bruno Zanin, Pupella Maggio, Armando Brancia; **D:** Federico Fellini; **W:** Federico Fellini, Tonino Guerra; **M:** Nino Rota. Academy Awards '74: Best Foreign Language Film; New York Film Critics Awards '74: Best Director (Fellini), Best Film; Nominations: Academy Awards '75: Best Director (Fellini), Best Original Screenplay. *HMV*

The Amateur 🎬½ 1982 (R)
Computer technologist for the CIA dives into a plot of international intrigue behind the Iron Curtain when he investigates the death of his girlfriend, murdered by terrorists. Confused and ultimately disappointing spy drama cursed with a wooden script written by Littell, based on his novel. **112m/C VHS, Beta.** John Savage, Christopher Plummer, Marthe Keller, Arthur Hill, Ed Lauter; **D:** Charles Jarrott; **W:** Robert Littell. *FOX*

Amateur 🎬🎬🎬 1994 (R)
Former nun Huppert, trying to make a living writing pornography, hooks up with an amnesiac (Donovan) who turns out to have a criminal past and a porno actress wife (Lowensohn) who wants him dead. Blackmail plot has oddball characters racing through dark and evocative settings while unfolding a tale loaded with offbeat oppositions and an irresistibly bizarre romantic triangle. Lively and playful without becoming pretentious, Hartley's self-described "action thriller... with one flat tire" evokes his typical deadpan subtle style.**CW:** Contains obscene language. **105m/C VHS, LV, Closed Caption.** Isabelle Huppert, Martin Donovan, Elina Lowensohn, Damian Young, Chuck Montgomery, David Simonds, Pamela Stewart; **D:** Hal Hartley; **W:** Hal Hartley; **C:** Michael Spiller; **M:** Jeff Taylor, Ned Rifle. *COL*

Amateur Night 🎬 1985
Sloppy musical comedy about the backstage bickering occuring during the amateur night at a famous nightclub. **91m/C VHS, Beta.** Geoffrey Deuel, Dennis Cole, Allen Kirk. *VES, ART*

Amazing Adventure 🎬🎬 1937
Romance and Riches; The Amazing Quest of Ernest Bliss; Riches and Romance A millionaire wins a bet when he rises from a chauffeur's position to the executive board room without using his wealth. Though not particularly amazing, lightweight English comedy has Grant working hard to charm over and above the demands of the dated formula, a performance he undertook during a vacation from Hollywood. Adapted from a novel by E. Phillips Oppenheim. **63m/C VHS, Beta.** Cary Grant, Mary Brian, Henry Kendall, Leon M. Lion, Ralph Richardson; **D:** Alfred Zeisler. *NOS, BAR, DVT*

The Amazing Colossal Man 🎬🎬 1957
A standard '50s sci-fi film about atomic radiation. Colonel Manning is exposed to massive doses of plutonium when an experiment backfires (literally). The former good-guy grows to 70 feet and starts taking out his anger on a helpless Las Vegas. Can anything stop his murderous rampages? Followed by "War of the Colossal Beast." **79m/B VHS.** Glenn Langan, Cathy Downs, William Hudson, James Seay, Russ Bender, Lyn Osborn; **D:** Bert I. Gordon; **C:** Joseph Biroc. *COL, FUS*

The Amazing Dobermans 🎬🎬 1976
(G) Family-oriented pooch performance piece featuring Astaire in one of his lesser roles. Ex-con man Astaire and his five trained Dobermans assist an undercover agent in foiling a small-time criminal's gambling and extortion racket. The last in a series that includes "The Daring Dobermans" and "The Doberman Gang." **96m/C VHS, Beta.** Fred Astaire, Barbara Eden, James Franciscus, Jack Carter, Billy Barty; **D:** Byron Ross Chudnow; **M:** Alan Silvestri.

Amazing Grace 🎬🎬 1974
Some righteous mothers led by Moms Mabley go up against corrupt city politics in this extremely dated comedy that was cast with a sense of the absurd. **99m/C VHS.** Moms Mabley, Slappy (Melvin) White, Moses Gunn, Rosalind Cash, Dolph Sweet, Butterfly McQueen, Stepin Fetchit; **D:** Stan Lathan. *NO*

Amazing Grace 🎬🎬 1992
Eighteen-year-old Jonathan leaves home to share his friend Mickey's apartment. He meets Thomas, who has just returned to Israel after years in New York, and they begin a tentative relationship. But Thomas is hiding the fact that he may be HIV-positive and tries to keep a distance from the eager Jonathan. Hebrew with subtitles. **95m/C VHS.** IS Rivka Michaely, Sharon Alexander, Gal Hoyberger, Hina Rozovska; **D:** Amos Gutman. *CCN*

Amazing Grace & Chuck 🎬🎬 1987
(PG) Perhaps the only anti-war/sports fantasy ever made. After a visit to a Minuteman missile site in Montana, 12-year-old Little Leaguer Chuck learns of the dangers of nuclear arms. He begins a protest by refusing to play until the nations come to a peace agreement. In a sudden surge of social conscience, athletes worldwide put down their equipment and join in droves, starting with pro-basketball star Amazing Grace Smith (Denver Nugget English). Capra-like fantasy has good intentions but ultimately lacks two key elements: coherency and plausibility. **115m/C VHS, Beta, LV, Closed Caption.** Jamie Lee Curtis, Gregory Peck, William L. Petersen, Joshua Zuehlke, Alex English; **D:** Mike Newell; **C:** Robert Elswit; **M:** Elmer Bernstein. *HBO*

The Amazing Howard Hughes 🎬🎬½ 1977
Reveals the full story of the legendary millionaire's life and career, from daring test pilot to inventor to Hollywood film producer to isolated wealthy paranoiac with a germ phobia. Lingers on the rich guy with big problems theme. Big-budget, made for television drama with a nice performance by Jones. **119m/C VHS, Beta.** Tommy Lee Jones, Ed Flanders, James Hampton, Tovah Feldshuh, Lee Purcell; **D:** William A. Graham. *FCT*

Amazing Mr. Blunden 🎬🎬½ 1972 (G)
Solid kidvid about two youngsters aided by a ghost who travel back in time to save the lives of two murdered children. Adapted by Jeffries from Antonia Barber's novel, "The Ghosts." **100m/C VHS, Beta.** Laurence Naismith, Lynne Frederick, Garry Miller, Marc Granger, Rosalyn London, Diana Dors; **D:** Lionel Jeffries; **M:** Elmer Bernstein.

The Amazing Mr. X 🎬🎬½ 1948
The Spiritualist When a woman's husband dies, she tries to contact him via a spiritualist. Things are not as they seem however, and the medium may just be part of an intricate scheme to defraud the woman. **79m/B VHS.** Turhan Bey, Lynn Bari, Cathy O'Donnell, Richard Carlson, Donald Curtis, Virginia Gregg; **D:** Bernard Vorhaus. *NOS, SNC, RXM*

The Amazing Panda Adventure 🎬🎬½ 1995 (PG)
Little Panda; The Amazing Panda Rescue Ryan (Slater) is off to China during his spring break to visit dad Michael (Lang), who's working on a project to rescue the dwindling panda population. But there's poacher trouble and Ryan and young translator Ling (Ding) decide to rescue the preserve's panda cub, which has been animal-napped (where's Ace Ventura when you need him). Family fare, with a mixture of totally adorable real and animatronic pandas; filmed in the Sichuan province of China, home to the Wolong Nature Reserve which is famous for its successful breeding of the endangered giant pandas. Slater, in his first starring role, is the younger brother of Christian. **84m/C VHS, LV, Closed Caption.** Ryan Slater, Stephen Lang, Yi Ding, Wang Fei; **D:** Christopher Cain; **W:** Laurice Elehwany, Jeff Rothberg; **C:** Jack N. Green; **M:** William Ross. *WAR*

The Amazing Spider-Man 🎬🎬 1977
Spider-Man The Marvel Comics superhero's unique powers are put to the test when he comes to the rescue of the government by preventing an evil scientist from blackmailing the government for big bucks. The wall-walking web-slinger has his origins probed (a grad student bit by a radioactive spider develops super-human powers) in his live-action debut, which was made for television and led to a short-lived series. **94m/C VHS, Beta, LV, Closed Caption.** Nicholas Hammond, David White, Lisa Eilbacher, Michael Pataki; **D:** E.W. Swackhamer. *FOX, IME*

Amazing Stories 1985
From the Steven Spielberg produced television series. "The Mission" sees a WWII tail gunner trapped in an unusual predicament. In "The Wedding Ring," a man gives his wife a strange ring and bizarre situations ensue. Additional episodes available. **70m/C VHS, LV.** Kevin Costner, Casey Siemaszko, Kiefer Sutherland, Danny DeVito, Rhea Perlman; **D:** Danny DeVito, Steven Spielberg. *USH, FCT, MOV*

The Amazing Transparent Man woof! 1960
A mad scientist makes a crook invisible in order to steal the radioactive materials he needs. The crook decides to rob banks instead. Shot at the Texas State Fair for that elusive futuristic look. For Ulmer fans only. **58m/B VHS.** Douglas Kennedy, Marguerite Chapman, James Griffith, Ivan Triesault; **D:** Edgar G. Ulmer. *NOS, SNC*

The Amazing Transplant woof! 1970
A sleaze-bag psycho has a "love enhancing" transplant, much to the pleasure of his sexual partners. Much to their and our dismay, however, he then kills them and bores us. **90m/C VHS, Beta.** Juan Fernandez, Linda Southern; **D:** Doris Wishman. *TPV*

Amazon 🎬🎬 1990 (R)
An adventure movie filmed in the Brazilian rainforest with an environmental message. A businessman being chased by the police in the Amazon jungle is rescued by a bush pilot who dreams of mining the Amazon's riches. A Brazilian woman enters the picture and persuades the businessman to help save the rainforest. Portions of the proceeds from the sale of this film go to the Rainforest Action Network. **88m/C VHS, LV, Closed Caption.** Kari Vaananen, Robert Davi, Rae Dawn Chong; **D:** Mika Kaurismaki. *ART*

Amazon Jail 🎬 1985
Scantily clad women go over the wall and promptly get caught by devil worshiping men in the jungle. They should have known better. Redeemed only by lingerie selection. **94m/C VHS, Beta.** Elisabeth Hartmann, Mauricio Do Valle, Sondra Graffi; **D:** Oswald De Oliveira. *NO*

Amazon Warrior 🎬🎬 1997
Tara is a mercenary in a future world ruled by violence. The last survivor of her Amazon tribe, she sells her fighting skills to the highest bidder while searching for the leader of the rebel Marauder army, which massacred her people. Tara's well-equipped when that final showdown comes. **85m/C VHS.** J.J. Rodgers, Christine Lydon, Jimmy Jerman, Al Spencer, Raymond Storti; **D:** Dennis Devine; **W:** Steve Jarvis; **M:** David De Palo. *CIN*

Amazon Women on the Moon 🐾🐾
1987 (R) A plotless, irreverent media spoof, depicting the programming of a slipshod television station as it crams weird commercials and shorts around a comical '50s' science fiction film. Inconsistent, occasionally funny anthology hangs together very loosely. Produced by Landis, with the usual amount of in-joke cameos and allusions to his other works of art. 85m/C VHS, Beta, LV. Rosanna Arquette, Steve Guttenberg, Steve Allen, B.B. King, Michelle Pfeiffer, Arsenio Hall, Andrew Dice Clay, Howard Hesseman, Lou Jacobi, Carrie Fisher, Griffin Dunne, Sybil Danning, Henny Youngman, Monique Gabrielle, Paul Bartel, Kelly Preston; **D:** John Landis, Joe Dante, Carl Gottlieb, Peter Horton, Robert Weiss; **W:** Michael Barrie, Jim Mulholland; **M:** Ira Newborn. USH

The Amazons 🐾½ **1984** Goofy made for television drama about a beautiful doctor who discovers an underground organization of Amazon-descended women bent on taking over the world or at least making life hard for men while investigating a Congressman's mysterious death. 100m/C VHS, Beta. Tamara Dobson, Jack Scalia, Stella Stevens, Madeleine Stowe, Jennifer Warren; **D:** Paul Michael Glaser; **M:** Basil Poledouris. NO

Amazons 🐾 **1986** (R) Tall, strong women who occasionally wander around nude search for a magical talisman that will overthrow an evil magician. 76m/C VHS, Beta. Windsor Taylor Randolph, Penelope Reed, Joseph Whipp, Willie Nelson, Danitza Kingsley; **D:** Alex Sessa. MGM

The Ambassador 🐾🐾½ *Peacemaker* **1984** An American ambassador (Mitchum) is sent to the Middle East to try to solve the area's deep political problems. He quickly becomes the target of terrorist attacks, and is blamed for the nation's unrest. To make matters worse, his wife is having an affair with a PLO leader. The President ignores him, forcing the ambassador to fend for himself. Talk about your bad days. Hudson's last feature. Based on Elmore Leonard's "52 Pickup," and remade a year later under its own title. 97m/C VHS, Beta. Robert Mitchum, Ellen Burstyn, Rock Hudson, Fabio Testi, Donald Pleasence; **D:** J. Lee Thompson. MGM

Ambassador Bill 🐾🐾 **1931** An Oklahoma rancher is appointed ambassador to a country in revolt. Rogers, of course, saves the day with his rustic witticisms. Based on the story "Ambassador from the United States" by Vincent Sheean. 68m/B VHS. Will Rogers, Marguerite Churchill, Greta Nissen; **D:** Sam Taylor. FOX, FCT

The Ambassador's Daughter 🐾🐾 **1956** The Parisian adventures of an American ambassador's daughter De Havilland and soldier Forsythe, who, unaware of her position, falls in love with her. Faltering comedy is supported by an expert cast (although nearly 40, De Havilland is charming as the young woman) with especially good performances from Menjou and Loy. 102m/C VHS. Olivia de Havilland, John Forsythe, Myrna Loy, Adolphe Menjou, Edward Arnold, Francis Lederer, Tommy Noonan, Minor Watson; **D:** Norman Krasna; **W:** Norman Krasna. MOV

Amber Waves 🐾🐾½ **1982** Credible made for television drama about a generation-gap conflict between a Midwestern farmer (Weaver) and an irresponsible male model (Russell) who has coasted through life on con and charm. 98m/C VHS, Beta. Dennis Weaver, Kurt Russell; **D:** Joseph Sargent. TLF

Ambition 🐾½ **1991** (R) Scriptwriter/star Phillips gets a bone for chutzpah by taking an unsavory lead role; his character torments a paroled psycho so that the killer will kill again and inspire a true-crime bestseller. The plot looks good on paper, but onscreen it's padded and unconvincing. **CW:** Language, violence, and sensuality. 99m/C VHS, Beta, LV, Closed Caption. Lou Diamond Phillips, Clancy Brown, Cecilia Peck, Richard Bradford, Willard Pugh, Grace Zabriskie, Katherine Armstrong, John Cullum, Haing S. Ngor; **D:** Scott Goldstein; **W:** Lou Diamond Phillips; **M:** Leonard Rosenman. VTR

The Ambulance 🐾🐾½ **1990** (R) A New York cartoonist witnesses a mysterious ambulance at work and decides to investigate. His probings uncover a plot to sell the bodies of dying diabetics. A surprisingly good no-money feature from low-budget king Cohen. Includes an appearance by Marvel Comics' Stan Lee as himself. 95m/C VHS, LV, Closed Caption. Eric Roberts, James Earl Jones, Megan Gallagher, Richard Bright, Janine Turner, Eric (Hans Gudegast) Braeden, Red Buttons, Laurene Landon, Jill Gatsby, Nicholas Chinlund; **D:** Larry Cohen; **W:** Larry Cohen. COL, EPC

Ambush at Tomahawk Gap 🐾🐾
1953 Three released prisoners go in search of hidden loot and tempers rise when the goods don't turn up. Then the Apaches show up. 73m/C VHS, Beta. John Hodiak, John Derek, David Brian, Maria Elena Marques, Ray Teal; **D:** Fred F. Sears. GKK

The Ambush Murders 🐾🐾½ **1982** True story of a stalwart white attorney defending a black activist accused of killing two cops. Not the compelling television it could be, but still enjoyable. From Ben Bradlee, Jr.'s novel. 100m/C VHS, Beta. James Brolin, James Earl Jones, Dorian Harewood, Alfre Woodard, Louis Giambalvo, John McLiam, Teddy Wilson, Antonio Fargas, Amy Madigan; **D:** Steven Hilliard Stern. ART

Ambush Trail 🐾🐾 **1946** Stranger-in-town Steele metes out justice to help local ranchers while sidekick Saylor leaves 'em laughing. 60m/B VHS. Bob Steele, Syd Saylor, I. Stanford Jolley, Lorraine Miller, Charles "Blackie" King, Kermit Maynard; **D:** Harry Fraser. NOS, GPV

The Ambushers woof! **1967** Martin's third Matt Helm farce finds him handling a puzzling case involving the first United States spacecraft. When the craft is hijacked with Rule on board, it's Matt to the rescue, regaining control before unfriendly forces can take it back to Earth. Tired formula seems to have worn Martin out while the remainder of the cast goes to camp. Followed by "The Wrecking Crew." 102m/C VHS, Beta, LV. Dean Martin, Janice Rule, James Gregory, Albert Salmi, Senta Berger; **D:** Henry Levin. COL

Amelia Earhart: The Final Flight 🐾🐾½ **1994** Investigates the mysterious disappearance of pioneering aviatrix Amelia Earhart's 1937 flight to become the first pilot to circumnavigate the globe. Earhart (Keaton) and her navigator Fred Noonan (Hauer) disappeared over the Pacific Ocean and their fate has never been determined. Dern plays Earhart's husband, publisher George B. Putnam, who served as Amelia's manager and publicist. Based on the biography by Doris L. Rich. Made for television. 95m/C VHS, LV, Closed Caption. Diane Keaton, Rutger Hauer, Bruce Dern, Paul Guilfoyle, Denis Arndt, David Carpenter, Diana Bellamy; **D:** Yves Simoneau; **W:** Anna Sandor; **M:** George S. Clinton. TTC

America 🐾🐾½ **1924** Young patriot Nathan Holden (Hamilton) is torn between his political beliefs and his love for the daughter of a Virginia Tory (Dempster). Meanwhile, evil redcoat Captain Butler (Barrymore) and his band of murderous Mohawks ruthlessly attack the colonists. 141m/B VHS. Neil Hamilton, Carol Dempster, Lionel Barrymore; **D:** D.W. Griffith. KIV

America 🐾½ **1986** (R) New York cable station receives worldwide fame when their signal bounces off of the moon. Uninspired piece of fluff from otherwise talented director Downey. 83m/C VHS. Zack Norman, Tammy Grimes, Michael J. Pollard, Monroe Arnold, Richard Belzer, Liz Torres, Howard Thomashefsky, Laura Ashton, Robert Downey Jr.; **D:** Robert Downey. NO

America at the Movies 🐾🐾½ **1976** Scenes from more than 80 of the finest American motion pictures fly by in an effort to tell the story of the cinema and provide a portrait of America as it has been seen on screen for half a century. Scenes from "The Birth of a Nation," "Citizen Kane," "Dr. Strangelove," "East of Eden," "The French Connection," and "From Here to Eternity,"

are among the many included. Some black and white scenes; produced by the American Film Institute. 116m/C VHS, Beta, LV. John Wayne, Orson Welles, Peter Sellers, James Dean, Gene Hackman, Burt Lancaster, Julie Harris, Deborah Kerr, Al Pacino, Robert De Niro. COL, IME

America First 🐾½ **1970** A group of seven travelers try to build an "Eden" with the inhabitants of an Appalachian hollow. 90m/C VHS, Beta. Michael Kennedy, Walter Keller, Pat Estrin, Lois McGuire. NO

America/The Fall of Babylon 🐾🐾🐾
1924 A double feature containing abridged versions; in "America," a Boston patriot and the daughter of an aristocratic Virginia Tory fall in love during the Revolutionary War; "The Fall of Babylon" is one of the stories in D.W. Griffith's "Intolerance." Silent. 56m/B VHS, Beta. Neil Hamilton, Lionel Barrymore, Constance Talmadge, Elmer Clifton, Alfred Paget. CCB

America 3000 🐾 **1986** (PG-13) Hundreds of years in the holocaust-torn future, men rebel against a brutal, overpowering race of women, with predictable results. 94m/C VHS, Beta. Chuck Wagner, Laurene Landon; **D:** David Engelbach. MGM

The American Angels: Baptism of Blood 🐾 **1989** (R) Three beautiful young women, each with a personal dream, strive to make it in the world of professional wrestling. Hackneyed plot devices, but those simply watching for the wrestling scenes won't be disappointed. 99m/C VHS, Beta, LV, Closed Caption. Jan MacKenzie, Tray Loren, Mimi Lesseos, Trudy Adams, Patricia Cavoti, Susan Sexton, Jean Kirkland, Jeff Lundy, Lee Marshall; **D:** Beverly Sebastian, Ferd Sebastian. PAR

American Anthem 🐾 **1986** (PG-13) A young gymnast must choose between family responsibilities or the parallel bars. Olympic gymnast Gaylord makes his movie debut but doesn't get the gold. Good fare for young tumblers, but that's about it. Followed by two of the films' music videos and tape-ads featuring Max Headroom. 100m/C VHS, Beta, LV, Closed Caption. Mitch Gaylord, Janet Jones, Michelle Phillips, Michael Pataki; **D:** Albert Magnoli; **W:** Evan P. Archerd, Jeff Benjamin; **M:** Alan Silvestri. ORI, WAR

American Aristocracy 🐾🐾½ **1917** A silent comic romp in which Fairbanks, an old moneyed dandy, wreaks havoc on an island resort whose clientele is composed of the nouveau wellto-do. 52m/B VHS, Beta. Douglas Fairbanks Sr., Jewel Carmen, Albert Parker; **D:** Lloyd Ingraham. GPV

American Autobahn 🐾½ **1984** A lowbudget independent actioner about a journalist who discovers an underworld weapons ring that hits the highway in pursuit of him. 90m/C VHS, Beta. Jan Jalenak, Michael von der Goltz, Jim Jarmusch; **D:** Andre Degas. NO

American Blue Note 🐾🐾 *Fakebook* **1989** (PG-13) Loosely plotted, bittersweet account of a struggling jazz quartet in the early 1960s, as its leader (MacNicol) must decide if their fruitless tours of sleazy bars and weddings are still worth it. The debut of Toporoff. 96m/C VHS, LV. Peter MacNicol, Carl Capotorto, Tim Guinee, Bill Christopher-Myers, Jonathan Walker, Charlotte d'Amboise, Louis Guss, Zohra Lampert, Trini Alvarado, Sam Behrens; **D:** Ralph Toporoff; **W:** Gilbert Girion, Larry Schanker. COL, BTV

American Born 🐾½ **1989** Murder Inc. returns to the dismay of one idealist who embarks on a battle he doesn't intend to lose. The mob had better look out. 90m/C VHS. Joey Travolta, Andrew Zeller; **D:** Raymond Martino; **W:** Raymond Martino. PMH

American Boyfriends 🐾🐾 **1989** (PG-13) An ostensible sequel to "My American Cousin," in which two Canadian girls go to California and discover innocent romance and friendship. 90m/C VHS, Beta, LV. CA Margaret Langrick, John Wildman, Jason Blicker, Lisa Repo Martell; **D:** Sandy Wilson; **W:** Sandy Wilson. ART

American Buffalo ♫♫½ 1995 (R) Somewhat lackluster but decent screen adaptation of a classic American drama. Franz's junk shop owner Donny plans to steal back a rare Buffalo-head nickel that he feels he was swindled out of, with the help of his protege Bobby (Nelson). Hoffman's ferret-like Teach, one of Donny's card-playing buddies and an arrogant opportunist, tries to weasel in on the plan that never comes to fruition. Set in Corrente's hometown of Pawtucket, the director's reverence for the material is obvious and he plays it too safe. Top-notch performances raise the level. Mamet adapts his play for the screen.**CW:** Language. **88m/C VHS, Closed Caption.** Dustin Hoffman, Dennis Franz, Sean Nelson; **D:** Michael Corrente; **W:** David Mamet; **C:** Richard Crudo; **M:** Thomas Newman. *EVE*

American Chinatown ♫½ 1996 Orphaned tough guy is taken in by a powerful Chinatown mob family but gets into trouble when he falls for the head man's sister. He has a chance to redeem himself when he learns about a plot to overthrow the triad clan but will he take it? **90m/C VHS.** Henry Lee, Robert Z'Dar, Liat Goodson; **D:** Richard W. Park. *HVF*

An American Christmas Carol ♫♫ 1979 Charles Dickens' classic story is retold with limited charm in a made for television effort. This time a greedy American financier (Winkler) learns about the true meaning of Christmas. **98m/C VHS, Beta.** Henry Winkler, David Wayne, Dorian Harewood; **D:** Eric Till; **M:** Hagood Hardy. *VES, ART*

American Cinema 1994 Ten-part series covering the roughly 100 years of cinema history through a look at the Hollywood film. Lots of clips and interviews with each part providing an overview of a particular feature of the movie industry from stars to studios to independent filmmakers. Available as a five-tape boxed set or individually. **500m/C VHS.** *FOX*

American Commandos ♫ *Hitman* 1984 (R) An ex-Green Beret slaughters the junkies who killed his son and raped his wife, and then joins his old buddies for a secret, Rambo-esque mission in Vietnam providing a tired rehash of Vietnam movie cliches. **96m/C VHS, Beta.** Chris Mitchum, John Phillip Law, Franco Guerrero; **D:** Bobby Suarez. *ART*

American Cop ♫½ 1994 (PG-13) Elmo La-Grange is an ordinary cop taking a vacation, when his layover in the Moscow airport becomes a lesson in mistaken identities. He teams up with the pre-requisite beautiful woman to outwit and outrun the Russian mafia.**CW:** Action violence. **91m/C VHS, LV.** Wayne Crawford, Ashley Laurence, Daniel Quinn, William Katt, Olga Vodin, Vladimir Shpoudeiko, Nickolai Nedovodin; **D:** Wayne Crawford; **W:** Carlos Brooks; **C:** Nicholas Von Sternberg. *APX*

American Cyborg: Steel Warrior ♫♫½ 1994 (R) Basic evil-machine-bent-on-mankind's-destruction movie—with a hero bent on rescuing the world. **95m/C VHS, LV.** Joe Lara, John P. Ryan; **D:** Boaz Davidson; **W:** Bill Crounse.

American Dream ♫♫♫ 1981 A midwestern family leaves the suburbs and moves into a Chicago inner-city neighborhood. Good TV-movie pilot for the short-lived series that was Emmy nominated for direction and writing. **90m/C VHS, Beta.** Stephen Macht, Karen Carlson, John Karlen, Andrea Smith, John Malkovich, John McIntire; **D:** Mel Damski; **M:** Artie Butler. *UNI*

American Dreamer ♫♫ 1984 (PG) A housewife wins a trip to Paris as a prize from a mystery writing contest. Silly from a blow on the head, she begins living the fictional life of her favorite literary adventure. Sporadic comedy with a good cast wandering about courtesy of a clumsy screenplay. **105m/C VHS, Beta, Closed Caption.** JoBeth Williams, Tom Conti, Giancarlo Giannini, Coral Browne, James Staley; **D:** Rick Rosenthal; **M:** Lewis Furey. *FOX*

American Eagle ♫½ 1990 (R) A veteran goes crazy and seeks sadistic, bloody revenge on his war buddies. Now his war buddies are the only ones who can stop him. **92m/C VHS, LV.** Asher Brauner, Robert F. Lyons, Vernon Wells, Kai Baker; **D:** Robert J. Smawley. *THV*

American Empire ♫♫½ *My Son Alone* 1942 Two Civil War heroes struggle to build a cattle empire in Texas and are hampered by rustlers, one of whom was their partner. A fine, veteran cast and a tight script keep things moving, including the cattle. **82m/B VHS, Beta.** Preston Foster, Richard Dix, Frances Gifford, Leo Carrillo; **D:** William McGann. *NOS, MRV, DVT*

American Fabulous ♫♫½ 1992 The posthumously released autobiography of an eccentric homosexual who lived life in the fast lane. Jeffrey Strouth performs his monologue from the back seat of a 1957 Cadillac, where the images of small-town America are seen to contrast sharply with his flamboyant style. His grotesque and candid recollections include his alcoholic Elvis-impersonator father, a stint as a teenage prostitute, drag queen friends, and drug addiction in New York. Strouth puts a comic twist on even the most brutal of his memories. He died of AIDS at the age of 33 in 1992. **105m/C VHS.** Jeffrey Strouth; **D:** Reno Dakota; **W:** Jeffrey Strouth. *FRF*

American Flyers ♫♫ 1985 (PG-13) Two competitive brothers train for a grueling three-day bicycle race in Colorado while tangling with personal drama, including the spectre that one of them may have inherited dad's tendency for cerebral aneurisms and is sure to drop dead during a bike race soon. Written by bike movie specialist Tesich ("Breaking Away") with a lot of the usual cliches (the last bike ride, battling bros, eventual understanding), which are gracefully overridden by fine bike-racing photography. Interesting performances, especially Chong as a patient girlfriend and Amos as the heavy. **113m/C VHS, Beta, LV, Closed Caption.** Kevin Costner, David Marshall Grant, Rae Dawn Chong, Alexandra Paul, John Amos, Janice Rule, Robert Townsend, Jennifer Grey, Luca Bercovici; **D:** John Badham; **W:** Steve Tesich; **M:** Lee Ritenour, Greg Mathieson. *WAR*

The American Friend ♫♫♫½ 1977 Tribute to the American gangster film helped introduce Wenders to American moviegoers. Young Hamburg picture framer thinks he has a terminal disease and is set up by American expatriate Hopper to become a hired assassin in West Germany. The lure is a promise of quick money that the supposedly dying man can then leave his wife and child. After the first assasination, the two bond. Hopper is the typical Wenders protagonist, a strange man in a strange land looking for a connection. Great, creepy thriller adapted from Patricia Highsmith's novel "Ripley's Game." Fuller and Ray (better known as directors) appear briefly as gangsters. **127m/C VHS, Beta, LV.** FR GE Bruno Ganz, Dennis Hopper, Elisabeth Kreuzer, Gerard Blain, Jean Eustache, Samuel Fuller, Nicholas Ray, Wim Wenders; **D:** Wim Wenders; **W:** Wim Wenders. *FCT, GLV, TPV*

American Friends ♫♫ 1991 (PG) Genteel story masquerades as high comedy. Palin is a fussy middle-aged Oxford classics tutor. On a holiday he meets American Hartley (Booth) and her adopted daughter, Elinor (Alvarado). Both women are immensely attracted to the don (for reasons that are unclear) and follow him back to Oxford, where he's engaged in a battle of succession with his rival Molina. Dismal screenplay lacks logic and urgency, making it difficult to care about the story or the characters. Script is said to have been inspired by an incident in the life of Palin's great-grandfather. If this sounds like your cup of tea, save your time and watch a Merchant Ivory film instead. **95m/C VHS, LV.** GB Michael Palin, Connie Booth, Trini Alvarado, Alfred Molina; **D:** Tristam Powell; **W:** Michael Palin, Tristam Powell; **M:** Georges Delerue. *THV, FCT*

The American Gangster 1992 Documentary look at the beginnings of organized crime and the rise of the gangster in American society. Includes vintage film and photographs. Profiles include Bugsy Siegel, Al Capone, John Dillinger, Pretty Boy Floyd, and Lucky Luciano. **45m/C VHS.** *COL*

American Gigolo ♫♫ 1979 (R) A Los Angeles loner who sexually services the rich women of Beverly Hills becomes involved with the wife of a California state senator and is then framed for a murder he did not commit. A highly stylized but empty view of seamy low lives marred by a contrived plot, with decent romp in the hay readiness displayed by Gere. **117m/C VHS, Beta, LV.** Richard Gere, Lauren Hutton, Hector Elizondo, Paul Schrader; **D:** Paul Schrader; **W:** Paul Schrader; **C:** John Bailey. *PAR*

American Gothic woof! *Hide and Shriek* 1988 (R) Three couples headed for a vacation are instead stranded on an island and captured by a demented family headed by Steiger and De Carlo, a scary enough proposition in itself. Even worse, Ma and Pa have three middle-aged moronic offspring who still dress as children and are intent on killing the thwarted vacationers (who are none too bright themselves) one by bloody one. A stultifying career low for all involved. **89m/C VHS, Beta, LV.** Rod Steiger, Yvonne De Carlo, Michael J. Pollard, Sarah Torgov, Fiona Hutchinson; **D:** John Hough. *THV*

American Graffiti ♫♫♫♫ 1973 (PG) Atmospheric, episodic look at growing up in the innocence of America before the Kennedy assassination and the Vietnam War. It all takes place on one hectic but typical night in the life of a group of recent California high school grads unsure of what the next big step in life is. So they spend their time cruising, listening to Wolfman Jack, and meeting at the drive-in. Slice of '60s life boasts a prudent script, great set design, authentic soundtrack, and consistently fine performances by the young cast. Catapulted Dreyfuss, Ford, and Somers to stardom, branded Lucas a hot directorial commodity with enough leverage to launch "Star Wars," and steered Howard and Williams towards continued age-of-innocence nirvana on "Happy Days." **112m/C VHS, Beta, LV.** Richard Dreyfuss, Ron Howard, Cindy Williams, MacKenzie Phillips, Paul LeMat, Charles Martin Smith, Suzanne Somers, Candy Clark, Harrison Ford, Bo Hopkins, Joe Spano, Kathleen Quinlan, Wolfman Jack; **D:** George Lucas; **W:** George Lucas, Gloria Katz, Willard Huyck. Golden Globe Awards '74: Best Film—Musical/Comedy, National Film Registry '95;; New York Film Critics Awards '73: Best Screenplay; National Society of Film Critics Awards '73: Best Screenplay; Nominations: Academy Awards '73: Best Director (Lucas), Best Film Editing, Best Picture, Best Story & Screenplay, Best Supporting Actress (Clark). *USH, FCT*

American Heart ♫♫♫½ 1992 (R) Jack (Bridges) is a suspicious ex-con, newly released from prison, with few prospects and little hope. He also has a teenage son, Nick (Furlong), he barely remembers but who desperately wants to have his father back in his life. Jack is reluctantly persuaded to let Nick stay with him in his cheap hotel where Nick befriends fellow resident, Molly, a teenage hooker, and other castoff street kids. Superb performances by both male leads—Furlong, both yearning and frustrated as he pursues his dream of having a family, and Bridges as the tough parolee, unwilling to open his heart. Hardboiled, poignant, and powerful. **114m/C VHS, LV.** Jeff Bridges, Edward Furlong, Lucinda Jenney, Tracey Kapisky, Don Harvey, Margaret Welsh; **D:** Martin Bell; **W:** Peter Silverman; **M:** James Newton Howard. Independent Spirit Awards '94: Best Actor (Bridges); Nominations: Independent Spirit Awards '94: Best Cinematography, Best First Feature, Best Supporting Actor (Furlong), Best Supporting Actress (Jenney). *ART, BTV*

An American in Paris ♫♫♫♫ 1951 Lavish, imaginative musical features a sweeping score, and knockout choreography by Kelly. Ex-G.I. Kelly stays on in Paris after the war to study painting, supported in his efforts by rich American

Foch, who hopes to acquire a little extra attention. But Kelly loves the lovely Caron, unfortunately engaged to an older gent. Highlight is an astonishing 17-minute ballet which holds the record for longest movie dance number—and one of the most expensive, pegged at over half a million for a month of filming. For his efforts, the dance king won a special Oscar citation. While it sure looks like Paris, most of it was filmed in MGM studios. ♫S'Wonderful; I Got Rhythm; Embraceable You; Love Is Here To Stay; Tra-La-La; I'll Build a Stairway to Paradise; Nice Work If You Can Get It; By Strauss; Concerto in F (3rd Movement). **113m/C VHS, Beta, LV, 8mm.** Gene Kelly, Leslie Caron, Oscar Levant, Nina Foch, Georges Guetary; *D:* Vincente Minnelli; *W:* Alan Jay Lerner; *C:* John Alton; *M:* George Gershwin, Ira Gershwin. Academy Awards '51: Best Art Direction/Set Decoration (Color), Best Color Cinematography, Best Costume Design (Color), Best Picture, Best Story & Screenplay, Scoring of a Musical; Golden Globe Awards '52: Best Film—Musical/Comedy, National Film Registry '93;; Nominations: Academy Awards '51: Best Director (Minnelli), Best Film Editing. *MGM, TLF, BTV*

American Justice ♂♂ *Jackals* 1986 (R) Two cops, one of whom looks suspiciously like a Simon of "Simon and Simon," fight political corruption and white slavery near the Mexican border. The chief white slaver bears a full resemblance to the other Simon. Sufficient action but less than original. **96m/C VHS, Beta.** Jameson Parker, Gerald McRaney, Wilford Brimley, Jack Lucarelli; *D:* Gary Grillo. *ART*

American Kickboxer 1 ♂½ 1991 (R) Barrett stars as B.J. Quinn, a down on his luck kickboxing champion who spends much of his time onscreen aimlessly wandering (apparently searching for the meaning of his life). Lackluster script and performances will make this one trying—even for kickboxing fans. Barrett is Chuck Norris' former workout partner, but there isn't enough action often enough for him to show off his formidable skills.*CW:* Language and kickboxing violence. **93m/C VHS, Beta.** John Barrett, Keith Vitali, Brad Morris, Terry Norton, Ted Leplat; *D:* Frans Nel; *W:* Emil Kolbe; *M:* Frank Becker.

American Kickboxer 2: To the Death ♂½ 1993 (R) Lillian must find a way to get her cop ex-husband and her kickboxer ex-lover to work together to save her kidnapped daughter's life.*CW:* Language, continous violence, and some sexuality. **91m/C VHS, LV, Closed Caption.** Dale "Apollo" Cook, Evan Lurie, Kathy Shower, Ted Markland; *D:* Jeno Hodi. *THV*

American Madness ♂♂½ 1932 Benevolent banker Dickson (Huston) has been making loans without sufficient collateral. The bank's board of directors give him a warning and then a robbery causes a run on the bank. The directors are ready to oust Dickson when the small businessmen he's helped rally to his defense. Tedious romantic subplot has Dickson's unhappy wife (Johnson) accusing him of neglect and dallying with unscrupulous bank clerk Cluett (Gordon). **75m/B VHS.** Walter Huston, Pat O'Brien, Kay Johnson, Gavin Gordon, Constance Cummings, Robert Ellis, Walter Walker, Arthur Hoyt; *D:* Frank Capra; *W:* Robert Riskin; *C:* Joseph Walker. *COL*

American Matchmaker ♂♂½ *Amerikaner Shadkhn* 1940 Nat Silver decides to go into the matchmaking business, after his own marriages fail miserably, hoping to experience happiness vicariously. However, he soon begins to realize that one of his clients is a better match for him than the man he chose for her. In Yiddish with English subtitles. **87m/B VHS.** Leo Fuchs, Judith Abarbanel, Rosetta Bialis, Yudel Dubinsky, Abe Lax; *D:* Edgar G. Ulmer. *ERG*

American Me ♂♂♂ 1992 (R) Violent and brutal depiction of more than 30 years of gang wars and drugs in East Los Angeles. Santana founded a street as a teenager, but has spent the last 18 years in prison, where he's the boss of the so-called Mexican Mafia, which oversees the

drugs, scams, murders, and violence that are an everyday fact of prison life. Released from Folsom, Santana goes back to his old neighborhood and attempts to distance himself from his old life but finds his gang ties are stronger than any other alliance. Unsparing and desolate directorial debut from Olmos.*CW:* Language, strong violence and drug content, and sensuality. **119m/C VHS, LV, Closed Caption.** Edward James Olmos, William Forsythe, Pepe Serna, Danny De La Paz, Evelina Fernandez, Sal Lopez, Daniel Villarreal, Cary-Hiroyuki Tagawa; *D:* Edward James Olmos; *W:* Floyd Mutrux, Desmond Nakano; *C:* Reynaldo Villalobos; *M:* Dennis Lambert. *USH*

American Nightmare ♂½ 1981 Young man searches for his missing sister against a background of pornography, drug peddling, and prostitution in the slums of a city. The usual titillating squalid urban drama. **85m/C VHS, Beta.** Lawrence S. Day, Lora Staley, Lenore Zann, Michael Ironside, Alexandra Paul; *D:* Don McBrearty.

American Ninja ♂♂ *American Warrior* 1985 (R) American Dudikoff is G.I. Joe, a martial-arts expert stationed in the Philippines who alienates most everyone around him (he's a rebel). Deadly black-belt war begins with Joe confronting the army which is selling stolen weapons to the South American black market. Aided by one faithful pal, Joe uses his head-kicking martial arts skills to stop hundreds of ninja combatants working for the corrupt arms dealer. In his spare time he romances the base chief's daughter. Efficient rib-crunching chop-socky action wrapped in no-brainer plot and performed by nonactors. Cannon epic mercilessly followed by at least three sequels. **96m/C VHS, Beta, Closed Caption.** Michael Dudikoff, Guich Koock, Judie Aronson, Steve James; *D:* Sam Firstenberg; *W:* Gideon Amir; *C:* Hanania Baer; *M:* Michael Linn. *MGM*

American Ninja 2: The Confrontation ♂♂ 1987 (R) Soldiers Dudikoff and James are back again using their martial arts skills (in any of any acting) to take on a Caribbean drug-lord. Apparently he has been kidnapping Marines and taking them to his island, where he genetically alters them to become fanatical ninja assassins eager to do his dirty work. The script hardly gets in the way of the rib-crunching action, but is an improvement upon Ninja Number One. **90m/C VHS, Beta, LV, Closed Caption.** Michael Dudikoff, Steve James, Larry Poindexter, Gary Conway; *D:* Sam Firstenberg; *W:* Gary Conway, James Booth. *VTR*

American Ninja 3: Blood Hunt woof! 1989 (R) Second sequel in the American Ninja series. Bradley replaces Dudikoff as the martial arts good guy fighting the martial arts bad guys on a Caribbean island. He's pursued by ex-evangelist Marjoe, who wants to inject him with a nasty virus before unloading the germs to bad buys worldwide. Less ninjitsu; more uninspired martial arts. **90m/C VHS, Beta, LV.** David Bradley, Steve James, Marjoe Gortner, Michele Chan, Calvin Jung; *D:* Cedric Sundstrom; *W:* Paul DeMielche, Gary Conway; *M:* George S. Clinton. *MGM*

American Ninja 4: The Annihilation woof! 1991 (R) Dudikoff returns after noticeable absence in last sequel. He should have stayed away from #4—it's a rehash of tired ideas that never gets off the ground. Forget this and see "American Ninja 2: The Confrontation," the best of this series. **99m/C VHS, Beta, LV, Closed Caption.** Michael Dudikoff, David Bradley, James Booth, Dwayne Alexandre, Robin Stille, Ken Gampu; *D:* Cedric Sundstrom; *W:* David Geeves; *M:* Nicolas Tenbroek.

American Pluck ♂♂ 1925 Before he can inherit anything, a playboy millionaire's son must go out into the world and prove he can make his own way. He meets a beautiful princess, who is pursued by a villainous count. Walsh, as the dashing hero, was the younger brother of director Raoul. Silent with original organ music. **91m/B VHS, Beta, 8mm.** George Walsh, Wanda Hawley, Frank Leigh, Sidney De Grey; *D:* Richard Stanton. *VYY*

American Pop ♂♂ 1981 (R) Animated story of four generations of men told in music. Immigrant Zalmie starts off in vaudeville and winds up involved in the mob, his pianist son Benny gets killed in WWII, Benny's son Tony winds up in the early psychedelic rock scene in Haight-Asbury, and Tony's son Little Pete becomes a rock idol. ♫A Hard Rain's A-Gonna Fall; Don't Think Twice It's All Right; People Are Strange; Purple Haze; Hell is for Children; Free Bird; I'm Waiting for the Man; Night Moves; You Send Me.*CW:* Mature themes, language. **95m/C VHS, LV, Closed Caption, DVD.** *D:* Ralph Bakshi; *W:* Ronni Kern; *M:* Lee Holdridge; *V:* Vincent Schiavelli, Marya Small, Lisa Jane Persky, Roz Kelly. *COL*

The American President ♂♂♂ 1995 (PG-13) Widower president Andrew Shepherd (Douglas) decides it's time to get back into the dating game. But just what woman wants to find her romance in the public eye? Well, it turns out to be feisty environmental lobbyist Sydney Wade (the ever-charming Bening). But the Prez also has to put up with nasty opponent Bob Rumson (Dreyfuss), who's using their courtship as political fodder, approval ratings, and a nosy press. Glossy fairytale material expertly handled by both cast and director.*CW:* Contains sexual situations and some strong language. **114m/C VHS, LV, Closed Caption.** Michael Douglas, Annette Bening, Martin Sheen, Michael J. Fox, David Paymer, Samantha Mathis, John Mahoney, Anna Deavere Smith, Nina Siemaszko, Wendie Malick, Shawna Waldron, Richard Dreyfuss; *D:* Rob Reiner; *W:* Aaron Sorkin; *C:* John Seale; *M:* Marc Shaiman. Nominations: Academy Awards '95: Best Original Score; Golden Globe Awards '96: Best Actor—Musical/Comedy (Douglas), Best Actress—Musical/Comedy (Bening), Best Director (Reiner), Best Film—Musical/Comedy, Best Screenplay; Writers Guild of America '95: Best Original Screenplay. *COL*

American Roulette ♂ 1988 (R) Garcia is the exiled president of a Latin American country living in London in this thin political thriller. A plot riddled with weaknesses and poor direction make this potentially interesting film dull and lifeless. **102m/C VHS, LV.** *GB AU* Andy Garcia, Kitty Aldridge, Robert Stephens, Al Matthews, Susannah York; *D:* Maurice Hatton; *M:* Michael Gibbs. *NO*

American Samurai ♂½ 1992 (R) Drew is the adopted son of a Japanese samurai, who gives him the family's sacred sword. This gesture angers his stepbrother who gets involved with Japanese gangsters and illegal live-blade fighting, and who also vows revenge on this American upstart. Lots of sword play to go with the chopsocky action.*CW:* Violence. **89m/C VHS, LV, Closed Caption.** David Bradley, Mark Dacascos, John Fujioka, Valarie Trapp; *D:* Sam Firstenberg; *W:* John Corcoran. *WAR, PMS*

The American Scream ♂½ 198? An innocent family vacationing in the mountains stumbles on to a satanic cult. And that can really ruin a vacation. **85m/C VHS, Beta.** Jennifer Darling, Pons Marr, Blackie Cammett, Kimberly Kramer, Jean Sapienza, Kevin Kaye, Matt Borlenghi, James Cooper; *D:* Mitchell Linden.

American Shaolin: King of the Kickboxers 2 ♂½ 1992 (PG-13) When Drew gets his butt kicked in a karate tournament he decides to head to China and learn some fightwinning moves from a group of warrior monks.*CW:* Martial arts violence. **103m/C VHS, Closed Caption.** Reese Madigan, Trent Bushy, Daniel Dae Kim, Billy Chang, Cliff Lenderman, Zhang Shi Yen, Kim Chan, Alice Zhang Hung; *D:* Lucas Lowe.

The American Soldier ♂♂½ *Der Amerikanische Soldat* 1970 Fassbinder's homage to the American gangster film tells the story of Ricky, a charismatic hit man. Ricky always wears a gun in a shoulder holster, sports a fedora and a white double-breasted suit, and drinks Scotch straight from the bottle. He also carries out his assigned murders with complete efficiency and no emotion. In German with English subtitles. **80m/C VHS.** *GE* Karl Scheydt, Elga Sorbas, Jan George; *D:* Rainer Werner

Fassbinder; **W:** Rainer Werner Fassbinder; **M:** Peer Raben. *NYF*

An American Story 🐾🐾½ 1992 (PG)
Earnest but predictable story based on an actual incident. Six WWII vets return to their small Texas town as heroes. But when they find a corrupt mayor and a brutal sheriff running things they decide to campaign to unseat the local politicos, in spite of some dire warnings. Meade (Johnson), their commanding officer in Europe, is the designated leader in the plan but his ambitious wife and father-in-law want him to align himself with the status quo instead. Hallmark Hall of Fame production is enjoyable and better than most made for TV movies, but fails to reach the heights of many other HHF offerings. **97m/C VHS, Closed Caption.** Brad Johnson, Kathleen Quinlan, Tom Sizemore, Josef Sommer, Patricia Clarkson, Lisa Blount, G.W. Bailey, John M. Jackson; **D:** John Gray; **W:** John Gray; **C:** Johnny E. Jensen. *REP*

American Strays 🐾½ 1996 (R)
Episodic black comedy about various oddballs (most of them violent) who cross paths (usually in Kane's roadside diner) in an isolated desert town. There's a masochist who wants help committing suicide, an unemployed family man on the verge of a breakdown, a serial killer, and more—mostly strange. **CW:** Strong language, some violence and sexuality. **97m/C VHS.** Carol Kane, Jennifer Tilly, Eric Roberts, John Savage, Luke Perry, Joe Viterelli, James Russo, Vonte Sweet, Sam Jones, Brion James, Toni Kalem, Melora Walters; **D:** Michael Covert; **W:** Michael Covert; **C:** Sead Mutarevic; **M:** John Graham. *APX*

American Streetfighter 🐾🐾 1996
Martial arts expert Jake Tanner gets involved with an illegal streetfighting ring to rescue his brother, Randy, who's the target of a drug courier. But what happens when his next opponent is his sibling? **80m/C VHS.** Gary Daniels, Ian Jacklin, Tracy Dali; **D:** Steve Austin. *SCP*

American Streetfighter 2: The Full Impact 🐾½ 1997
Ex-cop becomes a bounty hunter tracking a serial killer who likes to kill his victims with his bare hands. **90m/C VHS.** Gary Daniels, Graciela Casillas; **D:** Marc Messenger. *SCP*

An American Summer 🐾🐾 1990
A Chicago kid spends a summer with his aunt in beach-rich Los Angeles in this coming-of-age tale filled with '90s teen idols. **97m/C VHS, Closed Caption.** Brian Austin Green, Joanna Kerns, Michael Landes, Tony Crane. *NO*

An American Tail 🐾🐾½ 1986 (G)
While emigrating to New York in the 1880s, a young Russian mouse (Fievel) is separated from his family. He matures as he learns to live on the Big Apple's dirty boulevards. The bad guys are of course cats. Excellent animation and a high-minded (though sentimental and stereotypical) plot keep it interesting for adults. Produced by Spielberg and the first big hit for the Bluth factory, a collection of expatriate Disney artists. Knowing better than to let a money-making mouse tale languish, Bluth followed with "An American Tale: Fievel Goes West." **81m/C VHS, Beta, LV, Closed Caption. D:** Don Bluth; **M:** James Horner; **V:** Dom DeLuise, Madeline Kahn, Phillip Glasser, Christopher Plummer, Nehemiah Persoff, Will Ryan, John Finnegan, Cathianne Blore. Nominations: Academy Awards '86: Best Song ("Somewhere Out There"). *USH*

An American Tail: Fievel Goes West 🐾🐾 1991 (G)
Fievel and the Mousekewitz family continue their pursuit of the American dream by heading West, where the intrepid mouse seeks to become a famous lawman while his sister looks to make it big as a dance hall singer. The score is performed by the London Symphony Orchestra. Unfortunately released at the same time as "Beauty and the Beast," "Fievel Goes West" suffers from comparison. Worthwhile viewing for the whole family, but it won't ever reach the heights of "B&B." The laser edition is letterboxed and features chapter stops. **75m/C**

VHS, Beta, LV, Letterbox, Closed Caption. D: Phil Nibbelink, Simon Wells; **W:** Flint Dille; **M:** James Horner; **V:** John Cleese, Dom DeLuise, Phillip Glasser, Amy Irving, Jon Lovitz, Cathy Cavadini, Nehemiah Persoff, Erica Yohn, James Stewart. *USH*

American Tickler 🐾 Draws 1976 (R)
A thigh-slappin' (or is it head-whacking?) series of satirical pastiches in the grand style of "Kentucky Fried Movie," only more sophomoric. A tasteless collection of yearning to be funny sketches about American institutions. **77m/C VHS, Beta.** W.P. Dremak, Joan Sumner, Marlow Ferguson, Jeff Alin; **D:** Chuck Vincent. *GEM*

American Tiger 🐾🐾 American Rickshaw 1989 (R)
The collegiate hero of "American Tiger" is, like so many college students, framed for murder, and he applies himself to clearing his sullied name. Somewhere during this process, he finds himself in the middle of a battle between good and evil on a football field. About what you'd expect from a supernatural kung-fu teen-action drama. **CW:** Some language, violence, and sensuality. **93m/C VHS.** Mitch Gaylord, Donald Pleasence, Daniel Greene, Victoria Prouty; **D:** Martin Dolman.

An American Werewolf in London 🐾🐾🐾 1981 (R)
Strange, darkly humorous version of the classic man-into-wolf horror tale became a cult hit, but never clicked with most American critics. Two American college students (Naughton and Dunne) backpacking through England are viciously attacked by a werewolf one foggy night. Dunne is killed, but keeps appearing (in progressively decomposed form) before the seriously wounded Naughton, warning him of impending werewolfdom when the moon is full; Dunne advises suicide. Seat-jumping horror and gore, highlighted by intensive metamorphosis sequences orchestrated by Rick Baker, are offset by wry humor, though the shifts in tone don't always work. Great moon songs permeate the soundtrack, including CCR's "Bad Moon Rising" and Van Morrison's "Moondance." **97m/C VHS, Beta, LV.** David Naughton, Griffin Dunne, Jenny Agutter, Frank Oz, Brian Glover, Lila Kaye, David Schofield, John Woodvine, Don McKillop, Paul Kember, Colin Fernandes; **D:** John Landis; **W:** John Landis; **M:** Elmer Bernstein. Academy Awards '81: Best Makeup. *ART*

An American Werewolf in Paris 🐾🐾 1997 (R)
More of a remake than a sequel, horror-comedy fails to live up to the wit and quirkiness of the original. Andy (Scott) is on a daredevil tour of Europe along with buddies Brad (Vieluf) and Chris (Buckman). As he attempts to bungee jump off of the Eiffel Tower, he spots a French femme attempting to plunge jump nearby. He saves her and immediately falls in love with her. The girl, Serafine (Delpy) warns him to stay away, but he keeps sniffing around. They tail her to a creepy house she shares with a guy named Claude (Cosso), where Andy secures a date and his friends are invited to a dinner party. Claude, however, is top dog in a pack of racist werewolves, and Andy's pals end up as the main course. Bitten himself, Andy learns that he's now a werewolf. Brad and the other victims pop up now and again to remind Andy that they're doomed to walk the earth until the werewolves that killed them are destroyed. Special effects have advanced a long way since the original and it shows, although the computer generated wolves are difficult to tell apart. **CW:** Werewolf violence and gore, and for some sexuality/nudity. **100m/C VHS, LV, Closed Caption.** Julie Delpy, Tom Everett Scott, Julie Bowen, Pierre Cosso, Thierry Lhermitte, Vince Vieluf, Phil Buckman, Tom Novembre, Isabelle Constantini, Anthony Waller; **D:** Anthony Waller; **W:** Anthony Waller, Tim Burns, Tom Stern; **C:** Egon Werdin; **M:** Wilbert Hirsch. Nominations: MTV Movie Awards '98: Best Song ("Mouth"). *TOU*

American Yakuza 🐾🐾 1994 (R)
FBI agent Nick Davis (Mortensen) is sent to L.A. to infiltrate the American arm of the Yakuza, Japan's dangerous criminal underworld. He rises

through the ranks and is adopted into the powerful Tendo family. Now Davis finds himself caught between the FBI, the Yakuza, and the vengeful American mafia. **95m/C VHS, Closed Caption.** Viggo Mortensen, Michael Nouri; **D:** Frank Cappello; **W:** Max Strom, John Allen Nelson. *COL*

Americana 🐾🐾½ 1981 (PG)
A troubled Vietnam vet tries to restore himself by rebuilding a merry-go-round in a small midwestern town, while dealing with opposition from the local residents. Offbeat, often effective post-Nam editorial that was produced and directed in 1973 by Carradine and then shelved. Hershey and Carradine were a couple back then. **90m/C VHS, Beta.** David Carradine, Barbara Hershey, Michael Greene, John Blythe Barrymore Jr.; **D:** David Carradine; **W:** Richard Carr. *VES, ART*

The Americanization of Emily 🐾🐾🐾 1964
A happy-go-lucky American naval officer (Garner) with no appetite for war discovers to his horror that he may be slated to become the first casualty of the Normandy invasion as part of a military PR effort in this black comedy-romance. Meanwhile, he spreads the charisma in an effort to woo and uplift Emily (Andrews), a depressed English woman who has suffered the loss of her husband, father, and brother during the war. A cynical, often funny look at military maneuvers and cultural drift that was adapted by Paddy Chayefsky from William Bradford Huie's novel. Also available colorized. **117m/B VHS, LV, Letterbox.** James Garner, Julie Andrews, Melvyn Douglas, James Coburn, Joyce Grenfell, Keenan Wynn, Judy Carne, Liz Fraser, Edward Binns; **D:** Arthur Hiller; **W:** Paddy Chayefsky. Nominations: Academy Awards '64: Best Art Direction/Set Decoration (B & W), Best Black and White Cinematography. *MGM*

The Americano 🐾🐾½ 1917
Ever-suave Fairbanks frees a South American politician locked in a dungeon, returns him to political success, and captures the heart of his beautiful daughter. Based on Eugene P. Lyle, Jr.'s "Blaze Derringer." **58m/B VHS, Beta.** Douglas Fairbanks Sr., Alma Rubens, Spottiswoode Aitken, Lillian Langdon, Carl Stockdale, Tom Wilson; **D:** John Emerson. *GPV*

Americano 🐾🐾 1955
A cowboy travelling to Brazil with a shipment of Brahma bulls discovers the rancher he's delivering them to has been murdered. An odd amalgam of western cliches and a South American setting. **85m/C VHS.** Glenn Ford, Frank Lovejoy, Abbe Lane, Cesar Romero; **D:** William Castle. *REP*

The Americano/Variety 1925
The two silent classics in abridged form: "The Americano," (1917) about a soldier-of-fortune who aids a revolt-ridden Caribbean country, and "Variety," (1925) a classic German masterpiece about the career of a trapeze artist. **54m/B VHS, Beta.** Douglas Fairbanks Sr., Emil Jannings; **D:** John Emerson, E.A. Dupont. *CCB*

America's Deadliest Home Video 🐾🐾 1991
Camp spoof about America's obsession with videotaping everything in sight. Video enthusiast Doug is taken hostage by the Clint Dryer gang who want him to tape their crime spree. Every aspect is only seen through the lens of the video camera. **90m/C VHS.** Danny Bonaduce, Mick Wynhoff, Mollena Williams, Melora Walters; **D:** Jack Perez; **W:** Jack Perez. *FCT*

America's Dream 🐾🐾🐾 1995 (PG-13)
Trilogy of short stories covering black life from 1938 to 1958. In "Long Black Song," based on a short story by Richard Wright, Alabama farmer Silas (Glover) lives with lonely wife Sarah (Lifford), who succumbs to the charms of white travelling salesman, David (Donovan). "The Boy Who Painted Christ Black" is young Aaron (Golden), who gives the drawing to his teacher, Miss Williams (Calloway). But the portrait causes a great deal of controversy in Aaron's 1948 Georgia school, especially for ambitious principal George Du Vaul (Snipes). Based on a story by John Henrich Clarke. The last story is Maya Angelou's "The

Reunion," about Chicago jazz pianist Philomena (Toussaint), who encounters her childhood nemosis, Beth Ann (Thompson), the daughter of the white family who employed her parents as servants. **CW:** Scene of sexuality. **87m/C VHS.** Danny Glover, Tina Lifford, Tate Donovan, Dan Kamin, Wesley Snipes, Jasmine Guy, Vanessa Bell Calloway, Norman D. Golden II, Timothy Carhart, Yolanda King, Rae'ven Kelly, Lorraine Toussaint, Susanna Thompson, Carl Lumbly, Phyllis Cicero; **D:** Bill Duke, Kevin Rodney Sullivan, Paris Barclay; **W:** Ron Stacker Thompson, Ashley Tyler; **C:** Karl Herrmann; **M:** Patrice Rushen. *HBO*

Americathon woof! **1979 (PG)** It is the year 1998 and the United States is almost bankrupt, so President Chet Roosevelt decides to stage a telethon to keep the country from going broke. Interesting satiric premise with a diverse cast, but a poor script and slack pacing spoil all the fun. The soundtrack features music by The Beach Boys and Elvis Costello while the narration is by George Carlin. **85m/C VHS, Beta.** Peter Riegert, John Ritter, Nancy Morgan, Harvey Korman, Fred Willard, Meat Loaf, Elvis Costello, Chief Dan George, Howard Hesseman, Jay Leno; **Cameos:** Tommy Lasorda, Peter Marshall; **D:** Neal Israel; **W:** Monica Johnson; **M:** Earl Brown Jr. *ORI, WAR*

Amin: The Rise and Fall woof! **1982** Excessively violent and ultimately pointless dramatization of Idi Amin's eight-year reign of terror in Uganda, which resulted in the deaths of a half million people and the near ruin of a nation. **101m/C VHS, Beta.** Joseph Olita, Geoffrey Keen; **D:** Sharad Patel. *EMI*

Amistad ♦♦♦ **1997 (R)** Spielberg again creates an epic from another historic example of man's inhumanity, although not quite as effectively this time around. In 1839, African captives aboard the slaveship Amistad, led by a Mende tribesman named Cinque (Hounsou), free themselves and take over the ship in a bloody mutiny. Property attorney Robert Baldwin (McConaughey) must prove in lengthy court battles that the Africans were rightfully freed individuals in the eyes of the law. John Quincy Adams (Hopkins) presents the Africans' defense to the Supreme Court. Sequences depicting the horrors of slavery are bogged down with heavy handed musical orchestrations that elicit emotion, but at the price of storytelling. McConaughey seems a bit too Californian to be colonial and Morgan Freeman is reduced to periodic cameos as an abolitionist. Fortunately, thanks to an eye for rich detail and superb acting by dynamic newcomer Hounsou, the film nearly escapes the clutches of melodrama to emerge educational and moving. Film's release was marred by a French author accusing Spielberg and his Dreamworks studio of plagiarism. **CW:** Some scenes of strong brutal violence and some related nudity. **152m/C VHS.** Djimon Hounsou, Anthony Hopkins, Matthew McConaughey, Morgan Freeman, Nigel Hawthorne, David Paymer, Pete Postlethwaite, Stellan Skarsgard, Anna Paquin, Tomas Milian; **D:** Steven Spielberg; **W:** David Franzoni; **C:** Janusz Kaminski; **M:** John Williams. Broadcast Film Critics Association Awards '97: Best Supporting Actor (Hopkins); Nominations: Academy Awards '97: Best Cinematography, Best Costume Design, Best Supporting Actor (Hopkins), Best Original Score; Directors Guild of America Awards '97: Best Director (Spielberg); Golden Globe Awards '98: Best Actor (Hounsou), Best Director (Spielberg), Best Film—Drama, Best Supporting Actor (Hopkins); Screen Actors Guild Award '97: Best Supporting Actor (Hopkins). *USH*

The Amityville Horror ♦♦ **1979 (R)** Sometimes a house is not a home. Ineffective chiller that became a boxoffice biggie, based on a supposedly real-life occurrence in Amityville, Long Island. The Lutz family moves into the house of their dreams only to find it full of nightmares. Once the scene of a grisly mass murder, the house takes on a devilish attitude, plunging the family into supernatural terror. Pipes and walls ooze icky stuff, flies manifest in the strangest places, and doors mysteriously slam while exorcist Steiger staggers from room to room in scene-

chewing prayer. Based on the Jay Anson book and followed by a number of sequels. **117m/C VHS, Beta, LV.** James Brolin, Margot Kidder, Rod Steiger, Don Stroud, Murray Hamilton, Helen Shaver, Amy Wright, Val Avery; **D:** Stuart Rosenberg; **W:** Sandor Stern; **C:** Fred W. Koenekamp; **M:** Lalo Schifrin. Nominations: Academy Awards '79: Best Original Score. *WAR, OM*

Amityville 2: The Possession woof! **1982 (R)** More of a prequel than a sequel to "The Amityville Horror" (1979). Relates the story of the house's early years as a haven for demonic forces intent on driving a father to beat the kids, a mother to prayer, and a brother to lust after his sister (before he murders them all). Young etc. portray an obnoxious family that you're actually glad to see wasted by the possessed son. A stupid, clumsy attempt to cash in on the success of the first film, which was also stupid and clumsy but could at least claim novelty in the bad housing development genre. Followed by "Amityville 3: The Demon" in 1983. **110m/C VHS, Beta, LV.** James Olson, Burt Young, Andrew Prine, Moses Gunn, Rutanya Alda; **D:** Damiano Damiani; **W:** Tommy Lee Wallace; **C:** Franco Di Giacomo; **M:** Howard Blake.

Amityville 3: The Demon ♦½ *Amityville 3-D* **1983 (R)** America's worst real-estate value dupes another funky buyer. The infamous Amityville house is once again restless with terror and gore, though supported with even less plot than the usual smidgin. Cynical reporter Roberts moves in while trying to get to the bottom of the story by way of the basement. Courtesy of 3-D technology, monsters sprang at theatre patrons but the video version is strictly two-dimensional, forcing the viewer to press his or her face directly onto the television screen in order to derive similar effect. **98m/C VHS, Beta, LV.** Tony Roberts, Tess Harper, Robert Joy, Candy Clark, John Beal, Leora Dana, John Harkins, Lori Loughlin, Meg Ryan; **D:** Richard Fleischer; **W:** William Wales; **C:** Fred Schuler; **M:** Howard Blake. *VES, ART*

Amityville 4 ♦½ *The Amityville Horror: The Evil Escapes, Part 4* **1989 (R)** It's an unusual case of house-to-house transference as the horror from Amityville continues, now lodged in a Californian residence. The usual good house gone bad story has the place creating a lot of unusual creaks and rattles before deciding to use its inherited powers to attack and possess a little girl. Special effects from Richard Stutsman ("The Lost Boys" and "Jaws"). Made for television. **95m/C VHS.** Patty Duke, Jane Wyatt, Norman Lloyd, Frederic Lehne, Brandy Gold; **D:** Sandor Stern; **W:** Sandor Stern; **M:** Rick Conrad. *THV*

Amityville: A New Generation ♦½ **1993 (R)** And the bad sequels just go on and on and on. Terry is a young photographer who's given an old mirror by a crazy homeless man (tell me why he took it). He shares a loft with three friends and all begin experiencing vivid and terrifying dreams of murder. Seems the mirror is tied to Amityville and its evil legacy and Terry is the designated inheritor. **92m/C VHS, LV, Closed Caption.** Ross Partridge, Julia Nickson-Soul, David Naughton, Richard Roundtree, Terry O'Quinn; **D:** John Murlowski; **W:** Christopher DeFaria, Antonio Toro. *REP*

The Amityville Curse woof! **1990 (R)** The possessed house is yet again purchased by a pathetically uninformed family. The usual ghostly shenanigans occur with low-budget regularity in this fifth film in the series. Never released theatrically, for good reason. **91m/C VHS, LV.** CA Kim Coates, Dawna Wightman, Helen Hughes, David Stein, Cassandra Gava, Jan Rubes; **D:** Tom Berry; **W:** Michael Krueger, Norvell Rose. *VTR, THV*

Amityville Dollhouse ♦½ **1996 (R)** Family moves into their Victorian dream home in Amityville, which comes complete with a replica dollhouse that charms the daughter. But the Amityville curse inhabits the plaything and soon the poltergeists make their nasty appearance. **CW:** Horror violence, sensuality, and some language. **97m/C VHS, Closed Caption.** Robin Thomas, Starr Andreeff,

Allen Cutler, Rachel Duncan, Jarrett Lennon, Clayton Murray, Frank Ross, Lenora Kardorf, Lisa Robin Kelly; **D:** Steve White; **W:** Joshua Michael Stern. *REP*

Amityville 1992: It's About Time ♦♦ **1992 (R)** Time is of the essence in the sixth installment of the Amityville flicks. A vintage clock (from Amityville, of course), causes creepy goings-on in a family's house. Actually a halfway decent horror film with high-grade special effects, and much, much better than previous Amityville sequels, which isn't saying much. **CW:** Language, horror violence, and sensuality. **95m/C VHS, LV, Closed Caption.** Stephen Macht, Shawn Weatherly, Megan Ward, Damon Martin, Nita Talbot, Dick Miller; **D:** Tony Randel; **W:** Christopher DeFaria, Antonio Toro. *REP*

Amnesia ♦♦ **1996 (R)** Minister Paul Keller (Walker) is having an affair with his son's teacher, Veronica Dow (Tomanovich). Paul decides to fake his death, leaving wife Martha (Sheedy) with the insurance money, and allowing him to start a new life with Veronica. Only he has an accident that causes amnesia and runs into more trouble than he can imagine. Has more humor thank you might imagine, thanks to its wacky characters but as usual Kirkland is way over the top as a love-starved motel owner. **CW:** Sexual situations, violence, strong language. **92m/C VHS.** Nicholas Walker, Ally Sheedy, Sally Kirkland, John Savage, Dara Tomanovich, Vincent Berry; **D:** Kurt Voss. *PEG*

Among the Cinders ♦♦ **1983** Sometimes interesting coming of age drama about a 16-year-old New Zealand boy who runs away to his grandfather's farm to forget about his friend's accidental death. At the farm, he meets an older woman and compromises his virtue. **103m/C VHS, Beta, LV.** GE NZ Paul O'Shea, Derek Hardwick, Rebecca Gibney, Yvonne Lawley, Amanda Jones; **D:** Rolf Haedrich. *VTR*

Amongst Friends ♦♦ **1993 (R)** Three boyhood buddies, Trevor (McGaw), Billy (Lindsey), and Andy (Parlavecchio), from a nice Long Island neighborhood turn to crime out of boredom. Trevor gets busted and goes to prison for two years. Upon getting out, he finds his old cronies still share the taste for crime and general aimlessness but also still want that one big score. Trevor finally agrees to join Andy and Billy in a drug deal but the jealous Billy, who wants Trevor's old girlfriend Laura (Sorvino), plans a double-cross that will affect them all. Filled with cutting attacks on the society that spawns aimless youth. Debut of then 26-year-old writer/director Weiss. **CW:** Pervasive strong language, violence and drug use, and sexuality. **88m/C VHS, LV, Closed Caption.** Patrick McGaw, Steve Parlavecchio, Joseph Lindsey, Mira Sorvino, David Stepkin, Michael Artura; **D:** Rob Weiss; **W:** Rob Weiss; **C:** Michael Bonvillain; **M:** Mick Jones. *COL*

Amor Bandido ♦♦½ **1979** When cab drivers in Rio are turning up dead, a young prostitute is torn between her detective father and her prime suspect boyfriend. Drama based on a true story. In Portuguese with English subtitles. **95m/C VHS, LV.** BR Paulo Gracindo, Cristina Ache, Paulo Guarniero; **D:** Bruno Barreto. *FXL, IME, FCT*

Amore ♦♦♦ **1948** Rossellini's tribute to actress Magnani consists of the short films "The Human Voice" and "The Miracle." In "The Human Voice," Magnani is shown alone, speaking to her lover on the telephone. Based on Jean Cocteau's one-act drama. In "The Miracle," she is a simple peasant girl who believes her illegitimate child is acutally the new Messiah. In Italian with English subtitles. **78m/B VHS.** IT Anna Magnani; **D:** Roberto Rossellini. *FCT, CVC*

Amore! ♦♦½ **1993 (PG-13)** Wealthy investment banker Saul Schwartz (Scalia) hates his job, his wife, and his life. The only way he loses himself is by watching movies starring Italian matinee idol Rudolfo Carbonera (Hamilton). So Saul gets divorced and decides to change his life—by going to Hollywood and becoming an actor like his debonair idol. With the help of some newfound friends he transforms himself into suave leading man material (under the name of Salvatore Guiliano III) but promptly winds up falling for a writer (Ireland), who couldn't care less. *CW:* Sex-related scenes and dialogue. **93m/C VHS, LV, Closed Caption.** Jack Scalia, Kathy Ireland, Elliott Gould, George Hamilton, Brenda Epperson, James Doohan, Katherine Helmond, Betsy Russell, Norm Crosby, Frank Gorshin; *D:* Lorenzo Doumani; *W:* Lorenzo Doumani. *PMH*

The Amorous Adventures of Moll Flanders 🐾🐾 **1965** An amusing romp set in 18th century England focusing on a poor orphan girl who seeks wealth. Moll plots to get ahead through an advantageous series of romances and màrriages. Her plan is ruined when she falls in love and he turns out to be a wanted highwayman, landing her in prison. Not surprisingly, love (and money) conquers all. Based on the novel by Daniel Defoe. Novak tries in this female derivative of "Tom Jones," but this period piece isn't her style. **126m/C VHS.** Kim Novak, Richard Johnson, Angela Lansbury, Vittorio De Sica, Leo McKern, George Sanders, Lilli Palmer; *D:* Terence Young; *C:* Ted Moore; *M:* John Addison. *PAR*

Amos 🐾🐾½ **1985** Douglas is Amos, an aging baseball coach confined most reluctantly to a nursing home. He's disturbed by recent suspicious events there, his concern causing him to take on Montgomery, the staunch head nurse. Well-acted drama produced by Douglas's son Peter, offering an echo of "One Flew Over the Cuckoo's Nest," which Dad starred in on Broadway and son Michael helped produced as a movie classic. **100m/C VHS.** Kirk Douglas, Elizabeth Montgomery, Dorothy McGuire, Noriyuki "Pat" Morita, James Sloyan, Ray Walston; *D:* Michael Tuchner; *M:* Georges Delerue. *NO*

Amos and Andrew 🐾½ **1993 (PG-13)** Embarrassing attempt at comedy stops short of endorsing the stereotypes it tries to parody. Prizewinning African-American author Andrew Sterling (Jackson) is seen moving into a house on an island previously reserved for the uptight white, and the neighbors call the cops, assuming he's a thief. Chief of police (Coleman) eagerly gets into the act, then exploits drifter Amos (Cage) in a cover-up attempt when he realizes his mistake. Talented cast can't overcome lame jokes and transparent plot that serves as an opportunity to bring black and white together for a "see how much we have in common" bonding session. *CW:* Some language, drug content; mock violence, and sexual reference. **96m/C VHS, LV, Closed Caption.** Nicolas Cage, Samuel L. Jackson, Michael Lerner, Margaret Colin, Giancarlo Esposito, Dabney Coleman, Bob Balaban, Aimee Graham, Brad Dourif, Chelcie Ross, Jodi Long; *D:* E. Max Frye; *W:* E. Max Frye; *M:* Richard Gibbs. *COL, IME, NLC*

The Amphibian Man 🐾🐾 **1961** What does a scientist do once he's created a young man with gills? Plunge him in the real world of aqua pura to experience life and love, albeit underwater. Trouble is, the protagonist, who's come to be known as the Sea Devil, takes a dive for a young pretty he's snatched from the jaws of death. A '60s Soviet sci-fi romance originally seen on American television. **96m/C VHS.** *RU* K. Korieniev, M. Virzinskaya; *D:* Y. Kasancki. *SNC*

The Amsterdam Connection 🐾 **197?** Film company acts as a cover for prostitution and drug smuggling, with the girls acting as international couriers. **90m/C VHS, Beta.** *HK* Chen Shing, Kid Sherrif, Yeung Sze, Jason Pai Piu, Fang Mui San; *D:* Fang Mui San, Lo Ke. *NO*

The Amsterdam Kill 🐾🐾 **1978 (R)** A washed-up ex-agent of the U.S. Drug Enforcement Agency is hired by a desperate U.S. Drug Enforcement Agency to hunt down the kingpin of a narcotics syndicate in Hong Kong. Tedious pace with occasional spells of violence fails to awaken somnambulent Mitchum. Shot on location in Hong Kong. **93m/C VHS, Beta, LV.** *HK* Robert Mitc-

hum, Richard Egan, Keye Luke, Leslie Nielsen, Bradford Dillman; *D:* Robert Clouse; *W:* Robert Clouse. *GKK*

Amsterdamned 🐾🐾 **1988 (R)** A crime thriller taking place on the canals of Amsterdam featuring a serial skindiver killer who surfaces periodically to slash and splash. A steely detective fishes for clues. Dubbed. **114m/C VHS, Beta, LV, Letterbox.** *NL* Monique Van De Ven, Huub Stapel; *D:* Dick Maas. *VES, ART*

Amy 🐾🐾½ **1981 (G)** Set in the early 1900s, the story follows the experiences of a woman after she leaves her well-to-do husband to teach at a school for the deaf and blind. Eventually she organizes a football game between the handicapped kids and the other children in the neighborhood. Good Disney family fare. **100m/C VHS, Beta.** Jenny Agutter, Barry Newman, Kathleen Nolan, Margaret O'Brien, Nanette Fabray, Chris Robinson, Lou Fant; *D:* Vincent McEveety; *M:* Robert F. Brunner. *DIS*

The Amy Fisher Story 🐾🐾 **1993** Amy Fisher wishes she looked this good. Perhaps if she did, she could be acting in made-for-television movies like Barrymore instead of providing fodder for them. The ABC account draws from a variety of sources to dramatize the relationship between Amy and her married, ahem, friend, and Amy's subsequent attack on his wife. Although it tries not to take sides, it does include some pretty hot sex scenes which may be why this docudrama garnered the highest ratings of the three network productions released on TV. See also: "Casualties of Love: The 'Long Island Lolita' Story" and "Lethal Lolita—Amy Fisher: My Story." **96m/C VHS.** Drew Barrymore, Anthony John Denison, Harley Jane Kozak, Tom Mason, Laurie Paton, Ken Pogue, Linda Darlow; *D:* Andy Tennant; *W:* Janet Brownell.

Anaconda 🐾🐾½ **1996 (PG-13)** Snakes—lots and lots of snakes. Teeny baby snakes, little snakes, medium-sized snakes, large snakes, and one gigantic 40-foot long snake that likes to swallow people and then vomit them up again (the better to have room to swallow somebody else). Oh yeah, the minimal plot concerns a documentary film crew traveling the Amazon River looking for a legendary Indian tribe. They not only have to contend with the snakes but with crazy, snake-obsessed guide Paul Sarone (Voight). The actors react appropriately to becoming snake food. *CW:* Intense adventure violence, and for brief language and sensuality. **90m/C VHS, LV, Closed Caption.** Jon Voight, Jennifer Lopez, Ice Cube, Eric Stoltz, Owen C. Wilson, Kari Wuhrer, Jonathan Hyde, Vincent Castellanos; *D:* Luis Llosa; *W:* Jim Cash, Jack Epps Jr., Hans Bauer; *C:* Bill Butler; *M:* Randy Edelman. Nominations: Golden Raspberry Awards '97: Worst Picture, Worst Actor (Voight), Worst Director (Llosa), Worst Screenplay. *COL*

Anastasia 🐾🐾🐾½ **1956** Bergman won her second Oscar, and deservedly so, for her classic portrayal of the amnesia victim chosen by Russian expatriate Brynner to impersonate Anastasia, the last surviving member of the Romanoff dynasty. As such, she becomes part of a scam to collect millions of rubles deposited in a foreign bank by her supposed father, the now-dead Czar. But is she just impersonating the princess? Brynner as the scheming White General and Hayes as the Grand Duchess who needs to be convinced turn in fine performances as well. Based on Marcelle Maurette's play. **105m/C VHS, LV, Letterbox.** Ingrid Bergman, Yul Brynner, Helen Hayes, Akim Tamiroff; *D:* Anatole Litvak; *W:* Arthur Laurents; *C:* Jack Hildyard. Academy Awards '56: Best Actress (Bergman); Golden Globe Awards '57: Best Actress—Drama (Bergman); New York Film Critics Awards '56: Best Actress (Bergman); Nominations: Academy Awards '56: Best Original Dramatic/Comedy Score. *FXL*

Anastasia 🐾🐾½ **1997 (G)** Let's face it, this is a pretty weird story to turn into a cartoon fairy tale. Fox's first entry into the Disney-dominated full-length animated musical fray is the story of Princess Anastasia and the fall of the Romanov empire. She has been missing ever since the evil Rasputin put a curse on the Romanov family and started the Russian Revolution (Lenin must have

flunked the screen test. Not "toon" enough). Ten years later, con artist Dimitri and ex-aristocrat Vladimir try to convince orphaned 18-year-old Anya that she's the ex-royal so they can claim a reward from the princess' grandmother. Little do they know that she actually is the lost princess, but they must battle Rasputin and his albino bat henchman to put things right. Among the big names lending their voices are Meg Ryan, John Cusack (Cossack?) and Christopher Lloyd. Now let me tell you how the Katzenjammer Kids started World War II... **90m/C VHS.** *D:* Don Bluth, Gary Goldman; *W:* Bruce Graham, Susan Guathier, Bob Tzudiker, Noni White; *M:* David Newman; *V:* Meg Ryan, John Cusack, Kelsey Grammer, Angela Lansbury, Christopher Lloyd, Hank Azaria, Bernadette Peters, Kirsten Dunst, Liz Callaway, Jim Cummings, Lacey Chabert. Nominations: Academy Awards '97: Best Song ("Journey to the Past"), Best Original Musical/Comedy Score; Golden Globe Awards '98: Best Song ("Journey to the Past"), Best Song ("Once Upon a December"). *FXV*

Anastasia: The Mystery of Anna 🐾🐾½ **1986** Irving stars as Anna Anderson, a woman who claimed to be the Grand Duchess Anastasia, the sole surviving daughter of Russian Czar Nicholas II. A powerful epic reliving her experience of royalty, flight from execution, and struggle to retain her heritage. The story of Anastasia remains as one of the greatest dramatic mysteries of the 20th century. Adapted from the book "Anastasia: The Riddle of Anna Anderson" by Peter Kurth; originally broadcast on cable television. **190m/C VHS, LV.** Amy Irving, Olivia de Havilland, Jan Niklas, Nicolas Surovy, Susan Lucci, Elke Sommer, Edward Fox, Claire Bloom, Omar Sharif, Rex Harrison; *D:* Marvin J. Chomsky; *W:* James Goldman. *CAF, PBS, FUS*

Anatomy of a Murder 🐾🐾🐾🐾 **1959** Considered by many to be the best courtroom drama ever made. Small-town lawyer in northern Michigan faces an explosive case as he defends an army officer who has killed a man he suspects was his philandering wife's rapist. Realistic, cynical portrayal of the court system isn't especially concerned with guilt or innocence, focusing instead on the interplay between the various courtroom characters. Classic performance by Stewart as the down home but brilliant defense lawyer who matches wits with Scott, the sophisticated prosecutor; terse and clever direction by Preminger. Though tame by today's standards, the language used in the courtroom was controversial. Filmed in upper Michigan; based on the bestseller by judge Robert Traver. **161m/B VHS, Beta, LV.** James Stewart, George C. Scott, Arthur O'Connell, Ben Gazzara, Lee Remick, Eve Arden, Orson Bean, Kathryn Grant, Murray Hamilton, Joseph Welch; *Cameos:* Duke Ellington; *D:* Otto Preminger; *W:* Wendell Mayes; *C:* Sam Leavitt; *M:* Duke Ellington. New York Film Critics Awards '59: Best Actor (Stewart), Best Screenplay; Nominations: Academy Awards '59: Best Actor (Stewart), Best Adapted Screenplay, Best Black and White Cinematography, Best Film Editing, Best Picture, Best Supporting Actor (O'Connell, Scott). *COL*

Anatomy of a Psycho 🐾 **1961** A man plans to avenge his gas chambered brother by committing mass murder. Very cheaply and poorly produced. **75m/B VHS, Beta.** Ronnie Burns, Pamela Lincoln, Darrell Howe, Russ Bender; *D:* Brooke L. Peters. *SNC*

Anatomy of a Seduction 🐾🐾 **1979** Television formula melodrama of a middle-aged divorcee's affair with her son's best friend. Age knows no boundaries when it comes to television lust. **100m/C VHS, 8mm.** Susan Flannery, Jameson Parker, Rita Moreno, Ed Nelson, Michael Le Clair; *D:* Steven Hilliard Stern; *M:* Hagood Hardy. *HBO*

Anatomy of Terror 🐾 **1974** A made for television drama about an army vet going bonkers (what? really?) and revealing espionage secrets in his home life. **73m/C VHS, Beta.** Paul Burke, Polly Bergen, Dinsdale Landen, Basil Henson. *ART*

Anchors Aweigh 🎦🎦🎦 1945 Snappy big-budget (for then) musical about two horny sailors, one a girl-happy dancer and the other a shy singer. While on leave in Hollywood they return a lost urchin to his sister. The four of them try to infiltrate a movie studio to win an audition for the girl from maestro Iturbi. Kelly's famous dance with Jerry the cartoon Mouse (of "Tom and Jerry" fame) is the second instance of combining live action and animation. The young and handsome Sinatra's easy crooning and Grayson's near operatic soprano are blessed with music and lyrics by Styne and Cahn. Lots of fun, with conductor-pianist Iturbi contributing and Hollywood-style Little Mexico also in the brew. ♫We Hate to Leave; I Fall in Love Too Easily; The Charm of You; The Worry Song; Jalousie; All of a Sudden My Heart Sings; I Begged Her; What Makes the Sun Set?; Waltz Serenade. **139m/C VHS, Beta, LV, Closed Caption.** Frank Sinatra, Gene Kelly, Kathryn Grayson, Jose Iturbi, Sharon McManus, Dean Stockwell, Carlos Ramirez, Pamela Britton; **D:** George Sidney; **M:** Jule Styne, Sammy Cahn. Academy Awards '45: Scoring of a Musical; Nominations: Academy Awards '45: Best Actor (Kelly), Best Color Cinematography, Best Picture, Best Song ("I Fall in Love Too Easily"). *MGM*

And a Nightingale Sang 🎦🎦½ 1991 WWII England is the scene of this sweet romance, a sad and humorous tale of a woman who gives everything for the war effort. Stunning recreation of the final days of the Blitzkreig. Originally produced for Masterpiece Theatre. **90m/C VHS, Closed Caption.** Joan Plowright, Tom Watt, Phyllis Logan, John Woodvine. *PBS, FUS, VIF*

And Baby Makes Six 🎦🎦½ 1979 An unexpected pregnancy creates new challenges for a couple with grown children. Dewhurst is excellent as usual. Made for television. Followed by "Baby Comes Home." **100m/C VHS, 8mm.** Colleen Dewhurst, Warren Oates, Maggie Cooper, Mildred Dunnock, Timothy Hutton, Allyn Ann McLerie; **D:** Waris Hussein; **W:** Shelley List. *NO*

And God Created Woman 🎦🎦½ And Woman...Was Created; Et Dieu Crea la Femme 1957 (PG) Launching pad for Bardot's career as a sex siren, as she flits across the screen in a succession of scanty outfits and hangs out at the St. Tropez beach in what is euphemistically known as a swimsuit while turning up the heat for the males always in attendance. The plot concerns an 18-year-old nymphomaniac who is given a home by a local family with three handsome young sons. A cutting-edge sex film in its time that was boffo at the boxoffice. In French with English subtitles. **93m/C VHS, Beta.** *FR* Brigitte Bardot, Curt Jurgens, Jean-Louis Trintignant, Christian Marquand; **D:** Roger Vadim; **W:** Roger Vadim. *NO*

And God Created Woman 🎦½ 1988 (R) Loose, dull remake by Vadim of his own 1957 softcore favorite about a free-spirited woman dodging men and the law while yearning for rock and roll stardom. DeMornay is a prisoner who hopes to marry one of the local hunks (Spano) so she can be paroled. They marry, she strips, he frets, while political hopeful Langella smacks his lips in anticipation. Available in an unrated 100-minute version. **98m/C VHS, Beta, LV.** Rebecca DeMornay, Vincent Spano, Frank Langella, Donovan Leitch, Judith Chapman, Thelma Houston; **D:** Roger Vadim; **M:** Tom Chase, Steve Rucker. *VES, ART*

And God Said to Cain 🎦 196? Another Biblically titled western from the prolific Kinski, about a put-upon gunman who must fight for his life. **95m/C VHS, Beta.** Klaus Kinski. *UNI, CNG*

...And God Spoke 🎦🎦 1994 (R) Low budget spoof takes on both religion and moviemaking with two schlockmeisters filming a biblical epic. Since the duo have no budget and are basic hacks with pretensions, they have to settle...so Sales plays Moses, "The Incredible Hulk" Ferrigno gets cast as Cain, while Plumb ("Jan" on "The Brady Bunch") does Mrs. Noah. Has some lulls but also covers very recognizable territory. Directorial debut of Borman. **CW:** Language. **82m/C VHS.** Michael Riley, Stephen Rappaport, Soupy Sales, Lou Ferrigno, Eve Plumb, Andy Dick, R.C. Bates, Fred Kaz, Daniel Tisman; **D:** Arthur Borman; **W:** Gregory S. Malins, Michael Curtis. *WEA*

And Hope to Die 🎦🎦½ 1972 Moody, muddled crime drama with a good cast about a fleeing Frenchman who joins a gang of hardened criminals in Canada. They go ahead with their plans to kidnap a retarded girl even though she is already dead. Standard caper film is enhanced by arty camera work and some unusual directorial touches. **95m/C VHS, Beta.** *FR* Robert Ryan, Jean-Louis Trintignant, Aldo Ray, Tisa Farrow; **D:** Rene Clement. *NO*

And I Alone Survived 🎦🎦 1978 Made-for-television adaptation of the true story of a woman who survives a leisure-plane crash in the Sierra Nevadas and her struggle to get to the village below. Brown does her best to elevate the proceedings above the usual I-hope-I-don't-die cliches. **90m/C VHS, Beta.** Blair Brown, David Ackroyd, Vera Miles, G.D. Spradlin; **D:** William A. Graham; **C:** Jordan Cronenweth.

And Justice for All 🎦🎦½ 1979 (R) Earnest attorney Pacino questions the law and battles for justice in and out of the courtroom. He's hired to defend a detested judge in a rape charge, while dealing with a lost-soul caseload of eccentric and tragedy-prone clients. Overly melodramatic, an odd mix of satire, cynicism, and seemingly sincere drama that hits with a club when a stick will do. Jewison aims for black surrealism, permitting both Pacino and Warden (as a judge losing his sanity) to veer into histrionics, to the detriment of what is essentially a gripping behind-the-scenes story. Excellent cast creates sparks, including Lahti in her film debut. And Baltimore never looked lovelier. **120m/C VHS, Beta, LV, 8mm.** Al Pacino, Jack Warden, Christine Lahti, Thomas G. Waites, Craig T. Nelson, John Forsythe, Lee Strasberg; **D:** Norman Jewison; **W:** Barry Levinson, Valerie Curtin; **M:** Dave Grusin. Nominations: Academy Awards '79: Best Actor (Pacino), Best Original Screenplay. *COL*

And Nothing But the Truth 🎦🎦½ Giro City 1982 A multinational corporation is out to ruin the investigative television report team trying to do a story on the company. **90m/C VHS, Beta.** *GB* Glenda Jackson, Jon Finch, Kenneth Colley, James Donnelly; **D:** Karl Francis. *NO*

And Now for Something Completely Different 🎦🎦🎦 1972 (PG) A compilation of skits from BBC-television's "Monty Python's Flying Circus" featuring Monty Python's own weird, hilarious brand of humor. Sketches include "The Upper Class Twit of the Year Race," "Hell's Grannies" and "The Townswomen's Guild Reconstruction of Pearl Harbour." A great introduction to Python for the uninitiated, or a chance for the converted to see their favorite sketches again. **89m/C VHS, Beta, LV.** *GB* John Cleese, Michael Palin, Eric Idle, Graham Chapman, Terry Gilliam, Terry Jones; **D:** Ian McNaughton; **W:** John Cleese, Michael Palin, Graham Chapman, Terry Gilliam, Terry Jones. *COL, TVC*

And Now Miguel 🎦🎦 1966 Plodding tale of a young boy who wants to take over as head shepherd for his family's flock. Filmed in New Mexico, but the over-long outdoor shots make it drag a bit in spite of Cardi's competent performance. **95m/C VHS.** Pat Cardi, Michael Ansara, Guy Stockwell, Clu Gulager, Joe De Santis, Pilar Del Rey, Buck Taylor; **D:** James B. Clark. *NOS*

And Now My Love 🎦🎦½ 1974 (PG) A French couple endeavor to maintain their romance despite interfering socio-economic factors—she's a millionaire and he's an ex-con filmmaker. Keller plays three roles spanning three generations, as Lelouch invests autobiographical details to invent a highly stylized, openly sentimental view of French folks in love with love. Along the way he comments on social mores and changing attitudes through the years. Dubbed in English. **121m/C VHS, Beta.** *FR* Marthe Keller, Andre Dussollier, Carla Gravina; **D:** Claude Lelouch; **W:** Claude Lelouch. Los Angeles Film Critics Association Awards '75: Best Foreign Film; Nominations: Academy Awards '75: Best Original Screenplay. *COL*

And Now the Screaming Starts 🎦🎦½ Bride of Fengriffen; Fengriffen; I Have No Mouth But I Must Scream 1973 (R) The young bride-to-be of the lord of a British manor house is greeted by bloody faces at the window, a severed hand, and five corpses. Then Cushing shows up to investigate. Good-looking, sleek production with genuine chills. **87m/C VHS, Beta.** *GB* Peter Cushing, Herbert Lom, Patrick Magee, Ian Ogilvy, Stephanie Beacham, Geoffrey Whitehead, Guy Rolfe, Rosalie Crutchley, Gillian Lind, Janet Key; **D:** Roy Ward Baker; **W:** Roger Marshall; **C:** Denys Coop.

And Soon the Darkness 🎦🎦 1970 (PG) One of two vacationing young nurses disappears in France where a teenager was once murdered and the search is on. Predictable, ineffective suspenser. **94m/C VHS, Beta.** *GB* Pamela Franklin, Michele Dotrice, Sandor Eles, John Nettleton, Claire Kelly, Hanna-Marie Pravda; **D:** Robert Fuest; **W:** Brian Clemens. *NO*

And the Band Played On 🎦🎦🎦 1993 (PG-13) Randy Shilts' monumental, and controversial, 1987 book on the AIDS epidemic comes to television in an equally controversial made for cable movie. Details the intricate medical research undertaken by doctors in France and the U.S. who fought to isolate and identify the mystery virus despite governmental neglect, red tape, clashing egos, and lack of funding. Various aspects of gay life are shown objectively, without sensationalizing. Celebrity cameos are somewhat distracting though most acquit themselves well. The script went through numerous rewrites; director Spottiswoode reportedly objected to HBO interference at the editing stage. **CW:** Subject matter. **140m/C VHS, LV, Closed Caption.** Matthew Modine, Alan Alda, Ian McKellen, Lily Tomlin, Glenne Headly, Richard Masur, Saul Rubinek, Charles Martin Smith, Patrick Bauchau, Nathalie Baye, Christian Clemenson; **Cameos:** Richard Gere, David Clennon, Phil Collins, Alex Courtney, David Dukes, David Marshall Grant, Ronald Guttman, Anjelica Huston, Ken Jenkins, Richard Jenkins, Tcheky Karyo, Swoosie Kurtz, Jack Laufer, Steve Martin, Dakin Matthews, Peter McRobbie, Lawrence Monoson, B.D. Wong, Donal Logue, Jeffrey Nordling, Stephen Spinella; **D:** Roger Spottiswoode; **W:** Arnold Schulman; **C:** Paul Elliott; **M:** Carter Burwell. *HBO*

And the Children Shall Lead 1985 A young black girl is moved by the coming of the civil rights movement to her small Mississippi town. Part of the "Wonderworks" series. **60m/C VHS.** Danny Glover, LeVar Burton, Pam Potillo, Denise Nicholas, Andrew Prine; **D:** Michael Pressman. *PTB, HMV, FCT*

... And the Earth Did Not Swallow Him 🎦🎦½ ...Y No Se Lo Trago La Tierra 1994 Family trials of migrant farm workers from the perspective of 12-year-old Marcos, who travels with his parents on their annual (it's 1952) move from Texas throughout the midwest during harvest season. Balances their struggles with the strong family bonds that allow them to endure. Based on the semi-autobiographical novel by Tomas Rivera. **99m/C VHS.** Jose Alcala, Rose Portillo, Marco Rodriguez; **D:** Severo Perez; **W:** Severo Perez; **C:** Virgil Harper; **M:** Marcos Loya. *KIV, FCT*

And the Ship Sails On 🎦🎦🎦 El la Nave Va 1983 (PG) On the eve of WWI, a group of devoted opera lovers take a luxury cruise to pay their respects to a recently deceased opera diva. Also on board is a group of fleeing Serbo-Croation freedom fighters. A charming and absurd autumnal homage-to-life by Fellini shot entirely in the studio. **130m/C VHS, Beta, LV.** *IT* Freddie Jones, Barbara Jefford, Janet Suzman, Peter Cellier; **D:** Federico Fellini; **W:** Federico Fellini, Tonino Guerra. *COL*

And Then There Were None 🎬🎬🎬½ **1945** An all-star cast makes up the ten colorful guests invited to a secluded estate in England by a mysterious host. What the invitations do not say, however, is the reason they have been specifically chosen to visit—to be murdered, one by one. Cat and mouse classic based on Agatha Christie's book with an entertaining mix of suspense and black comedy. Remade in 1966 and again in 1975 as "Ten Little Indians," but lacking the force and gloss of the original. **97m/B VHS, LV.** Louis Hayward, Barry Fitzgerald, Walter Huston, Roland Young, Sir C. Aubrey Smith, Judith Anderson, Mischa Auer, June Duprez; **D:** Rene Clair. *EEL, VCI, TPV*

And Then You Die 🎬🎬🎬 **1988 (R)** An intense crime drama about a Canadian drug lord who amasses a fortune from the cocaine and marijuana trade. His empire is threatened as the Mafia, Hell's Angels, and the police try to bring him down. **115m/C VHS, Beta.** *CA* Kenneth Welsh, R.H. Thomson, Wayne Robson, Tom Harvey, George Bloomfield, Graeme Campbell; **D:** Francis Mankiewicz. *THV*

And You Thought Your Parents Were Weird! 🎬🎬½ **1991 (PG)** A pair of introverted, whiz kid brothers invent a lovable robot to provide fatherly guidance as well as companionship for their widowed mother. Surprisingly charming, sentimental film is only slightly hampered by low-budget special effects. **92m/C VHS, Closed Caption.** Marcia Strassman, Joshua Miller, Edan Gross, John Quade, Sam Behrens, Susan Gibney, Gustav Vintas, Eric Walker; **D:** Tony Cookson; **W:** Tony Cookson; **C:** Paul Elliott; **M:** Randy Miller; **V:** Alan Thicke, Richard Libertini. *THV*

The Anderson Tapes 🎬🎬🎬 **1971 (PG)** Newly released from prison, an ex-con assembles his professional pals and plans the million-dollar robbery of an entire luxury apartment house on NYC's upper east side. Of course, he's unaware that a hoard of law men from federal, state, and local agencies are recording their activities for a wide variety of reasons, though none of the surveillance is coordinated and it has nothing to do with the planned robbery. Based on the novel by Lawrence Sanders, the intricate caper is effectively shaped by Lumet, who skillfully integrates broad satire with suspense. Shot on location in New York City. Walken is The Kid, his first major role. **100m/C VHS, Beta, LV.** Sean Connery, Dyan Cannon, Martin Balsam, Christopher Walken, Alan King, Ralph Meeker, Garrett Morris, Margaret Hamilton; **D:** Sidney Lumet; **W:** Frank Pierson; **M:** Quincy Jones. *GKK, COL*

Andersonville 🎬🎬🎬 **1995** Andersonville was an infamous Confederate prison camp in Georgia that by August, 1864 contained more than 32,000 Union POWs—and was planned to hold 8,000 men. One in four soldiers died in the camp. The story is told through the eyes of Massachusetts Corporal Josiah Day (Emick), who is captured in 1864 and struggles to survive the hellish conditions. The commander of the Andersonville was a deranged German-Swiss captain named Wirz (Triska)—who became the only Civil War soldier to be hanged for war crimes (depicted in "The Andersonville Trial"). The TV miniseries was filmed some 150 miles from the original site. **168m/C VHS.** Jarrod Emick, Frederic Forrest, Ted Marcoux, Jan Triska, Cliff DeYoung, Tom Aldredge, Frederick Coffin, Justin Henry, Kris Kamm, William H. Macy, Gabriel Olds, William Sanderson, Natalie Radford, Carmen Argenziano, Peter Murnik; **D:** John Frankenheimer; **W:** David W. Rintels; **C:** Ric Waite; **M:** Gary Chang. *FCT, TTC*

The Andersonville Trial 🎬🎬🎬½ **1970** Details the atrocities experienced by captured Union soldiers who were held in the Confederacy's notorious Andersonville prison during the American Civil War. Provides an interesting account of the war-crimes trial of the Georgia camp's officials, under whom more than 14,000 prisoners died. Moving, remarkable television drama based on the Pulitzer-honored book by MacKinlay Kantor. **150m/C VHS, Beta, LV.** Martin Sheen, William Shatner, Buddy Ebsen, Jack Cassidy, Richard Basehart, Cameron Mitchell; **D:** George C. Scott. *ART*

Andre 🎬🎬½ **1994 (PG)** More human-animal interaction from the director of "The Man from Snowy River," telling the true story of an orphaned seal that was adopted by the local Maine harbormaster (Carradine) and his family. As they raise their houseguest, the question arises whether Andre should be returned to the wild. It'll remind you of "Free Willy" with an appealing smaller sea mammal and the equally appealing Majorino, as the youngster who befriends Andre. For those who are sticklers for accuracy, Andre is actually portrayed by a sea lion and not a seal. **94m/C VHS, Beta, Closed Caption.** Keith Carradine, Tina Majorino, Chelsea Field, Keith Szarabajka, Shane Meier; **D:** George Miller; **W:** Dana Baratta; **C:** Thomas Burstyn; **M:** Bruce Rowland. *PAR*

Andrei Rublev 🎬🎬🎬🎬 **1966** A 15th-century Russian icon painter must decide whether to record history or participate in it as Tartar invaders make life miserable. During the black and white portion, he becomes involved in a peasant uprising, killing a man in the process. After a bout of pessimism and a vow of silence, he goes forth to create artistic beauty as the screen correspondingly blazes with color. A brilliant historical drama censored by Soviet authorities until 1971. In Russian with English subtitles. **185m/C VHS, LV.** *RU* Anatoli Solonitzin, Ivan Lapikov, Nikolai Grinko, Nikolai Sergueiev; **D:** Andrei Tarkovsky; **W:** Andrei Tarkovsky, Andrei Konchalovsky. *FXL, NOS, FCT*

Androcles and the Lion 🎬🎬½ **1952** Stage-bound Hollywood version of the George Bernard Shaw story about a tailor in Imperial Rome who saves Christians from a hungry lion he had previously befriended. Sharp dialogue and a plot that's relatively (within the bounds of Hollywood) faithful help a great play become a semi-satisfying cinematic morsel. Harpo Marx was originally cast as Androcles, but was fired by producer Howard Hughes five weeks into the shooting. **105m/B VHS, Beta.** Jean Simmons, Alan Young, Victor Mature, Robert Newton, Maurice Evans; **D:** Chester Erskine; **C:** Harry Stradling. *COL*

Android 🎬🎬½ **1982 (PG)** When an android who has been assisting a quirky scientist in space learns that he is about to be permanently retired, he starts to take matters into his own synthetic hands. Combines science fiction, suspense and cloned romance. A must for Kinski fans. **80m/C VHS, Beta, LV.** Klaus Kinski, Don Opper, Brie Howard; **D:** Aaron Lipstadt.

The Android Affair 🎬🎬½ **1995 (PG-13)** Karen Garrett (Kozak) is studying at the Institute for Surgical Research where doctors practice experimental techniques on lifelike androids. Her next patient is William (Dunne), a handsome and charming android with a heart defect, who doesn't want to "die" during Karen's risky surgical procedure. What's worse is Karen finds this 'droid all too humanly appealing and decides to help him escape the Institute. From a story by Isaac Asimov and screenwriter Kletter. *CW:* Some sensuality and violence. **90m/C VHS, LV, Closed Caption.** Harley Jane Kozak, Griffin Dunne, Ossie Davis, Saul Rubinek, Peter Outerbridge, Harold Radford; **D:** Richard Kletter; **W:** Richard Kletter; **C:** Berhard Salzmann; **M:** Simon Boswell. *USH*

The Andromeda Strain 🎬🎬½ **1971 (G)** A satellite falls back to earth carrying a deadly bacteria that must be identified in time to save the population from extermination. The tension inherent in the bestselling Michael Crichton novel is talked down by a boring cast. Also available in letterbox format. **131m/C VHS, Beta, LV, Letterbox.** Arthur Hill, David Wayne, James Olson, Kate Reid, Paula Kelly; **D:** Robert Wise. Nominations: Academy Awards '71: Best Art Direction/Set Decoration, Best Film Editing. *USH*

Andy and the Airwave Rangers 🎬🎬 *Andy Colby's Incredibly Awesome Adventure* **1989** Andy is whisked into the TV!! He finds adventure and excitement—car chases, intergalactic battles, and cartoons. **75m/C VHS, LV.** Dianne Kay, Vince Edwards, Bo Svenson, Richard Thomas, Erik Estrada, Randy Josselyn, Jessica Puscas, Chuck Kovacic; **D:** Deborah Brock. *COL*

Andy Griffith Show **1960** Life in Mayberry with smalltown sheriff Andy (Griffith), inept deputy Barney Fife (Knotts), Andy's son Opie (Howard), Aunt Bee (Bavier) and all the other townsfolk in the first of the rural comedy series. Two episodes: "Barney's Sidecar" and "The Darlings Are Coming." Additional episodes are available. **52m/B VHS, Beta.** Andy Griffith, Don Knotts, Ron Howard, Jim Nabors, Frances Bavier, George Lindsey, Howard McNear, Hal Smith, Howard Morris. *MOV*

Andy Hardy Gets Spring Fever 🎬🎬 **1939** Andy falls for a beautiful acting teacher, and then goes into a funk when he finds she's engaged. Judge Hardy and the gang help heal the big wound in his heart. A lesser entry (and the seventh) from the popular series. **88m/B VHS, Beta.** Mickey Rooney, Lewis Stone, Ann Rutherford, Fay Holden, Cecilia Parker, Sara Haden, Helen Gilbert; **D:** Woodbridge S. Van Dyke. *MGM*

Andy Hardy Meets Debutante 🎬🎬½ **1940** Seems like there should be an article in that title. Garland's second entry in series, wherein Andy meets and falls foolishly for glamorous debutante Lewis with Betsy's help while family is on visit to New York. Judy/Betsy sings "I'm Nobody's Baby" and "Singing in Rain." Also available with "Love Finds Andy Hardy" on laserdisc. **86m/B VHS, Beta, LV, Closed Caption.** Mickey Rooney, Judy Garland, Lewis Stone, Ann Rutherford, Fay Holden, Sara Haden, Cecilia Parker, Diana Lewis, Tom Neal; **D:** George B. Seitz. *MGM*

Andy Hardy's Double Life 🎬🎬½ **1942** In this entertaining installment from the Andy Hardy series, Andy proposes marriage to two girls at the same time and gets in quite a pickle when they both accept. Williams makes an early screen splash. **91m/B VHS, Beta.** Mickey Rooney, Lewis Stone, Ann Rutherford, Fay Holden, Sara Haden, Cecilia Parker, Esther Williams, William Lundigan, Susan Peters, Robert (Bobby) Blake; **D:** George B. Seitz. *MGM, MLB*

Andy Hardy's Private Secretary 🎬🎬 **1941** After Andy fails his high school finals he gets help from a sympathetic faculty member. As the secretary, Grayson makes a good first impression in one of her early screen appearances. The Hardy series was often used as a training ground for new MGM talent. **101m/B VHS, Beta.** Mickey Rooney, Kathryn Grayson, Lewis Stone, Fay Holden, Ian Hunter, Gene Reynolds, Sara Haden; **D:** George B. Seitz. *MGM*

Andy Warhol's Bad 🎬🎬🎬 **1977 (R)** In the John Waters' school of "crime is beauty," a Queens housewife struggles to make appointments for both her home electrolysis clinic and her all-female murder-for-hire operation, which specializes in children and pets (who are thrown out of windows and knived, respectively). Her life is further complicated by a boarder (King) who's awaiting the go-ahead for his own assignment, an autistic child unwanted by his mother. One of Warhol's more professional-appearing films, and very funny if your tastes run to the tasteless. **100m/C VHS, Beta, LV.** Perry King, Carroll Baker, Susan Tyrrell, Stefania Cassini; **D:** Jed Johnson. *MLB*

Andy Warhol's Dracula 🎬🎬🎬 *Blood for Dracula; Young Dracula; Dracula Cerca Sangue di Vergine e...Mori de Sete; Dracula Vuole Vivere: Cerca Sangue de Vergina; Andy Warhol's Young Dracula* **1974 (R)** Sex and camp humor, as well as a large dose of blood, highlight Warhol's treatment of the tale. As Dracula can only subsist on the blood of pure, untouched maidens ("were-gins"), gardener Dallesandro rises to the occasion in order to make as many women as he can ineligible for Drac's purposes. Very reminiscent of Warhol's "Frankenstein," but with a bit more spoofery. Look for Roman Polanski in a cameo peek as a pub patron. Available in R and unrated versions. **CW:** Horror violence and sexuality. **106m/C VHS, Beta.** *IT FR* Udo Kier, Arno Juerging, Maxine McKendry, Joe Dallesandro, Vittorio De Sica, Milena Vukotic, Dominique Darel, Stefania Casini, Silvia Dionisio; *Cameos:* Roman Polanski; **D:** Paul Morrissey, Anthony (Antonio Margheriti) Dawson; **W:** Paul Morrissey; **C:** Luigi Kuveiller. *TRI*

Andy Warhol's Frankenstein ♂♂½
Flesh for Frankenstein; The Frankenstein Experiment; Up Frankenstein; The Devil and Dr. Frankenstein; Carne per Frankenstein; **Frankenstein 1974 (X)** A most outrageous parody of Frankenstein, featuring plenty of gore, sex, and bad taste in general. Baron von Frankenstein (Kier) derives sexual satisfaction from his corpses (he delivers a particularly thought-provoking philosphy on life as he lustfully fondles a gall bladder); his wife seeks her pleasure from the monster himself (Dallesandro). Originally made in 3-D, this is one of Warhol's campiest outings. Also available on video in an R-rated version. **95m/C VHS, Beta.** *GE FR IT* Udo Kier, Monique Van Vooren, Joe Dallesandro, Dalia di Lazzaro, Arno Juerging, Srdjan Zelenovic, Nicoletta Elmi, Marco Liofredi, Cristina Gaioni; **D:** Paul Morrissey; **W:** Paul Morrissey; **C:** Luigi Kuveiller. *TRI, MLB*

Angel ♂♂½ 1937
Melodrama finds Maria Barker (Dietrich) the bored wife of British diplomat Sir Frederick (Marshall). So she heads off to Paris to visit a friend and meets the dashing Anthony Halton (Douglas), with whom she has a fling. Too bad Halton's next stop is jolly old England where he runs into an old military chum (Sir Fred, of course). High gloss but no heart. **91m/B VHS.** Marlene Dietrich, Herbert Marshall, Melvyn Douglas, Edward Everett Horton, Laura Hope Crews; **D:** Ernst Lubitsch; **W:** Guy Bolton, Samson Raphaelson, Russell Medcroft; **C:** Charles B(ryant) Lang; **M:** Friedrich Hollander. *USH*

Angel ♂½ 1984 (R)
Low-budget leerer about a 15-year-old honor student who attends an expensive Los Angeles private school during the day and by night becomes Angel, a streetwise prostitute making a living amid the slime and sleaze of Hollywood Boulevard. But wait, all is not perfect. A psycho is following her, looking for an opportunity. **94m/C VHS, Beta.** Donna Wilkes, Cliff Gorman, Susan Tyrrell, Dick Shawn, Rory Calhoun, John Diehl, Elaine Giftos, Ross Hagen; **D:** Robert Vincent O'Neil; **W:** Joseph M. Cala. *VTR*

Angel 3: The Final Chapter woof!
1988 (R) Former hooker Angel hits the streets to save her newly discovered sister from a life of prostitution. Trashy sequel with a better cast to tepid "Avenging Angel," which was the inept 1985 follow-up to 1984's tasteless "Angel." **100m/C VHS, Beta, LV.** Maud Adams, Mitzi Kapture, Richard Roundtree, Mark Blankfield, Kin Shriner, Tawny Fere, Toni Basil; **D:** Tom De Simone; **M:** Eric Allaman. *VTR, IME*

Angel and the Badman ♂♂♂ 1947
When notorious gunslinger Wayne is wounded during a shoot-out, a pacifist family takes him in and nurses him back to health. While he's recuperating, the daughter in the family (Russell) falls for him. She begs him not to return to his previous life. But Wayne, though smitten, thinks that a Duke's gotta do what a Duke's gotta do. And that means finding the dirty outlaw (Cabot) who killed his pa. Predictable but nicely done, with a good cast and script. Wayne provides one of his better performances (and also produced). **100m/B VHS, LV.** John Wayne, Gail Russell, Irene Rich, Harry Carey Sr., Bruce Cabot; **D:** James Edward Grant; **W:** James Edward Grant; **C:** Archie Stout. *REP, CNG, MRV*

An Angel at My Table ♂♂♂♂ 1989
(R) New Zealand television mini-series chronicling the life of Janet Frame, New Zealand's premiere writer/poet. At once whimsical and tragic, the film tells of how a mischievious, free-spirited young girl was wrongly placed in a mental institution for eight years, yet was ultimately able to cultivate her incredible storytelling gifts, achieving success,

fame and happiness. Adapted from three of Frame's novels: "To the la land," "An Angel at My Table," and "The Envoy From Mirror City." Highly acclaimed the world over, winner of over 20 major international awards. **CW:** Language and sensuality. **157m/C VHS.** *NZ* Kerry Fox, Alexia Keogh, Karen Fergusson, Iris Churn, K.J. Wilson, Martyn Sanderson; **D:** Jane Campion; **W:** Laura Jones; **C:** Stuart Dryburgh. Independent Spirit Awards '92: Best Foreign Film. *COL, NLC*

Angel Baby ♂♂½ 1961
A mute girl struggles to re-define her faith when she is cured by preacher, but then sees him fail with others. Fine performances all around, notably Reynolds in his screen debut. Adapted from "Jenny Angel" by Elsie Oaks Barber. **97m/B VHS.** George Hamilton, Salome Jens, Mercedes McCambridge, Joan Blondell, Henry Jones, Burt Reynolds; **D:** Paul Wendkos, Hubert Cornfield; **C:** Haskell Wexler. *NO*

Angel Baby ♂♂♂ 1995 (R)
Psychiatric out patients Kate (McKenzie) and Harry (Lynch) fall in love and move in together despite some misgivings from family and the medical bureaucracy. When Kate becomes pregnant, they decide to stop taking their medication so the baby has a better chance of being born healthy. Kate's doctors believe she's not capable of dealing with a child, although she is equally determined to have her baby, while Harry struggles to make a life for all of them. Strong performances and an assured debut by writer/director Rymer. Film won all seven of the Australian Film Institute Awards for which it was nominated. **CW:** Strong sexuality and a traumatic childbirth. **101m/C VHS, LV, Closed Caption.** *AU* John Lynch, Jacqueline McKenzie, Colin Friels, Deborrah-Lee Furness, Robyn Nevin; **D:** Michael Rymer; **W:** Michael Rymer; **M:** Ellery Ryan; **C:** John Clifford Ryan. Australian Film Institute '95: Best Actor (Lynch), Best Actress (McKenzie), Best Cinematography, Best Director (Rymer), Best Film, Best Film Editing, Best Original Screenplay. *REP*

Angel City ♂♂½ 1980
A Florida labor camp is the setting for this made-for-TV drama. A family of rural West Virginia migrant workers find themselves trapped inside the camp and exploited by the boss-man. Adapted from Patricia Smith's book. **90m/C VHS.** Ralph Waite, Paul Winfield, Jennifer Warren, Jennifer Jason Leigh, Mitchell Ryan; **D:** Philip Leacock; **W:** James Lee Barrett. *XVC*

Angel City ♂♂ 1984
An experimental parody of film mysteries where a detective investigates the nature of visual truth in and about Hollywood. **75m/C VHS, Beta.** Bob Glaudini; **D:** Jon Jost. *FCT*

Angel Dust ♂♂ 1996
Nightmare noir about a serial killer who haunts Tokyo's subways. Setsuko (Minami) is a criminal psychologist investigating the murders of several young women, all committed during rush hour at various commuter stops. Each victim has been killed with a poisonous injection. Setsuko learns the first victim was psychologically deprogrammed after leaving a religious cult and contacts her ex-lover, Rei (Wakamatsu), who runs a clinic specializing in such deprogramming. But Rei also becomes the chief suspect when he begins to play sadistic mind games with Setsuko. Is she paranoid or truly in danger? Japanese with subtitles. **116m/C VHS.** *JP* Kaho Minami, Takeshi Wakamatsu; **D:** Sogo Ishii; **W:** Sogo Ishii, Yorozu Ikuta; **C:** Norimichi Kasamatsu; **M:** Hiroyuki Nagashima. *NYF*

An Angel for Satan ♂½ 1966
Steele plays a dual role in her last major, Italian horror film. She gives a strong performance as a woman obsessed by the spirit of a statue. In Italian with no subtitles. **?m/C VHS.** *IT* Barbara Steele, Anthony Steffen. *SNC*

Angel Heart ♂♂½ 1987 (R)
Exotic, controversial look at murder, voodoo cults, and sex in 1955 New Orleans. Bonet defiantly sheds her image as a young innocent (no more Cosby Show for you, young lady). Rourke is slimy as marginal NYC private eye Angel, hired by the devilish De Niro to track a missing big band singer who violated a "contract." His investigation leads him to the

bizarre world of the occult in New Orleans, where the blood drips to a different beat. Visually stimulating, with a provocative sex scene between Bonet and Rourke, captured in both R-rated and unrated versions. Adapted by Parker from "Falling Angel" by William Hjortsberg. **112m/C VHS, Beta, LV.** Mickey Rourke, Robert De Niro, Lisa Bonet, Charlotte Rampling, Michael Higgins, Charles Gordone, Kathleen Wilhoite, Stocker Fountelieu, Brownie McGhee; **D:** Alan Parker; **W:** Alan Parker; **C:** Michael Seresin; **M:** Trevor Jones. *ART, FCT*

Angel in a Taxi ♂♂ 1959
A six-year-old boy in an orphanage decides to choose his own mother, a beautiful ballerina he sees in a magazine, when an ugly couple try to adopt him. Italian film dubbed in English. **89m/B VHS, Beta, 8mm.** *IT* Wera Cecova, Ettore Manni, Vittorio De Sica, Marietto, Gabriele Ferzetti. *VYY, FCT*

Angel of Death woof! 1986 (R)
A small mercenary band of Nazi hunters attempt to track down Josef Mengele in South America. Stupid entry in the minor "let's find the darn Nazi before he really causes trouble" genre. Director Franco is also known as A. Frank Drew White. **92m/C VHS, Beta.** Chris Mitchum, Fernando Rey, Susan Andrews; **D:** Jess (Jesus) Franco. *VTR*

Angel of Destruction ♂½ 1994 (R)
Undercover cop is assigned to protect controversial rock star from psycho fan. Cop gets killed and cop's sister decides to go after the killer. **CW:** Language, violence, and sexuality. **80m/C VHS, LV.** Maria Ford, Charlie Spradling; **D:** Charles Philip Moore. *NHO*

Angel of Fury ♂♂½ 1993 (R)
Rothrock plays the head of security of a computer corporation who must battle terrorists after the company's top-secret computer. And there's no one she can trust. Lots of martial arts action with the competent Rothrock. **91m/C VHS, LV, Closed Caption.** Cynthia Rothrock, Christopher Barnes, Peter O'Brien; **D:** Ackyl Anwary. *IMP*

Angel of H.E.A.T. woof! *The Protectors, Book One* 1982 (R)
Porn-star Chambers is Angel, a female super-agent on a mission to save the world from total destruction. Sex and spies abound with trashy nonchalance. **90m/C VHS, Beta, LV.** Marilyn Chambers, Mary Woronov, Steve Johnson; **D:** Helen Sanford, Myrl A. Schreibman. *VES*

Angel on My Shoulder ♂♂♂ 1946
A murdered convict makes a deal with the Devil (Rains) and returns to earth for revenge as a respected judge who's been thinning Hell's waiting list. Occupying the good judge, the murderous Muni has significant problems adjusting. Amusing fantasy with Muni in a rare and successful comic role. Co-written by Segall, who scripted "Here Comes Mr. Jordan," in which Rains played an angel. Remade in 1980. **101m/B VHS, Beta.** Paul Muni, Claude Rains, Anne Baxter, Onslow Stevens; **D:** Archie Mayo; **W:** Harry Segall. *MRV, NOS, HHT*

Angel on My Shoulder ♂♂ 1980
A small-time hood wrongfully executed for murder comes back as district attorney. He owes the devil, but he's finding it tough to be evil enough to repay his debt. Okay television remake of the better 1946 film starring Paul Muni. **96m/C VHS, Beta.** Peter Strauss, Richard Kiley, Barbara Hershey, Janis Paige; **D:** John Berry; **M:** Artie Butler.

Angel Square ♂♂ 1992
A Canadian production from the director of the acclaimed "Bye Bye Blues." When the father of a neighborhood boy is brutally attacked, the community bands together to search for the culprit. **106m/C VHS.** *CA* Ned Beatty; **D:** Anne Wheeler; **W:** James DeFelice. *NO*

Angel Town ♂ 1989 (R)
A foreign exchange student, who happens to be a champion kick-boxer, is forced into combat with LA street gangs. **90m/C VHS, LV.** Olivier Gruner, Theresa Saldana, Frank Aragon, Tony Valentino, Peter Kwong, Mike Moroff; **D:** Eric Karson. *IMP*

Angel Unchained ✍½ 1970 Typical biker exploitation flick has bikers and hippies joining together to fend off small-town redneck hostility. **92m/C VHS.** Don Stroud, Tyne Daly, Luke Askew, Larry Bishop, Aldo Ray, Bill McKinney; **D:** Lee Madden; **W:** Jeffrey Alladin Fiskin. *ORI*

Angel with the Trumpet ✍✍ 1950 Depressing character study of a woman who marries to please her family, rather than herself. When the Gestapo finds out about her Jewish ancestry, she must make the most important decision of her life. **98m/B VHS.** *GB* Eileen Herlie, Basil Sydney, Norman Wooland, Maria Schell, Olga Edwards, Oskar Werner, Arnoul Bushell, Wilfrid Hyde-White; **D:** Anthony Bushell. *NOS*

Angela ✍ 1977 Twisted love story about a young man (Railsback) who jumps the bones of an older woman, unaware that she is the mother he's been separated from for 23 long years. Seems that way back when, the boy was kidnapped by crime boss Huston from mom Loren, an ex-prostitute, who then turned in the boy's dad, who was something of a criminal. Mom thought son was dead, dad vowed revenge from prison, and son went about his unwitting business. It all comes together insipidly, at the expense of the cast and viewer. **91m/C VHS, Beta.** *CA* Sophia Loren, Steve Railsback, John Huston, John Vernon; **D:** Boris Sagal; **M:** Henry Mancini. *SIM*

Angela ✍✍ 1994 Exceedingly mystical film focuses on religiously obsessed 10-year-old Angela (Rhyne), who tells her six-year-old sister Ellie (Blythe) that unless they are very good the Devil will come to take them away. Meanwhile, she tries to cope with volatile family relationships, including their unstable mother. Good performances in a sometimes sluggish and abstract drama. **105m/C VHS.** Miranda Stuart Rhyne, Charlotte Blythe, Anna Thomson, John Ventimiglia, Vincent Gallo; **D:** Rebecca Miller; **W:** Rebecca Miller; **C:** Ellen Kuras; **M:** Michael Rohatyn. Sundance Film Festival '95: Best Cinematography, Filmmakers Trophy. *NYR*

Angele ✍ 1934 A lovely, naive country girl is lured to the city by a cunning pimp who knows that she wants to escape her oppressive father. With her illegitimate baby, she's discovered in a whorehouse and taken in disgrace back home to dad, who promptly locks her in the barn. One special guy, however, appreciates her purity and plots to rescue her. What he lacks in material resources he makes up for in character. An overlong but moving story of lost innocence and intolerence. In French with English subtitles. Based on the novel "Un de Baumugnes" by Jean Giono. **130m/B VHS.** *FR* Orane Demazis, Fernandel, Henri Poupon, Edouard Delmont; **D:** Marcel Pagnol. *INT*

Angelo My Love ✍✍✍ 1983 (R) Compassionate docudrama about New York's modern gypsy community. Follows the adventures of 12-year-old Angelo Evans, the streetwise son of a fortune teller, who, with a fresh view, explores the ups and downs of his family's life. Duvall financed the effort and cast non-professional actors in this charming tale of reality and fairy-tale. **91m/C VHS, Beta, LV.** Angelo Evans, Michael Evans, Steve "Patalay" Tsiginoff, Cathy Kitchen, Millie Tsiginoff; **D:** Robert Duvall; **M:** Michael Kamen. *COL*

Angels and Insects ✍✍✍ 1995 (R) Very strange Victorian-era romantic drama is definitely an acquired taste. The mysteries of nature are nothing compared to the mysteries of human life as naturalist William Adamson (Rylance) comes to discover when he takes up a position at the home of amateur insect collector, Sir Harald Alabaster (Kemp). He falls in love and quickly marries blondly beautiful Eugenia (Kensit), whose outward propriety hides a sensual nature and some decadent family secrets. Based on A.S. Byatt's novella "Morpho Eugenia." Take particular note of the costumes by Paul Brown, which mimic the exoticness of insects. **CW:** Heavy sexual content, nudity. **116m/C VHS.** *GB* Mark Rylance, Patsy Ken-

sit, Kristin Scott Thomas, Jeremy Kemp, Douglas Henshall, Chris Larkin, Annette Badland, Anna Massey, Saskia Wickham; **D:** Philip Haas; **W:** Belinda Haas, Philip Haas; **C:** Bernard Zitzermann; **M:** Alexander Balanescu. Nominations: Academy Awards '96: Best Costume Design. *HMK*

Angel's Brigade ✍✍ 1979 (PG) Seven models get together to stop a big drug operation. Drive-in vigilante movie fare fit for a rainy night. **97m/C VHS, Beta.** Jack Palance, Peter Lawford, Jim Backus, Arthur Godfrey; **D:** Greydon Clark; **W:** Greydon Clark; **C:** Dean Cundey. *ART*

Angels Die Hard ✍✍ 1984 (R) Novel biker story with the cyclists as the good guys intent on helping a town during a mining disaster. Grizzly Adams makes an early film appearance. **86m/C VHS, Beta, LV.** Tom Baker, R.G. Armstrong, Dan Haggerty, William Smith; **D:** Richard Compton.

Angels from Hell ✍ 1968 Early application in the nutso 'Nam returnee genre. Disillusioned Vietnam veteran forms a massive biker gang for the sole purpose of wreaking havoc upon the Man, the Establishment and anyone else responsible for sending him off to war. The big gang invades a town, with predictably bloody results. Sort of a follow-up to "Hell's Angels on Wheels." **86m/C VHS.** Tom Stern, Arlene Martel, Ted Markland, Stephen Oliver, Paul Bertoya, James Murphy, Jack Starrett, Pepper Martin, Luana Talltree; **D:** Bruce Kessler. *NO*

Angels Hard as They Come ✍✍ 1971 (R) Opposing Hell's Angels leaders clash in a hippie-populated ghost town. A semi-satiric spoof of the biker genre's cliches features an early Glenn appearance and Busey's film debut. **86m/C VHS, Beta.** Gary Busey, Scott Glenn, James Iglehart, Gary Littlejohn, Sharon Peckinpah; **D:** Joe Viola; **W:** Jonathan Demme.

Angels in the Endzone ✍✍½ 1998 TV follow-up to Disney's 1994 "Angels in the Outfield" finds the heavenly troops trying to aid a failing high school football squad, especially the leading players (Gallagher and Lawrence) who are also trying to also handle the death of their father. **85m/C VHS, Closed Caption.** Matthew Lawrence, David Gallagher, Paul Dooley, Christopher Lloyd; **D:** Gary Nadeau. *TOU*

Angels in the Outfield ✍✍✍ 1951 Enjoyable comedy fantasy about the lowly Pittsburgh Pirates who get a little celestial help in their race for the pennant. Great performances all around, especially Douglas as the gruff manager of the losing baseball team. Based on a story by Richard Conlin. **102m/C VHS.** Paul Douglas, Janet Leigh, Keenan Wynn, Donna Corcoran, Lewis Stone, Spring Byington, Bruce (Herman Brix) Bennett, Marvin Kaplan, Ellen Corby, Jeff Richards; **D:** Clarence Brown; **W:** Dorothy Kingsley, George Wells; **C:** Paul Vogel. *MGM*

Angels in the Outfield ✍✍½ 1994 (PG) Remake of the 1951 fantasy about a lowly baseball team who, along with some heavenly animated help find themselves on a winning streak. The new lineup includes Glover as manager of the hapless California Angels, Danza as a washed-up pitcher, and Lloyd as captain of the celestial spirits. Gordon-Levitt plays the foster child who believes he'll get his family back together if the Angels win the pennant. Familar ground still yields good, heartfelt family fare. Oakland A's third baseman Carney Lansford served as technical advisor, molding actors into fair semblance of baseball team. **105m/C VHS, Closed Caption.** Danny Glover, Tony Danza, Christopher Lloyd, Brenda Fricker, Ben Johnson, Joseph Gordon-Levitt, Jay O. Sanders; **D:** William Dear; **W:** Holly Goldberg Sloan. *DIS*

Angels of the City ✍✍ 1989 What's a girl got to do to join a sorority? A house prank turns vicious when two coeds take a walk on the wild side and accidentally observe a murder, making them the next targets. Credible exploitation effort, if that's not an oxymoron. **90m/C VHS, Beta.** Lawrence-Hilton Jacobs, Cynthia Cheston, Kelly Galindo, Sandy Gershman; **D:** Lawrence-Hilton Jacobs; **W:** Lawrence-Hilton Jacobs, Raymond Martino, Joseph Merhi. *PMH*

Angels One Five ✍✍ 1954 A worm's-eye view of British air power in WWII. What little "excitement" there is, is generated by flashing lights, plotting maps, and status boards. Hawkins and Denison are the only bright spots. **97m/B VHS.** Jack Hawkins, Michael Denison, Dulcie Gray, John Gregson, Cyril Raymond, Veronica Hurst, Geoffrey Keen, Vida Hope. *NOS*

Angels Over Broadway ✍✍✍ 1940 Slick, fast-paced black comedy about con man Fairbanks, who plans to hustle suicidal thief Qualen during a poker game, but has a change of heart. With the help of call-girl Hayworth and drunken playwright Mitchell, he helps Qualen turn his life around. Ahead of its time with an offbeat morality, but a delight in the '90s. **80m/B VHS, LV.** Douglas Fairbanks Jr., Rita Hayworth, Thomas Mitchell, John Qualen, George Watts; **D:** Ben Hecht, Lee Garmes; **C:** Lee Garmes. Nominations: Academy Awards '40: Best Original Screenplay. *FCT, COL*

Angels' Wild Women woof! 1972 From the man who brought you "Dracula vs. Frankenstein" comes an amalgamation of hippies, motorcycle dudes, evil desert gurus and precious little plot. **85m/C VHS.** Kent Taylor, Regina Carrol, Ross Hagen, Maggie Bemby, Vicki Volante; **D:** Al Adamson. *NO*

Angels with Dirty Faces ✍✍✍✍ 1938 Rousing classic with memorable Cagney twitches and the famous long walk from the cell to the chair. Two young hoods grow up on NYC's lower East Side with diverse results—one enters the priesthood and the other opts for crime and prison. Upon release from the pen, famed gangster Cagney sets up shop in the old neighborhood, where Father O'Brien tries to keep a group of young toughs (the Dead End Kids) from following in his footsteps. Bogart's his unscrupulous lawyer and Bancroft a crime boss intent on double-crossing Cagney. Reportedly they were blasting real bullets during the big shootout, no doubt helping Cagney's intensity. Adapted from a story by Rowland Brown. **97m/B VHS, Beta, LV.** James Cagney, Pat O'Brien, Humphrey Bogart, Ann Sheridan, George Bancroft, Billy Halop, Leo Gorcey, Huntz Hall, Bobby Jordan, Dan Jesse, Gabriel Dell, J. Frank Burke, William Tracy, Bernard Punsley; **D:** Michael Curtiz; **W:** John Wexley, Warren Duff; **M:** Max Steiner. New York Film Critics Awards '38: Best Actor (Cagney); Nominations: Academy Awards '38: Best Actor (Cagney), Best Director (Curtiz), Best Story. *MGM, FOX, MLB*

Angie ✍✍ 1994 (R) Brassy Angie finds herself pregnant and unmarried. Tired of the advice and criticism she receives from her close knit neighborhood she strikes out of Brooklyn to find a new life for herself. Average "woman's movie" wrought with messages of pregnancy, childbirth, friendship, love, and family has far too much going on and relies too heavily on formula soap. Davis, in what could have been a juicy (read "Oscar") role is strong, but her performance is drowned by all the melodrama. Madonna was originally cast as Angie, but was bounced when the filming of "Snake Eyes" conflicted. Adapted from the book "Angie, I Says" by Avra Wing. **CW:** Language. **108m/C VHS, LV, Letterbox, Closed Caption.** Geena Davis, Aida Turturro, Stephen Rea, Philip Bosco, James Gandolfini, Jenny O'Hara; **D:** Martha Coolidge; **W:** Todd Graff. *HPH*

AngKor: Cambodia Express ✍ 1981 An American journalist travels back to Vietnam to search for his long lost love. **96m/C VHS, Beta.** Robert Walker Jr., Christopher George; **D:** Lek Kitiparaporn. *VES, ART*

Angry Harvest ✍✍✍ *Bittere Ernte* 1985 During the WWII German occupation of Poland, a gentile farmer shelters a young Jewish woman on the run, and a serious, ultimately interdependent relationship forms. Acclaimed; Holland's first film since her native Poland's martial law imposition made her an exile to Sweden. In German with English subtitles. Contains nudity and violence. **102m/C VHS, Beta.** *GE* Armin Mueller-Stahl, Elisabeth Trissenaar, Wojciech Pszoniak, Margit Carstensen, Kurt Raab,

Kathe Jaenicke, Hans Beerhenke, Isa Haller; **D:** Agnieszka Holland; **W:** Agnieszka Holland. Montreal World Film Festival '85: Best Actor (Mueller-Stahl). Nominations: Academy Awards '85: Best Foreign Language Film. *CTL, FCT, TPV*

Angry Joe Bass 🎬 1976 Contemporary Native American Joe Bass faces government officials who continually usurp his fishing rights. Something like "Billy Jack" without the intelligence. 82m/C VHS, Beta. Henry Bal, Molly Mershon; **D:** Thomas G. Reeves. *NO*

The Angry Red Planet 🎬🎬 1959 An unintentionally amusing sci-fi adventure about astronauts on Mars fighting off aliens and giant, ship-swallowing amoebas. Filmed using bizarre "Cinemagic" process, which turns almost everything pink. Wild effects have earned the film cult status. 83m/C VHS, Beta. Gerald Mohr, Les Tremayne, Jack Kruschen; **D:** Ib Melchior. *NO*

Anguish 🎬🎬½ 1988 (R) Well-done horror thriller about a lunatic who, inspired to duplicate the actions of an eyeball-obsessed killer in a popular film, murders a movie audience as they watch the movie. Violence and gore abound. 85m/C VHS, Beta, LV, Closed Caption. *SP* Zelda Rubinstein, Michael Lerner, Talia Paul, Clara Pastor; **D:** Bigas Luna; **W:** Bigas Luna; **M:** J.M. Pagan. *FOX*

Angus 🎬🎬 1995 (PG-13) Dull teen comedy about self-esteem revolves around the overweight Angus (Talbert), a friendly kid tormented by the usual school bullies. His best bud is twerp Troy (Owen), who tries to help Angus out with his crush on cute blonde Melissa (Ariana). There's even a schmaltzy prom scene. The profanity, though mild, and the boys sexual interests make this questionable for the pre-teen audience that could actually enjoy it. *CW:* Some coarse adolescent language. 87m/C VHS. Charlie Talbert, Kathy Bates, George C. Scott, Chris Owen, Ariana Richards, Lawrence Pressman, Rita Moreno, James Van Der Beek, Anna Thompson; **D:** Patrick Read Johnson; **W:** Jill Gordon; **C:** Alexander Grusynski; **M:** David E. Russo. *TTC*

Animal Behavior 🎬 1989 (PG) An animal researcher and a music professor fall in love on a college campus. Bowen's (she actually released it under the alias Riley N. Anne) comedy was filmed in 1985 and edited/shelved for over four years, with good reason. 79m/C VHS, Beta, LV. Karen Allen, Armand Assante, Holly Hunter, Josh Mostel, Richard Libertini; **D:** Jenny Bowen; **W:** Susan Rice; **C:** Richard Bowen; **M:** Cliff Eidelman. *HBO*

Animal Called Man 🎬 1987 Two crooked buddies join a big western gang in pillaging a small town and get in too deep. 83m/C VHS, Beta. Vassilli Karis, Craig Hill. *TWE*

Animal Crackers 🎬🎬🎬½ 1930 (G) The second and possibly the funniest of the 13 Marx Brothers films, "Animal Crackers" is a screen classic. Groucho is a guest at the house of wealthy matron Margaret Dumont and he, along with Zeppo, Chico, and Harpo, destroy the tranquility of the estate. Complete with the Harry Ruby music score—including Groucho's "Hooray for Captain Spaulding" with more quotable lines than any other Marx Brothers film: "One morning I shot an elephant in my pajamas. How he got into my pajamas, I'll never know." Based on a play by George S. Kaufman. 98m/B VHS, Beta, LV. Groucho Marx, Chico Marx, Harpo Marx, Zeppo Marx, Lillian Roth, Margaret Dumont, Louis Sorin, Hal Thompson, Robert Greig; **D:** Victor Heerman; **W:** Morrie Ryskind. *USH, FCT*

Animal Farm 🎬🎬🎬 1955 An animated version of George Orwell's classic political satire about a barnyard full of animals who parallel the growth of totalitarian dictatorships. Not entirely successful, but probably best translation of Orwell to film. 73m/C VHS, Beta, LV, 8mm. **D:** John Halas, Joy Batchelor; **V:** Maurice Denham, Gordon Heath. *VYY, KUI, VTR*

Animal Instincts 🎬🎬 1992 (R) A woman takes a prescription drug that makes her a nymphomaniac, and her police officer husband discovers that he's turned on by videotaping her in

bed with other men and women. One of the many in her constant stream of lovers is a politician whose campaign is based on shutting down all the town's sex clubs. Another in the string of sexual thrillers riding on the coattails of "Basic Instinct." *CW:* Strong language and strong sexuality. 94m/C VHS, Closed Caption. Maxwell Caulfield, Jan-Michael Vincent, Mitch Gaylord, Shannon Whirry, Delia Sheppard, John Saxon, David Carradine; **D:** Alexander Gregory Hippolyte.

Animal Instincts 2 🎬🎬 1994 (R) Joanna leaves her overbearing husband and moves into a supposedly quiet community. Neighbor Steve is a security expert—and a voyeur. He's hidden a camera in Joanna's bedroom but she knows he's watching. *CW:* Language, nudity, and sexual situations. 92m/C VHS, Beta, LV, Closed Caption. Shannon Whirry, Woody Brown, Elizabeth Sandifer, Al Sapienza; **D:** Alexander Gregory Hippolyte.

Animal Instincts 3: The Seductress 🎬 1995 (R) Joanna (Schumacher) finds a new kind of sexual excitement when she gets involved with rock music promoter Alex (Matthew), whose kicks include feining blindness. The unrated version contains 12 more minutes of footage. *CW:* Strong sexuality, and for language and some violence. 92m/C VHS. Wendy Schumacher, James Matthew; **D:** Alexander Gregory Hippolyte. *APX*

The Animal Kingdom 🎬🎬🎬 *The Woman in His House* 1932 A romantic triangle develops when Howard, married to Loy, has an affair with Harding. The problem is Harding acts more like a wife and Loy a mistress. Intelligently written and directed, with a marvelous performance from veteran character actor Gargan. 95m/B VHS. Ann Harding, Leslie Howard, Myrna Loy, Neil Hamilton, William Gargan, Henry Stephenson, Ilka Chase; **D:** Edward H. Griffith; **W:** Horace Jackson. *FCT, HEG*

Anita, Dances of Vice 🎬🎬 *Anita—Tanze des Lasters* 1987 German avant-garde film celebrates Anita Berber, the "most scandalous woman in 1920s Berlin." Berber was openly bisexual, used drugs, and danced nude in public. In von Praunheim's film, she rises from the dead and creates yet more scandal. 85m/C VHS, Beta. *GE* Lotti Huber, Ina Blum, Mikhael Honesseau; **D:** Rosa von Praunheim. *FRF, GLV, TPV*

The Ann Jillian Story 🎬½ 1988 Jillian stars as herself in this television melodrama recounting her battle with breast cancer. Several musical numbers are included. 96m/C VHS, Beta. Ann Jillian, Tony LoBianco, Viveca Lindfors, Leighton Bewley; **D:** Corey Allen. *NO*

Ann Vickers 🎬🎬½ 1933 A dashing young army captain wins over the heart of a dedicated social worker. Okay adaptation of a Sinclair Lewis novel, with Dunne suffering more than usual. 76m/B VHS, Beta. Irene Dunne, Walter Huston, Bruce Cabot, Conrad Nagel, Edna May Oliver; **D:** John Cromwell; **M:** Max Steiner. *TTC*

Anna 🎬🎬 1951 Novitiate nun Anna (Mangano) is forced to confront her sordid past (as a nightclub entertainer), and her love for two very different men, when her seriously injured former fiancee is brought to the hospital where she is a nurse. Anna must finally deal with her feelings and decide which path her life will take. Dubbed in English. 111m/B VHS. *IT* Silvana Mangano, Raf Vallone, Vittorio Gassman; **D:** Alberto Lattuada; **C:** Otello Martelli; **M:** Nino Rota. *FCT*

Anna 🎬🎬🎬 1987 (PG-13) Age, envy, and the theatrical world receive their due in an uneven but engrossing drama about aging Czech film star Anna, making a sad living in New York doing commercials and trying for off-Broadway roles. She takes in Krystyna, a young Czech peasant girl who eventually rockets to model stardom. Modern, strongly acted "All About Eve" with a story partially based on a real Polish actress. Kirkland drew quite a bit of flak for shamelessly self-promoting for the Oscar. She still lost. 101m/C VHS, Beta, LV, Closed Caption. Sally Kirkland, Paulina Porizko-

va, Robert Fields, Stefan Schnabel, Larry Pine, Ruth Maleczech; **D:** Yurek Bogayevicz; **W:** Yurek Bogayevicz, Agnieszka Holland; **C:** Bobby Bukowski; **M:** Greg Hawkes. Golden Globe Awards '88: Best Actress—Drama (Kirkland); Independent Spirit Awards '88: Best Actress (Kirkland); Los Angeles Film Critics Association Awards '87: Best Actress (Kirkland); Nominations: Academy Awards '87: Best Actress (Kirkland). *VES, ART*

Anna and the King of Siam 🎬🎬🎬½ 1946 Splendid adaptation, from the book by Margaret Landon, about the true life adventures of 33-year-old English widow Anna Leonowens. In 1862 Anna and her son travelled to the exotic kingdom of Siam to educate the harem and children of the king. Dunne is splendid as the strong-willed governess as is Harrison (in his first American film) as the authoritarian eastern ruler. Remade as the musical "The King and I." 128m/B VHS. Irene Dunne, Rex Harrison, Linda Darnell, Lee J. Cobb, Gale Sondergaard, Mikhail Rasumny, Dennis Hoey, Richard Lyon, John Abbott; **D:** John Cromwell; **W:** Sally Benson, Talbot Jennings; **C:** Arthur C. Miller; **M:** Bernard Herrmann. Academy Awards '46: Best Art Direction/Set Decoration (B & W), Best Black and White Cinematography; Nominations: Academy Awards '46: Best Screenplay, Best Supporting Actress (Sondergaard), Best Original Dramatic/Comedy Score. *FXV*

Anna Christie 🎬🎬🎬½ 1923 Silent production of Eugene O'Neill's play that even he liked. A young girl is sent away by her father, a seaman, and finds her way to Chicago, where she becomes a prostitute. Later she visits her father's barge and falls for a sailor. She shares her past life story, hoping they will understand. This film was acclaimed when it was released, and still remains a touching work of art. Remade in 1930. 75m/B VHS, Beta. Blanche Sweet, George F. Marion Sr., William Russell, Eugenie Besserer, Chester Conklin, George Siegmann, Victor Potel, Fred Kohler Sr.; **D:** John Wray. *GPV, FCT*

Anna Christie 🎬🎬½ 1930 Garbo is the ex-prostitute who finds love with sailor Bickford. Bickford is unaware of his lover's tarnished past and does her best to keep it that way. Garbo's first sound effort was advertised with the slogan "Garbo Talks." Adapted from the classic Eugene O'Neill play, the film is a slow but rewarding romantic drama. 90m/B VHS, Beta. Greta Garbo, Marie Dressler, Charles Bickford, George F. Marion Sr.; **D:** Clarence Brown; **C:** William H. Daniels. Nominations: Academy Awards '30: Best Actress (Garbo), Best Cinematography, Best Director (Brown). *MGM*

Anna Karenina 🎬🎬🎬½ 1935 Cinematic Tolstoy with Garbo as the sad, moody Anna willing to give up everything to be near Vronsky (March), the cavalry officer she's obsessed with. A classic Garbo vehicle with March and Rathbone providing excellent support. Interestingly, a remake of the Garbo and John Gilbert silent, "Love." 85m/B VHS, Beta. Greta Garbo, Fredric March, Freddie Bartholomew, Maureen O'Sullivan, May Robson, Basil Rathbone, Reginald Owen, Reginald Denny; **D:** Clarence Brown; **C:** William H. Daniels. New York Film Critics Awards '35: Best Actress (Garbo). *NOS, MGM, HEG*

Anna Karenina 🎬🎬½ 1948 Stiff version of Tolstoy's passionate story of illicit love between a married woman and a military officer. In spite of exquisite costumes, and Leigh and Richardson as leads, still tedious. 123m/C VHS, LV. *GB* Vivien Leigh, Ralph Richardson, Kieron Moore; **D:** Julien Duvivier. *MON, FCT, MRV*

Anna Karenina 🎬🎬½ 1985 (PG) Made for television version of Tolstoy's novel of betrayal, intrigue, and forbidden love. Anna, defying all social practices of the time, falls into the arms of a dashing count. Features an excellent performance from Paul "A Man For All Seasons" Scofield. 96m/C VHS, Beta, LV. Jacqueline Bisset, Christopher Reeve, Paul Scofield, Ian Ogilvy, Anna Massey, Judi Bowker; **D:** Simon Langton. *VES*

Anna to the Infinite Power 🎬🎬½ 1984 Sci fi based on the book of the same name follows a young girl with telepathic powers. When the girl discovers that she has sisters as the result of a strange scientific experiment, she sets out to find them, drawing on her own inner strength. 101m/C VHS, Beta. Dina Merrill, Martha Byrne, Mark Patton; *D:* Robert Wiemer. *COL*

Annabel Takes a Tour/Maid's Night Out 1938 A delightful comedy double feature. In "Annabel Takes a Tour," a fading movie star falls in love with a writer while on a tour to boost her career, and in "Maids Night Out," an heiress and a millionaire fall in love. 131m/B VHS, Beta. Lucille Ball, Jack Oakie, Ruth Donnelly, Joan Fontaine, Alan "Rocky" Lane, Hedda Hopper, Alice White; *D:* Lew (Louis Friedlander) Landers. *MLB, TTC*

Annapolis 🎬 1928 Life's in the pink for two guys at the U.S. naval academy until jealousy rears its loathsome head when they fall for the same gal. Just when it's beginning to look like love and honor is an either-or proposition, the lovelorn rivals find that although love transcends all, a guy's gotta do what a guy's gotta do, even if it means sticking up for his romantic nemesis. Lots of sub-par male bonding. 63m/B VHS, Beta. Johnny Mack Brown, Hugh Allan, Hobart Bosworth, William "Billy" Bakewell, Charlotte Walker, Jeanette Loff; *D:* Christy Cabanne. *GPV, FCT*

The Annapolis Story 🎬½ *Blue and the Gold* 1955 Cliche-ridden WWII drama about two naval cadets romancing the same lucky girl. Low-rent time for director Siegel which wastes a decent cast. 81m/C VHS, Beta. John Derek, Kevin McCarthy, Diana Lynn, Pat Dooley, L.Q. Jones; *D:* Donald Siegel. *FOX*

Anne of Avonlea 🎬🎬🎬½ *Anne of Green Gables: The Sequel* 1987 Equally excellent mini-series sequel to "Anne of Green Gables" in which the romantic heroine grows up and discovers romance. The same cast returns and Sullivan continues his tradition of lavish filming on Prince Edward Island and beautiful costumes. Based on the characters from L.M. Montgomery's classic novels "Anne of Avonlea," "Anne of the Island," and "Anne of Windy Poplars." CBC, PBS, and Disney worked together on this WonderWorks production. On two tapes. 224m/C VHS, Beta, LV, Closed Caption. *CA* Megan Follows, Colleen Dewhurst, Wendy Hiller, Frank Converse, Patricia Hamilton, Schuyler Grant, Jonathan Crombie, Rosemary Dunsmore; *D:* Kevin Sullivan; *W:* Kevin Sullivan; *M:* Hagood Hardy. *KUI, TOU, DIS*

Anne of Green Gables 🎬🎬🎬 1934 A lonely Canadian couple adopts an orphan who keeps them on their toes with her animated imagination, and wins a permanent place in their hearts. Warm (but loose) adaptation of Lucy Maud Montgomery's popular novel is entertaining although 1985 remake is far superior. Followed by "Anne of Windy Poplars." 79m/B VHS, Beta. Anne Shirley, Tom Brown, O.P. Heggie; *D:* George Nicholls Jr.; *M:* Max Steiner. *TTC*

Anne of Green Gables 🎬🎬🎬½ 1985 Splendid production of the famous Lucy Maud Montgomery classic about a young orphan girl growing to young adulthood with the help of a crusty brother and sister duo. The characters come to life under Sullivan's direction, and the movie is enhanced by the beautiful Prince Edward Island scenery and wonderful costumes. One of the few instances where an adaptation lives up to (if not exceeds) the quality of the original novel. A WonderWorks presentation that was made with the cooperation of the Disney channel, CBC, and PBS. Followed by "Anne of Avonlea." On two tapes. 197m/C VHS, Beta, LV, Closed Caption. *CA* Megan Follows, Colleen Dewhurst, Richard Farnsworth, Patricia Hamilton, Schuyler Grant, Jonathan Crombie, Marilyn Lightstone, Charmion King, Rosemary Radcliffe, Jackie Burroughs, Robert Collins, Joachim Hansen, Cedric Smith, Paul Brown, Miranda de Pencier, Jennifer Inch, Wendy Lyon, Christiane Krueger, Trish Nettleton, Morgan Chap-

man; *D:* Kevin Sullivan; *W:* Kevin Sullivan, Joe Weisenfeld; *C:* Rene Ohashi; *M:* Hagood Hardy. *KUI, TOU, IGP*

Anne of the Thousand Days 🎬🎬🎬½ 1969 (PG) Lavish re-telling of the life and loves of Henry the VIII. Henry tosses aside his current wife for the young and devastatingly beautiful Anne Boleyn. Burton's performance of the amoral king garnered him an Oscar nomination. Watch for Elizabeth Taylor as a masked courtesan at the costume ball. 145m/C VHS. Richard Burton, Genevieve Bujold, Irene Papas, Anthony Quayle, John Colicos, Michael Hordern; *D:* Charles Jarrott; *M:* Georges Delerue. Academy Awards '69: Best Costume Design; Directors Guild of America Awards '70: Best Director (Jarrott); Golden Globe Awards '70: Best Actress—Drama (Bujold), Best Director (Jarrott), Best Film—Drama, Best Screenplay; Nominations: Academy Awards '69: Best Actor (Burton), Best Actress (Bujold), Best Adapted Screenplay, Best Art Direction/Set Decoration, Best Cinematography, Best Picture, Best Sound, Best Supporting Actor (Quayle), Best Original Score. *USH*

Annie 🎬🎬 1982 (PG) Stagy big-budget adaption of the Broadway musical, which was an adaptation of the comic strip. A major financial disaster upon release, still it's an entertaining enterprise curiously directed by Huston and engagingly acted by Finney and Quinn. 🎵Tomorrow; It's the Hard Knock Life; Maybe; I Think I'm Gonna Like It Here; Little Girls; We Got Annie; Let's Go to the Movies; You're Never Fully Dressed Without a Smile; Easy Street. 128m/C VHS, Beta, LV, 8mm, Letterbox, Closed Caption. Aileen Quinn, Carol Burnett, Albert Finney, Bernadette Peters, Ann Reinking, Tim Curry; *D:* John Huston; *W:* Thomas Meehan; *M:* Ralph Burns. Golden Raspberry Awards '82: Worst Supporting Actress (Quinn); Nominations: Academy Awards '82: Best Art Direction/Set Decoration, Original Song Score and/or Adaptation. *COL, FCT, MLT*

Annie: A Royal Adventure 🎬🎬½ 1995 TV sequel to "Annie" finds the red-haired heroine (Johnson) traveling to England with her Daddy Warbucks (Hearn), who's about to be knighted in London. But the evil Lady Edwina Hogbottom (played to a high-camp hilt by Collins) has a plan to blow up Buckingham Palace and take over as queen. Naturally, it's up to Annie to defeat her and have a happy ending. 92m/C VHS. Ashley Johnson, George Hearn, Joan Collins, Emily Ann Lloyd, Camilla Bell, Ian McDiarmid. *COL*

Annie Hall 🎬🎬🎬 1977 (PG) Acclaimed coming-of-cinematic-age film for Allen is based in part on his own life. His love affair with Hall/Keaton is chronicled as an episodic, wistful comedy commenting on family, love, loneliness, communicating, maturity, driving, city life, careers, and various other topics. Abounds with classic scenes, including future star Goldblum and his mantra at a cocktail party; Allen and the lobster pot; and Allen, Keaton, a bathroom, a tennis racket, and a spider. The film operates on many levels, as does Keaton's wardrobe, which started a major fashion trend. Don't blink or you'll miss several future stars in bit parts. Expertly shot by Gordon Willis. 94m/C VHS, Beta, LV, Letterbox. Woody Allen, Diane Keaton, Tony Roberts, Paul Simon, Shelley Duvall, Carol Kane, Colleen Dewhurst, Christopher Walken, Janet Margolin, John Glover, Jeff Goldblum, Sigourney Weaver, Marshall McLuhan, Beverly D'Angelo, Shelley Hack; *D:* Woody Allen; *W:* Woody Allen, Marshall Brickman; *C:* Gordon Willis. Academy Awards '77: Best Actress (Keaton), Best Director (Allen), Best Original Screenplay, Best Picture; British Academy Awards '77: Best Actress (Keaton), Best Director (Allen), Best Film, Best Screenplay; Directors Guild of America Awards '77: Best Director (Allen); Golden Globe Awards '78: Best Actress—Musical/Comedy (Keaton); Los Angeles Film Critics Association Awards '77: Best Screenplay; National Board of Review Awards '77: Best Supporting Actress (Keaton), National Film Registry '92;; New York Film Critics Awards '77: Best Actress (Keaton), Best Director (Allen), Best Film, Best Screenplay; National Society of Film Critics Awards '77: Best Actress (Keaton), Best Film, Best Screenplay; Writers Guild of America Awards '77: Best Original Screenplay; Nominations: Academy Awards '77: Best Actor (Allen). *MGM, FOX, CRC*

Annie O 🎬🎬½ 1995 (PG) 15-year-old Annie Rojas (Yares) runs into problems when she joins the boys' basketball team (since her school doesn't have a girls team). Her teammates are jealous and so are her brother and boyfriend. 93m/C VHS, Closed Caption. Coco Yares, Chad Willet, Robert Stewart; *D:* Michael McClary. *HMK*

Annie Oakley 🎬🎬 1935 Energetic biographical drama based on the life and legend of sharpshooter Annie Oakley and her on-off relationship with Wild Bill Hickok. Stanwyck makes a great Oakley. Later musicalized as "Annie Get Your Gun." 90m/B VHS, Beta. Barbara Stanwyck, Preston Foster, Melvyn Douglas, Pert Kelton, Andy Clyde; *D:* George Stevens. *NOS, TTC*

The Annihilators woof! 1985 (R) A group of Vietnam vets band together in an extremely violent manner to protect their small town from a gang of thugs. 87m/C VHS, Beta. Gerrit Graham, Lawrence-Hilton Jacobs, Paul Koslo, Christopher Stone, Andy Wood, Sid Conrad, Dennis Redfield; *D:* Charles E. Sellier. *VTR*

The Anniversary 🎬🎬 1968 One-eyed monster mom Mrs. Taggart (Bette at her baddest) gives new meaning to the word "possessive." Thoroughly cowing her three grown sons, she manages to get them to come home each year on the wedding anniversary to the husband she despised. Only this time, the tell her they're going to live their own lives. Hah—not if mom has anything to do with it. Based on the play by Bill MacIlwraith. 93m/C VHS. *GB* Bette Davis, Jack Hedley, James Cossins, Christian Roberts, Sheila Hancock, Elaine Taylor; *D:* Roy Ward Baker; *W:* Jimmy Sangster; *C:* Henry Waxman; *M:* Philip Martell. *FXV*

Another Chance 🎬🎬 1988 (R) Girl-crazy bachelor is returned from heaven for a second chance and has to choose between a "bad" girl and a "good" girl. What a choice! 99m/C VHS, Beta. Bruce Greenwood, Frank Annese, Jeff East, Anne Ramsey, Barbara Edwards; *D:* Jerry Vint. *REP*

Another Country 🎬🎬½ 1984 Julian Mitchell's adaptation of his play about the true story of two English boarding school friends who wind up as spies for the Soviet Union. Based on the lives of Guy Burgess and Donald MacLean, whose youth is rather fancifully depicted in this loving recreation of 1930s English life. Although the film is inferior to the award-winning play, director Kanievska manages to transform a piece into a solid film, and Everett's performance as Burgess is outstanding. 90m/C VHS, Beta, LV. *GB* Rupert Everett, Colin Firth, Michael Jenn, Robert Addie, Anna Massey, Betsy Brantley, Rupert Wainwright, Cary Elwes, Arthur Howard, Tristan Oliver, Frederick Alexander, Adrian Ross-Magenty, Geoffrey Bateman, Philip Dupuy, Jeffrey Wickham, Gideon Boulting, Ivor Howard, Charles Spencer; *D:* Marek Kanievska; *W:* Julian Mitchell; *C:* Peter Biziou; *M:* Michael Storey.

Another 48 Hrs. 🎬½ 1990 (R) Continuing chemistry between Nolte and Murphy is one of the few worthwhile items in this stodgy rehash. Any innovation by Murphy seems lost, the story is redundant of any other cop thriller, and violence and car chases abound. Pointlessly energetic and occasionally fun for only the true devotee. 98m/C VHS, Beta, LV, 8mm, Closed Caption. Eddie Murphy, Nick Nolte, Brion James, Kevin Tighe, Bernie Casey, David Anthony Marshall, Ed O'Ross; *D:* Walter Hill; *W:* Jeb Stuart; *M:* James Horner. *PAR*

Another Man, Another Chance 🎬🎬 *Un Autre Homme, Une Autre Chance* 1977 (PG) Remake of Lelouch's "A Man and a Woman," set in the turn-of-the-century American West, pales by comparison to the original. Slow-moving tale casts widow Bujold and widower Caan as lovers. 132m/C VHS, Beta. *FR* James Caan, Genevieve Bujold, Francis Huster, Jennifer Warren, Susan Tyrrell; *D:* Claude Lelouch; *W:* Claude Lelouch. *NO*

Another 9 1/2 Weeks woof! 1996 (R) Uninteresting sequel finds suicidal John (Rourke) overwhelmed by his kinky memories of Elizabeth, so he flies to Paris determined to find her. Instead, he meets fashion designer Lea (Everhart), who claims to be Elizabeth's friend and who puts the sexual tease on the S/M devotee. Monotony sets in early and there's no real heat generated between the duo.**CW:** Strong sexuality and some language. **104m/C VHS, Closed Caption.** Mickey Rourke, Angie Everhart, Steven Berkoff, Agathe de la Fontaine, Dougray Scott; **D:** Anne Goursaud; **W:** Michael Paul Davis; **C:** Robert Alazraki; **M:** Stephen Parsons, Francis Haines. *THV*

Another Pair of Aces: Three of a Kind 🎬🎬🎬 1991 Nelson and Kristofferson team up to clear the name of Torn, a Texas Ranger accused of murder. Made for television; some scenes deemed too racy for TV were added to the video version. Sequel to "A Pair of Aces." **93m/C VHS.** Willie Nelson, Kris Kristofferson, Rip Torn, Dan Kamin, Ken Farmer; **D:** Bill Bixby. *THV*

Another Stakeout 🎬🎬½ *Stakeout 2* 1993 (PG-13) Sequel six years after the original finds Dreyfuss and Estevez partnered again for another stakeout, this time to keep an eye on Moriarty, a reluctant witness against the Mob. The two spying detectives find themselves in an upscale neighborhood where blending in is a hard thing to do. O'Donnell is a breath of fresh air as a wisecracking assistant district attorney. Stowe briefly reprises her role as Dreyfuss' girlfriend. Writer Kouf reportedly had difficulty penning the script, surprising since there isn't much new here.**CW:** Comic action violence. **109m/C VHS, LV, Closed Caption.** Richard Dreyfuss, Emilio Estevez, Rosie O'Donnell, Cathy Moriarty, Madeleine Stowe, John Rubinstein, Marcia Strassman, Dennis Farina, Miguel Ferrer; **D:** John Badham; **C:** Roy Wagner. *TOU*

Another Thin Man 🎬🎬½ 1939 Powell and Loy team up for the third in the delightful "Thin Man" series. Slightly weaker series entry takes its time, but has both Powell and Loy providing stylish performances. Nick Jr. is also introduced as the newest member of the sleuthing team. Sequel to "After the Thin Man;" followed by "Shadow of the Thin Man." **105m/B VHS, Closed Caption.** William Powell, Myrna Loy, Virginia Grey, Otto Kruger, Sir C. Aubrey Smith, Ruth Hussey; **D:** Woodbridge S. Van Dyke. *MGM*

Another Time, Another Place 🎬🎬 1958 Sappy melodrama about an American journalist who suffers an emotional meltdown when her married British lover is killed during WWII. So she heads for Cornwall to console the widow and family. **98m/B VHS, Beta.** *GB* Lana Turner, Barry Sullivan, Glynis Johns, Sean Connery, Terence Longdon; **D:** Lewis Allen; **C:** Jack Hildyard. *BAR, PAR*

Another Time, Another Place 🎬🎬🎬 1983 (R) Bored young Scottish housewife married to an older fella falls in love with an Italian prisoner-of-war who works on her farm during WWII. Occasionally quirky, always finely crafted view of wartime Britain and the little-known life of POWs in England. **101m/C VHS, Beta, LV, Closed Caption.** *GB* Phyllis Logan, Giovanni Mauriello, Gian Luca Favilla, Paul Young, Tom Watson; **D:** Michael Radford; **C:** Roger Deakins.

Another Way 🎬🎬🎬 *Olelkezo Tekintetek* 1982 The director of 1971's much-lauded "Love" sets this politically charged love story in Hungary in 1958. Opening with a view of a female corpse, the story flashes backward to look at the woman's journalistic career and her relationship with a women colleague. Candid love scenes between women in Hungary of 1958, considered a cinematic novelty in many places outside Hungary. In Hungarian with English subtitles. **100m/C VHS, Beta.** *HU* Jadwiga Jankowska Cieslak, Grazyna Szapolowska, Josef Kroner, Hernadi Judit, Andorai Peter; **D:** Karoly Makk. Cannes Film Festival '82: Best Actress (Cieslak). *NYF, FCT*

Another Woman 🎬🎬🎬 1988 (PG) The study of an intellectual woman whose life is changed when she begins to eavesdrop. What she hears provokes her to examine every relationship in her life, finding things quite different

than she had believed. Heavy going, with Rowlands effective as a woman coping with an entirely new vision of herself. Farrow plays the catalyst. Although Allen's comedies are more popular than his dramas, this one deserves a look. **81m/C VHS, Beta, LV, Closed Caption.** Gena Rowlands, Gene Hackman, Mia Farrow, Ian Holm, Betty Buckley, Martha Plimpton, Blythe Danner, Harris Yulin, Sandy Dennis, David Ogden Stiers, John Houseman, Philip Bosco, Frances Conroy, Kenneth Welsh, Michael Kirby; **D:** Woody Allen; **W:** Woody Allen; **C:** Sven Nykvist. *ORI*

Another You 🎬🎬 1991 (R) Con man Wilder takes pathological liar Pryor under his care and decides to use his talents to his fullest advantage. Posing as successful businessmen, the duo initiate a scam so complicated that they may end up being double-crossed or worse yet, dead! Can the pair see their plan through without losing their lives? Sad to see how far these two gifted comedians have fallen. Their collaboration is tired and the movie generally dreadful. **98m/C VHS, LV, 8mm, Closed Caption.** Richard Pryor, Gene Wilder, Mercedes Ruehl, Vanessa Williams, Stephen Lang, Kevin Pollak; **D:** Maurice Phillips. *COL*

Antarctica 🎬🎬 1984 Due to unfortunate circumstances, a group of scientists must leave their pack of huskies behind on a frozen glacier in the Antarctic. The film focuses on the dogs' subsequent struggle for survival. Dubbed. **112m/C VHS, Beta, Closed Caption.** *JP* Ken Takakura, Masako Natsume, Keiko Oginome; **D:** Koreyoshi Kurahara; **M:** Vangelis. *FOX*

Anthony Adverse 🎬🎬½ 1936 March is a young man in the 19th century who searches for manhood across America and Mexico. He grows slowly as he battles foes, struggles against adversity and returns home to find his lover in this romantic swashbuckler. A star-studded cast, lush costuming, and an energetic musical score. Highly acclaimed in its time, but now seems dated. Based on the novel by Hervey Allen. **141m/B VHS, Beta.** Fredric March, Olivia de Havilland, Anita Louise, Gale Sondergaard, Claude Rains, Louis Hayward, Scotty Beckett; **D:** Mervyn LeRoy; **C:** Gaetano Antonio "Tony" Gaudio. Academy Awards '36: Best Cinematography, Best Film Editing, Best Supporting Actress (Sondergaard), Best Score; Nominations: Academy Awards '36: Best Interior Decoration, Best Picture. *MGM, BTV, FHE*

Antonia and Jane 🎬🎬🎬 1991 (R) Enjoyable film tells the story of a longstanding, heavily tested friendship between two women. From the very beginning, they are a study in contrasts—Jane as rather plain, frumpy, and insecure; Antonia as glamorous, elegant, and successful. Both believe that each other's lives are more interesting and exciting than their own. Kidron, who directed this smart witty comedy for British television, offers an honest look into the often complex world of adult friendships.**CW:** Language and sensuality. **75m/C VHS, Beta, Closed Caption.** *GB* Imelda Staunton, Saskia Reeves, Patricia Leventon, Alfred Hoffman, Maria Charles, John Bennett, Richard Hope, Alfred Marks, Lila Kaye, Bill Nighy, Brenda Bruce; **D:** Beeban Kidron; **W:** Marcy Kahan; **M:** Rachel Portman. *PAR*

Antonia's Line 🎬🎬½ 1995 (R) 90-year-old Antonia (Van Ammelrooy) has decided that she is going to die today and so begins a 50-year-long flashback of her nonconformist life in a Dutch village. Her lesbian daughter Danielle (Dottermans) wants a child without bothering about a husband and Antonia obliging arranges a brief interlude that produces child prodigy Therese (Van Overloop), who eventually has her own daughter, Sarah (Ravesteijn). Lots of female bonding (the male characters are mostly on the periphery of the action) and a certain magic realism abound. Dutch with subtitles.**CW:** Strong sexual content and some violence, including a rape scene. **102m/C VHS.** *NL* Willeke Van Ammelrooy, Els Dottermans, Veerle Van Overloop, Thyrza Ravesteijn, Jan Decleir, Mil Seghers, Jan Steen, Marina De Graaf; **D:** Marleen Gorris; **W:** Marleen Gorris; **C:** Willy Stassen; **M:** Ilona Seckaz. Academy Awards '95: Best Foreign Language Film; Nominations: British Academy Awards '96: Best Foreign Film. *BMG*

Antonio 🎬🎬 1973 A Texas millionaire on the run from his wife and her divorce lawyer alights in a small Chilean village and turns it upside down. **89m/C VHS, Beta.** Larry Hagman, Trini Lopez, Noemi Guerrero, Pedro Becker; **D:** Claudio Guzman. *HEG*

Antonio Das Mortes 🎬🎬½ 1968 Antonio is a savage mercenary hired to kill rebels against the Brazilian government. Belatedly he realizes he sympathizes with the targets and turns his guns the other way for an incredible shootout finale. A visually lavish political polemic, espousing revolutionary guerrilla action within the format of a South American western. In Portuguese with English subtitles. **100m/C VHS.** *BR* Mauricio Do Valle, Odete Lara; **D:** Glauce Rocha; **W:** Glauce Rocha. *FCT*

Antony and Cleopatra 🎬🎬 1973 (PG) Heston wrote, directed, and starred in this long, dry adaptation of the Shakespeare play that centers on the torrid romance between Mark Antony and Cleopatra. **150m/C VHS, Beta.** Charlton Heston, Hildegarde Neil, Fernando Rey, Eric Porter; **D:** Charlton Heston.

Ants 🎬½ *Panic at Lakewood Manor; It Happened at Lakewood Manor* 1977 A mad bug parable for the planet-obsessed 90s. Insecticide-infected ants turn militant and check into a local hotel to vent their chemically induced foul mood on the unsuspecting clientele. The guest register includes a gaggle of celebrities who probably wish they'd signed on the Love Boat instead. Made for television (an ant farm would probably be just too horrible on the big screen). **100m/C VHS, Beta.** Suzanne Somers, Robert Foxworth, Myrna Loy, Lynda Day George, Gerald Gordon, Bernie Casey, Barry Van Dyke, Karen Lamm, Anita Gillette, Moosie Drier, Steve Franken, Brian Dennehy, Bruce French, Stacy Keach, Rene Enriquez, James Storm; **D:** Robert Scheerer. *ART*

Any Gun Can Play 🎬 *For a Few Bullets More* 1967 Typical spaghetti western. Three men (banker, thief, and bounty hunter) compete for a treasure of gold while wandering about the Spanish countryside. **103m/C VHS.** *IT SP* Edd Byrnes, Gilbert Roland, George Hilton, Kareen O'Hara, Pedro Sanchez, Gerard Herter; **D:** Enzo G. Castellari. *HHE*

Any Man's Death 🎬🎬 1990 (R) Savage is a globe-trotting reporter on the trail of a worldwide conspiracy who accidentally uncovers a Nazi war criminal in Africa. Well-meaning but confused tale. **105m/C VHS, Beta, LV.** John Savage, William Hickey, Mia Sara, Ernest Borgnine, Michael Lerner; **D:** Tom Clegg.

Any Number Can Play 🎬🎬½ 1949 Fast-moving drama about an ailing gambler who faces a series of crises. Gable gives a commanding performance as the noble dice-roller. Based on the novel by Edward Harris Heath. **102m/B VHS.** Clark Gable, Alexis Smith, Wendell Corey, Audrey Totter, Frank Morgan, Mary Astor, Lewis Stone, Barry Sullivan; **D:** Mervyn LeRoy; **W:** Richard Brooks. *MGM*

Any Place But Home 🎬🎬½ 1997 (PG-13) Roberta (Keller) and Lucas (Lando) Dempsey find themselves in big trouble when Roberta's sister Carrie Miller (Conway) and her low-life hubby Carl (Midkiff) try to involve them in a plan to kidnap 12-year-old John Danforth (Norris), figuring John's rich dad August (Thicke) will be happy to pay the ransom. Roberta manages to get the kid and the money away from the Millers but she and Lucas discover John is an abused child and terrified of his father. The threesome go on the run with the Millers, August's hired help, and the FBI on their trail. Cable thriller.**CW:** Thematic elements including child abuse and kidnapping, and for violence and brief sensuality. **90m/C VHS.** Joe Lando, Mary Page Keller, Alan Thicke, Dale Midkiff, Cristie Conway, Richard Roundtree; **D:** Rob Hedden; **W:** Bart Baker. *USH*

Any Wednesday 🎬🎬½ *Bachelor Girl Apartment* 1966 Okay sex farce about powerful industrialist Robards' use of his mistress's apartment as a tax write-off. When a young company executive learns of the "company" apartment, he meets Robards' nonchalant wife for a tryst of their own. Based on Muriel Resnik's Broadway play; similar to the 1960 "The Apartment." 110m/C VHS, Beta. Jane Fonda, Jason Robards Jr., Dean Jones, Rosemary Murphy; **D:** Robert Ellis Miller; **W:** Julius J. Epstein, Philip C. Epstein; **M:** George Duning. *WAR*

Any Which Way You Can 🐾🐾 1980 (PG) Bad brawler Philo Beddoe and his buddy Clyde, the orangutan, are back again in the sequel to "Every Which Way But Loose." This time Philo is tempted to take part in a big bout for a large cash prize. Clyde steals scenes, brightening up the no-brainer story. 116m/C VHS, Beta, LV. Clint Eastwood, Sondra Locke, Ruth Gordon, Harry Guardino; **D:** Buddy Van Horn. *WAR*

Anything for a Thrill 🐾 1937 Two kids save a cameraman's career, make friends with a millionairess, and foil some crooks. 59m/B VHS. Frankie Darro, Kane Richmond; **D:** Leslie Goodwins. *NOS, DVT, HEG*

Anything for Love 🐾½ 1993 Teen musician is the object of a school bully's rage so he decides to dress up as a girl to escape the guy's fists. 90m/C VHS. Corey Haim. *THV*

Anzacs: The War Down Under 🐾🐾🐾 1985 Well-made Australian TV miniseries about the Australian & New Zealand Army Corps during WWI. Follows the men from the time they enlist to the campaigns in Gallipoli and France. 165m/C VHS, Beta. AU Paul Hogan, Andrew Clarke, Jon Blake, Megan Williams; **D:** George Miller. *CEL*

Anzio 🐾🐾 *The Battle for Anzio; Lo Sbarco di Anzio* 1968 The historic Allied invasion of Italy during WWII as seen through the eyes of American war correspondent Mitchum. Fine cast waits endlessly to leave the beach, though big battle scenes are effectively rendered. Based on the book by Wynford Vaughan Thomas. 117m/C VHS, Beta. Robert Mitchum, Peter Falk, Arthur Kennedy, Robert Ryan, Earl Holliman, Mark Damon, Reni Santoni, Patrick Magee; **D:** Edward Dmytryk. *NO*

Apache 🐾🐾½ 1954 Lancaster is the only Indian in Geronimo's outfit who refuses to surrender in this chronicle of a bitter battle between the Indians and the U.S. cavalry in the struggle for the West. First western for Aldrich is a thoughtful piece for its time that had the original tragic ending reshot (against Aldrich's wishes) to make it more happy. Adapted from "Bronco Apache" by Paul I. Wellman. 91m/C VHS, Beta. Burt Lancaster, John McIntire, Jean Peters; **D:** Robert Aldrich; **C:** Ernest Laszlo. *MGM, FOX, FCT*

Apache Blood 🐾½ *Pursuit* 1975 (R) An Indian Brave, the lone survivor of an Indian massacre by the U.S. Army, squares off with a cavalry scout in the forbidding desert. 92m/C VHS. Ray Danton, DeWitt Lee, Troy Neighbors, Diane Taylor, Eva Kovacs, Jason Clark; **D:** Thomas Quillen.

Apache Chief 🐾 1950 Two Apache tribe leaders, one good, the other evil clash. Ultimately, and perhaps predictably, they face each other in hand-to-hand combat and peace prevails. 60m/B VHS, Beta, LV. Alan Curtis, Tom Neal, Russell Hayden, Carol Thurston; **D:** Frank McDonald. *NO*

Apache Kid's Escape 🐾 1930 The Apache Kid leads the cavalry on a wild chase across the plains in this saga of the old west. 60m/B VHS, Beta. Jack Perrin, Buzz Barton. *NOS, DVT, RXM*

Apache Rose 🐾🐾 1947 Gambling boat owner plots to gain control of oil found on Vegas Ranch. Roy and Dale oppose the idea. First of the series in color; the original, unedited version of the film. 75m/B VHS, Beta, LV. Roy Rogers, Dale Evans, Olin Howlin, George Meeker; **D:** William Witney. *FOX, NOS, VCN*

Apache Uprising 🐾½ 1966 A standard western with Calhoun as the lawman up against gunfighters and stagecoach robbers as well as the usual Indians. 60m/C VHS, **Closed Caption.** Rory Calhoun, Corinne Calvet, DeForest Kelley, John Russell, Lon Chaney Jr., Gene Evans, Richard Arlen, Robert Harris,

---

Arthur Hunnicutt, Jean Parker, Johnny Mack Brown; **D:** R.G. Springsteen. *PAR*

Apache Woman 🐾½ 1955 Bridges stars as a government agent sent to investigate some crimes committed by a group of Apache Indians. As he tries to calm the townspeople, Bridges discovers that the group is made up of white people led by an educated half-breed. He instigates the help of the half-breed's sister (and also Bridges' love interest) to stop the gang. Some good action, but lots of dull spots. 82m/C VHS. Lloyd Bridges, Joan Taylor, Lance Fuller, Morgan Jones, Paul Birch, Jonathan Haze, Paul Dubov, Lou Place; **D:** Roger Corman. *COL, FCT*

Apaches Last Battle 🐾🐾 *Old Shatterhand; Shatterhand* 1964 A boundary scout discovers that the ward of an Apache chief has been framed for murder by a cavalry officer who wants to start an Indian war in this exciting Euro western. ?m/C VHS. Lex Barker, Guy Madison, Pierre Brice. *SNC*

Aparajito 🐾🐾🐾½ *The Unvanquished* 1958 The second of the Apu trilogy, about a boy growing up in India, after "Pather Panchali," and before "The World of Apu." Apu is brought to Benares and his education seriously begins. The work of a master; in Bengali with English subtitles. 108m/B VHS, Beta. IN Pinaki Sen Gupta, Karuna Banerjee, Kanu Banerjee, Ramani Sen Gupta; **D:** Satyajit Ray. Venice Film Festival '57: Best Film. *FCT, MRV, TIM*

Apart from Hugh 🐾🐾 1994 Collin and Hugh have been living together for a year and to celebrate the occasion, Hugh decides to plan an anniversary party. Unfortunately, Collin hasn't told Hugh he's having second thoughts about their relationship. Directorial debut of FitzGerald. 87m/B VHS. **D:** Jon FitzGerald. *WBF*

The Apartment 🐾🐾🐾½ 1960 A lowly insurance clerk tries to climb the corporate ladder by "loaning" his apartment out to executives having affairs. Problems arise, however, when he unwittingly falls for the most recent girlfriend of the boss. Highly acclaimed social satire. 125m/B VHS, Beta, LV, **Letterbox.** Jack Lemmon, Shirley MacLaine, Fred MacMurray, Ray Walston, Jack Kruschen, Joan Shawlee, Edie Adams, Hope Holiday, David Lewis; **D:** Billy Wilder; **W:** I.A.L. Diamond, Billy Wilder; **C:** Joseph LaShelle. Academy Awards '60: Best Art Direction/Set Decoration (B & W), Best Director (Wilder), Best Film Editing, Best Picture, Best Story & Screenplay; British Academy Awards '60: Best Actor (Lemmon), Best Actress (MacLaine), Best Film; Directors Guild of America Awards '60: Best Director (Wilder); Golden Globe Awards '61: Best Actor—Musical/Comedy (Lemmon), Best Actress—Musical/Comedy (MacLaine), Best Film—Musical/Comedy, National Film Registry '94;; New York Film Critics Awards '60: Best Director (Wilder), Best Film, Best Screenplay; Nominations: Academy Awards '60: Best Actor (Lemmon), Best Actress (MacLaine), Best Black and White Cinematography, Best Sound, Best Supporting Actor (Kruschen). *MGM, BTV*

Apartment Zero 🐾🐾🐾½ 1988 (R) A decidedly weird, deranged psychological drama about the parasite/host-type relationship between two roommates in downtown Buenos Aires: one, an obsessive British movie nut, the other, a sexually mesmerizing stud who turns out to be a cold-blooded psycho. 124m/C VHS, Beta, LV. GB Hart Bochner, Colin Firth, Fabrizio Bentivoglio, Liz Smith; **D:** Martin Donovan; **W:** Martin Donovan, David Koepp. *FXL, FCT, IME*

The Ape 🐾🐾 1940 When his daughter dies of a crippling disease, Karloff becomes fixated with the mission to cure paralysis. Obviously distraught, he begins donning the hide of an escaped circus ape whose spinal fluid is the key to the serum. Hide-bedecked, he slays unknowing townspeople to tap them of their spinal fluid and cure his latest patient. 62m/B VHS, Beta. Boris Karloff, Maris Wrixon, Henry Hall, Gertrude Hoffman; **D:** William Nigh. *NOS, SNC, VYY*

A*P*E* woof! 1976 (PG) A*P*E* is 36 feet tall and ten tons of animal fury who destroys anything that comes between him and the actress he loves. Cheap rip-off of Kong. 87m/C VHS, Beta. Rod Arrants, Joanna DeVarona, Alex Nicol; **D:** Paul Leder.

The Ape Man 🐾🐾 *Lock Your Doors* 1943 With the aid of a secret potion, a scientist turns himself into a murderous ape. The only way to regain his human side is to ingest human spinal fluid. Undoubtedly inspired by Boris Karloff's 1940 film, "The Ape." 64m/B VHS, Beta. Wallace Ford, Bela Lugosi; **D:** William Beaudine. *NOS, MRV, SNC*

A.P.E.X. 🐾🐾 1994 (R) Nicholas Sinclair (Keats), a researcher from 2073, time travels back to 1973 to retrieve a faulty robot probe called A.P.E.X. (Advanced Prototype Extermination Unit). Unwittingly he has been infected with a mysterious virus and when he returns it's to a version of his own time where humans are dying from the virus and robots are sent to eradicate the few survivors. It also seems Sinclair is now a guerilla in an anti-robot army. Yes, it sounds like "The Terminator" but the action moves and though the budget is limited the special effects are still impressive. 103m/C VHS, **Closed Caption.** Richard Keats, Mitchell Cox, Lisa Ann Russell, Marcus Aurelius, Adam Lawson; **D:** Phillip J. Roth; **W:** Phillip J. Roth, Ronald Schmidt; **M:** Jim Goodwin. *REP*

The Apocalypse 🐾🐾 1996 (R) Two space salvage crews try to prevent an explosives-ladened spaceship from colliding with Earth. **CW:** Violence. 96m/C VHS, LV. Sandra Bernhard, Laura San Giacomo, Cameron Dye, Frank Zagarino, Matt McCoy; **D:** Hubert de la Bouillerie. *APX*

Apocalypse Now 🐾🐾🐾🐾 1979 (R) Coppola's $40 million epic vision of the Vietnam War was inspired by Joseph Conrad's novella "Heart of Darkness," and continues to be the subject of debate. Disillusioned Army captain Sheen travels upriver into Cambodia to assassinate overweight renegade colonel Brando. His trip is punctuated by surrealistic battles and a terrifying descent into a land where human rationality seems to have slipped away. Considered by some to be the definitive picture of war in its overall depiction of chaos and primal bloodletting; by others, overwrought and unrealistic. May not translate as well to the small screen, yet worth seeing if for nothing more than Duvall's ten minutes of scenery chewing as a battle-obsessed major ("I love the smell of napalm in the morning!"), a study in manic machismo. Stunning photography by Vittorio Storaro, awe-inspiring battle scenes, and effective soundtrack montage. Both Sheen and Coppola suffered emotional breakdowns during the prolonged filming, and that's a very young Fishburne in his major film debut. Available in widescreen format on laserdisc and in a remastered version in letterbox on VHS with a remixed soundtrack that features Dolby Surround stereo. In 1991 a documentary detailing the making of the film, "Hearts of Darkness: A Filmmaker's Apocalypse," was released. 153m/C VHS, Beta, LV, CD-I, **Letterbox.** Marlon Brando, Martin Sheen, Robert Duvall, Frederic Forrest, Sam Bottoms, Scott Glenn, Albert Hall, Laurence "Larry" Fishburne, Harrison Ford, G.D. Spradlin, Dennis Hopper, Colleen Camp, Tom Mason, R. Lee Ermey; **D:** Francis Ford Coppola; **W:** Francis Ford Coppola, John Milius; **C:** Vittorio Storaro; **M:** Carmine Coppola. Academy Awards '79: Best Cinematography, Best Sound; British Academy Awards '79: Best Director (Coppola), Best Supporting Actor (Duvall); Cannes Film Festival '79: Best Film; Golden Globe Awards '80: Best Director (Coppola), Best Supporting Actor (Duvall), Best Score; National Society of Film Critics Awards '79: Best Supporting Actor (Forrest); Nominations: Academy Awards '79: Best Adapted Screenplay, Best Art Direction/Set Decoration, Best Director (Coppola), Best Film Editing, Best Picture, Best Supporting Actor (Duvall). *PAR*

Apollo 13 🐾🐾🐾½ 1995 (PG) Realistic big-budget reenactment of the 1970 Apollo lunar mission that ran into a "problem" 205,000 miles from home reunites Hanks and Sinese from "F. Gump" and Howard and Hanks from "Splash." And an enjoyable reunion it is. Explosion in one of two oxygen tanks helping power the spacecraft leaves the three astronauts (led by Hanks) tumbling through space. With the electrical system kaput and oxygen running low, the men seek refuge in the Lunar Excursion Module. Since it's based on the real event and the outcome is known, director Howard concentrates on the personalities and the details of the seven-day adventure at Mission Control and in space, in the process delivering the dramatic payload. Weightless shots are the real deal as crew filmed for ten days and made 600 parabolic loops in a KC-135 jet, NASA's "Vomit Comet," the long plunge creating 25 seconds of weightlessness. Special effects (by James Cameron's Digital Domain) and set design do the rest; no NASA footage is used, though original TV footage is used to dramatic effect. Script, with an uncredited rewrite by John Sayles, is based on the 1994 book, "Lost Moon," written by 13's Jim Lovell (who has a cameo as the Navy captain welcoming the astronauts aboard the recovery ship), while Apollo 15 commander David Scott served as a consultant. **140m/C VHS, LV, Closed Caption, DVD.** Tom Hanks, Kevin Bacon, Bill Paxton, Gary Sinise, Ed Harris, Kathleen Quinlan, Brett Cullen, Emily Ann Lloyd, Miko Hughes, Max Elliott Slade, Jean Speegle Howard, Tracy Reiner, Michelle Little, David Andrews, Mary Kate Schellhardt; **D:** Ron Howard; **W:** William Broyles Jr., Al Reinert; **C:** Dean Cundey; **M:** James Horner. Academy Awards '95: Best Film Editing, Best Sound; Directors Guild of America Awards '95: Best Director (Howard); Screen Actors Guild Award '95: Best Supporting Actor (Harris); Cast; Blockbuster Entertainment Awards '96: Drama Actor, Theatrical (Hanks); Nominations: Academy Awards '95: Best Adapted Screenplay, Best Art Direction/Set Decoration, Best Picture, Best Supporting Actor (Harris), Best Supporting Actress (Quinlan), Best Original Dramatic/Comedy Score; British Academy Awards '95: Best Cinematography; Golden Globe Awards '96: Best Director (Howard), Best Film—Drama, Best Supporting Actor (Harris), Best Supporting Actress (Quinlan); MTV Movie Awards '96: Best Film, Best Male Performance (Hanks); Writers Guild of America '95: Best Adapted Screenplay. *USH*

Apology 🎞🎞 **1986** A psychotic killer stalks Warren, an experimental artist, in Manhattan while a detective stalks the killer. Made for cable, so expect a little more sex and violence than network TV movies. Written by Medoff, author of "Children of a Lesser God." **98m/C VHS.** Lesley Ann Warren, Peter Weller, John Glover, George Loros, Jimmie Ray Weeks, Christopher Noth, Harvey Fierstein; **D:** Robert Bierman; **W:** Mark Medoff; **M:** Maurice Jarre. *NO*

The Apostle 🎞🎞🎞 **1997 (PG-13)** No-holds-barred look at one man's search for religious redemption. Eulis Dewey (Duvall) is a devout, middle-aged, Pentecostal preacher in Texas, with a true gift for inspiring his congregation. Unfortunately, he's not so inspiring to his wife Jessie (Fawcett), who's cheating on him with younger minister, Horace (Allen). When Eulis discovers the infidelity, he strikes Horace with a bat, sending the man into a coma. Eulis escapes and winds up in the predominantly black town of Bayou Boutte, Louisiana, having shed his old identity for that of E.F., "The Apostle" of God. He zealously starts up a new church, seeking salvation, but his past comes back to haunt him.**CW:** Thematic elements and a related scene of violence. **134m/C VHS, Closed Caption, DVD.** Robert Duvall, Miranda Richardson, Farrah Fawcett, John Beasley, Todd Allen, June Carter Cash, Billy Bob Thornton, Rick Dial, Walton Goggins, Billy Joe Shaver; **D:** Robert Duvall; **W:** Robert Duvall; **C:** Barry Markowitz; **M:** David Mansfield. Independent Spirit Awards '98: Best Actor (Duvall), Best Director (Duvall), Best Film; Los Angeles Film Critics Association Awards '97: Best Actor (Duvall); National Society of Film Critics Awards '97: Best Actor (Duvall); Nominations: Academy Awards '97: Best Actor (Duvall); Independent Spirit Awards '98: Best Screenplay, Best Supporting Actress (Fawcett, Richardson); Screen Actors Guild Award '97: Best Actor (Duvall). *USH*

The Appaloosa 🎞🎞½ *Southwest to Sonora* **1966** A lamenting loner who decides to begin anew by breeding Appaloosas is ripped off by a desperate woman who steals his horse in order to get away from her abusive amour. Brando falls in love with the girl and the two amazingly survive a wealth of obstacles in their battle against Mexican

bandits. **99m/C VHS, Beta, LV.** Marlon Brando, Anjanette Comer, John Saxon; **D:** Sidney J. Furie; **W:** James Bridges; **C:** Russell Metty. *USH*

Applause 🎞🎞🎞 **1929** Morgan plays a down-and-out burlesque star trying to protect her fresh from the convent daughter. Definitely dated, but a marvelous performance by Morgan. Film buffs will appreciate this early talkie. **78m/B VHS.** Helen Morgan, Joan Peers, Fuller Mellish Jr., Henry Wadsworth, Dorothy Cumming; **D:** Rouben Mamoulian. *PAR*

The Apple 🎞½ **1980 (PG)** Futuristic musical filmed in Berlin that features a young, innocent, folk-singing couple who nearly become victims of the evil, glitzy record producer who tries to recruit the couple into a life of sex and drugs. **90m/C VHS, Beta.** Catherine Mary Stewart, Alan Love, Grace Kennedy, Joss Ackland; **D:** Menahem Golan. *NO*

The Apple Dumpling Gang 🎞🎞 **1975 (G)** Three frisky kids strike it rich and trigger the wildest bank robbery in the gold-mad West. Unmistakably Disney, a familial subplot and a wacky duo are provided. Mediocre yet superior to its sequel, "The Apple Dumpling Gang Rides Again." **100m/C VHS, Beta, Closed Caption.** Bill Bixby, Susan Clark, Don Knotts, Tim Conway, David Wayne, Slim Pickens, Harry (Henry) Morgan; **D:** Norman Tokar; **M:** Buddy Baker. *DIS*

The Apple Dumpling Gang Rides Again 🎞🎞 **1979 (G)** Two lovable hombres terrorize the West in their bungling attempt to go straight. Fans of Conway or Knotts may appreciate this sequel to Disney's "The Apple Dumpling Gang." **88m/C VHS, Beta.** Tim Conway, Don Knotts, Tim Matheson, Kenneth Mars, Harry (Henry) Morgan, Jack Elam; **D:** Vincent McEveety; **M:** Buddy Baker. *DIS*

The Applegates 🎞🎞½ *Meet the Applegates* **1989 (R)** Ecologically correct Amazonian beetles are more than a little miffed about the slash-and-burn tactics in their home and decide to establish a kinder, gentler habitat. Bug Begley and his brood transform themselves into average Americans, but then don't want to leave their decadent life: even insects aren't immune to the lure of sex, drugs, and cable shopping networks. Imaginative, often quite funny one-joke flick should've been shorter. Fits quite well as a double feature with Lehmann's earlier "Heathers." **90m/C VHS, Beta, LV, Closed Caption.** Ed Begley Jr., Stockard Channing, Dabney Coleman, Cami Cooper, Bobby Jacoby, Glenn Shadix, Susan Barnes, Adam Biesk, Savannah Smith Boucher; **D:** Michael Lehmann; **W:** Michael Lehmann, Redbeard Simmons. *FOX, VTR*

The Appointment woof! **1982** A supernatural force enters the bodies and minds of people and suddenly everyone begins going crazy. **90m/C VHS, Beta, 8mm.** Edward Woodward, Jane Merrow; **D:** Lindsey C. Vickers; **C:** Carlo DiPalma. *NO*

Appointment in Honduras 🎞🎞 **1953** An adventurer goes on a dangerous trek through the Central American jungles to deliver funds to the Honduran President. **79m/C VHS, Beta.** Glenn Ford, Ann Sheridan, Zachary Scott; **D:** Jacques Tourneur. *NO*

Appointment with Crime 🎞🎞½ **1945** After serving a prison sentence, an ex-con sets out to avenge himself against the colleagues who double crossed him. Well done, highlighted by superior characterizations. Based on the story by Michael Leighton. **91m/B VHS, Beta.** *GB* William Hartnell, Raymond Lovell, Robert Beatty, Herbert Lom, Joyce Howard, Alan Wheatley, Cyril Smith; **D:** John Harlow; **W:** John Harlow. *SNC*

Appointment with Death 🎞½ **1988 (PG)** Disappointing Agatha Christie mystery with Hercule Poirot solving the murder of a shrewish widow in 1937 Palestine. **103m/C VHS, Beta, LV, Closed Caption.** Peter Ustinov, Lauren Bacall, Carrie Fisher, John Gielgud, Piper Laurie, Hayley Mills, Jenny Seagrove, David Soul; **D:** Michael Winner; **W:** Anthony Shaffer, Peter Buckman, Michael Winner; **M:** Pino Donaggio. *WAR, FCT*

Appointment with Fear 🎞 **1985 (R)** A tough detective investigates a murder and all of the clues lead him mysteriously to a comatose asylum inmate. **95m/C VHS, Beta, LV.** Michael Wyle, Michelle Little, Kerry Remsen, Douglas Rowe, Garrick Dowhen, Deborah Voorhees; **D:** Alan Smithee, Razmi Thomas; **W:** Gideon Davis, Bruce Mead. *ART*

Apprentice to Murder 🎞🎞 **1988 (PG-13)** A small Pennsylvania Dutch town is shaken by a series of murders, thought to be associated with a bizarre local mystic and healer. Based on a true story, sort of. **97m/C VHS, Beta, LV, Closed Caption.** Donald Sutherland, Mia Sara, Chad Lowe, Eddie Jones; **D:** Ralph L. Thomas; **W:** Allan Scott, Wesley Moore. *VTR, HHE*

The Apprenticeship of Duddy Kravitz 🎞🎞🎞½ **1974 (PG)** Young Jewish man in Montreal circa 1948 is driven by an insatiable need to be the "somebody" everyone has always told him he will be. A series of get-rich-quick schemes backfire in different ways, and he becomes most successful at driving people away. Young Dreyfuss is at his best. Made in Canada with thoughtful detail, and great cameo performances. Script by Richler, from his novel. **121m/C VHS, Beta.** *CA* Richard Dreyfuss, Randy Quaid, Denholm Elliott, Jack Warden, Micheline Lanctot, Joe Silver; **D:** Ted Kotcheff; **W:** Mordecai Richler, Lionel Chetwynd. Berlin International Film Festival '74: Golden Berlin Bear; Writers Guild of America '74: Best Adapted Screenplay; Nominations: Academy Awards '74: Best Adapted Screenplay. *PAR*

April Fool 🎞🎞½ **1926** A man makes a fortune in the umbrella business and then discovers his daughter has fallen in love with the son of a nouveaux riche neighbor, resulting in all sorts of complications. **63m/B VHS.** Alexander Carr, Mary Alden, Raymond Keane, Snitz Edwards; **D:** Nat Ross; **W:** Zion Myers. *GPV, FCT*

April Fools 🎞🎞 **1969 (PG)** A bored stockbroker falls in love with a beautiful woman who turns out to be married to his boss. **95m/C VHS, Beta.** Jack Lemmon, Catherine Deneuve, Sally Kellerman, Peter Lawford, Charles Boyer, Myrna Loy, Harvey Korman; **D:** Stuart Rosenberg; **M:** Marvin Hamlisch. *FOX*

April Fool's Day 🎞 **1986 (R)** Rich girl Foreman invites eight college friends to spend the April Fool's weekend with her at her family's isolated island mansion. Everyone is subjected to an endless series of practical jokes when things apparently turn deadly and several of the kids begin disappearing. Lame spoof of "Friday the 13th" and other teenagers-in-peril slasher films. **90m/C VHS, Beta, LV, Closed Caption.** Deborah Foreman, Jay Baker, Pat Barlow, Lloyd Berry, Deborah Goodrich, Ken Olandt, Griffin O'Neal, Tom Heaton, Mike Nomad, Leah K. Pinsent, Clayton Rohner, Amy Steel, Thomas F. Wilson; **D:** Fred Walton; **W:** Danilo Bach; **M:** Charles Bernstein. *PAR*

April In Paris 🎞🎞 **1952** Dynamite Jackson (Day), a chorus girl accidentally sent by the State Department to perform in Paris, meets S. Winthrop Putnam (Bolger), a timid fellow trapped in an unpleasant marriage. They eventually sing and dance their way to warm feelings as they begin a lifelong romance and live happily ever after. **100m/C VHS.** Doris Day, Ray Bolger, Claude Dauphin, Eve Miller, George Givot, Paul Harvey; **D:** David Butler; **W:** Jack Rose, Melville Shavelson. *WAR, CCB, MVD*

The Arab Conspiracy 🎞🎞 *The Next Man; Double Hit* **1976 (R)** Sharpe plays a hit-woman conspiring with assassins from all over the world to kill Arab leaders. One problem—she falls in love with Saudi Arabian ambassador Connery as he tries to gain peace with Palestine. **108m/C VHS.** Sean Connery, Cornelia Sharpe, Albert Paulsen, Adolfo Celi, Charles Cioffi; **D:** Richard Sarafian; **W:** Alan R. Trustman; **C:** Michael Chapman; **M:** Michael Kamen. *SIM, QVD*

Arabesque 🎞🎞½ **1966** A college professor is drawn into international espionage by a beautiful woman and a plot to assassinate an Arab prince. Stylish and fast moving. From the novel "The Cipher" by Gordon Cotler. **105m/C VHS, Beta.** Gregory Peck, Sophia Loren, George Coulouris; **D:** Stanley Donen; **M:** Henry Mancini. *USH, FCT*

Arabian Nights 🎬🎬 1942 Two brothers fight for the throne of Turkey and the affection of the sultry dancing girl Scheherazade. Enchanting costumes and lavish sets augment the fantasy atmosphere. **87m/C VHS, Closed Caption.** Jon Hall, Maria Montez, Sabu, Leif Erickson, Edgar Barrier, Richard Lane, Turhan Bey; **D:** John Rawlins; **W:** Michael Hogan; **C:** Milton Krasner. Nominations: Academy Awards '42: Best Color Cinematography, Best Sound, Best Original Dramatic/Comedy Score. *USH, FCT*

Arabian Nights 🎬🎬🎬 1974 The third of Pasolini's epic, explicit adaptations of classic portmanteau, featuring ten of the old Scheherazade favorites adorned by beautiful photography, explicit sex scenes and homoeroticism. In Italian with English subtitles; available dubbed. **130m/C VHS, Beta, LV, Letterbox.** *IT* Ninetto Davoli, Franco Merli, Ines Pellegrini, Luigina Rocchi; **D:** Pier Paolo Pasolini; **M:** Ennio Morricone. *WBF*

Arachnophobia 🎬🎬½ 1990 (PG-13) Big-budget big-bug horror story has a few funny moments as lots and lots of spiders wreak havoc in a white picket fence community somewhere off the beaten track. Lethal South American spider makes a trek to sunny California, meets up with local spiders, and rapidly multiplies. Utterly arachnophobic (read: totally scared of spiders) town doctor Daniels pairs with gung-ho exterminator Goodman to try and track down the culprits. The script's a bit yawn-inspiring but the cast and effects will keep you from dozing off. Directorial debut for Marshall, a longtime friend and producer for Spielberg. **109m/C VHS, Beta, LV, Letterbox, Closed Caption.** Jeff Daniels, John Goodman, Harley Jane Kozak, Julian Sands, Roy Brocksmith, Stuart Pankin, Brian McNamara, Mark L. Taylor, Henry Jones, Peter Jason, James Handy; **D:** Frank Marshall; **W:** Wesley Strick, Don Jakoby; **C:** Mikael Salomon; **M:** Trevor Jones. *HPH*

Arcade 🎬½ 1993 (R) All the kids in town are desperate to play the new virtual reality game Arcade, only the game is just a little too real. Seems it can transport you into another world with its stunning graphics and sound effects but you really put your life on the line. Only Alex (Ward) worries when kids start to disappear and she decides to battle the game for their lives. **CW:** Violence. **85m/C VHS, Beta, Closed Caption.** Megan Ward, Peter Billingsley, John de Lancie, Sharon Farrell, Seth Green, Humberto Ortiz, Jonathan Fuller, Norbert Weisser; **D:** Albert Pyun; **W:** David S. Goyer; **M:** Alan Howarth. *PAR*

Arcadia of My Youth 1982 In the 30th century the evil Illumidus Empire has conquered Earth and only the heroic Captain Harlock and his friends can battle their tyranny. Based on Matsumoto Leiji's comic book series. Draws parallels to the post-WWII occupation of Japan. Animated; in Japanese with English subtitles. **130m/C VHS.** *JP ANI*

Arch of Triumph 🎬🎬🎬 1948 In Paris, an Austrian refugee doctor falls in love just before the Nazis enter the city. Big-budget boxoffice loser featuring fine cast but sluggish pace. Based on the Erich Maria Remarque novel and remade for television. **120m/B VHS.** Ingrid Bergman, Charles Boyer, Charles Laughton, Louis Calhern; **D:** Lewis Milestone; **W:** Harry Brown, Lewis Milestone; **C:** Russell Metty. *REP*

Arch of Triumph 🎬🎬½ 1985 A refugee doctor falls in love with a mystery woman as the Nazis enter Paris. Made for television remake of the 1948 film. **95m/C VHS.** Anthony Hopkins, Lesley-Anne Down, Donald Pleasence, Frank Finlay; **D:** Waris Hussein; **W:** Charles Israel; **M:** Georges Delerue. *FCT*

Archer: The Fugitive from the Empire 🎬 1981 A young warrior battles the forces of evil in this television movie. Lots of strange names to learn even if you already know who's going to win the final battle. **97m/C VHS, Beta.** Lane Caudell, Belinda Bauer, George Kennedy, Victor Campos, Kabir Bedi, George Innes, Marc Alaimo, Allen Rich, John Hancock, Priscilla Pointer, Sharon Barr; **D:** Nick Corea. *USH*

Archer's Adventure 🎬½ 1985 An Australian family film based on a true story. A horse-trainer's young apprentice delivers a prize racehorse to Melbourne, through 600 miles of tough frontier, devious bush rangers, and disaster. **120m/C VHS, Beta.** *AU* Brett Climo, Nicole Kidman; **D:** Denny Lawrence. *VTR, TVC*

Archie: Return to Riverdale 🎬🎬½ 1990 (PG) Archie, Reggie, Betty, Veronica, and Jughead return to Riverdale for their 15-year class reunion. Made for TV; based on the comic book. **85m/C VHS.** Christopher Rich, Lauren Holly, Karen Kopins, Sam Whipple, Gary Kroeger; **D:** Dick Lowry. *NHO*

Arctic Blue 🎬½ 1993 (R) Alaskan biologist Walsh gets stuck being the local lawman when he's the only one willing to escort Hauer, a homicidal trapper, to a Fairbanks jail. But nothing's that easy—their plane crashes atop a glacier and the duo must battle each other and the elements to survive, while Hauer's brutal partners hunt Walsh. **95m/C VHS, LV, Closed Caption.** Dylan Walsh, Rutger Hauer, Richard Bradford; **D:** Peter Masterson; **W:** Ross LaManna. *COL*

Are Parents People? 🎬🎬 1925 Lighthearted silent comedy about a young girl's successful attempts to reunite her feuding parents. It all begins as she runs away and spends the night in the office of a doctor she has grown to like. After a frantic night of searching, her parents are reunited through love for her. **60m/B VHS.** Betty Bronson, Adolphe Menjou, Florence Vidor. *GPV, PAR*

Are You in the House Alone? 🎬🎬 1978 Made for television adaptation of Richard Peck's award-winning novel. Story of a high school coed who becomes the target of a terror campaign. **100m/C VHS, Beta.** Blythe Danner, Kathleen Beller, Tony Bill, Scott Colomby; **D:** Walter Grauman; **M:** Charles Bernstein. *WOV, GKK*

Are You Lonesome Tonight 🎬🎬½ 1992 (PG-13) Suspense thriller casts Seymour as a wealthy socialite who discovers her husband is having an affair with a phone-sex girl. His sudden and mysterious disappearance forces her to hire a private detective (Stevenson) to track him down, with only the taped conversations as clues. Average made for cable television fare. **91m/C VHS, Beta, Closed Caption.** Jane Seymour, Parker Stevenson, Beth Broderick, Joel Brooks, Robert Pine; **D:** E.W. Swackhamer; **W:** Wesley Moore. *FCT*

Arena 🎬🎬 1989 (PG-13) Remember old boxing melodramas about good-natured palookas, slimy opponents, gangsters and dames? This puts those cliches in a garish sci-fi setting, with handsome Steve Armstrong battling ETs and the astro-mob to be the first human pugilistic champ in decades. A really cute idea (from the screenwriters of "The Rocketeer"), but it conks out at the halfway point. Worth a look for buffs. **97m/C VHS, LV, Closed Caption.** *IT* Paul Satterfield, Claudia Christian, Hamilton Camp, Marc Alaimo, Armin Shimerman, Shari Shattuck, Jack Carter; **D:** Peter Manoogian; **W:** Danny Bilson, Paul DeMeo; **M:** Richard Band. *COL*

Aria 🎬🎬 1988 (R) Ten directors were given carte blanche to interpret ten arias from well-known operas. Henry and D'Angelo star in Julian Temple's rendition of Verdi's "Rigoletto." In Fonda's film debut, she and her lover travel to Las Vegas and eventually kill themselves in the bathtub, just like "Romeo & Juliet." Jarman's piece (a highlight) shows an aged operatic star at her last performance remembering an early love affair. "I Pagliacci" is the one aria in which the director took his interpretation in a straightforward manner. **90m/C VHS, Beta.** *GB* Theresa Russell, Anita Morris, Bridget Fonda, Beverly D'Angelo, Buck Henry, John Hurt; **D:** Ken Russell, Charles Sturridge, Robert Altman, Bill Bryden, Jean-Luc Godard, Bruce Beresford, Nicolas Roeg, Franc Roddam, Derek Jarman, Julien Temple. *FCT, LTY*

Ariel 🎬🎬🎬 1989 Refreshing, offbeat Finnish comedy by highly praised newcomer Kaurismaki. Hoping to find work in Southern Finland, an out-of-work miner from Northern Finland (Pajala) jets off in his white Cadillac convertible given to him in a cafe by a friend, who promptly shoots himself. There's no linear progression toward a happy ending, although antiheroic subject does find employment and romances a meter maid. Mostly, though, he's one of those it's hell being me guys who wouldn't have any luck if it weren't for bad luck. Strange slice-of-life sporting film noir tendencies, although essentially anti-stylistic. **74m/C VHS.** *FI* Susanna Haavisto, Turo Pajala, Matti Pellonpaa; **D:** Aki Kaurismaki; **W:** Aki Kaurismaki. National Society of Film Critics Awards '90: Best Foreign Film. *KIV, FCT*

The Aristocats 🎬🎬🎬 1970 Typically entertaining Disney animated story about pampered pussy Duchess (Gabor) and her three kittens, who are left a fortune in their mistress' will. The fortune goes to the butler if the cats don't survive, so he dumps them in the country hoping they won't find their way home. The cats are aided by tough alley denizen O'Malley (Harris)—it's kind of the feline version of "Lady and the Tramp." Maurice Chevalier sings the title tune. **78m/C VHS. D:** Wolfgang Reitherman; **M:** George Bruns; **V:** Eva Gabor, Phil Harris, Sterling Holloway, Roddy Maude-Roxby, Bill Thompson, Hermione Baddeley, Carol Shelley, Pat Buttram, Nancy Kulp, Paul Winchell. *DIS*

Arizona 🎬🎬½ 1940 Arthur is a hellion in wild 1860 Tucson who falls for the wandering Holden. He's headed for California and she can't keep him in town so Arthur throws herself into business by establishing a freight line. Only warring Apaches try to burn her out and Holden rides in to save the day (with the cavalry and a stampeding cattle herd). Holden's first western is lively but long. **121m/B VHS.** Jean Arthur, William Holden, Warren William, Porter Hall, Paul Harvey, George Chandler, Regis Toomey, Edgar Buchanan; **D:** Wesley Ruggles; **W:** Claude Binyon; **M:** Victor Young. Nominations: Academy Awards '40: Best Original Score. *COL*

Arizona 🎬½ 1986 A group of illegal aliens struggle for survival after they cross the border into the harsh desert. **94m/C VHS, Beta.** *MX* Roberto "Flaco" Guzman, Juan Valentin.

Arizona Badman 🎬½ 1935 There is a bad man in Arizona, and he must be gotten rid of. **60m/B VHS, Beta.** Reb Russell; **D:** S. Roy Luby. *NOS, DVT*

Arizona Bound 🎬 1941 Mesa City is infested with a villain and our "Rough Rider" trio must rid the town of him. **57m/B VHS, Beta.** Buck Jones, Tim McCoy, Raymond Hatton, Dennis Moore, Luana Walters; **D:** Spencer Gordon Bennet. *NOS, VCN, DVT*

Arizona Bushwackers 🎬½ 1967 Routine western that has Confederate spy Keel taking job as sheriff in small Arizona town. Once there, he has to straighten out a few bad guys who have been selling weapons to the Apaches. Notable for presence of old western-movie veterans Ireland, Donlevy, Brady, and MacLane. Based on a story by Steve Fisher. **87m/C VHS, LV.** Howard Keel, Yvonne De Carlo, John Ireland, Marilyn Maxwell, Scott Brady, Brian Donlevy, Barton MacLane; **D:** Lesley Selander. *PAR*

Arizona Cowboy 🎬 1949 An ex-G.I., now the rodeo's big attraction, gets involved in a robbery. **57m/B VHS, Beta.** Rex Allen, Gordon Jones, Roy Barcroft; **D:** R.G. Springsteen. *DVT*

Arizona Days 🎬½ 1937 Cowboys join a minstrel group and rescue the show when a group of toughs try to break it up. **56m/B VHS, Beta.** Tex Ritter, Eleanor Stewart, Syd Saylor, Snub Pollard; **D:** John English. *NOS, VCI, VDM*

Arizona Dream 🎬🎬 1994 (R) Alex (Depp) is a New York drifter who gets stuck working for his uncle's (Lewis) car dealership in a small Arizona town. He meets an eccentric older woman (Dunaway) with a homemade plane and some dreams of her own. Tends toward the surreal and confusing. **CW:** Language; sexuality. **119m/C VHS, Closed Caption.** Johnny Depp, Faye Dunaway, Jerry Lewis, Lili Taylor, Paulina Porizkova, Tricia Leigh Fisher, Vincent Gallo; **D:** Emir Kusturica; **W:** Emir Kusturica, David Atkins; **C:** Vilko Filac. *WAR*

Arizona Gangbusters ⚔ 1940 Below-average oater has real-life cowboy McCoy fighting city hall in order to fight other baddies. Newfield directed under the pseudonym "Peter Stewart." 57m/B VHS. Tim McCoy, Pauline Hadden, Forrest Taylor, Julian Rivero, Curly Dresden; **D:** Sam Newfield. *DVT, HEG*

Arizona Gunfighter ⚔ 1937 A young cowhand seeks revenge against the man who murdered his father in this western. 60m/B VHS, Beta. Bob Steele, Ted Adams; **D:** Sam Newfield. *NOS, DVT*

Arizona Heat ⚔⚔ 1987 (R) A violent cop is teamed up with a tough, but tender female cop in this all-too-familiar tale of two cops chasing a cop killer. 91m/C VHS. Michael Parks, Denise Crosby, Hugh Farrington; **D:** John G. Thomas. *REP*

Arizona Kid ⚔ 1939 Another sagebrush saga featuring Roy in singin' and fightin' action. 54m/B VHS, Beta. Roy Rogers; **D:** Joseph Kane. *NOS, DVT, TIM*

Arizona Mahoney ⚔ 1936 Weird mixture of circus adventure and serious western doesn't work too well. Confused film with farfetched reasons for having the paths of circus performers and cowboys cross. Based on a Zane Grey novel. 58m/B VHS. Joe Cook, Robert Cummings, June Martel, Marjorie Gateson, John Miljan, James Mason; **D:** James Hogan; **W:** Robert Yost, Stuart Anthony. *MOV*

Arizona Raiders ⚔ 1965 Arizona rangers hunt down killers who have been terrorizing the territory. 88m/C VHS, Beta. Audie Murphy, Buster Crabbe, Gloria Talbott; **D:** William Witney. *NOS, VCI, VCN*

Arizona Roundup ⚔½ 1942 Good vs. bad amid tumbleweed, bleached-white chaps, bloodless shoot-outs and happy endings. 54m/B VHS, Beta. Tom George Duryea Keene, Sugar Dawn, Jack Ingram; **D:** Robert Emmett Tansey. *NOS, VDM*

Arizona Stagecoach ⚔ 1942 The Range Busters set out to bust a notorious, guiltless, devil-may-care outlaw gang. 58m/B VHS, Beta. Ray Corrigan, Max Terhune, Kermit Maynard, Charles "Blackie" King, John "Dusty" King; **D:** S. Roy Luby. *NOS*

Arizona Terror ⚔½ 1931 Our hero is on a quest for vengeance, seeking the posse that killed his partner. 64m/B VHS, Beta. Ken Maynard. *VCN*

Arizona Whirlwind ⚔ 1944 Our intrepid heroes must battle torrents of gunfire in order to prevent a stage hold-up in this western saga. 59m/B VHS, Beta. Ken Maynard, Hoot Gibson, Bob Steele. *NOS, DVT*

Ark of the Sun God ⚔ 1982 Another adventurer battles the Nazis and nutsies for a 2000-year-old ark buried in the Sahara. 95m/C VHS, Beta. David Warbeck, John Steiner, Susie Sudlow, Alan Collins, Riccardo Palacio; **D:** Anthony (Antonio Margheriti) Dawson. *TWE*

Armageddon 1998 (PG-13) A Texas-sized asteroid is hurtling towards earth, NASA gets nervous, and it's up to Willis and his misfit oil drillers turned astronaut crew to blow it up. Ya get a little romance as hotshot Affleck smooches with babe Tyler, who's playing Willis' daughter. The second "space rock hits earth" movie, following the somber "Deep Impact." Not yet reviewed. **CW:** Sci-fi disaster action, sensuality and brief language. ?m/C VHS. Bruce Willis, Ben Affleck, Steve Buscemi, Billy Bob Thornton, Liv Tyler, Will Patton, Peter Stormare, Keith David; **D:** Michael Bay; **W:** Jonathan Hensleigh. *NYR*

Armageddon: The Final Challenge ⚔½ 1994 After a nuclear holocaust, evil forces rule the Earth in the guise of "The Future Bank." They send out Fear-Permutator Clones to keep order and kill undesirables but naturally there's a rebel ready to do battle. 85m/C VHS. Todd Jensen, Graham Clarke, Tony Caprari, Joanna Rowlands; **D:** Michael Garcia; **W:** George Garcia, Michael Garcia; **M:** Johan Lass. *YHV*

Armed and Dangerous ⚔⚔ 1986 (PG-13) Candy and Levy are incompetent security guards assigned to a do-nothing job. Things get spiced up when a mobster tries to run a crime ring

under their nose. Candy catches on and winds up in a full-fledged chase. Not as funny as it sounds, though occasionally has moments of genuine comedy. 88m/C VHS, Beta, LV, Closed Caption. John Candy, Eugene Levy, Kenneth McMillan, Brion James, Robert Loggia, Meg Ryan, Don Stroud, Jonathan Banks, Steve Railsback, Bruce Kirby, Tony Burton, Larry Hankin, Judy Landers, David Wohl; **D:** Mark L. Lester; **W:** Harold Ramis, Peter Torokvei, James Keach, Brian Grazer. *COL*

Armed for Action ⚔⚔ 1992 Routine action thriller casts Estevez as Sgt. Phil Towers who gets more than he bargained for when his prisoner, Mafia hitman David Montel, escapes while en route from New York to Los Angeles. When he finally catches up with them, Towers leads a small army of locals on a brutal assault. 88m/C VHS, Closed Caption. Joe Estevez, Rocky Patterson, Barri Murphy, David Harrod, J. Scott Guy; **D:** Shane Spaulding.

Armed Response ⚔⚔ 1986 (R) Carradine leads a group of mercenaries in a battle against Chinatown mobsters. They race to locate a priceless jade statue before it can fall into the wrong hands. 86m/C VHS, Beta, LV. David Carradine, Lee Van Cleef, Mako, Lois Hamilton, Ross Hagen, Brent Huff; **D:** Fred Olen Ray; **C:** Paul Elliott. *NO*

Armistead Maupin's Tales of the City ⚔⚔½ *Tales of the City* 1993 Carefree '70s San Francisco is the setting for the interconnected stories of the inhabitants of 28 Barbary Lane. There's mysterious landlady Mrs. Madrigal (Dukakis); free-spirit Mona Ramsey (Webb); her gay roomie, Michael "Mouse" Tolliver (D'Amico); hetero lawyer-turned-waiter Brian (Gross); nerdy, secretive Norman (DeSantis); and the naively sweet Mary Ann Singleton (Linney). Definite time-warp factor in this pre-AIDS depiction of sex and drugs, but also the timeless search for love and happiness. Maupin first wrote the stories as an ongoing serial for the *San Francisco Chronicle* and they were later turned into six novels. Made for British TV. 360m/C VHS. *GB* Olympia Dukakis, Donald Moffat, Chloe Webb, Laura Linney, Marcus D'Amico, Paul Gross, Stanley DeSantis, Bill Campbell, Cynda Williams, Barbara Garrick, Thomas Gibson, Nina Foch, Paul Dooley, Belita Morena; *Cameos:* Karen Black, Edie Adams, Michael Jeter, Ian McKellen, Rod Steiger, Paul Bartel; **D:** Alastair Reid; **W:** Richard Kramer. *PGV*

Armored Car Robbery ⚔⚔ 1950 Talman and his buddies plot to rob an armored car but are foiled by McGraw and his crimefighters. Surprisingly good B-crime drama. 68m/B VHS. Charles McGraw, Adele Jergens, William Talman, Steve Brodie; **D:** Richard Fleischer. *NO*

Armored Command ⚔½ 1961 A beautiful German spy infiltrates an American outpost during the Battle of the Bulge. Tepid WWII fare made too long after the fact. 105m/B VHS, Beta. Burt Reynolds, Tina Louise, Howard Keel, Earl Holliman, Warner Anderson, Carleton Young; **D:** Byron Haskin. *FOX, FCT*

The Armour of God ⚔ 1986 Chan plays an adventurous thief who steals and sells pieces of a prized medieval armour set to collectors. When a criminal gang kidnaps his girl to get the entire set, Chan must come up with some spectacular saves of both the armour and the girl. In Cantonese with English subtitles. 100m/C VHS. *CH* Jackie Chan; **D:** Jackie Chan. *TAI, FCT*

Army Brats ⚔½ 1984 In this Dutch film a military family goes bloodily and comically to war with itself. Even in a welfare state, parents can't control their wee ones. 105m/C VHS, Beta. *NL* Akkemay, Frank Schaafsma, Peter Faber; **D:** Ruud Van Hemert. *WAR*

Army of Darkness ⚔⚔⚔ *Evil Dead 3; The Medieval Dead* 1992 (R) Campbell returns for a third "Evil Dead" round as the square-jawed, none too bright hero, Ash in this comic book extravaganza. He finds himself hurled back to the 14th-century through the powers of an evil book. There he romances a babe, fights an army of skeletons, and generally causes all those Dark Age knights a lot of grief, as he tries to get back to his own time.

Raimi's technical exuberance is apparent and, as usual, the horror is graphic but still tongue-in-cheek. **CW:** Violence and horror. 77m/C VHS, Beta, LV, Letterbox, Closed Caption. Bruce Campbell, Embeth Davidtz, Marcus Gilbert, Ian Abercrombie, Richard Grove, Michael Earl Reid, Tim Quill, Bridget Fonda, Patricia Tallman, Theodore (Ted) Raimi, Ivan Raimi; **D:** Sam Raimi; **W:** Sam Raimi, Ivan Raimi; **C:** Bill Pope; **M:** Joseph LoDuca, Danny Elfman. *USH, FCT*

Army of One ⚔½ 1994 (R) Santee (Lundgren) and his pal are hauling stolen cars across the desert when a cop pulls them over. Soon there's two dead bodies and Santee's in big trouble. An unrated version is also available. 102m/C VHS, LV. Dolph Lundgren, George Segal, Kristian Alfonso, Geoffrey Lewis, Michelle Phillips; **D:** Vic Armstrong; **W:** Steven Pressfield, Joel Goldsmith. *ART*

Arnold ⚔⚔½ 1973 (PG) Outrageous black comedy involving a woman who marries a cadaver to gain his large inheritance. Lots of bizarre and creative deaths in this horror spoof. Unusual wedding scene is a must-see. 96m/C VHS, Beta. Stella Stevens, Roddy McDowall, Elsa Lanchester, Victor Buono, Bernard Fox, Farley Granger, Shani Wallis, Jamie Farr, Patric Knowles, John McGiver, Norman Stuart; **D:** Georg Fenady; **W:** Jameson Brewer, John Fenton Murray; **C:** William B. Jurgensen; **M:** George Duning. *NO*

Around the World ⚔½ 1943 Kyser leads a USO-like tour to entertain troops. Interesting only in a historical sense. ♫Doodle-Ee-Doo; He's Got a Secret Weapon; Candlelight and Wine; Great News in the Making; They Chopped Down the Old Apple Tree; A Moke from Shamokin. 80m/B VHS. Kay Kyser, Ish Kabibble, Ginny Simms, Joan Davis, Mischa Auer; **D:** Allan Dwan. *TTC*

Around the World in 80 Days ⚔⚔⚔ 1956 (G) Niven is the unflappable Victorian Englishman who wagers that he can circumnavigate the earth in four-score days. With his faithful manservant Cantinflas they set off on a spectacular journey. A perpetual favorite providing ample entertainment. Star-gazers will particularly enjoy the more than 40 cameo appearances by many of Hollywood's biggest names. Adapted from the novel by Jules Verne. 178m/C VHS, Beta, LV, Closed Caption. David Niven, Shirley MacLaine, Cantinflas, Robert Newton, Charles Boyer, Joe E. Brown, Martine Carol, John Carradine, Charles Coburn, Ronald Colman; *Cameos:* Melville Cooper, Noel Coward, Andy Devine, Reginald Denny, Fernandel, Marlene Dietrich, Hermione Gingold, Cedric Hardwicke, Trevor Howard, Glynis Johns, Buster Keaton, Evelyn Keyes, Peter Lorre, Mike Mazurki, Victor McLaglen, John Mills, Robert Morley, Jack Oakie, George Raft, Cesar Romero, Gilbert Roland, Red Skelton, Frank Sinatra, Ava Gardner; **D:** Michael Anderson Sr.; **W:** James Poe, John Farrow, S.J. Perelman; **C:** Lionel Lindon; **M:** Victor Young. Academy Awards '56: Best Adapted Screenplay, Best Color Cinematography, Best Film Editing, Best Picture, Best Original Dramatic/Comedy Score; Golden Globe Awards '57: Best Actor—Musical/Comedy (Cantinflas), Best Film—Drama; New York Film Critics Awards '56: Best Film, Best Screenplay; Nominations: Academy Awards '56: Best Art Direction/Set Decoration (Color), Best Costume Design (Color), Best Director (Anderson). *WAR, BTV, HMV*

Around the World in 80 Days ⚔⚔½ 1989 TV adaptation of the Jules Verne adventure novel that finds Victorian gentleman Phineas Fogg (Brosnan) wagering that he can circle the globe in 80 days. He's pursued by private detective Fix (Ustinov), who suspects him of a daring bank robbery, and faces many trials and much excitement along the way. On two cassettes. 270m/C VHS. Pierce Brosnan, Peter Ustinov, Eric Idle, Arielle Dombasle, Henry Gibson, John Hillerman, Jack Klugman, Christopher Lee, Patrick Macnee, Roddy McDowall, Darren McGavin, John Mills, Robert Morley, Lee Remick, Pernell Roberts, James B. Sikking, Jill St. John, Robert Wagner, Julia Nickson-Soul; **D:** Buzz Kulik. *BFV*

Around the World in 80 Ways ⚔⚔½ 1986 (R) Sometimes clever, sometimes crude Australian comedy about an aging man rescued from a nursing home and taken on a phony trip around the world by his sons.

Odd, but genuinely funny at times. **90m/C VHS, LV.** *AU* Philip Quast, Alan Penney, Diana Davidson, Kelly Dingwall, Gosia Dobrowolska; *D:* Stephen MacLean; *W:* Stephen MacLean, Paul Leadon; *M:* Chris Neal. *NLC*

Around the World in a Daze 🐾🐾½

The Three Stooges Go Around the World in a Daze 1963 The Stooges are servants for Phileas Fogg's great-grandson, who has decided to repeat his ancestor's famous feat. Mayhem ensues when the three help out in their usual efficient, competent way. **93m/B VHS.** Moe Howard, Larry Fine, Joe DeRita, Jay Sheffield; *D:* Norman Maurer. *COL*

Around the World Under the Sea 🐾🐾

1965 Bunch of men and one woman scientist plunge under the ocean in an experiment to predict earthquakes. They plant earthquake detectors along the ocean floor and discover the causes of tidal waves. They have men-women battles. They see big sea critters. **111m/C VHS, Beta.** David McCallum, Shirley Eaton, Gary Merrill, Keenan Wynn, Brian Kelly, Lloyd Bridges; *D:* Andrew Marton. *MGM*

Aroused 🐾

1966 Hollister is an apparently dedicated policeman who commits a number of blunders in the pursuit of a serial killer, including leaving his wife with the sociopath while he cavorts with the prostitute assigned to his protection. Director Holden's psychothriller was gorily ahead of its time. Includes heart-stopping castration sequence. **78m/B VHS.** Janine Lenon, Steve Hollister, Fleurette Carter, Joanna Mills, Tony Palladino, Ted Gelanza; *D:* Anton Holden. *SMW, TPV*

The Arousers 🐾🐾½

Sweet Kill; A Kiss from Eddie 1970 **(R)** Cult item starring hunk Hunter as a handsome California psycho. Tab travels the coast searching for a woman he is able to make love to; those who fail to arouse him come to tragic, climactic ends. Definitely underground and moderately interesting. **85m/C VHS, Beta.** Tab Hunter, Nadyne Turney, Roberta Collins, Isabel Jewell, John Aprea, Angel Fox; *D:* Curtis Hanson.

The Arrangement 🐾½

1969 **(R)** Veteran advertising executive Douglas attempts suicide and then sets out to search for the meaning of life. Along the way he attempts to patch up his "arrangements" with his wife, his mistress and his father. Forced, slow, and self-conscious, though well acted. Adapted by Kazan from the director's own novel. **126m/C VHS, Beta.** Kirk Douglas, Faye Dunaway, Deborah Kerr, Richard Boone, Hume Cronyn, Elia Kazan; *D:* Elia Kazan; *C:* Robert L. Surtees; *M:* David Amram. *WAR*

Arrest Bulldog Drummond 🐾🐾

1938 Captain Drummond is accused of killing the inventor of a futuristic detonator machine and must track down the real killers. Part of the "Bulldog Drummond" series. **57m/B VHS, Beta.** John Howard, Heather Angel, George Zucco, H.B. Warner, E.E. Clive, Reginald Denny, John Sutton; *D:* James Hogan. *PAR, RXM, SNC*

The Arrival 🐾

1990 **(R)** An never-seen alien parasite turns an old man into a vampiric young stud after female blood. Plot and characterizations never do arrive. Horror director Stuart Gordon cameos as a hairy biker. **107m/C VHS, LV.** John Saxon, Joseph Culp, Robert Sampson, Michael J. Pollard; *Cameos:* David Schmoeller; *D:* David Schmoeller; *W:* David Schmoeller; *M:* Richard Band.

The Arrival 🐾🐾½

Shockwave 1996 **(PG-13)** Radio astronomer Zane (Sheen) picks up a message from deep space and discovers a planned alien invasion. When he brings evidence of such to his boss Gordian (Silver) he finds himself on the run from both government operatives and morphing aliens. Starts off slow, but an intelligent script and premise makes this a grade above cheesy. The aliens, with their kooky flaps of skin and back bending knees, are fun to watch. Directorial debut for Twohy. *CW:* Some sci-fi violence and terror, and for brief language. **109m/C VHS, LV, Closed Caption, DVD.** Charlie Sheen, Ron Silver, Lindsay Crouse, Teri Polo; *D:* David N. Twohy; *W:* David N. Twohy; *C:* Hiro Narita; *M:* Arthur Kempel. *ART*

Arrivederci, Baby! 🐾

1966 An unfunny sex comedy with Curtis as a modern Bluebeard who weds rich women and kills them for their money. His last mate plans to turn the tables and kill him first. **100m/C VHS, Closed Caption.** Tony Curtis, Rosanna Schiaffino, Lionel Jeffries, Zsa Zsa Gabor, Nancy Kwan, Fenella Fielding, Anna Quayle, Warren Mitchell, Mischa Auer; *D:* Ken Hughes; *W:* Ken Hughes. *PAR*

Arrowhead 🐾🐾½

1953 A long-running argument between a tough Cavalry scout and an Apache chief pits the cowboys against the Indians in this western fantasy. The personal battles that become all-out wars turn back to fist-fights before the matter is finally settled. **105m/C VHS, Beta, LV, Closed Caption.** Charlton Heston, Jack Palance, Katy Jurado, Brian Keith, Milburn Stone; *D:* Charles Marquis Warren; *C:* Ray Rennahan. *PAR*

Arrowsmith 🐾🐾½

1932 A small-town medical researcher battles his conscience as he juggles his selfish and unselfish motivations for the work he does. He travels to the West Indies to confront the issues of his life and come to terms with himself once and for all. A talented cast takes their time. Based on the classic Sinclair Lewis novel. Two edited versions available (99 and 89 minutes), both of which delete much of Loy. **95m/B VHS, Beta.** Ronald Colman, Helen Hayes, Myrna Loy; *D:* John Ford. Nominations: Academy Awards '32: Best Adapted Screenplay, Best Cinematography, Best Interior Decoration, Best Picture.

Arsenal 🐾🐾🐾

1929 Classic Russian propagandist drama about strikes affecting the Russian home front during WWI, marking Dovzhenko's first great achievement in the realm of Eisenstein and Pudovkin. Silent. **70m/B VHS, Beta.** *RU* Semyon Svashenko; *D:* Alexander Dovzhenko. *NOS, MRV, IHF*

The Arsenal Stadium Mystery 🐾🐾½

1939 Inspector Banks of Scotland Yard tracks down the killer of a football star in this clever but unassuming murder mystery. **85m/B VHS.** *GB* Leslie Banks, Greta Gynt, Ian MacLean, Liane Linden, Anthony Bushell, Esmond Knight; *D:* Thorold Dickinson. *SNC*

Arsenic and Old Lace 🐾🐾🐾½

1944 Set-bound but energetic adaptation of the classic Joseph Kesselring play. Easy-going drama critic Grant is caught in a sticky situation when he learns of his aunts' favorite pastime. Apparently the kind, sweet, lonely spinsters lure gentlemen to the house and serve them elderberry wine with a touch of arsenic, then they bury the bodies in the cellar—a cellar which also serves as the Panama Canal for Grant's cousin (who thinks he's Theodore Roosevelt). Massey and Lorre excel in their sinister roles. One of the best madcap black comedies of all time—a must-see. Shot in 1941 and released a wee bit later. Available colorized. **118m/B VHS, Beta, LV, Closed Caption.** Cary Grant, Josephine Hull, Jean Adair, Raymond Massey, Jack Carson, Priscilla Lane, John Alexander, Edward Everett Horton, John Ridgely, James Gleason, Peter Lorre; *D:* Frank Capra; *W:* Julius J. Epstein, Philip C. Epstein; *M:* Max Steiner. *MGM, FOX, HMV*

Art for Teachers of Children 🐾🐾

1995 Autobiographical account of 14-year-old Jennifer (McDonnell) who becomes a model for married photographer John (Hannah), who's also her boarding school dorm advisor. He's well-known for his nude portraits of young women as well as his affairs with his models and Jennifer's both confused and excited by her emerging sexuality as she and John become lovers. Remarkably detached considering the provocative subject matter. **82m/B VHS.** Caitlin Grace McDonnell, Duncan Hannah, Coles Burroughs, Bryan Keane; *D:* Jennifer Montgomery; *W:* Jennifer Montgomery; *C:* Jennifer Montgomery. *ZGI, WBF*

The Art of Crime 🐾🐾½

1975 A gypsy/detective is drawn into a homicide case when one of his fellow antique dealers is charged with murder. Maintains an atmospheric edge over others of the crime art genre. A pilot for a prospective television series based on the novel "Gypsy in Amber." **72m/C VHS.** Ron Leibman, Jose Ferrer, David Hedison, Jill Clayburgh; *D:* Richard Irving; *W:* Bill Davidson, Martin Smith. *MOV*

The Art of Dying 🐾🐾🐾

1990 A loony videophile decides to start staging productions of his all-time favorite scenes. Trouble is, his idea of a fabulous film moment calls for lots of blood and bile as he lures teenage runaways to his casting couch. Director Hauser stars as the cop who's none too impressed with the cinematic remakes, while cult favorite Pollard is his partner. If you like a little atmosphere and psychological depth in your slashers, you'll find this to be the stuff that populates film noir nightmares. **90m/C VHS, LV.** Wings Hauser, Michael J. Pollard, Sarah Douglas, Kathleen Kinmont, Sydney Lassick, Mitch Hara, Gary Werntz; *D:* Wings Hauser. *PMH*

Artemisia 🐾🐾🐾

1997 **(R)** Artemisia (Cervi) is the teenaged daughter of well-known artist Orazio Gentileschi (Serrault), who encourages her artistic pursuits. He bullies the local art academy to admit Artemisia, a no-no in 17th-century Rome, and she even tries the forbidden territory of the male nude. Soon her artistic passion is matched by a sexual passion for fellow artist Agostino Tassi (Manojlovic), but this time her father isn't so understanding and Artemisia becomes the center of a rape trial. The real Artemisia is considered to be the first known female artist. French with subtitles. *CW:* Strong, graphic sexuality and nudity. **102m/C VHS.** *FR* Valentina Cervi, Michel Serrault, Miki Manojlovic, Luca Zingaretti, Brigitte Catillon, Frederic Pierrot, Maurice Garrel, Yann Tregouet; *D:* Agnes Merlet; *W:* Agnes Merlet; *C:* Benoit Delhomme; *M:* Krishna Levy. Nominations: Golden Globe Awards '98: Best Foreign Language Film. *NYR*

Arthur 🐾🐾🐾

1981 **(PG)** Spoiled, alcoholic billionaire Moore stands to lose everything he owns when he falls in love with a waitress. He must choose between wealth and a planned marriage, or poverty and love. Surprisingly funny, with an Oscar for Gielgud as Moore's valet, and great performance from Minnelli. Arguably the best role Moore's ever had, and he makes the most of it, taking the one-joke premise to a nomination for Oscar actor. ♫ Arthur's Theme; Blue Moon; If You Knew Susie; Santa Claus is Coming to Town. **97m/C VHS, Beta, LV, 8mm, Closed Caption, DVD.** Dudley Moore, Liza Minnelli, John Gielgud, Geraldine Fitzgerald, Stephen Elliott, Jill Eikenberry, Lou Jacobi, Ted Ross, Barney Martin; *D:* Steve Gordon; *M:* Burt Bacharach. Academy Awards '81: Best Song ("Arthur's Theme"), Best Supporting Actor (Gielgud); Golden Globe Awards '82: Best Actor—Musical/Comedy (Moore), Best Film—Musical/Comedy, Best Song ("Arthur's Theme"), Best Supporting Actor (Gielgud); Los Angeles Film Critics Association Awards '81: Best Supporting Actor (Gielgud); New York Film Critics Awards '81: Best Supporting Actor (Gielgud); Writers Guild of America '81: Best Original Screenplay; Nominations: Academy Awards '81: Best Actor (Moore), Best Original Screenplay. *WAR, FCT, BTV*

Arthur 2: On the Rocks 🐾½

1988 **(PG)** When Arthur finally marries his sweetheart, it may not be "happily ever after" because the father of the girl he didn't marry is out for revenge. When Arthur discovers that he is suddenly penniless, a bit of laughter is the cure for the blues and ale serves well when the liquor runs out. A disappointing sequel with few laughs. **113m/C VHS, Beta, LV, 8mm, Closed Caption.** Dudley Moore, Liza Minnelli, John Gielgud, Geraldine Fitzgerald, Stephen Elliott, Ted Ross, Barney Martin, Jack Gilford; *D:* Bud Yorkin; *W:* Andy Breckman; *C:* Stephen Burum; *M:* Burt Bacharach. Golden Raspberry Awards '87: Worst Actress (Minnelli). *WAR, FCT*

Arthur's Hallowed Ground 🎥 1984 A cricket field caretaker battles the board of directors over the fate of his favorite plot of sod. **75m/C VHS, Beta.** Jimmy Jewel, Jean Bolt, Michael Elphick; **D:** Frederick A. (Freddie) Young. *MGM*

Article 99 🎥🎥 1992 (R) Doctors in a Kansas City Veteran's Administration hospital try to heal patients while putting up with bureaucratic red tape and a stingy administrator. When rogue physician Sturgess (Liotta) is dismissed, the patients hold a siege. Sort of son of "M.A.S.H." (Big Daddy Sutherland did Hawkeye) that gets its title from a fictional rule that says veterans can be treated only for conditions related to military service. Erstwhile cast labors to combine comedic and dramatic intentions of script. **100m/C VHS, LV, Closed Caption.** Ray Liotta, Kiefer Sutherland, Forest Whitaker, Lea Thompson, John C. McGinley, John Mahoney, Keith David, Kathy Baker, Eli Wallach, Noble Willingham, Julie Bovasso, Troy Evans, Lynne Thigpen, Jeffrey Tambor, Rutanya Alda; **D:** Howard Deutch; **W:** Ron Cutler; **C:** Rick Bota; **M:** Danny Elfman. *ORI*

Artists and Models 🎥🎥½ 1955 Martin is a struggling comic book artist and Lewis his idiot roommate. The pair become mixed up in both romance and intrigue when Lewis begins talking in his sleep about spys and such. One of the duo's more pleasant cinematic outings. ♫Innamorata; Lucky Song; You Look So Familiar; Why You Pretend. **109m/C VHS, Closed Caption.** Dean Martin, Jerry Lewis, Shirley MacLaine, Dorothy Malone, Eddie Mayehoff, Eva Gabor, Anita Ekberg, George Winslow, Jack Elam, Herbert Rudley, Nick Castle; **D:** Frank Tashlin; **W:** Frank Tashlin, Hal Kanter, Herbert Baker; **C:** Daniel F. Fapp. *PAR, MLB*

Artist's Studio Secrets 🎥 *The Story of an Artist's Studio Secrets; Artist Nude Secrets* 1964 An artist from Greenwich Village only gets aroused by clothed models, so his wife jealously arranges for him to only work with nude women. **78m/B VHS, Beta.** *VDM, TPV*

As Good as Dead 🎥🎥½ 1995 (PG-13) A young woman allows her sick friend to assume her identity but when her friend is murdered, she realizes the killer was really after her. **CW:** Violence. **88m/C VHS, Beta, Closed Caption.** Crystal Bernard, Traci Lords, Judge Reinhold; **D:** Larry Cohen; **W:** Larry Cohen. *PAR*

As Good As It Gets 🎥🎥🎥 *Old Friends* 1997 (PG-13) Entertaining and enjoyable outing from Brooks racked up an impressive list of Oscar noms (including Best Picture). Obsessive-compulsive romance novelist Melvin Udall (Nicholson) is also the meanest guy in New York, liked by nobody and hating all. The only exception is single-mother/waitress Carol (Hunt), who puts up with his annoying habits at the local restaurant where he dines. Forced to look after gay neighbor Kinnear's fussy-but-cute dog, Udall falls into an improbable quest for love, friendship, and a life as "normal as it gets" in this sort of extended-sitcom universe. Snappy dialogue by Brooks and co-writer Andrus, and an easy-going non-stereotypical performance by Kinnear are highlights, almost overshadowing both Hunt's Jodie Foster-like portrayal, and Nicholson's typical but delightful role (both of which won Oscars). **CW:** Strong language, thematic elements, nudity and a beating. **130m/C VHS, LV, DVD.** Jack Nicholson, Helen Hunt, Greg Kinnear, Cuba Gooding Jr., Skeet Ulrich, Shirley Knight, Yeardley Smith, Lupe Ontiveros, Bibi Osterwald, Brian Doyle-Murray, Shane Black, Randall Batinkoff, Danielle Brisebois, Tom McGowan; **Cameos:** Lawrence Kasdan, Harold Ramis, Jimmy Workman, Todd Solondz; **D:** James L. Brooks; **W:** Mark Andrus, James L. Brooks; **C:** John Bailey; **M:** Hans Zimmer. Academy Awards '97: Best Actor (Nicholson), Best Actress (Hunt); Golden Globe Awards '98: Best Actor—Musical/Comedy (Nicholson), Best Actress—Musical/Comedy (Hunt), Best Film—Musical/Comedy; National Board of Review Awards '97: Best Actor (Nicholson), Best Supporting Actor (Kinnear); Screen Actors Guild Award '97: Best Actor (Nicholson), Best Actress (Hunt); Writers Guild of America '97: Best Original Screenplay; Broadcast Film Critics Association Awards '97: Best Actor (Nicholson); Nomi-

nations: Academy Awards '97: Best Film Editing, Best Original Screenplay, Best Picture, Best Supporting Actor, Best Original Musical/Comedy Score; Directors Guild of America Awards '97: Best Director (Brooks); Golden Globe Awards '98: Best Director (Brooks), Best Screenplay; MTV Movie Awards '98: Best Female Performance (Hunt); Screen Actors Guild Award '97: Best Supporting Actor (Kinnear). *COL*

As If It Were Raining 🎥🎥 1963 Constantine gets involved in an embezzlement scheme in Spain in this espionage thriller. **85m/C VHS.** *FR* Eddie Constantine, Henri Cogan, Elisa Montes, Jose Nieto, Silvia Solar; **D:** Jose Monter. *SNC*

As Is 🎥½ 1985 Two gay New Yorkers deal with a troubled romance and AIDS. A cable television adaptation from the William M. Hoffman play. **86m/C VHS, Beta.** Jonathan Hadary, Robert Carradine; **D:** Michael Lindsay-Hogg. *ORI, WAR*

As Summers Die 🎥🎥 1986 Louisiana attorney Glenn fights in the late 1950s to protect the rights of a black family, against the wishes of a powerful local clan. Glenn finds support in surprising places, though. From Winston Groom's acclaimed novel. A cable television movie. **100m/C VHS, Beta.** Scott Glenn, Jamie Lee Curtis, Penny Fuller, Bette Davis, John Randolph, Beah Richards, Ron O'Neal, John McIntire; **D:** Jean-Claude Tramont. *CNG*

As You Desire Me 🎥🎥🎥 1932 Garbo plays an amnesia victim who returns to a husband she doesn't even remember after an abusive relationship with a novelist. An interesting, if not down-right bizarre movie, due to the pairing of the great Garbo and the intriguing von Stroheim. An adaption of Luigi Pirandello's play. **71m/B VHS, Beta.** Greta Garbo, Melvyn Douglas, Erich von Stroheim, Owen Moore, Hedda Hopper; **D:** George Fitzmaurice. *MGM, FCT*

As You Like It 🎥🎥½ 1936 A Duke's banished daughter poses as a man to win the attentions of one of her father's attendants in this highly stylized Shakespearean comedy adapted by J.M. Barrie and Robert Cullen. Early Shakespearean Olivier. **96m/B VHS, Beta, LV.** *GB* Elisabeth Bergner, Laurence Olivier, Henry Ainley, Felix Aylmer; **D:** Paul Czinner; **W:** J.M. Barrie, Robert Cullen. *NOS, MRV, VYY*

As You Were 🎥 1951 A girl with a photographic memory enlists in the Army, becoming both a nuisance and comedic victim to her sergeant. **57m/B VHS, Beta, LV.** Joseph Sawyer, William Tracy, Sondra Rogers, Joan Vohs. *NO*

As Young As You Feel 🎥🎥🎥 1951 A 65-year-old man is forced to retire from his job. He poses as the head of the conglomerate and convinces them to repeal their retirement policy. He then gains national publicity when he makes a speech about the dignity of man. Watch for Monroe as the boss's secretary. Fine comic performances enhance the script; based on a story by Chayefsky. **77m/C VHS.** Monty Woolley, Thelma Ritter, David Wayne, Jean Peters, Constance Bennett, Marilyn Monroe, Allyn Joslyn, Albert Dekker, Clinton Sundberg, Minor Watson; **D:** Harmon Jones; **W:** Paddy Chayefsky. *FXV*

The Ascent 🎥🎥½ 1994 (PG) Based on the true story of Franco (Spano), a WWII Italian POW who's held in a camp in Africa. The prisoners enjoy making fun of the camp commander (Cross), who consistently fails at his attempts to climb the 15,500 peak of Mt. Kenya. Meanwhile, Franco decides to escape and climb the mountain himself—with the commander right behind. Beware if you suffer from vertigo. **96m/C VHS, Closed Caption.** Vincent Spano, Ben Cross, Tony LoBianco, Rachel Ward; **D:** Donald Shebib; **C:** David Connell. *CAF*

Ash Wednesday 🎥 1973 (R) Taylor endures the pain of cosmetic surgery in an effort to rescue her floundering union with Fonda. Another undistinguished performance by Liz. Fonda is especially slimy as the philandering husband, but only appears in the latter stages of the film. **99m/C VHS, Closed Caption.** Elizabeth Taylor, Henry Fonda, Helmut Berger, Keith Baxter, Margaret Blye, Maurice Teynac, Monique Van Vooren; **D:** Larry Peerce; **M:** Maurice Jarre. *PAR, FCT, CCB*

Ashanti, Land of No Mcroy 🎥🎥 *Ashanti* 1979 Caine of the week movie with Michael portraying a doctor acting as a missionary in South Africa who finds himself alone in a battle to rescue his wife from a band of slave traders. The chase spans many Middle Eastern countries and begins to look bleak for our man. Talented cast and promising plot are undone by slow pace. Based on the novel "Ebano" by Alberto Vasquez-Figueroa. **117m/C VHS, Beta.** Michael Caine, Omar Sharif, Peter Ustinov, Rex Harrison, William Holden, Beverly Johnson; **D:** Richard Fleischer. *TWE*

Ashes and Diamonds 🎥🎥🎥½ *Popiol i Diament* 1958 In the closing days of WWII, a Polish resistance fighter assassinates the wrong man, tries to find love with the right women, and questions the meaning of struggle. A seminal Eastern European masterpiece that defined a generation of pre-solidarity Poles. Available in Polish with English subtitles or dubbed into English. The last installment of the trilogy that includes "A Generation" and "Kanal" and based on a novel by Jerzy Andrzewski. **105m/B VHS, Beta, LV.** *PL* Zbigniew Cybulski, Eva Krzyzewska, Adam Pawlikowski, Bogumil Kobiela, Waclaw Zastrzezynski; **D:** Andrzej Wajda. *ING, MRV, NLC*

Ashes and Embers 🎥🎥 1982 A black Vietnam vet in Los Angeles has trouble fitting into society, eventually running afoul of the police. Ethiopian-born director Gerima endows vital subject matter with a properly alienated mood. **120m/C VHS.** John Anderson, Evelyn Blackwell; **D:** Haile Gerima. *FCT*

Ashik Kerib 🎥🎥🎥 1988 Ashik Kerib is a wandering minstrel who is rejected by a rich merchant as his daughter's suitor. He then journeys for 1,000 days trying to earn enough money to marry his beloved. Along the way he's imprisoned by an evil sultan and rides a flying horse, among other adventures. Wonderful use of exotic makeup and costumes highlight this Arabian Nights tale. Adapted from a story by Mikhail Lermontov. Paradjanov's last film. In Russian with English subtitles. **75m/C VHS.** *RU* Yiur Mgoyan, Veronkia Metonidze, Levan Natroshvili, Sofiko Chiaureli; **D:** Dodo Abashidze, Sergei Paradjanov; **W:** Giya Badridze; **M:** Djavashir Kuliev. *KIV, FCT*

Ask Any Girl 🎥🎥½ 1959 Lighthearted fluff about a small-town girl who moves to Manhattan. MacLaine plays the bright Meg who gets a job at an ad agency and decides to set her sights on marrying her boss (Young). She asks his older brother's (Niven) help in her quest and the inevitable happens. **101m/C VHS.** Shirley MacLaine, David Niven, Gig Young, Rod Taylor, Jim Backus, Claire Kelly, Elisabeth Fraser; **D:** Charles Walters. British Academy Awards '59: Best Actress (MacLaine). *MGM, MOV*

Aspen Extreme 🎥 1993 (PG-13) Former Aspen ski instructor writes and directs a movie on (what else?) ski instructors in (where?) Aspen! Long on ski shots and short on plot, this movie never leaves the bunny hill. Two Detroiters leave Motown for Snowtown to pursue a life on the slopes. T.J (Gross) soon has his hands full with two beautiful women (Polo and Hughes) who encourage his dream of becoming a writer. His friend Dexter (Berg), however, acquires a few bad habits, and the whole movie just goes downhill from there. **CW:** Language, nudity, and drug content. **128m/C VHS, Beta, LV, Closed Caption.** Paul Gross, Peter Berg, Finola Hughes, Teri Polo, Martin Kemp, Nicolette Scorsese, William Russ; **D:** Patrick Hasburgh; **W:** Patrick Hasburgh; **C:** Steven Fierberg; **M:** Michael Convertino. *HPH, TOU*

The Asphalt Jungle 🎥🎥🎥🎥 1950 An aging criminal emerges from his forced retirement (prison) and assembles the old gang for one final heist. A very realistic storyline and a superb cast make this one of the best crime films ever made. Highly acclaimed; based on the work of W.R. Burnett. **112m/B VHS, Beta, LV.** Sterling Hayden, Louis Calhern, Jean Hagen, James Whitmore, Sam Jaffe, John McIntire, Marc Lawrence, Barry Kelley, Anthony Caruso, Teresa

Celli, Marilyn Monroe; **D:** John Huston; **W:** Ben Maddow; **M:** Miklos Rozsa. National Board of Review Awards '50: Best Director (Huston); Venice Film Festival '50: Best Actor (Hayden); Nominations: Academy Awards '50: Best Black and White Cinematography, Best Director (Huston), Best Screenplay, Best Supporting Actor (Jaffe).*MGM*

The Asphyx *🐾🐾🐾 Spirit of the Dead* 1972 (PG) Nineteenth century doctor Stephens is studying death when he discovers The Asphyx, an aura that surrounds a person just before they die. Stephens delves deeper into his research and finds the keys to immortality. However, his irresponsibility in unleashing the obscure supernatural power on the world brings a swarm of unforeseen and irreversible troubles. High-class sci fi. **98m/C VHS, Beta.** *GB* Robert Stephens, Robert Powell, Jane Lapotaire, Alex Scott, Ralph Arliss, Fiona Walker, John Lawrence; **D:** Peter Newbrook; **C:** Frederick A. (Freddie) Young.

Assassin *🐾* 1979 Athletic karate fighter poses as an underworld figure and infiltrates the largest gang in Japan where he is hired as a hit man. **86m/C VHS, Beta.** Sonny Chiba. *FOX*

Assassin *🐾🐾* 1986 (PG-13) Made for TV drama about a mad scientist who creates a bionic killer for a bizarre plot to take over the world. He programs the cyborg to assassinate the President and other key people to help carry out his plan. A retired CIA operative emerges to stop the scientist by trying to destroy the robot. **94m/C VHS, Beta.** Robert Conrad, Karen Austin, Richard Young, Jonathan Banks, Robert Webber; **D:** Sandor Stern.

Assassin *🐾🐾* 1989 (R) Fairly lame thriller about a CIA agent protecting a Senator who falls under suspicion when his charge is shot by an assassin. In investigating the killing the agent discovers the usual governmental conspiracy. **92m/C VHS, Beta, LV.** Steve Railsback, Nicholas Guest, Xander Berkeley, Elpidia Carrillo; **D:** Jon Hess. *NO*

Assassin of Youth *🐾🐾½* 1935 Girl is introduced to marijuana and soon becomes involved in "the thrills of wild parties," and the horrors of the "killer weed." Camp diversion. **70m/B VHS, Beta.** Luana Walters, Arthur Gardner; **D:** Elmer Clifton. *SNC, NOS, DVT*

Assassination *🐾* 1987 (R) A serious threat has been made to First Lady Ireland and no one is taking it lightly. Secret Service agent Bronson has been called as Ireland's personal bodyguard and suddenly they are both the target of terrorist attacks. Strangely though, the attacks seem to be directed from inside the White House. Bronson as you've seen him many times before. **93m/C VHS, Beta, LV, Closed Caption.** Charles Bronson, Jill Ireland, Stephen Elliott, Michael Ansara; **D:** Peter Hunt; **C:** Hanania Baer. *VTR*

The Assassination Bureau *🐾🐾🐾*
1969 Set in Victorian-era London, this amusing farce concerns a society of international assassins led by the charming Reed. Rigg is an intrepid reporter who pays Reed to have his own organization try to kill him. Reed in turn will try to get them first. A cross-European chase ends in a battle aboard a Zeppelin. Tongue-in-cheek whimsey with a fine cast. Based on a short story by Jack London. **106m/C VHS, LV, Closed Caption.** *GB* Oliver Reed, Diana Rigg, Telly Savalas, Curt Jurgens, Philippe Noiret, Warren Mitchell, Beryl Reid, Clive Revill, Kenneth Griffith, Vernon Dobtcheff, Annabella Incontrera; **D:** Basil Dearden; **C:** Geoffrey Unsworth. *PAR*

The Assassination File *🐾🐾* 1996 (R) FBI agent Lauren Jacobs (Fenn) quits the Bureau after the first African-American President (Winfield) is killed on her watch. But two years later, when she encounters former co-workers, there's talk of a conspiracy and things turn even more dangerous.*CW:* Violence, language and some nudity. **106m/C VHS.** Sherilyn Fenn, Daniel Butler, Tom Verica, Victor Love, Kevin Corrigan, Paul Winfield, Diedrich Bader; **D:** John Harrison; **W:** Bruce Miller. *USH*

The Assassination Game *🐾* 1992 (R) Rookie CIA agent teams up with a veteran KGB agent to prevent the assassination of a world leader. **90m/C VHS.** Robert Rusler, Theodore Bikel, Doug Wert, Denise Bixler; **D:** Jonathan Winfrey. *NHO*

Assassination of Trotsky *🐾🐾* 1972 Middling attempt to dramatize the last days of the Russian Revolutionary leader in Mexico before he's done in with an ice pick. **113m/C VHS, Beta, LV.** *FR GB IT* Richard Burton, Alain Delon, Romy Schneider, Valentina Cortese, Jean Desailly; **D:** Joseph Losey; **C:** Pasquale De Santis. *REP, FCT*

The Assassination Run *🐾* 1984 A retired British spy is involved against his will in an intricate plot of terrorism, counter-terrorism and espionage. **111m/C VHS, Beta.** *GB* Malcolm Stoddard, Mary Tamm; **D:** Ken Hannam. *FOX*

Assassins *🐾🐾½* 1995 (R) Stallone gets to play elder statesman in the very deadly rivalry between two contract killers. Robert Rath (Stallone) is the man—number one with a bullet—whose reputation has caught up with him. Hot-headed Miguel Bain (the ever-smoldering Banderas) wants to off Rath and assume the position of top hitman. Caught in the middle of this macho posturing is surveillance expert—and potential murderee—Electra (Moore). It's Stallone to the rescue but his character pays more attention to Pearl, Electra's pampered Persian cat than to the lovely lady herself. But then romance isn't what this film is about—and director Donner does know his action.*CW:* Violence and language. **132m/C VHS.** Sylvester Stallone, Antonio Banderas, Julianne Moore, Anatoly Davydov; **D:** Richard Donner; **W:** Brian Helgeland, Andy Wachowski, Larry Wachowski; **C:** Vilmos Zsigmond; **M:** Mark Mancina. Nominations: Golden Raspberry Awards '95: Worst Actor (Stallone). *WAR*

Assault *🐾🐾½ In the Devil's Garden; Tower of Terror; The Creepers* 1970 Violent sex murders in a girl's school have the police baffled. The school's pretty art teacher offers to act as bait in order to catch the murderer. **89m/C VHS, Beta.** *GB* Suzy Kendall, Frank Finlay, Freddie Jones, James Laurenson, Lesley-Anne Down, Tony Beckley; **D:** Sidney Hayers.

The Assault *🐾🐾🐾½ De Aanslag* 1986 (PG) Powerful and disturbing drama about a Dutch boy who witnesses the arbitrary murder of his family by Nazis. The memory tortures him and leaves him empty as he matures. Years later he meets other victims and also the perpetrators of the incident, each of them changed forever by it. Thought-provoking consideration of WWII and the horrors of living in Nazi Germany from many points of view. Based on a novel by Harry Mulisch. Dutch language dubbed into English. **149m/C VHS, Beta.** *NL* Derek De Lint, Marc Van Uchelen, Monique Van De Ven; **D:** Fons Rademakers. Academy Awards '86: Best Foreign Language Film; Golden Globe Awards '87: Best Foreign Film. *MGM, SWC*

Assault and Matrimony *🐾🐾½* 1987 Real-life married people Tucker and Eikenberry play a married couple fighting tooth and nail. Lots of slapstick and general nonsense. Television film based on James Anderson's novel. **100m/C VHS, Beta, LV, Closed Caption.** John Hillerman, Michelle Phillips, Joe Cortese, Michael Tucker, Jill Eikenberry; **D:** James Frawley. *THV*

Assault at West Point: The Court-Martial of Johnson Whittaker *🐾🐾½* 1994 (PG-13) In 1880, Johnson C. Whittaker, a black West Point cadet, is found beaten, mutilated, and tied to his bed. Instead of seeking his attackers, the Academy sets up a court martial to expel Whittaker, claiming he faked his own attack. Clashes also ignite between Whittaker's defense counsel—white abolitionist lawyer Chamberlain, whose own racism is thinly disguised, and black lawyer Greener, who originally encouraged Whittaker to enroll at the Point. Interesting case but a shallow production. Based on a true story and adapted from the book by John Marszalek. Made for television. **98m/C VHS, Closed Caption.** Seth Gil-

liam, Samuel L. Jackson, Sam Waterston, John Glover, Al Freeman Jr.; **D:** Harry Moses; **W:** Harry Moses; **M:** Terence Blanchard. *REP*

Assault of the Killer Bimbos *🐾🐾½*
1988 (R) A show girl gets framed for the murder of her boss and takes off for the border with a couple of girlfriends. On the way they get pursued by the expected dumb cops and meet up with horny, clean-cut hunks. In Mexico they encounter the villain and extract comic vengeance. Watchable mainly due to the likable female leads and pleasant, lightly camp execution, although it might prove too tame for most of its target audience. **85m/C VHS, Beta.** Patti Astor, Christina Whitaker, Elizabeth Kaitan, Griffin O'Neal, Nick Cassavetes, Clayton Landey, Eddie Deezen, Arell Blanton, David Marsh, Tammara Souza, Jamie Bozian, Mike Muscat, Jeffrey Orman, John Quern; **D:** Patti Astor; **W:** Patti Astor, Anita Rosenberg; **C:** Thomas Callaway; **M:** Fred Lapides, Marc Ellis. *AFE*

Assault of the Party Nerds *🐾* 1989 (R) Nerds throw a wild party to try and attract new members to their fraternity, while a jock frat plots against them. Sound familiar? Little more than a ripoff of "Revenge of the Nerds" made especially for video. **82m/C VHS, Beta.** Linnea Quigley, Troy Donahue, Richard Gabai, C. Paul Demsey, Marc Silverberg, Robert Mann, Richard Rifkin, Deborah Roush; **D:** Richard Gabai.

Assault of the Party Nerds 2: Heavy Petting Detective *🐾* 1995 Detective tries to save a beauty from her scheming husband. **87m/C VHS.** Linnea Quigley, Richard Gabai, Michelle (McClellan) Bauer, Arte Johnson, Burt Ward. *VCI*

Assault of the Rebel Girls *🐾½ Cuban Rebel Girls; Attack of the Rebel Girls* 1959 A reporter gets involved with smuggling in Castro's Cuba. Flynn's last film, saving the worst for last. **66m/B VHS, Beta.** Errol Flynn, Beverly Aadland, John McKay, Jackie Jackler, Marie Edmund; **D:** Barry Mahon; **W:** Errol Flynn.

Assault on a Queen *🐾* 1966 Stupid Sinatra vehicle about a group of con men who plot together to rob the Queen Mary on one of her trips. Their attack vessel is a renovated WWII German U-boat. The producers tried to capitalize on the popularity of "Ocean's Eleven," but they didn't even come close. Based on a novel by Jack Finney. **106m/C VHS, Closed Caption.** Frank Sinatra, Virna Lisi, Anthony (Tony) Franciosa, Richard Conte, Reginald Denny; **D:** Jack Donohue; **W:** Rod Serling; **C:** William H. Daniels. *PAR*

Assault on Agathon *🐾🐾* 1975 (PG) Amid the scenic Greek isles, an "executed" WWII guerilla leader returns to lead a revolution, and bloodshed and bombings ensue. **95m/C VHS, Beta.** *GB IT* Nina Van Pallandt, Marianne Faithfull, John Woodvine, Nico Minardos; **D:** Laslo Benedek. *GEM, MRV*

Assault on Precinct 13 *🐾🐾🐾* 1976 Urban horror invades LA. A sleepy police station in Los Angeles is suddenly under siege from a violent youth gang. Paranoia abounds as the police are attacked from all sides and can see no way out. Carpenter's musical score adds much to the setting of this unique police exploitation story that somehow stands as Carpenter's adaptation of Howard Hawks' "Rio Bravo." Semi-acclaimed and very gripping. **91m/C VHS, Beta, LV.** Austin Stoker, Darwin Joston, Martin West, Tony Burton, Nancy Loomis, Kim Richards, Henry Kleinbach Brandon; **D:** John Carpenter; **W:** John Carpenter; **M:** John Carpenter.

Assault with a Deadly Weapon *🐾* 1982 When the police budget is cutback, crime runs rampant in an unnamed American city. **86m/C VHS, Beta.** Sandra Foley, Richard Holliday, Lamont Jackson; **D:** Arthur Kennedy. *ART*

The Assignment *🐾🐾* 1978 The assassination of a high-ranking officer in an uneasy Latin American nation spurs violence and political instability. A Swedish diplomat is assigned the tremendous task of restoring peace and stability between the political factions. **92m/C VHS, Beta.** *SW*

Christopher Plummer, Thomas Hellberg, Carolyn Seymour, Fernando Rey; **D:** Mats Arehn.

The Assignment 🐾🐾½ **1997 (R)** Workmanlike thriller is a case of deadly impersonation. Infamous terrorist Carlos the Jackal (Quinn) is shown plying his trade in Europe under the nose of CIA counterterrorism expert Jack Shaw (Sutherland). Later, in Israel, Mossad agent Amos (Kingsley) captures a man whom he thinks is Carlos, only it's his double—U.S. Navy officer Annibal Ramirez (Quinn again). So Shaw and Amos decide to turn the seaman into the terrorist, in an elaborate plot to have Carlos' Russian handlers think the terrorist has betrayed them. There's a very long setup for a somewhat lame payoff.**CW:** Strong violence, sexuality and language. **115m/C VHS, LV, Closed Caption, DVD.** *CA* Aidan Quinn, Donald Sutherland, Ben Kingsley, Liliana Komorowska, Claudia Ferri, Celine Bonnier, Vlasta Vrana, Von Flores, Al Waxman; **D:** Christian Duguay; **W:** Don Gordon, Sabi H. Shabtai; **C:** David Franco; **M:** Normand Corbeil. COL

Assignment Outer Space 🐾 *Space Men* **1961** A giant spaceship with bytes for brains is on a collision course with Earth. A team of astronauts is sent to save the world from certain peril. Seems they take the task lightly, though, and their mission (and hence the plot) revolves more around saving sexy sultress Farinon from certain celibacy. If you're into stultifying Italian space operas with a gratuitous sex sub-plot then look up this assignment, but don't say we didn't warn you. Director Margheriti is also known as Anthony Dawson, not to be confused with the actor of the same name. **79m/B VHS.** *IT* Rik von Nutter, Gabriella Farinon, Archie Savage, Dave Montresor, Alan Dijon; **D:** Anthony (Antonio Margheriti) Dawson. NOS, SNC

Assignment Skybolt 🐾½ **198?** When terrorists get their hands on a hydrogen bomb, a special mission is detached to stop them before they start WWIII. **109m/C VHS, Beta. D:** Greg Tallas. BFV

The Assisi Underground 🐾🐾 **1984** True but boringly told story of how the Catholic Church helped to save several hundred Italian Jews from being executed by the Nazis during the 1943 German occupation of Italy. Edited from 178 minutes, a good-will gesture from the producers. **115m/C VHS, Beta.** James Mason, Ben Cross, Maximilian Schell, Irene Papas; **D:** Alexander Ramati; **M:** Pino Donaggio. MGM, IGP

The Associate 🐾🐾 *L'Associe* **1979 (R)** French farce about penniless financial consultant Julien Pardot (Serrault) who invents a fictitious partner, Mr. Davis, in order to get his business rolling. When his clients, his wife, and even his mistress are all more intrigued by the partner than Julien, he becomes so jealous he decides to "murder" his creation. Based on the novel "My Partner, Mr. Davis" by Jenaro Prieto. French with subtitles; remade in 1996 with Whoopi Goldberg. **93m/C VHS.** *FR* Michel Serrault, Claudine Auger, Catherine Alric, Matthieu Carriere; **D:** Rene Gainville; **W:** Jean-Claude Carriere. FRF

The Associate 🐾🐾 **1996 (PG-13)** Whoopi drags a 20-minute premise over almost two hours when she invents an elderly, white, male business partner to give her fledgling financial consulting business some prestige. After having all her moneymaking ideas appropriated by male colleagues, Laurel Ayres (Goldberg) starts her own business, only to find that no one wants to hire her. She creates the genius and the money comes rolling in. Everyone clamors to meet the mystery man, so she goes undercover as the elusive Robert S. Cutty. The sight of Goldberg in old white guy garb and makeup is jarring, and the payoff doesn't merit the overlong build up. Based on the French film "L'Associe" and the Jenaro Prieto novel "El Socio."**CW:** Sensuality and an exotic dance club scene. **113m/C VHS.** Whoopi Goldberg, Timothy Daly, Bebe Neuwirth, Dianne Wiest, Eli Wallach; **D:** Donald Petrie; **W:** Nick Thiel; **C:** Alex Nepomniaschy; **M:** Christopher Tyng. TOU

The Association 🐾½ **198?** A man and a woman go undercover to bust an international white slavery ring. **92m/C VHS, Beta.** *TW* Carter Huang, Angela Mao; **D:** Cheung Wo Chang. NO

Assunta Spina 🐾🐾 **1915** A very early, very rare Italian epic about ancient Rome, the prototype for the Italian silent epics to come. **70m/B VHS, Beta.** IT FCT

Asteroid 🐾🐾 **1997** Re-edited version of the NBC TV miniseries emphasises the special effects and action, which should help this routine disaster flick. Astronomer Lily McKee (Sciorra) discovers that several giant asteroids are on a collision course with Kansas City. She contacts FEMA and gets hotshot director Jack Wallach (Biehn) anxious to help out (and not just with the rock problem). Naturally, the citizens freak and one asteroid hits but there's an even bigger one on the way. **120m/C VHS.** Michael Biehn, Annabella Sciorra, Don Franklin, Anne-Marie Johnson, Anthony Zerbe, Carlos Gomez, Jensen Daggett; **D:** Bradford May; **C:** David Hennings, Thomas Del Ruth; **M:** Shirley Walker. ART

The Astounding She-Monster woof! *Mysterious Invader* **1958** How can you not love a movie with a title like this? A bad script and snail-paced plot are a good start. A geologist wanting only to be left alone with his rocks survives a brush with the kidnappers of a wealthy heiress only to happen upon an alien spacecraft that's crashed nearby. At the helm is a very tall, high-heeled fem-alien in an obligatory skintight space outfit. Excellent, our rock jock thinks, but it seems she kills with the slightest touch. For connoisseurs of truly bad movies. **77m/B VHS.** Robert Clarke, Kenne Duncan, Marilyn Harvey, Jeanne Tatum, Shirley Kilpatrick, Ewing Miles Brown; **D:** Ronnie Ashcroft. EEL, MRV, CNM

The Astro-Zombies woof! **1967** A contender as one of the worst movies of all time. Carradine plays a mad scientist creating zombies who eat people's guts. Cult favorite Satana stars. Co-written and co-produced by Rogers of "M*A*S*H" fame. **83m/C VHS, Beta.** Tura Satana, Wendell Corey, John Carradine, Tom Pace, Joan Patrick, Rafael Campos; **D:** Ted V. Mikels; **W:** Ted V. Mikels, Wayne Rogers. NO

Asylum 🐾🐾½ *House of Crazies* **1972 (PG)** Four strange and chilling stories weave together in this film. A murderer's victim seeks retribution. A tailor seems to be collecting his bills. A man who makes voodoo dolls...only to become one later on. A woman plagued by a double. A doctor visiting the asylum tells each tale. Horrifying and grotesque, not as humorless as American horror films. **100m/C VHS, Beta, LV.** *GB* Peter Cushing, Herbert Lom, Britt Ekland, Barbara Parkins, Patrick Magee, Barry Morse, Robert Powell, Richard Todd, Charlotte Rampling, Ann Firbank, Sylvia Syms, James Villiers, Geoffrey Bayldon, Megs Jenkins; **D:** Roy Ward Baker; **W:** Robert Bloch; **C:** Denys Coop.

Asylum 🐾🐾 **1997 (R)** Unstable investigator Nick Tordone (Patrick) looks into his shrink's supposed suicide by become a patient at the doctor's mental hospital. By what he finds is serial killer Sullivan Rane (McDowell) and a doctor (Gibson) doing dangerous mind control experiments. Tension holds up well until the unfortunate finale.**CW:** Violence and language. **92m/C VHS.** Robert Patrick, Malcolm McDowell, Henry Gibson, Sarah Douglas; **D:** James Seale. MNC

Asylum of Satan 🐾 **1972** A beautiful concert pianist is savagely tortured by a madman in the Asylum of Satan. Filmed on location in Louisville, Kentucky. **87m/C VHS, Beta.** Charles Kissinger, Carla Borelli, Nick Jolly, Sherry Steiner; **D:** William Girdler; **W:** William Girdler. VCI

At Close Range 🐾🐾🐾 **1986 (R)** Based on the true story of Bruce Johnston Sr. and Jr. in Brandywine River Valley, Pennsylvania. Father, Walken, tempts his teenaged son, Penn, into pursuing criminal activities with talk of excitement and high living. Penn soon learns that his father is extremely dangerous and a bit unstable, but he's still fascinated by his wealth and power. Some-

times overbearing and depressing, but good acting and fancy camera work. A young cast of stars includes Masterson as the girl Penn tries to impress. Features Madonna's "Live to Tell." **115m/C VHS, Beta, LV, Closed Caption.** Sean Penn, Christopher Walken, Christopher Penn, Mary Stuart Masterson, Crispin Glover, Kiefer Sutherland, Candy Clark, Tracey Walter, Millie Perkins, Alan Autry, David Strathairn, Eileen Ryan; **D:** James Foley; **W:** Nicholas Kazan; **C:** Juan Ruiz-Anchia; **M:** Patrick Leonard. VES, ART

At First Sight 🐾½ *Two Guys Talkin' About Girls* **1995 (R)** Yakky pedestrian comedy about schleppy Lenny (Silverman) and his best friend, macho Joey (Cortese), trying to help each other out with their romantic crises. Lenny meets cute when he picks up Rhonda (Smith) at the planetarium while Joey beds a string of girls, all of whom are named Cindy, in an effort to get over the first Cindy who broke his heart. It's been done before—and better.**CW:** Crude sexuality and language. **90m/C VHS.** Jonathan Silverman, Dan Cortese, Allison Smith, Monte Markham, Kathleen Freeman, Susan Walters; **D:** Steven Pearl; **W:** Ken Copel; **C:** Glenn Kershaw; **M:** Richard Gibbs. THV

At Gunpoint 🐾🐾 *Gunpoint* **1955** A store owner becomes the town hero when, by accident, he shoots and kills a bank robber. **81m/C VHS, Beta.** Fred MacMurray, Dorothy Malone, John Qualen, Walter Brennan; **D:** Alfred Werker; **C:** Ellsworth Fredericks. REP, HHE

At Gunpoint 🐾½ **1990** A no-account bank robber spends his six year stint in the slammer plotting his revenge. Having gone thoroughly stir-crazy, the vengeful criminal stalks the lawman who put him away, like so many vengeful criminals before him. Run of the mill addition to big list of bad-guy-hunting-for-revenge flicks. **90m/C VHS.** Frank Kanig, Tain Bodkin, Scott Claflin; **D:** Steven Harris; **W:** Steven Harris. CAF

At Home with the Webbers 🐾🐾 **1994 (R)** Gerald, Emma, Johnny, and Miranda Webber win a contest to star in a cable TV series about their lives. What they don't expect is that the series will become a hit or that all the family idosyncrasies will be exaggerated by stardom (the manipulative TV producer doesn't help). Over-the-top comedy requires tolerance but does have some amusing performances. **109m/C VHS, LV, Closed Caption.** Jeffrey Tambor, Rita Taggart, Jennifer Tilly, David Arquette, Robby Benson, Brian Bloom, Caroline Goodall; **D:** Brad Marlowe; **W:** Brad Marlowe. ART

At Midnight, I'll Take Your Soul 🐾 *A Meia-Noite Levarei Sua Alma* **1963** Brazilian import about sadistic gravedigger Coffin Joe (alter ego of director Jose Mojica Marins), who wanders the streets of his hometown in order to meet a desirable woman. His mission is to sire a son to continue his legacy and wiggle his lips at screaming women. A study in psycho-sexual horror, this makes "Apocalypse Now" look like a beach party. Coffin Joe, or "Ze do Caixao," is a kind of South American Freddy or Jason; Mojica Marin's movies—which are graphically sadistic—were banned by the Brazilian government. In Portugese with English subtitles. Followed by "Tonight I'll Be Incarnated in Your Corpse." **?m/B VHS.** *BR* Jose Mojica Marins; **D:** Jose Mojica Marins. SMW, FCT, TPV

At Play in the Fields of the Lord 🐾🐾🐾 **1991 (R)** A thoughtful epic that never quite lives up to its own self-importance—or length. Two yankee missionary couples try to evangelize a fearsome tribe of Brazilian rain-forest dwellers. One of the Christian families suffers a crisis of faith that's well-acted but not as powerful as a co-plot regarding a modern American Indian (Berenger) who joins the jungle natives with calamitous results. Based on the novel by Peter Matthiessen.**CW:** Language and sensuality. **186m/C VHS, Beta, LV, Closed Caption.** Tom Berenger, Aidan Quinn, Kathy Bates, John Lithgow, Daryl Hannah, Tom Waits, Stenio Garcia, Nelson Xavier, Jose Dumont, Niilo Kivirinta; **D:** Hector Babenco; **W:** Hector Babenco, Jean-Claude Carriere; **M:** Zbigniew Preisner. USH

At Sword's Point 🎬🎬 *Sons of the Musketeers* 1951 Adventure tale based on Alexandre Dumas' "The Three Musketeers," wherein the sons of the musketeers vie to save their queen from the evil plots of Duke Douglas. **81m/C VHS, Beta, LV.** Cornel Wilde, Maureen O'Hara, Robert Douglas, Dan O'Herlihy, Alan Hale Jr., Blanche Yurka; **D:** Lewis Allen. *TTC, FCT*

At the Circus 🎬🎬½ *The Marx Brothers at the Circus* 1939 Marx Brothers invade the circus to save it from bankruptcy and cause their usual comic insanity, though they've done it better before. Beginning of the end for the Marxes, a step down in quality from their classic work, though frequently darn funny. ♫Lydia the Tattooed Lady; Step Up and Take a Bow; Two Blind Loves; Blue Moon. **87m/B VHS, Beta, LV.** Groucho Marx, Chico Marx, Harpo Marx, Margaret Dumont, Kenny L. Baker, Florence Rice, Eve Arden, Nat Pendleton, Fritz Feld; **D:** Edward Buzzell. *MGM*

At the Earth's Core 🎬🎬 1976 **(PG)** A Victorian scientist invents a giant burrowing machine, which he and his crew use to dig deeply into the Earth. To their surprise, they discover a lost world of subhuman creatures and prehistoric monsters. Based on Edgar Rice Burrough's novels. **90m/C VHS, Beta.** **GB** Doug McClure, Peter Cushing, Caroline Munro, Cy Grant, Godfrey James, Keith Barron; **D:** Kevin Connor. *WAR, OM*

At War with the Army 🎬🎬 1950 Serviceable comedy from Martin and Lewis in their first starring appearance, as the recruits get mixed up in all kinds of wild situations at their army base. Based on the play by James Allardice. **93m/B VHS, Beta.** Dean Martin, Jerry Lewis, Polly Bergen, Mike Kellin; **D:** Hal Walker. *NOS, MRV, CAB*

Atalia 🎬🎬 1985 Relates the love between Atalia, a war widow, and the younger man she loves. The problem stems from the fact that she lives in a Kibbutz, and the lifestyle contradicts sharply from that of her beliefs in love, forcing her to eventually make a momentous decision. **90m/C VHS.** Michal Bat-Adam, Yftach Katzur, Dan Toren; **D:** Akiva Tevet. *ERG*

Athena 🎬🎬½ 1954 Two sisters (Powell and Reynolds) from an eccentric, health-faddist family fall in love with their opposites. Purdom is the stuffy Boston lawyer who goes off with Powell and Reynolds entices a TV crooner (Damone). Routine romance with routine songs. Reeves, who would become a star as a movie muscleman, appears in a brief role. ♫Love Can Change the Stars; The Girl Next Door; Imagine; Venezia; Chacun le Sait; I Never Felt Better; Vocalize. **96m/C VHS.** Jane Powell, Debbie Reynolds, Edmund Purdom, Vic Damone, Louis Calhern, Evelyn Varden, Linda Christian, Virginia Gibson, Nancy Kilgas, Dolores Starr, Jane Fischer, Cecile Rogers, Steve Reeves; **D:** Richard Thorpe; **W:** William Ludwig, Leonard Spigelgass; **M:** Hugh Martin, Ralph Blane. *MGM*

Atlantic City 🎬🎬🎬½ *Atlantic City U.S.A* 1981 **(R)** A small-time, aging Mafia hood falls in love with a young clam bar waitress, and they share the spoils of a big score against the backdrop of Atlantic City. Wonderful character study that becomes something more, a piercing declaration about a city's transformation and the effect on the people who live there. Lancaster, in a sterling performance, personifies the city, both of them fading with time. **104m/C VHS, Beta, LV.** **FR CA** Burt Lancaster, Susan Sarandon, Kate Reid, Michel Piccoli, Hollis McLaren; **D:** Louis Malle. British Academy Awards '81: Best Actor (Lancaster), Best Director (Malle); Genie Awards '81: Best Supporting Actress (Reid); Los Angeles Film Critics Association Awards '81: Best Actor (Lancaster), Best Film, Best Screenplay; New York Film Critics Awards '81: Best Actor (Lancaster), Best Screenplay; National Society of Film Critics Awards '81: Best Actor (Lancaster), Best Director (Malle), Best Film, Best Screenplay; Nominations: Academy Awards '81: Best Actor (Lancaster), Best Actress (Sarandon), Best Director (Malle), Best Original Screenplay, Best Picture. *PAR*

Atlantis, the Lost Continent 🎬 1961 If anything could sink the fabled lost continent of Atlantis it's this cheap fantasy flick. A greek sailor saves a princess and takes her back to her Atlantis home where he's promptly enslaved by the island's evil ruler. But this hero won't put up with any nonsense so he leads his fellow slaves in a revolt and gains his freedom before sinking both evil ruler and island (using atomic power no less!). **90m/C VHS.** Anthony Hall, Joyce Taylor, John Dall, Bill Smith, Edward Platt, Frank De Kova; **D:** George Pal. *MGM, FCT*

Atlas 🎬 1960 The mighty Atlas takes on massive armies, one of which includes director Corman, in a bid to win the hand of a princess. About as cheap as they come, although it is one of the few Sword & Sandal epics that isn't dubbed. **84m/C VHS.** Michael Forest, Frank Wolff, Barboura Morris, Walter Maslow; **D:** Roger Corman; **W:** Charles B. Griffith. *DVT, SNC, HEG*

Atlas in the Land of the Cyclops woof! *Atlas Against the Cyclops; Maciste Nella Terra dei Ciclopi* 1961 Atlas takes on a hideous one-eyed monster to save a baby from an evil queen. Not a divorce custody drama. **100m/C VHS.** **IT** Mitchell Gordon, Chelo Alonso, Vira Silenti; **D:** Antonio Leoniuola. *SNC*

Atom Age Vampire woof! *Seddok, l'Erede di Satana* 1961 Mad scientist doing research on Japanese nuclear bomb victims falls in love with a woman disfigured in an auto crash. To remove her scars, he treats her with a formula derived from the glands of freshly killed women. English dubbed. Not among the best of its kind (a low-rent district if ever there was one), but entertaining in a mischievous, boy-is-this-a-stupid-film sort of way. **71m/B VHS, Beta.** **IT** Alberto Lupo, Susanne Loret, Sergio Fantoni, Franca Parisi Strahl, Ivo Garrani, Andrea Scotti, Rina Franchetti; **D:** Anton Giulio Majano; **W:** Anton Giulio Majano, Alberto Bevilacqua, Gino De Santis; **C:** Aldo Giordani. *RHI*

Atom Man vs. Superman 1950 Superman saves Metropolis from the machinations of his deadly foe, Atom Man, in this long-unseen second theatrical serial. Contains all 15 episodes on two tapes. **251m/B VHS, Beta.** Kirk Alyn, Lyle Talbot, Noel Neill, Tommy "Butch" Bond, Pierre Watkin; **D:** Spencer Gordon Bennet. *WAR, MLB*

Atomic Attack 🎬 1950 Nuclear bomb is dropped on New York City and a family living 50 miles away must escape. Gentlemen, start your engines. **50m/B VHS.** Walter Matthau. *IHF*

The Atomic Brain woof! *Monstrosity* 1964 An old woman hires a doctor to transplant her brain into the body of a beautiful young girl. Of the three girls who are abducted, two become homicidal zombies and the third starts to act catty when she is given a feline brain. A must-see for badbrain movie fans. **72m/B VHS.** Frank Gerstle, Erika Peters, Judy Bamber, Marjorie Eaton, Frank Fowler, Margie Fisco; **D:** Joseph Mascelli. *NOS, SNC*

The Atomic Cafe 🎬🎬🎬 1982 A chillingly humorous compilation of newsreels and government films of the 1940s and '50s that show America's preoccupation with the A-Bomb. Some sequences are in black and white. Includes the infamous training film "Duck and Cover," which tells us what to do in the event of an actual bombing. **92m/C VHS, Beta.** **D:** Kevin Rafferty. *FRF*

The Atomic City 🎬🎬½ 1952 Barry plays a nuclear physicist at Los Alamos whose son is kidnapped by terrorists who want his bomb-making formulas. The bad guys hide out in the nearby mountains which at least makes for some pleasant scenery in this average thriller. **84m/B VHS, Closed Caption.** Gene Barry, Lee Aaker, Michael Moore, Lydia Clarke, Nancy Gates, Milburn Stone; **D:** Jerry Hopper. Nominations: Academy Awards '52: Best Story & Screenplay. *PAR*

The Atomic Kid 🎬½ 1954 A man survives an atomic blast because of a peanut butter sandwich he was eating. As a result, he himself becomes radioactive and discovers that he has acquired some strange new powers which get him into what pass for hilarious predicaments. **86m/B VHS.** Mickey Rooney, Robert Strauss, Elaine Davis, Bill Goodwin; **D:** Leslie Martinson; **W:** Blake Edwards; **M:** Van Alexander. *REP*

The Atomic Man 🎬½ *Timeslip* 1956 Owing to radioactive experimentation, a scientist exists for a short time in the future. Once there, both good and evil forces want to use him for their own purposes. **78m/B VHS.** **GB** Gene Nelson, Faith Domergue, Joseph Tomelty, Peter Arne; **D:** Ken Hughes. *NOS, SNC*

Atomic Submarine 🎬🎬 1959 Futuristic sci fi plots government agents against alien invaders. The battle, however, takes place in the ocean beneath the Arctic and is headed by an atomic-powered submarine clashing with a special alien underwater saucer. We all live on the atomic submarine: fun for devotees. **80m/C VHS, Beta.** Arthur Franz, Dick Foran, Bob Steele, Brett Halsey, Joi Lansing, Tom Conway, Paul Dubov; **D:** Spencer Gordon Bennet; **W:** Orville H. Hampton; **C:** Gilbert Warrenton. *SNC*

The Atonement of Gosta Berling 🎬🎬🎬 *Gosta Berling's Saga; The Legend of Gosta Berling; The Story of Gosta Berling; The Saga of Gosta Berling* 1924 A priest, forced to leave the priesthood because of his drinking, falls in love with a young married woman. Garbo shines in the first role which brought her critical acclaim; Hanson's performance also makes this a memorable drama. Adapted from the novel by Selma Lagerlof. **91m/B VHS.** **SW** Lars Hanson, Greta Garbo, Ellen Cederstrom, Mona Martenson, Jenny Hasselquist, Gerda Lundequist; **D:** Mauritz Stiller. *VYY, MRV, DVT*

Ator the Fighting Eagle woof! 1983 **(PG)** Styled after "Conan The Barbarian" this mythical action fantasy stars O'Keeffe as Ator, son of Thorn. Ator must put an end to the tragic Dynasty of the Spiders, thereby fulfilling the legend of his family at the expense of the viewer. Goofy low-budget sword and sandal stuff. Followed by "The Blade Master." **98m/C VHS, Beta.** **IT** Miles O'Keeffe, Sabrina Siani, Ritza Brown, Edmund Purdom, Laura Gemser; **D:** David Hills. *NO*

Attack Force Z 🎬🎬 1984 An elite corps of Australian military is Force Z. Volunteers are chosen for a dangerous mission: find the plane that crashed somewhere in the South Pacific and rescue the defecting Japanese government official on board, all before the end of WWII and the feature. Talented cast is effectively directed in low-key adventure featuring young Gibson. **84m/C VHS, Beta.** **AU** Sam Neill, Chris Haywood, Mel Gibson, John Phillip Law, John Waters; **D:** Tim Burstall. *MCG, MTX*

Attack of the Beast Creatures woof! 1985 The survivors of a wrecked ocean liner are stranded on a desert island overrun by savage creatures. This makes them anxious. **82m/C VHS, Beta.** Robert Nolfi, Robert Langyel, Julia Rust, Lisa Pak; **D:** Michael Stanley. *NO*

Attack of the 50 Foot Woman 🎬🎬½ 1958 A beautiful, abused housewife has a frightening encounter with a giant alien, causing her to grow to an enormous height. Then she goes looking for hubby. Perhaps the all-time classic '50s sci fi, a truly fun movie highlighted by the sexy, 50-foot Hayes in a giant bikini. Has intriguing psychological depth and social commentary done in a suitably cheezy manner. Also available with "House on Haunted Hill" on laserdisc. **72m/B VHS, Beta, LV.** Allison Hayes, William Hudson, Roy Gordon; **D:** Nathan (Hertz) Juran. *FOX, FCT*

Attack of the 50 Ft. Woman 🎬🎬½ 1993 Campy remake of the 1958 sci-fi cult classic features the statuesque Hannah in the title role. Nancy's a put-upon hausfrau with zero self-esteem thanks to her domineering father (Windom) and loutish hubby (Baldwin). They should have been sweet to her because after an encounter with a flying saucer Nancy starts to grow...and grow...and grow. And then she decides to get some revenge. Made for television. **90m/C VHS, LV.** Daryl Hannah, Daniel Baldwin, William Windom, Frances Fisher, Cristi Conaway, Paul Benedict, Lewis Arquette, Xander Berkeley, Hamilton Camp, Richard Edson, Victoria Haas, O'Neal Compton; **D:** Christopher Guest; **W:** Joseph Dougherty; **M:** Nicholas Pike. **HBO**

Attack of the Giant Leeches 🐾 *The Giant Leeches; She Demons of the Swamp* 1959 Cheapo Corman fare about giant leeches in a murky swamp who suddenly decide to make human flesh their new food supply. Perturbed inn keeper plays along by forcing his wife and lover into the murk. Leeches frolic. Sometimes tedious, sometimes chilling, always low budget and slimy. Although the special effects aren't top notch, this might be a fine choice for a late night scare/laugh. **62m/B VHS.** Ken Clark, Yvette Vickers, Gene Roth, Bruno Ve Sota, Michael Emmet; **D:** Bernard L. Kowalski; **W:** Leo Gordon; **C:** John M. Nickolaus Jr. **RHI**

Attack of the Killer Refrigerator woof! 1990 Chiller featuring a group of sleazy college students having a wild party. In the process, they abuse a hapless refrigerator. Fed up, the vengeful appliance goes on a rampage of murder and destruction. Certain to make you view kitchen appliances in a new light. Planned sequels in the newfound kitchen-utility horror genre include "Refrigerator II: Brutally Defrosted" and "Bloody, Bloody Coffee Maker." **?m/C VHS. BFA**

Attack of the Killer Tomatoes woof! 1977 (PG) Candidate for worst film ever made, deliberate category. Horror spoof that defined "low budget" stars several thousand ordinary tomatoes that suddenly turn savage and begin attacking people. No sci-fi cliche remains untouched in this dumb parody. A few musical numbers are performed in lieu of an actual plot. Followed by "Return of the Killer Tomatoes." Originally released at 87 minutes. **100m/C VHS, Closed Caption.** George Wilson, Jack Riley, Rock Peace, Eric Christmas; **D:** John DeBello; **W:** John DeBello. **TOU**

Attack of the Mayan Mummy woof! 1963 A greedy doctor gets his patient to channel her former self so that she can show him where to find an ancient tomb that is filled with treasure. Good idea. **77m/B VHS.** **MX** Richard Webb, Nina Knight, Norman Burton, Steve Conte; **D:** Jerry Warren. **NOS, LOO, SNC**

Attack of the Mushroom People 🐾🐾 *Matango; Fungus of Terror; Curse of the Mushroom People* 1963 Secluded island is the site where people eating mysterious mushrooms have been turning into oversized, killer 'shrooms' themselves. Trouble is, the only witness to this madness has gone insane. Will anyone believe him before it's too late? **70m/B VHS.** **JP** Akira Kubo, Kenji Sahara, Yoshio Tsuchiya, Hiroshi Koizumi, Kumi Mizuno, Miki Yashiro; **D:** Inoshiro Honda. **SMW**

Attack of the Robots 🐾½ *Cartes sur Table* 1966 Silly spy spoof about powerful government officials who are being killed off by a mad scientist's robots. Interpol agent Lemmy Caution comes to the rescue. **88m/B VHS, Beta.** **FR SP** Eddie Constantine, Fernando Rey; **D:** Jess (Jesus) Franco; **W:** Jean-Claude Carriere. **VYY**

Attack of the 60-Foot Centerfold 🐾½ 1995 (R) Angel Grace wants to be Centerfold of the Year so badly that she gets a doctor to enhance her endowments even more through a mystery formula. Only there's a little complication. Cheesy, with pretty women and no discernable acting (and a spoof of that '58 gem "Attack of the 50 Ft. Woman"). **CW:** Nudity; sexual situations; mild violence. **83m/C VHS.** J.J. North, Tammy Parks, John Lazar; **Cameos:** Russ Tamblyn, Michelle (McClellan) Bauer; **D:** Fred Olen Ray. **NHO**

Attack of the Swamp Creature woof! 1975 A deranged scientist transforms himself into a swamp critter and terrorizes a small town. **96m/C VHS, Beta.** Frank Crowell, David Robertson; **D:** Arnold Stevens. **ART**

Attack Squadron 🐾½ *Kamakazi* 197? Story of Japan's suicidal WWII pilots. **105m/C VHS, Beta.** **JP NO**

The Attic 🐾🐾½ 1980 (R) Psycho-drama about an overbearing invalid father and his insecure and unmarried daughter. The girl learns to escape her unhappy life by hiding in the attic. Not horrifying, but a clear analytical look into the game of control. **92m/C VHS, Beta.** Carrie Snodgress, Ray Milland, Rosemary Murphy, Ruth Cox, Francis Bay, Marjorie Eaton; **D:** George Edwards. **FOX**

The Attic: The Hiding of Anne Frank 🐾🐾½ 1988 Steenburgen is wonderful in the true story of Miep Gies, the Dutch woman who hid Otto Frank, her employer, and his family from the Nazis. Unusual because it is told from Gies' perspective, rather than from the more familiar Anne Frank story. Based on Gies' book, "Anne Frank Remembered." Made for television. **95m/C VHS, LV, Closed Caption.** Mary Steenburgen, Paul Scofield, Huub Stapel, Eleanor Bron, Miriam Karlin, Lisa Jacobs, Ronald Pickup; **D:** John Erman; **W:** William Hanley; **M:** Richard Rodney Bennett. **CAF**

Attica 🐾🐾🐾 1980 Tense made for television depiction of the infamous Attica prison takeover in 1971 and the subsequent bloodbath as state troops were called in. Although edited due to the searing commentary by Nelson Rockefeller, it remains powerful and thought-provoking. Adapted from the Tom Wicker bestseller "A Time to Die." **97m/C VHS, Beta.** George Grizzard, Charles Durning, Anthony Zerbe, Roger E. Mosley; **D:** Marvin J. Chomsky. **NLC**

Au Revoir Les Enfants 🐾🐾🐾🐾 *Goodbye, Children* 1987 (PG) During the Nazi occupation of France in the 1940s, the headmaster of a Catholic boarding school hides three Jewish boys among the other students by altering their names and identities. Two of the students, Julien (Manesse) and Jean (Fejto), form a friendship that ends tragically when Jean and the other boys are discovered and taken away by the Gestapo. Compelling and emotionally wrenching coming of age tale based on an incident from director Malle's childhood is considered to be his best film to date and quite possibly the best he will ever make. In French with English subtitles. Other 1987 movies with similar themes are "Hope and Glory" and "Empire of the Sun." **104m/C VHS, Beta, LV.** **FR** Gaspard Manesse, Raphael Fejto, Francine Racette, Stanislas Carre de Malberg, Philippe Morier-Genoud, Francois Berleand, Peter Fitz, Francois Negret, Irene Jacob; **D:** Louis Malle; **W:** Louis Malle; **C:** Renato Berta; **M:** Franz Schubert, Camille Saint-Saens. British Academy Awards '88: Best Director (Malle); Cesar Awards '88: Best Art Direction/Set Decoration, Best Cinematography, Best Director (Malle), Best Film, Best Sound, Best Writing; Los Angeles Film Critics Association Awards '87: Best Foreign Film; Venice Film Festival '87: Best Film; Nominations: Academy Awards '87: Best Foreign Language Film, Best Original Screenplay. **ORI, FCT, HMV**

Audrey Rose 🐾🐾 1977 (PG) Parents of a young girl are terrified when their darling daughter is having dreadful dreams. Mysterious friend Hopkins cements their fears when he declares that his dead daughter has been reincarnated in their child. The nightmares continue suggesting that none other than Lucifer could be at work. Good cast is hampered by slow-moving take-off on "The Exorcist" with a weak staged ending. Adapted by DeFelitta from his novel. **113m/C VHS, Beta.** Marsha Mason, Anthony Hopkins, John Beck, John Hillerman, Susan Swift, Norman Lloyd; **D:** Robert Wise; **W:** Frank de Felitta; **C:** Victor Kemper. **MGM**

August 🐾🐾½ 1995 (PG) Yet another version of Chekov's "Uncle Vanya," this time transported to 1890s Wales. Hopkins (who makes his directorial debut and composed the score) stars as Ieuan Davies, a bitter drinker who manages the

ootato of brother in law Alexander Blathwaite (Phillips). Blathwaite arrives for his annual summer stay with unhappy, young second wife Helen (Burton), who's the object of desire for both Ieuan and the local doctor, Michael Lloyd (Grainger). It's a perfectly adequate rendition but offers little that's new except a change of scenery. **93m/C VHS.** **GB** Anthony Hopkins, Kate Burton, Leslie Phillips, Gawn Grainger, Rhian Morgan, Hugh Lloyd, Rhoda Lewis, Menna Tussler; **D:** Anthony Hopkins; **W:** Julian Mitchell; **C:** Robin Vidgeon; **M:** Anthony Hopkins. **HMK**

Augustin 🐾🐾 1995 Very short comedy about aspiring actor Augustin (Sibertin-Blanc), who may just get his break when he hears about a part for a room-service waiter and prepares himself rigorously by actually getting a job in a Paris hotel. Pathetically earnest and dignified, at the actual audition he bewilders actor Lhermitte, when instead of just reading the scene, Augustin proceeds to act it out in detail. Very slight but charming thanks to a deadpan performance by Sibertin-Blanc (who's also director Fontaine's brother). French with subtitles. **61m/C VHS.** **FR** Jean-Chretien Sibertin-Blanc, Thierry Lhermitte; **D:** Anne Fontaine; **W:** Anne Fontaine; **C:** Jean-Marie Dreujou. **KIV**

Augustine of Hippo 🐾🐾🐾 *Agostino di Ippona* 1972 One of Rossellini's later historical epics, depicting the last years of St. Augustine and how they exemplify the growing conflicts between Church and State, Christian ethic and societal necessity. In Italian with subtitles. **120m/C VHS, Beta.** **IT D:** Roberto Rossellini. **FCT**

Auntie woof! 1980 (R) Entertainer must dress and act like his madam aunt who has died, in order to fool her former employees in a house of prostitution. **85m/C VHS, Beta.** **NO**

Auntie Lee's Meat Pies 🐾½ 1992 (R) Auntie Lee's meat pie business is booming thanks to her five beautiful nieces. They help keep their aunt supplied with the secret ingredient—gorgeous young men! Four Playboy Playmates are featured in this cannibalistic horror comedy. **CW:** Language, horror violence, and sexuality. **100m/C VHS, LV.** Karen Black, Noriyuki "Pat" Morita, Pat Paulsen, Huntz Hall, Michael Berryman, David Parry, Stephen Quadros; **D:** Joseph F. Robertson; **C:** Arledge Armenaki. **COL**

Auntie Mame 🐾🐾🐾 1958 A young boy is brought up by his only surviving relative—flamboyant and eccentric Auntie Mame. Mame is positive that "life is a banquet and most poor suckers are starving to death." Based on the Patrick Dennis novel about his life with "Auntie Mame." Part of the "A Night at the Movies" series, this tape simulates a 1958 movie evening, with a Road Runner cartoon, "Hook, Line and Stinker," a newsreel and coming attractions for "No Time for Sergeants" and "Chase a Crooked Shadow." **161m/C VHS, Beta, LV, Letterbox.** Rosalind Russell, Patric Knowles, Roger Smith, Peggy Cass, Forrest Tucker, Coral Browne; **D:** Morton DaCosta; **W:** Betty Comden, Adolph Green; **C:** Harry Stradling. Golden Globe Awards '59: Best Actress—Musical/Comedy (Russell); Nominations: Academy Awards '58: Best Actress (Russell), Best Art Direction/Set Decoration, Best Color Cinematography, Best Film Editing, Best Picture, Best Supporting Actress (Cass). **WAR**

Aurora 🐾🐾½ *Aurora by Night; Qualcosa di Biondo* 1984 Single mom Aurora (Loren) will do anything for her blind son Ciro (played by Loren's son Edoardo Ponti). When she discovers that there's a possible operation that could restore his sight, Aurora decides to call up all Ciro's possible fathers and get them to finance the surgery. This plan also reunites Aurora with the one man she truly loved. Made for Italian TV. **91m/C VHS.** **IT** Sophia Loren, Daniel J. Travanti, Ricardo Tognazzi, Philippe Noiret, Anna Strasberg, Franco Fabrizi; **D:** Maurizio Ponzi; **M:** Georges Delerue. **FCT**

The Aurora Encounter 🐾🐾 1985 (PG) Aliens surreptitiously infiltrate a small town in 1897, and spread benevolence everywhere. Family fare. **90m/C VHS, Beta.** Jack Elam, Peter Brown, Carol

Bagdasarian, Dottie West, George "Spanky" McFarland; **D:** Jim McCullough. *VTR, HHE*

Austin Powers: International Man of Mystery 🐾🐾🐾 1997 (PG-13) Hilarious
spoof of '60s spy and babe movies. Groovy '60s spy Austin Powers (Myers) discovers that his arch-enemy, Dr. Evil (Myers again) has frozen himself in order to elude capture, so the swingin' dentally challenged Brit decides to do the same. They awaken 30 years later in the same state: woefully out of touch. Dr. Evil is attempting to blackmail the British government and deal with his Gen-X son, Scott Evil (Green), who wants more quality time and less world conquest. Austin, on the other hand, is trying to "shag" every "groovy bird" he sees. He is teamed with Vanessa (Hurley), the daughter of his former partner, and they try to stop the evil machinations of...well..Evil. A festival of crushed velvet, political incorrectness, and female robots with lethal breasts. Myers revels in playing the fool, and he may step over the line every once in a while, but he gets plenty of mileage out of the one-joke premise.**CW:** Nudity, sex-related dialogue and humor. **88m/C VHS, LV, Closed Caption.** Mike Myers, Elizabeth Hurley, Michael York, Seth Green, Mimi Rogers, Tom Arnold, Carrie Fisher, Robert Wagner, Fabiana Udenio, Paul Dillon, Charles Napier; **D:** Jay Roach; **W:** Mike Myers; **C:** Peter Deming; **M:** George Clinton. MTV Movie Awards '98: Best Villain (Myers), Best Dance Sequence (Mike Myers/Londoners); Nominations: MTV Movie Awards '98: Best Film, Best Comedic Performance (Myers). *NLC*

Author! Author! 🐾🐾½ 1982 (PG) Sweet,
likable comedy about playwright Pacino who is about to taste success with his first big hit. Suddenly his wife walks out, leaving him to care for her four children and his own son. His views shift as he begins to worry about, among other things, who will watch the obnoxious kids on opening night. **100m/C VHS, Beta.** Al Pacino, Tuesday Weld, Dyan Cannon, Alan King, Andre Gregory; **D:** Arthur Hiller; **W:** Israel Horovitz; **M:** Dave Grusin. *FOX*

Autobiography of a Princess 🐾🐾
1975 A brief character study shot by Merchant-Ivory in six days. An East Indian princess, living in self-enforced exile in London, invites her father's former tutor to tea. They watch old movie footage of royal India together and dream of a happier past. **59m/C VHS, LV.** James Mason, Madhur Jaffrey; **D:** James Ivory; **W:** Ruth Prawer Jhabvala. *FCT, LUM, CVC*

The Autobiography of Miss Jane Pittman 🐾🐾🐾½ 1974 The history of blacks
in the South is seen through the eyes of a 110-year-old former slave. From the Civil War through the Civil Rights movement, Miss Pittman relates every piece of black history, allowing the viewer to experience the injustices. Tyson is spectacular in moving, highly acclaimed television drama. Received nine Emmy awards; adapted by Tracy Keenan Wynn from the novel by Ernest J. Gaines. **110m/C VHS, Beta.** Cicely Tyson, Odetta, Joseph Tremice, Richard Dysart, Michael Murphy, Katherine Helmond; **D:** John Korty.

Automatic 🐾½ 1994 (R) Renegade RobGen
Industries android Gruner saves Ashbrook from the loathsome sexual advances of the boss but kills the scum in the process. So the duo are targeted for death by company head Glover with killers, led by Kober, sent to do the mopping up.**CW:** Strong violence; language; a scene of nudity. **90m/ C VHS, LV, Closed Caption.** Olivier Gruner, Daphne Ashbrook, John Glover, Jeff Kober, Dennis Lipscomb; **D:** John Murlowski; **W:** Susan Lambert, Patrick Highsmith. *REP*

Autopsy 🐾½ 1978 (R) Rash of unexplainable, spontaneous suicides cause a college student to become emotionally upset. **89m/C VHS, Beta.** *IT* Mimsy Farmer, Barry Primus, Angela Goodwin, Ray Lovelock; **D:** Armando Crispino; **M:** Ennio Morricone. *MPI*

Autopsy 🐾 197? A young gold-digger and a
millionaire marry, and then cheat on each other, provoking blackmail and murder. **90m/C VHS, Beta.** Fernando Rey, Gloria Grahame, Christian Hay. *NO*

Autopsy 🐾½ 1986 A war correspondent in
Vietnam discovers the gruesome secret behind the doctors' autopsy methods at a military hospital. **90m/C VHS, Beta.** *NO*

Autopsy of a Ghost 🐾½ 1967 Comedy/
horror film stars Rathbone as a ghost and Mitchell as a mad scientist. Notable as Rathbone's last screen appearance. In Spanish with no subtitles. **?m/C VHS.** *SP* Basil Rathbone, John Carradine, Cameron Mitchell. *SNC*

An Autumn Afternoon 🐾🐾🐾½ 1962
Ozu's final film is a beautiful expression of his talent. In postwar Tokyo, an aging widower loses his only daughter to marriage and begins a life of loneliness. A heart-wrenching tale of relationships and loss. In Japanese with English subtitles. **112m/C VHS.** *JP* Chishu Ryu, Shima Iwashita, Shin-Ichiro Mikami, Mariko Okada, Keiji Sada; **D:** Yasujiro Ozu; **W:** Yasujiro Ozu. *NYF*

Autumn Born 🐾½ 1979 (R) Young heiress
is abducted by her guardian and imprisoned while she's taught to obey his will. Ill-fated ex-Playmate Dorothy Stratton's first film. **76m/C VHS, Beta.** Dorothy Stratten. *NO*

Autumn Leaves 🐾🐾½ 1956 Crawford
plays a middle-aged typist grasping at her last chance for love. She marries a younger man who's been romancing her, then finds him more and more unstable and violent. Weak story material that could turn melodramatic and tawdry, but doesn't because of Crawford's strength. **108m/B VHS, Beta.** Cliff Robertson, Joan Crawford, Vera Miles, Lorne Greene; **D:** Robert Aldrich; **W:** Robert Blees, Lewis Meltzer, Hugo Butler, Jean Rouveral; **C:** Charles B(ryant) Lang. Berlin International Film Festival '56: Best Director (Aldrich). *GKK*

Autumn Marathon 🐾🐾½ Osenny Marafon
1979 To say that this is one of the better Russian movies of the past three decades is sort of faint praise, given the state of Soviet cinema. Written by playwright Volodin, it's just another paint-by-number version of the philandering man who's really an OK Joe who loves his kids comedy. In Russian with English subtitles. **100m/C VHS.** *RU* Oleg Basilashvili, Natalia Gundareva, Marina Neyelova; **D:** Georgi Daniela; **W:** Alexander Volodin. *KIV, AUD*

Autumn Moon 🐾🐾 Qiuyue 1992 Young
Japanese tourist (Nagase) travels to Hong Kong to enjoy some sexual fun but instead he befriends a 15-year-old girl (Wai), who's afraid of her family's impending emigration to Canada. Not much happens but the Hong Kong setting is eye-catching. English and Cantonese with subtitles. **108m/C VHS.** *HK* Masatoshi Nagase, Li Pui Wai; **D:** Clara Law. *FRF*

Autumn Sonata 🐾🐾🐾 1978 Nordic family strife as famed concert pianist Bergman is
reunited with a daughter she has not seen in years. Bergman's other daughter suffers from a degenerative nerve disease and had been institutionalized until her sister brought her home. Now the three women settle old scores, and balance the needs of their family. Excellent performance by Bergman in her last feature film. **97m/C VHS, Beta, LV.** *SW* Ingrid Bergman, Liv Ullmann, Halvar Bjork, Lena Nyman, Gunnar Bjornstrand; **D:** Ingmar Bergman; **W:** Ingmar Bergman; **C:** Sven Nykvist. Golden Globe Awards '79: Best Foreign Film; National Board of Review Awards '78: Best Actress (Bergman), Best Director (Bergman); New York Film Critics Awards '78: Best Actress (Bergman); National Society of Film Critics Awards '78: Best Actress (Bergman); Nominations: Academy Awards '78: Best Actress (Bergman), Best Original Screenplay. *FOX*

Avalanche 🐾½ 1978 (PG) Disasterama as
vacationers at a new winter ski resort find themselves at the mercy of a monster avalanche leaving a so-called path of terror and destruction in its wake. Talented cast is buried by weak material, producing a snow-bound adventure yawn. **91m/C VHS, Beta.** Rock Hudson, Mia Farrow, Robert Forster, Rick Moses; **D:** Corey Allen; **W:** Corey Allen.

Avalanche Express 🐾 1979 (PG) Marvin
is a CIA agent who uses a defector (Shaw) to lure a scientist (Schell), specializing in biological warfare, aboard a European train. Marvin wants to eliminate Schell but all plans go awry when the snow begins to fall. Ineffective thriller. Director Robson's and actor Shaw's last film—much of Shaw's dialogue was dubbed due to his death before the film's soundtrack was completed. Based on a novel by Colin Forbes. **89m/C VHS.** Lee Marvin, Robert Shaw, Maximilian Schell, Linda Evans, Mike Connors, Joe Namath, Horst Buchholz, David Hess; **D:** Mark Robson; **W:** Abraham Polonsky; **C:** Jack Cardiff. *WAR*

Avalon 🐾🐾🐾 1990 (PG) Powerful but quiet
portrait of the break-up of the family unit as seen from the perspective of a Russian family settled in Baltimore at the close of WWII. Initally, the family is unified in their goals, ideologies and social lives. Gradually, all of this disintegrates; members move to the suburbs and television replaces conversation at holiday gatherings. Levinson based his film on experiences within his own family of Russian Jewish immigrants. **126m/C VHS, Beta, LV, 8mm, Letterbox, Closed Caption.** Armin Mueller-Stahl, Aidan Quinn, Elizabeth Perkins, Joan Plowright, Lou Jacobi, Leo Fuchs, Eve Gordon, Kevin Pollak, Israel Rubinek, Elijah Wood, Grant Gelt, Bernard Hiller; **D:** Barry Levinson; **W:** Barry Levinson; **C:** Allen Daviau; **M:** Randy Newman. Writers Guild of America '90: Best Original Screenplay; Nominations: Academy Awards '90: Best Cinematography, Best Costume Design, Best Original Screenplay, Best Original Score. *COL, FCT*

Avanti! 🐾🐾½ 1972 (R) Stuffy businessman
Wendell Armbruster (Lemmon) heads to Italy to claim his father's body when the old man dies while on vacation. Then he discovers dad has been visiting his mistress lo these many years. While trying to get through mountains of red tape, Wendell finds himself romancing the woman's daughter (Mills). Too long but still amusing. **144m/ C VHS.** Jack Lemmon, Juliet Mills, Clive Revill, Edward Andrews, Gianfranco Barra, Franco Angrisano; **D:** Billy Wilder; **W:** I.A.L. Diamond, Billy Wilder. *USH*

Ava's Magical Adventure 🐾🐾½ 1994
(PG) Ten-year-old Eddie decides to take Ava on a little adventure. Too bad she's a 2-ton elephant he's stolen from the circus. Based on the Mark Twain story "The Stolen White Elephant." **97m/C VHS, LV.** Timothy Bottoms, Georg Stanford Brown, Patrick Dempsey, Priscilla Barnes, David Lander, Kaye Ballard, Remi Ryan; **D:** Patrick Dempsey, Rocky Parker; **W:** Susan D. Nimm; **M:** Mark Holden.

The Avenger 🐾🐾½ 1960 The story of a
criminal who cuts off the heads of people and mails them off makes for a shocker. Graphic violence will appeal to those who like a good mail-order gorefest and are not employed by the post office. **102m/B VHS.** *GE* Ingrid van Bergen, Heinz Drache, Ina Duscha, Mario Litto, Klaus Kinski; **D:** Karl Anton. *SNC*

The Avenger 🐾 The Lost Glory of Troy 1962
This time muscleman Reeves plays Aeneas and leads the Trojans in battle against the Greeks. It's supposedly an adaptation of "The Aeneid" by Virgil. **108m/C VHS.** *FR IT* Steve Reeves, Giacomo "Jack" Rossi-Stuart, Carla Marlier, Gianni "John" Garko, Liana Orfei; **D:** Giorgio Rivalta. *SNC, NOS, VYY*

The Avengers 1998 (PG) It's the fads and
fashions of the swingin' sixties overlaid with cool nineties culture—all set in a surreal 1999 London. Scientist (and leather-girl) Mrs. Emma Peel (Thurman) teams up with dapper, bowler-wearing, umbrella-carrying secret agent John Steed (Fiennes) to defeat maximum baddie, Sir August de Wynter (Connery), who takes his last name very seriously. Seems de Wynter has a machine that can manipulate the world's weather—and he's not intending to do good deeds. Based on the culty sixties Brit TV series (with original Steed, Patrick MacNee, in a cameo). Not yet reviewed. **?m/C VHS.** Ralph Fiennes, Uma Thurman, Sean Connery, Jim Broadbent, Fiona Shaw, Eileen Atkins, John Wood, Eddie Izzard; **D:** Jeremiah S. Chechik; **W:** Don MacPherson. *NYR*

The Avenging 🎬🎬 1992 (PG) Horse comes home from college to run the family ranch but has problems with his two resentful brothers. **100m/C VHS, Closed Caption.** Michael Horse, Efrem Zimbalist Jr., Sherry Hursey, Joseph Runningfox, Taylor Lacher; **D:** Lyman Dayton; **W:** Lyman Dayton. IMP

Avenging Angel woof! 1985 (R) Law student Molly "Angel" Stewart is back on the streets to retaliate against the men who killed the policeman who saved her from a life of prostitution. Worthless sequel to 1984's "Angel," exploiting the original's exploitative intent. Followed listlessly by "Angel III: The Final Chapter." **94m/C VHS, Beta, LV, Closed Caption.** Betsy Russell, Rory Calhoun, Susan Tyrrell, Ossie Davis, Barry Pearl, Ross Hagen, Karin Mani, Robert Tessier; **D:** Robert Vincent O'Neil; **W:** Joseph M. Cala; **C:** Peter Collister; **M:** Paul Antonelli. VTR

The Avenging Angel 🎬🎬½ 1995 Unusual take on religion and western justice. Brigham Young (Heston) and his Mormon sect have established themselves in Utah—with the aid of some sharpshooting vigilantes, including Miles Utley (Berenger). When an assassination attempt is made on Young's life, Utley finds he's stumbled into an ever-widening church conspiracy that threatens to consume him. Based on the novel by Gary Stewart. **100m/C VHS.** Tom Berenger, Charlton Heston, James Coburn, Kevin Tighe, Jeffrey Jones, Tom Bower, Joanna Miles; **D:** Craig R. Baxley; **W:** Dennis Nemec; **C:** Mark Irwin; **M:** Gary Chang. TTC

Avenging Conscience 🎬🎬 Thou Shall Not Kill 1914 An early eerie horror film, based on tales of Edgar Allan Poe. D.W. Griffith's first large-scale feature. Silent. **78m/B VHS, Beta.** Henry B. Walthall, Blanche Sweet; **D:** D.W. Griffith. GPV, VYY, LSV

Avenging Disco Godfather 🎬½
Avenging Godfather; Disco Godfather 1976 (R) Moore parodies the "Godfather" and martial arts movies. **99m/C VHS, Beta.** Rudy Ray Moore, Lady Reed, Carol Speed, Jimmy Lynch; **D:** Rudy Ray Moore. XVC

Avenging Force 🎬🎬 1986 (R) Okay actioner about retired CIA agent Dudikoff returning to the force to help colleague James run for political office. A group of right-wing terrorists called "Pentangle" threatens James, so Dudikoff adds his name to their wanted list. Conflict leads to a forest manhunt where the avenging force does its avenging. **104m/C VHS, Beta, LV, Closed Caption.** Michael Dudikoff, Steve James, John P. Ryan; **D:** Sam Firstenberg; **W:** Mercer Ellington, James Booth; **M:** George S. Clinton. VTR

The Avenging Hand 🎬½ 1943 Leaden suspense story about a hotel filled with thieves all searching for stolen loot. **56m/B VHS.** Noah Beery Jr., Kathleen Kelly, Louis Borell, James Harcourt, Charles Oliver, Reginald Long; **D:** Victor Hanbury. HCV

The Average Woman 🎬🎬 1924 Gritty journalist consults plain Jane for "Modern Woman" story and finds a major rewrite in order when he falls with a thud for Miss Jane. **52m/B VHS, Beta.** Pauline Garon, David Powell, Harrison Ford, De Sacia Mooers; **D:** Christy Cabanne. GPV, GVV

The Aviator 🎬🎬 1985 (PG) Pilot Reeve, haunted by the memory of a fatal crash, tries to find a new line of work. Large sums of money persuade him to transport spoiled Arquette to Washington. When the biplane crashes in the mountain wilderness, the two fall in love between scavenging for food and fighting wild animals. From the director of "Man From Snowy River." **98m/C VHS, Beta.** Christopher Reeve, Rosanna Arquette, Jack Warden, Tyne Daly, Marcia Strassman, Sam Wanamaker, Scott Wilson; **D:** George Miller; **W:** Marc Norman; **C:** David Connell. MGM

The Awakening 🎬½ 1980 (R) An archeologist discovers the tomb of a murderous queen, but upon opening the coffin, the mummy's spirit is transferred to his baby daughter, born at that instant. They call that bad luck. **101m/C VHS.** GB Charlton Heston, Susannah York, Stephanie Zimbalist, Patrick Drury, Ian McDiarmid, Bruce Myers, Nadim Sawalha,

Jill Townsend; **D:** Mike Newell; **W:** Allan Scott, Chris Bryant, Clive Exton; **C:** Jack Cardiff; **M:** Claude Bolling. WAR

Awakening of Candra woof! 1981 Based on a real 1975 incident, a young couple honeymooning in the mountains is assaulted by a lunatic fisherman. The psycho kills the husband and rapes the girl, then he brainwashes poor Candra into thinking it was an accident. Intense subject matter should be horrifying, but falls short of the mark in this television flop. **96m/C VHS, Beta.** Blanche Baker, Cliff DeYoung, Richard Jaeckel; **D:** Paul Wendkos. GEM

Awakenings 🎬🎬🎬½ 1990 (PG-13) Marshall's first dramatic effort is based on the true story of Dr. Oliver Sacks, from his book of the same title. It details his experimentation with the drug L-dopa which inspired the "awakening" of a number of catatonic patients, some of whom had been "sleeping" for as long as 30 years. Occasionally over-sentimental, but still providing a poignant look at both the patients—who find themselves confronted with lost opportunities and faded youth—and at Sacks, who must watch their exquisite suffering as they slip away. De Niro's performance as the youngest of the group is heart-rending, while Williams offers a subdued, moving performance as the doctor. **120m/C VHS, Beta, LV, 8mm, Closed Caption.** Robin Williams, Robert De Niro, John Heard, Julie Kavner, Penelope Ann Miller, Max von Sydow, Anne Meara; **D:** Penny Marshall; **W:** Steven Zaillian; **M:** Randy Newman. National Board of Review Awards '90: Best Actor (De Niro), Best Actor (Williams); National Society of Film Critics Awards '90: Best Actor (De Niro); Nominations: Academy Awards '90: Best Actor (De Niro), Best Adapted Screenplay, Best Picture. COL, FCT

Awakenings of the Beast 🎬 Ritual Dos Sadicos; Ritual of the Maniacs 1968 Documents the protracted sufferings of an LSD drug user who is beset with hallucinatory visions and is prone to fits of frenzied violence. Director Jose Mojica Marins (AKA Coffin Joe) steps out of his Ze do Ciaxia character in this disjointed mix of drugs and sex intercut with Mojica Marins himself on trial for his offensive movies, followed by a case study on drugs and sexual behavior. By the end of the movie, there is a point—that drugs aren't the cause of evil behavior—but it's very painful getting there. In Portugese with English subtitles. **?m/ B VHS.** BR Jose Mojica Marins; **D:** Jose Mojica Marins. SMW, FCT

Away All Boats 🎬🎬½ 1956 The true story of one Captain Hawks, who led a crew of misfits to victory in WWII Pacific aboard transport USS Belinda. Battle scenes are well done; look for early (and brief) appearance by young Clint Eastwood. **114m/B VHS, Beta.** Jeff Chandler, George Nader, Richard Boone, Julie Adams, Keith Andes, Lex Barker; **D:** Joseph Pevney. USH

The Awful Dr. Orloff 🎬 Gritos en la Noche 1962 Set in a bygone era, Dr. Orloff (Vernon) is a retired prison physician who needs unblemished skin to remedy the horrible disfigurement of his daughter Melissa (Lorys), ravaged by fire. He abducts promising young women candidates with the help of his blind zombie henchman Morpho (Valle), who simply cannot be trusted with a scalpel. After several surgical mishaps, they kidnap the perfect specimen, a woman who bears an uncanny resemblance to Melissa. Unfortunately, she is engaged to suspicious police Inspector Tanner (San Martin). French version with English subtitles that includes more explicit gore is also available. **86m/B VHS, Letterbox.** SP Howard Vernon, Diana Lorys, Frank Wolff, Riccardo Valle, Conrado San Martin, Perla Cristal, Maria Silva, Mara Laso; **D:** Jess (Jesus) Franco; **W:** Jess (Jesus) Franco; **C:** Godofredo Pacheco; **M:** Jose Pagan, Antonio Ramirez Angel. SMW, TPV

The Awful Truth 🎬🎬🎬🎬 1937 Classic screwball comedy. Young couple discards their marriage made in heaven and go their separate ways in search of happiness. Meticulously sabotaging each others' new relationships, they discover they really were made for each other. First

on-screen pairing for Grant and Dunne: Grant is at his most charming with dead-on comic timing while Dunne is brilliant as his needling ex. The scene where Dunne poses as Grant's prodigal fan-dancing sister who pays a surprise cocktail-hour visit to the family of his stuffy, upper-class bride-to-be is among the most memorable screwball vignettes of all time. And don't miss the custody battle they have over the family dog (Asta of "The Thin Man" fame). Based on Arthur Richman's play. Preceded by 1925 and 1929 versions; remade in 1953 as "Let's Do It Again." **92m/B VHS, Beta, LV.** Irene Dunne, Cary Grant, Ralph Bellamy, Alexander D'Arcy, Cecil Cunningham, Molly Lamont, Esther Dale, Joyce Compton, Robert Allen, Robert Warwick, Mary Forbes; **D:** Leo McCarey; **W:** Vina Delmar. Academy Awards '37: Best Director (McCarey), National Film Registry '96;; Nominations: Academy Awards '37: Best Actress (Dunne), Best Film Editing, Best Picture, Best Screenplay, Best Supporting Actor (Bellamy). MLB, BTV, COL

An Awfully Big Adventure 🎬🎬 1994 (R) Coming-of-age saga set in postwar Liverpool around a provincial repertory company. Stagestruck 16-year-old Stella (Cates) gets work as a company apprentice, immediately getting a crush on arch, callous theatre manager Meredith Potter (a deliciously nasty Grant), who enjoys degrading everyone around him. The company's chance for success rests on a production of "Peter Pan," with visiting actor P.L. O'Hara (dashing Rickman), who immediately seduces Stella and has more than a few secrets of his own. Theatrically exaggerated; based on the novel by Beryl Bainbridge. **CW:** Sexuality; some language. **113m/C VHS, LV, Closed Caption.** GB Georgina Cates, Hugh Grant, Alan Rickman, Peter Firth, Alun Armstrong, Prunella Scales, Rita Tushingham, Alan Cox, Edward Petherbridge, Nicola Pagett, Carol Drinkwater, Clive Merrison, Gerard McSorley; **D:** Mike Newell; **W:** Charles Wood; **C:** Dick Pope; **M:** Richard Hartley. NLC

Ay, Carmela! 🎬🎬🎬 1990 During the Spanish Civil War, two vaudevillians with strong anti-Franco views are captured by Franco forces and sentenced to execution. They are reprieved when a theatre-loving Lieutenant offers to spare their lives if they will entertain the troops. Clever and entertaining farce, with poignant undertones. **105m/C VHS.** SP IT Carmen Maura, Andres Pajares, Gabino Diego, Maurizio De Razza, Miguel Rellan, Edward Zentara, Jose Sancho, Antonio Fuentes; **D:** Carlos Saura; **W:** Rafael Azcona; **C:** Jose Luis Alcaine. HBO

Baba 🎬🎬🎬 The Father 1973 A poor boatman agrees to be the fall guy in a murder in exchange for the actual murderer supporting his family. But after 24 years in prison, the boatman finds all his sacrificing has been in vain. His daughter has become a prostitute and his son is working as one of the murderer's henchman. In Turkish with English subtitles. **95m/C VHS.** TU **D:** Yilmaz Guney. FCT, HEG

Babar: The Movie 🎬🎬 1988 (G) The lovable Babar, king of the elephants, must devise a plan to outwit an angry hoard of attacking rhinos. Based on the characters of Jean and Laurent de Brunhoff. **75m/C VHS, Beta, LV, 8mm.** CA FR **D:** Alan Bunce; **W:** Alan Bunce, John deKlein; **V:** Gavin Magrath, Gordon Pinsent, Sarah Polley, Chris Wiggins, Elizabeth Hanna. FHE, IME

Babe! 🎬🎬🎬½ 1975 A fine television movie about the life of one of America's most famous woman athletes, Babe Didrickson. Adapted by Joanna Lee from Didrickson's autobiography, "The Life I've Led." The movie was nominated for Outstanding Special of 1975-76 and Clark won an Emmy for her work. **120m/C VHS.** Susan Clark, Alex Karras, Slim Pickens, Jeanette Nolan, Ellen Geer, Ford Rainey; **D:** Buzz Kulik; **M:** Jerry Goldsmith. NO

The Babe 🎬🎬½ 1992 (PG) Follows the life of legendary baseball player Babe Ruth, portrayed as a sloppy drunkard whose appetites for food, drink, and sex were as large as he was. Alvarado and McGillis do well as the Babe's first and second wives, but this is Goodman's show from start to finish. He's excellent as Ruth, and looks the part, but his fine performance can't make up for a lackluster script filled with holes. **115m/C VHS, LV, Closed Caption.** John Goodman, Kelly McGillis, Trini Alvarado, Bruce Boxleitner, Peter Donat, J.C. Quinn, Richard Tyson, James Cromwell, Joe Ragno, Bernard Kates, Michael McGrady, Stephen Caffrey; **D:** Arthur Hiller; **W:** John Fusco; **C:** Haskell Wexler; **M:** Elmer Bernstein. *USH*

Babe 🐾🐾🐾½ *Babe, the Gallant Pig* 1995 (G) Totally charming fable has intelligent piglet Babe being raised by matriarch sheepdog Fly, and learning the art of sheep herding along with his new canine brothers. Farmer Hoggett (Cromwell), Babe's owner by virtue of a winning raffle ticket, sees that he's more than just a ham, and enters them in the world sheepdog herding championship. Whimsy that never crosses the line into treacle. Four different special effects houses were used to make the barnyard animals talk and walk. Filmed on location in Australia; based on Dick King-Smith's book "The Sheep-Pig." **91m/C VHS, LV, Closed Caption, DVD.** AU James Cromwell, Magda Szubanski; **D:** Chris Noonan; **W:** Chris Noonan, George Miller; **C:** Andrew Lesnie; **M:** Nigel Westlake; **V:** Christine Cavanaugh, Miriam Margolyes, Danny Mann, Hugo Weaving. Academy Awards '95: Best Visual Effects; Golden Globe Awards '96: Best Film—Musical/Comedy; National Society of Film Critics Awards '95: Best Film; Nominations: Academy Awards '95: Best Adapted Screenplay, Best Art Direction/Set Decoration, Best Director (Noonan), Best Film Editing, Best Picture, Best Supporting Actor (Cromwell); British Academy Awards '95: Best Adapted Screenplay, Best Film; Writers Guild of America '95: Best Adapted Screenplay. *USH*

Babe Ruth Story 🐾🐾 1948 An overly sentimental biography about the famed baseball slugger. Bendix is miscast as the Bambino, but the actual film clips of the Babe are of interest. A movie to be watched during those infrequent bouts of sloppy baseball mysticism. **107m/B VHS, Beta, Closed Caption.** William Bendix, Claire Trevor, Charles Bickford, William Frawley, Sam Levene, Gertrude Niesen; **D:** Roy Del Ruth. *FOX*

Babes in Arms 🐾🐾½ 1939 The children of several vaudeville performers team up to put on a show to raise money for their financially impoverished parents. Loosely adapted from the Rodgers and Hart Broadway musical of the same name; features some of their songs as well as new additions. 🎵Babes in Arms; I Cried for You; Good Morning; You Are My Lucky Star; Broadway Rhythm; Where or When; Daddy Was a Minstrel Man; I'm Just Wild About Harry; God's Country. **91m/B VHS, Beta, LV.** Judy Garland, Mickey Rooney, Charles Winninger, Guy Kibbee, June Preisser; **D:** Busby Berkeley; **M:** George Bassman, Richard Rodgers, Lorenz Hart. Nominations: Academy Awards '39: Best Actor (Rooney), Best Score. *MGM*

Babes in Toyland 🐾🐾 1961 A lavish Disney production of Victor Herbert's timeless operetta, with Toyland being menaced by the evil Barnaby and his Bogeymen. Yes, Annette had a life after Mickey Mouse and before the peanut butter commercials. Somewhat charming, although the roles of the lovers seem a stretch for both Funicello and Kirk. But the flick does sport an amusing turn by Wynn. **105m/C VHS, Beta.** Annette Funicello, Ray Bolger, Tommy Sands, Ed Wynn, Tommy Kirk; **D:** Jack Donohue; **C:** Edward Colman; **M:** George Bruns. Nominations: Academy Awards '61: Best Costume Design (Color), Scoring of a Musical.*DIS*

Babes in Toyland 🐾½ 1986 Young girl must save Toyland from the clutches of the evil Barnaby and his monster minions. Bland TV remake of the classic doesn't approach the original. **96m/C VHS, LV.** Drew Barrymore, Noriyuki "Pat" Morita, Richard Mulligan, Eileen Brennan, Keanu Reeves, Jill Schoelen, Googy Gress; **D:** Clive Donner; **M:** Leslie Bricusse. *ORI*

Babes on Broadway 🐾🐾½ 1941 Mickey and Judy put on a show to raise money for a settlement house. Nearly the best of the Garland-Rooney series, with imaginative numbers staged by Berkeley. 🎵Babes on Broadway; Anything Can

Happen in New York; How About You?; Hoe Down; Chin Up! Cheerio! Carry On!; Mama Yo Quiero; F.D.R. Jones; Waiting for the Robert E. Lee. **118m/B VHS, Beta, LV.** Mickey Rooney, Judy Garland, Fay Bainter, Richard Quine, Virginia Weidler, Ray Macdonald, Busby Berkeley; **D:** Busby Berkeley; **M:** George Bassman. Nominations: Academy Awards '42: Best Song ("How About You?"). *MGM*

Babette's Feast 🐾🐾🐾½ 1987 A simple, moving pageant-of-life fable. A group of religiously zealous villagers are taught love and forgiveness through a lavish banquet prepared by one of their housemaids, who turns out to be a world-class chef. Adapted from a tale by Isak Dinesen. In French and Danish with English subtitles. **102m/C VHS, Beta, LV.** DK FR Stephane Audran, Bibi Andersson, Bodil Kjer, Birgitte Federspiel, Jean-Philippe LaFont, Ebbe Rode, Jarl Kulle; **D:** Gabriel Axel; **W:** Gabriel Axel. Academy Awards '87: Best Foreign Language Film; British Academy Awards '88: Best Foreign Film. *ORI, FCT, AUD*

The Baby 🐾🐾 1972 (PG) Bizarre story of a social worker who resorts to swinging an ax to cut the apron strings of "baby," a retarded man-child, from his over-protective and insane (bad combination) mother and sisters. Low-budget production looks and feels like a low-budget production, but any movie featuring a grown man wandering about in diapers can't be all bad. **85m/C VHS, Beta.** Anjanette Comer, Ruth Roman, Marianna Hill, Suzanne Zenor, David Manzy, Michael Pataki; **D:** Ted Post. *NO*

The Baby and the Battleship 🐾🐾½ 1956 The old baby out of (on the?) water plot. While on liberty in Italy, a sailor, after a series of complications, becomes custodian of a baby and attempts to hide the tyke aboard his battleship (hence the title). More complications ensue. Some funny moments. Great cast. **96m/C VHS.** GB John Mills, Richard Attenborough, Andre Morell, Bryan Forbes, Lisa Gastoni, Michael Hordern, Lionel Jeffries, Gordon Jackson, John Le Mesurier; **D:** Jay Lewis. *NOS, MOV, VEC*

Baby Boom 🐾🐾½ 1987 (PG) When a hard-charging female executive becomes the reluctant mother of a baby girl (a gift from a long-lost relative), she adjusts with great difficulty to motherhood and life outside the rat race and New York City (and Sam Shepard as the love interest). A fairly harmless collection of cliches bolstered by Keaton's usual nervous performance as a power-suited yuppie ad queen saddled with a noncareer-enhancing baby, moving from manic yuppie ad maven to jelly-packing Vermont store-owner/mom. To best appreciate flick, see it with a bevy of five- and six-year-olds (a good age for applauding the havoc that a baby creates). **103m/C VHS, Beta, LV, Closed Caption.** Diane Keaton, Sam Shepard, Harold Ramis, Sam Wanamaker, James Spader, Pat Hingle, Mary Gross, Victoria Jackson, Paxton Whitehead, Annie Golden, Dori Brenner, Robin Bartlett, Christopher Noth, Britt Leach; **D:** Charles Shyer; **W:** Charles Shyer, Nancy Meyers; **M:** Bill Conti. *FCT, FOX*

Baby Cart 1: Lend a Child...Lend an Arm 🐾 *Lone Wolf and Cub: Sword of Vengeance* 1972 First in a series of six from the sword-wielding samurai genre. Chronicles the events leading up to a samurai warrior's (Wakayama) expulsion from his native village along with his infant son (Tomikawa). Father's intense rivalry with the evil Shogun whom he was ousted by becomes an epic struggle of good vs. evil. The adorable little "Lone Cub" provides an effective counterpoint for Dad's sideline excursion into a local brothel. In Japanese with English subtitles in a letterbox format. **83m/C VHS, LV.** JP Tomisaburo Wakayama, Akihiro Tomikawa; **D:** Kenji Misumi. *ANI, VSM*

Baby Cart 4: Heart of a Parent...Heart of a Child 🐾 1972 Fourth in a series of six. A man (Wakayama) pushes his son (Tomikawa) across Japan in a baby cart loaded with deadly accessories including built-in guns and switchblades. Copious amounts of bloodshed. In Japanese with English

subtitles in a letterbox format. **80m/C VHS.** JP Tomisaburo Wakayama, Akihiro Tomikawa; **D:** Buichi Sato. *VSM*

Baby Cart at the River Styx 🐾 *Lone Wolf and Cub: Baby Cart at the River Styx; Baby Cart 2* 1972 Second of six parts in the "Kozure Ohkami" ("Sword of Vengeance") series about a man who wheels his motherless infant through the Chinese countryside in a baby cart armed with secret weapons, plotting his revenge on the warlord who expelled him. This one features the intro of Sayka and her fellow female assassins. Subtitled in English. **80m/C VHS.** JP Tomisaburo Wakayama, Akihiro Tomikawa; **D:** Kenji Misumi. *MOV*

Baby Cart to Hades 🐾 1972 The third "Kozure Ohkami" ("Sword of Vengeance") film once again finds samurai Itto Ogami and his son Diagoro embroiled in a power struggle between a regional landlord and a governor in feudal Japan. Subtitled in English. **88m/C VHS, Letterbox.** JP Tomisaburo Wakayama, Akihiro Tomikawa; **D:** Kenji Misumi. *VSM*

Baby Doll 🐾🐾🐾 1956 Suggestive sex at its best, revolving around the love of cotton in Mississippi. Nubile Baker is married to slow-witted Malden, who runs a cotton gin. His torching of Wallach's cotton gin begins a cycle of sexual innuendo and tension, brought to exhilarating life on screen, without a single filmed kiss. Performers and sets ooze during the steamy exhibition, which was considered highly erotic when released. Excellent performances from entire cast, with expert pacing by director Kazan. Screenplay is based on Tennessee Williams' "27 Wagons Full of Cotton." **115m/B VHS, Beta.** Eli Wallach, Carroll Baker, Karl Malden, Mildred Dunnock, Rip Torn; **D:** Elia Kazan; **W:** Tennessee Williams; **C:** Boris Kaufman. Golden Globe Awards '57: Best Director (Kazan); Nominations: Academy Awards '56: Best Actress (Baker), Best Adapted Screenplay, Best Black and White Cinematography, Best Supporting Actress (Dunnock). *WAR, FCT*

The Baby Doll Murders 🐾🐾 1992 (R) Someone in L.A. is killing beautiful young women and then leaving a broken baby doll at the scene of the crime. The gruesome murderer manages to elude everyone, until Detective Benz discovers a link between the victims and a pattern begins to form. He also discovers that his partner's wife is going to be the next victim unless he can stop this ruthless serial killer from striking again.*CW:* Language, violence, and sexuality. **90m/C VHS, Closed Caption.** Jeff Kober, Melanie Smith, John Saxon, Tom Hodges; **D:** Paul Leder; **W:** Paul Leder. *REP*

Baby Face 🐾🐾 1933 A small town girl moves to the city when her father dies. There she gets a job at a bank and sleeps her way to the top of the business world, discarding used men left and right. The Hays Office was extremely upset with the then risque material and forced Warner to trim the first cut. **70m/C VHS, Beta.** Barbara Stanwyck, George Brent, Donald Cook, John Wayne, Henry Kolker, Margaret Lindsay, Douglass Dumbrille, James Murray; **D:** Alfred E. Green. *MGM, FCT*

Baby Face Harry Langdon 🐾🐾½ 1926 Two silent shorts by the limpid-eyed comedian: "Saturday Afternoon" (1926), and "Lucky Stars" (1925). **60m/B VHS, Beta, 8mm.** Harry Langdon, Alice Ward, Natalie Kingston, Vernon Dent, Harry Edwards; **D:** Harry Edwards; **W:** Frank Capra, Arthur Ripley. *VYY*

Baby Face Morgan 🐾🐾 1942 Poor comedy about gangsters who attempt to take advantage of the FBI's preoccupation with saboteurs and spies by muscling in on an insurance firm. **60m/B VHS.** Mary Carlisle, Richard Cromwell, Robert Armstrong, Chick Chandler, James Judels, Warren Hymer, Vince Barnett, Ralf Harolde; **D:** Arthur Dreifuss. *SNC*

Baby Face Nelson 🐾½ 1997 (R) Lame Depression-era gangster flick with George "Baby Face" Nelson (Howell) and his moll Helen Womack (Zane) fighting rival Al Capone (Abraham) in Chicago. Kove comes off well as gangster John Dillinger.*CW:* Gangster violence, language and a sex scene. **80m/C VHS.** C. Thomas Howell, Lisa Zane, F. Murray Abraham, Doug Wert, Martin Kove; **D:** Scott Levy;

W: Joseph Farrugia, Craig J. Nevius; **C:** Christopher Raffa; **M:** Christopher Lennertz. *NHO*

Baby Girl Scott 🎬🎬½ 1987 Hurt and Lithgow play the parents of an extremely premature infant who is being kept alive by technology. They make a heartrending decision and then must battle doctors and the system to let their daughter die with dignity. Made for television. 97m/C VHS. John Lithgow, Mary Beth Hurt, Linda Kelsey; **D:** John Korty. *ART*

Baby It's You 🎬🎬🎬 1982 (R) In New Jersey in the '60s, the relationship between a smart, attractive Jewish girl who yearns to be an actress and a street-smart Catholic Italian boy puzzles their family and friends. It all works due to Arquette's strong acting and Sayles' script, which explores adolescent dreams, the transition to adulthood, class differences, and the late 1960s with insight and humor. Interesting period soundtrack (Woolly Bully and, for some reason, Bruce Springsteen) helps propel the film, a commercial job which helped finance Sayles' more independent ventures. 105m/C VHS, Beta, LV, Closed Caption. Rosanna Arquette, Vincent Spano, Jack Davidson, Joanna Merlin, Nick Ferrari, Leora Dana, Robert Downey Jr., Tracy Pollan, Matthew Modine; **D:** John Sayles; **W:** John Sayles; **C:** Michael Ballhaus. *PAR*

Baby Love woof! 1969 (R) A softcore fluff-fest about a trollop seducing a doctor's family. The doctor may or may not be her father. Hayden tantalizes the doctor, the doctor's son, and the doctor's wife, as well as the neighbors, leaving only those in adjoining communities untouched. Based on the novel by Tina Chad Christian. 98m/C VHS, Beta. *GB* Ann Lynn, Keith Barron, Linda Hayden, Derek Lamden, Diana Dors, Patience Collier; **D:** Alastair Reid. *NLC*

Baby Love woof! 1983 Nerds get revenge against the freshmen who run the local frat house. 80m/C VHS, Beta. *MGM*

The Baby Maker 🎬🎬 1970 (R) A couple who cannot have children because the wife is sterile decides to hire a woman to have a child for them. However, the relationship between the husband and the surrogate progresses beyond what either of them wanted. Hershey stars as the free-love surrogate mama (just before she underwent the supreme 60s transformation into Barbara Seagull) and Bridges makes his directorial debut. Flick is interesting as a combo critique/exploitation of those wild and groovy 1960s. 109m/C VHS. Barbara Hershey, Collin Wilcox-Horne, Sam Groom, Scott Glenn, Jeannie Berlin; **D:** James Bridges; **W:** James Bridges. Nominations: Academy Awards '70: Original Song Score and/or Adaptation. *WAR*

Baby Monitor: Sound of Fear 🎬🎬½ 1997 (R) Matt (Beghe) makes the mistake of falling in love with nanny Ann (Bissett), which makes his wife Carol (Tyson) go psychotic. She overhears everything thanks to that darn baby monitor and decides to have Ann killed in a botched kidnapping attempt. But Ann discovers the evil goings-on (because of the baby monitor, natch) and works to save the good guys. **CW:** Some violence/terror. 91m/C VHS, Closed Caption. Josie Bissett, Jason Beghe, Barbara Tyson, Jeffrey Noah, Vincent Gale, Gerard Plunkett; **D:** John L. Roman; **W:** Edgar van Cossart. *USH*

Baby of the Bride 🎬🎬½ 1991 Follow-up to "Children of the Bride," has McClanahan settling into wedded bliss with younger husband Shackleford when she discovers she's pregnant. Not only is she unsure about wanting to be a mom again at her age but then grown—and single—daughter McNichol announces she is also pregnant. The sheer silliness of this made-for-television fare makes it fun to watch. 93m/C VHS, Closed Caption. Rue McClanahan, Ted Shackleford, Kristy McNichol, John Wesley Shipp, Anne Bobby, Conor O'Farrell; **D:** Bill Bixby; **W:** Bart Baker. *TTC*

Baby on Board 🎬🎬 1992 (PG) Kane plays the wife of a Mafia bookkeeper who is accidentally killed in a gangland murder. Out for revenge, she tracks her husband's killer to JFK airport with her four year old daughter in tow. Just as she pulls the loaded gun from her purse and takes aim, a pickpocket snatches her purse, accidentally firing the gun. Now she's on the run and she jumps into the first cab she can find, driven by Reinhold. New York City is turned upside down as mother, daughter, and cabbie try to elude the mob in this funny but predictable comedy. 90m/C VHS, Beta, LV, Closed Caption. Carol Kane, Judge Reinhold, Geza Kovacs, Errol Slue, Alex Stapley, Holly Stapley; **D:** Francis Schaeffer.

Baby ... Secret of the Lost Legend 🎬🎬 1985 (PG) A sportswriter and his paleontologist wife risk their lives to reunite a hatching brontosaurus with its mother in the African jungle. Although this Disney film is not lewd in any sense, beware of several scenes displaying frontal nudity and some violence. 95m/C VHS, Beta, LV. William Katt, Sean Young, Patrick McGoohan, Julian Fellowes; **D:** Bill W.L. Norton. *TOU*

The Baby-Sitters Club 🎬🎬½ 1995 (PG) Centering on the summer vacation of seven enterprising Connecticut 13-year-olds and their teen trials with parents, boys, and babysitting, this film is sure to hit home with a crowd that is rarely featured, pre-teen girls. Director Mayron claims, "It's the 'Mystic Pizza' of their age." Young girls and girls young at heart should enjoy this touching look at the fragile years of our youth, leaving baby dolls behind and heading towards dating. Based on the best-selling book series by Ann Martin. Fisk, who plays club leader Kristy, is the daughter of actress Sissy Spacek and director Jack Fisk. 92m/C VHS, LV, Closed Caption. Schuyler Fisk, Bre Blair, Rachel Leigh Cook, Larisa Oleynik, Tricia Joe, Stacey Linn Ransower, Zelda Harris, Brooke Adams, Peter Horton, Bruce Davison, Ellen Burstyn, Austin O'Brien, Aaron Michael Metchik; **D:** Melanie Mayron; **W:** Dalene Young; **C:** Willy Kurant; **M:** David Michael Frank. *COL*

Baby Snakes: The Complete Version 1979 Concert footage of Zappa is interspersed with clay animation by Bruce Bickford. 166m/C VHS, Beta. Frank Zappa; **D:** Frank Zappa. *MVD*

Baby, Take a Bow 🎬🎬 1934 (PG) Temple's first starring role. As a cheerful Pollyanna-type she helps her father, falsely accused of theft, by finding the true thief. 76m/B VHS, Beta, Closed Caption. Shirley Temple, James Dunn, Claire Trevor, Alan Dinehart; **D:** Harry Lachman. *NO*

Baby, the Rain Must Fall 🎬🎬 1964 A rockabilly singer, paroled from prison after serving time for a knifing, returns home to his wife and daughter, but his outbursts of violence make the reunion difficult. Unsentimental with realistic performances, but script is weak (although written by Foote, based on his play, "The Traveling Lady"). Theme song was a Top 40 hit. 100m/B VHS, Beta, LV. Steve McQueen, Lee Remick, Don Murray; **D:** Robert Mulligan; **W:** Horton Foote; **C:** Ernest Laszlo; **M:** Elmer Bernstein. *COL, MOV*

Babycakes 🎬🎬½ 1989 A marshmellow romance between an overweight mortuary attendant who decides to follow her heart when she falls for a hunky ice skater. Can she make him appreciate her inner beauty instead of just her not-the-normal-beauty-standard outward appearance? (Happy ending guaranteed.) A made-for-television remake of the darker German film "Sugarbaby." 94m/C VHS, Closed Caption. Ricki Lake, Craig Sheffer, Paul Benedict, Betty Buckley, John Karlen, Nada Despotovich; **D:** Paul Schneider. *TTC*

Babyfever 🎬🎬½ 1994 (R) Women gather at a baby shower and tell stories about motherhood and related topics. May be viewed as a babblefest with video accompaniment or as an overdue cinematic exploration of a fairly important aspect of life (where would we be without mom?). That said, pace of the comedy drama is less than feverish, although director Jaglom captures the essence of the stories without disturbing their flow. Foyt, Jaglom's wife and co-screenwriter, makes her acting debut. 110m/C VHS. Matt Salinger, Eric Roberts, Frances Fisher, Victoria Foyt, Zack Norman, Dinah Lenney, Elaine Kagan; **D:** Henry Jaglom; **W:** Victoria Foyt, Henry Jaglom; **C:** Hanania Baer. *FXL*

The Babylon Story from "Intolerance" 🎬🎬🎬½ 1916 Lavishly produced vignette from Griffith's film "Intolerance" as it was released on its own in 1919, in order to recoup the studio losses incurred by that grandest of cinematic follies. Silent with organ score, tinted color. 25m/C VHS, Beta. Constance Talmadge, Alfred Paget; **D:** D.W. Griffith. *VYY*

Baby's Day Out 🎬🎬½ 1994 (PG) Poor man's "Home Alone" refits tired Hughes formula using little tiny baby for original spin. Adorable Baby Bink crawls his way onto the city streets, much to his frantic mother's dismay, and unwittingly outsmarts his would-be kidnappers. As in "HA I and II," the bad guys fall victim to all sorts of cataclysmic Looney Tunes violence. Small kids will get a kick out of this one. Particular problem for the moviemakers was that the nine-month old Worton twins were past the year mark by the end of the shoot, a world of difference in infantdom. Blue screens and out-of-sequence shooting were used to overcome the developmental gap. 99m/C VHS, Closed Caption. Adam Worton, Jacob Worton, Joe Mantegna, Lara Flynn Boyle, Joe Pantoliano, Fred Dalton Thompson, John Neville, Brian Haley, Matthew Glave; **D:** Patrick Read Johnson; **W:** John Hughes; **C:** Thomas Ackerman; **M:** Bruce Broughton. *FXV*

The Babysitter 🎬🎬 1980 A family hires the mysterious but ingratiating Johanna (Zimbalist) as live-in help without checking on her references (who'd all checked out). The babysitter is the answer to all their problems—Mom's an alcoholic, Dad's a workaholic, and their daughter's just plain maladjusted—but once Johanna's gained their trust (or, in Dad's case, lust), she sets out to manipulate and exploit the family for her own psychotic purposes. Houseman plays the nosy neighbor who's on to her evil plan. Fair made-for-TV treatment of a common suspense plot. 96m/C VHS, Beta, LV. William Shatner, Patty Duke, Stephanie Zimbalist, Quinn Cummings, John Houseman, David Wallace; **D:** Peter Medak. *NO*

The Babysitter 🎬🎬½ 1995 (R) All-American teen Jennifer (Silverstone) becomes the unexpected object of desire for family man Harry (Walsh), whose wife Dolly (Garlington) is fantasizing about having an affair with a neighbor (Segal). But then Jennifer's boyfriend (London) gets caught up in a malicious prank that turns bad for everyone involved. Based on a short story by Robert Coover. **CW:** Brief nudity, violence, adult situations, language. 90m/C VHS, LV, Closed Caption. Alicia Silverstone, Jeremy London, J.T. Walsh, Lee Garlington, Nicky Katt, Lois Chiles, George Segal; **D:** Guy Ferland; **W:** Guy Ferland; **M:** Loek Dikker. *REP*

The Bacchantes 🎬🎬 1963 Poorly dubbed account of a ballerina, her life and loves. Based on the play by Euripides. 100m/B VHS. *IT* Taina Elg, Pierre Brice, Alessandra Panaro, Alberto Lupo, Akim Tamiroff; **D:** Giorgio Ferroni. *FCT*

The Bachelor 🎬🎬🎬 1993 Beautiful, seductive period drama about a shy and solitary physician who is forced into a new life when a family tragedy changes everything he once took for granted. Richardson and Carradine give brilliant performances in this provocative story of one man's sexual awakening. Based on a novel by Arthur Schnitzler. 105m/C VHS. Keith Carradine, Miranda Richardson, Mari Torocsik, Max von Sydow, Kristin Scott Thomas, Sarah-Jane Fenton, Franco Diogene; **D:** Roberto Faenza; **W:** Roberto Faenza, Ennio de Concini, Hugh Fleetwood; **M:** Ennio Morricone. *TRI*

The Bachelor and the Bobby-Soxer 🎬🎬🎬 *Bachelor Knight* 1947 Playboy Grant is brought before Judge Loy for disturbing the peace and sentenced to court her teenage sister Temple. Cruel and unusual punishment? Maybe, but the wise Judge hopes that the dates will help Temple over her crush on handsome

Grant. Instead, Loy and Grant fall for each other. **95m/B VHS, Beta, LV.** Cary Grant, Myrna Loy, Shirley Temple, Rudy Vallee, Harry Davenport, Ray Collins, Veda Ann Borg; **D:** Irving Reis; **W:** Sidney Sheldon. Academy Awards '47: Best Original Screenplay. *CCB, MLB, TTC*

Bachelor Apartment 🗡🗡½ 1931 Once at the leading edge of the bachelor on the loose genre, this one's hopelessly dated. The scandalous womanizing of a wealthy '30s Lothario just doesn't have the same impact on the men just don't understand generation. Nevertheless, as vintage if-the-walls-could-talk fluff, it's good for a giggle. **77m/B VHS.** Lowell Sherman, Irene Dunne, Norman Kerry, Claudia Dell, Noel Francis, Charles Coleman; **D:** Lowell Sherman. *TTC, FCT*

Bachelor Bait 🗡½ 1934 A marriage license clerk who's tired of just handing out licenses opens a matrimonial service for men. **75m/B VHS, Beta.** Stuart Erwin, Rochelle Hudson, Pert Kelton, Richard "Skeets" Gallagher; **M:** Max Steiner. *CCB*

Bachelor in Paradise 🗡🗡½ 1969 Silly tale starring Hope as a writer of books to the love-lorn who decides to do firsthand research on the sexual goings-on of a suburban California community. All the married ladies find him charming (much to their husbands' disgust) and the lone single woman, Turner, isn't single by the end of the movie. **109m/C VHS, Closed Caption.** Bob Hope, Lana Turner, Janis Paige, Jim Hutton, Paula Prentiss, Don Porter, Virginia Grey, Agnes Moorehead, John McGiver; **D:** Jack Arnold; **W:** Hal Kanter, Valentine Davies; **M:** Henry Mancini. Nominations: Academy Awards '61: Best Song ("Bachelor in Paradise"). *MGM, FCT*

Bachelor Mother 🗡🗡🗡 1939 A single salesgirl causes a scandal when she finds an abandoned baby and is convinced by her boss to adopt the child. Smart, witty comedy with nice performance by Rogers. **82m/B VHS, Beta, LV.** Ginger Rogers, David Niven, Charles Coburn; **D:** Garson Kanin. Nominations: Academy Awards '39: Best Story. *CCB, FCT, TTC*

Bachelor of Hearts 🗡½ 1958 Sophomoric British comedy set at Cambridge University, with a German exchange student whose difficulty with English brings him to date several women in one evening. Notable for horror fans as the debut of femme fright fave Barbara Steele. **94m/C VHS.** *GB* Hardy Kruger, Sylvia Syms, Ronald Lewis; **D:** Wolf Rilla; **W:** Frederic Raphael, Leslie Bricusse. *NOS*

Bachelor Party 🗡🗡 1984 (R) He's silly, cute, and poor. She's intelligent, beautiful, and rich. It must be a marriage made in heaven, because no one in their right mind would put these two together. All is basically well, except that her parents hate him and his friends dislike her. Things are calm until right before the big event, when bride-to-be Kitaen objects to Hank's traditional pre-nuptial partying. Light and semi-entertaining with scattered laughs. **105m/C VHS, Beta, LV, Closed Caption.** Tom Hanks, Tawny Kitaen, Adrian Zmed, George Grizzard, Robert Prescott, William Tepper, Wendie Jo Sperber, Barry Diamond, Michael Dudikoff, Deborah Harmon, John Joe Bob Briggs Bloom, Toni Alessandra, Monique Gabrielle, Angela Aames, Rosanne Katon; **D:** Neal Israel; **W:** Pat Proft; **M:** Robert Folk. *FOX*

Back Door to Heaven 🗡🗡🗡½ 1939 Traces the path of a young boy who is born into a poor family and the reasons for his turning to a life of crime. A grim and powerful drama with many convincing performances. **85m/B VHS.** Wallace Ford, Aline MacMahon, Stuart Erwin, Patricia Ellis, Kent Smith, Van Heflin, Jimmy Lydon; **D:** William K. Howard. *NOS, MOV*

Back from Eternity 🗡🗡 1956 Eleven survivors of a plane crash are stranded in a headhunter region of South America's jungle. Remake of "Five Came Back" (1939), which was also directed by Farrow. **97m/B VHS, Beta, LV.** Robert Ryan, Rod Steiger, Anita Ekberg, Phyllis Kirk, Keith Andes, Gene Barry; **D:** John Farrow; **C:** William Mellor. *NO*

Back Home 🗡🗡½ 1990 A family reunion movie with pure Disney sentiment. A 12-year-old English girl, who has been living in America during WWII, is reunited with her family in postwar England. Made for cable television. **103m/C VHS, Closed Caption.** Hayley Carr, Hayley Mills, Jean Anderson, Rupert Frazer, Brenda Bruce, Adam Stevenson, George Clark; **D:** Piers Haggard. *DIS*

Back in Action 🗡½ 1994 (R) Veteran LA detective Rossi (Piper) is out to bust the ruthless drug gang who gunned down his partner. But he's got company—martial-arts expert Billy (Blanks) whose young sister has fallen prey to the same gang. So the two action junkies reluctantly team up to cause some major damage. **93m/C VHS, LV, Closed Caption.** Roddy Piper, Billy Blanks, Bobbie Phillips, Matt Birman, Nigel Bennett, Damon D'Oliveira, Kai Soremekun; **D:** Paul Ziller, Steve DiMarco; **W:** Karl Schiffman. *USH*

Back in Business 🗡🗡 1996 (R) Joe Elkhart's (Bosworth) life is down the drain. After failing to expose a fellow police officer as corrupt, he's kicked off the force, abandoned by his friends, and divorced by his wife. Now working as a mechanic, Joe gets pulled back into the action when his ex-partner, Tony (Torry), goes undercover to bring down a major drug dealer and Joe discovers the corrupt cops that framed him are also behind the current heroin deal. **CW:** Strong violence and language, and for sexuality. **93m/C VHS, Closed Caption.** Brian Bosworth, Joe Torry, Dara Tomanovich; **D:** Philippe Mora; **W:** Ed Decatur, Ash Staley. *COL*

Back in the USSR 🗡½ 1992 (R) Danger follows two lovers caught up in the Moscow underworld. When young American touring Russia unwittingly gets involved with a beautiful art thief. Lots of fast-paced action in an otherwise muddled film. The first American film shot entirely on location in Moscow. **CW:** Language, violence, and one scene of sensuality. **87m/C VHS.** Frank Whaley, Natalia Negoda, Roman Polanski, Claudia Robinson, Dey Young, Andrew Divoff, Brian Blessed, Ravil Issyanov; **D:** Deran Sarafian; **C:** Yuri Neyman. *FXV*

Back of Beyond 🗡🗡 1995 (R) Spectacular setting in the Australian outback can't make up for unfocused plot and characters with little impact. Tom (Mercutio) ran a remote desert gas station with his sister, Susan (Elmaloglou), before she was killed on his motorbike. When Connor's (Friels) car breaks down by the derelict station, he, girlfriend Charlie (Smart), and sidekick Nick (Polson) must wait while Tom tries to fix it. Only Connor is a diamond thief and patience isn't one of his virutes, especially when he notices the unhappy Charlie making friends with Tom. Mystical/supernatural elements involving ghosts and Aboriginal sites only add to the confusion. **CW:** Language and a scene of sexual assault. **85m/C VHS.** *AU* Paul Mercurio, Colin Friels, Dee Smart, John Polson, Rebekah Elmaloglou, Bob Maza, Terry Serio; **D:** Michael Robertson; **W:** Paul Leadon, A.M. Brooksbank, Richard I. Sawyer; **C:** Stephen Dobson; **M:** Mark Moffatt, Wayne Goodwin. *ART*

Back Roads 🗡🗡 1981 (R) Southern hooker meets a down-on-his-luck boxer and both head out for a better life in California, finding love along the way. Ritt road trip lacks any comedic rhythm and survives on Field and Jones working to entertain. **94m/C VHS, Beta.** Sally Field, Tommy Lee Jones, David Keith; **D:** Martin Ritt; **W:** Gary De Vore; **C:** John A. Alonzo; **M:** Henry Mancini. *FOX*

Back Street 1961 The forbidden affair between a married man and a beautiful fashion designer carries on through many anxious years to a tragic end. The lavish third film version of the Fannie Hurst novel. **107m/C VHS, Beta.** Susan Hayward, John Gavin, Vera Miles; **D:** David Miller; **C:** William H. Daniels. Nominations: Academy Awards '61: Best Costume Design (Color). *USH, MLB*

Back to Back 🗡 1990 (R) A beautiful young vigilante embarks on a rampage to clear her family's name and make her town's redneck crooks pay for their crimes. Never released in theatres. **95m/C VHS, Beta.** Bill Paxton, Todd Field, Apollonia, Luke Askew, Ben Johnson, David Michael-Standing, Susan Anspach, Sal Landi; **D:** John Kincade; **C:** James L. Carter. *MGM*

Back to Back 🗡🗡½ 1996 Ex-cop Malone (Rooker) must team up with hitman Koji (Ishibashi), who's holding Malone's daughter hostage, to double-cross a corrupt cop and stay alive while being hunted by the Mafia. **95m/C VHS, Closed Caption.** Michael Rooker, Ryo Ishibashi, John Laughlin, Danielle Harris, Bob(cat) Goldthwait, Vincent Schiavelli; **D:** Roger Nygard; **W:** Lloyd Keith; **C:** Mark W. Gray; **M:** Walter Werzowa. *BMG*

Back to Bataan 🗡🗡½ 1945 Colonel forms guerrilla army to raid Japanese in the Philippines and to help Americans landing on Leyte. Also available in a colorized version. **95m/B VHS, Beta, LV, Closed Caption.** John Wayne, Anthony Quinn, Beulah Bondi, Fely Franquelli, Richard Loo, Philip Ahn, Lawrence Tierney; **D:** Edward Dmytryk. *TTC*

Back to Hannibal: The Return of Tom Sawyer and Huckleberry Finn 🗡🗡½ 1990 Mark Twain's characters Tom Sawyer and Huckleberry Finn are reunited as adults to solve a murder mystery. Tom is a lawyer, Finn a newspaper man, and it's Becky Thatcher's husband who's been murdered. Did a freed slave really commit the crime? Made for television. **92m/C VHS.** Raphael Sbarge, Mitchell Anderson, Megan Follows, William Windom, Ned Beatty, Paul Winfield; **D:** Paul Krasny; **M:** Lee Holdridge. *DIS*

Back to School 🗡🗡½ 1986 (PG-13) Dangerfield plays an obnoxious millionaire who enrolls in college to help his wimpy son, Gordon, achieve campus stardom. His motto seems to be "if you can't buy it, it can't be had." At first, his antics embarrass his shy son, but soon everyone is clamoring to be seen with the pair as Gordon develops his own self confidence. **96m/C VHS, Beta, LV, Closed Caption.** Rodney Dangerfield, Keith Gordon, Robert Downey Jr., Sally Kellerman, Burt Young, Paxton Whitehead, Adrienne Barbeau, M. Emmet Walsh, Severn Darden, Ned Beatty, Sam Kinison, Kurt Vonnegut Jr., Robert Picardo, Terry Farrell, Edie McClurg, Jason Hervey; **D:** Alan Metter; **W:** Will Aldis, Steven Kampmann, Harold Ramis, Peter Torokvei; **C:** Thomas Ackerman; **M:** Danny Elfman. *NO*

Back to the Beach 🗡½ 1987 (PG) Frankie and Annette return to the beach as self-parodying, middle-aged parents with rebellious kids, and the usual run of sun-bleached, lover's tiff comedy ensues. Plenty of songs and guest appearances from television past. Tries to bring back that surf, sun, and sand feel of the orignal "Beach Party" movies, but fails. 🎵Absolute Perfection; California Sun; Catch a Ride; Jamaica Sky; Papa-Oom-Mow-Mow; Sign of Love; Sun, Sun, Sun, Sun; Surfin' Bird; Wooly Bully. **92m/C VHS, Beta, LV, Closed Caption.** Frankie Avalon, Annette Funicello, Connie Stevens, Jerry Mathers, Bob Denver, Barbara Billingsley, Tony Dow, Paul (Pee Wee Herman) Reubens, Edd Byrnes, Dick Dale, Don Adams, Lori Loughlin; **D:** Lyndall Hobbs; **C:** Bruce Surtees; **M:** Stephen Dorff. *PAR*

Back to the Future 🗡🗡🗡 1985 (PG) When neighborhood mad scientist Doc Brown constructs a time machine from a DeLorean, his youthful companion Marty accidentally transports himself to 1955. There, Marty must do everything he can to bring his parents together, elude the local bully, and get back...to the future. Solid fast-paced entertainment is even better due to Lloyd's inspired performance as the loony Doc while Fox is perfect as the boy completely out of his element. Soundtrack features Huey Lewis and the News. Followed by two sequels. **116m/C VHS, Beta, LV, Letterbox, Closed Caption, DVD.** Michael J. Fox, Christopher Lloyd, Lea Thompson, Crispin Glover, Wendie Jo Sperber, Marc McClure, Thomas F. Wilson, James Tolkan, Casey Siemaszko, Billy Zane, George DiCenzo, Courtney Gains, Claudia Wells, Jason Hervey, Harry Waters Jr., Maia Brewton, J.J. Cohen; *Cameos:* Huey Lewis; *D:* Robert Zemeckis; *W:* Robert Zemeckis, Bob Gale; *C:* Dean Cundey; *M:* Alan Silvestri. Nominations: Academy Awards '85: Best Original Screenplay, Best Song ("The Power of Love"), Best Sound. *USH, FCT, TLF*

Back to the Future, Part 2 🎬🎬½

1989 (PG) Taking up exactly where Part 1 left off, Doc Brown and Marty time-hop into the future (2015 to be exact) to save Marty's kids, then find themselves returning to 1955 to retrieve a sports almanac that causes havoc for the McFly family. Clever editing allows for Marty Part 2 to see Marty Part 1 at the school dance. Most of the cast returns, although Glover appears only in cuts from the original and Shue steps in as girlfriend Jennifer. Not up to the original, but still satisfying. Cliffhanger ending sets up Part 3, which was shot simultaneously with this. **107m/C VHS, Beta, LV, Letterbox, Closed Caption.** Michael J. Fox, Christopher Lloyd, Lea Thompson, Thomas F. Wilson, Harry Waters Jr., Charles Fleischer, Joe Flaherty, Elisabeth Shue, James Tolkan, Casey Siemaszko, Jeffrey Weissman, Flea, Billy Zane, J.J. Cohen, Darlene Vogel, Jason Scott Lee, Crispin Glover, Ricky Dean Logan; *D:* Robert Zemeckis; *W:* Robert Zemeckis, Bob Gale; *C:* Dean Cundey; *M:* Alan Silvestri. *USH*

Back to the Future, Part 3 🎬🎬🎬

1990 (PG) Picks up where Part 2 climaxed a la cliffhanger. Stuck in 1955, time-traveling hero Marty frantically searches for Doc Part 1 so he can return to 1985. Instead, he finds himself in the Wild West circa 1885, trying to save Doc's life. Plot is related to earlier BTTFs, so first time viewers might be confused. For those who've seen previous incarnations, the clever interconnections are really nifty. Nearly matches the original for excitement and offers some snazzy new special effects. Supposedly the last installment, though don't be surprised if another sequel follows. The complete trilogy is available as a boxed set. **118m/C VHS, Beta, LV, Letterbox, Closed Caption.** Michael J. Fox, Christopher Lloyd, Mary Steenburgen, Thomas F. Wilson, Lea Thompson, Elisabeth Shue, Matt Clark, Richard Dysart, Pat Buttram, Harry Carey Jr., Dub Taylor, James Tolkan, Marc McClure, Wendie Jo Sperber, J.J. Cohen, Ricky Dean Logan, Jeffrey Weissman; *D:* Robert Zemeckis; *W:* Robert Zemeckis, Bob Gale; *C:* Dean Cundey; *M:* Alan Silvestri. *USH*

Back to the Wall 🎬🎬

1956 Moreau is an adulturous wife whose web of deceit results in a suspenseful tale of murder and blackmail. **94m/B VHS.** *FR* Jeanne Moreau, Gerard Oury, Claire Maurier; *D:* Edouard Molinaro. *FCT*

Backbeat 🎬🎬🎬

1994 (R) Backed by the beat of early Beatle tunes as rendered by some of today's top alternative musicians, the debut for director Softley explores the Fab Four's beginnings in Hamburg's underground music scene. Storyline is driven by the complications of a romantic triangle between John Lennon, Astrid Kirchherr (the photographer who came up with the band's signature look) and Stu Sutcliffe, Lennon's best friend and the original bass player for the Beatles. Hart's dead-on as Lennon, playing him a second time (check out "The Hours and Times"). Energetic and enjoyable, particularly when the Was-produced music takes center stage.*CW:* Strong language, nudity, and sexuality. **100m/C VHS, LV, Letterbox, Closed Caption.** *GB* Stephen Dorff, Sheryl Lee, Ian Hart, Gary Bakewell, Chris O'Neill, Scot Williams, Kai Wiesinger, Jennifer Ehle; *D:* Iain Softley; *W:* Michael Thomas, Stephen Ward, Iain Softley; *M:* Don Was. *PGV*

Backdraft 🎬🎬½

1991 (R) High action story of Chicago firemen has some of the most stupendous incendiary special effects ever filmed. But then there's that plot, B-movie hokum about a mystery arsonist torching strategic parts of the community with the finesse of an expert and a brother-against-brother conflict. Straight-forward performances from most of the cast in spite of the weak storyline. Writer Widen wrote from experi-

ence—he used to be a fireman; real-life Chicago firefighters were reportedly very happy with the realistic and intense fire scenes. Forget the plot and just watch the fires. Also available in a letterboxed version.*CW:* Language and scene of sensuality. **135m/C VHS, Beta, LV, Letterbox, Closed Caption, DVD.** Kurt Russell, William Baldwin, Robert De Niro, Donald Sutherland, Jennifer Jason Leigh, Scott Glenn, Rebecca DeMornay, Jason Gedrick, J.T. Walsh, Tony Mockus Sr., Clint Howard, David Crosby; *D:* Ron Howard; *W:* Gregory Widen; *C:* Mikael Salomon; *M:* Hans Zimmer. Nominations: Academy Awards '91: Best Sound, Best Visual Effects.*USH*

Backfield in Motion 🎬🎬½

1991 Silly but harmless comedy about a widowed mom who tries to get closer to her high-schooler son by organizing a mother-son football game. But it's the boys' football coach who really wants to get close—to mom. Made for television movie debut of both Arnolds. **95m/C VHS, Beta, Closed Caption.** Roseanne, Tom Arnold, Colleen Camp, Conchata Ferrell, Johnny Galecki, Kevin Scannell; *D:* Richard Michaels. *TTC*

Backfire 🎬🎬

1922 If you're gonna rob a bank, you shouldn't let anyone hear you plan it, and if you're not gonna rob a bank, you shouldn't let anyone hear you plan one. This vintage "Lightning" Carson crime western has Carson and friend suspected of bank robbery because someone heard them planning one. The sheriff follows their every footstep as they search for the real perpetrators. **56m/B VHS, Beta.** Jack Hoxie, George Sowards, Lew Meehan, Florence Gilbert; *D:* Alan James. *GPV*

Backfire 🎬🎬

1988 (R) A mysterious stranger enters the lives of a disturbed 'Nam vet and his discontented wife, setting a pattern of murder and double-cross in motion. **90m/C VHS, Beta, LV.** Karen Allen, Keith Carradine, Jeff Fahey, Bernie Casey, Dinah Manoff, Dean Paul Martin; *D:* Gilbert Cates; *W:* Larry Brand; *M:* David Shire. *THV*

Backfire! 🎬½

1994 (PG-13) Silly spoof finds Jeremy (Mosby) wanting to join New York City's all-female fire brigade who are trying to stop an arsonist from blowing up the city's toilets. Mitchum is the fire marshal and Ireland the mayor's charming assistant.*CW:* Sensuality; crude humor. **88m/C VHS.** Josh Mosby, Kathy Ireland, Robert Mitchum, Shelley Winters; *D:* A. Dean Bell. *APX*

Background to Danger 🎬🎬🎬

1943 A suspenseful WWII actioner about American agent Raft who travels to Turkey to receive secret documents from the soon-to-be-murdered Massen. Greenstreet is the Nazi master spy who also wants the documents as do Russian spies, Lorre and Marshall. Somewhat confusing plot but fast-paced. Based on the thriller "Uncommon Danger" by Eric Ambler. This film was Warner Bros.' follow-up to "Casablanca" with Raft in the Bogie role he had turned down in that cinema classic. **80m/B VHS.** George Raft, Sydney Greenstreet, Peter Lorre, Brenda Marshall, Osa Massen, Turhan Bey, Kurt Katch; *D:* Raoul Walsh. *MGM, MOV*

Backlash 🎬🎬½

1986 (R) An aborigine barmaid is raped. When her assailant turns up dead, she's charged with murder and winds up in the custody of two police officers on a trip across the outback. Holes in the plot undermine this interesting, although graphic, drama with racial overtones. **88m/C VHS, Beta.** *AU* David Argue, Gia Carides, Lydia Miller, Brian Syron, Anne Smith; *D:* Bill Bennett; *W:* Bill Bennett; *M:* Michael Atkinson, Michael Spicer. *MCG*

Backlash: Oblivion 2 🎬🎬½

Oblivion 2 **1995 (PG-13)** Galactic supervillainess Lash stakes her claim to a rare derconium mine on the remote space outpost of Oblivion. Will cave monsters thwart her evil plan before space cowboys come to the town's rescue?*CW:* Some violence and sexual material. **82m/C VHS, LV, Closed Caption.** Andrew Divoff, Meg Foster, Isaac Hayes, Julie Newmar, Carel Struycken, George Takei, Musetta Vander, Jimmie F. Skaggs, Irwin Keyes, Maxwell Caulfield; *D:* Sam Irvin; *W:* Peter David; *M:* Pino Donaggio. *FLL*

Backstab 🎬🎬½

1990 (R) A spellbinding tale of work, lust, and murder. Architect Brolin finds himself unable to get over the death of his wife, until a seductive and mysterious woman helps him over his grief. They spend the night together, engulfed in passion, but in the morning he wakes to find himself sleeping with the corpse of his boss. Only the first twist in this intriguing thriller. **91m/C VHS, LV, Closed Caption.** James Brolin, Meg Foster, Isabelle Truchon; *D:* Jim Kaufman. *VTR*

Backstairs 🎬🎬

1921 An obscure German silent film about urban degradation and familial strife. **44m/B VHS, Beta.** *GE* Henny Porten, Fritz Kortner, William Dieterle; *D:* Leopold Jessner. *NOS, DVT, GLV*

Backstreet Dreams 🎬🎬

1990 (R) The young parents of an autistic child find themselves torn apart due to their feelings of guilt. The father has an affair with a specialist hired to help the boy, causing further strife. Interesting story possibilities never get far. **104m/C VHS, LV.** Brooke Shields, Jason O'Malley, Sherilyn Fenn, Tony Fields, Burt Young, Anthony (Tony) Franciosa, Nick Cassavetes, Ray "Boom Boom" Mancini; *D:* Rupert Hitzig; *M:* Bill Conti. *THV*

Backstreet Justice 🎬🎬½

1993 (R) Pittsburgh PI Keri Finnegan (Kozlowski) is investigating a series of murders in her neighborhood when she uncovers ties to police corruption dating back 30 years. This doesn't make her popular since it involves her dead cop father and a number of old friends (and enemies). Kozlowski is appropriately feisty and the plot twists will hold your attention. **91m/C VHS, LV.** Linda Kozlowski, Hector Elizondo, John Shea, Paul Sorvino, Viveca Lindfors, Tammy Grimes; *D:* Chris McIntyre; *W:* Chris McIntyre. *

Backtrack 🎬🎬🎬

Catchfire **1989 (R)** Foster co-stars in this thriller about an artist who accidentally witnesses a mob hit. The mob puts a hitman (Hopper) on her trail, and after studying her background and listening to audio tapes she recorded, he finds himself falling in love. Originally intended for a theatrical release, it hit the European screens in a different cut as "Catchfire;" Hopper restored his original version and it was released on cable TV in the U.S. **102m/C VHS, Closed Caption.** Dennis Hopper, Jodie Foster, Dean Stockwell, Vincent Price, John Turturro, Fred Ward, G. Anthony Sirico, Julie Adams, Frank Gio, Sy Richardson, Helena Kallianiotes, Bob Dylan; *Cameos:* Charlie Sheen, Joe Pesci; *D:* Dennis Hopper; *W:* Ann Louise Bardach; *M:* Michel Colombier. *ART*

Backwoods 🎬

1987 (R) Two campers wish they had never encountered a mountain man when he begins to stalk them with murder in mind. **90m/C VHS, Beta.** Jack O'Hara, Dick Kreusser, Brad Armacot; *D:* Dean Crow. *NO*

The Bad and the Beautiful 🎬🎬🎬½

1952 The story of a Hollywood producer, told from the eyes of an actress, a writer, and a director. Featuring what some consider Turner's best performance ever. Winner of five Oscars, a splendid drama. **118m/B VHS, LV, Closed Caption.** Kirk Douglas, Lana Turner, Dick Powell, Gloria Grahame, Barry Sullivan, Walter Pidgeon, Gilbert Roland; *D:* Vincente Minnelli; *C:* Robert L. Surtees. Academy Awards '52: Best Art Direction/Set Decoration (B & W), Best Black and White Cinematography, Best Costume Design (B & W), Best Screenplay, Best Supporting Actress (Grahame); Nominations: Academy Awards '52: Best Actor (Douglas). *MGM, BTV*

Bad Attitude 🎬🎬

1993 (R) Leon is a narcotics officer on a mission to restore his badge after his careless pistol work gets him booted off the force. The quick-tempered cop relentlessly pursues druglord Finque with the help of an open-minded preacher (De Veaux) and his sexy, street-wise assistant (Lim). **87m/C VHS.** Leon, Gina Lim, Nathaniel DeVeaux, Susan Finque; *D:* Bill Cummings. *XVC*

Bad Behavior 🎬🎬½

1992 (R) Unscripted character-driven drama. Gerry and Ellie McAllister are an Irish couple living in North London. He's tired of working for the local planning commission, she's bored being just a mum at home, and both are still a little uneasy living in England. When they decide to remodel the family bath, the unexpected problems lead to an emotional shakeup. Don't expect a lot of drama, the film works only if you accept the decency of the characters and the small moments of recognizable daily life. Director Blair wrote a basic script outline and had the actors improvise their dialogue, in character, over a long rehearsal period to develop their roles. **CW:** Language. **103m/C VHS, Closed Caption.** GB Stephen Rea, Sinead Cusack, Philip Jackson, Clare Higgins, Phil Daniels, Saira Todd; **D:** Les Blair; **M:** John Altman. THV

Bad Blood 🎬🎬 **1987** The true story of Stan Graham, who went on a killing spree in the New Zealand bush when his farm was foreclosed and his life ruined. **104m/C VHS, Beta.** NZ Jack Thompson, Carol Burns, Dennis Lill; **D:** Mike Newell.

Bad Blood 🎬½ **1994 (R)** Travis Blackstone (Lamas) will use any methods to protect his brother Franklin, who's targeted for death by a ruthless drug lord. Lots of action and violence. **CW:** Language, violence, nudity, sexual situations. **90m/C VHS, LV, Closed Caption.** Lorenzo Lamas, Hank Cheyne, Frankie Thorn, Kimberley Kates, Joe Son; **D:** Tibor Takacs; **W:** Neil Ruttenberg; **C:** Berhard Salzmann. WEA, ART

Bad Boy 🎬½ Branded **1939** A country boy goes to the big city, and succumbs to urban evils and temptations, but is eventually saved by motherly love. **60m/B VHS, Beta, LV.** Johnny Downs, Helen MacKellar, Rosalind Keith, Holmes Herbert; **D:** Kurt Neumann. NO

Bad Boy Bubby 🎬🎬 **1993** Bizarre black comedy about the extremely maladjusted Bubby (Hope), who becomes a pop culture phenomena. The 35-year-old childlike Bubby has been kept a virtual prisoner by his monstrous mom, who has told him the world outside is filled with poisonous gas. Wondering how his cat survived, Bubby wraps it in plastic wrap and is puzzled when it dies. Still, this gives Bubby an idea—he wraps mom in plastic and escapes outside, where he's soon adopted by a struggling rock band that writes a cult song hit about his experiences. It's even stranger than it sounds. **114m/C VHS.** IT AU Nicholas Hope, Claire Benito, Carmel Johnson, Ralph Cotterill, Norman Kaye, Paul Philpot, Graham Duckett, Bridget Walters; **D:** Rolf de Heer; **W:** Graham Tardiff. Australian Film Institute '94: Best Actor (Hope), Best Director (de Heer), Best Film Editing, Best Original Screenplay; Nominations: Australian Film Institute '94: Best Cinematography, Best Film. NYR

Bad Boys 🎬🎬🎬 **1983 (R)** When a gang member's little brother is killed in a rumble, the teen responsible (Penn, who else?) goes to a reformatory, where he quickly (though somewhat reluctantly) takes charge. Meanwhile, on the outside, his rival attacks Penn's girlfriend (Sheedy, in her feature film debut) in retaliation, is incarcerated, and ends up vying with Penn for control of the cell block. Backed into a corner by their mutual hatred and escalating peer pressure, the two are pushed over the brink into a final and shattering confrontation. Not as violent as it could be, to its credit; attempts to communicate a message. **104m/C VHS, Beta, LV.** Sean Penn, Esai Morales, Reni Santoni, Jim Moody, Eric Gurry, Ally Sheedy, Clancy Brown; **D:** Rick Rosenthal; **C:** Donald E. Thorin; **M:** Bill Conti. REP

Bad Boys 🎬🎬½ **1995 (R)** And you thought the old buddy-cop formula was played out. Well, Hollywood sticks with what works, and pairing the two television personalities definitely works at the minimalist level required. Mike (Smith) and Marcus (Lawrence) are Miami cops who must track down $100 million dollars worth of heroin stolen from their evidence room before internal affairs shuts down the precinct. The case leads them to a vicious thief and a beautiful female witness to his murderous handiwork. Plot lacks depth, but high energy and dazzling action sequences keep things moving. Loud adventure is made louder still by cranking soundtrack. Satisfying addition to the odd-couple cops genre with potential to spawn a "Lethal Weapon"-type franchise. Fea-

ture film debut for director Bay. **CW:** Intense violent action; pervasive strong language. **118m/C VHS, LV, Closed Caption, DVD.** Martin Lawrence, Will Smith, Tcheky Karyo, Tea Leoni, Theresa Randle, Marg Helgenberger, Joe Pantoliano, John Salley; **D:** Michael Bay; **W:** Michael Barrie, Jim Mulholland; **C:** Howard Atherton. Blockbuster Entertainment Awards '96: Male Newcomer, Theatrical (Smith); Nominations: MTV Movie Awards '96: Best On-Screen Duo (Martin Lawrence/Will Smith), Best Action Sequence. COL

Bad Bunch 🎬🎬 **1976** A white liberal living in Watts tries to befriend a ruthless black street gang, but is unsuccessful. **82m/C VHS, Beta.** Greydon Clark, Tom Johnigam, Pamela Corbett, Jacqulin Cole, Aldo Ray, Jock Mahoney; **D:** Greydon Clark. VCI

B.A.D. Cats 🎬 **1980** Two members of a police burglary auto detail team chase after a group of car thieves who are planning a million-dollar gold heist. **74m/C VHS, Beta, LV.** Asher Brauner, Michelle Pfeiffer, Vic Morrow, Jimmie Walker, Steve Hanks, LaWanda Page; **D:** Bernard L. Kowalski. ORI

Bad Channels 🎬🎬 **1992 (R)** Radio goes awry when female listeners of station KDUL are shrunk and put into speciman jars by a way-out disc jockey and a visiting alien, who plans to take the women back to his planet. Mildly amusing comedy features ex-MTV VJ Quinn and score by Blue Oyster Cult. Also available with Spanish subtitles. **CW:** Language. **88m/C VHS, Beta, Closed Caption.** Paul Hipp, Martha Quinn, Aaron Lustig, Ian Patrick Williams, Charlie Spradling, Tim Thomerson; **D:** Ted Nicolaou; **W:** Jackson Barr. PAR

Bad Charleston Charlie woof! **1973** **(PG)** Dud of a gangster comedy with terrible acting. A comedy? **91m/C VHS.** Ross Hagen, John Carradine; **D:** Ivan Nagy. NO

Bad Company 🎬🎬🎬½ **1972 (PG)** Thoughtful study of two very different Civil War draft dodgers roaming the Western frontier and eventually turning to a fruitless life of crime. Both the cast and script are wonderful in an entertaining film that hasn't been given the attention it's due. **94m/C VHS, Beta, LV.** Jeff Bridges, Barry Brown, Jim Davis, John Savage; **D:** Robert Benton; **W:** Robert Benton, David Newman; **C:** Gordon Willis. PAR

Bad Company 🎬🎬 **1994 (R)** Cynical thriller pits the bad against the worst. Vic Grimes (Langella) and Margaret Wells (Barkin) run a company of former secret agents who specialize in corporate dirty work. Nelson Crowe (Fishburne) is an ex-CIA agent who's their latest recruit. But maybe he's not so ex and maybe Margaret doesn't like sharing power and maybe the cold-blooded duo will get together to make some changes. Everything is stylish, including the leads, but there's a definite chill in the air. **CW:** Violence; sexual situations; some language. **118m/C VHS, LV, Closed Caption.** Ellen Barkin, Laurence "Larry" Fishburne, Frank Langella, Michael Beach, Gia Carides, David Ogden Stiers, Spalding Gray, James Hong, Daniel Hugh-Kelly; **D:** Damian Harris; **W:** Ross Thomas; **C:** Jack N. Green; **M:** Carter Burwell. TOU

Bad Day at Black Rock 🎬🎬🎬½ **1954** Story of a one-armed man uncovering a secret in a Western town. Wonderful performances from all concerned, especially Borgnine. Fine photography, shot using the new Cinemascope technique. Based on the novel by Howard Breslin. **81m/C VHS, LV, Letterbox.** Spencer Tracy, Robert Ryan, Anne Francis, Dean Jagger, Walter Brennan, John Ericson, Ernest Borgnine, Lee Marvin; **D:** John Sturges; **C:** William Mellor; **M:** Andre Previn. Cannes Film Festival '55: Best Actor (Tracy); Nominations: Academy Awards '55: Best Actor (Tracy), Best Director (Sturges), Best Screenplay. MGM, CRC, FCT

Bad Dreams 🎬½ **1988 (R)** The only surviving member of a suicidal religious cult from the '60s awakens in 1988 from a coma. She is pursued by the living-dead cult leader, who seeks to ensure that she lives up (so to speak) to the cult's pact. Blood begins flowing as her fellow therapy group members begin dying, but the only bad dreams you'd get from this flick would be over the money lost on the video rental. **84m/C VHS, Beta,**

LV, Closed Caption. Bruce Abbott, Jennifer Rubin, Richard Lynch, Harris Yulin, Dean Cameron, Elizabeth Daily, Susan Ruttan, Charles Fleischer, Sy Richardson; **D:** Andrew Fleming; **M:** Jay Michael Ferguson. FOX

Bad Georgia Road 🎬½ **1977 (R)** A New Yorker inherits a moonshine operation from her uncle, and fights off the syndicate for its profits. **85m/C VHS, Beta.** Gary Lockwood, Carol Lynley, Royal Dano, John Wheeler, John Kerry; **D:** John Broderick. VCI

Bad Girls 🎬🎬½ **1994 (R)** Latest in the current western craze turns the tables as women take their turns being the gunslingers. Four hooker chums hastily flee town after one kills a nasty customer—only to find the bank where their cash was stashed was robbed by baddies Loggia and Russo. Wearing stylish duds and with each hair perfectly in place the beauties manage to recover their loot. Unexciting script leaves a lot to be desired, but a strong performance from Stowe makes this nearly worthwhile. Lots of off-set drama with original director Tamra Davis fired, and the actresses reportedly having a less-than-bonding experience. **CW:** Mild profanity, brief nudity, western violence; suggested rape, and references to prostitution. **99m/C VHS, LV, Letterbox, Closed Caption.** Andie MacDowell, Madeleine Stowe, Mary Stuart Masterson, Drew Barrymore, James Russo, Dermot Mulroney, Robert Loggia, James LeGros; **D:** Jonathan Kaplan; **W:** Ken Friedman, Yolande Finch; **M:** Jerry Goldsmith. FOX

Bad Girls Do Cry woof! **1954** Unbelievably bad exploitation film. Idiotic plot with long scenes of girls stripping down to their undies. Although an American film, the voice track was dubbed in later. **?m/C VHS.** Bill Page, Misty Ayers, Heather English, Ben Frommer. SNC, TPV

Bad Girls Dormitory 🎬🎬 **1984 (R)** At the New York Female Juvenile Reformatory, suicide seems a painless and welcome escape. Utilizes standard genre identifiers, including rape, drugs, soapy showers, bad docs, and desperate young women trapped in a web of frustration and desire. Cheap and mindless titillation. **95m/C VHS, Beta.** Carey Zuris, Teresa Farley; **D:** Tim Kincaid.

Bad Girls from Mars woof! **1990 (R)** "B" movie sleaze-o-rama in which everyone is murdered, either before, after, or during sex, just like in real life. When the director of the film within this film hires an actress who is, shall we say, popular, to be the heroine of his latest sci-fier, the fun, slim as it is, begins. **CW:** Strong language, frontal nudity, and sensuality. **86m/C VHS.** Edy Williams, Brinke Stevens, Jay Richardson, Oliver Darrow; **D:** Fred Olen Ray; **W:** Sherman Scott, Mark Thomas McGee. THV

Bad Girls Go to Hell woof! **1965** From the sultana of sleaze, Wishman, comes this winning entry into Joe Bob Briggs' "Sleaziest Movies in the History of the World" series. A ditsy-but-sexy housewife accidentally commits murder and what follows is a plethora of perversion involving hirsute men and gender-bending women who are hell-bent on showing her how hot it is where bad girls go. **98m/B VHS.** **D:** Doris Wishman. VTR

Bad Girls in the Movies 🎬 **1986** A compilation of film clips depicting sleazy, criminal, female characters from women's prison films and other seedy sub-genres. **56m/C VHS, Beta.** David Carradine, Gene Autry, Yvonne De Carlo. ART

Bad Guys 🎬🎬 **1979** A goulash western about the outlaw days of Hungary in the 1860s. A gang of bandits terrorizes the Transdanubian countryside. In Hungarian with English subtitles. For those seeking the Eastern European Wild West experience. **93m/C VHS.** HU Janos Derzsi, Djoko Rosic, Mari Kiss, Gyorgy Dorner, Laszlo Szabo, Miklos Benedek; **D:** Gyorgy Szomjas. FCT

Bad Guys 🎬 **1986 (PG)** An inane comedy about two ridiculous policemen who decide to take the wrestling world by storm after being kicked off the police force. Featuring scenes with many of the world's most popular wrestlers. **86m/C VHS.** Adam Baldwin, Mike Jolly, Michelle Nicastro, Ruth Buzzi, James Booth, Gene LeBell, Norman Burton; **D:** Joel Silberg; **C:** Hanania Baer; **M:** William Goldstein. *ART*

Bad Influence ♂♂½ **1990 (R)** A lackluster effort in the evil-doppelganger school of psychological mystery, where a befuddled young executive (Spader) is led into the seamier side of life by a mysterious stranger (Lowe). **99m/C VHS, Beta, LV.** Rob Lowe, James Spader, Lisa Zane, Christian Clemenson, Kathleen Wilhoite; **D:** Curtis Hanson; **C:** Robert Elswit; **M:** Trevor Jones. *COL*

Bad Jim ♂♂½ **1989 (PG)** A cowpoke buys Billy the Kid's horse and, upon riding it, becomes an incorrigible outlaw himself. First feature film for Hollywood legend Clark Gable's son. **110m/C VHS, Beta, LV.** James Brolin, Richard Roundtree, John Clark Gable, Harry Carey Jr., Ty Hardin, Pepe Serna, Rory Calhoun; **D:** Clyde Ware. *COL*

Bad Lands ♂♂½ **1939** A small cowboy posse finds themselves trapped by a band of Apache Indians in the Arizona desert. A remake of "The Lost Patrol." **70m/B VHS, Beta.** Robert Barrat, Guinn "Big Boy" Williams, Douglas Walton, Andy Clyde, Addison Richards, Robert Coote, Paul Hurst, Noah Beery Jr.; **D:** Lew (Louis Friedlander) Landers. *TTC*

Bad Lieutenant ♂♂♂ **1992 (NC-17)** Social chaos and degeneration characterize story as well as nameless loner lieutenant Keitel, who is as corrupt as they come. Assigned to a case involving a raped nun, he's confronted by his own lagging Catholic beliefs and the need for saving grace. From cult filmmaker Ferrara ("Ms. 45") and filled with violence, drugs, and grotesque sexual situations. Tense, over-the-top, urban drama is not intended for seekers of the subtle. Rent it with "Reservoir Dogs" and prepare yourself for a long tense evening of top-rated Keitel and screen-splitting violence. "R" rated version is also available at 91 minutes.**CW:** Language, nudity, violence, and sensuality. **98m/C VHS, LV, Closed Caption.** Harvey Keitel, Brian McElroy, Frankie Acciario, Peggy Gormley, Stella Keitel, Victor Argo, Paul Calderone, Leonard Thomas, Frankie Thorn; **D:** Abel Ferrara; **W:** Zoe Tamerlaine Lund, Abel Ferrara; **M:** Joe Delia. Independent Spirit Awards '93: Best Actor (Keitel). *ART, FCT*

Bad Love ♂♂½ **1995 (R)** Unlucky Eloise (Gidley) stays true to nature when she falls for loser Lenny (Sizemore), who decides the big score lies with robbing the fading movie star (O'Neill) Eloise works for. Naturally, things go badly. Slick production for anyone who likes fringe romances.**CW:** Nudity, language, violence, sexual situations. **93m/C VHS.** Tom Sizemore, Pamela Gidley, Debi Mazar, Jennifer O'Neill, Margaux Hemingway, Richard Edson, Seymour Cassel; **D:** Jill Goldman. *APX*

Bad Man of Deadwood ♂♂ **1941** A man-with-a-past joins a circus as a sharp-shooter, and is threatened with disclosure. **56m/B VHS, Beta.** Roy Rogers, George "Gabby" Hayes. *DVT, NOS, RXM*

Bad Manners ♂ **1984 (R)** When an orphan is adopted by a wealthy but entirely selfish couple, a group of his orphan friends try to free him from his new home and lifestyle. **85m/C VHS, Beta.** Martin Mull, Karen Black, Anne DeSalvo, Murphy Dunne, Pamela Segall, Edy Williams, Susan Ruttan, Richard Deacon; **D:** Bobby Houston; **C:** Jan De Bont. *VTR*

Bad Man's River ♂♂ **1972** A Mexican revolutionary leader hires a gang of outlaws to blow up an arsenal used by the Mexican Army. **92m/C VHS, Beta.** *IT SP* Lee Van Cleef, James Mason, Gina Lollobrigida; **D:** Gene Martin; **W:** Philip Yordan. *NO*

Bad Medicine woof! **1985 (PG-13)** A youth who doesn't want to be a doctor is accepted by a highly questionable Latin American school of medicine. Remember that it was for medical students like these that the U.S. liberated Grenada. **97m/C VHS, Beta, Closed Caption.** Steve Guttenberg, Alan Arkin, Julie Hagerty, Bill Macy, Curtis Armstrong, Julie Kavner, Joe Grifasi, Robert Romanus, Taylor Negron, Gilbert Gottfried; **D:** Harvey Miller; **W:** Harvey Miller. *FOX*

Bad Men of the Border ♂½ **1945** Routine oater has Kirby posing as a bandit in order to infiltrate an outlaw band passing counterfeit money. He rounds up the bad guys and finds time to romance Armida too. **56m/B VHS.** Kirby Grant, Fuzzy Knight, Armida, John Eldridge, Francis McDonald; **D:** Wallace Fox; **W:** Adele Buffington. *MOV*

Bad Moon ♂½ **1996 (R)** Let's put it this way, the werewolf in this movie is not the only thing that bites. Shortest (mercifully) studio release in recent history is a horror (in more ways than one) film with Pare leading the pack as Ted, a photojournalist who comes back from the Amazon a different, more nocturnally hirsute man. Fleeing from the site of his nightly gore, Ted takes refuge with his loving sister Janet (Hemingway) and her son Brett (Gamble). The real hero (and best actor) is a German shepherd named Thor (Primo) who discovers that Ted's a werewolf. Dog steals the show paws down (naturally). Decent special FX. Adapted from Wayne Smith's novel "Thor."**CW:** Horror violence and gore, brief language and a scene of sexuality. **79m/C VHS, Closed Caption.** Mariel Hemingway, Michael Pare, Mason Gamble, Ken Pogue; **D:** Eric Red; **W:** Eric Red; **C:** Jan Kiesser; **M:** Daniel Licht. *WAR*

The Bad News Bears ♂♂♂ **1976 (PG)** Family comedy about a misfit Little League team that gets whipped into shape by a cranky, sloppy, beer-drinking coach who recruits a female pitcher. O'Neal and Matthau are top-notch. The kids' language is rather adult, and very titillating for younger viewers. Spawned two sequels and a television series. **102m/C VHS, Beta, LV, 8mm.** Walter Matthau, Tatum O'Neal, Vic Morrow, Joyce Van Patten, Jackie Earle Haley; **D:** Michael Ritchie; **C:** John A. Alonzo. Writers Guild of America '76: Best Original Screenplay. *PAR*

The Bad News Bears Go to Japan ♂ **1978 (PG)** The second sequel, in which the famed Little League team goes to the Little League World Series in Tokyo. Comic adventure features Curtis as a talent agent out to exploit the team's fame. **102m/C VHS, Beta, LV.** Tony Curtis, Jackie Earle Haley, Tomisaburo Wakayama, George Wyner; **D:** John Berry. *PAR*

The Bad News Bears in Breaking Training ♂½ **1977 (PG)** With a chance to take on the Houston Toros for a shot at the little league baseball Japanese champs, the Bears devise a way to get to Texas to play at the famed Astrodome. Disappointing sequel to "The Bad News Bears"; followed by "The Bad News Bears Go to Japan" (1978). **105m/C VHS, Beta, LV.** William Devane, Clifton James, Jackie Earle Haley, Jimmy Baio; **D:** Michael Pressman; **W:** Paul Brickman. *PAR*

Bad Ronald ♂♂♂ **1974** No, not a political biography of Ronald Reagan... Fascinating thriller about a disturbed teenager who kills a friend after being harassed repeatedly. The plot thickens after the boy's mother dies, and he is forced to hide out in a secret room when an unsuspecting family with three daughters moves into his house. The story is accurately recreated from the novel by John Holbrook Vance. **78m/C VHS.** Scott Jacoby, Pippa Scott, John Larch, Dabney Coleman, Kim Hunter, John Fiedler; **D:** Buzz Kulik. *ART*

The Bad Seed ♂♂½ **1956** A mother makes the tortuous discovery that her cherubic eight-year-old daughter harbors an innate desire to kill. Based on Maxwell Anderson's powerful Broadway stage play. Remade for television in 1985. **129m/B VHS, Beta.** Patty McCormack, Nancy Kelly, Eileen Heckart, Henry Jones, Evelyn Varden, Paul Fix; **D:** Mervyn LeRoy; **C:** Alex North. Golden Globe Awards '57: Best Supporting Actress (Heckart); Nominations: Academy Awards '56: Best Actress (Kelly), Best Black and White Cinematography, Best Supporting Actress (Heckart, McCormack). *WAR*

The Bad Seed ♂♂ **1985** Television remake of the movie with the same name. Story about a sadistic little child who kills for her own evil purposes. Acting is not up to par with previous

version. **100m/C VHS.** Blair Brown, Lynn Redgrave, David Carradine, Richard Kiley, David Ogden Stiers, Carrie Wells; **D:** Paul Wendkos. *NO*

The Bad Sleep Well ♂♂♂½ **1960** Japanese variation of the 1940 Warner Bros. crime dramas. A tale about corruption in the corporate world as seen through the eyes of a rising executive. **135m/B VHS.** *JP* Toshiro Mifune, Masayuki Kato, Masayuki Mori, Takashi Shimura, Akira Nishimura; **D:** Akira Kurosawa. *HMV, COL*

Bad Taste ♂♂♂ **1988** A definite pleaser for the person who enjoys watching starving aliens devour the average, everyday human being. Alien fast-food manufacturers come to earth in hopes of harvesting all of mankind. The earth's fate lies in the hands of the government who must stop these rampaging creatures before the whole human race is gobbled up. Terrific make-up jobs on the aliens add the final touch to this gory, yet humorous cult horror flick. **90m/C VHS, LV.** *NZ* Peter Jackson, Pete O'Herne, Mike Minett, Terry Potter, Craig Smith, Doug Wren, Dean Lawrie; **D:** Peter Jackson; **W:** Peter Jackson; **C:** Peter Jackson. *FCT*

Badge of the Assassin ♂♂ **1985** A television movie based on the true story of a New York assistant DA who directed a campaign to catch a pair of cop-killers from the '70s. **96m/C VHS, Beta, LV.** James Woods, Yaphet Kotto, Alex Rocco, David Harris, Pam Grier, Steven Keats, Richard Bradford, Rae Dawn Chong; **D:** Mel Damski. *THV*

Badge 373 ♂½ **1973 (R)** In the vein of "The French Connection," a New York cop is suspended and decides to battle crime his own way. **116m/C VHS, Beta.** Robert Duvall, Verna Bloom, Eddie Egan; **D:** Howard W. Koch. *PAR*

The Badlanders ♂♂♂ **1958** A western remake of the crime drama "The Asphalt Jungle." Ladd and Borgnine plan a gold robbery against Smith, who cheated them out of their share in a gold mine. Cross and double-cross follow the partners as does romance. **85m/C VHS.** Alan Ladd, Ernest Borgnine, Kent Smith, Katy Jurado, Claire Kelly, Nehemiah Persoff, Adam Williams; **D:** Delmer Daves. *MGM*

Badlands ♂♂♂½ **1974 (PG)** Based loosely on the Charlie Starkweather murders of the 1950s, this impressive debut by director Malick recounts a slow-thinking, unhinged misfit's killing spree across the midwestern plains, accompanied by a starry-eyed 15-year-old schoolgirl. Sheen and Spacek are a disturbingly numb, apathetic, and icy duo. **94m/C VHS, Beta, LV.** Martin Sheen, Sissy Spacek, Warren Oates; **D:** Terrence Malick; **W:** Terrence Malick. National Film Registry '93. *WAR*

Badman's Territory ♂♂♂ **1946** A straight-shooting marshal has to deal with such notorious outlaws as the James and Dalton boys in a territory outside of government control. **79m/B VHS, Beta.** Randolph Scott, Ann Richards, George "Gabby" Hayes, Steve Brodie; **D:** Tim Whelan. *TTC*

Badmen of Nevada ♂½ **1933** Badmen roam Nevada in the early days before law and order. **57m/B VHS, Beta.** Kent Taylor, Gail Patrick. *VCN*

Baffled ♂♂½ **1972** Nimoy is a race car driver who has visions of people in danger. He must convince an ESP expert (Hampshire) of the credibility of his vision, and then try to save the lives of the people seen with his sixth sense. Made for television. **90m/C VHS.** Leonard Nimoy, Susan Hampshire, Vera Miles, Rachel Roberts, Jewel Blanch, Christopher Benjamin; **D:** Philip Leacock. *FOX*

Bagdad ♂♂ **1949** Arabian nights story with the lovely O'Hara starring as Princess Marjan, the daughter of a sheik. She returns from England to find her father murdered and Hassan (Christian), the leader of a suspicious group known as The Black Riders, the main suspect. But then there's Turkish Pasha Al Nadim (Price) lurking sinisterly, as well. **83m/C VHS.** Maureen O'Hara, Paul Christian, Vincent Price, John Sutton, Jeff Corey, Frank Puglia, David Wolfe, Fritz Leiber; **D:** Charles Lamont; **C:** Russell Metty. *USH*

Bagdad Cafe 🎬🎬🎬 *Out of Rosenheim* **1988** **(PG)** A large German woman, played by Sagebrecht, finds herself stranded in the Mojave desert after her husband dumps her on the side of the highway. She encounters a rundown cafe where she becomes involved with the off-beat residents. A hilarious story in which the strange people and the absurdity of their situations are treated kindly and not made to seem ridiculous. Spawned a short-lived TV series with Whoopi Goldberg. **91m/C VHS, LV, Closed Caption.** *GE* Marianne Saegebrecht, CCH Pounder, Jack Palance, Christine Kaufmann, Monica Calhoun, Darron Flagg; **D:** Percy Adlon; **W:** Percy Adlon, Eleonore Adlon; **M:** Bob Telson. Cesar Awards '89: Best Foreign Film; Nominations: Academy Awards '88: Best Song ("Calling You"). *PGV, FCT*

Bahama Passage 🎬🎬½ **1942** Trite story of one lady's efforts to win the affection of a macho Bahamas stud. **83m/C VHS.** Madeleine Carroll, Sterling Hayden, Flora Robson, Leo G. Carroll; **D:** Edward H. Griffith. *PAR, MLB*

Bail Jumper 🎬🎬 **1989** A story of love and commitment against incredible odds; some of which happen to be a swarm of locusts, a tornado, and falling meteorites. Joe and Elaine are small-time hoods escaping their dreary lives in Murky Springs Missouri for that great bastion of idyllism and idealism—New York City. But even as the world starts to crumble around them, get the message that love prevails. **96m/C VHS, Beta.** Eszter Balint, B.J. Spalding, Tony Askin, Joie Lee; **D:** Christian Faber. *FXL*

Bail Out 🎬 **1990** **(R)** Three bounty hunters, armed to the teeth, run a car-trashing police gauntlet so they may capture a valuable crook. **88m/C VHS, Beta, LV.** David Hasselhoff, Linda Blair, John Vernon, Tom Rosales, Charlie Brill; **D:** Max Kleven. *VES, ART*

Bail Out at 43,000 🎬🎬 **1957** Movie about the lifestyles and love affairs of your average, everyday parachutist. **80m/B VHS.** John Payne, Karen Steele, Paul Kelly; **D:** Francis D. Lyon; **W:** Paul Monash. *MGM*

Baja 🎬🎬 **1995** **(R)** Bebe (Ringwald) hides out in Baja with her beau Alex (Logue) after a drug deal goes bad. They hold up in a sleazy motel while Bebe waits for dad, John (Bernsen), to bail her out. But instead, John persuades estranged hubby Michael (Nickles) to track down the runaways and Michael finds out that hitman Tom (Henriksen) is hunting for Alex. Must be the desert heat causing all the ensuing commotion. **CW:** Language, violence and brief strong sexuality. **92m/C VHS, LV, Closed Caption.** Molly Ringwald, Lance Henriksen, Michael A. Nickles, Donal Logue, Corbin Bernsen; **D:** Kurt Voss; **W:** Kurt Voss; **C:** Denis Maloney; **M:** Reg Powell. *REP*

Baja Oklahoma 🎬 **1987** A made-for-cable-television film about a country barmaid with dreams of being a country singer. Songs by Willie Nelson, Emmylou Harris and Billy Vera. **97m/C VHS, Beta, LV.** Lesley Ann Warren, Peter Coyote, Swoosie Kurtz, Willie Nelson, Julia Roberts; **D:** Bobby Roth; **W:** Bobby Roth; **C:** Michael Ballhaus. *WAR, ORI*

Baker's Hawk 🎬 **1976** A young boy befriends a red-tailed hawk and learns the meaning of family and caring. **98m/C VHS, Beta.** Clint Walker, Diane Baker, Burl Ives; **D:** Lyman Dayton. *FHE*

The Baker's Wife 🎬🎬🎬½ *La Femme du Boulanger* **1933** There's a new baker in town, and he brings with him to the small French village an array of tantalizing breads, as well as a discontented wife. When she runs off with a shepherd, her loyal and naive husband refuses to acknowledge her infidelity; however, in his loneliness, the baker can't bake, so the townspeople scheme to bring his wife back. Panned as overly cute Marcel Pagnol peasant glorification, and hailed as a visual poem full of wit; you decide. In French with subtitles. Also available for French students without subtitles; a French script booklet is also available. **101m/B VHS, Beta.** *FR* Raimu, Ginette LeClerc, Charles

Moulton, Charpin, Robert Vattier; **D:** Marcel Pagnol. New York Film Critics Awards '40: Best Foreign Film. *INT, MRV, DVT*

Bakery/Grocery Clerk 🎬🎬 **1921** A package of shorts featuring crazy comedian Larry Semon, getting tangled up in mayhem and molasses. Silent with piano score. **55m/B VHS, Beta.** Larry Semon, Oliver Hardy, Lucille Carlisle; **D:** Larry Semon. *CCB*

Balalaika 🎬🎬 **1939** Rather dull operetta about the Russian revolution with Eddy playing a Russian prince. Eddy masquerades as a member of the proletariat in order to romance Massey, who was expected to become the next Garbo. Didn't happen, though. Eddy's rendition of "Stille Nacht" ("Silent Night") is highlight of film. Based on the operetta by Eric Maschwitz, George Ponford, and Bernard Gruen. **102m/B VHS.** Nelson Eddy, Ilona Massey, Charlie Ruggles, Frank Morgan, Lionel Atwill, Sir C. Aubrey Smith, Joyce Compton; **D:** Reinhold Schunzel; **W:** Leon Gordon, Charles Bennett, Jacques Deval; **C:** Karl Freund. Nominations: Academy Awards '39: Best Sound. *MGM*

Balance of Power 🎬½ **1996** **(R)** Martial arts master Mako prepares fighter Blanks for a death match against a former student who's gone bad. **CW:** Strong violence and some language. **92m/C VHS, Closed Caption.** Billy Blanks, Mako, James Lew; **D:** Rick Bennet; **W:** Phil Good, Rick Bennet; **C:** Gilles Corbeil. *ART*

Balboa woof! **1982** Set on sun-baked Balboa Island, this is a melodramatic tale of high-class power, jealousy, and intrigue. Never-aired pilot for a television mini-series, in the night-time soap tradition (even features Steve Kanaly from TV's "Dallas"). Special appearance by Cassandra Peterson, also known as horror hostess Elvira; and if that interests you, look for Sonny Bono as well. **92m/C VHS, Beta.** Tony Curtis, Carol Lynley, Chuck Connors, Sonny Bono, Steve Kanaly, Jennifer Chase, Lupita Ferrer, Martine Beswick, Henry Jones, Cassandra Peterson; **D:** James Polakof. *VES, ART*

The Balcony 🎬🎬🎬 **1963** A film version of the great Jean Genet play about a surreal brothel, located in an unnamed, revolution-torn city, where its powerful patrons act out their fantasies. Scathing and rude. **87m/B VHS, Beta, LV.** Peter Falk, Shelley Winters, Lee Grant, Kent Smith, Peter Brocco, Ruby Dee, Jeff Corey, Leonard Nimoy, Joyce Jameson; **D:** Joseph Strick. Nominations: Academy Awards '63: Best Black and White Cinematography. *MFV*

Ball of Fire 🎬🎬🎬 **1941** A gang moll hides out with a group of mundane professors, trying to avoid her loathsome boyfriend. The professors are busy compiling an encyclopedia and Stanwyck helps them with their section on slang in the English language. Cooper has his hands full when he falls for this damsel in distress and must fight the gangsters to keep her. Stanwyck takes a personal liking to naive Cooper and resolves to teach him more than just slang. **111m/B VHS, Beta, LV.** Gary Cooper, Barbara Stanwyck, Dana Andrews, Gene Krupa, Oscar Homolka, Dan Duryea, S.Z. Sakall, Henry Travers; **D:** Howard Hawks; **W:** Billy Wilder, Charles Brackett; **C:** Gregg Toland. Nominations: Academy Awards '41: Best Actress (Stanwyck), Best Sound, Best Story, Best Original Dramatic/Comedy Score.

Ballad in Blue 🎬🎬 *Blues for Lovers* **1966** Real life story of Ray Charles and a blind child. Tearjerker also includes some of Charles' hit songs. 🎵I Got a Woman; What'd I Say?. **89m/B VHS, Beta.** *GB* Ray Charles, Tom Bell, Mary Peach, Dawn Addams, Piers Bishop, Betty McDowall; **D:** Paul Henreid. *ART*

Ballad of a Gunfighter 🎬 **1964** A feud between two outlaws reaches the boiling point when they both fall in love with the same woman. **84m/C VHS, Beta.** Marty Robbins, Bob Barron, Joyce Redd, Nestor Paiva, Laurette Luez; **D:** Bill Ward. *FHE*

Ballad of a Soldier 🎬🎬🎬½ **1960** As a reward for demolishing two German tanks, a 19-year-old Russian soldier receives a six-day pass so he can see his mother; however, he meets another woman. Well directed and photographed,

while avoiding propaganda. Russian with subtitles. **88m/B VHS.** *RU* Vladimir Ivashov, Shanna Prokhorenko; **D:** Grigori Chukrai. British Academy Awards '61: Best Film; Nominations: Academy Awards '61: Best Story & Screenplay. *NYF, HHT, IHF*

Ballad of Cable Hogue 🎬🎬🎬 **1970** **(R)** A prospector, who had been left to die in the desert by his double-crossing partners, finds a waterhole. A surprise awaits his former friends when they visit the remote well. Not the usual violent Peckinpah horse drama, but a tongue-in-cheek comedy romance mixed with tragedy. Obviously offbeat and worth a peek. **122m/C VHS, Beta, LV.** Jason Robards Jr., Stella Stevens, David Warner, L.Q. Jones, Strother Martin, Slim Pickens; **D:** Sam Peckinpah; **C:** Lucien Ballard; **M:** Jerry Goldsmith. *WAR*

Ballad of Gregorio Cortez 🎬🎬🎬 **1983** **(PG)** Tragic story based on one of the most famous manhunts in Texas history. A Mexican cowhand kills a Texas sheriff in self-defense and tries to elude the law, all because of a misunderstanding of the Spanish language. Olmos turns in a fine performance as Cortez. **105m/C VHS, Beta, LV.** Edward James Olmos, James Gammon, Tom Bower, Alan Vint, Barry Corbin, Rosana De Soto, Bruce McGill, Brion James, Pepe Serna, William Sanderson; **D:** Robert M. Young; **W:** Robert M. Young; **C:** Reynaldo Villalobos. *NLC*

The Ballad of Little Jo 🎬🎬½ **1993** **(R)** Inspired by a true story set during the 1866 gold rush. Easterner Josephine Monaghan is cast out of her wealthy family after she has a baby out of wedlock. Heading west, she passes herself off as a man—Little Jo—in an attempt to forestall harassment. Solemn and overly earnest attempt by Greenwald to demystify the old west and bring a feminist viewpoint to a familiar saga. **CW:** Some violence and sexuality. **110m/C VHS, Closed Caption.** Suzy Amis, Bo Hopkins, Ian McKellen, Carrie Snodgress, David Chung, Rene Auberjonois, Heather Graham, Anthony Heald, Sam Robards, Ruth Maleczech; **D:** Maggie Greenwald; **W:** Maggie Greenwald; **M:** David Mansfield. Nominations: Independent Spirit Awards '94: Best Actress (Amis). *COL*

The Ballad of Narayama 🎬🎬🎬🎬 *Narayama-Bushi-Ko* **1983** Director Imamura's subtle and vastly moving story takes place a vague century ago. In compliance with village law designed to control population among the poverty-stricken peasants, a healthy 70-year-old woman must submit to solitary starvation atop a nearby mountain. We follow her as she sets into motion the final influence she will have in the lives of her children and grandchildren, a situation described with detachment and without imposing a tragic perspective. In Japanese with English subtitles. **129m/C VHS.** *JP* Ken Ogata, Sumiko Sakamota, Takejo Aki, Tonpei Hidari, Shoichi Ozawa; **D:** Shohei Imamura; **W:** Shohei Imamura. Cannes Film Festival '83: Best Film. *HMV, FCT, KIV*

The Ballad of Paul Bunyan **1972** The good-humored, legendary American giant is pitted against a powerful lumber camp boss who likes to pick on the little guy. **30m/C VHS.** **D:** Arthur Rankin Jr., Jules Bass. *VTR*

The Ballad of the Sad Cafe 🎬🎬½ **1991** **(PG-13)** Unusual love story set in a small Southern town during the Depression. The everyday lives of its townspeople are suddenly transformed when a distant relation of the town's outcast (Redgrave) unexpectedly shows up. A moving story that tries to portray both sides of love and its power to enhance and destroy simultaneously. Emotion never seems to come to life in a movie that's nice to watch, but is ultimately disappointing. Adapted from the play by Edward Albee, which was based on the critically acclaimed novella by Carson McCullers. A British/U.S. co-production. **100m/C VHS, LV, Closed Caption.** *GB* Vanessa Redgrave, Keith Carradine, Cork Hubbert, Rod Steiger, Austin Pendleton, Beth Dixon, Lanny Flaherty, Mert Hatfield, Earl Hindman, Anne Pitoniak; **D:** Simon Callow; **W:** Michael Hirst; **C:** Walter Lassally; **M:** Richard Robbins. *COL*

Ballbuster 🎬½ **1989** Cops take on gangs in an all-out high-stakes battle to win back the streets. **100m/C VHS.** Ivan Rogers, Bonnie Paine, W. Randolph Galvin, Bill Shirk, Brenda Banet; **D:** Eddie Beverly Jr.; **W:** Eddie Beverly Jr. *XVC*

Ballet Shoes 🎬🎬½ **19??** The classic children's tale of three sisters living a very sheltered life with their guardian Sylvia, who is working to support all four of them. A story of hope and possibilities. From the BBC Television network. **120m/C VHS.** *GB VCO, HMV*

Ballistic 🎬½ **1994 (R)** L.A. cop Jesse Gavin (Holden) gets in trouble when the government witness she's supposed to be protecting gets murdered. So she teams up with her ex-con father and her boyfriend to track the mobster responsible for the hit.**CW:** Language; violence; nudity. **86m/C VHS, LV, Closed Caption.** Marjean Holden, Richard Roundtree, Sam Jones, Joel Beeson, Charles Napier; **D:** Kim Bass. *IMP, IME*

The Balloonatic/One Week 1923 "The Balloonatic" (1923) features Keaton in several misadventures. In "One Week" (1920), Keaton and his new bride, Seely, receive a new home as a wedding gift—the kind you have to assemble yourself. Silent. **48m/B VHS, Beta.** Buster Keaton, Phyllis Haver, Sybil Seely; **D:** Buster Keaton. *CCB*

Baltic Deputy 🎬🎬🎬½ **1937** An early forerunner of Soviet historic realism, where an aging intellectual deals with post-revolution Soviet life. In Russian with subtitles. **95m/B VHS, Beta.** *RU* Nikolai Cherkassov; **D:** Yosif Heifitz. *FCT, IHF*

The Baltimore Bullet 🎬🎬 **1980 (PG)** Two men make their living traveling through the country as pool hustlers, bilking would-be pool sharks. Features ten of the greatest pool players in the world. **103m/C VHS, Beta.** James Coburn, Omar Sharif, Bruce Boxleitner, Ronee Blakley, Jack O'Halloran; **D:** Robert Ellis Miller; **W:** Robert Vincent O'Neil, John F. Brascia. *NLC*

Balto 🎬🎬½ **1995 (G)** Animated adventure, based on a true story, of a half-husky, half-wolf sled dog, Balto, who faces overwhelming odds to bring life-saving medicine to Nome, Alsaka. It's 1925, there's a diptheria epidemic, and Balto is the lead team dog on the final leg of the race to get the serum to Nome in time. Balto and the rest of the team dogs became instant heroes and even journeyed to Hollywood to star in their own silent film "Balto's Race to Nome." **78m/C VHS, LV, Closed Caption.** **D:** Simon Wells; **W:** Cliff Ruby, Elana Lesser, David Steven Cohen, Roger S.H. Schulman; **M:** James Horner; **V:** Kevin Bacon, Bob Hoskins, Bridget Fonda, Jim Cummings, Phil Collins, Juliette Brewer, Danny Mann, Miriam Margolyes. *USH*

Bambi 🎬🎬🎬🎬 **1942 (G)** A true Disney classic, detailing the often harsh education of a newborn deer and his friends in the forest. Proves that Disney animation was—and still is—the best to be found. Thumper still steals the show and the music is delightful, including "Let's Sing a Gay Little Spring Song," "Love is a Song," "Little April Shower," "The Thumper Song," and "Twitterpated." Stands as one of the greatest children's films of all time; a genuine perennial from generation to generation. Based very loosely on the book by Felix Salten. **69m/C VHS, Beta, LV, Closed Caption. D:** David Hand; **W:** Larry Morey; **M:** Frank Churchill, Edward Plumb; **V:** Bobby Stewart, Peter Behn, Stan Alexander, Cammie King, Donnie Dunagan, Hardie Albright, John Sutherland, Tim Davis, Sam Edwards, Sterling Holloway, Ann Gillis, Perce Pearce. Nominations: Academy Awards '42: Best Song ("Love Is a Song"), Best Sound, Best Original Dramatic/Comedy Score.*DIS*

The Bamboo Saucer 🎬½ *Collision Course* **1968** Russian and American scientists race to find a U.F.O. in Red China. **103m/C VHS.** Dan Duryea, John Ericson, Lois Nettleton, Nan Leslie; **D:** Frank Telford. *REP*

Bananas 🎬🎬🎬 **1971 (PG-13)** Intermittently hilarious pre-"Annie Hall" Allen fare is full of the director's signature angst-ridden philosophical comedy. A frustrated product tester from New York runs off to South America, where he volunteers his support to the revolutionary force of a shaky Latin-American dictatorship and winds up the leader. Don't miss cameos by Stallone and Garfield. Witty score contributes much.**CW:** Comic sexuality including some pin-up nudity, some drug use and crude language. **82m/C VHS, Beta, LV.** Woody Allen, Louise Lasser, Carlos Montalban, Howard Cosell, Charlotte Rae, Conrad Bain; **Cameos:** Sylvester Stallone, Allen (Goorwitz) Garfield; **D:** Woody Allen; **W:** Woody Allen; **M:** Marvin Hamlisch. *MGM, FCT, FOX*

Bananas Boat woof! *What Changed Charley Farthing* **1978** A captain takes a man and his daughter away from the collapsing government of their banana republic. The cast and director take a few risks but fail in this would-be comedy. **91m/C VHS.** *GB* Doug McClure, Hayley Mills, Lionel Jeffries, Dilys Hamlett, Warren Mitchell; **D:** Sidney Hayers. *VCI*

Band of Angels 🎬🎬½ **1957** Orphaned Amantha (De Carlo) learns she has African-American blood and since it's the pre-Civil War era she promptly winds up on the auction block. She becomes both the property and the mistress of mysterious New Orleans landowner Hamish Bond (Gable). Then the Civil War comes along bringing threats and revelations. De Carlo looks properly sultry but this is a weak attempt at costume drama. Based on the novel by Robert Penn Warren. **127m/C VHS.** Clark Gable, Yvonne De Carlo, Sidney Poitier, Efrem Zimbalist Jr., Rex Reason, Patric Knowles, Torin Thatcher, Andrea King, Ray Teal; **D:** Raoul Walsh; **W:** John Twist, Ivan Goff; **M:** Max Steiner. *WAR, MOV*

Band of Gold 🎬🎬🎬 **1995** Unflinching British miniseries follows the lives of Yorkshire prostitutes Rosie (James), Carol (Tyson), and Gina (Gemmell). They try to survive the streets of Bradford while a serial killer is targeting the local hookers. On six cassettes. **312m/C VHS.** *GB* Geraldine James, Cathy Tyson, Ruth Gemmell, Barbara Dickson, David Schofield, Richard Moore, Rachel Davies, Samantha Morton; **D:** Richard Standeven, Richard Laxton; **W:** Kay Mellor; **C:** Peter Jessop; **M:** Hal Lindes. *CCB*

Band of Outsiders 🎬🎬½ *Bande a Part; The Outsiders* **1964** A woman hires a pair of petty criminals to rip off her aunt; Godard vehicle for exposing self-reflexive comments on modern film culture. In French with English subtitles. **97m/B VHS, Beta.** *FR* Sami Frey, Anna Karina, Claude Brasseur, Louisa Colpeyn; **D:** Jean-Luc Godard; **W:** Jean-Luc Godard. *HTV, NOS, MRV*

Band of the Hand 🎬 **1986 (R)** A "Miami Vice" type melodrama about five convicts who are trained to become an unstoppable police unit. The first feature film by Glaser, last seen as Starsky in "Starsky & Hutch." **109m/C VHS, Beta, LV.** Stephen Lang, Michael Carmine, Lauren Holly, Leon Robinson; **D:** Paul Michael Glaser; **W:** Jack Baran, Leo Garen. *NO*

The Band Wagon 🎬🎬🎬 **1953** A Hollywood song-and-dance man finds trouble when he is persuaded to star in a Broadway musical. Charisse has been called Astaire's most perfect partner, perhaps by those who haven't seen Rogers. ♫That's Entertainment; Dancing in the Dark; By Myself; A Shine On Your Shoes; Something to Remember You By; High and Low; I Love Louisa; New Sun in the Sky; I Guess I'll Have to Change My Plan. **112m/C VHS, Beta, LV.** Fred Astaire, Cyd Charisse, Oscar Levant, Nanette Fabray, Jack Buchanan, Bobby Watson; **D:** Vincente Minnelli; **W:** Betty Comden; **M:** Arthur Schwartz, Howard Dietz. National Film Registry '95;; Nominations: Academy Awards '53: Best Costume Design (Color), Best Story & Screenplay, Scoring of a Musical. *MGM, FCT*

Bandit King of Texas 🎬🎬½ **1949** A varmint is swindling unsuspecting settlers in a land scheme and then robbing and murdering them when they go to visit their supposed property. Rocky and friends come to the rescue. **60m/B VHS, Closed Caption.** Allan "Rocky" Lane, Eddy Waller,

Helene Stanley, Robert Bice, Harry Lauter, Jim Nolan, John Hamilton, Lane Bradford; **D:** Fred Brannon; **W:** Olive Cooper. *REP, GPV*

Bandit Queen 🎬½ **1951** Spanish girl forms a band to stop seizure of Spanish possessions by lawless Californians. **71m/B VHS, Beta.** Barbara Britton, Willard Parker, Philip Reed, Jack Perrin; **D:** William (Lester Williams) Berke. *RXM*

Bandit Queen 🎬🎬🎬 **1994** Phoolan Devi (Biswas) is a female Robin Hood in modern-day India. A lower-caste woman, Devi is sold into marriage at 11, brutalized by her husband (and many others throughout the film), and eventually winds up with an equally brutal group of hill bandits. Only this time around, Devi takes action by aiding the group in robbing, kidnapping (and murdering) the rich and higher castes. Devi surrendered to authorities in 1983 and spent 11 years in jail. Based on screenwriter Sen's biography "India's Bandit Queen: The True Story of Phoolan Devi" and Devi's diaries. In Hindi with subtitles. **119m/C VHS, LV.** *GB IN* Seema Biswas, Nirmal Pandey, Manoj Bajpai, Raghubir Yadav, Rajesh Vivek, Govind Namdeo; **D:** Shekhar Kapur; **W:** Mala Sen; **C:** Ashok Mehta. *HMK*

Bandits 🎬½ **1973** Three cowboys team up with a band of Mexican outlaws to fight a Mexican traitor. **83m/C VHS, Beta.** Robert Conrad, Jan-Michael Vincent, Roy Jenson; **D:** Robert Conrad, Alfredo Zacharias. *UNI*

Bandits 🎬🎬½ **1986** Simon Verini (Yanne), a sophisticated fence, is given the loot from a 10 million dollar Cartier heist to exchange for cash by Mozart (Bruel) the leader of the thieves. But two of Mozart's gang want to keep the jewels instead and kidnap Verini's wife as ransom. She's killed, even after he returns the goods, and Verini is then framed for the theft and spends 10 years in prison. He's sent his daughter Marie-Sophie to a Swiss boarding school and upon his release works to both establish a relationship with her and to find those responsible for his wife's death. Director Lelouch's wife portrays the adult Marie-Sophie. In French with English subtitles. **98m/C VHS. FR** Jean Yanne, Marie-Sophie L(elouch), Patrick Bruel, Charles Gerard, Corinne Marchand, Christine Barbelivien; **D:** Claude Lelouch; **W:** Pierre Uytterhoeven, Claude Lelouch. *FXL, FCT*

Bandits of Orgosolo 🎬🎬½ *Banditi a Orgosolo* **1961** An acclaimed, patient drama about a Sardinian shepherd who shelters a band of thieves from the police. When one of the cops is killed the shepherd panics and flees into the hills for survival. Dubbed in English. **98m/B VHS, Beta.** *IT* Michele Cossu, Peppeddu Cuccu; **D:** Vittorio de Seta. *NOS, FCT, VYY*

Bandolero! 🎬🎬½ **1968 (PG)** In Texas, Stewart and Martin are two fugitive brothers who run into trouble with their Mexican counterparts. **106m/C VHS, Beta, Closed Caption.** James Stewart, Raquel Welch, Dean Martin, George Kennedy, Will Geer, Harry Carey Jr., Andrew Prine; **D:** Andrew V. McLaglen; **C:** William Clothier; **M:** Jerry Goldsmith. *FOX*

Bang 🎬🎬 **1997** This $20,000 indie concerns a nameless, powerless Asian-American would-be actress (Narita) in L.A. She gets kicked out of her apartment, accosted by a homeless crazy (Greene), and sexually propositioned by a sleazy producer (Graff). Finally, she's accused of causing a public disturbance by a cop (Newland), who'll let her off in exchange for sexual favors. Instead, she grabs his gun, forces him to strip, ties him to a tree, puts on the cop's uniform, and steals his motorcycle. In uniform, she's suddenly viewed with authority and decides to take some time to see what that's like. **98m/C VHS.** Darling Narita, Peter Greene, Michael Newland, David Allen Graff; **D:** Ash; **W:** Ash; **C:** Dave Gasperik. Nominations: Independent Spirit Awards '98: Debut Performance (Narita). *NYR*

Bang Bang Kid 🎬🎬 *Bang Bang* **1967 (G)** A western spoof about a klutzy gunfighter defending a town from outlaws. **78m/C VHS, Beta.** Tom Bosley, Guy Madison, Sandra Milo; **D:** Stanley Prager. *NO*

Bang the Drum Slowly 🎬🎬 1956 The original television adaptation of a Mark Harris novel about baseball. A ball player stricken by a terminal illness strikes an unlikely friendship with a teammate. Interesting role for an actor (Newman) who claims to have been driven to acting by running away from the sporting goods business. **60m/B VHS.** Paul Newman, George Peppard, Albert Salmi. *NOS*

Bang the Drum Slowly 🎬🎬🎬 1973 **(PG)** The touching story of a major league catcher who discovers that he is dying of Hodgkins disease and wants to play just one more season. De Niro is the weakening baseball player and Moriarty is the friend who helps see it through. Based on a novel by Mark Harris. **97m/C VHS, Beta, LV.** Robert De Niro, Michael Moriarty, Vincent Gardenia, Phil Foster, Ann Wedgeworth, Heather MacRae, Selma Diamond, Danny Aiello; **D:** John Hancock. New York Film Critics Awards '73: Best Supporting Actor (De Niro); Nominations: Academy Awards '73: Best Supporting Actor (Gardenia). *PAR, FCT*

The Bank Dick 🎬🎬🎬🎬 *The Bank Detective* 1940 Fields wrote the screenplay (using an alias) and stars in this zany comedy about a man who accidentally trips a bank robber and winds up as a guard. Fields' last major role is a classic, a worthy end to his great career. Side two of the laserdisc is in CAV format, which allows single frame access to the frenetic cops and robbers chase sequence. **73m/B VHS, Beta, LV.** W.C. Fields, Cora Witherspoon, Una Merkel, Evelyn Del Rio, Jack Norton, Jessie Ralph, Franklin Pangborn, Shemp Howard, Grady Sutton, Russell Hicks, Richard Purcell, Reed Hadley; **D:** Eddie Cline; **W:** W.C. Fields; **C:** Milton Krasner. National Film Registry '92. *USH*

Bank Robber 🎬🎬 1993 **(R)** Billy (Dempsey) is a thief who will retire after one final bank heist, if only he hadn't forgotten to break that surveillance camera. Holed up in a New York hotel he's subjected to extortion schemes and finds himself a new outlaw celebrity to newshounds. Bonet is a sweet hooker who falls in love with him. Satire on crooks and fame is too mild-mannered for its own good but not without charm. Directorial debut of Mead. Unedited NC-17 version also available. **CW:** Explicit sex scenes. **94m/C VHS, LV, Closed Caption.** Patrick Dempsey, Lisa Bonet, Olivia D'Abo, James Garde, Forest Whitaker, Judge Reinhold, Michael Jeter, Joe Viterelli, John Chappoulis; **D:** Nick Mead; **W:** Nick Mead; **M:** Stewart Copeland. *ART*

Bank Shot 🎬🎬🎬 1974 Hilarious comedy about a criminal who plans to rob a bank by stealing the entire building. Based on the novel by Donald Westlake, and the sequel to "The Hot Rock." **83m/C VHS.** George C. Scott, Joanna Cassidy, Sorrell Booke, G. Wood, Clifton James, Bob Balaban, Bibi Osterwald; **D:** Gower Champion; **W:** Wendell Mayes; **C:** Harry Stradling Jr. *NO*

The Banker 🎬🎬 1989 **(R)** A cop, played by Forster, suspects a wealthy, highly influential banker of brutal serial killings. **90m/C VHS, Beta, LV.** Robert Forster, Jeff Conaway, Leif Garrett, Duncan Regehr, Shanna Reed, Deborah Richter, Richard Roundtree, Teri Weigel, E.J. Peaker; **D:** William Webb. *NO*

Banzai Runner 🎬🎬 1986 A cop whose brother was killed in an exclusive desert-highway race decides to avenge by joining the race himself. **88m/C VHS, Beta.** Dean Stockwell, John Shepherd, Charles Dierkop; **D:** John G. Thomas; **M:** Joel Goldsmith. *THV*

B.A.P.'s 🎬½ 1997 **(PG-13)** Ghetto to riches story about Georgia waitresses Nisi (Berry) and Mickey (Desselle) who dream about opening their own business—a combo restaurant and hair salon. An L.A. audition offering $10,000 gets them to the sunny coast and eventually into the Beverly Hills mansion of Mr. Blakemore (Landau), where Nisi's persuaded to pose as the granddaughter of his lost love by Blakemore's money-grubbing nephew, Isaac (Fried). Everybody bonds and butler Manley (Richardson) instructs the women in taste and etiquette. Good cast is wasted and the

comedy's lame when not offensive. **CW:** Brief strong language. **91m/C VHS.** Halle Berry, Natalie Desselle, Martin Landau, Ian Richardson, Troy Beyer, Luigi Amodeo, Jonathan Fried, A.J. Johnson; **D:** Robert Townsend; **W:** Troy Beyer; **C:** Bill Dill; **M:** Stanley Clarke. *NLC*

Bar Girls 🎬🎬 1995 **(R)** Mating rituals, set in L.A. wateringhole "The Girl Bar," finds usually tough cookie Loretta (Wolfe) spotting new face Rachael (D'Agostino) and deciding she likes what she sees. There's various mind games as they chart a rocky course to true love—with jealousy, possessiveness, and past romance all playing their parts. Hoffman adapted from her play and the staginess remains; film debut for director Giovanni. **CW:** Strong sexuality; nudity; language. **95m/C VHS, LV, Closed Caption.** Nancy Allison Wolfe, Liza D'Agostino, Justine Slater, Paula Sorge, Camila Griggs, Pam Raines; **D:** Marita Giovanni; **W:** Lauran Hoffman; **C:** Michael Ferris. *ORI*

Bar-20 🎬½ 1943 Stage hold-ups and jewel robberies abound in this Hopalong Cassidy western. **54m/B VHS, Beta.** George Reeves, Douglas Fowley, William Boyd, Andy Clyde, Robert Mitchum, Victor Jory; **D:** Lesley Selander. *NOS, MRV, GVV*

Barabbas 🎬🎬½ 1962 Barabbas, a thief and murderer, is freed by Pontius Pilate in place of Jesus. He is haunted by this event for the rest of his life. Excellent acting, little melodrama, lavish production make for fine viewing. Based on the novel by Lagerkvist. **144m/C VHS, Beta, LV.** Anthony Quinn, Silvana Mangano, Arthur Kennedy, Jack Palance, Ernest Borgnine, Katy Jurado; **D:** Richard Fleischer. *COL*

Baraka 🎬🎬🎬 1993 Time-lapse photography transforms a fascinating array of scenic panoramas into a thought-provoking experience. No dialogue, but the captivating visuals, shot in 24 countries, are a feast for the eyes. Points of interest include Iguacu Falls in Argentina, Ayers Rock in Australia, the temples of Angkor Wat in Cambodia, and the Grand Canyon. Also tours Auschwitz and the streets of Calcutta, in an effort to warn the viewer of the planet's fragility. Filmed in 70mm. **96m/C VHS, LV, Letterbox. D:** Ron Fricke; **W:** Ron Fricke, Mark Magidson, Bob Green; **C:** Ron Fricke; **M:** Michael Stearns. *MPI*

Barb Wire 🎬½ 1996 **(R)** "Don't call me babe!" That'll be difficult when the figure in question is Anderson Lee's big-screen take on Dark Horse comic book heroine Barb Wire. Barb runs the sleazy Hammerhead Bar & Grille in Steel Harbor, the only neutral city in an America torn by a second civil war, and reluctantly agrees to aid hunky resistance leader Axel (Morrison) on a dangerous peace mission. Pambo gives Stallone a fight for the action title—fetching in high heels and black leather—with lots of fire power and a take-no-prisoners attitude. Plot's secondary to pulchritude but, unfortunately, the movie's just not a lotta fun. **CW:** Violence and nudity/sexuality. **98m/C VHS, LV, Closed Caption.** Pamela Anderson, Temuera Morrison, Jack Noseworthy, Victoria Rowell, Xander Berkeley, Udo Kier, Steve Railsback, Clint Howard, Tony Bill; **D:** David Hogan; **W:** Ilene Chaiken, Chuck Pfarrer; **C:** Rick Bota; **M:** Michel Colombier. Golden Raspberry Awards '96: Worst New Star (Anderson); Nominations: MTV Movie Awards '97: Best Fight (Pamela Lee/A Guy); Golden Raspberry Awards '96: Worst Picture, Worst Screenplay, Worst Song ("Welcome to Planet Boom!"). *PGV*

Barbarella 🎬🎬½ *Barbarella, Queen of the Galaxy* 1968 **(PG)** Based on the popular French sci-fi comic strip drawn by Jean-Claude Forest, this cult classic details the bizarre adventures of a space nymphette (Fonda) encountering fantastic creatures and super beings. You'll see sides of Fonda you never saw before (not even in the workout videos). Notorious in its day; rather silly, dated camp now. Don't miss the elbow-sex scene. Terry Southern contributed to the script. **98m/C VHS, Beta, LV, Letterbox. FR IT** Jane Fonda, John Phillip Law, David Hemmings, Marcel Marceau, Anita Pallenberg, Milo O'Shea; **D:** Roger Vadim; **W:** Terry Southern; **C:** Claude Renoir; **M:** Charles Fox. *FUS, PAR*

Barbarian and the Geisha 🎬🎬 1958 The first US diplomat in Japan undergoes culture shock as well as a passionate love affair with a geisha, circa 1856. **104m/C VHS, Beta, Closed Caption.** John Wayne, Eiko Ando, Sam Jaffe, So Yamamura; **D:** John Huston; **M:** Hugo Friedhofer. *FOX*

Barbarian Queen 🎬 1985 **(R)** Female warriors led by beauteous babe seek revenge for the capture of their men in this sword-and-sorcery epic. Low-budget rip-off "Conan the Barbarian" is laughable. Also available in an unrated version. Followed by "Barbarian Queen 2: The Empress Strikes Back." **71m/C VHS, Beta, LV. IT** Lana Clarkson, Frank Zagarino, Katt Shea Ruben, Dawn Dunlap, Susana Traverso; **D:** Hector Olivera. *VES, ART*

Barbarian Queen 2: The Empress Strikes Back 🎬 1989 **(R)** Apparently one movie wasn't enough to tell the beautiful Princess Athalia's story. This time she fights her evil brother Ankaris. He throws her in prison, she escapes, joins a band of female rebels, and leads them into battle. No better than the first attempt. **87m/C VHS. IT** Lana Clarkson, Greg Wrangler, Rebecca Wood, Elizabeth Jaegen, Roger Cundy; **D:** Joe Finley. *ART*

The Barbarians 🎬 *The Barbarians and Co* 1987 **(R)** Two bodybuilder siblings in animal skins battle wizards and warlords in this dumb-but-fun U.S./Italian co-production. **88m/C VHS, Beta, LV. IT** David Paul, Peter Paul, Richard Lynch, Eva LaRue, Virginia Bryant, Sheeba Alahani, Michael Berryman; **D:** Ruggero Deodato; **M:** Pino Donaggio. *VTR*

Barbarians at the Gate 🎬🎬🎬½ 1993 **(R)** In the "greed is good" financial climate of the '80s, this made-for-cable movie chronicles the $25 billion dollar battle in 1988 for RJR Nabisco, which at the time was working on developing a "smokeless cigarette." Garner is CEO F. Ross Johnson, who is confident that their "smokeless cigarette" will boost the stock's value—until he gets the test-marketing results. Unwilling to risk the product's failure, Johnson decides to buy the company and is challenged by master dealer Kravis (Pryce). Fascinating social commentary on the nastiest mega-deal in history. Based on the book by Bryan Burrough and John Helyar. **CW:** Language. **107m/C VHS, Closed Caption.** James Garner, Jonathan Pryce, Peter Riegert, Joanna Cassidy, Fred Dalton Thompson, Leilani Sarelle Ferrer, Matt Clark, Jeffrey DeMunn; **D:** Glenn Jordan; **W:** Larry Gelbart; **M:** Richard Gibbs. Golden Globe Awards '94: Best Movie/Miniseries. *HBO, FCT, BTV*

Barbarosa 🎬🎬🎬 1982 **(PG)** Offbeat western about an aging, legendary outlaw constantly on the lam who reluctantly befriends a naive farmboy and teaches him survival skills. Nelson and Busey are a great team, solidly directed. Lovely Rio Grande scenery. **90m/C VHS, Beta, LV.** Willie Nelson, Gilbert Roland, Gary Busey, Isela Vega; **D:** Fred Schepisi; **C:** Ian Baker; **M:** Bruce Smeaton. *FOX*

Barbary Coast 🎬🎬🎬 1935 A ruthless club owner tries to win the love of a young girl by building her into a star attraction during San Francisco's gold rush days. **90m/B VHS, Beta, LV.** Edward G. Robinson, Walter Brennan, Brian Donlevy, Joel McCrea, Donald Meek, David Niven, Miriam Hopkins; **D:** Howard Hawks. Nominations: Academy Awards '35: Best Cinematography. *NO*

The Barbary Coast 🎬🎬 1974 A turn-of-the-century detective sleuths the streets of San Francisco in this average made-for-television movie. **100m/C VHS.** William Shatner, Dennis Cole, Lynda Day George, John Vernon, Charles Aidman, Michael Ansara, Neville Brand, Bill Bixby; **D:** Bill Bixby. *ORI*

The Barber Shop 🎬🎬🎬 1933 Fields portrays the bumbling, carefree barber Cornelius O'Hare, purveyor of village gossip and problem solver. Havoc begins when a gangster enters the shop and demands that Cornelius change his appearance. **21m/B VHS, Beta.** W.C. Fields, Elise Cavanna, Harry Watson, Dagmar Oakland, Frank Yaconelli. *CCB*

Barcelona 🎬🎬🎬 1994 (PG-13) Old-fashioned talkfest about two neurotic Americans experiencing sibling rivalry in Spain. Serious Ted (Nichols) is an American sales rep, posted to Barcelona, who can't quite get into the city's pleasure-loving rhythm. This is not a problem for Ted's cousin Fred (Eigeman), an obnoxious naval officer, with whom Ted has had a rivalry dating back to their boyhood. Set in the 1980s, the two must also deal with anti-Americanism, which leads both to violence and romantic developments. Tart dialogue, thoughtful performances, and exotic locales prove enticing in this low-budget sleeper that effectively mixes drama and dry comedy. Watch for Eigeman in Tom Cruise's uniform from "A Few Good Men." 102m/C VHS, LV. Taylor Nichols, Christopher Eigeman, Tushka Bergen, Mira Sorvino, Pep Munne, Francis Creighton, Thomas Gibson, Jack Gilpin, Nuria Badia, Hellena Schmied; **D:** Whit Stillman; **W:** Whit Stillman; **M:** Tom Judson, Mark Suozzo. Independent Spirit Awards '95: Best Cinematography. NLC, TTC, IME

The Barcelona Kill 🎬½ 1977 When a journalist and her boyfriend get in too deep with the Barcelona mob, their troubles begin. 86m/C VHS, Beta. Linda Hayden, John Astin, Simon Andreu, Maximo Valverde; **D:** Jose Antonio De La Loma. NO

Bare Essentials 🎬 1991 (PG) Made for TV yuppie Club Med nightmare in which a high-strung couple from New York find themselves marooned on a desert isle with only two other inhabitants. With no cellular telephoning ability and an absence of large-ticket consumer goods to purchase, the two turn their reluctant sights on each other, focusing on the bare essentials, as it were. Great soul-searching scenes for the inarticulate. 94m/C VHS, Closed Caption. Gregory Harrison, Lisa Hartman Black, Mark Linn-Baker, Charlotte Lewis; **D:** Martha Coolidge. REP

Bare Hunt 🎬 My Gun is Jammed; The Bear Hunt 1963 Detective Max T. Unimportant is dragged into the underground world of prospective nude actresses in this supposedly funny "nudie." 69m/B VHS, Beta. VDM, TPV

Bare Knees 🎬🎬 1928 A woman causes a scandal in her family when she arrives at her sister's birthday party with bare knees, cigarettes, and other flapper items. The quintessential flapper movie. 61m/B VHS, Beta. Virginia Lee Corbin, Donald Keith, Jane Winton, Johnnie Walker, Forrest Stanley, Maude Fulton; **D:** Erle C. Kenton. GPV

Bare Knuckles 🎬 1977 (R) The adventures of a low-rent bounty hunter. 90m/C VHS, Beta. Robert Viharo, Sherry Jackson, Michael Heit, Gloria Hendry, John Daniels; **D:** Don Edmunds; **C:** Dean Cundey. TWE

The Barefoot Contessa 🎬🎬🎬 1954 The story, told in flashback, of a Spanish dancer's rise to Hollywood stardom, as witnessed by a cynical director. Shallow Hollywood self-examination. 128m/C VHS, Beta. Ava Gardner, Humphrey Bogart, Edmond O'Brien, Valentina Cortese, Rossano Brazzi; **D:** Joseph L. Mankiewicz; **W:** Joseph L. Mankiewicz; **C:** Jack Cardiff. Academy Awards '54: Best Supporting Actor (O'Brien); Golden Globe Awards '55: Best Supporting Actor (O'Brien); Nominations: Academy Awards '54: Best Story & Screenplay. MGM, FOX, FCT

The Barefoot Executive 🎬🎬 1971 A mailroom boy who works for a national television network finds a chimpanzee that can pick hit shows in this Disney family comedy. 92m/C VHS, Beta. Kurt Russell, John Ritter, Harry (Henry) Morgan, Wally Cox, Heather North, Joe Flynn; **D:** Robert Butler; **M:** Robert F. Brunner. DIS, OM

Barefoot in Athens 🎬🎬 1966 Television presentation from "George Schaefer's Showcase Theatre" chronicles the last years of the philosopher Socrates who, barefoot and unkempt, an embarrassment to his wife, and a dangerous critic to the corrupt Athenian leaders, nevertheless believes that democracy and truth are all-important in his city. 76m/C VHS, Beta. Peter Ustinov, Geraldine Page, Anthony Quayle; **D:** George Schaefer. FHS

Barefoot in the Park 🎬🎬🎬 1967 Neil Simon's Broadway hit translates well to screen. A newly wedded bride (Fonda) tries to get her husband (Redford, reprising his Broadway role) to loosen up and be as free-spirited as she is. 106m/C VHS, Beta, LV. Robert Redford, Jane Fonda, Charles Boyer, Mildred Natwick; **D:** Gene Saks; **W:** Neil Simon; **C:** Joseph LaShelle. Nominations: Academy Awards '67: Best Supporting Actress (Natwick). PAR

Barfly 🎬🎬🎬 1987 (R) Bukowski's semi-autobiographical screenplay is the story of a talented writer who chooses to spend his time as a lonely barfly, hiding his literary abilities behind glasses of liquor. Dunaway's character is right on target as the fellow alcoholic. 100m/C VHS, Beta, LV, 8mm, Closed Caption. Mickey Rourke, Faye Dunaway, Alice Krige, Frank Stallone, J.C. Quinn, Jack Nance; **D:** Barbet Schroeder; **W:** Charles Bukowski. WAR, FCT

The Bargain 🎬½ 1915 Hart's first feature, in which he portrays a bandit desperately trying to go straight. Original titles with musical score. 50m/B VHS, Beta. William S. Hart. NOS, GPV, DVT

Baritone 🎬🎬 1985 Concerned Polish drama about a prominent opera singer who promises to deliver a grand concert upon returning to his small town, only to lose his voice just before the show is to start. Proof positive that the opera ain't over 'til the fat lady sings. 100m/C VHS. PL Zbigniew Zapasiewicz; **D:** Janusz Zaorski. FCT

Barjo 🎬🎬 1993 In a bland and isolated French suburb lives willful housewife Fanfan (Bouchet) with her older businessman husband Charles (Bohringer) and her eccentric twin brother Barjo (Girardot). Barjo is obsessed with lists and extraterrestrials and his sister's affair with their next-door neighbor, which he likes to spy on. Her husband naturally begins to go crazy. Deadpan satire based on the novel "Confessions of a Crap Artist" by Philip K. Dick. The post-WWII American setting of the novel makes a decidedly uneasy transistion to contemporary French life. In French with English subtitles. 85m/C VHS. FR Anne Brochet, Hippolyte Girardot, Richard Bohringer, Consuelo de Haviland, Renaud Danner, Nathalie Boutefeu; **D:** Jerome Boivin; **W:** Jerome Boivin, Jacques Audiard; **M:** Hugues LeBars. FXL

The Barkleys of Broadway 🎬🎬🎬 1949 The famous dancing team's last film together; they play a quarreling husband/wife showbiz team. ♫They Can't Take That Away From Me; The Sabre Dance; Swing Trot; Manhattan Downbeat; A Weekend in the Country; My One and Only Highland Fling; You'd Be Hard to Replace; Bouncin' the Blues; Shoes With Wings On. 109m/C VHS, Beta, LV. Fred Astaire, Ginger Rogers, Gale Robbins, Oscar Levant, Jacques Francois, Billie Burke; **D:** Charles Walters; **W:** Adolph Green, Betty Comden; **C:** Harry Stradling; **M:** Ira Gershwin, Harry Warren. Nominations: Academy Awards '49: Best Color Cinematography. MGM

Barn of the Naked Dead woof! Terror Circus; Nightmare Circus 1973 Prine plays a sicko who tortures women while his radioactive monster dad terrorizes the Nevada desert. Rudolph's first film, directed under the pseudonym Gerald Comier. 86m/C VHS. Andrew Prine, Manuella Thiess, Sherry Alberoni, Gylian Roland, Al Cormier, Jennifer Ashley; **D:** Alan Rudolph. NO

Barnaby and Me 🎬🎬 1977 Australian star Barnaby the Koala Bear joins an international con-man in this romantic adventure. The mob is chasing the con-man when he meets and falls for a lovely young woman and her daughter. 90m/C VHS, Beta. AU Sid Caesar, Juliet Mills, Sally Boyden; **D:** Norman Panama.

Barney's Great Adventure 🎬🎬 1998 (G) First the bad news: that big purple dweebosaur made a movie and your three-year-old is going to make you buy the video. Now the good news: since it's on video you can cue it up for the young-uns and run screaming from the room. You see, they don't care what you think about Barney, who looks a little out of place away from his cheesy video set. Kinda like a big lug in a purple felt suit, actually. In this extravaganza of not so special effects, Barney and two little girls chase a magical egg around town and encounter a parade, a circus and other allegedly wonderful things, all while trying to convince the older Kyle that Barney is "cool." In a surprise move, the egg hatches to reveal....that new stuffed animal you're going to have to buy! 75m/C VHS. George Hearn, Shirley Douglas, Kyla Pratt, Trevor Morgan, Bob West, Renee Madeleine Le Guerrier; **D:** Steve Gomer; **W:** Stephen White; **C:** Sandi Sissel; **V:** Diana Rice, Julie Johnson. NYR

Barnum 🎬🎬½ 1986 P.T. Barnum's life is focused upon in this biography about the man who helped to form "The Greatest Show On Earth." 100m/C VHS, Beta, LV. Burt Lancaster, Hanna Schygulla, Jenny Lind, John Roney; **D:** Lee Philips.

Barocco 🎬🎬 1976 Crook kills his lookalike and takes his place and his girlfriend. Together the duo try blackmail to get the money they need to start a new life. Self-conscious would-be film noir. French with subtitles. 102m/C VHS. FR Gerard Depardieu, Isabelle Adjani, Marie-France Pisier, Jean-Claude Brialy; **D:** Andre Techine; **W:** Andre Techine, Marilyn Goldin; **C:** Bruno Nuytten; **M:** Philippe Sarde. CVC

The Baron 🎬½ 1988 Vengeance is the name of the game when an underworld boss gets stiffed on a deal. Fast-paced no-brainer street drama. 88m/C VHS. Calvin Lockhart, Charles McGregor, Joan Blondell, Richard Lynch, Marlene Clark; **D:** Philip Fently. NO

The Baron and the Kid 🎬 1984 A pool shark finds out that his opponent at a charity exhibition game is his long-lost son. Based on Johnny Cash's song. Made for TV. 100m/C VHS, Beta, Closed Caption. Johnny Cash, Darren McGavin, June Carter Cash, Richard Roundtree; **D:** Gary Nelson; **M:** Brad Fiedel. FOX

Baron Munchausen 🎬🎬🎬 1943 The German film studio UFA celebrated its 25th anniversary with this lavish version of the Baron Munchausen legend, starring a cast of top-name German performers at the height of the Third Reich. Filmed in Agfacolor; available in English subtitled or dubbed versions. 120m/C VHS, Beta. GE Hans Albers, Kaethe Kaack, Hermann Speelmanns, Leo Slezak; **D:** Josef von Baky. VCD, GLV, TPV

Baron of Arizona 🎬🎬🎬 1951 Land office clerk almost succeeds in convincing the U.S. that he owned the state of Arizona. 99m/B VHS, Beta. Vincent Price, Ellen Drew, Beulah Bondi, Reed Hadley, Vladimir Sokoloff; **D:** Samuel Fuller; **W:** Samuel Fuller; **C:** James Wong Howe. RXM

Barracuda woof! The Lucifer Project 1978 (R) Lots of innocent swimmers are being eaten by crazed killer barracudas. 90m/C VHS, Beta. Wayne Crawford, Jason Evers, Roberta Leighton; **D:** Harry Kerwin. NO

The Barretts of Wimpole Street 🎬🎬🎬 Forbidden Alliance 1934 The moving, almost disturbing, account of poetess Elizabeth Barrett, an invalid confined to her bed, with only her poetry and her dog to keep her company. She is wooed by poet Robert Browning, in whose arms she finds true happiness and a miraculous recovery. Multi-faceted drama expertly played by all. 110m/B VHS, LV. Fredric March, Norma Shearer, Charles Laughton, Maureen O'Sullivan, Katherine Alexander, Una O'Connor, Ian Wolfe; **D:** Sidney Franklin; **W:** William H. Daniels. Nominations: Academy Awards '34: Best Actress (Shearer), Best Picture. MGM, CCB

Barry Lyndon 🎬🎬🎬½ 1975 (PG) Ravishing adaptation of the classic Thackeray novel about the adventures of an Irish gambler moving from innocence to self-destructive arrogance in the aristocracy of 18th Century England. Visually opulent. Kubrick received excellent performances from all his actors, and a stunning display of history, but the end result still overwhelms. O'Neal has seldom been better. 185m/C VHS, Beta, LV, Letterbox. Ryan O'Neal, Marisa Berenson, Patrick Magee, Hardy Kruger, Guy Hamilton; **D:** Stanley Kubrick. Academy

Awards '75: Best Art Direction/Set Decoration, Best Cinematography, Best Costume Design, Original Song Score and/or Adaptation; British Academy Awards '75: Best Director (Kubrick); Los Angeles Film Critics Association Awards '75: Best Cinematography; National Board of Review Awards '75: Best Director (Kubrick); National Society of Film Critics Awards '75: Best Cinematography; Nominations: Academy Awards '75: Best Adapted Screenplay, Best Director (Kubrick), Best Picture. *WAR*

Barry McKenzie Holds His Own 🐾🐾 1974
In this sequel to "The Adventures of Barry McKenzie," we find that after a young man's aunt is mistaken for the Queen of England, two emissaries of Count Plasma of Transylvania kidnap her to use as a Plasma tourist attraction. Based on the 'Private Eye' comic strip, this crude Australian film is as disappointing as the first of the Barry McKenzie stories. 93m/C VHS, Beta. *AU* Barry Humphries, Barry Crocker, Donald Pleasence; *D:* Bruce Beresford; *W:* Barry Humphries, Bruce Beresford. *NO*

Bartleby 🐾🐾½ 1970
A new version of the classic Herman Melville short story. McEnery is Bartleby the clerk, who refuses to leave his job even after he's fired; Scofield is his frustrated boss. 79m/C VHS, LV. Paul Scofield, John McEnery, Colin Jeavons, Thorley Walters; *D:* Anthony Friedman; *W:* Rodney Carr-Smith. *WST, TVC*

Barton Fink 🐾🐾🐾 1991 (R)
This eerie comic nightmare comes laden with awards (including the Palme D'Or from Cannes) but only really works if you care about the time and place. Fink is a trendy New York playwright staying in a seedy Hollywood hotel in the 1940s, straining to write a simple B-movie script. Macabre events, both real and imagined, compound his writer's block. Superb set design from Dennis Gassner complements an unforgettable cast of grotesques. *CW:* Language and some violence. 116m/C VHS. John Turturro, John Goodman, Judy Davis, Michael Lerner, John Mahoney, Tony Shalhoub, Jon Polito, Steve Buscemi, David Warrilow, Richard Portnow, Christopher Murney; *D:* Joel Coen; *W:* Joel Coen, Ethan Coen; *C:* Roger Deakins; *M:* Carter Burwell. Cannes Film Festival '91: Best Actor (Turturro), Best Director (Coen); Los Angeles Film Critics Association Awards '91: Best Cinematography, Best Supporting Actor (Lerner); New York Film Critics Awards '91: Best Cinematography, Best Supporting Actress (Davis); National Society of Film Critics Awards '91: Best Cinematography; Nominations: Academy Awards '91: Best Art Direction/Set Decoration, Best Costume Design, Best Supporting Actor (Lerner). *CCB*

Baseball 1994
Ken Burns' follow-up to "The Civil War" is an equally epic history of the great American pastime, spanning 150 years. On nine tapes, released in a collector's edition or individually. 1080m/C VHS. *D:* Ken Burns. *WAR, PBS*

Based on an Untrue Story 🐾🐾½ 1993
Campy spoof of popular "true story" television docudramas in which powerful Satin Chau (Fairchild), a perfume mogul, loses her sense of smell. Satin leaves her mentor Varda (Cannon) to discovery herself but finds that only her two separated-at-birth sisters, Velour (Lake) and Corduroy (Jackson), hold the secrets to the past. It's hard to spoof a genre that's become a cliche but this television movie does its best. 90m/C VHS, Closed Caption. Morgan Fairchild, Dyan Cannon, Victoria Jackson, Ricki Lake, Harvey Korman, Robert Goulet, Dan Hedaya; *D:* Jim Drake. *FOX*

BASEketball 1998
Dude! Three slacker buddies ("South Park"'s Parker and Stone plus Bachar) invent a new game in their driveway—a combo of basketball with baseball rules—and see it turn into big business. Based on a game that director Zucker invented with friends. Not yet reviewed. ?m/C VHS. Trey Parker, Matthew Stone, Yasmine Bleeth, Jenny McCarthy, Ernest Borgnine, Robert Stack, Robert Vaughn, Dian Bachar; *D:* David Zucker; *W:* David Zucker, Robert Locash, Jeffrey Wright, Lewis Friedman. *NYR*

The Bashful Bachelor 🐾🐾 1942
Yokel joker Abner trades his delivery car for a race horse, hoping to win a big race. 78m/B VHS. Chester Lauck, Norris Goff, ZaSu Pitts, Grady Sutton, Louise Currie, Irving Bacon, Earle Hodgins, Benny Rubin; *D:* Malcolm St. Clair. *NOS, RXM*

Basic Instinct 🐾🐾½ 1992 (R)
Controversial thriller had tongues wagging months before its theatrical release. Burnt-out detective Douglas falls for beautiful, manipulative murder suspect Stone, perfectly cast as a bisexual ice queen who may or may not have done the deed. Noted for highly erotic sex scenes and an expensive (3 million bucks) script; ultimately the predictable plot is disappointing. Gay activists tried to interrupt filming because they objected to the depiction of Stone's character but only succeeded in generating more free publicity. The American release was edited to avoid an "NC-17" rating, but an uncut, unrated video version is also available. *CW:* Language, strong violence and drug use, and strong sensuality. 123m/C VHS, Beta, Closed Caption, DVD. Michael Douglas, Sharon Stone, George Dzundza, Jeanne Tripplehorn, Denis Arndt, Leilani Sarelle Ferrer, Bruce A. Young, Chelcie Ross, Dorothy Malone, Wayne Knight, Stephen Tobolowsky; *D:* Paul Verhoeven; *W:* Joe Eszterhas; *C:* Jan De Bont; *M:* Jerry Goldsmith. MTV Movie Awards '93: Best Female Performance (Stone), Most Desirable Female (Stone); Nominations: Academy Awards '92: Best Film Editing, Best Original Score. *ART, PMS*

Basic Training WOOF! 1986 (R)
Three sexy ladies wiggle into the Pentagon in their efforts to clean up the government. 85m/C VHS, Beta. Ann Dusenberry, Rhonda Shear, Angela Aames, Walter Gotell; *D:* Andrew Sugarman. *ART, VES*

Basileus Quartet 🐾🐾🐾 1982
The replacement for a violinist in a well-established quartet creates emotional havoc. Beautiful music, excellent and evocative photography. 118m/C VHS, LV. *FR IT* Pierre Malet, Hector Alterio, Omero Antonutti, Michel Vitold, Alain Cuny, Gabriele Ferzetti, Elisabeth Kreuzer; *D:* Fabio Carpi. *TPV*

Basket Case 🐾🐾🐾 1982
A gory horror film about a pair of Siamese twins—one normal, the other gruesomely deformed. The pair is surgically separated at birth, and the evil disfigured twin is tossed in the garbage. Fraternal ties being what they are, the normal brother retrieves his twin—essentially a head atop shoulders—and totes him around in a basket (he ain't heavy). Together they begin twisted and deadly revenge, with the brother-in-a-basket in charge. Very entertaining, if you like this sort of thing. Followed by two sequels, if you just can't get enough. 89m/C VHS, Beta, LV. Kevin Van Hentenryck, Terri Susan Smith, Beverly Bonner, Robert Vogel, Diana Browne, Lloyd Pace, Bill Freeman, Joe Clarke, Ruth Neuman, Richard Pierce; *D:* Frank Henenlotter; *W:* Frank Henenlotter; *C:* Bruce Torbet.

Basket Case 2 🐾🐾½ 1990 (R)
Surgically separated teenage mutant brothers Duane and Belial are back! This time they've found happiness in a "special" family—until they're plagued by the paparazzi. Higher production values make this sequel slicker than its low-budget predecessor, but it somehow lacks the same charm. *CW:* Language, graphic monster violence, and sensuality. 90m/C VHS, Beta, LV, Closed Caption. Kevin Van Hentenryck, Annie Ross, Kathryn Meisle, Heather Rattray, Jason Evers, Ted Sorel, Matt Mitler; *D:* Frank Henenlotter; *W:* Frank Henenlotter; *C:* Robert Baldwin; *M:* Joe Renzetti. *VTR, IME, SGE*

Basket Case 3: The Progeny 🐾🐾½ 1992 (R)
In this sequel to the cult horror hits "Basket Case" and "Basket Case 2," Belial is back and this time he's about to discover the perils of parenthood as the mutant Mrs. Belial delivers a litter of bouncing mini-monsters. Everything is fine until the police kidnap the little creatures and chaos breaks out as Belial goes on a shocking rampage in his newly created mechanical body. Weird special effects make this a cult favorite for fans of the truly outrageous. 90m/C VHS, Closed Caption. Annie Ross, Kevin Van Hentenryck, Gil Roper,

Tina Louise Hilbert, Dan Biggers, Jim O'Doherty, Jackson Faw, Jim Grimshaw; *D:* Frank Henenlotter; *W:* Frank Henenlotter, Robert Martin; *C:* Bob Paone; *M:* Joe Renzetti. *USH, SGE*

The Basketball Diaries 🐾🐾 1994 (R)
Disappointing adaptation of undeground writer/ musician Jim Carroll's 1978 cult memoirs, with DiCaprio starring as the teen athlete whose life spirals into drug addiction and hustling on the New York streets. Carroll and friends Mickey (Wahlberg), Neutron (McGaw), and Pedro (Madio), form the heart of St. Vitus' hot hoopster team. But the defiant quartet really get their kicks from drugs, dares, and petty crime—leading to an ever-downward turn. The book takes place in the '60s but the film can't make up its mind what the decade is, although DiCaprio (and Wahlberg) are particularly effective in a self-conscious first effort from Kalvert. *CW:* Graphic depiction of drug addiction with related strong violence, sexuality and language. 102m/C VHS. Leonardo DiCaprio, Mark Wahlberg, Patrick McGaw, James Madio, Bruno Kirby, Ernie Hudson, Lorraine Bracco, Juliette Lewis, Josh Mostel, Michael Rapaport, Michael Imperioli; *Cameos:* Jim Carroll; *D:* Scott Kalvert; *W:* Bryan Goluboff; *C:* David Phillips; *M:* Graeme Revell. *PGV*

Basquiat 🐾🐾🐾 Build a Fort Set it on Fire 1996 (R)
First-time writer/director and reknowned '80s pop artist Schnabel paints a celluloid portrait of African-American artist Jean Michel Basquiat, who went from graffiti artist to overnight sensation in the mid-1980s before dying of a drug overdose at 27. Schnabel's first-hand knowledge provides details of the painters, the dealers, and the patrons of the whirlwind New York art scene of the time using an all-star cast (no mean feat on a $3 million budget). Making the move from stage to screen, Wright is an aptly deep and elusive Basquiat and Bowie stands out in a marvelously conceived portrayal of Basquiat's pseudo-mentor, the equally sensational Warhol. Features authentic works of the artists portrayed and some very convincing Basquiat reproductions done by Schnabel. *CW:* Drug use and strong language. 108m/C VHS, LV, Closed Caption. Jeffrey Wright, David Bowie, Dennis Hopper, Gary Oldman, Christopher Walken, Michael Wincott, Benicio Del Toro, Parker Posey, Elina Lowensohn, Courtney Love, Claire Forlani, Willem Dafoe, Paul Bartel, Tatum O'Neal, Chuck Pfeiffer; *D:* Julian Schnabel; *W:* Julian Schnabel; *C:* Ron Fortunato; *M:* John Cale. Independent Spirit Awards '97: Best Supporting Actor (Del Toro); Nominations: Independent Spirit Awards '97: Debut Performance (Wright). *MAX*

The Bastard 🐾🐾½ The Kent Chronicles 1978
Dashing (but alas, illegitimate) nobleman roams Europe on futile, Roots-like search, then settles for America during the Revolutionary War in this longwinded television adaptation of John Jakes' equally cumbersome bestseller (part of his popular Bicentennial series). Stevens stars, along with many supporting performers merely keeping active. Followed by "The Rebels" and "The Seekers." 189m/C VHS, Closed Caption. Andrew Stevens, Tom Bosley, Kim Cattrall, Buddy Ebsen, Lorne Greene, Olivia Hussey, Cameron Mitchell, Harry (Henry) Morgan, Patricia Neal, Eleanor Parker, Donald Pleasence, William Shatner, Barry Sullivan, Noah Beery Jr., William Daniels, Keenan Wynn; *D:* Lee H. Katzin; *M:* John Addison. *USH*

Bastard out of Carolina 🐾🐾 1996 (R)
Huston's steeped-in-controversy directorial debut tells the story of young mom Anney (Leigh), who lives a hardscrabble life in Greenville, South Carolina, with an illegitimate daughter nicknamed Bone (Malone). Working as a waitress, Anney's eager to find love and succumbs to the charms of laborer Glen (Eldard), despite his nasty temper. Eleven-year-old Bone and Glen are immediately at odds and he begins to beat her, with Anney unwilling to face the truth, until a final horrific event. Based on the 1992 semiautiobiographical novel by Dorothy Allison, the film was originally made for Ted Turner's TNT network but was rejected as unsuitable because of its graphic depic-

tion of child abuse. **CW:** Strong depiction of sexual and violent abuse, including a rape scene involving a young girl. **97m/C VHS.** Jennifer Jason Leigh, Jena Malone, Ron Eldard, Glenne Headly, Lyle Lovett, Dermot Mulroney, Christina Ricci, Michael Rooker, Diana Scarwid, Susan Traylor, Grace Zabriskie; **D:** Anjelica Huston; **W:** Anne Meredith; **C:** Anthony B. Richmond; **M:** Van Dyke Parks. Nominations: Independent Spirit Awards '97: Debut Performance (Malone). *BMG*

The Bat 🐾🐾🐾 1926 A bat-obsessed killer stalks the halls of a spooky mansion in this early film version of the Mary Roberts Rinehart novel. 81m/B VHS, Beta. Andre de Beranger, Charles Herzinger, Emily Fitzroy, Louise Fazenda, Arthur Houseman, Robert McKim, Jack Pickford, Jewel Carmen; **D:** Roland West; **W:** Roland West. *SNC, FUS*

The Bat 🐾🐾 1959 A great plot centering around a murderer called the Bat, who kills hapless victims by ripping out their throats when he isn't busy searching for a million dollars worth of securities stashed in the old house he is living in. Adapted from the Mary Roberts Rinehart. 80m/B VHS, Beta. Vincent Price, Agnes Moorehead, Gavin Gordon, John Sutton, Lenita Lane, Darla Hood; **D:** Crane Wilbur. *NOS, SNC, DVT*

The Bat People 🐾 *It Lives By Night* 1974 (R) Less-than-gripping horror flick in which Dr. John Bech is bitten by a bat while on his honeymoon. He then becomes a sadistic bat creature, compelled to kill anyone who stumbles across his path. The gory special effects make for a great movie if you've ever been bitten by that sort of thing. 95m/C VHS, Beta. Stewart Moss, Marianne McAndrew, Michael Pataki, Paul Carr; **D:** Jerry Jameson. *HBO*

Bat 21 🐾🐾 1988 (R) Hackman, an American officer, is stranded in the wilds of Vietnam alone after his plane is shot down. He must rely on himself and Glover, with whom he has radio contact, to get him out. Glover and Hackman give solid performances in this otherwise average film. 112m/C VHS, Beta, LV, Closed Caption. Gene Hackman, Danny Glover, Jerry Reed, David Marshall Grant, Clayton Rohner, Erich Anderson, Joe Dorsey; **D:** Peter Markle; **W:** Marc Norman, William C. Anderson. *VTR, LUM*

The Bat Whispers 🐾🐾½ 1930 A masked madman is stalking the halls of a creepy mansion; eerie tale that culminates in an appeal to the audience to keep the plot under wraps. Unusually crafted film for its early era. Comic mystery based on the novel and play by Mary Roberts Rinehart and Avery Hopwood. 82m/B VHS, LV. Chester Morris, Chance Ward, Richard Tucker, Wilson Benge, DeWitt Jennings, Una Merkel, Spencer Charters; **D:** Roland West; **W:** Roland West. *NOS, DVT, MLB*

Bataan 🐾🐾½ 1943 A rugged war-time combat drama following the true story of a small platoon in the Philippines endeavoring to blow up a pivotal Japanese bridge. Also available in a colorized version. 115m/B VHS, Beta. Robert Taylor, George Murphy, Thomas Mitchell, Desi Arnaz Sr., Lee Bowman, Lloyd Nolan, Robert Walker; **D:** Tay Garnett. *MGM, TLF*

Bathing Beauty 🐾🐾½ 1944 This musical stars Skelton as a pop music composer with the hots for college swim teacher Williams. Rathbone is a music executive who sees the romance as a threat to Skelton's career and to his own profit margin. Full of aquatic ballet, Skelton's shtick, and wonderful original melodies. The first film in which Williams received star billing. ♫I Cried for You; Bim, Bam, Boom; Tico-Tico; I'll Take the High Note; Loch Lomond; By the Waters of Minnetonka; Magic is the Moonlight; Trumpet Blues; Hora Staccato. 101m/C VHS, LV. Red Skelton, Esther Williams, Basil Rathbone, Bill Goodwin, Jean Porter, Carlos Ramirez, Donald Meek, Ethel Smith, Helen Forrest; **D:** George Sidney; **C:** Harry Stradling; **M:** Xavier Cugat. *MGM, TTC, FCT*

Batman 🐾🐾½ 1966 Holy television camp, Batman! Will the caped crusader win the Bat-tle against the combined forces of the Joker, the Riddler, the Penguin, and Catwoman? Will Batman and Robin save the United World Security Council from dehydration? Will the Bat genius ever figure

out that Russian journalist Miss Kitka and Catwoman are one and the same? Biff! Thwack! Socko! Not to be confused with the Michael Keaton version of the Dark Knight, this is the pot-bellied Adam West Batman, teeming with Bat satire and made especially for the big screen. 104m/C VHS, Beta, LV, Closed Caption. Burt Ward, Adam West, Burgess Meredith, Cesar Romero, Frank Gorshin, Lee Meriwether; **D:** Leslie Martinson. *FOX*

Batman 🐾🐾🐾½ 1989 (PG-13) The blockbuster fantasy epic that renewed Hollywood's faith in media blitzing. The Caped Crusader is back in Gotham City, where even the criminals are afraid to walk the streets alone. There's a new breed of criminal in Gotham, led by the infamous Joker. Their random attacks via acid-based make-up are just the beginning. Keaton is surprisingly good as the dual personality hero though Nicholson steals the show. Marvelously designed and shot. Much better on the big screen. Followed in 1992 by "Batman Returns." 126m/C VHS, Beta, LV, Letterbox, Closed Caption, DVD. Michael Keaton, Jack Nicholson, Kim Basinger, Robert Wuhl, Tracey Walter, Billy Dee Williams, Pat Hingle, Michael Gough, Jack Palance, Jerry Hall; **D:** Tim Burton; **W:** Sam Hamm, Warren Skaaren; **M:** Danny Elfman, Prince. Academy Awards '89: Best Art Direction/Set Decoration. *FOX, WAR*

Batman and Robin 🐾🐾 1997 (PG-13) Includes lots of flash but, as usual, not much substance in this fourth adventure, which features a less angst-ridden caped crusader in the charming persona of Clooney. O'Donnell, who apparently knows a good gig when he's got one, returns as Robin. They must battle evil industrialist, Mr. Freeze (an impressively costumed Schwarzenegger), and his partner-with-the-deadly-kiss (but what a way to go!), Poison Ivy (Thurman), who have plans to freeze Gotham City. Our heroes have some additional help in the person of Batgirl (Silverstone), who's now butler Alfred's (Gough) ward (she was Commissioner Gordon's daughter in the comics). Story's simplified but the secondary characters still get lost in the crowd. Director Schumacher's already agreed to helm a fifth film although the comic book hero's more fanatic followers keep complaining about the films' camp, high-gloss tone. **CW:** Strong stylized action and some innuendos. 125m/C VHS, LV, Closed Caption, DVD. George Clooney, Chris O'Donnell, Arnold Schwarzenegger, Uma Thurman, Alicia Silverstone, Michael Gough, Pat Hingle, John Glover, Elle Macpherson, Vivica A. Fox, Vendela Thommessen, Jeep Swenson; **D:** Joel Schumacher; **W:** Joel Schumacher, Akiva Goldsman; **C:** Stephen Goldblatt; **M:** Elliot Goldenthal. Golden Raspberry Awards '97: Worst Supporting Actress (Silverstone); Nominations: Golden Raspberry Awards '97: Best Song ("The End is The Beginning is The End"), Worst Picture, Worst Remake/Sequel, Worst Supporting Actor (O'Donnell, Schwarzenegger), Worst Supporting Actress (Thurman), Worst Director (Schumacher), Worst Screenplay. *WAR*

Batman Forever 🐾🐾🐾 1995 (PG-13) Holy franchise, Batman! Third-time actioner considerably lightens up Tim Burton's dark vision for a more family-oriented Caped Crusader (now played by Kilmer, who fills out lip requirement nicely). The Boy Wonder also makes a first-time appearance in the bulked-up form of O'Donnell, a street-smart Robin with revenge on his mind. Naturally, the villains still steal the show in the personas of maniacal Carrey (the Riddler) and the sartorially splendid Jones as Harvey "Two-Face" Dent. Rounding out this charismatic cast is Kidman's slinky psychologist Chase Meridian, who's eager to find the man inside the bat (and who can blame her). Lots of splashy toys for the boys and awe-inspiring sets to show you where the money went. A Gotham City gas that did $53 million at it's opening weekend boxoffice—breaking the "Jurassic Park" record, testimony to the power of aggressive marketing. **CW:** Strong stylized action. 121m/C VHS, LV, Closed Caption, DVD. Val Kilmer, Tommy Lee Jones, Jim Carrey, Chris O'Donnell, Nicole Kidman, Drew Barrymore, Debi Mazar, Michael Gough, Pat Hingle; **D:** Joel Schumacher; **W:** Janet Scott Batchler, Akiva Golds-

man, Lee Batchler; **C:** Stephen Goldblatt; **M:** Elliot Goldenthal. Blockbuster Entertainment Awards '96: Action Actress, Theatrical (Kidman); Nominations: Academy Awards '95: Best Cinematography, Best Sound; Golden Globe Awards '96: Best Song ("Hold Me, Thrill Me, Kiss Me, Kill Me"); MTV Movie Awards '96: Most Desirable Male (Kilmer), Best Villain (Carrey, Jones), Best Song ("Kiss from a Rose", "Hold Me, Thrill Me, Kiss Me, Kill Me"). *WAR*

Batman: Mask of the Phantasm 🐾🐾½ *Batman: The Animated Movie* 1993 (PG) Based on the Fox television series with the animated Batman fending off old enemy the Joker, new enemy the Phantasm, and dreaming of his lost first love. Cartoon film noir set in the 1940s but filled with '90s sarcasm. Complicated storyline with a stylish dark look may be lost on the kiddies but adults will stay awake. 77m/C VHS, LV, Letterbox, Closed Caption. **D:** Eric Radomski, Bruce W. Timm; **W:** Michael Reeves, Alan Burnett, Paul Dini, Martin Pako; **M:** Shirley Walker; **V:** Kevin Conroy, Dana Delany, Mark Hamill, Stacy Keach, Hart Bochner, Abe Vigoda, Efrem Zimbalist Jr., Dick Miller. *WAR*

Batman Returns 🐾🐾½ 1992 (PG-13) More of the same from director Burton, with Batman more of a supporting role overshadowed by provocative villains. DeVito is the cruelly misshapen Penguin who seeks to rule over Gotham City; Pfeiffer is the exotic and dangerous Catwoman—who has more than a passing purr-sonal interest in Batman; Walken is the maniacal tycoon Max Shreck. Pfeiffer fares best in her wickedly sexy role and second-skin costume (complete with bullwhip). Plot is secondary to special effects and nightmarish settings. Despite a big budget, this grandiose sequel is of the love it or leave it variety. 126m/C VHS, Closed Caption. Michael Keaton, Danny DeVito, Michelle Pfeiffer, Christopher Walken, Michael Gough, Michael Murphy, Cristi Conaway, Pat Hingle, Vincent Schiavelli, Jan Hooks, Paul (Pee Wee Herman) Reubens, Andrew Bryniarski; **D:** Tim Burton; **W:** Daniel Waters; **C:** Stefan Czapsky; **M:** Danny Elfman. Nominations: Academy Awards '92: Best Makeup, Best Visual Effects. *WAR*

Baton Rouge 🐾🐾 1988 Gigolo Antonio (Banderas) gets together with psychiatrist Anao (Abril) in a scheme to seduce one of her patients, the wealthy Isabel (Maura), who suffers from terrible nightmares. They plan to kill her wealthy ex-husband and accuse her of the crime in order to get her fortune. But there's an elaborate doublecross and things go back for all concerned. The spanish trio, all veterans of director Pedro Almodovar's films, certainly know how to steam up the screen. Spanish with subtitles. 90m/C VHS. *SP* Antonio Banderas, Victoria Abril, Carmen Maura; **D:** Rafael Moleon; **W:** Rafael Moleon, Augustin Diaz Yanes; **C:** Angel Fernandez. *NYF, FCT*

*batteries not included 🐾🐾½ 1987 (PG) As a real estate developer fights to demolish a New York tenement, the five remaining residents are aided by tiny metal visitors from outer space in their struggle to save their home. Each resident gains a renewed sense of life in this sentimental, wholesome family film produced by Spielberg. Cronyn and Tandy keep the schmaltz from getting out of hand. Neat little space critters. 107m/C VHS, Beta, LV. Hume Cronyn, Jessica Tandy, Frank McRae, Michael Carmine, Elizabeth Pena, Dennis Boutsikaris; **D:** Matthew Robbins; **W:** Matthew Robbins, Brad Bird, Brent Maddock, S.S. Wilson; **M:** James Horner. *USH*

Battle Beneath the Earth 🐾🐾 1968 The commies try to undermine democracy once again when American scientists discover a Chinese plot to invade the U.S. via a series of underground tunnels. Perhaps a tad jingoistic. 112m/C VHS, Beta. **GB** Kerwin Mathews, Peter Arne, Viviane Ventura, Robert Ayres; **D:** Montgomery Tully. *MGM*

Battle Beyond the Stars 🐾🐾½ 1980 (PG) The planet Akir must be defended against alien rapscallions in this intergalactic Corman creation. Sayles authored the screenplay and co-authored the story on which it was based. 105m/C VHS, Beta, LV. Richard Thomas, Robert Vaughn, George

Peppard, Sybil Danning, Sam Jaffe, John Saxon, Darlanne Fluegel; *D:* Jimmy T. Murakami; *W:* John Sayles; *M:* James Horner. *VES, ART*

Battle Beyond the Sun 🎬🎬 1963 Former Russian movie "Nebo Zowet" is Americanized. Everyone is trying to send a mission to Mars. Roger Corman was the producer, Thomas Colchart is a pseudonym for Francis Ford Coppola. **75m/C VHS.** Edd Perry, Arla Powell, Bruce Hunter, Andy Stewart; *D:* Francis Ford Coppola; *M:* Les Baxter. *NOS, SNC*

Battle Circus 🎬½ 1953 Sappy drama casts Bogart as a surgeon at a M*A*S*H unit during the Korean War. Allyson is a combat nurse who finds love amongst the harsh reality of a war zone. Bogart was badly miscast and his performance proves it. Weak script and uninspired performances don't help this depressing story. **90m/B VHS, Closed Caption.** Humphrey Bogart, June Allyson, Keenan Wynn, Robert Keith, William Campbell; *D:* Richard Brooks; *W:* Richard Brooks; *C:* John Alton. *MGM*

Battle Cry 🎬🎬🎬 1955 A group of U.S. Marines train, romance, and enter battle in WWII. Based on the novel by Leon Uris. Part of the "A Night at the Movies" series, this tape simulates a 1955 movie evening, with a cartoon, "Speedy Gonzales," a newsreel, and coming attractions for "Mr. Roberts" and "East of Eden." **169m/C VHS, Beta, LV, Letterbox, Closed Caption.** Van Heflin, Aldo Ray, Mona Freeman, Tab Hunter, Dorothy Malone, Anne Francis, James Whitmore, Raymond Massey; *D:* Raoul Walsh. Nominations: Academy Awards '55: Best Original Dramatic/Comedy Score. *WAR*

Battle for the Planet of the Apes 🎬🎬 1973 (G) A tribe of human atomic bomb mutations are out to make life miserable for the peaceful ape tribe. The story is told primarily in flashback with the opening and closing sequences taking place in the year 2670 A.D. Final chapter in the five-movie simian saga. **96m/C VHS, Beta, Closed Caption.** Roddy McDowall, Lew Ayres, John Huston, Paul Williams, Claude Akins, Severn Darden, Natalie Trundy; *D:* J. Lee Thompson; *W:* John W. Corrington, Joyce H. Corrington. *FOX*

Battle Hell 🎬🎬 *Yangtse Incident* 1956 The true story of how a British ship was attacked by the Chinese Peoples Liberation Army on the Yangtze River in 1949. **112m/B VHS, Beta.** *GB* Richard Todd, Akim Tamiroff, Keye Luke; *D:* Michael Anderson Sr. *NO*

Battle Hymn 🎬🎬½ 1957 After accidentally bombing an orphanage as a WWII fighter pilot, Dean Hess (Hudson) becomes a minister. He returns to the Air Force in 1950 to train Korean pilots in Seoul and winds up building a home for the local orphans. True story on which the real Hess served as technical advisor. **109m/C VHS, Closed Caption.** Rock Hudson, Dan Duryea, Martha Hyer, Anna Kashfi, Don DeFore, Jock Mahoney, Carl Benton Reid, Alan Hale Jr., Richard Loo, Philip Ahn; *D:* Douglas Sirk; *W:* Charles Grayson, Vincent B. Evans; *C:* Russell Metty; *M:* Frank Skinner. *USH*

The Battle of Algiers 🎬🎬🎬½ 1966 Famous, powerful, award-winning film depicting the uprisings against French Colonial rule in 1954 Algiers. A seminal documentary-style film which makes most political films seem ineffectual by comparison in its use of non-professional actors, gritty photography, realistic violence, and a boldly propagandistic sense of social outrage. **123m/B VHS, Beta, LV.** *AL IT* Yacef Saadi, Jean Martin, Brahim Haggiag, Tommaso Neri, Samia Kerbash, Fawzia el Kader, Michele Kerbash, Mohamed Ben Kassen; *D:* Gillo Pontecorvo; *W:* Franco Solinas; *M:* Ennio Morricone. Venice Film Festival '66: Best Film; Nominations: Academy Awards '66: Best Foreign Language Film; Academy Awards '68: Best Director (Pontecorvo), Best Story & Screenplay. *IHF, TPV*

The Battle of Austerlitz 🎬🎬 *Austerlitz* 1960 (PG) Ambitious but numbing costume drama about the events leading up to the epic battle between Napoleon and the overwhelming forces of the Czar and the Austrian Emperor at Austerlitz. Napoleon won. Film has been drastically cut from original 166 minute release. Watch director

Gance's silent version, "Napoleon," for a truly epic experience. **123m/C VHS.** *FR IT YU* Claudia Cardinale, Martine Carol, Leslie Caron, Vittorio De Sica, Jean Marais, Ettore Manni, Jack Palance, Orson Welles; *D:* Abel Gance. *ART, TPV*

The Battle of Blood Island 🎬 1960 Two G.I.s, one Christian and one Jewish, face death at the hands of the Japanese during WWII. Still, they bicker incessantly before finally pulling together to save themselves. **64m/B VHS, Beta.** Richard Devon, Ron Kennedy; *D:* Joel Rapp. *NOS, SNC*

Battle of Britain 🎬🎬 1969 (G) A powerful retelling of the most dramatic aerial combat battle of WWII, showing how the understaffed Royal Air Force held off the might of the German Luftwaffe. **132m/C VHS, Beta, LV, Letterbox, Closed Caption.** Michael Caine, Laurence Olivier, Trevor Howard, Kenneth More, Christopher Plummer, Robert Shaw, Susannah York, Ralph Richardson, Curt Jurgens, Michael Redgrave, Nigel Patrick, Edward Fox; *D:* Guy Hamilton; *C:* Frederick A. (Freddie) Young. *MGM, FOX*

Battle of China 1944 A look at the people, culture, and industry of China, and Japan's total commitment to conquer the country during WWII, through authentic newsreel footage. **67m/B VHS, Beta.** *D:* Frank Capra. *MPI, MRV, HHT*

The Battle of El Alamein 🎬🎬 1968 Action filled movie about the alliance of Italy and Germany in a war against the British, set in a North African desert in the year 1942. **105m/C VHS, Beta.** *IT FR* Frederick Stafford, Ettore Manni, Robert Hossein, Michael Rennie, George Hilton, Ira Furstenberg; *D:* Calvin Jackson Padget. *CNG, MRV, GEM*

Battle of Elderbush Gulch 1913 An ancient pioneering western short famous for innocently employing the now-established cliches of bad guy, good guy, and helpless frontier heroine. One of Gish's first films. **22m/B VHS, Beta.** Lillian Gish; *D:* D.W. Griffith. *VCN, PYR, GVV*

Battle of Neretva 🎬🎬 1969 During WWII, Yugoslav partisans are facing German and Italian troops and local Chetniks as they battle for freedom. Big budget war film lost continuity with U.S. cut. **106m/C VHS.** *YU* Yul Brynner, Curt Jurgens, Orson Welles, Hardy Kruger, Franco Nero, Sergei Bondarchuk; *D:* Veljko Bulajic. Nominations: Academy Awards '69: Best Foreign Language Film. *REP*

The Battle of Russia 1944 Hitler's forces are victorious in Moscow and Leningrad but are thoroughly defeated at the battle of Stalingrad. Authentic newsreel footage. **83m/B VHS, Beta.** *D:* Frank Capra. *HHT, MRV, CCB*

Battle of the Bulge 🎬🎬 1965 A recreation of the famous offensive by Nazi Panzer troops on the Belgian front during 1944-45, an assault that could have changed the course of WWII. **141m/C VHS, Beta, LV, Letterbox, Closed Caption.** Henry Fonda, Robert Shaw, Robert Ryan, Dana Andrews, Telly Savalas, Ty Hardin, Pier Angeli, George Montgomery, Charles Bronson; *D:* Ken Annakin; *W:* Philip Yordan; *C:* Jack Hildyard. *WAR*

Battle of the Bullies woof! 1985 A made-for-television special about an unsalvageable nerd who plots a high-tech revenge upon a slew of high school bullies. **45m/C VHS, Beta.** Manny Jacobs, Christopher Barnes, Sarah Inglis.

Battle of the Commandos 🎬 *Legion of the Damned* 1971 A tough Army colonel leads a group of convicts on a dangerous mission to destroy a German-built cannon before it's used against the Allied Forces. **94m/C VHS.** *IT* Jack Palance, Curt Jurgens, Thomas Hunter, Robert Hunter; *D:* Umberto Lenzi. *REP*

Battle of the Eagles 🎬½ 1981 Follows the true adventures of the "Partisan Squadron," the courageous airmen known as the "Knights of the Sky" during WWII in Yugoslavia. **102m/C VHS, Beta.** Bekim Fehmiu, George Taylor, Gloria Samara, Frank Phillips; *D:* Tom Raymonth. *NO*

The Battle of the Japan Sea 🎬🎬 1970 (G) A Japanese epic, dubbed in English, centering around the historic WWII battle between Japan and Russia. **120m/C VHS, Beta.** *JP* Toshiro Mifune. *VCD*

The Battle of the Sexes 🎬🎬🎬 1960 Sophisticated British comedy has mild-mannered Sellers trying to prevent a business takeover by the brash American Cummings. A good supporting cast and the impeccable Sellers make this one unique. Adapted from the James Thurber short story "The Catbird Seat." **88m/B VHS, Beta.** *GB* Peter Sellers, Robert Morley, Constance Cummings, Jameson Clark, Ernest Thesiger, Donald Pleasence, Moultrie Kelsall, Alex Mackenzie, Roddy McMillan, Michael Goodliffe, Norman MacOwen, William Mervyn; *D:* Charles Crichton; *W:* Monja Danischewsky; *C:* Freddie Francis; *M:* Stanley Black. *MRV*

Battle of the Worlds 🎬 *Il Pianeta Degli Uomini Spenti; Planet of the Lifeless Men* 1961 Typical low-budget science fiction. A scientist tries to stop an alien planet from destroying the Earth. Even an aging Rains can't help this one. Poorly dubbed in English. **84m/C VHS.** *IT* Claude Rains, Maya Brent, Bill Carter, Marina Orsini, Jacqueline Derval; *D:* Anthony (Antonio Margheriti) Dawson. *SNC, NO*

Battle of Valiant 🎬 1963 Thundering hordes of invading barbarians trample the splendor of ancient Rome beneath their grimy sandals. **90m/C VHS, Beta.** Gordon Mitchell, Ursula Davis, Massimo Serato; *D:* John Gentil. *NO*

Battle Shock 🎬½ *A Woman's Devotion; War Shock* 1956 Painter is accused of murdering a cantina waitress while on his honeymoon in Mexico. **88m/C VHS.** Ralph Meeker, Janice Rule, Paul Henreid; *D:* Paul Henreid; *M:* Les Baxter. *REP*

Battleforce 🎬 *The Battle of the Mareth Line; The Greatest Battle* 1978 Exciting battle scenes lose their power in the confusion of this mixed-up WWII film about Rommel's last days. Dubbed sequences, news-reel vignettes and surprise performances by big name stars are incomprehensibly glued together. **97m/C VHS, Beta.** *GE YU* Henry Fonda, Stacy Keach, Helmut Berger, Samantha Eggar, Giuliano Gemma, John Huston; *D:* Umberto Lenzi. *QVD, TLF*

Battleground 🎬🎬🎬 1949 A tightly conceived post-WWII character drama, following a platoon of American soldiers through the Battle of the Bulge. Available in a Colorized version. **118m/B VHS, Beta, LV, Closed Caption.** Van Johnson, John Hodiak, James Whitmore, George Murphy, Ricardo Montalban, Marshall Thompson, Jerome Courtland, Don Taylor, Bruce Cowling, Leon Ames, Douglas Fowley, Richard Jaeckel, Scotty Beckett; *D:* William A. Wellman; *W:* Robert Pirosh; *C:* Paul Vogel. Academy Awards '49: Best Black and White Cinematography, Best Story & Screenplay; Golden Globe Awards '50: Best Screenplay, Best Supporting Actor (Whitmore); Nominations: Academy Awards '49: Best Director (Wellman), Best Film Editing, Best Picture, Best Supporting Actor (Whitmore). *MGM*

The Battleship Potemkin 🎬🎬🎬🎬 *Potemkin; Bronenosets Potemkin* 1925 Eisenstein's best work documents mutiny aboard the Russian battleship Potemkin in 1905 which led to a civilian uprising against the Czar in Odessa, and the resulting crackdown by troops loyal to the Czar. Beautiful cinematography, especially the use of montage sequences, changed filmmaking. In particular, a horrifying sequence depicting the slaughter of civilians on an Odessa beach by soldiers coming down the stairs leading to it is exceptional; many movies pay homage to this scene including "The Untouchables" and "Love and Death." Viewers should overlook obvious Marxist overtones and see this film for what it is: a masterpiece. **71m/B VHS, Beta, LV.** *RU* Alexander Antonov, Vladimir Barsky, Grigori Alexandrov, Mikhail Gomorov, Sergei Eisenstein; *D:* Sergei Eisenstein; *M:* Eric Allaman. *REP, MRV, NOS*

Battlestar Galactica 🎬🎬½ 1978 (PG) Plot episode of the sci-fi television series which was later released in the theatres. The crew of the spaceship Galactica must battle their robot enemies in an attempt to reach Earth. Contains special effects designed by John "Otal Wars" Dykstra. Individual episodes of the series are also available. **125m/C VHS, Beta, LV.** Lorne Greene, Dirk Benedict, Maren Jensen, Jane Seymour, Patrick Macnee, Terry Carter, John Colicos, Richard A. Colla, Laurette Spang, Richard Hatch; *D:* Richard A. Colla. *USH, MOV*

Battling Bunyon 🎬🎬½ 1924 A wily youngster becomes a comedy boxer for profit, and eventually gets fed up and battles the champ. Silent. **71m/B VHS, Beta.** Chester Conklin, Wesley Barry, Mollie Malone, Jackie Fields. *GPV, VYY*

Battling Butler 🎬🎬½ 1926 Rich young Keaton tries to impress a young lady by impersonating a boxer. All goes well until he has to fight the real thing. Mostly charming if uneven; one of Keaton's more unusual efforts, thought to be somewhat autobiographical. Silent. **70m/B VHS.** Buster Keaton, Sally O'Neil, Snitz Edwards, Francis McDonald, Mary O'Brien, Tom Wilson, Walter James; *D:* Buster Keaton. *NO*

Battling for Baby 🎬🎬 1992 It's the war of the Grandmas. New mother Katherine decides to return to work and both her mother and mother-in-law want to look after the little tyke. Silly made-for-TV fluff. **93m/C VHS, Closed Caption.** Courteney Cox, Suzanne Pleshette, Debbie Reynolds, John Terlesky, Doug McClure, Leigh Lawson, Mary Jo Catlett; *D:* Art Wolff; *W:* Walter Lockwood, Nancy Silvers. *TTC*

Battling Marshal 🎬½ 1948 Fast-moving action western starring Carson. **52m/B VHS, Beta.** Sunset Carson, Lee Roberts; *D:* Oliver Drake. *VCN*

Battling Orioles 1924 The once scrappy baseball team is now a bunch of grumpy old men, that is until Glenn whips them into shape. Silent. **58m/B VHS, Beta, 8mm.** Glenn Tryon, Blanche Mehaffey, Noah Young; *D:* Ted Wilde, Fred Guiol. *GVV*

Battling Outlaws 🎬½ 194? Western featuring the American cowboy Bob Steele. **64m/B VHS, Beta.** Bob Steele. *NOS, VCN*

Battling with Buffalo Bill 1931 Twelve episodes of the vintage serial concerning the exploits of the legendary Indian fighter. **180m/B VHS, Beta.** Tom Tyler, Rex Bell, Franklyn Farnum. *VCN*

The Bawdy Adventures of Tom Jones 🎬½ 1976 (R) An exploitive extension of the Fielding novel about the philandering English lad, with plenty of soft-core skin and lewdness. **89m/C VHS, Beta.** *GB* Joan Collins, Trevor Howard, Terry-Thomas, Arthur Lowe, Murray Melvin; *D:* Cliff Owen. *USH*

Baxter 🎬🎬½ 1989 A bull terrier lives his life with three different sets of masters. He examines all of humankind's worst faults and the viewer quickly realizes that Baxter's life depends on his refusal to obey like a good dog should. Based on the novel by Ken Greenhall. Funny, sometimes erotic, quirky comedy. In French with English subtitles. **82m/C VHS, LV.** *FR* Lisa Delamare, Jean Mercure, Jacques Spiesser, Catherine Ferran, Jean-Paul Roussillon, Sabrina Leurquin; *D:* Jerome Boivin; *W:* Jerome Boivin, Jacques Audiard; *M:* Marc Hillman, Patrick Roffe. *FXL, PMS*

The Bay Boy 🎬🎬½ 1985 (R) Set in the 1930s in Nova Scotia, this period piece captures the coming-of-age of a rural teenage boy. Young Sutherland's adolescent angst becomes a more difficult struggle when he witnesses a murder, and is tormented by the secret. **107m/C VHS, Beta, LV, Closed Caption.** *CA* Liv Ullmann, Kiefer Sutherland, Peter Donat, Matthieu Carriere, Joe MacPherson, Isabelle Mejias, Alan Scarfe, Chris Wiggins, Leah K. Pinsent; *D:* Daniel Petrie; *M:* Claude Bolling. Genie Awards '85: Best Film, Best Supporting Actor (Scarfe). *ORI*

Bayou Romance 🎬 1986 Painter inherits a Louisiana plantation, moves in, and falls in love with a young gypsy. **90m/C Beta.** Annie Potts, Michael Ansara, Barbara Horan.

Baywatch the Movie: Forbidden Paradise 🎬🎬½ 1995 (PG) The "Baywatch" babes and their fellow lifesaving hunks-in-trunks head off to Hawaii to study the latest search and rescue techniques from the state's premier lifeguard team. **90m/C VHS.** David Hasselhoff, Pamela Anderson, Alexandra Paul, Yasmine Bleeth, David Charvet, Gregory Alan-Williams, Jeremy Jackson; *D:* Douglas Schwartz. *ART*

Be My Valentine, Charlie Brown 1975 The Peanuts gang endures the follies of the heart on St. Valentine's Day. Animated. **30m/C VHS, Beta.** *D:* Phil Roman.

Be the Man 1998 Cable TV character Super Dave Osborne (Einstein) comes to the big screen as Super Dave comes out of retirement for one last megastunt. He and protege Van Wormer plot a death-defying leap to raise money for neighbor Carides who has an ill son (Lindner). Not yet reviewed. **?m/C VHS.** Bob Einstein, Gia Carides, Carl Michael Lindner, Steve Van Wormer, Dan Hedaya; *D:* Peter Macdonald; *W:* Lorne Cameron, Don Lake. *NYR*

Beach Babes from Beyond Infinity 🎬 1993 (R) "HOT. TAN. ALIEN." Three words that would send shivers through the body of any red-blooded American boy. And as if alien silicone isn't enough to draw a crowd, this piece of fluff also features the relatives of big name stars hoping to cash in on the family name. Typical Hollywood cheese and sleaze should be fun for those who still can't get this kind of quality entertainment on cable. *CW:* Nudity and stong sexuality. **78m/C VHS, Closed Caption.** Joe Estevez, Don Swayze, Joey Travolta, Burt Ward, Jacqueline Stallone, Linnea Quigley, Sara Bellomo, Tamara Landry, Nicole Posey; *D:* Ellen Cabot. *PAR*

Beach Blanket Bingo 🎬🎬🎬 1965 Fifth entry in the "Beach Party" series (after "Pajama Party") is by far the best and has achieved near-cult status. Both Funicello and Avalon are back, but this time a very young Evans catches Avalon's eye. Throw in a mermaid, some moon-doggies, skydiving, sizzling beach parties, and plenty of nostalgic golly-gee-whiz fun and you have the classic '60s beach movie. Totally implausible, but that's half the fun when the sun-worshipping teens become involved in a kidnapping and occasionally break into song. Followed by "How to Stuff a Wild Bikini." 🎵Beach Blanket Bingo; The Cycle Set; Fly Boy; The Good Times; I Am My Ideal; I Think You Think; It Only Hurts When I Cry; New Love; You'll Never Change Him. **96m/C VHS, Beta, LV.** Frankie Avalon, Annette Funicello, Linda Evans, Don Rickles, Buster Keaton, Paul Lynde, Harvey Lembeck, Deborah Walley, John Ashley, Jody McCrea, Marta Kristen, Timothy Carey, Earl Wilson, Bobbi Shaw; *D:* William Asher; *W:* William Asher, Sher Townsend, Leo Townsend; *M:* Les Baxter. *NO*

Beach Girls 🎬 1982 (R) Three voluptuous coeds intend to re-educate a bookish young man and the owner of a beach house. **91m/C VHS, Beta, LV.** Debra Blee, Val Kline, Jeana Tomasina, Adam Roarke; *D:* Patrice Townsend. *PAR*

The Beach Girls and the Monster 🎬 *Monster in the Surf* 1965 Here's one on the cutting edge of genre bending: while it meticulously maintains the philosophical depth and production values of 60s beach bimbo fare, it manages to graft successfuly with the heinous critter from the sea genre to produce a hybrid horror with acres o' flesh. **70m/B VHS.** Jon Hall, Sue Casey, Walker Edmiston; *D:* Jon Hall; *M:* Frank Sinatra Jr. *SNC, EEL*

Beach House 🎬 1982 In this boring comedy, adolescents frolic on the beach, get inebriated, and listen to rock 'n' roll. **76m/C VHS, Beta.** Kathy McNeil, Richard Duggan, Ileana Seidel, John Cosola, Spence Waugh, Paul Anderson, John A. Gallagher; *W:* Marino Amaruso. *NO*

Beach Party 🎬🎬 1963 Started the "Beach Party" series with the classic Funicello/Avalon combo. Scientist Cummings studying the mating habits of teenagers intrudes on a group of surfers, beach bums, and bikers, to his lasting regret. Typical beach party bingo, with sand, swimsuits, singing, dancing, and bare minimum in way of a plot. Followed by "Muscle Beach Party." 🎵Beach Party; Don't Stop Now; Promise Me Anything; Secret Surfin' Spot; Surfin' and a Swingin'; Treat Him Nicely. **101m/C VHS, Beta.** Frankie Avalon, Annette Funicello, Harvey Lembeck, Robert Cummings, Dorothy Malone, Morey Amsterdam, Jody McCrea, John Ashley, Candy Johnson, Dolores Wells, Yvette Vickers, Eva Six; *D:* William Asher; *W:* Lou Rusoff; *M:* Les Baxter. *NO*

Beachcomber 🎬🎬🎬 *Vessel of Wrath* 1938 Comedy set in the Dutch East Indies about a shiftless beachcomber (Laughton) who falls in love with a missionary's prim sister (Lanchester), as she attempts to reform him. The real-life couple of Laughton and Lanchester are their usual pleasure to watch. Remade in 1954. Story by W. Somerset Maugham. **88m/B VHS, Beta.** *GB* Charles Laughton, Elsa Lanchester, Robert Newton, Tyrone Guthrie; *D:* Erich Pommer. *NOS, MRV, DVT*

Beaches 🎬🎬🎬½ 1988 (PG-13) Based on the novel by Iris Rainer Dart about two girls whose friendship survived the test of time. The friendship is renewed once more when one of the now middle-aged women learns that she is dying slowly of a fatal disease. **123m/C VHS, Beta, LV, 8mm.** Bette Midler, Barbara Hershey, John Heard, Spalding Gray, Lainie Kazan, James Read, Mayim Bialik; *D:* Garry Marshall; *W:* Mary Agnes Donoghue; *C:* Dante Spinotti; *M:* Georges Delerue. Nominations: Academy Awards '88: Best Art Direction/Set Decoration. *TOU*

Beaks: The Movie woof! *Birds of Prey* 1987 (R) Two television reporters try to figure out why birds of prey are suddenly attacking humans. Owes nothing to Hitchcock's "The Birds." **86m/C VHS, Beta.** Christopher Atkins, Michelle Johnson; *D:* Rene Cardona Jr. *ART*

Bean 🎬🎬🎬 1997 (PG-13) Big screen adaption of rubber-faced Atkinson's Mr. Bean character finds our disaster-magnet hero working as a guard in London's National Gallery. When a famous painting is purchased by a museum in L.A., the Gallery's curators jump at the chance to send Bean along with the painting as an "expert," although he is nearly mute and definitely not qualified. David (MacNicol), the American curator, invites him to stay at his house, much to the dismay of his wife and children. Bean, of course, wrecks the painting, ruins David's marriage and career, and generally makes an ass out of himself. He then resourcefully (and sometimes accidentally) puts things right. Atkinson proves himself a master of the almost lost art of slapstick comedy. *CW:* Moments of risque humor. **92m/C VHS.** *GB* Rowan Atkinson, Peter MacNicol, Pamela Reed, Harris Yulin, Burt Reynolds, Larry Drake, Johnny Galecki, Richard Gant, Tom McGowan, Dakin Matthews, Peter Capaldi, Sandra Oh, Tricia Vessey, Peter Egan; *D:* Mel Smith; *W:* Richard Curtis, Robin Driscoll; *C:* Francis Kenny; *M:* Howard Goodall. *PGV*

Beanstalk 🎬🎬½ 1994 (PG) Modern-day version of the fairytale finds young Jack Taylor (Daniels) scheming to make it big to help his hardworking single mom. He meets up with a wacky scientist (Kidder), who gives Jack some recently discovered seeds that naturally grow into an enormous beanstalk. And what does Jack find when he climbs the beanstalk—an entire family of silly giants. **80m/C VHS, Beta, Closed Caption.** J.D. Daniels, Margot Kidder, Richard Moll, Amy Stock-Poynton, Patrick Renna, Richard Paul, David Naughton, Stuart Pankin, Cathy McAuley; *D:* Michael Paul Davis; *W:* Michael Paul Davis; *M:* Kevin Bassinson. *PAR*

The Bear 🎬🎬🎬 1989 (PG) Breathtaking, effortlessly entertaining family film about an orphaned bear cub tagging after a grown male and dealing with hunters. The narrative is essentially from the cub's point of view, with very little dialogue. A huge money-maker in Europe. Based on a novel by James Oliver Curwood. **92m/C VHS, Beta, LV, Letterbox, Closed Caption.** *FR* Jack Wallace, Tcheky Karyo, Andre Lacombe; *D:* Jean-Jacques Annaud; *W:* Gerard Brach, Michael Kane; *C:* Philippe Rousselot; *M:* Bill Conti. Nominations: Academy Awards '89: Best Film Editing. *COL, RDG, HMV*

Bear Island 🎬½ **1980 (PG)** Group of secret agents cleverly disguising themselves as U.N. weather researchers converge upon Bear Island in search of a Nazi U-Boat. Looks like rain. **118m/C VHS, Beta.** Donald Sutherland, Richard Widmark, Barbara Parkins, Vanessa Redgrave, Christopher Lee, Lloyd Bridges; **D:** Don Sharp. *NO*

The Bears & I 🎬🎬 **1974 (G)** A young Vietnam war helps Indians regain their land rights while raising three bear cubs. Beautiful photography in this Disney production. **89m/C VHS.** Patrick Wayne, Chief Dan George, Andrew Duggan, Michael Ansara; **D:** Bernard McEveety; **M:** Buddy Baker. *DIS*

The Beast 🎬🎬½ *The Beast of War* **1988 (R)** Violent and cliche-driven war drama notable for its novel twist: wild Russian tank officer becomes lost in the Afghanistan wilderness while being tracked by Afghan rebels with revenge in mind. Filmed in the Israel desert and adapted by William Mastrosimone from his play. **93m/C VHS, Beta, Closed Caption.** George Dzundza, Jason Patric, Steven Bauer, Stephen Baldwin, Don Harvey, Kabir Bedi, Erik Avari, Haim Gerafi; **D:** Kevin Reynolds; **W:** William Mastrosimone; **M:** Mark Isham. *COL*

The Beast 🎬🎬 **1996 (PG-13)** Peter Benchley once again terrorizes a coastal community wih a giant sea creature that preys on sailors and divers. When a poacher's attempts to capture the creature result in further disaster, a fishing boat captain, a Coast Guard officer, and a marine biologist set sail to kill the critter. **116m/C VHS, Closed Caption.** William L. Petersen, Karen Sillas, Charles Martin Smith, Ronald Guttman, Missy Crider, Sterling Macer, Denis Arndt, Larry Drake; **D:** Jeff Bleckner; **W:** J.B. White. *USH*

The Beast from Haunted Cave 🎬🎬 **1960** Gold thieves hiding in a wilderness cabin encounter a spiderlike monster. Surprisingly good performances from Sinatra (Frank's nephew) and Carol. Produced by Gene Corman, Roger's brother. **64m/B VHS.** Michael Forest, Sheila Carol, Frank Wolff, Richard Sinatra, Wally Campo; **D:** Monte Hellman; **W:** Charles B. Griffith. *DVT, MRV, SNC*

The Beast from 20,000 Fathoms 🎬🎬½ **1953** Atomic testing defrosts a giant dinosaur in the Arctic; the hungry monster proceeds onwards to its former breeding grounds, now New York City. Oft-imitated saurian-on-the-loose formula is still fun, brought to life by Ray Harryhausen special effects. Based loosely on the Ray Bradbury story "The Foghorn." **80m/B VHS, Beta, LV.** Paul Christian, Paula Raymond, Cecil Kellaway, Kenneth Tobey, Donald Woods, Lee Van Cleef, Steve Brodie, Mary Hill; **D:** Eugene Lourie; **W:** Fred Freiberger, Louis Morheim. *WAR, FCT, MLB*

Beast in the Cellar 🎬½ *Are You Dying Young Man?* **1970 (R)** Every family has something to hide, and in the case of two spinster sisters, it's their murderous inhuman brother, whom they keep chained in the cellar. Like all brothers, however, the "beast" rebels against his sisters' bossiness and escapes to terrorize their peaceful English countryside. The sisters' (Reid and Robson) performances aren't bad, but rest of effort is fairly disappointing. **85m/C VHS, Beta.** GB Beryl Reid, Flora Robson, T.P. McKenna; **D:** James Kelly. *NO*

Beast of Morocco 🎬🎬 *Hand of Night* **1966** Interesting vampire film about a Morrocan vampire princess who sets her sights on seducing a noted archaeologist. Of course his girlfriend ends up being abducted by the vampire's servant. **88m/C VHS.** GB William Sylvester, Alizia Gur, Terence de Marney. *SNC*

Beast of the Yellow Night woof! **1970 (R)** A dying soldier sells his soul to Satan at the close of WWII. Years later, existing without aging, he periodically turns into a cannibal monster. Although the first half is tedious, the monster turns things around when he finally shows up. Decent gore effects. **87m/C VHS, Beta.** PH John Ashley, Mary Wilcox, Eddie Garcia, Vic Diaz; **D:** Eddie Romero. *VCI, INC*

The Beast of Yucca Flats woof! **1961** A really cheap, quasi-nuclear protest film. A Russian scientist is chased by communist agents into a nuclear testing area and is caught in an atomic blast. As a result, he turns into a club-weilding monster. Voice over narration is used in lieu of dialogue as that process proved too expensive. **53m/B VHS.** Tor Johnson, Douglas Mellor, Larry Aten, Barbara Francis; **D:** Coleman Francis; **W:** Coleman Francis. *SNC, CNM, MLB*

The Beast that Killed Women 🎬🎬½ **1965** Colonists at a sunny Florida nudist camp have their beach party interrupted by an escaped gorilla. Director Mahon, in his first color effort, stretches this panicky moment into an hour of fleshy fun and games. **60m/C VHS. D:** Barry Mahon. *SMW, TPV*

The Beast with Five Fingers 🎬🎬½ **1946** After a pianist mysteriously dies and leaves his fortune to his private nurse, the occupants of his villa are terrorized by a creature that turns out to be the pianist's hand which was severed by his personal secretary (Lorre). Lorre is also terrorized by hallucinations of the hand, and no matter what he does to stop it (nail it to a desk, throw it in the fire, etc.), nothing can keep the hand from carrying out its mission. A creepy thriller with inventive shots of the severed hand. **88m/B VHS, Closed Caption.** Robert Alda, Andrea King, Peter Lorre, Victor Francen, J. Carrol Naish, Charles Dingle; **D:** Robert Florey; **W:** Curt Siodmak; **M:** Max Steiner. *MGM*

The Beast Within 🎬🎬 **1982 (R)** Young woman has the misfortune of being raped by an unseen creature in a Mississippi swamp. Seventeen years later, her son conceived from that hellish union begins to act quite strange, developing a penchant for shedding his skin before turning into an insect-like critter with a cannibalistic appetite. First film to use the air "bladder" type of prosthetic make-up popularized in later, and generally better, horror films. Contains some choice cuts in photo editing: the juxtaposition of hamburger and human "dead meat" is witty. Based on Edward Levy's 1981 novel. **98m/C VHS, Beta.** Ronny Cox, Bibi Besch, L.Q. Jones, Paul Clemens, Don Gordon, Katherine Moffat, John Dennis Johnston; **D:** Philippe Mora; **W:** Tom Holland; **C:** Jack L. Richards; **M:** Les Baxter. *MGM*

Beastmaster 🎬🎬 **1982 (PG)** Adventure set in a wild and primitive world. The Beastmaster is involved in a life-and-death struggle with overwhelming forces of evil. Campy neanderthal flesh flick. **119m/C VHS, Beta, LV.** Marc Singer, Tanya Roberts, Rip Torn, John Amos, Josh Milrad, Billy Jacoby; **D:** Don A. Coscarelli; **W:** Don A. Coscarelli; **C:** John Alcott. *MGM*

Beastmaster 2: Through the Portal of Time 🎬½ **1991 (PG-13)** This time the laughs are intentional as the Beastmaster follows an evil monarch through a dimensional gate to modern-day L.A., where the shopping is better for both trendy clothes and weapons. Fun for genre fans, with a behind-the-scenes featurette on the tape. **107m/C VHS, LV, Closed Caption.** Marc Singer, Kari Wuhrer, Sarah Douglas, Wings Hauser, James Avery, Robert Fieldsteel, Arthur Malet, Robert Z'Dar, Michael Berryman; **D:** Sylvio Tabet; **M:** Robert Folk. *REP*

Beastmaster 3: The Eye of Braxus 🎬🎬½ **1995 (PG)** Heroic hunk Dar the Beastmaster (Singer) returns to battle evil. Lord Agon (Warner) needs to obtain a jeweled eye that will bring the demon Braxus back to life—and he'll stop at nothing, including kidnapping Dar's brother King Tal (Van Dien), to reach his terrifying goal. But Dar isn't alone—he's got the bewitching sorceress Morgana (Down), tempting warrioress Shada (Hess), and loyal advisor Seth (Todd) to help him out. **92m/C VHS, LV, Closed Caption.** Marc Singer, David Warner, Lesley-Anne Down, Tony Todd, Caspar Van Dien, Keith Coulouris, Sandra Hess, Patrick Kilpatrick; **D:** Gabrielle Beaumont; **W:** David Wise; **C:** Barbara Claman; **M:** Jan Hammer. *USH*

Beasts 🎬 **1983** A young couple's plans for a romantic weekend in the Rockies are slightly changed when the pair are savagely attacked by wild beasts. **92m/C VHS, Beta.** Tom Babson, Kathy Christopher, Vern Potter.

The Beat 🎬 **1988** Unrealistic film about a bookish new kid who intercedes in the tension between two rival street gangs, changing their lives in his literary way. **101m/C VHS, Beta, LV.** John Savage, Kara Glover, Paul Dillon, David Jacobson, William McNamara; **D:** Peter Mones; **W:** Peter Mones; **M:** Carter Burwell. *ART, VES*

Beat Girl 🎬🎬 *Wild for Kicks* **1960** Pouty rebellious teen Jennifer (Hill) spends her days in art school and her nights at a London beat hangout. She's jealous when daddy (Farrar) marries sexy French Nichole (Adam) and plots to break them up. When Jennifer discovers Nichole's sordid past she winds up in a burlesque club, attracting the unsavory attentions of owner Kenny (Lee). Then Kenny winds up dead. Singer Adam Faith performs and Reed has a bit as a youthful tough. **85m/B VHS.** GB Gillian Hills, David Farrar, Noelle Adam, Christopher Lee, Shirley Anne Field, Oliver Reed; **D:** Edmond T. Greville; **M:** John Barry. *KIV, FCT, SNC*

Beat Street 🎬🎬½ **1984 (PG)** Intended as a quick cash-in on the break dancing trend, this essentially plotless musical features kids trying to break into local show biz with their rapping and dancing skills. Features the music of Afrika Bambaata and the Soul Sonic Force, Grand Master Melle Mel and the Furious Five, and others. ♫*Beat Street Breakdown; Baptize the Beat; Stranger in a Strange Land; Beat Street Strut; Us Girls; This Could Be the Night; Breakers Revenge; Tu Carino (Carmen's Theme); Frantic Situation.* **106m/C VHS, Beta, LV.** Rae Dawn Chong, Leon Grant, Saundra Santiago, Guy Davis, Jon Chardiet, Duane Jones, Kadeem Hardison; **D:** Stan Lathan; **W:** Andrew Davis. *VES, ART*

Beat the Devil 🎬🎬🎬 **1953** Each person on a slow boat to Africa has a scheme to beat the other passengers to the uranium-rich land that they all hope to claim. An unusual black comedy which didn't fare well when released, but over the years has come to be the epitome of spy-spoofs. **89m/C VHS, Beta, LV, Closed Caption.** Humphrey Bogart, Gina Lollobrigida, Peter Lorre, Robert Morley, Jennifer Jones, Edward Underdown, Ivor Barnard, Bernard Lee, Marco Tulli; **D:** John Huston; **W:** John Huston, Truman Capote; **C:** Oswald Morris. *MRV, NOS, COL*

Beatlemania! The Movie 🎬 *Beatlemania* **1981** Boring look at the Fab Four. Not the real Beatles, but impersonators who do a very inadequate job. Based on the equally disappointing stage show. **86m/C VHS, Beta, LV.** Mitch Weissman, Ralph Castelli, David Leon, Tom Teeley; **D:** Joseph Manduke. *IME*

The Beatniks 🎬 **1960** Story about the dark secrets of the beat generation in which a man is promised fame and fortune by an agent, but his dreams are dashed when his friend commits murder. A big waste of time. **78m/B VHS.** Tony Travis, Peter Breck, Karen Kadler, Joyce Terry; **D:** Paul Frees. *SNC, TPV*

Beatrice 🎬🎬🎬½ *La Passion Beatrice* **1988 (R)** In France during the Middle Ages, a barbaric soldier of the Hundred Years' War returns to his estate that his daughter has maintained, only to brutalize and abuse her. In French with English subtitles. **132m/C VHS, Beta, LV.** FR Julie Delpy, Bernard Pierre Donnadieu, Nils Tavernier; **D:** Bertrand Tavernier; **W:** Colo Tavernier O'Hagan; **C:** Bruno de Keyzer; **M:** Lili Boulanger. Cesar Awards '88: Best Costume Design. *NO*

Beau Brummel 🎬🎬½ **1924** The famous silent adaptation of the Clyde Fitch play about an ambitious English dandy's rise and fall. **80m/B VHS, Beta.** John Barrymore, Mary Astor, Willard Louis, Irene Rich, Carmel Myers, Alec B. Francis, William Humphreys; **D:** Harry Beaumont. *NOS, HHT, VYY*

Beau Brummel 🎬🎬🎬 1954 Lavish production casts Granger in the role of the rags-to-riches dandy and chief adviser to the Prince of Wales. Born into a life of poverty, George Bryan Brummel uses wit and intelligence to meet the vain Prince and ingratiate himself to the future king (George IV). He also manages to catch the eye of Taylor, who falls in love with him. Outstanding period piece cinematography, sets, and costumes. Shot on location in England's beautiful countryside, many of the interior shots are from a 15th-century mansion, Ockwell Manor, located near Windsor Castle. Remake of the 1924 silent film starring John Barrymore. Based on the play by Clyde Fitch. **113m/C VHS.** Stewart Granger, Elizabeth Taylor, Peter Ustinov, Robert Morley, James Donald, James Hayter, Rosemary Harris, Paul Rogers, Noel Willman, Peter Dyneley, Charles Carson; **D:** Curtis Bernhardt; **W:** Karl Tunberg; **C:** Oswald Morris. *MGM*

Beau Geste 🎬🎬🎬½ 1939 The classic Hollywood adventure film based on the Percival Christopher Wren story about three brothers who join the Foreign Legion after nobly claiming responsibility for a jewel theft they didn't commit. Once enlisted, they must face desert wars and the most despicable commanding officer ever, before clearing their family name. A rousing, much-copied epic. **114m/B VHS.** Gary Cooper, Ray Milland, Robert Preston, Brian Donlevy, Donald O'Connor, J. Carrol Naish, Susan Hayward, James Stephenson; **D:** William A. Wellman. Nominations: Academy Awards '39: Best Interior Decoration, Best Supporting Actor (Donlevy). *USH*

Beau Pere 🎬🎬🎬 *Stepfather* 1981 Bittersweet satiric romp from Blier about the war zone of modern romance, wherein a 30-year-old widower falls madly in love with his 14-year-old stepdaughter. Sharp-edged and daring. In French with subtitles. **125m/C VHS, Beta.** *FR* Patrick Dewaere, Nathalie Baye, Ariel Besse, Maurice Ronet; **D:** Bertrand Blier; **W:** Bertrand Blier; **C:** Sacha Vierny.

Beau Revel 🎬🎬🎬½ 1921 Critically acclaimed romantic drama of the silent era. A passionate dancing girl played by Vidor, one of the '20s more prolific romantic leads (and erstwhile wife of director King Vidor) is the object of romantic interest of a father and son, which leaves the threesome lovelorn, suicidal, and emotionally scarred. You might recognize Stone from his later role as Judge Hardy in the MGM "Hardy Family" series. **70m/B VHS, Beta.** Lewis Stone, Florence Vidor, Lloyd Hughes, Katherine Kirkham, William Conklin; **D:** John Wray. *GPV, FCT*

Beaumarchais the Scoundrel 🎬🎬½ *Beaumarchais L'Insolent* 1996 Adapted from an unpublished play by Sacha Guitry. Beautifully filmed romp of the social-climbing and political-spying gadfly Pierre Augustin Caron de Beaumarchais. Molinaro has simplified the fantastic life of the 18th-century dramatist, courtier, and watchmaker to Louis XV (and author of the comic masterpieces "The Barber of Seville" and "The Marriage of Figaro") but the result is still dizzying. French with subtitles. **100m/C VHS.** *FR* Fabrice Luchini, Jacques Weber, Michel Piccoli, Claire Nebout, Jean-Francois Balmer, Florence Thomassin, Michel Serrault, Dominique Besnehard, Jean-Claude Brialy, Murray Head, Jeff Nuttal, Jean Yanne, Manuel Blanc, Sandrine Kiberlain, Axelle Laffont; **D:** Edouard Molinaro; **W:** Edouard Molinaro, Jean-Claude Brisville; **C:** Michael Epp; **M:** Jean-Claude Petit. *NYF*

The Beautician and the Beast 🎬🎬 1997 (PG) Evita meets Lucille Ball when TV's "Nanny" enters Eastern Europe whining to conquer fictional "Slovetzia" royalty. Camp comedy casts Drescher as Joy, a beautician who becomes a local hero after a fire in her beauty class and is subsequently hired by a visiting emissary to tutor the children of despotic dictator Pochenko (Dalton). Overridingly well-known caricatures, loosely based on the fairy tale "Beauty and the Beast," as well as a host of old-time, culture clash movies ("The King and I," "Sound of Music"), where the humble nanny attempts to bring joy (get it?) into the life of a man who carries the weight of the world on his shoulders. Lensed in Prague inside a Gothic, 17th-century castle. Pleasant enough, if not original, time-killer. **105m/C VHS, Beta, Closed Caption.** Fran Drescher, Timothy Dalton, Ian McNeice, Patrick Malahide, Lisa Jakub, Michael Lerner, Phyllis Newman, Todd Graff; **D:** Ken Kwapis; **W:** Todd Graff; **C:** Peter Collister; **M:** Cliff Eidelman. Nominations: Golden Raspberry Awards '97: Worst Actress (Drescher). *PAR*

Beauties of the Night 🎬🎬 *Night Beauties; Les Belles de Nuit* 1952 Dreamy fantasy finds a shy music teacher (Philipe) escaping from his boring life into romantic adventures with beautiful women. But his dreams slowly turn nightmarish and he's forced to deal with reality—and real love. French with subtitles. **89m/B VHS.** *FR* Gerard Philipe, Gina Lollobrigida, Martine Carol, Magali Vendeuil, Paolo Stoppa, Raymond Bussieres, Raymond Cordy; **D:** Rene Clair; **W:** Rene Clair; **C:** Armand Thirard; **M:** Georges Van Parys. *WBF*

The Beautiful Blonde from Bashful Bend 🎬🎬½ 1949 Charming comedy-western gets better with age. Grable is the pistol packing mama mistaken for the new school teacher. Fun performances by all, especially Herbert. **77m/C VHS, LV, Closed Caption.** Betty Grable, Cesar Romero, Rudy Vallee, Olga San Juan, Hugh Herbert, Porter Hall, Sterling Holloway, El Brendel; **D:** Preston Sturges. *FOX*

Beautiful Dreamers 🎬½ 1992 (PG-13) Maurice Bucke is a young Canadian physician who runs the London Insane Asylum. After a chance meeting with poet Walt Whitman, both men discover their mutual outrage for current treatment of the mentally ill. Bucke persuades Whitman to visit his asylum in order to try Whitman's theory of human compassion on the asylum's inmates. However, Bucke runs into opposition from the local townspeople, scandalized by Whitman's radical reputation. Fairly humdrum with a larger-than-life performance by Torn as Whitman. Based on Whitman's visit to Canada in 1880. **108m/C VHS, LV, Letterbox, Closed Caption.** *CA* Rip Torn, Colm Feore, Wendel Meldrum, Sheila McCarthy, Colin Fox; **D:** John Kent Harrison; **W:** John Kent Harrison. *FCT*

Beautiful Girls 🎬🎬½ 1996 (R) Slow but easy-going film highlights the differences between men, women, and relationships. A 10-year high school reunion brings together buddies Tommy (Dillon), Kev (Perlich), Paul (Rapaport), Mo (Emmerich), and Willie (Hutton). They ice-fish, drink, and talk about women (about whom they haven't a clue). All are smitten by Andera (Thurman), the gorgeous visiting cousin of another friend, and Willie becomes intrigued by Marty (Portman), his precociously tantalizing 13-year-old neighbor. The guys whining gets annoying and the women are strictly secondary characters, but O'Donnell's tirade about fake femininity is amusing. The Afghan Whigs are featured as the bar band. **CW:** Strong language and nude pin-ups. **110m/C VHS, LV, Closed Caption.** Matt Dillon, Timothy Hutton, Michael Rapaport, Max Perlich, Noah Emmerich, Lauren Holly, Uma Thurman, Natalie Portman, Mira Sorvino, Martha Plimpton, Rosie O'Donnell, Annabeth Gish, Pruitt Taylor Vince, Sam Robards, David Arquette, Anne Bobby, Richard Bright; **D:** Ted Demme; **W:** Scott Rosenberg; **C:** Adam Kimmel; **M:** David A. Stewart. *TOU*

The Beautiful, the Bloody and the Bare 🎬 1969 Sordid screamer in the Herschell Gordon Lewis tradition. Set in New York City in the 60s, a depraved artist kills the nude models who pose for him. **?m/C VHS.** *MOV*

Beautiful Thing 🎬🎬🎬 1995 (R) Sweet, fairytalish, gay coming-of-age story set in a working-class southeast London housing estate. Shy teenager Jamie (Berry) lives with his barmaid mum, Sandra (Henry), and her lover, Tony (Daniels). Next-door is his best mate, the stoic Ste (Neal), who's regularly abused by his father and brother. But when things get too bad, he sleeps over with Jamie. And one night, nature hesitantly takes its course. Their tart-tongued, Mama Cass fanatic, friend Leah (Empson) starts rumors about the twosome that lead to some uneasy (but ultimately conciliatory) confrontations. Fine performances; Harvey adapted from his play. **CW:** Sexuality, pervasive strong language and some drug content. **89m/C VHS, Closed Caption.** *GB* Glen Berry, Scott Neal, Linda Henry, Tameka Empson, Ben Daniels; **D:** Hettie Macdonald; **W:** Jonathan Harvey; **C:** Chris Seager. *COL*

Beauty and the Beast 🎬🎬🎬 *La Belle et Laete* 1946 The classic medieval fairy tale is brought to life on the big screen for the first time. Beauty takes the place of her father after he is sentenced to die by the horrible Beast and falls in love with him. Cocteau uses the story's themes and famous set-pieces to create a cohesive and captivating surreal hymn to romantic love that is still the definitive version of B&B. In French with subtitles. **90m/B VHS, Beta, LV, DVD.** *FR* Jean Marais, Josette Day, Marcel Andre, Mila Parely, Nane Germon, Michel Auclair, Georges Auric; **D:** Jean Cocteau. *HMV, MLB, CRC*

Beauty and the Beast 1983 From "Faerie Tale Theatre" comes the story of a Beauty who befriends a Beast and learns a lesson about physical appearance and true love. **60m/C VHS, Beta, LV, Closed Caption.** Susan Sarandon, Anjelica Huston, Klaus Kinski, Stephen Elliott; **D:** Roger Vadim. *FOX, FCT*

Beauty and the Beast 🎬🎬🎬🎬 1991 (G) Wonderful Disney musical combines superb animation, splendid characters, and lively songs about a beautiful girl, Belle, and the fearsome and disagreeable Beast. Supporting cast includes the castle servants (a delightful bunch of household objects). Notable as the first animated feature to be nominated for the Best Picture Oscar. Destined to become a classic. The deluxe video version features a work-in-progress rough film cut, a compact disc of the soundtrack, a lithograph depicting a scene from the film, and an illustrated book. 🎵Beauty and the Beast; Belle; Something There; Be Our Guest. **84m/C VHS, LV, Letterbox. D:** Kirk Wise, Gary Trousdale; **M:** Alan Menken, Howard Ashman; **V:** Paige O'Hara, Robby Benson, Rex Everhart, Richard White, Jesse Corti, Angela Lansbury, Jerry Orbach, David Ogden Stiers, Bradley Michael Pierce, Jo Anne Worley, Kimmy Robertson. Academy Awards '91: Best Song ("Beauty and the Beast"), Best Original Score; Golden Globe Awards '92: Best Film—Musical/Comedy; Nominations: Academy Awards '91: Best Picture, Best Song ("Belle", "Be Our Guest"), Best Sound. *DIS, OM*

Beauty and the Beast, Episode 1: Once Upon a Time in New York 1987 When socialite attorney Catherine Chandler is brutally attacked in New York, Vincent, a mysterious man/beast, rescues and befriends her, taking her to his fantastical subterranean world. Pilot for the popular television series. Additional episodes are available. **48m/C VHS, LV.** Ron Perlman, Linda Hamilton, Roy Dotrice, Ray Wise. *REP, MOV*

Beauty and the Beast: Though Lovers Be Lost 1989 The love affair of Vincent and Catherine takes a tragic turn when she is kidnapped by a crime lord. Feature-length drama from the television series. **90m/C VHS, LV, Closed Caption.** Linda Hamilton, Ron Perlman. *REP*

Beauty and the Devil 🎬🎬 *La Beaute du Diable* 1950 Ambitious retelling of the Faust legend finds old Faust (Simon) willing to sell his soul to the Devil, courtesy of his agent Mephistopheles (Philipe), in return for youth and beauty to pursue the beautiful woman he loves. Clair has his actors trade roles midway through as Faust makes his bargain. French with subtitles. **97m/B VHS.** *FR* Michel Simon, Gerard Philipe, Simone Valere, Raymond Cordy, Gaston Modot, Paolo Stoppa, Nicole Besnard; **D:** Rene Clair; **W:** Rene Clair, Armand Salacrou; **C:** Michel Kelber; **M:** Roman Vlad. *WBF*

Beauty for the Asking ⚟ 1939 It sounds like a workable Lucille Ball vehicle—a beautician develops a bestselling skin cream—and even the title sounds like something you'd like to love Lucy in. But somehow the numerous plot implausibilities managed to get by the story's five writers, and the idea of a jilted woman making millions while being financed by her ex's wife just doesn't fly (perhaps it was an idea ahead of its time). Die-hard Lucy fans may find this interesting. 68m/B VHS. Lucille Ball, Patric Knowles, Donald Woods, Frieda Inescort, Frances Mercer; D: Glenn Tryon. TTC, FCT

Beauty on the Beach ⚟ 196? A comedy about a mad psychologist, his bizarre experiments with women, and his eventual descent into insanity. In Italian with English subtitles. 90m/C VHS, Beta. IT Valeria Fabrizi. NO

Beauty School ⚟ Sylvia Kristel's Beauty School 1993 (R) The promise of an advertising contract pits the owners of rival beauty schools against each other. 95m/C VHS, LV. Sylvia Kristel, Kevin Bernhardt, Kimberly Taylor, Jane Hamilton; D: Ernest G. Sauer; W: Mike MacDonald, Merrill Friedman; M: Jonathan Hannah. IMP

Beavis and Butt-Head Do America ⚟⚟½ 1996 (PG-13) Moronic MTV metalheads go on the road in search of their stolen TV and are somehow mistaken for criminal masterminds. Okay, enough about plot. If you're thinking of renting this one, you don't care about that stuff anyway. Director/writer/voice of B&B Judge is smart enough not to change our "heroes" just because they're on a bigger screen. They're still stupid, obsessed with chicks, (Yeah! Chicks are cool!) and blissfully unaware of what's happening around them. The opening sequence, a parody of 70s cop shows, is hilarious (and cool). For those who like the show, and for people who just don't admit that they do, the boys' movie debut (he said "but") doesn't suck. CW: Continuous crude sex-related humor and language, and a drug-related scene. 82m/C VHS, Beta, Closed Caption. D: Mike Judge; W: Mike Judge, Joe Stillman; M: John Frizzell; V: Mike Judge, Robert Stack, Cloris Leachman, Demi Moore, Eric Bogosian, Richard Linklater. Nominations: MTV Movie Awards '97: Best On-Screen Duo (Beavis/Butt-head). PAR

Bebe's Kids ⚟⚟½ 1992 (PG-13) When ladies' man Robin falls for the lovely Jamika, he gets some unexpected surprises when he takes her out on a first date to an amusement park—and she brings along four kids. Animated comedy takes some funny pot-shots at both black and white culture and Disneyland. The children are amusing, especially baby PeeWee, a tot with chronically dirty diapers and Tone Loc's gravelly voice. Based on characters created by the late comedian Robin Harris. The video includes the seven-minute animated short "Itsy Bitsy Spider." 74m/C VHS, Beta, Closed Caption. D: Bruce Smith; W: Reginald Hudlin; M: John Barnes; V: Faizon Love, Vanessa Bell Calloway, Wayne Collins, Jonell Green, Marques Houston, Tone Loc, Nell Carter, Myra J. PAR

Because of the Cats ⚟½ 1974 Police inspector uncovers an evil cult within his seaside village while investigating a bizarre rape and burglary. 90m/C VHS, Beta. Bryan Marshall, Alexandra Stewart, Alex Van Rooyen, Sylvia Kristel, Sebastian Graham Jones; D: Fons Rademakers.

Because You're Mine ⚟⚟ 1952 Lanza plays an opera star who is drafted and falls in love with Morrow, his top sergeant's sister. Plenty of singing—maybe too much at times, but Lanza's fans will enjoy it nonetheless. ♫ All the Things You Are; Because You're Mine; Be My Love; Granada; Lee-Ah-Loo; The Lord's Prayer; The Song Angels Sing; You Do Something to Me. 103m/C VHS. Mario Lanza, James Whitmore, Doretta Morrow, Dean Miller, Rita (Paula) Corday, Jeff Donnell, Spring Byington; D: Alexander Hall. Nominations: Academy Awards '52: Best Song ("Because You're Mine"). MGM

Becket ⚟⚟⚟ 1964 Adaptation of Jean Anouilh's play about the tumultuous friendship between Henry II of England and the Archbishop of Canterbury Thomas Becket. Becket views his position in the church of little relation to the sexual and emotional needs of a man, until he becomes archbishop. His growing concern for religion and his shrinking need of Henry as friend and confidant eventually cause the demise of the friendship and the resulting tragedy. Flawless acting from every cast member, and finely detailed artistic direction make up for the occasional slow moment. 148m/C VHS, Beta, LV, Letterbox. Richard Burton, Peter O'Toole, John Gielgud, Donald Wolfit; D: Peter Glenville; W: Edward Anhalt; C: Geoffrey Unsworth. Academy Awards '64: Best Adapted Screenplay; Golden Globe Awards '65: Best Actor—Drama (O'Toole), Best Film—Drama; Nominations: Academy Awards '64: Best Actor (Burton), Best Actor (O'Toole), Best Art Direction/Set Decoration (Color), Best Color Cinematography, Best Costume Design (Color), Best Director (Glenville), Best Film Editing, Best Picture, Best Sound, Best Supporting Actor (Gielgud), Best Original Score. MPI, TVC

Becky Sharp ⚟⚟½ 1935 This premiere Technicolor film tells the story of Becky Sharp, a wicked woman who finally performs one good deed. 83m/C VHS, Beta. Miriam Hopkins, Frances Dee, Cedric Hardwicke, Billie Burke, Nigel Bruce, Pat Nixon; D: Rouben Mamoulian; C: Ray Rennahan. Nominations: Academy Awards '35: Best Actress (Hopkins). NOS, MRV, HEG

Becoming Colette ⚟⚟ 1992 (R) Tedious flashbacking bio of French writer Colette, from her innocent days in the country to her (bad) marriage to writer/publisher Willy and on and on to her own growing career as a writer. She begins writing stories, using an alter-ego character, Claudine, which detail her sexual escapades. Lots of naked flesh but little passion. A postscript notes that Colette wrote "Gigi" and was the first woman to receive the French Legion of Honor. CW: Strong sexuality. 97m/C VHS, Closed Caption. Mathilda May, Klaus Maria Brandauer, Virginia Madsen, Paul Rhys, Jean-Pierre Aumont, John van Dreelen, Lucienne Hamon; D: Danny Huston; W: Ruth Graham; M: John Scott.

Bed & Breakfast ⚟⚟½ 1992 (PG-13) Three generations of women lead quiet lives while running a failing Nantucket bed and breakfast. When a mystery man washes up on their beach, he charms them all, but it seems that he has a past that could endanger everyone. Lightweight final role for Dewhurst, though she provides some sparks as the strong and loving matriarch. Gentle romantic comedy skims the surface, but is still enjoyable. 97m/C VHS, LV, Closed Caption. Roger Moore, Talia Shire, Colleen Dewhurst, Nina Siemaszko, Ford Rainey, Stephen Root, Jamie Walters, Victor Slezak; D: Robert Ellis Miller; W: Cindy Myers; M: David Shire.

Bed and Sofa ⚟⚟⚟½ 1927 Adultery, abortion, and women's rights are brought about by a housing shortage which forces a man to move in with a married friend. Famous, groundbreaking Russian silent. 73m/B VHS, Beta. RU Nikolai Batalov, Vladimar Fogel; D: Abram Room. IHF

Bed of Roses ⚟⚟½ Amelia and the King of Plants 1995 (PG) Wistful romance finds workaholic investment banker Lisa Walker (Masterson) receiving lavish floral tributes from an unknown admirer. When Lisa tracks her giver down, it turns out to be lovestruck widowed florist Lewis Farrell (Slater), who noticed Lisa crying through her apartment window and sent the flowers to cheer her up. Best friend Kim (Seagall) urges Lisa to go for Lewis but a problematic past has Lisa distrusting her emotions and their romantic path has a few bumps (easily overcome). Appealing leads, lots of cliches. Goldenberg's debut. 88m/C VHS, LV, Closed Caption. Christian Slater, Mary Stuart Masterson, Pamela Segall, Josh Brolin, Ally Walker, Debra Monk; D: Michael Goldenberg; W: Michael Goldenberg; C: Adam Kimmel; M: Michael Convertino. NLC

The Bed You Sleep In ⚟⚟ 1993 Ray (Blair) is a struggling lumber mill owner, living with his wife Jean (McLaughlin) in a small Oregon town. The couple are torn apart when they receive a letter from their daughter, who's away at college, accusing her father of sexual abuse. The secrets and lies of the family soon echo throughout their community. 117m/C VHS, Letterbox. Tom Blair, Ellen McLaughlin, Kathryn Sannella; D: Jon Jost; W: Jon Jost; C: Jon Jost. VNG

Bedazzled ⚟⚟⚟ 1968 (PG) In the process of hanging himself, Stanley, a short-order cook is approached by the devil with an offer: seven wishes in exchange for his soul. Each of Stanley's wishes is granted with surprising consequences. Cult comedy is a sometimes uneven, but thoroughly entertaining and funny retelling of the Faustian story. 107m/C VHS, Beta, LV, Letterbox. GB Dudley Moore, Peter Cook, Eleanor Bron, Michael Bates, Raquel Welch, Bernard Spear, Parnell McGarry, Howard Goorney, Daniele Noel, Barry Humphries, Robert Russell, Lockwood West, Robin Hawdon, Evelyn Moore, Charles Lloyd Pack; D: Stanley Donen; W: Dudley Moore, Peter Cook; C: Austin Dempster; M: Dudley Moore. FOX

Bedford Incident ⚟⚟½ 1965 The U.S.S. Bedford discovers an unidentified submarine in North Atlantic waters. The Bedford's commander drives his crew to the point of exhaustion as they find themselves the center of a fateful controversy. 102m/B VHS, Beta, LV. Richard Widmark, Sidney Poitier, James MacArthur, Martin Balsam, Wally Cox, Donald Sutherland, Eric Portman; D: James B. Harris. COL, IME

Bedknobs and Broomsticks ⚟⚟½ 1971 (G) A novice witch and three cockney waifs ride a magic bedstead and stop the Nazis from invading England during WWII. Celebrated for its animated art. 117m/C VHS, Beta, LV. Angela Lansbury, Roddy McDowall, David Tomlinson, Bruce Forsyth, Sam Jaffe; D: Robert Stevenson. Academy Awards '71: Best Visual Effects; Nominations: Academy Awards '71: Best Art Direction/Set Decoration, Best Costume Design, Best Song ("The Age of Not Believing"), Original Song Score and/or Adaptation. DIS

Bedlam ⚟⚟⚟ 1945 Creeper set in the famed asylum in 18th-century London. A woman, wrongfully committed, tries to stop the evil doings of the chief (Karloff) of Bedlam, and endangers herself. Fine horror film co-written by producer Lewton. 79m/B VHS, Beta, LV. Jason Robards Sr., Ian Wolfe, Glenn Vernon, Boris Karloff, Anna Lee, Billy House, Richard Fraser; D: Mark Robson. TTC, FCT, MLB

Bedroom Eyes ⚟⚟ 1986 (R) A successful businessman becomes a voyeur by returning nightly to a beautiful woman's window, until she is killed and he is the prime suspect. Part comic, part disappointing thriller. 90m/C VHS, Beta, LV. Kenneth Gilman, Dayle Haddon, Christine Cattall; D: William Fruet. FOX

Bedroom Eyes 2 ⚟⚟ 1989 (R) After discovering his wife has had an affair, a stockbroker takes a lover. When she turns up dead, he and his wife become murder suspects. Provides some suspenseful moments. 85m/C VHS, LV. Wings Hauser, Kathy Shower, Linda Blair, Jane Hamilton, Jennifer Delora; D: Chuck Vincent. THV, IME

The Bedroom Window ⚟⚟½ 1987 (R) Guttenberg is having an illicit affair with his boss' wife (Huppert), who witnesses an assault on another woman (McGovern) from the bedroom window. To keep the affair secret Guttenberg reports the crime, but since it is secondhand, the account is flawed and he becomes a suspect. Semi-tight thriller reminiscent of Hitchcock mysteries isn't always believable, but is otherwise interesting. 113m/C VHS, Beta, LV, Closed Caption. Steve Guttenberg, Elizabeth McGovern, Isabelle Huppert, Wallace Shawn, Paul Shenar, Carl Lumbly, Frederick Coffin, Brad Greenquist; D: Curtis Hanson; W: Curtis Hanson; M: Patrick Gleeson, Michael Shrieve, Felix Mendelssohn. FHE, VES, ART

Bedtime for Bonzo 🎬🎬½ **1951** A professor adopts a chimp to prove that environment, not heredity, determines a child's future. Fun, lighthearted comedy that stars a future president. Followed by "Bonzo Goes to College." **83m/B VHS, Beta.** Ronald Reagan, Diana Lynn, Walter Slezak, Jesse White, Bonzo the Chimp; **D:** Fred de Cordova. *USH, FCT*

Bedtime Story 🎬🎬 **1963** Two con artists attempt to fleece an apparently wealthy woman and each other on the French Riviera. Re-made in 1988 as "Dirty Rotten Scoundrels." One of Brando's thankfully few forays into comedy. **99m/C VHS, Beta.** Marlon Brando, David Niven, Shirley Jones, Dody Goodman, Marie Windsor; **D:** Ralph Levy. *USH*

Beer 🎬 **1985 (R)** A female advertising executive devises a dangerous sexist campaign for a cheap beer, and both the beer and its nickname become nationwide obsessions. Not especially amusing. **83m/C VHS, Beta, Closed Caption.** Loretta Swit, Rip Torn, Dick Shawn, David Alan Grier, William Russ, Kenneth Mars, Peter Michael Goetz; **D:** Patrick Kelly; **C:** Bill Butler; **M:** Bill Conti. *NO*

The Bees woof! **1978 (PG)** Sting of a poor movie is painful. A strain of bees have ransacked South America and are threatening the rest of the world. The buzz is that no one is safe. Cheap rip-off of "The Swarm," which is saying something. **93m/C VHS, Beta.** John Saxon, John Carradine, Angel Tompkins, Claudio Brook, Alicia Encinas; **D:** Alfredo Zacharias. *WAR*

Beethoven 🎬🎬 *Beethoven's Great Love; The Life and Loves of Beethoven; Un Grand Amour de Beethoven* **1936** Startling biography of the musical genius, filled with opulent, impressionistic visuals. French with subtitles. **116m/B VHS.** *FR* Harry Baur, Jean-Louis Barrault, Marcel Dalio; **D:** Abel Gance. **W:** Abel Gance. *CVC, TPV*

Beethoven 🎬🎬½ **1992 (PG)** Adorable St. Bernard puppy escapes from dognappers and wanders into the home of the Newtons, who, over dad's objections, adopt him. Beethoven grows into a huge, slobbering dog who sorely tries dad's patience. To make matters worse, two sets of villains also wreak havoc on the Newton's lives. Evil veterinarian Dr. Varnick plots to steal Beethoven for lab experiments, and yuppie couple Brad and Brie plot to take over the family business. Enjoyable cast, particularly Grodin as dad and Chris as Beethoven enable this movie to please more than the milk and cookies set. Followed by "Beethoven's 2nd." **89m/C VHS, LV, Closed Caption, DVD.** Charles Grodin, Bonnie Hunt, Dean Jones, Oliver Platt, Stanley Tucci, Nicholle Tom, Christopher Castile, Sarah Rose Karr, David Duchovny, Patricia Heaton, Laurel Cronin; **D:** Brian Levant; **W:** John Hughes, Amy Holden Jones. *USH, FCT*

Beethoven Lives Upstairs 🎬🎬½ **1992** In 19th century Vienna 10 year-old Christoph's life is turned upside-down when the family's eccentric new tenant turns out to be composer Ludwig Van Beethoven. In time, Christoph comes to appreciate the beauty of the music and the tragedy of the composer's deafness. Features more than 25 excerpts of Beethoven's works. **52m/C VHS, Closed Caption.** Neil Munro, Illya Woloshyn, Fiona Reid, Paul Soles, Sheila McCarthy, Albert Schultz; **D:** David Devine; **W:** Heather Conkie. *BMG, MVD*

Beethoven's Nephew 🎬½ *Le Neveu de Beethoven* **1988** A tepid pseudo-historical farce about Beethoven's strange obsession with his only nephew. Directed by erstwhile Warhol collaborator Morrissey. **103m/C VHS, Beta, LV.** *FR* Wolfgang Reichmann, Ditmar Prinz, Jane Birkin, Nathalie Baye; **D:** Paul Morrissey; **W:** Paul Morrissey, Matthieu Carriere. *VTR*

Beethoven's 2nd 🎬🎬½ **1993 (PG)** Sequel has awwww factor going for it as new daddy Beethoven slobbers over four adorable and appealing St. Bernard pups and his new love Missy. Same basic kid subplot as the first, with wicked kidnappers replacing evil vet. During the upheaval, the Newtons take care of the little yapping troublemakers, providing the backdrop for endless puppy mischief and exasperation on Grodin's part. Silly subplots and too many human moments tend to drag, but the kids will find the laughs (albeit stupid ones). **87m/C VHS, LV, Letterbox, Closed Caption, DVD.** Charles Grodin, Bonnie Hunt, Nicholle Tom, Christopher Castile, Sarah Rose Karr, Debi Mazar, Christopher Penn, Ashley Hamilton; **D:** Rod Daniel; **W:** Len Blum; **C:** Bill Butler; **M:** Randy Edelman. Nominations: Academy Awards '93: Best Song ("The Day I Fall in Love"); Golden Globe Awards '94: Best Song ("The Day I Fall in Love"). *USH*

Beetlejuice 🎬🎬🎬½ **1988 (PG)** The after-life is confusing for a pair of ultra-nice novice ghosts who are faced with chasing an obnoxious family of post-modern art lovers who move into their house. Then they hear of a poltergeist who promises to rid the house of all trespassers for a price. Things go from bad to impossible when the maniacal Keaton (as the demonic "Betelgeuse") works his magic. The calypso scene is priceless. A cheesy, funny, surreal farce of life after death with inventive set designs popping continual surprises. Ryder is striking as the misunderstood teen with a death complex, while O'Hara is hilarious as the yuppie art poseur. **92m/C VHS, Beta, LV, 8mm, Closed Caption, DVD.** Michael Keaton, Geena Davis, Alec Baldwin, Sylvia Sidney, Catherine O'Hara, Winona Ryder, Jeffrey Jones, Dick Cavett, Glenn Shadix, Robert Goulet; **D:** Tim Burton; **W:** Michael McDowell, Warren Skaaren; **C:** Thomas Ackerman; **M:** Danny Elfman. Academy Awards '88: Best Makeup; National Society of Film Critics Awards '88: Best Actor (Keaton). *WAR, FCT, TLF*

Before and After 🎬½ **1995 (PG-13)** Disjointed drama depicts well-off suburban couple, Carolyn (Streep) and Ben (Neeson), who are thrown into chaos when their teenaged son Jacob (Furlong) is accused of murdering his girlfriend. Upon notification by the police that his son is the prime suspect and on the lam, Ben finds what seems to be bloody evidence in the family's car, which he destroys. The story loses steam from there. Based on the novel by Rosellen Brown, the focus is on the effect the death has on this picture book Massachusetts family. Neeson and Streep fall short of usually deliverable goods and director Schroeder takes the middle-of-the-road sentimental approach. **CW:** Some disturbing images of violence, brief strong language and some sensuality. **107m/C VHS, LV, Closed Caption.** Meryl Streep, Liam Neeson, Edward Furlong, Alfred Molina, John Heard, Julia Weldon, Daniel von Bargen, Ann Magnuson, Alison Folland, Kaiulani Lee; **D:** Barbet Schroeder; **W:** Ted Tally; **C:** Luciano Tovoli; **M:** Howard Shore. *TOU*

Before I Hang 🎬🎬🎬 **1940** When a doctor invents a youth serum from the blood of a murderer, he'll stop at nothing to keep his secret. Karloff himself stands the test of time, and is satisfying as the mad scientist, giving this horror flick its appeal. **60m/B VHS, Beta.** Boris Karloff, Evelyn Keyes, Bruce (Herman Brix) Bennett, Edward Van Sloan, Ben Taggart, Pedro de Cordoba, Wright Kramer, Bertram Marburgh, Don Beddoe, Robert Fiske; **D:** Nick Grinde; **W:** Robert D. Andrews; **C:** Benjamin Kline. *COL*

Before Morning 🎬½ **1933** Police officer poses as a blackmailer to find out which of the two women in the murder victim's life are guilty. **68m/B VHS, Beta, LV.** Leo Carrillo, Lora Baxter, Taylor Holmes. *NO*

Before Sunrise 🎬🎬½ **1994 (R)** Light, "getting-to-know-you," romance unfolds as two 20-somethings share an unlikely 14-hour date. Gen-Xer Jesse (Hawke) and French beauty (Delpy) meet on the Eurail and he convinces her to join him in exploring Vienna and their mutual attraction before he heads back to the States in the morning. The two exchange life experiences and philosophies in the typical Linklater conversational fashion, but the film strays from the comical accounts of earlier works "Slacker" and "Dazed and Confused." Cinematographer Daniel captures the Old World with finesse, especially in the inevitable "first kiss" atop the Ferris wheel made famous in Orson Welles' "The Third Man." **CW:** Some strong language. **101m/C VHS, LV, Closed Caption.** Ethan Hawke, Julie Delpy; **D:** Richard Linklater; **W:** Richard Linklater, Kim Krizan; **C:** Lee Daniel. Berlin International Film Festival '94: Best Director (Linklater); Nominations: MTV Movie Awards '95: Best Kiss (Ethan Hawke/Julie Delpy). *COL*

Before the Rain 🎬🎬🎬 *Po Dezju; Pred dozhdot* **1994** War-torn Macedonia is the backdrop for Manchevski's first film (and first made in the newly declared republic of Macedonia). Powerful circular narrative joins three stories about the freedom of love and the pervasiveness of violence. "Words" finds young Macedonian monk Kiril (Colin) distracted from his spiritual duties by young Albanian Muslim Zamira (Mitevska), who takes refuge in his monastery. In "Faces," pregnant picture editor Anne (Cartlidge) is torn between her estranged husband and her lover, Aleksander (Serbedzija), a London-based war photographer who left his native Macedonia years before. "Pictures" finds Aleksandar returning to his old village—now torn by ethnic strife. In Macedonian, Albanian, and English, with subtitles. **120m/C VHS.** *GB FR MA* Rade Serbedzija, Katrin Cartlidge, Gregoire Colin, Labina Mitevska, Phyllida Law; **D:** Milcho Manchevski; **W:** Milcho Manchevski; **C:** Manuel Teran; **M:** Anastasia. Independent Spirit Awards '96: Best Foreign Film; Venice Film Festival '94: Golden Lion; Nominations: Academy Awards '94: Best Foreign Language Film. *PGV*

Before the Revolution 🎬🎬 **1965** One of Bertolucci's first films. Love and politics are mixed when the young Fabrizio, who is dabbling in communism, is also flirting with his young aunt. Striking and powerful film that has yet to lose its effect despite the times. Italian with subtitles. **115m/C VHS.** *IT* Francesco Barilli, Adrianna Asti, Alain Midgette, Morando Morandini, Domenico Alpi; **D:** Bernardo Bertolucci; **W:** Bernardo Bertolucci; **M:** Ennio Morricone, Gato Barbieri. *NYF*

Beggars in Ermine 🎬🎬 **1934** A handicapped, impoverished man organizes all the beggars in the world into a successful corporation. Unusual performance from Atwill. **70m/B VHS, Beta.** Lionel Atwill, Henry B. Walthall, Betty Furness, Jameson Thomas, James Bush, Astrid Allwyn, George "Gabby" Hayes; **D:** Phil Rosen. *VYY, SNC*

Beginning of the End 🎬½ **1957** Produced the same year as "The Deadly Mantis," Gordon's effort adds to 1957's harvest of bugs on a rampage "B"-graders. Giant, radiation-spawned grasshoppers attack Chicago causing Graves to come to the rescue. Easily the best giant grasshopper movie ever made. **73m/B VHS.** Peggy Castle, Peter Graves, Morris Ankrum, Richard Benedict, James Seay; **D:** Bert I. Gordon. *NO*

The Beguiled 🎬🎬🎬 **1970 (R)** During the Civil War a wounded Union soldier is taken in by the women at a girl's school in the South. He manages to seduce both a student and a teacher, and jealousy and revenge ensue. Decidedly weird psychological melodrama from action vets Siegel and Eastwood. **109m/C VHS, Beta, LV, DVD.** Clint Eastwood, Geraldine Page, Elizabeth Hartman, Jo Ann Harris; **D:** Donald Siegel; **C:** Bruce Surtees; **M:** Lalo Schifrin. *USH*

Behave Yourself! 🎬½ **1952** A married couple adopts a dog who may be the key for a million-dollar hijacking setup by a gang of hoodlums. **81m/B VHS, Beta.** Shelley Winters, Farley Granger, William Demarest, Lon Chaney Jr., Hans Conried, Elisha Cook Jr., Francis L. Sullivan; **D:** George Beck. *NOS*

Behind Enemy Lines 🎬½ **1985 (R)** Special Forces soldier goes on a special mission to eliminate a possible Nazi spy. Made for television. **83m/C VHS, Beta.** Hal Holbrook, Ray Sharkey, David McCallum, Tom Isbell, Anne Twomey, Robert Patrick; **D:** Sheldon Larry.

Behind Enemy Lines 🎬🎬 **1996 (R)** Ex-Marine Mike Weston (Griffith) believes he was responsible for the death of his friend Jones (Mulkey) during assignment in Vietnam. When Weston discovers Jones is actually being hostage, he decides on a rescue mission. **CW:** Commando violence and language. **89m/C VHS, Closed Caption.**

Thomas Ian Griffith, Chris Mulkey, Courtney Gains; **D:** Mark Griffiths; **W:** Andrew Osborne, Dennis Cooley; **C:** Blake T. Evans; **M:** Arthur Kempel. *ORI*

Behind Locked Doors ✯✯½ 1948 A journalist fakes mental illness to have himself committed to an asylum, where he believes a crooked judge is in hiding. A superior "B" mystery/suspense feature, with some tense moments. **61m/B VHS.** Lucille Bremer, Richard Carlson, Tor Johnson, Douglas Fowley, Herbert Heyes, Ralf Harolde; **D:** Budd Boetticher. *VDM*

Behind Office Doors ✯✯ 1931 Astor stars as the secretarial "power behind the throne" in this look at who really wields power in an office. Her boss takes her for granted until things go wrong. **82m/B VHS.** Mary Astor, Robert Ames, Ricardo Cortez, Charles Sellon; **D:** Melville Brown. *NOS, HEG*

Behind Prison Walls ✯✯ *Youth Takes a Hand* 1943 A steel tycoon and his son are sent to prison, and the son tries to convert his dad to socialism. A fun, light hearted film, the last for veteran Tully. **64m/B VHS.** Alan Baxter, Gertrude Michael, Tully Marshall, Edwin Maxwell, Jacqueline Dalya, Matt Willis; **D:** Steve Sekely. *SNC*

Behind the Front ✯✯½ 1926 Two friends tumble in and out of trouble in this comic Army film. One of the most profitable films of the late '20s. **60m/B VHS.** Wallace Beery, Raymond Hatton, Richard Arlen, Mary Brian, Chester Conklin; **D:** Edward Sutherland. *GPV*

Behind the Mask ✯✯½ 1946 Lamont Cranston, better known as do-gooder "The Shadow," finds himself accused of murdering a blackmailing newspaper reporter. Based on the radio serial. **68m/C VHS.** Kane Richmond, Barbara Read, George Chandler, Dorothea Kent, Robert Shayne, June Clyde; **D:** Phil Karlson. *GPV, ADL*

Behind the Rising Sun ✯✯½ 1943 A Japanese publisher's political views clash with those of his American-educated son in 1930s Japan. Well done despite pre-war propaganda themes. **88m/B VHS, Beta.** Tom Neal, J. Carrol Naish, Robert Ryan, Mike Mazurki, Margo, Gloria Holden, Don Douglas; **D:** Edward Dmytryk. *NO*

Behold a Pale Horse ✯✯½ 1964 A Spanish police captain attempts to dupe Peck into believing that his mother is dying and he must visit her on her deathbed. Loyalist Spaniard Peck becomes privy to the plot against him, but goes to Spain anyway in this post Spanish Civil War film. **118m/B VHS, Beta.** Gregory Peck, Anthony Quinn, Omar Sharif, Mildred Dunnock; **D:** Fred Zinnemann; **M:** Maurice Jarre. *GKK*

The Being ✯ 1983 (R) People in Idaho are terrorized by a freak who became abnormal after radiation was disposed in the local dump. Another dull monster-created-by-nuclear-waste non-event. Of limited interest is Buzzi. However, you'd be more entertained (read: amused) by Troma's "The Toxic Avenger," which takes itself much (much!) less seriously. **82m/C VHS, Beta.** Ruth Buzzi, Martin Landau, Jose Ferrer; **D:** Jackie Kong. *NO*

Being at Home with Claude ✯✯ 1992 Yves (Godin) is a 22-year-old Montreal hustler being interrogated by a nameless inspector (Dupuis) for the murder of his lover, Claude (Pichette). Yves has admitted his guilt but the inspector wants to reconstruct the event and determine a motive. Lots of black-and-white flashbacks as Yves dwells on his work and his psychologically love-death relationship with Claude. Rather pretentious and long-winded. Based on the play by Rene-Daniel DuBois. In French with English subtitles. **86m/C VHS.** CA Roy Dupuis, Jacques Godin, Jean-Francois Pichette, Gaston Lepage; **D:** Johanne Boisvert; **W:** Jean Boudin. Genie Awards '92: Best Score. *FXL, FCT*

Being Human ✯✯½ 1994 (PG-13) Ambitious comedy drama promises more than it delivers, and shackles Williams in the process. Hector (Williams) is a regular guy continuously reincarnated throughout the milennia. He plays a cave-

man, a Roman slave, a Middle Ages nomad, a crew member on a 17th century new world voyage, and a modern New Yorker in separate vignettes that echo and/or extend the main themes of family, identity, and random fate. But he manages to emerge from each sketch as an unassuming everyman who never learns his lesson. One of Williams' periodic chancy ventures away from his comedic roots occasionally strikes gold, but often seems overly restrained. **CW:** Language, elements of violence, and elements of sensuality. **122m/C VHS, LV, Letterbox, Closed Caption.** Robin Williams, John Turturro, Anna Galiena, Vincent D'Onofrio, Hector Elizondo, Lorraine Bracco, Lindsay Crouse, Kelly Hunter, William H. Macy, Grace Mahlaba, Theresa Russell, Charles Miller, Helen Miller; **D:** Bill Forsyth; **W:** Bill Forsyth; **C:** Michael Coulter; **M:** Michael Gibbs. *WAR*

Being There ✯✯✯½ 1979 (PG) A feebleminded gardener, whose entire knowledge of life comes from watching television, is sent out into the real world when his employer dies. Equipped with his prize possession, his remote control unit, the gardener unwittingly enters the world of politics and is welcomed as a mysterious sage. Sellers is wonderful in this satiric treat adapted by Jerzy Kosinski from his novel. **130m/C VHS, Beta, LV, Closed Caption.** Peter Sellers, Shirley MacLaine, Melvyn Douglas, Jack Warden, Richard Dysart, Richard Basehart; **D:** Hal Ashby; **C:** Caleb Deschanel. Academy Awards '79: Best Supporting Actor (Douglas); Golden Globe Awards '80: Best Actor—Musical/Comedy (Sellers), Best Supporting Actor (Douglas); Los Angeles Film Critics Association Awards '79: Best Supporting Actor (Douglas); National Board of Review Awards '79: Best Actor (Sellers); New York Film Critics Awards '79: Best Supporting Actor (Douglas); National Society of Film Critics Awards '79: Best Cinematography; Writers Guild of America '79: Best Adapted Screenplay; Nominations: Academy Awards '79: Best Actor (Sellers). *FOX, FCT, WAR*

Being Two Isn't Easy ✯✯½ 1962 Director Ichikawa shows the world through the eyes of a two-year-old as a young couple struggle to raise their son. In Japanese with English subtitles. **88m/C VHS.** JP Fujiko Yamamoto, Eiji Funakoshi; **D:** Kon Ichikawa. *HMV, FCT*

Bela Lugosi Meets a Brooklyn Gorilla woof! *The Boys from Brooklyn* 1952 Two men who look like Dean Martin and Jerry Lewis (but aren't) get lost in the jungle, where they meet mad scientist Lugosi. Worse than it sounds. Real Jerry sued for unflattering imitation. **74m/B VHS, Beta.** Bela Lugosi, Duke Mitchell, Sammy Petrillo; **D:** William Beaudine. *NOS, SNC, AOV*

Belfast Assassin ✯ 1984 A British anti-terrorist agent goes undercover in Ireland to find an IRA assassin who shot a British cabinet minister. **130m/C VHS, Beta.** Derek Thompson, Ray Lonnen.

The Believers ✯✯½ 1987 (R) Tense horror mystery set in New York city about a series of gruesome, unexplained murders. A widowed police psychologist investigating the deaths unwittingly discovers a powerful Santeria cult that believes in the sacrifice of children. Without warning he is drawn into the circle of the "Believers" and must free himself before his own son is the next sacrifice. Gripping (and grim), unrelenting horror. **114m/C VHS, Beta, LV, Closed Caption.** Martin Sheen, Helen Shaver, Malick Bowens, Harris Yulin, Robert Loggia, Jimmy Smits, Richard Masur, Harley Cross, Elizabeth Wilson, Lee Richardson, Carla Pinza; **D:** John Schlesinger; **W:** Mark Frost; **C:** Robby Muller; **M:** J. Peter Robinson. *HBO*

Belizaire the Cajun ✯✯½ 1986 (PG) 19th-century Louisiana love story. White prejudice against the Cajuns is rampant and violent, but that doesn't stop sexy faith healer Assante from falling in love with the inaccessible Cajun wife (Youngs) of a rich local. Made with care on a tight budget. Worthwhile, though uneven. **103m/C VHS, Beta, Closed Caption.** Armand Assante, Gail Youngs, Will Patton, Stephen McHattie, Michael Schoeffling, Robert Duvall, Nancy Barrett; **D:** Glen Pitre; **W:** Glen Pitre; **C:** Richard Bowen; **M:** Michael Doucet, Howard Shore. *FOX*

Bell, Book and Candle ✯✯½ 1958 A young witch makes up her mind to refrain from using her powers. When an interesting man moves into her building, she forgets her decision and enchants him with a love spell. **106m/C VHS, Beta, LV.** James Stewart, Kim Novak, Jack Lemmon, Elsa Lanchester, Janice Rule, Hermione Gingold; **D:** Richard Quine; **W:** Daniel Taradash; **C:** James Wong Howe; **M:** George Duning. Nominations: Academy Awards '58: Best Art Direction/Set Decoration, Best Costume Design. *COL, FCT, MLB*

Bell Diamond ✯✯ 1981 A study by the experimental filmmaker of a Vietnam vet surviving in a bankrupt mining town. Created without a script using non-professional actors. **96m/C VHS, Beta. D:** Jon Jost. *FCT*

Bell from Hell ✯✯ 1974 A tale of insanity and revenge, wherein a young man, institutionalized since his mother's death, plots to kill his aunt and three cousins. **80m/C VHS, Beta.** Viveca Lindfors, Renaud Verley, Alfredo Mayo; **D:** Claudio Guerin Hill. *UNI*

The Bell Jar ✯½ 1979 (R) Based on poet Sylvia Plath's acclaimed semi-autobiographical novel, this is the story of a young woman who becomes the victim of mental illness. Not for the easily depressed and a disjointed and disappointing adaptation of Plath's work. **113m/C VHS, Beta.** Marilyn Hassett, Julie Harris, Barbara Barrie, Anne Bancroft, Robert Klein, Anne Jackson; **D:** Larry Peerce. *VES*

Bell Ringer of Antigua ✯✯ 1946 Inspirational story by Royer, one of Hollywood's pioneering women. Shot on location in Guatemala. **?m/C VHS. D:** Fanchon Royer; **W:** Fanchon Royer. *LOO*

Bella Mafia ✯✯½ 1997 (R) Over-the-top trash and that's meant in the finest possible way. This lurid melodrama, originally a two-part miniseries, concerns the Sicilian mob family, the Lucianos, who have suffered the loss of father Roberto (Farina) and three sons. Widowed matriarch Graziella (Redgrave) decides to join with her three daughters-in-law, Sophia (Kinski), Teresa (Douglas), and Moyra (Tilly), and avenge their deaths. Oh yes, there's also Sophia's secret son Luca (Marsden), a killer who turns up to insinuates himself into family life. Adapted by La Plante from her novel. **CW:** Some violence. **117m/C VHS, Closed Caption.** Vanessa Redgrave, Nastassia Kinski, Illeana Douglas, Jennifer Tilly, James Marsden, Peter Bogdanovich, Dennis Farina, Gina Philips; **D:** David Greene; **W:** Lynda La Plante. *THV*

Bellamy ✯ 1980 Murderous madman massacres masseuses, and Bellamy is the cop out to get him. **92m/C VHS, Beta.** John Stanton, Timothy Elston, Sally Conabere; **D:** Colin Eggleston, Pino Amenta. *NO*

The Bellboy ✯✯½ 1960 Lewis makes his directorial debut in this plotless but clever outing. He also stars as the eponymous character, a bellboy at Miami's Fountainbleau Hotel. Cameos from Berle and Winchell are highlights. **72m/B VHS, Beta, LV, Letterbox.** Jerry Lewis, Alex Gerry, Bob Clayton, Sonny Sands; **Cameos:** Milton Berle, Walter Winchell; **D:** Jerry Lewis; **W:** Jerry Lewis. *ART*

The Bellboy and the Playgirls woof! *The Playgirls and the Bellboy; Mit Eva Fing Die Sunde An* 1962 Early Coppola effort adds new film footage to a 1958 German movie. Stars Playboy playmate June "The Body" Wilkinson, with other centerfolds of the time. **93m/C VHS.** June Wilkinson; **D:** Francis Ford Coppola; **W:** Francis Ford Coppola. *NO*

Belle Americaine ✯✯ *What a Chassis!* 1961 Title refers to the Cadillac car young Parisian factory worker Dhery buys at a suspiciously bargain price. Naturally, this deal is too good to be true and trouble follows. Dubbed in English. **97m/C VHS.** FR Robert Dhery, Louis de Funes, Collette Brosset, Alfred Adam, Bernard Lavelette, Annie Ducaux; **D:** Robert Dhery; **W:** Robert Dhery, Alfred Adam, Pierre Tchernia; **C:** Ghislan Cloquet; **M:** Gerard Calvi. *FCT*

Belle de Jour 🐾🐾🐾½ 1967 **(R)** Based on Joseph Kessel's novel, one of director Bunuel's best movies has all his characteristic nuances: the hypocrisy of our society; eroticism; anti-religion. Deneuve plays Severine, a chic, frigid Parisian newlywed, who decides to become a daytime prostitute, unbeknownst to her husband. Bunuel blends reality with fantasy, and the viewer is never sure which is which in this finely crafted movie. French with subtitles. **CW:** Language, sensuality, nudity, violence. **100m/C VHS, LV.** *FR* Catherine Deneuve, Jean Sorel, Genevieve Page, Michel Piccoli, Francesco Rabal, Pierre Clementi, Georges Marchal, Francoise Fabian; **D:** Luis Bunuel; **W:** Luis Bunuel, Jean-Claude Carriere; **C:** Sacha Vierny. *TOU*

Belle Epoque 🐾🐾🐾 *The Age of Beauty* 1992 **(R)** Young army deserter Fernando (Sanz) embarks on a personal voyage of discovery when he meets Manolo (Gomez), an eccentric old man, and father to four beautiful daughters. Fernando can't believe his luck—and the sisters share his interest, resulting in an amusing round of musical beds. Lighthearted romp set in 1930s Spain with a terrific screenplay that tastefully handles the material without stooping to the obvious leering possibilities. In addition to Oscar, won nine Spanish Goyas, including best picture, director, actress (Gil), and screenplay. Spanish with English subtitles or dubbed. **CW:** Brief nudity and sexual situations. **108m/C VHS, LV.** *SP* Jorge Sanz, Fernando Gomez, Ariadna Gil, Maribel Verdu, Penelope Cruz, Miriam Diaz-Aroca, Mary Carmen Ramirez, Michel Galabru, Gabino Diego; **D:** Fernando Trueba; **W:** Rafael Azcona. Academy Awards '93: Best Foreign Language Film. *-COL*

The Belle of New York 🐾🐾 1952 A turn-of-the-century bachelor falls in love with a Salvation Army missionary in this standard musical. ♫Naughty But Nice; Baby Doll; Oops; I Wanna Be a Dancin' Man; Seeing's Believing; Bachelor's Dinner Song; When I'm Out With the Belle of New York; Let a Little Love Come In. **82m/C VHS, Beta.** Fred Astaire, Vera-Ellen, Marjorie Main, Keenan Wynn, Alice Pearce, Gale Robbins, Clinton Sundberg; **D:** Charles Walters. *MGM, FHE*

Belle of the Nineties 🐾🐾½ 1934 West struts as a 1890s singer who gets involved with a boxer. Her trademark sexual innuendos were already being censored but such lines as "It's better to be looked over than overlooked," done in West style, get the point across. **73m/B VHS.** Mae West, Roger Pryor, Johnny Mack Brown, John Miljan, Katherine DeMille, Harry Woods, Edward Gargan; **D:** Leo McCarey; **W:** Mae West; **C:** Karl Struss. *USH, BTV*

Belle Starr 🐾½ 1979 The career of Wild West outlaw Belle Starr is chronicled in this strange western pastiche about lawlessness and sexual agression. Wertmuller directed under the pseudonym Nathan Wich. Dubbed in English. **90m/C VHS, Beta.** *IT* Elsa Martinelli, Robert Wood, George Eastman, Dan Harrison; **D:** Lina Wertmuller. *FCT*

The Belles of St. Trinian's 🐾🐾🐾 1953 Sim is priceless in a dual role as the eccentric headmistress of a chaotic, bankrupt girls' school and her bookie twin brother who scheme the school into financial security. The first in a series of movies based on a popular British cartoon by Ronald Searles about a girls' school and its mischievous students. Followed by "Blue Murder at St. Trinian's," "The Pure Hell of St. Trinian's," and "The Great St. Trinian's Train Robbery." **86m/B VHS, Beta.** *GB* Alastair Sim, Joyce Grenfell, Hermione Baddeley, George Cole, Eric Pohlmann, Renee Houston, Beryl Reid, Balbina, Jill Braidwood, Annabelle Covey, Betty Ann Davies, Diana Day, Jack Doyle, Irene Handl, Arthur Howard, Sidney James, Lloyd Lamble, Jean Langston, Belinda Lee, Vivian Martin, Andree Melly, Mary Merrall, Guy Middleton, Joan Sims, Jerry Verno, Richard Wattis; **D:** Frank Launder; **W:** Frank Launder, Sidney Gilliat, Val Valentine; **C:** Stanley Pavey; **M:** Malcolm Arnold, Malcolm Arnold. *REP*

Bellhop/The Noon Whistle 1922 Two comedic shorts back to back, separately featuring the famous comics Laurel and Hardy. **46m/B VHS, Beta.** Stan Laurel, Oliver Hardy. *CCB*

Bellissima 🐾🐾🐾 1951 A woman living in an Italian tenement has unrealistic goals for her plain but endearing daughter when a famous director begins casting a role designed for a child. The mother's maternal fury and collision with reality highlight a poignant film. Italian with subtitles. **130m/B VHS.** *IT* Anna Magnani; **D:** Luchino Visconti; **W:** Luchino Visconti, Cesare Zavattini, Francesco Rosi, Suso Cecchi D'Amico. *CIG*

Bellman and True 🐾🐾½ 1988 **(R)** Rewarding, but sometimes tedious character study of a mild mannered computer whiz who teams with a gang of bank robbers. Fine performances, especially subtle dangerous gang characters. **112m/C VHS, Beta.** *GB* Bernard Hill, Kieran O'Brien, Richard Hope, Frances Tomelty, Derek Newark, John Kavanagh, Ken Bones; **D:** Richard Loncraine; **M:** Colin Towns. *VTR, VES, MGM*

Bells Are Ringing 🐾🐾🐾 1960 A girl who works for a telephone answering service can't help but take an interest in the lives of the clients, especially a playwright with an inferiority complex. Based on Adolph Green and Betty Comden's Broadway musical. Special letterboxed edition along with the original trailer available on laserdisc format. ♫Just in Time; The Party's Over; It's a Perfect Relationship; Do It Yourself; It's a Simple Little System; Better Than a Dream; I Met a Girl; Drop That Name; I'm Going Back. **126m/C VHS, Beta, LV, Letterbox.** Judy Holliday, Dean Martin, Fred Clark, Eddie Foy Jr., Jean Stapleton; **D:** Vincente Minnelli; **W:** Betty Comden, Adolph Green; **C:** Milton Krasner; **M:** Andre Previn. Nominations: Academy Awards '60: Scoring of a Musical. *MGM*

Bells of Coronado 🐾🐾 1950 Rogers and Evans team up to expose the murderer of the owner of a profitable uranium mine. A gang of smugglers trying to trade the ore to foreign powers is thwarted. The usual thin storyline, but filled with action and riding stunts. **67m/B VHS.** Roy Rogers, Dale Evans, Pat Brady, Grant Withers; **D:** William Witney. *REP*

Bells of Death 🐾½ 1990 A young martial arts student infiltrates the gang that killed his family and kidnapped his sister, finishing them off one by one. **91m/C VHS.** Chun Ping, Chang Yi, Chao Hsin Yen; **D:** Yueh Fung.

Bells of Rosarita 🐾🐾½ 1945 Roy helps foil an evil plan to swindle Evans out of the circus she inherited. All-star western cast under the big top. **54m/B VHS, Beta.** Roy Rogers, Dale Evans, George "Gabby" Hayes, Sunset Carson, Adele Mara, Grant Withers, Roy Barcroft; **D:** Frank McDonald. *NOS, MRV, VCN*

The Bells of St. Mary's 🐾🐾🐾½ 1945 An easy-going priest finds himself in a subtle battle of wits with the Mother Superior over how the children of St. Mary's school should be raised. It's the sequel to "Going My Way." Songs include the title tune and "Aren't You Glad You're You?" Also available in a colorized version. **126m/B VHS, Beta, LV, Closed Caption.** Bing Crosby, Ingrid Bergman, Henry Travers; **D:** Leo McCarey; **C:** George Barnes. Academy Awards '45: Best Sound; Golden Globe Awards '46: Best Actress—Drama (Bergman); New York Film Critics Awards '45: Best Actress (Bergman); Nominations: Academy Awards '45: Best Actor (Crosby), Best Actress (Bergman), Best Director (McCarey), Best Film Editing, Best Picture, Best Song ("Aren't You Glad You're You"), Best Original Dramatic/Comedy Score. *REP, IGP*

Bells of San Angelo 🐾 1947 Roy foils thieves' attempts to steal a girl's inherited ranch. **54m/C VHS, Beta.** Roy Rogers, Dale Evans; **D:** William Witney. *NOS, DVT, TIM*

Bells of San Fernando 🐾 1947 An Irish seaman wanders into California during early Spanish rule and confronts a cruel overseer in this lackluster Western drama. Scripted by "Cisco Kid" Renaldo. **75m/B VHS.** Donald Woods, Gloria War-

ren, Byron Foulger; **D:** Terry Morse; **W:** Jack DeWitt, Duncan Renaldo. *MOV*

The Belly of an Architect 🐾🐾🐾½ 1991 **(R)** A thespian feast for the larger-than-life Dennehy as blustering American architect whose personal life and health both crumble as he obsesssively readies an exhibition in Rome. A multitiered, carefully composed tragicomedy from the ideosyncratic filmmaker Greenaway, probably his most accessible work for general audiences. **119m/C VHS, LV.** *GB IT* Brian Dennehy, Chloe Webb, Lambert Wilson; **D:** Peter Greenaway; **W:** Peter Greenaway; **C:** Sacha Vierny. *NO*

Beloved Enemy 🐾🐾🐾 1936 A romantic tragedy set in Civil War-torn Ireland in the 1920s. A rebel leader and a proper English lady struggle to overcome the war's interference with their burgeoning relationship. **86m/B VHS.** David Niven, Merle Oberon, Brian Aherne, Karen Morley, Donald Crisp; **D:** H.C. Potter; **C:** Gregg Toland. *HBO, CAB, NOS*

Beloved Infidel 🐾🐾½ 1959 Sudsy, lavish romancer, based on the book by gossip queen Sheilah Graham, about her brief romance with novelist F. Scott Fitzgerald. Fitzgerald (a badly miscast Peck) was in Hollywood trying to write screenplays when he meets young, English, aspiring writer Graham (an equally miscast Kerr). She becomes his mistress, putting up with Fitzgerald's drinking and insults, while he interferes with her career. Story is slanted towards Graham nobly trying to rescue Fitzgerald from himself (he did actually die from a heart attack while with Graham). **123m/C VHS.** Gregory Peck, Deborah Kerr, Eddie Albert, Philip Ober, Herbert Rudley, John Sutton, Karin Booth; **D:** Henry King; **W:** Sy Bartlett; **C:** Leon Shamroy; **M:** Franz Waxman. *FXV*

The Beloved Rogue 🐾🐾🐾 1927 Crosland—who gained a reputation for innovation, having directed "Don Juan" the previous year (noted for the debut of synchronized music), and "The Jazz Singer" the following year (noted for the first talkie bits)—mounted this well-designed and special effect-laden medieval costumer. Barrymore is in high profile as a swashbuckling caricature of French poet Francois Villon, who battles mightily (and verbally) with Louis XI (played by Veidt, in his first US film). Marked by the excesses typical of Barrymore's prestige days, it flouts history, taking generous poetic license when the facts ain't fab enough. In short, it's great entertainment. **110m/B VHS, Beta, LV.** John Barrymore, Conrad Veidt, Marceline Day, Henry Victor, Mack Swain, Slim Summerville; **D:** Alan Crosland. *GPV, FCT, CRC*

Below the Belt 🐾🐾 1980 **(R)** Almost interesting tale of street-smart woman from New York City who becomes part of the blue-collar "circus" of lady wrestlers. Ex-wrestling champ Burke plays herself. **98m/C VHS, Beta.** Regina Baff, Mildred Burke, John C. Becher; **D:** Robert Fowler. *TPV*

Below the Border 🐾½ 1942 The Rough Riders go undercover to straighten out some cattle rustlers. **57m/B VHS.** Buck Jones, Tim McCoy, Raymond Hatton, Linda Brent, Roy Barcroft, Charles "Blackie" King; **D:** Howard Bretherton. *NOS, DVT, VDM*

Below the Deadline 🐾 1929 A man framed for embezzlement is set free and allowed to clear his name by a sympathetic detective. **79m/B VHS.** Frank Leigh, Barbara Worth, Arthur Rankin, Walter Merrill; **D:** J.P. McGowan. *SNC, VYY*

The Belstone Fox 🐾🐾 1973 Orphaned fox goes into hiding, and is hunted by the hound he has befriended and his former owner. **103m/C VHS, Beta.** Eric Porter, Rachel Roberts, Jeremy Kemp; **D:** James Hill.

Ben 🐾½ 1972 **(PG)** Sequel to "Willard" finds police Detective Kirtland still on the hunt for a killer rat pack led by Ben, king of the rodents. Title song by young Michael Jackson hit the top of the charts. **95m/C VHS, Beta, LV.** Joseph Campanella, Lee Montgomery, Arthur O'Connell, Rosemary Murphy, Meredith Baxter, Norman Alden, Paul Carr, Kaz Garas, Kenneth Tobey, Richard Van Heet; **D:** Phil Karlson; **W:** Gilbert Ralston; **C:** Russell Metty. Golden Globe Awards '73: Best Song ("Ben"); Nominations: Academy Awards '72: Best Song ("Ben"). *NO*

Ben-Hur ♫♫♫♫ 1926 Second film version of the renowned story of Jewish and Christian divisiveness in the time of Jesus. Battle scenes and chariot races still look good, in spite of age. Problems lingered on the set and at a cost of over $4,000,000 it was the most expensive film of its time and took years to finish. A hit at the boxoffice, it still stands as the all-time silent classic. In 1931, a shortened version was released. Based on the novel by Lewis Wallace. 148m/B VHS, Beta, LV. Ramon Novarro, Francis X. Bushman, May McAvoy, Betty Bronson, Claire McDowell, Carmel Myers, Nigel de Brulier, Ferdinand P. Earle; **D:** Fred Niblo; **C:** Clyde De Vinna. National Film Registry '97. *MGM*

Ben-Hur ♫♫♫♫ 1959 The third film version of the Lew Wallace classic stars Heston in the role of a Palestinian Jew battling the Roman empire at the time of Christ. Won a record 11 Oscars. The breathtaking chariot race is still one of the best screen races today. Perhaps one of the greatest pictures of all time. Also available in letterbox format. 212m/C VHS, Beta, LV, Letterbox, Closed Caption. Charlton Heston, Jack Hawkins, Stephen Boyd, Haya Harareet, Hugh Griffith, Martha Scott, Sam Jaffe, Cathy O'Donnell, Finlay Currie; **D:** William Wyler; **W:** Karl Tunberg; **C:** Robert L. Surtees; **M:** Miklos Rozsa. Academy Awards '59: Best Actor (Heston), Best Art Direction/Set Decoration (Color), Best Color Cinematography, Best Costume Design (Color), Best Director (Wyler), Best Film Editing, Best Picture, Best Sound, Best Special Effects, Best Supporting Actor (Griffith), Best Original Dramatic/Comedy Score; British Academy Awards '59: Best Film; Directors Guild of America Awards '59: Best Director (Wyler); Golden Globe Awards '60: Best Director (Wyler), Best Film—Drama, Best Supporting Actor (Boyd); New York Film Critics Awards '59: Best Film; Nominations: Academy Awards '59: Best Adapted Screenplay. *MGM, BTV, RDG*

Ben Turpin: An Eye for an Eye 1924 Two silent Ben Turpin comedies: "He Looked Crooked, or Why Ben Bolted" (1917) and "Ten Dollars or Ten Days" (1924). 77m/B VHS, Beta, 8mm. Ben Turpin, Harry Gribbon. *VYY*

Bend of the River ♫♫♫ *Where the River Bends* 1952 A haunted, hardened guide leads a wagon train through Oregon territory, pitting himself against Indians, the wilderness and a former comrade-turned-hijacker. 91m/C VHS, Beta. James Stewart, Arthur Kennedy, Rock Hudson, Harry (Henry) Morgan, Royal Dano; **D:** Anthony Mann. *USH*

Beneath Arizona Skies/Paradise Canyon ♫♫½ 1935 A package of John Wayne westerns filled with lots of rumble tumble action. 109m/B VHS, Beta. John Wayne. *REP*

Beneath the Planet of the Apes ♫♫½ 1970 (G) In the first sequel, another Earth astronaut passes through the same warp and follows the same paths as Taylor, through Ape City and to the ruins of bomb-blasted New York's subway system, where warhead-worshipping human mutants are found. The strain of sequelling shows instantly, and gets worse through the next three films; followed by "Escape from the Planet of the Apes." 108m/C VHS, Beta, LV, Letterbox, Closed Caption. Charlton Heston, James Franciscus, Kim Hunter, Maurice Evans, James Gregory, Natalie Trundy, Jeff Corey, Linda Harrison, Victor Buono; **D:** Ted Post; **C:** Milton Krasner. *FOX, FUS*

Beneath the 12-Mile Reef ♫♫ 1953 Two rival groups of divers compete for sponge beds off the Florida coast. Lightweight entertainment notable for underwater photography and early Cinemascope production, as well as Moore in a bathing suit. 102m/C VHS, Beta, LV, Letterbox. Robert Wagner, Terry Moore, Gilbert Roland, Richard Boone, Peter Graves, J. Carrol Naish; **D:** Robert D. Webb. Nominations: Academy Awards '53: Best Color Cinematography. *NOS, FCT, GEM*

Beneath the Valley of the Ultra-Vixens ♫ 1979 Sex comedy retread directed by the man with an obsession for big. Scripted by Roger Ebert, who also scripted the cult classic "Beyond the Valley of the Dolls." Explicit nudity. 90m/C VHS. Francesca "Kitten" Natividad, Ann Marie, Ken Kerr, Stuart Lancaster; **D:** Russ Meyer; **W:** Roger Ebert. *RMF*

Benefit of the Doubt ♫♫ 1993 (R) Excon Sutherland, released from prison after 22 years, attempts to repaint his family a la Norman Rockwell. Grown-up daughter Irving, who testified against him in her mother's murder, wants to put a crimp in those plans since daddy's new vision of family fondness frankly makes her stomach turn. Aside from the sexual shenanigans, and the haunting Monument Valley backdrop, an extended chase scene would seem to be the film's only hope of salvation. Unfortunately, it fails to deliver, being both implausible and boring. Based on a story by Michael Lieber. **CW:** Language, violence, and sexuality. 92m/C VHS, Beta, Closed Caption. Donald Sutherland, Amy Irving, Christopher McDonald, Rider Strong, Graham Greene, Theodore Bikel, Gisele Kovach, Ferdinand "Ferdy" Mayne; **D:** Jonathan Heap; **W:** Jeffrey Polman, Christopher Keyser; **M:** Hummie Mann. *PAR*

The Beniker Gang ♫♫½ 1983 (G) Five orphans, supported by the eldest who writes a syndicated advice column, work together as a family. A made-for-television film. 87m/C VHS, Beta. Andrew McCarthy, Jennie Dundas, Danny Pintauro, Charlie Fields; **D:** Ken Kwapis. *WAR*

Benji ♫♫♫ 1974 (G) In the loveable mutt's first feature-length movie, he falls in love with a female named Tiffany, and saves two young children from kidnappers. Kiddie classic that was a boxoffice hit when first released. Followed by "For the Love of Benji." 87m/C VHS, Beta. Benji, Peter Breck, Christopher Connelly, Patsy Garrett, Deborah Walley, Cynthia Smith; **D:** Joe Camp; **W:** Joe Camp; **M:** Euel Box. Golden Globe Awards '75: Best Song ("I Feel Love"); Nominations: Academy Awards '74: Best Song ("Benji's Theme (I Feel Love)"). *VES, FCT, BFV*

Benji the Hunted ♫½ 1987 (G) The heroic canine, shipwrecked off the Oregon coast, discovers a litter of orphaned cougar cubs, and battles terrain and predators to bring them to safety. 89m/C VHS, Beta, LV, Closed Caption. Benji, Red Steagall, Frank Inn; **D:** Joe Camp; **W:** Joe Camp; **M:** Euel Box. *DIS*

Benji's Very Own Christmas Story 1983 Benji and his friends go on a magic trip and meet Kris Kringle and learn how Christmas is celebrated around the world. Also included: "The Phenomenon of Benji," a documentary about Benji's odyssey from the animal shelter to international stardom. 60m/C VHS, Beta. *BFV*

Benny & Joon ♫♫½ 1993 (PG) Depending on your tolerance for cute eccentrics and whimsy this will either charm you with sweetness or send you into sugar shock. Masterson is Joon, a mentally disturbed young woman who paints and has a habit of setting fires. She lives with overprotective brother Benny (Quinn). Sam (Depp) is the outsider who charms Joon, a dyslexic loner who impersonates his heroes Charlie Chaplin and Buster Keaton with eery accuracy. Depp is particularly fine with the physical demands of his role, but the film's easy dismissal of Joon's mental illness is a serious flaw. The laserdisc version is letterboxed. 98m/C VHS, Beta, LV, Letterbox, Closed Caption. Johnny Depp, Mary Stuart Masterson, Aidan Quinn, Julianne Moore, Oliver Platt, CCH Pounder, Dan Hedaya, Joe Grifasi, William H. Macy, Eileen Ryan; **D:** Jeremiah S. Chechik; **W:** Barry Berman; **M:** Rachel Portman. Nominations: Golden Globe Awards '94: Best Actor—Musical/Comedy (Depp); MTV Movie Awards '94: Best On-Screen Duo (Johnny Depp/Mary Stuart Masterson), Best Comedic Performance (Depp), Best Song ("I'm Gonna Be 500 Miles"). *MGM*

The Benny Goodman Story ♫♫ 1955 The life and music of Swing Era bandleader Benny Goodman is recounted in this popular biopic. Covering Benny's career from his child prodigy days to his monumental 1938 Carnegie Hall Jazz Concert, the movie's soggy plot machinations are redeemed by a non-stop music track featuring the real Benny and an all-star lineup. ♫Don't Be That Way; Memories of You; Sing, Sing, Sing; Slipped Disc. 116m/C VHS, Beta. Steve Allen, Donna Reed, Gene Krupa, Lionel Hampton, Kid Ory, Ben Pollack, Harry James, Stan Getz, Teddy Wilson, Martha Tilton; **D:** Valentine Davies; **M:** Henry Mancini. *USH, FCT*

Benny Hill's Crazy World 1974 The British comedian delivers some of his best material with the help of "Hill's Angels." 55m/C VHS, Beta. *GB* Benny Hill. *HBO*

Bent ♫♫ 1997 (NC-17) Theatre director Mathias makes his film debut with Sherman's adaptation of his 1979 play. Gay playboy Max (Owen) is enjoying the nightlife in decadent Berlin—until the Nazi crackdown. Soon, Max is in a cattle car on his way to Dachau, where he passes himself off as Jewish, thinking he'll be treated better. However Horst (Bluteau), who befriended Max on the train, is openly part of the pink triangle prisoners. Still, Max gets Horst assigned to the same meaningless hard labor and the duo fall in love—without ever be allowed to touch. Good performances (with Jagger notable in a brief role as a drag star) but the lingering staginess is to the film's detriment. **CW:** Strong scene of graphic sexuality. 104m/C VHS. *GB* Clive Owen, Lothaire Bluteau, Ian McKellen, Brian Webber, Mick Jagger; *Cameos:* Jude Law, Rupert Graves; **D:** Sean Mathias; **W:** Martin Sherman; **C:** Yorgos Arvanitis; **M:** Philip Glass. *NYR*

Beretta's Island ♫♫ 1992 (R) When Interpol operative Beretta comes out of retirement to track his friend's killer, the chase leads him back to his homeland of Sardinia, which has been overrun by drugs. **CW:** Some nudity and violence and drug use. 97m/C VHS. Franco Columbu, Ken Kercheval; *Cameos:* Arnold Schwarzenegger. *ART*

Bergonzi Hand ♫ 1970 Drama about two art scoundrels who are astonished when an immigrant admits to painting a forged "Bergonzi." 62m/C VHS, Beta. Keith Mitchell, Gordon Jackson, Martin Miller. *VYY*

The Berlin Affair ♫♫ 1985 (R) A sordid tale from "The Night Porter" director about a Japanese woman seducing various parties in pre-WWII Germany. 97m/C VHS, Beta. *IT GE* Mio Takaki, Gudrun Landgrebe, Kevin McNally; **D:** Liliana Cavani; **M:** Pino Donaggio. *MGM*

Berlin Alexanderplatz ♫♫♫½ 1980 Fassbinder's 15 1/2-hour epic follows the life, death, and resurrection of Franz Biberkof, a former transit worker who has just finished a lengthy prison term and must learn to adjust in the harsh social atmosphere of Berlin in the 1920s. Melodramatic parable with Biblical overtones considered by some to be a masterpiece. Based on the novel by Alfred Doblin; originally aired as a miniseries on German television. On eight tapes. 930m/C VHS, Beta. *GE* Gunter Lamprecht, Hanna Schygulla, Barbara Sukowa, Gottfried John, Elisabeth Trissenaar, Brigitte Mira, Karin Baal, Ivan Desny; **D:** Rainer Werner Fassbinder. *FCT, MGM*

Berlin Blues 1989 (PG-13) A nightclub singer is torn between two men. 90m/C VHS, LV. Julia Migenes-Johnson, Keith Baxter; **D:** Richardo Franco.

The Berlin Conspiracy ♫♫ 1991 (R) Espionage/action potboiler does an imaginative job of setting its action against the fall of the Berlin Wall and the end of the Cold War. A CIA agent forms a shaky alliance with his East German spymaster rival to prevent germ warfare technology from falling into terrorist hands. **CW:** Violence and sensuality. 83m/C VHS, LV. Marc Singer, Mary Crosby, Stephen Davies, Richard Leparmentier, Terence Henry; **D:** Terence H. Winkless. *COL*

Berlin Express ✈✈✈½ 1948 Battle of wits ensues between the Allies and the Nazis who are seeking to keep Germans divided in post-WWII Germany. Espionage and intrigue factor heavily. 86m/B VHS, Beta, LV. Robert Ryan, Merle Oberon, Paul Lukas, Charles Korvin; **D:** Jacques Tourneur. *TTC, FCT*

Berlin Tunnel 21 ✈½ 1981 Based on the novel by Donald Lindquist, five American soldiers attempt a daring Cold War rescue of a beautiful German girl. The plan is to construct a tunnel under the Berlin Wall. A better-than-average film that was made for television. 150m/C VHS, Beta. Richard Thomas, Jose Ferrer, Horst Buchholz; **D:** Richard Michaels. *NO*

Bernadette ✈✈½ 1990 A French-made version of the legend of St. Bernadette, who endured persecution after claiming to have seen the Virgin Mary. Beautiful in its simplicity, but overly long. 120m/C VHS, Beta. FR Sydney Penny, Roland LeSaffre, Michele Simonnet, Bernard Dheran, Arlette Didier; **D:** Jean Delannoy. *IGP*

Bernard and the Genie ✈✈½ 199? (G) It seems Bernard Bottle is not going to have a happy Christmas—he's been fired from his job and his girlfriend has left him. But things take a turn for the better when he discovers an antique lamp and its resident Genie. But with the Genie granting his every wish, Bernard's sudden wealth is causing some suspicions among both his greedy ex-employer and the police. Meanwhile, the Genie discovers the delights of modern-day England and poses as a department store Santa to truly fulfill a child's Christmas wish. Amusing family fare. 70m/C VHS, Closed Caption. GB Alan Cumming, Lenny Henry, Rowan Atkinson; **D:** Paul Weiland. *FOX, BTV, VCO*

Berserk! ✈½ 1967 A seedy traveling circus is beset by a series of murders. Not heralded as one of Crawford's best pieces. 95m/C VHS, Beta. Joan Crawford, Diana Dors, Judy Geeson, Ty Hardin; **D:** James O'Connolly. *COL*

Berserker ✈ 1987 (R) Six camping college students are attacked by a bloodthirsty psychotic out of a Nordic myth, who takes the shape of a badder-than-the-average bear. 85m/C VHS, Beta. Joseph Alan Johnson, Valerie Sheldon, Greg Dawson; **D:** Jef Richard.

Bert Rigby, You're a Fool ✈✈½ 1989 (R) A starstruck British coal miner finds his way to Hollywood singing old showtunes, only to be rebuffed by a cynical industry. Available with Spanish subtitles. 94m/C VHS, Beta, LV, Closed Caption. Robert Lindsay, Robbie Coltrane, Jackie Gayle, Bruno Kirby, Cathryn Bradshaw, Corbin Bernsen, Anne Bancroft; **D:** Carl Reiner; **W:** Carl Reiner; **C:** Jan De Bont; **M:** Ralph Burns. *WAR, MVD*

Best Buns on the Beach woof! 1987 Sexploitation movie about 10 beautiful girls in a bikini contest, that ends up with them going topless. Ridiculous plot, for mature (??) audiences. 60m/C VHS, LV. *IME*

The Best Christmas Pageant Ever 1986 The meanest kids in town just decided to participate in the town's Christmas pageant and something special happens when the curtain finally goes up. 60m/C VHS. Dennis Weaver, Karen Grassle. *RHV*

Best Defense ✈ 1984 (R) A U.S. Army tank operator is sent to Kuwait to test a new state-of-the-art tank in a combat situation. Although the cast is popular, the movie as a whole is not funny and the story frequently is hard to follow. 94m/C VHS, Beta, LV, Closed Caption. Dudley Moore, Eddie Murphy, Kate Capshaw, George Dzundza, Helen Shaver; **D:** Willard Huyck; **W:** Willard Huyck, Gloria Katz. *PAR*

Best Enemies ✈½ 1986 An English film about a man suffering the trials of the 1960s, including Vietnam, and how it affects his relationships with his friends and wife. 96m/C VHS, Beta. GB Sigrid Thornton, Paul Williams, Judy Morris, Brandon Burke; **D:** David Baker.

Best Foot Forward ✈✈½ 1943 Vintage musical about a movie star who agrees to accompany a young cadet to a military ball. Based on the popular Broadway show. The film debuts of Walker, Allyson, and DeHaven. ♫Buckle Down, Winsocki; The Three B's (Barrelhouse, Boogie Woogie, and the Blues); Alive and Kicking; Two O'Clock Jump; Ev'ry Time; Three Men on a Date; Wish I May; Shady Lady; My First Promise. 95m/C VHS, Beta. Lucille Ball, June Allyson, Tommy Dix, Nancy Walker, Virginia Weidler, Gloria De Haven, Harry James; **D:** Edward Buzzell; **W:** Irving Brecher; **M:** George Bassman. *MGM*

Best Friends ✈✈ 1982 (PG) A pair of screenwriters decide to marry after years of living and working together. Story based on the lives of screenwriters Barry Levinson and Valerie Curtin. 109m/C VHS, Beta, LV. Goldie Hawn, Burt Reynolds, Jessica Tandy, Barnard Hughes, Audra Lindley, Keenan Wynn, Ron Silver; **D:** Norman Jewison; **W:** Valerie Curtin, Barry Levinson; **C:** Jordan Cronenweth. Nominations: Academy Awards '82: Best Song ("How Do You Keep the Music Playing"). *WAR*

The Best Intentions ✈✈✈½ 1992 Ingmar Bergman wrote the screenplay chronicling the early years of the stormy relationship of his parents. Set in Sweden at the turn of the century, the film focuses on the class differences that divide his mother and father, while portrayal of little Bergy is limited to a bundle under his mother's maternity dress. Inspired performances and directing illuminates the emotionally complex relationship, revealing truths about the universal human condition along the way. Six-hour version was shot for television in Europe and Japan. 182m/C VHS. SW Samuel Froler, Pernilla August, Max von Sydow, Ghita Norby, Mona Malm, Lena Endre, Bjorn Kjellman; **D:** Bille August; **W:** Ingmar Bergman. Cannes Film Festival '92: Best Actress (August), Best Film. *FCT*

Best Kept Secrets ✈✈½ 1988 A feisty woman discovers corruption and blackmail in the police department where her husband is an officer. 104m/C VHS, Beta. Patty Duke, Frederic Forrest, Peter Coyote; **D:** Jerrold Freedman. *THV*

Best Legs in the 8th Grade ✈✈ 1984 A handsome attorney bumps into the gorgeous homeroom angel who had ignored his nebbishly dull countenance in grade school. Lightweight made for TV comedy. 60m/C VHS, Beta. Tim Matheson, James Belushi, Annette O'Toole, Kathryn Harrold; **D:** Tom Patchett. *NO*

The Best Little Girl in the World ✈✈✈ 1981 Exceptional made for TV tale of an apparently perfect teenager suffering from anorexia. Slow starvation is her only cry for help. Fine performances from Durning and Saint. 96m/C VHS, Beta. Charles Durning, Eva Marie Saint, Jennifer Jason Leigh, Melanie Mayron, Viveca Lindfors, Jason Miller, David Spielberg, Lisa Pelikan, Ally Sheedy; **D:** Sam O'Steen; **M:** Billy Goldenberg. *NO*

The Best Little Whorehouse in Texas ✈✈ 1982 (R) Parton is the buxom owner of The Chicken Ranch, a house of ill-repute that may be closed down unless Sheriff-boyfriend Reynolds can think of a way out. Strong performances don't quite make up for the erratically comic script. Based on the long-running Broadway musical, in turn based on a story by Larry McMurtry. Available in a letterboxed edition on laserdisc. 115m/C VHS, Beta, LV, Letterbox. Dolly Parton, Burt Reynolds, Dom DeLuise, Charles Durning, Jim Nabors, Lois Nettleton; **D:** Colin Higgins. Nominations: Academy Awards '82: Best Supporting Actor (Durning). *USH, FCT*

The Best Man ✈✈✈½ 1964 An incisive, darkly satiric political tract, based on Gore Vidal's play, about two presidential contenders who vie for the endorsement of the aging ex-president, and trample political ethics in the process. 104m/B VHS, Beta. Henry Fonda, Cliff Robertson, Lee Tracy, Margaret Leighton, Edie Adams, Kevin McCarthy, Ann Sothern, Gene Raymond, Shelley Berman, Mahalia Jackson; **D:** Franklin J. Schaffner; **W:** Gore Vidal; **C:** Haskell Wexler. Nominations: Academy Awards '64: Best Supporting Actor (Tracy). *MGM*

The Best of Abbott & Costello Live 1954 A compilation of vintage live-television routines by the duo, naturally including "Who's on First," along with their other celebrated bits. 58m/B VHS, Beta. Bud Abbott, Lou Costello, George Raft, Charles Laughton. *WAR*

The Best of Bogart ✈✈✈ 1943 A two-cassette gift pack of the Bogie classics "The Maltese Falcon" and "Casablanca." 204m/B VHS, Beta. Humphrey Bogart, Ingrid Bergman, Mary Astor, Sydney Greenstreet. *MGM*

Best of Bugs Bunny & Friends 1940 This collection includes classics from great cartoon stars Bugs Bunny, Daffy Duck, Tweetie Pie and Porky Pig. Includes "Duck Soup to Nuts," "A Feud There Was" and "Tweetie Pie." 53m/C VHS, Beta. **D:** Isadore "Friz" Freleng, Chuck Jones, Robert McKimson. Academy Awards '47: Best Animated Short Film ("Tweetie Pie"). *MGM*

The Best of Chaplin 1918 Three Chaplin comedies when he worked with Mutual. Includes "The Rink," "One A.M.," and "The Floorwalker." 60m/B VHS. Charlie Chaplin; **D:** Charlie Chaplin. *MVC, VRS*

The Best of Cracker Mysteries ✈✈✈ 1993 Coltrane stars as brilliant-but-abrasive forensic psychologist Dr. Eddie Fitzgerald. His insatiable desires for smoking, drinking, and gambling have blown apart his marriage and caused him grief at work. But Fitz's brilliant at "cracking" cases by reading clues (and people) to nail wrongdoers. In "The Mad Woman in the Attic," a murder suspect, claiming to have amnesia, may be a serial killer. "To Say I Love You," finds a loan shark getting murdered and a recently paroled hijacker and his girlfriend being involved. And in "One Day a Lemming Will Fly," a teen suicide turns out to be murder. On three cassettes. 350m/C VHS. GB Robbie Coltrane, Andrew Tiernan, Susan Lynch, Christopher Eccleston, Beryl Reid, Adrian Dunbar, Barbara Flynn, Geraldine Somerville, Lorcan Cranitch, Frances Tomelty; **D:** Simon Cellan Jones, Michael Winterbottom, Andy Wilson; **W:** Jimmy McGovern. *PBS, AEH, TVC*

Best of Eddie Murphy ✈½ 1989 A compilation of Murphy's funniest bits from his three seasons on "Saturday Night Live," including appearances as Stevie Wonder, Buckwheat, Bill Cosby and Little Richard. 78m/C VHS, Beta, Closed Caption. Eddie Murphy, Joe Piscopo, Robin Duke, Tim Kazurinsky, Mary Gross, Gary Kroeger, Brad Hall, Julia Louis-Dreyfus. *PAR*

Best of Ernie Kovacs 1956 A compilation of some of the best moments from Ernie Kovacs' television programs that features such memorable characters as Percy Dovetonsils and the Nairobi Trio. 60m/B VHS, Beta. Ernie Kovacs, Edie Adams, Ernie Hatrak, Bill Wendell, Peter Hanley. *WST, DVT, TVC*

The Best of Everything ✈✈✈ 1959 Trashy sexist soap opera about women seeking success and love in the publishing world of N.Y.C. Several stories take place, the best being Crawford's hard-nosed editor who's having an affair with a married man. Look for Evans as a philandering playboy (he went on to become the producer of "Chinatown," among others.) Based on the novel by Rona Jaffe. 121m/C VHS, Closed Caption. Hope Lange, Stephen Boyd, Suzy Parker, Diane Baker, Martha Hyer, Joan Crawford, Brian Aherne, Robert Evans, Louis Jourdan; **D:** Jean Negulesco; **W:** Edith Sommer, Mann Rubin; **C:** William Mellor; **M:** Alfred Newman. Nominations: Academy Awards '59: Best Costume Design (Color), Best Song ("The Best of Everything"). *FXV*

The Best of John Candy on SCTV 198? Some of Candy's most memorable characters, including Johnny LaRue, Yosh Schmenge, and the grown up Theodore "Beaver" Cleaver, are featured on this compilation of his years on SCTV (Second City Television). **62m/C VHS, LV.** John Candy, Eugene Levy, Rick Moranis, Catherine O'Hara, Harold Ramis, Martin Short. *COL*

The Best of Lovejoy Mysteries 1993 Four-tape series features the best adventures of irrepressible (if untrustworthy) antiques dealer Lovejoy (McShane). What he usually discovers are forgeries, dirty dealing, and other assorted mayhem. Based on the mysteries by Jonathan Gash; made for British TV. **200m/C VHS.** *GB* Ian McShane, Phyllis Logan, Dudley Sutton, Chris Jury. *TVC, AEH*

The Best of Soap: Jessica's Wonderful Life 197? From the camp TV sitcom comes this take-off on "It's a Wonderful Life." Jessica Tate (Helmond) finds herself at the stairway to heaven, pleading with an angel (Arthur) to return to aid her very dysfunctional family. **70m/C VHS.** Katherine Helmond, Beatrice Arthur, Robert Mandan, Cathryn Damon, Richard Mulligan, Billy Crystal. *REP*

The Best of Soap: Who Killed Peter? 1977 From the outrageous comedy TV series, featuring the eccentric and rich Tate family and the equally eccentric, but working-class, Campbell family. When Jessica Tate (Helmond) is convicted of murdering her tennis pro, brother-in-law Burt (Mulligan) decides to investigate. Crystal gained attention as gay son Jodie Dallas. **72m/C VHS.** Katherine Helmond, Richard Mulligan, Diana Canova, Robert Urich, Robert Mandan, Ted Wass, Billy Crystal, Robert Guillaume. *REP*

Best of the Badmen ✍️✍️½ 1950 A whole bunch of outlaws, although seemingly quite nice, are brought together by an ex-Union general who is being framed. Too much talk, not enough action. **84m/B VHS, Beta.** Robert Ryan, Claire Trevor, Jack Buetel, Robert Preston, Walter Brennan, Bruce Cabot, John Archer, Lawrence Tierney; *D:* William D. Russell. *TTC*

Best of the Best ✍️½ 1989 (PG-13) An interracial kick-boxing team strives to win a world championship. **95m/C VHS, Beta, LV.** Eric Roberts, Sally Kirkland, Christopher Penn, Phillip Rhee, James Earl Jones, John P. Ryan, John Dye, David Agresta, Tom Everett, Louise Fletcher, Simon Rhee; *D:* Robert Radler. *COL*

Best of the Best 2 ✍️½ 1993 (R) The Coliseum is a notorious martial-arts venue owned by the champion fighter Brackus and his manager Weldon. No rules death matches are the norm and when their friend is killed Tommy and Alex set up a grudge match with Brackus.*CW:* Strong martial arts violence. **100m/C VHS, LV, Letterbox, Closed Caption.** Eric Roberts, Phillip Rhee, Christopher Penn, Ralph Moeller, Wayne Newton, Edan Gross, Sonny Landham, Meg Foster, Simon Rhee, Claire Stansfield, Betty Carvalho; *D:* Robert Radler; *W:* John Allen Nelson, Max Strom; *M:* David Michael Frank. *FOX*

Best of the Best 3: No Turning Back ✍️✍️ 1995 (R) Asian-American Tommy Lee (Rhee) discovers a band of racist vigilantes are trying to take over the rural community of Liberty, where his sister lives. But with the help of his brother-in-law Jack (McDonald), who' also the sheriff, and school teacher Margo (Gershon), Tommy is going to fight back.*CW:* Shootings and martial arts violence. **102m/C VHS, LV, Closed Caption.** Phillip Rhee, Gina Gershon, Christopher McDonald, Mark Rolston, Peter Simmons, Dee Wallace Stone; *D:* Phillip Rhee; *W:* Deborah Scott. *TOU*

The Best of the Kenny Everett Video Show 1981 Scenes from the popular British late-night television show combining new wave rock music, outrageous dancing and innovative video special effects. **104m/C VHS, Beta.** Kenny Everett. *NO*

The Best of the Kids in the Hall 1993 Features some of the best clips of the hot Canadian comedy ensemble "The Kids in the Hall." Executive producer Lorne Michaels is best known for producing "Saturday Night Live." **120m/ C VHS.** *CA* Dave Foley, Bruce McCulloch, Kevin McDonald, Mark McKinney, Scott Thompson. *COL*

The Best of the Two Ronnies 197? A selection of skits from the well-loved BBC comedy series. **45m/C VHS, Beta, Closed Caption.** *GB* Ronnie Barker, Ronnie Corbett. *FOX*

The Best of Times ✍️✍️ 1986 (PG) Slim story of two grown men who attempt to redress the failures of the past by reenacting a football game they lost in high school due to a single flubbed pass. With this cast, it should have been better. **105m/C VHS, Beta, LV, 8mm, Closed Caption.** Robin Williams, Kurt Russell, M. Emmet Walsh, Pamela Reed, Holly Palance, Donald Moffat, Margaret Whitton, Kirk Cameron; *D:* Roger Spottiswoode; *W:* Ron Shelton. *NLC*

Best of W.C. Fields 1933 Three of W.C. Field's Mack Sennett shorts are presented in their complete, uncut form: "The Dentist," "The Fatal Glass of Beer," and "The Golf Specialist." **58m/B VHS.** W.C. Fields, Elise Cavanna. *REP*

Best Revenge ✍️✍️ 1983 (R) Two aging hippies engage in a Moroccan drug deal in order to free a kidnapped friend from a sleazy gangster. They get caught by the police, but escape, searching for the engineers of the frame-up. **92m/ C VHS, Beta.** John Heard, Levon Helm, Alberta Watson, John Rhys-Davies, Moses Znaimer; *D:* John Trent; *M:* Keith Emerson. *ORI, WAR*

Best Seller ✍️✍️✍️ 1987 (R) Interesting, subtext-laden thriller about a cop/bestselling author with writer's block, and the strange symbiotic relationship he forms with a slick hired killer, who wants his own story written. Dennehy is convincing as the jaded cop, and is paired well with the psychotic Woods. **112m/C VHS, Beta, LV.** James Woods, Brian Dennehy, Victoria Tennant, Paul Shenar, Seymour Cassel, Allison Balson, George Coe, Anne Pitoniak; *D:* John Flynn; *W:* Larry Cohen; *M:* Jay Michael Ferguson. *VES*

The Best Way ✍️✍️½ *The Best Way to Walk; La Meilleure Facon de Marcher* 1976 Two summer camp counselors discover they might be gay and desirous of each other. Miller's first film; in French with English subtitles. **85m/C VHS, Beta.** *FR* Patrick Dewaere, Patrick Bouchitey, Christine Pascal, Claude Pieplu; *D:* Claude Miller; *W:* Luc Beraud, Claude Miller; *C:* Bruno Nuytten; *M:* Alain Jomy. *FCT*

The Best Years of Our Lives ✍️✍️✍️✍️ 1946 Three WWII vets return home to try to pick up the threads of their lives. A film that represented a large chunk of American society and helped it readjust to the modern postwar ambience is now considered an American classic. Supporting actor Russell, an actual veteran, holds a record for winning two Oscars for a single role. In addition to his Best Supporting Actor award, Russell was given a special Oscar for bringing hope and courage to fellow veterans. Based on the novella by MacKinlay Kantor. Remade for television as "Returning Home" in 1975. **170m/B VHS, Beta, LV.** Fredric March, Myrna Loy, Teresa Wright, Dana Andrews, Virginia Mayo, Harold Russell, Hoagy Carmichael, Gladys George, Roman Bohnen, Steve Cochran, Charles Halton; *D:* William Wyler; *W:* Robert Sherwood; *C:* Gregg Toland; *M:* Hugo Friedhofer. Academy Awards '46: Best Actor (March), Best Director (Wyler), Best Film Editing, Best Picture, Best Screenplay, Best Supporting Actor (Russell), Best Original Dramatic/Comedy Score; British Academy Awards '47: Best Film; Golden Globe Awards '47: Best Film—Drama; National Board of Review Awards '46: Best Director (Wyler), National Film Registry '89;; New York Film Critics Awards '46: Best Director (Wyler), Best Film; Nominations: Academy Awards '46: Best Sound. *HBO, FCT, BTV*

Bethune ✍️✍️½ 1977 The life story of a Canadian doctor who started a practice in Communist China. **88m/C VHS, Beta.** Donald Sutherland, Kate Nelligan, David Gardner, James Hong; *D:* Eric Till. *TWE*

Betrayal ✍️ 1974 Psycho-thriller pits an unhappy widow against her seemingly innocent hired companion. Seems this girl has a boyfriend who has a plan to murder the lonely lady for her money. Routine and predictable. **78m/C VHS.** Amanda Blake, Dick Haymes, Tisha Sterling, Sam Groom; *D:* Gordon Hessler; *M:* Ernest Gold. *JEF*

Betrayal ✍️½ 1978 Telefilm based on the book by Lucy Freeman and Julie Roy about a historic malpractice case involving a psychiatrist and one of his female patients. The doctor convinced the female patient that sex with him would serve as therapy. **95m/C VHS, Beta.** Lesley Ann Warren, Rip Torn, Ron Silver, Richard Masur, Stephen Elliott, John Hillerman, Peggy Ann Garner; *D:* Paul Wendkos. *NO*

Betrayal ✍️✍️½ 1983 (R) An unusual adult drama, beginning at the end of a seven-year adulterous affair and working its way back in time to finally end at the start of the betrayal of a husband by his wife and his best friend. Kingsley and Irons make Pinter's adaptation of his own play work. **95m/C VHS, Beta.** *GB* Ben Kingsley, Patricia Hodge, Jeremy Irons; *D:* David Jones; *W:* Harold Pinter. Nominations: Academy Awards '83: Best Adapted Screenplay. *FOX*

Betrayal from the East ✍️✍️ 1944 A carnival barker saves the Panama Canal from the vicious Japanese war machine in this rather silly wartime drama. **82m/B VHS, Beta.** Lee Tracy, Nancy Kelly, Richard Loo, Abner Biberman, Regis Toomey, Philip Ahn, Addison Richards, Victor Sen Yung, Drew Pearson; *D:* William (Lester Williams) Berke. *TTC*

Betrayal of the Dove ✍️✍️ 1992 (R) Slater stars as a divorced woman set-up on a blind date by best friend Le Brock. Zane is the dashing doctor who sweeps Slater off her feet but things are never quite what they seem. He may not be Mr. Right and the best friend has her own hidden agenda.*CW:* Language, violence, and sexuality. **93m/C VHS.** Helen Slater, Kelly Le Brock, Billy Zane, Alan Thicke, Harvey Korman, Stuart Pankin, David Lander; *D:* Strathford Hamilton; *W:* Robby Benson.

Betrayed ✍️✍️✍️ 1954 Bombshell Turner and strongman Gable star in this story of WWII intrigue. Suspected of being a Nazi informer, Turner is sent back to Holland for a last chance at redemption. Her cover as a sultry nightclub performer has the Nazis drooling and ogling (can you spell h-o-t?), but her act may be blown by an informant. Can luscious Lana get out of this one intact? **107m/C VHS, Beta.** Clark Gable, Lana Turner, Victor Mature, Louis Calhern, O.E. Hasse, Wilfrid Hyde-White, Ian Carmichael, Niall MacGinnis, Nora Swinburne, Roland Culver; *D:* Gottfried Reinhardt; *C:* Frederick A. (Freddie) Young. *MGM, CCB*

Betrayed ✍️✍️ 1988 (R) A rabid political film, dealing with an implausible FBI agent infiltrating a white supremacist organization via her love affair with a handsome farmer who turns out to be a murderous racist. Winger is memorable in her role as the FBI agent, despite the film's limitations, and admirers of Costa-Gavras's directorial work and political stances will want to see how the director botched this one. **112m/C VHS, Beta, LV, Closed Caption.** Tom Berenger, Debra Winger, John Mahoney, John Heard, Albert Hall, Jeffrey DeMunn; *D:* John Mahoney, John Heard, Albert Hall, Jeffrey DeMunn; *D:* Constantin Costa-Gavras; *W:* Joe Eszterhas; *C:* Patrick Blossier. *MGM*

The Betsy ✍️✍️ *Harold Robbins' The Betsy* 1978 (R) A story of romance, money, power, and mystery centering around the wealthy Hardeman family and their automobile manufacturing business. Loosely patterned after the life of Henry Ford as portrayed in the Harold Robbins' pulp-tome. Olivier is the redeeming feature. **132m/C VHS, Beta.** Laurence Olivier, Kathleen Beller, Robert Duvall, Lesley-Anne Down, Edward Herrmann, Tommy Lee Jones, Katharine Ross, Jane Alexander; *D:* Daniel Petrie; *W:* William Bast, Walter Bernstein; *M:* John Barry. *FOX*

Betsy's Wedding ✍️✍️½ 1990 (R) Betsy wants a simple wedding, but her father has other, grander ideas. Then there's the problem of paying for it, which Dad tries to take care of in a not-so-typical manner. Alda at his hilarious best. **94m/C VHS, Beta, LV, Closed Caption.** Alan Alda, Joey Bishop, Madeline Kahn, Molly Ringwald, Catherine O'Hara, Joe Pesci, Ally Sheedy, Burt Young, Anthony LaPaglia, Julie Bovasso, Nicolas Coster, Bibi Besch, Dylan Walsh; *D:* Alan Alda; *W:* Alan Alda; *M:* Bruce Broughton. *TOU*

Better Late Than Never 🎬🎬 1979
Fun television tale of senior citizens in revolt at an old-age home. Fine characters portrayed by some of the best in the business. **100m/C VHS.** Harold Gould, Tyne Daly, Strother Martin, Harry (Henry) Morgan, Victor Buono, George Gobel, Lou Jacobi, Donald Pleasence, Larry Storch; *D:* Richard Crenna; *M:* Charles Fox. *FOX*

Better Late Than Never 🎬🎬½ 1983
Two penniless old fools vie for the acceptance of a bratty 10-year-old millionairess, who must choose one as her guardian. Niven's last film. **95m/C VHS, Beta.** David Niven, Art Carney, Maggie Smith, Kimberly Partridge, Catherine Hicks, Melissa Prophet; *D:* Bryan Forbes; *M:* Henry Mancini. *FOX*

Better Off Dead 🎬🎬½ 1985 (PG)
A compulsive teenager's girlfriend leaves him and he decides to end it all. After several abortive attempts, he decides instead to out-ski his ex-girlfriend's obnoxious new boyfriend. Uneven but funny. **97m/C VHS, Beta, LV, Closed Caption.** John Cusack, Curtis Armstrong, Diane Franklin, Kim Darby, David Ogden Stiers, Dan Schneider, Amanda Wyss, Taylor Negron, Vincent Schiavelli, Demian Slade, Scooter Stevens; *D:* Steve Holland; *W:* Steve Holland; *M:* Rupert Hine. *FOX*

Better Off Dead 🎬🎬½ 1994
Preachy, manipulative TV movie redeemed by good performances. Kit (Winningham) is an unrepentant white-trash thief who kills a black police officer and is sentenced to death. Cutter Dubuque (Ferrell) is the ambitious black district attorney who prosecuted the case but comes to doubt the wisdom of the death penalty and slowly begins to try to help Kit. **91m/C VHS.** Mare Winningham, Tyra Ferrell, Kevin Tighe, Don Harvey; *D:* M. Neema Barnette; *W:* Marlane X. Meyer; *C:* Ueli Steiger; *M:* John Barnes. *TTC*

A Better Tomorrow 🎬🎬½
Yingxiong Bense 1986 Former hit men (Leung and Fat) team up to bring down the mob boss who double-crossed them and sent one to prison and the other to the streets. One of them also has to protect his younger brother, a cop, from the gang. Considered one of the best of Woo's Hong Kong efforts, there's plenty of his hallmark balletic action and an interesting story. In Cantonese with English subtitles. **95m/C VHS.** CH Chow Yung Fat, Leslie Cheung, Ti Lung; *D:* John Woo. *REP, FCT*

A Better Tomorrow, Part 2 🎬½ 1988
A smooth-talking gangster, who was killed in Part I, returns in Part II as the dead man's twin brother (unmentioned in Part I). He teams up with a cop and a reformed gangster to fight the forces of evil. In Cantonese with English subtitles. **100m/C VHS.** HK Chow Yung Fat, Leslie Cheung; *D:* John Woo. *FCT*

A Better Tomorrow, Part 3 🎬🎬
Love and Death in Saigon 1989 Prequel set in 1974 finds detective Mark Gor (Fat) and his cousin (Leung) seeking to escape from Saigon. Unfortunately, they both fall for the same sultry babe (Mui), who's also a gangster's moll. Mandarin with subtitles. **114m/C VHS.** HK Chow Yung Fat, Tony Leung, Anita Mui; *D:* Tsui Hark. *FCT*

Betty 🎬🎬 1992
Sulky, drunken Betty (Trintignant) is doing her best to destroy her bourgeois life, escaping from her marriage into adultery and debasement. She meets the concerned middle-aged widow Laure (Audran), who inexplicably takes her to her hotel room, cleans her up, and spends the remainder of the movie as Betty's sounding-board. Betty's passive personality offers little to explain her appeal to either Laure or the viewer. Based on the novel by Georges Simenon. French with subtitles. **103m/C VHS.** FR Marie Trintignant, Stephane Audran, Jean-Francoise Garreau, Yves Lambrecht, Christiane Minazolli, Pierre Vernier; *D:* Claude Chabrol; *W:* Claude Chabrol; *M:* Matthieu Chabrol. *NYF*

Betty Blue 🎬🎬🎬 1986 (R)
A vivid, intensely erotic film about two young French lovers and how their inordinately strong passion for each other destroys them, leading to poverty, violence, and insanity. English subtitles. From the director of "Diva." Based on the novel "37.2 Le Matin" by Philippe Djian. **121m/C VHS, Beta, LV, Closed Caption.** FR Beatrice Dalle, Jean-Hugues Anglade, Gerard Darmon, Consuelo de Haviland, Clementine Celarie, Jacques Mathou, Vincent Lindon; *D:* Jean-Jacques Beineix; *W:* Jean-Jacques Beineix; *M:* Gabriel Yared. Nominations: Academy Awards '86: Best Foreign Language Film; Cesar Awards '86: Best Actor (Anglade). *FOX*

Between Fighting Men 🎬½ 1932
The orphaned daughter of a shepherd is adopted by the cowpoke who caused her father's death. The cowpoke's sons fall in love with, and compete for, the love of the girl. **62m/B VHS.** Ken Maynard, Ruth Hall, Josephine Dunn, Wallace MacDonald; *D:* Forrest Sheldon. *NOS, DVT*

Between Friends 🎬🎬½ 1983
Two women with only their respective divorces in common, meet and become fast friends. The rapport between Burnett and Taylor makes for a touching drama. Adapted for cable television from the book "Nobody Makes Me Cry," by Shelley List, one of the producers. **105m/C VHS, Beta.** Elizabeth Taylor, Carol Burnett; *D:* Lou Antonio; *M:* James Horner. *VES*

Between God, the Devil & a Winchester 🎬 1972
Violent western with plenty of shooting and dust. Lots of cowboys are hot on the trail of some stolen loot from a church but apparently God isn't on their side since the majority bite the dust and become a snack for the vultures. **98m/C VHS, Beta.** Gilbert Roland, Richard Harrison; *D:* Dario Silvester. *UNI*

Between Heaven and Earth 🎬🎬
1993 Maria (Maura) is an ambitious television journalist, prone to surreal dreams, who becomes pregnant after a one-night stand. After witnessing a violent protest, Maria becomes convinced that she can communicate with her unborn baby and that the child is unwilling to be born into such a violent world. So Maria must try to convince her baby otherwise. In French with English subtitles. **80m/C VHS.** BE FR SP Carmen Maura, Jean-Pierre Cassel, Didier Bezace, Samuel Mussen, Andre Delvaux; *D:* Marion Hansel; *W:* Marion Hansel. *FCT*

Between Heaven and Hell 🎬🎬🎬
1956 Prejudiced Southern gentleman Wagner finds how wrong his misconceptions are, as he attempts to survive WWII on a Pacific Island. Ebsen is exceptional, making this rather simplistic story a meaningful classic. **94m/C VHS.** Robert Wagner, Terry Moore, Broderick Crawford, Buddy Ebsen, Robert Keith, Brad Dexter, Mark Damon, Kenneth Clark, Harvey Lembeck, Frank Gorshin, Scatman Crothers; *D:* Richard Fleischer. Nominations: Academy Awards '56: Best Original Dramatic/Comedy Score. *FOX*

Between Men 🎬🎬 1935
A father kills a man he believes killed his son and flees. Later in life, the son meets his father. For father and son, this causes some major concern. **59m/B VHS, Beta.** Johnny Mack Brown, Beth Marion, William Farnum, Earl Dwire, Lloyd Ingraham, Milburn Morante; *D:* Robert North Bradbury. *NOS, DVT, GPV*

Between the Lines 🎬🎬🎬½ 1977 (R)
A witty, wonderfully realized ensemble comedy about the staff of a radical post-'60s newspaper always on the brink of folding, and its eventual sell-out. **101m/C VHS, Beta.** John Heard, Lindsay Crouse, Jeff Goldblum, Jill Eikenberry, Stephen Collins, Lewis J. Stadlen, Michael J. Pollard, Marilu Henner, Bruno Kirby; *D:* Joan Micklin Silver; *W:* Fred Barron; *M:* Michael Kamen. *VES*

Between Two Women 🎬🎬 1986
A television movie about a wife's rocky relationship with her bossy mother-in-law, until the latter has a stroke and needs care. Dewhurst won an Emmy for her portrayal of the mother-in-law. **95m/C VHS, Beta.** Farrah Fawcett, Michael Nouri, Colleen Dewhurst, Steven Hill, Bridgette Anderson, Danny Corkill; *D:* Jon Avnet. *WAR*

Between Wars 🎬🎬 1974
Young doctor in Australia's Medical Corps encounters conflict when he tries to introduce Freud's principles into his work. **97m/C VHS, Beta.** AU Corin Redgrave, Arthur Dignam, Judy Morris, Patricia Leehy, Gunter Meisner; *D:* Michael Thornhill. *NO*

Beulah Land 🎬½ 1980
A television mini-series about 45 years in the lives of a Southern family, including the Civil War. Based on the novels "Beulah Land" and "Look Away, Beulah Land" by Lonnie Coleman. **267m/C VHS, Beta, LV.** Lesley Ann Warren, Michael Sarrazin, Don Johnson, Meredith Baxter, Dorian Harewood, Eddie Albert, Hope Lange, Paul Rudd; *D:* Virgil W. Vogel, Harry Falk. *COL, TVC*

The Beverly Hillbillies 1962
The successful sitcom series, which ran from 1962-71, features Jed Clampett and his Ozark clan striking oil, getting rich, and heading for the good life in California. Two episodes per tape. **51m/B VHS.** Buddy Ebsen, Irene Ryan, Donna Douglas, Max Baer Jr., Nancy Kulp, Raymond Bailey, Phil Silvers; *Cameos:* John Wayne. *FXV, MOV*

The Beverly Hillbillies 🎬🎬½ 1993 (PG)
Big-screen transfer of the long-running TV show may appeal to fans. Ozark mountaineer Jed Clampett discovers oil, becomes an instant billionaire, and packs his backwoods clan off to the good life in California. Minimal plot finds dim-bulb nephew Jethro and daughter Elly May looking for a bride for Jed. Not that any of it matters. Everyone does fine by their impersonations, particularly Varney as the good-hearted Jed and Leachman as stubborn Granny. Ebsen, the original Jed, reprises another of his TV roles, detective Barnaby Jones. And yes, the familiar strains of the "Ballad of Jed Clampett" by Jerry Scoggins starts this one off, too. **93m/C VHS, LV, Closed Caption.** Jim Varney, Erika Eleniak, Diedrich Bader, Cloris Leachman, Dabney Coleman, Lily Tomlin, Lea Thompson, Rob Schneider, Linda Carlson, Penny Fuller, Kevin Connolly; *Cameos:* Buddy Ebsen, Zsa Zsa Gabor, Dolly Parton; *D:* Penelope Spheeris; *W:* Larry Konner, Mark Rosenthal, Jim Fisher, Jim Staahl; *C:* Robert Brinkmann; *M:* Lalo Schifrin. *FOX*

Beverly Hills Bodysnatchers 🎬½
1989 (R) A mad scientist and a greedy mortician plot to get rich, but their plan backfires when they bring a Mafia godfather back to life and he terrorizes Beverly Hills. **85m/C VHS, LV.** Vic Tayback, Frank Gorshin, Brooke Bundy, Seth Jaffe, Art Metrano; *D:* Jonathan Mostow. *IME*

Beverly Hills Brats 🎬 1989 (PG-13)
A spoiled, rich Hollywood brat hires a loser to kidnap him, in order to gain his parents' attention, only to have both of them kidnapped by real crooks. **90m/C VHS, Beta, LV, Closed Caption.** Martin Sheen, Burt Young, Peter Billingsley, Terry Moore; *D:* Dimitri Sotirakis; *M:* Barry Goldberg. *ART, IME, VTR*

Beverly Hills Cop 🎬🎬½ 1984 (R)
When a close friend of smooth-talking Detroit cop Axle Foley is brutally murdered in L.A., he traces the murderer to the posh streets of Beverly Hills. There he must stay on his toes to keep one step ahead of the killer and two steps ahead of the law. Better than average Murphy vehicle. **105m/C VHS, Beta, LV, 8mm, Closed Caption.** Eddie Murphy, Judge Reinhold, John Ashton, Lisa Eilbacher, Ronny Cox, Steven Berkoff, James Russo, Jonathan Banks, Stephen Elliott, Bronson Pinchot, Paul Reiser, Damon Wayans, Rick Overton; *D:* Martin Brest; *W:* Danilo Bach, Dan Petrie Jr.; *C:* Bruce Surtees; *M:* Harold Faltermeyer. Nominations: Academy Awards '84: Best Original Screenplay. *PAR*

Beverly Hills Cop 2 🎬½ 1987 (R)
The highly successful sequel to the first profitable comedy, with essentially the same plot, this time deals with Foley infiltrating a band of international munitions smugglers. **103m/C VHS, Beta, LV, 8mm, Closed Caption.** Eddie Murphy, Judge Reinhold, Juergen Prochnow, Ronny Cox, John Ashton, Brigitte Nielsen, Allen (Goorwitz) Garfield, Paul Reiser, Dean Stockwell; *D:* Tony Scott; *W:* Larry Ferguson, Warren Skaaren; *M:* Harold Faltermeyer. Golden Raspberry Awards '87: Worst Song ("I Want Your Sex"); Nominations: Academy Awards '87: Best Song ("Shakedown"). *PAR*

Beverly Hills Cop 3 🎬½ **1994 (R)** Yes, Detroit cop Axel Foley (Murphy) just happens to find another case that takes him back to his friends on the Beverly Hills PD. This time he uncovers a criminal network fronting WonderWorld, an amusement park with a squeaky-clean image. Fast-paced action, lots of gunplay, and Eddie wisecracks his way through the slow spots. Reinhold returns as the still impossibly naive Rosewood, with Bronson briefly reprising his role as Serge of the undeterminable accent. Critically panned boxoffice disappointment relies too heavily on formula and is another disappointing followup. **CW:** Language and some violence. 105m/C VHS, Beta, Closed Caption. Eddie Murphy, Judge Reinhold, Hector Elizondo, Timothy Carhart, Stephen McHattie, Theresa Randle, John Saxon, Alan Young, Bronson Pinchot; **Cameos:** Al Green, Gil Hill; **D:** John Landis; **W:** Steven E. de Souza; **C:** Mac Ahlberg; **M:** Nile Rodgers. PAR

Beverly Hills Knockouts **1989** A bevy of beautiful boxers pummel each other with both fists. 60m/C VHS, Beta. CEL

Beverly Hills Madam 🎬 **1986 (PG-13)** In this routine plot, a stable of elite call girls struggle with their lifestyle and their madam, played by Dunaway. Made for television. 97m/C VHS, Beta, LV. Faye Dunaway, Louis Jourdan, Donna Dixon, Robin Givens, Marshall Colt, Melody Anderson, Terry Farrell; **D:** Harvey Hart. ORI

Beverly Hills 90210 **1990** In the pilot episode for the immensely popular series, the world is introduced to the exciting teens who wander the halls of West Beverly High. Join Brandon and Brenda Walsh as they move from Minneapolis to Beverly Hills and experience all the trials and tribulations that come with the new zip code. Includes 25 minutes of previously unseen footage. 90m/C VHS, LV. Jason Priestley, Shannen Doherty, Jennie Garth, Brian Austin Green, Tori Spelling, Ian Ziering, Gabrielle Carteris. WOV, MOV

Beverly Hills 90210: The Graduation **1993** The 1993 end-of-the-season episode of the hit TV series finds the group finally getting out of Beverly Hills High. As they graduate the friends share plans for the summer (and the future) and you'll see lots of flashbacks as well as their final graduation prank. Includes interviews with the cast and music videos from the series soundtrack. 90m/C VHS. Jason Priestley, Shannen Doherty, Luke Perry, Jennie Garth, Brian Austin Green, Tori Spelling, Ian Ziering, Gabrielle Carteris. WOV

Beverly Hills Ninja 🎬½ **1996 (PG-13)** Farley plays Haru, a pathetically inept adopted son of a ninja, who is, nevertheless, sent to Beverly Hills on a rescue mission to break up an international counterfeiting ring. There, second-time spoof siren Sheridan hires the "great white ninja" to follow her no-good boyfriend and becomes the object of Haru's desire. Farley's extraordinary gift for physical comedy is exploited to the hilt, and the increase in Haru's tripping and stumbling (and in one harrowing scene, stripping) usually coincides with the fumbling of the plot. Rock's talents are squandered on a poorly conceived bellboy character. Farley's first feature sans fellow SNL alumni Spade suffers for his absence. Director Duggan, who also helmed Adam Sandler's "Happy Gilmore," might want to start screening his calls. **CW:** Sex-related humor, martial arts violence, and a humorous drug related scene. 88m/C VHS, LV, Closed Caption. Chris Farley, Nicolette Sheridan, Robin Shou, Nathaniel Parker, Chris Rock, Soon-Teck Oh, Francois Chau, Keith Cooke Hirabayashi; **D:** Dennis Dugan; **W:** Mark Feldberg, Mitch Klebenoff; **C:** Arthur Albert; **M:** George S. Clinton. Nominations: MTV Movie Awards '97: Best Comedic Performance (Farley). COL

Beverly Hills Vamp 🎬🎬 **1988 (R)** A madame and her girls are really female vampires with a penchant for hot-blooded men. 88m/C VHS, Beta. Britt Ekland, Eddie Deezen, Debra Lamb; **D:** Fred Olen Ray. THV

Beware 🎬½ **1946** A black singer saves a college from bankruptcy and makes off with the gym teacher. The photography may be a bit harsh, but the all-black cast made this a pioneering but impressive film. 64m/B VHS. Louis Jordan, Frank Wilson, Emory Richardson, Valerie Black, Milton Woods; **D:** Bud Pollard. NOS, RXM

Beware! Children at Play woof! **1995 (R)** Cult leader kidnaps kids and introduces them to cannibalism. Bleech! As if this didn't sound grim enough, there's also an unrated version. **CW:** Violence and gore, and for some sexuality. 90m/C VHS. Michael Robinson, Eric Tonken, Jamie Krause, Mik Cribben; **D:** Mik Cribben; **C:** Mik Cribben. TTV

Beware, My Lovely 🎬🎬½ **1952** Taut chiller. Lonely widow Lupino hires a new handyman. He's great with screen doors and storm windows, but has a problem with sharp tools. Intense and gripping with fine performances. 77m/B VHS, LV. Ida Lupino, Robert Ryan, Taylor Holmes, O.Z. Whitehead, Barbara Whiting, Dee Pollock; **D:** Harry Horner. REP

Beware of a Holy Whore 🎬🎬 Warnung Vor Einer Heiligen Nutte **1970** German film crew sits around a Spanish resort—complaining, drinking, and making love—as they wait for financial support from Bonn. Provocative and self-indulgently honest look at filmmaking. Filmed on location in Sorrento, Italy; German with subtitles. 103m/C VHS. GE Lou Castel, Eddie Constantine, Hanna Schygulla, Marquard Bohm, Ulli Lommel, Margarethe von Trotta, Kurt Raab, Ingrid Caven, Werner Schroeter, Rainer Werner Fassbinder; **D:** Rainer Werner Fassbinder; **W:** Rainer Werner Fassbinder; **C:** Michael Ballhaus; **M:** Peer Raben. ORI

Beware of Pity 🎬🎬½ **1946** A crippled baroness thinks she's found true love with a military officer, but it turns out his marriage proposal grew out of pity for her, not passion. A quality but somber British-made historical drama, based on a novel by Stefan Zweig. 129m/B VHS. Lilli Palmer, Albert Lieven, Cedric Hardwicke, Gladys Cooper, Ernest Thesiger, Freda Jackson, Linden Travers, Ralph Truman, Peter Cotes, Jenny Laird, Emrys Jones, Gerhard Kempinski, John Salew, Kenneth Warrington; **D:** Maurice Elvey; **W:** W.P. Lipscomb, Elizabeth Barron, Margaret Steen. HMK

Bewitched **1985** A made-for-British-television horror story about an elderly couple ostensibly plagued by the witch-like conniving of a dead woman. 60m/C VHS, Beta. GB Eileen Atkins, Alfred Lynch; **D:** Edmund Oboler.

Beyond a Reasonable Doubt 🎬🎬 **1956** In order to get a behind-the-scenes glimpse at the judicial system, a man plays the guilty party to a murder. Alas, when he tries to vindicate himself, he is the victim of his own folly. Not as interesting as it sounds on paper. 80m/B VHS. Dana Andrews, Joan Fontaine, Sidney Blackmer, Philip Bourneuf, Barbara Nichols, Shepperd Strudwick, Arthur Franz, Edward Binns; **D:** Fritz Lang; **W:** Douglas S. Morrow. NO

Beyond Atlantis woof! **1973 (PG)** An ancient underwater tribe is discovered when it kidnaps land-lubbin' women with which to mate. 91m/C VHS, Beta. PH John Ashley, Patrick Wayne, George Nader; **D:** Eddie Romero. VCI

Beyond Darkness 🎬½ **1992 (R)** When Peter and his family move into their New England home they are immediately beset by some unknown terror. With the help of Father George, Peter learns his house was built upon the graves of 20 witches burned for heresy. The witches have decided to seek revenge by kidnapping Peter's young son and sacrificing him to an evil demon. Can Peter destroy the evil spirits before they destroy his son? **CW:** Horror violence. 111m/C VHS, Closed Caption. Gene Le Brock, David Brandon, Barbara Bingham, Michael Stephenson, Stephen Brown; **D:** Clyde Anderson. IMP

Beyond Desire 🎬🎬½ **1994 (R)** Elvis Ray (Forsythe) is released after 14 years in prison and gets picked up by corvette-driving prison groupie and Las Vegas prostitute Rita (Wuhrer) but more than sex is on both their minds. **CW:** Strong sexuality, violence, and language. 87m/C VHS, Closed Caption. William Forsythe, Kari Wuhrer, Leo Rossi, Sharon Farrell; **D:** Dominique Othenin-Girard; **W:** Dale Trevillion; **M:** Mark Holden. ART

Beyond Dream's Door 🎬 **1988** A young, All-American college student's childhood nightmares come back to haunt him, making dreams a horrifying reality. 86m/C VHS, Beta. Nick Baldasare, Rick Kesler, Susan Pinsky, Norm Singer; **D:** Jay Woelfel. NO

Beyond Erotica **1979** After being cut out of his father's will, a sadistic young man takes out his rage on his mother and a peasant girl. 90m/C VHS. David Hemmings, Alida Valli, Andrea Rau.

Beyond Evil woof! **1980 (R)** Relatively dim-witted newlywed couple moves into an old island mansion despite rumors that the house is haunted. Sure enough, wife George becomes possessed by the vengeful spirit of a woman murdered 200 years earlier, and a reign of pointless terror begins. Poor rip-off of hybrid Amityville/Exorcist paranormality. 98m/C VHS, Beta. John Saxon, Lynda Day George, Michael Dante, Mario Milano; **D:** Herb Freed; **W:** Herb Freed; **M:** Pino Donaggio.

Beyond Fear 🎬🎬½ **1975** Compelling drama about a man forced to aid a gang in robbery while they hold his wife and son captive. 92m/C VHS, Beta. Michael Boquet.

Beyond Fear 🎬🎬½ **1993 (R)** Tipper Taylor (Lesseos) is a wilderness tour guide who's also a martial arts expert. This is going to come in handy when her tour group is stalked by two men who are after a videotape innocently filmed by someone in Tipper's group. It seems the tape shows the men committing a murder. 84m/C VHS. Mimi Lesseos. MNC

Beyond Forgiveness 🎬🎬½ **1994 (R)** Basic maverick cop goes after his brother's killers and winds up involved in an international black market in transplantable human organs. 95m/C VHS, LV, Closed Caption. Thomas Ian Griffith, Rutger Hauer, John Rhys-Davies; **D:** Bob Misiorowski; **W:** Charles Cohen. REP

Beyond Innocence 🎬 **1987** A 17-year-old lusts after a mature married woman. Ostensibly based on Raymond Radiguet's "Devil in the Flesh." 87m/C VHS, Beta. Keith Smith, Katia Caballero, John Morris; **D:** Scott Murray; **C:** Andrzej Bartkowiak. NO

Beyond Justice 🎬🎬 **1992 (PG-13)** High action-adventure with the prolific Hauer starring as an ex-CIA agent who is hired to rescue the kidnapped son of a beautiful executive. **CW:** Action violence. 113m/C VHS, LV, Closed Caption. Rutger Hauer, Carol Alt, Omar Sharif, Elliott Gould; **M:** Ennio Morricone. THV

Beyond Obsession 🎬🎬 **1982** The strange relationship between a political prisioner, his daughter, and her obsession with a mysterious American is provocatively explored. 116m/C VHS. IT Marcello Mastroianni, Elenora Giorgi, Tom Berenger, Michel Piccoli; **D:** Liliana Cavani. FCT

Beyond Rangoon 🎬🎬 **1995 (R)** Sisters Laura (Arquette) and Andy (McDormand) Bowman travel to Burma to unwind, only to have political unrest and a repressive regime spoil the holiday. Dr. Laura (yeah, right) loses her passport and must flee from trigger-happy soldiers with a political dissident (Ko, a real-life exiled Burmese activist) who befriends her. The search for her passport soon becomes a imperiled trek of survival and self-discovery. Tense, well-crafted action sequences hint at a potential for excitement and intrigue; too bad Arquette isn't the least bit convincing. Filmed in Malaysia. **CW:** Depiction of violent political oppression. 100m/C VHS, LV, Closed Caption. Patricia Arquette, Frances McDormand, Spalding Gray, U Aung Ko, Victor Slezak; **D:** John Boorman; **W:** Alex Lasker, Bill Rubenstein; **C:** John Seale; **M:** Hans Zimmer. COL

Beyond Reason 🎬 1977 A psychologist uses unorthodox methods by treating the criminally insane with dignity and respect. 88m/C VHS, Beta. Telly Savalas, Laura Johnson, Diana Muldaur, Marvin Laird, Priscilla Barnes; *D:* Telly Savalas; *C:* John A. Alonzo.

Beyond Reasonable Doubt 🎬🎬½ 1980 Chilling true-life murder mystery which shattered the peaceful quiet of a small New Zealand town and eventually divided the country. An innocent farmer (Hargreaves) was convicted of a grisly double murder based on evidence planted by a local cop (Hemmings, in a superb role). It wasn't until Yallop's book questioned the facts of the case that it was reopened. Yallop also wrote the screenplay. 127m/C VHS, Beta. *NZ* David Hemmings, John Hargreaves, Martyn Sanderson, Grant Tilly, Diana Rowan, Ian Watkin; *D:* John Laing; *W:* David Yallop. NO

Beyond Silence 🎬🎬 *Jenseits der Stille* 1996 (PG-13) Lara (Trieb/Testud), the daughter of deaf parents, has been their guide to the outside world since childhood. When her Aunt Clarissa (Canonica) gives her a clarinet, it opens Lara's life to music and gives her the courage to move beyond the limits of her family. German with subtitles. *CW:* Scene of sexuality. 109m/C VHS. *GE* Sylvie Testud, Tatjana Trieb, Howie Seago, Emmanuelle Laborit, Sibylle Canonica; *D:* Caroline Link; *W:* Caroline Link; *C:* Gernot Roll; *M:* Niki Reiser. Nominations: Academy Awards '97: Best Foreign Language Film. NYR

Beyond the Bermuda Triangle 🎬½ 1975 Unfortunate and flat television flick. Businessman MacMurray, now retired, doesn't have enough to do. He begins an investigation of the mysterious geometric island area when his friends and fiancee disappear. Silly. 78m/C VHS. Fred MacMurray, Sam Groom, Donna Mills, Suzanne Reed, Dana Plato, Woody Woodbury; *D:* William A. Graham. NO

Beyond the Call 🎬🎬½ 1996 (R) Connecticut housewife Pam O'Brien (Spacek) learns from the paper that her high-school sweetheart Russell Cates (Strathairn) is on death row in South Carolina for killing a cop and his execution has been scheduled within weeks. Pam writes Russell and then hears from his sister Fran (Wright), who urges Pam to visit her brother and get him to apply for a clemency hearing. Husband Keith (Howard) becomes angry and alarmed as Pam gets more involved with Russell and his case, which hinges on Russell's Vietnam experiences and post-traumatic shock syndrome. Cable movie. *CW:* Strong language and some violence. 101m/C VHS, LV, Closed Caption. David Strathairn, Sissy Spacek, Arliss Howard, Janet Wright; *D:* Tony Bill; *W:* Doug Magee; *C:* Jean Lepine; *M:* George S. Clinton. HMK

Beyond the Call of Duty 🎬🎬½ 1992 (R) Renegade U.S. Army Commander Len Jordan (Vincent) is after a particularly deadly Vietcong enemy. Aided by the head of a special forces naval unit he tracks his quarry through the notorious Mekong River Delta. But Jordan's mission may be hindered, both personally and professionally, by a beautiful American journalist after a hot story. *CW:* Language and war violence. 92m/C VHS, LV. Jan-Michael Vincent, Eb Lottimer, Jillian McWhirter; *D:* Cirio H. Santiago. NHO

Beyond the Carribean 🎬🎬 1936 Bizarre jungle thriller featuring voodoo and native crucifixion. Also known as "Manhunters of the Carribean." Andre Roosevelt. SNC

Beyond the Door WOOF! *Beyond Obsession; Chi Sei; The Devil within Her* 1975 (R) San Francisco woman finds herself pregnant with a demonic child. One of the first "Exorcist" ripoffs; skip this one and go right to the sequel, "Beyond the Door 2." In Italian; dubbed. 97m/C VHS, Beta, LV, Closed Caption. *IT* Juliet Mills, Richard Johnson, David Colin Jr.; *D:* Richard Barrett, Oliver Hellman; *W:* Richard Barrett, Oliver Hellman. NO

Beyond the Door 2 🎬🎬½ *Shock; Shock (Transfer Suspense Hypnos); Suspense; Al 33 di Via Orologio fa Sempre Freddo* 1979 (R) Better treatment of the possession theme, but this time the door is to the home of a new family: Colin (from the original) plays a boy possessed by his dead father, who seeks revenge on his widow and her new husband. Director Bava's last feature. 90m/C VHS, Beta. *IT* John Steiner, Daria Nicolodi, David Colin Jr., Ivan Rassimov, Nicola Salerno; *D:* Mario Bava; *W:* Lamberto Bava, Franco Barbieri, Dardano Sacchetti, Paolo Brigenti; *C:* Alberto Spagnoli.

Beyond the Door 3 WOOF! 1991 (R) Fool American students in Yugoslavia board a hellish locomotive which speeds them toward a satanic ritual. Demonic disaster-movie stuff (with poor miniatures) isn't as effective as the on-location filming; Serbian scenery and crazed peasants impart an eerie pagan aura. What this has to do with earlier "Beyond the Door" movies only the marketing boys can say. Some dialogue in Serbo-Croat with English subtitles. 94m/C VHS, LV, Closed Caption. Mary Kohnert, Sarah Conway Ciminera, William Geiger, Renee Rancourt, Alex Vitale, Victoria Zinny, Savina Gersak, Bo Svenson; *D:* Jeff Kwitny. COL

Beyond the Forest 🎬½ 1949 Camp diva Davis, in her last role for Warner Bros., really turns on the histrionics as a big-city gal married to a small-town guy (Cotten) and bored out of her mind. Although the most memorable line, "What a dump," has become larger-than-life, the film itself is rather small and muddled (interestingly, Vidor directed "The Fountainhead" the same year.) A trashy melodrama full of ennui, envy, unwanted pregnancy, and murder, it's definitely high on camp and low on art. 96m/B VHS. Bette Davis, Joseph Cotten, David Brian, Ruth Roman, Minor Watson, Regis Toomey; *D:* King Vidor; *C:* Robert Burks; *M:* Max Steiner. Nominations: Academy Awards '49: Best Original Dramatic/Comedy Score. MGM, FCT

Beyond the Law 🎬🎬 *Bloodsilver; Al Di La Della Legge* 1968 Spaghetti western with Van Cleef as the too smart bad guy. He becomes sheriff, picks up the stack of silver at the depot, and disappears. Humorous and clever, with fine location photography. 91m/C VHS. *IT* Lee Van Cleef, Antonio Sabato Jr., Lionel Stander, Bud Spencer, Gordon Mitchell, Ann Smyrner; *D:* Giorgio Stegani. IMP, QVD

Beyond the Law 🎬½ *Fixing the Shadow* 1992 (R) Ex-undercover cop Danny Saxon (Sheen) is recruited by the FBI to infiltrate a biker gang involved in drugs and gun smuggling. But Saxon finds himself drawn too close into the unconventional biker lifestyle and into an uneasy friendship with leader Blood (Madsen). Clumsy and exploitative. *CW:* Pervasive strong language, violence and drug use, and sexuality. 101m/C VHS, LV. Charlie Sheen, Michael Madsen, Linda Fiorentino, Courtney B. Vance, Leon Rippy, Rip Torn; *D:* Larry Ferguson; *W:* Larry Ferguson; *M:* John D'Andrea, Cory Lerios. ART

Beyond the Limit 🎬🎬½ *The Honorary Consul* 1983 (R) The story of an intense and darkly ominous love triangle which takes place in the South American coastal city of Corrientes. Based on Graham Greene's novel "The Honorary Consul." 103m/C VHS, Beta. Michael Caine, Richard Gere, Bob Hoskins, Elpidia Carrillo; *D:* John MacKenzie; *W:* Christopher Hampton; *C:* Phil Meheux. PAR

Beyond the Next Mountain 🎬 1987 (PG) A missionary in China attempts to convert all those he meets. Thin plot and marginal acting will likely make viewers fall asleep. 97m/C VHS, Beta. Alberto Isaac, Jon Lormer, Bennett Ohta, Richard Lineback, Edward Ashley, Barry Foster; *D:* James F. Collier, Rolf Forsberg. NO

Beyond the Poseidon Adventure 🎬 1979 (PG) A sequel to the 1972 film in which salvage teams and ruthless looting vandals compete for access to the sunken ocean liner. Sinking ships should be abandoned. 115m/C VHS, Beta. Michael Caine, Sally Field, Telly Savalas, Peter Boyle, Jack Warden, Slim Pickens, Shirley Knight, Shirley Jones, Karl Malden, Mark Harmon; *D:* Irwin Allen; *C:* Joseph Biroc. WAR

Beyond the Rockies 🎬🎬⅓ 1932 Keene and a group of cowboys battle cattle rustlers in this action-packed sagebrush saga. Solid script with good direction by Allen. 55m/B VHS. Tom George Duryea Keene, Rochelle Hudson, Ernie Adams, Julian Rivero, Hank Bell, Tom London; *D:* Fred Allen; *W:* John P. McCarthy. MOV

Beyond the Silhouette 🎬 *Ultimate Desires* 1990 It starts out as another sleazy video sex thriller, as the lawyer heroine discovers her sensuality and poses a lot in her underclothes. Then in the third act it become a hyper-paranoid political-conspiracy assassination-o-rama. Pretty weird junk. 90m/C VHS, Beta. *CA* Tracy Scoggins, Marc Singer, Brion James; *D:* Lloyd A. Simanol. NO

Beyond the Stars 🎬 1989 A sci-fi adventure directed by the author of "Cocoon," wherein a whiz-kid investigates the NASA cover-up of a deadly accident that occurred on the moon during the Apollo 11 landing. Unfortunately, the interesting cast can't make up for the script. 94m/C VHS, Beta, LV. Martin Sheen, Christian Slater, Olivia D'Abo, F. Murray Abraham, Robert Foxworth, Sharon Stone; *D:* David Saperstein. ART

Beyond the Time Barrier 🎬🎬½ 1960 Air Force test pilot gets more than he bargained for when his high speed plane carries him into the future. There he sees the ravages of an upcoming plague, to which he must return. 75m/B VHS, Beta. Robert Clarke, Darlene Tompkins, Arianne Arden, Vladimir Sokoloff; *D:* Edgar G. Ulmer. SNC, CNM

Beyond the Trail 1926 One of Bill Patton's most entertaining and funny films. In this comedic Western adventure he must face Black Mike and his gang and rescue Mary from their clutches. 50m/C VHS. Bill Patton, Sheldon Lewis, Stuart Holmes, Eric Wayne, Janet Dawn, Clara Horton, James F. Fulton; *D:* Al(bert) Herman. GPV

Beyond the Valley of the Dolls 🎬🎬½ 1970 (NC-17) Sleazy, spirited nonsequel to "Valley of the Dolls." Meyer ("Faster, Pussycat! Kill! Kill!") directed this Hollywood parody ("BVD," as it came to be known) about an all-girl rock combo and their search for stardom. Labeled the first "exploitation horror camp musical"—how can you pass that up? Screenplay by film critic Ebert, from an original story by Ebert and Meyer. Mondo trasho. 109m/C VHS, Beta, LV. Edy Williams, Dolly Reed; *D:* Russ Meyer; *W:* Roger Ebert. BTV

Beyond the Walls 🎬🎬½ *Meachorei Hasoragim* 1984 (R) The opposing factions of a hellish Israeli prison unite to beat the system. Brutal with good characterizations. Available in both subtitled and dubbed versions. 104m/C VHS, Beta. *IS* Arnon Zadok, Muhamad Bakri; *D:* Uri Barbash; *W:* Benny Barbash. Venice Film Festival '85: Best Film; Nominations: Academy Awards '84: Best Foreign Language Film. WAR

Beyond Therapy 🎬½ 1986 (R) A satire on modern psychotherapy, from the play by Christopher Durang, about a confused, crazily neurotic couple and their respective, and not any saner, analysts. Unfortunately, comes off as disjointed and confused. 93m/C VHS, Beta, Closed Caption. Jeff Goldblum, Tom Conti, Julie Hagerty, Glenda Jackson, Christopher Guest; *D:* Robert Altman; *W:* Robert Altman. VTR

Beyond Tomorrow 🎬🎬 1940 Young romance is guided from the spirit world during the Christmas season, as two "ghosts" come back to help young lovers. 84m/B VHS, Beta. Richard Carlson, Sir C. Aubrey Smith, Jean Parker, Charles Winninger, Harry Carey Sr., Maria Ouspenskaya, Rod La Rocque; *D:* Edward Sutherland. SNC, NOS, DVT

Bhaji on the Beach 🎬🎬½ 1994 (R) Amusing comedy-drama about a group of Indian women who organize a bus outing from Birmingham to the seaside resort town of Blackpool. They range from sari-clad elders to feminist Gen Xers and a couple of teenagers looking for romance. There's bonding and gossiping and secrets galore before the story is tidily wrapped up. *CW:* Language; scene of domestic abuse. **100m/C VHS, Closed Caption. GB** Kim Vithana, Jimmi Harkishin, Sarita Khajuria, Mo Sesay, Lalita Ahmed, Shaheen Khan; **D:** Gurinder Chadha; **W:** Meera Syal; **C:** John Kenway; **M:** John Altman, Craig Preuss. *COL*

Bhowani Junction 🐾🐾 **1956** A half-Indian, half-English woman is torn between her country and the British officer she loves in post-colonial India. Great cinematography. Based on a book by John Masters. **110m/C VHS, LV, Letterbox.** Ava Gardner, Stewart Granger, Bill Travers, Abraham Sofaer, Francis Matthews, Marne Maitland, Peter Illing, Edward Chapman, Freda Jackson, Lionel Jeffries; **D:** George Cukor; **C:** Frederick A. (Freddie) Young; **M:** Miklos Rozsa. *MGM*

The Bible 🐾 **1966** Bloated, even by religious epic standards, Huston's drama covers the first 22 chapters of Genesis. So you get the Creation, Adam and Eve, Noah and the ark, the flood, the Tower of Babel, and Abraham, among other would-be spectacles. **174m/C VHS.** Michael Parks, Ulla Bergryd, Richard Harris, Stephen Boyd, George C. Scott, Ava Gardner, Peter O'Toole, Franco Nero, John Huston; **D:** John Huston; **W:** Christopher Fry, Vittorio Bonicelli; **C:** Giuseppe Rotunno; **M:** Toshiro Mayuzumi. Nominations: Academy Awards '66: Best Original Score. *FOX*

The Bible and Gun Club 🐾🐾 **1996** Foul-mouthed look at the wasted lives of five middle age traveling salesmen who sell, you guessed it, bibles and guns. There's a turf war between the Anaheim, CA and the Las Vegas branches of the club, there's a sales convention, the salesmen try to sell their goods to the real-life denizens of a poor trailer park, there's a porn shoot. There's a number of shoot-outs and to say the least, the salesmen are not politically correct—they're racist, sexist losers. It's depressing and disturbing and highlighted by some spot-on acting. Harris' debut feature. **87m/B VHS.** Andy Kallok, Don Yanan, Julian Ott, Al Schuerman, Robert Blumenthal; **D:** Daniel J. Harris; **W:** Daniel J. Harris; **C:** Alex Vendler; **M:** Shawn Patterson. Nominations: Independent Spirit Awards '98: Best Cinematography, Best First Feature. *NYR*

The Bible...In the Beginning 🐾🐾🐾 **1966** The book of Genesis is dramatized, including the stories of Adam and Eve, Cain and Abel, and Noah and the flood. **155m/C VHS, Beta, LV, IT** George C. Scott, Richard Harris, Stephen Boyd, John Huston, Peter O'Toole, Franco Nero, Ava Gardner; **D:** John Huston; **C:** Giuseppe Rotunno. *FOX*

The Bicycle Thief 🐾🐾🐾🐾 *Ladri di Biciclette* **1948** A world classic and indisputable masterpiece about an Italian workman who finds a job, only to have the bike he needs for work stolen; he and his son search Rome for it. A simple story that seems to contain the whole of human experience, and the masterpiece of Italian neo-realism. Based on the book by Luigi Bartolini. In Italian with English subtitles. **90m/B VHS, Beta, LV. IT** Lamberto Maggiorani, Lianella Carell, Enzo Staiola, Elena Altieri, Vittorio Antonucci, Gino Saltamerenda, Fausto Guerzoni; **D:** Vittorio De Sica; **W:** Cesare Zavattini. Academy Awards '49: Best Foreign Language Film; British Academy Awards '49: Best Film; Golden Globe Awards '50: Best Foreign Film; National Board of Review Awards '49: Best Director (De Sica); New York Film Critics Awards '49: Best Foreign Film; Nominations: Academy Awards '49: Best Screenplay. *NOS, MRV, FCT*

Big 🐾🐾🐾½ **1988 (PG)** A 13-year-old boy makes a wish at a carnival fortune-teller to be "big." When he wakes up the next morning he finds that he suddenly won't fit into his clothes and his mother doesn't recognize him. Until he finds a cure, he must learn to live in the adult world—complete with job, apartment, and romance. Perkins is wonderful as a warming cynic while Hanks is totally believable as the little boy inside a man's body. Marshall directs with authority and the whole thing clicks from the beginning. **98m/C VHS, Beta, LV.** Tom Hanks, Elizabeth Perkins, John Heard, Robert Loggia, Jared Rushton, David Moscow, Jon Lovitz, Mercedes Ruehl; **D:** Penny Marshall; **W:** Gary Ross; **M:** Howard Shore. Golden Globe Awards '89: Best Actor—Musical/Comedy (Hanks); Los Angeles Film Critics Association Awards '88: Best Actor (Hanks); Nominations: Academy

Awards '88: Best Actor (Hanks), Best Original Screenplay. *FOX, HMV*

Big Bad John 🐾½ **1990 (PG-13)** Some good ol' boys ride around in trucks as they get into a variety of shootouts. The soundtrack includes music by Willie Nelson, The Charlie Daniels Band, and others. **91m/C VHS, Beta, LV.** Jimmy Dean, Ned Beatty, Jack Elam, Bo Hopkins, Romy Windsor, Doug English. *IME*

Big Bad Mama 🐾🐾½ **1974 (R)** Tough and sexy machine-gun toting mother moves her two nubile daughters out of Texas during the Depression, and they all turn to robbing banks as a means of support while creating sharp testosterone increases among the local men. "Wild Palm" Dickinson has notable nude scene with Captain Kirk. "Big Bad Mama 2" arrived some 13 years later. **83m/C VHS, Beta.** Angie Dickinson, William Shatner, Tom Skerritt, Susan Sennett, Robbie Lee, Sally Kirkland, Noble Willingham, Royal Dano, Dick Miller; **D:** Steve Carver; **W:** William W. Norton Sr. *NHO*

Big Bad Mama 2 🐾½ **1987 (R)** Belated Depression-era sequel to the 1974 Roger Corman gangster film, where the pistol-packin' matriarch battles a crooked politician with the help of her two daughters. **85m/C VHS, Beta.** Angie Dickinson, Robert Culp, Danielle Brisebois, Julie McCullough; **D:** Jim Wynorski; **W:** Jim Wynorski, R.J. Robertson. *MGM*

The Big Bet 🐾 **1985 (R)** High school sex comedy about a guy who is challenged by the school bully to get the gorgeous new girl into bed. Energetic romp is for adults. **CW:** Language and strong sexuality. **90m/C VHS, Beta.** Sylvia Kristel, Kimberly Evenson, Ron Thomas; **D:** Bert I. Gordon. *NO*

The Big Bird Cage 🐾🐾 *Women's Penitentiary 2* **1972 (R)** Prison spoof sequel to "The Big Doll House." Horny females incarcerated in a rural jail decide to defy their homosexual guards and plan an escape. They are aided by revolutionaries led by a Brooklynese expatriate and his lover. **93m/C VHS, Beta.** Pam Grier, Sid Haig, Anitra Ford, Candice Roman, Teda Bracci, Carol Speed, Karen McKevic; **D:** Jack Hill. *WAR*

The Big Blue 🐾½ *Le Grand Bleu* **1988 (PG)** Vapid, semi-true tale about competing free-divers, who descend deep into the big blue without the aid of any kind of breathing apparatus. Arquette is the ditz who makes them come up for air. **122m/C VHS, Beta, LV, Closed Caption.** Rosanna Arquette, Jean Reno, Jean-Marc Barr, Paul Shenar, Sergio Castellitto, Marc Duret, Griffin Dunne; **D:** Luc Besson; **W:** Luc Besson; **M:** Bill Conti. Cesar Awards '89: Best Sound, Best Score. *COL*

Big Bluff 🐾🐾 *Worthy Deceivers* **1955** Disappointing result from an interesting premise: fatally ill woman finds love, but when she surprisingly recovers, her new husband decides to help her back along the path to death. Uneven and melodramatic. **70m/B VHS. SI** John Bromfield, Martha Vickers, Robert Hutton, Rosemary Bowe; **D:** W. Lee Wilder. *NOS, MOV, HEG*

Big Boss 🐾½ *Mr. Scarface* **1977 (R)** A hoodlum climbs to the top of a crime syndicate. An Italian film previously titled "Mr. Scarface." **90m/C Beta. IT** Jack Palance, Edmund Purdom, Al Cliver, Harry Baer, Gisela Hahn. *NO*

The Big Brawl 🐾½ **1980 (R)** Chicago gangster recruits a martial arts expert to fight in a free-for-all match in Texas. **95m/C VHS, Beta.** Jackie Chan, Jose Ferrer, Mako, Rosalind Chao; **D:** Robert Clouse; **W:** Robert Clouse; **M:** Lalo Schifrin. *WAR*

The Big Broadcast of 1938 🐾½ **1938** Fields is the owner of an ocean liner which he enters in a race. Supposedly, the ship can convert the electricity from radio broadcasts into power for the propellers. No, it doesn't make sense, as it's just an excuse for various radio stars to show off their routines in the ship's entertainment room. Hope, in his first feature, gets to sing his Oscar-winning signature tune "Thanks for the Memories." **94m/B VHS.** W.C. Fields, Martha Raye, Dorothy Lamour, Shirley Ross, Russell Hicks, Bob Hope, Ben Blue,

Leif Erickson; **D:** Mitchell Leisen; **W:** Walter DeLeon, Francis Martin. Academy Awards '38: Best Song ("Thanks for the Memories"). *USH*

Big Bully 🐾🐾 **1995 (PG)** David Leary (Moranis) is an aspiring novelist who moves back to the town where he was picked on as a kid. His son immediately starts bullying a smaller child, whose father happens to be Roscoe "Fang" Bigger (Arnold), David's former tormentor. The timid henpecked Roscoe's sadistic streak is awakened with the reappearance of his old prey, leading to a barrage of wet willies and indian burns. The slapstick quickly escalates to danger before all is tied up in a syrupy sweet ending. With Moranis playing the nerdy bespectacled underdog and Arnold playing the loud obnoxious guy (although that might not be acting), it may be time to call the typecasting cops. Don Knotts (looking very un-Barney-like) makes an appearance as the high school principal. **93m/C VHS.** Tom Arnold, Rick Moranis, Julianne Phillips, Don Knotts, Carol Kane, Jeffrey Tambor, Curtis Armstrong, Faith Prince, Tony Pierce, Blake Bashoff; **D:** Steve Miner; **W:** Mark Steven Johnson; **C:** Daryn Okada; **M:** David Newman. Golden Raspberry Awards '96: Worst Actor (Arnold). *WAR*

The Big Bus 🐾🐾 **1976 (PG)** The wild adventures of the world's first nuclear-powered bus as it makes its maiden voyage from New York to Denver. Clumsy disaster-movie parody. **88m/C VHS, Beta.** Joseph Bologna, Stockard Channing, Ned Beatty, Ruth Gordon, Larry Hagman, John Beck, Jose Ferrer, Lynn Redgrave, Sally Kellerman, Stuart Margolin, Richard Mulligan, Howard Hesseman, Richard B. Shull; **D:** James Frawley; **W:** Lawrence J. Cohen; **C:** Harry Stradling Jr.; **M:** David Shire. *PAR*

Big Business 🐾🐾 **1988 (PG)** Strained high-concept comedy about two sets of identical twins, each played by Tomlin and Midler, mismatched at birth by a near-sighted country nurse. The city set of twins intends to buy out the factory where the country set of twins work. So the country twins march up to the big city to stop the sale and destruction of their beloved home. Both set of twins stay in the Plaza Hotel and zany consequences ensue. Essentially a one-joke outing with some funny moments, but talented comediennes Midler and Tomlin are somewhat wasted. Great technical effects. **98m/C VHS, Beta, LV, 8mm, Closed Caption.** Bette Midler, Lily Tomlin, Fred Ward, Edward Herrmann, Michele Placido, Barry Primus, Michael Gross, Mary Gross, Daniel Gerroll, Roy Brocksmith; **D:** Jim Abrahams; **C:** Dean Cundey. *TOU*

Big Business Girl 🐾🐾 **1931** Less than remarkable comedy starring Young as a corporate climber who must dodge her boss' advances and save her troubled marriage when her jazz singer husband is called away to perform in Paris. Based on a story by Patricia Reilly and Harold N. Swanson. **72m/B VHS.** Loretta Young, Frank Albertson, Ricardo Cortez, Joan Blondell, Dorothy Christy; **D:** William A. Seiter; **W:** Robert Lord. *MGM*

The Big Bust Out woof! **1973 (R)** Several female convicts escape from prison only to be sold into slavery and face additional torture. Nothing redeeming about this exploitative film. **75m/C VHS, Beta.** Vonetta McGee, Monica Taylor, Linda Fox, Karen Carter, Gordon Mitchell; **D:** Karen Carter.

Big Calibre 🐾 **1935** A rancher is inches away from being lynched for his dad's murder before he is found to be innocent. **59m/B VHS, Beta.** Bob Steele, Bill Quinn, Earl Dwire, Peggy Campbell, John Elliott, Georgia O'Dell; **D:** Robert North Bradbury. *SNC, DVT, HEG*

The Big Cat 🐾🐾 **1949** Mountain valley in Utah is ravaged by a cougar, while two ranchers fuss and feud. Big cat, bickering, help make okay adventure. **75m/C VHS, Beta.** Lon McCallister, Peggy Ann Garner, Preston Foster, Forrest Tucker; **D:** Phil Karlson; **C:** William Howard Greene. *NOS, MRV, DVT*

Big Chase 🐾 **1954** A rookie cop chases down a mob of payroll thieves in this early action film. **60m/B VHS, Beta, LV.** Glenn Langan, Adele Jergens, Lon Chaney Jr., Jim Davis. *NO*

The Big Chill 🎬🎬🎬½ 1983 (R) Seven former '60s radicals, now coming upon middle age and middle class affluence, reunite on the occasion of an eighth friend's suicide and use the occasion to re-examine their past relationships and commitments. A beautifully acted, immensely enjoyable ballad to both the counter-culture and its Yuppie descendants. Great period music. Kevin Costner is the dead man whose scenes never made it to the big screen. 108m/C VHS, Beta, LV, 8mm, Letterbox, Closed Caption. Tom Berenger, Glenn Close, Jeff Goldblum, William Hurt, Kevin Kline, Mary Kay Place, Meg Tilly, JoBeth Williams; **D:** Lawrence Kasdan; **W:** Lawrence Kasdan, Barbara Benedek; **C:** John Bailey. Writers Guild of America '83: Best Original Screenplay; Nominations: Academy Awards '83: Best Original Screenplay, Best Picture, Best Supporting Actress (Close). COL, CRC

The Big City 🎬🎬 Mahanagar 1963 When debts threaten to overwhelm the Mazumdar family, Arati does the unthinkable and gets a job as a saleswoman. She soon begins to realize she not only likes to work but enjoys the freedom and respect her job brings. Bengali with subtitles. 131m/B VHS. **IN** Anil Chatterjee, Majhabi Mukherjee; **D:** Satyajit Ray. COL

The Big Clock 🎬🎬🎬 1948 George Stroud (Milland) is the editor of the successful Crimeways magazine, owned by tyrannical publisher Earl Janoth (Laughton). Forced to miss a vacation with his wife Georgette (O'Sullivan), George winds up spending time with lovely Pauline (Johnson), whom he inadvertently discovers is the boss' mistress. Pauline's murdered and George is quick to realize all the clues are deliberately pointed in his direction. Classic crime melodrama adapted from Kenneth Fearing's novel. Remade as "No Way Out" (1987). 95m/B VHS, Closed Caption. Ray Milland, Charles Laughton, Maureen O'Sullivan, George Macready, Rita Johnson, Dan Tobin, Elsa Lanchester, Harry (Henry) Morgan; **D:** John Farrow; **W:** Jonathan Latimer; **C:** John Seitz; **M:** Victor Young. USH

Big Combo 🎬🎬🎬 1955 A gangster's ex-girlfriend helps a cop to smash a crime syndicate. Focuses on the relationship between Wilde's cop and the gangster Conte in an effective film noir, with some scenes of torture that were ahead of their time. 87m/B VHS, Beta. Cornel Wilde, Richard Conte, Jean Wallace, Brian Donlevy, Earl Holliman, Lee Van Cleef, Helen Walker; **D:** Joseph H. Lewis; **W:** Philip Yordan; **C:** John Alton.

The Big Country 🎬🎬½ 1958 (R) Ex-sea captain Peck heads west to marry fiance Baker and live on her father's (Bickford) ranch. Peck immediately clashes with ranch foreman Heston and finds out there's a vicious feud with neighbor Ives. Then Peck decides he and Baker aren't meant to be and he falls for schoolmarm Simmons instead. It's too long but if you like sprawling western sagas, this one has its moments. 168m/C VHS, Beta. Gregory Peck, Charlton Heston, Burl Ives, Jean Simmons, Carroll Baker, Chuck Connors; **D:** William Wyler. Academy Awards '58: Best Supporting Actor (Ives); Golden Globe Awards '59: Best Supporting Actor (Ives); Nominations: Academy Awards '58: Best Original Dramatic/Comedy Score. MGM, BTV

The Big Crimewave 🎬🎬 1986 A cast of unknowns in a comedy about a loner who takes a bus to Kansas City (Kansas City?) to become a screenwriter, with comic adventures along the way. A feast of jabs at genre films. 80m/C VHS, Beta. **CA** John Paizs, Eva Covacs, Darrel Baran; **D:** John Paizs. HHE

Big Deadly Game 🎬½ 1954 A vacationing American gets caught up in a complicated espionage plot by helping a mysterious wartime buddy. 63m/B VHS, Beta, LV. Lloyd Bridges, Simone Silva, Finlay Currie. NO

Big Deal on Madonna Street 🎬🎬🎬½ The Usual Unidentified Thieves 1958 A band of inept crooks plan to make themselves very rich when they attempt to rob a jewelry store. Their elaborate plans cause numerous (and hilarious) disasters. In Italian with English subtitles. Remade as "Crackers." 90m/B VHS, Beta. IT Marcello Mastroianni, Vittorio Gassman, Claudia Cardinale; **D:** Mario Monicelli. Nominations: Academy Awards '58: Best Foreign Language Film. CVC, MRV, DVT

The Big Dis 🎬🎬 1989 An interracial comedy about a young black soldier on a weekend pass who's looking for a willing sexual partner. His confidence is shattered when 12 possibilities turn him down. Feature debut of Eriksen and O'Brien. 88m/B VHS. **D:** Gordon Eriksen, John O'Brien. FCT, FRF

The Big Doll House 🎬🎬 Women's Penitentiary 1; Women in Cages 1971 (R) Roger Corman-produced prison drama about a group of tormented female convicts who decide to break out. Features vintage Grier, and a caliber of women's-prison sleaziness that isn't equalled in today's films. 93m/C VHS, Beta. Judy Brown, Roberta Collins, Pam Grier, Brooke Mills, Pat Woodell, Sid Haig, Christianne Schmidtmer, Kathryn Loder; **D:** Jack Hill; **M:** Les Baxter. NLC

The Big Easy 🎬🎬🎬½ 1987 (R) A terrific thriller. A slick New Orleans detective uncovers a heroin-based mob war while romancing the uptight assistant DA who's investigating corruption on the police force. An easy, Cajun-flavored mystery, a fast-moving action-comedy, a very sexy romance, and a serious exploration of the dynamics of corruption. 101m/C VHS, Beta, LV, Closed Caption. Dennis Quaid, Ellen Barkin, Ned Beatty, John Goodman, Ebbe Roe Smith, Charles Ludlam, Lisa Jane Persky, Tom O'Brien, Grace Zabriskie, Marc Lawrence; **D:** Jim McBride; **W:** Dan Petrie Jr.; **C:** Alfonso Beato; **M:** Brad Fiedel. Independent Spirit Awards '88: Best Actor (Quaid).HBO, FCT

The Big Fall 🎬🎬 1996 (R) L.A. private investigator (Howell) is hired by a mystery babe to find her brother. **CW:** Violence and language. ?m/C VHS. C. Thomas Howell, Sophie Ward, Jeff Kober, Justin Lazard; **D:** C. Thomas Howell. PMH

Big Fella 🎬🎬½ 1937 Musical drama starring Robeson as Joe, a Marseilles dockworker (a familiar film occupation for the actor), who's asked by the police to help find a young boy (Grant) missing from an ocean liner. When Joe locates the boy, he discovers the child ran away from his wealthy family and doesn't want to return. Joe takes the boy to his cafe singer girlfriend, Miranda (Welch), and the two become his surrogate parents. Loose adapatation of the 1929 novel, "Banjo," by Claude McKay. ♪Lazin'; Roll Up Sailorman; You Didn't Ought to Do Such Things; All God's Chillun Got a Robe; My Curly Headed Baby; River Steals My Folks from Me. 73m/B VHS. GB Paul Robeson, Elizabeth Welch, Eldon Grant; **D:** J. Elder Wills. KIV

The Big Fix 🎬🎬🎬 1978 (PG) Private investigator Moses Wine finds himself in an ironic situation: searching for a fugitive alongside whom he'd protested in the 60s. Based on a Roger Simon novel. 108m/C VHS, Beta. Richard Dreyfuss, Susan Anspach, Bonnie Bedelia, John Lithgow, F. Murray Abraham, Fritz Weaver, Mandy Patinkin; **D:** Jeremy Paul Kagan; **M:** Bill Conti. USH

Big Foot woof! 1972 Even genre devotees will be disappointed with this one. Sasquatch, who has procreation on his mind, searches rather half-heartedly for a human mate. A horror flick that forgot to include the horror. 92m/C VHS, Beta. Chris Mitchum, Joi Lansing, John Carradine, John Mitchum; **D:** Bob Slatzer. NO

The Big Gag 🎬 1987 (R) An international group of comedians travel the world and pull gags on people. Lame. 84m/C VHS, Beta. TWE, HHE

Big Girls Don't Cry...They Get Even 🎬½ 1992 (PG) A teenage girl decides to run away from home after she's driven crazy by her eccentric new stepfamily. Comic confusion ensues as various family members set out to find her. Hackneyed script and annoying characters hinder this comedy. 98m/C VHS, LV, Closed Caption. Hillary Wolf, Griffin Dunne, Margaret Whitton, David Strath-

aim, Don Savage, Adrienne Shelly, Patricia Kalember; **D:** Joan Micklin Silver. COL, NLC

The Big Grab 🎬🎬½ Any Number Can Win 1963 A dark big caper thriller about a couple of aging French thugs determined to rip off a casino at Cannes. In French with English subtitles. 118m/B VHS, Beta. FR Jean Gabin, Alain Delon, Viviane Romance, Maurice Biraud, Carla Marlier; **D:** Henri Verneuil. FCT

The Big Green 🎬½ 1995 (PG) British teacher Anna Montgomery (D'Abo) blows into a small Texas town determined to give the deprived kiddies a boost of self-esteem. With help from the town sheriff (Guttenberg), Anna organizes a soccer team that's supposed to give the kids a reason to live. Problems abound when the star player disappears just before the face-off with the biggest, nastiest team in the league. Sound familiar? This is the soccer version of "The Bad News Bears," "The Little Giants," and "The Mighty Ducks." The formula is less successful in this case, but some mildly amusing moments and a few fresh performances from the kids offer minor bright spots in this tired scenario. 100m/C VHS, LV, Closed Caption. Olivia D'Abo, Steve Guttenberg, Jay O. Sanders, John Terry, Chauncey Leopardi, Patrick Renna, Billy L. Sullivan, Yareli Arizmendi, Bug Hall; **D:** Holly Goldberg Sloan; **W:** Holly Goldberg Sloan; **C:** Ralf Bode; **M:** Randy Edelman. TOU

A Big Hand for the Little Lady 🎬🎬½ Big Deal at Dodge City 1966 Fonda and Woodward, playing two West-headed country bumpkins, get involved in a card game in Laredo against high rollers Robards and McCarthy. Fonda risks their savings, finds himself stuck with a losing hand, and has a bit of heart trouble; that's where the little lady comes in. Fine performances and a nifty twist ending don't entirely compensate for the overly padded script (which evolved from a 48-minute TV play drafted by Sydney Carroll). 95m/C VHS, Beta. Henry Fonda, Joanne Woodward, Jason Robards Jr., Charles Bickford, Burgess Meredith, Kevin McCarthy; **D:** Fielder Cook; **C:** Lee Garmes. WAR, FCT

The Big Hangover 🎬🎬 1950 Odd story about a man whose allergy to alcohol makes him drunk at the most inopportune moments. Johnson stars as the attorney with the peculiar problem and Taylor plays the boss' daughter who helps him overcome the allergy. Good supporting cast can't help this otherwise boring and predictable film. 82m/B VHS. Van Johnson, Elizabeth Taylor, Percy Waram, Fay Holden, Leon Ames, Edgar Buchanan, Selena Royle, Gene Lockhart; **D:** Norman Krasna; **W:** Norman Krasna. MGM

The Big Heat 🎬🎬🎬½ 1953 When detective Ford's wife (played by Jocelyn Brando, sister of Marlon) is killed in an explosion meant for him, he pursues the gangsters behind it and uncovers a police scandal. His appetite is whetted after this discovery and he pursues the criminals even more vigorously with the help of gangster moll Gloria Grahame. Definitive film noir. 90m/B VHS, Beta, LV. Glenn Ford, Lee Marvin, Gloria Grahame, Jocelyn Brando, Alexander Scourby, Carolyn Jones; **D:** Fritz Lang; **C:** Charles B(ryant) Lang. COL

The Big Hit 🎬🎬🎬 1998 (R) Combustible mixture of extravagent stunts, cartoon violence, hip-hop soundtrack, and a colorful cast serve up an explosively funny look at organized crime. When not executing their skills as ruthless hitmen, Melvin, Cisco, Vince, and Crunch (Wahlberg, Phillips, Sabato, Jr., and Woodbine) are regular working Joes with regular problems. For Melvin, financial and female problems force him to partner with Cisco in the kidnapping of a Chinese heiress. Said heiress turns out to be the goddaughter of their own crime boss. Much hilarity ensues. Phillips brings gusto to his flamboyant homeboy character and Wahlberg is his equal as the sappy gun for hire with a heart of gold. Big plot holes and fickle storyline, but bigger laughs make you not care so much. American directorial debut of Hong Kong import Che-Kirk Wong. **CW:** Violence, pervasive language and some sexuality. **91m/C VHS.** Mark Wahlberg, Lou Diamond Phillips, Bokeem Woodbine, Antonio Sabato Jr., Christina Applegate, Avery Brooks, China Chow, Lainie Kazan, Elliott Gould, Lela Rochon, Sab Shimono; **D:** Kirk Wong; **W:** Ben Ramsey; **C:** Danny Nowak; **M:** Graeme Revell. *NYR*

The Big House 🐾🐾🐾 1930 Prison melodrama at its best follows top con Beery as he plans a big breakout—and is betrayed. Life in the pen is depicted as brutal and futile, with sadistic guards and a hapless warden. Spawned numerous imitators. **80m/B VHS.** Wallace Beery, Chester Morris, Robert Montgomery, Lewis Stone, Leila Hyams, George F. Marion Sr., Karl Dane, DeWitt Jennings; **D:** George Hill; **W:** Frances Marion. Academy Awards '30: Best Writing; Nominations: Academy Awards '30: Best Actor (Beery), Best Picture. *MGM*

The Big Hurt 🐾½ 1987 (R) A reporter investigating a bizarre double murder discovers a secret government agency involved in torture and mind-control. **90m/C VHS, Beta, LV.** *AU* David Bradshaw, Lian Lunson, Simon Chilvers, Nick Wateres; **D:** Barry Peak. *NO*

Big Jake 🐾🐾 1971 (PG) An aging Texas cattle man who has outlived his time swings into action when outlaws kidnap his grandson and wound his son. He returns to his estranged family to help them in the search for Little Jake. O'Hara is once again paired up with Wayne and the chemistry is still there. **90m/C VHS, Beta, LV, Letterbox, Closed Caption.** John Wayne, Richard Boone, Maureen O'Hara, Patrick Wayne, Chris Mitchum, Bobby Vinton; **D:** George Sherman; **C:** William Clothier; **M:** Elmer Bernstein. *FOX*

Big Jim McLain 🐾🐾 1952 Wayne and Arness are federal agents working on behalf of the House Un-American Activities Committee to eliminate communist terrorism in Hawaii. And there's a suspicious psychiatrist, too: Wayne falls for a babe whose boss is a shrink who doesn't quite seem on the level. Definitely not a highpoint in the Duke's career. **90m/C VHS, LV, Closed Caption.** John Wayne, Nancy Olson, James Arness, Veda Ann Borg; **D:** Edward Ludwig; **C:** Archie Stout. *WAR, FCT*

The Big Knife 🐾🐾🐾 1955 Palance plays a Hollywood superstar who refuses to renew his studio contract, which enrages studio boss Steiger. It seems Steiger knows a very damaging secret about the star and is willing to go to any lengths to have Palance re-sign or wind up destroying himself. A ruthless, emotional look at fame and power, with excellent performances by all. Based on the play by Clifford Odets. **113m/B LV.** Jack Palance, Rod Steiger, Ida Lupino, Shelley Winters, Wendell Corey, Jean Hagen, Ilka Chase, Everett Sloane, Wesley Addy, Paul Langton; **D:** Robert Aldrich; **C:** Ernest Laszlo. *FCT*

The Big Lebowski 🐾🐾🐾½ 1997 (R) Jeff Lebowski (Bridges), a stuck-in-the-'70s stoner who insists on being called "the Dude" and loves to go bowling, is mistaken for a wheelchair-bound millionaire of the same name, and suffers a beating at the hands of thugs who are after money owed by the rich Lebowski's slutty wife. Dude is drawn into kidnapping, the attempted scamming of payoff money, and more bowling. While this may seem like plot-a-plenty, it's mainly a showcase for the Coen brothers' unique texturing of style and quirky-but-deep characters. Goodman is loud and funny as a Vietnam vet who takes any opportunity to pull a gun or explode into DI-like obscenities. Turturro steals his scenes as a pervert rival bowler who loves skintight lilac jumpsuits and polishing his ball. The showpiece is an amazing musical-bowling-fantasy sequence that would've made Busby Berkeley proud. **CW:** Pervasive strong language, drug content, sexuality and brief violence. **117m/C VHS, LV.** Jeff Bridges, John Goodman, Steve Buscemi, Julianne Moore, Peter Stormare, David Huddleston, Philip S. Hoffman, Flea, Leon Russom, Sam Elliott, John Turturro, David Thewlis, Tara Reid; **D:**

Joel Coen; **W:** Joel Coen, Ethan Coen; **C:** Roger Deakins; **M:** Carter Burwell. *PGV*

The Big Lift 🐾🐾½ 1950 Two G.I.'s assigned to the Berlin airlift ally themselves in counter-intelligence when they discover that their mutual girlfriend is a spy. **119m/B VHS, Beta.** Montgomery Clift, Paul Douglas, Cornell Borchers, Bruni Lobel, O.E. Hasse; **D:** George Seaton. *NOS, MRV, DVT*

The Big Man: Crossing the Line 🐾🐾🐾 *Crossing the Line* 1991 (R) Neeson shines as a down on his luck Scottish miner who loses his job during a union strike. Desperate for cash and unable to resolve his bitterness at being unable to support his family, he's enticed by a Glasgow loan boss to fight in an illegal bare-knuckled boxing match. What follows is an overlong and extremely brutal fight. Good performances from a talented cast overcome a rather preachy script that doesn't disguise its contempt for the Thatcher government, but also allows a glimpse into the tough times that many Brits suffered during the '80s. Based on the novel by William McIlvanney. **93m/C VHS, LV.** *GB* Liam Neeson, Joanne Whalley, Ian Bannen, Billy Connolly, Hugh Grant, Maurice Roeves, Rob Affleck; **D:** David Leland; **W:** Don MacPherson; **M:** Ennio Morricone. *COL*

Big Man on Campus 🐾 1989 (PG-13) A modern-day Quasimodo makes his home in an affluent university's belltower. Of course he falls in love with one of the pretty young co-eds and races out of his tower only to be captured by the psychology department. Really, really bad. **102m/C VHS, Beta, LV.** Tom Skerritt, Corey Parker, Allan Katz, Cindy Williams, Melora Hardin, Jessica Harper; **D:** Jeremy Paul Kagan; **C:** Bojan Bazelli. *VES*

Big Meat Eater 🐾🐾 1985 A musical gore-comedy about extraterrestrials using radioactive butcher's discards for ship fuel. Deliberate camp that is so bad its funny! **81m/C VHS, Beta.** *CA* George Dawson, Big Miller, Andrew Gillies; **D:** Chris Windsor.

Big Mo 🐾🐾 *Mauri* 1973 (G) True story of the friendship that developed between Cincinnati Royals basketball stars Maurice Stokes and Jack Twyman after a strange paralysis hit Stokes. **110m/C VHS, Beta.** Bernie Casey, Bo Svenson, Stephanie Edwards, Janet MacLachlan; **D:** Daniel Mann. *VES*

Big Mouth 🐾 1967 A dopey fisherman gets ahold of a treasure map and is pursued by cops and gangsters. Standard Lewis fare, with the requisite infantile histrionics; must be French to appreciate. **107m/C VHS, Beta.** Jerry Lewis, Jeannine Riley, Harold J. Stone, Charlie Callas, Buddy Lester, Susan Bay; **D:** Jerry Lewis; **W:** Jerry Lewis; **M:** Harry Betts. *COL*

Big News 🐾🐾 1929 Based on the play "For Two Cents" by George S. Brooks, this early talkie uses sound to great advantage. Fired for going after a gangster who's a big advertiser (Hardy), reporter Armstrong nevertheless keeps after the crook. When the intrepid reporter pushes too far, murder enters the picture. **75m/B VHS.** Robert Armstrong, Carole Lombard, Tom Kennedy, Warner Richmond, Wade Boteler, Sam Hardy, Lew Ayres; **D:** Gregory La Cava. *NOS*

Big Night 🐾🐾½ 1995 (R) Set in '50s New Jersey, film provides an Old World/New World look at Italian brothers Primo (Shalhoub) and Secondo (Tucci) Pilaggi and their elegant but failing restaurant. Primo is the perfectionist chef who hates compromise while Secondo wants to Americanize the place in an effort to make it a success. (He knows the customer is always right even if they can't appreciate Primo's exquisitely authentic Italian dishes). In order to get attention, Secondo arranges a special night in honor of jazz great Louis Prima, with Primo out to cook the feast of a lifetime—if they can pull it off. Another food film guaranteed to make you hungry. **CW:** Language. **109m/C VHS, LV, Closed Caption, DVD.** Tony Shalhoub, Stanley Tucci, Ian Holm, Minnie Driver, Campbell Scott, Isabella Rossellini, Mark Anthony, Allison Janney; **D:** Stanley Tucci, Campbell Scott; **W:** Stanley Tucci, Joseph Tropiano; **C:** Ken Kelsch. National Society of Film Critics Awards

'96: Best Supporting Actor (Shalhoub); Sundance Film Festival '96: Best Screenplay; Nominations: Independent Spirit Awards '97: Best First Feature, Best First Feature (Shalhoub, Tucci). *COL*

The Big One 🐾🐾 1998 (PG-13) Moore once again takes his populist, CEO-baiting act on the road in search of corporate evil-doers, this time on Random House's dime. Documentary lovingly follows Moore on his 1996 book promo tour, as he highlights plant closings, verbally spars with Nike boss Phil Knight, plays pranks on his "handlers," and mugs for his adoring fans. His style is still the same as in "Roger & Me," but since he's joined the celebrity ranks, Moore isn't going to sneak up on anybody. To his credit, he doesn't try, but to his discredit, he ends up haranguing the very working people he claims to be standing up for, mostly exasperated receptionists and secretaries. Corporate greed and apathy are still squarely in Moore's crosshairs, but this time his own ego prevents him from getting a clear shot at his target. **CW:** Some strong language. **96m/C VHS.** **D:** Michael Moore. *NYR*

The Big Parade 🐾🐾🐾🐾 1925 Wonderful WWI silent, considered to be one of the best war flicks of all time. Gilbert and Adoree are exceptional as lovers torn apart by the conflict. Interesting and thoughtful picture of the trauma and trouble brought to men and their loved ones in wartime. Battle scenes are compelling and intense; Vidor's masterpiece. **141m/B VHS, LV.** John Gilbert, Renee Adoree, Hobart Bosworth, Claire McDowell, Claire Adams, Karl Dane; **D:** King Vidor. National Film Registry '92. *MGM*

The Big Picture 🐾🐾½ 1989 (PG-13) A hilarious, overlooked comedy by and starring a variety of Second City/National Lampoon alumni, about a young filmmaker who is contracted by a big studio, only to see his vision trampled by formula-minded producers, crazed agents, hungry starlets, and every other variety of Hollywood predator. **95m/C VHS, Beta, LV, Closed Caption.** Kevin Bacon, Jennifer Jason Leigh, Martin Short, Michael McKean, Emily Longstreth, J.T. Walsh, Eddie Albert, Richard Belzer, John Cleese, June Lockhart, Stephen Collins, Roddy McDowall, Kim Miyori, Teri Hatcher, Dan Schneider, Jason Gould, Tracy Brooks Swope; **D:** Christopher Guest; **W:** Christopher Guest, Michael McKean, Michael Varhol; **M:** David Nichtern. *COL*

The Big Push 🐾½ *Timber Tramps* 1975 (PG) Motley bunch of Alaskan lumberjacks get together to save a poor widow's logging camp from a pair of greedy mill owners. **98m/C VHS, Beta.** Joseph Cotten, Claude Akins, Cesar Romero, Tab Hunter, Roosevelt Grier, Leon Ames, Stubby Kaye, Patricia Medina; **D:** Tay Garnett. *GEM*

Big Red 🐾🐾½ 1962 Set amid the spectacular beauty of Canada's Quebec Province, an orphan boy protects a dog which later saves him from a mountain lion. **89m/C VHS, Beta.** Walter Pidgeon, Gilles Payant; **D:** Norman Tokar; **C:** Edward Colman. *DIS*

The Big Red One 🐾🐾🐾½ 1980 (PG) Fuller's harrowing, intense semi-autobiographical account of the U.S. Army's famous First Infantry Division in WWII, the "Big Red One." A rifle squad composed of four very young men, led by the grizzled Marvin, cut a fiery path of conquest from the landing in North Africa to the liberation of the concentration camp at Falkenau, Czechoslovakia. In part a tale of lost innocence, the film scores highest by bringing the raw terror of war down to the individual level. **113m/C VHS, Beta, LV.** Lee Marvin, Robert Carradine, Mark Hamill, Stephane Audran, Bobby DiCicco, Perry Lang; **D:** Samuel Fuller; **W:** Samuel Fuller. *FOX, WAR*

The Big Scam 🐾🐾½ *A Nightingale Sang in Berkeley Square; The Mayfair Bank Caper* 1979 Criminal mastermind Niven recruits ex-con Jordan to pull off a massive bank heist. **102m/C VHS.** Richard Jordan, David Niven, Oliver Tobias, Elke Sommer, Gloria Grahame, Hugh Griffith, Richard Johnson; **D:** Ralph Thomas. *SIM*

Big Score 🎬 1983 (R) When a policeman is falsely accused and dismissed from the Chicago Police Department, he goes after the men who really stole the money from a drug bust. Script was originally intended to be a Dirty Harry flick; too bad it wasn't. 88m/C VHS, Beta. Fred Williamson, John Saxon, Richard Roundtree, Nancy Wilson, Ed Lauter, Ron Dean, D'Urville Martin, Michael Dante, Joe Spinell; **D:** Fred Williamson; **C:** Joao Fernandes. VES

Big Shots 🎬 1987 (PG-13) Two kids, one naive and white, the other black and streetwise, search for a stolen watch. 91m/C VHS, Beta, LV, **Closed Caption.** Ricky Busker, Darius McCrary, Robert Joy, Paul Winfield, Robert Prosky, Jerzy Skolimowski; **D:** Robert Mandel; **W:** Joe Eszterhas; **M:** Bruce Broughton. ORI, WAR

Big Show 🎬🎬 Home in Oklahoma 1937 A western adventure about the making of a western adventure. Autry jangles spurs aplenty in duel role. 54m/B VHS, Beta. Gene Autry, Smiley Burnette; **D:** Mack V. Wright. NOS, VCN, VDM

The Big Sky 🎬🎬🎬 1952 It's 1830, and a rowdy band of fur trappers embark upon a back breaking expedition up the uncharted Missouri River. Based on the A.B. Guthrie Jr. novel, it's an effortlessly enjoyable and level-headed Hawksian American myth, with a streak of gentle gallows humor. Also available colorized. 122m/C VHS, Beta, **Closed Caption.** Kirk Douglas, Dewey Martin, Arthur Hunnicutt, Elizabeth Threatt, Buddy Baer, Steve Geray, Jim Davis; **D:** Howard Hawks. Nominations: Academy Awards '52: Best Black and White Cinematography, Best Supporting Actor (Hunnicutt). FCT, TTC

The Big Sleep 🎬🎬🎬🎬 1946 Private eye Philip Marlowe, hired to protect a young woman from her own indiscretions, falls in love with her older sister while uncovering murders galore. A dense, chaotic thriller that succeeded in defining and setting a standard for its genre. The very best Raymond Chandler on film combining a witty script with great performances, especially from Bogart and Bacall. 114m/B VHS, Beta, LV. Humphrey Bogart, Lauren Bacall, John Ridgely, Martha Vickers, Louis Jean Heydt, Regis Toomey, Peggy Knudsen, Dorothy Malone, Bob Steele, Elisha Cook Jr.; **D:** Howard Hawks; **W:** William Faulkner, Jules Furthman, Leigh Brackett; **M:** Max Steiner. National Film Registry '97. FCT, TLF

The Big Sleep 🎬🎬 1978 (R) A tired remake of the Raymond Chandler potboiler about exhausted Los Angeles private dick Marlowe and his problems in protecting a wild young heiress from her own decadence and mob connections. Mitchum appears to need a rest. 99m/C VHS, Beta, LV. Robert Mitchum, Sarah Miles, Richard Boone, Candy Clark, Edward Fox, Joan Collins, John Mills, James Stewart, Oliver Reed, Harry Andrews, James Donald, Colin Blakely, Richard Todd; **D:** Michael Winner; **W:** Michael Winner. COL

The Big Slice 🎬½ 1990 (R) Two would-be crime novelists want to improve their fiction. One masquerades as a cop, the other as a crook, and they infiltrate the underworld from both ends. Clever comedy premise, but vaudeville-level jokes fall flat.**CW:** Sexual dialogue. 86m/C VHS, LV. Casey Siemaszko, Leslie Hope, Justin Louis, Heather Locklear, Kenneth Welsh, Nicholas Campbell, Henry Ramer; **D:** John Bradshaw; **W:** John Bradshaw; **M:** Mychael Danna, Jeff Danna.

The Big Sombrero 🎬🎬½ 1949 Autry takes a stand against the marriage between an unsuspecting, wealthy Mexican girl and the fortune-seeking bridegroom who wants her land. 77m/C VHS. Gene Autry, Elena Verdugo, Steve Dunne, George Lewis; **D:** Frank McDonald. NO

The Big Squeeze 🎬🎬½ 1996 (R) Married bartender Tanya (Boyle) is displeased to find out her born-again hubby Henry (Bercovici) has been holding out a large wad of cash from an insurance settlement, apparently about to donate it to a local Spanish mission. Enter Benny (Dobson), a cocky con man willing to help Tanya get her share of the dough for his own cut; sweet bartender Jesse (Nucci), who's secretly in love in Tanya; and fellow barmaid Cece (Dispina), who catches Ben-

ny's wandering eye. All get caught up in the frantic double-dealing. **CW:** Sexuality and some language. 100m/C VHS. Lara Flynn Boyle, Peter Dobson, Luca Bercovici, Danny Nucci, Teresa Dispina, Sam Vlahos, Valente Rodriguez; **D:** Marcus De Leon; **C:** Marcus De Leon; **C:** Jacques Haitkin; **M:** Mark Mothersbaugh. BMG

Big Stakes 🎬 1922 Extremely rare Western feature that has a Texas cowboy falling for a Mexican senorita. Plenty of action as complications ensue. ?m/B VHS. H.B. Warner, Elinor Fair, Les Bates; **D:** Clifford S. Elfelt; **W:** Frank Howard Clark. GVV

The Big Stampede 🎬🎬 1932 Twenty-five-year-old Wayne stars in this action-packed Western that was a remake of "Land Beyond the Law" from Ken Maynard's silent. Based on a story by Marion Jackson. 63m/B VHS, **Closed Caption.** John Wayne, Noah Beery Sr., Luis Alberni, Berton Churchill, Paul Hurst, Lafe McKee, Frank Ellis, Hank Bell; **D:** Tenny Wright; **W:** Kurt Kempler. MGM, GPV

Big Steal 🎬🎬🎬 1949 An Army officer recovers a missing payroll and captures the thieves after a tumultuous chase through Mexico. 72m/B VHS, Beta, LV. Robert Mitchum, William Bendix, Jane Greer, Ramon Novarro, Patric Knowles; **D:** Donald Siegel.

Big Store 🎬🎬½ 1941 Late Marx Brothers in which they are detectives in a large metropolitan department store, foiling a hostile takeover and preventing a murder. Their last MGM effort, with some good moments between the Tony Martin song numbers which include "If It's You" and the immortal "Tenement Symphony." Groucho also leads the "Sing While You Sell" number. 96m/b VHS, Beta. Groucho Marx, Harpo Marx, Chico Marx, Tony Martin, Margaret Dumont, Virginia Grey, Virginia O'Brien; **D:** Charles Riesner; **M:** George Bassman. MGM, CCB

Big Street 🎬🎬½ 1942 A timid busboy, in love with a disinterested nightclub singer, gets to prove his devotion when she is crippled in a fall. Based on a Damon Runyon story, "Little Pinks." 88m/B VHS, Beta, LV. Henry Fonda, Lucille Ball, Agnes Moorehead, Louise Beavers, Barton MacLane, Eugene Pallette, Ozzie Nelson; **D:** Irving Reis. TTC

The Big Sweat 🎬 1990 Maybe you've heard this one before: a man who has been framed by the mob escapes from prison and heads for Mexico. But first, he's got to get past the mobsters and police who are hot on his trail. And maybe you've seen some of it before: some of the same stock footage appears in Lommel's "Cold Heat." Not surprisingly, this one bypassed theatres and went straight to video. 85m/C VHS, LV. Robert Z'Dar, Steve Molone, Kevin McBride, William Roebuck, Cheri Caspari, David Rushing, Joanne Watkins, Ken Letner; **D:** Ulli Lommel; **W:** Max Bolt; **M:** John Massari.

The Big Switch 🎬½ Strip Poker 1970 (R) Gambler is framed for murder and becomes embroiled in a plot to reinstate an old gangster kingpin. 68m/C VHS, Beta. Sebastian Breaks, Virginia Wetherell, Erika Raffael; **D:** Pete Walker. NO

Big Top Pee Wee 🎬🎬 1988 (PG) Pee Wee's second feature film following the success of "Pee Wee's Big Adventure." This time Pee Wee owns a farm, has a girlfriend (!) and lives the good life until a weird storm blows a traveling circus onto his property. Cute, but not the manic hilarity the first one was. 86m/C VHS, Beta, LV, 8mm, **Closed Caption.** Paul (Pee Wee Herman) Reubens, Kris Kristofferson, Susan Tyrrell, Penelope Ann Miller; **D:** Randal Kleiser; **W:** Paul (Pee Wee Herman) Reubens; **C:** Steven Poster; **M:** Danny Elfman. PAR

Big Town 🎬 Guilty Assignment 1947 A newspaper is saved by a new editor who brings integrity to the once scandalous paper. The editor and his reporters also solve a series of murders. Some action, but weak dialogue and direction hold it back. Based on the radio program of the same name. 59m/B VHS. Philip Reed, Hillary Brooke, Robert Lowery, Byron Barr, Veda Ann Borg, Nana Bryant, Charles Arnt; **D:** William C. Thomas. SNC

Big Town 🎬🎬 1987 (R) A farmboy, lucky with dice, hits Chicago to claim his fortune when he meets floozies, criminals, and other streetlife. Look for Lane's strip number. 109m/C VHS, Beta, LV. Matt Dillon, Diane Lane, Tommy Lee Jones, Bruce Dern, Tom Skerritt, Lee Grant, Suzy Amis; **D:** Ben Bolt; **C:** Ralf Bode. VES, ART

Big Town After Dark 🎬🎬 Underworld After Dark 1947 Daring journalists search for the bottom-line story on a gang of criminals. They find themselves caught behind the firing lines when the sun goes down. Slightly better than average thriller. 69m/B VHS. Philip Reed, Hillary Brooke, Richard Travis, Ann Gillis; **D:** William C. Thomas. NOS, SNC, RXM

Big Trail 🎬🎬🎬 1930 This pioneering effort in widescreen cinematography was Wayne's first feature film. A wagon train on the Oregon trail encounters Indians, buffalo, tough terrain, and romantic problems. 110m/B VHS, Beta, **Closed Caption.** John Wayne, Marguerite Churchill, El Brendel, Tully Marshall, Tyrone Power Sr., Ward Bond, Helen Parrish; **D:** Raoul Walsh. FOX

Big Trees 🎬🎬🎬 1952 A ruthless lumberman attempts a takeover of the California Redwood Timberlands that are owned by a group of peaceful homesteaders. 89m/C VHS, Beta. Kirk Douglas, Patrice Wymore, Eve Miller, Alan Hale Jr., Edgar Buchanan; **D:** Felix Feist. NOS, MRV, DVT

Big Trouble 🎬🎬 1986 (R) An insurance broker endeavors to send his three sons to Yale by conspiring with a crazy couple in a fraud scheme that goes awry in every possible manner. Look for the cameo by screenwriter Bergman as Warren Bogle. 93m/C VHS, Beta, LV. Alan Arkin, Peter Falk, Beverly D'Angelo, Charles Durning, Robert Stack, Paul Dooley, Valerie Curtin, Richard Libertini; **Cameos:** Andrew Bergman; **D:** John Cassavetes; **W:** Andrew Bergman; **C:** Bill Butler; **M:** Bill Conti. COL

Big Trouble in Little China 🎬🎬½ 1986 (PG-13) A trucker plunges beneath the streets of San Francisco's Chinatown to battle an army of spirits. An uproarious comic-book-film parody with plenty of action and a keen sense of sophomoric sarcasm. 99m/C VHS, Beta, LV, Letterbox, **Closed Caption.** Kurt Russell, Suzee Pai, Dennis Dun, Kim Cattrall, James Hong, Victor Wong, Kate Burton; **D:** John Carpenter; **W:** David Weinstein, Gary Goldman, W.D. Richter; **C:** Dean Cundey; **M:** John Carpenter, Alan Howarth. FXV, FOX

Big Valley 1968 The western television series's two feature-length episodes: "Explosion," and "Legend of a General." 90m/C VHS, Beta. Richard Long, Linda Evans, Barbara Stanwyck, Lee Majors. NO

Big Wednesday 🎬🎬½ Summer of Innocence 1978 (PG) Three California surfers from the early '60s get back together after the Vietnam war to reminisce about the good old days and take on the big wave. 120m/C VHS, LV, Letterbox. Jan-Michael Vincent, Gary Busey, William Katt, Lee Purcell, Patti D'Arbanville; **D:** John Milius; **W:** John Milius; **M:** Basil Poledouris. WAR

The Big Wheel 🎬🎬½ 1949 Old story retold fairly well. Rooney is young son determined to travel in his father's tracks as a race car driver, even when dad buys the farm on the oval. Good acting and direction keep this a cut above average. 92m/B VHS. Mickey Rooney, Thomas Mitchell, Spring Byington, Mary Hatcher, Allen Jenkins, Michael O'Shea; **D:** Edward Ludwig. GPV

Big Zapper 🎬½ 1973 Violent P.I. Marlowe and masochistic assistant Rock work together in this British comic strip film. 94m/C VHS. GB Linda Marlowe, Gary Hope, Sean Hewitt, Richard Monette, Penny Irving; **D:** Lindsay Shonteff. VCD

The Bigamist 🎬½ 1953 Have you heard the one about the traveling salesman in this movie? He has one wife in Los Angeles, another in San Francisco, and they inevitably find out about each other. A maudlin soap opera with a do-it-yourself ending, only shows why bigamy was done better as farce in the later "Micki and Maude." 79m/B VHS. Edmond O'Brien, Joan Fontaine,

Ida Lupino, Edmund Gwenn, Jane Darwell, Kenneth Tobey; *D:* Ida Lupino. *DVT, NOS, HEG*

Bigfoot: The Unforgettable Encounter 🐾🐾½ 1994 (PG) Young boy
heads off into the woods, comes face to face with Bigfoot, and sets off a media frenzy and a band of ruthless bounty hunters determined to capture his hairy friend. 89m/C **VHS, Closed Caption.** Zachery Ty Bryan, Matt McCoy, Barbara Willis Sweete, Clint Howard, Rance Howard, David Rasche; *D:* Corey Michael Eubanks; *W:* Corey Michael Eubanks; *M:* Shimon Arama. *REP*

Biggles 🐾🐾 *Biggles: Adventures in Time* 1985
(PG) Time-travel fantasy in which a young businessman from present-day New York City is inexplicably transferred into the identity of a 1917 WWI flying ace. He suddenly finds himself aboard a fighter plane over Europe during WWI. 100m/C **VHS, Beta, LV, Closed Caption.** *GB* Neil Dickson, Alex Hyde-White, Peter Cushing; *D:* John Hough. *VTR*

Bikers, Blondes, and Blood 1993 A
montage of the sleaze genre's greatest moments including a clip from Jayne Mansfield's "Single Room Furnished." Suitable for dorm keggers, frat parties or any other venue where the audience has supplementary amusements available. Some clips in black and white. 90m/B **VHS.** *SMW, TPV*

Bikini Beach 🐾🐾½ 1964 Surfing teenag-
ers of the "Beach Party" series follow up "Muscle Beach Party" with a third fling at the beach and welcome a visitor, British recording star "Potato Bug" (Avalon in a campy dual role). But, golly gee, wealthy Wynn wants to turn their sandy, surfin' shores into a retirement community. What to do? Sing a few songs, dance in your bathing suits, and have fun. Classic early '60s nostalgia is better than the first two efforts; followed by "Pajama Party." ♫Because You're You; Love's a Secret Weapon; Bikini Drag. 100m/C **VHS, Beta.** Annette Funicello, Frankie Avalon, Martha Hyer, Harvey Lembeck, Don Rickles, Stevie Wonder, John Ashley, Keenan Wynn, Jody McCrea, Candy Johnson, Danielle Aubry, Meredith MacRae, Dolores Wells, Donna Loren, Timothy Carey; *D:* William Asher; *W:* William Asher, Leo Townsend, Robert Dillon; *C:* Floyd Crosby; *M:* Les Baxter.

Bikini Bistro 🐾 1994 (R) A boring vegetari-
an cafe gets turned into a gourmet restaurant but, faced with an eviction notice, the female owners decide to increase business by waitressing in bikinis. Also available in an unrated version at 84 minutes.*CW:* Numerous sex-related situations. 80m/C **VHS.** Marilyn Chambers, Amy Lynn Baxter, Joan Gerardi, Isabelle Fortea, John Altamura, Joseph Pallister; *D:* Ernest G. Sauer; *W:* Matt Unger. *AVI*

The Bikini Car Wash
Company woof! *California Hot Wax* 1990 (R)
Babes in bikinis in Los Angeles. A young man is running his uncle's carwash when he meets a business major who persuades him to let her take over the business for a cut of the profits. She decides that a good gimmick would be to dress all the female employees in the tiniest bikinis possible. The story is of course secondary to the amount of flesh on display. Also available in an unrated version.*CW:* Language, nudity, and sexuality. 87m/C **VHS, Closed Caption.** Joe Dusic, Neriah Napaul, Suzanne Browne, Kristie Ducati; *D:* Ed Hansen. *IMP*

The Bikini Car Wash Company
2 🐾 1992 (R) Entrepreneur Melissa and the oth-
er lovely ladies of the Bikini Car Wash Co. find themselves a big success, so much so that a greedy businessman wants to buy them out. In order to get money to fight the takeover, the ladies take to the airwaves of a cable-access station. Their new business adventure involves selling sexy lingerie which means the flesh quotient is as great as ever. An unrated version is also available.*CW:* Nudity and sexual situations. ?m/C **VHS, LV, Closed Caption.** Kristie Ducati, Suzanne Browne, Neriah Napaul, Rikki Brando, Greg Raye, Larry De Russy; *D:* Gary Orona; *W:* Bart B. Gustis; *M:* Michael Smith. *IMP*

Bikini Drive-In 🐾½ 1994 (R) Babe (Rhey)
inherits grandad's decrepit drive-in, which is wanted by a mall mogul, but she refuses to sell. So to raise some cash, Rhey stages a B-movie marathon with in-person, bikini-clad scream queens.*CW:* Strong sexual content. 85m/C **VHS.** Ashlie Rhey, Richard Gabai, Ross Hagen, Sara Bellomo, Steve Barkett, Conrad Brooks; *D:* Fred Olen Ray. *AVI*

Bikini Island 🐾 1991 (R) Beautiful swimsuit
models gather on a remote tropical island for a big photo shoot, each vying to be the next cover girl of the hottest swimsuit magazine. Before long, scantily clad lovelies are turning up dead and full out madness ensues. Will the mystery be solved before they run out of models, or will the magazine have no choice but to grace its cover with a bikinied cadaver? Low-budget trash that has few, if any, redeeming qualities.*CW:* Violence and sensuality. 85m/C **VHS, Beta.** Holly Floria, Alicia Anne, Jackson Robinson, Shannon Stiles, Cyndi Pass, Sherry Johnson; *D:* Anthony Markes; *W:* Emerson Bixby; *M:* Marc David Deeker.

Bikini Summer 🐾½ 1991 Laughs, music,
and skin are the order of the day as two nutty guys and a few beautiful girls form an unlikely friendship on the beach. Konop was Julia Roberts's "Pretty Woman" body double. Sort of the '90s version of the old '60s Frankie and Annette beach parties. 90m/C **VHS, LV.** David Millburn, Melinda Armstrong, Jason Clow, Shelley Michelle, Alex Smith, Kent Lipham, Kelly Konop, Carmen Santa Maria; *D:* Robert Veze; *W:* Robert Veze, Nick Stone; *M:* John Gonzalez. *PMH*

Bikini Summer 2 🐾 1992 (R) An eccentric
family decides to stage a bikini contest to raise money to help the homeless. 94m/C **VHS, LV.** Jeff Conaway, Jessica Hahn, Melinda Armstrong, Avalon Anders; *D:* Jeff Conaway; *M:* Jim Halfpenny. *PMH*

Bikini Summer 3: South Beach
Heat 🐾 1997 (R) Babes in bikinis frolic on Mi-
ami's fashionable South Beach for the chance to become the spokesmodel for Mermaid Body Splash.*CW:* Pervasive nudity and some strong sexuality. 84m/C **VHS.** Heather-Elizabeth Parkhurst, Tiffany Turner. *PMH*

Bilitis 🐾½ 1977 (R) A young girl from a private
girls' school is initiated into the pleasures of sex and the unexpected demands of love. One of director Hamilton's exploitative meditations on nudity. 95m/C **VHS, Beta.** *FR* Patti D'Arbanville, Bernard Giraudeau, Mona Kristensen; *D:* David Hamilton.

Bill 🐾🐾🐾 1981 A made-for-television movie
based on a true story about a mentally retarded man who sets out to live independently after 44 years in an institution. Rooney gives an affecting performance as Bill and Quaid is strong as the filmmaker who befriends him. Awarded Emmys for Rooney's performance and the well written script. Followed by "Bill: On His Own." 97m/C **VHS, Beta.** Mickey Rooney, Dennis Quaid, Largo Woodruff, Harry Goz; *D:* Anthony Page. *ART*

Bill and Coo 🐾🐾 1947 An unusual love
story with a villian and hero using an all bird cast. 61m/C **VHS, Beta, 8mm.** *D:* Dean Riesner. *VYY, MRV, NOS*

Bill & Ted's Bogus Journey 🐾🐾
1991 (PG) Big-budget sequel to B & T's first movie has better special effects but about the same quota of laughs. Slain by lookalike robot duplicates from the future, the airhead heroes pass through heaven and hell before tricking the Grim Reaper into bringing them back for a second duel with their heinous terminators. Most excellent closing-credit montage. Non-fans still won't think much of it. 98m/C **VHS, Closed Caption.** Keanu Reeves, Alex Winter, William Sadler, Joss Ackland, Pam Grier, George Carlin, Amy Stock-Poynton, Hal Landon Jr., Annette Azcuy, Sarah Trigger, Chelcie Ross, Taj Mahal, Roy Brocksmith, William Shatner; *D:* Pete Hewitt; *W:* Chris Matheson, Edward Solomon; *M:* David Newman. *ORI*

Bill & Ted's Excellent
Adventure 🐾🐾½ 1989 (PG) Excellent prem-
ise: when the entire future of the world rests on whether or not two '80s dudes pass their history final, Rufus comes to the rescue in his time-travelling telephone booth. Bill and Ted share an adventure through time as they meet and get to know some of history's most important figures. 105m/C **VHS, Beta, LV, 8mm, Closed Caption.** Keanu Reeves, Alex Winter, George Carlin, Bernie Casey, Dan Shor, Robert Barron, Amy Stock-Poynton, Ted Steedman, Terry Camillieri, Rod Loomis, Al Leong, Tony Camilieri; *D:* Stephen Herek; *W:* Chris Matheson, Edward Solomon; *M:* David Newman. *COL, NLC*

A Bill of Divorcement 🐾🐾½ 1932
Hepburn's screen debut, as the daughter of a shell-shocked WWI vet, who requires her care after her mother decides to divorce him. Creaky early talker. 76m/B **VHS, Beta, LV, Closed Caption.** John Barrymore, Katharine Hepburn, Billie Burke, Henry Stephenson, David Manners, Paul Cavanagh, Elizabeth Patterson; *D:* George Cukor; *M:* Max Steiner. *FOX*

Bill: On His Own 🐾🐾🐾 1983 Rooney is
again exceptional in this sequel to the Emmy-winning TV movie "Bill." After 44 years in an institution, a mentally retarded man copes more and more successfully with the outside world. Fine supporting cast and direction control the melodramatic potential. 100m/C **VHS.** Mickey Rooney, Helen Hunt, Teresa Wright, Dennis Quaid, Largo Woodruff, Paul Leiber, Harry Goz; *D:* Anthony Page. *ART*

Billie 🐾½ 1965 Duke stars as a tomboy ath-
lete who puts the boys' track team to shame. Some amusing but very predictable situations, plus a few songs from Miss Duke. Based on Ronald Alexander's play "Time Out for Ginger." 86m/C **VHS, Beta, LV, Letterbox.** Patty Duke, Jim Backus, Jane Greer, Warren Berlinger, Billy DeWolfe, Charles Lane, Dick Sargent, Susan Seaforth Hayes, Ted Bessell, Richard Deacon; *D:* Don Weis; *W:* Ronald Alexander. *MGM*

The Billion Dollar Hobo 🐾½ 1978 (G)
Poor, unsuspecting heir of a multimillion dollar fortune must duplicate his benefactor's experience as a hobo during the Depression in order to collect his inheritance. Slow-moving family stuff. 96m/C **VHS, Beta.** Tim Conway, Will Geer, Eric Weston, Sydney Lassick; *D:* Stuart E. McGowan. *FOX*

A Billion for Boris 🐾🐾½ 1990 Boris'
TV gives a sneak preview of the future and Boris plans to make some money off of it. Zany comedy in the vein of "Let It Ride." 89m/C **VHS, Beta.** Lee Grant, Tim Kazurinsky; *D:* Alex Grasshof; *W:* Mary Rogers. *IMP*

Billionaire Boys Club 🐾🐾½ 1987
Chilling look at greed in the '80s. Nelson plays Joe Hunt, who gets together with a group of rich, preppie friends to manipulate investments in the commodities markets. When a slick con man (Silver) gets in their way he's murdered to keep their schemes intact. Based on a true story and adapted from the book by Sue Horton. Originally shown on television in two parts, the video version is considerably pared down. 94m/C **VHS.** Judd Nelson, Frederic Lehne, Brian McNamara, Raphael Sbarge, John Stockwell, Barry Tubb, Stan Shaw, Jill Schoelen, Ron Silver, James Sloyan, James Karen; *D:* Marvin J. Chomsky. *ART*

Billy Bathgate 🐾🐾½ 1991 (R) Uneven but
well acted drama set in 1935 New York. A streetwise young man decides getting ahead during the Depression means gaining the attention of mobster Dutch Schultz and joining his gang. As Billy becomes the confidant of the racketeer he learns the criminal life is filled with suspicion and violence; in order to stay alive he must rely on every trick he's learned. Willis has a small role as a rival mobster who gets fitted for cement overshoes. Kidman does well as Dutch's girlfriend with Hill fine as the gang's number man. Based on the novel by E.L. Doctorow.*CW:* Language and gangster violence. 107m/C **VHS, Beta, LV, Letterbox, Closed Caption.** Dustin Hoffman, Nicole Kidman, Loren Dean, Bruce Willis, Steven Hill, Steve Buscemi, Stanley

Tucci, Tim Jerome, Billy Jaye, Katharine Houghton, Mike Otari, John Oostelive, Moira Kelly, **D.** Robert Benton; **W:** Tom Stoppard; **C:** Nestor Almendros; **M:** Mark Isham. Nominations: Golden Globe Awards '91: Best Supporting Actress (Kidman). *TOU*

Billy Budd 🎬🎬🎬 1962 The classic Melville good-evil allegory adapted to film, dealing with a British warship in the late 1700s and its struggle between evil master-at-arms and innocent shipmate. Stamp's screen debut as the naive Billy who is tried for the murder of the sadistic first mate. Well directed and acted. 123m/B VHS, Beta, LV. *GB* Terence Stamp, Peter Ustinov, Robert Ryan, Melvyn Douglas, Paul Rogers, John Neville, Ronald Lewis, David McCallum, John Meillon; **D:** Peter Ustinov; **W:** Peter Ustinov, Robert Rossen; **C:** Robert Krasker. Nominations: Academy Awards '62: Best Supporting Actor (Stamp). *FOX*

Billy Galvin 🎬🎬½ 1986 (PG) A bullheaded ironworker tries to straighten out the turbulent relationship he has with his rebellious son. 95m/C VHS, Beta. Karl Malden, Lenny Von Dohlen, Joyce Van Patten, Toni Kalem, Keith Szarabajka, Alan North, Paul Guilfoyle, Barton Heyman; **D:** John Gray; **W:** John Gray; **M:** Joel Rosenbaum. *ART, VES*

Billy Jack 🎬🎬 1971 (PG) On an Arizona Indian reservation, a half-breed ex-Green Beret with pugnacious martial arts skills (Laughlin) stands between a rural town and a school for runaways. Laughlin stars with his real-life wife Taylor. Features the then-hit song "One Tin Soldier," sung by Coven. The movie and its marketing by Laughlin inspired a "Billy Jack" cult phenomenon. A Spanish-dubbed version of this film is also available. Followed by a sequel in 1974, "Trail of Billy Jack," which bombed. 112m/C VHS, Beta, LV. Tom Laughlin, Delores Taylor, Clark Howat; **D:** Tom Laughlin; **W:** Tom Laughlin. *WAR*

Billy Liar 🎬🎬🎬 1963 A young Englishman dreams of escaping from his working class family and dead-end job as an undertaker's assistant. Parallels James Thurber's story, "The Secret Life of Walter Mitty." 94m/B VHS, Beta. *GB* Tom Courtenay, Julie Christie, Finlay Currie; **D:** John Schlesinger; **M:** Richard Rodney Bennett. *REP*

Billy Madison 🎬½ 1994 (PG-13) Wealthy slacker Billy (Sandler) must prove to Dad he is capable of running the family hotel business by undertaking the obvious challenge of repeating grades 1-12 in six months. Ponder a few bodily function gags, and you'll have exhausted the humor in this lame attempt at creating a feature-length movie out of what would barely pass as a Saturday Night Live sketch.*CW:* Language; crude humor. 90m/C VHS, LV, Closed Caption. Adam Sandler, Darren McGavin, Bridgette Wilson, Bradley Whitford, Josh Mostel, Norm MacDonald, Mark Beltzman, Larry Hankin, Theresa Merritt; *Cameos:* Chris Farley, Steve Buscemi; **D:** Tamra Davis; **W:** Adam Sandler; **M:** Randy Edelman. Nominations: MTV Movie Awards '95: Best Comedic Performance (Sandler). *USH*

Billy: Portrait of a Street Kid 🎬🎬 1977 A ghetto youngster tries to pry himself up and out of his bleak surroundings through education, but complications arise when he gets his girlfriend pregnant. 96m/C VHS, Beta. LeVar Burton, Tina Andrews, Ossie Davis, Michael Constantine; **D:** Steven Gethers. *WOV*

Billy Rose's Jumbo 🎬🎬🎬 *Jumbo* 1962 Better-than-average update of the circus picture. Durante and Raye are terrific, as are the Rodgers and Hart songs. Fun, with lively production numbers in the inimitable Berkeley style. ♫Over and Over Again; Circus on Parade; Why Can't I?; This Can't Be Love; The Most Beautiful Girl in the World; My Romance; Little Girl Blue; What is a Circus; Sawdust, Spangles and Dreams. 125m/C VHS, LV, Letterbox. Doris Day, Stephen Boyd, Jimmy Durante, Martha Raye, Dean Jagger; **D:** Charles Walters; **W:** Sidney Sheldon. Nominations: Academy Awards '62: Best Adapted Score. *MGM*

Billy the Kid 🎬🎬½ 1941 Billy Bonney joins up with a group of outlaws in a Southwest town where he bumps into his old friend Jim Sherwood, now the marshal. Attempting to change his ways, he falls back into the life of a bandit when an outlaw friend is murdered. Although an entertaining western, the story bears no resemblance to the actual last days of Billy the Kid. Based on a story by Howard Emmett Rogers and Bradbury Foote, suggested by the book "The Saga of Billy the Kid" by Walter Noble Burns. 94m/C VHS, Closed Caption. Robert Taylor, Brian Donlevy, Ian Hunter, Mary Howard, Gene Lockhart, Lon Chaney Jr., Guinn "Big Boy" Williams, Cy Kendall, Henry O'Neill, Ted Adams, Frank Puglia, Mitchell Lewis, Dick Curtis, Grant Withers, Joe Yule, Eddie Dunn, Kermit Maynard, Chill Wills, Olive Blakeney, Carl Pitti; **D:** David Miller; **W:** Gene Fowler Jr.; **M:** David Snell. Nominations: Academy Awards '41: Best Color Cinematography. *MGM*

Billy the Kid in Texas 🎬½ 1940 The famed outlaw takes on trouble and makes sure the Texans never forget that he has been there. 52m/B VHS, Beta. Bob Steele. *NOS, VCN*

Billy the Kid Returns 🎬½ 1938 While trying to clean up a town of its criminal element, Rogers is mistaken for the legendary Billy. Complications ensue. 60m/B VHS, Beta. Roy Rogers, George "Gabby" Hayes, Smiley Burnette, Lynn (Mary Hart) Roberts; **D:** Joseph Kane. *NOS, HHT, VCN*

Billy the Kid Trapped 🎬½ 1942 Billy and his partner are rescued from hanging by an outlaw band. 59m/B VHS. Buster Crabbe, Al "Fuzzy" St. John, Bud McTaggart, Anne Jeffreys, Glenn Strange; **D:** Sam Newfield. *NOS, MRV, DVT*

Billy the Kid Versus Dracula 🎬🎬 1966 The title says it all. Dracula travels to the Old West, anxious to put the bite on a pretty lady ranch owner. Her fiance, the legendary outlaw Billy the Kid, steps in to save his girl from becoming a vampire herself. A Carradine camp classic. 95m/C VHS, Beta. Chuck Courtney, John Carradine, Melinda Plowman, Walter Janovitz, Harry Carey Jr., Roy Barcroft, Virginia Christine, Bing Russell, Olive Carey; **D:** William Beaudine; **W:** Carl K. Hittleman; **C:** Lothrop Worth. *VYY*

Billy Two Hats 🎬🎬½ *The Lady and the Outlaw* 1974 (PG) Grizzled Scottish bandit Deans (Peck) teams up with young half-breed Billy (Arnaz Jr.) to pull off a robbery that results in an accidental death and Billy's capture. Deans is shot while breaking the kid out of jail and must rely on Billy to get them through, while being pursued by the law. It ain't happy. Mainly notable as the first western shot in Israel. 139m/C VHS. Gregory Peck, Desi Arnaz Jr., Jack Warden, Sian Barbara Allen, David Huddleston; **D:** Ted Kotcheff; **W:** Alan Sharp; **C:** Brian West; **M:** John Scott. *MGM*

Billyboy 1979 Coming of age film with the world of boxing as background. Excellent fight scenes. 94m/C VHS, Beta. Duane Bobrick, Kim Braden. *BFV*

Biloxi Blues 🎬🎬½ *Neil Simon's Biloxi Blues* 1988 (PG-13) Eugene Morris Jerome has been drafted and sent to boot camp in Biloxi, Mississippi where he encounters a troubled drill sergeant, hostile recruits, and a skillful prostitute. Walken is the drill sergeant from hell. Some good laughs from the ever-wry Broderick. A sequel to Neil Simon's "Brighton Beach Memoirs" and adapted by Simon from his play. Followed by "Broadway Bound." 105m/C VHS, Beta, LV. Matthew Broderick, Christopher Walken, Casey Siemaszko, Matt Mulhern, Corey Parker, Penelope Ann Miller, Michael Dolan, Park Overall; **D:** Mike Nichols; **W:** Neil Simon; **C:** Bill Butler; **M:** Georges Delerue. *USH*

Bimini Code 🎬 1984 Two female adventurers accept a dangerous mission where they wind up on Bimini Island in a showdown with the mysterious Madame X. 95m/C VHS, Beta. Vickie Benson, Krista Richardson, Frank Alexander, Rosanna Simanaitis; **D:** Barry Clark.

Bingo 🎬🎬½ 1991 (PG) Mediocre spoof of hero-dog movies. The heroic title mutt roams from Denver to Green Bay in search of his absent-minded master, with numerous absurd adventures en route. Some cute moments, but sometimes Bingo is just lame-o. Good family fare. 90m/C VHS, LV, Closed Caption. Cindy Williams, David Rasche, Robert J. Steinmiller Jr., David French, Kurt Fuller, Joe Guzaldo, Glenn Shadix; **D:** Matthew Robbins; **W:** Jim Strain; **M:** Richard Gibbs. *COL*

Bingo Long Traveling All-Stars & Motor Kings 🎬🎬🎬 1976 (PG) Set in 1939, this film recounts the comedic adventures of a lively group of black ball players who have defected from the old Negro National League. The All-Stars travel the country challenging local white teams. 111m/C VHS, Beta. Billy Dee Williams, James Earl Jones, Richard Pryor, Stan Shaw; **D:** John Badham; **W:** Matthew Robbins, Hal Barwood; **C:** Bill Butler; **M:** William Goldstein. *USH, FCT*

Bio-Dome 🎬 1996 (PG-13) Pauly Shore in a hermetically sealed environment separated from the rest of society? Great! Where do I sign? Unfortunately, it's only a movie, and a typically useless one, at that. Shore brings his lame schtick to a scientifically created "perfect environment" that he and his college (yeah, right) buddy Doyle (Baldwin) mistake for a mall and eventually destroy. In Bloom's not-too-auspicious directorial debut, bodily function jokes found in Jim Carrey's wastebasket masquerade as a script, while the supporting cast wanders aimlessly, perhaps pondering a switch in agents.*CW:* Crude language, sex-related material and some drug content. 94m/C VHS, LV, Closed Caption. Pauly Shore, Stephen Baldwin, William Atherton, Henry Gibson, Joey Lauren Adams, Teresa Hill, Kylie Minogue, Kevin West, Denise Dowse, Dara Tomanovich; **D:** Jason Bloom; **W:** Kip Koenig, Scott Marcano; **C:** Phedon Papamichael; **M:** Andrew Gross. Golden Raspberry Awards '96: Worst Actor (Shore). *MGM*

Bio Hazard 🎬 1985 (R) A toxic monster needs human flesh to survive and consequently goes on a rampage. 84m/C VHS, Beta. Angelique Pettyjohn, Carroll Borland, Richard Hench, Aldo Ray; **D:** Fred Olen Ray. *MTX*

Biohazard: The Alien Force 🎬½ 1995 (R) Reptilian mutant, the result of a genetic experiment gone awry, must be hunted down before it can reproduce. Sounds like a rip-off of "Species."*CW:* Sci-fi violence and gore, and for some sexuality and language. 88m/C VHS. Steve Zurk, Chris Mitchum, Susan Fronsoe, Tom Ferguson, Patrick Moran, John Maynard; **D:** Steve Latshaw. *THV*

The Bionic Woman 🎬🎬 1975 Sky-diving accident leaves tennis pro Jaimie Somers crippled and near death. Her bionic buddy, Steve Austin, gets his friends to rebuild her and make her better than she was before. The pilot for the television series. 96m/C VHS, Beta. Lindsay Wagner, Lee Majors, Richard Anderson, Alan Oppenheimer; **D:** Richard Moder. *USH*

The Birch Interval 🎬🎬 1978 (PG) A chronicle of a young Amish girl growing up and experiencing adult passions and fears when she visits her kin in their isolated Pennsylvania community. 104m/C VHS, Beta. Eddie Albert, Rip Torn, Ann Wedgeworth; **D:** Delbert Mann; **W:** Joanna Crawford.

Bird 🎬🎬🎬 1988 (R) The richly textured, though sadly one-sided biography of jazz sax great Charlie Parker, from his rise to stardom to his premature death via extended heroin use. A remarkably assured, deeply imagined film from Eastwood that never really shows the Bird's genius of creation. The soundtrack features Parker's own solos re-mastered from original recordings. 160m/C VHS, Beta, LV, Closed Caption. Forest Whitaker, Diane Venora, Michael Zelniker, Samuel E. Wright, Keith David, Michael McGuire, James Handy, Damon Whitaker, Morgan Nagler, Peter Crook; **D:** Clint Eastwood; **W:** Joel Oliansky; **C:** Jack N. Green; **M:** Lennie Niehaus. Academy Awards '88: Best Sound; Cannes Film Festival '88: Best Actor (Whitaker); Golden Globe Awards '89: Best Director

(Eastwood); New York Film Critics Awards '88: Best Supporting Actress (Venora). *MVD, WAR, FCT*

Bird of Paradise 🎬🎬½ **1932** An exotic South Seas romance in which an adventurer is cast onto a remote Polynesian island when his yacht haphazardly sails into a coral reef. There he becomes enamored of an exotic island girl, and nature seems to disapprove. **80m/B VHS, Beta, 8mm.** Joel McCrea, Dolores Del Rio, Lon Chaney Jr.; **D:** King Vidor; **M:** Max Steiner. *NOS, MRV, VYY*

Bird of Prey 🎬🎬½ **1995 (R)** Nick Milev (Milushev) has just been released from a Bulgarian prison for attacking Jonathan Griffith (Chamberlain), the drugs-and-arms dealer who was responsible for the death of Milev's policeman father. But Milev still wants revenge, though matters get complicated by Kily (Tilly), Griffith's naive daughter, with whom he falls in love. Plot's so-so but characters make up for some of the routiness. Filmed on location in Sofia, Bulgaria. **102m/C VHS, Closed Caption.** Boyan Milushev, Jennifer Tilly, Richard Chamberlain, Lenny Von Dohlen, Robert Carradine, Lesley Ann Warren; **D:** Temistocles Lopez; **W:** Boyan Milushev; **C:** David Knaus. *CAF*

Bird on a Wire 🎬🎬 **1990 (PG-13)** After suddenly being forced to emerge from a prolonged period under the Witness Protection Program, an ex-hood and his ex-girlfriend are pursued by old enemies. **110m/C VHS, Beta, LV, Letterbox, Closed Caption, DVD.** Mel Gibson, Goldie Hawn, David Carradine, Bill Duke, Stephen Tobolowsky; **D:** John Badham; **W:** David Seltzer; **C:** Robert Primes; **M:** Hans Zimmer. *USH*

The Bird with the Crystal Plumage 🎬🎬½ *L'Ucello dalle Plume di Cristallo; The Phantom of Terror* **1970 (PG)** An American writer living in Rome witnesses a murder. He becomes involved in the mystery when the alleged murderer is cleared because the woman believed to be his next victim is shown to be a psychopathic murderer. Vintage Argento mayhem. **98m/C VHS, Beta, LV.** *IT* Tony Musante, Suzy Kendall, Eva Renzi; **D:** Dario Argento; **W:** Dario Argento; **M:** Ennio Morricone. *VCI, MRV*

The Birdcage 🎬🎬🎬 *Birds of a Feather* **1995 (R)** Somewhat overlong but well-played remake of "La Cage aux Folles" features Williams suppressing his usual manic schtick to portray Armand, the subdued half of a longtime gay couple living in Miami. His partner is the ever-hysterical-but-loving drag queen Albert (Lane), whose presence provides a distinct challenge when Armand's son Val (Futterman) announces his engagement to the daughter of family values, right-wing senator Kevin Keeley (Hackman). When the Senator and family arrive for dinner, Armand tries to play it straight while Albert opts for a matronly mom impersonation (think Barbara Bush). Highlights include Armand's initial attempts to teach Albert to be butch (walk like John Wayne) and Hackman congoing in drag. **CW:** Language. **120m/C VHS, LV, Closed Caption.** Robin Williams, Nathan Lane, Gene Hackman, Dianne Wiest, Hank Azaria, Dan Futterman, Christine Baranski, Calista Flockhart, Tom McGowan; **D:** Mike Nichols; **W:** Elaine May; **C:** Emmanuel Lubezki. Screen Actors Guild Award '96: Cast; Nominations: Academy Awards '96: Best Art Direction/Set Decoration; Golden Globe Awards '97: Best Actor—Musical/Comedy (Lane), Best Film—Musical/Comedy; MTV Movie Awards '97: Best On-Screen Duo (Robin Williams/Nathan Lane), Best Comedic Performance (Williams); Screen Actors Guild Award '96: Best Supporting Actor (Azaria), Best Supporting Actor (Lane); Writers Guild of America '96: Best Adapted Screenplay. *MGM*

Birdman of Alcatraz 🎬🎬🎬 **1962** Robert Stroud, convicted of two murders and sentenced to life imprisonment on the Island, becomes an internationally accepted authority on birds. Lovingly told, with stunning performance from Lancaster, and exceptionally fine work from the supporting cast. The confinement of Stroud's prison cell makes the film seem claustrophobic and tedious at times, just as the imprisonment must have been. Ritter played Stroud's mother,

who never stops trying to get him out of prison. **143m/B VHS.** Burt Lancaster, Karl Malden, Thelma Ritter, Betty Field, Neville Brand, Edmond O'Brien, Hugh Marlowe, Telly Savalas; **D:** John Frankenheimer; **C:** Burnett Guffey, Robert Krasker; **M:** Elmer Bernstein. British Academy Awards '62: Best Actor (Lancaster); Nominations: Academy Awards '62: Best Actor (Lancaster), Best Black and White Cinematography, Best Supporting Actor (Savalas), Best Supporting Actress (Ritter). *COL, FCT*

The Birds 🎬🎬🎬½ **(PG-13)** **1963** Hitchcock attempted to top the success of "Psycho" with this terrifying tale of Man versus Nature, in which Nature alights, one by one, on the trees of Bodega Bay to stage a bloody act of revenge upon the civilized world. Only Hitchcock can twist the harmless into the horrific while avoiding the ridiculous; this is perhaps his most brutal film, and one of the cinema's purest, horrifying portraits of apocalypse. Based on a short story by Daphne Du Maurier; screenplay by novelist Evan Hunter (aka Ed McBain). **120m/C VHS, Beta, LV.** Rod Taylor, Tippi Hedren, Jessica Tandy, Veronica Cartwright, Suzanne Pleshette, Ethel Griffies, Charles McGraw, Ruth McDevitt; **D:** Alfred Hitchcock; **W:** Evan Hunter; **C:** Robert Burks. *USH*

The Birds 2: Land's End woof! **1994 (R)** Unfortunate rip-off of the Hitchcock fright classic. Killer seagulls begin attacking the inhabitants of east coast Gull Island. Seems they're tired of being oil slick victims. Hedren's the town shopkeeper in a role that's nothing like the one she played in the original. Definitely for the birds—even the director refuses to acknowledge it by officially using the film industry pseudonym "Alan Smithee." Made for TV. **87m/C VHS, LV, Closed Caption.** Brad Johnson, Chelsea Field, Tippi Hedren, James Naughton, Jan Rubes, Megan Gallagher; **D:** Rick Rosenthal; **W:** Jim Wheat, Ken Wheat. *USH*

Birds & the Bees 🎬🎬 **1956** A millionaire falls in love with an alluring card shark, and then calls it all off when he learns of her profession, only to fall in love with her again when she disguises herself. A remake—and poor shade—of Preston Sturge's 1941 classic "The Lady Eve." **94m/C VHS, Beta.** Mitzi Gaynor, David Niven, George Gobel, Reginald Gardiner, Hans Conried; **D:** Norman Taurog; **W:** Sidney Sheldon. *BAR*

Birds of Prey 🎬🎬 **1972** Made-for-television action film pits an ex-WWII army pilot against a group of kidnapping thieves in an airborne chopper chase. **81m/C VHS, Beta.** David Janssen, Ralph Meeker, Elayne Heilveil; **D:** William A. Graham; **C:** Jordan Cronenweth.

Birdy 🎬🎬🎬½ **1984 (R)** An adaptation of the William Wharton novel about two Philadelphia youths, one with normal interests, the other obsessed with birds, and their eventual involvement in the Vietnam War, wrecking one physically and the other mentally. A hypnotic, evocative film, with a compelling Peter Gabriel soundtrack. **120m/C VHS, Beta, LV, Closed Caption.** Matthew Modine, Nicolas Cage, John Harkins, Sandy Baron, Karen Young, Bruno Kirby; **D:** Alan Parker; **W:** Jack Behr, Sandy Kroopf; **M:** Peter Gabriel. Cannes Film Festival '85: Grand Jury Prize. *COL*

Birgitt Haas Must Be Killed 🎬🎬½ **1983** A ruthless secret agent (Noiret) plots to murder a German female terrorist and make it appear that her boyfriend was the killer. Never quite hits the mark, despite novel premise and strong cast. **105m/C VHS, Beta.** Philippe Noiret, Jean Rochefort, Elisabeth Kreuzer; **D:** Laurent Heynemann. *GLV*

The Birth of a Nation 🎬🎬🎬 *The Clansman* **1915** Lavish Civil War epic in which Griffith virtually invented the basics of film grammar. Gish and Walthall have some of the most moving scenes ever filmed and the masterful battle choreography brought the art of cinematography to new heights. Griffith's positive attitude toward the KKK notwithstanding, this was the first feature length silent, and it brought credibility to an entire industry. Based on the play "The Clansman" and the book "The Leopard's Spots" by Thomas Dixon, it is still a rouser, and of great historical inter-

est. Silent with music score. Also available in a 124-minute version. **175m/B VHS, LV.** Lillian Gish, Mae Marsh, Henry B. Walthall, Robert "Bobbie" Harron, Wallace Reid, Joseph Henabery, Donald Crisp, Raoul Walsh, Erich von Stroheim, Eugene Pallette; **D:** D.W. Griffith. National Film Registry '92. *VYY, MRV, REP*

Birth of the Blues 🎬🎬½ **1941** Songman Crosby starts a band in New Orleans in the midst of the jazz boom. Help from partner Martin and real-life trombonist Teagarden, with comic relief from Eddie "Rochester" Anderson, make for a fun-filled story. Plot is riddled with some unbelievable gangster scenes, but the music and laughs will keep you amused. In B&W with color segments. 🎵St. Louis Blues; St. James Infirmary; Melancholy Baby; Birth of the Blues. **76m/B VHS, Closed Caption.** Bing Crosby, Mary Martin, Brian Donlevy, Eddie Anderson, J. Carrol Naish, Cecil Kellaway, Warren Hymer, Horace McMahon, Carolyn Lee, Jack Teagarden; **D:** Victor Schertzinger; **W:** Harry Tugend, Walter DeLeon; **C:** William Mellor; **M:** Robert Emmett Dolan. Nominations: Academy Awards '41: Scoring of a Musical. *USH*

Birthday Boy 🎬🎬 **1985** A cable comedy about a buffoonish salesman's 30th birthday, on which he takes an ill-fated business trip. Written by Belushi. **33m/C VHS, Beta.** James Belushi; **D:** Claude Conrad; **W:** James Belushi. *VES, ART*

The Bishop's Wife 🎬🎬🎬 **1947** An angel comes down to earth at Christmas to help a young bishop, his wife and his parishioners. Excellent performances by the cast make this an entertaining outing. **109m/B VHS, Beta, LV.** Cary Grant, Loretta Young, David Niven, Monty Woolley, Elsa Lanchester, James Gleason, Gladys Cooper, Regis Toomey; **D:** Henry Koster; **C:** Gregg Toland. Academy Awards '47: Best Sound; Nominations: Academy Awards '47: Best Director (Koster), Best Film Editing, Best Picture, Best Original Dramatic/Comedy Score. *HBO, FCT, MLB*

The Bitch woof! **1978 (R)** High-camp follies are the rule in this lustful continuation of "The Stud" as it follows the erotic adventures of a beautiful divorcee playing sex games for high stakes on the international playgrounds of high society. A collaborative effort by the sisters Collins: written by Jackie, with sister Joan well cast in the title role. **90m/C VHS, Beta.** *GB* Joan Collins, Kenneth Haigh, Michael Coby, Ian Hendry, Carolyn Seymour, Sue Lloyd, John Ratzenberger; **D:** Gerry O'Hara. *NO*

Bite the Bullet 🎬🎬🎬½ **1975 (PG)** Moralistic western tells of a grueling 600-mile horse race where the participants reluctantly develop respect for one another. Unheralded upon release and shot in convincing epic style by Harry Stradling, Jr. Excellent cast. **131m/C VHS, Beta, LV.** Gene Hackman, James Coburn, Candice Bergen, Dabney Coleman, Jan-Michael Vincent, Ben Johnson, Ian Bannen, Paul Stewart, Sally Kirkland; **D:** Richard Brooks; **W:** Richard Brooks; **C:** Harry Stradling Jr.; **M:** Alex North. Nominations: Academy Awards '75: Best Sound, Best Original Score. *COL*

Bitter Harvest 🎬🎬🎬 **1981** Emmy-nominated made-for-television movie concerning a dairy farmer frantically trying to discover what is mysteriously killing off his herd. Howard is excellent as the farmer battling the bureaucracy to find the truth. Based on a true story. **98m/C VHS, Beta.** Ron Howard, Art Carney, Tarah Nutter, Richard Dysart, Barry Corbin, Jim Haynie, David Knell; **D:** Roger Young. *ART*

Bitter Harvest 🎬🎬 **1993 (R)** Rubin and Kensit are the femme fatales who turn their considerable wiles on the innocent Baldwin. He's more than happy to be their lover but does he want to be their victim as well? **CW:** Violent language, violent action, and strong sexual scenes. **98m/C VHS, Closed Caption.** Stephen Baldwin, Patsy Kensit, Jennifer Rubin, Adam Baldwin, M. Emmet Walsh; **D:** Duane Clark; **W:** Randall Fontana; **C:** Remi Adefarasin.

Bitter Moon 🎬🎬 **1992 (R)** Polanski effort looks promising, but ultimately disappoints. Bored British couple (Grant and Scott Thomas) meet up with sexual devilants (Coyote and Seigner, aka Mrs. Polanski) on a cruise and learn that passion and cruelty often share the same path to destruction. Masquerades as high class art, but whenever substance is lacking expect a silly, kinky sex scene. Needless to say, there isn't much substance, so erotic mischief abounds. Scott Thomas manages to hold her own, but Coyote is almost embarrassingly over the top. Based on the Pascal Bruckner novel "Lunes de Fiel." **139m/C VHS, LV, Letterbox.** Peter Coyote, Emmanuelle Seigner, Hugh Grant, Kristin Scott Thomas, Victor Banerjee; **Cameos:** Stockard Channing; **D:** Roman Polanski; **W:** Roman Polanski, Gerard Brach, John Brownjohn; **C:** Tonino Delli Colli; **M:** Vangelis. *COL*

Bitter Rice 🎞🎞🎞 *Riso Amaro* 1949 Mangano became a star with her sultry performance about survival in postwar Italy. She scrapes by, working in the rice fields of the Po Valley, loved by the down-to-earth Vallone, who provides her with little excitement. Gassman is the rotten-to-the-core thief who meets up with Mangano while he's running from the police. He mistreats her, she steals his money and betrays his friends, and both destroy each other. In Italian with English subtitles. **96m/C VHS.** *IT* Silvana Mangano, Vittorio Gassman, Raf Vallone; **D:** Guiseppe de Santis. Nominations: Academy Awards '50: Best Story.*FCT*

Bitter Sugar 🎞🎞🎞 *Azucar Amarga* 1996 Young, idealistic communist Gustavo (Lavan) is a Havana university student who still believes that the Castro regime can make things better. His rock musician brother Bobby (Villanueva) is a radical, defying government policies, and his psychiatrist father Tomas (Gutierrez) makes more money playing piano at a tourist hotel than in his practice. But Gustavo's eyes are opened, not only by his family situation, but when he falls in love with cynical dancer Yolanda (Vilan), who longs to escape to Miami. Serious politics bolstered by excellent performances and sharp cinematography. Spanish with subtitles. **102m/B VHS.** *CU* Rene Lavan, Mayte Vilan, Miguel Gutierrez, Larry Villanueva; **D:** Leon Ichaso; **W:** Leon Ichaso, Orestes Matacena; **C:** Claudio Chea; **M:** Manuel Tejada. *NYF*

Bitter Sweet 🎞🎞½ 1933 Tragic tale of a woman who finally marries the man she loves, only to find that he is a compulsive gambler. Written by Coward, adapted from his operetta. **76m/B VHS.** *GB* Anna Neagle, Fernand Graavey, Esme Percy, Clifford Heatherly, Hugh Williams; **D:** Herbert Wilcox; **W:** Noel Coward. *NOS, MRV, DVT*

Bitter Sweet 🎞🎞 1940 The second version of the Noel Coward operetta, about young romance in 1875 Vienna. Creaky and overrated, but the lush Technicolor and Coward standards help to compensate. 🎵Ziguener; I'll See You Again. **94m/C VHS, Beta.** Jeanette MacDonald, Nelson Eddy, George Sanders, Felix Bressart, Ian Hunter, Sig Rumann, Herman Bing, Fay Holden, Curt Bois, Edward Ashley; **D:** Woodbridge S. Van Dyke; **W:** Lesser Samuels, Noel Coward. Nominations: Academy Awards '40: Best Color Cinematography, Best Interior Decoration. *MGM*

The Bitter Tea of General Yen 🎞🎞🎞 1933 Stanwyck arrives in Shanghai to marry a missionary (Gordon) during the threatening days of China's civil war. Unexpectedly swept into the arms of an infamous warlord (Asher), she becomes fascinated, although his attempts to seduce her fail. She even remains with him while his enemies close in. Exotic and poetic, if melodramatic by today's standards. The interracial aspects were considered very daring for their time. Adapted from the book by Grace Zaring Stone. **89m/B VHS.** Barbara Stanwyck, Nils Asther, Gavin Gordon, Walter Connolly, Lucien Littlefield, Toshia Mori, Richard Loo, Clara Blandick; **D:** Frank Capra; **W:** Edward Paramore. *COL, FCT, BTV*

The Bitter Tears of Petra von Kant 🎞🎞½ *Die Bitteren Traenen der Petra von Kant* 1972 Dark German story of lesbian love, the fashion world, obsession and anger. Claustrophobic settings and slow pace may frustrate some viewers. In German with English subtitles. **124m/C VHS.** *GE* Margit Carstensen, Hanna Schygulla, Irm Hermann,

Eva Mattes, **D:** Rainer Werner Fassbinder; **C:** Michael Ballhaus. *NYF, FCT*

Bitter Vengeance 🎞🎞 1994 (R) Security guard Jack Westford (Greenwood) pulls off a bank heist with his lover Isabella (Hocking) and plans to frame his wife Annie (Madsen) for the crime. Only Annie finds out and sets out to get them before the police get her. Made for cable TV.*CW:* Some violence and sexuality. **90m/C VHS, Beta, Closed Caption.** Virginia Madsen, Bruce Greenwood, Kristen Hocking, Eddie Velez, Gordon Jump, Carlos Gomez, Tim Russ; **D:** Stuart Cooper; **W:** Pablo F. Fenjves; **M:** David Michael Frank. *PAR*

Bittersweet Love 🎞½ 1976 (PG) Two young people fall in love and marry, only to have the bride's mother and the groom's father confess a 30-year-old affair, disclosing that the two newlyweds are actually half-siblings. **92m/C VHS, Beta.** Lana Turner, Robert Lansing, Celeste Holm, Robert Alda, Meredith Baxter; **D:** David Miller.

Bix 1990 Based on the brief life of legendary Jazz Age cornetist Leon Bix Beiderbecke, who died at age 28. Story unfolds in flashbacks through friend Joe Venuti memories of the dissipated genius and the music he created with Hoagy Carmichael, Pee Wee Russell, Paul Whiteman, and others. **100m/C VHS.** *IT* Bryant Weeks, Emile Levisetti, Mark Collver, Sally Groth; **D:** Pupi Avati; **W:** Pupi Avati, Antonio Avati, Lino Patruno. *RHP*

Bizarre 🎞 1987 When a wife escapes her perverse, psychologically threatening marriage, she finds her husband still haunts her literally and figuratively, and plots psychological revenge. Dubbed. **93m/C VHS, Beta.** *IT* Florence Guerin, Luciano Bartoli, Robert Egon Spechtenhauser, Stefano Sabelli.

Bizarre Bizarre 🎞🎞🎞 *Drole de Drame* 1939 A mystery writer is accused of murder and disappears, only to return in disguise to try to clear his name. Along the way, a number of French comedians are introduced with a revue of comedy-farce sketches that include slapstick, burlesque, black humor, and comedy of the absurd. In French with English subtitles. **90m/B VHS, Beta.** *FR* Louis Jouvet, Michel Simon, Francoise Rosay; **D:** Marcel Carne. *NOS, HHT, DVT*

The Black Abbot 🎞🎞 1963 A mysterious black-hooded figure is seen entering a ruined Abbey tower that leads to a country house with buried treasure. Based on an Edgar Wallace story. **95m/C VHS.** *GE* Joachim Fuchsberger, Dieter Borsche, Gritt Bottcher, Eva Scholtz, Franz Gottlieb; **D:** Franz Gottlieb. *SNC*

Black and White as Day and Night 🎞🎞 1963 A man's talent for the game of chess becomes a destructive obsession. In German with English subtitles. **?m/C VHS.** Bruno Ganz. *SNC*

Black and White in Color 🎞🎞🎞 *La Victoire en Chantant* 1976 (PG) Award-winning satire about a French soldier at an African outpost, who, upon hearing the news of the beginning of WWI, takes it upon himself to attack a neighboring German fort. Calamity ensues. In French, with English subtitles. **100m/C VHS, Beta, LV.** *FR* Jean Carmet, Jacques Dufilho, Catherine Rouvel, Jacques Spiesser, Dora Doll, Jacques Perrin; **D:** Jean-Jacques Annaud; **W:** George Conchon, Jean-Jacques Annaud; **M:** Pierre Bachelet. Academy Awards '76: Best Foreign Language Film. *ORI, WAR*

Black Angel 🎞🎞🎞 1946 Catherine Bennett (Vincent) tries to clear the name of estranged husband Kirk (Phillips), who's accused of murdering his lover, blackmailing chanteuse Mavis Marlowe (Dowling). Catherine enlists the aid of Mavis' husband, drunken songwriter Martin Blair (Duryea), whom she suspects actually did the deed. Another suspect is sleazy nightclub owner Marko (Lorre), where the duo get a job to check things out. Blair falls for Catherine and goes on another bender when she rejects him, as Kirk's execution day draws ever closer. Atmospheric noir is based on the novel by Cornell Woolrich. **80m/B VHS.** June Vincent, Dan Duryea, Peter Lorre, Broderick Crawford, John

Phillips, Constance Dowling, Wallace Ford, Hobart Cavanaugh; **D:** Roy William Neill; **W:** Roy Chanslor; **C:** Paul Ivano; **M:** Frank Skinner. *USH*

Black Arrow 🎞🎞🎞 *Black Arrow Strikes* 1948 Original adventure film of the famous Robert Louis Stevenson novel. Upon return from 16th century's War of the Roses, a young man must avenge his father's murder by following a trail of clues in the form of black arrows. Well made and fun. **76m/B VHS, Beta.** Louis Hayward, Janet Blair, George Macready, Edgar Buchanan, Paul Cavanagh; **D:** Gordon Douglas. *DIS*

The Black Arrow 🎞🎞 1984 Exiled bowman returns to England to avenge the injustices of a villainous nobleman. Made-for-cable version of the Robert Louis Stevenson medieval romp is not as well done as the 1948 adaptation. **93m/C VHS, Beta.** Oliver Reed, Benedict Taylor, Georgia Slowe, Stephan Chase, Donald Pleasence; **D:** John Hough. *DIS*

Black Beauty 🎞🎞 1946 In this adaptation of Anna Sewell's familiar novel, a young girl develops a kindred relationship with an extraordinary horse. **74m/B VHS, Beta.** Mona Freeman, Richard Denning, Evelyn Ankers; **D:** Max Nosseck. *CCB, VTR*

Black Beauty 🎞🎞 1971 (G) International remake of the classic horse story by Anna Sewell. **105m/C VHS, Beta, LV.** *GB GE SP* Mark Lester, Walter Slezak; **D:** James Hill; **C:** Chris Menges; **M:** Lionel Bart. *PAR, FCT*

Black Beauty 🎞🎞🎞 1994 (G) Remake of the classic Anna Sewell children's novel about an oft-sold horse whose life has its shares of ups and downs. Timeless tale still brings children and adults to tears. Six-year-old quarterhorse named Justin gives a nuanced portrayal as the Black Beauty, recalling Olivier in "Hamlet." Directorial debut of "Secret Garden" screenwriter Thompson. **88m/C VHS, LV, Closed Caption.** Andrew Knott, Sean Bean, David Thewlis, Jim Carter, Alun Armstrong, Eleanor Bron, Peter Cook, Peter Davison, John McEnery, Nicholas Jones; **D:** Caroline Thompson; **W:** Caroline Thompson. *WAR*

Black Beauty/Courage of Black Beauty 🎞🎞 1957 Two feature-length films based on Anna Sewell's novel about the love of a child for a black stallion. "Black Beauty" was first released in 1946; "Courage of Black Beauty" in 1957. Excellent for children who love horses, of course. **145m/C VHS, Beta.** Mona Freeman, Johnny Crawford; **D:** Max Nosseck, Harold Schuster.

Black Belt 🎞 1992 (R) A private detective is hired to protect a rock star from a fanatic Vietnam vet. **80m/C VHS, Closed Caption.** Don "The Dragon" Wilson, Richard Beymer, Alan Blumenfeld, Matthias Hues; **D:** Charles Philip Moore; **W:** Charles Philip Moore. *NHO*

Black Belt Jones 🎞 1974 (R) Martial arts expert fights the mob to save a school of self-defense in Los Angeles' Watts district. **87m/C VHS, Beta.** Jim Kelly, Gloria Hendry, Scatman Crothers; **D:** Robert Clouse. *WAR*

Black Bikers from Hell 🎞½ *Black Angels* 1970 (R) Black gang-members infiltrate and wreak havoc on their rivals. Who can stop these brutal young men? Cast with real bikers and biker chicks. **87m/C VHS, Beta.** King John III, Des Roberts, Linda Jackson, James Whitworth, James Young-El, Clancy Syrko, Beverly Gardner; **D:** Lawrence Merrick; **W:** Lawrence Merrick. *TPV, JEF*

Black Bird 🎞🎞 1975 (PG) In this satiric "sequel" to "The Maltese Falcon," detective Sam Spade, Jr. searches for the mysterious black falcon statuette that caused his father such trouble. Features appearances by Elisha Cook Jr. and Lee Patrick, who starred in the 1941 classic "The Maltese Falcon" with Humphrey Bogart. **98m/C VHS, Beta.** George Segal, Stephane Audran, Lionel Stander, Lee Patrick, Elisha Cook Jr., Connie Kreski; **D:** David Giler. *GKK*

Black Box Affair ♂½ **1966** An American secret agent must find a black box lost in a B-52 plane crash before it falls into the wrong hands. **95m/C VHS, Beta.** Craig Hill, Teresa Gimpera, Luis Martin, Jorge Rigaud. *NO*

Black Brigade ♂♂ **1969** Pryor and Williams star in this low budget movie as leaders of an all-black outfit assigned to a suicide mission behind Nazi lines during WWII. Their force wreaks havoc and earns them the respect of military higher-ups. Lots of action and climactic finish. **90m/C VHS.** Richard Pryor, Billy Dee Williams, Stephen Boyd. *QVD*

Black Caesar ♂♂ **1973 (R)** A small-time hood climbs the ladder to be the head of a Harlem crime syndicate. Music by James Brown. Followed by the sequel "Hell Up in Harlem." **92m/C VHS, Beta, LV.** Fred Williamson, Julius W. Harris, Val Avery, Art Lund, Gloria Hendry; *D:* Larry Cohen; *M:* James Brown. *ORI*

The Black Castle ♂♂ **1952** MacNally plays an 18th-century Austrian count whose guests tend to disappear after a visit. This happens to two of Greene's friends and he decides to investigate. Uninspired and melodramatic, not enough horror. Karloff doesn't have enough to do. **81m/B VHS, Closed Caption.** Richard Greene, Boris Karloff, Stephen McNally, Rita (Paula) Corday, Lon Chaney Jr., John Hoyt; *D:* Nathan (Hertz) Juran. *USH*

The Black Cat ♂♂♂½ *House of Doom; Vanishing Body* **1934** The first of the Boris and Bela pairings stands up well years after release. Polished and taut, with fine sets and interesting acting. Confrontation between architect and devil worshipper acts as plot, with strange twists. Worth a look. Also available with "The Raven" (1935) on laserdisc. **65m/B VHS, LV.** Boris Karloff, Bela Lugosi, David Manners, Jacqueline Wells, Lucille Lund, Henry Armetta; *D:* Edgar G. Ulmer; *W:* Edgar G. Ulmer; *C:* John Mescall. *MLB, USH*

The Black Cat woof! *Il Gatto Nero* **1981** Spaghetti splatter-meister Fulci, best known for his unabashed ripoffs "Zombie" and "Gates of Hell," tones down the gore this time in a vaguely Poe-ish tale of a medium with some marbles loose (Magee) whose kitty provides the temporary habitat for spirits its master calls up. The dreary English village setting and the downright myopic camerawork add up to an oppressive viewing experience. **92m/C VHS.** *IT GB* Patrick Magee, Mimsy Farmer, David Warbeck, Al Cliver, Dagmar Lassander, Geoffrey Copleston, Daniela Dorio; *D:* Lucio Fulci; *W:* Lucio Fulci, Biagio Proietti; *C:* Sergio Salvati; *M:* Pino Donaggio. *RHI*

Black Cat ♂½ **1990** Filmmakers find lots of action in a haunted house. Chock full of references to the works of spaghetti horror dons Mario Bava and Dario Argento. **?m/C VHS, Beta.** *IT* Caroline Munro, Brett Halsey; *D:* Lewis (Luigi Cozzi) Coates; *W:* Lewis (Luigi Cozzi) Coates. *COL*

The Black Cauldron ♂♂½ **1985 (PG)** Disney's 25th full-length animated movie follows the adventures of pig-keeper Taran, who discovers his psychic pig Hen Wen is the key to keeping a magical cauldron out of the hands of the evil Horned King. Based on the "Chronicles of Prydain" novels by Lloyd Alexander. **82m/C VHS.** *D:* Ted Berman, Richard Rich; *W:* Ted Berman, Richard Rich; *M:* Elmer Bernstein; *V:* Grant Bardsley, Susan Sheridan, John Hurt, Freddie Jones, Nigel Hawthorne, John Byner, Arthur Malet. *DIS*

Black Christmas ♂♂½ *Silent Night, Evil Night; Stranger in the House* **1975 (R)** A college sorority is besieged by an axe-murderer over the holidays. **98m/C VHS.** *CA* Olivia Hussey, Keir Dullea, Margot Kidder, John Saxon; *D:* Bob (Benjamin) Clark. *WAR*

Black Cobra woof! **1983 (R)** A lesbian ex-acts revenge for her lover's snake-bite murder by trapping the guilty party with his own snakes. **97m/C VHS, Beta.** Laura Gemser, Jack Palance. *GEM*

The Black Cobra woof! **1987 (R)** After photographing a psychopath in the process of killing someone, a beautiful photographer seeks the help of a tough police sergeant to protect her. The leader of the Black Cobras gang gives chase. **90m/C VHS, Beta.** *IT* Fred Williamson, Karl Landgren, Eva Grimaldi. *TWE*

Black Cobra 2 ♂♂ **1989 (R)** A mismatched team of investigators tracks a notorious terrorist. They find him holding a school full of children as hostage. **95m/C VHS.** Fred Williamson.

Black Cobra 3: The Manila Connection ♂♂½ **1990 (R)** Interpol turns to police lieutenant Robert Malone (Williamson) when a team of high-tech weapons thieves threatens the world. Malone attacks like a cyclone on the terrorists' jungle haven. They won't know what hit 'em! **92m/C VHS, Beta.** Fred Williamson, Forry Smith, Debra Ward; *D:* Don Edwards.

The Black Coin **1936** A 15-episode adventure serial about a cursed silver piece from the Middle Ages and the ill luck that has followed its possessors through the years. **316m/B VHS, Beta, LV.** Ralph Graves, Ruth Mix, Dave O'Brien, Matthew Betz. *VYY, NOS, MLB*

Black Day Blue Night ♂♂ **1995 (R)** Rinda (Forbes) and Hallie (Sara) take a road trip from Utah to Phoenix and pick up the handsome Dodge (Bellows). Turns out he's being pursued by cop John Quinn (Walsh) as a suspect in a murder/robbery. Women-in-peril-who-help-themselves type story. *CW:* Violence, sexuality, and language. **99m/C VHS, LV, Closed Caption.** Michelle Forbes, Mia Sara, Gil Bellows, J.T. Walsh, Tim Guinee, John Beck; *D:* J.S. Cardone; *W:* J.S. Cardone; *C:* Michael Cardone; *M:* Johnny Lee Schell, Joe Sublett. *REP*

Black Devil Doll from Hell ♂ **1984** This shot-on-video movie deals with a nasty little voodoo doll that likes to kill its owners. **70m/C VHS, Beta.** Shirley Jones, Rickey Roach, Marie Sainvilvs; *D:* Chester Turner. *HHT*

The Black Devils of Kali ♂ *Mystery of the Black Jungle* **1955** Adventurers in the Indian jungle discover a lost race of idol-worshipping primitives. Racist garbage produced near the end of Republic Pictures' existence. Based on a novel by Emillio Salgari. **72m/B VHS.** Lex Barker, Jane Maxwell, Luigi Tosi, Paul Muller; *D:* Ralph Murphy. *SNC, MLB*

Black Dog ♂ **1998 (PG-13)** Not since the '70s heyday of CBs and C.W. McCall have 18-wheelers been so lovingly portrayed. Too bad the rest of the characters weren't given the same attention. Swayze (resurrecting his sensitive butt-kicker persona from "Roadhouse") plays disgraced trucker Jack Crews, recently released from prison after a vehicular manslaughter rap. With no driver's license and an overdue mortgage, he agrees to an "off books" run for his shady boss (Beckel). The cargo turns out to be guns, which attracts the attention of the FBI, ATF, and a scuzzy band of hijackers led by the Bible-quoting Red (Meatloaf). Of course, the paint-by-numbers plot puts Jack's family in harm's way, and gives him a soulful, country-croonin' ally (Travis). Avoid this mutt like three-day-old roadkill unless you're a big-rig fetishist. *CW:* Intense scenes of action violence, and for language. **88m/C VHS.** Patrick Swayze, Randy Travis, Meat Loaf, Gabriel Casseus, Graham Beckel, Stephen Tobolowsky, Charles S. Dutton, Brian Vincent, Brenda Strong, Erin Broderick; *D:* Kevin Hooks; *W:* William Mickelberry, Dan Vining; *C:* Buzz Feitshans IV; *M:* George S. Clinton. *NYR*

Black Dragon ♂ **1974 (R)** Young farm boy moves to the city and teams up with an undercover narcotics agent to infiltrate and destroy the underworld syndicate. **93m/C VHS.** Ron Van Cliff, Jason Rai Pow, Jorge Estraga, Nancy Veronica. *SUN*

The Black Dragons ♂ **1942** Weird and fairly stupid war drama involving sabotage by the Japanese. Lugosi is the plastic surgeon who deftly cuts and pastes Japanese face parts to permit agents to pass as Americans. Also available co-

lorized. **62m/B VHS, Beta.** Bela Lugosi, Joan Barclay, George Pembroke, Clayton Moore; *D:* William Nigh. *VYY, MRV, SNC*

Black Dragon's Revenge ♂ **1975 (R)** The Black Dragon arrives in Hong Kong to investigate the death of a great kung fu master. **90m/C VHS.** Ron Van Cliff, Charles Bonet, Jason Rai Pow. *SUN*

Black Eagle ♂♂ **1988 (R)** Pre-Glasnost, anti-Soviet tale of two high-kicking spies. CIA and KGB agents race to recover innovative equipment in the Mediterranean. **93m/C VHS, Beta, LV.** Bruce Doran, Jean-Claude Van Damme, Sho Kosugi; *D:* Eric Karson. *NO*

Black Eliminator ♂ **197?** A black cop struggles to stop a maniacal secret agent who plans to destroy the world. **84m/C VHS, Beta.** Jim Kelly, George Lazenby, Harold Sakata, Bob Minos, Patch MacKenzie, Aldo Ray. *NO*

Black Eyes ♂½ **1939** A lowly waiter, working in a Moscow restaurant, manages to overhear a number of stock tips from the wealthy patrons and makes a tidy pile of rubles to improve his daughter's life. The daughter already thinks he's a successful businessman and is disillusioned when she discovers dad's true profession. All comes out right in the end. **72m/B VHS.** *GB* Otto Kruger, Mary Maguire, Walter Rilla, George L. Baxt, Marie Wright; *D:* Herbert Brenon. *HCV*

Black Force ♂♂ **1975** Brothers who fight crime with violent actions, are called for assistance in the recovery of an African artifact. Originally known as "Force Four." **82m/C VHS, Beta.** Malachi Lee, Warhawk Tanzania, Owen Watson, Judie Soriano; *D:* Michael Fink. *NO*

Black Force 2 ♂♂ **1978 (R)** The brothers are back on the scene in another violent, cartilage-shattering adventure. **90m/C VHS.** Terry Carter, James B. Sikking. *NO*

Black Fox: Blood Horse ♂♂½ **1994** Alan Johnson (Reeve) and Britt (Todd) try to maintain an uneasy peace with the local Kiowas until evil Ralph Holtz (Wiggins) tries to stir things up and have some vigilantes attack the tribe. The second episode in the three-part series. **90m/C VHS, Closed Caption.** Christopher Reeve, Raoul Trujillo, Tony Todd, Chris Wiggins; *D:* Steven Hilliard Stern; *C:* Frank Tidy, Eric N. Robertson. *CAF*

Black Fox: Good Men and Bad ♂♂½ **1994** Britt (Todd) accepts a job as a federal marshall while Alan (Reeve) goes after desperado Carl Glenn (Fox) and his gang. During a stagecoach robbery, the outlaws take Hallie (Rowan) hostage, thinking she's the wife of a tycoon and Alan manages to use her to get to Glenn. The third episode in the sagebrush series. **90m/C VHS, Closed Caption.** Christopher Reeve, David Fox, Tony Todd, Kim Coates, Kelly Rowan; *D:* Steven Hilliard Stern; *C:* Frank Tidy; *M:* Eric N. Robertson. *CAF*

Black Fox: The Price of Peace ♂♂½ **1994** Former plantation owner Alan Johnson (Reeve) and childhood friend Britt (Todd), whom he frees from slavery, try to forge a new life in 1860s Texas. But there's trouble when abusive bigot Ralph Holtz (Wiggins) threatens the peace between settlers and Indians when he goes after his wife delores (Holtz) who left him for a Kiowa warrior, Running Dog (Trujillo). Based on the novel by Matt Braun; made for TV. **90m/C VHS, Closed Caption.** Christopher Reeve, Raoul Trujillo, Tony Todd, Chris Wiggins, Cyndy Preston; *D:* Steven Hilliard Stern; *C:* Frank Tidy; *M:* Eric N. Robertson. *CAF*

Black Friday ♂♂½ **1940** Karloff is a surgeon who saves the life of his college professor friend (Ridges) by transplanting part of the brain of a gangster (involved in the same car crash) into the man's body. This results in a Jekyll/Hyde complex with the gangster's evil portion taking over and seeking revenge on rival mobster Lugosi. Horror stars Karloff and Lugosi never have any scenes together. **70m/B VHS, Closed Caption.** Boris Karloff, Stanley Ridges, Bela Lugosi, Anne Nagel, Anne Gwynne, Paul Fix, Virginia Brissac, James Craig; *D:* Arthur

Lubin; **W:** Curt Siodmak, Eric Taylor; **C:** Woody Bredell. *VOI I*

Black Fury 🎬🎬🎬 1935 A coal miner's efforts to protest working conditions earn him a beating by the company goons who also kill his friend. He draws national attention to this brutal plight of the workers when he barricades himself inside the mine. Muni's carefully detailed performance adds authenticity to this powerful drama, but it proved too depressing to command a big boxoffice. 95m/B VHS, **Beta.** Paul Muni, Barton MacLane, Henry O'Neill, John Qualen, J. Carrol Naish; **D:** Michael Curtiz. *FOX*

Black Gestapo woof! 1975 (R) Black-exploitation film about a vigilante army taking over a Los Angeles ghetto, first to help residents, but later to abuse them. Extremely violent. 89m/C VHS, **Beta.** Rod Perry, Charles Robinson, Phil Hoover, Ed Gross. *UNI*

Black Glove 🎬 *Face the Music* 1954 A trumpet star defends himself against charges of murdering a Spanish singer by tracking down the real killer. 84m/B VHS, Beta, LV. Alex Nicol, Eleanor Summerfield. *NOS*

Black God & White Devil 🎬🎬 1964 Another Brazilan socio-political commentary by Rocha, an oft-incendiary filmmaker whose left-leaning works are steeped in mysticism, obscure folklore, and powerful images. An impoverished man transforms from a religious zealot to a bandit, his tale underscored by conflict between poor masses and wealthy landowners. Portuguese with subtitles. 102m/C VHS. *BR* **D:** Glauce Rocha. *FCT*

Black Godfather 🎬 1974 (R) The grueling story of a hood clawing his way to the top of a drug-selling mob. Features an all-black cast. 90m/C VHS, **Beta.** Rod Perry, Damu King, Don Chastain, Jimmy Witherspoon, Diane Summerfield; **D:** John Evans. *NO*

Black Gold 🎬🎬 1936 Oil field suspense thriller by "B" movie king Hopton. 57m/B VHS. Frankie Darro, Leroy Mason; **D:** Russell Hopton. *SNC, VYY*

The Black Hand 🎬🎬🎬 1950 Kelly plays well against character in this atmospheric turn-of-the-century thriller. The evil society of the Black Hand murders his father, and he seeks revenge. Well-made drama. 93m/B VHS. Gene Kelly, J. Carrol Naish, Teresa Celli, Marc Lawrence, Frank Puglia; **D:** Richard Thorpe; **C:** Paul Vogel. *NO*

Black Hand 🎬½ 1976 Unemployed Italian immigrant is drawn into a web of murder and betrayal after he is attacked by an Irish gang. 90m/C VHS, **Beta.** Lionel Stander, Mike Placido. *NO*

Black Hills 🎬 1948 Dull oater with Dean and his sidekick Ates out to avenge the murder of a struggling ranch owner. 60m/B VHS. Eddie Dean, Roscoe Ates, Shirley Patterson, Terry Frost, Nina Bara, William "Bill" Fawcett; **D:** Ray Taylor. *MOV*

The Black Hole 🎬½ 1979 (G) A high-tech, computerized Disney space adventure dealing with a mad genius who attempts to pilot his craft directly into a black hole. Except for the top quality special effects, a pretty creaky vehicle. 97m/C VHS, Beta, LV. Maximillian Schell, Anthony Perkins, Ernest Borgnine, Yvette Mimieux, Joseph Bottoms, Robert Forster; **D:** Gary Nelson; **W:** Gerry Day; **M:** John Barry. Nominations: Academy Awards '79: Best Cinematography. *DIS, OM*

Black Ice 🎬🎬 1992 (R) After an affair with a popular politician ends violently, Vanessa (Pacula) realizes her boss set up his death—and she's next in line. She finds the nearest taxi and offers the driver plenty of cash if he can quickly get her out of the country. It's going to be the ride of her life. Also available in an unrated version.**CW:** Language, violence, and sexuality. 90m/C VHS, Beta, **Closed Caption.** Michael Nouri, Michael Ironside, Joanna Pacula; **D:** Neill Fearnley; **M:** Amin Bhatia.

Black Jesus 🎬🎬 *Seduta Alla Sua Destra; Seated At His Right* 1968 Lalubi (Strode) ia an African leader using passive resistance to save his people from a dictatorial regime that's supported by European colonialism. When he's betrayed by a

follower, Lalubi's imprisoned and tortured, along with a thief who gains a greater understanding after contact with the leader. Film is a thinly disguised depiction of Zaire and its history. ?m/C VHS. *IT* Woody Strode, Jean Servais; **D:** Valerio Zurlini. *IVY*

The Black King 🎬½ *Harlem Hot Shot* 1932 Prejudiced propaganda based on the life of Marcus Garvey, black leader of the '20s, who advocated black superiority and a return to Africa. A black con man takes advantage of fellow blacks by organizing a phony back-to-Africa movement, enriching himself in the process. When one man's girlfriend deserts him for the bogus leader, the jilted one blows the whistle. 70m/B VHS. A.B. Comethiere, Vivianne Baber, Knolly Mitchell, Dan Michaels, Mike Jackson; **D:** Bud Pollard. *FCT, BTV, HEG*

The Black Klansman 🎬 *I Crossed the Line* 1966 A black man masquerades as a white extremist in order to infiltrate the KKK and avenge his daughter's murder. In the interest of racial harmony, he seduces the Klan leader's daughter. As bad as it sounds. 88m/B VHS, Beta. Richard Gilden, Rima Kutner, Harry Lovejoy; **D:** Ted V. Mikels. *UNI*

The Black Lash 🎬 1952 Two lawmen go undercover to break a silver hijacking gang. 55m/B VHS, Beta. Lash LaRue, Al "Fuzzy" St. John, Peggy Stewart, Kermit Maynard; **D:** Ron Ormond. *NOS, DVT, GPV*

Black Lemons 🎬 198? While in prison, a convict is stalked by the Mafia because of what he knows. He eventually spills the beans to the cops, putting himself in unavoidable jeopardy. 93m/C VHS, Beta. *IT* Peter Carsten, Antonio Sabato Jr., Florinda Bolkan; **D:** Camillo Bazzoni. *UNI*

Black Like Me 🎬½ 1964 Based on John Howard Griffin's successful book about how Griffin turned his skin black with a drug and traveled the South to experience prejudice firsthand. Neither the production nor the direction enhance the material. 107m/B VHS, Beta. James Whitmore, Roscoe Lee Browne, Will Geer, Walter Mason, John Marriott, Clifton James, Dan Priest; **D:** Carl Lerner. *RHI, UND, PTB*

Black Limelight 🎬½ 1938 Massey plays a fugitive from justice and Marion the loyal wife who clears her husband of the murder of his mistress. Distracting lead performance by Marion who insists on shouting her lines. Based on the play by Gordon Sherry. 60m/B VHS. *GB* Raymond Massey, Joan Marion, Walter Hudd, Henry Oscar, Dan Tobin; **D:** Paul Stein; **W:** Walter Summers. *DVT*

Black Lizard 🎬🎬 1968 A camp spectacle set in the Japanese underworld. The Lizard is the glamorous queen of Tokyo crime who plots to steal a famous diamond by first kidnapping the owner's daughter. Complications arise when she falls for a detective. The Lizard is played by female impersonator Maruyama. Mishima, who wrote the original drama and the screenplay, has a cameo as an embalmed corpse. Style is all. In Japanese with English subtitles. 112m/C VHS. *JP* Akihiro Maruyama, Isao Kimura; **Cameos:** Yukio Mishima; **D:** Kinji Fukasaku; **W:** Yukio Mishima. *CCN*

Black Magic 🎬🎬 1949 Cagliostro the magician becomes involved in a plot to supply a double for Marie Antoinette. 105m/B VHS, Beta. Orson Welles, Akim Tamiroff, Nancy Guild, Raymond Burr; **D:** Gregory Ratoff; **W:** Charles Bennett.

Black Magic 🎬🎬½ 1992 (PG-13) Insomniac Alex, haunted by the nightly appearances of his dead cousin Ross, goes to Ross' hometown to see if he can find a way to make the apparition disappear. On the way, he runs into his cousin's ex-girlfriend Lilian and falls in love. Problem is, Lilian's a witch, maybe. Lightweight made for cable TV fare. 94m/C VHS, LV, Closed Caption. Rachel Ward, Judge Reinhold, Brion James, Anthony LaPaglia; **D:** Daniel Taplitz; **W:** Daniel Taplitz. *USH*

Black Magic Terror 🎬 1979 Jilted by her lover, the old queen of black magic has everybody under her spell. Trouble starts, however, when she turns her back on one of her subjects. 85m/C VHS, Beta. *JP* Suzanna, W.D. Mochtar, Alan Nuary; **D:** L. Sudjio. *TWE*

Black Magic Woman woof! 1991 (R) An art gallery owner has an affair with a beautiful and exotic woman but starts to get cold feet when he's plagued by inexplicable phenomena. Seems that black magic woman has put a voodoo spell on him. Listless companion to director Warren's "Blood Spell" that gives away the ending, has a wretched script, and poor acting.**CW:** Violence and sensual scenes. 91m/C VHS, Closed Caption. Mark Hamill, Amanda Wyss, Apollonia, Abadah Viera, Larry Hankin, Victor Rivers, Bonnie Ebson; **D:** Deryn Warren; **W:** Gerry Daly; **M:** Randy Miller. *THV*

The Black Maid woof! 1974 A scantily clad, sassy black maid cleans, cooks, cusses, and drives her racist employer to the brink of insanity. 90m/C VHS, Beta. *IT NO*

The Black Marble 🎬🎬🎬 1979 (PG) A beautiful policewoman is paired with a policeman who drinks too much, is divorced, and is ready to retire. Surrounded by urban craziness and corruption, they eventually fall in love. Based on the Joseph Wambaugh novel. 110m/C VHS, Beta. Paula Prentiss, Harry Dean Stanton, Robert Foxworth, James Woods, Michael Dudikoff, Barbara Babcock, John Hancock, Judy Landers, Anne Ramsey, Christopher Lloyd; **D:** Harold Becker; **M:** Maurice Jarre. *NLC*

Black Market Rustlers 🎬½ 1943 The Range Busters are at it again. This time they break up a cattle rustling syndicate. 60m/B VHS, Beta. Ray Corrigan, Dennis Moore, Max Terhune; **D:** S. Roy Luby. *VDM, RXM*

Black Moon Rising 🎬½ 1986 (R) Based on an idea by John Carpenter ("Halloween"), this film deals with the theft of a new jet-powered car and its involvement in an FBI investigation. Solid performances and steady action enhance this routine effort. 100m/C VHS, Beta, LV, Closed Caption. Tommy Lee Jones, Linda Hamilton, Richard Jaeckel, Robert Vaughn; **D:** Harley Cokliss; **W:** John Carpenter; **M:** Lalo Schifrin. *VTR*

Black Narcissus 🎬🎬🎬½ 1947 A group of Anglican nuns attempting to found a hospital and school in the Himalayas confront native distrust and human frailties amid beautiful scenery. Adapted from the novel by Rumer Godden. Stunning cinematography. Crucial scenes were cut from the American release by censors. 101m/C VHS, Beta, LV. *GB* Deborah Kerr, David Farrar, Sabu, Jean Simmons, Kathleen Byron, Flora Robson, Esmond Knight, Jenny Laird, Judith Furse, May Hallatt, Nancy Roberts; **D:** Michael Powell, Emeric Pressburger; **C:** Jack Cardiff. Academy Awards '47: Best Art Direction/Set Decoration (Color), Best Color Cinematography; New York Film Critics Awards '47: Best Actress (Kerr). *MLB*

Black Oak Conspiracy 🎬🎬 1977 (R) Based on a true story, this film deals with a mining company conspiracy discovered by an inquisitive stuntman. 92m/C VHS, Beta. Jesse Vint, Karen Carlson, Albert Salmi, Seymour Cassel, Robert F. Lyons; **D:** Bob Kelljan. *NLC*

Black Orchid 🎬🎬½ 1959 A businessman and a crook's widow fall in love and try to persuade their children it can work out. 96m/B VHS, Beta. Sophia Loren, Anthony Quinn, Ina Balin, Peter Mark Richman, Jimmie Baird; **D:** Martin Ritt; **W:** Joseph Stefano; **C:** Robert Burks. *PAR*

Black Orpheus 🎬🎬🎬½ *Orfeu Negro* 1958 The legend of Orpheus and Eurydice unfolds against the colorful background of the carnival in Rio de Janeiro. In the black section of the city, Orpheus is a street-car conductor and Eurydice, a country girl fleeing from a man sworn to kill her. Dancing, incredible music, and black magic add to the beauty of this film. Based on the play "Orfeu da Conceica." In Portuguese with English subtitles or dubbed. 103m/C VHS, Beta, LV. *BR FR PT* Breno Mello, Marpessa Dawn, Lea Garcia, Fausto Guerzoni, Lourdes De Oliveira; **D:** Marcel Camus; **C:** Jean Bourgoin; **M:** Antonio Carlos Jobim, Luis Bonfa. Academy Awards '59: Best Foreign Language Film; Cannes Film Festival '59: Best Film; Golden Globe Awards '60: Best Foreign Film. *CVC, FOX, FCT*

Black Out 🐾½ 1996 (R) John Grey (Bosworth), who's suffering from amnesia after a car crash, becomes desperate to remember his life after his wife (DuBois) is murdered. 98m/C VHS. Brian Bosworth, Brad Dourif, Claire Yarlett, Marta DuBois; **D:** Allan Goldstein. THV

Black Panther 🐾½ 1977 True story of psycho-killer Donald Neilson, who murdered heiress Lesley Whittle in England in the 1970s. 90m/C VHS, Beta. Donald Sumpter, Debbie Farrington; **D:** Ian Merrick; **W:** Michael Armstrong. VES, ART

The Black Pirate 🐾½ Rage of the Buccaneers; The Black Buccaneer; Gordon il Pirata Nero 1926 A shipwrecked mariner vows revenge on the pirates who destroyed his father's ship. Quintessential Fairbanks, this film features astounding athletic feats and exciting swordplay. Silent film with music score. Also available in color. 122m/B VHS, Beta, LV. IT Douglas Fairbanks Sr., Donald Crisp, Billie Dove; **D:** Albert Parker. National Film Registry '93. KIV, MRV, REP

Black Pit of Dr. M 🐾 Misterios del Ultratumba 1947 The ghost of a doctor who has been unjustly executed for murder seeks revenge on employees of an insane asylum. The horror is not just confined to the asylum. 90m/B VHS, Beta. MX Gaston Santos, Rafael Bertrand, Mapita Cortes; **D:** Fernando Mendez; **W:** Ramon Obon. MAD, SMW

Black Rain 🐾 Kuroi Ame 1988 Erstwhile Ozu assistant Imamura directs this powerful portrait of a post-Hiroshima family five years after the bombing. Tanaka plays a young woman who, having been caught in a shower of black rain (radioactive fallout) on an ill-timed visit to Hiroshima, returns to her village to find herself ostracized by her peers and no longer considered marriage-worthy. Winner of numerous awards (including five Japanese Academy Awards). In Japanese with English subtitles. 123m/B VHS. JP Kazuo Kitamura, Yoshiko Tanaka, Etsuko Ichihara, Shoichi Ozawa, Norihei Miki; **D:** Shohei Imamura. FXL, FCT

Black Rain 🐾½ 1989 (R) Douglas portrays a ruthless American cop chasing a Japanese murder suspect through gang-controlled Tokyo. Loads of action and stunning visuals from the man who brought you "Blade Runner." 125m/C VHS, Beta, LV, 8mm, Letterbox, Closed Caption. Michael Douglas, Andy Garcia, Kate Capshaw, Ken Takakura, Yusaku Matsuda, John Spencer, Shigeru Koyama; **D:** Ridley Scott; **W:** Craig Bolotin, Warren Lewis; **C:** Jan De Bont; **M:** Hans Zimmer. Nominations: Academy Awards '89: Best Sound. PAR

Black Rainbow 🐾🐾🐾 1991 (R) Surprisingly good thriller that's relatively unknown, haunted by a menacing mood. Robards and Arquette are a father/daughter duo who perform clairvoyance scams at carnival sideshows. Suddenly, without warning, Arquette's former cons become real: she sees murder victims—before their demise. Quirky sleeper filmed on location in North Carolina. **CW:** Language, violence, and sensual scene. 103m/C VHS, Beta, LV, Closed Caption. Rosanna Arquette, Jason Robards Jr., Tom Hulce, Ron Rosenthal, John Bennes, Linda Pierce, Mark Joy; **D:** Mike Hodges; **W:** Mike Hodges. VTR

The Black Raven 🐾½ 1943 An action film that combines several plots into one. The Black Raven is an inn that sees more excitement than any other—not the least of which is murder! 64m/B VHS, Beta. George Zucco, Wanda McKay, Glenn Strange, I. Stanford Jolley; **D:** Sam Newfield. SNC, MLB, RXM

Black Robe 🐾🐾🐾½ 1991 (R) In 1634 a young Jesuit priest journeys across the North American wilderness to bring the word of God to Canada's Huron Indians. The winter journey is brutal and perilous and he begins to question his mission after seeing the strength of the Indian's native ways. Stunning cinematography, a good script, and fine acting combine to make this superb. Portrays the Indians in a realistic manner, the only flaw being that Beresford portrays the white culture with very few redeeming qualities

and as the only reason for the Indian's downfall. Moore adapted his own novel for the screen. **CW:** Violence and sensuality. 101m/C VHS, LV, Letterbox. AU CA Lothaire Bluteau, Aden Young, Sandrine Holt, August Schellenberg, Tantoo Cardinal, Billy Two Rivers, Lawrence Bayne, Harrison Liu; **D:** Bruce Beresford; **W:** Brian Moore; **M:** Georges Delerue. Australian Film Institute '92: Best Cinematography; Genie Awards '91: Best Director (Beresford), Best Film. THV

The Black Room 🐾🐾🐾 1935 As an evil count lures victims into his castle of terror, the count's twin brother returns to fulfill an ancient prophecy. Karloff is wonderful in his dual role as the twin brothers. 70m/B Beta, LV. Boris Karloff, Marian Marsh, Robert Allen, Katherine DeMille, John Buckler, Thurston Hall; **D:** Roy William Neill; **W:** Henry Myers, Arthur Strawn; **C:** Allen Siegler. COL, MLB

The Black Room 🐾 1982 (R) Couples are lured to a mysterious mansion where a brother and his sister promise to satisfy their sexual desires. Not much to recommend unless you're a fan of the vampire as psychology test case. 90m/C VHS, Beta, LV. Linnea Quigley, Stephen Knight, Cassandra Gaviola, Jim Stathis; **D:** Norman Thaddeus Vane. VES, ART

Black Roses 🐾 1988 (R) A disgusting band of rockers shows up in a small town, and the local kids start turning into monsters. Coincidence? 90m/C VHS, Beta, LV. Carmine Appice, Sal Viviano, Carla Ferrigno, Julie Adams, Ken Swofford, John Martin; **D:** John Fasano. IMP

Black Sabbath 🐾🐾🐾 I Tre Volti della Paura; Black Christmas; The Three Faces of Terror; The Three Faces of Fear 1964 An omnibus horror film with three parts, climaxing with Karloff as a Wurdalak, a vampire who must kill those he loves. Also available with "Black Sunday" on laserdisc. 99m/C VHS, Beta. IT Boris Karloff, Jacqueline Pierreux, Michele Mercier, Lidia Alfonsi, Susy Anderson, Mark Damon, Rika Dialina; **D:** Mario Bava; **W:** Marcello Fondato, Alberto Bevilacqua, Mario Bava; **C:** Ubaldo Terzano; **M:** Les Baxter. SNC

Black Samurai 🐾 1977 (R) When his girlfriend is held hostage, a martial arts warrior will stop at nothing to destroy the organization that abducted her. 84m/C VHS, Beta. Jim Kelly; **D:** Al Adamson. NO

The Black Scorpion 🐾½ 1957 Two geologists in Mexico unearth a nest of giant scorpions living in a dead volcano. Eventually one of the oversized arachnids escapes to wreak havoc on Mexico City. 85m/B VHS. Richard Denning, Mara Corday, Carlos Rivas; **D:** Edward Ludwig; **W:** Robert Blees. WAR, MLB, FRG

Black Scorpion 🐾🐾½ Roger Corman Presents: Black Scorpion 1995 (R) Darcy Walker (Severance) is an ex-cop-turned-superhero (the scorpion is her symbol), who dons a mask and fetching (and tight) black vinyl to fight crime and avenge her dad's death. She's got the prerequisite sidekick—an ex-chop shop operator (Morris)—and a supervillain—the asthmatic Breathtaker (Siemaszko) who threatens to annihilate the city with toxic gas. Campy, schlock fun. **CW:** Violence, sexuality and some language. 92m/C VHS. Joan Severance, Garrett Morris, Casey Siemaszko, Rick Rossovich; **D:** Jonathan Winfrey. NHO

Black Scorpion 2: Ground Zero 🐾🐾 1996 (R) Fetching crimefighter Darcy Walker (Severance) returns to battle villains Gangster Prankster and AfterShock, who are set on destroying the City of Angels by earthquake. Made for cable. **CW:** Sexuality, violence and some language. 85m/C VHS. Joan Severance, Whip Hubley, Stoney Jackson; **D:** Jonathan Winfrey. NHO

Black Shampoo woof! 1976 A black hairdresser on the Sunset Strip fights the mob with a chainsaw. 90m/C VHS, Beta. John Daniels, Tanya Boyd, Joe Ortiz; **D:** Greydon Clark. VCI

Black Sheep 🐾½ 1996 (PG-13) Isn't there a five-day waiting period for remakes? The previously viewed copies of "Tommy Boy" hadn't even hit the sale bin before Spade and Farley went in

search of more property to destroy. The twist here? Spade is assigned to keep the oafish brother (not son) of a gubernatorial candidate (not auto parts dealer) out of trouble until after the election (not so he can save the family business). In an effort to provide humor, plot points, and character development, Farley falls out of, off of or onto every prop in sight while Spade smirks. **CW:** Crude language and humor, drug-related material and sexual innuendo. 87m/C VHS, Beta, Closed Caption. Chris Farley, David Spade, Tim Matheson, Christine Ebersole, Gary Busey, Grant Heslov, Timothy Carhart, Bruce McGill; **D:** Penelope Spheeris; **W:** Fred Wolf; **C:** Daryn Okada; **M:** William Ross. PAR

Black Sister's Revenge 🐾🐾 Emma Mae 1976 Poorly selected video title mars this intelligent drama about a young black woman's struggle to adjust to the big city after growing up in the deep South. 100m/C VHS, Beta. Jerri Hayes, Ernest Williams II, Charles D. Brook III, Eddie Allen; **D:** Jamaa Fanaka; **W:** Jamaa Fanaka. UNI

The Black Six 🐾 1974 (R) Six black Vietnam veterans are out to punish the white gang who killed the brother of one of the black men. 91m/C VHS, Beta. Gene Washington, Carl Eller, Lem Barney, Mercury Morris, Joe "Mean Joe" Greene, Willie Lanier, Rosalind Miles, John Isenbarger, Ben Davidson, Maury Wills; **D:** Matt Cimber. UNI

Black Snow 🐾½ 1993 The mob is off on a violent search for 50 million bucks in cocaine. 90m/C VHS, LV. Jane Badler, Peter Sherayko, Julia Montgomery, Randy Brooks; **D:** Frank Patterson.

The Black Stallion 🐾🐾🐾 1979 (PG) A young boy and a wild Arabian Stallion are the only survivors of a shipwreck, and they develop a deep affection for each other. When rescued, they begin training for an important race. Exceptionally beautiful first half. Rooney plays a horse trainer, again. Great for adults and kids. 120m/C VHS, Beta, LV, Closed Caption. Kelly Reno, Mickey Rooney, Teri Garr, Clarence Muse; **D:** Carroll Ballard; **W:** William D. Wittliff, Melissa Mathison, Jeanne Rosenberg; **C:** Caleb Deschanel; **M:** Carmine Coppola. Academy Awards '79: Best Sound Effects Editing; Los Angeles Film Critics Association Awards '79: Best Cinematography; National Society of Film Critics Awards '79: Best Cinematography; Nominations: Academy Awards '79: Best Film Editing, Best Supporting Actor (Rooney). MGM, FOX, TLF

The Black Stallion Returns 🐾🐾½ 1983 (PG) Sequel to "The Black Stallion" follows the adventures of young Alec as he travels to the Sahara to search for his beautiful horse, which was stolen by an Arab chieftain. Unfortunately lacks much of the charm that was present in the first film. Adapted from the stories by Walt Farley. 103m/C VHS, Beta, LV, Closed Caption. Kelly Reno, Teri Garr, Vincent Spano; **D:** Robert Dalva; **C:** Carlo DiPalma; **M:** Georges Delerue. FOX

Black Starlet 🐾½ Black Gauntlet 1974 (R) A girl from the projects of Chicago travels to Hollywood in search of fame. She winds her way through a world of sleaze and drugs in order to make it to the top. 90m/C VHS. Juanita Brown, Eric Mason, Rockne Tarkington, Damu King, Diane Holden; **D:** Chris Munger. GEM

Black Sunday 🐾🐾🐾 La Maschera del Demonio; The Demon's Mask; House of Fright; Revenge of the Vampire 1960 Executed one hundred years previously, a witch returns with her vampire servant to do the bidding of Satan. A must see for horror fans; firsts for Steele as star and Bava as director. Also available with "Black Sabbath" on laserdisc. 83m/B VHS. IT Barbara Steele, John Richardson, Ivo Garrani, Andrea Checchi, Arturo Dominici, Enrico Olivieri, Clara Bindi, Enrico Olivieri, Germana Dominici; **D:** Mario Bava; **W:** Mario Bava, Ennio de Concini, Mario Serandrei; **C:** Mario Bava, Ubaldo Terzano; **M:** Les Baxter. SMW, SNC, MRV

Black Sunday 🐾🐾½ 1977 (R) An Arab terrorist group plots to steal the Goodyear Blimp and load it with explosives. Their intent is to explode it over a Miami Super Bowl game to assassinate the U.S. president and to kill all the fans. Based on Thomas Harris' novel. **143m/C VHS, Beta, LV.** Robert Shaw, Bruce Dern, Marthe Keller, Frita Weaver, Steven Keats, Michael V. Gazzo, William Daniels; **D:** John Frankenheimer; **W:** Ernest Lehman; **C:** John A. Alonzo; **M:** John Williams. *PAR*

The Black Swan 🐾🐾🐾 1942 Swashbuckling pirate film, based on the novel by Rafael Sabatini, stars Power as James Waring, compatriot of notorious buccaneer Henry Morgan (Cregar). Morgan is pardoned and sent to Jamaica as its new governor—if he can prevent his from associates from continuing their criminal ways. He enlists Waring to help him fight the renegades; meanwhile Waring falls in love with former governor's daughter Margaret (O'Hara). Lots of derring do. **85m/C VHS, Closed Caption.** Tyrone Power, Maureen O'Hara, Laird Cregar, Thomas Mitchell, George Sanders, Anthony Quinn, George Zucco, Edward Ashley, Fortunio Bonanova; **D:** Henry King; **W:** Ben Hecht, Seton I. Miller; **C:** Leon Shamroy; **M:** Alfred Newman. Academy Awards '42: Best Color Cinematography; Nominations: Academy Awards '42: Best Original Dramatic/Comedy Score. *FXV*

Black Terrorist 1985 Terrorists take over a ranch and slay the inhabitants. They keep a young boy alive and the mother tries to rescue him. **81m/C VHS, Beta.** Allan Granville, Vera Jones; **D:** Neil Hetherington. *NO*

Black Tide 🐾🐾 *Stormy Crossing* 1958 Suspicions arise that a drowning may have actually been a murder. **69m/C VHS.** John Ireland, Derek Bond. *SNC, VYY*

Black Tights 🐾🐾½ *Un, Deux, Trois, Quatre!* 1960 Chevalier introduces four stories told in dance by Roland Petit's Ballet de Paris company: "The Diamond Crusher," "Cyrano de Bergerac," "A Merry Mourning," and "Carmen." A keeper for dance fans. Shearer's Roxanne in "Cyrano" was her last performance before retirement. **120m/C VHS, Beta.** *FR* Cyd Charisse, Zizi Jeanmarie, Moira Shearer, Dirk Sanders, Roland Petit; **D:** Terence Young. *VYY, NOS, VAI*

Black Tower 🐾🐾 1950 An interesting murder mystery telling the story of a desperately impoverished medical student. **54m/B VHS, Beta.** Peter Cookson, Warren William, Anne Gwynne, Charles Calvert. *VYY*

Black Vampire 🐾½ *Blood Couple; Ganja and Hess; Double Possession; Black Out: The Moment of Terror; Black Evil* 1973 (R) Jones plays a professor of African studies who is turned into a vampire by another vampire. He then marries the villain's ex-wife, played by Clark, a veteran of Russ Meyer films. Not much of a story but the acting is actually quite good and there are some creepy moments thanks mainly to an interesting score. **83m/C VHS, Beta.** Duane Jones, Marlene Clark, Bill Gunn, Sam Waymon, Leonard Jackson, Candice Tarpley, Mabel King; **D:** Bill Gunn; **W:** Bill Gunn. *GEM*

A Black Veil for Lisa 🐾🐾 1968 A man attempts to exact revenge upon his unfaithful wife, but things go horribly awry. **87m/C VHS.** *IT GE* John Mills, Luciana Paluzzi, Robert Hoffman; **D:** Massimo Dallamano. *REP*

The Black Velvet Gown 🐾🐾½ 1992 Riah Millican (McTeer) is a poor miner's widow living in rural 1834 England with her three children. She finds work as a housekeeper to the reclusive Miller (Peck), who agrees to educate her children and even gives Riah the titular gown, which was once his mother's. Now educated out of their working-class, the Millican's lives provide unexpected love and tragedy for all concerned. Based on the novel by Catherine Cookson; made for British TV. **103m/C VHS.** *GB* Janet McTeer, Bob Peck, Geraldine Somerville; **D:** Norman Stone. *TVC*

Black Venus woof! 1983 (R) A soft-core epic, starring the former Miss Bahamas, Josephine Jacqueline Jones, about the 18th-century French aristocracy. Laughably based upon the stories of Balzac. European film dubbed in English. **80m/C VHS, Beta.** Josephine Jacqueline Jones, Emiliano Redondo; **D:** Claude Mulot. *MGM*

Black Water 🐾🐾½ 1994 Tennessee fishing trip turns into a nightmare for an innocent man accused of murder. Based on the novel "Minnie" by Hans Werner Kettenbach. **105m/C VHS, Closed Caption.** Julian Sands, Stacey Dash, Ned Beatty, Ed Lauter, Denise Crosby, Billy McNamara, Rod Steiger; **D:** Nicolas Gessner; **W:** Nicolas Gessner, Laird Koenig; **M:** Gabriel Yared.

Black Water Gold 🐾🐾½ 1969 Television movie about a search for sunken Spanish gold. **75m/C VHS.** Ricardo Montalban, Keir Dullea, Lana Wood, Bradford Dillman, France Nuyen; **D:** Alan Landsburg. *NO*

Black Werewolf 🐾🐾 *The Beast Must Die* 1975 (PG) A millionaire sportsman invites a group of men and women connected with bizarre deaths or the eating of human flesh to spend the cycle of a full moon at his isolated lodge. **93m/C VHS, Beta, LV.** *GB* Peter Cushing, Calvin Lockhart, Charles Gray, Anton Diffring, Marlene Clark, Ciaran Madden, Tom Chadbon, Michael Gambon; **D:** Paul Annett; **W:** Michael Winder; **C:** Jack Hildyard; **M:** Douglas Gamley.

The Black Widow *Sombra, the Spider Woman* 1947 A fortune-teller plots to steal scientific secrets and take over the world. Serial in 13 episodes. **164m/B VHS.** Bruce Edwards, Carol Forman, Anthony Warde; **D:** Spencer Gordon Bennet. *VCN, REP, MLB*

Black Widow 🐾🐾🐾 1987 (R) A federal agent pursues a beautiful murderess who marries rich men and then kills them, making the deaths look natural. The agent herself becomes involved in the final seduction. The two women are enticing and the locations picturesque. **101m/C VHS, Beta, LV, Closed Caption.** Debra Winger, Theresa Russell, Sami Frey, Nicol Williamson, Terry O'Quinn, Dennis Hopper, D.W. Moffett, Lois Smith, Mary Woronov, Rutanya Alda, James Hong, Diane Ladd; **Cameos:** David Mamet; **D:** Bob Rafelson; **W:** Ronald Bass; **C:** Conrad Hall; **M:** Michael Small. *FOX*

The Black Windmill 🐾🐾½ 1974 (PG) An English spy is caught between his service and the kidnapping of his family by rival spies. **102m/C VHS, Beta.** Michael Caine, Donald Pleasence, Delphine Seyrig, Clive Revill, Janet Suzman, John Vernon; **D:** Donald Siegel. *USH*

Blackbeard the Pirate 🐾🐾 1952 The 18th-century buccaneer is given the full-blooded, Hollywood treatment. **99m/C VHS, Beta, LV.** Robert Newton, Linda Darnell, Keith Andes, William Bendix, Richard Egan; **D:** Raoul Walsh. *TTC*

Blackbeard's Ghost 🐾🐾 1967 Disney comedy in which the famed 18th-century pirate's spirit (Ustinov) is summoned to wreak havoc in order to prevent an old family home from being turned into a casino. **107m/C VHS, Beta, LV.** Peter Ustinov, Dean Jones, Suzanne Pleshette, Elsa Lanchester, Richard Deacon; **D:** Robert Stevenson; **C:** Edward Colman; **M:** Robert F. Brunner. *DIS*

Blackbelt 2: Fatal Force 🐾½ 1993 (R) A man seeks to avenge his brother's murder by going after his killers. **?m/C VHS.** Blake Bahner, Roxanne Baird, Michael Vlastas. *NHO*

Blackboard Jungle 🐾🐾🐾½ 1955 Well-remembered urban drama about an idealistic teacher in a slum area who fights doggedly to connect with his unruly students. Bill Hailey's "Rock Around the Clock" over the opening credits was the first use of rock music in a mainstream feature film. Based on Evan Hunter novel. **101m/B VHS, Beta, Closed Caption.** Glenn Ford, Anne Francis, Louis Calhern, Sidney Poitier, Vic Morrow, Richard Kiley, Margaret Hayes, John Hoyt, Warner Anderson; **D:** Richard Brooks; **W:** Richard Brooks. Nominations: Academy Awards '55: Best Art Direction/Set Decoration (B & W), Best Black and White Cinematography, Best Film Editing, Best Screenplay. *MGM*

Blackenstein woof! *Black Frankenstein* 1973 (R) Doctor into nouveau experimentation restores a man's arms and legs. But a jealous assistant gives our man a wrong injection, causing him to become "Blackenstein," a large African American with chip on hulking shoulder who enjoys killing people and otherwise causing big trouble. Ripe

blaxploitation 87m/C VHS, Beta. John Hart, Ivory Stone, Andrea King, Liz Renay, Joe DiSue; **D:** William A. Levey.

Blackjack 🐾🐾 1978 (R) Las Vegas is the scene for action and excitement as the mob puts the hit on tough guy William Smith! **104m/C VHS.** William Smith, Tony Burton, Paris Earl, Damu King, Diane Summerfield, Angela May; **D:** John Evans. *TPV*

Blackjack 🐾🐾½ 1997 (R) Former U.S. Marshal Jack Devlin (Lundgren), who has a pathological fear of the color white, becomes the bodyguard of a young supermodel (Haskin) who's the target of a psycho killer (Mackenzie). To highlight Devlin's phobia, Woo sets one of his big action scenes in a dairy flooded with milk. **CW:** Violence. **113m/C VHS, Closed Caption.** Dolph Lundgren, Kam Haskin, Saul Rubinek, Fred Williamson, Phillip MacKenzie; **D:** John Woo. *TOU*

Blackmail 🐾🐾🐾 1929 This first sound film for Great Britain and director Hitchcock features an early visualization of some typical Hitchcockian themes. The story follows the police investigation of a murder, and a detective's attempts to keep his girlfriend from being involved. Look for Hitchcock's screen cameo. Made as a silent, this was reworked to become a talkie. **86m/B VHS, Beta, LV.** *GB* Anny Ondra, John Longden, Sara Allgood, Charles Paton, Cyril Richard, Donald Calthrop, Charles Paton, Hannah Jones, Percy Parsons, Johnny Butt, Harvey Braban, Phyllis Monkman; **Cameos:** Alfred Hitchcock; **D:** Alfred Hitchcock; **W:** Alfred Hitchcock, Charles Bennett, Benn W. Levy, Garnett Weston. *REP, MRV, NOS*

Blackmail 🐾🐾🐾 1991 (R) Familiar story is given new life in this suspenseful movie originally made for cable TV. Blakely is a lonely woman who succumbs to Midkiff's attentions. She doesn't suspect that he's conning her with the help of his lover, Toussaint. Engaging thriller adapted from a short story by Bill Crenshaw. **CW:** Violence and sensuality. **87m/C VHS, Beta, LV, Closed Caption.** Susan Blakely, Dale Midkiff, Beth Toussaint, John Saxon, Mac Davis; **D:** Ruben Preuss. *PAR*

Blackout 🐾½ 1950 Blind man recovers his sight and finds that the brother of his girlfriend, once thought dead, is actually alive and well and running a smuggling ring. Routine. **73m/B VHS, Beta.** *GB* Maxwell Reed, Dinah Sheridan, Patric Doonan, Eric Pohlmann; **D:** Robert S. Baker. *SNC*

Blackout 🐾🐾 *Murder by Proxy* 1954 A drunken private eye is offered a murder case, and is subsequently framed for the crime. **87m/B VHS, Beta, LV.** Dane Clark, Belinda Lee, Betty Ann Davies; **D:** Terence Fisher. *MLB*

Blackout 🐾🐾 1978 (R) Four killers terrorize an office building during the 1977 New York electrical blackout. Soon the police enter, confront them, and the fun starts. Comic touches provide some relief from the violence here. **86m/C VHS, Beta.** Jim Mitchum, Robert Carradine, Ray Milland, June Allyson, Jean-Pierre Aumont, Belinda J. Montgomery; **D:** Eddy Matalon; **W:** Joseph Stefano. *NLC*

Blackout 🐾🐾½ 1985 Made-for-cable-TV thriller. An aging police chief suspects a disfigured amnesiac is responsible for past killings, in spite of the fact that he now leads a subdued family life. **99m/C VHS, Beta.** Richard Widmark, Keith Carradine, Kathleen Quinlan, Michael Beck, Gerald Hiken; **D:** Douglas Hickox; **W:** David Ambrose.

Blackout 🐾🐾 1988 (R) Strange memories from childhood come back to her as a woman fights for her life. **91m/C VHS, Beta, LV.** Carol Lynley, Gail O'Grady, Michael Keys Hall, Joseph Gian, Joanna Miles; **D:** Doug Adams; **C:** Arledge Armenaki. *NO*

Blackrock 🐾🐾 1997 Cliched though dramatic saga, inspired by a true story, and adapted by Enright from his play. Uncommunicative teenager Jared (Bruels) throws a bash upon the return to town of his mates best the surfing bud Ricko (Lyndon). The party gets out of control and Jared witnesses a group of his mates beating and raping Tracey (Novakovitch), who's discovered dead the next morning. Her death attracts rabid media attention and divides the community while Jared is filled with guilt for doing nothing to stop the act. But his conflicts increase when he realizes the extent of Ricko's involvement and he tries to decide where his loyalties lie. **100m/C VHS.** *AU* Laurence Breuls, Simon Lyndon, Linda Cropper, Rebecca Smart, David Field, Chris Haywood, Boyana Novakovitch; *D:* Steven Vidler; *W:* Nick Enright; *C:* Martin McGrath, George Greenough; *M:* Steve Kilbey. Nominations: Australian Film Institute '97: Best Adapted Screenplay, Best Cinematography, Best Film, Best Supporting Actor (Lyndon), Best Supporting Actress (Smart). NYR

The Blacksmith/The Balloonatic 1923 Two Buster Keaton shorts: "The Blacksmith" (1922) features Buster as the local blacksmith's apprentice who suddenly finds himself in charge. "The Balloonatic" (1923) presents Buster trapped in a runaway hot air balloon. Both films include music score. **57m/B VHS, Beta.** Buster Keaton, Virginia Fox, Phyllis Haver; *D:* Buster Keaton. VYY

The Blacksmith/The Cops 1922 "The Blacksmith" is a burlesque of Longfellow's famous poem "The Village Blacksmith." In "Cops" Buster tries a new business venture to win his girl's hand. Chaos ensues. Silent comedy at its most adroit. **38m/B VHS, Beta.** Buster Keaton, Virginia Fox. CCB

Blacksnake! woof! 1973 (R) Overheated sex and race tale, set in 1835, finds a British lord travelling to a Caribbean island in search of his brother. What he finds is his sadistic sister-in-law and her evil overseer using violence to keep the slaves in line. *CW:* Nudity, violence, mature themes. **83m/C VHS.** Anouska Hempel, David Warbeck, Percy Herbert, David Prowse; *D:* Russ Meyer. RMF

Blackwater Trail ♂♂ 1995 (R) Novelist Matt Curran (Nelson) travels from L.A. to Michelton, Australia, to attend the funeral of his best friend Andy, a cop who supposedly committed suicide. But Andy's sister (and Matt's former lover) Cathy (Smart) thinks he was murdered because of a case involving a serial killer. Matt decides to snoop around and finds out the killer likes to leave behind body parts and biblical quotations. Contrived plotting but some good performances and some spectacular scenery. **100m/C VHS, Closed Caption.** *AU* Judd Nelson, Dee Smart, Peter Phelps, Mark Lee, Brett Climo; *D:* Ian Barry; *W:* Andrew Russell; *C:* John Stokes; *M:* Stephen Rae. WAR

Blacula ♂♂ 1972 (PG) The African Prince Mamuwalde stalks the streets of Los Angeles trying to satisfy his insatiable desire for blood. Mildly successful melding of blaxploitation and horror that spawned a sequel, "Scream, Blacula, Scream." **92m/C VHS, Beta, LV.** William Marshall, Thalmus Rasulala, Denise Nicholas, Vonetta McGee, Gordon Pinsent, Emily Yancy, Charles Macaulay, Ted Harris; *D:* William Crain; *W:* Raymond Koenig, Joan Torres; *C:* John Stevens. ORI

Blade ♂♂ 1972 (PG) An honest cop challenges a dirty cover-up in killer-stalked New York. **79m/C VHS, Beta.** Steve Landesburg, John Schuck, Kathryn Walker; *D:* Ernie Pintoff. GEM, MRV

Blade 1998 Blade (Snipes) is half-vampire, half-human, who's intent on preventing evil Deacon Frost (Dorff) from unleashing the blood tide upon humanity. Helping out Blade are vampire hunter Abraham Whistler (Kristofferson) and Dr. Karen Jansen (Wright), who's searching for a cure for vampirism. Adapted from the Marvel comic book character. Not yet reviewed. **?m/C VHS.** Wesley Snipes, Stephen Dorff, Kris Kristofferson, N'Bushe Wright, Donal Logue, Udo Kier, Traci Lords; *D:* Stephen Norrington; *W:* David S. Goyer. NYR

Blade Boxer ♂ 1997 Police detectives go undercover to expose an illegal fight ring that has its combatants battling to the death, and equipped with deadly steel talons. **91m/C VHS.** Kevin King, Todd McKee, Andrew Martino, Cass Magda, Dana Plato; *D:* Bruce Reisman. MTH

Blade in Hong Kong ♂♂½ 1985 Made-for-TV action outing. Investigator travels to Hong Kong, finds trouble and romance in the underbelly of the city. Pilot for un-sold series. **100m/C VHS.** Terry Lester, Keye Luke, Mike Preston, Jean-Marie Hon, Leslie Nielsen, Nancy Kwan, Anthony Newley, Ellen Regan; *D:* Reza Badiyi. NO

A Blade in the Dark ♂♂ *La Casa Con La Scala Nel Buio; House of the Dark Stairway* 1983 A young man composing a score for a horror film moves into a secluded villa and is inspired and haunted by the mysterious murder he witnesses. **99m/C VHS, Beta.** Andrea Occhipinti, Anny Papa; *D:* Lamberto Bava. VES, ART

Blade Master ♂½ *Ator the Invincible* 1984 (PG) In this sequel to "Ator the Fighting Eagle," O'Keeffe as Ator is back as the Blade Master. Ator defends his people and his family name in a battle against the "Geometric Nucleus": a primitive bomb. His quest leads him and his small band of men to the castle of knowledge. **92m/C VHS, Beta.** Miles O'Keeffe, Lisa Foster; *D:* David Hills.

Blade of the Ripper woof! *The Next Victim; Next!; Lo Strano Vizio della Signora Ward* 1970 A madman armed with a razor slashes his way through the lovelies of the international jet set. **90m/C VHS, Beta.** George Hilton, Edwige Fenech, Alberto De Mendoza, Ivan Rassimov; *D:* Sergio Martino; *W:* Ernesto Gastaldi, Eduardo Brochero. NO

Blade Runner ♂♂♂½ 1982 (R) Los Angeles, the 21st century. World-weary cop tracks down a handful of renegade "replicants" (synthetically produced human slaves who, with only days left of life, search madly for some way to extend their prescribed lifetimes). Moody, beautifully photographed, dark thriller with sets from an architect's dream. Based on "Do Androids Dream of Electric Sheep" by Philip K. Dick. Laser edition features restored footage, information about special effects, and production sketches. Director's cut, released at 117 minutes, removes Ford's narration and the last scene of the film, which Scott considered too "up," and inserts several short scenes, including a dream sequence. *CW:* Violence. **122m/C VHS, Beta, LV, 8mm, Letterbox, DVD.** Harrison Ford, Rutger Hauer, Sean Young, Daryl Hannah, M. Emmet Walsh, Edward James Olmos, Joe Turkel, Brion James, Joanna Cassidy, William Sanderson; *D:* Ridley Scott; *W:* Hampton Fancher, David Peoples; *C:* Jordan Cronenweth; *M:* Vangelis. Los Angeles Film Critics Association Awards '82: Best Cinematography, National Film Registry '93; Nominations: Academy Awards '82: Best Art Direction/ Set Decoration. COL, WAR, CRC

Blades ♂ 1989 (R) Another junk heap from Troma, dealing with the efforts of three golfers who try to stop a maniacal power mower that's been grinding duffers with regularity. **101m/C VHS, Beta, LV.** Robert North, Jeremy Whelan, Victoria Scott, Jon McBride.

Blades of Courage ♂♂ *Skate!* 1988 A made-for-television biography of Olympic skater Lori Larouche. Choreographed by Debbi Wilkes. **98m/C VHS, Beta.** *CA* Lynn Nightingale, Christianne Hirt, Colm Feore, Rosemary Dunsmore; *D:* Randy Bradshaw.

Blaise Pascal ♂♂♂½ 1971 Another of Rossellini's later historical portraits, detailing the life and times of the 17th-century philosopher, seen as a man whose scientific ideas conflicted with his own religious beliefs. Made for Italian television. In Italian with subtitles. **131m/C VHS, Beta.** *IT D:* Roberto Rossellini. FCT

Blake of Scotland Yard 1936 Blake, the former Scotland Yard inspector, battles against a villain who has constructed a murderous death ray. Condensed version of the 15 episode serial (originally at 180 minutes). **70m/B VHS, Beta.** Ralph Byrd, Herbert Rawlinson, Joan Barclay, Lloyd Hughes; *D:* Robert F. "Bob" Hill. VYY, DVT, NOS

Blake's Seven 1978 Freedom-fighter Blake and his crew battle against a totalitarian superpower in this futuristic space adventure series from Great Britain. Created by Terry Nation of

"Doctor Who" fame. Each volume contains two episodes and is available individually. **105m/C VHS.** *GB* Gareth Thomas, Sally Knyvette, Paul Darrow, Michael Keating, David Jackson, Jan Chappell; *D:* Michael E. Briant, Vere Lorrimer. VCO, TVC, MOV

Blame It on Rio ♂♂ 1984 (R) A middle-aged man has a ridiculous fling with his best friend's daughter while on vacation with them in Rio de Janeiro. Caine and Johnson are amusing, but the script is somewhat weak. Remake of the French film "One Wild Moment." **90m/C VHS, Beta, LV.** Michael Caine, Joseph Bologna, Demi Moore, Michelle Johnson, Valerie Harper; *D:* Stanley Donen; *W:* Charlie Peters, Larry Gelbart. VES, GKT

Blame It on the Bellboy ♂♂½ 1992 (PG-13) Wild farce set in Venice about a hotel bellboy who confuses three similarly named visitors—sending the wrong ones to meet corporate bigwigs, date women, or even kill. The brisk pace loses it towards the end and devolves into chase scenes. **79m/C VHS, Beta, Closed Caption.** Dudley Moore, Bryan Brown, Richard Griffiths, Andreas Katsulas, Patsy Kensit, Alison Steadman, Bronson Pinchot, Lindsay Anderson, Penelope Wilton; *D:* Mark Herman; *W:* Mark Herman; *M:* Trevor Jones. HPH

Blame It on the Night ♂♂ 1984 (PG-13) A rock star gets to take care of the military cadet son he never knew after the boy's mother suddenly dies. Mick Jagger helped write the story. Available in VHS and Beta Hi-Fi. **85m/C VHS, Beta.** Nick Mancuso, Byron Thames, Leslie Ackerman, Billy Preston, Merry Clayton; *D:* Gene Taft. FOX

Blanche Fury ♂♂½ 1948 Governess Blanche (Hobson) marries her wealthy widowed cousin but the man she truly desires is the illegitimate Philip Thorn (Granger), who manages the estate for her husband. So Blanche decides to get rid of the man she doesn't love. Based on England's 19th-century Rush murder and adapted from the novel by Joseph Shearing. **95m/C VHS.** *GB* Valerie Hobson, Stewart Granger, Walter Fitzgerald, Michael Gough, Maurice Denham, Sybilla Binder; *D:* Marc Allegret; *W:* Hugh Mills; *C:* Guy Green, Geoffrey Unsworth; *M:* Clifton Parker. FCT

Blank Check ♂ *Disney's Blank Check* 1993 (PG) Parents may want to verify the whereabouts of their checkbooks after this one. Eleven-year-old Preston receives a blank check from a mobster on the run, cashes it for a million bucks, and goes on a spending orgy under an assumed name. Where are his parents? Apparently they don't have a problem with a shadowy benefactor taking their son under his wing. Sound familiar? And who thought it would be a good idea to have the little twerp mooning after a comely bank teller? Formula aside, this blatant rip-off of "Home Alone" tries to throw in an ending moral but probably won't fool the kids either. **93m/C VHS, LV, Closed Caption.** Brian Bonsall, Miguel Ferrer, Michael Lerner, Tone Loc, Rick Ducommun, Karen Duffy; *D:* Rupert Wainwright; *W:* Colby Carr, Blake Snyder; *M:* Nicholas Pike. DIS

Blankman ♂♂ 1994 (PG-13) Self-appointed superhero (Wayans), who makes up in creativity what he lacks in superpowers, fights crime in his underwear and a cape made from his grandmother's bathrobe. Life is simple, until an ambitious TV reporter (Givens) finds out about him. Silly one-joke premise is carried a little too far; didn't similar "Meteor Man" crash? Gifted comedian Wayans tries, but can't make this guy fly. **96m/C VHS, LV, Closed Caption.** Damon Wayans, Robin Givens, David Alan Grier, Jason Alexander, Jon Polito; *D:* Mike Binder; *W:* Damon Wayans, J.F. Lawton. COL

Blast ♂♂ 1996 Terrorists take a group of spectators hostage at the Atlanta Summer Olympics. **98m/C VHS.** Linden Ashby, Andrew Divoff, Rutger Hauer, Tim Thomerson; *D:* Albert Pyun. WAR

Blast-Off Girls ♂ 1967 A scuzzball promoter sets out to avenge himself for being blacklisted by the rock 'n' roll industry. He discovers a fresh group, but without corporate backing he can only pay them with groovy clothes and mini-skirted girls. Trouble ensues when they unexpectedly hit the charts and want real money. **83m/C VHS.** Ray Sager, Dan Conway; **D:** Herschell Gordon Lewis. *MOV, SMW*

Blastfighter woof! **1985 (R)** After local hoodlums kill his daughter, an ex-con cop goes on a spree of violence and revenge. Director Bava uses the pseudonym "John Old, Jr.," as his father Mario Bava occasionally credited himself as John Old. Italian film shot in Atlanta. **93m/C VHS, Beta.** *IT* Michael Sopkiw, Valerie Blake, George Eastman; **D:** Lamberto Bava. *VES, ART*

Blaze 🐾🐾½ **1989 (R)** The true story of Louisiana governor Earl Long who became involved with a stripper, Blaze Starr, causing a political scandal of major proportions. Robust, good-humored bio-pic featuring a fine character turn by Newman. **117m/C VHS, Beta, LV, Closed Caption.** Paul Newman, Lolita Davidovich, Jerry Hardin, Robert Wuhl, Gailard Sartain, Jeffrey DeMunn, Richard Jenkins, Garland Bunting; **D:** Ron Shelton; **W:** Ron Shelton; **C:** Haskell Wexler. Nominations: Academy Awards '89: Best Cinematography. *TOU*

Blazing Across the Pecos 🐾½ **1948** The Durango Kid (Starrett) is after Pecos Flats mayor Ace Brockaway (Wilson), who's secretly selling guns to the local Indian tribe so they'll attack the supply wagons of his business rivals. **54m/B VHS.** Charles Starrett, Smiley Burnette, Charles C. Wilson, Chief Thundercloud; **D:** Ray Nazarro. *COL*

Blazing Guns 🐾 *Marshal of Heldorado* **1950** A marshal, masquerading inexplicably as a tenderfoot, enters a lawless town and is immediately hired as a deputy. **54m/B VHS, Beta, LV.** Raymond Hatton, Russell Hayden, Fuzzy Knight, Julie Adams. *NOS, HEG*

Blazing Saddles 🐾🐾🐾½ **1974 (R)** Wild, wacky spoof by Brooks of every cliche in the western film genre. Little is Black Bart, a convict offered a reprieve if he will become a sheriff and clean up a nasty frontier town; the previous recipients of this honor have all swiftly ended up in shallow graves. A crazy, silly film with a cast full of lovable loonies including comedy greats Wilder, Kahn, and Korman. Watch for the Count Basie Orchestra. A group writing effort, based on an original story by Bergman. Was the most-viewed movie in its first year of release on HBO cable. **90m/C VHS, Beta, LV, DVD.** Cleavon Little, Harvey Korman, Madeline Kahn, Gene Wilder, Mel Brooks, John Hillerman, Alex Karras, Dom DeLuise, Liam Dunn; **D:** Mel Brooks; **W:** Mel Brooks, Norman Steinberg, Andrew Bergman, Richard Pryor; **C:** Joseph Biroc; **M:** John Morris. Writers Guild of America '74: Best Original Screenplay; Nominations: Academy Awards '74: Best Film Editing, Best Song ("Blazing Saddles"), Best Supporting Actress (Kahn). *WAR*

Blazing Stewardesses woof! **1975 (R)** The Hound salutes the distributor for truth in advertising, as they stamped this as one of the world's worst videos. Lusty, busty stewardesses relax at a western guest ranch under siege from hooded riders and the aging gags of the Ritz Brothers. **95m/C VHS.** Yvonne De Carlo, Bob Livingston, Donald (Don "Red") Barry, Regina Carrol; *Cameos:* The Ritz Brothers; **D:** Al Adamson. *NO*

Bleak House 🐾🐾½ **1985** The British television mini-series adaptation of the Charles Dickens tome about an interminable lawsuit and the decadent, criminal ruling class of 19th-century England. On three tapes. **391m/C VHS, Beta, Closed Caption.** *GB* Denholm Elliott, Diana Rigg, Philip Franks, Peter Vaughan, T.P. McKenna; **D:** Ross Devenish; **M:** Geoffrey Burgon. *FOX, SIG, TVC*

Bleak Moments 🐾🐾 *Loving Moments* **1971** Bored secretary Sylvia (Raitt) tries to work her flirtatious charms on a repressed teacher (Allan) and an eccentric musician (Bradwell) in order to escape the pressures of caring for a mentally retarded sister. **110m/C VHS.** *GB* Anne Raitt, Eric Allen, Mike Bradwell, Joolia Cappleman; **D:** Mike Leigh; **W:** Mike Leigh; **C:** Bahram Manocheri; **M:** Eric Allen. *WBF*

Bleeding Hearts 🎵🎵½ **1994** A liberal white professor falls in love with the teenaged black student he's tutoring and then becomes aware of the vast differences between them. Their problems increase when the young woman becomes pregnant. **95m/C VHS.** Gregory Hines, Mark Evan Jacobs, Ranjit Chowdhry, Elliott Gould, Robert Levine, Peter Riegert, Lorraine Toussaint; **D:** Gregory Hines. *YHV*

Bless the Beasts and Children 🐾🐾½ **1971 (PG)** A group of six teenage boys at a summer camp attempt to save a herd of buffalo from slaughter at a national preserve. Treacly Kramer backwater. Based on the novel by Glendon Swarthout. **109m/C VHS, Beta.** Billy Mumy, Barry Robins, Miles Chapin, Darel Glaser, Bob Kramer, Ken Swofford, Jesse White; **D:** Stanley Kramer; **M:** Perry Botkin. Nominations: Academy Awards '71: Best Song ("Bless the Beasts and the Children"). *COL*

Blessed Event 🐾🐾🐾 **1932** Fast-moving, entertaining film about a Broadway gossip columnist with a poison pen. Tracy has the role of a lifetime as a Walter Winchell prototype who thinks no one is exempt from his juicy column. Powell makes film debut as a crooner after a brief career as a band singer. Based on a play by Manuel Seff and Forrest Wilson. **77m/B VHS, Closed Caption.** Lee Tracy, Mary Brian, Dick Powell, Allen Jenkins, Ruth Donnelly, Emma Dunn, Walter Miller, Tom Dugan, Isabel Jewell; **D:** Roy Del Ruth; **W:** Howard J. Green. *MGM*

Blessing 🐾🐾 **1994** It's an unhappy time down on the Wisconsin dairy farm in this tale of family life. Embittered patriarch Jack (Griffis) can barely make a go of it and takes his frustrations out by beating his cows and climbing to the top of the silo. Despairing wife Arlene (Glynn) enters newspaper lotteries and collects religious statues while daughter Randi (Griffis) keeps delaying leaving the farm because of a nagging sense of responsibility. Claustrophobic atmosphere. **94m/C VHS.** Guy Griffis, Carlin Glynn, Melora Griffis, Gareth Williams, Clovis Siemon; **D:** Paul Zehrer; **W:** Paul Zehrer; **C:** Stephen Kazmierski; **M:** Joseph S. DeBeasi. *LEO*

Blind Ambition 🐾🐾½ **1982** Television mini-series docu-drama traces the career of John Dean, special counsel to President Richard M. Nixon. Focuses on his fractured personal life and touches on virtually all of the Watergate headlines. **95m/C VHS, Beta.** Martin Sheen, Rip Torn. *TLF*

Blind Date 🐾½ **1984 (R)** Blind man agrees to have a visual computer implanted in his brain in order to help the police track down a psychopathic killer. Violent scenes may be disturbing to some. **100m/C VHS, Beta, LV.** Joseph Bottoms, Kirstie Alley, Keir Dullea, James Daughton, Lana Clarkson, Marina Sirtis; **D:** Nico Mastorakis; **W:** Nico Mastorakis. *VES, ART*

Blind Date 🐾🐾 **1987 (PG-13)** A blind date between a workaholic yuppie and a beautiful blonde starts off well, but when she drinks too much at dinner, things get out of hand. In addition to embarrassing her date and destroying the restaurant, she has a jealous ex-boyfriend who must be dealt with. **95m/C VHS, Beta, LV.** Kim Basinger, Bruce Willis, John Larroquette, William Daniels, George Coe, Mark Blum, Phil Hartman, Stephanie Faracy, Alice Hirson, Graham Stark; **D:** Blake Edwards; **C:** Harry Stradling Jr.; **M:** Henry Mancini. *COL*

Blind Faith 🐾 **1989 (R)** Action and adventure take a turn for the horrific when several men find themselves in captivity. **?m/C VHS.** Eric Gunn, Kevin Yon, Lynne Browne; **D:** Dean Wilson; **W:** Dean Wilson. *HHE*

Blind Faith 🐾🐾½ **1998 (R)** In 1957, John Williams (Vance) is a struggling new lawyer, living with older sibling Charles (Dutton) and his family in a Bronx neighborhood. The first black NYPD sergeant, Charles has an uneasy relationship with his eldest son, Charlie (Whitt). The family's shocked when Charlie's accused of murdering a white boy during a robbery attempt, especially when he confesses. John thinks the cops beat the confession out of the boy and becomes determined to defend him but he gradually becomes suspicious of the story Charlie is telling. **CW:** Language. **122m/C VHS.** Courtney B. Vance, Charles S. Dutton, Garland Whitt, Kadeem Hardison, Lonette McKee, Karen Glave, Dan Lett; **D:** Ernest R. Dickerson; **W:** Frank Military; **C:** Rodney Charters; **M:** Ron Carter. *EVE*

Blind Fear 🐾½ **1989 (R)** A blind woman is stalked by three killers in an abandoned country inn. **98m/C VHS, Beta, LV.** Shelley Hack, Jack Langedijk, Kim Coates, Jan Rubes, Heidi von Palleske; **D:** Tom Berry; **W:** Sergio D. Altieri.

Blind Fists of Bruce 🐾½ **197?** A rich, idle young man learns the techniques of kung fu from a former warrior. **92m/C VHS, Beta.** Bruce Li; **D:** Kam Bo. *NO*

Blind Fools 🐾½ **1940** A scathing indictment of children neglected by ambitious parents. **66m/B VHS, Beta, LV.** Herbert Rawlinson, Claire Whitney, Russell Hicks, Miriam Battista. *NO*

Blind Fury 🐾🐾½ **1990 (R)** A blind Vietnam vet enlists the aid of a Zen master and a sharpshooter to tackle the Mafia. Hauer works well in the lead, but unfortunately, the movie doesn't. **86m/C VHS, Beta, LV, Closed Caption.** Rutger Hauer, Terry O'Quinn, Brandon Call, Lisa Blount, Randall "Tex" Cobb, Noble Willingham, Meg Foster, Sho Kosugi, Nick Cassavetes, Charles Cooper, Rick Overton; **D:** Phillip Noyce; **W:** Charles Robert Carner; **C:** Don Burgess; **M:** J. Peter Robinson. *COL, FCT*

Blind Husbands 🐾🐾🐾½ **1919** An Austrian officer is attracted to the pretty wife of a dull surgeon. Controversial in its day, this lurid, sumptuous melodrama instigated many stubborn Hollywood myths, including the stereotype of the brusque, jodhpur-clad Prussian officer. This was von Stroheim's first outing as director. **98m/B VHS, Beta.** Erich von Stroheim, Fay Wray; **D:** Erich von Stroheim. *VYY, GVV*

Blind Justice 🐾🐾 **1986** An innocent man is identified as a rapist, and the accusation ruins his life. Made for television. **94m/C VHS, Beta.** Tim Matheson, Lisa Eichhorn, Mimi Kuzyk, Philip Charles MacKenzie, Tom Atkins; **D:** Rod Holcomb; **M:** Miles Goodman. *FOX*

Blind Justice 🐾🐾½ **1994 (R)** Gunfighter gets blinded in battle and rides into a small town where he's nursed back to health by an attractive lady doctor. While he recovers, he learns the town is trying to protect a cache of government silver from being stolen by bandits. Made for cable TV. **CW:** Some language; graphic western violence. **85m/C VHS.** Armand Assante, Elisabeth Shue, Robert Davi; **D:** Richard Spence. *HBO*

Blind Man's Bluff 🐾🐾 **1991 (PG-13)** A blind professor is accused of murdering his neighbor, but as he tries to solve the mystery, evidence points to his ex-girlfriend who may have framed him for the murder. Surprisingly suspenseful made for cable TV movie is hampered by a stock Hollywood ending. **86m/C VHS, Beta, Closed Caption.** Robert Urich, Lisa Eilbacher, Patricia Clarkson, Ken Pogue, Ron Perlman; **D:** James Quinn; **W:** Joel Gross; **M:** Richard Bellis. *PAR*

Blind Rage 🐾 **1978 (R)** When the United States government transports $15 million to the Philippines, five blind kung fu masters want a piece of the action. **81m/C VHS, Beta.** *PH* D'Urville Martin, Leo Fong, Tony Ferrer, Dick Adair, Darnell Garcia, Leila Hermosa, Fred Williamson; **D:** Efren C. Pinon. *MGM*

Blind Side 🐾½ **1993 (R)** DeMornay and Silver are a married couple whose Mexican vacation turns into trouble when they get into a hit-and-run accident which they don't report. Back home, they're frightened by the sudden appearance of Hauer, who's also just back from Mexico. They think he's after blackmail but he's really just a run-of-the-mill psycho intrigued by DeMornay, who at least keeps her character in control. Silver and Hauer have a great time chewing scenery. Made for cable television. Also available in an unrated version which will run 98 minutes. **CW:** Violence and terror and sexuality. **92m/C VHS.** Rebecca DeMornay,

Ron Silver, Rutger Hauer; **D:** Geoff Murphy; **W:** John Carlen. *HBO*

Blind Spot 🎬🎬½ **1993** Okay family drama which works because of the performances and not the script. Woodward stars as Nell Harrington, a take-charge U.S. Representative long married to Simon (Weaver). Her troubled, pregnant daughter Phoebe (Linney) is married to Nell's aide Charlie (Diamond). Charlie is killed and Phoebe injured in a car crash but the real tragedy is when Nell discovers what caused the accident—drugs—and that her daughter is a cocaine addict. Lots of suffering. Made for television. 99m/ C VHS, **Closed Caption.** Joanne Woodward, Laura Linney, Fritz Weaver, Reed Edward Diamond, Cynthia Martells, Patti Yasutake, Patti D'Arbanville; **D:** Michael Toshiyuki Uno; **W:** Nina Shengold; **M:** Patrick Williams. *REP*

Blind Vengeance 🎬🎬½ **1990 (R)** A man whose son was murdered by white supremacists decides to take his own special revenge when they are acquitted by the local jury. But this isn't your usual bloodbath, instead he plays psychological games with the men, waiting for them to break. Made for cable television. 93m/C VHS. Gerald McRaney, Marg Helgenberger; Thalmus Rasulala, Lane Smith, Don Hood, Grand Bush; **D:** Lee Philips; **W:** Henri Simoun, Curt Allen. *USH*

Blind Vision 🎬½ **1991** Von Dohlen stars as William Dalton, a mail clerk who is in love with his beautiful neighbor Leanne (Shelton). Suffering from extreme shyness, Dalton can only spy on her through a telephoto lens. Things start to get complicated for him when one of Leanne's boyfriends turns up dead outside her apartment. Soon afterwards, their landlady and a local police detective uncover a shocking sexual secret that forces Dalton into a deadly game of obsession and desire. 92m/C VHS, LV, **Closed Caption.** Lenny Von Dohlen, Deborah Shelton, Ned Beatty, Robert Vaughn, Louise Fletcher; **D:** Shuki Levy. *WOV*

Blind Witness 🎬🎬½ **1989** Routine story about a blind woman who's the only witness to her husband's murder during a robbery. Made for television. 92m/C VHS, **Closed Caption.** Victoria Principal, Paul LeMat, Stephen Macht, Matt Clark, Tim Choate; **D:** Richard A. Colla; **M:** Robert Alcivar. *WOV*

Blinded by the Light 🎬🎬 **1982** Young woman tries to save her brother from attachment to a quasi-religious cult, The Light of Salvation. Real-life brother and sister McNichol team up in this made-for-television drama, one of the earlier examinations of cult behavior. 90m/C VHS, Beta. Kristy McNichol, Jimmy McNichol, Anne Jackson, Michael McGuire; **D:** John Alonzo. *TLF*

Blindfold: Acts of Obsession 🎬🎬 **1994 (R)** Madeline's (Doherty) marriage is boring so she consults therapist Jennings (Nelson). He suggests a number of sexual fantasies Madeline plays out with hubby Woods only to have murder enter the picture. Then Madeline's older sister Chris (Alfonso) is assigned to investigate and lets out lots of family secrets. Shannen in the buff, murder, infidelity, deception, and sex. An unrated version is also available.**CW:** Language, nudity, violence, and sexual situations. 93m/C VHS. Shannen Doherty, Judd Nelson, Michael Woods, Kristian Alfonso, Shell Danielson, Drew Snyder; **D:** Lawrence L. Simeone; **W:** Lawrence L. Simeone; **M:** Shuki Levy. *AVE*

Blindside 🎬🎬 **1988 (R)** A surveillance hobbyist who owns a motel spies on his tenants until a murder involves him in a big-scale drug war. 98m/C VHS, Beta, LV. Harvey Keitel, Lori Hallier, Lolita Davidovich, Alan Fawcett, Michael Rudder; **D:** Paul Lynch. *NLC*

Blindsided 🎬🎬½ **1993 (PG-13)** A former police officer temporarily loses his sight when he plays the middle man in a bank robbery. Sight improving, he falls for a woman who draws him into another crime. 93m/C VHS, LV. Jeff Fahey, Mia Sara, Rudy Ramos, Jack Kehler, Ben Gazzara; **D:** Tom Donnelly. *USH*

Blink 🎬🎬½ **1993 (R)** Recent corneal transplants allow blind musician Emma (Stowe) to regain her sight, but until they "settle" what she sees may not register in her mind immediately, a phenomenon the script dubs "retroactive vision." This poses a problem for Chicago cop Quinn when he falls for Emma—the only one who can recognize a sadistic killer. Average thriller has been done better before, but adds two attractive leads, enough suspense, and a unique twist to the typical woman-in-jeopardy tale to keep things interesting. The distorted images in Stowe's blurry vision were created by computer. Stowe also learned fiddle for her place as the fictional member of the real-life Irish-American band, The Drovers.**CW:** Nudity, graphic violence, and sexual content. 106m/C VHS, LV, **Letterbox, Closed Caption.** Madeleine Stowe, Aidan Quinn, Laurie Metcalf, James Remar, Bruce A. Young, Peter Friedman, Paul Dillon, Michael Kirkpatrick; **D:** Michael Apted; **W:** Dana Stevens; **C:** Dante Spinotti; **M:** Brad Fiedel. *NLC*

Blink of an Eye 🎬½ **1992 (R)** Special agent Sam Browning (Pare) must use his psychic powers and military skills against the terrorists who have kidnapped the CIA director's daughter.**CW:** Violence. 90m/C VHS, LV, **Closed Caption.** Michael Pare. *THV*

Bliss 🎬🎬🎬½ **1985 (R)** A savage, surreal Australian comedy about an advertising executive who dies suddenly for a few minutes, and upon his awakening he finds the world maniacally, bizarrely changed. Based on the Peter Carey novel, and one of the most inspired absurdist films of the decade. 112m/C VHS, Beta, LV. **AU** Barry Otto, Lynette Curran, Helen Jones; **D:** Ray Lawrence; **W:** Peter Carey. Australian Film Institute '85: Best Film. *VTR*

Bliss 🎬½ **1996 (R)** Creepy feature-length sexed lecture delves deeply into sexual problems in modern society. So deeply, in fact, that it could've been called "Ouch, You're on my Hair." Clueless yuppies Joseph (Sheffer) and Maria's (Lee) sexual dysfunctions lead her to seek aid from unconventional therapist Baltazar (Stamp), who does things like compare women to violins (hint: they're not really the same. Unless you REALLY like wood). Joseph has his doubts, but soon becomes a chanting tantric goofball. Too clinical to be sexy, but too sexy to be used as an Army training film.**CW:** Graphic sex scenes with strong sex-related dialogue, and for language. 103m/C VHS, **Closed Caption.** Sheryl Lee, Craig Sheffer, Terence Stamp, Casey Siemaszko, Spalding Gray, Leigh Taylor-Young, Lois Chiles; **D:** Lance Young; **W:** Lance Young; **C:** Mike Molloy; **M:** Jan A.P. Kaczmarek. *COL*

The Bliss of Mrs. Blossom 🎬🎬🎬 **1968** Three's a crowd in this light-hearted romp through the machinations of a brassiere manufacturer (Attenborough) and his neglected wife (MacLaine). Mrs. Blossom finds sewing machine repairman Booth so appetizing that she hides him in the attic of the Blossom home. He reads books and redecorates, until, several plot twists later, Attenborough discovers the truth. Witty and wise, with fine supporting cast and excellent pacing. 93m/C LV, **Closed Caption.** **GB** Shirley MacLaine, Richard Attenborough, James Booth, Freddie Jones, John Cleese; **D:** Joseph McGrath. *PAR, MOV*

Blithe Spirit 🎬🎬🎬½ **1945** Charming and funny adaptation of Coward's famed stage play. A man re-marries and finds his long-dead wife is unhappy enough about it to come back and haunt him. Clever supporting cast, with Rutherford exceptional as the medium. Received Oscar for its Special Effects. 96m/C VHS. **GB** Rex Harrison, Constance Cummings, Kay Hammond, Margaret Rutherford, Hugh Wakefield, Joyce Carey, Jacqueline Clarke; **D:** David Lean; **C:** Ronald Neame; **M:** Richard Addinsell. Academy Awards '46: Best Special Effects. *MLB, FCT*

The Blob 🎬🎬½ **1958** Sci-fi thriller about a small town's fight against a slimy jello invader from space. Slightly rebellious McQueen (in his first starring role) redeems himself when he saves the town with quick action. Low-budget, horror/teen-fantasy became a camp classic. Other names considered included "The Glob," "The Glob that Girdled the Globe," "The Meteorite Monster," "The Molten Meteorite," and "The Night of the Creeping Dead." Followed by a worthless sequel in 1972, "Son of Blob," and a worthwhile remake in 1988. Laserdisc contains an additional 15 minutes of McQueen interviews and the trailers for both the original and the 1988 remake. 83m/C VHS, Beta, LV, **Letterbox.** Steve McQueen, Aneta Corsaut, Olin Howlin, Earl Rowe, Steve Chase, John Benson; **D:** Irvin S. Yeaworth Jr.; **W:** Kate Phillips, Theodore Simonson; **C:** Thomas E. Spalding; **M:** Burt Bacharach, Hal David. *GEM, MLB, CRC*

The Blob 🎬🎬🎬 **1988 (R)** A hi-tech remake of the 1958 camp classic about a small town beset by a fast-growing, man-eating mound of glop shot into space by scientists, irradiated into an unnatural being, and then returned to earth. Well-developed characters make this an excellent tribute to the first film. 92m/C VHS, Beta, LV, **Closed Caption.** Kevin Dillon, Candy Clark, Joe Seneca, Shawnee Smith, Donovan Leitch, Jeffrey DeMunn, Ricky Paull Goldin, Del Close; **D:** Chuck Russell; **W:** Chuck Russell, Frank Darabont; **C:** Mark Irwin. *COL*

Block-heads 🎬🎬🎬 **1938** Twenty years after the end of WWI, soldier Stan is found, still in his foxhole, and brought back to America, where he moves in with old pal Ollie. Also includes a 1934 Charley Chase short "I'll Take Vanilla." 75m/ B VHS, Beta. Stan Laurel, Oliver Hardy, Billy Gilbert, Patricia Ellis, James Finlayson, Charley Chase; **D:** John Blystone. *CCB, MLB*

Blockhouse woof! **1973** Four men are entombed in a subterranean stronghold for six years after the D-Day invasion of Normandy. Encourages claustrophobic feeling in viewer. Based on Jean Paul Cleberts' novel "Le Blockhaus." 88m/C VHS, Beta. **GB** Peter Sellers, Charles Aznavour, Per Oscarsson, Peter Vaughan, Leon Lissek, Alfred Lynch, Jeremy Kemp; **D:** Clive Rees. *NO*

Blonde Blackmailer 🎬 **1958** Boring story about an innocent man who serves time for the murder of a female blackmailer. When he's released, he searches for the real killer. 69m/B VHS. **GB** Richard Arlen, Susan Shaw, Vincent Ball, Constance Leigh; **D:** Charles Deane; **W:** Charles Deane. *RXM*

Blonde Crazy 🎬🎬½ *Larceny Lane* **1931** A charming grifter hooks up with a gorgeous blonde as he works the territory of a big wheel criminal. Escapist fare, with fun performances from Cagney and Blondell. 81m/B VHS. James Cagney, Joan Blondell, Louis Calhern, Ray Milland, Nat Pendleton; **D:** Roy Del Ruth. *MGM*

Blonde in Black Leather 🎬½ **1977** A bored Italian housewife takes up with a leather-clad lady biker, and together they cavort about. 88m/C VHS, Beta. Claudia Cardinale, Monica Vitti; **D:** Carlo DiPalma. *NLC*

Blonde Savage 🎬 **1947** Charting African territories, an adventurer encounters a white jungle queen swinging amongst the vines. Essentially a cheap, distaff "Tarzan." 62m/B VHS, Beta. Leif Erickson, Gale Sherwood, Veda Ann Borg, Douglass Dumbrille, Frank Jenks, Matt Willis, Ernest Whitman; **D:** Steve Sekely. *SNC*

Blonde Venus 🎬🎬🎬½ **1932** A German cafe singer marries an Englishman, but their marriage hits the skids when he contracts radiation poisoning and she gets a nightclub job to pay the bills. Sternberg's and Dietrich's fourth film together, and characteristically beautiful, though terribly strange. Dietrich's cabaret number "Hot Voodoo," in a gorilla suit and blonde afro, attains new heights in early Hollywood surrealism. 94m/B VHS, Beta. Marlene Dietrich, Herbert Marshall, Cary Grant, Dickie Moore, Hattie McDaniel, Sidney Toler; **D:** Josef von Sternberg. *USH*

Blondes Have More Guns 🎞🎞 1996 (R) Very dumb detective Harry Bates (McGaharin) is investigating a chainsaw murder and falls for the mysterious Montana (Key), who's possibly a serial killer, or maybe it's her half-sister, Dakota (Lusiak). Spoof of "Basic Instinct" and others of that ilk, done in the usual Troma fashion. **CW:** Language, nudity, sexual situations, violence. 90m/C VHS. Michael McGahern, Elizabeth Key, Gloria Lusiak, Richard Neil; **D:** George Merriweather. TTV

Blondie 🎞🎞½ 1938 Chic Young's famous comic strip debuted on the big screen with Singleton in the title role, Lake as the bumbling Dagwood, and Simms as Baby Dumpling (son Alexander, when he grows up). The couple are about to celebrate their 5th wedding anniversary when Dagwood loses his job and Blondie suspects him of infidelity. The series eventually contained 28 films. 68m/B VHS. Penny Singleton, Arthur Lake, Larry Simms, Gene Lockhart, Ann Doran, Jonathan Hale, Gordon Oliver, Stanley Andrews; **D:** Frank Strayer; **W:** Richard Flournoy. MOV

Blondie Has Trouble 🎞🎞½ Blondie Has Servant Trouble 1940 Mr. Dithers has a property he just can't sell because of rumors that the house is haunted. So he offers to let the Bumsteads stay in it to prove that the rumors are false. The Bumsteads also find the creepy mansion comes complete with two equally creepy servants. 6th film in the series. 70m/B VHS. Penny Singleton, Arthur Lake, Larry Simms, Danny Mummert, Jonathan Hale, Arthur Hohl, Esther Dale, Irving Bacon; **D:** Frank Strayer; **W:** Richard Flournoy. MOV

Blondie Hits the Jackpot 🎞½ 1949 Dagwood is fired for the umpteenth time after he makes a mistake in a construction deal and tries frantically to get his job back. Meanwhile, Blondie wins the big prize on a radio quiz show. The 26th film in the series. 66m/B VHS. Penny Singleton, Arthur Lake, Larry Simms, Marjorie Kent, Jerome Cowan, Lloyd Corrigan, Danny Mummert, James Flavin; **D:** Edward L. Bernds; **W:** Jack Henley. MOV

Blondie in Society 🎞½ 1941 A weak entry (the ninth) in the comedic series. Dagwood brings home a pedigreed Great Dane and Blondie decides to enter the pooch in the local dog show. Then an important client of Dagwood's decides he wants the dog. 77m/B VHS. Penny Singleton, Arthur Lake, Larry Simms, William Frawley, Edgar Kennedy, Jonathan Hale, Danny Mummert, Chick Chandler; **D:** Frank Strayer; **W:** Karen De Wolf. MOV

Blondie Knows Best 🎞½ 1946 Dagwood impersonates his boss, Mr. Dithers, and causes all sorts of problems. Howard, one of the Three Stooges, has a cameo as a myopic process-server. The 18th film in the series. 66m/B VHS. Penny Singleton, Arthur Lake, Larry Simms, Marjorie Kent, Jonathan Hale, Steve Geray, Jerome Cowan, Danny Mummert; **Cameos:** Shemp Howard; **D:** Abby Berlin; **W:** Edward L. Bernds, Al Martin. MOV

Blondie Takes a Vacation 🎞🎞½ 1939 Third in the series of fluff films adapted from Chic Young's comic strip. After the Bumstead family is snubbed at a snobby mountain resort they move to a friendlier nearby hotel where they try to help out the owners who are in danger of losing their investment. Baby Dumpling does his bit by unleashing a skunk in the ventilation system of the competing hotel. 68m/B VHS. Penny Singleton, Arthur Lake, Larry Simms, Danny Mummert, Donald Meek, Donald MacBride, Thomas Ross, Robert Wilcox, Irving Bacon; **D:** Frank Strayer; **W:** Richard Flournoy. MOV

Blondie's Blessed Event 🎞🎞½ 1942 Cookie is born, causing even more chaos in the Bumstead household. Meanwhile, Dagwood gets into trouble at work when he hires a cynical playwright to write an important speech for him. 11th entry in series. 69m/B VHS. Penny Singleton, Arthur Lake, Larry Simms, Norma Jean Wayne, Jonathan Hale, Danny Mummert, Hans Conried, Irving Bacon, Stanley Brown, Mary Wickes, Paul Harvey, Arthur O'Connell; **D:** Frank Strayer; **W:** Richard Flournoy, Karen De Wolf, Connie Lee. MOV

Blood Alley 🎞🎞 1955 A seasoned merchant Marine captain takes on a cargo of refugee Chinese to smuggle through enemy territory. Middling, mid-career Wayne vehicle. 115m/C VHS, Beta, LV, Letterbox, Closed Caption. John Wayne, Lauren Bacall, Paul Fix, Joy Kim, Berry Kroeger, Mike Mazurki, Anita Ekberg; **D:** William A. Wellman; **C:** William Clothier. WAR, FCT

Blood and Black Lace 🎞 1964 Beautiful models are being brutally murdered and an inspector is assigned to the case, but not before more gruesome killings occur. Bava is, as usual, violent and suspenseful. Horror fans will enjoy this flick. 90m/C VHS, Beta. IT FR GE Cameron Mitchell, Eva Bartok, Mary Arden; **D:** Mario Bava.

Blood & Concrete: A Love Story 🎞🎞 1990 (R) Bizarre, violent and stylish film-noir spoof, definitely not for all tastes. The innocent hero gets drawn into a maelstrom of intrigue over a killer aphrodisiac drug. Beals, an addicted punk rocker, gets to perform a few songs. **CW:** Language, violence and drug content, and sensuality. 97m/C VHS, LV, Letterbox. Billy Zane, Jennifer Beals, Darren McGavin; **D:** Jeff Reiner; **W:** Jeff Reiner. COL

Blood & Donuts 🎞🎞 1995 (R) Hungry vampire Boya (Currie) is looking for a rat snack when he stumbles across an all-night donut shop where pretty cashier Molly (Clarkson) and friendly cabbie Earl (Louis) seek his help with a local crime boss. Mild horror mixed with comedy and limited gore. **CW:** Language, violence, sexual situations. 89m/C VHS, LV, Closed Caption. CA Gordon Currie, Justin Louis, Helene Clarkson, Fiona Reid, Frank Moore; **Cameos:** David Cronenberg; **D:** Holly Dale; **W:** Andrew Rai Berzins; **C:** Paul Sarossy. Nominations: Genie Awards '96: Best Actress (Clarkson), Best Costume Design, Best Original Screenplay. ART

Blood and Guns 🎞½ 1979 (R) Romance, revenge, and action abound in post-revolutionary Mexico. 96m/C VHS, Beta. Orson Welles, Tomas Milian, John Steiner; **D:** Giulio Petroni. MRV

Blood and Roses 🎞🎞 Et Mourir de Plaisir 1961 A girl who is obsessed with her family's vampire background becomes possessed by a vampire and commits numerous murders. The photography is good, but the plot is hazy and only effective in certain parts. Based on the story "Carmilla" by Sheridan Le Fanu. Later remade as "The Vampire Lovers" and "The Blood-Spattered Bride." 74m/C VHS, Closed Caption. FR IT Mel Ferrer, Elsa Martinelli, Annette Vadim, Marc Allegret, Jacques-Rene Chauffard; **D:** Roger Vadim; **W:** Roger Vadim, Claude Martin, Roger Vailand, Claude Brule; **C:** Claude Renoir. PAR

Blood and Sand 🎞🎞½ 1922 Vintage romance based on Vicente Blasco Ibanez's novel about the tragic rise and fall of a matador, and the women in his life. The film that made Valentino a star. Remade in 1941. Silent. 87m/B VHS, Beta. Rudolph Valentino, Nita Naldi, Lila Lee, Walter Long; **D:** Fred Niblo. REP, NOS, CAB

Blood and Sand 🎞🎞🎞 1941 Director Mamoulian "painted" this picture in the new technicolor technique, which makes it a veritable explosion of color and spectacle. Power is the matador who becomes famous and then falls when he is torn between two women, forsaking his first love, bullfighting. Based on the novel "Sangre y Arena" by Vicente Blasco Ibanez. This movie catapulted Hayworth to stardom, primarily for her dancing, but also for her sexiness and seductiveness (and of course, her acting). Remake of the 1922 silent classic. Made again in 1989. 123m/C VHS, Beta, LV. Tyrone Power, Linda Darnell, Rita Hayworth, Alla Nazimova, Anthony Quinn, J. Carrol Naish, John Carradine, George Reeves; **D:** Rouben Mamoulian; **W:** Jo Swerling; **C:** Ernest Palmer, Ray Rennahan; **M:** Alfred Newman. Academy Awards '41: Best Color Cinematography; Nominations: Academy Awards '41: Best Interior Decoration. FXL

Blood and Sand 🎞🎞 1989 (R) A bullfighter on the verge of super-stardom risks it all when he falls under the spell of a sexy, seductive woman. Will she destroy his one opportunity for fame? Interesting for people who actually enjoy watching the "sport" of bullfighting. Originally made in 1922 and remade in 1941. **CW:** Drug use and strong sensuality. 96m/C VHS, LV. Christopher Rydell, Sharon Stone, Ana Torrent, Jose-Luis De Villalonga, Simon Andrew; **D:** Javier Elorrieta. THV

Blood and Sand/Son of the Sheik 1926 A double feature containing two abridged versions; in "Blood and Sand," an idolized matador meets another woman just before his wedding; in "Son of the Sheik," a man believes he has been betrayed by a dancing girl, and he abducts her to seek revenge. Silent. 56m/B VHS, Beta. Rudolph Valentino, Lila Lee, Vilma Banky. CCB

Blood and Steel 1925 The railroad tycoon's daughter and the construction foreman wind up together on an exciting train ride. Silent. ?m/B VHS, Beta, 8mm. Helen Holmes, William Desmond; **D:** J.P. McGowan. GVV

Blood & Wine 🎞🎞½ 1996 (R) Miami wine merchant Alex (Nicholson) gets involved with terminally ill safecracker Victor (Caine) to steal a necklace worth a cool million. Meanwhile he must deal with his crumbling marriage to Suzanne (Davis) and the bitter relationship with his stepson Jason (Dorff), who has eyes for both the necklace and his Cuban mistress (Lopez). Characterizations and strong performances (particularly by Nicholson and Caine) haul the sometimes lumbering plot to its violent conclusion. Promoted as the third part of a "dysfunctional family trilogy" with "Five Easy Pieces" and "The King of Marvin's Gardens." Seventh time Nicholson has worked with director Rafelson. **CW:** Violence and language. 100m/C VHS. Jack Nicholson, Michael Caine, Judy Davis, Stephen Dorff, Jennifer Lopez, Harold Perrineau Jr.; **D:** Bob Rafelson; **W:** Nick Villiars, Allison Cross; **C:** Newton Thomas Sigel; **M:** Stephen Cohen. NYR

Blood at Sundown 🎞½ 1988 Routine oater where man returns home after the Civil War to find his wife kidnapped by a group of Mexican outlaws who have also taken over his village. 92m/C VHS, Beta. Giuliano Gemma, Hally Hamond, Nieves Navarro, Antonio Casas, Fernando Sancho, Pajarito, George Martin; **D:** Duccio Tessari. IMP

Blood Beach woof! 1981 (R) A group of teenagers are devoured by menacing sand, which keeps people from getting to the water by swallowing them whole. Weak parody with some humorous moments; more silly than scary. 92m/C VHS, Beta. David Huffman, Marianna Hill, John Saxon, Burt Young, Otis Young, Pamela McMyler, Bobby Bass, Darrell Fetty, Stefan Gierasch, Harriet Medin; **D:** Jeffrey Bloom; **W:** Jeffrey Bloom; **C:** Steven Poster.

Blood Beast Terror 🎞½ The Vampire-Beast Craves Blood; Deathshead Vampire 1967 An entomologist transforms his own daughter into a Deathshead Moth and she proceeds to terrorize and drink innocent victims' blood. 81m/C VHS, Beta. GB Peter Cushing, Robert Flemyng, Wanda Ventham, Vanessa Howard; **D:** Vernon Sewell. MON

Blood Bride 🎞½ 19?? A lonely young woman finally finds happiness with her new husband but her world comes crashing about her with soul-mangling ferocity when she discovers he is actually a bloodthirsty maniac. 90m/C VHS, Beta. Ellen Barber, Philip English. NO

Blood Brothers 🎞🎞 1974 (R) A young man who dreams of becoming a lawyer is disturbed when he discovers that his family has mafia ties. 148m/C VHS, Beta. IT Claudia Cardinale, Franco Nero, Lina Polito; **D:** Pasquale Squitieri. NO

Blood Brothers 1977 James Grizzly Adams, who lives in the mountains of the American wilderness, relives the story of how he met his Indian blood brother, Nakuma. Beautiful scenery. 50m/C VHS, Beta. Dan Haggerty, Denver Pyle, Don Shanks. MCG

Blood Brothers 🎬🎬 1997 Darryl has always looked up to older brother Sylvester. And then one day he witnesses a gang murder and Sylvester is one of the killers. The District Attorney senses Darryl knows more than he's saying and the gang bangers want to shut him up permanently, so each brother must look to his conscience and decide how best to be his brother's keeper. 91m/C VHS. Clark Johnson, Richard Chevolleau, Mia Korf, Richard Yearwood, Ron White, Amir Williams, Ndehru Roberts, Timothy Stickney, Bill Nunn; **D:** Bruce Pittman; **W:** Paris Qualles; **M:** Harold Wheeler. PEG

Blood Clan 🎬½ 1991 (R) Based on the true story of Katy Bane, daughter of notorious Scottish cult leader, Sawney Bane, in whose lair were found the remains of over 1000 killed and cannibalized followers. When found, Bane's entire family was sentenced to death with the exception of Katy, who left to make a new start in Canada. When a rash of mysterious deaths break out in Katy's new home, she must defend herself from rumors that her father's murderous cult is resurfacing. **CW:** Violence and sensuality. 91m/C VHS. Gordon Pinsent, Michelle Little, Robert Wisden; **D:** Charles Wilkinson. FXL

Blood Cult 🎬 1985 A bizarre series of murder-mutilations take place on a small midwestern campus. Contains graphic violence that is not for the squeamish. This film was created especially for the home video market. 92m/C VHS, Beta. Chuck Ellis, Julie Andelman, Jim Vance, Joe Hardt; **D:** Christopher Lewis. VCI

Blood Debts 1983 A father is out for revenge after he saves his daughter from some hunters who raped her and also killed her boyfriend. 91m/C VHS, Beta. Richard Harrison, Mike Manty, Jim Gaines, Anne Jackson, Anne Milhench; **D:** Teddy Page. NO

Blood Diner woof! 1987 Two spirit-possessed, diner-owning brothers kill countless young girls for demonic rituals, and serve their corpses as gourmet food in their restaurant. Some funny moments mixed in with the requisite gore. Cult potential. 88m/C VHS, Beta. Rick Burks, Carl Crew; **D:** Jackie Kong. VES, ART

Blood Feast 🎬 Feast of Flesh 1963 The first of Lewis' gore-fests, in which a demented caterer butchers hapless young women to splice them together in order to bring back an Egyptian goddess. Dated, campy, and gross; reportedly shot in four days (it shows). 70m/C VHS, Beta. Connie Mason, Thomas Wood, Mal Arnold, Scott H. Hall, Lyn Bolton, Toni Calvert, Gene Courtier; **D:** Herschell Gordon Lewis; **W:** Allison Louise Downe; **C:** Herschell Gordon Lewis. SMW, FCT

Blood Feud 🎬🎬 Revenge 1979 (R) In Italy preceding Europe's entry into WWII, a young widow is in mourning over the brutal murder of her husband by the Sicilian Mafia. In the meantime she must contend with the rivalry between Mastroianni as a lawyer and Giannini as a small-time crook both vying for her affections. Dubbed. 112m/C VHS, Beta. IT Sophia Loren, Marcello Mastroianni, Giancarlo Giannini; **D:** Lina Wertmuller; **W:** Lina Wertmuller. FOX

Blood for a Silver Dollar 🎬½ 1966 Action-filled western, littered with murder, revenge and romance. 98m/C VHS, Beta. Montgomery Wood, Evelyn Stewart. VYY

Blood for Blood 🎬½ 1995 (R) Cop must take up the martial arts skills he learned in childhood in order to protect his family from assassination. 93m/C VHS, LV, Closed Caption. Lorenzo Lamas, James Lew, Mako, Eric Pierpont, James Shigeta, James Callahan; **D:** John Weidner; **M:** Joel Goldsmith. ART

Blood Freak woof! Blood Freaks 1972 An absolutely insane anti-drug, Christian splatter film. A Floridian biker is introduced to drugs by a young woman and eventually into a poultry-monster who drinks the blood of junkies. Narrated by a chain smoker who has a coughing fit. Don't miss it. 86m/C VHS, Beta. Steve Hawkes, Dana Cullivan, Randy Grinter Jr., Tina Anderson, Heather Hughes; **D:** Brad Grinter, Steve Hawkes.

Blood Frenzy 🎬 1987 Psychologist's patients take a therapeutic trip to the desert. The sun and heat take their toll, and everyone gets violent. This kind of therapy we don't need, and the movie's a waste, as well. Made for video. Loring was Wednesday on TV's "The Addams Family." 90m/C VHS, Beta. John Montero, Lisa Loring, Hank Garrett, Wendy MacDonald; **D:** Hal Freeman. NO

Blood Games woof! 1990 (R) Buxom baseball team bats 1000 against the home team and the winning babes find out just how poor losers can be. Diamonds aren't always a girl's best friend. 90m/C VHS, LV, Closed Caption. Gregory Cummings, Laura Albert, Shelly Abblett, Luke Shay, Ross Hagen; **D:** Tanya Rosenberg. COL

Blood Hook 🎬½ 1986 A self-parodying teenage-slasher film about kids running into a backwoods fishing tournament while on vacation, complete with ghouls, cannibalism and grotesquerie. 85m/C VHS, Beta. Mark Jacobs, Lisa Todd, Patrick Danz; **D:** James Mallon. PAR

Blood In ... Blood Out: Bound by Honor 🎬½ Bound by Honor 1993 (R) Three-hour epic about Chicano gang culture focuses on three buddies whose lives evolve into a drug-addicted artist, a narc, and a prison regular. Written by acclaimed poet Baca, the film touches on issues such as poverty, racism, drugs, and violence as they pertain to Hispanic life. Unfortunately, the extreme violence (shootings, stabbings, and garrotings) completely overwhelms the rest of the story. Contains profanity, nudity, and sexual innuendo. Based on a story by Ross Thomas. **CW:** Strong language, strong violence and drug content, and sexuality. 180m/C VHS, Beta, LV, Closed Caption. Damian Chapa, Jesse Borrego, Benjamin Bratt, Enrique Castillo, Victor Rivers, Delroy Lindo, Tom Towles; **D:** Taylor Hackford; **W:** Floyd Mutrux, Jimmy Santiago Baca, Jeremy Iacone; **M:** Bill Conti. HPH, TOU

Blood Island 🎬🎬 The Shuttered Room 1968 A couple inherits an old house on a remote New England island where the woman grew up. They discover that this old house needs more than a paint job to make it livable; seems there's something evil in them there walls. Based on an H.P. Lovecraft story. Greene, who's best known for later directing "Godspell," and the solid cast fail to animate the inert script. 100m/C VHS. GB Gig Young, Carol Lynley, Oliver Reed, Flora Robson; **D:** David Greene. ACE

Blood Legacy 🎬🎬 Legacy of Blood 1973 (R) Four heirs must survive a night in a lonely country estate to collect their money; what do you think happens? Average treatment of the haunted house theme. 77m/C VHS, Beta. John Carradine, John Russell, Faith Domergue, Merry Anders, Richard Davalos, Jeff Morrow, Roy Engle; **D:** Carl Monson; **W:** Eric Norden; **C:** Jack Beckett. CNG, MRV, GEM

Blood Mania 🎬 1970 (R) A retired surgeon's daughter decides to murder her father to collect her inheritance prematurely, but soon learns that crime doesn't pay as well as medicine. Low-budget, low-interest flick. 90m/C VHS, Beta. Peter Carpenter, Maria de Aragon, Alex Rocco; **D:** Robert Vincent O'Neil. NO

Blood Money 🎬½ 1980 (PG) A dying ex-criminal returns to Australia to redeem his name and die with dignity. 64m/C VHS, Beta. AU Bryan Brown, John Flaus, Chrissie James; **D:** Christopher Fitchett. NO

Blood Money: The Story of Clinton and Nadine 🎬🎬½ Clinton & Nadine 1988 A confusing action/thriller with a good cast. Garcia is a small-time exotic bird smuggler whose gun-running brother has been murdered. He uses high-class hooker Barkin to get close to his brother's contacts, who turn out to be running guns to the Nicaraguan contras and involved in a dangerous government conspiracy. Made for cable television. 95m/C VHS, Beta. Andy Garcia, Ellen Barkin, Morgan Freeman; **D:** Jerry Schatzberg. FCT

The Blood of a Poet Le Sang d'un Poete 1930 Cocteau's first film, a practically formless piece of poetic cinema, detailing all manner of surreal events occurring in the instant a chimney falls. In French with English subtitles. 55m/B VHS, Beta. Jean Cocteau; **D:** Jean Cocteau; **C:** Georges Perinal. VYY, MRV, HHT

Blood of Dracula 🎬½ Blood Is My Heritage; Blood of the Demon 1957 They don't make 1950s rock 'n' roll girls' school vampire movies like this anymore, for which we may be grateful. Hypnotism, an amulet, and a greasepaint makeup job turn a shy female student into a bloodsucker. 71m/B VHS. Sandra Harrison, Louise Lewis, Gail Ganley, Jerry Blaine, Heather Ames, Malcolm Atterbury, Richard Devon, Thomas B. Henry; **D:** Herbert L. Strock; **W:** Ralph Thornton; **C:** Monroe Askins. COL, OM

Blood of Dracula's Castle 🎬🎬 Dracula's Castle 1969 Couple inherits an allegedly deserted castle, but upon moving in discover Mr. and Mrs. Dracula have settled there. The vampires keep young women chained in the dungeon for continual blood supply. Also present are a hunchback and a werewolf. Awesome Adamson production is highlighted by the presence of the gorgeous Volante. Early cinematography effort by the renowned Laszlo Kovacs. 84m/C VHS, Beta. John Carradine, Alexander D'Arcy, Paula Raymond, Ray Young, Vicki Volante, Robert Dix, John Cardos; **D:** Al Adamson, Jean Hewitt; **W:** Rex Carlton; **C:** Laszlo Kovacs. NO

Blood of Ghastly Horror woof! The Fiend with the Atomic Brain; Psycho a Go Go!; The Love Maniac; The Man with the Synthetic Brain; The Fiend with the Electronic Brain 1972 A young man thinks he has a new lease on life when he is the happy recipient of a brain transplant, but his dreams are destroyed when he evolves into a rampaging killer. This movie is so awful it hides behind numerous but rather creative aliases. 87m/C VHS. John Carradine, Kent Taylor, Tommy Kirk, Regina Carrol; **D:** Al Adamson. MOV

The Blood of Heroes 🎬🎬 The Salute of the Jugger 1989 (R) A post-apocalyptic action flick detailing the adventures of a battered team of "juggers," warriors who challenge small village teams to a brutal sport (involving dogs' heads on sticks) that's a cross between jousting and football. 97m/C VHS, Beta, LV, Closed Caption. Rutger Hauer, Joan Chen, Vincent D'Onofrio, Anna Katarina; **D:** David Peoples; **W:** David Peoples; **C:** David Eggby; **M:** Todd Boekelheide. HBO

Blood of Jesus 🎬🎬 1941 A sinful husband accidentally shoots his newly baptized wife, causing an uproar in their rural town. Williams later starred as Andy on the "Amos 'n' Andy" television series. 50m/C VHS. Spencer Williams Jr., Kathryn Craviness; **D:** Spencer Williams Jr.; **W:** Spencer Williams Jr. National Film Registry '91. FCT, HEG, BTV

The Blood of Others 🎬 1984 A driveling adaptation of the Simone de Beauvoir novel about a young French woman at the outbreak of WWII torn between her absent boyfriend in the Resistance and a kind, wealthy German. Made for French television, it stars Jodie Foster and Michael Ontkean as the Gallic pair. 130m/C VHS, Beta. FR Jodie Foster, Sam Neill, Michael Ontkean, Stephane Audran, Lambert Wilson, John Vernon, Kate Reid, Jean-Pierre Aumont; **D:** Claude Chabrol; **W:** Brian Moore.

Blood of the Hunter 🎬🎬½ 1994 (PG-13) Psycho-killer holds postman's wife captive in a remote cabin in the Canadian wilderness. Turns out hubby and psycho share a mysterious past. **CW:** Violence, scene of nudity. 92m/C VHS. Michael Biehn, Alexandra Vandernoot, Gabriel Arcand; **D:** Gilles Carle. THV, FCT

Blood of the Vampire 🎬½ 1958 A Transylvanian doctor is executed for being a vampire and his hunchbacked assistant brings him back to life. 84m/C VHS, Beta. GB Donald Wolfit, Vincent

Ball, Barbara Shelley, Victor Maddern; *D:* Henry Case; *W:* Jimmy Sangster. *MPI, MLB*

The Blood on Satan's Claw 🎬🎬🎬
Satan's Skin; Satan's Claw 1971 Graphic tale centering on the Devil himself. Townspeople in an English village circa 1670 find the spirit of Satan taking over their children, who begin to practice witchcraft. Well made with lots of attention to period details. Not for the faint-hearted. 90m/C VHS, Beta. *GB* Patrick Wymark, Linda Hayden, Barry Andrews, Michele Dotrice, James Hayter, Avice Landon, Simon Williams, Tamara Ustinov; *D:* Piers Haggard; *C:* Dick Bush. *MGM, FCT*

Blood on the Badge 🎬½ 1992 Illegal
arms have been stolen from a military arsenal and fall into the hands of Libyan Nationalists who begin a terrorist campaign. Detective Neal Farrow is assigned to stop them. 92m/C VHS. Ramon Estevez, David Harrod, Rocky Patterson, Desiree Laforge, Dean Nolen, Melissa Deleon, Todd Everett; *D:* Bret McCormick.

Blood on the Moon 🎬🎬½ 1948 Well-
acted film about a cowboy's involvement in a friend's underhanded schemes. Based on a Luke Short novel, this dark film revolves around a western land dispute between cattlemen and homesteaders. 88m/B VHS, Beta, LV. Robert Mitchum, Robert Preston, Walter Brennan, Barbara Bel Geddes; *D:* Robert Wise. *TTC*

Blood on the Mountain 🎬 1988 After
escaping from prison, Jim plots revenge against his accomplice, only to kill an innocent man instead. 71m/C VHS. Stracker Edwards, Tim Jones, Paula Preston, Cliff Turknett, Rich Jury; *D:* Donald W. Thompson. *RDF*

Blood on the Sun 🎬🎬½ 1945 Newspa-
perman in Japan uncovers plans for world dominance as propaganda, violence, and intrigue combine in this action-adventure. Also available colorized. 98m/B VHS, LV. James Cagney, Sylvia Sidney, Robert Armstrong, Wallace Ford; *D:* Frank Lloyd; *M:* Miklos Rozsa. Academy Awards '45: Best Interior Decoration. *NOS, MRV, HHT*

Blood Orgy of the She-
Devils woof! 1974 (PG) Exploitative gore nonsense about female demons, beautiful witches, and satanic worship. Some movies waste all their creative efforts on their titles. 73m/C VHS, Beta. Lila Zaborin, Tom Pace, Leslie McRae, Ray Myles, Victor Izay, William Bagdad; *D:* Ted V. Mikels; *W:* Ted V. Mikels; *C:* Anthony Salinas. *NO*

Blood Rage woof! *Nightmare at Shadow
Woods* 1987 (R) A maniacal twin goes on a murderous rampage through his brother's neighborhood. AKA "Nightmare at Shadow Woods." Only for diehard "Mary Hartman" fans. 87m/C VHS, Beta. Louise Lasser, Mike Soper; *D:* John Grissmer; *M:* Richard Einhorn.

Blood Red 🎬½ 1988 (R) In 1895 Northern
California, an Italian immigrant and his family give bloody battle to a powerful industrialist who wants their land in wine-growing country. Watch for the scenes involving veteran Roberts and his then-newcomer sister, pretty woman Julia. 91m/C VHS, Beta, LV, 8mm. Eric Roberts, Dennis Hopper, Giancarlo Giannini, Burt Young, Carlin Glynn, Lara Harris, Susan Anspach, Julia Roberts, Elias Koteas, Frank Campanella, Aldo Ray, Horton Foote Jr.; *D:* Peter Masterson; *W:* Ron Cutler. *COL*

Blood Relations 🎬½ 1987 (R) A woman is
introduced to her fiance's family only to find out that they, as well as her fiance, are murdering, perverted weirdos competing for an inheritance. 88m/C VHS, Beta, LV. *CA* Jan Rubes, Ray Walston, Lydie Denier, Kevin Hicks, Lynne Adams, Sam Malkin, Steven Saylor, Carrie Leigh; *D:* Graeme Campbell. *NLC*

Blood Relatives 🎬 *Les Liens de Sang* 1977
Langlois admits she saw her brother kill her cousin, with whom he had been carrying on an incestuous relationship. But the discovery of the dead girl's diary by police inspector Sutherland reveals many more layers of intrigue than were initially evident. Based on a novel by Ed McBain. 94m/C VHS. *CA* Lisa Langlois, Donald Sutherland, Ste-

phane Audran, David Hemmings, Donald Pleasence, Laurent Malet, Micheline Lanctot, Aude Landry; *D:* Claude Chabrol; *W:* Claude Chabrol. *NO*

Blood Ring 🎬½ 1993 When Sue's boxer
husband goes missing she enlists old friend Max to help find him. They uncover a gambling ring run by drug lords where the kickboxing matches are to the death. Naturally, Max decides to use his expert kickboxing skills to get a violent revenge. 90m/C VHS. Dale "Apollo" Cook, Andrea Lamatsch, Don Nakaya Neilsen, Steve Tartalia; *D:* Irvin Johnson; *W:* Ron Davies.

Blood Salvage 🎬 *Mad Jake* 1990 (R) A crazy
junkman kidnaps beautiful girls, selling their organs to the highest bidder. He meets his match when a potential target refuses to become a victim in spite of her wheelchair. Interesting plot twists keep this Grade B thriller above average. 90m/C VHS, Beta, LV. Danny Nelson, Lori Birdsong, John Saxon, Ray Walston, Christian Hesler, Ralph Pruitt Vaughn, Laura Whyte, Evander Holyfield; *D:* Tucker Johnson; *W:* Tucker Johnson, Ken Sanders; *C:* Michael Karp. *TTC*

Blood Screams woof! 1988 (R) Nosy peo-
ple drop in on an old town in Mexico and attempt to uncover the secrets hidden there, but bizarre entities throw out the unwelcome mat and terrorize them. Lots of blood and screaming. 75m/C VHS, Beta. Ran Sands, James Garnett. *WAR*

Blood Simple 🎬🎬🎬½ 1985 (R) A jealous
husband hires a sleazy private eye to murder his adulterous wife and her lover. A dark, intricate, morbid morality tale that deviates imaginatively from the standard murder mystery thriller. First film scripted by the Coen brothers. 96m/C VHS, Beta, LV, Closed Caption. John Getz, M. Emmet Walsh, Dan Hedaya, Frances McDormand, Samm-Art Williams; *D:* Joel Coen; *W:* Joel Coen, Ethan Coen; *C:* Barry Sonnenfeld; *M:* Carter Burwell. Independent Spirit Awards '86: Best Actor (Walsh), Best Director (Coen); Sundance Film Festival '85: Grand Jury Prize. *USH*

Blood Sisters woof! 1986 (R) Sorority
babes intend to spend a giggle-strewn night in a haunted house but end up decapitated, butchered, and cannibalized. 85m/C VHS, Beta. Amy Brentano, Marla MacHart, Brigete Cossu, Randy Mooers; *D:* Roberta Findlay. *COL*

Blood Song 🎬 *Dream Slayer* 1982 A patient
(yester-decade teen throb Frankie Avalon) escapes into the night from a mental institution after murdering an attendant. He takes his only possession with him, a carved wooden flute. A young woman sees him burying his latest victim, and now he's on a hunt to play his "blood song" for her. Pretty bad, but fun to see Avalon play a less-than-squeaky-clean role. 90m/C VHS, Beta. Frankie Avalon, Donna Wilkes, Richard Jaeckel, Dane Clark, Antoinette Bower; *D:* Alan J. Levi. *NO*

The Blood Spattered Bride 🎬 *Blood
Castle; La Novia Esangrentada; Bloody Fiance; Till Death Us Do Part* 1972 Newlywed couple honeymoons in a remote castle in southern Spain. They are visited by a mysterious young woman who begins to influence the bride in the ways of lesbian bloodsucking. O.K. '70s Euro-eroti-horror based on Sheridan Le Fanu's "Carmilla." 82m/C VHS, Beta. *SP* Simon Andreu, Maribel Martin, Alexandra Bastedo, Dean Selmier, Rosa Ma Rodriguez, Montserrat Julio, Angel Lombarte, Maria Rosa Rodriguez; *D:* Vicente Aranda; *W:* Vicente Aranda; *C:* Fernando Arribas. *MPI*

Blood Thirst 🎬 1965 Obscure horror film
about a woman who stays young by indulging in ritual killings and strange experiments. ?m/C VHS. Robert Winston, Yvonne Nielson; *D:* Newton Arnold. *SNC*

Blood Tide 🎬 *The Red Tide* 1982 (R) A dis-
gusting, flesh-eating monster disrupts a couple's vacation in the Greek isles. Beautiful scenery, good cast, bad movie. 82m/C VHS, Beta. James Earl Jones, Jose Ferrer; *D:* Richard Jeffries; *W:* Nico Mastorakis. *NO*

Blood Ties 🎬½ 1987 An American naval
engineer in Sicily gets involved with the Mob in order to save his father's life. 98m/C VHS, Beta. *IT* Brad Davis, Tony LoBianco, Vincent Spano, Barbara DeRossi, Maria Conchita Alonso; *D:* Giacomo Battiato. *TWE*

Blood Ties 🎬🎬 1992 Reporter Harry
Martin belongs to an unusual family—modern-day vampires (who prefer to be known as Carpathian-Americans). But they have an age-old problem with a band of fanatical vampire hunters. This time around you'll root for the bloodsuckers. Made for television. 90m/C VHS. Harley Venton, Patrick Bauchau, Kim Johnston-Ulrich, Michelle Johnson, Jason London, Bo Hopkins, Grace Zabriskie, Salvator Xuereb; *D:* Jim McBride; *W:* Richard Shapiro.

Blood Tracks 🎬½ 1986 A woman kills her
abusive husband, then hides out in the mountains with her kids until they turn into cannibalistic savages. Years later, people show up to shoot a music video. Blood runs in buckets. 82m/C Beta. Jeff Harding, Michael Fitzpatrick, Naomi Kaneda; *D:* Mike Jackson. *NO*

Blood Vows: The Story of a Mafia
Wife 🎬🎬 1987 TV's Laura Ingalls (Gilbert) leaps from the prairie to modern-day mafia in this warped Cinderella story. She meets the man of her dreams, whom she slowly finds is her worst nightmare as she becomes trapped within the confines of her new-found "family." Made for television soaper is way over the top in terms of melodrama. 100m/C VHS. Melissa Gilbert, Joe Penny, Eileen Brennan, Talia Shire, Anthony (Tony) Franciosa; *D:* Paul Wendkos; *M:* William Goldstein.

Blood Voyage woof! 1977 (R) A crewman
aboard a pleasure yacht must find out who is killing off his passengers one by one. 80m/C VHS, Beta. Jonathon Lippe, Laurie Rose, Midori, Mara Modair; *D:* Frank Mitchell. *NO*

Blood Warriors 🎬½ 1993 An ex-Marine
finds out a old buddy is leading a private army of mercenaries. When he refuses to join up their friendship turns violent. 93m/C VHS, LV, Closed Caption. David Bradley, Frank Zagarino; *D:* Sam Firstenberg. *IMP, IME*

Blood Wedding 🎬🎬🎬 *Bodas de Sangre*
1981 A wonderfully passionate dance film from Saura and choreographed by Gades, based on the play by famed author Federico Garcia Lorca. A young bride runs off with her married lover on her wedding day and her jilted husband comes after them. If you like flamenco, there are two more: "Carmen" and "El Amor Brujo." In Spanish with English subtitles. 71m/C VHS, Beta. *SP* Antonio Gades, Christina Hoyos, Marisol, Carmen Villena; *D:* Carlos Saura. *XVC, CTH*

Bloodbath 19?? Drugs, sex and terrorism—
Hopper is typecast as an American degenerate who, along with his expatriate friends, is persecuted by local religious cults who need sacrifices. 89m/C VHS, Beta. Dennis Hopper, Carroll Baker, Richard Todd, Faith Brook, Win Wells; *D:* Silvio Narizzano. *HHE*

Bloodbath at the House of
Death 🎬🎬 1985 Price and his compatriots fight a team of mad scientists in this parody of popular horror films. Fun to see Price spoofing his own genre; die-hard horror camp fans will be satisfied. Best line: "Wanna fork?". 92m/C VHS, Beta. *GB* Kenny Everett, Pamela Stephenson, Vincent Price, Gareth Hunt; *D:* Ray Cameron.

Bloodbath in Psycho Town 🎬 1989
(R) A film crew is marked for death by a hooded man when it enters a remote little village. 87m/C VHS. Ron Arragon, Donna Baltron, Dave Elliott; *D:* Alessandro DeGaetano; *W:* Alessandro DeGaetano. *NO*

Bloodbeat 🎬 1985 A supernatural being ter-
rorizes a family as they gather at their country home to celebrate Christmas. 84m/C VHS, Beta. Helen Benton, Terry Brown, Claudia Peyton; *D:* Fabrice A. Zaphiratos. *TWE*

Bloodbrothers 🎞️½ 1978 (R) Portrayal of working-class Italian men's lives—if that's possible without the benefit of Italian writers, producers, or director. Still, lots of cussing and general intensity, as Gere's character struggles between staying in the family construction business and doing what he wants to do—work with children. Re-cut for television and re-titled "A Father's Love." 120m/C VHS. Richard Gere, Paul Sorvino, Tony LoBianco, Kenneth McMillan, Marilu Henner, Danny Aiello, Lelia Goldoni, Yvonne Wilder; **D:** Robert Mulligan; **C:** Robert L. Surtees; **M:** Elmer Bernstein. Nominations: Academy Awards '78: Best Adapted Screenplay. WAR

Bloodfight 🎞️ 1990 (PG-13) Exciting kick-boxing and martial arts tournament turns sour when champ offends the sense of honor of the master. Now the champ must battle the master, and only one will remain standing! ?m/C VHS. Bolo Yeung. IMP

Bloodfist 🎞️🎞️ 1989 (R) A kickboxer tears through Manila searching for his brother's killer. A Roger Corman production. 85m/C VHS, Beta. Don "The Dragon" Wilson, Rob Kaman, Billy Blanks, Kris Aguilar, Riley Bowman, Michael Shaner; **D:** Terence H. Winkless. MGM

Bloodfist 2 🎞️🎞️½ 1990 (R) Six of the world's toughest martial artists find themselves kidnapped and forced to do the bidding of the evil Su. The mysterious recluse stages a series of incredible fights between the experts and his own army of drugged warriors. 85m/C VHS, Beta, Closed Caption. Don "The Dragon" Wilson, Maurice Smith, James Warring, Timothy Baker, Richard Hill, Rina Reyes; **D:** Andy Blumenthal. MGM

Bloodfist 3: Forced to Fight 🎞️½ 1992 (R) Just as long as nobody's forced to watch, real-life world champion kickboxer Wilson thrashes his way through another showdown-at-the-arena plot. Better-than-average fight choreography. **CW:** Language, violence, and sensuality. 90m/C VHS. Don "The Dragon" Wilson, Richard Roundtree, Laura Stockman, Richard Paul, Rick Dean, Peter "Sugarfoot" Cunningham; **D:** Oley Sassone; **W:** Allison Burnett; **C:** Rick Bota; **M:** Nigel Holton. NHO

Bloodfist 4: Die Trying 🎞️½ 1992 (R) To rescue his daughter, a fighter must do battle with the FBI, the CIA, and an international arms cartel. **CW:** Language and violence. 86m/C VHS, LV. Don "The Dragon" Wilson, Catya Sassoon, Amanda Wyss, James Tolkan, Liz Torres; **D:** Paul Ziller. NHO

Bloodfist 5: Human Target 🎞️½ 1993 (R) When undercover FBI agent Jim Roth (Wilson) attempts to unravel an international arms deal he's found out and left for dead. He comes to with no memory only to find himself caught between the arms dealers and the FBI, who think he's turned double-agent. Both sides want Roth dead. ?m/C VHS. Don "The Dragon" Wilson, Denice Duff, Yuji Okumoto, Don Stark, Danny Lopez, Steve James, Michael Yama; **D:** Jeff Yonis; **W:** Jeff Yonis. NHO

Bloodfist 6: Ground Zero 🎞️½ 1994 (R) Nick Corrigan (Wilson) must battle terrorists who have a nuclear missile aimed at New York City. **CW:** Violence; language; nudity. 86m/C VHS, LV. Don "The Dragon" Wilson, Cat Sasson, Steve Garvey; **D:** Rick Jacobson. NHO

Bloodfist 7: Manhunt 🎞️🎞️ 1995 (R) Martial arts expert Jim Trudell is accused by corrupt cops of murder and is forced on the run while he tries to prove his innocence. **CW:** Brutal martial arts violence; some bloody shootings; scene of sexuality; strong language. 95m/C VHS. Don "The Dragon" Wilson, Jonathan Penner, Jillian McWhirter, Stephen Davies, Cyril O'Reilly, Eb Lottimer, Steven Williams; **D:** Jonathan Winfrey. NHO

Bloodhounds 🎞️🎞️ 1996 (R) Detective Harnos, who's skilled in the martial arts, reluctantly agrees to team up with writer Bernsen, whose specialty is criminal cases, to catch a killer. Made for cable. **CW:** Violent content. 86m/C VHS, Beta, Closed Caption. Corbin Bernsen, Christina Harnos, Marcus Flanagan, Gina Mastrogiacomo, James Pickens Jr., Kirk Baltz; **D:** Michael Katleman; **W:** Pablo F. Fenjves. PAR

Bloodhounds 2 🎞️🎞️ 1996 (PG-13) True-crime writer Harrison Coyle (Bersen) teams up with PI Nikki Cruz (Peeples) to nab serial killer Matthew Standing (Tracey), who hunts down convicted rapists he thinks haven't been punished enough. Turns out the killer is also a fan of Coyle's and begins contacting him about them writing a book together. Made for cable. **CW:** Violence and thematic elements. 89m/C VHS, Closed Caption. Corbin Bernsen, Nia Peeples, Ian Tracey, Amy Yasbeck, Jim Byrnes, Suki Kaiser, Tom Cavanagh. PAR

Bloodhounds of Broadway 🎞️🎞️½ 1989 (PG) A musical tribute to Damon Runyon, detailing the cliched adventures of an assortment of jazz-age crooks, flappers, chanteuses, and losers. 90m/C VHS, Beta, LV, Letterbox, Closed Caption. Madonna, Rutger Hauer, Randy Quaid, Matt Dillon, Jennifer Grey, Julie Hagerty, Esai Morales, Anita Morris, Josef Sommer, William S. Burroughs, Ethan Phillips, Stephen McHattie, Dinah Manoff, Googy Gress, Tony Azito, Tony Longo, Madeleine Potter; **D:** Howard Brookner; **W:** Howard Brookner, Colman DeKay; **C:** Elliot Davis; **M:** Jonathan Sheffer. COL

Bloodknot 🎞️🎞️ 1995 (R) The Reaves' are devastated when their son Martin is killed in a military accident. So they're an easy target when Kaye (Vernon) shows up, claiming to be Martin's girlfriend. Mom Evelyn (Kidder) and brother Tom (Dempsey) are only too eager to welcome Kaye into the family but it wouldn't be a thriller if devious Kaye didn't have some deadly ulterior motives. Made for cable. **CW:** Strong sexuality, language, and some violence. 98m/C VHS, Beta, Closed Caption. Patrick Dempsey, Kate Vernon, Margot Kidder, Craig Sheffer; **D:** Jorge Montesi; **W:** Randy Kornfield; **C:** Philip Linzey; **M:** Ian Thomas. PAR

Bloodlink 🎞️½ 1986 (R) A well-to-do doctor has a recurring nightmare about killing an elderly woman. This prompts him to explore his past, discovering that he was separated at birth from a twin brother. Naturally, only by searching frantically for his long-lost sibling can the good doctor hope to solve the mystery of the recurring nightmare. A somnolent tale indeed. 98m/C VHS, Beta. Michael Moriarty, Penelope Milford, Geraldine Fitzgerald, Cameron Mitchell, Sarah Langenfeld; **D:** Alberto De Martino. VTR

Bloodlust 🎞️ 1959 More teenagers fall prey to yet another mad scientist, who stores their dead bodies in glass tanks. Low-budget ripoff of "The Most Dangerous Game" and other such films. A must for Mike Brady (Robert Reed) fans though. 89m/B VHS. Wilton Graff, June Kennedy, Robert Reed, Lilyan Chauvin; **D:** Ralph Brooke; **W:** Ralph Brooke. SNC, NOS

Bloodlust: Subspecies 3 🎞️½ 1993 (R) Subspecies 3 Equally gory followup to "Bloodstone: Subspecies 2." Sadistic vampire Radu is still battling for Michelle's soul, this time against Michelle's sister Becky, aided by his disgusting Mummy and the demonic Subspecies. Castle Vladislas is awash is blood and Becky discovers more than Michelle's fate is at risk. **CW:** Gory vampire violence and some sexuality. 83m/C VHS, Beta, LV, Closed Caption. Anders Hove, Kevin Blair, Denice Duff, Pamela Gordon, Ion Haiduc, Michael DellaFemina; **D:** Ted Nicolaou; **W:** Ted Nicolaou. FLL

Bloodmatch 🎞️ 1991 (R) A whodunit, martial-arts-style: the "sleuth" kidnaps all the suspects in a corruption case and kickboxes each to death until somebody confesses. Not exactly Agatha Christie, and artsy camera moves fail to exploit the fancy footwork. **CW:** Language, pervasive violence, and strong sex scene. 85m/C VHS, LV, Closed Caption. Thom Mathews, Michel Qissi, Benny "The Jet" Urquidez, Marianne Taylor, Hope Marie Carlton, Dale Jacoby, Thunder Wolf, Vincent Klyn, Peter "Sugarfoot" Cunningham, Hector Pena; **D:** Albert Pyun; **W:** K. Mannah; **M:** Tony Riparetti. HBO

Bloodmoon woof! 1990 The setting is Australia but the sleazy story's all too familiar: an insane killer employs knives and other sharp objects to prevent sex-crazed students from getting past third base. 104m/C VHS, Beta, LV. AU Leon Lissek, Christine Amor, Ian Patrick Williams, Helen Thomson, Hazel Howson, Craig Cronin, Anya Molina; **D:** Alec Mills; **W:** Richard Brennan; **M:** Brian May. ART

Bloodmoon 🎞️½ 1997 A New York serial killer is quite a specialist—he only kills fighters, and he kills with his bare hands. So it's up to Ken O'Hara (Daniels), who specializes in tracking murderers, to find this guy before he kills again. 105m/C VHS. Gary Daniels, Chuck Jeffreys, Darren Shahlavi, Nina Repeta, Frank Gorshin, Jeffrey Pillars, Joe Hess; **D:** Tony Leung; **W:** Keith W. Strandberg; **C:** Derek M.K. Wan; **M:** Richard Yuen. BMG

Bloodshed 🎞️ 1983 (R) A psychotic harbors a girl's dead body, and systematically kills anyone who discovers his secret. 88m/C VHS, Beta. Laslo Papas, Beverly Ross; **D:** Richard Cassidy. NO

Bloodspell 🎞️ 1987 (R) A student with an evil power unleashes it on those who cross his path. 87m/C VHS, Beta. Anthony Jenkins, Aaron Teich, Alexandra Kennedy, John Reno; **D:** Deryn Warren. MCG

Bloodsport 🎞️½ 1988 (R) American soldier Van Damme endeavors to win the deadly Kumite, an outlawed martial arts competition in Hong Kong. Lots of kick-boxing action and the sound of bones cracking. 92m/C VHS, Beta, LV, Closed Caption. Jean-Claude Van Damme, Leah Ayres, Roy Chiao, Donald Gibb, Bolo Yeung, Norman Burton, Forest Whitaker; **D:** Newton Arnold; **W:** Christopher Cosby. WAR, TLF

Bloodsport 2: The Next Kumite 🎞️½ 1995 (R) Old-fashioned kickfest has Alex (Bernhardt) stealing antiquities in Thailand. He's left to take the fall by his partner in the theft of an ancient sword belonging to powerful businessman Leung (Morita) and is sent to a prison where sadistic head guard Demon (Han) takes an instant dislike to him. Alex learns about a sacred fighting competition, the Kumite, from wise prison sage Sun (Hong) and naturally, once Alex manages to get into the contest, his opponent is—you guessed it—Demon. **CW:** Non-stop martial arts violence. 87m/C VHS. Daniel Bernhardt, Ong Soo Han, Noriyuki "Pat" Morita, James Hong; **D:** Alan Mehrez. FEI

Bloodsport 3 🎞️½ 1995 Alex must avenge the death of his mentor and regain the Kumite sword. 92m/C VHS. Daniel Bernhardt, John Rhys-Davies, James Hong, Noriyuki "Pat" Morita; **D:** Alan Mehrez; **W:** James Williams. FEI

Bloodstalkers woof! 1976 Two vacationers in Florida meet up with a band of slaughtering, swamp-based lunatics. 91m/C VHS, Beta. Kenny Miller, Celea Ann Cole, Jerry Albert; **D:** Robert W. Morgan. THV

Bloodstone 🎞️🎞️ 1988 (PG-13) A couple honeymooning in the Middle East unexpectedly become involved in a jewel heist when they discover a valuable ruby amongst their luggage. Non-stop action and humor. 90m/C VHS, Beta. Charlie Brill, Christopher Neame, Jack Kehler, Brett Stimely; **D:** Dwight Little; **W:** Nico Mastorakis, Curt Allen. MCG

Bloodstone: Subspecies 2 🎞️½ 1992 (R) Subspecies 2 A gory sequel to "Subspecies" finds Radu the vampire pursuing the luscious Michelle. Radu gets some help from his ghoulish mother and yucky demonic spawn. Filmed on location in Romania. **CW:** Vampire violence. 107m/C VHS, LV, Closed Caption. Anders Hove, Denice Duff, Kevin Blair, Michael Denish, Pamela Gordon, Ion Haiduc; **D:** Ted Nicolaou; **W:** Ted Nicolaou. FLL

The Bloodsuckers 🎞️🎞️ Incense for the Damned; Doctors Wear Scarlet 1970 British horror tale set on a Greek Island. An Oxford don is seduced into an ancient vampire cult. Director Michael Burrowes replaces Hartford-Davis in the credits due to a dispute over post-production editing. 90m/C VHS, Beta. GB Patrick Macnee, Peter Cushing, Patrick Mower, Edward Woodward, Alex Davion, Imogen Hassall, Madeline Hinde, Johnny Sekka; **D:** Robert Hartford-Davis; **W:** Julian More; **C:** Desmond Dickinson. SNC

Bloodsuckers from Outer Space

woof! 1983 Via an alien invasion, Texas farmers becoming bloodsucking zombies. 80m/C VHS, Beta. Thom Meyer, Laura Ellis, Billie Keller, Kim Braden; **D:** Glenn Coburn. ORI, WAR

Bloodsucking Freaks

woof! *The Incredible Torture Show* 1975 (R) Virtually plotless Troma gagfest full of torture, cannibalistic dwarfs, and similar debaucheries, all played out on a Soho Grand Guignol stage (horror shows that allegedly contained real torture and death). Features "The Caged Sexoids," if that tells you anything (a cage of naked cannibal women tended by a dwarf). Not to mention the woman who has her brain sucked out through a straw. Filmed in "Ghoulovision" and originally rated X. Intolerable for most. 89m/C VHS, Beta, DVD. Seamus O'Brian, Niles McMaster; **D:** Joel M. Reed. VES

Bloodsucking Nazi Zombies

Oasis of the Zombies; Treasure of the Living Dead 1982 European students set out to find buried treasure in Saharan oasis but instead find bevy of hungry Nazis with eating disorders. 75m/C VHS, Beta. SP FR Manuel Gelin, France Jordan, Jeff Montgomery, Miriam Landson, Eric Saint-Just, Caroline Audret, Henry Lambert; **D:** Jess (Jesus) Franco, A.M. Frank; **W:** A. L. Mariaux. NO

Bloodsucking Pharoahs of Pittsburgh

woof! 1990 (R) Pittsburgh is plagued by crazed cannibals who think eternal life is in Pennsylvania. Two detectives on the case are mystified.**CW:** Language, strong violence, and sensuality. 89m/C VHS, Beta, Closed Caption. Jake Dengel, Joe Sharkey, Suzanne Fletcher, Beverly Penberthy, Shawn Elliott, Pat Logan, Jane Hamilton; **D:** Alan Smithee; **W:** Dean Tschetter. PAR, FCT

Bloody Avenger

1987 A trio of detectives search for a murderer in the streets of Philadelphia. 100m/C VHS, Beta. Jack Palance, George Eastman, Jenny Tamburi; **D:** Al Bradley. THV

Bloody Birthday

🐾½ *Creeps* 1980 (R) Three youngsters, bound together by their eerie birth during an eclipse (you know what that means), kill everyone around them that ever gave them problems. Typical "and the fun continues" ending; standard fare. 92m/C VHS, Beta. Susan Strasberg, Jose Ferrer, Lori Lethin, Melinda Cordell, Joe Penny, Ellen Geer, Julie Brown, Michael Dudikoff, Billy Jacoby, Elizabeth Hoy, Andy Freeman; **D:** Edward Hunt; **W:** Edward Hunt, Barry Pearson.

The Bloody Brood

woof! 1959 Really bad flick about a drug-dealing beatnik gang who commit nasty crimes, like feeding messenger boys hamburgers filled with ground glass. Yuck. 80m/C VHS. CA Jack Betts, Barbara Lord, Peter Falk, Robert Christie; **D:** Julian Hoffman. SNC, TPV

The Bloody Fight

🐾 197? Two young people learn the cost of courage and the high price of justice when they avenge a murderer. 90m/C VHS, Beta. Alan Tang, Yu In Yin, Tan Chin, Pai Ying, Lui Ran In; **D:** N.G. Tien Tsu. NO

Bloody Mama

🐾🐾½ 1970 (R) Corman's violent, trashy story of the infamous Barker Gang of the 30s, led by the bloodthirsty and sex-crazed Ma Barker (Winters, can't you just picture it?) and backed by her four perverted sons. De Niro is the space cadet sibling, Walden the homosexual ex-con, Stroud the sadistic mama lover, and Kimbrough the lady killer. They're joined by Walden's prison lover, Dern, who also has a thing for Ma Barker. Winters is a riot in this perverse stew of crime, violence, and, of course, sentimental blood bonding (the family that slays together, stays together). First of the Corman-produced (and sometimes directed) mama movies, followed by "Big Bad Mama" and "Crazy Mama". 90m/C VHS, Beta, LV. Shelley Winters, Robert De Niro, Don Stroud, Pat Hingle, Bruce Dern, Diane Varsi, Robert Walden, Clinton Kimbrough, Scatman Crothers; **D:** Roger Corman; **C:** John A. Alonzo. VES, ART

Bloody Moon

woof! *Die Saage des Todes* 1983 Tourists are being brutally attacked and murdered during a small Spanish village's Festival of the Moon. 84m/C VHS, Beta. GE Olivia Pascal, Christopher Brugger, Ann-Beate Engelke, Antonia Garcia, Nadja Gerganoff, Corinna Gillwald, Jasmin Losensky, Maria Rubio, Alexander Waechter; **D:** Jess (Jesus) Franco; **W:** Jess (Jesus) Franco, Rayo Casablanca; **C:** Juan Soler. TWE

Bloody New Year

🐾 *Time Warp Terror* 1987 (R) Corpses stalk the living as a group of teens happen upon an impromptu New Year's Eve party on a deserted island. Auld acquaintance shouldn't be forgot, just this flick. 90m/C VHS, Beta. **D:** Norman J. Warren.

The Bloody Pit of Horror

🐾½ *Crimson Executioner; The Red Hangman* 1965 While wife Jayne Mansfield was in Italy filming "Primitive Love," bodybuilder Hargitay starred in this sado-horror epic. He owns a castle that is visited by a group of models for a special shoot. While in the dungeon, Hargitay becomes possessed by the castle's former owner, a sadist, and begins torturing the models. Supposedly based on the writings of the Marquis de Sade. 87m/B VHS. IT Mickey Hargitay, Louise Barrett, Walter Brandi, Moa Thai, Ralph Zucker, Albert Gordon; **D:** Max (Massimo Pupillo) Hunter. SNC

Bloody Trail

🐾 1972 A Union soldier who chooses the recently pummeled South as the venue for postwar R-and-R is, for some reason, pursued by Confederates. And his good ol' boy pursuers don't have a sudden change of heart when he teams up with a former slave. Lots of violence and nudity; little plot and entertainment. 91m/C VHS. Paul Harper, Rance Howard, John Mitchum; **D:** Richard Robinson.

The Bloody Vampire

🐾½ 1962 Atmospheric and chilling Mexican vampire film. Sequel to "Invasion of the Vampires." ?m/C VHS. MX Carlos Agosti. SNC

Bloody Wednesday

🐾🐾½ 1987 It's sanity check-out time when a hotel caretaker is driven mad by tormentors...or is he driving himself mad? What is it about vacant hotels that make men lose their minds? If you can remove "The Shining" from yours, this flick's worthwhile. 89m/C VHS, Beta. Raymond Elmendorf, Pamela Baker, Navarre Perry; **D:** Mark Gilhuis; **W:** Philip Yordan; **M:** Al Sendry.

Blossoms in the Dust

🐾🐾 1941 The true story of Edna Gladney is told as she starts the Texas Children's Home and Aid Society of Fort Worth. Major league Garson tear-jerker. 100m/B VHS, Beta, Closed Caption. Greer Garson, Walter Pidgeon, Felix Bressart, Marsha Hunt, Fay Holden, Samuel S. Hinds, Kathleen Howard; **D:** Mervyn LeRoy. Academy Awards '41: Best Interior Decoration; Nominations: Academy Awards '41: Best Actress (Garson), Best Color Cinematography, Best Picture. MGM

The Blot

🐾🐾 1921 A story about a poorly paid professor and his family, whose lifestyle contrasts with that of an affluent neighbor, a butcher. 55m/B VHS, Beta. Louis Calhern, Claire Windsor; **D:** Lois Weber. GPV, GVV, DVT

Blow Out

🐾🐾🐾 1981 (R) When a prominent senator is killed in a car crash, a sound effects engineer becomes involved in political intrigue as he tries to expose a conspiracy with the evidence he has gathered. An intricate mystery and homage to Antonioni's "Blow-Up." 108m/C VHS, Beta, LV. John Travolta, Nancy Allen, John Lithgow, Dennis Franz; **D:** Brian DePalma; **W:** Brian DePalma; **C:** Vilmos Zsigmond; **M:** Pino Donaggio. WAR, OM

Blow-Up

🐾🐾🐾½ 1966 A young London photographer takes some pictures of a couple in the park and finds out he may have recorded evidence of a murder. Though marred by badly dated 1960s modishness, this is Antonioni's most accessible film, a sophisticated treatise on perception and the film-consumer-as-voyeur, brilliantly assembled and wrought. 111m/C VHS, Beta, LV, Letterbox. GB IT David Hemmings, Vanessa Redgrave, Sarah Miles, Jane Birkin, Veruschka; **D:** Michelangelo Antonioni; **W:** Tonino Guerra, Michelangelo Antonioni; **C:**

Carlo DiPalma, **M:** Herbie Hancock. Cannes Film Festival '67: Best Film; National Society of Film Critics Awards '66: Best Director (Antonioni), Best Film; Nominations: Academy Awards '66: Best Director (Antonioni), Best Story & Screenplay. MGM, FCT

Blowing Wild

🐾½ 1954 Filmed in Mexico, this Quinn-Stanwyck-Cooper love triangle, set in the early thirties, speaks of lust and vengeance, rashness and greed. Stanwyck, married to oil tycoon Quinn, lusts after one-time lover wildcatter Cooper. 92m/B VHS, LV. Gary Cooper, Barbara Stanwyck, Anthony Quinn, Ruth Roman, Ward Bond; **D:** Hugo Fregonese; **W:** Philip Yordan. REP, FCT

Blown Away

🐾 1990 (R) A mafia wife goes up against her husband in order to retrieve her kidnapped child.**CW:** Language, violence, and strong sexuality. 92m/C VHS, Beta. Loni Anderson, John Heard, James Naughton; **D:** Michael Miller.

Blown Away

🐾½ 1993 (R) Haim and Feldman are brothers working at a ski resort where Haim falls for rich teenager Eggert. She's a young femme fatale who manages to get Haim all hot and bothered but she's actually using the unsuspecting dupe in a murder plot. Also available in an unrated version at 93 minutes. 91m/C VHS, LV, Closed Caption. Nicole Eggert, Corey Haim, Corey Feldman. ART

Blown Away

🐾🐾 1994 (R) Boston Irish bomb-squad cop Jimmy Dove (Bridges) is after former compatriot Ryan Gaerity (Jones), an Irish radical who's taken his bombing expertise onto Jimmy's new turf. Meanwhile, Jimmy wants to keep his unsavory past from unsuspecting wife Amis. Real life dad Lloyd plays Jeff's uncle. While Jones seems adequately obsessed with making things go boom and Bridges significantly concerned that they don't, thriller moves on predictable path toward explosive climax. Special effects create the suspense, as everyday objects become lethal in Gaerity's knowledgeable hands. The final explosion was more than even the special effects coordinator desired—windows were unintentionally blown out in nearby buildings.**CW:** Some language and violence. 121m/C VHS, LV, Letterbox, Closed Caption. Jeff Bridges, Tommy Lee Jones, Suzy Amis, Lloyd Bridges, Forest Whitaker; **D:** Stephen Hopkins; **W:** Joe Batteer, John Rice; **C:** Gregory McClatchy. Nominations: MTV Movie Awards '95: Best Villain (Jones), Best Action Sequence. MGM

Blue

🐾 1968 A dull western about an American boy (Stamp) raised by Mexicans who doesn't trust another living soul until he finds himself face to face with his former gang, led by his adoptive father (Montalban). 113m/C VHS, Closed Caption. Terence Stamp, Joanna Pettet, Karl Malden, Ricardo Montalban, Joe De Santis, Sally Kirkland; **D:** Silvio Narizzano; **W:** Ronald M. Cohen; **M:** Manos Hadjidakis. PAR

Blue

🐾🐾 1993 (R) Meditation/memoir of director Jarman's deteriorating AIDS condition consists of narration and a soundtrack set against an unvaried blue screen. Jarman ponders the associations with the color blue (sky, ocean, blindness, heaven, eternity) and his own physical problems, alternately expressed with dreamy vagueness or incendiary contempt. Limited in appeal, depending highly on boredom tolerance and ability to suspend visual expectations.**CW:** Some sexuality. 76m/C VHS. GB **D:** Derek Jarman; **W:** Derek Jarman; **M:** Simon Fisher Turner. KIV

The Blue and the Gray

🐾🐾 1985 Epic television mini-series about love and hate inflamed by the Civil War. Keach plays a Pinkerton's secret service agent in this loosely based historical romance. The uncut version is available on three cassettes; the 295 minute version is on two cassettes. 398m/C VHS, Beta, LV. Gregory Peck, Lloyd Bridges, Colleen Dewhurst, Stacy Keach, John Hammond, Sterling Hayden, Warren Oates; **D:** Andrew V. McLaglen; **M:** Bruce Broughton. COL, TVC, FCT

The Blue Angel 🎭🎭🎭🎭 *Der Blaue Engel* 1930 Tale of a man stripped of his dignity. A film classic filled with sensuality and decay, which made Dietrich a European star and led to her discovery in Hollywood. When a repressed professor (Jannings) goes to a nightclub hoping to catch some of his students in the wrong, he's taken by Lola, the sultry singer portrayed by Dietrich. After spending the night with her, losing his job, and then marrying her, he goes on tour with the troupe, peddling indiscreet photos of his wife. Versions were shot in both German and English, with the German version sporting English subtitles. ♫Falling in Love Again; They Call Me Wicked Lola. 90m/B VHS, Beta, 8mm. **GE** Marlene Dietrich; Emil Jannings; Kurt Gerron; Rosa Valetti; Hans Albers; **D:** Josef von Sternberg; **W:** Karl Vollmoller, Robert Liebmann, Carl Zuckmayer; **M:** Friedrich Hollander. *NOS, FCT, BAR*

The Blue Bird 🎭🎭🎭 1940 (G) A weird, dark fantasy about two children who search for the blue bird of happiness in various fantasy lands, but find it eventually at home. Overlooked and impressively fatalistic. 98m/C VHS, Beta, Closed Caption. Shirley Temple, Gale Sondergaard, John Russell, Eddie Collins, Nigel Bruce, Jessie Ralph, Spring Byington, Sybil Jason; **D:** Walter Lang; **C:** Arthur C. Miller. Nominations: Academy Awards '40: Best Color Cinematography. *MLB*

Blue Blazes Rawden 1918 Hart plays a lumberjack who gains control of a local saloon after shooting its villainous proprietor. ?m/B VHS, Beta, 8mm. William S. Hart. *GPV, GVV*

Blue Blood 🎭 1973 A demonic butler inflicts nightmares upon a family to gain possession of its mansion. 90m/C VHS, Beta. **GB** Oliver Reed, Derek Jacobi, Fiona Lewis; **D:** Andrew Sinclair. *NO*

Blue Canadian Rockies 🎭½ 1952 Autry's employer sends him to Canada to discourage his daughter from marrying a fortune hunter. The daughter has turned the place into a dude ranch and wild game preserve. When Autry arrives, he encounters some mysterious killings. 58m/B VHS, Beta. Gene Autry, Pat Buttram, Gail Davis, Ross Ford, Tom London; **D:** George Archainbaud. *CCB*

Blue Chips 🎭🎭½ 1994 (PG-13) Nolte does Bobby Knight in this saga of Western U basketball coach Pete Bell, suffering through his first losing season. What follows is a tug of war between rich alumni who want to win at any cost and his ethics as he recruits for a new season. Larger than life hoopster O'Neal's film debut. McDonnell and Woodard are merely afterthoughts, but look for cameos from many real life b-ballers, including Dick Vitale and Larry Bird. Average script is bolstered by exciting game footage, shot during real games for authenticity.**CW:** Profanity. 108m/C VHS, Beta, LV, Letterbox, Closed Caption. Nick Nolte, Shaquille O'Neal, Mary McDonnell, Ed O'Neill, J.T. Walsh, Alfre Woodard; **Cameos:** Larry Bird, Bobby Knight, Rick Pitino; **D:** William Friedkin; **W:** Ron Shelton; **M:** Nile Rodgers, Jeff Beck, Jed Leiber. *PAR*

Blue City 🎭½ 1986 (R) A young man returns to his Florida hometown to find his father murdered, and subsequently vows to solve and avenge the matter. Based on a Ross MacDonald thriller. 83m/C VHS, Beta, LV, Closed Caption. Judd Nelson, Ally Sheedy, Paul Winfield, Anita Morris, David Caruso, Julie Carmen, Scott Wilson; **D:** Michelle Manning; **W:** Walter Hill, Lukas Heller; **M:** Ry Cooder. *PAR*

Blue Collar 🎭🎭🎭 1978 (R) An auto assembly line worker, tired of the poverty of his life, hatches a plan to rob his own union. A study of the working class and the robbing of the human spirit. 114m/C VHS, Beta, LV. Richard Pryor, Harvey Keitel, Yaphet Kotto, Ed Begley Jr.; **D:** Paul Schrader; **W:** Paul Schrader, Leonard Schrader; **M:** Jack Nitzsche. *USH, FCT*

Blue Country 🎭🎭½ *Le Pays Bleu* 1977 (PG) A joyful romantic comedy about a pair of free souls who leave their stagnant lives behind to seek out a more idyllic existence. Subtitled in English. 104m/C VHS, Beta. **FR** Brigitte Fossey, Jacques Serres, Ginette Garcin, Armand Meffre, Ginette Mathieu,

Roger Crouzet; **D:** Jean-Charles Tacchella; **W:** Jean-Charles Tacchella; **C:** Edmond Sechan; **M:** Gerard Anfosso. *COL*

The Blue Dahlia 🎭🎭🎭½ 1946 Classic film noir finds Navy vet Johnny Morrison (Ladd) returning home to discover his wife Helen (Dowling) has been keeping the home fires burning—with Eddie Harwood (Da Silva), owner of the Blue Dahlia nightclub. After a nasty fight, Johnny takes off and is picked up by sultry blonde Joyce (Lake). The next day Johnny discovers he's wanted by the cops for the murder of his wife and decides to hide out until he can find the real killer, with Joyce's help. Very stylish and fast-paced with excellent performances; Chandler's first original screenplay. 100m/B VHS, Closed Caption. Alan Ladd, Veronica Lake, William Bendix, Howard da Silva, Doris Dowling, Tom Powers, Hugh Beaumont, Howard Freeman, Don Costello; **D:** George Marshall; **W:** Raymond Chandler; **C:** Lionel Lindon; **M:** Victor Young. Nominations: Academy Awards '46: Best Original Screenplay.*USH*

Blue De Ville 🎭🎭 1986 (PG) Two young women buy a '59 Cadillac and journey from St. Louis to New Mexico, having adventures on the way. The rambling, free-spirited movie was a pilot for a prospective series that never set sail—but when "Thelma & Louise" hit big this superficially similar item was hauled out on video. 96m/C VHS, Closed Caption. Jennifer Runyon, Kimberly Pistone, Mark Thomas Miller, Alan Autry, Robert Prescott; **D:** Jim Johnston. *THV*

Blue Desert 🎭🎭🎭 1991 (R) Cox is strong in her performance as Lisa Roberts, a comic book artist who leaves New York City for small town Arizona life after surviving a traumatic rape. Once there, she's befriended by Sheffer and Sweeney, a local cop. Battersby does a good job of keeping the suspense level high (in his directorial debut) as Cox finds that there's danger in small towns, too. Fine performances keep this slightly above average.**CW:** Sexual scene. 98m/C VHS, Beta. D.B. Sweeney, Courteney Cox, Craig Sheffer, Philip Baker Hall, Sandy Ward; **D:** Bradley Battersby; **W:** Bradley Battersby, Arthur Collis; **M:** Jerry Goldsmith.

Blue Fin 🎭🎭 1978 (PG) When their tuna boat is shipwrecked, and the crew disabled, a young boy and his father learn lessons of love and courage as the son tries to save the ship. 93m/C VHS, Beta. **AU** Hardy Kruger, Greg Rowe; **D:** Carl Schultz; **C:** Geoff Burton.

Blue Fire Lady 🎭🎭 1978 The heartwarming story of a young girl and her love of horses which endures even her father's disapproval. Good family fare. 96m/C VHS, Beta. Cathryn Harrison, Mark Holden, Peter Cummins.

Blue Flame 🎭🎭 1993 (R) Vigilante cop is hired to track down two humanoid aliens who have escaped captivity in futuristic L.A. They evade him by time-traveling through alternate realities, infiltrating the cop's mind, and using his fantasies against him. 88m/C VHS, Beta. Brian Wimmer, Ian Buchanan, Kerri Green, Cecilia Peck, Jad Mager; **D:** Cassian Elwes; **W:** Cassian Elwes. *COL*

Blue Hawaii 🎭🎭 1962 (PG) A soldier, returning to his Hawaiian home, defies his parents by taking a job with a tourist agency. Presley sings "Can't Help Falling in Love." For Elvis fans. 101m/C VHS, Beta, LV. Elvis Presley, Angela Lansbury, Joan Blackman, Roland Winters, Iris Adrian, John Archer, Steve Brodie; **D:** Norman Taurog; **W:** Hal Kanter. *FOX, MVD*

Blue Heaven 🎭 1984 A couple struggles through problems with their marriage and alcohol abuse. 100m/C VHS, Beta. Leslie Denniston, James Eckhouse; **D:** Kathleen Dowdey. *VES, ART*

The Blue Hour 🎭🎭 1991 Theo is a Berlin hustler whose business is so good he can pick his clients. Marie, his next-door neighbor, lives with her boyfriend Paul until he just walks out one day. Marie is shattered and refuses to leave her apartment until Theo takes an interest in her plight. Just when it seems that the improbable couple

could find true love, Paul comes back. In German with English subtitles. 87m/C VHS. **GE** Andreas Herder, Dina Leipzig, Cyrill Rey-Coquais; **D:** Marcel Gisler. *WBF, FCT*

Blue Ice 🎭🎭½ 1992 (R) Harry Anders (Caine) is an ex-spy with an eye for the ladies and a loyalty to his friends. When his friends start winding up dead, Harry decides to investigate—a very dangerous decision, especially when a mysterious woman (Young) takes an interest. Made for cable television.**CW:** Strong language, nudity, and violence. 96m/C VHS, LV, Closed Caption. Michael Caine, Sean Young, Ian Bannen, Bob Hoskins; **D:** Russell Mulcahy; **W:** Ron Hutchinson; **M:** Michael Kamen. *HBO*

Blue Iguana 🎭🎭 1988 (R) An inept bounty hunter travels south of the border to recover millions from a crooked South American bank, and meets up with sexy women, murderous thugs, and corruption. 88m/C VHS, Beta, LV, Closed Caption. Dylan McDermott, Jessica Harper, James Russo, Dean Stockwell, Pamela Gidley, Tovah Feldshuh; **D:** John Lafia. *PAR*

Blue in the Face 🎭🎭½ 1995 (R) Wang and Auster's immediate follow-up to "Smoke," shot in five days, recycles the same Brooklyn cigar shop setting and contains a dozen fast-paced, loosely scripted or wholly improvised scenes that they couldn't cram into "Smoke," led by Reed's deadpan riff on eyewear, New York, and smoking. The action again centers around Auggie (Keitel), the shop manager, who hangs out with the mostly eccentric, and sometimes famous clientele. Jarmusch idly waxes philosophic on smoking technique, while puffing on what he claims is his last. Scenes are woven together with videotaped interviews from actual Brooklyn residents, creating a tribute to life in the borough with a documentary feel. Improv lovers will enjoy watching what sometimes seems more like outtakes than finished performances.**CW:** Language; scene of nudity. 83m/C VHS, LV, Closed Caption. Harvey Keitel, Lou Reed, Michael J. Fox, Roseanne, Jim Jarmusch, Lily Tomlin, Mel Gorham, Jared Harris, Giancarlo Esposito, Victor Argo, Madonna, Keith David, Mira Sorvino, Malik Yoba; **D:** Wayne Wang, Paul Auster; **W:** Wayne Wang, Paul Auster. *TOU*

Blue Jeans 🎭🎭½ 1978 A young French boy experiences sexual awakening and humiliation in a British school. In French with English subtitles. 80m/C VHS, Beta. **FR D:** Hugues des Roziers. *FCT*

Blue Jeans and Dynamite 🎭🎭 198? A stuntman is hired to lift the "Golden Mask of the Duct Tomb" and is followed on land, water, and air. Great chase scenes and action-filled finale. 90m/C VHS. Robert Vaughn, Simon Andrew, Katia Kristine. *NO*

The Blue Kite 🎭🎭🎭 1993 Fifteen years of political and cultural upheaval in China is shown through the eyes of young troublemaker Tietou, who certainly earns his nickname of "Iron Head" after his 1954 birth. Soon his father is sent to a labor reform camp and his mother remarries—only to be faced with more struggles as the years go by. The kite is Tietou's cherished toy, which keeps getting lost or destroyed but is always being rebuilt, offering one token of hope. Chinese with subtitles. 138m/C VHS. **CH** Lu Liping, Zhang Wenyao, Pu Quanxin; **D:** Tian Zhuangzhuang; **W:** Xiao Mao. Nominations: Independent Spirit Awards '95: Best Foreign Film. *KIV*

The Blue Knight 🎭🎭½ 1975 Kennedy brings energy and care to this basically standard story. Policeman waiting for retirement searches for his partner's killer. Unexceptional treatment made palatable by actors. Made for television movie. 72m/C VHS. George Kennedy, Alex Rocco, Glynn Turman, Verna Bloom, Michael Margotta, Seth Arnold; **D:** J. Lee Thompson. *ART*

The Blue Lagoon woof! 1980 (R) Useless remake of 1949 film of the same name. An adolescent boy and girl marooned on a desert isle discover love (read: sex) without the restraints of society. Not too explicit, but nonetheless intellectually offensive. Gorgeous photography of island paradise is wasted on this Shields vehicle. **105m/C VHS, Beta, LV.** Brooke Shields, Christopher Atkins, Leo McKern, William Daniels; *D:* Randal Kleiser; *C:* Nestor Almendros; *M:* Basil Poledouris. Golden Raspberry Awards '80: Worst Actress (Shields); Nominations: Academy Awards '80: Best Cinematography. *FCT*

The Blue Lamp 🎟🎟🎟 **1949** Action-adventure fans familiar with the hoary plot where a cop must avenge the wrongful death of his partner will appreciate this suspenseful British detective effort. It's one of the very first in the genre to explore buddy cop revenge in a very British sort of way. Also sports a concluding chase scene which has stood the test of time. Led to the long-running British TV series "Dixon of Dock Green." **84m/B VHS.** *GB* Dirk Bogarde, Jimmy Hanley, Jack Warner, Bernard Lee, Robert Flemyng, Patric Doonan, Bruce Seton, Frederick Piper, Betty Ann Davies, Peggy Evans; *D:* Basil Dearden. British Academy Awards '50: Best Film. *FCT*

The Blue Light 🎟🎟🎟 *Das Blaue Licht* **1932** Fairy-tale love story, based on an Italian fable about a mysterious woman, thought to be a witch, and a painter. Riefenstahl's first film which brought her to the attention of Adolf Hitler, who requested she make films glorifying the Nazi Party. In German with English subtitles. **77m/B VHS, Beta.** *GE* Leni Riefenstahl, Matthias Wieman, Max Holsboer; *D:* Leni Riefenstahl; *W:* Leni Riefenstahl. *VYY, MRV, FCT*

The Blue Lightning 🎟🎟½ **1986** Investigator Elliott travels to Australia to retrieve the priceless Blue Lightening gem. He must fight the crime lord in his Aussie encampment. Nice scenery, but unexceptional television story. **95m/C VHS.** Sam Elliott, Rebecca Gilling, Robert Culp, John Meillon, Robert Coleby, Max Phipps; *D:* Lee Philips.

The Blue Max 🎟🎟½ **1966** During WWI a young German, fresh out of aviation training school, competes for the coveted "Blue Max" flying award with other members of a squadron of seasoned flyers from aristocratic backgrounds. Based on a novel by Jack D. Hunter. **155m/C VHS, Beta, LV, Letterbox.** George Peppard, James Mason, Ursula Andress; *D:* John Guillermin; *M:* Jerry Goldsmith. *FOX*

Blue Money 🎟🎟 **1984** A wild, comedic caper film about a cab-driving nightclub impressionist who absconds with a briefcase packed with cash and is pursued by everyone, even the I.R.A. Originally made for British television. **82m/C VHS, Beta.** *GB* Tim Curry, Dabby Bishop, Billy Connolly, Frances Tomelty; *D:* Colin Bucksey. *NO*

Blue Monkey 🎟 *Green Monkey* **1987 (R)** A mysterious alien plant impregnates a man, who gives birth to a huge, man-eating insect larva. It subsequently grows up into a giant bug, and roams around a quarantined hospital looking for patients to eat. What made you think it had anything to do with monkeys? **97m/C VHS, Beta.** Steve Railsback, Susan Anspach, Gwynyth Walsh, John Vernon, Joe Flaherty; *D:* William Fruet. *COL*

Blue Movies woof! **1988 (R)** A couple of jerks try their hand at making porn films with predictable results. **92m/C VHS, Beta.** Larry Linville, Lucinda Crosby, Steve Levitt, Darien Mathias, Larry Poindexter; *D:* Paul Koval.

Blue Murder at St. Trinian's 🎟🎟🎟 **1956** The second of the madcap British comedy series (based on cartoons by Ronald Searle) about an incredibly ferocious pack of schoolgirls. This time they travel to the European continent and make life miserable for a jewel thief. Highlight: fantasy sequence in ancient Rome showing the girls thrown to the lions—and scaring the lions. **86m/B VHS.** *GB* Joyce Grenfell, Terry-Thomas, George Cole, Alastair Sim, Lionel Jeffries, Thorley Walters; *D:* Frank Launder; *M:* Malcolm Arnold. *VYY, VDM, FUS*

Blue Paradise woof! **1986** A depiction of Adam and Eve as they peruse the primal landscape and each other. **90m/C VHS, Beta.** Mark Gregory, Andrea Goldman. *TWE, MLB*

Blue River 🎟🎟½ 1995 (PG-13) Flashbacks highlight this saga of a troubled family. Successful doctor Edward Sellers (McDonough) is dismayed when his derelict older brother Lawrence (O'Connell), whom he hasn't seen in 15 years, suddenly appears on his doorstep. A gifted teenager, Lawrence once built his world around science and logic after their father deserted the family but his only purpose turns out to be getting even with everyone he feels has betrayed him. Young Edward (Stahl) tried to be the "good" son, while Mom (Dey) retreated into religion and an affair with self-righteously nasty school principal Henry Howland (Elliott). TV adaptation of the novel by Ethan Canin. *CW:* Thematic material, sensuality and a scene of violence. **90m/C VHS.** Jerry O'Connell, Nick Stahl, Susan Dey, Sam Elliott, Neal McDonough, Jean Marie Barnwell, Patrick Renna; *D:* Larry Elikann; *W:* Maria Nation; *C:* Eric Van Haren Noman; *M:* Lawrence Shragge. *HMK*

Blue Skies 🎟🎟🎟 **1946** Former dancer turned radio personality Astaire flashes back to his friendship with singer Crosby and the gal (Caulfield) that came between them. Flimsy plot is just an excuse for some 20 Irving Berlin songs and Astaire's split-screen dance number, "Puttin' on the Ritz." 🎵 All By Myself; Always; Any Bonds Today?; Blue Skies; A Couple of Song and Dance Men; Everybody Step; Getting Nowhere; Heat Wave; I'll See You in C-U-B-A. **104m/C VHS, LV, Closed Caption.** Fred Astaire, Bing Crosby, Joan Caulfield, Billy DeWolfe, Olga San Juan, Frank Faylen; *D:* Stuart Heisler; *W:* Arthur Sheekman; *C:* Charles B(ryant) Lang. Nominations: Academy Awards '46: Best Song ("You Keep Coming Back Like a Song"), Scoring of a Musical. *USH*

Blue Skies Again 🎟½ **1983 (PG)** Spunky young woman determined to play major league baseball locks horns with the chauvinistic owner and the gruff manager of her favorite team. **91m/C VHS, Beta.** Robyn Barto, Harry Hamlin, Mimi Rogers, Kenneth McMillan, Dana Elcar, Andy Garcia; *D:* Richard Michaels. *WAR*

Blue Sky 🎟🎟🎟 **1991 (PG-13)** Carly Marshall (Lange) is an irrepressible beauty, long married to adoring but uptight military scientist Hank (Jones). Things are barely in control when they're stationed in Hawaii but after Hank's transfer to a backwater base in Alabama, Carly's emotional mood swings go wildly out of control. Hell truly breaks loose when Carly attracts the attention of the camp's commander (Boothe), who's only too willing to take advantage. Set in 1962, a nuclear radiation subplot (Hank's new project) proves a minor distraction. Exceptional performance by Lange with Jones providing a quiet counterpoint as a man still deeply in love with his disturbed wife. Director Richardson's final film. Release date was delayed to 1994 due to Orion's financial problems. *CW:* Glimpse of nudity; strong language; sexual situations; some violence. **101m/C VHS, LV, Closed Caption.** Jessica Lange, Tommy Lee Jones, Powers Boothe, Carrie Snodgress, Amy Locane, Chris O'Donnell, Mitchell Ryan, Dale Dye; *D:* Tony Richardson; *M:* Jack Nitzsche. Academy Awards '94: Best Actress (Lange); Golden Globe Awards '95: Best Actress—Drama (Lange); Los Angeles Film Critics Association Awards '94: Best Actress (Lange); Nominations: Screen Actors Guild Award '94: Best Actress (Lange). *ORI*

Blue Steel 🎟🎟 **1934** A young Wayne saves a town from financial ruin by leading the citizens to a gold strike. Also available with "Man From Utah" on laserdisc. **59m/B VHS, Beta, LV.** John Wayne, George "Gabby" Hayes; *D:* Robert North Bradbury. *COL, NOS, MRV*

Blue Steel 🎟🎟 **1990 (R)** Director Bigelow's much-heralded, proto-feminist cop thriller. A serious female rookie's gun falls into the hands of a Wall Street psycho who begins a killing spree. Action film made silly with over-anxious sub-text and patriarchy-directed rage. **102m/C VHS, Beta, LV, 8mm, Closed Caption.** Jamie Lee Curtis, Ron Silver, Clancy Brown, Louise Fletcher, Philip Bosco, Elizabeth Pena,

Tom Sizemore; *D:* Kathryn Bigelow; *W:* Kathryn Bigelow, Eric Red; *M:* Brad Fiedel. *MGM*

Blue Sunshine 🎟🎟½ **1978 (R)** A certain brand of L.S.D. called Blue Sunshine starts to make its victims go insane. **94m/C VHS, Beta.** Zalman King, Deborah Winters, Mark Goddard, Robert Walden, Charles Siebert, Ann Cooper, Ray Young, Alice Ghostley; *D:* Jeff Lieberman; *W:* Jeff Lieberman. *VES*

Blue Thunder 🎟🎟½ **1983 (R)** Police helicopter pilot Scheider is chosen to test an experimental high-tech chopper that can see through walls, record a whisper, and level a city block. Seems anti-terrorist supercopter is needed to ensure security during 1984 Olympics. Bothered by Vietnam flashbacks, Scheider then battles wacky McDowell in the skies over L.A. High-techy police drama with satisfying aerial combat scenes nearly crashes with storyline. **110m/C VHS, Beta, LV, Letterbox, Closed Caption.** Roy Scheider, Daniel Stern, Malcolm McDowell, Candy Clark, Warren Oates; *D:* John Badham; *W:* Dan O'Bannon, Don Jakoby; *C:* John A. Alonzo. Nominations: Academy Awards '83: Best Film Editing. *COL*

Blue Tiger 🎟🎟 **1994 (R)** Gina Hayes (Madsen) is shopping with her young son when a masked gunman enters the store and opens fire. When Gina realizes her son has been killed she becomes obsessed with finding the assailant. Her one clue—a blue tiger tattoo. *CW:* Language; some sexuality; strong, brutal violence. **88m/C VHS, LV, Closed Caption.** Virginia Madsen, Toru Nakamura, Harry Dean Stanton, Ryo Ishibashi; *D:* Norberto Barba; *W:* Joel Soisson. *COL*

Blue Tornado 🎟 **1990 (PG-13)** An eerie bright light, emitted from a mountain, makes supersonic jets disappear into thin air. A beautiful researcher and a cocky pilot set out to solve the mystery. Better-than-average aerial sequences don't make up for goofy story and ludicrous dialogue. **96m/C VHS.** Dirk Benedict, Patsy Kensit, Ted McGinley, David Warner; *D:* Tony B. Dobb. *THV*

Blue Velvet 🎟🎟🎟 **1986 (R)** Disturbing, unique exploration of the dark side of American suburbia, involving an innocent college youth who discovers a severed ear in an empty lot, and is thrust into a turmoil of depravity, murder, and sexual deviance. Brutal, grotesque, and unmistakably Lynch; an immaculately made, fiercely imagined film that is unlike any other. Mood is enhanced by the Badalamenti soundtrack. Graced by splashes of Lynchian humor, most notably the movie's lumber theme. Hopper is riveting as the chief sadistic nutcase and Twin Peaks' MacLachlan is a study in loss of innocence. **121m/C VHS, Beta, LV, Letterbox, Closed Caption.** Brad Dourif, Kyle MacLachlan, Isabella Rossellini, Dennis Hopper, Laura Dern, Hope Lange, Jack Nance, Dean Stockwell, George Dickerson, Priscilla Pointer; *D:* David Lynch; *W:* David Lynch; *C:* Frederick Elmes; *M:* Angelo Badalamenti. Independent Spirit Awards '87: Best Actress (Rossellini); Los Angeles Film Critics Association Awards '86: Best Director (Lynch), Best Supporting Actor (Hopper); Montreal World Film Festival '86: Best Supporting Actor (Hopper); National Society of Film Critics Awards '86: Best Cinematography, Best Director (Lynch), Best Film, Best Supporting Actor (Hopper); Nominations: Academy Awards '86: Best Director (Lynch). *WAR*

The Blue Yonder 🎟½ *Time Flyers* **1986** In this made-for-video feature, a young boy travels back in time to meet the grandfather he never knew, risking historical integrity. **89m/C VHS, Beta, Closed Caption.** Art Carney, Peter Coyote, Huckleberry Fox; *D:* Mark Rosman. *DIS*

Bluebeard 🎟🎟½ **1944** Tormented painter with a psychopathic urge to strangle his models is the basis for this effective, low-budget film. One of Carradine's best vehicles. **73m/B VHS, Beta.** John Carradine, Jean Parker, Nils Asther; *D:* Edgar G. Ulmer. *NOS, MRV, SNC*

Bluebeard 🎟🎟🎟 *Landru* **1963** French biography of Henri-Desire Landru, who seduced and murdered 11 women and was subsequently beheaded. Dubbed into English. **108m/C VHS, Beta.** *FR*

Charles Denner, Danielle Darrieux, Michele Morgan, Hildegarde Neff; **D:** Claude Chabrol. *NLC*

Bluebeard 🎬½ **1972 (R)** Lady killer Burton knocks off series of beautiful wives in soporific remake of the infamous story. **128m/C VHS.** Richard Burton, Raquel Welch, Joey Heatherton, Nathalie Delon, Virna Lisi, Sybil Danning; **D:** Edward Dmytryk; **M:** Ennio Morricone. *ART*

Bluebeard's Eighth Wife 🎬🎬 **1938** Problematic comedy set on the French Riviera about a spoiled millionaire (Cooper) who's been married seven times and wants to go for eight with Colbert, the daughter of a destitute aristocrat. Good for a few laughs, but Coop seemed out of place in his role. Based on the play by Alfred Savoir, American version by Charlton Andrews. **86m/B VHS, Closed Caption.** Claudette Colbert, Gary Cooper, David Niven, Edward Everett Horton, Elizabeth Patterson, Herman Bing, William Hymer, Franklin Pangborn; **D:** Ernst Lubitsch; **W:** Charles Brackett, Billy Wilder. *USH*

Blueberry Hill 🎬½ **1988 (R)** While her mother struggles with the grief over husband's death, a young girl in a small town learns about life, music, and her late father from a jazz singer. Good soundtrack. **93m/C VHS, Beta.** Jennifer Rubin, Carrie Snodgress, Margaret Avery; **D:** Strathford Hamilton. *FOX*

The Blues Brothers 🎬🎬🎬 **1980 (R)** As an excuse to run rampant on the city of Chicago, Jake and Elwood Blues attempt to raise $5,000 for their childhood orphanage by putting their old band back together. Good music, quotable dialogue, lots of wrecked cars, plenty of cameos. A classic. **133m/C VHS, Beta, LV.** John Belushi, Dan Aykroyd, James Brown, Cab Calloway, Ray Charles, Henry Gibson, Aretha Franklin, Carrie Fisher, John Candy; **Cameos:** Frank Oz, Steven Spielberg, Twiggy, Paul (Pee Wee Herman) Reubens, Steve Lawrence, John Lee Hooker; **D:** John Landis; **W:** Dan Aykroyd, John Landis; **M:** Ira Newborn. *USH*

Blues Brothers 2000 🎬🎬 **1998 (PG-13)** Eighteen years after the original caper, Landis, Aykroyd, and most of the original cast return to the scene of the crime. Jake's died but Elwood's (Aykroyd) still around. He gets the band back together, recruits a Blues cousin (Goodman), a half-foster-brother (Morton), and an orphan (Bonifant) in need of mentoring, and heads for a battle of the bands between New Orleans and Chicago. The music, performed by the original Blues Brothers Band as well as a rock and blues all-star lineup, is the highlight. As for the rest of the flick, watch the original instead.**CW:** Exotic dancing and some language. **123m/C VHS.** Dan Aykroyd, John Goodman, Joe Morton, Evan Bonifant, Nia Peeples, Kathleen Freeman, Frank Oz, Steve Lawrence, Aretha Franklin; **Cameos:** Wilson Pickett; **D:** John Landis; **W:** John Landis, Dan Aykroyd. *NYR*

Blues Busters 🎬🎬½ **1950** Another entry in the "Bowery Boys" series. When Sach emerges from a tonsillectomy with the velvety voice of a crooner, Slip cashes in by turning Louie's Sweet Shop into a nightclub, the better to showcase his buddy's talents. Sach's singing voice provided by John Lorenz. **68m/B VHS.** Leo Gorcey, Huntz Hall, Adele Jergens, Gabriel Dell, Craig Stevens, Phyllis Coates, Bernard Gorcey, David Gorcey; **D:** William Beaudine. *WAR*

Bluffing It 🎬 **1987** A made-for-television movie about an older man who has been disguising his illiteracy for years. **120m/C VHS.** Dennis Weaver, Janet Carroll, Michelle Little, Robert Sean Leonard, Cleavant Derricks, Victoria Wauchope; **D:** James Sadwith; **M:** Brad Fiedel. *NO*

The Blum Affair 🎬🎬 **1948** In post-WWI Germany, a Jewish man is framed for the murder of an accountant and uncovers in his capture and prosecution a rat's nest of corruption and anti-Semitism. In German with English subtitles. **109m/B VHS, Beta.** *GE* Hans-Christian Blech, Gisela Trowe, Kurt Ehrhardt, Paul Bildt, Klaus Becker; **D:** Erich Engel. *NOS, FCT, GLV*

Blume in Love 🎬🎬🎬 **1973 (R)** An ironic comedy/drama about a man who falls hopelessly in love with his ex-wife who divorced him for cheating on her while they were married. **115m/C VHS, Beta.** George Segal, Susan Anspach, Kris Kristofferson, Shelley Winters, Marsha Mason; **D:** Paul Mazursky; **W:** Paul Mazursky; **C:** Bruce Surtees; **M:** Bill Conti. *WAR*

Blush 🎬🎬 *Hongfen* **1995** Shanghai prostitutes and friends Quiyi (Ji) and Xiao (Saifei) are stripped of their vocation by the communist takeover in 1949. Quiyi manages to take refuge with her favorite customer, wealthy Lao Pu (Zhiwen), while Xiao is re-educated and becomes a worker in a silk factory. Eventually thrown out of the house by Lao's disapproving mother, Quiyi learns to make her own way. Xiao meets Lao after his family has lost their money and winds up marrying him, unhappily since Lao continually pines for Quiyi. Based on the novel by Su Tong; Cantonese with subtitles. **119m/C VHS.** *CH* Wang Ji, He Saifei, Wang Zhiwen, Wang Rouli; **D:** Li Shaohong; **W:** Li Shaohong, Ni Zhen; **C:** Zeng Nianping; **M:** Guo Wenjing. *FRF*

BMX Bandits 🎬🎬 **1983** Three adventurous Aussie teens put their BMX skills to the test when they witness a crime and are pursued by the criminals. Much big air. **92m/C VHS.** Nicole Kidman, David Argue, John Ley, Angelo D'Angelo; **D:** Brian Trenchard-Smith; **W:** Patrick Edgeworth. *IMP*

Boarding House 🎬 **1983 (R)** Residents of a boardinghouse discover sinister doings in the basement. It does not occur to any of them to move to another house. **90m/C VHS, Beta.** Hank Adly, Kalassu, Alexandra Day; **D:** John Wintergate. *MRV*

Boarding School 🎬🎬 *The Passion Flower Hotel* **1983 (R)** Basic teen sex comedy about students at a proper Swiss boarding school for girls who devise a plan to seduce the boys at a nearby school by posing as prostitutes. Kinski stars as the American girl who masterminds the caper. **100m/C VHS, Beta.** *GE* Nastassia Kinski; **D:** Andre Farwagi. *VES, ART*

Boardinghouse Blues 🎬🎬 **1948** A showbiz musical centered around a boarding house with tenant troubles. It's an excuse for popular black entertainers of the day to perform, including Lucky Millinder, Bull Moose Jackson, Una Mae Carlisle, and Stumpy and Stumpy. **90m/C VHS.** Dusty Fletcher, Moms Mabley; **D:** Josh Binney. *FCT, RXM*

The Boat Is Full 🎬🎬🎬 **1981** A group of refugees pose as a family in order to escape from Nazi Germany as they seek asylum in Switzerland. Available in German with English subtitles or dubbed into English. **104m/C VHS, Beta.** *SI* Tina Engel, Curt Bois, Renate Steiger, Mathias Gnaedinger; **D:** Markus Imhoof. Berlin International Film Festival '81: Best Director (Imhoof); Nominations: Academy Awards '81: Best Foreign Language Film. *FRF, GLV, SWC*

The Boatniks 🎬🎬½ **1970 (G)** An accident-prone Coast Guard ensign finds himself in charge of the "Times Square" of waterways: Newport Harbor. Adding to his already "titanic" problems is a gang of ocean-going jewel thieves who won't give up the ship! **99m/C VHS, Beta.** Robert Morse, Stefanie Powers, Phil Silvers, Norman Fell, Wally Cox, Don Ameche; **D:** Norman Tokar; **M:** Robert F. Brunner. *DIS*

Bob & Carol & Ted & Alice 🎬🎬½ **1969 (R)** Two California couples have attended a trendy therapy session and, in an attempt to be more in touch with sexuality, resort to applauding one another's extramarital affairs and swinging. Wacky and well-written, this is a farce on free love and psycho-speak. Mazursky's directorial debut. **104m/C VHS, Beta, LV.** Natalie Wood, Robert Culp, Dyan Cannon, Elliott Gould; **D:** Paul Mazursky; **W:** Paul Mazursky, Larry Tucker; **C:** Charles B(ryant) Lang; **M:** Quincy Jones. New York Film Critics Awards '69: Best Screenplay, Best Supporting Actress (Cannon); National Society of Film Critics Awards '69: Best Screenplay; Writers Guild of America '69: Best Original Screenplay; Nominations: Academy Awards '69: Best Cinematography, Best Story & Screenplay, Best Supporting Actor (Gould), Best Supporting Actress (Cannon). *GKK*

Bob Dylan: Don't Look Back 🎬🎬🎬 **1991** A famous documentary about Bob Dylan at the beginning of his career: on the road, in performance and during private moments. From the director of "Monterey Pop." **95m/B VHS, Beta, LV.** Bob Dylan, Joan Baez, Donovan; **D:** D.A. Pennebaker. *WRV, MVD, PAR*

Bob le Flambeur 🎬🎬🎬 *Bob the Gambler* **1955** Wonderful film noir of a compulsive gambler who decides to take a final fling by robbing the casino at Deauville. French with subtitles. **97m/C VHS, Beta, LV.** *FR* Roger Duchesne, Isabel Corey, Daniel Cauchy; **D:** Jean-Pierre Melville. *COL, CVC, ING*

Bob Roberts 🎬🎬🎬 **1992 (R)** Pseudo-documentary satire about a 1990 Pennsylvania senatorial race between Robbins' right-wing folk singer/entrepreneur versus Vidal's aging liberal incumbent. Roberts seems like a gee-whiz kinda guy but he'll stop at nothing to get elected and he knows a lot about political dirty tricks and, even more important, manipulating the media to get what he wants. Robbins directorial debut turned out to be very timely in view of the 1992 presidential campaign. Features a number of cameos. Line to remember: "Vote first. Ask questions later."**CW:** Momentary language. **105m/C VHS, LV, Closed Caption.** Tim Robbins, Giancarlo Esposito, Ray Wise, Rebecca Jenkins, Harry J. Lennix, John Ottavino, Robert Stanton, Alan Rickman, Gore Vidal, Brian Doyle-Murray, Anita Gillette, David Strathairn; **Cameos:** Susan Sarandon, James Spader, John Cusack, Fred Ward, Pamela Reed; **D:** Tim Robbins; **W:** Tim Robbins; **M:** David Robbins. *ART, BTV*

Bobbie Jo and the Outlaw 🎬½ **1976 (R)** Wonderwoman Carter is a bored carhop who yearns to be a country singer. She becomes involved with Marjoe, who fancies himself as a contemporary Billy the Kid. Together, they do their Bonnie and Clyde thing, to a significantly lesser dramatic effect than the original, though a glut of violence keeps the bodies dropping. **89m/C VHS, Beta.** Lynda Carter, Marjoe Gortner, Jesse Vint; **D:** Mark L. Lester. *VES, ART*

Bobby Deerfield 🎬🎬 **1977 (PG)** Cold-blooded Grand Prix driver comes face to face with death each time he races, but finally learns the meaning of life when he falls in love with a critically ill woman. Even with race cars, soap opera stalls. **124m/C VHS, Beta.** Al Pacino, Marthe Keller, Anny Duperey, Romolo Valli; **D:** Sydney Pollack; **W:** Alvin Sargent; **C:** Henri Decae; **M:** Dave Grusin. *WAR*

Bobo 🎬½ **1967** Lousy bullfighter tries to lure a gorgeous woman into romance. Filmed in Spain and Italy. **103m/C VHS, Beta, LV, Letterbox.** *GB* Peter Sellers, Britt Ekland, Rossano Brazzi, Adolfo Celi; **D:** Robert Parrish. *WAR, FCT*

Boca 🎬🎬 **1994 (R)** American journalist J.J. (Chong) arrives in Rio during Carnival to investigate a story about random killings throughout the Brazilian streets. She gets stonewalled asking questions, until she meets an up-from-poverty criminlord named Boca De Ouro (Meira). Now, our noisy journalist may learn too much to keep her alive. Filmed in Rio de Janiero.**CW:** Strong violence and sexuality; language; some drug content. **92m/C VHS, Closed Caption.** Rae Dawn Chong, Martin Kemp, Tarcisio Meira, Martin Sheen; **D:** Sandra Werneck, Walter Avancini; **W:** Ed Silverstein. *REP*

Boccaccio '70 🎬🎬 **1962** Three short bawdy/comedy/pageant-of-life films inspired by "The Decameron," each pertaining to ironically twisted sexual politics in middle class life. A fourth story, "Renzo and Luciana," by Mario Monicelli, has been cut. Dubbed. **145m/C VHS, Beta.** *IT* Anita Ekberg, Romy Schneider, Tomas Milian, Sophia Loren, Peppino de Filippo; **D:** Vittorio De Sica, Luchino Visconti, Federico Fellini, Mario Monicelli; **W:** Federico Fellini, Mario Monicelli; **M:** Nino Rota. *NO*

Bodies, Rest & Motion 🎬🎬 **1993 (R)** Stagnant 20-something movie in which four young people basically do nothing in the sun-baked town of Enfield, Arizona. Similar to the movie "Singles," but without the Seattle grunge scene. The title's reference to Newton is fitting: "A body in rest or motion remains in that state unless acted upon by an outside force." Appealing cast is wasted in listless film that's content to just drift along. Based on the play by Roger Hedden. **CW:** Language and sexuality. **94m/C VHS, LV, Closed Caption.** Phoebe Cates, Bridget Fonda, Tim Roth, Eric Stoltz, Scott Frederick, Scott Johnson, Alicia Witt, Rich Wheeler, Peter Fonda; **D:** Michael Steinberg; **W:** Roger Hedden; **M:** Michael Convertino. *NLC, BTV*

Bodily Harm 🐾🐾 **1995 (R)** By-the-numbers neo-noir features Fiorentino as Vegas detective Rita Cates, who's investigating the murders of two women with ties to ex-cop Sam McKeon (Baldwin), not incidentally Rita's former lover. She rekindles their lust but then begins to have second thoughts about Sam's innocence. Unconvincing despite the expert cast. **CW:** Scenes of violence, sex and nudity, and for some language. **91m/C VHS.** Linda Fiorentino, Daniel Baldwin, Greg Henry, Bill Smitrovich, Troy Evans, Joe Regalbuto, Millie Perkins, Todd Susman, Shannon Kenny; **D:** James Lemmo; **W:** James Lemmo, Joseph Whaley, Ronda Barendse; **M:** Robert Sprayberry. *AVE*

Body and Soul 🐾🐾 **1924** The first screen appearance of Robeson has him cast in a dual role as a conniving preacher and his good brother. The preacher preys on the heroine, making her life a misery. Objections by censors to the preacher's character caused him to be redeemed and become worthy of the heroine's love. **102m/B VHS.** Paul Robeson, Julia Theresa Russell, Mercedes Gilbert; **D:** Oscar Micheaux. *KIV, FCT*

Body and Soul 🐾🐾🐾½ *An Affair of the Heart* 1947 A young boxer fights his way unscrupulously to the top. Vintage '40s boxing film that defines the genre. Remade in 1981. **104m/B VHS, LV.** John Garfield, Lilli Palmer, Hazel Brooks, Anne Revere, William Conrad, Canada Lee; **D:** Robert Rossen; **W:** Abraham Polonsky; **C:** James Wong Howe. Academy Awards '47: Best Film Editing; Nominations: Academy Awards '47: Best Actor (Garfield), Best Original Screenplay. *REP*

Body & Soul 🐾🐾½ **1981 (R)** Interesting remake of 1947 gem about a boxer who loses his perspective in the world of fame, fast cars, and women. **109m/C VHS, Beta.** Leon Isaac Kennedy, Jayne Kennedy, Peter Lawford, Muhammad Ali, Perry Lang; **D:** George Bowers. *MGM*

Body & Soul 🐾🐾🐾 **1993** After spending 16 years as a cloistered nun in a Welsh convent, with vows of poverty, chastity, and obedience, Anna Gibson (Scott Thomas) must return to the outside world. Following her brother's suicide, Anna is forced to deal with his pregnant widow (Redman) and two children and her family's failing Yorkshire mill. Anna suffers a crisis of faith as both the secular and the religious exert their strong influences and she's drawn as well to two very different men—younger Hal (Mavers), the mill's supervisor, and divorced bank manager Daniel Stern (Bowe). Based on the 1991 novel by Marcelle Bernstein; British TV miniseries. **312m/C VHS. GB** Kristin Scott Thomas, Amanda Redman, Gary Mavers, Anthony Valentine, Sandra Voe, John Bowe, Dorothy Tutin, Patrick Allen; **D:** Moira Armstrong; **W:** Paul Hines; **C:** Peter Middleton; **M:** Jim Parker. *WMI, VIF*

Body Armor 🐾🐾 **1997 (R)** Special agent Conway (McColm) is recruited by an ex-girlfriend (Schofield) to find a missing scientist. This leads our hero to nutball virologist Dr. Krago (Perlman) who's using germ warfare for personal gain. For the action junkie (who doesn't mind a little eye candy as well). **CW:** Violence, language, nudity, sexual situations. **90m/C VHS.** Matt McColm, Ron Perlman, Annabel Schofield, Carol Alt, Clint Howard, Morgan Brittany, Shauna O'Brien; **D:** Jack Gill. *APX*

Body Bags 🐾🐾½ *John Carpenter Presents Body Bags* 1993 (R) Three gory, though humorous, made for cable stories hosted by horrormeister Carpenter as your friendly local coroner. "The Gas Station" finds the young female overnight attendant menaced by a psycho. "Hair" is about a

balding yuppie who'll do anything for a full head of hair. Then he meets the sinister Dr. Lock and his magical new-hair growth treatment. The grisly "Eye" concerns a ballplayer who loses the aforementioned appendage and finds that his transplanted eyeball, taken from an executed serial killer, is subject to ghastly visions. Several fellow horror directors have cameos. **CW:** Horror violence and sexuality. **95m/C VHS, LV, Closed Caption.** Alex Datcher, Robert Carradine, Stacy Keach, David Warner, Mark Hamill, Twiggy, John Agar, Deborah Harry, Sheena Easton, David Naughton, John Carpenter; *Cameos:* Wes Craven, Sam Raimi, Roger Corman, Tobe Hooper; **D:** Tobe Hooper, John Carpenter; **W:** Billy Brown, Dan Angel; **M:** John Carpenter, Jim Lang. *REP*

Body Beat 🐾🐾 **1988 (PG)** Wild jazz and rock dancers are integrated into a previously classical ballet academy. While the students become fast friends, the teachers break off into two rival factions. **90m/C VHS, Beta.** Tony Fields, Galyn Gorg, Scott Grossman, Eliska Krupka. *THV*

The Body Beneath WOOF! **1970** A livingdead ghoul survives on the blood of innocents and is still preying on victims today. **85m/C VHS, Beta.** Gavin Reed, Jackie Skarvellis, Susan Heard, Colin Gordon; **D:** Andy Milligan. *NO*

Body Chemistry 🐾 **1990 (R)** A married sexual-behavior researcher starts up a passionate affair with his lab partner. When he tries to end the relationship, his female associate becomes psychotic. You've seen it all before in "Fatal Attraction." And you'll see it again in "Body Chemistry 2." **84m/C VHS, Beta, LV.** Marc Singer, Mary Crosby, Lisa Pescia, Joseph Campanella, David Kagen; **D:** Kristine Peterson; **W:** Jackson Barr, Thom Babbes; **C:** Phedon Papamichael. *COL*

Body Chemistry 2: Voice of a Stranger 🐾½ **1991 (R)** An ex-cop (Harrison) obsessed with violent sex gets involved with a talk-radio psychologist (Pescia) whose advice could prove deadly in this erotic sequel. **CW:** Language, violence, and strong sensuality. **84m/C VHS, LV, Closed Caption.** Gregory Harrison, Lisa Pescia, Morton Downey Jr., Robin Riker; **D:** Adam Simon. *COL*

Body Chemistry 3: Point of Seduction 🐾🐾 **1993 (R)** TV producer Alan Clay (Stevens) finds himself caught in a business and sexual triangle when he okays the making of a movie about the life of a TV sex therapist (Shattuck). Seems the lady's lovers have a nasty habit of getting murdered which doesn't prevent Clay from getting personally involved. His actress wife (Fairchild), who wants to star in the movie, is not pleased. Lives up to its title. **CW:** Nudity and sexual situations. **90m/C VHS, LV.** Andrew Stevens, Morgan Fairchild, Shari Shattuck; **D:** Jim Wynorski. *NHO*

Body Chemistry 4: Full Exposure 🐾½ **1995 (R)** When sex psychologist Claire Archer (Tweed) is accused of murder she hires Simon Mitchell (Poindexter), the best criminal defense attorney around. But Simon becomes just a little too closely involved with his possibly psycho client and it could cost him not only his career and marriage but his life. Also available unrated. **CW:** Strong graphic sex scenes, and some violence and language. **89m/C VHS, LV.** Shannon Tweed, Larry Poindexter, Andrew Stevens, Chick Vennera, Larry Manetti, Stella Stevens; **D:** Jim Wynorski; **W:** Karen Kelly; **C:** Zoran Hochstatter. *NHO*

Body Count 🐾½ *The 11th Commandment* 1987 A weird and wealthy family will stop at nothing, including murder and cannibalism, to enhance their fortune. Rather than bodies, count the minutes 'til the movie's over. **90m/C VHS, Beta.** Marilyn Hassett, Dick Sargent, Steven Ford, Greg Mullavey, Thomas Ryan, Bernie White; **D:** Paul Leder. *MCG*

Body Count 🐾½ **1995 (R)** Professional killer Makoto (Chiba) and his partner Sybil (Nielsen) seek revenge on the New Orleans cops who set them up. Opposing them are special crime unit partners, Eddie Cook (Davi) and Vinnie Rizzo (Bauer). Lots of shootouts and macho brava-

do. **CW:** Violence, sexuality and language. **93m/C VHS, LV.** Sonny Chiba, Brigitte Nielsen, Robert Davi, Steven Bauer; **D:** Talun Hsu. *APX*

Body Count 🐾🐾 **1997 (R)** Daniel (Theroux) takes fiancee Suzanne (Milano) home to meet his wealthy family and they just happen to be out of the line of immediate mayhem when a gang of thieves (led by Ice-T) break in to steal the art collection. Now, they're playing a very serious game of hide-and-seek in order to stay alive. **CW:** Strong violence and pervasive strong language. **88m/C VHS, Closed Caption.** Ice-T, Alyssa Milano, Justin Theroux, Tommy (Tiny) Lister; **D:** Kurt Voss; **W:** David Diamond; **C:** Denis Maloney; **M:** Joseph Williams. *ART*

Body Count 🐾🐾 **1997 (R)** Fiorentino and Caruso are reteamed (after "Jade") in a crime saga about a heist gone bad. There is no honor among thieves as driver Hobbs (Caruso) learns when he plans a job with some unreliable associates at the Boston Museum of Fine Arts and things go very wrong. The gang decide to drive to Miami in order to sell their ill-gotten gains, squabbling all the way. Then mystery woman Natalie (Fiorentino) comes aboard, to cause more friction between the gun-happy boys. **84m/C VHS, LV.** David Caruso, Linda Fiorentino, John Leguizamo, Ving Rhames, Donnie Wahlberg, Forest Whitaker; **D:** Robert Patton-Spruill; **W:** Theodore Witcher; **C:** Charles Mills; **M:** Curt Sobel. *PGV*

Body Double 🐾🐾🐾 **1984 (R)** A voyeuristic unemployed actor peeps on a neighbor's nightly disrobing and sees more than he wants to. A grisly murder leads him into an obsessive quest through the world of pornographic films. **114m/C VHS, Beta, LV, Letterbox, Closed Caption.** Craig Wasson, Melanie Griffith, Greg Henry, Deborah Shelton, Guy Boyd, Dennis Franz, David Haskell, Rebecca Stanley, Barbara Crampton; **D:** Brian DePalma; **W:** Brian DePalma, Robert J. Avrech; **C:** Stephen Burum; **M:** Pino Donaggio. National Society of Film Critics Awards '84: Best Supporting Actress (Griffith). *COL*

Body Heat 🐾🐾🐾 **1981 (R)** During a Florida heat wave, a none-too-bright lawyer becomes involved in a steamy love affair with a mysterious woman and then in a plot to kill her husband. Hurt and Turner (in her film debut) became stars under Kasdan's direction (the three would reunite for "The Accidental Tourist"). Hot love scenes supplement a twisting mystery with a surprise ending. Rourke's arsonist and Danson's soft shoe shouldn't be missed. **113m/C VHS, Beta, LV.** William Hurt, Kathleen Turner, Richard Crenna, Ted Danson, Mickey Rourke; **D:** Lawrence Kasdan; **W:** Lawrence Kasdan; **M:** John Barry. *WAR*

The Body in the Library 🐾½ *Agatha Christie's Miss Marple: The Body In the Library* 1987 A British television-produced Miss Marple mystery, based on Agatha Christie's 1942 novel, involving the septuagenarian detective investigating the murder of a young woman in a wealthy British mansion. **155m/C VHS, Beta, Closed Caption. GB** Joan Hickson; **D:** Silvio Narizzano. *FOX, HMV, VCO*

Body Language 🐾🐾 **1992 (R)** A successful businesswoman, with a man problem, hires a super secretary with answers to all life's questions—and a deadly agenda all her own. **CW:** Violence. **93m/C VHS, Beta, Closed Caption.** Heather Locklear, Linda Purl, Edward Albert, James Acheson; **D:** Arthur Seidelman; **W:** Dan Gurskis, Brian Ross; **C:** Hanania Baer. *PAR*

Body Language 🐾🐾½ **1995 (R)** Criminal defense attorney Gavin St. Claire (Berenger) falls for a topless dancer (Schanz), which leads him into all sorts of trouble, including murder. **CW:** Violence, language and strong sexuality. **95m/C VHS, Closed Caption.** Tom Berenger, Heidi Schanz, Nancy Travis; **D:** George Case. *HBO*

Body Melt 🐾🐾½ **1993** When a crazed doctor unleashes an experimental drug on an unsuspecting town, the residents begin to literally melt away. **82m/C VHS, LV. AU** Gerard Kennedy, Andrew Daddo, Ian Smith, Vincent Gil, Regina Gaigalas; **D:** Philip Brophy; **W:** Philip Brophy, Rod Bishop; **M:** Philip Brophy.

Body Moves 🎞🎞 **1990 (PG-13)** Romantic entanglements heat up the competition when two couples enter a steamy dance contest. Not apt to move you. **98m/C VHS, Beta.** *IT* Kirk Rivera, Steve Messina, Dianne Granger, Linsley Allen, Philip Spruce, Nicole Kolman, Susan Gardner; **D:** Gerry Lively; **W:** Daniel Steel.

Body of Evidence woof! **1992 (R)** Bad movie with pretensions takes "Basic Instinct" a step further. Instead of an ice pick and sex, sex itself is used as the weapon in a murder trial featuring Madonna as the defendant, Dafoe as her lawyer, and Mantegna as the prosecutor. The plot is, of course, secondary to the S&M sex scenes with Dafoe which feature hot wax and broken glass. Madonna's lack of performance is the least of the film's problems since everyone seems to have forgotten any acting talent they possess. Director Edel fails to direct—the film even looks bad. "Body" was the subject of another NC-17 ratings flap but this film shouldn't be seen by anybody. An unrated version is also available. **CW:** Language, violence, and strong sexuality. **99m/C VHS, Beta, LV, Letterbox, Closed Caption.** Madonna, Willem Dafoe, Joe Mantegna, Anne Archer, Michael Forest, Charles Hallahan, Mark Rolston, Richard Riehle, Julianne Moore, Frank Langella, Juergen Prochnow, Stan Shaw; **D:** Uli Edel; **W:** Graeme Revell. Golden Raspberry Awards '93: Worst Actress (Madonna). *MGM*

Body of Influence 🎞🎞 **1993 (R)** A Beverly Hills psychiatrist gets overly involved with a beautiful female patient. But she not only wants his love—she wants his life. Also available in an unrated version. **CW:** Strong language and strong language. **96m/C VHS, Closed Caption.** Nick Cassavetes, Shannon Whirry, Sandahl Bergman, Don Swayze, Anna Karin, Catherine Parks, Diana Barton, Richard Roundtree; **D:** Andrew Garroni; **W:** David Schreiber.

Body of Influence 2 🎞 **1996 (R)** Shrink Dr. Benson (Anderson) finds he's using his couch for more than professional purposes with his latest patient, Leza (Fisher), whose seductive charms prove more than the doc can handle. The unrated version is 94 minutes. **CW:** Strong sexuality, language and some violence. **88m/C VHS.** Daniel Anderson, Jodie Fisher, Steve Poletti, Jonathan Goldstein, Pat Brennan; **D:** Brian J. Smith; **W:** Brian J. Smith; **C:** Azusa Ohno; **M:** Ron Sures. *APX*

Body Parts 🎞 **1990** For fans of the demented dismemberer niche. Body Parts, a sleazy skin club, loses some of its star talent when the strippers start turning up in cameo video appearances. Seems there's a psycho killer on the loose who videotapes the dismemberment of his stripper-victims. The police decide they've got to meet this guy when he sends them a sample of his work. **90m/C VHS, LV.** Teri Lee, Dick Monda, Johnny Mandel. *NO*

Body Parts 🎞🎞 **1991 (R)** A crime psychologist loses his arm in an auto accident and receives a transplant from an executed murderer. Does the limb have an evil will of its own? Poorly paced horror goes off the deep end in gore with its third act. Based on the novel "Choice Cuts" by French writers Pierre Boileau and Thomas Narcejac, whose work inspired some of the greatest suspense films. **CW:** Language, violence and gore, and sensual scene. **88m/C VHS, Beta, LV, Letterbox, Closed Caption.** Jeff Fahey, Kim Delaney, Lindsay Duncan, Peter Murnik, Brad Dourif, Zakes Mokae, Johnny Walsh, Paul Benevictor; **D:** Eric Red; **W:** Eric Red, Norman Snider, Larry Gross; **M:** Loek Dikker. *PAR*

Body Rock woof! **1984 (PG-13)** Brooklyn breakdancer Lamas deserts his buddies to work at a chic Manhattan nightclub. Watching Lamas as the emcee/breakdancing fool is a hoot. 🎵Body Rock; Team Work; Why Do You Want to Break My Heart?; One Thing Leads to Another; Let Your Body Rock; Vanishing Point; Sharpshooter; The Jungle; Deliver. **93m/C VHS, Beta.** Lorenzo Lamas, Vicki Frederick, Cameron Dye, Michelle Nicastro, Ray Sharkey, Grace Zabriskie, Carole Ita White; **D:** Marcelo Epstein. *NO*

The Body Shop woof! *Doctor Gore* **1972** Unorthodox love story in which a man decides to patch up his relationship with his dead wife by piecing together her dismembered body. For lovers only. Under "Doctor Gore" title the film includes an intro by horror director Herschell Gordon Lewis. **91m/C VHS.** Pat Patterson, Jenny Driggers, Roy Mehaffey, Linda Faile, Candy Furr; **D:** Pat Patterson. *NO*

Body Shot 🎞🎞½ **1993 (R)** Celebrity shutterbug Mickey Dane (Patrick) is fingered in the murder of a rock star after it turns out he did a kinky layout for a look-alike. When police find out he had an obsession for the dead woman, he employs his photographic expertise in the search for the real killer. Effective tension-builder with fast-paced chases through the seamy side of Los Angeles. **CW:** Language and nudity. **98m/C VHS, LV.** Robert Patrick, Michelle Johnson, Ray Wise, Jonathan Banks, Kim Miyori; **D:** Dimitri Logothetis; **W:** Robert Strauss; **C:** Nicholas Von Sternberg. *TRI*

Body Slam 🎞½ **1987 (PG)** A small-time talent monger hits it big with a rock and roll/ professional wrestling tour. Piper's debut; contains some violence and strong language. **100m/C VHS, Beta.** Roddy Piper, Captain Lou Albano, Dirk Benedict, Tanya Roberts, Billy Barry, Charles Nelson Reilly, John Astin, Wild Samoan, Tonga Kid, Barry Gordon; **D:** Hal Needham; **W:** Steven H. Burkow; **M:** John D'Andrea. *NLC*

The Body Snatcher 🎞🎞🎞½ **1945** Based on Robert Louis Stevenson's story about a grave robber who supplies corpses to research scientists. Set in Edinburgh in the 19th century, this Lewton production is superior. One of Karloff's best vehicles. **77m/B VHS, Beta, LV.** Edith Atwater, Russell Wade, Rita (Paula) Corday, Boris Karloff, Bela Lugosi, Henry Daniell, Sharyn Moffett, Donna Lee; **D:** Robert Wise; **W:** Philip MacDonald, Val Lewton, Carlos Keith; **C:** Robert De Grasse. *TTC*

Body Snatcher from Hell 🎞½ *Goke,* *Body Snatcher from Hell; Goke the Vampire; Kyuketsuki Gokemidoro* **1969** An airliner passes through a mysterious cloud and crashes in a desert. One by one, the passengers are turned into vampires. Some interesting special effects. **84m/C VHS.** *JP* Hideo Ko, Teruo Yoshida, Tomomi Sato, Eizo Kitamura, Masay Takahashi, Cathy Horlan, Kazuo Kato, Yuko Kusunoki; **D:** Hajime Sato. *SNC*

Body Snatchers 🎞🎞 **1993 (R)** Yet another version of "Invasion of the Body Snatchers." An innocent family arrive at an Army base which turns out to be infested with pod people. This time around the heroine is angst-ridden teenager Marti (Anwar) and the pods have something to do with a mysterious toxic spill. The 1978 remake was well done; this so-so version takes advantage of the advances in special effects (particularly in Anwar's bathtub scene) and sound technology but is slow-paced with few jolts of terror. **CW:** Nudity and violence. **87m/C VHS, LV, Closed Caption.** Gabrielle Anwar, Meg Tilly, Terry Kinney, Forest Whitaker, Billy Wirth, R. Lee Ermey, Reilly Murphy; **D:** Abel Ferrara; **W:** Stuart Gordon, Dennis Paoli, Nicholas St. John; **C:** Bojan Bazelli; **M:** Joe Delia. *WAR*

Body Strokes 🎞 **1995** Blocked artist Leo Kessler (Johnston) is aroused by the wild fantasies of his beautiful models Beth (Knittle) and Claire (Weber). But it's just fantasy and it also helps get Leo's marriage back on track when manager/wife Karen (Beck) gets jealous. Also available unrated. **99m/C VHS.** Bobby Johnston, Dixie Beck, Kristen Knittle, Catherine Weber; **D:** Edward Holzman; **M:** Richard Bronskill. *APX*

Body Trouble 🎞½ *Joker's Wild* **1992 (R)** After being attacked by sharks while vacationing in the Caribbean, a man washes ashore in Miami and then somehow makes his way to New York City. There he meets Vera Vin Rouge and her friends Cinnamon, Spice, Paprika, and Johnny Zero, a gangster. Zero decides he doesn't like the man, so he chases him back to the Caribbean. Supposedly this all happens in only one day.

Hmmm... **CW:** Language and sexuality. **98m/C VHS.** Dick Van Patten, Priscilla Barnes, Frank Gorshin, James Hong, Marty Rackham, Michael Unger, Jonathan Soloman, Brit Helfer, Leigh Clark, Patricia Cardell, Richie Barathy; **D:** Bill Milling; **W:** Bill Milling. *TRI*

The Body Vanished 🎞🎞 **1939** Murder mystery featuring a corpse that disappears from the scene of the crime. **?m/C VHS.** *GB* Lewis Wilson, Frances Dubay, Dana Wilson. *SNC*

Body Waves 🎞½ **1992 (R)** Beach comedy starring Calvert as a teenager who bets his father that he can raise money on his own. In typical teen movie fashion, he invents a sex cream that drives boys and girls wild. Brain candy featuring lots of skimpy bikinis. **CW:** Language, drug content, and sensuality. **80m/C VHS, Closed Caption.** Bill Calvert, Leah Lail, Larry Linville, Dick Miller, Jim Wise; **D:** P.J. Pesce. *NHO*

The Bodyguard 🎞½ **1976 (R)** The Yakuza, Japan's mafia, and New York's big crime families face off in this martial arts extravaganza. **89m/C VHS, Beta.** Sonny Chiba, Aaron Banks, Bill Louie, Judy Lee; **D:** Maurice Sarli.

The Bodyguard 🎞🎞 **1992 (R)** Buttoned-down, ex-Secret Service agent turned private bodyguard reluctantly takes on a wildly successful singer/actress as a client. Houston, in her acting debut as the over-indulged diva, doesn't have to stretch too far but acquits herself well. Costner has really bad hair day but easily portrays the tightly wound Frank. Critically trashed, a boxoffice smash, and too long. Originally scripted by producer Kasdan over a decade ago, with Steve McQueen in mind. Predictable romantic melodrama is kept moving by the occasional sharp dialog and a few action pieces. Songs include the smash hit "I Will Always Love You," written and originally performed by Dolly Parton. **CW:** Language and violence. **130m/C VHS, LV, Closed Caption, DVD.** Kevin Costner, Whitney Houston, Gary Kemp, Bill Cobbs, Ralph Waite, Tomas Arana, Michele Lamar Richards, Mike Starr, Christopher Birt, DeVaughn Nixon, Charles Keating, Robert Wuhl; **Cameos:** Debbie Reynolds; **D:** Mick Jackson; **W:** Lawrence Kasdan; **M:** Alan Silvestri. MTV Movie Awards '93: Best Song ("I Will Always Love You"); Nominations: Academy Awards '92: Best Song ("I Have Nothing"), Best Song ("Run to You"). *WAR, BTV*

Boeing Boeing 🎞🎞½ **1965** A dated but still amusing sex farce about a bachelor newspaperman (Curtis) in Paris, his three stewardess girlfriends, and the elaborate plots he resorts to in trying to keep them from finding out about each other. When the new Boeing jet makes air travel faster all Curtis' schemes may come crashing down. Ritter is fun as the exasperated housekeeper and Lewis amazingly subdued as Curtis' business rival. **102m/C VHS, LV, Closed Caption.** Tony Curtis, Jerry Lewis, Dany Saval, Christianne Schmidtmer, Suzanna Leigh, Thelma Ritter; **D:** John Rich; **W:** Edward Anhalt. *PAR*

Bog 🎞 **1984 (PG)** Boggy beast from the Arctic north awakens to eat people. Scientists mount an anti-monster offense. **90m/C VHS, Beta.** Gloria De Haven, Marshall Thompson, Leo Gordon, Aldo Ray.

Boggy Creek II 🎞½ *The Barbaric Beast of Boggy Creek, Part II* **1983 (PG)** The continuing saga of the eight-foot-tall, 300 pound monster from Texarkana. Third in a series of low-budget movies including "The Legend of Boggy Creek" and "Return to Boggy Creek." **93m/C VHS, Beta, LV.** Charles B. Pierce, Cindy Butler, Serene Hedin; **D:** Charles B. Pierce; **W:** Charles B. Pierce.

Bogie: The Last Hero **1980** Television biography of Humphrey Bogart, populated by almost-lookalikes who can almost act. **100m/C VHS, Beta.** Kevin J. O'Connor, Kathryn Harrold, Ann Wedgeworth, Patricia Barry, Alfred Ryder, Donald May, Richard Dysart, Arthur Franz; **D:** Vincent Sherman; **M:** Charles Bernstein.

Bogus 🎬🎬 1996 (PG) Aptly named fantasy-comedy has orphan Albert (Osment) sent to foster aunt Harriet (Goldberg) after his magician's assistant mom (Travis) dies in a car accident. He brings along an imaginary friend, the eponymous Bogus (Depardieu) to ease the transition. Harriet is your typical workaholic easterner and isn't too thrilled with the arrangement. Goldberg and Depardieu are fine, but predictability drains most of the magic. 112m/C VHS, LV, Closed Caption. Whoopi Goldberg, Gerard Depardieu, Haley Joel Osment, Nancy Travis, Andrea Martin, Denis Mercier, Ute Lemper, Sheryl Lee Ralph, Al Waxman, Fiona Reid, Don Francks; **D:** Norman Jewison; **W:** Alvin Sargent; **C:** David Watkin; **M:** Marc Shaiman. Nominations: Golden Raspberry Awards '96: Worst Actress (Goldberg). *WAR*

Bohemian Girl 🎬🎬🎬 1936 The last of Laurel and Hardy's comic operettas finds them as guardians of a young orphan (Hood, famous for her roles in the Our Gang comedies), whom no one realizes is actually a kidnapped princess. 74m/B VHS, Beta. Stan Laurel, Oliver Hardy, Mae Busch, Darla Hood, Jacqueline Wells, Thelma Todd, James Finlayson; **D:** James W. Horne. *CCB*

Boiling Point 🎬1/2 1932 Lawman proves once again that justice always triumphs. 67m/B VHS, Beta. Hoot Gibson. *NOS, VCI, DVT*

Boiling Point 🎬🎬1/2 1993 (R) Darkly flavored action drama delves into the personalities of its two main characters before setting up a final confrontation. Treasury agent Jimmy Mercer (Snipes) is trying to solve his partner's murder, relentlessly pursuing the murderers in cold and methodical fashion. Sleazy Red Diamond (Hopper), just out of prison, owes the mob and has one week to pay them back. Lawman and crook both come home to women (Davidovich and Perrine) graduates of the Hollywood school of female martyrdom, selflessly supportive of their men. Grim but cliched. Adapted from the Gerald Petievich novel "Money Men." **CW:** Language and violence. 93m/C VHS, Beta, LV, Letterbox. Wesley Snipes, Dennis Hopper, Lolita Davidovich, Viggo Mortensen, Dan Hedaya, Valerie Perrine, Seymour Cassel, Jonathan Banks, Tony LoBianco, Christine Elise, James Tolkan, Paul Gleason; **D:** James B. Harris; **W:** James B. Harris; **M:** Cory Lerios, John D'Andrea. *WAR*

The Bold Caballero 🎬1/2 *The Bold Cavalier* 1936 Rebel chieftain Zorro overthrows oppressive Spanish rule in the days of early California. 69m/B VHS, Beta. Bob Livingston, Heather Angel, Sig Rumann, Robert Warwick; **D:** Wells Root. *NOS, VDM, VCN*

The Boldest Job in the West 🎬 *El Mas Fabulosi Golpe del Far West* 1971 Italian western about bankrobbers who meet to divide their spoils. Problem is, the guys with the loot don't show. Dubbed in English. 200m/C VHS, Beta. *IT* Mark Edwards, Frank Sancho, Carmen Sevilla; **D:** Joseph Loman. *NO*

Bolero 🎬🎬1/2 1982 Beginning in 1936, this international epic traces the lives of four families across three continents and five decades, highlighting the music and dance that is central to their lives. 173m/C VHS, Beta. James Caan, Geraldine Chaplin, Robert Hossein, Nicole Garcia, Jacques Villeret; **D:** Claude Lelouch; **W:** Claude Lelouch. *VES*

Bolero woof! *Bolero: An Adventure in Ecstasy* 1984 (R) What sounds like a wet dream come true is really just a good snooze: Bo Derek plays a beautiful young woman who goes on a trip around the world in hopes of losing her virginity; in Spain, she meets a bullfighter who's willing to oblige. Too bad Bo cannot act as good as she looks. 106m/C VHS, Beta. Bo Derek, George Kennedy, Andrea Occhipinti, Anna Obregon, Olivia D'Abo; **D:** John Derek; **W:** John Derek; **M:** Peter Bernstein, Elmer Bernstein. Golden Raspberry Awards '84: Worst Picture, Worst Actress (Derek), Worst Director (Derek), Worst Screenplay, Worst New Star (D'Abo). *ART*

Bomb at 10:10 🎬🎬 1967 An American pilot escapes from a German POW camp and plots to assassinate a camp commandant. 87m/C VHS, Beta. George Montgomery, Rada Popovic, Peter Banicevic; **D:** Charles Damic. *GEM*

Bombardier 🎬🎬1/2 1943 A group of cadet bombardiers discover the realities of war on raids over Japan during WWII. Also available colorized. 99m/B VHS, Beta. Pat O'Brien, Randolph Scott, Robert Ryan, Eddie Albert, Anne Shirley, Barton MacLane; **D:** Richard Wallace. *TTC*

Bombay Talkie 🎬🎬1/2 1970 (PG) A bored British writer (Kendal) heads to India to gather "experiences" and becomes involved with an Indian movie actor (Kapoor). Early clash-of-cultures film from Merchant Ivory has it's dull spots; the behind-the-scenes look at the Indian film industry is more interesting than the romance. 110m/C VHS, Beta. *IN* Jennifer Kendal, Shashi Kapoor, Zia Mohyeddin, Aparna Sen; **D:** James Ivory; **W:** Ruth Prawer Jhabvala. *NLC*

Bombs Away! 🎬 1986 An atomic bomb is mistakenly shipped to a seedy war surplus store in Seattle, and causes much chicanery. 90m/C VHS, Beta. Michael Huddleston, Pat McCormick; **D:** Bruce Wilson. *COL, NLC*

Bombshell 🎬🎬🎬 *Blonde Bombshell* 1933 Wry insightful comedy into the Hollywood of the 1930s. Harlow plays a naive young actress manipulated by her adoring press agent. He thwarts her plans until she finally notices and begins to fall in love with him. Brilliant satire with Harlow turning in perhaps the best performance of her short career. 96m/B VHS, Beta. Jean Harlow, Lee Tracy, Pat O'Brien, Una Merkel, Sir C. Aubrey Smith, Franchot Tone; **D:** Victor Fleming. *MGM, BTV, FCT*

Bombshell 🎬🎬 1997 (R) Scientist Buck Hogan (Thomas) discovers a deadly flaw in the world's first cancer-killing drug, which he publicly reveals, much to the dismay of the manufacturer's head honcho (James). But then Hogan and his girlfriend (Amick) are abducted by a terrorist group, and Buck's implanted with a device that will kill him unless he does as they say. **CW:** Sexuality, violence and language. 95m/C VHS. Henry Thomas, Frank Whaley, Madchen Amick, Brion James, Pamela Gidley, Shawnee Smith, Martin Hewitt; **D:** Paul Wynne. *THV*

Bon Voyage! 🎬1/2 1962 A family's long-awaited European "dream" vacation turns into a series of comic misadventures in this very Disney, very family, very predictable comedy. 131m/C VHS, Beta, LV. Fred MacMurray, Jane Wyman, Deborah Walley, Michael Callan, Tommy Kirk, Jessie Royce Landis; **D:** James Neilson. Nominations: Academy Awards '62: Best Costume Design (Color), Best Sound. *DIS*

Bon Voyage, Charlie Brown 🎬🎬🎬 1980 (G) The "Peanuts" comic strip group becomes exchange students in Europe, led by Charlie Brown, Linus, Peppermint Patty, Marcie, and the irrepressible beagle, Snoopy. 76m/C VHS, Beta, LV. **D:** Bill Melendez; **W:** Charles M. Schulz; **M:** Ed Bogas; **V:** Arrin Skelley, Laura Planting, Casey Carlson, David Anderson, Annalisa Bartolin, Scott Beads. *PAR*

Bonanza 1964 This western series about the Cartwright clan and their Ponderosa ranch ran on TV from 1959-73, second only to "Gunsmoke." In "The Pure Truth," Hoss escapes from jail after being unjustly accused of robbing the bank. An eccentric recluse comes to his aid. Additional episodes are available. 50m/C VHS. Lorne Greene, Pernell Roberts, Dan Blocker, Michael Landon, Glenda Farrell. *REP, MOV*

Bonanza: The Return 🎬1/2 1993 (PG) In 1905, the children of various members of the Cartwright clan work to see the Ponderosa is safe from an unscrupulous businessman. Lame update of the classic family western series. Made for television. 96m/C VHS, LV, Closed Caption. Michael Landon Jr., Dirk Blocker, Emily Warfield, Alistair MacDou-

gall, Brian Leckner, Dean Stockwell, Ben Johnson, Richard Roundtree, Linda Gray, Jack Elam. *THV*

Bonanza Town 🎬1/2 1951 Steve Ramsey (Starrett), aka The Durango Kid, and sidekick Smiley (Burnette) are hired to locate the loot stolen in a Dodge City hold-up. Marked money leads our heroes to Bonanza Town, where the Kid tracks down outlaws and corrupt officials. 56m/B VHS. Charles Starrett, Smiley Burnette, Myron Healey, Fred F. Sears; **D:** Fred F. Sears; **C:** Henry Freulich. *COL*

The Bone Yard 🎬 1990 (R) A weird mortuary is the setting for strange goings on when a murder is investigated. 98m/C VHS, Beta. Ed Nelson, Deborah Rose, Norman Fell, Jim Eustermann, Denise Young, Willie Stratford Jr., Phyllis Diller; **D:** James Cummins; **W:** James Cummins.

The Bonfire of the Vanities 🎬1/2 1990 (R) If you liked Tom Wolfe's viciously satirical novel, chances are you won't like this version. If you didn't read the book, you probably still won't like it. Miscast and stripped of the book's gutsy look inside its characters, the film's sole attribute is Vilmos Zsigmond's photography. Hanks is all wrong as wealthy Wall Street trader Sherman McCoy who, lost in the back streets of the Bronx, panics and accidentally kills a young black kid. Willis' drunken journalist/narrator, Griffith's mistress, and Freeman's righteous judge are all awkward and thinly written. If you're still awake, look for F. Murray Abraham's cameo as the Bronx D.A. **CW:** Language. 126m/C VHS, Beta, LV, 8mm, Letterbox, Closed Caption. Tom Hanks, Melanie Griffith, Bruce Willis, Morgan Freeman, Alan King, Kim Cattrall, Saul Rubinek, Clifton James, Donald Moffat, Richard Libertini, Andre Gregory, Robert Stephens; **Cameos:** F. Murray Abraham; **D:** Brian DePalma; **W:** Michael Cristofer; **C:** Vilmos Zsigmond; **M:** Dave Grusin. *WAR, FCT*

Bonjour Tristesse 🎬🎬🎬 1957 An amoral French girl (Seberg) conspires to break up her playboy father's (Niven) upcoming marriage to her stuffy godmother (Kerr) in order to maintain her decadent freedom. Preminger attempted, unsuccessfully, to use this soaper to catapult Seberg to stardom. Based on the novel by Francoise Sagan. 94m/B VHS. *FR* Deborah Kerr, David Niven, Jean Seberg, Mylene Demongeot, Geoffrey Horne, Walter Chiari, Jean Kent; **D:** Otto Preminger; **W:** Arthur Laurents; **C:** Georges Perinal. *COL*

Bonnie & Clyde 🎬🎬🎬1/2 1967 Based on the biographies of the violent careers of Bonnie Parker and Clyde Barrow, who roamed the Southwest robbing banks. In the Depression era, when any job, even an illegal one, was cherished, money, greed, and power created an unending cycle of violence and fury. Highly controversial and influential, with pronounced bloodshed that spurred mainstream cinematic proliferation. Established Dunaway as a star; produced by Beatty in one of his best performances. 111m/C VHS, Beta, LV, Closed Caption, DVD. Warren Beatty, Faye Dunaway, Michael J. Pollard, Gene Hackman, Estelle Parsons, Denver Pyle, Gene Wilder, Dub Taylor; **D:** Arthur Penn; **W:** David Newman, Robert Benton; **C:** Burnett Guffey. Academy Awards '67: Best Cinematography, Best Supporting Actress (Parsons), National Film Registry '92;; New York Film Critics Awards '67: Best Screenplay; National Society of Film Critics Awards '67: Best Screenplay, Best Supporting Actor (Hackman); Writers Guild of America '67: Best Original Screenplay; Nominations: Academy Awards '67: Best Actor (Beatty), Best Actress (Dunaway), Best Costume Design, Best Director (Penn), Best Picture, Best Story & Screenplay, Best Supporting Actor (Hackman, Pollard). *WAR, BTV*

Bonnie Prince Charlie 🎬🎬1/2 1948 Historical epic opening in 1745 and romanticizing the title pretender to the British throne, who united Scottish clans in a doomed campaign against King George. Talky and rather slow-moving except for stirring battle scenes. A notorious boxoffice flop in its native Britain, where the original running time was 140 minutes. 114m/C VHS, Closed Caption. David Niven, Margaret Leighton, Judy Campbell, Jack Hawkins, Morland Graham, Finlay Currie, Elwyn Brook-Jones, John Laurie; **D:** Anthony Kimmins. *NOS, REP*

Bonnie Scotland 🎬🎬½ 1935 Laurel & Hardy accidentally join an India-bound Scottish regiment. Laughs aplenty. **81m/B VHS, Beta.** Stan Laurel, Oliver Hardy, James Finlayson, Daphne Pollard, June Lang; *D:* James W. Horne. *MGM, MLB*

Bonnie's Kids 🎬½ 1973 (R) Two sisters become involved in murder, sex, and stolen money. **107m/C VHS, Beta.** Tiffany Bolling, Robin Mattson, Scott Brady, Alex Rocco; *D:* Arthur Marks. *NO*

The Boogey Man 🎬🎬 1980 (R) Through the reflection in a mirror, a girl witnesses her brother murder their mother's lover. Twenty years later this memory still haunts her; the mirror is now broken, revealing its special powers. Who will be next? Murder menagerie; see footage from this flick mirrored in "The Boogey Man 2." **93m/C VHS, Beta, LV.** John Carradine, Suzanna Love, Ron James; *D:* Ulli Lommel. *HHE*

Boogey Man 2 woof! 1983 The story continues; same footage, new director but with Lommel, the director of the original "Boogey Man," co-writing the script and appearing in the film. **90m/C VHS, Beta.** John Carradine, Suzanna Love, Shannah Hall, Ulli Lommel, Sholto Von Douglas; *D:* Bruce Starr. *VHE*

Boogie Nights 🎬🎬🎬½ 1997 (R) Epic tale covering the rise and fall of porn star Eddie Adams (Wahlberg). The protege of director Jack Horner (Reynolds), 17-year-old Eddie jumps in a hot tub at an industry bash, christens himself Dirk Diggler, and goes on to become the toast of the adult entertainment industry. Brilliantly spanning the decadent disco-era 70s and the excess of the 80s, 27-year-old writer/director Anderson boldly delves into fresh, albeit dangerous, territory most successfully in this lengthy sophomore outing. What Tarantino did for Travolta, Anderson does here for Reynolds, who plays the past-his-prime but touchingly ambitious auteur with a dream to make a legitimately legendary skin flick. Wahlberg proves himself a serious and seriously good actor in his turn, surrounded by equally fine performances of the ensemble cast. Details such as wardrobe, bits of dialogue, and music are deftly used, avoiding parody. Nonstop disco and early 80s music, often with a message, and energetic camera work make you shake your booty.*CW:* Strong sex scenes with explicit dialogue, nudity, drug use, language and violence. **155m/C VHS, LV, Closed Caption.** Mark Wahlberg, Burt Reynolds, Julianne Moore, Don Cheadle, William H. Macy, Heather Graham, John C. Reilly, Luis Guzman, Philip S. Hoffman, Alfred Molina, Philip Baker Hall, Robert Ridgely, Joanna Gleason, Thomas Jane, Ricky Jay, Nicole Parker, Melora Walters, Michael Jace, Jack Wallace, John Doe; *Cameos:* Robert Downey, Michael Penn; *D:* Paul Thomas Anderson; *W:* Paul Thomas Anderson; *C:* Robert Elswit; *M:* Michael Penn. Golden Globe Awards '98: Best Supporting Actor (Reynolds); Los Angeles Film Critics Association Awards '97: Best Supporting Actor (Reynolds), Best Supporting Actress (Moore); MTV Movie Awards '98: Breakthrough Performance (Graham); New York Film Critics Awards '97: Best Supporting Actor (Reynolds); National Society of Film Critics Awards '97: Best Supporting Actor (Reynolds), Best Supporting Actress (Moore); Nominations: Academy Awards '97: Best Original Screenplay, Best Supporting Actor (Reynolds), Best Supporting Actress (Moore); British Academy Awards '97: Best Original Screenplay, Best Supporting Actor (Reynolds); Golden Globe Awards '98: Best Supporting Actress (Moore); MTV Movie Awards '98: Best Dance Sequence (Mark Wahlberg/cast); Screen Actors Guild Award '97: Best Supporting Actor (Reynolds), Best Supporting Actress (Moore), Cast; Writers Guild of America '97: Best Original Screenplay. *WAR*

Book of Love 🎬🎬 1991 (PG-13) "Zany" hijinks as a teenager struggles with friendship, girls, and those all-important hormones when he moves to a new neighborhood in the mid-'50s. Average rehash of every '50s movie and TV show cliche in existence. Surprise! There's a classic rock 'n' roll soundtrack. Adapted by Kotzwinkle from his novel "Jack in the Box." **88m/C VHS, LV, 8mm, Closed Caption.** Chris Young, Keith Coogan, Aeryk Egan, Josie Bissett, Tricia Leigh Fisher, Danny Nucci, Mi-

chael McKean, John Cameron Mitchell, Lewis Arquette; *D:* Robert Shaye; *W:* William Kotzwinkle; *M:* Stanley Clarke. *COL*

Boom in the Moon woof! *A Modern Bluebeard* 1946 Keaton fares poorly in this sci-fi comedy. He's trapped on a space ship to the moon. Poor production, with uneven direction and acting. **83m/C VHS.** Buster Keaton, Angel Garasa, Virginia Serret, Fernando Soto, Luis Barreiro; *D:* Jaime Salvador. *NO*

Boom Town 🎬🎬½ 1940 A lively vintage comedy/drama/romance about two oil-drilling buddies competing amid romantic mix-ups and fortunes gained and lost. **120m/B VHS, Beta, Closed Caption.** Clark Gable, Spencer Tracy, Claudette Colbert, Hedy Lamarr, Frank Morgan, Lionel Atwill, Chill Wills, Curt Bois; *D:* Jack Conway. Nominations: Academy Awards '40: Best Black and White Cinematography.*MGM, CCB*

Boomerang 🎬🎬🎬 1947 Film noir based on actual events features the murder of a Connecticut clergyman and the quick arrest of vagrant John Waldron (Kennedy). Prosecuting attorney Henry Harvey (Andrews) is told by his political bosses to get an equally quick conviction to stem public outrage. The evidence seems overwhelming but Harvey begins his own investigation and suddenly switches to the defense to prove Waldron's innocence in dramatic courtroom style. Kazan filmed on location in Bridgeport, CT in a successful semi-documentary style that heightened the tension. **88m/B VHS, Closed Caption.** Dana Andrews, Arthur Kennedy, Lee J. Cobb, Jane Wyatt, Cara Williams, Sam Levene, Ed Begley Sr., Karl Malden, Taylor Holmes, Robert Keith; *D:* Elia Kazan; *W:* Richard Murphy; *C:* Norbert Brodine; *M:* David Buttolph. Nominations: Academy Awards '47: Best Screenplay. *FXV*

Boomerang 🎬½ 1976 A father rescues his wrongly convicted son from prison. Dubbed. **101m/C VHS, Beta, Closed Caption.** *IT* Alain Delon, Carla Gravina, Dora Doll; *D:* Jose Giovanni. *UNI*

Boomerang 🎬🎬 1992 (R) Successful, womanizing marketing exec for a cosmetics company (Murphy) meets his match when he falls for a colleague (Givens) who is as vain and sexually predatory as he is. She treats him the way he treats women (as a sex object), and he's shocked into the arms of a nice girl (Berry). Although it's refreshing to see this sexual role reversal, the typical Murphy-style humor is in play with sexist jokes and a couple of vulgar female characters. Grier and Lawrence are great as Murphy's best friends. Blaustein and Sheffield are the same guys who wrote Murphy's "Coming to America."*CW:* Language and sexuality. **118m/C VHS, Beta, LV, Letterbox, Closed Caption.** Eddie Murphy, Halle Berry, Robin Givens, David Alan Grier, Martin Lawrence, Grace Jones, Geoffrey Holder, Eartha Kitt, Chris Rock, Tisha Campbell, John Witherspoon, Melvin Van Peebles; *D:* Reginald Hudlin; *W:* Barry W. Blaustein, David Sheffield. *PAR*

The Boost 🎬½ 1988 (R) A feverish, messy melodrama about a young couple's spiraling decline from yuppie-ish wealth in a haze of cocaine abuse. **95m/C VHS, Beta, LV.** James Woods, Sean Young, John Kapelos, Steven Hill, Kelle Kerr, John Rothman, Amanda Blake, Grace Zabriskie; *D:* Harold Becker; *W:* Darryl Ponicsan; *C:* Howard Atherton. *HBO*

Boot Hill 🎬½ 1969 (PG) Two guys mess with western baddies and wild women in spaghetti oater. **97m/C VHS, Beta.** *IT* Terence Hill, Bud Spencer, Woody Strode, Victor Buono, Lionel Stander; *D:* Giuseppe Colizzi. *NO*

Boot Hill Bandits 🎬🎬½ 1942 "Crash" Corrigan fights on the side of right in this classic western as he helps corral Wells Fargo bandits. **58m/B VHS.** Ray Corrigan, John "Dusty" King, Max Terhune, Jean Brooks, John Merton, Glenn Strange; *D:* S. Roy Luby. *NOS, HEG*

Boothill Brigade 🎬🎬 1937 Former football-er Brown rides to the rescue when criminals steal land from homesteaders. **58m/B VHS.** Johnny Mack Brown, Claire Rochelle, Dick Curtis, Horace Murphy, Frank LaRue, Edward Cassidy, Bobby Nelson, Frank Ball, Steve Clark; *D:* Sam Newfield. *NOS, MRV*

Bootleg 🎬🎬 1989 A detective is on a case that leads to crooked politics and espionage. **82m/C VHS.** Ray Meagher; *D:* John Prescott.

Boots & Saddles 🎬½ 1937 A young English lord wants to sell the ranch he has inherited but Autry is determined to make him a real Westerner. **54m/B VHS.** Gene Autry, Judith Allen, Smiley Burnette; *D:* Joseph Kane. *NOS, MRV, VYY*

Boots Malone 🎬🎬½ 1952 An old down-on-his-luck gambling addict and a young, rich kid fascinated by the sordid atmosphere of the racetrack stumble upon one another and form a symbiotic relationship. All goes well for while, but there'd be no movie unless a collection of obstacles suddenly threatens their success, friendship, and even their lives. A rather melodramatic buddy tale, but Holden and Stewart hold interest. **103m/C VHS.** William Holden, John Stewart, Ed Begley Sr., Harry (Henry) Morgan, Whit Bissell; *D:* William Dieterle; *W:* Harold Buchman, Milton Holmes; *M:* Elmer Bernstein. *GKK*

Boots of Destiny 🎬 1937 Cheap western with Maynard and his sidekick Barnett on the lam and coming to the aid of ranch owner Dell. Based on a story by E. Morton Hough. **59m/B VHS.** Ken Maynard, Claudia Dell, Vince Barnett, Edward Cassidy, Martin Garralaga; *D:* Arthur Rosson; *W:* Arthur Rosson. *MOV*

Booty Call 🎬🎬½ 1996 (R) Reserved Rushon (Davidson) and conservative Nikki (Jones) have been dating for a couple of months and Rushon's decided they should consummate their relationship. Nikki's more ambivalent and first sets up a double date with her vivacious best friend Lysterine (Fox) and Rushon's bragging buddy Bunz (Foxx). The duos do pair up but since the "no glove, no love" rule prevails, first the guys have to find some condoms. Raunch rules as might be expected but it's an appealing cast.*CW:* Non-stop sexuality including sex-related dialogue and humor, and for strong language. **120m/C VHS, LV, Closed Caption, DVD.** Jamie Foxx, Tommy Davidson, Vivica A. Fox, Tamala Jones, Art Malik, Gedde Watanabe, Scott LaRose, Ammie Sin, Bernie Mac, David Hemblen; *D:* Jeff Pollack; *W:* Takashi Bufford; *C:* Ronald Orieux; *M:* Robert Folk. *COL*

Bopha! 🎬🎬🎬 1993 (PG-13) Father-son strife set against the anti-apartheid movement. In the Senior township police officer Mikah takes pride in his peaceful community, particularly in light of the growing unrest in the other townships. Son Zweli has become an activist and wife Rosie must be the family peacemaker. Then a prominent freedom movement member is arrested and two officers of the secret police make their sinister appearance. Well acted; directorial debut of Freeman. Adapted from the play by Percy Mtwa, although the hopeful ending has been changed in the movie. The title, a Zulu word, stands for arrest or detention. Filmed on location in Zimbabwe. **121m/C VHS, Beta, LV, Closed Caption.** Danny Glover, Maynard Eziashi, Alfre Woodard, Malcolm McDowell, Marius Weyers, Malick Bowens, Robin Smith, Michael Chinyamurindi, Christopher John Hall, Grace Mahlaba; *D:* Morgan Freeman; *W:* Brian Bird, John Wierick; *M:* James Horner. *PAR*

Bordello 🎬 1979 A made-for-television western spoof about cowboys and shady ladies. **90m/C VHS, Beta.** Chuck Connors, Michael Conrad, John Ireland, Isela Vega, George Rivero.

The Border 🎬🎬🎬 1982 (R) A border guard faces corruption and violence within his department and tests his own sense of decency when the infant of a poor Mexican girl is kidnapped. Excellent cast, fine cinematography, unusual Nicholson performance. **107m/C VHS, Beta, LV.** Jack Nicholson, Harvey Keitel, Valerie Perrine, Warren Oates, Elpidia Carrillo; *D:* Tony Richardson; *W:* Deric Washburn, Walon Green; *M:* Ry Cooder. *USH*

Border Badmen 🎬½ 1945 It's just another tired old western, even if it does appropriate the classic mystery-thriller plot; following the reading of a silver baron's will, someone starts killing off the relatives. 59m/B VHS, Beta. Buster Crabbe, Lorraine Miller, Charles "Blackie" King, Ray Bennett, Archie Hall, Budd Buster, Bud Osborne; **D:** Sam Newfield. GPV, MRV

Border Bandits ✍ 1946 Plodding oater has Brown going after the bad guys. Not only is it a dirty job, but apparently pretty boring. **57m/B VHS.** Johnny Mack Brown, Raymond Hatton, John Merton, Frank LaRue, Steve Clark, Charles Stevens, Bud Osborne; **D:** Lambert Hillyer. DVT, HEG

Border Caballero ✍½ 1936 Western star McCoy and lady cowpoke January shoot out the skies in this lackluster McCoy vehicle. Based on a story by Norman S. Hall. **57m/B VHS.** Tim McCoy, Lois January, Ralph Byrd, Ted Adams; **D:** Sam Newfield; **W:** Joseph O'Donnell. MOV

Border Devils ✍ 1932 A boy is pursued by a ruthless gang of outlaws, until he is saved by the good guys. **60m/B VHS, Beta, LV.** Harry Carey Sr., Art Mix, George "Gabby" Hayes; **D:** William Nigh. NO

Border Feud ✍ 1947 LaRue endeavors to prevent someone who, by instigating a family feud, will claim large gold mine rights. **54m/B VHS, Beta.** Lash LaRue, Al "Fuzzy" St. John, Bob Duncan; **D:** Ray Taylor. COL

Border Law ✍✍½ 1931 Jones plays a heroic Texas Ranger who goes undercover to find the man who killed his brother. One of Jones' finest outings and far better than most B westerns. **62m/B VHS.** Buck Jones, Lupita Tovar, James Mason, Frank Rice, Glenn Strange; **D:** Louis King; **W:** Stuart Anthony. MOV, GVV

The Border Legion ✍½ 1940 Sappy retelling of Grey's novel about an outlaw sacrificing himself for a pair of young lovers. This time Rogers is the outlaw with a heart of gold. Originally filmed in 1930 with Jack Holt, Richard Arlen, and Fay Wray. **58m/B VHS.** Roy Rogers, George "Gabby" Hayes, Carol Hughes, Joseph Sawyer, Maude Eburne, Jay Novello; **D:** Joseph Kane; **W:** Olive Cooper, Louis Stevens. MOV

Border Patrol ✍✍ 1943 Another installment in the Hopalong Cassidy series. This time there's a villainous owner of a silvermine to reckon with. A man so low he's abducting hapless Mexicans as they cross the border, forcing them to work his mines. Hoppy is saddled with the task of persuading him that the town ain't big enough for the both of them. Robert Mitchum makes his perfectly forgettable film debut as one of the bad guys. Not one of the best in the series, but plenty of action. **63m/B VHS.** William Boyd, Andy Clyde, Jay Kirby, Russell Simpson, Claudia Drake, George Reeves, Duncan Renaldo; **D:** Lesley Selander. NOS

Border Phantom ✍✍ 1937 Steele (whom you might recognize as Canino in "The Big Sleep"), takes on a suave Chinese businessman who heads a mail order business: seems he's smuggling mail-order brides from Mexico in this vintage "B"-grade horse opera. **60m/B VHS.** Bob Steele, Harley Wood, Don Barclay, Karl Hackett, Horace Murphy, Miki Morita; **D:** S. Roy Luby. NOS, MRV, VTR

Border Radio woof! 1988 A rock singer decides to steal a car and try to outrun some tough thugs hot on his trail. **88m/B VHS, Closed Caption.** Chris D, Luana Anders; **D:** Allison Anders, Kurt Voss; **W:** Allison Anders, Kurt Voss; **M:** Dave Alvin. FCT

Border Rangers ✍ 1950 A man joins the Rangers in order to avenge the murders of his brother and sister-in-law. **57m/B VHS, Beta, LV.** Robert Lowery, Donald (Don "Red") Barry, Lyle Talbot, Pamela Blake; **D:** William (Lester Williams) Berke. NO

Border Romance ✍½ 1930 Three Americans have their horses stolen by bandits while riding through Mexico. Trouble with the locals follows in this early sound western. **58m/B VHS, Beta.** Don Terry, Armida, Marjorie Kane. VYY

Border Roundup ✍ 1941 The "Lone Rider" uncovers a gang of thieving crooks. **57m/B VHS, Beta.** George Houston, Al "Fuzzy" St. John, Dennis Moore; **D:** Sam Newfield. VDM

Border Saddlemates ♪ 1952 U.S. government veterinarian Allen is asked to sub for the local doc in the Canadian border town of Pine Rock. But he learns that a gang is using silver fox pelts to smuggle illegal goods into the U.S. and it's up to Allen and the Rhythm Riders to stop them. **67m/B VHS, Closed Caption.** Rex Allen. REP

Border Shootout ✍✍ 1990 (PG) A trigger-happy sheriff battles a rich young cattle rustler. **110m/C VHS, Beta, Closed Caption.** Glenn Ford, Charlene Tilton, Jeff Kaake, Michael Horse, Russell Todd, Cody Glenn, Sergio Calderon, Michael Ansara; **D:** C.T. McIntyre. TTC

Border Vengeance ✍✍½ 1935 Reb is a member of a family of outlaws. He aims to improve himself and steer his family to the straight and narrow trail. **45m/B VHS.** Reb Russell, Mary Jane Carey, Kenneth MacDonald, Hank Bell, Glenn Strange, Norman Feusier, Charles "Slim" Whitaker; **D:** Ray Heinz. GPV

Border Vigilantes ✍✍ 1941 Hoppy and pals try to rid a town of outlaws that even the vigilantes can't run off. The big surprise comes when they find out who the leader of the outlaws is. **61m/B VHS.** William Boyd, Russell Hayden, Andy Clyde, Victor Jory, Morris Ankrum, Frances Gifford, Ethel Wales, Hal Taliaferro; **D:** Derwin Abrahams. NOS

Borderline ✍✍ 1950 MacMurray and Trevor play undercover agents trying to infiltrate a Mexican drug ring. With their real identities hidden, they fall for each other and make a run for the border. Although the leads work well together, they're hindered by an occasionally confusing script. Unfortunately, director Seiter never decides whether the material is of a comedic or dramatic nature. **88m/B VHS.** Fred MacMurray, Claire Trevor, Raymond Burr, Roy Roberts, Jose Torvay, Morris Ankrum, Charles Lane, Don Diamond, Nacho Galindo, Pepe Hern, Richard Irving; **D:** William A. Seiter. HEG

Borderline ✍✍ 1980 (PG) Bronson is a border patrol guard in pursuit of a murderer in this action flick. Meanwhile, he gets caught up in trying to help an illegal alien and her young child. **106m/C VHS, Beta, Closed Caption.** Charles Bronson, Wilford Brimley, Bruno Kirby, Benito Morales, Ed Harris, Kenneth McMillan; **D:** Jerrold Freedman. FOX

Bordertown Gunfighters ✍½ 1943 A cowboy breaks up a vicious lottery racket and falls in love in the process. **56m/B VHS, Beta.** Wild Bill Elliott, Anne Jeffreys. DVT

Boris and Natasha: The Movie ✍½ 1992 (PG) The two inept spies from the classic television cartoon "The Adventures of Rocky and Bullwinkle" star in this mediocre live-action comedy. These nogoodniks are sent by "Fearless Leader" to America and encounter the usual misadventures. For true fun watch the original animated versions. Never released theatrically, it aired for the first time on cable television. **88m/C VHS, Closed Caption.** Sally Kellerman, Dave Thomas, Paxton Whitehead, Andrea Martin, Alex Rocco, Larry Cedar, Arye Gross, Christopher Neame, Anthony Newley; **Cameos:** John Candy, John Travolta, Charles Martin Smith; **D:** Charles Martin Smith. NLC

B.O.R.N. ✍½ 1988 (R) Hagen uncovers an underground network of doctors who kill people and sell the body parts and organs. **90m/C VHS, Beta.** Ross Hagen, P.J. Soles, William Smith, Hoke Howell, Russ Tamblyn, Amanda Blake, Clint Howard, Rance Howard, Debra Lamb; **D:** Ross Hagen.

Born Again 1978 This is the filmed adaptation of Charles Colson's biography of why he became a born again Christian. **110m/C VHS, Beta.** Dean Jones, Anne Francis, Dana Andrews, George Brent; **D:** Irving Rapper; **C:** Harry Stradling Jr.; **M:** Les Baxter.

Born American ✍ Arctic Heat 1986 (R) Pre-Glasnost flick about teenagers vacationing in Finland who "accidentally" cross the Russian border. There they battle the Red Plague. Melodramatic and heavily politicized. Original release banned in Finland. **95m/C VHS, Beta.** Mike Norris, Steve Durham, David Coburn, Thalmus Rasulala, Albert Salmi; **D:** Renny Harlin. NO

Born Beautiful ✍✍½ 1982 Made for TV. Beautiful young women come to New York, hoping to strike it rich in the world of modeling. At the same time, a still beautiful, but older and overexposed model comes to grips with a change in her career. Well-told, but sugar-coated. **100m/C VHS.** Erin Gray, Ed Marinaro, Polly Bergen, Lori Singer, Ellen Barber, Judith Barcroft, Michael Higgins; **D:** Harvey Hart; **M:** Brad Fiedel. WAR

Born Free ✍✍✍ 1966 The touching story of a game warden in Kenya and his wife raising Elsa the orphaned lion cub. When the cub reaches maturity, they work to return her to life in the wild. Great family entertainment based on Joy Adamson's book. Theme song became a hit. ♫Born Free. **95m/C VHS, Beta, LV.** Virginia McKenna, Bill Travers; **D:** James Hill; **W:** Lester Cole; **M:** John Barry. Academy Awards '66: Best Song ("Born Free"), Best Original Score. COL, HMV

Born in America ✍ Dead Aim 1990 A young orphan is adopted by an undertaker. The boy grows up enveloped by his guardian's business and, when things are slow, works to bring in business himself. **90m/C VHS.** James Westerfield, Glen Lee, Virgil Frye, Venetia Vianello; **D:** Jose Antonio Bolanos. NO

Born in East L.A. ✍✍ 1987 (R) Marin brings his Bruce Springsteen-parody song to life as he plays a mistakenly deported illegal alien who struggles to return to the U.S. Suprisingly resolute effort by the usually self-exploiting Mexican-American. Stern is the American expatriate who helps him get back and Lopez is the love interest who stalls him. **85m/C VHS, Beta, LV.** Richard "Cheech" Marin, Daniel Stern, Paul Rodriguez, Jan-Michael Vincent, Kamala Lopez, Tony Plana, Vic Trevino, A. Martinez; **D:** Richard "Cheech" Marin. USH, FCT

Born in Flames ✍ 1983 An acclaimed futuristic feminist film about women who band together in an effort to gain control of the state owned media. **90m/C VHS. D:** Lizzie Borden; **W:** Lizzie Borden. ICA

Born Innocent ✍½ 1974 As if "The Exorcist" weren't bad enough, Blair is back for more abuse-on-film, this time as a 14-year-old runaway from a dysfunctional family who lands in a reform school for girls. There, she must struggle to be as brutal as her peers in order to survive. Fairly tame by today's standards, but controversial at its made-for-TV premiere, chiefly due to a rape scene involving a broom handle. First trip up the river for Blair. **92m/C VHS, Beta, LV.** Linda Blair, Joanna Miles, Kim Hunter, Richard Jaeckel; **D:** Donald Wrye. NO

Born Invincible ✍ 1976 A Kung Fu master avenges the kick-death of a student by randomly kick-killing suspects. **90m/C VHS, Beta.** Lo Lieh, Carter Wong, Nancy Yan; **D:** Joseph Kuo. GEM

Born Killer ✍½ 1989 Teenagers in the woods meet up with murderous escaped convicts. **90m/C VHS, Beta.** Francine Lapensee, Fritz Matthews, Ted Prior, Adam Tucker; **D:** Kimberly Casey.

Born Losers ✍✍ 1967 (PG) The original "Billy Jack" film in which the Indian martial arts expert takes on a group of incorrigible bikers bothering some California babes and runs afoul of the law. Classic drive-in fare. **112m/C VHS, Beta, LV.** Tom Laughlin, Elizabeth James, Jeremy Slate, William Wellman Jr., Robert Tessier, Jane Russell; **D:** Tom Laughlin; **W:** Tom Laughlin. VES, ART

Born of Fire ✍½ 1987 (R) A flutist investigating his father's death seeks the Master Musician; his search leads him to the volcanic (and supernatural) mountains of Turkey. **84m/C VHS, Beta, LV.** Peter Firth, Susan Crowley, Stephan Kalipha; **D:** Jamil Dehlavi; **M:** Colin Towns. THV

Born on the Fourth of July ✍✍✍½ 1989 (R) A riveting meditation on American life affected by the Vietnam War, based on the real-life, bestselling experiences of Ron Kovic, though some facts are subtly changed. The film follows him as he develops from a naive recruit to an angry, wheelchair-bound paraplegic to an active antiwar protestor. Well-acted and generally lauded; Kovic co-wrote the screenplay and appears as a war veteran in the opening parade sequence. **145m/C VHS, Beta, LV, Letterbox, Closed Caption, DVD.** Tom Cruise, Kyra Sedgwick, Raymond J. Barry, Jerry Levine, Tom Berenger, Willem Dafoe, Frank Whaley, John Getz, Caroline Kava, Bryan Larkin, Abbie Hoffman, Stephen Baldwin, Josh Evans; **D:** Oliver Stone; **W:** Oliver Stone; **C:** Robert Richardson; **M:** John Williams. Academy Awards '89: Best Director (Stone), Best Film Editing; Directors Guild of America Awards '89: Best Director (Stone); Golden Globe Awards '90: Best Actor—Drama (Cruise), Best Director (Stone), Best Film—Drama, Best Screenplay; Nominations: Academy Awards '89: Best Actor (Cruise), Best Adapted Screenplay, Best Cinematography, Best Picture, Best Sound, Best Original Score. *USH, FCT, BTV*

Born Reckless 🎬½ 1959 Van Doren plays a singer working the rodeo circuit who falls for aging rider Richards. Not bad enough to be funny, however, Van Doren shows an incredible lack of talent while singing several tunes. ♫Song of the Rodeo; Born Reckless; A Little Longer; Home Type Girl; Separate the Men from the Boys; Something to Dream About; You, Lovable You. **79m/B VHS.** Mamie Van Doren, Jeff Richards, Arthur Hunnicutt, Carol Ohmart, Donald (Don "Red") Barry, Nacho Galindo; **D:** Howard W. Koch. *MOV*

Born to Be Bad 🎬🎬½ 1950 Fontaine, an opportunistic woman who was b-b-born to be b-b-bad, attempts to steal a wealthy business man away from his wife while carrying on an affair with a novelist. Ray's direction (he's best known for "Rebel Without a Cause," filmed five years later) prevents the film from succumbing to standard Hollywood formula. **93m/B VHS, Beta, LV.** Joan Fontaine, Robert Ryan, Zachary Scott, Joan Leslie, Mel Ferrer; **D:** Nicholas Ray. *TTC*

Born to Be Wild 🎬🎬 1938 A pair of truck drivers are commissioned to deliver a shipment of dynamite. The dynamite will be used to destroy a dam, preventing the surrounding land from falling into the hands of unscrupulous land barons. Good action picture thanks to the cast. **66m/B VHS, Beta.** Ralph Byrd, Doris Weston, Ward Bond, Robert Emmett Keane, Bentley Hewlett, Charles Williams; **D:** Joseph Kane. *SNC, RXM*

Born to Be Wild 🎬½ 1995 (PG) Rebellious teenager Rick (Hornoff) befriends Katie, the three-year-old gorilla his behaviorial scientist mom (Shaver) is studying. When Katie's owner (Boyle) decides she would make a better sideshow attraction than science project, Rick busts her out and they head for the Canadian border. Animal slapstick and bodily function jokes ensue as the chase continues. "Free Willy"-inspired plot and primate hijinks should keep young kids interested, but anyone over the age of nine probably won't be too impressed. **98m/C VHS, LV, Closed Caption.** Wil Horneff, Helen Shaver, Peter Boyle, Jean Marie Barnwell, John C. McGinley, Marvin J. McIntyre; **D:** John Gray; **W:** John Bunzel, Paul Young; **C:** Donald M. Morgan. *WAR*

Born to Boogie 🎬🎬 1972 A concert, a chronicle, and a tribute, "Born To Boogie" is about Marc Bolan and his band T. Rex. The film, which features concert footage from a 1972 concert at the Wembley Empire Pool in London, chronicles the glitter rock era and the next wave of British rock and roll, and pays tribute to Bolan, who died in 1977 just as he was starting a comeback. Ringo Starr and Elton John join T. Rex in the studio for "Children of the Revolution" and "Tutti-Frutti" as well as a psychadelic soiree where Bolan plays acoustic versions of his hits. This film was never released in the United States. **75m/C VHS.** Marc Bolan, Elton John, Ringo Starr; **D:** Ringo Starr. *MPI, MVD*

Born to Dance 🎬🎬½ 1936 A quintessential MGM 1930s dance musical, wherein a beautiful dancer gets a sailor and a big break in a show. Great songs by Cole Porter sung in a less than great manner by a gangly Stewart. Powell's first starring vehicle. ♫Love Me Love My Pekinese;

I've Got You Under My Skin; Hey Babe Hey; Easy to Love; Rolling Home; Rap Tap on Wood; Entrance of Lucy James; Swingin' the Jinx Away. **108m/B VHS, Beta, LV.** Eleanor Powell, James Stewart, Virginia Bruce, Una Merkel, Frances Langford, Sid Silvers, Raymond Walburn, Reginald Gardiner, Buddy Ebsen; **D:** Roy Del Ruth; **M:** Cole Porter, Cole Porter. Nominations: Academy Awards '36: Best Song ("I've Got You Under My Skin"). *MGM, MLB*

Born to Kill 🎬🎬🎬 *Lady of Deceit* 1947 A ruthless killer marries a girl for her money. Minor tough-as-nails film noir exemplifying Tierney's stone-faced human-devil persona. **92m/B VHS, Beta.** Lawrence Tierney, Claire Trevor, Walter Slezak, Elisha Cook Jr.; **D:** Robert Wise. *TTC*

Born to Race 🎬 1988 (R) In the world of competitive auto racing, a beautiful engineer is kidnapped for her new controversial engine design. **95m/C VHS, Beta.** Joseph Bottoms, George Kennedy, Marc Singer, Marla Heasly; **D:** James Fargo. *FOX*

Born to Ride 🎬🎬 1991 (PG) A biker rebel joins the Army prior to WWII in order to escape a prison term after a good ol' boy brush with the law. He shuns Army discipline, but proves himself in action as the leader of a scout troup for the Army's motorcycle cavalry brigade. Available with Spanish subtitles. **88m/C VHS, Beta, Closed Caption.** John Stamos, John Stockwell, Teri Polo, Kris Kamm; **D:** Graham Baker. *WAR*

Born to Run 🎬🎬½ 1993 Nicky Donatello (Grieco) is a Brooklyn street drag racer who gets mixed up with the mob while trying to rescue his no-account brother. But he still finds time to fall for an uptown model who also happens to be the mobster's girlfriend. Made for television. **97m/C VHS, LV.** Richard Grieco, Jay Acovone, Shelli Lether, Christian Campbell, Brent Stait, Martin Cummins, Wren Roberts, Joe Cortese; **D:** Albert Magnoli; **W:** Randall Badat. *FXV*

Born to Win 🎬🎬½ *Addict* 1971 (R) A New York hairdresser with an expensive drug habit struggles through life in this well made comedy drama. Excellent acting from fine cast, well-paced, and interestingly photographed. Not well received when first released, but worth a look. **90m/C VHS.** George Segal, Karen Black, Paula Prentiss, Hector Elizondo, Robert De Niro, Jay Fletcher; **D:** Ivan Passer; **C:** Jack Priestley. *QVD, MDM*

Born Wild 🎬🎬½ 1995 (PG) Documentary filmmaker Christine Shaye (Shields) has just gotten her first important assignment from overbearing boss Dan Walker (Sheen), which is to capture the beauty of Africa. Christine arrives at the South African game preserve of Londolozi where she meets passionate conservationist John Varty (who plays himself). Varty has filmed one leopard family for 12 years but when the mother leopard is killed, he violates his own ethical code when he rescues her two orphaned cubs. **98m/C VHS, LV, Closed Caption.** Brooke Shields, Martin Sheen, John Varty, David Keith; **D:** Duncan McLachlan; **W:** Duncan McLachlan, Andrea Buck. *COL*

Born Yesterday 🎬🎬🎬½ 1950 Ambitious junk dealer Harry Brock is in love with smart but uneducated Billie Dawn. He hires newspaperman Paul Verrall to teach her the finer points of etiquette. During their sessions, they fall in love and Billie realizes how she has been used by Brock. She retaliates against him and gets to deliver that now-famous line: "Do me a favor, drop dead." Based on the Broadway play. **103m/B VHS, Beta, LV, Closed Caption.** Judy Holliday, Broderick Crawford, William Holden; **D:** George Cukor. Academy Awards '50: Best Actress (Holliday); Golden Globe Awards '51: Best Actress—Musical/Comedy (Holliday); Nominations: Academy Awards '50: Best Costume Design (B & W), Best Director (Cukor), Best Picture, Best Screenplay. *COL, FCT, BTV*

Born Yesterday 🎬🎬 1993 (PG) Remake of the 1950 classic suffers in comparison, particularly Griffith, who has the thankless task of surpassing (or even meeting) Judy Holliday's Oscar-winning mark as not-so-dumb blonde Billie Dawn. Her intellectual inadequacies are glaring when

she hits the political world of D.C. with obnoxious tycoon boyfriend Goodman. To save face, he hooks her up with a journalist (Johnson) willing to coach her in Savvy 101, a la Eliza Doolittle. What worked well in post-WWII America seems sadly outdated today; stick with the original. **102m/C VHS, Beta, LV, Letterbox, Closed Caption.** Melanie Griffith, John Goodman, Don Johnson, Edward Herrmann, Max Perlich, Fred Dalton Thompson, Nora Dunn, Benjamin C. Bradlee, Sally Quinn, Michael Ensign, William Frankfather, Celeste Yarnall, Meg Wittner; **D:** Luis Mandoki; **W:** Douglas McGrath; **C:** Lajos Koltai; **M:** George Fenton. *TOU, HPH*

The Borrower 🎬🎬 1989 (R) An exiled unstable mutant insect alien serial killer (you know the type) must switch heads with human beings regularly to survive. This colorful, garish gorefest has humor and attitude, but never develops behind the basic grossout situation. **97m/C VHS, LV.** Rae Dawn Chong, Don Gordon, Antonio Fargas, Tom Towles; **D:** John McNaughton. *WAR*

The Borrowers 🎬🎬🎬 1993 Excellent made for television adaptation of the May Norton childrens classics "The Borrowers" and "The Borrowers Afield." This miniature family (about mouse-size) live beneath the floorboards of an English house and borrow what they need to survive from the normal-sized human inhabitants. Problems come when the teeny family are discovered and must make their way to a new home. Sweet and humorous. On two cassettes. **199m/C VHS, Closed Caption.** *GB* Ian Holm, Penelope Wilton, Rebecca Callard; **D:** John Henderson; **W:** Richard Carpenter. *TTC*

The Borrowers 🎬🎬½ 1997 (PG) Charming big-screen, big-budget tale about the little people who live under the floor. The British, elfin, and about four inch tall Clock family, headed by papa Pod (Broadbent) lives hidden in the walls of the home of the normal-sized American Lenders and exist by "borrowing" objects from their human's household. When an evil lawyer (Goodman), also American, threatens their happiness, the Borrowers bond with young Peter Lender (Pierce) who "discovers" them and volunteers to help them save their way of life. This remake focuses mainly on the impressive special effects, lending a modern look and appeal. Goodman is lovably evil in that wonderfully Snidely Whiplash way. Based on the children's books of Mary Norton. **83m/C VHS.** *GB* John Goodman, Hugh Laurie, Jim Broadbent, Mark Williams, Celia Imrie, Bradley Michael Pierce, Raymond Pickard, Aden Gillett, Ruby Wax, Flora Newbigin, Tom Felton, Doon Mackichan; **D:** Peter Hewitt; **W:** John Camps, Gavin Scott; **C:** John Fenner, Trvor Brooker; **M:** Harry Gregson-Williams. Nominations: British Academy Awards '97: Best Film. *NYR*

Borsalino 🎬🎬🎬 1970 (R) Delon and Belmondo are partners in crime in this seriocomic film about gang warfare in 1930s Marseilles. The costumes, settings, and music perfectly capture the mood of the period. Followed by a sequel "Borsalino and Co." Based on "The Bandits of Marseilles" by Eugene Saccomano. ***CW:** Strong gangster violence.* **124m/C VHS.** *FR* Jean-Paul Belmondo, Alain Delon, Michel Bouquet, Catherine Rouvel, Francoise Christophe, Corinne Marchand; **D:** Jacques Deray; **W:** Jacques Deray, Claude Sautet, Jean-Claude Carriere; **M:** Claude Bolling. *PAR*

Bosom Buddies 1980 Sitcom features best friends Hanks and Scolari who, desperate for cheap rent in New York City, dress in drag in order to move into the women-only Susan B. Anthony hotel. Naturally, this causes some confusion in their love lives. Two episodes per tape. **51m/C VHS, Closed Caption.** Tom Hanks, Peter Scolari, Donna Dixon, Wendie Jo Sperber, Holland Taylor, Telma Hopkins. *PAR*

Boss 🎬½ *The Black Bounty Killer; Boss Nigger* 1974 (PG) Blaxploitation western parody with Williamson and Martin as a couple of bounty hunters tearing apart a town to find a fugitive. Relatively non-violent. **87m/C VHS.** Fred Williamson, D'Urville Marith, R.G. Armstrong, William Smith, Carmen Hayworth, Barbara Leigh; **D:** Jack Arnold; **W:** Fred Williamson. NO

Boss Cowboy ✗ 1935 A cowboy shows who wears the chaps in his family when he kidnaps his girlfriend to prevent her from moving East. 51m/B VHS, Beta. Buddy Roosevelt, Frances Morris, Sam Pierce, Fay McKenzie, Lafe McKee; **D:** Victor Adamson. GPV

Boss Foreman WOOF! 1939 A languorous, entwining comedy of errors about a construction foreman and his misadventures with the mob. 58m/B VHS, Beta. Henry Armetta. VYY

The Boss Is Served ✗✗ 196? A mother (Berger) and three daughters, racked with debt, are forced to take in boarders. The lascivious man and teenage son want to be more than just boarders to the lovely Berger. In Italian with English subtitles. 95m/C VHS, Beta. IT Senta Berger, Maurizio Arena, Bruno Zanin. NO

Boss of Big Town ✗✗ 1943 Gangsters try to infiltrate the milk industry in this standard crime drama. 65m/B VHS, Beta. John Litel, Florence Rice, H.B. Warner, Jean Brooks, John Miljan, Mary Gordon, John Maxwell; **D:** Arthur Dreifuss. SNC, RXM

Boss of Bullion City ✗✗½ 1941 A crooked sheriff is exposed by Brown and sidekick Knight in this sagebrush saga. Based on a story by Arthur St. Claire. 61m/B VHS. Johnny Mack Brown, Fuzzy Knight, Maria Montez, Earle Hodgins, Harry Woods; **D:** Ray Taylor; **W:** Victor McLeod, Arthur St. Claire. MOV

Boss of Rawhide ✗ 1944 The Texas Rangers fight for law and order in the old west despite odds against them. 60m/B VHS, Beta. Dave O'Brien, James Newill. NOS, DVT

Boss' Son ✗✗✗ 1978 Worthwhile coming-of-age tale about a young man who learns more than he bargained for about life when he goes to work for his father in the family carpet business. Dad feels he should work his way up through the ranks and makes him a delivery man. The young man meets reality head on and must deal with the injustices of the world around him. Independently filmed by director/writer Roth. 97m/C VHS, Beta. Rita Moreno, James Darren, Asher Brauner, Rudy Solari, Henry Sanders, Richie Havens, Piper Laurie, Elena Verdugo; **D:** Bobby Roth; **W:** Bobby Roth; **C:** Alfonso Beato. VES, ART

The Boss' Wife ✗✗ 1986 A young stockbroker attempts to fix what's wrong with his life by maneuvering sexually with the boss' wife, and complications set in. 83m/C VHS, Beta, Closed Caption. Daniel Stern, Arielle Dombasle, Christopher Plummer, Martin Mull, Melanie Mayron, Lou Jacobi; **D:** Ziggy Steinberg; **M:** Bill Conti. FOX

Boston Kickout ✗✗ 1995 A quartet of teenaged friends/losers struggle to grow up in a bleak concrete town outside London. There are neglected girlfriends, dysfunctional families, menial jobs, petty crime, emotional disasters—and some faint glimmer of hope for at least a couple of the lads. Title refers to a destructive game the boys play. 105m/C VHS. GB John Simm, Andrew Lincoln, Richard Hanson, Nathan Valente, Emer McCourt, Marc Warren, Derek Martin, Vincent Phillips, Natalie Davies; **D:** Paul Hills; **W:** Paul Hills, Diane Whitley, Roberto Troni; **C:** Roger Bonnici; **M:** Robert Hartshorne. BMG

The Boston Strangler ✗✗½ 1968 Based on Gerold Frank's bestselling factual book about the deranged killer who terrorized Boston for about a year and a half. Traces events from first killing to prosecution. Curtis, going against type, is compelling in title role. 116m/C VHS, Closed Caption. Tony Curtis, Henry Fonda, George Kennedy, Murray Hamilton, Mike Kellin, George Voskovec, William Hickey, James Brolin, Hurd Hatfield, William Marshall, Jeff Corey, Sally Kellerman; **D:** Richard Fleischer; **W:** Edward Anhalt. FOX

The Bostonians ✗✗½ 1984 (PG) A faith healer's daughter is forced to choose between the affections of a militant suffragette and a young lawyer in 19th Century Boston. Based on Henry James' classic novel. 120m/C VHS, Beta, LV. Christopher Reeve, Vanessa Redgrave, Madeleine Potter, Jessica

Tandy, Nancy Marchand, Wesley Addy, Linda Hunt, Wallace Shawn; **D:** James Ivory; **W:** Ruth Prawer Jhabvala; **C:** Walter Lassally. National Society of Film Critics Awards '84: Best Actress (Redgrave); Nominations: Academy Awards '84: Best Actress (Redgrave), Best Costume Design. VES, ART

Botany Bay ✗✗ 1953 A rousing costumer about a convict ship in the 1700s that, after a trying voyage, lands in Australia, wherein a framed doctor conquers the local plague. From the novel by Charles Nordoff. 99m/C VHS, Beta. Alan Ladd, James Mason, Patricia Medina, Cedric Hardwicke; **D:** John Farrow. BAR

Bottle Rocket ✗✗½ 1995 (R) A trio of inexperienced but aspiring criminals attempt to make their mark on the world in suburban Dallas. Newcomers Wilson, who plays the group's ambitious leader Dignan, and Anderson penned this smart ensemble piece first as a 13-minute black and white short. A subsequent showing at the Sundance Film Festival got the attention of producer James L. Brooks ("Broadcast News"). Film got the backing to go feature length with Anderson directing, and deservedly so, with its fresh dialogue and surprising warmth. **CW:** Language. 91m/C VHS, LV, Closed Caption. Owen C. Wilson, Luke Wilson, Robert Musgrave, Lumi Cavazos, James Caan, Teddy Wilson, Andrew Wilson, Jim Ponds; **D:** Wes Anderson; **W:** Owen C. Wilson, Wes Anderson; **C:** Robert Yeoman; **M:** Mark Mothersbaugh. MTV Movie Awards '96: Best New Filmmaker Award (Anderson). COL

Bottoms Up WOOF! 1987 Three nymphomaniacs seduce a virginal mechanic and turn him into an insatiable womanizer. Skin aplenty. 90m/C VHS, Beta. Adam Janas, Sparky Abbrams, Kathleen Johnson.

Boudu Saved from Drowning ✗✗✗½ Boudu Sauve des Eaux 1932 A suicidal tramp completely disrupts the wealthy household of the man that saves him from drowning. A gentle but sardonic farce from the master filmmaker. Remade in 1986 as "Down and Out In Beverly Hills." 87m/B VHS, Beta. FR Michel Simon, Charles Granval, Jean Daste; **D:** Jean Renoir. INT, MRV, DVT

Boulevard ✗½ 1994 (R) Jennefer (Wuhrer) is forced to give her baby up for adoption, after escaping from an abusive husband, and make her way on the city's mean streets. She meets prostitute Ola (Chong), who decides to look after the naif and protect Jennefer from violent pimp Hassan (Phillips). But Ola gets into trouble with tough cop Claren (Henriksen) and soon Jennefer must survive on her own—against both Hassan and her vengeful husband. Woman empowerment, complete with standard cliches. **CW:** Violence, sexual situations, nudity. 96m/C VHS, LV, Closed Caption. Kari Wuhrer, Rae Dawn Chong, Lou Diamond Phillips, Lance Henriksen, Joel Bissonnette; **D:** Penelope Buitenhuis; **W:** Rae Dawn Chong; **M:** Ian Thomas. ART

Boulevard Nights ✗✗ 1979 (R) A young Latino man tries to escape his neighborhood's streetgang violence, until his older brother is sucked into it. Music by Schifrin, known for the "Mission: Impossible" theme. 102m/C VHS, Beta. Richard Yniguez, Danny De La Paz, Marta DuBois, Carmen Zapata, Victor Millan; **D:** Michael Pressman; **C:** John Bailey; **M:** Lalo Schifrin. WAR

Boulevard of Broken Dreams ✗✗ 1988 (PG-13) Successful Hollywood screenwriter Tom Garfield (Waters) returns to his native Australia to figure out how his life got so screwed up. His estranged wife is living with someone else and his daughter barely remembers him. Affecting look at personal priorities versus success. 95m/C VHS. AU John Waters, Kim Gyngell, Penelope Stewart; **D:** Pino Amenta.

Bound ✗✗ 1996 (R) Ex-con Corky (Gershon) is busy fixing up her new apartment after serving five years for robbery. Her next-door neighbors are Caesar (Pantoliano), a neurotic, money-laundering mobster, and his sexy girlfriend, a seemingly dumb brunette named Violet (Tilly). The

femme twosome hook up (in and out of bed) and hatch a plan to steal two million freshly laundered dollars from Caesar, who goes ballistic when he discovers the money gone. It's a flashy—but not substantive—thriller. Directorial debut for the brothers Wachowski. **CW:** Strong sexuality, violence and language. 107m/C VHS, LV, Closed Caption. Gina Gershon, Jennifer Tilly, Joe Pantoliano, John P. Ryan, Barry Kivel, Christopher Meloni, Peter Spellos, Richard Sarafian, Mary Mara, Susie Bright, Ivan Kane, Kevin M. Richardson, Gene Borkan; **D:** Andy Wachowski, Larry Wachowski; **W:** Andy Wachowski, Larry Wachowski; **C:** Bill Pope; **M:** Don Davis. Nominations: Independent Spirit Awards '97: Best Cinematography; MTV Movie Awards '97: Best Kiss (Jennifer Tilly/Gina Gershon). REP

Bound and Gagged: A Love Story ✗ 1993 (R) For some reason, Elizabeth (Saltarelli), who is desperate for a husband, thinks that she might increase her chances of finding one if she kidnaps her friend Leslie (Allen) and goes on a weird wild goose chase through Minnesota with the hostage and her hopeless partner-in-crime, Cliff (Denton). Go figure. **CW:** Language and strong sexuality. 96m/C VHS, LV. Ginger Lynn Allen, Karen Black, Chris Denton, Elizabeth Saltarelli, Mary Ella Ross, Chris Mulkey; **D:** Daniel Appleby; **W:** Daniel Appleby; **M:** William Murphy. TRI

Bound for Glory ✗✗✗½ 1976 (PG) The award-winning biography of American folk singer Woody Guthrie set against the backdrop of the Depression. Superb portrayal of the spirit and feelings of the period featuring many of his songs encased in the incidents that inspired them. Haskell Wexler's award-winning camera work is superbly expressive. 149m/C VHS, Beta, LV. David Carradine, Ronny Cox, Melinda Dillon, Randy Quaid; **D:** Hal Ashby; **W:** Robert Getchell; **C:** Haskell Wexler. Academy Awards '76: Best Cinematography, Original Song Score and/or Adaptation; Los Angeles Film Critics Association Awards '76: Best Cinematography; National Board of Review Awards '76: Best Actor (Carradine); National Society of Film Critics Awards '76: Best Cinematography; Nominations: Academy Awards '76: Best Adapted Screenplay, Best Costume Design, Best Film Editing, Best Picture. MGM

The Bounty ✗✗½ 1984 (PG) A new version of "Mutiny on the Bounty," with emphasis on a more realistic relationship between Fletcher Christian and Captain Bligh—and a more sympathetic portrayal of the captain, too. The sensuality of Christian's relationship with a Tahitian beauty also receives greater importance. 130m/C VHS, Beta, LV. Mel Gibson, Anthony Hopkins, Laurence Olivier, Edward Fox, Daniel Day-Lewis, Bernard Hill, Philip Davis, Liam Neeson; **D:** Roger Donaldson; **W:** Robert Bolt; **M:** Vangelis. VES, ART

Bounty Hunter 2002 ✗½ 2002: The Rape of Eden 1994 A rogue virus kills most of the world's population and few of those remaining are completely immune. So slave trading in the capture and sale of immune survivors is a lucrative business and a bounty's hunter's last assignment is to bring in a beautiful but deadly woman. 90m/C VHS, LV. Phil Nordell, Francine Lapensee, Vernon Wells, Jeff Conaway; **D:** Sam Auster; **W:** Sam Auster.

Bounty Hunters ✗✗ 1989 (R) A man hunts down his friend's killer. 91m/C VHS, Beta. Robert Ginty, Bo Hopkins, Loeta Waterdown; **D:** Robert Ginty.

Bounty Hunters ✗✗ 1996 (R) Rival bounty hunters (and ex-lovers) Jersey Bellini (Dudikoff) and B.B. Mitchell (Howard) join forces to capture bail-jumping, stolen-car king Delmos (Ratner), who's also the target of mob hitmen. Gunplay and car chases. **CW:** Violence and brief sexuality. 98m/C VHS, Closed Caption. Michael Dudikoff, Lisa Howard, Benjamin Ratner; **D:** George Erschbamer. TOU

The Bounty Man ✗✗ 1972 A bounty hunter brings an outlaw in, robbing him of his freedom and his girlfriend. 74m/C VHS, Beta. Clint Walker, Richard Basehart, Margot Kidder, Arthur Hunnicutt, John Ericson, Gene Evans; **D:** John Llewellyn Moxey. FOX

Bounty Tracker ♪♪½ 1993 (R) Johnny Damone (Lamas) is a bounty-hunter in pursuit of the killer-for-hire who murdered his brother. This personal vendetta leads to an action-packed martial arts showdown between Johnny and his cold-blooded prey. **90m/C VHS, LV, Closed Caption.** Lorenzo Lamas, Matthias Hues, Eugene Glazer. *REP*

Bouquet of Barbed Wire ♪♪½ 1976 Overlong soaper revolves around a weathly family and their hidden secrets: incest and infidelity. On three tapes. **330m/C VHS.** Frank Finlay, Susan Penhaligon, Deborah Grant, Sheila Allen, James Aubrey; *D:* Tom Wharmby. *NO*

The Bourne Identity ♪♪♪ 1988 Chamberlain stars as an amnesiac trying to piece together the fragments of his memory. Is he U.S. espionage agent Jason Bourne or an international terrorist? Aided by Smith (the kidnap victim who falls in love with her captor), the two traverse Europe trying to escape the spy network out to assassinate the mystery man who knows too little. Exciting adaptation of the Robert Ludlum thriller. Originally a two-part television miniseries. **185m/C VHS.** Richard Chamberlain, Jaclyn Smith, Denholm Elliott, Anthony Quayle, Donald Moffat, Yorgo Voyagis; *D:* Roger Young; *W:* Carol Sobieski. *WAR, BTV*

Bowery at Midnight ♪♪ 1942 Lugosi plays a man who recycles criminals into zombies that commit crimes for his benefit. Bela and an intense mood can't quite save this pic. **60m/B VHS, Beta.** Bela Lugosi, Tom Neal, Dave O'Brien, Wanda McKay; *D:* Wallace Fox. *NOS, MRV, SNC*

Bowery at Midnight/Dick Tracy vs. Cueball 1942 On one tape, the vintage Lugosi grade-C thriller about zombies in the Bowery, and a standard Dick Tracy entry. **125m/B VHS, Beta.** Bela Lugosi, Morgan Conway, Dick Wessel, Skelton Knaggs. *AOV*

Bowery Blitzkrieg ♪ *Stand and Deliver* 1941 This lesser "East Side Kids" entry has Gorcey opting to enter the boxing ring rather than turn to crime. Needs more Huntz. **62m/B VHS.** Leo Gorcey, Huntz Hall, Bobby Jordan, Warren Hull, Charlotte Henry, Keye Luke; *D:* Wallace Fox. *NOS, VEC, HEG*

Bowery Boys Meet the Monsters 1954 The infamous Bowery Boys display their usual hilarious hijinks in this comedy in which they confront a group of transplant-happy scientists. **65m/C VHS.** Leo Gorcey, Huntz Hall, Bernard Gorcey, Bennie Bartlett, Lloyd Corrigan; *D:* Edward L. Bernds. *GPV*

Bowery Buckaroos ♪ 1947 The Bowery Boys take their act West in search of gold, meeting up with the usual amounts of goofy characters and hilarious misunderstandings. **66m/B VHS.** Leo Gorcey, Huntz Hall, Bobby Jordan, Gabriel Dell, Billy Benedict, David Gorcey, Julie Briggs, Bernard Gorcey, Chief Yowlachie, Iron Eyes Cody; *D:* William Beaudine. *WAR*

Box of Moonlight ♪♪ 1996 (R) Hardworking, by-the-book electrical systems engineer Al Fountain (Turturo) feels mysteriously compelled to play hookey from his family and career while on an out-of-town business trip. Lost and confused, Al meets up with the Kid, a quirky recluse played with energy and appeal by Rockwell. Through a series of mix-ups, the nice-but-stuffy Al and the wild-but-well-meaning Kid end up spending the fourth of July weekend together. Al's inability to see the point of his journey long after the audience probably has makes the film a bit predictable and stale. DeCillo's third feature was six years in the making and financed by the success of his second feature, Living in Oblivion. **111m/C VHS, LV, Closed Caption.** John Turturro, Sam Rockwell, Catherine Keener, Lisa Blount, Annie Corley, Dermot Mulroney; *D:* Tom DiCillo; *W:* Tom DiCillo; *C:* Paul Ryan; *M:* Jim Farmer. Nominations: Independent Spirit Awards '98: Best Actor (Turturro). *THV*

Boxcar Bertha ♪♪½ 1972 (R) Scorsese's vivid portrayal of the South during the 1930s' Depression casts Hershey as a woman who winds up in cahoots with an anti-establishment train rob- ber. Based on the book "Sister of the Road" by Boxcar Bertha Thomson. **90m/C VHS, Beta, LV.** Barbara Hershey, David Carradine, John Carradine; *D:* Martin Scorsese; *W:* John W. Corrington, Joyce H. Corrington. *VES, ART*

Boxcar Blues ♪ 1990 Bird (Coufos) is a down and out fighter who decides to fight "The Man" (Ventura), a bare knuckle fighter who enjoys beating his opponents to death. On the way to the fight, in New Orleans, he meets up with his girl Casey (Langrick), along with some other shady characters, including a truck driving preacher. **96m/C VHS.** Paul Coufos, Margaret Langrick, Jesse Ventura, M. Emmet Walsh, Donny Lalonde; *D:* Damian Lee. *VHE, VTR*

The Boxer ♪♪½ 1997 (R) Affecting, if predictable, romance set in Ulster, Northern Ireland. Having served 14 years in prison Danny Flynn (Day-Lewis) wants nothing more to do with politics and violence. But his return to his old neighborhood—where he hopes to get back to his boxing career—finds him in the thick of both. Danny manages to persuade his ex-trainer, the alcoholic Ike (Stott), to help him re-open the local gym but resentment is high. Particularly from hard-liner Harry (McSorley), who doesn't like Danny's live-and-let-live attitude and is incensed that he's interested in rekindling his lost-but-never-forgotten love for Maggie (Watson), who's the daughter of local IRA boss Joe (Cox), and the wife of another IRA prisoner. Things quickly turn ugly but the emotionally fragile Danny and Maggie continue to fight to be together against formidable odds. *CW:* Language and some violence. **113m/C VHS, Closed Caption, DVD.** GB IR Daniel Day-Lewis, Emily Watson, Brian Cox, Gerard McSorley, Ken Stott, Ciaran Fitzgerald, Kenneth Cranham; *Cameos:* Tom Bell; *D:* Jim Sheridan; *W:* Jim Sheridan, Terry George; *C:* Chris Menges; *M:* Gavin Friday, Maurice Seezer. Nominations: Golden Globe Awards '98: Best Actor (Day-Lewis), Best Director (Sheridan), Best Film—Drama. *USH*

The Boxer and Death ♪♪♪ 1963 A new-wave Czech film about a boxer in a Nazi concentration camp who interests the boxing-obsessed commandant in a match. In Czech with subtitles. **120m/B VHS, Beta.** Stefan Kvietik; *D:* Peter Solan. *NOS, FCT, DVT*

Boxing Helena ♪♪ 1993 (R) Highly publicized as the film that cost Basinger almost $9 million in damages, the debut of director/writer Jennifer Lynch (daughter of David) explores the dark side of relationships between men and women. Sands is Dr. Nick Cavanaugh, a surgeon who becomes dangerously obsessed with the beautiful, yet unattainable Helena (Fenn). When she is hit by a car near his home, he performs emergency surgery and amputates her arms and legs, forcing her to be dependent on him. Metaphorically a situation, albeit an extreme one, that mirrors the power struggle in any sexual relationship. Problematic in some aspects, although equally fascinating as it is disturbing. *CW:* Strong language and strong sexuality. **107m/C VHS, LV, Closed Caption.** Julian Sands, Sherilyn Fenn, Bill Paxton, Kurtwood Smith, Betsy Clark, Nicolette Scorsese, Art Garfunkel; *D:* Jennifer Lynch; *W:* Jennifer Lynch; *M:* Graeme Revell. Golden Raspberry Awards '93: Worst Director (Lynch). *ORI*

A Boy and His Dog ♪♪½ 1975 (R) In the post-holocaust world of 2024, a young man (Johnson) and his telepathic canine (McIntire supplies narration of the dog's thoughts) cohort search for food and sex. They happen upon a community that drafts Johnson to repopulate their largely impotent race; Johnson is at first ready, willing, and able, until he discovers the mechanical methods they mean to employ. Based on a short story by Harlan Ellison. The dog was played by the later of "The Brady Bunch." *CW:* Adult situations, brief nudity. **87m/C VHS, Beta, LV, DVD.** Don Johnson, Susanne Benton, Jason Robards Jr., Charles McGraw, Alvy Moore; *D:* L.Q. Jones; *V:* Tim McIntire. *FRF, MRV, CCB*

A Boy Called Hate ♪♪ 1995 (R) Troubled teen Steve (Caan)—whose nickname is "Hate" after his tattoo—lives with his divorced dad in an L.A. suburb. Steve's on a latenight motorcycle ride, taking potshots at billboards with his trusty handgun, when he stumbles onto what he thinks is an attempted rape. So Steve shoots at the rapist, Richard (Gould), and takes off with would-be victim Cindy (Crider). Turns out Richard is the assistant D.A. and he tells the cops he's been robbed, so the teen duo are now on the run. Familiar tale with some good twists and believable performances. Caan is the son of James (seen in a cameo as the dad). Debut for director Marcus. *CW:* Language; sexuality; violence. **98m/C VHS, Beta, Closed Caption.** Scott Caan, Missy Crider, Elliott Gould, Adam Beach; *Cameos:* James Caan; *D:* Mitch Marcus; *W:* Mitch Marcus; *C:* Paul Holahan. *PAR*

Boy, Did I Get a Wrong Number! ♪ 1966 A real estate agent gets more than he bargained for when he accidentally dials a wrong number. Zany comedy persists as Hope gets entangled in the life of sexy starlet Sommer. **100m/C VHS, Beta.** Bob Hope, Phyllis Diller, Marjorie Lord, Elke Sommer, Cesare Danova; *D:* George Marshall. *MGM, FCT*

The Boy Friend ♪♪♪ 1971 (G) Russell pays tribute to the Busby Berkeley Hollywood musical. Lots of charming dance numbers and clever parody of plot lines in this adaptation of Sandy Wilson's stage play. Fun! ♫The Boy Friend; I Could Be Happy; Won't You Charleston With Me?; Fancy Forgetting; Sur La Plage; A Room in Bloomsbury; Safety in Numbers; It's Never Too Late to Fall in Love; Poor Little Pierette. **135m/C VHS.** GB Twiggy, Christopher Gable, Moyra Fraser, Max Adrian, Vladek Sheybal, Georgina Hale, Tommy Tune; *D:* Ken Russell; *W:* Ken Russell; *C:* David Watkin. Golden Globe Awards '72: Best Actress—Musical/Comedy (Twiggy); Nominations: Academy Awards '71: Original Song Score and/or Adaptation. *MGM*

The Boy God ♪ 1986 Rocco here describes his trials and everyday shenanigans; he the young demi-God, battling evil on a fantasy land. **100m/C VHS, Beta.** Nino Muhlach; *D:* Erastheo J. Navda. *VCD*

Boy in Blue ♪½ 1986 (R) A "Rocky"-esque biography of Canadian speed-rower Ned Hanlan, who set aside lackluster pursuits to turn to rowing. **97m/C VHS, Beta, Closed Caption.** CA Nicolas Cage, Christopher Plummer, David Naughton; *D:* Charles Jarrott; *W:* Douglas Bowie. *FOX*

The Boy in the Plastic Bubble ♪♪½ 1976 Well-made, sensitive television drama about a young man born with immunity deficiencies who must grow up in a specially controlled plastic environment. Travolta is endearing as the boy in the bubble. **100m/C VHS, Beta.** John Travolta, Robert Reed, Glynnis O'Connor, Diana Hyland, Ralph Bellamy, Anne Ramsey; *D:* Randal Kleiser.

Boy Meets Girl ♪♪♪ 1938 Cagney and O'Brien play screenwriters whose every film is a variation on the boy meets girl theme. Trouble is they're running out of ideas and their scripts get increasingly outlandish. A fading cowboy actor is supposed to star in the duo's next film—if they can ever settle down to work. Then they get the idea to feature their friend Wilson's baby in the movie—and guess who becomes a new star. Good satire on moviemaking and movie moguls, which made fine use of the Warner studio back lots, sound stages, and offices. Based on the play by Bella and Samuel Spewack who also wrote the screenplay. **86m/B VHS.** James Cagney, Pat O'Brien, Ralph Bellamy, Dick Foran, Marie Wilson, Frank McHugh, Bruce Lester, Ronald Reagan, Penny Singleton, James Stephenson; *D:* Lloyd Bacon; *W:* Bella Spewack, Samuel Spewack. *MGM, FCT*

Boy Meets Girl ♪♪♪ 1984 A French Holden Caulfield type character cruises the seamier side of Paris in this acclaimed film. Carax's directoral debut at age 22. In French with English subtitles. 100m/B VHS. *FR* Denis Lavant, Mireille Perrier. *D:* Leos Carax; *W:* Jim Brady. *FCT, MGM*

A Boy Named Charlie Brown 🐾🐾🐾 1970 Charlie Brown enters the National Spelling Bee in New York and makes the final rounds with one other contestant. Based on Charles Schultz's popular comic strip characters from "Peanuts." Music by the Vince Guaraldi trio is, as always, a treat. 86m/C VHS, Beta, LV, Closed Caption. *D:* Bill Melendez; *W:* Charles M. Schulz; *M:* Vince Guaraldi, Rod McKuen. Nominations: Academy Awards '70: Original Song Score and/or Adaptation. *FOX*

Boy of Two Worlds 🐾½ 1970 (G) Because he is of a lineage foreign to his late father's town, a boy is exiled to the life of a junior Robinson Crusoe. 103m/C VHS, Beta. Jimmy Sternman, Edvin Adolphson; *D:* Astrid Henning Jensen. *GEM*

Boy Takes Girl 🐾🐾 1983 A little girl finds it hard adjusting to life on a farming cooperative during a summer recess. 93m/C VHS, Beta. Gabi Eldor, Hillel Neeman, Dina Limon; *D:* Michal Bat-Adam. *MGM*

Boy! What a Girl 🐾🐾 1945 Moore (in drag) is mistaken for a woman, and is fought over by a couple of suitors. 60m/B VHS, Beta. Tim Moore, Duke Williams, Sheila Guyse, Beth Mays, Elwood Smith; *D:* Arthur Leonard. *FCT, GVV, DVT*

The Boy Who Could Fly 🐾🐾🐾 1986 (PG) After a plane crash kills his parents, a boy withdraws into a fantasy land where he can fly. The young daughter of a troubled family makes friends with him and the fantasy becomes real. A sweet film for children, charming though melancholy for adults, too. Fine cast, including Savage, Dewhurst, and Bedelia keep this from becoming sappy. 120m/C VHS, Beta, LV, Closed Caption. Lucy Deakins, Jay Underwood, Bonnie Bedelia, Colleen Dewhurst, Fred Savage, Fred Gwynne, Louise Fletcher, Jason Priestley; *D:* Nick Castle; *W:* Nick Castle; *C:* Steven Poster; *M:* Bruce Broughton. *WAR, ORI*

The Boy Who Left Home to Find Out About the Shivers 1981 From "Faerie Tale Theatre" comes this tale about a boy who learns about fear. 60m/C VHS, Beta, LV. Peter MacNicol, Christopher Lee, David Warner, Dana Hill, Frank Zappa; *D:* Graeme Clifford; *V:* Vincent Price. *FOX*

The Boy Who Loved Trolls 1984 Paul's fantastic dreams come true when he meets Ofoeti, a real, live troll. The only problem is Ofoeti only has a day to live, and Paul must find a way to save him. Aired on PBS as part of the "Wonderworks" series. 58m/C VHS, Beta, Closed Caption. Sam Waterston, Susan Anton, Matt Dill; *D:* Harvey Laidman. *HMV, FCT*

The Boy with the Green Hair 🐾🐾🐾 1948 When he hears that his parents were killed in an air raid, a boy's hair turns green. The narrow-minded members of his community suddenly want nothing to do with him and he becomes an outcast. Thought-provoking social commentary. 82m/C VHS, Beta, LV. Pat O'Brien, Robert Ryan, Barbara Hale, Dean Stockwell; *D:* Joseph Losey. *IME*

Boyfriends 🐾🐾 1996 Gay sexual roundelay that takes place over a weekend spent in the English countryside. Paul (Dreyfus) and Ben (Sands) are on the verge of splitting up after five years, orderly Matt's (Urwin) in love with philandering Owen (Ableson), and social worker Will (Coffey) wants more than a one-nighter with working-class pickup Adam (Petrucci). They all head to James's (McGrath) house and the sexual games begin. Low-budget first feature from Hunter and Hunsinger. 82m/C VHS. *GB* James Dreyfus, Mark Sands, Andrew Ableson, Michael Urwin, David Coffey, Darren Petrucci, Michael McGrath, Russell Higgs; *D:* Neil Hunter, Tom Hunsinger; *W:* Neil Hunter, Tom Hunsinger; *C:* Richard Tisdall. *FRF*

Boyfriends & Girlfriends 🐾🐾½ *My Girlfriend's Boyfriend; Ami de Mon Ami* 1988 (PG) Another one of Rohmer's "Comedies and Proverbs," in which two girls with boyfriends fade in and out of interest with each, casually reshuffling their relationships. Typical, endless-talks-at-cafes Rohmer,

the most happily consistent of the aging French New Wave. In French with subtitles. 102m/C VHS, Beta, LV. *FR* Emmanuelle Chaulet, Sophie Renoir, Eric Viellard, Francois-Eric Gendron; *D:* Eric Rohmer; *W:* Eric Rohmer. *ORI*

Boys 🐾 *The Girl You Want* 1995 (PG-13) Seems like only yesterday we saw Haas as that big-eared, doe-eyed Amish kid from "Witness," but now, in this dry love story, he has grown into a big-eared, doe-eyed teenager lusting after older woman Ryder. John (Haas) saves Patty (Ryder) after a riding accident leaves her unconscious near his New England prep school. Immediately taken by her beauty and mystery, John decides to hide her in his dorm room and a romance blossoms between the unlikely pair. But John isn't the only one hiding something. Patty has a terrible secret from her past (gasp!), but when it's finally revealed, you'll be too bored to care. Based on the short story "Twenty Minutes" by James Salter. 86m/C VHS, LV, Closed Caption. Winona Ryder, Lukas Haas, John C. Reilly, William Sage, Skeet Ulrich; *D:* Stacy Cochran; *W:* Stacy Cochran; *C:* Robert Elswit; *M:* Stewart Copeland. *TOU*

The Boys Club 🐾🐾 1996 (R) Teens-in-trouble film is given a tough core by first time director Fawcett. Excitement-craving 14-year-olds Kyle (Zamprogna), Eric (Sawa), and Brad (Stone) spend all their free time at an abandoned shack at the outskirts of their small town. Only one day they discover it occupied by gun-pointing criminal Luke Cooper (Penn), who tells the boys he's actually a good cop who's been shot and is on the run from some bad cops. The boys are willing to buy into the story at first but Cooper is quick to show his psycho colors, taking Eric hostage, and precipitating a violent finale. *CW:* Violence including a scene of sexual intimidation, language and some nude pin-ups. 92m/C VHS. *CA* Christopher Penn, Stuart Stone, Devon Sawa, Dominic Zamprogna, Nicholas Campbell, Jarred Blanchard; *D:* John Fawcett; *W:* Peter Wellington; *C:* Thom Best; *M:* Michael Timmins. Nominations: Genie Awards '96: Best Actor (Penn), Best Art Direction/Set Decoration, Best Director (Fawcett), Best Film Editing, Best Original Screenplay. *APX*

The Boys from Brazil 🐾🐾½ 1978 (R) Based on Ira Levin's novel, a thriller about Dr. Josef Mengele endeavoring to reconstitute the Nazi movement from his Brazilian sanctuary by cloning a brood of boys from Hitler's genes. 123m/C VHS, Beta, LV. Gregory Peck, James Mason, Laurence Olivier, Uta Hagen, Steve Guttenberg, Denholm Elliott, Lilli Palmer; *D:* Franklin J. Schaffner; *W:* Heywood Gould; *C:* Henri Decae; *M:* Jerry Goldsmith. National Board of Review Awards '78: Best Actor (Olivier); Nominations: Academy Awards '78: Best Actor (Olivier), Best Film Editing, Best Original Score. *FOX*

The Boys in Company C 🐾🐾 1977 (R) A frank, hard-hitting drama about five naive young men involved in the Vietnam War. 127m/C VHS, Beta, LV. Stan Shaw, Andrew Stevens, James Canning, Michael Lembeck, Craig Wasson, R. Lee Ermey, James Whitmore Jr., Scott Hylands; *D:* Sidney J. Furie; *W:* Sidney J. Furie. *COL*

Boys in Love 🐾🐾 1995 Four gay shorts about young men in love. "Death in Venice, CA" finds a repressed academic drawn to his landlady's stepson. The animated "Achilles" features the Greek heros Achilles and Petroclus at the battle of Troy. A young man becomes determined to conquer "My Polish Waiter" and a rejected Latin lover finds love again (with some help from a dog) in "Miguel, Ma Belle." 83m/C VHS. *D:* Barry Purves, P. David Ebersole. *FRF*

The Boys in the Band 🐾🐾½ 1970 (R) A group of gay friends get together one night for a birthday party. A simple premise with a compelling depiction of friendship, expectations, and lifestyle. One of the first serious cinematic presentations to deal with the subject of homosexuality. The film was adapted from Mart Crowley's play using the original cast. 120m/C VHS, Beta, LV. Frederick Combs, Cliff Gorman, Laurence Luckinbill, Kenneth Nel-

son, Leonard Frey; *D:* William Friedkin; *W:* Matt Crowley. *FOX*

Boys Life 🐾🐾 1994 Three shorts about gay teenagers coming of age. "Pool Days" has 17-year-old Justin (Weinstein) taking a summer job as a lifeguard at a health spa. Still clueless as to his sexual preferences, Justin is flustered when cruised by a charming male swimmer but it does get him to thinking. "A Friend of Dorothy" finds NYU student Winston (O'Connell) seeking freedom in Greenwich Village as he looks for like-minded friends (and a little romance). "The Disco Years" takes place in California during the Nixon era as casually gay-bashing high-schooler Tom (Nolan) gradually realizes his true nature. 90m/C VHS. Josh Weinstein, Nick Poletti, Kimberly Flynn, Richard Salamanca, Raoul O'Connell, Kevin McClatchy, Greg Lauren, Anne Zupa, Matt Nolan, Russell Scott Lewis, Gwen Welles, Dennis Christopher; *D:* Brian Sloan, Raoul O'Connell, Robert Lee King; *W:* Brian Sloan, Raoul O'Connell, Robert Lee King. *SHV, MOV*

The Boys Next Door 🐾🐾½ 1985 (R) Two California lads kill and go nuts during a weekend in Los Angeles. Sheen overacts as a budding psychotic, not an easy thing to do. Apparently is trying to show what a particular lifestyle can lead to. Violent. 90m/C VHS, Beta, LV. Maxwell Caulfield, Charlie Sheen, Christopher McDonald, Hank Garrett, Patti D'Arbanville, Moon Zappa; *D:* Penelope Spheeris; *W:* Glen Morgan, James Wong; *C:* Arthur Albert; *M:* George S. Clinton. *VTR*

The Boys Next Door 🐾🐾½ 1996 (PG) Gentle comedy/drama, based on Tom Griffin's play, about four mentally disabled men—Norman (Lane), Barry (Leonard), Arnold (Jeter), and Lucien (Vance)—who share a house under the supervision of too-dedicated social worker Jack (Goldwyn). In fact, Jack's devotion is causing enough problems in his marriage to have him consider changing careers, even as each of "the boys" struggle with their daily lives. TV movie is overly sweet but the performances are very good. 99m/C VHS, Closed Caption. Nathan Lane, Tony Goldwyn, Robert Sean Leonard, Michael Jeter, Courtney B. Vance, Mare Winningham, Jenny Robertson, Elizabeth Wilson, Richard Jenkins, Lynne Thigpen; *D:* John Erman; *W:* William Blinn; *C:* Frank Tidy; *M:* John Kander. *HMK*

Boys' Night Out 🐾🐾🐾 1962 Amusing comedy about four businessmen who desperately want to escape the suburban doldrums by setting up an apartment equipped with plaything Novak. Little do they know, but Novak is a sociology student studying the American male, and they are merely her guinea pigs in an experiment beyond their control. Blair, Page, and Gabor provide comic relief. Based on a story by Marvin Worth and Arne Sultan. 113m/C VHS. Kim Novak, James Garner, Tony Randall, Howard Duff, Janet Blair, Patti Page, Jessie Royce Landis, Oscar Homolka, Zsa Zsa Gabor; *D:* Michael Gordon; *W:* Ira Wallach. *MGM*

The Boys of St. Vincent 🐾🐾🐾🐾 1993 Outstanding, and heartbreaking, story of sexual abuse by Catholic clergy that was inspired by actual events. Divided into two segments, the drama begins in 1975 with 10-year-old Kevin Reevey (Morina) living at the St. Vincent orphanage in an eastern Canadian town. The orphanage is run by charismatic and terrifying Brother Lavin (Czerny), who it turns out has a special fondness for "his boy" Kevin. Nor is Brother Lavin alone—a fact eventually revealed by a police investigation, although the matter is hushed up by both the church and the government. Until 15 years later. In 1990, the case is reopened and Lavin, having married and fathered two sons, is returned to face charges. Now the young men must open wounds that have never truly healed and confront their tormentors in a court of law, amidst a blaze of publicity. Czerny gives a truly inspired performance as the self-loathing monster. The emotional agony is excruciating to watch and be forewarned that the depiction of the sexual abuse is unflinching. Made for Canadian TV; on two cassettes. **186m/C VHS. CA** Henry Czerny, Johnny Morina, Sebastian Spence, Brian Dodd, David Hewlett, Jonathan Lewis, Jeremy Keefe, Phillip Dinn, Brian Dooley, Greg Thomey, Michael Wade, Lise Roy, Timothy Webber, Kristine Demers, Ashley Billard, Sam Grana; **D:** John N. Smith; **W:** Sam Grana, John N. Smith, Des Walsh; **C:** Pierre Letarte; **M:** Neil Smolar. Nominations: Independent Spirit Awards '95: Best Foreign Film. *NYF*

Boys of the City 🎬🎬 *The Ghost Creeps*
1940 The East Side Kids run amuck in an eerie mansion while trying to solve the murder of a judge. **63/B VHS, Beta.** Leo Gorcey, Bobby Jordan; **D:** Joseph H. Lewis. *NOS, SNC, DVT*

Boys on the Side 🎬🎬½ 1994 (R)
It's "Thelma & Louise" come to "Terms of Endearment" by way of "Philadelphia." Goldberg is Jane, an unemployed lesbian singer, who connects with Ms. Priss real estate agent Robin (Parker) for a road trip to California. The two become a female version of the Odd Couple as Jane tags Robin as "the whitest woman in America." They stop off to pick up addle-brain friend Holly (Barrymore) who has just knocked her drug-crazed abusive beau in the head with a baseball bat. Holly's accident turns fatal and the threesome are on the run from cops. They bond like crazy glue and become a family as they face two huge setbacks—one's pregnant, another has AIDS. Strong performances by the lead actresses and a cool soundtrack may make up for this often trite movie of the week premise. **CW:** Strong language; some sexuality. **117m/C VHS, LV, Closed Caption.** James Remar, Anita Gillette, Matthew McConaughey, Whoopi Goldberg, Mary-Louise Parker, Drew Barrymore; **D:** Herbert Ross; **W:** Don Roos; **C:** Donald E. Thorin. *WAR*

Boy's Reformatory 🎬½ 1939
Brothers are framed. One takes the rap, goes to the title institution, breaks out, and hunts the real bad guys. Creaky and antiquated. **62m/B VHS.** Frankie Darro, Grant Withers, David Durand, Warren McCollum; **D:** Howard Bretherton. *NOS, LOO*

Boys Town 🎬🎬🎬½ 1938
Righteous portrayal of Father Flanagan and the creation of Boys Town, home for juvenile soon-to-be-ex-delinquents. **93m/B VHS, Beta, LV, Closed Caption.** Spencer Tracy, Mickey Rooney, Henry Hull, Gene Reynolds, Sidney Miller, Frankie Thomas Jr.; **D:** Norman Taurog. Academy Awards '38: Best Actor (Tracy), Best Story; Nominations: Academy Awards '38: Best Director (Taurog), Best Picture. *MGM, BTV, IGP*

Boys Will Be Boys 🎬🎬½ 1997 (PG)
With their parents away at a company party, Matt and Robbie are home alone for the first time. Expect chaos when the boys discover that their father's business rival has something nasty in store and the brothers will use anything around to defeat him. **89m/C VHS.** Randy Travis, Julie Hagerty, Jon Voight, Michael DeLuise, Catherine Oxenberg, Mickey Rooney, Ruth Buzzi, Dom DeLuise; **D:** Dom DeLuise. *APX*

Boyz N the Hood 🎬🎬🎬½ 1991 (R)
Singleton's debut as a writer and director is an astonishing portrait of young black men, four high school students with different backgrounds, aims, and abilities trying to survive Los Angeles gangs and bigotry. Excellent acting throughout, with special nods to Fishburne and Gooding, Jr. Violent outbreaks outside theatres where this ran only proves the urgency of its passionately nonviolent, pro-family message. Hopefully those viewers scared off at the time will give this a chance in the safety of their VCRs. Singleton was the youngest director ever nominated for an Oscar. The laserdisc version includes two extra scenes and an interview with Singleton. **CW:** Language, violence, and sensuality. **112m/C VHS, Beta, LV, 8mm, Letterbox, Closed Caption.** Laurence "Larry" Fishburne, Ice Cube, Cuba Gooding Jr., Nia Long, Morris Chestnut, Tyra Ferrell, Angela Bassett; **D:** John Singleton; **W:** John Singleton; **M:** Stanley Clarke. MTV Movie Awards '92: Best New Filmmaker Award (Singleton); Nominations: Academy Awards '91: Best Director (Singleton), Best Original Screenplay. *COL, CRC, FCT*

Braddock: Missing in Action 3 🎬
1988 (R) The battle-scarred, high-kicking 'Nam vet battles his way into the jungles once more, this time to rescue his long-lost Vietnamese family. A family effort, Chuck co-wrote the script; his brother directed. **104m/C VHS, Beta, LV, Closed Caption.** Chuck Norris, Aki Aleong, Roland Harrah III; **D:** Aaron Norris; **W:** Chuck Norris, James Bruner; **C:** Joao Fernandes. *CCB, VTR*

The Brady Bunch 1969
Relive classic moments with TV's grooviest family—two episodes per tape—including "The Honeymoon," the premiere episode explaining how Mike and his three boys get hitched to Carol and her three girls. Additional episodes available. **51m/C VHS, Closed Caption.** Robert Reed, Florence Henderson, Ann B. Davis, Maureen McCormick, Barry Williams, Eve Plumb, Christopher Knight, Michael Lookinland, Susan Olsen. *PAR*

The Brady Bunch Movie 🎬🎬🎬 1995
(PG-13) Grunge and CDs may be the norm in the '90s, but the Bradys still live in the eight-track world of the '70s, where Davy Jones rocks and every day is a sunshine day. Then greedy developer McKean schemes to cash in on Mike and Carol's financial woes. (Hawaii! The Grand Canyon! What were they thinking?) Great ensemble cast capably fills the white platform shoes of the originals—Cole sounds just like Mr. Brady, Cox hilariously channels Jan's tormented middle child angst, and Taylor's self-absorbed Marcia, Marcia, Marcia is dead-on, right down to the frosty pursed lips. Look for neat-o cameos from some original Bradys and most of the Monkees. Followed by "A Very Brady Sequel." **CW:** Sly references to sex that most kids probably won't understand; Marcia's girlfriend has a crush on her, Alice wears a leather teddy during the final credits, and Jan hears inner voices. "Hey there, groovy chick" is about as offensive as the language gets. Cast wears dangerously high levels of bad polyester without much thought for taste. Florence Henderson says "crap!" **88m/C VHS, Beta, Closed Caption.** Shelley Long, Gary Cole, Michael McKean, Jean Smart, Henriette Mantel, Christopher Daniel Barnes, Christine Taylor, Paul Sutera, Jennifer Elise Cox, Jesse Lee, Olivia Hack, David Graf, Jack Noseworthy, Shane Conrad, RuPaul; **Cameos:** Ann B. Davis, Florence Henderson, Davy Jones, Barry Williams, Christopher Knight, Michael Lookinland, Mickey Dolenz, Peter Tork; **D:** Betty Thomas; **W:** Bonnie Turner, Terry Turner, Laurice Elehwany, Rick Copp; **C:** Mac Ahlberg; **M:** Guy Moon. Nominations: MTV Movie Awards '95: Best Dance Sequence (The Brady Kids). *PAR*

Brady's Escape 🎬½ *The Long Ride* 1984
American WWII pilot is shot down in the Hungarian countryside and befriended by Hungarian csikos (cowboys) in this made-for-cable television movie. **92m/C VHS, Beta, LV.** *HU* John Savage, Kelly Reno; **D:** Pal Gabor. *CAF*

The Brain 🎬🎬½ *Vengeance* 1962
A scientist learns that a mind isn't always a terrible thing to waste when he finds himself being manipulated by the brain of a dead man he's trying to keep alive. Remake of "Donovan's Brain" (1953). **83m/B VHS, Beta, LV. GB GE** Anne Heywood, Peter Van Eyck, Bernard Lee, Cecil Parker, Jack MacGowran; **D:** Freddie Francis. *NOS, SNC*

The Brain 🎬🎬 *Le Cerveau* 1969 (G)
Run of the mill comedy caper has Niven planning to heist millions from a NATO train. The caper begins when lots of other crooks decide to rob the same train. The cast holds this one together. **100m/C VHS, Closed Caption. FR** David Niven, Jean-Paul Belmondo, Bourvil, Eli Wallach, Silvia Monti, Fernand Valois; **D:** Gerard Oury; **M:** Georges Delerue. *PAR*

The Brain 🎬½ 1988 (R)
Dr. Blake, host of a popular TV talk-show, is in league with a power-hungry alien brain. Viewers of his show kill themselves and others in the midst of many special effects. The ratings go down. **94m/C VHS, Beta.** Tom Breznahan, Cyndy Preston, David Gale; **D:** Edward Hunt. *ART*

Brain Damage 🎬🎬 1988 (R)
A tongue-in-bloody-cheek farce about a brain-sucking parasite. The parasite in question, Aylmer, addicts our dubious hero to the euphoria induced by the blue liquid the parasite injects into his brain, paving the way for the bloody mayhem that follows. Poor shadow of Henenlotter's far-superior "Basket Case." In fact, it even includes an inside-joke cameo by Van Hentenryck, reprising his "Basket Case" character; look for him on the subway. **89m/C VHS, Beta, Closed Caption.** Rick Herbst, Gordon MacDonald, Jennifer Lowry, Theo Barnes, Lucille Saint Peter; **Cameos:** Kevin Van Hentenryck, Beverly Bonner; **D:** Frank Henenlotter; **W:** Frank Henenlotter; **C:** Bruce Torbet; **V:** John Zacherle. *PAR*

Brain Dead 🎬🎬🎬½ 1989 (R)
Low-budget but brilliantly assembled puzzle-film about a brain surgeon who agrees to perform experimental surgery on a psychotic to retrieve some corporately valuable data—his first mistake, which begins a seemingly endless cycle of nightmares and identity alterations. A mind-blowing sci-fi feast from ex-"Twilight Zone" writer Charles Beaumont. **85m/C VHS, Beta.** Bill Pullman, Bill Paxton, Bud Cort, Patricia Charbonneau, Nicholas Pryor, George Kennedy; **D:** Adam Simon; **W:** Charles Beaumont. *MGM*

Brain Donors 🎬🎬½ 1992 (PG)
Goofy, uneven film starring Turturro as a sleazy lawyer trying to take over the Oglethorpe Ballet Company by sweet-talking its aged patronness. He is helped by two eccentric friends, and together the three crack a lot of bad but witty jokes. The film culminates into a hilarious ballet scene featuring someone giving CPR to the ballerina playing the dying swan, an actor in a duck suit, duck hunters, and a pack of hounds. This trio reminds us of second-rate Marx Brothers (or the Three Stooges) but the movie has enough funny moments to be worth a watch. **79m/C VHS, Beta, LV, Letterbox, Closed Caption.** John Turturro, Bob Nelson, Mel Smith, Nancy Marchand, John Savident, George de la Pena, Juli Donald, Spike Alexander, Teri Copley; **D:** Dennis Dugan; **W:** Pat Proft; **M:** Ira Newborn. *PAR*

The Brain Eaters 🎬🎬 1958
A strange ship from inside the Earth invades a small town, and hairy monsters promptly attach themselves to people's necks in a daring bid to control the planet. The imaginative story compensates somewhat for the cheap special effects. Watch for Nimoy before he grew pointed ears. **60m/B VHS.** Edwin Nelson, Alan Frost, Jack Hill, Joanna Lee, Jody Fair, Leonard Nimoy; **D:** Bruno Ve Sota. *NOS, CNM*

The Brain from Planet Arous 🎬
1957 Lassie meets Alien when an evil alien brain appropriates the body of a scientist in order to take over planet Earth. His plans are thwarted, however, by a good alien brain that likewise inhabits the body of the scientist's dog. High camp and misdemeanors. **80m/B VHS, LV.** John Agar, Joyce Meadows, Robert Fuller, Henry Travis; **D:** Nathan (Hertz) Juran. *EEL, SNC, CNM*

Brain of Blood woof! *The Creature's Revenge* 1971
Deals with a scientist who transplants the brain of a politician into the body of a deformed idiot. The change is minimal. **107m/C VHS, Beta.** Kent Taylor, John Joe Bob Briggs Bloom, Regina Carrol, Angelo Rossitto, Grant Williams, Reed Hadley, Vicki Volante, Zandor Vorkov; **D:** Al Adamson. *NO*

Brain Smasher...A Love Story 🎬
1993 (PG-13) A bouncer and a super model become the targets of a gang of killer ninjas who want the mysterious blood-red lotus the model's been given. Of course they do. What's the lovely Hatcher doing in such a stupid movie? **88m/C VHS, LV, Closed Caption.** Andrew Dice Clay, Teri Hatcher; **D:** Albert Pyun. *THV*

The Brain that Wouldn't Die 🎬🎬½
The Head That Wouldn't Die 1963 Love is a many-splattered thing when a brilliant surgeon keeps the decapitated head of his fiancee alive after an auto accident while he searches for a suitably stacked body onto which to transplant the head.

Absurd and satiric (head talks so much that Doc tapes her/its mouth shut) adding up to major entry in trash film genre; much of the gore was slashed for the video, however. **92m/B VHS, Beta.** Herb Evers, Virginia Leith, Adele Lamont, Leslie Daniel; **D:** Joseph Green; **W:** Joseph Green. *RHI, FCT*

The Brainiac 🎬½ 1961 Sorcerer sentenced for black magic returns to strike dark deeds upon the descendants of those who judged him. He turns himself into a hideous monster, feeding on his victims' brains and blood. Yuck. **75m/B VHS, Beta.** *MX* Abel Salazar, Ariadne Welter, Mauricio Garces, Rosa Maria Gallardo. *SNC, MRV, HHT*

Brainscan 🎬 1994 (R) Teenage loner takes a trip in virtual reality and finds that murder is the first stop. Furlong ("Terminator 2") is the troubled youth whose voyage is led by Smith as Trickster, the Freddy Krueger meets David Bowie tour guide from virtual hell. Langella turns in a straight performance as a local cop hot on the trail. Hard-core horror fans will be disappointed by the lack of onscreen violence, and special effects buffs won't see anything new. Lame effort tries to appeal to a wide audience and is bland as a result. The end is left wide open, so expect a sequel or two or three. **96m/C VHS, LV, Closed Caption.** Edward Furlong, Frank Langella, T. Ryder Smith, David Hemblen, Amy Hargreaves, Jamie Marsh, Victor Ertmanis; **D:** John Flynn; **W:** Andrew Kevin Walker; **M:** George S. Clinton. *COL*

Brainstorm 🎬🎬½ 1983 (PG) Husband-and-wife scientist team invents headphones that can record dreams, thoughts, and fantasies (VCR-style) and then allow other people to experience them by playing back the tape. Their marriage begins to crumble as the husband becomes more and more obsessed with pushing the limits of the technology; things get worse when the government wants to exploit their discovery. Special effects and interesting camerawork punctuate this sci-fi flick. Wood's last film; in fact, she died before production was completed. **106m/C VHS, Beta, LV, Letterbox.** Natalie Wood, Christopher Walken, Cliff Robertson, Louise Fletcher; **D:** Douglas Trumbull; **W:** Bruce Joel Rubin; **M:** James Horner. *MGM*

Brainwaves 🎬🎬 1982 (R) A young woman has disturbing flashbacks after her brain is electrically revived following a car accident. Curtis is the demented doctor who jump-starts her. **83m/C VHS, Beta.** Suzanna Love, Tony Curtis, Keir Dullea, Vera Miles; **D:** Ulli Lommel; **W:** Ulli Lommel.

Bram Stoker's Dracula 🎬🎬 *Dracula* 1992 (R) Coppola's highly charged view of the vampire classic is visually stunning, heavy on eroticism and violence, and weak in plot and performance. Oldman, in a number of amazing transformations, portrays the deadly bloodsucker as a lonely soul determined to reunite with his lost love, the innocent Ryder. Hopkins cheerfully chews the scenery as nemesis Van Helsing, newcomer Frost is fetching, Reeves is lightweight, and Ryder goes way over the top. Musician Waits is great as bug-eating madman Renfield. Filmed entirely on soundstages with beautiful costumes and some amazing visual effects and sets. Laserdisc includes "The Making of Bram Stoker's Dracula."**CW:** Horror violence and sexuality. **128m/C VHS, Beta, LV, Letterbox, Closed Caption, DVD.** Gary Oldman, Winona Ryder, Anthony Hopkins, Keanu Reeves, Richard E. Grant, Cary Elwes, Bill Campbell, Sadie Frost, Tom Waits; **D:** Francis Ford Coppola; **W:** Jim V. Hart; **C:** Michael Ballhaus. Academy Awards '92: Best Costume Design, Best Makeup, Best Sound Effects Editing; Nominations: Academy Awards '92: Best Art Direction/Set Decoration. *COL*

Bram Stoker's The Mummy 🎬🎬 *The Mummy* 1997 (R) Modern retelling of the horror tale focuses on the savage incident that left Egyptologist Abel Trelawny in a coma. Now his daughter seeks the help of her father's colleague to uncover the connection between Trewlawny and an Egyptian ritual to raise a queen from her tomb. Based on Stoker's book "The Jewel of the Seven Stars."**CW:** Some violence, sexuality and lan-

guage. **100m/C VHS.** Louis Gossett Jr., Amy Locane, Victoria Tennant, Eric Lutes, Richard Karn, Lloyd Bochner, Mark Lindsay Chapman; **D:** Jeffrey Obrow. *APX*

The Bramble Bush 🎬🎬½ 1960 Guy (Burton) is a doctor who returns to his New England hometown to care for a dying friend, Larry (Drake). Unfortunately, Guy falls for Larry's wife Mar (Rush) and they have an affair. When Guy pulls the plug on his friend's suffering, suspicious townspeople (who of course know what's going on) wonder just how "merciful" the doctor was really being and he's tried for murder. Tawdry "Peyton Place"-ish soap opera based on the novel by Charles Mergendahl. **104m/C VHS.** Richard Burton, Barbara Rush, Tom Drake, Jack Carson, Angie Dickinson, James Dunn, Henry Jones, Frank Conroy, Carl Benton Reid; **D:** Daniel Petrie; **W:** Philip Yordan. *WAR*

Bramwell 1995 British miniseries stars Redgrave as the determined Eleanor Bramwell. In 1895, she manages to follow in her physician father's footsteps but it's a battle to gain respect from her sexist colleagues and to overcome her own class prejudices as she works with London's poor. Seven episodes on four cassettes. **360m/C VHS.** *GB* Jemma Redgrave, David Calder, Kevin McMonagle, Keeley Gainey, Cliff Parisi, Ruth Sheen, Michele Dotrice, Robert Hardy; **D:** David Tucker, Laura Sims; **W:** Lucy Gannon. *FCT, ATS*

Brand New Life 🎬 1972 A childless couple in their 40s are unexpectedly confronted by the wife's first pregnancy. Both have careers and well-ordered lives that promise to be disrupted. **74m/C VHS, Beta.** Cloris Leachman, Martin Balsam, Wilfrid Hyde-White, Mildred Dunnock; **D:** Sam O'Steen; **M:** Billy Goldenberg. *BFA*

Brand of Fear 🎬½ 1949 Crooning cowpoke Wakely puts down his guitar long enough to chase rustlers off the land of an innocent lady in this average oater. **56m/B VHS.** Jimmy Wakely, Dub Taylor, Gail Davis, Tom London; **D:** Oliver Drake; **W:** Basil Dickey. *MOV*

Brand of Hate 🎬 1934 A good cowboy rustles up a gang of rustlers. **61m/B VHS, Beta.** Bob Steele, George "Gabby" Hayes, Lucille Browne, James Flavin; **D:** Lewis D. Collins. *NOS, RXM*

Brand of the Outlaws 🎬 1936 A cowboy becomes an unwitting aid to rustlers in this early western. **56m/B VHS, Beta.** Bob Steele, Margaret Marquis, Virginia True Boardman, Jack Rockwell; **D:** Robert North Bradbury. *NOS, DVT*

Branded 🎬🎬½ 1950 Ladd (pre-"Shane") impersonates the long-gone son of rich rancher Bickford, with unusual results. Nicely balanced action and love scenes makes this old Max Brand story a better-than-average western. Filmed in Technicolor. **95m/C VHS, LV, Closed Caption.** Alan Ladd, Mona Freeman, Charles Bickford, Joseph Calleia, Milburn Stone; **D:** Rudolph Mate. *PAR*

Branded a Bandit 🎬 1924 Yakima must avoid the sheriff while tracking down the killers of an old miner so that he can clear himself of the crime. **58m/C VHS.** Yakima Canutt; **D:** Paul Hurst. *GPV*

Branded a Coward 🎬 1935 A man whose parents were killed seeks revenge via his trusty six-shooters. **56m/B VHS, Beta.** Johnny Mack Brown, Billie Seward, Yakima Canutt; **D:** Sam Newfield. *NOS, DVT*

Branded Men 🎬🎬 1931 A couple of oddballs become mixed up in a number of zany, western-type adventures. **60m/B VHS.** Ken Maynard, June Clyde, Irving Bacon, Billy Bletcher, Charles "Blackie" King, Donald Keith; **D:** Phil Rosen. *NOS*

Branded to Kill 🎬🎬 *Koroshi no Rakuin* 1967 Visual tricks, including animated graphics, and a blues score highlight this gangster story, which follows No. 3 Killer, who's bungled his last hit. Now he's the target of No. 1 Killer. Japanese with subtitles. **91m/B VHS.** *JP* Joe Shishido, Mari Annu, Koji Nambara; **D:** Seijun Suzuki. *HMV*

Brannigan 🎬🎬½ 1975 (PG) The Duke stars in the somewhat unfamiliar role of a rough and tumble Chicago police officer. He travels across the Atlantic to arrest a racketeer who has fled the States rather than face a grand jury indictment. Humor and action abound. **111m/C VHS, Beta.** John Wayne, John Vernon, Mel Ferrer, Daniel Pilon, James Booth, Ralph Meeker, Lesley-Anne Down, Richard Attenborough; **D:** Douglas Hickox; **W:** Michael Butler, William W. Norton Sr. *MGM, FOX*

Brass 🎬 1985 (PG) First post-Archie Bunker role for O'Connor, who plods through this average police drama at a snail's pace, dragging everything else down with him. Made-for-TV pilot for a series that never aired. **94m/C VHS, LV.** Carroll O'Connor, Lois Nettleton, Jimmie Baird, Paul Shenar, Vincent Gardenia, Anita Gillette; **D:** Corey Allen. *ORI*

The Brass Bottle 🎬🎬½ 1963 Silly but amusing comedy that served as the inspiration for the TV series "I Dream of Jeannie," although Eden plays the girlfriend in this movie. Ives stars as jovial genie Fakrash, whose antique bottle is bought by architect Harold Ventimore (Randall). Fakrash wants nothing more than to make his new master happy but his efforts cause constant crises for the bewildered man, who'd prefer his life return to normal. Based on the novel by F. Anstey. **90m/C VHS, Closed Caption.** Tony Randall, Burl Ives, Barbara Eden, Edward Andrews, Ann Doran, Kamala Devi, Howard Smith, Parley Baer; **D:** Harry Keller; **W:** Oscar Brodney; **C:** Clifford Stine; **M:** Bernard Green. *USH*

Brass Target 🎬½ 1978 (PG) Hypothetical thriller about a plot to kill George Patton in the closing days of WWII for the sake of $250 million in Nazi gold stolen by his staff. Interesting cast can't find story. **111m/C VHS, Beta, LV.** Sophia Loren, George Kennedy, Max von Sydow, John Cassavetes, Patrick McGoohan, Robert Vaughn, Bruce Davison, Edward Herrmann, Ed Bishop; **D:** John Hough; **W:** Alvin Boretz. *MGM*

Brassed Off 🎬🎬½ 1996 (R) Bittersweet tale of despair and hope in the fictional coal mining town of Grimly in Yorkshire, England. Set in 1992, when sweeping closures of British coal mines devastated the area, the sole respite of these workers is playing in the pit's brass band. Secretly suffering from black lung disease, the band's leader (Postlethwaite) dreams of winning a competition in Albert Hall. Fitzgerald plays the flugelhorn-tooting vixen who returns to the small town, inspiring the music (and virility) of the formerly all male band. She resumes her relationship with former flame MacGregor, but all is on shaky ground with the imminent closure of the mine. Fine performances brighten the generally gloomy proceedings. The band is played by the real-life Grimethorpe Colliery Brass Band.**CW:** Language. **100m/C VHS, LV, Closed Caption.** *GB* Pete Postlethwaite, Ewan McGregor, Tara Fitzgerald, Jim Carter, Philip Jackson, Peter Martin, Stephen Tompkinson; **D:** Mark Herman; **W:** Mark Herman; **C:** Andy Collins; **M:** Trevor Jones. Cesar Awards '98: Best Foreign Film; Nominations: British Academy Awards '96: Best Original Screenplay. *TOU*

The Bravados 🎬🎬🎬 1958 A rough, distressing Western revenge tale, wherein a man is driven to find the four men who murdered his wife. In tracking the perpetrators, Peck realizes that he has been corrupted by his vengeance. **98m/C VHS, Beta, Closed Caption.** Gregory Peck, Stephen Boyd, Joan Collins, Albert Salmi, Henry Silva, Lee Van Cleef, George Voskovec, Barry Coe; **D:** Henry King; **W:** Philip Yordan; **C:** Leon Shamroy. National Board of Review Awards '58: Best Supporting Actor (Salmi). *FOX*

The Brave Bunch 🎬½ 1970 A courageous Greek soldier tries to save his men and country during WWII. **110m/C VHS, Beta.** *GR* Peter Funk, John Miller; **D:** Costa Carayiannis. *ART*

The Brave One 🎬🎬🎬 1956 A love story between a Spanish boy and the bull who saves his life. The animal is later carted off to the bullring. Award-winning screenplay by the then-blacklisted Trumbo, credited as "Robert Rich." **100m/C**

VHS, Beta, LV, DVD. Michel Ray, Rodolfo Hoyos, Joi Lansing; *D:* Irving Rapper; *W:* Dalton Trumbo; *C:* Jack Cardiff; *M:* Victor Young. Academy Awards '56: Best Story; Nominations: Academy Awards '56: Best Film Editing, Best Sound. *VCI, LUM*

Braveheart 1925 When a Native American adapts to the white man's world, he alienates his own people. He eventually chooses to renounce his love for a white woman, and returns to lead his people. Silent. **62m/B VHS, Beta, 8mm.** Rod La Rocque; *D:* Alan Hale. *GVV, FCT*

Braveheart 🐾🐾🐾½ **1995 (R)** Producer-director-star Gibson does it all in this bold, ferocious, reasonably accurate epic about the passion and cost of freedom. Charismatic 13th-century Scottish folk hero William Wallace leads his desperate and outnumbered clansmen in revolt against British oppression. Sweeping, meticulous battle scenes fit suprisingly well with moments of stirring romance and snappy wit. Among the mostly unknown (in the States, anyway) cast, Marceau and McCormack are elegant as Wallace's lady loves, and McGoohan is positively hateful as King Edward I. Gory and excessively violent (as medieval warfare tends to be) and a bit too long (as historical epics tend to be), but rewarding entertainment for those who stick it out—where else can you see the king's army get mooned en masse? Script was based on 300 pages of rhyming verse attributed to a blind poet known as Blind Harry. Gibson put up $15 million of his own money to complete the film. *CW:* Brutal medieval warfare. **178m/C VHS, Beta, Closed Caption.** Mel Gibson, Sophie Marceau, Patrick McGoohan, Catherine McCormack, Brendan Gleeson, James Cosmo, David O'Hara, Angus McFadyen, Peter Hanly; *D:* Mel Gibson; *W:* Randall Wallace; *C:* John Toll; *M:* James Horner. Academy Awards '95: Best Cinematography, Best Director (Gibson), Best Makeup, Best Picture; British Academy Awards '95: Best Cinematography; Golden Globe Awards '96: Best Director (Gibson); MTV Movie Awards '96: Best Action Sequence; Writers Guild of America '95: Best Original Screenplay; Broadcast Film Critics Association Awards '95: Best Director (Gibson); Nominations: Academy Awards '95: Best Costume Design, Best Film Editing, Best Original Screenplay, Best Sound, Best Original Dramatic/Comedy Score; British Academy Awards '95: Best Director (Gibson); Best Score; Directors Guild of America Awards '95: Best Director (Gibson); Golden Globe Awards '96: Best Film—Drama, Best Screenplay, Best Score; MTV Movie Awards '96: Best Film, Best Male Performance (Gibson), Most Desirable Male (Gibson). *PAR*

Brazil 🐾🐾🐾½ **1985 (R)** The acclaimed nightmare comedy about an Everyman trying to survive in a surreal paper-choked bureaucratic society. There are copious references to "1984" and "The Trial," fantastic mergings of glorious fantasy and stark reality, and astounding visual design. *CW:* Strong violence. **131m/C VHS, Beta, LV, Letterbox, Closed Caption, DVD.** *GB* Jonathan Pryce, Robert De Niro, Michael Palin, Katherine Helmond, Kim Greist, Bob Hoskins, Ian Holm, Peter Vaughan, Ian Richardson; *D:* Terry Gilliam; *W:* Terry Gilliam, Tom Stoppard; *M:* Michael Kamen. Los Angeles Film Critics Association Awards '85: Best Director (Gilliam), Best Film, Best Screenplay; Nominations: Academy Awards '85: Best Art Direction/Set Decoration, Best Original Screenplay. *USH, FCT*

Breach of Conduct 🐾½ **1994 (PG-13)** Colonel Bill Case (Coyote) is the commander of the Fort Benton, Utah Army base where Helen Lutz's (Thorne-Smith) husband Tom (Verica) has just been transferred. At first there's a mutual attraction between Helen and Case, but then hubby is assigned a mission off base and, when Helen refuses Case's overtures, things turn very nasty. Made for cable TV. *CW:* Mature thematic material. **93m/C VHS, LV, Closed Caption.** Peter Coyote, Courtney Thorne-Smith, Tom Verica, Beth Toussaint; *D:* Tim Matheson; *W:* Scott Abbott; *C:* Gideon Porath. *USH*

Breach of Trust 🐾🐾½ **1995 (R)** Small-time crook Casey (Biehn) winds up in big trouble when he steals a computer disc with access codes to millions in drug cartel money. He goes on the lam and meets Madeline (Ferrer), an

undercover cop who thinks that some police are on the cartel's payroll. So the daring duo decide to take on the drug lords and the dirty cops. *CW:* Violence, a scene of sexuality, language and some drug use. **96m/C VHS, LV, Closed Caption.** Michael Biehn, Matt Craven, Leilani Sarelle Ferrer, Miguel Sandoval, Kim Coates, Ed Lauter; *D:* Charles Wilkinson; *W:* Gordon Basichis, Raul Inglis; *C:* Michael Slovis; *M:* Graeme Coleman. *REP*

Bread and Chocolate 🐾🐾🐾 *Pane e Cioccolata* **1974** Uneducated Italian immigrant Manfredi works a series of odd jobs in complacently bourgeois Switzerland and tries desperately to fit in and better himself (which he fails utterly to do). Culture clash satire, with an engaging everyman lead. Italian with subtitles. **109m/C VHS.** *IT* Nino Manfredi, Anna Karina, Johnny Dorelli, Paolo Turco; *D:* Franco Brusati; *W:* Nino Manfredi, Franco Brusati, Iaia Fiastri; *C:* Luciano Tovoli; *M:* Daniele Patrucchi. New York Film Critics Awards '78: Best Foreign Film. *HTV*

The Break 🐾🐾 **1995 (PG-13)** Clumsy teen tennis hopeful Ben (Jorgensen) refuses to give up his dreams even after his bookie dad Robbins (Sheen) hires washed-up player Nick Irons (Van Patten) as a coach to show Ben the error of his game. *CW:* Some racy sexuality and brief strong language. **104m/C VHS.** Vincent Van Patten, Martin Sheen, Ben Jorgensen, Rae Dawn Chong, Valerie Perrine; *W:* Vincent Van Patten, Dan Jenkins. *THV*

The Break 🐾🐾½ *A Further Gesture* **1997 (R)** Disillusioned IRA gunman Dowd (Rea) breaks out of prison and escapes to New York to find a new life. Instead, he befriends (and falls in love with one of) a group of Guatemalan refugees who plan to kill the dictator who persecuted them. Appalled by their inability, he agrees to help them. This is definitely Rea's film (it's based on an idea of his), mainly because his is the only character that's really fleshed out. Character study of a man who's lost whatever passion he had for the cause but can't give up the life doesn't delve into specific Irish or Guatemalan politics, and loses some impact as a result. *CW:* Violence, language and some sexuality. **97m/C VHS.** Stephen Rea, Rosana Pastor, Brendan Gleeson, Pruitt Taylor Vince, Maria Doyle Doyle Kennedy, Jorge Sanz, Carolyn Seymour, Sean McGinley, Paul Giamatti; *D:* Robert Dornhelm, Alfred Molina; *W:* Ronan Bennett; *C:* Andrzej Sekula; *M:* John Keane. *NYR*

Break of Hearts 🐾🐾½ **1935** Hepburn marries Boyer, who becomes an alcoholic, and then more troubles arise. Very soapy, but well-made. **78m/B VHS, Beta, LV.** Katharine Hepburn, Charles Boyer, Jean Hersholt, John Beal, Sam Hardy; *D:* Philip Moeller; *M:* Max Steiner. *TTC*

Breakaway 🐾 **1995 (R)** Myra (Thompson) decides to get away from her drop-woman job with $300,000 of mob money. Naturally, she's pursued by a hit man (Estevez) and then betrayed by a boyfriend (De Rose), who steals the cash and hides it in the apartment of the other woman he's seeing (Harding). Thompson does fine but to describe Harding's debut performance as wooden is to be very, very kind. *CW:* Sex scene, violence and some nudity. **94m/C VHS.** Teri Thompson, Joe Estevez, Chris De Rose, Tonya Harding; *D:* Sean Dash; *W:* Sean Dash. *NYR*

Breakdown 🐾 **1953** A boxer is set up by his girlfriend's father to take the rap for a murder. Lackluster effort. **76m/B VHS, Beta.** Ann Richards, William Bishop, Anne Gwynne, Sheldon Leonard, Wally Cassell, Richard Benedict; *D:* Edmond Angelo. *NOS, SNC*

Breakdown 🐾🐾🐾 **1996 (R)** Jeff (Russell) and Amy (Quinlan) are high-falootin' Easterners on their way to San Diego when their car breaks down somewhere in the vast Southwest. When a trucker (Walsh) stops and offers to take Amy to the next stop while Jeff guards their yuppie treasure trove, they accept willingly. Inconvenience soon turns to terror when Jeff gets the car started, drives to meet his wife and finds her nowhere in sight. Spotting the truck by the side of the road,

he confronts the trucker with the cops only to have him deny ever having seen them before. Thus begins the frantic hunt. Russell's descent from dismay to panic to resolve is grippingly played. You may know where it's going, but the fun is in getting there. *CW:* Strong violence/terror and language. **93m/C VHS.** Kurt Russell, Kathleen Quinlan, J.T. Walsh, M.C. Gainey, Jack Noseworthy, Rex Linn, Ritch Brinkley, Kim Robillard; *D:* Jonathan Mostow; *W:* Jonathan Mostow; *C:* Doug Milsome; *M:* Basil Poledouris. *PAR*

Breaker! Breaker! 🐾 **1977 (PG)** Convoy of angry truck drivers launch an assault on the corrupt and sadistic locals of a small Texas town. Goofy entry in "mad or sex-crazed trucker armed with a CB radio" genre. **86m/C VHS, Beta.** Chuck Norris, George Murdock; *D:* Don Hulette.

Breaker Morant 🐾🐾🐾½ **1980 (PG)** In 1901 South Africa, three Australian soldiers are put on trial for avenging the murder of several prisoners. Based on a true story which was then turned into a play by Kenneth Ross, this riveting, popular antiwar statement and courtroom drama heralded Australia's film renaissance. Rich performances by Woodward and Waters. **107m/C VHS, Beta, LV, 8mm.** *AU* Edward Woodward, Jack Thompson, John Waters, Bryan Brown; *D:* Bruce Beresford; *W:* Jonathon Hardy, David Stevens, Bruce Beresford. Australian Film Institute '80: Best Actor (Thompson), Best Film; Nominations: Academy Awards '80: Best Adapted Screenplay. *CCB, COL, HMV*

Breakfast at Tiffany's 🐾🐾🐾½ **1961** Truman Capote's amusing story of an endearingly eccentric New York City playgirl and her shaky romance with a young writer. Hepburn lends Holly Golightly just the right combination of naivete and worldly wisdom with a dash of melancholy. A wonderfully offbeat romance. 🎵 Moon River. **114m/C VHS, Beta, LV, 8mm.** Audrey Hepburn, George Peppard, Patricia Neal, Buddy Ebsen, Mickey Rooney, Martin Balsam, John McGiver; *D:* Blake Edwards; *W:* George Axelrod; *M:* Henry Mancini. Academy Awards '61: Best Song ("Moon River"), Best Original Dramatic/Comedy Score; Nominations: Academy Awards '61: Best Actress (Hepburn), Best Adapted Screenplay, Best Art Direction/Set Decoration (Color). *PAR, FCT*

The Breakfast Club 🐾🐾🐾 **1985 (R)** Five students from different cliques at a Chicago suburban high school spend a day together in detention. Rather well done teenage culture study; these characters delve a little deeper than the standard adult view of adolescent stereotypes. One of John Hughes' best movies. Soundtrack features Simple Minds and Wang Chung. **97m/C VHS, Beta, LV, Closed Caption, DVD.** Ally Sheedy, Molly Ringwald, Judd Nelson, Emilio Estevez, Anthony Michael Hall, Paul Gleason, John Kapelos; *D:* John Hughes; *W:* John Hughes; *M:* Gary Chang, Keith Forsey. *USH, FCT*

Breakfast in Hollywood 🐾½ *The Mad Hatter* **1946** Movie about the popular morning radio show of the 1940s hosted by Tom Breneman, a coast-to-coast coffee klatch. **93m/B VHS, Beta.** Tom Breneman, Bonita Granville, Eddie Ryan, Beulah Bondi, Billie Burke, ZaSu Pitts, Hedda Hopper, Spike Jones; *D:* Harold Schuster. *NO*

Breakfast in Paris 🐾½ **1981** Two American professionals in Paris, both crushed from past failures in the love department, find each other. **85m/C VHS, Beta.** *AU* Rod Mullinar, Barbara Parkins, Jack Lenoir; *D:* John Lamond.

Breakheart Pass 🐾🐾 **1976 (PG)** A governor, his female companion, a band of cavalrymen, and a mysterious man travel on a train through the mountains of Idaho in 1870. The mystery man turns out to be a murderer. Based on a novel by Alistair MacLean. **92m/C VHS, Beta, LV, Closed Caption.** Charles Bronson, Ben Johnson, Richard Crenna, Jill Ireland, Charles Durning, Ed Lauter, Archie Moore, Sally Kirkland; *D:* Tom Gries; *C:* Lucien Ballard; *M:* Jerry Goldsmith. *MGM, FOX*

Breakin' 🐾🐾 *Breakdance* **1984 (PG)** Dance phenomenon break dancing along with the hit songs that accompanied the fad. 🎵 Tibetan Jam; Heart of the Beat; Breakin...There's No Stopping

Us; Street People; Showdown; 99 1/2. **87m/C VHS, Beta, LV.** Lucinda Dickey, Adolfo "Shabba Doo" Quinones, Michael "Boogaloo Shrimp" Chambers, Ben Lokey, Christopher McDonald, Phineas Newborn III; *D:* Joel Silberg; *W:* Allen N. DeBevoise; *C:* Hanania Baer; *M:* Michael Boyd. *MGM*

Breakin' 2: Electric Boogaloo 🎬
Breakdance 2: Electric Boogaloo; Electric Boogaloo "Breakin' 2" **1984 (PG)** Breakdancers hold a benefit concert to preserve an urban community center. 🎵Electric Boogaloo; Radiotron; Action; When I.C.U. **94m/C VHS, Beta, LV.** Lucinda Dickey, Adolfo "Shabba Doo" Quinones, Michael "Boogaloo Shrimp" Chambers, Susie Bono; *D:* Sam Firstenberg; *C:* Hanania Baer. *MGM*

Breakin' Through 🎬 1984
The choreographer of a troubled Broadway-bound musical decides to energize his shows with a troupe of street dancers. **73m/C VHS, Beta.** Ben Vereen, Donna McKechnie, Reid Shelton; *D:* Peter Medak. *DIS*

Breaking All the Rules 🎬½ 1985 (R)
Comedy about two teenage lovers who find themselves embroiled in a slapdash jewel robbery at an amusement park during the last day of summer break. **91m/C VHS, Beta.** Carolyn Dunn, Carl Marotte, Thor Bishopric, Rachel Hayward; *D:* James Orr; *W:* James Orr, Jim Cruickshank. *VTR*

Breaking Away 🎬🎬🎬 1979 (PG)
A lighthearted coming-of-age drama about a high school graduate's addiction to bicycle racing, whose dreams are tested against the realities of a crucial race. An honest, open look at present Americana with tremendous insight into the minds of average youth; shot on location at Indiana University. Great bike-racing photography. Quaid, Barrie, and Christopher give exceptional performances. Basis for television series. **100m/C VHS, Beta, LV.** Dennis Christopher, Dennis Quaid, Daniel Stern, Jackie Earle Haley, Barbara Barrie, Paul Dooley, Amy Wright; *D:* Peter Yates; *W:* Steve Tesich. Academy Awards '79: Best Original Screenplay; Golden Globe Awards '80: Best Film—Musical/Comedy; National Board of Review Awards '79: Best Supporting Actor (Dooley); New York Film Critics Awards '79: Best Screenplay; National Society of Film Critics Awards '79: Best Screenplay; Writers Guild of America '79: Best Original Screenplay; Nominations: Academy Awards '79: Best Director (Yates), Best Picture, Best Supporting Actress (Barrie), Original Song Score and/or Adaptation. *FOX, HMV*

Breaking Free 🎬🎬½ 1995 (PG)
Teenaged loser forms an unlikely friendship with a bitter gymnast who's been blinded and forced to give up her dreams. **106m/C VHS.** Jeremy London, Gina Philips, Christine Taylor, Megan Gallagher. *AVE*

Breaking Glass 🎬🎬½ 1980 (PG)
A "New Wave" musical that gives an insight into the punk record business and at the same time tells of the rags-to-riches life of a punk rock star. **94m/C VHS, Beta.** GB Hazel O'Connor, Phil Daniels, Jon Finch, Jonathan Pryce; *D:* Brian Gibson. *PAR*

Breaking Home Ties 🎬🎬½ Norman Rockwell's Breaking Home Ties 1987
Norman Rockwell's illustration is the basis for this coming of age story set in a small Texas town. A young man is eager to be off to college and lessen his family ties but his mother's serious illness may prevent both. Good performances help overcome the sentimentality. Originally made for television. **95m/C VHS.** Jason Robards Jr., Eva Marie Saint, Doug McKeon, Claire Trevor, Erin Gray; *D:* John Wilder; *W:* John Wilder. *CAF*

Breaking In 🎬🎬🎬 1989 (R)
A semi-acclaimed comedy about a professional thief who takes a young amateur under his wing and shows him the ropes. Under-estimated Reynolds is especially charming. Witty and innovative script, with intelligent direction from Forsyth. **95m/C VHS, Beta, LV, Closed Caption.** Burt Reynolds, Casey Siemaszko, Sheila Kelley, Lorraine Toussaint, Albert Salmi, Harry Carey Jr., Maury Chaykin, Stephen Tobolowsky, David Frishberg; *D:* Bill Forsyth; *W:* John Sayles; *C:* Michael Coulter; *M:* Michael Gibbs. *HBO, WAR*

Breaking Loose 🎬½ 1990 (R)
A surfer is on the run from a vicious motorcycle gang that kidnapped his girlfriend, but turns to fight eventually, board in hand. **88m/C VHS.** Peter Phelps, Vince Martin, Abigail, David Ngcombujarra; *D:* Rod Hay.

Breaking Point 🎬🎬½ 1994 (R)
Ex-cop Dwight Meadows (Busey) retired from the force when he was nearly killed by a scalpel-wielding mass murderer known as "The Surgeon." Now the psycho is back and Meadows returns to active duty, paired with relentless officer Dana Preston (Fluegel), who wants the killer caught—at any cost. Vancouver, British Columbia fills in for the Seattle, Washington setting. *CW:* Language; violence; nudity. **95m/C VHS, LV, Closed Caption.** Gary Busey, Darlanne Fluegel, Jeff Griggs, Kim Cattrall; *D:* Paul Ziller; *M:* Graeme Coleman. *REP*

Breaking the Code 🎬🎬½ 1995
Alan Turing (Jacobi) is a British mathematical genius whose work leads to the birth of the digital computer and who is instrumental in enabling the allies to crack the German WWII Enigma code. An active homosexual when homosexuality was illegal, Turing's personal behavior was tolerated because of the importance of his work but after the gay spy scare of the '50s, Turing was regarded as a security risk and his life increasingly restricted. British TV adaptation based on the play by Hugh Whitemore (Jacobi also played the role on stage) and the book "Alan Turing: The Enigma" by Andrew Hodges. **90m/C VHS.** GB Derek Jacobi, Amanda Root, Prunella Scales, Harold Pinter, Julian Kerridge, Richard Johnson; *D:* Herbert Wise; *W:* Hugh Whitemore. *VTR, VIF, WMI*

Breaking the Ice 🎬🎬 1938
Unlikely mixture of Mennonites and a big city ice skating show. Young man leaves the farm to get a job singing at the rink. Musical numbers abound with backing by Victor Young and his Orchestra. **79m/B VHS, Beta.** Bobby Breen, Charlie Ruggles, Dolores Costello, Billy Gilbert, Margaret Hamilton. Nominations: Academy Awards '38: Best Original Score. *NOS, VYY, DVT*

Breaking the Rules 🎬🎬½ 1992 (PG-13)
Predicatable buddy-road movie with a tearjerking premise and comedic overtones. Rob, Gene, and Phil were best buds growing up in Cleveland but young adulthood has separated them. They are reunited by Phil, who is dying of leukemia, and whose last wish is a cross-country road trip to California so he can appear as a contestant on "Jeopardy." Along the way they meet brassy waitress Mary, who impulsively decides to join them and winds up bringing the trio's shaky friendship back together. Potts does well as the big-haired, big-hearted Mary but the actors must work hard to maintain any dignity given the story's melodrama. **100m/C VHS, LV, Closed Caption.** Jason Bateman, C. Thomas Howell, Jonathan Silverman, Annie Potts, Kent Bateman, Shawn Phelan; *D:* Neal Israel; *W:* Paul Shapiro; *M:* David Kitay. *HBO*

Breaking the Surface: The Greg Louganis Story 🎬🎬½ 1996
Trials and tribulations of the gold-medal winning Olympic diver, including his overbearing father, abusive lover, and his own HIV-positive status. Based on Louganis' autobiography; made for TV. **95m/C VHS.** Mario Lopez, Michael Murphy, Jeffrey Meek, Bruce Weitz, Rosemary Dunsmore; *D:* Steven Hilliard Stern; *W:* Alan Hines. *PHO*

Breaking the Waves 🎬🎬🎬 1995 (R)
Sacrificial journey of shy, religious Bess (Watson), who's living in an austere northern Scotland coastal village in the '70s. Bess, who regularly talks to God, marries Jan (Skarsgard), an adventurer working on a North Sea oil rig. It must be a case of opposites attracting but the couple are happy until Jan is paralyzed from the neck down in a rig accident. Bess, who blames herself, begins sleeping around, believing her actions can somehow help Jan, and slides ever deeper into mental instability. Powerful story is divided into seven chapters and an epilogue. *CW:* Strong graphic sexuality, nudity, language and some violence. **152m/C VHS, Letterbox, Closed Caption.** DK FR Emily Watson, Stellan Skarsgard, Katrin Cartlidge, Adrian Rawlins, Jean-Marc Barr, Sandra Voe, Udo Kier, Mikkel Gaup; *D:* Lars von Trier; *W:* Lars von Trier; *C:* Robby Muller; *M:* Joachim Holbek. Cannes Film Festival '96: Grand Jury Prize; Cesar Awards '97: Best Foreign Film; New York Film Critics Awards '96: Best Actress (Watson), Best Cinematography, Best Director (von Trier); National Society of Film Critics Awards '96: Best Actress (Watson), Best Cinematography, Best Director (von Trier), Best Film; Nominations: Academy Awards '96: Best Actress (Watson); British Academy Awards '96: Best Actress (Watson); Golden Globe Awards '97: Best Actress—Drama (Watson), Best Film—Drama; Independent Spirit Awards '97: Best Foreign Film. *EVE*

Breaking Up 🎬🎬½ 1978
A woman fights to rediscover her personal identity after her 15-year marriage crumbles. Made for television. Emmy nominated. **90m/C VHS, Beta.** Lee Remick, Granville Van Dusen, David Stambaugh; *D:* Delbert Mann. *TLF*

Breaking Up 🎬½ 1997 (R)
What steamy sheet action brings together, dreary day to day living easily pulls apart. That is the basic message of this bland romantic comedy that brings nothing new to the tired genre. Typical opposites attract but can't stay together (yet can't stay apart) plot finds photographer Crowe and teacher Hayek madly in lust and impulsively marrying. Hayek had more to work with when she played this role in "Fools Rush In," and Crowe seems uncomfortable as the lackluster boyfriend. Told in a chatty style with frequent asides to the audience by the main characters and a string of flashback sequences, director Greenwald's theatre background is apparent here. Clever camera work and editing are highlights. Adapted from Michael Cristofer's Pulitzer Prize-winning play. *CW:* Language and sexuality. **90m/C VHS.** Salma Hayek, Russell Crowe; *D:* Robert Greenwald; *W:* Michael Cristofer; *M:* Mark Mothersbaugh. *WAR*

Breaking Up Is Hard to Do 🎬 1979
Six men leave their wives and shack up together on Malibu for a summer of partying and introspection. Made for television; edited down from its original 201 minute length. **96m/C VHS, Beta, LV.** Billy Crystal, Bonnie Franklin, Ted Bessell, Jeff Conaway, Tony Musante, Robert Conrad, Trish Stewart, David Ogden Stiers, George Gaynes; *D:* Lou Antonio; *M:* Richard Bellis. *THV*

Breakout 🎬🎬 1975 (PG)
The wife of a man imprisoned in Mexico hires a Texas bush pilot (Bronson) to help her husband (Duvall) escape. **96m/C VHS, Beta, LV.** Charles Bronson, Robert Duvall, John Huston, Sheree North, Randy Quaid; *D:* Tom Gries; *C:* Lucien Ballard; *M:* Jerry Goldsmith. *COL*

Breakthrough 🎬🎬 Sergeant Steiner 1978 (PG)
German soldier, broken at the end of WWII, sets out to negotiate with the Allies. Average at best. **96m/C VHS, Beta.** Richard Burton, Robert Mitchum, Rod Steiger, Michael Parks, Curt Jurgens; *D:* Andrew V. McLaglen. *WOV*

Breast Men 🎬🎬½ 1997 (R)
A campy fictional look into the lives and careers of the two doctors who invented the silicone breast implant in 1960s Texas. Struggling Kevin Saunders (Schwimmer) is an ambitious geek who works with grumpy plastic surgeon mentor, Dr. William Larson (Cooper), to develop a prosthetic breast, made from Dow-Corning's silicone gel. It's an immediate success and the doctors become rich, successful, and ever more obnoxious. Then come the lawsuits and life is suddenly no longer so sweet. And yes, you will see a lot of naked breasts. *CW:* Sexuality and nudity, language and drug use. **95m/C VHS, Closed Caption.** David Schwimmer, Chris Cooper, Louise Fletcher, Emily Procter, Matt Frewer; *D:* Lawrence O'Neil; *W:* John Stockwell; *C:* Robert Stevens; *M:* Dennis McCarthy. *HBO*

Breath of Scandal 🐾🐾 1960 An American diplomat in Vienna rescues a princess when she is thrown off a horse; he falls for her like a ton o' bricks. Viennese politics complicate things. Based on a play by Molnar. **98m/C VHS, Closed Caption.** Sophia Loren, John Gavin, Maurice Chevalier, Angela Lansbury; **D:** Michael Curtiz. *PAR, BAR*

Breathing Fire 🐾🐾 1991 (R) A Vietnamese teenager and his American brother find out their ex-GI father is behind an armed bank robbery and murder. They join together to protect the only eyewitness—a young girl—against the ruthless gang of criminals and their own father. Lots of kickboxing action for martial arts fans. **CW:** Martial arts violence. **86m/C VHS, Closed Caption.** Bolo Yeung, Jonathan Ke Quan, Jerry Trimble; **D:** Lou Kennedy. *IMP*

Breathing Lessons 🐾🐾🐾 1994 (PG) Sweet look at a long-term marriage that renews itself on a road trip. Flighty Maggie and pragmatic Ira have been married for 28 squabbling but loving years. They're driving from their Baltimore home to a funeral in Pennsylvania and the road stops provide some small adventures and a great deal of conversation. Drama rests easily on the capable shoulders of the veteran performers. Based on the novel by Anne Tyler. Made for TV. **98m/C VHS, Closed Caption.** James Garner, Joanne Woodward, Paul Winfield, Kathryn Erbe, Joyce Van Patten, Eileen Heckart, Tim Guinee, Henry Jones, Stephi Lineburg, Jean Louisa Kelly, John Considine; **D:** John Erman; **W:** Robert W. Lenski. *REP*

Breathing Room 🐾🐾 *'Til Christmas* 1996 (R) New Yorker David (Futterman) has trouble with commitment to girlfriend Kathy (Floyd) and the duo break up again at Thanksgiving when he won't tell her he loves her. Kathy decides they need a break and refuses to see David until Christmas. She plays at seeing her boss, both get too much advice from friends and family, they attend the same holiday party—and the inevitable happens. Nothing new here. **CW:** Language and some sexuality. **90m/C VHS.** Dan Futterman, Susan Floyd, David Thornton; **D:** Jon Sherman; **W:** Jon Sherman, Tom Hughes; **C:** Jim Denault; **M:** Pat Irwin. *AVI*

Breathless 🐾🐾🐾🐾 *A Bout de Souffle* 1959 Godard's first feature catapulted him to the vanguard of French filmmakers. A carefree Parisian crook, who emulates Humphrey Bogart, falls in love with an American girl with tragic results. Wonderful scenes of Parisian life. Established Godard's Brechtian, experimental style. Belmondo's film debut. Mistitled "Breathless" for American release, the film's French title actually means "Out of Breath"; however, the fast-paced, erratic musical score leaves you breathless. French with English subtitles. Remade with Richard Gere in 1983 with far less intensity. **90m/B VHS, Beta.** *FR* Jean-Paul Belmondo, Jean Seberg, Daniel Boulanger, Jean-Pierre Melville, Liliane Robin; **D:** Jean-Luc Godard; **W:** Jean-Luc Godard. Berlin International Film Festival '60: Best Director (Godard). *NOS, MRV, CVC*

Breathless 🐾🐾 1983 (R) Car thief turned cop killer has a torrid love affair with a French student studying in Los Angeles as the police slowly close in. Glossy, smarmy remake of the Godard classic that concentrates on the thin plot rather than any attempt at revitalizing the film syntax. **105m/C VHS, Beta, LV.** Richard Gere, Valerie Kaprisky, Art Metrano, John P. Ryan, Lisa Jane Persky; **D:** Jim McBride; **W:** Jim McBride, L.M. Kit Carson; **M:** Jack Nitzsche. *VES*

A Breed Apart 🐾🐾 1984 (R) An on-going battle over a rare eagle's eggs strikes sparks between a reclusive conservationist and a scheming adventurer hired by a billionaire collector. **95m/C VHS, Beta.** Kathleen Turner, Rutger Hauer, Powers Boothe, Donald Pleasence, Brion James, John Dennis Johnston; **D:** Philippe Mora.

Breed of the Border 🐾 *Speed Brent Wins* 1933 Tough-fisted cowboys must take the law into their own hands. **60m/B VHS, Beta.** Bob Steele, Marion Byron, George "Gabby" Hayes, Ernie Adams; **D:** Robert North Bradbury. *NOS, DVT*

Breeders WOOF! 1997 (R) Alien on a mating mission terrorizes a Boston womens' college. Doesn't deliver on its exploitation premise, so why bother. **CW:** Violence/gore, language and some sexuality. **92m/C VHS.** Todd Jensen, Samantha Janus, Kadamba Simmons, Oliver Tobias; **D:** Paul Matthews.

Brenda Starr 🐾 1986 (PG) Amateurish adaptation of the comic strip by Dale Messick. Shields stars as girl reporter Brenda Starr, who is once again risking her life to get the scoop. She finds herself in the jungles of South America searching for a mad scientist who is creating a rocket fuel that could destroy the world. The most entertaining thing about this film is the costumes designed by Bob Mackie. **94m/C VHS.** Brooke Shields, Timothy Dalton, Tony Peck, Diana Scarwid, Nestor Serrano, Jeffrey Tambor, June Gable, Charles Durning, Eddie Albert, Henry Gibson, Ed Nelson; **D:** Robert Ellis Miller; **W:** James David Buchanan. *COL*

The Bretts 🐾🐾🐾 1988 Amusing two-part British miniseries follows the egos and eccentricities of the British theatrical dynasty, the Bretts. Part 1 is set in the '20s and introduces the family heads, Charles (Rodway) and Lydia (Murray), who enjoy performing off-stage almost as well as they enjoy performing on. Also introduced are their five children and loyal (if opinionated) servants. Part 2 follows the family into the '30s with son Edwin (Yelland) having become a film star, actress daughter Martha (Lang) falling for a politician, and son Tom (Winter) continuing to write his gloomy social dramas. Each part is on six cassettes. **600m/C VHS.** *GB* Barbara Murray, Norman Rodway, David Yelland, Belinda Lang, George Winter, Janet Maw, Tim Wylton, Bert Parnaby, Lysette Anthony, Clive Francis, Frank Middlemass, John Castle, Hugh Fraser, Patrick Ryecart, Sally Cookson, Billy Boyle; **W:** Rosemary Anne Sisson. *SIG, VCO*

Brewster McCloud 🐾🐾🐾½ 1970 (R) Altman's first picture after M*A*S*H reunites much of the cast and combines fantasy, black comedy, and satire in the story of a young man whose head is in the clouds or at least in the upper reaches of the Houston Astrodome. Brewster (Cort) lives covertly in the Dome and dreams of flying. He also has a guardian angel (Kellerman) who watches over him and may actually be killing people who give him a hard time. Murphy is a cop obsessed with catching the killer. And there's a circus allegory as well. Hard to figure what it all means and offbeat as they come, but for certain tastes, exquisite. **101m/C VHS, Beta, LV, Letterbox.** Bud Cort, Sally Kellerman, Shelley Duvall, Michael Murphy, William Windom, Rene Auberjonois, Stacy Keach, John Schuck, Margaret Hamilton; **D:** Robert Altman; **W:** Doran William Cannon; **C:** Jordan Cronenweth. *MGM*

Brewster's Millions 🐾🐾½ 1945 If Brewster, an ex-GI, can spend a million dollars in one year, he will inherit a substantially greater fortune. Originally a 1902 novel, this is the fifth of seven film adaptations. **79m/B VHS, Beta.** Dennis O'Keefe, June Havoc, Eddie Anderson, Helen Walker, Gail Patrick, Mischa Auer; **D:** Allan Dwan. Nominations: Academy Awards '45: Best Original Dramatic/Comedy Score.

Brewster's Millions 🐾½ 1985 (PG) An aging minor league baseball player must spend $30 million in order to collect an inheritance of $300 million. He may find that money can't buy happiness. Seventh remake of the story. **101m/C VHS, Beta, LV, Closed Caption.** Richard Pryor, John Candy, Lonette McKee, Stephen Collins, Jerry Orbach, Pat Hingle, Tovah Feldshuh, Hume Cronyn, Rick Moranis; **D:** Walter Hill; **W:** Herschel Weingrod, Timothy Harris; **M:** Ry Cooder. *USH*

Brian's Song 🐾🐾🐾🐾 1971 (G) The story of the unique relationship between Gale Sayers, the Chicago Bears' star running back, and his teammate Brian Piccolo. The friendship between the Bears' first interracial roommates ended suddenly when Brian Piccolo lost his life to cancer. Made for television. Incredibly well received in its time. **74m/C VHS, Beta, LV, Closed Caption.** James Caan, Billy Dee Williams, Jack Warden, Shelley Fabares, Judy Pace; **D:** Buzz Kulik; **C:** Joseph Biroc. *COL*

The Bride 🐾🐾½ 1985 (PG-13) Re-telling of "The Bride of Frankenstein." Sting's Dr. Frankenstein has much more success in creating his second monster (Beals). She's pretty and intelligent and he may even be falling in love with her. When she begins to gain too much independence, though, the awful truth about her origins comes out. Fans of the two leads will want to see this one, but for a true classic see Elsa Lanchester's bride. **118m/C VHS, Beta, LV, Closed Caption.** Sting, Jennifer Beals, Anthony Higgins, David Rappaport, Geraldine Page, Clancy Brown, Phil Daniels, Veruschka; **D:** Franc Roddam; **W:** Lloyd Fonvielle; **C:** Stephen Burum; **M:** Maurice Jarre. *COL*

The Bride & the Beast WOOF! *Queen of the Gorillas* 1958 While on an African safari honeymoon, a big game hunter's new bride is carried off by a gorilla. Ludicrous jungle tale. **78m/B VHS, Beta.** Charlotte Austin, Lance Fuller, William Justine; **D:** Adrian Weiss; **W:** Edward D. Wood Jr.; **M:** Les Baxter. *AOV*

The Bride Came C.O.D. 🐾🐾 1941 Rough'n'tough pilot Cagney is hired by a rich Texas oil man to prevent his daughter (the one with the Bette Davis eyes) from marrying cheesy bandleader Carson. The payoff: $10 per pound if she's delivered unwed. What a surprise when Cagney faces the timeworn dilemma of having to choose between love and money. A contemporary issue of "Time" magazine trumpeted: "Screen's most talented tough guy rough-houses one of screen's best dramatic actresses." That tells you right there it's a romantic comedy. Cagney and Davis—a likely pairing, you'd think—are essentially fish out of water, bothered and bewildered by a weak script. **92m/B VHS.** Bette Davis, James Cagney, Stuart Erwin, Jack Carson, George Tobias, Eugene Pallette, William Frawley; **D:** William Keighley; **W:** Julius J. Epstein, Philip C. Epstein; **M:** Max Steiner. *MGM, FCT*

The Bride Is Much Too Beautiful 🐾🐾½ 1958 Bardot, playing a French farm girl, becomes a renowned model. Dubbed. **90m/C VHS, Beta.** *FR* Brigitte Bardot, Louis Jourdan, Micheline Presle, Marcel Amont; **D:** Fred Surin. *NOS, FCT, HEG*

The Bride of Frankenstein 🐾🐾🐾🐾 1935 The classic sequel to the classic original in which Dr. F. seeks to build a mate for his monster. More humor than the first, but also more pathos, including the monster's famous but short-lived friendship with a blind hermit. Lanchester plays both the bride and Mary Shelley in the opening sequence. **75m/B VHS, Beta, LV.** Boris Karloff, Elsa Lanchester, Ernest Thesiger, Colin Clive, Una O'Connor, Valerie Hobson, Dwight Frye, John Carradine, E.E. Clive, O.P. Heggie, Gavin Gordon, Douglas Walton; **D:** James Whale; **W:** John L. Balderston, William Hurlbut; **C:** John Mescall. Nominations: Academy Awards '35: Best Sound. *USH, MLB*

Bride of Killer Nerd 🐾 1991 Harold Kunkel, left over from the original "Killer Nerd," finds his opposite sex nirvana in the person of Thelma, also a nerd in mind, body, and soul. They relentlessly pursue revenge on the rockers who humiliate them at a campus beer bash. **75m/C VHS.** Toby Radloff, Wayne A. Harold, Heidi Lohr; **D:** Mark Steven Bosko. *TEM*

Bride of Re-Animator 🐾🐾½ *Re-Animator 2* 1989 Herbert West is back, and this time he not only re-animates life but creates life—sexy female life—in this sequel to the immensely popular "Re-Animator." High camp and blood curdling gore make this a standout in the sequel parade. Available in a R-rated version as well. **99m/C VHS, Beta, LV, Closed Caption.** Bruce Abbott, Claude Earl Jones, Fabiana Udenio, Jeffrey Combs, Kathleen Kinmont, David Gale, Mel Stewart; **D:** Brian Yuzna; **W:** Rick Fry, Woody Keith; **C:** Rick Fichter; **M:** Richard Band. *AHV*

Bride of the Gorilla 🐾🐾 1951 Burr travels to the jungle where he finds a wife, a plantation, and a curse in this African twist on the werewolf legend. Chaney is the local policeman on his trail. Burr's physical changes are fun to watch. **76m/B VHS.** Raymond Burr, Barbara Payton, Lon Chaney Jr., Tom Conway, Paul Cavanagh; **D:** Curt Siodmak; **W:** Curt Siodmak. *NOS, MRV, SNC*

Bride of the Monster woof! *Bride of the Atom* 1956 Lugosi stars as a mad scientist trying to create a race of giants. Classic Woodian badness. **70m/B VHS, Beta.** Bela Lugosi, Tor Johnson, Loretta King, Tony McCoy, Harvey B. Dunn, George Becwar, Paul Marco, Billy Benedict, Dolores Fuller; **D:** Edward D. Wood Jr.; **W:** Edward D. Wood Jr., Alex Gordon; **C:** William C. Thompson. *SNC, VYY, HHT*

The Bride Walks Out 🐾🐾 1936 Newlywed crisis: a woman with rich taste learns how to adjust to living on her husband's poor salary, but not before she samples the life of the wealthy. Interesting in a sociological sort of way. **81m/B VHS, Beta.** Barbara Stanwyck, Gene Raymond, Robert Young, Ned Sparks, Willie Best, Helen Broderick, Hattie McDaniel; **D:** Leigh Jason. *TTC*

The Bride with White Hair 🐾🐾 1993 Operatic martial arts fable based on a novel by Leung Yu-Sang. A young warrior revives a beautiful witch (also a champion warrior) who was killed by jealous Siamese twins. Now the duo, who have fallen in love, must battle the evil twins who rule the corrupt Mo Dynasty. Available dubbed or in Chinese with subtitles. **92m/C VHS, Letterbox.** *HK* Leslie Cheung, Brigitte Lin Ching Hsia; **D:** Ronny Yu. *TAI*

The Bride with White Hair 2 🐾🐾 1993 The magic saga continues with the massacre of the followers of the Eight Lineages. Powerful and obsessed with vengeance, the Bride can only be stopped by the one man who loves her. Chinese with subtitles or dubbed. **80m/C VHS, LV, Letterbox.** *HK* Brigitte Lin Ching Hsia, Leslie Cheung, Christy Chung; **D:** David Wu. *TAI*

The Bride Wore Black 🐾🐾🐾 *La Mariee Etait en Noir* 1968 Truffaut's homage to Hitchcock, complete with Bernard Herrmann score. A young woman exacts brutal revenge on the five men who accidentally killed her husband. Adapted from a novel by Cornell Woolrich. **107m/C VHS, LV.** *FR* Jeanne Moreau, Claude Rich, Jean-Claude Brialy, Michel Bouquet, Michael Lonsdale; **D:** Francois Truffaut; **C:** Raoul Coutard; **M:** Bernard Herrmann. *MGM, MLB, FCT*

The Bride Wore Red 🐾🐾 1937 Crawford stars as a cabaret singer who masquerades as a socialite in an attempt to break into the upper crust. When a wealthy aristocrat invites her to spend two weeks at a posh resort in Tyrol, Crawford plays her part to the hilt, managing to charm both a rich gentleman and the village postman. Typical "love conquers all" melodrama. **103m/B VHS, Closed Caption.** Joan Crawford, Franchot Tone, Robert Young, Billie Burke, Reginald Owen, Lynne Carver, George Zucco; **D:** Dorothy Arzner. *MGM*

Brides of Christ 🐾🐾½ 1991 Set in the Australian Santo Spirito Convent during the Vatican II upheaval of the 1960s. Explores the tensions between old and new religious ideas by focusing on novices, older nuns, and the Reverend Mother of the convent as they try to cope with a changing world. TV miniseries. **300m/C VHS.** Brenda Fricker, Sandy Gore, Josephine Byrnes, Lisa Hensley, Naomi Watts, Kym Wilson, Melissa Thomas; **D:** Ken Cameron; **W:** John Alsop, Sue Smith. *AEH, NEW*

The Brides of Dracula 🐾🐾½ 1960 A young French woman unknowingly frees a vampire. He wreaks havoc, sucking blood and creating more of the undead to carry out his evil deeds. One of the better Hammer vampire films. **86m/C VHS, LV.** *GB* Peter Cushing, Martita Hunt, Yvonne Monlaur, Freda Jackson, David Peel, Mona Washbourne, Miles Malleson, Henry Oscar, Michael Ripper, Andree Melly; **D:** Terence Fisher; **W:** Peter Bryan, Edward Percy, Jimmy Sangster; **C:** Jack Asher. *USH, FCT*

Brides of the Beast woof! *Brides of Blood; Grave Desires; Island of the Living Horror* 1968 Filipino radiation monsters get their jollies by eating beautiful young naked women. Newly arrived research scientist and his bride oppose this custom. First in a series of "Blood Island" horrors. **85m/C VHS, Beta.** *PH* John Ashley, Kent Taylor, Beverly Hills, Eva Darren, Mario Montenegro; **D:** Eddie Romero, Gerardo (Gerry) De Leon. *NO*

Brideshead Revisited 🐾🐾🐾 1981 The acclaimed British miniseries based on the Evelyn Waugh classic about an Edwardian young man who falls under the spell of a wealthy aristocratic family and struggles to retain his integrity and values. On six tapes. **540m/C VHS, Beta, Closed Caption.** *GB* Jeremy Irons, Anthony Andrews, Diana Quick, Laurence Olivier, John Gielgud, Claire Bloom, Stephane Audran, Mona Washbourne, John Le Mesurier, Charles Keating; **D:** Charles Sturridge, Michael Lindsay-Hogg; **M:** Geoffrey Burgon. *MOV, FUS, FCT*

The Bridge 🐾🐾 *Die Brucke* 1959 In 1945, two days before the end of WWII, seven German schoolboys are drafted to defend an unimportant bridge from American tanks. Emotional anti-war film based on the autobiographical novel of Manfred Gregor. German with subtitles. **102m/B VHS.** *GE* Fritz Wepper, Volker Bohnet, Franz Glaubrecht, Karl Michael Balzer, Gunther Hoffman; **D:** Bernhard Wicki; **W:** Michael Mansfield, Karl-Wilhelm Vivier; **C:** Gerd Von Bonen; **M:** Hans-Martin Majewski. Nominations: Academy Awards '59: Best Foreign Language Film. *FCT*

The Bridge at Remagen 🐾🐾½ 1969 (PG) Based on the true story of allied attempts to capture a vital bridge before retreating German troops destroy it. For war-film buffs. **115m/C VHS, Beta.** George Segal, Robert Vaughn, Ben Gazzara, Bradford Dillman, E.G. Marshall; **D:** John Guillermin; **W:** William Roberts; **M:** Elmer Bernstein. *NO*

The Bridge of San Luis Rey 🐾🐾🐾 1944 A priest investigates the famous bridge collapse in Lima, Peru that left five people dead. Based upon the novel by Thornton Wilder. **89m/B VHS, Beta, LV.** Lynn Bari, Francis Lederer, Louis Calhern, Akim Tamiroff, Donald Woods, Alla Nazimova, Blanche Yurka; **D:** Rowland V. Lee. Nominations: Academy Awards '44: Best Original Dramatic/Comedy Score. *IME*

The Bridge on the River Kwai 🐾🐾🐾🐾 1957 Award-winning adaptation of the Pierre Bouelle novel about the battle of wills between a Japanese POW camp commander and a British colonel over the construction of a rail bridge, and the parallel efforts by escaped prisoner Holden to destroy it. Holden's role was originally cast for Cary Grant. Memorable too for whistling "Colonel Bogey March." Because the writers were blacklisted, Bouelle (who spoke no English) was originally credited as the screenwriter. **161m/C VHS, Beta, LV, Letterbox.** *GB* William Holden, Alec Guinness, Jack Hawkins, Sessue Hayakawa, James Donald, Geoffrey Horne, Andre Morell, Ann Sears; **D:** David Lean; **W:** Michael Wilson, Carl Foreman; **C:** Jack Hildyard; **M:** Malcolm Arnold. Academy Awards '57: Best Actor (Guinness), Best Adapted Screenplay, Best Cinematography, Best Director (Lean), Best Film Editing, Best Picture, Best Score; British Academy Awards '57: Best Actor (Guinness), Best Film, Best Screenplay; Directors Guild of America Awards '57: Best Director (Lean); Golden Globe Awards '58: Best Actor—Drama (Guinness), Best Director (Lean), Best Film—Drama; National Board of Review Awards '57: Best Actor (Guinness), Best Director (Lean), Best Supporting Actor (Hayakawa), National Film Registry '97;; New York Film Critics Awards '57: Best Actor (Guinness), Best Director (Lean), Best Film; Nominations: Academy Awards '57: Best Supporting Actor (Hayakawa). *COL, BTV, HMV*

Bridge to Hell 🐾½ 1987 A group of allied P.O.W.s try to make their way to the American front during WWII in Yugoslavia. A heavily guarded bridge occupied by Nazi troops stands between them and freedom. A special introduction by Michael Dudikoff doing martial arts. **94m/C VHS.** Jeff Connors, Francis Ferre, Andy Forrest, Paky Valente; **D:** Umberto Lenzi.

The Bridge to Nowhere 🐾🐾 1986 Five city kids go hunting and back-packing in the New Zealand wilderness, and are hunted by a maniacal backwoodsman. **82m/C VHS, Beta.** *NZ* Bruno Lawrence, Alison Routledge, Margaret Umbers, Philip Gordon; **D:** Ian Mune. *NLC*

Bridge to Silence 🐾🐾 1989 A young hearing-impaired mother's life begins to crumble following the death of her husband in a car crash. Her mother tries to get custody of her daughter and a friend applies romantic pressure. Made for TV melodrama features Matlin in her first television speaking role. **95m/C VHS, Closed Caption.** Marlee Matlin, Lee Remick, Josef Sommer, Michael O'Keefe, Allison Silva, Candice Brecker; **D:** Karen Arthur.

Bridge to Terabithia 1985 An imaginative girl and a young boy learn the joys of friendship in a magic make-believe kingdom called Terabithia. Adapted from the novel by Katherine Paterson. Originally aired by PBS for the "Wonderworks" television series. **58m/C VHS, Closed Caption.** Annette O'Toole, Julian Coutts, Julie Beaulieu; **D:** Eric Till. *HMV, FCT*

A Bridge Too Far 🐾🐾 1977 (PG) A meticulous recreation of one of the most disastrous battles of WWII, the Allied defeat at Arnhem in 1944. Misinformation, adverse conditions, and overconfidence combined to prevent the Allies from capturing six bridges that connected Holland to the German border. **175m/C VHS, Beta, LV, Letterbox, Closed Caption.** *GB* Sean Connery, Robert Redford, James Caan, Michael Caine, Elliott Gould, Gene Hackman, Laurence Olivier, Ryan O'Neal, Liv Ullmann, Dirk Bogarde, Hardy Kruger, Arthur Hill, Edward Fox, Anthony Hopkins; **D:** Richard Attenborough; **W:** William Goldman; **C:** Geoffrey Unsworth; **M:** John Addison. British Academy Awards '77: Best Supporting Actor (Fox); National Society of Film Critics Awards '77: Best Supporting Actor (Fox). *MGM, FOX*

The Bridges at Toko-Ri 🐾🐾🐾½ 1955 Based on the James A. Michener novel, the rousing war-epic about a lawyer being summoned by the Navy to fly bombing missions during the Korean War. A powerful anti-war statement. **103m/C VHS, Beta, LV.** William Holden, Grace Kelly, Fredric March, Mickey Rooney, Robert Strauss, Earl Holliman, Keiko Awaji, Charles McGraw; **D:** Mark Robson; **W:** Valentine Davies; **C:** Loyal Griggs. Academy Awards '55: Best Special Effects; Nominations: Academy Awards '55: Best Film Editing. *PAR*

The Bridges of Madison County 🐾🐾🐾 1995 (PG-13) Robert Kincaid (Eastwood) is on assignment in 1965 Iowa to photograph Madison County's scenic covered bridges. Only problem is he gets lost and stops for directions at Francesca Johnson's (Streep) farmhouse. There's an immediate attraction between the repressed Italian war-bride-turned-farm-wife and the charismatic world traveler, which they act on in four short days. Much of the treacle from Robert James Waller's novel has been fortunately abandoned but the mature romance remains. 64-year-old Eastwood exudes low-key sexiness while Streep (with a light Italian accent) is all earthy warmth. Fans of both book and stars should be pleased, though the leisurely paced film takes too long to get started.**CW:** Some sexuality; brief strong language. **135m/C VHS, LV, Closed Caption, DVD.** Clint Eastwood, Meryl Streep, Victor Slezak, Annie Corley, Jim Haynie; **D:** Clint Eastwood; **W:** Richard LaGravenese; **C:** Jack N. Green; **M:** Lennie Niehaus. Nominations: Academy Awards '95: Best Actress (Streep); Golden Globe Awards '96: Best Actress—Drama (Streep), Best Film—Drama; Screen Actors Guild Award '95: Best Actress (Streep). *WAR*

Brief Encounter 🐾🐾🐾🐾 1946 Based on Noel Coward's "Still Life" from "Tonight at 8:30," two middle-aged, middle-class people become involved in a short and bittersweet romance in WWII England. Intensely romantic, underscored with Rachmaninoff's Second Piano Concerto. **86m/B VHS, Beta.** *GB* Celia Johnson, Trevor Howard, Stanley Holloway, Cyril Raymond, Joyce Carey, Everley Gregg, Margaret Barton, Dennis Harkin, Valentine Dyall,

Marjorie Mars, Irene Handl; **D:** David Lean; **W:** Noel Coward; **C:** Robert Krasker. New York Film Critics Awards '46: Best Actress (Johnson); Nominations: Academy Awards '46: Best Actress (Johnson), Best Director (Lean), Best Screenplay. *PAR, HMV*

A Brief History of Time 🎬🎬🎬 1992
(G) A stunning documentary about physicist Stephen Hawking, the author of the popular book "Brief History of Time." Crippled by Lou Gehrig's Disease, Hawking narrates the film in the computer-synthesized voice he uses to speak. Interviews with family, friends, and colleagues, bring Hawking's scientific theories to light. 85m/C VHS, Beta, Closed Caption. Stephen Hawking; **D:** Errol Morris; **W:** Stephen Hawking; **C:** John Bailey; **M:** Philip Glass. Sundance Film Festival '92: Filmmakers Trophy. *PAR, BTV, WSH*

The Brig 🎬🎬🎬 1964
A film by Jonas Mekas documenting the Living Theatre's infamous performance of Kenneth H. Brown's experimental play. Designed by Julian Beck. 65m/B VHS, Beta. Adolfas Mekas, Jim Anderson, Warren Finnerty, Henry Howard, Tom Lillard, James Tiroff, Gene Lipton; **D:** John Mekas. *MFV, FCT, TPV*

Brigadoon 🎬🎬🎬 1954
The story of a magical, 18th century Scottish village which awakens once every 100 years and the two modern-day vacationers who stumble upon it. Main highlight is the Lerner and Loewe score. ♫Brigadoon; Almost Like Being in Love; I'll Go Home With Bonnie Jean; Wedding Dance; From This Day On; Heather on the Hill; Waitin' For My Dearie; Once in the Highlands. 108m/C VHS, Beta, LV, Letterbox, DVD. Gene Kelly, Van Johnson, Cyd Charisse; **D:** Vincente Minnelli; **C:** Joseph Ruttenberg; **M:** Alan Jay Lerner, Frederick Loewe. Nominations: Academy Awards '54: Best Art Direction/Set Decoration (Color), Best Costume Design (Color), Best Sound. *MGM, TLF*

Brigham Young: Frontiersman 🎬🎬 1940
Somewhat interesting story about the pioneering Mormons and their founding of Salt Lake City. Under the leadership of Brigham Young (Jagger), they set out across the plains, battling hardships and starvation along the way. An emphasis was placed on the historical rather than the religious in an effort not to scare off moviegoers, but the picture failed at the boxoffice anyway. Based on the story by Louis Bromfield. 114m/C VHS. Tyrone Power, Linda Darnell, Dean Jagger, Brian Donlevy, John Carradine, Jane Darwell, Jean Rogers, Mary Astor, Vincent Price; **D:** Henry Hathaway; **W:** Lamar Trotti; **C:** Arthur C. Miller. *FXV*

Bright Angel 🎬🎬½ 1991 (R)
Road movie pairs an unconventional team: George wants to visit his aunt to see if she's heard from his mother who ran off with another man; Luey is a free-spirit trying to free her brother from jail. Good performances by Mulroney, Taylor, & Pullman. Ford adapted two of his short stories, "Childern" and "Great Falls" for the gritty and uncompromising script of life in the modern west. 94m/C VHS, Closed Caption. Dermot Mulroney, Lili Taylor, Sam Shepard, Valerie Perrine, Burt Young, Bill Pullman, Benjamin Bratt, Mary Kay Place, Delroy Lindo, Kevin Tighe, Sheila McCarthy; **D:** Michael Fields; **W:** Richard Ford; **M:** Christopher Young. *HBO*

Bright Eyes 🎬🎬 1934 (PG)
Shirley Temple stars as an adorable orphan caught between foster parents. Submitted for an MPAA rating when the video was released. Also available colorized. 84m/B VHS, Beta, Closed Caption. Shirley Temple, James Dunn, Lois Wilson, Jane Withers, Judith Allen; **D:** David Butler. *FOX, MLT*

Bright Lights, Big City 🎬🎬 1988 (R)
Based on Jay McInerney's popular novel, Fox plays a contemporary yuppie working in Manhattan as a magazine journalist. As his world begins to fall apart, he embarks on an endless cycle of drugs and nightlife. Fox is poorly cast and his character is hard to care for as he becomes more and more dissolute. Although McInerney wrote his own screenplay, the intellectual abstractness of the novel can't be captured on film. 110m/C VHS,

Beta, LV, Closed Caption. Michael J. Fox, Kiefer Sutherland, Phoebe Cates, Frances Sternhagen, Swoosie Kurtz, Tracy Pollan, Jason Robards Jr., John Houseman, Dianne Wiest, Charlie Schlatter, William Hickey; **D:** James Bridges; **C:** Gordon Willis. *MGM*

Bright Smiler 🎬½ 1985
A made-for-British-television mystery about a writer who retires to her favorite spa and falls into the hands of a malevolent masseuse. 60m/C VHS, Beta. GB Janet Suzman.

Brighton Beach Memoirs 🎬🎬½ Neil Simon's Brighton Beach Memoirs 1986 (PG-13)
The film adaptation of the popular (and semiautobiographical) Neil Simon play. Poignant comedy/drama about a young Jewish boy's coming of age in Depression-era Brooklyn. Followed by "Biloxi Blues" and "Broadway Bound." 108m/C VHS, Beta, LV, Closed Caption. Blythe Danner, Bob Dishy, Judith Ivey, Jonathan Silverman, Brian Drillinger, Stacey Glick, Lisa Waltz, Jason Alexander; **D:** Gene Saks; **W:** Neil Simon; **C:** John Bailey; **M:** Michael Small. *USH, FCT*

Brighton Rock 🎬🎬🎬 Young Scarface 1947
Sterling performances highlight this seamy look at the British underworld. Attenborough is Pinkie Brown, a small-time hood who ends up committing murder. He manipulates a waitress to get himself off the hook, but things don't go exactly as he plans. Based on the novel by Graham Greene. 92m/B VHS. GB Richard Attenborough, Hermione Baddeley, William Hartnell, Carol Marsh, Nigel Stock, Wylie Watson, Alan Wheatley, George Carney, Reginald Purdell; **D:** John Boulting. *DVT, HEG*

Brighton Strangler 🎬🎬 1945
An actor who plays a murderer assumes the role of the strangler after suffering from a concussion. Decent psychodrama. 67m/B VHS, Beta. John Loder, June Duprez, Miles Mander; **D:** Max Nosseck. *NO*

The Brighton Strangler/Before Dawn 🎬🎬 1945
A mystery double feature: In "The Brighton Strangler," an actor takes his part too seriously as he murders Londoners at night; in "Before Dawn" a brilliant scientist turns to a life of murderous crime. 128m/B VHS, Beta. John Loder, June Duprez, Miles Mander, Stuart Oland, Dorothy Wilson. *TTC*

Brighty of the Grand Canyon 🎬½ 1967
The spunky donkey Brighty roams across the Grand Canyon in search of adventure. He finds friendship with a gold-digging old prospector who hits pay dirt. 90m/C VHS, Beta. Joseph Cotten, Pat Conway, Dick Foran, Karl Swenson; **D:** Norman Foster. *KAR*

A Brilliant Disguise 🎬½ 1993 (R)
Sportswriter gets involved with an artist who turns out to have multiple personality disorder and a sinister psychiatrist. Then his friends start to turn up dead but things aren't exactly what they seem. 97m/C VHS, LV. Lysette Anthony, Anthony John Denison, Corbin Bernsen, Gregory McKinney, Robert Shafer; **D:** Nick Vallelonga; **W:** Nick Vallelonga.

Brilliant Lies 🎬🎬½ 1996
Susy Connor (Gia Carides) has brought an official complaint of sexual harassment against former boss Gary Fitzgerald (LaPaglia), who denies the charge. She claims her sister Katie (Zoe Carides) will substantiate her story, which she will, even though Katie knows it's a lie. As a matter of fact, Susy's a consummate liar though, in a way, she also turns out to be telling the truth. Fine performances from the Carides sisters, as well as LaPaglia (who's married to Gia) and Barrett, who plays the self-pitying Connor patriarch. Adapted from the play by David Williamson. 93m/C VHS. AU Gia Carides, Anthony LaPaglia, Zoe Carides, Ray Barrett, Michael Veitch, Neil Melville, Catherine Wilkin, Grant Tilly; **D:** Richard Franklin; **W:** Richard Franklin, Peter Fitzpatrick; **C:** Geoff Burton; **M:** Nevida Tyson-Chew. Nominations: Australian Film Institute '96: Best Actress (Carides), Best Supporting Actor (Barrett), Best Supporting Actress (Carides). *PEG*

Brimstone & Treacle 🎬🎬 1982 (R)
Weird, obsessive psychodrama in which a young rogue (who may or may not be an actual agent of the Devil) infiltrates the home of a staid British

family caring for their comatose adult daughter. 85m/C VHS, Beta. GB Sting, Denholm Elliott, Joan Plowright, Suzanna Hamilton; **D:** Richard Loncraine; **W:** Dennis Potter. Montreal World Film Festival '82: Best Film. *MGM*

Bring Me the Head of Alfredo Garcia 🎬🎬 1974 (R)
Peckinpah falters in this poorly paced outing. American piano player on tour in Mexico finds himself entwined with a gang of bloodthirsty bounty hunters. Bloody and confused. 112m/C VHS. Warren Oates, Isela Vega, Gig Young, Robert Webber, Helmut Dantine, Emilio Fernandez, Kris Kristofferson; **D:** Sam Peckinpah; **W:** Sam Peckinpah, Gordon Dawson. *MGM*

Bring Me the Vampire 🎬 1961
A wealthy baron must endure a night of terror in order to receive an inheritance. 100m/B VHS. MX Maria Eugenia San Martin, Hector Godoy, Joaquin Vargas. *SNC, MOV*

Bringing Up Baby 🎬🎬🎬🎬 1938
The quintessential screwball comedy, featuring Hepburn as a giddy socialite with a "baby" leopard, and Grant as the unwitting object of her affections. One ridiculous situation after another adds up to high speed fun. Hepburn looks lovely, the supporting actors are in fine form, and director Hawks manages the perfect balance of control and mayhem. From a story by Hagar Wilde, who helped Nichols with the screenplay. Also available in a colorized version. 103m/B VHS, Beta, LV. Katharine Hepburn, Cary Grant, May Robson, Charlie Ruggles, Walter Catlett, Fritz Feld, Jonathan Hale, Barry Fitzgerald, Ward Bond; **D:** Howard Hawks; **W:** Dudley Nichols; **C:** Russell Metty. National Film Registry '90. *TTC, HMV, BTV*

Brink of Life 🎬🎬½ Nara Livet 1957
Three pregnant women in a hospital maternity ward await the impending births with mixed feelings. Early Bergman; in Swedish with English subtitles. 82m/B VHS, Beta. SW Eva Dahlbeck, Bibi Andersson, Ingrid Thulin, Babro Ornas, Max von Sydow, Erland Josephson, Gunnar Sjoberg; **D:** Ingmar Bergman. Cannes Film Festival '58: Best Actress (Dahlbeck), Best Actress (Andersson, Thulin), Best Director (Bergman). *VYY*

Brink's Job 🎬🎬🎬 1978 (PG)
Recreates the "crime of the century," Tony Pino's heist of 2.7 million dollars from a Brink's truck. The action picks up five days before the statute of limitations is about to run out. 103m/C VHS, Beta. Peter Falk, Peter Boyle, Warren Oates, Gena Rowlands, Paul Sorvino, Sheldon Leonard, Allen (Goorwitz) Garfield; **D:** William Friedkin; **W:** Walon Green; **M:** Richard Rodney Bennett. Nominations: Academy Awards '78: Best Art Direction/Set Decoration. *USH*

Britannia Hospital 🎬🎬½ 1982 (R)
This is a portrait of a hospital at its most chaotic: the staff threatens to strike, demonstrators surround the hospital, a nosey BBC reporter pursues an anxious professor, and the eagerly anticipated royal visit degenerates into a total shambles. 111m/C VHS, Beta. GB Malcolm McDowell, Leonard Rossiter, Graham Crowden, Joan Plowright, Mark Hamill, Alan Bates; **D:** Lindsay Anderson. *REP*

British Intelligence 🎬½ 1940
Silly American-made film about British espionage. Boris Karloff plays a butler (who is also a spy) trapped by an agent who visits the home of a British bureaucrat. Half-baked story that doesn't hold up. 62m/B VHS. Boris Karloff, Margaret Lindsay, Maris Wrixon, Holmes Herbert, Leonard Mudie, Bruce Lester; **D:** Terry Morse. *NOS, SNC, MLB*

A Brivele der Mamen 🎬🎬🎬 A Letter to Mother; A Letter to Mama 1938
A Jewish mother does her best to hold her fragile family together, in spite of the ravages of war and poverty. Her travails take her and her family from the Polish Ukraine to New York City. In Yiddish with English subtitles. 90m/C VHS, Beta. PL Berta Gersten, Lucy Gerhman, Misha Gerhman, Edmund Zayenda; **D:** Joseph Green. *ERG*

Broadcast News 🎬🎬🎬½ 1987 (R)
The acclaimed, witty analysis of network news shows, dealing with the three-way romance of a driven career-woman producer, an ace nebbish reporter and a brainless, popular on-screen anchorman. Incisive and funny, though often simply

idealistic. **132m/C VHS, Beta, LV, Closed Caption.** William Hurt, Albert Brooks, Holly Hunter, Jack Nicholson, Joan Cusack, Robert Prosky, Lois Chiles, Gennie James; *Cameos:* John Cusack; *D:* James L. Brooks; *W:* James L. Brooks; *C:* Michael Ballhaus; *M:* Bill Conti, Michael Gore. Los Angeles Film Critics Association Awards '87: Best Actress (Hunter); National Board of Review Awards '87: Best Actress (Hunter); New York Film Critics Awards '87: Best Actress (Hunter), Best Director (Brooks), Best Film, Best Screenplay; Nominations: Academy Awards '87: Best Actor (Hurt), Best Actress (Hunter), Best Cinematography, Best Film Editing, Best Original Screenplay, Best Picture, Best Supporting Actor (Brooks). *FOX*

Broadway Bill 🎬🎬🎬 *Strictly Confidential*
1934 A man decides to abandon his nagging wife and his job in her family's business for the questionable pleasures of owning a racehorse known as Broadway Bill. This racetrack comedy was also remade by Frank Capra in 1951 as "Riding High." **90m/C VHS, Beta, LV.** Warner Baxter, Myrna Loy, Walter Connolly, Helen Vinson, Margaret Hamilton, Frankie Darro; *D:* Frank Capra. *PAR*

Broadway Bound 🎬🎬½ *Neil Simon's Broadway Bound* **1992** The final film in Simon's trilogy (preceded by "Brighton Beach Memoirs" and "Biloxi Blues"). This time the playwright's alter ego, Eugene Morris Jerome, is ready to leave Brooklyn for good, hoping to make it as a comedy writer for a radio show. Meanwhile, his mother decides what to do about her unfaithful father. Made for television. **90m/C VHS, Closed Caption.** Jonathan Silverman, Anne Bancroft, Jerry Orbach, Corey Parker, Hume Cronyn, Michele Lee; *D:* Paul Bogart; *W:* Neil Simon.

Broadway Danny Rose 🎬🎬🎬½ **1984**
(PG) One of Woody Allen's best films, a hilarious, heart-rending anecdotal comedy about a third-rate talent agent involved in one of his client's infidelities. The film magically unfolds as show business veterans swap Danny Rose stories at a delicatessen. Allen's Danny Rose is pathetically lovable. **85m/B VHS, Beta, LV.** Woody Allen, Mia Farrow, Nick Apollo Forte, Sandy Baron, Milton Berle, Howard Cosell; *D:* Woody Allen; *W:* Woody Allen; *C:* Gordon Willis. British Academy Awards '84: Best Original Screenplay; Writers Guild of America '84: Best Original Screenplay; Nominations: Academy Awards '84: Best Director (Allen), Best Original Screenplay. *VES*

The Broadway Drifter 🎬🎬 **1927** A silent Jazz Age drama about a playboy who repents his decadent ways by opening a girls' health school. Complications ensue. **90m/B VHS, Beta, 8mm.** George Walsh, Dorothy Hall, Bigelow Cooper, Arthur Donaldson; *D:* Bernard McEveety Sr. *VYY*

Broadway Limited 🎬🎬 *The Baby Vanishes*
1941 Three aspiring actors head for the Great White Way with a baby to use as a prop. Thinking the baby kidnapped, the police make things tough for the trio. McLaglen was wasted on this one, which was apparently made to show off the considerable assets of Woodworth. **75m/B VHS.** Victor McLaglen, Marjorie Woodworth, Dennis O'Keefe, Patsy Kelly, ZaSu Pitts, Leonid Kinskey, George E. Stone; *D:* Gordon Douglas. *NOS*

Broadway Melody 🎬🎬½ **1929** Early musical in which two sisters hope for fame on Broadway, and encounter a wily song and dance man who traps both their hearts. Dated, but still charming, with a lovely score. Considered the great granddaddy of all MGM musicals; followed by three more melodies in 1935, 1937, and 1940. 🎵Broadway Melody; Give My Regards to Broadway; Truthful Parson Brown; The Wedding of the Painted Doll; The Boy Friend; You Were Meant For Me; Love Boat; Broadway Babies. **104m/B VHS, Beta.** Bessie Love, Anita Page, Charles King, Jed Prouty, Kenneth Thomson, Edward Dillon, Mary Doran; *D:* Harry Beaumont; *M:* Nacio Herb Brown, Arthur Freed. Academy Awards '29: Best Picture; Nominations: Academy Awards '29: Best Actress (Love), Best Director (Beaumont). *MGM, BTV*

Broadway Melody of 1936 🎬🎬🎬
1935 Exceptional musical comedy with delightful performances from Taylor and Powell. Benny is a headline-hungry columnist who tries to entrap Taylor by using Powell. 🎵Broadway Melody; Broadway Rhythm; You Are My Lucky Star; I've Got A Feeling You're Fooling; All I Do Is Dream of You; Sing Before Breakfast; On a Sunday Afternoon. **110m/B VHS, Beta.** Jack Benny, Eleanor Powell, Robert Taylor, Una Merkel, Sid Silvers, Buddy Ebsen; *D:* Roy Del Ruth; *C:* Charles Rosher; *M:* Nacio Herb Brown, Arthur Freed. Nominations: Academy Awards '35: Best Picture, Best Story. *MGM, MLB, CCB*

Broadway Melody of 1938 🎬🎬½
1937 Third entry in the melody series lacks the sparkle of "Broadway Melody of 1936" despite the all-star cast. Lots of singing and dancing without much charm. Two bright spots: a young Garland singing the now famous "Dear Mr. Gable" and the always lovely Powell's dance numbers. 🎵Broadway Rhythm; Dear Mr. Gable (You Made Me Love You); A New Pair of Shoes; Yours and Mine; I'm Feeling Like a Million; Everybody Sing; Follow in My Footsteps; Your Broadway and My Broadway; Sun Showers. **110m/B VHS, Beta, Closed Caption.** Eleanor Powell, Sophie Tucker, George Murphy, Judy Garland, Robert Taylor, Buddy Ebsen, Binnie Barnes; *D:* Roy Del Ruth; *C:* William H. Daniels; *M:* Nacio Herb Brown, Arthur Freed. *MGM*

Broadway Melody of 1940 🎬🎬½
1940 The last entry in the melody series features the only screen teaming of Astaire and Powell. The flimsy plot is just an excuse for a potent series of Cole Porter musical numbers. 🎵I Concentrate on You; I've Got My Eye on You; Begin the Beguine; I am the Captain; Please Don't Monkey With Broadway; Between You and Me; Il Bacio. **103m/B VHS, Beta, LV.** Fred Astaire, Eleanor Powell, George Murphy, Frank Morgan, Ian Hunter; *D:* Norman Taurog. *MGM, TTC, FCT*

Broadway Rhythm 🎬🎬½ **1944** A too-long look at Broadway behind-the-scenes. Murphy plays a Broadway producer who hopes to land a Hollywood star for his new show. She rejects his offer in favor of a show being produced by his father. Just a chance to showcase a number of popular vaudeville acts, songs, and the music of Tommy Dorsey and his orchestra. 🎵All the Things You Are; That Lucky Fellow; In Other Words; Seventeen; All In Fun; Brazilian Boogie; What Do You Think I Am?; Somebody Loves Me; Milkman Keep Those Bottles Quiet. **111m/C VHS.** George Murphy, Ginny Simms, Charles Winninger, Gloria De Haven, Nancy Walker, Ben Blue, Lena Horne, Eddie Anderson; *D:* Roy Del Ruth; *W:* Dorothy Kingsley, Harry Clork. *MGM*

Broadway Serenade 🎬🎬½ **1939** Melodramatic musical in which a songwriter (Ayres) and his wife, singer MacDonald, make career choices that destroy their marriage. 🎵Broadway Serenade for the Lonely Heart; High Flyin'; One Look at You; Time Changes Everything; Un Bel Di; No Time to Argue; Italian Street Song; Les Filles de Cadiz; Musical Contract. **114m/B VHS.** Jeanette MacDonald, Lew Ayres, Ian Hunter, Frank Morgan, Wally Vernon, Rita Johnson, Virginia Grey, William Gargan; *D:* Robert Z. Leonard; *W:* Charles Lederer. *MGM*

Broadway to Cheyenne 🎬 *From Broadway to Cheyenne* **1932** A group of big city gangsters try to take over a small western town but are opposed by heroic cowboys. **53m/B VHS, Beta.** Rex Bell, George "Gabby" Hayes, Marceline Day, Robert Ellis, Alan Bridge, Matthew Betz; *D:* Harry Fraser. *GPV, RXM, VDM*

Broken Angel 🎬½ **1988** Jamie seemed to be such a nice girl, with good looks and great grades—and membership in a notorious street gang. When Jamie disappears, her family discovers her secret activities and dad tries to find his wayward little girl. Melodramatic made for television goo. **94m/C VHS, Closed Caption.** William Shatner, Susan Blakely, Erika Eleniak, Roxann Biggs-Dawson; *D:* Richard T. Heffron. *MGM*

Broken Arrow 🎬🎬½ **1950** A U.S. scout befriends Cochise and the Apaches, and helps settlers and Indians live in peace together in the 1870s. Acclaimed as the first Hollywood film to side with the Indians, and for Chandler's portrayal of Cochise. Based on the novel "Blood Brother" by Elliot Arnold. **93m/C VHS, Beta, Closed Caption.** James Stewart, Jeff Chandler, Will Geer, Debra Paget, Basil Ruysdael, Arthur Hunnicutt, Jay Silverheels; *D:* Delmer Daves; *W:* Albert Maltz; *C:* Ernest Palmer. Nominations: Academy Awards '50: Best Color Cinematography, Best Screenplay, Best Supporting Actor (Chandler). *FOX*

Broken Arrow 🎬🎬 **1995 (R)** Air Force pilot Vic Deakins (Travolta) rips off a couple of nuclear weapons during a routine exercise over the Utah desert. Deakins' ex-co-pilot Riley Hale (Slater), with help from spunky park ranger Terry Carmichael (Mathis), sets out to find and retrieve the warheads before the big bang. Hong Kong action king Woo once again tries his hand at the big-budget Hollywood action extravaganza, with mixed results. Triple script whammy of cheesy dialogue, continuity problems, and predictability undercuts, but doesn't obscure, his talent for choreographing mayhem. Travolta plays the All-American Boy as creepily charming psychotic to great effect.*CW:* Contains strong action violence and language. **108m/C VHS, Closed Caption.** John Travolta, Christian Slater, Samantha Mathis, Delroy Lindo, Bob Gunton, Frank Whaley, Howie Long; *D:* John Woo; *W:* Graham Yost; *C:* Peter Levy; *M:* Hans Zimmer. Nominations: MTV Movie Awards '96: Best Villain (Travolta), Best Action Sequence. *FXV*

Broken Badge 🎬🎬🎬 *The Rape of Richard Beck* **1985** Crenna stars as a macho, chauvinistic cop whose attitude towards rape victims changes dramatically after he himself is raped by a couple of thugs. Excellent TV movie. **100m/C VHS.** Richard Crenna, Meredith Baxter, Pat Hingle, Frances Lee McCain, Cotter Smith, George Dzundza, Joanna Kerns; *D:* Karen Arthur; *W:* James G. Hirsch; *M:* Peter Bernstein. *SIM, VTR*

Broken Blossoms 🎬🎬🎬½ **1919** One of Griffith's most widely acclaimed films, about a young Chinaman in London's squalid Limehouse district hoping to spread the peaceful philosophy of his Eastern religion. He befriends a pitiful street waif who is mistreated by her brutal father, resulting in tragedy. Silent. Revised edition contains introduction from Gish and a newly recorded score. **89m/B VHS, Beta, LV.** Lillian Gish, Richard Barthelmess, Donald Crisp; *D:* D.W. Griffith; *C:* Billy Bitzer. National Film Registry '96.*MRV, HHT, FST*

The Broken Chain 🎬🎬½ **1993** In the mid 18th-century Joseph Brant (Schweig), a member of the Mohawk tribe, is sent away to be educated by the British. When he returns, his loyalties are divided between his Native American roots and his English mentor, Sir William Johnson (Brosnan). His boyhood friend Lohaheo (White Shirt) disdains Joseph's white man ways, leading to tragic consequences. Historical background features the French and Indian Wars, the splintering of the Iroquois Confederacy, and the coming of the American Revolution. Filmed on location in Virginia. Made for television. **93m/C VHS, Closed Caption.** Eric Schweig, Wes Studi, Buffy Saint Marie, Pierce Brosnan, J.C. White Shirt, Floyd "Red Crow" Westerman, Graham Greene, Elaine Bilstad, Kim Snyder; *D:* Lamont Johnson; *W:* Earl W. Wallace; *M:* Charles Fox. *TTC*

Broken English 🎬🎬½ **1996 (NC-17)** Ethnically diverse New Zealand is the setting for this story of young lovers and the parents who don't understand them. Croatian refugee Nina (Vujcic) and Maori cook Eddie (Arahanga) meet in the Chinese restaurant where they both work and quickly fall in love. Nina's menacing father Ivan (Serbedzija) objects to their passion, sometimes with a baseball bat. Film deals honestly with immigration and racial issues. Engaging debut for Vujcic, a Croatian refugee director Nicholas met in a bar. Also available in an R-rated version.*CW:* Strong sexual content. **92m/C VHS.** *NZ* Aleksandra Vujcic, Julian (Sonny) Arahanga, Rade Serbedzija, Marton

Csokas, Jing Zhao, Yang Li, Madeline McNamara; **D:** Gregor Nicholas; **W:** Gregor Nicholas, Johanna Pigott, Jim Salter; **C:** John Toon. COL

Broken Glass 🎞🎞½ **1996** Set in Brooklyn in 1938 and adapted from a play by Arthur Miller. Jewish housewife, Sylvia Gellberg (Leicester), has been stricken by a mysterious paralysis and Dr. Harry Hyman (Patinkin) is called in to treat her. Her illness is apparently psychosomatic and Sylvia gradually reveals her anxiety about her unhappy marriage and her obsessive fears with newspaper reports concerning Jewish persecution in Germany. Hyman and his wife Margaret (McGovern) soon find themselves drawn in deeper than could have imagined. Made for TV. **120m/C VHS, Closed Caption.** Mandy Patinkin, Margot Leicester, Henry Goodman, Elizabeth McGovern; **D:** David Thacker; **W:** David Thacker, David Holman. PBS

Broken Harvest 🎞🎞½ **1994** Jimmy O'Leary remembers his youth in rural 1950s Ireland when a poor wheat harvest led to his family's financial demise and a feud between his father (Lane) and neighbor Josie McCarthy (O'Brien) threatened to destroy their lives. The men fought side by side for Ireland's independence, but the friendship dissolved when they took different sides during the ensuing civil war, and fought over Jimmy's mother. Strong performances and the beautiful West Cork and Wicklow location shots provide a nice balance to the uneven narrative. The black and white scenes were actually filmed in the mid-'80s when the independently financed project was begun. Adapted from O'Callaghan's own story "The Shilling." **101m/C VHS.** *IR* Colin Lane, Niall O'Brien, Marian Quinn, Darren McHugh, Joy Florish, Joe Jeffers, Pete O'Reilly, Michael Crowley; **D:** Maurice O'Callaghan; **W:** Maurice O'Callaghan; **C:** Jack Conroy; **M:** Patrick Cassidy. KIT, FCT

Broken Hearts of Broadway 🎞🎞 **1923** Stories of heartbreak and success along the Great White Way. **85m/B VHS.** Colleen Moore, John Walker, Alice Lake, Tully Marshall, Creighton Hale; **D:** Irving Cummings. GPV

Broken Lance 🎞🎞🎞½ **1954** Western remake of "House of Strangers" that details the dissolution of a despotic cattle baron's family. Beautifully photographed. **96m/C VHS, Beta, LV, Letterbox, Closed Caption.** Spencer Tracy, Richard Widmark, Robert Wagner, Jean Peters, Katy Jurado, Earl Holliman, Hugh O'Brian, E.G. Marshall; **D:** Edward Dmytryk; **W:** Philip Yordan. Academy Awards '54: Best Story; Nominations: Academy Awards '54: Best Supporting Actress (Jurado). FOX

The Broken Mask 🎞🎞 **1928** A doctor performs remarkable plastic surgery on a patient, but when the patient becomes attracted to his sweetheart, he throws the Hippocratic oath to the wind, and his patient's spiffy new look has got to go. A ground-breaker amid plastic surgery-gone-amok pieces. **58m/B VHS, Beta.** Cullen Landis, Barbara Bedford, Wheeler Oakman, James Marcus; **D:** James Hogan. GPV, FCT

Broken Melody 🎞½ *Vagabond Violinist* **1934** An opera singer sent to prison by mistake must escape in order to return to the woman of his dreams. **62m/B VHS.** *GB* John Garrick, Margot Grahame, Merle Oberon, Austin Trevor, Charles Carson, Harry Terry; **D:** Bernard Vorhaus. FCT

Broken Mirrors 🎞🎞½ *Gebroken Spiegels* **1985** A disturbing film which intertwines two stories of violence against women: prostitutes go about their daily business in Amsterdam, while a twisted serial killer who imprisons, photographs, and ultimately destroys his victims, draws near. An independently made chiller with staunch feminist agenda. **110m/C** *NL* Lineke Rijxman, Henriette Tol, Edda Barends, Coby Brugman, Coby Stunnenberg; **D:** Marleen Gorris; **W:** Marleen Gorris. ICA

Broken Strings 🎞 **1940** All-black musical in which a concert violinist must come to terms with himself after an auto accident limits the use of his left hand. **50m/B VHS, Beta.** Clarence Muse, Sybil

Lewis, William Washington, Matthew "Stymie" Beard; **D:** Bernard B. Ray. VYY, NOS, VCN

Broken Trust 🎞🎞 **1993** Erica inherits her fabulously weathy uncle's estate but she has problems knowing who to trust now that she has all this money. Seems her husband is greedy and her sister resentful but just how far will they go to get what Erica has? **85m/C VHS.** Kimberly Foster, Nick Cassavetes, Kathryn Harris, Don Swayze, Edward Albert, Wendy MacDonald; **D:** Rafael Portillo. MNC

Broken Trust 🎞🎞½ **1995** Municipal judge Timothy Nash (Selleck) is recruited for a sting operation, designed to ensnare fellow judges, by two slightly less-than-ethical feds (Atherton and McGovern). When Nash decides he doesn't like what's going on he discovers it's not going to be so easy to get out. Selleck's stoic, McGovern provides attractive ornamentation, and Atherton excels as the smarmy villain. From the novel "Court of Honor" by William P. Wood; made for cable. **90m/C VHS.** Tom Selleck, Elizabeth McGovern, William Atherton, Fritz Weaver, Marsha Mason, Charles Haid, Stanley DeSantis, Cynthia Martells; **D:** Geoffrey Sax; **W:** Joan Didion, John Gregory Dunne; **C:** Ronald Orieux; **M:** Richard Horowitz. TTC

Broken Vows 🎞🎞½ **1987** Made for TV thriller with Jones as ghetto priest Father Joseph, who has doubts about his calling. When he gives last rites to a murder victim, he decides to help the victim's girlfriend find his killers. Based on the novel "Where the Dark Secrets Go" by Dorothy Salisbury Davis. **95m/C VHS, Closed Caption.** Tommy Lee Jones, Annette O'Toole, M. Emmet Walsh, Milo O'Shea, David Groh, Madeline Sherwood, Jean De Baer, David Strathairn; **D:** Jud Taylor; **C:** Thomas Burstyn. CAF

Bronco Billy 🎞🎞 **1980 (PG)** Eastwood stars as a New Jersey shoe clerk who decides to fulfill his dream of being a cowboy hero by becoming the proprietor of a rag-tag wild west show. Locke's one-note performance as a spoiled rich girl who joins up is a problem and the film's charm is as ragged as the acts. Good if you want to see Eastwood in something other than a shoot-'em-up. **117m/C VHS, Beta, LV.** Clint Eastwood, Sondra Locke, Bill McKinney, Scatman Crothers, Sam Bottoms, Geoffrey Lewis, Dan Vadis, Sierra Pecheur; **D:** Clint Eastwood; **M:** Stephen Dorff. WAR, TLF, RXM

Bronson Lee, Champion 🎞🎞 **1978 (PG)** Kung-fu and karate highlight this action adventure. **81m/C VHS, Beta.** Tadashi Yamashita. NO

Bronson's Revenge 🎞½ **1979 (R)** Two frontier soldiers face constant danger as they attempt to transport death row prisoners, a large quantity of gold, and a stranded woman across the Rocky Mountains territory. **90m/C VHS.** Robert Hundar, Roy Hill, Emma Cohen. SUN

The Bronx Executioner 🎞 **1986** Android, robot, and human interests clash in futuristic Manhattan and all martial arts hell breaks loose. Special introduction by martial arts star Michael Dudikoff. **88m/C VHS, Beta.** Rob Robinson, Margie Newton, Chuck Valenti, Gabriel Gori; **D:** Bob Collins.

A Bronx Tale 🎞🎞🎞 **1993 (R)** Vivid snapshot of a young Italian-American boy growing up in the '60s among neighborhood small-time wiseguys. As a nine-year-old Calogero witnesses mobster Sonny kill a man but doesn't rat to the police, so Sonny takes the kid under his wing. His upright bus-driving father Lorenzo doesn't approve but the kid is drawn to Sonny's apparent glamor and power. At 17, he's gotten both an education in school and on the streets but he needs to make a choice. Good period detail and excellent performances. Palminteri shows both Sonny's charisma and violence and De Niro handles the less-showy father role with finesse. Based on Palminteri's one-man play; De Niro's directorial debut. **CW:** Strong language and several scenes of violence. **122m/C VHS, LV, Closed Caption.** Robert De Niro, Chazz Palminteri, Lillo Brancato, Francis Capra, Taral Hicks, Kathrine Narducci, Clem Caserta, Alfred Sauchelli Jr., Frank Pietrangolare, Joseph D'Onofrio; **Cameos:**

Joe Pesci; **D:** Robert De Niro; **W:** Chazz Palminteri; **C:** Reynaldo Villalobos; **M:** Butch Barbella. HBO

The Bronx War 🎞🎞 **1990 (R)** Rival gangs take to the streets in this film from the director of "Hangin' with the Homeboys." A malicious gang leader tricks his gang into going to war over a girl he wants. Very violent; an unrated version available. **CW:** Language, nudity, and gang violence and drug content. **91m/C VHS.** Joseph B. Vasquez, Fabio Urena, Charmaine Cruz, Andre Brown, Marlene Forte, Francis Colon, Miguel Sierra, Kim West; **D:** Joseph B. Vasquez.

Bronze Buckaroo 🎞🎞 **1939** Horse opera in which a cowpoke seeks revenge for his pa's death. Commendable performances from the all-black cast and crew. **57m/B VHS.** Herbert Jeffries, Artie Young, Rellie Hardin, Spencer Williams Jr., Clarence Brooks, F.E. Miller; **D:** Richard C. Kahn; **W:** Richard C. Kahn. NOS, MRV, TPV

The Brood 🎞🎞½ **1979 (R)** Cronenberg's inimitable biological nightmares, involving an experimentally malformed woman who gives birth to murderous demon-children that kill every time she gets angry. Extremely graphic. Not for all tastes. **92m/C VHS, Beta, LV.** CA Samantha Eggar, Oliver Reed, Art Hindle, Susan Hogan, Nuala Fitzgerald, Cindy Hinds, Robert A. Silverman; **D:** David Cronenberg; **W:** David Cronenberg; **C:** Mark Irwin; **M:** Howard Shore.

Broth of a Boy 🎞🎞½ **1959** A hungry British producer decides to film a birthday party of the oldest man in the world. The old Irishman wants a portion of the profits. Well made and thought provoking. **77m/B VHS.** *IR* Barry Fitzgerald, Harry Brogan, Tony Wright, June Thorburn, Eddie Golden; **D:** George Pollock. NOS, HEG, FCT

Brother Cadfael 🎞🎞½ **1994** Four episodic mysteries featuring a 12th-century Welsh soldier-turned-Benedictine monk (Jacobi), combining medieval atmosphere and politics with murder. Adapted from the novels by Ellis Peters. Hungary substitutes for the no-longer green and rural English setting of Shrewsbury. Made for British TV. Tapes available individually or as a boxed set. **300m/C VHS.** *GB* Derek Jacobi, Sean Pertwee, Tara Fitzgerald, Jonathan Firth, Norman Eshley; **D:** Graham Theakston. SIG, TVC

Brother Cadfael 2 1995 Brother Cadfael (Jacobi), the medieval, mystery-solving, man-of-the-world turned man-of-the-cloth returns in three more adventures. "The Virgin in the Ice" finds the monk's novice accused of rape and murder. Cadfael also discovers a young squire is the son he never knew about. At "St. Peter's Fair" a disagreeable merchant is murdered but Cadfael doesn't believe greed is the motive. In "The Devil's Novice" a young man confesses to murder but is actually hiding family secrets. Based on the mystery series by Ellis Peters. On three cassettes. **75m/C VHS.** *GB* Derek Jacobi. ATS, FCT, VIF

The Brother from Another Planet 🎞🎞🎞 **1984** A black alien escapes from his home planet and winds up in Harlem, where he's pursued by two alien bounty hunters. Independently made morality fable by John Sayles before he hit the big time; features Sayles in a cameo as an alien bounty hunter. **109m/C VHS, Beta, Closed Caption.** Joe Morton, Dee Dee Bridgewater, Ren Woods, Steve James, Maggie Renzi, David Strathairn; **Cameos:** John Sayles; **D:** John Sayles; **W:** John Sayles; **M:** Mason Daring. FOX, FCT

Brother Future 1991 T.J., a black, streetsmart city kid who thinks school and helping others is all a waste of time gets knocked out in a car accident. As he's lying unconscious, he is transported back in time to a slave auction block in the Old South. There the displaced urbanite is forced to work on a cotton plantation, and watch the stirrings of a slave revolt. T.J. sees the light and realizes how much opportunity he's been wasting in his own life. He comes to just a few moments later, but worlds away from who he was before. Part of the "Wonderworks" series. **110m/C VHS.**

Phill Lewis, Frank Converse, Carl Lumbly, Vonetta McGee. *HMV, BTV, FCT*

Brother John *♂♂♂* 1970 (PG-13) An early look at racial tensions and labor problems. An angel goes back to his hometown in Alabama to see how things are going. **CW:** Thematic elements and some language. **94m/C VHS, Beta.** Sidney Poitier, Will Geer, Bradford Dillman, Beverly Todd, Paul Winfield; **D:** James Goldstone; **M:** Quincy Jones. *COL, FCT*

Brother of Sleep *♂♂♂ Schlafes Bruder* **1995 (R)** Elias (Eisermann), the illegitimate son of the local priest, is discovered to have perfect pitch, a beautiful voice, and a special symbiosis with nature. Which does nothing to endear him to the superstitious inhabitants of his 19th-century Austrian mountain village. Elias doesn't know whether his gift is a blessing or a curse but he'd give it up if he could win the love of his cousin Elspeth (Vavrova). Schneider scripted from his 1992 novel, which has previously been adapted as a ballet and opera. German with subtitles. **CW:** Violent and disturbing images, and for some sexuality. **133m/C VHS, LV.** *GE* Andre Eisermann, Dana Vavrova, Ben Becker; **D:** Joseph Vilsmaier; **W:** Robert Schneider; **C:** Joseph Vilsmaier; **M:** Norbert J. Schneider. Nominations: Golden Globe Awards '96: Best Foreign Language Film. *COL*

Brother Orchid *♂♂♂* 1940 Mobster puts a henchman in charge of his gang while he vacations in Europe. Upon his return, he is deposed and wounded in an assassination attempt. Hiding out in a monastary, he plots to regain control of the gang, leading to fish outta water episodes and a change in his outlook on life. Fine cast fans through farce intelligently. **87m/B VHS, Beta.** Edward G. Robinson, Humphrey Bogart, Ann Sothern, Donald Crisp, Ralph Bellamy, Allen Jenkins, Charles D. Brown, Cecil Kellaway; **D:** Lloyd Bacon; **C:** Gaetano Antonio "Tony" Gaudio. *MGM, CCB*

Brother Sun, Sister Moon *♂♂½* 1973 (PG) Post-'60s costume epic depicting the trials of St. Francis of Assisi as he evaluates his beliefs in Catholicism. **120m/C VHS, Beta.** Graham Faulkner, Judi Bowker, Alec Guinness, Leigh Lawson, Kenneth Cranham, Lee Montague, Valentina Cortese; **D:** Franco Zeffirelli; **M:** Donovan. Nominations: Academy Awards '73: Best Art Direction/Set Decoration. *PAR, TVC, WSH*

The Brotherhood *♂♂½* 1968 Two hotheaded brothers in a Mafia syndicate clash over old vs. new methods and the changing of the Family's guard. **96m/C VHS, Beta, LV.** Kirk Douglas, Alex Cord, Irene Papas, Luther Adler, Susan Strasberg, Murray Hamilton; **D:** Martin Ritt; **W:** Lewis John Carlino; **C:** Boris Kaufman; **M:** Lalo Schifrin. *PAR*

Brotherhood of Death *♂½* 1976 (R) Three black Vietnam veterans return to their southern hometown to get even with the Klansmen who slaughtered all of the townspeople. **85m/C VHS, Beta.** Roy Jefferson, Larry Jones, Mike Bass, Le Tari, Haskell V. Anderson; **D:** Bill Berry. *MPI*

Brotherhood of Justice *♂♂* 1986 Young men form a secret organization to rid their neighborhood of drug dealers and violence. As their power grows, their propriety weakens, until all are afraid of the "Brotherhood of Justice." Exciting made-for-television feature. **97m/C VHS.** Keanu Reeves, Kiefer Sutherland, Billy Zane, Joe Spano, Darren Dalton, Evan Mirand, Don Michael Paul; **D:** Charles Braverman; **M:** Brad Fiedel. *THV, VTR*

The Brotherhood of Satan *♂♂½* 1971 (PG) In an isolated southern town, a satanic coven persuades children to join in their devil-may-care attitude. Worthwhile. **92m/C VHS, Beta, LV.** Strother Martin, L.Q. Jones, Charles Bateman, Ahna Capri, Charles Robinson, Alvy Moore, Geri Reischl; **D:** Bernard McEveety; **W:** William Welch; **C:** John Morrill. *GKK, IME*

The Brotherhood of the Rose *♂½* 1989 (PG-13) Too many twists and turns mar the otherwise mediocre plot of this murky adaption of a book by David (First Blood) Morrell. Strauss and Morse are the C.I.A. agents marked for death and

running for their lives after uncovering their boss's (Mitchum) plot of world domination. Though almost every scene takes place in a different country, the movie was in fact filmed entirely in New Zealand. Convoluted and frustratingly difficult to follow. **103m/C VHS, Closed Caption.** Robert Mitchum, Peter Strauss, Connie Sellecca, James B. Sikking, David Morse, M. Emmet Walsh, James Hong; **D:** Marvin J. Chomsky. *THV*

Brotherly Love *♂½* 1985 Good twin/bad twin made-for-TV mystery about an escaped psychopath who's out to get his businessman twin brother (Hirsch in both roles). **94m/C VHS, Beta, Closed Caption.** Judd Hirsch, Karen Carlson, George Dzundza, Barry Primus, Lori Lethin; **D:** Jeff Bleckner. *FOX*

Brothers in Arms *♂♂* 1988 (R) Savage mountainmen have developed a weird religion that requires them to hunt down and mercilessly massacre human prey. **95m/C VHS, LV.** Todd Allen, Jack Starrett, Dedee Pfeiffer; **D:** George J. Bloom III. *REP*

Brothers in Law *♂♂* 1957 Wry British humor in this tale of a rookie lawyer up against a veteran judge who forces him to sink or swim. **94m/B VHS.** *GB* Richard Attenborough, Ian Carmichael, Terry-Thomas, Miles Malleson, John Le Mesurier; **D:** Roy Boulting; **W:** Roy Boulting. *NOS*

Brothers in Trouble *♂♂* 1995 Illegal Pakistani immigrants occupy a squalid boardinghouse in '60s Yorkshire, including newly-arrived Amir (Malhotra). He settles in, befriending young student Sakib (Kumar), and learning the ropes from house leader Hossein Shah (Puri). But Shah brings unexpected problems to the group when his pregnant, white English girlfriend Mary (Ball) comes to stay and his nephew Irshad (Bhatti) arranges a paper marriage with the young woman. Based on the novel "Return Journey" by Abdullah Hussein. **104m/C VHS.** *GB* Om Puri, Pavan Malhotra, Pravesh Kumar, Angeline Ball, Ahsen Bhatti; **D:** Udayan Prasad; **W:** Robert Buckler; **C:** Alan Almond; **M:** Stephen Warbeck. *FRF*

The Brothers Karamazov *♂♂♂ Karamazov; The Murderer Dmitri Karamazov; Der Morder Dimitri Karamasoff* **1958** Hollywood adaptation of the classic novel by Dostoyevsky, in which four 19th-Century Russian brothers struggle with their desires for the same beautiful woman and with the father who brutalizes them. Incredible performances from every cast member, especially Cobb. Long and extremely intense, with fine direction from Brooks. Marilyn Monroe tried desperately to get Schell's part. **147m/C VHS, Beta.** Yul Brynner, Claire Bloom, Lee J. Cobb, William Shatner, Maria Schell, Richard Basehart; **D:** Richard Brooks; **W:** Richard Brooks; **C:** John Alton. Nominations: Academy Awards '58: Best Supporting Actor (Cobb). *MGM*

Brother's Keeper *♂♂♂* 1992 Filmmakers Berlinger and Sinofsky document the story of the eccentric and reclusive Ward brothers, four bachelor dairy farmers who shared the same two-room shack for more than 60 years in rural New York. When Bill Ward dies, brother Delbert is accused of murder and goes to trial. The film covers a year's span in preparation for the trial and how the media attention changed the Ward's lives. **104m/C VHS, LV.** *D:* Joe Berlinger, Bruce Sinofsky. Directors Guild of America Awards '92: Best Feature Documentary (Berlinger), Best Feature Documentary (Sinofsky); National Board of Review Awards '92: Best Feature Documentary; New York Film Critics Awards '92: Best Feature Documentary; Sundance Film Festival '92: Audience Award. *FXL, BTV*

A Brother's Kiss *♂♂* 1997 (R) Growing up in an East Harlem neighborhood with an alcoholic mother (Moriarty), two brothers are set on different paths that strain their brotherly love. Lex (Chinlund) is a never-was ex-basketball player with a bad marriage and an even worse drug problem. Mick (Raynor) is a tightly wound, obsessive, and sexually dysfunctional cop. Both of their problems stem from a childhood trauma that neither is able or willing to discuss with the other. Starts out strong but runs out of energy by the

second half. Expanded from a one-act play by director Rosenfeld. **CW:** Strong sexuality, pervasive strong language, drug use and violence. **92m/C VHS.** Nicholas Chinlund, Michael Raynor, Justin Pierce, Cathy Moriarty, Rosie Perez, Marisa Tomei, Joshua Danowsky; **D:** Seth Zvi Rosenfeld; **W:** Seth Zvi Rosenfeld; **C:** Fortunato Procopio; **M:** Frank London. *BMG*

Brothers Lionheart *♂♂½* 1985 (G) The Lion brothers fight for life, love and liberty during the Middle Ages. **120m/C VHS, Beta.** Staffan Gotestam, Lars Soderdahl, Allan Edwall; **D:** Olle Hellbron. *NO*

The Brothers McMullen *♂♂♂* 1994 (R) Slice of life drama finds three Irish-American brothers suddenly living under the same Long Island roof for the first time since childhood. Eldest brother Jack (Mulcahy) is a stolid high-school basketball coach married to teacher Molly (Britton) who's pressing him to have children. Cynical middle brother Barry (Burns), a writer, has just broken up with free-spirited Ann (McKay), and earnest young Patrick (McGlone) is engaged to Jewish girlfriend Susan (Albert). All three find their romantic relationships, as well as their belief in each other, tested. Generally good performances and dialogue, with Burns proving himself a triple threat as actor/writer/director. **CW:** Language and some sexuality. **98m/C VHS, Closed Caption.** Edward Burns, Jack Mulcahy, Mike McGlone, Connie Britton, Shari Albert, Elizabeth P. McKay, Maxine Bahns, Jennifer Jostyn, Catharine Bolt, Peter Johansen; **D:** Edward Burns; **W:** Edward Burns; **M:** Seamus Egan. Independent Spirit Awards '96: Best First Feature; Sundance Film Festival '95: Grand Jury Prize. *FXV*

Brothers of the West *♂½* 1937 Cowboy saves his brothers from being lynched by proving the guilt of the real outlaws. **56m/B VHS, Beta.** Tom Tyler, Bob Terry, Lois Wilde, Dorothy Short. *NOS, VCN, DVT*

Brothers O'Toole *♂♂* 1973 (G) The misadventures of a pair of slick drifters who, by chance, ride into a broken-down mining town in the 1890s. **94m/C VHS, Beta.** John Astin, Steve Carlson, Pat Carroll, Hans Conried, Lee Meriwether; **D:** Richard Erdman. *NO*

The Browning Version *♂♂♂½* 1951 A lonely, unemotional classics instructor at a British boarding school realizes his failure as a teacher and as a husband. From the play by Terrence Rattigan. **89m/B VHS, Beta.** *GB* Michael Redgrave, Jean Kent, Nigel Patrick, Wilfrid Hyde-White, Bill Travers; **D:** Anthony Asquith. Cannes Film Festival '51: Best Actor (Redgrave). *HMV, MOV, FUS*

The Browning Version *♂♂½* 1994 (R) Mediocre remake of the Terence Rattigan play, previously filmed in 1951. Austere classics professor (Finney) at prestigious British boys school is disillusioned with both his floundering career and marriage. His emotional chill drives his younger wife (Scacchi) into an affair with a visiting American science teacher (Modine). Unfortunately updated to contemporary times, which can't hide apparent mustiness. Worth seeing for Finney's superb work as the out-of-touch prof. **CW:** Some language. **97m/C VHS, Beta, Closed Caption.** Albert Finney, Greta Scacchi, Matthew Modine, Michael Gambon, Julian Sands, Ben Silverstone, Maryam D'Abo; **D:** Mike Figgis; **W:** Ronald Harwood; **M:** Mark Isham. *PAR*

Brubaker *♂♂♂* 1980 (R) A sanctimonious drama about a reform warden who risks his life to replace brutality and corruption with humanity and integrity in a state prison farm. Powerful prison drama. **131m/C VHS, Beta, LV.** Robert Redford, Jane Alexander, Yaphet Kotto, Murray Hamilton, David Keith, Morgan Freeman, Matt Clark, M. Emmet Walsh, Everett McGill; **D:** Stuart Rosenberg; **W:** W.D. Richter, Arthur Ross; **M:** Lalo Schifrin. Nominations: Academy Awards '80: Best Original Screenplay. *FOX*

Bruce Lee: Curse of the Dragon *♂♂♂ The Curse of the Dragon* **1993** A behind the scenes look at the continuing mystery surrounding the life and untimely death of the martial arts superstar who died in 1973 at the age of 32. Highlights the spectacular fight sequences from Lee's movies as well as footage from his funeral and an interview with his son Brandon Lee, whose own death in 1993 raised further comment about a Lee family curse. **90m/C VHS, Beta, LV.** *WAR, BTV*

Bruce Lee Fights Back From the Grave 🐾 1976 (R)
Bruce Lee returns from the grave to fight the Black Angel of Death with his feet and to wreak vengeance on the evil ones who brought about his untimely demise. **97m/C VHS, Beta.** Deborah Chaplin, Anthony Bronson; **D:** Umberto Lenzi.

Bruce Lee's Ways of Kung Fu 🐾
198? Copious head-kicking film in honor of the long-dead star. Brings together the best from Shaolin: White Crane, Wu-Deng, Dragon-Fist, Kwun-Lun, Eagle Claws, Tiger, and Leopard in a fight against the Dragon. **87m/C VHS, Beta.** Bruce Lei, Philip Cheung, Pearl Lin. *UNI*

Bruce Le's Greatest Revenge 🐾
1980 (R) Bruce Le, one e. Kung-fu action and martial arts fighting occur when a martial arts student gets involved in a clash between Chinese and a discriminatory European Club. **94m/C VHS, Beta.** Bruce Le. *GEM*

Bruce Li in New Guinea 🐾 1980 (PG)
Bruce Li, i, not ee. The tribe of a remote island worships the legendary Snake Pearl. Two masters of Kung-fu visit the isle and discover they must defend the daughter of the murdered chief against a cruel wizard. **98m/C VHS, Beta.** Bruce Li, Ho Chung Dao, Chen Sing; **D:** C.Y. Yang. *MGI, GEM, MRV*

Bruce Li the Invincible 🐾 1980
Cheng, the Kung-Fu killer, is pursued by the vengeance-minded Bruce. **93m/C VHS.** Bruce Li, Ho Chung Dao, Chen Sing. *MGI, MRV, GEM*

Bruce the Superhero 🐾 1979
Chopsocky action as the coattails-riding Bruce Le takes on the Black Dragon Society. **88m/C VHS, Beta.** Bruce Le. *BFV, MRV*

Bruce's Deadly Fingers 🐾 1980 (R)
Bruce Lee kept a book of deadly finger techniques for kung fu killing. When a vicious gangster kidnaps the Master's ex-girlfriend, one of his followers must rescue her and maintain the book's integrity. **90m/C VHS, Beta.** Bruce Le, Lo Lieh, Chan Wai, Nora Miao, Rose Marie, Yuen Man Chi, Chang Leih, Young Zee, Wuk Ma No Hans. *GEM*

Bruce's Fists of Vengeance 🐾 1984
Le and Lee guard master Bruce Lee's kicking secrets from an evil adversary. **87m/C VHS, Beta.** Bruce Le, Jack Lee, Ken Watanabe, Romano Kristoff, Don Gordon. *GEM*

Brussels Transit 🐾🐾🐾 1980
The story of a Yiddish family's arrival and adjustment to the new world of Brussels, Belgium, after WWII. In Yiddish with English subtitles. **80m/B VHS. D:** Samy Szlingerbaum. *NO*

Brutal Fury 🐾 1992
Detective Molly Griffin goes undercover at a local high school and discovers a secret female vigilante group, called the "Fury," which goes after the drug dealers and rapists preying on the school's students. Teenagers with an attitude. **97m/C VHS.** Tom Campitelli, Lisa-Gabrielle Greene, Annette Gerbon, Karen Eppers, Jennifer Winder, Allen Arkus; **D:** Frederick P. Watkins.

Brutal Glory 🐾 1989
Set in New York City in 1918 and based on the true story of the boxer known as "The Real McCoy." Fascinating and detailed history of a period, a champion, and the man who made it happen. **96m/C VHS.** Robert Vaughn, Timothy Brantley, Leah K. Pinsent; **D:** Koos Roets. *NO*

The Brute Man 🐾🐾 1946
A young man who had been disfigured by his school mates goes out on a trail of revenge. Hatton is convincing in the title role, as in real life he was afflicted with acromegly, an ailment that produces an enlargment of the bones in the face, hands, and feet. **62m/B VHS, Beta, LV.** Rondo Hatton, Tom Neal, Jane Adams; **D:** Jean Yarbrough. *AOV, MLB, COL*

The Brylcreem Boys 🐾🐾 1996 (PG-13)
In September, 1941, Canadian pilot Miles Keogh (Campbell) and his crew are forced to bail out of their plane. They land in neutral southern Ireland, where they're interned in the local POW camp run by Sean O'Brien (Byrne). The camp holds both Allies and Germans—separated by only a thin wire fence. Keogh figures it's his patriotic duty to try to escape as does German officer Rudolph von Stegenbeck (Macfadyen), and problems compound when both soldiers are let out on day-release passes and, naturally, fall for the same lovely local colleen, Mattie (Butler). It's pleasant but unmemorable. **CW:** Language, violence and sensuality. **105m/C VHS.** GB Bill Campbell, Angus McFadyen, William McNamara, Gabriel Byrne, Jean Butler, Gordon John Sinclair, Oliver Tobias; **D:** Terence Ryan; **W:** Terence Ryan, Jamie Brown; **C:** Gerry Lively; **M:** Richard Hartley. *BMG*

The Buccaneer 🐾🐾 1958
A swashbuckling version of the adventures of pirate Jean LaFitte and his association with President Andrew Jackson during the War of 1812. Remake of Cecille B. DeMille's 1938 production. **121m/C VHS, Beta, LV, Closed Caption.** Yul Brynner, Charlton Heston, Claire Bloom, Inger Stevens, Charles Boyer, Henry Hull, E.G. Marshall, Lorne Greene; **D:** Anthony Quinn; **C:** Loyal Griggs; **M:** Elmer Bernstein. Nominations: Academy Awards '58: Best Costume Design. *BAR, FCT, RXM*

The Buccaneers 🐾🐾🐾 1995
Lavish adaptation of the Edith Wharton novel follows the adventures of four American girls in 1870s society. Nouveaux riche, the young ladies are unable to crack New York snobbery and, after vivacious Brazilian Conchita (Sorvino) manages to snag Lord Richard (Vibert), the others are encouraged by English governess Laura Testvalley (Lunghi) to try their luck in London. There, Virginia (Elliott), sister Nan (Gugino), their friend Lizzy (Kihlstedt), and Conchita all find hope and heartbreak among the English aristocracy. Wharton's novel was unfinished at her death and, though she left story notes, scripter Wadey concedes to changes. Made for TV. **288m/C VHS.** GB Carla Gugino, Mira Sorvino, Alison Elliott, Rya Kihlstedt, Cherie Lunghi, Connie Booth, Mark Tandy, Ronan Vibert, Jenny Agutter, Richard Huw, Greg Wise, James Frain, Michael Kitchen, Sheila Hancock, Rosemary Leach, Elizabeth Ashley, Conchata Ferrell, Peter Michael Goetz, James Rebhorn, E. Katherine Kerr; **D:** Philip Saville; **W:** Maggie Wadey; **C:** Maggie Wadey; **M:** Colin Towns. *FOX*

Buck and the Magic Bracelet 🐾🐾½ 1997 (PG-13)
In the old west a teen and his dog escape an attack on their prospecting camp. They're aided in bringing the bad guys to justice by a shaman's magic bracelet. **CW:** Frontier violence. **99m/C VHS.** Matt McCoy, Abby Dalton, Felton Perry, Conrad Nichols. *PMH*

Buck and the Preacher 🐾🐾½ 1972 (PG)
A trail guide and a con man preacher join forces to help a wagon train of former slaves who are seeking to homestead out West. Poitier's debut as a director. **102m/C VHS, Beta.** Sidney Poitier, Harry Belafonte, Ruby Dee, Cameron Mitchell, Denny Miller; **D:** Sidney Poitier. *COL*

Buck Privates 🐾🐾½
Rookies 1941 Abbott and Costello star as two dim-witted tie salesmen, running from the law, who become buck privates during WWII. The duo's first great success, and the film that established the formula for each subsequent film. **84m/B VHS, Beta, LV.** Bud Abbott, Lou Costello, Shemp Howard, Lee Bowman, Alan Curtis, The Andrews Sisters; **D:** Arthur Lubin; **C:** Milton Krasner. Nominations: Academy Awards '41: Best Song ("Boogie Woogie Bugle Boy of Company B"), Scoring of a Musical. *USH*

Buck Privates Come Home 🐾🐾🐾
Rookies Come Home 1947 Abbott and Costello return to their "Buck Privates" roles as two soldiers trying to adjust to civilian life after the war. They also try to help a French girl sneak into the United States. Funny antics culminate into a wild chase scene. **77m/B VHS.** Bud Abbott, Lou Costello, Tom Brown, Joan Shawlee, Nat Pendleton, Beverly Simmons,

Don Beddoe, Don Porter, Donald MacBride; **D:** Charles T. Barton. *USH*

Buck Rogers Conquers the Universe 🐾🐾 1939
The story of Buck Rogers, written by Phil Nolan in 1928, was the first science-fiction story done in the modern superhero space genre. Many of the "inventions" seen in this movie would actually come into existence—spaceships, ray guns (lasers), anti-gravity belts—a testament to Nolan's almost psychic farsightedness. **91m/B VHS, Beta.** Buster Crabbe, Constance Moore, Jackie Moran; **D:** Ford Beebe, Saul Goodkind. *FOX*

Buck Rogers in the 25th Century 🐾🐾 1979 (PG)
An American astronaut, preserved in space for 500 years, is brought back to life by a passing Draconian flagship. Outer space adventures begin when he is accused of being a spy from Earth. Based on the classic movie serial. Made for TV movie that began the popular series. Additional series episodes are available. **90m/C VHS, Beta, LV.** Gil Gerard, Pamela Hensley, Erin Gray, Henry Silva; **D:** Daniel Haller; **V:** Mel Blanc. *USH, MOV*

A Bucket of Blood 🐾🐾🐾 1959
Cult favorite Dick Miller stars as a sculptor with a peculiar "talent" for lifelike artwork. Corman fans will see thematic similarities to his subsequent work, "Little Shop of Horrors" (1960). "Bucket of Blood" was made in just five days, while "Little Shop of Horrors" was made in a record breaking two days. Corman horror/spoof noted for its excellent beatnik atmosphere. **66m/B VHS, Beta.** Dick Miller, Barboura Morris, Antony Carbone, Julian Burton, Ed Nelson, Bert Convy, Judy Bamber, John Brinkley; **D:** Roger Corman; **W:** Charles B. Griffith; **C:** Jack Marquette. *RHI, SNC*

Buckeye and Blue 🐾½ 1987 (PG)
A hero turned outlaw, his 14 year-old female sidekick, and a gang known as the McCoys are all on the lam from the law in this western adventure. **94m/C VHS, Beta.** Robin Lively, Jeffery Osterhage, Rick Gibbs, Will Hannah, Kenneth Jensen, Patrick Johnston, Stuart Rogers, Michael Horse; **D:** J.C. Compton.

Buckskin 🐾½ 1968
Slowmoving western about a marshall protecting townspeople from a greedy, land-grabbing cattle baron. **98m/C VHS, LV, Closed Caption.** Barry Sullivan, Wendell Corey, Joan Caulfield, Lon Chaney Jr., John Russell, Barbara Hale, Barton MacLane, Bill Williams; **D:** Michael Moore. *PAR*

Buckskin Frontier 🐾½ 1943
Story is built around Western railroad construction and cattle empires in the 1860s. Cobb tries to stop the railroad from coming through by hiring Jory to do his dirty work. **75m/B VHS, Beta.** Richard Dix, Jane Wyatt, Lee J. Cobb, Albert Dekker, Victor Jory, Lola Lane, Max Baer Sr.; **D:** Lesley Selander. *NOS, MRV, GPV*

Bucktown 🐾½ 1975 (R)
A black man who reopens his murdered brother's bar fights off police corruption and racism in a Southern town. **95m/C VHS, Beta.** Fred Williamson, Pam Grier, Bernie Hamilton, Thalmus Rasulala, Art Lund; **D:** Arthur Marks. *ORI*

Bud and Lou 🐾½ 1978
Comedy/drama recounts Abbott & Costello's rise in Hollywood. While the story, based on the book by Bob Thomas, is interesting, the two funnymen in the leads can't pull off the old classic skits. **98m/C VHS, Beta, LV.** Harvey Korman, Buddy Hackett, Michele Lee, Arte Johnson, Robert Reed; **D:** Robert C. Thompson. *JTC*

Buddha Assassinator 🐾 1982
Young Kung-Fu enthusiast challenges a Ming dynasty lord to a duel to the death. **93m/C VHS, Beta.** Hwang Jang Lee, Mang Hai, Lung Fei, Chien Yueh Sheng. *WVE*

The Buddha of Suburbia 🐾🐾🐾 1992
Satire set in late '70s suburban London follows the coming of age adventures of Karim (Andrews), the handsome son of an Indian father and English mother. His gleeful father Haroon (Seth) exploits the vogue for eastern philosophies he knows nothing about with lectures to the upper-middle classes while he carries on with devotee Eva (Fleetwood). When his mother finds out, Kar-

im and his father move into central London with Eva, where Karim decides to take up acting in fringe theatre and sex while his friend, Eva's son Charlie (Mackintosh), experiments with the punk music scene. TV miniseries adapted by Kureishi from his novel. **220m/C VHS.** *GB* Naveen Andrews, Roshan Seth, Susan Fleetwood, Steven Mackintosh, Brenda Blethyn, John McEnery, Janet Dale, David Bamber, Donald Sumpter, Jemma Redgrave; **D:** Roger Michell; **W:** Hanif Kureishi, Roger Michell; **C:** John McGlashan; **M:** David Bowie. *FOX*

Buddy 🎞🎞½ **1997 (PG)** Animals run amok in the Lintz household. Mother hen Gertrude Lintz (Russo) raises just about everything from mischievous chimps to impressionable parrots on her estate. A baby gorilla (named Buddy, short for Budha) becomes part of the family, but as he grows in size, so does the difficulty in caring for him. Amiable tale of one woman's motherly bond with a gorilla that includes convincing performances by Russo and an animatronic gorilla courtesy of Jim Henson's Creature Shop. Well-paced and very touching at moments, children will definitely enjoy the zany animal antics, and adults should be moved by the unusual relationship. Based on the book by Lintz. **84m/C VHS, LV, Closed Caption.** Rene Russo, Robbie Coltrane, Irma P. Hall; **D:** Caroline Thompson; **W:** Caroline Thompson; **C:** Steve Mason; **M:** Elmer Bernstein. *COL*

Buddy Buddy 🎞🎞½ **1981 (R)** A professional hitman's well-ordered arrangement to knock off a state's witness keeps being interrupted by the suicide attempts of a man in the next hotel room. **96m/C VHS, Beta.** Jack Lemmon, Walter Matthau, Paula Prentiss, Klaus Kinski; **D:** Billy Wilder; **W:** Billy Wilder, I.A.L. Diamond; **C:** Harry Stradling Jr.; **M:** Lalo Schifrin. *MGM*

The Buddy Holly Story 🎞🎞🎞½ **1978 (PG)** An acclaimed biography of the famed 1950s pop star, spanning the years from his meteoric career's beginnings in Lubbock to his tragic early death in the now famous plane crash. Busey performs Holly's hits himself. ♫ Rock Around the Ollie Vee; That'll Be the Day; Oh, Boy; It's So Easy; Well All Right; Chantilly Lace; Peggy Sue. **113m/C VHS, Beta, LV, Closed Caption.** Gary Busey, Don Stroud, Charles Martin Smith, Conrad Janis, William Jordan; **D:** Steve Rash; **M:** Joe Renzetti. Academy Awards '78: Original Song Score and/or Adaptation; National Society of Film Critics Awards '78: Best Actor (Busey); Nominations: Academy Awards '78: Best Actor (Busey), Best Sound. *COL*

The Buddy System 🎞🎞 **1983 (PG)** A tale of contemporary love and the modern myths that outline the boundaries between lovers and friends. **110m/C VHS, Beta, Closed Caption.** Richard Dreyfuss, Susan Sarandon, Jean Stapleton, Nancy Allen, Wil Wheaton, Ed Winter, Keene Curtis; **D:** Glenn Jordan; **W:** Mary Agnes Donoghue. *FOX*

Buddy's Song 🎞🎞 **1991 (R)** A '60s coming of age tale, only in this case it's the father and not the son who needs to grow up. Dad (Daltrey) is more interested in hanging out with his no-account musician friends than in looking after his family. Although he's not above meddling in his teenage son's musical career, which could be the success his father's never was. Based on the novel by Nigel Hinton who also did the screenplay. British teen idol Hawkes (in his film debut) had a top ten hit song from the film with "The One and Only." **106m/C VHS, LV, Closed Caption.** *GB* Roger Daltrey, Chesney Hawkes; **W:** Nigel Hinton. *THV, BTV*

Buffalo Bill 🎞🎞 **1944** A light, fictionalized account of the life and career of Bill Cody, from frontier hunter to showman. **89m/C VHS, Beta, Closed Caption.** Joel McCrea, Maureen O'Hara, Linda Darnell, Thomas Mitchell, Edgar Buchanan, Anthony Quinn, Moroni Olsen, Sidney Blackmer; **D:** William A. Wellman; **C:** Leon Shamroy. *FOX*

Buffalo Bill & the Indians 🎞🎞🎞 *Sitting Bull's History Lesson* **1976 (PG)** A perennially underrated Robert Altman historical pastiche, portraying the famous Wild West character as a charlatan and shameless exemplar of encroaching im-

perialism. Great all-star cast amid Altman's signature mise-en-scene chaos. **135m/C VHS, Beta.** Paul Newman, Geraldine Chaplin, Joel Grey, Will Sampson, Harvey Keitel, Burt Lancaster, Kevin McCarthy; **D:** Robert Altman; **W:** Robert Altman, Alan Rudolph; **M:** Richard Baskin. *FOX*

Buffalo Bill Rides Again 🎞½ **1947** With an Indian uprising on the horizon, Buffalo Bill is called in. Mr. Bill finds land swindlers pitting natives against ranchers, but there's precious little action or interest here. **68m/C VHS, Beta.** Richard Arlen, Jennifer Holt, Edward Cassidy, Edmund Cobb, Charles Stevens; **D:** Bernard B. Ray. *GPV*

Buffalo Girls 🎞🎞½ **1995** Western saga, set in the 1870s, tells of the lifelong friendship between hard-drinking, hard-living Calamity Jane (Huston—who's not exactly any plain Jane) and buxom, soft-hearted madam Dora DuFran (Griffith). Dora's in love (but refuses to marry) rancher Teddy Blue (Byrne) while Calamity has a daughter by Wild Bill Hickok (Elliott) that she gives up for adoption. There's lots of rambling and commiserating over the changing and civilizing of the west and various man trouble. Based on the novel by Larry McMurty; originally a two-part TV miniseries. **180m/C VHS, Closed Caption.** Anjelica Huston, Melanie Griffith, Gabriel Byrne, Peter Coyote, Jack Palance, Sam Elliott, Reba McEntire, Floyd "Red Crow" Westerman, Tracey Walter, Russell Means, Charlaine Woodard, John Diehl, Liev Schreiber, Andrew Bicknell, Paul Lazar; **D:** Rod Hardy; **W:** Cynthia Whitcomb; **C:** David Connell; **M:** Lee Holdridge. *CAF*

Buffalo Heart: The Pain of Death 🎞½ **1996** Buffalo Heart decides to avenge the rape and murder of his daughter by tracking down her killers. **85m/C VHS.** Daniel Matmor, Alex Wexo, Craig Eisner; **D:** Daniel Matmor; **W:** Daniel Matmor; **C:** Paul DeGruccio. *TPV*

Buffalo Jump 🎞🎞🎞 **1990** An independent woman, working as a lounge singer in Toronto, returns to her home in Alberta when her father dies. To her surprise he has left her the family ranch and, to the surprise of everyone else, she decides to stay and run it. She hires a good-looking local man to help her out and they both discover that they want more than a working relationship. However, the fireworks really start when he proposes a marriage of convenience. Engaging performances and beautiful scenery help raise this romantic tale of opposites above the average. **97m/C VHS.** *CA* Wendy Crewson, Paul Gross, Marion Gilsenan, Kyra Harper, Victoria Snow; **D:** Eric Till.

Buffalo Rider 🎞½ **1978** An adventure film depicting the real-life experiences of C.J. "Buffalo" Jones who worked to save the American buffalo from extinction. **90m/C VHS, Beta.** Rick Guinn, John Freeman, Pricilla Lauris, George Sager, Rich Scheeland; **D:** George Lauris. *NO*

Buffalo Soldiers 🎞🎞🎞 **1997** Post-Civil War western about the all-black Cavalry troops, created by Congress in 1866 to patrol the west. They received their nickname from the Indians, who thought the black soldiers on horseback looked like buffalo. A former slave and by-the-book Army man, Sgt. Washington Wyatt (Glover) leads the chase for Apache warrior Victorio (Lowe) across the New Mexico Territory while trying tp deal with the common degradation suffered by his troops at the hands of white officers. Lots of cruelty and explicit violence. **120m/C VHS.** Danny Glover, Carl Lumbly, Bob Gunton, Tom Bower, Harrison Lowe, Glynn Turman, Michael Warren, Mykelti Williamson, Timothy Busfield, Gabriel Casseus; **D:** Charles Haid; **W:** Frank Military, Susan Rhinehart; **C:** William Wages; **M:** Joel McNeely. *WAR*

Buffalo Stampede 🎞 **1933** Our heroes are involved in a plot to round up buffalo to sell for meat. **60m/B VHS, Beta.** Randolph Scott, Buster Crabbe, Harry Carey Sr., Noah Beery Sr., Raymond Hatton. *NOS, VCN, MRV*

Buffet Froid 🎞🎞🎞½ **1979** Surreal black comedy about a group of bungling murderers. First rate acting and directing makes this film a hilarious treat. From the director of "Menage." In French with English subtitles. **95m/C VHS, LV.** *FR* Gerard Depardieu, Bernard Blier, Jean Carmet, Genevieve Page, Denise Gence, Carole Bouquet, Jean Benguigui, Michel Serrault; **D:** Bertrand Blier; **W:** Bertrand Blier. Cesar Awards '80: Best Writing. *FXL, INT, TPV*

Buffy the Vampire Slayer 🎞🎞🎞 **1992 (PG-13)** Funny, near-camp teen genre spoof. Buffy is a typical mall gal concerned with shopping and cheerleading, until the mysterious Sutherland proclaims it her destiny to slay the vampires who have suddenly infested Los Angeles. Like, really. Buffy requires some convincing, but eventually takes up the challenge, fighting off the vamps and their seductive leader Hauer, aided by perpetual guy-in-distress Perry. "Pee Wee" Reubens is unrecognizable and terribly amusing as the vampire king's sinister henchman, engaging in one of the longer death scenes of film history. Check out Cassandra (Wagner), Natalie Wood's daughter. **98m/C VHS, LV.** Kristy Swanson, Donald Sutherland, Luke Perry, Paul (Pee Wee Herman) Reubens, Rutger Hauer, Michele Abrams, Randall Batinkoff, Hilary Swank, Paris Vaughan, David Arquette, Candy Clark, Natasha Gregson Wagner; **D:** Fran Rubel Kazui; **W:** Joss Whedon; **C:** James Hayman; **M:** Carter Burwell. *FXV*

Buford's Beach Bunnies 🎞 **1992 (R)** Harry Buford has made a fortune selling barbecued rabbit sandwiches served by the sexiest waitresses around. Harry wants to leave the business to his son Jeeter—if Jeeter can overcome his overwhelming fear of women. So three of Harry's waitresses decide to show Jeeter a very good time. Lots of pretty girls in not much clothing. **CW:** Language, nudity, and sex scenes. **90m/C VHS, Closed Caption.** Jim Hanks, Rikki Brando, Monique Parent, Amy Page, Barrett Cooper, Ina Rogers, Charley Rossman, David Robinson; **D:** Mark Pirro; **W:** Mark Pirro. *IMP*

Bug WOOF! *The Bug* **1975 (PG)** The city of Riverside is threatened with destruction after a massive earth tremor unleashes a super-race of ten-inch mega-cockroaches that belch fire, eat raw meat, and are virtually impervious to Raid. Produced by gimmick-king William Castle, who wanted to install windshield wiper-like devices under theatre seats that would brush against the patrons' feet as the cockroaches crawled across the screen; unfortunately, the idea was squashed flat. **100m/C VHS, Beta.** Bradford Dillman, Joanna Miles, Richard Gilliland, Jamie Smith-Jackson, Alan Fudge, Jesse Vint, William Castle, Patty McCormack, Jesse Vint; **D:** Jeannot Szwarc; **W:** William Castle; **C:** Michael Hugo; **M:** Charles Fox. *PAR*

Bugged! 🎞 **1996 (PG-13)** Flesh-eating insects attack a beautiful homemaker and a group of bumbling exterminators who have only one hope. **CW:** Comic sci-fi violence/gore, and for brief strong language. **90m/C VHS.** Ronald K. Armstrong, Priscilla Basque, Jeff Lee, Derek C. Johnson, Billy Graham; **D:** Ronald K. Armstrong; **W:** Ronald K. Armstrong; **C:** S. Torriano Berry; **M:** Boris Elkis. *TTV*

Bugles in the Afternoon 🎞🎞 **1952** Life in the army during Custer's last days, with a love triangle, revenge and the Little Big Horn for added spice. **85m/C VHS.** Ray Milland, Hugh Marlowe, Helena Carter, Forrest Tucker, Barton MacLane, George Reeves; **D:** Roy Rowland. *REP, FCT*

Bugs & Daffy: The Wartime Cartoons **1945** A compilation of Daffy and Bugs classics made during WWII, often dominated by propaganda and Axis-baiting. **120m/C VHS, Beta, LV.** **D:** Robert McKimson, Chuck Jones, Isadore "Friz" Freleng. *MGM*

The Bugs Bunny/Road Runner Movie *Great American Bugs Bunny-Road Runner Chase* **1979 (G)** A compilation of classic Warner Bros. cartoons, starring Bugs Bunny, Daffy Duck, Elmer Fudd, the Road Runner, Wile E. Coyote, Porky Pig, and Pepe Le Pew, including some all-new animated sequences. Also available with Spanish dubbing. 98m/C VHS, Beta. *D:* Chuck Jones, Phil Monroe; *V:* Mel Blanc. **WAR**

Bugs Bunny Superstar 1975 (G) A collection of nine animated classics starring everybody's favorite "wascally wabbitt." Includes fascinating interviews and behind the scenes moments featuring the men and women who brought Bugs to life. 91m/C VHS, LV. *D:* Larry Jackson, Bob Clampett, Tex Avery, Isadore "Friz" Freleng; *V:* Mel Blanc. **MGM**

Bugsy 🐾🐾🐾½ 1991 (R) Beatty is Benjamin "Bugsy" Siegel, the 40s gangster who built the Flamingo Hotel in Las Vegas when it was still a virtual desert, before it became a gambling mecca. Bening is perfect as Bugsy's moll, Virginia Hill, who inspired him to carry out his dream of building the Flamingo (which was her nickname). Beatty and Bening heat up the screen and their off-screen relationship was no different. Fans anticipated their seemingly imminent marriage almost as much as the release of this movie. Almost nothing mars this film which Toback adapted from a novel by Dean Jennings, "We Only Kill Each Other: The Life and Bad Times of Bugsy Siegel." *CW:* Language, violence, and sensuality. 135m/C VHS, Beta, LV, 8mm, **Closed Caption.** Warren Beatty, Annette Bening, Harvey Keitel, Ben Kingsley, Elliott Gould, Joe Mantegna, Richard Sarafian, Bebe Neuwirth, Wendy Phillips, Robert Beltran, Bill Graham, Lewis Van Bergen, Debrah Farentino; *D:* Barry Levinson; *W:* James Toback; *C:* Allen Daviau; *M:* Ennio Morricone. Academy Awards '91: Best Art Direction/Set Decoration, Best Costume Design; Golden Globe Awards '92: Best Film—Drama; Los Angeles Film Critics Association Awards '91: Best Director (Levinson), Best Film, Best Screenplay; National Board of Review Awards '91: Best Actor (Beatty); Nominations: Academy Awards '91: Best Actor (Beatty), Best Cinematography, Best Director (Levinson), Best Original Screenplay, Best Picture, Best Supporting Actor (Keitel, Kingsley), Best Original Score. **COL**

Bugsy Malone 🐾🐾½ 1976 (G) Delightful musical features an all-children's cast highlighting this spoof of 1930s' gangster movies. 94m/C VHS, Beta, LV. *GB* Jodie Foster, Scott Baio, Florrie Augger, John Cassisi, Martin Lev; *D:* Alan Parker; *W:* Alan Parker; *C:* Peter Biziou; *M:* Paul Williams. British Academy Awards '76: Best Screenplay; Nominations: Academy Awards '76: Best Original Score. **PAR**

Bull Durham 🐾🐾🐾½ 1988 (R) Lovable American romantic comedy, dealing with a very minor minor-league team and three of its current constituents: an aging baseball groupie that beds one player each season; a cocky, foolish new pitcher; and the older, weary catcher brought in to wise the rookie up. The scene in which Sarandon tries poetry out on the banal rookie is a hoot. Highly acclaimed, the film sears with Sarandon and Costner's love scenes. 107m/C VHS, Beta, LV, **Closed Caption.** Kevin Costner, Susan Sarandon, Tim Robbins, Trey Wilson, Robert Wuhl, Jenny Robertson; *D:* Ron Shelton; *W:* Ron Shelton; *M:* Michael Convertino. Los Angeles Film Critics Association Awards '88: Best Screenplay; New York Film Critics Awards '88: Best Screenplay; National Society of Film Critics Awards '88: Best Screenplay; Writers Guild of America '88: Best Original Screenplay; Nominations: Academy Awards '88: Best Original Screenplay. **ORI, HMV**

Bull of the West 🐾½ 1989 Cattlemen battle for land in the wide open spaces of the old West. 90m/C VHS. Charles Bronson, Lee J. Cobb, Brian Keith, George Kennedy, DeForest Kelley, Doug McClure. **NO**

Bulldance 🐾 *Forbidden Son* 1988 At a gymnastic school in Crete, a girl's obsession with Greek mythological ritual leads to murder. 105m/C VHS, Beta. Lauren Hutton, Cliff DeYoung, Renee Estevez; *D:* Zelda Barron.

Bulldog Courage 🐾🐾 1935 Young man is out to avenge his father's murder. 66m/B VHS, Beta. Tim McCoy, Lois January, Joan Woodbury, John Elliott; *D:* Sam Newfield. **NOS, VCN, DVT**

Bulldog Drummond 🐾🐾½ 1929 The Bulldog Drummond character, created by "Sapper" (Herman Cyril McNeile), underwent a number of different incarnations from 20s silents through the 40s, and even occassionally in the 50s and 60s. A suave ex-British officer (a precursor to the glib shaken-not-stirred gentleman-spy variety), Bulldog has been played by the likes of Colman, Ralph Richardson, and Tom Conway, among others. In this, the first installment in the long-standing series, a WWI vet, bored with civilian life, is enlisted by a beautiful woman to help her father in various adventures. 85m/B VHS, Beta, LV. Ronald Colman, Joan Bennett, Montagu Love; *D:* F. Richard Jones. Nominations: Academy Awards '30: Best Actor (Colman), Best Interior Decoration, Best Interior Decoration. **RXM**

Bulldog Drummond at Bay 🐾 1937 Drummond searches for a group of foreign agents who are trying to steal the plans for a top-secret warplane. Poor British entry to the "Bulldog Drummond" series. 63m/B VHS. *GB* John Lodge, Dorothy Mackaill, Victor Jory, Claud Allister, Hugh Miller; *D:* Norman Lee. **SNC**

Bulldog Drummond Comes Back 🐾🐾 1937 Drummond, aided by Colonel Nielson, rescues his fiancee from the hands of desperate kidnappers. 119m/B VHS, Beta. John Howard, John Barrymore, Louise Campbell, Reginald Denny, Guy Standing; *D:* Louis King. **SNC, NOS, DVT**

Bulldog Drummond Escapes 🐾🐾 1937 Drummond, aided by his side-kick and valet, rescues a beautiful girl from spies. He then falls in love with her. 67m/B VHS, Beta. Ray Milland, Heather Angel, Reginald Denny, Guy Standing, Porter Hall, E.E. Clive; *D:* James Hogan. **SNC, NOS, VYY**

Bulldog Drummond in Africa/Arrest Bulldog Drummond 🐾🐾 1938 Two midseries Bulldog Drummond films, with two new villains. 115m/B VHS, Beta. John Howard, H.B. Warner, George Zucco. **RXM**

Bulldog Drummond's Bride 🐾🐾 1939 Ace detective Bulldog Drummond has to interrupt his honeymoon in order to pursue a gang of bank robbers across France and England. The last of the Bulldog Drummond film series. 69m/B VHS, Beta. John Howard, Heather Angel, H.B. Warner, E.E. Clive, Reginald Denny, Eduardo Ciannelli; *D:* James Hogan. **DVT, MRV, RXM**

Bulldog Drummond's Peril 🐾🐾 1938 Murder and robbery drag the adventurous Drummond away from his wedding and he pursues the villains until they are behind bars. One in the film series. 77m/B VHS, Beta. John Barrymore, John Howard, Louise Campbell, Reginald Denny, E.E. Clive, Porter Hall; *D:* James Hogan. **SNC, RXM, MRV**

Bulldog Drummond's Revenge 🐾🐾½ 1937 Bulldog's "Revenge" was made during the series' heyday and was the second to star Howard as Drummond; Barrymore revels in the character of Inspector Neilson of Scotland Yard, and Denny is Algy. In this typically fast-paced installment, suave sleuth Drummond stalks the master criminal responsible for stealing the formula to an explosive. 55m/B VHS. John Howard, John Barrymore, Reginald Denny, Louise Campbell, Frank Puglia, Nydia Westman, Lucien Littlefield; *D:* Louis King. **SNC, MOV**

Bulldog Drummond's Revenge/ Bulldog Drummond's Peril 1938 Once again, Bulldog Drummond becomes entangled with diamond counterfeiters, secret explosives, and other crime and criminals. Two episodes in a series. 118m/B VHS, Beta. John Howard, John Barrymore, Louise Campbell, Reginald Denny, E.E. Clive, Porter Hall.

Bulldog Drummond's Secret Police 🐾🐾 1939 The 15th Drummond film, adapted from Herman Cyril McNeile's famed detective novels featuring a million-pound treasure stashed in the Drummond manor and the murderous endeavors to retrieve it. 54m/B VHS, Beta. John Howard, Heather Angel, H.B. Warner, Reginald Denny, E.E. Clive, Leo G. Carroll; *D:* James Hogan. **SNC, VYY, RXM**

Bulldog Edition 🐾🐾 1936 Two newspapers engage in an all-out feud to be number one in the city, even going so far as to employ gangsters for purposes of sabotage. 57m/B VHS, Beta. Ray Walker, Evalyn Knapp, Regis Toomey, Cy Kendall, Billy Newell, Oscar Apfel, Betty Compson, Robert Warwick; *D:* Charles Lamont. **SNC**

Bulldog Jack 🐾🐾🐾 *Alias Bulldog Drummond* 1935 Fine entry in the series has Drummond's colleague battling it out with Richardson, the leader of gang of jewel thieves. 62m/B VHS, Beta. *GB* Fay Wray, Jack Hulbert, Claude Hulbert, Ralph Richardson, Paul Graetz, Gibb McLaughlin; *D:* Walter Forde. **NOS, SNC**

The Bulldozer Brigade 🐾🐾½ 1985 Young friends fight city hall in an effort to save their secret wooded playground from land developers. 86m/C VHS, **Closed Caption.** **FHE, BTV**

Bullet 🐾½ 1994 (R) Butch (Rourke) gets released from prison and immediately returns to his old drug and burglary ways on New York's mean streets. And he's got a score to settle with crazy drug kingpin Tank (Shakur). Has little to recommend it, except to those who like violence, with lackluster performances and a dull script. *CW:* Strong violence, drug use, pervasive language and a graphic sex scene. 96m/C VHS, LV, **Closed Caption.** Mickey Rourke, Tupac Shakur, Ted Levine, Adrien Brody, John Enos; *D:* Julien Temple; *W:* Bruce Rubenstein; *C:* Crescenzo G.P. Notarile. **NLC**

Bullet Code 🐾🐾 1940 It's quick-shooting shenanigans when O'Brien chases a pack of angry rustlers off his neighbor's land. 56m/B VHS. George O'Brien, Virginia Vale, Howard Hickman, Harry Woods, Charles "Slim" Whitaker; *D:* David Howard; *W:* Doris Schroeder. **MOV**

Bullet for Sandoval 🐾🐾 1970 (PG) An ex-Confederate renegade loots and pillages the north Mexican countryside on his way to murder the grandfather of the woman he loves. 96m/C VHS, Beta. *SP IT* Ernest Borgnine, George Hilton; *D:* Julio Buchs. **VCI**

A Bullet for the General 🐾 *Quien Sabe?* 1968 An American mercenary joins with rebel forces during the Mexican Revolution. 95m/C VHS, Beta. *IT* Martine Beswick, Lou Castel, Gian Marie Volonte, Klaus Kinski; *D:* Damiano Damiani; *M:* Luis Bacalov. **COL, NLC**

A Bullet in the Head 🐾🐾🐾 1990 Violent (no surprise there) tale of friendship finds Frank (Cheung), Ben (Leung), and Paul (Lee) heading out of 1967 Hong Kong for Saigon, where they hope to make money selling contraband goods in the city. They wind up on the wrong side of the Vietnamese Army, steal a fortune in gold from a local crime lord, and end up the prisoners of the Viet Cong. There's betrayal and death and a final moral reckoning and—did we mention lots and lots of (over-the-top) violence? Chinese with subtitles. 85m/C VHS. *HK* Tony Leung, Jacky Cheung, Waise Lee; *D:* John Woo. **FCT**

A Bullet Is Waiting 🐾🐾 1954 A diligent sheriff finally catches his man only to be trapped in a blinding snowstorm with the hardened criminal. 83m/C VHS, Beta. Jean Simmons, Rory Calhoun, Stephen McNally, Brian Aherne; *D:* John Farrow. **GKK**

Bullet to Beijing 🐾🐾½ *Len Deighton's Bullet to Beijing* 1995 (R) After some 30 years, Caine returns to his role as intelligence agent Harry Palmer. Forced into retirement, Harry finds himself privately recruited by a Russian businessman (Gambon) to retrieve a stolen chemical weapon being transported on a train headed for China. Harry gets a little help (from Connery and Sara) but treachery is all around. Follows "The Ipcress File," "Funeral in Berlin," and "Billion Dollar Brain"; based on the novel by Len Deighton. *CW:* Violence, nudity and language. 105m/C VHS, **Closed Caption.** *GB* Michael Caine, Michael Gambon, Jason Connery, Mia Sara, Patrick Allen, Burt Kwouk, Michael Sarrazin,

Sue Lloyd; **D:** George Mihalka; **W:** Peter Welbeck; **C:** Terence Cole; **M:** Rick Wakeman. *PAR*

Bulletproof 🎬 1988 (R) An unstoppable ex-CIA agent battles to retrieve a high-tech nuclear tank from terrorist hands. 93m/C VHS, Beta, LV. Gary Busey, Darlanne Fluegel, Henry Silva, Thalmus Rasulala, L.Q. Jones, R.G. Armstrong, Rene Enriquez; **D:** Steve Carver; **W:** Steve Carver. *COL*

Bulletproof 🎬 1996 (R) Desperately trying to be a male buddy bonding movie, "Bulletproof" fails miserably in every respect. Keats (Wayans) and Moses (Sandler) are an unlikely pair of car thieves with an equally unlikely bond to each other. Turns out Keats is really undercover cop Jack Carter, who is trying to infiltrate a drug cartel via his pal Moses. When the bust goes bad, Carter must bring Moses in unharmed to testify. Meanwhile the two rejuvenate their tainted relationship amid many homoerotic innuendoes. It's an embarrassment all around, especially for ex-Spike Lee cinematographer Dickerson on his first directing outing.**CW:** Strong violence and language, some sexuality and drug use. 85m/C VHS, LV, **Closed Caption, DVD.** Damon Wayans, Adam Sandler, James Caan, Kristen Wilson, James Farentino, Bill Nunn, Mark Roberts, Xander Berkeley, Alan Covert, Jeep Swenson, McCoy Larry; **D:** Ernest R. Dickerson; **W:** Joe Gayton, Lewis Colick; **C:** Steven Bernstein; **M:** Elmer Bernstein. Nominations: Golden Raspberry Awards '96: Worst Actor (Sandler). *USH*

Bulletproof Heart 🎬🎬🎬 Killer 1995 (R) Mick (LaPaglia), a hit man with a severe case of burnout, is assigned to kill Fiona (Rogers), a beautiful socialite who, conveniently, wants to die. Despite being warned by his boss (Boyle) that Fiona has a habit of making men weak, he falls in love and can't bring himself to kill her. First-time director Malone takes great care to establish the noir look and feel, capitalizing on the all-in-one-night timeframe to raise the tension level. LaPaglia and Rogers turn in riveting performances, but can't stop the film from losing momentum when it becomes self-consciously melodramatic near the end.**CW:** Strong graphic sex scene; language. 95m/C VHS, LV, **Closed Caption.** Anthony LaPaglia, Mimi Rogers, Peter Boyle, Matt Craven, Monika Schnarre, Joseph Maher; **D:** Mark Malone; **W:** Gordon Melbourne, Mark Malone; **C:** Tobias Schliessler; **M:** Graeme Coleman. *REP*

Bullets or Ballots 🎬🎬🎬 1938 Tough New York cop goes undercover to join the mob in order to get the goods on them. Old-fashioned danger and intrigue follow, making for some action-packed thrills. 82m/B VHS, Beta. Edward G. Robinson, Humphrey Bogart, Barton MacLane, Joan Blondell, Frank McHugh, Louise Beavers; **D:** William Keighley; **C:** Hal Mohr. *MGM, CCB*

Bullets Over Broadway 🎬🎬🎬½ 1994 (R) Mediocre playwright David Shayne (Cusack, in the Allen role) talks up the virtues of artistic integrity to his pretentious hothouse contemporaries, then sells out to a gangster who agrees to finance his latest play provided his no-talent, brassy moll (Tilly) gets a part. And it's her hit-man bodyguard's (Palminteri) unexpected artistic touches that redeem Shayne's otherwise lousy work. Wiest as the eccentric diva, Ullman as the aging ingenue, Reiner as the Greenwich Village sage, and Broadbent as the increasingly plump matinee idol lead a collection of delicious, over-the-top performances in this smart and howlingly funny tribute to Jazz Age New York City that showcases Woody at his self-conscious best. 106m/C VHS, LV, **Closed Caption.** Dianne Wiest, John Cusack, Jennifer Tilly, Rob Reiner, Chazz Palminteri, Tracey Ullman, Mary-Louise Parker, Joe Viterelli, Jack Warden, Jim Broadbent, Harvey Fierstein, Annie-Joe Edwards; **D:** Woody Allen; **W:** Woody Allen, Douglas McGrath; **C:** Carlo DiPalma. Academy Awards '94: Best Supporting Actress (Wiest); Golden Globe Awards '95: Best Supporting Actress (Wiest); Independent Spirit Awards '95: Best Supporting Actor (Palminteri), Best Supporting Actress (Wiest); Los Angeles Film Critics Association Awards '94: Best Supporting Actress (Wiest); New York Film Critics Awards '94: Best Supporting Actress (Wiest); National Society of Film Critics Awards '94: Best Sup-

porting Actress (Wiest); Screen Actors Guild Award '94: Best Supporting Actress (Wiest); Nominations: Academy Awards '94: Best Art Direction/Set Decoration, Best Costume Design, Best Director (Allen), Best Original Screenplay, Best Supporting Actor (Palminteri), Best Supporting Actress (Tilly); British Academy Awards '95: Best Original Screenplay; Independent Spirit Awards '95: Best Film, Best Screenplay; Writers Guild of America '94: Best Original Screenplay. *MAX*

Bullfighter & the Lady 🎬🎬½ 1950 An American goes to Mexico to learn the fine art of bullfighting in order to impress a beautiful woman. 87m/B VHS, LV. Robert Stack, Gilbert Roland, Virginia Grey, Katy Jurado; **D:** Budd Boetticher. Nominations: Academy Awards '51: Best Story.*REP*

Bullfighters 🎬🎬 1945 Stan and Ollie are in hot pursuit of a dangerous criminal which leads them to Mexico where Stan winds up in a bull ring. 61m/B VHS, Beta. Stan Laurel, Oliver Hardy, Margo Woode, Richard Lane; **D:** Malcolm St. Clair. *FOX, MLB*

Bullies woof! 1986 (R) A woodland-transplanted young man decides to fight back against an ornery mountain clan who have raped his mother, tortured his father, and beat up his girlfriend. Brutal and unpalatable. 96m/C VHS, Beta, LV, **Closed Caption.** CA Janet-Laine Green, Dehl Berti, Stephen Hunter, Jonathan Crombie, Olivia D'Abo; **D:** Paul Lynch. *USH*

Bullitt 🎬🎬🎬 1968 (PG) A detective assigned to protect a star witness for 48 hours senses danger; his worst fears are confirmed when his charge is murdered. Based on the novel, "Mute Witness" by Robert L. Pike, and featuring one of filmdom's most famous car chases. 105m/C VHS, Beta, LV. Steve McQueen, Robert Vaughn, Jacqueline Bisset, Don Gordon, Robert Duvall, Norman Fell, Simon Oakland; **D:** Peter Yates; **W:** Alan R. Trustman; **C:** William A. Fraker; **M:** Lalo Schifrin. Academy Awards '68: Best Film Editing; National Society of Film Critics Awards '68: Best Cinematography; Nominations: Academy Awards '68: Best Sound. *WAR*

Bullseye! 🎬½ 1990 (PG-13) Knockabout farce is a letdown considering the talents involved. Shady scientists (Moore and Caine) pursue/are pursued by lookalike con-artists (Caine and Moore), who are pursued in turn by international agents. Full of inside jokes and celebrity cameos, but nothing exceptional. 95m/C VHS, LV. Michael Caine, Roger Moore, Sally Kirkland, Patsy Kensit, Jenny Seagrove, John Cleese, Lee Patterson, Deborah Barrymore, Mark Burns, Deborah Leng, Alexandra Pigg; **Cameos:** Lynn Nesbitt, Steffanie Pitt; **D:** Michael Winner; **W:** Michael Winner, Leslie Bricusse; **M:** John Du Prez. *COL*

Bullshot 🎬🎬½ 1983 (PG) Zany English satire sends up the legendary Bulldog Drummond. In the face of mad professors, hapless heroines, devilish Huns and deadly enemies, our intrepid hero remains distinctly British. 84m/C VHS, Beta. GB Alan Shearman, Diz White, Ron House, Frances Tomelty, Michael Aldridge, Ron Pember, Christopher Good; **D:** Dick Clement; **M:** John Du Prez. *NO*

Bullwhip 🎬🎬 1958 A man falsely accused of murder saves himself from the hangman's noose by agreeing to a shotgun wedding. 80m/C VHS. Guy Madison, Rhonda Fleming, James Griffith, Peter Adams; **D:** Harmon Jones. *REP*

Bulworth 🎬🎬🎬 1998 (R) No-holds barred look at the political process. Senator John Jay Bulworth (Beatty), bored and disillusioned by the banality of his own political career, hires a hitman to end his misery. During his last days on earth fulfilling re-election duties, and with nothing to loose, he starts spewing the truth about politics and big business, much to the dismay of his constituents and assistants. Morphing into a hip-hop political prophet, he becomes entranced and invigorated by beautiful South Central resident Nina (Berry). Beatty (in an engaging and funny performance) tackles his fiery subject matter of dwindling racial harmony and corporate deceit with a brazen and winning sense of humor lost in contemporary films. Fine script and enjoyable supporting performances by Platt as Bulworth's pan-

ic-stricken aide and Cheadle as an enterprising drug lord.**CW:** Pervasive strong language and some drug content. 107m/C VHS. Warren Beatty, Halle Berry, Oliver Platt, Paul Sorvino, Don Cheadle, Jack Warden, Christine Baranski, Isaiah Washington, Joshua Malina, Richard Sarafian, Amiri Baraka, Sean Astin, Laurie Metcalf, Wendell Pierce, Michele Morgan, Ariyan Johnson, Graham Beckel, Nora Dunn, Jackie Gayle; **D:** Warren Beatty; **W:** Jeremy Pikser, Warren Beatty; **C:** Vittorio Storaro; **M:** Ennio Morricone. *NYR*

Bummer woof! 1973 (R) Rock band's wild party turns into tragedy when the bass player goes too far with two groupies. It's a bad scene, man. 90m/C VHS, Beta. Kipp Whitman, Dennis Burkley, Carol Speed, Connie Strickland; **D:** William Allen Castleman. *NO*

Bums 🎬🎬 1993 Sergeant Andrew Holloman is a military officer in search of his long lost brother. It turns out his brother was homeless and is now dead at the hands of a skid row killer. Holloman recruits a platoon of other homeless people to help him track the killer but what he discovers is a multimillion conspiracy behind the murders. 94m/C VHS. Christopher McDonald, Haskell Phillips, Dawn Evans; **D:** Andy Galler; **W:** Pat Allee, Ben Hurst. *MNC*

Bunco 🎬 1983 Two policemen working for the Los Angeles Police Department's Bunco Squad discover a college for con artists complete with tape-recorded lessons and on-the-job training. 60m/C VHS, Beta. Tom Selleck, Robert Urich, Donna Mills, Will Geer, Arte Johnson, Alan Feinstein. *ORI, WAR*

Bundle of Joy 🎬🎬½ 1956 Salesgirl who saves an infant from falling off the steps of a foundling home is mistaken for the child's mother. Remake of 1939's "Bachelor Mother." 🎵Bundle of Joy; I Never Felt This Way Before; Lullaby in Blue; Worry About Tomorrow; All About Love; Someday Soon; What's So Good About Morning?; You're Perfect In Every Departmant. 98m/C VHS, Beta, LV. Debbie Reynolds, Eddie Fisher, Adolphe Menjou; **D:** Norman Taurog. *NO*

A Bunny's Tale 🎬🎬 1985 The story of Gloria Steinem's undercover journey into the Playboy Club as a fledgling journalist. It is here that she discovered her dedication as a feminist. Based on the book by Steinem. 97m/C VHS, Beta, **Closed Caption.** Kirstie Alley, Cotter Smith, Deborah Van Valkenburgh, Joanna Kerns, Delta Burke, Diana Scarwid; **D:** Karen Arthur.

Buona Sera, Mrs. Campbell 🎬🎬½ 1968 The lovely Lollobrigida and some fast-paced plot moves are the main highlights of this comedy. Mrs. Campbell convinced her three American WWII lovers that each of them had fathered her daughter. All three have supported mother and child through the years, unbeknust to each other and their wives. When their 20-year reunion brings them back to Italy, Mrs. Campbell must do some fast-thinking and some quick-stepping to keep everyone happy. 113m/C VHS, LV, **Letterbox.** Gina Lollobrigida, Shelley Winters, Phil Silvers, Peter Lawford, Telly Savalas, Lee Grant, Janet Margolin, Marian Moses; **D:** Melvin Frank. *MGM*

The 'Burbs 🎬🎬½ 1989 (PG) A tepid satire about suburbanites suspecting their creepy new neighbors of murderous activities. Well-designed and sharp, but light on story. 101m/C VHS, Beta, LV. Tom Hanks, Carrie Fisher, Rick Ducommun, Corey Feldman, Brother Theodore, Bruce Dern, Gale Gordon, Courtney Gains; **D:** Joe Dante; **W:** Dana Olsen; **M:** Jerry Goldsmith. *USH, CCB*

Burden of Dreams 1982 The landmark documentary chronicling the berserk circumstances behind the scenes of Werner Herzog's epic "Fitzcarraldo." Stuck in the Peruvian jungles, the film crew was subjected to every disaster imaginable while executing Herzog's vision, including disease, horrendous accident, warring local tribes and the megalomaniacal director himself. Considered better than "Fitzcarraldo," although both films discuss a man's obsession. 94m/C VHS, Beta, LV. Klaus Kinski, Mick Jagger, Jason Robards Jr., Werner Herzog; **D:** Les Blank. *TPV, FFM, BTV*

Bureau of Missing Persons ⅛⅛½
1933 Comedy-drama about big-city bureau of missing persons, in which the hardened Stone is in charge. O'Brien plays a tough cop who is transferred to the bureau and Davis stars as the mystery woman with whom he gets involved. Although fast-paced and intriguing, the film is somewhat confusing and never stays in one direction for very long. **75m/B VHS, Closed Caption.** Bette Davis, Lewis Stone, Pat O'Brien, Glenda Farrell, Allen Jenkins, Ruth Donnelly, Hugh Herbert; **D:** Roy Del Ruth. *MGM*

Burglar ⅛⅛
1987 (R) A cat burglar moves to the right side of the law when she tries to solve a murder case. Whoopi's always a treat, but this movie's best forgotten; Goldberg's fans should watch "Jumpin' Jack Flash" again instead. Co-star Goldthwait elevates the comedic level a bit. **103m/C VHS, Beta, LV, Closed Caption.** Whoopi Goldberg, Bob(cat) Goldthwait, Lesley Ann Warren, John Goodman, G.W. Bailey, James Handy, Anne DeSalvo; **D:** Hugh Wilson; **W:** Hugh Wilson. *WAR, KIV*

Burglar ⅛⅛⅛
Vzlomschik **1987** Not to be confused with the Whoopi Goldberg vehicle, this Russian film relates a story no less American than apple pie and teenage angst. Senka and would-be punk star Kostya are two neglected and disaffected brothers whose father is a drunken womanizer best known for absentee paternalism. When Howmuch, a serious heavy metalloid, pressures Kostya to steal a synthesizer, brother Senka steps in to steal the Community Center's property himself. In Russian with English subtitles, the solid performances hold their own against the heavy musical content. **89m/C VHS.** *RU* Konstantin Kinchev, Oleg Yelykomov; **D:** Valery Orgorodnikov. *FCT, KIV*

Burial Ground ⅛
1985 A classically grisly splatter film in which the hungry dead rise and proceed to kill the weekend denizens of an isolated aristocratic mansion. **85m/C VHS, Beta.** Karen Well, Peter Bark; **D:** Andrew Bianchi. *VES, ART*

Burial of the Rats ⅛½
Roger Corman Presents Burial of the Rats; Bram Stoker's Burial of the Rats **1995 (R)** Based on a short story by Bram Stoker, this cable campiness features young Bram (Alber) himself being kidnapped while traveling in Eastern Europe. He's taken to the "Queen of Vermin" (Barbeau), who heads a bloodthirsty cult that hate men, worship rats, and live by violence. Fortunately, the Queen decides to spare Bram so he can write of their exploits and he falls for the fleshy charms of rat-woman Madeleine (Ford). **CW:** Nudity; a sex scene; horror violence/gore. **85m/C VHS.** Adrienne Barbeau, Maria Ford, Kevin Alber; **D:** Dan Golden. *NHO*

Buried Alive ⅛
1939 A man is sent to prison on trumped up charges. Only the prison nurse believes he is innocent as a crooked politician strives to keep him behind bars. **74m/B Beta.** Beverly Roberts, Robert Wilcox, George Pembroke, Ted Osborn, Paul McVey, Alden Chase; **D:** Victor Halperin. *NOS, MRV, LOO*

Buried Alive ⅛⅛
1981 Director d'Amato reaps his finest gore-fest to date, incorporating the well-established taxidermist gone loony motif in his repertoire of appalling bad taste. Not for the squeamish, this bloodier-than-thou spaghetti spooker is chock full of necrophilia, cannibalism, and more. **90m/C VHS.** *IT* Kieran Canter, Cinzia Monreale, Franca Stoppi; **D:** Joe D'Amato. *NO*

Buried Alive ⅛⅛
1989 (R) Once Ravenscroft Hall was an asylum for the incurably insane. Now, the isolated mansion is a school for troubled teenage girls, run by a charismatic psychiatrist. Captivated by his charm, a young woman joins the staff. Soon, she is tormented by nightmare visions of the long-dead victims of a nameless killer. When the students begin to disappear, she realizes he still lives...and she may be his next victim. Carradine's last role. **97m/C VHS, LV.** Robert Vaughn, Donald Pleasence, Karen Witter, John Carradine, Ginger Lynn Allen; **D:** Gerard Kikoine. *COL*

Buried Alive ⅛⅛½
1990 (PG-13) One of the many horror flicks entitled "Buried Alive," this one is not bad, injecting a bit of levity into the time-worn genre. Schemestress Leigh and her paramour poison her husband. Or so they think, only to discover that he's not quite dead. Made for cable. **93m/C VHS.** Tim Matheson, Jennifer Jason Leigh, William Atherton, Hoyt Axton; **D:** Frank Darabont; **W:** Mark Patrick Carducci, Jake Clesi; **M:** Michel Colombier. *USH*

Buried Alive 2 ⅛⅛½
1997 (PG-13) Randy (Caffrey) wants to get rid of rich wife Laura (Sheedy) so he and girlfriend Roxanne (Needham) can enjoy her cash. So he slips some blowfish venom into her wine and buries her. But the venom only simulated death and after clawing her way out of the grave, Laura is one angry gal. Clint Goodman (Matheson), who was buried in the first movie, shows up to help out the wronged wife. Made for cable. **CW:** Terror/violence and some sensuality. **92m/C VHS, Closed Caption.** Ally Sheedy, Stephen Caffrey, Tracey Needham, Tim Matheson; **D:** Tim Matheson; **W:** Walter Klenhard. *USH*

Burke & Wills ⅛⅛½
1985 (PG-13) A lush, big-budgeted true story of the two men who first crossed Australia on foot, and explored its central region. Popular Australian film. **120m/C VHS, Beta, LV, Closed Caption.** *AU* Jack Thompson, Nigel Havers, Greta Scacchi, Ralph Cotterill, Drew Forsythe, Chris Haywood, Matthew Fargher; **D:** Graeme Clifford; **W:** Michael Thomas; **C:** Russell Boyd; **M:** Peter Sculthorpe. *NLC*

Burlesque of Carmen ⅛⅛
1916 A silent pastiche of the Bizet opera, with Charlie as Don Schmose. Interesting early work. **30m/B VHS, Beta.** Charlie Chaplin, Ben Turpin, Edna Purviance; **D:** Charlie Chaplin. *NOS, DVT, GVV*

The Burmese Harp ⅛⅛⅛⅛
Harp of Burma; Birumano Tategoto **1956** At the end of WWII, a Japanese soldier is spiritually traumatized and becomes obsessed with burying the masses of war casualties. A searing, acclaimed anti-war statement, in Japanese with English subtitles. Remade by Ichikawa in 1985. **115m/B VHS, Beta, LV.** *JP* Shoji Yasui, Rentaro Mikuni, Tatsuya Mihashi, Tanie Kitabayashi, Yunosuke Ito; **D:** Kon Ichikawa. Nominations: Academy Awards '56: Best Foreign Language Film. *CVC, TPV*

Burn! ⅛⅛⅛½
Quemimada! **1970 (PG)** An Italian-made indictment of imperialist control by guerrilla-filmmaker Pontecorvo, depicting the efforts of a 19th century British ambassador to put down a slave revolt on a Portuguese-run Caribbean island. Great Brando performance. **112m/C VHS, Beta, LV, Letterbox.** *IT* Marlon Brando, Evarist Marquez, Renato Salvatori; **D:** Gillo Pontecorvo; **M:** Ennio Morricone. *MGM, CRC, FCT*

Burn 'Em Up Barnes
1934 Twelve episodes each depicting the adventures of "Burn'Em Up" Barnes, a racer, and his buddy, Bobbie. **40m/B VHS, Beta.** Frankie Darro, Lola Lane, Jack Mulhall. *SNC, NOS, VCN*

Burn Witch, Burn! ⅛⅛⅛
Night of the Eagle **1962** A college professor proudly finds himself rapidly rising in his profession. His pride turns to horror though when he discovers that his success is not due to his own abilities, but to the efforts of his witchcraft practicing wife. Excellent, atmospheric horror with a genuinely suspenseful climax. **89m/B VHS.** *GB* Peter Wyngarde, Janet Blair, Margaret Johnston, Anthony Nicholls, Colin Gordon, Kathleen Byron, Reginald Beckwith, Jessica Dunning, Norman Bird, Judith Scott; **D:** Sidney Hayers; **W:** Richard Matheson, Charles Beaumont, George L. Baxt; **C:** Reg Wyer. *VTR*

Burndown ⅛
1989 (R) Victims of a serial killer in a town with a large nuclear reactor are themselves radioactive, which leads the Police Chief and a beautiful reporter to the truth and the hidden conspiracy. **98m/C VHS, Beta, LV.** Cathy Moriarty, Peter Firth; **D:** James Allen. *NO*

The Burning ⅛
1982 (R) Story of macabre revenge set in the dark woods of a seemingly innocent summer camp. **90m/C VHS, Beta.** Brian Matthews, Leah Ayres, Brian Backer, Larry Joshua, Jason Alex-

ander, Ned Eisenberg, Garrick Glenn, Carolyn Houlihan, Fisher Stevens, Lou David, Holly Hunter; **D:** Tony Maylam; **W:** Bob Weinstein, Peter Lawrence; **C:** Harvey Harrison; **M:** Rick Wakeman. *NO*

The Burning Bed ⅛⅛⅛½
1985 A made for television dramatic expose (based on a true story) about wife-beating. Fawcett garnered accolades for her performance as the battered wife who couldn't take it anymore. Highly acclaimed and Emmy-nominated. **95m/C VHS, Beta, Closed Caption.** Farrah Fawcett, Paul LeMat, Penelope Milford, Richard Masur; **D:** Robert Greenwald. *FOX*

The Burning Court ⅛½
1962 Unusual horror film involving occultism, possession, and family curses. Dubbed into English. Based on a story by John Dickson Carr. **102m/C VHS.** Nadja Tiller, Jean-Claude Brialy, Edith Scob. *SNC*

Burning Daylight ⅛⅛
1928 Alaskan real estate baron loses everything to a group of San Francisco sharpies. Based on the story by Jack London. **72m/B VHS.** Milton Sills, Arthur Stone, Doris Kenyon, Guinn "Big Boy" Williams; **D:** Richard A. Rowland. *GPV*

The Burning Hills ⅛½
1956 Unexceptional cow flick based on a Louis L'Amour novel. Hunter hides from cattle thieves in a barn and, eventually, in the arms of a half-breed Mexican girl (Wood). Tedious and unsurprising. **94m/C VHS.** Tab Hunter, Natalie Wood, Skip Homeier, Eduard Franz; **D:** Stuart Heisler. *WAR, MLB*

Burning Rage ⅛
1984 A blazing, abandoned coal mine threatens to wreak havoc in the Appalachians. The government sends geologist Mandrell to help prevent a disaster. Made for television. **100m/C VHS, LV.** Barbara Mandrell, Tom Wopat, Bert Remsen, John Pleshette, Carol Kane, Eddie Albert; **D:** Gilbert Cates. *VTR*

The Burning Season ⅛⅛⅛
1994 In one of his last performances, Julia inspires as Chico Mendes, a socialist union leader who fought to protect the homes and land of Brazilian peasants in the western Amazon rain forest. With Mendes' help the peasants form a union and struggle to prevent the building of a road that will provide easy access to forest land for speculators and cattlemen. Naturally, they are violently opposed by corruption-ridden capitalist powers in the government. Julia provides a haunting portrayal of the heroic figure who was assassinated in 1990. Based in part on the book by Andrew Revkin. Filmed on location in Mexico. **123m/C VHS, Closed Caption.** Raul Julia, Edward James Olmos, Sonia Braga, Luis Guzman, Nigel Havers, Kamala Dawson, Tomas Milian, Esai Morales, Tony Plana, Carmen Argenziano; **D:** John Frankenheimer; **W:** William Mastrosimone, Michael Tolkin, Ron Hutchinson; **M:** Gary Chang. *WAR*

Burning Secret ⅛⅛
Brennendes Geheimnis **1989 (PG)** After WWI, a widow in Austria (Dunaway) meets a baron (Brandauer) who has befriended her son. Mutual seduction ensues but the sparks don't fly. Adapted from Stefan Zweig story. **107m/C VHS, Beta, LV.** *GB* Faye Dunaway, Klaus Maria Brandauer, Ian Richardson, David Eberts; **D:** Andrew Birkin; **W:** Andrew Birkin; **M:** Hans Zimmer. *VES, IME, ART*

The Burns and Allen Show **1950**
George and Gracie's classic vaudeville routines are a highlight of this sitcom series, with George the perpetually harried husband to the scatterbrained Gracie. Additional episodes are available. **115m/B VHS, Beta, LV, Closed Caption.** Gracie Allen, George Burns. *SHO, COL, MOV*

Burnt by the Sun ⅛⅛⅛
Outomlionnye Solntsem **1994 (R)** Masterful evocation of '30s Stalinist Russia, covering a day in the life of Soviet revolutionary hero Serguei (Mikhalkov) and his family, far from the purges and gulags. Enjoying a country existence with wife Moroussia (Dapkounaite) and daughter Nadia (played by Mikhalkov's daughter), his idyll is disturbed by mystery man Dimitri (Menchikov), and Serguei realizes that their fates are bound by the difference between their Communist dreams and reality. Symbolism is a

little heavy but film delivers emotionally. Russian with subtitles. **CW:** Some language and sexuality. 134m/C VHS, LV. *RU FR* Nikita Mikhalkov, Ingeborga Dapkounaite, Oleg Menshikov, Nadia Mikhalkov, Andre Oumansky, Viatcheslav Tikhonov, Svetlana Krioutchkova, Vladimir Ilyine; *D:* Nikita Mikhalkov; *W:* Nikita Mikhalkov, Rustam Ibragimbekov; *M:* Eduard Artemyev. Academy Awards '94: Best Foreign Language Film; Cannes Film Festival '94: Grand Jury Prize; Nominations: Australian Film Institute '96: Best Foreign Film; British Academy Awards '95: Best Foreign Film. COL

Burnt Offerings 🎬🎬 1976 (PG) A family rents an old mansion for the summer and they become affected by evil forces that possess the house. Based on the novel by Robert Marasco. 116m/C VHS, Beta. Oliver Reed, Karen Black, Bette Davis, Burgess Meredith; *D:* Dan Curtis; *W:* Dan Curtis. MGM

Bury Me an Angel 🎬 1971 A female biker sets out to seek revenge against the men who killed her brother. 85m/C VHS, Beta, LV. Dixie Peabody, Terry Mace, Clyde Ventura, Dan Haggerty, Stephen Whittaker, Gary Littlejohn; *D:* Barbara Peeters. HHT

Bury Me Not on the Lone Prairie 🎬🎬 1941 When his brother is murdered in cold blood by claim jumpers, mining engineer Brown goes to avenge the dead. Based on a story by Sherman Lowe. 57m/B VHS. Johnny Mack Brown, Fuzzy Knight, Nell O'Day, Frank O'Connor, Kermit Maynard; *D:* Ray Taylor; *W:* Sherman Lowe, Victor McLeod. MOV

The Bus Is Coming 🎬🎬 1972 A love story entwined with the problems of blacks in a small town. 95m/C VHS, Beta. Mike Sims, Stephanie Faulkner, Morgan Jones; *D:* Horace Jackson. NO

Bus Stop 🎬🎬🎬 *The Wrong Kind of Girl* 1956 Murray plays a naive cowboy who falls in love with Monroe, a barroom singer, and decides to marry her without her permission. Considered by many to be the finest performance by Marilyn Monroe; she sings "That Old Black Magic" in this one. Very funny with good performances by all. Based on the William Inge play. 96m/C VHS, Beta, LV. Marilyn Monroe, Arthur O'Connell, Hope Lange, Don Murray, Betty Field, Max Casey Adams Showalter, Hans Conried, Eileen Heckart; *D:* Joshua Logan; *W:* George Axelrod; *C:* Milton Krasner. Nominations: Academy Awards '56: Best Supporting Actor (Murray). FOX

The Busby Berkeley Disc 1992 A collection of the innovative dance director's work at Warner Bros. studio covering 1933-37. Berkeley was known for his elaborate production numbers, beautiful women, military precision, and kaleidoscopic patterns in such films as "42nd Street," "Footlight Parade," and the "Gold Diggers" series. 176m/B LV. MGM

Bush Mama 🎬🎬 1976 A hallucinatory film about a black woman on welfare trying to care for her daughter in a Los Angeles ghetto. Street violence varies with fantasy scenes in a loose narrative filled with flashbacks. 100m/C VHS. *D:* Haile Gerima. FCT

The Bushbaby 🎬½ 1970 The young Brooks is given a tiny bushbaby while visiting Africa with her father. Because of her pet she misses her ship home and finds herself with former servant Gossett, who agrees to take her to a family friend. Unfortunately, the authorities think he's kidnapped the girl and the two, along with the trouble-causing pet, are pursued by the police. Simple-minded kiddie fare. 100m/C VHS. Margaret Brooks, Louis Gossett Jr., Donald Houston, Laurence Naismith, Marne Maitland, Geoffrey Bayldon, Jack Gwillim; *D:* John Trent. MGM, FCT

The Busher 🎬½ 1919 All-American pitcher's romance is interrupted by a gratuitous Mr. Moneybags. Minor-league conflict with little real hardball. 54m/B VHS, Beta. Charles Ray, Colleen Moore, John Gilbert. GPV, FCT, GVV

The Bushido Blade 🎬🎬¼ *The Bloody Bushido Blade* 1980 An action-packed samurai thriller of adventure and betrayal set in medieval Japan. 92m/C VHS, Beta. *JP* Richard Boone, James Earl Jones, Frank Converse; *D:* Tom Kotani. NO

The Bushwackers 🎬½ *The Rebel* 1952 Ireland plays a veteran of the Confederate army who wishes only to put his violent past behind him. He is forced to reconsider his vow when old-west bullies threaten his family. 70m/B VHS. Dorothy Malone, John Ireland, Wayne Morris, Lawrence Tierney, Jack Elam, Lon Chaney Sr., Myrna Dell; *D:* Rod Amateau. NOS, LOO, SNC

Bushwhacked 🎬🎬½ *Tenderfoots; The Tenderfoot* 1995 (PG-13) Crude, rude, dim-witted, kid-hating Max Grabelski (Stern) is falsely accused of murder and forced to become a fugitive. While not to be confused with Harrison Ford, he is mistaken for the leader of a group of Cub Scouts out on their maiden camping trip and soon finds himself in an unlikely partnership with the boys. Together they encounter everything from grizzly bears to whitewater rapids. Light-hearted, goofy comedy continues Stern's tendency toward kid-intensive, family-oriented fare in the "Rookie of the Year" vein. **CW:** Crude dialogue. 85m/C VHS, Closed Caption. Daniel Stern, Jon Polito, Brad Sullivan, Ann Dowd, Anthony Heald, Thomas Wood; *D:* Greg Beeman; *W:* Tommy Swerdlow, Michael Goldberg, John Jordan, Danny Byers; *M:* Bill Conti. FXV

A Business Affair 🎬🎬½ *D'Une Femme a L'Autre* 1993 (R) Kate Swallow (the ravishing Bouquet), the neglected wife of temperamental author Alex Bolton (Pryce), begins an affair with her flamboyant American publisher Vanni Corso (Walken). While the men posture between themselves for her affections, Kate, who has literary aspirations, decides to strike out on her own. Based on the romantic triangle of British writers Barbara Skelton and Cyril Connolly and his publisher George Weidenfeld and taken from Skelton's memoirs "Tears Before Bedtime" and "Weep No More." **CW:** Language and some sexuality. 102m/C VHS. Carole Bouquet, Jonathan Pryce, Christopher Walken, Sheila Hancock; *D:* Charlotte Brandstrom; *W:* William Stadiem; *C:* Willy Kurant; *M:* Didier Vasseur. THV

Business as Usual 🎬🎬 1988 (PG) A meek boutique manager in Liverpool defends a sexually harassed employee, is fired, fights back, and creates a national furor over her rights as a woman. 89m/C VHS, Beta, Closed Caption. Glenda Jackson, Cathy Tyson, John Thaw, Craig Charles, Eamon Boland; *D:* Lezli-Ann Barrett; *W:* Lezli-Ann Barrett. WAR

Busted Up 🎬 1986 (R) A young, hard-luck urban street-fighter battles for the sake of his family and neighborhood against local crimelords. 93m/C VHS, Beta, Closed Caption. *CA* Irene Cara, Paul Coufos, Tony Rosato, Stan Shaw, Gordon Judges; *D:* Conrad Palmisano; *M:* Charles P. Barnett. USH

Buster 🎬🎬 1988 (R) The story of Buster Edwards, the one suspect in the 1963 Great Train Robbery who evaded being captured by police. Collins makes his screen debut as one of Britain's most infamous criminals. Collins also performs on the film's soundtrack, spawning two hit singles, "Two Hearts" and "Groovy Kind of Love." 102m/C VHS, Beta, LV, Closed Caption. *GB* Phil Collins, Julie Walters, Larry Lamb, Stephanie Lawrence, Ellen Beaven, Michael Attwell, Ralph Brown, Christopher Ellison, Sheila Hancock, Martin Jarvis, Anthony Quayle; *D:* David Green; *M:* Anne Dudley. Nominations: Academy Awards '88: Best Song ("Two Hearts"). HBO

Buster and Billie 🎬½ 1974 (R) Tragedy ensues when a popular high school student falls in love with the class tramp in rural Georgia in 1948. Serious, decently appointed period teen drama. 100m/C VHS, Beta. Jan-Michael Vincent, Joan Goodfellow, Clifton James, Pamela Sue Martin, Robert Englund; *D:* Daniel Petrie. COL

Buster Keaton Rides Again/The Railrodder 1965 "The Railrodder" is a silent comedy short that returns Buster Keaton to the type of slapstick he made famous in his legendary 1920s films. "Buster Keaton Rides Again" (in black and white) is a documentary-style look at Keaton filmed during the making of "The Railrodder." Besides scenes of Keaton at work, there is also a capsule rundown of his career. 81m/C VHS, Beta, LV. Buster Keaton. GPV

Bustin' Loose 🎬🎬🎬 1981 (R) A fast-talking ex-con reluctantly drives a bus load of misplaced kids and their keeper cross-country. 94m/C VHS, LV. Richard Pryor, Cicely Tyson, Robert Christian, George Coe, Bill Quinn; *D:* Oz Scott; *W:* Richard Pryor, Lonnie Elder III. USH

Busting 🎬🎬½ 1974 (R) Gould and Blake play a pair of slightly off-the-wall L.A. cops. The pair are forced "to bust" local addicts and prostitutes instead of the real crime bosses because much of the police department is on the take. Plenty of comedy and action as well as highly realistic drama. 92m/C VHS. Elliott Gould, Robert (Bobby) Blake, Allen (Goorwitz) Garfield, Antonio Fargas, Michael Lerner, Sid Haig, Cornelia Sharpe; *D:* Peter Hyams; *W:* Peter Hyams; *M:* Billy Goldenberg. MGM, USH

But Not for Me 🎬🎬½ 1959 Gable stars as a middled-aged entertainment executive who thinks he can forestall maturity by carrying on with his youthful secretary. 105m/B VHS, Closed Caption. Clark Gable, Carroll Baker, Lilli Palmer, Lee J. Cobb, Barry Coe, Thomas Gomez, Charles Lane; *D:* Walter Lang; *W:* John Michael Hayes; *C:* Robert Burks. PAR

But Where Is Daniel Wax? 🎬🎬 1974 At a class reunion, a doctor and a popular singing star reminisce about their youth and Daniel Wax, their one-time hero. Hebrew with English subtitles. 95m/C VHS, Beta. Lior Yaeni, Michael Lipkin, Esther Zevko; *D:* Avram Heffner. ERG

Butch and Sundance: The Early Days 🎬🎬½ 1979 (PG) Traces the origins of the famous outlaw duo. It contains the requisite shoot-outs, hold-ups, and escapes. A "prequel" to "Butch Cassidy and the Sundance Kid." 111m/C VHS, Beta. Tom Berenger, William Katt, John Schuck, Jeff Corey, Jill Eikenberry, Brian Dennehy, Peter Weller; *D:* Richard Lester; *W:* Allan Burns. Nominations: Academy Awards '79: Best Costume Design. FOX

Butch Cassidy and the Sundance Kid 🎬🎬🎬🎬 1969 (PG) Two legendary outlaws at the turn of the century take it on the lam with a beautiful, willing ex-school teacher. With a clever script, humanly fallible characters, and warm, witty dialogue, this film was destined to become a boxoffice classic. Featured the hit song "Raindrops Keep Falling on My Head" and renewed the buddy film industry, as Newman and Redford trade insult for insult. Look for the great scene where Newman takes on giant Ted Cassidy in a fist fight. 🎵Raindrops Keep Fallin' on My Head; On a Bicycle Built for Joy. 110m/C VHS, Beta, LV. Paul Newman, Robert Redford, Katharine Ross, Jeff Corey, Strother Martin, Cloris Leachman, Kenneth Mars, Ted Cassidy, Henry Jones, George Furth, Sam Elliott; *D:* George Roy Hill; *W:* William Goldman; *C:* Conrad Hall; *M:* Burt Bacharach. Academy Awards '69: Best Cinematography, Best Song ("Raindrops Keep Fallin' on My Head"), Best Story & Screenplay, Best Original Score; British Academy Awards '70: Best Actor (Redford), Best Actress (Ross), Best Director (Hill), Best Film, Best Screenplay; Golden Globe Awards '70: Best Score; Writers Guild of America '69: Best Adapted Screenplay; Nominations: Academy Awards '69: Best Director (Hill), Best Picture, Best Sound. NO

The Butcher's Wife 🎬🎬 1991 (PG-13) Charming tale of a young psychic (Moore) who brings romance to a Greenwich Village neighborhood that never quite gets off the ground. Moore stars as the clairvoyant whose mystical powers bring magic into the lives of everyone around her, including the local psychiatrist (Daniels), who falls under her spell. Talented cast is virtually wasted with a script that is lightweight; excepting Steenburgen and Dzundza who shine. 107m/C VHS, Beta,

LV, Letterbox, Closed Caption. Demi Moore, Jeff Daniels, George Dzundza, Frances McDormand, Margaret Colin, Mary Steenburgen, Max Perlich, Miriam Margolyes, Christopher Durang, Diane Salinger; **D:** Terry Hughes; **W:** Ezra Litwack, Marjorie Schwartz; **M:** Michael Gore. *PAR*

Butler's Dilemma *🎞🎞* 1943 A jewel thief and a playboy both claim the identity of a butler who never existed, with humorous results. 75m/B VHS, Beta. *GB* Richard Hearne, Francis L. Sullivan, Hermione Gingold, Ian Fleming. *VYY*

Butterfield 8 *🎞🎞🎞* 1960 A seedy film of the John O'Hara novel about a prostitute that wants to go straight and settle down. Taylor won an Oscar, perhaps because she was ill and had lost in the two previous years in more deserving roles. 108m/C VHS, Beta, LV, Letterbox. Elizabeth Taylor, Laurence Harvey, Eddie Fisher, Dina Merrill, Mildred Dunnock, Betty Field, Susan Oliver, Kay Medford; **D:** Daniel Mann; **W:** John Michael Hayes, Charles Schnee; **C:** Joseph Ruttenberg. Academy Awards '60: Best Actress (Taylor); Nominations: Academy Awards '60: Best Color Cinematography. *MGM, BTV*

Butterflies 1975 Ria, a middle-aged housewife with two lazy sons, is beginning to feel her age, and like a butterfly, feeling like she has too much to do and not enough time. Then Leonard appears in her life—divorced, lonely and romantic. Made for British television. 60m/C VHS. *GB VCO*

Butterflies Are Free *🎞🎞🎞* 1972 (PG) Fast-paced humor surrounds the Broadway play brought to the big screen. Blind youth Albert is determined to be self-sufficient. A next-door-neighbor actress helps him gain independence from his over-protective mother (Heckart). 109m/C VHS, Beta. Goldie Hawn, Edward Albert, Eileen Heckart, Michael Glaser; **D:** Milton Katselas; **C:** Charles B(ryant) Lang; **M:** Robert Alcivar. Academy Awards '72: Best Supporting Actress (Heckart); Nominations: Academy Awards '72: Best Cinematography, Best Sound. *GKK*

Butterfly *🎞½* 1982 (R) Based on James M. Cain's novel about an amoral young woman (Pia, who'd you think?) who uses her beauty and sensual appetite to manipulate the men in her life, including her father. Set in Nevada of the 1930s, father and daughter are drawn into a daring and forbidden love affair by their lust and desperation. 105m/C VHS, Beta, LV. Pia Zadora, Stacy Keach, Orson Welles, Edward Albert, James Franciscus, Lois Nettleton, Stuart Whitman, June Lockhart, Ed McMahon; **D:** Matt Cimber; **W:** Matt Cimber; **M:** Ennio Morricone. Golden Raspberry Awards '82: Worst Actress (Zadora), Worst Supporting Actor (McMahon), Worst New Star (Zadora). *VES, ART*

Butterfly Affair *🎞* 1971 (PG) Beautiful singer, involved in a scheme to smuggle two million dollars worth of gems, plots to double-cross her partners in crime. 75m/C VHS, Beta. Claudia Cardinale, Henri Charriere, Stanley Baker; **D:** Jean Herman. *NO*

Butterfly Ball *🎞* 1976 Retelling of the 19th century classic combines the rock music of Roger Glover, live action and animation by Halas and Batchelor. Only for the brain-cell depressed. 85m/C VHS, Beta. *GB* Twiggy, Ian Gillian, David Coverdale; **D:** Tony Klinger. *NO*

Butterfly Kiss *🎞🎞* 1994 Strange psychodrama/road tale finds drifter Eunice (Plummer) wandering the motorways of northern England. At one service station she meets Miriam (Reeves)—the two, immediately drawn together, make love at Miriam's that night. When Eunice hitches a ride with a trucker next morning, Miriam decides to follow and discovers Eunice with the truck and the driver's dead body. It's soon not the only dead body Miriam encounters as she discovers Eunice is a serial killer—not that this seems to worry Miriam a great deal as she herself gets into the spirit of their crimes. Grim all the way 'round. 90m/C VHS. *GB* Amanda Plummer, Saskia Reeves, Paul Brown, Des McAleer, Ricky Tomlinson; **D:** Michael Winterbottom; **W:** Frank Cottrell Boyce; **C:** Seamus McGarvey; **M:** John Harle. *FRF*

Butterfly Wings *🎞🎞* *Alas de Mariposa* 1991 The tragedy of a dysfunctional family. Pregnant Carmen longs for a boy to carry on her husband's name but she's afraid to tell her shy six-year-old daughter Ami about the baby. Maybe with reason, since the child's brith triggers a series of nightmarish events. Spanish with subtitles. 105m/C VHS. SP **D:** Juanma Bajo Ulloa. *FCT*

Buy & Cell *🎞½* 1989 (R) A stockbroker attempts to set up a business while serving a prison sentence. An assortment of amusing inmates doesn't help matters much. Fans of Malcolm McDowell will enjoy his performance as the shady warden. 95m/C VHS, LV. Robert Carradine, Michael Winslow, Malcolm McDowell, Ben Vereen, Lise Cutter, Randall "Tex" Cobb, Roddy Piper; **D:** Robert Boris.

Buying Time *🎞* 1989 (R) Two teenagers are arrested when they try to pry their money away from a dishonest bookie, and the police use their connections to solve a drug-related murder. 97m/C VHS, Beta. Dean Stockwell, Jeff Schultz, Michael Rudder, Tony De Santis, Leslie Toth, Laura Cruickshank; **D:** Mitchell Gabourie. *FOX*

Buzzy Rides the Range *🎞🎞* 1940 Average "B" western with a kid saving the day. 60m/C VHS. Robert "Buzzy" Henry, Dave O'Brien. *LOO*

By Dawn's Early Light *🎞🎞* 1989 Made-for-cable-TV thriller about two Air Force pilots who must decide whether or not to drop the bombs that would begin WWIII. 100m/C VHS, Beta, LV. Powers Boothe, Rebecca DeMornay, James Earl Jones, Martin Landau, Rip Torn, Darren McGavin; **D:** Jack Sholder; **M:** Trevor Jones. *HBO*

By Design *🎞* 1982 (R) Two cohabiting women want to have a baby, so they embark on a search for the perfect stud. Not one of Astin's better performances. 90m/C VHS, Beta. CA Patty Duke, Sara Botsford; **D:** Claude Jutra. *NO*

By Love Possessed *🎞🎞½* 1961 Can a seemingly typical, quiet, New England town stay quiet when Lana Turner is your neighbor? Vintage romantic melodrama about an attorney who is drawn into an affair when he realizes his home life is not all it could be. 115m/C VHS. Lana Turner, Efrem Zimbalist Jr., Jason Robards Jr., George Hamilton, Thomas Mitchell; **D:** John Sturges; **C:** Russell Metty; **M:** Elmer Bernstein. *MGM*

By the Blood of Others *🎞🎞🎞* 1973 In a small French town, a psycho holds two women hostage in a farmhouse, and the townspeople try to figure out a solution without getting anyone killed. In French with English subtitles. 90m/C VHS, Beta. FR Mariangela Melato; **D:** Marc Simenon. *FCT*

By the Light of the Silvery Moon *🎞🎞½* 1953 The equally old-fashioned sequel to "On Moonlight Bay" finds Day engaged to MacRae, who's just returned from Army service in WWI. He wants to postpone their marriage until he gets financially secure and the waiting causes some jealous misunderstandings (naturally resolved by movie's end). Based on Booth Tarkington's "Penrod" stories. 🎵By the Light of the Silvery Moon; I'll Forget You; Your Eyes Have Told Me So; Be My Little Baby Bumble Bee; If You Were the Only Girl in the World; Ain't We Got Fun; King Chanticleer. 101m/C VHS, LV. Doris Day, Gordon MacRae, Leon Ames, Billy Gray, Rosemary DeCamp, Mary Wickes, Russell Arms, Maria Palmer; **D:** David Butler; **W:** Robert O'Brien, Irving Elinson; **M:** Max Steiner. *WAR, MVD*

By the Sword *🎞½* 1993 (R) Maximilian Suba (Abraham) is a one-time fencing whiz who has spent the last 25 years in prison for the murder of his mentor during a fencing match. Upon his release, Suba heads back to his old fencing grounds to see what's become of the murdered man's now-grown son and discovers Alexander (Roberts) is as ruthless and ambitious as Suba once was. Incoherent plot leaves both actors and viewers in the dark. **CW:** Vulgar language and some violence. 91m/C VHS, Closed Caption. F. Murray Abraham, Eric Roberts, Mia Sara, Christopher Rydell; **D:** Jeremy Paul Kagan; **W:** John McDonald, James Donadio; **C:** Arthur Albert; **M:** Bill Conti. *COL*

By Way of the Stars *🎞🎞½* 1992 (PG) Young man is pursued by a killer while he searches for his father on the 19th-century Canadian frontier. Made for TV. 150m/C VHS. CA Zachary Bennett, Tantoo Cardinal, Gema Zamprogna, Jan Rubes, Michael Mahonen; **D:** Allan King. *HMK*

Bye-Bye *🎞🎞* 1996 Ismael (Bouajila), 25, and his 14-year-old brother Mouloud (Embarek) are French-born Arabs whose parents have abruptly returned to their Tunisian homeland after a family tragedy. The brothers have travelled from Paris to stay with their uncle (Ahourari) and his family in the port city of Marseilles. Their cousin Rhida (Mammeri), a petty criminal involved with drugs, takes the innocent Mouloud under his wing and hides him away so the boy won't be sent back to his parents. Ismael desperately roams the city trying to find his brother while he also struggles to make a fresh start amidst much societal hostility. French and Arabic with subtitles. 105m/C VHS. FR Sami Bouajila, Ouassini Embarek, Benhaissa Ahourari, Sofiane Mammeri, Jamila Darwich-Farah, Nozha Khouadra; **D:** Karim Dridi; **W:** Karim Dridi; **C:** Jon Mathieson; **M:** Jimmy Oihid, Steve Shehan. *FXL*

Bye Bye Baby *🎞* 1988 (R) Two luscious young women cavort amid lusty Italian men on various Mediterranean beaches. 80m/C VHS, LV. IT Carol Alt, Brigitte Nielsen, Jason Connery, Luca Barbareschi; **D:** Enrico Oldoini; **M:** Manuel De Sica. *PAR*

Bye, Bye, Birdie *🎞🎞🎞* 1963 Energized and sweet film version of the Broadway musical about a teen rock and roll idol (Pearson doing Elvis) coming to a small town to see one of his fans before he leaves for the army. The film that made Ann-Margret a star. 🎵Bye Bye Birdie; The Telephone Hour; How Lovely to be a Woman; Honestly Sincere; One Boy; Put on a Happy Face; Kids; One Last Kiss; A Lot of Livin' to Do. 112m/C VHS, Beta, LV, Letterbox. Dick Van Dyke, Janet Leigh, Ann-Margret, Paul Lynde, Bobby Rydell, Maureen Stapleton, Ed Sullivan, Trudi Ames; **D:** George Sidney; **W:** Irving Brecher; **C:** Joseph Biroc. Nominations: Academy Awards '63: Best Adapted Score, Best Sound. *COL*

Bye Bye Blues *🎞🎞½* 1989 (PG) The lives of the Cooper family are disrupted when the husband is called to service during WWII and is then taken prisoner by the Japanese. In need of money, wife Daisy (Jenkins) joins a local swing band and begins charming all who watch her, especially the band's trombone player (Reilly). A sweet-spirited tale of love, loyalty, and the search for inner strength. Jenkins gives a strong performance as the shy wife who becomes an independent woman during her husband's absence. 110m/C VHS. CA Rebecca Jenkins, Michael Ontkean, Luke Reilly, Stuart Margolin, Robyn Stevan, Kate Reid, Wayne Robson; **D:** Anne Wheeler; **W:** Anne Wheeler; **M:** George Blondheim. Genie Awards '90: Best Actress (Jenkins), Best Supporting Actress (Stevan). *MNC*

Bye Bye Brazil *🎞🎞½* 1979 A changing Brazil is seen through the eyes of four wandering gypsy minstrels participating in a tent show traveling throughout the country. Lots of Brazilian charm. In Portuguese with English subtitles. 115m/C VHS, Beta, LV. BR Jose Wilker, Betty Faria, Fabio Junior, Zaira Zambello; **D:** Carlos Diegues; **W:** Carlos Diegues. *FXL, TPV*

Bye Bye, Love *🎞🎞½* 1994 (PG-13) Forty-eight hours in the lives of three divorced buddies starts at the local Mickey D's for the biweekly exchange of their kids. The dads don't offer any surprises: Donny (Reiser) still loves his ex, Vic (Quaid) hates his, and Dave (Modine) loves anything in a skirt. Sometimes witty, but just as often sadly poignant, the plot is as shallow as a TV sitcom, with an easy answer for every difficult question about divorce. The three leads are likeable enough, but Garofalo is the gem in an otherwise dull flick. She looks like she's having a blast, stealing scenes with abandon as Vic's blind date from hell. **CW:** Brief language; sensuality. 107m/C

VHS, LV, Closed Caption. Matthew Modine, Randy Quaid, Paul Reiser, Rob Reiner, Janeane Garofalo, Ed Flanders, Lindsay Crouse, James Whitworth, Maria Pitillo; **D:** Sam Weisman; **W:** Gary David Goldberg, Brad Hall; **M:** J.A.C. Redford. FXV

The C-Man 🎬🎬 1949 Customs agent Jagger finds work isn't so dull after all. Murder and theft on an international scale make for a busy week as he follows jewel smugglers from Paris to New York. Docu-style though routine crime story. 75m/B VHS. Dean Jagger, John Carradine, Harry Landers, Rene Paul; **D:** Joseph Lerner. SNC

Cabaret 🎬🎬🎬½ 1972 (PG) Hitler is rising to power, racism and anti-Semitism are growing, and the best place to hide from it all is the cabaret. With dancing girls, androgynous master of ceremonies Grey and American expatriate and singer Minnelli, you can laugh and drink and pretend tomorrow will never come. Minnelli does just that. Face to face with the increasing horrors of Nazism, she persists in the belief that the "show must go on." Based on the John Kander's hit Broadway musical (taken from the Christopher Isherwood stories), the film is impressive, with excellent direction and cinematography. ♫Cabaret; Wilkommen; Mein Herr; Maybe This Time; Two Ladies; Money, Money; Hieraten; Tomorrow Belongs to Me; If You Could See Her. 128m/C VHS, Beta, LV, Closed Caption. Liza Minnelli, Joel Grey, Michael York, Marisa Berenson; **D:** Bob Fosse; **W:** Jay Presson Allen; **C:** Geoffrey Unsworth; **M:** Ralph Burns. Academy Awards '72: Best Actress (Minnelli), Best Art Direction/Set Decoration, Best Cinematography, Best Director (Fosse), Best Film Editing, Best Sound, Best Supporting Actor (Grey), Original Song Score and/or Adaptation; British Academy Awards '72: Best Actress, Best Director (Fosse), Best Film; Golden Globe Awards '73: Best Actress—Musical/Comedy (Minnelli), Best Film—Musical/Comedy, Best Supporting Actor (Grey); National Board of Review Awards '72: Best Director (Fosse), Best Supporting Actor (Grey), Best Supporting Actress (Berenson), National Film Registry '95; National Society of Film Critics Awards '72: Best Supporting Actor (Grey); Writers Guild of America '72: Best Adapted Screenplay; Nominations: Academy Awards '72: Best Adapted Screenplay, Best Picture. FOX, BTV, CCB

Cabeza de Vaca 🎬🎬🎬 1990 (R) In 1528, a Spanish expedition shipwrecks in unknown territory off the Florida coast. Only survivor Cabeza de Vaca is captured by the Iguase Indian tribe and made a slave to their shaman. He's later freed, but leaves with respect for their culture. Spanish soldiers find him and want his help in capturing the natives, but he is outraged by their cruelty and must confront his own people. Strong visual style easily brings the audience deeply into this uncharted world. Based on Cabeza de Vaca's book "Naufragios." Director Echevarria's feature film debut. Spanish and Indian with subtitles. **CW:** Nudity and violence. 111m/C VHS. MX SP Juan Diego, Daniel Gimenez Cacho, Roberto Sosa, Carlos Castanon, Gerardo Villarreal, Roberto Cobo, Jose Flores, Ramon Barragan; **D:** Nicolas Echevarria; **W:** Guillermo Sheridan, Nicolas Echevarria; **M:** Mario Lavista. NHO, FCT

Cabin Boy woof! 1994 (PG-13) Obnoxious "fancy lad" Elliott mistakenly boards the wrong boat and becomes the new cabin boy for a ridiculous bunch of mean, smelly sailors. Fish out of water saga is so bad it's—bad, a blundering attempt at parody that's just plain stupid. Surprisingly produced by Tim Burton, this effort will disappoint even diehard fans. Look for Chris' real life dad Bob as the lad's dad; good friend Letterman appears briefly as nasty "Old Salt," but uses the alias Earl Hofert in the final credits. As usual, the acerbic Letterman gets the best line, "Man, oh, man do I hate them fancy lads." We know how you feel, Dave. **CW:** Strong language and sexual humor. 80m/C VHS, LV, Closed Caption. Chris Elliott, Ann Magnuson, Ritch Brinkley, James Gammon, Brian Doyle-Murray, Russ Tamblyn, Brion James, Ricki Lake, Bob Elliott; **Cameos:** David Letterman; **D:** Adam Resnick; **W:** Adam Resnick; **M:** Steve Bartek. TOU

The Cabin in the Cotton 🎬🎬½ 1932 Davis stars as a rich, ruthless Southern belle in this dated melodrama about sharecroppers. Barthelmess is cast as a poor sharecropper who is almost brought to ruin when he falls for the sexy Southern vamp. Contains Davis's most famous line, "Ah'd love t'kiss you, but ah jes washed mah hair." 77m/B VHS, Closed Caption. Bette Davis, Richard Barthelmess, Dorothy Jordan, Henry B. Walthall, Tully Marshall; **D:** Michael Curtiz; **W:** Paul Green. MGM

Cabin in the Sky 🎬🎬🎬 1943 A poor woman fights to keep her husband's soul out of the devil's clutches. Based on a Broadway show and featuring an all-Black cast. Lively dance numbers and a musical score with contributions from Duke Ellington. Minnelli's first feature film. ♫Cabin in the Sky; Happiness Is Just a Thing Called Joe; Taking a Chance on Love; Life's Full of Consequence; Li'l Black Sheep; Shine; Honey in the Honeycomb. 99m/C VHS, Beta, LV. Ethel Waters, Eddie Anderson, Lena Horne, Rex Ingram, Louis Armstrong, Duke Ellington; **D:** Vincente Minnelli; **M:** Duke Ellington, Harold Arlen, E.Y. Harburg, George Bassman. Nominations: Academy Awards '43: Best Song ("Happiness Is a Thing Called Joe"). MGM, MLB, FHE

The Cabinet of Dr. Caligari 🎬🎬🎬🎬 Das Cabinet des Dr. Caligari 1919 A pioneering film in the most extreme expressionistic style about a hypnotist in a carnival and a girl-snatching somnambulist. Highly influential in its approach to lighting, composition, design and acting. Much imitated. Silent. 92m/B VHS, Beta, LV. GE Conrad Veidt, Werner Krauss, Lil Dagover, Friedrich Feher, Hans von Twardowski, Rudolf Klein-Rogge, Rudolf Lettinger; **D:** Robert Wiene; **W:** Carl Mayer, Hans Janowitz; **C:** Willy Hameister. KIV, REP, MRV

Cabiria 🎬🎬½ 1914 The pioneering Italian epic about a Roman and a slave girl having a love affair in Rome during the Second Punic War. Immense sets and set-pieces; an important influence on Griffith and DeMille. Silent. 123m/B VHS, Beta, 8mm. IT **D:** Giovanni Pastrone. KIV, FCT

The Cable Guy 🎬🎬½ 1996 (PG-13) Carrey's first $20 million paycheck finds cable subscriber Broderick in for a comedic nightmare when he accepts the offer of free movie channels. The overeager installer (Carrey, naturally) turns his life upside down. A little darker humor than Carrey fans may be used to, and don't expect any bodily ventriloquism. Carrey (did we mention he's in it?) gets to act with real life people. Director Stiller does a nice job of reining in his more manic impulses when necessary. Broderick holds his own as the reluctant pal. Original scripter Holtz won a Writer's Guild arbitration for sole writing credit from producer-writer Judd Apatow. **CW:** Dark thematic elements and crude humor. 95m/C VHS, LV, 8mm, Closed Caption, DVD. Jim Carrey, Matthew Broderick, Leslie Mann, George Segal, Diane Baker, Jack Black, Janeane Garofalo, Andy Dick, Charles Napier; **D:** Ben Stiller; **W:** Judd Apatow, Lou Holtz Jr.; **C:** Robert Brinkmann; **M:** John Ottman. MTV Movie Awards '97: Best Villain (Carrey), Best Comedic Performance (Carrey); Nominations: MTV Movie Awards '97: Best Fight (Jim Carrey/Matthew Broderick). COL

Cabo Blanco 🎬🎬 1981 (R) A bartender and a variety of other characters, including an ex-Nazi and a French woman searching for her lover, assemble in Peru after WWII. Nazi Robards controls police chief Rey, while American Bronson runs the local watering hole and eyes French woman Sanda. Hey, this sounds familiar. Everyone shares a common interest: finding a missing treasure of gold, lost in a ship wreck. Remaking "Casablanca" via "The Treasure of Sierra Madre" is never easy. 87m/C VHS, Beta. Charles Bronson, Jason Robards Jr., Dominique Sanda, Fernando Rey, Gilbert Roland, Simon MacCorkindale; **D:** J. Lee Thompson; **M:** Jerry Goldsmith.

Cactus 🎬🎬½ 1986 Melodrama about a young French woman, separated from her husband, who faces the reality of losing her sight after a car accident. She experiences a growing relationship with a blind man and contemplates the thought of risky surgery which may improve her eyesight or cause complete blindness. Countering all that blindness and tangled romance is a camera that pans lush Australian landscapes and humorously focuses on the small telling details of daily life. 95m/C VHS, Beta. AU Isabelle Huppert, Robert Menzies, Monica Maughan, Sheila Florence, Norman Kaye, Banduk Marika; **D:** Paul Cox; **W:** Norman Kaye, Paul Cox, Bob Ellis; **M:** Giovanni Pergolese, Yannis Markopolous, Elsa Davis. ORI

Cactus Flower 🎬🎬 1969 (PG) Good cast doesn't quite suffice to make this adaptation of a Broadway hit work. A middle-aged bachelor dentist gets involved with a kookie mistress, refusing to admit his real love for his prim and proper receptionist. Hawn's big leap to stardom. 103m/C VHS, Beta, LV. Walter Matthau, Goldie Hawn, Ingrid Bergman, Jack Weston, Rick Lenz; **D:** Gene Saks; **C:** Charles B(ryant) Lang; **M:** Quincy Jones. Academy Awards '69: Best Supporting Actress (Hawn); Golden Globe Awards '70: Best Supporting Actress (Hawn). COL

Cactus in the Snow 🎬½ 1972 A virginal Army private serving during the Vietnam War era tries to find sex on a 72-hour leave and instead discovers love. Some guys have all the luck. Melodrama never grabs where it ought to. 90m/C VHS, Beta, LV. Richard Thomas, Mary Layne, Lucille Benson; **D:** Martin Zweiback. NO

Caddie 🎬🎬½ 1976 Based on an autobiographical story of a woman who leaves her unfaithful husband in 1930s Australia. Struggling to raise her two children, she works as a waitress in a bar where she finds romance with one of the regulars. Average script bolstered by Morse's performance. 107m/C VHS, Beta. AU Helen Morse, Jack Thompson, Takis Emmanuel, Jacki Weaver; **D:** Donald Crombie; **W:** Joan Long; **C:** Peter James; **M:** Patrick Flynn. HBO

The Caddy 🎬🎬 1953 Lewis plays frantic caddy prone to slapstick against Martin's smooth professional golfer with a bent toward singing. Mostly a series of Martin and Lewis sketches that frequently land in the rough. Introduces several songs, including a classic Martin and Lewis rendition of "That's Amore." Look for cameos by a host of professional golfers. 95m/C VHS, Beta. Dean Martin, Jerry Lewis, Donna Reed, Barbara Bates, Joseph Calleia, Marshall Thompson, Fred Clark; **Cameos:** Ben Hogan, Sam Snead, Byron Nelson, Julius Boros, Jimmy Thomson, Harry E. Cooper; **D:** Norman Taurog; **W:** Danny Arnold. Nominations: Academy Awards '53: Best Song ("That's Amore"). PAR

Caddyshack 🎬🎬🎬½ 1980 (R) Inspired performances by Murray and Dangerfield drive this sublimely moronic comedy onto the green. The action takes place at Bushwood Country Club, where caddy O'Keefe is bucking to win the club's college scholarship. Characters involved in various sophomoric set pieces include obnoxious club president Knight, a playboy who is too laid back to keep his score (Chase), a loud, vulgar, and extremely rich golfer (Dangerfield), and Murray as a filthy gopher-hunting groundskeeper. Occasional dry moments are followed by scenes of pure (and tasteless) anarchy, so watch with someone immature. Does for golf what "Major League" tried to do for baseball. 99m/C VHS, Beta, LV, DVD. Chevy Chase, Rodney Dangerfield, Ted Knight, Michael O'Keefe, Bill Murray, Sarah Holcomb, Brian Doyle-Murray; **D:** Harold Ramis; **W:** Brian Doyle-Murray, Doug Kenney, Harold Ramis. WAR

Caddyshack 2 🎬½ 1988 (PG) Obligatory sequel to "Caddyshack," minus Bill Murray who wisely avoided further encroachment of gopher holes and director Ramis who opted for the screenwriting chore. Mason is the star of the show as a crude self-made millionaire who tangles with the snobs at the country club. Although it occasionally earns a side-splitting chuckle, "Shack 2" has significantly fewer guffaws than the original, proving once again that funny guys are always undone by lousy scripts and weak direction. **103m/C VHS, Beta, LV, 8mm, Closed Caption.** Jackie Mason, Chevy Chase, Dan Aykroyd, Dyan Cannon, Robert Stack, Dina Merrill, Randy Quaid, Jessica Lundy, Jonathan Silverman, Chynna Phillips; **D:** Allan Arkush; **W:** Harold Ramis, Peter Torokvei; **C:** Harry Stradling Jr.; **M:** Ira Newborn. Golden Raspberry Awards '88: Worst Supporting Actor (Aykroyd), Worst Song ("Jack Fresh"). **WAR**

Cadence 🎬🎬 1989 (PG-13) The directorial debut of actor Martin Sheen, this fitful melodrama stars son Charlie as an unruly trooper on a 1960s army base. Placed in an all-black stockade for punishment, he bonds with his brother prisoners by defying the hardcase sergeant (played by Sheen the elder). Characters and situations are intriguing but not rendered effectively. Based on the novel "Count a Lonely Cadence" by Gordon Weaver. **97m/C VHS, LV, Closed Caption.** Charlie Sheen, Martin Sheen, Laurence "Larry" Fishburne, Michael Beach, Ramon Estevez; **D:** Martin Sheen; **M:** Georges Delerue. **REP**

Cadillac Girls 🎬½ 1993 Page is a self-destructive teenager who is arrested for car theft. To avoid jail, Page is placed in her single mom's custody and moves to her family's straitlaced hometown in Nova Scotia. Mom isn't exactly good at parenting and Page's adolescent anger extends to putting the moves on mom's potential new beau. **99m/C VHS.** Jennifer Dale, Gregory Harrison, Mia Kirshner. Genie Awards '93: Best Score. **MNC**

Cadillac Man 🎬🎬 1990 Williams is the quintessential low-life car salesman in this rather disjointed comedy. A lesser comedic talent might have stalled and been abandoned, but Williams manages to drive away despite the flat script and direction. One storyline follows his attempt to sell 12 cars in 12 days or lose his job, while another follows his confrontation with a gun-toting, mad-as-hell cuckolded husband. Williams and Robbins are often close to being funny in a hyperkinetic way, but the situations are dumb enough to rob most of the scenes of their comedy. Watch for a movie-stealing bit by the spunky waitress at the local Chinese restaurant. **95m/C VHS, Beta, LV, Closed Caption.** Robin Williams, Tim Robbins, Pamela Reed, Fran Drescher, Zack Norman, Annabella Sciorra, Lori Petty, Paul Guilfoyle; **D:** Roger Donaldson; **W:** Ken Friedman. **ORI**

Cadillac Ranch 🎬🎬½ 1996 (R) CJ (Amis), Frances (Feeney), and Mary Katharine (Humphrey) Crowley are three squabbling Texas sisters who have reunited to celebrate Mary K.'s upcoming marriage. CJ works in a strip club owned by greedy ex-Texas Ranger Wood (Lloyd), who sent their long-gone daddy, Travis (Metzler), to prison for a heist Wood was involved in. When CJ gets fired, the threesome steal a key from Wood that will supposedly access money from the heist and the vengeful Wood goes after them. **CW:** Language and some nudity. **104m/C VHS.** Suzy Amis, Renee Humphrey, Caroleen Feeney, Christopher Lloyd, Jim Metzler, Linden Ashby; **D:** Lisa Gottlieb; **W:** Jennifer Cecil; **C:** Bruce Douglas Johnson; **M:** Christopher Tyng. **BMG**

Caesar and Cleopatra 🎬🎬½ 1946 Based on the classic George Bernard Shaw play. Caesar meets the beautiful Cleopatra in ancient Egypt and helps her gain control of her life. Remains surprisingly true to Shaw's adaptation, unlike many other historical films of the same era. **135m/C VHS, Beta. GB** Claude Rains, Vivien Leigh, Stewart Granger, Flora Robson, Francis L. Sullivan, Cecil Parker; **D:** Gabriel Pascal; **C:** Robert Krasker. Nominations: Academy Awards '46: Best Interior Decoration. **NO**

Cafe au Lait 🎬🎬🎬 *Metisse* 1994 Actor/director/writer Kassovitz scores in his debut feature about an interracial menage a trois. Beautiful mulatto Lola (Mauduech) is pregnant but she's not sure by which of her two contrasting lovers (who don't yet know about each other). It could be white, Jewish, easy-going bicycle messenger Felix (Kassovitz) or stuffy, wealthy, black Moslem student Jamal (Kounde). Both men desire the fatherhood role and both move in with Lola to share responsibility. This is not without complications.

Generally light and frothy without ignoring racial tensions. French with subtitles. **94m/C VHS. FR** Mathieu Kassovitz, Julie Mauduech, Hubert Kounde, Vincent Cassel, Tadek Lokcinski, Jany Holt; **D:** Mathieu Kassovitz; **W:** Mathieu Kassovitz; **C:** Pierre Aim; **M:** Marie Daulne, Jean-Louis Daulne. **NYF**

Cafe Express 🎬🎬½ 1983 A con artist (he sells coffee illegally aboard an Italian train) stays one step ahead of the law as he raises money to help his ailing son. As in "Bread and Chocolate," Manfredi is again the put-upon working class hero comedically attempting to find a better way of life in this bittersweet tale. **90m/C VHS, Beta. IT** Nino Manfredi, Gigi Reder, Adolfo Celi, Vittorio Mezzogiorno; **D:** Nanni Loy. **NO**

Cafe Romeo 🎬🎬 1991 (R) Tale of 20-something friendships forged in the neighborhood coffeehouse of a heavily Italian community. Lia (Stewart) is a waitress who dreams of becoming a fashion designer, but her marriage to a small time hood holds her back. Crombie, her cousin by marriage, is a dental student confused about his future, but very much in love with Lia. Quiet movie boasts average script that's helped along by strong performances. Originally broadcast on Canadian TV. **CW:** Language. **93m/C VHS, LV, Closed Caption. CA** Catherine Mary Stewart, Jonathan Crombie; **D:** Rex Bromfield. **REP**

Cafe Society 🎬🎬½ 1997 (R) The fictional nightclub El Casbah is the setting for director De Felitta's debut take on a 1952 New York prostitution scandal. Wealthy young playboy Mickey Jelke (Whaley) prefers to mix with lowlifes rather than high society. Newcomer Jack Kale (Gallagher) is working the scene and turns out to be an undercover cop investigating a prostitution ring operating out of the clubs. Jack befriends both Mickey and his latest girlfriend, in-the-know Patricia Ward (Boyle), who's not above selling her favors. Then patsy Jelke gets indicted as a pimp and all cafe society's tawdriness is exposed. **CW:** Strong sexuality and some language. **104m/C VHS, Closed Caption.** Peter Gallagher, Frank Whaley, Lara Flynn Boyle, John Spencer, Anna Thomson, David Patrick Kelly, Paul Guilfoyle; **D:** Raymond De Felitta; **W:** Raymond De Felitta; **C:** Mike Mayers; **M:** Chris Guardino. **COL**

The Cage 🎬 1989 (R) Gangsters enlist a brain-damaged Vietnam vet played by Ferrigno to participate in illegal "cage fights," enclosed wrestling matches fought to the death. Crude and annoying. **101m/C VHS, Beta, LV, Closed Caption.** Lou Ferrigno, Reb Brown, Michael Dante, Mike Moroff, Marilyn Tokuda, James Shigeta, Al Ruscio; **D:** Hugh Kelley. **ORI**

The Cage 🎬🎬🎬 1990 Sent to prison for murdering his girlfriend, Jive has no idea what the pen has in store for him. The inmates stage a mock trial, the defendant is found guilty and the sentence is too horrible to imagine. From a stage play by the San Quentin Drama Workshop and co-starring Hayes, author of "Midnight Express." **90m/C VHS, Beta.** Rick Cluchey, William Hayes; **D:** Rick Cluchey; **W:** Rick Cluchey. **NO**

Cage 2: The Arena of Death 🎬½ 1994 (R) Billy Thomas (Ferrigno) is kidnapped by a vicious mobster and forced to battle martial arts experts in a steel cage battle to the death. But his best friend (Brown) plans to infiltrate the show and put a stop to the carnage. **CW:** Violence; brief nudity; language. **94m/C VHS.** Lou Ferrigno, Reb Brown; **D:** Lang Elliott. **PAR**

Caged Fear 🎬½ 1992 (R) Young Krissie (Cloke) is mistakenly put behind bars in a brutal, high-security prison for a shootout caused by her outlaw husband Tommy (Keith) during their honeymoon. Tommy comes up with an outrageous scheme to rescue her. Not quite as bad as it sounds, but close. **CW:** Language, violence, and sexuality. **94m/C VHS, LV.** David Keith, Deborah May, Ray Sharkey, Loretta Devine, Karen Black, Kristen Cloke; **D:** Bobby Houston; **W:** Bobby Houston. **NLC**

Caged Fury 🎬 1980 (R) American women being held captive in Southeast Asia are brainwashed into becoming walking time bombs. Yes, that dame's gonna blow. Made in the Philippines with the best of intentions. **90m/C VHS, Beta. PH** Bernadette Williams, Taaffe O'Connell, Jennifer Laine; **D:** Cirio H. Santiago. **NO**

Caged Fury 🎬 1990 Two Los Angeles women allegedly commit sexual crimes and are sent to prison. Cheap, exploitive women's prison rehash. **85m/C VHS, Beta, LV.** Erik Estrada, Richie Barathy, Roxanna Michaels, Paul Smith, James Hong, Greg Cummins; **D:** Bill Milling. **COL**

Caged Hearts 🎬 1995 (R) Chicks-behind-bars flick finds Kate (Genzel) and Sharon (McClure) framed for murder by a shady organization called "The Shield." Cliches abound. **CW:** Nudity; sexuality; violence; language. **87m/C VHS.** Tane McClure, Carrie Genzel, Taylor Leigh, Nick Wilder; **D:** Henri Charr. **PMH**

Caged Heat 🎬🎬 *Renegade Girls; Caged Females* 1974 (R) Low-budget babes-behind-bars film touted as the best sexploitation film of the day. Demme's directorial debut is a genre-altering installment in Roger Corman's formulaic cellblock Cinderella cycle. Recycled plot—innocent woman is put behind bars, where she loses some of her innocence—boasts an updated treatment. These babes may wear hot pants and gratuitously bare their midriffs, but they're not brainless bimbos. They're strong individuals who work together to liberate themselves. Reached cult status. Cult diva Steele returned to the big screen after six years to play the wheelchair-ridden prison warden, written specifically for her. **83m/C VHS, LV.** Juanita Brown, Erica Gavin, Roberta Collins, Barbara Steele, Ella Reid, Cheryl "Rainbeaux" Smith; **D:** Jonathan Demme; **W:** Jonathan Demme.

Caged Heat 2: Stripped of Freedom 🎬½ 1994 (R) Women-in-prison formula with a princess thrown into the pen following a political coup. CIA agent is sent undercover as an inmate to bust her out. Usual sadistic guards, rape, and revenge scenes. From Roger Corman's direct-to-video factory. **CW:** Language, nudity, violence, and sexual situations. **84m/C VHS, LV.** Jewel Shepard, Chanel Akiko Hirai, Pamella D'Pella, Vic Diaz; **D:** Cirio H. Santiago. **NHO**

Caged Heat 3000 🎬 1995 (R) Yes, it's a sci-fi chicks-in-prison movie! Innocent Kira Murphy (Leigh) is wrongly condemned to an underground prison located 45 lightyears from Earth where there are lots of racial tensions and evil prison officials. Prerequisite shower scenes and sadistic guards also add to the standard exploitation. **84m/C VHS.** Cassandra Leigh, Kena Land, Debra Beatty; **D:** Cirio H. Santiago; **W:** Paul Ziller. **NHO**

Caged in Paradiso 🎬½ 1989 (R) A convicted criminal and his wife are dumped onto a remote prisoner's isle to live out their lives. When Cara loses contact with her husband, she must fend for herself. Survival tale boringly told. **90m/C VHS, Beta, LV.** Irene Cara; **D:** Michael Snyder. **THV, IME**

Caged Terror woof! 1972 Two urbanites hit the countryside for a weekend and meet a band of crazy rapists who ravage the wife and set the husband raging with bloodthirsty revenge. Squalid stroll through the ruins. **76m/C VHS, Beta.** Percy Harkness, Elizabeth Suzuki, Leon Morenzie.

Caged Women 🎬 *Women's Penitentiary 4* 1984 (R) Undercover journalist enters a women's prison and gets the usual eyeful. **97m/C VHS, Beta. FR IT** Laura Gemser, Gabriele Tinti, Lorraine De Selle, Maria Romano; **D:** Vincent Dawn. **VES, ART, DMP**

Cahill: United States Marshal 🎬🎬 1973 (PG) The aging Duke in one of his lesser moments, portraying a marshal who comes to the aid of his sons. The boys are mixed up with a gang of outlaws, proving that no matter how good a parent you are, sometimes the kids just lean toward the wayward. Turns out, though, that the boys harbor a grudge against the old man due to years of workaholic neglect. Will Duke see the error of his ways and reconcile with the delinquent boys? Will he catch the outlaw leader? Will he go on to star in other Duke vehicles? **103m/C VHS, Beta, LV, Letterbox.** John Wayne, Gary Grimes, George Kennedy, Neville Brand, Marie Windsor, Harry Carey Jr.; **D:** Andrew V. McLaglen; **M:** Elmer Bernstein. WAR, TLF

The Caine Mutiny 🏆🏆🏆🏆 1954 A group of naval officers revolt against a captain they consider mentally unfit. Bogart is masterful as Captain Queeg, obsessed with cleanliness while onboard and later a study in mental meltdown during the court-martial of a crew member who participated in the mutiny. Based on the Pulitzer-winning novel by Herman Wouk, the drama takes a close look at the pressure-filled life aboard ship during WWII. **125m/C VHS, Beta, LV, 8mm, Closed Caption, DVD.** Humphrey Bogart, Jose Ferrer, Van Johnson, Fred MacMurray, Lee Marvin, Claude Akins, E.G. Marshall, Robert Francis, May Wynn, Tom Tully; **D:** Edward Dmytryk; **W:** Stanley Roberts; **M:** Max Steiner. Nominations: Academy Awards '54: Best Actor (Bogart), Best Film Editing, Best Picture, Best Screenplay, Best Sound, Best Supporting Actor (Tully), Best Original Dramatic/Comedy Score. COL, HMV

The Caine Mutiny Court Martial 🏆🏆🏆 1988 (PG) A young lieutenant is up for a court-martial after taking control of the U.S.S. Caine in the midst of a typhoon. In order to save him, his lawyer must discredit the paranoid Commander Queeg. As the events of the mutiny unfold, it becomes clear that Queeg's obsession with discipline had become a threat to everyone aboard. Good performances, particularly by Bogosian as the lawyer. Based on the Pulitzer Prize-winning novel by Herman Wouk. Made for television. **100m/C VHS, LV, Closed Caption.** Jeff Daniels, Eric Bogosian, Brad Davis, Peter Gallagher, Michael Murphy, Kevin J. O'Connor, Daniel H. Jenkins; **D:** Robert Altman. THV

Cain's Cutthroats 🏆 Cain's Way; The Blood Seekers 1971 (R) A former Confederate army captain and a bounty hunting preacher team up to settle the score with soldiers on a gang-raping, murdering spree. **87m/C VHS, Beta.** Scott Brady, John Carradine, Robert Dix.

Cairo 🏆🏆 1942 War correspondent Young lands in Cairo where he is supposed to pass along classified information to a Nazi spy posing as a Brit. He meets and falls in love with American movie queen thought to be enemy agent (MacDonald) and a race across the desert follows when Young is trapped in a pyramid. Catchy tunes can't save this cheesy WWII spy spoof that marked the end of MacDonald's MGM contract. **101m/B VHS.** Jeanette MacDonald, Robert Young, Ethel Waters, Reginald Owen, Grant Mitchell, Lionel Atwill, Eduardo Ciannelli, Mitchell Lewis; **D:** Woodbridge S. Van Dyke; **W:** John McClain; **M:** Herbert Stothart. MGM

Cal 🏆🏆🏆 1984 (R) Cal (Lynch), a young Catholic man, is reluctantly recruited into the Irish Republican Army. He falls in love with the older Marcella (Mirren), the widow of a Protestant policeman whom he helped kill while acting as the getaway driver for his fellow Republicans. Thoughtful and tragic, with excellent performances; set in Northern Ireland. **104m/C VHS, Beta, LV.** IR Helen Mirren, John Lynch, Donal McCann, Kitty Gibson, Ray McAnally, John Kavanagh; **D:** Pat O'Connor; **W:** Bernard MacLaverty; **M:** Mark Knopfler. Cannes Film Festival '84: Best Actress (Mirren). WAR, FCT

Calamity Jane 🏆🏆🏆 1953 In one of her best Warner musicals, Day stars as the rip-snortin', gun-totin' Calamity Jane of Western lore, in an on-again, off-again romance with Wild Bill Hickok. 🎵Secret Love; Just Blew in From the Windy City; The Black Hills of Dakota; The Deadwood Stage (Whip-Crack-Away!). **101m/C VHS, Beta, LV.** Doris Day, Howard Keel, Allyn Ann McLerie; **D:** David Butler; **M:** Sammy Fain, Paul Francis Webster. Academy Awards '53: Best Song ("Secret Love"); Nominations:

Academy Awards '53: Best Sound, Scoring of a Musical. WAR, FCT

Calamity Jane 🏆🏆½ 1982 A made-for-television biography of the famous lady crack shot. Alexander is cast as the tough-as-nails woman who considered herself on a par with any man. **96m/C VHS, Beta.** Jane Alexander, Frederic Forrest, Ken Kercheval, Talia Balsam, David Hemmings; **D:** James Goldstone. FOX

Calendar 🏆🏆🏆 1993 A Canadian photographer (Egoyan) is hired to take pictures of ancient Armenian churches for a calendar. His wife (Egoyan's real-life spouse Khanjian) accompanies him, serving as a translator, and they hire a driver (Adamian) who turns out to be an architectural expert. Told in flashback, the film gradually reveals a romantic triangle—with the photographer becoming so caught up in his work that he fails to realize his wife, increasingly drawn to her ethnic heritage, and their driver are having an affair. This romantic puzzle also includes the photographer, having returned to Canada wifeless and apparently seeking a replacement, having dinner with a series of women he's meet through the personals. In English and Armenian. **78m/C VHS.** CA Atom Egoyan, Arsinee Khanjian, Ashot Adamian; **D:** Atom Egoyan; **W:** Atom Egoyan; **M:** Norayr Kasper. KIV

Calendar Girl 🏆🏆½ 1993 (PG-13) In 1962 three high-school best friends borrow a convertible and travel from their Nevada homes to Hollywood to meet their pinup idol, Marilyn Monroe. Roy's (Priestley) a rebel, Ned's (Olds, in his film debut) sensitive, and Scott's (O'Connell) just a nice guy. They stay with Roy's Uncle Harvey (Pantoliano), an aspiring actor, and work to meet their dream girl. Which they finally do, in a notably weak sequence which fits in with this notably uninspired film. The three actors at least have enough comradery to make realistic buddies—one of the few true touches in the film. **CW:** Language, nudity, and drug content. **86m/C VHS, LV, 8mm, Closed Caption.** Jason Priestley, Gabriel Olds, Jerry O'Connell, Joe Pantoliano, Stephen Tobolowsky, Kurt Fuller, Steve Railsback, Emily Warfield, Stephanie Anderson; **Cameos:** Chubby Checker; **D:** John Whitesell; **W:** Paul Shapiro; **M:** Hans Zimmer. COL

Calendar Girl Murders 🏆🏆½ 1984 Minor mystery about the murder of some girlie magazine pinups. Made for television. **104m/C VHS.** Robert Culp, Tom Skerritt, Barbara Parkins, Sharon Stone; **D:** William A. Graham; **M:** Brad Fiedel.

California Casanova woof! 1989 (R) Mirthless, semi-musical farce about a nerdy stagehand learning to be a great lover to win a beautiful singer's heart who's being blackmailed by a cruel gangster. Nice cast; nobody's home. **CW:** Sensuality. **94m/C VHS.** Jerry Orbach, Audrey Landers, Tyrone Power Jr., Bryan Genesse, Ken Kercheval, Ted Davis, Joyce Blair; **D:** Nathaniel Christian; **W:** Nathaniel Christian.

California Dreaming 🏆🏆 1979 (R) Nerdy young man heads west to California where he tries to fit in with the local beach crowd. Reminiscent of the popular beach movies of the '60s. **93m/ C VHS, Beta.** Dennis Christopher, Tanya Roberts, Glynnis O'Connor, John Calvin, Seymour Cassel; **D:** John Hancock. VES, ART

California Girls 🏆 1984 Radio station stages a beauty contest and three sexy ladies prove to be tough competition. Features women in little swimsuits, minimal plot, and a soundtrack by the Police, Kool & the Gang, Blondie, Queen, and 10cc. **83m/C VHS, Beta.** Al Music, Mary McKinley, Alicia Allen, Lantz Douglas, Barbara Parks; **D:** Rick Wallace; **C:** Gil Hubbs. NO

California Gold Rush 🏆🏆 1981 Hays portrays young aspiring writer, Bret Harte, who, in search of adventure in 1849, arrives in Sutter's Fort and takes on a job at the local sawmill. When gold is found, Sutter's Fort is soon overrun with fortune hunters whose greed, violence and corruption threaten to tear apart the peaceful com-

munity. Made for television. 100m/C VHS, Beta. Robert Hays, John Dehner, Dan Haggerty, Ken Curtis; **D:** Jack B. Hively. NO

California Joe 🏆 1943 California is being eyed by Confederate sympathizers and also by their leader, who wants it for his own plans. Enter California Joe, a Union officer in disguise, who will save the day. Standard western. **55m/B VHS, Beta.** Donald (Don "Red") Barry, Lynn Merrick, Helen Talbot. DVT

California Straight Ahead 🏆🏆 1925 Denny—whose niche in the '20s was silent action comedies, and who had teamed with director Pollard earlier in the decade to produce "The Leatherpushers" series—stars in this silent actioner which features a cross-country road trip, zoo animals-on-a-rampage, and a car-racing conclusion (sounds like an action formula ahead of its time). Audiences didn't revel until the talkies that the All-American manly man was in fact played by a Brit. For those who revel in trivia, Denny appeared in the 1961 "Batman." **77m/B VHS, Beta.** Reginald Denny, Gertrude Olmsted, Tom Wilson, Lucille Ward, John Steppling; **D:** Harry Pollard. GPV, FCT

California Suite 🏆🏆🏆 1978 (PG) The posh Beverly Hills Hotel is the setting for four unrelated Neil Simon skits, ranging from a battling husband and wife to feuding friends. Simonized dialogue is crisp and funny. **103m/C VHS, Beta, LV.** Alan Alda, Michael Caine, Bill Cosby, Jane Fonda, Walter Matthau, Richard Pryor, Maggie Smith, Elaine May; **D:** Herbert Ross; **W:** Neil Simon; **M:** Claude Bolling. Academy Awards '78: Best Supporting Actress (Smith); Golden Globe Awards '79: Best Actress—Musical/Comedy (Smith); Nominations: Academy Awards '78: Best Adapted Screenplay, Best Art Direction/Set Decoration. COL

Caligari's Cure 🏆🏆🏆 1982 Palazzolo's first film is a satiric, non-narrative stab at his Catholic upbringing via German expressionism and modern performance art. **70m/C VHS, Beta. D:** Tom Palazzolo. FCT

Caligula woof! 1980 Infamous, expensive, extremely graphic, and sexually explicit adaptation of the life of the mad Roman emperor, Caligula. Scenes of decapitation, necrophilia, rape, bestiality, and sadomasochism abound. Biggest question is why Gielgud, O'Toole, and McDowell lent their talents to this monumentally abhorred film (not to mention Gore Vidal on the writing end, who didn't want the credit). Adult magazine publisher Bob Guccione coproduced and didn't particularly want to release it. Also available in a censored, "R" rated version. **143m/C VHS, Beta, LV.** IT Malcolm McDowell, John Gielgud, Peter O'Toole, Helen Mirren; **D:** Tinto Brass; **W:** Gore Vidal. NO

Call Him Mr. Shatter 🏆 Shatter 1974 (R) A hired killer stalks a tottering Third World president and becomes embroiled in international political intrigue. **90m/C VHS, Beta.** GB Stuart Whitman, Peter Cushing, Anton Diffring; **D:** Michael Carreras. NLC

Call Me 🏆🏆 1988 (R) Psycho-drama about a lusty young woman who responds positively to an obscene telephone caller until she witnesses him murder another person. Doubt creeps into the relationship. **98m/C VHS, Beta, LV.** Patricia Charbonneau, Patti D'Arbanville, Sam Freed, Boyd Gaines, Stephen McHattie; **D:** Sollace Mitchell. VES

Call Me Bwana 🏆½ 1963 Pure cornpone with Hope as a bumbling explorer sent with CIA agent Adams to track down a lost American space capsule in deepest Africa. Enemy agents Ekberg and Jeffries try to make things difficult. **103m/C VHS.** Bob Hope, Edie Adams, Anita Ekberg, Lionel Jeffries, Percy Herbert, Paul Carpenter, Orlando Martins; **D:** Gordon Douglas; **W:** Nate Monaster, Johanna Harwood. MGM, FCT

Call Northside 777 🏆🏆🏆½ Calling Northside 777 1948 Chicago reporter Stewart finds himself in the crux of a decade-old murder investigation when he follows up a newspaper ad offering $5,000 for any information leading to the arrest and conviction of a police killer. The cunning reporter discovers police coverups and missing evidence pointing to an imprisoned man's innocence. Powerful performance from Stewart directs this docu-drama based on the real-life story of Chicago's Joe Majczek, unjustly imprisoned for 11 years, and the Pulitzer Prize winning reporter Jim McGuire who, through a clever investigation, found enough evidence to have the case reopened. **111m/B VHS, Closed Caption.** James Stewart, Richard Conte, Lee J. Cobb, Helen Walker, Betty Garde, Moroni Olsen, E.G. Marshall, Howard Smith, John McIntire, Paul Harvey, George Tyne, Michael Chapin, Addison Richards, Richard Rober, Eddie Dunn, Charles Lane, Walter Greaza, William Post Jr., George Melford, Charles Miller, Lionel Stander, Jonathan Hale; *D:* Henry Hathaway; *M:* Alfred Newman. *FXV*

Call of the Canyon ♫½ 1942 A crooked agent for a local meat packer won't pay a fair price, so Gene goes off to talk to the head man to set him straight. **71m/B VHS, Beta.** Gene Autry, Smiley Burnette, Ruth Terry, Thurston Hall, Pat Brady; *D:* Joseph Santley. *CCB, VCN, GPV*

Call of the Forest ♫½ 1949 Bobby makes friends with a beautiful wild black stallion which is captured and tamed by his father. The father has found a goldmine, also desired by an villain, and Bobby and his horse must come to his father's aid. Black Diamond (the horse) has the best role. **74m/B VHS.** Robert Lowery, Ken Curtis, Martha Sherrill, Chief Thundercloud, Charles Hughes; *D:* John F. Link. *NOS, DVT, VYY*

Call of the Rockies ♫♫ 1944 Action-packed oater in which Carson and Burnette ride across country to save Placer City's mine from crooked townsmen. **54m/B VHS, Closed Caption.** Sunset Carson, Smiley Burnette. *REP*

Call of the Wild ♫♫ 1972 (PG) Jack London's famous story about a man whose survival depends upon his knowledge of the Alaskan wilderness almost comes to life. Filmed in Finland. **105m/C VHS, Beta.** Charlton Heston, Michele Mercier, George Eastman; *D:* Ken Annakin. *KUI, SIM, MPI*

Call of the Wild ♫♫½ 1993 Another of Jack London's survival tales is dramatized for television. John Thornton (Schroder) is a rich greenhorn seeking adventure during the 1897 Klondike gold rush. Buck is a German shepherd, sold as a sled dog, who finds adventures of his own in the frozen North until man and dog are united to search for a legendary gold mine. The book is more exciting but the film is more violent. Filmed on location in British Columbia. **97m/C VHS, Closed Caption.** Rick Schroder, Gordon Tootoosis, Mia Sara, Duncan Fraser, Richard Newman, Brent Stait. *CAF*

Call Out the Marines ♫♫ 1942 A group of army buddies re-enlist to break up a spy ring. Two of the guys fall in love with the same girl, not realizing that she's one of the spies. McLaglen and Lowe's last comedy together. Mediocre outing isn't redeemed by below average musical numbers. ♫Call Out the Marines; Zana Zaranda; The Light of My Life; Beware; Hands Across the Border. **67m/B VHS, Beta.** Edmund Lowe, Victor McLaglen, Binnie Barnes, Paul Kelly, Dorothy Lovett, Franklin Pangborn; *D:* William Hamilton, Frank Ryan. *NO*

Call to Glory ♫♫½ 1984 Pilot for the critically praised television series. An Air Force pilot and his family face turbulent times during the Cuban missile crisis. **96m/C VHS, Beta, LV.** Craig T. Nelson, Cindy Pickett, Gabriel Damon, Keenan Wynn, Elisabeth Shue, G.D. Spradlin. *PAR*

A Call to Remember ♫♫½ 1997 (R) Paula Rubinek (Danner) and David Tobias (Mantegna) are concentration camp survivors who both had their spouses and children killed by the Nazis. They've married, moved to America, and are living in the suburbs with their two sons and trying to forget the past. But Paula's quiet world explodes when she receives a phone call notifying her that a son she thought died in the war has in fact survived and is eager to be reunited with his shocked mother. Writer Eisenberg based this cable drama on his parents' history. *CW:* Lan-

guage and sexuality. **105m/C VHS.** Blythe Danner, Joe Mantegna, David Lascher, Kevin Zegers; *W:* Max Eisenberg. *USH*

The Caller ♫♫ 1987 (R) A strange man enters the house of a lone woman and sets off a long night of suspense and an almost longer evening of inept movie-making. **90m/C VHS, Beta.** Malcolm McDowell, Madolyn Smith; *D:* Arthur Seidelman; *M:* Richard Band. *TWE*

Callie and Son ♫♫ *Rags to Riches* 1981 Details the sordid story of a waitress who works her way up to become a Dallas socialite and her obsessive relationship with her illegitimate son. **97m/C VHS, VHS, Beta.** Lindsay Wagner, Dabney Coleman, Jameson Parker, Andrew Prine, James Sloyan, Michelle Pfeiffer; *D:* Waris Hussein; *M:* Billy Goldenberg. *WAR*

Calling Dr. Death/Strange Confession *Strange Confession* 1943 In 1943's "Calling Dr. Death," Chaney plays a neurologist with an unfaithful wife who gets herself murdered. Naturally, Chaney's the primary suspect. In 1944's "Strange Confession" idealistic writer Chaney is made a fool of by publishing mogul Naish, who not only distorts his work but steals his wife. So Chaney plans an appropriate revenge. Based on the "The Inner Sanctum Mysteries" radio show. **124m/B VHS.** Lon Chaney Jr., J. Carrol Naish, Brenda Joyce, Patricia Morison, Ramsay Ames, David Bruce, Milburn Stone, Lloyd Bridges; *D:* Reginald LeBorg, John Hoffman; *W:* Edward Dein, M. Coates Webster. *USH*

Calling Paul Temple ♫♫½ 1948 The wealthy patients of a nerve doctor have been dying and a detective is called in to investigate. **92m/B VHS, Beta.** *GB* John Bentley, Dinah Sheridan, Margaretta Scott, Abraham Sofaer, Celia Lipton, Alan Wheatley, Wally Patch; *D:* Maclean Rogers. *SNC*

Calling Wild Bill Elliott ♫½ 1943 The crooked territorial governor is exposed by hero Elliott and sidekick Hayes and justice is restored in this typical B-western. Elliott's first film for Republic; he went on to star in 16 Red Ryder films as well as other westerns for the studio. **55m/B VHS.** Wild Bill Elliott, George "Gabby" Hayes, Herbert Heyes, Anne Jeffreys, Fred Kohler Jr., Roy Barcroft, Yakima Canutt; *D:* Spencer Gordon Bennet. *REP*

Calm at Sunset ♫♫½ 1996 (PG) James Pfeiffer (Facinelli) drops out of college to pursue his dream of becoming a commercial fisherman, much to the dismay of his parents (Moriarty, Nelligan) who already know how rough that life can be. But James gets his chance when he rescues a seaman (Conway) and the two become partners. Still, James must deal with secrets, a tragedy, and some hard decisions. TV drama with some solid performances. **98m/C VHS.** Peter Facinelli, Michael Moriarty, Kate Nelligan, Kevin Conway, Gretchen Mol, Melvin Van Peebles; *D:* Daniel Petrie. *HMK*

Came a Hot Friday ♫♫ 1985 (PG) Two cheap conmen arrive in a 1949 southern New Zealand town, run various scams and pursue women. **101m/C VHS, Beta, Closed Caption.** *NZ* Peter Bland, Philip Gordon, Billy T. James; *D:* Ian Mune; *C:* Alun Bollinger. *NLC*

Camel Boy ♫½ 1984 True story of a young Arabian boy who befriends a camel and their treacherous trek across the desert. **78m/C VHS, Beta.** *AU D:* Yoram Gross; *V:* Michael Pate, Ron Haddrick, John Meillon. *VES, ART*

Camelot ♫♫ 1967 The long-running Lerner and Loewe Broadway musical about King Arthur, Guinevere, and Lancelot was adapted from T.H. White's book, "The Once and Future King." Redgrave and Nero have chemistry as the illicit lovers, Harris is strong as the king struggling to hold together his dream, but muddled direction undermines the effort. Laserdisc edition contains 28 minutes of previously edited footage, trailers and backstage info. ♫I Wonder What the King is Doing Tonight; The Simple Joys of Maidenhood; Camelot; C'est Moi; The Lusty Month of May; Follow Me; How To Handle a Woman; Then You May

Take Me to the Fair; If Ever I Would Leave You. **150m/C VHS, Beta, LV, Letterbox, Closed Caption.** Richard Harris, Vanessa Redgrave, David Hemmings, Franco Nero, Lionel Jeffries; *D:* Joshua Logan; *M:* Frederick Loewe, Alan Jay Lerner. Academy Awards '67: Best Adapted Score, Best Art Direction/Set Decoration, Best Costume Design; Golden Globe Awards '68: Best Actor—Musical/Comedy (Harris), Best Song ("If Ever I Should Leave You"), Best Score; Nominations: Academy Awards '67: Best Cinematography, Best Sound. *WAR, RDG, HMV*

Camera Buff ♫♫ *Amator* 1979 Satire on bureaucracy finds a factory worker buying a home-movie camera to film his new baby but becoming obsessed with his new toy. So he begins recording everything he sees—even things the authorities don't want shown. Polish with subtitles. **108m/C VHS.** *PL* Jerzy Stuhr, Malgorzata Zajaczkowska, Ewa Pokas, Krzysztof Zanussi; *D:* Krzysztof Kieslowski; *W:* Jerzy Stuhr, Krzysztof Kieslowski; *M:* Krzysztof Knittel. *NYF*

The Cameraman ♫♫♫♫ 1928 After moving to MGM, Keaton made his first feature with a major studio, giving up the artistic control he had enjoyed in his previous films. Spared from the vilification of studio politics (not the case with later Keaton films) "The Cameraman" enjoyed both critical and popular success. Keaton's inept tintype portrait-maker has a heart that pitter-patters for an MGM office girl. He hopes to impress her by joining the ranks of the newsreel photographers. Fortuitously poised to grab a photo scoop on a Chinese tong war, he is forced to return empty-handed when an organ-grinder's monkey absconds with his firsthand footage. Silent with a musical score. **78m/B VHS, LV.** Buster Keaton, Marceline Day, Harold Goodwin, Harry Gribbon, Sidney Bracy, Edward Brophy, Vernon Dent, William Irving; *D:* Edward Sedgwick. *MGM, FCT*

Cameron's Closet ♫½ 1989 (R) Every child's nightmare comes true. A young boy is convinced that a monster lives in his closet due to his perverse father's psychological tortures. Only this time the monster is real! **86m/C VHS, LV.** Cotter Smith, Mel Harris, Scott Curtis, Chuck McCann, Leigh McCloskey, Kim Lankford, Tab Hunter; *D:* Armand Mastroianni; *W:* Gary Brandner; *C:* Russell Carpenter. *COL*

Camila ♫♫♫ 1984 The true story of the tragic romance between an Argentinian socialite and a Jesuit priest in 1847. The two lovers escape to a small provincial village where they live together as man and wife. Eventually they are recognized and condemned to death. Available in Spanish with English subtitles or dubbed into English. **105m/C VHS.** *AR SP* Susu Pecoraro, Imanol Arias, Hector Alterio, Elena Tasisto; *D:* Maria-Luisa Bemberg. Nominations: Academy Awards '84: Best Foreign Language Film. *COL, MFI*

Camilla ♫♫½ 1994 (PG-13) Tandy is delightful in her last starring role as a former violinist on the run with frustrated musician Fonda. Oafish son (Chaykin) and insensitive husband (Koteas) just don't understand, so its time to head to Toronto, site of a fondly, if perhaps incorrectly, remembered triumph. Sort of a May-December female-bonding roadtrip with lots of conversation and comic asides. An inevitably poignant pairing of Tandy and real-life husband Cronyn offers the chance to experience one of America's greatest acting teams one last time. Lack of stereotyping and fairly novel twist on the road movie keep this one on the highway. *CW:* Contains profanity, brief nudity, and some sensuality. **91m/C VHS, LV, Closed Caption.** Jessica Tandy, Bridget Fonda, Hume Cronyn, Elias Koteas, Maury Chaykin, Graham Greene; *D:* Deepa Mehta; *W:* Paul Quarrington; *M:* Daniel Lanois. *MAX*

Camille ♫♫ 1921 Dying courtesan falls in love with innocent young man in the Dumas classic. Valentino in his prime. **55m/B VHS.** Rudolph Valentino, Alla Nazimova; *D:* Fred Niblo. *FCT*

Camille ♫♫♫½ 1936 The classic Alexandre Dumas story about a dying French courtesan falling in love with a shallow young nobleman. A clean, romantic adaptation that somehow escapes the cliches and stands as one of the most telling monuments to Garbo's unique magic and presence on film. **108m/B VHS, Beta.** Greta Garbo, Robert Taylor, Lionel Barrymore, Henry Daniell, Elizabeth Allan, Rex O'Malley, Lenore Ulric, Laura Hope Crews; **D:** George Cukor; **C:** William H. Daniels. New York Film Critics Awards '37: Best Actress (Garbo); Nominations: Academy Awards '37: Best Actress (Garbo). *MGM*

Camille Claudel 🎬🎬🎬 1989 (R) A lushly romantic version of the art world at the turn of the century, when art was exploding in new forms and independence for women was unheard of. Sculptor Claudel's tragic love for art, Auguste Rodin (for whom she modeled), and independence clash, costing her sanity. Very long, it requires an attentive and thoughtful viewing. In French with English subtitles. **149m/C VHS, Beta, LV.** *FR* Isabelle Adjani, Gerard Depardieu, Laurent Grevill, Alain Cuny, Madeleine Robinson, Katrine Boorman; **D:** Bruno Nuytten; **W:** Bruno Nuytten, Marilyn Goldin; **M:** Gabriel Yared. Cesar Awards '89: Best Actress (Adjani), Best Art Direction/Set Decoration, Best Cinematography, Best Costume Design, Best Film; Nominations: Academy Awards '89: Best Actress (Adjani), Best Foreign Language Film. *ORI, IME*

Camorra: The Naples Connection 🎬🎬 *Un Complicato Intrigo Di Donne, Vicoli E Delitti* 1985 (R) A prostitute and an American drug dealer find themselves embroiled in the murders of Neapolitan Mafia heads. Violent, overblown, minor Wertmuller. *IT* Harvey Keitel, Angela Molina, Lorraine Bracco, Francesco Rabal; **D:** Lina Wertmuller; **W:** Lina Wertmuller. *MGM*

Camp Cucamonga: How I Spent My Summer Vacation 🎬 1990 Zany antics at summer camp abound when Camp Cucamonga's owner mistakes the new handyman for the camp inspector. Well known stars from TV's "Cheers," "The Jeffersons," "The Wonder Years," and "The Love Boat" are featured in this silly made for television flick. **100m/C VHS.** John Ratzenberger, Sherman Hemsley, Josh Saviano, Danica McKellar, Chad Allen, Dorothy Lyman, Lauren Tewes, G. Gordon Liddy; **D:** Roger Duchonwny. *GKK*

Camp Nowhere 🎬🎬 1994 (PG) Video fodder for the juniors in the household as kids turn tables on parents. Instead of trudging off to summer camp for the umpteenth time, a group of upscale kids create their own with the help of laid-off drama teacher Lloyd, who must first con their parents into believing that Camp Nowhere is legit. What follows is that very special summer camp in the Hollywood tradition with lots of junk food, video games galore, and of course, no rules. Camp beserko formula good for a few laughs. **106m/C VHS, LV, Closed Caption.** Christopher Lloyd, Wendy Makkena, M. Emmet Walsh, Peter Scolari, Peter Onorati, Ray Baker, Kate Mulgrew, Jonathan Jackson, Romy Walthall, Maryedith Burrell, Tom Wilson, Nathan Cavaleri, Andrew Keegan, Melody Kay; **D:** Jonathan Prince; **W:** Andrew Kurtzman, Eliot Wald; **C:** Sandi Sissel. *TOU*

The Campus Corpse 🎬 1977 (PG) Young man stumbles into deadly college frat hazing and discovers he and rest of cast are utterly devoid of acting ability. **92m/C VHS, Beta.** Charles Martin Smith, Jeff East, Brad Davis; **D:** Douglas Curtis. *VES*

Campus Knights 🎬 1929 If you're a serious student of the campus caper film, this is one of the earliest (though not one of the best) of the genre (if such a distinction can be made). The story involves twin brothers—one a tweedy highbrowed professor, the other a bon vivant man about town—who wreak fraternal chaos on the quads. **70m/B VHS, Beta.** Raymond McKee, Shirley Palmer, Marie Quillen, Jean Laverty, Sybil Grove; **D:** Albert Kelly. *GPV, FCT*

Campus Man 🎬 1987 (PG) An entrepreneurial college student markets a beefcake calendar featuring his best friend, until the calendar's sales threaten his friend's amateur athletic status. **94m/C VHS, Beta, LV.** John Dye, Steve Lyon, Kim Delaney, Miles O'Keeffe, Morgan Fairchild, Kathleen Wilhoite; **D:** Ron Casden; **W:** Geoffrey Baere; **M:** James Newton Howard. *PAR*

Can-Can 🎬🎬 1960 Lackluster screen adaptation of the Cole Porter musical bears little resemblance to the stage version. MacLaine is a cafe owner who goes to court to try and get the "Can-Can," a dance considered risque in gay Paree at the end of the 19th century, made legal. Love interest Sinatra happens to be a lawyer. ♪C'est Manifique; Let's Do It; I Love Paris; You Do Something to Me; It's All Right With Me; Live and Let Live; Come Along With Me; Just One of Those Things. **131m/C VHS, Beta, LV, Letterbox, Closed Caption.** Frank Sinatra, Shirley MacLaine, Maurice Chevalier, Louis Jourdan, Juliet Prowse, Marcel Dalio, Leon Belasco; **D:** Walter Lang; **C:** William H. Daniels. Nominations: Academy Awards '60: Best Costume Design (Color), Scoring of a Musical. *FOX, FCT*

Can I Do It...Till I Need Glasses? WOOF! 1977 More to the point, can you stay awake till the end? Prurient juvenile junk. Brief Williams footage was grafted to this mess during 15 minutes of Mork fame. **72m/C VHS, Beta.** Robin Williams, Roger Behr, Debra Klose, Moose Carlson, Walter Olkewicz; **D:** I. Robert Levy.

Can She Bake a Cherry Pie? 🎬🎬 1983 Two offbeat characters meet and fall in love in an odd sort of way. Slow-moving and talky but somewhat rewarding. One of Black's better performances. **90m/C VHS, Beta, Closed Caption.** Karen Black, Michael Emil, Michael Margotta, Frances Fisher, Martin Frydberg; **D:** Henry Jaglom; **W:** Henry Jaglom; **M:** Karen Black. *PAR, FCT*

Can You Feel Me Dancing? 🎬🎬 1985 Family-happy lightweight entertainment co-produced by Kent Bateman and starring Bateman progeny Jason and Justine as brother and sister, a novel premise that only a father could love. A blind independence-impaired teenager tries to liberate herself from her overbearing family, and finds the secret to conquering her fears and to standing up for herself when she falls in love. Written by spouse-team Steven and J. Miyoko Hensley. **95m/C VHS.** Jason Bateman, Justine Bateman; **D:** Michael Miller; **W:** Steven Hensley, J. Miyoko Hensley. *NO*

Can You Hear the Laughter? The Story of Freddie Prinze 🎬🎬 1979 Heartstring tugging biography of the late Puerto Rican comedian whose troubled life lead to suicide in spite of his apparent success. He was most noted for his starring role in "Chico and the Man." **100m/C VHS, Beta.** Ira Angustain, Kevin Hooks, Randee Heller, Devon Ericson, Julie Carmen, Stephen Elliott; **D:** Burt Brinckerhoff. *GEM*

Canada's Sweetheart: The Saga of Hal C. Banks 🎬🎬 *Sweetheart!* 1985 True story of Banks, hired by the Canadian government to break up a strike among the communist-led seaman's union which had put a stranglehold on Canadian commerce, and who was eventually convicted of strong-arm tactics. **115m/C VHS, Beta.** *CA* Maury Chaykin. Toronto-City Award '85: Best Canadian Feature Film. *NO*

Canadian Bacon 🎬½ 1994 (PG) Regrettably amateurish satire (with some sharp observations) serves as the feature film debut for Moore, who irritated many with "Roger and Me." Title refers to the military code name for a campaign to whip up anti-Canadian hysteria and justify a U.S. invasion of its neighbor to the north. Evil political advisor Pollak convinces well-meaning but inept President Alda that it's just the thing to get the presidential popularity up and those defense industries humming. Ugly Americans abound, at expense of polite Canadians, eh? Filmed in Toronto, which is shown to good advantage. Candy in one of last roles is the superpatriotic sheriff of Niagara Falls, New York. **110m/C VHS.** Alan Alda, Kevin Pollak, John Candy, Rhea Perlman, Rip Torn, Bill Nunn, Kevin J. O'Connor, Steven Wright, G.D. Spradlin; **Cameos:** Michael Moore; **D:** Michael Moore; **W:** Michael Moore; **C:** Haskell Wexler; **M:** Elmer Bernstein. *PGV*

Canadian Mounties vs. Atomic Invaders 🎬🎬½ 1953 Mountie Don Roberts and undercover agent Kay Conway chase foreign agents and face natural disasters (avalanches and reindeer stampedes) to keep atomic missiles away from Canada and the U.S. Part of "The Cliffhanger Serials" series. 12 chapters. **169m/B VHS.** William Henry, Susan Morrow, Arthur Space. *REP, MOV*

Cancel My Reservation 🎬 1972 (G) New York talk show host Hope sets out for a vacation on an Arizona ranch, but winds up in trouble due to a mysterious corpse, a rich rancher, and an enigmatic mystic. Even more muddled than it sounds. Based on the novel "Broken Gun" by Louis L'Amour, with pointless cameos by Crosby, Wayne, and Wilson. **99m/C VHS, Beta.** Bob Hope, Eva Marie Saint, Ralph Bellamy, Anne Archer, Forrest Tucker, Keenan Wynn, Flip Wilson, Noriyuki "Pat" Morita, Chief Dan George; **Cameos:** John Wayne, Bing Crosby, Doodles Weaver; **D:** Paul Bogart; **W:** Arthur Marx; **C:** Russell Metty. *COL, FCT*

The Candidate 🎬🎬🎬 1972 (PG) Realistic, satirical look at politics and political campaigning. A young, idealistic lawyer is talked into trying for the Senate seat and learns the truth about running for office. Ritchie's other efforts include "Downhill Racer" and "Bad News Bears." **105m/C VHS, Beta, LV.** Robert Redford, Peter Boyle, Don Porter, Allen (Goorwitz) Garfield, Karen Carlson, Melvyn Douglas, Michael Lerner; **D:** Michael Ritchie; **W:** Jeremy Larner. Academy Awards '72: Best Story & Screenplay; Writers Guild of America '72: Best Original Screenplay; Nominations: Academy Awards '72: Best Sound. *WAR*

Candles at Nine 🎬½ 1944 An innocent showgirl must spend a month in her late uncle's creepy mansion In order to inherit it, much to the malevolent chagrin of the rest of the family who want the place and the loot for themselves. Uninspired. **84m/B VHS, Beta.** *GB* Jessie Matthews, John Stuart, Reginald Purdell; **D:** John Harlow. *SNC, VYY, MLB*

Candleshoe 🎬🎬 1978 (G) A Los Angeles street urchin poses as an English matron's long lost granddaughter in order to steal a fortune hidden in Candleshoe, her country estate, where Niven butlers. Somewhat slapsticky Disney fare. **101m/C VHS, Beta, Closed Caption.** Vivian Pickles, Helen Hayes, David Niven, Jodie Foster, Leo McKern; **D:** Norman Tokar. *DIS*

Candy Mountain 🎬🎬 1987 (R) Guitar playin' O'Connor roadtrips across America and Canada in search of a legendary guitar maker Yulin. Occasional interest derives from musician cameos from the likes of Buster Poindexter, Dr. John and Redbone. **90m/C VHS.** *FR SI CA* Kevin J. O'Connor, Harris Yulin, Tom Waits, Bulle Ogier, Roberts Blossom; **Cameos:** David Johansen, Leon Redbone, Joe Strummer, Rita MacNeil, Laurie Metcalf; **D:** Robert Frank; **W:** Rudy Wurlitzer. *REP, FCT*

Candy Stripe Nurses 🎬 *Sweet Candy* 1974 Even hard-core Roger Corman fans might find his final installment in the nursing comedy pentad to be a lethargic exercise in gratuitous "sexual situations." Bet those uniforms don't meet hospital standards. The previous films in the series are: "The Student Nurses," "Private Duty Nurses," "Night Call Nurses," and "The Young Nurses." **80m/C VHS, Beta.** Candice Rialson, Robin Mattson, Maria Rojo, Kimberly Hyde, Dick Miller, Stanley Ralph Ross, Monte Landis, Tom Baker; **D:** Allan Holleb.

Candy Tangerine Man 🎬 1975 Respectable businessman leads a double life as loving father and LA pimp. **88m/C VHS, Beta.** John Daniels, Tom Hankerson, Eli Haines, Marva Farmer, George Flower; **D:** Matt Cimber. *UNI*

Candyman 🎬🎬 1992 (R) Terrifying tale from horror maven Clive Barker is an effective combination of American gothic, academia, and urban squalor. A search for dissertation material leads graduate student Helen Lyle (Madsen) into gang-infested housing. There she encounters the urban myth of Candyman, the son of a former slave who was lynched and is now back with a hook and a vendetta. Filled with the appropriate amount of yucky stuff, yet successfully employs subtle scare tactics and plausible characters.**CW:** Violence and gore. 98m/C **VHS, Beta, LV, 8mm, Letterbox, Closed Caption.** Virginia Madsen, Tony Todd, Xander Berkeley, Kasi Lemmons, Vanessa Williams, DeJuan Guy, Michael Culkin, Gilbert Lewis, Stanley DeSantis; **D:** Bernard Rose; **W:** Bernard Rose; **C:** Anthony B. Richmond; **M:** Philip Glass. *COL*

Candyman 2: Farewell to the Flesh ⚔ 1994 (R) Explains the origins of the urban bogeyman called Candyman—the man, the hook, and the bees. Rehashes the same old scare tactics from previous and better horror movies and uses cheesy special effects. The sensual background of New Orleans during Mardi Gras can't help this stale sequel. Embrace this "Farewell" from a distance. Based on stories by Clive Barker.**CW:** Violence and gore; some sexuality and language. 99m/C **VHS.** Tony Todd, Kelly Rowan, Veronica Cartwright, Timothy Carhart, William O'Leary, Bill Nunn, Fay Hauser; **D:** Bill Condon; **W:** Rand Ravich, Mark Kruger; **C:** Tobias Schliessler; **M:** Philip Glass. *PGV*

Cannery Row ⚔⚔½ 1982 (PG) Baseball has-been Nolte lives anonymously among the downtrodden in the seamy part of town and carries on with working girl girlfriend Winger. Based on John Steinbeck's "Cannery Row" and "Sweet Thursday." 120m/C **VHS, Beta.** Nick Nolte, Debra Winger, Audra Lindley, M. Emmet Walsh, Frank McRae, James Keane, Sunshine Parker; **D:** David S. Ward; **W:** David S. Ward; **C:** Sven Nykvist; **M:** Jack Nitzsche. *MGM*

Cannes Man ⚔⚔ 1996 (R) Features legendary Hollywood producer Sy Lerner (Cassel), who vows to make unknown cabbie/screenwriter Frank Rhinoslavsky (Quinn) a star, all while being schmoozed at Cannes by stars who want to be in his latest epic, while he tries to find backers for his unwritten script.**CW:** Adult themes, language, brief nudity. 88m/C **VHS.** Seymour Cassel, Francesco Quinn, Rebecca Broussand; **D:** Richard Martini. *ROC*

Cannibal Campout ⚔ 1988 Crazed orphans with eating disorders make square meal of coed babes getting back to nature. 89m/C **VHS, Beta.** Carrie Lindell, Richard Marcus, Amy Chludzinski, Jon McBride; **D:** Jon McBride, Tom Fisher. *DMP*

Cannibal! The Musical ⚔ 1996 (R) Only those wacky people at Troma could offer a horror/musical about a group of 1883 gold miners who get lost in the Colorado Rockies, have some strange adventures, and eventually wind up as dinner to cannibal Alferd Packer (who's telling his version of the story to a female reporter while in prison). Seven rather tedious musical numbers lead up to the gore-splashed finale. From director Trey Parker, who also repulses (and amuses us) with TV's "South Park."**CW:** Comic gore/violence and some language. 105m/C **VHS.** Ian Hardin, Jason McHugh, Matt Stone, Trey Parker, Juan Schwartz; **D:** Trey Parker; **W:** Trey Parker. *TTV*

Cannibal Women in the Avocado Jungle of Death ⚔⚔½ 1989 (PG-13) Tongue-in-cheek cult classic features erstwhile playmate Tweed as feminist anthropologist who searches with ditzy student and mucho macho male guide for lost tribe of cannibal women who dine on their mates. Lawton directed under the alias "J.D. Athens." 90m/C **VHS, Beta, LV, Closed Caption.** Shannon Tweed, Adrienne Barbeau, Karen Mistal, Barry Primus, Bill Maher; **D:** J.F. Lawton; **W:** J.F. Lawton. *PAR*

Cannon Ball/Eyes Have It 1915 Conklin stars in "The Cannon Ball" (1915), as an explosives expert in the Boom Powder Factory. "The Eyes Have It" (1928), stars Turpin involved in another misunderstanding with wife and mother-in-law. Silent. 41m/B **VHS, Beta.** Chester Conklin, Ben Turpin, Georgia O'Dell, Helen Gilmore, Jack Lipson. *CCB*

Cannon Movie Tales: Red Riding Hood ⚔⚔½ 1989 (G) Bright re-telling of the little girl in red and that nasty wolf. 84m/C **VHS.** Craig T. Nelson, Isabella Rossellini; **D:** Adam Brooks. *WAR*

Cannon Movie Tales: Sleeping Beauty ⚔⚔½ 1989 (G) Fairchild stars in this version of the sleeping princess and the evil witch. 90m/C **VHS.** Morgan Fairchild, Tracy Welch, Nicholas Clay, Sylvia Miles, Kenny Baker, David Holliday; **D:** David Irving. *WAR*

Cannon Movie Tales: The Emperor's New Clothes ⚔⚔½ 1989 Caesar stars in this version of vain despot and the crafty tailors. 85m/C **VHS.** Sid Caesar, Robert Morse, Clive Revill; **D:** David Irving. *WAR*

Cannonball ⚔⚔ *Carquake* 1976 (PG) Assorted ruthless people leave patches of rubber across the country competing for grand prize in less than legal auto race. Not top drawer New World but nonetheless a cult fave. Inferior to Bartel's previous cult classic, "Death Race 2000." Most interesting for plethora of cult cameos, including Scorsese, Dante, and grandmaster Corman. 93m/C **VHS, Beta.** David Carradine, Bill McKinney, Veronica Hamel, Gerrit Graham, Robert Carradine, Sylvester Stallone, Jonathan Kaplan; **Cameos:** Martin Scorsese, Roger Corman, Joe Dante; **D:** Paul Bartel; **W:** Paul Bartel; **M:** David A. Axelrod. *NO*

Cannonball/Dizzy Heights and Daring Hearts 1916 Two classic comedies featuring Conklin, the Keystone Kops, and wacky aeroplanes from the irrepressible Sennett. 71m/B **VHS, Beta.** Chester Conklin; **D:** Mack Sennett. *VYY*

Cannonball Run ⚔½ 1981 (PG) So many stars, so little plot. Reynolds and sidekick DeLuise disguise themselves as paramedics to foil cops while they compete in cross-country Cannonball race. Shows no sign of having been directed by an ex-stuntman. One of 1981's top grossers—go figure. Followed by equally languid sequel "Cannonball Run II." 95m/C **VHS, Beta, LV.** Burt Reynolds, Farrah Fawcett, Roger Moore, Dom DeLuise, Dean Martin, Sammy Davis Jr., Jack Elam, Adrienne Barbeau, Peter Fonda, Molly Picon, Bert Convy, Jamie Farr; **D:** Hal Needham. *VES*

Cannonball Run 2 ⚔ 1984 (PG) More mindless cross-country wheel spinning with gratuitous star cameos. Director Needham apparently subscribes to the two wrongs make a right school of sequels. 109m/C **VHS, Beta, LV, Closed Caption.** Burt Reynolds, Dom DeLuise, Jamie Farr, Marilu Henner, Shirley MacLaine, Jim Nabors, Frank Sinatra, Sammy Davis Jr., Dean Martin, Telly Savalas, Susan Anton, Catherine Bach, Jack Elam, Sid Caesar, Ricardo Montalban, Charles Nelson Reilly; **Cameos:** Henry Silva, Tim Conway, Don Knotts, Molly Picon; **D:** Hal Needham; **W:** Harvey Miller; **M:** Stephen Dorff. *WAR*

Can't Buy Me Love ⚔½ 1987 (PG-13) Unpopular high school nerd Dempsey buys a month of dates with teen babe Peterson for $1000 in order to win friends and influence people. Previously known as "Boy Rents Girl." 94m/C **VHS, Beta, LV, Closed Caption.** Patrick Dempsey, Amanda Peterson, Dennis Dugan, Courtney Gains; **D:** Steve Rash; **C:** Peter Collister; **M:** Robert Folk. *TOU*

Can't Hardly Wait *The Party* 1998 (PG-13) Graduation is over and it's time for the fun to begin as shy writer Preston (Embry) decides to make a move on class beauty Amanda (Hewitt) before things change forever. Not yet reviewed.**CW:** Teen drinking and sexuality, and for language. ?m/C **VHS.** Ethan Embry, Jennifer Love Hewitt, Peter Facinelli, Adam Hann-Byrd, Seth Green, Jerry O'Connell, Melissa Joan Hart, Charlie Korsmo, Jenna Elfman; **D:** Harry Elfont, Deborah Kaplan; **W:** Harry Elfont, Deborah Kaplan. *NYR*

Can't Help Singing ⚔⚔½ 1945 In 1849, willful heiress Caroline (Durbin) ignores her senator father's (Collins) wishes and heads west to marry her Army sweetheart (Bruce). But on the wagon train she falls for wagon master Lawlor (Paige), who's a better guy anyway. Durbin's first

color musical. 90m/C **VHS.** Deanna Durbin, Robert Paige, David Bruce, Akim Tamiroff, Leonid Kinskey, Ray Collins, June Vincent, Thomas Gomez; **D:** Frank Ryan; **W:** Frank Ryan, Lewis R. Foster; **C:** Woody Bredell, William Howard Greene; **M:** Hans J. Salter, Jerome Kern, E.Y. Harburg. Nominations: Academy Awards '45: Best Song ("More and More"), Scoring of a Musical. *USH*

Can't Stop the Music WOOF! 1980 (PG) Retired model invites friends from Greenwich Village to a party to help the career of her roommate, an aspiring composer. Disco inferno that nearly reaches heights of surreal ineptness. Put it in a time capsule and let the people of the future decide what the heck was going on in the '70s. Features two of the top hits by the Village People. ♫Y.M.C.A.; Macho Man; Give Me a Break; The Sound of the City; Samantha; I'm a Singing Juggler; Sophistication; Liberation; I Love You to Death. 120m/C **VHS, Beta.** Valerie Perrine, Bruce Jenner, Steve Guttenberg, Paul Sand, Leigh Taylor-Young, Village People; **D:** Nancy Walker; **W:** Allan Carr; **C:** Bill Butler. Golden Raspberry Awards '80: Worst Picture, Worst Screenplay. *REP*

A Canterbury Tale ⚔⚔⚔ 1944 Writer-director team Powell and Pressburger have loosely modeled a retelling of Chaucer's famous tale of a pilgrimage to the cathedral in Canterbury. Set in Nazi-threatened Britain in 1944, the story follows the pilgrimage of three Brits and an American GI to the eponymous cathedral. Strange, effective, worth looking at. The 95-minute American version, with added footage of Kim Hunter, is inferior to the 124-minute original. 124m/B **VHS.** GB Eric Portman, Sheila Sim, Dennis Price, Esmond Knight, Charles Hawtrey, Hay Petrie; **D:** Michael Powell, Emeric Pressburger. *HMV*

The Canterbury Tales ⚔⚔ 1971 Four Chaucer tales, most notably "The Merchant's Tale" and "The Wife of Bath," are recounted by travelers, with director Pasolini as the bawdy poet. Deemed obscene by the Italian courts, it's the second entry in Pasolini's medieval "Trilogy of Life," preceded by "The Decameron" and followed by "The Arabian Nights." In Italian with English subtitles. 109m/C **VHS, Beta.** IT Laura Betti, Ninetto Davoli, Pier Paolo Pasolini, Hugh Griffith, Josephine Chaplin, Michael Balfour, Jenny Runacre; **D:** Pier Paolo Pasolini. Berlin International Film Festival '72: Golden Berlin Bear.*WBF*

The Canterville Ghost ⚔⚔½ 1944 Laughton, a 300-year-old ghost with a yellow streak, is sentenced to spook a castle until he proves he's not afraid of his own shadow. American troops stay at the castle during WWII and, as luck would have it, soldier Young is distantly related to spunky young keeper of the castle O'Brien, ghost Laughton's descendant. Once Young is acquainted with his cowardly ancestor, he begins to fear a congenital yellow streak, and both struggle to be brave despite themselves. Vaguely derived from an Oscar Wilde tale. 95m/B **VHS, Beta, Closed Caption.** Charles Laughton, Robert Young, Margaret O'Brien, William Gargan, Reginald Owen, Rags Ragland, Una O'Connor, Peter Lawford, Mike Mazurki; **D:** Jules Dassin; **W:** Edwin Blum; **M:** George Bassman. *MGM*

The Canterville Ghost 1991 During a family's vacation in an old English manor, they run into a ghost who is doomed to haunt the place until he can overcome his fears. Problems start when the family tries to scare him away. From the "Wonderworks" family movie series. 58m/C **VHS.** Richard Kiley, Mary Wickes. *HMV, FCT*

The Canterville Ghost ⚔⚔½ 1996 (PG) Stewart is the highlight of this updated TV version of the Oscar Wilde short story. He's the cursed Elizabethan spirit of Sir Simon de Canterville, doomed to haunt the family mansion until a prophecy is fulfilled. But he's not happy with a family of American intruders, until teenager Virginia (Campbell) discovers Sir Simon and realizes she may hold the key to freeing the unhappy ghost. 91m/C **VHS.** Patrick Stewart, Neve Campbell, Ed Wiley, Cherie Lunghi, Donald Sinden, Joan Sims, Leslie

Phillips, Ciaran Fitzgerald, Daniel Betts, Raymond Pickard; **D:** Syd Macartney; **W:** Robert Benedetto; **C:** Denis Lewiston; **M:** Ernest Troost. *HMK*

The Cantor's Son 🐾½ Dem Khann's Zindl

1937 Real-life story based on Moishe Oysher's life, vaguely influenced by Jolson's "Jazz Singer." Runaway Oysher joins troupe of performers as a youth, travels to the shores of America, and finds fame once his beautiful voice is discovered. Returning to his mother country to celebrate his parents' golden anniversary, he encounters his childhood sweetheart and falls in love, but another woman is written into the plot to complicate matters. Poorly acted, laughable staging. In Yiddish with English subtitles. **90m/B VHS, Beta.** Judith Abarbanel, Florence Weiss, Moishe Oysher, Isadore Cashier; **D:** Ilya Motyleff. *ERG, HEG*

Canvas: The Fine Art of Crime 🐾🐾

1992 (R) A ruthless, underhanded art gallery owner recruits a desperate young artist into his art stealing schemes. The artist learns how to steal, but decides he wants out after his burglary partner has a brush with death. The gallery owner, however, wants one last job completed. *CW:* Language, violence and drug content, and some sexuality. **94m/C VHS.** Gary Busey, John Rhys-Davies, Vittorio Rossi, Nick Cavaiola, Cary Lawrence; **D:** Alain Zaloum. *ART*

Canyon Passage 🐾🐾🐾

1946 Rip-roarin' western set in the Oregon Territory in 1856. Stuart (Andrews) is a former scout turned store owner who falls for Lucy (Hayward), who happens to be the fiancee of banker/gambler Camrose (Donlevy). Camrose gets into money troubles, there's a villain named Bragg (Bond), and a pretty spectacular Indian attack. Carmichael serves as the wandering minstrel to the action, singing four songs. Director Tourneur was best known for his horror films. **92m/C VHS, Closed Caption.** Dana Andrews, Brian Donlevy, Susan Hayward, Ward Bond, Hoagy Carmichael, Lloyd Bridges, Andy Devine, Patricia Roc; **D:** Jacques Tourneur; **W:** Ernest Pascal; **C:** Edward Cronjager; **M:** Frank Skinner. *USH*

Cape Fear 🐾🐾🐾½

1961 Former prosecutor turned small-town lawyer Peck and his family are plagued by the sadistic attentions of criminal Mitchum, who just finished a six year sabbatical at the state pen courtesy of prosecutor Peck. Taut and creepy; Mitchum's a consummate psychopath. Based on (and far superior to) John MacDonald's "The Executioners." Don't pass this one up in favor of the Scorsese remake. **106m/B VHS, Beta.** Gregory Peck, Robert Mitchum, Polly Bergen, Martin Balsam, Telly Savalas, Jack Kruschen; **D:** J. Lee Thompson; **C:** Sam Leavitt. *USH*

Cape Fear 🐾🐾🐾

1991 (R) Scorsese takes on this terrifying tale of brutality and manipulation (previously filmed in 1961) and cranks it up a notch as a paroled convict haunts the lawyer who put him away. Great cast, a rollercoaster of suspense. Note the cameos by Mitchum, Peck, and Balsam, stars of the first version. Original source material was "The Executioners" by John D. MacDonald. Breath-taking rollercoaster of a film. Elmer Bernstein adapted the original score by Bernard Herrmann. *CW:* Language and strong violence. **128m/C VHS, LV, Letterbox, Closed Caption.** Robert De Niro, Nick Nolte, Jessica Lange, Juliette Lewis, Joe Don Baker, Illeana Douglas, Fred Dalton Thompson; **Cameos:** Robert Mitchum, Gregory Peck, Martin Balsam; **D:** Martin Scorsese; **W:** Wesley Strick; **C:** Freddie Francis; **M:** Bernard Herrmann, Elmer Bernstein. Nominations: Academy Awards '91: Best Actor (De Niro), Best Supporting Actress (Lewis). *USH*

Caper of the Golden Bulls 🐾 Carnival

of Thieves 1967 Former bank robber Boyd is blackmailed into joining a group of safecrackers who plan to assault the Royal Bank of Spain during the annual Santa Maria bull run. More like siesta of the golden bulls. **104m/C VHS, Beta.** Stephen Boyd, Yvette Mimieux, Giovanna Ralli, Walter Slezak, Vito Scotti; **D:** Russel Rouse. *NLC*

Capital Punishment 🐾½ 1996 Martial

arts expert James Thayer (Daniels) is recruited by the DEA to go undercover and stop Nakata (Yamashita), the supplier of a new illegal drug. His operation turns up a corrupt police chief (Carradine), who frames him for murder, and lots of action. **90m/C VHS.** Gary Daniels, Tadashi Yamashita, David Carradine, Mel Novak, Ian Jacklin, Ava Fabian; **D:** David Hue; **W:** David Hue; **C:** David Swett. *SCP*

Capone 🐾🐾½ 1989 (R) This is the story of

the gangster after Elliot Ness put him in a Chicago jail. That didn't stop Capone from running his crime empire until a single FBI agent worked to sent the crime boss to Alcatraz, where his power would be useless. Exuberant performances from Sharkey and Carradine. Made for television. *CW:* Violence and sexuality. **96m/C VHS, LV, Closed Caption.** Ray Sharkey, Keith Carradine, Debrah Farentino. *THV*

Capricorn One 🐾🐾🐾 1978 (R) Astronauts

Brolin, Simpson and Waterston follow Mission Controller Holbrook's instructions to fake a Mars landing on a soundstage when their ship is discovered to be defective. When they find out they're supposed to expire in outer space so that the NASA scam won't become public knowledge, they flee to the desert, while reporter Gould sniffs out the cover up. Based on a pseudonymous novel by Ken Follett. **123m/C VHS, Beta, LV.** Elliott Gould, James Brolin, Brenda Vaccaro, O.J. Simpson, Hal Holbrook, Sam Waterston, Karen Black, Telly Savalas; **D:** Peter Hyams; **W:** Peter Hyams; **C:** Bill Butler; **M:** Jerry Goldsmith. *FOX*

Captain America The Return of Captain America

1944 Captain America battles a mad scientist in this 15-episode serial based on the comic book character. **240m/B VHS, Beta.** Dick Purcell, Adrian Booth, Lionel Atwill; **D:** John English; **W:** Elmer Clifton. *VCN, MLB, VTR*

Captain America 🐾½ 1979 Marvel Comic

character steps into feature film and flounders. The patriotic superhero son of WWII hero fights bad guy with contraband nuclear weapon. Made for television. Followed the same year with "Captain America II: Death Too Soon." **98m/C VHS, Beta.** Reb Brown, Len Birman, Heather Menzies, Steve Forrest, Robin Mattson, Joseph Ruskin, Michael McManus; **D:** Rod Holcomb. *USH*

Captain America 🐾½ 1989 (PG-13) Based

on the Marvel Comics superhero. It's 1941 and Steve Rogers has just been recruited to join a top secret experimental government program after flunking his army physical. Injected with a serum, Steve becomes super strong, fast, and smart but is matched in all three by an evil Nazi counterpart, Red Skull. The two battle to a WWII standstill and while Red Skull goes on with his evil plots, the next 40 years finds Captain America fast frozen in the Alaskan tundra. Finally, our hero is thawed in time to do a final battle with his evil nemesis. This one is ridiculous even by comic book standards but it may amuse the kids. **103m/C VHS, LV.** Matt Salinger, Scott Paulin, Ronny Cox, Ned Beatty, Darren McGavin, Melinda Dillon; **D:** Albert Pyun; **W:** Stephen Tolkin. *COL*

Captain America 2: Death Too Soon 🐾

1979 Terrorists hit America where it hurts, threatening to use age accelerating drug. Sequelized superhero fights chronic crow lines and series also slow, painful death. Made for television. **98m/C VHS, Beta.** Reb Brown, Connie Sellecca, Len Birman, Christopher Lee, Katherine Justice, Lana Wood, Christopher Carey; **D:** Ivan Nagy. *USH*

Captain Apache 🐾 1971 Union intelli-

gence officer Van Cleef investigates murder of Indian commissioner and discovers fake Indian war landscam. As clever as the title. **95m/C VHS, Beta.** Lee Van Cleef, Carroll Baker, Stuart Whitman; **D:** Alexander Singer; **W:** Philip Yordan. *MRV*

Captain Blackjack 🐾🐾 Black Jack 1951 All

star cast craps out in wannabe thriller about drug smuggling on the French Riviera. Social butterfly Moorehead directs drug traffic, detective Marshall undercovers as doctor, and Sanders looks bored in a British sort of way. **90m/B VHS.** *FR* George Sanders, Herbert Marshall, Agnes Moorehead, Patricia Roc, Marcel Dalio; **D:** Julien Duvivier. *NO*

Captain Blood 🐾🐾🐾½ 1935 Sabatini ad-

venture story launched then unknown 26-year-old Flynn and 19-year-old De Havilland to fame in perhaps the best pirate story ever. Exiled into slavery by a tyrannical governor, Irish physician Peter Blood is forced into piracy but ultimately earns a pardon for his swashbuckling ways. Love interest De Havilland would go on to appear in seven more features with Flynn, who took the part Robert Donat declined for health reasons. Cleverly budgeted using ship shots from silents, and miniature sets when possible. First original film score by composer Korngold. Also available colorized. **120m/B VHS, Beta, Closed Caption.** Errol Flynn, Olivia de Havilland, Basil Rathbone, J. Carrol Naish, Guy Kibbee, Lionel Atwill; **D:** Michael Curtiz; **C:** Hal Mohr. Nominations: Academy Awards '35: Best Picture, Best Sound. *MGM, FCT, MLB*

Captain Boycott 🐾🐾½ 1947 In 1880 Ire-

land, Boycott (Parker) is the despised rent collector for an aristocratic English landlord. When the poor tenant farmers can't pay, he's quick to throw them off the land. The farmers then band together to get rid of Boycott. Granger and Ryan are the prerequisite young lovers. Adapted from the novel by Philip Rooney. **94m/B VHS.** *GB* Cecil Parker, Stewart Granger, Kathleen Ryan, Niall McGinnis, Robert Donat, Mervyn Johns, Alastair Sim, Noel Purcell, Maurice Denham; **D:** Frank Launder; **W:** Frank Launder, Wolfgang Wilhelm; **C:** Wilkie Cooper, Oswald Morris; **M:** William Alwyn. *HMK*

Captain Caution 🐾🐾 1940 Young girl

throws caution to the wind when dad dies during the War of 1812, assisting young Mature to take over the old man's ship to do battle with the British. Watch for then unknown sailor Ladd. **84m/B VHS, Beta.** Victor Mature, Louise Platt, Bruce Cabot, Alan Ladd, Robert Barrat, Vivienne Osborne; **D:** Richard Wallace. Nominations: Academy Awards '40: Best Sound.

Captain Conan 🐾🐾🐾 Capitaine Conan 1996

On the Bulgarian border in 1918, during the last clashes of WWI, Conan (Torreton) is a fearless, impulsive warrior, reserving his respect only for his men. Although armistice is finally declared, the troops stationed in the Balkans are not demobilized and become increasingly fractious. This causes a rift between Conan and his educated friend Norbert (Le Bihan), who's been appointed a military legal representative. They are warily reunited in defense of a soldier (Val) charged with desertion, while still dealing with the ravages of the long conflict. Adapted from the book by Roger Vercel; French with subtitles. **129m/C VHS.** *FR* Philippe Torreton, Samuel Lebihan, Bernard Le Coq, Pierre Val, Francois Berleand, Claude Rich, Catherine Rich; **D:** Bertrand Tavernier; **W:** Bertrand Tavernier, Jean Cosmos; **C:** Alain Choquart; **M:** Oswald D'Andrea. Cesar Awards '97: Best Actor (Torreton), Best Director (Tavernier), Best Film. *NYR*

Captain from Castile 🐾🐾🐾 1947 Excit-

ing saga finds 16th-century Spanish nobleman Pedro De Vargas (Power) forced to flee the wrath of Inquisition chief De Silva (Sutton). He takes peasant girl Cantana (Peters), who's helped him, and joins Cortez's expedition to Mexico and the search for Aztec riches. Lots of adventures and old-fashioned pageantry. Peters' screen debut. **141m/C VHS, Closed Caption.** Tyrone Power, Jean Peters, Cesar Romero, Lee J. Cobb, John Sutton, Antonio Moreno, Thomas Gomez, Alan Mowbray; **D:** Henry King; **W:** Lamar Trotti; **C:** Charles Clarke, Arthur E. Arling; **M:** Alfred Newman. Nominations: Academy Awards '47: Best Original Dramatic/Comedy Score. *FXV*

The Captain from Koepenick 🎬🎬½ *Der Hauptmann von Koepenick* 1956 Popular true life comedy about a Berlin cobbler in 1906 who rebels against military bureaucracy by impersonating a Prussian officer and wreaking havoc on his town, arresting authorities and capturing soldiers, only to enjoy folk herodom when his ruse is discovered. Remake of Richard Oswald's 1931 classic. In German with subtitles. **93m/B VHS, Beta.** *GE* Heinz Ruehmann, Hannelore Schroth, Martin Held, Erich Schellow; *D:* Helmut Kaeutner. *NOS, FCT*

Captain Horatio Hornblower 🎬🎬🎬 1951 A colorful drama about the life and loves of the British sea captain during the Napoleonic wars. Peck is rather out of his element as the courageous, swashbuckling hero (Errol Flynn was originally cast) but there's enough fast-paced derring-do to make this a satisfying saga. Based on the novel by C.S. Forester. **117m/C VHS, Beta, LV.** *GB* Gregory Peck, Virginia Mayo, Robert Beatty, Denis O'Dea, Christopher Lee; *D:* Raoul Walsh; *W:* Ivan Goff; *C:* Guy Green. *WAR*

Captain January 🎬🎬½ 1936 (G) Crusty old lighthouse keeper rescues little orphan girl with curly hair from drowning and everyone breaks into cutesy song and dance, interrupted only when the authorities try to separate the two. Also available colorized. ♫*At the Codfish Ball; Early Bird; The Right Somebody to Love.* **81m/B VHS, Closed Caption.** Shirley Temple, Guy Kibbee, Buddy Ebsen, Slim Summerville, Jane Darwell, June Lang, George Irving, Si Jenks; *D:* David Butler. *FXV*

Captain Kidd 🎬½ 1945 Laughton huffs and puffs and searches for treasure on the high seas, finds himself held captive with rest of cast in anemic swashbuckler. **83m/B VHS, Beta.** Charles Laughton, John Carradine, Randolph Scott, Reginald Owen, Gilbert Roland, Barbara Britton, John Qualen, Sheldon Leonard; *D:* Rowland V. Lee; *W:* Norman Reilly Raine; *C:* Archie Stout. Nominations: Academy Awards '45: Best Original Dramatic/Comedy Score. *MRV, NOS, HHT*

Captain Kronos: Vampire Hunter 🎬🎬🎬 *Kronos; Vampire Castle* 1974 (R) Captain Kronos fences thirsty foes in Hammer horror hybrid. Artsy, atmospheric and atypical, it's written and directed with tongue firmly in cheek by Clemens, who penned many an "Avengers" episode. **91m/C VHS, Beta.** *GB* Horst Janson, John Carson, Caroline Munro, Ian Hendry, Shane Briant, Wanda Ventham, John Cater, Lois Daine; *D:* Brian Clemens; *C:* Ian Wilson. *NO*

Captain Newman, M.D. 🎬🎬½ 1963 Three army guys visit stiff shrink Peck during the final months of WWII in VA ward for the mentally disturbed. Much guilt and agonizing, with comic relief courtesy of Curtis. Peck is sub par, the direction flounders and there's something unsettling about quicksilver shifts from pathos to parody. Nonetheless touching with fine performance from Darin as guilt ridden hero. Based on the novel by Leo Rosten. **126m/C VHS, Beta.** Gregory Peck, Bobby Darin, Tony Curtis, Angie Dickinson, Eddie Albert, James Gregory, Jane Withers, Larry Storch, Robert Duvall; *D:* David Miller. Nominations: Academy Awards '63: Best Adapted Screenplay, Best Sound, Best Supporting Actor (Darin). *USH*

Captain Nuke and the Bomber Boys 🎬½ *Demolition Day* 1995 (PG) Three teenagers, who've stumbled across an atomic bomb, decide to use the device to get school called off. Instead, they wind up with the FBI and a couple of crooks after them. **?m/C VHS, Closed Caption.** Joe Mantegna, Martin Sheen, Joe Piscopo, Joanna Pacula, Rod Steiger. *NHO*

Captain Ron 🎬½ 1992 (PG-13) Harried couple Short and Place inherit a large boat and, with their two smart-mouthed kids, go to the Caribbean to sail the boat back to the U.S. Of course they know nothing about sailing, so they hire Captain Ron (Russell), a one-eyed, Long John Silver-talking boat captain. From there, numerous mishaps occur. Amusing sounding premise sinks like a

stone. Russell looks great in his teeny-weeny bikini, and the scenery is beautiful, but that's about it. *CW:* Some language and sensual situations. **104m/C VHS, Beta, LV, Closed Caption.** Kurt Russell, Martin Short, Mary Kay Place, Meadow Sisto, Benjamin Salisbury; *D:* Thom Eberhardt; *W:* Thom Eberhardt. *TOU*

Captain Scarlett 🎬½ 1953 Formulaic swashbuckler has nobleman Greene and highway guy Young fighting nasty French Royalists who've been putting the pressure on impecunious peasants. Runaway Spanish damsel in distress courtesy of Amar. Most novel aspect of the production is that the post-Napoleon French terrain has that vaguely south of the border feel. **75m/C VHS, Beta.** Richard Greene, Leonora Amar, Isobel Del Puerto, Nedrick Young, Manolo Fabregas; *D:* Thomas Carr. *NOS, MRV, GEM*

Captain Sinbad 🎬🎬½ 1963 Captain Sinbad must destroy the evil El Kerim, but first he must tackle a many-headed ogre, man-eating fish and crocodiles, a large fist clad in a spiked glove, an invisible monster, and more. To kill the villain, Sinbad must destroy his heart, which is kept in a tower with no entrance. A huge, witty, epic production with lots of special effects. This one is fun. **85m/C VHS.** Guy Williams, Heidi Bruhl, Pedro Armendariz Sr., Abraham Sofaer, Bernie Hamilton, Helmut Schneider; *D:* Byron Haskin; *W:* Ian McLellan Hunter, Guy Endore. *MGM*

Captain Swagger 🎬½ 1925 A man on the brink of thievery experiences some changes that keep him on the right side of the law. **50m/B VHS, Beta.** Rod La Rocque, Sue Carol, Richard Tucker, Victor Potel, Ullrich Haupt; *D:* Edward H. Griffith. *GPV*

Captains Courageous 🎬🎬🎬 1937 Rich brat Bartholomew takes a dip sans life jacket while leaning over an ocean liner railing to relieve himself of the half dozen ice cream sodas imprudently consumed at sea. Picked up by a Portuguese fishing boat, he at first treats his mandatory three month voyage as an unscheduled cab ride, but eventually, through a deepening friendship with crewman Tracy, develops a hitherto unheralded work ethic. The boy's filial bond with Tracy, of course, requires that the seaman meet with watery disaster. Based on the Rudyard Kipling novel. Director Fleming went on to "Gone With the Wind" and "The Wizard of Oz." **116m/B VHS, Beta.** Spencer Tracy, Lionel Barrymore, Freddie Bartholomew, Mickey Rooney, Melvyn Douglas, Charley Grapewin, John Carradine, Bobby Watson, Jack LaRue; *D:* Victor Fleming. Academy Awards '37: Best Actor (Tracy); Nominations: Academy Awards '37: Best Film Editing, Best Picture, Best Screenplay. *MGM, BMV, BTV*

Captains Courageous 🎬🎬½ 1995 TV adaptation of the 1897 novel by Rudyard Kipling finds pampered rich kid Vadas learning to become a man at the hands of stalwart sea captain Urich. **93m/C VHS.** Robert Urich, Kenny Vadas, Kaj-Erik Eriksen, Robert Wisden, Duncan Fraser; *D:* Michael Anderson Jr.; *W:* John McGreevey; *C:* Glen MacPherson; *M:* Eric N. Robertson, Claude Desjardins. *CAF*

Captains of the Clouds 🎬🎬½ 1942 Unabashedly patriotic film starring Cagney as a daredevil, independent Canadian bush pilot who makes his own flying rules. When WWII begins he joins the Royal Canadian Air Force but washes out when he can't follow orders. However, he finds a way to prove himself a hero as a civilian pilot ferrying a bomber to England. Cagney's first Technicolor film. **113m/C VHS.** James Cagney, Dennis (Stanley Morner) Morgan, Brenda Marshall, Alan Hale, George Tobias, Reginald Gardiner, Reginald Denny, Russell Arms, Paul Cavanagh, Charles Halton; *D:* Michael Curtiz; *M:* Max Steiner. Nominations: Academy Awards '42: Best Color Cinematography. *MGM, FCT*

Captain's Paradise 🎬🎬🎬 1953 Golden Fleece captain Guinness chugs between wives in Gibraltar and North Africa, much to the adulation of chief officer Goldner. While Gibraltar's little woman Johnson is homegrown homebody, little woman de Carlo is paint the town red type, allowing Guinness to have cake and eat it too, it

seems, except that he's inconveniently positioned in front of a firing squad at movie's start. **89m/B VHS, Beta.** *GB* Alec Guinness, Yvonne De Carlo, Celia Johnson, Miles Malleson, Nicholas Phipps, Ferdinand "Ferdy" Mayne, Sebastian Cabot; *D:* Anthony Kimmins; *M:* Malcolm Arnold. Nominations: Academy Awards '53: Best Story. *FCT*

The Captain's Table 🎬🎬 1960 Former cargo vessel captain Gregson is given luxury liner to command, and fails to revise his cargo captain style to fit new crew and clientele. British cast saves unremarkable script from mediocrity. **90m/C VHS.** *GB* John Gregson, Peggy Cummins, Donald Sinden, Nadia Gray; *D:* Jack Lee. *PAR*

Captive 🎬½ 1987 (R) Spoiled heiress is kidnapped by terrorist trio and brainwashed into anti-establishment Hearst-like creature. **98m/C VHS, Beta.** Oliver Reed, Irina Brook, Xavier DeLuc, Hiro Arai; *D:* Paul Mayersberg. *VTR*

Captive Heart 🎬🎬🎬 1947 Czech soldier Redgrave assumes the identity of a dead British officer in order to evade Nazis in WWII. Captured and imprisoned in camp reserved for British POWs, his stalagmates think they smell a spy, but he manages to convince them he's an OK Joe. Meanwhile, he's been writing letters home to the little missus, which means he's got a little explaining to do when he's released from prison. Especially fine Redgrave performance. **86m/B VHS, Beta.** *GB* Michael Redgrave, Basil Radford, Jack Warner, Jimmy Hanley, Rachel Kempson, Mervyn Johns; *D:* Basil Dearden. *NOS, DVT, VEC*

Captive Hearts 🎬 1987 (PG) Well frayed story holds cast captive in sushi romance. Two American flyers are shot down and taken prisoner in isolated Japanese mountain village, and one is shot by Cupid's arrow. **97m/C VHS, Beta, Closed Caption.** Noriyuki "Pat" Morita, Michael Sarrazin, Chris Makepeace; *D:* Paul Almond; *M:* David Benoit. *MGM, FOX*

A Captive in the Land 🎬½ 1991 (PG) Routine survival pic pits two strangers against the frozen Arctic tundra. Potapov is a Soviet airman who's too injured to walk when he's discovered by American meteorologist Waterston. When a rescue seems unlikely, the two are forced to try for a trek to civilization. Based on the novel by James Aldridge. **96m/C VHS.** Sam Waterston, Alexander Potapov; *D:* John Berry; *M:* Bill Conti, Lee Gold. *ART*

Captive Planet 🎬 1978 Bargain basement FX and really atrocious acting hold audience captive in routine earth on the verge of obliteration yarn. **95m/C VHS, Beta.** Sharon Baker, Chris Auram, Anthony Newcastle; *D:* Al Bradley. *NO*

Captive Rage 🎬 1988 (R) South American general Reed hijacks planeful of girlies to encourage US to release his son, who's in trouble because he swaps money for white powder. Violence lives up to title, all else disappoints. **99m/C VHS, Beta.** Oliver Reed, Robert Vaughn, Claudia Udy; *D:* Cedric Sundstrom. *MCG*

The Captive: The Longest Drive 2 🎬🎬 1976 (PG-13) Matheson and Russell play two recently reunited brothers in search of their sister, whom they believe is still a captive of the Cheyenne Indians who also raised Russell. Along the way the two come to the aid of a pioneer woman and her young son. This western was actually a brief television series known as "The Quest," and is a continuation of the pilot episode released on video as "The Longest Drive." **80m/C VHS, LV, Closed Caption.** Kurt Russell, Tim Matheson. *THV*

Captive Wild Woman 🎬🎬½ 1943 Mad scientist Dr. Sigmund Walters (Carradine) transforms an ape into the beautiful Paula Depress (Aquanetta), who promptly joins the circus as a mysterious animal trainer. Unfortunately, she falls in love with fellow trainer Fred (Stone), who already has a gal, bringing back the beast in the pretty Paula. Sequelled by "Jungle Captive" and "Jungle Woman." **61m/B VHS, Closed Caption.** Acquanetta, John Carradine, Milburn Stone, Evelyn Ankers,

Lloyd Corrigan, Vince Barnett, Paul Fix; **D:** Edward Dmytryk; **W:** Griffin Jay, Henry Sucher. *USH*

Captives 🎬🎬½ **1994 (R)** Middle-class dentist Rachel Clifford (Ormond), recently separated from her husband, takes a part-time job at a local prison where she becomes attracted to her patient, Cockney charmer Philip Chaney (Roth). He's coming to the end of a 10-year sentence and the lusty duo manage to consummate their relationship during one of Philip's day-releases. Only problem is fellow con Towler (Salmon) notices what's happening and blackmails and threatens Rachel—leading to a violent confrontation. Roth and Ormond click believably as opposites-attract partners though the script has some weak elements.**CW:** Strong sex scene, and for language and some violence. 100m/C VHS, LV, **Closed Caption.** *GB* Tim Roth, Julia Ormond, Colin Salmon, Keith Allen, Siobhan Redmond, Peter Capaldi, Richard Hawley, Annette Badland, Jeff Nuttal; **D:** Angela Pope; **W:** Frank Deasy; **C:** Remi Adefarasin; **M:** Colin Towns. *TOU*

The Capture 🎬🎬🎬 **1950** Above-average story told in flashback has Ayres hiding out in Mexico because he thought he killed an innocent man. He seeks out the widow to question her about him and they wind up marrying. When he finds the real culprit, the man is killed and the evidence points to Ayres. Ayres and Wright are great, as is the native Mexican musical score. 67m/B VHS. Lew Ayres, Teresa Wright, Victor Jory, Jacqueline White, Jimmy Hunt, Duncan Renaldo, William "Billy" Bakewell; **D:** John Sturges. *NOS*

The Capture of Bigfoot 🎬 **1979 (PG)** Barefoot monster tracks footprints around town after 25 years of peace, and evil businessman attempts to capture creature for personal gain. 92m/C VHS, Beta. Stafford Morgan, Katherine Hopkins, Richard Kennedy, Otis Young, George Flower, John Goff; **D:** Bill Rebane.

The Capture of Grizzly Adams 🎬½ **1982** Framed for murder, Adams and his everfaithful companion Ben the bear must not only clear his name but outwit a band of outlaws who are holding his young daughter captive. Made for television. 96m/C VHS. Dan Haggerty, Chuck Connors, June Lockhart, Kim Darby, Noah Beery Jr., Keenan Wynn. *WOV*

Captured in Chinatown 🎬 **1935** Dog chases bad guys in Chinatown. Bow wow. 53m/B VHS, Beta, LV. Marion Shilling, Charles Delaney, Philo McCullough, Robert Ellis; **D:** Elmer Clifton. *SNC*

Car Crash 🎬 **19??** Organized crime hits stock car racing head on to produce crashing bore. 103m/C VHS. Joey Travolta, Anna Obregon, Vittorio Mezzogiorno. *NO*

Car 54, Where Are You? **1961** The first situation comedy about police officers ran on television from 1961-63. Join offbeat New York cops Gunther Toody and Francis Muldoon of the beleaguered 53rd Precinct. Each cassette contains two episodes. Eight cassettes. 50m/B VHS. Fred Gwynne, Joe E. Ross, Nipsey Russell, Al Lewis; **D:** Stanley Prager, Nat Hiken. *REP, FCT, MOV*

Car 54, Where Are You? 🎬 **1994 (PG-13)** Exceedingly lame remake of the exceedingly lame television series, which ran for only two seasons, 1961-63. This time, Toody (Johansen) and Muldoon (McGinley) are protecting a mafia stool pigeon (Piven), while vampy Velma Velour (Drescher) sets her sights on Muldoon. Not many laughs and a waste of a talented cast. Sat on the shelf at Orion for three years (with good reason).**CW:** Language and sexual suggestiveness. 89m/C VHS, LV, **Closed Caption.** David Johansen, Fran Drescher, Rosie O'Donnell, John C. McGinley, Nipsey Russell, Al Lewis, Daniel Baldwin, Jeremy Piven; **D:** Bill Fishman; **W:** Ebbe Roe Smith, Erik Tarloff, Peter McCarthy, Peter Crabbe; **M:** Bernie Worrell, Pray For Rain. Golden Raspberry Awards '94: Worst Supporting Actress (O'Donnell). *ORI*

Car Trouble 🎬🎬½ **1986 (R)** Young English husband buys new Jaguar and wife's not so minor car trouble causes major marital trouble. Funnybone-tickling pairing of Walters and Charleson. 93m/C VHS, Beta, LV. Julie Walters, Ian Charleson; **D:** David Green; **M:** Meat Loaf. *MCG*

Car Wash 🎬🎬½ **1976 (PG)** L.A. carwash provides a soap-opera setting for disjointed comic bits about owners of dirty cars and people who hose them down for a living. Econo budget and lite plot, but serious comic talent. A sort of disco carwash version of "Grand Hotel." 97m/C VHS, Beta. Franklin Ajaye, Sully Boyer, Richard Brestoff, George Carlin, Richard Pryor, Melanie Mayron, Ivan Dixon, Antonio Fargas; **D:** Michael A. Schultz; **W:** Joel Schumacher. *USH, FCT*

Caravaggio 🎬🎬🎬 **1986** Controversial biography of the late Renaissance painter famous for his bisexuality, fondness for prostitute models, violence and depravity. Photography by Gabriel Beristain reproduces the artist's visual style. 97m/C VHS, Beta, LV. *GB* Nigel Terry, Sean Bean, Tilda Swinton; **D:** Derek Jarman; **W:** Derek Jarman. *TPV, FCT, CCN*

Caravan to Vaccares 🎬 **1974 (PG)** French Duke hires young American to sneak Eastern European scientist into the States, and little suspense ensues. Based on Alistair MacLean novel. 98m/C VHS, Beta. David Birney, Charlotte Rampling; **D:** Geoffrey Reeve.

The Caravan Trail 🎬🎬 **1946** A cowboy becomes marshal in order to bring to justice those who have stolen land and murdered his friend. This was shot in color, which was rare for the 1940s. 53m/C VHS, Beta. Eddie Dean, Lash LaRue, Emmett Lynn, Jean Carlin, Charles "Blackie" King, Bob Barron, Lloyd Ingraham, Bud Osborne; **D:** Robert Emmett Tansey. *NOS, RXM, HEG*

Carbon Copy 🎬🎬 **1981 (PG)** Successful white executive has life turned inside out when his 17-year-old illegitimate son, who happens to be black, decides it's time to look up dear old dad. Typical comedy-with-a-moral. 92m/C VHS, Beta, LV. George Segal, Susan St. James, Jack Warden, Paul Winfield, Dick Martin, Vicky Dawson, Tom Poston, Denzel Washington; **D:** Michael A. Schultz; **W:** Stanley Shapiro; **M:** Bill Conti. *COL*

Cardiac Arrest 🎬 **1974 (PG)** Lunatic eviscerates victims in trolley town. They left their hearts in San Francisco. 95m/C VHS, Beta. Garry Goodrow, Mike Chan, Max Gail; **D:** Murray Mintz.

The Cardinal 🎬🎬½ **1963** Priestly young Tryon rises through ecclesiastical ranks to become Cardinal, struggling through a plethora of tests of faith, none so taxing as the test of the audience's patience. Had Preminger excised some 60 minutes of footage, he might have had a compelling portrait of faith under fire, but as it stands, the cleric's life is epic confusion. Fine acting, even from Tryon, who later went on to bookish fame, and from Huston who's normally on the other side of the camera. McNamara's final performance. Based on the Henry Morton Robinson novel. 175m/C VHS, Beta, LV, Letterbox. Tom Tryon, Carol Lynley, Dorothy Gish, Maggie McNamara, Cecil Kellaway, John Huston, John Saxon, Burgess Meredith; **D:** Otto Preminger; **C:** Leon Shamroy. Golden Globe Awards '64: Best Film—Drama, Best Supporting Actor (Huston); Nominations: Academy Awards '63: Best Art Direction/Set Decoration (Color), Best Color Cinematography, Best Costume Design (Color), Best Director (Preminger), Best Film Editing, Best Supporting Actor (Huston). *WAR, IME, VTR*

The Care Bears Movie 🎬🎬 **1984 (G)** The Care Bears leave their cloud home in Care-a-lot to try and teach earthlings how to share their feelings of love and caring for each other. 75m/C VHS, Beta, **Closed Caption.** **D:** Arna Selznick; **V:** Mickey Rooney, Georgia Engel, Harry Dean Stanton. *ART, VES, FCT*

The Care Bears Movie 2: A New Generation 🎬🎬 **1986 (G)** Sequel to the sweet adventures of the animated bear family and their new offspring. 77m/C VHS, Beta, Closed

Caption. D: Dale Schott; **V:** Maxine Miller, Pam Hyatt, Hadley Key. *COL*

Career 🎬🎬½ **1959** An overwrought, depressing drama about the trials and tribulations of an actor trying to make it on Broadway. He'll try anything to succeed. Good direction, but so-so acting. 105m/B VHS, LV, **Closed Caption.** Dean Martin, Anthony (Tony) Franciosa, Shirley MacLaine, Carolyn Jones, Joan Blackman, Robert Middleton, Donna Douglas; **D:** Joseph Anthony; **C:** Joseph LaShelle. Golden Globe Awards '60: Best Actor—Drama (Franciosa); Nominations: Academy Awards '59: Best Art Direction/Set Decoration (B & W), Best Black and White Cinematography, Best Costume Design (B & W).*PAR*

Career Opportunities 🎬½ **1991 (PG-13)** "Home Alone" clone for teenagers from John Hughes' factory. Whaley is an unsuccessful conartist who finally gets a job as the night janitor of the local department store. He fools around at company expense until he finds the town's beauty (Connelly) asleep in a dressing room. The pair then play make-believe until its time to thwart some small-time thieves. Unexciting and unrealistic in the worst way; no wonder Candy isn't billed—he probably didn't want to be. 83m/C VHS, LV, **Closed Caption.** Frank Whaley, Jennifer Connelly, Dermot Mulroney, Kieran Mulroney, John M. Jackson, Jenny O'Hara, Noble Willingham, Barry Corbin, Denise Galik, William Forsythe; **Cameos:** John Candy; **D:** Bryan Gordon; **W:** John Hughes; **M:** Thomas Newman. *USH*

Carefree 🎬🎬🎬 **1938** Dizzy radio singer Rogers can't make up her mind about beau Bellamy, so he sends her to analyst Astaire. Seems she can't even dream a little dream until shrink Astaire prescribes that she ingest some funny food, which causes her to dream she's in love with the Fredman. Au contraire, says he, it's a Freudian thing, and he hypnotically suggests that she really loves Bellamy. The two line up to march down the aisle together, and Fred stops dancing just long enough to realize he's in love with Ginger. A screwball comedy with music. 🎵I Used to be Colorblind; The Night is Filled With Music; Change Partners; The Yam. 83m/B VHS, Beta, LV. Fred Astaire, Ginger Rogers, Ralph Bellamy, Jack Carson, Franklin Pangborn, Hattie McDaniel; **D:** Mark Sandrich; **M:** Irving Berlin. Nominations: Academy Awards '38: Best Interior Decoration, Best Song ("Change Partners and Dance with Me"), Best Score. *TTC, IME*

Careful 🎬🎬 **1994** Butler-in-training Neale courts Neville in an alpine mountain village where silence is golden, or at least being quiet will lessen the chance of an avalanche. Dig a little deeper and you find incest, repression and other nasty things. Highly individualistic black comedy parodies German Expressionism and Freudian psychology to the point of absurdity, dealing with snow, sex, sleep, spirits, and obsessive/compulsive personality disorders. Third film from Canadian cult director Maddin is awash in vivid primary colors when it suits the scene's mood and employs between-scenes titles in a homage to cinematic antiquity. 100m/C VHS. Kyle McCulloch, Gosia Dobrowolska, Jackie Burroughs, Sarah Neville, Brent Neale, Paul Cox, Victor Cowie, Michael O'Sullivan, Vince Rimmer, Katya Gardner; **D:** Guy Maddin; **W:** Guy Maddin, George Toles; **M:** John McCulloch. *KIV*

Careful, He Might Hear You 🎬🎬🎬 **1984 (PG)** Abandoned by his father, six-year-old P.S. becomes a pawn between his dead mother's two sisters, one working class and the other wealthy, and his worldview is further overturned by the sudden reappearance of his prodigal father. Set in Depression-era Australia, Schultz's vision is touching and keenly observed, and manages a sort of child's eye sense of proportion. Based on a novel by Sumner Locke Elliott. 113m/C VHS, Beta, **Closed Caption.** *AU* Nicholas Gledhill, Wendy Hughes, Robyn Nevin, John Hargreaves; **D:** Carl Schultz. Australian Film Institute '83: Best Actress (Hughes), Best Film. *FOX*

Caribe ⬥½ **1987** Caribbean travelogue masquerades as spy thriller. Arms smuggling goes awry, and neither voodoo nor bikinied blondes can prevent audience from dozing. Never released theatrically. **96m/C VHS, Beta, LV.** John Savage, Kara Glover, Stephen McHattie, Sam Malkin; *D:* Michael Kennedy. ART, VES

The Cariboo Trail ⬥⬥ **1950** Two prospecting men seek their fortune in British Columbia, the golden West of Canada in the 1890s. But they find themselves opposed by a ruthless rancher and claim-jumpers. Actually filmed in Colorado with excellent cinematography and solid performances from some big names, it's still a run-of-the-mill entry. Made the same year that the Gabby Hayes' show first aired. **80m/C VHS, LV, Closed Caption.** Randolph Scott, George "Gabby" Hayes, Bill Williams, Victor Jory; *D:* Edwin L. Marin. IME

Carlito's Way ⬥⬥⬥ **1993 (R)** Puerto Rican crime czar Carlito Brigante (Pacino) has just gotten out of jail and wants to go straight. But his drug underworld cohorts don't believe he can do it. Penn (barely recognizable) is great as a sleazy coked-out lawyer who's way out of his league. Remarkably subdued violence given DePalma's previous rep—it's effective without being gratuitous, especially the final shootout set in Grand Central Station. Pacino's performance is equally subdued, with controlled tension and lots of eye contact rather than grandiose emotions. Based on the novels "Carlito's Way" and "After Hours" by Edwin Torres. Pacino and DePalma previously teamed up for "Scarface." *CW:* Drug content and language, strong violence, and sexuality. **145m/C VHS, LV, Letterbox, Closed Caption, DVD.** Al Pacino, Sean Penn, Penelope Ann Miller, Luis Guzman, John Leguizamo, Ingrid Rogers, James Rebhorn, Viggo Mortensen, Jorge Porcel, Joseph Siravo, Adrian Pasdar; *D:* Brian DePalma; *W:* David Koepp; *C:* Stephen Burum; *M:* Patrick Doyle. Nominations: Golden Globe Awards '94: Best Supporting Actor (Penn), Best Supporting Actress (Miller).USH

Carlton Browne of the F.O. ⬥⬥½ *Man in a Cocked Hat* **1959** Bumbling Brit diplomat Thomas visits tiny Pacific island of Gallardia, forgotten by the mother country for some 50 years, to insure tenuous international agreement after the island's king dies. Not sterling Sellers but some shining moments. **88m/C VHS, Beta.** *GB* Peter Sellers, Terry-Thomas, Luciana Paluzzi, Ian Bannen; *D:* Roy Boulting, Jeffrey Dell; *W:* Roy Boulting; *M:* John Addison. FCT

Carmen ⬥⬥⬥ **1983 (R)** Choreographer casts Carmen and finds life imitates art when he falls under the spell of the hotblooded Latin siren. Bizet's opera lends itself to erotically charged flamenco context. Well acted, impressive scenes including cigarette girls' dance fight and romance between Carmen and Don Jose. In Spanish with English subtitles. **99m/C VHS, Beta.** *SP* Antonio Gades, Laura Del Sol, Paco DeLucia, Christina Hoyos; *D:* Carlos Saura; *C:* Pasquale De Santis. British Academy Awards '84: Best Foreign Film; Nominations: Academy Awards '83: Best Foreign Language Film. CTH

Carmen Jones ⬥⬥⬥ **1954** Bizet's tale of fickle femme fatale Carmen heads South with an all black cast and new lyrics by Hammerstein II. Soldier Belafonte falls big time for factory working belle Dandridge during the war, and runs off with miss thang after he kills his C.O. and quits the army. Tired of prettyboy Belafonte, Dandridge's eye wanders upon prize pugilist Escamillo, inspiring ex-soldier beau to wring her throaty little neck. Film debuts of Carroll and Peters. More than a little racist undertone to the direction. Actors' singing is dubbed. ♪Dat's Love; Dere's a Cafe on de Corner; Beat Out Dat Rhythm on a Drum; You Talk Just Like My Maw; Stand Up and Fight; Dis Flower; My Joe. **105m/C VHS, LV, Letterbox, Closed Caption.** Dorothy Dandridge, Harry Belafonte, Pearl Bailey, Roy Glenn, Diahann Carroll, Brock Peters; *D:* Otto Preminger; *C:* Sam Leavitt. Golden Globe Awards '55: Best Film—Musical/Comedy, National Film Registry '92;; Nominations:

Academy Awards '54: Best Actress (Dandridge), Scoring of a Musical. FXL

Carmilla **1989** An adaptation of the Sheridan Le Fanu lesbian vampire tale. From Shelley Duvall's cable television series "Nightmare Classics." **60m/C VHS, Beta.** Meg Tilly, Ione Skye, Roddy McDowall, Roy Dotrice; *D:* Gabrielle Beaumont. NO

Carnage ⬥ **1984** Hungry house consumes inhabitants. **91m/C VHS, Beta.** Leslie Den Dooven, Michael Chiodo, Deeann Veeder; *D:* Andy Milligan.

Carnal Crimes ⬥½ **1991 (R)** Well-acted upscale softcore trash about a sensuous woman, ignored by her middle-aged lawyer husband and drawn to a young stud photographer with a shady past and S&M tendencies. Available in a sexy unrated version also.*CW:* Language, violence, and strong sensuality. **103m/C VHS.** Martin Hewitt, Linda Carol, Rich Crater, Alex Kubik, Yvette Stefens, Paula Trickey; *D:* Alexander Gregory Hippolyte; *W:* Jon Robert Samsel; *M:* Matthew Ross, Jeff Fishman. NO

Carnal Knowledge ⬥⬥⬥ **1971 (R)** Carnal knowledge of the me generation. Three decades in the sex-saturated lives of college buddies Nicholson and Garfunkel, chronicled through girlfriends, affairs, and marriages. Controversial upon release, it's not a flattering anatomy of Y-chromosome carriers. Originally written as a play. Kane's debut. **96m/C VHS, Beta, LV, 8mm, Letterbox.** Jack Nicholson, Candice Bergen, Art Garfunkel, Ann-Margret, Rita Moreno, Carol Kane; *D:* Mike Nichols; *W:* Jules Feiffer; *C:* Giuseppe Rotunno. Golden Globe Awards '72: Best Supporting Actress (Ann-Margret); Nominations: Academy Awards '71: Best Supporting Actress (Ann-Margret). COL, FOX, CRC

Carnival in Flanders ⬥⬥⬥½ *La Kermesse Heroique* **1935** When Spanish invaders enter a small 17th century Flemish village they discover all the men have diappeared. So it's up to the women to save the town from destruction—and they decide to do it by seducing the invaders. Classic French costume farce with a witty script and fine performances. In French with English subtitles. **90m/B VHS, Beta.** *FR* Francoise Rosay, Louis Jouvet, Jean Murat, Andre Aleme, Micheline Cheirel; *D:* Jacques Feyder; *C:* Harry Stradling. New York Film Critics Awards '36: Best Foreign Film; Venice Film Festival '36: Best Director (Feyder). HTV, MRV, HHT

Carnival Lady ⬥ **1933** Silver spooner Vincent is scheduled to tie the knot until little lady-to-be discovers he's a bit out of pocket after the stock market takes a wee dip. Jilted and impecunious, he heads for the big top, where he horns in on the high diver's turf, and it's all downhill from there. **66m/B VHS, Beta.** Patricia "Boots" Mallory, Allen Vincent. VCN

Carnival of Blood ⬥ *Death Rides a Carousel* **1971 (PG)** Boring talky scenes punctuated by Coney Island murder mayhem followed by more boring talky scenes. Young's debut, not released for five years. The question's not why they delayed release, but why they bothered at all. A carnival of cliches. **80m/C VHS, Beta.** Earle Edgerton, Judith Resnick, Martin Barlosky, John Harris, Burt Young, Kaly Mills, Gloria Spivak; *D:* Leonard Kirtman; *W:* Leonard Kirtman. NO

Carnival of Souls ⬥⬥⬥ **1962** Cult-followed zero budget zombie opera has young Hilligoss and girlfriends take wrong turn off bridge into river. Mysteriously unscathed, Hilligoss rents room and takes job as church organist, but she keeps running into dancing dead people, led by director Harvey. Spooky, very spooky. Laserdisc version offers restored picture quality and a refined audio track, as well as introductory feature on the movie's background. **80m/B VHS, LV.** Candace Hilligoss, Sidney Berger, Frances Feist, Stan Levitt, Art Ellison, Harold (Herk) Harvey; *D:* Harold (Herk) Harvey; *W:* John Clifford; *C:* Maurice Prather. EEL, MRV, SNC

Carnival Rock ⬥½ **1957** Story of love triangular in seedy nightclub. Club owner Stewart loves chanteuse Cabot who loves card playin' Hutton. Who cares? Maybe hard-core Corman

devotees. Good tunes from the Platters, the Blockbusters, Bob Luman and David Houston. **80m/B VHS, Beta.** Susan Cabot, Brian Hutton, David J. Stewart, Dick Miller; *D:* Roger Corman. RHI, AOV, FCT

Carnival Story ⬥½ **1954** Yet another melodramatic cliche about love triangular under the big top. German girl joins American-owned carnival and two guys start acting out unbecoming territorial behavior. Filmed in Germany. **94m/C VHS, Beta.** Anne Baxter, Steve Cochran, Lyle Bettger, George Nader; *D:* Kurt Neumann. NOS, GEM, DVT

Carnosaur ⬥⬥ **1993 (R)** Straight from the Corman film factory, this exploitive quickie about dinosaurs harkens back to '50s-style monster epics. Predictable plot with extremely cheap effects. Genetic scientist Dr. Jane Tiptree (Ladd) is hatching diabolic experiments with chickens when things go awry. The experiments result in a bunch of lethal prehistoric creatures wrecking havoc among the community.*CW:* Language and monster violence. **82m/C VHS.** Diane Ladd, Raphael Sbarge, Jennifer Runyon, Harrison Page, Clint Howard, Ned Bellamy; *D:* Adam Simon; *W:* Adam Simon; *M:* Nigel Holton. NHO

Carnosaur 2 ⬥½ **1994 (R)** Technicians investigating a power shortage at a secret military mining facility encounter deadly dinos. Entertaining schlock.*CW:* Language; violence; gore. **90m/C VHS, LV.** John Savage, Cliff DeYoung, Arabella Holzbog, Ryan Thomas Johnson; *D:* Louis Morneau. NHO

Carnosaur 3: Primal Species ⬥½ **1996** Terrorists get big surprise when the cargo they hijack turns out to be three very hungry dinos who make snacks of them all. Then it's up to commando Valentine, scientist Gunn, and some soldiers to get rid of the beasts. **82m/C VHS.** Scott Valentine, Janet Gunn, Rick Dean, Rodger Halstead, Tony Peck; *D:* Jonathan Winfrey; *M:* Kevin Kiner. NHO

Carny ⬥⬥⬥ **1980 (R)** Hothead carnival bozo Busey and peacemaker Robertson experience friendship difficulties when runaway Foster rolls in hay with one and then other. Originally conceived as a documentary by "Derby" filmmaker Kaylor, it's a candid, unsavory, behind-the-scenes anatomy. Co-written by "The Band" member Robertson. **102m/C VHS, Beta.** Gary Busey, Robbie Robertson, Jodie Foster, Meg Foster, Kenneth McMillan, Elisha Cook Jr., Craig Wasson; *D:* Robert Kaylor; *W:* Robbie Robertson, Thomas Baum; *C:* Harry Stradling Jr.; *M:* Alex North. FOX, WAR

Caro Diario ⬥⬥⬥ *Dear Diary* **1993** Three offbeat chapters from director Moretti's own life. "On My Vespa" has the director taking off on a personal tour of Rome, including its cinemas and their influence on him. In "Islands" Moretti and friend Gerardo travel to a series of island communities, including Salina, dominated by only children to whom their parents defer obsessively. "Doctors" finds Moretti experiencing a misdiagnosed medical crisis. Lots of charm and a certain shameless romanticism. Italian with subtitles. **100m/C VHS, LV.** *IT* Renato Carpentieri; *D:* Nanni Moretti; *W:* Nanni Moretti; *M:* Nicola Piovani. Cannes Film Festival '94: Best Director (Moretti). NLC

Carolina Skeletons ⬥⬥ **1992 (R)** As a child in a small southern town, Gossett watched as his brother was accused of a vicious double murder and quickly tried and executed. Thirty years later, the ex-Green Beret returns home to find the real killer and clear his brother's name. But there are those in the town who will do anything to stop their secrets from being revealed.*CW:* Violence to children. **94m/C VHS, LV.** Louis Gossett Jr., Bruce Dern, Melissa Leo, Paul Roebling, G.D. Spradlin, Bill Cobbs; Henderson Forsythe, Clifton James; *D:* John Erman; *W:* Tracy Keenan Wynn; *M:* John Morris. TRI

Caroline? ⬥⬥⬥ **1990 (PG)** A wealthy young woman is presumed dead in a plane crash. Now 15 years later a stranger appears at the family home claiming to be Caroline—and wanting her inheritance. Is it possible that what she says is true or is it all an elaborate ruse? An especially good performance by Zimbalist. Made for television as a "Hallmark Hall of Fame" presentation. Based on the novel "Father's Arcane Daughter" by E.L. Konigsburg. **100m/C VHS, LV, Closed Caption.** Stephanie Zimbalist, Pamela Reed, George Grizzard, Dorothy McGuire, Patricia Neal, Shawn Phelan, Jenny Jacobs; **D:** Joseph Sargent; **M:** Charles Bernstein. REP

Caroline at Midnight 🎞️ **1993** (R) After a reporter's former girlfriend, Caroline, dies in a mysterious auto accident he winds up falling for her girlfriend Victoria. Then he discovers both women are connected to drug-dealing cops. Good cast in this atmospheric erotic thriller with plenty of puzzles. **CW:** Language, violence and drug content, and sexuality. **92m/C VHS, LV.** Clayton Rohner, Mia Sara, Timothy Daly, Judd Nelson, Virginia Madsen, Zach Galligan; **D:** Scott McGinnis. NHO

Carousel 🎞️🎞️🎞️ **1956** Much-loved Rodgers & Hammerstein musical based on Ferenc Molnar's play "Liliom" (filmed by Fritz Lang in 1935) about a swaggering carnival barker (MacRae) who tries to change his life after he falls in love with a good woman. Killed while attempting to foil a robbery he was supposed to help commit, he begs his heavenly hosts for the chance to return to the mortal realm just long enough to set things straight with his teenage daughter. Now indisputably a classic, the film lost $2 million when it was released. 🎵If I Loved You; Soliloquy; You'll Never Walk Alone; What's the Use of Wond'rin; When I Marry Mister Snow; When the Children Are Asleep; A Real Nice Clambake; Carousel Ballet; Carousel Waltz. **128m/C VHS, Beta, LV, Closed Caption.** Gordon MacRae, Shirley Jones, Cameron Mitchell, Gene Lockhart, Barbara Ruick, Robert Rounseville, Richard Deacon, Tor Johnson; **D:** Henry King; **M:** Richard Rodgers, Oscar Hammerstein. FOX, RDG, HMV

The Carpathian Eagle 🎞️ **1981** Police wonder why murdered victims have hearts ripped out while audience wonders what weird title has to do with anything. Routine evisceration fest, part of Elvira's Thriller Video. **60m/C VHS, Beta.** Suzanne Danielle, Sian Phillips, Pierce Brosnan, Anthony Valentine; **D:** Francis Megahy. ART

The Carpenter 🎞️ **1989** (R) Post-nervous breakdown woman receives nightly visits from guy who builds stuff with wood. Very scary stuff. Also available in slightly longer unrated version. **85m/C VHS, LV.** CA Wings Hauser, Lynne Adams, Pierce Lenoir, Barbara Ann Jones, Beverly Murray; **D:** David Wellington; **W:** Doug Taylor; **C:** David Franco. REP

Carpet of Horror 🎞️🎞️ **1964** The city of London is terrorized by a small ball emitting poison gas in this schlock horror film. Death results when the ball is rolled into the living rooms of intended victims. **?m/C VHS.** Joachim Berger, Carl Lange, Karin Dor. SNC

The Carpetbaggers 🎞️🎞️ **1964** (PG) Uncannily Howard Hughesian Peppard wallows in wealth and women in Hollywood in the 1920s and 1930s. Spayed version of the Harold Robbins novel. Ladd's final appearance. Followed by the prequel "Nevada Smith." Introduced by Joan Collins. **150m/C VHS, Beta.** George Peppard, Carroll Baker, Alan Ladd, Elizabeth Ashley, Lew Ayres, Martha Hyer, Martin Balsam, Robert Cummings, Archie Moore, Audrey Totter; **D:** Edward Dmytryk; **W:** John Michael Hayes; **M:** Elmer Bernstein. National Board of Review Awards '64: Best Supporting Actor (Balsam). PAR

Carpool 🎞️🎞️ **1996** (PG) Dumb but amiable comedy finds harried dad Daniel Miller stuck driving a minivan filled with kids to school. Too bad he gets sidetracked and hijacked by bumbling would-be bank robber Franklin Laszlo (Arnold) who takes them hostage and on a really wild ride through the streets and shopping malls of Seattle (except it's filmed in Vancouver). **92m/C VHS, LV, Closed Caption.** Tom Arnold, David Paymer, Rhea Perlman, Rod Steiger, Kim Coates, Rachel Leigh Cook, Mikey Kovar, Micah Gardener, Blake Warkol; **D:** Arthur Hiller; **W:** Don Rhymer; **C:** David M. Walsh; **M:** John Debney. Golden Raspberry Awards '96: Worst Actor (Arnold). MGM

Carrie 🎞️🎞️🎞️ **1952** In a part turned down by Cary Grant, Olivier plays a married American who self destructs as the woman he loves scales the heights to fame and fortune. The manager of a posh epicurean mecca, Olivier deserts wife Hopkins and steals big bucks from his boss to head east with paramour Jones, a country bumpkin transplanted to Chicago. Once en route to thespian fame in the Big Apple, Jones abandons her erstwhile beau, who crumbles pathetically. Adapted from Theodore Dreiser's "Sister Carrie," it's mega melodrama, but the performances are above reproach. **118m/B VHS, Beta, LV, Closed Caption.** Laurence Olivier, Jennifer Jones, Miriam Hopkins, Eddie Albert, Basil Ruysdael, Ray Teal, Barry Kelley, Sara Berner, William Reynolds, Mary Murphy, Charles Halton; **D:** William Wyler; **C:** Victor Milner. Nominations: Academy Awards '52: Best Art Direction/Set Decoration (B & W), Best Costume Design (B & W). PAR, FCT

Carrie 🎞️🎞️🎞️ **1976** (R) Overprotected by religious fanatic mother Laurie and mocked by the in-crowd, shy, withdrawn high school girl Carrie White is asked to the prom. Realizing she's been made the butt of a joke, she unleashes her considerable telekinetic talents. Travolta, Allen, and Irving are teenagers who get what they deserve. Based on the Stephen King novel. Laserdisc version features the original movie trailer, an interview with screenwriter Lawrence D. Cohen, publicity shots, a study of De Palma's film-making techniques, and commentary by film expert Laurent Bouzereau. **98m/C VHS, Beta, LV.** Sissy Spacek, Piper Laurie, John Travolta, William Katt, Amy Irving, Nancy Allen, Edie McClurg, Betty Buckley, P.J. Soles, Sydney Lassick, Stefan Gierasch; **D:** Brian DePalma; **W:** Lawrence D. Cohen; **C:** Mario Tosi; **M:** Pino Donaggio. National Society of Film Critics Awards '76: Best Actress (Spacek); Nominations: Academy Awards '76: Best Actress (Spacek), Best Supporting Actress (Laurie). MGM, CRC

Carried Away 🎞️🎞️½ Acts of Love **1995** (R) Exposing his middle-aged bod, as well as the myth that he can play only psycho toughs, Hopper, as the Midwestern teacher Joseph, is seduced by a 17-year-old student (Locane) in their small conservative town. Based on Harrison's novel "Farmer," it's a sexually active slice of life with the injured Joseph limping through the care of his dying mother, the fate of the small country school where he teaches and his relationship with longtime lover Rosealee (Amy Irving). Hopper's not the only one playing against type, as Irving turns in a fine performance as the widowed schoolmarm. Director Barreto (and Irving's husband) pushes the envelope with full frontal nudity. **CW:** Nudity, strong sexuality, and language. **109m/C VHS, LV, Closed Caption.** Dennis Hopper, Amy Locane, Gary Busey, Hal Holbrook, Amy Irving, Julie Harris, Christopher Pettiet, Priscilla Pointer, Gail Cronauer; **D:** Bruno Barreto; **W:** Ed Jones; **C:** Declan Quinn; **M:** Bruce Broughton. NLC

The Carrier 🎞️🎞️ **1987** (R) Smalltown Sleepy Rock is ideal family-raising turf until plague mysteriously blights inhabitants, and townspeople are out to exterminate all potential carriers. Silverman is standout as local spiritual leader; well orchestrated crowd scenes. Best park your IQ before watching. Filmed on location in Manchester, Michigan. **99m/C VHS, Beta.** Gregory Fortescue, Steve Dixon, Paul Silverman; **D:** Nathan J. White. NO

Carrington 🎞️🎞️½ **1995** (R) England's artistic Bloomsbury group is examined through the eccentric relationship of artist Dora Carrington (Thompson) and her love for homosexual Lytton Strachey (Pryce), celebrated author of "Eminent Victorians." There's many a menage as the duo live together with Carrington's husband (Waddington), on whom Strachey has a crush, and both their various amours (though Carrington's heart is reserved for Lytton). Film is distractingly divided into titled segments (from 1915 to 1932) and, while Pryce gives a bravura performance, Thompson is merely enigmatic. Based on Michael Holroyd's biography "Lytton Strachey." Hampton's directorial debut. **CW:** Strong sexuality and language, nudity. **120m/C VHS, LV.** FR GB Emma Thompson, Jonathan Pryce, Steven Waddington, Sam West, Rufus Sewell, Penelope Wilton, Jeremy Northam, Peter Blythe, Janet McTeer, Alex Kingston, Sebastian Harcombe, Richard Clifford; **D:** Christopher Hampton; **W:** Christopher Hampton; **C:** Denis Lenoir; **M:** Michael Nyman. Cannes Film Festival '95: Special Jury Prize, Best Actor (Pryce); National Board of Review Awards '95: Best Actress (Thompson); Nominations: British Academy Awards '95: Best Actor (Pryce), Best Film. PGV

Carrington, V.C. 🎞️🎞️🎞️ Court Martial **1954** British army major Niven is brought up for a court-martial on embezzlement charges because he arranges, without official permission, to be reimbursed for money owed to him. A former war hero, he decides to defend himself in court, and, once an affair comes to light, his vindictive wife joins the opposition. Good cast, superlative Niven performance. **100m/B VHS, Beta.** GB David Niven, Margaret Leighton, Noelle Middleton, Laurence Naismith; **D:** Anthony Asquith. NO

Carry Me Back 🎞️½ **1982** Two brothers carry dead dad back to Australian ranch in order to inherit mucho dinero. **93m/C VHS, Beta.** AU Grant Tilly, Kelly Johnson. ART

Carry On Admiral 🎞️½ The Ship was Loaded **1957** Weak British comedy about two friends who get drunk and decide it would be fun to switch identities. One has an easy job as a public relations exec but the other is supposedly the captain of a ship. His lack of sea knowledge causes wacky catastrophes. Unrelated to the "Carry On" series of comedies. **85m/B VHS.** GB David Tomlinson, Brian Reece, Peggy Cummins, Eunice Gayson, A.E. Matthews, Lionel Murton, Joan Sims; **D:** Val Guest; **W:** Val Guest. FUS

Carry On at Your Convenience 🎞️½ **1971** Low-brow humor in and around a toilet factory. **86m/C VHS, Beta.** GB Sidney James, Kenneth Williams, Charles Hawtrey, Joan Sims, Kenneth Kope; **D:** Gerald Thomas. NO

Carry On Behind 🎞️🎞️ **1975** "Carry On" crew heads for archeological dig and find themselves sharing site with holiday caravan. **95m/C VHS, Beta.** GB Sidney James, Kenneth Williams, Elke Sommer, Joan Sims; **D:** Gerald Thomas.

Carry On Camping 🎞️🎞️½ **1971** Another entry in the silly series finds James and Bresslaw trying to persuade their girlfriends to go on a camping trip to what the men hope is a nudist colony. They don't find nudists but they do find a group of sex-starved schoolgirls. **88m/C VHS.** GB Sidney James, Bernard Bresslaw, Kenneth Williams, Joan Sims, Charles Hawtrey, Barbara Windsor; **D:** Gerald Thomas; **W:** Talbot Rothwell. TVC

Carry On Cleo 🎞️🎞️½ **1965** "Carry On" spoof of Shakespeare's "Antony and Cleopatra." **91m/C VHS, Beta.** GB Sidney James, Amanda Barrie, Kenneth Williams, Kenneth Connor, Jim Dale, Charles Hawtrey, Joan Sims; **D:** Gerald Thomas. NO

Carry On Cowboy 🎞️🎞️ Rumpo Kid **1966** "Carry On" Western parody of "High Noon." **91m/C VHS, Beta.** GB Sidney James, Kenneth Williams, Jim Dale. NO

Carry On Cruising 🎞️ **1962** "Carry On" gang attacks sailing world with low humor and raunchiness. **89m/C VHS, Beta.** GB Sidney James, Kenneth Williams, Liz Fraser; **D:** Gerald Thomas. NO

Carry On Dick 🎞️🎞️ **1975** What made the seemingly endless "Carry On" series of super-low-budget British farces such a hit is a mystery not to be solved. Low production values, scripts that peter out midway, and manifest humor don't normally a classic make; and yet the gang has its following. "Dick," a detective movie spoof, was preceded by some 20-odd carryings on; suffice it to say that the series, which began in 1958 with "Carry on Sergeant," has not improved with age in subsequent incarnations. **95m/C VHS.** GB Sidney James, Joan Sims; **D:** Gerald Thomas. NO

Carry On Doctor 🐾🐾🐾 1968 British series continues as characters of questionable competence join the medical profession. Hospital staff gets caught in battle over secret weight loss formula. 95m/C VHS. *GB* Frankie Howerd, Kenneth Williams, Jim Dale, Barbara Windsor; *D:* Gerald Thomas. *PAR*

Carry On Emmanuelle 🐾 1978 Bedroom diplomat Emmanuelle enters international politics by taking on foreign legion. Part of the British "Carry On" series. 104m/C VHS, Beta. *GB* Suzanne Danielle, Kenneth O'Connor, Kenneth Williams, Beryl Reid; *D:* Gerald Thomas. *NO*

Carry On England 🐾 1976 Mercifully, the gang didn't carry on much beyond this entry, in which a WWII antiaircraft fleet captain bumbles through the usual pranks and imbroglios. 89m/C VHS. *GB* Kenneth Connor, Patrick Mower, Judy Geeson; *D:* Gerald Thomas. *NO*

Carry On Henry VIII 🐾🐾½ 1971 Slapstick sex humor with Henry marrying the French Marie of Normandie and having to deal with both her addiction to garlic and the fact that she's pregnant by her lover. 88m/C VHS. *GB* Sidney James, Kenneth Williams, Joan Sims, Charles Hawtrey, Barbara Windsor, Kenneth Connor, Julian Holloway; *D:* Gerald Thomas; *W:* Talbot Rothwell. *TVC*

Carry On Nurse 🐾🐾 1959 Men's ward in a British hospital declares war on nurses and the rest of the hospital. The second of the "Carry On" series. 86m/B VHS, Beta. *GB* Shirley Eaton, Kenneth Connor, Hattie Jacques, Wilfrid Hyde-White; *D:* Gerald Thomas. *NOS, VYY, VDM*

Carry On 'Round the Bend 🐾½ 1972 Williams, who played in the original ("Carry On Sergeant"), and Carry On regulars (charpei-mugged James and ever-zaftig Jacques), go 'round the bend in yet another installment of the British spoof. 89m/C VHS. *GB* Sidney James, Kenneth Williams, Hattie Jacques; *D:* Gerald Thomas. *NO*

Carry On Screaming 🐾🐾 1966 "Carry On" does horror. A pair of goofy detectives trail monsters suspected in kidnapping. 97m/C VHS. *GB* Harry H. Corbett, Kenneth Williams, Fenella Fielding, Joan Sims, Charles Hawtrey, Jim Dale, Angela Douglas, Jon Pertwee; *D:* Gerald Thomas. *MOV*

The Cars That Ate Paris 🐾🐾🐾 *The Cars That Eat People* 1974 (PG) Parasitic town in the Parisian (Australia) outback preys on car and body parts generated by deliberate accidents inflicted by wreck-driving wreckless youths. Weir's first film released internationally, about a small Australian town that survives economically via deliberately contriving car accidents and selling the wrecks' scrap parts. A broad, bitter black comedy with some horror touches. 91m/C VHS, Beta. *AU* Terry Camilleri, Kevin Miles, John Meillon, Melissa Jaffe; *D:* Peter Weir; *W:* Peter Weir. *COL*

Carson City Kid 🐾½ 1940 Typical western which has Rogers trying to exact revenge on the man who killed his brother. 54m/B VHS, Beta. Roy Rogers. *NOS, VCN, DVT*

Cartel woof! 1990 (R) O'Keeffe, "B" actor extraordinaire, plays the wrong man to pick on in this rancid dope opera. Hounded by drug lord Stroud and framed for murder, pilot O'Keeffe decides the syndicate has gone too doggone far when they kill his sister. Exploitive and otherwise very bad. 106m/C VHS, LV. Miles O'Keeffe, Don Stroud, Crystal Carson, William Smith; *D:* John Stewart; *C:* Thomas Callaway. *IME*

Carthage in Flames 🐾🐾 *Cartagine in Fiamme; Carthage en Flammes* 1960 A graphic portrayal of the destruction of ancient Carthage in a blood and guts battle for domination of the known world. A tender love story is a welcome aside in this colorful Italian-made epic. 96m/C VHS, Beta. *IT* Anne Heywood, Jose Suarez, Pierre Brasseur; *D:* Carmine Gallone. *NO*

Cartier Affair 🐾 1984 A beautiful television actress unwittingly falls in love with the man who wants to steal her jewels. Collins designed her own wardrobe. Made for television. 120m/C VHS, Beta. Joan Collins, David Hasselhoff, Telly Savalas, Ed Lauter, Joe La Due; *D:* Rod Holcomb; *C:* Hanania Baer. *ORI, WAR*

Cartouche 🐾🐾🐾 *Swords of Blood* 1962 A swashbuckling action-comedy set in 18th-century France. Belmondo plays a charming thief who takes over a Paris gang, aided by the lovely Cardinale. When he is captured, she sacrifices her life to save him and Belmondo and his cohorts vow to have their revenge. Based on a French legend and a well-acted combination of tragedy, action, and farce. In French with English subtitles. 115m/C VHS. *FR IT* Jean-Paul Belmondo, Claudia Cardinale, Odile Versois, Philippe Lemaire; *D:* Philippe de Broca; *W:* Philippe de Broca; *M:* Georges Delerue. *FCT, HTV*

Carve Her Name with Pride 🐾🐾½ 1958 The true story of Violette Szabo who at age 19 became a secret agent with the French Resistance in WWII. 119m/B VHS, Beta. Virginia McKenna, Paul Scofield. *BFA*

Carver's Gate 🐾🐾 1996 Thanks to an environmental disaster, earth is in big trouble and its inhabitants take refuge in a virtual reality game called Afterlife. But when an engineer tries to improve the game by heightening its reality, the game's computer-generated demons get loose and it's up to cybercop Pare to stop them by traveling between virtual reality and the actual world. 97m/C VHS. Michael Pare, Kevin Stapleton. *YHV*

Casablanca 🐾🐾🐾🐾 1942 (PG) Can you see George Raft as Rick? Jack Warner did, but producer Hal Wallis wanted Bogart. Considered by many to be the best film ever made and one of the most quoted movies of all time, it rocketed Bogart from gangster roles to romantic leads as he and Bergman (who never looked lovelier) sizzle on screen. Bogart runs a gin joint in Morocco during the Nazi occupation, and meets up with Bergman, an old flame, but romance and politics do not mix, especially in Nazi-occupied French Morocco. Greenstreet, Lorre, and Rains all create memorable characters, as does Wilson, the piano player to whom Bergman says the oft-misquoted, "Play it, Sam." Without a doubt, the best closing scene ever written; it was scripted on the fly during the end of shooting, and actually shot several ways. Written from an unproduced play. See it in the original black and white. Laserdisc edition features restored imaging and sound and commentary by film historian Ronald Haver about the production, the play it was based on, and the famed evolution of the screenplay on audio track two. 50th Anniversary Edition contains a restored and remastered print, the original 1942 theatrical trailer, a film documentary narrated by Lauren Bacall, and a booklet. 102m/B VHS, Beta, LV, 8mm, Closed Caption. Humphrey Bogart, Ingrid Bergman, Paul Henreid, Claude Rains, Peter Lorre, Sydney Greenstreet, Conrad Veidt, S.Z. Sakall, Dooley Wilson, Marcel Dalio, John Qualen, Helmut Dantine; *D:* Michael Curtiz; *W:* Julius J. Epstein, Philip G. Epstein, Howard Koch; *M:* Max Steiner. Academy Awards '43: Best Director (Curtiz), Best Picture, Best Screenplay, National Film Registry '89;; Nominations: Academy Awards '43: Best Actor (Bogart), Best Black and White Cinematography, Best Film Editing, Best Supporting Actor (Rains), Best Original Dramatic/Comedy Score. *MGM, FOX, TLF*

Casablanca Express 🐾 1989 Nazi commandos hijack Churchill's train in this action-adventure drama. 90m/C VHS, Beta. Glenn Ford, Donald Pleasence, Jason Connery; *D:* Sergio Martino. *NO*

Casanova 🐾🐾 1987 (PG-13) A comedic romp through the bedrooms of 18th-century Europe with Chamberlain as the legendary lover. Lots of lovely ladies and hammy performances. Made for television. 124m/C VHS, Beta, LV, Closed Caption. Richard Chamberlain, Faye Dunaway, Sylvia Kristel, Ornella Muti, Hanna Schygulla, Sophie Ward, Frank Finlay, Ken-

neth Colley; *D:* Simon Langton; *W:* George MacDonald Fraser; *C:* Giuseppe Rotunno. *TTC*

Casanova Brown 🐾🐾½ 1944 Lighthearted comedy about a shy California professor (Cooper) who learns that his recent ex-wife (Wright) has had a baby (guess whose). When Cooper learns Wright has decided to give their daughter up for adoption he kidnaps the tyke and attempts fatherhood in a hotel room. When Wright finds out where he is, the twosome (who have really been in love all along) decide to remarry and be a family. Cooper, with baby and surrounded by diapers, makes a comedic sight. Based on the play "The Little Accident" by Floyd Dell and Thomas Mitchell. 94m/B VHS, Beta. Gary Cooper, Teresa Wright, Frank Morgan, Anita Louise, Patricia Collinge, Edmund Breon, Jill Esmond, Emory Parnell, Isobel Elsom, Mary Treen, Halliwell Hobbes; *D:* Sam Wood; *W:* Nunnally Johnson; *M:* Arthur Lange. Nominations: Academy Awards '44: Best Interior Decoration, Best Sound, Best Original Dramatic/Comedy Score. *MGM, FCT*

Casanova '70 🐾🐾½ 1965 Mastroianni plays a handsome soldier who has a knack for enticing liberated women in this comic rendition of the much-cinematized legendary yarn. Trouble is, he's in the mood only when he believes that he's in imminent danger. In Italian with English subtitles. 113m/C VHS. *IT* Marcello Mastroianni, Virna Lisi, Michele Mercier, Guido Alberti, Margaret Lee, Bernard Blier, Liana Orfei; *D:* Mario Monicelli; *W:* Tonino Guerra. Nominations: Academy Awards '65: Best Story & Screenplay. *FOX*

Casanova's Big Night 🐾🐾½ 1954 Classic slapstick comedy stars Hope masquerading as Casanova to test Fontaine's virtue before her marriage to a duke. The all-star cast provides one hilarious scene after another in this dated film. Price has a cameo as the "real" Casanova. Based on a story by Aubrey Wisberg. 85m/C VHS, LV. Bob Hope, Joan Fontaine, Audrey Dalton, Basil Rathbone, Hugh Marlowe, Vincent Price, John Carradine, Raymond Burr; *D:* Norman Z. McLeod; *W:* Hal Kanter, Edmund Hartmann; *C:* Lionel Lindon. *PAR, CCB*

A Case for Murder 🐾🐾½ 1993 (R) Jack Hammet has just become the youngest full partner ever at his Chicago law firm, with a knack for winning impossible cases. His next one's a beaut. Seems an envious colleague has gotten himself murdered and his estranged wife is the prime suspect. Jack decides to work with newly arrived lawyer Kate Weldon but as the two become personally involved, Kate begins to question Jack's ethics. Seems the evidence is more than a little shady and Jack isn't telling all. 94m/C VHS, LV, Closed Caption. Peter Berg, Jennifer Grey, Belinda Bauer; *D:* Duncan Gibbins; *W:* Duncan Gibbins, Pablo F. Fenjves. *USH*

A Case of Deadly Force 🐾🐾🐾 1986 Based on the true story of a black man wrongfully killed by Boston's Tactical Police Force who mistook him for a robber. The police investigation calls it self-defense but the family and the attorney they hire fight to change the verdict. Excellent cast, great dramatic story. Originally made for television. 95m/C VHS, LV. Richard Crenna, John Shea, Lorraine Toussaint, Frank McCarthy, Tom Isbell; *D:* Michael Miller. *CAF*

A Case of Libel 🐾🐾½ 1983 A made for television dramatization based on attorney Louis Nizer's account of Quentin Reynolds' libel suit against columnist Westbrook Pegler. 90m/C VHS, Beta. Daniel J. Travanti, Ed Asner; *D:* Eric Till. *ART*

Case of the Baby Sitter 🐾 1947 A private eye investigates jewel thieves posing as nobility. 40m/B VHS, Beta, LV. Tom Neal, Allen Jenkins, Pamela Blake. *SNC*

The Case of the Frightened Lady 🐾 *The Frightened Lady* 1939 A homicidal family does its collective best to keep its dark past a secret in order to collect some inheritance money. Watch, if you're still awake, for the surprise ending. 80m/B VHS, Beta. *GB* Marius Goring, Helen Haye, Penelope Dudley Ward, Felix Aylmer, Patrick Barr; *D:* George King. *SNC*

The Case of the Lucky Legs 🎬🎬½
1935 Yes, there was a Perry Mason before Raymond Burr. Erle Stanley Gardner's sleuthing litigator's first appearance was 1934's "The Case of the Howling Dog," which initiated Warner Bros' "A"-grade (but soon-to-be "B"-grade) series. More akin to Nick Charles than to Gardner's character or to his later TV incarnation, the "Lucky Legs" Perry is a high-living, interminably hungover tippler who winces and wisecracks as he unravels the case of the corpse of a crooked con man. William, who left shortly after the series was downgraded to "B" status, plays the esquire; Tobin plays his smart-mouthed secretary, and Ellis is the tomato suspected of murder. **76m/B VHS, Beta.** Warren William, Genevieve Tobin, Patricia Ellis, Lyle Talbot, Allen Jenkins, Barton MacLane, Peggy Shannon, Porter Hall; **D:** Archie Mayo. *SNC, RXM*

The Case of the Missing Lady 🎬½
1983 A famous Arctic explorer asks Tommy and Tuppence to find his missing fiancee. Based on the Christie story. **51m/C VHS, Beta. GB** Francesca Annis, James Warwick. *TPV*

The Case of the Mukkinese Battle Horn 🎬🎬 1956 The cast of Britain's "The Goon Show" takes over in a zany, slapdash featurette-length mystery spoof. **27m/C VHS, Beta, 8mm. GB** Peter Sellers, Spike Milligan, Dick Emery; **M:** Edwin Astley. *VYY*

Casey at the Bat 1985 From Shelley Duvall's made for cable television "Tall Tales and Legends" series, in which the immortal poem is brought to life. Rousing comedy for the whole family. **52m/C VHS, Beta, Closed Caption.** Bill Macy, Hamilton Camp, Elliott Gould, Carol Kane, Howard Cosell; **D:** David Steinberg. *FOX*

Casey Jones and Fury (Brave Stallion) 1957 An episode from each of these early adventure series. **60m/B VHS, Beta.** Alan Hale Jr., Peter Graves. *NOS, DVT*

Casey's Shadow 🎬🎬 1978 (PG) The eight-year-old son of an impoverished horse trainer raises a quarter horse and enters it in the world's richest horse race. **116m/C VHS, Beta.** Walter Matthau, Alexis Smith, Robert Webber, Murray Hamilton; **D:** Martin Ritt; **C:** John A. Alonzo. *COL*

Cash McCall 🎬🎬½ 1960 McCall (Garner) is a corporate raider who just loves making money. But problems come in when he falls for the lovely daughter (Wood) of his latest takeover target, failing businessman Jagger. Based on the novel by Cameron Hawley. **116m/C VHS.** James Garner, Natalie Wood, Dean Jagger, Nina Foch, E.G. Marshall, Henry Jones, Otto Kruger, Roland Winters, Parley Baer, Dabbs Greer; **D:** Joseph Pevney; **W:** Lenore Coffee, Marion Hargrove; **M:** Max Steiner. *WAR*

Casino 🎬½ 1980 A made-for-television thriller about back-stabbings and ritzy romance aboard a high-priced gambling liner. **100m/C VHS, Beta.** Mike Connors, Lynda Day George, Bo Hopkins, Gary Burghoff, Joseph Cotten, Robert Reed, Barry Sullivan; **D:** Don Chaffey.

Casino 🎬🎬🎬 1995 (R) Final part of the Scorsese underworld crime trilogy that began with "Mean Streets" and continued in "GoodFellas." Casino boss Sam "Ace" Rothstein (De Niro), his ex-hustler wife Ginger (Stone), and his loose-cannon enforcer pal Nicky (Pesci) are the principals in this lengthy, fictionalized account of how the mob lost Las Vegas in a haze of drugs, sex, coincidence and betrayal. Flashy, intriguing, and unflinchingly violent account of mob-run '70s Vegas clicks when exploring the inner workings of a major casino and its hierarchy. Although Stone shines as a hedonistic money chaser, visuals are great and the soundtrack is a killer, story line suffers from deja vu. Pileggi again adapted the screenplay from his own book. **CW:** Brutal violence, pervasive strong language, drug use and some sexuality. **177m/C VHS, LV, Closed Caption, DVD.** Robert De Niro, Joe Pesci, Sharon Stone, James Woods, Don Rickles, Alan King, Kevin Pollak, L.Q. Jones,

Dick Smothers, John Joe Bob Briggs Bloom; **Cameos:** Frankie Avalon, Steve Allen, Jayne Meadows, Jerry Vale; **D:** Martin Scorsese; **W:** Nicholas Pileggi, Martin Scorsese; **C:** Robert Richardson. Golden Globe Awards '96: Best Actress—Drama (Stone); Nominations: Academy Awards '95: Best Actress (Stone); Golden Globe Awards '96: Best Director (Scorsese); MTV Movie Awards '96: Best Female Performance (Stone), Best Villain (Pesci). *USH*

Casino Royale 🎬 1967 The product of five directors, three writers and a mismatched cast of dozens, this virtually plotless spoof of James Bond films can stand as one of the low-water marks for 1960s comedy. And yet, there are some marvelous bits within, scenes of bizarre hilarity. Welles and Sellers literally couldn't stand the sight of one another, and their scenes together were filmed separately, with stand-ins. **130m/C VHS, Beta, LV.** David Niven, Woody Allen, Peter Sellers, Ursula Andress, Orson Welles, Jacqueline Bisset, Deborah Kerr, Peter O'Toole, Jean-Paul Belmondo, Charles Boyer, Joanna Pettet, John Huston, William Holden, George Raft; **D:** John Huston, Ken Hughes, Robert Parrish, Val Guest, Joseph McGrath; **C:** Jack Hildyard; **M:** Burt Bacharach. Nominations: Academy Awards '67: Best Song ("The Look of Love"). *MRV, COL*

Casper 🎬🎬🎬 1995 (PG) World's friendliest ghost appears on the big screen with outstanding visual trickery (from Industrial Light and Magic) and a lively, if hokey, story. Evilish Carrigan Crittenden (Moriarty) inherits ghost-infested Whiplash Manor and hires scatterbrained "ghost therapist" Dr. Harvey (Pullman) to get rid of its unwanted occupants. His daughter Kat (Ricci) is soon the object of Casper's friendly attention while the good doc must contend with Casper's mischievous uncles—Stinkie, Fatso, and Stretch. Exec producer Spielberg shows his influence with numerous topical gags and screen references that help amuse the adults while the ghosts work their magic on the kiddies. Silberling's directorial debut; based on the comic-book and television cartoon character created more than 30 years ago. **95m/C VHS, LV, Closed Caption, DVD.** Christina Ricci, Bill Pullman, Cathy Moriarty, Eric Idle, Amy Brenneman, Ben Stein; **Cameos:** Don Novello, Rodney Dangerfield, Clint Eastwood, Mel Gibson, Dan Aykroyd; **D:** Brad Silberling; **W:** Sherri Stoner, Deanna Oliver; **C:** Dean Cundey; **M:** James Horner; **V:** Malachi Pearson, Joe Nipote, Joe Alaskey, Brad Garrett. *USH*

Casque d'Or 🎬🎬🎬 *Golden Marie* 1952 Crime passionnel in turn-of-the-century Paris as an honest carpenter (Reggiani) gets drawn into the netherworld of pimps and thieves. He's finally driven to murder—all for love of gangster's moll Marie (a very sultry Signoret). French with subtitles. **96m/B VHS. FR** Serge Reggiani, Simone Signoret, Claude Dauphin, Raymond Bussieres, Gaston Modot; **D:** Jacques Becker; **W:** Jacques Becker, Jacques Companeez; **C:** Robert Le Febvre; **M:** Georges Van Parys. *FCT*

Cass 🎬 1978 Disenchanted filmmaker returns home to Australia to experiment with alternative lifestyles. **90m/C VHS, Beta.** Michelle Fawden, John Waters, Judy Morris, Peter Carroll. *NO*

Cass Timberlane 🎬🎬½ 1947 Scandalous story of a May-December romance set in a small Midwestern town. Tracy stars as Cass Timberlane, a widowed judge who falls for a voluptuous young girl from the wrong side of the tracks (Turner). They marry and experience problems when she is shunned by his snobbish friends. Good performances, especially from the supporting cast, dominate this fairly predictable film. Based on the novel by Sinclair Lewis. **119m/B VHS.** Spencer Tracy, Lana Turner, Zachary Scott, Tom Drake, Mary Astor, Albert Dekker, Margaret Lindsay, John Litel, Mona Barrie, Josephine Hutchinson, Rose Hobart, Selena Royle; **Cameos:** Walter Pidgeon; **D:** George Sidney; **W:** Donald Ogden Stewart. *MGM*

Cassandra 🎬 1987 (R) A fragile young woman has dreams that foretell the future—specifically, a series of grisly murders. **94m/C VHS, Beta, LV.** Shane Briant, Brionny Behets, Tessa Humphries, Kit Taylor, Lee James; **D:** Colin Eggleston. *VTR*

The Cassandra Crossing 🎬½ 1976 (R) A terrorist with the plague causes havoc on a transcontinental luxury train. Turgid adventure filmed in France and Italy. **129m/C VHS, Beta. GB** Sophia Loren, Richard Harris, Ava Gardner, Burt Lancaster, Martin Sheen, Ingrid Thulin, Lee Strasberg, John Phillip Law, Lionel Stander, O.J. Simpson, Ann Turkel, Alida Valli; **D:** George P. Cosmatos; **W:** George P. Cosmatos, Tom Mankiewicz; **M:** Jerry Goldsmith. *FOX*

Cassie 🎬 1987 (R) Follows the rise of Cassie, a successful country and western singer, and documents all her trials along the way. **75m/C VHS, Beta.** Marilyn Chambers; **D:** Godfrey Daniels. *NO*

Cast a Dark Shadow 🎬🎬🎬 1955 Bogarde is the charmer who decides to reap his reward by marrying and murdering elderly women for their fortunes. But Bogarde meets his match when he plots against his latest intended (Lockwood). Tidy thriller with effective performances. Based on the play "Murder Mistaken" by Janet Green. **82m/B VHS. GB** Dirk Bogarde, Margaret Lockwood, Mona Washbourne, Kay Walsh, Kathleen Harrison, Robert Flemyng, Walter Hudd; **D:** Lewis Gilbert; **W:** John Cresswell. *FCT*

Cast a Deadly Spell 🎬🎬🎬 1991 (R) A bubbly, flavorful witch's brew of private-eye and horror cliches, set in a fantasy version of 1948 Los Angeles where sorcery and voodoo abound, but gumshoe Harry P. Lovecraft uses street smarts instead of magic to track down a stolen Necronomicon—and if you know what that is you'll want to watch. Wild creatures and f/x wizardry complement this made-for-cable-TV trick and treat. **CW:** Some language and horror violence. **93m/C VHS, LV, Closed Caption.** Fred Ward, David Warner, Julianne Moore, Clancy Brown, Alexandra Powers; **D:** Martin Campbell; **W:** Joseph Dougherty, Dave Edison. *HBO, FCT*

Cast a Giant Shadow 🎬🎬 1966 Follows the career of Col. David "Mickey" Marcus, an American Jew and WWII hero who helped turn Israel's army into a formidable fighting force during the 1947-48 struggle for independence. **142m/C VHS, Beta, Closed Caption.** Kirk Douglas, Senta Berger, Angie Dickinson, John Wayne, James Donald, Chaim Topol, Frank Sinatra, Yul Brynner; **D:** Melville Shavelson; **W:** Melville Shavelson; **M:** Elmer Bernstein. *MGM, FCT*

Cast the First Stone 🎬🎬 1989 Made for TV soaper based on the true story of a former nun who becomes a small town schoolteacher. After being raped, Diane Martin discovers she's pregnant and when she decides to keep the baby the school board dismisses her. The plot centers around her fight to regain her job and dignity—while trying to convince everybody that she doesn't deserve to lose her job simply because she is an unwed mother. Eikenberry gives a strong performance, but it can't carry this lackluster film. **94m/C VHS, LV.** Jill Eikenberry, Richard Masur, Joe Spano, Lew Ayres, Holly Palance; **D:** John Korty; **M:** Ira Newborn. *COL*

Castaway 🎬🎬½ 1987 (R) Based on the factual account by Lucy Irvine. The story of Michael Wilmington, who placed an ad for a young woman to spend a year on a Pacific atoll with him, and the battle of the sexes that followed. **118m/C VHS, Beta, Closed Caption.** Oliver Reed, Amanda Donohoe, Tony Rickards, Georgina Hale, Frances Barber, Todd Rippon; **D:** Nicolas Roeg; **W:** Allan Scott; **M:** Stanley Myers. *WAR*

The Castaway Cowboy 🎬🎬 1974 (G) A shanghaied cowboy becomes partners with a widow when he turns her Hawaiian potato farm into a cattle ranch. Good, clean "family fare." **91m/C VHS, Beta.** James Garner, Robert Culp, Vera Miles; **D:** Vincent McEveety; **M:** Robert F. Brunner. *DIS, OM*

The Castilian 🎬🎬½ *Valley of the Swords* 1963 Some very odd casting in this historical tale of heroism and swordplay about a Spanish nobleman who leads his followers against the invading Moors and their evil king (Crawford). Based on a 13th century poem. **128m/C VHS, Beta.** Cesar Romero, Broderick Crawford, Alida Valli, Frankie Avalon, Espartaco Santoni, Fernando Rey, Jorge Rigaud; **D:** Javier Seto; **W:** Sidney Pink. *WAR, FCT*

The Castle 🎬🎬🎬 *Das Schloss* 1968 A man is summoned by the seemingly invisible occupants of a castle to their village. All his efforts to meet with those inhabiting the castle are futile and the task gradually becomes his obsession. Both wonderfully acted and shot, this is a well-executed adaptation of Franz Kafka's novel. **90m/C VHS, Beta.** *GE SI* Maximilian Schell, Cordula Trantow, Trudik Daniel, Helmut Qualtinger; **D:** Rudolf Noelte. *NO*

The Castle 🎬🎬 1997 The Kerrigans are a working class clan who happily live directly adjacent to Melbourne's Tullamarine airport. But when the airport decides to expand, their house is subject to a compulsory acquisition order. However, Daryl Kerrigan (Caton) decides to fight and takes their case all the way to the High Court in Canberra. It's a David vs. Goliath comedy with an Aussie disdain for authority figures. Cultural references may not travel overseas but the film was a hit on its home turf. **93m/C VHS.** *AU* Michael Caton, Charles Tingwell, Sophie Lee, Robyn Nevin, Anne Tenney, Stephen Curry, Anthony Simcoe, Wayne Hope, Tiriel Mora, Eric Bana; **D:** Rob Sitch; **W:** Rob Sitch, Santo Cilauro, Tom Gleisner, Jane Kennedy; **C:** Miriana Marusic; **M:** Craig Harnath. Australian Film Institute '97: Best Original Screenplay; Nominations: Australian Film Institute '97: Best Actor (Caton), Best Supporting Actor (Tingwell), Best Supporting Actress (Lee). *NYR*

Castle Freak 🎬🎬 1995 (R) Italian countess leaves her creepy haunted castle to her American nephew and his family. They find an unwelcome surprise lurking in the cellar.**CW:** Some strong violence and gore, a scene of sexuality and some language. **90m/C VHS, LV.** Jeffrey Combs, Barbara Crampton, Jonathan Fuller, Jessica Dollarhide; **D:** Stuart Gordon; **W:** Dennis Paoli; **C:** Mario Vulpiani; **M:** Richard Band. *FLL*

Castle in the Desert 🎬🎬½ 1942 Charlie Chan investigates murder and other strange goings-on in a spooky old castle. One of the last in the series. **62m/B VHS, Closed Caption.** Sidney Toler, Arleen Whelan, Richard Derr, Douglass Dumbrille, Henry Daniell, Victor Sen Yung; **D:** Harry Lachman. *FOX*

Castle of Blood 🎬🎬 *Castle of Terror; Coffin of Terror; Danza Macabra* 1964 Staying overnight in a haunted castle, a poet is forced to deal with a number of creepy encounters. Cult favorite Steele enhances this atmospheric chiller. Dubbed in English. **85m/B VHS.** *IT FR* Barbara Steele, George Riviere, Margrete Robsahm, Henry Kruger, Montgomery Glenn, Sylvia Sorente; **D:** Anthony (Antonio Margheriti) Dawson. *SNC*

The Castle of Cagliostro 1980 An animated Japanese adventure tale featuring a hero named Wolf, who's a thief. Wolf infiltrates the suspicious country of Cagliostro, whose one industry is conterfeiting money, and winds up rescuing a princess. Lots of violence to go with the action. In Japanese with English subtitles. **100m/C VHS.** *JP STP*

Castle of Evil woof! 1966 Group of heirs gathers on a deserted isle to hear the reading of the will of your basic mad scientist. One by one, they fall victim to a humanoid created by the loony doc in his own image. Inspired moments of unintentional fun. **81m/C VHS.** Scott Brady, Virginia Mayo, Lisa Gaye, David Brian, Hugh Marlowe, William Thourlby, Shelly Morrison; **D:** Francis D. Lyon. *REP, FCT*

The Castle of Fu Manchu 🎬 *Assignment: Istanbul; Die Folterkammer des Dr. Fu Manchu* 1968 **(PG)** The final chapter in a series starring Lee as the wicked doctor. This time, Lee has developed a gadget which will put the earth into a deep freeze, and at his mercy. To fine tune this contraption, he enlists the help of a gifted scientist by abducting him. However, the helper/hostage has a bad ticker, so Lee must abduct a heart surgeon to save his life, and thus, the freezer project. Most critics felt this was the weakest installment in the series. **92m/C VHS.** *GE SP IT GB* Christopher Lee, Richard Greene, H. Marion Crawford, Tsai Chin, Gunther Stoll,

Rosalba (Sara Bay) Neri, Maria Perschy; **D:** Jess (Jesus) Franco. *MRV*

Castle of the Creeping Flesh woof! 1968 A surgeon's daughter is brutally murdered. Vowing to bring her back he begins ripping out the organs of innocent people and transplanting them into her body. Has the dubious honor of being one of the few movies to sport actual open heart surgery footage. So bad it's...just bad. **85m/C VHS, Beta.** Adrian Hoven, Janine Reynaud, Howard Vernon; **D:** Percy G. Parker. *NO*

Castle of the Living Dead 🎬🎬 *Il Castello de Morti Vivi* 1964 Evil Count Drago's hobbies include mummifying a traveling circus group visiting his castle. Lee is as evil as ever, but be sure to look for Sutherland's screen debut. In a dual role, he plays not only the bumbling inspector, but also a witch, in drag. **90m/B VHS.** *IT FR* Christopher Lee, Gaia Germani, Phillipe LeRoy, Jacques Stanislawsky, Donald Sutherland; **D:** Herbert Wise. *SNC, MRV*

Casual Sex? 🎬½ 1988 (R) Two young women, looking for love and commitment, take a vacation at a posh resort where they are confronted by men with nothing on their minds but sex, be it casual or the more formal black-tie variety. Supposedly an examination of safe sex in a lightly comedic vein, though the comic is too light and the morality too limp. Adapted from the play by Wendy Goldman and Judy Toll. **87m/C VHS, Beta, LV.** Lea Thompson, Victoria Jackson, Stephen Shellan, Jerry Levine, Mary Gross, Andrew Dice Clay; **D:** Genevieve Robert. *USH*

Casualties 🎬🎬 1997 (R) Annie's got very unfortunate luck with men. Her abusive husband's a cop and can't safely get away from home, then she meets a seemingly nice guy, Tommy, at her cooking class, who offers to help Annie out. But when Tommy's behavior becomes obsessive, Annie figures she just has to rely on herself.**CW:** Strong violence and some language. **86m/C VHS.** Mark Harmon, Caroline Goodall, Michael Beach, Jonathan Gries, John Diehl; **D:** Alex Graves. *THV*

Casualties of Love: The "Long Island Lolita" Story 🎬🎬 1993 (PG-13) Told from the Buttafuoco's point of view, Amy Fisher was nothing but a wacko fatally attracted teenager who misunderstood Joey's harmless flirtations and deliberately went after his wife with a gun. The Buttafuocos received $300,000 from CBS to tell their side of the story which features Milano, who resembles Amy not in the least, as the lead. One of three competing network television versions of the sordid story. See also: "The Amy Fisher Story" and "Lethal Lolita—Amy Fisher: My Story."**CW:** Violence and drug use and sexual subject matter. **94m/C VHS.** Jack Scalia, Alyssa Milano, Phyllis Lyons, Jack Kehler, Michael Bowen, J.E. Freeman, Nicky Corello, Lawrence Tierney, Peter Van Norden, Anne DeSalvo; **D:** John Herzfeld; **W:** John Herzfeld. *COL*

Casualties of War 🎬🎬🎬 1989 (R) A Vietnam war morality play about army private Fox in the bush who refuses to let his fellow soldiers and commanding sergeant (Penn) skirt responsibility for the rape and murder of a native woman. Fox achieves his dramatic breakthrough. Based on the true story by Daniel Lang. **120m/C VHS, Beta, LV, 8mm, Letterbox, Closed Caption.** Sean Penn, Michael J. Fox, Don Harvey, Thuy Thu Le, John Leguizamo, Sam Robards, John C. Reilly, Erik King; **D:** Brian DePalma; **W:** David Rabe; **C:** Stephen Burum; **M:** Ennio Morricone. *COL*

A Casualty of War 🎬🎬½ 1990 (R) Made-for-TV adaptation of Frederick Forsyth's thriller about modern-day arms smuggling (Libya to Ireland) and espionage. Well-acted, with the exception of Hack. **96m/C VHS.** Shelley Hack, David Threlfall, Richard Hope, Alan Howard, Clarke Peters; **D:** Tom Clegg; **W:** Frederick Forsyth. *NO*

The Cat 🎬 1966 A boy and a tamed mountain lion become friends on the run from a murderous poacher. **95m/C VHS, Beta.** Peggy Ann Garner, Roger Perry, Barry Coe; **D:** Ellis Kadison. *COL, NLC*

Cat and Mouse 🎬🎬🎬½ 1978 (PG) A very unorthodox police inspector is assigned to investigate a millionaire's mysterious death. Who done it? French dialogue with English subtitles. **107m/C VHS, Beta.** *FR* Michele Morgan, Serge Reggiani, Jean-Pierre Aumont, Philippe Labro, Philippe Leotard, Valerie Lagrange, Michel Perelon, Christine Laurent; **D:** Claude Lelouch; **W:** Claude Lelouch; **C:** Andre Perlstein; **M:** Francis Lai. *COL*

The Cat and the Canary 🎬🎬🎬 1927 A great silent film about the ghost of a madman that wanders nightly through the corridors of an old house. Remade twice, once in 1939 and again in 1979. **70m/B VHS, Beta.** Laura La Plante, Creighton Hale, Tully Marshall, Gertrude Astor, Arthur Edmund Carewe, Lucien Littlefield; **D:** Paul Leni; **W:** Robert F. "Bob" Hill, Alfred A. Cohn; **C:** Gilbert Warrenton. *MRV, VYY, HHT*

The Cat and the Canary 🎬🎬 1979 (PG) A stormy night, a gloomy mansion, and a mysterious will combine to create an atmosphere for murder. An entertaining remake of the 1927 silent film. **96m/C VHS, Beta.** *GB* Carol Lynley, Michael Callan, Wendy Hiller, Olivia Hussey, Daniel Massey, Honor Blackman, Edward Fox, Wilfrid Hyde-White, Beatrix Lehmann, Peter McEnery; **D:** Radley Metzger; **W:** Radley Metzger; **C:** Alex Thomson. *COL, OM*

The Cat and the Fiddle 🎬🎬🎬 1934 Lovely Jerome Kern-Oscar Hammerstein operetta in which Novarro plays a struggling composer who forces his affections on MacDonald. She sings in response to his romantic proposals. The final sequence is in color. ♫The Night Was Made for Love; She Didn't Say 'Yes'; A New Love is Old; Try to Forget; One Moment Alone; Don't Ask Us Not To Sing; I Watch the Love Parade; The Breeze Kissed Your Hair; Impressions in a Harlem Flat. **90m/B VHS.** Ramon Novarro, Jeanette MacDonald, Frank Morgan, Charles Butterworth. *MGM*

Cat Ballou 🎬🎬🎬½ 1965 At the turn of the century, a schoolmarm turns outlaw with the help of a drunken gunman. Marvin played Kid Shelleen and his silver-nosed evil twin Tim Strawn in this cheery spoof of westerns. Cole and Kaye sing the narration in a one of a kind Greek chorus. **96m/C VHS, Beta.** Jane Fonda, Lee Marvin, Michael Callan, Dwayne Hickman, Reginald Denny, Nat King Cole, Stubby Kaye; **D:** Elliot Silverstein; **W:** Frank Pierson. Academy Awards '65: Best Actor (Marvin); Berlin International Film Festival '65: Best Actor (Marvin); British Academy Awards '65: Best Actor (Marvin); Golden Globe Awards '66: Best Actor—Musical/Comedy (Marvin); National Board of Review Awards '65: Best Actor (Marvin); Nominations: Academy Awards '65: Best Adapted Score, Best Adapted Screenplay, Best Film Editing, Best Song ("The Ballad of Cat Ballou"). *COL, BTV*

Cat Chaser 🎬🎬 1990 Weller walks listlessly through the role of an ex-soldier in Miami who has an affair with the wife of an exiled—but still lethal—military dictator. Surpisingly low-key, sometimes effective thriller that saves its energy for sex scenes, also available in a less steamy, 90-minute "R" rated version. Based on an Elmore Leonard novel. **97m/C VHS.** Kelly McGillis, Peter Weller, Charles Durning, Frederic Forrest, Tomas Milian, Juan Fernandez; **D:** Abel Ferrara; **W:** Elmore Leonard, Jim Borrelli; **M:** Chick Corea. *VES*

The Cat from Outer Space 🎬🎬 1978 (G) An extraterrestrial cat named Jake crashes his spaceship on Earth and leads a group of people on endless escapades. Enjoyable Disney fare. **103m/C VHS, Beta.** Ken Berry, Sandy Duncan, Harry (Henry) Morgan, Roddy McDowall, McLean Stevenson; **D:** Norman Tokar. *DIS, OM*

Cat Girl 🎬 1957 A young bride on her honeymoon finds she has inherited the family curse—she has a psychic link to a ferocious leopard. Numerous murders ensue. Poor production value and a weak script, despite Shelley's fine acting, make this an unworthwhile film. **69m/B VHS.** Barbara

Shelley, Robert Ayres, Kay Callard, Paddy Webster; **D:** Alfred Shaughnessy. *PAR, COL*

Cat in the Cage 🐾½ **1968** A young man finds many things have changed at home while he was in a mental institution. Dad has remarried, the housekeeper is practicing witchcraft, the chauffeur is after his mistress, and the cat is gone. So where'd that cat go? **96m/C VHS, Beta.** Colleen Camp, Sybil Danning, Mel Novak, Frank De Kova; **D:** Tony Zarin Dast.

The Cat o' Nine Tails 🐾 **1971 (PG)** A blind detective and a newsman team up to find a sadistic killer. A gory murder mystery. **112m/C VHS, 8mm. GE FR IT** Karl Malden, James Franciscus, Catherine Spaak, Cinzia de Carolis, Carlo Alighiero; **D:** Dario Argento; **W:** Dario Argento; **M:** Ennio Morricone. *SIM*

Cat on a Hot Tin Roof 🐾🐾🐾½ **1958** Tennessee Williams' powerful play about greed and deception in a patriarchal Southern family. Big Daddy (Ives) is dying. Members of the family greedily attempt to capture his inheritance, tearing the family apart. Taylor is a sensual wonder as Maggie the Cat, though the more controversial elements of the play were toned down for the film version. Intense, believable performances from Ives and Newman. **108m/C VHS, Beta, LV.** Paul Newman, Burl Ives, Elizabeth Taylor, Jack Carson, Judith Anderson; **D:** Richard Brooks; **W:** Richard Brooks, James Poe; **C:** William H. Daniels. Nominations: Academy Awards '58: Best Actor (Newman), Best Actress (Taylor), Best Adapted Screenplay, Best Color Cinematography, Best Director (Brooks), Best Picture. *MGM, FCT, CCB*

Cat on a Hot Tin Roof 🐾🐾 **1984** In this adaptation of the Tennessee Williams play, fights over the family inheritance tear a family apart. **122m/C VHS, Beta, LV.** Jessica Lange, Tommy Lee Jones, Rip Torn, David Dukes; **D:** Jack Hofsiss. *MGM, ART, VES*

Cat People 🐾🐾🐾 **1942** A young dress designer is the victim of a curse that changes her into a deadly panther who must kill to survive. A classic among the horror genre with unrelenting terror from beginning to end. First horror film from producer Val Lewton. **73m/B VHS, Beta, LV.** Simone Simon, Kent Smith, Jane Randolph, Jack Holt, Elizabeth Russell, Alan Napier, Tom Conway; **D:** Jacques Tourneur; **W:** DeWitt Bodeen; **C:** Nicholas Musuraca. National Film Registry '93. *TTC, BTV*

Cat People 🐾🐾½ **1982 (R)** A beautiful young woman learns that she has inherited a strange family trait—she turns into a vicious panther when sexually aroused. The only person with whom she can safely mate is her brother, a victim of the same genetic heritage. Kinski is mesmerizing as the innocent, sensual woman. Remake of the 1942 film. **118m/C VHS, Beta, LV, Letterbox.** Nastassia Kinski, Malcolm McDowell, John Heard, Annette O'Toole, Ruby Dee, Ed Begley Jr., John Larroquette; **D:** Paul Schrader; **W:** Alan Ormsby; **C:** John Bailey; **M:** Giorgio Moroder. *USH, FCT*

Cat Women of the Moon 🐾🐾 *Rocket to the Moon* **1953** Scientists land on the moon and encounter an Amazon-like force of skimpily attired female chauvinists. Remade as "Missile to the Moon." Featuring the Hollywood Cover Girls as various cat women. Available in its original 3-D format. **65m/B VHS, Beta.** Sonny Tufts, Victor Jory, Marie Windsor, Bill Phipps, Douglas Fowley, Carol Brewster, Suzanne Alexander, Susan Morrow; **D:** Arthur Hilton; **M:** Elmer Bernstein. *RHI, SNC, EEL*

Cataclysm 🐾🐾½ *Satan's Supper* **1981 (R)** A swell flick about a sadistic demon who spends his time either finding people willing to join him or killing the people who won't. **94m/C VHS, Beta.** Cameron Mitchell, Marc Lawrence, Faith Clift, Charles Moll; **D:** Tom McGowan, Greg Tallas, Philip Marshak. *FOX*

Catacombs 🐾 **1989 (R)** An investigative monk and a beautiful photographer stumble across a mysterious, centuries-old evil power. **112m/C VHS, Beta.** Timothy Van Patten, Laura Schaefer, Ian Abercrombie, Jeremy West; **D:** David Schmoeller; **W:** C. Courtney Joyner; **M:** Pino Donaggio. *TWE*

The Catamount Killing 🐾½ **1974 (PG)** The story of a small town bank manager and his lover. They decide to rob the bank and run for greener pastures only to find their escape befuddled at every turn. **82m/C VHS, Beta. GE** Horst Buchholz, Ann Wedgeworth; **D:** Krzysztof Zanussi. *NO*

Catch as Catch Can 🐾 *Lo Scatenato* **1968** An Italian male model is comically besieged by animals of every type, making a mess of his life and career. Dubbed. **95m/C VHS, Beta. IT** Vittorio Gassman, Martha Hyer, Gila Golan; **D:** Franco Indovina; **M:** Luis Bacalov. *NLC*

Catch Me a Spy 🐾½ *To Catch a Spy* **1971** A foreign agent attempts to lure an innocent man into becoming part of a swap for an imprisoned Russian spy. **94m/C VHS, Beta. GB FR** Kirk Douglas, Tom Courtenay, Trevor Howard, Marlene Jobert, Bernard Blier, Patrick Mower, Bernadette LaFont; **D:** Dick Clement; **W:** Dick Clement, Ian LaFrenais; **M:** Claude Bolling.

Catch Me...If You Can 🐾🐾 **1989 (PG)** High school class president Melissa doesn't want to see the school torn down. To raise fast cash, she teams up with a drag racer and the fun begins. **105m/C VHS, LV, Closed Caption.** Matt Lattanzi, Loryn Locklin, M. Emmet Walsh, Geoffrey Lewis; **D:** Stephen Sommers. *MCG*

Catch the Heat 🐾 *Feel the Heat* **1987 (R)** Alexandra is an undercover narcotics agent sent to infiltrate Steiger's South American drug operation. **90m/C VHS, Beta, Closed Caption.** Tiana Alexandra, David Dukes, Rod Steiger; **D:** Joel Silberg; **W:** Stirling Silliphant; **M:** Tom Chase, Steve Rucker. *VTR*

Catch-22 🐾🐾🐾 **1970 (R)** Buck Henry's adaptation of Joseph Heller's black comedy about a group of fliers in the Mediterranean during WWII. A biting anti-war satire portraying the insanity of the situation in both a humorous and disturbing manner. Perhaps too literal to the book's masterfully chaotic structure, causing occasional problems in the "are you following along department?" Arkin heads a fine and colorful cast. **121m/C VHS, Beta, LV.** Alan Arkin, Martin Balsam, Art Garfunkel, Jon Voight, Richard Benjamin, Buck Henry, Bob Newhart, Paula Prentiss, Martin Sheen, Charles Grodin, Anthony Perkins, Orson Welles, Jack Gilford; **D:** Mike Nichols; **W:** Buck Henry; **C:** David Watkin. *NO*

The Catered Affair 🐾🐾🐾 *Wedding Breakfast* **1956** Davis, anti-typecast as a Bronx housewife, and Borgnine, as her taxi-driving husband, play the determined parents of soon-to-be-wed Reynolds set on giving her away in a style to which she is not accustomed. Based on Paddy Chayefsky's teleplay, the catered affair turns into a familial trial, sharing the true-to-life poignancy that marked "Marty," the Oscar-winning Chayefsky drama of the previous year. **92m/B VHS.** Bette Davis, Ernest Borgnine, Debbie Reynolds, Barry Fitzgerald, Rod Taylor, Robert Simon; **D:** Richard Brooks; **W:** Gore Vidal; **C:** John Alton; **M:** Andre Previn. *MGM, FCT, CCB*

Catherine & Co. 🐾½ **1976 (R)** Lonely, penniless girl arrives in Paris and "opens shop" on the streets of Paris. As business booms, she takes a cue from the big corporations and sells stock in herself. **91m/C VHS, Beta. FR IT** Jane Birkin, Patrick Dewaere, Jean-Pierre Aumont, Jean-Claude Brialy; **D:** Michel Boisrond. *NO*

Catherine Cookson's The Wingless Bird 🐾🐾½ *The Wingless Bird* **1997** Agnes Conway (Skinner) is the strong-minded daughter of a Newcastle shop-owner in class-conscious England in December, 1913. Managing her unhappy father's store, Claire waits on two members of the wealthy Farrier family and is soon drawn into their lives when the younger Farrier son, Charles (Atterton), falls in love with her, despite their class differences. But the Conway's have their own class problems—Agnes' younger sister Jessie becomes pregnant by a lower-class lad and her father's fury is murderous. Still as Agnes' love for Charlie grows, she must also deal with the outbreak of WWI, which will bring changes for all concerned. **?m/C VHS. GB** Claire Skinner, Edward Atter-

ton, Julian Wadham, Frank Grimes, Moira Hedmond, Elspet Gray, Dinsdale Landen, Anne Reid; **D:** David Wheatley; **W:** Alan Seymour; **M:** Colin Towns. *VTR*

Catherine the Great 🐾🐾½ *The Rise of Catherine the Great* **1934** Slow but lavish and engrossing British dramatization of the tortured and doomed love affair between Catherine, Empress of Russia, and her irrational, drunken husband Peter. **88m/B VHS, Beta, LV. GB** Douglas Fairbanks Jr., Elisabeth Bergner, Flora Robson; **D:** Paul Czinner; **C:** Georges Perinal. *BAR, VYY, HEG*

Catholic Hour 🐾🐾 **1960** A dramatized version of the life story of Thomas Frederick Price who co-founded the Maryknoll Missionaries in the early 1900s. **30m/B VHS, Beta.** Edward Cullen, Arthur Gary. *VYY*

Catholics 🐾🐾🐾 *The Conflict* **1973** A sensitive exploration of contemporary mores and changing attitudes within the Roman Catholic church. Sheen is sent by the Pope to Ireland to reform some priests. Based on Brian Moore's short novel and made for television. **86m/C VHS, Beta.** Martin Sheen, Trevor Howard; **D:** Jack Gold; **M:** Carl Davis. *NO*

Cathy's Curse 🐾 *Cauchemares* **1977** The spirit of her aunt, who died as a child, possesses a young girl in this Canadian-French collaboration. Tries to capitalize on the popularity of "The Exorcist," but falls seriously short. **90m/C VHS, Beta. FR CA** Alan Scarfe, Beverly Murray; **D:** Eddy Matalon. *NO*

Catlow 🐾🐾½ **1971 (PG-13)** A comedic western with Brynner aiming to steal 2 million dollars in gold from under the nose of his friend, lawman Crenna. Based on the novel by Louis L'Amour. **103m/C VHS.** Yul Brynner, Richard Crenna, Leonard Nimoy, JoAnn Pflug, Jeff Corey, Michael Delano, David Ladd, Bessie Love; **D:** Sam Wanamaker; **W:** Scot Finch, J.J. Griffith. *MGM*

Cats Don't Dance 🐾🐾 **1997 (G)** Animated musical/comedy finds Danny (Bakula) a hoofer wannabe trying to break into '30s Hollywood. Only problem is that he's a cat and can't understand why he only gets parts playing animals. He gets into trouble with bratty human star Darla Dimple (Peldon) and nearly sees his chance at a career vanish. Combines "Singin' in the Rain" and "Who Framed Roger Rabbit," with some showbiz cynicism from "The Player" to create a cartoon that will most likely sail over the heads of its target audience. Most of the time, as in the old Warner Bros. classics, that's a good thing. Not in this case, however. **77m/C VHS, LV, Closed Caption. D:** Mark Dindal; **W:** Cliff Ruby, Roberts Gannaway, Elana Lesser, Theresa Pettengill; **M:** Steve Goldstein, Randy Newman; **V:** Scott Bakula, Jasmine Guy, Ashley Peldon, Kathy Najimy, John Rhys-Davies, George Kennedy, Rene Auberjonois, Hal Holbrook, Don Knotts, Frank Welker, David Johansen, Natalie Cole. *WAR*

Cat's Eye 🐾🐾 *Stephen King's Cat's Eye* **1985 (PG-13)** An anthology of three Stephen King short stories connected by a stray cat who wanders through each tale. **94m/C VHS, Beta, LV, Closed Caption.** Drew Barrymore, James Woods, Alan King, Robert Hays, Candy Clark, Kenneth McMillan, James Naughton, Charles S. Dutton; **D:** Lewis Teague; **W:** Stephen King; **C:** Jack Cardiff; **M:** Alan Silvestri. *FOX, FCT*

Cat's Play 🐾🐾 *Mascskajatek* **1974** A widowed music teacher makes a ceremonial occasion of a weekly dinner with an old flame. Then an old friend from her youth suddenly reappears and begins an affair with the gentleman, causing self-destructive passions to explode. In Hungarian with English subtitles. **115m/C VHS. HU** Margit Dayka, Margit Makay, Elma Bulla; **D:** Karoly Makk. Nominations: Academy Awards '74: Best Foreign Language Film. *CVC*

Cattle Queen of Montana 🐾🐾½ **1954** Reagan stars as an undercover federal agent investigating livestock rustlings and Indian uprisings. **88m/C VHS, Beta, LV.** Ronald Reagan, Barbara Stanwyck, Jack Elam, Gene Evans, Lance Fuller, Anthony Caruso; **D:** Allan Dwan; **W:** Robert Blees. *NO*

Caught 🐾🐾🐾 **1949** A woman marries for wealth and security and is desperately unhappy. She runs away and takes a job with a struggling physician, and falls in love with him. Her husband finds her, forcing her to decide between a life of security or love. **90m/B VHS.** James Mason, Barbara Bel Geddes, Robert Ryan, Curt Bois, Natalie Schafer, Art Smith; **D:** Max Ophuls; **C:** Lee Garmes. *REP*

Caught 🐾 **1996 (R)** Homeless Irishman Nick (Verveen) winds up in the New Jersey fish shop run by Joe (Olmos) and his wife Betty (Alonso). Betty takes a liking to the good-looking young man and encourages Joe to offer him a job and even invites Nick to stay with them in departed son Danny's (Schub) old room. Soon, room and board isn't all the spicy Betty is offering and Nick's willing to please, especially since Joe turns a blind eye. Too bad cocaine-addicted Danny, a failed comedian, returns home and immediately becomes jealous of the interloper. He's also too willing to drag secrets out into the open, whatever the cost. Based on Pomerantz's novel "Into It."**CW:** Strong sexuality and language, and for some violence and drug use. **109m/C VHS, LV, Closed Caption.** Edward James Olmos, Maria Conchita Alonso, Arie Verveen, Steven Schub, Bitty Schram, Shawn Elliot; **D:** Robert M. Young; **W:** Edward Pomerantz; **C:** Michael Barrow; **M:** Chris Botti. Nominations: Independent Spirit Awards '97: Best Actress (Alonso), Best Director (Young), Debut Performance (Verveen). *COL*

Caught in the Act 🐾🐾½ **1993 (PG-13)** Scott McNally (Harrison) is an out-of-work actor who teaches acting classes to make a buck. Into one of his classes walks the sultry Rachel (Hope) and they start a hot affair. Then Rachel calls Scott, claiming to be kidnapped, he suddenly finds 10 million dollars in his bank account, and his landlord is murdered. Scott finds himself the pawn in an embezzlement scheme and framed for murder. But this is one role Scott doesn't want and he intends to work with a new script of his own devise. Made for cable television. **93m/C VHS, LV, Closed Caption.** Gregory Harrison, Leslie Hope, Patricia Clarkson, Kevin Tighe; **D:** Deborah Reinisch; **W:** Ken Hixon. *USH*

Caught in the Draft 🐾🐾🐾 **1941** Hope's funniest role has him as a Hollywood star trying to evade the draft in WW II, but he ends up accidentally enlisting himself. Lamour plays the daughter of a colonel in the Army whom Hope plans to marry, thinking it will get him out of the service. Very funny military comedy and one of Hope's best. Based on a story by Harry Tugend. **82m/B VHS, Closed Caption.** Bob Hope, Dorothy Lamour, Lynne Overman, Eddie Bracken, Clarence Kolb, Paul Hurst, Ferike Boros, Irving Bacon; **D:** David Butler; **W:** Harry Tugend. *USH, BTV*

Caught Up 🐾🐾 **1998 (R)** Directorial debut for Darin Scott follows the luckless path of ex-con Daryl (Woodbine). After serving five years as an unwitting accomplice to a bank robbery, he meets Vanessa (Williams) who is a dead ringer for his ex-girlfriend. She gets him a job as a limo driver that caters to thugs and gangsters. Unfortunately for Daryl, Vanessa has stolen some diamonds from a Rastafarian named Ahmad (Wallace), and he is tangled in a web of deceit and violence. He is also tangled in a plot that twists and turns a little too much for its own good. Director Scott tries a few too many fancy tricks, although some of them work reasonably well. Cameos from Snoop Doggy Dog and LL Cool J. **95m/C VHS.** Bokeem Woodbine, Cynda Williams, Snoop Doggy Dogg, Joseph Lindsey, Clifton Powell, Basil Wallace, Tony Todd, L.L. Cool J., Jeffrey Combs, Damon Saleem, Shedric Hunter Jr.; **D:** Darin Scott; **W:** Darin Scott; **C:** Thomas Callaway; **M:** Marc Bonilla. *NYR*

Cauldron of Blood 🐾½ *Blind Man's Bluff; El Coleccionista de Cadaveres* **1967 (PG)** Blind sculptor Karloff unwittingly uses human skeletons supplied by his crazed wife Lindfors as the framework of his art pieces. **95m/C VHS.** *SP* Boris Karloff, Viveca Lindfors, Jean-Pierre Aumont, Rosenda Monteros, Ruben

Rojo, Dianik Zurakowska; **D:** Edward Mann; **W:** Edward Mann. *REP, VDC, FCT*

Cause for Alarm 🐾🐾½ **1951** A jealous husband recovering from a heart attack begins to lose his mind. He wrongly accuses his wife of having an affair and attempts to frame her for his own murder. A fast-paced thriller with a nifty surprise ending. **74m/B VHS.** Loretta Young, Barry Sullivan, Bruce Cowling, Margalo Gillmore, Irving Bacon, Carl "Alfalfa" Switzer; **D:** Tay Garnett; **M:** Andre Previn. *NOS, SNC, MGM*

Cause of Death 🐾½ **1990 (R)** After the accidental death of his brother, Colombian drug lord Manuel Ramirez is lured to L.A. to collect his millions in blood money. **90m/C VHS.** Michael Barak, Sydney Coale Phillips, Daniel Martine; **D:** Philip Jones. *VSE*

Cavalcade 🐾🐾🐾 **1933** Traces the lives of the British Marryot family from the death of Queen Victoria, through WWI, the Jazz Age, and the Depression. A wistful adaptation of the hit play by Noel Coward with its touching portrayal of one family trying to weather good times and bad together. **110m/B VHS.** Diana Wynyard, Clive Brook, Herbert Mundin, Una O'Connor, Ursula Jeans, Beryl Mercer, Merle Tottenham, Frank Lawton, John Warburton, Margaret Lindsay, Billy Bevan; **D:** Frank Lloyd; **C:** Ernest Palmer. Academy Awards '33: Best Director (Lloyd), Best Interior Decoration, Best Picture; Nominations: Academy Awards '33: Best Actress (Wynyard). *FXV, BTV*

Cavalcade of the West 🐾🐾 **1936** Typical western with two brothers, separated by a kidnapping, growing up on opposite sides of the law. Much later they meet, and the question is: will the outlaw be reformed and reunited with his happy family? **70m/B VHS, Beta.** Hoot Gibson, Rex Lease, Marion Shilling, Earl Dwire; **D:** Harry Fraser. *GPV, DVT, VCN*

The Cavalier 🐾 **198?** Chinese cavalier faces love, danger and intrigue while deploying martial arts skills. **90m/C VHS, Beta.** Tang Wei, Lung Fei, Yeh Yuen, Tseng Tsao. *UNI*

Cavalier of the West 🐾 **1931** An Army captain is the only negotiating force between the white man and a primitive Indian tribe. **66m/B VHS, Beta, LV.** Harry Carey Sr., Kane Richmond, George "Gabby" Hayes; **D:** John P. McCarthy. *NOS*

Cavalry 🐾½ **1936** A Union Army Lieutenant is reunited with his family after the Civil War, bringing them happiness and joy. **60m/B VHS, Beta.** Bob Steele, Frances Grant, Karl Hackett, Hal Price; **D:** Robert North Bradbury. *NOS, DVT*

Cavalry Charge 🐾🐾½ *The Last Outpost* **1951** Vance Britton (Reagan) is the captain of a brigade of Confederate troops wreaking havoc on Union outposts. His brother Jeb (Bennett) is a Union soldier sent to the western frontier to take care of the Confederate problem. Vance's former fiance Julie (Fleming) is also living in the territories with her new husband. All three converge when the Union fort, where Julie is living and Jeb is defending, is attacked by Apaches. Brother Vance rides to the rescue. Lots of action. **72m/C VHS.** Ronald Reagan, Bruce (Herman Brix) Bennett, Rhonda Fleming, Noah Beery Jr., Bill Williams, Peter Hanson, Hugh Beaumont, John Ridgely, Lloyd Corrigan, James Burke, Richard Crane, Ewing Mitchell; **D:** Lewis R. Foster; **W:** Geoffrey Homes, George Worthing Yates, Winston Miller; **C:** Loyal Griggs. *IVY*

Cavalry Command 🐾½ *Cavalleria Commandos* **1963** Good will and integrity characterize the U.S. soldiers called into a small village to quiet a guerrilla rebellion. **77m/C VHS, Beta.** John Agar, Richard Arlen, Myron Healey, Alicia Vergel, William Phipps, Eddie Infante; **D:** Eddie Romero; **W:** Eddie Romero. *RHI*

Cave Girl woof! *Cavegirl* **1985 (R)** After falling through a time-warp during a high-school field trip, a social pariah makes a hit with a pre-historic honey. Sexist teen exploitation film, with few original ideas and a not-so-hot cast. **85m/C VHS, Beta, LV.** Daniel Roebuck, Cindy Ann Thompson, Saba Moor, Jeff Chayette; **D:** David Oliver; **W:** David Oliver. *COL*

Cave of the Living Dead woof! *Der Fluch Der Gruenen Augen; Night of the Vampire; The Curse of Green Eyes* **1965** Mad professor with a past is up to something in a cave under castle. Villagers summon Inspector Doren of Interpol to solve a rash of nasty murders that they've blamed on green-eyed, cave-dwelling vampires. A challenge to watch till the end. Filmed in Sepiatone. **87m/B VHS, Beta.** *GE YU* Adrian Hoven, Erika Remberg, Carl Mohner, Wolfgang Preiss, Karin Field, John Kitzmiller, Akos Von Rathony; **D:** Akos Von Rathony.

Caveman 🐾🐾 **1981 (PG)** Starr stars in this prehistoric spoof about a group of cavemen banished from different tribes who band together to form a tribe called "The Misfits." **92m/C VHS, Beta.** Ringo Starr, Barbara Bach, John Matuszak, Dennis Quaid, Jack Gilford, Shelley Long, Cork Hubbert; **D:** Carl Gottlieb; **W:** Carl Gottlieb, Rudy DeLuca; **M:** Lalo Schifrin. *MGM, FOX*

CB4: The Movie 🐾½ **1993 (R)** Falling somewhere between a serious attempt and parody, CB4 tries to do both and succeeds at neither. Written in the key of "Wayne's World" by "Saturday Night Live's" Rock, it starts out as a "rockumentary" (please refer to "This is Spinal Tap"), but quickly turns into a sitcom after two gangsta rap friends assume the identity of a local club owner when he is in jail. Hartman, also of SNL, appears as a right-wing city councilman. Chock full of violence, sexism, and profanity tucked into a wandering plot.**CW:** Strong language, drug content, and sexuality. **83m/C VHS, LV, Letterbox, Closed Caption.** Chris Rock, Allen Payne, Deezer D, Phil Hartman, Charlie Murphy, Khandi Alexander, Art Evans, Chris Elliott, Willard Pugh, Theresa Randle; **D:** Tamra Davis; **W:** Chris Rock, Nelson George, Robert Locash; **M:** John Barnes. *USH*

Cease Fire 🐾🐾 **1985 (R)** The story of a troubled Vietnam vet who finds solace in a veterans' therapy group. Adapted from the play by George Fernandez. **97m/C VHS, Beta.** Don Johnson, Robert F. Lyons, Lisa Blount; **D:** David Nutter; **M:** Gary Fry. *CNG*

Ceiling Zero 🐾🐾🐾 **1935** Cagney is an irrepressible pilot who does as he pleases and loves to aggravate his soft-hearted boss O'Brien. He falls for aviatrix Travis and neglects his duties to woo her, which leads to tragedy. Naturally, this sobers Cagney up and he volunteers for a dangerous test flight. Lots of fast-paced action and Cagney is at his swaggering best. Based on a play by Frank Wead, who also wrote the screenplay. Remade in 1941 as "International Squadron." **95m/B VHS.** James Cagney, Pat O'Brien, June Travis, Stuart Erwin, Henry Wadsworth, Isabel Jewell, Barton MacLane; **D:** Howard Hawks; **W:** Frank Wead. *MGM, FCT*

Celebrity 🐾½ **1985** In this television film, a tragic childhood secret must be confronted by three friends when one is charged with murder. Based on the Thomas Thompson novel. **313m/C VHS, Beta.** Michael Beck, Ben Masters, Joseph Bottoms; **D:** Paul Wendkos. *NO*

Celeste 🐾🐾🐾 **1981** Adlon (who later made the offbeat comedy "Sugarbaby") directed this longish but finely detailed and beautifully photographed biographical look at French writer Marcel (Remembrance of Things Past) Proust. Based on the memoirs of Proust's housekeeper, Celeste Albaret, an uneducated farmgirl, portraying the woman's devoted relationship ('til death did them part) with the middle-aged, homosexual author. It does so with wit, poignancy, and insight, but is not entirely successful in its attempt to render Proust's verbal literary style into a visual medium. In German with English subtitles. **107m/C VHS.** *GE* Eva Mattes, Jurgen Arndt, Norbert Wartha, Wolf Euba; **D:** Percy Adlon; **W:** Percy Adlon. *NYF, FCT*

Celestial Clockwork 🐾🐾½ *Mecaniques Celestes* **1994** Runaway Venezuelan bride Ana (Gil), an aspiring opera singer, takes off for Paris clutching her Maria Callas poster. God must protect the innocent because she meets a friendly cabbie, immediately finds a place to live, and gets the perfect singing teacher, a cranky Russian emigre named Grigorief (Debrane). In fact, the only problem in this Cinderella's life is jealous would-be star Celeste (Dombasle), who wants the same lead theatrical role that Ana is also interested in. French with subtitles. **85m/C VHS.** *FR* Ariadna Gil, Arielle Dombasle, Evelyne Didi, Frederic Longbois, Lluis Homar, Michel Debrane; *D:* Fina Torres; *W:* Fina Torres; *C:* Ricardo Aronvich. *EVE*

Celia: Child Of Terror 🎬🎬 **1989** Set in the 1950s, this film deals with the awful results of a young girl's inability to handle disappointment. **110m/C VHS, Beta.** *AU* Rebecca Smart, Nicholas Eadie, Victoria Longley, Mary-Anne Fahey; *D:* Ann Turner. *NO*

Celine and Julie Go Boating 🎬🎬 **1974** Strange fantasy follows magician Celine (Berto) and her librarian friend, Julie (Labourier). Celine sometimes works as a governess for a little girl who lives with her widowed father in a possibly haunted house. Two women are in love with the father but he'd promised his wife never to re-marry as long as their invalid daughter was still alive. Celine and Julie become worried for the little girl and decide to rescue her. An adaptation of the Henry James story "A Romance of Certain Old Clothes." French with subtitles. **193m/C VHS.** Juliet Berto, Dominique Labourier, Bulle Ogier, Marie-France Pisier, Barbet Schroeder, Philippe Clevenot, Nathalie Asnor; *D:* Jacques Rivette; *W:* Jacques Rivette, Eduardo Di Gregorio; *C:* Jacques Renard; *M:* Jean-Marie Senia. *NYF*

The Cellar 🎬½ **1990 (PG-13)** A young boy finds an ancient Comanche monster spirit in the basement of his home. His parents, as usual, don't believe him, so he must battle the monster alone. **90m/C VHS.** Patrick Kilpatrick, Suzanne Savoy, Chris Miller, Ford Rainey; *D:* Kevin S. Tenney.

Cellar Dweller woof! **1987** A cartoonist moves into an old house and soon discovers it's haunted by a demonic cartoonist who killed himself 30 years earlier. What a coincidence. Low-budget scare-'em-uper filmed on one set and lit by a floodlamp. **78m/C VHS, Beta, LV.** Pamela Bellwood, Deborah Muldowney, Brian Robbins, Vince Edwards, Jeffrey Combs, Yvonne De Carlo; *D:* John Carl Buechler.

Cellblock Sisters: Banished Behind Bars 🎬½ **1995 (R)** Biker babe Harris reunites with college girl sis Wood to off their disgusting stepfather who separately sold them to adoptive families after killing their junkie mom. Harris does the crime but Wood does the time—until her guilty sibling deliberately gets thrown behind bars in order to protect her. Has all the standard jail chicks elements.**CW:** Violence, sexuality, and language. **95m/C VHS.** Gail Harris, Annie Wood, Ace Ross; *D:* Henri Charr. *PMH*

The Celluloid Closet 🎬🎬🎬½ **1995 (R)** Terrific documentary on how Hollywood films have depicted homosexual characters, subliminally and otherwise. Working chronologically and in an historical context, beginning with silent films, there are clips from more than 100 films, along with interviews from writers and actors. (Notable is writer Gore Vidal's comments on the gay subtext in 1959's "Ben-Hur"). Based on Vito Russo's 1981 book.**CW:** Some graphic footage of sexuality and violence, and for language. **102m/C VHS, LV, Closed Caption.** *D:* Robert Epstein, Jeffrey Friedman; *W:* Armistead Maupin; *C:* Nancy Schreiber; *M:* Carter Burwell. *COL*

Celtic Pride 🎬🎬 **1996 (PG-13)** Mike O'Hara (Stern) and Jimmy Flaherty (Aykroyd) are the worst kind of crazy. They're sports nuts. They are so consumed with passion for their beloved Celtics that they kidnap foul-mouthed superstar Lewis Scott (Wayans) of the Utah Jazz before game seven of the NBA finals. If this sounds far fetched, well...it is, unless you have an ESPN junkie in your life. There's not as much court action as you would expect, since most of the story revolves around intermittent trash-talking and escape attempts. If you're a Celtic hater, stick around for

the end, when the Boston Garden is demolished using special effects.**CW:** Language and an abundance of crude humor. **90m/C VHS, LV, Closed Caption.** Damon Wayans, Daniel Stern, Dan Aykroyd, Gail O'Grady, Adam Hendershott, Paul Guilfoyle, Deion Sanders, Christopher McDonald, Gus Williams, Ted Rooney, Vladimir Cuk; *Cameos:* Bill Walton, Larry Bird; *D:* Tom DeCerchio; *W:* Judd Apatow; *C:* Oliver Wood; *M:* Basil Poledouris. *TOU*

The Cement Garden 🎬🎬 **1993** Fatherless 15-year-old Jack (Robertson) and 16-year-old sister Julie (Gainsbourg) are afraid that they and their two younger siblings Sue (Coulthard) and Tom (Birkin) will be taken into foster care after their mother dies at home. So to keep their secret, they bury her in the basement and try to assume a normal family life. Not that this works for long—Jack and Julie give into an incestuous fascination and the household slowly sinks into chaotic squalor around them. Gainsbourg is the director's niece and the young Birkin is his son. Based on Ian McEwan's 1978 novel. **105m/C VHS.** *FR GE GB* Charlotte Gainsbourg, Andrew Robertson, Alice Coulthard, Ned Birkin, Sinead Cusack, Hanns Zischler, Jochen Horst; *D:* Andrew Birkin; *W:* Andrew Birkin; *C:* Stephen Blackman; *M:* Ed Shearmur. *NYF*

The Cemetery Club 🎬🎬½ **1993 (PG-13)** Story of three Jewish widows who make weekly visits to their husbands' graves while attempting to cope with their lives. Doris (Dukakis) is loyal to the memory of her husband and acts as the moral conscience of the trio. Lucille (Ladd) is a merry widow who wears clothes more suitable for younger women, but she also harbors a painful secret. Esther (Burstyn) struggles with her loneliness until a widowed cab driver begins to woo her. Commendably, the characters are given more dimension than Hollywood usually grants women of a certain age. Based on the play "The Cemetary Club" by Menchell, who also wrote the screenplay.**CW:** Some language and sensuality. **114m/C VHS, Beta, LV, Closed Caption.** Ellen Burstyn, Olympia Dukakis, Diane Ladd, Danny Aiello, Lainie Kazan, Christina Ricci, Bernie Casey, Alan Mason, Sam Schwartz, Jeff Howell, Robert Costanzo, Wallace Shawn, Louis Guss; *D:* Bill Duke; *W:* Ivan Menchell; *C:* Steven Poster; *M:* Elmer Bernstein. *TOU, BTV*

Cemetery High 🎬 **1989** Beautiful high school girls decide to lure the local boys into a trap and kill them. **80m/C VHS, Beta.** Debi Thibeault, Karen Nielsen, Lisa Schmidt, Ruth Collins, Simone, Tony Kruk, David Coughlin, Frank Stewart; *D:* Gorman Bechard; *W:* Gorman Bechard, Carmine Capobianco. *UNI, HHE*

Cemetery Man 🎬🎬 *Dellamorte Delamore; Of Death, of Love* **1995 (R)** Grotesque little saga about zombies and necrophilia set in a small Italian cemetery. Thanks to a weird post-death plague the corpses refuse to stay quietly in their graves, forcing watchman Francisco Dellamorte (Everett) and mute gravedigger Gnaghi (Hadji-Lazaro) to split their heads open. But when Francisco's dead sweetheart (Falchi) rises from her grave, he's a little slow to rebury the still-active corpse. Based on the Italian graphic novel "Dellamorte Dellamore," from the "Dylan Dog" series by Tiziano Sclavi.**CW:** Macabre violence and gore, strong sexuality, some language. **100m/C VHS, Closed Caption.** *IT* Rupert Everett, Anna Falchi, Francois Hadji-Lazaro; *D:* Michele (Michael) Soavi; *W:* Gianni Romoli; *C:* Mauro Marchetti; *M:* Manuel De Sica. *FOX*

Centennial 🎬🎬🎬 **1978** Epic 12-part TV miniseries, based on the 1974 novel by James Michener, about the building of the Rocky Mountain town of Centennial, Colorado, from 1795 to the present. There are trappers and Indians, immigrants and cattlemen, soldiers, conservationists, and politicians all with their own stories to tell. **1258m/C VHS.** Robert Conrad, Richard Chamberlain, Raymond Burr, Sally Kellerman, Barbara Carrera, Michael Ansara, Gregory Harrison, Stephanie Zimbalist, Christina Raines, Stephen McHattie, Kario Salem, Chad Everett, Alex Karras, Mark Harmon, Dennis Weaver, Timothy Dalton, Richard Crenna, Cliff DeYoung, Glynn Turman, Brian Keith,

Les Lannom, Rafael Campos, Anthony Zerbe, Doug McKeon, Lynn Redgrave, William Atherton, A. Martinez, Lois Nettleton, David Janssen, Robert Vaughn, Andy Griffith, Sharon Gless; *D:* Virgil W. Vogel, Harry Falk, Paul Krasny, Bernard McEveety; *W:* John Wilder. *USH*

Center of the Web 🎬🎬 **1992 (R)** John Phillips is a victim of mistaken identity—someone thinks he's a professional hit man. After surviving an apparent mob attempt on his life, Phillips is persuaded by a CIA operative to go along with the deception in order to capture a potential political assassin. At least that's what Phillips is told, but he soon realizes that the deeper he gets into his new role, the deadlier the plot becomes. Davi is one of the best bad guys around and the fast-paced stunts and plot twists make this watchable.**CW:** Language and violence. **88m/C VHS, LV.** Ted Prior, Robert Davi, Tony Curtis, Charlene Tilton, Bo Hopkins, Charles Napier; *D:* David A. Prior.

The Centerfold Girls woof! **1974 (R)** Microscopic storyline involves a deranged man who is determined to kill all the voluptuous young women who have posed nude for a centerfold. **93m/C VHS, Beta.** Andrew Prine, Tiffany Bolling, Aldo Ray, Jeremy Slate, Ray Danton, Francine York; *D:* John Peyser.

Century 🎬🎬 **1994 (R)** Ambitious young doctor Paul Reisner (Owen), the son of a prosperous Jewish father (Stephens), gets a position at a London research hospital headed by the charismatic Professor Mandry (Dance). Paul manages to disgrace himself by provoking Mandry and is dismissed but finds out some disturbing information and is determined to discredit his former mentor. Anti-Semitism lurks as does the change from Victorian mores to the challenging dawn of the 20th century. Complex performances are somewhat undermined by the static direction.**CW:** Some scenes of sexuality. **112m/C VHS.** *GB* Clive Owen, Charles Dance, Miranda Richardson, Robert Stephens, Joan Hickson, Lena Headey, Neil Stuke; *D:* Stephen Poliakoff; *W:* Stephen Poliakoff; *C:* Witold Stok; *M:* Michael Gibbs. *PGV*

A Century of Women **1994** Three-part look at the lives and accomplishments of American women over the past 100 years, including the changing role of women in the workplace and the home. The documentary segments are interspersed with a fictional story spanning five generations of women who reunite for a weekend. On three cassettes. **360m/C VHS.** Teresa Wright, Olympia Dukakis, Justine Bateman, Talia Shire, Madge Sinclair, Jasmine Guy, Brooke Smith. *TTC*

Certain Fury 🎬 **1985 (R)** Two timid women go on the lam when they are mistaken for escaped prostitutes who shot up a courthouse. The sooner they get caught, the better. **88m/C VHS, Beta, LV.** Tatum O'Neal, Irene Cara, Peter Fonda, Nicholas Campbell, Moses Gunn; *D:* Stephen Gyllenhaal. *VTR*

Certain Sacrifice 🎬 **1980** Nineteen-year-old Madonna expresses herself in her film debut. Seeking revenge on the man who raped her, she murders him in a strange ritualistic manner underneath the Brooklyn Bridge. Poor is the man whose pleasures depend on the permission of another? **60m/C VHS, Beta.** Madonna, Jeremy Pattnosh, Charles Kurtz; *D:* Stephen Lewicki. *WOV, MVD*

Cesar 🎬🎬🎬🎬 **1936** This is the third and most bittersweet part of Pagnol's famed trilogy based on his play depicting the lives and loves of the people of Provence, France. Marius returns after a 20-year absence to his beloved Fanny and his now-grown son, Cesariot. The first two parts of the trilogy are "Marius" and "Fanny" and were directed by Alexander Korda and Marc Allegret respectively. In French with English subtitles. **117m/B VHS, Beta, LV.** *FR* Raimu, Pierre Fresnay, Orane Demazis, Charpin, Andre Fouche, Alida Rauffe; *D:* Marcel Pagnol; *W:* Marcel Pagnol; *M:* Vincent Scotto. *NOS, MRV, INT*

Cesar & Rosalie ✂✂✂ 1972 (PG) Acclaimed French comedy depicts the love triangle between a beautiful divorcee, her aging live-in companion and a younger man. Engaging portrait of how their relationship evolves over time. In French with English subtitles. 110m/C VHS, Beta, LV. *FR* Romy Schneider, Yves Montand, Sami Frey, Umberto Orsini; *D:* Claude Sautet. *TPV*

Cesare Borgia ✂✂ 1923 Veidt stars in this bloodthirsty saga as the ruthless son of Pope Alexander VI who'll let nothing come between him and his desires. 83m/B VHS. *GE* Conrad Veidt; *D:* Richard Oswald. *FCT*

Chain Gang Killings ✂ 1985 Pair of shackled prisoners, one black, the other white, escape from a truck transporting them to prison. 99m/C VHS, Beta. Ian Yule, Ken Gampu. *NO*

Chain Gang Women woof! 1972 (R) Sordid violence. Two escaped convicts plunder, rob, and rape until a victim's husband comes looking for revenge. 85m/C VHS. Robert Lott, Barbara Mills, Michael Stearns, Linda York; *D:* Lee Frost. *NO*

Chain Lightning ✂✂ 1950 Bogart stars as a bomber pilot who falls in love with a Red Cross worker (Parker) while fighting in Europe in 1943. They lose touch after the war until Bogie goes to work as a test pilot for the same shady airplane manufacturer (Massey) where Parker works. He is given the chance to test a new plane, which has already cost the life of one of his friends. Bogart has more success, along with rekindling the flames of romance. Average script but the flying sequences are well-done. 94m/B VHS. Humphrey Bogart, Eleanor Parker, Raymond Massey, Richard Whorf; *D:* Stuart Heisler; *W:* Liam O'Brien, Vincent B. Evans. *MGM*

Chain of Command ✂✂ 1995 (R) Anti-terrorist agent Merrill Ross (Dudikoff) goes up against hired mercenaries trying to overthrow the government of the oil-rich Republic of Qumir. Then Ross realizes he's being manipulated and it could be by any number of players.*CW:* Language, violence, brief nudity. 97m/C VHS. Michael Dudikoff, R. Lee Ermey. *AVE*

Chain of Desire ✂✂ 1993 Nightclub inside Manhattan's Chrysler Building is the spot for numerous folk to have lot of meaningless sexual encounters and look at the emptiness of their lives. 107m/C VHS, Beta, LV. Linda Fiorentino, Elias Koteas, Malcolm McDowell, Grace Zabriskie, Tim Guinee, Assumpta Serna, Patrick Bauchau, Seymour Cassel, Kevin Conroy, Angel Aviles, Holly Marie Combs, Jamie Harold, Dewey Weber, Suzanne Douglas; *D:* Temistocles Lopez; *W:* Temistocles Lopez; *C:* Nancy Schreiber; *M:* Nathan Birnbaum. Nominations: Independent Spirit Awards '94: Best Cinematography.

Chain Reaction ✂½ *Nuclear Run* 1980 When a nuclear scientist is exposed to radiation after an accident at an atomic power plant, he must escape to warn the public of the danger. 87m/C VHS, Beta, LV. Steve Bisley, Ross Thompson; *D:* Ian Barry; *C:* Russell Boyd. *NO*

Chain Reaction ✂✂½ *Dead Drop* 1996 (PG-13) Government/scientific conspiracy chase story finds Chicago lab tech Eddie Kasalivich (Reeves) a member of a research team that's discovered the formula for cheap, pollution-free energy. This doesn't sit well with someone since the team's leader is murdered and the lab destroyed in an explosion. Eddie and scientist Lily Sinclair (Weisz) become prime suspects and are pursued by the feds as they try to find the real culprits. Old pro Freeman, as money man Paul Shannon, is the best reason to watch (as usual). Davis did "The Fugitive," so he knows his tension-filled chases but this is just more same old-same old.*CW:* Some intense action/violence. 107m/C VHS, LV, Closed Caption. Keanu Reeves, Morgan Freeman, Rachel Weisz, Fred Ward, Brian Cox, Kevin Dunn, Joanna Cassidy, Chelcie Ross, Tzi Ma, Nicholas Rudall; *D:* Andrew Davis; *W:* J.F. Lawton, Michael Bortman; *C:* Frank

Tidy; *M:* Jerry Goldsmith. Nominations: Golden Raspberry Awards '96: Worst Actor (Reeves). *FXV*

Chained ✂✂½ 1934 Crawford and Gable star in this love triangle that somehow never sizzles. Crawford, in love with married businessman Kruger, takes a South American cruise to get away from it all, meets Gable, and of course falls in love. Seems simple enough, but wait! Crawford goes back to New York City and marries Kruger (his wife grants him a divorce) and is miserable. But then Gable shows up, further complicating matters. Choices, choices. Predictable script was not helped by half-hearted performances. 73m/B VHS, Beta. Joan Crawford, Clark Gable, Otto Kruger, Stuart Erwin, Una O'Connor; *D:* Clarence Brown. *MGM, CCB*

Chained for Life woof! 1951 Daisy and Violet Hilton, real life Siamese twins, star in this old-fashioned "freak" show. When a gigolo deserts one twin on their wedding night, the other twin shoots him dead. The twins go on trial and the judge asks the viewer to hand down the verdict. Exploitative and embarrassing to watch. 81m/B VHS, Beta. Daisy Hilton, Violet Hilton; *D:* Harry Fraser. *SNC, NOS, RHI*

Chained Heat ✂✂ 1983 (R) Seamy tale of the vicious reality of life for women behind bars. Naive Blair is imprisoned again (after another bad jailhouse gig in "Born Innocent") and has usual assortment of negative experiences with domineering prisoners, degenerate guards, and the creepy warden who maintains a prison bachelor pad equipped with hot tub. Needless to say, she grows up in a hurry. Trashifying, archetypal women-in-prison effort that aims to satisfy full range of low-quality audience demands. Sequel to 1982 "Concrete Jungle." 97m/C VHS, Beta, LV. Linda Blair, Stella Stevens, Sybil Danning, Tamara Dobson, Henry Silva, John Vernon, Nita Talbot, Louisa Moritz; *D:* Paul Nicholas; *C:* Mac Ahlberg. Golden Raspberry Awards '83: Worst Supporting Actress (Danning).*VES*

Chained Heat 2 ✂½ 1992 (R) Another sordid tale of women behind bars. Nielsen stars as the psychotic stiletto-heeled warden of an infamous prison, complete with sadistic heroin-smuggling guards. This drug ring also deals in prostitution, which results in two imprisoned sisters (innocent, naturally) being separated from one another. One sister is determined to find true justice. 98m/C VHS, LV, Closed Caption. Brigitte Nielsen, Paul Koslo, Kari Whitman, Kimberley Kates; *D:* Lloyd A. Simandl; *W:* Chris Hyde. *NLC*

Chains ✂✂ 1989 (R) A Chicago gangland feud entraps two couples in its web, and the innocents must take care of themselves when the situation goes from bad to worse. 93m/C VHS, LV. Jimi Jourdan, Michael Dixon, John L. Eves; *D:* Roger J. Barski. *IMP*

Chains of Gold ✂✂ 1992 (R) Kind social worker (Travolta) befriends teen who wants to get out of the crack-dealing gang in which he's involved. He infiltrates the gang and risks his life helping the boy get out. Originally aired on cable television. 95m/C VHS, Closed Caption. John Travolta, Marilu Henner, Bernie Casey, Hector Elizondo, Joey Lawrence; *D:* Rod Holcomb; *M:* Trevor Jones.

The Chair ✂✂ *Hot Seat* 1987 (R) The penitentiary where an evil superintendent was fried in his own electric chair during an inmate uprising is reopened after two decades. The new warden (Benedict), who used to be a subordinate to the dead man, believes in rigid control of the inmates and locks horns with the big-house shrink (Coco), who on the surface is an intelligent humanitarian, but may have a darker side. This acrimonious dispute takes a back seat, when it appears that the spirit of the late warden has come back to make the inmates pay for his untimely death.*CW:* Language and strong violence. 90m/C VHS, LV, Closed Caption. James Coco, Paul Benedict, Stephen Geoffreys, Trini Alvarado, John Bentley; *D:* Waldemar Korzeniowsky. *IMP*

Chairman of the Board woof! 1997 (PG-13) Some studio executive decided to take a bad prop comic named after a vegetable and give him a major motion picture. If this movie accomplishes one thing, it may be the abolition of Friday afternoon twelve-martini lunches in Hollywood. Carrot Top plays Edison, a wacky surfer/inventor who befriends an old eccentric man. After the old guy heads for the big wave in the sky, it turns out that he was fabulously wealthy and left his company to Edison. This doesn't sit well with the conniving Bradford (Miller). Courtney Thorne-Smith plays Natalie (although this does not stop Mr. Top from calling her Courtney in one scene) as the standard love interest. Also appearing are Jack Warden, Raquel Welch and M. Emmet Walsh. Why? That's what they're asking their agents. Rent it only if every single video, including the instructional mime section, is already out.*CW:* Crude and sex-related humor and language. 95m/C VHS, Closed Caption, DVD. Carrot Top, Courtney Thorne-Smith, Larry Miller, Raquel Welch, Jack Warden, Estelle Harris, Bill Erwin, M. Emmet Walsh, Jack McGee, Glenn Shadix, Fred Stoller, Mystro Clark, Jack Plotnick; *D:* Alex Zamm; *W:* Al Septien, Turi Meyer, Alex Zamm; *C:* David Lewis; *M:* Chris Hajian. *THV*

The Chalk Garden ✂✂✂ 1964 A woman with a mysterious past takes on the job of governess for an unruly 14-year-old girl, with unforseen consequences. An excellent adaptation of the Enid Bagnold play although not as suspenseful as the stage production. 106m/C VHS, Beta. *GB* Deborah Kerr, Hayley Mills, Edith Evans, John Mills, Elizabeth Sellars, Felix Aylmer; *D:* Ronald Neame; *W:* John Michael Hayes; *M:* Malcolm Arnold. National Board of Review Awards '64: Best Supporting Actress (Evans); Nominations: Academy Awards '64: Best Supporting Actress (Evans). *USH*

The Challenge ✂✂✂ 1938 Story of the courageous party of explorers who conquered the Matterhorn. Incredible avalanche scenes. 77m/B VHS, Beta. Luis Trenker, Robert Douglas. *DVT, VYY*

Challenge woof! 1974 (PG) When his entire family is killed, dad decides to seek revenge with his shotgun. Very bloody and violent and very nearly plotless. 90m/C VHS. Earl Owensby, William T. Hicks, Katheryn Thompson, Johnny Popwell; *D:* Martin Beck. *FOX*

The Challenge ✂✂½ 1982 (R) A contemporary action spectacle which combines modern swordplay with the mysticism and fantasy of ancient Samurai legends. 108m/C VHS, Beta. Scott Glenn, Toshiro Mifune; *D:* John Frankenheimer; *W:* John Sayles, Richard Maxwell; *M:* Jerry Goldsmith. *FOX*

Challenge of a Lifetime ✂✂½ 1985 Marshall stars as a divorcee whose dream is to compete in the Hawaiian Ironman Triathlon. Cult favorite; Woronov has a substantial supporting role. 100m/C VHS. Penny Marshall, Richard Gilliland, Jonathan Silverman, Mary Woronov, Paul Gleason, Mark Spitz, Cathy Rigby; *D:* Russ Mayberry. *TTC, MOV*

Challenge of McKenna ✂✂ 1983 Run-of-the-prairie horse opera has drifter Ireland stumble upon danger and intrigue when he enters a mysterious town. 90m/C VHS. John Ireland, Robert Woods. *PMH*

Challenge of the Masters ✂ 1989 A young Kung-Fu artist wins a new tutor in a contest. Soon he's fighting for a friend to protect his family's honor. 97m/C VHS. Liu Chia Hui, Liu Chia-Yung, Chen Kuan-Tai, Chiang Yang; *D:* Lu Chia-Liang.

Challenge the Ninja ✂ 198? One talented fighter defends a town from high-kicking hordes. Lots of kung fu action for martial arts fans. 92m/C VHS, Beta. Bruce Baron, Pierre Tremblay, Richard Berman, Eric Redner. *TWE*

Challenge To Be Free ✂✂ *Mad Trapper of the Yukon* 1976 (G) Action adventure geared toward a young audience depicting the struggles of a man being pursued by 12 men and 100 dogs across a thousand miles of frozen wilderness. The last film directed by Garnett, who has a cameo as Marshal McGee. Produced in 1972, the release wasn't until 1976. **90m/C VHS, Beta.** Mike Mazurki, Jimmy Kane; *Cameos:* Tay Garnett; *D:* Tay Garnett. *VTR*

Challenge to Lassie 🎞🎞½ 1949 (G)
When Lassie's Scottish master dies, the faithful pup remains at his grave. An unsympathetic policeman orders Lassie to leave the premises, inspiring a debate among the townsfolk as to the dog's fate. Based on a true story (although the original hero was a Skye Terrier); remade as "Greyfriar's Bobby." **76m/C VHS, Beta.** Edmund Gwenn, Donald Crisp, Geraldine Brooks, Reginald Owen, Alan Webb, Henry Stephenson, Alan Napier, Sara Allgood; *D:* Richard Thorpe; *M:* Andre Previn. *MGM, FCT*

Challenge to White Fang 🎞½ 1986
(PG) A courageous dog prevents a scheming businessman from taking over an old man's gold mine. **89m/C VHS, Beta.** Harry Carey Jr., Franco Nero; *D:* Lucio Fulci. *TWE*

The Challengers 🎞🎞½ 1993
Young Mackie wants to join local rock band The Challengers, only to discover their main rule is no girls. So Mackie disguises herself as her male cousin Mac—getting ever more confused as she tries to juggle her dual identities. Then she gets found out. **97m/C VHS.** Gema Zamprogna, Gwynyth Walsh, Eric Christmas, Eric Till; *W:* Clive Endersby. *TRI*

The Chamber 🎞🎞 1996 (R)
Dull retelling of yet another John Grisham legal thriller fails to engross. White supremacist Sam Cahill (Hackman) is on Mississippi's death row for killing two Jewish boys in a 1967 bombing. Young Chicago lawyer Adam Hall (O'Donnell), looking to find out more about his family's odious past, volunteers to work on his grandfather's case and win a stay of execution. Sam's an unrepentent racist but there's some question about whether he was the only culprit. Hackman and Dunaway (as his alcoholic daughter) devour their usual professional selves while the charming O'Donnell seems out of his depth. Co-screenwriter Robinson used the pen name Chris Reese. *CW:* Violent images and some language. **113m/C VHS, LV, Closed Caption, DVD.** Gene Hackman, Chris O'Donnell, Faye Dunaway, Lela Rochon, Robert Prosky, Raymond J. Barry, Bo Jackson, David Marshall Grant, Millie Perkins; *D:* James Foley; *W:* Phil Alden Robinson, William Goldman; *C:* Ian Baker; *M:* Carter Burwell. Nominations: Golden Raspberry Awards '96: Worst Supporting Actress (Dunaway). *USH*

Chamber of Horrors 🎞🎞½ *The Door with Seven Locks* 1940
A family is brought together at an English castle to claim a fortune left by an aristocrat. However, there's a catch—seven keys may open the vault with the fortune, or leave the key turner dead. Based on the work by Edgar Wallace. **80m/B VHS, Beta.** *GB* Leslie Banks, Lilli Palmer; *D:* Norman Lee. *VCI, MRV, SNC*

Chameleon 1981
A freeform dramatic examination of a day in the life of a Los Angeles pusher. **90m/C VHS, Beta.** Bob Glaudini; *D:* Jon Jost. *FCT*

Chameleon 🎞🎞 1995 (R)
Undercover agent, and master of disguise, Willie Serling (LaPaglia), had his wife and daughter murdered by drug smuggler Alberto Cortese (Mandola) and he naturally wants revenge. Willie poses as a bank auditor to learn if Cortese is behind a money-laundering scheme and things get increasingly complex. Talky thriller with lots of cliches. *CW:* Some violence. **108m/C VHS.** Anthony LaPaglia, Kevin Pollak, Melora Hardin, Wayne Knight, Tony Mandola, Derek McGrath, Andy Romano, Robin Thomas, Richard Brooks; *D:* Michael Pavone; *W:* Michael Pavone; *C:* Ross Berryman; *M:* John Debney. *AVE*

Chameleon Street 🎞🎞🎞 1989 (R)
Entertaining fact-based account of William Douglas Street, a Detroit man who successfully impersonated, among others, a Time magazine reporter and a surgeon until he was caught and sent to prison. He escaped and went to Yale, faked his identity as a student, and then returned to Michigan to impersonate a lawyer for the Detroit Hu-

man Rights Commission. Harris wrote and directed this insightful look into the man who fooled many people, including the mayor of Detroit, Coleman A. Young, who appears briefly as himself. *CW:* Language and sexual dialogue. **95m/C VHS, LV.** Wendell B. Harris Jr., Angela Leslie, Amina Fakir, Paula McGee, Mano Breckenridge, David Kiley, Anthony Ennis; *Cameos:* Coleman A. Young; *D:* Wendell B. Harris Jr.; *W:* Wendell B. Harris Jr.; *C:* Daniel S. Noga; *M:* Peter S. Moore. Sundance Film Festival '90: Grand Jury Prize. *FCT*

The Champ 🎞🎞🎞 1932
A washed out boxer dreams of making a comeback and receives support from no one but his devoted son. Minor classic most notorious for jerking the tears and soiling the hankies, this was the first of three Beery/Cooper screen teamings. **87m/B VHS, Beta, LV.** Wallace Beery, Jackie Cooper, Irene Rich, Roscoe Ates, Edward Brophy, Hale Hamilton, Jesse Scott, Marcia Mae Jones; *D:* King Vidor; *W:* Frances Marion. Academy Awards '32: Best Actor (Beery), Best Story; Nominations: Academy Awards '32: Best Director (Vidor), Best Picture. *MGM, FCT, BTV*

The Champ 🎞½ 1979 (PG)
An ex-fighter with a weakness for gambling and drinking is forced to return to the ring in an attempt to keep custody of his son. Excessive sentiment may cause cringing. Remake of the 1931 classic. **121m/C VHS, Beta, LV, Letterbox.** Jon Voight, Faye Dunaway, Rick Schroder, Jack Warden, Arthur Hill, Strother Martin, Joan Blondell, Elisha Cook Jr.; *D:* Franco Zeffirelli; *C:* Fred W. Koenekamp; *M:* Dave Grusin. Nominations: Academy Awards '79: Best Original Score. *MGM*

Champagne 🎞🎞 1928
A socialite's father fakes bankruptcy to teach his irresponsible daughter a lesson. Early, silent endeavor from Hitchcock is brilliantly photographed. **93m/B VHS.** *GB* Betty Balfour, Gordon Harker, Ferdinand von Alten, Clifford Heatherly, Jack Trevor; *D:* Alfred Hitchcock; *W:* Alfred Hitchcock. *GPV, MLB, VEC*

Champagne for Breakfast 🎞 1935 (R)
Sex comedy follows the fun-filled adventures of "Champagne," a free-spirited beauty living life to the fullest. **69m/B VHS.** Mary Carlisle, Hardie Albright, Joan Marsh, Lila Lee, Sidney Toler, Bradley Page, Emerson Treacy; *D:* Melville Brown. *NO*

Champagne for Caesar 🎞🎞🎞 1950
The laughs keep coming in this comedy about a self-proclaimed genius-on-every-subject who goes on a television quiz show and proceeds to win everything in sight. The program's sponsor, in desperation, hires a femme fatale to distract the contestant before the final program. Wonderful spoof of the game-show industry. **99m/B VHS, LV.** Ronald Colman, Celeste Holm, Vincent Price, Art Linkletter, Barbara Britton; *D:* Richard Whorf. *EEL, VCI*

Champion 🎞🎞🎞½ 1949
An ambitious prizefighter alienates the people around him as he desperately fights his way to the top. When he finally reaches his goal, he is forced to question the cost of his success. From a story by Ring Lardner. Certainly one of the best films ever made about boxing, with less sentiment than "Rocky" but concerned with sociological correctness. **99m/B VHS, Closed Caption.** Kirk Douglas, Arthur Kennedy, Marilyn Maxwell, Ruth Roman, Lola Albright, Paul Stewart; *D:* Mark Robson; *W:* Carl Foreman; *C:* Franz Planer; *M:* Dimitri Tiomkin. Academy Awards '49: Best Film Editing; Nominations: Academy Awards '49: Best Actor (Douglas), Best Black and White Cinematography, Best Screenplay, Best Supporting Actor (Kennedy), Best Original Dramatic/Comedy Score. *REP*

The Champion/His New Job 🎞🎞🎞
Champion Charlie 1915 Two classic silent shorts by Chaplin, with music; the first is alternately entitled "Champion Charlie." **53m/B VHS, Beta, 8mm.** Charlie Chaplin, Edna Purviance, Ben Turpin, Gloria Swanson, Mack Swain, "Broncho" Billy Anderson; *D:* Charlie Chaplin. *VYY*

Champion Operation 🎞 1987
Hong Kong heavies pose as police officers. The action follows them from the slums to the red-light district. Lots of martial arts action. **100m/C VHS.** Tong Chun Chung, Yu Ka Hei, Tang Ho Kwong. *MGI*

Champions 🎞🎞 1984
Moving but cliched story of Bob Champion, a leading jockey who overcame cancer to win England's Grand National Steeplechase. A true story, no less. **113m/C VHS, Beta, LV, Closed Caption.** GB John Hurt, Gregory Jones, Mick Dillon, Ann Bell, Jan Francis, Peter Barkworth, Edward Woodward, Ben Johnson, Kirstie Alley, Alison Steadman; *D:* John Irvin; *W:* Evan Jones; *M:* Carl Davis. *NLC*

Chan Is Missing 🎞🎞🎞 1982
Two cab drivers try to find the man who stole their life savings. Wry, low-budget comedy filmed in San Francisco's Chinatown was an art-house smash. The first full-length American film produced exclusively by an Asian-American cast and crew. **80m/B VHS.** Wood Moy, Marc Hayashi, Laureen Chew, Judy Mihei, Peter Wang, Presco Tabios, Frankie Allarcon, Virginia Cerenio, Roy Chan, George Woo, Emily Yamasaki, Ellen Yeung; *D:* Wayne Wang; *W:* Wayne Wang, Terrel Seltzer, Isaac Cronin; *C:* Michael G. Chin; *M:* Robert Kikuchi-Yngojo. National Film Registry '95. *NYF*

Chance 🎞½ 1989
With over a million dollars in diamonds missing, Haggerty and Jacobs throw out all the stops to recover them in this action thriller. **90m/C VHS.** Dan Haggerty, Lawrence-Hilton Jacobs, Addison Randall, Roger Rudd, Charles Gries, Pamela Dixon; *D:* Addison Randall, Charles Kanganis. *PMH*

Chances Are 🎞🎞🎞 1989 (PG)
After her loving husband dies in a chance accident, a pregnant woman remains unmarried, keeping her husband's best friend as her only close male companion. Years later, her now teenage daughter brings a friend home for dinner, but due to an error in heaven, the young man begins to realize that this may not be the first time he and this family have met. A wonderful love-story hampered only minimally by the unbelievable plot. **108m/C VHS, Beta, LV, 8mm, Closed Caption, DVD.** Cybill Shepherd, Robert Downey Jr., Ryan O'Neal, Mary Stuart Masterson, Josef Sommer, Christopher McDonald, Joe Grifasi, James Noble, Susan Ruttan, Fran Ryan; *D:* Emile Ardolino; *W:* Perry Howze, Randy Howze; *M:* Maurice Jarre. Nominations: Academy Awards '89: Best Song ("After All"). *COL, FCT*

Chandu on the Magic Island 🎞🎞 1934
Chandu the Magician takes his powers of the occult to the mysterious lost island of Lemuri to battle the evil cult of Ubasti. Sequel to "Chandu the Magician" and just as campy. **67m/B VHS, Beta.** Bela Lugosi, Maria Alba, Clara Kimball Young. *NOS, SNC, VYY*

Chandu the Magician 🎞🎞 1932
Bad guy searches desperately for the secret of a powerful death ray so he can (surprise!) destroy civilization. Not well received in its day, but makes for great high-camp fun now. One of Lugosi's most melodramatic performances. **70m/B VHS, Beta.** Edmund Lowe, Bela Lugosi, Irene Ware, Henry B. Walthall; *D:* William Cameron Menzies, Marcel Varnel; *C:* James Wong Howe. *MLB, RXM*

Chanel Solitaire 🎞🎞 1981 (R)
Uninspiring biography follows the fabulous (simply fabulous) career of dress designer Gabrielle "Coco" Chanel. Ah, go sew something. **124m/C VHS, Beta.** Marie-France Pisier, Rutger Hauer, Timothy Dalton, Karen Black, Brigitte Fossey; *D:* George Kaczender. *FCT*

Chang: A Drama of the Wilderness 🎞🎞🎞½ 1927
A farmer and his family has settled a small patch of ground on the edge of the jungle and must struggle for survival against numerous wild animals. The climatic elephant stampede is still thrilling. Shot on location in Siam. **67m/B VHS.** *W:* Merian C. Cooper, Ernest B. Schoedsack. *MIL*

Change of Habit 🎞🎞 1969 (G)
Three noviatiates undertake to learn about the world before becoming full-fledged nuns. While working at a ghetto clinic a young doctor forms a strong, affectionate relationship with one of them. Presley's last feature film. ♫ Change of Habit; Let Us Pray; Rubberneckin'. **93m/C VHS, Beta.** Elvis Presley, Mary Tyler Moore, Barbara McNair, Ed Asner, Ruth McDevitt, Regis Toomey; *D:* William A. Graham; *C:* Russell Metty; *M:* Billy Goldenberg. *USH, GKK*

A Change of Seasons 🐾🐾 1980 (R)
One of them so-called sophisticated comedies that look at the contemporary relationships and values of middle-class, middle-aged people who should know better. The wife of a college professor learns of her husband's affair with a seductive student and decides to have a fling with a younger man. The situation reaches absurdity when the couples decide to vacation together. 102m/C VHS, **Beta.** Shirley MacLaine, Bo Derek, Anthony Hopkins, Michael Brandon, Mary Beth Hurt; **D:** Richard Lang; **W:** Erich Segal; **M:** Henry Mancini. FOX

The Changeling 🐾🐾½ 1980 (R) A music teacher moves into an old house and discovers that a young boy's ghostly spirit is his housemate. The ghost wants revenge against the being that replaced him upon his death. Scary ghost story with some less than logical leaps of script. 114m/C VHS, Beta, LV. **CA** George C. Scott, Trish Van Devere, John Russell, Melvyn Douglas, Jean Marsh, John Colicos, Barry Morse, Roberta Maxwell, James B. Douglas; **D:** Peter Medak; **W:** William Gray, Diana Maddox; **C:** John Coquillon. Genie Award '80: Best Film. VES

Changes 🐾 1969 (PG) A young man leaves home and thumbs across the California coast in order to find himself. On the road again. 103m/C VHS, Beta. Kent Lane, Michele Carey, Jack Albertson, Marcia Strassman; **D:** Hall Bartlett.

Changing Habits 🐾½ 1996 (R) Starving artist Soosh (Kelly) moves into a nunnery, in exchange for doing chores, in order to save money. She's so broke, she's taken to stealing art supplies, but salesman Felix (Walsh) are more interested in romancing Soosh than turning her in. Dull, dull, dull, and a waste of a talented cast. 92m/C VHS, LV, Closed Caption. Moira Kelly, Christopher Lloyd, Teri Garr, Shelley Duvall, Dylan Walsh, Marissa Ribisi, Frances Bay, Bob Gunton, Anne Haney, Eileen Brennan; **D:** Lynn Roth; **W:** Scott Davis Jones; **C:** Mike Mayers; **M:** David McHugh. APX

The Channeler 🐾 1989 The traditional dopey students probe an old Colorado mine and encounter black-robed, demon whazzits. A spunky cast and nice scenery didn't stop the Hound from switching channels on this one. 90m/C VHS, Beta. Dan Haggerty, Richard Harrison, Jay Richardson, David Homb, Oliver Darrow, Robin Sims, Charles Solomon; **D:** Grant Austin Waldman. NO

Chantilly Lace 🐾🐾½ 1993 (R) Ensemble cast tries hard in this story of modern American women and friendship in the nineties. Val (Eilenberry) gathers a group of seven close friends at her new house in Sundance. Turns out trying to "have it all" is causing some emotional crises to surface, which are explored over the course of a year. Actresses improvised their dialogue from basic character information. Lots of weeping and bonding. Made for cable television.**CW:** Strong language and scene of sexuality. 102m/C VHS, Closed Caption. Jill Eikenberry, Ally Sheedy, Helen Slater, Lindsay Crouse, JoBeth Williams, Martha Plimpton, Talia Shire; **D:** Linda Yellen; **W:** Linda Yellen, Rosanne Ehrlich; **M:** Patrick Seymour. COL

Chapayev 🐾🐾🐾 1934 Striking propagandist drama dealing with the exploits of a legendary Red Army commander during the 1919 battle with the White Russians. Stunning, and carefully choreographed, battle scenes. Adapted from a biographical novel by Dmitri Furmanov. In Russian with English subtitles. 101m/B VHS, Beta. **RU** Boris Babochkin, Leonid Kmit; **D:** Sergei Vasiliev, Gregory Vasiliev. VYY, AUD, IHF

Chaplin 🐾🐾🐾 1992 (PG-13) The life and career of "The Little Tramp" is chronicled by director Attenborough and brilliantly portrayed by Downey, Jr. as Chaplin. A flashback format traces his life from its poverty-stricken Dickensian origins in the London slums through his directing and acting career, to his honorary Oscar in 1972. Slow-moving at parts, but captures Chaplin's devotion to his art and also his penchant towards jailbait. In a clever casting choice, Chaplin's own daughter from his fourth marriage to Oona O'Neill, Geraldine Chap-

lin, plays her own grandmother who goes mad.**CW:** Language and nudity. 135m/C VHS, LV, **Letterbox, Closed Caption.** GB Robert Downey Jr., Dan Aykroyd, Geraldine Chaplin, Kevin Dunn, Anthony Hopkins, Milla Jovovich, Moira Kelly, Kevin Kline, Diane Lane, Penelope Ann Miller, Paul Rhys, John Thaw, Marisa Tomei, Nancy Travis, James Woods, David Duchovny, Deborah Maria Moore, Bill Paterson, John Standing, Robert Stephens, Peter Crook; **D:** Richard Attenborough; **W:** Bryan Forbes, William Boyd, William Goldman; **C:** Sven Nykvist; **M:** John Barry. British Academy Awards '92: Best Actor (Downey); Nominations: Academy Awards '92: Best Actor (Downey), Best Art Direction/Set Decoration, Best Original Score. ART, MOV, FCT

The Chaplin Revue 1958 The "Revue," put together by Chaplin in 1958, consists of three of his best shorts: "A Dog's Life" (1918), the WWI comedy "Shoulder Arms" (1918), and "The Pilgrim," in which a convict hides out in a clerical guise (1922). Chaplin added self-composed score, narration, and some documentary on-the-set material. 121m/B VHS, Beta. Charlie Chaplin, Edna Purviance, Sydney Chaplin, Mack Swain; **D:** Charlie Chaplin. FOX

Chapter in Her Life 🐾🐾½ 1923 An early silent film by Lois Weber which examines the relationships between an orphaned child and the adults in her life. 87m/B VHS, Beta. **D:** Lois Weber. GVV

Chapter Two 🐾🐾 1979 (PG) Loosely based on Neil Simon's marriage to Mason and his Broadway hit of the same name. A writer, griefstricken over the death of his first wife, meets the woman who will become his second. Witty dialogue in first half deteriorates when guilt strikes. 124m/C VHS, Beta, LV, Closed Caption. James Caan, Marsha Mason, Valerie Harper, Joseph Bologna; **D:** Robert Moore; **W:** Neil Simon. Nominations: Academy Awards '79: Best Actress (Mason). COL

Character 🐾🐾 Karakter 1997 (R) Based on the 1938 novel by F. Bordewijk, which follows the troubled relationship of young lawyer Jacob Willem Katadreuffe (van Huet) and his overbearing father in 1920's Rotterdam. Dreverhaven (Declier) is a powerful bailiff who has an illegitimate son with his servant, Joba (Schuurman), who turns down his marriage proposal. Still, Dreverhaven is determined to control his son's life, even if it means ruining him first. No wonder the old man gets murdered. Dark and unsentimental. Dutch with subtitles.**CW:** Violence. 120m/C VHS, LV. **NL** Fredja Van Huet, Jan Decleir, Betty Schuurman, Victor Low, Tamar van den Dop, Hans Kestig; **D:** Mike van Diem; **W:** Mike van Diem; **C:** Rogier Stoffers; **M:** Paleis Van Boem. Academy Awards '97: Best Foreign Language Film. NYR

Charade 🐾🐾 1953 Mason and wife Pamela star in this trilogy of love and violence. "Portrait of a Murderer" has a young artist sketching the picture of the man who—unknown to her—has just murdered her girlfriend. "Duel at Dawn" concerns an 1880s Austrian officer who steals a woman from another officer and is then challenged to a duel. "The Midas Touch" revolves around a successful but dissatisfied man who abandons his riches to find the meaning of life. Mason himself had said he hoped "this curiosity" would disappear. 83m/B VHS. James Mason, Pamela Mason, Scott Forbes, Paul Cavanagh, Bruce Lester, Sean McClory, Vince Barnett; **D:** Roy Kellino. NOS

Charade 🐾🐾🐾½ 1963 After her husband is murdered, a young woman finds herself on the run from crooks and double agents who want the $250,000 her husband stole during WWII. Hepburn and Grant are charming and sophisticated as usual in this stylish intrigue filmed in Paris. Based on the story "The Unsuspecting Wife" by Marc Behm and Peter Stone. 113m/C VHS, Beta. Cary Grant, Audrey Hepburn, Walter Matthau, James Coburn, George Kennedy; **D:** Stanley Donen; **W:** Peter Stone; **C:** Charles B(ryant) Lang; **M:** Henry Mancini. British Academy Awards '64: Best Actress (Hepburn); Nominations: Academy Awards '63: Best Song ("Charade"). CNG, MRV, USH

The Charge of the Light Brigade 🐾🐾🐾 1936 (PG-13) A British army officer stationed in India deliberately starts the Balaclava charge to even an old score with Surat Khan, who's on the other side. Still an exciting film, though it's hardly historically accurate. De Havilland is along to provide the requisite romance with Flynn. Also available colorized.**CW:** Epic battle scenes. 115m/B VHS, Beta, LV, Closed Caption. Olivia de Havilland, Errol Flynn, David Niven, Nigel Bruce, Patric Knowles, Donald Crisp, Sir C. Aubrey Smith, J. Carrol Naish, Henry Stephenson, E.E. Clive, Scotty Beckett; **D:** Michael Curtiz; **M:** Max Steiner. Nominations: Academy Awards '36: Best Sound, Best Score. MGM, FCT, FOX

The Charge of the Light Brigade 🐾🐾½ 1968 (PG-13) Political indictment of imperialistic England in this revisionist retelling of the notorious British defeat by the Russians at Balaclava. Battle scenes are secondary to this look at the stupidity of war. Fine cast; notable animation sequences by Richard Williams. 130m/C VHS. GB Trevor Howard, John Gielgud, David Hemmings, Vanessa Redgrave, Harry Andrews, Jill Bennett, Peter Bowles, Mark Burns, Alan Dobie, T.P. McKenna, Corin Redgrave, Norman Rossington, Rachel Kempson, Donald Wolfit; **D:** Tony Richardson; **W:** Charles Wood; **C:** David Watkin; **M:** John Addison. MGM

Charge of the Model T's 🐾½ 1976 (G) Comedy about a WWI German spy who tries to infiltrate the U.S. army. 90m/C VHS, Beta. Louis Nye, John David Carson, Herb Edelman, Carol Bagdasarian, Arte Johnson; **D:** Jim McCullough.

Chariots of Fire 🐾🐾🐾½ 1981 (PG) A lush telling of the parallel stories of Harold Abraham and Eric Liddell, English runners who competed in the 1924 Paris Olympics. One was compelled by a hatred of anti-Semitism, the other by the love of God. Outstanding performances by the entire cast. 123m/C VHS, Beta, LV, DVD. GB Ben Cross, Ian Charleson, Nigel Havers, Ian Holm, Alice Krige, Brad Davis, Dennis Christopher, Patrick Magee, Cheryl Campbell, John Gielgud, Lindsay Anderson, Nigel Davenport; **D:** Hugh Hudson; **W:** Colin Welland; **C:** David Watkin; **M:** Vangelis. Academy Awards '81: Best Costume Design, Best Original Screenplay, Best Picture, Best Original Score; British Academy Awards '81: Best Film, Best Supporting Actor (Holm); Golden Globe Awards '82: Best Foreign Film; New York Film Critics Awards '81: Best Cinematography; Nominations: Academy Awards '81: Best Director (Hudson), Best Film Editing, Best Supporting Actor (Holm). WAR, FCT, BTV

Charlemagne 🐾🐾½ 1995 British miniseries follows the life of the royal conqueror who civilized western Europe and ruled as emperor from 800-814. On five cassettes. 250m/C VHS. GB Christian Brendel, Anna Dupery; **D:** Clive Donner. TVC

Charles & Diana: A Palace Divided 🐾🐾½ 1993 Trashy scandalous tale of the disintegration of the fairytale romance and marriage of Prince Charles and Princess Diana. Oxenberg stars as Princess Di, a role she played a decade ago in "The Royal Romance of Charles and Diana," and Rees does a fine job playing the conservative Prince Charles. Although the film covers all of the couple's highly publicized troubles, it's such a quick superficial treatment that it's often hard to follow. Nonetheless, it's a flashingly inviting look into the privileged House of Windsor. 92m/C VHS, Closed Caption. Roger Rees, Catherine Oxenberg, Benedict Taylor, Tracy Brabin, Amanda Walker, David Quilter, Jane How; **D:** John Power. TTC

Charles et Lucie 🐾🐾🐾 1979 A has-been couple are ripped off, pursued, persecuted, and saddled with very bad luck in the South of France. Essentially a character study; semi-acclaimed. In French with subtitles. 96m/C VHS, Beta. FR Daniel Ceccaldi, Ginette Garcin, Jean-Marie Proslier, Samson Fainsilber; **D:** Nelly Kaplan. FCT

Charleston 🐾🐾🐾 1926 Renoir's third film, a simple erotic dance fantasy that caused much controversy in its day. Silent, with jazz score and historical introduction. 30m/B VHS, Beta. Catherine Hessling; **D:** Jean Renoir. FCT

Charley and the Angel ♪♪ℐ½ 1973 (G)
Touching story of a man who changes his cold ways with his family when informed by an angel that he hasn't much time to live. Amusing Disney movie set in the Great Depression. 93m/C VHS. Fred MacMurray, Cloris Leachman, Harry (Henry) Morgan, Kurt Russell, Vincent Van Patten, Kathleen Cody; D: Vincent McEveety. DIS, OM

Charley Chase Festival, Vol. 1 ℐℐ 1923 Six classic Charley Chase comedies: "At First Sight" (1923), "Fighting Fluid" (1924), "Young Oldfield" (1924), "Ten Minute Egg" (1924), "Stolen Goods" (1924), and "Long Fliv the King" (1926). 70m/B VHS, Beta. Charley Chase. VDM

Charley Varrick ℐℐℐ 1973 (PG) Matthau, a small-town hood, robs a bank only to find out that one of its depositors is the Mob. Baker's the vicious hit-man assigned the job of getting the loot back. A well-paced, on-the-mark thriller. 111m/C VHS, Beta. Walter Matthau, Joe Don Baker, Felicia Farr, John Vernon, Sheree North, Norman Fell, Andrew (Andy) Robinson, Jacqueline Scott; D: Donald Siegel; M: Lalo Schifrin. USH

Charley's Aunt ℐℐ½ 1925 Amusing Victorian farce in which two young male students convince an older fellow student to dress up as their female chaperon so they can pitch woo to two local lovelies. Fun performances and well-paced direction by Sidney. Based on the Brandon Thomas farce, the movie was remade in 1930, starring Charles Ruggles, and again in 1941, with Jack Benny. 75m/B VHS, Beta. Sydney Chaplin, Ethel Shannon, Lucien Littlefield, Alec B. Francis, Mary Akin, Priscilla Bonner, Jimmy Harrison, David James, Eulalie Jensen, James E. Page, Phillips Smalley; D: Scott Sidney; W: F. McGrew Willis, Joe Farnham; C: Gus Peterson, Paul Garnett. GPV, FCT

Charlie and the Great Balloon Chase ℐℐ 1982 When a grandfather takes his grandson on a cross-country balloon trip, they are hotly pursued by the boy's mother, her stuffy fiance (who wants the boy in military school), the FBI, a reporter, and the Mafia. Made for television. 98m/C VHS, Beta. Jack Albertson, Adrienne Barbeau, Slim Pickens, Moosie Drier; D: Larry Elikann. TLF

Charlie Boy ℐ½ 1981 The new owner of an ancient African idol enters the world of the supernatural when he casts a death spell on six people. 60m/C VHS, Beta. Leigh Lawson, Angela Bruce, Marius Goring; D: Robert M. Young. ART

Charlie Bravo ℐ 198? (R) A commando group is commanded to rescue a captured nurse in Vietnam. Dubbed. 94m/C VHS, Beta. FR Bruno Pradal, Karen Verlier, Jean-Francois Poron; D: Rene Demoulin. GEM

A Charlie Brown Celebration 1984 The Peanuts gang in an extended adventure in which Lucy courts Schroeder, Patty goes to obedience school, and Charlie Brown finally kicks the football. 49m/C VHS, Beta. D: Bill Melendez. BAR

A Charlie Brown Christmas 1965 Disillusioned by the commercialization of the holiday season, Charlie Brown sets out to find the true meaning of Christmas. 30m/C VHS, Beta, Closed Caption. D: Bill Melendez. FCT

A Charlie Brown Thanksgiving 1981 The Peanuts gang learns that Thanksgiving is more than just turkey and stuffing in this family favorite. 25m/C VHS, Beta. D: Bill Melendez, Phil Roman. BAR, KAR

Charlie Brown's All-Stars 1966 Charlie Brown and the whole Peanuts gang is here to delight young and old alike. 26m/C VHS, Closed Caption. D: Bill Melendez.

Charlie Chan and the Curse of the Dragon Queen ℐ½ 1981 (PG) The famed Oriental sleuth confronts his old enemy the Dragon Queen, and reveals the true identity of a killer. 97m/C VHS, Beta. Peter Ustinov, Lee Grant, Angie Dickinson, Richard Hatch, Brian Keith, Roddy McDowall, Michelle

Pfeiffer, Rachel Roberts; D: Clive Donner; W: David Axelrod, Stanley Burns.

Charlie Chan at the Opera ℐℐℐ 1936 The great detective investigates an amnesiac opera star (Karloff) who may have committed murder. Considered one of the best of the series. Interesting even to those not familiar with Charlie Chan. 66m/B VHS, LV, Closed Caption. Warner Oland, Boris Karloff, Keye Luke, Charlotte Henry, Thomas Beck, Nedda Harrigan, William Demarest; D: H. Bruce Humberstone. FOX

Charlie Chan at the Wax Museum ℐℐ½ 1940 Charlie and number one son must find a criminal hiding out in a wax museum. Chills abound when the fugitive heads for the chamber of horrors. 63m/B VHS, LV, Closed Caption. Sidney Toler, Victor Sen Yung, C. Henry Gordon, Marc Lawrence, Joan Valerie, Marguerite Chapman, Ted Osborn, Michael Visaroff; D: Lynn Shores. FOX

Charlie Chan in Paris ℐℐ½ 1935 Chan scours the city of lights to track down a trio of counterfeiters. Top-notch plot and plenty of suspense will please all. 72m/B VHS, LV, Closed Caption. Warner Oland, Mary Brian, Thomas Beck, Erik Rhodes, John Miljan, Minor Watson, John Qualen, Keye Luke, Henry Kolker; D: Lewis Seiler. FOX

Charlie Chan in Rio ℐℐ 1941 Local police call on Chan to help solve a double murder. One of the series' weaker entries but with fine setting and music. 60m/B VHS, LV, Closed Caption. Sidney Toler, Mary Beth Hughes, Cobina Wright Jr., Ted North, Victor Jory, Harold Huber, Victor Sen Yung; D: Harry Lachman. FOX

Charlie Chan in the Secret Service ℐ½ 1944 Toler's Chan is now a government agent who is assigned to find the killer of an inventor. Moreland joins up as Chan's taxi-driving, constantly terrified sidekick. The series moved from 20th-century Fox to low-budget Monogram Pictures with this entry, with an ensuing drop in production quality. 64m/B VHS. Sidney Toler, Mantan Moreland, Gwen Kenyon, Arthur Loft, Marianne Quon, Lela Tyler, Benson Fong; D: Phil Rosen. MGM

Charlie Chan's Secret ℐℐ 1935 Chan must solve the murder of the heir to a huge fortune. A good, logical script with plenty of suspects to keep you guessing. 72m/B VHS, Closed Caption. Warner Oland, Rosina Lawrence, Charles Quigley, Henrietta Crosman, Edward Trevor, Astrid Allwyn; D: Gordon Wiles. FOX

Charlie Chaplin: Night at the Show ℐℐℐ 1915 Chaplin plays two different mugs, both out for a night on the town. Mr. Pest, a sharp-dressed upper-cruster, clings to his disgusting habits, and Mr. Rowdy is his working-class doppleganger. Both obnoxious Chaplins-in-disguise collaborate to wreak havoc on a local theatre. Contains original organ score. ?m/B VHS, Beta. Charlie Chaplin, Edna Purviance; D: Charlie Chaplin; W: Charlie Chaplin. VYY

Charlie Chaplin: The Early Years, Vol. 1 1917 Package includes Chaplin's "The Immigrant," "The Count," and "Easy Street." Silent. 62m/B VHS, LV. Charlie Chaplin, Edna Purviance, John Rand, Eric Campbell. REP, FCT, KIV

Charlie Chaplin: The Early Years, Vol. 2 1917 Package includes Chaplin's "The Pawnshop" (1916), "The Adventurer" (1917), and "One A.M." (1916). 61m/B VHS, LV. Charlie Chaplin, Edna Purviance, Eric Campbell, Albert Austin, Henry Bergman, John Rand. REP, FCT, KIV

Charlie Chaplin: The Early Years, Vol. 3 1916 Package includes Chaplin's "The Cure" (1916), "The Floorwalker" (1916), and "The Vagabond." 64m/B VHS, LV. Charlie Chaplin, Edna Purviance, Eric Campbell, Albert Austin. REP, FCT, KIV

Charlie Chaplin: The Early Years, Vol. 4 1916 Package includes Chaplin's "Behind the Screen," "The Fireman" (1916), and "The Rink" (1916). 63m/B VHS, Beta, LV. Charlie

Chaplin, Edna Purviance, Eric Campbell, Lloyd Bacon, Albert Austin. REP, FCT, KIV

Charlie Chaplin...Our Hero! 1915 Two shorts from 1915 written and directed by Chaplin, "Night at the Show" and "In the Park," as well as a 1914 film, "Hot Finish," in which Charlie plays the villain. 58m/B VHS, Beta, 8mm. Charlie Chaplin, Edna Purviance, Lloyd Bacon, Mabel Normand, Chester Conklin, Mack Sennett; D: Charlie Chaplin. VYY

Charlie Chaplin's Keystone Comedies #1 1914 Six one-reelers which Chaplin filmed in 1914, his first movie-making year: "Making a Living," Chaplin's first, in which he plays a villain; "Kid Auto Races," in which Charlie now sports baggy pants, bowler hat and cane; "A Busy Day," featuring Charlie in drag; "Mabel's Married Life"; "Laughing Gas"; and "The New Janitor." Silent with musical score. 59m/B VHS, Beta. Charlie Chaplin, Mabel Normand, Mack Swain. VYY, KIV

Charlie Chaplin's Keystone Comedies #2 1914 Three hilarious early Chaplin shorts, "His Trysting Place," "Getting Acquainted" and "The Fatal Mallet." Silent with musical score. 60m/B VHS, Beta. Charlie Chaplin, Mabel Normand, Mack Swain, Mack Sennett. VYY, KIV

Charlie Chaplin's Keystone Comedies #3 1914 Three more vintage early Chaplin shorts: "Caught in a Cabaret," "The Masquerader," and "Between Showers." Silent, includes a musical score. 59m/B VHS, Beta. Charlie Chaplin, Mack Swain, Mabel Normand, Chester Conklin; D: Charlie Chaplin. VYY, KIV

Charlie Chaplin's Keystone Comedies #4 1914 Four classic silent shorts featuring Chaplin in 1914, Including "Caught in the Rain (in the Park)," "His Million Dollar Job," "Mabel's Busy Day," and "The Face on the Bar Room Floor." With musical score. 54m/B VHS, Beta, 8mm. Charlie Chaplin, Mack Swain, Alice Davenport, Fatty Arbuckle, Mabel Normand, Chester Conklin, Slim Summerville, Cecile Arnold, Alice Howell. VYY, KIV

Charlie Chaplin's Keystone Comedies #5 1914 Four classic silent features: "Mabel's Strange Predicament," "The Rounders," "Tango Tangles," and "The Star Border." 57m/B VHS. Charlie Chaplin; D: Charlie Chaplin. VYY, KIV

Charlie Chase and Ben Turpin 1921 Three silent comedy classics, "All Wet," "Publicity Pays," and "A Clever Dummy." 67m/B VHS, Beta. Ben Turpin, Charley Chase, Wallace Beery, Juanita Hansen. VYY

Charlie Grant's War ℐℐ 1980 The true story of a Canadian businessman who hears of Nazi brutality and determines to save European Jews from persecution during the Holocaust. Not among the more distinguished works of its kind. 130m/C VHS, Beta. GB Jan Rubes, R.H. Thomson. MOV

Charlie, the Lonesome Cougar ℐℐ 1967 (G) Life for a rugged logger will never be the same after he adopts an orphaned cougar. From the Disney factory. 75m/C VHS, Beta. Linda Wallace, Jim Wilson, Ron Brown, Brian Russell, Clifford Peterson; D: Winston Hibler. DIS

Charlie's Ghost: The Secret of Coronado ℐℐ½ Charlie's Ghost Story 1994 (PG) Kid who has trouble fitting in is befriended by the ghost of a Spanish conquistador. 92m/C VHS. Richard "Cheech" Marin, Trenton Knight, Anthony Edwards, Linda Fiorentino, Daphne Zuniga.

Charlotte Forten's Mission: Experiment in Freedom ℐℐℐ Half Slave, Half Free 2 1985 Fact-based story, set during the Civil War. A wealthy, educated black woman, determined to prove to President Lincoln that blacks are equal to whites, journeys to a remote island off the coast of Georgia. There she teaches freed slaves to read and write. Part of the "American Playhouse" series on PBS. Preceded by "Solomon Northrup's Odyssey." 120m/C VHS. Melba

Moore, Mary Alice, Ned Beatty, Carla Borelli, Micki Grant, Moses Gunn, Anna Maria Horsford, Bruce McGill, Glynn Turman, Roderick Wimberly; **D:** Barry Crane; **W:** Samm-Art Williams. *FCT, PTB, XVC*

Charlotte's Web 🐾🐾½ 1979 (G) E.B. White's classic story of a friendship between a spider and a pig is handled only adequately by Hanna-Barbera studios. Some okay songs. **94m/C VHS, Beta, LV. D:** Charles A. Nichols; **V:** Debbie Reynolds, Agnes Moorehead, Paul Lynde, Henry Gibson. *PAR, FCT, HMV*

Charly 🐾🐾🐾 1968 A retarded man becomes intelligent after brain surgery, then romances a kindly caseworker before slipping back into retardation. Moving account is well served by leads Robertson and Bloom. Adapted from the Daniel Keyes novel "Flowers for Algernon." **103m/C VHS, Beta, LV.** Cliff Robertson, Claire Bloom, Lilia Skala, Leon Janney, Dick Van Patten, William Dwyer; **D:** Ralph Nelson; **W:** Stirling Silliphant. Academy Awards '68: Best Actor (Robertson); Golden Globe Awards '69: Best Actor (Robertson); National Board of Review Awards '68: Best Actor (Robertson). *FOX, BTV*

Charm of La Boheme 🐾🐾½ 1936 A vintage German musical based on the Puccini opera. With English subtitles. **90m/B VHS, Beta.** *GE* Jan Kiepura, Martha Eggerth, Paul Kemp; **D:** Geza von Bolvary. *NOS, DVT, GLV*

The Charmer 🐾🐾½ 1989 Havers stars as Ralph Gorse, a charming but amoral con man who uses any means to get what he wants. This includes using the affection (and money) of an older woman, blackmail, and even murder. Set in the late '30s. Made for British television miniseries on six cassettes. **312m/C VHS.** *GB* Nigel Havers, Rosemary Leach, Bernard Hepton, Fiona Fullerton, Abigail McKern, George Baker, Judy Parfitt; **D:** Alan Gibson; **W:** Allan Prior. *FCT, VCO, SIG*

Charro! 🐾 1969 (G) Presley in a straight role as a reformed bandit hounded by former gang members. Western fails on nearly all accounts, with Presley hopelessly acting outside the bounds of his talent. Furthermore, he sings only one song. **98m/C VHS.** Elvis Presley, Ina Balin, Victor French, Lynn Kellogg, Barbara Werle, Paul Brinegar, James B. Sikking; **D:** Charles Marquis Warren; **W:** Charles Marquis Warren; **M:** Hugo Montenegro. *WAR*

Charulata 🐾🐾 *The Lonely Wife* 1964 Charulata is a loyal and dutiful wife taken for granted by her husband. But when his young cousin Amal comes to live with them, Charulata glimpses what true love could be. Adapted from the novella by Rabindranath Tagore. Bengali with subtitles. **117m/B VHS.** *IN* Majhabi Mukherjee, Soumitra Chatterjee; **D:** Satyajit Ray. *COL*

The Chase 🐾🐾½ 1946 Not realizing that his boss-to-be is a mobster, Cummings takes a job as a chauffeur. Naturally, he falls in love with the gangster's wife (Morgan), and the two plan to elope. Somewhat miffed, the cuckolded mafioso and his bodyguard (Lorre) pursue the elusive couple as they head for Havana. The performances are up to snuff, but the story's as unimaginative as the title, with intermittent bouts of suspense. **86m/B VHS, Beta, LV.** Robert Cummings, Michele Morgan, Peter Lorre, Steve Cochran, Lloyd Corrigan, Jack Holt, Don Wilson; **D:** Arthur Ripley; **W:** Philip Yordan. *NOS, MRV, SNC*

The Chase 🐾🐾½ 1966 Southern community is undone when rumors circulate of a former member's prison escape and return home. Excellent cast only partially shines. Brando is outstanding as the beleaguered, honorable sheriff, and Duvall makes a splash in the more showy role of a cuckold who fears the escapee is returning home to avenge a childhood incident. Reliable Dickinson also makes the most of her role as Brando's loving wife. Fonda, however, was not yet capable of fashioning complex characterizations, and Redford is under-utilized as the escapee. Adapted from the play by Horton Foote. Notorious conflicts among producer, director, and writer kept it from being a winner. **135m/C VHS, Beta,**

LV, Letterbox. Marlon Brando, Robert Redford, Angie Dickinson, E.G. Marshall, Jane Fonda, James Fox, Janice Rule, Robert Duvall, Miriam Hopkins, Martha Hyer; **D:** Arthur Penn; **W:** Lillian Hellman, Horton Foote; **M:** John Barry. *COL*

Chase 🐾½ 1985 A big-city lawyer returns to her small hometown to defend a killer and ends up at odds with the town, including an ex-lover. Routine made for television drama. **104m/C VHS, Beta.** Jennifer O'Neill, Robert Woods, Richard Farnsworth, Michael Parks; **D:** Rod Holcomb; **M:** Charles Bernstein. *FOX*

The Chase 🐾🐾 1991 (PG-13) Routine made for television actioner. An ex-con killer leads a ruthless cop and a TV news team on a wild chase. Loosely based on a true story. **93m/C VHS, LV, Closed Caption.** Casey Siemaszko, Ben Johnson, Gerry Bamman, Robert Beltran, Barry Corbin, Ricki Lake, Megan Follows. *THV*

The Chase 🐾🐾½ 1993 (PG-13) Heiress Natalie Voss (Swanson) is in the wrong place at the wrong time when she's carjacked by escaped con Jack Hammond (Sheen) who uses a Butterfinger for his weapon. Frantic chases ensue as it turns out that Daddy Voss is a media hungry millionaire and he's followed by not only the cops but the media as well. One-dimensional characters aren't helped by a one-dimensional script, but slick film-making and a little charm helps. Skewers the media hype that surrounds crime, taking on news programs that offer immediate coverage and reality based shows with glee.**CW:** Some language, violence, and scene of sensuality. **87m/C VHS, LV, Closed Caption.** Joao Fernandes, Kristy Swanson, Charlie Sheen, Josh Mostel, Ray Wise, Henry Rollins, Flea; **D:** Adam Rifkin; **W:** Adam Rifkin; **M:** Richard Gibbs. *FXV*

Chasers 🐾🐾 1994 (R) Gruff Navy petty officer Rock Reilly (Berenger) and his conniving partner Eddie Devane (McNamara) are stuck escorting maximum security prisoner Toni Johnson (Eleniak) to a Charleston naval base. Imagine their surprise when Toni turns out to be a beautiful blonde whose one purpose is to escape her jail-sentence for going AWOL. Considering how dumb her jailers are this shouldn't be too difficult. Lots of sneering, leering, and macho posturing.**CW:** Strong language and one scene of sexuality. **100m/C VHS, LV, Letterbox, Closed Caption.** Tom Berenger, William McNamara, Erika Eleniak; **Cameos:** Gary Busey, Crispin Glover, Dean Stockwell, Seymour Cassel, Frederic Forrest, Marilu Henner, Dennis Hopper; **D:** Dennis Hopper; **W:** Joe Batteer, John Rice, Dan Gilroy; **M:** Dwight Yoakam, Pete Anderson. *WAR*

Chasing Amy 🐾🐾½ 1997 (R) Holden (Affleck) and best friend Banky (Lee), New Jersey comic book artists, attend a convention in New York where Holden is immediately attracted to fellow artist Alyssa (Adams). His ego is quickly deflated when Alyssa lets him know she's a lesbian. They try for friendship, head into a rocky romance, and then Holden discovers Alyssa's had a wild (and heterosexual) past, which pushes all his emotional buttons. Writer/director Smith supplies his trademark sharp dialogue, and the leads all contribute fine performances. Jay (Mewes) and Silent Bob (Smith), from Smith's earlier pics, make another appearance and supply the story that gives the film its title.**CW:** Strong graphic sex-related dialogue, language, sexuality and drug content. **113m/C VHS, LV, Closed Caption.** Ben Affleck, Joey Lauren Adams, Jason Lee, Dwight Ewell, Jason Mewes, Kevin Smith, Matt Damon; **D:** Kevin Smith; **W:** Kevin Smith; **C:** David Klein; **M:** David Pirner. Independent Spirit Awards '97: Best Screenplay, Best Supporting Actor (Lee); Nominations: Golden Globe Awards '98: Best Actress—Musical/Comedy (Adams); Independent Spirit Awards '98: Best Film; MTV Movie Awards '98: Breakthrough Performance (Adams), Best Kiss (Joey Lauren Adams/Carmen Llywelyn). *TOU*

Chasing Butterflies 🐾🐾 *La Chasse aux Papillons* 1994 Society's decline is represented by a once-grand, now-decaying chateau, located in a small French village, and its equally decaying in-

habitants. Marie-Agnes, confined to a wheelchair, is attended to by her cousin Solange and sullen maid Valerie. When Marie-Agnes suddenly dies, the greedy relatives descend, as well as untrustworthy antiques dealers, and Japanese businessmen interested in acquiring foreign real estate. The film is also an acquired taste. French with subtitles. **115m/C VHS.** *FR* Thamar Tarassashvili, Narda Blanchet, Pierrette Pompom Bailhache, Alexandre Tcherkassoff; **D:** Otar Iosseliani; **W:** Otar Iosseliani. *NYF, FCT*

Chasing Dreams 🐾½ 1981 (PG) Sickly melodrama about a farmboy who finds fulfillment as a baseball player. Lame film promoted as Costner baseball vehicle, but the star of "Bull Durham" and "Field of Dreams" appears only briefly in a secondary role. **96m/C VHS, Beta.** David G. Brown, John Fife, Jim Shane, Lisa Kingston, Matt Clark, Kevin Costner; **D:** Sean Roche, Therese Conte.

Chasing the Deer 🐾🐾 1994 In 1745, Scotland's Bonnie Prince Charlie (Carrara) has returned from France intent on resurrecting the Jacobite cause and regaining the English throne. Reluctant Alistair Campbell (Zajac) joins the army only to protect his son Euan (Rae), who's supposedly being held prisoner for shooting a Highlander. Euan's actually fallen into the hands of a sympathetic Englishman, Major Elliot (Blessed), advisor to the government's troops. The Jacobites begin their march south until that fateful day on Culloden Moor, which will determine all their futures. **92m/C VHS.** *GB* Brian Blessed, Matthew Zajac, Iain Cuthbertson, Lewis Rae, Dominique Carrara, Fish; **D:** Graham Holloway; **W:** Jerome Vincent, Bob Carruthers, Steve Gillham; **C:** Alan M. Trow; **M:** John Wetton. *VIF*

Chasing Those Depression Blues 1935 Four '30s comedy shorts: "Money on Your Life," "Dental Follies," "Any Day in Hollywood" and "Art in the Raw." **58m/B VHS, Beta.** Danny Kaye, Pinky Lee, Edgar Kennedy, Ben Turpin. *VYY*

Chato's Land 🐾🐾½ 1971 (PG) An Indian is tracked by a posse eager to resolve a lawman's death. Conventional violent Bronson vehicle is bolstered by presence of masterful Palance. **100m/C VHS, Beta, Closed Caption.** Charles Bronson, Jack Palance, Richard Basehart, James Whitmore, Simon Oakland, Richard Jordan, Ralph Waite, Victor French, Lee Patterson; **D:** Michael Winner. *MGM, VTR*

Chattahoochee 🐾🐾½ 1989 A man suffering from post-combat syndrome lands in a horrifying institution. Strong cast, with Oldman fine in the lead, and Hopper memorable in extended cameo. Fact-based film is, unfortunately, rather conventionally rendered. **97m/C VHS.** Gary Oldman, Dennis Hopper, Frances McDormand, Pamela Reed, Ned Beatty, M. Emmet Walsh, William De Acutis, Lee Wilkof, Matt Craven, Gary Klar; **D:** Mick Jackson; **W:** James Cresson. *HBO, IME, FCT*

Chattanooga Choo Choo 🐾½ 1984 (PG) A football team owner must restore the Chattanooga Choo Choo and make a 24-hour run from Chattanooga to New York in order to collect one-million dollars left to him in a will. The train never leaves the station. **102m/C VHS, Beta.** Barbara Eden, George Kennedy, Melissa Sue Anderson, Joe Namath, Bridget Hanley, Christopher McDonald, Clu Gulager, Tony Azito; **D:** Bruce Bilson. *HBO*

Chatterbox 🐾🐾 1976 A starlet's life and career are severely altered when her sex organs begin speaking. So why didn't they warn her about movies like this? Plenty of B-queen Rialson on view. Good double bill with "Me and Him." **73m/C VHS, Beta.** Candice Rialson, Larry Gelman, Jean Kean, Perry Bullington; **D:** Tom De Simone. *ART, VES*

The Cheap Detective 🐾🐾🐾 1978 (PG) Neil Simon's parody of the "Maltese Falcon" gloriously exploits the resourceful Falk in a Bogart-like role. Vast supporting cast—notable Brennan, De-Luise, and Kahn—equally game for fun in this consistently amusing venture. **92m/C VHS.** Peter Falk, Ann-Margret, Eileen Brennan, Sid Caesar, Stockard Channing, James Coco, Dom DeLuise, Louise Fletcher, John Houseman, Madeline Kahn, Fernando Lamas, Marsha

Mason, Phil Silvers, Vic Tayback, Abe Vigoda, Paul Williams, Nicol Williamson; **D:** Robert Moore; **W:** Neil Simon; **C:** John A. Alonzo. COL

Cheap Shots 🐾½ **1991 (PG-13)** Cheap best describes this. Two guys running a sleazy New York State resort motel plot to videotape patrons having sex, but capture an apparent mob murder instead. More of a character study than sexploitation, but who needs these characters? Not a stellar writing/directing debut for Ureles and Stoeffhaas. **90m/C VHS.** Louis Zorich, David Patrick Kelly, Mary Louise Wilson, Michael Twaine, Patience Moore; **D:** Jeff Ureles; **W:** Jeff Ureles, Jerry Stoeffhaas; **M:** Jeff Beal.

Cheaper by the Dozen 🐾🐾🐾 **1950** Turn-of-the-century family comedy based on the book by Frank B. Gilbreth, Jr., and Ernestine Gilbreth Carey, which chronicled life in the expansive Gilbreth household—12 children, efficiency expert father Frank (Webb), and psychologist mother Lillian (Loy). Stern dad likes to test his theories on the family (and have everything his own way) while nuturing mom easily manages him as well as their large household. There are various family crises (times 12) but it's all very heartwarming. Followed by "Belles on Their Toes." **85m/C VHS.** Clifton Webb, Myrna Loy, Jeanne Crain, Edgar Buchanan, Mildred Natwick, Sara Allgood, Betty Lynn, Barbara Bates, Norman Ollestad; **D:** Walter Lang; **W:** Lamar Trotti; **C:** Leon Shamroy; **M:** Cyril Mockridge. FXV

Cheaper to Keep Her woof! **1980 (R)** Alleged comedy about a private detective hired to track likely alimony dodgers. Loathsome, repellent fare, with Davis hopeless in the lead. **92m/C VHS, Beta.** Mac Davis, Tovah Feldshuh, Jack Gilford, Rose Marie; **D:** Ken Annakin; **W:** Herschel Weingrod, Timothy Harris.

The Cheat 🐾🐾🐾 **1915** Ward plays a frivolous socialite heavily indebted to Hayakawa as the Japanese money lender. Hayakawa makes Ward pay with her honor and her flesh by branding her. A dark and captivating drama. Silent with piano score. **55m/B VHS, Beta.** Fannie Ward, Sessue Hayakawa; **D:** Cecil B. DeMille. National Film Registry '93. GPV, KIV

The Cheaters 🐾 **1976 (R)** A young gambler runs away with his boss's son's girlfriend, and is pursued therein. **91m/C VHS, Beta.** IT Dayle Haddon, Luc Merenda, Lino Troisi, Enrico Maria Salerno; **D:** Sergio Martino.

Cheaters 🐾½ **1984** Two middle class couples are having affairs with each other's spouses. Complications arise when their respective children decide to marry each other. **103m/C VHS, Beta.** Peggy Cass, Jack Kruschen. NO

Cheatin' Hearts 🐾🐾½ **1993 (R)** Kirkland is a woman beset by woe: she's about to lose her house, her philandering husband (Brolin) wanders back to town with his latest bimbo in tow, and her daughter's getting married. This should be a good thing, except hubby makes a fool of himself at the wedding and nearly ruins everything. Well, at least local rancher Kristofferson is around to lift a woman's spirits. And yes, there's a (predictably) happy ending. **88m/C VHS, LV, Closed Caption.** Sally Kirkland, James Brolin, Kris Kristofferson, Pamela Gidley, Laura Johnson; **D:** Rod McCall. THV

Check & Double Check 🐾 **1930** Radio's original Amos 'n' Andy (a couple of blackfaced white guys) help solve a lover's triangle in this film version of the popular radio series. Interesting only as a novelty. Duke Ellington's band plays "Old Man Blues" and "Three Little Words." **85m/B VHS, Beta, LV.** Freeman Gosden, Charles Correll, Duke Ellington; **D:** Melville Brown; **M:** Max Steiner. NOS, MRV, VYY

Check Is in the Mail 🐾½ **1985 (R)** Lame comedy about a financier determined to make his home entirely independent from the rat-race of capitalist society. Dependables Dennehy and Archer are wasted. **83m/C VHS, Beta.** Brian Dennehy, Anne Archer, Dick Shawn; **D:** Joan Darling. VTR

Check Your Guns 🐾🐾 **1948** A crooked judge and a gang of outlaws team up to prey on law-abiding folk and cause headaches for the new sheriff, who's pushing an unsuccessful Old West version of gun control. Nothing really noteworthy here. **55m/B VHS.** Eddie Dean, Roscoe Ates, Nancy Gates, George Chesebro, I. Stanford Jolley, Mikel Conrad, William "Bill" Fawcett; **D:** Ray Taylor. NOS

The Checkered Flag 🐾 **1963** Lame auto-racing drama about an aging, millionaire race car driver with an alcoholic wife who would like nothing more than to see him dead. She talks a young rookie into helping her dispose of hubby. Plans go awry—with horrifying results. Racing scenes overshadow incredibly weak script and performances. **110m/C VHS.** Joe Morrison, Evelyn King, Charles G. Martin, Peggy Vendig; **D:** William Grefe; **W:** William Grefe. SNC

Checking Out 🐾½ **1989 (R)** Black comedy about a manic hypochondriac who is convinced that his demise will soon occur. You'll pray that he's right. Daniels can't make it work, and supporters Mayron and Magnuson also have little chance in poorly conceived roles. **95m/C VHS, Beta, LV.** Jeff Daniels, Melanie Mayron, Michael Tucker, Kathleen York, Ann Magnuson, Allen Havey, Jo Harvey Allen, Felton Perry, Alan Wolfe; **D:** David Leland; **W:** Joe Eszterhas; **M:** Carter Burwell. NO

Cheech and Chong: Still Smokin' 🐾½ Still Smokin' **1983 (R)** Not really. More like still trying to make a buck. Veteran marijuana-dazed comedy duo travel to Amsterdam to raise funds for a bankrupt film festival group by hosting a dope-a-thon. Lots of concert footage used in an attempt to hold the slim plot together. Only for serious fans of the dopin' duo. **91m/C VHS, Beta, LV.** Richard "Cheech" Marin, Thomas Chong; **D:** Thomas Chong; **W:** Richard "Cheech" Marin, Thomas Chong; **M:** George S. Clinton. PAR

Cheech and Chong: Things Are Tough All Over 🐾🐾 **1982 (R)** Stoner comedy team are hired by two rich Arab brothers (also played by Cheech and Chong in acting stretch) and unwittingly drive a car loaded with money from Chicago to Las Vegas. Tired fourth in the series. **87m/C VHS, Beta.** Richard "Cheech" Marin, Thomas Chong, Shelby Fiddis, Rikki Marin, Evelyn Guerrero, Rip Taylor; **D:** Tom Avildsen; **W:** Richard "Cheech" Marin, Thomas Chong. COL

Cheech and Chong's Next Movie 🐾🐾 **1980 (R)** A pair of messed-up bumblers adventure into a welfare office, massage parlor, nightclub, and flying saucer, while always living in fear of the cops. Kinda funny, like. Sequel to "Up in Smoke." **95m/C VHS, Beta, LV.** Richard "Cheech" Marin, Thomas Chong, Evelyn Guerrero, Edie McClurg, Paul (Pee Wee Herman) Reubens, Phil Hartman; **D:** Thomas Chong; **W:** Richard "Cheech" Marin, Thomas Chong. USH

Cheech and Chong's Nice Dreams 🐾🐾 **1981 (R)** The spaced-out duo are selling their own "specially mixed" ice cream to make cash and realize their dreams. Third in the series. **97m/C VHS, Beta, LV.** Richard "Cheech" Marin, Thomas Chong, Evelyn Guerrero, Stacy Keach, Paul (Pee Wee Herman) Reubens; **D:** Thomas Chong; **W:** Richard "Cheech" Marin, Thomas Chong; **M:** Harry Betts. COL

Cheech and Chong's The Corsican Brothers woof! **1984 (PG)** Wretched swashbuckler features the minimally talented duo in a variety of worthless roles. Dumas would vomit in his casket if he knew about this. Fifth in the series. **91m/C VHS, LV.** Richard "Cheech" Marin, Thomas Chong, Roy Dotrice, Rae Dawn Chong, Shelby Fiddis, Rikki Marin, Edie McClurg; **D:** Thomas Chong; **W:** Richard "Cheech" Marin, Thomas Chong. ART

Cheech and Chong's Up in Smoke 🐾🐾½ **1979 (R)** A pair of free-spirited burn-outs team up for a tongue-in-cheek spoof of sex, drugs, and rock and roll. First and probably the best of the dopey duo's cinematic adventures.

A boxoffice bonanza when released and still a cult favorite. **87m/C VHS, Beta, LV.** Richard "Cheech" Marin, Thomas Chong, Stacy Keach, Tom Skerritt, Edie Adams, Strother Martin, Cheryl "Rainbeaux" Smith; **D:** Lou Adler; **W:** Richard "Cheech" Marin, Thomas Chong. PAR

The Cheerful Fraud 🐾🐾½ **1927** Denny, who appeared in some two hundred-odd films in his career, masquerades as a butler to be near the girl he loves. A fool for love is a cheerful fraud. A zanily romantic silent comedy. **64m/B VHS, Beta.** Reginald Denny, Gertrude Olmsted, Emily Fitzroy, Gertrude Astor; **D:** William A. Seiter. GPV

Cheering Section woof! **1973 (R)** High school football teams compete for the grand prize—the privilege of ravishing the losing school's cheerleaders. Rah, rah, rah. **84m/C VHS.** Rhonda Foxx, Tom Leindecker, Gregg D'Jah, Patricia Michelle, Jeff Laine; **D:** Harry Kerwin. NO

Cheerleader Camp woof! Bloody Pom Poms **1988 (R)** Nubile gals are stalked by a psychopath while they cavort semi-clad at summer camp. **89m/C VHS, Beta.** Betsy Russell, Leif Garrett, Lucinda Dickey, Lorie Griffin, George Flower, Teri Weigel, Rebecca Ferratti; **D:** John Quinn. PAR

The Cheerleaders woof! **1972 (R)** Dimwitted exploitation effort has the usual suspects—moronic jocks and lamebrained gals—cavorting exuberantly. Followed by "Revenge of the Cheerleaders." **84m/C VHS, Beta, LV.** Stephanie Fondue, Denise Dillaway, Jovita Bush, Debbie Lowe, Sandy Evans; **D:** Paul Glickler. IME

Cheerleaders' Wild Weekend woof! **1985 (R)** Group of cheerleaders are held captive by a disgruntled former football star. Pom poms wave. **87m/C VHS, Beta.** Jason Williams, Kristine DeBell; **D:** Jeff Werner. ART, VES

Cheers for Miss Bishop 🐾🐾½ **1941** The story of a woman who graduates from college then teaches at the same institution for the next 50 years. Somewhat moving. Based on Bess Streeter Aldrich's novel. **95m/B VHS, Beta.** Martha Scott, William Gargan, Edmund Gwenn, Sterling Holloway, Rosemary DeCamp; **D:** Tay Garnett; **M:** Edward Ward. Nominations: Academy Awards '41: Best Original Dramatic/Comedy Score. NOS, MRV, VYY

Cheetah 🐾🐾 **1989 (G)** Two California kids visiting their parents in Kenya embark on the adventure of their lives when, with the help of a young Masai, they adopt and care for an orphaned cheetah. Usual Disney kids and animals story. **80m/C VHS, LV, Closed Caption.** Keith Coogan, Lucy Deakins, Collin Mothupi; **D:** Jeff Blyth; **W:** John Cotter; **C:** Thomas Burstyn. DIS

A Chef in Love 🐾🐾 Les Mille et Une Recettes du Cuisinier Amoureux; The Cook in Love **1996 (PG-13)** In 1920, Parisian Pascal Ishac (Richard) meets Georgian Princess Cecilia (Kirtadze) while travelling and decides to stay and open a French restaurant in the capital of Tbilisi. When the capital is invaded by the Red Army in 1921, communist leader Zigmund (Kahmhadze) forces Cecilia to marry him and shuts down Pascal's eatery. With his great love and his restaurant both gone, Pascal writes a master cookbook and memoir that is later discovered and translated by Cecilia's son Anton (Gautier), who also discovers that Pascal is his father. French, Russian and Georgian with subtitles. **CW:** Nudity, sexual situations and some images of violence. **95m/C VHS.** FR Pierre Richard, Nino Kirtadze, Temur Kahmhadze, Jean-Yves Gautier, Vladimir Ilyine, Danielle Darrieux, Micheline Presle; **D:** Nana Dzhordzadze; **W:** Irakli Kvirikadze; **C:** Georgi Beridze; **M:** Goran Bregovic. Nominations: Academy Awards '96: Best Foreign Language Film. COL

The Cherokee Kid 🐾🐾½ **1996 (PG-13)** Cable western/comedy about a novice gunslinger (Sinbad) avenging his family. There's a corrupt banker (Coburn), a bounty hunter (Hines), a Mexican freedom fighter (Martinez), and a gang of bankrobbing nuns to keep things interesting while the Kid learns his outlaw ways. **CW:** Wild West violence, language and some sex-related material. **?m/C VHS.** Sinbad, James Coburn, Burt Reynolds, Gregory Hines, A. Martinez, Ernie Hudson; *D:* Paris Barclay; *W:* Tim Kazurinsky, Denise DeClue; *M:* Stanley Clarke. *HBO*

Cherry Hill High woof! 1976 (R) Five teen girls compete for former-virgin status. Pass on this one. **92m/C VHS, Beta.** Linda McInerney, Carrie Olsen, Nina Carson, Lynn Hastings, Gloria Upson, Stephanie Lawlor; *D:* Alex E. Goiten. *USH*

Cherry 2000 �♫☫ 1988 (PG-13) Futuristic flick concerns a man who short-circuits his sex-toy robots and embarks on a search for replacement parts across treacherous territory, only to meet a real female—Griffith. Offbeat, occasionally funny. **94m/C VHS, Beta, LV, Closed Caption.** Melanie Griffith, David Andrews, Ben Johnson, Tim Thomerson, Michael C. Gwynne; *D:* Steve DeJarnatt; *W:* Michael Almereyda; *M:* Basil Poledouris. *ORI*

Chesty Anderson USN ☫ *Anderson's Angels* 1976 Ultra-lame sexploitation about female naval recruits. Minimal nudity. **90m/C VHS, Beta.** Shari Eubank, Dorri Thompson, Rosanne Katon, Marcie Barkin, Scatman Crothers, Frank Campanella, Fred Willard; *D:* Ed Forsyth. *NO*

Cheyenne Autumn ☫☫½ 1964 The newly restored version of the ambitious, ultimately hit-and-miss western epic about three hundred Cheyenne Indians who migrate from Oklahoma to their Wyoming homeland in 1878. The cavalry, for once, are not the good guys. Widmark is strong in the lead. Stewart is memorable in his comic cameo as Wyatt Earp. Last film from genre master Ford, capturing the usual rugged panoramas. Based on a true story as told in the Mari Sandoz novel. **156m/C VHS, Beta.** Richard Widmark, Carroll Baker, Karl Malden, Dolores Del Rio, Sal Mineo, Edward G. Robinson, Ricardo Montalban, Gilbert Roland, Arthur Kennedy, John Carradine, Victor Jory, Mike Mazurki, George O'Brien, John Qualen; *Cameos:* James Stewart; *D:* John Ford; *C:* William Clothier. Nominations: Academy Awards '64: Best Color Cinematography. *WAR, FCT*

Cheyenne Kid ☫½ 1933 Determined bronco buster is up against a gang of bad guys. **40m/B VHS, Beta.** Tom George Duryea Keene, Mary Mason, Roscoe Ates; *M:* Max Steiner. *NOS, DVT*

Cheyenne Rides Again ☫½ 1938 Cheyenne poses as an outlaw to hunt a gang of rustlers. **60m/B VHS, Beta.** Tom Tyler, Lucille Browne, Lon Chaney Jr., Roger Williams, Charles "Slim" Whitaker; *D:* Robert F. "Bob" Hill. *NOS, VYY, VCN*

The Cheyenne Social Club ☫☫ 1970 (PG) Stewart inherits a brothel and Fonda helps him operate it. Kelly directs, sort of. Some laughs, but this effort is beneath this trio. **103m/C VHS.** Henry Fonda, James Stewart, Shirley Jones, Sue Ane Langdon, Elaine Devry; *D:* Gene Kelly; *C:* William Clothier. *WAR*

Cheyenne Takes Over ☫ 1947 Lash sniffs out the bad guy in the case of a murdered ranch heir. **56m/B VHS, Beta.** Lash LaRue, Al "Fuzzy" St. John, George Chesebro; *D:* Ray Taylor. *COL*

Cheyenne Warrior ☫☫½ 1994 (PG) Pregnant young bride Rebecca heads west with a husband who soons winds up dead, leaving her stranded at an isolated trading post. She takes in a wounded Cheyenne warrior, nurses him back to health, and he tries to convince her to let his tribe care for her. Respectable performances if unexciting. **90m/C VHS, LV.** Kelly Preston, Pato Hoffmann, Bo Hopkins, Dan Haggerty, Charles Powell, Rick Dean, Clint Howard; *D:* Mark Griffiths; *W:* Michael B. Druxman. *NHO*

Chicago Joe & the Showgirl ☫☫ 1990 (R) A London-based GI befriends a loopy showgirl and helps her in various crimes during WWII. Appealing Lloyd overwhelms Sutherland, who shows only limited acting ability here. Kensit and Pigg are fine in smaller roles. **105m/C VHS, LV, Closed Caption.** Emily Lloyd, Kiefer Sutherland, Patsy Kensit, Keith Allen, Liz Fraser, Alexandra Pigg, Ralph Nossek, Colin Bruce; *D:* Bernard Rose; *M:* Hans Zimmer. *ART, IME*

The Chicken Chronicles ☫ 1977 (PG) An affluent high school dude longs to get horizontal with his dream girl. Set in the 1960s. First feature film appearance for Guttenberg. **94m/C VHS, Beta.** Phil Silvers, Ed Lauter, Steve Guttenberg, Lisa Reeves, Meredith Baer; *D:* Francis Simon. *COL*

Chiefs ☫☫ 1983 A police chief in a Southern town discovers a series of murders concealed by town big wigs. Made for TV film boasts a surprisingly strong cast, but provides otherwise conventional entertainment. **200m/C VHS, Beta.** Charlton Heston, Paul Sorvino, Keith Carradine, Brad Davis, Billy Dee Williams, Wayne Rogers, Stephen Collins, Tess Harper, Victoria Tennant; *D:* Jerry London. *VTR*

Child Bride of Short Creek ☫☫½ 1981 A young Korean war veteran returns to his community where polygamy is allowed, to find that his father intends to marry again, this time to a 15-year-old. Conflict ensues. Made for television. Based on an actual event that occurred in the 1950s. **100m/C VHS, Beta.** Diane Lane, Conrad Bain, Christopher Atkins, Kiel Martin, Helen Hunt; *D:* Robert Lewis.

Child in the Night ☫☫ 1990 (R) A shaken eight-year-old boy is a witness to murder in his family, and a psychologist must get him to testify. First film for Wood. Middling TV-movie suspense. **93m/C VHS, Beta.** Tom Skerritt, JoBeth Williams, Darren McGavin, Season Hubley, Elijah Wood; *D:* Mike Robe. *TRI*

A Child Is Waiting ☫☫☫ 1963 Poignant and provocative story of teachers in an institution for the mentally retarded. Fine performances include Lancaster as the institution's administrator and Garland as a teacher who cares too much for everyone's good. Cassavetes incorporates footage using handicapped children as extras—not entirely seamlessly—providing a sensitive and candid edge. **105m/B VHS, Beta.** Burt Lancaster, Judy Garland, Gena Rowlands, Steven Hill, Bruce Ritchey; *D:* John Cassavetes; *W:* Abby Mann; *M:* Ernest Gold. *MGM*

Child of Darkness, Child of Light ☫½ 1991 (PG-13) A priest is sent to investigate two virgin pregnancies and discovers that one child will be a savior and the other the Anti-Christ. Totally mindless brain candy resembling the "Omen" movies and "Rosemary's Baby." Made for cable television. Adapted from James Patterson's book "Virgin." **85m/C VHS, Beta, Closed Caption.** Anthony John Denison, Brad Davis, Paxton Whitehead, Claudette Nevins, Sydney Penny, Kristin Datillo, Viveca Lindfors, Sela Ward, Alan Oppenheimer, Eric Christmas; *D:* Marina Sargenti; *W:* Brian Taggert. *PAR*

Child of Glass ☫☫ 1978 (G) A young boy's family moves into a huge New Orleans mansion, and soon after encounters a young girl's ghost and lost treasure from the Civil War. A Disney made for TV movie. **93m/C VHS, Beta.** Barbara Barrie, Biff McGuire, Anthony Zerbe, Nina Foch, Steve Shaw, Katy Kurtzman, Olivia Barash; *D:* John Erman. *DIS*

Child of the Prairie ☫ 1918 An early Mix film about a young cowboy and his city-loving wife down on their luck in a western town. Silent with music score. **63m/B VHS, Beta, 8mm.** Tom Mix. *VYY*

The Children woof! 1980 (R) Familiar nuclear leak leads to monster mutants down to a novel (though extremely low-budget) turn: after a school bus passes through radioactive fog, the kiddies inside assume the ability to incinerate whoever they hug. They also assume a certain zombie-like demeanor and sport black fingernails. None of this is noted by their uncaring and less-than-observant parents, many of whom are enticed into a very warm hug. This may be intended as social satire. Not only are the little microwaves extremely dangerous, the only way to kill them is to chop off their hands, leading to a wild limbless finale. **89m/C VHS, Beta.** Martin Shaker, Gale Garnett, Gil Rogers; *D:* Max Kalmanowicz. *VES, FCT, RHI*

The Children ☫☫½ 1990 Kingsley stars as a middle-aged engineer who finds himself caring for seven children in this touching love story from novelist Edith Wharton. Shot on location in Venice, the cinematography is excellent and the cast is superb, but the film lags in places. A remake of "The Marriage Playground." **90m/C VHS.** *GB GE* Ben Kingsley, Kim Novak, Siri Neal, Geraldine Chaplin, Joe Don Baker, Britt Ekland, Donald Sinden, Karen Black, Robert Stephens, Rupert Graves, Rosemary Leach; *D:* Tony Palmer.

The Children Are Watching Us ☫☫☫ *The Little Martyr; I Bambini Ci Guardano* 1944 Sobering drama of a family dissolution as seen by a child. A four-year-old boy drifts unloved by his suicidal father and by his mother, who's only interested in her own love affair. Worthy example of Italian neo-realism marks the first collaboration between Zavattini and De Sica. In Italian with subtitles. **92m/B VHS.** *IT* Luciano de Ambrosis, Isa Pola, Emilio Cigoli; *D:* Vittorio De Sica; *W:* Cesare Zavattini, Vittorio De Sica. *FCT, HMV*

Children in the Crossfire ☫☫½ 1984 When youngsters from war-torn Northern Ireland spend a summer in America with children from the Republic of Ireland, both sides find their nationalistic prejudices falling away. But a great challenge awaits them when they return home from their summer of fun. Nicely done drama made for television. **96m/C VHS, LV.** Charles Haid, Karen Valentine, Julia Duffy, David Hoffman; *D:* George Schaefer; *M:* Brad Fiedel. *ART, VES*

Children of a Lesser God ☫☫☫½ 1986 (R) Based upon the play by Mark Medoff, this sensitive, intelligent film deals with an unorthodox speech teacher at a school for the deaf, who falls in love with a beautiful and rebellious ex-student. Inarguably romantic; the original stage production won the Best Play Tony in 1980. Hurt and Matlin reportedly continued their romance off-screen as well. **119m/C VHS, Beta, LV, 8mm, Closed Caption.** William Hurt, Marlee Matlin, Piper Laurie, Philip Bosco, E. Katherine Kerr; *D:* Randa Haines; *W:* Hesper Anderson, Mark Medoff; *C:* John Seale; *M:* Michael Convertino. Academy Awards '86: Best Actress (Matlin); Golden Globe Awards '87: Best Actress—Drama (Matlin); Nominations: Academy Awards '86: Best Actor (Hurt), Best Adapted Screenplay, Best Picture, Best Supporting Actress (Laurie). *PAR, BTV*

The Children of An Lac ☫☫½ 1980 Three women attempt to rescue hundreds of Vietnamese orphans before Saigon falls to the communists. The film derives from actress Balin's actual wartime experience. Made for television. **100m/C VHS, Beta.** Shirley Jones, Ina Balin, Beulah Quo, Alan Fudge, Ben Piazza, Lee Paul, Kieu Chinh, Vic Diaz.

Children of Divorce ☫½ 1980 Made-for-television drama shows divorce from the children's point of view. Standard fare. **96m/C VHS, Beta.** Barbara Feldon, Lance Kerwin, Stacey Nelkin, Billy Dee Williams; *D:* Joanna Lee; *M:* Minette Alton. *ART*

Children of Fury ☫☫ *In the Line of Duty: Siege at Marion* 1994 (PG-13) Fact-based TV movie covers the death (at police hands) of self-proclaimed prophet, Utah polygamist John Singer (Weisser), whose wife Vickie (Harper) and children vow revenge. When fundamentalist Addam Swapp (Secor) joins their group, he soon begins intimidating the locals and bombs a building in the town of Marion. Authorities call in the FBI and chief agent Bill Bryant (Franz) sets up a siege of the property. *CW:* Some violent content. **85m/C VHS.** Kyle Secor, Tess Harper, Dennis Franz, Ed Begley Jr., Paul LeMat, Norbert Weisser, William H. Macy, Rex Linn; *D:* Charles Haid; *W:* Rich Husky; *C:* William Wages; *M:* Gary Chang. *NHO*

Children of Nature ☫☫½ *Born Natturunnar* 1991 A 78-year-old man unwillingly enters a nursing home where he meets a long-ago sweetheart. The two fall in love again and decide to escape from the home and return to their childhood village. Sweet love story about late-blooming passions laced with fantasy and humor. Iceland's first Academy Award nomination. **85m/C VHS.** *IC* Gisli Halldorsson, Sigridur Hagalin, Bruno Ganz; *D:* Fridrik Thor Fridriksson; *W:* Fridrik Thor Fridriksson, Einar Mar Gudmundsson; *M:* Hilmar Orn Hilmarsson. Nominations: Academy Awards '92: Best Foreign Language Film. *FXL, ING*

The Children of Noisy Village 🎬🎬½ 1995
Noisy Village is a small town in the Swedish countryside consisting of three red frame houses. In the town, a group of adventurous children discover a multitude of fantasy lands right in their own backyard—their backyard being the beautiful pastures, ponds, and fields of Sweden. Based on the stories of Astrid "Pippi Longstocking" Lindgren. Dubbed. **88m/C VHS.** *SW* Linda Bergstrom, Anna Sahlin, Ellem Demerus, Harsald Lonnbro; *D:* Lasse Hallstrom. *FRF*

Children of Paradise 🎬🎬🎬🎬 *Les Enfants du Paradise* 1944
Considered by many to be the greatest film ever made, certainly one of the most beautiful. In the Parisian theatre district of the 1800s an actor falls in love with a seemingly unattainable woman. Although circumstances keep them apart, their love never dies. Produced in France during WWII right under the noses of Nazi occupiers; many of the talent (including the writer, poet Jacques Prevert) were active resistance fighters. Laserdisc version features: interview with director Marcel Carne, production photos, analysis of influences of French painting on the film, and audio essay by film authority Brian Stonehill. In French with English subtitles. **188m/B VHS, LV.** *FR* Jean-Louis Barrault, Arletty, Pierre Brasseur, Maria Casares, Albert Remy, Leon Larive, Marcel Herrand, Pierre Renoir, Jeanne Marken, Gaston Modot; *D:* Marcel Carne; *W:* Jacques Prevert; *C:* Roger Hubert; *M:* Maurice Thiriet, Joseph Kosma. Nominations: Academy Awards '46: Best Original Screenplay. *HMV, CRC, FCT*

Children of Rage 🎬🎬½ 1975 (PG)
High-minded and long-winded drama dealing with the Israeli/Palestinian war and terrorism from the viewpoint of an Israeli doctor yearning for peace. **106m/C VHS, Beta.** *GB* IS Simon Ward, Cyril Cusack, Helmut Griem, Olga Georges-Picot; *D:* Arthur Seidelman; *W:* Richard Alfieri.

Children of Sanchez 🎬🎬 1979 (PG)
Mexican man attempts to provide for his family with very little except faith and love. U.S./Mexican production based on Oscar Lewis' novel. **103m/C VHS, Beta.** *MX* Anthony Quinn, Dolores Del Rio, Katy Jurado, Lupita Ferrer; *D:* Hall Bartlett; *W:* Hall Bartlett; *M:* Chuck Mangione. *MON*

Children of the Corn 🎬½ 1984 (R)
Young couple lands in a small Iowa town where children appease a demon by murderously sacrificing adults. Time to move or dispense with some major spankings. Infrequently scary. Another feeble attempt to translate the horror of a Stephen King book to film. **93m/C VHS, Beta, LV.** Peter Horton, Linda Hamilton, R.G. Armstrong, John Franklin, Courtney Gains, Robbie Kiger; *D:* Fritz Kiersch; *W:* George Goldsmith; *C:* Raoul Lomas; *M:* Jonathan Elias. *VTR*

Children of the Corn 2: The Final Sacrifice 🎬½ 1992 (R)
Reporter working for a tabloid paper gets more than he bargained for when he decides to do a story on the adults murdered in the town of Gatlin, Nebraska. Gatlin's surviving children, who killed their parents in the first film, are now living in a neighboring town and free to kill again. This youthful satanic cult does in authority figures in a number of sacrificial ways, working ever more smartly to create the prime attraction—blood flow. Not based on anything written by Stephen King. *CW:* Language and horror violence. **93m/C VHS, Closed Caption.** Terence Knox, Paul Scherrer, Rosalind Allen, Christie Clark, Ned Romero, Ryan Bollman, Ed Travelstead; *D:* David F. Price; *W:* Gilbert Adler, A.L. Katz. *PAR*

Children of the Corn 3: Urban Harvest 🎬🎬 1995 (R)
Joshua (Melendez) and younger brother Eli (Cerny) are adopted by a wealthy couple and transplanted from Nebraska to Chicago's suburbia. But when Eli grows a corn patch that resurrects an evil force, only Joshua can stop his reign of terror. Contrived premise but lots of nifty special effects. *CW:* Horror violence and gore; language. **103m/C VHS, LV, Closed Caption.** Daniel Cerney, Ron Melendez, Mari Morrow, Duke Stroud, Jim Metzler, Nancy Lee Grahn; *D:* James D.R. Hickox; *W:* Dode Levenson; *C:* Gerry Lively; *M:* Daniel Licht. *TOU*

Children of the Corn 4: The Gathering 🎬 *Deadly Harvest* 1996 (R)
Medical student Grace Rhodes (Watts) seeks to free the children of her Nebraska hometown from a mysterious plague and a shadowy figure. **85m/C VHS, LV, Closed Caption.** Naomi Watts, Brent Jennings, Jaime Renee Smith, William Windom, Karen Black; *D:* Greg Spence; *W:* Stephen Berger, Greg Spence; *C:* Richard Clabaugh; *M:* David Williams. *TOU*

Children of the Damned 🎬🎬 1963
Six children, who are a sample of what man will evolve to in a million years, are born all around the world with genius IQs, ray-gun eyes, and murderous dispositions. Two investigators bring the children together, and while they are being examined by scientists they escape. The children hide out in a church, but they are doomed because their destiny is to be destroyed to teach a lesson to modern man. A sequel to "Village of the Damned" based loosely on the novel "The Midwich Cuckoos" by John Wyndham. **90m/B VHS, LV.** *GB* Ian Hendry, Alan Badel, Barbara Ferris, Alfred Burke, Sheila Allen, Clive Powell, Frank Summerscales, Mahdu Mathen, Gerald Delsol, Roberta Rex, Franchesca Lee, Harold Goldblatt, Ralph Michael, Martin Miller, Lee Yoke-Moon; *D:* Anton Leader; *W:* John Briley. *MGM*

Children of the Full Moon 🎬 1984
A young couple find themselves lost in a forest that is the home of a family of werewolves. Earns praise only for brevity. Even bad movie aficionados will want to skip this howler. **60m/C VHS, Beta.** *GB* Christopher Cazenove, Celia Gregory, Diana Dors, Jacof Witken, Robert Urquhart; *D:* Tom Clegg. *ART*

Children of the Night 🎬½ 1992 (R)
Allburg seems like a typically quiet small town far removed from any danger—until a vampire is released from an underground crypt and decides to make the town his bloodthirsty target. When a teacher, whose girlfriend is visiting Allburg, learns of the supernatural goings on he decides to investigate, which may be a deadly mistake. *CW:* Language and horror violence. **92m/C VHS.** Peter DeLuise, Karen Black, Ami Dolenz, Maya McLaughlin, Evan Mackenzie, David Sawyer, Garrett Morris; *D:* Tony Randel; *W:* Nicolas Falacci; *C:* Richard Michalak. *COL*

Children of the Revolution 🎬🎬 1995 (R)
Mockumentary covering 45 years of Australian history and politics, beginning in 1951 when the conservative Prime Minister attempts to ban the Australian Communist Party. Party member (and Stalin admirer) Joan Fraser (Davis) helps to prevent the ban, bringing her to the Russian leader's attention, and she's invited to Moscow. There, Joan winds up in bed with Stalin (Abraham) and comes home pregnant. Eventually, son Joe (Rush) makes an entry into the Australian political scene, resulting in chaos. There's almost too much more for the film to handle, although the actors don't seem to have any problems. *CW:* Some strong sexuality and language. **101m/C VHS, LV, Closed Caption.** *AU* Judy Davis, Sam Neill, Richard Roxburgh, Rachel Griffiths, Geoffrey Rush, F. Murray Abraham; *D:* Peter Duncan; *W:* Peter Duncan; *C:* Martin McGrath; *M:* Nigel Westlake. Australian Film Institute '96: Best Actress (Davis), Best Art Direction/Set Decoration, Best Costume Design; Nominations: Australian Film Institute '96: Best Director (Duncan), Best Film. *TOU*

Children of the Wild 🎬🎬½ *Killers of the Wild* 1937
Adventure story about a pack of dogs surviving in the Rocky Mountain wilderness. Splendid scenery and some interesting sequences. **65m/B VHS.** Patsy Moran. *VYY*

The Children of Theatre Street 1977
Absorbing documentary follows three children attending the renowned Kirov Ballet School. A show for all ages that may be especially enjoyed by kids who are interested in ballet. Kelly's last film appearance. **92m/C VHS, Beta.** *RU* Angelina Armeiskaya, Alec Timoushin, Lena Voronzova, Michaela Cerna, Galina Messenzeva, Konstantin Zaklinsky; *D:* Robert Dornhelm; *W:* Beth Gutcheon; *C:* Karl Kofler. Nominations: Academy Awards '77: Best Feature Documentary. *MVD, PBC, KUL*

The Children of Times Square 🎬🎬 1986
A mother pursues her son who has fled home and joined a gang of drug dealers in New York City's seedy Times Square. Ordinary television film despite strong casting of Cassidy and Rollins. **95m/C VHS, Beta, Closed Caption.** Joanna Cassidy, Howard E. Rollins Jr., Brandon Douglas, David Ackroyd, Griffin O'Neal, Danny Nucci, Larry B. Scott; *D:* Curtis Hanson; *M:* Patrick Gleeson.

Children Shouldn't Play with Dead Things 🎬🎬½ *Revenge of the Living Dead* 1972
A band of foolhardy hippie filmmakers on an island cemetary skimp on special effects by using witchcraft to revive the dead. The plan works. Soon the crew has an island full of hungry ghouls to contend with. Film strives for yucks, frequently succeeds. A late night fave, sporting some excellent dead rising from their grave scenes as well as a selection of groovy fashions. Screenwriter/star Ormsby went on to write the remake of "Cat People," while director Clark would eventually helm "Porky's." **85m/C VHS, Beta.** Alan Ormsby, Valerie Mamches, Jeff Gillen, Anya Ormsby, Paul Cronin, Jane Daly, Roy Engelman, Robert Philip, Bruce Solomon, Alecs Baird, Seth Sklarey; *D:* Bob (Benjamin) Clark; *W:* Bob (Benjamin) Clark, Alan Ormsby; *C:* Jack McGowan. *VTR*

The Children's Hour 🎬🎬 *The Loudest Whisper* 1961
The teaching careers of two women are ruined when girls begin circulating vicious rumors. Only an occasionally taut drama despite forceful handling of a lesbian theme. Updated version of Lillian Hellman's play (adapted by Hellman) is more explicit, but less suspenseful in spite of excellent performances from the talented cast. Remake of Wyler's own "These Three." **107m/C VHS, LV, Closed Caption.** Shirley MacLaine, Audrey Hepburn, James Garner, Miriam Hopkins, Veronica Cartwright, Fay Bainter; *D:* William Wyler; *W:* John Michael Hayes; *M:* Alex North. Nominations: Academy Awards '61: Best Art Direction/Set Decoration (B & W), Best Black and White Cinematography, Best Costume Design (B & W), Best Sound, Best Supporting Actress (Bainter). *MGM, BTV, FCT*

Child's Christmas in Wales 1988
A film of Dylan Thomas's Christmas story about an old, traditional Christmas in Wales circa 1910. **55m/C VHS, Beta.** Mathonwy Reeves; *D:* Don McBrearty. *ART, VES, HMV*

Child's Play 🎬🎬½ 1988 (R)
A boy discovers that his new doll named Chucky is actually the embodiment of a deranged killer. His initially skeptical mom and a police officer come around after various killings. Exciting, if somewhat moronic, fare, with fine special effects. Followed by "Child's Play 2." **95m/C VHS, Beta, LV, Closed Caption.** Catherine Hicks, Alex Vincent, Chris Sarandon, Dinah Manoff, Brad Dourif, Tommy Swerdlow, Jack Colvin; *D:* Tom Holland; *W:* Don Mancini, John Lafia, Tom Holland; *C:* Bill Butler; *M:* Joe Renzetti. *MGM*

Child's Play 2 WOOF! 1990 (R)
Chucky lives. Basic doll-on-a-rampage story, a metaphor for the Reagan years, lives on in the sequel (you remember: somehow guy-doll Chucky made it past the quality control people with a highly inflammable temper). A little dotty from playing with dolls, young Vincent finds himself fostered by two new parents, and plagued by an obnoxious and very animated doll that fosters ill will toward all. What's worse is the doll is transmigratory, craving the boy's body as his next address. Chef d'effects Kevin Yagher's new toy is bad, real bad, and so are the other part two FX. Little Chucky's saga, however grows a tad tiresome. A bad example for

small children. **84m/C VHS, Beta, LV, Closed Caption.** Alex Vincent, Jenny Agutter, Gerrit Graham, Christine Elise, Grace Zabriskie; **D:** John Lafia; **W:** Don Mancini; **C:** Stefan Czapsky; **M:** Graeme Revell; **V:** Brad Dourif. *USH*

Child's Play 3 *♂* **1991 (R)** Possessed doll Chucky returns to life again in search of a new child to control, and luckily finds his old pal (Whalin) at a military school filled with the usual stereotypes. Gory sequel in a mostly awful series. "Don't F— With the Chuck" was its catch phrase; that should indicate the level of this junk.**CW:** Language and horror violence. **89m/C VHS, Beta, LV, Closed Caption.** Justin Whalin, Perrey Reeves, Jeremy Sylvers, Peter Haskell, Dakin Matthews, Travis Fine, Dean Jacobson, Matthew Walker, Andrew (Andy) Robinson; **D:** Jack Bender; **M:** Cory Lerios, John D'Andrea; **V:** Brad Dourif. *USH*

Chill Factor *♂♂* **1990 (R)** A television reporter for an investigative news show uncovers evidence of an international conspiracy. Plot twists abound. **?m/C VHS.** Paul Williams, Patrick Macnee, Andrew Prine, Carrie Snodgress, Patrick Wayne, Gary Crosby; **D:** David L. Stanton. *NO*

Chillers *♂* **1988** Travellers waiting for a bus are besieged by carnivorous zombies and voracious vampires. How this is different from the standard bus trip is unclear. **90m/C VHS, Beta.** Jesse Emery, Marjorie Fitzsimmons, Laurie Pennington, Jim Wolfe, David Wohl; **D:** Daniel Boyd; **W:** Daniel Boyd.

The Chilling woof! *Gamma 693* **1989 (R)** Corpses preserved in a deep freeze come alive and plague Kansas City as flesh-chomping zombies. Utterly worthless film doesn't even provide convincing effects.**CW:** Horror violence and one sensual scene. **91m/C VHS.** Linda Blair, Dan Haggerty, Troy Donahue, Jack A. De Rieux, Ron Vincent; **D:** Deland Nuse, Jack A. Sunseri.

Chilly Scenes of Winter *♂♂½* *Head Over Heels* **1979 (PG)** Quirky comedy with a cult following about a man obsessed with regaining the love of a former girlfriend who is now married. He must also deal with an insane mom and various other problems. Strong, subtle performances from Heard and Riegert. Hurt is somewhat less satisfying as the supposedly fascinating woman. Released with a different, inferior ending as "Head Over Heels." Adapted by Joan Micklin Silver from Ann Beattie's first novel. Watch for Beattie's cameo as a waitress. **96m/C VHS, Beta.** John Heard, Mary Beth Hurt, Peter Riegert, Kenneth McMillan, Gloria Grahame, Nora Heflin, Griffin Dunne; **Cameos:** Ann Beattie; **D:** Joan Micklin Silver; **W:** Joan Micklin Silver. *MGM*

Chimes at Midnight *♂♂♂♂* *Falstaff, Campanadas a Medianoche* **1967** Classic tragedy—derived by Welles from five Shakespeare plays—about a corpulent blowhard and his friendship with a prince. Crammed with classic sequences, including a battle that is both realistic and funny. The love scene between massive Welles and a nonetheless willing Moreau also manages to be both sad and amusing. Great performances all around, but Welles understandably dominates. The film's few flaws (due to budget problems) are inconsequential before considerable strengths. This one ranks among Welles', and thus the entire cinema's, very best. **115m/B VHS, Beta.** *SP SI* Orson Welles, Jeanne Moreau, Margaret Rutherford, John Gielgud, Marina Vlady, Keith Baxter, Fernando Rey, Norman Rodway; **D:** Orson Welles; **W:** Orson Welles; **M:** Angelo Francesco Lavagnino. *FCT*

China *♂♂½* **1943** David Jones (Ladd) is an unfeeling profiteer who's making money off the Japanese invading China (it's 1941). But he and buddy Johnny Sparrow (Bendix) have their truck hijacked by a group of Chinese guerrillas, lead by China-born American teacher Carolyn Grant (Young), who need a group of schoolgirls driven to safety through enemy lines. Naturally, Jones has a change of heart (and sides) and battles the Japanese troops. Typically fervent propaganda film. Based on the play by Archibald Forbes. **79m/ B VHS, Closed Caption.** Alan Ladd, Loretta Young, William Bendix, Philip Ahn, Victor Sen Yung, Marianne Quon, Rich-

ard Loo; **D:** John Farrow; **W:** Frank Butler; **C:** Leo Tover. *USH*

China Beach *♂♂♂* **1988** TV movie/pilot launched the acclaimed series about American military women behind the lines during the chaos of the Vietnam War. Nurse McMurphy has only seven days left on her first tour of duty, and in spite of her hate of the brutality of the war, she has mixed feelings about leaving her friends and her work. A USO singer on a one week tour finds her search for men brings the war too close for comfort. Cherry, a new Red Cross volunteer, shows up at the Beach. Skillfully introduces the viewer to all the characters, their problems and joys, without melodrama or redundancy. **95m/C VHS, Beta, Closed Caption.** Dana Delany, Chloe Webb, Robert Picardo, Nan Woods, Michael Boatman, Marg Helgenberger, Tim Ryan, Concetta Tomei, Jeff Kober, Brian Wimmer; **D:** Rod Holcomb; **W:** John Sacret Young. *WAR*

China Cry *♂♂½* **1991 (PG-13)** Based on the true story of Sung Negn Yee who escaped from Communist China to the freedom of Hong Kong in the early '60s. Fine portrayal of the young woman from a privileged background who witnessed some of the atrocities of Mao's government policies. **103m/C VHS.** Julia Nickson-Soul, Russell Wong, James Shigeta, France Nuyen; **D:** James F. Collier. *IGP*

China Gate *♂♂♂* **1957** A band of multi-national troops follows a French officer against a communist stronghold in Indochina. Conventional fare bolstered considerably by director Fuller's flair for action. Weak male leads, but Dickinson shines. **97m/B VHS.** Gene Barry, Angie Dickinson, Nat King Cole, Paul Dubov, Lee Van Cleef, George Givot, Marcel Dalio; **D:** Samuel Fuller; **W:** Samuel Fuller; **M:** Max Steiner. *REP*

China Girl *♂♂½* **1987 (R)** An Italian-American boy and a Chinese-American girl romance despite a war between gangs in their respective NYC communities. This often violent drama is enriched by director Ferrara's slick, high-energy approach. **90m/C VHS, Beta, LV.** Richard Panebianco, James Russo, Sari Chang, Russell Wong, David Caruso, Joey Chin; **D:** Abel Ferrara; **W:** Nicholas St. John; **C:** Bojan Bazelli; **M:** Joe Delia. *VES*

The China Lake Murders *♂♂½* **1990 (PG-13)** A made for cable crazy cop on the loose fable in which a serial killer disguised as a highway patrolman practices population control on the inhabitants of a small town in the Mojave desert. Meanwhile the local sheriff (Skerritt), unwittingly befriends the killer-patrolman. **100m/C VHS, Beta, Closed Caption.** Tom Skerritt, Michael Parks, Nancy Everhard, Lauren Tewes, Bill McKinney, Lonny Chapman; **D:** Alan Metzger; **W:** Nevin Schreiner. *USH*

China Moon *♂♂½* **1991 (R)** Convoluted police thriller, set in Florida, about beautiful Rachel (Stowe), who's married to rich-but-abusive Rupert (Dance). Kyle (Harris) is the lonely homicide detective who's besotted by Rachel and conveniently helps her dispose of her murdered husband's body. Kyle's problems increase when his rookie partner (Del Toro) turns out to be smarter than anyone thinks. Good performances but the suspense is only average.**CW:** Language, violence, and sensuality. **99m/C VHS, LV, Closed Caption.** Ed Harris, Madeleine Stowe, Benicio Del Toro, Charles Dance; **D:** John Bailey; **W:** Roy Carlson; **M:** George Fenton. *ORI*

China, My Sorrow *♂♂½* *Chine, Ma Douleur* **1989** Thirteen-year-old "Little Four Eyes" is sent to a Chinese re-education camp for the crime of playing a love song to a girl. There he befriends another enemy of the revolution and a Buddhist monk who help him maintain his familial traditions and identity. Tragi-comic look at how freedom's spirit survived the Cultural Revolution. Mandarin with subtitles. **86m/C VHS.** *CH* Guo Yiang Yi, Tieu Quan Nghieu, Vong Han Lai, Chi-Vy Sam, Chang Cheung Siang; **D:** Dai Sijie; **W:** Dai Sijie, Shan Yuan Zhu; **M:** Chen Qi Gang. *CVC, FCT*

China O'Brien *♂½* **1988 (R)** Gorgeous police officer with martial arts expertise returns home for a little R & R, but finds she has to kick some major butt instead. Violent, dimwitted action drama proves only that cleavage can be macho too.**CW:** Martial arts violence. **90m/C VHS, Closed Caption.** Cynthia Rothrock, Richard Norton, Patrick Adamson, David Blackwell, Steven Kerby, Robert Tiller, Lainie Watts, Keith Cooke; **D:** Robert Clouse; **M:** Paul Antonelli. *IMP, BTV*

China O'Brien 2 *♂½* **1989 (R)** The unbreakable China, now a sheriff, battles the standard-issue Vietnam-vet druglord who invades her little town. Made back-to-back with the first film (note that both pics' bad guys have the same gang of henchman!), and in both films Rothrock is basically invincible, so there's no suspense.**CW:** Violence. **85m/C VHS, Closed Caption.** Cynthia Rothrock, Richard Norton, Keith Cooke; **D:** Robert Clouse. *IMP*

China Seas *♂♂♂* **1935** The captain of a commercial steamship on the China route has to fight off murderous Malay pirates, a spurned woman, and a raging typhoon to reach port safely. Fast-moving romantic action taken from Crosbie Garstin's novel. **89m/B VHS, Beta.** Clark Gable, Jean Harlow, Wallace Beery, Rosalind Russell, Lewis Stone, Sir C. Aubrey Smith, Dudley Digges, Robert Benchley; **D:** Tay Garnett. *MGM*

China Sky *♂♂* **1944** An American doctor fights alongside Chinese guerilas against the Japanese during WWII. Drama, to its credit, often opts for character conflict instead of warfare, but this makes it merely dull instead of cliched. Adapted from a Pearl S. Buck novel. **78m/B VHS, Beta, LV.** Randolph Scott, Ellen Drew, Ruth Warrick, Anthony Quinn, Carol Thurston, Richard Loo, Philip Ahn; **D:** Ray Enright. *TTC*

The China Syndrome *♂♂♂½* **1979 (PG)** A somewhat unstable executive at a nuclear plant uncovers evidence of a concealed accident, takes drastic steps to publicize the incident. Lemmon is excellent as the anxious exec, while Fonda and Douglas are scarcely less distinguished as a sympathetic TV journalist and camera operator, respectively. Tense, prophetic thriller that ironically preceded the Three Mile Island accident by just a few months. Produced by Douglas. **123m/C VHS, Beta, LV, Closed Caption.** Jane Fonda, Jack Lemmon, Michael Douglas, Scott Brady, James Hampton, Peter Donat, Wilford Brimley, James Karen; **D:** James Bridges; **W:** Mike Gray, T.S. Cook, James Bridges. British Academy Awards '79: Best Actor (Lemmon), Best Actress (Fonda); Cannes Film Festival '79: Best Actor (Lemmon); Writers Guild of America '79: Best Original Screenplay; Nominations: Academy Awards '79: Best Actor (Lemmon), Best Actress (Fonda), Best Art Direction/Set Decoration, Best Original Screenplay. *COL*

China White **1991 (R)** Violence erupts in the streets of Paris, Amsterdam, and Bangkok, when international drug cartels battle over the ownership of China White—premium heroin, its sources and its outlets. Rousing, realistic action.**CW:** Language and strong violence and drug content. **?m/C VHS, Closed Caption.** Billy Drago, Russell Wong, Lisa Schrage, Steven Leigh; **D:** Ronny Yu. *IMP*

Chinatown *♂♂♂♂* **1974 (R)** Private detective finds himself overwhelmed in a scandalous case involving the rich and powerful of Los Angeles. Gripping, atmospheric mystery excels in virtually every aspect, with strong narrative drive and outstanding performances from Nicholson, Dunaway, and Huston. Director Polanski also appears in a suitable unsettling cameo. Fabulous. A sneaky, snaking delight filled with seedy characters and plots-within-plots. Followed more than 15 years later by "The Two Jakes." **131m/C VHS, Beta, LV, 8mm, Letterbox, Closed Caption.** Jack Nicholson, Faye Dunaway, John Huston, Diane Ladd, John Hillerman, Burt Young, Perry Lopez, Darrell Zwerling; **Cameos:** Roman Polanski; **D:** Roman Polanski; **W:** Robert Towne; **C:** John A. Alonzo; **M:** Jerry Goldsmith. Academy Awards '74: Best Original Screenplay; British Academy Awards '74: Best Actor (Nicholson), Best Director (Polanski), Best Screenplay; Golden Globe Awards '75: Best Actor—Drama (Nicholson); Best Director (Polanski); Best Film—Drama, Best Screenplay, National Film Registry '91;; New York Film Critics Awards '74: Best Actor (Nicholson); National Society of Film Critics Awards '74: Best Actor (Nicholson); Writers Guild of America '74: Best Original Screenplay; Nominations: Academy Awards '74: Best Actor (Nicholson), Best Actress (Dunaway), Best Art Direction/Set Decoration, Best Cinematography, Best Costume Design, Best Director (Polanski), Best Film Editing, Best Picture, Best Sound, Best Original Dramatic/Comedy Score. *PAR*

Chinatown After Dark *🐾* 1931 Ludicrous, inane melodrama about a white girl raised by the Chinese. 50m/B VHS. Rex Lease, Barbara Kent, Carmel Myers; *D:* Stuart Paton. *SNC, NOS, DVT*

Chinatown Connection *🐾* 1990 (R) For some inexplicable reason, local drug dealers start selling poisoned cocaine. Two renegade cops discover the super-secret organization doing the poisoning, arm themselves heavily, and kill lots of people while putting an end to the poisonings. Violent, foolish film with dull performances. 94m/C VHS. Bruce Ly, Lee Majors, Pat McCormick, Art Camacho, Susan Frailey, Scott Richards; *D:* Jean-Paul Ouellette. *NO*

The Chinatown Kid *🐾* 1978 Tan Tung escapes from Red China on a ship bound for San Francisco. There he becomes involved in a local extortion racket and he'll need all his martial arts skills to overcome the two gangs fighting for power. 115m/C VHS. Alexander Fu Sheng, Sun Chein, Shirley Yu, Shaw Yin-Yin; *D:* Chen Chen. *FXL*

The Chinatown Murders: Man Against the Mob *🐾🐾* 1992 (R) A tough cop is up against the Chinese mafia and his own corrupt police force as he tries to stay alive and find some justice. 96m/C VHS, Closed Caption. George Peppard, Charles Haid, Richard Bradford, Ursula Andress. *THV*

Chinese Box *🐾🐾½* 1997 Hong Kong's return to Chinese rule is the backdrop for Wang's story of a dying British journalist (Irons) and a former bar girl turned nightclub owner (Li). In the months before the 1997 handover, business writer John learns he is dying of leukemia and decides to pursue Vivian, the woman he has secretly loved for some time. He also sets out to discover the "meaning" of Hong Kong itself. This quest is personified by Jean (Cheung), a street hustler with stories to tell. Metaphors abound as Wang tries to convey the everyday chaos and impenetrability of Hong Kong life. Striking visuals provide cues and clues to the not-always-subtle symbolism. Mandarin and English dialogue. 109m/C VHS. *FR JP* Jeremy Irons, Gong Li, Maggie Cheung, Ruben Blades, Michael Hui; *D:* Wayne Wang; *W:* Wayne Wang, Jean-Claude Carriere, Larry Gross, Paul Theroux; *C:* Vilko Filac; *M:* Graeme Revell. *THV*

Chinese Boxes *🐾🐾½* 1984 An American man in Berlin is framed in a murder and becomes caught in an international web of crime and intrigue. Low budget but interesting thriller. 87m/C VHS, Beta. *GE GB* Will Patton, Adelheid Arndt, Robbie Coltrane; *D:* Christopher Petit; *W:* L.M. Kit Carson. *ART, VES*

The Chinese Cat *🐾* 1944 Poorly scripted formula mystery has the younger Chan smitten with a girl who needs the elder Chan's detective skills in finding her father's killer. 65m/B VHS. Sidney Toler, Benson Fong, Mantan Moreland, Weldon Heyburn, Joan Woodbury, Ian Keith, Sam Flint; *D:* Phil Rosen. *MGM*

Chinese Connection *🐾🐾½* 1973 *Fist of Fury; The Iron Hand* (R) A martial arts expert tracks sadistic brutes who slew his instructor. Wild action sequences provide a breathtaking view of Lee's skill. Dubbed. 90m/C VHS, Beta, LV, Letterbox. *CH* Bruce Lee, James Tien, Robert Baker; *D:* Lo Wei. *FOX, MRV, REP*

Chinese Connection 2 *🐾🐾* 1984 A martial-arts expert learns that the school where he trained is now run by an unappealing master. Conflict ensues. Bruce Li is not Bruce Lee, but he

is fairly good in action portions of this otherwise dull, sloppy venture. 96m/C VHS, Beta. Bruce Li. *TWE*

Chinese Roulette *🐾🐾½* 1986 A host of unappealing characters convene at a country house for sexual shenanigans and a cruel game masterminded by a sadistic crippled girl. Cold effort from German master Fassbinder. In German with English subtitles. 96m/C VHS, Beta, LV, Letterbox. *GE* Anna Karina, Margit Carstensen, Ulli Lommel, Brigitte Mira, Macha Meril, Andrea Schober, Volker Spengler; *D:* Rainer Werner Fassbinder; *W:* Rainer Werner Fassbinder; *C:* Michael Ballhaus. *CVC*

Chinese Web *🐾* 1978 Spiderman adventure in which Spidey becomes entwined in international intrigue and corrupt officials. 95m/C VHS, Beta, Closed Caption. Nicholas Hammond, Robert F. Simon, Rosalind Chao, Ted Danson; *D:* Donald McDougall. *FOX*

Chino *🐾🐾* *Valdez the Half Breed; The Valdez Horses* 1975 (PG) A half-Indian horse rancher struggles to maintain his livelihood in this spaghetti western. Not among Bronson's stronger—that is, more viscerally effective—films. Adapted from Lee Hoffman's novel. 97m/C VHS, Beta. *IT* Charles Bronson, Jill Ireland, Vincent Van Patten; *D:* John Sturges. *MPI, MRV, VTR*

The Chipmunk Adventure *🐾🐾* 1987 The three animated chipmunks, Simon, Theodore and Alvin, get involved with a diamond smuggling ring. Original songs. In HiFi Stereo. 76m/C VHS, Beta, LV, Closed Caption. *D:* Janice Karman; *W:* Janice Karman, Ross Bagdasarian; *M:* Randy Edelman. *ORI, WAR*

Chips, the War Dog *🐾🐾½* 1990 A WWII Army recruit, who's scared of dogs, is assigned to train a German shepherd for duty. Made for cable television. 90m/C VHS. Brandon Douglas, Ned Vaughn, Paxton Whitehead, Ellie Cornell, Robert Miranda, William Devane; *D:* Ed Kaplan. *DIS*

The Chisholms *🐾🐾½* 1979 If you're into oaters, here's a high fiber six-hour serial: Chisolm (Preston) leads the family as they head west and find trouble with a capital "T" en route from Virginia to Califor-i-a. Originally a network miniseries, it's now a two-cassette rentable; adapted by Evan Hunter from his novel. 300m/C VHS, Beta. Robert Preston, Rosemary Harris, Brian Keith, Ben Murphy, Charles Frank; *D:* Mel Stuart; *M:* Elmer Bernstein. *ART*

Chisum *🐾½* 1970 (G) Cattle baron faces various conflicts, including a confrontation with Billy the Kid. Lame Wayne vehicle contributes nothing to exhausted western genre. Laserdisc available in widescreen letterbox edition. 111m/C VHS, Beta, LV, Letterbox. John Wayne, Forrest Tucker, Geoffrey Deuel, Christopher George, Ben Johnson, Bruce Cabot, Patric Knowles, Richard Jaeckel, Glenn Corbett; *D:* Andrew V. McLaglen; *W:* Andrew J. Fenady; *C:* William Clothier. *WAR, TLF*

Chitty Chitty Bang Bang *🐾🐾* 1968 (G) An eccentric inventor spruces up an old car and, in fantasy, takes his children to a land where the evil rulers have forbidden children. Poor special effects and forgettable score stall effort. Loosely adapted by Roald Dahl and Hughes from an Ian Fleming story. ♫Chitty Chitty Bang Bang; Hushabye Mountain; Truly Scrumptious; You Two; Toot Sweet; Me Ol' Bam-Boo; Lovely Lonely Man; Posh; The Roses of Success. 142m/C VHS, Beta, LV, Closed Caption. *GB* Dick Van Dyke, Sally Ann Howes, Lionel Jeffries, Gert Frobe, Anna Quayle, Benny Hill; *D:* Ken Hughes; *W:* Ken Hughes, Roald Dahl. Nominations: Academy Awards '68: Best Song ("Chitty Chitty Bang Bang"). *FOX, MGM, TLF*

Chloe in the Afternoon *🐾🐾🐾* 1972 (R) A married man finds himself inexplicably drawn to an ungainly young woman. Sixth of the "Moral Tales" series is typical of director Rohmer's talky approach. Not for all tastes, but rewarding for those who are drawn to this sort of thing. In French with English subtitles. 97m/C VHS, Beta. *FR* Bernard Verley, Zouzou, Francoise Verley, Daniel Ceccaldi, Malvina Penne, Babette Ferrier, Suze Randall,

Marie-Christine Barrault; *D:* Eric Rohmer; *W:* Eric Rohmer; *C:* Nestor Almendros. *FCT*

Chocolat *🐾🐾🐾½* 1988 (PG-13) A woman recalls her childhood spent in French West Africa and the unfulfilled sexual tension between her mother and black servant. Vivid film provides a host of intriguing characters and offers splendid panoramas of rugged desert landscapes. Profound, if somewhat personal filmmaking from novice director Denis. In French with English subtitles. 105m/C VHS, Beta, LV. Mireille Perrier, Emmet Judson Williamson, Cecile Ducasse, Giulia Boschi, Francois Cluzet, Isaach de Bankole, Kenneth Cranham; *D:* Claire Denis; *W:* Claire Denis, Jean-Pol Fargeau. *ORI*

The Chocolate Soldier *🐾* 1941 Dull musical in which an opera star tests his wife's fidelity. Lovers of the musical genre will find that this one has too much talking, not enough singing. Lovers of fine films will realize that more singing would hardly improve things. Based loosely on Molnar's play "The Guardsman." 102m/B VHS. Nelson Eddy, Rise Stevens, Nigel Bruce, Florence Bates, Dorothy Gilmore, Nydia Westman; *D:* Roy Del Ruth; *C:* Karl Freund. Nominations: Academy Awards '41: Best Black and White Cinematography, Best Sound, Scoring of a Musical. *MGM*

The Chocolate War *🐾🐾🐾* 1988 (R) An idealistic student and a hardline headmaster butt heads at a Catholic boys' school over an unofficial candy business in this tense, unsettling drama. Glover is notable in his familiar villain role, and Gordon is effective in his first effort as director. Based on the Robert Cormier novel. 95m/C VHS, Beta, LV, Closed Caption. John Glover, Jenny Wright, Wally Ward, Bud Cort, Ilan Mitchell-Smith, Adam Baldwin; *D:* Keith Gordon; *W:* Keith Gordon. *MCG*

The Choice *🐾🐾* 1981 A young woman must make the choice between aborting or keeping her baby in this fairly insipid television drama. 96m/C VHS, Beta. Susan Clark, Jennifer Warren, Mitchell Ryan, Largo Woodruff; *D:* David Greene. *ART*

Choice of Arms *🐾🐾½* 1983 A gangster's rural retirement is undone by a dimwitted criminal in this sometimes gripping drama. Montand and Deneuve are serviceable in undemanding roles of the gangster and his glamorous wife; Depardieu is more impressive as the trouble-making punk. In French with English subtitles. 114m/C VHS, Beta. *FR* Gerard Depardieu, Catherine Deneuve, Yves Montand; *D:* Alain Corneau.

Choice of Weapons *🐾🐾* *A Dirty Knight's Work; Trial by Combat* 1976 Ex-cop trying to solve murders focuses on a curious group of 20th-century men who live within a 12th-century fantasy—jousting for sport and chivalrous honor. Offbeat lance thruster notable for incongruity and all-star cast. 88m/C VHS, Beta. *GB* David Birney, Peter Cushing, Donald Pleasence, Barbara Hershey, John Mills, Margaret Leighton; *D:* Kevin Connor; *W:* Julian Bond. *NO*

Choices *🐾½* 1981 A hearing-impaired athlete suffers alienation when banned from the football squad. What? Controversial covergirl Moore is a supporting player in this, her first film. 90m/C VHS, Beta. Paul Carafotes, Victor French, Lelia Goldoni, Val Avery, Dennis Patrick, Demi Moore; *D:* Rami Alon. *VHE, HHE, VTR*

Choices *🐾🐾½* 1986 Scott is a 62-year-old man with a lovely second wife (Bisset) and a rebellious grown daughter (Gilbert), who announces she's pregnant and is getting an abortion. Meanwhile, his wife also discovers she's pregnant and wants the child, although Scott is adamantly opposed to raising a second family at his age. Family strife carried by fine performances. Made for television. 95m/C VHS. George C. Scott, Jacqueline Bisset, Melissa Gilbert; *D:* David Lowell Rich. *CAF*

The Choirboys *🐾* 1977 (R) Thoroughly mediocre production about overbearing L.A. cops and their off-hours handling of job stress. Few of the strong cast emerge unscathed. Based on the Joseph Wambaugh novel. 120m/C VHS, Beta. Charles Durning, Louis Gossett Jr., Perry King, Clyde Kusatsu, Stephen Macht, Tim McIntire, Randy Quaid, Chuck Sacci, Don Stroud, James Woods, Burt Young, Robert Webber, Barbara Rhoades, Vic Tayback, Blair Brown, Charles Haid, Jim Davis; **D:** Robert Aldrich; **C:** Joseph Biroc. *USH*

Choke Canyon ✍️✍️ 1986 (PG) An environmentalist thwarts the henchmen of an industrialist eager to coverup a nuclear dump in a picturesque canyon. Good intentions do not necessarily make for a good movie. **95m/C VHS, Beta.** Stephen Collins, Bo Svenson, Lance Henriksen; **D:** Chuck Bail.

C.H.O.M.P.S. ✍️½ 1979 (PG) Comedy in which a youthful inventor and a popular robot guard dog become the target of a business takeover. Harmless but unfunny and unfun. **90m/C VHS, Beta.** Jim Backus, Valerie Bertinelli, Wesley Eure, Conrad Bain, Chuck McCann, Red Buttons; **D:** Don Chaffey. *NO*

Choose Me ✍️✍️✍️½ 1984 (R) Comedy-drama about sad, lonely, and often quirky characters linked to an unlikely L.A. radio sex therapist. Moody, memorable fare features especially strong playing from Bujold as a sexually inexperienced sex therapist and Warren as one of her regular listeners. Typically eccentric fare from director Rudolph. **106m/C VHS, Beta, LV.** Keith Carradine, Genevieve Bujold, Lesley Ann Warren, Rae Dawn Chong, John Larroquette, John Considine; **D:** Alan Rudolph; **W:** Alan Rudolph.

Chopper Chicks in Zombietown ✍️✍️ 1991 (R) Tough but sexy Chopper Chicks show up in that American vacation mecca, Zombietown, for a little rest and relaxation. Little do they know that a mad mortician has designs on turning our hot heroines into mindless zombie slaves. Can the buxom biker babes thwart the evil embalmer before it's too late, or will they abandon their Harleys to shuffle about in search of human flesh? From the Troma Team, featuring Oscar-winner Billy Bob Thornton as "Donny." **86m/C VHS, LV, Closed Caption.** Jamie Rose, Catherine Carlen, Lycia Naff, Vicki Frederick, Kristina Loggia, Gretchen Palmer, Whitney Reis, Nina Peterson, Ed Gale, David Knell, Billy Bob Thornton, Don Calfa, Martha Quinn; **D:** Dan Hoskins; **W:** Dan Hoskins; **C:** Tom Fraser; **M:** Daniel May. *COL, NLC*

The Choppers ✍️ 1961 Naw, not a fable about false teeth. Teen punk Hall operates a car theft ring made up of fellow punksters. Rock'n'roll tunes by the Hall-meister include the much-overlooked "Monkey in my Hatband." **66m/B VHS, Beta.** Arch Hall Jr., Marianne Gaba, Robert Paget, Tom Brown, Rex Holman, Bruno Ve Sota; **D:** Leigh Jason. *SNC*

Chopping Mall ✍️½ *Killbots* 1986 (R) A freak electric storm unleashes killer security robots on a band of teens trapped inside the mall. Nobody shops. Premise undone by obscure humor, lack of flair, action, or horror. Updated imitation of the 1973 TV movie "Trapped." **77m/C VHS, Beta.** Kelli Maroney, Tony O'Dell, Suzee Slater, Russell Todd, Paul Bartel, Mary Woronov, Dick Miller, Karrie Emerson, Barbara Crampton, Nick Segal, John Terlesky, Gerrit Graham; **D:** Jim Wynorski; **W:** Jim Wynorski, Steve Mitchell; **C:** Tom Richmond. *ART*

A Chorus Line ✍️✍️ 1985 (PG-13) A range of performers reveal their insecurities and aspirations while auditioning before a hardnosed director in this adaptation of the popular, overblown Broadway musical. Singing and dancing is rarely rousing. Director Attenborough probably wasn't the right choice for this one. ♫Dance 10, Looks 3; What I Did for Love; At the Ballet; I Can Do That; Let Me Dance For You; I Hope I Get It; Nothing; The Music and the Mirror; And.. **118m/C VHS, Beta, LV, 8mm, Closed Caption.** Michael Douglas, Audrey Landers, Gregg Burge, Alyson Reed, Janet Jones, Michael Blevins, Terrence Mann, Cameron English, Vicki Frederick, Nicole Fosse, Michelle Johnson; **D:** Richard Attenborough; **W:** Arnold Schulman; **M:** Marvin Hamlisch, Ralph Burns. Nominations: Academy Awards '85: Best Film Editing, Best Song ("Surprise, Surprise"), Best Sound.*NLC*

A Chorus of Disapproval ✍️½ 1989 (PG) Adaptation of prolific Alan Ayckbourn's play about a withdrawn, somewhat dimwitted British widower who attempts social interaction by joining community theatre, then finds himself embroiled in romantic shenanigans and theatrical intrigue. Irons is fine in the lead, but Hopkins sparkles in the more spectacular role of the musical production's demanding but beleaguered director. Seagrove is impressive as an amoral sexpot. Sharper focus from director Winner would have improved this one, but the film is fun even when it isn't particularly funny. **105m/C VHS, Beta.** GB Jeremy Irons, Anthony Hopkins, Jenny Seagrove, Lionel Jeffries, Patsy Kensit, Gareth Hunt, Prunella Scales, Sylvia Syms, Richard Briers, Barbara Ferris; **D:** Michael Winner; **W:** Michael Winner, Alan Ayckbourn; **M:** John Du Prez. *NO*

The Chosen woof! *Holocaust 2000* 1977 (R) Executive of a nuclear power facility located in the Sahara Desert realizes that his son is the Anti-Christ bent on the world's destruction. This truly horrible film provides nothing in terms of entertainment. It's rarely even laughably bad. **102m/C VHS, Beta.** Kirk Douglas, Simon Ward, Agostina Belli, Anthony Quayle, Virginia McKenna, Alexander Knox; **D:** Alberto De Martino; **M:** Ennio Morricone. *FOX, ART, VES*

The Chosen ✍️✍️✍️ 1981 Set in 1940s Brooklyn about the friendship between two teenagers—Benson, the Hassidic son of a rabbi, and Miller, whose father is a Zionist professor. Based on the novel by Chaim Potok. **108m/C VHS.** Robby Benson, Barry Miller, Maximilian Schell, Rod Steiger, Hildy Brooks, Ron Rifkin, Val Avery; **D:** Jeremy Paul Kagan; **M:** Elmer Bernstein. *FXV*

The Chosen One: Legend of the Raven ✍️✍️ 1998 (R) McKenna Ray ("Baywatch" babe Electra) wants payback after her sister is murdered and is transformed into a superheroine avenger (guided by her shaman father) so she can rid the world of scum. Electra has a provocative costume but the nude scenes are courtesy of a body-double.**CW:** Violence, language, sexual situations, nudity. **105m/C VHS, DVD.** Carmen Electra, David Stadvec, David Oliver; **D:** Lawrence Lanoff. *TTV*

Christ Stopped at Eboli ✍️✍️✍️✍️ *Eboli* 1979 Subdued work about an anti-Fascist writer exiled to rural Italy in the 1930s. Excellent performances from the lead Volonte and supporting players Papas and Cuny. Slow, contemplative film is probably director Rosi's masterpiece. Adapted from Carlo Levi's book. In Italian with English subtitles. **118m/C VHS, Beta.** IT FR Gian Maria Volonte, Irene Papas, Paolo Bonacelli, Francois Simon, Alain Cuny, Lea Massari; **D:** Francesco Rosi; **W:** Francesco Rosi; **C:** Pasquale De Santis. British Academy Awards '82: Best Foreign Film; National Board of Review Awards '80: Best Foreign Film. *COL*

Christabel ✍️✍️ 1989 Condensed version of the BBC mini-series based on the true-life WWII exploits of Christabel Bielenberg, a British woman who battled to save her German husband from the horrors of the Ravensbruck concentration camp. **148m/C VHS, Beta, Closed Caption.** GB Elizabeth Hurley, Stephen Dillon, Nigel le Vaillant, Geoffrey Palmer; **W:** Dennis Potter. *FOX*

Christian the Lion ✍️✍️½ 1976 (G) The true story of Christian, a lion cub raised in a London zoo, who is transported to Africa to learn to live with other lions. With the principals from "Born Free." **87m/C VHS, Beta.** GB Virginia McKenna, Bill Travers, George Adamson, James Hill; **D:** Bill Travers. *UNI*

Christiane F. ✍️✍️✍️ 1982 (R) Gripping, visually impressive story of a bored German girl's decline into drug use and prostitution. Based on a West German magazine article. Sobering and dismal look at a milieu in which innocence and youth have run amok. The film's impact is only somewhat undermined by poor dubbing. Bowie appears in a concert sequence. **120m/C VHS, Beta.** GE Natja Brunkhorst, Thomas Haustein, David Bowie; **D:** Uli Edel; **M:** David Bowie. *GLV*

Christina ✍️✍️½ 1974 (PG) Gloomy suspense fare in which a beautiful woman pays a forlorn fellow $25,000 to marry her, then disappears as he begins to actually fall in love with her. His search takes him to various gothic settings. Intriguing, but not really fulfilling. Parkins, however, is appropriately mysterious in the lead. **95m/C VHS, Beta.** CA Barbara Parkins, Peter Haskell; **D:** Paul Krasny. *MPI*

Christine ✍️✍️½ 1984 (R) Unassuming teen gains posession of a classic auto equipped with a murderous will. The car more than returns the care and consideration its owner provides it. Are you listening GMC? Based on a novel by Stephen King. **110m/C VHS, Beta, LV, 8mm, Closed Caption.** Keith Gordon, John Stockwell, Alexandra Paul, Robert Prosky, Harry Dean Stanton, Kelly Preston, Christine Belford, Roberts Blossom, William Ostrander, David Spielberg, Robert Darnell; **D:** John Carpenter; **W:** Bill Phillips; **C:** Donald M. Morgan; **M:** John Carpenter, Alan Howarth. *COL*

The Christmas Box ✍️✍️½ 1995 Tearjerking Christmas drama based on Richard Paul Evans' surprising 1992 bestseller, which started out as a story for the author's children. Richard (Thomas) and Keri (O'Toole) Evans have money troubles so they and their five-year-old daughter Jenna (Mulrooney) move into the mansion of elderly widow Mary Parkin (O'Hara) as caretakers. Richard keeps seeing an angel in a recurring dream and hears a familiar tune—all of which leads to a music box hidden in the attic, a series of love letters, and Mary's unhappy past. **92m/C VHS.** Maureen O'Hara, Richard Thomas, Annette O'Toole, Kelsey Mulrooney; **D:** Marcus Cole; **W:** Greg Taylor; **C:** John Newby. *CAF*

A Christmas Carol ✍️✍️✍️ 1938 An early version of Dickens' classic tale about miser Scrooge, who is instilled with the Christmas spirit after a grim evening with some ghosts. Good playing from Owen as Scrooge and Lockhart as the hapless Bob Cratchit. Scary graveyard sequence too. **70m/B VHS, Beta, LV.** Reginald Owen, Gene Lockhart, Terence Kilburn, Leo G. Carroll, Lynne Carver, Ann Rutherford; **D:** Edwin L. Marin. *MGM*

A Christmas Carol ✍️✍️✍️✍️ *Scrooge* 1951 A fine retelling of the classic tale about a penny-pinching holiday hater who learns appreciation of Christmas following a frightful, revealing evening with supernatural visitors. Perhaps the best rendering of the Dickens classic. "And God bless Tiny Tim!" **86m/B VHS, Beta, LV.** GB Alastair Sim, Kathleen Harrison, Jack Warner, Michael Hordern, Patrick Macnee, Mervyn Johns, Hermione Baddeley, Clifford Mollison, George Cole, Carol Marsh, Miles Malleson, Ernest Thesiger, Hattie Jacques, Peter Bull, Hugh Dempster; **D:** Brian Desmond Hurst; **W:** Noel Langley; **M:** Richard Addinsell. *MLB, HMV*

A Christmas Carol ✍️✍️ 1954 Musical version of the Dickens' classic about a stingy old man who is visited by three ghosts on Christmas Eve. **54m/B VHS, Beta.** Fredric March, Basil Rathbone, Ray Middleton, Bob Sweeney, Christopher Cook. *CFV*

A Christmas Carol ✍️✍️ 1984 (PG) Excellent TV adaptation of the Dickens Christmas classic features a memorable Scott as miserly misanthrope Ebenezer Scrooge, who gets a scary look at his life thanks to a Christmas Eve visit from the ghosts of Christmas Past, Present, and Future. Terrific supporting cast; filmed on location in Shrewsbury, England. **100m/C VHS, Closed Caption.** George C. Scott, Nigel Davenport, Edward Woodward, Frank Finlay, Lucy Gutteridge, Angela Pleasence, Roger Rees, David Warner, Susannah York; **D:** Clive Donner; **W:** Roger O. Hirson. *NO*

The Christmas Coal Mine Miracle ✍️½ *Christmas Miracle in Caulfield, U.S.A* 1977 Syrupy made-for-television story about miners struggling for survival in a collapsed mine on Christmas Eve. **98m/C VHS, Beta, Closed Caption.** Mitchell Ryan, Kurt Russell, Andrew Prine, John Carradine,

Barbara Babcock, Melissa Gilbert, Don Porter, Shelby Leverington; **D:** Jud Taylor. FOX

Christmas Comes to Willow Creek 🐾🐾 1987
Mutually antagonistic brothers are enlisted to deliver Christmas gifts to an isolated Alaskan community. Can brotherly love be far off? Two leads played together in the rowdy TV series "Dukes of Hazzard." This is hardly an improvement. **96m/C VHS, Beta.** John Schneider, Tom Wopat, Hoyt Axton, Zachary Ansley, Kim Delaney; **D:** Richard Lang; **M:** Charles Fox. ART, FHE

Christmas in Connecticut 🐾🐾🐾
Indiscretion **1945** Lightweight comedy about a housekeeping magazine's successful columnist who isn't quite the expert homemaker she presents herself to be. When a war veteran is invited to her home as part of a publicity gimmick, she must master the ways of housekeeping or reveal her incompetence. Stanwyck is winning in the lead role. Also available in a colorized version. **101m/B VHS, Beta, LV.** Barbara Stanwyck, Reginald Gardiner, Sydney Greenstreet, Dennis (Stanley Morner) Morgan, S.Z. Sakall, Una O'Connor, Robert Shayne, Joyce Compton; **D:** Peter Godfrey. MGM

Christmas in Connecticut 🐾🐾 1992
Cannon hosts a weekly television show as America's favorite homemaker/hostess. A local forest ranger (Kristofferson) becomes a hero by saving a little boy's life and her network stages a media event by inviting him to her home for a traditional Christmas dinner. There's only one problem: she can't cook. Schwarzenegger's directorial debut lacks challenge in this fluffy remake. See the original instead. Made for cable television. **93m/C VHS, Closed Caption.** Dyan Cannon, Kris Kristofferson, Tony Curtis, Richard Roundtree, Kelly Cinnante, Gene Lithgow, Vivian Bonnell; **D:** Arnold Schwarzenegger; **W:** Janet Brownell. TTC

Christmas in July 🐾🐾🐾½ 1940
A young man goes on a spending spree when he thinks he's won a sweepstakes. Things take a turn for the worse when he finds out that it was all a practical joke. Powell provides a winning performance in this second film from comic master Sturges. **67m/B VHS, Beta, LV.** Dick Powell, Ellen Drew, Raymond Walburn, William Demarest, Franklin Pangborn; **D:** Preston Sturges. USH, FCT

The Christmas Kid 🐾½ 1968
A desperado struggles to determine his true identity while stopping in a frontier town. Gunplay ensues. Don't bother with this one. **87m/C VHS.** SP Jeffrey Hunter, Louis Hayward, Gustavo Rojo, Perla Cristal, Luis Prendes; **D:** Sidney Pink. NO

Christmas Lilies of the Field 🐾🐾½ 1984
This made-for-television sequel to "Lilies of the Field" follows an ex-soldier who returns to the church he helped build. This time he sets out to build an orphanage. **98m/C VHS, Beta.** Billy Dee Williams, Maria Schell, Fay Hauser, Judith Piquet; **D:** Ralph Nelson. MPI

A Christmas Reunion 🐾🐾½ 1993 (PG)
Young boy, still trying to adjust to his parents' death, runs away from his grandfather's house. But they're reunited thanks to street corner Santa and an enchanted book. **92m/C VHS.** James Coburn, Edward Woodward, Meredith Edwards; **D:** David Hemmings. AVE

A Christmas Story 🐾🐾🐾 1983 (PG)
Unlikely but winning comedy of a boy's single-minded obsession to acquire a Red Ryder BB-gun for Christmas. Particularly great sequence involving an impatient department-store Santa. Fun for everyone. Based on "In God We Trust, All Others Pay Cash," an autobiographical story by Shepherd. **95m/C VHS, Beta, LV.** Peter Billingsley, Darren McGavin, Melinda Dillon, Ian Petrella; **D:** Bob (Benjamin) Clark; **W:** Bob (Benjamin) Clark, Leigh Brown, Jean Shepherd. Genie Awards '84: Best Director (Clark). MGM

The Christmas That Almost Wasn't 🐾½ Il Natale Che Quasi Non Fu 1966 (G)
Loathsome humbug decides to destroy Christmas forever by removing Santa Claus from the North

Pole. Crude Italian made children's film nonetheless remembered fondly by a generation of kids. ♫The Christmas That Almost Wasn't; Christmas is Coming; Hustle Bustle; I'm Bad; Kids Get All the Breaks; The Name of the Song is Prune; Nothing to do But Wait; Santa Claus; Time For Christmas. **95m/C VHS, Beta.** IT Rossano Brazzi, Paul Tripp, Lidia Brazzi, Sonny Fox, Mischa Auer; **D:** Rossano Brazzi. HBO

A Christmas to Remember 🐾🐾½ 1978 (G)
Depression-era Minnesota farmer who has lost his son in WWI brings his city-bred grandson to the farm for a holiday visit. Somber, occasionally poignant film buoyed by Robards presence, and Saint's as well. Made for television. **96m/C VHS, Beta.** Jason Robards Jr., Eva Marie Saint, Joanne Woodward; **D:** George Englund. NO

The Christmas Wife 🐾🐾½ 1988
A lonely man pays a woman to be his holiday companion at a mountain retreat. Sturdy performances by Robards and Harris manage to keep this one from going to the dogs. Based on a story by Helen Norris. Made for cable television. **73m/C VHS, Beta, Closed Caption.** Jason Robards Jr., Julie Harris, Don Francks, Patricia Hamilton, Deborah Grover, James Eckhouse; **D:** David Jones. HBO

A Christmas Without Snow 🐾🐾½ 1980
Made-for-television film about a lonely divorced woman finding communal happiness within a local church choir led by a crusty choir master. **96m/C VHS, Beta, Closed Caption.** Michael Learned, John Houseman, Ramon Bieri, James Cromwell, Valerie Curtin, Ruth Nelson, Beah Richards, Calvin Levels; **D:** John Korty; **M:** Ed Bogas. FOX

Christopher Columbus 🐾🐾½ 1949
Step-by-step biography of the 15th-century explorer, his discovery of America, the fame that first greeted him, and his last days. **103m/C VHS.** GB Fredric March, Florence Eldridge, Francis L. Sullivan; **D:** David MacDonald. FCT, IGP, BFA

Christopher Columbus 🐾🐾½ 1985
The man who explored the New World is shown in all his flawed complexity in this film that takes a contemporary approach to the discoveries and character of Christopher Columbus. Shot on location in Spain, Malta, and the Dominican Republic, the film features an exact replica of Columbus' flagship, the Santa Maria. Originally aired as a six-hour television miniseries. **128m/C VHS.** Gabriel Byrne, Faye Dunaway, Oliver Reed, Max von Sydow, Eli Wallach, Nicol Williamson, Jose Ferrer, Virna Lisi, Raf Vallone; **D:** Alberto Lattuada. WAR

Christopher Columbus: The Discovery 🐾 1992 (PG-13)
The 500th anniversary of Columbus' voyage brought this lame excursion in historical biography to the screen briefly. Columbus is portrayed as a swashbuckling adventurer who finally gets the Queen of Spain to agree to finance his voyage of discovery (which primarily consists of discovering a lot of bare-breasted native women). Story is secondary to the banality of the entire production, including the acting. Brando is briefly seen as Torquemada—another film in which he took his substantial paycheck and ran. **CW:** Nudity and action violence. **120m/C VHS, Beta, LV, Closed Caption.** Georges Corraface, Rachel Ward, Tom Selleck, Marlon Brando, Robert Davi, Oliver Cotton, Benicio Del Toro, Catherine Zeta-Jones, Matthieu Carriere, Nigel Terry, Branscombe Richmond; **D:** John Glen; **W:** John Briley, Mario Puzo, Cary Bates; **M:** Cliff Eidelman. Golden Raspberry Awards '92: Worst Supporting Actor (Selleck). WAR

Christopher Strong 🐾🐾½ 1933
Interesting Hepburn turn as a daredevil aviatrix who falls in love with a married British statesman. **77m/B VHS, Beta, LV.** Katharine Hepburn, Billie Burke, Colin Clive, Helen Chandler; **D:** Dorothy Arzner; **M:** Max Steiner. TTC

Christy 1994
Pilot movie for the TV series finds 19-year-old Christy Huddleston (Martin) leaving her privileged Southern life to teach school in the Great Smoky Mountains. It's 1912 in Cutter Gap,

Tennessee and her students are literally dirt poor, with ignorance and superstition the norm. Christy's inspiration in Miss Alice (Daly), a middle-aged Quaker who runs the mission school. And Christy needs encouragement as she struggles to cope with her new life and responsibilities. Based on the novel by Catherine Marshall, which is a fictional biography of her mother. **90m/C VHS.** Kellie Martin, Tyne Daly, Tess Harper, Randall Batinkoff, Annabelle Price, Stewart Finlay-McLennan; **D:** Michael Rhodes; **M:** Ron Ramin. GKK

Chrome and Hot Leather 🐾½ 1971 (PG)
A Green Beret is out for revenge after vicious bikers kill his fiance. Conventional, tasteless genre fare notable only as Gaye's first film. **91m/C VHS, Closed Caption.** William Smith, Tony Young, Michael Haynes, Peter Brown, Marvin Gaye, Michael Stearns, Katherine Baumann, Wes Bishop, Herbert Jeffries; **D:** Lee Frost. ORI

Chrome Hearts 🐾 C.C. & Company 1970 (R)
Rebel biker rescues a buxom gal from a fate worse than death, than vies for control of the gang. Laughable, with Namath hopeless in his film debut. Redeemed only by Ann-Margret in continual disarray. **91m/C VHS, Beta.** Joe Namath, Ann-Margret, William Smith, Jennifer Billingsley, Teda Bracci, Greg Mullavey, Sid Haig, Bruce Glover; **D:** Seymour Robbie. COL, SIM

Chrome Soldiers 🐾🐾 1992
Five Vietnam veterans come together to avenge a friend's murder in a town controlled by drug dealers. Busey, as the murdered man's brother, leads the "Chrome Soldiers" in their battle to expose the killers and end local corruption. **92m/C VHS, Beta, Closed Caption.** Gary Busey, Ray Sharkey, William Atherton, Yaphet Kotto, Nicholas Guest, Kim Robillard, Norman Skaggs, D. David Morin; **D:** Thomas J. Wright; **W:** Nick Randall; **C:** Billy Dickson. PAR

Chronicle of a Boy Alone 🐾🐾 Chronicle of a Lonely Child; Cronica de un Nino Solo 1964
Eleven-year-old Polin is abandoned by his family and sent to live in a state-run orphanage where well-meaning administrators succeed in destroying the childrens' lives. Spanish with subtitles. **86m/C VHS.** AR Oscar Espindola, Beto Gianola, Victoriano Moreira, Leonardo Favio; **D:** Leonardo Favio; **W:** Leonardo Favio; **C:** Ignacio Souto. FCT

The Chronicles of Narnia 1989
Exceptional BBC production of the C.S. Lewis fantasy about four brave children who battle evil in a mythical land where the animals talk and strange creatures roam the countryside. In three volumes; aired on PBS as part of the "Wonderworks" family movie series. **180m/C VHS, Closed Caption.** GB Barbara Kellerman, Jeffery Perry, Richard Dempsey, Sophie Cook, Jonathan Scott, Sophie Wilcox, David Thwaites, Tom Baker; **D:** Alex Kirby. FCT, HMV, TVC

Chu Chu & the Philly Flash woof! 1981 (PG)
A has-been baseball player and a lame dance teacher meet while hustling the same corner; he sells hot watches, she's a one-woman band. A briefcase full of government secrets soon involves them with the feds, the mob, and a motley collection of back-alley bums. Insipid comedy is actually worse than its title, with Burnett and Arkin both trying too hard. Supporters Warden, Aiello, and Glover don't help either. **102m/C VHS, Beta.** Alan Arkin, Carol Burnett, Jack Warden, Danny Aiello, Ruth Buzzi, Danny Glover, Lou Jacobi; **D:** David Lowell Rich; **W:** Barbara Dana. FOX

Chuck Amuck: The Movie 1991
An in-depth look at legendary animator/director Chuck Jones. **51m/C VHS.** Chuck Jones. WAR, FCT

Chuck Berry: Hail! Hail! Rock 'n' Roll 🐾🐾🐾 1987 (PG)
Engaging, energetic portrait of one of rock's founding fathers, via interviews, behind-the-scenes footage and performance clips of Berry at 60. Songs featured: "Johnny B. Goode," "Roll Over Beethoven," "Maybelline," and more. Appearances by Eric Clapton, Etta James, John and Julian Lennon, Roy Orbison, Linda Ronstadt, Bo Diddley and

Bruce Springsteen among others. **121m/C VHS, Beta.** Chuck Berry, Eric Clapton, Etta James, Robert Cray, Julian Lennon, Keith Richards, Linda Ronstadt, John Lennon, Roy Orbison, Bo Diddley, Jerry Lee Lewis, Bruce Springsteen, Kareem Abdul-Jabbar; **D:** Taylor Hackford. *USH, MVD, FCT*

C.H.U.D. woof! 1984 (R) Cannibalistic Humanoid Underground Dwellers are what it's about. Exposed to toxic wastes, a race of flesh-craving, sewer-dwelling monstrosities goes food shopping on the streets of New York. Don't be fooled by the presence of real actors, this one is inexcusable. Followed by a sequel. **90m/C VHS, Beta, LV.** John Heard, Daniel Stern, Christopher Curry, Kim Greist, John Goodman, Jay Thomas; **D:** Douglas Cheek; **W:** Parnell Hall. *VTR*

C.H.U.D. 2: Bud the Chud woof! 1989 (R) Asinine teens steal a corpse that is actually a zombie cannibal capable of passing the trait to anyone it bites (but doesn't eat entirely). Graham excels as the kidnapped corpse, but this horror-comedy is consistently repellent. Contains one of Jagger's few film appearances, a situation of no despair. **84m/C VHS, Beta, LV.** Brian Robbins, Bill Calvert, Gerrit Graham, Tricia Leigh Fisher, Bianca Jagger, Robert Vaughn, Larry Cedar; **D:** David Irving. *ART*

Chuka 🎬🎬½ 1967 A gunfighter tries to resolve a conflict between Indians and unlikeable troops while simultaneously romancing the fort's beautiful occupant. Pedestrian western features convincing playing from the always reliable Taylor. **105m/C VHS, Closed Caption.** Rod Taylor, Ernest Borgnine, John Mills, Luciana Paluzzi, James Whitmore, Angela Dorian, Louis Hayward, Michael Cole, Hugh Reilly; **D:** Gordon Douglas. *PAR, FCT*

A Chump at Oxford 🎬🎬½ 1940 Two street cleaners foil a bank robbery and receive an all-expenses-paid education at Oxford as their reward. This loopy Laurel and Hardy vehicle provides regular amusement in detailing the duo's exploits in Britain. **63m/B VHS, Beta, LV.** Stan Laurel, Oliver Hardy, James Finlayson, Wilfrid Lucas, Peter Cushing, Charlie Hall; **D:** Alfred Goulding. *CCB, FCT, THA*

Chungking Express 🎬🎬🎬 1995 (PG-13) Director Kar-wai presents two quirky tales of loneliness and love, loosely linked by a snack bar in the tourist section of Hong Kong. Cops and drugs are still a part of the storyline, but this is no chopsocky action movie. Both male protagonists are cops, identified only by their badge numbers, who have recently been dumped by their girlfriends. One has a fixation for canned pineapple and expiration dates, the other talks to the inanimate objects in his apartment. The women they eventually fall for are a blonde-wigged heroin dealer and a shy counter girl who bops to "California Dreaming" after breaking in and cleaning the cop's apartment without his knowledge. Shot commando-style in 23 days during the hiatus of Wong's "Ashes of Time" without permits or professional lighting. The high energy is reflected in the pacing and acting performances. Chosen by Quentin Tarantino as the first release of his Miramax-backed Rolling Thunder imprint.**CW:** Some violence, sexuality and drug content. **102m/C VHS, LV, Closed Caption.** HK Bridget Lin, Takeshi Kaneshiro, Tony Leung, Faye Wang, Valerie Chow, Piggy Chan; **D:** Wong Kar-Wai; **W:** Wong Kar-Wai; **C:** Christopher Doyle, Lau Wai-Keung; **M:** Frankie Chan, Roel A. Garcia. Nominations: Independent Spirit Awards '97: Best Foreign Film. *MAX*

The Church 🎬🎬🎬 *La Chiesa* 1990 Italian thrill-meister Argento scripted and produced this ecclesiastical gorefest. A gargoyle-glutted gothic cathedral which happens to stand on the site of a gruesome mass murder is renovated, and the kirk-cleaning turns into a special-effects loaded demonic epiphany. It'll have you muttering your pater noster. Unrated, it's also available in an R-rated version imprint. **110m/C VHS.** IT Tomas Arana, Hugh Quarshie, Feodor Chaliapin Jr, Barbara Cupisti, Antonella Vitale, Asia Argento; **D:** Michele (Michael) Soavi; **W:** Dario Argento, Michele (Michael) Soavi, Franco Ferrini; **C:** Renato Tafuri; **M:** Keith Emerson. *NO*

Churchill and the Generals 🎬🎬 1981 The true story of how Winston Churchill led England away from the bleak Dunkirk battle and rallied the Allied generals to a D-Day victory. Based upon Churchill's memoirs. **180m/C VHS, Beta.** Timothy West, Joseph Cotten, Arthur Hill, Eric Porter, Richard Dysart.

C.I.A.: Code Name Alexa 🎬½ 1992 (R) Alexa is the beautiful and deadly protege of Victor, who heads an international crime ring. A CIA agent decides the best way to stop Victor is to turn Alexa against her boss. Lots of action and violence.**CW:** Language, violence, and sexuality. **93m/C VHS, LV, Closed Caption.** Kathleen Kinmont, Lorenzo Lamas, Alex Cord, O.J. Simpson, Stephen Quadros, Pamela Dixon, Michael Smith; **D:** Joseph Merhi. *PMH*

C.I.A. 2: Target Alexa 🎬🎬 1994 When a nuclear guidance system is stolen from a government facility CIA agent Mark Graver (Lamas) reteams with former terrorist Alexa (Kinmont) to retrieve the system from international terrorist Franz Klug (Savage). Complicating things are ex-CIA agent Straker (Ryan), who now heads his own commando army and wants to sell the device to the highest bidder. **90m/C VHS, LV.** Lorenzo Lamas, Kathleen Kinmont, John Savage, John P. Ryan, Pamela Dixon, Larry Manetti; **D:** Lorenzo Lamas; **W:** Michael January. *PMH*

Ciao Federico! Fellini Directs Satyricon 1969 A documentary of Frederico Fellini's filming of Petronius' "Satyricon." Portrays the Italian filmmaker's larger-than-life directorial approach and relationship with his actors. In English and Italian, with English subtitles. **60m/C VHS, Beta.** Federico Fellini, Martin Potter, Hiram Keller, Roman Polanski, Sharon Tate; **D:** Gideon Bachmann. *MFV, TPV*

Ciao, Professore! 🎬🎬½ *Io Speriamo Che Me La Cavo* 1994 (R) Okay comedy about conventional teacher Marco Sperelli (Villaggio), from northern Italy, who is mistakenly sent to a ramshackle village school in Naples, populated by poor, wily, unruly students. Both, of course, manage to learn from each other. Humor derived from northern vs. southern Italian culture clash may bypass most viewers although the cast of amateur kid actors provide charm. Italian with subtitles. **91m/C VHS, LV.** IT Paolo Villaggio, Isa Danieli, Ciro Esposito; **D:** Lina Wertmuller; **W:** Leo Benvenuti, Piero De Bernardi, Alessandro Bencivenni, Domenico Saverni, Lina Wertmuller. *MAX*

The Cigarette Girl of Mosselprom 🎬🎬½ 1924 A lowly cigarette girl is thrust into the world of moviemaking in this sharp Russian satire. Silent with orchestral score. **78m/B VHS.** RU Yuri Zhelyabuzhsky. *KIV, FCT*

Cimarron 🎬🎬 1931 Hopelessly overblown saga of an American frontier family from 1890 to 1915. Hokey, cliched, with only sporadic liveliness. How did this one win an Oscar? An adaptation of Edna Ferber's novel, featuring Dunne in an early major role. Remade in 1960. **130m/B VHS, Beta.** Richard Dix, Irene Dunne, Estelle Taylor, Nance O'Neil, William Collier Jr., Roscoe Ates, George E. Stone, Stanley Fields, Edna May Oliver, Dennis O'Keefe; **D:** Wesley Ruggles; **M:** Max Steiner. Academy Awards '31: Best Adapted Screenplay, Best Interior Decoration, Best Picture; Nominations: Academy Awards '31: Best Actor (Dix), Best Actress (Dunne), Best Cinematography, Best Director (Ruggles). *MGM, BTV*

Cimarron 🎬🎬½ 1960 Director Mann's remake of the 1931 Academy Award-winning film about frontier life in Oklahoma. This version features Ford as a carefree survivor of the Old West with an extreme case of wanderlust. Schell plays his civilizing wife. Based on Edna Ferber's novel. **140m/C VHS, Letterbox.** Glenn Ford, Maria Schell, Anne Baxter, Arthur O'Connell, Russ Tamblyn, Mercedes McCambridge, Vic Morrow, Robert Keith, Charles McGraw; **D:** Anthony Mann; **W:** Arnold Schulman; **M:** Franz Waxman. Nominations: Academy Awards '60: Best Art Direction/Set Decoration (Color), Best Sound.*MGM*

The Cincinnati Kid 🎬🎬½ 1965 Cardsharks gather for a major stakes poker game, with some romance on the side. Conventional fare helped along by serviceable performances and some stunning cinematography. Sam Peckinpah was dismissed as director from this one. Guess he took the script with him. **104m/C VHS, Beta, LV.** Steve McQueen, Edward G. Robinson, Ann-Margret, Tuesday Weld, Karl Malden, Joan Blondell, Rip Torn, Jack Weston, Cab Calloway; **D:** Norman Jewison; **W:** Ring Lardner Jr., Terry Southern; **M:** Lalo Schifrin. National Board of Review Awards '65: Best Supporting Actress (Blondell). *MGM*

The Cinder Path 🎬🎬½ 1994 Coming-of-age story begins in 1913 with unassuming Charlie MacFell (Owen) forced to take over the family farm. Charlie (who needs a spine transplant) also goes along with an arranged marriage to local lovely Victoria (Jones), a disaster since she's little more than a well-bred tart and it's her younger sister Nellie (Miles) who's really in love with Charlie anyway. As if Charlie didn't have enough to cope with, he's soon an army soldier as WWI begins and up against vindictive Ginger (Byrne), a former farmhand who resents the monied classes Charlie represents. Based on the novel by Catherine Cookson. **145m/C VHS.** GB Lloyd Owen, Catherine Zeta-Jones, Maria Miles, Antony Byrne, Tom Bell; **D:** Simon Langton; **W:** Alan Seymour; **M:** Barrington Pheloung. *VCO*

Cinderella 🎬🎬🎬½ 1950 Classic Disney animated fairytale about the slighted beauty who outshines her evil stepsisters at a royal ball, then returns to her grim existence before the handsome prince finds her again. Engaging film, with a wicked stepmother, kindly fairy godmother, and singing mice. 🎵Cinderella; Bibbidy-Bobbidi-Boo; So This Is Love; A Dream Is a Wish Your Heart Makes; The Work Song; Oh Sing, Sweet Nightingale. **76m/C VHS, Beta.** **V:** Ilene Woods, William Phipps, Verna Felton, James MacDonald. Venice Film Festival '50: Special Jury Prize; Nominations: Academy Awards '50: Best Song ("Bibbidy-Bobbidi-Boo"), Best Sound, Scoring of a Musical. *DIS*

Cinderella 🎬🎬 1964 A made-for-television rendition of the fairy tale as scored by Rodgers and Hammerstein. Songs include "The Loveliness of Evening," "Ten Minutes Ago" and "Do I Love You (Because You're Beautiful?)." **83m/C VHS, Beta, LV, Closed Caption.** Lesley Ann Warren, Ginger Rogers, Walter Pidgeon, Stuart Damon, Celeste Holm; **D:** Charles S. Dubin; **M:** Richard Rodgers, Oscar Hammerstein. *FOX, FCT*

Cinderella 1984 From the "Faerie Tale Theatre" comes the classic tale of a poor girl who goes to a ball to meet the man of her dreams, despite her nasty stepmother and stepsisters. **60m/C VHS, Beta, LV, Closed Caption.** Jennifer Beals, Jean Stapleton, Matthew Broderick, Eve Arden; **D:** Mark Cullingham. *FOX, FCT, HMV*

Cinderella 🎬🎬½ *Rodgers & Hammerstein's Cinderella* 1997 Disney does some multiracial casting in this lavish, latest TV version of the fairytale. Norwood is sweetly sincere in the title role, with Houston as her diva-like Fairy Godmother. Peters' camps as wicked stepmama, Goldberg's the Prince's mother, and the Prince is handsome newcomer Montalban. And Alexander gets the role of comic relief as the princely confidante, Lionel. The Rodgers and Hammerstein score, written for the 1957 TV version, has been augmented with other Richard Rodgers tunes. 🎵The Sweetest Sounds; Impossible; Do I Love You Because You're Beautiful?; Falling in Love with Love. **92m/C VHS, Closed Caption.** Brandy Norwood, Whitney Houston, Paolo Montalban, Jason Alexander, Bernadette Peters, Whoopi Goldberg, Victor Garber; **D:** Robert Iscove; **W:** Robert Freedman; **M:** Richard Rodgers, Oscar Hammerstein. *DIS*

Cinderella Liberty 🎬🎬🎬 1973 (R) Bittersweet romance in which a kindly sailor falls for a brash hooker with a son. Sometimes funny, sometimes moving, with sometimes crude direction overcome by truly compelling performances from Caan and Mason. Story written by Darryl Ponicsan from his novel. **117m/C VHS, Beta.** James Caan, Marsha Mason, Eli Wallach, Kirk Calloway, Burt Young, Bruce Kirby, Dabney Coleman, Sally Kirkland; **D:** Mark Rydell; **W:** Darryl Ponicsan; **C:** Vilmos Zsigmond; **M:** John Williams. Golden Globe Awards '74: Best Actress—Drama (Mason); Nominations: Academy Awards '73: Best Actress (Mason), Best Song ("You're So Nice to Be Around"), Best Original Dramatic/Comedy Score. *FOX*

Cinderella 2000 🎞🎞 1978 (R)
Soft-core musical version of the classic fairy tale. It's the year 2047 and sex is outlawed, except by computer. Strains of Sugarman's score, including "Doin' Without" and "We All Need Love," set the stage for Erhardt's Cinderella to meet her Prince Charming at that conventional single prince romance venue, a sex orgy. Trouble is, it wasn't a shoe Cinderella lost before she fled, and the charming one must interface, as it were, with the local pretenders to the throne in order to find his lost princess. Touching. **86m/C VHS.** Catharine Erhardt, Jay B. Larson, Vaughn Armstrong; **D:** Al Adamson; **M:** Sparky Sugarman. *NO*

Cinderfella 🎞🎞½ 1960
This twist on the classic children's fairy tale features Lewis as the hapless buffoon guided by his fairy godfather. Somewhat overdone, with extended talking sequences and gratuitous musical interludes. Lewis, though, mugs effectively. **88m/C VHS, Beta.** Jerry Lewis, Ed Wynn, Judith Anderson, Anna Maria Alberghetti, Henry Silva, Count Basie, Robert Hutton; **D:** Frank Tashlin; **W:** Frank Tashlin. *ART*

Cinema Paradiso 🎞🎞🎞 Nuovo Cinema Paradiso 1988
Memoir of a boy's life working at a movie theatre in small-town Italy after WWII. Film aspires to both majestic sweep and stirring poignancy, but only occasionally hits its target. Still manages to move the viewer, and it features a suitably low-key performance by the masterful Noiret. Autobiographically inspired script written by Tornatore. The version shown in America is approximately a half-hour shorter than the original Italian form. **123m/C VHS, LV, 8mm.** *IT* Philippe Noiret, Jacques Perrin, Salvatore Cascio, Marco Leonardi, Agnes Nano, Leopoldo Trieste; **D:** Giuseppe Tornatore; **W:** Giuseppe Tornatore; **M:** Ennio Morricone. Academy Awards '89: Best Foreign Language Film; British Academy Awards '90: Best Actor (Noiret), Best Foreign Film, Best Original Screenplay, Best Supporting Actor (Cascio); Cannes Film Festival '89: Grand Jury Prize; Golden Globe Awards '90: Best Foreign Film. *HBO*

Circle Canyon 🎞 1933
In a remote canyon two opposing outlaw gangs battle to the death. **48m/B VHS, Beta.** Buddy Roosevelt. *NO*

Circle Man 🎞 1987
A made-for-video action drama about the underground sporting phenomenon, bare-knuckle fighting. **90m/C VHS, Beta.** William Sanderson. *NO*

Circle of Death 🎞½ 1936
Average formula western about a white boy who is raised as an Indian. Later he falls in love with a white girl and leaves the tribe. **55m/B VHS, Beta.** Monte Montana, Yakima Canutt. *NOS, VDM*

Circle of Deceit 🎞🎞½ 1994
SAS officer John Neil (Waterman) is called back into service in Belfast two years after his wife and child were killed by terrorists. His assignment is to assume the identity of recently deceased IRA soldier Jackie O'Connell and learn about an arms shipment headed for Northern Ireland. But can his disguise hold against local IRA commander Liam McAuley (Vaughan)? Made for British TV. **103m/C VHS.** *GB* Dennis Waterman, Peter Vaughan, Derek Jacobi, Clare Higgins; **W:** Jean-Claude Carriere. *VCO*

Circle of Fear 🎞½ 1989 (R)
An ex-hitman who worked for the Mob upends the black market for sex and drugs in the Philippines while looking for his daughter who was sold into a sex slave ring. El cheapo exploiter. **90m/C VHS, Beta.** *PH* Patrick Dollaghan, Welsey Pfenning, Joey Aresco, Vernon Wells; **D:** Clark Henderson. *MGM*

Circle of Friends 🎞🎞½ 1994 (PG-13)
Nostalgic Irish coming-of-ager focuses on three friends and the trials and tribulations they face when hearts and hormones conflict with a strict Catholic upbringing. Small-town teenager Benny (Driver), overweight and slightly awkward, reunites with her friends at university in Dublin. Benny begins a romance with gentle, doe-eyed Jack Foley (O'Donnell) and endures the humorous but sometimes painful passage from adolescence to womanhood. Sentimental moments can be too sticky-sweet at times, but humor, disappointment, and small triumphs are convincingly portrayed, offering a universal appeal. Adapted from the Maeve Binchy novel. **CW:** Contains sexual situations. **96m/C VHS.** Chris O'Donnell, Minnie Driver, Geraldine O'Rawe, Saffron Burrows, Colin Firth, Alan Cumming, Aidan Gillen; **D:** Pat O'Connor; **W:** Andrew Davies; **M:** Michael Kamen. *HBO*

Circle of Iron 🎞🎞½ The Silent Flute 1978 (R)
Plenty of action and martial arts combat abound in this story of one man's eternal quest for truth. Originally co-written by and intended for Bruce Lee as a rib-crunching vehicle, until he died before production began and was replaced by Kung-Fu Carradine. A cut above most chop-socky actioners. Filmed in Israel. **102m/C VHS, Beta.** *GB* Jeff Cooper, David Carradine, Roddy McDowall, Eli Wallach, Christopher Lee; **D:** Richard Moore; **W:** Bruce Lee, James Coburn, Stirling Silliphant; **M:** Bruce Smeaton.

Circle of Love 🎞🎞 1964
Episodic melodrama drifts from romance to romance in contemporary Paris. A somewhat pretentious remake of Ophuls classic "La Ronde," which was in turn adapted from Arthur Schnitzler's play. Credible performers are undone by Vadim's strained direction. **110m/C VHS, Beta.** *FR* Jane Fonda, Francine Berge, Marie DuBois, Jean-Claude Brialy, Catherine Spaak, Claude Giraud; **D:** Roger Vadim; **W:** Jean Anouilh. *JEF*

Circle of Passion 🎞🎞 Never Ever 1997 (R)
Devoted hubby Thomas Murray (Finch) works for his father-in-law at a London bank. But when Thomas is transferred to Paris and his socialite wife (March) refuses to go with him, devotion falls by the wayside when he falls in love with the free-spirited Katherine (Bonnaire). Now Thomas has to choose between money and love. **CW:** Language, sexual situations. **94m/C VHS.** Charles Finch, Sandrine Bonnaire, Jane March, Julian Sands, James Fox; **D:** Charles Finch. *THV*

Circle of Power 🎞½ Brainwash; The Naked Weekend; Mystique 1983 (R)
Mimieux must cure various business men of their problems (homosexuality, alcoholism and the like) to help them become better executives. Intriguing and somewhat disturbing, supposedly based on a true story. **103m/C VHS.** *GB* Yvette Mimieux, John Considine, Terence Knox, Cindy Pickett, Christopher Allport; **D:** Bobby Roth; **W:** Stephen F. Bello; **C:** Alfonso Beato.

Circle of Two 🎞🎞 1980 (PG)
A platonic friendship between an aging artist and a young girl is misunderstood by others. Well, of course they do meet in a porno theatre. Pedestrian fare adapted from a story by Marie Therese Baird. **90m/C VHS, Beta.** *CA* Richard Burton, Tatum O'Neal, Kate Reid; **D:** Jules Dassin. *VES, VTR*

Circonstances Atténuantes 🎞🎞½ Extenuating Circumstances 1936
French classic about a retired judge who moves to the outskirts of Paris with his wife and attempts to convert the locals from disreputable to law-abiding citizens. Also available dubbed. **90m/B VHS.** *FR* Michel Simon, Arletty; **D:** Jean Boyer. *FRA, FCT*

Circuit Breaker 🎞½ 1996 (R)
Traveling repairman Foster Carver (Bernsen) and his wife (Harris) encounter a broken-down spaceship with a lone survivor (Grieco). Then they discover he's a cyborg trying to create a new breed of humans. It's "Dead Calm" in space without the talent or suspense and with a whiny would-be heroine and some boring action sequences. **CW:** Strong sexuality, sci-fi violence and some language. **88m/C VHS.** Richard Grieco, Corbin Bernsen, Lara Harris, Edie McClurg; **D:** Victoria Musspratt; **W:** Victoria Musspratt. *NHO*

Circuitry Man 🎞🎞½ 1990 (R)
Post-apocolyptic saga of future American life as a woman tries to deliver a briefcase full of computer chips to the underground Big Apple. Along the way she runs into Plughead, a humanoid with electrical outlets that allow him to "plug in" to other people's fantasies. Intelligent retelling of a standard tale with an inspired soundtrack by Deborah Holland. Witty and original. **85m/C VHS, LV, Letterbox.** Jim Metzler, Dana Wheeler-Nicholson, Lu Leonard, Vernon Wells, Barbara Alyn Woods, Dennis Christopher; **D:** Steven Lovy; **W:** Steven Lovy; **M:** Deborah Holland. *COL*

Circumstances Unknown 🎞½ 1995 (R)
Paul Kinsey (Nelson) is a serial killer who drowns his victims, including a woman who happens to be the fiance of his friend Tim (Moses). Years later, Tim has married and Paul decides to stalk him and wife Deena (Glasser). Too many loose ends since you never know why Paul kills. Based on the novel by Jonellen Heckler. **CW:** Some violence/terror. **91m/C VHS, Beta, Closed Caption.** Judd Nelson, Isabel Glasser, William R. Moses; **D:** Robert Lewis; **W:** Thomas Hood, Emily Shoemaker; **C:** Bruce Worrall. *PAR*

Circumstantial Evidence 🎞🎞 1935
Newspaper reporter (Chandler) goes to extremes for a story and nearly dies as a result. Chandler sets it up to look like he's murdered a colleague, and he's tried and convicted on, you guessed it, circumstantial evidence. The colleague's then supposed to come forward but there's a problem. **69m/B VHS.** Chick Chandler, Shirley Grey, Dorothy Revier, Arthur Vinton; **D:** Charles Lamont; **W:** Ewart Adamson. *SNC*

The Circus 🎞🎞🎞½ 1919
Classic comedy silent details the tramp's exploits as a member of a traveling circus, including a romance with the bareback rider. Hilarious, less sentimental than most of Chaplin's feature films. Chaplin won a special Academy Award for "versatility and genius in writing, acting, directing and producing" for this one. Outrageous final scenes. **105m/B VHS, Closed Caption.** Charlie Chaplin, Merna Kennedy; **D:** Charlie Chaplin. Nominations: Academy Awards '28: Best Actor (Chaplin), Best Director (Chaplin). *FOX*

Circus Angel 🎞🎞🎞 1965
The renowned director of "The Red Balloon" creates a fantasy about a klutzy burglar transformed by a found nightgown into an angel. He begins to serve the dreams and actions of an odd lot of characters. Subtitled in English. **80m/C VHS, Beta.** *FR* Philippe Avron, Mirielle Negre; **D:** Albert Lamorisse. *NLC*

Circus of Fear 🎞½ Psycho-Circus 1967
A travelling troupe is stalked by a murderer. The unedited version is occasionally scary. **92m/C VHS, Beta.** *GB GE* Christopher Lee, Leo Genn, Anthony Newlands, Heinz Drache, Eddi Arent, Klaus Kinski, Margaret Lee, Suzy Kendall; **D:** John Llewellyn Moxey. *INC, SNC, NOS*

Circus of Horrors 🎞🎞½ 1960
Nip 'n' tuck horror about a plastic surgeon who takes over a circus to escape a disfigured patient bent on revenge. The circus is staffed by former patients with new faces who, one by one, fall victim in fine circus style. A bloody one-ring extravaganza. **87m/C VHS, Beta.** *GB* Donald Pleasence, Anton Diffring, Erika Remberg, Yvonne Monlaur, Jane Hylton, Kenneth Griffith; **D:** Sidney Hayers; **W:** George L. Baxt. *REP*

Circus World 🎞🎞½ The Magnificent Showman 1964
A circus boss tries to navigate a reckless, romancing crew through a European tour while searching for aerialist he loved 15 years before and whose daughter he has reared. Too long and too familiar, but nonetheless well done with an excellent finale. **132m/C VHS, Beta, LV, Letterbox.** John Wayne, Rita Hayworth, Claudia Cardinale, Lloyd Nolan, Richard Conte; **D:** Henry Hathaway; **W:** Ben Hecht, James Edward Grant, Julian Zimet; **C:** Jack Hildyard. Golden Globe Awards '65: Best Song ("Circus World"). *NO*

The Cisco Kid 1950 Renaldo is the heroic Cisco, a do-gooder who, with his sidekick Pancho, championed the poor and downtrodden. The first TV series shown in color. Features two episodes: "Quarterhorse" and "The Postmaster." Additional episodes are available. **60m/C VHS.** Duncan Renaldo, Leo Carrillo. *HEG, MOV*

The Cisco Kid ✓✓½ 1994 The Cisco Kid and his sidekick Pancho went from O. Henry's short story, to silent movies, talkies, a '50s TV series, and now this made for TV movie. Benito Juarez is leading an uprising to overthrow the French-backed Emperor Maximilian in 1867 Mexico. Cisco's (Smits) supplying the rebels with guns while carrying on romantic escapades (watch for the tango). Meanwhile, true-believer Pancho tries to convince his friend to become a revolutionary. Light-hearted with pedestrian action shots. Filmed on location in Mexico. **96m/C VHS, LV, Closed Caption.** Jimmy Smits, Richard "Cheech" Marin, Sadie Frost, Tim Thomerson, Bruce Payne; **D:** Luis Valdez; **W:** Michael Kane, Luis Valdez. *TTC*

The Citadel ✓✓✓ 1938 From the A.J. Cronin novel, the intelligent and honest Hollywood drama about a young British doctor who is morally corrupted by his move from a poor mining village to a well-off practice treating wealthy hypochondriacs. Somewhat hokey but still consistently entertaining, with Donat fine in the lead. **114m/C VHS, Beta.** GB Robert Donat, Rosalind Russell, Rex Harrison, Ralph Richardson, Emlyn Williams, Penelope Dudley Ward; **D:** King Vidor; **C:** Harry Stradling. New York Film Critics Awards '38: Best Film; Nominations: Academy Awards '38: Best Actor (Donat), Best Director (Vidor), Best Picture, Best Screenplay. *MGM, HMV*

Citizen Cohn ✓✓ 1992 (R) An appallingly fascinating look at a human monster. Told in hallucinatory flashbacks, as he lays dying from AIDS, Roy Cohn is a lawyer and power broker, probably best-remembered as the malevolent sidekick to Communist-hunting Senator Joseph McCarthy. But his contempt also extended to antisemitism and gay-bashing (though Cohn was both homosexual and Jewish), and his past comes, literally, back to haunt him. Woods does an exceptional job in bringing this sociopathic heel to wretched life. Adapted from the biography by Nicholas von Hoffman. Made for cable television. **CW:** Strong language. **112m/C VHS, LV, Closed Caption.** James Woods, Joe Don Baker, Joseph Bologna, Ed Flanders, Frederic Forrest, Lee Grant, Pat Hingle; **D:** Frank Pierson; **W:** David Franzoni; **C:** Paul Elliott. *HBO, BTV*

Citizen Kane ✓✓✓✓ 1941 Extraordinary film is an American tragedy of a newspaper tycoon (based loosely on William Randolph Hearst) from his humble beginnings to the solitude of his final years. One of the greatest films ever made—a stunning tour-de-force in virtually every aspect, from the fragmented narration to breathtaking, deep-focus cinematography; from a vivid soundtrack to fabulous ensemble acting. Welles was only 25 when he co-wrote, directed, and starred in this masterpiece. Three-disc laser edition was reproduced from a superior negative and features liner notes and running commentary from film historian Robert J. Carringer. Watch for Ladd and O'Connell as reporters. **119m/B VHS, Beta, LV, 8mm, Closed Caption.** Orson Welles, Joseph Cotten, Everett Sloane, Dorothy Comingore, Ruth Warrick, George Coulouris, Ray Collins, William Alland, Paul Stewart, Erskine Sanford, Agnes Moorehead, Alan Ladd, Gus Schilling, Philip Van Zandt, Harry Shannon, Sonny Bupp, Arthur O'Connell; **D:** Orson Welles; **W:** Orson Welles, Herman J. Mankiewicz; **C:** Gregg Toland; **M:** Bernard Herrmann. Academy Awards '41: Best Original Screenplay, National Film Registry '89'; New York Film Critics Awards '41: Best Film; Nominations: Academy Awards '41: Best Actor (Welles), Best Black and White Cinematography, Best Director (Welles), Best Film Editing, Best Interior Decoration, Best Picture, Best Sound, Best Original Dramatic/Comedy Score. *CRC, FCT, TTC*

Citizen Ruth ✓✓½ *Precious; Meet Ruth Stoops* 1996 (R) Glue-sniffing, pregnant Ruth Stoops (Dern) has already borne four children and been declared an unfit mother. In trouble again, Ruth's quietly told it's in her best interests to get an abortion but a couple (Smith and Place) from the pro-life community bail her out and give her a place to stay, while the group uses her as a propaganda symbol. Added to the commotion is a smarmy televangelist (Reynolds) and tough pro-choice Diane (Kurtz), who manages to get Ruth to stay with her while Ruth ineffectually tries to get some control over her wayward life. Doesn't take sides—both the pro-choice and pro-life camps are tweaked, with neither willing to compromise. **CW:** Substance abuse, strong language and a sex scene. **104m/C VHS, LV, Closed Caption.** Laura Dern, Swoosie Kurtz, Mary Kay Place, Kurtwood Smith, Kelly Preston, Burt Reynolds, M.C. Gainey, Kenneth Mars, Kathleen Noone, David Graf, Tippi Hedren, Alicia Witt, Diane Ladd; **D:** Alexander Payne; **W:** Alexander Payne, Jim Taylor; **C:** James Glennon; **M:** Rolfe Kent. Montreal World Film Festival '95: Best Actress (Dern). *TOU*

Citizen X ✓✓✓ 1995 (R) Based on the true story of '80s Russian serial killer Andrei Chikatilo (DeMunn) and his 52 victims. Viktor Burakov (Rea) is a beleaguered rural forensics expert who is blatantly told by party officials that the Soviet state does not have serial killers—in spite of a rising body count. His only ally is Col. Fetisov (Sutherland), who's adept at political maneuvering, but it takes the duo eight frustrating years to bring the grisly killer to justice. Fine performances highlight a literate script from Robert Cullen's book "The Killer Department." Filmed on location in Budapest, Hungary. Made for cable television. **CW:** Strong, graphic violence and related language. **100m/C VHS.** Stephen Rea, Donald Sutherland, Jeffrey DeMunn, John Wood, Joss Ackland, Max von Sydow, Ralph Nossek, Imelda Staunton; **D:** Chris Gerolmo; **W:** Chris Gerolmo; **C:** Robert Fraisse; **M:** Randy Edelman. *HBO*

Citizens Band ✓✓✓ *Handle With Care* 1977 (PG) Episodic, low-key comedy about people united by their CB use in a midwestern community. Notable performance from Clark as a soft-voiced guide for truckers passing through. Demme's first comedy is characteristically idiosyncratic. **98m/C VHS, Beta.** Paul LeMat, Candy Clark, Ann Wedgeworth, Roberts Blossom, Charles Napier, Marcia Rodd, Bruce McGill, Ed Begley Jr., Alix Elias; **D:** Jonathan Demme; **W:** Paul Brickman; **C:** Jordan Cronenweth; **M:** Bill Conti. National Society of Film Critics Awards '77: Best Supporting Actress (Wedgeworth). *PAR*

The City ✓ 1976 Police desperately search for a psychotic determined to kill a country singer. He shouldn't be too hard to find. Made for television. **78m/C VHS, Beta.** Don Johnson, Robert Forster, Ward Costello, Jimmy Dean, Mark Hamill; **D:** Harvey Hart. *WOV*

The City and the Dogs ✓✓✓ *La Ciudad y los Perros* 1985 A brutal, cynical adaptation of Mario Vargas Llosa's novel. A young military recruit rebels against the authority establishments around him. In Spanish with English subtitles. **135m/C VHS, Beta.** SP **D:** Francisco J. Lombardi Pery. *FCT*

City Boy ✓✓✓ 1993 At the turn of the century the orphaned Nick makes his way from Chicago to the Pacific Northwest in search of his natural father. He takes a job guarding Limberlost, a valuable old-growth forest, from thieves and is torn between the ideals of two new friends. His mentor Tom sees the forest as timber that will build homes and provide jobs, while Angelica sees the forest as an irreplaceable sanctuary. Filmed on location in Vancouver, British Columbia. Adaptation of "Freckles" by Gene Stratton Porter. **120m/C VHS, Closed Caption.** GB CA Christian Campbell, James Brolin, Sarah Chalke, Wendel Meldrum, Christopher Bolton; **D:** John Kent Harrison; **W:** John Kent Harrison. *BTV, HMV*

City for Conquest ✓✓✓ 1940 Two lovers go their separate ways to pursue individual careers. He attempts to become a boxing champ, but is blinded in the ring and ends up selling newspapers. She takes a shot at a dancing career but hooks up with an unscrupulous partner. Will the ill-fated pair find happiness again? **101m/B VHS, Beta.** James Cagney, Ann Sheridan, Frank Craven, Donald Crisp, Arthur Kennedy, Frank McHugh, George Tobias, Anthony Quinn, Blanche Yurka, Elia Kazan, Bob Steele; **D:** Anatole Litvak; **C:** James Wong Howe; **M:** Max Steiner. *MGM, CCB*

City Girl ✓✓½ *Our Daily Bread* 1930 Friedrich Murnau, who directed the silent vampire classic "Nosferatu," was removed from the director's chair before "City Girl" was completed and it shows. But so do the marks of his inimitable camera direction. The story concerns a Minnesota grain grower who visits the Windy City and returns with a waitress as his wife. Frustratingly inconsistent, leading you to wonder what could have been had Murnau remained behind the camera (he died the following year). Silent. **90m/B VHS, Beta.** Charles Farrell, Mary Duncan; **D:** F.W. Murnau. *GPV, FCT*

City Hall ✓✓✓ 1995 (R) Investigating the deaths of a heroic cop, a drug dealer, and six-year old boy in a shoot-out, idealistic deputy mayor Cusack uncovers a web of corruption and deceit in the Big Apple. Pacino excels as charismatic mayor John Pappas by showing the crafty string-puller behind the glossy image of the modern politico. Supporting cast is also strong, including Aiello as a Rodgers and Hammerstein-loving Brooklyn boss, and Fonda as the police union lawyer and standard issue love interest. Screenplay was conceived by Ken Lipper, who was once deputy mayor under Ed Koch, but the involvement of three other scripters causes confusion over what type of picture it's aiming to be. Cash-strapped New York rented its actual city hall out for filming at a price of $50,000. **CW:** Language and some violence. **111m/C VHS, LV, Closed Caption.** Al Pacino, John Cusack, Bridget Fonda, Danny Aiello, David Paymer, Martin Landau, Anthony (Tony) Franciosa, Lindsay Duncan, Nestor Serrano, Mel Winkler, Richard Schiff; **D:** Harold Becker; **W:** Paul Schrader, Nicholas Pileggi, Bo Goldman, Ken Lipper; **C:** Michael Seresin; **M:** Jerry Goldsmith. *COL*

City Heat ✓✓½ 1984 (PG) A hardnosed cop and a plucky private eye berate each other while opposing the mob in this overdone comedy. Both Eastwood and Reynolds spoof their screen personas, but the results are only slightly satisfactory. Good back-up, though, from Alexander and Kahn as the dames. Screenplay written by Blake Edwards under the pseudonym Sam O. Brown. **98m/C VHS, Beta, LV, Closed Caption.** Clint Eastwood, Burt Reynolds, Jane Alexander, Irene Cara, Madeline Kahn, Richard Roundtree, Rip Torn, Tony LoBianco, William Sanderson; **D:** Richard Benjamin; **W:** Blake Edwards; **M:** Lennie Niehaus. *WAR*

City in Fear ✓✓✓ 1980 Stellar cast lights up a made-for-television drama about a tired newspaper columnist (Janssen) who communicates directly with a murdering psychotic (Rourke), as publisher Vaughn applauds and hypes. Rourke's first role, Janssen's last, and Smithee is actually Jud Taylor. **135m/C VHS, Beta.** David Janssen, Robert Vaughn, Mickey Rourke, William Daniels, Perry King, Susan Sullivan, William Prince; **D:** Alan Smithee. *ART, HHE*

City in Panic ✓ 1986 A detective and radio talk show host try to catch a psychotic mass murderer busy offing homosexuals throughout the city. Violent with no redeeming social qualities. **85m/C VHS, Beta.** Dave Adamson, Ed Chester, Leeann Westegard; **D:** Robert Bouvier. *TWE*

City Killer ✓ 1987 A lunatic tries to blackmail the girl he loves into going out on a few dates by committing huge destructive acts of inner-city terrorism (flowers won't do). Made for television. **120m/C VHS, Beta.** Heather Locklear, Gerald McRaney,

Terence Knox, Peter Mark Richman, John Harkins; **D:** Robert Lewis.

City Lights 🐾🐾🐾🐾 1931 Masterpiece that was Chaplin's last silent film. The "Little Tramp" falls in love with a blind flower seller. A series of lucky accidents permits him to get the money she needs for a sight-restoring surgery. One of the most eloquent movies ever filmed, due to Chaplin's keen balance between comedy and tragedy. **86m/B VHS, Beta, LV.** Charlie Chaplin, Virginia Cherrill, Florence Lee, Hank Mann, Harry Myers, Henry Bergman, Jean Harlow; **D:** Charlie Chaplin. National Film Registry '91. FOX

City Limits 🐾 1985 **(PG-13)** In a post-apocalyptic city, gangs of young people on choppers clash. **85m/C VHS, Beta, LV.** John Stockwell, Kim Cattrall, Darrell Larson, Rae Dawn Chong, Robby Benson, James Earl Jones, Jennifer Balgobin; **D:** Aaron Lipstadt. VES, ART, HHE

City of Angels 🐾🐾½ 1998 **(PG-13)** Weepy American remake of Wim Wenders' "Wings of Desire" finds guardian angel Seth (Cage) falling in love with heart surgeon Maggie (Ryan) and then trying to decide whether he wants to become mortal in order to join her. Subtle, it is not. Cage does his doe-eyed best to convey Seth's longing and innocence to earthly ways, and the chemistry with Ryan really clicks. Overly sappy and sentimental, especially near the end, but that won't stop the intended audience from loving it. Big Hollywood flick that wears its art-house aspirations on its sleeve.**CW:** Sexuality including language, and some nudity. **117m/C VHS.** Nicolas Cage, Meg Ryan, Andre Braugher, Dennis Franz, Colm Feore, Robin Bartlett, Joanna Merlin; **D:** Brad Silberling; **W:** Dana Stevens; **C:** John Seale; **M:** Gabriel Yared. NYR

City of Blood 🐾🐾½ 1988 **(R)** A South African doctor is embroiled in mystery with racial overtones when prostitutes are being killed with a spiked club. Packaged as a horror film, this movie actually deals with the questions of South African racial tensions in a sophisticated, ultimately tragic manner. **96m/C VHS, Beta.** SA Joe Stewardson, Ian Yule, Susan Coetzer; **D:** Darrell Roodt. NO

City of Hope 🐾🐾🐾 1991 **(R)** The picture that "Bonfire of the Vanities" wanted to be, an eventful few days in the fictional metropolis of Hudson: an ugly racial incident threatens to snowball, the corrupt mayor pushes a shady real-estate deal, and a botched robbery has profound implications. Some of the subplots resolve too easily, but this cynical, crazy-quilt of urban life is worthy of comparison with "American Graffiti" and "Nashville" as pure Americana.**CW:** Strong language and one sensual scene. **132m/C VHS, LV, 8mm, Closed Caption.** Vincent Spano, Tony LoBianco, Joe Morton, Todd Graff, David Strathairn, Anthony John Denison, Barbara Williams, Angela Bassett, Gloria Foster, Lawrence Tierney, John Sayles, Maggie Renzi, Kevin Tighe, Chris Cooper, Jace Alexander, Frankie Faison, Michael Mantell, Josh Mostel, Joe Grifasi, Louis Zorich, Gina Gershon, Rose Gregorio, Bill Raymond, Maeve Kinkead, Ray Aranha; **D:** John Sayles; **W:** John Sayles; **C:** Robert Richardson; **M:** Mason Daring. Independent Spirit Awards '92: Best Supporting Actor (Strathairn). COL

City of Industry 🐾🐾 1996 **(R)** Efficient contemporary noir that doesn't always live up to its promise. Old pro thief Roy Egan (Keitel), now retired, is drawn into the final jewel heist of his younger brother, Lee (Hutton), who's also vowed to get out of the game. Unfortunately for him, Lee's picked one wrong partner in volatile wheelman Skip Kovich (Ulrich). When the violent Skip decides he doesn't want to share the goods it starts an elaborate cat-and-mouse hunt through the seedier sides of L.A.**CW:** Strong language, violence and some sexuality. **97m/C VHS, LV, Closed Caption.** Harvey Keitel, Stephen Dorff, Famke Janssen, Timothy Hutton, Michael Jai White, Wade Dominguez, Reno Wilson; **D:** John Irvin; **W:** Ken Solarz; **C:** Thomas Burstyn; **M:** Stephen Endelman. ORI

City of Joy 🐾🐾 1992 **(PG-13)** Disillusioned American heart surgeon Swayze flees to India after losing a patient. In Calcutta he is beaten by a street gang and loses his money and passport, but finds help from a farmer (Puri) who takes him to a nearby clinic in the City of Joy, one of Calcutta's poorest areas. Collins runs the clinic and recruits the reluctant doctor, who undergoes a life-changing transformation. The squalor of Calcutta is shown, but the city's portrayal as a magical place where problems miraculously disappear is unrealistic. Swayze lacks the emotional range for his part, but Collins and Puri are excellent in their roles. Adapted from the book by Dominique Lapierre. **134m/C VHS, LV, Letterbox.** GB FR Patrick Swayze, Pauline Collins, Om Puri, Shabana Azmi, Art Malik, Ayesha Dharker, Santu Chowdhury, Imran Badsah Khan, Shyamanand Jalan; **Cameos:** Sam Wanamaker; **D:** Roland Joffe; **W:** Mark Medoff; **C:** Peter Biziou; **M:** Ennio Morricone. COL

The City of Lost Children 🐾🐾🐾 La Cite des Enfants Perdus 1995 **(R)** Weird not-for-the-kiddies fairytale finds crazed inventor Krank (Emilfork) getting his evil one-eyed minions, the appropriately named Cyclops, to kidnap local children so that he can steal their dreams (because Krank himself is incapable of dreaming). The latest victim is young Denree (Lucien), the adopted brother of sideshow strongman One (Perlman), who single-mindedly pursues a way to get Denree back—aided by nine-year-old feral child Miette (Vittet) and a band of orphan thieves. Freaks galore with avant-garde designer Jean-Paul Gaultier in charge of costumes. French with subtitles or dubbed.**CW:** Disturbing and grotesque images of violence and menace. **114m/C VHS, LV, Closed Caption.** FR Ron Perlman, Daniel Emilfork, Joseph Lucien, Judith Vittet, Dominique Pinon, Jean Claude Dreyfus, Odile Mallet, Genevieve Brunet, Mireille Mosse; **D:** Jean-Pierre Jeunet, Marc Caro; **W:** Jean-Pierre Jeunet, Marc Caro, Gilles Adrien; **C:** Darius Khondji; **M:** Angelo Badalamenti; **V:** Jean-Louis Trintignant. Cesar Awards '96: Best Art Direction/Set Decoration; Nominations: Cesar Awards '96: Best Cinematography, Best Costume Design, Best Score; Independent Spirit Awards '96: Best Foreign Film. COL

City of Shadows 🐾🐾 1986 **(R)** Twins separated at birth are reunited by a criminal mind with evil intentions. Double trouble? **97m/C VHS, Beta.** John P. Ryan, Paul Coufos, Tony Rosato; **D:** David Mitchell; **M:** Tangerine Dream. VTR

City of the Walking Dead 🐾 Nightmare City; Nightmare 1983 Eco-misery as a community must contend with prowling, radiation-zapped zombies who enjoy chewing through human flesh. **92m/C VHS.** IT SP Mel Ferrer, Hugo Stiglitz, Laura Trotter, Francesco Rabal; **D:** Umberto Lenzi. NO

City of Women 🐾🐾 1981 **(R)** Visually stunning, but otherwise thin fantasy/drama about a man smothered with women. A journalist wanders through a feminist theme park replete with a roller rink and screening room. Some worthwhile adventures are mixed in with rather dull stretches. Not among the best from either Mastroianni, who is under utilized, or Fellini, who here seems incapable of separating good ideas from bad. Plenty of buxom babes, but otherwise undistinguished. In Italian with English subtitles. **140m/C VHS, Beta.** IT Marcello Mastroianni, Ettore Manni, Anna Prucnall, Bernice Stegers; **D:** Federico Fellini; **W:** Federico Fellini; **C:** Giuseppe Rotunno; **M:** Luis Bacalov. NYF, FCT

City on Fire woof! 1978 **(R)** An arsonist starts a fire that could engulf an entire city. Flaming bore. **101m/C VHS, Beta.** CA Barry Newman, Susan Clark, Shelley Winters, Leslie Nielsen, Henry Fonda, Ava Gardner; **D:** Alvin Rakoff.

City Slickers 🐾🐾🐾 1991 **(PG-13)** Three men with mid-life crises leave New York City for a cattle-ranch vacation that turns into an arduous, character-building stint. Many funny moments supplied by leads Crystal, Stern, and Kirby, but Palance steals the film as a salty, wise cowpoke. Slater is fetching as the lone gal vacationer on the cattle drive. Boxoffice winner notable for a realis-

tic calf birthing scene, one of few in cinema history. From an idea by Crystal, who also produced. Palance stole the show from Oscar ceremonies host Crystal a second time when he accepted his award and suddenly started doing one-arm push-ups, startling the audience into laughter. **114m/C VHS, Beta, LV, 8mm, Letterbox, Closed Caption.** Billy Crystal, Daniel Stern, Bruno Kirby, Patricia Wettig, Helen Slater, Jack Palance, Noble Willingham, Tracey Walter, Josh Mostel, David Paymer, Bill Henderson, Jeffrey Tambor, Phill Lewis, Kyle Secor, Yeardley Smith, Jayne Meadows; **D:** Ron Underwood; **W:** Lowell Ganz, Babaloo Mandel; **C:** Dean Semler; **M:** Marc Shaiman. Academy Awards '91: Best Supporting Actor (Palance); Golden Globe Awards '92: Best Supporting Actor (Palance); MTV Movie Awards '92: Best Comedic Performance (Crystal). COL, NLC

City Slickers 2: The Legend of Curly's Gold 🐾🐾½ 1994 **(PG-13)** Mid-life crisis meets the wild west, part deux. Crystal and his fellow urban dudes discover a treasure map in the hat of departed trail boss Curly and decide to go a-huntin'. Palance is back as Curly's seafarin', equally cantankerous, twin brother. Lovitz occupies the screen as Crystal's ne'er-do-well brother, replacing sidekick Bruno Kirby. A bit of a rehash, formulaic and occasionally straining for a punchline, it's still pretty darn funny, especially when the boys start to improvise.**CW:** Off-color humor and comic sex scene. **116m/C VHS, LV, Closed Caption.** Billy Crystal, Daniel Stern, Jon Lovitz, Jack Palance, Patricia Wettig, Pruitt Taylor Vince, Bill McKinney, Lindsay Crystal, Noble Willingham, David Paymer, Josh Mostel; **D:** Paul Weiland; **W:** Billy Crystal, Lowell Ganz, Babaloo Mandel; **M:** Marc Shaiman. COL

City That Never Sleeps 🐾🐾½ 1953 A Chicago cop must decide whether or not to run off with an entertainer, or continue his life with his family. Decisions, decisions. Moody but dated melodrama that's finely acted and indecisively directed, with good use of dim city lights. Nothing new here. **90m/B VHS.** Gig Young, Mala Powers, Edward Arnold, Paula Raymond, Chill Wills, Marie Windsor; **D:** John H. Auer. REP

City Unplugged 🐾🐾 Darkness in Tallinn 1995 Heist film with some twists. $970 million in gold, in Paris for safekeeping since WWII, has been returned to the treasury in the newly independent Republic of Estonia. The thieves, who belong to the Russian mob, plan to cut all electricity in the capital city of Tallinn, break into the bank, and move the gold to a nearby cigarette factory where it can be melted down and repackaged as cigarettes. The mob's use of local electrician Toivo proves to be their undoing in a comedy of errors. Estonian with subtitles. **99m/C VHS.** Peter Oja, Ivo Uukkivi, Milena Gulbe, Monika Mager; **D:** Ilkka Jarvilaturi; **W:** Paul Kolsby; **C:** Rein Kotov. LEO

City Without Men 🐾½ 1943 Melodramatic story about a boarding house near a prison where the women tenants await the release of their imprisoned men. Little plot, no suspense. **75m/B VHS, Beta.** Linda Darnell, Sara Allgood, Michael Duane, Edgar Buchanan, Leslie Brooks, Glenda Farrell, Margaret Hamilton, Sheldon Leonard; **D:** Sidney Salkow. RXM

The City's Edge 🐾½ 1983 A young man becomes involved with the mysterious residents of a boarding house on the edge of the ocean. **86m/C VHS, Beta.** AU Mark Lee; **D:** Ken Quinnell. MGM

Civil War Diary Across Five Aprils 1990 Too young to go to war, a young man struggles for the survival of his family amidst harsh winters, the devastation of the Civil War and his own personal nightmares. Winner of the International Heritage Award in 1990. Based on the Newberry Award winning young people's novel "Across Five Aprils." **82m/C VHS.** RHI

The Civil War, Episode 1: The Cause—1861 1990 The blowout PBS hit mini-series, five years in the making by author and filmmaker Ken Burns, is a staggering historical achievement. Episode 1 focuses on the causes of the Civil War from the schism created by Lincoln's election, John Brown's assault on

Harper's Ferry, and the firing on Fort Sumpter. Also available as a set for $179.95. **99m/C VHS, Closed Caption. D:** Ken Burns; **W:** Ken Burns. WAR, SIG, PBS

The Civil War, Episode 2: A Very Bloody Affair—1862 🎞🎞🎞 1990 Second in the enormously popular PBS series looks at the unexpectedly extreme costs in human life of the War Between the States. **69m/C VHS, Closed Caption. D:** Ken Burns; **W:** Ken Burns. WAR, SIG, PBS

The Civil War, Episode 3: Forever Free—1862 🎞🎞🎞 1990 Third volume in the PBS Emmy-nominated mini-series covers Antietam, Robert E. Lee and Stonewall Jackson planning Confederate strategy, and Lincoln's decision to free the slaves. **76m/C VHS, Closed Caption. D:** Ken Burns; **W:** Ken Burns. WAR, SIG, PBS

The Civil War, Episode 4: Simply Murder—1863 🎞🎞🎞 1990 Union forces meet disaster at Fredericksburg, and Gen. Lee wins a victory but loses Stonewall Jackson in the fourth episode of the Emmy-nominated PBS mini-series. **62m/C VHS, Closed Caption. D:** Ken Burns; **W:** Ken Burns. WAR, SIG, PBS

The Civil War, Episode 5: The Universe of Battle—1863 🎞🎞🎞🎞 1990 Gettysburg, the battleground which claimed 150,000 American lives, is examined in the 5th episode of the Emmy-nominated PBS mini-series. **95m/C VHS, Closed Caption. D:** Ken Burns; **W:** Ken Burns. WAR, SIG, PBS

The Civil War, Episode 6: Valley of the Shadow of Death—1864 🎞🎞🎞 1990 Profiles of Grant and Lee are offered, plus Sherman's assault on Atlanta, in this volume from the Emmy-nominated PBS mini-series. **70m/C VHS, Closed Caption. D:** Ken Burns; **W:** Ken Burns. WAR, SIG, PBS

The Civil War, Episode 7: Most Hallowed Ground—1864 🎞🎞🎞🎞 1990 The nation re-elects Abraham Lincoln, and the North turns General Lee's mansion into Arlington National Cemetery in this episode of the Emmy-nominated PBS mini-series. **72m/C VHS, Closed Caption. D:** Ken Burns; **W:** Ken Burns. WAR, SIG, PBS

The Civil War, Episode 8: War Is All Hell—1865 🎞🎞🎞🎞 1990 Sherman marches to the sea and Lee surrenders to Grant in this episode from the Emmy-nominated PBS mini-series. **69m/C VHS, Closed Caption. D:** Ken Burns; **W:** Ken Burns. WAR, SIG, PBS

The Civil War, Episode 9: The Better Angels of Our Nature—1865 🎞🎞🎞🎞 1990 In this final episode of the Emmy-nominated PBS mini-series, Lincoln's assasination is examined, and the central characters of the war are summarized. **68m/C VHS, Closed Caption. D:** Ken Burns; **W:** Ken Burns. WAR, SIG, PBS

Civilization 🎞🎞🎞 1916 A silent epic about the horrors and immorality of war as envisioned by the ground-breaking film pioneer Ince, who was later murdered. Famous scene involves Christ walking through body-ridden battlefields. **80m/B VHS, Beta.** Howard Hickman, Enid Markey, Lola May; **D:** Thomas Ince, Reginald Barker, Raymond B. West. GPV, VYY, GVV

Claire of the Moon 🎞🎞 1992 Famous satirist Claire goes to a women writers retreat in the Pacific Northwest where she's assigned a room with Noel, a solemn sex therapist. Noel's recovering from a disasterous love affair while Claire is promiscuous and unwilling to commit. Inspite of their differences, the two women find themselves drawn together. Too many philosophical debates slow the story down but the gentle romance works well. **102m/C VHS, Closed Caption.** Trisha Todd, Karen Trumbo, Faith McDevitt, Damon Craig; **D:** Nicole Conn; **W:** Nicole Conn; **M:** Michael Allen Harrison. FXL, FCT, BTV

Claire's Knee 🎞🎞🎞½ 1971 A grown man about to be married goes on a holiday and develops a fixation on a young girl's knee. Another of Rohmer's Moral Tales exploring sexual and erotic obsessions. Lots of talk, little else. You'll either find it fascinating or fail to watch more than 10 minutes. Most, however, consider it a classic. Sophisticated dialogue, lovely visions of summer on Lake Geneva. In French with English subtitles. **105m/C VHS, Beta, LV.** *FR* Jean-Claude Brialy, Aurora Cornu, Beatrice Romand; **D:** Eric Rohmer; **C:** Nestor Almendros. National Society of Film Critics Awards '71: Best Film. FCT

Clambake 🎞 1967 Noxious Elvis vehicle about a rich man's son who wants success on his own terms, so he trades places with a water-skiing teacher. Inane, even in comparison to other Elvis ventures. ♫Clambake; The Girl I Never Loved; Hey, Hey, Hey; Confidence; Who Needs Money?; A House That Has Everything. **98m/C VHS, Beta.** Elvis Presley, Shelley Fabares, Bill Bixby, James Gregory, Gary Merrill, Will Hutchins, Harold Peary; **D:** Arthur Nadel. MGM

The Clan of the Cave Bear 🎞½ 1986 (R) A scrawny cavegirl is taken in by Neanderthals after her own parents are killed. Hannah is lifeless as a primitive gamine, and the film is similarly DOA. Ponderous and only unintentionally funny. Based on the popular novel by Jean M. Auel. **100m/C VHS, Beta, LV, Closed Caption.** Daryl Hannah, James Remar, Pamela Reed, John Doolittle, Thomas G. Waites; **D:** Michael Chapman; **W:** John Sayles; **C:** Jan De Bont; **M:** Alan Silvestri. Nominations: Academy Awards '86: Best Makeup. FOX

Clara's Heart 🎞 1988 (PG-13) A Jamaican maid enriches the lives of her insufferable, bourgeois employers and their particularly repellent son. A kinder, gentler waste of film and Goldberg; sentimental clap-trap which occasionally lapses into comedy. **108m/C VHS, Beta, LV, Closed Caption.** Whoopi Goldberg, Michael Ontkean, Kathleen Quinlan, Neil Patrick Harris, Spalding Gray, Beverly Todd, Hattie Winston; **D:** Robert Mulligan; **W:** Mark Medoff; **M:** Dave Grusin. WAR, FCT

Clarence 🎞🎞½ 1991 (G) Clarence, the benevolent angel from the classic "It's a Wonderful Life" is back, risking his wings for a beautiful young woman. Made for cable. **92m/C VHS, Closed Caption.** Robert Carradine, Kate Trotter; **D:** Eric Till; **W:** Lorne Cameron. REP

Clarence Darrow 🎞🎞🎞 1978 Riveting one-man stage performance shot for television and based on Darrow's writings, adapted from the play by Irving Stone. **81m/C VHS, Beta, LV.** Henry Fonda; **D:** John Rich. KAR, IME

Clarence, the Cross-eyed Lion 🎞🎞🎞 1965 Follows the many adventures of a cross-eyed lion and his human compatriots. Great family viewing from the creator of "Flipper." **98m/C VHS.** Marshall Thompson, Betsy Drake, Richard Haydn, Cheryl Miller, Rockne Tarkington, Maurice Marsac; **D:** Andrew Marton; **W:** Alan Caillou. MGM, FCT

Clark & McCullough 🎞🎞½ 1933 The zany duo, a hit in burlesque and night clubs, transferred some of their crazy antics onto film. Their comedy shorts include "Fits in a Fiddle" (1933), "Love and Kisses" (1934), "Alibi Bye Bye" (1935), and a rehearsal of "Mademoiselle from New Rochelle" from "Strike Up the Band" (with George Gershwin on piano). **53m/B VHS, Beta.** Bobby Clark, Paul McCullough, George Gershwin, James Finlayson. GVV, DVT, VYY

Clash by Night 🎞🎞🎞½ 1952 A wayward woman marries a fisherman, then beds his best friend. Seamy storyline is exploited to the hilt by master filmmaker Lang. An utterly unflinching melodrama. Early Monroe shines in a supporting role too. Based on the Clifford Odets play. **105m/B VHS.** Barbara Stanwyck, Paul Douglas, Marilyn Monroe, Robert Ryan, J. Carrol Naish; **D:** Fritz Lang. TTC

Clash of the Ninja 🎞½ 1986 Evil Occidental ninja runs medical smuggling operation. Interpol ninja sets out to stop him. Wild ninja nonsense includes ninja with rotating head and exploding ninja. Dubbed poorly. **90m/C VHS, Beta.** *HK* Paul Torcha, Louis Roth, Eric Neff, Bernie Junker, Joe Redner, Klaus Mutter, Eddie Chan, Max Kwan, Tom Allen, Stanley Tong; **D:** Wallace Chan; **W:** Kurt Spielberg. TWE

Clash of the Titans WOOF! 1981 (PG) Mind-numbing fantasy derived from Greek legends about heroic Perseus, who slays the snakehaired Medusa and rescues a semi-clad maiden from the monstrous Kraken. Wooden Hamlin plays Perseus and fares better than more accomplished Olivier and Smith, who seem in need of enemas as they lurch about Mt. Olympus. Only Bloom seems truly godlike in a supporting role. Some good, some wretched special effects from pioneer Harryhausen. **118m/C VHS, Beta, LV, Letterbox.** *GB* Laurence Olivier, Maggie Smith, Claire Bloom, Ursula Andress, Burgess Meredith, Harry Hamlin, Sian Phillips, Judi Bowker; **D:** Desmond Davis; **W:** Beverley Cross; **C:** Ted Moore. MGM, MLB

Class 🎞🎞 1983 (R) A prep school student discovers that his mother is the lover whom his roommate has bragged about. Lowe is serviceable as the stunned son of sexy Bisset, who woos McCarthy, even in an elevator. Too ludicrous to be enjoyed, but you may watch just to see what happens next. **98m/C VHS, Beta, LV.** Jacqueline Bisset, Rob Lowe, Andrew McCarthy, Cliff Robertson, John Cusack, Stuart Margolin, Casey Siemaszko; **D:** Lewis John Carlino; **M:** Elmer Bernstein. VES

Class Act 🎞🎞½ 1991 (PG-13) Rappers Kid 'N' Play team up once again in this role reversal comedy. A straight-laced brain and a partying, macho bully find their school records and identifications switched when they enroll in a new high school. This turns out to be good for the character of both young men, as the egghead learns to loosen up and the bully learns what it feels like to be respected for his ideas rather than a fierce reputation. Comedy is very uneven but the duo are energetic and likable. **98m/C VHS, LV, Letterbox.** Christopher Reid, Christopher Martin, Meshach Taylor, Karyn Parsons, Doug E. Doug, Rick Ducommun, Lamont Jackson, Rhea Perlman; **D:** Randall Miller; **M:** Vassal Benford. WAR

Class Action 🎞🎞🎞 1991 (R) 1960s versus 1990s ethics clash when a father and daughter, both lawyers, wind up on opposing sides of a litigation against an auto manufacturer. Hackman and Mastrantonio give intense, exciting performances, almost surmounting the melodramatic script. **110m/C VHS, Beta, LV, Closed Caption.** Mary Elizabeth Mastrantonio, Gene Hackman, Joanna Merlin, Colin Friels, Laurence "Larry" Fishburne, Donald Moffat, Jan Rubes, Matt Clark, Fred Dalton Thompson, Jonathan Silverman, Dan Hicks; **D:** Michael Apted; **W:** Samantha Shad, Christopher Ames; **M:** James Horner. FXL

Class of Fear 🎞½ 1991 (R) The new kid in school is having a particularly rough time. He's been framed for murdering a teacher and must prove his innocence before he winds up in prison. **105m/C VHS.** Julianne McNamara, Noah Blake. MOV

Class of '44 🎞½ 1973 (PG) The sequel to "Summer of '42" finds insufferable boys becoming insufferable men at miltary school. Worse than its predecessor, and notable only in that it is Candy's film debut. **95m/C VHS, Beta.** Gary Grimes, Jerry Houser, Oliver Conant, Deborah Winters, William Atherton, Sam Bottoms, John Candy; **D:** Paul Bogart; **M:** David Shire. WAR

The Class of Miss MacMichael 🎞🎞 1978 (R) A dedicated instructor inherits and ultimately inspires a class of high school misfits and malcontents. Derivative venture is beneath considerable talents of Jackson. Based on a novel by Sandy Hutson. **95m/C VHS, Beta, Closed Caption.** *GB* Glenda Jackson, Oliver Reed, Michael Murphy, Rosalind Cash; **D:** Silvio Narizzano; **W:** Judd Bernard. FOX

Class of 1004 woof! 1982 (R) Teacher King must face a motley crew of teenagers in the classroom. Ring leader and student psychopath Van Patten leads his groupies on a reign of terror through the high school halls, stopping to gang rape King's wife. Teacher attempts revenge. Bloody and thoughtless update of "Blackboard Jungle." Early Fox appearance. Followed by "Class of 1999." **93m/C VHS, Beta, LV.** *CA* Perry King, Roddy McDowall, Timothy Van Patten, Michael J. Fox, Merrie Lynn Ross, Stefan Arngrim, Al Waxman; *D:* Mark L. Lester; *W:* Mark L. Lester, Tom Holland; *M:* Lalo Schifrin. *VES*

Class of 1999 🎬 1990 (R) Freewheeling sci-fi set in the near future where teen gangs terrorize seemingly the entire country. A high school principal determines to enforce law and order by installing human-like robots with rocket launchers for arms. Violent, crude entertainment. Class dismissed. Sequel to "Class of 1984" and available in an unrated version. **98m/C VHS, Beta.** Bradley Gregg, Traci Lind, Malcolm McDowell, Stacy Keach, Patrick Kilpatrick, Pam Grier, John P. Ryan, Darren E. Burrows, Joshua Miller; *D:* Mark L. Lester; *W:* C. Courtney Joyner. *VES, ART*

Class of 1999 2: The Substitute 🎬½ 1993 (R) High school in 1999 is filled with violent gangs who murder at random. Enter substitute teacher John Bolen, who has his own ideas of discipline—leading to an even higher body count. John just doesn't seem human and when a CIA agent starts investigating, school may never be the same. **90m/C VHS, LV, Closed Caption.** Sasha Mitchell, Nick Cassavetes, Caitlin Dulany, Jack Knight, Gregory West, Rick Hill; *D:* Spiro Razatos; *W:* Mark Sevi. *THV*

Class of Nuke 'Em High 🎬½ 1986 (R) Team Troma once again experiments with the chemicals, with violent results. Jersey high school becomes a hotbed of mutants and maniacs after a nuclear spill occurs. Good teens Chrissy and Warren succumb, the school blows, life goes on. High camp, low budget, heavy gore. Followed by "Class of Nuke 'Em High Part 2." **84m/C VHS, Beta, DVD.** Janelle Brady, Gilbert Brenton, Robert Prichard; *D:* Richard W. Haines, Lloyd (Samuel Weil) Kaufman.

Class of Nuke 'Em High 2: Subhumanoid Meltdown 🎬 1991 (R) The Troma team brings us back into the world of the strange. In this adventure, the evil Nukamama Corporation holds secret experiments at their "college" and create sub-humanoids as slave labor, swelling unemployment and wrecking the economy. This does not fare too well with the rest of society, including our heroes Roger the reporter, Professor Holt, and the scantily clad sub-humanoid Victoria. *CW:* Language, nudity, comic horror violence and grossness, and sexuality. **96m/C VHS, Beta, LV, Closed Caption.** Lisa Gaye, Brick Bronsky, Leesa Rowland; *D:* Eric Louzil. *VTR*

Class of Nuke 'Em High 3: The Good, the Bad and the Subhumanoid woof! 1994 (R) Revisit Tromie the nuclear rodent and the other disaster-prone denizens of Tromaville, USA. Admire the classic good twin vs. evil subhumanoid twin plot as they battle against each other, aided by chicks with guns and tin undergarments. Supposedly inspired by Shakespeare's Comedy of Errors. Tip: stick to the BBC production for your senior thesis. *CW:* Gross presentation of sex, language, and gore. **95m/C VHS.** Brick Bronsky, Lisa Gaye, Lisa Star; *D:* Eric Louzil; *W:* Lloyd (Samuel Weil) Kaufman. *TTV*

Class of '61 🎬🎬½ 1992 1861, that is, as this class of West Point cadets prepares for the outbreak of war. Three close friends find themselves on opposing sides and with romantic entanglements, as well. Illustrated history, complete with voiceover passages from soldiers' letters, tend to slow the action, although the battles scenes are well done. Made for TV. **95m/C VHS, Closed Caption.** Dan Futterman, Clive Owen, Joshua

---

Lucas, Sophie Ward, Laura Linney, Andre Braugher, Len Cariou, Dana Ivey, Scott Burkholder, Niall O'Brien, Christien Anholt, Paul Guilfoyle, Beverly Todd, Ed Wiley, Sue-Ann Leeds; *D:* Gregory Hoblit; *W:* Jonas McCord; *C:* Janusz Kaminski. *USH*

Class of '63 🎬🎬 1973 An unfulfilled woman finally discovers the lover she lost nearly ten years ago at her college reunion. Nearly average made for television drama. **74m/C VHS, Beta.** James Brolin, Joan Hackett, Cliff Gorman, Ed Lauter; *D:* John Korty. *ORI*

Class Reunion woof! 1987 (X) Sexual highjinks are the order of the day at a 10-year high school reunion. Insipid softcore effort. It's cheaper just to cut out heads from yearbooks and paste 'em to skin mags torsos. Not to be confused with "National Lampoon's Class Reunion," equally bad but nonetheless distinct. **90m/C VHS, Beta, LV.** Marsha Jordan, Renee Bond, Terry Johnson.

Class Reunion Massacre woof! *The Redeemer* 1977 (R) Typically lame-brained horror about the mysterious deaths of former school jerks who've reconvened for the 10-year reunion. Worthless flick stars someone named Finkbinder. Contains graphic violence that is not for the squeamish. **87m/C VHS, Beta.** T.K. Finkbinder, Damien Knight, Nick Carter. *NO*

Claudia 🎬🎬 1985 (R) A wealthy woman who's part of London's high society falls for a lowly musician while trying to escape her dominating husband. Melodramatic meanderings not likely to move you. *CW:* Strong sexuality. **88m/C VHS.** Deborah Raffin, Nicholas Ball; *D:* Anwar Kawadri. *TTC*

The Claw 1927 A young British profligate goes to Africa to prove his manhood to the woman who rejected him. Silent. **?m/B VHS, Beta, 8mm.** Claire Windsor, Norman Kerry; *D:* Sidney Olcott. *GVV*

Claws 🎬 1977 (PG) A woodsman, a game commissioner, and an Indian band together to stop a grizzly bear who is killing residents of a small Alaskan town. **100m/C VHS, Beta.** Leon Ames, Jason Evers, Anthony Caruso, Glenn Sipes, Carla Layton, Myron Healey; *D:* Richard Bansbach, R.E. Pierson. *GEM*

Claws woof! 1985 A lone farmboy is subjected to repeated attacks by feline mutants. Meow, baby. **84m/C VHS, Beta.** Jason Roberts, Brian O'Shaughnessy, Sandra Prinsloo. *NO*

The Clay Pigeon 🎬🎬½ 1949 Seaman comes to in the hospital after a long coma and discovers he's about to be court-martialed for treason and murder. Effective suspense as he goes after the man who incriminated him. **63m/B VHS, Beta.** Bill Williams, Barbara Hale, Richard Loo; *D:* Richard Fleischer. *NO*

Clayton County Line 🎬 198? Plucky buddies decide to end a cruel sheriff's reign of terror. Derivative and unredeeming. **80m/C VHS.** Kelly Bradish, Vince Csapos, Michael Heinz, Donald Kenney, Kathy Kenney, Gregg Schultz, Dan Quine, Steve Szilagyi, Dean Wilson; *D:* Dean Wilson. *NO*

Clean and Sober 🎬🎬🎬½ 1988 (R) A drug addict hides out at a rehabilitation clinic and actually undergoes treatment. A serious, subtle, and realistic look at the physical/emotional detoxification of an obnoxious, substance-abusing real estate broker; unpredictable and powerful without moralizing. Keaton is fine in unsympathetic lead, with both Baker and Freeman excelling in lesser roles. Not for all tastes, but it's certainly a worthwhile work. Caron, creator of TV's "Moonlighting," debuts here as director. **124m/C VHS, Beta, LV, 8mm, Letterbox, Closed Caption.** Michael Keaton, Kathy Baker, Morgan Freeman, M. Emmet Walsh, Claudia Christian, Pat Quinn, Ben Piazza, Brian Benben, Luca Bercovici, Tate Donovan, Henry Judd Baker, Mary Catherine Martin; *D:* Glenn Gordon Caron; *W:* Tod Carroll; *C:* Jan Kiesser. National Society of Film Critics Awards '88: Best Actor (Keaton). *WAR, FCT*

Clean, Shaven 🎬🎬 1993 Schizophrenic Peter Winter (Greene in a stunning performance) is searching bleak Miscou Island, off the New Brunswick coast, for the younger daughter his

---

mother put up for adoption after Peter was institutionalized and his wife died. Peter's being tailed by Detective McNally (Albert), who suspects him of a child's murder, and his tenuous hold on reality slowly disintegrates into torment and self-mutilation. Debut for director/writer Kerrigan. **80m/C VHS.** Peter Greene, Robert Albert, Jennifer MacDonald, Megan Owen, Molly Castelloe; *D:* Lodge Kerrigan; *W:* Lodge Kerrigan; *C:* Teodoro Maniaci; *M:* Hahn Rowe. Nominations: Independent Spirit Awards '95: Best First Feature. *ORI*

Clean Slate 🎬🎬 1994 (PG-13) Private-eye Maurice Pogue (Carvey) sustains injuries that cause a rare type of amnesia making every day seem like the first day of his life. As the only witness to a crime, he bumbles through mix-ups with the mob and his job as a bodyguard. Lightweight comedy fare is good for a few yuks but doesn't work as well as the similar "Groundhog Day." Barkley the sight-impaired dog steals nearly every scene he's in. *CW:* Language. **106m/C VHS, Beta, LV, Closed Caption.** Dana Carvey, Valeria Golino, James Earl Jones, Kevin Pollak, Michael Murphy, Michael Gambon, Jayne Brook, Vyto Ruginis, Olivia D'Abo, Peter Crook; *D:* Mick Jackson; *W:* Robert King; *M:* Alan Silvestri. *MGM*

Clear and Present Danger 🎬🎬½ 1994 (PG-13) Ford returns for a second go at CIA agent Jack Ryan in the third installment of Tom Clancy's bestselling adventures. With the Cold War over, the U.S. government is the bad guy as Ryan discovers a link between a South American drug cartel and a Presidential advisor. Viewers will also finally get an answer to that nagging question at the end of "Patriot Games:" is it a boy or a girl? Archer's back as Ryan's annoying wife, and Birch and Jones also return. Keep alert for complex plot twists in lieu of tons of action, though there's enough to keep action fans happy. *CW:* Language and intense action; violence. **141m/C VHS, Beta, Closed Caption.** Harrison Ford, Anne Archer, James Earl Jones, Willem Dafoe, Thora Birch, Henry Czerny, Harris Yulin, Raymond Cruz, Joaquim de Almeida, Miguel Sandoval, Donald Moffat, Theodore (Ted) Raimi, Dean Jones; *D:* Phillip Noyce; *W:* Steven Zaillian, Donald Stewart, John Milius. Blockbuster Entertainment Awards '95: Action Actor, Theatrical (Ford); Blockbuster Entertainment Awards '96: Action Actor, Video (Ford); Nominations: Academy Awards '94: Best Sound; MTV Movie Awards '95: Best Action Sequence. *PAR*

Clearcut 🎬🎬½ 1992 (R) Progressive lawyer finds his liberalism and his survival skills tested among modern Canadian Indians, when a militant native resorts to kidnapping the businessman who threatens their land. Well-acted, brutal drama that asks tough questions; it includes what purports to be the first authentic sweat-lodge ceremony ever filmed. *CW:* Language and strong torture and violence. **98m/C VHS.** *CA* Graham Greene, Ron Lea, Michael Hogan, Floyd "Red Crow" Westerman, Rebecca Jenkins; *D:* Richard Bugajski.

Clearing the Range 🎬½ 1931 Hoot wants the bad guy who knocked off his brother so he poses as a cringing coward in the hopes of uncovering the villain. Eilers is the love interest as well as his real-life wife. **64m/B VHS, Beta.** Hoot Gibson, Sally Eilers, Hooper Atchley; *D:* Otto Brower. *NOS, VCN, DVT*

Cleo from 5 to 7 🎬🎬🎬½ *Cleo de 5 a 7* 1961 A singer strolls through Paris for 90 minutes, and reconsiders her life while awaiting the results of medical tests for cancer. Typical documentary-like effort from innovative filmmaker Varda, who constructed the film in real time. Look for a brief appearance of master director Jean-Luc Godard. In French with English subtitles. **90m/B VHS.** *FR* Corinne Marchand, Antoine Bourseiller, Dorothee Blanck, Michel Legrand, Jean-Claude Brialy, Jean-Luc Godard, Anna Karina, Eddie Constantine, Sami Frey; *D:* Agnes Varda; *W:* Agnes Varda. *HMV, FCT*

Cleo/Leo 🎬 1989 (R) Crude and sexist jerk Leo gets chased into the East River by a gun-toting feminist. Reincarnated, Leo returns as Cleo and endures the same Neanderthal remarks and attitudes that "he" used to dish out. Tasteless, exploitive comedy only cynically explores the sex reversal theme. **94m/C VHS.** Jane Hamilton, Scott Thompson Baker, Kevin Thomas, Alan Naggar, Ginger Lynn Allen; **D:** Chuck Vincent. *VTR*

Cleopatra 🎬🎬 1934 Early Hollywood DeMille version of the Egyptian temptress's lust for Marc Antony after Julius Caesar's death. Intermittently interesting extravaganza. Colbert seems to be enjoying herself in the lead role in this hokey, overdone epic. Includes the original theatrical trailer on laser-track 2. Remade in 1963. **100m/B VHS, Beta, LV, Closed Caption.** Claudette Colbert, Henry Wilcoxon, Warren William, Gertrude Michael, Joseph Schildkraut, Sir C. Aubrey Smith; **D:** Cecil B. DeMille; **C:** Victor Milner. Academy Awards '34: Best Cinematography; Nominations: Academy Awards '34: Best Film Editing, Best Picture, Best Sound. *USH*

Cleopatra 🎬 1963 And we thought DeMille's version was extravagant. After the death of Julius Caesar, Cleopatra, Queen of Egypt, becomes infatuated with Mark Antony. Costly four-hour epic functions like a blimp-sized, multi-colored sleeping tablet. Historical characters are utterly dwarfed by the film's massive scope, and audiences are benumbed by a spectacle of crowd scenes and opulent, grotesque interiors. Taylor looks and often acts like a sex bomb ruler, while Harrison has some notion of Caesar's majesty. Burton, however, is hopelessly wooden. Hard to believe this came from director Mankiewicz. **246m/C VHS, Beta, LV, Letterbox.** Elizabeth Taylor, Richard Burton, Rex Harrison, Roddy McDowall, Martin Landau, Pamela Brown, Michael Hordern, Kenneth Haigh, Andrew Keir, Hume Cronyn, Carroll O'Connor; **D:** Joseph L. Mankiewicz; **W:** Joseph L. Mankiewicz; **C:** Leon Shamroy; **M:** Alex North. Academy Awards '63: Best Art Direction/Set Decoration (Color), Best Color Cinematography, Best Costume Design (Color), Best Visual Effects; National Board of Review Awards '63: Best Actor (Harrison); Nominations: Academy Awards '63: Best Actor (Harrison), Best Film Editing, Best Picture, Best Sound, Best Original Score. *FOX*

Cleopatra Jones 🎬🎬 1973 (PG) Lean and lethal government agent with considerable martial arts prowess takes on loathsome drug lords. Dobson is fetching as the lead performer in this fast-paced, violent flick. Followed by "Cleopatra Jones and the Casino of Gold." **89m/C VHS, Beta.** Tamara Dobson, Shelley Winters, Bernie Casey, Brenda Sykes; **D:** Jack Starrett. *WAR*

Cleopatra Jones & the Casino of Gold 🎬🎬 1975 (R) Dobson returns as the lethal, physically imposing federal agent to Hong Kong to take on a powerful druglord in this sequel to "Cleopatra Jones." Watch for sexy Stevens as the Dragon Lady. **96m/C VHS, Beta.** Tamara Dobson, Stella Stevens, Norman Fell; **D:** Chuck Bail. *WAR*

The Clergyman's Daughter 🎬½ 1984 A clergyman's daughter calls upon detectives Tommy and Tuppence to investigate some murders at the family's country house. Made for British television and based on the Agatha Christie story. **60m/C VHS, Beta.** *GB* James Warwick, Francesca Annis. *TPV*

Clerks 🎬🎬🎬 1994 (R) "What kind of convenience store do you run here?" Day in the life of a convenience store clerk is an often hilarious lesson in the profane from first time writer/director Smith (who has a cameo as Silent Bob). Twenty-two-year-old Dante Hicks (O'Halloran) is a disaffected New Jersey Quick Stop employee who spends most of his time bored and dealing with borderline crazies. The next-door video store is clerked by his best friend Randal (Anderson), who derives equal delight from tormenting his customers and debating absolutely anything (especially anything sexual). Nothing much actually happens but the very low-budget ($27,575) production has a decidedly scuzzy charm and a cult following. Based on the director's four years of clerking at the Quick Stop and shot on location.**CW:** Explicit sex-related dialogue. **89m/B VHS, LV, Closed Caption.** Brian O'Halloran, Jeff Anderson, Marilyn Ghiglotti,

Lisa Spoonhauer, Jason Mewes; **Cameos:** Kevin Smith; **D:** Kevin Smith; **W:** Kevin Smith; **C:** David Klein; **M:** Scott Angley. Sundance Film Festival '94: Filmmakers Trophy; Nominations: Independent Spirit Awards '95: Best First Feature, Debut Performance (Anderson). *MAX*

The Client 🎬🎬½ 1994 (PG-13) Another legal thriller from the Grisham factory. Reggie Love (Sarandon) is a troubled attorney hired by 11-year-old Mark (Renfro), who witnessed the suicide of a Mafia attorney and now knows more than he should. Ambitious federal prosecutor Foltrigg's (Jones) willing to risk the boy's life in exchange for career advancement. Lacks the mega-big Hollywood names of "The Firm" and "The Pelican Brief" but gains solid acting in return with Renfro a find in his film debut. No frills, near-faithful adaptation by Schumacher basically travels down the path of least resistance. Filmed on location in Memphis.**CW:** Brief language and child in jeopardy. **121m/C VHS, LV, 8mm, Letterbox, Closed Caption.** Susan Sarandon, Tommy Lee Jones, Brad Renfro, Mary-Louise Parker, Anthony LaPaglia, Bradley Whitford, Anthony Edwards, Ossie Davis, Walter Olkewicz, J.T. Walsh, Will Patton, Anthony Heald; **D:** Joel Schumacher; **W:** Robert Getchell, Akiva Goldsman; British Academy Awards '94: Best Actress (Sarandon); Nominations: Academy Awards '94: Best Actress (Sarandon); Screen Actors Guild Award '94: Best Actress (Sarandon). *WAR*

Cliffhanger 🎬🎬🎬 1993 (R) Action-packed thriller. Expert climber Gabe Walker (Stallone) faces his greatest challenge when criminal mastermind Lithgow and his henchman appear on the scene. Turner plays fellow climber and love interest. Lithgow makes a particularly convincing, if not downright chilling, murderous thief. Filmed in the Italian Alps with a budget of $70 million-plus; boasts stunning cinematography and breathtaking footage of the Dolomite mountain range. Harlin's expert pacing and direction combine to produce maximum thrills and suspense. The hit Stallone's been waiting for, placing eighth on the list of top 1993 boxoffice grossers.**CW:** Language and violence. **113m/C VHS, Beta, LV, Letterbox, Closed Caption, DVD.** Sylvester Stallone, John Lithgow, Michael Rooker, Janine Turner, Rex Linn, Caroline Goodall, Leon, Paul Winfield, Ralph Waite, Craig Fairbrass, Michelle Joyner, Max Perlich; **D:** Renny Harlin; **W:** Sylvester Stallone, Michael France; **C:** Alex Thomson; **M:** Trevor Jones. Nominations: Academy Awards '93: Best Sound, Best Sound Effects Editing, Best Visual Effects; MTV Movie Awards '94: Best Action Sequence. *COL, BTV, FCT*

Clifford woof! 1992 (PG) Short plays a 10-year-old in an effort delayed by Orion's financial crisis. Creepy little Clifford's uncle Martin (Grodin) rues the day he volunteered to babysit his nephew to prove to his girlfriend (Steenburgen) how much he likes kids. Clifford terrorizes Grodin in surprisingly nasty ways when their plans for visiting Dinosaurworld fall through, although Grodin sees to well-deserved revenge. Not just bad in the conventional sense, but bad in a bizarre sort of alien fashion that raises questions about who was controlling the bodies of the producers. To create the effect of Short really being short, other actors stood on boxes and sets were built slightly larger. **90m/C VHS, LV, Closed Caption.** Martin Short, Charles Grodin, Mary Steenburgen, Dabney Coleman, Sonia Jackson; **D:** Paul Flaherty; **W:** Bobby Von Hayes, Jay Dee Rock, Steven Kampmann, Will Aldis; **C:** John A. Alonzo; **M:** Richard Gibbs. *ORI*

A Climate for Killing 🎬🎬½ 1991 (R) Arizona police are baffled when a woman murdered 16 years earlier is again found dead. Case open? Hunks Bauer and Beck are earnest in leads, and Ross and Sara are foxy. Passable entertainment.**CW:** Language, violence, and sensuality. **104m/C VHS, Beta, LV, Closed Caption.** Steven Bauer, John Beck, Katharine Ross, Mia Sara, John Diehl, Phil Brock, Dedee Pfeiffer, Lu Leonard, Jack Dodson, Eloy Casados; **D:** J.S. Cardone; **W:** J.S. Cardone; **M:** Robert Folk.

The Climax 🎬🎬½ 1944 Technicolor highlights this horror saga of obsession. House physician for Vienna's Royal Theatre, Dr. Hohner (Karloff) kills opera singer Marcellina (Vincent) when she rejects him. Twenty years later, Hohner hears the beautiful voice of Angela (Foster), a near duplicate of Marcellina's, and hypnotizes her to prevent her singing. Now, it's up to Angela's composer friend Franz (Bey) to overcome the doctor's evil influence. Adapted from a play by Edward Locke. Waggner directed this "The Phantom of the Opera" clone using the same sets as the 1943 "Phantom" remake. **86m/C VHS, Closed Caption.** Boris Karloff, Susanna Foster, Turhan Bey, Gale Sondergaard, Thomas Gomez, June Vincent, Jane Farrar, Scotty Beckett; **D:** George Waggner; **W:** Curt Siodmak, Lynn Starling; **C:** Hal Mohr, William Howard Greene; **M:** Edward Ward. *USH*

The Climb 🎬🎬½ 1987 (PG) German mountain climbers attempt to conquer the Himalayan Nanga Parbat, the world's fifth highest peak. Sometimes compelling film based on 1953 expedition in which only one member succeeded in reaching the summit. **90m/C VHS, Beta, LV.** Bruce Greenwood, James Hurdle, Kenneth Welsh; **D:** Donald Shebib; **W:** Donald Shebib; **M:** Peter Jermyn. *IME*

Clipped Wings 🎬🎬½ 1953 The Bowery Boys are at their best as they inadvertently join the army while visiting a friend and in the process of their usual bumblings, uncover a Nazi plot. **62m/B VHS.** Leo Gorcey, Huntz Hall, Bernard Gorcey, David Condon, Bennie Bartlett, June Vincent, Mary Treen, Philip Van Zandt, Elaine Riley, Jeanne Dean, Lyle Talbot; **D:** Edward L. Bernds. *WAR*

Cloak and Dagger 🎬🎬 1946 An American physicist joins the secret service during WWII and infiltrates Nazi territory to release a kidnapped scientist who is being forced to build a nuclear bomb. Disappointing spy show with muted anti-nuclear tone. **106m/B VHS, LV.** Gary Cooper, Lilli Palmer, Robert Alda, James Flavin, Vladimir Sokoloff, J. Edward Bromberg, Marc Lawrence, Ludwig Stossel; **D:** Fritz Lang; **W:** Ring Lardner Jr., Albert Maltz; **M:** Max Steiner. *REP, FCT*

Cloak & Dagger 🎬🎬½ 1984 (PG) A young boy, last seen befriending E.T., depends upon his imaginary super-friend to help him out when some real-life agents are after his video game. Coleman is particularly fun as both dad and fantasy hero in an interesting family adventure. **101m/C VHS, Beta, LV, Closed Caption.** Dabney Coleman, Henry Thomas, Michael Murphy, John McIntire, Jeanette Nolan; **D:** Richard Franklin; **W:** Tom Holland; **M:** Brian May. *USH*

The Clock 🎬🎬🎬 *Under the Clock* 1945 Appealing romance about an office worker who meets and falls in love with a soldier on two-day leave in New York City. Charismatic Walker and likeable Garland make a fine screen couple, and Wynn is memorable as the drunk. The original theatrical trailer is included on the laserdisc format. **91m/B VHS, LV.** Judy Garland, Robert Walker, James Gleason, Marshall Thompson, Keenan Wynn; **D:** Vincente Minnelli; **M:** George Bassman. *BTV, MGM, FCT*

Clockers 🎬🎬🎬 1995 (R) Strike (Phifer), leader of a group of bottom-feeding drug dealers ("clockers"), engages in a power struggle with his boss (Lindo), his do-the-right-thing brother Victor (Washington), and his own conscience. He's also suspected of murder by relentless narcotics cop Rocco Klein (Keitel). Supported by an excellent cast, first-timer Phifer surprises with a fierce and powerful performance. Lindo, in particular, stands out as the paternally evil Rodney. Aggressively edited, with Turturro's performance mostly lost on the cutting room floor. Critically lauded cinematography is marred by the occasional boom shot. Poignant and compelling street drama is based on the Richard Price novel. Lee took over after Scorsese and De Niro dropped out to make "Casino."**CW:** Strong graphic violence; strong language; drug content. **128m/C VHS, LV, Closed Caption.** Mekhi Phifer, Harvey Keitel, Delroy Lindo, Isaiah

Washington, John Turturro, Keith David; **D:** Spike Lee; **W:** Richard Price, Spike Lee; **C:** Malik Hassan Sayeed; **M:** Terence Blanchard. *USH*

The Clockmaker 🎞🎞🎞½ **1976** Contemplative drama about a clockmaker whose life is shattered when his son is arrested as a political assassin. Tavernier regular Noiret excels in the lead. In French with English subtitles. 105m/C VHS, Beta, LV. **FR** Philippe Noiret, Jean Rochefort, Jacques Denis, William Sabatier, Christine Pascal; **D:** Bertrand Tavernier. *FCT, LUM*

Clockwatchers 🎞½ **1997 (PG-13)** Decent cast gets wasted in a slice of life story that goes nowhere. Meek temp Iris's (Collette) new assignment is at a big, faceless credit company. Iris is taken in hand by fellow temps Margaret (Posey), Paula (Kudrow), and Jane (Ubach), who like to complain about how badly they're treated by management. Things gets worse when the company makes an announcement about a rash of petty thefts and the temps get blamed. That's it. **CW:** Brief language. 105m/C VHS. Toni Collette, Parker Posey, Lisa Kudrow, Alanna Ubach, Stanley DeSantis, Jamie Kennedy, David James Elliott, Kevin Cooney, Bob Balaban, Paul Dooley; **D:** Jill Sprecher; **W:** Jill Sprecher, Karen Sprecher; **C:** Jim Denault. *BMG*

Clockwise 🎞🎞½ **1986 (PG)** Monty Python regular Cleese is a teacher preoccupied by punctuality. His neurosis proves his undoing when he falls victim to misadventure while traveling to deliver a speech. Cleese is acceptable, dialogue and story is less so, though sprinkled with a fair amount of humor. 96m/C VHS, LV, Closed Caption. **GB** John Cleese, Penelope Wilton, Alison Steadman, Stephen Moore, Sharon Maiden; **D:** Christopher Morahan; **W:** Michael Frayn; **M:** George Fenton. *REP*

A Clockwork Orange 🎞🎞🎞🎞 **1971 (R)** In the Britain of the near future, a sadistic punk leads a gang on nightly rape and murder sprees, then is captured and becomes the subject of a grim experiment to eradicate his violent tendencies in this extraordinary adaptation of Anthony Burgess's controversial novel. The film is an exhilarating experience, with an outstanding performance by McDowell as the funny, fierce psychopath. Many memorable, disturbing sequences, including a rape conducted while assailant McDowell belts "Singing in the Rain." Truly outstanding, provocative work from master filmmaker Kubrick. 137m/C VHS, Beta, LV, Letterbox, Closed Caption. **GB** Malcolm McDowell, Patrick Magee, Adrienne Corri, Michael Bates, Warren Clarke, Aubrey Morris, James Marcus, Steven Berkoff, David Prowse, John Clive, Carl Duering, Miriam Karlin; **D:** Stanley Kubrick; **W:** Stanley Kubrick; **C:** John Alcott. New York Film Critics Awards '71: Best Director (Kubrick); Nominations: Academy Awards '71: Best Adapted Screenplay, Best Director (Kubrick), Best Film Editing, Best Picture. *WAR, FCT, FUS*

Clodhopper 🎞🎞 **1917** A farmboy decides to head out for New York where he achieves fame on Broadway for his dance number, the "Clophooper Glide." He stays true to his hometown girl, however, and returns to save his father's farm from financial ruin. 47m/B VHS, Beta. Charles Ray, Margery Wilson; **D:** Victor Schertzinger. *GPV, CCB, DVT*

The Clones 🎞🎞 **1973 (PG)** A doctor discovers a government experiment engineered to murder him with a perfect clone. 90m/C VHS, Beta. Michael Greene, Gregory Sierra; **D:** Paul Hunt, Lamar Card. *ART, HHE*

Clones of Bruce Lee 🎞🎞 **1980 (R)** It's a martial arts free-for-all as bold masters from throughout the world duel for supremacy in the realm of self defense. If you like martial arts movies, you'll probably like this one. If you don't know if you like martial arts movies, find out with one of the actual Bruce Lee's flicks. 87m/C VHS, Beta. Dragon Lee, Bruce Le, Bruce Lai, Bruce Thai; **D:** Joseph Kong.

The Clonus Horror 🎞½ **Parts:** *The Clonus Horror* **1979** A scientist discovers a government plot to clone the population by freezing bodies alive and using their parts in surgery. 90m/C VHS, Beta.

Tim Donnelly, Keenan Wynn, Peter Graves, Dick Sargent, Paulette Breen; **D:** Robert S. Fiveson. *AHT*

Close Encounters of the Third Kind 🎞🎞🎞🎞 **1977 (PG)** Middle-American strangers become involved in the attempts of benevolent aliens to contact earthlings. Despite the sometimes mundane nature of the characters, this Spielberg epic is a stirring achievement. Studded with classic sequences; the ending is an exhilarating experience of special effects and peace-on-earth feelings. Dreyfuss and Dillon excel as friends who are at once bewildered and obsessed by the alien presence, and French filmmaker Truffaut is also strong as the stern, ultimately kind scientist. Laserdisc includes formerly edited scenes, live interviews with Spielberg, special effects man Douglas Trumbull, and composer Williams, publicity materials, and over 1,000 production photos. 152m/C VHS, Beta, LV, Letterbox, Closed Caption. Richard Dreyfuss, Teri Garr, Melinda Dillon, Francois Truffaut, Bob Balaban, Cary Guffey, J. Patrick McNamara; **D:** Steven Spielberg; **W:** Steven Spielberg; **C:** Vilmos Zsigmond; **M:** John Williams. Academy Awards '77: Best Cinematography, Best Sound Effects Editing; Nominations: Academy Awards '77: Best Art Direction/Set Decoration, Best Director (Spielberg), Best Film Editing, Best Sound, Best Supporting Actress (Dillon), Best Original Score. *COL, CRC, FUS*

Close My Eyes 🎞🎞 **1991 (R)** A hot, steamy summer arouses vibrant passions in a brother and sister, and neither marriage nor blood relation can halt the inevitable. **CW:** Language and strong sensuality. 105m/C VHS. Alan Rickman, Clive Owen, Saskia Reeves; **D:** Stephen Poliakoff.

Close to Eden 🎞🎞 *Urga* **1990 (PG)** A peasant couple living in inner Mongolia with their three children are prevented by strict Chinese law from having a fourth. The husband sets out from his village to obtain birth control from the nearby town. While on his way, the farmer (Bayaertu) saves a Russian truck driver (Gostukhin) after he drives into a lake. Sergei is introduced to another way of life when he's taken home by his rescuer to meet the family and becomes accustomed to the tranquility of farm life in the rural Mongolian steppe. Essentially a story about the changes modern civilization can bring to a rural way of life. Filmed in Mongolia. In Russian with English subtitles. 109m/C VHS, Beta. **RU** Baoyinhexige, Badema, Nikita Mikhalkov; **D:** Nikita Mikhalkov; **W:** Rustam Ibragimbekov; **M:** Eduard Artemyev. Venice Film Festival '91: Best Film; Nominations: Academy Awards '92: Best Foreign Language Film. *PAR, FCT*

Close to Home 🎞🎞 **1986** A runaway fleeing a home life of abuse and neglect befriends a TV journalist doing a story on similar girls. She turns to him for support after she is arrested and returned home. Merely mediocre. 93m/C VHS, Beta. **CA** Daniel Allman, Jillian Fargey, Anne Petrie; **D:** Rick Beairsto. *TWE*

Closely Watched Trains 🎞🎞🎞½ **1966** A novice train dispatcher attempts to gain sexual experience in German-occupied Czechoslovakia during WWII. Many funny scenes in this film regarded by some as a classic. Based upon the Czech novel by Bohumil Hrabal. In Czech with English subtitles. 89m/B VHS, Beta, LV. **CZ** Vaclav Neckar, Jitka Bendova, Vladimir Valenta, Josef Somr; **D:** Jiri Menzel; **W:** Jiri Menzel. Academy Awards '67: Best Foreign Language Film. *FXL, COL*

The Closer 🎞🎞½ **1991 (R)** Aiello is "The Closer," a high-powered salesman whose world is falling apart. Somewhere between the money and the power, he's lost touch with his family and the truly important things in life. Is it too late to get them back? **CW:** Language. 87m/C VHS, LV. Danny Aiello, Michael Pare, Joe Cortese, Justin Bateman, Diane Baker, James Karen, Rick Aiello, Michael Lerner; **D:** Dimitri Logothetis; **W:** Robert Keats, Louis LaRusso II; **M:** Al Kasha.

Closet Land 🎞½ **1990 (R)** Severe, stylized political allegory aims high but falls to convincingly distill totalitarian repression into just two characters—a government inquisitor and his captive, a woman subjected to hideous mental and physical torture. Child-molesting emerges as an ill-advised subtheme. A better video on the same subject: "Interrogation," from Poland. **CW:** Language and psychological torture. 95m/C VHS, Beta, LV, Closed Caption. Madeleine Stowe, Alan Rickman; **D:** Radha Bharadwaj; **W:** Radha Bharadwaj; **M:** Richard Einhorn. *VTR*

Cloud Dancer 🎞🎞 **1980 (PG)** A self-absorbed acrobat uses and abuses those around him, including his girlfriend. Carradine and O'Neill fail to distinguish themselves in this mediocre film. 107m/C VHS, Beta. David Carradine, Jennifer O'Neill, Joseph Bottoms, Colleen Camp; **D:** Barry Brown; **W:** William Goodhart.

Cloud Waltzing 🎞🎞½ **1987** The screen version of a Harlequin romance about a journalist who arrives in France to interview a vintner and finds romance and danger. Melodrama bolstered by the presence of photogenic Beller. 103m/C VHS, Beta. Kathleen Beller, Francois-Eric Gendron, Paul Maxwell, Therese Liotard, Claude Gensac, David Baxt; **D:** Gordon Flemyng. *PAR*

The Clouded Yellow 🎞🎞🎞 **1951** Young, lovely, and a little unstable, Sophie Malraux (Simmons) is accused of murdering the handyman who worked for her guardians (Jones and Dresdel). Ex-British Secret Service agent David Somers (Howard), who's in love with Sophie, helps her escape from jail and the two head for Liverpool and a ship to Mexico. But the police (hoping to find the real killer) are hot on their trail. Romantic suspense with good lead pairing. 95m/B VHS. **GB** Jean Simmons, Trevor Howard, Sonia Dresdel, Barry Jones, Maxwell Reed, Kenneth More, Andre Morell, Geoffrey Keen; **D:** Ralph Thomas; **W:** Eric Ambler; **C:** Geoffrey Unsworth. *HMV*

Clouds Over Europe 🎞🎞🎞 *Q Planes* **1939** A test pilot and a man from Scotland Yard team up to find out why new bomber planes are disappearing. 82m/B VHS, Beta, LV. Laurence Olivier, Valerie Hobson, Ralph Richardson, George Curzon, George Merritt, Gus McNaughton, David Tree, Sandra Storme, Hay Petrie, Frank Fox, Gordon McLeod, John Longden, Reginald Purdell, John Laurie, Pat Aherne; **D:** Tim Whelan; **W:** Ian Dalrymple; **C:** Harry Stradling.

Clown 🎞🎞½ **1953** A broken-down funny man with a worshipful son obtains one last career opportunity. This "Champ"-derived tearjerker features credible playing from Skelton and Considine as father and son, respectively. 91m/B VHS, Beta. Red Skelton, Jane Greer, Tim Considine, Steve Forrest; **D:** Robert Z. Leonard; **C:** Paul Vogel. *MGM*

Clown House 🎞 **1988 (R)** Young brothers are stalked in their home by three demonic clowns. 95m/C VHS, Beta, LV, Closed Caption. Nathan Forrest Winters, Brian McHugh, Sam Rockwell, Viletta Skillman, Timothy Enos, Tree; **D:** Victor Salva. *COL*

Clown Murders 🎞½ **1983** Posh Halloween party is undone when a cruel group fakes a kidnapping to ruin a too-prosperous pal's business deal. Awkward thriller boasts little suspense. Candy plays it straight, mostly, in this one. 94m/C VHS, Beta. John Candy, Al Waxman, Susan Keller, Lawrence Dane; **D:** Martyn Burke. *TWE*

Clowning Around 🎞🎞½ **1992** Simon, who has lived in foster homes all his life, dreams of becoming a famous circus clown. When he's sent to a new home, his new foster parents think his idea is silly, so he runs away and joins the circus. There he meets Anatole, a European clown has-been who can no longer perform because of injuries. Simon believes Anatole can teach him about clowning, so he follows Anatole to Paris to help make his dream come true. Part of the "Wonderworks" series. 165m/C VHS. **AU** Clayton Williamson, Jean-Michel Dagory, Ernie Dingo. *HMV, BTV, FCT*

Clowning Around 2 ⚬⚬½ **1993** The continuing story of Sim, whose dream is to become a world-famous clown. Now a member of the Winter Circus in Paris, he is still training with his mentor Anatole. But Sim is dissatisfied and when he befriends Eve, another young clown, he learns an experimental style of clowning which gets them both fired. He first follows Eve to her home in Montreal but then returns to his own home in Australia where he has been left the co-owner of a less-than-successful circus by a former employer. Filmed on location in Paris, France and Perth, Australia. **120m/C VHS.** *AU* Clayton Williamson, Jean-Michel Dagory, Ernie Dingo, Frederique Fouche; *D:* George Whaley. *HMV, BTV*

The Clowns ⚬⚬⚬½ **1971 (G)** An idiosyncratic documentary about circus clowns. Director Fellini has fashioned an homage that is sincere, entertaining, and personal. Contains some truly poignant sequences. Made for Italian television with English subtitles. **90m/C VHS, Beta.** *IT* ⊃ Federicò Fellini; *W:* Federico Fellini; *M:* Nino Rota. *HTV, NOS, MRV*

The Club ⚬⚬⚬ *Players* **1981 (PG)** A soccer coach tries to train and motivate a mediocre squad into one worth playing for—and perhaps even winning—the league cup. Conventional sports story is significantly improved by Thompson's rendering of the coach. **99m/C VHS, Beta.** *AU* Jack Thompson, Graham Kennedy, John Wood, John Howard, Alan Cassell; *D:* Bruce Beresford; *W:* David Williamson.

The Club ⚬ **1994 (R)** Typical teens-in-peril flick finds the high school prom held in a mysterious old castle with ghouls out to get the unfortunate seniors. Visuals are decent but frights are tepid. **88m/C VHS, LV.** Kim Coates, Joel Wyner, Andrea Roth, Rino Romano, Zack Ward, Kelli Taylor, Matthew Ferguson; *D:* Benton Spencer; *W:* Robert Cooper; *M:* Paul Zaza. *IMP*

Club Extinction ⚬⚬½ *Docteur M* **1989 (R)** A near-future thriller in which Berlin is plagued by a wave of suicides. An investigator suspects a spa representative and a media tycoon of being involved. Features a fine international cast, but the film is a lesser venture from prolific master Chabrol. *CW:* Language, violence, and sensuality. **105m/C VHS, Beta.** *GE* Alan Bates, Andrew McCarthy, Jennifer Beals, Jan Niklas, Hanns Zischler, Benoit Regent, Peter Fitz, Wolfgang Preiss, Isolde Barth; *D:* Claude Chabrol. *FCT*

Club Fed ⚬⚬½ **1990 (PG-13)** A rigid prison warden's plot to impose greater discipline is undone by inmate highjinks. Crude laughs and one-dimensional play from a cast of recognizable names and faces. **93m/C VHS, Beta.** Judy Landers, Sherman Hemsley, Karen Black, Burt Young, Rick Schmidt, Allen (Goorwitz) Garfield, Joseph Campanella, Lyle Alzado, Mary Woronov, Debbie Lee Carrington; *D:* Nathaniel Christian; *C:* Arledge Armenaki.

Club Havana ⚬½ **1946** A benevolent nightclub owner tries to save one of his singers from the depths of despair by reuniting her with her boyfriend. Minor musical with mild musical numbers. ♫Besame Mucho; Tico Tico. **62m/B VHS, Beta.** Tom Neal, Margaret Lindsay, Don Douglas, Isabelita, Dorothy Morris, Ernest Truex; *D:* Edgar G. Ulmer. *SNC*

Club Life ⚬ **1986 (R)** A hardened biker finds sex, drugs, and violence on the Hollywood streets. What did he expect? Peace, love, and understanding? **93m/C VHS, Beta.** Tony Curtis, Dee Wallace Stone, Tom Parsekian, Michael Parks, Jamie Barrett; *D:* Norman Thaddeus Vane.

Club Med ⚬⚬ **1983 (PG)** An insecure comedian and his goofy friend try to make the most of a ski vacation. Perhaps your only chance to see Thicke, Killy, and Coolidge together. **60m/C VHS, Beta.** Alan Thicke, Jim Carrey, Jean-Claude Killy, Rita Coolidge, Ronnie Hawkins; *D:* David Mitchell; *M:* Peter Bernstein.

Club Paradise ⚬⚬½ **1986 (PG-13)** A Chicago fireman flees the big city for a faltering tropical resort and tries to develop some night life. Somewhat disappointing with Williams largely playing the straight man. Most laughs provided by Martin, particularly when she is assaulted by a shower, and Moranis, who gets lost while windsurfing. **96m/C VHS, Beta, LV, Closed Caption.** Robin Williams, Peter O'Toole, Rick Moranis, Andrea Martin, Jimmy Cliff, Brian Doyle-Murray, Twiggy, Eugene Levy, Adolph Caesar, Joanna Cassidy, Mary Gross, Carey Lowell, Robin Duke, Simon Jones; *D:* Harold Ramis; *W:* Harold Ramis, Brian Doyle-Murray; *M:* David Mansfield, Van Dyke Parks. *WAR*

Clubhouse Detectives ⚬⚬½ **1996 (PG)** When Billy witnesses a crime at a neighbor's no one believes him—except his friends, so the clubhouse detectives decide to investigate. **85m/C VHS, LV.** Michael Ballem, Michael Galeota, Jimmy Galeota, Suzanne Barnes; *D:* Eric Hendershot. *APX*

Clue ⚬⚬½ **1985 (PG)** The popular boardgame's characters must unravel a night of murder at a spooky Victorian mansion. The entire cast seems to be subsisting on sugar, with wild eyes and frantic movements the order of the day. Butler Curry best survives the uneven script and direction. Warren is appealing too. The theatrical version played with three alternative endings, and the video version shows all three successively. **96m/C VHS, Beta, LV, Closed Caption.** Lesley Ann Warren, Tim Curry, Martin Mull, Madeline Kahn, Michael McKean, Christopher Lloyd, Eileen Brennan, Howard Hesseman, Lee Ving, Jane Wiedlin, Colleen Camp, Bill Henderson; *D:* Jonathan Lynn; *W:* Jonathan Lynn, John Landis; *M:* John Morris. *PAR*

Clueless ⚬⚬⚬ *I Was a Teenage Teenager; No Worries* **1995 (PG-13)** Watch out "Beverly Hills 90210," here comes Cher. No, not the singer Cher, but ultra-filthy-rich brat Cher, who's out to make over her classmates and teachers, specifically flannel-shirted transfer student Tai (Murphy). Aerosmith vamp Silverstone stars as the teenage manipulator who knows all too well how to spend her trust fund. The only person who can match her wits is disapproving stepbrother Josh (Rudd). (Ah, love.) Loosely based on Jane Austen's "Emma," Heckerling, of "Fast Times at Ridgemont High" fame, knows this territory and directs a bright, surprisingly satirical romp. *CW:* Sex related dialogue; some teen use of alcohol and drugs. **113m/C VHS.** Alicia Silverstone, Stacey Dash, Paul Rudd, Brittany Murphy, Donald A. Faison, Julie Brown, Jeremy Sisto, Dan Hedaya, Wallace Shawn, Breckin Meyer, Elisa Donovan, Aida Linares; *D:* Amy Heckerling; *W:* Amy Heckerling; *C:* Bill Pope; *M:* David Kitay. MTV Movie Awards '96: Best Female Performance (Silverstone), Most Desirable Female (Silverstone); National Society of Film Critics Awards '95: Best Screenplay; Blockbuster Entertainment Awards '96: Female Newcomer, Theatrical (Silverstone); Nominations: MTV Movie Awards '96: Best Film, Best Comedic Performance (Silverstone); Writers Guild of America '95: Best Original Screenplay. *PAR*

The Clutching Hand ⚬⚬ **1936** The Clutching Hand seeks a formula that will turn metal into gold and detective Craig Kennedy is out to prevent him from doing so. A serial in 15 chapters on three cassettes. **268m/B VHS, Beta.** Jack Mulhall, Rex Lease; *D:* ; *SNC, NOS, VDM*

Coach ⚬½ **1978 (PG)** Sexy woman is unintentionally hired to coach a high school basketball team and mold rookies into lusty young champions. Low-grade roundball fever. **100m/C VHS, Beta.** Cathy Lee Crosby, Michael Biehn, Keenan Wynn, Sidney Wicks; *D:* Bud Townsend.

Coal Miner's Daughter ⚬⚬⚬ **1980 (PG)** A strong bio of country singer Loretta Lynn, who rose from Appalachian poverty to Nashville riches. Spacek is perfect in the lead, and she even provides acceptable rendering of Lynn's tunes. Band drummer Helm shines as Lynn's father, and Jones is strong as Lynn's downhome husband. Uneven melodrama toward the end, but the film is still a good one. ♫Coal Miner's Daughter; Sweet Dreams of You; I'm a Honky-Tonk Girl; You're Lookin' at Country; One's On the Way; You Ain't Woman Enough to Take My Man; Back in My Baby's Arms. **125m/C VHS, Beta, LV.** Sissy Spacek, Tommy Lee Jones, Levon Helm, Beverly D'Angelo; *D:* Michael Apted; *C:* Ralf Bode. Academy Awards '80: Best Actress (Spacek); Golden Globe Awards '81: Best Actress—Musical/Comedy (Spacek), Best Film—Musical/Comedy; Los Angeles Film Critics Association Awards '80: Best Actress (Spacek); National Board of Review Awards '80: Best Actress (Spacek); New York Film Critics Awards '80: Best Actress (Spacek); National Society of Film Critics Awards '80: Best Actress (Spacek); Nominations: Academy Awards '80: Best Adapted Screenplay, Best Art Direction/Set Decoration, Best Cinematography, Best Film Editing, Best Picture, Best Sound. *USH, BTV*

The Coast Patrol ⚬⚬½ **1925** B. Reeves Eason, responsible for the chariot scene in the silent "Ben Hur" and the action scenes in "The Charge of the Light Brigade," directed Fay in one of her earliest parts, eight years before the role that prompted her to say "I didn't realize that King Kong and I were going to be together for the rest of our lives, and longer... " Much Eason-style high action when smugglers meet the coast patrol. **63m/B VHS, Beta.** Kenneth McDonald, Claire De Lorez, Fay Wray; *D:* Bud Barsky. *NOS, GPV, FCT*

Coast to Coast ⚬⚬ **1980 (PG)** A wacky woman escapes from a mental institution and teams with a pugnacious trucker for a cross-country spree. Ostensibly freewheeling comedy is only occasionally worthwhile despite appropriate playing from leads Cannon and Blake, who deserve better. **95m/C VHS, Beta, LV.** Dyan Cannon, Robert (Bobby) Blake, Quinn Redeker, Maxine Stuart, William Lucking; *D:* Joseph Sargent; *M:* Charles Bernstein. *PAR*

Cobb ⚬⚬⚬ **1994 (R)** Biography of Ty Cobb (Jones), the universally acknowledged "most hated man in baseball" who, near the end of his life, realizes he doesn't want to be remembered in that way. So he hires sportswriter Al Stump (Wuhl) to ghostwrite (read: sugarcoat) his life story. As seen through Stump's eyes, Cobb is an unrelenting, petty, bigoted, hateful, paranoid, drunken, and yet compelling man. They form an uneasy bond as Stump duty records the fiction Cobb is feeding him, secretly deciding to write the truth after the legend's death. Jones is at his scene-chewing, antagonistic best, while Wuhl seems both overwhelmed and overshadowed as the embattled Stump. Shelton has something to say about American hero worship and a celebrity's desire for posterity, but with the focus intent on portraying Cobb's meanness, it's hard to say what. Surprisingly stellar baseball action for a baseball bio. Based on Stump's "Cobb: A Biography." *CW:* Strong language; scenes of nudity and violent behavior. **128m/C VHS, LV, Closed Caption.** Tommy Lee Jones, Robert Wuhl, Lolita Davidovich; *D:* Ron Shelton; *W:* Ron Shelton; *C:* Russell Boyd. *WAR*

Cobra ⚬ **1925** To pay off the debts incurred by his profligate playboyance, Valentino takes a job with an antique dealer, falls for the dealer's secretary and arranges an assignation with the dealer's wife, who is inconveniently killed at the designated rendezvous. Complications abound as Valentino finds himself Sheik out of luck. Lesser Valentino effort was released a year before the famous heartthrob's untimely death and enjoyed a rather acrid critical reception. Which isn't to say the public didn't flock to see the Italian stallion flare his nostrils. **70m/B VHS, Beta.** Rudolph Valentino, Nita Naldi, Casson Ferguson, Gertrude Olmsted; *D:* Joseph Henabery. *VYY, FCT, GPV*

The Cobra ⚬ *Il Cobra; El Cobra* **1968** A tight-lipped U.S. agent ogles a voluptuous siren when not fighting opium smugglers from the Middle East. A must for all admirers of Ekberg. **93m/C VHS.** Dana Andrews, Anita Ekberg; *D:* Mario Sequi. *NO*

Cobra 🎬🎬½ *le Sant de l'Ange* **1971** A hired killer destroys most of a mob family and becomes the target of revenge for the lone survivor. Moody thriller boasts an international cast. **93m/C VHS, Beta.** *FR IT* Sterling Hayden, Senta Berger, Jean Yanne; **D:** Yves Boisset. *UNI*

Cobra 🎬 **1986 (R)** A cold-blooded cop protects a model from a gang of deranged killers. Lowbrow, manipulative action fare void of feeling. Truly exploitive, with little expression from the leads. Highlight is the extended chase sequence. Based on the Paula Gosling novel "Fair Game," which was remade under the book's title (and in a more faithful adaptation) in 1995. **87m/C VHS, Beta, LV, Closed Caption.** Sylvester Stallone, Reni Santoni, Brigitte Nielsen, Andrew (Andy) Robinson; **D:** George P. Cosmatos; **W:** Sylvester Stallone. *WAR*

Cobra Against Ninja 🎬 **1987** Once again, two martial arts experts try to kill each other. Can't be many of these fellas left. **88m/C VHS.** Jimmy Bosco, Paul Branney, Gary Carter, Alan Friss, Alfred Pears; **D:** Joseph Lai. *IMP*

The Cobra Strikes 🎬½ **1948** Nosey thief gets more than he bargained for when he works his way through an inventor's studio. Low-budget and unexceptional. **62m/B VHS.** Sheila Ryan, Richard Fraser, Leslie Brooks, Herbert Heyes; **D:** Charles F. Reisner. *NOS, MOV, RXM*

Cobra Woman 🎬🎬½ **1944** Technicolor adventure fantasy about the jungle queen (Montez) of a cobra-worshiping cult and her evil twin sister who wants the throne for herself. **70m/C VHS.** Maria Montez, Jon Hall, Sabu, Edgar Barrier, Lois Collier, Lon Chaney Jr.; **D:** Robert Siodmak; **C:** Gene Lewis, Richard Brooks; **C:** William Howard Greene. *NO*

The Cobweb 🎬🎬 **1955** Shady goings on are uncovered at a psychiatric ward run by a bunch of neurotic administrators. A strong cast, director and producer do not add much to this dull outing. **125m/C LV.** Lauren Bacall, Richard Widmark, Gloria Grahame, Charles Boyer, Lillian Gish, John Kerr, Susan Strasberg, Oscar Levant, Tommy Rettig, Paul Stewart, Adele Jergens, Bert Freed, Sandy Descher, Fay Wray, Virginia Christine; **D:** Vincente Minnelli. *MGM*

The Coca-Cola Kid 🎬🎬🎬½ **1984 (R)** A smug sales executive treks to Australia to improve regional sales and becomes embroiled in sexual and professional shenanigans. Roberts is strong in the difficult lead role, and Scacchi is compelling in an awkwardly constructed part. Ambitious satire is somewhat scattershot, with more storylines than it needs. Still, filmmaker Makavejev is usually capable of juggling the entire enterprise. **94m/C VHS, Beta, LV, Closed Caption.** *AU* Eric Roberts, Greta Scacchi, Bill Kerr; **D:** Dusan Makavejev. *ART, VES, FCT*

Cocaine Cowboys 🎬½ **1979 (R)** Lame rockers support themselves between gigs by peddling drugs then find out they've run afoul of the mob. Palance is the only worthwhile aspect of this rambling venture produced at Andy Warhol's home. **90m/C VHS, Beta.** Jack Palance, Andy Warhol, Tom Sullivan, Suzanna Love; **D:** Ulli Lommel. *GEM, OM*

Cocaine Fiends 🎬🎬 *The Pace That Kills* **1936** Drug use leads siblings into a squalid life of addiction, crime, prostitution, and eventually suicide. Ostensibly straight morality tale functions better as loopy camp. Features memorable slang. **74m/B VHS, Beta.** Lois January, Noel Madison; **D:** William O'Connor. *SNC, NOS, HHT*

Cocaine: One Man's Seduction 🎬🎬½ **1983** Made-for-television film documents one man's degeneration into drug addiction. Weaver snorts convincingly in lead. **97m/C VHS, Beta.** Dennis Weaver, Karen Grassle, Pamela Bellwood, David Ackroyd; **D:** Paul Wendkos; **M:** Brad Fiedel.

Cocaine Wars 🎬 **1986 (R)** An undercover U.S. agent kills dozens while trying to rescue his kidnapped girlfriend from an evil South American drug tycoon. Violent, but otherwise unaffecting.

Cockeyed Cavaliers 🎬🎬 **1934** Wheeler and Woolsey are stockaded for stealing the Duke's horses and carriage. To escape jail they swap clothes with some drunken royalty. **70m/B VHS, Beta.** Bert Wheeler, Robert Woolsey, Dorothy Lee, Thelma Todd; **D:** Mark Sandrich. *CCB*

Cockfighter 🎬🎬🎬 *Gamblin' Man; Born to Kill; Wild Drifters* **1974 (R)** A unique, grim portrait of a cockfighting trainer. Oates, in the lead, provides voiceover narrations, but the film otherwise remains silent until the end. Strong support from Stanton. Interesting, violent fare. **84m/C VHS, Beta.** Warren Oates, Harry Dean Stanton, Richard B. Shull, Troy Donahue, Millie Perkins; **D:** Monte Hellman; **C:** Nestor Almendros; **M:** Michael Franks.

Cocktail 🎬🎬½ **1988 (R)** A smug young man finds fame and fortune as a proficient, flashy bartender, charming the ladies with his bottle and glass juggling act. Slick, superficial film boasts a busy soundtrack and serviceable exchanges between male leads Cruise and Brown. There's less chemistry between Cruise and love interest Shue. Filmed in a high-tech rock video style. **103m/C VHS, Beta, LV, 8mm, Closed Caption.** Tom Cruise, Bryan Brown, Elisabeth Shue, Lisa Banes, Laurence Luckinbill, Kelly Lynch, Gina Gershon, Ron Dean, Paul Benedict; **D:** Roger Donaldson; **W:** Heywood Gould; **C:** Dean Semler; **M:** J. Peter Robinson. Golden Raspberry Awards '88: Worst Picture, Worst Screenplay. *TOU*

The Cocoanuts 🎬🎬½ **1929** In their film debut, the Marx Brothers create their trademark, indescribable mayhem. Stagey, technically crude comedy nonetheless delights with zany, free-for-all exchanges, antics. Includes famous "viaduct" exchange. **96m/B VHS, Beta, LV.** Groucho Marx, Chico Marx, Harpo Marx, Zeppo Marx, Margaret Dumont, Kay Francis, Oscar Shaw, Mary Eaton; **D:** Robert Florey, Joseph Santley; **W:** George S. Kaufman, Morrie Ryskind; **M:** Irving Berlin. *USH*

Cocoon 🎬🎬🎬 **1985 (PG-13)** Humanist fantasy in which senior citizens discover their fountain of youth is actually a breeding ground for aliens. Heartwarming, one-of-a kind drama showcases elderly greats Ameche, Brimley, Gilford, Cronyn, and Tandy. A commendable, recommendable venture. Based on David Saperstein's novel and followed by "Cocoon: The Return." **117m/C VHS, Beta, LV, Closed Caption.** Wilford Brimley, Brian Dennehy, Steve Guttenberg, Don Ameche, Tahnee Welch, Jack Gilford, Hume Cronyn, Jessica Tandy, Gwen Verdon, Maureen Stapleton, Tyrone Power Jr., Barret Oliver, Linda Harrison, Herta Ware, Clint Howard; **D:** Ron Howard; **W:** Tom Benedek; **M:** James Horner. Academy Awards '85: Best Supporting Actor (Ameche), Best Visual Effects. *FOX, FCT, BTV*

Cocoon: The Return 🎬🎬 **1988 (PG)** Old timers who left with aliens in "Cocoon" return to earth and face grave problems. Less compelling sequel misses guiding hand of earlier film's director, Ron Howard. Still, most of cast from the original is on board here, and the film has its moments. **116m/C VHS, Beta, LV, Closed Caption.** Don Ameche, Wilford Brimley, Steve Guttenberg, Maureen Stapleton, Hume Cronyn, Jessica Tandy, Gwen Verdon, Jack Gilford, Tahnee Welch, Courteney Cox, Brian Dennehy, Barret Oliver; **D:** Daniel Petrie; **C:** Tak Fujimoto; **M:** James Horner. *FOX*

C.O.D. 🎬 **1983 (PG)** Bosom buddies must develop advertising campaign for brassiere producer or find their careers are bust. Premise milked for all its worth, so you may want to keep abreast of this one. On the other hand, you may not give a hoot. Oh well, tit for tat. **96m/C VHS, Beta.** Chris Lemmon, Olivia Pascal, Jennifer Richards, Corinne Alphen, Teresa Ganzel, Carole Davis; **D:** Chuck Vincent; **W:** R.J. Marx. *VES, ART*

Code Name Alpha 🎬🎬 *Red Dragon; A-009 Missione Hong Kong* **1967** You don't have to have a federal case of intelligence to figure out where this FBI story's going and how it's going to get there. Someone's smuggling sophisticated electrical components to the communists, and a team of

intelligence agents, including Granger and Schiaffino, hike over to Hong Kong to break up the party. Based on the story "Le Riviere des Trois Jonques" by Georges Godefroy. **89m/C VHS.** *IT GE* Stewart Granger, Rosanna Schiaffino, Harald Juhnke, Paul Klinger, Helga Sommerfeld, Horst Frank; **D:** Ernest Hofbauer. *SNC*

Code Name: Chaos 🎬🎬 *Spies, Lies, and Alibis* **1990 (R)** A political spoof featuring a group of renegade spies trying to come up with a get-rich-quick scheme. It involves inventing a global crisis in a small Asian country that comes under the scrutiny of a CIA agent who's not in on the scheme. **CW:** Language. **96m/C VHS.** Robert Loggia, Diane Ladd, David Warner, Alice Krige, Brian Kerwin; **D:** Antony Thomas. *ART, MOV, ART*

Code Name: Dancer **1987** A retired spy leaves her peaceful life, husband and family to take care of business in Cuba. Made for television. **93m/C VHS.** Kate Capshaw, Jeroen Krabbe, Gregory Sierra, Cliff DeYoung. *THV*

Code Name: Diamond Head 🎬 **1977** In Hawaii, a secret agent is assigned to retrieve a deadly chemical that has been hidden by a master of disguises. Made for television. **78m/C VHS, Beta.** Roy Thinnes, France Nuyen, Zulu, Ian McShane; **D:** Jeannot Szwarc. *WOV*

Code Name: Emerald 🎬 **1985 (PG)** WWII drama in which an American agent must stop an enemy spy with knowledge of impending D-Day invasion. Conventional TV fare boasts a fine performance by von Sydow, but Stolz is hopelessly miscast as an adult. Perhaps the only film featuring both Buchholz and Berger. First feature film by NBC-TV network. **95m/C VHS, Beta, LV, Closed Caption.** Ed Harris, Max von Sydow, Eric Stoltz, Horst Buchholz, Helmut Berger, Cyrielle Claire, Patrick Stewart, Graham Crowden; **D:** Jonathan Sanger; **W:** Ronald Bass; **M:** John Addison. *FOX*

Code Name: Zebra 🎬½ **1984** The Zebra Force helps the cops put bad guys away. When the bad guys get out, they want revenge. The result: lots of violence and action. Wasn't released theatrically. **96m/C VHS, Beta.** Jim Mitchum, Mike Lane, Tim Brown, Joe Dante, Deana Jurgens, Frank Sinatra Jr.; **D:** Joe Tornatore. *TWE*

Code of Honor 🎬🎬½ *Sweet Revenge* **1984** A young woman vows revenge on the military commanders who caused her brother's demise. Neatly made psychological thriller is surprisingly good for a TV movie. **105m/C VHS.** Kevin Dobson, Wings Hauser, Alec Baldwin, Merritt Butrick, Kelly McGillis, Alfre Woodard, Savannah Smith, Helen Hunt, Dana Elcar; **D:** David Green. *XVC, VTR*

Code of Honor 🎬 **1988** Prominent businessman embarks on mission of revenge when police fail to apprehend his wife's rapist. No surprise here. You either enjoy this sort of thing or you lead a reasonably fulfilling life. **90m/C VHS.** Cameron Mitchell, Mark Sabin. *NO*

Code of Silence 🎬🎬 **1985 (R)** A police loner must contend with both a gang war and police department corruption. Hectic, violent action-drama with some wild stunts. **100m/C VHS, Beta, LV.** Chuck Norris, Henry Silva, Bert Remsen, Molly Hagan, Nathan Davis, Dennis Farina; **D:** Andrew Davis; **W:** Michael Butler, Mike Gray. *NO*

Code of the Fearless 🎬 **1939** A cowboy wins the heart of a beautiful maiden while bringing evildoers to justice. **56m/B VHS.** Fred Scott, Claire Rochelle, John Merton, Harry Harvey, Walter McGrail, Roger Williams; **D:** Raymond K. Johnson. *NOS, DVT*

Codename: Foxfire 🎬🎬 *Slay It Again, Sam* **1985** An attractive secret agent is framed for wrongdoing and must clear her name by tracking the enemy spy lurking within the intelligence network. Always interesting Cassidy is an asset, but this by-the-numbers TV film is otherwise a misappropriation of the term "intelligence" in relation to espionage. **99m/C VHS, Beta.** Joanna Cassidy, John

McCook, Sheryl Lee Ralph, Henry Jones, Luke Andreas; **D:** Corey Allen. *USH*

Codename: Icarus ♂♂ 1985 A young mathematical genius, enrolled at a special school for accelerated study uncovers evil government plots to use the students for espionage. Made for British television. 106m/C VHS, Beta, Closed Caption. *GB* Barry Angel, Jack Galloway; **D:** Marilyn Fox. *FOX, TVC, VCO*

Codename Kyril ♂♂½ 1991 (R) Woodward plays a British spy pitted against Soviet assassin Kyril (Charleson) who's been sent to England by the KGB to rout out a double agent. Turns out there's more to it than Kyril knows, and nobody loves an assassin. Based on John Trenhaile's "A Man Called Kyril," the script is slow from the gun, but eventually builds something akin to momentum. Made for cable TV. 115m/C VHS. Edward Woodward, Ian Charleson, Denholm Elliott, Joss Ackland, Richard E. Grant, Sven-Bertil Taube, Catherine Nielson, John McEnery, Peter Vaughan, James Laurenson; **D:** Ian Sharp; **W:** John Hopkins. *TTC*

Codename: Terminate ♂½ 1990 Title says it all in this tender exploration of the human condition. Jungle-trained mercenaries grab their guns and go after an American pilot shot down behind enemy lines. 84m/C VHS. Robert Mason, Jim Gaines. *NO*

Codename: Vengeance ♂ 1987 (R) A macho fellow tries to stop a killer holding the shah's wife and son hostage. Dated. 97m/C VHS. Robert Ginty, Cameron Mitchell, Shannon Tweed; **D:** David Winters. *VTR, MCG*

Codename: Wildgeese ♂½ *Geheimecode Wildgänse* 1984 (R) The big-name cast of this meandering mercenary macho-rama probably wish they'd been credited under code names; solid histrionics cannot a silly script save. A troop of commandos-for-hire are engaged by the Drug Enforcement Administration to obliterate an opium operation in Asia's infamous Golden Triangle, and much mindless agitation ensues. 101m/C VHS. *IT GE* Lewis Collins, Lee Van Cleef, Ernest Borgnine, Klaus Kinski, Mimsy Farmer; **D:** Anthony (Antonio Margheriti) Dawson. *VTR*

Cody ♂ 1967 A former bronco buster wants his son to "take it like a man" when the boy's dog dies. Then a mystical goose arrives to mellow the old man. That's really the plot. 82m/C VHS, Beta. Tony Becker, Terry Evans. *NO*

A Coeur Joie ♂♂ *Two Weeks in September* 1967 Sixties set piece about a gorgeous woman who must choose between her much older lover or her newfound stud. Bardot and U.K. scenery keep this one from sinking entirely. In French with English subtitles. 100m/C VHS, Beta. *FR* Brigitte Bardot, Laurent Terzieff; **D:** Serge Bourguignon. *BAR*

Coffy ♂♂ 1973 (R) A beautiful woman feigns drug addiction to discover and destroy the evil dealers responsible for her sister's death. Grier is everything in this exploitative flick full of violence and nudity. 91m/C VHS, Beta, LV. Pam Grier, Booker Bradshaw, Robert DoQui, Allan Arbus; **D:** Jack Hill; **M:** Roy Ayers. *ORI, FCT*

Cohen and Tate ♂♂ 1988 (R) Two antagonistic mob hitmen kidnap a nine-year-old who witnessed his parent's recent murder by the mob. In order to survive, the boy begins to play one psycho off the other. 113m/C VHS, Beta, LV, Closed Caption. Roy Scheider, Adam Baldwin, Harley Cross, Cooper Huckabee; **D:** Eric Red; **W:** Eric Red; **M:** Bill Conti. *NLC*

Cold Around the Heart ♂♂ 1997 (R) Familiar crime/road movie finds sensitive jewel thief Ned (Caruso) partnering up (both in and out of the sack) with tough cookie Jude (Lynch). Only in their latest heist, Jude takes off with the diamonds and Ned's in pursuit across the southwest but, nice guy that Ned is, he stops to help out pregnant, black hitchhiker Bec (Dash). If you don't expect much, you won't be disappointed.**CW:** Strong violence and language, and for sexuality. 96m/C VHS, Closed Caption. David Caruso, Kelly Lynch,

Stacey Dash, Christopher Noth, John Spencer; **D:** John Ridley; **W:** John Ridley; **C:** Malik Hassan Sayeed; **M:** Mason Daring. *FOX*

Cold Blood ♂½ 197? (R) A small dubbed Dutch film about a pair of kidnap victims who turn the tables on their captors. 90m/C VHS, Beta. *NL* Rutger Hauer. *SIM*

Cold Comfort ♂♂½ 1990 (R) A father arranges his teen daughter's romance, but finds his plans going awry in this Canadian thriller. Nominated for several Canadian television awards, including Best Actress, Best Actor, Best Picture and Best Musical Score. 90m/C VHS. *CA* Margaret Langrick, Maury Chaykin, Paul Gross; **D:** Vic Sarin; **W:** Richard Beattie, Elliot L. Sims; **C:** Vic Sarin. *REP*

Cold Comfort Farm ♂♂♂ 1994 (PG) Stella Gibbons classic 1932 comedic novel is brought to life in this TV adaptation, which finds orphaned London lass Flora Poste (Beckinsdale) trying to take charge of the lives of her very odd country cousins, the Starkadders. The rowdy family and their dilapidated farm are putty in practical Flora's hands as she works to make everybody happy (including herself). Terrific ensemble cast, with a fast pace and wicked humor. 104m/C VHS, LV, Closed Caption. *GB* Kate Beckinsale, Eileen Atkins, Ian McKellen, Sheila Burrell, Rufus Sewell, Maria Miles, Freddie Jones, Ivan Kaye, Miriam Margolyes, Joanna Lumley, Stephen Fry, Christopher Bowen; **D:** John Schlesinger; **W:** Malcolm Bradbury; **C:** Chris Seager; **M:** Robert Lockhart. *USH*

Cold Days ♂♂½ 1966 Four men await execution for their part in the WWII massacre of Jews and Serbs. Their reminiscences and justifications, if any, are examined. Stunning cinematography and unusual theme for 1960s Hungarian political climate. 102m/C VHS. *HU* **D:** Andras Kovacs. *FCT*

Cold Eyes of Fear ♂ 197? A man and his girlfriend are besieged by a raving convict whom his uncle, a judge, had put away years before. Shades of "Cape Fear" on a low budget. 88m/C VHS, Beta. Fernando Rey, Frank Wolfe, Karin Schubert; **D:** Enzo G. Castellari; **M:** Ennio Morricone. *TWE*

Cold Feet ♂♂½ 1984 (PG) Light romantic comedy about a television director just recovering from a failed marriage and his fall for a lab researcher who just went through a break-up herself. 96m/C VHS, Beta, Closed Caption. Griffin Dunne, Marissa Chibas, Blanche Baker, Mark Cronogue; **D:** Bruce Van Dusen. *FOX*

Cold Feet ♂♂½ 1989 (R) Modern-day western in which a trio of loopy desperados smuggle jewels inside a racehorse's stomach. Quirky comedy offers wild performances from Waits and sexbomb Kirkland, but could use a few more laughs. Filmed largely on McGuane's ranch. 94m/C VHS, Beta, LV. Keith Carradine, Tom Waits, Sally Kirkland, Rip Torn, Kathleen York, Bill Pullman, Vincent Schiavelli, Jeff Bridges; **D:** Robert Dornhelm; **W:** Thomas McGuane, Jim Harrison; **C:** Bryan Duggan; **M:** Tom Bahler. *ART*

Cold Fever ♂ 1995 Japanese yuppie Atsushi Hirata (Nagase) is expecting to vacation in the tropical paradise of Hawaii not the frozen reaches of Iceland. But instead he must perform a memorial ritual on the remote Icelandic spot where his parents died some time before. He arrives in a blizzard and things just go downhill from there. Some quirky characters but the film loses focus. 85m/C VHS. *IC* Masatoshi Nagase, Gisli Halldorsson, Lili Taylor, Fisher Stevens; **D:** Fridrik Thor Fridriksson; **W:** Fridrik Thor Fridriksson, Jim Stark; **M:** Hilmar Orn Hilmarsson. *FXL*

Cold Front ♂½ 1989 (R) A hired assassin turned serial killer is hunted by two dedicated cops. 94m/C VHS, Beta, LV. *CA* Martin Sheen, Michael Ontkean, Beverly D'Angelo, Kim Coates; **D:** Allan Goldstein; **C:** Thomas Burstyn. *HBO*

Cold Heat ♂♂ 1990 When a custody battle rocks a crime boss' world, he pulls out all the stops in the war against his wife. 85m/C VHS, Beta. John Phillip Law, Britt Ekland, Robert Sacchi, Roy Summer-

set, Joanne Watkins, Chance Michael Corbitt; **D:** Ulli Lommel.

Cold Heaven ♂½ 1992 (R) Alex and Marie Davenport are on vacation when an accident occurs and Alex dies—or does he? The next day his body disappears and his unfaithful wife begins to have paranoid delusions that he is returning to exact retribution for her affair. But these aren't her only visions, for during the past year Marie has also had religious visions she believes are part of a personal battle with God. Harmon does what he can with his role as the alleged corpse but Russell is uncharacteristically whiny and bland. Convoluted story of marriage, death, and spirituality; doesn't pan out on any accounts. Based on a novel by Brian Moore.**CW:** Language and sensuality. 103m/C VHS, LV, Closed Caption. Theresa Russell, Mark Harmon, James Russo, Talia Shire, Will Patton, Richard Bradford; **D:** Nicolas Roeg; **W:** Allan Scott. *FCT*

Cold Justice ♂♂ 1989 (R) An ex-prizefighter (Daltrey) and his friends welcome an English priest into their tough southside Chicago neighborhood. The good father seems too good to be true as he befriends the locals—even raising funds for the children's hospital. When the funds never make it to the hospital and the neighborhood begins to experience a number of violent tragedies, the residents decide to take their own revenge.**CW:** Language. 106m/C VHS, LV. Dennis Waterman, Roger Daltrey, Penelope Milford, Ron Dean, Bert Rosario; **D:** Terry Green; **W:** Terry Green. *COL*

Cold Light of Day ♂♂ 1995 Police officer Victor Marek (Grant) is hunting a serial killer of young children in the English countryside—and he'll do anything, including using a young girl as bait. Marek seduces single mother Milena (Baxter) to use her young daughter to set a trap for the killer but can he catch the madman before it's too late? 101m/C VHS. *GB* Richard E. Grant, Lynsey Baxter, Simon Cadell, Perdita Weeks, James Laurenson, Heathcote Williams; **D:** Rudolf Van Den Berg; **W:** Doug Magee. *PGV*

Cold River ♂♂½ 1981 (PG) An experienced guide takes his two children on an extended trip through the Adirondacks. For the children, it's a fantasy vacation until their father succumbs to a heart attack in the chilly mountains. "Cold River" is a journey of survival, and an exploration of human relationships. 94m/C VHS, Beta. Pat Petersen, Richard Jaeckel, Suzanne Weber; **D:** Fred G. Sullivan. *FCT*

Cold Room ♂½ *The Prisoner* 1984 College student on vacation with her father in East Berlin discovers the horrors hidden in an antiquated hotel room next to hers. Made for cable television. From the novel by Jeffrey Caine. 95m/C VHS, Beta. George Segal, Renee Soutendijk, Amanda Pays, Warren Clarke, Anthony Higgins; **D:** James Dearden; **M:** Michael Nyman. *FOX*

Cold Sassy Tree ♂♂♂½ 1989 Endearing romance of a scandalous May-December marriage as perceived by the younger woman's teenage son. Dunaway and Widmark shine, and small town pettiness is vividly rendered. Adapted from the books by Olive Ann Burns. A superior made-for-cable production. 95m/C VHS. Faye Dunaway, Richard Widmark, Neil Patrick Harris, Frances Fisher, Lee Garlington, John M. Jackson; **D:** Joan Tewkesbury; **W:** Joan Tewkesbury; **M:** Brad Fiedel. *TTC*

Cold Steel ♂½ 1987 (R) Standard revenge drama about a hardnosed Los Angeles cop tracking his father's disfigured psycho-killer. Cast includes the always intense Davis, ex-pop star Ant, and screen scorchstress Stone. Still it's predictable, low-grade fare. 91m/C VHS, Beta. Brad Davis, Jonathan Banks, Adam Ant, Sharon Stone; **D:** Dorothy Ann Puzo. *COL*

Cold Steel for Tortuga ♂ 1965 An Italian epic about a mercenary rescuing his woman and his gold from an evil governor. Dubbed. 95m/C VHS, Beta. *IT* Guy Madison, Rick Battaglia, Ingeborg Schoener; **D:** Luigi Capuano. *NO*

Cold Sweat 🎬🎬 *L'Uomo Dalle Due Ombre; De la Part des Copains* 1974 (PG) A brutal drug trader takes his ultra-violent revenge after his wife is captured by a drug boss' moronic henchmen. Typical Bronson flick boasts superior supporting cast of Ullmann and Mason. Writing and direction, however, are mediocre. 94m/C VHS, Beta. *IT FR* Charles Bronson, Jill Ireland, Liv Ullmann, James Mason; *D:* Terence Young. *GEM, MRV*

Cold Sweat 🎬🎬 1993 (R) A professional hit man (Cross) is literally haunted by the ghost of his last victim (who happens to be female and usually appears naked), so he decides his next assignment will be his last. A ruthless businessman suspects his very sexy wife (Tweed) has been unfaithful but she has lots of other secrets to hide. *CW:* Language, violence, and strong sexuality. 93m/C VHS, Beta, Closed Caption. Ben Cross, Shannon Tweed, Adam Baldwin, Dave Thomas; *D:* Gail Harvey; *W:* Richard Beattie. *PAR, VTR*

Cold Turkey 🎬🎬 1971 (PG) Often witty satire about what happens when an entire town tries to stop smoking for a contest. Van Dyke is fine as the anti-smoking minister; newscasters Bob and Ray are riotous; oldtimer Horton's swansong. Wholesome, somewhat tame fare. 99m/C VHS, Beta, LV. Dick Van Dyke, Pippa Scott, Tom Poston, Bob Newhart, Vincent Gardenia, Barnard Hughes, Jean Stapleton, Graham Jarvis, Edward Everett Horton; *D:* Norman Lear; *M:* Randy Newman. *MGM*

Cold War Killers 🎬1/2 1986 (PG) Soviet and British agents vie for control of prized cargo plane recently retrieved from the sea floor. 85m/C VHS, Beta. *GB* Terence Stamp; *D:* William Brayne. *NO*

Coldblooded 🎬1/2 1994 (R) Minor mob flunky (and dim bulb) Cosmo (Priestley) is unwillingly promoted to the position of hit man by his mobster boss. He's tutored by the organization's primo professional (Riegert) and finds out he has a real knack for murder. More sophomoric than satiric and a waste of Riegert's talents; Williams is attractive as Priestley's clueless girlfriend. Directorial debut of Wolodarsky. *CW:* Some graphic violence, sexual dialogue and language. 92m/C VHS. Jason Priestley, Peter Riegert, Kimberly Williams, Robert Loggia, Janeane Garofalo, Josh Charles, David Anthony Higgens, Doris Grau; *Cameos:* Talia Balsam, Michael J. Fox; *D:* M. Wallace Wolodarsky; *W:* M. Wallace Wolodarsky; *C:* Robert Yeoman; *M:* Steve Bartek. *PGV*

Coldfire 🎬1/2 1990 Two rookie cops work to undo the havoc unleashed on the streets of LA because of a deadly new drug sought for its powerful high. Not many surprises here. 90m/C VHS, LV. Wings Hauser, Kamar Reyes, Robert Viharo, Gary Swanson; *D:* Wings Hauser. *PMH*

The Colditz Story 🎬🎬1/2 1955 Prisoners of war from the Allied countries join together in an attempt to escape from Colditz, an allegedly escape-proof castle-prison deep within the Third Reich. 93m/B VHS, Beta. John Mills, Eric Portman, Lionel Jeffries, Bryan Forbes, Ian Carmichael, Anton Diffring; *D:* Guy Hamilton. *REP, CNG*

Cole Justice 🎬🎬 1989 An older man, haunted by the memory of his girlfriend's rape and murder 35 years earlier, takes to the streets to protect innocent citizens from lowlife criminals. Somewhat unusual revenge pic filmed in and around Tulsa, Oklahoma. 90m/C VHS, Beta. Carl Bartholomew, Keith Andrews, Mike Wiles, Nick Zickefoose; *D:* Carl Bartholomew. *NO*

The Collector 🎬🎬🎬1/2 1965 Compelling adaptation of the John Fowles novel about a withdrawn butterfly collector who decides to add to his collection by kidnapping a beautiful girl he admires. He locks her in his cellar hoping she will fall in love with him. Chilling, unsettling drama with Stamp unnerving, yet sympathetic in lead. 119m/C VHS, Beta, LV. *GB* Terence Stamp, Samantha Eggar, Maurice Dalton, Mona Washbourne; *D:* William Wyler; *C:* Robert Krasker, Robert L. Surtees; *M:* Maurice Jarre. Cannes Film Festival '65: Best Actor (Stamp), Best Actress (Eggar); Golden Globe Awards '66: Best Actress—Drama (Eggar); Nominations: Academy Awards '65: Best Actress

(Eggar), Best Adapted Screenplay, Best Director (Wyler). *COL*

Collector's Item 🎬🎬🎬 1989 Two lovers reunite after 16 years and a flurry of memories temporarily rekindles their passion, which comes dangerously close to obsession. Casting of the physically bountiful Antonelli helps this effective erotic drama. 99m/C VHS, Beta. *IT* Tony Musante, Laura Antonelli, Florinda Bolkan; *D:* Giuseppe Patroni Griffi. *NO*

College 🎬🎬🎬1/2 1927 A high school valedictorian tries out for every sport in college, hoping to win the girl. Vintage Keaton antics, including disaster as a soda jerk, an attempt to be a track star, and the pole vault through a window to rescue the damsel in distress. 60m/B VHS, Beta, LV. Buster Keaton, Anne Cornwall, Harold Goodwin; *D:* James W. Horne; *M:* John Muri. *DVT, MRV, CCB*

College Swing 🎬1/2 *Swing, Teacher, Swing* 1938 Lightweight, lackluster musical about Allen inheriting a small town college which she turns into a hangout for her vaudeville pals. Top cast is basically wasted performing many forgettable songs and familiar routines. Based on an adaptation by Frederick Hazlitt Brennan from a story by Ted Lesser. ♫College Swing; What Did Romeo Say to Juliet?; I Fall In Love With You Every Day; You're a Natural; The Old School Bell; Moments Like This; How D'ja Like to Love Me?; What a Rumba Does to Romance. 86m/B VHS, Beta, Closed Caption. George Burns, Gracie Allen, Martha Raye, Bob Hope, Edward Everett Horton, Ben Blue, Betty Grable, Jackie Coogan, John Payne; *D:* Raoul Walsh. *USH, BTV*

Collision Course 🎬 1989 (PG) A wisecracking cop from Detroit teams up with Japan's best detective to nail a ruthless gang leader. Release was delayed until 1992 due to a lawsuit, but it was resolved in time to coordinate the release with Leno's debut as the host of "The Tonight Show." Pretty marginal, but diehard fans of Leno may appreciate it. Filmed on location in Detroit. 99m/C VHS, Beta, LV, Closed Caption. Noriyuki "Pat" Morita, Jay Leno, Chris Sarandon, Al Waxman; *D:* Lewis Teague. *HBO*

The Colombian Connection 🎬1/2 1991 America's best undercover agent battles a powerful cocaine empire deep in the jungles of the Amazon, where slave labor and political corruption abound. 90m/C VHS, Beta. Miles O'Keeffe, Henry Silva. *NO*

Colonel Chabert 🎬🎬 1994 In the 1807 Battle of Eylau, French officer Chabert (Depardieu) is thought dead and stripped of all he possesses. After 10 years of imprisonment, a man shows up in the office of Paris lawyer Derville (Luchini), claiming to be the dead Chabert. His remarried wife (Ardant), now the Countess Ferraud, has used his fortune to bolster the political aspirations of her second husband (Dussolier) and refuses to acknowledge this stranger's claims. Is Chabert a fraud? And what exactly are the motives of all the players? Based on the novel by Honore de Balzac. Directorial debut of Angelo. French with subtitles. 111m/C VHS. *FR* Gerard Depardieu, Fanny Ardant, Fabrice Luchini, Andre Dussollier; *D:* Yves Angelo; *W:* Yves Angelo, Jean Cosmos, Veronique Lagrange; *C:* Bernard Lutic. Nominations: Cesar Awards '94: Best Actor (Depardieu). *REP*

Colonel Effingham's Raid 🎬🎬1/2 *Man of the Hour* 1945 A retired army colonel uses military tactics to keep an old historical courthouse open, while defeating some crooked politicians in the process. 70m/B VHS, Beta. Joan Bennett, Charles Coburn, William Eythe, Donald Meek; *D:* Irving Pichel. *NOS, HEG*

Colonel Redl 🎬🎬🎬🎬 1984 (R) Absorbing, intricately rendered psychological study of an ambitious officer's rise and fall in pre-WWI Austria. Brandauer is excellent as the vain, insecure homosexual ultimately undone by his own ambition and his superior officer's smug loathing. Muller-Stahl and Landgrebe are particularly distinguished among the supporting players. The sec-

ond in the Szabo/Brandauer trilogy, after "Mephisto" and before "Hanussen." In German with English subtitles. 114m/C VHS, Beta, LV. *GE HU* Klaus Maria Brandauer, Armin Mueller-Stahl, Gudrun Landgrebe, Jan Niklas, Hans-Christian Blech, Laszlo Mensaros, Andras Balint; *D:* Laszlo Szabo; *C:* Lajos Koltai. British Academy Awards '85: Best Foreign Film; Cannes Film Festival '85: Special Jury Prize; Nominations: Academy Awards '85: Best Foreign Language Film. *FCT, GLV, TPV*

Colonel Wolodyjowski 🎬🎬1/2 1969 An adaptation of the monumental novels by Henryk Sinkiewicz chronicling the attack on Poland's eastern border by the Turks in 1668. In Polish with English subtitles. 160m/C VHS. *PL* Tadeusz Loniski, Magdalena Zawadzka, Daniel Olbrychski; *D:* Jerzy Hoffman. *FCT*

The Colony 🎬🎬1/2 1995 (PG-13) "The Colony" is a luxurious and exclusive gated community owned by secretive billionaire developer Phillip Denning (Linden). Newest residents, security expert Rick Knowlton (Ritter), wife Leslie (Keller) and their two children, find out things are just too good to be true—and that trying to leave could be the very last thing they'll ever do. *CW:* Some violence. 93m/C VHS, Closed Caption. John Ritter, Hal Linden, Mary Page Keller, Marshall Teague, Frank Bonner, Michelle Scarabelli, June Lockhart, Todd Jeffries, Alexandra Picatto, Cody Dorkin; *D:* Rob Hedden; *W:* Rob Hedden; *C:* David Geddes. *USH*

Color Me Blood Red WOOF! *Model Massacre* 1964 Artist decides that the red in his paintings is best rendered with human blood. He even manages to continue his art career—when not busy stabbing and mutilating the unsuspecting citizenry. Short and shoddy. 74m/C VHS, Beta. Don Joseph, Candi Conder, Elyn Warner, Scott H. Hall, Jerome Eden, Patricia Lee, James Jackel; *D:* Herschell Gordon Lewis; *W:* Herschell Gordon Lewis; *C:* Herschell Gordon Lewis. *SMW*

Color Me Dead 🎬1/2 1969 (R) A victim of an extremely slow-acting poison frantically spends his final days trying to uncover his killer. Another inferior remake of B-thriller "D.O.A." Rent that one instead. 97m/C VHS. *AU* Tom Tryon, Carolyn Jones, Rick Jason, Patricia Connolly, Tony Ward; *D:* Eddie Davis. *REP*

Color of a Brisk and Leaping Day 🎬🎬 1995 While living in L.A. at the end of WWII, Chinese-American John Lee (Alexander) learns that the Yosemite Valley Railroad is being scrapped and he becomes determined to save it—in part as a homage to his grandfather who emigrated to work as a railroad laborer. A romantic train fanatic himself, Lee arranges financing from wealthy businessman Pinchot (Diehl) but must make the railroad pay within a year—unlikely as the automobile rapidly takes over as preferred transportation. Well-captures a '40s atmosphere but pacing and dialogue are uneven. 87m/B VHS. Peter Alexander, Jeri Arredondo, Henry Gibson, Michael Stipe, John Diehl, David Chung, Diana Larkin, Bok Yun Chon; *D:* Christopher Munch; *W:* Christopher Munch; *C:* Rob Sweeney. Sundance Film Festival '96: Best Cinematography; Nominations: Independent Spirit Awards '97: Best Cinematography. *NYR*

The Color of Evening 🎬🎬 1995 Aging painter Landau tries to regain his youth by pursuing his young model Skye, but it's the older Burstyn who really inspires his imagination. ?m/C VHS. Martin Landau, Ellen Burstyn, Ione Skye. *YHV*

The Color of Money 🎬🎬🎬1/2 1986 (R) Flashy, gripping drama about former pool hustler Fast Eddie Felsen (Newman) who, after years off the circuit, takes a brilliant but immature pool shark (Cruise) under his wing. Strong performances by Newman as the grizzled veteran, Cruise as the showboating youth, and Mastrantonio and Shaver as the men's worldly girlfriends. Worthy sequel to "The Hustler." 119m/C VHS, Beta, LV. Paul Newman, Tom Cruise, Mary Elizabeth Mastrantonio, Helen Shaver, John Turturro, Forest Whitaker; *D:* Martin Scorsese; *W:* Richard Price; *C:* Michael Ballhaus. Academy Awards '86: Best Actor (Newman); National Board of

Review Awards '86: Best Actor (Newman); Nominations: Academy Awards '86: Best Adapted Screenplay, Best Art Direction/Set Decoration, Best Supporting Actress (Mastrantonio). TOU, BTV

Color of Night 🐾½ **1994 (R)** Psychologist Dr. Bill Capa (Willis) takes over a murdered colleague's therapy group hoping to find out the killer's identity. Then he meets temptress Rose (March) and gets involved in a hot affair, but she's not what she seems—nor is anyone else. Preposterous thriller fails to deliver necessary suspense although the eroticism could spark some interest, particularly in the director's cut, which puts the sex back in the sex scenes between Willis and March (and is 15 minutes longer than the theatrical release). **136m/C VHS.** Bruce Willis, Jane March, Scott Bakula, Ruben Blades, Lesley Ann Warren, Lance Henriksen, Kevin J. O'Connor, Andrew Lowery, Brad Dourif, Eriq La Salle, Jeff Corey, Shirley Knight, Kathleen Wilhoite; **D:** Richard Rush; **W:** Matthew Chapman, Billy Ray, Richard Rush; **M:** Dominic Frontiere. Golden Raspberry Awards '94: Worst Picture; Nominations: Golden Globe Awards '95: Best Song ("The Color of the Night"); Golden Raspberry Awards '94: Worst Actor (Willis). HPH

The Color of Pomegranates 🐾🐾🐾 *Sayat Nova; Tsvet Granata* **1969** Paradjanov's depiction of the life of Armenian poet Arutiun Sayadin, known as Sayat Nova, who rises from carpet weaver to court minstrel to archbishop. Eloquent imagery and symbols are derived from Armenian paintings, poetry and history. In Armenian with English subtitles. Also includes "Hagop Hovnatanian," a 12-minute short on the artist. **80m/C VHS.** RU Sofiko Chiaureli, M. Aleksanian, V. Galstian; **D:** Sergei Paradjanov; **W:** Sergei Paradjanov. NYF, FCT, CVC

The Color Purple 🐾🐾🐾½ **1985 (PG-13)** Celie is a poor black girl who fights for her self-esteem when she is separated from her sister and forced into a brutal marriage. Spanning 1909 to 1947 in a small Georgia town, the movie chronicles the joys, pains, and people in her life. Adaptation of Alice Walker's acclaimed book features strong lead from Goldberg (in her screen debut), Glover, Avery, and talk-show host Winfrey (also her film debut). It's hard to see director Spielberg as the most suited for this one, but he acquits himself nicely, avoiding the facileness that sometimes flaws his pics. Brilliant photography by Allen Daviau and musical score by Jones (who co-produced) compliment this strong film. **154m/C VHS, Beta, LV, Letterbox, Closed Caption, DVD.** Whoopi Goldberg, Danny Glover, Oprah Winfrey, Margaret Avery, Adolph Caesar, Rae Dawn Chong, Willard Pugh, Akosua Busia; **D:** Steven Spielberg; **C:** Allen Daviau; **M:** Chris Boardman, Quincy Jones. Directors Guild of America Awards '85: Best Director (Spielberg); Golden Globe Awards '86: Best Actress—Drama (Goldberg); National Board of Review Awards '85: Best Actress (Goldberg); Nominations: Academy Awards '85: Best Actress (Goldberg), Best Adapted Screenplay, Best Art Direction/Set Decoration, Best Cinematography, Best Costume Design, Best Makeup, Best Picture, Best Song ("Miss Celie's Blues (Sister)"), Best Supporting Actress (Avery, Winfrey), Best Original Score. WAR, FCT

Colorado 🐾½ **1940** Roy tries to find his brother, a Union deserter, during the Civil War. **54m/B VHS, Beta.** Roy Rogers, George "Gabby" Hayes, Milburn Stone; **D:** Joseph Kane. NOS, DVT, TIM

Colorado Serenade 🐾🐾 **1946** Standard oater has Dean, Sharpe and Ates trying to prevent a young outlaw from bullying the local citizenry. Sharpe shows off his athletic prowess, and King provides some laughs. Other than that, it's pretty routine stuff. **68m/C VHS.** Eddie Dean, David Sharpe, Roscoe Ates, Forrest Taylor, Dennis Moore, Warner Richmond, Bob Duncan, Charles "Blackie" King; **D:** Robert Emmett Tansey. NOS, RXM, HEG

Colorado Sundown 🐾 **1952** A conniving brother and sister attempt to cheat a man out of his inheritance. **67m/B VHS.** Rex Allen, Mary Ellen Kay, Slim Pickens, June Vincent, Koko; **D:** William Witney. NOS, DVT

Colors 🐾🐾🐾½ **1988 (R)** Vivid, realistic cop drama pairs sympathetic veteran Duvall and trigger-tempered rookie Penn on the gang-infested streets of East Los Angeles. Fine play from leads is one of the many assets in this controversial, unsettling depiction of deadly streetlife. Colorful, freewheeling direction from the underrated Hopper. Rattling rap soundtrack too. Additional footage has been added for video release. **120m/C VHS, Beta, LV, Closed Caption.** Sean Penn, Robert Duvall, Maria Conchita Alonso, Trinidad Silva, Randi Brooks, Grand Bush, Don Cheadle, Rudy Ramos; **D:** Dennis Hopper; **W:** Michael Schiffer; **C:** Haskell Wexler; **M:** Herbie Hancock. ORI, FCT

Colossus and the Amazon Queen 🐾½ **1964** Idle gladiators are unwillingly recruited for service to Amazons. Doesn't seem like the worst way to make a living. But lead actor Taylor—so notable in comedies, thrillers, and action flicks—is too good for this sort of thing. Dubbed. **94m/C VHS, Beta, 8mm.** IT Rod Taylor, Dorian Gray, Ed Fury. VYY

Colossus of the Arena 🐾🐾 **1960** In 4th century Rome, Forest plays a mighty gladiator who uncovers a plot to imprison a beautiful princess. Through an incredible series of feats and combats, he exposes an evil duke as a traitor. **?m/C VHS.** Mark Forest, Scilla Gabel. SNC

Colossus: The Forbin Project 🐾🐾🐾 *The Forbin Project* **1970** A computer designed to manage U.S. defense systems teams instead with its Soviet equal and they attempt world domination. Wire-tight, suspenseful film seems at once dated yet timely. Based on the novel by D.F. Jones. **100m/C VHS, Beta.** Eric (Hans Gudegast) Braeden, Susan Clark, Gordon Pinsent, William Schallert, Georg Stanford Brown; **D:** Joseph Sargent; **W:** James Bridges; **C:** Gene Polito; **M:** Michel Colombier. USH

Colt Comrades 🐾🐾 **1943** A bad guy's monopoly on water rights is jeopardized when Boyd and Clyde strike water while drilling for oil. Nothing really notable here, except for Bob (Robert) Mitchum and George ("Superman") Reeves in minor roles. **67m/B VHS.** William Boyd, Andy Clyde, Jay Kirby, George Reeves, Gayle Lord, Earle Hodgins, Victor Jory, Douglas Fowley, Herbert Rawlinson, Robert Mitchum; **D:** Lesley Selander. NOS

Columbo: Murder By the Book 🐾🐾½ **1971** The rumpled, cigar-smoking television detective investigates the killing of a mystery writer. Scripted by Bochco of "Hill Street Blues" and "L.A. Law" fame. **79m/C VHS, Beta.** Peter Falk, Jack Cassidy, Rosemary Forsyth, Martin Milner; **D:** Steven Spielberg; **W:** Steven Bochco. USH

Columbo: Prescription Murder **1967** Falk's debut as the raincoat-clad lieutenant who always has just one more question. In the TV series pilot he investigates the death of a psychiatrist's wife. Rich with subplots. Good mystery fare. **99m/C VHS, Beta.** Peter Falk, Gene Barry, Katherine Justice, William Windom, Nina Foch, Anthony James, Virginia Gregg; **D:** Richard Irving; **W:** Richard Levinson, William Link. USH

Coma 🐾🐾🐾 **1978 (PG)** A doctor discovers murder and corpse-napping at her Boston hospital, defies her male bosses, and determines to find out what's going on before more patients die. Exciting, suspenseful fare, with Bujold impressive in lead. Based on the novel by Robin Cook. **113m/C VHS, Beta, LV.** Genevieve Bujold, Michael Douglas, Elizabeth Ashley, Rip Torn, Richard Widmark, Lois Chiles, Hari Rhodes, Tom Selleck, Ed Harris; **D:** Michael Crichton; **W:** Michael Crichton; **M:** Jerry Goldsmith. MGM

Comanche Station 🐾🐾½ **1960** Loner Jefferson Cody (Scott) agrees to rescue Mrs. Lowe (Gates), a senator's wife who's been captured by the Comanches. After Cody achieves her rescue, they fall in with outlaw Ben Lane (Akins) and his two young proteges, who insist on accompanying them back to the Lowe homestead, saying that they'll need additional protection. But Cody soon realizes that Lane is after the reward

money and is planning an ambush. **73m/C VHS.** Randolph Scott, Nancy Gates, Claude Akins, Skip Homeier, Richard Rust, Rand Brooks; **D:** Budd Boetticher; **W:** Burt Kennedy; **C:** Charles Lawton Jr. COL

Comanche Territory 🐾🐾 **1950** Western frontiersman Jim Bowie travels to Comanche country and helps the Indians save their land from settlers. Routine oater. Based on a story by Meltzer. **76m/C VHS, Closed Caption.** Maureen O'Hara, MacDonald Carey, Will Geer, Charles Drake; **D:** George Sherman; **W:** Oscar Brodney, Lewis Meltzer. USH

The Comancheros 🐾🐾 **1961** Texas Ranger Wayne and his prisoner fight with the Comancheros, an outlaw gang who is supplying guns and liquor to the dreaded Comanche Indians. Musical score adds flavor. Last film by Curtiz. **108m/C VHS, Beta, LV, Letterbox, Closed Caption.** John Wayne, Ina Balin, Stuart Whitman, Nehemiah Persoff, Lee Marvin, Bruce Cabot; **D:** Michael Curtiz; **C:** William Clothier; **M:** Elmer Bernstein. FOX

Combat! **1962** Morrow and Jason starred in this gritty series about an Army platoon in Europe during the final years of WWII. In "The Bridge at Chalons" Marvin guest stars as a demolitions expert. Additional episodes available. **50m/B VHS, Beta.** Vic Morrow, Rick Jason, Lee Marvin. GKK, MOV

Combat Academy 🐾 **1986** Weak comedy about two goofballs sent to a military academy to straighten out, but instead turn the academy on its ear with their antics. Unremarkable. **96m/C VHS, LV.** Keith Gordon, Jamie Farr, Sherman Hemsley, John Ratzenberger, Bernie Kopell, Charles Moll; **D:** Neal Israel. VTR

Combat Killers 🐾🐾 **1980** A WWII Army captain grabs for individual glory on the battlefield, and jeopardizes the lives of his platoon. **96m/C VHS, Beta.** Paul Edwards, Marlene Dauden, Claude Wilson; **D:** Ken Loring.

Combat Shock 🐾 *American Nightmares* **1984 (R)** A Vietnam veteran returns home and can't cope with the stresses of modern life, including the lowlifes who have been taking over the streets. So he goes after some scum who have been trying to kill him, succeeds, but things don't end well. Familiar plot handled in a conventional manner. **85m/C VHS, Beta.** Ricky Giovinazzo, Nick Nasta, Veronica Stork; **D:** Buddy Giovinazzo.

Combination Platter 🐾🐾½ **1993** Anxious young immigrant Robert (Lau), newly arrived from Hong Kong, becomes a waiter at the Szechuan Inn in Queens, New York, where he gets a crash course in American culture and romance (as well as tipping). Gentle comedy works best with little details that ring true: overheard customer conversations, staff banter, the kitchen scenes. Lau's earnest, but effort feels like a series of small vignettes rather than a complete story. Still, a worthy first effort for the then 24-year-old Chan, who directed on a $250,000 budget, using his parents restaurant after hours for a set. **84m/C VHS.** Jeff Lau, Colleen O'Brien, Lester Chan, Thomas S. Hsiung, David Chung, Colin Mitchell, Kenneth Lu, Eleonara Khilberg, James DuMont; **D:** Tony Chan; **W:** Tony Chan, Edwin Baker; **C:** Yoshifumi Hosoya; **M:** Brian Tibbs. Sundance Film Festival '93: Best Screenplay; Nominations: Independent Spirit Awards '94: Best First Feature, Best Screenplay, Best Supporting Actor (Chung). AVI

Come Along with Me 🐾🐾½ **1984** A made-for-television adaptation of Shirley Jackson's unfinished novel about a woman who sells all and leaves her hometown when her husband dies, determined to start a new career as a seer. **60m/C VHS, Beta.** Estelle Parsons, Barbara Baxley, Sylvia Sidney; **D:** Joanne Woodward. MON, KAR

Come and Get It 🐾🐾🐾 *Roaring Timber* **1936** A classic adaptation of the Edna Ferber novel about a lumber king battling against his son for the love of a woman. Farmer's most important Hollywood role. **99m/B VHS, Beta.** Frances Farmer, Edward Arnold, Joel McCrea, Walter Brennan, Andrea Leeds, Charles Halton; **D:** William Wyler, Howard Hawks. Academy

Awards '36: Best Supporting Actor (Brennan); Nominations: Academy Awards '36: Best Film Editing. *HBO, DTV*

Come and See *IIII* ~Idi i Smotri; Go and See~ 1985 Harrowing, unnerving epic which depicts the horrors of war as a boy soldier roams the Russian countryside during the Nazi invasion. Some overwhelming sequences, including tracer-bullets flashing across an open field. War has rarely been rendered in such a vivid, utterly grim manner. Outstanding achievement from Soviet director Klimov. In Russian with English subtitles. 142m/C VHS. *RU* Alexei Kravchenko, Olga Mironova, Lubomiras Lauciavicus; *D:* Elem Klimov. *KIV, FCT, TPV*

Come Back, Little Sheba *IIII½* 1952 Unsettling drama about a worn-out housewife, her abusive, alcoholic husband and a comely boarder who causes further marital tension. The title refers to the housewife's despairing search for her lost dog. Booth, Lancaster, and Moore are all excellent. Based on the play by William Inge, this film still packs an emotional wallop. 99m/B VHS, Beta, LV, Closed Caption. Burt Lancaster, Shirley Booth, Terry Moore, Richard Jaeckel, Philip Ober, Lisa Golm, Walter Kelley; *D:* Daniel Mann; *C:* James Wong Howe. Academy Awards '52: Best Actress (Booth); Cannes Film Festival '53: Best Actress (Booth); Golden Globe Awards '53: Best Actress (Booth); New York Film Critics Awards '52: Best Actress (Booth); Nominations: Academy Awards '52: Best Film Editing, Best Supporting Actress (Moore). *PAR, FCT, BTV*

Come Back to the Five & Dime Jimmy Dean, Jimmy Dean *IIII* 1982 (PG) Five women convene at a run-down Texas drugstore for a 20-year reunion of a local James Dean fan club. The women recall earlier times and make some stunning revelations. Altman's filming of Ed Graczyk's sometimes funny, sometimes wrenching play proves fine vehicle for the actresses. Cher is probably the most impressive, but Dennis and Black are also memorable. 109m/C VHS, Beta, LV. Sandy Dennis, Cher, Karen Black, Kathy Bates, Sudie Bond, Marta Heflin; *D:* Robert Altman.

Come Blow Your Horn *III* 1963 Neil Simon's first major Broadway success is a little less successful in its celluloid wrapper, suffering a bit from a familiar script. Sinatra's a playboy who blows his horn all over town, causing his close-knit New York Jewish family to warp a bit. Dad's not keen on his son's pledge of allegiance to the good life, and kid brother Bill would like to be his sibling's understudy in playboyhood. 115m/C VHS, Beta, Closed Caption. Frank Sinatra, Lee J. Cobb, Tony Bill, Molly Picon, Barbara Rush, Jill St. John; *D:* Bud Yorkin; *W:* Norman Lear; *C:* William H. Daniels. Nominations: Academy Awards '63: Best Art Direction/Set Decoration (Color). *PAR*

Come On, Cowboys *II½* 1937 The Three Mesquiteers rescue an old circus friend from certain death. Part of "The Three Mesquiteers" series. 54m/B VHS, Beta. Bob Livingston, Ray Corrigan. *DVT*

Come On Danger! *II½* 1932 Keene makes his "B" Western debut, out to avenge the death of his brother and battle an outlaw gang. Haydon is forced into a life of crime in order to save her ranch from villain Ellis and only Texas Ranger Keene can set her free. 60m/B VHS. Tom Keene, Julie Haydon, Roscoe Ates, Robert Ellis, Wade Boteler; *D:* Robert F. "Bob" Hill; *W:* Bennett Cohen. *MOV*

Come On Rangers *II* ~Come On Ranger~ 1938 Rogers and his friends go to Texas to avenge the death of a comrade. 54m/B VHS, Beta. Roy Rogers, George "Gabby" Hayes. *NOS, DVT, RXM*

Come On Tarzan *II½* 1932 Maynard and his trusty horse Tarzan save wild horses from the bad guys who want to turn them into dog food. 60m/B VHS, Beta. Ken Maynard. *NOS, VDM, DVT*

Come See the Paradise *III* 1990 (R) Jack McGurn (Quaid) takes a job at a movie theatre in Los Angeles' Little Tokyo and falls for owner's daughter Lily (Tomita). They marry, but after the bombing of Pearl Harbor all Japanese Americans are interned. Told in flashback, the story offers a candid look at the racism implicit in the relocations and the hypocrisy that often lurks beneath the surface of the pursuit of liberty and justice for all. Sometimes melodramatic script indulges a bit too much in the obvious, but the subject is worthwhile, one that has not yet been cast into the vast bin of Hollywood cliches. The cast, apart from Quaid's misguided attempt at seriousness, is excellent. 135m/C VHS, Beta, LV, Letterbox, Closed Caption. Dennis Quaid, Tamlyn Tomita, Sab Shimono, Shizuko Hoshi, Stan Egi, Ronald Yamamoto, Akemi Nishino, Naomi Nakano, Brady Tsurutani, Pruitt Taylor Vince, Joe Lisi; *D:* Alan Parker; *W:* Alan Parker; *M:* Randy Edelman. *FOX, FCT, CCB*

Come September *II½* 1961 American business tycoon Robert Talbot (Hudson) maintains a holiday villa on the Italian Riviera. But the only time he uses the place is the month of September, so when Talbot arrives in July he discovers his enterprising major domo Maurice (Slezak) has been managing the place as a hotel the rest of the year. Talbot finds his home filled with tourists and, to make matters worse, discovers his Italian lover Lisa (Lollobrigida) about to get married. Darin and Dee are the film's romantic ingenues and wound up getting married after filming wrapped; his screen debut. 114m/C VHS, Closed Caption. Rock Hudson, Gina Lollobrigida, Sandra Dee, Bobby Darin, Walter Slezak, Joel Grey, Brenda de Banzie; *D:* Robert Mulligan; *W:* Stanley Shapiro, Maurice Richlin; *C:* William H. Daniels; *M:* Hans J. Salter. *USH*

Come to the Stable *III* 1949 Warm, delightful story about two French nuns, Young and Holm, who arrive in New England and set about building a children's hospital. Although Catholic in intent, pic demonstrates that faith and tenacity can move mountains. (This film must have been Fox's response to Paramount's "Going My Way" and "The Bells of Saint Mary's.") Based on a story by Clare Boothe Luce. 94m/B VHS. Loretta Young, Celeste Holm, Hugh Marlowe, Elsa Lanchester, Regis Toomey, Mike Mazurki; *D:* Henry Koster; *W:* Oscar Millard, Sally Benson; *C:* Joseph LaShelle; *M:* Cyril Mockridge. Nominations: Academy Awards '49: Best Actress (Young), Best Art Direction/Set Decoration (B & W), Best Black and White Cinematography, Best Song ("Through a Long and Sleepless Night"), Best Story, Best Supporting Actress (Holm, Lanchester). *FXV*

The Comeback *I* ~The Day the Screaming Stopped~ 1977 A singer attempting a comeback in England finds his wife murdered. 100m/C VHS, Beta. *GB* Jack Jones, Pamela Stephenson, David Doyle, Bill Owen, Sheila Keith, Richard Johnson; *D:* Pete Walker. *ORI*

Comeback *II½* 1983 The story of a disillusioned rock star, played by Eric Burdon (the lead singer of the Animals), who gives up his life in the fast lane and tries to go back to his roots. 105m/C VHS, Beta. Eric Burdon; *D:* Christel Bushmann; *M:* Eric Burdon. *MGM*

Comeback Kid *II* 1980 An ex-big league baseball player is conned into coaching an urban team of smarmy street youths, and falls for their playground supervisor. Made for television. 97m/C VHS, Beta. John Ritter, Susan Dey; *D:* Peter Levin. *NLC*

The Comedians *II½* 1967 Disturbing and powerful drama of political intrigue set against the murderous dictatorship of "Papa Doc" Duvalier. Burton plays the cynical owner of a resort hotel in Haiti as his German mistress. Ustinov is great as he does his usual scene-stealing in his role as a South American ambassador married to Taylor. Excellent cast was somewhat held back by sluggish direction and an uninspired script. Based on the novel of the same name by Graham Greene. 148m/C VHS. Elizabeth Taylor, Richard Burton, Alec Guinness, Peter Ustinov, Paul Ford, Lillian Gish, Raymond St. Jacques, Zakes Mokae; *D:* Peter Glenville; *W:* Graham Greene. National Board of Review Awards '67: Best Supporting Actor (Ford). *MGM*

The Comedy of Terrors *III* 1964 Comedy in which some deranged undertakers take a hands-on approach to insuring their continued employment. Much fun is supplied by the quartet of Price, Lorre, Karloff, and Rathbone, all veterans of the horror genre. 84m/C VHS, LV. Vincent Price, Peter Lorre, Boris Karloff, Basil Rathbone, Joe E. Brown, Joyce Jameson; *D:* Jacques Tourneur; *W:* Richard Matheson; *C:* Floyd Crosby; *M:* Les Baxter. *MOV*

Comes a Horseman *II½* 1978 (PG) Robards is a cattle baron, attempting to gobble up all the oil-rich land his neighbor owns. Neighbor Fonda has the courage to stand up to him, with the help of a WWII veteran and the local old timer Farnsworth, in this slow-moving but intriguing western drama. 119m/C VHS, Beta. James Caan, Jane Fonda, Jason Robards Jr., George Grizzard, Richard Farnsworth, Jim Davis, Mark Harmon; *D:* Alan J. Pakula; *W:* Dennis Lynton Clark; *C:* Gordon Willis. National Board of Review Awards '78: Best Supporting Actor (Farnsworth); National Society of Film Critics Awards '78: Best Supporting Actor (Farnsworth); Nominations: Academy Awards '78: Best Supporting Actor (Farnsworth). *MGM*

Comfort and Joy *III½* 1984 (PG) After his kleptomaniac girlfriend deserts him, a Scottish disc jockey is forced to reevaluate his life. He becomes involved in an underworld battle between two mob-owned local ice cream companies. Another odd comedy gem from Forsyth, who did "Gregory's Girl" and "Local Hero." Music by Dire Straits guitarist Knopfler. 93m/C VHS, Beta. *GB* Bill Paterson, Eleanor David, C.P. Grogan, Alex Norton, Patrick Malahide, Rikki Fulton, Roberto Berrardi; *D:* Bill Forsyth; *C:* Chris Menges; *M:* Mark Knopfler. National Society of Film Critics Awards '84: Best Cinematography. *USH*

The Comfort of Strangers *III* 1991 (R) Atmospheric psychological thriller. Mary and Colin (Richardson and Everett), a handsome young British couple, take a Venetian holiday to rediscover the passion in their relationship. Lost in the city, they chance, it seems, upon Robert (Walken), a sort of Virgil in an Armani suit. He later reappears, and, abetted by his wife Caroline (Mirren), gradually leads the couple on an eerie tour of urbane decadence that hints at danger. Psychologically tantalizing and horrifyingly erotic, the movie's based on Ian McEwan's novel. *CW:* Obsessive and perverse sexuality. 102m/C VHS, Beta, Closed Caption. Christopher Walken, Natasha Richardson, Rupert Everett, Helen Mirren; *D:* Paul Schrader; *W:* Harold Pinter; *C:* Dante Spinotti; *M:* Angelo Badalamenti. *PAR, FCT*

The Comic *III* 1969 (PG) Van Dyke is terrific as a silent screen comedian (a composite of several real-life screen comics) whose ego destroys his career. Recreations of silent films, and the blend of comedy and pathos, are especially effective. 96m/C VHS, Beta, LV. Dick Van Dyke, Mickey Rooney, Michele Lee, Cornel Wilde, Nina Wayne, Pert Kelton, Jeannine Riley; *D:* Carl Reiner; *W:* Carl Reiner. *COL*

The Comic *I* 1985 In a future police state, a young comedian kills the star and takes his place in the show. His future rises, but who cares? 90m/C VHS, Beta. Steve Munroe, Bernard Plant, Jeff Pirie; *D:* Richard Driscoll. *NO*

Comic Book Kids *II½* 1982 (G) Two youngsters enjoy visiting their friend's comic strip studio, since they have the power to project themselves into the cartoon stories. Viewers will be less impressed. 90m/C VHS, Beta. Joseph Campanella, Mike Darnell, Robyn Finn, Jim Engelhardt, Fay De Witt. *GEM*

Comic Cabby woof! 1987 A day in the life of an introvert cabby seems to last forever. From "New York City Cab Driver's Joke Book" by Jim Pietsch. 59m/C VHS, Beta. Bill McLaughlin, Al Lewis. *VES, ART*

Comin' Round the Mountain *II½* 1951 The duo are caught in a Kentucky family feud while seeking a fortune in gold. Funniest bit has backwoods witch Hamilton squaring off with Costello when he refuses to pay for the love po-

tion she's made him. **77m/B VHS, Closed Caption.** Bud Abbott, Lou Costello, Dorothy Shay, Kirby Grant, Joseph Sawyer, Margaret Hamilton, Glenn Strange, Guy Wilkerson; *D:* Charles Lamont; *W:* John Grant, Robert Lees, Frederic Rinaldo. *USH*

Coming Home 🎬🎬🎬½ **1978 (R)** Looks at the effect of the Vietnam War on home front. The wife of a gung-ho Marine officer volunteers as an aide in a Veteran's Hospital, befriends and eventually falls in love with a Vietnam vet, paralyzed from war injuries. His attitudes, pain, and firsthand knowledge of the war force her to re-examine her previously automatic responses. Honest look at the everyday life of disabled veterans, unusual vision of the possibilities of simple friendship between men and women. Fonda and Voight are great; Dern's character suffers from weak scriptwriting late in the film. Critically acclaimed. Compelling score from late '60s music. **130m/C VHS, Beta, LV, Closed Caption.** Jane Fonda, Jon Voight, Bruce Dern, Penelope Milford, Robert Carradine, Robert Ginty; *D:* Hal Ashby; *W:* Robert C. Jones; *C:* Haskell Wexler. Academy Awards '78: Best Actor (Voight), Best Actress (Fonda), Best Original Screenplay; Cannes Film Festival '78: Best Actor (Voight); Golden Globe Awards '79: Best Actor—Drama (Voight), Best Actress—Drama (Fonda); Los Angeles Film Critics Association Awards '78: Best Actor (Voight), Best Actress (Fonda), Best Film; New York Film Critics Awards '78: Best Actor (Voight); Writers Guild of America '78: Best Original Screenplay; Nominations: Academy Awards '78: Best Director (Ashby), Best Film Editing, Best Picture, Best Supporting Actor (Dern), Best Supporting Actress (Milford).*MGM, FOX, FCT*

The Coming of Amos 🎬🎬🎬 **1925** A wonderful send-up of all those Fairbanks-style melodramas, with La Rocque as an Aussie on vacation on the French Riviera falling for and eventually rescuing Goudal, as the Russian princess held captive by the lustful Beery. **60m/B VHS, Beta.** Rod La Rocque, Jetta Goudal, Noah Beery Sr., Florence Vidor; *D:* Paul Sloane. *GVV*

Coming Out Alive 🎬🎬½ **1984** Tense thriller about a woman and her hired mercenary who try to rescue her kidnapped son from her estranged father—a radical is involved in an assassination plot. Hylands is especially compelling. **73m/C VHS, Beta.** Helen Shaver, Scott Hylands, Michael Ironside, Monica Parker. *TWE*

Coming Out of the Ice 🎬🎬🎬 **1982 (PG)** Engrossing true story of Victor Herman, an outstanding American athlete who worked in Russia in the 1930s. He was imprisoned in Siberia (for 38 years!) for refusing to renounce his American citizenship. Made for television. **100m/C VHS, Beta, Closed Caption.** John Savage, Willie Nelson, Ben Cross, Francesca Annis, Peter Vaughan; *D:* Waris Hussein; *M:* Maurice Jarre. *FOX*

Coming Through 🎬🎬½ **1985** Writer D.H. Lawrence meets the married Frieda von Richthofer and begins a scandalous affair which intertwines with his own writings, and the life of a young man in the present day. Made for British television production lacks passion. **78m/C VHS.** *GB* Kenneth Branagh, Helen Mirren, Alison Steadman, Philip Martin Brown, Norman Rodway; *D:* Peter Barber-Fleming; *W:* Alan Plater. *TVC, VCO*

Coming to America 🎬🎬🎬 **1988 (R)** An African prince (Murphy) decides to come to America in search of a suitable bride. He lands in Queens, and quickly finds American women to be more confusing than he imagined. Sometimes overly cute entertainment relieved by clever costume cameos by Murphy and Hall. Later lawsuit resulted in columnist Art Buchwald being given credit for story. **116m/C VHS, Beta, LV, 8mm, Closed Caption.** Eddie Murphy, Arsenio Hall, James Earl Jones, John Amos, Madge Sinclair, Shari Headley, Don Ameche, Louie Anderson, Paul Bates, Allison Dean, Eriq La Salle, Calvin Lockhart, Samuel L. Jackson, Cuba Gooding Jr., Vanessa Bell, Frankie Faison, Vondie Curtis-Hall; *D:* John Landis; *W:* David Sheffield, Barry W. Blaustein; *M:* Nile Rodgers. Nominations: Academy Awards '88: Best Costume Design. *PAR, FCT*

Coming Up Roses 🎬🎬½ *Rhosyn A Rhith* **1987 (PG)** Pleasant comedy about the residents of a small mining village in the South of Wales who fight to keep their local movie house from being shut down. In Welsh with English subtitles. **95m/C VHS, Beta.** *GB* Dafydd Hywel, Iola Gregory, Olive Michael, Mari Emlyn, Bill Paterson; *D:* Stephen Bayly; *W:* Ruth Carter; *M:* Michael Storey. *FCT*

Command Decision 🎬🎬½ **1948** Upon realizing he must send his men on missions-of-no-return to destroy German jet production, Gable's WWII flight commander becomes tactically at odds with his political superior, Pidgeon (who's not keen to have his precision bombing plans placed in an unflattering light). Based on the stage hit by William Wister Haines, it's a late war pic by Wood, who earlier directed such diverse efforts as "A Night at the Opera," "The Devil and Miss Jones," and "Our Town." Vintage war-is-hell actioner. **112m/B VHS.** Clark Gable, Walter Pidgeon, Van Johnson, Brian Donlevy, Charles Bickford, John Hodiak; *D:* Sam Wood; *M:* Miklos Rozsa. *MGM, FCT*

Commandments 🎬🎬 **1996 (R)** When Seth Warner (Quinn) loses his wife (Going), job, and even his dog, he finds no solace in faith and decides to test why God would make a good man suffer by breaking every one of the 10 commandments. Rachel (Cox), his wife's sister, persuades him to move in with her and her jerk husband Harry (LaPaglia), who can't really be bothered by Seth's problems. The three leads certainly have presence but given the ambivalence of the material, the movie doesn't hang together.*CW:* Language and sexuality. **92m/C VHS, LV, Closed Caption.** Aidan Quinn, Courteney Cox, Anthony LaPaglia, Louis Zorich, Pat McNamara, Tom Aldredge, Pamela Gray, Alice Drummond, Jack Gilpin; *Cameos:* Joanna Going; *D:* Daniel Taplitz; *W:* Daniel Taplitz; *C:* Slawomir Idziak; *M:* Joseph Vitarelli. *USH*

Commando 🎬🎬🎬 **1985 (R)** An ex-commando leader's daughter is kidnapped in a blackmail scheme to make him depose a South American president. He fights instead, and proceeds to rescue his daughter amid a torrential flow of falling bodies. Violent action spiced with throwaway comic lines. **90m/C VHS, Beta, LV, Closed Caption.** Arnold Schwarzenegger, Rae Dawn Chong, Dan Hedaya, Vernon Wells, James Olson, David Patrick Kelly, Alyssa Milano, Bill Duke; *D:* Mark L. Lester; *W:* Steven E. de Souza; *M:* James Horner. *TLF*

Commando Attack 🎬½ **1967** A tough sergeant leads a group of misfit soldiers to blow up a German radio transmitter the day before D-Day. **90m/C VHS, Beta.** Michael Rennie, Monica Randall, Bob Sullivan. *UNI*

Commando Invasion 🎬 **1987** When an army captain is accused of murder, he hunts down the man he knows is responsible for the crime. Jungle revenge mayhem is confusing. Set in Viet Nam. **90m/C VHS, Beta.** Michael James, Gordon Mitchell, Carol Roberts, Pat Vance, Ken Watanabe; *D:* John Gale. *NO*

Commando Squad 🎬 **1976 (R)** During WWII, soldiers go to prevent the development of a device that re-animates flesh. The script stays dead. **82m/C VHS, Beta.** Chuck Alford, Peter Owen, April Adams; *D:* Charles Nizet.

Commando Squad 🎬 **1987 (R)** Story of drug agents undercover in Mexico, and a female agent who rescues her kidnapped lover. Firepower is wasted, but Shower is a former "Playboy" Playmate of the Year. **90m/C VHS, Beta.** Brian Thompson, William Smith, Kathy Shower, Sid Haig, Robert Quarry, Ross Hagen, Mel Welles, Marie Windsor, Russ Tamblyn; *D:* Fred Olen Ray. *TWE*

Commandos 🎬½ **1973 (PG)** Commando operation against Rommel's forces in North Africa during WWII. Too much said, not enough action. Also know as "Sullivan's Marauders." **100m/C VHS, Beta.** *GE IT* Lee Van Cleef, Jack Kelly; *D:* Armando Crispino. *GEM, MRV, CNG*

Commandos Strike at Dawn 🎬🎬½ **1943** Norwegian villagers, including Muni, fight the invading Nazis, and eventually help the British Navy battle them over an Arctic supply line. Okay script helped along by veteran actors Muni and Gish. Based on a C.S. Forester story. **100m/B VHS, Beta.** Paul Muni, Lillian Gish, Cedric Hardwicke, Anna Lee, Ray Collins, Robert Coote, Alexander Knox, Rosemary DeCamp; *D:* John Farrow; *W:* Irwin Shaw; *C:* William Mellor. Nominations: Academy Awards '43: Best Original Dramatic/Comedy Score. *COL*

Comment Ca Va? 🎬🎬 *How Is It Going?* **1976** The boss and workers in a Communist publishing house decide to make a simple film about how information is manufactured. But Odette, one of the workers, has some strange ideas about filmmaking. In French with English subtitles. **76m/C VHS.** *FR* Anne-Marie Mieville; *D:* Jean-Luc Godard. *FCT*

The Commies Are Coming, the Commies Are Coming 🎬🎬 *Red Nightmare* **1957** Cult classic will leave viewers red from laughing in disbelief. Webb narrates this anticommunist movie about the Russians taking over the United States. Filmed in a documentary style, it captures the paranoia of the times. Re-released in 1984, just before the Evil Empire collapsed. **60m/B VHS, Beta.** Jack Webb, Andrew Duggan, Robert Conrad, Jack Kelly, Peter Brown; *D:* George Waggner. *RHI*

Commissar 🎬🎬🎬🎬 *Komissar* **1968** Before the Soviet Union ended up in the ashcan of history, this film was labeled as "treason" and shelved in Red Russia. Now, even Americans can view the story of a female Soviet soldier who becomes pregnant during the civil war of 1922. The Soviet military has no policy regarding pregnancy, so the woman is dumped on a family of outcast Jews to complete her pregnancy. This film makes the strong statement that women were just as discriminated against in the U.S.S.R. as were many races or creeds, especially Jews. In Russian with English subtitles. Released in the U.S. in 1988. **105m/B VHS.** *RU* Nonna Mordyukova, Rolan Bykov; *D:* Alexander Askoldov. *KIV*

The Commitments 🎬🎬🎬 **1991 (R)** Convinced that they can bring soul music to Dublin, a group of working-class youth form a band. High-energy production paints an interesting, unromanticized picture of modern Ireland and refuses to follow standard showbiz cliches, even though its lack of resolution hurts. Honest, whimsical dialog laced with poetic obscenities, delivered by a cast of mostly unknowns. Very successful soundtrack features the music of Wilson Pickett, James Brown, Otis Redding, Aretha Franklin, Percy Sledge, and others, and received a Grammy nomination. Based on the book "The Commitments" by Roddy Doyle, part of a trilogy which includes "The Snapper" and "The Van." **116m/C VHS, Beta, LV, Closed Caption.** *IR* Andrew Strong, Bronagh Gallagher, Glen Hansard, Michael Aherne, Dick Massey, Ken McCluskey, Robert Arkins, Dave Finnegan, Johnny Murphy, Angeline Ball, Felim Gormley, Maria Doyle, Colm Meaney; *D:* Alan Parker; *W:* Dick Clement, Roddy Doyle, Ian LaFrenais. British Academy Awards '91: Best Adapted Screenplay, Best Director (Parker), Best Film; Nominations: Academy Awards '91: Best Film Editing. *CCB, IME*

Committed 🎬½ **1991 (R)** Schlock-meister Levey's latest directorial effort is a step above his earlier "Slumber Party" and "Happy Hooker Goes to Washington," a statement ringing with the faintest of praise. Thinking she's applying for a job at an asylum, a nurse discovers she has committed herself. Try as she may, not even a committed nurse can snake her way out of the pit of madness they call "The Institute." **93m/C VHS, Closed Caption.** Jennifer O'Neill, William Windom, Robert Forster, Ron Palillo, Sydney Lassick; *D:* William A. Levey. *VTR*

The Committee 🎬🎬 **1968 (PG)** Comedy film of the seminal comedy troupe "The Committee," specialists in short, punchy satire. Dated, but of interest to comedy buffs. **88m/C VHS, Beta.**

Wolfman Jack, Howard Hesseman, Barbara Bosson, Peter Bonerz, Garry Goodrow, Carl Gottlieb; **D:** Jack Del. *NO*

Common Bonds 🎬🎬½ 1991 (PG) After being put together in an experimental outreach program, two mismatched partners struggle to break free from a system that threatens to destroy them both. 109m/C VHS, Beta, Closed Caption. Rae Dawn Chong, Michael Ironside, Brad Dourif; **D:** Allan Goldstein; **M:** Graeme Coleman.

Common Law Wife 🎬 1963 (R) Made-for-the-drive-in flick about a man whose common law marriage is threatened by his niece, who wants his money. Murder and mayhem abound when the man's moonshine is poisoned. Cheap and exploitative. 81m/B VHS. Lacy Kelly, Shugfoot Rainey, Annabelle Lee, Jody Works, Anne MacAdams, George Edgely; **D:** Eric Sayers. *SNC*

Common Threads: Stories from the Quilt 1989 The heavily awarded, made-for-cable-TV documentary about the Quilt: an immense 14-acre blanket created by the survivors of AIDS victims as a monument to their loved ones' premature deaths. All proceeds from the sale of this tape go to the NAMES Project Foundation in support of the Quilt and AIDS service providers. 79m/C VHS, Beta, LV, Closed Caption. **D:** Robert Epstein, Jeffrey Friedman. Academy Awards '89: Best Feature Documentary. *WAR, HBO, IME*

Communion 🎬🎬 1989 (R) A serious adaptation of the purportedly nonfictional bestseller by Whitley Strieber about his family's abduction by extraterrestrials. Spacey new age story is overlong and hard to swallow. 103m/C VHS, Beta, LV. Christopher Walken, Lindsay Crouse, Frances Sternhagen, Joel Carlson, Andreas Katsulas, Basil Hoffman; **D:** Philippe Mora; **M:** Eric Clapton. *NO*

The Companion 🎬🎬 1994 (R) In 2015 romance novelist Gillian Tanner (Harrold) decides to hide out at a remote mountain cabin to get over a broken love affair. For safety's sake, Gillian takes along custom-designed android companion Geoffrey (Greenwood). But then Gillian decides to tinker with Geoffrey's programming, turning him from domestic guardian to devoted lover. Unfortunately, Geoffrey doesn't understand the difference between fantasy and reality (especially since he's getting his ideas from Gillian's romance novels) and becomes lethally obsessed. **CW:** Some violence; sexuality. 94m/C VHS, LV, Closed Caption. Kathryn Harrold, Bruce Greenwood, Talia Balsam, Brion James, Bryan Cranston, Joely Fisher; **D:** Gary Fleder; **W:** Ian Seeberg, Valerie Bennett; **C:** Rick Bota; **M:** David Shire. *USH*

Company Business 🎬½ 1991 (PG-13) Sam Boyd is a retired CIA agent who's brought back to swap Pyiotr Grushenko (Baryshnikov), a Russian mole in the State Department, for a U-2 pilot being held in Moscow. The swap is to be made in Berlin and also involves two million dollars of what turns out to be Colombian drug money. When things inevitably go wrong (both intelligence agencies would like them out of the way permanently) the two men find they must depend on each other if they want to stay alive. An unimaginative plot wastes a stalwart cast in this old-fashioned spy drama. 104m/C VHS. Gene Hackman, Mikhail Baryshnikov, Kurtwood Smith, Terry O'Quinn; **D:** Nicholas Meyer; **W:** Nicholas Meyer. *MGM*

The Company of Wolves 🎬🎬🎬 1985 (R) A young girl on the threshold of womanhood listens to her grandmother tell fairy tales and dreams of a medieval fantasy world inhabited by wolves and werewolves. An adult "Little Red Riding Hood" type comedy heavy on Freudian symbolism. Not really for kids. 95m/C VHS, Beta, LV, Closed Caption. Angela Lansbury, David Warner, Stephen Rea, Tusse Silberg, Sarah Patterson, Brian Glover, Danielle Dax, Graham Crowden, Kathryn Pogson, Georgia Slowe; **D:** Neil Jordan; **W:** Neil Jordan, Angela Carter; **C:** Bryan Loftus; **M:** George Fenton. *VES, ART*

The Competition 🎬🎬🎬 1980 (PG) Two virtuoso pianists meet at an international competition and fall in love. Will they stay together if one of them wins? Can they have a performance career and love too? Is he trying to distract her with sex, so he can win? Dreyfuss and Irving are fine (they practiced for four months to look like they were actually playing the pianos), and Remick's character has some interesting insights into the world of art. 125m/C VHS, Beta, LV. Richard Dreyfuss, Amy Irving, Lee Remick, Sam Wanamaker, Joseph Cali, Ty Henderson, Priscilla Pointer, James B. Sikking; **D:** Joel Oliansky; **M:** Lalo Schifrin. Nominations: Academy Awards '80: Best Film Editing, Best Song ("People Alone"). *COL, TVC*

The Compleat Beatles 🎬🎬🎬 1982 Music, interviews, film clips, animation and live performances make up this "rockumentary" on the Beatles. New interviews are featured, as well as vintage film clips and studio footage with narration by Malcolm McDowell. The first U.S. press conference, legendary Hamburg footage, and an in-depth interview with George Martin are highlights. 120m/C VHS, Beta, LV. John Lennon, Paul McCartney, Ringo Starr, George Harrison, George Martin, Brian Epstein, Billy Preston, Milt Oken, Bruce Johnston, Roger McGuinn, Mike McCartney, Mick Jagger; **D:** Patrick Montgomery. *MVD, MGM*

Complex World 🎬½ 1992 (R) The Heartbreak Hotel is a notorious rock club which may not be around much longer. It seems the young owner's father is an ex-CIA redneck who is running for President and his son's profession is a political liability. Meanwhile, the town's mayor wants to replace the club with a shopping mall. A bomb is planted in the club's basement, terrorists lurk, and a gang of bikers is spoiling for a fight but the crowd at the Heartbreak just rocks on. **CW:** Language and drug use. 81m/C VHS. Dan Welch, Bob Owczarek, Jay Charbonneau, Tilman Gandy Jr., David P.B. Stephens; **D:** James Wolpaw; **W:** James Wolpaw. *NO*

Compromising Positions 🎬🎬 1985 (R) A philandering dentist is killed on Long Island, and a bored housewife begins to investigate, uncovering scandal after scandal. Black comedy mixed unevenly with mystery makes for unsatisfying brew. However, Ivey is a standout as Sarandon's best friend. Screenplay was written by Susan Isaacs, based on her novel of the same title. 99m/C VHS, Beta, LV, Closed Caption. Susan Sarandon, Raul Julia, Edward Herrmann, Judith Ivey, Mary Beth Hurt, Joe Mantegna, Josh Mostel, Anne DeSalvo; **D:** Frank Perry; **M:** Brad Fiedel. *PAR*

Compulsion 🎬🎬🎬½ 1959 Artie Strauss (Dillman) is a mother-dominated sadist who, along with submissive friend Judd Steiner (Stockwell), plan and execute a cold-blooded murder. Flamboyant lawyer Jonathan Wilk (brilliantly portrayed by Welles) knows he has no defense so he attacks the system and establishment, seeking to at least save his clients from death. A suspenseful shocker with taut direction and a tight script. Based on the notorious 1924 Leopold and Loeb murder trial, also filmed as "Rope" and "Swoon." 103m/B VHS. Orson Welles, Bradford Dillman, Dean Stockwell, Diane Varsi, E.G. Marshall, Martin Milner, Richard Anderson, Robert Simon, Edward Binns, Robert Burton, Wilton Graff, Gavin MacLeod; **D:** Richard Fleischer; **W:** Richard Murphy; **C:** William Mellor. *FXV*

Computer Beach Party 🎬 1988 A couple of surf-head college computer hackers foil their mayor's plans to develop their favorite beach. The title, at least, is original. 97m/C VHS, Beta. Hank Amigo, Stacey Nemour, Andre Chimene; **D:** Gary A. Troy. *VES, ART*

Computer Wizard 🎬 1977 (G) Boy genius builds a powerful electronic device. His intentions are good, but the invention disrupts the town and lands him in big trouble. Not the "Thomas Edison Story." 91m/C VHS, Beta. Henry Darrow, Kate Woodville, Guy Madison, Marc Gilpin; **D:** John Florea. *NO*

The Computer Wore Tennis Shoes 🎬½ 1969 (G) Disney comedy (strictly for the kids) about a slow-witted college student who turns into a genius after a "shocking" encounter with the campus computer. His new brains give the local gangster headaches. Sequel: "Now You See Him, Now You Don't." 87m/C VHS, Beta. Kurt Russell, Cesar Romero, Joe Flynn, William Schallert, Alan Hewitt, Richard Bakalayan; **D:** Robert Butler; **M:** Robert F. Brunner. *DIS, OM*

Comrade X 🎬🎬½ 1940 Gable is an American correspondent in Moscow who is blackmailed into marrying die-hard Communist Lamarr in this comedic spinoff of "Ninotchka." The two stars failed to create any sparks as a love duo, although their previous film "Boom Town" was a hit. Based on a story by Walter Reisch. 87m/B VHS. Clark Gable, Hedy Lamarr, Oscar Homolka, Felix Bressart, Eve Arden, Sig Rumann, Natasha Lytess, Vladimir Sokoloff; **D:** King Vidor; **W:** Ben Hecht, Charles Lederer. Nominations: Academy Awards '40: Best Story. *MGM*

Comrades in Arms 🎬½ 1991 (R) When an international drug cartel threatens to take over the world, the United States and Russia must set their differences aside and team up to stop them. **CW:** Language and strong action violence. 91m/C VHS, Closed Caption. Lyle Alzado, Rick Washburne, John Christian, Lance Henriksen; **D:** J. Christian Ingvordsen; **W:** J. Christian Ingvordsen. *REP*

The Comrades of Summer 🎬🎬½ 1992 (R) Mantegna plays big-league baseball coach Sparky Smith, whose fiery temper gets him into big trouble. Out of a job, he discovers the only team willing to take a chance on him happens to be Russian. Sparky finds the players of the Russian National team need a lot of help—and not just with their English. Made for cable television. **CW:** Language. 90m/C VHS, LV, Closed Caption. Joe Mantegna, Natalia Negoda, Mark Rolston, John Fleck, Eric Allen Kramer, Michael Lerner, Ian Tracey; **D:** Tommy Lee Wallace; **W:** Robert Rodat; **M:** William Olvis. *HBO*

Con Air 🎬🎬🎬 1997 (R) Producer Bruckheimer flies solo for the first time, and has a very successful flight. Cage re-ups as former Ranger Cameron Poe, jailed for manslaughter, who gets paroled just in time to catch a ride home aboard a plane filled with the worst of America's criminals. Led by Cyrus "The Virus" Grissom (Malkovich), the first-class psycho passengers take over the plane, and Cameron must save the day. Among the snappy one-liners, chases, shoot-outs, and stuff blowin' up real good, comes Federal Marshal Larkin (Cusack) to help Poe from the ground. Cusack can't shake his indie-film, quirky-kid image enough to really pass as an action hero, but he gives it his all. Flick supplies everything you'd expect from a summer blockbuster actioner, but it's best seen on a big-screen with surround sound to get the full effect. **CW:** Strong violence and language. 105m/C VHS, LV, Closed Caption. Nicolas Cage, John Malkovich, John Cusack, Mykelti Williamson, Ving Rhames, Steve Buscemi, Colm Meaney, Rachel Ticotin, Dave Chappelle, M.C. Gainey, Danny Trejo, Nicholas Cinnlund, Jesse Borrego, Angela Featherstone, Monica Potter, John Roselius, Renoly, Landry Allbright, Jose Zuniga; **D:** Simon West; **W:** Scott Rosenberg; **C:** David Tattersall; **M:** Mark Mancina, Trevor Rabin. Nominations: Academy Awards '97: Best Song ("How Do I Live"), Best Sound; Golden Raspberry Awards '97: Best Song ("How Do I Live"). *TOU*

The Con Artists 🎬½ *The Con Man* 1980 After con man Quinn is sprung from prison, he and his protege set up a sting operation against the beautiful Capucine. Not clever or witty enough for the caper to capture interest. 86m/C VHS, Beta. Anthony Quinn, Adriano Celentano, Capucine, Corinne Clery; **D:** Sergio Corbucci. *HHE*

Con Man 🎬 1992 Robin Mitchell is a small-time con man on the fringes of London's underworld, which means they want him dead, and his girlfriend has decided it's just too dangerous being a part of his life. But Mitchell is convinced his luck will change for the better as he puts together a million-dollar long-shot that could secure him for life—if he survives. **91m/C VHS.** Ian McShane, Gayle Hunnicutt, Keith Barron, Alan Lake, Luan Peters; **D:** Francis Megahy. *NO*

Conagher 🎬🎬½ *Louis L'Amour's Conagher* **1991** A lyrical, if poorly plotted Western about a veteran cowboy who takes the whole movie to decide to end up in the arms of the pretty widow lady. Cable-TV adaptation of Louis L'Amour's novel doesn't have much intensity, though Elliott captures his character well. **94m/C VHS, Beta, Closed Caption.** Sam Elliott, Katharine Ross, Barry Corbin, Buck Taylor, Dub Taylor, Daniel Quinn, Anndi McAfee, Billy Green Bush, Ken Curtis; **D:** Reynaldo Villalobos. *TTC*

Conan the Barbarian 🎬🎬🎬 **1982 (R)** A fine sword and sorcery tale featuring brutality, excellent production values, and a rousing score. Conan's parents are killed and he's enslaved. But hardship makes him strong, so when he is set free he can avenge their murder and retrieve the sword bequeathed him by his father. Sandahl Bergman is great as The Queen of Thieves, and Schwarzenegger maintains an admirable sense of humor throughout. Jones is dandy, as always. Based on the character created by Robert E. Howard. Sequel: "Conan the Destroyer." **115m/C VHS, Beta, LV, Letterbox, Closed Caption, DVD.** Arnold Schwarzenegger, James Earl Jones, Max von Sydow, Sandahl Bergman, Mako, Ben Davidson, Valerie Quennessen, Cassandra Gaviola, William Smith; **D:** John Milius; **W:** John Milius, Oliver Stone; **M:** Basil Poledouris. *USH*

Conan the Destroyer 🎬🎬½ **1984 (PG)** Conan is manipulated by Queen Tamaris into searching for a treasure. In return she'll bring Conan's love Valeria back to life. On his trip he meets Jones and Chamberlain, who later give him a hand. Excellent special effects, good humor, camp fun, somewhat silly finale. Sequel to the better "Conan the Barbarian." **101m/C VHS, Beta, LV, Closed Caption.** Arnold Schwarzenegger, Grace Jones, Wilt Chamberlain, Sarah Douglas, Mako, Jeff Corey, Olivia D'Abo, Tracey Walter; **D:** Richard Fleischer; **C:** Jack Cardiff; **M:** Basil Poledouris. Golden Raspberry Awards '84: Worst New Star (D'Abo). *USH*

Concealed Weapon 🎬½ **1994 (R)** A struggling actor gets the part of a lifetime but then becomes the prime suspect in a brutal crime. **CW:** Violence; sexuality; language. **80m/C VHS.** Daryl Haney, Suzanne Wouk, Monica Simpson, Mark Driscoll, Karen Stone; **D:** Dave Payne, Milan Zivkovich. *NHO*

The Concentratin' Kid 🎬🎬 **1930** An unusual horse opera sans shootouts and fisticuffs. Hoot's fiancee is kidnapped and taken to the range so that the renegade cowpokes can, uh, benefit from a female perspective on home decorating. Despite being outnumbered, Hoot concentrates and sets the rescue in motion, taking on the gang of rustlers without firing a shot. **54m/B VHS, Beta.** Hoot Gibson, Kathryn Crawford, Duke Lee, Robert E. Homans, James Mason; **D:** Arthur Rosson. *GPV*

The Concorde: Airport '79 🎬 *Airport '79* **1979 (PG)** A supersonic film in the "Airport" tradition has the Concorde chased by missiles and fighter aircraft before it crashes in the Alps. Incredibly far-fetched nonsense with an all-star cast doesn't fly. **103m/C VHS, Beta.** Alain Delon, Susan Blakely, Robert Wagner, Sylvia Kristel, John Davidson, Charo, Sybil Danning, Jimmie Walker, Eddie Albert, Bibi Andersson, Monica Lewis, Andrea Marcovicci, Martha Raye, Cicely Tyson, Mercedes McCambridge, George Kennedy, David Warner; **D:** David Lowell Rich; **W:** Eric Roth; **M:** Lalo Schifrin. *USH*

Concrete Angels 🎬 **1987 (R)** A poignant glimpse at the influence of rock music in its infancy. A group of deprived teens in Toronto form a band and audition to open for the Beatles. Lack of nostalgia is refreshing, but too much of this is amateurish. **97m/C VHS, Beta.** CA Joseph Dimambro, Luke McKeehan, Omie Craden, Dean Bosacki.

Concrete Beat 🎬½ **1984** A newspaper reporter simultaneously searches for a murderer, tries to win his ex-wife back, and writes front page stories for his editor/ex-father-in-law. Tough assignment. Made for television. **74m/C VHS, Beta.** Kenneth McMillan, John Getz, Darlanne Fluegel, Rhoda Gemignani; **D:** Robert Butler.

The Concrete Cowboys 🎬½ *Ramblin' Man* **1979** Two bumbling cowboys from Montana come to the metropolis of Nashville and promptly turn detective to foil a blackmail scheme and locate a missing singer. Barbara Mandrell and Roy Acuff play themselves. Silly made-for-TV pilot of short-lived series. **100m/C VHS.** Jerry Reed, Tom Selleck, Morgan Fairchild, Claude Akins, Gene Evans, Roy Acuff, Barbara Mandrell; **D:** Burt Kennedy. *FOX, HHE, MTX*

The Concrete Jungle 🎬🎬 *The Criminal* **1982 (R)** After being set up by her no-good boyfriend, Bregman is sent to a correctional facility for drug smuggling. There she must learn to fend for herself (or else). Typical prison for gals fare with cute babes in revealing outfits, a topless riot, the bad warden, and a concerned social worker. Followed by "Chained Heat." **106m/C VHS, Beta.** Tracy Bregman, Jill St. John, Barbara Luna, Peter Brown, Aimee Eccles, Nita Talbot, Sondra Currie; **D:** Tom De Simone; **W:** Alan J. Adler. *COL*

Condemned to Hell woof! **198?** A tough-as-iron street punk gets thrown into a women's prison, where she must fight for her existence. Low-brow violence galore. **97m/C VHS, Beta.** *IT* Leonor Benedetto. *TWE*

Condemned to Live 🎬🎬 **1935** Mild-mannered doctor Ralph Morgan and his fiancee Maxine Doyle seem like your average early 20th Century Middle-European couple...but the doctor's hunchbacked servant Mischa Auer is a tipoff that this is a horror movie of some sort. Like many men, the doctor has suffered from a vampire curse all his life. And, like many men, he is unaware of his blood-sucking habit, thanks to the concealment efforts of his loyal (hunchback) servant. Doyle discovers her fiance's sanguine secret, but not before she finds out she really loves Gleason, anyway. Answers the question: just how do you jilt a vampire? **68m/B VHS.** Ralph Morgan, Maxine Doyle, Russell Gleason, Pedro de Cordoba, Mischa Auer, Lucy Beaumont, Carl Stockdale; **D:** Frank Strayer. *SNC, LSV*

Condition Red 🎬🎬 **1995 (R)** Philadelphia prison guard Dan Capelli's (Russo) illicit involvement with inmate Gidell (Williams) turns into big trouble and double-crosses thanks to her drug-dealing boyfriend Angel (Calderon). **CW:** Violence, sexuality, language and drug use. **85m/C VHS.** James Russo, Cynda Williams, Paul Calderone; **D:** Mika Kaurismaki; **W:** Andre Degas; **C:** Ken Kelsch; **M:** Mauri Sumen. *AVI*

Condorman 🎬🎬½ **1981 (PG)** Woody Wilkins, an inventive comic book writer, adopts the identity of his own character, Condorman, in order to help a beautiful Russian spy defect. A Disney film, strictly for the small fry. **90m/C VHS, Beta.** Michael Crawford, Oliver Reed, Barbara Carrera, James Hampton, Jean-Pierre Kalfon, Dana Elcar; **D:** Charles Jarrott; **W:** Glenn Gordon Caron; **M:** Henry Mancini. *DIS*

Conduct Unbecoming 🎬🎬½ **1975 (PG)** Late 19th-century India is the setting for a trial involving the possible assault of a British officer's wife. Ambitious production based on a British stage play suffers from claustrophobic atmosphere but is greatly redeemed by the first rate cast. **107m/C VHS.** GB Michael York, Richard Attenborough, Trevor Howard, Stacy Keach, Christopher Plummer, Susannah York, James Faulkner, Michael Culver, Persis Khambatta; **D:** Michael Anderson Sr. *CRV*

The Conductor 🎬🎬 *Dyrygent* **1980** A famous Polish-born conductor (Gielgud) returns to his birthplace after 50 years of living in the U.S. A dying man, he decides to work with a struggling provincial orchestra, much to the dismay of their own conductor. But the conductor finds himself

being used in government schemes to take advantage of his return. In English and Polish with subtitles. **101m/C VHS.** PL John Gielgud, Krystyna Janda, Andrzej Seweryn, Jan Ciercierski, Tadeusz Czechowski; **D:** Andrzej Wajda; **W:** Andrzej Kijowski. *NYF, ING*

Coneheads 🎬🎬½ **1993 (PG)** Comedy inspired by once popular characters from "Saturday Night Live" coasts in on the coattails of "Wayne's World." Aykroyd and Curtin reprise their roles as Beldar and Prymaat, the couple from the planet Remulak who are just trying to fit in on Earth. Newman, who created the role of teenage daughter Connie, appears as Beldar's sister, while Burke takes over as Connie (toddler Connie is Aykroyd's daughter, in her film debut). One-joke premise is a decade late and a dime short, though cast of comedy all-stars provides a lift. **86m/C VHS, Beta, Closed Caption.** Dan Aykroyd, Jane Curtin, Laraine Newman, Jason Alexander, Michelle Burke, Chris Farley, Michael Richards, Lisa Jane Persky, Sinbad, Shishir Kurup, Michael McKean, Phil Hartman, David Spade, Dave Thomas, Jan Hooks, Chris Rock, Adam Sandler, Julia Sweeney, Danielle Aykroyd; **D:** Steven Barron; **W:** Dan Aykroyd, Tom Davis, Bonnie Turner, Terry Turner. *PAR, BTV*

Confessing to Laura 🎬🎬 *Confesion a Laura* **1990** Set in Colombia after the 1948 assassination of liberal leader Jorge Elieser Gaitain, which begets a violent civil war. Two people are trapped at Laura's house by the riots—setting up a night of volatile emotion. Spanish with subtitles. **90m/C VHS.** CL D: Jaime Osorio Gomez. *FCT*

The Confession 🎬🎬½ **1920** A priest hears a killer's confession and must protect the oath of confidentiality, even as his own brother is being convicted of the murder. **78m/B VHS.** Henry B. Walthall, Francis McDonald, William H. Clifford, Margaret McWade, Margaret Landis; **D:** Bertram Bracken. *GPV*

The Confessional 🎬 *House of Mortal Sin* **1975 (R)** A mad priest unleashes a monster from his confessional to wreak havoc upon the world. Pray for your VCR. **108m/C VHS, Beta.** GB Anthony Sharp, Susan Penhaligon, Stephanie Beacham, Norman Eshley, Sheila Keith; **D:** Pete Walker.

The Confessional 🎬🎬½ *Le Confessionnal* **1995** Ambiguous psychological drama that's, in part, a homage to Alfred Hitchcock's 1952 film "I Confess," which was filmed in the same Quebec City locations. Pierre (Bluteau) returns to Quebec in 1989 for his father's funeral and to reunite with his adoptive brother Marc (Goyette). Marc's mother Rachel (who committed suicide shortly after his birth) refused to name his father, thought to be a priest, perhaps at the church where Hitchcock filmed his movie. Flashbacks depict the rotund director (Burrage) and his assistant (Scott Thomas) and their production. Lots of intriguing visuals, thanks to director Lepage's innovative stage background. French with subtitles. **100m/C VHS.** CA FR GB Lothaire Bluteau, Patrick Goyette, Jean-Louis Millette, Kristin Scott Thomas, Ron Burrage, Richard Frechette, Francois Papineau, Marie Gignac; **D:** Robert Lepage; **W:** Robert Lepage; **C:** Alan Dostie; **M:** Sacha Puttnam. Genie Awards '95: Best Art Direction/Set Decoration, Best Director (Lepage), Best Film; Nominations: Genie Awards '95: Best Actor (Bluteau). *NYR*

Confessions of a Hit Man 🎬🎬 **1994 (R)** Nephew who stole millions from his mobster uncle must amend his sordid past. **CW:** Language. **93m/C VHS, LV.** James Remar, Michael Wright, Emily Longstreth; **D:** Larry Leahy; **W:** Tony Cinciripini, Larry Leahy; **M:** Billy Talbot.

Confessions of a Police Captain 🎬🎬 **1972 (PG)** A dedicated police captain tries to wipe out the bureaucratic corruption that is infecting his city. Balsam gives a fine performance in a heavy-going tale. **104m/C VHS, Beta.** IT Martin Balsam, Franco Nero, Marilu Tolo; **D:** Damiano Damiani.

Confessions of a Serial Killer 🎬🎬 **1987** True story based on the life of Henry Lee Lucas, one of the nation's most vicious killers. Burns plays Lucas in this grisly account of his most violent murders. Shocking realistic look inside the mind of a serial killer. 85m/C VHS, **Closed Caption.** Robert Burns, Dennis Hill; **D:** Mark Blair. *NHO*

Confessions of a Vice Baron *&*

1942 Vice Baron Lombardo makes it big as a drug dealer and flesh peddler, then loses it all when he falls in love. Sleazy exploitation. 70m/B VHS, Beta. Willy Castello; **D:** John Melville. *SNC*

Confessions of Tom Harris *&* *Tale of the Cock; Childish Things*

1972 (PG) Somewhere between all the prize-fighting, leg-breaking for the mob, and jail terms for rape, Tom Harris finds time for a life-changing encounter with love. Based on true story. 90m/C VHS, Beta. Don Murray, Linda Evans, David Brian, Gary Clarke, Logan Ramsey, Angelique Pettyjohn; **D:** John Derek, David Nelson; **W:** Don Murray. *NO*

Confidential *&&½*

1935 A G-man goes under cover to infiltrate a crime ring. Well made and full of action, fun array of character actors. Naish particularly good as nasty killer. 67m/B VHS. Donald Cook, Evalyn Knapp, Warren Hymer, J. Carrol Naish, Herbert Rawlinson, Morgan Wallace, Kane Richmond, Theodore von Eltz, Reed Howes; **D:** Edward L. Cahn. *VYY*

Confidential woof!

1986 (R) A '40s detective tries to solve a decades-old axe murder, only to disappear himself. Horrible fare from our friends north of the border. 95m/C VHS, Beta. *CA* Neil Munro, August Schellenberg, Chapelle Jaffe, Tom Butler; **D:** Bruce Pittman. *NO*

Confidentially Yours *&&&* *Vivement Dimanche!; Finally, Sunday*

1983 (PG) Truffaut's homage to Hitchcock, based on Charles Williams' "The Long Saturday Night." A hapless small-town real estate agent is framed for a rash of murders and his secretary, who is secretly in love with him, tries to clear his name. Truffaut's last film is stylish and entertaining. In French with English subtitles. 110m/B VHS, Beta, LV. *FR* Fanny Ardant, Jean-Louis Trintignant, Philippe Morier-Genoud, Philippe Laudenbach, Caroline Sihol; **D:** Francois Truffaut; **W:** Suzanne Schiffman; **C:** Nestor Almendros; **M:** Georges Delerue. *FOX, HMV*

Conflict *&&&*

1945 Bogart falls for his sister-in-law and asks his wife for a divorce. She refuses, he plots her murder, and thinks up the alibi. When the police fail to notify him of her death, Bogart is forced to report his wife missing. But is she dead? Her guilty husband smells her perfume, sees her walking down the street, and discovers the body is missing from the scene of the crime. Suspenseful thriller also features Greenstreet as a psychologist/family friend who suspects Bogart knows more than he's telling. 86m/B VHS. Humphrey Bogart, Alexis Smith, Sydney Greenstreet, Rose Hobart, Charles Drake, Grant Mitchell; **D:** Curtis Bernhardt. *MGM*

Conflict of Interest *&½*

1992 (R) Gideon (Nelson) is a thug who runs stolen cars, drugs, and women from his heavy-metal club on the wrong side of town. Mickey Flannery (McDonald) is the new cop determined to get Gideon behind bars, especially after Gideon kills Mickey's wife, sets up his son on a phony murder rap, and kidnaps his son's girlfriend. Now it's personal and Mickey will stop at nothing to get his revenge. Over-the-top performance by Nelson will have the viewer hoping he gets it soon and puts the film out of its misery. *CW:* Language, violence, and strong sexuality. 88m/C VHS. Judd Nelson, Christopher McDonald, Alyssa Milano, Dey Young, Gregory Alan Harris; **D:** Gary Davis; **W:** Gregory Miller, Michael Angeli; **C:** Bryan England. *HBO*

The Conformist *&&&&* *Il Conformist*

1971 (R) Character study of young Italian fascist, plagued by homosexual feelings, who must prove his loyalty by killing his old professor. Decadent and engrossing story is brilliantly acted. Based on the novel by Alberto Moravia. 108m/C VHS, Beta, LV. *IT FR GE* Jean-Louis Trintignant, Stefania Sandrelli, Dominique Sanda, Pierre Clementi, Gastone Moschin, Pasquale Fortunato; **D:** Bernardo Bertolucci; **W:** Bernardo Bertolucci; **C:** Vittorio Storaro; **M:** Georges Delerue. National Society of Film Critics Awards '71: Best Cinematography (Storaro),

Best Director (Bertolucci); Nominations: Academy Awards '71: Best Adapted Screenplay. *PAR*

Congo *&&*

1995 (PG-13) Communications company supervisor jets off to the African jungle along with a primatologist to search for a lost city's priceless diamonds, and to return Amy, a gorilla who communicates with sign language to her natural habitat. Why she would want to return to volcanoes and bloodthirsty mutant gray gorillas is anybody's guess. This appropriately technology-laden adaptation of Michael Crichton's novel delivers all the cliches of the old B-movie jungle flicks, but none of the thrills or fun of other Crichton adaptations.*CW:* Jungle adventure terror and action; brief strong language. 109m/C VHS, Beta, **Closed Caption.** Dylan Walsh, Laura Linney, Ernie Hudson, Tim Curry, Grant Heslov, Joe Don Baker; **D:** Frank Marshall; **W:** John Patrick Shanley; **C:** Allen Daviau; **M:** Jerry Goldsmith. Nominations: Golden Raspberry Awards '95: Worst Picture. *NYR*

Congress Dances *&&* *Der Kongress Tanzt*

1931 A rare German musical about a romance in old Vienna. Popular in its day, it was subsequently banned by the Nazis in 1937. In German with English subtitles. 92m/B VHS, Beta. *GE* Lilian Harvey, Conrad Veidt, Willy Fritsch; **D:** Erik Charell. *NOS, HHT, GLV*

A Connecticut Yankee *&&&*

1931 A charming, if somewhat dated, version of the popular Mark Twain story, "A Connecticut Yankee in King Arthur's Court." Rogers is a radio shop owner who dreams his way back to the Knights of the Round Table. Story rewritten to fit Rogers' amiable style and to make then-current wisecracks. Great cast overcomes weak points in the script. 96m/B VHS. Will Rogers, Myrna Loy, Maureen O'Sullivan, William Farnum; **D:** David Butler. *FOX, FCT*

A Connecticut Yankee in King Arthur's Court *&&½* *A Yankee in King Arthur's Court*

1949 A pleasant version of the famous Mark Twain story about a 20th century man transported to Camelot and mistaken for a dangerous wizard. This was the third film version of the classic, which was later remade as "Unidentified Flying Oddball," a made for television movie and an animated feature. *♫Once and For Always; Busy Doin' Nothin'; If You Stub Your Toe on the Moon; When Is Sometime?; Twixt Myself and Me.* 108m/C VHS, Beta, LV. Bing Crosby, Rhonda Fleming, William Bendix, Cedric Hardwicke, Henry Wilcoxon, Murvyn Vye, Virginia Field; **D:** Tay Garnett; **C:** Ray Rennahan. *USH*

A Connecticut Yankee in King Arthur's Court *&&½*

1989 The Mark Twain classic has had a gender switch in this TV version, with Pulliam as the time-travelling heroine who winds up in the royal court. 100m/C VHS. Keisha Knight Pulliam, Jean Marsh, Rene Auberjonois, Emma Samms, Whip Hubley, Michael Gross; **D:** Mel Damski. *FHE*

The Connection *&&&½*

1961 The Living Theatre's ground-breaking performance of Jack Gelber's play about heroin addicts waiting for their connection to arrive, while a documentary filmmaker hovers nearby with his camera. 105m/B VHS, Beta. Warren Finnerty, Carl Lee, William Redfield, Roscoe Lee Browne, Garry Goodrow, James Anderson, Jackie McLean; **D:** Shirley Clarke. *MFV, FCT*

The Connection *&&½*

1973 During steps in to work a deal between hotel jewel thieves and the insurance company. Complex plot handled deftly by all concerned. Made for television. 74m/C VHS, Beta. Charles Durning, Ronny Cox, Dennis Cole, Zohra Lampert, Heather MacRae, Dana Wynter; **D:** Tom Gries. *THV*

The Conqueror woof!

1956 Wayne in pointed helmet and goatee is convincingly miscast as Genghis Khan in this woeful tale of the warlord's early life and involvement with the kidnapped daughter of a powerful enemy. Rife with stilted, unintentionally funny dialogue, whose "Oriental western was very expensive to make (with backing by Howard Hughes), and is now listed in the "Fifty Worst Films of All Time." No matter; it's

surreal enough to enable viewer to approximate an out-of-body experience. Even those on the set suffered; filming took place near a nuclear test site in Utah and many members of the cast and crew eventually developed cancer. 111m/C VHS, Beta. John Wayne, Susan Hayward, William Conrad, Agnes Moorehead, Lee Van Cleef, Pedro Armendariz Sr., Thomas Gomez, John Hoyt; **D:** Dick Powell; **W:** Oscar Millard; **C:** Joseph LaShelle. *USH*

Conqueror & the Empress woof!

1964 Low-budget tale of English explorers who roust an island prince from his throne, motivating him to engage in inspired blood-letting. 89m/C VHS, Beta. Guy Madison, Ray Danton, Mario Petri, Alberto Farnese. *NO*

The Conqueror Worm *&&&* *Witchfinder General; Edgar Allan Poe's Conqueror Worm*

1968 Price turns in a fine performance portraying the sinister Matthew Hopkins, a real-life 17th century witchhunter. No "ham" in this low-budget, underrated thriller, based on Ronald Bassett's novel. The last of three films from director Reeves, who died from an accidental overdose in 1969. Also available with "Tomb of Ligeia" on laserdisc. 95m/C VHS. *GB* Vincent Price, Ian Ogilvy, Hilary Dwyer, Rupert Davies, Robert Russell, Patrick Wymark, Wilfrid Brambell; **D:** Michael Reeves; **W:** Michael Reeves, Louis M. Heyward, Michael Reeves, Tom Baker; **C:** John Coquillon. *ORI, FCT*

Conquest *&&&* *Marie Walewska*

1937 Garbo, as the Polish countess Marie Walewska, tries to persuade Napoleon (Boyer) to free her native Poland from the Russian Tsar. Garbo, Boyer, and Ouspenskaya are outstanding, while the beautiful costumes and lavish production help, but the script is occasionally weak. A boxoffice flop in the U.S., which ended up costing MGM more than any movie it had made up until that time. 115m/B VHS, Beta. Greta Garbo, Charles Boyer, Reginald Owen, Alan Marshal, Henry Stephenson, Leif Erickson, May Whitty, Maria Ouspenskaya, Vladimir Sokoloff, Scotty Beckett; **D:** Clarence Brown; **C:** Karl Freund. Nominations: Academy Awards '37: Best Actor (Boyer). *MGM, FCT*

Conquest *&½*

1983 (R) Sword and sorcery tale of two mighty warriors against an evil sorceress who seeks world domination. Excellent score. 92m/C VHS, Beta. *IT SP MX* Jorge Rivero, Andrea Occhipinti, Violeta Cela, Sabrina Siani; **D:** Lucio Fulci; **M:** Claudio Simonetti.

Conquest of Cochise *&&*

1953 Mediocre oater about a cavalry officer who must stop the war between the Apache and Comanche tribes and a group of Mexicans in the Southwest of the 1850s. 70m/C VHS, Beta. John Hodiak, Robert Stack, Joy Page; **D:** William Castle. *GKK*

Conquest of Mycene *&½* *Ercole Contro Molock*

1963 Hercules battles an evil queen and this time he may actually lose! Muscleman mayhem will entertain the kids. 102m/C VHS. *IT FR* Gordon Scott, Rosalba (Sara Bay) Neri, Jany Clair; **D:** Giorgio Ferroni. *SNC*

Conquest of Space *&½*

1955 A spaceship sets off to explore Mars in spite of the commander's attempts to sabotage the voyage. He believes the flight is an heretical attempt to reach God. An uneasy mixture of religion and space exploration detracts from the nifty special effects which are the only reason to watch. 81m/C VHS, **Closed Caption.** Walter Brooke, Eric Fleming, Mickey Shaughnessy, Phil Foster, William Redfield, William Hopper, Benson Fong, Ross Martin; **D:** Byron Haskin; **C:** Lionel Lindon. *PAR*

Conquest of the Normans *&*

1962 During the Norman invasion of England, Oliver is accused of kidnapping the King. To save his life, Oliver must find the true identity of the abductors. With so much plot, there should have been some suspense. 83m/C Beta. Cameron Mitchell.

Conquest of the Planet of the Apes *&&½*

1972 (PG) The apes turn the tables on the human Earth population when they lead a revolt against their cruel masters in the distant year of 1990. Sure, there's plenty of cliches—but the story drags you along. The 4th film in the series. Followed by "Battle for the Planet of the Apes." **87m/C VHS, Beta, LV, Closed Caption.** Roddy McDowall, Don Murray, Ricardo Montalban, Natalie Trundy, Severn Darden, Hari Rhodes; **D:** J. Lee Thompson; **C:** Bruce Surtees. *FOX*

Conrack 🐾🐾🐾 **1974 (PG)** The true story of Pat Conroy, who tried to teach a group of illiterate Black children in South Carolina by using common-sense teaching techniques to inspire their interest. Voight is convincing as the earnest teacher. Based on Conroy's novel "The Water Is Wide." **111m/C VHS, Beta, Closed Caption.** Jon Voight, Paul Winfield, Madge Sinclair, Hume Cronyn, Martin Ritt; **D:** Martin Ritt; **W:** Harriet Frank Jr., Irving Ravetch; **C:** John A. Alonzo; **M:** John Williams. *FOX*

Conseil de Famille 🐾🐾 **1986** Hallyday returns to his family from a five-year prison stint, ready to resume his safe-cracking career. Then he discovers the real talent lies with his son Francois (Martin), whose expertise raises the family to middleclass prosperity. But just as dad decides to affiliate with a bigger crime organization, Francois decides to get a straight job because he's fallen in love. Based on a novel by Francis Ryck. French with subtitles. **111m/C VHS.** *FR* Johnny Hallyday, Remi Martin, Fanny Ardant, Guy Marchand; **D:** Constantin Costa-Gavras; **W:** Constantin Costa-Gavras; **C:** Robert Alazraki; **M:** Georges Delerue. *WBF*

Consenting Adult 🐾🐾½ **1985** Made for television movie about a distressed family coming to terms with a favorite son's homosexuality. Restrained exploration of the controversial subject. Based on Laura Z. Hobson's novel. **100m/C VHS.** Marlo Thomas, Martin Sheen, Barry Tubb, Talia Balsam, Ben Piazza, Corinne Michaels; **D:** Gilbert Cates; **W:** John McGreevey. *NO*

Consenting Adults 🐾🐾 **1992 (R)** Cookie-cutter thriller capitalizes on popular "psycho-destroys-your-normal-life" theme. Average yuppie couple (Kline and Mastrantonio) are startled and then seduced by the couple moving in next door (Spacey and Miller), who conduct a considerably less-restrained lifestyle. Wife-swapping leads to murder and an innocent man is framed. Plot and characters are underdeveloped yet manage to hold interest through decent performances. **CW:** Language, violence, and sexuality. **100m/C VHS, Beta, LV, Closed Caption.** Kevin Kline, Mary Elizabeth Mastrantonio, Kevin Spacey, Rebecca Miller, Forest Whitaker, E.G. Marshall, Billie Neal; **D:** Alan J. Pakula; **W:** Matthew Chapman. *HPH, IME*

Consolation Marriage 🐾🐾½ *Married in Haste* **1931** A couple meet and marry after being jilted by others, then must make a choice when their old flames return. Dunne and O'Brien make a charming couple in this early talkie. One of Dunne's early starring roles. **82m/B VHS, Beta.** Irene Dunne, Pat O'Brien, John Halliday, Matt Moore, Myrna Loy, Lester Vail; **D:** Paul Sloane. *TTC*

Conspiracy 🐾 **1989 (R)** Defense Secretary William Baine is haunted by a past sexual encounter, and a top secret team moves in to avert any hint of what could become a "sex scandal." Based on a true story. **87m/C VHS, Beta.** James Wilby, Kate Hardie, Glyn Houston; **D:** Christopher Barnard.

Conspiracy of Hearts 🐾🐾🐾 **1960** A convent of nuns hide Jewish children in 1943 Italy despite threats to their personal safety. Suspenseful tale despite the familiar plot. **113m/B VHS, Beta.** *GB* Lilli Palmer, Yvonne Mitchell, Sylvia Syms, Ronald Lewis; **D:** Ralph Thomas; **W:** Robert Presnell. *BFA*

A Conspiracy of Love 🐾 **1987** A made-for-television movie about three generations of a divorce-torn family trying to pull itself back together. Sugary domestic tale tries to be uplifting, succeeds in being cliche-ridden. **93m/C VHS.** Robert Young, Drew Barrymore, Glynnis O'Connor, Elizabeth Wilson, Michael Laurence, John Fujioka, Alan Fawcett; **D:** Noel Black. *VTR*

Conspiracy of Terror 🐾🐾 **1975** Married detectives investigate a series of murders and unearth a grisly cult in a quiet suburb. Standard fare with a few too cute lines concerning the leads' mixed-faith marriage. Made for television pilot. **78m/C VHS.** Michael Constantine, Barbara Rhoades, Mariclare Costello, Roger Perry, David Opatoshu, Logan Ramsey; **D:** John Llewellyn Moxey. *ART*

Conspiracy: The Trial of the Chicago Eight 🐾🐾🐾 **1987** Courtroom drama focuses on the rambunctious trial of the Chicago Eight radicals, charged with inciting a riot at the Democratic National Convention of 1968. Dramatized footage mixed with interviews with the defendants. Imaginative reconstruction of history. **118m/C VHS, Beta.** Peter Boyle, Elliott Gould, Robert Carradine, Martin Sheen, David Clennon, David Kagen, Michael Lembeck, Robert Loggia; **D:** Jeremy Paul Kagan. *NO*

Conspiracy Theory 🐾🐾🐾 **1997 (R)** Whacked-out New York cabbie Jerry Fletcher (Gibson) writes a newsletter on conspiracy theories, which he finds in every possible place and situation. Naturally, he doesn't keep his thoughts to himself and exasperated Justice Department attorney Alice Sutton (Roberts) is stuck listening to the love-struck fool. But as the saying goes just because you're paranoid doesn't mean they're not out to get you. Sure enough, one of Jerry's conspiracies turns out to be true and suddenly he and Alice are being pursued by CIA shrink Dr. Jonas (Stewart), who's not what he seems to be either. Gibson's more geek than hero but appealing regardless, as is heroine Roberts. Another successful, enjoyable, and highly profitable, teaming of Donner, Gibson and producer Joel Silver.**CW:** Some violence. **135m/C VHS, LV, Closed Caption.** Mel Gibson, Julia Roberts, Patrick Stewart, Cylk Cozart; **D:** Richard Donner; **W:** Brian Helgeland; **C:** John Schwartzman; **M:** Carter Burwell. *WAR*

Conspirator 🐾🐾½ **1949** Somewhat engrossing drama about a beautiful young girl who discovers that her new husband, a British army officer, is working with the Communists. Elizabeth Taylor stars as the naive American wife and Robert Taylor plays her Russkie agent husband. Although madly in love with his wife, he is given orders to kill her. Picture falls apart at end due to weak script. Based on the novel by Humphrey Slater. **85m/B VHS.** *GB* Robert Taylor, Elizabeth Taylor, Robert Flemyng, Harold Warrender, Honor Blackman, Marjorie Fielding, Thora Hird; **D:** Victor Saville; **W:** Sally Benson, Gerard Fairlie; **C:** Frederick A. (Freddie) Young. *MGM*

Consuming Passions 🐾½ **1988 (R)** A ribald, food-obsessed English comedy about a young idiot who rises within the hierarchy of a chocolate company via murder. You'll never guess what the secret ingredient in his wonderful chocolate is. Based on a play by Michael Palin and Terry Jones (better known as part of the Monty Python troupe), the film is sometimes funny, more often gross, and takes a single joke far beyond its limit. **95m/C VHS, Beta, LV.** *GB* Vanessa Redgrave, Jonathan Pryce, Tyler Butterworth, Freddie Jones, Prunella Scales, Sammi Davis, Thora Hird; **D:** Giles Foster; **W:** Michael Palin, Andrew Davies. *NO*

Contact 🐾🐾½ **1997 (PG)** Thought-provoking (if overlong) drama rather than sci-fi spectacular (though it has its fair share of special effects). Radio astronomer Dr. Ellie Arroway (Foster) discovers signals being transmitted from the distant star Vega. When they're deciphered, the signals turn out to be blueprints for a craft that will take its occupant into space and a first meeting with aliens. Ellie fights to become that first spokesperson for Earth's inhabitants. More philosophical than the usual sci-fi alien encounter epic, but the excellent cast, led by Foster, pulls it off nicely. Based on the novel by Carl Sagan. **150m/C VHS, LV, Closed Caption.** Jodie Foster, Matthew McConaughey, James Woods, Tom Skerritt, Angela Bassett, John Hurt, David Morse, Rob Lowe, Jake Busey, William Fichtner, Geoffrey Blake, Jena Malone; **D:** Robert Zemeckis; **W:** Michael Goldenberg; **C:** Don Burgess; **M:** Alan Silvestri. Nomi-

nations: Academy Awards '97: Best Sound; Golden Globe Awards '98: Best Actress (Foster). *WAR*

Contagion 🐾½ **1987** Innocent real estate agent meets a reclusive, eccentric millionaire who offers him unlimited wealth and beautiful women, but only if he kills someone. Interesting ethical premise loses its philosophic purity. **90m/C VHS, Beta.** *AU* John Doyle, Nicola Bartlett, Roy Barrett, Nathy Gaffney, Pamela Hawksford; **D:** Karl Zwicky. *NO*

Contagious 🐾🐾½ **1996 (PG-13)** A doctor (Wagner) discovers that passengers aboard a flight from Latin American have been exposed to cholera and could cause an epidemic. She teams with a detective (Pena), who's tracking an infected drug smuggler, to find the source of the disease. Made for cable.**CW:** Drug content and brief violence. **90m/C VHS, Closed Caption.** Lindsay Wagner, Elizabeth Pena, Tom Wopat. *PAR*

Contempt 🐾🐾🐾½ *Le Mepris; Il Disprezzo* **1964** A film about the filming of a new version of "The Odyssey," and the rival visions of how to tell the story. Amusing look at the film business features Fritz Lang playing himself, Godard as his assistant. Bardot is pleasant scenery. Adapted from Moravia's "A Ghost at Noon." **102m/C VHS, Beta, LV.** *IT FR* Brigitte Bardot, Jack Palance, Fritz Lang, Georgia Moll, Michel Piccoli; **D:** Jean-Luc Godard; **W:** Jean-Luc Godard; **M:** Georges Delerue. *COL*

Continental Divide 🐾🐾 **1981 (PG)** A hard-nosed political columnist takes off for the Colorado Rockies on an "easy assignment"—interviewing a reclusive ornithologist, with whom he instantly falls in love. A city slicker, he first alienates her, but she eventually falls for him, too. But it's not exactly a match made in heaven. Story meanders to a conclusion of sorts. Probably the most normal Belushi ever was on screen. **103m/C VHS, Beta, LV.** John Belushi, Blair Brown, Allen (Goorwitz) Garfield, Carlin Glynn, Val Avery, Tony Ganios, Tim Kazurinsky; **D:** Michael Apted; **W:** Lawrence Kasdan; **C:** John Bailey. *USH*

Contraband 🐾½ **1986** The leader of a smuggling gang escapes from an ambush in which his brother was murdered. He searches for a haven of safety while his cronies seek brutal revenge. Average crime yarn lacks much excitement. Dubbed into English. **95m/C VHS, Beta.** *IT* Fabio Testi, Ivana Monti; **D:** Lucio Fulci. *NO*

Control 🐾½ **1987** Tedious tale of 15 volunteers for a 20-day fallout shelter habitation experiment who become trapped when a real nuclear emergency occurs. Filmed in Rome. Made for cable TV. **83m/C VHS, Beta.** *IT* Burt Lancaster, Kate Nelligan, Ben Gazzara, Andrea Ferreol, Lavinia Segurini, Andrea Occhipinti, Cyrielle Claire, Jean Benguigui, Kate Reid, Erland Josephson, Ingrid Thulin; **D:** Guiliano Montaldo. *CNG, HBO*

The Convent 🐾🐾 **1995** Idiosyncratic saga of Paris-based American scholar Michael Padovic (Malkovich) and his French wife Helene (Deneuve) who travel to an ancient Portuguese monastery so Michael may do research at their library. The convent's guardian is the charming and sinister Baltar (Cintra), who flirts with neglected Helene, while playing Mephistopheles to Michael's Faust. Lots of mysticism and religious iconography. Portuguese, French, and English dialogue. **90m/C VHS.** *PT FR* John Malkovich, Catherine Deneuve, Luis Miguel Cintra, Leonor Silveira; **D:** Manoel de Oliveira; **W:** Manoel de Oliveira; **C:** Mario Barroso. *FXL*

The Conversation 🐾🐾🐾½ **1974 (PG)** Hackman plays a surveillance expert increasingly uneasy about his job as he begins to suspect he is an accomplice to murder. Powerful statement about privacy, responsibility and guilt. One of the best movies of the '70s. **113m/C VHS, Beta, LV.** Gene Hackman, John Cazale, Frederic Forrest, Allen (Goorwitz) Garfield, Cindy Williams, Robert Duvall, Teri Garr, Michael Higgins, Elizabeth McRae, Harrison Ford; **D:** Francis Ford Coppola; **W:** Francis Ford Coppola; **C:** Bill Butler; **M:** David Shire. Cannes Film Festival '74: Best Film; National Board of Review Awards '74: Best Actor (Hackman), Best Director (Coppola), National Film Registry '95;; National Society of

Film Critics Awards '74: Best Director (Coppola); Nominations: Academy Awards '74: Best Original Screenplay, Best Picture, Best Sound. *PAR*

Conversation Piece 🐾🐾🐾 *Violence et Passion; Gruppo di Famiglia in un Interno* 1975 (R) An aging art historian's life is turned upside down when a Countess and her daughters rent out the penthouse in his estate. Sometimes-talky examination of scholarly pretensions. 112m/C VHS, Beta. *IT FR* Burt Lancaster, Silvana Mangano, Helmut Berger, Claudia Cardinale; *D:* Luchino Visconti; *C:* Pasquale De Santis. *NO*

Convict Cowboy 🐾🐾½ 1995 (R) Hardbitten professional rodeo cowboy Ry Weston (Voight) killed a man and now works the Montana prison rodeo circuit. Newcomer greenhorn Clay Treyton (Chandler) wants to get out of kitchen duty and decides Ry is the perfect ridin' and ropin' teacher. Only Ry isn't interested in wasting his time (at first). It's a predictable bonding experience in a melodramatic cable movie. *CW:* Strong language; some violence. 106m/C VHS. Jon Voight, Kyle Chandler, Ben Gazzara, Marcia Gay Harden, Glenn Plummer, Stephen McHattie; *D:* Rod Holcomb; *C:* James L. Carter. *MGM*

Convicted 🐾🐾½ 1932 Lean thriller about a woman cleared of a murder charge, but only when a second, identical murder occurs while she is jailed. 57m/B VHS, Beta, LV. Aileen Pringle, Jameson Thomas, Harry Myers, Dorothy Christy, Richard Tucker; *D:* Christy Cabanne. *NOS*

Convicted 🐾🐾½ 1986 Solid story of innocent man imprisoned for rape, and his wife's determined efforts to free him. Larroquette does well in unexpected role. Based on a true story. Made for television. 94m/C VHS, Beta. John Larroquette, Carroll O'Connor, Lindsay Wagner; *D:* David Lowell Rich; *M:* Stephen Dorff. *TTC*

Convicted: A Mother's Story 🐾 1987 Jillian embezzles cash from her employer, all for the sake of a bum of a boyfriend, and goes to jail. Odd casting hinders a ho-hum plot. Made for television. 95m/C VHS, Beta. Ann Jillian, Kiel Martin, Fred Savage, Gloria Loring, Christa Denton; *D:* Richard T. Heffron; *M:* David Shire. *JTC*

Convicts at Large 🐾 1938 An escaped convict steals the clothes of a inept architect. Left with only prison duds, the architect stumbles into the bad side of town and gets involved with the mob. Inane. 58m/B VHS, Beta, LV. Ralph Forbes, Paula Stone. *NO*

Convoy 🐾🐾½ 1940 Life aboard a convoy ship in the North Sea during WWII. The small cruiser is picked on by a German U-Boat. Will a rescuer appear? Noted for technical production values. 95m/B VHS. Clive Brook, John Clements, Edward Chapman, Judy Campbell, Edward Rigby, Stewart Granger, Michael Wilding, George Benson; *D:* Pen Tennyson. *NOS*

Convoy 🐾🐾 1978 (R) A defiant trucker leads an indestructible truck convoy to Mexico to protect high gasoline prices. Lightweight stuff was inspired by the song "Convoy" by C.W. McCall. 106m/C VHS, Beta. Kris Kristofferson, Ali MacGraw, Ernest Borgnine, Burt Young, Madge Sinclair, Franklin Ajaye, Cassie Yates; *D:* Sam Peckinpah; *C:* Harry Stradling Jr. *NO*

Coogan's Bluff 🐾🐾🐾 1968 (PG) An Arizona deputy sheriff (Eastwood) travels to New York in order to track down a killer on the loose. First Eastwood/Siegel teaming is tense actioner. The television series "McCloud" was based on this film. 100m/C VHS, Beta, LV. Clint Eastwood, Lee J. Cobb, Tisha Sterling, Don Stroud, Betty Field, Susan Clark, Tom Tully; *D:* Donald Siegel; *M:* Lalo Schifrin. *USH*

The Cook, the Thief, His Wife & Her Lover 🐾🐾🐾½ 1990 (R) An exclusive restaurant houses four disturbing characters. Greenaway's powerful study of greed, love, and violence may be too strong for some tastes. Available in several different versions: the standard unrated theatrical release, the unrated version in a letterboxed format, an R-rated cut which runs half an hour shorter, and a Spanish-subtitled version. *GW:* Psychological intensity/violence. 123m/C VHS, Letterbox. *GB* Richard Bohringer, Michael Gambon, Helen Mirren, Alan Howard, Tim Roth; *D:* Peter Greenaway; *W:* Peter Greenaway; *C:* Sacha Vierny; *M:* Michael Nyman. *THV*

Cookie 🐾🐾½ 1989 (R) Light comedy about a Mafia don's daughter trying to smart mouth her way into the mob's good graces. A character-driven vehicle, this plot takes a backseat to casting. Wiest is superb as Falk's moll. 93m/C VHS, 8mm, Closed Caption. Emily Lloyd, Peter Falk, Dianne Wiest, Jerry Lewis, Brenda Vaccaro, Ricki Lake, Lionel Stander, Michael V. Gazzo, Adrian Pasdar, Bob Gunton, Rockets Redglare, G. Anthony Sirico; *D:* Susan Seidelman; *W:* Alice Arlen, Nora Ephron; *M:* Thomas Newman. *WAR*

Cooking Up Trouble 🐾🐾 1944 The crazy trio become foster dads in this "Stooge" type comedy. ?m/C VHS. Shemp Howard, Billy Gilbert, Maxie "Slapsie" Rosenbloom. *LOO*

Cool As Ice 🐾 1991 (PG) "Rapper" Vanilla Ice makes his feature film debut as a rebel with an eye for the ladies, who motors into a small, conservative town. Several so-so musical segments. For teenage girls only. 92m/C VHS, Beta, LV, Closed Caption. Vanilla Ice, Kristin Minter, Michael Gross, Sydney Lassick, Dody Goodman, Naomi Campbell, Candy Clark; *D:* David Kellogg; *C:* Janusz Kaminski; *M:* Stanley Clarke. Golden Raspberry Awards '91: Worst New Star (Vanilla Ice). *USH*

Cool Blue 🐾½ 1988 (R) An unsuccessful painter meets the woman of his dreams, has a brief affair, then tries to locate her in the greater Los Angeles metro area. Good luck. Watch for Penn's cameo. 93m/C VHS, Beta, LV, Closed Caption. Woody Harrelson, Hank Azaria, Ely Pouget, John Diehl; *Cameos:* Sean Penn; *D:* Mark Mullin, Richard Shepard. *COL*

Cool Hand Luke 🐾🐾🐾½ 1967 One of the last great men-in-chains films. A man (Newman) sentenced to sweat out a term on a prison farm refuses to compromise with authority. Martin shines in his supporting role as the oily warden, uttering that now-famous phrase, "What we have here is a failure to communicate." Kennedy's performance as leader of the chain gang won him an Oscar. Based on the novel by Donn Pearce. 126m/C VHS, Beta, LV, DVD. Paul Newman, George Kennedy, J.D. Cannon, Strother Martin, Dennis Hopper, Anthony Zerbe, Lou Antonio, Wayne Rogers, Harry Dean Stanton, Ralph Waite, Joe Don Baker, Richard Davalos, Jo Van Fleet; *D:* Stuart Rosenberg; *W:* Frank Pierson; *C:* Conrad Hall; *M:* Lalo Schifrin. Academy Awards '67: Best Supporting Actor (Kennedy); Nominations: Academy Awards '66: Best Adapted Screenplay, Best Original Score; Academy Awards '67: Best Actor (Newman). *WAR, BTV*

Cool Mikado 🐾🐾 1963 A jazzy modernization of the Gilbert-Sullivan operetta, in which an American soldier is kidnapped by the gangster fiance of the Japanese girl he loves. 81m/C VHS, Beta. *GB* Stubby Kaye, Frankie Howerd, Dennis Price; *D:* Michael Winner. *JEF*

Cool Runnings 🐾🐾½ 1993 (PG) Bright, slapstick comedy based on the true story of the Jamaican bobsled team's quest to enter the 1988 Winter Olympics in Calgary. Candy is recruited to coach four unlikely athletes who don't quite exemplify the spirit of the Games. He accepts the challenge not only because of its inherent difficulty but because he needs to reconcile himself to past failures as a former sledder. When our heroes leave their sunny training ground for Calgary, their mettle is tested by serious sledders from more frigid climes who pursue the competition with a stern sense of mission. An upbeat story which will appeal to children, its target audience. 98m/C VHS, LV, Closed Caption. Leon, Doug E. Doug, John Candy, Marco Brambilla, Malik Yoba, Rawle Lewis, Raymond J. Barry, Peter Outerbridge, Larry Gilman, Paul Coeur; *D:* Jon Turteltaub; *W:* Tommy Swerdlow, Lynn Siefert, Michael Goldberg; *C:* Phedon Papamichael; *M:* Hans Zimmer. *DIS*

The Cool Surface 🐾🐾 1992 (R) Sex and ambition, Hollywood style. Dani, a wannbe actress, and Jarvis, an aspiring screenwriter become lovers. Jarvis turns their hot affair into a sizzling novel and then a script. Dani may have inspired the lead role but that doesn't mean she'll get the part. But it won't be for lack of trying (anything). *CW:* Language, nudity, violence, and sexual situations. 88m/C VHS. Robert Patrick, Teri Hatcher, Matt McCoy, Cyril O'Reilly, Ian Buchanan; *D:* Erik Anjou; *W:* Erik Anjou; *M:* Dave Kopplin. *COL*

The Cool World 🐾🐾½ 1963 Tough-talking docudrama, set on the streets of Harlem, focuses on a 15-year-old black youth whose one ambition in life is to own a gun and lead his gang. 107m/B VHS, Beta. Gloria Foster, Hampton Clanton, Carl Lee; *D:* Shirley Clarke. National Film Registry '94. *NO*

Cool World 🐾🐾 1992 (PG-13) Underground cartoonist Jack Deebs enters his own adult cartoon "Cool World," lured by his sex-kitten character "Holli Would," who needs him to leave her animated world and become human. Holli's plan is opposed by the only other human to occupy Cool World, a slick detective whose main job is to prevent noids (humans) and doodles (cartoons) from having sex and destroying the balance between the two existences. A mixture of live-action and wild animation. Director Bakshi's creations are not intended for children but this is less explicit than usual, which may be one of the problems. Little humor and a flat script leave this film too uninvolving. 101m/C VHS, Beta, LV, Closed Caption. Gabriel Byrne, Kim Basinger, Brad Pitt, Michele Abrams, Deirdre O'Connell, Carrie Hamilton, Frank Sinatra Jr.; *D:* Ralph Bakshi; *C:* John A. Alonzo. *PAR, PMS*

Cooley High 🐾🐾🐾 1975 (PG) Black high school students in Chicago go through the rites of passage in their senior year during the '60s. Film is funny, smart and much acclaimed. Great soundtrack featuring Motown hits of the era is a highlight. Sequel to the TV series "What's Happening." 107m/C VHS, LV. Glynn Turman, Lawrence-Hilton Jacobs, Garrett Morris, Cynthia Davis; *D:* Michael A. Schultz; *W:* Eric Monte. *ORI, FCT, PTB*

Cooperstown 🐾🐾½ 1993 Harry (Arkin) is a former major-league pitcher who now works as a baseball scout in Florida. He's been angry for 30 years over giving up a home-run pitch that kept his team (the ficitional Chicago Barons) out of the World Series. Harry's feels this error cost him his chance at induction into the Baseball Hall of Fame in Cooperstown, New York, and he's always blamed ex-friend and former catcher Raymond (Greene), who's just had the gall to be elected. Only Raymond's just died—but his ghostly figure visits Harry and urges him to take a road trip not only to the baseball shrine but into his past. Made for cable television. 100m/C VHS. Alan Arkin, Graham Greene, Hope Lange, Josh Charles, Ed Begley Jr., Maria Pitillo, Ann Wedgeworth, Paul Dooley, Joanna Miles, Charles Haid; *D:* Charles Haid; *W:* Lee Blessing. *NO*

Cop 🐾🐾½ 1988 (R) Left by his wife and child, a ruthless and work-obsessed detective goes after a twisted serial killer. Woods' exceptional ability to play sympathetic weirdos is diluted by a script—based on James Ellroys's novel "Blood on the Moon"—that warps the feminist theme, is violent, and depends too heavily on coincidence. 110m/C VHS, Beta, LV, Closed Caption. James Woods, Lesley Ann Warren, Charles Durning, Charles Haid, Raymond J. Barry, Randi Brooks, Annie McEnroe, Victoria Wauchope; *D:* James B. Harris; *W:* James B. Harris; *M:* Michel Colombier. *PAR*

Cop and a Half 🐾½ 1993 (PG) Streetwise eight-year-old (Golden) accidentally witnesses a murder and then bullies police into letting him join the force (for a day) when he withholds key information. Enter his partner for the day—hard-edged detective Reynolds, who claims to hate kids, but who we know will learn to love them. Meanwhile, the outlaw (Sharkey) knows Devon saw him and is trying to silence him permanently. Predictable fantasy may appeal to kids, but will make most adults yawn. One of Sharkey's last roles. **87m/C VHS, LV, Letterbox, Closed Caption.** Norman D. Golden II, Burt Reynolds, Ruby Dee, Ray Sharkey, Holland Taylor, Frank Sivero, Marc Macaulay, Rocky Giordani, Sammy Hernandez; *D:* Henry Winkler; *W:* Arne Olsen; *C:* Bill Butler; *M:* Alan Silvestri. Golden Raspberry Awards '93: Worst Actor (Reynolds). *USH*

The Cop & the Girl ⊃ 1986 A cop falls for a teenage runaway, ends up on the lam. Confused story overpowered by camera work. Lots of violence and strong language. Dubbed. **94m/C VHS, Beta.** GE Juergen Prochnow, Annette Von Klier; *D:* Peter Keglevic. *NO*

Cop in Blue Jeans ⊃ 1978 Undercover cop goes after a mob kingpin in this violent, badly dubbed crime yarn. **92m/C VHS, Beta.** Tomas Milian, Jack Palance, Maria Rosaria Omaggio, Guido Mannari; *D:* Bruno Corbucci. *THV*

Cop Land ⊃⊃⊃ 1997 (R) Partially deaf sheriff (Stallone), whose small New Jersey town is home to a number of New York cops, has divided loyalties when a criminal investigation could implicate his department and the cops he idolizes. Stallone wanted to put "actor" back on his resume, and made the ultimate sacrifice of his physique for the role by gaining some 35 pounds and letting his muscles go. Writer-director Mangold, who grew up in an upstate New York town populated by NYC cops and firemen, pairs his earnest morality tale with a Western feel to provide the excellent, Method-Actors All-Star Team cast a chance to do what they do best. Welcome departure from the usual summer bombast. *CW:* Violence, strong language, and brief nudity. **105m/C VHS, LV, Closed Caption.** Sylvester Stallone, Robert De Niro, Annabella Sciorra, Harvey Keitel, Peter Berg, Janeane Garofalo, Michael Rapaport, Ray Liotta, Cathy Moriarty, Robert Patrick, Noah Emmerich, John Spencer, Malik Yoba; *D:* James Mangold; *W:* James Mangold; *C:* Eric Alan Edwards; *M:* Howard Shore. *MAX*

Cop-Out ⊃⊃ 1991 A cop is framed. His brother is mad. Teamed up with a sexy lawyer, he exposes the filth that is corrupting the city. Okay melodrama. **102m/C VHS, Beta, LV.** David Buff, Kathryn Luster, Dan Ranger, Reggie DeMorton, Lawrence L. Simeone; *D:* Lawrence L. Simeone; *W:* Lawrence L. Simeone.

Copacabana ⊃ 1947 A shady theatrical agent (Groucho) books a nightclub singer into two shows at the same time at New York's ritzy nightclub. Lots of energy spent trying to enliven a routine script. Also available colorized. ♫Tico Tico; Stranger Things Have Happened; Je Vous Amie; My Heart Was Doing a Bolero; Let's Do the Copacobana; I Haven't Got a Thing to Sell; We've Come to Copa. **91m/B VHS, LV.** Groucho Marx, Carmen Miranda, Steve Cochran, Gloria Jean, Andy Russell, Earl Wilson; *D:* Alfred E. Green. *REP, FCT, MLB*

Copkillers woof! 1977 (R) Two men desperate for an easy way to make money embark on a murderous shooting spree. Mostly blanks. **93m/C VHS, Beta.** Jason Williams, Bill Osco. *TWE*

Copper Canyon ⊃⊃½ 1950 Milland plays a Confederate Army officer who heads West after the Civil War, meets up with Lamarr, and sparks a romance. Good chemistry between the leads in this otherwise standard western. **84m/B VHS, Closed Caption.** Ray Milland, Hedy Lamarr, MacDonald Carey, Mona Freeman, Harry Carey Jr., Frank Faylen, Taylor Holmes, Peggy Knudsen; *D:* John Farrow. *PAR, FCT*

Copperhead ⊃ 1984 (R) A group of copperhead snakes attack a family who possess a stolen Incan gold necklace. This one bites. **90m/C VHS, Beta.** Jack Renner, Gretta Ratliff, David Fritts, Cheryl Nickerson. *VCI*

Cops and Robbers ⊃⊃½ 1973 (PG) Two cops use a Wall Street parade for returning astronauts as a cover for a multi-million dollar heist. Exceptional caper film thanks to the likable leads and genuine suspense. **89m/C VHS.** Joseph Bologna, Dick Ward, Shepperd Strudwick, John P. Ryan, Ellen Holly, Dolph Sweet, Joe Spinell, Cliff Gorman; *D:* Aram Avakian; *W:* Donald E. Westlake. *MGM*

Cops and Robbersons ⊃ 1994 (PG) Bored, dim-witted dad Chase, a TV cop-show junkie, wishes his life had a little more danger and excitement. How lucky for him when hard-nosed cop Palance sets up a command post in his house to stake out the mobster living next door (Davi). Predictable plot isn't funny and drags Chase's bumbling idiot persona on for too long; Wiest and Davi are two bright spots, but their talents are wasted, while Palance does little more than reincarnate his "City Slickers" character. Poor effort for otherwise notable director Ritchie. **93m/C VHS, LV, 8mm, Closed Caption.** Chevy Chase, Jack Palance, Dianne Wiest, Robert Davi, Jason James Richter, Fay Masterson, Miko Hughes, Richard Romanus, David Barry Gray; *D:* Michael Ritchie; *W:* Bernie Somers; *M:* William Ross. *COL*

Cops/One Week 1922 Two vintage Keaton shorts, with original organ score. **51m/B VHS, Beta, 8mm.** Buster Keaton; *D:* Buster Keaton, Eddie Cline. *VYY*

Copycat ⊃⊃ 1995 (R) Crowded serial killer genre yields crooner Connick as southern psychopath stuck on murder. Soon he's in jail, advising the police in their hunt for another serial killer who imitates the murders of other infamous serial killers. Agoraphobic, boozing criminal psychologist Helen Hudson (Weaver), still suffering the after effects of an attack by sicko subject Darryl Lee Cullum (Connick), is enlisted to help detective M.J. Monahan (Hunter) catch the homage specialist. Weaver and Hunter bring sparks to the usually testosterone-laden formula, helping mask the preponderance of serial killer cliches and giant holes in the script. Connick's turn as a nut-job killer won't make you forget Anthony Hopkins, or even Frank Sinatra. Exploitative and imitative, and always faithful to the formula. *CW:* Violence, language. **124m/C VHS, Closed Caption.** Sigourney Weaver, Holly Hunter, Dermot Mulroney, Harry Connick Jr., William McNamara, Will Patton, John Rothman, David Michael Silverman; *D:* Jon Amiel; *W:* Ann Biderman, David Madsen; *C:* Laszlo Kovacs; *M:* Christopher Young. *WAR*

Coquette ⊃⊃½ 1929 Pickford's first talkie portrays her as a flirtatious flapper from a well-to-do family who falls in love with a poor man her father despises. So much in fact that daddy kills the young man and then commits suicide, leaving his daughter to face the world alone. Pickford and Brown get to share a melodramatic death scene and audiences flocked to hear "America's Sweetheart" speak onscreen. Based on a play by George Abbott and Anne Preston. **75m/B VHS.** Mary Pickford, Johnny Mack Brown, Matt Moore, John St. Polis, Henry Kolker, George Irving, Louise Beavers, William Janney; *D:* Sam Taylor; *C:* Karl Struss. Academy Awards '29: Best Actress (Pickford). *MGM*

Cord & Dischords/Naughty Nurse ⊃⊃ 1928 Two vintage silent shorts featuring some lesser known slapstick clowns cavorting in blackface. **50m/B VHS, Beta.** Fred Parker, Jack Cooper, Ella MacKenzie, Spencer Williams Jr. *VYY*

Coriolanus, Man without a Country ⊃ 1964 When the Romans begin to abuse their rights, the Plebians call upon the brave and mighty Coriolanus to lead them into battle against their oppressors. Predictable muscle man outing. **?m/C VHS, Beta.** IT Gordon Scott, Alberto Lupo, Lilla Brignone. *SNC*

Corleone ⊃ 1979 (R) Limp tale about two boyhood friends who grow up to fight the evil landowners who dominate Italy. To accomplish this, one becomes a mobster, the other a politician. **115m/C VHS, Beta.** IT Claudia Cardinale, Giuliano Gemma; *D:* Pasquale Squitieri. Montreal World Film Festival '79: Best Actor (Gemma). *MGM*

The Corn Is Green ⊃⊃⊃ 1945 Touching story of a school teacher in a poor Welsh village who eventually sends her pet student to Oxford. Davis makes a fine teacher, though a little young, while the on-site photography provides atmosphere. Based on the play by Emlyn Williams. Remade in 1979. **115m/B VHS, Beta.** Bette Davis, John

Dall, Nigel Bruce, Joan Lorring, Arthur Shields, Mildred Dunnock, Rhys Williams, Rosalind Ivan; *D:* Irving Rapper; *M:* Max Steiner. Nominations: Academy Awards '45: Best Supporting Actor (Dall), Best Supporting Actress (Lorring). *MGM, FCT*

Cornbread, Earl & Me ⊃⊃ 1975 (R) A high school basketball star from the ghetto is mistaken for a murderer by cops and shot, causing a subsequent furor of protest and racial hatred. Superficial melodrama. **95m/C VHS, Beta.** Moses Gunn, Rosalind Cash, Bernie Casey, Tierre Turner, Madge Sinclair, Keith Wilkes, Antonio Fargas; *D:* Joseph Manduke; *M:* Donald Byrd. *NO*

Cornered ⊃ 1932 McCoy is a sheriff, chasing bad guys, whose life is saved by Welch. Basically boring. **62m/B VHS.** Tim McCoy, Niles Welch, Raymond Hatton, Noah Beery Sr., Shirley Grey, Walter Long; *D:* B. Reeves Eason. *GPV*

Cornered ⊃⊃⊃ 1945 Tough Powell plays an airman released from a German prison camp who pursues a Nazi war criminal to avenge the death of his wife and child. **102m/B VHS, Beta, LV.** Dick Powell, Walter Slezak, Micheline Cheirel, Luther Adler; *D:* Edward Dmytryk. *TTC*

Coroner Creek ⊃⊃½ 1948 Chris Danning's (Scott) fiancee commits suicide after being held hostage during an Indian attack on her stagecoach and a payroll robbery. Danning sets out to trace the loot and exact his revenge. A superior production, notable for being one of the first westerns with an adult theme. **89m/B VHS.** Randolph Scott, Marguerite Chapman, George Macready, Sally Eilers, Edgar Buchanan, Wallace Ford, Forrest Tucker; *D:* Ray Enright. *COL*

Corporate Affairs ⊃⊃ 1990 (R) A ruthless business woman climbing her way to the top literally seduces her boss to death. **92m/C VHS.** Peter Scolari, Mary Crosby, Chris Lemmon, Ken Kercheval; *D:* Terence H. Winkless; *W:* Terence H. Winkless, Geoffrey Baere. *MGM*

The Corporation ⊃½ Subliminal Seduction; *Roger Corman Presents Subliminal Seduction* 1996 (R) Darrin Danver (Ziering), the new exec at a computer game company, discovers the games are controlling their users with powerful, subliminal messages. So he tries to expose his employers' lethal manipulations before they can kill him. Standard-issue made-for-TV movie doesn't bring anything new new to the "evil company" genre. Shot on location in L.A. and Las Vegas. **?m/C VHS.** Ian Ziering, Andrew Stevens, Katherine Kelly Lang, Dee Wallace Stone, Larry Manetti, Kim Morgan Greene, Kin Shriner, Stella Stevens; *D:* Andrew Stevens; *W:* Karen Kelly; *C:* Gary Graver; *M:* Terry Plumeri. *NHO*

The Corpse Grinders woof! 1971 (R) Low-budget bad movie classic in which a cardboard corpse-grinding machine makes nasty cat food that makes cats nasty. Sets are cheap, gore effects silly, and cat attacks ridiculous. **73m/C VHS, Beta.** Sean Kenney, Monika Kelly, Sandford Mitchell; *D:* Ted V. Mikels; *W:* Ted V. Mikels. *NO*

The Corpse Vanishes ⊃⊃½ 1942 Lugosi at his chilling best as a diabolical scientist who snatches young brides and drains their blood in an effort to keep his 70-year-old wife eternally youthful. Not for newlyweds! **64m/B VHS, Beta.** Bela Lugosi, Luana Walters, Tristram Coffin, Elizabeth Russell, Vince Barnett, Joan Barclay, Angelo Rossitto; *D:* Wallace Fox. *NOS, MRV, SNC*

Corregidor ⊃⊃ 1943 A love triangle develops between doctors treating the wounded during the WWII battle. A poor propaganda piece which contains only shaky stock footage for its "action" sequences. **73m/B VHS.** Otto Kruger, Elissa Landi, Donald Woods, Rick Vallin, Frank Jenks, Wanda McKay, Ian Keith; *D:* William Nigh. *NOS, MOV, HEG*

The Corridor: Death 1989 Two Americans are involved in a car accident in Israel which triggers a debate on the Jewish perspective of death and the afterlife. Filmed on location at Hadassah Hospital on St. Scopus, Jerusalem. The final part of the trilogy preceded by "The Eighth

Day: Circumcision" and "The Journey: Bar Mitzvah." 25m/C VHS, Beta. *ERG*

Corridors of Blood 🎞🎞½ *The Doctor from Seven Dials* 1958 Karloff is a doctor, in search of a viable anesthetic, who accidently becomes addicted to drugs, then turns to grave robbers to support his habit. Karloff plays usual threatening doctor to perfection. 86m/C VHS, Beta. **GB** Boris Karloff, Betta St. John, Finlay Currie, Christopher Lee, Francis Matthews, Adrienne Corri, Nigel Green; **D:** Robert Day. *MPI*

Corrina, Corrina 🎞🎞½ 1994 (PG) Newly widowed jingle-writer Liotta needs someone to care for his withdrawn eight-year-old daughter. Enter Whoopi, as housekeeper and eventual love interest. Sweet, nostalgic romance set in the 1950s. Goldberg also found off-screen romance (again), this time with the film's union organizer Lyle Trachtenberg. Last role for Ameche. 115m/C VHS, LV, Closed Caption. Whoopi Goldberg, Ray Liotta, Don Ameche, Tina Majorino, Wendy Crewson, Jenifer Lewis, Larry Miller, Erica Yohn; **Cameos:** Anita Baker; **D:** Jessie Nelson; **W:** Jessie Nelson. *NLC, TTC*

Corrupt 🎞🎞🎞 *Order of Death; Cop Killers* 1984 (PG) Bad narcotics cop goes after murderer, but mysterious Lydon gets in the way. An acquired taste, best if you appreciate Lydon, better known as Johnny Rotten of the Sex Pistols. 99m/C VHS, Beta. **IT** Harvey Keitel, John (Johnny Rotten) Lydon, Sylvia Sidney, Nicole Garcia, Leonard Mann; **D:** Roberto Faenza; **M:** Ennio Morricone. *NO*

The Corrupt Ones 🎞🎞½ *Il Sigillo de Pechino; Die Holle von Macao; Les Corrompus; The Peking Medallion; Hell to Macao* 1967 Everyone's after a photographer who has a medallion that will lead to buried treasure in China. Great characters hampered by pedestrian script. 87m/C VHS, Beta. Robert Stack, Elke Sommer, Nancy Kwan, Christian Marquand, Werner Peters; **D:** James Hill; **W:** Brian Clemens. *NLC*

Corruption woof! 1989 (R) Mostly soft-porn. Alleged plot: The Mob is interested in having Shea work for them, and makes it worth his while. 80m/C VHS. Mary McGee, Patrick Shea. *NO*

Corsair 🎞🎞 1931 Actioner about a gorgeous debutante and a handsome gangster who find themselves caught up with a gang of bootlegging pirates. Todd is always worth watching. 73m/B VHS, Beta. Chester Morris, Thelma Todd, Frank McHugh, Ned Sparks, Mayo Methot; **D:** Roland West. *GPV, RXM, HEG*

The Corsican Brothers 🎞🎞½ 1942 Alexander Dumas' classic about twins who, although separated, remain spiritually tied throughout their various adventures. Fairbanks takes on dual roles in this entertaining swashbuckler. Remade for television in 1984. 111m/B VHS, Beta, LV. Douglas Fairbanks Jr., Akim Tamiroff, Ruth Warrick, J. Carrol Naish, H.B. Warner, Henry Wilcoxon, Veda Ann Borg; **D:** Gregory Ratoff; **C:** Harry Stradling. Nominations: Academy Awards '42: Best Original Dramatic/Comedy Score. *VTR, ART*

Corvette Summer 🎞 *The Hot One* 1978 (PG) After spending a semester restoring a Corvette in his high school shop class, an L.A. student must journey to Las Vegas to recover the car when it is stolen. There he meets a prostitute, falls in love, and steps into the "real world" for the first time. Potts intriguing as the low-life love interest, but she can't save this one. 104m/C VHS, Beta. Mark Hamill, Annie Potts, Eugene Roche, Kim Milford, Richard McKenzie, William Bryant; **D:** Matthew Robbins; **W:** Matthew Robbins, Hal Barwood. *MGM*

Cosh Boy woof! *The Slasher* 1961 Vicious male youths stalk women on the streets of London in this low-budget Jack the Ripper rip-off. 90m/B VHS, Beta. Joan Collins, James Kennedy. *NO*

Cosi 🎞🎞🎞 1995 (R) Amiable Lewis (Mendelsohn) is hired to help with drama therapy at the local Sydney mental institution. Pressured by long-term patient Roy (Otto), Lewis finds himself agreeing to stage a production of Mozart's opera "Cosi Fan Tutte" though none of the patients can speak Italian or sing. Rehearsals prove a challenge, there are numerous setbacks, and then it's show time. Fine ensemble cast delivers; adapted from Nowra's play. Friels stepped into the role of security guard Errol when Bruno Lawrence died before filming was completed; pic is dedicated to Lawrence. **CW:** Language. 100m/C VHS, LV, Closed Caption. **AU** Ben Mendelsohn, Barry Otto, Aden Young, Toni Collette, Rachel Griffiths, Colin Friels, Paul Chubb, Pamela Rabe, Jacki Weaver, David Wenham, Colin Hay, Tony Llewellyn-Jones; **Cameos:** Greta Scacchi, Paul Mercurio; **D:** Mark Joffe; **W:** Louis Nowra; **C:** Ellery Ryan; **M:** Stephen Endelman. Australian Film Institute '96: Best Adapted Screenplay, Best Supporting Actress (Collette); Nominations: Australian Film Institute '96: Best Supporting Actor (Otto). *TOU*

The Cosmic Eye 🎞🎞🎞 1971 Animated tale of three musicians from outer space who come to earth to spread the message of worldwide peace and harmony. A variety of cultural perspectives about the origins and destiny of the Earth are offered. Rather moralizing but the animation is impressive. 71m/C VHS, Beta, LV. **D:** Faith Hubley; **V:** Dizzy Gillespie, Maureen Stapleton, Benny Carter. *LTY, DIS, BTV*

The Cosmic Man 🎞½ 1959 An alien arrives on Earth with a message of peace and restraint. He is regarded with suspicion by us nasty Earthlings. Essentially "The Day the Earth Stood Still" without the budget, but interesting nonetheless. 72m/B VHS, Beta. Bruce (Herman Brix) Bennett, John Carradine, Angela Greene, Paul Langton, Scotty Morrow; **D:** Herbert Greene. *SNC*

The Cosmic Monsters 🎞½ *The Strange World of Planet X* 1958 Scientist accidentally pops a hole in the ionosphere during a magnetism experiment. Then huge, mean insects arrive to plague mankind. Coincidence? You figure it out. 75m/B VHS, Beta. Forrest Tucker, Gaby Andre, Alec Mango, Hugh Latimer, Martin Benson; **D:** Gilbert Gunn. *MRV, SNC, EEL*

Cosmic Slop 🎞🎞 1994 (R) Three-part anthology. "Space Traders," based on a story by Derrick Bell, finds a fleet of aliens offering to solve all of U.S. society's most pressing social ills if they can have the entire black population in return (for what purpose is never explained). "The First Commandment" features a Catholic priest in a Latino parish who comes up against his parishoners pagan beliefs in Santeria. "Tang," based on a story by Chester Himes, finds a poor, desperately unhappy married couple dreaming about what they'll do with the rifle mysteriously delivered in a flower carton to their door. **CW:** Some strong language. 87m/C VHS, Closed Caption. Robert Guillaume, Jason Bernard, Nicholas Turturro, Richard Herd, Paula Jai Parker, Chi McBride; **D:** Reginald Hudlin, Warrington Hudlin, Kevin Sullivan; **W:** Warrington Hudlin, Trey Ellis, Kyle Baker; **C:** Peter Deming. *HBO*

Cosmo Jones, Crime Smasher 🎞🎞 1943 Murder mystery based on a '40s radio program. ?m/C VHS. Mantan Moreland, Frank Graham. *SNC*

Cosmos: War of the Planets woof! *Cosmo 2000: Planet Without a Name; War of the Planets* 1980 (PG) The ultimate battle for survival is fought in outer space, though not very well and on a small budget. Special effects especially laughable. 90m/C VHS, Beta. **IT** Katia Christine, West Buchanan, John Richardson, Yanti Somer; **D:** Al Bradley. *NO*

Cottage to Let 🎞½ *Bombsight Stolen* 1941 Propaganda thriller about a Nazi plot to kidnap the inventor of a new bombsight. Focused cast struggles with lackluster script. 90m/B VHS, Beta. **GB** Leslie Banks, Alastair Sim, John Mills, Jeanne de Casalis, Carla Lehmann, George Cole, Michael Wilding, Frank Cellier, Wally Patch, Catherine Lacey; **D:** Anthony Asquith. *SNC*

Cotter 🎞 1972 A Native American rodeo clown feels responsible for a cowboy's death, returns home to reflect on his life. Fair story, best at the small town feeling. 94m/C VHS, Beta. Don Murray, Carol Lynley, Rip Torn, Sherry Jackson; **D:** Paul Stanley. *XVC*

Cotton Candy 🎞🎞 1982 Follows the faintly interesting trials and tribulations of a high school senior who tries to form a rock band. At first he meets failure, but is ultimately successful with the band and romance. Made for television. Joint script-writing venture by brothers Clint and Ron Howard. 97m/C VHS, Beta. Charles Martin Smith, Clint Howard, Leslie King; **D:** Ron Howard; **W:** Clint Howard, Ron Howard. *TLF*

The Cotton Club 🎞🎞🎞 1984 (R) With $50 million in his pocket, Francis reaches for an epic and delivers: handsome production, lots of dance, bit of singing, confused plot, uneven performances, tad too long. A musician playing at The Cotton Club falls in love with gangster Dutch Schultz's girlfriend. A black tap dancer falls in love with a member of the chorus line who can pass for white. These two love stories are told against a background of mob violence and music. Excellent performances by Hoskins and Gwynne. ♫Minnie the Moocher; Ill Wind; The Mooch; Ring Dem Bells; Drop Me Off in Harlem; Cotton Club Stomp; Truckin; Mood Indigo; Copper Colored Gal. 121m/C VHS, Beta, LV, 8mm, Closed Caption. Diane Lane, Richard Gere, Gregory Hines, Lonette McKee, Bob Hoskins, Fred Gwynne, James Remar, Nicolas Cage, Lisa Jane Persky, Allen (Goorwitz) Garfield, Gwen Verdon, Joe Dallesandro, Jennifer Grey, Tom Waits, Diane Venora; **D:** Francis Ford Coppola; **W:** Francis Ford Coppola, William Kennedy, Mario Puzo; **M:** John Barry. Nominations: Academy Awards '84: Best Art Direction/Set Decoration, Best Film Editing. *NLC*

Cotton Comes to Harlem 🎞🎞🎞 1970 (R) Cambridge and St. Jacques star as Harlem plainclothes detectives Grave Digger Jones and Coffin Ed Johnson in this successful mix of crime and comedy. They're investigating a suspicious preacher's back-to-Africa scheme which they suspect is a swindle. Directorial debut of Davis. Filmed on location in Harlem, New York. Based on the novel by Chester Himes. Followed by a weak sequel, "Come Back, Charleston Blue." 97m/C VHS. Godfrey Cambridge, Raymond St. Jacques, Calvin Lockhart, Judy Pace, Redd Foxx, John Anderson, Emily Yancy, J.D. Cannon, Teddy Wilson, Eugene Roche, Cleavon Little, Lou Jacobi; **D:** Ossie Davis; **W:** Ossie Davis. *MGM*

Cotton Queen 🎞½ *Crying Out Loud* 1937 Romance and light intrigue plague the children of two rival textile mill owners. 80m/B VHS, Beta, 8mm. Will Fyffe, Stanley Holloway; **D:** Bernard Vorhaus. *VYY, FCT*

A Couch in New York 🎞🎞 *Un Divan a New York* 1995 (R) Limp romantic comedy features that old standby—opposites attracting. French dancer Beatrice (Binoche) responds to an ad for a temporary Paris-New York apartment switch placed by a stuffy psychoanalyst, Henry Harriston (Hurt). Henry's patients presume Beatrice is his replacement (he works at home) and the free-spirit begins giving them ad hoc advice. Meanwhile in Paris, Henry's plagued by all Beatrice's heartsick boyfriends and decides to come back early. When he arrives unannounced, she assumes he's a new patient and he's intrigued enough to go along. Lots of yakking, not too many sparks, and a strained artificiality make for a dull mix. 104m/C VHS. **FR BE GE** William Hurt, Juliette Binoche, Paul Guilfoyle, Stephanie Buttle, Richard Jenkins, Kent Broadhurst, Henry Bean, Barbara Garrick; **D:** Chantal Akerman; **W:** Chantal Akerman, Jean-Louis Benoit; **C:** Dietrich Lohmann; **M:** Paolo Conte, Sonia Atherton. *BMG*

The Couch Trip 🎞½ 1987 (R) Aykroyd is an escapee from a mental institution who passes himself off as a radio psychologist and becomes a media sensation. There are a few laughs and some funny characters but for the most part this one falls flat. 98m/C VHS, Beta, LV, Closed Caption. Dan Aykroyd, Walter Matthau, Charles Grodin, Donna Dixon, Richard Romanus, Arye Gross, David Clennon, Mary Gross; **D:** Michael Ritchie; **W:** Will Aldis, Steven Kampmann; **M:** Michel Colombier. *ORI*

Could It Happen Here? 🎬 198? A lurid Italian spectacle about a metropolis thrown into a state of chaotic martial law by terrorism. Dubbed. 90m/C VHS, Beta. IT Luc Merenda, Marcella Michelangeli; *D:* Massimo Pirri. *NO*

The Count 🎬🎬½ 1916 Chaplin pretends to be the secretary of his boss, who in turn is posing as a count. Silent with musical soundtrack added. 20m/B VHS, Beta. Charlie Chaplin; *D:* Charlie Chaplin. *CAB*

Count/Adventurer 1917 Two Chaplin two-reelers: "The Count (The Phoney Nobleman)" (1916), in which Charlie impersonates a count at the home of Miss Moneybags, and "The Adventurer" (1917), Chaplin's final film for Mutual, in which he plays an escaped convict with the law relentlessly on his trail. Silent with musical score. 52m/B VHS, Beta. Charlie Chaplin, Eric Campbell, Edna Purviance, Frank Coleman; *D:* Charlie Chaplin. *VYY*

Count Dracula 🎬🎬½ *Bram Stoker's Count Dracula; Il Conte Dracula; Dracula 71; Nachts wenn Dracula Erwacht; The Nights of Dracula* 1971 (R) Passable version of the Dracula legend (based on the novel by Bram Stoker) has Lee as the thirsty count on the prowl for fresh blood. Starts out as one of the most faithful adaptations, but loses momentum because Franco was running out of money. 90m/C VHS. *SP GE IT* Christopher Lee, Herbert Lom, Klaus Kinski, Frederick Williams, Maria Rohm, Soledad Miranda, Paul Mueller; *D:* Jess (Jesus) Franco; *W:* Jess (Jesus) Franco, Augusto Finochi, Peter Welbeck, Milo G. Cuccia, Carlo Fadda; *C:* Manuel Merino. *REP, FCT*

Count Dracula's Great Love 🎬🎬 1972 European horror superstar Naschy plays Dracula; stylishly done in the Hammer tradition. Considered by many to be Naschy's best horror film. ?m/C VHS. Paul Naschy. *SNC, SMW*

The Count of Monte Cristo 🎬🎬½ 1912 One of the first full-length features starring popular stage stars of the day. The first truly American feature, it was based on the classic tale of revenge by Alexander Dumas. Silent. Remade many times. Lead actor O'Neill was the father of famed American playwright, Eugene O'Neill, who covered his father's success in this role in his own family drama "Long Day's Journey Into Night." 90m/B VHS, Beta. James O'Neill; *D:* Edwin S. Porter. *NOS, VYY, DVT*

The Count of Monte Cristo 🎬🎬🎬 1934 A true swashbuckling revenge tale about Edmond Dantes, who unjustly spends years in prison. After escaping, he gains ever so sweet and served quite cold revenge. Adaptation of the Alexandre Dumas classic. 114m/B VHS, Beta. Robert Donat, Elissa Landi, Louis Calhern, Sidney Blackmer, Irene Hervey, Raymond Walburn, O.P. Heggie; *D:* Rowland V. Lee. *CCB, MOV, VTR*

The Count of Monte Cristo 🎬🎬½ 1974 The Alexander Dumas classic about an innocent man (Chamberlain) who is imprisoned, escapes, and finds the treasure of Monte Cristo, which he uses to bring down those who wronged him. Good version of the historical costumer. Originally shown in theatres in Europe, but broadcast on television in the U.S. 104m/C VHS, Beta. *GB* Richard Chamberlain, Kate Nelligan, Donald Pleasence, Alessio Orano, Tony Curtis, Louis Jourdan, Trevor Howard, Taryn Power; *D:* David Greene. *ART, FUS*

The Count of the Old Town 🎬🎬 *Munkbrogreven* 1934 Feisty townsfolk settle the score after a gang of booze smugglers trick them out of their money. Bergman's film debut as a maid swept off her feet by a mysterious young stranger. Adapted from the play "Greven fran Gamla Sta'n" by Arthur and Sigfried Fischer. In Swedish with English subtitles. 90m/B VHS, Beta. *SW* Edvin Adolphson, Ingrid Bergman, Sigurd Wallen, Valdemar Dahlquist; *D:* Edvin Adolphson, Sigurd Wallen; *W:* Gosta Stevens. *WAC*

Count Yorga, Vampire 🎬🎬½ 1970 (PG) The vampire Count Yorga is practicing his trade in Los Angeles, setting up a coven and conducting seances. Good update of the traditional character, with Quarry suitably solemn and menacing. Followed by "The Return of Count Yorga." Also available with "Cry of the Banshee" on laserdisc. 90m/C VHS, Beta. Robert Quarry, Roger Perry, Michael Murphy, Michael Macready, Donna Anders, Judith Lang, Marsha Jordan, Julie Conners, Paul Hansen; *D:* Bob Kelljan; *W:* Bob Kelljan; *C:* Arch Archambault. *NO*

Countdown 🎬🎬½ 1968 Documentary-type fictional look at the first moon mission and its toll on the astronauts and their families. Timely because the U.S. was trying to send a man to the moon in 1968. Interesting as a look at the developing Altman style. 99m/B VHS, Beta. James Caan, Robert Duvall, Michael Murphy, Ted Knight, Joanna Moore, Barbara Baxley, Charles Aidman, Steve Ihnat, Robert Altman; *D:* Robert Altman. *WAR*

Counter Attack 🎬½ 1984 Story of murder and insurance fraud takes place on the back lots of the Hong Kong film industry. As good as these get. 105m/C VHS, Beta. Bruce Li, Dan Inosanto, John Ladalski, Young Kong; *D:* Bruce Li. *WVE*

Counter Measures 🎬 198? A helicopter pilot stumbles on to a bizarre chain of crimes and disasters. 98m/C VHS, Beta. Monte Markham; *D:* Gerban Ceth. *NO*

Counter Punch 🎬🎬½ *Ripped Off; The Boxer; Uomo Dalla Pelle Dura* 1971 (R) Blake is a boxer framed for the murder of his manager who sets out to clear his name by finding the killers. Fair rendition of a familiar plot. 72m/C VHS, Beta. *IT* Robert (Bobby) Blake, Ernest Borgnine, Gabriele Ferzetti, Catherine Spaak, Tomas Milian; *D:* Franco Prosperi. *SIM, ART*

Counterblast 🎬🎬 *The Devil's Plot* 1948 A Nazi spy assumes the role of a British scientist in order to gain classified information for the Fatherland. The trouble begins when he refuses to carry out an order to execute a pretty young assistant. Appealing performances distract from the somewhat confusing plot. 99m/B VHS, Beta. *GB* Robert Beatty, Mervyn Johns, Nova Pilbeam, Margaretta Scott, Sybilla Binder, Marie Lohr, Karel Stepanek, Alan Wheatley; *D:* Paul Stein. *SNC, RXM*

The Counterfeit Traitor 🎬🎬🎬½ 1962 Suspense thriller with Holden playing a double agent in Europe during WWII. Based on the true adventures of Eric Erickson, the top Allied spy of WW II, who was captured by the Gestapo but escaped. 140m/C VHS, Beta, Closed Caption. William Holden, Lilli Palmer, Hugh Griffith, Werner Peters, Eva Dahlbeck; *D:* George Seaton; *W:* George Seaton; *C:* Jean Bourgoin. *PAR*

Counterforce 🎬 1987 (R) A rough group of mercenaries is hired to guard a Mideastern leader being chased by his country's ruling despot. Mild action with predictable plot. 98m/C VHS, Beta, LV. George Rivero, George Kennedy, Andrew Stevens, Isaac Hayes, Louis Jourdan, Kevin Bernhardt, Hugo Stiglitz, Robert Foster, Susana Dosamantes; *D:* J. Anthony Loma. *ART*

A Countess from Hong Kong 🎬 1967 (G) Very bad romantic comedy features impoverished Russian countess Natasha (would you believe Loren is Russian?) stowing away in the luxury liner suite of stuffy American diplomat Ogden Mears (equally miscast Brando). The ship is sailing from Hong Kong to Honolulu and Natasha has until then to persuade Ogden to assist her. Chaplin's final film. 108m/C VHS, Closed Caption. Marlon Brando, Sophia Loren, Sydney Chaplin, Tippi Hedren, Patrick Cargill, Michael Medwin, Oliver Johnston, Margaret Rutherford; *D:* Charlie Chaplin; *W:* Charlie Chaplin; *C:* Arthur Ibbetson; *M:* Charlie Chaplin. *USH*

Country 🎬🎬🎬 1984 (PG) Strong story of a farm family in crisis when the government attempts to foreclose on their land. Good performances all around and an excellent portrayal of the wife by Lange. "The River" and "Places In the Heart," both released in 1984, also dramatized the plight of many American farm families in the early 1980s. 109m/C VHS, Beta, LV. Jessica Lange, Sam Shepard, Wilford Brimley, Matt Clark, Therese Graham, Levi L. Knebel; *D:* Richard Pearce; *W:* William D. Wittliff. Nominations: Academy Awards '84: Best Actress (Lange). *TOU*

Country Gentlemen 🎬🎬 1936 Vaudeville team, Olsen and Johnson, play fast-talking conmen who sell shares in a worthless oil field to a bunch of WWI veterans. What a surprise when oil is actually found there. Not one of the duo's better performances. 54m/B VHS, Beta. Ole Olsen, Chic Johnson, Joyce Compton, Lila Lee, Ray Corrigan, Donald Kirke, Pierre Watkin; *D:* Ralph Staub. *NOS, MRV, VYY*

Country Girl 🎬🎬🎬½ 1954 In the role that completely de-glamorized her (and won her an Oscar), Kelly plays the wife of alcoholic singer Crosby who tries to make a comeback with the help of director Holden. One of Crosby's four dramatic parts, undoubtedly one of his best. Seaton won an Oscar for his adaptation of the Clifford Odets play. Remade in 1982. ♫The Search is Through; Dissertation on the State of Bliss; It's Mine, It's Yours; The Land Around Us. 104m/B VHS, Beta. Bing Crosby, Grace Kelly, William Holden, Gene Reynolds, Anthony Ross; *D:* George Seaton; *W:* George Seaton. Academy Awards '54: Best Actress (Kelly), Best Screenplay; Golden Globe Awards '55: Best Actress—Drama (Kelly); National Board of Review Awards '54: Best Actress (Kelly); New York Film Critics Awards '54: Best Actress (Kelly); Nominations: Academy Awards '54: Best Actor (Crosby), Best Art Direction/Set Decoration (B & W), Best Black and White Cinematography, Best Director (Seaton), Best Picture. *PAR, BTV*

Country Girl 🎬 1982 Aging, alcoholic actor is desperate for a comeback. His director blames his fiercely loving wife for the downfall. Poor cable TV remake of 1954 version with Bing Crosby. 137m/C VHS, Beta. Dick Van Dyke, Faye Dunaway, Ken Howard. *NO*

The Country Kid 🎬🎬🎬 1923 A freckle-faced teenager and his two brothers are beset by a wicked uncle out to steal their inheritance. One of Barry's best-remembered films. 60m/B VHS, Beta. Wesley Barry, "Spec" O'Donnell, Bruce Guerin, Kate Toncray, Helen Jerome Eddy, George Nicholls Jr.; *D:* William Beaudine. *NO*

Country Life 🎬🎬 1995 (PG-13) Down Under adaptation of Chekov's "Uncle Vanya," has Blakemore returning to Aussie farm roots after 22-year stint as unsuccessful London theatre critic. His bored young wife (Scacchi) upsets the business-as-usual life of her husband's brother-in-law (Hargreaves) and abandoned daughter, Sally (Fox), who is also jealous of the attention paid the beautiful Deborah by both her uncle and longtime crush, Dr. Askey (Neill). Exchanges Chekov's emotional exploration for a light comedy of manners and a message of Australian independence from England.*CW:* Some sex-related scenes. 107m/C VHS, LV, Closed Caption. *AU* Sam Neill, Greta Scacchi, Kerry Fox, John Hargreaves, Googie Withers, Patricia Kennedy, Michael Blakemore; *D:* Michael Blakemore; *W:* Michael Blakemore; *C:* Stephen Windon; *M:* Peter Best. *TOU*

Countryman 🎬🎬 1983 (R) A dope-smuggling woman crashes her plane in Jamaica and is rescued by Countryman, a rasta super hero. Not very good, but at least there's great music by Bob Marley and others. 103m/C VHS, Beta. Hiram Keller, Kristine Sinclair; *D:* Dickie Jobson. *MVD*

County Fair 🎬🎬 1920 This early silent film is an adaptation of Neil Burgess' play about life in New England. 60m/B VHS, Beta. Helen Jerome Eddy, David Butler. *NOS, DVT, HEG*

Coup de Grace 🎬🎬½ 1978 Engaging political satire about a wealthy aristocratic woman in Latvia during the 1919-20 Civil War, and how she attempts to maintain her lifestyle as German soldiers are housed on her estate. Her unrequited love for a German officer adds to her troubles. In German with English subtitles. Co-written by von Trotta and based on the novel by Marguerite

Yourcenar. **96m/B Beta.** *GE FR* Margarethe von Trotta, Matthias Habich, Rudiger Kirschstein, Matthieu Carriere; **D:** Volker Schlondorff; **W:** Margarethe von Trotta. *COL, GLV*

Coup de Torchon ✶✶✶ *Clean Slate* 1981 Set in 1938 French West Africa, Noiret plays corrupt police chief Lucien Cordier who is consistently harrassed by his community, particularly by the town pimp. He usually overlooks the pimp's crimes, but when Cordier catches him and a friend shooting at plague victims' bodies floating down the river he decides to murder them in cold blood. Based on the novel "POP 1280" by Jim Thompson. In French with English subtitles. **128m/C VHS.** *FR* Philippe Noiret, Isabelle Huppert, Guy Marchand, Stephane Audran, Eddy Mitchell, Jean-Pierre Marielle, Irene Skobline; **D:** Bertrand Tavernier; **W:** Bertrand Tavernier. Nominations: Academy Awards '82: Best Foreign Language Film. *HMV*

Coupe de Ville ✶✶½ 1990 (PG-13) Three brothers are forced by their father to drive mom's birthday present from Detroit to Florida in the summer of '63. Period concerns and music keep it interesting. **98m/C VHS, Beta, LV, Closed Caption.** Patrick Dempsey, Daniel Stern, Arye Gross, Joseph Bologna, Alan Arkin, Annabeth Gish, Rita Taggart, James Gammon; **D:** Joe Roth; **W:** Mike Binder; **M:** James Newton Howard. *USH*

Courage ✶✶✶ 1986 Based on fact, a television movie about a Hispanic mother in New York City who, motivated by her drug-troubled children, goes undercover and exposes a multimillion-dollar drug ring. Loren is great in a decidedly non-glamorous role. **141m/C VHS, Beta, Closed Caption.** Sophia Loren, Billy Dee Williams, Hector Elizondo, Val Avery, Dan Hedaya, Ron Rifkin, Jose Perez; **D:** Jeremy Paul Kagan. *VTR*

Courage Mountain ✶ 1989 (PG) If you're looking for a good sequel to Johanna Spyri's classic "Heidi" this isn't it. Europe is on the brink of WWI when teenage Heidi leaves her beloved mountain for an exclusive boarding school in Italy. Not surprisingly it's a war zone, the military takes over and the kids are sent to an orphanage run by nasties (see also "Oliver!"). The girls escape to the mountains and are saved by none other than Sheen as Heidi's pal Peter (who cast the 20-something Sheen as a teenager? Bad mistake.) Ridiculous sequel to the classic tale will appeal to kids despite what the critics say. **92m/C VHS, Beta, LV, Closed Caption.** Juliette Caton, Joanna Clarke, Nicola Stapleton, Charlie Sheen, Jan Rubes, Leslie Caron, Jade Magri, Kathryn Ludlow, Yorgo Voyagis; **D:** Christopher Leitch; **W:** Weaver Webb; **M:** Sylvester Levay. *COL, FCT*

Courage of Black Beauty ✶½ 1957 Another version of the perennial heart warmer about a boy and his horse. **80m/C VHS, Beta.** Johnny Crawford, Mimi Gibson, John Bryant, Diane Brewster, J. Pat O'Malley; **D:** Harold Schuster. *ART*

Courage of Lassie ✶✶½ *Blue Sierra* 1946 (G) Fourteen-year-old Taylor is the heroine in this girl loves dog tale. In this case, the dog is actually called Bill, not Lassie, in spite of the film's title. Bill is found wounded by Taylor and she nurses him back to health. He proves to be loving, loyal, and useful, so much so that, through a complicated plotline, he winds up in the Army's K-9 division and returns home with the doggie version of shell-shock. Taylor's still there to nurse him back to his old kind self again. **93m/C VHS.** Elizabeth Taylor, Frank Morgan, Tom Drake, Selena Royle, Harry Davenport; **D:** Fred M. Wilcox. *MGM*

Courage of Rin Tin Tin ✶✶ 1983 Rusty and his faithful dog Rin Tin Tin help the cavalry soldiers of Fort Apache keep law and order in a small Arizona town. The perennial kid-pleasing German Shepherd comes through again. **90m/C VHS, Beta.** James Brown, Lee Aaker. *MON*

Courage of the North ✶½ 1935 The Mounties break up a fur-stealing ring with the help of Captain Dog and Dynamite Horse. Bound to set your hair on end. **55m/B VHS, Beta.** John Preston, June Love, William Desmond, Tom London, Jimmy Aubrey. *NO*

Courage Under Fire ✶✶✶ 1996 (R) Army Lt. Col. Nat Serling (Washington) is unexpectedly assigned to review the candidacy of Capt. Karen Emma Walden (Ryan, seen only in flashbacks) to receive the posthumous Medal of Honor for bravery in combat. A Gulf War Medevac pilot, Walden would be the first woman awarded the honor if Serling can figure out the truth from her surviving crew's wildly conflicting reports. Ironically, Serling's dealing with a guilt complex since four members of his tank unit died in the war under friendly fire. Stellar performances, including a frightening one by Phillips. Based on the novel by Duncan, who also did the screenplay; Washington and director Zwick previously worked together on "Glory."**CW:** War violence and language. **120m/C VHS.** Denzel Washington, Meg Ryan, Matt Damon, Lou Diamond Phillips, Michael Moriarty, Scott Glenn, Bronson Pinchot, Seth Gilliam, Sean Astin, Regina Taylor, Tim Guinee, Ken Jenkins, Kathleen Widdoes; **D:** Edward Zwick; **W:** Patrick Sheane Duncan; **C:** Roger Deakins; **M:** James Horner. *FXV*

Courageous Avenger ✶ 1935 A sheriff brings a treacherous ore mine foreman to justice. **59m/B VHS, Beta, LV.** Johnny Mack Brown. *MLB*

Courageous Dr. Christian ✶✶ 1940 Dr. Christian is faced with an epidemic of meningitis among the inhabitants of a shanty town. Typical entry in the "Dr. Christian" series. **66m/B VHS, Beta.** Jean Hersholt, Dorothy Lovett, Tom Neal, Robert Baldwin, Maude Eburne; **D:** Bernard Vorhaus; **C:** John Alton. *NOS, VYY, DVT*

The Courageous Mr. Penn ✶✶ *Penn of Pennsylvania* 1941 Slow-moving British film, outlining the achievements of William Penn, the Quaker founder of Pennsylvania. **79m/B VHS, Beta.** *GB* Clifford Evans, Deborah Kerr, Dennis Arundell, Aubrey Mallalieu, D.J. Williams, O.B. Clarence, Charles Carson, Henry Oscar, J.H. Roberts; **D:** Lance Comfort. *NOS, VYY, VEC*

The Courier ✶✶ 1988 (R) A former drug addict seeks revenge on the dealers who killed his friend. Only thing that saves it are the songs by U2, The Pogues, and Hothouse Flowers. Musical score by Elvis Costello. **85m/C VHS, Beta, LV.** *IR* Gabriel Byrne, Ian Bannen, Padraig O'Loingsigh, Cait O'Riordan, Patrick Bergin; **D:** Frank Deasy, Joe Lee; **M:** Elvis Costello. *VES, ART*

Courier of Death ✶ 1984 A courier is embroiled in a mob war/struggle over a locked briefcase with mysterious contents. **77m/C VHS, Beta.** Joey Johnson, Barbara Garrison; **D:** Tom Shaw. *VES, ART*

Court Jester ✶✶✶½ 1956 Swashbuckling comedy stars Danny Kaye as a former circus clown who teams up with a band of outlaws trying to dethrone a tyrant king. Kaye poses as the court jester so he can learn of the evil king's intentions. Filled with more color, more song, and more truly funny lines than any three comedies put together, this is Kaye's best performance. ♫They'll Never Outfox the Fox; Baby, Let Me Take You Dreaming; My Heart Knows a Lovely Song; The Maladjusted Jester. **101m/C VHS, Beta, LV.** Danny Kaye, Glynis Johns, Basil Rathbone, Angela Lansbury, Cecil Parker, John Carradine, Mildred Natwick, Robert Middleton; **D:** Norman Panama, Melvin Frank; **W:** Norman Panama. *PAR*

The Court Martial of Billy Mitchell ✶✶✶ *One-Man Mutiny* 1955 Terrific courtroom drama depicts the secret trial of Billy Mitchell, head of the Army Air Service in the 1920s, who predicted the role of airpower in subsequent warfare and the danger of war with Japan. Mitchell incurred the wrath of the military by publicly faulting the lack of U.S. preparedness for invasion. Steiger is outstanding as the attorney; Cooper is great as Mitchell. Debut for Montgomery. **100m/C VHS, LV, Letterbox.** Gary Cooper, Charles Bickford, Ralph Bellamy, Rod Steiger, Elizabeth Montgomery, Fred Clark, Jack Lord, Peter Graves, Darren McGavin, Robert Simon, Jack Perrin, Charles Dingle; **D:** Otto Preminger; **C:** Sam Leavitt. Nominations: Academy Awards '55: Best Story & Screenplay.*REP*

The Court Martial of Jackie Robinson ✶✶✶½ 1990 (R) True story of a little known chapter in the life of the famous athlete. During his stint in the Army, Robinson refused to take a back seat on a bus and subsequently faced the possibility of court martial. Originally made for cable television. **94m/C VHS, Beta, Closed Caption.** Andre Braugher, Daniel Stern, Ruby Dee, Stan Shaw, Paul Dooley, Bruce Dern; **D:** Larry Peerce; **W:** Dennis Lynton Clark; **C:** Don Burgess. *TTC, FCT*

The Courtesans of Bombay ✶✶✶ 1985 Gritty docudrama, set in Pavanpul, the poverty-stricken brothel section of Bombay, looks at how the impoverished women support themselves through a combination of prostitution and performing. Made for British television. **74m/C VHS, Beta.** *GB* Kareem Samar, Zohra Segal, Saeed Jaffrey; **D:** Ismail Merchant, James Ivory, Ruth Prawer Jhabvala. *NLC*

Courtin' Wildcats ✶½ 1929 Early Gibson programmer in which he plays a frail eastern college boy who was sent west by his father to toughen up. Once there, he meets Gilbert and ends up marrying her. **56m/B VHS.** Hoot Gibson, Eugenia Gilbert, Monte Montague; **D:** Jerome Storm. *GPV*

The Courtney Affair ✶✶½ *The Courtneys of Curzon Street* 1947 An aristocratic young Britisher causes a stir when he marries an Irish maid. As a result, the couple must face terrific social ostracism. Classy soap opera family saga was a big money maker in England. **112m/B VHS.** *GB* Anna Neagle, Michael Wilding, Gladys Young, Michael Medwin, Coral Browne, Jack Watling, Bernard Lee; **D:** Herbert Wilcox. *VYY*

Courtship ✶✶✶ 1987 From renowned playwright Horton Foote comes this touching story about a sheltered, upper-crust young girl who shocks her family and friends by eloping with a traveling salesman. Made for television. **84m/C VHS, Beta.** Hallie Foote, William Converse-Roberts, Amanda Plummer, Rochelle Oliver, Michael Higgins; **D:** Howard Cummings. *ORI, WAR*

The Courtship of Eddie's Father ✶✶✶ 1962 A clever nine-year-old boy plays matchmaker for his widowed dad in this rewarding family comedy-drama (the inspiration for the TV series). Some plot elements are outdated, but young Howard's performance is terrific; he would later excel at direction. Based on the novel by Mark Toby. **117m/C VHS.** Glenn Ford, Shirley Jones, Stella Stevens, Dina Merrill, Ron Howard, Jerry Van Dyke; **D:** Vincente Minnelli; **W:** John Gay; **C:** Milton Krasner. *MGM, FCT*

The Courtyard ✶✶ 1995 (R) Jonathan Hoffman (McCarthy) seems to have the perfect life—a great job, great girl, great California apartment. But then his apartment complex is bedeviled by a series of sinister crimes and Jonathan becomes the prime suspect.**CW:** Language, sexuality and some violence. **103m/C VHS, Closed Caption.** Andrew McCarthy, Madchen Amick, Richard "Cheech" Marin, Vincent Schiavelli; **D:** Fred Walton; **W:** Christopher Hawthorne. *REP*

Cousin, Cousine ✶✶✶½ 1976 (R) Pleasant French comedy about distant cousins who meet at a round of family parties, funerals and weddings and become friends, but their relationship soon becomes more than platonic. Remade in the U.S. in 1989 as "Cousins." In French with English subtitles. **95m/C VHS, Beta, LV.** *FR* Marie-Christine Barrault, Marie-France Pisier, Victor Lanoux, Guy Marchand, Ginette Garcin, Sybil Maas; **D:** Jean-Charles Tacchella; **W:** Jean-Charles Tacchella; **M:** Gerard Anfosso. Cesar Awards '76: Best Supporting Actress (Pisier); Nominations: Academy Awards '76: Best Actress (Barrault), Best Foreign Language Film, Best Original Screenplay. *TPV, IME, FOX*

The Cousins ✶✶✶ *Les Cousins* 1959 Set against the backdrop of Parisian student life, two very different cousins (one twisted, the other saintly) vie for the hand of Mayniel. This country mouse, city mouse adult fable ultimately depicts the survival of the fittest. Chabrol's lovely but sad second directorial effort. **112m/B VHS.** *FR* Jean-Claude Brialy, Gerard Blain, Juliette Mayniel, Claude Cerval, Genevieve Cluny; *D:* Claude Chabrol; *W:* Claude Chabrol. *PAR*

Cousins 🎬🎬🎬½ **1989 (PG-13)** An American remake of "Cousin, Cousine," in which two distant cousins-by-marriage meet at a wedding and, due to their respective spouses' infidelities, fall in love with each other's arms. A gentle love story with a humorous and biting look at the foibles of extended families. **110m/C VHS, Beta, LV, Closed Caption.** Isabella Rossellini, Sean Young, Ted Danson, William L. Petersen, Norma Aleandro, Lloyd Bridges, Keith Coogan; *D:* Joel Schumacher; *C:* Ralf Bode; *M:* Angelo Badalamenti. *PAR, FCT, HMV*

Cover Girl 🎬🎬🎬 **1944** A vintage wartime musical about a girl who must decide between a nightclub career and a future as a cover model. Hayworth is beautiful, Kelly dances like a dream, and Silvers and Arden are hilarious. 🎵Cover Girl; Sure Thing; Make Way For Tomorrow; Put Me to the Test; Long Ago and Far Away; That's the Best of All; The Show Must Go On; Who's Complaining?; Poor John. **107m/C VHS, Beta, LV.** Rita Hayworth, Gene Kelly, Phil Silvers, Otto Kruger, Lee Bowman, Jinx Falkenberg, Eve Arden, Edward Brophy, Anita Colby; *D:* Charles Vidor; *C:* Rudolph Mate; *M:* Ira Gershwin, Jerome Kern. Academy Awards '44: Best Original Dramatic/Comedy Score; Nominations: Academy Awards '44: Best Color Cinematography, Best Interior Decoration, Best Song ("Long Ago and Far Away"), Best Sound. *COL*

Cover Girl Models 🎬 **1975** An action-packed '70s adventure in which beautiful models are forced to fight for survival. **82m/C VHS, Beta.** Lindsay Bloom, Pat Anderson, John Kramer, Rhonda Leigh Hopkins, Mary Woronov; *D:* Cirio H. Santiago. *NO*

The Cover Girl Murders 🎬🎬½ **1993 (PG-13)** Six beautiful models have been brought together on a remote island to shoot a magazine's popular swimsuit issue. Each one wants to be the cover model—but someone is willing to kill to get the job. **87m/C VHS, Beta, Closed Caption.** Lee Majors, Jennifer O'Neill, Adrian Paul, Beverly Johnson, Vanessa Angel; *D:* James A. Contner; *W:* Douglas Barr, Bernard Maybeck; *M:* Rick Marotta. *PAR*

Cover Me 🎬🎬 **1995 (R)** When beautiful models turn up dead, L.A. detectives Bobby Colter (Rossovich) and J.J. Davis (Sorvino) discover they were all on the cover of L.A. Erotica magazine. So detective Holly Jacobsen, Colter's girlfriend, (Taylor) goes undercover at the magazine and learns more about the seamy sex underworld than the killer wants her to know. *CW:* Strong sexuality; language; violence. **94m/C VHS, Beta, Closed Caption.** Courtney Taylor, Rick Rossovich, Paul Sorvino, Elliott Gould, Corbin Bernsen; *D:* Michael Schroeder; *W:* Steve Johnson. *PAR*

Cover Story 🎬½ **1993** Journalist Matt McKendree falls in love with a mystery woman whose story he's investigating. Too bad she's dead—or is she. **93m/C VHS.** William Wallace, Tuesday Knight, Robert Forster, Christopher McDonald. *AVI*

Cover-Up 🎬½ **1991 (R)** Terrorist attacks on U.S. military bases in Israel are just a smokescreen for a greater threat. The below-par actioner stands out only for the hokey religious symbolism in its Good Friday climax. *CW:* Language, strong violence, and sensuality. **89m/C VHS, LV, Closed Caption.** Dolph Lundgren, Louis Gossett Jr., John Finn; *D:* Manny Coto. *ART, IME*

The Covered Wagon 🎬🎬½ **1923** Prototypical silent Western began the genre. Wagon train moves cross-country, battling weather and wild Indians. By today's standards, somewhat bucolic and uneventful, but the location photography holds up quite well. Big budget film in its day, and enormously popular. **98m/B VHS, LV.** Warren Kerigan, Lois Wilson, Alan Hale, Ernest Torrence; *D:* James Cruze. *PAR*

Covered Wagon Days 🎬🎬 **1940** The Three Mesquiteers set out after silver smugglers who have framed Rico's brother for murder. **54m/B VHS.** Bob Livingston, Raymond Hatton, Duncan Renaldo, John Merton, Reed Howes; *D:* George Sherman. *REP*

Covered Wagon Trails 🎬 **1940** Substandard Western has good guy Randall dealing with the shifty cattleman's association and making the West safe for the hardworking locals. Future Frankenstein monster Strange plays the hired muscle. **52m/B VHS.** Jack Randall, Sally Cairns, David Sharpe, Lafe McKee, Budd Buster, Glenn Strange; *D:* Raymond K. Johnson; *W:* Tom Gibson. *MOV*

Covergirl 🎬½ *Dreamworld* **1983 (R)** Wealthy man seeks to relieve his boredom by molding a young woman into a supermodel. She finds the glamorous life isn't always what it's cracked up to be. TV-type melodrama. **98m/C VHS, Beta, Closed Caption.** *CA* Jeff Conaway, Irena Ferris, Cathie Shirriff, Roberta Leighton, Deborah Wakeham; *D:* Jean-Claude Lord. *VTR*

Covert Action 🎬½ **1988** A drug kingpin who desires to protect his business tries to frame a captain for a crime he did not commit. **85m/C VHS, Beta.** Rick Washburne, John Christian, Stuart Garrison Day, Amanda Zinsser, Johnny Stumper; *D:* J. Christian Ingvordson. *MCG*

Covert Assassin 🎬🎬 **1994 (R)** Anti-terrorist specialist is hired by wealthy widow to avenge her husband's murder. Adapted from the novel "Wild Justice" by Wilbur Smith. *CW:* Terrorist violence. **114m/C VHS.** Roy Scheider, Sam Wanamaker, Ted McGinley, Christopher Buchholz; *D:* Tony Wharmby. *THV*

Cow Town 🎬🎬 **1950** A range war results when ranchers begin fencing in their land to prevent cattle rustling. Autry's 72nd film has some good songs and a dependable cast. **70m/B VHS, Beta.** Gene Autry, Gail Davis, Jock Mahoney, Harry Shannon; *D:* John English. *CCB*

The Coward 🎬🎬 **1962** A schoolteacher and his wife are living in a remote Slovak village during the last days of WWII. The wife supports the anti-Nazi partisans while her husband collaborates with the Germans that occupy the village. Eventually, he finds the courage to save some innocent victims of the Nazi purge. Czech with subtitles. **113m/C VHS.** *CZ* Jiri Weiss. *FCT*

Coward of the County 🎬🎬½ **1981** A devout pacifist is put to the test when his girlfriend is raped. Good performances by all concerned. Based on the lyrics of Kenny Rogers' hit song of the same name. Made for television. **115m/C VHS, Beta.** Kenny Rogers, Frederic Lehne, Largo Woodruff, Mariclare Costello, Ana Alicia, Noble Willingham; *D:* Dick Lowry. *ORI, WAR*

Cowboy 🎬🎬🎬 **1958** Western roundup based on the memoirs of tenderfoot-turned-cowpoke Frank Harris. Harris (Lemmon) is a Chicago hotel clerk who meets cattle boss Tom Reece (Ford) who's in the city on business. Losing his money in a poker game, Reece reluctantly accepts a loan from Harris in exchange for a piece of his cattle business. So Harris and Reece hit the dusty trail on a cattle drive that takes them into Mexico where Harris falls in love with Maria (Kashfi), the daughter of a wealthy rancher, and gradually turns from city slicker into hardened trail boss. Good cast, no fuss. From the book "Reminiscences As a Cowboy" by Harris. **92m/C VHS.** Jack Lemmon, Glenn Ford, Anna Kashfi, Brian Donlevy, Dick York, Victor Manuel Mendoza, Richard Jaeckel, King Donovan; *D:* Delmer Daves; *W:* Edmund H. North; *C:* Charles Lawton Jr.; *M:* George Duning. Nominations: Academy Awards '58: Best Film Editing. *COL*

The Cowboy & the Ballerina 🎬🎬 **1984** A television movie about an aging rodeo star who falls in love with a petite ballerina defecting from a Russian Dance Company. Good cast makes it watchable. **96m/C VHS, Beta.** Lee Majors, Leslie Wing, Christopher Lloyd, Anjelica Huston, George de la Pena; *D:* Jerry Jameson; *M:* Bruce Broughton.

Cowboy & the Bandit 🎬 **1935** A cowboy comes to the aid of a widow being victimized by outlaws. **58m/B VHS, Beta.** Rex Lease, Bobby Nelson, William Desmond; *D:* Al(bert) Herman. *NOS*

The Cowboy and the Lady 🎬🎬½ **1938** Oberon plays a madcap heiress who is deposited by her politician father on their Florida estate to keep her out of trouble while he seeks the Presidential nomination. She is bored and decides to go to a local rodeo where she meets cowboy Cooper. Both are instantly smitten and marry on impulse. Cooper doesn't know about her wealth and when her father finds out about the marriage he's appalled that his daughter has married beneath her. Since this is a comedy all comes out right in the end. Good cast, weak story. **91m/B VHS.** Gary Cooper, Merle Oberon, Patsy Kelly, Walter Brennan, Fuzzy Knight, Mabel Todd, Henry Kolker, Harry Davenport; *D:* H.C. Potter; *C:* Gregg Toland. Academy Awards '38: Best Sound; Nominations: Academy Awards '38: Best Song ("The Cowboy and the Lady"), Best Original Score. *FCT, HBO*

Cowboy & the Senorita 🎬🎬 **1944** A cowboy solves the mystery of a missing girl and wins his lovely cousin. The first film that paired Rogers and Evans, who went on to become a winning team, on and offscreen. **56m/B VHS, Beta.** Roy Rogers, John Hubbard, Dale Evans. *NOS, MRV, DVT*

Cowboy Commandos 🎬½ **1943** Improbable plot has cowboys riding out after Nazi spies, who want to steal valuable ore. **53m/B VHS.** Ray Corrigan, Dennis Moore, Max Terhune, Budd Buster, John Merton; *D:* S. Roy Luby. *DVT, RXM, HEG*

Cowboy Counselor 🎬 **1933** Cowboy Hoot Gibson helps an enchanting girl clear her innocent brother's name. **60m/B VHS, Beta.** Hoot Gibson. *VCI*

Cowboy Millionaire 🎬🎬½ **1935** An Englishwoman comes to an American dude ranch and falls in love with one of the ranch hands. Entertaining Western comedy. **65m/B VHS.** George O'Brien, Evalyn Bostock, Edgar Kennedy, Alden Chase; *D:* Eddie Cline. *NOS, DVT, RXM*

The Cowboy Way 🎬½ **1994 (PG-13)** A mess from start to finish made somewhat watchable by cowpoke charm of the leads and one good horse chase. Two rodeo stars (Harrelson and Sutherland) from New Mexico ride into New York City to avenge a buddy's death, with Hudson as a mounted NYC cop who always yearned to be a cowboy. Great premise is overcome by tasteless humor and a patched-up plot shot full of holes. Good for a gander is the 90-foot Times Square billboard of Harrelson's character as a Calvin Klein underwear model, which stopped traffic even in jaded New York. *CW:* Some language, violence, and comic sensuality. **106m/C VHS, LV, Closed Caption.** Woody Harrelson, Kiefer Sutherland, Dylan McDermott, Ernie Hudson, Cara Buono, Marg Helgenberger, Tomas Milian, Joaquin Martinez; *Cameos:* Travis Tritt; *D:* Gregg Champion; *W:* William D. Wittliff, Rob Thompson; *M:* David Newman. *USH*

The Cowboys 🎬🎬🎬 **1972 (PG)** Wayne stars as a cattle rancher who is forced to hire 11 schoolboys to help him drive his cattle 400 miles to market. Clever script makes this one of Wayne's better Westerns. Carradine's film debut. Inspired the television series. Laserdisc available in widescreen letterbox edition. **128m/C VHS, Beta, LV, Letterbox.** John Wayne, Roscoe Lee Browne, A. Martinez, Bruce Dern, Colleen Dewhurst, Slim Pickens, Robert Carradine, Clay O'Brien; *D:* Mark Rydell; *W:* Harriet Frank Jr., Irving Ravetch; *C:* Robert L. Surtees; *M:* John Williams. *WAR, TLF*

Cowboys Don't Cry 🎬🎬 **1988** When a modern cowboy's wife is killed in an automobile accident, he must change his immature ways and build a solid future with his teenage son or perish in loneliness. **96m/C VHS, Beta.** Rebecca Jenkins, Ron White, Janet-Laine Green. *USH*

Cowboys from Texas 🎬½ **1939** The Three Mesquiteers bring about a peaceful settlement to a fight between cattlemen and homesteaders. Part of "The Three Mesquiteers" series. **54m/B VHS, Beta.** Bob Livingston, Raymond Hatton, Duncan Renaldo, Carole Landis.

Cowboys of the Saturday Matinee **1984** The history of B-movie westerns is traced from the beginning of the sound era. **75m/B VHS, Beta.** Gene Autry, Tex Ritter, Roy Rogers. *ORI, FCT, WAR*

Coyote Trails 🎬½ **1935** Standard western adventure has cowboy Tyler helping a damsel in distress. **68m/B VHS, Beta.** Tom Tyler. *NOS, VCN, RXM*

Crack House 🎬🎬 **1989 (R)** A man seeks revenge for the murder of a relative by drug dealers. Average exploitation flick. **91m/C VHS, Beta, LV.** Jim Brown, Richard Roundtree, Anthony Geary, Angel Tompkins, Greg Gomez Thomsen, Clyde Jones, Cheryl Kay; *D:* Michael Fischa; *C:* Arledge Armenaki. *MGM, WAR*

Crack Shadow Boxers 🎬 **197?** Through a series of misadventures, Wu Lung and Chu San battle to protect the inhabitants of a small village from the onslaught of relentless bandits. **91m/C VHS, Beta.** HK Ku Feng, Chou Li Lung, Han Guo Gai; *D:* Weng Yao Hai. *MGI*

Crack-Up 🎬🎬½ **1946** Largely ignored at the time of its release, this tense tale is now regarded as a minor classic of film noir. An art expert suffers a blackout while investigating a possible forgery and must piece together the missing hours to uncover a criminal conspiracy. **70m/B VHS, Beta, LV.** Pat O'Brien, Claire Trevor, Herbert Marshall, Ray Collins, Wallace Ford, Damian O'Flynn, Erskine Sanford; *D:* Irving Reis. *TTC*

Cracker: Brotherly Love 🎬🎬🎬 **1995** Everyone carries lots of emotional baggage in this entry of the British series. Detective Jane Penhaligon (Somerville) is still suffering from the aftereffects of rape, which she believes was by colleague Jimmy Beck (Cranitch), who's just returned to duty following a breakdown. Meanwhile, Fitz's (Coltrane) mother has died bringing him into contact with his stodgy brother Danny (Russell). And yes, there are murders to investigate—a killer who likes prostitutes to dress up as little girls. **150m/C VHS.** GB Robbie Coltrane, Geraldine Somerville, Lorcan Cranitch, Ricky Tomlinson, Barbara Flynn, Clive Russell, Kieran O'Brien, Tess Thompson, Brid Brennan, David Calder, Mark Lambert; *D:* Roy Battersby; *W:* Jimmy McGovern. *AEH*

The Cracker Factory 🎬🎬½ **1979** Wood is impressive as a woman committed to a mental institution who attempts to charm her way out of treatment. Made for television. **90m/C VHS, Beta.** Natalie Wood, Perry King, Shelley Long, Vivian Blaine, Juliet Mills, Peter Haskell; *D:* Burt Brinckerhoff; *M:* Billy Goldenberg. *NO*

Cracker: Men Should Weep 🎬🎬½ **1994** Fitz's skills are called into play when he must deal with a serial rapist (Aggrey). However, things become personal when Detective Jane Penhaligon (Somerville) is raped. **150m/C VHS.** GB Robbie Coltrane, Geraldine Somerville, Lorcan Cranitch, Graham Aggrey; *D:* Jean Stewart; *W:* Jimmy McGovern. *AEH*

Cracker: The Big Crunch 🎬🎬½ **1994** The leader of a Christian fundamentalist sect has an affair with a schoolgirl and then plots her murder to avoid a scandal. But what he can't avoid is Fitz (Coltrane). **150m/C VHS.** GB Robbie Coltrane, Jim Carter, Samantha Morton, James Fleet, Cherith Mellor; *D:* Julian Jarrold; *W:* Jimmy McGovern, Ted Whitehead. *AEH*

Cracker: To Be a Somebody 🎬🎬 **1994** The murder of an Asian shopkeeper first prompts the Manchester police to look for their suspect in the violent world of skinheads. But when the professor helping to profile the killer is murdered, the cops are forced to call in irascible forensic psychologist "Fitz" Fitzgerald (Coltrane) to aid in their investigation. Made for TV. **150m/C VHS.** GB Robbie Coltrane, Robert Carlyle, Barbara Flynn, Christopher Eccleston, Geraldine Somerville, Lorcan Cranitch; *D:* Tim Fywell; *W:* Jimmy McGovern. *AEH*

Crackerjack 🎬🎬 **1994 (R)** Chicago cop Jack Wild (Griffith) agrees to join his brother's family at a vacation resort in the Rocky Mountains. Coincidentally, a team of mercenaries are determined to hijack $50 million in diamonds from the resort and it's up to Jack to stop them. **96m/C VHS, LV, Closed Caption.** Thomas Ian Griffith, Nastassia Kinski, Christopher Plummer; *D:* Michael Mazo; *W:* Jonas Quastel, Michael Bafaro; *C:* Danny Nowak; *M:* Peter Allen. *REP*

Crackers 🎬🎬 **1984 (PG)** The offbeat story of two bumbling thieves who round up a gang of equally inept neighbors and go on the wildest crime spree you have ever seen. A would-be comic remake of "Big Deal on Madonna Street." **92m/C VHS, Beta, LV.** Donald Sutherland, Jack Warden, Sean Penn, Wallace Shawn, Larry Riley, Trinidad Silva, Christine Baranski, Charlaine Woodard, Tasia Valenza; *D:* Louis Malle. *USH*

Cracking Up 🎬½ *Smorgasbord* **1983 (PG)** Accident-prone misfit's mishaps on the road to recovery create chaos for everyone he meets. Lewis plays a dozen characters in this overboard comedy with few laughs. **91m/C VHS, Beta.** Jerry Lewis, Herb Edelman, Foster Brooks, Milton Berle, Sammy Davis Jr., Zane Buzby, Dick Butkus, Buddy Lester; *D:* Jerry Lewis. *WAR*

The Crackler 🎬🎬 **1984** During the '20s, a husband-and-wife private investigation team (Tommy and Tuppence) set out to find a gang of forgers operating in high society circles. Based on a story by Agatha Christie. Made for British television. **60m/C VHS, Beta.** GB James Warwick, Francesca Annis. *TPV*

The Cradle Will Fall woof! **1983** A made-for-television adaptation of the pulpy bestselling mystery by Mary Higgins Clark about a woman who cannot convince anyone she witnessed a murder. The cast of "The Guiding Light" appear. Poor script and poor direction do not a thriller make. **103m/C VHS, Beta.** Lauren Hutton, Ben Murphy, James Farentino, Charita Bauer, Peter Simon; *D:* John Llewellyn Moxey. *ORI, WAR*

The Craft 🎬🎬½ **1996 (R)** Call it "Heathers" with hexes. Troubled 17-year-old Sarah (Tunney) moves to L.A. and begins her senior year at St. Benedict's Academy. She takes up with three rebels—Nancy (Balk), Bonnie (Campbell), and Rochelle (True)—who like to dabble in witchcraft. Now, with the addition of would-be witch Sarah, these black magic women start slinging spells at their uppity classmates. Works best when concentrating on the girls and their problems, but degenerates into a special effects barrage toward the end. Alas, no one is turned into a newt. *CW:* Some terror and violence, and for brief language. **100m/C VHS, LV, 8mm, Closed Caption, DVD.** Robin Tunney, Fairuza Balk, Neve Campbell, Rachel True, Skeet Ulrich, Helen Shaver, Cliff DeYoung, Christine Taylor, Assumpta Serna; *D:* Andrew Fleming; *W:* Andrew Fleming, Peter Filardi; *C:* Alexander Grusynski; *M:* Graeme Revell. MTV Movie Awards '97: Best Fight (Fairuza Balk/Robin Tunney). *COL*

Craig's Wife 🎬🎬🎬 **1936** A classic soap opera about a pitiful woman driven to total ruin by her desire for social acceptance and material wealth. Russell makes her surprisingly sympathetic. Based on a Pulitzer Prize-winning George Kelly play. Remake of a silent film, was also remade as "Harriet Craig." **75m/B VHS, Beta.** Rosalind Russell, John Boles, Alma Kruger, Jane Darwell, Billie Burke; *D:* Dorothy Arzner. *NO*

Crainquebille 🎬🎬🎬 **1923** The classic satire based on the Anatole France story about a street merchant in Paris unfairly imprisoned and eventually surviving peacefully as a tramp. Silent. **50m/B VHS, Beta.** FR Maurice Feraudy; *D:* Jacques Feyder. *FCT, GPV*

The Cranes Are Flying 🎬🎬🎬½ *Letyat Zhuravit* **1957** When her lover goes off to fight during WWII, a girl is seduced by his cousin. Touching love story is free of politics. Filmed in Russia;

English subtitles. **91m/B VHS, Beta, LV, Letterbox.** RU Tatyana Samoilova, Alexei Batalov, Vasily Merkuryev, A. Shvorin; *D:* Mikhail Kalatozov. Cannes Film Festival '58: Best Film. *IHF, CVC*

Crash 🎬🎬 **1995 (NC-17)** You can always expect surreal kinkiness from Cronenberg and this film, awarded a Special Jury Prize at Cannes for "daring, originality, and audacity," won't prove the exception. It's "auto" erotica taken to the max, with car crashes and bodily injury turned into fetishes. James (Spader) lands in the hospital after an accident, which injured Helen (Hunter), a passenger in the other car. Helen and James' shared experience soon leads to a sexual relationship, which doesn't bother James' wife, Catherine (Unger). Then there's Vaughan (Koteas) and his group, who like to reenact famous auto crashes (like those of James Dean and Jayne Mansfield). Oh yes, there's lots more sex (in various combinations). Based on J.G. Ballard's 1973 cult novel. An R-rated version clocks in at 90 minutes. *CW:* Numerous explicit sex scenes, accident gore, some graphic language. **98m/C VHS, LV, Closed Caption.** CA James Spader, Holly Hunter, Elias Koteas, Deborah Kara Unger, Rosanna Arquette, Peter MacNeill; *D:* David Cronenberg; *W:* David Cronenberg; *C:* Peter Suschitzsky; *M:* Howard Shore. Cannes Film Festival '96: Special Jury Prize; Genie Awards '96: Best Adapted Screenplay, Best Cinematography, Best Director (Cronenberg), Best Film Editing; Nominations: Genie Awards '96: Best Film, Best Sound. *NLC, CRC*

Crash and Burn 🎬🎬½ **1990 (R)** Rebels in a repressive future police state reactivate a huge, long-dormant robot to battle the establishment's army of powerful androids. Special effects by David Allen make the mayhem interesting. **85m/C VHS, Beta, LV, Closed Caption.** Ralph Waite, Paul Ganus, Eva LaRue, Bill Moseley, Jack McGee; *D:* Charles Band; *W:* J.S. Cardone; *M:* Richard Band. *PAR*

Crash Dive 🎬🎬½ **1943** WWII glory film provides comic relief in the form of romance. Second-in-command Power falls hopelessly in love with school teacher Baxter, only to find out later that she is Lt. Commander Andrews' fiance. Once this little tidbit of information is disclosed, the two officers embark on a mission to destroy a Nazi U-Boat responsible for laying mines in the North Atlantic. Fantastic special effects and sound. Based on the story by W.R. Burnett. **105m/C VHS.** Tyrone Power, Anne Baxter, Dana Andrews, James Gleason, May Whitty, Harry (Henry) Morgan, Ben Carter, Frank Conroy, Florence Lake, John Archer, Minor Watson, Kathleen Howard, Stanley Andrews, Thurston Hall, Trudy Marshall; *D:* Archie Mayo; *W:* Jo Swerling; *C:* Leon Shamroy; *M:* David Buttolph. Academy Awards '44: Best Special Effects (Sersen). *FXV*

Crash Dive 🎬🎬 **1996 (R)** An atomic submarine is taken hostage by Richter (Schone) and his band of terrorists, who demand a billion dollars in gold or Washington D.C. will become a nuclear disaster. Naturally, there's one hero—sub designer James Carter (Dudikoff)—who manages to sneak aboard and plots to save the day. Fast pace and top special effects make this one watchable. *CW:* Violence, a scene of sexuality, and brief language. **90m/C VHS.** Michael Dudikoff, Reiner Schone, Frederic Forrest, Jay Acovone; *D:* Andrew Stevens; *W:* William Martell; *C:* Michael Slovis; *M:* Eric Wurst, David Wurst. *CAF*

The Crash of Flight 401 🎬½ **1978** A plane, full of recognizable TV stars, crashes in the Florida Everglades. "Airport" for a smaller screen. Based on a real event. Made for television. **97m/C VHS, Beta.** William Shatner, Adrienne Barbeau, Eddie Albert, Brooke Bundy, Christopher Connelly, Lorraine Gary, Ron Glass, Sharon Gless, Brett Halsey, George Maharis, Gerald S. O'Loughlin; *D:* Barry Shear.

Crashout 🎬🎬½ **1955** Six men break out of prison in this entertaining melodrama. Bendix plays the gang's leader to nasty perfection. **82m/B VHS.** William Bendix, Gene Evans, Arthur Kennedy, Luther Adler, William Talman, Marshall Thompson, Beverly Michaels; *D:* Lewis R. Foster. *REP*

The Crater Lake Monster woof! 1977 (PG) The dormant egg of a prehistoric creature hatches after a meteor rudely awakens the dozing dino. He's understandably miffed and begins a revenge campaign. Prehistoric yawner. 85m/C VHS, Beta. Richard Cardella, Glenn Roberts, Mark Siegel, Bob Hyman, Kacey Cobb; *D:* William R. Stromberg. *VCI, MRV*

The Craving ⅆ *Return of the Wolfman; El Retorno del Hombre-Lobo* 1980 (R) Naschy returns as El Hombre Lobo for the umpteenth time and once again battles a female vampire (see "Werewolf vs. the Vampire Woman"). Although continental Europe's biggest horror star, this film was such a boxoffice disaster that Naschy went bankrupt. He was then forced to turn to Japan for financing (see "The Human Beasts"). Naschy also directed under a pseudonym. 93m/C VHS, Beta. *SP* Paul Naschy, Julie Saly, Silvia Aquilar, Azucena Hernandez, Beatriz Elorietta, Pilar Alcon; *D:* Jack Molina, Paul Naschy. *VES, ART*

The Crawlers ⅆ 1993 (R) Illegal radioactive dumping has caused a living, lethal organism to invade in a small western town. Seems the local sheriff and the nuclear plant manager were partners in a toxic dumping scheme that went awry and two teenagers are the only ones willing to expose the truth. More to the point—scary monster attacks woman with artistically enhanced cleavage. 94m/C VHS, Closed Caption. Jason Saucier, Mary Sellers; *D:* Martin Newlin; *W:* Dan Price, Martin Newlin. *COL*

The Crawling Eye ⅆⅆ *The Trollenberg Terror* 1958 Hidden in a radioactive fog on a mountaintop, the crawling eye decapitates its victims and returns these humans to Earth to threaten mankind. Average acting, but particularly awful special effects. Based on a British TV series. 87m/B VHS, LV. *GB* Forrest Tucker, Laurence Payne, Janet Munro, Jennifer Jayne, Warren Mitchell; *D:* Quentin Lawrence; *W:* Jimmy Sangster; *M:* Stanley Black. *EEL, MRV, MLB*

The Crawling Hand woof! 1963 An astronaut's hand takes off without him on an unearthly spree of stranglings. Silly stuff is a hands-down loser. 98m/B VHS, Beta, LV. Alan Hale Jr., Rod Lauren, Richard Arlen, Peter Breck, Kent Taylor, Arline Judge, Allison Hayes, Sirry Steffen; *D:* Herbert L. Strock. *RHI, GEM, FCT*

Crawlspace ⅆ 1986 (R) Beautiful girls lease rooms from a murdering, perverted doctor who spies on them, then kills. You may find Kinski amusing but not terrifying. 86m/C VHS, Beta. Klaus Kinski, Talia Balsam, Joyce Van Patten, Sally Brown, Barbara Whinnery; *D:* David Schmoeller; *W:* David Schmoeller; *M:* Pino Donaggio. *VES, ART*

Craze ⅆⅆ *The Infernal Idol; Demon Master* 1974 (R) Tongue-in-cheek tale of a crazed antique dealer who slays a number of women as sacrifices to an African idol named Chuku. 96m/C VHS, Beta. Jack Palance, Diana Dors, Julie Ege, Suzy Kendall, Michael Jayston, Edith Evans, Hugh Griffith, Trevor Howard; *D:* Freddie Francis. *MRV*

Crazed woof! 1982 Dull plodder about a psychopath who keeps a dead girl's body in his boarding house and kills all intruders to keep his secret. 88m/C VHS, Beta. Laslo Papas, Belle Mitchell, Beverly Ross; *D:* Richard Cassidy. *TWE*

Crazed Cop ⅆ *One Way Out* 1988 A man's mind snaps when his wife is found raped and murdered, and nothing will stop him on his quest for revenge. Low budget and violent. 85m/C VHS, Beta. Ivan Rogers, Sandy Brooke, Rich Sutherlin, Doug Irk, Abdulah the Great; *D:* Paul Kyriazi. *UNI*

The Crazies ⅆⅆ *Code Name: Trixie* 1973 (R) A poisoned water supply makes the residents of a small town go on a chaotic, murderous rampage. When the army is called into to quell the anarchy, a small war breaks out. Message film about the military is muddled and derivative. 103m/C Beta. Lane Carroll, W.G. McMillan, Harold W. Jones, Lloyd Hollar, Lynn Lowry; *D:* George A. Romero; *W:* George A. Romero. *VTR*

Crazy Fat Ethel II woof! 1985 A fat, hungry, homicidal female psychopath gets released from the asylum and goes on a cannabilistic rampage. Offensive junk. Sequel to "Criminally Insane." 90m/C VHS, Beta. Priscilla Alden, Michael Flood, Jane Lambert, Robert Copple; *D:* Nick Phillips. *NO*

Crazy for Love ⅆⅆ½ 1952 A village idiot stands to inherit the town inn if he can get a diploma within a year. With English subtitles. 80m/B VHS, Beta. *FR* Brigitte Bardot, Bourvil, Jane Marken, Nadine Basile. *DVT, GVV*

Crazy from the Heart ⅆⅆⅆ 1991 Sweet made-for-cable TV tale of a high school principal in a small south Texas town who discovers the romance of her life one weekend with a Mexican janitor. Strong, nuanced performances from Lahti and Blades make this chestnut of a story work beautifully, with able help from supporting actors. 104m/C VHS, Closed Caption. Christine Lahti, Ruben Blades, Mary Kay Place, Brent Spiner, William Russ, Louise Latham, Tommy Muntz, Robin Lively, Bibi Besch, Kamala Lopez; *D:* Thomas Schlamme. *TTC*

Crazy Horse ⅆⅆⅆ 1996 TV bio of the Oglala Sioux warrior (Greyeyes) whose home in the Black Hills of South Dakota was threatened by western expansion and the constant breaking of government treaties. As war chief, Crazy Horse, along with Teton Sioux leader Sitting Bull (Schellenberg), lead the Cheyenne and Sioux against Custer (Horton) at the battle of Little Bighorn. They elude capture but constant harassment by troops lead to Crazy Horse's surrender and death in 1877, betrayed by both the whites and some of his own people. Gripping story with a fine cast. 120m/C VHS. Michael Greyeyes, Jimmy Herman, Wes Studi, Irene Bedard, Peter Horton, John Finn, Steve Reevis, Gordon Tootoosis, August Schellenberg, Sheldon Peters Wolfchild, Ned Beatty; *D:* John Irvin; *W:* Robert Schenkkan; *C:* Thomas Burstyn; *M:* Lennie Niehaus. *TTC*

Crazy Horse and Custer: "The Untold Story" ⅆ 1990 (R) Long before Little Big Horn, two legendary enemies find themselves trapped together in deadly Blackfoot territory. George Armstrong Custer and Crazy Horse are forced to form a volatile alliance in their life-or-death struggle against the murderous Blackfoot Tribe. History takes a back seat to Hollywood scriptwriting. 120m/C VHS. Slim Pickens, Wayne Maunder, Mary Ann Mobley, Michael Dante. *NO*

Crazy in Love ⅆⅆ½ 1992 Three generations of women live on an island in the home that has been in their family for years. Hunter is wildly in love with her husband, but misses (and doesn't quite trust) him when he is away on business. Enter Sands, who showers her with affection and fills the void in her life. The supporting cast fleshes out the story nicely and illustrates the reasons behind Hunter's insecurity. Enjoyable romantic comedy doesn't throw out anything heavy. Adapted from the novel by Luanne Rice; made for television. 93m/C VHS, LV, Closed Caption. Holly Hunter, Gena Rowlands, Bill Pullman, Julian Sands, Frances McDormand, Herta Ware, Joannne Baron; *D:* Martha Coolidge; *W:* Gerald Ayres. *TTC*

Crazy Mama ⅆⅆ½ 1975 (PG) Three women go on a crime spree from California to Arkansas, picking up men and having a hoot. Crime and comedy in a campy romp. Set in the 1950s and loaded with period kitsch. 81m/C VHS, Beta. Cloris Leachman, Stuart Whitman, Ann Sothern, Jim Backus, Linda Purl; *D:* Jonathan Demme.

Crazy Moon ⅆⅆ½ *Huggers* 1987 (PG-13) A rich high school nerd falls in love with a deaf girl, and must struggle against his domineering father's and older brother's prejudices. The viewer must struggle against the romantic cliches and heavy-handed message to enjoy a basically tender tale of romance. 89m/C VHS, Beta, LV, Closed Caption. Kiefer Sutherland, Vanessa Vaughan, Peter Spence, Ken Pogue, Eve Napier; *D:* Allan Eastman; *W:* Tom Berry, Stefan Wodoslowsky; *M:* Lou Forestieri. *NLC*

Crazy People ⅆ½ 1990 (R) Advertising exec Emory Leeston (Moore) writes commercials that describe products with complete honesty, and is committed to a mental hospital as a result. He meets a variety of characters at the hospital, including Hannah, with whom he falls in love. Tepid boxoffice blunder sounds funnier than it is. We give half a bone for the ad slogans, the funniest part of the movie. Our favorite: "Most of our passengers arrive alive" for an airline. 91m/C VHS, Beta, LV, Closed Caption. Dudley Moore, Daryl Hannah, Paul Reiser, Mercedes Ruehl, J.T. Walsh, Ben Hammer, Dick Cusack, Alan North, David Paymer, Danton Stone, Doug Yasuda, Bill Smitrovich, Paul Bates, Floyd Vivino; *D:* Tony Bill; *W:* Mitch Markowitz; *M:* Cliff Eidelman. *PAR*

The Crazy Ray ⅆⅆⅆ *Paris Qui Dort* 1922 The classic silent fantasy about a mad scientist who endeavors to put the whole population of Paris in a trance. Vintage Clair nonsense. 60m/B VHS, Beta. *FR* Henri Rollan, Albert Prejean, Marcel Vallee, Madeleine Rodrigue; *D:* Rene Clair. *SNC, FCT, MRV*

The Crazysitter ⅆⅆ½ 1994 (PG-13) Edie (D'Angelo), a petty thief recently released from jail, is hired as a sitter to the twins-from-hell. So, she decides to sell the little monsters.*CW:* Crude humor, thematic material. 97m/C VHS, LV. Beverly D'Angelo, Ed Begley Jr., Carol Kane, Phil Hartman, Brady Bluhm, Rachel Duncan; *Cameos:* Nell Carter, Steve Landesburg; *D:* Michael James McDonald; *C:* Christopher Baffa. *NHO*

Creation of Adam ⅆⅆ 1993 Weirdly mystical Russian drama finds Andrey's marriage in trouble because his wife thinks he's gay. She may be right because during a business meeting, Andrey is drawn to the charasmatic Philip, who, it turns out, is some sort of angelic messenger whose mission seems to be to give Andrey confidence in love. Good performances although the plot lacks coherence and is not improved by the poor subtitling. Russian with subtitles. 93m/C VHS. *RU* Alexander Strizhenov, Anzhelika Nevolina, Saulus Balandis, Serghei Vinogradov, Irina Metlitshkaya; *D:* Yuri Pavlov. *WBF*

The Creation of the Humanoids woof! 1962 Set in the familiar post-holocaust future, this is a tale of humans outnumbered by androids and the resulting struggle for survival. Slow and silly low-budget sets. For some reason, Andy Warhol was reported to love this film. 84m/C VHS, Beta. Don Megowan, Frances McCann, Erica Elliot, Don Doolittle, Dudley Manlove; *D:* Wesley E. Barry. *MRV, SNC*

Creator ⅆⅆ 1985 (R) A Frankenstein-like scientist plans to clone a being based on his wife, who died 30 years ago. As his experiments begin to show positive results, his romantic attention turns towards his beautiful lab assistant. O'Toole as the deranged scientist almost saves this one. Based on a novel by Jeremy Leven. 108m/C VHS, Beta, LV. Peter O'Toole, Mariel Hemingway, Vincent Spano, Virginia Madsen, David Ogden Stiers, John Dehner, Karen Kopins, Jeff Corey; *D:* Ivan Passer; *C:* Robbie Greenberg. *NO*

Creature ⅆ *Titan Find* 1985 (R) A two thousand-year-old alien life form is killing off astronauts exploring the planet Titan. "Alien" rip-off has its moments, but not enough of them. Kinski provides some laughs. 97m/C VHS, Beta, LV, Closed Caption. Klaus Kinski, Stan Ivar, Wendy Schaal, Lyman Ward, Annette McCarthy, Diane Salinger; *D:* William Malone; *M:* Tom Chase, Steve Rucker.

Creature from Black Lake ⅆ 1976 (PG) Two anthropology students from Chicago travel to the Louisiana swamps searching for the creature from Black Lake. Predictably, they find him. McClenny, incidentally, is Morgan Fairchild's sister. 95m/C VHS, Beta. Jack Elam, Dub Taylor, Dennis Fimple, John David Carson, Bill Thurman, Catherine McClenny; *D:* Joy Houck Jr. *MRV, VES, ART*

Creature from the Black Lagoon *♫♫♫* **1954** An anthropological expedition in the Amazon stumbles upon the Gill-Man, a prehistoric humanoid fish monster who takes a fancy to fetching Adams, a coed majoring in "science," but the humans will have none of it. Originally filmed in 3-D, this was one of the first movies to sport top-of-the-line underwater photography and remains one of the most enjoyable monster movies ever made. Gershenson's score became a "Creature Features" standard. Based on a story by Maurice Zimm. Sequels: "Revenge of the Creature" and "The Creature Walks Among Us." **79m/B VHS, Beta, LV.** Richard Carlson, Julie Adams, Richard Denning, Antonio Moreno, Whit Bissell, Nestor Paiva, Ricou Browning; **D:** Jack Arnold; **W:** Arthur Ross; **M:** Hans J. Salter. *USH*

Creature from the Haunted Sea *♫♫* **1960** Monster movie satire set in Cuba shortly after the revolution and centering around an elaborate plan to loot the Treasury and put the blame on a strange sea monster. Corman comedy is predictably low budget but entertaining. "Wain" is really Robert Towne, winner of an Oscar for screenwriting. Remake of "Naked Paradise." **76m/B VHS, Beta.** Antony Carbone, Betsy Jones-Moreland, Beach Dickerson, Edward Wain, Edmundo Rivera Alvarez, Robert Bean, Sonya Noemi Gonzalez; **D:** Roger Corman; **W:** Charles B. Griffith; **C:** Jacques Marquette. *VYY, MRV, SNC*

Creature of Destruction *♫* **1967** A beautiful young woman is hypnotized and inadvertently reverted to her past life as a hideous sea monster. Buchanan's remake of his own 1956 production, "The She Creature." **?m/B VHS.** Les Tremayne, Aron Kincaid, Pat Delaney, Neil Fletcher, Ann McAdams; **D:** Larry Buchanan. *NO*

Creature of the Walking Dead *♫*½ *La Marca del Muerto* **1960** Scientist brings his grandfather back to life with horrifying results for the cast and the audience. Made cheaply and quickly in Mexico in 1960, then released with added footage directed by Warren. **74m/B VHS.** *MX* Rock Madison, Ann Wells, George Todd, Willard Gross, Bruno Ve Sota; **D:** Frederic Corte, Jerry Warren. *NOS, MRV, SNC*

The Creature Walks Among Us *♫*½ **1956** Sequel to "Revenge of the Creature" has the Gill-Man once again being captured by scientists for studying purposes. Through an accidental lab fire, the creature's gills are burned off and he undergoes surgery in an attempt to live out of water. Final entry in the Creature series has little magic of the original. Also shot in 3-D. Available on laserdisc as part of a special Encore Edition Double Feature with "Revenge of the Creature." **79m/B VHS, LV, Closed Caption.** Jeff Morrow, Rex Reason, Leigh Snowden, Gregg Palmer, Ricou Browning, Don Megowan, Maurice Manson, Frank Chase; **D:** John Sherwood; **W:** Arthur Ross; **M:** Henry Mancini. *USH, FCT*

Creature with the Blue Hand *♫♫* **1970** A German horror film based on a passable Edgar Wallace story about a man unjustly convicted of murders actually committed by a lunatic. Dubbed. **92m/C VHS, Beta.** *GE* Klaus Kinski, Harald Leopold, Hermann Leschau, Diana Kerner, Carl Lange, Ilse Page; **D:** Alfred Vohrer. *NO*

Creatures the World Forgot **woof!** **1970** A British-made bomb about two tribes of cavemen warring over power and a cavewoman. No special effects, dinosaurs, or dialogue. **96m/C VHS, Beta.** Julie Ege, Robert John, Tony Bonner, Rosalie Crutchley, Sue Wilson; **D:** Don Chaffey; **W:** Michael Carreras. *COL, MLB*

The Creeper *♫♫* **1948** After experimenting with a variety of serums, a doctor turns into a murderous monster with feline paws. **65m/B VHS, Beta.** Eduardo Ciannelli, Onslow Stevens, June Vincent, Ralph Morgan; **D:** Jean Yarbrough. *MLB*

Creepers *♫♫*½ *Phenomena* **1985 (R)** A young girl talks to bugs and gets them to follow her instructions, which comes in handy when she battles the lunatic who is killing her school chums.

Argento weirdness—and graphic gore—may not be for all tastes. **82m/C VHS, Beta.** *IT* Jennifer Connelly, Donald Pleasence, Daria Nicolodi, Elenora Giorgi, Dalia di Lazzaro, Patrick Bauchau, Fiore Argento, Federica Mastroianni, Michele (Michael) Soavi, Gavin Friday; **D:** Dario Argento; **W:** Dario Argento, Franco Ferrini; **C:** Romano Albani; **M:** Simon Boswell. *NLC*

The Creeping Flesh *♫♫*½ **1972 (PG)** A scientist decides he can cure evil by injecting his patients with a serum derived from the blood of an ancient corpse. Some truly chilling moments will get your flesh creeping. **89m/C VHS, Beta, LV.** *GB* Peter Cushing, Christopher Lee, Lorna Heilbron, George Benson, Kenneth J. Warren, Duncan Lamont, Harry Locke, Hedger Wallace, Michael Ripper, Jenny Runacre; **D:** Freddie Francis; **W:** Peter Spenceley, Jonathan Rumbold; **C:** Norman Warwick. *COL, IME, MLB*

Creeping Terror **woof!** *The Crawling Monster; Dangerous Charter* **1964** Gigantic alien carpet monster (look for the tennis shoes sticking out underneath) devours slow-moving teenagers. Partially narrated because some of the original soundtrack was lost, with lots of bad acting, a worse script, laughable sets, and a ridiculous monster. Beware of the thermometer scene. **81m/B VHS, Beta.** Vic Savage, Shannon O'Neal, William Thourlby, Louise Lawson, Robin James; **D:** John Sherwood. *NO*

Creepozoids *♫* **1987** In the near future, a monster at an abandoned science complex stalks army deserters hiding out there. Violent nonsense done better by others. **72m/C Beta, LV.** Linnea Quigley, Ken Abraham, Michael Aranda; **D:** David DeCoteau. *NO*

The Creeps *♫♫* **1997 (PG-13)** A horror-film obsessed scientist steals the original manuscript of Mary Shelley's "Frankenstein" to use in his wacky experiment. He decides to reanimate his four favorite movie monsters but when Anna the librarian steals the book back before the experiment is complete, Dracula, the Mummy, the Wolfman, and the Monster wind up only three feet tall. Not pleased by their diminutive size, the creeps work to restore themselves to the proper height (and cause a little mayhem as well). **CW:** Language. **80m/C VHS.** Phil Fondacaro, Rhonda Griffin, Justin Lauer, Bill Moynihan, Kristin Norton, Jon Simanton, Joe Smith, Thomas Wellington; **D:** Charles Band; **W:** Benjamin Carr. *AFE*

Creepshow *♫♫*½ **1982 (R)** Stephen King's tribute to E.C. Comics, those pulp horror comic books of the 1950s that delighted in grisly, grotesque, and morbid humor. The film tells five horror tales, and features King himself in one segment, as a none-too-bright farmer who unknowingly cultivates a strange, alien-origin moss. With despicable heroes and gory monsters, this is sure to delight all fans of the horror vein. Those easily repulsed by cockroaches beware! **120m/C VHS, Beta, LV, Closed Caption.** Hal Holbrook, Adrienne Barbeau, Viveca Lindfors, E.G. Marshall, Stephen King, Leslie Nielsen, Carrie Nye, Fritz Weaver, Ted Danson, Ed Harris, John Amplas; **D:** George A. Romero; **W:** Stephen King; **C:** Michael Gornick. *WAR*

Creepshow 2 *♫*½ **1987 (R)** Romero adapted three Stephen King stories for this horror anthology which presents gruesome looks at a hit-and-run driver, a wooden Indian, and a vacation gone wrong. Gory and childish stuff from two masters of the genre. Look for King as a truck driver. **92m/C VHS, Beta, LV, Closed Caption.** Lois Chiles, George Kennedy, Dorothy Lamour, Tom Savini, Domenick John, Frank S. Salsedo, Holt McCallany, David Holbrook, Page Hannah, Daniel Beer, Stephen King, Paul Satterfield, Jeremy Green, Tom Wright; **D:** Michael Gornick; **W:** George A. Romero; **C:** Richard Hart, Tom Hurwitz. *VTR*

The Cremators **woof!** **1972** A meteorite carrying an alien lands at a seaside resort and everyone begins bursting into flames. Low budget effort from the scripter of "It Came from Outer Space." **90m/C VHS, Beta.** Marvin Howard, Maria de Aragon; **D:** Harry Essex. *NO*

The Crew *♫♫* **1995 (R)** Sometimes it doesn't pay to be a good samaritan—as a boatload of pleasure cruisers discover when they rescue two psychopaths from a burning boat in the Bahamas. **CW:** Strong language. **99m/C VHS, Closed Caption.** Viggo Mortensen, Jeremy Sisto, Pamela Gidley, Donal Logue, Laura Del Sol, Grace Zabriskie, John Philbin; **D:** Carl Colpaert; **W:** Carl Colpaert. *ART*

Cria *♫♫♫* *Cria Cuervos; Raise Ravens* **1976 (PG)** The award-winning story of a nine-year-old girl's struggle for maturity in a hostile adult world. In Spanish with English subtitles. **115m/C VHS, Beta, LV, Letterbox.** *SP* Geraldine Chaplin, Ana Torrent, Conchita Perez; **D:** Carlos Saura. Cannes Film Festival '76: Grand Jury Prize. *INT, TPV*

Cricket on the Hearth *♫♫* **1923** An adaptation of Charles Dickens' short story about a mail carrier and his bride, who find the symbol of good luck, a cricket on the hearth, when they enter their new home. Silent with organ score. **68m/B VHS, Beta.** Paul Gerson, Virginia Brown Faire, Paul Moore, Joan Standing. *CCB*

Cries and Whispers *♫♫♫* *Viskingar Och Rop* **1972 (R)** As a woman dies slowly of tuberculosis, three women care for her: her two sisters, one sexually repressed, the other promiscuous, and her servant. The sisters remember family love and closeness, but are too afraid to look death in the face to aid their sister. Only the servant can touch her in her dying and only the servant believes in God and his will. Beautiful imagery, focused through a nervous camera, which lingers on the meaningless and whisks away from the meaningful. Absolute mastery of cinematic art by Bergman. **91m/C VHS, Beta, LV.** *SW* Harriet Andersson, Ingrid Thulin, Liv Ullmann, Kary Sylway, Erland Josephson, Henning Moritzen; **D:** Ingmar Bergman; **W:** Ingmar Bergman; **C:** Sven Nykvist. Academy Awards '73: Best Cinematography; National Board of Review Awards '73: Best Director (Bergman); New York Film Critics Awards '72: Best Actress (Ullmann), Best Director (Bergman), Best Film, Best Screenplay; National Society of Film Critics Awards '72: Best Cinematography, Best Screenplay; Nominations: Academy Awards '73: Best Costume Design, Best Director (Bergman), Best Picture, Best Story & Screenplay. *HMV, WAR, BTV*

Cries of Silence *♫♫* **1997** In 1969 a teenaged girl (Buchanan) is found along a remote Mississippi island shore in the aftermath of Hurricane Camille. Young doctor Dorrie Walsh (York) brings the girl to her mother's (Black) home after the locals swear they don't know who she is and the girl herself is mute from trauma. Dorrie calls her Camille and struggles to communicate with her in the face of community opposition. It seems learning Camille's identity could reveal the truth behind more than one local secret. **109m/C VHS.** Kathleen York, Karen Black, Erin Buchanan, Ed Nelson, Ellen Crawford, Guy Boyd; **D:** Avery Crounse; **W:** Avery Crounse; **C:** Michael Barnard; **M:** Nigel Holton. *SHE*

Crime & Passion *♫*½ **1975 (R)** Two scheming lovers plan to get rich by having the woman marry a multimillionaire and sue for a quick divorce. The multimillionaire is no patsy, however, and seeks a deadly revenge. Three scripts by six writers were combined to create this story. That explains the many problems. **92m/C VHS, Beta.** Omar Sharif, Karen Black, Joseph Bottoms, Bernhard Wicki; **D:** Ivan Passer. *VES, ART*

Crime and Punishment *♫♫♫* **1935** Pared down but well-executed version of the Dostoyevski novel. Lorre is superb as Raskolnikov, who robs and murders an elderly pawnbroker. Believing he has committed the perfect murder, he accepts the invitation of police inspector Porfiry (Arnold) to observe the investigation. Gradually Raskolnikov's conscience begins to overwhelm him as Porfiry slowly works to wring a confession from the killer. Von Sternberg's subdued directorial approach worked well to explore the psychological aspects of guilt, although the melodramatic French film version (released at the same time) scored better with the critics. **88m/B VHS.** Peter

Lorre, Edward Arnold, Marian Marsh, Tala Birell, Elisabeth Risdon, Robert Allen, Douglass Dumbrille, Gene Lockhart; *D:* Josef von Sternberg; *W:* S.K. Lauren, Joseph Anthony. COL

Crime and Punishment 🗡🗡🗡🗡 *Crime et Chatiment* 1935 Original French production (preceding the American version by just one week) of Dostoyevski's novel, the tale of a young murderer, his crime, and ultimately, his confession. Generally considered better than the American version, the French throw out all that is not dramatic, keeping the psychology and suspense. Remade in 1958. 110m/B VHS. Harry Baur, Pierre Blanchar, Madeleine Ozeray, Marcelle Geniat, Lucienne Lemarchand; *D:* Pierre Chenal; *W:* Marcel Ayme, Chenal, Christian Stengel, Wladimir Strijewski; *M:* Arthur Honegger. FCT

Crime and Punishment 🗡🗡 1970 Ponderous, excruciatingly long adaptation of the Dostoyevski classic involving a haunted murderer and the relentless policeman who seeks to prove him guilty. In Russian with English subtitles. 200m/B VHS. RU Georgi Taratorkin, Victoria Fyodorova; *D:* Lev Kulijanov; *W:* Lev Kulijanov. DVT, HEG, TPV

Crime Broker 🗡🗡 1994 A respected judge (Bisset) decides to experience life on the other side of the bench for a change. So she hooks up with a handsome partner to execute a series of high-profile robberies of bank vaults and museums. Implied sex so don't look for this under erotic thrillers. 93m/C VHS. Jacqueline Bisset, Massaya Kato, Gary Day; *D:* Ian Barry; *W:* Tony Morphett; *C:* Dan Burstall; *M:* Roger Mason. APX

Crime Busters 🗡½ 1978 (PG) Two guys attempt to pull off a bank heist but accidentally join the Miami police force instead. Hill and Spencer are enjoyable as usual but the film suffers from poor dubbing. Remake of "Two Supercops." 114m/C VHS, Beta. IT Terence Hill, Bud Spencer, Laura Gemser, Luciana Catenacci, David Huddleston; *D:* E.B. Clucher. WAR

Crime Killer 🗡 1985 Confusing shenanigans about an explosive ex-CIA agent enlisted by the FBI to battle a brutal crime syndicate shipping guns to nasty Arabs. 90m/C VHS, Beta. George Pan-Andreas, Leo Morrell, Althan Karras; *D:* George Pan-Andreas; *C:* Arledge Armenaki. VTR

Crime Lords 🗡🗡 1991 (R) When a pair of cops are suspended from the force for committing a blunder, they travel to Hong Kong to continue their investigation. Little do they know their sleuthing has drawn them into a confrontation with one of largest crime syndicates in the world. Lots of action, beautiful women, and exotic locations keep this basic buddy plot moving well.*CW:* Language, strong violence, and sensuality. 96m/C VHS. Wayne Crawford, Martin Hewitt, Susan Byun, Mel Castelo, James Hong; *D:* Wayne Crawford.

The Crime of Dr. Crespi 🗡🗡 1935 A doctor takes his revenge on a man who is after his girlfriend by injecting him with suspended animation serum. Extremely campy performance from von Stroheim; Frye's biggest role in terms of screen time. 64m/B VHS, Beta. Erich von Stroheim, Dwight Frye, Paul Guilfoyle, Harriett Russell, John Bohn; *D:* John H. Auer. NOS, SNC, MLB

Crime of Honor 🗡 1985 A European executive goes public with his company's corruption, and his family suffers predictable ruin as a result. Based on a true story. 95m/C VHS, Beta. Maria Schneider, David Suchet; *D:* John Goldschmidt.

The Crime of Monsieur Lange 🗡🗡🗡 *Le Crime de Monsieur Lange* 1936 Charming French socialist fantasy where workers at a publishing company turn the business into a thriving cooperative while their evil boss is gone. When he returns, worker Lefevre plots to kill him. Rather talky, but humorous. In French with subtitles. French script booklet also available. 90m/B VHS, Beta. FR Rene Lefevre, Jules Berry, Florelle, Sylvia Bataille, Jean Daste, Nadia Sibirskaia; *D:* Jean Renoir; *W:* Jacques Prevert. FCT, INT

Crime of Passion 🗡🗡½ 1957 Stanwyck plays a femme fatale whose ambitions for detective hubby lead to murder. Good performances from Stanwyck, Hayden, and Burr make this an above-average, although outlandish, crime-drama. 85m/B VHS, Closed Caption. Barbara Stanwyck, Sterling Hayden, Raymond Burr, Fay Wray, Royal Dano, Virginia Grey, Dennis Cross, Robert Griffin, Jay Adler, Malcolm Atterbury, S. John Launer, Brad Trumbull, Skipper McNally, Jean Howell, Peg La Centra, Nancy Reynolds, Marjorie Owens, Robert Quarry, Joe Conley, Stuart Whitman; *D:* Gerd Oswald; *W:* Jo Eisinger; *C:* Joseph LaShelle; *M:* Paul Dunlap. MGM, FCT

Crime of the Century 🗡🗡½ 1996 (PG-13) Another look at the 1932 kidnapping and death of Charles Lindbergh's 18-month-old son. Based on the 1985 book "The Airman and the Carpenter" by Ludovic Kennedy, it's clear the author regards Bruno Richard Hauptmann (Rea), who was executed in 1936, as an innocent scapegoat essentially railroaded thanks to media and political pressures. Made for cable.*CW:* Some intense thematic elements, including an execution scene. 116m/C VHS. Stephen Rea, J.T. Walsh, David Paymer, John Harkins, Michael Moriarty, Isabella Rossellini, Bert Remsen, Allen (Goorwitz) Garfield, Don Harvey, Gerald S. O'Loughlin, Barry Primus; *D:* Mark Rydell; *W:* William Nicholson; *C:* Toyomichi Kurita; *M:* John Frizzell. HBO

Crime Story 🗡🗡 *Hard to Die* 1993 (R) Police Inspector Eddie Chan (Chan) tries to crack a kidnapping case and discovers his partner, Detective Hung (Cheng), is not on the up-and-up. Usual acrobatic stunts from Chan and company. Cantonese with subtitles.*CW:* Martial arts violence, shootings and a sex scene. 104m/C VHS, LV, Closed Caption. HK Jackie Chan, Kent Cheng, Law Hang Kang, Christine Ng; *D:* Kirk Wong; *C:* Arthur Wong, Ardy Lam. TOU

Crime Story: The Complete Saga 1986 All 42 episodes of the 1986-88 NBC cops-vs.-mobsters series set first in Chicago in 1963, and later in Las Vegas. The series was created by Michael Mann, the executive producer of "Miami Vice." Del Shannon updated the lyrics to his hit "Runaway" for the series theme. Available as a boxed set of ten tapes or individually. ?m/C VHS. Dennis Farina, Anthony John Denison, Bill Smitrovich, Steve Ryan, Bill Campbell, Paul Butler, Stephen Lang, Darlanne Fluegel. VTR, MOV

Crime Zone 🗡🗡½ 1988 (R) In a totalitarian, repressive, future society, two young lovers try to beat the system and make it on their own. A well-made, if occasionally muddled, low-budget film shot in Peru, of all places. 96m/C VHS. David Carradine, Peter Nelson, Sherilyn Fenn, Orlando Sacha, Don Manor, Michael Shaner; *D:* Luis Llosa; *W:* Daryl Haney; *M:* Rick Conrad. MGM

Crimebusters 🗡½ 1979 (PG) A man exacts revenge against a government conspiracy that kidnapped his loved ones. 90m/C VHS, Beta. Henry Silva, Antonio Sabato Jr.; *D:* Michael Tarantini. NO

Crimes & Misdemeanors 🗡🗡🗡 1989 (PG-13) One of Allen's most mature films, exploring a whole range of moral ambiguities through the parallel and eventually interlocking stories of a nebbish filmmaker—who agrees to make a profile of a smug Hollywood television comic and then sabotages it—and an esteemed ophthalmologist who is being threatened with exposure by his neurotic mistress. Intriguing mix of drama and comedy few directors could pull off. Look for Daryl Hannah in an unbilled cameo. 104m/C VHS, Beta, LV, Closed Caption. Martin Landau, Woody Allen, Alan Alda, Mia Farrow, Joanna Gleason, Anjelica Huston, Jerry Orbach, Sam Waterston, Claire Bloom, Jenny Nichols, Caroline Aaron; *Cameos:* Daryl Hannah, Nora Ephron, Jerry Zaks; *D:* Woody Allen; *W:* Woody Allen; *C:* Sven Nykvist. National Board of Review Awards '89: Best Supporting Actor (Alda); New York Film Critics Awards '89: Best Supporting Actor (Alda); Writers Guild of America '89: Best Original Screenplay; Nominations: Academy Awards '89: Best Director (Allen), Best Original Screenplay, Best Supporting Actor (Landau). ORI

Crimes at the Dark House 🗡🗡🗡 1939 In this campy, melodramatic adaptation of Wilkie Collins's novel "The Woman in White," a man kills his rich wife and puts a disguised mental patient in her place. Later remade using the book's title. 69m/B VHS. GB Tod Slaughter, Hilary Eaves, Sylvia Marriott, Hay Petrie, Geoffrey Wardwell; *D:* George King. NOS, MRV, SNC

Crimes of Dr. Mabuse 🗡🗡🗡½ *The Testament of Dr. Mabuse; The Last Will of Dr. Mabuse* 1932 Supernatural horror classic about the evil Dr. Mabuse controlling an underworld empire while confined to an insane asylum. One of the best "mad doctor" movies ever made. 120m/B VHS. GE Rudolf Klein-Rogge, Otto Wernicke, Gustav Diesl, Karl Meixner; *D:* Fritz Lang. SNC

Crimes of Passion 🗡🗡🗡 1984 Vintage whacked-out Russell, not intended for the kiddies. A business-like fashion designer becomes a kinky prostitute at night. A disturbed street preacher makes her the heroine of his erotic fantasies. A dark terrifying vision of the underground sex world and moral hypocrisy. Sexually explicit and violent, with an extremely black comedic center. Turner's portrayal is honest and believable, Perkins over-acts until he nearly gets a nosebleed, but it's all for good effect. Cut for "R" rating to get it in the theatres; this version restores some excised footage. Also available in rated version. 101m/C VHS, Beta, LV, Closed Caption. Kathleen Turner, Anthony Perkins, Annie Potts, John Laughlin, Bruce Davison, Norman Burton; *D:* Ken Russell; *W:* Barry Sandler; *M:* Rick Wakeman. Los Angeles Film Critics Association Awards '84: Best Actress (Turner). VTR

The Crimes of Stephen Hawke 🗡🗡 *Strangler's Morgue* 1936 The world knows Stephen Hawke as a big-hearted money lender. What they don't know is his favorite hobby is breaking peoples' spines. An entertaining thriller set in the 1800s. 65m/B VHS, Beta. GB Tod Slaughter, Marjorie Taylor, D.J. Williams, Eric Portman, Ben Soutten; *D:* George King. SNC, MRV, HEG

Crimes of the Heart 🗡🗡½ 1986 (PG-13) Based on Beth Henley's acclaimed play. A few days in the lives of three very strange Southern sisters, one of whom has just been arrested for calmly shooting her husband after he chased her black lover out of town. Spacek as the suicidal sister is a lark. A tart, black comedy that works better as a play than a film. 105m/C VHS, Beta, LV, Closed Caption. Sissy Spacek, Diane Keaton, Jessica Lange, Sam Shepard, Tess Harper, Hurd Hatfield; *D:* Bruce Beresford; *W:* Beth Henley; *C:* Dante Spinotti; *M:* Georges Delerue. Golden Globe Awards '87: Best Actress—Musical/Comedy (Spacek); New York Film Critics Awards '86: Best Actress (Spacek); Nominations: Academy Awards '86: Best Actress (Spacek), Best Adapted Screenplay, Best Supporting Actress (Harper). ORI, WAR

Crimetime 🗡½ 1996 (R) Silly thriller has actor Bobby (Baldwin) finding unexpected success portraying a serial killer in a crime re-enactment TV show called "Crimetime." Meanwhile, Sydney (Postlethwaite), who's the real killer Bobby's character is based on, becomes seduced by the media frenzy surrounding the crimes and seeing them re-enacted on television. He goes on killing, so the show can literally go on.*CW:* Violence, sexuality, and language. 118m/C VHS, Closed Caption. Stephen Baldwin, Pete Postlethwaite, Sadie Frost, Geraldine Chaplin, Karen Black, James Faulkner; *Cameos:* Marianne Faithfull; *D:* George Sluizer; *W:* Brendan Somers; *C:* Jules Van Den Steenhoven. THV

Crimewave 🗡🗡 *The XYZ Murders; Broken Hearts and Noses* 1985 (PG-13) Zany spoof about serial killers set in Detroit (director Raimi's hometown). A rhapsody to comic book style, short on plot and long on style. With such credentials you expect more. 83m/C VHS, Beta, Closed Caption. Louise Lasser, Paul Smith, Brion James, Bruce Campbell, Reed Birney, Sheree J. Wilson, Edward R. Pressman, Julius W. Harris; *D:* Sam Raimi; *W:* Ethan Coen, Joel Coen, Sam Raimi. NLC

Criminal Act 🐾½ 1988 A newspaper editor hits the street to prove she's still a tough reporter, but uncovers a dangerous scandal in the process. 94m/C VHS, Beta. Catherine Bach, Charlene Dallas, Nicholas Guest, John Saxon, Vic Tayback; *D:* Mark Byers.

Criminal Code 🐾🐾½ 1931 Aging melodrama about a young man who's jailed for killing in self-defense. His life worsens at the hands of a prison warden when the head guy's daughter falls for him. Remade as "Penitentiary" and "Convicted." 98m/B VHS, Beta. Walter Huston, Phillips Holmes, Boris Karloff, Constance Cummings, Mary Doran, DeWitt Jennings, John Sheehan; *D:* Howard Hawks. Nominations: Academy Awards '31: Best Adapted Screenplay. COL, MLB

Criminal Court 🐾🐾 1946 A man accused of murdering his blackmailer hires the real killer as his attorney. Hard to follow, with an interesting premise that turns flat. 63m/B VHS, Beta. Tom Conway, Martha O'Driscoll, Robert Armstrong, Addison Richards, June Clayworth, Pat Gleason, Steve Brodie; *D:* Robert Wise. NO

Criminal Hearts 🐾🐾 1995 (R) Keli (Locane) is driving to Phoenix when she picks up the hitchhiking Rafe (Dillon), who's just robbed a gas station. Turns out the stations are laundering mob drug money and when the store owners are killed, Rafe gets the blame for the murders as well. The killers are actually corrupt FBI agents Martin (Walsh) and Tierney (McDonald) who are soon of the trail of the twosome.*CW:* Violence, sexuality, and language. 92m/C VHS. Kevin Dillon, Amy Locane, Morgan Fairchild, M. Emmet Walsh, Michael James McDonald, Don Stroud; *D:* Dave Payne; *W:* Dave Payne; *C:* Christopher Baffa. AVE

Criminal Justice 🐾🐾🐾 1990 (R) A black man is accused of a crime by a woman with whom he was involved. Is it justice or revenge? Strong cast in important story. Made for cable TV. 92m/C VHS, Closed Caption. Forest Whitaker, Jennifer Grey, Rosie Perez, Anthony LaPaglia, Tony Todd; *D:* Andy Wolk; *W:* Andy Wolk; *C:* Steven Fierberg. HBO

Criminal Law 🐾🐾 1989 (R) An ambitious young Boston lawyer gets a man acquitted for murder, only to find out after the trial that the man is guilty and renewing his killing spree. Realizing he's the only one privy to the killer's trust, the lawyer decides to stop him himself. A white-knuckled thriller burdened by a weak script. 113m/C VHS, Beta, LV. Kevin Bacon, Gary Oldman, Karen Young, Joe Don Baker, Tess Harper; *D:* Martin Campbell; *W:* Mark Kasden; *M:* Jerry Goldsmith. HBO, WAR

The Criminal Life of Archibaldo de la Cruz 🐾🐾🐾 *Ensayo de un Crimen; Rehearsal for a Crime* 1955 Seeing the death of his governess has a lasting effect on a boy. He grows up to be a demented cretin whose failure with women leads him to conspire to kill every one he meets, a task at which he also fails. Hilarious, bitter Bunuelian diatribe. In Spanish with English subtitles. 95m/B VHS, Beta. MX SP Ernesto Alonso, Ariadne Welter, Rita Macedo, Rodolfo Landa, Andrea Palma, Miroslava Stern; *D:* Luis Bunuel. FCT, WBF

The Criminal Mind 🐾🐾 1993 (R) L.A. District Attorney Nick August (Rossi) reunites with his long-lost brother (Cross), whom he discovers is very familiar with the other side of the law. Tied up with the mob, Cross forces his bro to watch a hit and then Rossi winds up the next target for a group of assassins and some corrupt cops. 93m/C VHS, Closed Caption. Ben Cross, Frank Rossi, Tahnee Welch, Lance Henriksen, Joseph Ruskin, Lynn-Holly Johnson; *D:* Joseph Vittorie; *W:* Sam A. Scribner. COL

Criminally Insane 🐾 1975 Authorities release 250 pounds of cleaver-wielding maniacal fury from the loony bin. She seeks food and human blood. They should have known better. Followed by "Crazy Fat Ethel II." 61m/C VHS, Beta. Priscilla Alden, Michael Flood; *D:* Nick Phillips. NO

Criminals Within 🐾 *Army Mystery* 1941 A scientist working on a top secret formula is murdered and a detective tries to nail the spy ring responsible. Very confusing, poor usage of some fine female cast members. 67m/B VHS, Beta. Eric Linden, Ann Doran, Constance Worth, Donald Curtis, Weldon Heyburn, Ben Alexander; *D:* Joseph H. Lewis. SNC

The Crimson Cult 🐾 *The Crimson Altar; Curse of the Crimson Altar* 1968 (PG) Eden and his girlfriend are invited to a mysterious mansion. They discover that Lee is out to enact revenge as his ancestor was burned for witchcraft by Eden's. An all-star horror disaster. Karloff was 80 and confined to a wheelchair. Despite ads claiming this as his last film, he made four more in Mexico. Highlights include the scantily clad Steele in sado-masochistic sequences and a psychedelic party with strippers and body painters. 87m/C VHS. GB Boris Karloff, Christopher Lee, Mark Eden, Barbara Steele, Virginia Wetherell, Michael Gough, Rupert Davies; *D:* Vernon Sewell. MOV

Crimson Pirate 🐾🐾🐾½ 1952 An 18th-century buccaneer pits his wits and brawn against the might of a ruthless Spanish nobleman. Considered by many to be one of the best swashbucklers, laced with humor and enthusiastically paced. Showcase for Lancaster and Cravat's acrobatic talents. 104m/C VHS, Beta, LV. GB Burt Lancaster, Eva Bartok, Torin Thatcher, Christopher Lee, Nick Cravat; *D:* Robert Siodmak. WAR

Crimson Romance 🐾🐾 1934 Two unemployed American pilots in Europe decide to join the German airforce for want of anything better to do. Conflicts revolve around a warmongering Commandant and his pilot. 70m/B VHS, Beta, 8mm. Ben Lyon, Sari Maritza, James Bush, Erich von Stroheim, Jason Robards Sr., Herman Bing, Vince Barnett; *D:* David Howard. NOS, VYY, RXM

Crimson Tide 🐾🐾🐾 1995 (R) Mutiny erupts aboard the submarine USS Alabama as Captain Ramsey (Hackman) and his Executive Officer Hunter (Washington) clash over the validity of orders to launch the sub's missiles. Ramsey, who wants to fire the missiles, and Hunter, who refuses to comply until the message is verified, battle for control of the sub. Suspenseful and well-paced thriller lets Hackman and Washington show off their considerable screen presence, while Bruckheimer, Simpson, and Scott show that they haven't lost any of their trademark big-budget, testosterone-laden flash. Original screenplay went under the knife of a number of script doctors, most notably Quentin Tarantino.*CW:* Strong language. 116m/C VHS, LV, Closed Caption. Gene Hackman, Denzel Washington, George Dzundza, Viggo Mortensen, James Gandolfini, Matt Craven, Lillo Brancato, Danny Nucci, Steve Zahn, Rick Schroder, Vanessa Bell Calloway, Rocky Carroll; *Cameos:* Jason Robards Jr.; *D:* Tony Scott; *W:* Michael Schiffer, Richard P. Henrick; *C:* Darius Wolski; *M:* Hans Zimmer. Nominations: Academy Awards '95: Best Film Editing, Best Sound; MTV Movie Awards '96: Best Male Performance (Washington). TOU

The Crimson Trail 🐾🐾½ 1935 Buck believes his uncle may be involved in cattle rustling. Lots of action, minimal plot. 56m/B VHS. Buck Jones, Polly Ann Young, Carl Stockdale, Charles French, Ward Bond, Robert F. (Bob) Kortman, Bud Osborne, Charles Brinley, Robert Walker; *D:* Al Raboch; *W:* Jack Natteford. GPV

The Crippled Masters 🐾🐾 1982 (R) After Li Ho's (Shum) arms are cut off by an evil warlord, he wanders the countryside facing ridicule until he teams up with disfigured Dax Oh Jen (Conn). Helped by an elderly yoga master, the duo unite to seek revenge. Features kung-fu masters with real-life disabilities.*CW:* Violence. 90m/C VHS. Frankie Shum, Jack Conn; *D:* Joe Law. NLC

Crisis at Central High 🐾🐾🐾 1980 A dramatic television recreation of the events leading up to the 1957 integration of Central High in Little Rock, Arkansas. Based on teacher Elizabeth Huckaby's journal. Emmy-nominated performance by Woodward as Huckaby. 120m/C VHS, Beta. Joanne Woodward, Charles Durning, William Ross, Henderson Forsythe; *D:* Lamont Johnson; *M:* Billy Goldenberg. NO

Criss Cross 🐾🐾🐾 1949 A classic grade-B film noir, in which an armored car driver is suckered into a burglary by his ex-wife and her hoodlum husband. Multiple back-stabbings and double-crossings ensue. 98m/B VHS, Beta. Burt Lancaster, Yvonne De Carlo, Dan Duryea, Stephen McNally, Richard Long, Tony Curtis; *D:* Robert Siodmak; *W:* Daniel Fuchs; *M:* Miklos Rozsa. USH

Crisscross 🐾🐾½ *Alone Together* 1992 (R) It's 1969 and Tracy Cross is a divorced mom whose ex-husband is a traumatized Vietnam vet who has left her alone to raise their 12 year-old son Chris during some hard times. She works two jobs, as a waitress and, unbeknownst to her son, as a stripper in a local club. When Chris sneaks into the club and sees her act he takes drastic measures to help out—by selling drugs. Film is sluggish and relies too much on voice-overs to explain thoughts but Hawn gives a convincing and restrained performance as the mother.*CW:* Language, drug-related scenes, and one strong sensual scene. 107m/C VHS, LV, Closed Caption. Goldie Hawn, David Arnott, Arliss Howard, James Gammon, Keith Carradine, J.C. Quinn, Steve Buscemi, Paul Calderone; *D:* Chris Menges; *M:* Trevor Jones. MGM

Critical Care 🐾½ 1997 (R) Spader is a doctor in a high-tech intensive care unit dealing with the ethics of modern health care, such as insurance scams, euthanasia, and a drunken administrator (Brooks) whose only concern is the hospital's profits. Two sisters (Sedgwick and Martindale) fight over the fate of their terminally ill, near-vegetable father. Spader finds his career on the line after bedding Sedgwick and backing her attempts to pull the plug. Given the meatiness of the subject, director Lumet could have made a much more scathing satire. Schwartz's script is lame even for a first time effort, and the usually interesting Shawn falls horribly flat with an embarrassing bit of dialogue. Occasional laughs (this was supposed to be a dark comedy) and good performances from Brooks and Mirren can't keep this one from flatlining. Watch an episode of "ER" instead.*CW:* Language and a scene of sexuality. 105m/C VHS, LV, DVD. James Spader, Albert Brooks, Kyra Sedgwick, Helen Mirren, Margo Martindale, Jeffrey Wright, Wallace Shawn, Anne Bancroft, Philip Bosco, Edward Herrmann, Colm Feore, James Lally, Al Waxman, Harvey Atkin; *D:* Sidney Lumet; *W:* Steven S. Schwartz; *C:* David Watkin; *M:* Michael Convertino. ART

Critical Choices 🐾🐾 1997 (R) The Women's Health Clinic in Milwaukee, Wisconsin, provides safe and legal abortions. Run by Dr. Margaret Ludlow (Buckley) and her pro-choice supporter, Diana Johnson (Scarwid), the clinic becomes the focal point for right-wing evangelist Bobby Ray Flood (Kerwin) and his supporters, including Arlene Dickens (Reed). Tensions mount and violence erupts as everyone believes they're doing the right thing.*CW:* Language and depiction of an abortion procedure. 88m/C VHS, Closed Caption. Betty Buckley, Pamela Reed, Diana Scarwid, Terry Kinney, Brian Kerwin; *D:* Claudia Weill; *W:* Susan Cuscuna, Robin Green, Mitchell Burgess; *M:* Patrick Seymour. PAR

Critical Condition 🐾 1986 (R) During a blackout, a criminal masquerades as a doctor in a city hospital. Limp comedy embarrassing for Pryor. 99m/C VHS, Beta, LV, Closed Caption. Richard Pryor, Rachel Ticotin, Ruben Blades, Joe Mantegna; *D:* Michael Apted; *C:* Ralf Bode; *M:* Alan Silvestri. PAR

Critters 🐾🐾½ 1986 (PG-13) A gang of furry, razor-toothed aliens escapes from its prison ship to Earth with their bounty hunters right behind them. They make it to a small town in Kansas where they begin to attack anything that moves. Not just a thrill-kill epic, but a sarcastic otherworldly thrill-kill epic. 86m/C VHS, Beta, LV. Dee Wallace Stone, M. Emmet Walsh, Billy Green Bush, Scott Grimes, Nadine Van Der Velde, Terrence Mann, Billy Zane, Don Opper, Don Opper, Terrence Mann; *D:* Stephen Herek; *W:* Stephen Herek, Dominic Muir; *C:* Tim Suhrstedt; *M:* David Newman. COL

Critters 2: The Main Course 🐾🐾 **1988 (PG-13)** Sequel to the hit horror-comedy, wherein the voracious alien furballs return in full force to Grovers Bend, Kansas, from eggs planted two years before. Occasionally inspired "Gremlins" rip. **93m/C VHS, Beta, LV, Closed Caption.** Scott Grimes, Liane Curtis, Don Opper, Barry Corbin, Terrence Mann; **D:** Mick Garris; **W:** Mick Garris, David N. Twohy; **C:** Russell Carpenter. *COL*

Critters 3 🐾🐾 **1991 (PG-13)** The not-so-loveable critters are back, terrorizing the occupants of a tenement building. **86m/C VHS, Closed Caption.** Frances Bay, Aimee Brooks, Leonardo DiCaprio, Don Opper; **D:** Kristine Peterson; **W:** David J. Schow. *COL, NLC*

Critters 4 🐾🐾 **1991 (PG-13)** The ghoulish critters are back, and this time a strain of genetically engineered mutant critters (what's the difference?) wants to take over the universe. **94m/C VHS, LV, Closed Caption.** Don Opper, Paul Whitthorne, Angela Bassett, Brad Dourif, Terrence Mann; **D:** Rupert Harvey; **W:** David J. Schow. *NLC, COL*

Crocodile woof! **1981 (R)** Giant crocodile attacks a beach town, killing and devouring dozens of people. The locals sit around trying to figure a way to stop the critter. Special effects include rear-projected croc. Lots of blood but lacking humor of "Alligator." Filmed in Thailand and Korea. **95m/C VHS, Beta.** Nat Puvanai, Tany Tim, Angela Wells, Kirk Warren; **D:** Sompote Sands. *NO*

Crocodile Dundee 🐾🐾🐾½ **1986 (PG-13)** New York reporter Sue Charlton is assigned to the Outback to interview living legend Mike Dundee. When she finally locates the man, she is so taken with him that she brings him back to New York with her. There, the naive Aussie wanders about, amazed at the wonders of the city and unwittingly charming everyone he comes in contact with, from high-society transvestites to street hookers. One of the surprise hits of 1986. **98m/C VHS, Beta, LV, 8mm, Closed Caption.** AU Paul Hogan, Linda Kozlowski, John Meillon, David Gulpilil, Mark Blum; **D:** Peter Faiman; **W:** Paul Hogan, John Cornell; **C:** Russell Boyd; **M:** Peter Best. Golden Globe Awards '87: Best Actor—Musical/Comedy (Hogan); Nominations: Academy Awards '86: Best Original Screenplay. *PAR*

Crocodile Dundee 2 🐾🐾½ **1988 (PG)** In this sequel Mike Dundee, the loveable rube, returns to his native Australia looking for new adventure, having "conquered" New York City. He inadvertently gets involved in stopping a gang of crooks active in Australia and New York. Lacks the charm and freshness of the first film. **110m/C VHS, Beta, LV, Closed Caption.** Paul Hogan, Linda Kozlowski, Kenneth Welsh, John Meillon, Ernie Dingo, Juan Fernandez, Charles S. Dutton; **D:** John Cornell; **W:** Paul Hogan; **C:** Russell Boyd; **M:** Peter Best. *PAR*

Crocodiles in Amsterdam 🐾🐾 *Krokodillen in Amsterdam* **1989** Lunatic girl-meets-girl movie about flighty Gino and would-be terrorist Nina who team up to rob Gino's rich uncle. Dutch with subtitles. **88m/C VHS.** NL Joan Nederlof, Yolanda Entius; **D:** Annette Apon; **W:** Yolanda Entius, Annette Apon. *WBF*

Cromwell 🐾🐾½ **1970 (G)** A lavish British-made spectacle about the conflict between Oliver Cromwell and Charles I, and the British Civil War. History is twisted as Cromwell becomes the liberator of the oppressed. Harris gives a commanding performance and the battle scenes are stunners. **139m/C VHS, Beta, LV.** GB Richard Harris, Alec Guinness, Robert Morley, Frank Finlay, Patrick Magee, Timothy Dalton; **D:** Ken Hughes; **W:** Ken Hughes; **C:** Geoffrey Unsworth. Academy Awards '70: Best Costume Design; Nominations: Academy Awards '70: Best Original Score. *COL, TVC*

Cronos 🐾🐾 *Chronos* **1994 (R)** Stylish Mexican variation of the vampire tale. Aged antiques dealer Jesus Gris (Luppi) comes across the mysterious title object—a 14th century golden egg possessing magical powers to grant eternal life. But can its possessor stand the consequences, which include a developing taste for blood? Another problem is Gris isn't the only one to know about the device. First feature for writer/director del

Toro. Spanish with subtitles. **CW:** Language; horror violence. **92m/C VHS, LV.** MX Federico Luppi, Ron Perlman, Claudio Brook, Tamara Shanath, Margarita Isabel; **D:** Guillermo del Toro; **W:** Guillermo del Toro; **C:** Guillermo Navarro; **M:** Ian Deardon. *THV*

The Crooked Circle 🐾½ **1932** More comedy than mystery as slapstick policeman Gleason goes under cover as a swami. Not helped at all by a weak script and poor photography. **68m/B VHS.** Ben Lyon, ZaSu Pitts, James Gleason, C. Henry Gordon, Raymond Hatton, Roscoe Karns; **D:** H. Bruce Humberstone. *SNC, NOS*

Crooked Hearts 🐾🐾 **1991 (R)** Dysfunctional family drama means well but lays it on too thick, as a father/son rivalry threatens to sunder the tight-knit Warrens. Based on a novel by Robert Boswell. **CW:** Language and one sensual scene. **113m/C VHS, Beta, LV, Closed Caption.** Peter Coyote, Jennifer Jason Leigh, Peter Berg, Cindy Pickett, Vincent D'Onofrio; **D:** Michael Bortman; **W:** Michael Bortman. *MGM*

Crooked Trail 🐾 **1936** A lawman and bad guy become friends. **58m/B VHS, Beta, LV.** Johnny Mack Brown. *NO*

Crooklyn 🐾🐾🐾 **1994 (PG-13)** Director Lee turns from the life of Malcolm X to the early lives of Generation X in this profile of an African-American middle-class family growing up in 1970s Brooklyn. Lee's least politically charged film to date is a joint effort between him and sibs Joie and Cinque, and profiles the only girl in a family of five children coming of age. Tender and real performances from all, especially newcomer Harris, propel the sometimes messy, music-laden trip to nostalgia land. **CW:** Drug content. **112m/C VHS, LV, Letterbox, Closed Caption.** Alfre Woodard, Delroy Lindo, Zelda Harris, David Patrick Kelly, Carlton Williams, Sharif Rashed, Tse-March Washington, Christopher Knowings, Jose Zuniga, Isaiah Washington, Ivelka Reyes, N. Jeremi Duru, Frances Foster, Norman Matlock, Patriece Nelson, Joie Lee, Vondie Curtis-Hall, Tiasha Reyes, Spike Lee; **D:** Spike Lee; **W:** Joie Lee, Cinque Lee; **M:** Terence Blanchard. *USH*

Crooks & Coronets 🐾½ *Sophie's Place* **1969 (PG)** Two-bit crooks plot to rob the country estate of an eccentric British dowager. **106m/C VHS, Beta.** GB Cesar Romero, Telly Savalas, Warren Oates, Edith Evans; **D:** James O'Connolly. *WAR*

The Cross & the Switchblade 🐾½ **1972 (PG)** An idealistic priest tries to bring the message of religion to the members of a vicious street gang. They don't wanna listen. Spanish language version available. **105m/C VHS, Beta.** Pat Boone, Erik Estrada, Jackie Giroux, Jo-Ann Robinson; **D:** Don Murray. *VBL*

Cross Country 🐾½ **1983 (R)** Action revolves around the brutal murder of a call girl, with initial suspicion falling on a television advertising director involved with the woman. The story twists and turns from the suspect to investigating detective Ironside without becoming particularly interesting. **95m/C VHS, Beta, LV.** CA Richard Beymer, Nina Axelrod, Michael Ironside; **D:** Paul Lynch; **W:** Logan N. Danforth. *NLC*

Cross Creek 🐾🐾½ **1983 (PG)** Based on the life of Marjorie Kinnan Rawlings, author of "The Yearling," who, after 10 years as a frustrated reporter/writer, moves to the remote and untamed Everglades. There she meets colorful local characters and receives the inspiration to write numerous bestsellers. Well acted though overtly sentimental at times. **115m/C VHS, Beta.** Mary Steenburgen, Rip Torn, Peter Coyote, Dana Hill, Alfre Woodard, Malcolm McDowell; **D:** Martin Ritt; **C:** John A. Alonzo. Nominations: Academy Awards '83: Best Costume Design, Best Supporting Actor (Torn), Best Supporting Actress (Woodard), Best Original Score. *REP*

Cross Examination 🐾½ **1932** A boy is charged with his father's murder, and a defense attorney struggles to acquit him. **61m/B VHS, Beta, LV.** H.B. Warner, Sally Blane, Sarah Padden. *NO*

Cross Mission 🐾 **1989 (R)** Predictable actioner about a photographer and a soldier who are captured by the enemy. Packed with a bit of ninja, ammo, and occult. **90m/C VHS.** Richard Randall; **D:** Al Bradley.

Cross My Heart 🐾🐾 **1988 (R)** Light comedy about two single people with complicated, post-divorce lives who go on a date and suffer accordingly. Will true love prevail? **91m/C VHS, Beta.** Martin Short, Annette O'Toole, Paul Reiser, Joanna Kerns; **D:** Armyan Bernstein; **W:** Armyan Bernstein; **M:** Bruce Broughton. *USH*

Cross My Heart 🐾🐾 **1991** A group of school children conspire to hide the death of one of the group's mothers. This will prevent his placement in the state orphanage. Interesting premise is blandly treated by Fansten. Child actors don't seem realistic, photography is without flair. In French with English subtitles. **?m/C VHS, Beta.** FR Sylvain Copans; **D:** Jacques Fansten. *FXL*

Cross of Iron 🐾🐾½ **1976 (R)** During WWII, two antagonistic German officers clash over personal ideals as well as strategy in combating the relentless Russian attack. Followed by "Breakthrough." **120m/C VHS, Beta.** James Coburn, Maximilian Schell, James Mason, David Warner, Senta Berger; **D:** Sam Peckinpah; **W:** Julius J. Epstein; **M:** Ernest Gold.

Crossbar 🐾🐾 **1979** Aaron Kornylo is determined to reach Olympic qualifications in the high jump despite having only one leg. Inspired by a true story, this program dramatically shows how far determination and work can take a person. **77m/C VHS, Beta.** John Ireland, Brent Carver, Kate Reid; **D:** John Trent. *TWE, BFA*

Crosscut 🐾 **1995 (R)** Mob hitman Martin Niconi (Mandylor) makes a mistake that could cost him his life when a barroom brawl leads him to shooting the son of a Mafia don. He escapes to a small California logging town, changes his identity, and falls for single mom Anna (Gallagher) but the mob manages to track him down. Big shootout. **CW:** Strong violence and language, and for some drug use and brief nudity. **90m/C VHS, LV.** Costas Mandylor, Megan Gallagher, Casey Sander, Allen Cutler, Zack Norman, George Murdock; **D:** Paul Raimondi; **W:** Paul Raimondi, David Masiel, Scott Phillips; **C:** David Bridges; **M:** Christopher Tyng. *APX*

Crossfire 🐾🐾🐾½ **1947** A Jewish hotel guest is murdered and three soldiers just back from Europe are suspected of the crime. The first Hollywood film that explored racial bigotry. Due to the radical nature of its plot, the director and the producer were eventually black-listed for promoting "un-American" themes. Loosely based on Richard Brooks' "The Brick Foxhole." **86m/B VHS, Beta.** Robert Young, Robert Mitchum, Robert Ryan, Gloria Grahame, Paul Kelly; **D:** Edward Dmytryk. Nominations: Academy Awards '47: Best Director (Dmytryk), Best Picture, Best Screenplay, Best Supporting Actor (Ryan), Best Supporting Actress (Grahame). *TTC*

Crossfire 🐾 *The Bandit* **1967 (PG)** Two bandits are almost hung in the midst of the Mexican revolution. Released in the U.S. in 1979. **82m/C VHS, Beta.** MX Robert Conrad, Jan-Michael Vincent, Manuel Lopez Ochoa, Roy Jenson; **D:** Robert Conrad, Alfredo Zacharias.

Crossfire 🐾🐾 **1989 (R)** A rescue team heads to Vietnam to pick up their MIA comrades. With no help from the government and the enemy at every turn, can they possibly succeed? **99m/C VHS, LV.** Richard Norton, Michael Meyer, Daniel Dietrich, Don Pemrick, Eric Hahn, Wren Brown, Steve Young; **D:** Anthony Maharaj; **W:** Noah Blough. *NO*

The Crossing 🐾🐾 **1992 (R)** Powerful coming-of-age story with which Meg, a sheltered young woman, falls in love with an ambitious artist named Sam. When he decides to leave their small town to pursue his career, she turns to his best friend for comfort and companionship. However, when Sam unexpectedly returns, Meg is forced to make a choice that could drastically change all of their lives. *CW:* Language and sensuality. 92m/C VHS, LV, **Closed Caption.** *AU* Russell Crowe, Danielle Spencer, Robert Mammone; *W:* Ranald Allan; *M:* Martin Armiger. *REP*

Crossing Delancey 🎦🎦🎦 1988 (PG)

Jewish woman (Bozyk), in old world style, plays matchmaker to her independent 30-something granddaughter. Charming modern-day New York City fairy tale deftly manipulates cliches and stereotypes. Lovely performance from Irving as the woman whose heart surprises her. Riegert is swell playing the gentle but never wimpy suitor. Perfectly cast Bozyk was a star on the Yiddish vaudeville stage; this is her film debut. Appealing music by the Roches, with Suzzy Roche giving a credible performance as Irving's friend. Adapted for the big screen by Sandler from her play of the same name. 97m/C VHS, Beta, LV, 8mm, **Closed Caption.** Amy Irving, Reizl Bozyk, Peter Riegert, Jeroen Krabbe, Sylvia Miles, Suzzy Roche, George Martin, John Bedford Lloyd, Rosemary Harris, Amy Wright, Claudia Silver, David Hyde Pierce; *D:* Joan Micklin Silver; *W:* Susan Sandler. *WAR, FCT, HMV*

The Crossing Guard 🎦🎦🎦 1994 (R)

Nicholson headlines as Freddy Gale, a revenge-minded father who hunts down a drunk driver (Morse), who killed his daughter five years previous. Story focuses on dual emotions of the two men: Gale seeks an end to his grief and rage; Booth attempts to deal with guilt and regret. Writer Penn pairs one-time lovers Nicholson and Huston (playing ex-spouses here) in his sophomore directorial effort with explosive results. Focus is, accordingly, on emotional performances while narrative and directorial finesse take a back seat. Dedicated to the late chronicler of the curbside, Charles Bukowski. *CW:* Sexuality and strong language. 111m/C VHS, LV, **Closed Caption.** Jack Nicholson, Anjelica Huston, David Morse, Robin Wright Penn, Robbie Robertson, Piper Laurie, Richard Bradford, John Savage, Priscilla Barnes, Kari Wuhrer, Jennifer Leigh Warren, Richard Sarafian, Jeff Morris, Joe Viterelli, Eileen Ryan, Ryo Ishibashi, Michael Ryan, Nicky Blair, Gene Kirkwood, Jason Kristofer, Hadda Brooks; *D:* Sean Penn; *W:* Sean Penn; *C:* Vilmos Zsigmond; *M:* Jack Nitzsche. Nominations: Golden Globe Awards '96: Best Supporting Actress (Huston); Independent Spirit Awards '96: Best Supporting Actor (Morse); Screen Actors Guild Award '95: Best Supporting Actress (Huston). *TOU*

Crossing the Bridge 🎦🎦 1992 (R)

An after high-school tale of three buddies and their restless lives as they take their uncertain steps towards adulthood. It's 1975 in Detroit and Mort, Danny, and Tim cling to high-school memories as they pass time on petty jobs, drinking, and cruising across the Ambassador Bridge to check out the Canadian strip joints. Their big moment—for better or worse—comes when they are offered the chance to make a lot of quick cash if they'll smuggle hash from Toronto to Detroit. Directorial debut of Binder. *CW:* Language and drug use. 105m/C VHS, Beta, LV, **Closed Caption.** Josh Charles, Jason Gedrick, Stephen Baldwin, Cheryl Pollak, Jeffrey Tambor; *D:* Mike Binder; *W:* Mike Binder. *TOU*

Crossing the Line 🎦 1990 (R)

Two motocross racers battle it out for the championship. 90m/C VHS, Beta, LV. Jon Stafford, Rick Hearst, Paul Smith, Cameron Mitchell, Vernon Wells, Colleen Morris, John Saxon; *D:* Gary Graver. *COL*

Crossover 🎦½ 1982 (R)

A devoted male nurse works the graveyard shift in the psychiatric ward and neglects his personal life. 96m/C VHS, Beta. James Coburn, Kate Nelligan; *D:* John Guillermin. *VES, ART*

Crossover Dreams 🎦🎦½ 1985

Actor and musician Blades moves this old story along. Sure that he has at last made the international Big Time, a salsa artist becomes a self-important back-stabber after cutting an album. Great music. Blades's first film. ♫Good For Baby; Liz's Theme; Sin Fe; Todos Vuelven; Libra Timbero; Elegua; Merecumbe; Judy, Part 2; Yiri Yiri Bon. 86m/C VHS, Beta. Ruben Blades, Shawn Elliott, Elizabeth Pena, Virgilio

Marti, Tom Signorelli, Frank Robico, Joel Diamond, Amanda Barber, John Hammil; *D:* Leon Ichaso; *W:* Ruben Blades, Leon Ichaso, Manuel Arce; *M:* Mauricio Smith. *CNG*

Crossroads 🎦🎦½ 1986 (R)

A blues-loving young white man, classically trained at Juilliard, befriends an aging black blues-master. After helping the old man escape from the nursing home, the two hop trains to the South where it's literally a duel with the devil. Fine performances by Macchio, Gertz, Seneca, and Morton. Wonderful score by Ry Cooder, with some help from Steve Vai in the final showdown. 100m/C VHS, Beta, LV, **Closed Caption.** Ralph Macchio, Joe Seneca, Jami Gertz, Joe Morton, Robert Judd, Harry Carey Jr., Steve Vai; *D:* Walter Hill; *W:* John Fusco; *C:* John Bailey; *M:* Steve Vai, Ry Cooder. *COL*

Crossworlds 🎦🎦 1996 (PG-13)

All dimensions of the universe collide in the mystical valley of Crossworlds. When alien night riders attack Joe Talbolt (Charles), he escapes with girlfriend Laura (Roth) and they meet up with mercenary A.T. (Hauer). Turns out the crystal pendant Joe's father left him is one of the keys that unlock the boundaries between the worlds. Along with a scepter, they give the owner unlimited power. So the trio enter Crossworlds to fight a battle between good and evil. *CW:* Action violence and brief strong language. 91m/C VHS, LV, **Closed Caption.** Rutger Hauer, Josh Charles, Andrea Roth, Stuart Wilson; *D:* Krishna Rao; *W:* Raman Rao, Krishna Rao; *M:* Christophe Beck. *THV*

The Crow 🎦🎦½ 1993 (R)

Revenge-fantasy finds Eric Draven (Lee) resurrected on Devil's Night, a year after his death, in order to avenge his own murder and that of his girlfriend. 90% of the scenes are at night, in the rain, or both, and it's not easy to tell what's going on (a blessing considering the violence level). Very dark, but with good performances, particularly from Lee, in his last role before an unfortunate on set accident caused his death. That footage has been destroyed, but use of a stunt double and camera trickery allowed for the movie's completion. Film was dedicated to Lee and his fiance Eliza. Based on the comic strip by James O'Barr. The video release includes Brandon Lee's final interview. 100m/C VHS, LV, **Closed Caption.** Brandon Lee, Ernie Hudson, Michael Wincott, David Patrick Kelly, Rochelle Davis, Angel David, Michael Massee, Bai Ling, Lawrence Mason, Bill Raymond, Marco Rodriguez, Anna Thomson, Sofia Shinas, Jon Polito, Tony Todd; *D:* Alex Proyas; *W:* David J. Schow, John Shirley; *C:* Darius Wolski; *M:* Graeme Revell. MTV Movie Awards '95: Best Song ("Big Empty"); Nominations: MTV Movie Awards '95: Best Film, Best Male Performance (Lee). *TOU*

The Crow 2: City of Angels 🎦🎦

1996 (R) James O'Barr's cult graphic-novel "hero" returns in a new incarnation. It's eight years later (in film time) and the setting's changed from Detroit to L.A. but the horror remains. Ashe (Perez) and his young son witness a murder and are killed themselves by scumbags working for drug lord Judah (Brooks). So the Crow brings back Ashe to get revenge. Also involved is Sarah (Kirshner), who retains her role as story narrator but is now a grown-up tattoo artist who falls in love with Ashe. Lots of kink and flash—no substance—and confusing as well. The eerie sepia-toned look is created with sodium lighting. *CW:* Strong violence, drug content, language and sexuality. 93m/C VHS, LV, **Closed Caption.** Vincent Perez, Mia Kirshner, Iggy Pop, Richard Brooks, Ian Dury, Thuy Trang, Thomas Jane, Vincent Castellanos, Tracey Ellis; *D:* Tim Pope; *W:* David S. Goyer; *C:* Jean-Yves Escoffier; *M:* Graeme Revell. *TOU*

Crow Hollow 🎦🎦 1952

A Victorian mansion inhabited by three whacko sisters is the site of a murder committed in an attempt to cash in on an inheritance. When a young woman investigates, eyebrows are raised. 69m/B VHS, Beta. GB Donald Houston, Nastasha Parry, Nora Nicholson, Esma Cannon, Melissa Stribling; *D:* Michael McCarthy. *SNC, RXM*

The Crowd 🎦🎦🎦🎦 1928

A look at the day-to-day trials of a working-class family set against the backdrop of wealthy society. True-to-life, it's peppered with some happy moments, too. One of the best silent films. Available on laserdisc as a double feature with another '20s classic, "The Wind." 104m/B VHS, Beta, LV. Eleanor Boardman, James Murray, Bert Roach, Daniel G. Tomlinson, Dell Henderson, Lucy Beaumont; *D:* King Vidor. National Film Registry '89;; Nominations: Academy Awards '28: Best Director (Vidor). *MGM*

Crows and Sparrows 🎦🎦🎦 *Wuya Yu Maque* 1949

Poor tenants of a Shanghai boardinghouse are about to lose their home when their greedy landlord decides to sell and move to Taiwan. But the advancing Red Army causes a change in plans and they're saved! Sounds politically turgid but isn't, thanks to naturalistic acting and dialog. Completed just before the revolution, the film was censored by the Nationalist Kuomintang government but cuts were restored when the Communists came to power. Mandarin with subtitles. 108m/B VHS. CH Zhao Dan, Wu Yin, Wei Heling, Sun Dao-Lin, Li Tianji, Ouyang Yunzhu; *D:* Zheng Junli; *W:* Zhao Dan, Zheng Junli; *C:* Miao Zhenhua, Hu Zhenhua; *M:* Wang Yunjie. *HTV, FCT*

The Crucible 🎦🎦🎦 *The Witches of Salem* 1957

Signoret is outstanding in this version of Arthur Miller's play about the Salem witch trials in 17th-century New England. Miller's depiction of witch hunts was written as a searing commentary on McCarthyism and the anti-communist panic that swept America in the 1950s. Film was made in France because Miller was blacklisted in America and blackballed by Hollywood at the time. In French with English subtitles. 108m/B VHS. FR Simone Signoret, Yves Montand, Mylene Demongeot, Jean Debucourt; *D:* Raymond Rouleau; *W:* Jean-Paul Sartre. *HTV*

The Crucible 🎦🎦🎦 1996 (PG-13)

Mass hysteria reigns in 17th century Salem, Mass., when a group of teenaged girls, caught performing heathen rituals in the woods, concoct an elaborate story to exonerate themselves by whipping the town into a witch-hunting frenzy. Chief liar is Abigail Williams (Ryder), who was cast aside by married farmer John Proctor (Day-Lewis), for whom she still lusts. The deranged lass puts her dubious talents into getting Proctor's wife (Allen) out of the picture. Director Hytner demanded authentic period reproduction, down to the finest detail. Impressive cast does justice to the story, especially Scofield's delightfully odious Judge Danforth. Based on Miller's 1953 play which, not so coincidentally, opened during the communist witch hunts of the early 1950s. Screenwriter Miller willingly slashed dialogue from his original work for cinematic purposes. Filmed at the remote wildlife sanctuary of Hog Island, Massachusetts. *CW:* Intense depiction of the Salem witch trials. 123m/C VHS, LV, **Closed Caption.** Daniel Day-Lewis, Winona Ryder, Paul Scofield, Joan Allen, Bruce Davison, Jeffrey Jones, Rob Campbell, Peter Vaughan, Karron Graves, Charlaine Woodard, Frances Conroy, Elizabeth Lawrence, George Gaynes; *D:* Nicholas Hytner; *W:* Arthur Miller; *C:* Andrew Dunn; *M:* George Fenton. British Academy Awards '96: Best Supporting Actor (Scofield); Broadcast Film Critics Association Awards '96: Best Supporting Actress (Allen); Nominations: Academy Awards '96: Best Adapted Screenplay, Best Supporting Actress (Allen); British Academy Awards '96: Best Adapted Screenplay; Golden Globe Awards '97: Best Supporting Actor (Scofield), Best Supporting Actress (Allen). *FXV*

Crucible of Horror 🎦🎦 *Velvet House; The Corpse* 1969

Chilling story of a terrorized wife, who, along with her daughter, plots to murder her sadistic husband to end his abusive treatment of them. However, he isn't yet ready to die and comes back to drive them mad. 91m/C VHS, Beta. GB Michael Gough, Yvonne Mitchell, Sharon Gurney, David Butler, Simon Gough, Nicholas Jones, Olaf Pooley, Mary Hignett; *D:* Viktors Ritelis; *W:* Olaf Pooley; *C:* John Mackey. *MGM, FCT*

Crucible of Terror woof! 1972 Mad sculptor covers beautiful models with hot wax, then imprisons them in a mold of bronze. **95m/C VHS, Beta.** *GB* Mike Raven, Mary Maude, James Bolam, John Arnatt, Ronald Lacey, Judy Matheson, Me Me Lay, Melissa Stribling, Beth Morris; *D:* Ted Hooker; *W:* Ted Hooker, Tom Parkinson; *C:* Peter Newbrook. *MRV, GEM*

The Crucifer of Blood ✗✗½ 1991 A disappointing Sherlock Holmes yarn, made for cable TV. Heston is adequate as the Baker Street sleuth, but the mystery—about two retired British soldiers who share an accursed secret and a vengeful comrade—unreels clumsily in the form of flashbacks that give away most of the puzzle from the start. Interesting only in that Dr. Watson has a love affair, more or less. Adapted from a play (and looking like it) by Paul Giovanni, inspired by Arthur Conan Doyle's "The Sign of Four." **105m/C VHS, Beta, Closed Caption.** Charlton Heston, Richard Johnson, Susannah Harker, John Castle, Clive Wood, Simon Callow, Edward Fox; *D:* Fraser Heston. *TTC*

The Crucified Lovers ✗✗✗½ *Chikamatsu Monogatari* 1954 A shy scrollmaker falls in love with his master's wife. Excellent Japanese tragedy with fine performances all around. **100m/B VHS.** *JP* Kazuo Hasegawa, Kyoko Kagawa, Yoko Minamida, Eitaro Shindo, Sakae Ozawa; *D:* Kenji Mizoguchi. *FCT*

The Crude Oasis ✗✗½ 1995 (R) Shot in 14 days on a $25,000 budget, producer/writer/director Graves' debut is an aggressively moody suspenser. Karen (Taylor) is a neglected, suicidal Kansas housewife who is haunted by dreams of a mystery man. He turns up in the form of Shields, the pump jockey at a local gas station. Obsessed by the stranger, Karen begins following him, leading to situations paralleling her dream. Adept at setting up an atmosphere of small-town menace and constructing a plot with surprising twists and turns, Graves can't quite deliver the payoff required.*CW:* Language. **82m/C VHS, Beta, Closed Caption.** Jennifer Taylor, Aaron Shields, Robert Peterson, Mussef Sibay, Lynn Bieler, Roberta Eaton; *D:* Alex Graves; *W:* Alex Graves; *C:* Steven Quale. *PAR*

Cruel Sea ✗✗✗ 1953 Well-made documentary-like account of a Royal Navy corvette on convoy duty in the Atlantic during WWII. **121m/B VHS, Beta.** *GB* Jack Hawkins, Stanley Baker, Denholm Elliott, Virginia McKenna; *D:* Charles Frend. Nominations: Academy Awards '53: Best Screenplay. *REP, BMV, HMV*

The Cruel Story of Youth ✗✗✗ *Seishun Zanoku Monogatari; Naked Youth; A Story of the Cruelties of Youth* 1960 A teenage girl and her criminal boyfriend use sex to get money out of rich, middle-aged men in this controversial look at the disillusionment of youth and the breaking of old values and traditions in Japan after WWII. In Japanese with English subtitles. **96m/C VHS.** *JP* Yusuke Kawazu, Miyuki Kuwano, Yoshiko Kuga; *D:* Nagisa Oshima; *W:* Nagisa Oshima. *NYF*

Cruise into Terror woof! 1978 A sarcophagus brought aboard a pleasure cruise ship unleashes an evil force that slowly starts to kill off the ship's passengers, most of whom likely thought they were on the Love Boat. Made for television. **100m/C VHS, Beta.** Ray Milland, Hugh O'Brian, John Forsythe, Christopher George, Dirk Benedict, Frank Converse, Lynda Day George, Stella Stevens; *D:* Bruce Kessler.

Cruise Missile ✗ 1978 Unique task force is on a mission to keep the world from nuclear holocaust. **100m/C VHS, Beta.** Peter Graves, Curt Jurgens, Michael Dante; *D:* Ted V. Mikels. *NO*

Cruisin' High ✗ 1975 (R) Two city street gangs battle it out. **109m/C VHS, Beta.** David Kyle, Kelly Yaegermann, Rhodes Reason. *VES, ART*

Cruising ✗✗ 1980 (R) Rookie cop Pacino is deep undercover investigating the bizarre murders of homosexuals in New York's West Village. Sexually explicit but less than suspenseful mystery. Release was sensationalized, with many gay rights groups voicing loud disapproval of the sor-

did gay characterization, while others feared copy-cat crimes. Excellent NYC cinematography. **102m/C VHS, Beta.** Al Pacino, Paul Sorvino, Karen Allen, Powers Boothe; *D:* William Friedkin; *W:* William Friedkin; *M:* Jack Nitzsche. *WAR*

Crumb ✗✗✗½ 1994 (R) Countercultural documentary looking at the life of underground cartoonist Robert Crumb—'60s satirist and social misfit who created such drug and sex characters as Fritz the Cat and Mr. Natural. Crumb's extraordinarily dysfunctional family play a significant role, with his mother and two brothers, elder brother Charles and younger brother Max, also interviewed as well as Crumb's friends and current and former wives. The dead abusive father also plays a part. Director Zwigoff spent six years filming his material, and gained wider distribution for his work after taking the Grand Jury prize at Sundance.*CW:* Graphic sex-related cartoons; language. **119m/C VHS, LV, Closed Caption.** *D:* Terry Zwigoff. Directors Guild of America Awards '95: Best Feature Documentary (Zwigoff); National Society of Film Critics Awards '95: Best Feature Documentary; Sundance Film Festival '95: Best Cinematography, Grand Jury Prize. *COL*

The Crusades ✗✗½ 1935 Typical DeMille extravaganza, loosely based on the Third Crusade, which finds Richard the Lionheart (Wilcoxon) and the armies of Europe battling Saladin and the Mahommedan horde in order to reclaim Jerusalem. Meanwhile, Richard marries by proxy in order to gain supplies for his men—something that enrages his bride Berengaria (Young). Once he realizes how beautiful she is, Richard tries to win her love. Obviously, not historically accurate and it's all secondary to the battle scenes, anyway. Based on the Harold Lamb book "The Crusade: Iron Men and Saints." **126m/B VHS, Closed Caption.** Henry Wilcoxon, Loretta Young, Sir C. Aubrey Smith, Ian Keith, Katherine DeMille, Joseph Schildkraut, Alan Hale, C. Henry Gordon, George Barbier, Lumsden Hare, William Farnum, Hobart Bosworth, Montagu Love, Pedro de Cordoba, Mischa Auer; *D:* Cecil B. DeMille; *W:* Waldemar Young, Dudley Nichols, Harold Lamb; *C:* Victor Milner; *M:* Rudolph Kopp. Nominations: Academy Awards '35: Best Cinematography. *USH*

The Crush ✗✗½ 1993 (R) Wealthy 14-year-old temptress Silverstone (in her debut) develops an obsessive crush on handsome 28-year-old Elwes, who rents her family's guest house. In an attempt to win his heart, she rewrites his poorly composed magazine articles. This doesn't convince him they should mate for life, so she sabotages his apartment to vent her rage. Sound familiar? The plot's lifted right out of "Fatal Attraction" and Shapiro doesn't offer viewers anything inventively different. He does manage to substitute new methods for the spurned lover to snare her prey. Limp plot would have been exciting if we hadn't seen it so many times before.*CW:* Language and terror violence. **89m/C VHS, Beta, LV, Letterbox, Closed Caption.** Cary Elwes, Alicia Silverstone, Jennifer Rubin, Kurtwood Smith, Gwynyth Walsh, Amber Benson; *D:* Alan Shapiro; *W:* Alan Shapiro; *M:* Graeme Revell. MTV Movie Awards '94: Breakthrough Performance (Silverstone), Best Villain (Silverstone). *WAR*

Crush ✗✗ 1993 Christina is a local New Zealand literary critic on her way to interview Colin, a reclusive novelist. Along for the ride is her seductive American friend Lane who manages to crash the car but walk away with hardly a scratch. Christina appears to be dead and Lane abandons her, finding her way to the home Colin shares with his teenage daughter Angela. Lane promptly sets out to seduce Colin, making Angela jealous, (oh, and Christina's not dead after all). Poor script finds the characters actions baffling and why Lane is so wildly attractive is never apparent. **97m/C VHS.** *NZ* Marcia Gay Harden, Donough Rees, William Zappa, Caitlin Bossley; *D:* Alison Maclean; *W:* Alison Maclean, Anne Kennedy. *FXL, ORI*

Crusoe ✗✗½ 1989 (PG-13) A lushly photographed version of the Daniel Defoe classic. Crusoe is an arrogant slave trader stranded on a desert island populated by unfriendly natives. Themes of prejudice, fear, and choice appear in this never-padded, thoughtful film. Quinn gives an excellent performance as the stranded slave-trader. **94m/C VHS, Beta, LV.** Aidan Quinn, Ade Sapara, Jimmy Nail, Timothy Spall, Colin Bruce, Michael Higgins, Shane Rimmer, Hepburn Grahame; *D:* Caleb Deschanel; *W:* Walon Green, Christopher Logue; *M:* Michael Kamen. *NO*

Cry-Baby ✗✗✗ 1990 (PG-13) An homage and spoof of '50s teen-rock melodramas by the doyen of cinematic Bad Taste, involving a terminal bad-boy high schooler who goes with a square blond and starts an inter-class rumble. Musical numbers, throwaway gags and plenty of knee-bending to Elvis, with a weak story supported by offbeat celeb appearances. **85m/C VHS, Beta, LV, Closed Caption.** Johnny Depp, Amy Locane, Polly Bergen, Traci Lords, Ricki Lake, Iggy Pop, Susan Tyrrell, Patty Hearst, Kim McGuire, Darren E. Burrows, Troy Donahue, Willem Dafoe, David Nelson, Mink Stole, Joe Dallesandro, Joey Heatherton, Robert Walsh; *D:* John Waters; *W:* John Waters; *M:* Patrick Williams. *USH*

Cry Danger ✗✗✗ 1951 A falsely imprisoned man is released from jail, and he searches for those who framed him. **80m/B VHS.** Dick Powell, Rhonda Fleming, William Conrad, Richard Erdman; *D:* Robert Parrish; *C:* Joseph Biroc. *REP*

A Cry for Love ✗✗ 1980 An amphetamine addict and an alcoholic meet, fall in love, and help each other recover. Based on the best seller by Jill Schary Robinson, "Bedtime Story." **96m/C VHS, Beta.** Susan Blakely, Powers Boothe, Gene Barry, Charles Siebert, Herb Edelman, Fern Fitzgerald, Lainie Kazan; *D:* Paul Wendkos.

Cry Freedom ✗✗½ 1987 (PG) A romantic look at the short life of South African activist Steven Biko, and his friendship with the white news editor, Donald Woods. The film focuses on Woods' escape from Africa while struggling to bring Biko's message to the world. Based on a true story. **157m/C VHS, Beta, LV.** Kevin Kline, Denzel Washington, Penelope Wilton, Kevin McNally, John Thaw, Timothy West, John Hargreaves, Alec McCowen, Zakes Mokae, Ian Richardson, Juanita Waterman; *D:* Richard Attenborough; *W:* John Briley; *M:* George Fenton, Jonas Gwangwa. Nominations: Academy Awards '87: Best Song ("Cry Freedom"), Best Supporting Actor (Washington), Best Original Score. *USH, KUI, FCT*

A Cry from the Mountain ✗ 1985 (PG) Heavily religious film about a father and son who go on a kayak trip through Alaska's wilderness so the father can break the news of his impending divorce. A series of events occurs that change their lives, and they meet a mysterious mountain man who relies on his faith in God to get by in the wilderness. Features an appearance by Rev. Billy Graham. **78m/C VHS, Beta, LV.** James Cavan, Wes Parker, Rita Walter, Chris Kidd, Coleen Gray, Jerry Ballew, Allison Argo, Glen Alsworth, Myrna Kidd; *D:* James F. Collier. *ART*

A Cry from the Streets ✗✗ 1957 Drama about the plight of orphan children and dedicated social workers in England. **100m/C VHS.** *GB* Max Bygraves, Barbara Murray, Kathleen Harrison, Colin Petersen; *D:* Lewis Gilbert; *M:* Larry Adler. *FCT*

A Cry in the Dark ✗✗✗½ *Evil Angels* 1988 (PG-13) Tight film story of the infamous Australian murder trial of Lindy Chamberlain, who was accused of killing her own baby, mostly because of the intensely adverse public opinion, aroused by vicious press, that surrounded the case. Chamberlain blamed the death on a wild dingo dog. Near-documentary style, with Streep excellent as the religious, unknowable mother. Based on the book "Evil Angels" by John Bryson. This case was also detailed in the film "Who Killed Baby Azaria?" **120m/C VHS, Beta, LV, 8mm, Closed Caption.** *AU* Meryl Streep, Sam Neill, Bruce Myles, Charles Tingwell, Nick Tate, Neil Fitzpatrick, Maurice Fields,

Lewis Fitz-gerald; *D:* Fred Schepisi; *W:* Fred Schepisi, Robert Caswell; *C:* Ian Baker; *M:* Bruce Smeaton. Australian Film Institute '89: Best Actor (Neill), Best Actress (Streep), Best Film; Cannes Film Festival '89: Best Actress (Streep); New York Film Critics Awards '88: Best Actress (Streep); Nominations: Academy Awards '88: Best Actress (Streep). *WAR, FCT*

A Cry in the Night 🎬🎬½ 1993 (PG-13) After Jenny (Higgins Clark) marries an internationally acclaimed artist, she thinks her life is complete. However, once she and her two daughters move into his country estate, her life takes a tragic turn as she's haunted by the mysterious deaths of her ex-husband and newborn child. King plays the new husband who turns out to have a few psychological quirks of his own. Based on the bestselling novel by Mary Higgins Clark. Actress Higgins Clark is the novelist's daughter. Made for television.*CW:* Violence. 99m/C VHS, Closed Caption. Perry King, Carol Higgins Clark; *D:* Robin Spry; *W:* Robin Spry. *REP*

A Cry in the Wild 🎬🎬🎬 1990 (PG) A 14-year-old boy must find his way back to civilization when he's the lone survivor of an airplane crash. Strong acting from Rushton, excellent nature photography make this well used story work again. 93m/C VHS, Closed Caption. Jared Rushton, Ned Beatty, Pamela Sue Martin, Stephen Meadows; *D:* Mark Griffiths; *W:* Catherine Cyran. *MGM*

Cry of a Prostitute: Love Kills 🎬 1972 (R) Former prostitute joins with a professional assassin in an effort to pacify rival gangsters in Italy. 86m/C VHS, Beta. Henry Silva, Barbara Bouchet; *D:* Andrew Bianchi.

Cry of Battle 🎬🎬½ *To Be a Man* 1963 Anxious for the challenges of manhood, a well-heeled young man joins a guerrilla militia in the Philippines. 99m/B VHS, Beta. Van Heflin, Rita Moreno, James MacArthur; *D:* Irving Lerner. *MRV, FGF, BMV*

Cry of the Banshee 🎬🎬½ 1970 (PG) Witch-hunter Price and family are tormented by Satanic powers seeking revenge. Superior horror period piece. Also available with "Count Yorga, Vampire" on Laserdisc. 87m/C VHS, Beta. *GB* Vincent Price, Elisabeth Bergner, Essy Persson, Hugh Griffith, Hilary Dwyer, Sally Geeson, Patrick Mower, Marshall Jones, Michael Elphick, Pamela Fairbrother, Robert Hutton; *D:* Gordon Hessler; *W:* Christopher Wicking, Tim Kelly; *C:* John Coquillon; *M:* Les Baxter. *HBO*

Cry of the Innocent 🎬🎬🎬 1980 An action-packed thriller about a Vietnam veteran who is out to find a group of Irish terrorists that killed his family. 93m/C VHS, Beta. Cyril Cusack, Alexander Knox, Rod Taylor, Joanna Pettet, Nigel Davenport; *D:* Michael O'Herlihy. *NO*

The Cry of the Owl 🎬🎬 *Le Cri du Hibou* 1992 Robert (Malavoy) has divorced the dreadful Veronique (Thevenet) and struck up a friendship with Juliette (May). He admires the way her life seems so satisfied and orderly but Juliette decides she doesn't like this idea of herself and impulsively drops her swinish fiance Patrick (Penot) and pursues Robert instead. But Robert is only interested in friendship, leading to some very twisted revenge plots. Suspenseful look at what obsessions can drive people to do. Adapted from the novel by Patricia Highsmith. In French with English subtitles. 102m/C VHS. *FR IT* Christophe MaLavoy, Mathilda May, Virginie Thevenet, Jacques Penot, Jean-Pierre Kalfon, Patrice Kerbrat; *D:* Claude Chabrol; *W:* Claude Chabrol, Odile Barski; *M:* Matthieu Chabrol. *CVC*

Cry of the Penguins 🎬🎬½ *Mr. Forbush and the Penguins* 1971 Womanizing biologist Forbush (Hurt) heads off on an Antartic expedition to study penguins when his would-be romance with Tara (Mills) comes to naught. Beautiful photography, shallow story. Adapted from the novel "Mr. Forbush and the Penguins" by Graham Billing. Note the similarities with "Never Cry Wolf." 105m/ C VHS. *GB* John Hurt, Hayley Mills, Dudley Sutton, Tony Britton, Thorley Walters, Judy Campbell, Joss Ackland, Nicholas Pennell; *D:* Albert T. Viola; *W:* Anthony Shaffer; *M:* John Addison. *TVC*

Cry of the Werewolf 🎬🎬 1944 A beautiful New Orleans gypsy protects her mother's mummified remains by periodically turning into a werewolf and killing people. 63m/B VHS. Nina Foch, Stephen Crane, Osa Massen, Blanche Yurka, Barton MacLane, Ivan Triesault, John Abbott, Fritz Leiber; *D:* Henry Levin; *W:* Charles "Blackie" O'Neal. *MOV*

Cry Panic 🎬🎬 1974 A man is thrown into a strange series of events after accidentally running down a man on a highway. Made for television. 74m/C VHS, Beta. John Forsythe, Anne Francis, Earl Holliman, Claudia McNeil, Ralph Meeker; *D:* James Goldstone.

Cry Terror 🎬🎬 1974 Two escaped convicts take two beautiful women hostage hoping to gain their own freedom. Only a quick-thinking undercover police officer can save the girls. Made for television. 71m/C VHS, Beta. *GB* Bob Hoskins, Susan Hampshire, Gabrielle Drake. *NO*

Cry, the Beloved Country 🎬🎬🎬½ *African Fury* 1951 A black country minister travels to Johannesberg to be with his son after the youth is accused of killing a white man. Through the events of the trial, the horror, oppression, and destruction of South Africa's apartheid system are exposed. Startling and moving, the first entertainment feature set against the backdrop of apartheid. Still trenchant; based on the novel by Alan Paton. 111m/B VHS. *GB* Canada Lee, Charles Carson, Sidney Poitier, Joyce Carey, Geoffrey Keen; *D:* Zoltan Korda; *W:* John Howard Lawson, Alan Paton; *C:* Robert Krasker. *MON, FCT*

Cry, the Beloved Country 🎬🎬🎬 1995 (PG-13) Alan Paton's classic South African apartheid novel (first filmed in 1951) depicts a Zulu Christian pastor and a wealthy white farmer finding common ground through personal loss—both of their sons were killed in regional violence. Rural black minister Stephen Kumalo (Jones), travels to Johannesburg only to discover his sister (Kente) is a prostitute, his younger brother John (Dutton) no longer believes in Christianity and his son is in prison for the murder of a white man. That man turns out to be the son of rich farmer James Jarvis (Harris), from Kumalo's own village. Both Jones and Harris turn in wonderfully understated performances in this hopeful tale of potential racial harmony.*CW:* Emotional thematic elements and brief language. 120m/C VHS, LV, Closed Caption. *SA* James Earl Jones, Charles S. Dutton, Leleti Khumalo, Dambisa Kente, Vusi Kunene, Eric Miyeni, Ian Robers; *D:* Darrell Roodt; *W:* Ronald Atwood; *C:* Paul Gilpin; *M:* John Barry. Nominations: Screen Actors Guild Award '95: Best Actor (Jones).*TOU*

Cry Uncle 🎬½ 1971 (R) Comic account of a private eye who investigates a blackmailing case involving a film of orgies in which, much to his chagrin, he participated. 85m/C VHS. Allen (Goorwitz) Garfield, Paul Sorvino, Devin Goldenberg, Madeleine Le Roux; *D:* John G. Avildsen; *W:* David Odell; *C:* John G. Avildsen. *TTV*

Cry Vengeance 🎬🎬½ 1954 A falsely imprisoned detective gets out of jail and searches for the people who framed him and killed his family. 83m/B VHS, Beta. Mark Stevens, Joan Vohs, Martha Hyer, Skip Homeier; *D:* Mark Stevens. *REP*

Cry Wolf 🎬🎬 1947 Weak mystery thriller places Stanwyck in creepy environs when she goes to claim her inheritance from her late husband's estate. Based on the novel by Marjorie Carleton. 83m/B VHS. Errol Flynn, Barbara Stanwyck, Richard Basehart, Geraldine Brooks, Jerome Cowan, John Ridgely, Patricia White; *D:* Peter Godfrey; *W:* Catherine Turney. *MGM*

The Crying Child 🎬½ 1996 (PG-13) Madeline Jeffreys (Hemingway) and her husband Ran (DelHoyo) retreat to their 19th-century island vacation cottage after the stillbirth of their first child. Madeline begins to hear a child crying in the house and sees a ghostly apparition—now she has to discover what the spirit wants (and convince everyone she's not just going crazy). TV movie based on the novel by Barbara Mi-

chaels.*CW:* Supernatural terror and thematic elements. 93m/C VHS, Closed Caption. Mariel Hemingway, George DelHoyo, Finola Hughes, Kin Shriner, Collin Wilcox Paxton; *D:* Robert Lewis; *W:* Rob Gilmer; *C:* Stephen Lighthill; *M:* Shirley Walker. *USH*

The Crying Game 🎬🎬🎬½ 1992 (R) PR lesson in how to launch a small movie into the hypersphere and ensure critical silence on salient characterization. Jordan's gritty drama is on par with his best, a complex blend of violence, love, betrayal, guilt, and redemption and is not about what it seems to be about much of the time. Wonderful performances by all, including Rea as the appealing, conscience-stricken Fergus; Richardson as the cold, violent IRA moll Jude; and Davidson, in a film debut, as the needy, charismatic Dil. Whitaker is terrific in his 15 minutes of intense screen time. Filled with definite surprises and unexpected pleasures. Title is taken from a top-5 British hit of 1964, three versions of which are heard.*CW:* Language, full frontal nudity, strong violence, and sexuality. 112m/C VHS, LV, Letterbox, Closed Caption, DVD. *IR* Stephen Rea, Jaye Davidson, Miranda Richardson, Forest Whitaker, Adrian Dunbar, Jim Broadbent, Ralph Brown, Breffini McKenna, Joe Savino, Birdie Sweeney, Andre Bernard; *D:* Neil Jordan; *W:* Neil Jordan; *C:* Ian Wilson; *M:* Anne Dudley. Academy Awards '92: Best Original Screenplay; Australian Film Institute '93: Best Foreign Film; Independent Spirit Awards '93: Best Foreign Film; Los Angeles Film Critics Association Awards '92: Best Foreign Film; New York Film Critics Awards '92: Best Screenplay, Best Supporting Actress (Richardson); National Society of Film Critics Awards '92: Best Actor (Rea); Writers Guild of America '92: Best Original Screenplay; Nominations: Academy Awards '92: Best Actor (Rea), Best Director (Jordan), Best Film Editing, Best Picture, Best Supporting Actor (Davidson). *ART, MOV, BTV*

Crypt of Dark Secrets 🎬 1976 (R) Vietnam veteran recovering from wounds in the Louisiana swamps encounters a friendly Indian spirit who saves him from death. 100m/C VHS, Beta. Maureen Chan, Ronald Tanet, Wayne Mack, Herbert G. Jahncke; *D:* Jack Weis. *NO*

Crypt of the Living Dead woof! 1973 (PG) An undead woman from the 13th century makes life miserable for visitors on Vampire Island. 75m/C VHS, Beta. Andrew Prine, Mark Damon, Teresa Gimpera, Patty Shepard, Francisco (Frank) Brana; *D:* Ray Danton. *NO*

Crystal Heart 🎬 1987 (R) A medically isolated songwriter with an incurable disease falls in love with a lovely rock singer. 103m/C VHS, Beta. Lee Curreri, Tawny Kitaen, Lloyd Bochner; *D:* Gil Bettman; *M:* Joel Goldsmith. *VTR*

Crystalstone 🎬🎬 1988 (PG) A wooden cross leads a pair of orphans on a dangerous search for the legendary Crystalstone. 103m/C VHS, Beta. Frank Grimes, Kamlesh Gupta, Laura Jane Goodwin, Sydney Bromley; *D:* Antonio Pelaez. *MCG*

Cthulhu Mansion woof! 1991 (R) The oldest-looking juvenile delinquents you've ever seen release evil spirits when they take over a magician's estate. Not very special effects and abominable dialogue; it claims to be based on H.P. Lovecraft stories, but that's a load of dung.*CW:* Language and horror violence/drug related scenes. 95m/C VHS, Closed Caption. Frank Finlay, Marcia Layton, Brad Fisher, Melanie Shatner, Luis Fernando Alves, Kaethe Cherney, Paul Birchard, Francisco (Frank) Brana; *D:* J. Piquer Simon; *W:* J. Piquer Simon. *REP*

Cuba 🎬🎬🎬 1979 (R) Cynical, satirical adventure/love story. Mercenary soldier rekindles an old affair during the Castro revolution. Charismatic cast and good direction make for an entertaining, if overlooked, Connery vehicle. 121m/C VHS, Beta. Sean Connery, Brooke Adams, Jack Weston, Hector Elizondo, Denholm Elliott, Chris Sarandon, Lonette McKee; *D:* Richard Lester; *W:* Charles Wood; *C:* David Watkin. *MGM, FOX*

Cujo 🐾🐾 1983 (R) A rabid dog goes berserk and attacks a mother and her child who are trapped inside a broken-down Pinto. Frighteningly realistic film is based on Stephen King's bestseller. **94m/C VHS, Beta, LV.** Dee Wallace Stone, Daniel Hugh-Kelly, Danny Pintauro, Ed Lauter, Christopher Stone, Kaiulani Lee, Mills Watson, Jerry Hardin, Billy Jacoby, Sandy Ward; **D:** Lewis Teague; **W:** Lauren Currier, Don Carlos Dunaway; **C:** Jan De Bont; **M:** Charles Bernstein. *WAR*

Cul de Sac 🐾🐾🐾 1966 A macabre, psychological thriller set in a dreary castle on a small island off the British coast. Pleasence is an eccentric, middle-aged hermit living acrimoniously with his young, nympho wife (Dorleac) when their home is invaded by two wounded gangsters (Stander and MacGowran), who proceed to hold the couple hostage. MacGowran soon dies of his wounds, leaving Stander and Pleasence to fight it out, encouraged by the luscious Dorleac, who finds her fun where she can. A bleak, sinister film considered one of Polanski's best. **111m/C VHS.** *GB* Donald Pleasence, Francoise Dorleac, Lionel Stander, Jack MacGowran, Jacqueline Bisset; **D:** Roman Polanski; **W:** Roman Polanski, Gerard Brach. *FCT*

Culpepper Cattle Co. 🐾🐾½ 1972 (PG) A young, starry-eyed yokel wants to be a cowboy and gets himself enlisted in a cattle drive, where he learns the harsh reality of the West. **92m/C VHS, Beta.** Gary Grimes, Billy Green Bush, Bo Hopkins, Charles Martin Smith, Geoffrey Lewis; **D:** Dick Richards; **M:** Jerry Goldsmith. *FOX*

Cult of the Cobra 🐾🐾 1955 Mysterious horror film that became minor camp classic. It seems ex-servicemen are being killed by exotic snake-lady Domergue. Cheesy film that can be fun. Based on a story by Jerry Davis. **75m/B VHS, Closed Caption.** Faith Domergue, Richard Long, Marshall Thompson, William Reynolds, Jack Kelly, Kathleen Hughes; **D:** Francis D. Lyon; **W:** Jerry Davis. *USH*

Cult People 🐾½ 1989 Interviews and film clips featuring a host of filmmaking's favorite cult personalities. **60m/C VHS.** Patrick Macnee, Cameron Mitchell, James Karen, Russ Meyer, Curtis Harrington, Waris Hussein, Michael Sarne. *FCT*

Cup Final 🐾🐾 *G'mar Giviya* 1992 The similarities and contradictions in war and sports, where passions and competition run high, are depicted in this emotional drama. Set in 1982 during Israel's invasion of Lebanon. Cohen is an Israeli soldier passionately interested in the World Cup soccer tournament. When he is taken prisoner by the PLO he discovers his captor Ziad shares his interest in the Italian national team. This common interest brings the two antagonists reluctantly together. In Hebrew and Arabic with English subtitles. **107m/C VHS.** *IS* Moshe Ivgi, Muhamad Bacri, Suheil Haddad; **D:** Eran Riklis; **W:** Eyal Halfon; **M:** Raviv Gazil. *FRF, BTV*

Cupid 🐾½ 1996 (R) Eric (Galligan) develops a deadly obsession for beautiful Jennifer (Laurence), who discovers that Jack and his equally crazy sister Dana (Crosby) have a nasty habit of killing the women that don't measure up to Jack's fantasies. **CW:** Language, violence, adult themes. **94m/C VHS, LV, Closed Caption.** Zach Galligan, Ashley Laurence, Mary Crosby, Joseph Kell, Michael Bowen; **D:** Doug Campbell; **W:** David Benullo; **C:** M. David Mullen. *ART*

Curdled 🐾🐾½ 1995 (R) And you thought your job sucked. Tarantino-funded dark comedy arouses interest with that tag line alone. Gore-obsessed Gabriela (Jones) gets her dream job cleaning up blood and guts with the Post-Forensic Cleaning Service and becomes obsessed with serial killer to the rich Paul (Baldwin), who is keeping her company hopping with one beheading after another. Cultishly violent pic culminates in a tango by the gruesome twosome around a murder scene. Tarantino spotted Jones, starring in Braddock's original student short, while touring with "Reservoir Dogs" and borrowed her for "Pulp Fiction," only to return the favor by exec producing

this interesting feature debut. Soundtrack adds spice to the formaldehyde flavor. **CW:** Violence/ gore, brief language. **87m/C VHS, LV, Closed Caption.** Angela Jones, William Baldwin, Mel Gorham, Barry Corbin, Bruce Ramsey, Daisy Fuentes, Lois Chiles, Carmen Lopez; **D:** Reb Braddock; **W:** John Maass, Reb Braddock; **C:** Steven Bernstein; **M:** Joseph Julian Gonzalez. *TOU*

The Cure 1917 Chaplin arrives at a spa to take a rest cure, accompanied by a trunk full of liquor that somehow gets dumped into the water at the resort. Silent with music track. **20m/B VHS, Beta.** Charlie Chaplin, Edna Purviance, Eric Campbell, Albert Austin; **D:** Charlie Chaplin. *VYY, GVV, CAB*

The Cure 🐾🐾½ 1995 (PG-13) Erik (Renfro), the neighborhood bad kid, befriends Dexter (Mazzello), a boy with AIDS. As Dexter's health weakens, Erik decides they must go on a quest for a cure, Huck Finn style, by floating along the Mississippi River to New Orleans. Despite film's preposterous plot, the performances of the two young leads do inspire a level of sentiment. **CW:** Emotional thematic elements, language. **99m/C VHS, LV, Closed Caption.** Brad Renfro, Joseph Mazzello, Annabella Sciorra, Diana Scarwid, Bruce Davison; **D:** Peter Horton; **W:** Robert Kuhn; **C:** Andrew Dintenfass; **M:** Dave Grusin. *USH*

Curfew 🐾🐾 1988 (R) A young woman rushes home so she doesn't break her curfew, only to find two killers with time on their hands waiting for her. Violent. **86m/C VHS, Beta, LV.** John Putch, Kyle Richards, William Wellman Jr., Bert Remsen; **D:** Gary Winick. *VTR*

The Curfew Breakers 🐾 1957 Dim teen-exploitation/message-movie finds a pair of community workers investigating the murder of a gas station attendent by a drug-crazed youth. **78m/B VHS.** Regis Toomey, Paul Kelly, Cathy Downs, Marilyn Madison, Sheila Urban; **D:** Alex Wells. *SNC, SMW, TPV*

Curiosity Kills 🐾½ 1990 (R) Young people find more than they bargained for when they begin to investigate the death of a fellow tenant. Tense made-for-cable thriller. **CW:** Violence. **86m/ C VHS.** Rae Dawn Chong, C. Thomas Howell, Courteney Cox, Paul Guilfoyle, Jeff Fahey; **D:** Colin Bucksey; **W:** Joe Batteer, John Rice; **C:** Bojan Bazelli. *USH*

The Curious Dr. Humpp 🐾 1970 A mad scientist (Barbero) kidnaps exotic dancers and extracts their libidos to preserve his youth. Under the guise of research, he encourages his victims to engage in trysts so that their carnal energies will increase. Everything is hunky dory until a reporter (Bauleo) starts snooping around the laboratory, discovering Dr. Humpp observing multiple couplings via closed-circuit television. Boldly exploitative, the American distributor added about 10 minutes of raunchy hard-core footage of exotic dance routines. **87m/B VHS.** *AR* Ricardo Bauleo, Aldo Barbero; **D:** Emilio Vieyra. *SMW, TPV*

Curley 🐾🐾 1947 High-spirited youngsters play pranks on their schoolteacher. A part of the Hal Roach Comedy Carnival. **53m/C VHS, Beta.** Larry Olsen, Frances Rafferty, Eilene Janssen, Walter Abel; **D:** Bernard Carr. *DVT, NOS, HHT*

Curly Sue 🐾🐾 1991 (PG) Adorable, homeless waif Porter and her scheming, adoptive father Belushi plot to rip off single, career-minded female attorney Lynch in order to take in some extra cash. Trouble is, all three heartstrings are tugged, and the trio develop a warm, caring relationship. A throwback to the Depression era's Shirley Temple formula films met with mixed reviews. Undiscriminating younger audiences should have a good time, though. Available in widescreen format on laserdisc. **102m/C VHS, Beta, LV, 8mm, Closed Caption.** James Belushi, Kelly Lynch, Alison Porter, John Getz, Fred Dalton Thompson; **D:** John Hughes; **W:** John Hughes; **M:** Georges Delerue. *WAR, CCB*

Curly Top 🐾🐾½ 1935 (G) Orphan Temple helps land a husband for her beautiful sister. Along the way, she sings "Animal Crackers in My Soup." Remake of the silent "Daddy Long Legs,"

which was remade again in 1955. **74m/B VHS, Beta, Closed Caption.** Shirley Temple, John Boles, Rochelle Hudson, Jane Darwell, Esther Dale, Arthur Treacher, Rafaela Ottiano; **D:** Irving Cummings. *FOX, MLT*

The Curse 🐾 *The Farm* 1987 (R) After a meteorite lands near a small farming community and contaminates the area, a young boy tries to prevent residents from turning into slime-oozing mutants. Remake of "Die, Monster, Die." **92m/C VHS, Beta, LV, Closed Caption.** Wil Wheaton, Claude Akins, Malcolm Danare, Cooper Huckabee, John Schneider, David Keith, Amy Wheaton, John Chaskin, Kathleen Jordan Gregory; **D:** David Keith; **W:** David Chaskin; **C:** Robert D. Forges. *UNI*

Curse 2: The Bite 🐾 1988 (R) Radiation affected snakes are transformed into deadly vipers whose bites change their unsuspecting victims into horrible creatures. **97m/C VHS, Beta.** Jill Schoelen, J. Eddie Peck, Jamie Farr, Savina Gersak, Bo Svenson, Sydney Lassick, Marianne Muellerleile, Terrence Evans; **D:** Fred Goodwin; **W:** Fred Goodwin, Susan Zelouf; **C:** Roberto D'Ettorre Piazzoli. *TWE*

Curse 3: Blood Sacrifice *Panga* 1990 (R) An African sugar cane plantation becomes host to a horrible nightmare when a voodoo curse is placed on the owners. The monstrous God of the Sea is summoned to avenge the accidental death of a baby, and the hellish journey into insanity begins. **91m/C VHS, LV, Closed Caption.** Christopher Lee, Jenilee Harrison, Henry Cele; **D:** Sean Barton. *COL*

Curse 4: The Ultimate Sacrifice 🐾½ *Catacombs* 1990 (R) Beneath the monastery at San Pietro lies buried the beast of the Apocalypse. For 400 years the secret has been kept and then an American priest and a lovely school teacher unwittingly break the seal and unleash the cursed beast upon an unsuspecting world. **84m/C VHS, LV, Closed Caption.** Timothy Van Patten, Laura Schaefer, Jeremy West, Ian Abercrombie; **D:** David Schmoeller. *COL*

The Curse of Frankenstein 🐾🐾½ 1957 Young Victor Frankenstein reenacts his father's experiments with creating life from the dead resulting in a terrifying, hideous creature. The first in Hammer's Frankenstein series and followed by "Revenge of Frankenstein." From the Shelley story. Make-up by Jack Pierce, who also created the famous make-up for Universal's Frankenstein monster. **83m/C VHS, Beta.** *GB* Peter Cushing, Christopher Lee, Hazel Court, Robert Urquhart, Valerie Gaunt, Noel Hood; **D:** Terence Fisher; **W:** Jimmy Sangster; **C:** Jack Asher; **M:** James Bernard. *WAR, MLB*

The Curse of King Tut's Tomb 🐾½ 1980 Made-for-television movie is set in 1922 where archaeologists have just opened Tutankhamen's tomb. The curse of the boy king is unleashed as tragic events bring the adventurers uncommon gloom. Oh boy. **98m/C VHS, Beta.** Robin Ellis, Harry Andrews, Eva Marie Saint, Raymond Burr, Wendy Hiller; **D:** Philip Leacock. *GKK*

The Curse of the Aztec Mummy woof! *La Maldicion de la Momia Azteca* 1959 A mad scientist schemes to rob a Mayan pyramid of its treasure but the resident mummy will have none of it. Sequel to "Robot vs. the Aztec Mummy" and followed by "Wrestling Women vs. the Aztec Mummy." **65m/B VHS.** *MX* Ramon Gay, Rosita Arenas, Crox Alvarado; **D:** Rafael Portillo. *SNC*

Curse of the Aztec Mummy/Robot vs. the Aztec Mummy woof! 1959 Vengeful mummy of an Aztec warrior stalks those who attempt to steal a fabulous treasure. A mad criminal scientist wants the treasure and uses gangsters and a human robot to get what he wants. **130m/B VHS, Beta.** Ramon Gay, Rosita Arenas, Crox Alvarado, Luis Aceves Cantaneda; **D:** Rafael Portillo. *HHT*

Curse of the Black Widow 🐾🐾 *Love Trap* 1977 An investigator follows a trail of brutal murders to the lair of a supernatural gigantic spider in the middle of Los Angeles. Made for television. **100m/C VHS, Beta.** Patty Duke, Anthony (Tony)

Francisca, Donna Mills, June Lockhart, Sid Caesar, Vic Morrow, June Allyson, Roz Kelly, Jeff Corey; **D:** Dan Curtis. *NO*

Curse of the Blue Lights woof! 1988
(R) Mysterious lights begin appearing at the local romantic spot. Little do the young lovers know, it hails the arrival of a ghoul, intent on raising the dead. Also available in an unedited version. Unfortunately, nothing can resurrect this film. **93m/C VHS, Beta.** Brent Ritter; **D:** John H. Johnson. *NO*

Curse of the Cat People *♂♂♂* 1944
A young sensitive girl is guided by the vision of her dead mother. Sequel to "Cat People." Available in a colorized version. **70m/B VHS, Beta, LV.** Simone Simon, Kent Smith, Jane Randolph, Elizabeth Russell, Ann Carter; **D:** Robert Wise, Gunther Von Fritsch. *TTC*

The Curse of the Crying Woman *♂♂½* La Maldicion de a Llorona; La Casa Embrujada 1961
Unknowing descendant of a witch is lured to her aunt's home to perform the act that will revive the monstrous crying woman and renew a reign of evil. **74m/B VHS, Beta.** MX Rosita Arenas, Abel Salazar, Rita Macedo. *SNC, HHT*

Curse of the Crystal Eye *♂♂* 1993
(PG-13) A gunrunner tries to get the treasure of Ali Baba aided by the requisite lovely lady and opposed by your usual bad guys. **CW:** Depiction of a burning man. **90m/C VHS.** Jameson Parker, Cynthia Rhodes, Mike Lane, David Sherwood, Andre Jacobs; **D:** Joe Tornatore. *NHO*

Curse of the Demon *♂♂♂½* Night of the Demon; The Haunted 1957
A famous psychologist investigates a colleague's mysterious death and enters a world of demonology and the occult, climaxing in a confrontation with a cult's patron demon. Superb thriller based upon the story "Casting the Runes" by M.R. James. **81m/B VHS, Beta, LV.** GB Dana Andrews, Peggy Cummins, Niall MacGinnis, Maurice Denham, Athene Seyler, Liam Redmond, Reginald Beckwith, Ewan Roberts, Peter Elliott, Brian Wilde; **D:** Jacques Tourneur; **W:** Charles Bennett, Hal E. Chester; **C:** Edward Scaife. *GKK, MLB*

Curse of the Devil *♂♂½* El Retorno de la Walpurgis 1973
(R) This time Naschy is turned into a werewolf by annoyed gypsies whose ancestors were slain by his. **73m/C VHS.** MX SP Paul Naschy, Maria Silva, Patty Shepard, Fay Falcon; **D:** Carlos Aured; **W:** Paul Naschy. *SNC*

Curse of the Headless Horseman 1972
The headless horseman rides again, bringing terror to all who cross his path! **80m/C VHS.** Don Carrara, Claudia Dean, B.G. Fisher, Margo Dean, Lee Byers, Joe Cody; **D:** John Kirkland. *NO*

Curse of the Living Corpse *♂* 1964
A millionaire comes back to rotting life to kill his negligent relatives. Scheider's first film. **84m/C VHS, Beta.** Candace Hilligoss, Roy Scheider, Helen Warren, Margot Hartman; **D:** Del Tenney.

Curse of the Living Dead *♂* 1989
Two siblings are forced to eat flesh for eternity after their witch-doctor mother puts a curse on them. **90m/C VHS, Beta. D:** Lawrence Foldes. *ELV, HHE*

Curse of the Pink Panther *♂♂* 1983
(PG) Clifton Sleigh, an inept New York City detective played by Wass, is assigned to find the missing Inspector Clouseau. His efforts are complicated by an assortment of gangsters and aristocrats who cross paths with the detective. So-so attempt to keep popular series going after Seller's death. Niven's last film. **110m/C VHS, Beta, Closed Caption.** Ted Wass, David Niven, Robert Wagner, Herbert Lom, Joanna Lumley, Capucine, Robert Loggia, Harvey Korman, Leslie Ash, Denise Crosby; **D:** Blake Edwards; **W:** Blake Edwards; **M:** Henry Mancini. *MGM*

Curse of the Puppet Master *♂♂½* 1998
(R) The little guys have been taking a break since 1994's "Puppet Master 5" but they're baaaack. This time they're trying to prevent their new master, evil Dr. Magrew, from transforming more victims into living dolls. **CW:** Horror violence/gore and language. **90m/C VHS.** George Peck, Emily Harrison, Michael Guerin; **D:** Victoria Sloan. *AFE*

Curse of the Queerwolf *♂♂* 1987 A
man is bitten on the butt by gay werewolf and transforms into the title character. Filmed in Santa Barbara in 8mm; some funny moments. From the director of "A Polish Vampire in Burbank." **90m/C VHS.** Michael Palazzolo, Kent Butler, Taylor Whitney; **D:** Mark Pirro. *HHE*

Curse of the Starving Class *♂♂* 1994
(R) Ineffective adaptation of Sam Shepard's 1977 play exploring family disintegration. Weston (Woods) is the alcoholic, irresponsible patriarch of a decaying farm. His unhappy wife, Ella (Bates), wants to sell out to land speculator Taylor (Quaid) and move to Paris while rebellious teenager Emma (Fiorella) plans to run off to Mexico and sullen older brother Wesley (Thomas) desires to stay and make a go of things. One-dimensional characterizations don't translate well from stage to screen. **CW:** Language; scene of nudity. **102m/C VHS, LV, Closed Caption.** James Woods, Kathy Bates, Henry Thomas, Kristin Fiorella, Randy Quaid, Louis Gossett Jr.; **D:** Michael McClary; **W:** Bruce Beresford; **C:** Dick Quinlan. *THV*

Curse of the Stone Hand woof! 1964
A pair of stone hands causes folks to do suicidal things. A mutation of a Mexican and a Chilean horror film, each purchased and monster-mashed into one by Warren. **72m/B VHS.** MX John Carradine, Ernest Walch, Sheila Bon, Katherine Victor, Lloyd Nelson; **D:** Jerry Warren. *NOS, LOO*

Curse of the Swamp Creature *♂* 1966
A mad scientist in the Everglades attempts to create half human/half alligator monsters. In turn, a geologic expeditionary force attempts to stop his experimentation. Low budget thrills courtesy of Larry Buchanan. **80m/C VHS.** John Agar, Francine York, Shirley McLine, Bill Thurman, Jeff Alexander; **D:** Larry Buchanan. *MOV, VDM*

Curse of the Undead *♂♂½* Affairs of the Vampire; Mark of the West; Mark of the Beast; The Invisible Killer; Le Teur Invisible; Les Griffes du Vampire; The Grip of the Vampire 1959
Mediocre vampire western finds a small town suffering from the deaths of several young women—all with small wounds in the neck. Suspicions fall on gunslinger Drake Robey (Pate) and it's up to preacher Dan Young (Fleming) to take care of the blood-sucking miscreant. **89m/B VHS, Closed Caption.** Eric Fleming, Michael Pate, Kathleen Crowley, John Hoyt, Bruce Gordon, Edward Binns, Jimmy Murphy, Jay Adler; **D:** Edward Dein; **W:** Edward Dein, Mildred Dein; **C:** Ellis W. Carter; **M:** Irving Gertz. *USH*

The Curse of the Werewolf *♂♂½* 1961
Horror film about a 19th-century European werewolf that is renowned for its ferocious departure from the stereotypical portrait of the beast. **91m/C VHS, Beta.** GB Oliver Reed, Clifford Evans, Yvonne Romain, Catherine Feller, Anthony Dawson, Michael Ripper, Peter Sallis; **D:** Terence Fisher; **W:** Anthony John Elder Hinds; **C:** Arthur Grant. *USH, TLF, MLB*

Curse of the Yellow Snake *♂♂* 1963
Voluminous yarn features a running battle over an ancient Chinese artifact, with crazed Chinese cultists running through foggy London streets. **98m/C VHS, Beta.** GE Joachim Berger, Werner Peters; **D:** Franz Gottlieb. *VYY*

The Cursed Mountain Mystery *♂½* 1993
(R) Two petty thieves steal a legendary precious gem rumored to cursed. The immortal warrior supposed to guard the gem lures the crooks to Sher Mountain, where he intends to eliminate them and return the stone to its keeper. **87m/C VHS.** Phillip Avalon, Tom Richards, Joe Bugner; **D:** Vince Martin; **W:** Denis Whitburn. *COL*

Curtain Up *♂♂* 1953
"Little theatre" dramatics and the exasperating temperaments of amateur theatricals are exposed in this adaptation of the play "On Monday Next," by Philip King. **82m/C VHS, Beta.** GB Robert Morley, Margaret Rutherford, Olive Sloane; **D:** Ralph Smart; **W:** Jack Davies; **M:** Malcolm Arnold. *BFA*

Curtains woof! 1983 (R)
Director has a clash of wills with a film star that spells "Curtains" for a group of aspiring actresses gathered together at a haunted house for an audition. Hamfest with no thrills, chills, gore, or gratuitous skin. No wonder why director Richard Ciupka hides behind pseudonym Stryker. **90m/C VHS, Beta.** CA John Vernon, Samantha Eggar; **D:** Jonathan Stryker; **W:** Robert Guza Jr. *VES*

Curtis's Charm *♂½* 1996
Thanks to his drug paranoia, crack addict Curtis (Wint) believes his wife Cookie (Crawford) and mother-in-law (Barnes-Hopkins) have put a voodoo spell on him. His friend Jim (Callum Rennie), a former addict, tries to help Curtis by coming up with some magic of his own, intended to convince the addled druggie that it will protect him. Lots of narration does little to make the character's friendship convincing. Based on a short story by Jim Carroll. **74m/B VHS.** CA Maurice Dean Wint, Callum Keith Rennie, Rachael Crawford, Barbara Barnes-Hopkins; **D:** John L'Ecuyer; **W:** John L'Ecuyer; **C:** Harald Bachmann; **M:** Mark Korven. Genie Awards '96: Best Score; Nominations: Genie Awards '96: Best Adapted Screenplay. *NYR*

Custer's Last Fight *♂½* 1912
Re-enactment of the American West period when the Sioux and Cheyenne Indian tribes bitterly opposed the white man. Silent. **50m/B VHS, Beta. D:** Francis Ford. *NOS, DVT, CCP*

Custer's Last Stand *♂½* 1936
Feature-length version of the Mascot serial recounting the last days of the famous General. **70m/B VHS, Beta.** Frank McGlynn, Rex Lease, Nancy Caseell, Lona Andre, William Farnum, Reed Howes, Jack Mulhall, Josef Swickard, Ruth Mix; **D:** Elmer Clifton. *VCN, GPV*

The Custodian *♂♂* 1994
(R) Honest cop must battle corruption of Australian police precinct while dealing with numerous personal problems. Good cast goes a long way in routine story. **CW:** Language, violence, and sexuality. **110m/C VHS, LV.** AU Anthony LaPaglia, Hugo Weaving, Barry Otto, Bill Hunter, Kelly Dingwall, Gosia Dobrowolska, Naomi Watts; **D:** John Dingwall.

Cut and Run *♂* 1985
(R) Two journalists follow a lead to the former South American home of Jim Jones, and are instantly captured by local guerrillas. **87m/C VHS, Beta.** Michael Berryman, Willie Aames, Lisa Blount, Karen Black. *VTR*

The Cut Throats *♂* 1989
(R) Americans stumble upon an isolated Nazi outpost stocked with gold and beautiful women. Exploitation at its worst. **80m/C VHS.** Jay Scott, Joanne Douglas, Jeff Letham, Pat Michaels, Barbara Lane; **D:** John Hayes; **W:** John Hayes. *TPV*

Cutter's Way *♂♂½* Cutter and Bone 1981
(R) An embittered and alcoholic disabled Vietnam vet and his small-time crook/gigolo friend wrestle with justice and morality when the drifter uncovers a murder but declines to get involved. An unusually cynical mystery from the novel by Newton Thorburg. **105m/C VHS, Beta, LV.** Jeff Bridges, John Heard, Lisa Eichhorn, Ann Dusenberry, Stephen Elliott, Nina Van Pallandt, George Dickerson; **D:** Ivan Passer; **C:** Jordan Cronenweth; **M:** Jack Nitzsche. *MGM*

Cutthroat Island *♂♂½* 1995
(PG-13) Big-budget swashbuckling adventure—long on action and short on plot and character. Female pirate captain Morgan Adams (Davis) is left part of a treasure map by her father and "persuades" educated slave/thief William Shaw (Modine), who has lots of charm and no morals, to assist her. Her scurvy Uncle Dawg (despically well-played by Langella) also has a portion of the map and is willing to let Morgan find the treasure—on Cutthroat Island—before taking it for himself. Director Harlin likes lots of big, noisy explosions (when he doesn't know what else to do) but Davis' exuberance for her pirate queen role is appealing. **CW:** Some strong pirate action/violence and brief sensuality. **123m/C VHS, LV, Closed Caption, DVD.** Geena Davis, Matthew Modine, Frank Langella, Patrick Malahide, Stan Shaw, Maury Chaykin, Harris Yulin, George Murcell;

D: Renny Harlin; **W:** Robert King, Marc Norman; **C:** Peter Levy; **M:** John Debney. *ART*

Cutting Class 🎬 1989 (R) Murders proliferate in a high school, where a student with a history of mental illness is number one on the suspect list. Tongue-in-cheek mayhem. **91m/C VHS, LV.** Jill Schoelen, Roddy McDowall, Donovan Leitch, Martin Mull, Brad Pitt; **D:** Rospo Pallenberg. *REP*

The Cutting Edge 🎬🎬½ 1992 (PG) Spoiled figure skater's lifelong quest for Olympic gold is seriously hampered by her inability to be nice to her partners. In a final effort to snag the medal she teams up with a cocky guy who thinks the only sport on ice is hockey, but whose own dreams of NHL stardom were cut short by an injury. Saddled with a predictable and thin plot, it sometimes looks and feels like a TV movie. So why bother? Because the chemistry between photogenic leads Kelly and Sweeney is terrific. Add half a bone for the flying sparks and snappy dialogue, sit back, and enjoy. **101m/C VHS, LV, Closed Caption.** D.B. Sweeney, Moira Kelly, Roy Dotrice, Terry O'Quinn, Dwier Brown, Rachelle Ottley, Jo Jo Starbuck; **D:** Paul Michael Glaser; **W:** Tony Gilroy; **C:** Elliot Davis; **M:** Patrick Williams. *MGM*

Cyber Bandits 🎬½ 1994 (R) In a future society, navigator Jack Morris (Kemp) has just sailed a pleasure craft to the island city of Pacifica. His passengers included wealthy Morgan Wells (Hays), whose scientists have developed a deadly virtual reality weapon, and Wells' mistress Rebecca (Paul). Rebecca steals the plans for the weapon and seduces Jack into having the data digitally transferred onto his back in the form of a tattoo. Then Rebecca disappears and Jack finds himself in big trouble. **86m/C VHS, LV, Closed Caption.** Martin Kemp, Alexandra Paul, Robert Hays, Adam Ant, George Jones; **D:** Erik Fleming; **W:** James Robinson, Winston Beard; **M:** Steve Hunter. *COL*

Cyber Ninja 🎬🎬½ 1994 Warrior princess Saki is captured by the Dark Overlord, who plans to sacrifice her. It's up to a mercenary to come to her rescue. Lightweight, action-oriented Japanese mix of samurais and science fiction. Dubbed. **80m/C VHS.** JP Hanbel Kawai, Hiroki Ida. *FXL*

Cyber-Tracker 🎬½ 1993 (R) In the judicial system of the future androids hunt down vicious criminals and execute them immediately. When secret service agent Eric Phillips is framed for murder, he's also marked for death. His only chance is to link up with rebels fighting the mechanized monsters. **?m/C VHS, LV, Closed Caption.** Don "The Dragon" Wilson, Richard Norton, Joseph Ruskin, Abby Dalton, John Aprea; **D:** Richard Pepin. *PMH*

Cyber-Tracker 2 🎬½ 1995 (R) An international weapons dealer has gotten control of the cybertracker technology and created cyborg lookalikes of secret agent Eric Phillips (Wilson) and his newscaster wife Connie (Foster). When the cyborgs commit murder on live TV, the human duo become fugitives who must expose the real killers.**CW:** Non-stop violence, and for language. **97m/C VHS, Closed Caption.** Don "The Dragon" Wilson, Stacie Foster, Stephen Burton. *PMH*

Cyberstalker 🎬½ 1996 Detective twosome must track down a serial killer who uses the Internet to select his victims. **96m/C VHS.** Blake Bahner, Jeffrey Combs, Annie Biggs, Schnele Wilson. *SDE*

Cyberzone 🎬½ 1995 (R) Intergalactic investigator pursues four dangerous androids who are hiding on earth.**CW:** Nudity, a strong sex scene, and some violence. **95m/C VHS.** Marc Singer, Matthias Hues. *NHO*

Cyborg 🎬 1989 (R) In a deathly, dirty, post-holocaust urban world, an able cyborg battles a horde of evil mutant thugs. Poorly made action flick. **85m/C VHS, Beta, LV, Letterbox.** Jean-Claude Van Damme, Deborah Richter, Vincent Klyn, Dayle Haddon; **D:** Albert Pyun; **W:** Kitty Chalmers; **M:** Kevin Bassinson. *MGM*

Cyborg 2 🎬🎬 1993 (R) In the year 2074 cyborgs have replaced humans at all levels. A devious company which manufactures cyborgs decides to get rid of its chief competition by literally killing them off. They plan to inject cyborg Cash Reese (Jolie) with a liquid explosive that will detonate her and everything else in sight. Tech-master Mercy (Palance) clues Cash in and she escapes with the help of the human Colton (Koteas) but they've become prey to a group of ruthless hunters. **99m/C VHS, LV, Closed Caption.** Angelina Jolie, Elias Koteas, Jack Palance, Billy Drago. *THV*

Cyborg 3: The Recycler 🎬🎬 1995 (R) Female cyborg has been programmed to become a creator—essentially making mankind useless.**CW:** Non-stop violence, some nudity. **90m/C VHS.** Khrystyne Haje, Zach Galligan, Andrew Bryniarski, Richard Lynch, Malcolm McDowell; **D:** Michael Schroeder; **W:** Barry Victor, Troy Bolotnick. *AVE*

Cyborg Cop 🎬½ 1993 (R) DEA agent Phillip (Jenson) is captured during a foreign drug raid and is turned into a half-man, half-machine by mad scientist Kessel (Rhys-Davies), who wants to sell his cyborgs as unstoppable hitmen. Phillip's brother Jack (Bradley) tries to come to his rescue. Lots of stunts and car chases and even a minor romantic subplot with Sharon (Shaw). **97m/C VHS, LV, Closed Caption.** David Bradley, John Rhys-Davies, Todd Jensen, Alonna Shaw; **W:** Glenn A. Bruce. *THV*

Cyborg Soldier 🎬🎬½ *Cyborg Cop 2* 1994 (R) Loose cannon cop Jack Ryan (Bradley) is up against psycho killer Starkraven (Hunter) who gets turned into a new-model cyborg by your basic suspicious government agency. But when the cyborg decides to go on an unplanned human killing spree, Ryan gets to break out the heavy artillery to mow him down. Also available in an unrated version. **96m/C VHS, LV, Closed Caption.** David Bradley, Morgan Hunter, Jill Pierce; **D:** Sam Firstenberg; **W:** Jon Stevens. *NLC*

Cycle Psycho woof! *Numbered Days; Savage Abduction* 1972 (R) Serial killer blackmails the businessman whose wife he was contracted to kill into bringing him young girls to slaughter. The businessman hires out the job to sleazy motorcycle gang. **80m/C VHS, Beta.** Joe Turkel, Tom Drake, Stephen Oliver; **D:** John Lawrence; **W:** John Lawrence.

Cycle Vixens woof! *The Young Cycle Girls* 1979 (R) Three girls jump on their hogs and head from Colorado to California. Much leather, motor revving and other obligatory motorcycle-trash trimmings. **90m/C VHS.** Loraine Ferris, Daphne Lawrence, Deborah Marcus, Lonnie Pense, Kevin O'Neill, Bee Lechat, Billy Bullet; **D:** Peter Perry. *SIM*

Cyclo 🎬🎬 *Xich Lo* 1995 An orphaned 18-year-old (Van Loc), known only by his profession of cyclo (pedal-taxi) driver, struggles on the streets of Ho Chi Minh City. When his vehicle is stolen, he's forced by his boss to repay its value and takes small-time jobs from local crime boss, The Poet (Leung), who, unbeknownst to the cyclo, is also his sister's (Yen-Khe) pimp. The deeper the young man gets into the criminal world, the closer he also gets to tragedy. Vietnamese with subtitles. **123m/C VHS.** VT Le Van Loc, Tran Nu Yen-Khe, Tony Leung, Nguyen Nhu Quynh; **D:** Tran Anh Hung; **W:** Tran Anh Hung; **C:** Benoit Delhomme; **M:** Ton That Tiet. *NYF*

Cyclone 🎬🎬 1987 (R) The girlfriend of a murdered scientist must deliver a secretly devised motorcycle into righteous government hands, much to the dismay of evil agents and corrupt officials. Good fun, sparked by a stellar "B" cast. **89m/C VHS, Beta, LV.** Heather Thomas, Jeffrey Combs, Ashley Ferrare, Dar Robinson, Martine Beswick, Robert Quarry, Martin Landau, Huntz Hall, Troy Donahue, Michael Reagan, Dawn Wildsmith, Bruce Fairbairn, Russ Tamblyn; **D:** Fred Olen Ray; **C:** Paul Elliott. *COL*

Cyclone Cavalier 1925 A dauntless hero travels through Central America on an adventurous spree. **58m/B VHS, Beta.** Reed Howes; **D:** Albert Rogell. *GPV, GVV*

Cyclone of the Saddle 🎬 1935 Typical Western about a range war. **53m/B VHS, Beta.** Rex Lease, Bobby Nelson, William Desmond, Yakima Canutt; **D:** Elmer Clifton. *NO*

Cyclops 🎬🎬 1956 When an expedition party searches throughout Mexico for a woman's long lost fiance, they are shocked when they find out that radiation has turned him into a one-eyed monster. **72m/B VHS, Beta.** Tom Drake, Gloria Talbott, Lon Chaney Jr., James Craig; **D:** Bert I. Gordon. *ART, MLB*

Cyclotrode "X" *The Crimson Ghost* 1946 The Crimson Ghost attempts to kidnap the inventor of the title machine, which would enable him to rule the world. Moore (The Lone Ranger) plays a bad guy. Serial in 12 episodes. Also available in a 93-minute colorized edition. **100m/B VHS, Beta.** Charles Quigley, Linda Stirling, I. Stanford Jolley, Clayton Moore, Kenne Duncan; **D:** William Witney, Fred Brannon. *VCN, REP, MLB*

Cyrano de Bergerac 🎬🎬🎬 1925 Silent version of Edmond Rostand's novel about romantic Cyrano who fears to reveal his love to Roxanne because he feels his enormous nose makes him unattractive. So, he serves as a surrogate lover by encouraging another man's attentions to her. Color-tinted. **114m/C VHS.** IT FR Pierre Magnier, Linda Moglia, Angelo Ferrari; **D:** Augusto Genina; **M:** Carlo Moser. *KIV*

Cyrano de Bergerac 🎬🎬🎬🎬 1950 Edmund Rostand's famous story of a large-nosed yet poetic cavalier, who finds himself too ugly to be loved. He bears the pain of his devotion to Roxanne from afar, and helps the handsome but tongue-tied Christian to romance her. Ferrer became famous for this role, which won him an Oscar. Based on Brian Hooke's translation of the play. Also available colorized. **112m/B VHS, LV.** Jose Ferrer, Mala Powers, William Prince, Elena Verdugo, Morris Carnovsky; **D:** Michael Gordon; **W:** Carl Foreman; **M:** Dimitri Tiomkin. Academy Awards '50: Best Actor (Ferrer); Golden Globe Awards '51: Best Actor—Drama (Ferrer). *MON, MRV, NOS*

Cyrano de Bergerac 🎬🎬🎬 1985 Edmond Rostand's gallant poet and swordsman, with the extraordinary nose, is well-portrayed by Jacobi in this Royal Shakespeare Company production. Translated and adapted by Anthony Burgess. **177m/C VHS.** GB Derek Jacobi, Sinead Cusack. *TVC, TTC*

Cyrano de Bergerac 🎬🎬🎬🎬 1990 (PG) Depardieu brings to exhilarating life Rostand's well-loved play about the brilliant but grotesque-looking swordsman/poet, afraid of nothing—except declaring his love to the beautiful Roxanne. One of France's costliest modern productions, a multi-award winner for its cast, costumes, music and sets. English subtitles (by Anthony Burgess) are designed to capture the intricate rhymes of the original French dialogue. **135m/C VHS, LV.** FR Gerard Depardieu, Jacques Weber, Anne Brochet, Vincent Perez, Roland Bertin, Josiane Stoleru, Phillipe Volter, Phillippe Morier-Genoud, Pierre Maguelon; **D:** Jean-Paul Rappeneau; **W:** Jean-Claude Carriere, Jean-Paul Rappeneau. Academy Awards '90: Best Costume Design; Cannes Film Festival '90: Best Actor (Depardieu); Cesar Awards '91: Best Actor (Depardieu), Best Art Direction/Set Decoration, Best Cinematography, Best Costume Design, Best Director (Rappeneau), Best Film, Best Sound, Best Supporting Actor (Weber); Golden Globe Awards '91: Best Foreign Film; Nominations: Academy Awards '90: Best Actor (Depardieu), Best Art Direction/Set Decoration, Best Foreign Language Film, Best Makeup. *ORI, FCT, BTV*

D-Day on Mars 🎬🎬 1945 Alien invader the Purple Monster is bent on taking over Earth. Originally a 15-part Republic serial titled "The Purple Monster Strikes." **100m/B VHS.** Dennis Moore, Linda Stirling, Roy Barcroft, James Craven, Bud Geary, Mary Moore; **D:** Spencer Gordon Bennet, Fred Brannon. *REP*

D-Day, the Sixth of June 🎬🎬🎬 *The Sixth of June* 1956 An American soldier has an affair with a Englishwoman weeks before D-Day, where he unhappily finds himself fighting side by side with her husband. Based on the novel by Lionel

Shapiro. **106m/C VHS, Beta.** Richard Todd, Dana Winter, Robert Taylor, Edmond O'Brien, John Williams, Jerry Paris, Richard Stapley; **D:** Henry Koster; **C:** Lee Garmes. *NO*

Da ✶✶½ **1988 (PG)** A middle-aged man returns to Ireland for his father's funeral. As he sorts out his father's belongings, his father returns as a ghostly presence to chat with him about life, death, and their own relationship. Based on the Hugh Leonard play with Hughes recreating his Tony-award winning role. **102m/C VHS, Beta, LV, Closed Caption.** Barnard Hughes, Martin Sheen, William Hickey, Hugh O'Conor; **D:** Matt Clark; **W:** Hugh Leonard; **M:** Elmer Bernstein. *NO*

Dad ✶✶½ **1989 (PG)** Hoping to make up for lost time, a busy executive rushes home to take care of his father who has just had a heart attack. What could have easily become sappy is made bittersweet by the convincing performances of Lemmon and Danson. Based on the novel by William Wharton. **117m/C VHS, Beta, LV, Closed Caption.** Jack Lemmon, Ted Danson, Ethan Hawke, Olympia Dukakis, Kathy Baker, Zakes Mokae, J.T. Walsh, Kevin Spacey, Chris Lemmon; **D:** Gary David Goldberg; **W:** Gary David Goldberg; **M:** James Horner. Nominations: Academy Awards '89: Best Makeup. *USH*

Daddy Long Legs ✶✶✶ **1955** Far from the great musicals, but enjoyable. An eccentric millionaire glimpses a French orphan and becomes her anonymous benefactor. Her musing over his identity spawns some surreal (often inexplicable) dance numbers, but love conquers all, even lesser Johnny Mercer songs. From a story by Jean Webster, also done in 1919 with Mary Pickford, 1931 with Janet Gaynor and 1935 with Shirley Temple as "Curly Top." ♫Daddy Long Legs; Something's Got To Give; Sluefoot; Dream; History of the Beat; C-A-T Spells Cat; Welcome Egghead. **126m/C VHS, LV, Letterbox, Closed Caption.** Fred Astaire, Leslie Caron, Terry Moore, Thelma Ritter, Fred Clark, Charlotte Austin, Larry Keating; **D:** Jean Negulesco; **C:** Leon Shamroy; **M:** Alex North. Nominations: Academy Awards '55: Best Art Direction/Set Decoration (Color), Best Song ("Something's Gotta Give"), Scoring of a Musical. *FCT*

Daddy Nostalgia ✶✶✶ *These Foolish Things* **1990** Birkin plays the estranged daughter of Bogarde, who rushes from her home in England to France to be with her seriously ill father. She must come to terms with her feelings for him just as Bogarde must deal with his own mortality. Wonderful performances, with Bogarde a charming and dominating presence. In French with English subtitles. **105m/C VHS. FR** Dirk Bogarde, Jane Birkin, Odette Laure; **D:** Bertrand Tavernier; **W:** Colo Tavernier O'Hagan; **M:** Antoine Duhamel. *FCT*

Daddy-O ✶ *Out on Probation* **1959** Drag racer Daddy-O traps the killers of his best friend and lands the blonde bombshell Jana. It might seem bad since it's dated, but, hey, it may have been bad in 1959, too! **74m/B VHS.** Dick Contino, Sandra Giles; **D:** Lou Place; **W:** David Moessinger. *COL*

Daddy's Boys ✶½ **1987 (R)** Since farming during the Depression is a rather low-paying endeavor, this family turns to thieving instead. But all-for-one and one-for-all is not the credo for one of the sons who decides to branch out on his own. Produced by Roger Corman. **90m/C VHS, Beta, LV.** Daryl Haney, Laura Burkett, Raymond J. Barry, Dan Shor; **D:** Joe Minion; **W:** Daryl Haney. *COL*

Daddy's Dyin'...Who's Got the Will? ✶✶½ **1990 (PG-13)** Based on the critically acclaimed play, this bittersweet comedy stars Bridges and D'Angelo as two members of the spiteful Turnover clan. When Daddy is on his deathbed, the entire family uses the opportunity to stab each other in the back. Non-stop humor and deep-hearted honesty carries this delightful adaptation quickly from beginning to end. **95m/C VHS, Beta, LV, Closed Caption.** Beau Bridges, Beverly D'Angelo, Tess Harper, Judge Reinhold, Amy Wright, Keith Carradine, Patrika Darbo, Molly McClure, Bert Remsen; **D:**

Jack Fisk; **W:** Del Shores; **C:** Paul Elliott; **M:** David Mullugh. *MGM*

Daddy's Girl ✶½ **1996 (R)** When adopted Jody's new family is threatened she'll stop at nothing to protect herself and them. **CW:** For violence and menace perpetrated by a child. **95m/C VHS, LV, Closed Caption.** William Katt, Michele Greene, Roxana Zal, Mimi Craven, Whip Hubley, Gabrielle Boni; **D:** Martin Kitrosser; **W:** Steve Pesce. *ART*

Daddy's Gone A-Hunting ✶✶✶ **1969 (PG)** It's an eye for an eye, a baby for a baby in this well-done psychological thriller. A happily married woman is stalked by her deranged ex-boyfriend, whose baby she aborted years before. Now he wants the life of her child as just compensation for the loss of his. **108m/C VHS.** Carol White, Paul Burke, Scott Hylands, Rachel Ames, Mala Powers, James B. Sikking; **D:** Mark Robson; **W:** Larry Cohen; **C:** Ernest Laszlo; **M:** John Williams. *WAR*

Daens ✶✶½ **1992** Looks at the disparity between rich and poor at the turn of the century. Daens, a priest, returns home to Flanders to find desperate poverty among the Flemish-speaking workers of the local textile mill. The French-speaking mill owners are supported by the local Catholic church while Daens believes in the rights of the workers. Decleir makes his priest a complex and troubled man, who must choose between his conscience and social reform and the dictates of his church. Marred by somewhat cardboard villains and a complex political/social situation that isn't adequately explained. Based on the novel by Louis Paul Boon. Flemish and French with English subtitles. **134m/C VHS. FR BE NL.** Jan Decleir, Gerard Desarthe, Antje De Boeck, Michael Pas, Johan Leysen, Idwig Stephane, Linda Van Dijck, Wim Meuwissen; **D:** Stijn Coninx; **W:** Francois Chevallier, Stijn Coninx; **M:** Dirk Brosse. Nominations: Academy Awards '92: Best Foreign Language Film. *FXL*

Daffy Duck's Movie: Fantastic Island **1983 (G)** A compilation of classic Warner Bros. cartoons, starring Daffy Duck, Speedy Gonzales, Bugs Bunny, Porky Pig, Sylvester, Tweety, Pepe Le Pew, Pirate Sam, Granny, Foghorn Leghorn, and the Tasmanian Devil. **78m/C VHS, Beta, LV. D:** Isadore "Friz" Freleng; **V:** Mel Blanc, June Foray, Les Tremayne. *WAR, FCT*

Daffy Duck's Quackbusters **1989 (G)** Daffy, with help from pals Bugs and Porky, sets up his own "ghostbusting" service. Good compilation of old classics such as "Night of the Living Duck," plus a new feature, "The Duxcorcist." Video is also available in Spanish. **79m/C VHS, Beta, LV, Closed Caption. D:** Greg Ford, Terry Lennon; **V:** Mel Blanc. *WAR, FCT*

Dagger Eyes ✶½ **198?** A political assassin at work is inadvertently captured on film by a photographer. The assassin's mob employers will go to any lengths to destroy the film. Say cheeeeeese! **84m/C VHS, Beta.** Carole Bouquet, Philip Coccioletti, John Steiner; **D:** Carlo Vanzina. *NO*

The Dagger of Kamui ✶✶½ **1985** Jiro is pursued by minions of the evil Tenkai as he races from Japan to the American Old West and back again. He's trying to avenge the murder of his father and Jiro's only weapon is the mysterious Dagger of Kamui, which holds the secret to a treasure and the future of Japan. In Japanese with English subtitles. **132m/C VHS, LV. JP ANI, CPM**

Dagora, the Space Monster woof! *Dagora; Space Monster Dagora; Uchudai Dogora; Uchu Daikaiju Dogora* **1965** Giant, slimy, pulsating mass from space lands on Earth and begins eating everything in sight. Scientists join together in a massive effort to destroy the creature. Believe it or not, it's sillier than most of the Japanese sci-fi genre. **80m/C VHS, Beta. JP** Yosuke Natsuki, Yoko Fujiyama, Akiko Wakabayashi, Hiroshi Koizumi; **D:** Inoshiro Honda; **W:** Shinichi Sekizawa; **C:** Hajime Koizumi. *VYY*

The Dain Curse ✶✶ *Dashiell Hammett's The Dain Curse* **1978** In 1928, private eye Hamilton Nash must recover stolen diamonds, solve a millionaire's suicide, avoid being murdered, and end a family curse. Based on the novel by Dashiell Hammett. Made-for-television as a 312-minute miniseries. **138m/C VHS, Beta.** James Coburn, Jason Miller, Jean Simmons, Beatrice Straight, Hector Elizondo, Nancy Addison; **D:** E.W. Swackhamer. *VTR*

Daisy Miller ✶✶½ **1974 (G)** Shepherd portrays the title character in this adaptation of the Henry James novella about a naive young American woman travelling through Europe and getting a taste of the Continent during the late 19th century. Though it is intelligently written and has a good supporting cast, the film seems strangely flat, due in large part to Shepherd's hollow performance. **93m/C VHS, Beta.** Cybill Shepherd, Eileen Brennan, Cloris Leachman, Mildred Natwick; **D:** Peter Bogdanovich; **W:** Frederic Raphael. Nominations: Academy Awards '74: Best Costume Design. *PAR*

Dakota ✶✶ **1945** Fine cast becomes embroiled in railroad land dispute. In the meantime, love strikes The Duke. Standard Wayne western saga never quite gets on track. **82m/B VHS, LV.** John Wayne, Vera Ralston, Walter Brennan, Ward Bond, Ona Munson; **D:** Joseph Kane. *REP*

Dakota ✶✶ **1988 (PG)** A troubled half-breed teenager works for a rancher, romances his daughter, and befriends his crippled 12-year-old son. A well-meaning, but predictable drama. **96m/C VHS, Beta, LV, Closed Caption.** Lou Diamond Phillips, Dee Dee Norton, Eli Cummins, Herta Ware; **D:** Fred Holmes. *HBO*

Dakota Incident ✶✶ **1956** Decent western about stagecoach passengers travelling through Dakota Territory who must defend themselves against an Indian attack. **88m/C VHS.** Dale Robertson, Ward Bond, Linda Darnell, John Lund; **D:** Lewis R. Foster. *REP*

Daleks—Invasion Earth 2150 A.D. ✶✶½ *Invasion Earth 2150 A.D* **1966** A sequel to "Dr. Who and the Daleks," wherein the popular British character endeavors to save the Earth from a robotic threat. **81m/C VHS, Beta. GB** Peter Cushing, Andrew Keir, Jill Curzon, Ray Brooks; **D:** Gordon Flemyng. *NO*

The Dallas Connection ✶ **1994 (R)** Three of the four scientists working on a satellite weapons system are assassinated by a trio of sexy but lethal females. Now the remaining scientist is under federal protection in Dallas while he continues his work. Lots of T&A. **CW:** Nudity; sexual situations; violence; language. **90m/C VHS.** Julie Strain, Samantha Phillips, Julie K. Smith, Wendy Hamilton; **D:** Andy Sidaris. *MNC*

Dalva ✶½ **1995** Dull TV movie finds restless Dalva Northridge (Fawcett) deciding to search for the son she was forced to give up for adoption some 20 years before. But she gets sidetracked juggling two love affairs—with Sam Creekmouth (Boothe), whose Indian heritage is tied to Dalva's family, and alcoholic university professor Michael (Coyote) who wants the Northridge family diaries for his research on the Great Plains. Based on the novel by Jim Harrison. **?m/C VHS.** Farrah Fawcett, Powers Boothe, Peter Coyote, Rod Steiger, Carroll Baker. *NYR*

Dam Busters ✶✶✶½ **1955** Well-done and exciting film details the efforts of British scientists trying to devise a method of destroying a strategic dam in Nazi Germany during WWII. Definitely one of the better in the war movie genre. **119m/B VHS, Beta.** Michael Redgrave, Richard Todd, Ursula Jeans, Basil Sydney; **D:** Michael Anderson Sr. *HMV, CNG*

Damage ✶✶✶ **1992 (R)** The elegant Irons portrays Stephen, a middle-aged, married British politican who has always been completely in control of his life, especially where his feelings are concerned. Then he meets Anna (Binoche), his son's less-than-innocent fiance, and immediately begins an obsessive, wildly sexual affair with her. Stephen should have listened to Anna's warning about herself "Damaged people are dangerous, they know they can survive," because their passion leads to betrayal and tragedy. Binoche is more icon than human being but the film still hypnotizes as an exploration of passion. Based on the novel by Josephine Hart. An unrated version is also available. **CW:** Language and strong sexuality. **111m/C VHS, LV, Letterbox, Closed Caption.** *GB FR* Jeremy Irons, Juliette Binoche, Rupert Graves, Miranda Richardson, Ian Bannen, Leslie Caron, Peter Stormare, Gemma Clark, Julian Fellowes; **D:** Louis Malle; **W:** David Hare; **C:** Peter Biziou; **M:** Zbigniew Preisner. British Academy Awards '92: Best Supporting Actress (Richardson); Los Angeles Film Critics Association Awards '92: Best Score; Nominations: Academy Awards '92: Best Supporting Actress (Richardson). **COL, IME, MOV**

Dames ✍✍✍ **1934** A millionaire with fanatically religious beliefs tries to stop the opening of a Broadway show. In the last of the grand budget-breaking spectacles before the "production code" came into being, distinguished choreographer Busby Berkeley took his imagination to the limit: watch for the dancing clothes on an ironing board and dancing girls with puzzle pieces on their backs which form the real Keeler. ♫Dames; I Only Have Eyes For You; When You Were a Smile on Your Mother's Lips and a Twinkle in Your Father's Eye; Try To See It My Way; The Girl at the Ironing Board. **95m/B VHS, Beta, LV.** Dick Powell, Joan Blondell, Ruby Keeler, ZaSu Pitts, Guy Kibbee, Busby Berkeley; **D:** Ray Enright; **W:** Delmer Daves; **C:** George Barnes. **MGM, FOX**

Dames Ahoy ✍ **1930** Three sailors on shore leave try to find the blonde who tricked one of them out of his pay. This is the original silent version with a piano score. **52m/B VHS.** Glenn Tryon, Otis Harlan, Eddie Gribbon, Helen Wright, Gertrude Astor; **D:** William James Craft. **GPV, FCT**

Damien: Omen 2 ✍✍ **1978 (R)** Sequel to "The Omen" about Damien, a young boy possessed with mysterious demonic powers, who kills those people who anger him. Followed by "The Final Conflict." **110m/C VHS, Beta, LV, Letterbox.** William Holden, Lee Grant, Lew Ayres, Robert Foxworth, Sylvia Sidney, Lance Henriksen, Jonathan Scott-Taylor, Nicholas Pryor, Allan Arbus, Meshach Taylor; **D:** Don Taylor; **W:** Mike Hodges; **C:** Bill Butler; **M:** Jerry Goldsmith. **FOX**

Damien: The Leper Priest ✍✍ *Father Damien: The Leper Priest* **1980** True story of a Roman Catholic priest who doomed himself by voluntarily serving on a leper colony one hundred years ago. Somewhat disappointing considering the dramatic material. Originally a vehicle for David Janssen, who died prior to filming. Made for television. **100m/C VHS, Beta.** Ken Howard, Mike Farrell, Wilfrid Hyde-White, William Daniels, David Ogden Stiers; **D:** Steven Gethers. **ART**

Damn the Defiant ✍✍✍ *HMS Defiant* **1962** Adventure abounds when Guinness, as captain of the HMS Defiant during the Napoleonic wars, finds himself up against not only the French but his cruel second-in-command (Bogarde) and a mutinous crew as well. In the end, both a fleet-wide mutiny and a French invasion of England are avoided. Much attention is paid to period detail in this well-crafted film. **101m/C VHS, Beta, LV.** *GB* Alec Guinness, Dirk Bogarde, Maurice Denham, Anthony Quayle; **D:** Lewis Gilbert. **COL, FCT**

Damn Yankees ✍✍✍ *What Lola Wants* **1958** Musical feature adapted from the Broadway hit. A baseball fan frustrated by his team's lack of success makes a pact with the devil to become the team's new star. Verdon is dynamite as the devil's accomplice. Great Bob Fosse choreography. ♫Whatever Lola Wants; (You Gotta Have) Heart; Shoeless Joe From Hannibal Mo; Goodbye, Old Girl; A Little Brains, a Little Talent; Who's Got the Pain; Two Lost Souls; There's Something About an Empty Chair; Those Were the Good Old Days. **110m/C VHS, Beta, LV, Closed Caption.** Gwen Verdon,

Ray Walston, Tab Hunter, Jean Stapleton, Russ Brown; **D:** George Abbott, Stanley Donen. Nominations: Academy Awards '58: Scoring of a Musical. **WAR, FCT, HMV**

Damnation Alley ✍1/2 **1977 (PG)** A warrior, an artist, and a biker jump in tank and set off in search of civilization after Armageddon. They go to Albany instead. So-so attempt to revive the post-nuclear holocaust genre which was more successfully accomplished by the "Mad Max" series. Adapted from Roger Zelazny's novel. **87m/C VHS, Beta.** George Peppard, Jan-Michael Vincent, Paul Winfield, Dominique Sanda, Jackie Earle Haley; **D:** Jack Smight; **W:** Alan Sharp, Lukas Heller; **C:** Harry Stradling Jr.; **M:** Jerry Goldsmith. **FOX**

The Damned ✍✍1/2 **1969 (R)** Depicts the Nazi takeover of a German industrialist family and their descent into greed, lust, and madness. Comes in dubbed or subtitled formats. **146m/C VHS, Beta.** *IT GE* Dirk Bogarde, Ingrid Thulin, Helmut Griem, Charlotte Rampling, Helmut Berger; **D:** Luchino Visconti; **M:** Maurice Jarre. Nominations: Academy Awards '69: Best Story & Screenplay. **WAR**

Damned River ✍1/2 **1989 (R)** Four friends take a guided tour down Zimbabwe's Zambezi River, only to find midway down that their guide is a murderous psycho. Survival becomes a priority. **93m/C VHS, Beta, Closed Caption.** Stephen Shellan, Lisa Aliff, John Terlesky, Marc Poppel, Bradford Bancroft; **D:** Michael Schroeder; **W:** John Crowther. **FOX**

A Damsel in Distress ✍✍✍ **1937** Astaire falls for an upper-class British girl, whose family wants her to have nothing to do with him. Features memorable songs from the Gershwins. ♫A Foggy Day in Londontown; Nice Work If You Can Get It; Stiff Upper Lip; Put Me to the Test; I Can't Be Bothered Now; The Jolly Tar and the Milkmaid; Things Are Looking Up; Sing of Spring; Ah Che a Voi Perdoni Iddio. **101m/B VHS, Beta, LV.** Fred Astaire, Joan Fontaine, George Burns, Gracie Allen, Ray Noble, Montagu Love, Reginald Gardiner; **D:** George Stevens; **M:** George Gershwin, George Bassman, Ira Gershwin. Nominations: Academy Awards '37: Best Interior Decoration. **CCB, TTC**

Dan Candy's Law ✍1/2 *Alien Thunder* **1973** A Canadian mountie becomes a driven hunter, and then desperate prey, when he tries to track down the Indian who killed his partner. **90m/C VHS, Beta.** *CA* Donald Sutherland, Gordon Tootoosis, Chief Dan George, Kevin McCarthy; **D:** Claude Fournier; **M:** Georges Delerue. **SIM**

Dance ✍1/2 **1990** Two ballet dancers struggle to find love amidst the backstage treacheries and demanding schedules of their profession. **90m/C VHS, Beta.** John Revall, Ellen Troy, Carlton Wilborn, Charlene Campbell; **D:** Robin Murray.

Dance Fools Dance ✍✍✍ **1931** Fast-paced drama has Crawford and Bakewell as a pair of spoiled rich kids who are forced to face poverty when the stock market crashes. He meets up with Gable, who's producing liquor illegally, while she gets a job at a newspaper. When Gable arranges something akin to the St. Valentine's Day Massacre, Bakewell's investigative reporting of the situation produces fatal results. The Hays Office had a problem with Crawford and friends appearing in their underwear. Cast notes: Gable was just starting out at MGM, which is why he was billed sixth; the William Holden here is not THE William Holden, and Edwards went on to provide the voice of Jiminy Cricket in "Pinocchio." **82m/B VHS, Beta.** Joan Crawford, Lester Vail, Cliff Edwards, William "Billy" Bakewell, Clark Gable; **D:** Harry Beaumont; **C:** Charles Rosher. **MGM, FCT**

Dance, Girl, Dance ✍✍ **1940** The private lives and romances of a wartime nightclub dance troupe. Standard Hollywood potpourri of dance, drama, comedy. ♫Mother, What Do I Do Now?; Jitterbug Bite; Morning Star. **88m/B VHS, Beta, LV.** Maureen O'Hara, Louis Hayward, Lucille Ball, Virginia Field, Ralph Bellamy, Maria Ouspenskaya, Mary Carlisle, Katherine Alexander, Edward Brophy; **D:** Dorothy Arzner. **TTC**

The Dance Goes On ✍✍ **1992** After the death of an uncle, Keach and his estranged son Almond reunite at the old Quebec family farm left to them. The father is country-bred and appreciates the property but his Los Angeles-reared son wants to sell for a quick profit. Director Almond cast his own son in the starring role as well as ex-wife Bujold, who plays the ambitious showbiz mother. **104m/C VHS.** James Keach, Matt Almond, Genevieve Bujold, Cary Lawrence; **D:** Paul Almond; **W:** Paul Almond. **MNC**

Dance Hall ✍1/2 **1941** A Pennsylvania dance hall owner is propelled into romantic confusion with the introduction of a sultry blond dancer into his club. **73m/B VHS, Beta.** Cesar Romero, Carole Landis, William Henry, June Storey, Charles Halton; **D:** Irving Pichel. **NOS, BAR, HEG**

Dance Hall Racket ✍✍ **1958** A sleazy, stilted expose of dance hall vice featuring a brief appearance by Bruce and his wife, Harlow. **60m/B VHS, Beta.** Lenny Bruce, Honey Harlow; **D:** Phil Tucker. **DVT, HEG**

Dance Macabre ✍ **1991 (R)** Englund takes on a dual role as a man with a split personality—one of whom is deadly. Jessica, an American ballerina, enrolls in a Russian dance academy and meets mesmerizing choreographer, Anthony. Unfortunately for Jessica she happens to look exactly like Anthony's long-dead lover and he becomes obsessed with her. Also, her fellow dancers are being brutally murdered. Are the events connected? **CW:** Violence and sensuality. **97m/C VHS, LV.** Robert Englund, Michelle Zeitlin, Marianna Moen, Julene Renee, Alexander Sergeyev; **D:** Greydon Clark; **W:** Greydon Clark. **COL**

Dance Me Outside ✍✍1/2 **1995 (R)** Native Canadian teens look for some excitement on their Northern Ontario reservation and find themselves cut off from their tradition-bound parents in this slice of life drama. Friends Silas and Blackie plot revenge against a white who murdered a native girl while Silas' sister Illiana comes to visit from Toronto, with her Yuppie lawyer husband, just as her ex-boyfriend returns from a prison stint. Based on the novel by W.P. Kinsella. **CW:** Language, brief violence. **91m/C VHS, LV.** *CA* Ryan Black, Adam Beach, Michael Greyeyes, Lisa Lacroix; **D:** Bruce McDonald; **W:** Bruce McDonald, Don McKellar, John Frizzell. Genie Awards '95: Best Film Editing. **APX**

Dance of Death woof! *House of Evil; Macabre Serenade* **1968** Just before his death, Karloff agreed to appear in footage for four Mexican cheapies that were practically thrown together (Karloff actually filmed his scenes in Los Angeles). If they had mixed the footage instead of matched it, the flicks couldn't be any worse. This one concerns a lunatic toy-maker whose toys kill and maim his heirs. **89m/C VHS, Beta.** *MX* Boris Karloff, Julissa, Andres Garcia, Jack Hill; **D:** Juan Ibanez. **SNC, MPI**

Dance of Death ✍ **1984** A girl learns kung fu and kills many warriors by kicking them in the ribs and head. **81m/C VHS, Beta.** Mao Ying, Shih Tien, Shiao Bou-Lo, Chien Pay, Chia Kai, Noh Tikki. **UNI**

Dance of Life ✍✍1/2 **1929** A look at the backstage goings-on at a burlesque theatre. A successful entertainer's life goes down the tubes when he hits the bottle. His wife leaves him because of his philandering, but returns when she sees how much he really needs her. One scene of the Ziegfeld Follies uses two-tone Technicolor technology. This was re-made twice: as "Swing High, Swing Low" in 1937 and as "When My Baby Smiles at Me" in 1948. Carroll replaced the stage lead, who was said to have no "name recognition"—Barbara Stanwyck. ♫True Blue Lou; King of Jazzmania; Cuddlesome Baby; Flippity Flop; Ladies of the Dance; The Mightiest Matador; Sweet Rosie O'Grady; In the Gloaming; Sam, the Accordion Man. **115m/B VHS.** Nancy Carroll, Hal Skelly, Ralph Theadore, Charles D. Brown, Dorothy Revier, Al

"Fuzzy" St. John, Oscar Levant; **D:** John Cromwell. *NOS, MLD*

Dance of the Damned 🎔🎔 1988 **(R)** A case where low-budget isn't synonymous with bomb. Fascinating noir-ish plot concerning a vampire who wants to learn more about the life of his next victim, a deep-thinking stripper, who has lost the will to live it. Surprisingly well-done and acted; above-par for this genre. 83m/C **VHS, Beta, LV.** Cyril O'Reilly, Starr Andreeff, Deborah Ann Nassar, Maria Ford; **D:** Katt Shea Ruben; **W:** Katt Shea Ruben, Andy Ruben; **C:** Phedon Papamichael; **M:** Gary Stockdale. *NO*

Dance or Die 🎔 1987 Just goes to show that in Las Vegas you can't have your dance and drugs too, because if the Mob doesn't get you, the Feds will. Made for video (though maybe it shouldn't have been made at all). In HiFi Stereo. 90m/C VHS, Beta. Ray Kieffer, Rebecca Barrington; **D:** Richard W. Munchkin. *NO*

Dance with a Stranger 🎔🎔🎔½ 1985 **(R)** The engrossing and factual story of Ruth Ellis who gained notoriety as the last woman hanged in Great Britain. This emotional and sometimes violent film mirrors the sensationalism produced in the 1950s. The film follows Ellis's pre-trial life and her perpetual struggle to maintain her independence. Newcomer Richardson portrays the Marilyn Monroe look-alike barmaid. 101m/C VHS, Beta, LV, **Closed Caption.** *GB* Miranda Richardson, Rupert Everett, Ian Holm, Joanne Whalley, Matthew Carroll, Tom Chadbon, Jane Bertish, David Trughton, Paul Mooney, Stratford Johns, Susan Kyd, Leslie Manville, Sallie-Anne Field, Martin Murphy, Michael Jenn, Daniel Massey; **D:** Mike Newell; **W:** Shelagh Delaney; **C:** Peter Hannan; **M:** Richard Hartley. Cannes Film Festival '85: Best Film. *VES, ART*

Dance with Death 🎔 1991 **(R)** When strippers turn up brutally murdered, a young journalist goes undercover to solve the case. **CW:** Language, strong violence, and strong sensuality. 90m/C VHS, LV, **Closed Caption.** Maxwell Caulfield, Barbara Alyn Jones, Martin Mull, Drew Snyder, Catya Sassoon; **D:** Charles Philip Moore. *HBO*

Dance With Me *Shut Up and Dance* 1998 **(PG)** Cuban emigre Rafael (Chayanne) winds up in Houston, teaching at the fading Excelsior Dance Studio. Instructor Ruby (Williams) is looking for a partner who can help her enter the competitive ballroom dance world but she's not looking for love. But at the World Open Dance Championships in Las Vegas, she may find both. Not yet reviewed. **?m/C VHS.** Vanessa L(ynne) Williams, Chayanne, Kris Kristofferson, Joan Plowright, J.E. Freeman; **D:** Randa Haines. *NYR*

Dance with Me, Henry 🎔½ 1956 When Lou becomes involved with Bud's gambling debts and the local district attorney turns up dead, Lou's not only wanted by the law, but by the mafia as well. This was the great comedy duo's last picture together and it's clear the pair are not happy about working with each other, even on this mediocre effort. 89m/B VHS. Bud Abbott, Lou Costello, Gigi Perreau, Rusty Hamer, Mary Wickes, Ted de Corsia; **D:** Charles T. Barton. *MGM*

Dancer, Texas - Pop. 81 🎔🎔🎔 1998 **(PG)** Four buddies have to decide if they're going to fulfill the pact they made when they were 11 to leave the eponymous town upon graduating from high school. Each one has a reason to consider sticking around: Keller (Meyer) tkaes care of his widowed grandfather; Terrell Lee (Facinelli) is expected to join the family's failing oil business; Squirrel (Embry) thinks he should care for his alcoholic father; and John (Mills) is a natural at cattle ranching. Coming-of-age comedy deals in honest emotion and humor, and doesn't resort to syrupy sentiment or small-town stereotyping. Texas-born writer-director McCanlies' feature debut. 95m/C VHS. *NYR*

Dancers 🎔½ 1987 **(PG)** During the filming of the ballet "Giselle" in Italy, a famous, almost-over-the-hill dancer (Baryshnikov, ten years after his role in "The Turning Point") coaches a young,

inexperienced starlet. He hopes to revitalize his life and his dancing. Features dancers from the Baryshnikov-led American Ballet Theatre. 99m/C **VHS, Beta, LV, Closed Caption.** Mikhail Baryshnikov, Leslie Browne, Julie Kent, Mariangela Melato, Alessandra Ferri, Lynn Seymour, Victor Barbee, Tommy Rall; **D:** Herbert Ross; **M:** Pino Donaggio. *CTH, WAR, FCT*

Dances with Wolves 🎔🎔🎔½ 1990 **(PG-13)** The story of a U.S. Army soldier, circa 1870, whose heroism in battle allows him his pick of posts. His choice, to see the West before it disappears, changes his life. He meets, understands and eventually becomes a member of a Lakota Sioux tribe in the Dakotas. Costner's first directorial attempt proves him a talent of vision and intelligence. This sometimes too objective movie lacks a sense of definitive character, undermining its gorgeous scenery and interesting perspective on the plight of Native Americans. Lovely music and epic proportions. Adapted by Blake from his novel. 181m/C VHS, Beta, LV, **Letterbox, Closed Caption.** Kevin Costner, Mary McDonnell, Graham Greene, Rodney Grant, Floyd "Red Crow" Westerman, Tantoo Cardinal, Robert Pastorelli, Charles Rocket, Maury Chaykin, Jimmy Herman, Nathan Lee Chasing His Horse, Wes Studi; **D:** Kevin Costner; **W:** Michael Blake; **C:** Dean Semler; **M:** John Barry. Academy Awards '90: Best Adapted Screenplay, Best Cinematography, Best Director (Costner), Best Film Editing, Best Picture, Best Sound, Best Original Score; Directors Guild of America Awards '90: Best Director (Costner); Golden Globe Awards '91: Best Director (Costner), Best Film—Drama, Best Screenplay; National Board of Review Awards '90: Best Director (Costner); Writers Guild of America '90: Best Adapted Screenplay; Nominations: Academy Awards '90: Best Actor (Costner), Best Art Direction/Set Decoration, Best Costume Design, Best Supporting Actor (Greene), Best Supporting Actress (McDonnell). *ORI, FCT, IME*

Dancing in the Dark 🎔🎔½ 1986 **(PG-13)** An interesting but slow-moving Canadian film about the perfect housewife who learns that after 20 years of devotion to him, her spouse has been unfaithful. Realizing how her life has been wasted she murders her husband and, in the end, suffers a mental breakdown. 93m/C VHS, Beta. *CA* Martha Henry, Neil Munro, Rosemary Dunsmore, Richard Monette; **D:** Leon Marr; **W:** Leon Marr; **M:** Erik Satie. Genie Awards '87: Best Actress (Henry). *VTR*

Dancing Lady 🎔🎔½ 1933 Rarely seen film is MGM's answer to "42nd Street," with Crawford as a small-time hoofer trying to break into Broadway. The screen debuts of Astaire and Eddy. 🎵Everything I Have Is Yours; Heigh-Ho! The Gang's All Here; Hold Your Man; That's the Rhythm of the Day; My Dancing Lady; Let's Go Bavarian; Hey Young Fella. 93m/B VHS, Beta. Clark Gable, Joan Crawford, Fred Astaire, Franchot Tone, Nelson Eddy, Ted Healy, Moe Howard, Shemp Howard, Larry Fine; **D:** Robert Z. Leonard. *MGM, TTC, FCT*

Dancing Man 🎔½ 1933 A gigolo romances both mother and daughter and winds up implicated in murder as a result. Dismissable. 65m/B VHS, Beta, 8mm. Judith Allen, Reginald Denny, Natalie Moorhead; **D:** Albert Ray. *VYY*

Dancing Mothers 🎔🎔½ 1926 A fast-living woman becomes involved with her mother's roguish boyfriend in this silent film with accompanying musical score. 85m/B VHS, Beta. Clara Bow, Alice Joyce, Conway Tearle, Donald Keith; **D:** Herbert Brenon. *NOS, MRV, DVT*

Dancing Pirate 🎔🎔 1936 A Boston dance instructor is kidnapped by pirates and jumps ship in Mexico, where he romances a mayor's daughter. The silly story boasts some Rodgers and Hart tunes, plus the early use of Technicolor, exploited here for all it was worth and then some. 🎵Are You My Love?; When You're Dancing the Waltz. 83m/C **VHS.** Charles Collins, Frank Morgan, Steffi Duna, Luis Alberni, Victor Varconi, Jack LaRue; **D:** Lloyd Corrigan. *NOS, LOO*

The Dancing Princesses 1984 When five naughty princesses wear the soles of their slippers out every night, their father the King must foot the bill. He soon tires of this expense and offers a reward to the person who can discover how this happens. A handsome prince becomes invisible to follow the lovely ladies and discover their secret. From the "Faerie Tale Theatre" series. Made for television. 60m/C VHS, Beta, **Closed Caption.** Lesley Ann Warren, Peter Weller, Sachi Parker, Roy Dotrice; **D:** Peter Medak. *FOX, FCT*

Dancing with Danger 🎔🎔½ 1993 **(PG-13)** A private investigator is hired to find out why a taxi dancer's customers all end up dead. Soon the PI's employer is the next victim of a serial killer whose ultimate target is the dancer herself. 90m/C VHS, Beta, **Closed Caption.** Cheryl Ladd, Ed Marinaro, Miguel Sandoval, Pat Skipper; **D:** Stuart Cooper; **W:** Elisa Bell. *PAR*

Dandelions 🎔 1974 German soft-core flick starring Hauer in an early role as a man jilted by his wife. To make himself feel better he decides to explore the sleazier side of life. Meaningless film evokes no sympathy but some may appreciate the titillation. Dubbed. 92m/C VHS, Beta. *GE* Rutger Hauer, Dagmar Lassander; **D:** Adrian Hoven. *NO*

Dandy in Aspic 🎔½ 1968 **(R)** A double-agent is assigned to kill himself in this hard to follow British spy drama. The film is based on Derek Marlowe's novel. Mann died midway through shooting and Harvey finished direction. 107m/C VHS, Beta, LV, Letterbox. *GB* Laurence Harvey, Tom Courtenay, Lionel Stander, Mia Farrow, Harry Andrews, Peter Cook, Per Oscarsson; **D:** Anthony Mann; **M:** Quincy Jones. *COL*

Danger Ahead 🎔 1940 Newill stars again as Renfrew of the Mounties—this time he tries to rid the north woods of the baddies who are trying to take over. 57m/B VHS. James Newill, Dorothea Kent, Guy Usher, Dave O'Brien, Bob Terry; **D:** Ralph Staub. *DVT, HEG*

Danger: Diabolik 🎔 *Diabolik* 1968 **(PG-13)** A superthief called Diabolik (Law) continuously evades the law while performing his criminal antics. 99m/C VHS, **Closed Caption.** *IT* John Phillip Law, Marisa Mell, Michel Piccoli, Terry-Thomas; **D:** Mario Bava; **M:** Ennio Morricone. *PAR*

Danger in the Skies 🎔½ *The Pilot* 1979 **(PG)** An alcoholic airline pilot tries to straighten out his life when he nearly loses everything while drinking on the job. Made for cable television. 99m/C VHS, Beta. Cliff Robertson, Diane Baker, Dana Andrews, Gordon MacRae, Milo O'Shea, Frank Converse, Edward Binns; **D:** Cliff Robertson; **C:** Walter Lassally. *HHE*

Danger Lights 🎔½ 1930 Depicts the railroads and the railroad men's dedication to each other and their trains. 73m/B VHS, Beta. Jean Arthur, Louis Wolheim, Robert Armstrong; **D:** George B. Seitz. *PEN, MRV, NOS*

Danger Man 1961 British tv series starring McGoohan as NATO agent John Drake. Half-hour episodes were known as "Danger Man" in England, when the series went to 60 minutes the title was changed to "Secret Agent" with the premise remaining the same. Additional episodes available. 30m/C VHS. *GB* Patrick McGoohan. *MPI, MOV*

Danger of Love 🎔½ 1995 **(R)** Married teacher Michael Carlin (Penny) has an affair with seductive colleague Carolyn Warmus (Robertson) but when he's about to end it, his wife is murdered. The detective (Bologna) thinks Michael is guilty but it's Carolyn who's hiding all the secrets. Based on a true story; made for TV. **CW:** Violence and some sexual material. 95m/C VHS. Joe Penny, Jenny Robertson, Joseph Bologna, Richard Lewis, Fairuza Balk, Deborah Benson, Sydney Walsh; **D:** Joyce Chopra. *THV*

Danger on the Air 🎔🎔 1938 A radio program sponsor—a much-despised misogynist—is murdered, and the sound engineer attempts to solve the mystery. Features Cobb in one of his earliest roles; Garrett also directed

"Lady in the Morgue" that year. **70m/B VHS, Beta.** Donald Woods, Nan Grey, Berton Churchill, Jed Prouty, William Lundigan, Richard "Skeets" Gallagher, Edward Van Sloan, George Meeker, Lee J. Cobb, Johnny Arthur, Linda Hayes, Louise Stanley; **D:** Otis Garrett. *SNC*

Danger Trails *♂♂½* **1935** Rehashed western programmer. Features the hero who must save the rancher's honor as well as the ranch, while fighting detestable hombres with the traditional fare as an arsenal. **55m/B VHS.** Guinn "Big Boy" Williams, Marjorie Gordon, Wally Wales, John Elliott, Ace Cain, Edmund Cobb; **D:** Robert F. "Bob" Hill. *NOS, DVT, GPV*

Danger UXB *♂♂½* **1981** During the 1940 London blitz "Danger UXB" was scrawled wherever there was, or thought to be, an unexploded German bomb. This miniseries covers the exploits of the Royal Engineers whose job it was, with little training and lots of nerve, to defuse the bombs. Based on the memoirs of Major A.B. Hartley of the Royal Engineers. On five cassettes. Made for television. **660m/C VHS.** *GB* Anthony Andrews, Judy Geeson, Maurice Roeves, Kenneth Cranham, Jeremy Sinden, Iain Cuthbertson, George Innes, Norman Chappell, Kenneth Farrington, Gordon Kane, Ken Kitson, Robert Longden, Robert Pugh, Deborah Watling. *SIG, TVC, FUS*

Danger Zone *♂♂* **1951** A man is hired to bid for a saxophone at an auction and then has the instrument stolen from him. He discovers it contained stolen jewelry and tries to recover it. **56m/B VHS, Beta, LV.** Hugh Beaumont, Tom Neal, Richard Travis, Virginia Dale. *NO*

Danger Zone woof! **1987 (R)** A low-budget, low-brow flick about an all-female rock band whose bus breaks down in the middle of the desert, leaving the girls to defend themselves against a merciless motorcycle gang. You'll wish this one was a mirage. **90m/C VHS, Beta.** Robert Canada, Jason Williams, Kriss Braxton, Dana Dowell, Jamie Ferreira; **D:** Henry Vernon. *NLC*

Danger Zone *♂♂* **1995 (R)** An American mining expert uncovers a worldwide nuclear plot when he's lured to East Africa to supposedly contain a toxic spill. Instead, he's being used to recover a load of plutonium. *CW:* Commando violence. **92m/C VHS, LV, Closed Caption.** Billy Zane, Ron Silver, Robert Downey Jr., Cary-Hiroyuki Tagawa; **D:** Allan Eastman; **W:** Jeff Albert; **C:** Yossi Wein. *ART*

Danger Zone 2 *♂* **1989 (R)** A pernicious biker is released from prison on a technicality and decides to pay a social call to the undercover cop who set him up. **95m/C VHS.** Jason Williams, Robert Random; **D:** Geoffrey G. Bowers; **W:** Dulany Ross Clements. *MCG*

Danger Zone 3: Steel Horse War *♂* **1990 (R)** The "Danger Zone" dude is back and this time he's taken on a bevy of bikertypes in a most gruesome battle to make our deserts safe. **91m/C VHS, Beta.** Jason Williams, Robert Random, Barne Suboski, Juanita Ranney, Rusty Cooper, Giles Ashford; **D:** Douglas Bronco. *PMR*

Dangerous *♂♂½* **1935** Davis won her first Oscar for her rather overdone portrayal of a has-been alcoholic actress reformed by a smitten architect who recognizes her from her days as a star. **72m/B VHS, Beta, LV.** Bette Davis, Franchot Tone, Margaret Lindsay, Alison Skipworth, John Eldridge, Dick Foran; **D:** Alfred E. Green. Academy Awards '35: Best Actress (Davis). *MGM, BTV*

The Dangerous *♂½* **1995 (R)** New Orleans' seamy underworld is the setting for a hot-headed cop (Pare), a mystery man (Davi) and the beauty (Barbieri) they're both interested in. Also available unrated. *CW:* Strong brutal violence, sexuality and language. **96m/C VHS, LV, Closed Caption.** Robert Davi, Michael Pare, Paula Barbieri, Elliott Gould, John Savage, Joel Grey; **D:** Maria Dante, Rod Hewitt; **W:** Rod Hewitt. *ORI*

A Dangerous Age *♂♂½* **1957** A young girl, hoping to marry her lover, runs away from boarding school. **?m/C VHS.** Ben Piazza, Ann Pearson. *SNC*

Dangerous Appointment *♂♂* **1934** Story of an innocent store clerk accused of theft and attempted murder. **?m/C VHS.** Charles Starrett, Dorothy Wilson. *SNC*

Dangerous Beauty *♂♂♂* *The Honest Courtesan; Indiscretion; Venice; Courtesan* **1998 (R)** In 16th-century Venice, poor but beautiful Veronica (McCormack) gains wealth and power by becoming a sought after courtesan. The bewigged, bewitched and bewildered heads of state fall as hard for the comely courtesan as victims to the plague that strikes Venice later in the film. The one man she wants, however, Marco Venier (Sewell), comes from a wealthy family that looks down on the common Veronica. Director Herskovitz mixes the strong feminist messages with humor and a modern sensibility that sometimes make you forget you're watching a period film. Based on the biography of the real Veronica Franco by Margaret Rosenthal. *CW:* Some scenes of strong sexuality, and for nudity and language. **112m/C VHS.** Catherine McCormack, Rufus Sewell, Moira Kelly, Jacqueline Bisset, Oliver Platt, Fred Ward, Naomi Watts, Jeroen Krabbe, Joanna Cassidy, Daniel Lapaine, Jake Weber, Simon Dutton, Michael Culkin, Peter Eyre; **D:** Marshall Herskovitz; **W:** Jeannine Dominy; **C:** Bojan Bazelli; **M:** George Fenton. *NYR*

Dangerous Charter *♂♂½* **1962** A group of fishermen discover a deserted yacht and man its helm. But their good fortune takes a decided turn for the worst as they become caught in mob-propelled danger. **76m/C VHS, Beta.** Chris Warfield, Sally Fraser, Richard Foote, Peter Foster, Wright King; **D:** Robert Gottschalk. *NOS*

Dangerous Curves *♂♂½* **1988 (PG)** Two friends are assigned to deliver a new Porsche to a billionaire's daughter—one of them talks the other into taking a little detour, and the trouble begins. This one went straight to video. **93m/C VHS, Beta.** Robert Stack, Tate Donovan, Danielle von Zerneck, Robert Klein, Elizabeth Ashley, Leslie Nielsen; **D:** David Lewis. *VES, ART*

Dangerous Game *♂♂½* **1990 (R)** A computer hacker leads his friends through a department store's security system, only to find they can't get out until morning. They soon discover they are not alone when one of the group turns up dead. **102m/C VHS, Beta, LV, Closed Caption.** Miles Buchanan, Sandy Lillingston, Kathryn Walker, John Polson; **D:** Stephen Hopkins.

Dangerous Game *♂♂* *Snake Eyes* **1993 (R)** Abrasive filmmaker Eddie Israel's (Keitel) new movie is about a couple's disintegrating marriage turning violent. Stars Sarah (Madonna) and Francis (Russo) find the on-camera violence spilling over into their tangled private lives while Eddie finds his personal traumas intruding more and more into the fictional material. Very raw movie within a movie features volatile Keitel (who also worked with Ferrera on "Bad Lieutenant") and suitably histrionic Russo; Madonna manages to hold her own in the least showy role, a cinematic first. Eddie's betrayed and bewildered wife is sympathetically portrayed by Ferrara, director Abel's wife. Also available in an unrated version. *CW:* Language and sexuality. **107m/C VHS, LV, Closed Caption.** Harvey Keitel, James Russo, Madonna, Nancy Ferrara; **D:** Abel Ferrara; **W:** Nicholas St. John. *MGM*

Dangerous Ground *♂♂* **1996 (R)** Hackneyed thriller has expatriate South African Vusi (Cube) returning to his homeland to find his younger brother Steven, who has double-crossed the head of a drug cartel. Since Vusi's departure 12 years ago, apartheid's been replaced by gangs and drugs, and while combing the dangerous streets of Johannesburg, the graduate student implausibly turns into a gun-wielding hero. Rhames's sinister drug lord Muki is pic's best

character. Lead Cube shows just how limited his acting ability is while Hurley displays the picture's clearly limited wardrobe budget. Interracial relationships are glossed over, while South Africa's sociological problems are used as plot devices and then ignored. Filmed on location in South Africa, this shoot-em-up's locale could easily be Anytown, USA. *CW:* Strong violence, drug use and language, and for some nudity. **92m/C VHS, LV, Closed Caption.** Ice Cube, Elizabeth Hurley, Ving Rhames, Eric Miyeni, Sechaba Morojele; **D:** Darrell Roodt; **W:** Darrell Roodt, Greg Latter; **C:** Paul Gilpin; **M:** Stanley Clarke. *NLC*

Dangerous Heart *♂♂* **1993 (R)** A crooked undercover cop steals a bundle from a drug dealer and gets himself killed for his troubles. Only the dealer doesn't know where the money is. So he decides to befriend the cop's widow, get romantically involved, and see what she knows. **93m/C VHS, LV, Closed Caption.** Timothy Daly, Lauren Holly, Jeffrey Nordling, Alice Carter, Joe Pantoliano; **D:** Michael Scott; **W:** Patrick Cirillo. *USH*

Dangerous Holiday *♂♂* **1937** A young violin prodigy would rather be just "one of the boys" than be forced to practice all the time. He decides to run away but has everyone in an uproar thinking he's been kidnapped. **54m/B VHS, Beta.** Hedda Hopper, Guinn "Big Boy" Williams, Jack LaRue, Franklin Pangborn, Grady Sutton. *VYY*

Dangerous Hours *♂♂* **1919** An anti-communist propaganda film with Hughes as the innocent young college boy who gets duped by the evil Marxists until he realizes the truth of his all-American upbringing. Silent with original organ score. **88m/B VHS, Beta, 8mm.** Lloyd Hughes; **D:** Fred Niblo; **C:** George Barnes. *VYY, FCT, GPV*

Dangerous Indiscretion *♂♂* **1994 (R)** Ad exec finds his girlfriend is actually a woman married to a very powerful man, who's not going to be happy to find out about their liaison. *CW:* Strong sexuality. **81m/C VHS, Closed Caption.** Joan Severance, C. Thomas Howell, Malcolm McDowell; **D:** Richard Kletter; **W:** Richard Kletter, Jack Tarpon; **M:** Richard Gibbs. *PAR*

Dangerous Liaisons *♂♂* *Les Liaisons Dangereuses; Dangerous Love Affairs* **1960** A couple take each other to the brink of destruction via their insatiable desire for extra-marital affairs. Vadim attempted to repeat his success with Brigitte Bardot by featuring wife Annette as a new sex goddess, but lightning didn't strike twice. **111m/B VHS, LV.** *FR IT* Gerard Philipe, Jeanne Moreau, Jeanne Valeri, Annette Vadim, Simone Renant, Jean-Louis Trintignant, Nikolas Vogel; **D:** Roger Vadim; **W:** Roger Vadim. *INT, TPV*

Dangerous Liaisons *♂♂♂* **1988 (R)** Stylish and absorbing, this adaptation of the Laclos novel and the Christopher Hampton play centers around the relationship of two decadent members of 18th-century French nobility. The two, Close and Malkovich, spend their time testing and manipulating the loves of others. They find love often has a will of its own. Possibly the best of the several versions available. Interesting to comparison-view with director Milos Forman's version of this story, 1989's "Valmont." **120m/C VHS, Beta, LV, 8mm, Letterbox, Closed Caption.** John Malkovich, Glenn Close, Michelle Pfeiffer, Uma Thurman, Keanu Reeves, Swoosie Kurtz, Mildred Natwick, Peter Capaldi; **D:** Stephen Frears; **W:** Christopher Hampton; **C:** Philippe Rousselot; **M:** George Fenton. Academy Awards '88: Best Adapted Screenplay, Best Art Direction/Set Decoration, Best Costume Design; British Academy Awards '89: Best Adapted Screenplay, Best Supporting Actress (Pfeiffer); Cesar Awards '90: Best Foreign Film; Writers Guild of America '88: Best Adapted Screenplay; Nominations: Academy Awards '88: Best Actress (Close), Best Picture, Best Supporting Actress (Pfeiffer), Best Original Score. *WAR, FCT*

Dangerous Life *♂♂* **1989** Explosive drama brings to the screen the story of the Philippine uprising. It shows the horrible events that lead to the fall of Marcos and permitted the rise of Corazon Aquino. **163m/C VHS, Beta, LV.** Gary Busey; *W:* David Williamson. *NO*

Dangerous Love woof! **1987** Advice to the lovelorn: Avoid this one. Female members of a video dating service are being filmed in a death scene—their own. **87m/C VHS, Beta.** Lawrence Monoson, Brenda Bakke, Peter Marc, Elliott Gould, Anthony Geary; *D:* Marty Ollstein.

A Dangerous Man: Lawrence after Arabia 🎬🎬🎬 **1991** At the 1919 Paris Peace Conference, T.E. Lawrence serves as the liaison to the Hashemite delegation in an effort to have the Allies agree to Arab independence. He finds the diplomatic fields more treacherous than anything he encountered during WWI. Fiennes does well in the difficult role of the reluctant, ambivalent hero. Made for television. **104m/C VHS, Closed Caption.** *GB* Ralph Fiennes, Denis Quilley, Alexander Siddig, Nicholas Jones, Roger Hammond, Peter Copley, Paul Freeman, Polly Walker; *D:* Christopher Menaul; *W:* Tim Rose Price. *VTR*

Dangerous Minds 🎬🎬½ *My Posse Don't Do Homework* **1995 (R)** Based on the autobiography of LouAnne Johnson (Pfeiffer), a 10-year Marine turned inspirational inner-city high school English teacher. Naturally, Johnson has to take on the establishment educational system to fight for her kids. If you can buy Pfeiffer as an ex-jarhead, a tough teacher should be no problem. A subplot romance involving Pfeiffer and Andy Garcia was cut from the film to focus on the teacher/student byplay (which seems a real shame); Elaine May did a uncredited script rewrite. Kinda squishy and surprisingly successful.*CW:* Language. **99m/C VHS, LV, Closed Caption.** Michelle Pfeiffer, George Dzundza, Courtney B. Vance, Robin Bartlett, Renoly Santiago, Lorraine Toussaint; *Cameos:* John N. Smith; *W:* Ronald Bass; *C:* Pierre Letarte. Blockbuster Entertainment Awards '96: Drama Actress, Theatrical (Pfeiffer); Nominations: MTV Movie Awards '96: Best Film, Best Female Performance (Pfeiffer), Most Desirable Female (Pfeiffer), Best Song ("Gangsta's Paradise"). *TOU*

Dangerous Mission 🎬½ **1954** A young woman witnesses a mob murder in New York and flees to the Midwest, pursued by killers and the police. Good cast couldn't do much with this one. **75m/B VHS, Beta.** Victor Mature, Piper Laurie, Vincent Price, William Bendix; *D:* Louis King; *W:* W.R. Burnett, Charles Bennett.

Dangerous Moonlight 🎬🎬🎬 *Suicide Squadron* **1941** Polish concert pianist becomes a bomber pilot for the British in WWII, though his wife wants him to stay at the piano. Great battle and music sequences; the piece "Warsaw Concerto" became a soundtrack hit. **97m/B VHS.** *GB* Anton Walbrook, Sally Gray, Derrick DeMarney, Cecil Parker, Percy Parsons, Keneth Kent, Guy Middleton, John Laurie, Frederick Valk; *D:* Brian Desmond Hurst. *TTC*

Dangerous Moves 🎬🎬🎬 *La Diagonale du Fou* **1984 (PG)** A drama built around the World Chess championship competition between a renowned Russian master and a young, rebellious dissident. The chess game serves as both metaphor and background for the social and political tensions it produces. With English subtitles. **96m/C VHS, Beta, LV.** *SI* Liv Ullmann, Michel Piccoli, Leslie Caron, Alexandre Arbatt; *D:* Richard Dembo; *W:* Richard Dembo; *C:* Raoul Coutard. Academy Awards '84: Best Foreign Language Film. *ORI, IME*

Dangerous Obsession 🎬 *Divine Obsession; Mortal Sins* **1988 (R)** A woman kidnaps the doctor she blames for her boyfriend's death and instead of exacting revenge, she makes him her personal sex slave. In the case of this flick, it's really a fate worse than death.*CW:* Language and strong sexuality. **81m/C VHS.** *IT* Corinne Clery, Brett Halsey; *D:* Lucio Fulci; *M:* Simon Boswell.

Dangerous Orphans 🎬½ **1986 (R)** Not completely awful tale of three brothers, orphaned as boys when their father is murdered before their very eyes, and the vendetta they have against the killer. **90m/C VHS, Beta.** *NZ* Peter Stevens, Peter Bland,

Ian Mune, Ross Girven, Jennifer Ward-Lealand; *D:* John Laing.

Dangerous Passage 🎬🎬 **1944** A ne'er-do-well inherits 200 grand but gets in trouble before he can collect it. He ends up falling in with assorted misfits aboard a tramp steamer. **60m/B VHS, Beta, 8mm.** Robert Lowery, Phyllis Brooks, Jack LaRue, Victor Kilian; *D:* William (Lester Williams) Berke. *VYY*

Dangerous Passion 🎬🎬½ **1995** Ruthless Lou (Williams) kills an intruder and tries to force his mechanic, Kyle (Weathers), to take the fall for him. But instead Kyle escapes with Lou's mistreated wife (and Kyle's lover) Meg (McKee), with Lou's henchman Frank (Boswell) on their tail. **94m/C VHS.** Billy Dee Williams, Carl Weathers, Lonette McKee, Charles Boswell, Elpidia Carrillo, Tony DiBenedetto, Dan Ziskie; *D:* Michael Miller; *W:* Brian Taggert; *C:* Steve Shaw; *M:* Rob Mounsey. *ART*

A Dangerous Place 🎬🎬½ **1994 (R)** Teenaged Ethan (Roberts) joins a karate team to prove his older brother's death was not a suicide. But the Scorpion's leader (Feldman) has a definite mean streak.*CW:* Violence. **97m/C VHS, LV, Closed Caption.** Ted Jan Roberts, Corey Feldman, Mako, Erin Gray, Dick Van Patten; *D:* Jerry P. Jacobs. *PMH*

Dangerous Prey 🎬½ **1995 (R)** Young woman, looking for adventure while vacationing in Europe, gets more than she bargained for when she gets mixed up with a high-tech training school for female mercenaries.*CW:* Nudity, sexual situations, violence, language. **93m/C VHS, Beta.** Shannon Whirry, Ciara Hunter; *D:* Lloyd A. Simanol. *MNC*

Dangerous Pursuit 🎬🎬 **1989** A woman discovers that a man she slept with years ago is an assassin. Knowing too much, she finds herself next on his hit list. Decent psycho-thriller that was never released theatrically. **95m/C VHS, Beta, LV, Closed Caption.** Gregory Harrison, Alexandra Powers, Scott Valentine, Brian Wimmer, Elena Stiteler; *D:* Sandor Stern. *PAR*

Dangerous Relations 🎬🎬½ *Father & Son: Dangerous Relations* **1993 (PG-13)** Made-for-TV drama with Gossett as a tough convict at the end of 15-year prison sentence whose authority is challenged by young punk prisoner Underwood. Imagine his surprise when the old con realizes the punk is the son he hasn't seen since he started his time behind bars. Things don't improve (well, not at first) when they are paroled into each other's custody.*CW:* Language, urban violence, and scene of sensuality. **93m/C VHS.** Louis Gossett Jr., Blair Underwood, Rae Dawn Chong, Clarence Williams III, Rigg Kennedy.

Dangerous Summer 🎬🎬 *The Burning Man* **1982** In Australia, an American businessman building a resort is the victim of elaborate arson/murder insurance schemes. **100m/C VHS, Beta.** *AU* Tom Skerritt, James Mason, Ian Gilmour, Wendy Hughes; *D:* Quentin Masters; *W:* David Ambrose. *NO*

Dangerous Touch 🎬½ **1994 (R)** A very charming sociopath seduces a radio host/therapist into a willing, if kinky, sexual relationship. But everything she values is put at risk when he threatens to show an incriminating video tape if she doesn't continue to do as he demands. An unrated version is also available. **101m/C VHS, LV, Closed Caption.** Lou Diamond Phillips, Kate Vernon; *D:* Lou Diamond Phillips. *THV*

Dangerous When Wet 🎬🎬 **1953** A typical Williams water-musical. A farm girl dreams of fame by swimming the English Channel. One famous number pairs Williams with cartoon characters Tom & Jerry in an underwater frolic. ♫I Got Out of Bed on the Right Side; Ain't Nature Grand; I Like Men; Fifi; In My Wildest Dreams. **96m/C VHS, Beta, LV.** Esther Williams, Fernando Lamas, Charlotte Greenwood, William Demarest, Jack Carson; *D:* Charles Walters; *M:* Arthur Schwartz, Johnny Mercer. *MGM*

A Dangerous Woman 🎬🎬 **1993 (R)** No, this isn't the femme fatale romance the word "dangerous" suggests. Instead, the eponymous character is a mildly retarded woman, Martha

(Winger), whose simplistic view on life places her in ethically compromising positions. When a hunky Irish handyman (Byrne) comes on the scene and seduces both her and the aunt with whom she lives (Hershey), Martha awakens to feelings she has never experienced. Winger's performance is both sensitive and provocative, but is wasted in a film filled with two-dimensional characters, and really, not too much of a point. Adapted from a novel by Mary McGarry Morris. Screenplay by Foner, wife of director Gyllenhaal.*CW:* Sexuality. **101m/C VHS, LV, Closed Caption.** Debra Winger, Barbara Hershey, Gabriel Byrne, David Strathairn, Chloe Webb, John Terry, Jan Hooks, Paul Dooley, Viveka Davis, Richard Riehle, Laurie Metcalf; *D:* Stephen Gyllenhaal; *W:* Naomi Foner; *C:* Robert Elswit; *M:* Carter Burwell. Nominations: Golden Globe Awards '94: Best Actress—Drama (Winger). *USH*

Dangerous Youth 🎬 *These Dangerous Years* **1958** Would-be Liverpool rocker Vaughan is drafted into the army where he becomes a man. He gets into trouble, goes AWOL, but manages to set things right. The Brit version of the troubled-teen exploitation flick. **97m/B VHS.** *GB* Frankie Vaughan, George Baker, Carole Lesley, Jackie Lane, Eddie Byrne, Thora Hird; *D:* Herbert Wilcox; *W:* Jack Trevor Story. *SNC*

Dangerously Close 🎬½ **1986 (R)** A group of anti-crime high school students organize a hall monitoring gang that becomes a group of neo-fascist disciplinarian elite. **96m/C VHS, Beta, Closed Caption.** John Stockwell, Carey Lowell, J. Eddie Peck; *D:* Albert Pyun; *C:* Walt Lloyd.

Daniel 🎬🎬½ **1983 (R)** The children of a couple who were executed for espionage (patterned after the Rosenbergs) struggle with their past in the dissident 1960s. So-so adaptation of E.L. Doctorow's "The Book of Daniel." **130m/C VHS, Beta.** Timothy Hutton, Amanda Plummer, Mandy Patinkin, Lindsay Crouse, Ed Asner, Ellen Barkin; *D:* Sidney Lumet; *C:* Andrzej Bartkowiak. *PAR*

Daniel and the Towers **199?** Daniel and his friends enjoy making fun of Sam, the man who is building glass towers in Watts, California. But when Daniel must pay for the repairs of a shopkeeper's window, he turns to Sam for help. Sam agrees to fix the windows if Daniel helps him collect glass for the towers. In the process, Sam and Daniel become friends and Sam teaches Daniel valuable lessons about beauty and determination. Although this story is fictional, the glass towers, built by Sam Rodia, really stand in Watts. A viewers' guide is included. Part of the "Wonderworks" series. **58m/C VHS.** Allan Arbus, Michael McKean, Carmen Zapata, Miguel Alamo; *D:* Paul Schneider. *HMV, BTV*

Daniel Boone 🎬🎬½ **1934** Daniel Boone guides a party of settlers from North Carolina to the fertile valleys of Kentucky, facing Indians, food shortages and bad weather along the way. O'Brien turns in a fine performance as the early American frontier hero. **75m/B VHS, Beta.** George O'Brien, Heather Angel, John Carradine; *D:* David Howard. *NOS, MRV, VCN*

Daniel Boone: Trail Blazer 🎬🎬½ **1956** Low-budget, though surprisingly well-acted rendition of the frontiersman's heroics, filmed in Mexico. **75m/B VHS.** Bruce (Herman Brix) Bennett, Lon Chaney Jr., Faron Young, Damian O'Flynn, Fred Kohler Jr., Claudio Brook, Kem Dibbs; *D:* Ismael Rodriguez, Albert C. Gannaway; *W:* John Patrick, Tom Hubbard. *NOS, MRV, REP*

Daniella by Night 🎬🎬 **1961** French model Daniella (Sommer) gets a contract to work for an Italian fashion house in Rome and she's soon attracting a lot of attention, including some that involves a spy plot. This leads to a chase through a Paris cabaret and a nude scene of Sommer, so how much does the story really matter, anyway. French with subtitles. **83m/B VHS.** *FR* Elke Sommer, Ivan Desny; *D:* Max Pecas; *M:* Charles Aznavour. *FRF*

Danielle Steel's Changes 🦴🦴½ *Changes* 1991 Ladd is a successful, divorced New York television anchorwoman who turns her life upside-down when she marries an equally successful, widowed Los Angeles surgeon (Nouri). Can they overcome their bicoastal careers to make things work? What do you think. Made for television. **96m/C VHS, Closed Caption.** Cheryl Ladd, Michael Nouri, Christopher Gartin, Randee Heller, Charles Frank, James Sloyan, Cynthia Bain; *D:* Charles Jarrott. *CMB, WOV*

Danielle Steel's "Daddy" 🦴🦴½ *Daddy* 1991 Ad exec Oliver Watson (Duffy) is happily married to Sarah (Mulgrew) and living the good life with their three kids—or so he thinks. Then Sarah announces she's leaving and Oliver's left to cope with family crisis as a single parent. A move to a new job in LA finds Oliver falling for an actress (Carter) and wondering if his family can ever be put back together again. Made for television. **95m/C VHS, Closed Caption.** Patrick Duffy, Lynda Carter, Kate Mulgrew; *D:* Michael Miller. *CMB, WOV*

Danielle Steel's Heartbeat 🦴🦴½ *Heartbeat* 1993 Shameless soap opera with Draper as Adrian Townsend, an L.A. TV-news producer with a self-involved ad-exec hubby (Kilner) who never wants children because of his own lousy childhood. When Adrian gets preggers the louse dumps her and she's left to weep prettily. That is until lovable divorced dad Bill Grant (Ritter) comes along to dry her eyes. Predictable and glossy adaptation of the Steel best-seller. Made for television. **95m/C VHS.** Polly Draper, John Ritter, Kevin Kilner, Michael Lembeck, Nancy Morgan, Victor DiMattia, Christian Cousins; *D:* Michael Miller; *W:* Jan Worthington. *CMB*

Danielle Steel's Kaleidoscope 🦴🦴½ *Kaleidoscope* 1990 Three sisters are separated in childhood, after the mysterious deaths of their parents. Then a detective is hired to reunite the adult siblings. But Hilary, the eldest, has secrets she doesn't want her sisters to share. Made for television. **96m/C VHS, Closed Caption.** Jaclyn Smith, Perry King, Colleen Dewhurst, Donald Moffat; *D:* Jud Taylor. *CMB, WOV*

Danielle Steel's Palomino 🦴🦴½ *Palomino* 1991 Bittersweet romance with Frost as an ambitious photojournalist who gets involved with a headstrong cowboy (Horsley). Their differences drive them apart and tragedy strikes when Frost becomes a paraplegic after a horse-riding accident. This leads her to new goals and the eventual return of her old flame. Between the palomino's blond mane and the equally impressive blond locks of Frost, there's a lot of streaming in the wind hair shots. Horsley's merely tall, dark, and handsome. Made for television. **90m/C VHS.** Lindsay Frost, Lee Horsley, Eva Marie Saint, Rod Taylor, Michele Greene, Beau Gravitte. *CMB*

Danielle Steel's Star 🦴½ *Star* 1993 Garth is the country girl with big dreams of a singing career but an unhappy love life. She falls for an idealist lawyer (Bierko) but their romance is put on hold by career ambitions. She goes to Hollywood and gets discovered, becoming a singing/acting sensation who's under the thumb of her increasingly obsessed manager, Wass. Meanwhile, Bierko's trapped in a miserable marriage to the wealthy, influential Farrell. Do the true lovers get together? (Take a guess). Although the story spans 15 years and lots of tribulations the young Garth never ages a day. Made for television. **90m/C VHS.** Jennie Garth, Craig Bierko, Ted Wass, Terry Farrell, Penny Fuller, Mitchell Ryan, Jim Haynie; *D:* Michael Miller; *W:* Claire Labine. *CMB*

Danny 🦴🦴½ 1979 (G) Charming story of a lonely young girl who receives an injured horse that was no longer fit for the spoiled daughter of the rich owners. **90m/C VHS, Beta.** Rebecca Page, Janet Zarish, Barbara Jean Earhardt, Gloria Maddox, George Luce; *D:* Gene Feldman. *MON, WOM, HHE*

Danny Boy 🦴½ 1946 Veteran dog, returning from the war, has difficulty adjusting to life back home. Things get worse for him and his young master when Danny Boy is assumed to be shell-shocked and dangerous. One of the few shell-shocked dog stories ever filmed. **67m/B VHS, Beta.** *VYY*

Danny Boy 🦴🦴🦴 1984 (R) Takes place in Ireland where a young saxaphonist witnesses a murder and, in an effort to understand it, sets out to find the killer. Thought-provoking film is meant to highlight the continuing struggles in Ireland. **92m/C VHS, Beta.** *IR* Stephen Rea, Veronica Quilligan, Honor Heffernan, Marie Kean, Donal McCann, Ray McAnally; *D:* Neil Jordan; *W:* Neil Jordan. *COL*

Dante's Inferno 🦴🦴🦴 1924 Abandon all hope you who watch this film. A one-time friend sends his ruthless capitalist nemesis a copy of Dante's "Inferno," and the man reads the book and dreams he's gone to hell (would that be the dress circle?) A silent film that was controversial in its day: the body-stockinged actors were believed to be nude (which would have made it the first nudie Comedy). **54m/B VHS.** Lawson Butt, Howard Gaye, Ralph Lewis, Pauline Starke, Josef Swickard; *D:* Henry Otto. *CNM*

Dante's Inferno: Life of Dante Gabriel Rossetti 🦴🦴 1969 The flamboyant life of mid-19th century English Pre-Raphaelite artist/poet Dante Gabriel Rossetti is depicted with the usual Russell flair. The drunken, drug-taking, womanizing Rossetti was part of the leading intellectual group of his age, which included Swinburne, Morris, Ruskin, and Rossetti's sister, the poet Christina Rossetti. **90m/B VHS.** *GB* Oliver Reed; *D:* Ken Russell. *TPV*

Dante's Peak 🦴🦴½ 1997 (PG-13) Northwest volcano serves up a smorgasbord of molten disaster in the second most desirable town in the U.S.—the titular Dante's Peak. Brosnan is the intuitive scientist who comes to Washington to match wits with the conical adversary and joins forces with the town's tres femme mayor Wando (Hamilton). Ashes fall like snow in January, computer generated lava flows profusely, poisonous gases leak out and water turns to acid, all with desired nail-biting effect. Wando's two kids, dog and grandma lend folksy charm and the requisite loved-ones-in-grave-danger, but this heated disaster flick is not exactly for the whole family. Cliched and predictable, flick runs the Disaster Movie Playbook page by page as plot takes a backseat to nonstop action.*CW:* Disaster related peril and gore. **112m/C VHS, LV, Closed Caption, DVD.** Pierce Brosnan, Linda Hamilton, Charles Hallahan, Grant Heslov, Elizabeth Hoffman, Jaime Renee Smith, Arabella Field, Tzi Ma, Jeremy Foley, Brian Reddy, Kirk Trutner; *D:* Roger Donaldson; *W:* Leslie Bohem; *C:* Andrzej Bartkowiak; *M:* John Frizzell. *USH*

Danton 🦴🦴🦴🦴 1982 (PG) A sweeping account of the reign of terror following the French Revolution. Focuses on the title character (wonderfully portrayed by Depardieu) and is directed with searching parallels to modern-day Poland by that country's premier filmmaker, Andrzej Wajda. Well-acted period sets round out a memorable film. In French with English subtitles. **136m/C VHS, Beta, LV.** *PL FR* Gerard Depardieu, Wojciech Pszoniak, Patrice Chereau, Angela Winkler, Boguslaw Linda; *D:* Andrzej Wajda; *W:* Jean-Claude Carriere, Agnieszka Holland, Boleslaw Michalek, Jacek Gasiorowski, Andrzej Wajda. British Academy Awards '83: Best Foreign Film; Cesar Awards '83: Best Director (Wajda); Montreal World Film Festival '83: Best Actor (Depardieu). *COL*

Danzon 🦴🦴🦴½ 1991 (PG) Julia (Rojo), a single, working-class mom escapes the drudgery of her simple existence by going to a Mexico City dance hall every Wednesday. There she loses herself to the movement of the danzon, a dance with Haitian roots, popular in Mexico for over 100 years. When her partner of six years, Carmelo (Rergis), doesn't show up one night, her life is turned upside down. So begins a search for Carmelo—and herself. Quiet and restrained, like the ballroom-style danzon at the center of the plot. Applauded at Cannes. In Spanish with English subtitles. **103m/C VHS.** *SP* Maria Rojo, Carmen Salinas, Blanca Guerra, Tito Vasconcelos, Victor Carpinteiro, Victor Vasconcelos; *D:* Maria Novaro; *W:* Maria Novaro, Betriz Novaro. *COL, FCT*

Darby O'Gill & the Little People 🦴🦴🦴½ 1959 (G) Set in Ireland, a roguish old story teller tumbles into a well and visits the land of leprechauns who give him three wishes in order to rearrange his life. When he tries to tell his friends what happened, they think that it is only another one of his stories. A wonderful Disney production (despite its disappointing boxoffice performance) with wit, charm and an ounce or two of terror. **93m/C VHS, Beta, LV.** Albert Sharpe, Janet Munro, Sean Connery, Estelle Winwood; *D:* Robert Stevenson; *C:* Winton C. Hoch. *DIS*

Darby's Rangers 🦴🦴½ *Young Invaders* 1958 WWII pot-boiler with Garner as the leader of a commando team put together for covert operations in North Africa and Italy. Successful battle sequences combine with slow-paced romantic scenes as the soldiers chase women when not chasing the enemy. **122m/B VHS.** James Garner, Jack Warden, Edd Byrnes, Peter Brown, Stuart Whitman, David Janssen, Etchika Choureau, Venetia Stevenson, Torin Thatcher, Joan Elan, Corey Allen, Murray Hamilton; *D:* William A. Wellman; *W:* Guy Trosper; *C:* William Clothier; *M:* Max Steiner. *WAR*

Daredevils of the Red Circle 1938 Three young men set out to free a man held prisoner by an escaped convict. A serial in 12 chapters. **195m/B VHS.** Charles Quigley, Bruce (Herman Brix) Bennett, Carole Landis; *D:* John English, William Witney. *REP, VCN, MLB*

Daring Danger 🦴½ 1932 McCoy is nearly killed in a fight with the villainous Alexander. When he recovers he finds Alexander has joined forces with a rustler (Ellis), so McCoy battles both of them—while his horse goes for help. **58m/B VHS.** Tim McCoy, Richard Alexander, Robert Ellis, Alberta Vaughn, Wallace MacDonald, Murdock McQuarrie, Max Davidson; *D:* David Ross Lederman. *GPV*

Daring Dobermans 🦴🦴 1973 (PG) In this sequel to "The Doberman Gang," the barking bank-robbers have a new set of crime-planning masters. A young Indian boy who loves the dogs enters the picture and may thwart their perfect crime. **88m/C VHS, Beta, Closed Caption.** Charles Robinson, Tim Considine, David Moses, Claudio Martinez, Joan Caulfield; *D:* Byron Ross Chudnow. *FOX*

Daring Game 🦴🦴 1968 A group of scuba divers nicknamed the Flying Fish attempt to rescue a woman's husband and daughter from an island dictatorship. Failed series pilot by producer Ivan Tors, better known for "Sea Hunt" and "Flipper." **100m/C VHS, Beta.** Lloyd Bridges, Brock Peters, Michael Ansara, Joan Blackman; *D:* Laslo Benedek; *M:* George Bruns. *NO*

Dario Argento's Trauma 🦴🦴 *Trauma* 1993 (R) When a teenage girl's parents are decapitated, she and an artist friend start following the clues to a psychotic killer known as "The Headhunter." Trademark horror work for Italian cult director Argento with high suspense quotient and equally high gore. An unrated version is also available.*CW:* Nudity, extreme violence, and sexual situations. **106m/C VHS, Closed Caption.** Christopher Rydell, Asia Argento, Laura Johnson, James Russo, Brad Dourif, Frederic Forrest, Piper Laurie; *D:* Dario Argento; *W:* T.E.D. Klein, Dario Argento. *REP*

The Dark 🦴½ *The Mutilator* 1979 (R) A supernatural beast commits a string of gruesome murders. **92m/C VHS, Beta.** William Devane, Cathy Lee Crosby, Richard Jaeckel, Keenan Wynn, Vivian Blaine, Biff Elliot, Warren Kemmerling, Casey Kasem; *D:* John Cardos; *W:* Stanford Whitmore; *C:* John Morrill.

The Dark ♂½ 1994 (R) Cop and scientist ~~assit a mysterious graveyard creature~~ who holds both the power to heal and destroy. One man wants to kill it, one man wants to save it, and they race to be the first to find it. **CW:** Horror violence. **90m/C VHS, LV, Closed Caption.** Brion James, Jaimz Woolvett, Cynthia Belliveau, Stephen McHattie, Dennis O'Connor, Neve Campbell, Christopher Bondy, William Lynn; **D:** Craig Pryce; **W:** Robert Cooper. *IMP*

A Dark Adapted Eye ♂♂♂ 1993 Sinister TV mystery adapted from the psychological thriller by Ruth Rendell (writing as Barbara Vine). In 1951 Vera Hillyard (Imrie) is hung for murdering her younger sister Eden (Ward)—an act that has profound effects on the family, including young niece Faith (Bonham Carter). Long haunted by the "why" of the crime, Faith later begins an investigation into her family's past—and discovers very dark and disturbing secrets dating back to WWII. Title refers to a vision problem caused by remaining in darkness too long. **150m/C VHS.** *GB* Helena Bonham Carter, Celia Imrie, Sophie Ward, Robin Ellis, Ciaran Hinds, Pip Torrens, William Gaminara, Polly Adams, Bernice Stegers, Steven Mackintosh, Jason Durr; **D:** Tim Fywell; **W:** Sandy Welch; **M:** David Ferguson. *FOX*

Dark Age ♂♂½ 1988 (R) An Australian conservationist must track down a rampaging, giant, semi-mythical alligator before it is killed by bounty hunters. Based on the novel (and Aboriginal legend) "Numunwari." **90m/C VHS, Beta, LV.** *AU* John Jarratt, David Gulpilil, Max Phipps, Ray Meagher, Nikki Coghill, Burnam Burnam; **D:** Arch Nicholson. *NLC*

The Dark Angel ♂♂♂ 1991 Maud is the young and innocent heiress to a fortune in this gothic mystery of creeping unease. She is intrigued by the romantic portrait of her youthful and unknown Uncle Silas. But her mysterious uncle is no longer the Byronic hero. What secret wickedness does his ravaged face hide? And what about Maud's drug-addicted governess and the brutish young man in the cemetary? Does Uncle Silas just want Maud's fortune or Maud herself? Excellent performances by O'Toole as the decadent uncle and Edney as the innocent-but-not-stupid Maud. Based on the novel "Uncle Silas" by Sheridan Le Fanu. Made for British TV. **150m/C VHS.** *GB* Peter O'Toole, Beatie Edney, Jane Lapotaire, Tim Woodward, Alan MacNaughton, Barbara Shelley, Guy Rolfe; **D:** Peter Hammond. *FOX, VCO*

Dark Angel: The Ascent ♂♂½ 1994 (R) She-devil gets tired of hell and decides to get a look at the world upstairs. She also decides to turn vigilante and dispatch some bad guy souls to her former home. **CW:** Language, horror violence, and sexuality. **80m/C VHS, Beta, Closed Caption.** Charlotte Stewart, Daniel Markel, Michael C. Mahon, Nicholas Worth, Milton James, Angela Featherstone; **D:** Linda Hassani; **W:** Matthew Bright; **M:** Fuzzbee Morse. *FLL*

Dark August ♂♂ 1976 (PG) A New Yorker drops out and transplants to rural Vermont, where he accidentally kills a young girl and then suffers numerous horrors as a result of a curse put on him by the girl's grandfather. **87m/C VHS, Beta.** J.J. Barry, Carole Shelyne, Kim Hunter, William Robertson; **D:** Martin Goldman. *VES, ART*

The Dark Backward ♂♂½ 1991 (R) A dark, subversive comedy about a garbage man who dreams of making it big in show biz as a stand-up comedian. He's terrible until a third arm starts growing out of his back and the sheer grotesqueness of his situation makes him a temporary star. Caan and Newton are interestingly cast, but young, first-time director Rifkin's foray into David Lynch territory was not well received by critics. **CW:** Bizarre comic sensuality. **97m/C VHS, LV, Letterbox.** Judd Nelson, Bill Paxton, Wayne Newton, Lara Flynn Boyle, James Caan, Rob Lowe, Claudia Christian; **D:** Adam Rifkin; **W:** Adam Rifkin. *COL*

Dark Before Dawn ♂♂½ 1989 (R) American farmers and Vietnam veterans team up against corrupt government officials and ruthless businessmen in this violent film about the plight of the underdog. **95m/C VHS, Beta, LV.** Doug MaClure, Sonny Gibson, Ben Johnson, Billy Drago, Rance Howard, Morgan Woodward, Buck Henry, Jeffery Osterhage, Rod Steagall, John Martin, Gary Cooper; **D:** Robert Totten. *VES, ART*

Dark Breed ♂♂ 1996 (R) Ewww, yuck, it's sci-fi infestation time once again as Nick Saxon (Scalia) is assigned to find the bodies of six astronauts whose top secret space craft has mysteriously crashed. He discovers that the bodies are playing host to reptilian parasites with designs on world domination. **104m/C VHS.** Jack Scalia, Jonathan Banks, Robin Curtis, Donna W. Scott; **D:** Richard Pepin. *PMH*

Dark City ♂♂ *Dark Empire; Dark World* 1997 (R) Brooding city of gloom floats in a sunless world, with skylines nightmarishly changing as its residents sleep. The city seems to belong to no era, looking at times like a neo-goth music video and at others like a work of German expressionism. Sometimes it just looks like '60s Cleveland. Director Proyas seems to have wanted to make a futuristic film noir like "Blade Runner," but gets lost somewhere along the way. He does however, keep the style. Disfigured Dr. Schreber (Sutherland) is forced by a dying race of pasty-faced long-coated aliens to use humans as guinea pigs in an attempt to find out what makes them tick. John Murdoch (Sewell) wakes up in a hotel room with a dead body and no memory of his life. Searching for his past, he wanders through one incredible set after another, but is it real or is it hypodermically injected? Hurt is a detective who only wants to stop the grisly murders. Garbled story rewards persistence at the end. **CW:** Violent images and some sexuality. **103m/C VHS, LV, Closed Caption.** Kiefer Sutherland, William Hurt, Rufus Sewell, Richard O'Brien, Jennifer Connelly, Ian Richardson, Colin Friels, Frank Gallacher, Bruce Spence, John Bluthal, Mitchell Butel, Melissa George; **D:** Alex Proyas; **W:** Alex Proyas, Lem Dobbs, David S. Goyer; **C:** Darius Wolski; **M:** Trevor Jones. *WAR*

Dark Command ♂♂♂ 1940 The story of Quantrell's Raiders who terrorized the Kansas territory during the Civil War until one man came along to put a stop to it. Colorful and talented cast add depth to the script. Also available colorized. **95m/B VHS, Beta.** John Wayne, Walter Pidgeon, Claire Trevor, Roy Rogers, Marjorie Main, George "Gabby" Hayes; **D:** Raoul Walsh. Nominations: Academy Awards '40: Best Interior Decoration, Best Original Score. *REP, FCT*

Dark Corner ♂♂♂ 1946 Gripping, intricate film noir about a detective, already framed once, who may go up the river yet again—this time for the murder of his ex-partner, the guy who framed him the first time. Loyal secretary Ball helps to extricate him from his tangled web. **99m/B VHS, Beta, Closed Caption.** Lucille Ball, Mark Stevens, Clifton Webb, William Bendix, Cathy Downs, Reed Hadley, Constance Collier, Kurt Kreuger; **D:** Henry Hathaway. *FOX*

The Dark Crystal ♂♂♂ 1982 (PG) Jen and Kira, two of the last surviving Gelflings, attempt to return a crystal shard (discovered with the help of a sorceress) to the castle where the Dark Crystal lies, guarded by the cruel and evil Skeksis. Designed by Brian Froud. From the creators of the Muppets. **93m/C VHS, Beta, LV.** **D:** Jim Henson, Frank Oz; **W:** David Odell; **C:** Oswald Morris; **M:** Trevor Jones; **V:** Jim Henson, Frank Oz, Kathryn Mullen, Dave Goelz. *TOU*

The Dark Dancer ♂½ 1995 (R) Psychology prof Maggie (Tweed), who authors books on feminine sexual behavior, gets her experience first-hand by working in a strip club. Now, she's also the target of a police investigation. Also available unrated. **CW:** Numerous strong sex scenes, language and brutal violence. **?m/C VHS.** Shannon Tweed. *TCE*

The Dark Dealer ♂♂ 1995 Three terror tales find the Devil's assistant dealing a deadly game of blackjack to a trio in limbo, with the cards propelling each man to a horrific adventure. Provides some real scares along with effective (if low-budget) special effects. **85m/C VHS.** Mark Fickert, Richard Hull, Vincent Gaskins, Rocky Patterson, Gordon Fox; **D:** Tom Alexander. *SDE*

Dark Eyes ♂♂♂½ *Les Yeux Noirs; Oci Ciornie* 1987 An acclaimed Italian film based on a several short stories by Anton Chekov. Mastroianni is a weak-willed Italian, trapped in a marriage of convenience, who falls in love with a mysterious, also married, Russian beauty he meets in a health spa. He embarks on a journey to find her and, perhaps, his lost ideals. Hailed as Mastroianni's consummate performance. In Italian with English subtitles. **118m/C VHS, Beta.** *IT* Marcello Mastroianni, Silvana Mangano, Elena Sofonova, Marthe Keller; **D:** Nikita Mikhalkov; **C:** Franco Di Giacomo. Cannes Film Festival '87: Best Actor (Mastroianni); Nominations: Academy Awards '87: Best Actor (Mastroianni). *FOX*

Dark Forces ♂♂ *Harlequin* 1983 (PG) A faithhealer promises to help a senator's dying son and finds the politician's wife also desires his assistance. This Australian film is uneven and predictable. Though rated "PG," beware of two rather brief, but explicit, nudity scenes. **96m/C VHS, Beta.** *AU* Robert Powell, David Hemmings, Broderick Crawford, Carmen Duncan; **D:** Simon Wincer.

Dark Habits ♂♂½ *Entre Tinieblas* 1984 An early Almodovar farce about already-demented nuns in a failing convent trying to raise funds with the help of a nightclub singer who is on the run. Although certainly irreverant, it doesn't quite have the zing of his later work. In Spanish with subtitles. **116m/C VHS, Beta, LV, Letterbox.** *SP* Carmen Maura, Cristina Pascual, Julieta Serrano, Marisa Paredes; **D:** Pedro Almodovar; **W:** Pedro Almodovar. *CCN, TPV*

The Dark Half ♂♂ 1991 (R) Flawed chiller based on a Stephen King novel. Thad Beaumont's serious novels have been failures, but writing as George Stark, he's had phenomenal success with grisly horror stories. In a publicity stunt Thad kills off and publicly buries George (who doesn't want to stay dead). Soon everyone who's crossed Thad is brutally murdered. Hutton acquits himself well in a change of pace dual role. Otherwise, the psychological thrills are few and the gore is plentiful. Pittsburgh serves as location double for King's usual New England territory. Film's release was delayed due to Orion's bankruptcy problems. **CW:** Language and violence. **122m/C VHS, Closed Caption.** Timothy Hutton, Amy Madigan, Michael Rooker, Julie Harris, Robert Joy, Kent Broadhurst, Beth Grant, Rutanya Alda, Tom Mardirosian, Chelsea Field, Royal Dano; **D:** George A. Romero; **W:** George A. Romero; **M:** Christopher Young. *ORI*

Dark Horse ♂♂½ 1992 (PG) Meyers is a young woman distraught over the death of her mother. She gets into trouble and is assigned to do community service work at a horse farm where she finds herself caring for a prize-winning horse. **98m/C VHS.** Ari Meyers, Mimi Rogers, Ed Begley Jr., Donovan Leitch, Samantha Eggar; **D:** David Hemmings. *ART, MOV, FCT*

The Dark Hour ♂½ 1936 Two detectives team up to solve a murder in which multiple suspects are involved. Based on Sinclair Gluck's "The Last Trap." **72m/B VHS, Beta.** Ray Walker, Irene Ware, Berton Churchill, Hedda Hopper, Hobart Bosworth, E.E. Clive; **D:** Charles Lamont. *NOS, LOO, SNC*

Dark Journey ♂♂ *The Anxious Years* 1937 WWI Stockholm is the setting for a love story between a double agent and the head of German Intelligence. Clever, sophisticated production; Leigh is stunning. **82m/B VHS.** *GB* Vivien Leigh, Conrad Veidt, Joan Gardner, Anthony Bushell, Ursula Jeans; **D:** Victor Saville. *HMV, MRV, CAB*

Dark Justice ♂♂½ 1991 Judge by day, avenger by night in this actioner created from three episodes of the late-night television series. Judge Nicholas Marshall is disgusted by the criminals sprung on legal loopholes and backroom deals. So he decides to take justice into his own hands. **99m/C VHS.** Ramy Zada, Dick O'Neill, Clayton Prince, Begona Plaza. *WAR*

Dark

Dark Mirror 🎬🎬🎬 1946 A psychologist
and a detective struggle to determine which twin
sister murdered a prominent physician. Good and
evil siblings finely acted by de Havilland. **85m/B
VHS.** Olivia de Havilland, Lew Ayres, Thomas Mitchell, Garry Owen; **D:** Robert Siodmak; **C:** Milton Krasner. Nominations: Academy Awards '46: Best Story. *REP*

Dark Mountain 🎬½ 1944 A forest ranger
rescues his gal from the clutches of a hardened
criminal. **56m/B VHS.** Robert Lowery, Ellen Drew, Regis
Toomey, Eddie Quillan, Elisha Cook Jr.; **D:** William (Lester
Williams) Berke, William C. Thomas. *NOS, DVT*

Dark Night of the Scarecrow 🎬🎬½
1981 Thriller with a moral. Prejudiced townspeople execute a retarded man who was innocently
befriended by a young girl. After his death unusual things begin to happen. Slow to start but effective. Made for television. **100m/C VHS, Beta, Closed
Caption.** Charles Durning, Tanya Crowe, Larry Drake; **D:**
Frank de Felitta. *FOX, HHE*

Dark Obsession 🎬🎬 *Diamond Skulls* 1990
(R) Byrne portrays a husband who lives out his
dark erotic fantasies with his wife (Donohoe), and
is involved in a hit-and-run accident. Driven by
guilt, madness slowly begins to take him. Ugly
and depressing. Based on a true scandal. Available in an "NC-17" rated version. **CW:** Language
and strong sensuality. **97m/C VHS, Beta.** Gabriel
Byrne, Amanda Donohoe, Michael Hordern, Judy Parfitt,
Douglas Hodge, Sadie Frost, Ian Carmichael; **D:** Nick
Broomfield; **W:** Tim Rose Price; **C:** Michael Coulter; **M:**
Hans Zimmer.

Dark Odyssey 🎬🎬 1957 Metzger's first
feature tells the tragic tale of a young Greek seaman who jumps ship in New York in order to
avenge his sister's rape. He finds himself conflicted between his masculine sense of family honor
and love when he falls for a Greek-American
woman. Director's cut includes the original theatrical trailer. **85m/B VHS.** David Hooks, Edward Brazier,
Jeanne Jerrems; **D:** William Kyriakis, Radley Metzger. *FRF*

Dark of the Night 🎬🎬½ *Mr. Wrong* 1985
A young woman, new to the city, purchases a
used Jaguar and finds she must share it with the
car's former owner—a woman murdered inside
the Jag. Decent psycho-thriller with some suspenseful and amusing moments. **88m/C VHS, Beta.**
NZ Heather Bolton, David Letch, Gary Stalker, Michael
Haigh, Danny Mulheron, Kate Harcourt; **D:** Gaylene Preston; **W:** Gaylene Preston, Geoff Murphy, Graham Tetley;
C: Thomas Burstyn; **M:** Jonathan Crayford. *ART*

Dark of the Sun 🎬🎬½ *The Mercenaries*
1968 (PG) Lots of action; routine plot. Taylor is a
tough mercenary hired to retrieve a supply of uncut diamonds from a besieged town in the Congo
during the 1950s rebellion. Oh, and if he can help
out the town's inhabitants, that's okay too. Based
on the novel by Wilbur A. Smith. **101m/C VHS.** *GB*
Rod Taylor, Jim Brown, Yvette Mimieux, Kenneth More,
Peter Carsten, Calvin Lockhart, Andre Morell; **D:** Jack Cardiff; **W:** Quentin Werty, Adrian Spies; **M:** Jacques Loussier.
MGM

Dark Passage 🎬🎬½ 1947 Bogart plays a
convict who escapes from San Quentin to prove
he was framed for the murder of his wife. He undergoes plastic surgery and is hidden and aided
by Bacall as he tries to find the real killer. Stars
can't quite compensate for a far-fetched script
and so-so direction. **107m/B VHS, Beta, LV.** Humphrey
Bogart, Lauren Bacall, Agnes Moorehead, Bruce (Herman
Brix) Bennett, Tom D'Andrea; **D:** Delmer Daves. *MGM*

The Dark Past 🎬🎬🎬 1949 A crazy, escaped convict holds a psychologist and his family
hostage, and the two men engage in psychological cat-and-mouse combat. An underrated thriller
with off-beat casting. **75m/B VHS, Beta.** William Holden, Lee J. Cobb, Nina Foch, Adele Jergens; **D:** Rudolph
Mate; **M:** George Duning. *COL*

Dark Places 🎬🎬 1973 (PG) Masquerading
as a hospital administrator, a former mental patient inherits the ruined mansion of a man who
had killed his wife and children and died insane.

As he lives in the house, the spirit of its former
owner seems to overcome him with a need to
repeat the crime. Meanwhile, Lee, Collins, and
Lom think the nut is hiding money they would like
to get their collective hands on. Low-budget but
fairly effective. **91m/C VHS, Beta.** *GB* Joan Collins,
Christopher Lee, Robert Hardy; **D:** Don Sharp.

Dark Planet 🎬🎬 1997 (R) In the year 2131,
Earth is in the middle of WW6 and it's up to rebel
commander Hawke to search for the Dark Planet
and complete a secret assignment that is humanity's last hope. **CW:** Violence. **99m/C VHS, LV.** Paul
Mercurio, Harley Jane Kozak, Michael York, Maria Ford, Ed
O'Ross; **D:** Albert Magnoli. *APX*

The Dark Power 🎬 1985 Ex-cowboy La-
Rue and his trusty whip provide this flick with its
only excitement. As sheriff, he must deal with the
dead Mexican warriors who rise to wreak havoc
when a house is built on their burial ground. **87m/C
VHS, Beta.** Lash LaRue, Anna Lane Tatum; **D:** Phil Smoot.
NO

The Dark Ride 🎬½ 1984 Lunatic picks up
women with the intention of raping and killing
them. Ugly thriller based on the evil deeds of serial murderer Ted Bundy. **83m/C VHS, Beta.** James Luisi, Susan Sullivan, Martin Speer; **D:** Jeremy Hoenack.

Dark Rider 1991 Dark Rider is a mysterious,
motorcycle riding hero who comes to the rescue
of a small town. Besieged by a gangster who buys
up all their land, the townspeople must abandon
their homes and indeed, their very dreams. That
is until Dark Rider rolls into to town to enact his
own unique brand of vengeance. **94m/C VHS.** Joe
Estevez, Doug Shanklin, Alicia Kowalski, David Shark,
Chuck Williams; **W:** Chuck Williams, Bob Ivy.

**Dark River: A Father's
Revenge** 🎬🎬 1990 When his daughter is
killed in a toxic waste dump accident, a man be-
gins revenge on the company and its managers.
Tense, with important message. **95m/C VHS.** Helen
Hunt, Mike Farrell, Tess Harper. *TTC*

Dark Sanity WOOF! *Straight Jacket* 1982 Uninvolving attempt at horror has a recently de-institu-
tionalized woman envisioning death and destruction (something you'll wish the film would do)
while everyone else just thinks she's losing her
marbles. Problem is we don't really care. **89m/C
VHS, Beta.** Aldo Ray, Kory Clark, Andy Gwyn, Bobby Holt;
D: Martin Greene.

**The Dark Secret of Harvest
Home** 🎬🎬½ 1978 An urban couple confront a
pagan cult in the New England town into which
they've moved. Based upon the Thomas Tryon
novel. Made for television. **118m/C VHS, Beta.** Bette
Davis, Rosanna Arquette, David Ackroyd, Rene Auberjonois, Michael O'Keefe, Joanna Miles; **D:** Leo Penn; **W:** Jennifer Miller, Jack Guss. *USH*

Dark Secrets 🎬 1995 (R) Reporter Claire
(Parent) wants to get a hot story on sex club mogul Justin DeVille (Carroll) and winds up falling
prey to his charms. But Justin's not the trusting
kind and sets up some loyalty tests for Claire. The
unrated version is 99 minutes. **CW:** Strong sexuality and graphic nudity, and for language. **90m/C
VHS, Closed Caption.** Monique Parent, Julie Strain, Justin
Carroll; **D:** John Bowen; **W:** Steve Tymon. *APX*

Dark Shadows 1967 "Dark Shadows" had
already been on television for about eight months
when the character of Barnabas Collins was introduced. This volume serves to familiarize the viewer with characters and situations that were running on the series at that time. These are the first
five episodes that feature Barnabas. Original air
dates are April 17 to May 1, 1967. Contains both
B&W and color episodes. Additional episodes
available. **120m/B VHS.** Joan Bennett, Kathryn Leigh
Scott, John Karlen, Alexandra Moltke, Jonathan Frid, David
Selby, Kate Jackson; **D:** John Sedwick. *MPI, MOV*

Dark Shadows: Episode 1 1991 The
short-lived primetime remake of the 1960s camp
television classic about eerie Collinwood mansion
and the mysterious and tragic Collins family, including cousin Barnabas who happens to be a
vampire. The revival featured more explicit sex
and violence and a darker tone. In 12 parts. **105m/
C VHS.** Ben Cross, Jean Simmons, Roy Thinnes, Barbara
Steele, Joanna Going, Lysette Anthony, Michael T. Weiss;
D: Dan Curtis. *MPI, TPV*

Dark Side of Genius 🎬🎬 1994 (R) Jennifer Cole (Hughes), a reporter for an L.A. arts
weekly, tries to get the story on artist Julian Jons
(Fraser), who's just been paroled after being imprisoned for the murder of his model. Now his
lurid new paintings of a sultry nude model hint at
some obsessive behavior and Jennifer's reporter
instincts may be the death of her. **86m/C VHS, Beta,
Closed Caption.** Finola Hughes, Brendan Fraser, Glenn
Shadix, Moon Zappa, Patrick Richwood, Seymour Cassel;
D: Phedon Papamichael; **W:** Fred Stroppel; **C:** Phedon Papamichael; **M:** Tom Hiel. *PAR*

The Dark Side of Love 🎬½ 1979 A
young girl gets involved with the rougher side of
New Orleans society, gets pregnant, and realizes
how she's been degraded. **94m/C VHS, Beta.** James
Stacy, Glynnis O'Connor, Jan Sterling, Mickey Rooney.
GEM

Dark Side of Midnight 🎬½ *The Creeper*
1986 (R) A super-detective tracks down a psychopathic killer. **108m/C VHS, Beta.** James Moore, Wes Olsen, Sandy Schemmel, Dave Bowling.

The Dark Side of the Heart 🎬🎬 *El
Lado Oscuro del Corazon* 1992 Magic realism features
in this story of struggling Buenos Aires poet Oliv-
erio (Grandinetti) who falls in love with prostitute
Ana (Ballesteros). She wants to keep things busi-
nesslike but when a man finds a woman whose
lovemaking causes them to actually levitate, he's
not about to make things easy. Spanish with subtitles. **127m/C VHS.** *CA AR* Dario Grandinetti, Sandra Ballesteros, Nacha Guevara; **D:** Eliseo Subiela; **W:** Eliseo Subiela; **C:** Hugo Colace; **M:** Osvaldo Montes. Montreal World
Film Festival '92: Best Film. *NYF*

Dark Side of the Moon 🎬🎬 1990 (R)
Members of a space ship sent on a routine mission to the far side of the moon, discover an unknown force that feeds on human emotion and
consumes the soul. Lukewarm science fiction/hor-
ror. **96m/C VHS.** William Bledsoe, Alan Blumenfeld,
John Diehl, Robert Sampson, Wendy MacDonald, Camilla
More, Joe Turkel; **D:** D.J. Webster. *THV*

Dark Star 🎬🎬🎬 1974 (G) John Carpenter's
directorial debut is a low-budget, sci-fi satire
which focuses on a group of scientists whose mission is to destroy unstable planets. During their
journey, they battle their alien mascot (who closely resembles a walking beach ball), as well as a
"sensitive" and intelligent bombing device which
starts to question the meaning of its existence.
Enjoyable early feature from John "Halloween"
Carpenter and Dan "Aliens" O'Bannon. Fun,
weird, and unpredictable. **95m/C VHS, Beta, LV,
Letterbox.** Dan O'Bannon, Brian Narelle; **D:** John Carpenter; **W:** Dan O'Bannon, John Carpenter; **M:** John Carpenter.
HHT, IME, VCI

Dark Tide 🎬🎬 1993 (R) Erotic action thriller
about a pair of deep sea divers whose love life is
disturbed when their boat captain becomes sexually fixated on the woman. Also available in an
uncut, unrated version. **92m/C VHS, LV.** Brigitte Bako,
Richard Tyson, Chris Sarandon. *THV*

Dark Tower 🎬 1987 (R) Decent cast is
wasted in yet another inept attempt at horror. An
architect is dismayed to learn that an evil force is
inhabiting her building and it might just be the
ghost of her dearly departed husband. **91m/C VHS,
Beta, LV.** Michael Moriarty, Jenny Agutter, Theodore Bikel,
Carol Lynley, Anne Lockhart, Kevin McCarthy; **D:** Ken Barnett, Freddie Francis, Ken Wiederhorn; **W:** Robert J. Avrech, Kenneth G. Blackwell. *VTR, IME*

Dark Universe 🎬½ 1993 (R) An alien terror wants to conquer the Earth and make its inhabitants their new food source. 83m/C VHS, Beta. Blake Pickett, Cherie Scott, Bently Tittle, John Maynard, Paul Austin Saunders, Tom Ferguson, Steve Barkett, Joe Estevez, Patrick Moran; **D:** Steve Latshaw; **W:** Patrick Moran.

Dark Victory 🎬🎬🎬½ 1939 A spoiled young heiress discovers she is dying from a brain tumor. She attempts to pack a lifetime of parties into a few months, but is rescued by her doctor, with whom she falls in love. Classic final scene with Davis at the top of her form. Bogart plays an Irish stable hand, but not especially well. Also available in a colorized version. 106m/B VHS, Beta, LV, Closed Caption. Bette Davis, George Brent, Geraldine Fitzgerald, Humphrey Bogart, Ronald Reagan, Henry Travers; **D:** Edmund Goulding; **M:** Max Steiner. Nominations: Academy Awards '39: Best Actress (Davis), Best Picture, Best Original Score. MGM

Dark Waters 🎬🎬 1944 The drowning death of her parents has left a young woman mentally unstable. She returns to her family home in the backwaters of Louisiana with her peculiar aunt and uncle to serve as guardians. It eventually becomes apparent that someone is trying to drive her insane. This one tends to be rather murky and it's not simply due to the plentiful scenes of misty swampland. 93m/B VHS, Beta, LV. Merle Oberon, Franchot Tone, Thomas Mitchell, Fay Bainter, Elisha Cook Jr., John Qualen, Rex Ingram; **D:** Andre de Toth; **M:** Miklos Rozsa. VTR

The Dark Wind 🎬½ 1991 (R) The first of Tony Hillerman's popular Native American mysteries comes to the screen in a lame adaptation. Phillips stars as the Navaho cop investigating a murder on a New Mexico Indian reservation. Since the Navaho believe a "dark wind" enters a man's soul when he does evil, expect some "spirited" goings-on as well. 111m/C VHS, LV, Closed Caption. Lou Diamond Phillips; **D:** Errol Morris; **W:** Eric Bergren. ART

Darker than Amber 🎬🎬 1970 (R) John D. MacDonald's houseboat-dwelling detective Travis McGee (Taylor) rescues a girl (Kendall) he's fallen for, and soon discovers that the mugs who thugged her were part of a collection racket. A violent action melodrama upgraded from its original "R" rating. 96m/C VHS, Beta. Rod Taylor, Suzy Kendall, Theodore Bikel, Jane Russell, James Booth, Janet MacLachlan, William Smith, Ahna Capri, Chris Robinson; **D:** Robert Clouse. NO

Darkest Africa Batmen of Africa; King of the Jungleland 1936 Legendary animal trainer Beatty is the hero of this 15 episode cliffhanger serial as he vies with beasts—both animal and human. 270m/B LV. Clyde Beatty, Manuel King, Elaine Shepard; **D:** Joseph Kane, B. Reeves Eason. REP, MOV

Darkman 🎬🎬🎬 1990 (R) Raimi's disfigured-man-seeks-revenge suspenser is comicbook kitsch cross-pollinated with a strain of gothic horror. Neeson plays a scientist who's on the verge of discovering the key to cloning body parts; brutally attacked by the henchmen of a crooked politico, his lab is destroyed and he's left for dead. Turns out he's not dead—just horribly disfigured and a wee bit chafed—and he stalks his deserving victims from the shadows, using his lab know-how to disguise his rugged bad looks. Exquisitely violent. Montage by Pablo Ferro. 96m/C VHS, Beta, LV, Closed Caption, DVD. Liam Neeson, Frances McDormand, Larry Drake, Colin Friels, Nelson Mashita, Jenny Agutter, Rafael H. Robledo, Nicholas Worth; **D:** Sam Raimi; **W:** Sam Raimi, Ivan Raimi, Daniel Goldin, Joshua Goldin, Chuck Pfarrer; **C:** Bill Pope; **M:** Danny Elfman. USH, CCB

Darkman 2: The Return of Durant 🎬🎬½ 1994 (R) The first in a series of direct-to-video adventures about disfigured scientist Peyton "Darkman" Westlake (now played by Vosloo), who's continuing his liquid skin research in the hopes of transforming his grotesque appearance. He finds an ally in scientist David Brinkman but Westlake's nemesis, crime boss Robert G. Durant (Drake), wants the property

where Brinkman's lab is located. And what Durant wants, he takes. Sam Raimi, who directed the original film, is one of the series producers. **CW:** Language; brutal violence. 93m/C VHS, LV, Letterbox, Closed Caption. Arnold Vosloo, Larry Drake, Kim Delaney, Renee O'Connor, Rod Wilson; **D:** Bradford May; **W:** Steven McKay, Chuck Pfarrer; **C:** Bradford May; **M:** Randy Miller. USH

Darkman 3: Die Darkman Die 🎬🎬½ 1995 (R) The second direct-to-video Darkman saga finds Dr. Peyton Westlake (Vosloo) disrupting the drug-dealing activities of underworld boss Peter Rooker (Fahey). The obsessed Rooker is determined to figure out the secret to Darkman's enormous strength, employing the feminine wiles of his mistress, Dr. Bridget Thorne (Fluegel). Then Westlake/Darkman finds himself drawn to Rooker's neglected wife and young daughter. Our hero suffers a lot (as usual) and there's lots of action (as usual). **CW:** Violent action and some violence. 87m/C VHS, LV, Letterbox, Closed Caption. Arnold Vosloo, Jeff Fahey, Darlanne Fluegel, Nigel Bennett, Roxann Biggs-Dawson; **D:** Bradford May; **W:** Mike Werb; **M:** Randy Miller. USH

Darkroom 🎬½ 1990 An unstable young man devises a scheme to photograph his father in bed with his mistress, and then use the pics to blackmail dear ol' dad. 90m/C VHS. Jill Pierce, Jeffrey Allen Arbaugh, Sara Lee Wade, Aaron Teich; **D:** Terrence O'Hara. NO

The Darkside 🎬½ 1987 (R) In this frightening drama, a young prostitute and an innocent cabbie attempt to escape the clutches of a maniacal film producer with a secret he won't let them reveal. 95m/C VHS. Tony Galati, Cyndy Preston; **D:** Constantino Magnatta. THV

Darktown Strutters 🎬 Get Down and Boogie 1974 (PG) Effort to satirize racial stereotypes is humorless and ineffective. Black female motorcycle gang searches for the kidnapped mother of one of the members. 85m/C VHS, Beta. Trina Parks, Roger E. Mosley, Shirley Washington; **D:** William Witney. NLC

Darling 🎬🎬🎬½ 1965 Young amoral model tries to hold boredom at bay by having a number of love affairs. She joins the international jet set and manages to reach the top of European society by marrying a prince. She then learns what an empty life she has. Christie won an Oscar for her portrayal of the disillusioned, cynical young woman. 122m/B VHS, Beta, LV. GB Julie Christie, Dirk Bogarde, Laurence Harvey; **D:** John Schlesinger; **W:** Frederic Raphael. Academy Awards '65: Best Actress (Christie), Best Costume Design (B & W), Best Story & Screenplay; British Academy Awards '65: Best Actor (Bogarde), Best Actress (Christie), Best Screenplay; Golden Globe Awards '66: Best Foreign Film; National Board of Review Awards '65: Best Actress (Christie), Best Director (Schlesinger); New York Film Critics Awards '65: Best Actress (Christie), Best Director (Schlesinger), Best Film; Nominations: Academy Awards '65: Best Director (Schlesinger), Best Picture. COL, BTV

Darling Lili 🎬🎬½ 1970 Big-budget WWI spy comedy/musical with Andrews as a German agent posing as an English music hall performer, who falls in love with squadron leader Hudson and finds she can't betray him. A critical flop when first released, film has its charms though director Edwards did much better for Andrews in "Victor/Victoria." ♫Whistling Away the Dark; The Girl In No Man's Land; Smile Away Each Rainy Day; I'll Give You Three Guesses; Your Good Will Ambassador; Darling Lili; The Little Birds. 136m/C VHS. Julie Andrews, Rock Hudson, Jeremy Kemp, Jacques Marin, Michael Witney, Vernon Dobtcheff; **D:** Blake Edwards; **W:** Blake Edwards, William Peter Blatty; **M:** Henry Mancini, Johnny Mercer. Golden Globe Awards '71: Best Song ("Whistling Away the Dark"); Nominations: Academy Awards '70: Best Costume Design, Best Song ("Whistling Away the Dark"), Original Song Score and/or Adaptation. PAR

D.A.R.Y.L. 🎬🎬 1985 (PG) The little boy found by the side of the road is too polite, too honest and too smart. His friend explains to him the necessity of imperfection (If you don't want the grown-ups to bother you too much) and he begins to become more like a real little boy. But the American military has a top-secret interest in this child, since he is in fact the combination of a cloned body and a computer brain. More interesting when it's involved with the human beings and less so when it focuses on science. 100m/C VHS, Beta, LV, Closed Caption. Mary Beth Hurt, Michael McKean, Barret Oliver, Colleen Camp, Danny Corkill; **D:** Simon Wincer; **W:** David Ambrose, Allan Scott; **M:** Marvin Hamlisch. PAR

Das Boot 🎬🎬🎬🎬 The Boat 1981 (R) Superb detailing of life in a German U-boat during WWII. Intense, claustrophobic atmosphere complemented by nail-biting action provides a realistic portrait of the stressful conditions that were endured on these submarines. Excellent performances, especially from Prochnow. In German with subtitles. From the novel by Lothar-Guenther Buccheim. Originally a six-hour special made for German television. The director's cut is released at 209 minutes on two cassettes. **CW:** Some war violence and brief language. 210m/C VHS, Beta, LV. GE Juergen Prochnow, Herbert Gronemeyer, Klaus Wennemann, Hubertus Bengsch, Martin Semmelrogge, Bernd Tauber, Erwin Leder, Martin May, Heinz Honig, U. A. Ochsen, Claude-Oliver Rudolph, Jan Fedder, Ralph Richer, Joachim Bernhard, Oliver Stritzel, Konrad Becker, Lutz Schnell, Martin Hemme; **D:** Wolfgang Petersen; **W:** Wolfgang Petersen; **C:** Jost Vacano; **M:** Klaus Doldinger. Nominations: Academy Awards '82: Best Adapted Screenplay, Best Cinematography, Best Director (Petersen), Best Film Editing, Best Sound. COL, GLV, HMV

Das Testament des Dr. Mabuse 🎬🎬🎬½ The Testament of Dr. Mabuse 1933 The third, and only sound, Mabuse film by Lang. The infamous crime lord/megalomaniac plots the world's destruction from the confines of an asylum cell. In German, with English subtitles. Released as "The Last Will of Dr. Mabuse" in the U.S. in 1943. 122m/B VHS, Beta. GE Rudolf Klein-Rogge, Otto Wernicke, Gustav Diesl, Karl Meixner; **D:** Fritz Lang. SNC, GLV

Date Bait 🎬 1960 When a teen couple decides—much to their parents' chagrin—to elope, they find themselves on a date with danger when their post-nuptials are plagued by pushers and assorted other bad guys. 71m/B VHS, Beta. Gary Clarke, Marlo Ryan, Richard Gering, Danny Logan; **D:** O'Dale Ireland. SNC

Date with an Angel 🎬½ 1987 (PG) When aspiring musician Knight fishes a beautiful angel out of the swimming pool, he is just trying to rescue her. But the beauty of the angel overwhelms him and he finds himself questioning his upcoming wedding to Cates, a cosmetic mogul's daughter. Sickeningly cute and way too sentimental, though Beart's beauty is other-wordly. 114m/C VHS, Beta, LV. Emmanuelle Beart, Michael E. Knight, Phoebe Cates, David Dukes, Bibi Besch, Albert Macklin, David Hunt, Michael Goodwin; **D:** Tom McLoughlin. NO

A Date with Judy 🎬🎬 1948 Standard post-war musical dealing with teenage mix-ups in and around a big high school dance. Choreography by Stanley Donen. ♫Cuanto La Gusto; Strictly on the Corny Side; It's a Most Unusual Day; Judaline; I've Got a Date with Judy; I'm Gonna Meet My Mary; Temptation; Mulligatawny. 114m/C VHS, Beta, LV, Closed Caption. Jane Powell, Elizabeth Taylor, Carmen Miranda, Wallace Beery, Robert Stack, Xavier Cugat, Selena Royle, Leon Ames; **D:** Richard Thorpe; **C:** Robert L. Surtees. MGM, MLB

Dating the Enemy 🎬🎬 1995 War between the sexes comedy about two instantaneous lovers who have nothing in common. Tash (Karvan) is a serious journalist who falls for easy-going Brett (Pearce), the host of a musicvideo program. After a year of togetherness, Tash wishes macho Brett could understand what it's like to be a woman. Surprise! The duo mysteriously switch bodies and find their new sexual (and job) roles aren't easy. **104m/C VHS.** *AU* Claudia Karvan, Guy Pearce, Matt Day, Lisa Hensley, Pippa Grandison, John Howard; **D:** Megan Simpson; **W:** Megan Simpson; **C:** Steve Arnold; **M:** David Hirschfelder. Nominations: Australian Film Institute '96: Best Actress (Karvan). *NYR*

Daughter of Darkness 🐾🐾½ 1989 (R)
A young woman goes to Hungary in search of her family tree, only to discover vampires nestled there.**CW:** Violence; sexuality. **93m/C VHS.** Mia Sara, Anthony Perkins, Robert Reynolds, Jack Coleman; **D:** Stuart Gordon. *THV*

Daughter of Death 🐾 *Julie Darling* 1982 (R)
A little mentally off-center since she witnessed the gruesome rape and murder of her mother, a teenage girl doesn't bond well with her new mom when dad remarries. **100m/C VHS.** *CA GE* Anthony (Tony) Franciosa, Isabelle Mejias, Sybil Danning, Cindy Gurling, Paul Hubbard, Benjamin Schmoll; **D:** Paul Nicholas. *FCT*

The Daughter of Dr. Jekyll 🐾½ 1957
The doc's daughter believes she may have inherited her father's evil curse when several of the locals are found dead. Originally released in theaters on a double bill with "Dr. Cyclops." **71m/C VHS, Beta.** John Agar, Arthur Shields, John Dierkes, Gloria Talbott; **D:** Edgar G. Ulmer. *FOX*

Daughter of Don Q 🐾🐾½ 1946 Delores' father is very rich with a huge real estate empire and she is his only heir. Greedy cousin Carlos would like to change that—by killing Delores. Delores must dodge speeding cars, hurling harpoons, and more to escape Carlos' evil plot. Part of "The Cliffhanger Serials" series. **166m/B VHS.** Adrian Booth, Kirk Alyn, Leroy Mason. *REP, MOV*

Daughter of Horror 🐾🐾 *Dementia* 1955 A young woman finds herself involved with a porcine mobster who resembles her abusive father. Trouble is, Dad's dead, and daughter dearest abetted his departure. Obscure venture into expressionism that was initially banned by the New York State Board of Censors. Shot on a low budget (how low was it? So low that McMahon narrated because shooting with sound was too expensive). The 55 minutes tend to lag, although the film should be intriguing to genre enthusiasts and to fans of things pseudo-Freudian. **60m/B VHS.** Adrienne Barrett, Bruno Ve Sota, Ben Roseman; **D:** John Parker; **W:** John Parker. *NOS, SNC, MRV*

Daughter of the Dragon 🐾🐾 1931 Fu Manchu is again on the prowl, this time sending his daughter to murder Fletcher to avenge the death of his wife and son during China's Boxer Rebellion. Based on a Sax Rohmer story. **70m/B VHS.** Anna May Wong, Warner Oland, Sessue Hayakawa, Bramwell Fletcher, Holmes Herbert; **D:** Lloyd Corrigan. *NOS*

Daughter of the Tong 🐾 1939 FBI agent gets tong twisted when he tries to put a lid on a smuggling ring headed by a woman (who's beautiful, of course). Something that resembles acting is wasted in a mess of a movie. **56m/B VHS, Beta.** Evelyn Brent, Grant Withers, Dorothy Short, Dave O'Brien; **D:** Raymond K. Johnson. *NOS, SNC*

Daughters of Darkness 🐾🐾🐾 *Le Rouge aux Levres; Blut an den Lippen; Erzebeth; The Promise of Red Lips; The Red Lips* 1971 (R) Newlyweds on their way to England stop at a posh French hotel. There they meet a beautiful woman whom the hotel owner swears had been there 40 years ago, even though she hasn't aged a bit. When she introduces herself as Countess of Bathory (the woman who bathed in the blood of virgins to stay young) folks begin to wonder. A really superb erotic vampire film charged with sensuality and a sense of dread. **87m/C VHS, Beta.** *BE GE IT FR* Delphine Seyrig, John Karlen, Daniele Ouimet, Andrea Rau, Paul Esser, Georges Jamin, Joris Collet, Fons Rademakers; **D:** Harry Kumel; **W:** Harry Kumel, Pierre Drouot, Jean Ferry; **C:** Eddy van den Enden. *FCT, VTR*

Daughters of Satan 🐾🐾 1972 (R) Selleck, in an early role as a virile museum buyer, antagonizes a coven of witches when he purchases a painting. His wife, played by Grant, becomes a target of the witches' revenge and salacious shenanigans ensue. **96m/C VHS, Beta.** Tom Selleck, Barra Grant, Paraluman, Tani Phelps Guthrie; **D:** Hollingsworth Morse. *NO*

Daughters of the Dust 🐾🐾🐾½ 1991
Five women of a Gullah family living on the Sea Islands off the Georgia coast in 1902 contemplate moving to the mainland in this emotional tale of change. The Gullah are descendants of West African slaves and their isolation has kept their superstitions and native dialect (a mixture of Western African, Creole, and English) intact. Family bonds and memories are celebrated with a quiet narrative and beautiful cinematography in Dash's feature-film directorial debut. **113m/C VHS.** Cora Lee Day, Barbara O, Alva Rogers, Kaycee Moore, Cheryl Lynn Bruce, Adisa Anderson, Eartha D. Robinson, Bahni Turpin, Tommy Redmond Hicks, Malik Farrakhan, Cornell (Kofi) Royal, Vertamae Crosvenor, Umar Abdurrahman, Sherry Jackson, Rev. Ervin Green; **D:** Julie Dash; **W:** Julie Dash; **C:** A. Jafa Fielder; **M:** John Barnes. Sundance Film Festival '91: Best Cinematography. *KIV, FCT, PMS*

Dave 🐾🐾🐾 1993 (PG-13) Regular guy Dave Kovic (Kline) is a dead ringer for the President, launching him into the White House after the prez suffers a stroke in embarrassing circumstances. Seamless comedy prompts lots of hearty laughs and the feel-good faith that despite the overwhelming odds, everything will turn out just fine. Political cameos abound: look for real-life Senators Alan Simpson, Paul Simon, Howard Metzenbaum, Tom Harkin, and Christopher Dodd as well as the commentators from TV's "The McLaughlin Group," and Stone, poking fun at himself on "Larry King Live," as he tries to convince the public there's a conspiracy going on.**CW:** Brief profanity and over sexual situation. **110m/C VHS, Beta, LV, Letterbox, Closed Caption.** Kevin Kline, Sigourney Weaver, Frank Langella, Kevin Dunn, Ving Rhames, Ben Kingsley, Charles Grodin, Faith Prince, Laura Linney, Bonnie Hunt, Parley Baer, Stefan Gierasch, Anna Deavere Smith, Bonnie Bartlett, Ben Stein; **Cameos:** Jay Leno, Larry King, Oliver Stone, Arnold Schwarzenegger; **D:** Ivan Reitman; **W:** Gary Ross; **M:** James Newton Howard. Nominations: Academy Awards '93: Best Original Screenplay; Golden Globe Awards '94: Best Actor—Musical/Comedy (Kline), Best Film—Musical/Comedy; Writers Guild of America '93: Best Original Screenplay. *WAR, BTV, FCT*

David 🐾🐾🐾½ 1979 A haunting portrait of the survival of a Jewish teenager in Berlin during the Nazi reign of terror, based on the novel by Joel Koenig. Universally acclaimed, this was the first film about the Holocaust made in Germany by a German Jew. In German with English subtitles. **106m/C VHS, Beta.** *GE* Mario Fischel, Walter Taub, Irene Vrkijan, Torsten Hentes, Eva Mattes; **D:** Peter Lilienthal. Berlin International Film Festival '79: Golden Berlin Bear. *KIV, GLV*

David 🐾🐾½ 1997 TNT's Old Testament biblical series continues with the story of shepherd boy David (Turner) who succeeds Saul (Pryce) to become king over the tribes of Israel. When King David (Parker) becomes smitten with the married Bathsheba (Lee), he sends her husband into battle, soon leaving her a comely widow (although not for long). And there's also subplots involving three of David's children: Absalom (Rowan), Amnon (Hall), and Tamar (Bellar). Lots of action. **?m/C VHS.** Nathaniel Parker, Sheryl Lee, Jonathan Pryce, Leonard Nimoy, Dominic Rowan, Edward Hall, Clara Bellar, Marco Leonardi, Franco Nero, Ben Daniels, Maurice Roeves, Gina Bellman, Gideon Turner; **D:** Robert Markowitz; **W:** Larry Gross; **C:** Raffaele Mertes; **M:** Carlo Siliotto. *TTC*

David and Bathsheba 🐾🐾🐾 1951 The Bible story comes alive in this lush and colorful Fox production. Peck and Hayward are great together and Peck is properly concerned about the wrath of God over his transgressions. Terrific costumes and special effects, lovely music and a fine supporting cast keep this a notch above other Biblical epics. **116m/C VHS, LV, Closed Caption.** Gregory Peck, Susan Hayward, Raymond Massey, Kieron Moore, James Robertson Justice, Jayne Meadows, John Sutton, Dennis Hoey, Francis X. Bushman, George Zucco; **D:** Henry King; **W:** Philip Dunne; **C:** Leon Shamroy. Nominations: Academy Awards '51: Best Art Direction/Set Decoration (Color), Best Color Cinematography, Best Costume Design (Color), Best Story & Screenplay, Best Original Dramatic/Comedy Score. *FOX*

David and Lisa 🐾🐾🐾 1962 Director Perry was given an Oscar for this sensitive independently produced film. Adapted from Theodore Isaac Rubin's true case history novel concerning a young man and woman who fall in love while institutionalized for mental illness. Dullea and Margolin are excellent in the title roles of this sleeper. **94m/B VHS, Beta, LV.** Keir Dullea, Janet Margolin, Howard da Silva, Neva Patterson, Clifton James; **D:** Frank Perry. Nominations: Academy Awards '62: Best Adapted Screenplay, Best Director (Perry). *COL, MRV*

David Copperfield 🐾🐾🐾 1935 Superior adaptation of Charles Dickens' great novel. An orphan grows to manhood in Victorian England with a wide variety of help and harm. Terrific acting by Bartholomew, Fields, Rathbone, and all the rest. Lavish production, lovingly filmed. **132m/B VHS, Beta, LV.** Lionel Barrymore, W.C. Fields, Freddie Bartholomew, Maureen O'Sullivan, Basil Rathbone, Lewis Stone, Frank Lawton, Madge Evans, Roland Young, Edna May Oliver, Lennox Pawle, Elsa Lanchester, Una O'Connor, Arthur Treacher; **D:** George Cukor; **W:** Howard Estabrook, Hugh Walpole; **M:** Herbert Stothart. Nominations: Academy Awards '35: Best Film Editing, Best Picture. *MGM*

David Copperfield 🐾🐾½ 1970 This British made-for-television production is more faithful to the Dickens classic than any of its predecessors. The added material, however, fails to highlight any one character as had the successful 1935 MGM version. Still, the exceptional (and largely stage-trained) cast do much to redeem the production. **118m/C VHS, Closed Caption.** Richard Attenborough, Cyril Cusack, Edith Evans, Pamela Franklin, Susan Hampshire, Wendy Hiller, Ron Moody, Laurence Olivier, Robin Phillips; **D:** Delbert Mann; **M:** Malcolm Arnold. *FOX, TVC*

David Holzman's Diary 🐾🐾🐾 1967
Director McBride helmed this fake underground movie, a legendary put-on focusing on film student pretensions. Holzman is a sincere geek who seeks the meaning of life by filming his own existence in oh-so-chic grainy black-and-white verite. He learns reality is more important than film. Drolly captures the state of the art in late '60s America. **71m/B VHS, LV.** L.M. Kit Carson; **D:** Jim McBride; **W:** L.M. Kit Carson, Jim McBride. National Film Registry '91. *FXL*

DaVinci's War 🐾🐾 1992 (R) Frank DaVinci's sister is murdered and he wants revenge. So he hooks up with a professional killer and a bunch of Vietnam vets and gets the firepower he needs to blow the bad guys away.**CW:** Language, strong violence, and strong sexuality. **94m/C VHS.** Joey Travolta, Michael Nouri, Vanity, Richard Foronjy, Branscombe Richmond, Sam Jones, Jack Bannon; **Cameos:** Brian Robbins, James Russo; **D:** Raymond Martino; **W:** Raymond Martino; **M:** Jeff Lass. *TRI*

Davy Crockett and the River Pirates 🐾🐾½ 1956 (G) Another Disney splice and dice of two episodes from the television series, chronicling the further adventures of our frontier hero. Davy meets up with Mike Fink, the King of the Ohio River, and the two engage in a furious keelboat race, and then unite to track down a group of thieves masquerading as Indians and threatening the peace. **81m/C VHS, Beta, LV.** Fess Parker, Buddy Ebsen, Jeff York; **D:** Norman Foster; **M:** George Bruns. *DIS*

Davy Crockett, King of the Wild Frontier 🐾🐾🐾 1955 (PG) Three episodes of the popular Disney television series are blended together here to present the life and some of the adventures of Davy Crockett. These include his days as an Indian fighter and his gallant stand in defense of the Alamo. Well-done by a splendid cast, the film helped to spread Davy-mania among the children of the 1950s. **93m/C VHS, Beta, Closed Caption.** Fess Parker, Buddy Ebsen, Hans Conried, Ray Whiteside, Pat Hogan, William "Billy" Bakewell, Basil Ruysdael, Kenneth Tobey; **D:** Norman Foster; **M:** George Bruns. *DIS, BTV*

Dawn! 🎬🎬 1983 True story of Dawn Fraser, an Olympic champion swimmer and an unfulfilled woman willing to fight for her happiness. **114m/C VHS, Beta.** Bronwyn MacKay-Payne, Tom Richards. *NO*

Dawn Express 🎬½ 1942 Nazi spies infiltrate the U.S. in search of a secret formula designed to enhance the power of gasoline. Another film made to contribute to the war effort that doesn't make much sense. **63m/B VHS, Beta.** Michael Whalen, Anne Nagel, William "Billy" Bakewell, Constance Worth, Hans von Twardowski, Jack Mulhall, George Pembroke, Kenneth Harlan, Robert Frazer; **D:** Al(bert) Herman. *SNC*

Dawn of the Dead 🎬🎬🎬½ *Zombie; Zombies* 1978 Romero's gruesome sequel to his "Night of the Living Dead." A mysterious plague causes the recently dead to rise from their graves and scour the countryside for living flesh. Very violent, gory, graphic, and shocking, yet not without humor. Gives interesting consideration to the violence created by the living humans in their efforts to save themselves. **126m/C VHS, Beta, LV.** David Emge, Ken Foree, Gaylen Ross, Scott H. Reiniger, David Crawford, David Early, Tom Savini, George A. Romero; **D:** George A. Romero; **W:** George A. Romero; **C:** Michael Gornick. *VTR, FCT*

Dawn of the Mummy woof! 1982 Lousy plot and bad acting—not to mention gore galore—do this one in. A photographer and a bevy of young fashion models travel to Egypt for a special shoot. They unwittingly stumble upon an ancient tomb, teeming with vengeance-minded mummies. **93m/C VHS, Beta.** Brenda King, Barry Sattels, George Peck, Joan Levy; **D:** Frank Agrama. *NO*

Dawn on the Great Divide 🎬🎬½ 1942 Jones' last film before his tragic and untimely death trying to save people from a fire at the Coconut Grove in Boston. Wagon train has to battle not only Indians, but bad guys as well. Plot provides more depth than the usual western fare. **57m/B VHS, Beta.** Buck Jones, Tim McCoy, Raymond Hatton, Mona Barrie, Robert Lowery, Betty Blythe, Jan Wiley, Harry Woods, Roy Barcroft; **D:** Howard Bretherton. *NOS, MRV, VCN*

Dawn Patrol 🎬🎬🎬 1938 Flynn plays a flight commander whose nerves are shot in this story of the British Royal Flying Corps during WWI. The focus is on the effects that the pressures and deaths have on all those concerned. Fine performances from all in this well-done remake of the 1930 film. **103m/B VHS, Beta.** Errol Flynn, David Niven, Basil Rathbone, Donald Crisp, Barry Fitzgerald, Melville Cooper; **D:** Edmund Goulding; **C:** Gaetano Antonio "Tony" Gaudio; **M:** Max Steiner. *FOX, MGM*

Dawn Rider 🎬🎬 1935 Formula western has all the right ingredients: Wayne as a cowboy out to get revenge on the gang that murdered his father. Features stuntman Canutt in rare acting role. **60m/B VHS.** John Wayne, Marion Burns, Yakima Canutt; **D:** Robert North Bradbury. *COL, REP, MRV*

Dawn Rider/Frontier Horizon 1939 A double feature of two of Wayne's earliest western films. **114m/B VHS, Beta.** John Wayne, Jennifer Jones, Marion Burns; **D:** Robert North Bradbury, George Sherman. *REP*

The Dawning 🎬🎬½ 1988 An Irish revolutionary in the 1920s draws a young woman into his dangerous world of romance, intrigue, and death. Howard's last film. Based on the novel "Old Jest" by Jennifer Johnston. **97m/C VHS, LV.** *GB* Anthony Hopkins, Jean Simmons, Trevor Howard, Rebecca Pidgeon, Hugh Grant, Tara MacGowran; **D:** Robert Knights. *ART, PMS*

The Dawson Patrol 🎬½ 1978 Royal Canadian Mountie dog-sled race turns into a dramatic battle for survival. **75m/C VHS, Beta.** George R. Robinson, Tim Henry, Neil Dainaro, James B. Douglas; **D:** Peter Kelly. *TWE*

The Day After 🎬🎬🎬 1983 Powerful drama graphically depicts the nuclear bombing of a midwestern city and its after-effects on the survivors. Made for television, and very controversial when first shown, gathering huge ratings and vast media coverage. **122m/C VHS, Beta, LV.** Jason Robards Jr., JoBeth Williams, John Lithgow, Steve Guttenberg, John Cullum; **D:** Nicholas Meyer. *PAR*

The Day and the Hour 🎬🎬½ *Today We Live; Le Jour et l'Heure; Il Giorno e L'Ora; Viviamo Oggi* 1963 A woman becomes accidentally involved in the resistance movement during the Nazi occupation of France in WWII. **110m/C VHS, Beta.** *FR JP* Simone Signoret, Stuart Whitman, Genevieve Page, Michel Piccoli, Reggie Nalder, Pierre Dux, Billy Kearns; **D:** Rene Clement; **M:** Claude Bolling. *MGM, CCB*

A Day at the Races 🎬🎬🎬½ 1937 Though it seems labored at times, the brilliance of the brothers Marx still comes through in this rather weak tale of a patient in a sanitorium who convinces horse doctor Groucho to take on running the place. 🎵A Message from the Man in the Moon; On Blue Venetian Waters; Tomorrow is Another Day; All God's Chillun Got Rhythm. **111m/B VHS, Beta, LV.** Groucho Marx, Harpo Marx, Chico Marx, Sig Rumann, Douglass Dumbrille, Margaret Dumont, Allan Jones, Maureen O'Sullivan; **D:** Sam Wood; **C:** Joseph Ruttenberg; **M:** George Bassman. *MGM, CCB*

Day for Night 🎬🎬🎬🎬 *La Nuit Americaine* 1973 (PG) A wryly affectionate look at the profession of moviemaking—its craft, character, and the personalities that interact against the performances commanded by the camera. In French with English subtitles. **116m/C VHS, Beta.** *FR* Jean-Pierre Leaud, Jacqueline Bisset, Jean-Pierre Aumont, Valentina Cortese, Alexandra Stewart, Dani, Nathalie Baye, Francois Truffaut; **D:** Francois Truffaut; **W:** Suzanne Schiffman, Jean-Louis Richard, Francois Truffaut; **M:** Georges Delerue. Academy Awards '73: Best Foreign Language Film; British Academy Awards '73: Best Director (Truffaut), Best Film, Best Supporting Actress (Cortese); New York Film Critics Awards '73: Best Director (Truffaut), Best Film, Best Supporting Actress (Cortese); National Society of Film Critics Awards '73: Best Director (Truffaut), Best Film, Best Supporting Actress (Cortese); Nominations: Academy Awards '74: Best Director (Truffaut), Best Original Screenplay, Best Supporting Actress (Cortese). *WAR*

A Day for Thanks on Walton's Mountain 🎬🎬 1982 Many of the original television-show cast members returned for this sentimental Thanksgiving reunion on Walton's Mountain. Made for television. **97m/C VHS.** Ralph Waite, Ellen Corby, Judy Norton-Taylor, Eric Scott, Jon Walmsley, Robert Wightman, Mary McDonough, David W. Harper, Kami Cotler, Joe Conley, Ronnie Clair Edwards, Richard Gilliland, Melinda Naud; **D:** Harry Harris. *WAR*

A Day in October 🎬🎬½ 1992 (PG-13) 1943, Copenhagen, Denmark. There are signs the Jewish population is in danger from occupying Nazi officials and the resistance movement is active. Wounded resistance fighter Sweeney is rescued by the Jewish Sara (Wolf), and their relationship deepens as the realities of WWII change their lives. Based on historical fact, but there's little explanation of the politics or the fierce nationalism and intense loyalty most Danes felt towards their fellow countrymen, a loyalty that ultimately saved most of the Danish Jews from the Holocaust. Good performances, particularly Benzali as Sara's father, help overcome the script weaknesses. Filmed on location in Denmark. **CW:** Some violence. **96m/C VHS, Closed Caption.** D.B. Sweeney, Kelly Wolf, Tovah Feldshuh, Daniel Benzali, Ole Lemmeke, Kim Romer, Anders Peter Bro, Lars Oluf Larsen; **D:** Kenneth Madsen; **W:** Damian F. Slattery; **M:** Jens Lysdal. *FOX*

A Day in the Country 🎬🎬🎬½ *Une Partie de Campagne* 1946 The son of the famed painter gives us the moving tale of a young woman's sudden and intense love for a man she meets while on a picnic with her family. Beautifully adapted from a story by Guy de Maupassant. Renowned photographer Henri Cartier-Bresson contributed to the wonderful cinematography. In French with English subtitles. **40m/B VHS, Beta.** *FR* Sylvia Bataille, Georges Darnoux, Jane Marken, Paul Temps; **D:** Jean Renoir; **C:** Henri Cartier-Bresson. *NOS, MRV, DVT*

A Day in the Death of Joe Egg 🎬🎬🎬 1971 (R) Based on the Peter Nichols play, an unlikely black comedy about a British couple trying to care for their retarded/autistic child, nearly destroying their marriage in the process. They begin to contemplate euthanasia as a solution. Well-acted, but potentially offensive to some. **106m/C VHS, Beta.** *GB* Alan Bates, Janet Suzman, Elizabeth Robillard, Peter Bowles, Joan Hickson, Sheila Gish; **D:** Peter Medak; **W:** David Deutsch. *COL*

The Day It Came to Earth woof! 1977 (PG) Completely silly and unbelievable sci-fi flick has meteor crashing into the watery grave of a mobster. The decomposed corpse is revived by the radiation and plots to take revenge on those who fitted him with cement shoes. **89m/C VHS.** Roger Manning, Wink Roberts, Bob Ginnaven, Rita Wilson, Delight de Bruine; **D:** Harry Z. Thomason. *EEL*

The Day My Parents Ran Away 🎬🎬½ 1993 (PG) Rebellious 16-year-old gets a tough lesson in responsibility when his parents get tired of his antics and decide to leave home in search of a new life. He finds out things aren't so easy on your own. **95m/C VHS, LV, Closed Caption.** Matt Frewer, Bobby Jacoby, Brigid Conley Walsh, Blair Brown, Martin Mull; **D:** Martin Nicholson; **W:** Handel Glassberg; **M:** J. Peter Robinson. *COL, IME*

Day of Atonement 🎬🎬½ 1993 (R) It's a war for power between rival druglords when Hanin is released from prison and finds out his son and cousin are battling over turf. Then Walken is dragged into the fracas. Beals is the government agent trying to regain some control of the dangerous situation. **CW:** Strong language and strong violence. **127m/C VHS, LV, Closed Caption.** Christopher Walken, Jennifer Beals, Jill Clayburgh, Roger Hanin, Richard Berry. *THV*

Day of Judgment 🎬½ 1981 A mysterious stranger arrives in a town to slaughter those people who violate the Ten Commandments. **101m/C VHS, Beta.** William T. Hicks, Harris Bloodworth, Brownlee Davis; **D:** C.D.H. Reynolds. *NO*

Day of the Animals 🎬 *Something is Out There* 1977 (PG) Nature gone wild. It seems a depleted ozone layer has exposed the animals to the sun's radiation, turning Bambi and Bugs into brutal killers. A group of backpackers trek in the Sierras, unaware of the transformation. Farfetched and silly (we hope). **95m/C VHS.** Christopher George, Leslie Nielsen, Lynda Day George, Richard Jaeckel, Michael Ansara, Ruth Roman, Jon Cedar, Susan Backlinie, Andrew Stevens, Gil Lamb; **D:** William Girdler; **W:** William W. Norton Sr.

Day of the Assassin 🎬 1981 A Mideast shah's yacht explodes, sending a huge fortune to the bottom of a murky bay. This sets off a rampage of treasure hunting by a variety of ruthless mercenaries. **94m/C VHS, Beta.** Glenn Ford, Chuck Connors, Richard Roundtree, Henry Silva, Jorge Rivero; **D:** Brian Trenchard-Smith.

Day of the Cobra 🎬½ 1984 A corrupt narcotics bureau official hires an ex-cop to find a heroin kingpin on the back streets of Genoa, Italy. **95m/C VHS, Beta.** *IT* Franco Nero, Sybil Danning, Mario Maranzana, Licinia Lentini, William Berger; **D:** Enzo G. Castellari.

Day of the Dead 🎬½ 1985 The third in Romero's trilogy of films about flesh-eating zombies taking over the world. Romero hasn't thought up anything new for the ghouls to do, and the humans are too nasty to care about this time around. For adult audiences. **91m/C VHS, Beta, LV.** Lori Cardille, Terry Alexander, Joe Pilato, Jarlath Conroy, Richard Liberty; **D:** George A. Romero; **W:** George A. Romero; **C:** Michael Gornick. *VTR, IME*

The Day of the Dolphin 🐾🐾 1973 **(PG)** Research scientist, after successfully working out a means of teaching dolphins to talk, finds his animals kidnapped; espionage and assassination are involved. Dolphin voices by Henry, who also wrote the screenplay. **104m/C VHS, Beta, LV.** George C. Scott, Trish Van Devere, Paul Sorvino, Fritz Weaver, Jon Korkes, John Dehner, Edward Herrmann, Severn Darden; **D:** Mike Nichols; **W:** Buck Henry; **M:** Georges Delerue; **V:** Buck Henry. Nominations: Academy Awards '73: Best Sound, Best Original Dramatic/Comedy Score. *NLC*

The Day of the Jackal 🐾🐾🐾½ 1973 **(PG)** Frederick Forsyth's best-selling novel of political intrigue is splendidly brought to the screen by Zinnemann. A brilliant and ruthless assassin hired to kill Charles de Gaulle skirts the international intelligence pool, while intuitive police work try to stop him. Tense, suspenseful, beautiful location photography. Excellent acting by Fox, Cusack and Britton. **142m/C VHS, Beta, LV, DVD.** Edward Fox, Alan Badel, Tony Britton, Derek Jacobi, Cyril Cusack, Olga Georges-Picot; **D:** Fred Zinnemann; **M:** Georges Delerue. Nominations: Academy Awards '73: Best Film Editing. *USH*

The Day of the Locust 🐾🐾🐾½ 1975 **(R)** Compelling adaptation of Nathaniel West's novel concerning the dark side of 1930s' Hollywood. A no-talent amoral actress's affair with a meek accountant leads to tragedy and destruction. Told from the view of a cynical art director wise to the ways of Hollywood. **140m/C VHS, Beta, LV.** Donald Sutherland, Karen Black, Burgess Meredith, William Atherton, Billy Barty, Bo Hopkins, Richard Dysart, Geraldine Page; **D:** John Schlesinger; **C:** Conrad Hall; **M:** John Barry. Nominations: Academy Awards '75: Best Cinematography, Best Supporting Actor (Meredith). *PAR*

Day of the Maniac 🐾½ 1977 **(R)** Psychotic drug addict will stop at nothing to support his growing habit. **89m/C VHS, Beta.** George Hilton, Susan Scott; **D:** Sergio Martino. *REP*

Day of the Panther 🐾½ 1988 The Panthers—the world's most formidable martial artists—are mighty torqued when panther-Linda is pithed, and they're not known to turn the other cheek. Much chop-socky kicking and shrilling. **86m/C VHS, Beta.** John Stanton, Eddie Stazak; **D:** Brian Trenchard-Smith. *CEL*

Day of the Triffids 🐾🐾🐾 1963 The majority of Earth's population is blinded by a meteor shower which also causes plant spores to mutate into giant carnivores. Well-done adaptation of John Wyndham's science fiction classic; Philip Yordan acknowledged "fronting" for blacklisted screenwriter Gordon, who finally received credit in 1996. **94m/C VHS, Beta, LV, Letterbox.** Howard Keel, Janet Scott, Nicole Maurey, Kieron Moore, Mervyn Johns, Alison Leggatt, Ewan Roberts, Janina Faye; **D:** Freddie Francis, Steve Sekely; **W:** Bernard Gordon. *MRV, VTR, HHT*

Day of the Warrior 🐾🐾 1996 **(R)** Babes who belong to a paramilitary law-and-order group infiltrate crime lord, the Warrior's, smuggling operations, strip joints and porn palaces. **96m/C VHS.** Julie Strain, Marcus Bagwell; **D:** Andy Sidaris. *MNC*

Day of Triumph 1954 A dynamic version of the life of Christ as seen through the eyes of the apostles Andrew and Zadok, the leaders of the Zealot underground. **110m/C VHS.** Lee J. Cobb, Robert Wilson, Ralph Freud; **D:** Irving Pichel. *REP*

Day of Wrath 🐾🐾🐾🐾 *Vredens Dag* 1943 An involving psychological thriller based on records of witch trials from the early 1600s. An old woman, burned at the stake as a witch, puts a curse on the local parson and his family. Grim and unrelentingly pessimistic, moving from one horrific scene to another, director Dreyer creates a masterpiece of terror. Based on a play by Hans Wiers Jenssen. In Danish with English subtitles. **110m/B VHS. DK** Thorkild Roose, Sigrid Neiiendam, Lisbeth Movin, Preben Lerdorff, Anna Svierker; **D:** Carl Theodor Dreyer; **W:** Carl Theodor Dreyer; **M:** Poul Schierbeck. *HTV, NOS, SNC*

Day One 🐾🐾🐾 1989 Vivid recreation of one of the most turbulent periods of American history—the WWII race to build the atomic bomb. Chronicles the two year top-secret efforts of the Manhattan Project, with General Leslie Groves (Dennehy) having to supervise the project and contain the scientific rivalries. Outstanding cast, with Strathairn notable as physicist J. Robert Oppenheimer. Adapted from "Day One: Before Hiroshima and After" by Peter Wyden. Made for television. **141m/C VHS, Closed Caption.** Brian Dennehy, David Strathairn, Michael Tucker, Hume Cronyn, Richard Dysart, Barnard Hughes, Hal Holbrook, David Ogden Stiers, John McMartin; **D:** Joseph Sargent; **W:** David W. Rintels; **M:** Mason Daring. *WOV*

The Day That Shook the World 🐾🐾 1978 **(R)** Slow-moving but intriguing account of events surrounding the assassination of Archduke Ferdinand of Austria that triggered WWI. Garnered an R-rating due to some disturbingly graphic scenes. **111m/C VHS.** Christopher Plummer, Florinda Bolkan, Maximilian Schell; **D:** Veljko Bulajic. *NO*

Day the Bookies Wept 🐾🐾 1939 Decent yarn about cabbies tricked into buying a "racehorse." Turns out she's old as the hills and hooked on alcohol to boot, but they enter her in the big race anyway. **50m/B VHS, Beta.** Betty Grable, Joe Penner, Tom Kennedy, Richard Lane; **D:** Leslie Goodwins. *CCB*

The Day the Earth Caught Fire 🐾🐾🐾½ 1961 The earth is knocked out of orbit and sent hurtling toward the sun when nuclear testing is done simultaneously at both the North and South Poles. Realistic and suspenseful, this is one of the best of the sci-fi genre. **95m/B VHS, Beta.** Janet Munro, Edward Judd, Leo McKern; **D:** Val Guest; **W:** Val Guest, Wolf Mankowitz. British Academy Awards '61: Best Screenplay. *REP, KAR*

The Day the Earth Froze 🐾🐾 1959 Witch steals the sun because she couldn't have a magical mill that produced grain, salt, and gold. Everything on Earth freezes. Based on a Finnish epic poem. **67m/B VHS.** Nina Anderson, Jon Powers, Ingrid Elhardt, Paul Sorenson; **D:** Gregg Sebelious. *SNC*

The Day the Earth Stood Still 🐾🐾🐾½ 1951 A gentle alien lands on Earth to deliver a message of peace and a warning against experimenting with nuclear power. He finds his views echoed by a majority of the population, but not the ones who are in control. In this account based loosely on the story of Christ, Rennie is the visitor backed by the mighty robot Gort. One of the greatest science fiction films of all time. **92m/B VHS, Beta, LV.** Michael Rennie, Patricia Neal, Hugh Marlowe, Sam Jaffe, Frances Bavier, Lock Martin, Billy Gray; **D:** Robert Wise; **W:** Edmund H. North; **C:** Leo Tover; **M:** Bernard Herrmann. National Film Registry '95. *FOX, FCT, MLB*

The Day the Sky Exploded 🐾½ *Death From Outer Space; La Morte Viene Dalla Spazio; Le Danger Vient de l'Escape* 1957 Sci-fi disaster drama doesn't live up to the grandiose title, as a runaway rocket ship hits the sun, unleashing an asteroid shower that threatens Earth with tidal waves, earthquakes, heat waves and terrible dialogue. The highlight of this Franco-Italian effort is the cinematography for director Mario Bava. **80m/B VHS. FR IT** Paul Hubschmid, Madeleine Fischer, Fiorella Mari, Ivo Garrani, Dario Michaelis; **D:** Richard Benson; **C:** Mario Bava. *NOS, FCT*

The Day the Sun Turned Cold 🐾🐾🐾 *Tianguo Niezi* 1994 In an apparent crisis of conscience a young man (Zhong Hua) enters a police station and tries to convince a weary captain (Hu) that his mother (Gowa) murdered his cruel father (Jingwu) 10 years before in order to marry another man. The detective eventually concludes he should investigate the supposed crime, which happened in a remote village, but Zhong Hua's accusations naturally stir up a great deal of resentment and anger. There's lots of questions about guilt, innocence, and motives—on everybody's part. Mandarin with subtitles. **99m/C VHS. HK** Siqin Gowa, Tuo Zhong Hua, Wai Zhi, Ma Jingwu, Li Hu; **D:** Yim Ho; **W:** Yim Ho; **C:** Hou Yong; **M:** Yoshihide Otomo. *KIV*

The Day the Women Got Even 🐾½ 1980 Four suburban homemakers take up the life of vigilantes to save unsuspecting actresses from a talent agent's blackmail scheme. Made for television. **98m/C VHS, Beta.** JoAnn Pflug, Tina Louise, Georgia Engel, Barbara Rhoades, Julie Hagerty, Ed O'Neill; **D:** Burt Brinckerhoff; **M:** Brad Fiedel. *TLF*

Day the World Ended 🐾 1955 The first science fiction film of exploitation director Roger Corman. Five survivors of nuclear holocaust discover a desert ranch house fortress owned by a survivalist (Birch) and his daughter (Nelson). With relatively abundant supplies, they fatuously wallow in false misery until a disfigured visitor, wasting away from radiation, stumbles into their paradise. His mutation into an alien being confronts them with the horror that lurks outside. **79m/B VHS, Letterbox.** Paul Birch, Lori Nelson, Adele Jergens, Raymond Hatton, Paul Dubov, Richard Denning, Mike Connors; **D:** Roger Corman; **W:** Lou Rusoff. *COL*

Day Time Ended 🐾🐾 *Vortex; Timewarp* 1980 A pair of glowing UFO's streaking across the sky and an alien mechanical device with long menacing appendages are only two of the bizarre phenomena witnessed from a lone house in the desert. Good special effects. Also released as "Time Warp" (1978). **80m/C VHS, Beta, LV.** Chris Mitchum, Jim Davis, Dorothy Malone; **D:** John Cardos; **W:** David Schmoeller, J. Larry Carroll; **M:** Richard Band. *MRV*

The Day Will Dawn 🐾🐾🐾 *The Avengers* 1942 Suspenseful British-made WWII thriller about a reporter and a young Norwegian girl who plot to sabotage a secret Nazi U-boat base near the girl's town. **100m/B VHS, Beta, 8mm. GB** Deborah Kerr, Hugh Williams, Griffith Jones, Ralph Richardson, Francis L. Sullivan, Roland Culver, Niall MacGinnis, Finlay Currie, Patricia Medina; **D:** Harold French; **W:** Terence Rattigan. *VYY*

Day with Conrad Green 1980 Set in 1927, this program presents a somewhat farcical look at a successful Broadway producer as he attempts to cope with a full schedule of personal and business problems on the day of the funeral of his longtime assistant. **60m/C VHS, Beta.** Fred Gwynne. *MTP*

Daybreak 🐾🐾½ 1993 **(R)** In the near future America has been decimated by a nameless, sexually transmitted disease (read AIDS parable) and public policy is to quarantine the infected in concentration camp-like prisons. This leads to a quasi-official group of green-shirted thugs roaming the streets and imprisoning or killing anyone they suspect has the disease. A small resistance movement is lead by Torch (Gooding, Jr.), who happens to fall in love with Blue (Kelly), the sister of one of the fascist leaders. Based on Alan Bowne's play "Beirut, Daybreak." Made for cable television. **91m/C VHS.** Cuba Gooding Jr., Moira Kelly, Omar Epps, Martha Plimpton, Alice Drummond, David Eigenberg, John Savage; **Cameos:** Phil Hartman; **D:** Stephen Tolkin; **W:** Stephen Tolkin. *HBO*

The Daydreamer 🐾🐾½ *Absent-Minded; Le Distrait* 1975 Actor/director/writer Richard stars as a bumbling fool let loose in the French corporate world with comical results. In French with subtitles. **90m/C VHS, Beta. FR** Pierre Richard, Bernard Blier, Maria Pacome, Marie-Christine Barrault; **D:** Pierre Richard; **W:** Pierre Richard; **M:** Vladimir Cosma. *FCT*

Daylight 🐾🐾 1996 **(PG-13)** After a massive explosion seals both ends of New York's Holland Tunnel (The Tunneling Inferno?), a small band of stock disaster flick survivors are trapped under the waters of the Hudson River. Fortunately, a cab driver with a really square jaw who, conveniently, is an ex-emergency rescue worker AND who knows the entire layout of the tunnel happens to be driving toward the tunnel at the exact moment of the disaster. Coincidence? Nope, just Hollywood. Kit Latura (Stallone) leads the survivors through cave-ins, floods, fire, rats, and poison gas (The Poison-Hiding Adventure!) only to discover to their dismay that they have emerged in New Jersey. Long on special effects but short on character development, this nod to the catastrophe movies of the '70s is still enjoyable for those who like to watch things go boom. **CW:** Disaster-related peril, death and destruction. **109m/C VHS, LV, Closed Caption, DVD.** Sylvester Stallone, Viggo Mortensen, Amy Brenneman, Stan Shaw, Claire Bloom, Renoly Santiago, Sage Stallone, Dan Hedaya, Jay O. Sanders, Karen Young, Vanessa Bell Calloway, Colin Fox, Danielle Harris, Jo Anderson, Mark Rolston, Rosemary Forsyth, Barry Newman; **D:** Rob Cohen; **W:** Leslie Bohem; **C:** David Eggby; **M:** Randy Edelman. Nominations: Academy Awards '96: Best Sound Effects Editing; Golden Raspberry Awards '96: Worst Actor (Stallone), Worst Song ("Whenever There is Love"). *USH*

Days and Nights in the Forest 🎬🎬½ 1970 Four men living in Calcutta decide to leave the city for a brief vacation. Each has a different emotional experience which will change him forever, including a brief love affair and finding true romance. In Bengali with English subtitles. **120m/C VHS.** *IN D;* Satyajit Ray. *FCT*

Days of Glory 🎬🎬½ 1943 Peck's screen debut finds him as a Russian peasant bravely fighting the Nazi blitzkrieg almost single-handedly. **86m/B VHS, Beta.** Tamara Toumanova, Gregory Peck, Alan Reed, Maria Palmer, Lowell Gilmore, Hugo Haas; **D:** Jacques Tourneur; **C:** Gaetano Antonio "Tony" Gaudio. *TTC*

Days of Heaven 🎬🎬🎬½ 1978 (PG) Drifter Gere, his younger sister, and a woman he claims is his sister become involved with a Texas sharecropper. Told through the eyes of the younger girl, this is a sweeping vision of the U.S. before WWI. Loss and loneliness, deception, frustration, and anger haunt these people as they struggle to make the land their own. Deservedly awarded an Oscar for breathtaking cinematography. **95m/C VHS, Beta, LV.** Richard Gere, Brooke Adams, Sam Shepard, Linda Manz, Stuart Margolin; **D:** Terrence Malick; **W:** Terrence Malick; **C:** Nestor Almendros; **M:** Ennio Morricone. Academy Awards '78: Best Cinematography; Cannes Film Festival '79: Best Director (Malick); Los Angeles Film Critics Association Awards '78: Best Cinematography; New York Film Critics Awards '78: Best Director (Malick); National Society of Film Critics Awards '78: Best Cinematography, Best Director (Malick), Best Film; Nominations: Academy Awards '78: Best Costume Design, Best Sound, Best Original Score. *PAR*

Days of Hell 🎬 *I Giorni Dell'Inferno* 1984 Forgettable tale of four mercenaries who are hired to rescue a doctor and his daughter held captive by guerrillas somewhere in Afghanistan only to find out they're pawns in an even bigger scheme. **90m/C VHS, Beta.** Conrad Nichols, Richard Raymond, Stephen Elliott, Kinako Harada; **D:** Anthony Richmond. *NO*

Days of Thrills and Laughter 🎬🎬🎬½ 1961 Delightful compilation of clips from the era of silent films, showcasing the talents of the great comics as well as daring stuntman. **93m/B VHS, Beta.** Buster Keaton, Charlie Chaplin, Harold Lloyd, Stan Laurel, Oliver Hardy, Douglas Fairbanks Sr.; **D:** Robert Youngson. *MPI*

Days of Thunder 🎬🎬 1990 (PG-13) "Top Gun" in race cars! Cruise follows the same formula he has followed for several years now (with the notable exception of "Born on the Fourth of July.") Cruise and Towne co-wrote the screenplay concerning a young kid bursting with talent and raw energy who must learn to deal with his mentor, his girlfriend, and eventually the bad guy. First film that featured cameras that were actually on the race cars. If you like Cruise or race cars then

this is the movie for you. **109m/C VHS, Beta, LV, Letterbox, Closed Caption.** Tom Cruise, Robert Duvall, Randy Quaid, Nicole Kidman, Cary Elwes, Michael Rooker, Fred Dalton Thompson, John C. Reilly; **D:** Tony Scott; **W:** Tom Cruise, Robert Towne; **M:** Hans Zimmer. Nominations: Academy Awards '90: Best Sound. *PAR*

Days of Wine and Roses 🎬🎬½ 1958 The original "Playhouse 90" television version of J.P. Miller's story which was adapted for the big screen in 1962. An executive on the fast track and his young wife, initially only social drinkers, find themselves degenerating into alcoholism. A well-acted, stirring drama. **89m/B VHS, Beta.** Cliff Robertson, Piper Laurie; **D:** John Frankenheimer. *RHI, MGM, BTV*

Days of Wine and Roses 🎬🎬🎬½ 1962 A harrowing tale of an alcoholic advertising man who gradually drags his wife down with him into a life of booze. Part of the "A Night at the Movies" series, this tape simulates a 1962 movie evening with a Bugs Bunny cartoon, "Martian Through Georgia," a newsreel, and coming attractions for "Gypsy" and "Rome Adventure." Big screen adaptation of the play originally shown on television. ♫Days of Wine and Roses. **138m/B VHS, Beta, LV.** Jack Lemmon, Lee Remick, Charles Bickford, Jack Klugman, Jack Albertson; **D:** Blake Edwards; **M:** Henry Mancini, Johnny Mercer. Academy Awards '62: Best Song ("Days of Wine and Roses"); Nominations: Academy Awards '62: Best Actor (Lemmon), Best Actress (Remick), Best Art Direction/Set Decoration (B & W), Best Costume Design (B & W). *WAR*

Dayton's Devils 🎬🎬 1968 Nielsen is the leader of a motley crew of losers who plan to rob a military base bank in this action-packed heist flick. **107m/C VHS, Beta.** Rory Calhoun, Leslie Nielsen, Lainie Kazan, Eric (Hans Gudegast) Braeden, Georg Stanford Brown, Rigg Kennedy; **D:** Jack Shea. *NO*

The Daytrippers 🎬🎬½ 1996 Happily married Eliza D'Amico is living on Long Island while husband Louis (Tucci) goes to work in Manhattan. That is she's happy until she finds what appears to be a love letter addressed to her husband. Frantic, Eliza runs to aggressive mom Rita (Meara), who decides that her daughter should immediately confront her possibly erring husband at his office. So Eliza, her mom and dad (McNamara), sarcastic younger sister Jo (Posey), and Jo's pretentious boyfriend Carl (Schreiber) all pile into the family station wagon and head into the city. Only Louis isn't at his office and they scour Manhattan to track him down. **88m/C VHS, Closed Caption.** Hope Davis, Anne Meara, Parker Posey, Liev Schreiber, Pat McNamara, Stanley Tucci, Campbell Scott, Marcia Gay Harden, Andy Brown; **D:** Greg Mottola; **W:** Greg Mottola; **C:** John Inwood. *COL*

Dazed and Confused 🎬🎬🎬 1993 (R) A day in the life of a bunch of high schoolers should prove to be a trip back in time for those coming of age in the '70s. Eight seniors facing life after high school have one last year long hurrah, as they search for Aerosmith tickets and haze the incoming freshmen. Keen characterization by writer/director Linklater captures the spirit of a generation shaped by Watergate, the Vietnam War, feminism, and marijuana. Groovy soundtrack features Alice Cooper, Deep Purple, KISS, and Foghat. **CW:** Extremely vulgar language; sex talk and substance abuse. **97m/C VHS, LV, Letterbox, Closed Caption, DVD.** Jason London, Rory Cochrane, Sasha Jensen, Wiley Wiggins, Michelle Burke, Adam Goldberg, Anthony Rapp, Marissa Ribisi, Parker Posey, Joey Lauren Adams, Ben Affleck; **D:** Richard Linklater; **W:** Richard Linklater. *USH*

D.C. Cab 🎬🎬½ 1984 (R) A rag-tag group of Washington, D.C. cabbies learn a lesson in self-respect in this endearing comedy. Though not without flaws, it's charming all the same. **100m/C VHS, Beta, LV, Closed Caption.** Mr. T, Leif Erickson, Adam Baldwin, Charlie Barnett, Irene Cara, Anne DeSalvo, Max Gail, Gloria Gifford, Gary Busey, Jill Schoelen, Marsha Warfield; **D:** Joel Schumacher; **W:** Joel Schumacher, Topper Carew; **C:** Dean Cundey. *USH*

De Mayerling a Sarajevo 🎬🎬½ *Mayerling to Sarajevo; Sarajevo* 1940 Looks at the romance and marriage, as well as royal pomp and circumstance, of the Countess Sophie (Feuillere) and the Archduke Franz-Ferdinand (Lodge). The assassination of these innocuous rulers at Sarajevo would lead to the outbreak of WWI. French with subtitles. **89m/B VHS.** *FR* Edwige Feuillere, John Lodge, Aime Clairmond, Gabrielle Dorziat; **D:** Max Ophuls; **W:** Kurt Alexander; **C:** Curt Courant, Otto Heller; **M:** Oscar Straus. *WBF*

The Dead 🎬🎬🎬½ 1987 (PG) The poignant final film by Huston, based on James Joyce's short story. At a Christmas dinner party in turn-of-the-century Dublin, a man discovers how little he knows about his wife when a song reminds her of a cherished lost love. Beautifully captures the spirit of the story while providing Huston an opportunity to create a last lament on the fickle nature of time and life. **82m/C VHS, Beta, LV, Closed Caption.** *GB* Anjelica Huston, Donal McCann, Marie Kean, Donal Donnelly, Dan O'Herlihy, Helen Carroll, Frank Patterson; **D:** John Huston; **C:** Fred Murphy; **M:** Alex North. Independent Spirit Awards '88: Best Director (Huston), Best Supporting Actress (Huston); National Society of Film Critics Awards '87: Best Film; Nominations: Academy Awards '87: Best Adapted Screenplay, Best Costume Design. *ART, VES, TVC*

Dead Again 🎬🎬🎬½ 1991 (R) Branagh's first film since his brilliant debut as the director/star of "Henry V" again proves him a visionary force on and off camera. As the smart L.A. detective hired to discover the identity of a beautiful, but mute woman, he's realistic, clever, tender and cynical. He finds that he's apparently trapped in a nightmarish cycle of murder begun years before. Literate, lovely to look at, suspenseful, with a sense of humor to match its high style. **107m/C VHS, LV, Letterbox, Closed Caption.** Kenneth Branagh, Emma Thompson, Andy Garcia, Lois Hall, Richard Easton, Derek Jacobi, Hanna Schygulla, Campbell Scott, Wayne Knight, Christine Ebersole; **Cameos:** Robin Williams; **D:** Kenneth Branagh; **W:** Scott Frank; **C:** Matthew F. Leonetti; **M:** Patrick Doyle. *PAR, CCB*

Dead Ahead 🎬🎬 1996 (PG-13) Skilled archer Maura Loch (Zimbalist) is enjoying a camping trip with her family until four bankrobbers on the lam stumble across them and take Maura's son hostage. Armed with her bow, Maura tracks the criminals to save her child. Made for cable TV. **CW:** Violence, drug use. **92m/C VHS, Closed Caption.** Stephanie Zimbalist, Sarah Chalke, Tom Butler, Brendan Fletcher, Peter Onorati, John Tench, Michael Tayles, Douglas Arthurs; **D:** Stuart Cooper; **W:** David Alexander. *PAR*

Dead Ahead: The Exxon Valdez Disaster 🎬🎬🎬 *Disaster at Valdez* 1992 (PG-13) Focuses on the first crucial days after the March 24, 1989 oil spill when the Exxon Valdez ran aground off Alaska in Prince William Sound. Portrays the inadequate precautions, incompetence, greed, and petty bureaucracy that made an appalling situation even worse. Lloyd stars as Exxon official Frank Iarossi, in charge of the official cleanup, caught between onsite confusion and corporate bungling while Heard is outraged environmentalist Dan Lawn. News and home videotapes of the actual spill are used to enhance the dramatization. Filmed in Vancouver, British Columbia. Made for cable television. **CW:** Strong language used once. **90m/C VHS.** Christopher Lloyd, John Heard, Rip Torn, Michael Murphy, Don S. Davies, Ken Walsh, Bob Gunton, Mark Metcalf, Paul Guilfoyle, David Morse, Jackson Davies; **D:** Paul Seed; **W:** Michael Baker; **M:** David Ferguson. *NO*

Dead Aim woof! 1987 (R) A dud about Soviet spies who introduce even more drugs into New York City, ostensibly to bring about the downfall of the U.S. Obviously a completely farfetched plot. **91m/C VHS, LV.** Ed Marinaro, Isaac Hayes, Corbin Bernsen; **D:** William Vanderkloot. *ART, HHE*

Dead Air 🎬🎬 1994 (PG-13) Atmospheric murder mystery finds radio deejay Hines getting calls from a mystery woman who says she knows him well and has kidnapped his new girlfriend. Meanwhile, a woman claiming to be a reporter wants to interview him and things around the radio station start looking decidedly sinister. *CW:* Violence and views of murder victims. **91m/C VHS, LV, Closed Caption.** Gregory Hines, Debrah Farentino, Gloria Reuben, Beau Starr, Laura Harrington, Michael Harris, W. Earl Brown, Veronica Cartwright; *D:* Fred Walton; *W:* David Amann; *M:* Dana Kaproff. *USH*

Dead Alive 🎬🎬 *Braindead* 1993 This outrageously over-the-top horror flick from New Zealand is a gore aficionado's delight (think "Evil Dead" movies for comparison). Set in 1957 and satirizing the bland times, the "plot" has the mom of a nerdy son getting bitten by an exotic monkey, which promptly turns her into a particularly nasty ghoul. This condition is apparently contagious (except for her son who tries to hide the fact mom is literally a monster) and calls for lots of spurting blood and body parts which take on lives of their own. For those with strong stomachs and senses of humor. Also available in an 85-minute R-rated version. **97m/C VHS, LV, Closed Caption.** *NZ* Timothy Balme, Elizabeth Moody, Diana Penalver, Ian Watkin, Breanda Kendall, Stuart Devenie; *D:* Peter Jackson; *W:* Peter Jackson. *THV, FCT*

Dead and Buried 🎬🎬½ 1981 (R) Farentino is the sheriff who can't understand why the victims of some pretty grisly murders seem to be coming back to life. Eerily suspenseful. **95m/C VHS, Beta.** James Farentino, Jack Albertson, Melody Anderson, Lisa Blount, Bill Quinn, Michael Pataki, Robert Englund, Barry Corbin, Lisa Marie; *D:* Gary Sherman; *W:* Dan O'Bannon, Ronald Shusett. *NO*

Dead as a Doorman 🎬½ 1985 A young writer takes a part-time post as a doorman and becomes the target of a murderous lunatic. **83m/C VHS, Beta.** Bradley Whitford, Sharon Schlarth, Bruce Taylor; *D:* Gary Youngman. *ART, VES*

Dead Badge 🎬🎬½ 1994 (R) An honest cop is reassigned to a corrupt precinct and becomes targeted for death. **95m/C VHS, Closed Caption.** Brian Wimmer, Olympia Dukakis, Yaphet Kotto, M. Emmet Walsh, James B. Sikking, Marta DuBois. *CAF*

Dead Bang 🎬🎬½ 1989 (R) A frustrated cop uncovers a murderous white supremacist conspiracy in L.A. Frankenheimer's deft directorial hand shapes a somewhat conventional cop plot into an effective vehicle for Johnson. **102m/C VHS, Beta, LV, 8mm.** Don Johnson, Bob Balaban, William Forsythe, Penelope Ann Miller, Tim Reid, Frank Military, Michael Higgins, Michael Jeter, Evans Evans, Tate Donovan; *D:* John Frankenheimer; *W:* Robert Foster; *M:* Gary Chang, Michael Kamen. *WAR*

Dead Beat 🎬🎬½ 1994 (R) Teen love and lust—and murder—all set in Albuquerque, New Mexico, circa 1965. Womanizer Kit (Ramsey) will use any tale to score with his dates—and is happy to pass on tips to adoring disciple Rudy (Getty). When Kit meets up with rebellious rich girl Kirsten (Wagner), he demands proof of his love and he confides he once murdered a girl. Kirsten tries to tighten her stranglehold on Kit with this info and force Rudy from his life but Kit's dark side doesn't stay hidden either. *CW:* Language; sociopathic behavior, including violence and sexuality. **94m/C VHS, Closed Caption.** Bruce Ramsay, Natasha Gregson Wagner, Balthazar Getty, Meredith Salenger, Sara Gilbert, Deborah Harry, Max Perlich, Alex Cox; *D:* Adam Dubov; *W:* Adam Dubov. *WEA, ART*

Dead Boyz Can't Fly 🎬🎬 1993 (R) Disturbing look at urban violence. Dysfunctional punk leads his equally amoral cohorts on a looting spree in a near-empty highrise in revenge against a patronizing businessman. The unrated version contains 10 more minutes of violence. **92m/C VHS.** Delia Sheppard, Sheila Kennedy, Ruth Collins, Mark McCulley, Brad Friedman; *D:* Howard Winters. *NO*

Dead Calm 🎬🎬🎬 1989 (R) A taut Australian thriller based on a novel by Charles Williams. A young married couple is yachting on the open seas when they happen upon the lone survivor of a sinking ship. They take him on board only to discover he's a homicidal maniac. Makes for some pretty suspenseful moments that somewhat make up for the weak ending. **97m/C VHS, Beta, LV, 8mm, Letterbox, Closed Caption.** *AU* Sam Neill, Billy Zane, Nicole Kidman, Rod Mullinar; *D:* Phillip Noyce; *W:* Terry Hayes; *C:* Dean Semler; *M:* Graeme Revell. *WAR, FCT*

Dead Center 🎬🎬 *Crazy Joe* 1994 (R) Street punk gets trained as assassin by secret government agency that frames him for the murder of a U.S. senator. So now he has to stay alive long enough to prove his innocence. **90m/C VHS, LV, Closed Caption.** Justin Lazard, Eb Lottimer, Rachel York; *D:* Steve Carver. *THV*

Dead Certain 🎬 1992 (R) A "Silence of the Lambs" rip-off. Dourif (again specializing in weirdos) is the jailed serial killer providing tantalizing clues to the identity of a new killer on the loose. **93m/C VHS.** Brad Dourif, Francesco Quinn, Karen Russell, Joel Kaiser; *D:* Anders Palm; *W:* Anders Palm.

Dead Cold 🎬🎬½ 1996 (R) Screenwriter Eric Thornsen (Mulkey) decides he and wife Alicia (Anthony) need a second honeymoon at a remote cabin. But their privacy is disturbed by homicidal fugitive Kale (Dobson), who drugs and dumps Eric's body down a ravine. Turns out Alicia wants hubby's insurance money and she and the disgusting Kale are very intimate friends. But of course Eric's not really dead. Decent thriller is slow to start but picks up speed in the second half. *CW:* Violence, sexuality, and language. **91m/C VHS, LV, Closed Caption.** Lysette Anthony, Chris Mulkey, Peter Dobson, Alina Thompson, Michael Champion; *D:* Kurt Anderson; *W:* Richard Brandes; *C:* M. David Mullen. *ART*

Dead Connection 🎬🎬 1994 (R) Beautiful reporter Bonet is in cahoots with cop Madsen to see justice brought to the "phone sex killer" who is terrorizing Los Angeles. **93m/C VHS, Closed Caption.** Michael Madsen, Lisa Bonet, Gary Stretch; *D:* Nigel Dick; *W:* Larry Grolin; *M:* Rolfe Kent. *PGV*

The Dead Don't Die 🎬 1975 Unbelievable plot set in the 1930s has Hamilton as a detective trying to prove his brother was wrongly executed for murder. He ultimately clashes with the madman who wants to rule the world with an army of zombies. Perhaps if they had cast Hamilton as Master of the Zombies. Made for television. **74m/C VHS, Beta.** George Hamilton, Ray Milland, Linda Cristal, Ralph Meeker, Joan Blondell, James McEachin; *D:* Curtis Harrington. *WOV, GKK*

Dead Easy 🎬🎬 1982 Livin' ain't easy for a Sydney sleaze-club owner, his working-girl girlfriend, and a slandered cop when they're caught between machete-wielding enemy gangs (it seems somebody made the crime boss REALLY mad). The three fight in that quintessential escape vehicle—a two-ton truck—to qualify the effort as an Australian contender for greatest chase scene ever (heavy chassis category). **92m/C VHS, Beta.** *AU* Scott Burgess, Rosemary Paul; *D:* Bert Deling. *MCG*

Dead End 🎬🎬🎬½ *Cradle of Crime* 1937 Sidney Kingsley play, adapted for the big screen by Lillian Hellman, traces the lives of various inhabitants of the slums on New York's Lower East Side as they try to overcome their surroundings. Gritty drama saved from melodrama status by some genuinely funny moments. Film launched the Dead End Kids. **92m/B VHS, Beta, LV.** Sylvia Sidney, Joel McCrea, Humphrey Bogart, Wendy Barrie, Claire Trevor, Allen Jenkins, Marjorie Main, Leo Gorcey, Charles Halton; *D:* William Wyler; *C:* Gregg Toland. Nominations: Academy Awards '37: Best Cinematography, Best Interior Decoration, Best Picture, Best Supporting Actress (Trevor). *MGM, MLB*

Dead End City 🎬½ 1988 Street-wise resident of L.A. organizes fellow citizens into a vigilante force to fight the gangs for control of the city. **88m/C VHS, Beta.** Dennis Cole, Greg Cummins, Christine Lunde, Robert Z'Dar, Darrell Nelson, Alena Downs; *D:* Peter Yuval; *W:* Michael Bogert.

Dead End Drive-In 🎬🎬 1986 (R) In a surreal, grim future a man is trapped at a drive-in theatre-cum-government-run concentration camp, where those considered to be less than desirable members of society are incarcerated. **92m/C VHS, Beta, Closed Caption.** *AU* Ned Manning, Natalie McCurry, Peter Whitford; *D:* Brian Trenchard-Smith. *VTR*

Dead End Street 🎬 1983 Young prostitute attempts to change her self-destructive lifestyle. It's not easy. **86m/C VHS, Beta.** *IS* Anat Atzman, Yehoram Gaon. *TWE*

Dead Eyes of London 🎬🎬½ *Dark Eyes of London; Die Toten Augen von London* 1961 Blind old German men are dying to lower their premiums in this geriatric thriller: someone (perhaps the director of the home for the blind?) is killing off the clientele for their insurance money, and a Scotland Yard inspector aims to expose the scam. Relatively early vintage Kinski, it's a remake of the eerie 1939 Lugosi vehicle, "The Human Monster" (originally titled "Dark Eyes of London"), adapted from Edgar Wallace's "The Testament of Gordon Stuart." **95m/B VHS.** *GE* Joachim Fuchsberger, Karin Baal, Dieter Borsche, Ady Berber, Klaus Kinski, Eddi Arent, Wolfgang Lukschy; *D:* Alfred Vohrer. *SNC*

Dead for a Dollar 🎬½ 197? A Colonel, a con man, and a mysterious woman team up in the Old West to search for the two hundred thousand dollars they stole from a local bank. **92m/C VHS, Beta.** John Ireland, George Hilton, Piero Vida, Sandra Milo. *UNI, MOV*

Dead Funny 🎬🎬 1994 (R) Vivian (Pena) returns to her Manhattan walk-up to find boyfriend Reggie (McCarthy) dead on her kitchen table, skewered by a Samurai sword. Instead of calling the police, Viv gets gal pal Louise (Turco) to come over to figure out who did Reg in. Instead, they get drunk and discuss Reggie's (who seen in flashbacks) immaturity and penchant for practical jokes. Good performances, twist ending, but situation runs out of steam. *CW:* Language, some sexuality. **91m/C VHS, LV.** Elizabeth Pena, Andrew McCarthy, Paige Turco, Blanche Baker, Lisa Jane Persky, Michael Mantell; *D:* John Feldman; *W:* John Feldman; *M:* Sheila Silver. *APX*

Dead Girls 🎬 1990 (R) A rock group whose lyrics focus on suicide goes on vacation. The members find themselves stalked by a serial killer who decides to take matters out of the musicians' hands and into his own. Graphic violence. **105m/C VHS.** Diana Karanikas, Angela Eads; *D:* Dennis Devine. *HHE*

Dead Heart 🎬🎬🎬 1996 Culture clash story set in the 1930s is highlighted by a terrific lead performance by Brown. He's cop Ray Lorkin, whose territory is the tiny community of Wala Wala in Australia's outback. This remote spot just happens to be a focal point for the local aboriginals, who regard the area as a spiritual place. Trouble erupts when an aboriginal prisoner is found hanged in his cell and tradition demands revenge—from there every other situation in the community just gets worse. First-timer Parsons directs from his stage play. **103m/C VHS.** *AU* Bryan Brown, Ernie Dingo, Angie Milliken, Aaoron Pedersen, Lewis Fitz-gerald, John Jarratt, Anne Tenney, Gnarnayarrahe Waitaire, Lafe Charlton; *D:* Nick Parsons; *W:* Nick Parsons; *C:* James Bartle; *M:* Stephen Rae. *FXL*

Dead Heat 🎬½ 1988 (R) Some acting talent and a few funny moments unfortunately don't add up to a fine film, though they do save it from being a complete woofer. In this one even the cops are zombies when one of them is resurrected from the dead to help his partner solve his murder and rid the city of the rest of the undead. **86m/C VHS, Beta, LV, Closed Caption.** Joe Piscopo, Treat Williams,

Lindsay Frost, Darren McGavin, Vincent Price, Keye Luke, Clare Kirkconnell; **D:** Mark Goldblatt; **W:** Terry Black; **C:** Robert Yeoman; **M:** Ernest Troost. *VTR*

Dead Heat on a Merry-Go-Round 🐾🐾🐾 1966 (R)
Coburn turns in a great performance as the ex-con who masterminds the heist of an airport safe. Intricately woven plot provides suspense and surprises. The film is also notable for the debut of Ford in a bit part (he has one line as a hotel messenger). 108m/C VHS, Beta. James Coburn, Camilla Sparv, Aldo Ray, Nina Wayne, Robert Webber, Rose Marie, Todd Armstrong, Marian Moses, Severn Darden, Harrison Ford; **D:** Bernard Girard; **C:** Lionel Lindon. *COL*

Dead in the Water 🐾½ 1991 (PG-13)
Brown is Charlie Deegan, a big-time lawyer with a rich wife that he'd rather see dead. Charlie and his mistress plot the perfect murder to dispose of his spouse and collect her money. When plans go awry, he ends up as a suspect for the wrong murder in this story of infidelity and greed. 90m/C VHS, Beta, Closed Caption. Bryan Brown, Teri Hatcher, Anne DeSalvo, Veronica Cartwright; **D:** Bill Condon; **W:** Eleanor Gaver, Robert Seidenberg, Walter Klenhard. *USH*

Dead Lucky 🐾½ 1960
A novice tries gambling and wins a fortune, but his luck leads him into an entanglement with an assassin, a scam artist, and a beautiful woman. Based on the novel "Lake of Darkness." 91m/B VHS, Beta. Alan Vincent Ball, Betty McDowall, John Le Mesurier, Alfred Burke, Michael Ripper; **D:** Montgomery Tully. *FCT, VCO*

Dead Man 🐾🐾 1995 (R)
Depp wanders throughs the 19th-century American west as William Blake, an Ohio accountant who runs afoul of the law. Hooking up with a Native American named Nobody (Farmer), who envisions Blake as the famous English poet, the two try to stay one step ahead of the hired guns and lawmen out to get him. Action is sporadic and pace is all over the road in this offbeat and long-winded western, while Farmer's performance and Jarmusch's polished visuals are high points. **CW:** Moments of strong violence, a graphic sex scene and some language. 121m/B VHS, LV, Closed Caption. Johnny Depp, Gary Farmer, Lance Henriksen, Michael Wincott, Mili Avital, Crispin Glover, Gabriel Byrne, Iggy Pop, Billy Bob Thornton, Jared Harris, Jimmie Ray Weeks, Mark Bringleson, John Hurt, Alfred Molina, Robert Mitchum; **D:** Jim Jarmusch; **W:** Jim Jarmusch; **C:** Robby Muller; **M:** Neil Young. New York Film Critics Awards '96: Best Cinematography; National Society of Film Critics Awards '96: Best Cinematography; Nominations: Independent Spirit Awards '97: Best Cinematography, Best Film, Best Screenplay, Best Supporting Actor (Farmer). *TOU*

Dead Man on Campus 🐾🐾 1997 (R)
Failing college freshmen Scott and Gosselaar learn that if your roomie commits suicide, you get a straight-A average for the year. So they decide to find a new roommate who's on the edge and make certain to push him over. Anyone who's ever done time in the dorms has heard this rumor, so it was only a matter of time before someone turned it into a screenplay. The wait wasn't long enough. One-joke premise can't sustain a whole movie, and Gosselaar goes a long way toward duplicating "Saved By the Bell" co-star Elizabeth Berkley's um, success. **CW:** Drug use, language and crude sexual humor. ?m/C VHS. Tom Everett Scott, Mark Paul Gosselaar; **D:** Alan Cohn. *NYR*

Dead Man Out 🐾🐾🐾 1989
Both Glover and Blades turn in exceptional performances in this thought-provoking drama. A convict on Death Row (Blades) goes insane and therefore cannot be executed. The state calls in a psychiatrist (Glover) to review the case and determine whether he can be cured so that the sentence can be carried out. Powerful and riveting morality check. 87m/C VHS, Beta, LV. Danny Glover, Ruben Blades, Tom Atkins, Larry Block, Sam Jackson, Maria Ricossa; **D:** Richard Pearce; **M:** Cliff Eidelman. *HBO*

Dead Man Walking 🐾🐾 1988 (R)
In a post-holocaust future, half the population has been stricken with a deadly plague. Hauser is a mercenary, dying from the disease, who is hired to rescue a young woman who was kidnapped and is being held in the plague zone. 90m/C VHS. Wings Hauser, Brion James, Pamela Ludwig, Sy Richardson, Leland Crooke, Jeffrey Combs; **D:** Gregory Brown; **W:** R.J. Marx. *REP*

Dead Man Walking 🐾🐾🐾½ 1995 (R)
True story of a nun whose anti-death penalty beliefs put her in moral crisis with grieving victims when she becomes the spiritual advisor to a death-row murderer. Based on the book by Sister Helen Prejean, Sarandon stars as the nun who develops a relationship of understanding with inmate Poncelet (Penn), unwavering in her Christian beliefs even though Penn's character shows little or no remorse for the two young lovers he was accused of murdering. Penn offers one of the best performances (but worst hair-dos) of his career, while writer/director Robbins presents both sides of the death-penalty issue mingled with simple human compassion. **CW:** Depiction of a rape and murder. 122m/C VHS, LV, DVD. Susan Sarandon, Sean Penn, Robert Prosky, Raymond J. Barry, R. Lee Ermey, Celia Weston, Lois Smith, Scott Wilson, Roberta Maxwell, Margo Martindale, Barton Heyman, Larry Pine; **D:** Tim Robbins; **W:** Tim Robbins; **C:** Roger Deakins; **M:** David Robbins. Academy Awards '95: Best Actress (Sarandon); Independent Spirit Awards '96: Best Actor (Penn); Screen Actors Guild Award '95: Best Actress (Sarandon); Nominations: Academy Awards '95: Best Actor (Penn), Best Director (Robbins), Best Song ("Dead Man Walking"); Australian Film Institute '96: Best Foreign Film; Golden Globe Awards '96: Best Actor—Drama (Penn), Best Actress—Drama (Sarandon), Best Screenplay, Independent Spirit Awards '96: Best Supporting Actress (Weston); MTV Movie Awards '96: Best Female Performance (Sarandon); Screen Actors Guild Award '95: Best Actor (Penn). *PGV*

Dead Man's Eyes/Pillow of Death
Pillow of Death 1944 In 1944's "Dead Man's Eyes" artist Chaney is accidentally blinded but may get a second chance through an eye operation. His father-in-law offers his own eyes after he dies—and then he's murdered. In 1945's "Pillow of Death" attorney Chaney is accused of smothering various family members to death. Based on radio's "The Inner Sanctum Mysteries." 130m/B VHS, Beta. Acquanetta, J. Edward Bromberg, Rosalind Ivan, Wilton Graff, Bernard B. Thomas, Lon Chaney Jr., Brenda Joyce, George Cleveland, Clara Blandick, Paul Kelly, Jean Parker, George Meeker; **D:** Wallace Fox, Reginald LeBorg; **W:** George Bricker, Dwight V. Babcock. *USH*

Dead Man's Revenge 🐾🐾½ 1993 (PG-13)
Ruthless railroad mogul Payton McCay (Dern) doesn't let anyone stand in his way—even if it means framing innocent homesteader Hatcher (Ironside) in order to get his land. Hatcher escapes from jail and goes after McCay, trailed by bounty hunter Bodeen (Couloris). But Bodeen's not what he seems and has his own plans on getting even with the villainous McCay. 92m/C VHS, LV, Closed Caption. Bruce Dern, Michael Ironside, Keith Coulouris, Randy Travis; **D:** Alan J. Levi; **W:** Jim Byrnes, David Chisholm. *USH*

Dead Mate 🐾 1988
A woman marries a mortician after a whirlwind romance only to discover that, to her husband, being an undertaker is not just a job, it's a way of life. 93m/C VHS, Beta. Elizabeth Mannino, David Gregory, Lawrence Bockus, Adam Wahl; **D:** Straw Weisman.

Dead Men Can't Dance 🐾🐾 1997 (R)
CIA agent Victoria Ellis (York) gets sent to South Korea to train with a women-only group of Army Rangers. Meanwhile, Vic's boyfriend (Biehn) and his buddy (Paul) are trying to steal nuclear detonators from the demilitarized zone. Things go bad and the women are forced to take things into their own more than capable hands. Lots of action. 97m/C VHS, LV, Closed Caption. Kathleen York, Michael Biehn, Adrian Paul; **D:** Stephen Anderson; **W:** Mark Sevi; Bill Kerby, Paul Sinor; **C:** Levie Isaacks; **M:** Rick Marvin. *ART*

Dead Men Don't Die 🐾½ 1991 (PG-13)
An anchorman is slain by criminals but resurrected as a shambling voodoo zombie. Few viewers notice the difference in this inoffensive but repetitious farce. The living-dead Gould appears to be having a lot of fun. 94m/C VHS. Elliott Gould, Melissa Anderson, Mark Moses, Philip Bruns, Jack Betts, Mabel King; **D:** Malcolm Marmorstein; **W:** Malcolm Marmorstein.

Dead Men Don't Wear Plaid 🐾🐾½ 1982 (PG)
Martin is hilarious as a private detective who encounters a bizarre assortment of suspects while trying to find out the truth about a scientist's death. Ingeniously interspliced with clips from old Warner Bros. films. Features Humphrey Bogart, Bette Davis, Alan Ladd, Burt Lancaster, Ava Gardner, Barbara Stanwyck, Ray Milland, and others. Its only flaw is that the joke loses momentum by the end of the film. 89m/B VHS, Beta, LV. Steve Martin, Rachel Ward, Reni Santoni, George Gaynes, Frank McCarthy, Carl Reiner; **D:** Carl Reiner; **W:** Steve Martin, Carl Reiner; **C:** Michael Chapman; **M:** Miklos Rozsa. *USH, FCT, HMV*

Dead Men Walk 🐾🐾 *Creatures of the Devil* 1943
A decent, albeit low budget, chiller about twin brothers (Zucco in a dual role); one a nice, well-adjusted member of society, the other a vampire who wants to suck his bro's blood. Sibling rivalry with a bite. 65m/B VHS, Beta. George Zucco, Mary Carlisle, Dwight Frye, Nedrick Young, Al "Fuzzy" St. John, Fern Emmett, Robert Strange; **D:** Sam Newfield; **W:** Fred Myton; **C:** Jack Greenhalgh. *VCI, MRV, SNC*

The Dead Next Door 🐾 1989
Eerily reminiscent of "Night of the Living Dead." A scientist manufactures a virus which inhabits corpses and multiplies while replacing the former cells with its own. But the newly living corpses need human flesh to survive. In response, the government creates "The Zombie Squad" who do heroic battle with the stiffs. When a bizarre cult whose goal is the eradication of the human race befriend the dead, the battle gets ugly. 84m/C VHS. Scott Spiegel, Peter Terry; **W:** J.R. Bookwalter. *TEM, MOV*

Dead of Night 🐾🐾🐾🐾 1945
The template for episodic horror films, this suspense classic, set in a remote country house, follows the individual nightmares of five houseguests. Redgrave turns in a chillingly convincing performance as a ventriloquist terrorized by a demonic dummy. Not recommended for light-sleepers. Truly spine-tingling. 102m/B VHS, Beta. GB Michael Redgrave, Mervyn Johns, Sally Ann Howes, Basil Radford, Naunton Wayne, Roland Culver, Googie Withers, Frederick Valk, Antony Baird, Judy Kelly, Miles Malleson, Ralph Michael, Mary Merrall, Renee Gadd, Michael Allan, Robert Wyndham, Esme Percy, Peggy Bryan, Hartley Power, Elizabeth Welch, Magda Kun, Carry Marsh; **D:** Alberto Cavalcanti, Charles Crichton, Basil Dearden, Robert Hamer; **W:** T.E.B. Clarke, John Baines, Angus MacPhail; **C:** Stanley Pavey, Douglas Slocombe; **M:** Georges Auric. *NO*

Dead of Night 🐾½ 1977
This trilogy features Richard Matheson's tales of the Supernatural: "Second Chance," "Bobby," and "No Such Thing As a Vampire," all served up by your hostess, Elvira. 76m/C VHS, Beta, LV. Joan Hackett, Ed Begley Jr., Patrick Macnee, Anjanette Comer; **D:** Dan Curtis. *ART*

Dead of Winter 🐾🐾🐾 1987 (R)
A young actress is suckered into a private screen test for a crippled old director, only to find she is actually being remodeled in the guise of a murdered woman. Edge-of-your-seat suspense as the plot twists. 100m/C VHS, Beta, LV, Closed Caption. Mary Steenburgen, Roddy McDowall, Jan Rubes, Ken Pogue, William Russ; **D:** Arthur Penn; **W:** Mark Shmuger, Mark Malone; **M:** Richard Einhorn. *MGM, FOX*

Dead On 🐾½ 1993 (R)
Illicit lovers want to get rid of their inconvenient spouses so they can be together always. But their perfect plan doesn't work out as expected. Also available in an unrated version. 87m/C VHS, LV, Closed Caption. Matt McCoy, Shari Shattuck, David Ackroyd, Tracy Scoggins, Thomas Wagner; **D:** Ralph Hemecker; **W:** April Wayne. *ORI*

Dead on Sight 🎬🎬½ 1994 (R) A college student dreams of a masked man, a knife, a bound woman, and other terrors. Too bad her nightmares match the actions of a serial killer. 96m/C VHS, Closed Caption. Jennifer Beals, Daniel Baldwin, Kurtwood Smith, William H. Macy; D: Ruben Preuss; W: Lewis Green; M: Harry Manfredini. PAR

Dead on the Money 🎬🎬½ 1991 Adequate made for TV suspenser about a woman who believes her lover plots a dire fate for her cousin. But nothing is what it seems here. Confusing, droopy in spots, but fun. 92m/C VHS, Beta, Closed Caption. Corbin Bernsen, Amanda Pays, John Glover, Eleanor Parker, Kevin McCarthy; D: Mark Cullingham; W: Gavin Lambert. TTC

Dead or Alive 🎬½ 1941 Tex and the Texas Rangers pretend to be outlaws in order to join a gang terrorizing a town. 54m/B VHS, Beta. Tex Ritter, Dave O'Brien, Guy Wilkerson, Charles "Blackie" King, Bud Osborne, Reed Howes; D: Elmer Clifton. GPV, RXM, VCN

Dead Pigeon on Beethoven Street 🎬🎬½ 1972 (PG) Sandy (Corbett) is a detective whose partner gets murdered while investigating blackmailers who take compromising pictures of international big-wigs. So Sandy goes undercover joined by a gang. Cheeky paranoia from Fuller. 92m/C VHS. Glenn Corbett, Christa Lang, Anton Diffring, Alexander D'Arcy; D: Samuel Fuller; W: Samuel Fuller. FCT

Dead Pit woof! 1989 (R) Leave this one in the pit it crawled out of. Twenty years ago a mad scientist was killed as a result of horrible experiments he was conducting on mentally ill patients at an asylum. A young woman stumbles across his experiments, awakening him from the dead. 90m/C VHS, Beta. Jeremy Slate, Steffen Gregory Foster; D: Brett Leonard. IMP

Dead Poets Society 🎬🎬🎬½ 1989 (PG) An idealistic English teacher inspires a group of boys in a 1950s' prep school to pursue individuality and creative endeavor, resulting in clashes with school and parental authorities. Williams shows he can master the serious roles as well as the comic with his portrayal of the unorthodox educator. Big boxoffice hit occasionally scripted with a heavy hand in order to elevate the message. The ensemble cast is excellent. 128m/C VHS, Beta, LV, 8mm. Robin Williams, Ethan Hawke, Robert Sean Leonard, Josh Charles, Gale Hansen, Kurtwood Smith, James Waterson, Dylan Kussman, Lara Flynn Boyle, Melora Hardin; D: Peter Weir; W: Tom Schulman; C: John Seale; M: Maurice Jarre. Academy Awards '89: Best Original Screenplay; British Academy Awards '89: Best Film; Cesar Awards '91: Best Foreign Film; Nominations: Academy Awards '89: Best Actor (Williams), Best Director (Weir), Best Picture. TOU

The Dead Pool 🎬½ 1988 (R) Dirty Harry Number Five features a new twist on the sports pool: a list of celebrities is distributed and bets are placed on who will be first to cross the finish line, literally. Unfortunately someone seems to be hedging their bet by offing the celebs themselves. When Harry's name appears on the list, he decides to throw the game. 92m/C VHS, Beta, LV, 8mm, Closed Caption. Clint Eastwood, Liam Neeson, Patricia Clarkson, Evan C. Kim, David Hunt, Michael Currie, Michael Goodwin; D: Buddy Van Horn; M: Lalo Schifrin. WAR, TLF

Dead Presidents 🎬🎬½ 1995 (R) Sophomore release for the Hughes brothers falls short of impact of "Menace II Society," but not for lack of ambition. Combination coming of age tale, war story, period piece and caper film follows Anthony ("Menace" veteran Tate) from his Bronx neighborhood in 1968 to Vietnam (for "Platoon" adventures in the wilds of Florida) and then back to the 'hood, where his life continues to spiral downward. Desperate to escape, he becomes involved in an armoured car heist to grab some cash (the "dead presidents") Supported by hard-edged and effective acting, the Hughes continue to develop their control of cinematic imagery, displaying genius for staging violent, confrontational scenes. But the script, based on a story by the

brothers, fails to live up to the vision, with characterization and dialogue lagging. Pounding period soundtrack with contributions by Curtis Mayfield, James Brown, and Marvin Gaye keeps things humming. CW: Strong graphic violence, language, a sex scene, some drug use. 120m/C VHS, LV, Closed Caption. Larenz Tate, Keith David, Chris Tucker, Freddy Rodriguez, N'Bushe Wright, Bokeem Woodbine, Rose Jackson, Clifton Powell; D: Albert Hughes, Allen Hughes; W: Michael Henry Brown; C: Lisa Rinzler; M: Danny Elfman. TOU

Dead Reckoning 🎬🎬🎬 1947 Bogart and Prince are two WWII veterans en route to Washington when Prince disappears. Bogart trails Prince to his Southern hometown and discovers he's been murdered. Blackmail and more murders follow as Bogie tries to uncover the truth. Suspenseful with good performances from all, especially Bogart. 100m/B VHS, Beta, LV, Closed Caption. Humphrey Bogart, Lizabeth Scott, Morris Carnovsky, Charles Cane, Wallace Ford, William Prince, Marvin Miller; D: John Cromwell. CCB, COL

Dead Reckoning 🎬½ 1989 (R) A plastic surgeon and his lovely wife embark on a cruise aboard his new luxury yacht. The intrigue begins with a storm, an isolated island, and the discovery that the captain is the wife's former lover. 95m/C VHS, LV. Cliff Robertson, Susan Blakely, Rick Springfield; D: Robert Lewis. USH

Dead Right 🎬½ If He Hollers, Let Him Go 1968 A black man is unjustly put into prison in the Deep South. He manages to escape in order to try and prove his innocence. 111m/C VHS, Beta. Raymond St. Jacques, Dana Wynter, Kevin McCarthy, Barbara McNair.

Dead Ringers 🎬🎬🎬 1988 (R) A stunning, unsettling film, based loosely on a real case and the bestseller by Bari Wood and Jack Geasland. Irons, in an excellent dual role, is effectively disturbing as the twin gynecologists who descend into madness when they can no longer handle the fame, fortune, drugs, and women in their lives. Acutely upsetting film made all the more so due to its graphic images and basis in fact. 117m/C VHS, Beta, LV. CA Jeremy Irons, Genevieve Bujold, Heidi von Palleske, Barbara Gordon, Shirley Douglas, Stephen Lack, Nick Nichols; D: David Cronenberg; W: David Cronenberg, Norman Snider; C: Peter Suschitzky; M: Howard Shore. Genie Awards '89: Best Actor (Irons), Best Director (Cronenberg), Best Film; Los Angeles Film Critics Association Awards '88: Best Film (Cronenberg), Best Supporting Actress (Bujold); New York Film Critics Awards '88: Best Actor (Irons). VTR, CRC

Dead Silence 1990 (R) Screenwriter Cliff Morgan has written a classic film noir screenplay... with the money, it seems all Cliff's problems are solved... or are they? CW: Language. 92m/C VHS, Closed Caption. Clete Keith, Doris Anne Soyka, Joseph Scott, Craig Fleming; D: Harrison Ellenshaw. NO

Dead Silence 🎬🎬½ 1996 (R) Three escaped convicts, including ruthless Ted Handy (Coates), have hijacked a busload of deaf children and their teacher (Matlin) and are holding them hostage in an abandoned slaughterhouse. Veteran FBI agent John Cooper (Garner) is called in but he not only has to deal with a tense and possibly tragic situation but with a grandstanding politician (Smith) who's criticizing his every action and the last-minute arrival of another hostage negotiator (Davidovich). Cable movie based on the novel "A Maiden's Grave" by Jeffery Deaver. CW: Strong violence and language. 105m/C VHS, Closed Caption. James Garner, Kim Coates, Marlee Matlin, Charles Martin Smith, Lolita Davidovich, Kenneth Welsh, Linda Thorson; D: Dan Petrie Jr.; W: Donald Stewart; M: Jonathan Goldsmith. HBO

Dead Sleep 🎬🎬 1991 (R) A nurse discovers that comatose patients at a private clinic have been used as guinea pigs by an overzealous doctor. This minor-league chiller from Down Under is said to have been inspired by an actual medical scandal. CW: Sensuality. 95m/C VHS. Linda Blair, Tony Bonner; D: Alec Mills. VES

Dead Solid Perfect 🎬🎬 1988 Quaid stars as a golf pro whose life on the PGA tour is handicapped by his taste for scotch and his eye for the ladies. Based on the book by Dan Jenkins. 97m/C VHS, Beta. Randy Quaid, Kathryn Harrold, Jack Warden, Larry Riley, Brett Cullen, Corinne Bohrer; D: Bobby Roth; W: Dan Jenkins, Bobby Roth. WAR, BTV

Dead Space 🎬 1990 (R) Dead space lay between the ears of whoever thought we needed this remake of 1982's "Forbidden World." At a lab on a hostile planet an experimental vaccine mutates into a prickly puppet monster who menaces the medicos. Needed: a vaccine against cheapo "Alien" ripoffs. CW: Violence and sensuality. 72m/C VHS, LV. Marc Singer, Laura Tate, Bryan Cranston, Judith Chapman; D: Fred Gallo. COL

Dead Tides 🎬🎬 1997 (R) Former Navy SEAL Mick (Piper) is hired by Nola (Kitaen) to pilot a sailboat from California to Mexico. But Mick soon realizes that Nola's the wife of a powerful drug dealer and he's in more trouble than he can imagine. CW: Nudity, violence, language. 100m/C VHS, LV. Roddy Piper, Tawny Kitaen, Trevor Goddard, Miles O'Keeffe, Juan Fernandez; D: Serge Rodnunsky; W: Serge Rodnunsky. ART

Dead to Rights 🎬🎬½ Donato and Daughter 1993 (R) TV movie finds veteran LAPD cop Donato (Bronson) on the trail of a serial killer along with his new partner—who's not only his daughter but his superior officer. Based on the novel by Jack Early. CW: Some violence. 90m/C VHS. Charles Bronson, Dana Delany, Xander Berkeley, Bonnie Bartlett, Jenette Goldstein, Louis Giambalvo; D: Rod Holcomb; W: Robert Roy Pool; C: Thomas Del Ruth; M: Sylvester Levay. THV

Dead Weekend 🎬🎬 1995 (R) Made for cable sci fier finds Lt. Weed (Baldwin) given the task of finding and destroying a seductively dangerous female alien. Turns out she has the ability to physically change into a number of different women—all of whom attract the willing-and-eager soldier. CW: Violence, language, nudity, sexual situations. 82m/C VHS, Closed Caption. Stephen Baldwin, David Rasche, Alexis Arquette, Bai Ling, Tom Kenny, Jennifer MacDonald, Barbara Alyn Woods; D: Amos Poe; W: Joel Rose; C: Gary Tieche; M: Steve Hunter. PAR

Dead Women in Lingerie woof! 1990 (R) When beautiful models are turning up dead, a detective is called in to solve the mystery. Perhaps they committed suicide to avoid being in this picture any longer than necessary. Title sounds like the next episode of "Geraldo." 87m/C VHS. June Lockhart, Lyle Waggoner, John Romo, Jerry Orbach, Maura Tierney; D: Erika Fox. NO

Dead Wrong 🎬½ 1983 Undercover agent falls in love with the drug smuggler she's supposed to bring to justice. 93m/C VHS, Beta, Closed Caption. Britt Ekland, Winston Rekert, Jackson Davies.

Dead Zone 🎬🎬🎬 1983 (R) A man gains extraordinary psychic powers following a near-fatal accident. He is forced to decide between seeking absolute seclusion in order to escape his frightening visions, or using his "gift" to save mankind from impending evil. A good adaptation of the Stephen King thriller. 104m/C VHS, Beta, LV, Closed Caption. Christopher Walken, Brooke Adams, Tom Skerritt, Martin Sheen, Herbert Lom, Anthony Zerbe, Colleen Dewhurst; D: David Cronenberg; W: Jeffrey Boam; C: Mark Irwin; M: Michael Kamen. PAR

Deadbolt 🎬🎬 1992 (R) Divorced med student Marty Hiller (Bateman) desperately needs a roommate and Alec Danz (Baldwin) seems perfect. Soon they're sharing more than the rent, until Danz kills her friends and imprisons her in the apartment (equipped of course with soundproof walls and bulletproof glass—one wonders why she doesn't bang on the floor to gain attention). Predictable and silly would-be thriller attempts to capitalize on the roommate-from-hell theme that started with "Single White Female," but isn't nearly as effective. Went straight to video and showed up on network TV several months later. CW:

Strong violence. 95m/C VHS, LV. Justine Bateman, Adam Baldwin, Michelle Scarabelli, Chris Mulkey, Cyndi Pass, Isabelle Truchon; **D:** Douglas Jackson. *NLC*

Deadfall 🐾🐾½ 1993 (R) Father/son grifters plan an elaborate scam that goes wrong when son Joe (Biehn) inadvertently kills dear old dad (Coburn). When Joe is going through his father's effects he finds out about an unknown twin uncle, who also turns out to be a racketeer. Along with Uncle Lou's mistrustful henchman Eddie (Cage), they plan another con but swindles and vendettas abound. 99m/C VHS, LV, Closed Caption. Michael Biehn, Sarah Trigger, Nicolas Cage, James Coburn, Charlie Sheen, Peter Fonda; **D:** Christopher Coppola; **W:** Christopher Coppola, David Peoples. *THV*

Deadline 🐾½ 1981 Journalist must find out the truth behind a minor earthquake in Australia. 94m/C VHS, Beta. Barry Newman, Trisha Noble, Bill Kerr. *WOV*

Deadline 🐾🐾 1982 Eerie tale of horror writer's life as it begins to reflect his latest story in this play on the "truth is stranger than fiction" adage. 85m/C VHS, Beta. Stephen Young, Sharon Masters, Cindy Hinds, Phillip Leonard; **D:** Mario Azzopardi. *NO*

Deadline 🐾🐾 1987 (R) Walken is a cynical American journalist assigned to cover the warring factions in Beirut. He finds himself becoming more and more involved in the events he's supposed to report when he falls in love with a German nurse who is aiding the rebel forces. Tense, though sometimes murky drama. 110m/C VHS, Beta, LV. GE Christopher Walken, Hywel Bennett, Marita Marschall; **D:** Nathaniel Gutman. *VTR*

Deadline Assault 🐾½ *Act of Violence* 1990 (R) Kate McSweeny is a beautiful young reporter who is brutally attacked and raped by a gang of savage youths. Kate must now face the unsettling facts; they're still on the streets and they may be stalking her again. 90m/C VHS. Elizabeth Montgomery, James Sloyan, Sean Frye, Biff McGuire, Michael Goodwin, Linden Chiles; **D:** Paul Wendkos. *ELV, HHE*

Deadline at Dawn 🐾🐾 1946 Hayward is an aspiring actress who tries to help a sailor (Williams) prove that he is innocent of murder. Based on a novel by Cornell Woolrich. 82m/B VHS, Beta. Bill Williams, Susan Hayward, Lola Lane, Paul Lukas, Joseph Calleia; **D:** Harold Clurman; **W:** Clifford Odets. *MLB, TTC*

Deadline Auto Theft 🐾 1983 A fun lovin' guy drives fast cars and meets beautiful women. Nudge, nudge, wink, wink. 90m/C VHS, Beta. H.B. Halicki, Hoyt Axton, Marion Busia, George Cole, Judi Gibbs, Lang Jeffries Jr.; **D:** H.B. Halicki. *IMP*

Deadlock 🐾🐾½ 1991 (R) Hauer and Rogers star as inmates in a prison of the future. This prison has no walls, no fences and no guards—and no one EVER escapes. Each prisoner wears an explosive collar that is tuned to the same frequency as one of the other prisoner's. Should the two separate by more than 100 yards, the collars explode. When Rogers convinces Hauer that they are on the same frequency, the two escape. Trouble is, they are being pursued not only by the police, but by Hauer's former partners in crime as well. Can the two find the freedom they are looking for—without losing their heads? Originally made for cable television.**CW:** Language and strong violence. 103m/C VHS, Beta, LV, Closed Caption. Rutger Hauer, Mimi Rogers, Joan Chen, James Remar, Stephen Tobolowsky, Basil Wallace; **D:** Lewis Teague. *VTR*

Deadlock 2 🐾🐾 *Deadlocked: Escape from Zone 14* 1994 (R) Same basic plot as in the first TV movie. Tony Archer (Morales) and Allie Thompson (Peeples), two strangers who have been set up by the same corrupt businessman, are being held in a violent correctional facility. Inmates wear electronic collars programmed to explode if they venture too far apart. But Tony figures a way around this trap only to discover he and Allie are caught in another.**CW:** Strong sexuality, violence and language. 120m/C VHS. Esai Morales, Nia Peeples,

Stephen McHattie, Jon Cuthbert; **D:** Graeme Campbell. *HMK*

Deadly Advice 🐾🐾 1993 (R) Meek bookseller Jodie (Horrocks) and her sister are constantly humiliated by their overbearing mother (Fricker), who also objects to Jodie's romance with the local doctor (Pryce). As life becomes increasingly unbearable, Jodie discovers a book on infamous killers and is visited by their ghosts, including Jack the Ripper, who is happy to suggest ways to get rid of mom.**CW:** Some sexuality, violence and language. 91m/C VHS. Jane Horrocks, Imelda Staunton, Brenda Fricker, Jonathan Pryce; **D:** Mandie Fletcher. *HMK*

Deadly Alliance 🐾 1978 Two impecunious filmmakers (who happen to be hunks) and a babe (for good measure) poke their noses in where they're not wanted (in the shady business of an international oil cartel). "Deadly Dull" would be a more appropriate moniker. 90m/C VHS, Beta. Kathleen Arc, Tony de Fonte, Michele Marsh, Walter Prince; **D:** Paul S. Parco. *NO*

The Deadly and the Beautiful 🐾
Wonder Women 1973 (PG) Dr. Tsu sends her "deadly but beautiful" task force to kidnap the world's prime male athletes for use in her private business enterprise. 82m/C VHS, Beta. PH Nancy Kwan, Ross Hagen, Maria de Aragon, Roberta Collins, Tony Lorea, Sid Haig, Vic Diaz, Shirley Washington, Gale Hansen; **D:** Robert Vincent O'Neil.

Deadly Bet 🐾½ 1991 (R) A made-for-video saga of a kickboxer who loses his money and his girl when he loses the big match. Lots of fight sequences as he works to regain his career.**CW:** Kickboxing violence. 93m/C VHS, LV. Jeff Wincott, Charlene Tilton, Steven Leigh; **D:** Richard W. Munchkin. *PMH*

Deadly Blessing 🐾🐾 1981 (R) A young, recently widowed woman is visited in her rural Pennsylvania home by some friends from the city. Something's not quite right about this country life and they become especially suspicious after meeting their friend's very religious in-laws. 104m/C VHS, Beta. Maren Jensen, Susan Buckner, Sharon Stone, Ernest Borgnine, Jeff East, Lisa Hartman Black, Lois Nettleton, Colleen Riley, Douglas Barr, Michael Berryman; **D:** Wes Craven; **W:** Wes Craven, Glenn Benest, Matthew F. Barr; **C:** Robert C. Jessup; **M:** James Horner.

Deadly Breed 🐾½ 1989 Beware your friendly neighborhood cop. A band of white supremacists has infiltrated the local police force, intent on causing violence, not keeping the peace. 90m/C VHS. William Smith, Addison Randall, Blake Bahner, Joe Vance; **D:** Charles Kanganis. *PMH*

Deadly Business 🐾🐾🐾 1986 The true story of a man who turned from crime to become a government informant. As a garbage man, he works to stop the illegal dumping of chemicals in New Jersey. An interesting made-for-televison drama. 100m/C VHS. Alan Arkin, Armand Assante, Michael Learned, Jon Polito, George Morfogen, James Rebhorn; **D:** John Korty. *REP*

Deadly Business 🐾½ 19?? Hard-nosed collection man for a lethal loan shark finds he is the one with the debt to pay as he's stalked through the city street by hit men. 95m/C VHS, Beta. David Peterson, John Lazarus, Leo Gabrowski.

Deadly Companions 🐾🐾½ 1961 Keith is an ex-gunslinger who agrees to escort O'Hara through Apache territory in order to make up for inadvertently killing her son. Director Peckinpah's first feature film. 90m/C VHS, Beta, LV. Maureen O'Hara, Brian Keith, Chill Wills, Steve Cochran; **D:** Sam Peckinpah; **C:** William Clothier. *VTR*

Deadly Conspiracy 🐾 1991 (R) Saxon plays a corrupt businessman who kills an employee about to blow the whistle on his shady dealings. Hauser is the good cop, with the bad personal life, who makes it his mission to bring Saxon to justice. The prolific Hauser brings some fast-paced action to this routine story.**CW:** Language, violence, and sexuality. 92m/C VHS, Closed

Caption. Wings Hauser, John Saxon, Frances Fisher, Patti D'Arbanville, Margaux Hemingway, Greg Mullavey; **D:** Paul Leder. *MNC*

Deadly Currents 🐾🐾 1993 (R) Scott plays a former sea captain who owns a bar on the island of Curacao and enjoys regaling his patrons with his sea-going tales. Petersen is the exiled CIA agent stuck as the security officer of the American consulate. The dangerous pasts of both men catch them up and find them caught in a web of international intrigue. Based on the novel "The Prince of Malta" by James David Buchanan. 93m/C VHS, Closed Caption. George C. Scott, William L. Petersen, Julie Carmen, Alexei Sayle, Trish Van Devere, Philip Anglim, Maria Ellingsen; **D:** Carl Schultz; **W:** James David Buchanan. *COL*

Deadly Dancer 🐾½ 1990 It's up to a lone cop to find out who's been offing the hoofers in L.A. 88m/C VHS. Adolfo "Shabba Doo" Quinones, Smith Wordes, Walter W. Cox, Steve Jonson; **D:** Kimberly Casey; **W:** David A. Prior.

Deadly Daphne's Revenge 🐾½ 1993 Gory story of rape and revenge from the Troma Team. Hitchhiker Cindy is beaten and raped by Charlie Johnson. When she seeks justice via the local police, Johnson makes plans to have her snuffed out. Meantime, another of his victims escapes from the asylum she's been in and comes looking for him with murder on her mind. 98m/C VHS, LV.

Deadly Darling woof! 1985 Muddled, completely awful tale centering on two different rapes with no discernible attempt made to link the two or establish a plot. 91m/C VHS, Beta. Fonda Lynn, Warren Chan, Bernard Tsui, Cherry Kwok; **D:** Karen Young. *UNI*

Deadly Desire 🐾🐾 1991 (R) Seduced by the beautiful Harrold, security guard Scalia finds himself putting his life on the line when Harrold asks him to help cheat her husband out of millions in an insurance scam. Trouble begins when they try to outsmart Harrold's powerful entrepreneurial husband.**CW:** Sensuality. 93m/C VHS, Closed Caption. Jack Scalia, Kathryn Harrold, Will Patton, Joe Santos; **D:** Charles Correll. *PAR, HHE*

Deadly Diamonds 🐾½ 1991 Cop is on the trail of diamond smugglers who leave a trail of death in their wake. 90m/C VHS, Beta. Dan Haggerty, Troy Donahue, Eli Rich, Kathleen Kane, Kenna Grob, Nicholas Mercer; **D:** Thomas Atcheson; **W:** Ron Herbst. *DMP, HHT*

Deadly Dreams 🐾🐾 1988 (R) A young boy's parents are killed by a maniac who then commits suicide. Years later, he dreams that he is being stalked anew by the same killer. Nightmares turn into reality in this decent horror/suspense flick. 79m/C VHS, Beta, LV. Mitchell Anderson, Xander Berkeley, Thom Babbes, Juliette Cummins; **D:** Kristine Peterson; **W:** Thom Babbes. *NO*

Deadly Embrace woof! 1988 (R) Sordid tale of wealthy man (Vincent) who wants to get rid of his wife—permanantly. He enlists the aid of a beautiful young coed. Soft-core sleaze with nary a redeemable quality. 82m/C VHS, Beta. Jan-Michael Vincent, Jack Carter, Ty Randolph, Linnea Quigley, Michelle (McClellan) Bauer, Ken Abraham; **D:** Ellen Cabot.

Deadly Encounter 🐾🐾🐾 1972 Thrilling actioner in which Hagman portrays a helicopter pilot—a former war ace—who allows an old flame to talk him into helping her escape from the mobsters on her trail. Terrific edge-of-your-seat aerial action. 90m/C VHS, Beta. Larry Hagman, Susan Anspach, Michael C. Goetz, James Gammon; **D:** William A. Graham. *NO*

Deadly Encounter woof! 1978 (R) Lacking any redeemable qualities, this film shows just how low some people go. Merrill hosts a dinner to garner financial support for a budding playwright, but what we get is a look at the lifestyles of the rich and perverse. 90m/C VHS, Beta. Dina Merrill, Carl Betz, Leon Ames, Vicki Powers, Mark Rasmussen, Susan Logan; **D:** R. John Hugh. *CNG*

Deadly Exposure ♂♂ 1993 (R) Benson stars as a burned-out journalist doing his own investigation of the right-wing extremist group that killed his father. Aspiring reporter Johnson helps out and turns up a conspiracy between the extremists, the government, and a plot to assassinate a U.S. senator. Also available in an unrated version. **CW:** Strong sexuality and violence; brief language. 100m/C VHS, Closed Caption. Robby Benson, Laura Johnson, Paul Hampton, Andrew Prine, Bentley Mitchum, Isaac Hayes; **D:** Lawrence Mortorff; **W:** Asher Brauner. AVE

Deadly Eyes ♂½ The Rats 1982 (R) After eating grain laced with steroids a group of rats grows to mammoth proportions (dachshunds in rat drag were used). Their appetites grow accordingly—now they crave humans. Amid the nibbling by the giant rat-dogs, romance blooms. Silly adaptation by Charles Eglee of Frank Herbert's "The Rats." 93m/C VHS, Beta. Sam Groom, Sara Botsford, Scatman Crothers, Lisa Langlois, Cec Linder; **D:** Robert Clouse. WAR

Deadly Fieldtrip ♂½ 1974 Four female students and their teacher are abducted by a biker gang and held hostage on a deserted farm. 91m/C VHS, Beta. Zalman King, Brenda Fogarty, Robert Porter; **D:** Earl Barton. NO

Deadly Force ♂½ 1983 (R) Ex-cop turned private detective stalks a killer in Los Angeles who has left an "X" carved in the forehead of each of his 17 victims. If he had just signed his name, things could have been tidied up much earlier. 95m/C VHS, Beta. Wings Hauser, Joyce Ingalls, Paul Shenar, Al Ruscio, Arlen Dean Snyder, Lincoln Kilpatrick; **D:** Paul Aaron; **W:** Robert Vincent O'Neil, Barry Schneider. NLC

Deadly Friend ♂♂ 1986 (R) A well-meaning horror flick? That's what Wes Craven has tried to provide for us. When the girlfriend of a lonely teenage genius is accidentally killed, he decides to insert his robot's "brain" in her body, though the results aren't entirely successful. The same can be said for the film which was based on Diana Henstell's more effective novel "Friend." 91m/C VHS, Beta, LV, Closed Caption. Matthew Laborteaux, Kristy Swanson, Michael Sharrett, Anne Twomey, Richard Marcus, Anne Ramsey; **D:** Wes Craven; **W:** Bruce Joel Rubin; **C:** Philip Lathrop; **M:** Charles Bernstein. WAR

Deadly Game ♂♂ 1982 (R) A reunion at a remote hotel leads to an ordeal of psychological terror and murderous intrigue. **CW:** Strong action violence. 108m/C VHS, Beta. George Segal, Robert Morley, Trevor Howard, Emlyn Williams, Alan Webb; **D:** George Schaefer.

Deadly Game ♂½ 1983 Much-maligned and preyed-upon witness is protected by a weary cop, who speaks with the use of English subtitles. 90m/C VHS, Beta. GE Mel Ferrer, Helmut Berger, Barbara Sukowa; **D:** Karoly Makk, Dieter Geissler. VCD, GLV

The Deadly Game ♂♂ 198? East-West intrigue prior to the fall of the Berlin Wall finds a Western operative returning a dangerous mission, only to walk into a trap set by his own side. 104m/C VHS. GB David Hemmings. FCT

Deadly Game ♂½ 1991 (R) Horribly burned, a vengeful millionaire invites seven people he believes have wronged him to spend the weekend on his isolated island. He has promised them each a reward for their good deeds, but instead plans to have a big-game hunt with his "guests" as the prey. 93m/C VHS, Beta, Closed Caption. Roddy McDowall, Jenny Seagrove, Marc Singer, Michael Beck; **D:** Thomas J. Wright; **W:** Wes Claridge. PAR

Deadly Games ♂½ 1980 Ineffective cop involving a series of murders in a small town is seemingly played out by the principal characters in a horror board game. Film is saved from being a complete waste by Groom's good performance as the local cop. 94m/C VHS, Beta. Sam Groom, Jo Ann Harris, Steve Railsback, Dick Butkus, June Lockhart, Colleen Camp; **D:** Scott Mansfield. MON

Deadly Harvest ♂ 1972 (PG) Scientists' worst fears have been realized—due to ecological abuse and over-development of the land, food has become extremely scarce. This in turn has caused people to become a bit savage. They are particularly nasty to a farmer and his family. Not a bad plot, but a poorly acted film. 86m/C VHS, Beta. Clint Walker, Nehemiah Persoff, Kim Cattrall, David G. Brown, Gary Davies; **D:** Timothy Bond. VTR

Deadly Hero ♂♂♂ 1975 (R) Gripping tale of a young woman who becomes the prey of a New York City cop after questioning the brutal methods he employed while saving her from being assaulted, ultimately killing her attacker. Williams makes film debut in this chilling suspenser. 102m/C VHS, Beta. Don Murray, James Earl Jones, Diahn Williams, Lilia Skala, Conchata Ferrell, George S. Irving, Treat Williams, Josh Mostel; **D:** Ivan Nagy; **C:** Andrzej Bartkowiak; **M:** Brad Fiedel. VTR

Deadly Heroes ♂♂ 1996 (R) Terrorists highjack an American plane at Athens International Airport with the demand that their leader, Carlos (Drago), who's jailed in Miami, be delivered to them. CIA agent and ex-Navy SEAL, Captain Cody Grant (Vincent), is forced to take Carlos to Athens but having captured Carlos once, Grant is determined that the terrorist and his associates won't be free for long. 104m/C VHS, Closed Caption. Jan-Michael Vincent, Billy Drago, Michael Pare, Claudette Mink; **D:** Menahem Golan; **W:** Damian Lee, Gregory Lee. COL

Deadly Illusion ♂♂ Love You to Death 1987 (R) Williams is a private detective who manages to get himself tangled in a complex web of intrigue and winds up framed for murder. Decent outing for all. 95m/C VHS, Beta, LV, Closed Caption. Billy Dee Williams, Morgan Fairchild, Vanity, John Beck, Joe Cortese; **D:** William Tannen, Larry Cohen; **W:** Larry Cohen; **M:** Patrick Gleeson. COL

Deadly Impact ♂½ 1984 Las Vegas casinos are targeted for rip-off by means of a computer. Svenson and Williamson give good performances, but that's not enough to save this one. 90m/C VHS, Beta. IT Bo Svenson, Fred Williamson, Marcia Clingan, John Morghen, Vincent Conti; **D:** Larry Ludman. ART, VES

Deadly Innocence ♂½ 1988 (R) A shy, lonely girl works at an isolated gas station. After her father's death, she takes in a boarder—a mysterious woman being chased by her past. 90m/C VHS. Mary Crosby, Andrew Stevens, Amanda Wyss; **D:** John D. Patterson, Hugh Parks. NO

Deadly Intent ♂♂ 1988 The widow of a murdered archeologist becomes the target of fortune hunters when they try to get their hands on the priceless jewel her husband brought back from a dig. 83m/C VHS. Lisa Eilbacher, Steve Railsback, Maud Adams, Lance Henriksen, Fred Williamson, Persis Khambatta; **D:** Nigel Dick.

Deadly Intruder ♂½ 1984 Quiet vacation spot is being terrorized by an escapee from a mental institution. So much for the sedate R and R. 86m/C VHS, Beta. Chris Holder, Molly Creek. NO

Deadly Lessons ♂♂ 1994 Misfit Ann gets shunned by the college "in" crowd but then a childhood friend comes to her aid and decides to take revenge on the nasty students. 90m/C VHS. Andrea Gall, Mat McGinnis, Dana Wise; **D:** Leslie Delano. SWI

The Deadly Mantis ♂½ The Incredible Praying Mantis 1957 A gigantic praying mantis lies in a million-year-old sleep in the frozen reaches of the Arctic. Then a volcanic eruption releases the critter and the flying beastie does it's destructive best on Washington, D.C., and New York City until the military can gas it into oblivion. Typically silly '50s sci-fi with decent special effects. 79m/B VHS, Closed Caption. Craig Stevens, William Hopper, Alix Talton, Pat Conway, Donald Randolph; **D:** Nathan (Hertz) Juran; **W:** Martin Berkeley. USH

Deadly Mission ♂½ 1978 (R) Five soldiers in WWII France are convicted of crimes against the Army, only to escape from lock-up and become focal points in a decisive battle. 99m/C VHS, Beta. Bo Svenson, Peter Hooten, Fred Williamson. ART

Deadly Neighbor ♂♂ 1991 New neighbor moves in, dead neighborhood housewives move out. Another neighbor becomes suspicious and investigates. 90m/C VHS. Don Leifert, George Stover, Lydia Laurans; **D:** Donald M. Dohler. VCI

Deadly Obsession ♂½ 1988 (R) A disfigured lunatic stalks a young co-ed hoping to extort $1 million from the wealthy dean of the school. 93m/C VHS. Jeffrey R. Iorio; **D:** Jeno Hodi; **W:** Brian Cox. REP, FCT

Deadly Outbreak ♂♂ 1996 (R) A chemical weapons facility is taken over by a renegade colonel who threatens to unleash a deadly plague. Now it's up to one man (Speakman) to free the hostage scientist who knows the formula for the antidote. **CW:** Non-stop violence, language. 94m/C VHS, LV, Closed Caption. Jeff Speakman, Ron Silver, Rochelle Swanson, Jonathan Sagalle; **D:** Rick Avery; **M:** Harvey W. Mason. ART

Deadly Passion ♂½ 1985 (R) A James Cain-like thriller about a private eye getting carnally involved with a beautiful and treacherous woman who is manipulating her late husband's estate through murder and double-crossing. 100m/C VHS, Beta. SA Brent Huff, Ingrid Boulting, Harrison Coburn, Lynn Maree; **D:** Larry Larson. ART

Deadly Past ♂½ 1995 (R) Predictable story finds dumb ex-con bartender (Marquette) making the mistake of getting involved with a femme fatale (Alt) from his past. Also available in an unrated version. **CW:** Some strong sexuality; some violence and language. 90m/C VHS. Ron Marquette, Carol Alt, Dedee Pfeiffer, Mark Dacascos. AVE

Deadly Possession ♂♂ 1988 A college student plays amateur detective when she tries to clear her ex-husband's name after he is accused of the horrible murder of a fellow student. 99m/C VHS, Beta, LV. AU Penny Cook, Anna-Maria Winchester, Liddy Clark, Olivia Hamnett; **D:** Craig Lahiff. ART, VES

Deadly Prey woof! 1987 (R) Prior is up against a fully outfitted army of bloodthirsty mercenaries who are using innocent people as "live targets" at their secret bootcamp. Plot lifted from "The Most Dangerous Game" has more than its share of gruesome violence. 87m/C VHS, Beta. Cameron Mitchell, Troy Donahue, Ted Prior, Fritz Matthews; **D:** David A. Prior; **W:** David A. Prior. NO

Deadly Reactor ♂♂ 1989 In a post-nuclear future a lone preacher turns into an armed vigilante to protect the people of a town being terrorized by a vicious motorcycle gang. 88m/C VHS, Beta. David Heavener, Stuart Whitman, Darwyn Swalve, Allyson Davis; **D:** David Heavener.

Deadly Recruits ♂½ 1986 The Russians did it! The Russians did it! Stamp is convinced that the downfall of several top students at Oxford, amid scandal and rumor, is due to a KGB conspiracy. 92m/C VHS, Beta. GB Terence Stamp, Michael Culver, Carmen Du Sautoy, Robin Sachs; **D:** Roger Tucker. NO

Deadly Revenge ♂ 1983 (R) Action-adventure pic with not much adventure and even less action. Small-town reporter finds himself up against a mob boss when he takes over the nightclub business of a friend killed by the mobsters. Dubbed. 90m/C VHS, Beta. IT Rodolfo Ranni, Julio de Grazia, Silvia Montanari, Fred Commoner; **D:** Juan Carlos Sesanzo. UNI

Deadly Rivals ♂♂ 1992 (R) Stevens plays a laser specialist in Miami for a top-secret weapons conference. A beauty takes a interest in him but then she's first accused of being a spy and then mistaken for a courier in the pay of a ruthless crime boss. Can Stevens find the truth? **CW:** Language, violence, and sexuality. 93m/C VHS, LV, Closed Caption. Andrew Stevens, Cela Wise, Joseph Bologna, Margaux Hemingway, Richard Roundtree, Francesco Quinn, Randi Ingerman; *O:* James Dodson; *W:* Hedye Mahaffey; *M:* Ashley Irwin. *USH*

Deadly Sanctuary woof! 1968 Censors stopped production of this film several times. The Marquis de Sade's writings provided the inspiration (though there's nothing inspired about it) for this tale of two recently orphaned young women who get caught up in prostitution, an S&M club, and murder. 92m/C VHS, Beta. Jack Palance, Mercedes McCambridge, Sylva Koscina, Klaus Kinski, Akim Tamiroff, Romina Power; *D:* Jess (Jesus) Franco. *NO*

The Deadly Secret 🐾🐾 1994 Randall Parks is a successful real estate agent with a past he has managed to hide for 20 years. When he is blackmailed, he decides to take matters into his own hands and track down his accusers. 98m/C VHS. Joe Estevez, Tracy Spaulding, Reggie Cale, Douglas Stalgren; *D:* Jason Hammond; *W:* Douglas Stalgren; *M:* Erik Hansen.

Deadly Sins 🐾🐾½ 1995 (R) Deputy sheriff Jack Gates (Keith) hooks up with P.I. Christina Herrera (Milano) to investigate a murder in a Catholic girls school. Christina poses as a student and uncovers sinister secrets. *CW:* Strong sexuality; violence; language. 98m/C VHS. David Keith, Alyssa Milano, Corrie Clark; *D:* Michael Robison; *W:* John Langley, Malcolm Barbour. *AVE*

Deadly Spygames 1989 A special agent for the United States Special Operations Bureau finds himself in deep trouble. ?m/C VHS. Troy Donahue, Tippi Hedren; *D:* Jack M. Sell; *W:* Jack M. Sell. *UNI*

Deadly Sting 🐾½ 1982 Silva devises an intricate scheme to gain revenge on the men who cheated him out of his share of a gold bullion heist. 90m/C VHS, Beta. *FR* Henry Silva, Philip Clay, Andre Pousse; *D:* Jean-Claude Roy. *NO*

Deadly Stranger *Border Heat* 1988 Fluegel's talents could have been put to much better use than as the selfish mistress of a plantation owner who is taking advantage of the migrant workers toiling on his land. Moore is a drifter and hired hand who rallies the workers to stand up to the owner. 93m/C VHS. Darlanne Fluegel, Michael J. Moore, John Vernon, Ted White; *D:* Max Kleven. *MCG*

Deadly Strangers 🐾🐾 1982 Two people meet up on the road and decide to share a ride. We discover that one of them is an insane killer who's escaped from a mental institution. Suspense builds nicely, but the ending is flawed. 89m/C VHS, Beta. *GB* Hayley Mills, Simon Ward, Sterling Hayden, Ken Hutchison; *D:* Sidney Hayers. *NO*

Deadly Sunday 🐾½ 1982 A family's weekly Sunday drive turns terrifying when desperate jewel thieves detour them and hold them hostage. 85m/C VHS, Beta. Dennis Ely, Henry Sanders, Gylian Roland, Douglas Alexander; *D:* Donald M. Jones. *ART*

Deadly Surveillance 🐾🐾 1991 (R) Two tough policemen investigate a series of drug-related murders and stake out a possible suspect—a beautiful woman who's the lover of one of the lawmen. Tension in this Canadian-made cop opera evaporates in the third act for a standard buddy-buddy action finale. Made for television. *CW:* Language, violence, and sensuality. 92m/C VHS, Closed Caption. Michael Ironside, Christopher Bondy, Susan Almgren, Vlasta Vrana, David Carradine; *D:* Paul Ziller. *REP*

Deadly Target 🐾½ 1994 (R) Detective Charles Prince (Daniels) is sent to L.A. to return a notorious Chinese gangster to Hong Kong for trial. But Prince finds out his would-be prisoner's escaped and soon he's involved in martial arts mayhem. 90m/C VHS. Gary Daniels, Kenneth McLeod, Max Gail, Susan Byun. *PMH*

Deadly Thief 🐾🐾 *Shalimar* 1978 A former jewel thief comes out of retirement to challenge those who are now tops in the profession to try and steal the world's most precious ruby from him. Of course all they have to lose is their lives. What could have been an exciting adventure is

made curiously boring. 90m/C VHS, Beta. *IN* Rex Harrison, John Saxon, Sylvia Miles, Dharmendra, Zenat Aman, Shammi Kapoor; *D:* Krishna Shah.

The Deadly Trackers 🐾 1973 (PG) If gorey oaters are your thing, this one's definitely for you; if not, make tracks. Harris plays a spiteful sheriff who heads south of the border to get his pound of flesh from the outlaws who slew his family in a bank robbery. Overlong revenge-o-rama based on Samuel Fuller's short story, "Riata"; might have been bearable if Fuller hadn't been bumped from the director's chair (as it is, he and other contributors refused to be listed in the credits). 104m/C VHS, LV, Closed Caption. Richard Harris, Rod Taylor, Al Lettieri, Neville Brand, William Smith, Paul Benjamin, Pedro Armendariz Jr.; *D:* Barry Shear. *WAR, FCT*

The Deadly Trap 🐾 *Death Scream* 1971 (PG) Confusing thriller that couldn't. Dunaway is the mentally unstable wife of an ex-spy. His former employers have targeted him with plans to use her and her fragile state-of-mind to their advantage. 96m/C VHS. *FR IT* Faye Dunaway, Frank Langella, Barbara Parkins, Maurice Ronet; *D:* Rene Clement. *FCT*

Deadly Twins woof! 1985 After being beaten and gang-raped, twin sister singers are out to get revenge. Nothing new here; don't waste your time. 87m/C VHS, Beta. Audrey Landers, Judy Landers, Ellie Russell, Wayne Allison; *D:* Joe Oaks.

Deadly Vengeance 🐾 1981 It's strictly low budget as the mob kills Jones's boyfriend, forcing her to mount a vengeful but inexpensive offensive against the crime syndicate's bigwigs. 84m/C VHS, Beta. Grace Jones, Alan Marlowe, Arthur Roberts. *NO*

Deadly Voyage 🐾🐾½ 1996 (R) In 1992, nine Ghanaian dockworkers are discovered hiding aboard a Ukrainian freighter bound for New York. Since each stowaway would cost the shipping company a hefty fine, sadistic first officer Ion (Pertwee) orders them killed. Only one, Kingsley (Epps), manages to survive and reveal the truth. Made for cable. *CW:* Graphic violence, strong language and some nudity. 92m/C VHS. Omar Epps, Sean Pertwee, Joss Ackland, David Suchet, Jean LaMarre, Andrew Divoff; *D:* John MacKenzie; *C:* Stuart Urban; *M:* John Scott. *HBO*

Deadly Weapon 🐾 1988 (PG-13) It's a bit of nerdish wish fulfillment when 15-year-old geek Eastman finds a secret anti-matter weapon conveniently lost by the military in an Arizona stream. You won't like the kid any more than you'll like the story of this low rent boy-gets-back-at-bullies sci fiasco. 89m/C VHS. Rodney Eastman, Gary Frank, Michael Horse, Ed Nelson, Kim Walker; *D:* Michael Miner; *W:* Michael Miner; *C:* James L. Carter. *TWE, HHE*

Deadly Weapons 🐾 1970 (R) Chesty Morgan, she of the 73-inch bustline, takes on the mob using only her God-given abilities. One of Joe Bob Brigg's "Sleaziest Movies in the History of the World" series, and he is welcome to it. 90m/C VHS. Chesty Morgan, Harry Reems; *D:* Doris Wishman. *NO*

Deadman's Curve 🐾🐾 1978 Decent bio pic detailing the lives of Jan Berry and Dean Torrence who, as Jan and Dean, started the surf music wave only to wipe out after an almost-fatal car wreck. Shows how they deal with and recover from the tragedy. Made for television. 100m/C VHS. Richard Hatch, Bruce Davison, Pamela Bellwood, Susan Sullivan, Dick Clark, Wolfman Jack; *D:* Richard Compton. *GEM*

Deadtime Stories 🐾½ 1986 Mother Goose it's not. Fairy tales "Little Red Riding Hood" and "Goldilocks and the Three Bears," among others, are presented like you've never before seen them—as low-budget horror tales. 93m/C VHS, Beta, LV. Michael Mesmer, Brian DePersia, Scott Valentine, Phyllis Craig, Melissa Leo, Nicole Picard; *D:* Jeffrey Delman. *NO*

Deadwood 🐾½ 1965 In the untamed West, a young cowboy is mistaken for the notorious Billy the Kid. 100m/C VHS, Beta. Arch Hall Jr., Jack Lester, Melissa Morgan, Robert Dix; *D:* James Landis; *C:* Vilmos Zsigmond. *RHI, FCT*

Deadwood Pass 🐾 1933 Below-standard fare has Tyler rescuing Monti more times than seems reasonable. Monti was once an all-around helper to W.C. Fields. 62m/B VHS. Tom Tyler, Alice Dahl, Wally Wales, Buffalo Bill Jr., Lafe McKee, Bud Osborne, Charles "Slim" Whitaker, Charlotte (Carlotta) Monti; *D:* J.P. McGowan. *DVT, HEG, GPV*

Deal of the Century 🐾🐾 1983 (PG) A first-rate hustler and his cohorts sell second-rate weapons to third-world nations; unfortunately, their latest deal threatens to blow up in their faces—literally. 99m/C VHS, Beta, LV. Chevy Chase, Sigourney Weaver, Gregory Hines, Richard Libertini, Wallace Shawn; *D:* William Friedkin; *W:* Paul Brickman. *WAR*

Dealers 🐾½ 1989 (R) Two money-hungry stock traders mix business and pleasure, then set their sights on one final all or nothing score. 92m/C VHS, Beta, LV. *GB* Rebecca DeMornay, Paul McGann, Derrick O'Connor; *D:* Colin Bucksey. *IME*

Dear America: Letters Home from Vietnam 🐾🐾🐾½ 1988 (PG) Acclaimed documentary featuring pictures and film of the war with voice-overs by dozens of Hollywood stars reading the words of American GIs. Initially made for cable television. 84m/C VHS, Beta, Closed Caption. *D:* Bill Couturie; *W:* Bill Couturie; *M:* Todd Boekelheide. *HBO, AMB*

Dear Boys 🐾🐾 1980 A stylized film of sexual fantasies and romance between a moody writer and a carefree young man who relentlessly pursues excitement. Based on the novel by Gerald Reve. *NL* Hugo Netsers, Hans Dagelet, Bill Van Dijk, Albert Mol; *D:* Paul de Lussanet. *FCT*

Dear Brigitte 🐾🐾 1965 A young American kid ("Lost in Space" tyke Mumy) writes a love letter to Brigitte Bardot and travels to Paris to meet her in person. Based on the novel "Erasmus with Freckles" by John Haase. 100m/C VHS, Beta, Closed Caption. James Stewart, Billy Mumy, Glynis Johns, Fabian, Cindy Carol, John Williams, Jack Kruschen, Brigitte Bardot, Ed Wynn, Alice Pearce; *D:* Henry Koster; *W:* Hal Kanter. *FOX*

Dear Dead Delilah 🐾½ 1972 Moorehead is Delilah, the matriarch of a southern family, who is on her deathbed. Her heirs are fighting to the bitter—and bloody—end to be the first to find Delilah's money, buried somewhere on her land. 90m/C VHS, Beta. Agnes Moorehead, Will Geer, Michael Ansara, Patricia Carmichael, Dennis Patrick; *D:* John Farris.

Dear Detective 🐾🐾 *Dear Inspector; Tendre Poulet* 1977 Comedy/thriller/romance finds female police inspector (Girandot) investigating a murder while romancing a somewhat pompous professor of Greek (Noiret). French with subtitles. 105m/C VHS. *FR* Annie Girardot, Philippe Noiret, Catherine Alric, Guy Marchand, Simone Renant; *D:* Philippe de Broca; *W:* Philippe de Broca, Michel Audiard; *M:* Georges Delerue. *FRA*

Dear Detective 🐾🐾 1978 Vaccaro is the head of the police homicide unit who is trying to track down the killer of several politicians. In the midst of her investigation, she falls for an old friend, a professor of Greek language. Made for television and based on a French television series. 90m/C VHS. Brenda Vaccaro, Arlen Dean Snyder, Michael MacRae, John Dennis Johnston, Jack Ging, Stephen McNally, M. Emmet Walsh, Constance Forslund, R.G. Armstrong; *D:* Dean Hargrove; *M:* Georges Delerue. *FCT*

Dear God 🐾 1996 (PG) TV vets Marshall (director) and Kinnear team up for a sappy and predictable "Miracle on Melrose," a little piece of Capra-corn that feels like it lodged in your tooth. Cynical con man Tom (Kinnear) goes to work for the post office and gets stuck with a group of misfits at the Dead Letter Office, sorting mail for the likes of Elvis, Santa, and God. Even though he's merely working the ultimate angle for easy cash, the oddball team of postal workers think he's on a mission from the Lord and joins him in aiding the needy. Most unbelievable is the premise that single mom and love interest Gloria (Pitillo) can give the hardened criminal an instant psychological makeover. Broadly characterized supporting cast, including Conway and Metcalf, suffer at the hands of script. Strictly a star vehicle for Kinnear's budding movie career, it won't help. It also won't do anything for Marshall's downward-spiraling reputation. Ironic cameo from Christopher Darden as a reporter outside the courtroom, and Marshall himself as Postmaster General. **112m/C VHS, Beta, Closed Caption.** Greg Kinnear, Laurie Metcalf, Maria Pitillo, Hector Elizondo, Tim Conway, Roscoe Lee Browne, Jon Seda, Anna Maria Horsford, Donal Logue, Nancy Marchand, Larry Miller, Rue McClanahan, Toby Huss, Jack Klugman; **Cameos:** Garry Marshall; **D:** Garry Marshall; **W:** Ed Kaplan, Warren Leight; **C:** Charles Minsky. *PAR*

Dear Murderer 🐾🐾 1947 A husband suspects his wife of having an affair, and devises an ingenious, if complicated, trap for her. Inspired performances from the leads, but the plot is grim and confusing. **94m/B VHS, Beta.** *GB* Eric Portman, Greta Gynt, Dennis Price, Jack Warner, Maxwell Reed, Hazel Court, Andrew Crawford, Jane Hylton; **D:** Arthur Crabtree. *SNC*

Dear Wife 🐾🐾½ 1949 Comedy about those ties that bind. Even though her father is runnning for reelection to the State Senate, Freeman wants her brother-in-law (Holden) to run against him. Sequel to "Dear Ruth." **88m/B VHS, Beta.** William Holden, Joan Caulfield, Edward Arnold, Billy DeWolfe, Mona Freeman; **D:** Richard Haydn. *BAR*

Death and Desire 🐾🐾 1997 (R) Fashion photographer Jeff Reed isn't tempted by the beautiful models he shoots because he's happily married. But when his wife is killed in an accident, the vulnerable Jeff becomes the target of fashion mag editor, Lynn, who desperately wants to offer him comfort. Too desperately. Soon Lynn's obsessed and Jeff's fighting for his life. Unrated version runs 88 minutes. **84m/C VHS.** Tane McClure, Tim Abell, Jennifer Burton. *MTH*

Death and the Maiden 🐾🐾🐾 1994 (R) Former political prisoner and torture victim (Weaver) turns the tables on the man she believes was her tormentor 15 years before. Pressing her civil rights lawyer husband (Wilson) into duty as defense attorney, she becomes prosecutor, judge, and jury. The accused (Kingsley) learns the dangers of picking up stranded motorists, as he is bound, gagged, and roughed up by the now empowered and vengeful Paulina. Tense, claustrophobic political thriller features a talented ensemble both on screen and behind the scenes. From an Ariel Dorfman play. **CW:** Contains strong language, violence, and graphic descriptions of rape and torture. **103m/C VHS, LV, Closed Caption.** Sigourney Weaver, Ben Kingsley, Stuart Wilson; **D:** Roman Polanski; **W:** Rafael Yglesias, Ariel Dorfman; **C:** Tonino Delli Colli; **M:** Wojciech Kilar. Nominations: Independent Spirit Awards '95: Best Director (Polanski). *TTC, NLC, IME*

The Death Artist 🐾½ 1995 (R) Struggling busboy and would-be artist Walter Paisley (Hall) finds fame creating sculptures from dead bodies. Gruesome plot is a remake of Corman's 1960 "A Bucket of Blood" but the same premise was done much better with Vincent Price in 1953's "House of Wax." **79m/C VHS.** Anthony Michael Hall, Darcy Demoss, Shadoe Stevens, Paul Bartel, Mink Stole; **D:** Michael James McDonald; **W:** Michael James McDonald, Brendan Broderick; **C:** Christopher Baffa; **M:** David Wurst, Eric Wurst. *NHO*

Death at Love House 🐾½ 1975 A screen writer becomes obsessed when he is hired to write the life story of a long dead silent movie queen. Filmed at the Harold Lloyd estate. Made for television. **74m/C VHS, Beta.** Robert Wagner, Kate Jackson, Sylvia Sidney, Joan Blondell, John Carradine; **D:** E.W. Swackhamer.

Death Be Not Proud 🐾🐾🐾 1975 Based on the book by John Gunther detailing the valiant battle fought by his son against the brain tumor that took his life at the age of 17. Wonderfully acted by the three principals, especially Alexander, this film leaves us feeling hopeful despite its subject. Made for television. **74m/C VHS, Beta.** Arthur Hill, Robby Benson, Jane Alexander, Linden Chiles, Wendy Phillips; **D:** Donald Wrye. *BFA*

Death Becomes Her 🐾🐾🐾 1992 (PG-13) Aging actress Streep will do anything to stay young and beautiful, especially when childhood rival Hawn shows up, 200 pounds lighter and out to revenge the loss of her fiance, Streep's henpecked hubby. Doing anything arrives in the form of a potion that stops the aging process (and keeps her alive forever). Watch for the hilarious party filled with dead celebrities who all look as good as the day they died. Great special effects and fun performances by Streep and Hawn playing their glamour-girl roles to the hilt add merit to this biting commentary on Hollywood's obsession with beauty and youth. **105m/C VHS, Beta, LV, Letterbox, Closed Caption, DVD.** Meryl Streep, Bruce Willis, Goldie Hawn, Isabella Rossellini, Sydney Pollack, Michael Caine, Ian Ogilvy, Adam Storke, Nancy Fish, Alaina Reed Hall, Michelle Johnson, Mimi Kennedy, Jonathan Silverman; **Cameos:** Fabio Lanzoni; **D:** Robert Zemeckis; **W:** Martin Donovan, David Koepp; **C:** Dean Cundey; **M:** Alan Silvestri. Academy Awards '92: Best Visual Effects. *MGM, PMS*

Death Before Dishonor 🐾½ 1987 (R) Formula actioner stars Dryer as a tough Marine sergeant who battles ruthless Middle Eastern terrorists after they slaughter his men and kidnap his commanding officer (Keith). **95m/C VHS, Beta, LV, Closed Caption.** Fred Dryer, Brian Keith, Joanna Pacula, Paul Winfield; **D:** Terry J. Leonard; **C:** Don Burgess. *VTR*

Death Benefit 🐾🐾½ 1996 (PG-13) Corporate attorney Steven Keeney (Horton) takes on the case of Lou Anne Wilkins (Ruscio), who's having trouble getting her insurance company to cover the funeral expenses for her teenaged daughter Melissa, who died in a fall. The more Steven investigates, the more suspicious Melissa's death becomes—and he discovers money is the root of all evil. Based on the book "Death Benefit" by David Heilbroner. Made for cable. **CW:** Scene of sensuality and thematic elements. **89m/C VHS, Closed Caption.** Peter Horton, Carrie Snodgress, Wendy Makkena, Elizabeth Ruscio, Belita Morena, Lee De-Broux; **D:** Mark Piznarski; **W:** Philip Rosenberg; **C:** Christopher Taylor. *USH*

Death Blow 🐾½ 1987 (R) The victims of a violent rapist team together to stop the criminal after he repeatedly skirts conviction. **90m/C VHS, Beta.** Martin Landau, Frank Stallone, Jerry Van Dyke, Terry Moore, Henry Darrow, Jack Carter, Peter Lapis, Don Swayze, Donna Denton; **D:** Raphael Nussbaum. *NO*

Death by Dialogue 🐾 1988 (R) Muddled story of some teenagers who discover an old film script from a project never produced because it was haunted by tragic accidents. **90m/C VHS, Beta.** Laura Albert, Ken Sagoes; **D:** Tom Dewier. *NO*

Death by Prescription 🐾 198? After adjusting his patients' wills to benefit himself, an evil physician sees to their mysterious deaths. **75m/C VHS, Beta.** Timothy West, Nigel Davenport. *MOV*

Death Challenge 🐾½ 1980 Gangs battle without weapons, order or discretion in this kung fu extravaganza. **94m/C VHS, Beta.** Steve Leving, Susan Wong. *UNI*

Death Chase 🐾½ 1987 An average Joe, just jogging down the street, is thrown into a desperate game of cat-and-mouse when a body lands at his feet. **86m/C VHS, Beta.** William Zipp, Paul Smith, Jack Starrett, Bainbridge Scott; **D:** David A. Prior. *NO*

Death Collector 🐾½ 1989 (R) In the future when insurance companies run the world, if you don't pay your premium, you die. **CW:** Language, violence, and sensuality. **90m/C VHS, Beta.** Daniel Chapman, Ruth Collins; **D:** Tom Gniazdowski. *VTR*

Death Cruise 🐾½ 1974 The six winners of a free cruise find that there is a fatal catch to the prize in this made-for-TV movie. **74m/C VHS, Beta.** Kate Jackson, Celeste Holm, Tom Bosley, Edward Albert, Polly Bergen, Michael Constantine, Richard Long; **D:** Ralph Senensky.

The Death Curse of Tartu woof! 1966 Another aspiring cult classic. (Read: A low-budget flick so bad it's funny). Students accidentally disturb the burial ground of an Indian medicine man who comes to zombie-like life with a deadly prescription. **84m/C VHS, Beta.** Fred Pinero, Doug Hobart, William Grefe. *NO*

Death Dreams 🐾🐾 1992 Crista thinks she has a perfect life with her wealth, beautiful daughter Jennie, and handsome new husband George. Then Jennie tragically drowns. It appears to be an accident until Jennie contacts her mother from beyond the grave to tell what really happened. Is the tragedy turning Crista's mind or is there truly something sinister going on—something that involves George? Based on the novel by William Katz. Routine suspenser originally appeared on cable television. **94m/C VHS, LV.** Marg Helgenberger, Christopher Reeve, Fionnula Flanagan; **D:** Martin Donovan; **W:** Robert Glass. *NLC*

Death Driver 🐾½ 1978 In order to make a comeback, a stuntman attempts to do a stunt that was responsible for ending his career ten years earlier. Obviously brave but none too smart. **93m/C VHS, Beta.** Earl Owensby, Mike Allen, Patty Shaw, Mary Ann Hearn; **D:** Jimmy Huston. *NO*

Death Drug 🐾½ 1983 Cliched alarmist film about a talented musician ruining his career by becoming addicted to the drug angel dust. **73m/C VHS, Beta.** Philip Michael Thomas, Vernee Watson-Johnson, Rosalind Cash; **D:** Oscar Williams.

Death Feud 1989 A man tries to save the woman he loves from the man who would destroy her and her former pimp. **98m/C VHS, Beta.** Karen Mayo Chandler, Chris Mitchum, Frank Stallone.

Death Force 🐾½ 1978 When a Vietnam veteran comes to New York City, he becomes a hitman for the Mafia. **90m/C VHS, Beta.** Jayne Kennedy, Leon Isaac Kennedy, James Iglehart, Carmen Argenziano; **D:** Cirio H. Santiago. *NO*

Death from a Distance 🐾½ 1936 A reporter and a detective put the moves on a group of astronomers who may be responsible for a murder. **73m/B VHS, Beta.** Russell Hopton, Lola Lane, George F. Marion Sr., John St. Polis, Lee Kohlmar, Lew Kelly, Wheeler Oakman, Robert Frazer, Cornelius Keefe; **D:** Frank Strayer. *SNC*

Death Games 🐾½ 1982 Two young men shooting a documentary about an influential music promoter ask too many wrong questions, causing the powers-that-be to want them out of the picture for good. **78m/C VHS, Beta.** Lou Brown, David Clendenning, Jennifer Cluff. *NO*

Death Goes to School 🐾🐾 1953 A strangler is loose in a girl's school, and the music teacher has a hunch as to who it is. **65m/B VHS, Beta.** *GB* Barbara Murray, Gordon Jackson, Pamela Allan, Jane Aird, Beatrice Varley; **D:** Stephen Clarkson. *SNC*

Death House 🐾½ 1988 Derek Keillor is on Death Row at Townsend State Prison when he discovers a plot to use inmates for scientific experiments in biological warfare. He decides the best way to get out is to volunteer, which means convincing the man who put him in prison that they're now on the same side. **92m/C VHS.** Dennis Cole, Anthony (Tony) Franciosa, Michael Pataki, John Saxon; **D:** John Saxon.

Death Hunt 🐾🐾 1981 (R) A man unjustly accused of murder pits his knowledge of the wilderness against the superior numbers of his pursuers. **98m/C VHS, Beta, LV.** Charles Bronson, Lee Marvin, Ed Lauter, Andrew Stevens, Carl Weathers, Angie Dickinson; **D:** Peter Hunt; **W:** Mark Victor, Michael Grais. *FOX*

Death in Brunswick 🐾🐾 *Nothing to Lose* 1990 (R) Carl Fitzgerald (Neill) seems to be one of life's born losers—his wife's left him, his mother nags him, his house is falling apart, and he's unemployed. At least until he gets a job as a chef in a sleazy rock 'n' roll club and finds Sophie (Carides), the lovely barmaid, who just happens to be engaged to the club's owner. Of course, with Carl's luck, things go from bad to downright dangerous. Based on the novel by Boyd Oxlade. **CW:** Language; some sexuality. 106m/C VHS. *AU* Sam Neill, Zoe Carides, Yvonne Lawley, Boris Brkic, John Clarke; **D:** John Ruane; **W:** John Ruane, Boyd Oxlade; **C:** Ellery Ryan. *COL*

Death in Deep Water 🐾🐾 1974 A sensuous woman lures a man into a plot to kill her incredibly rich husband. 71m/C VHS, Beta. Bradford Dillman, Suzan Farmer. *ART*

Death in the Garden 🐾🐾 *La Mort en Ce Jardin; Evil Eden* 1956 Surreal film, filled with symbolism, about a group of French people, living in a South American settlement, who must flee a riot between soldiers and striking miners. Local adventurer, Chark (Marchal), agrees to lead them to safety but their trek through the jungle is fraught with peril (and not just from the animal life). French with subtitles. 90m/C VHS. *MX FR* Georges Marchal, Simone Signoret, Charles Vanel, Michele Girardon, Michel Piccoli, Tito Junco; **D:** Luis Bunuel; **W:** Luis Bunuel, Luis Alcoriza, Raymond Queneau; **C:** Jorge Stahl Jr.; **M:** Paul Misraki. *INT*

Death in Venice 🐾🐾🐾½ *Morte a Venezia* 1971 (PG) A lush, decadent adaptation of the Thomas Mann novella about an aging and jaded composer, here suggested to be Gustav Mahler, tragically obsessed with ideal beauty as personified in a young boy. 124m/C VHS, Beta. *IT* Dirk Bogarde, Mark Burns, Bjorn Andresen, Marisa Berenson, Silvana Mangano; **D:** Luchino Visconti; **M:** Gustav Mahler. Nominations: Academy Awards '71: Best Costume Design. *WAR*

Death Is Called Engelchen 🐾🐾🐾½ *For We Too Do Not Forgive* 1963 An influential, important work of the Czech new wave. A survivor of WWII remembers his experiences with the SS leader Engelchen in a series of flashbacks. In Czech with subtitles. 111m/B VHS, Beta. *CZ* **D:** Jan Kadar, Elmar Klos. *FCT*

Death Journey 🐾½ 1976 (R) Producer and director Williamson portrays private eye Jesse Crowder, hired by the New York D.A. to escort a key witness cross-country. A regular Williamsonfest. 90m/C VHS, Beta. Fred Williamson, D'Urville Martin, Bernie Kuby, Heidi Dobbs, Stephanie Faulkner; **D:** Fred Williamson. *UNI*

The Death Kiss 🐾🐾½ 1933 Creepy thriller about eerie doings at a major Hollywood film studio where a sinister killer does away with his victims while a cast-of-thousands movie spectacular is in production. 72m/B VHS, Beta, 8mm. Bela Lugosi, David Manners, Adrienne Ames, Edward Van Sloan, Vince Barnett; **D:** Edwin L. Marin. *NOS, SNC, CAB*

Death Kiss 🐾½ 1977 (R) When a man hires a psychopath to murder his wife, his plan doesn't proceed exactly as expected. 90m/C VHS, Beta. Larry Daniels, Dorothy Moore. *LSV*

Death Machine 🐾½ 1995 (R) New company exec Hayden Cale (Pouget) uncovers questionable scientific project at weapons technology company and scientist in charge Jack Dante (Dourif) decides to get even by testing his death machine, which works by sensing fear, in corporate headquarters. **CW:** Sci-fi terror and violence; language; brief sexuality. 99m/C VHS, LV, Closed Caption. Brad Dourif, Ely Pouget, William Hootkins; **D:** Stephen Norrington; **W:** Stephen Norrington; **C:** John de Borman. *THV*

Death Machines 🐾½ 1976 (R) Young karate student must face the "Death Machines," a team of deadly assassins who are trained to kill on command. 93m/C VHS, Beta. Ron Marchini, Michael Chong, Joshua Johnson; **D:** Paul Kyriazi. *NO*

Death Magic 🐾½ 1992 A group of five ceremonial magicians performs a spell to bring someone back from the dead, but the man they bring back, a soldier from the Civil War, decides to go on a vicious murdering spree to kill the descendants of the people who convicted him of murder in 1875. A suspenseful first entry from director Clinco. 93m/C VHS. Anne Coffrey, Keith DeGreen, Jack Dunlap, Danielle Frons, Norman Stone; **D:** Paul E. Clinco; **W:** Paul E. Clinco. *NO*

Death Mask of the Ninja 🐾½ 198? Two princes, separated at birth, reunite and kick everyone in the head. Dubbed. 95m/C VHS, Beta. Joey Lee, Tiger Tung, Jon Chen. *MOV*

Death Match 🐾 1994 (R) John Larson gives up kickboxing after a tragedy but when his friend disappears, John is forced into a fighting bout with no rules and only one outcome. **CW:** Strong martial arts violence. 90m/C VHS. Matthias Hues, Martin Kove, Ian Jacklin, Nick Hill, Renee Ammann; **D:** Joe Coppoletta. *MNC*

The Death Merchant 🐾 1991 Foundering attempt at a nuclear thriller. A modern mad man hopes to sell a computer chip to third world countries but is thwarted by a secret agent. Confusing, illogical plot highlighted by mediocre performances. 90m/C VHS. Lawrence Tierney, Martina Castle, Melody Munyan, Monika Schnarre; **D:** James R. Winburn; **W:** Kari Holman.

Death Nurse 🐾🐾 1987 Fresh from "Crazy Fat Ethel II," aspiring Queen of Camp Alden takes up residence in a health care establishment, much to the dismay of the patients who give up their lives in exchange for their money. 80m/C VHS. Priscilla Alden, Michael Flood; **D:** Nick Phillips. *VCD*

Death of a Bureaucrat 🐾🐾🐾 1966 A Cuban hero dies, and in tribute, the Communist government buries him with his union card. His widow, however, needs the card in order to collect a pension, and she enlists her nephew's help to retrieve it. The nephew soon finds himself buried in red tape, and digs himself in ever-deeper as he seeks to disinter his late uncle. A wry satire of the communist bureaucracy in Cuba, brimming with comedic tributes to Harold Lloyd, Buster Keaton and Laurel & Hardy. Alea's film was only briefly released in 1966 and was promptly banned, eventually finding its way to the U.S. in 1979. In Spanish with English subtitles. 87m/B VHS, Beta. *CU* Salvador Wood, Silvia Planas, Manuel Estanillo, Gaspar de Santelices, Carlos Ruiz de la Tejera, Omar Alfonso, Ricardo Suarez, Luis Romay, Elsa Montero; **D:** Tomas Gutierrez Alea. *NYF, FCT*

Death of a Centerfold 🐾🐾 1981 Drama based on the life and tragic death of Playboy model and actress Dorothy Stratten. More effectively handled in Bob Fosse's "Star 80." 96m/C VHS, Beta. Jamie Lee Curtis, Bruce Weitz, Robert Reed, Mitchell Ryan, Bibi Besch; **D:** Gabrielle Beaumont. *MGM*

Death of a Gunfighter 🐾🐾 1969 (PG) A western town courting eastern investors and bankers seeks a way to kill their ex-gunslinger sheriff. 94m/C VHS, Beta. Richard Widmark, Lena Horne, Carroll O'Connor, John Saxon, Larry Gates; **D:** Donald Siegel; **W:** Robert Totten. *USH*

Death of a Salesman 🐾🐾🐾½ 1986 A powerful made-for-television adaptation of the famous Arthur Miller play. Hoffman won an Emmy (as did Malkovich) for his stirring portrayal of Willy Loman, the aging salesman who realizes he's past his prime and tries to come to grips with the life he's wasted and the family he's neglected. Reid also turns in a fine performance as his long-suffering wife. 135m/C VHS, Beta, LV, Closed Caption. Dustin Hoffman, John Malkovich, Charles Durning, Stephen Lang, Kate Reid, Louis Zorich; **D:** Volker Schlondorff; **M:** Michael Ballhaus; **M:** Alex North. *ORI, FCT, WAR*

Death of a Scoundrel 🐾🐾½ *Loves of a Scoundrel* 1956 A womanizing entrepreneur is murdered and the culprit could be any one of his many jealous romantic conquests. 119m/B VHS,

Beta, LV. George Sanders, Zsa Zsa Gabor, Yvonne De Carlo, Victor Jory; **D:** Charles Martin; **M:** Max Steiner. *NO*

Death of a Soldier 🐾🐾 1985 (R) During WWII, the uneasy U.S.-Australian alliance explodes when a psychotic American soldier murders three Melbourne women. The lawyer hired to defend him has to fight political as well as legal influences. Based on a true story. 93m/C VHS, Beta, Closed Caption. *AU* James Coburn, Reb Brown, Maurie Field, Belinda Darey; **D:** Philippe Mora. *FOX*

The Death of Adolf Hitler 🐾🐾½ 1984 British made-for-television film depicting Hitler's last ten days in an underground bunker. Drug-addled, suicidal, and Eva Braun-haunted, he receives the news of the fall of the Third Reich. While the film avoids cliche, it lacks emotional depth. 107m/C VHS, Beta. *GB* Frank Finlay, Caroline Mortimer; **D:** Rex Firlin. *ORI, TLF, WAR*

Death of an Angel 🐾🐾½ 1986 When her crippled daughter runs away to join a cult in Mexico, a recently ordained priest (Bedelia) follows her, only to become caught up herself with the leader of the group. 95m/C VHS, Beta, LV. Bonnie Bedelia, Nick Mancuso, Pamela Ludwig, Alex Colon; **D:** Petru Popescu; **M:** Jay Michael Ferguson. *NO*

The Death of Richie 🐾🐾 *Richie* 1976 Gazzara does a fine job as a father driven to kill his drug-addicted teenage son, portrayed by Benson. Occasionally lapses into melodrama, but all-in-all a decent adaptation of Thomas Thompson's book "Richie" which was based on a true story. Made for television. 97m/C VHS, Beta. Ben Gazzara, Robby Benson, Eileen Brennan, Clint Howard; **D:** Paul Wendkos. *BFA*

Death of the Incredible Hulk 🐾½ 1990 Scientist David Banner's new job just may provide the clues for stopping his transformation into the monstrous Incredible Hulk. But first there are terrorists after the Hulk who need to be defeated and Banner's new romance to contend with. Made for television. 96m/C VHS. Bill Bixby, Lou Ferrigno, Elizabeth Gracen, Philip Sterling; **D:** Bill Bixby. *RHI*

Death on the Nile 🐾🐾½ 1978 (PG) Agatha Christie's fictional detective, Hercule Poirot, is called upon to interrupt his vacation to uncover who killed an heiress aboard a steamer cruising down the Nile. Ustinov's first stint as the Belgian sleuth. Anthony Powell's costume design won an Oscar. 135m/C VHS, Beta, LV. *GB* Peter Ustinov, Jane Birkin, Lois Chiles, Bette Davis, Mia Farrow, David Niven, Olivia Hussey, Angela Lansbury, Jack Warden, Maggie Smith, George Kennedy, Simon MacCorkindale, Harry Andrews, Jon Finch; **D:** John Guillermin; **W:** Anthony Shaffer; **C:** Jack Cardiff; **M:** Nino Rota. Academy Awards '78: Best Costume Design; National Board of Review Awards '78: Best Supporting Actress (Lansbury). *REP*

Death Promise 🐾 1978 (R) Ho-hum excuse for a horror flick has murderous landlord trying to evict his tenants using whatever means are necessary. 90m/C VHS, Beta. Charles Bonet. *NO*

Death Race 2000 🐾🐾½ 1975 (R) In the 21st century, five racing car contenders challenge the national champion of a cross country race in which drivers score points by killing pedestrians. Gory fun. Based on the 1956 story by Ib Melchior, and followed by "Deathsport." Made for television. 80m/C VHS. David Carradine, Simone Griffeth, Sylvester Stallone, Mary Woronov; **D:** Paul Bartel; **W:** Charles B. Griffith, Robert Thom. *NHO*

Death Rage 🐾½ 1977 (R) A hitman comes out of retirement to handle the toughest assignment he has ever faced: search for and kill the man who murdered his brother. He finds out he's the victim of a Mafia doublecross. 92m/C VHS, Beta. *IT* Yul Brynner, Martin Balsam; **D:** Anthony (Antonio Margheriti) Dawson. *NO*

Death Ray woof! 19?? It's a race to the finish as terrorists threaten to unleash the world's most powerful weapon. A very poor James Bond rip-off. 93m/C VHS, Beta. Gordon Scott; **D:** Frank G. Carroll. *BFV, MRV*

Death Ray 2000 ♂½ *T.R. Sloane* 1981 Bondian superspy T.R. Sloane must search out the whereabouts of a stolen military device that could kill all life on Earth. TV pilot for the series "A Man Called Sloane." **100m/C VHS, Beta.** Robert F. Logan, Ann Turkel, Maggie Cooper, Dan O'Herlihy; **D:** Lee H. Katzin. *WOV, MOV*

Death Rides the Plains ♂♂ 1944 Western with a twist. A man lures prospective buyers to his ranch, kills them, and steals their money. It's up to our heroes to ride to the rescue. **53m/B VHS, Beta.** Robert Livingston, Al "Fuzzy" St. John, Nica Doret, Ray Bennett; **D:** Sam Newfield. *VYY, VDM*

Death Rides the Range ♂½ 1940 Russian spies start a range war as a cover for an operation to pipe helium off a ranch and over the border. Maynard, an undercover FBI agent posing as a cowboy, is out to stop them. **58m/B VHS.** Ken Maynard, Fay McKenzie, Ralph Peters, Julian Rivero, Charles "Blackie" King, John Elliott, Bud Osborne; **D:** Sam Newfield. *GPV, NOS, DVT*

Death Ring ♂ 1993 (R) Basic action/martial arts tale about three men who must battle the bad guys to ensure their own survival. **CW:** Language, strong violence, and sexuality. **91m/C VHS, LV.** Mike Norris, Chad McQueen, Isabel Glasser; **D:** Robert J. Kizer; **W:** George T. LeBrun. *COL, NLC*

Death Row Diner ♂½ 1988 A movie mogul, executed for a crime he didn't commit, is brought back to life by a freak electrical storm. Nothing will stop him from exacting revenge. **90m/C VHS.** Jay Richardson, Michelle (McClellan) Bauer, John Content, Tom Schell, Dennis Mooney, Frank Sarcinello Sr., Dana Mason. *NO*

Death Scream ♂♂ *Street Kill* 1975 Drama based on the New York murder of Kitty Genovese, whose cries for help while being assaulted went ignored by her neighbors. Good casting but the pacing deteriorates. Made for television. **100m/C VHS.** Raul Julia, John P. Ryan, Lucie Arnaz, Ed Asner, Art Carney, Diahann Carroll, Kate Jackson, Cloris Leachman, Tina Louise, Nancy Walker, Eric (Hans Gudegast) Braeden, Allyn Ann McLerie, Tony Dow, Sally Kirkland, Helen Hunt; **D:** Richard T. Heffron; **W:** Stirling Silliphant. *ACE*

Death Screams ♂ 1983 (R) Attractive college coeds have a party and get hacked to pieces for their troubles by a machete-wielding maniac. **88m/C VHS, Beta.** Susan Kiger, Jennifer Chase, Jody Kay, William T. Hicks, Martin Tucker. *GEM*

Death Sentence ♂½ *Murder One* 1974 When a woman juror on a murder case finds out that the wrong man is on trial, she is stalked by the real killer. Made for television. **74m/C VHS, Beta.** Cloris Leachman, Laurence Luckinbill, Nick Nolte, William Schallert; **D:** E.W. Swackhamer.

Death Ship ♂ 1980 (R) A luxury liner is destroyed by an ancient, mysterious freighter on open seas, leaving the survivors to confront the ghost ship's inherent evil in this slow-going horror flick. **91m/C VHS, Beta.** GB CA George Kennedy, Richard Crenna, Nick Mancuso, Sally Ann Howes, Saul Rubinek, Kate Reid, Victoria Burgoyne, Danny Higham, Jennifer McKinney; **D:** Alvin Rakoff; **W:** John Robins; **C:** Rene Verzier. *NLC*

Death Shot ♂ 1973 Two plainclothes detectives (who seem just as sleazy as the criminals they're trying to bust) try to break up a drug ring and find that, with a little coercion, their best sources of information are the pimps and junkies they want to stop. Senseless attempt to make an action pic. **90m/C VHS.** Richard C. Watt, Frank Himes; **D:** Mitch Brown. *NO*

Death Spa woof! 1987 (R) A health club is possessed by the spirit of a vengeful woman. The fitness craze takes on a campy new twist. **87m/C VHS.** William Bumiller, Brenda Bakke, Merritt Butrick; **D:** Michael Fischa. *MPI*

Death Sport ♂♂ 1978 (R) In this sequel to the cult hit "Death Race 2000," a group of humans play a game of death in the year 3000. The object is to race cars and kill as many competitors as possible. Not as good as the original, but still watchable. **83m/C VHS, Beta.** David Carradine, Claudia Jennings, Richard Lynch, William Smithers, Will Walker, David McLean, Jesse Vint; **D:** Henry Suso, Allan Arkush. *WAR, OM*

The Death Squad ♂½ 1973 A police commissioner hires an ex-cop to find a group of vigilante cops who are behind a series of gangland-style executions. Good cast, though that's about all this flick has got going for it. Made for television. **74m/C VHS, Beta.** Robert Forster, Melvyn Douglas, Michelle Phillips, Mark Goddard, Bert Remsen, Claude Akins; **D:** Harry Falk.

Death Stalk ♂½ 1974 Dream vacation turns nightmarish for two couples when the wives are taken hostage by several escaped convicts. Made for television. **90m/C VHS, Beta.** Vince Edwards, Vic Morrow, Anjanette Comer, Robert Webber, Carol Lynley, Neville Brand, Norman Fell; **D:** Robert Day. *CNG, GEM, HHE*

Death Target ♂½ 1983 Three former mercenaries team up for one last mission that gets sidetracked when one of the soldiers-of-fortune falls for a worker with a habit. **72m/C VHS, Beta.** Jorge Montesi, Elaine Lakeman; **D:** Peter Hyams.

Death Tide ♂♂ 1958 Hoodlums pirate a ship full of diamonds in this story of death and crime on the high seas. **?m/C VHS.** Frank Silvera. *SNC*

Death Train ♂½ 1979 Dead man seems to have been struck by a train, but clueless investigator can't figure out where the train came from. **96m/C VHS, Beta.** Hugh Keays-Byrne, Ingrid Mason, Max Meldrum; **D:** Igor Auzins. *NO*

Death Valley ♂½ 1946 Greed turns gold prospectors in Death Valley against each other. **70m/C VHS, Beta.** Robert Lowery, Helen Gilbert, Sterling Holloway; **D:** Lew (Louis Friedlander) Landers. *NO*

Death Valley ♂½ 1981 (R) Good cast, lousy plot. Youngster (Billingsley) gets caught up with a psycho cowpoke while visiting mom in Arizona. **90m/C VHS, Beta.** Paul LeMat, Catherine Hicks, Peter Billingsley, Wilford Brimley, Edward Herrmann, Stephen McHattie; **D:** Dick Richards; **C:** Stephen Burum. *USH*

Death Valley Days: No Gun Behind His Badge 1965 Western anthology series which ran on television from 1952-70 and was noted for its longtime sponsor, 20 Mule Team Borax, as well as its hosts, including Stanley Andrews, Ronald Reagan, Robert Taylor, and Dale Robertson. On this tape: the premiere episode plus "Halo for a Bad Man." Each additional tape contains two episodes. **55m/C VHS.** Robert Taylor, Ronald Reagan. *NO*

Death Valley Manhunt ♂♂ 1943 A marshal hired to protect a man's oil wells discovers that the company manager is keeping the profits for himself. **55m/B VHS, Beta.** Wild Bill Elliott, George "Gabby" Hayes, Anne Jeffreys; **D:** John English. *DVT*

Death Valley Rangers ♂½ 1944 The hero pretends to be an outlaw to expose a gang robbing gold-laden stagecoaches. **59m/B VHS, Beta.** Ken Maynard, Hoot Gibson, Bob Steele, Linda Brent, Kenneth Harlan; **D:** Robert Emmett Tansey. *NOS, DVT*

Death Warmed Up ♂½ 1985 A crazed brain surgeon turns ordinary people into bloodthirsty mutants, and a small group of young people travel to his secluded island to stop him. **83m/C VHS, Beta.** Michael Hurst, Margaret Umbers, David Letch; **D:** David Blyth. *ART, VES*

Death Warrant ♂♂ 1990 (R) Van Damme whams and bams a little less than usual in this cop-undercover-in-prison testosterone fest. As a Royal Canadian Mountie undercover in prison— where inmates are perishing under mysterious circumstances—the pectoral-perfect Muscles from Brussels is on the brink of adding two plus two when an inmate transferee threatens his cover. Contains the requisite gratuitous violence, prison bromide, and miscellaneous other Van Dammages. **111m/C VHS, LV, Closed Caption.** Jean-Claude Van Damme, Robert Guillaume, Cynthia Gibb, George Dickerson, Patrick Kilpatrick; **D:** Deran Sarafian; **C:** Russell Carpenter. *MGM*

Death Watch ♂♂♂ 1980 (R) In the future, media abuse is taken to an all time high as a terminally ill woman's last days are secretly filmed by a man with a camera in his head. Intelligent, adult science fiction with an excellent cast. **128m/C VHS, LV.** FR GE Romy Schneider, Harvey Keitel, Harry Dean Stanton, Max von Sydow; **D:** Bertrand Tavernier; **W:** Bertrand Tavernier, David Rayfiel.

Death Weekend ♂½ *House by the Lake* 1976 A woman is stalked by a trio of murderous, drunken hoodlums who seek to spoil her weekend. **89m/C VHS, Beta.** CA Brenda Vaccaro, Don Stroud, Chuck Shamata, Richard Ayres, Kyle Edwards; **D:** William Fruet. *ART, VES*

Death Wish ♂♂½ 1974 (R) A middle-aged businessman turns vigilante after his wife and daughter are violently attacked and raped by a gang of hoodlums (one is Goldblum in his film debut). He stalks the streets of New York seeking revenge on other muggers, pimps, and crooks, making the neighborhood safer for those less macho. **93m/C VHS, Beta, LV.** Charles Bronson, Vincent Gardenia, William Redfield, Hope Lange, Jeff Goldblum, Stuart Margolin, Olympia Dukakis; **D:** Michael Winner; **W:** Wendell Mayes; **M:** Herbie Hancock. *MGM, PAR*

Death Wish 2 woof! 1982 (R) Bronson recreates the role of Paul Kersey, an architect who takes the law into his own hands when his family is victimized once again. Extremely violent sequel to the successful 1974 movie. Followed by "Death Wish 3" (1985) and 4 (1987) in which Bronson continues to torture the street scum and the viewers as well. **89m/C VHS, Beta, LV.** J.D. Cannon, Charles Bronson, Jill Ireland, Vincent Gardenia, Anthony (Tony) Franciosa; **D:** Michael Winner; **M:** Jimmy Page. *WAR, OM*

Death Wish 3 ♂½ 1985 (R) Once again, Charles Bronson blows away the low lifes who have killed those who were dear to him and were spared in the first two films. **100m/C VHS, Beta, LV.** Charles Bronson, Martin Balsam, Deborah Raffin, Ed Lauter, Alex Winter, Marina Sirtis; **D:** Michael Winner; **M:** Jimmy Page. *MGM*

Death Wish 4: The Crackdown ♂ 1987 (R) The four-times-weary urban vigilante hits crack dealers this time, hard. **100m/C VHS, Beta, LV, Closed Caption.** Charles Bronson, John P. Ryan, Kay Lenz; **D:** J. Lee Thompson. *VTR*

Death Wish 5: The Face of Death woof! 1994 (R) Paul Kersey (Bronson) returns to vigilantism when his clothing manufacturer fiancee Olivia (Downs) has her business threatened by mobsters, one of whom turns out to be her sadistic ex (Parks). Bronson looks bored with the rehashed material. Lots of explicit and grisly violence. **CW:** Strong language, nudity, and extreme violence & cruelty. **95m/C VHS, LV, Closed Caption.** Charles Bronson, Lesley-Anne Down, Michael Parks, Kenneth Welsh; **D:** Allan Goldstein; **W:** Allan Goldstein; **M:** Terry Plumeri. *THV*

Death Wish Club ♂½ *Carnival of Fools* 1983 Young woman gets involved in a club with an unusual mission—suicide. **93m/C VHS, Beta.** Meridith Haze, Rick Barns, J. Martin Sellers, Ann Fairchild; **D:** John Carr. *NO*

Deathcheaters ♂½ 1976 (G) Australian Secret Service offers two stuntmen a top secret mission in the Philippines. **96m/C VHS, Beta.** John Hargreaves, Grant Page, Noel Ferrer; **D:** Brian Trenchard-Smith; **W:** Michael Cove. *VES*

Deathdream ♂♂½ *Dead of Night; Night Walk; The Veteran* 1972 In this reworking of the "Monkey's Paw" tale, a mother wishes her dead son would return from Vietnam. He does, but he's not quite the person he used to be. Gripping plot gives new meaning to the saying, "Be careful what you wish for—it might come true." 98m/C VHS, Beta. CA John Morley, Richard Backus, Lynn Carlin; D: Bob (Benjamin) Clark; W: Alan Ormsby. MPI

Deathfight 🎬½ 1993 (R) Let's face it, no one watches these movies because they have a plot. This is a fast-paced B-grade martial arts flick with numerous butts getting kicked. Oh, all right, if you insist on a plot—Norton's evil half-brother (Guerrero) is trying to turn their legitimate family business into a criminal front by framing Norton for murder. 92m/C VHS, Closed Caption. Richard Norton, Franco Guerrero, Karen Moncrieff, Chuck Jeffreys, Ron Vreeken, Tetchie Agbayani, Joe Mari Avellana; D: Anthony Maharaj; W: Tom Huckabee.

Deathhead Virgin 🎬½ 1974 (R) An evil virgin spirit is waiting to possess one of two men eager to find a sunken fortune. The fate of the fortunate one is only death! 94m/C VHS, Beta. Jock Gaynor, Larry Ward, Diane McBain, Vic Diaz. NO

Deathmask 🎬🎬 1969 A four-year-old boy's corpse is found buried in a cardboard box, and a medical examiner—whose daughter met a similar fate—investigates the murder. Could've been done more tastefully. 102m/C VHS, Beta. Farley Granger, Ruth Warrick, Danny Aiello; D: Richard S. Friedman. PRD

Deathmoon 🎬½ 1978 A businessman plagued by recurring werewolf nightmares goes on a Hawaiian vacation to try to forget his troubles. Made for television. 90m/C VHS, Beta. Robert Foxworth, Joe Penny, Debralee Scott, Dolph Sweet, Charles Haid; D: Bruce Kessler. NO

Deathrow Gameshow 🎬½ 1988 Condemned criminals can either win their freedom or die in front of millions on a new television show that doesn't win the host many friends. 78m/C VHS, Beta, LV. John McCafferty, Robin Bluthe, Beano, Mark Lasky; D: Mark Pirro; W: Mark Pirro.

Deathstalker woof! El Cazador de la Muerte 1983 (R) Deathstalker sets his sights on seizing the evil wizard Munkar's magic amulet so he can take over Munkar's castle. The only excuse for making such an idiotic film seems to have been to fill it with half-naked women. Filmed in Argentina and followed by two sequels that were an improvement. 80m/C VHS, Beta, LV. Richard Hill, Barbi Benton, Richard Brooker, Victor Bo, Lana Clarkson; D: John Watson; W: Howard R. Cohen. ART, VES

Deathstalker 2: Duel of the Titans 🎬🎬 1987 (R) Campy fantasy comically pits the lead character against an evil wizard. Sword-and-sorcery spoof doesn't take itself too seriously. 85m/C VHS, Beta, LV. John Terlesky, Monique Gabrielle, John Lazar, Toni Naples, Maria Socas, Queen Kong; D: Jim Wynorski; W: Jim Wynorski. ART, VES

Deathstalker 3 🎬½ Deathstalker 3: The Warriors From Hell 1989 (R) Another humorous entry in the Deathstalker saga. This time there's action, romance, magic and the Warriors From Hell. 85m/C VHS, Beta, LV. John Allen Nelson, Carla Herd, Terri Treas, Thom Christopher; D: Alfonso Corona. ART, VES, HHE

Deathstalker 4: Match of Titans 🎬 1992 (R) The sword and sorcery epic continues, with our hero revealing yet more musculature in his efforts to defeat an evil queen and her legion of stone warriors. CW: Adventure violence and sensuality. 85m/C VHS. Richard Hill, Maria Ford, Michelle Moffett, Brent Baxter Clark; D: Howard R. Cohen. NHO

Deathtrap 🎬🎬 1982 (PG) A creatively blocked playwright, his ailing rich wife, and a former student who has written a sure-fire hit worth killing for, are the principals in this compelling comedy-mystery. Cross and double-cross are explored in this film based on the Broadway hit by Ira Levin. 118m/C VHS, Beta. Henry Jones, Michael Caine, Christopher Reeve, Dyan Cannon, Irene Worth; D: Sidney Lumet; W: Jay Presson Allen; C: Andrzej Bartkowiak. WAR

The Decameron 🎬🎬🎬½ 1970 (R) Pasolini's first epic pageant in his "Trilogy of Life" series. An acclaimed, sexually explicit adaptation of a handful of the Boccaccio tales. In Italian with English subtitles. CW: Some language and sensuality. 111m/C VHS, Beta, LV, Letterbox. FR IT GE Franco Citti, Ninetto Davoli, Angela Luce, Patrizia Capparelli, Jovan Jovanovich, Silvana Mangano, Pier Paolo Pasolini; D: Pier Paolo Pasolini; C: Tonino Delli Colli; M: Ennio Morricone. Berlin International Film Festival '71: Silver Prize. WBF

Decameron Nights 🎬🎬½ 1953 Story of Boccaccio's pursuit of a recently widowed young women is interwoven amongst the three of the 14th century Italian writer's bawdy tales. 87m/C VHS, Beta. GB Louis Jourdan, Joan Fontaine, Binnie Barnes, Joan Collins, Marjorie Rhodes; D: Hugo Fregonese. NOS, MRV, GEM

Deceit 🎬🎬 1993 (R) A sci-fi sex comedy with an environmental premise. Bailey and Brick are two aliens working for their planet's Environmental Protection Agency, whose idea of protection is to vaporize polluter planets. Guess which planet is next on their hit list. But before they get down to business, our two alien studs want to do the horizontal bop with two of the local lovelies, who decide that isn't how they want to spend their last moments on earth. It has a happy ending. 92m/C VHS. Scott Paulin, Norbert Weisser, Samantha Phillips; D: Albert Pyun; W: Kitty Chalmers. COL

Deceived 🎬🎬½ 1991 (PG-13) A successful career woman with a passionate husband and a young daughter feels she has it all until her husband is apparently killed in a bizarre tragedy. But just how well did she know the man she married? Who was he really and what secrets are hidden in his past? As she struggles to solve these mysteries, her own life becomes endangered in this psychological thriller. 115m/C VHS, Beta, Closed Caption. Goldie Hawn, John Heard, Ashley Peldon, Jan Rubes, Amy Wright, Maia Filar, Robin Bartlett, Tom Irwin, Beatrice Straight, Kate Reid; D: Damian Harris; W: Mary Agnes Donoghue, Derek Saunders; C: Jack N. Green; M: Thomas Newman. TOU

Deceiver 🎬🎬 Liar 1997 (R) Contrived psychological thriller starts out with the requisite dead prostitute (Zellwegger, in a questionable career move) and the rounding up of the usual suspects, settling on disturbed but brainy Princeton grad Wayland (indie film icon Roth). Wayland uses his superior I.Q. and penchant for mind games to send head detectives Kennesaw and Braxton (Rooker and Penn) into a tailspin of deceit and lies, turning the investigation around on the gritty cops. Flashy camera work only adds to the tangled mayhem. Fine performances from talented cast bring this up a notch. Twin directors Jonas and Joshua Pate's convoluted spin on a noirish murder mystery follows up their 1996 debut, "Grave." CW: Violence, language and some sexual content. 102m/C VHS, Closed Caption. Renee Zellweger, Tim Roth, Christopher Penn, Michael Rooker, Ellen Burstyn, Rosanna Arquette; D: Jonas Pate, Josh Pate; W: Jonas Pate, Josh Pate; C: Bill Butler; M: Harry Gregson-Williams. MGM

The Deceivers 🎬🎬 1988 (PG-13) Brosnan stars as a British officer sent on a dangerous undercover mission in 1820s India. He's to infiltrate the notorious Thuggee cult, known for robbing and murdering unwary travelers. Interesting premise falters due to slow pacing and Brosnan's lack of believability. 112m/C VHS, Beta, LV, Closed Caption. IN GB Pierce Brosnan, Saeed Jaffrey, Shashi Kapoor, Keith Michell; D: Nicholas Meyer; C: Walter Lassally. MGM

December 🎬🎬 1991 (PG) Four prep-school students in New Hampshire must confront the reality of war when the Japanese bomb Pearl Harbor. A touching story of courage and friendship that takes place in one night during the surpise-attack. 92m/C VHS, Beta, LV, Closed Caption. Wil Wheaton, Chris Young, Brian Krause, Balthazar Getty, Jason London; D: Gabe Torres; W: Gabe Torres. NO

December Bride 🎬🎬½ 1991 Determined young woman (Reeves) becomes the housekeeper to two taciturn Irish farmer/brothers (Hinds and McCann) and proceeds to bully them into prosperity in early 20th century rural Ireland. She also scandalizes the community by sleeping with both men and refusing to marry either—even after she becomes pregnant. Based on the novel by Sam Hanna Bell. 88m/C VHS. IR Saskia Reeves, Ciaran Hinds, Donal McCann, Patrick Malahide, Brenda Bruce; D: Thaddeus O'Sullivan; W: David Rudkin; C: Bruno de Keyzer; M: Jurgen Knieper. FXL

December Flower 🎬🎬½ 19?? A young woman arrives at her aunt's estate so she can nurse her back to health, but she finds her aunt a bit down in the mouth: seems someone is trying to kill her, and she could be next in line. 65m/C VHS. Jean Simmons, Mona Washbourne, Bryan Forbes. FCT, MOV

December 7th: The Movie 🎬🎬½ 1991 Banned for 50 years by the U.S. Government, this planned Hollywood explanation to wartime audiences of the Pearl Harbor debacle offers such "offensive" images as blacks fighting heroically alongside whites, loyal Japanese-Americans, and Uncle Sam asleep on the morning of the attack. The Chief of Naval Operations confiscated the original film, claiming it demeaned the Navy. The battle scenes were so realistic they fooled even documentarians. This isn't the most incisive video on the event—just an unforgettable snapshot. 82m/B VHS. Walter Huston, Harry Davenport; D: John Ford. KIT, CPM, FUS

Deception 🎬🎬🎬 1946 Davis is a pianist torn between two loves: her intensely jealous sponsor (Rains) and her cellist boyfriend (Henreid). Plot in danger of going over the melodramatic edge is saved by the very effective performances of the stars. 112m/B VHS, Beta. Bette Davis, Paul Henreid, Claude Rains, John Abbott, Benson Fong; D: Irving Rapper. MGM

Deception 🎬½ Ruby Cairo 1992 (PG-13) Talented cast is wasted in an old-fashioned mystery that lacks a coherent script. MacDowell is married to Mortensen, the owner of an aircraft salvage company. He's supposedly killed in a plane crash but she thinks he's just pulled a fast one and sets off to find him. Tracking her hubby's secret bank accounts takes her all over the world, and finally to Cairo, Egypt where she meets Neeson. Together they discover Mortensen's scam involves smuggling poison gas and the duo then try to outwit the hoods on their trail. Film was originally released at 110 minutes. CW: Brief language and a shooting. 90m/C VHS, LV, Closed Caption. Andie MacDowell, Liam Neeson, Viggo Mortensen, Jack Thompson, Jeff Corey, Miriam Reed, Luis Cortes, Paco Mauri; D: Graeme Clifford; W: Robert Dillon, Michael Thomas; M: John Barry. ART

Deceptions 🎬🎬 1990 (R) A risque, semi-erotic thriller about a wealthy society woman (Sheridan) who kills her husband. Sheridan claims that she acted in self-defense, but macho cop Hamlin has a different view. He interrogates her, grows increasingly attracted, and is drawn into her web of seduction. 105m/C VHS, LV, Closed Caption. Harry Hamlin, Nicolette Sheridan. REP

Deceptions 2: Edge of Deception 🎬½ 1994 (R) Voyeur detective becomes obsessed with his comely neighbor, leading to unpleasant consequences. CW: Strong sexuality; violence; language. 100m/C VHS. Mariel Hemingway, Jennifer Rubin, Stephen Shellan; D: George Mihalka. AVE

The Decline of the American Empire 🎬🎬🎬½ Le Declin De L'Empire Americain 1986 (R) The critically acclaimed French-Canadian film about eight academic intellectuals who spend a weekend shedding their sophistication and engaging in intertwining sexual affairs. Examines the differing attitudes of men and women in regards to sex and sexuality. In French with English subtitles. **102m/C VHS, Beta.** *CA* Dominique Michel, Dorothee Berryman, Louise Portal, Genevieve Rioux; **D:** Denys Arcand; **W:** Denys Arcand. Genie Awards '87: Best Director (Arcand), Best Film, Best Supporting Actor (Arcand), Best Supporting Actress (Portal); New York Film Critics Awards '86: Best Foreign Film; Toronto-City Award '86: Best Canadian Feature Film; Nominations: Academy Awards '86: Best Foreign Language Film. *USH*

Decline of Western Civilization

1 🎬🎬🎬 **1981** The L.A. hard core punk scene. Music by X, Circle Jerks, Black Flag, Fear and more. **100m/C VHS, Beta, LV. D:** Penelope Spheeris. *MVD*

Decline of Western Civilization 2: The Metal Years

1988 (R) Following Spheeris's first documentary about hardcore punk, she in turn delves into the world of heavy metal rock. We are given a look at some of the early rockers, as well as some of the smaller bands still playing L.A. clubs. Features appearances by Alice Cooper, Ozzy Osbourne, Poison, Gene Simmons, and Megadeth. **90m/C VHS, Beta, Closed Caption.** Alice Cooper, Ozzy Osbourne, Gene Simmons, Lizzie Borden; **D:** Penelope Spheeris. *COL, MVD, FCT*

Deconstructing Harry 🎬🎬½ **1997 (R)**

Interesting idea has Allen as a successful author, Harry Block, whose thinly-veiled autobiographical fiction spills the beans on his ex-wives, lovers, friends, and family, thereby pissing them all off. Toggles back and forth between Harry's "real" life and scenes from his books, giving characters and situations two versions: one slanted to suit Harry and one more real than Harry wants or knows how to deal with. Infidelity, divorce, and art all get their usual treatment. Another not bad, but not great project by Allen that may be too self-absorbed for most. Features an elaborate, star-studded cast, mostly delegated to minor roles.**CW:** Strong language and some sexuality. **96m/C VHS.** Woody Allen, Billy Crystal, Judy Davis, Elisabeth Shue, Kirstie Alley, Caroline Aaron, Bob Balaban, Richard Benjamin, Eric Bogosian, Mariel Hemingway, Amy Irving, Julie Kavner, Eric Lloyd, Julia Louis-Dreyfus, Tobey Maguire, Demi Moore, Stanley Tucci, Robin Williams, Philip Bosco, Gene Saks, Hazelle Goodman; **D:** Woody Allen; **W:** Woody Allen; **C:** Carlo DiPalma. Nominations: Academy Awards '97: Best Original Screenplay. *NLC*

Deconstructing Sarah 🎬🎬 **1994 (R)**

Sarah Vincent (Ticotin) is a high-powered but bored ad exec who assumes an alter-ego, Ruth, when she heads for the wrong side of the tracks in her pursuit of casual sex. Her secret life is discovered when Sarah is murdered and best friend Elizabeth (Kelley) begins to turn up some likely suspects. Fast-paced whodunnit with good cast work. Made for cable TV.**CW:** Some sexuality. **120m/C VHS, LV, Closed Caption.** Rachel Ticotin, Sheila Kelley, A. Martinez, David Andrews, John Vickery, Jenifer Lewis, Dwier Brown, Peter Jason; **D:** Craig R. Baxley; **W:** Lee Rose; **C:** Joao Fernandes; **M:** Tom Scott. *USH*

Decoration Day 🎬🎬🎬 **1990 (PG)** Garner

plays a retired Southern judge who aids an angry childhood friend who has refused to accept his long-overdue Medal of Honor. Investigating the past leads to a decades-old mystery and a tragic secret that has repercussions for everyone involved. Based on the novel by John William Corrington. A Hallmark Hall of Fame presentation. **99m/C VHS, LV, Closed Caption.** James Garner, Bill Cobbs, Judith Ivey, Ruby Dee, Laurence "Larry" Fishburne, Jo Anderson; **D:** Robert Markowitz. *REP*

Decoy 🎬🎬½ **1995 (R)** Two ex-government

operatives, Baxter (Weller) and Travis (Patrick), are hired by their former commanding officer, Wellington (Breck), to protect his daughter Diana (Vogel) from business rival Jensen (Hylands) who's got a grudge against dad. But then it turns out the job's a set up, and Wellington and Jensen have their own deadly agenda.**CW:** Strong violence; some language. **98m/C VHS, LV.** Peter Weller, Robert Patrick, Darlene Vogel, Charlotte Lewis, Peter

Breck, Scott Hylands; **D:** Victor Rambaldi; **W:** Robert Sarno; **C:** Jon Kranhouse; **M:** Mark Adler. *TTC*

Dedee d'Anvers 🎬🎬½ *Dedee; Woman of*

Antwerp **1949** A gritty dockside melodrama about a drunken prostitute abused by her pimp. A sailor and a local barkeep don't like it. In French with subtitles. **95m/B VHS, Beta.** Simone Signoret, Marcel Dalio, Bernard Blier, Marcel Pagliero, Jane Marken; **D:** Yves Allegret; **C:** Jean Bourgoin. *NOS, FCT*

A Dedicated Man **1986** A lonely woman

agrees to act as a wife for a businessman to lend him credibility. A British "Romance Theater" presentation. **60m/C VHS.** *GB* Alec McCowen, Joan Plowright; **D:** Robert Knights.

The Deep 🎬🎬 **1977 (PG)** An innocent cou-

ple get involved in an underwater search for a shipwreck, and they quickly find themselves in over their heads. Gorgeous photography manages to keep this slow mover afloat. Famous for Bisset's wet T-shirt scene. Based on the novel by Peter Benchley. The laserdisc edition offers widescreen format. **123m/C VHS, Beta, LV, Letterbox.** Nick Nolte, Jacqueline Bisset, Robert Shaw, Louis Gossett Jr., Eli Wallach; **D:** Peter Yates; **W:** Peter Benchley, Tracy Keenan Wynn; **M:** John Barry. Nominations: Academy Awards '77: Best Sound.*GKK*

Deep Cover 🎬½ **1988 (R)** A man dares to

go beyond the walls of a mysterious English manor in order to expose the secrets that lie within the manor. **81m/C VHS, Beta.** Tom Conti, Donald Pleasence, Denholm Elliott, Kika Markham, Phoebe Nicholls; **D:** Richard Loncraine. *PAR*

Deep Cover 🎬🎬½ **1992 (R)** Fishburne

plays Russell Stevens Jr., a straight-arrow cop who goes undercover to infiltrate a Latin American cocaine cartel. While undercover, he becomes partners with drug dealer David Jason (Goldblum), and undergoes an inner transformation until he realizes he is betraying his cause. Confusing and commercial, yet marked with a moral rage.**CW:** Language, violence and drug use, and sensuality. **107m/C VHS, LV, Letterbox, Closed Caption.** Laurence "Larry" Fishburne, Jeff Goldblum, Victoria Dillard, Charles Martin Smith, Sydney Lassick, Clarence Williams III, Gregory Sierra, Roger Guenveur Smith, Cory Curtis, Glynn Turman, Def Jef; **D:** Bill Duke; **W:** Michael Tolkin, Henry Bean; **C:** Bojan Bazelli; **M:** Michel Colombier. *NLC*

Deep Down 🎬½ **1994 (R)** When young

Andy (Young) moves into a new apartment, he discovers his neighbor (Roberts) is a gorgeous married woman just looking for a little fun on the side. Too bad her husband (Segal) is a violent psychopath, totally suspicious of his wife's fidelity. Just how far will everyone go to get what they want? Also available in an unrated version.**CW:** Strong sexuality; language; some violence. **86m/C VHS, Closed Caption.** Tanya Roberts, Chris Young, George Segal. *IMP*

Deep End 🎬🎬🎬 **1970** A 15-year-old boy

working as an attendant in a bath house falls in love with a 20-year-old woman in this tragic tale of a young man obsessed. Good British cast and music by Cat Stevens. **88m/C VHS.** *GB GE* Jane Asher, John Moulder-Brown, Diana Dors, Karl Michael Vogler, Christopher Sandord; **D:** Jerzy Skolimowski; **W:** Jerzy Skolimowski, Jerzy Gruza, Bloeslav Sulik; **C:** Charly Steinberger; **M:** Cat Stevens. *NO*

Deep Impact 🎬🎬½ **1998 (PG-13)** Poor Mor-

gan Freeman. He gets a chance to play the President of the United States only to have his term shortened by a dastardly comet the size of the Grand Canyon. Although his presidency would have been more interesting, the destruction's the star of this show, as well as the touchy-feely interaction of various two-dimensional characters. There's the astronauts (led by Duvall) sent into space to nuke the thing; ordinary teenager Leo (Wood) who initially discovered the rock; and career-conscious news anchor (Leoni), who first breaks the story. The all-star cast is underused, but lend the film a sense of gravity by their pres-

ence. The remaining stick figure characters evoke more yawns than tears. Good thing the comet comes along to, ironically, inject a little life into the flick. The special effects are the best in recent film history, and worth the long, laborious wait.**CW:** Intense disaster related elements and brief language. **120m/C VHS.** Morgan Freeman, Robert Duvall, Tea Leoni, Elijah Wood, Vanessa Redgrave, Maximilian Schell, James Cromwell, Blair Underwood, Ron Eldard, Jon Favreau, Leelee Sobieski, Mary McCormack, Dougray Scott, Alexander Baluyev, Charles Martin Smith; **D:** Mimi Leder; **W:** Michael Tolkin, Bruce Joel Rubin; **C:** Dietrich Lohmann; **M:** James Horner. *NYR*

Deep in My Heart 🎬🎬½ **1954** A musical

biography of the life and times of composer Sigmund Romberg, with guest appearances by many MGM stars. 🎵Leg of Mutton; You Will Remember Vienna; Softly, as in a Morning Sunrise; Mr. & Mrs.; I Love to Go Swimmin' with Wimmin; The Road to Paradise; Will You Remember; It; Serenade. **132m/C VHS, Beta.** Jose Ferrer, Merle Oberon, Paul Henreid, Walter Pidgeon, Helen Traubel, Rosemary Clooney, Jane Powell, Howard Keel, Cyd Charisse, Gene Kelly, Ann Miller; **D:** Stanley Donen. *MGM*

Deep in the Heart 🎬🎬 *Handgun* **1983 (R)**

When a young teacher is raped at gunpoint on a second date, she takes the law into her own hands. Just-off-the-target film tries to take a stand against the proliferation of guns in the U.S. Thought-provoking all the same. **99m/C VHS, Beta.** *GB* Karen Young, Clayton Day, Ben Jones, Suzie Humphreys; **D:** Tony Garnett; **W:** Tony Garnett. *NO*

Deep Red 🎬🎬 **1994 (R)** When a young girl

has an encounter with an extra-terrestrial spacecraft her blood chemistry is mysteriously altered. Now the proteins her body manufactures can lead to immortality and ruthless scientist Newmeyer wants to take advantage of the fact—any way he can.**CW:** Violence. **85m/C VHS, LV, Closed Caption.** Michael Biehn, Joanna Pacula, John de Lancie; **D:** Craig R. Baxley; **W:** D. Brent Mote. *USH*

Deep Red: Hatchet Murders 🎬🎬½

The Hatchet Murders; Profundo Rosso; Dripping Deep Red; The Sabre Tooth Tiger; Deep Red **1975** A stylish but gruesome rock music-driven tale of a composer who reads a book on the occult which happens to relate to the sadistic, sangfroid murder of his neighbor. When he visits the book's author, he discovers that she has been horribly murdered as well. **100m/C VHS, Beta.** *IT* David Hemmings, Daria Nicolodi, Gabriele Lavia, Macha Meril, Eros Pagni, Giuliana Calandra, Erykah Badu, Clara Calamai, Nicoletta Elmi; **D:** Dario Argento; **W:** Dario Argento, Barnardino Zapponi; **C:** Luigi Kuveiller. *QVD*

Deep Rising 🎬🎬½ **1998 (R)** Huge sea ser-

pents cause massive destruction to the cruise ship Argonautica and put major dinks in the plans of mercenaries, led by Finnegan (Williams), who board the ship for greedy motives. Sticks to a reliable action-horror formula with the good sense to not take its characters or slimy creatures too seriously. Sea critters have inventive ways of disposing of extraneous cast members, resulting in gore aplenty. Slacker humor provided by Finnegan's sidekick Pantucci (Kevin J. O'Connor) injects the film with a certain goofiness. Typical B-movie fare that leans more toward guilty pleasure than quality entertainment.**CW:** Sci-fi violence and gore. **106m/C VHS.** Treat Williams, Famke Janssen, Anthony Heald, Kevin J. O'Connor, Wes Studi, Derrick O'Connor, Jason Flemyng, Djimon Hounsou; **D:** Stephen Sommers; **W:** Stephen Sommers; **C:** Howard Atherton; **M:** Jerry Goldsmith. *TOU*

Deep Six 🎬🎬½ **1958** A WWII drama that

examines the conflict between pacifism and loyalty. A staunch Quaker is called to active duty as a lieutenant in the U.S. Navy, where his beliefs put him into disfavor with shipmates. **110m/C VHS, Beta.** Alan Ladd, William Bendix, James Whitmore, Keenan Wynn, Efrem Zimbalist Jr., Joey Bishop; **D:** Rudolph Mate. *NO*

Deep Space 🎬½ 1987 A flesh-eating alien lands on earth and, after devouring a cop, is stalked by his partner. An "Alien" rip-off. Some humorous moments keep us from thinking too hard about how much the monster resembles our friend from "Alien." 90m/C VHS, Beta. Charles Napier, Ann Turkel, Ron Glass, Bo Svenson, Julie Newmar; *D:* Fred Olen Ray. *TWE*

Deepstar Six 🎬½ 1989 (R) When futuristic scientists try to set up an undersea research and missile lab, a group of subterranean monsters get in the way. 97m/C VHS, Beta, LV. Taurean Blacque, Nancy Everhard, Greg Evigan, Miguel Ferrer, Matt McCoy, Nia Peeples, Cindy Pickett, Marius Weyers; *D:* Sean S. Cunningham; *W:* Lewis Abernathy, Geof Miller. *ART*

The Deer Hunter 🎬🎬🎬🎬 1978 (R) A powerful and vivid portrait of Middle America with three steel-working friends who leave home to face the Vietnam War. Controversial, brutal sequences in Vietnam are among the most wrenching ever filmed; the rhythms and rituals of home are just as purely captured. Neither pro- nor anti-war, but rather the perfect evocation of how totally and forever altered these people are by the war. Emotionally shattering; not to be missed. 183m/C VHS, Beta, LV, Letterbox, DVD. Robert De Niro, Christopher Walken, Meryl Streep, John Savage, George Dzundza, John Cazale, Chuck Aspegren, Rutanya Alda, Shirley Stoler, Amy Wright; *D:* Michael Cimino; *W:* Deric Washburn, Michael Cimino; *C:* Vilmos Zsigmond; *M:* John Williams. Academy Awards '78: Best Director (Cimino), Best Film Editing, Best Picture, Best Sound, Best Supporting Actor (Walken); Directors Guild of America Awards '78: Best Director (Cimino); Golden Globe Awards '79: Best Director (Cimino); Los Angeles Film Critics Association Awards '78: Best Director (Cimino), National Film Registry '96;; New York Film Critics Awards '78: Best Film, Best Supporting Actor (Walken); National Society of Film Critics Awards '78: Best Supporting Actress (Streep); Nominations: Academy Awards '78: Best Actor (De Niro), Best Cinematography, Best Original Screenplay, Best Supporting Actress (Streep). *USH, FCT, BTV*

The Deerslayer 🎬½ 1978 Low-budget snoozer based on the classic novel by James Fenimore Cooper. Frontiersman Hawkeye and his Indian companion Chingachgook set out to rescue a beautiful Indian maiden and must fight bands of hostile Indians and Frenchmen along the way. 98m/C VHS, Beta. Steve Forrest, Ned Romero, John Anderson, Joan Prather; *D:* Richard Friedenberg; *M:* Andrew Belling. *NO*

Def by Temptation 🎬🎬 1990 (R) A potent horror fantasy about a young black theology student who travels to New York in search of an old friend. There he meets an evil woman who is determined to seduce him and force him to give in to temptation. Great soundtrack. 95m/C VHS, Beta, LV, DVD. James Bond III, Kadeem Hardison, Bill Nunn, Samuel L. Jackson, Minnie Gentry, Rony Clanton, Cynthia Bond, John Canada Terrell; *D:* James Bond III; *W:* James Bond III; *C:* Ernest R. Dickerson. *TTV*

Def-Con 4 🎬½ 1985 (R) Three marooned space travelers return to a holocaust-shaken Earth to try to start again, but some heavy-duty slimeballs are in charge and they don't want to give it up. Good special effects bolster a weak script. 85m/C VHS, Beta. Maury Chaykin, Kate Lynch, Tim Choate; *D:* Paul Donovan. *VTR*

Def Jam's How to Be a Player 🎬
How to Be a Player 1997 (R) Dray (Bellamy) thinks that monogamy is a wood used to build furniture. Although he has steady girlfriend Lisa (Voorhies), he also has several other ladies in waiting. He is, in fact, a player. He even teaches others to play. What he needs, however, is a screenplay. His sister Jenny (Desselle), who has been hurt in love, cracks the numerical code to his organizer, and invites all of Dray's harem to one party. The result of this booty intervention is Dray's abandonment of his promiscuous ways. The stand-up comedy roots of much of the cast translate into clunky performances, and the direction is pretty played out, too. *CW:* Strong sexual content and language. 93m/C VHS, LV. Bill Bellamy, Natalie Desselle, Mari Morrow, Jermaine Hopkins, A.J. Johnson, Max Julien, Beverly Johnson, Gilbert Gottfried, Bernie Mac, Elise Neal, Amber Smith, Lark Voorhies; *D:* Lionel C. Martin; *W:* Mark Brown, Demetria Johnson; *M:* Darren Floyd. *PGV*

The Defender 🎬🎬½ 1957 CBS "Studio One" presentation of a live courtroom drama. First shown in 1957. Made for television. 112m/B VHS, Beta. Steve McQueen, William Shatner, Ralph Bellamy, Martin Balsam. *FCT, RHI*

Defenders of the Law 🎬🎬 1931 Early action talkie concerned with gang warfare and law enforcement. 64m/B VHS. John Holland, Mae Busch, Alan Cooke, Joseph Girard, Edmund Breese, Catherine Dale Owen, Robert Gleckler; *D:* Joseph Levering. *GPV*

Defending Your Life 🎬🎬🎬 1991 (PG) Brooks' cock-eyed way of looking at the world travels to the afterlife in this uneven comedy/romance. In Judgment City, where everyone goes after death, past lives are examined and judged. If you were a good enough person you get to stay in heaven (where you wear funny robes and eat all you want without getting fat). If not, it's back to earth for another go-round. Brooks plays an L.A. advertising executive who crashes his new BMW and finds himself defending his life. When he meets and falls in love with Streep, his interest in staying in heaven multiplies. Occasionally charming, seldom out-right hilarious. 112m/C VHS, LV, 8mm, Letterbox, Closed Caption. Albert Brooks, Meryl Streep, Rip Torn, Lee Grant, Buck Henry, George Wallace, Lillian Lehman, Peter Schuck, Susan Walters; *D:* Albert Brooks; *W:* Albert Brooks; *C:* Allen Daviau; *M:* Michael Gore. *WAR*

The Defense Never Rests 🎬🎬 1990 Perry Mason, the lawyer who never loses a case, aids his friend and secretary, Della Street, in this made-for-television movie. 95m/C VHS, Beta. Raymond Burr, Barbara Hale, Al Freeman Jr., William Katt, Patrick O'Neal. *MCG*

Defense of the Realm 🎬🎬🎬½ 1985 (PG) A British politician is accused of selling secrets to the KGB through his mistress and only a pair of dedicated newspapermen believe he is innocent. In the course of finding the answers they discover a national cover-up conspiracy. An acclaimed, taut thriller. 96m/C VHS, Beta, LV, Closed Caption. *GB* Gabriel Byrne, Greta Scacchi, Denholm Elliott, Ian Bannen, Bill Paterson, Fulton Mackay, Robbie Coltrane; *D:* David Drury; *C:* Roger Deakins. British Academy Awards '85: Best Supporting Actor (Elliott). *COL*

Defense Play 🎬½ 1988 (PG) Two teenagers are unwittingly stuck in the middle of a Soviet plot to steal the plans that created a technologically advanced helicopter. 95m/C VHS, Beta. David Oliver, Susan Ursitti, Monte Markham, William Frankfather, Patch MacKenzie; *D:* Monte Markham. *TWE*

Defenseless 🎬🎬 1991 (R) Hershey tries hard in an unplayable part as a giddy attorney who finds herself trapped in a love-affair/legal case that turns murderous. Good cast and interesting twists contend with a sexist sub-text, which proves a woman can't "have it all." 106m/C VHS, LV, Closed Caption. Barbara Hershey, Sam Shepard, Mary Beth Hurt, J.T. Walsh, Sheree North; *D:* Martin Campbell; *W:* James Cresson; *M:* Trevor Jones. *ART*

Defiance 🎬🎬 1979 (PG) A former merchant seaman moves into a tenement in a run-down area of New York City. When a local street gang begins terrorizing the neighborhood, he decides to take a stand. Familiar plotline handled well in this thoughtful film. 101m/C VHS, Beta. Jan-Michael Vincent, Art Carney, Theresa Saldana, Danny Aiello; *D:* John Flynn; *W:* Tom Donnelly; *M:* John Beal, Basil Poledouris. *ORI, ART, VES*

Defiant 🎬½ *The Wild Pack; The Sandpit Generals* 1970 Two rival street gangs clash when one admits a young orphan boy in. 93m/C VHS, Beta. Kent Lane, John Rubinstein, Tisha Sterling; *D:* Hall Bartlett. *ART*

The Defiant Ones 🎬🎬🎬½ 1958 Thought-provoking story about racism revolves around two escaped prisoners (one black, one white) from a chain gang in the rural South. Their societal conditioning to hate each other dissolves as they face constant peril together. Critically acclaimed. 97m/B VHS, Beta, Closed Caption. Tony Curtis, Sidney Poitier, Theodore Bikel, Lon Chaney Jr., Charles McGraw, Cara Williams; *D:* Stanley Kramer; *W:* Nedrick Young, Harold Jacob Smith; *C:* Sam Leavitt; *M:* Stephen Dorff. Academy Awards '58: Best Black and White Cinematography, Best Story & Screenplay; British Academy Awards '58: Best Actor (Poitier); Golden Globe Awards '59: Best Film—Drama; New York Film Critics Awards '58: Best Director (Kramer), Best Film, Best Screenplay; Nominations: Academy Awards '58: Best Actor (Curtis), Best Actor (Poitier), Best Director (Kramer), Best Film Editing, Best Picture, Best Supporting Actor (Bikel), Best Supporting Actress (Williams). *MGM*

The Defilers 🎬 1965 (R) Disturbing, low-budget J.D. movie in which two thugs imprison a young girl in a basement and force her to be their love slave. ?m/B VHS. Byron Mabe, Jerome Eden, Mae Johnson; *D:* David Friedman. *SNC, TPV*

Deja Vu 🎬 1984 (R) A lame romantic thriller about the tragic deaths of two lovers and their supposed reincarnation 50 years later. 95m/C VHS, Beta, LV. *GB* Jaclyn Smith, Nigel Terry, Claire Bloom, Shelley Winters; *D:* Anthony Richmond; *W:* Ezra D. Rappaport; *M:* Pino Donaggio. *MGM*

Deja Vu 🎬🎬 1989 Thriller set in 1925 and moving between Chicago and Odessa. A Chicago hitman is hired by the mob to kill a traitor who has fled to Odessa. Niczypur, the traitor, has been using the newly opened Chicago-Constantinople-Odessa shipping line for his own smuggling operation. Filled with shoot-outs, brawls, and chases. In English, Russian, and Polish with English subtitles. 108m/C VHS. *PL* Jerzy Stuhr, Galina Pietrowa, Nikolai Karaczencow, Wladimir Golowin; *D:* Juliusz Machulski. *FCT*

The Deli 🎬🎬 1997 Johnny Amico (Starr) runs a New York deli, has a bad gambling habit and a big debt to mobster Tommy Tomatoes (Vincent), an outspoken Mama (Malina), and a colorful clientele. Not much happens, the budget is small, but the actors charm. 98m/C VHS. Mike Starr, Judith Malina, Matt Keeslar, Frank Vincent, Ice-T, Heather Matarazzo, Iman, Jerry Stiller; *D:* John A. Gallagher; *W:* John A. Gallagher, John Dorrian; *C:* Robert Lechterman; *M:* Ernie Mannix. *FCT*

The Deliberate Stranger 🎬🎬🎬 1986 Harmon is engrossing as charismatic serial killer Ted Bundy, sentenced to death for several Florida murders and suspected in the killings of a least 25 women in several states. After eluding police for five years Bundy was finally arrested in Florida in 1979. His case became a cause celebre on capital punishment as it dragged on for nine years. Bundy was finally executed in 1989. Based on the book "Bundy: The Deliberate Stranger" by Richard W. Larsen. Made for television. 188m/C VHS, Beta. Mark Harmon, M. Emmet Walsh, Frederic Forrest, John Ashton, George Grizzard, Ben Masters, Glynnis O'Connor, Bonnie Bartlett, Billy Green Bush, Lawrence Pressman; *D:* Marvin J. Chomsky. *WAR, PMS*

The Delicate Delinquent 🎬🎬½ 1956 Lewis's first movie without Dean Martin finds him in the role of delinquent who manages to become a policeman with just the right amount of slapstick. 101m/B VHS, Beta, LV, Closed Caption. Jerry Lewis, Darren McGavin, Martha Hyer, Robert Ivers, Horace McMahon; *D:* Don McGuire; *W:* Don McGuire. *PAR*

Delicatessen 🎬🎬🎬 1992 (R) Set in 21st-century Paris, this hilarious debut from directors Jeunot and Caro focuses on the lives of the oddball tenants of an apartment building over a butcher shop. Although there is a famine, the butcher shop is always stocked with fresh meat—made from the building's tenants. Part comedy, part horror, part romance, this film merges a cacophony of sights and sounds with intriguing results. Watch for the scene involving a symphony of creaking bed springs, a squeaky bicycle pump, a cello, and clicking knitting needles. In French with English subtitles. **95m/C VHS, Beta, LV, Closed Caption.** *FR* Marie-Laure Dougnac, Dominique Pinon, Karin Viard, Jean Claude Dreyfus, Ticky Holgado, Anne Marie Pisani, Edith Ker, Patrick Paroux, Jean-Luc Caron; *D:* Jean-Pierre Jeunet, Marc Caro; *W:* Gilles Adrien; *C:* Darius Khondji; *M:* Carlos D'Alessi. Cesar Awards '92: Best Art Direction/Set Decoration, Best Writing. *PAR, BTV*

Delightfully Dangerous 🎞🎞 1945
Often Deadly Dull. A farfetched musical rooted in yesteryear about mismatched sisters, one a 15-year-old farm girl, the other a New York burlesque dancer, in competition on Broadway. 🎵 I'm Only Teasin'; In a Shower of Stars; Mynah Bird; Through Your Eyes to Your Heart; Delightfully Dangerous; Once Upon a Song. **92m/B VHS.** Jane Powell, Ralph Bellamy, Constance Moore, Arthur Treacher, Louise Beavers; *D:* Arthur Lubin. *DVT, NOS, VDM*

Delinquent Daughters 🎞½ 1944
Slow-paced drama about a high school girl who commits suicide and the cop and reporter who try to find out why so darn many kids are getting into trouble. **71m/B VHS, Beta.** June Carlson, Fifi d'Orsay, Teala Loring; *D:* Al(bert) Herman. *SNC, VYY, DVT*

Delinquent Parents 🎞½ 1938
A wayward girl gives up her baby for adoption. She turns her life around and becomes a juvenile court judge. Years later, who should come up before her for misdeeds but her long-lost daughter. The Hound cannot improve on a contemporary critic who renamed this "Delinquent Producers." **62m/B VHS.** Doris Weston, Maurice Murphy, Helen MacKellar, Terry Walker, Richard Tucker, Morgan Wallace; *D:* Nick Grinde. *NOS, LOO*

Delinquent School Girls woof! *Bad Girls* 1984 (R)
Three escapees from an asylum get more than they bargained for when they visit a Female Correctional Institute to fulfill their sexual fantasies. Buys into just about every conceivable stereotype. **89m/C VHS, Beta.** Michael Pataki, Bob Minos, Stephen Stucker; *D:* Gregory Corarito. *ART, VES*

Delirious 🎞½ 1991 (PG)
A writer for a television soap opera wakes from a bash on the head to find himself inside the story where murder and mayhem are brewing. Can he write himself back to safety, and find romance along the way? Somehow Candy just isn't believeable as a romantic lead and the film has few laughs. **96m/C VHS, Beta, LV, 8mm, Closed Caption.** John Candy, Mariel Hemingway, Emma Samms, Raymond Burr, David Rasche, Dylan Baker, Charles Rocket, Jerry Orbach, Renee Taylor, Robert Wagner; *D:* Tom Mankiewicz; *W:* Lawrence J. Cohen; *M:* Cliff Eidelman. *MGM*

Delirium woof! *Psycho Puppet* 1977
Homicidal maniac goes on a killing spree and has just one thing in mind—women. Angry group of citizens inadvertently includes the demonic villain in their vigilante club. Nothing redeeming here. **94m/C VHS, Beta.** Turk Cekovsky, Debi Shanley, Terry Ten Broeck; *D:* Peter Maris. *NO*

Deliverance 🎞🎞🎞🎞 1972 (R)
Terrifying exploration of the primal nature of man and his alienation from nature, based on the novel by James Dickey, which he adapted for the film (he also makes an appearance as a sheriff). Four urban professionals, hoping to get away from it all for the weekend, canoe down a southern river, encounter crazed backwoodsmen, and end up battling for survival. Excellent performances all around, especially by Voight. Debuts for Beatty and Cox. Watch for O'Neill as a sheriff, and director Boorman's son Charley as Voight's son. "Dueling Banjos" scene and tune are memorable as is scene where the backwoods boys promise to make the fellows squeal like pigs. **109m/C VHS, Beta, LV, Letterbox.** Jon Voight, Burt Reynolds, Ronny Cox, Ned Beatty, James Dickey, Bill McKinney, Ed O'Neill, Charley Boorman; *D:* John Boorman; *W:* James Dickey; *C:* Vilmos Zsigmond; *M:* Eric Weissburg. Nominations: Academy Awards '72: Best Director (Boorman), Best Film Editing, Best Picture. *WAR, FCT*

Delivery Boys 🎞½ 1984 (R)
The "Delivery Boys," three breakdancers aiming to win the $10,000 New York City Break-Off, find unusual perils that may keep them from competing. **94m/C VHS, Beta.** Joss Marcano, Tom Sierchio, Jim Soriero, Mario Van Peebles, Samantha Fox; *D:* Ken Handley. *VTR*

Delos Adventure 🎞 1986 (R)
A geological expedition in South America stumbles upon covert Russian activities and must battle to survive in this overly violent actioner. **98m/C VHS, Beta.** Roger Kern, Jenny Neumann, Kevin Brophy; *D:* Joseph Purcell. *TWE*

The Delta 🎞🎞 1997
White, middleclass Memphis teenager Lincoln Bloom (Gray) is leading a double life. He parties with his girlfriend Monica (Huss) and macho buddies but also sneaks off to cruise the city's gay pick-up spots. Which is where he meets the older John (Chan), an Amerasian immigrant from Vietnam, whose unknown father was a black soldier. The two have a brief romantic idyll but while the openly gay John is desperate for love, Lincoln is still uncertain about his sexual identity and the disparity between their lives. Feature debut for both Sachs and his two lead actors. **85m/C VHS.** Shayne Gray, Thang Chan, Rachel Zan Huss, Ricky Little; *D:* Ira Sachs; *W:* Ira Sachs; *C:* Benjamin P. Speth; *M:* Michael Rohatyn. *NYR*

Delta Force 🎞🎞 1986 (R)
Based on the true hijacking of a TWA plane in June 1985. Arab terrorists take over an airliner; the Delta Force, led by Lee Marvin and featuring Norris as its best fighter, rescue the passengers in ways that cater directly to our nationalistic revenge fantasies. Average thriller, exciting and tense at times, with fine work from Marvin, Norris, and Forster. **125m/C VHS, Beta, LV, Closed Caption.** Lee Marvin, Chuck Norris, Shelley Winters, Martin Balsam, George Kennedy, Hanna Schygulla, Susan Strasberg, Bo Svenson, Joey Bishop, Lainie Kazan, Robert Forster, Robert Vaughn, Kim Delaney; *D:* Menahem Golan; *W:* James Bruner; *M:* Alan Silvestri. *VTR*

Delta Force 2: Operation Stranglehold 🎞½ 1990 (R)
Delta Force is back with martial artist and military technician Norris at the helm. Action-packed and tense. **110m/C VHS, Beta, LV, Closed Caption.** John P. Ryan, Chuck Norris, Billy Drago, Richard Jaeckel, Paul Perri; *D:* Aaron Norris; *W:* Lee Reynolds; *C:* Joao Fernandes. *BTV, VTR*

Delta Force 3: The Killing Game 🎞½ *Young Commandos* 1991 (R)
A terrorist mastermind plants an atomic bomb in an American city, and the President has only one choice...call in the Delta Force. The leading men in this lackluster thriller are the sons of some of Hollywood's biggest stars. **CW:** Language and war violence. **97m/C VHS, LV.** Nick Cassavetes, Eric Douglas, Mike Norris, Matthew Penn, John P. Ryan, Sandy Ward; *D:* Sam Firstenberg; *W:* Boaz Davidson.

Delta Force Commando 🎞½ 1987 (R)
Two U.S. Fighter pilots fight against terrorism in the deadly Nicaraguan jungle. **90m/C VHS.** Fred Williamson, Bo Svenson. *VES, RHI*

Delta Force Commando 2 🎞 *Priority Red One* 1990 (R)
The celluloid was hardly dry on the first "Delta Force Commando" before the resourceful Italians began grinding out this follow-up, with the lead commando getting the Force entangled in a deadly international conspiracy. **CW:** Some language and strong violence. **100m/C VHS.** *IT* Richard Hatch, Fred Williamson, Giannina Facio, Van Johnson; *D:* Frank Valenti. *ART*

Delta Fox 🎞🎞 1977
Delta Fox is carrying a million dollars for the mob, but the mob is carrying a grudge and the chase is on. **90m/C VHS, Beta.** Priscilla Barnes, Richard Lynch, Stuart Whitman, John Ireland; *D:* Beverly Sebastian, Ferd Sebastian. *NO*

Delta Heat 🎞🎞 1992 (R)
A new designer drug hits L.A. and detective Mike Bishop (Edwards) follows his partner to the drug's source in Louisiana. When Bishop arrives he discovers his partner has been tortured and murdered in order to keep the drug lord's foes in line. Bishop must then save himself and find justice in the steamy streets of New Orleans. Routine lone guy vs. bad guys actioner. **CW:** Language and violence. **91m/C VHS, Closed Caption.** Anthony Edwards, Lance Henriksen, Betsy Russell, Linda Dona, Rod Masterson, John McConnell, Clyde Jones; *D:* Michael Fischa.

Delta of Venus 🎞½ 1995 (R)
Paris, 1940—beautiful young American Elena (England), an aspiring author, falls for handsome Lawrence (Mandylor), a writer of dirty books. But she finds out Lawrence isn't faithful and winds up supporting herself as a nude model and writing her own erotic tales. Lots of sex scenes and an equal amount of pretensions. Based on the erotic novel "Delta of Venus" by Anais Nin. Prague substitutes for Paris as the film location. Also availble unrated; the theatrical version came out as NC-17. **CW:** Strong erotic content. **100m/C VHS, LV, Closed Caption.** Audie England, Costas Mandylor, Erick Da Silva, Raven Snow; *D:* Zalman King; *W:* Patricia Louisianna Knop, Elisa Rothstein; *C:* Eagle Egilsson; *M:* George S. Clinton. *NLC*

Deluge 🎞🎞 1933
Tidal waves causd by earthquakes have destroyed most of New York (though some may think this is no great loss) in this early sci-fi pic. **72m/B VHS, Beta.** Edward Van Sloan, Peggy Shannon, Sidney Blackmer, Fred Kohler Sr., Matt Moore, Samuel S. Hinds, Lane Chandler; *D:* Felix Feist. *EEL*

The Deluge 🎞🎞 *Potop* 1973
Romance woven around the Polish-Swedish war in the 17th century. Adapted from the 1886 novel by Nobel prize-winning author Henryk Sienkiewicz, and filmed largely on location in authentic castles of the era. Polish with subtitles. **185m/C VHS.** *PL* Daniel Olbrychski, Malgorzata Braunek, Wladyslaw Hancza, Leszek Herdegen, Andrzej Lapicki; *D:* Jerzy Hoffman; *C:* Jerzy Wojcik; *M:* Kazimierz Serocki. Nominations: Academy Awards '73: Best Foreign Language Film. *FCT*

Delusion 🎞½ *The House Where Death Lives* 1984 (R)
Gothic thriller in which invalid Cotten and family are harassed by a possibly supernatural killer as told by Cotten's nurse. Filmed in 1980. Ending is a let-down. **93m/C VHS, Beta.** Patricia Pearcy, David Hayward, John Dukakis, Joseph Cotten, Simone Griffeth; *D:* Alan Beattie.

Delusion 🎞🎞½ 1991 (R)
A yuppie with an embezzled fortune is held up in the Nevada desert by a psycho hood with a showgirl lover. But who's really in charge here? The snappy, hip, film-noir thriller takes a few unlikely twists and has an open Lady-or-the-Tiger finale that may infuriate. Available in a widescreen edition on laserdisc. **CW:** Language and sensuality. **100m/C VHS, LV, Letterbox.** Jim Metzler, Jennifer Rubin, Kyle Secor, Robert Costanzo, Tracey Walter, Jerry Orbach; *D:* Carl Colpaert; *W:* Carl Colpaert, Kurt Voss; *M:* Barry Adamson. *COL*

Delusions of Grandeur 🎞🎞½ *La Folle des Grandeurs* 1976
A French comedy of court intrigue set in 17th-century Spain. In French with English subtitles. Based loosely on Victor Hugo's "Ruy Blas." **85m/C VHS, Beta.** *FR* Yves Montand, Louis de Funes, Alice Sapritch, Karin Schubert, Gabriele Tinti; *D:* Gerard Oury. *FCT*

Demented 🎞 1980 (R)
Beautiful and talented woman is brutally gang-raped by four men, but her revenge is sweet and deadly as she entices each to bed and gives them a big dose of their own medicine. All-too-familiar plot offers nothing new. **92m/C VHS, Beta.** Sallee Elyse, Bruce Gilchrist.

Dementia 13 🎞🎞½ *The Haunted and the Hunted* 1963
This eerie thriller, set in a creepy castle, is an early Coppola film about the members of an Irish family who are being offed by an axe murderer one by one. **75m/B VHS, Beta.** William Campbell, Luana Anders, Bart Patton, Patrick Magee, Barbara Dowling; *D:* Francis Ford Coppola; *W:* Francis Ford Coppola; *C:* Ethne Dunn. *VYY, MRV, SNC*

Demetrius and the Gladiators 🎬🎬½ 1954 A sequel to "The Robe," wherein the holy-robe-carrying slave is enlisted as one of Caligula's gladiators and mixes with the trampy empress Messalina. **101m/C VHS, Beta, LV, Closed Caption.** Victor Mature, Susan Hayward, Michael Rennie, Debra Paget, Anne Bancroft, Jay Robinson, Barry Jones, Richard Egan, William Marshall, Ernest Borgnine; **D:** Delmer Daves; **W:** Philip Dunne; **C:** Milton Krasner. *FOX*

The Demi-Paradise 🎬🎬🎬 *Adventure for Two* 1943 Tongue-in-cheek look at people's perceptions of foreigners has Olivier as a Russian inventor (?!) who comes to England with some trepidation. Though the Brits are plenty quirky, he manages to find romance with Ward in this charming look at British life. **110m/B VHS, Beta.** *GB* Laurence Olivier, Penelope Dudley Ward, Margaret Rutherford, Wilfrid Hyde-White; **D:** Anthony Asquith. *NOS, VDM, DVT*

Demolition 🎬½ 1977 Ex-international courier finds that the "simple" task he has consented to do for his old employers is deceptively hazardous. **90m/C VHS, Beta.** John Waters, Belinda Giblin, Fred Steele, Vincent Ball; **D:** Kevin J. Dobson. *NO*

Demolition High 🎬🎬½ 1995 (R) Standard actioner finds New York kid Lenny (Haim) having problems adjusting to his new California high school, where he's labeled a troublemaker. But real trouble comes along when a group of terrorists, fleeing police after a robbery, take over the school and hold the teachers and students as hostages. Fortunately, Lenny is able to lead a secret counterattack. **CW:** Violence and some language. **85m/C VHS, Closed Caption.** Corey Haim, Alan Thicke, Jeff Kober, Dick Van Patten; **D:** Jim Wynorski; **W:** Steve Jankowski; **C:** Zoran Hochstatter; **M:** Kevin Kiner. *CAF*

Demolition Man 🎬🎬 1993 (R) No-brain sci-fier rests on the action skills of Stallone and Snipes. Psychovillain Snipes (sporting a Dennis Rodman 'do) is pursued by equally violent cop Stallone in the late 1990s. Then they're cryogenically frozen, defrosted in 2032, and back to their old tricks. One problem. This is not a fun future: virtual reality sex is the only kind allowed and puritan ethics and political correctness are enforced to the max. Cop and bad guy get to show this highly orderly society some really violent times. Implausible plot and minimal acting, but lots of action and violence for fans. **CW:** Strong language, partial nudity, and non-stop action violence. **115m/C VHS, Beta, LV, 8mm, Letterbox, Closed Caption.** Sylvester Stallone, Wesley Snipes, Sandra Bullock, Nigel Hawthorne, Benjamin Bratt, Bob Gunton, Glenn Shadix, Denis Leary; **D:** Marco Brambilla; **W:** Daniel Waters, Robert Reneau, Peter M. Lenkov; **M:** Elliot Goldenthal. Nominations: MTV Movie Awards '94: Best Villain (Snipes). *WAR*

The Demolitionist 🎬🎬 1995 (R) Tough undercover cop Alyssa Lloyd (Eggert) is killed by crimelord Mad Dog Burne (Grieco) and then resurrected by scientist Jack Crowley (Abbott) as a hard-hitting futuristic superheroine who's out to save Metro City from evil. **CW:** Strong violence, some nudity and language. **100m/C VHS, LV.** Nicole Eggert, Richard Grieco, Bruce Abbott, Susan Tyrrell, Peter Jason, Sarah Douglas, Andras Jones, Heather Langenkamp, David Anthony Marshall, Jack Nance, Tom Savini; **D:** Robert Kurtzman; **W:** Brian DiMuccio, Dino Vindeni; **C:** Marcus Hahn; **M:** Leland Hahn. *APX*

The Demon 🎬🎬½ 1981 (R) A small town may be doomed to extinction, courtesy of a monster's thirst for the blood of its inhabitants. **94m/C VHS, Beta.** Cameron Mitchell, Jennifer Holmes. *NO*

Demon Barber of Fleet Street 🎬🎬½ *Sweeney Todd: The Demon Barber of Fleet Street* 1936 Loosely based on an actual event, this film inspired the 1978 smash play "Sweeney Todd." Slaughter stars as a mad barber who doesn't just cut his client's hair. He happens to have a deal cooked up with the baker to provide him with some nice 'juicy' filling for his meat pies.

Manages to be creepy and funny at the same time. **68m/B VHS, Beta.** *GB* Tod Slaughter, Eve Lister, Bruce Seton; **D:** George King. *VYY, MRV, SNC*

Demon City Shinjuku 🎬🎬½ 1993 In the near future the evil Levih Rah has created a Demon City in Shinjuku, located in the heart of Tokyo, where he commands his army of thugs and monsters. Sayama and the streetwise Kyoya venture into Shinjuku in search of Sayama's kidnapped father. They encounter the mystical Mephisto, who may be able to help them, but time is running out—Levih Rah is set to destroy the entire planet in three days! In Japanese with English subtitles. **82m/C VHS, LV.** *JP CPM*

Demon for Trouble 🎬 1934 Outlaws are murdering land buyers in this routine western. **58m/B VHS, Beta.** Bob Steele. *NOS, RXM*

Demon Hunter 🎬½ 1988 Terror reigns while a deranged killer stalks his next victim. **90m/C VHS, Beta.** George Ellis, Erin Fleming, Marrianne Gordon; **D:** Massey Cramer; **W:** Bob Corley.

A Demon in My View 🎬🎬½ 1992 (R) In a role similar to his infamous Norman Bates in "Psycho," Perkins stars as a man who hides a terrible secret—he is a former serial killer. When a fellow tenant in his apartment house accidentally destroys his doll, Perkins' tenuous sanity is shaken and he begins killing again. A smart thriller. Perkins last big-screen role. **CW:** Violence and some sexuality. **98m/C VHS, LV, Closed Caption.** Anthony Perkins, Sophie Ward, Stratford Johns; **D:** Petra Haffter; **W:** Petra Haffter. *THV, MOV*

The Demon Lover woof! *Devil Master; Master of Evil* 1977 (R) Leader of a satanic cult calls forth the devil when he doesn't get his way. Poorly acted and badly produced. Features comic book artists Val "Howard the Duck" Mayerick and Gunnar "Leatherface" Hansen. **87m/C VHS, Beta.** Christmas Robbins, Val Mayerick, Gunnar Hansen, Tom Hutton, David Howard; **D:** Donald G. Jackson, Jerry Younkins; **W:** Donald G. Jackson, Jerry Younkins. *UNI, PMR*

Demon Lust 🎬 19?? A couple's lovely country vacation is turned into a nightmare when two drifters terrorize them. **76m/C VHS, Beta. D:** Bernard Buys.

Demon of Paradise woof! 1987 (R) Dynamite fishing off the coast of Hawaii unearths an ancient, man-eating lizard-man. Uneven, unexciting horror attempt. **84m/C VHS, Beta.** Kathryn Witt, William Steis, Leslie Huntly, Laura Banks, Frederick Bailey; **D:** Cirio H. Santiago; **W:** Frederick Bailey; **C:** Ricardo Remias. *WAR*

Demon Possessed 🎬½ 1993 (R) When Tom is critically injured in a snowmobile race in a remote woods, he and his friends find shelter in a deserted children's camp. It turns out the camp was run by a secret religious cult that practiced occult murder and the demon that haunted the place has never left. When Tom dies this satanic spirit finds the perfect host to return to human form and continue its bloody work. **97m/C VHS, LV.** Dawn Laurrie, Aaron Kjenass, David Fields, Eve Montgomery; **D:** Christopher Webster; **W:** Julian Weaver; **M:** John Tatgenhorst.

Demon Queen 🎬 1980 A vampirish woman seduces, then murders, many men. **70m/C VHS, Beta.** Mary Fanaro, Dennis Stewart, Cliff Dance; **D:** Donald Farmer. *NO*

Demon Rage 🎬½ *Satan's Mistress; Fury of the Succubus; Dark Eyes* 1982 (R) Neglected housewife drifts under the spell of a phantom lover. **98m/C VHS, Beta.** Britt Ekland, Lana Wood, Kabir Bedi, Don Galloway, John Carradine, Sherry Scott; **D:** James Polakof. *HHE*

Demon Seed 🎬🎬🎬 1977 (R) When a scientist (Weaver) and his wife (Christie) separate so he can work on "Proteus," a somewhat biological supercomputer, the terminal within his computer-controlled home allows Proteus to infiltrate, taking over the house and his wife. Proteus' intent? To procreate. Bizarre and taut; based on a Dean Koontz novel. **97m/C VHS, Beta, LV.** Julie Christie, Fritz

Weaver, Gerrit Graham, Berry Kroeger, Ron Hays, Lisa Lu, Larry J. Blake; **D:** Donald Cammell; **W:** Robert Jaffe, Roger O. Hirson; **C:** Bill Butler; **V:** Robert Vaughn. *MGM*

Demon Wind 🎬½ 1990 (R) A gateway to Hell opens up on a secluded farm and various heroic types try to close it. Meanwhile, demons attempt to possess those humans in their midst. Zombies abound in this near-woof. **97m/C VHS, Beta, LV.** Eric Larson, Francine Lapensee, Rufus Norris; **D:** Charles Philip Moore. *PAR*

Demon with a Glass Hand 🎬½ 1964 In the vein of "The Terminator," a man goes back two hundred years in time to escape the evil race that rules the planet. **63m/B VHS, Beta.** Robert Culp, Arlene Martel, Abraham Sofaer. *MGM*

Demonic Toys 🎬½ 1990 (R) The possessed play-things attack a bunch of unfortunates in a warehouse, and pumped-up lady cop Scoggins deserves an award for keeping a straight face. Skimpily scripted gore from the horror assembly-line at Full Moon Productions. Far more entertaining are the multiple behind-the-scenes featurettes on the tape. **CW:** Language and fantasy/horror violence. **86m/C VHS, Beta, LV, Closed Caption.** Tracy Scoggins, Bentley Mitchum, Michael Russo, Jeff Weston, Daniel Cerney, Pete Schrum; **D:** Peter Manoogian. *PAR*

Demonoid, Messenger of Death 🎬 *Macabra* 1981 (R) Discovery of an ancient temple of Satan worship drastically changes the lives of a young couple when the husband becomes possessed by the Demonoid, which initially takes on the form of a severed hand. Poor script needs hand, producing a number of unintentionally laughable moments. **85m/C VHS, Beta.** Samantha Eggar, Stuart Whitman, Roy Cameron Jenson; **D:** Alfredo Zacharias.

The Demons 🎬 *Les Demons; Los Demonios* 1974 (R) As she slips into death, a tortured woman curses her torturers. **CW:** Contains graphic violence, nudity, and sexual content. **116m/C VHS, Beta.** *FR PT* Anne Libert, Britt Nichols, Doris Thomas, Howard Vernon, Karin Field, Luis Barboo; **D:** Jess (Jesus) Franco, Clifford Brown; **W:** Jess (Jesus) Franco. *UNI, VSM*

Demons 🎬½ *Demoni* 1986 (R) A horror film in a Berlin theatre is so involving that its viewers become the demons they are seeing. The new monsters turn on the other audience members. Virtually plotless, very explicit. Rock soundtrack by Accept, Go West, Motley Crue, and others. Revered in some circles, blasted in others. Followed by "Demons 2." **89m/C VHS, Beta, LV.** *IT* Urbano Barberini, Natasha Hovey, Paolo Cozza, Karl Zinny, Fiore Argento, Fabiola Toledo, Nicoletta Elmi; **D:** Lamberto Bava; **W:** Lamberto Bava, Dario Argento, Franco Ferrini, Dardano Sacchetti; **C:** Gianlorenzo Battaglia.

Demons 2 🎬½ 1987 Inferior sequel to "Demons." The son of horror-meister Mario Bava, Lamberto collaborated with Italian auteur Argento (who co-wrote and produced) to create an improbable sequel (storywise) which seems to have been edited by some kind of crazed cutting room slasher with equally hackneyed dubbing. Residents of a chi-chi high rise watching a documentary about the events of "Demons"—a sort of high-tech play-within-a-play ploy—when a demon emerges from the TV, spreads his creepy cooties, and causes the tenants to sprout fangs and claws and nasty tempers. Lots of blood drips from ceilings, plumbing fixtures, and various body parts. **88m/C VHS, LV.** *IT* David Knight, Nancy Brill, Coralina Cataldi Tassoni, Bobby Rhodes, Asia Argento, Virginia Bryant; **D:** Lamberto Bava; **W:** Dario Argento, Lamberto Bava; **M:** Simon Boswell. *IMP*

Demons in the Garden 🎬🎬🎬 *Demonios En El Jardin* 1982 (R) Centers on the disintegration of a family after the end of the Spanish Civil War, due to sibling rivalries and a variety of indiscretions. Problems mount as two brothers become involved with their stepsister. Story takes on poignancy in its narration by a young boy. Beautiful cinematography. In Spanish with English subtitles. **100m/C VHS.** *SP* Angela Molina, Ana Belen, Encarna Paso, Imanol Arias; *D:* Manuel Gutierrez Aragon; *C:* Jose Luis Alcaine. *CVC, TPV, FCT*

Demons of Ludlow *woof!* 1975 Demons attend a small town's bicentennial celebration intent on raising a little hell of their own. **83m/C VHS, Beta.** Paul von Hauser, Stephanie Cushna, James Robinson, Carol Perry; *D:* Steven Kuether. *TWE*

Demons of the Mind *AA* *Blood Evil; Blood Will Have Blood* 1972 (R) A sordid psychological horror film about a baron in 19th century Austria who imprisons his children, fearing that mental illness is a family trait. **85m/C VHS, Beta.** *GB* Michael Hordern, Patrick Magee, Yvonne Mitchell, Robert Hardy, Gillian Hills, Virginia Wetherell, Shane Briant, Paul Jones, Thomas Heathcote, Kenneth J. Warren; *D:* Peter Sykes; *W:* Christopher Wicking; *C:* Arthur Grant. *REP, MLB*

Demonstone *A* *Heartstone* 1989 (R) A television reporter becomes possessed by a Filipino demon and carries out an ancient curse against the family of a corrupt government official. **90m/C VHS, Beta, LV.** R. Lee Ermey, Jan-Michael Vincent, Nancy Everhard; *D:* Andrew Prowse.

Demonstrator *AA½* 1971 A father and son are at odds when dad heads an Asian military coalition and junior protests. Notable for being one of the first major Australian films to use an entirely native cast. **82m/C VHS.** *AU* Joe James, Irene Inescort, Gerard Maguire, Wendy Lingham, Harold Hopkins; *D:* Warwick Freeman.

Demonwarp *woof!* 1987 A vengeance-minded hunter journeys into an evil, primeval forest to kill the monsters that abducted his daughter. **91m/C VHS, Beta.** George Kennedy, Emmett Alston. *THV*

Dempsey *AA* 1983 In this made for television film based on Jack Dempsey's autobiography, Williams plays the role of the famed world heavyweight champ. His rise through the boxing ranks as well as his personal life are chronicled. A bit slow-moving considering the pounding fists and other action. **110m/C VHS, Beta.** Treat Williams, Sam Waterston, Sally Kellerman, Victoria Tennant, Peter Mark Richman, Jesse Vint, Bonnie Bartlett, James Noble; *D:* Gus Trikonis; *M:* Billy Goldenberg.

Denial: The Dark Side of Passion *AA* 1991 (R) A strong-willed woman tries to put a destructive love affair behind her—but if she succeeded there'd be no movie. Torrid stuff with a watchable cast. *CW:* Sensuality. **103m/ C VHS, LV, Closed Caption.** Robin Wright Penn, Jason Patric, Barry Primus, Christina Harnos, Rae Dawn Chong; *D:* Eric Dignam; *W:* Eric Dignam. *REP*

Denise Calls Up *AA½* 1995 (PG-13) Comedy about futility and complications of urban relationships among overworked professionals. A group of six work-at-home city friends socialize, romance, and date entirely via phone, fax, and computer without ever meeting or leaving their homes, even for a close friend's funeral (who dies, oddly enough, while on the phone). Subplot involves title character, Denise (Ubach) tracking down sperm donor Martin (Gunther) and eventually giving birth, with the help of her cellular coaches. Funny premise is executed well, but doesn't hold up over a (barely) feature length film. *CW:* Sexual references and nudity. **79m/C VHS, LV, Closed Caption.** Dana Wheeler-Nicholson, Caroleen Feeney, Liev Schreiber, Dan Gunther, Aida Turturro, Alanna Ubach, Sylvia Miles; *D:* Hal Salwen; *W:* Hal Salwen; *M:* Mike Mayers; *M:* Lynne Geller. *COL*

Dennis the Menace *AA½* 1993 (PG) Straight from the Hughes kiddie farm comes Kevin McAllister —oops!— Dennis Mitchell (newcomer Gamble), curious, crafty, and blond five-year-old. He dreams and schemes, but everything he does manages to be a threat to the physical and mental well being of hot-head neighbor Mr. Wilson (Matthau, perfectly cast as the grump). Lloyd is very nasty as protagonist Switchblade Sam; Plowright, Thompson, and Stanton round out the cast as Mrs. Wilson and the Mitchell parents, respective-

ly. Sure to please young kids, but parents may be less enthralled with this adaptation of the popular '50s comic strip and subsequent TV series. **96m/C VHS, Beta, LV, 8mm, Letterbox, Closed Caption.** Walter Matthau, Mason Gamble, Joan Plowright, Christopher Lloyd, Lea Thompson, Robert Stanton, Billie Bird, Paul Winfield, Amy Sakasitz, Kellen Hathaway, Arnold Stang; *D:* Nick Castle; *W:* John Hughes; *C:* Thomas Ackerman; *M:* Jerry Goldsmith. *WAR*

Dennis the Menace: Dinosaur Hunter *AA½* 1993 (G) Another version of Hank Ketcham's mischievious cartoon character brought to life to have adventures and disturb his neighbor Mr. Wilson. This time Dennis discovers a huge, primitive bone in his backyard and when an archaeologist declares it's a dinosaur bone, news crews, tourists, and scientists are suddenly everywhere. This badly disturbs Mr. Wilson's retirement and Dennis and his friends must save the day (and their neighborhood). **118m/C VHS, LV, Closed Caption.** Victor Dimattia, William Windom, Pat Estrin, Jim Jansen, Patsy Garrett. *THV*

Dennis the Menace Strikes Again *AA½* 1998 (G) Direct-to-video sequel finds hyperactive Dennis (Cooper) trying to save curmudgeonly Mr. Wilson (Rickles) from a pair of con men. **75m/C VHS.** Justin Cooper, Don Rickles, George Kennedy, Betty White, Brian Doyle-Murray, Carrot Top; *D:* Charles Kanganis; *W:* Tim McCanlies; *C:* Christopher Faloona; *M:* Graeme Revell. *WAR*

The Dentist *AAA½* 1932 Fields treats several oddball patients in his office. After watching the infamous tooth-pulling scene, viewers will be sure to brush regularly. **22m/B VHS, Beta.** W.C. Fields, Elise Cavanna, Babe Kane, Bud Jamison, Zedna Farley. *CCB, GVV*

The Dentist *AA½* 1996 (R) After seeing this movie, you may never want to sit in that dental chair again. When his marriage falls apart, L.A. dental specialist Dr. Alan Feinstone (Bernsen) takes to pill popping and psychotic behavior, including demonic drilling and particularly bloody oral surgery. *CW:* Graphic violence including scenes of dental torture, sexuality and some language. **93m/C VHS.** Corbin Bernsen, Ken Foree, Linda Hoffman, Michael Stadvec; *D:* Brian Yuzna; *W:* Charles Finch, Stuart Gordon, Dennis Paoli; *C:* Levie Isaacks; *M:* Alan Howarth. *THV*

The Denver & Rio Grande *AA½* 1951 Action-packed western about two rival railroads competing to be the first to complete a line through the Royal Gorge. Plot is predictable, but the scene featuring two trains crashing into each other is worth it (Haskin used actual trains for this stunt). **89m/C VHS, Closed Caption.** Edmond O'Brien, Sterling Hayden, Dean Jagger, ZaSu Pitts, J. Carrol Naish; *D:* Byron Haskin. *PAR*

Department Store *A* *Bargain Basement* 1935 Confusing crime-drama involving a store manager who mistakes an ex-convict for his employer's heir. Based on a story by H. F. Maltby. **65m/B VHS.** *GB* Garry Marsh, Eve Gray, Sebastian Shaw, Geraldine Fitzgerald, Jack Melford; *D:* Leslie Hiscott. *DVT*

Depraved *A½* 1998 Opella and Dan spice up their sex lives by acting out their fantasies. But they start to go too far for Dan and he has a fight with his fiance, who storms out. Only the next morning Dan discovers Opella's dead body. Naturally, instead of calling the cops, Dan calls his brother, and they decide to dispose of the body and come up with an alibi. Can you spell trouble? **90m/C VHS.** Mario Lopez, Seidy Lopez, Barbara Niven. *PEG*

The Deputy Drummer *A½* 1935 Second-rate early British musical, notable as a later vehicle for silent-era star Lane. He plays a penniless composer who impersonates an aristocrat to attend a party, and catches jewel robbers in the act. **71m/B VHS.** *GB* Lupino Lane, Jean Denis, Kathleen Kelly, Wallace Lupino, Margaret Yarde, Syd Crossley. *NOS*

Deputy Marshall *A½* 1950 Hall trails a pair of bankrobbers, fights off landgrabbers, and finds romance as well. **75m/B VHS, Beta.** Jon Hall, Frances Langford, Dick Foran. *RXM*

Der Purimshpiler *AA½* *The Purim Player; The Jester; The Jewish Jester* 1937 A drifter embarks on a quest for happiness, which takes him to various small towns. In one, he meets and falls in love with a shoemaker's daughter. In Yiddish with English subtitles. **90m/B VHS, Beta.** *PL* Miriam Kressyn, Zygmund Turkow, Hymie Jacobsen; *D:* Joseph Green. *ERG*

Deranged *AAA* 1974 (R) Of the numerous movies based on the cannibalistic exploits of Ed Gein ("Psycho," "The Texas Chainsaw Massacre," etc.), this is the most accurate. A dead-on performance by Blossom and a twisted sense of humor help move things along nicely. The two directors, Gillen and Ormsby, previously worked together on the classic "Children Shouldn't Play with Dead Things." An added attraction is the early special effect work of gore wizard Tom Savini. **82m/C VHS.** *CA* Roberts Blossom, Cosette Lee, Robert Warner, Marcia Diamond, Brian Sneagle, Leslie Carlson, Marion Waldman, Micki Moore, Pat Orr, Robert McHeady; *D:* Jeff Gillen, Alan Ormsby; *W:* Jeff Gillen, Alan Ormsby. *FRG, MRV*

Deranged *A½* 1987 (R) A mentally unstable, pregnant woman is attacked in her apartment after her husband leaves town. She spends the rest of the movie engaged in psychotic encounters, real and imagined. Technically not bad, but extremely violent and grim. Not to be confused with 1974 movie of the same name. **85m/C VHS.** Jane Hamilton, Paul Siederman, Jennifer Delora, James Gillis, Jill Cumer, Gary Goldman; *D:* Chuck Vincent. *REP*

Derby *AAA* 1971 (R) The documentary story of the rise to fame of roller-derby stars on the big rink. **91m/C VHS, Beta.** Charlie O'Connell, Lydia Gray, Janet Earp, Ann Colvello, Mike Snell; *D:* Robert Kaylor. *FAF*

Dersu Uzala *AAA½* 1975 An acclaimed, photographically breathtaking film about a Russian surveyor in Siberia who befriends a crusty, resourceful Mongolian. They begin to teach each other about their respective worlds. Produced in Russia; one of Kurosawa's stranger films. **124m/C VHS, Beta.** *JP RU* Yuri Solomin, Maxim Munzuk; *D:* Akira Kurosawa. Academy Awards '75: Best Foreign Language Film. *KIV*

Descending Angel *AAA* 1990 (R) The premise is familiar: a swastika-friendly collaborator is forced out of the closet. But the cast and scripting make this made-for-cable there's-a-Nazi-in-the-woodwork suspenser better than average, despite its flawed finale. Scott plays a well-respected Romanian refugee—active in the community, in the church, and in Romanian-American activities—whose daughter's fiance (Roberts) suspects him of Nazi collusion. *CW:* Language and sensuality. **96m/C VHS, LV, Closed Caption.** George C. Scott, Diane Lane, Eric Roberts, Mark Margolis, Vyto Ruginis, Amy Aquino, Richard Jenkins, Jan Rubes; *D:* George C. Scott, Jeremy Paul Kagan; *W:* George C. Scott. *HBO*

Desert Bloom *AAA* 1986 (PG) On the eve of a nearby nuclear bomb test, a beleaguered alcoholic veteran and his family struggle through tensions brought on by a promiscuous visiting aunt and the chaotic, rapidly changing world. Gish shines as the teenage daughter through whose eyes the story unfolds. From a story by Corr and Linda Ramy. **103m/C VHS, Beta, LV.** Jon Voight, JoBeth Williams, Ellen Barkin, Annabeth Gish, Allen (Goorwitz) Garfield, Jay Underwood; *D:* Eugene Corr; *W:* Eugene Corr; *C:* Reynaldo Villalobos; *M:* Brad Fiedel. *NO*

Desert Commandos *A* 196? When the Allies appear to be winning WWII, the Nazis devise a plan to eliminate all of the opposing forces' leaders at once. **?m/C VHS.** Kenneth Clark, Horst Frank, Jeanne Valeri, Carlo Hinterman, Gianni Rizzo. *NO*

The Desert Fox 🎬🎬🎬 *Rommel—Desert Fox* 1951 Big-budgeted portrait of German Army Field Marshal Rommel, played by Mason, focuses on the soldier's defeat in Africa during WWII and his subsequent, disillusioned return to Hitler's Germany. Mason played Rommel again in 1953's "Desert Rats." 87m/B **VHS, Beta, LV.** James Mason, Cedric Hardwicke, Jessica Tandy, Luther Adler; **D:** Henry Hathaway. FOX, TLF

Desert Gold 🎬½ 1936 A fierce Indian chief battles a horde of greedy white men over his tribe's gold mine. Based on a novel by Zane Grey. 58m/B **VHS, Beta.** Buster Crabbe, Robert Cummings, Marsha Hunt, Tom George Duryea Keene, Raymond Hatton, Monte Blue, Leif Erickson; **D:** Charles T. Barton. NOS, DVT

Desert Guns/Six-Shootin' Sheriff 🎬 1936 Double feature includes a rare Tearle "B" film and a Maynard oater from 1938. ?m/C **VHS.** Conway Tearle, Ken Maynard. RXM

Desert Hearts 🎬🎬🎬 1986 (R) An upstanding professional woman travels to Reno, Nevada in 1959 to obtain a quick divorce, and slowly becomes involved in a lesbian relationship with a free-spirited casino waitress. 93m/C **VHS, Beta, LV.** Helen Shaver, Audra Lindley, Patricia Charbonneau, Andra Akers, Dean Butler, Jeffrey Tambor, Denise Crosby, Gwen Welles; **D:** Donna Deitch; **W:** Natalie Cooper; **C:** Robert Elswit. ART, VES

Desert Kickboxer 🎬🎬 1992 (R) A border guard takes on a cocaine dealer and his henchmen, fighting for gold and, of course, a beautiful woman. Lots of kickboxing action.**CW:** Violence and some sexuality. 86m/C **VHS, LV, Closed Caption.** John Haymes Newton, Judie Aronson, Sam DeFrancisco, Paul Smith; **D:** Isaac Florentine. HBO

Desert of the Lost 🎬🎬½ 1927 Wales flees to Mexico after shooting a man in self-defense. He's aided by Montgomery and, in turn, helps save her from a forced marriage. 58m/B **VHS.** Wally Wales, Peggy Montgomery, William J. Dyer, Edward Cecil, Richard Neill, Kelly Cafford, Ray Murro, George Magrill, Charles "Slim" Whitaker; **D:** Richard Thorpe. GPV

The Desert of the Tartars 🎬 *Le Desert des Tartares* 1976 (PG) Story of a young soldier who dreams of war and discovers that the real battle for him is with time. 140m/C **VHS, Beta.** Jacques Perrin; **M:** Ennio Morricone.

Desert Phantom 🎬½ 1936 Villains threaten to rob a woman of her ranch until a stranger rescues her. 66m/B **VHS, Beta, LV.** Johnny Mack Brown, Sheila Mannors, Charles "Blackie" King, Ted Adams, Hal Price, Nelson McDowell; **D:** S. Roy Luby. GPV

The Desert Rats 🎬🎬🎬 1953 A crusty British captain (Burton) takes charge of an Australian division during WWII. Thinking they are inferior to his own British troops, he is stiff and uncaring to the Aussies until a kind-hearted drunk and the courage of the division win him over. Crack direction from Wise and Newton's performance (as the wag) simply steal the movie. Mason reprises his role as Germany Army Field Marshal Rommel from "The Desert Fox." 88m/B **VHS, Beta.** Richard Burton, Robert Newton, Robert Douglas, Torin Thatcher, Chips Rafferty, Charles Tingwell, James Mason; **D:** Robert Wise. Nominations: Academy Awards '53: Best Story & Screenplay. FCT

Desert Snow 🎬🎬 1989 (R) Here's a non-formulaic dope opera oater: cowboys 'n' drug runners battle it out for an out-of-the-way, underpopulated western town. About as clever as the title. 90m/C **VHS, Beta.** Frank Capizzi, Flint Carney, Shelley Hinkle, Sam Incorvia, Carolyn Jacobs; **D:** Paul de Cruccio. NO

The Desert Song 🎬🎬½ 1953 MacRae secretly leads a band of do-gooders against the evil forces of a dastardly sheik. Grayson is the general's daughter who falls in love with our disguised hero. Third filmed version of the Sigmund Romberg operetta creaks along with the talents of MacRae and Grayson rising about the hackneyed plot. ♫The Desert Song; Gay Parisienne; Long Live the Night; One Alone; One Flower; The Riff Song; Romance. 96m/C **VHS.** Gordon MacRae, Kathryn

Grayson, Raymond Massey, Steve Cochran, Dick Wesson, Allyn Ann McLerie, Ray Collins, William Conrad; **D:** H. Bruce Humberstone; **W:** Roland Kibbee; **C:** Robert Burks; **M:** Max Steiner. FCT

Desert Steel 🎬½ 1994 (PG) Rival racers risk their lives in the big off-road race. 89m/C **VHS.** David Naughton, Brian Skinner, Amanda Wyss, Russ Tamblyn; **D:** Glenn Gebhard. MNC

Desert Trail 🎬½ 1935 Wayne is a championship rodeo rider accused of bank robbery. 57m/B **VHS, Beta.** John Wayne, Paul Fix, Mary Kornman; **D:** Robert North Bradbury. COL, REP, MRV

Desert Warrior 🎬 1988 (PG-13) Earth becomes a waste site after a nuclear war. Ferrigno stars as a post-nuke hero in this low-budget action film. Very bad acting. 89m/C **VHS, Beta.** Lou Ferrigno, Shari Shattuck, Kenneth Peer, Anthony East; **D:** Jim Goldman; **W:** Frederick Bailey.

The Deserters 🎬½ 198? Sergeant Hawley, a Vietnam-era hawk, hunts deserters and draft-dodgers in Canada. There, he confronts issues of war and peace head-on. 110m/C **VHS, Beta.** Alan Scarfe, Dermot Hennelly, Jon Bryden, Barbara March; **M:** Michael Conway Baker. MOV

The Designated Mourner 🎬½ 1997 (R) Adapted from the play by Wallace Shawn, this pointy-headed inaction movie laments the passing of the class of people who "appreciate the poetry of John Donne" and other forms of high art. It's probably the same class that would like this movie. Set in an unnamed politically repressive country that resembles a large table, Nichols plays the eponymous mourner Jack, a journalist who once ran with a literary crowd but betrayed their ideals for survival. Richardson plays his wife Judy, the daughter of final talking head Howard (de Keyser), who is a humanist poet who doesn't like people. If you need a lecture on culture written by a man who was in "Mom and Dad Save the World" and played the geeky social studies teacher in "Clueless," then this is your movie. To quote Shawn: "Inconceivable!"**CW:** Some language. 94m/C **VHS.** GB Mike Nichols, Miranda Richardson, David de Keyser; **D:** David Hare; **W:** Wallace Shawn; **C:** Oliver Stapleton; **M:** Richard Hartley. NYR

Designing Woman 🎬🎬🎬 1957 Bacall and Peck star in this mismatched tale of romance. She's a chic high-fashion designer, he's a rumpled sports writer. The fun begins when they try to adjust to married life together. Neither likes the other's friends or lifestyle. Things get even crazier when Bacall has to work with her ex-lover Helmore on a fashion show and Peck's former love Gray shows up as well. And as if that weren't enough, Peck is being hunted by the mob because of a boxing story he's written. It's a fun, quick, witty tale that is all entertainment and no message. Bacall's performance is of note because Bogart was dying of cancer at the time. 118m/C **VHS, Beta, LV, Letterbox.** Gregory Peck, Lauren Bacall, Dolores Gray, Sam Levene, Tom Helmore, Mickey Shaughnessy, Jesse White, Chuck Connors, Edward Platt, Alvy Moore, Jack Cole; **D:** Vincente Minnelli; **W:** George Wells; **C:** John Alton; **M:** Andre Previn. Academy Awards '57: Best Story & Screenplay.MGM

Desire 🎬🎬🎬 1936 Jewel thief Madeleine (Dietrich) manages to involve innocent tourist Tom (Cooper) into carrying her ill-gotten goods across the Spanish border. Then she entices him into joining her at the country estate of her partner-in-crime. By this time Tom is in love—and so is Madeleine but she doesn't think she's good enough for him. Lots of lying until the twosome can figure out what to do. Cooper manages to hold his own with the sophisticated Dietrich in their second film together (after "Morocco"). 96m/B **VHS.** Marlene Dietrich, Gary Cooper, John Halliday, William Frawley, Ernest Cossart, Akim Tamiroff, Alan Mowbray; **D:** Frank Borzage; **W:** Edwin Justus Mayer, Waldemar Young; **M:** Friedrich Hollander. USH, FCT

Desire 🎬🎬 1993 (R) A free-spirited woman finds herself attracted to a local fisherman. Hardly her intellectual equal but then what she really wants is his body.**CW:** Strong language and sexuality. 108m/C **VHS.** Greta Scacchi, Vincent D'Onofrio; **D:** Andrew Birkin.

Desire 🎬🎬 1995 (R) Security consultant Lauren Allen (Hodge) is working for a perfume manufacturer whose fragrance, Desire, is the fave of a Beverly Hills serial killer who likes to douse his victims in the scent. The prime suspect is scent expert Gordon Lewis (Kemp) and naturally Lauren falls for him. Standard erotic thriller fare.**CW:** Sexuality, violence, and some language. 90m/C **VHS.** Kate Hodge, Martin Kemp, Deborah Shelton, Robert Miranda. MNC

Desire and Hell at Sunset Motel 🎬½ 1992 (PG-13) Low-budget thriller takes place at the Sunset Motel in 1950s Anaheim. Fenn is the bombshell wife of a toy salesman who's in town for a sales meeting, while she just wants to visit Disneyland. She's soon fooling around with another guy and her husband hires a psychotic criminal to spy on her as her new lover plots to kill hubby. Very confusing plot isn't worth figuring out. Film's only redeeming quality is the imaginative and creative work used in the visuals. Castle's directorial debut. 90m/C **VHS, Beta, LV, Closed Caption.** Sherilyn Fenn, Whip Hubley, David Hewlett, David Johansen, Paul Bartel; **D:** Alien Castle; **W:** Alien Castle. FXV, VTR

Desire Under the Elms 🎬🎬½ 1958 Ives, the patriarch of an 1840s New England farming family, takes a young wife (Loren) who promptly has an affair with her stepson. Loren's American film debut. Based on the play by Eugene O'Neill. 114m/B **VHS, Beta, LV, Closed Caption.** Sophia Loren, Anthony Perkins, Burl Ives, Frank Overton; **D:** Delbert Mann; **C:** Daniel F. Fapp; **M:** Elmer Bernstein. Nominations: Academy Awards '58: Best Black and White Cinematography. BAR, FCT, PAR

Desiree 🎬🎬½ 1954 A romanticized historical epic about Napoleon and his 17-year-old mistress, Desiree. Based on the novel by Annemarie Selinko. Slightly better than average historical fiction piece. 110m/C **Beta, LV, Letterbox, Closed Caption.** Marlon Brando, Jean Simmons, Merle Oberon, Michael Rennie, Cameron Mitchell, Elizabeth Sellars, Cathleen Nesbitt; **D:** Henry Koster; **W:** Daniel Taradash; **C:** Milton Krasner; **M:** Alex North. Nominations: Academy Awards '54: Best Art Direction/Set Decoration (Color), Best Costume Design (Color). FOX, IME

Desk Set 🎬🎬🎬 *His Other Woman* 1957 One of the later and less dynamic Tracy/Hepburn comedies, about an efficiency expert who installs a giant computer in an effort to update a television network's female-run reference department. Still, the duo sparkle as they bicker, battle, and give in to love. Based on William Marchant's play. 103m/C **VHS, Beta, LV, Closed Caption.** Spencer Tracy, Katharine Hepburn, Joan Blondell, Gig Young, Dina Merrill, Neva Patterson; **D:** Walter Lang; **C:** Leon Shamroy. FOX, FCT

Desolation Angels 🎬🎬 1995 Nick Adams (Rodrick) returns to New York after a month spent unhappily visiting his mother and discovers his girlfriend Mary (Thomas) has been raped by his best friend Sid (Bassett). At least that's how Nick interprets the situation after an unwilling Mary admits they had sex. Nick goes after Sid, gets beaten up, hires a couple of thugs who botch a retaliation, and just gets increasingly enraged over his inability to settle the situation. The focus is on Nick and Rodrick is more than up to the director McCann's demands. 90m/C **VHS.** Michael Rodrick, Peter Bassett, Jennifer Thomas; **D:** Tim McCann; **W:** Tim McCann; **C:** Matt Howe. FXL

Despair 🎬🎬 1978 A chilling and comic study of a victimized chocolate factory owner's descent into madness, set against the backdrop of the Nazi rise to power in the 1930s. Adapted from the Nabokov novel by Tom Stoppard. 120m/C **VHS, Beta.** GE Dirk Bogarde, Andrea Ferreol, Volker Spengler, Klaus Lowitsch; **D:** Rainer Werner Fassbinder; **W:** Tom Stoppard; **C:** Michael Ballhaus; **M:** Peer Raben. *GLV*

Desperado 🎬🎬🎬 *El Mariachi 2* 1995 (R) Rodriguez's nameless guitar player-turned-gunman returns—this time in the persona of heartthrob Banderas. The director also has a studio budget to play with (a sizable increase over the $7000 for "El Mariachi"), so the action's on a bigger, more violent scale (you'll quickly lose count of flying bodies and bullets) as El Mariachi tracks infamous drug lord Bucho (de Almeida). Gringo Buscemi provides assistance, beautiful bookstore owner Carolina (Hayek) offers solace, and Tarantino meets his well-deserved cameo demise. You'll also find original Mariachi, Gallardo, in a cameo role as a musician/gunslinger amigo of the hero. Filmed in Mexico. **CW:** Strong bloody violence; strong sex sequence; language. 103m/C VHS, LV, 8mm, Closed Caption, DVD. Antonio Banderas, Salma Hayek, Joaquim de Almeida, Steve Buscemi, Richard "Cheech" Marin, Carlos Gomez; *Cameos:* Quentin Tarantino, Carlos Gallardo; **D:** Robert Rodriguez; **W:** Robert Rodriguez; **C:** Guillermo Navarro. Nominations: MTV Movie Awards '96: Most Desirable Male (Banderas), Best Kiss (Antonio Banderas/Salma Hayek). *COL*

The Desperadoes 🎬🎬½ 1943 Sheriff Steve Upton (Scott) has a peaceful little Utah town but things change when his old friend, outlaw Cheyenne Rodgers (Ford), comes to visit. Claiming to have gone straight, Rodgers falls for the lovely Allison (Keyes) but is soon accused of robbing the local bank. However, Sheriff Upton believes in his old friend's innocence, helps him escape jail, and together they go after the real criminals. Based on a story by Max Brand. 85m/C VHS. Randolph Scott, Glenn Ford, Evelyn Keyes, Claire Trevor, Edgar Buchanan, Raymond Walburn, Porter Hall, Guinn "Big Boy" Williams; **D:** Charles Vidor; **W:** Robert Carson. *COL*

Desperados 🎬🎬½ 1969 (PG) After the Civil War, a murderous renegade and two of his sons go on a looting rampage, eventually kidnapping the child of the third son who just wants to live in peace. Made in Spain. 90m/C VHS, Beta. SP Jack Palance, Vince Edwards, Christian Roberts, George Maharis, Neville Brand, Sylvia Syms; **D:** Henry Levin; **W:** Walter Brough; **C:** Sam Leavitt. *COL*

The Desperados 🎬½ 198? When a young woman is raped by outlaws robbing her stagecoach, a bevy of western heroes band together to avenge her. 86m/C VHS. Keenan Wynn, Henry Silva, Michele Carey, John Anderson, Joe Turkel; **D:** Ron Joy. *SIM, COL*

Desperate 🎬🎬½ 1947 An honest truck driver witnesses a mob crime and must escape with his wife in this minor film noir. Eventually, the law is on his tail, too. 73m/B VHS, Beta. Steve Brodie, Audrey Long, Raymond Burr, Jason Robards Sr., Douglas Fowley, William Challee, Ilka Gruning, Nan Leslie; **D:** Anthony Mann. *TTC*

Desperate Cargo 🎬½ 1941 Two show-girls stranded in a Latin American town manage to get aboard a clipper ship with hoodlums who are trying to steal the vessel's cargo. 69m/B VHS, Beta. Ralph Byrd, Carol Hughes, Jack Mulhall. *NOS, DVT, HEG*

Desperate Characters 🎬🎬🎬 1971 (R) A slice-of-city-life story about a middle-class couple living in a once-fashionable section of Brooklyn, New York, who watch their neighborhood disintegrate around them. Their marriage on remote control, the two find their lives a series of small disappointments, routine work, uncertain friendships, and pervasive violence. Excellent performances, especially by MacLaine as the harried wife, but the film's depressing nature made it a complete boxoffice flop. 87m/C VHS, Closed Caption. Shirley MacLaine, Kenneth Mars, Gerald S. O'Loughlin, Sada Thompson, Michael Higgins, Rose Gregorio, Jack Somack, Chris Gampel, Mary Alan Hokanson, Patrick McVey, Carol Kane; **D:** Frank D. Gilroy; **W:** Frank D. Gilroy. *PAR*

Desperate Crimes 🎬🎬 1993 Two rival mobs battle over the prostitution and drug trade. When an innocent woman is murdered her brother looks for revenge with the help of a beautiful prostitute. 92m/C VHS. Traci Lords, Denise Crosby, Franco Columbu, Van Quattro, Rena Niehaus, Nicoletta Boris, Elizabeth Kaitan, Randi Ingerman; **D:** Andreas Marfori.

Desperate Hours 🎬🎬🎬 1955 A tough, gritty thriller about three escaped convicts taking over a suburban home and holding the family hostage. Plenty of suspense and fine acting. Based on the novel and play by Joseph Hayes. 112m/B VHS, Beta. Humphrey Bogart, Fredric March, Martha Scott, Arthur Kennedy, Gig Young, Dewey Martin, Mary Murphy, Robert Middleton, Richard Eyer; **D:** William Wyler; **C:** Lee Garmes. National Board of Review Awards '55: Best Director (Wyler). *PAR*

Desperate Hours 🎬🎬 1990 (R) An escaped prisoner holes up in a suburban couple's home, waiting for his lawyer/accomplice to take him to Mexico. Tensions heighten between the separated couple and the increasingly nerve-wracked criminals. Terrific, if not downright horrifying, performance by Rourke in an overall tepid remake of the 1955 thriller. 105m/C VHS, Beta, LV, Closed Caption. Mickey Rourke, Anthony Hopkins, Mimi Rogers, Kelly Lynch, Lindsay Crouse, Elias Koteas, David Morse, Shawnee Smith, Danny Gerard, Matt McGrath; **D:** Michael Cimino; **W:** Mark Rosenthal. *MGM, FHE*

Desperate Journey 🎬🎬½ 1942 Flynn and Reagan are two of five Allied fighters shot down over Nazi occupied Poland. They go through various tight squeezes such as stealing Goering's car in Berlin, and eliminating a few Nazis at a chemical factory to get back to the safety of England. All the while they are hunted by Massey as Nazi Major Otto Baumester, who of course bumbles and fumbles the whole affair. Strictly propaganda intended to keep up morale on the homefront. Flynn was not pleased about having Reagan as his co-star, seeing as he was usually paired with female leads. 108m/B VHS, Beta. Errol Flynn, Ronald Reagan, Raymond Massey, Nancy Coleman, Alan Hale, Arthur Kennedy, Helmut Dantine; **D:** Raoul Walsh; **M:** Max Steiner. *MGM*

Desperate Lives 🎬🎬 1982 High school siblings come into contact with drugs and join their guidance counselor in the war against dope. Average made for TV fare. 100m/C VHS, Beta. Diana Scarwid, Doug McKeon, Helen Hunt, William Windom, Art Hindle, Tom Atkins, Sam Bottoms, Diane Ladd, Dr. Joyce Brothers; **D:** Robert Lewis; **M:** Bruce Broughton. *ART*

Desperate Living 🎬🎬½ 1977 Typical John Waters trash. A mental patient (Stole) is released and becomes paranoid that her family may be out to kill her. After aiding in the murder of her husband (the hefty maid, Hill, suffocates him by sitting on him), Stole and Hill escape to Mortville, a town populated by outcasts such as transsexuals, murderers, and the woefully disfigured. 90m/C VHS, Beta. Jean Hill, Mink Stole, Edith Massey, Mary Vivian Pearce, Liz Renay, Susan Lowe; **D:** John Waters; **W:** John Waters. *NLC*

Desperate Measures 🎬½ 1998 (R) Police officer Frank Connor (Garcia) desperately searches for a bone marrow donor for his dying son. Turns out the perfect match is vicious murderer and prison inmate Pete McCabe (Keaton). McCabe seizes the opportunity to unleash an elaborate and violent prison escape in a San Francisco hospital. Keaton, as a poor man's Hannibal Lecter, offers this movie's only entertainment. If not for the dying child to propel its already ludicrous story along, it would be a great source for slapstick comedy. Film was held back for several months before its final release and you'll find out why the studio wanted to hide this one. **CW:** Violence and language. 100m/C VHS, LV, Closed Caption, DVD. Andy Garcia, Michael Keaton, Marcia Gay Harden, Brian Cox; **D:** Barbet Schroeder; **W:** Neal Jimenez, David Klass, Henry Bean; **M:** Trevor Jones. *COL*

Desperate Motives 🎬🎬 *Distant Cousins* 1992 (R) Keith and his fiancee Helgenberger are a charming couple who arrive to stay with Keith's distant cousin (Katt) and his family. Only what the family doesn't realize is that the duo have escaped from an asylum for the criminally insane and want to take over their lives. **CW:** Language and violence. 92m/C VHS, LV. David Keith, Marg Helgenberger, William Katt, Mel Harris, Mary Crosby, Brian Bonsall, Cyndi Pass; **D:** Andrew Lane; **W:** C. Courtney Joyner. *NLC*

Desperate Moves 🎬🎬 1986 An Oregon-transplanted geek in San Francisco sets out to make himself over in order to win his dream girl. Sometimes effective, often sappy treatment of his coming to terms with the big city. 90m/C VHS, Beta. Isabel Sanford, Steve Tracy, Paul Benedict, Christopher Lee, Eddie Deezen; **D:** Oliver Hellman. *TWE*

Desperate Prey 🎬½ *Redheads* 1994 (R) Lucy (Karvan) videotapes herself having sex with lawyer Brewster (Hembrow) and then accidentally films his murder. So she's stalked by the killer. 102m/C VHS, Closed Caption. AU Claudia Karvan, Catherine McClements, Mark Hembrow; **D:** Danny Vendramini; **W:** Danny Vendramini. *APX*

Desperate Remedies 🎬🎬 1993 (R) Enjoyment will rest on the viewer's appreciation of campy melodrama. In a Victorian-era New Zealand town, regal shop owner Dorothea Brook (Ward-Lealand) is trying to find a husband for her difficult younger sister Rose (Mills)—who happens to be pregnant and a drug addict. She spots handsome sailor Lawrence (Smith) and decides he'll do but Lawrence is instantly smitten with Dorothea (who's also having heart palpitations over the hunk). Unfortunately, her current lover is Anne (Chappell) and Dorothea has also decided on a marriage of convenience with ambitious politician William (Hurst). It's all very operatic. **CW:** Some graphic sexuality. 92m/C VHS, Beta, Closed Caption. NZ Jennifer Ward-Lealand, Kevin Smith, Lisa Chappell, Michael Hurst, Kiri Mills, Clifford Curtis; **D:** Stewart Main, Peter Wells; **W:** Stewart Main, Peter. Wells; **C:** Leon Narbey; **M:** Peter Scholes. *PAR*

Desperate Scoundrel/The Pride of Pikeville 1922 Two classic comedy films back to back featuring the best of the early silent comics. 44m/B VHS, Beta. Ford Sterling, Ben Turpin, The Keystone Cops. *CCB*

Desperate Target 🎬½ 1980 Courageous people fight against all odds to survive. 90m/C VHS, Beta. Chris Mitchum. *NO*

Desperate Teenage Lovedolls 🎬 1984 A trashy view of the formation of a tacky all-girl punk group. 60m/C VHS, Beta. Jennifer Schwartz, Hilary Rubens, Steve McDonald, Tracy Lea; **D:** David Markey. *HHT*

The Desperate Trail 🎬🎬½ 1994 (R) Prostitute, convicted of killing an abusive client, manages to escape from the marshal who's escorting her to her hanging. She teams up with a con man in a plot to rob a bank while the marshal enlists a posse to track her down. Strong performances augmented by blazing guns, hobbled by weak writing. Made for cable television. **CW:** Strong western violence; some nudity. 93m/C VHS. Sam Elliott, Linda Fiorentino, Craig Sheffer, Frank Whaley; **D:** P.J. Pesce; **W:** P.J. Pesce, Tom Abrams; **C:** Michael Bonvillain; **M:** Stephen Endelman. *TTC*

Desperate Women 🎬½ 1978 Made for television western about three unjustly accused female convicts rescued en route to prison by an ex-hired gun. 98m/C VHS, Beta. Susan St. James, Dan Haggerty, Ronee Blakley, Ann Dusenberry, Susan Myers; **D:** Earl Bellamy. *ART*

Desperately Seeking Susan 🎬🎬 1985 (PG-13) A bored New Jersey housewife gets her kicks reading the personals. When she becomes obsessed with a relationship between two lovers who arrange their meetings through the columns, she decides to find out for herself who they are. But when she is involved in an accident the housewife loses her memory and thinks she is Susan, the free-spirited woman in the personals. Unfortunately, Susan is in a lot of trouble with all sorts of unsavory folk and our innocent housewife finds herself caught in the middle. Terrific characters, with special appeal generated by Arquette and Madonna. Quinn winningly plays the romantic interest. 104m/C VHS, Beta, LV. Rosanna Arquette, Madonna, Aidan Quinn, Mark Blum, Robert Joy, Laurie Metcalf, Steven Wright, John Turturro, Will Patton, Richard Hell, Annie Golden, Ann Magnuson, Richard Edson; *D:* Susan Seidelman; *W:* Leora Barish; *M:* Thomas Newman. British Academy Awards '85: Best Supporting Actress (Arquette); National Board of Review Awards '85: Best Supporting Actress (Arquette).*FCT*

Destination Moon 🎬🎬½ 1950
Story of man's first lunar voyage contains Chesley Bonstell's astronomical artwork and a famous Woody Woodpecker cartoon. Includes previews of coming attractions from classic science fiction films. 91m/C VHS, LV. Warner Anderson, Tom Powers, Dick Wesson, Erin O'Brien Moore; *D:* Irving Pichel; *C:* Lionel Lindon. Academy Awards '50: Best Special Effects; Nominations: Academy Awards '50: Best Art Direction/Set Decoration (Color). *EEL, SNC*

Destination Moonbase Alpha 🎬🎬
1975 In the 21st century, an explosion has destroyed half the moon, causing it to break away from the Earth's orbit. The moon is cast far away, but the 311 people manning Alpha, a research station on the moon, must continue their search for other life forms in outer space. A thankless task. Pilot for the television series "Space: 1999." 93m/C VHS, Beta. Martin Landau, Barbara Bain, Barry Morse. *FOX*

Destination Saturn 🎬🎬 Buck Rogers 1939
Buck Rogers awakens from suspended animation in the 25th century. 90m/B VHS, Beta. Buster Crabbe, Constance Moore; *D:* Ford Beebe. *NOS, CAB, VYY*

Destination Tokyo 🎬🎬 1943
A weathered WWII submarine actioner, dealing with the search-and-destroy mission of a U.S. sub sent into Tokyo harbor. Available in a colorized version. 135m/B VHS, Beta. Cary Grant, John Garfield, Alan Hale, Dane Clark, John Ridgely, Warner Anderson, William Prince, Robert Hutton, Tom Tully, Peter Whitney, Faye Emerson, John Forsythe; *D:* Delmer Daves. Nominations: Academy Awards '43: Best Story. *MGM*

The Destiny of Marty Fine 🎬 1996
Lame low-budget drama about washed-up boxer Marty Fine (Gelfant), who witnesses the murder of mob boss Capelli (Ironside). He promises old-time gangster Daryl (Fell) he'll keep quiet but Daryl orders a hit anyway. So lowlife Marty tries to get out of L.A. 85m/B VHS. Alan Gelfant, Norman Fell, James LeGros, Catherine Keener, Michael Ironside, Glenn Plummer, John Diehl, Sandra Seacat; *D:* Michael Hacker; *W:* Mark Ruffalo, Michael Hacker; *C:* Melinda Sue Gordon. *PZA*

Destiny Turns on the Radio 🎬🎬
1995 (R) Mystic figure Johnny Destiny (Tarantino) dabbles in the lives of various stock characters in Las Vegas after emerging from a glowing swimming pool. Three years after this grand entrance, he enlists escaped con Julian and partner Thoreau (McDermott and Le Gros, respectively) to help him return to his place of origin. Julian has other plans, which involve getting his ex, Lucille (Travis), back from sleazy casino owner Tuerto (Belushi). Aggressively cheezy, dime novel dialogue and threadbare, convoluted plot wastes talents of interesting cast. Too much time and energy spent trying to be hip. Sadly, Tarantino's only participation was in front of the camera.*CW:* Language, brief nudity. 101m/C VHS, Closed Caption. Dylan McDermott, Nancy Travis, James LeGros, Quentin Tarantino, Allen (Goorwitz) Garfield, James Belushi, Tracey Walter, Bob(cat) Goldthwait, Richard Edson; *D:* Jack Baran; *W:* Robert Ramsey, Matthew Stone; *C:* James L. Carter; *M:* Steven Soles. *HBO*

Destroy All Monsters 🎬🎬½ Kaiju Soshingeki 1968 (G)
When alien babes take control of Godzilla and his monstrous colleagues, it looks like all is lost for Earth. Adding insult to injury, Ghidra is sent in to take care of the loose ends. Can the planet possibly survive this madness? Classic Toho monster slugfest also features Mothra, Rodan, Son of Godzilla, Angila, Varan, Baragon, Spigas and others. 88m/C VHS. JP Akira Kubo, Jun Tazaki, Yoshio Tsuchiya, Kyoko Ai, Yukiko Kobayashi, Kenji Sahara, Andrew Hughes; *D:* Inoshiro Honda. *FRG*

Destroy All Planets 🎬🎬 Gamera Tai Viras; Gamera Tai Uchukaiju Bairasu; Gamera Vs. Viras; Gamera Vs. Outer Space Monster Viras 1968
Aliens whose spaceships turn into giant flying squids are attacking Earth. It's up to Gammera, the flying, fire-breathing turtle to save the day. ?m/C VHS. JP Peter Williams, Kojiro Hongo, Toru Takatsuka; *D:* Noriaki Yuasa. *SNC*

Destroyer 🎬🎬🎬 1943
Trials and tribulations aboard a WWII destroyer result in tensions, but when the time comes for action, the men get the job done. 99m/B VHS, Beta. Edward G. Robinson, Glenn Ford, Marguerite Chapman, Edgar Buchanan, Leo Gorcey, Regis Toomey, Edward Brophy, Larry Parks; *D:* William A. Seiter. *NO*

Destroyer 🎬 1988 (R)
Small-budget film crew goes to an empty prison to shoot, and are stalked by the ghost/zombie remains of a huge serial killer given the electric chair 18 months before. 94m/C VHS, Beta, LV. Anthony Perkins, Deborah Foreman, Lyle Alzado; *D:* Robert Kirk. *NO*

The Destructors 🎬🎬 The Marseille Contract 1974 (PG)
An American narcotics enforcement officer in Paris seeks the help of a hitman in order to catch a druglord. 89m/C VHS, Beta. GB Anthony Quinn, Michael Caine, James Mason, Maureen Kerwin, Alexandra Stewart; *D:* Robert Parrish; *W:* Judd Bernard. *ART, VES, HHE*

Destry Rides Again 🎬🎬🎬🎬 Justice Rides Again 1939
An uncontrollably lawless western town is whipped into shape by a peaceful, unarmed sheriff. A vintage Hollywood potpourri with Dietrich's finest post-Sternberg moment; standing on the bar singing "See What the Boys in the Back Room Will Have." The second of three versions of this Max Brand story. First was released in 1932; the third in 1954. 94m/B VHS, Beta, LV. James Stewart, Marlene Dietrich, Brian Donlevy, Charles Winninger, Mischa Auer, Irene Hervey, Una Merkel, Billy Gilbert, Jack Carson, Samuel S. Hinds, Allen Jenkins; *D:* George Marshall; *W:* Gertrude Purcell, Felix Jackson, Henry Myers; *C:* Hal Mohr; *M:* Frank Skinner. National Film Registry '96. *USH, FCT*

Details of a Duel: A Question of Honor 🎬🎬½ 1989
A butcher and a teacher collide in this comedy, and prodded by the church, militia and town officals, must duel before the entire town. In Spanish with English subtitles. 97m/C VHS. SP *D:* Sergio Cabrera. *FRF, FCT*

The Detective 🎬🎬🎬 Father Brown 1954
Based on G.K. Chesterton's "Father Brown" detective stories, a slick, funny English mystery in which the famous priest tracks down a notorious, endlessly crafty antique thief. 91m/B VHS, Beta. GB Alec Guinness, Peter Finch, Joan Greenwood, Cecil Parker, Bernard Lee; *D:* Robert Hamer; *M:* Jerry Goldsmith. *COL*

The Detective 🎬🎬🎬 1968
A New York detective investigating the mutilation murder of a homosexual finds political and police department corruption. Fine, gritty performances prevail in this suspense thriller. Based on the novel by Roderick Thorpe. 114m/C VHS, Beta, LV, Letterbox. Frank Sinatra, Lee Remick, Ralph Meeker, Jacqueline Bisset, William Windom, Robert Duvall, Tony Musante, Jack Klugman, Al Freeman Jr.; *D:* Gordon Douglas; *W:* Abby Mann; *C:* Joseph Biroc. *FOX*

Detective Sadie & Son 🎬 1984
A television movie about an elderly detective and her young son cracking a case. 96m/C VHS, Beta. Debbie Reynolds, Sam Wanamaker, Brian McNamara. *NO*

Detective School Dropouts 🎬🎬 Dumb Dicks 1985 (PG)
Since they couldn't pass detective school, are they smart enough to outwit a kidnapper? Find out and get a few laughs at the same time. 92m/C VHS, Beta. Lorin Dreyfuss, David Landsberg, Christian de Sica, George Eastman; *D:* Filippo Ottoni. *MGM*

Detective Story 🎬🎬🎬½ 1951
Intense drama about a New York City police precinct with a wide array of characters led by a disillusioned and bitter detective (Douglas). Excellent casting is the strong point, as the film can be a bit dated. Based on Sydney Kingsley's Broadway play. 103m/B VHS. Kirk Douglas, Eleanor Parker, Lee Grant, Horace McMahon, William Bendix, Craig Hill, Cathy O'Donnell, Bert Freed, George Macready, Joseph Wiseman, Gladys George, Frank Faylen, Warner Anderson, Gerald Mohr; *D:* William Wyler; *W:* Philip Yordan, Robert Wyler; *C:* Lee Garmes. Cannes Film Festival '52: Best Actress (Grant); Nominations: Academy Awards '51: Best Actress (Parker), Best Director (Wyler), Best Screenplay, Best Supporting Actress (Grant). *PAR*

Detonator 🎬🎬 Alistair MacLean's Death Train; Death Train 1993 (R)
A renegade Russian general has stolen a nuclear bomb and is transporting it from Germany to Iraq via a hijacked train commandeered by his hired band of mercenaries. Stewart is the U.N. troubleshooter delegated to stop the plot, aided by a commando team featuring Brosnan and Paul. Based on the novel "Death Train" by Alistair MacLean. Made for cable television.*CW:* Some language and violence. 98m/C VHS, Closed Caption. Pierce Brosnan, Patrick Stewart, Ted Levine, Alexandra Paul, Christopher Lee; *D:* David S. Jackson; *W:* David S. Jackson. *NLC*

Detonator 2: Night Watch 🎬🎬½ Alistair MacLean's Night Watch; Night Watch 1995 (R)
Made-for-cable movie finds Brosnan and Paul returning as operatives for the secret United Nations Anti-Crime Organization (UNACO). Mike Graham and Sabrina Carver are teamed by their boss Nick Caldwell (Devane) when it's discovered that Rembrandt's "Night Watch" has been replaced by a forgery. This takes our intrepid duo to Hong Kong, a shady computer expert/art collector (Shannon), and a suspicious satellite about to be launched by North Korea. Based on a story by Alistair MacLean.*CW:* Some violence. 99m/C VHS, LV, Closed Caption. Pierce Brosnan, Alexandra Paul, William Devane, Michael J. Shannon, Lim Kay Siu, Irene Ng; *D:* David S. Jackson; *W:* David S. Jackson; *M:* John Scott. *NLC*

Detour 🎬🎬🎬 1946
Considered to be the creme de la creme of "B" movies, a largely unacknowledged but cult-followed noir downer. Well-designed, stylish, and compelling, if a bit contrived and sometimes annoyingly shrill. Shot in only six days with six indoor sets. Down-on-his-luck pianist Neal hitches cross-country to rejoin his fiancee. His first wrong turn involves the accidental death of the man who picked him up, then he's en route to Destiny with a capital "D" when he picks up fatal femme Savage, as vicious a vixen as ever ruined a good man. Told in flashback, it's also been called the most despairing of all "B"-pictures. As noir as they get. 67m/B VHS, LV. Tom Neal, Ann Savage, Claudia Drake, Edmund MacDonald, Tim Ryan, Esther Howard; *D:* Edgar G. Ulmer; *W:* Martin Goldsmith; *M:* Erdody. National Film Registry '92. *EEL, MRV, SNC*

Detour to Danger woof! 1945
Two young men set out on a fishing expedition and run into crooks and damsels in distress. Unintentionally hilarious "acting" by the no-name cast make this a grade-Z "B" movie. Of interest only because it was filmed in the three-color Kodachrome process used primarily in documentaries. 56m/C VHS, Beta, 8mm. Britt Wood, John Day, Nancy Brinckman; *D:* Richard Talmadge. *VYY*

Detroit 9000 🎬½ Detroit Heat 1973 (R)
A pair of Detroit policemen investigate a robbery that occurred at a black congressman's fundraising banquet. 106m/C VHS, Beta. Alex Rocco, Scatman Crothers,

Hari Rhodes, Lonette McKee, Herbert Jefferson Jr.; **D:** Arthur Marks. *NO*

Deutschland im Jahre Null 🎬🎬🎬½
1947 The acclaimed, unsettling vision of post-war Germany as seen through the eyes of a disturbed boy who eventually kills himself. Lyrical and grim, in German with subtitles. **75m/B VHS, Beta.** *GE* Franz Gruber; **D:** Roberto Rossellini. *FCT, GLV*

Devastator 🎬 *Kings Ransom; The Destroyers*
1985 (R) A Vietnam vet exacts violent revenge on the murderer of an old army buddy. **79m/C VHS, Beta.** Richard Hill, Katt Shea Ruben, Crofton Hardester; **D:** Cirio H. Santiago. *MGM*

Devi 🎬🎬🎬½ *The Goddess* **1960** A minor film in the Ray canon, it is, nonetheless, a strange and compelling tale of religious superstition. An Indian farmer becomes convinced that his beautiful daughter-in-law is the reincarnation of the goddess Kali. The girl is then pressured into accepting a worship that eventually drives her mad. In Bengali with English subtitles. **93m/B VHS.** *IN* Chhabi Biswas, Sharmila Tagore, Soumitra Chatterjee; **D:** Satyajit Ray. *COL, WFV, DVT*

Devices and Desires 🎬🎬🎬 *P.D. James'*
Devices & Desires **1991** Typically complicated mystery adapted from the novel by P.D. James. Scotland Yard Commander Adam Dalgliesh (Marsden) is on holiday on the east coast of England where, of course, there's blackmail, murder, suicide, and trouble at a nearby nuclear power station for him to contend with. Made for TV; on six cassettes. **312m/C VHS.** *GB* Roy Marsden, Susannah York, Gemma Jones, James Faulkner, Tony Haygarth, Tom Georgeson, Tom Chadbon, Nicola Cowper, Suzan Crowley, Robert Hines, Harry Burton, Helena Michell; **D:** John Davies; **W:** Thomas Ellice. *TVC, AEH*

The Devil & Daniel Webster 🎬🎬🎬½ *All That Money Can Buy; Here Is a Man; A Certain Mr. Scratch* **1941** In 1840s New Hampshire, a young farmer, who sells his soul to the devil, is saved from a trip to Hell when Daniel Webster steps in to defend him. This classic fantasy is visually striking and contains wonderful performances. Adapted from the story by Stephen Vincent Benet who based it on Goethe's Faust. **106m/B VHS, Beta, LV.** James Craig, Edward Arnold, Walter Huston, Simone Simon, Gene Lockhart, Jane Darwell, Anne Shirley, John Qualen, H.B. Warner; **D:** William Dieterle; **M:** Bernard Herrmann. Academy Awards '41: Best Original Dramatic/Comedy Score; Nominations: Academy Awards '41: Best Actor (Huston). *HMV, CRC, FCT*

Devil & Leroy Basset 🎬 **1973 (PG)**
Keema Gregwolf kills a deputy, breaks from jail with the Basset brothers, hijacks a church bus, kidnaps a family, and gets into other troublesome situations while on a posse-eluding cross-country adventure. **85m/C VHS, Beta.** Cody Bearpaw, John Goff, George Flower; **D:** Robert E. Pearso; **M:** Les Baxter.

The Devil & Max Devlin 🎬🎬½ **1981 (PG)**
Good cast wanders aimlessly in Disney family fantasy. The recently deceased Max Devlin strikes a bargain with the devil. He will be restored to life if he can convince three mortals to sell their souls. **95m/C VHS, Beta.** Elliott Gould, Bill Cosby, Susan Anspach, Adam Rich, Julie Budd; **D:** Steven Hilliard Stern; **W:** Jimmy Sangster; **M:** Marvin Hamlisch, Buddy Baker. *DIS, OM*

The Devil & Miss Jones 🎬🎬🎬½
1941 Engaging romantic comedy finds a big business boss posing as an ordinary salesclerk to weed out union organizers. He doesn't expect to encounter the wicked management or his beautiful co-worker, however. **90m/B VHS.** Jean Arthur, Robert Cummings, Charles Coburn, Edmund Gwenn, Spring Byington, William Demarest, S.Z. Sakall; **D:** Sam Wood; **C:** Harry Stradling. Nominations: Academy Awards '41: Best Original Screenplay, Best Supporting Actor (Coburn). *REP*

The Devil at 4 O'Clock 🎬🎬 **1961**
An alcoholic missionary and three convicts work to save a colony of leper children from a South Seas volcano. Quality cast barely compensates for mediocre script. **126m/B VHS, Beta, LV.** Spencer

Tracy, Frank Sinatra, Kerwin Mathews, Jean-Pierre Aumont; **D:** Mervyn LeRoy; **C:** Joseph Biroc; **M:** George Duning. *GKK, IME*

The Devil Bat 🎬🎬 *Killer Bats* **1941** Madman Lugosi trains a swarm of monstrous blood-sucking bats to attack whenever they smell perfume. Followed by the sequel "Devil Bat's Daughter." DVD release is paired with the Lugosi vehicle "Scared to Death" (1946). **67m/B VHS, Beta, DVD.** Bela Lugosi, Dave O'Brien, Suzanne Kaaren, Yolande Donlan; **D:** Jean Yarbrough. *NOS, SNC, DVT*

The Devil Bat's Daughter 🎬½ **1946** A young woman, hoping to avoid becoming insane like her batty father, consults a psychiatrist when she starts to have violent nightmares. Unsuccessful sequel to "The Devil Bat." **66m/B VHS, Beta.** Rosemary La Planche, Michael Hale, John James, Molly Lamont; **D:** Frank Wisbar. *COL, MRV*

Devil Diamond 🎬 **1937** Mystery-suspense yarn about two amateur detectives who find themselves facing danger after tracking down a gang of evil jewel thieves. **?m/C VHS.** Kane Richmond, Frankie Darro. *SNC, VYY*

Devil Dog: The Hound of Hell 🎬
1978 A family has trouble with man's best friend when they adopt a dog that is the son of the "Hound of Hell" in this made-for-television movie. **95m/C VHS, Beta.** Richard Crenna, Yvette Mimieux, Kim Richards, Victor Jory; **D:** Curtis Harrington. *NO*

Devil Dogs of the Air 🎬🎬½ **1935**
Cagney and O'Brien team up in another air drama with Cagney once again the cocky pilot who, this time, joins the Marine Air Corp. O'Brien plays his flying idol (and later rival). Cagney finds all his wisecracking and luck are no match for knowledge and experience but he learns. Good stunt flying; shot on location at the San Diego naval air base. **85m/B VHS.** James Cagney, Pat O'Brien, Margaret Lindsay, Frank McHugh, Robert Barrat, Russell Hicks, Ward Bond; **D:** Lloyd Bacon. *MGM, FCT*

Devil Doll 🎬🎬🎬 **1936** An escaped convict uses a mad scientist's human-shrinking formula to evil ends—he sends out miniature assassins in the guise of store-bought dolls. Rarely seen horror oldie. **80m/B VHS, Beta.** Lionel Barrymore, Maureen O'Sullivan, Frank Lawton, Rafaela Ottiano, Henry B. Walthall, Arthur Hohl, Grace Ford; **D:** Tod Browning; **W:** Tod Browning, Erich von Stroheim, Guy Endore, Garrett Fort; **C:** Leonard Smith. *MGM, MLB*

Devil Doll 🎬🎬 **1964** Ventriloquist's dummy, which contains the soul of a former performer, eyes a beautiful victim in the crowd. Newspaper guy senses trouble. Cut above the usual talking, stalking dummy story. **80m/B VHS, Beta.** *GB* Bryant Holiday, William Sylvester, Yvonne Romain, Sandra Dorne, Karel Stepanek, Francis De Wolff; **D:** Lindsay Shonteff; **W:** Lance Z. Hargreaves, George Barclay; **C:** Gerald Gibbs. *NO*

Devil Girl from Mars 🎬½ **1954** Sexy female from Mars and her very large robot arrive at a small Scottish inn to announce that a Martian feminist revolution has occurred. The distaff aliens then undertake a search of healthy Earth males for breeding purposes. Believe it or not, the humans don't want to go and therein lies the rub. A somewhat enjoyable space farce. **76m/B VHS.** *GB* Hugh McDermott, Hazel Court, Patricia Laffan, Peter Reynolds, Adrienne Corri, Joseph Tomelty, Sophie Stewart, John Laurie, Anthony Richmond; **D:** David MacDonald; **W:** John C. Mather, James Eastwood. *EEL, MRV, SNC*

Devil Horse 🎬🎬 **1932** A boy's devotion to a wild horse marked for destruction as a killer leads him into trouble. A serial in 12 chapters of 13 minutes each. **156m/B VHS, Beta.** Frankie Darro, Harry Carey Sr., Noah Beery Sr.; **D:** Otto Brower, Richard Talmadge. *GPV, VCN, DVT*

Devil in a Blue Dress 🎬🎬🎬 **1995 (R)**
Down-on-his-luck Easy Rawlins (Washington) is an out of work aircraft worker in 1948 LA. He's hired to find mystery woman Daphne (Beals) by a shady businessman (Sizemore). What he finds are the usual noir staples: government corruption backed by thugs who want him to mind his own

business. Easy and Daphne's torrid romance featured in the Walter Mosley novel is missing but the racism and violence are intact. Realism and accuracy in period detail enhance solid performance by Washington, though the deliberate, literary pace is at times lulling. Cheadle takes over whenever he shows up as Mouse, Rawlins' loyal friend and muscle.**CW:** Violence; sexuality; language. **102m/C VHS, LV, Closed Caption.** Denzel Washington, Jennifer Beals, Don Cheadle, Tom Sizemore, Maury Chaykin, Terry Kinney, Mel Winkler, Albert Hall; **D:** Carl Franklin; **W:** Carl Franklin; **C:** Tak Fujimoto; **M:** Elmer Bernstein. Los Angeles Film Critics Association Awards '95: Best Supporting Actor (Cheadle); National Society of Film Critics Awards '95: Best Cinematography, Best Supporting Actor (Cheadle); Nominations: Screen Actors Guild Award '95: Best Supporting Actor (Cheadle).*COL*

The Devil in Silk 🎬🎬 **1956** A composer marries a woman, not knowing that she is psychotically jealous. After she commits suicide, he must prove to the police that he did not kill her. Original dialogue in German. **102m/B VHS, Beta.** *GE* Lilli Palmer, Curt Jurgens, Winnie Markus; **D:** Rolf Hansen. *NOS, SNC*

Devil in the Flesh 🎬🎬🎬 *Le Diable au Corps* **1946** Acclaimed drama about a French soldier's wife having a passionate affair with a high school student while her husband is away fighting in WWI. From the novel by Raymond Radiguet. Dubbed. Updated and remade in 1987. **112m/B VHS, Beta.** *FR* Gerard Philipe, Micheline Presle, Denise Grey; **D:** Claude Autant-Lara. *NOS, FCT*

Devil in the Flesh 🎬🎬 *Il Diavolo in Corpo* **1987 (R)** A angst-ridden, semi-pretentious Italian drama about an obsessive older woman carrying on an affair with a schoolboy, despite her terrorist boyfriend and the objections of the lad's psychiatrist father, who had treated her. In Italian with subtitles. Famous for a graphic sex scene, available in the unrated version. Updated remake of the 1946 French film.**CW:** Strong language and strong sexuality. **110m/C VHS, Beta, LV.** *IT* Maruschka Detmers, Federico Pitzalis; **D:** Marco Bellocchio; **W:** Marco Bellocchio. *ORI*

Devil Kiss 🎬 **1977** Gothic horror including zombies, virgins, sorcery, and the inevitable living dead. **93m/C VHS, Beta.** Oliver Mathews, Evelyn Scott. *HMV*

Devil Monster 🎬 **1946** A world-weary traveler searches for a girl's fiance in the South Pacific, and is attacked by a large manta. **65m/B VHS, Beta, LV.** Barry Norton, Blanche Mehaffey; **D:** S. Edwin Graham. *SNC*

Devil of the Desert Against the Son of Hercules 🎬🎬½ **1962** The grandson of Zeus ventures into the wasteland to take on a feisty foe. **?m/C VHS, Beta.** *IT* Kirk Morris, Michele Girardon; **D:** Riccardo (Robert Hampton) Freda. *SNC*

Devil on Horseback 🎬🎬 **1954** A miner's son journeys to London to become a jockey in this comedy/drama. As he tries to bully his way into the racing circuit, he succeeds, but not in the way he anticipated. **88m/B VHS, Beta, 8mm.** *GB* Googie Withers, John McCallum, Jeremy Spenser, Liam Redmond; **D:** Cyril Frankel; **M:** Malcolm Arnold. *VYY*

The Devil on Wheels 🎬🎬 **1947** Inspired by his dad's reckless driving, a teenager becomes a hot rodder and causes a family tragedy. A rusty melodrama that can't be described as high-performance. **67m/B VHS.** James B. Cardwell, Noreen Nash, Darryl Hickman, Jan Ford, Damian O'Flynn, Lenita Love. *NOS, LOO*

The Devil, Probably 🎬🎬 *Le Diable, Probablement* **1977** Ennui among Parisian youth, lost in their polluted, consumer society. Charles (Monnier) spins deeper into depression, despite the efforts of his friends, and finally makes a bargain with a junkie to shoot him in Pere Lachaise cemetery. French with subtitles. **95m/C VHS.** *FR* Antoine Monnier, Tina Irissari, Henri De Maublanc; **D:** Robert Bresson; **W:** Robert Bresson; **C:** Pasquale De Santis; **M:** Philippe Sarde. *NYF*

Devil Rider *Woof½* 1001 A monster from Hell, the Devil Rider, once rode the plains in search of human fodder. In the present day, a pleasure ranch is built on his old territory, and people begin dying in the most horrific manners. Could this mean the return of the Devil Rider? **90m/C VHS. NO**

Devil Riders *Woof½* 1944 Unspectacular horse opera has a crooked lawyer trying to get his grubby hands on some choice land. Enter Crabbe to set things straight. **56m/B VHS.** Buster Crabbe, Al "Fuzzy" St. John, Patti McCarty, Charles "Blackie" King, John Merton, Kermit Maynard, Frank LaRue, Jack Ingram, George Chesebro, Edward Cassidy; **D:** Sam Newfield. *NOS, MRV*

The Devil Thumbs a Ride *Woof Woof Woof* 1947 A naive traveller picks up a hitchhiker, not knowing he's wanted for murder. Will history repeat itself in this interesting noir? **63m/B VHS, Beta.** Ted North, Lawrence Tierney, Nan Leslie; **D:** Felix Feist. *NO*

The Devil Thumbs a Ride/Having Wonderful Crime 1947 A mystery double feature. In "Devil Thumbs a Ride," a ruthless killer-bank robber hitches a ride from an inebriated travelling salesman. In "Having Wonderful Crime," a criminal lawyer investigates the disappearance of a magician. **132m/B VHS, Beta.** Lawrence Tierney, Pat O'Brien, George Murphy, Carole Landis, Nan Leslie, George Zucco; **D:** Felix Feist, Edward Sutherland. *NO*

Devil Times Five *Woof½ People Toys; The Horrible House on the Hill* 1974 (R) To take revenge for being incarcerated in a mental hospital, five children methodically murder the adults who befriend them. **87m/C VHS, Beta.** Gene Evans, Sorrell Booke, Shelly Morrison; **D:** Sean McGregor.

Devil Wears White *Woof* 1986 (R) A student's vacation is disrupted when he becomes involved in a war with an insane arms dealer who wants to take over a Latin American Republic. **92m/C VHS, Beta.** Robert Livesy, Jane Higginson, Guy Ecker, Anthony Cordova; **D:** Steven A. Hull. *TWE*

Devil Woman woof! 1976 (R) A Filipino Gorgon-woman seeks reptilian revenge on the farmers who killed her family. Bad news. **79m/C VHS.** PH Rosemarie Gil; **D:** Albert Yu, Felix Vilars. *SNC*

Devilfish *Woof* 1984 A small seaside community is ravaged by berserk manta rays in this soggy saga. **92m/C VHS, Beta.** IT **D:** Lamberto Bava. *THV*

The Devils *Woof Woof Woof* 1971 (R) In 1631 France, a priest is accused of commerce with the devil and sexual misconduct with nuns. Since he is also a political threat, the accusation is used to denounce and eventually execute him. Based on Aldous Huxley's "The Devils of Loudun," the movie features masturbating nuns and other excesses—shocking scenes typical of film director Russell. Supposedly this was Russell's attempt to wake the public to their desensitization of modern horrors of war. Controversial and flamboyant. **109m/C VHS, Beta.** GB Vanessa Redgrave, Oliver Reed, Dudley Sutton, Max Adrian, Gemma Jones, Murray Melvin, Michael Gothard, Georgina Hale, Christopher Logue, Andrew Faulds; **D:** Ken Russell; **W:** Ken Russell; **C:** David Watkin. National Board of Review Awards '71: Best Director (Russell). *WAR*

The Devil's Advocate *Woof Woof½* 1997 (R) Forget the actors, this film belongs to cinematographer Bartkowiak and production designer Bruno Rubeo, who offer a lush, rich look that's very enticing. And it's all about enticement—young Florida lawyer Kevin Lomax (Reeves) is seduced by the power and money of a position at an influential New York law firm run by the mysterious John Milton (Pacino). But soon Kevin's beautiful wife Mary Ann (Theron) is having a breakdown, his religious mother (Ivey) is prophesizing doom, and Kevin learns the boss is Satan—literally. Reeves is earnest, Pacino relishes his showy role, and the visual effects provide some much needed jolts. Based on the novel by Andrew Neiderman. **144m/C VHS, LV, Letterbox, Closed Caption.** Al Pacino, Keanu

Reeves, Charlize Theron, Judith Ivey, Craig T. Nelson, Jeffrey Jones, Connie Nielsen, Ruben Santiago-Hudson, Debra Monk, Tamara Tunie, Vyto Ruginis, Laura Harrington, Pamela Gray, Heather Matarazzo, Delroy Lindo; **D:** Taylor Hackford; **W:** Tony Gilroy, Jonathan Lemkin; **C:** Andrzej Bartkowiak; **M:** James Newton Howard. Nominations: MTV Movie Awards '98: Best Villain (Pacino). *WAR*

Devil's Angels *Woof* 1967 A motorcycle gang clashes with a small-town sheriff. Cheap 'n' sleazy fare. **84m/C VHS.** John Cassavetes, Beverly Adams, Mimsy Farmer, Salli Sachse, Nai Bonet, Leo Gordon; **D:** Daniel Haller; **W:** Charles B. Griffith. *NO*

The Devil's Brigade *Woof Woof* 1968 "Dirty Dozen" style film with Holden as the leader of special commando brigade consisting of the usual misfits and oddballs. The team is trained to take on the Nazis in Scandanavia but has their assignment cancelled. Instead, they take them on in the Italian Alps, making for some perilous adventures. Non-acting notables include former football great Hornung and former boxing champ Gene Fullmer. **130m/C VHS, Beta.** William Holden, Cliff Robertson, Vince Edwards, Michael Rennie, Dana Andrews, Gretchen Wyler, Andrew Prine, Claude Akins, Carroll O'Connor, Richard Jaeckel, Jack Watson, Paul Hornung, Jeremy Slate, Don Megowan, Patric Knowles, James Craig, Richard Dawson, Tom Stern, Luke Askew; **D:** Andrew V. McLaglen; **W:** William Roberts; **C:** William Clothier; **M:** Alex North. *MGM*

The Devil's Brother *Woof Woof Fra Diavolo; Bogus Bandits; The Virtuous Tramps* 1933 In one of their lesser efforts, Laurel and Hardy star as bumbling bandits in this comic operetta based on the 1830 opera by Daniel F. Auber. Also available with "Laurel & Hardy's Laughing '20s" on laserdisc. **88m/B VHS.** Stan Laurel, Oliver Hardy, Dennis King, Thelma Todd, James Finlayson, Lucille Browne; **D:** Charles R. Rogers, Hal Roach. *MGM, MLB, CCB*

Devil's Canyon *Woof Woof* 1953 An ex-lawman, serving time in an Arizona prison, is beset by a jailed killer seeking vengeance for his own incarceration. Filmed in 3-D. **92m/B VHS, Beta.** Dale Robertson, Virginia Mayo, Stephen McNally, Arthur Hunnicutt, Robert Keith, Jay C. Flippen, Whit Bissell; **D:** Alfred Werker. *TTC*

The Devil's Cargo *Woof½* 1948 When a man is accused of killing a racetrack operator, he calls in the Falcon to clear his name. The master detective finds this to be a most difficult task however, especially when the accused is found poisoned in his cell. One of the final three "Falcon" films, in which Calvert replaced Tom Conway. **61m/B VHS, Beta.** John Calvert, Rochelle Hudson, Roscoe Karns, Lyle Talbot, Tom Kennedy; **D:** John F. Link. *SNC*

The Devil's Commandment *Woof Woof I, Vampiri; Lust of the Vampires* 1956 A lurid melodrama about a Parisian newspaperman's journey into a network of crime and perversion. **90m/B VHS, Beta, LV.** FR Gianna Maria Canale, Dario Michaelis, Carlo D'Angelo, Wandisa Guida, Paul Muller, Renato Tontini; **D:** Riccardo (Robert Hampton) Freda; **C:** Mario Bava. *SNC*

Devil's Crude *Woof* 1971 Adventurous sailor and a young oil heir uncover a conspiracy within a giant corporation. **85m/C VHS, Beta.** IT Franco Nero. *TWE*

The Devil's Daughter *Woof½ Pocomania; Poncomania* 1939 A sister's hatred and voodoo ceremonies play an important part in this all-black drama. **60m/B VHS, Beta.** Nina Mae McKinney, Jack Carter, Ida James, Hamtree Harrington. *SNC, VYY, DVT*

The Devil's Daughter 1991 (R) Satan, in a desperate bid to take over the planet, orders his minions to flood the earth with horrific evil. Only one woman can prevent the HellMaster from succeeding, and she may be too late! **CW:** Horror violence. **112m/C VHS, Closed Caption.** IT Kelly Curtis, Herbert Lom, Maria Angela Giordano, Michel Hans Adatte, Carla Cassola, Angelika Maria Boeck, Tomas Arana; **D:** Michele (Michael) Soavi; **W:** Dario Argento; **M:** Pino Donaggio. *REP*

The Devil's Disciple *Woof Woof Woof* 1959 Entertaining adaptation of George Bernard Shaw play set during the American Revolution. Standout performances by Douglas as a romantic rogue, Lancaster as a New England pastor, and Olivier as British General Burgoyne. Film suffers from choppy direction, but the excellent cast more than makes up for it. **82m/B VHS, Closed Caption.** GB Burt Lancaster, Kirk Douglas, Laurence Olivier, Janet Scott, Eva LeGallienne, Harry Andrews, Basil Sydney, George Rose; **D:** Guy Hamilton; **C:** Jack Hildyard; **M:** Richard Rodney Bennett. *MGM*

The Devil's Eye *Woof Woof Djavulens Oga* 1960 The devil dispatches Don Juan to tempt and seduce a young virgin bride-to-be, a reverend's daughter, no less. Based on the Danish radio play "Don Juan Returns." **90m/B VHS, Beta.** SW Bibi Andersson, Jarl Kulle; **D:** Ingmar Bergman; **W:** Ingmar Bergman. *NLC*

Devil's Gift woof! 1984 A young boy's toy is possessed by a demon and havoc ensues. **112m/C VHS, Beta.** Bob Mendlesolin, Vicki Saputo, Steven Robertson; **D:** Kenneth Berton. *ART, VES*

The Devil's Hand *Woof Devil's Doll; The Naked Goddess; Live to Love* 1961 When Alda finds a doll that represents his ideal woman in a curio shop, the shop's owner (Hamilton, aka Commissioner Gordon), tells him the dream girl who modeled for the doll lives nearby. Trouble is, she's part of a voodoo cult, and guess who's head voodoo-man. Big trouble for Alda; big snooze for you. **71m/B VHS.** Linda Christian, Robert Alda, Neil Hamilton, Ariadne Welter; **D:** William Hole Jr. *NOS, SNC, LOO*

The Devil's Mistress *Woof½* 1968 A gang of criminals on a pillaging spree murder a man and rape his Indian wife, only to find out she's a she-demon who won't let bygones be bygones. Lame. **66m/C VHS.** Joan Stapleton, Robert Gregory, Forrest Westmoreland, Douglas Warren, Oren Williams, Arthur Resley; **D:** Orville Wanzer; **W:** Orville Wanzer. *SNC*

The Devil's Nightmare *Woof½ Succubus; The Devil Walks at Midnight* 1971 (R) A woman leads seven tourists (representing the seven deadly sins) on a tour of a medieval European castle. There they experience demonic tortures. Lots of creepy moments. Euro-horror/sex star Blanc is fantastic in this otherwise mediocre production. **88m/C VHS, Beta.** BE IT Erika Blanc, Jean Servais, Daniel Emilfork, Lucien Raimbourg, Jacques Monseau, Colette Emmanuelle, Ivana Novak, Shirley Corrigan, Frederique Hender; **D:** Jean Brismee. *APP*

The Devil's Own *Woof Woof Woof* 1996 (R) Irish-American New York cop Tom O'Meara (Harrison) and wife Sheila (Colin) take charming Irish emigre Rory Devaney (Pitt) into their home and make him part of the family. But Rory, AKA Frankie McGuire, turns out to be an IRA terrorist who has hustled out of trouble in Belfast and now has a bloody purpose for coming to America. When Tom discovers just what it is, he tries to stop Rory before he destroys any more lives—including his own. More a low-key character study than a slam-bang actioner, with Pitt cooly charismatic as the troubled gunman while Ford does his usual professional work as a good cop caught up in a bad situation. **CW:** Strong brutal violence, and for language. **110m/C VHS, Closed Caption, DVD.** Harrison Ford, Brad Pitt, Margaret Colin, Ruben Blades, Treat Williams, George Hearn, Natascha McElhone, Mitchell Ryan, Simon Jones, Paul Ronan; **D:** Alan J. Pakula; **W:** Kevin Jarre, David Aaron Cohen, Vincent Patrick; **C:** Gordon Willis; **M:** James Horner. *COL*

The Devil's Partner *Woof½* 1958 Yet another uninspired devil yarn in which an old-timer trades in his senior citizenship by dying and coming back in the form of his younger self. Young again, he takes a new wife and indulges in multiple ritual sacrifices. Noteworthy only by virtue of the cast's later TV notoriety—Buchanan and Foulger would later appear on "Petticoat Junction," Nelson played Dr. Rossi on "Peyton Place," and Crane beached a role on "Hawaiian Eye." **75m/B**

VHS. Ed Nelson, Jean Allison, Edgar Buchanan, Richard Crane, Spencer Carlisle, Byron Foulger, Claire Carleton; *D:* Charles R. Rondeau. *SNC, MRV, CNM*

Devil's Party 🎬🎬 **1938** A tenement boy's reunion party turns into a night of horror when one of the guests is killed. As a result, the childhood friends band together to uncover the murderer's identity. 65m/B VHS, Beta. Victor McLaglen, Paul Kelly, William Gargan, Samuel S. Hinds, Scotty Beckett; *D:* Ray McCarey. *NOS, MRV, DVT*

The Devil's Playground 🎬🎬🎬 **1976** Sexual tension rises in a Catholic seminary, distracting the boys from their theological studies. The attentions of the priests only further their sexual confusion. Winner of many Australian film awards. 107m/C Beta. *AU* Arthur Dignam, Nick Tate, Simon Burke, Charles Frawley, Jonathon Hardy, Gerry Dugan, Thomas Keneally; *D:* Fred Schepisi; *W:* Fred Schepisi; *C:* Ian Baker; *M:* Bruce Smeaton. Australian Film Institute '76: Best Actor (Tate), Best Actor (Burke), Best Film.

The Devil's Possessed 🎬½ **1974** A Middle Ages despot tortures and maims the peasants in his region until they rise up and enact an unspeakable revenge. 90m/C VHS, Beta. AR SP Paul Naschy; *D:* Leon Klimovsky. *NO*

Devil's Rain 🎬½ **1975 (PG)** The rituals and practices of devil worship, possession, and satanism are gruesomely related. Interesting cast. 85m/C VHS, Beta, LV. Ernest Borgnine, Ida Lupino, William Shatner, Eddie Albert, Keenan Wynn, John Travolta, Tom Skerritt; *D:* Robert Fuest; *W:* James Ashton, Gabe Essoe, Gerald Hopman; *C:* Alex Phillips Jr. *NO*

The Devil's Sleep 🎬 **1951** When a crusading woman sets out to break up a teen narcotics ring, the threatened thugs attempt to draw her daughter into their sleazy affairs, thus assuring the mother's silence. 81m/B VHS, Beta. Lita Grey Chaplin, Timothy Farrell, John Mitchum, William Thomason, Tracy Lynn; *D:* W. Merle Connell. *SNC*

Devil's Son-in-Law woof! **1977 (R)** A black stand-up comic makes a deal with a devil. 95m/C VHS, Beta. Rudy Ray Moore; *D:* Cliff Roguemore. *NO*

The Devil's Undead 🎬🎬½ **1975 (PG)** When a Scottish orphanage is besieged by a rash of cold-blooded murders, the detectives Lee and Cushing are summoned to investigate. Interesting spin on that old possessed by demons theme. 90m/C VHS, Beta. *GB* Christopher Lee, Peter Cushing; *D:* Peter Sasdy. *MLB*

Devil's Wanton 🎬🎬½ *Fangelse; Prison* **1949** A young girl tries to forget an unhappy relationship by beginning a new romance with an equally frustrated beau. Gloomy, but hopeful. 80m/B VHS, Beta. *SW* Doris Svedlund, Eva Henning, Hasse Ekman; *D:* Ingmar Bergman; *W:* Ingmar Bergman. *VYY, MRV, DVT*

The Devil's Web 🎬½ **1974 (PG)** A demonic nurse infiltrates, manipulates, and corrupts three beautiful sisters. 73m/C VHS, Beta. Diana Dors, Andrea Marcovicci, Ed Bishop, Cec Linder, Michael Culver. *ART*

Devil's Wedding Night woof! *El Returno de la Drequessa Dracula; The Return of the Duchess Dracula; Full Moon of the Virgins* **1973 (R)** An archaeologist and his twin brother fight over a ring that lures virgins into Count Dracula's Transylvanian castle. Vampire queen Bay seduces the dimwit twins and strips at every chance she gets. 85m/C VHS, Beta. Mark Damon, Rosalba (Sara Bay) Neri, Frances Davis; *D:* Paul Solvay. *NO*

Devlin 🎬🎬 **1992 (R)** Devlin is a tough cop with an alcohol problem and a bad marriage. His father-in-law, Brennan, is a powerful local political boss. When Brennan's son is murdered, Devlin is the fall guy. Seeking to clear himself, he discovers a conspiracy going back 30 years. Made for cable television.*CW:* Language, violence and drug use, and sexuality. 110m/C VHS, Beta, LV. Bryan Brown, Roma Downey, Lloyd Bridges; *D:* Rick Rosenthal; *M:* Minette Alton. *FXV, VTR*

The Devlin Connection 🎬🎬 **1982** Retired private investigator helps his son learn the ropes as he embarks on a Los Angeles crime fighting career. Hudson's last starring television series, excluding his "Dynasty" role. All 13 episodes are available separately. 50m/C VHS, Beta. Rock Hudson, Jack Scalia, Louis Giambalvo, Leigh Taylor-Young, Jack Kruschen; *D:* Christian Nyby. *TWE*

Devonsville Terror 🎬🎬 **1983 (R)** Strange things begin to happen when a new school teacher arrives in Devonsville, a town that has a history of torture, murder, and witchcraft. The hysterical townspeople react by beginning a 20th-century witchhunt. 97m/C VHS, Beta. Suzanna Love, Donald Pleasence, Deanna Haas, Mary Walden, Robert Walker Jr., Paul Wilson; *D:* Ulli Lommel; *W:* Ulli Lommel.

Devotion 🎬🎬½ **1931** A lovesick British miss disguises herself as a governess so she can be near the object of her affection, a London barrister. 80m/B VHS. Ann Harding, Leslie Howard, Robert Williams, O.P. Heggie, Louise Closser Hale, Dudley Digges; *D:* Robert Milton. *TTC*

D.I. 🎬🎬 **1957** A tough drill sergeant is faced with an unbreakable rebellious recruit, threatening his record and his platoon's status. Webb's film features performances by actual soldiers. 106m/B VHS, Beta. Jack Webb, Don Dubbins, Jackie Loughery, Lin McCarthy, Virginia Gregg; *D:* Jack Webb. *WAR*

The Diabolical Dr. Z 🎬🎬 **1965** *Miss Muette; Dans les Griffes du Maniaque* When dad dies of cardiac arrest after the medical council won't let him make the world a kinder gentler place with his personality-altering technique, his dutiful daughter—convinced the council brought on dad's demise—is out to change some personalities in a big way. 86m/B VHS. *SP FR* Mabel Karr, Fernando Montes, Estella Blain, Antonio J. Escribano, Howard Vernon; *D:* Jess (Jesus) Franco. *SNC*

Diabolically Yours 🎬🎬½ *Diaboliquement Votre* **1967** A French thriller about an amnesiac who struggles to discover his lost identity. Tensions mount when his pretty spouse and friends begin to wonder if it's all a game. Dubbed. 94m/C VHS, Beta. *FR* Alain Delon, Senta Berger; *D:* Julien Duvivier. *UNI*

Diabolique 🎬🎬🎬½ *Les Diabolique* **1955** The mistress and the wife of a sadistic schoolmaster conspire to murder the man, carry it out, and then begin to wonder if they have covered their tracks effectively. Plot twists and double-crosses abound. In French with English subtitles. Remade for television as "Reflections of Murder." 107m/B VHS, Beta, LV, 8mm. *FR* Simone Signoret, Vera Clouzot, Paul Meurisse, Charles Vanel, Michel Serrault; *D:* Henri-Georges Clouzot. New York Film Critics Awards '55: Best Foreign Film. *VYY, NOS, SNC*

Diabolique 🎬½ **1996 (R)** Remake of the 1955 French noir classic, updated for '90s sensibilities, finds timid teacher Mia (Adjani) married to overbearing school head Guy (Palminteri), who's having an affair with fellow teacher Nicole (Stone). The two women, who loathe Guy equally, plot to kill him. But when a P.I. (Bates) investigates, it seems possible that Guy isn't dead after all. If you're having trouble accessorizing with leopard skin, watch Stone. Otherwise, watch the far superior original. The usually publicity hungry Stone refused to have anything to do with this picture after its release due to a spat with director Chechik.*CW:* Violence/terror, sexuality and language. 105m/C VHS, LV. Sharon Stone, Isabelle Adjani, Chazz Palminteri, Kathy Bates, Spalding Gray, Shirley Knight, Adam Hann-Byrd, Allen (Goorwitz) Garfield; *D:* Jeremiah S. Chechik; *W:* Don Roos; *C:* Peter James; *M:* Randy Edelman. *WAR*

Dial Help 🎬½ *Ragno Gelido; Minaccia d'Amore* **1988 (R)** A lame Italian-made suspenser about a model plagued by ghostly phone calls. 94m/C VHS, Beta. *IT* Charlotte Lewis, Marcello Modugno, Mattia Sbragia, Victor Cavallo, William Berger, Carlo Monni, Carola Stagnaro; *D:* Ruggero Deodato; *C:* Renato Tafuri.

Dial "M" for Murder 🎬🎬🎬 **1954** An unfaithful husband devises an elaborate plan to murder his wife for her money, but when she accidentally stabs the killer-to-be, with scissors no less, he alters his methods. Part of the "A Night at the Movies" series, this tape simulates a 1954 movie evening with a Daffy Duck cartoon, "My Little Duckaroo," a newsreel, and coming attractions for "Them" and "A Star Is Born." Filmed in 3-D. Based on the play by Frederick Knotts. 123m/C VHS, Beta, LV. Ray Milland, Grace Kelly, Robert Cummings, John Williams, Anthony Dawson; *D:* Alfred Hitchcock; *C:* Robert Burks; *M:* Dimitri Tiomkin. *WAR, TLF*

Diamond Fleece 🎬🎬½ **1992** Rick (Cross) is a convicted diamond thief who's given a parole just so he can guard the world's largest uncut gemstone. But Inspector Outlaw (Dennehy) figures Rick will never be able to resist stealing the gem himself and the law can finally lock Rick away for good. Oh, and Holly, she thinks a maybe-ex-diamond thief will bring a little romance to her life. 93m/C VHS. Ben Cross, Brian Dennehy, Kate Nelligan; *D:* Al Waxman; *W:* Michael Norell.

Diamond Head 🎬🎬½ **1962** A Hawaiian landowner brings destruction and misery to his family via his stubbornness. Based on the Peter Gilman novel. 107m/C VHS, Beta, LV. Charlton Heston, Yvette Mimieux, George Chakiris, France Nuyen, James Darren; *D:* Guy Green; *C:* Sam Leavitt; *M:* John Williams. *COL*

Diamond Run 🎬½ **1990 (R)** A streetwise American expatriate frantically searches for his girlfriend after unwittingly involving her in an assassination plot. 89m/C VHS, Beta, LV. William Bell Sullivan, Ava Lazar, Ayu Azhari, David Thornton, Peter Fox; *D:* Robert Chappell. *NO*

Diamond Trail 🎬½ **1933** East Coast jewel thieves bring their operation to the West, trailed by a New York reporter. 58m/B VHS, Beta. Rex Bell, Frances Rich, Bud Osborne, Lloyd Whitlock, Norman Feusier; *D:* Harry Fraser. *NOS, DVT*

The Diamond Trap 🎬🎬 **1991 (PG)** A Manhattan detective finds himself in the middle of a diamond heist and involved with a con artist. Made for television. 93m/C VHS, LV, Closed Caption. Howard Hesseman, Brooke Shields, Ed Marinaro, Twiggy; *D:* Don Taylor; *W:* David Peckinpah. *THV*

Diamonds 🎬🎬 **1972 (PG)** A tense film in which the Israel Diamond Exchange is looted by a motley array of criminal heisters. Shaw plays a dual role as twin brothers. 108m/C VHS, Beta. *IS* Robert Shaw, Richard Roundtree, Barbara Harvey, Shelley Winters; *D:* Menahem Golan. *NLC*

Diamonds Are Forever 🎬🎬🎬½ **1971 (PG)** 007 once again battles his nemesis Blofeld, this time in Las Vegas. Bond must prevent the implementation of a plot to destroy Washington through the use of a space-orbiting laser. Fabulous stunts include Bond's wild drive through the streets of Vegas in a '71 Mach 1. Connery returned to play Bond in this film after being offered the then record-setting salary of one million dollars. 120m/C VHS, Beta, LV, Letterbox, Closed Caption. *GB* Sean Connery, Jill St. John, Charles Gray, Bruce Cabot, Jimmy Dean, Lana Wood, Bruce Glover, Putter Smith, Norman Burton, Joseph Furst, Bernard Lee, Desmond Llewelyn, Laurence Naismith, Leonard Barr, Lois Maxwell, Margaret Lacey, Joe Robinson, Donna Garrat, Trina Parks; *D:* Guy Hamilton; *W:* Tom Mankiewicz; *C:* Ted Moore; *M:* John Barry. Nominations: Academy Awards '71: Best Sound. *MGM, TLF*

Diamond's Edge 🎬🎬 *Just Ask for Diamond* **1988 (PG)** An adolescent private eye and his juvenescent brother snoop into the affairs of the Fat Man, and find out that the opera ain't over until they find out what's in the Fat Man's mysterious box of bon-bons. A genre-parodying kid mystery, written by Horowitz, based on his novel, "The Falcon's Malteser." 83m/C VHS, Beta, Closed Caption. Susannah York, Peter Eyre, Patricia Hodge, Nickolas Grace; *D:* Stephen Bayly; *W:* Anthony Horowitz; *M:* Trevor Jones. *HBO*

Diamonds of the Night 🐕🐕🐕🐕 *Demanty Noci* 1964 A breakthrough masterpiece of the Czech new wave, about two young men escaping from a transport train to Auschwitz and scrambling for survival in the countryside. Surreal, powerfully expressionistic film, one of the most important of its time. In Czech with English subtitles. Accompanied by Nemec's short "A Loaf of Bread." 71m/B VHS, Beta. *CZ* Ladislav Jansky, Antonin Kumbera, Ilse Bischofova; *D:* Jan Nemec; *W:* Arnost Lustig, Jan Nemec. *FCT*

Diana: Her True Story 🐕🐕½ 1993 Britain's royals are held up to scandalous review in this made for tv adaptaion of Andrew Morton's sympathetic bio of the Princess of Wales. Taking Diana from her lonely childhood to her "fairytale" nuptials and subsequent disillusion with being a royal, including her bulimia and half-hearted suicide attempts. Charles is portrayed as an arrogant, emotional cold fish, only interested in farming and continuing his liaison with Camilla Parker-Bowles. Handsome production with appropriate inpersonations by the cast. 180m/C VHS, Closed Caption. Serena Scott Thomas, David Threlfall, Elizabeth Garvie, Jemma Redgrave, Tracy Hardwick, Anne Stallybrass, Jeffrey Harmer, Donald Douglas; *D:* Kevin Connor; *W:* Stephen Zito. *NO*

Diane 🐕🐕 1955 Overstuffed medieval drama featuring Turner as Diane de Poitier, the mistress of a 16th century French King. Moore plays the king in his Hollywood debut. Gorgeous sets and costumes couldn't boost this film at the boxoffice, which had disappointing figures in spite of the expense bestowed upon it. Based on the novel "Diane de Poitier" by John Erskine. 110m/C VHS, LV, Letterbox. Lana Turner, Pedro Armendariz Sr., Roger Moore, Marisa Pavan, Cedric Hardwicke, Torin Thatcher, Taina Elg, John Lupton, Henry Daniell, Sean McClory, Michael Ansara; *D:* David Miller; *W:* Christopher Isherwood; *M:* Miklos Rozsa. *MGM*

Diary of a Chambermaid 🐕🐕🐕 1946 A chambermaid wants to marry a rich man and finds herself the object of desire of a poor servant willing to commit murder for her. Excellent comic drama, but very stylized in direction and set design. Produced during Renoir's years in Hollywood. Adapted from a story by Octave Mirbeau, later turned into a play. Remade in 1964 by Luis Bunuel. 86m/B VHS. Paulette Goddard, Burgess Meredith, Hurd Hatfield, Francis Lederer, Judith Anderson, Florence Bates, Almira Sessions, Reginald Owen; *D:* Jean Renoir. *REP, FCT*

Diary of a Chambermaid 🐕🐕🐕½ *Le Journal d'une Femme de Chambre; Il Diario di una Cameriera* 1964 Vintage Bunuelian social satire about a young girl taking a servant's job in a provincial French family, and easing into an atmosphere of sexual hypocrisy and decadence. In French with English subtitles. Remake of the 1946 Jean Renoir film. 97m/C VHS, Beta, LV. *FR* Jeanne Moreau, Michel Piccoli, Georges Geret, Francoise Lugagne, Daniel Ivernel; *D:* Luis Bunuel; *W:* Luis Bunuel, Jean-Claude Carriere. *IME, XVC*

Diary of a Country Priest 🐕🐕🐕½ *Le Journal d'un Cure de Campagne* 1950 With "Balthazar" and "Mouchette," this is one of Bresson's greatest, subtlest films, treating the story of an alienated, unrewarded young priest with his characteristic austerity and Catholic humanism. In French and English subtitles. 120m/B VHS, Beta. *FR* Claude Layou, Jean Riveyre, Nicole Ladmiral; *D:* Robert Bresson; *W:* Robert Bresson. *DVT, IGP, FCT*

Diary of a Hitman 🐕🐕½ 1991 (R) A hitman is hired to knock off the wife and child of a commodities broker who claims his wife is a drug addict and the infant is a crack baby and not his. The hired killer wants out of the business, but needs to pull off one more job for a down payment on his apartment. Beset by doubts, he breaks conduct by conversing with the victim and discovers the broker lied. Based on the play "Insider's Price" by Pressman. *CW:* Language and sensuali-

tv, 90m/C VHS, LV, Closed Caption. Forest Whitaker, James Belushi, Sherilyn Fenn, Sharon Stone, Seymour Cassel, Lewis Smith, Lois Chiles, John Bedford-Lloyd; *D:* Roy London; *W:* Kenneth Pressman; *M:* Michel Colombier. *COL*

Diary of a Lost Girl 🐕🐕🐕½ 1929 The second Louise Brooks/G.W. Pabst collaboration (after "Pandora's Box") in which a frail but mesmerizing German girl plummets into a life of hopeless degradation. Dark and gloomy, the film chronicles the difficulties she faces, from rape to an unwanted pregnancy and prostitution. Based on the popular book by Margarete Boehme. Silent. Made after flapper Brooks left Hollywood to pursue greater opportunities and more challenging roles under Pabst's guidance. 99m/B VHS, Beta, LV. *GE* Louise Brooks, Fritz Rasp, Josef Rovensky, Sybille Schmitz; *D:* G.W. Pabst. *GPV, MRV, VDM*

Diary of a Mad Housewife 🐕🐕🐕 1970 (R) Despairing of her miserable family life, a housewife has an affair with a writer only to find him to be even more selfish and egotistical than her no-good husband. Snodgress plays her character perfectly, hearing the insensitive absurdity of her husband and her lover over and over again, enjoying her martyrdom even as it drives her crazy. 94m/C VHS, Beta. Carrie Snodgress, Richard Benjamin, Frank Langella; *D:* Frank Perry. Golden Globe Awards '71: Best Actress—Musical/Comedy (Snodgress); National Board of Review Awards '70: Best Supporting Actor (Langella); Nominations: Academy Awards '70: Best Actress (Snodgress). *GKK*

Diary of a Mad Old Man 🐕🐕 *Dagboek Van Een Oude Dwaas* 1988 (PG-13) A wistful drama about an old man who's lost everything except his desire for his daughter-in-law, which sends him into fits of nostalgia. 93m/C VHS, Beta. Derek De Lint, Ralph Michael, Beatie Edney.

Diary of a Madman 🐕🐕 1963 Price is once again possessed by an evil force in this gothic thriller. Fairly average Price vehicle, based on Guy de Maupassant's story. 96m/C VHS, Beta. Vincent Price, Nancy Kovack, Chris Warfield, Ian Wolfe, Nelson Olmstead, Elaine Devry, Stephen Roberts; *D:* Reginald LeBorg; *W:* Robert Kent; *C:* Ellis W. Carter. *MGM, FCT*

Diary of a Rebel 🐕 1984 A fictional account of the rise of Cuban rebel leader Che Guevara. 89m/C VHS, Beta. John Ireland, Francesco Rabal. *NO*

Diary of a Seducer 🐕🐕 *Le Journal du Seducteur; The Seducer's Diary* 1995 Claire's (Mastroianni) a bored 20-year-old Parisian whose ennui is lifted when she meets philosophy student Gregoire (Poupaud), who lends her a rare copy of Soren Kierkegaard's "Diary of a Seducer." The volume apparently has seductive powers and manages to affect everyone within Claire's orbit. French with subtitles. 98m/C VHS, Letterbox. *FR* Danielle Dubroux, Chiara Mastroianni, Melvil Poupaud, Mathieu Amalric, Micheline Presle, Hubert Saint Macary, Jean-Pierre Leaud; *D:* Danielle Dubroux; *W:* Danielle Dubroux; *C:* Laurent Machuel; *M:* Jean-Marie Senia. *FXL, FCT*

Diary of a Serial Killer 🐕🐕 1997 (R) Down-on-his-luck journalist Nelson Keece (Busey) witnesses a murder and then is invited by the killer, Stefan (Vosloo), to conduct an exclusive interview. Stefan keeps killing and Nelson keeps writing, but the cops begin to think that Keece is the killer. Then Stefan decides to target Keece's girlfriend Juliette (Campbell) as his next victim. *CW:* Mature themes, language, violence. 92m/C VHS, LV. Gary Busey, Arnold Vosloo, Michael Madsen, Julia Campbell; *D:* Alan Jacobs. *APX*

Diary of a Teenage Hitchhiker 🐕 1982 Teen girl ignores family restrictions and police warnings about a homicidal rapist stalking the area and continues to thumb rides to her job at a beach resort. One night she's picked up for ride she'll never forget. 96m/C VHS, Beta. Charlene Tilton, Dick Van Patten; *D:* Ted Post. *NO*

Diary of a Young Comic 🐕🐕 1979 New York comedian searches for the meaning of lunacy. He finds it after Improvisation in Los Angeles. 74m/C VHS, Beta. Stacy Keach, Dom DeLuise, Richard Lewis, Bill Macy, George Jessel, Gary Muledeer, Nina Van Pallandt; *D:* Gary Weis. *NO*

The Diary of Anne Frank 🐕🐕🐕½ 1959 In June 1945, a liberated Jewish refugee returns to the hidden third floor of an Amsterdam factory where he finds the diary kept by his youngest daughter, Anne. The document recounts their years in hiding from the Nazis. Based on the actual diary of 13-year-old Anne Frank, killed in a death camp during WWII. 150m/B VHS, Beta, LV, Letterbox, Closed Caption. Millie Perkins, Joseph Schildkraut, Shelley Winters, Richard Beymer, Gusti Huber, Ed Wynn, Lou Jacobi, Diane Baker; *D:* George Stevens; *C:* William Mellor. Academy Awards '59: Best Art Direction/Set Decoration (B & W), Best Black and White Cinematography, Best Supporting Actress (Winters); Nominations: Academy Awards '59: Best Costume Design (B & W), Best Director (Stevens), Best Picture, Best Supporting Actor (Wynn), Best Original Dramatic/Comedy Score. *KUI, FOX, BTV*

Diary of Forbidden Dreams 🐕🐕🐕 *What?; Che?* 1973 (R) A beautiful young girl finds herself drawn into bizarre incidents at an eccentric millionaire's mansion that cause her to go insane. Set on the Italian Riviera, it's the most off-beat rendition of "Alice in Wonderland" you're apt to find. Unfortunately, the convoluted plot lessens its appeal. Unedited version, under the original title "What!," released at 113 minutes, is also available. 94m/C VHS, Beta, Letterbox. *IT* Marcello Mastroianni, Hugh Griffith, Sydne Rome, Roman Polanski; *D:* Roman Polanski; *W:* Roman Polanski, Gerard Brach. *VDM, TWE, FCT*

Diary of the Dead 🐕 198? (PG) A newlywed kills his aggravating mother-in-law, only to have her repeatedly return from the grave. 93m/C Beta. Hector Elizondo, Geraldine Fitzgerald, Salome Jens; *D:* Arvin Brown. *NO*

Dick Barton, Special Agent 🐕 1948 Dick Barton is called in when a mad scientist threatens to attack London with germ-carrying bombs. The first film production for Hammer Studios, later to be known for its horror classics. 70m/B VHS, Beta. *GB* Don Stannard, Geoffrey Ford, Jack Shaw; *D:* Alfred Goulding. *SNC, VYY*

Dick Barton Strikes Back 🐕🐕½ 1948 "Mr. French" Cabot has a nuclear weapon and is willing to use it; that is, until Dick Barton arrives to put the Frenchman out of commission. Generally considered the best of the Dick Barton film series. 73m/B VHS, Beta. *GB* Don Stannard, Sebastian Cabot, Jean Lodge; *D:* Godfrey Grayson. *SNC, VYY*

Dick Tracy 1937 Serial, based on the comic-strip character, in 15 chapters. Tracy tries to find his kidnapped brother as he faces the fiend "Spider." The first chapter is 30 minutes and each additional chapter is 20 minutes. 310m/B VHS, Beta, LV. Ralph Byrd, Smiley Burnette, Irving Pichel, Jennifer Jones; *D:* John English. *SNC, VYY, VCI*

Dick Tracy 🐕🐕🐕½ 1990 (PG) Beatty wears the caps of producer, director, and star, performing admirably on all fronts. One minor complaint: his Tracy is somewhat flat in comparison to the outstanding performances and makeup of the unique villains, especially Pacino. Stylistically superior, shot in only seven colors, the timeless sets capture the essence rather than the reality of the city, successfully bringing the comic strip to life. Madonna is fine as the seductive Breathless Mahoney, belting out Stephen Sondheim like she was born to do it. People expecting the gothic technology of "Batman" may be disappointed, but moviegoers searching for a memory made real will be thrilled. ♫ Sooner or Later. 105m/C VHS, Beta, LV, Letterbox, Closed Caption. Warren Beatty, Madonna, Charlie Korsmo, Glenne Headly, Al Pacino, Dustin Hoffman, James Caan, Mandy Patinkin, Paul Sorvino, Charles Durning, Dick Van Dyke, R.G. Armstrong, Catherine O'Hara, Estelle Parsons, Seymour Cassel, Michael J. Pollard, William Forsythe, Kathy Bates, James Tolkan; **D:** Warren Beatty; **W:** Jim Cash, Jack Epps Jr.; **M:** Danny Elfman, Stephen Sondheim. Academy Awards '90: Best Art Direction/Set Decoration, Best Makeup, Best Song ("Sooner or Later"); Nominations: Academy Awards '90: Best Cinematography, Best Costume Design, Best Sound, Best Supporting Actor (Pacino). TOU, FCT, IME

Dick Tracy, Detective 🎬🎬 1945 The first Dick Tracy feature film, in which Splitface is on the loose, a schoolteacher is murdered, the Mayor is threatened, and a nutty professor uses a crystal ball to give Tracy the clues needed to connect the crimes. 62m/B VHS, Beta. Morgan Conway, Anne Jeffreys, Mike Mazurki, Jane Greer, Lyle Latell; **D:** William (Lester Williams) Berke. SNC, VYY, GPV

Dick Tracy, Detective/The Corpse Vanishes 🎬🎬½ 1942 On one tape, the first Dick Tracy feature film and Lugosi's minor epic about a mad scientist using virgin's blood to restore youth to an aging countess. 126m/B VHS, Beta. Bela Lugosi, Morgan Conway, Luana Walters, Tristram Coffin, Mike Mazurki, Jane Greer, Lyle Latell; **D:** William (Lester Williams) Berke. AOV

Dick Tracy Double Feature #1 1945 Mystery-adventure double feature presents Chester Gould's popular comic strip hero in live action. Includes "Dick Tracy, Detective" and "Dick Tracy's Dilemma." 122m/B VHS, Beta. Ralph Byrd, Lyle Latell, Morgan Conway, Anne Jeffreys. VCI

Dick Tracy Double Feature #2 🎬🎬 1947 Chester Gould's famous comic strip character is personified in "Dick Tracy Meets Gruesome" and "Dick Tracy vs. Cueball," a double-feature videocassette featuring Dick Tracy battling two of his arch-enemies. 127m/B VHS, Beta. Boris Karloff, Ralph Byrd, Morgan Conway, Anne Jeffreys. VCI

Dick Tracy Meets Gruesome 🎬🎬 Dick Tracy's Amazing Adventure; Dick Tracy Meets Karloff 1947 Gruesome and his partner in crime, Melody, stage a bank robbery using the secret formula of Dr. A. Tomic. Tracy has to solve the case before word gets out and people rush to withdraw their savings, destroying civilization as we know it. 66m/B VHS, Beta. Boris Karloff, Ralph Byrd, Lyle Latell; **D:** John Rawlins. NOS, MRV, SNC

Dick Tracy Returns 1938 15-chapter serial. Public Enemy Paw Stark and his gang set out on a wave of crime that brings them face to face with dapper Dick. 100m/B VHS, Beta, LV. Ralph Byrd, Charles Middleton; **D:** William Witney. VCI, IME, MLB

Dick Tracy: The Original Serial, Vol. 1 🎬🎬🎬 1937 The first seven parts of the original popular serial. The comic strip character comes to life and tries to stop the spider, a dangerous criminal. 150m/B VHS, Beta. Ralph Byrd, Smiley Burnette, Kay Hughes, Francis X. Bushman, Lee Van Atta; **D:** Ray Taylor; **W:** Alan James. GKK

Dick Tracy: The Original Serial, Vol. 2 🎬🎬🎬 1937 The last eight chapters of the highly acclaimed serial. Tracy is still tracking down the spider in this action-packed adventure. 160m/B VHS, Beta. Ralph Byrd, Smiley Burnette, Kay Hughes, Francis X. Bushman, Lee Van Atta; **D:** Ray Taylor; **W:** Alan James. GKK

Dick Tracy: The Spider Strikes 1937 Dick Tracy, his bumbling sidekick, and his beautiful, brainy assistant go up against the master criminal, The Spider. 60m/B VHS, Beta. Ralph Byrd, Francis X. Bushman. KAR

Dick Tracy vs. Crime Inc. 1941 Dick Tracy encounters many difficulties when he tries to track down a criminal who can make himself invisible. A serial in 15 chapters. 100m/B VHS, Beta, LV. Ralph Byrd, Ralph Morgan, Michael Owen; **D:** William Witney; **W:** John English. VCI, IME, MLB

Dick Tracy vs. Cueball 🎬🎬 1946 Dick Tracy has his work cut out for him when the evil gangster Cueball appears on the scene. Based on Chester Gould's comic strip. 62m/B VHS, Beta. Morgan Conway, Anne Jeffreys; **D:** Gordon Douglas. NOS, VCI, VYY

Dick Tracy's Dilemma 🎬🎬 Mark of the Claw 1947 The renowned police detective Dick Tracy tries to solve a case involving the Claw. Based on the Chester Gould comic strip. 60m/B VHS, Beta. Ralph Byrd, Lyle Latell, Kay Christopher, Jack Lambert, Ian Keith, Jimmy Conlin; **D:** John Rawlins. MRV, VCI, VYY

Dick Turpin 🎬🎬½ 1925 In this rare film, Mix plays the famed English highwayman who seeks adventure in historical Britain. 60m/B VHS, Beta. Tom Mix, Alan Hale; **D:** John Blystone. GVV

Didn't You Hear? 🎬 1983 (PG) An alienated college student discovers that dreams have a life of their own when he becomes immersed in his own fantasy world. 94m/C VHS, Beta. Dennis Christopher, Gary Busey, Cheryl Waters, John Kauffman.

Die! Die! My Darling! 🎬½ Fanatic 1965 A young widow visits her mad ex-mother-in-law in a remote English village, and is imprisoned by the mourning woman as revenge for her son's death. Bankhead's last role. Based on Anne Blaisdell's novel. 97m/C VHS, Beta, Letterbox. GB Tallulah Bankhead, Stefanie Powers, Peter Vaughan, Maurice Kaufman, Donald Sutherland, Gwendolyn Watts, Yootha Joyce, Winifred Dennis; **D:** Silvio Narizzano; **W:** Richard Matheson; **C:** Arthur Ibbetson. COL, MLB

Die Grosse Freiheit Nr. 7 🎬½ 1945 A man tries to stop his niece's love affair with a sailor. Nazi propaganda minister Goebbels banned this film in Germany, since it showed German soldiers getting drunk and also had Hildebrand cast as a prostitute. After the war, however, it enjoyed great popularity throughout Germany. Albers sings the classic "Auf der Reeperbahn." In German with no English translation. 100m/C VHS, Beta. GE Hans Albers, Hilde Hildebrand. IHF

Die Hard 🎬🎬🎬 1988 (R) High-voltage action thriller pits a lone New York cop against a band of ruthless high-stakes terrorists who attack and hold hostage the employees of a large corporation as they celebrate Christmas in a new L.A. high rise. It's just as unbelievable as it sounds, but you'll love it anyway. Rickman, who later charmed audiences as the villain in "Robin Hood: Prince of Thieves," turns in a marvelous performance as the chief bad guy. Based on the novel "Nothing Lasts Forever" by Roderick Thorp. 114m/C VHS, Beta, LV, Letterbox, Closed Caption. Bruce Willis, Bonnie Bedelia, Alan Rickman, Alexander Godunov, Paul Gleason, William Atherton, Reginald Vel Johnson, Hart Bochner, James Shigeta, Mary Ellen Trainor, De'voreaux White, Robert Davi, Rick Ducommun; **D:** John McTiernan; **W:** Jeb Stuart, Steven E. de Souza; **C:** Jan De Bont; **M:** Michael Kamen. Nominations: Academy Awards '88: Best Film Editing, Best Sound. FOX

Die Hard 2: Die Harder 🎬🎬🎬 1990 (R) Fast, well-done sequel brings another impossible situation before the wise-cracking, tough-cookie cop. Our hero tangles with a group of terrorists at an airport under siege, while his wife remains in a plane circling above as its fuel dwindles. Obviously a repeat of the plot and action of the first "Die Hard," with references to the former in the script. While the bad guys lack the fiendishness of their predecessors, this installment features energetic and finely acted performances. Fairly gory, especially the icicle-in-the-eyeball scene. Adapted from the novel "58 Minutes" by Walter Wager and characters created by Roderick Thorp. 124m/C VHS, LV, Letterbox, Closed Caption. Bruce Willis, William Atherton, Franco Nero, Bonnie Bedelia, John Amos, Reginald Vel Johnson, Dennis Franz, Art Evans, Fred Dalton Thompson, William Sadler, Sheila McCarthy, Robert Patrick, John Leguizamo, Robert Costanzo, Tom Verica; **D:** Renny Harlin; **W:** Doug Richardson, Steven E. de Souza; **M:** Michael Kamen. FOX

Die Hard: With a Vengeance 🎬🎬½ Die Hard 3 1995 (R) Third time is not a charm in the "Die Hard" series. McClane (Willis) is back home in the Big Apple and having another bad day. More Eurotrash terrorists, led by the brilliant and vengeful Simon (Irons), are out to blow things up, snag some gold, and make life miserable for

McClane and his reluctant partner, Zeus Carver (Jackson). The claustrophobic settings of the first two outings have been replaced by the exhausting expanse of New York City, to good effect, but frenetic action scenes and good chemistry between Willis and Jackson don't quite compensate for a lackluster script and more cartoony feel. Jackson brings a fresh perspective and vitality to what will probably be the last ride of John McClane. **CW:** Strong violence; pervasive strong language. 131m/C VHS, LV, Closed Caption. Bruce Willis, Samuel L. Jackson, Jeremy Irons, Graham Greene, Colleen Camp, Larry Bryggman, Tony Peck, Nick Wyman, Sam Phillips; **D:** John McTiernan; **W:** Jonathan Hensleigh; **C:** Peter Menzies Jr.; **M:** Michael Kamen. Nominations: MTV Movie Awards '96: Best Action Sequence. FXV

Die Laughing woof! 1980 (PG) A cab driver unwittingly becomes involved in murder, intrigue, and the kidnapping of a monkey that has memorized a scientific formula that can destroy the world. Writer/actor/composer Benson might consider renaming it "Die from Embarrassment." 108m/C VHS, Beta. Robby Benson, Charles Durning, Bud Cort, Elsa Lanchester, Peter Coyote; **D:** Jeff Werner; **W:** Robby Benson, Scott Parker; **M:** Robby Benson. WAR

Die, Monster, Die! 🎬🎬 Monster of Terror 1965 A reclusive scientist experiments with a radioactive meteorite and gains bizarre powers. Karloff is great in this adaptation of H.P. Lovecraft's "The Color Out of Space." 80m/C VHS, LV. GB Boris Karloff, Nick Adams, Suzan Farmer, Patrick Magee, Freda Jackson, Terence de Marney, Leslie Dwyer, Paul Farrell; **D:** Daniel Haller; **W:** Jerry Sohl; **C:** Paul Beeson; **M:** Don Banks. NO

Die Screaming, Marianne 🎬 Die, Beautiful Marianne 1973 A girl is on the run from her father, a crooked judge, who wants to kill her before her 21st birthday, when she will inherit evidence that will put him away for life. 81m/C VHS, Beta. GB Michael Rennie, Susan George, Karin Dor; **D:** Pete Walker. UNI

Die Sister, Die! 🎬 1974 Thriller about a gothic mansion with an eerie secret in the basement features a battle between a senile, reclusive sister and her disturbed, tormenting brother. 88m/C VHS, Beta. Jack Ging, Edith Atwater, Antoinette Bower, Kent Smith, Robert Emhardt; **D:** Randall Hood. NO

Die Watching 🎬½ 1993 (R) Sleazy erotic thriller about a video director (Atkins) who not only likes to film some hot Hollywood babes but may also like to kill them as well. His latest discovery just could be the next victim. 92m/C VHS. Christopher Atkins, Vali Ashton, Tim Thomerson, Carlos Palomino, Mike Jacobs Jr.; **D:** Charles Davis; **W:** Kenneth J. Hall. TRI

Different for Girls 🎬🎬🎬 1996 (R) Boyish motorcycle dispatch rider Paul Prentice (Graves) nearly gets run over by a London taxi whose passenger Kim Foyle (Mackintosh) seems strangely familiar. Then Paul discovers Kim used to be his boyhood school chum Karl. After a shaky start, the duo discover a genuine attraction but when they get into an argument that leads to a police call and Paul gets thrown in jail, Kim's first instincts are to retreat to her sister's (Reeves) family and back into her quiet life. Director Spence refrains from camping up the situation and some fine performances, especially from the engaging Graves, make this quirky film well worth a watch. **CW:** Nudity, brief graphic sexuality and strong language. 101m/C VHS. GB Rupert Graves, Steven Mackintosh, Miriam Margolyes, Saskia Reeves, Neil Dudgeon, Charlotte Coleman; **D:** Richard Spence; **W:** Tony Merchant; **C:** Sean Van Hales; **M:** Stephen Warbeck. Montreal World Film Festival '95: Best Film. FXL

A Different Kind of Love 🎬 1985 A romantic novel on tape, in modern settings. Love, frustration, tragedy. 60m/C Beta. Joyce Redman.

Different Story 🎬🎬½ 1978 (PG) Romance develops when a lesbian real estate agent offers a homosexual chauffeur a job with her firm. Resorts to stereotypes when the characters decide to marry. 107m/C VHS, Beta. Perry King, Meg Foster,

Valerie Curtin, Peter Donat, Richard Bull; **D:** Paul Aaron. *NLC*

Digby, the Biggest Dog in the World
🐾 **1973 (G)** Poor comedy-fantasy about Digby, a sheepdog, who wanders around a scientific laboratory, drinks an experimental fluid, and grows and grows and grows. 88m/C **VHS, Beta.** *GB* Jim Dale, Angela Douglas, Spike Milligan, Dinsdale Landen; **D:** Joseph McGrath; **M:** Edwin Astley.

Digger
🐾🐾½ **1994 (PG)** Digger (Hann-Byrd) arrives at a Pacific Northwest island to stay with relatives, including his Grandma (Dukakis) who's being romanced by the fun-loving Arthur (Nielsen). He makes friends with another youth who turns out to have a terminal heart ailment. 92m/C **VHS, Closed Caption.** Adam Hann-Byrd, Olympia Dukakis, Leslie Nielsen, Joshua Jackson, Barbara Williams, Timothy Bottoms; **D:** Robert Turner; **W:** Rodney Gibbons; **M:** Todd Boekelheide. *PAR*

Digging Up Business
woof! **1991 (PG)** Johnson tries to save the family funeral home business from financial ruin with some unique interment services. This film needs a decent burial. 89m/C **VHS.** Lynn-Holly Johnson, Billy Barty, Ruth Buzzi, Murray Langston, Yvonne Craig, Gary Owens; **D:** Mark Byers. *NO*

Diggstown
🐾🐾½ **1992 (R)** Lightweight, good-natured sports comedy about a boxing scam. Con man Gabriel Caine (Woods), fresh out of prison, heads for Diggstown and the unregulated boxing matches arranged by town boss, John Gillon (Dern). The bet is that Caine's one boxer can beat any 10 boxers, chosen by Gillon, in a 24-hour period. So Caine decides to hook up with an old friend, former prizefighter "Honey" Roy Palmer (Gosset Jr.), to run the scam of his life. Dern is sufficiently nasty and Woods his usual nervy self but it's Gossett Jr. who manages to hold everything together as the aging boxer. Based on the novel "The Diggstown Ringers" by Leonard Wise. **CW:** Language. 97m/C **VHS, Beta, LV, Closed Caption.** James Woods, Louis Gossett Jr., Bruce Dern, Oliver Platt, Heather Graham, Randall "Tex" Cobb, Thomas Wilson Brown, Duane Davis, Willie Green, George Wallace; **D:** Michael Ritchie; **W:** Steven McKay; **M:** James Newton Howard. *MGM*

Digital Man
🐾½ **1994 (R)** High-tech military super-soldier prototype has his programming sabotaged and a team of human and robotic commandoes must prevent him from starting WWIII. **CW:** Futuristic military violence; some sexuality. 95m/C **VHS, Closed Caption.** Ken Olandt, Adam Baldwin, Ed Lauter, Matthias Hues, Kristen Dalton, Paul Gleason; **D:** Phillip J. Roth; **W:** Phillip J. Roth, Ronald Schmidt. *REP*

Dillinger
🐾🐾🐾 **1945** John Dillinger's notorious career, from street punk to public enemy number one, receives a thrilling fast-paced treatment. Tierney turns in a fine performance in this interesting account of the criminal life. 70m/C **VHS, Beta.** Lawrence Tierney, Edmund Lowe, Anne Jeffreys, Elisha Cook Jr.; **D:** Max Nosseck; **W:** Philip Yordan. Nominations: Academy Awards '45: Best Original Screenplay. *FOX, FCT*

Dillinger
🐾🐾½ **1973 (R)** The most colorful period of criminality in America is brought to life in this story of bank-robber John Dillinger, "Baby Face" Nelson, and the notorious "Lady in Red." 106m/C **VHS, Beta, LV.** Warren Oates, Michelle Phillips, Richard Dreyfuss, Cloris Leachman, Ben Johnson, Harry Dean Stanton; **D:** John Milius; **W:** John Milius. *ART, VES*

Dillinger
🐾🐾½ *The Last Days of John Dillinger* **1991** Harmon stars as the Depression-era bank robber, who became public enemy number one, in this TV gangster story. Fenn's girlfriend Billy Frenchette, with Patton particularly beady-eyed as G-man Melvin Purvis. 95m/C **VHS, Closed Caption.** Mark Harmon, Sherilyn Fenn, Will Patton, Patricia Arquette, Vince Edwards, Bruce Abbott; **D:** Rupert Wainwright; **C:** Donald M. Morgan. *WAR*

Dillinger and Capone
🐾🐾½ **1995 (R)** Supposedly the FBI has killed the wrong Dillinger and the gangster (Sheen) decides to make a new life. But his old friend Al Capone (Abraham), newly released from prison, is holding Dillinger's wife (Hicks) and son hostage as insurance that first he'll retrieve $15 million from a mob-owned Chicago bank. **CW:** Language, violence, brief nudity. 95m/C **VHS, LV.** Martin Sheen, F. Murray Abraham, Catherine Hicks, Stephen Davies, Don Stroud, Clint Howard; **D:** Jon Purdy; **W:** Michael B. Druxman. *NHO*

Dim Sum: A Little Bit of Heart
🐾🐾🐾 **1985 (PG)** The second independent film from the director of "Chan Is Missing." A Chinese-American mother and daughter living in San Francisco's Chinatown confront the conflict between traditional Eastern ways and modern American life. Gentle, fragile picture made with humor and care. In English and Chinese with subtitles. 88m/C **VHS, Beta, LV.** Laureen Chew, Kim Chew, Victor Wong, Ida F.O. Chong, Cora Miao, John Nishio, Joan Chen; **D:** Wayne Wang; **W:** Terrel Seltzer; **M:** Todd Boekelheide. *FCT, IME, TPV*

Dimples
🐾🐾½ **1936 (PG)** When Shirley's pickpocket grandfather is caught red-handed, she steps in, takes the blame, and somehow ends up in show business. Re-issued version is rated. Also available colorized. ♫Hey, What Did the Bluebird Say?; He Was a Dandy; Picture Me Without You; Oh Mister Man Up in the Moon; Dixie-Anna; Get On Board; Swing Low Sweet Chariot. 78m/B **VHS, Beta, Closed Caption.** Shirley Temple, John Carradine, Frank Morgan, Helen Westley, Berton Churchill, Robert Kent, Delma Byron; **D:** William A. Seiter. *FOX*

Diner
🐾🐾🐾½ **1982 (R)** A group of old high school friends meet at "their" Baltimore diner to find that more has changed than the menu. A bittersweet look at the experiences of a group of Baltimore post-teenagers growing up, circa 1959. Particularly notable was Levinson's casting of "unknowns" who have since become household names. Features many humorous moments and fine performances. 110m/C **VHS, Beta, LV, Letterbox.** Steve Guttenberg, Daniel Stern, Mickey Rourke, Kevin Bacon, Ellen Barkin, Timothy Daly, Paul Reiser, Michael Tucker; **D:** Barry Levinson; **C:** Peter Sova. National Society of Film Critics Awards '82: Best Supporting Actor (Rourke); Nominations: Academy Awards '82: Best Original Screenplay. *MGM*

Dingaka
🐾🐾½ **1965** A controversial drama from the writer and director of "The Gods Must Be Crazy" about a South African tribesman who avenges his daughter's murder by tribal laws, and is then tried by white man's laws. A crusading white attorney struggles to acquit him. 96m/C **VHS, Beta.** Stanley Baker, Juliet Prowse, Ken Gampu; **D:** Jamie Uys. *COL, NLC, FCT*

Dingo
🐾🐾½ **1990** In Davis' only film appearance he's, what else, a famous jazz trumpeter. Paris-based Billy Cross (Davis) and his combo are on tour in 1969 and momentarily stuck at a remote Australian airstrip. They give an impromptu concert heard by John "Dingo" Anderson (Friels), who instantly decides that music is the life for him. Over the years Dingo keeps in touch with his idol as he works outback bars and secretly saves to go to Paris and check out the scene—even if it means sacrificing his wife and family. 108m/C **VHS.** FR AU Colin Friels, Miles Davis, Helen Buday, Bernadette LaFont; **D:** Rolf de Heer; **W:** Marc Rosenberg; **C:** Denis Lenoir; **M:** Miles Davis, Michel Legrand. *GRE*

The Dining Room
🐾🐾½ **1986** Six performers play more than 50 roles in this adaptation of A. R. Gurney Jr.'s play set in a dining room, where people live out dramatic and comic moments in their lives. From the "American Playhouse" series. 90m/C **VHS, Beta.** Remak Ramsay, Pippa Perthree, John Shea, Frances Sternhagen; **D:** Allan Goldstein. *PBS*

Dinner at Eight
🐾🐾🐾 **1933** A social-climbing woman and her husband throw a dinner party for various members of the New York elite. During the course of the evening, all of the guests reveal something about themselves. Special performances all around, especially Barrymore, Dressler, and Harlow. Superb comedic direction by Cukor. Adapted from the play by Edna Ferber and George Kaufman. 110m/C **VHS, Beta, LV, 8mm.** John Barrymore, Lionel Barrymore, Wallace Beery, Madge Evans, Jean Harlow, Billie Burke, Marie Dressler, Phillips Holmes, Jean Hersholt, Lee Tracy, Edmund Lowe, Karen Morley, May Robson; **D:** George Cukor; **W:** Herman J. Mankiewicz, Frances Marion, Donald Ogden Stewart; **C:** William H. Daniels. *MGM*

Dinner at Eight
🐾🐾 **1989** A social-climbing romance novelist throws an elegant dinner party. Made for television remake of the 1933 film does not compare well. 100m/C **VHS, Beta.** Lauren Bacall, Charles Durning, Ellen Greene, Harry Hamlin, John Mahoney, Marsha Mason, Tim Kazurinsky; **D:** Ron Lagomarsino. *TTC*

Dinner at the Ritz
🐾🐾½ **1937** Daughter of a murdered Parisian banker vows to find his killer with help from her fiance. 78m/B **VHS, Beta.** *GB* David Niven, Annabella, Paul Lukas, Patricia Medina; **D:** Harold Schuster. *NOS, MRV, VYY*

Dino
🐾½ **1957** Social worker joins a young woman in helping a 17-year-old delinquent re-enter society. 96m/B **VHS, Beta.** Sal Mineo, Brian Keith, Susan Kohner; **D:** Thomas Carr. *REP*

Dinosaur Island
🐾 **1993 (R)** Five military men survive a plane crash and discover an island where scantily clad (leather bikinis being the fashion choice) lascivious ladies live. Will the awesome power of testosterone overcome the fierce dinosaurs which stand between the men and their objects of desire? **CW:** Abundant nudity and sexuality. 85m/C **VHS.** Ross Hagen, Richard Gabai, Antonia Dorian, Peter Spellos, Tom Shell, Griffin Drew, Steve Barkett, Toni Naples; **D:** Jim Wynorski, Fred Olen Ray; **W:** Bob Sheridan, Christopher Wooden. *NHO, HVL*

Dinosaur Valley Girls
🐾½ **1996** Hollywood action hero Tony Markham comes into possession of a magic stone that hurls him backwards through time to a prehistoric world. That just happens to be populated by fierce, beautiful babes in animal-print bikinis. A PG version is also available. 94m/C **VHS.** Ron Jeffries; **Cameos:** Karen Black, William D. Russell; **D:** Don Glut; **W:** Don Glut. *Ell*

Dinosaurus!
🐾 **1960** Large sadistic dinosaurs appear in the modern world. They eat, burn, and pillage their way through this film. Also includes a romance between a Neanderthal and a modern-age woman. 85m/C **VHS, Beta.** Ward Ramsey, Kristina Hanson, Paul Lukather; **D:** Irvin S. Yeaworth Jr. *SNC*

Diplomaniacs
🐾🐾½ **1933** Wheeler and Woolsey, official barbers on an Indian reservation, are sent to the Geneva peace conference to represent the interests of their tribe. Slim plot nevertheless provides quite a few laughs. Fun musical numbers. 62m/B **VHS, Beta, LV.** Bert Wheeler, Robert Woolsey, Marjorie White, Hugh Herbert; **D:** William A. Seiter; **W:** Joseph L. Mankiewicz, Henry Myers; **M:** Max Steiner. *CCB, IME, TTC*

Diplomatic Courier
🐾🐾🐾 **1952** Cold-war espionage saga has secret agent Power attempting to re-steal sensitive documents from the hands of Soviet agents. Involved and exciting thriller. Michael Ansara, Charles Bronson and Lee Marvin made brief appearances. 97m/B **VHS.** Tyrone Power, Patricia Neal, Stephen McNally, Hildegarde Neff, Karl Malden; **D:** Henry Hathaway; **C:** Lucien Ballard. *FXL*

Diplomatic Immunity
🐾½ **1991 (R)** Vicious killer gets off scot-free due to his diplomatic immunity. That is, until the victim's ex-soldier father follows this low-life to the jungles of Paraguay to exact revenge. A heap o' action. **CW:** Language, violence, and sensuality. 95m/C **VHS, Beta, LV, Closed Caption.** Bruce Boxleitner, Billy Drago, Meg Foster, Robert Forster; **D:** Peter Maris. *IME*

Direct Hit 🎬🎬½ **1993 (R)** A CIA assassin discovers retiring is not an option. John Hatch (Forsythe) decides he wants out, particularly when his next kill, Savannah (Champa), turns out to be an innocent pawn. So Hatch turns protector and decides to best the agency at its own deadly game. **CW:** Language, plentiful violence, and some sexuality. **91m/C VHS, LV, Closed Caption.** William Forsythe, Richard Norton, Jo Champa, John Aprea, Juliet Landau, George Segal; **D:** Joseph Merhi; **W:** Jacobsen Hart. REP

Dirkham Detective Agency 🎬½ **1983** Three children team up to form the Dirkham Detective Agency and are hired by a veterinarian to recover two dognapped poodles. **60m/C VHS, Beta.** Sally Kellerman, Stan Shaw, John Quade, Gordon Jump, Randy Morton. NO

Dirt Bike Kid 🎬½ **1986 (PG)** A precocious brat is stuck with a used motorbike that has a mind of its own. Shenanigans follow in utterly predictable fashion as he battles bankers and bikers with his bad bike. **91m/C VHS, Beta, LV, 8mm, Closed Caption.** Peter Billingsley, Anne Bloom, Stuart Pankin, Patrick Collins, Sage Parker, Chad Sheets; **D:** Hoite C. Caston; **W:** Lewis Colick, David Brandes. COL, NLC

Dirt Gang 🎬 **1971 (R)** A motorcycle gang terrorizes the members of a film crew on location in the desert. **89m/C VHS, Beta.** Paul Carr, Michael Pataki, Michael Forest; **D:** Jerry Jameson. MPI

Dirty Dancing 🎬🎬🎬 **1987 (PG-13)** An innocent 17-year-old (Grey) is vacationing with her parents in the Catskills in 1963. Bored with the program at the hotel, she finds the real fun at the staff dances. Falling for the sexy dance instructor (Swayze), she discovers love, sex, and rock and roll dancing. An old story, with little to save it, but Grey and Swayze are appealing, the dance sequences fun, and the music great. Swayze, classically trained in ballet, also performs one of the sound-track songs. 🎵(I've Had) the Time of My Life; Be My Baby; Big Girls Don't Cry; Cry to Me; Do You Love Me?; Hey Baby; Hungry Eyes; In the Still of the Nite; Love is Strange. **97m/C VHS, Beta, LV, Closed Caption, DVD.** Patrick Swayze, Jennifer Grey, Cynthia Rhodes, Jerry Orbach, Jack Weston, Jane Brucker, Kelly Bishop, Lonny Price, Charles "Honi" Coles, Bruce Morrow; **D:** Emile Ardolino; **W:** Eleanor Bergstein; **M:** John Morris. Academy Awards '87: Best Song ("(I've Had) the Time of My Life"); Golden Globe Awards '88: Best Song ("(I've Had) the Time of My Life"); Independent Spirit Awards '88: Best First Feature. ART, SNL

Dirty Dishes 🎬🎬🎬 **1982 (R)** A French film sardonically examining the fruitless life of the average housewife as she confronts a series of bizarre but pointless experiences during the day. Dubbed and subtitled versions available. The director is the American daughter-in-law of the late Luis Bunuel. **99m/C VHS, Beta.** FR Carol Laurie, Pierre Santini; **D:** Joyce Bunuel.

The Dirty Dozen 🎬🎬🎬 **1967 (PG)** A tough Army major is assigned to train and command 12 hardened convicts offered absolution if they participate in a suicidal mission into Nazi Germany in 1944. Well made movie is a standout in its genre. Rough and gruff Marvin is good as the group leader. Three made-for-television sequels followed in the '80s. **149m/C VHS, Beta, LV, Letterbox.** Lee Marvin, Ernest Borgnine, Charles Bronson, Jim Brown, George Kennedy, John Cassavetes, Clint Walker, Donald Sutherland, Telly Savalas, Robert Ryan, Ralph Meeker, Richard Jaeckel, Trini Lopez; **D:** Robert Aldrich. Academy Awards '67: Best Sound Effects Editing; Nominations: Academy Awards '67: Best Film Editing, Best Sound, Best Supporting Actor (Cassavetes). MGM, TLF

The Dirty Dozen: The Deadly Mission 🎬🎬½ **1987** A second made-for-TV sequel to the '67 movie finds Borgnine ordering another suicide mission. Savalas (killed in the original, he's playing a new character) must pick 12 convicted army prisoners for an assault on a Nazi-held French monastery. Their mission is to rescue six scientists who are working on a deadly new nerve gas. Followed by "The Dirty Dozen: The Fatal Mission." **96m/C VHS.** Ernest Borgnine, Telly Savalas, Vince Edwards, Gary Graham, James Van Patten, Vincent Van Patten, Bo Svenson; **D:** Lee H. Katzin. MGM

The Dirty Dozen: The Fatal Mission 🎬🎬½ **1988** This third TV sequel has Borgnine learning of a plan to bring a group of high-ranking Nazis to Instanbul via the Orient Express. Naturally, he assigns Savalas the task of getting his motley gang together to thwart the Nazi schemes. To add intrigue, a female has joined the ranks of the Dirty Dozen and a spy may also have infiltrated the group. **91m/C VHS.** Ernest Borgnine, Telly Savalas, Hunt Block, Jeff Conaway, Erik Estrada, Ray "Boom Boom" Mancini, Heather Thomas, Alex Cord; **D:** Lee H. Katzin. MGM

The Dirty Dozen: The Next Mission 🎬½ **1985** Disappointing made for television sequel to the 1967 hit, with Marvin reprising his role as the leader of the motley pack. In this installment, the rag-tag toughs are sent on yet another suicide mission inside Nazi Germany, this time to thwart an assassination attempt of Hitler. Followed by two more sequels. **97m/C VHS, Beta, Closed Caption.** Lee Marvin, Ernest Borgnine, Richard Jaeckel, Ken Wahl, Larry Wilcox, Sonny Landham, Ricco Ross; **D:** Andrew V. McLaglen. MGM

Dirty Games 🎬½ **1993** Nicola Kendra is part of a team sent to Africa to inspect a nuclear waste site. Once there, the scientists discover terrorists are plotting to blow up the nuclear complex unless Nicola and her new allies can prevent it. **97m/C VHS.** Jan-Michael Vincent, Valentina Vargas, Ronald France, Michael McGovern; **D:** Gray Hofmeyr.

Dirty Gertie from Harlem U.S.A. 🎬🎬 **1946** All-black cast performs a variation of W. Somerset Maugham's "Rain." Gertie goes to Trinidad to hide out from her jilted boyfriend. **60m/B VHS, Beta.** Gertie LaRue, Spencer Williams Jr., Francine Everett. VYY, DVT, VYY

Dirty Hands 🎬🎬 *Les Innocents aux Mains Sales* **1976** A woman and her lover conspire to murder her husband. A must for fans of the sexy Schneider. Cinematography provides moments that are both interesting and eerie. **102m/C VHS.** FR Rod Steiger, Romy Schneider, Paul Giusti, Jean Rochefort, Hans-Christian Blech; **D:** Claude Chabrol. FCT

Dirty Harry 🎬🎬🎬½ **1971 (R)** Rock-hard cop Harry Callahan attempts to track down a psychopathic rooftop killer before a kidnapped girl dies. Harry abuses the murderer's civil rights, however, forcing the police to return the criminal to the streets, where he hijacks a school bus and Harry is called on once again. The only answer to stop this vicious killer seems to be death in cold blood, and Harry is just the man to do it. Taut, suspenseful direction by Siegel, who thoroughly understands Eastwood's on-screen character. Features Callahan's famous "Do you feel lucky?" line, the precursor to his "Go ahead, make my day." **103m/C VHS, Beta, LV, 8mm, Letterbox.** Clint Eastwood, Harry Guardino, John Larch, Andrew (Andy) Robinson, Reni Santoni, John Vernon; **D:** Donald Siegel; **C:** Bruce Surtees; **M:** Lalo Schifrin. WAR, TLF

Dirty Heroes 🎬🎬 *Dalle Ardenne All'Inferno* **1971 (R)** A band of escaped WWII POWs battle the Nazis for a precious treasure in the war's final days. **117m/C VHS, Beta.** John Ireland, Curt Jurgens, Adolfo Celi, Daniela Bianchi, Michael Constantine; **D:** Alberto De Martino; **M:** Ennio Morricone. NO

Dirty Laundry woof! **1987 (PG-13)** Insipid wreck of a comedy about a klutz who accidentally gets his laundry mixed up with $1 million dollars in drug money. Features Olympians Lewis and Louganis. Never released theatrically. **81m/C VHS, Beta.** Leigh McCloskey, Jeanne O'Brien, Frankie Valli, Sonny Bono, Carl Lewis, Greg Louganis, Nicholas Worth; **D:** William Webb. NO

Dirty Mary Crazy Larry 🎬🎬🎬 **1974 (PG)** A racecar driver, his mechanic, and a sexy girl hightail it from the law after pulling off a heist. Great action, great fun, and an infamous surprise ending. **93m/C VHS, Beta, LV.** Peter Fonda, Susan

George, Adam Roarke, Vic Morrow, Roddy McDowall; **D:** John Hough; **W:** Leigh Chapman. FOX

Dirty Mind of Young Sally woof! **1972 (R)** Sally's erotic radio program broadcasts from a mobile studio, which must stay one step ahead of the police. **84m/C VHS, Beta.** Sharon Kelly. TPV

Dirty Rotten Scoundrels 🎬🎬🎬 **1988 (PG)** A remake of the 1964 "Bedtime Story," in which two confidence tricksters on the Riviera endeavor to rip off a suddenly rich American woman, and each other. Caine and Martin are terrific, Martin has some of his best physical comedy ever, and Headly is charming as the prey who's always one step ahead of them. Fine direction from Oz, the man who brought us the voice of Yoda in "The Empire Strikes Back." **112m/C VHS, Beta, LV, Closed Caption.** Steve Martin, Michael Caine, Glenne Headly, Anton Rodgers, Barbara Harris, Dana Ivey; **D:** Frank Oz; **W:** Dale Launer, Stanley Shapiro; **C:** Michael Ballhaus; **M:** Miles Goodman. ORI

Dirty Tricks 🎬½ **1981 (PG)** History professor Gould fights with bad guys for a letter written by George Washington. Thoroughly forgettable comedy lacking in laughs. **91m/C VHS, Beta.** CA Elliott Gould, Kate Jackson, Arthur Hill, Rich Little; **D:** Alvin Rakoff; **W:** William W. Norton Sr.; **M:** Hagood Hardy. COL

Dirty Work 🎬🎬 **1992 (R)** A drug-dealing bail bondsman (Ashton) steals counterfeit money from the mob and then sets up his partner (Dobson) as the fall guy. Can Dobson survive long enough to set things straight? **CW:** Violence. **88m/C VHS, Beta, Closed Caption.** John Ashton, Kevin Dobson, Roxann Biggs-Dawson, Donnelly Rhodes, Jim Byrnes, Mitchell Ryan; **D:** John McPherson; **W:** Aaron Julien. PAR

Disappearance 🎬🎬 **1981 (R)** A hired assassin discovers an ironic link between his new target and his missing wife. **80m/C VHS, Beta.** CA Donald Sutherland, David Hemmings, John Hurt, Christopher Plummer, David Warner, Virginia McKenna; **D:** Stuart Cooper. VES, RHI

The Disappearance of Aimee 🎬🎬🎬 **1976** Dramatic recreation of events surrounding the 1926 disappearance of evangelist Aimee Semple McPherson. She claimed she was abducted, but her mother insisted she ran away to have an affair. Excellent made for television movie with an exceptional cast. Originally to star Ann-Margret. **110m/C VHS, Beta.** Faye Dunaway, Bette Davis, James Sloyan, James Woods, John Lehne, Lelia Goldoni, Barry Brown, Severn Darden; **W:** Anthony Harvey. ART

The Disappearance of Christina 🎬🎬½ **1993 (PG-13)** Successful entrepreneur Joe Seldon (Stamos) is married to heiress Christina (Yarlett) and they seem to be the perfect couple. But when Christina mysteriously vanishes during a sailing trip, was it really an accident? Detective Nora Davis (Pounder) doesn't think so and naturally, Joe is suspect numero uno. **93m/C VHS, LV, Closed Caption.** John Stamos, Kim Delaney, Robert Carradine, Claire Yarlett, CCH Pounder; **D:** Karen Arthur; **W:** Camille Thomasson. USH

The Disappearance of Garcia Lorca 🎬🎬½ *Death in Granada; Lorca* **1996 (R)** In 1954, Spanish-born journalist Ricardo Fernandez (Morales) returns to Granada to look into the death of his idol, poet/playwright Gabriel Garcia Lorca (Garcia). Ricardo's family fled Spain for Puerto Rico in 1936, at the start of the Spanish Civil War, when anti-fascist Lorca was executed. Ricardo wants to find out just who Lorca's killers were but Franco's Spain is a country eager to bury its past. Based on two books by Ian Gibson. **CW:** Bloody violence and a scene of sexuality. **114m/C VHS, Closed Caption.** SP Esai Morales, Andy Garcia, Edward James Olmos, Jeroen Krabbe, Miguel Ferrer, Giancarlo Giannini, Marcela Wallerstein, Jose Coronado; **D:** Marcos Zurinaga; **W:** Marcos Zurinaga, Neil Cohen, Juan Antonio Ramos; **C:** Juan Ruiz-Anchia; **M:** Mark McKenzie. COL

The Disappearance of Kevin Johnson ♂♂½ 1995 (R) Mockumentary about a British TV crew, doing a film about successful Brits in Hollywood, stumbling across the disappearance of wannabe producer and wealthy Englishman, Kevin Johnson. So they begin asking questions of the agents, executives, stars, business associates, and women in Johnson's life. So just who is—or was—Kevin Johnson? **105m/C VHS, Closed Caption.** Michael Brandon, Bridget Baiss, Keely Sims, Rick Peters, Kari Wuhrer, John Hillard, Heather Stephens, Richard Beymer, Richard Neil, Michael Laskin, Ian Ogilvy, Stoney Jackson; *Cameos:* Pierce Brosnan, James Coburn, Dudley Moore; *D:* Francis Megahy; *W:* Francis Megahy; *C:* John Newby; *M:* John Coda. COL

Disaster at Silo 7 ♂♂ 1988 When the engine of a Titan missile goes on the fritz, the Air Force tries to prevent a nuclear disaster. Based on an actual Titan II missile incident near Little Rock, Arkansas. Made for television. **92m/C VHS.** Peter Boyle, Patricia Charbonneau, Perry King, Michael O'Keefe, Joe Spano, Dennis Weaver; *D:* Larry Elikann; *W:* Douglas Lloyd McIntosh; *C:* Roy Wagner. TRI

The Disciple ♂½ 1915 Vintage silent western wherein Hart's unsmiling good-bad guy tries to clean up a lawless town and win back his wife, who has shamelessly fallen in with a corrupt saloon-keeper. **80m/B VHS, Beta, 8mm.** William S. Hart, Dorothy Dalton, Robert McKim, Jean Hersholt; *D:* William S. Hart; *W:* Thomas Ince. VYY, GPV

Disciple of Death ♂ 1972 (R) Raven plays "The Stranger," a ghoul who sacrifices virgins to the Devil. **82m/C VHS, Beta.** GB Mike Raven, Ronald Lacey, Stephen Bradley, Virginia Wetherell; *D:* Tom Parkinson. UNI

Disclosure ♂♂ 1994 (R) Likable, responsible executive and family man (Douglas) finds himself sexually harassed by his ex-lover turned dragon-lady boss (Moore). But when he rejects her lusty come-on, she points the finger at him. One-dimensional characters and hollow material turn sexual harassment into a trivial issue. High-tech saga of corporate politics, while flashy, is nothing we haven't seen before. Douglas just can't pass up these "Regular Joe meets beautiful, horny babe, bad things happen" roles, can he? Based on the Michael Crichton novel. *CW:* Contains strong language, sexual references, and one sexual episode. **129m/C VHS, LV, Closed Caption.** Michael Douglas, Demi Moore, Donald Sutherland, Caroline Goodall, Dylan Baker, Dennis Miller, Rosemary Forsyth, Roma Maffia; *D:* Barry Levinson; *W:* Paul Attanasio; *M:* Ennio Morricone. Blockbuster Entertainment Awards '95: Drama Actress, Theatrical (Moore); Blockbuster Entertainment Awards '96: Drama Actress, Video (Moore); Nominations: MTV Movie Awards '95: Most Desirable Female (Moore), Best Villain (Moore). WAR

Disconnected ♂½ 1987 "Sorry, Wrong Number" is updated, with more than ample doses of sex and violence. **81m/C VHS, Beta.** Mark Walker. NO

Discontent ♂½ 1916 An early silent film by Lois Weber in which a cantankerous old vet goes to live with his wealthy nephew. The harmonious family life is disrupted by his meddling ways. **30m/B VHS, Beta.** *D:* Lois Weber. GVV

The Discovery Program ♂♂½ 1989 Four award-winning short films on one video: "Ray's Male Heterosexual Dance Hall," "Greasy Lake," "The Open Window," and "Hearts of Stone." The subjects range from humorous and offbeat to tragic and deadly serious. **106m/C VHS, Beta.** FCT

The Discreet Charm of the Bourgeoisie ♂♂♂♂ Le Charme Discret de la Bourgeoisie 1972 (R) Bunuel in top form, satirizing modern society. These six characters are forever sitting down to dinner, yet they never eat. Dreams and reality, actual or contrived, prevent their feast. **100m/C VHS, Beta, LV.** FR Fernando Rey, Delphine Seyrig, Jean-Pierre Cassel, Bulle Ogier, Michel Piccoli, Stephane Audran, Luis Bunuel; *D:* Luis Bunuel; *W:* Luis Bunuel, Jean-Claude Carriere. Academy Awards '72: Best For-

eign Language Film; British Academy Awards '73: Best Actress (Seyrig), Best Screenplay; National Society of Film Critics Awards '72: Best Director (Bunuel), Best Film; Nominations: Academy Awards '72: Best Story & Screenplay.

Discretion Assured ♂♂½ 1993 (R) Successful businessman Trevor McCabe (York) finds himself in a romantic quandry with three women, leading to his involvement in embezzlement and murder. *CW:* Language and sexuality. **97m/C VHS.** Michael York, Jennifer O'Neill, Dee Wallace Stone, Elizabeth Gracen; *D:* Odorico Mendes. MNC

Dishonored ♂♂½ 1931 Dated spy drama has Dietrich playing secret agent X-27 in WWI and masquerading on the side as a peasant girl. Although not one of the more famous Dietrich-Sternberg productions, its camp plot and Dietrich's lavish performance make it worth watching. Based on the infamous spy Mata Hari, who was shot by the French in 1917 for espionage. **91m/B VHS, Closed Caption.** Marlene Dietrich, Victor McLaglen, Lew Cody, Gustav von Seyffertitz, Warner Oland, Barry Norton, Davison Clark, Wilfrid Lucas; *D:* Josef von Sternberg; *W:* Josef von Sternberg, Daniel N. Rubin; *C:* Lee Garmes. USH, FCT

Dishonored Lady ♂½ 1947 After her ex-boyfriend is murdered, a female art director finds that she's the number one suspect. When put on trial for the dastardly deed, she takes the fifth in this mediocre melodrama. **85m/B VHS, Beta.** Hedy Lamarr, Dennis O'Keefe, William Lundigan, John Loder; *D:* Robert Stevenson. SNC, NOS, CAB

Disney's Storybook Classics 1982 A collection of classic children's fables, featuring "Little Toot" (1948, excerpted from "Melody Time"), the story of a little harbor tugboat; "Chicken Little" (1943); "The Grasshopper and the Ant" (1934, a "Silly Symphony"); and "Peter and the Wolf" (1946, excerpted from "Make Mine Music"), a Disneyized version of Prokofiev's famous concert piece. **121m/C VHS, Beta.** Sterling Holloway, The Andrews Sisters. DIS

Disorderlies ♂ 1987 (PG) Members of the popular rap group cavort as incompetent hospital orderlies assigned to care for a cranky millionaire. Fat jokes abound with performances by the Fat Boys. **86m/C VHS, Beta, LV, Closed Caption.** The Fat Boys, Ralph Bellamy; *D:* Michael A. Schultz; *M:* Anne Dudley. WAR

Disorderly Orderly ♂½ 1964 When Jerry Lewis gets hired as a hospital orderly, nothing stands upright long with him around. Vintage slapstick Lewis running amuck in a nursing home. **90m/C VHS, Beta.** Jerry Lewis, Glenda Farrell, Everett Sloane, Kathleen Freeman, Susan Oliver; *D:* Frank Tashlin. PAR

Disorganized Crime ♂♂ 1989 (R) On the lam from the law, Bernsen attempts to organize a group of his ex-con buddies to pull off the perfect heist. Before the boys can organize, however, the cops are hot on Bernsen's trail, and he must vacate the meeting place. Good cast attempts to lift this movie beyond script. **101m/C VHS, Beta, LV, Closed Caption.** Lou Diamond Phillips, Fred Gwynne, Corbin Bernsen, Ruben Blades, Hoyt Axton, Ed O'Neill, Daniel Roebuck, William Russ; *D:* Jim Kouf; *M:* David Newman. TOU

Disraeli ♂♂♂ 1930 Arliss deservedly won the Best Actor Oscar for his title role as the famed British prime minister to Queen Victoria. This particular slice of the cunning statesman's life depicts his efforts to secure the Suez Canal for England against the Russians. Arliss' wife also played his screen spouse. One of Warner's earliest and best biographical pictures. Based on a play by Louis Napoleon Parker. **87m/B VHS.** George Arliss, Joan Bennett, Florence Arliss, Anthony Bushell, David Torrence, Doris Lloyd, Ivan Simpson, Gwendolyn Logan; *D:* Alfred E. Green; *C:* Lee Garmes. Academy Awards '30: Best Actor (Arliss); Nominations: Academy Awards '30: Best Picture, Best Writing. MGM

Distant Drums ♂♂ 1951 A small band of adventurers tries to stop the Seminole War in the Florida Everglades. **101m/C VHS.** Gary Cooper, Mari Aldon, Robert Barrat, Richard Webb, Ray Teal, Arthur Hunnicutt; *D:* Raoul Walsh; *M:* Max Steiner. REP, FCT

Distant Justice ♂½ 1992 (R) Tokyo police inspector Rio (Sugawara) is vacationing in Boston with his wife and daughter, where he can also visit old friend, Chief Bradfield (Kennedy). But Rio's wife is murdered and his daughter kidnapped by vicious drug dealer Roy Pennola (Carradine) and Bradfield assigns young officer Charlie Givens (Lutes) to see that Rio doesn't get himself killed as well. *CW:* Strong violence; a rape; sexuality; some language. **91m/C VHS.** Bunta Sugawara, George Kennedy, David Carradine, Eric Lutes; *D:* Toru Murakawa. COL

Distant Thunder ♂♂♂½ 1973 A bitter, unrelenting portrait of a small Bengali neighborhood as the severe famines of 1942, brought about by the "distant thunder" of WWII, take their toll. A mature achievement from Ray; in Bengali with English subtitles. **92m/C VHS, Beta.** IN Soumitra Chatterjee, Sandhya Roy, Babita, Gobinda Chakravarty, Romesh Mukerji; *D:* Satyajit Ray. Berlin International Film Festival '73: Golden Berlin Bear. FCT

Distant Thunder ♂♂ 1988 (R) A scarred Vietnam vet, who has become a recluse, and his estranged son reunite in the Washington State wilderness, causing him to reflect on his isolation. Strong premise and cast watered down by weak script. **114m/C VHS, Beta, LV, Closed Caption.** CA John Lithgow, Ralph Macchio, Kerrie Keane, Janet Margolin, Rick Rosenthal; *D:* Rick Rosenberg; *C:* Ralf Bode; *M:* Maurice Jarre. PAR

Distant Voices, Still Lives ♂♂♂ 1988 A profoundly executed, disturbing film chronicling a British middle-class family through the maturation of the three children, under the dark shadow of their abusive, malevolent father. An evocative, heartbreaking portrait of British life from WWII on, and of the rhythms of dysfunctional families. A film festival favorite. **87m/C VHS, Beta, LV.** GB Freda Dowie, Pete Postlethwaite, Angela Walsh, Dean Williams, Lorraine Ashbourne; *D:* Terence Davies; *W:* Terence Davies. Los Angeles Film Critics Association Awards '89: Best Foreign Film. ART

The Distinguished Gentleman ♂♂ 1992 (R) A small-time con man (Murphy) manages to scam his way into a political career and winds up in Congress. The other characters serve mostly as foils for Murphy's comedic talent. Viewers will laugh despite the story's predictablity. *CW:* Language and one sexual scene. **122m/C VHS, LV, Closed Caption.** Eddie Murphy, Lane Smith, Sheryl Lee Ralph, Joe Don Baker, Victoria Rowell, Grant Shaud, Kevin McCarthy, Charles S. Dutton, James Garner; *D:* Jonathan Lynn; *W:* Marty Kaplan; *M:* Randy Edelman. TOU

Distortions ♂♂ 1987 (PG) Hussey is a widow whose evil aunt (Laurie) is holding her hostage. What the film lacks in suspense throughout most of the movie is made up for in the end. **90m/C VHS, Beta.** Piper Laurie, Steve Railsback, Olivia Hussey, Edward Albert, Rita Gam, Terence Knox; *D:* Armand Mastroianni.

Disturbance ♂½ 1989 The two personas of a young schizophrenic get him entangled in a mysterious string of murders. **81m/C VHS, Beta.** Timothy Greeson, Lisa Geoffreion; *D:* Cliff Guest. NO

Disturbed ♂ 1990 (R) Lusty mental hospital director McDowell meets sex starved and suicidal Gidley in this less-than-stellar erotic creeper. Redeemed only by McDowell's performance and more evidence that the droog's career hasn't been just peachy since "Clockwork Orange." **96m/C VHS, LV.** Malcolm McDowell, Geoffrey Lewis, Priscilla Pointer, Pamela Gidley, Clint Howard; *D:* Charles Winkler; *W:* Emerson Bixby, Charles Winkler. ART

Disturbing Behavior 1998 Newcomer Steve (Marsden) moves to Cradle Bay and finds his high school classmates are too good to be true. He teams up with rebellious Rachel

(Holmes) and Gavin (Stahl) to figure out what's wrong. Think "Stepford." Not yet reviewed. **?m/C VHS.** James Marsden, Nick Stahl, Katie Holmes, Bruce Greenwood, William Sadler; **D:** David Nutter; **W:** Scott Rosenberg. *NYR*

Diva 🎞🎞🎞½ 1982 (R) While at a concert given by his favorite star, a young French courier secretly tapes a soprano who has refused to record. The film follows the young man through Paris as he flees from two Japanese recording pirates, and a couple of crooked undercover police who are trying to cover-up for the chief who not only has a mistress, but runs a prostitution ring. Brilliant and dazzling photography compliment the eclectic soundtrack. **123m/C VHS, Beta, LV.** *FR* Frederic Andrei, Roland Bertin, Richard Bohringer, Gerard Darmon, Jacques Fabbri, Wilhelmenia Wiggins Fernandez, Dominique Pinon; **D:** Jean-Jacques Beineix; **W:** Jean-Jacques Beineix; **C:** Philippe Rousselot; **M:** Vladimir Cosma. Cesar Awards '82: Best Cinematography, Best Sound, Best Score; National Society of Film Critics Awards '82: Best Cinematography. *MGM*

The Dive 🎞🎞 1989 (PG-13) Two North Sea oil-rig workers are trapped far below the waves when the lifeline to their diving bell snaps in rough seas. **90m/C VHS, Beta, LV, Closed Caption.** Bjorn Sundquist, Frank Grimes, Einride Eidsvold, Michael Kitchen; **D:** Tristan De Vere Cole. *NO*

Dive Bomber 🎞🎞🎞 1941 Exciting aviation film that focuses on medical problems related to flying. Flynn stars as an aviator-doctor who conducts experiments to eliminate pilot-blackout. MacMurray, Toomey, and Heydt perform well as three flyboys stationed in Hawaii. Great flying sequences filmed at San Diego's naval base with extra scenes shot at Pensacola. Warner Bros. released this film just months before the Japanese attacked Pearl Harbor. Based on the story "Beyond the Blue Sky" by Frank Wead. **130m/B VHS, Closed Caption.** Errol Flynn, Fred MacMurray, Ralph Bellamy, Alexis Smith, Regis Toomey, Robert Armstrong, Allen Jenkins, Craig Stevens; **D:** Michael Curtiz; **W:** Frank Wead, Robert Buckner; **M:** Max Steiner. Nominations: Academy Awards '41: Best Color Cinematography. *MGM*

Divided by Hate 🎞🎞 1996 (PG-13) In 1984, struggling farmer Louis Gibbs (Walsh), wife Carol (Roth), and their children fall under the spell of charismatic preacher Steve Riordan (Skerritt) whose anti-government sentiments lead to the forming of a local militia. Naturally, the FBI gets involved and there's a struggle between the feds and the militia, with the family caught in the middle. If it sounds familiar that's because it's based on the 1995 Branch Davidian incident. **CW:** Thematic elements and some violence. **92m/C VHS, Closed Caption.** Dylan Walsh, Andrea Roth, Tom Skerritt; **D:** Tom Skerritt. *USH*

Divine 🎞🎞½ 1990 Two Divine flicks from Waters. First, Divine plays a naughty girl who, not surprisingly, since this one is titled "The Diane Linkletter Story," ends up a successful suicide. "The Neon Woman" is a rare live performance, with Divine a woman who owns a strip joint and has a slew of problems you won't read about in Dear Abby. **110m/C VHS.** Divine; **D:** John Waters. *FCT*

The Divine Enforcer 🎞½ 1991 A monsignor in a crime-ridden L.A. neighborhood reaches his wit's end in trying to stave off perpetrators of injustice. Fortunately, help arrives in the form of a mysterious priest who is equally handy with his fists, nunchakus, and guns. From then on it's no more mister nice guy, and the criminals haven't a prayer. **90m/C VHS, Beta.** Jan-Michael Vincent, Erik Estrada, Jim Brown, Judy Landers, Don Stroud, Robert Z'Dar, Michael Foley, Carrie Chambers, Hiroko; **D:** Robert Rundle.

Divine Nymph 🎞½ 1971 (R) Charts the erotic adventures of the beautiful and young Manuela, who is dangerously pursued by two cousins. **100m/C VHS, Beta.** *IT* Laura Antonelli, Marcello Mastroianni, Terence Stamp; **D:** Giuseppe Patroni Griffi; **M:** Ennio Morricone. *MPI*

Diving In 🎞🎞 1990 (PG-13) Have you heard the one about the acrophobic diver? It seems a paralyzing fear of heights is the only thing between a young diver and Olympic gold. Much splashing about and heartstring-tugging. **92m/C VHS, Beta, Closed Caption.** Burt Young, Matt Adler, Kristy Swanson, Matt Lattanzi, Richard Johnson, Carey Scott, Yolanda Jilot; **D:** Strathford Hamilton; **C:** Hanania Baer; **M:** Guy Moon, Paul Buckmaster. *PAR, FCT*

Divorce American Style 🎞🎞½ 1967 Dated but still amusing look at love, marriage, and the big D. Richard (Van Dyke) and Barbara (Reynolds) Harmon find their longtime marriage in a tailspin as they spend all their time arguing. They split but find single life and the dating game have their own pitfalls. **103m/C VHS.** Dick Van Dyke, Debbie Reynolds, Jason Robards Jr., Jean Simmons, Van Johnson, Lee Grant, Joe Flynn, Shelley Berman, Martin Gabel, Tom Bosley, Dick Gautier, Eileen Brennan; **D:** Bud Yorkin; **W:** Norman Lear; **C:** Conrad Hall; **M:** Dave Grusin. Nominations: Academy Awards '67: Best Story & Screenplay. *COL*

Divorce His, Divorce Hers 🎞🎞 1972 The first half of this drama shows the crumbling of a marriage through the husband's eyes. The second half offers the wife's perspective. Made for television. **144m/C VHS, Beta.** Richard Burton, Elizabeth Taylor; **D:** Waris Hussein. *NO*

Divorce—Italian Style 🎞🎞🎞½ *Divorzio All'Italiana* 1962 A middle-aged baron bored with his wife begins directing his amorous attentions to a teenage cousin. Since divorce in Italy is impossible, the only way out of his marriage is murder—and the baron finds a little-known law that excuses a man from murdering his wife if she is having an affair (since he would merely be defending his honor). A hilarious comedy with a twist ending. Available in Italian with English subtitles or dubbed in English. **104m/B VHS.** *IT* Marcello Mastroianni, Daniela Rocca, Leopoldo Trieste; **D:** Pietro Germi; **W:** Pietro Germi, Ennio de Concini, Alfredo Giannetti. Academy Awards '62: Best Story & Screenplay; British Academy Awards '63: Best Actor (Mastroianni); Golden Globe Awards '63: Best Actor—Musical/Comedy (Mastroianni), Best Foreign Film; Nominations: Academy Awards '62: Best Actor (Mastroianni), Best Director (Germi). *HTV*

The Divorce of Lady X 🎞🎞½ 1938 A spoiled British debutante, in the guise of "Lady X," makes a woman-hating divorce lawyer eat his words through romance and marriage. Based on the play by Gilbert Wakefield. **92m/C VHS, Beta, LV.** *GB* Merle Oberon, Laurence Olivier, Ralph Richardson, Binnie Barnes; **D:** Tim Whelan; **C:** Harry Stradling; **M:** Miklos Rozsa. *NOS, MRV, UNI*

The Divorcee 🎞🎞½ 1930 Early Leonard film (he'd later direct "The Great Ziegfeld" and "Pride and Prejudice") casts Shearer as a woman out to beat her husband at philandering. Married to a journalist, she cavorts with her husband's best friend and a discarded old flame as only a pre-production code gal could. Shearer—who Lillian Hellman described as having "a face unclouded by thought"—grabbed an Oscar. Based on the novel "Ex-Wife" by Ursula Parrott. **83m/B VHS.** Norma Shearer, Chester Morris, Conrad Nagel, Robert Montgomery, Mary Doran, Tyler Brooke, George Irving, Helen Johnson; **D:** Robert Z. Leonard. Academy Awards '30: Best Actress (Shearer); Nominations: Academy Awards '30: Best Director (Leonard), Best Picture, Best Writing. *MGM, FCT, BTV*

Dixiana 🎞½ 1930 A Southern millionaire falls for a circus performer shortly before the start of the Civil War. Part color. 🎵Dixiana; Here's to the Old Days; A Tear, a Kiss, a Smile; My One Ambition is You; A Lady Loved a Soldier; Mr. & Mrs. Sippi; Guiding Star. **99m/B VHS, Beta.** Bebe Daniels, Bert Wheeler, Robert Woolsey, Dorothy Lamour, Bill Robinson; **D:** Luther Reed; **M:** Max Steiner. *NOS, DVT*

Dixie: Changing Habits 🎞🎞🎞 1985 A New Orleans madam and a Mother Superior go head to head in this amusing made-for-television movie. In the end all benefit as the nuns discover business sense and pay off a debt, while the for-mer bordello owner cleans up her act. Above-average scripting and directing for the medium. **100m/C VHS.** Suzanne Pleshette, Cloris Leachman, Kenneth McMillan, John Considine, Geraldine Fitzgerald, Judith Ivey; **D:** George Englund. *ART*

Dixie Dynamite 🎞 1976 (PG) The two daughters of a Georgia moonshiner set out to avenge the murder of their father. The music is performed by Duane Eddy and Dorsey Burnette. **88m/C VHS, Beta.** Warren Oates, Christopher George, Jane Anne Johnstone, Kathy McHaley, R.G. Armstrong, Wes Bishop; **D:** Lee Frost. *VCI*

Dixie Jamboree 🎞 1944 Low-budget musical has gangster on the lam using an unusual method to escape from St. Louis—the last Mississippi Showboat. 🎵Dixie Showboat; No, No, No; If It's a Dream; You Ain't Right with the Lord; Big Stuff. **69m/B VHS, Beta.** Guy Kibbee, Frances Langford, Louise Beavers, Charles Butterworth; **D:** Christy Cabanne. *NOS, VYY, DVT*

Dixie Lanes 🎞 1988 A relentlessly nostalgic comedy set in a small town at the end of WWII. A woman, troubled by her nephew's restless antics, puts him to work. Unfortunately she adds to his plight, as her business involves the Black Market. **92m/C VHS, Beta.** Hoyt Axton, Karen Black, Art Hindle, John Vernon, Ruth Buzzi, Tina Louise, Pamela Springsteen, Nina Foch; **D:** Don Cato. *CEL*

Django 🎞🎞½ 1968 (PG) Django is a stranger who arrives in a Mexican-border town to settle a dispute between a small band of Americans and Mexicans. **90m/C VHS, Beta.** Franco Nero, Loredana Nusciak, Angel Alvarez; **D:** Sergio Corbucci. *NO*

Django Shoots First 🎞½ 1974 Spaghetti western with usual amount of action and plot twists. **96m/C VHS, Beta.** Glen Saxson, Evelyn Stewart, Alberto Lupo. *VYY*

DNA 🎞½ 1997 (R) Idealistic doctor Ash Mattley (Dacascos) reveals his radical DNA theories to creepy scientist Wessinger (Prochonow), who uses the knowledge in mutant experiments. One mutant, an insect-like creature with super powers, lurks in the rain forest, waiting for prey, while Mattley sets out to destroy it. **CW:** Violence, language. **94m/C VHS, Closed Caption.** Mark Dacascos, Juergen Prochnow, Robin McKee; **D:** William Mesa; **W:** Nick Davis; **C:** Gerry Lively; **M:** Christopher Stone. *CAF*

Do or Die 🎞½ 1991 (R) Former "Playboy" centerfolds Speir and Vasquez team up as a couple of federal agent babes who take on international crime boss Morita. But the crimelord is ready for our scantily clad heroines with a sick game of revenge—and the stakes are their very lives! **CW:** Nudity and sensuality. **97m/C VHS, LV.** Erik Estrada, Dona Speir, Roberta Vasquez, Noriyuki "Pat" Morita, Bruce Penhall, Carolyn Liu, Stephanie Schick; **D:** Andy Sidaris; **W:** Andy Sidaris. *COL*

Do the Right Thing 🎞🎞🎞½ 1989 (R) An uncompromising, brutal comedy about the racial tensions surrounding a white-owned pizzeria in the Bed-Stuy section of Brooklyn on the hottest day of the summer, and the violence that eventually erupts. Ambivalent and, for the most part, hilarious; Lee's coming-of-age. **120m/C VHS, Beta, LV, Closed Caption, DVD.** Spike Lee, Danny Aiello, Richard Edson, Ruby Dee, Ossie Davis, Giancarlo Esposito, Bill Nunn, John Turturro, John Savage, Rosie Perez, Frankie Faison; **D:** Spike Lee; **W:** Spike Lee. Los Angeles Film Critics Association Awards '89: Best Director (Lee), Best Film, Best Supporting Actor (Aiello); New York Film Critics Awards '89: Best Cinematography; Nominations: Academy Awards '89: Best Original Screenplay, Best Supporting Actor (Aiello). *USH, FCT*

D.O.A. 🎞🎞🎞 1949 A man is given a lethal, slow-acting poison. As his time runs out, he frantically seeks to learn who is responsible and why he was targeted for death. Dark film noir remade in 1969 as "Color Me Dead" and in 1988 with Dennis Quaid and Meg Ryan. Also available colorized. **83m/B VHS.** Edmond O'Brien, Pamela Britton, Luther Adler, Neville Brand, Beverly Garland, Lynne Baggett, William Ching, Henry Hart, Laurette Luez, Virginia Lee,

Jess Kirkland, Cay Forrester, Michael Ross; **D:** Rudolph Mate; **W:** Russel Rouse, Clarence Green; **C:** Ernest Laszlo; **M:** Dimitri Tiomkin. *EEL, NOS, VYY*

D.O.A. 🎬🎬½ **1988 (R)** Well-done remake of the 1949 thriller with Quaid portraying a college professor who is poisoned and has only 24 hours to identify his killer. His search for the suspect is further complicated by the fact that he is being sought by the police on phony charges of murder. Directed by the same people who brought "Max Headroom" to television screens. **98m/C VHS, Beta, LV, Closed Caption.** Dennis Quaid, Meg Ryan, Charlotte Rampling, Daniel Stern, Jane Kaczmarek, Christopher Neame, Jay Patterson; **D:** Rocky Morton, Annabel Jankel; **W:** Charles Edward Pogue; **M:** Chaz Jankel. *TOU*

The Doberman Gang 🎬🎬 **1972 (PG)** Clever thieves train a gang of Dobermans in the fine art of bank robbery. Sequelled by "The Daring Dobermans." **85m/C VHS, Beta, Closed Caption.** Byron Mabe, Hal Reed, Julie Parrish, Simmy Bow, JoJo D'Amore; **D:** Byron Ross Chudnow; **W:** Frank Ray Perilli. *FOX*

Doc Hollywood 🎬🎬½ **1991 (PG-13)** A hot-shot young physician on his way to a lucrative California practice gets stranded in a small Southern town. Will the wacky woodsy inhabitants persuade the city doctor to stay? There aren't many surprises in this fish-out-of-water comedy, but the cast injects it with considerable charm. Adapted from Neil B. Shulman's book "What?...Dead Again?" **104m/C VHS, Beta, LV, 8mm, Letterbox, Closed Caption.** Michael J. Fox, Julie Warner, Woody Harrelson, Barnard Hughes, David Ogden Stiers, Frances Sternhagen, Bridget Fonda, George Hamilton, Roberts Blossom, Helen Martin, Macon McCalman, Barry Sobel; **D:** Michael Caton-Jones; **W:** Daniel Pyne, Jeffrey Price, Peter S. Seaman; **C:** Michael Chapman; **M:** Carter Burwell. *WAR*

Doc Savage 🎬🎬½ **1975 (PG)** Doc and "The Amazing Five" fight a murderous villain who plans to take over the world. Based on the novels of Kenneth Robeson. **100m/C VHS, Beta,** Ron Ely, Pamela Hensley, Paul Gleason, Paul Wexler, William Lucking; **D:** Michael Anderson Sr.; **W:** George Pal, Joe Morhaim; **C:** Fred W. Koenekamp. *WAR*

Docks of New York 🎬🎬🎬 **1928** Von Sternberg made his mark in Hollywood with this silent drama about two dockside losers finding love amid the squalor. A rarely seen, early masterpiece. **60m/B VHS, Beta.** George Bancroft, Betty Compson, Olga Baclanova; **D:** Josef von Sternberg; **M:** Gaylord Carter. *PAR*

The Doctor 🎬🎬½ **1991 (PG-13)** A hotshot doctor develops throat cancer and gets treated at his own hospital, an ordeal that teaches him a respect and compassion for patients that he formerly lacked. Potential melodrama is saved by fine acting and strong direction. Based on the autobiographical book "A Taste of My Own Medicine" by Dr. Edward Rosenbaum. **125m/C VHS, Beta, LV, Letterbox, Closed Caption.** William Hurt, Elizabeth Perkins, Christine Lahti, Mandy Patinkin, Wendy Crewson, Charlie Korsmo, Adam Arkin, Bill Macy; **D:** Randa Haines; **W:** Robert Caswell; **C:** John Seale; **M:** Michael Convertino. *TOU*

Dr. Alien 🎬 **1988 (R)** Alien poses as beautiful scientist and turns a college freshman into a sex-addicted satyr. Likewise, the cast turns this flick into a dog. **90m/C VHS, Beta, LV, Closed Caption.** Billy Jacoby, Olivia Barash, Stuart Fratkin, Troy Donahue, Arlene Golonka, Judy Landers; **D:** David DeCoteau. *PAR*

The Doctor and the Devils 🎬🎬½ **1985 (R)** Based on an old screenplay by Dylan Thomas, this is a semi-Gothic tale about two criminals who supply a physician with corpses to study, either digging them up or killing them fresh. **93m/C VHS, Beta.** *GB* Timothy Dalton, Julian Sands, Jonathan Pryce, Stephen Rea, Beryl Reid, Sian Phillips, Patrick Stewart, Phyllis Logan, T.P. McKenna; **D:** Freddie Francis; **W:** Ronald Harwood; **M:** John Morris. *FOX*

Doctor at Large 🎬🎬½ **1957** A fledgling doctor seeks to become a surgeon at a hospital for the rich. Humorous antics follow. The third of the "Doctor" series. **98m/C VHS, Beta.** *GB* Dirk Bo-

garde, Muriel Pavlow, James Robertson Justice, Shirley Eaton, Donald Sinden, Anne Heywood; **D:** Ralph Thomas. *NO*

Doctor at Sea 🎬🎬½ **1956** To escape a troublesome romantic entanglement and the stresses of his career, a London physician signs on a cargo boat as a ship's doctor and becomes involved with French bombshell Bardot. The second of the "Doctor" series. **93m/C VHS, Beta.** *GB* James Robertson Justice, Dirk Bogarde, Brigitte Bardot; **D:** Ralph Thomas; **W:** Jack Davies. *FCT*

Dr. Bethune 🎬 *Bethune, The Making of a Hero* **1990** Canadian surgeon Norman Bethune was a larger-than-life hero with equally great flaws. A crusader for socialized medicine and an outspoken opponent of Fascism (as well as an alcoholic womanizer), he worked for the Loyalist forces in the Spanish Civil War and was instrumental in developing mobile medical units for treating battlefield wounded. He's also credited with bringing modern medical care to China, where he attended to Mao's revolutionary forces. Sutherland's strong performance shows the intensity and vision of a complicated man; he previously played the doctor in 1977's "Bethune." Awkward jumps in time and place rob the story of narrative drive. **115m/C VHS.** *CA FR* Donald Sutherland, Helen Mirren, Helen Shaver, Colm Feore, Anouk Aimee, Ronald Pickup, Harrison Liu; **D:** Phillip Borsos; **W:** Ted Allan; **C:** Raoul Coutard; **M:** Alan Reeves. *FXL, ING*

Dr. Black, Mr. Hyde 🎬 *Dr. Black and Mr. White; The Watts Monster* **1976 (R)** Not-so-horrifying tale of a black Jekyll who metamorphoses into a white monster with the help of the special potion. Unintended laughs lessen suspense. **88m/C VHS, Beta.** Rosalind Cash, Stu Gilliam, Bernie Casey, Marie O'Henry; **D:** William Crain. *VCI*

Doctor Blood's Coffin 🎬🎬½ **1962** The aptly named doctor performs hideous experiments on the unsuspecting denizens of a lonely village. Good cast in this effective chiller. **92m/C VHS.** *GB* Kieron Moore, Hazel Court, Ian Hunter; **D:** Sidney J. Furie. *SNC*

Doctor Butcher M.D. woof! *Queen of the Cannibals* **1980 (R)** Mad doctor's deranged dream of creating "perfect people" by taking parts of one person and interchanging them with another backfires as his monstrosities develop strange side effects. The M.D., by the way, stands for "Medical Deviate". Dubbed. **81m/C VHS, Beta.** *IT* Ian McCulloch, Alexandra Cole, Peter O'Neal, Donald O'Brien; **D:** Frank Martin. *NO*

Dr. Caligari 🎬🎬 **1989 (R)** The granddaughter of the original Dr. Caligari promotes "better living through chemistry" in her insane asylum while using her patients as guinea pigs in her bizarre sexual experiments. Nothing outstanding here in terms of story or performance, but "Dick Tracy" has nothing on the visually compelling set designs and make-up. **80m/C VHS, LV.** Madeleine Reynal, Fox Harris, Laura Albert, Jennifer Balgobin, John Durbin, Gene Zerna, David Parry, Barry Phillips; **D:** Stephen Sayadian. *FCT*

Dr. Christian Meets the Women 🎬½ **1940** This entry in the "Dr. Christian" series of films has the small-town physician once again exposing a con man trying to filch the townspeople. **63m/B VHS, Beta, 8mm.** Jean Hersholt, Edgar Kennedy, Rod La Rocque, Dorothy Lovett, Veda Ann Borg; **D:** William McGann. *VYY*

Dr. Cyclops 🎬🎬½ **1940** The famous early Technicolor fantasia about a mad scientist miniaturizing a group of explorers who happen upon his jungle lab. Landmark F/X and a slow-moving story. **76m/C VHS, Beta, LV.** Albert Dekker, Janice Logan, Victor Kilian, Thomas Coley, Charles Halton, Frank Yaconelli, Paul Fix, Frank Reicher; **D:** Ernest B. Schoedsack; **W:** Tom Kilpatrick; **C:** Winton C. Hoch, Henry Sharp. *USH, FCT, MLB*

Dr. Death, Seeker of Souls 🎬 **1973 (R)** Evil doctor discovers a process for transmigrating his soul into the bodies of people he murdered 1000 years ago. Now he seeks to revive his

wife. Final role for 77-year-old "Stooge" Moe Howard. **93m/C VHS, Beta.** John Considine, Barry Coe, Cheryl Miller, Stewart Moss, Leon Askin, Jo Morrow, Florence Marly, Sivi Aberg, Athena Lorde, Moe Howard; **D:** Eddie Saeta.

Doctor Detroit 🎬🎬 **1983 (R)** Aykroyd is funny in thin film, portraying a meek college professor who gets involved with prostitutes and the mob, under the alias "Dr. Detroit." Aykroyd later married actress Donna Dixon, whom he worked with on this film. Features music by Devo, James Brown, and Pattie Brooks. **91m/C VHS, Beta, LV.** Dan Aykroyd, Howard Hesseman, Donna Dixon, T.K. Carter, Lynn Whitfield, Lydia Lei, Fran Drescher, Kate Murtagh, George Furth, Andrew Duggan, James Brown, Glenne Headly; **D:** Michael Pressman; **W:** Carl Gottlieb, Robert Boris; **M:** Lalo Schifrin. *USH*

Doctor Dolittle 🎬🎬 **1967** An adventure about a 19th century English doctor who dreams of teaching animals to speak to him. Realistic premise suffers from poor script. Based on Hugh Lofting's acclaimed stories. ♫ Doctor Dolittle; My Friend the Doctor; Talk to the Animals; I've Never Seen Anything Like It; Beautiful Things; When I Look in Your Eyes; After Today; Fabulous Places; Where Are the Words?. **144m/C VHS, Beta, LV, Letterbox, Closed Caption.** Rex Harrison, Samantha Eggar, Anthony Newley, Richard Attenborough, Geoffrey Holder, Peter Bull; **D:** Richard Fleischer; **W:** Leslie Bricusse; **C:** Robert L. Surtees; **M:** Leslie Bricusse. Academy Awards '67: Best Song ("Talk to the Animals"), Best Visual Effects; Golden Globe Awards '68: Best Supporting Actor (Attenborough); Nominations: Academy Awards '67: Best Art Direction/Set Decoration, Best Cinematography, Best Film Editing, Best Picture, Best Sound, Best Original Score. *FOX, FCT, MLT*

Dr. Dolittle **1998 (PG-13)** Murphy goes the remake route again, this time taking the title role of the doctor who talks (but does not sing) to the animals. Now they talk back, expressively, thanks to numerous comedic vocal talents. **CW:** Crude humor and language. **?m/C VHS, Closed Caption.** Eddie Murphy, Oliver Platt, Peter Boyle, Jeffrey Tambor; **D:** Betty Thomas; **V:** Albert Brooks, Chris Rock, John Leguizamo, Garry Shandling, Norm MacDonald, Paul (Pee Wee Herman) Reubens, Jean Stapleton, Dennis Franz, Julie Kavner. *NYR*

Doctor Faustus 🎬½ **1968** A stilted, stagy, but well-meaning adaptation of the Christopher Marlowe classic about Faust, who sold his soul to the devil for youth and the love of Helen of Troy. **93m/C VHS, Beta.** Richard Burton, Andreas Teuber, Elizabeth Taylor, Ian Marter; **D:** Richard Burton, Nevill Coghill. *COL*

Dr. Frankenstein's Castle of Freaks 🎬 **1974 (PG)** Dr. Frankenstein and his dwarf assistant reanimate a few Neanderthals that are terrorizing a nearby Rumanian village. **87m/C VHS, Beta.** *IT* Rossano Brazzi, Michael Dunn, Edmund Purdom, Christiane Royce; **D:** Robert Oliver. *SNC*

Dr. Giggles 🎬 **1992 (R)** Drake plays the psycho-genius Dr. Giggles, an escaped mental patient who sets out to avenge the death of his psycho-genius father (dementia runs in the family). He returns to his family home to procure the necessary medical instruments, most notably a hypodermic needle, and starts killing people—on screen with the tools and in the audience with remarkably stupid one-liners. Opening scenes are especially mired in gore. **CW:** Language and horror violence and gore. **96m/C VHS, Beta, LV, Letterbox, Closed Caption.** Larry Drake, Holly Marie Combs, Glenn Quinn, Keith Diamond, Cliff DeYoung; **D:** Manny Coto; **W:** Manny Coto, Graeme Whifler; **M:** Brian May. *USH*

Dr. Goldfoot and the Bikini Machine 🎬🎬 **1966** A mad scientist employs gorgeous female robots to seduce the wealthy and powerful, thereby allowing him to take over the world. Title song by the Supremes. **90m/C VHS.** Vincent Price, Frankie Avalon, Dwayne Hickman, Annette Funicello, Susan Hart, Kay Elkhardt, Fred Clark, Deanna Lund, Deborah Walley; **D:** Norman Taurog; **M:** Les Baxter.

Dr. Hackenstein 🎬½ 1988 (R) A doctor tries to revive his wife by "borrowing" parts from unexpected (and unsuspecting) guests. 88m/C VHS, Beta. David Muir, Stacy Travis, Catherine Davis Cox, Dyanne DiRosario, Anne Ramsey, Logan Ramsey; **D:** Richard Clark. MCG

Dr. Heckyl and Mr. Hype 🎬🎬 1980 (R) A naughty, comical version of the Jekyll and Hyde story. Exuberantly wicked performances from Reed and Coogan; stellar cast of "B" veterans. 100m/C VHS, Beta. Oliver Reed, Sunny Johnson, Maia Danzinger, Mel Welles, Virgil Frye, Kedrick Wolfe, Jackie Coogan, Corinne Calvet, Dick Miller, Lucretia Love; **D:** Charles B. Griffith; **W:** Charles B. Griffith; **M:** Richard Band. NO

Doctor in Distress 🎬🎬½ 1963 Aging chief surgeon falls in love for the first time. His assistant tries to further the romance as well as his own love life. Comedic fourth in the six-film "Doctor" series. 102m/C VHS, Beta. GB Dirk Bogarde, James Robertson Justice, Leo McKern, Samantha Eggar; **D:** Ralph Thomas. NO

Doctor in the House 🎬🎬🎬½ 1953 Four medical student/roommates seek only to examine lovely women and make lots of cash. In the process, they are also tempted by the evils of drink, but rally to make their grades. A riotous British comedy with marvelous performances all around. Led to six sequels and a television series. 92m/C VHS. GB Dirk Bogarde, Muriel Pavlow, Kenneth More, Donald Sinden, Kay Kendall, James Robertson Justice, Donald Houston, Geoffrey Keen, George Coulouris, Shirley Eaton, Joan Hickson, Richard Wattis; **D:** Ralph Thomas. British Academy Awards '54: Best Actor (More). PAR, HMV

Dr. Jack/For Heaven's Sake 1926 In "Dr. Jack" (1922) and "For Heaven's Sake" (1926) Lloyd acts respectively as an unorthodox doctor and as a debonair millionaire who falls in love with a poor girl. Silent comedy shorts from Lloyd. 88m/B VHS, Beta. Harold Lloyd, Jobyna Ralston; **D:** Sam Taylor. TLF

Dr. Jekyll and Ms. Hyde 🎬🎬½ 1995 (PG-13) Chemist Richard Jacks (Daly) stumbles across the secret formula of great-grandad Dr. Jekyll and, after trying to improve the potion, he finds himself transformed into wicked woman Helen Hyde (Young). Cheap cross-gender gags abound.**CW:** Crude sex-related scenes and humor, nudity, and brief strong language. 89m/C VHS, Beta. Timothy Daly, Sean Young, Lysette Anthony, Stephen Tobolowsky, Harvey Fierstein, Polly Bergen, Stephen Shellan; **D:** David F. Price; **W:** William Davies, William Osborne, Tim John, Oliver Butcher; **M:** Mark McKenzie. HBO

Dr. Jekyll and Mr. Hyde 🎬🎬🎬 1920 The first American film version of Robert Louis Stevenson's horror tale about a doctor's experiments that lead to his developing good and evil sides to his personality. Silent. Kino Video's edition also contains the rarely seen 1911 version of the film, as well as scenes from a different 1920 version. 96m/B VHS, LV. John Barrymore, Martha Mansfield, Brandon Hurst, Charles Lane, J. Malcolm Dunn, Nita Naldi, Louis Wolheim; **D:** John S. Robertson; **W:** Clara Beranger; **C:** Karl Struss, Roy F. Overbaugh. KIV, REP, MRV

Dr. Jekyll and Mr. Hyde 🎬🎬🎬 1932 The hallucinatory, feverish classic version of the Robert Louis Stevenson story, in which the good doctor becomes addicted to the formula that turns him into a sadistic beast. Possibly Mamoulian's and March's best work, and a masterpiece of subversive, pseudo-Freudian creepiness. Eighteen minutes from the original version, lost until recently, have been restored, including the infamous whipping scene. 96m/B VHS, Beta, LV. Fredric March, Miriam Hopkins, Halliwell Hobbes, Rose Hobart, Holmes Herbert, Edgar Norton; **D:** Rouben Mamoulian; **W:** Samuel Hoffenstein, Percy Heath; **C:** Karl Struss. Academy Awards '32: Best Actor (March); Venice Film Festival '31: Best Actor (March); Nominations: Academy Awards '32: Best Adapted Screenplay, Best Cinematography. MGM, BTV

Dr. Jekyll and Mr. Hyde 🎬🎬🎬 1941 Strangely cast adaptation of the Robert Louis Stevenson story about a doctor's experiment on himself to separate good and evil. 113m/B VHS, Beta, LV. Spencer Tracy, Ingrid Bergman, Lana Turner, Donald Crisp, Ian Hunter, Barton MacLane, Sara Allgood, Billy Bevan; **D:** Victor Fleming; **W:** John Lee Mahin; **C:** Joseph Ruttenberg; **M:** Franz Waxman. Nominations: Academy Awards '41: Best Black and White Cinematography, Best Film Editing, Best Original Dramatic/Comedy Score. MGM

Dr. Jekyll and Mr. Hyde 🎬🎬🎬 1968 Yet another production of Robert Louis Stevenson's classic story of a split-personality. 90m/C VHS, Beta. Jack Palance. ART

Dr. Jekyll and Mr. Hyde 🎬🎬 1973 Dr. Jekyll discovers a potion that turns him into the sinister Mr. Hyde. Based on the classic story by Robert Louis Stevenson. 90m/C VHS, Beta, LV. Kirk Douglas, Michael Redgrave, Susan George, Donald Pleasence; **D:** David Winters. IME

Dr. Jekyll and Sister Hyde 🎬🎬½ 1971 (R) A tongue-in-cheek variation on the split-personality theme, which has the good doctor transforming himself into a sultry, knife-wielding woman who kills prostitutes. 94m/C VHS, Beta. GB Ralph Bates, Martine Beswick, Gerald Sim; **D:** Roy Ward Baker; **W:** Brian Clemens. MLB

Dr. Jekyll and the Wolfman 🎬 Dr. Jekyll y el Hombre Lobo 1971 (R) Naschy's sixth stint as El Hombre Lobo. This time he visits a mysterious doctor in search of a cure but ends up turning into Mr. Hyde, a man who likes to torture women. 85m/C VHS. SP Paul Naschy, Shirley Corrigan, Jack Taylor; **D:** Leon Klimovsky. SNC

Dr. Jekyll vs. the Werewolf 🎬½ 1971 A man afflicted with the characteristics of a wolf seeks a cure from Dr. Jekyll's grandson. ?m/C VHS. Paul Naschy, Jack Taylor. SNC

Dr. Jekyll's Dungeon of Death 🎬 1982 (R) Dr. Jekyll and his lobotomized sister, Hilda, scour the streets of San Francisco looking for human blood to recreate his great-grandfather's secret serum. 90m/C VHS, Beta. James Mathers, Dawn Carver Kelly, John Kearney, Jake Pearson; **D:** James Wood.

Dr. Kildare's Strange Case 🎬🎬 1940 Dr. Kildare administers a daring treatment to a man suffering from a mental disorder of a dangerous nature. One in the film series. 76m/B VHS, Beta. Lew Ayres, Lionel Barrymore, Laraine Day; **D:** Harold Bucquet. NOS, HHT, DVT

Dr. Mabuse, Parts 1 & 2 🎬🎬🎬½ Doktor Mabuse der Spieler 1922 The massive, two-part crime melodrama, introducing the raving mastermind/extortionist/villain to the world. The film follows Dr. Mabuse through his life of crime until he finally goes mad. Highly influential and inventive. Lang meant this to be a criticism of morally bankrupt post-WWI Germany. Followed some time later by "Testament of Doctor Mabuse" and "The Thousand Eyes of Dr. Mabuse." Silent. 242m/B VHS, Beta. GE Rudolf Klein-Rogge, Aud Egede Nissen, Alfred Abel, Gertrude Welcker, Lil Dagover, Paul Richter; **D:** Fritz Lang. SNC, MRV, NOS

Dr. Mabuse vs. Scotland Yard 🎬🎬½ 1964 A sequel to the Fritz Lang classics, this film features the arch-criminal attempting to take over the world with a mind-controlling camera. 90m/B VHS, Beta. GE Sabine Bethmann, Peter Van Eyck; **D:** Paul May. VYY, SNC, GLV

Doctor Mordrid: Master of the Unknown 🎬🎬 1990 (R) Two immensely powerful sorcerers from the 4th dimension cross over into present time with two very different missions—one wants to destroy the Earth, one wants to save it.**CW:** Language and one sexual scene. 102m/C VHS, Beta, Closed Caption. Jeffrey Combs, Yvette Nipar, Jay Acovone, Brian Thompson; **D:** Albert Band, Charles Band; **M:** Richard Band. PAR

Dr. No 🎬🎬🎬 1962 (PG) The world is introduced to British secret agent 007, James Bond, when it is discovered that a mad scientist is sabotaging rocket launchings from his hideout in Jamaica. The first 007 film is far less glitzy than any of its successors but boasts the sexiest "Bond girl" of them all in Andress, and promptly made stars of her and Connery. On laserdisc, the film is in widescreen transfer and includes movie bills, publicity photos, location pictures, and the British and American trailers. The sound effects and musical score can be separated from the dialogue. Audio interviews with the director, writer, and editor are included as part of the disc. 111m/C VHS, Beta, LV, Letterbox, Closed Caption. GB Sean Connery, Ursula Andress, Joseph Wiseman, Jack Lord, Zena Marshall, Eunice Gayson, Margaret LeWars, John Kitzmiller, Lois Maxwell, Bernard Lee, Anthony Dawson; **D:** Terence Young; **C:** Ted Moore; **M:** John Barry. MGM, CRC, TLF

Dr. Orloff's Invisible Horror 🎬½ 1972 In this horror film, Dr. Orloff creates an invisible ape-monster that escapes and goes on a rampage. ?m/C VHS. Howard Vernon. SNC

Dr. Orloff's Monster woof! 1964 As if "The Awful Dr. Orloff" wasn't awful enough, the doctor is back, this time eliminating his enemies with his trusty killer robot. Awful awful. 88m/B VHS. SP Jose Rubio, Agnes Spaak; **D:** Jess (Jesus) Franco. SNC, VYY

Dr. Otto & the Riddle of the Gloom Beam 🎬½ 1986 (PG) Ernest is in your face again. Fresh from the TV commercials featuring "Ernest" comes Varney playing a villain out to wreck the global economy. He also plays all the other characters, too. Way bizarre. "Know whut I mean?" 92m/C VHS, Beta. Jim Varney; **D:** John R. Cherry III. GKK

Dr. Petiot 🎬🎬 Le Docteur Petiot 1990 Based on the true life story of a French WWII doctor who promised to smuggle Jews to freedom but instead killed them for their money and possessions. He was executed in 1946—accused of 60 murders and convicted of 27. The gruesome details are left to the imagination rather than shown. In French with subtitles. 102m/C VHS. FR Michel Serrault, Berangere Bonvoisin, Aurore Prieto, Nita Klein, Dominique Marcas, Andre Lacombe; **D:** Christian de Chalonge; **W:** Christian de Chalonge, Dominique Garnier; **C:** Patrick Blossier; **M:** Michel Portal. WAC, FCT

Doctor Phibes Rises Again 🎬🎬½ 1972 (PG) The despicable doctor contines his quest to revive his beloved wife. Fun, superior sequel to "The Abominable Dr. Phibes." 89m/C VHS, Beta. GB Vincent Price, Robert Quarry, Peter Cushing, Beryl Reid, Hugh Griffith, Terry-Thomas; **D:** Robert Fuest; **W:** Robert Fuest, Robert Blees. ORI

Doctor Satan's Robot 🎬🎬½ 1940 Indestructible robot is battled by insane Dr. Satan in reedited serial, "Mysterious Dr. Satan." 100m/B VHS. Eduardo Ciannelli, Robert Wilcox, William Newell, Ella Neal; **D:** William Witney, John English. VCN

Dr. Strange 🎬½ 1978 A made-for-television pilot based upon the Marvel Comics character who, with the help of a sorcerer, practices witchcraft in order to fight evil. 94m/C VHS, Beta. Peter Hooten, Clyde Kusatsu, Jessica Walter, Eddie Benton, John Mills; **D:** Philip DeGuere. USH

Dr. Strangelove, or: How I Learned to Stop Worrying and Love the Bomb 🎬🎬🎬🎬 1964 Sellers plays a tour-de-force triple role in Kubrick's classic black anti-war comedy. While a U.S. President (Sellers) deals with the Russian situation, a crazed general (Hayden) implements a plan to drop the A-bomb on the Soviets. Famous for Pickens' wild ride on the bomb, Hayden's character's "purity of essence" philosophy, Scott's gumchewing militarist, and a soft-drink vending machine dispute, and countless other scenes. Based on the novel "Red Alert" by Peter George. 93m/B VHS, Beta, LV, Letterbox, DVD. GB Peter Sellers, George C. Scott, Sterling Hayden, Keenan Wynn, Slim Pickens, James Earl Jones, Peter Bull; **D:**

Stanley Kubrick; **W:** Terry Southern, Peter George, Stanley Kubrick; **M:** Laurie Johnson. British Academy Awards '64: Best Film, National Film Registry '89'; New York Film Critics Awards '64: Best Director (Kubrick); Nominations: Academy Awards '64: Best Actor (Sellers), Best Adapted Screenplay, Best Director (Kubrick), Best Picture.**COL, HMV**

Dr. Syn ✓✓ **1937** The story of a seemingly respectable vicar of Dymchurch who is really a former pirate. The last film of George Arliss. **90m/B VHS, Beta. GB** George Arliss, Margaret Lockwood, John Loder; **D:** Roy William Neill. **NOS, MRV, CAB**

Dr. Syn, Alias the Scarecrow ✓✓½ **1964 (G)** A mild-mannered minister is, in reality, a smuggler and pirate avenging King George III's injustices upon the English people. Originally broadcast in three parts on the Disney television show. **129m/C VHS, Beta.** Patrick McGoohan, George Cole, Tony Britton, Michael Hordern, Geoffrey Keen, Kay Cole; **D:** James Neilson. **DIS**

Doctor Takes a Wife ✓✓✓ **1940** A fast, fun screwball comedy wherein two ill-matched career people are forced via a publicity mix-up to fake being married. **89m/B VHS, Beta.** Ray Milland, Loretta Young, Reginald Gardiner, Gail Patrick, Edmund Gwenn, George Metaxa, Charles Halton; **D:** Alexander Hall; **W:** George Seaton. **COL**

Dr. Tarr's Torture Dungeon woof!
Dr. Jekyll's Dungeon of Darkness **1975 (R)** A mysterious man is sent to the forest to investigate the bizarre behavior of Dr. Tarr who runs a torture asylum. **90m/C VHS, Beta.** Claudio Brook, Ellen Sherman, Robert Dumont. **NO**

Dr. Terror's House of Horrors ✓✓½ *The Blood Suckers* **1965** On a train, six traveling companions have their fortunes told by a mysterious doctor. Little do they realize that their final destination has changed. Creepy and suspenseful, especially the severed-hand chase sequence. Amazingly, Christopher Lee and Peter Cushing manage to appear in the movie but not the vampire story. **92m/C VHS. GB** Christopher Lee, Peter Cushing, Donald Sutherland; **D:** Freddie Francis. **REP, MLB**

Doctor Who ✓✓½ **1996** The late British sci-fi series, which ended in 1989, has been resurrected in this TV movie. The TARDIS is forced down in 1999 San Francisco and renegade Time Lord The Master's sluglike remains escape from the Doctor (McCoy) and into a temporary host body (Roberts). Meanwhile, the Doctor's been hospitalized and a botched operation by Dr. Grace Holloway (Ashbrook) leaves him clinically dead—until he manages to regenerate once again (as McGann). With Grace's help, the Doctor tries to stop his enemy from destroying the world on New Year's Eve in a plot that will also give the Master the Doctor's body as his new home. Production design and special effects are lavish (particularly in relation to the cheesiness of the series). **?m/C VHS. GB CA** Paul McGann, Eric Roberts, Daphne Ashbrook, Yee Jee Tso, Sylvester McCoy; **D:** Geoffrey Sax; **W:** Matthew Jacobs; **C:** Glen MacPherson; **M:** John Debney. **NYR**

Doctor Who: An Unearthly Child **1963** In the long-running British series' first episode, Doctor Who and his granddaughter travel to prehistoric times to witness the discovery of fire. Additional episodes are available. **98m/B VHS. GB** William Hartnell; **D:** Waris Hussein. **FXV, MOV**

Doctor Who and the Daleks **1965** The Time Lord and his two grandchildren accidentally transport themselves to a futuristic planet inhabited by the Daleks, who capture the travelers and hold them captive. A feature film version of the long-running British television show. **78m/C VHS, Beta, Closed Caption. GB** Peter Cushing, Roy Castle; **D:** Gordon Flemyng. **REP**

Doctor X ✓✓½ **1932** An armless mad scientist uses a formula for "synthetic flesh" to grow temporary limbs and commit murder. A classic, rarely seen horror oldie, famous for its very early use of two-color Technicolor. **77m/C VHS, Beta, LV.**

Lionel Atwill, Fay Wray, Lee Tracy, Preston Foster, Arthur Edmund Carewe, Leila Bennett, Mae Busch; **D:** Michael Curtiz; **W:** Earl Baldwin, Robert Tasker; **C:** Ray Rennahan, Richard Towers. **MGM, MLB**

Doctor Zhivago ✓✓✓ **1965 (PG-13)** Sweeping adaptation of the Nobel Prize-winning Boris Pasternak novel. An innocent Russian poet-intellectual is caught in the furor and chaos of the Bolshevik Revolution. Essentially a poignant love story filmed as a historical epic. Panoramic film popularized the song "Lara's Theme." Overlong, with often disappointing performances, but gorgeous scenery. Lean was more successful in "Lawrence of Arabia," where there was less need for ensemble acting.**CW:** Mature themes. **197m/C VHS, Beta, LV, Letterbox, Closed Caption.** Omar Sharif, Julie Christie, Geraldine Chaplin, Rod Steiger, Alec Guinness, Klaus Kinski, Ralph Richardson, Rita Tushingham, Siobhan McKenna, Tom Courtenay; **D:** David Lean; **W:** Robert Bolt; **C:** Frederick A. (Freddie) Young; **M:** Maurice Jarre. Academy Awards '65: Best Adapted Screenplay, Best Art Direction/Set Decoration (Color), Best Color Cinematography, Best Costume Design (Color), Best Original Score; Golden Globe Awards '66: Best Actor—Drama (Sharif), Best Director (Lean), Best Film—Drama, Best Screenplay, Best Score; National Board of Review Awards '65: Best Actress (Christie); Nominations: Academy Awards '65: Best Director (Lean), Best Film Editing, Best Picture, Best Sound, Best Supporting Actor (Courtenay). **MGM, RDG, HMV**

Doctors and Nurses ✓✓ **1982** A children's satire of soap operas wherein the adults play the children and vice-versa. **90m/C VHS, Beta.** Rebecca Rigg, Drew Forsythe, Graeme Blundell; **D:** Maurice Murphy. **NO**

Doctors' Wives ✓½ **1970 (R)** An adaptation of the Frank Slaughter potboiler about a large city hospital's doctors, nurses, and their respective spouses, with plenty of affairs, medical traumas, and betrayals. **102m/C VHS, Beta.** Dyan Cannon, Richard Crenna, Gene Hackman, Carroll O'Connor, Rachel Roberts, Janice Rule, Diana Sands, Ralph Bellamy, John Colicos; **D:** George Schaefer; **W:** Daniel Taradash; **C:** Charles B(ryant) Lang; **M:** Elmer Bernstein. **COL**

Dodes 'ka-den ✓✓✓½ *Clickety Clack* **1970** In this departure from his samurai-genre films, Kurosawa depicts a throng of fringe-dwelling Tokyo slum inhabitants in a semi-surreal manner. Fascinating presentation and content. **140m/C VHS, Beta. JP** Yoshitaka Zushi, Junzaburo Ban, Kiyoko Tange; **D:** Akira Kurosawa. Nominations: Academy Awards '71: Best Foreign Language Film. **NO**

Dodge City ✓✓✓ **1939** Flynn stars as Wade Hutton, a roving cattleman who becomes the sheriff of Dodge City. His job: to run a ruthless outlaw and his gang out of town. De Havilland serves as Flynn's love interest, as she did in many previous films. A broad and colorful shoot-em-up! **104m/C VHS, Beta, LV, Closed Caption.** Errol Flynn, Olivia de Havilland, Bruce Cabot, Ann Sheridan, Alan Hale, Frank McHugh, Victor Jory, Henry Travers, Charles Halton; **D:** Michael Curtiz; **M:** Max Steiner. **MGM, FOX, FCT**

Dodsworth ✓✓✓½ **1936** The lives of a self-made American tycoon and his wife are drastically changed when they take a tour of Europe. The success of their marriage seems questionable as they re-evaluate their lives. Huston excels as does the rest of the cast in this film, based upon the Sinclair Lewis novel. **101m/B VHS, Beta, LV.** Walter Huston, David Niven, Paul Lukas, John Payne, Mary Astor, Ruth Chatterton, Maria Ouspenskaya, Charles Halton; **D:** William Wyler. Academy Awards '36: Best Interior Decoration, National Film Registry '90;; New York Film Critics Awards '36: Best Actor (Huston); Nominations: Academy Awards '36: Best Actor (Huston), Best Director (Wyler), Best Picture, Best Screenplay, Best Sound, Best Supporting Actress (Ouspenskaya). **HBO**

Does This Mean We're Married? ✓✓ **1990 (PG-13)** A stand-up comedian is trying to find success in the comedy clubs of Paris but without her green card she may soon be deported. She finds a sleazy marriage broker who fixes her up with a womanizing songwriter who needs money. As usual, immigration

officials suspect that the marriage is a fake and the mismatched couple must live together to prove them wrong. **93m/C VHS, LV.** Patsy Kensit, Stephane Freiss; **D:** Carol Wiseman. **COL, NLC**

Dog Day ✓✓½ *Canicule* **1983** An American traitor, who is on the lam from the government, and his cronies, takes refuge on a small farm. A surprise awaits him when the farmers come up with an unusual plan to bargain for his life. **101m/C VHS, Beta. FR** Lee Marvin, Miou-Miou, Victor Lanoux; **D:** Yves Boisset. **ART**

Dog Day Afternoon ✓✓✓½ **1975 (R)** Based on a true story, this taut, yet fantastic thriller centers on a bi-sexual and his slow-witted buddy who rob a bank to obtain money to fund a sex change operation for the ringleader's lover. Pacino is breathtaking in his role as the frustrated robber, caught in a trap of his own devising. Very controversial for its language and subject matter when released, it nevertheless became a huge success. Director Lumet keeps up the pace, fills the screen with pathos without gross sentiment. **124m/C VHS, Beta, LV, Closed Caption.** Al Pacino, John Cazale, Charles Durning, James Broderick, Chris Sarandon, Carol Kane, Lance Henriksen, Dick Williams; **D:** Sidney Lumet; **W:** Frank Pierson. Academy Awards '75: Best Original Screenplay; British Academy Awards '75: Best Actor (Pacino); National Board of Review Awards '75: Best Supporting Actor (Durning); Writers Guild of America '75: Best Original Screenplay; Nominations: Academy Awards '75: Best Actor (Pacino), Best Director (Lumet), Best Film Editing, Best Picture, Best Supporting Actor (Sarandon). **WAR**

Dog Eat Dog ✓ *Einer Frisst den Anderen; La Morte Vestita di Dollar* **1964** Centering on a heist scheme by Mitchell, this one has nothing to offer except Mansfield's attributes. **86m/B VHS, Beta, 8mm.** Cameron Mitchell, Jayne Mansfield, Isa Miranda; **D:** Ray Nazarro. **VYY, HEG**

A Dog of Flanders ✓✓½ **1959** A young Dutch boy and his grandfather find a severely beaten dog and restore it to health. **96m/C VHS, Beta.** David Ladd, Donald Crisp, Theodore Bikel, Max Croiset, Monique Ahrens; **D:** James B. Clark. **PAR**

Dog Pound Shuffle ✓✓✓ *Spot* **1975 (PG)** Two drifters form a new song-and-dance act in order to raise the funds necessary to win their dog's freedom from the pound. Charming Canadian production. **98m/C VHS, Beta, Closed Caption. CA** Ron Moody, David Soul; **D:** Jeffrey Bloom; **W:** Jeffrey Bloom. **FOX**

Dog Star Man ✓✓✓ **1964** The silent epic by the dean of experimental American film depicts man's spiritual and physical conflicts through Brakhage's characteristically freeform collage techniques. **78m/C VHS, Beta. D:** Stan Brakhage. National Film Registry '92. **MFV, FCT, TPV**

The Dog Who Stopped the War ✓✓ **1984 (G)** A Canadian children's film about a dog who puts a halt to an escalating snowball fight between rival gangs. **90m/C VHS, Beta. CA D:** Andre Melancon. **NO**

Dogfight ✓✓✓ **1991 (R)** It's 1963 and a baby-faced Marine and his buddies are spending their last night in San Francisco before leaving the U.S. for a tour of duty in Vietnam. They agree to throw a "dogfight," a competition to see who can bring the ugliest date to a party. Birdlace (Phoenix) chooses Taylor, a shy, average-looking waitress who dreams of becoming a folk singer and realizes too late that she doesn't deserve the treatment he's about to subject her to. This quiet film didn't see a wide release, but is worth renting due to an above average script which is held up by the splendid performances of Phoenix and Taylor.**CW:** Pervasive strong language and one sexual scene. **94m/C VHS, Beta, LV, 8mm.** River Phoenix, Lili Taylor, Richard Panebianco, Anthony Clark, Mitchell Whitfield, E.G. Daily, Holly Near, Brendan Fraser, Peg Phillips; **D:** Nancy Savoca; **W:** Bob Comfort. **WAR**

The Dogfighters 🐾🐾 1995 (R) Ex-Air Force pilot Rowdy Wells (Davi) is blackmailed into trying to destroy a plutonium plant in an eastern European country. That is, if Rowdy can survive an air battle with nemisis Lothar Krasna (Godunov). Small budget is reflected in the mediocre aerial sequences. *CW:* Language, nudity, violence. **96m/C VHS, LV, Closed Caption.** Robert Davi, Alexander Godunov, Ben Gazzara, Lara Harris; *D:* Barry Zetlin; *W:* Sean Smith, Anthony Stark; *C:* Levie Isaacks; *M:* Jimmie Haskell. *ART*

Dogs in Space 🐾🐾 1987 A low-budget Australian film about a clique of aimless Melbourne rock kids in 1978, caught somewhere between post-hippiedom and punk, free love and heroin addiction. Acclaimed. Includes music by Hutchence, Brian Eno, Iggy Pop, and others. **109m/C VHS, Beta.** *AU* Michael Hutchence, Saskia Post, Nique Needles, Tony Helou, Deanna Bond; *D:* Richard Lowenstein; *W:* Richard Lowenstein. *FOX*

Dogs of Hell 🐾½ 1983 (R) The sheriff of an idyllic resort community must stop a pack of killer dogs from terrorizing the residents. **90m/C VHS, Beta.** Earl Owensby, Bill Gribble, Jerry Rushing; *D:* Worth Keeter.

The Dogs of War 🐾🐾½ 1981 (R) A graphic depiction of a group of professional mercenaries, driven by nothing but their quest for wealth and power, hired to overthrow the dictator of a new West African nation. Has some weak moments which break up the continuity of the movie. Based on the novel by Frederick Forsyth. **102m/C VHS, Beta, LV.** *GB* Christopher Walken, Tom Berenger, Colin Blakely, Paul Freeman, Hugh Millais, Victoria Tennant, JoBeth Williams; *D:* John Irvin; *W:* Gary De Vore; *C:* Jack Cardiff; *M:* Geoffrey Burgon. *MGM*

Dogwatch 🐾🐾 1997 (R) San Francisco police detective Elliott tries to avenge his partner's murder but kills the wrong man. Then he learns dirty cops are behind the crime. Cable thriller takes the easy road by solving everything with violence. **100m/C VHS.** Sam Elliott, Esai Morales, Paul Sorvino, Dan Lauria; *D:* John Langley. *REA*

Doin' Time 🐾 1985 (R) At the John Dillinger Memorial Penitentiary, the inmates take over the prison under the supervision of warden "Mongo." Silliness prevails. **80m/C VHS, Beta.** Jeff Altman, Dey Young, Richard Mulligan, John Vernon, Colleen Camp, Melanie Chartoff, Graham Jarvis, Pat McCormick, Eddie Velez, Jimmie Walker, Judy Landers, Nicholas Worth, Mike Mazurki, Muhammad Ali, Melinda Fee, Francesca "Kitten" Natividad, Ron Palillo; *D:* George Mendeluk; *W:* Dee Caruso; *M:* Charles Fox. *WAR*

Doin' Time on Planet Earth 🐾🐾½ 1988 (PG-13) A young boy feels out of place with his family and is convinced by two strange people (aliens themselves?) that he is really an extraterrestrial. Amusing, aimless fun directed by the son of Walter Matthau. **83m/C VHS, Beta, Closed Caption.** Adam West, Candice Azzara, Hugh O'Brian, Matt Adler, Timothy Patrick Murphy, Roddy McDowall, Maureen Stapleton, Andrea Thompson; *D:* Charles Matthau. *WAR*

Doing Time for Patsy Cline 🐾🐾🐾 1997 Humor and charm highlight this country music/road/jailhouse comedy. Hitchhiking, country music-loving teenager Ralph (Day) has a ticket for his dream trip to Nashville when he's picked up in a stolen Jag by drug-runner Boyd (Roxburgh) and the beautiful Patsy (Otto), who tells Ralph she was named for Patsy Cline. When the cops pull them over, Patsy gets away and Boyd lays all their crimes on the innocent Ralph. While the pair are in lockup, Ralph befriends three brothers who are equally interested in country tunes. This fractured fairytale does manage to come together and, of course, has a happy ending. **93m/C VHS.** *AU* Matt Day, Richard Roxburgh, Miranda Otto, Tom Long, Tony Barry, Kiri Paramore, Laurence Coy, Annie Byron, Roy Billing; *D:* Chris Kennedy; *W:* Chris Kennedy; *C:* Andrew Lennie; *M:* Peter Best. Australian Film Institute '97: Best Actor (Roxburgh), Best Cinematography, Best Costume Design; Nominations: Australian Film Institute '97: Best Art Direction/Set Decoration, Best Director (Kennedy), Best Film, Best Original Screenplay, Best Sound, Best Supporting Actress (Byron), Best Score. *NYR*

Dolemite 🐾½ 1975 (R) An ex-con attempts to settle the score with some of his former inmates. He forms a band of kung-fu savvy ladies. Strange combination of action and comedy. **88m/C VHS.** Rudy Ray Moore, Jerry Jones; *D:* D'Urville Martin. *XVC*

Dolemite 2: Human Tornado 🐾½
The Human Tornado 1976 (R) Nobody ever said Moore was for everybody's taste. But, hey, when blaxploitation movies were the rage, Rudy the standup comic was out there rapping through a series of trashy movies that, when viewed today, have survived the test of time. This one's just as vile, violent, and sexist as the day it was released. When Rudy is surprised in bed with a white sheriff's wife, he flees and meets up with a madam and a house of kung-fu-skilled girls who are embroiled in a fight with a local mobster. **98m/C VHS.** Rudy Ray Moore, Lady Reed. *XVC*

The Doll 🐾🐾 *La Poupee; He, She or It* 1962 A lonely night watchman happens upon two burglars and, in the chase, the thieves knock over a mannequin. The watchman reports the mannequin stolen, brings it home and begins to have conversations with it. Soon, the doll's needs cause him to steal jewelry and clothes, until his brutish neighbor discovers his secrets. In Swedish with English subtitles. **96m/B VHS.** *SW* Per Oscarsson, Gio Petre, Tor Isedal, Elsa Prawitz; *D:* Arne Mattson. *FCT, DVT, AUD*

Doll Face 🐾🐾½ *Come Back to Me* 1946 Story of a stripper who wants to go legit and make it on Broadway. Film was adapted from the play "The Naked Genius" by tease queen Gypsy Rose Lee. ♫Dig You Later; Here Comes Heaven Again; Chico-Chico; Somebody's Walkin' In My Dreams; Red Hot and Beautiful. **80m/B VHS, Beta, LV.** Vivian Blaine, Dennis O'Keefe, Perry Como, Carmen Miranda, Martha Stewart, Reed Hadley; *D:* Lewis Seiler. *NOS, HHT, DVT*

The Doll Squad 🐾 *Hustler Squad* 1973 (PG) Three voluptuous special agents fight an ex-CIA agent out to rule the world. **93m/C VHS, Beta.** Michael Ansara, Francine Yorke, Anthony Eisley, Tura Satana; *D:* Ted V. Mikels. *MRV*

Dollar 🐾🐾 1938 The actress wife of an industrialist, convinced that he is having an affair, follows him to a ski lodge in attempt to catch him in the act. In Swedish with English subtitles. **74m/B VHS, Beta, LV.** *SW* Georg Rydeberg, Ingrid Bergman, Kotti Chave, Tutta Rolf, Hakan Westergren, Elisa Burnett, Edvin Adolphson, Gosta Cederlund, Eric Rosen; *D:* Gustaf Molander. *WAC*

Dollars 🐾🐾🐾 *The Heist* 1971 (R) A bank employee and his dizzy call-girl assistant plan to steal the German facility's assets while installing its new security system. Lighthearted fun. **119m/C VHS, Beta, LV.** Warren Beatty, Goldie Hawn, Gert Frobe, Scott Brady, Robert Webber; *D:* Richard Brooks; *W:* Richard Brooks; *M:* Quincy Jones. *GKK*

The Dollmaker 🐾🐾½ 1984 Excellent made for television adaptation of Harriette Arnow's novel. A strong-willed Kentucky mother of five helps move her family to Detroit in the 1940s. Petrie's direction moves the story along and creates a lovely period vision. **140m/C VHS, Beta, Closed Caption.** Jane Fonda, Levon Helm, Geraldine Page, Amanda Plummer, Susan Kingsley; *D:* Daniel Petrie. *FOX*

Dollman 🐾½ 1990 (R) An ultra-tough cop from an Earth-like planet (even swear words are the same) crashes in the South Bronx—and on this world he's only 13 inches tall. The filmmakers squander a great premise and cast with bloody shootouts and a sequel-ready non-ending. *CW:* Language and sci-fi violence. **86m/C VHS, Beta, LV, Closed Caption.** Tim Thomerson, Jackie Earle Haley, Kamala Lopez, Humberto Ortiz, Nicholas Guest, Michael Halsey, Eugene Glazer, Judd Omen, Frank Collison, Vincent Klyn; *D:* Albert Pyun. *PAR*

Dollman vs Demonic Toys 🐾🐾 1993 (R) Let's combine elements from three separate films and make one disgusting sequel: "Dollman," the 13-inch cop from the planet Arturus; his new girlfriend, Dollchick, who was shrunk to a diminutive 10 inches in "Bad Channels"; and tough cop Judith Grey, who's once again battling those loathsome playthings from "Demonic Toys." If you feel the need for a plot—Dollchick is kidnapped by Baby Doll and needs to be rescued. *CW:* Language, violence, and sexuality. **84m/C VHS, Beta, Closed Caption.** Tim Thomerson, Tracy Scoggins, Melissa Behr, Phil Brock, Phil Fondacaro; *D:* Charles Band; *W:* Craig Hamann; *M:* Richard Band. *PAR*

The Dolls woof! 1983 A tropically located photographer recruits an area beauty into the fashion world with his winning smile and macho charm, only to learn native traditions forbid her to follow him. **96m/C VHS, Beta, LV.** Tetchie Agbayani, Max Thayer, Carina Schally, Richard Seward; *D:* Hubert Frank. *ART, VES*

Dolls 🐾🐾½ 1987 (R) A group of people is stranded during a storm in an old, creepy mansion. As the night wears on, they are attacked by hundreds of antique dolls. Tongue-in-cheek. **77m/C VHS, Beta.** Ian Patrick Williams, Carolyn Purdy-Gordon, Carrie Lorraine, Stephen Lee, Guy Rolfe, Bunty Bailey, Cassie Stuart, Hilary Mason; *D:* Stuart Gordon; *W:* Ed Naha; *M:* Richard Band. *ART, VES*

A Doll's House 🐾🐾½ 1959 An all-star cast is featured in this original television production of Henrik Ibsen's classic play about an independent woman's quest for freedom in 19th-century Norway. **89m/B VHS, Beta.** Julie Harris, Christopher Plummer, Jason Robards Jr., Hume Cronyn, Eileen Heckart, Richard Thomas. *MGM, FCT*

A Doll's House 🐾🐾½ 1973 (G) Fonda plays Nora, a subjugated 19th-century housewife who breaks free to establish herself as an individual. Based on Henrik Ibsen's classic play; some controversy regarding Fonda's interpretation of her role. **98m/C Beta.** Jane Fonda, Edward Fox, Trevor Howard, David Warner, Delphine Seyrig; *D:* Joseph Losey; *W:* Christopher Hampton; *M:* John Barry.

A Doll's House 🐾🐾🐾 1989 (G) A Canadian production of the Henrik Ibsen play about a Norwegian woman's search for independence. **96m/C VHS, Beta, LV.** *CA* Claire Bloom, Anthony Hopkins, Ralph Richardson, Denholm Elliott, Anna Massey, Edith Evans; *D:* Patrick Garland.

Dolly Dearest 🐾½ 1992 (R) Strange things start happening after an American family takes over a run-down Mexican doll factory. They create a new doll called "Dolly Dearest" with deadly results. In the same tradition as the "Chucky" series. *CW:* Horror violence. **94m/C VHS, LV, Closed Caption.** Rip Torn, Sam Bottoms, Denise Crosby; *D:* Maria Lease. *THV*

The Dolly Sisters 🐾🐾½ 1946 Competent musical about sisters Jenny (Grable) and Rosie (Haver), who become turn-of-the-century vaudeville stars and also find romance. Good songs, extravagent costuming, fine support work, and the charms of the two leading actresses provide simple enjoyment. ♫I Can't Begin to Tell You; I'm Always Chasing Rainbows; Powder, Lipstick and Rouge; Give Me the Moonlight; On the Mississippi; We Have Been Around; Carolina In the Morning; Arrah Go On, I'm Gonna Go Back to Oregon; The Darktown Strutter's Ball. **114m/C VHS, Closed Caption.** Betty Grable, June Haver, John Payne, Frank Latimore, S.Z. Sakall, Reginald Gardiner, Gene Sheldon, Sig Rumann; *D:* Irving Cummings; *W:* Marian Spitzer, John Larkin; *C:* Ernest Palmer. Nominations: Academy Awards '46: Best Song ("I Can't Begin to Tell You"). *FXV*

Dolores Claiborne 🐾🐾🐾 1994 (R) Stephen King gets the Hollywood treatment again (the check cleared, King approved), with better results than previous outings (remember "Needful Things"?). Successful but neurotic New York journalist Selena (Leigh) confronts her troubled past when coarse, hard-talking mom Dolores (Bates) is accused of murdering her wealthy employer (Parfitt). Plummer is vengeful detective John Mackey who, like everyone else on the fictitious Maine island, believes Dolores murdered her husband 15 years before. Top-notch performances by Bates and Leigh highlight this sometimes manipulative tale. Straithairn is wonderfully despicable as the stereotypically deadbeat dad. **CW:** Language; domestic abuse; nudity. **132m/C VHS, LV, Closed Caption.** Kathy Bates, Jennifer Jason Leigh, Christopher Plummer, Judy Parfitt, David Strathairn, John C. Reilly; **D:** Taylor Hackford; **W:** Tony Gilroy; **M:** Danny Elfman. *COL*

The Dolphin 🐾🐾½ 1987 A dolphin visits a Brazilian fishing village each full moon, turns himself into a man, and casts a spell of seduction over the women. Villagers are both enchanted and angered by the dolphin-man, since his presence creates desire in local women but scares fish from the waters. In Portuguese with English subtitles. **95m/C VHS.** *BR* Carlos Alberto Riccelli, Cassia Kiss, Ney Latorraca; **D:** Walter Lima Jr.; **W:** Walter Lima Jr. *FXL, FCT*

Dominick & Eugene 🐾🐾🐾 1988 (PG-13) Dominick is a little slow, but he makes a fair living as a garbageman—good enough to put his brother through medical school. Both men struggle with the other's faults and weaknesses, as they learn the meaning of family and friendship. Well-acted, especially by Hulce, never melodramatic or weak. **96m/C VHS, Beta, LV, Closed Caption.** Ray Liotta, Tom Hulce, Jamie Lee Curtis, Todd Graff, Bill Cobbs, David Strathairn; **D:** Robert M. Young; **W:** Alvin Sargent, Corey Blechman; **M:** Trevor Jones. *ORI, FCT*

Dominion 🐾🐾½ 1994 (R) Six buddies take off for a weekend hunting trip that turns deadly when a murderous hunter believes they've trespassed on his territory and begins stalking them. **CW:** Strong violence; language. **98m/C VHS, Closed Caption.** Brad Johnson, Brion James, Tim Thomerson, Woody Brown, Glen Morshower, Richard Riehle, Geoffrey Blake; **D:** Michael Kehoe; **W:** Woody Brown, Michael Kehoe. *TTC*

Dominique Is Dead 🐾🐾 1979 (PG) A woman is driven to suicide by her greedy husband; now someone is trying to drive him mad. A.K.A. "Dominique" and "Avenging Spirit." **95m/C VHS, Beta.** Cliff Robertson, Jean Simmons, Jenny Agutter, Simon Ward, Ron Moody; **D:** Michael Anderson Sr.

Domino 🐾 1988 (R) A beautiful woman and a mysterious guy link up for sex, murder and double-crosses. Dubbed. Tries to be arty and avant-garde, but only succeeds in being a piece of softcore fluff. **95m/C VHS, Beta, LV.** *IT* Brigitte Nielsen, Tomas Arana, Daniela Alzone; **D:** Ivana Massetti. *ART*

The Domino Principle 🐾½ *The Domino Killings* 1977 (R) It's got nothing to do with pizza. Viet vet Hackman is a doltish convict sprung from the joint by a government organization to do some dirty work: working as a political assassin. Heavy-handed direction and lack of suspense make it less than it should be. **97m/C VHS, Beta.** Gene Hackman, Candice Bergen, Richard Widmark, Mickey Rooney, Edward Albert, Eli Wallach; **D:** Stanley Kramer; **C:** Fred W. Koenekamp; **M:** Billy Goldenberg. *CCB, FOX*

Don Amigo/Stage to Chino 194? A western double feature: The Cisco Kid and Pancho ride together again in "Don Amigo," and in "Stage to Chino," a postal inspector investigates a gang who robs rival stage lines. **122m/B VHS, Beta.** Duncan Renaldo, Leo Carrillo, George O'Brien, Roy Barcroft; **D:** Edward Killy. *TTC*

Don Daredevil Rides Again 🐾 1951 A greedy political boss tries to take over homesteaders' claims for their mineral rights. One settler adopts the identity of an ancestor (Don Daredevil), and a black mask, and becomes a frontier avenger. A 12-episode serial. **180m/B VHS, Beta.** Ken Curtis, Aline Towne, Roy Barcroft. *REP, MLB, MOV*

The Don Is Dead 🐾½ *Beautiful But Deadly* 1973 (R) A violent Mafia saga wherein a love triangle interferes with Family business, resulting in gang wars. **96m/C VHS, Beta.** Anthony Quinn, Frederic Forrest, Robert Forster, Al Lettieri, Ina Balin, Angel Tompkins, Charles Cioffi; **D:** Richard Fleischer; **W:** Michael Butler; **M:** Jerry Goldsmith. *USH*

Don Juan 🐾🐾🐾½ 1926 Barrymore stars as the swashbuckling Italian duke with Spanish blood who seduces a castleful of women in the 1500s. Many exciting action sequences, including classic sword fights in which Barrymore eschewed a stunt double. Great attention is also paid to the detail of the costumes and settings of the Spanish-Moor period. Noted for employing fledgling movie sound effects and music-dubbing technology, which, ironically, were responsible for eclipsing the movie's reputation. Watch for Loy as an Asian vamp and Oland as a pre-Charlie Chan Cesare Borgia. **90m/B VHS, LV.** John Barrymore, Mary Astor, Willard Louis, Estelle Taylor, Helene Costello, Myrna Loy, June Marlowe, Warner Oland, Montagu Love, Hedda Hopper, Gustav von Seyffertitz; **D:** Alan Crosland. *MGM, FCT*

Don Juan DeMarco 🐾🐾½ 1994 (PG-13) Burned-out clinical psychiatrist Dr. Jack Meckler (Brando) is romantically inspired by a cape-wearing, suicidal man-child from Queens (Depp), who thinks he's legendary lover Don Juan. Delusional Depp recounts, in a convincing Castilian accent, thousands of conquests as the sympathetic shrink decides it's time to bring some spice to his own ho-hum life and marriage (to Dunaway). Depp turns in a sincere, engaging performance that avoids the huge potential for melodrama and compensates for inconsistent pacing. Brando and Dunaway make a charmingly quirky couple. Watch for slain Tejano queen Selena in a musical interlude. **CW:** Sexual content; brief nudity; suggestive dialogue. **92m/C VHS, LV, Closed Caption.** Marlon Brando, Johnny Depp, Faye Dunaway, Geraldine Pailhas, Rachel Ticotin, Bob Dishy, Talisa Soto; **D:** Jeremy Leven; **W:** Jeremy Leven; **C:** Ralf Bode. Nominations: Academy Awards '95: Best Song ("Have You Ever Really Loved a Woman?"); Golden Globe Awards '96: Best Song ("Have You Ever Really Loved a Woman?"), Best Score. *TTC, NLC*

Don Juan, My Love 🐾🐾🐾 *Don Juan, Mi Querido Fantasma* 1990 Sexy comedy finds the ghost of Don Juan given a chance, after 450 years in Purgatory, to perform a good deed and free his soul. In Spanish with English subtitles. **96m/C VHS, LV.** *SP* Juan Luis Galiardo, Rossy de Palma, Maria Barranco, Loles Leon; **D:** Antonio Mercero; **M:** Bernardo Bonazzi. *FXL, FCT*

Don King: Only in America 🐾🐾½ 1997 (R) Rhames reigns in this cable bio of flamboyant, notorious boxing promoter Don King. King starts off as a Cleveland numbers runner at ease with violence, which eventually sends him to a four-year prison term for manslaughter. Released in 1971, King uses his friendship with R&B singer Lloyd Price (Curtis-Hall) to meet Muhammed Ali (McCrary), leading to his set-up of the 1974 Ali-Foreman fight in Zaire. From there it's just more self-promotion. **CW:** Strong language, some violence and nudity. **112m/C VHS, Closed Caption.** Ving Rhames, Vondie Curtis-Hall, Jeremy Piven, Darius McCrary, Keith David, Bernie Mac, Loretta Devine, Lou Rawls, Ron Leibman; **D:** John Herzfeld; **W:** Kario Salem; **C:** Bill Butler; **M:** Anthony Marinelli. *HBO*

Don Q., Son of Zorro 🐾🐾 1925 Zorro's son takes up his father's fight against evil and injustice. Silent sequel to the 1920 classic. **111m/B VHS, Beta, LV.** Douglas Fairbanks Sr., Mary Astor. *NOS, WFV, CCB*

Don Quixote 🐾🐾🐾🐾 1935 Miguel de Cervantes' tale of the romantic who would rather be a knight in shining armor than shining armor at night. Chaliapin stars as the knight-errant on his nightly errands, tilting at windmills and charging flocks of sheep. Certain scenes were adapted to fit the pre-WWII atmosphere, as it was filmed during the same time that the Nazis were burning

books. 73m/B VHS. Feodor Chaliapin, George Robey, Sidney Fox, Miles Mander, Oscar Asche, Emily Fitzroy, Wally Patch; **D:** G.W. Pabst; **W:** Paul Morand, Alexandre Arnoux; **M:** Jacques Ibert. *NOS, MLB, VEC*

Don Quixote 🐾🐾🐾½ 1957 The lauded, visually ravishing adaptation of the Cervantes classic, with a formal integrity inherited from Eisenstein and Dovshenko. In Russian with English subtitles. **110m/C VHS, Beta.** *SP RU* Nikolai Cherkassov, Yuri Tobubeyev; **D:** Grigori Kosintsev. *FCT*

Don Segundo Sombra 🐾🐾½ 1969 An interesting film seen through the eyes of an old gaucho, who is the mentor of a young boy growing to manhood. Based on the novel by Ricardo Guiraldes. In Spanish with English subtitles. **110m/C VHS, Beta.** *SP* Juan Carballido, Juan Carlos Gene, Soledad Silveyra, Alejandra Boero; **D:** Manuel Antin. *CVC*

Don Winslow of the Coast Guard 1943 Serial in 13 episodes features comic-strip character Winslow as he strives to keep the waters of America safe for democracy. **234m/B VHS, Beta.** Don Terry, Elyse Knox; **D:** Ford Beebe, Ray Taylor. *NOS, VDM*

Don Winslow of the Navy 1943 Thirteen episodes centered around the evil Scorpion, who plots to attack the Pacific Coast, but is thwarted by comic-strip hero Winslow. **234m/B VHS, Beta.** Don Terry, Walter Sande, Anne Nagel; **D:** Ford Beebe, Ray Taylor. *VYY, MLB, VDM*

Dona Flor and Her Two Husbands 🐾🐾🐾 *Dona Flor e Seus Dois Maridos* 1978 A woman becomes a widow when her philandering husband finally expires from drink, gambling, and ladies. She remarries, but her new husband is so boring and proper that she begins fantasizing spouse number one's return. But is he only in her imagination? Based on the novel by Jorge Amado. In Portuguese with English subtitles. Remade as "Kiss Me Goodbye." **106m/C VHS, Beta, LV.** *BR* Sonia Braga, Jose Wilker, Mauro Mendonca; **D:** Bruno Barreto; **W:** Bruno Barreto; **M:** Chico Buarque. *FXL, IME, TPV*

Dona Herlinda & Her Son 🐾🐾 *Dona Herlinda y Su Hijo* 1986 A Mexican sex comedy about a mother who manipulates her bisexual son's two lovers (one male, one female), until all four fit together into a seamless unit. In Spanish with English subtitles. Slow, but amusing. **90m/C VHS, Beta, LV.** *MX* Guadalupe Del Toro, Arturo Meza, Marco Antonio Trevino, Leticia Lupersio; **D:** Jaime Humberto Hermosillo. *TPV, CCN*

Donkey Skin 🐾🐾🐾 *Peau d'Ane* 1970 A charming, all-star version of the medieval French fairy tale about a king searching for a suitable wife in a magical realm after his queen dies. In his quest for the most beautiful spouse, he learns that his daughter is that woman. She prefers Prince Charming, however. In French with English subtitles. **89m/C VHS, Beta.** *FR* Catherine Deneuve, Jean Marais, Delphine Seyrig, Jacques Perrin; **D:** Jacques Demy; **C:** Ghislan Cloquet. *NO*

Donner Pass: The Road to Survival 🐾 1984 Tame retelling of the western wagon-train pioneers who were forced to resort to cannibalism during a brutal snowstorm in the Rockies. The tragedy is lightly implied, keeping the film suitable for family viewing. **98m/C VHS, Beta.** Robert Fuller, Diane McBain, Andrew Prine, John Anderson, Michael Callan; **D:** James L. Conway. *VTR, HHE*

Donnie Brasco 🐾🐾🐾 1996 (R) Excellent look at the unglamourous working end of the mob and an undercover operation. In the late '70s, FBI agent Joe Pistone (Depp) infiltrates the New York Bonanno crime family, under the alias of Donnie Brasco, where he's mentored by aging low-level hood Lefty (Pacino). As Joe/Donnie gets deeper into the wiseguy life, Lefty takes a fatherly pride in his protege and the agent also becomes ensnared by his new identity—to the possible detriment of both feds and family. Terrific lead performances. Based on a true story and adapted from the book by Pistone and Richard Woodley. **CW:**

Some strong graphic violence, pervasive strong language and brief nudity and sexuality. 126m/C VHS, LV, Closed Caption. Johnny Depp, Al Pacino, Anne Heche, Michael Madsen, Bruno Kirby, James Russo, Zeljko Ivanek, Gerry Becker, Zach Grenier, Robert Miano; **D:** Mike Newell; **W:** Paul Attanasio; **C:** Peter Sova; **M:** Patrick Doyle. National Board of Review Awards '97: Best Supporting Actress (Heche); Nominations: Academy Awards '97: Best Adapted Screenplay; Writers Guild of America '97: Best Adapted Screenplay. COL

The Donor 🎞½ 1994 (R) Cartel stalks victims and kills them for a human organ black market.*CW:* Sexuality and some language. 94m/C VHS. Jeff Wincott, Michelle Johnson, Gordon Thomson; **D:** Damian Lee; **W:** Neal Dobrofsky, Tippi Dobrofsky. AVE

Donor Unknown 🎞🎞 1995 (R) Driven businessman Nicholas Stillman (Onorati) has always put work before his family—and both wife Alice (Krige) and teenaged daughter Danielle (Herbst) have suffered from his attitude. When Nick is hit by a massive heart attack and gets a transplant, he insists on knowing everything about the donor. What he uncovers is a black market in organ procurement and Nash Creed (Brown), who'll do anything to stop Nick from exposing his lucrative business. Based on the novel "Corazon" by William H. Mooney.*CW:* Violence and a scene of sexuality. 93m/C VHS, Closed Caption. Peter Onorati, Alice Krige, Clancy Brown, Becky Herbst, Sam Robards, Richard Portnow, T.J. Castranovo, Leo Garcia, John Dorman; **D:** John Harrison; **W:** John Harrison; **C:** Zoltan David; **M:** David Bergeaud. USH

Donovan's Brain 🎞🎞🎞 1953 A scientist maintains the still-living brain of a dead millionaire and begins to be controlled by its powerful force. Based on Curt Siodmak's novel. 85m/B VHS, Beta, LV. Lew Ayres, Gene Evans, Nancy Davis, Steve Brodie; **D:** Felix Feist; **C:** Joseph Biroc. MGM, IME, MLB

Donovan's Reef 🎞🎞🎞 1963 Two WWII buddies meet every year on a Pacific atoll to engage in a perpetual bar-brawl, until a stuck-up Bostonian maiden appears to find her dad, a man who has fathered a brood of lovable half-casts. A rollicking, good-natured film from Ford. 109m/C VHS, Beta, LV. John Wayne, Lee Marvin, Jack Warden, Elizabeth Allen, Dorothy Lamour, Mike Mazurki, Cesar Romero; **D:** John Ford; **C:** William Clothier. PAR, TLF

Don's Party 🎞🎞🎞 1976 A rather dark comedy focusing on Australian Yuppie-types who decide to watch the election results on television as a group. A lot more goes on at this party, however, than talk of the returns. Sexual themes surface. Cast members turn fine performances, aided by top-notch script and direction. 90m/C VHS, Beta. AU Pat Bishop, Graham Kennedy, Candy Raymond, Veronica Lang, John Hargreaves, Ray Barrett, Claire Binney, Graeme Blundell, Jeanie Drynan; **D:** Bruce Beresford; **W:** David Williamson; **C:** Donald McAlpine. Australian Film Institute '77: Best Actress (Bishop). FCT

Don't Answer the Phone 🎞 The Hollywood Strangler 1980 (R) Deeply troubled photographer stalks and attacks the patients of a beautiful psychologist talk-show hostess. 94m/C VHS, Beta. James Westmoreland, Flo Gerrish, Ben Frank; **D:** Robert Hammer; **M:** Byron Allred.

Don't Be a Menace to South Central While Drinking Your Juice in the Hood 🎞🎞 1995 (R) Parody of "life in the hood" movies pokes fun at the attitudes and characters that are quickly becoming cliches in the genre. Shawn Wayans plays G-next-door Ashtray, sent by his mother to discover "what it is to be a man" from his father in South Central L.A. He hooks up with his homey Loc Dog (Marlon Wayans), a gun-crazed beer-swilling gangsta who packs a nuclear warhead. As the title implies, almost every major black film in recent memory is given the Wayans' drive-by treatment, with a majority of the plot lifted from "Boyz N the Hood." Fans of the TV series "In Living Color" will love this twisted look at ghetto life, but others may be offended.*CW:* Strong language, sexuality, some drug content and violence. 88m/C VHS, LV, Closed

Caption. Shawn Wayans, Marlon Wayans, Tracey Cherelle Jones, Chris Spencer, Suli McCullough, Darrell Heath, Helen Martin, Isaiah Barnes, Lahmard Tate; **Cameos:** Keenen Ivory Wayans; **D:** Paris Barclay; **W:** Shawn Wayans, Marlon Wayans, Phil Beauman; **C:** Russ Brandt; **M:** John Barnes. TOU

Don't Be Afraid of the Dark 🎞🎞½ 1973 A young couple move into their dream house only to find that demonic little critters are residing in their basement and they want more than shelter. Made for TV with creepy scenes and eerie makeup for the monsters. 74m/C VHS, Beta. Kim Darby, Jim Hutton, Barbara Anderson, William Demarest, Pedro Armendariz Jr.; **D:** John Newland. ART

Don't Bother to Knock 🎞🎞½ 1952 As a mentally unstable hotel babysitter, Monroe meets a pilot (Widmark) and has a brief rendezvous with him. When the little girl she is babysitting interrupts, Monroe is furious, and later tries to murder the girl. This is one of Monroe's best dramatic roles. Bancroft's film debut as the Widmark's girlfriend. 76m/B VHS. Richard Widmark, Marilyn Monroe, Anne Bancroft, Elisha Cook Jr., Jim Backus, Lurene Tuttle, Jeanne Cagney, Donna Corcoran; **D:** Roy Ward Baker; **W:** Daniel Taradash. FXV

Don't Change My World 🎞½ 1983 (G) To preserve the natural beauty of the north woods, a wildlife photographer must fight a villainous land developer and a reckless poacher. Eco-correct. 89m/C VHS, Beta. Roy Tatum, Ben Jones, Edie Kramer, George Macrenais, Paul Newmark, David Eidson; **D:** Robert Rector. ART

Don't Cry, It's Only Thunder 🎞🎞½ 1982 (PG) A young army medic who works in a mortuary in Saigon becomes involved with a group of Vietnamese orphans and a dedicated army doctor. Based on a true story. 108m/C VHS, Beta. Dennis Christopher, Susan St. James, Roger Brown, Li Lu, Thu Thuy, James Whitmore; **D:** Peter Werner; **M:** Maurice Jarre. COL

Don't Do It 🎞🎞½ 1994 (PG-13) Three 20-something couples, attempting to find love, all wind up in the same cafe and try to tell the truth about how they feel and whom they desire.*CW:* Language, mild sexual situations. 90m/C VHS. James Marshall, James LeGros, Sheryl Lee, Esai Morales, Alexis Arquette, Balthazar Getty, Sarah Trigger, Heather Graham; **D:** Eugene Hess; **W:** Eugene Hess. TRI

Don't Drink the Water 🎞🎞½ 1969 (G) Based on Woody Allen's hit play, this film places an average Newark, New Jersey, family behind the Iron Curtain, where their vacation photo-taking gets them accused of spying. 100m/C VHS, Beta. Jackie Gleason, Estelle Parsons, Joan Delaney, Ted Bessell, Michael Constantine; **D:** Howard Morris. COL

Don't Go in the House 🎞 1980 (R) Long-dormant psychosis is brought to life by the death of a young man's mother. 90m/C VHS. Dan Grimaldi, Robert Osth, Ruth Dardick; **D:** Joseph Ellison; **M:** Richard Einhorn.

Don't Go in the Woods woof! 1981 (R) Routine exercise in "don't do that" terror genre (includes warnings about going into houses, answering phones, looking into basements, opening windows, etc.). This time, four young campers are stalked by a crazed killer armed with prerequisite ax. 88m/C VHS, Beta. VES

Don't Go Near the Water 🎞🎞 1957 Somewhat amusing comedy about the happenings at a Naval installation on a South Pacific tropical paradise. Clark outshines the others in his role as a frustrated officer. Based on the novel by William Brinkley. 107m/C VHS. Glenn Ford, Gia Scala, Earl Holliman, Anne Francis, Keenan Wynn, Fred Clark, Eva Gabor, Russ Tamblyn; **D:** Charles Walters; **W:** Dorothy Kingsley, George Wells. MGM

Don't Go to Sleep 🎞🎞 1982 After a fatal car crash, a young girl misses mom and dad so much she returns from the grave to take them where they can be one big happy family again. Better than most made-for-TV junk-food frightfests, written by Keenan Wynn's son, Ned. 93m/C

VHS. Dennis Weaver, Valerie Harper, Robin Ignico, Kristin Cummings, Ruth Gordon, Robert Webber; **D:** Richard Lang; **W:** Ned Wynn. UNI

Don't Hang Up 🎞🎞½ 1990 Handicapped New York actress Sarah (Arquette) wants to do a production of agoraphobic London writer Joe's (Suchet) play. So she calls him up to get his permission and the two begin a phone relationship that develops from business to romance. 84m/C VHS. GB Rosanna Arquette, David Suchet. WBF

Don't Let Your Meat Loaf 🎞 1995 Three struggling comedians take their act on the road, including subway stations and street corners, in order to get the money to open their own comedy club. 82m/C VHS. Leander Sales, Dana S. Hubbard, Brad Albright; **D:** Leander Sales. SDE

Don't Look Back 🎞🎞🎞 1996 (R) Musician and heroin addict Jesse Parish (Stoltz) stumbles across a suitcase full of cash after witnessing a drug deal gone bad. He heads back to family and friends in Texas so he can kick his habit, but is marked for death by the dealers who want their money back. Strong script and performances: made for cable TV.*CW:* Strong violence, language and drug content. 91m/C VHS, Closed Caption. Eric Stoltz, John Corbett, Josh Hamilton, Annabeth Gish, Dwight Yoakam, Amanda Plummer; **D:** Geoff Murphy; **W:** Billy Bob Thornton, Tom Epperson. HBO

Don't Look Back: The Story of Leroy "Satchel" Paige 🎞🎞½ 1981 Drama of the legendary baseball pitcher who helped break down racial barriers, based on his autobiography. Made-for-TV fare. Gossett hits a home run in the lead, but the overall effort is a ground-rule double. 98m/C VHS. Louis Gossett Jr., Beverly Todd, Cleavon Little, Clifton Davis, Jim Davis, Ossie Davis, Hal Williams; **D:** George C. Scott, Richard A. Colla.

Don't Look in the Attic woof! 1981 A couple finds a haunted house with cows in the attic. 90m/C VHS, Beta. Beba Loncar, Jean-Pierre Aumont; **D:** Carl Ausino. NO

Don't Look in the Basement 🎞½ 1973 (R) Things get out of hand at an isolated asylum and a pretty young nurse is caught in the middle. Straight-jacketed by a low budget. 95m/C VHS, Beta. Rosie Holotik, Anne MacAdams, William Bill McGhee, Rhea MacAdams, Gene Ross, Betty Chandler, Camilla Carr, Robert Dracup, Jessie Kirby, Hugh Feagin, Harryete Warren, Jessie Lee Fulton, Michael Harvey; **D:** S.F. Brownrigg. MPI

Don't Look Now 🎞🎞🎞 1973 (R) A psychological thriller about a couple's trip to Venice after their child drowns. Notable for a steamy love scene and a chilling climax. Based on the novel by Daphne Du Maurier. 110m/C VHS, Beta, LV. Donald Sutherland, Julie Christie, Hilary Mason, Clelia Matania, Massimo Serato, Leopoldo Trieste, Adelina Porrio; **D:** Nicolas Roeg; **W:** Chris Bryant, Allan Scott; **C:** Anthony B. Richmond; **M:** Pino Donaggio. PAR

Don't Mess with My Sister! 🎞🎞½ 1985 A married, New York junkyard worker falls in love with a belly dancer he meets at a party. The affair leads to murder and subsequently, revenge. An interesting, offbeat film from the director of "I Spit on Your Grave." 90m/C VHS, Beta, LV. Joe Perce, Jeannine Lemay, Jack Gurci, Peter Sapienza, Laura Lanfranchi; **D:** Mier Zarchi. NO

Don't Open the Door! woof! 1974 (PG) A young woman is terrorized by a killer located inside her house. 90m/C VHS, Beta. Susan Bracken, Gene Ross, Jim Harrell; **D:** S.F. Brownrigg. GEM

Don't Open Till Christmas woof! 1984 A weirdo murders various Santa Clauses in assorted gory ways. Best to take this one back to the department store. 86m/C VHS, Beta. GB Edmund Purdom, Caroline Munro, Alan Lake, Belinda Mayne, Gerry Sundquist, Mark Jones; **D:** Edmund Purdom. ART, VES

Don't Raise the Bridge, Lower the River 🎞🎞 1968 (G) After his wife leaves him, an American with crazy, get-rich-quick schemes turns his wife's ancestral English home into a Chinese discotheque. Domestic farce that comes and goes; if mad for Lewis, rent "The Nutty Professor." **99m/C VHS, Beta.** Jerry Lewis, Terry-Thomas, Jacqueline Pearce; **D:** Jerry Paris. COL

Don't Shove/Two Gun Gussie 1919 Two early Harold Lloyd shorts feature the comedian's embryonic comic style as a young fellow impressing his date at a skating rink ("Don't Shove") and a city slicker out West ("Two Gun Gussie"). Silent with piano scores. **27m/B VHS, Beta.** Harold Lloyd, Bebe Daniels, Noah Young, Snub Pollard. CCB

Don't Talk to Strangers 🎬🎬½ 1994 (R) Formula thriller has Brosnan marrying divorcee Reed and becoming instant father to her nine-year-old son. But someone appears to be a whacko—is it the kid's real dad (Quinn) or is Brosnan just too good to be true?**CW:** Some terror and violence. **94m/C VHS.** Pierce Brosnan, Shanna Reed, Terry O'Quinn; **D:** Robert Lewis; **W:** Neill D. Hicks, Jon George, Nevin Schreiner. USH

Don't Tell Her It's Me 🎬 *The Boyfriend School* 1990 (PG-13) Guttenberg is determined to win the heart of an attractive writer. With the assistance of his sister, he works to become a dream man. Clever premise, promising cast, lame comedy. From the novel by Sarah Bird. **101m/C VHS, Beta, LV, Closed Caption.** Steve Guttenberg, Jami Gertz, Shelley Long, Kyle MacLachlan, Madchen Amick; **D:** Malcolm Mowbray; **W:** Sarah Bird; **M:** Michael Gore. HBO

Don't Tell Mom the Babysitter's Dead 🎬½ 1991 (PG-13) Their mother traveling abroad, the title situation leaves a houseful of teenagers with the whole summer to themselves. Eldest daughter Applegate cons her way into the high-powered business world while the metalhead son parties hardy. Many tepid comic situations, not adding up to very much. **105m/C VHS, Beta, LV, 8mm, Closed Caption.** Christina Applegate, Keith Coogan, Joanna Cassidy, John Getz, Josh Charles, Concetta Tomei, Eda Reiss Merin; **D:** Stephen Herek. HBO

The Doolins of Oklahoma 🎬🎬½ *The Great Manhunt* 1949 Scott is the leader of the last of the southwestern outlaw gangs, pursued by lawmen and changing times with the onset of the modern age. Fast-paced and intelligent. **90m/B VHS, Beta.** Randolph Scott, George Macready, Louise Allbritton, John Ireland, Virginia Huston, Charles Kemper, Noah Beery Jr.; **D:** Gordon Douglas; **M:** George Duning. GKK

Doom Asylum woof! 1988 (R) Several sex kittens wander into a deserted sanatorium and meet up with the grisly beast wielding autopsy instruments. The people involved with this spoof should have been (more) committed. **77m/C VHS, Beta.** Patty Mullen, Ruth Collins, Kristen Davis, William Hay, Kenny L. Price, Harrison White, Dawn Alvan, Michael Rogan; **D:** Richard S. Friedman.

The Doom Generation 🎬🎬🎬 1995 (R) Alienated trio on the road trip to hell (doubling as L.A.). Beautiful 17-year-old druggie Amy Blue (McGowan), her sweetly dim boyfriend Jordan White (Duval), and hot-tempered stud/drifter Xavier Red (Schaech) flee after Red kills a store clerk. They're basically from nowhere, going nowhere, and finding sex and (lots of gruesomely depicted) violence along the way. The subtitle, "A Heterosexual Movie by Gregg Araki," may be technically accurate but the homoerotic subtext is very clear. Terrific performances. Second film in Araki's teen trilogy, following "Totally F***ked Up," and preceding "Nowhere." An unrated version is also available.**CW:** Violence, language, nudity, sexual situations. **84m/C VHS.** Rose McGowan, James Duval, Johnathon Schaech; *Cameos:* Parker Posey, Lauren Tewes, Christopher Knight, Margaret Cho, Skinny Puppy; **D:** Gregg Araki; **W:** Gregg Araki; **C:** Jim Fealy. Nominations: Independent Spirit Awards '96: Debut Performance (McGowan). THV

Doomed at Sundown 🎬🎬½ 1937 Decent Steele vehicle has the tough cowpoke as a sheriff's son known for playing practical jokes. When his father gets knifed, it's no laughing matter and he takes off after the killers. Based on a story by Fred Myton. **55m/B VHS.** Bob Steele, Laraine Day, Warner Richmond, Harold Daniels, David Sharpe; **D:** Sam Newfield; **W:** George Plympton. GPV, DVT

Doomed Caravan 🎬🎬🎬 1941 Hoppy and his pals lend a hand when some villains try to monopolize the wagon train business. Location shooting was done in the valleys of central California. **60m/B VHS.** William Boyd, Russell Hayden, Andy Clyde, Minna Gombell, Morris Ankrum, Georgia Hawkins, Trevor Bardette, Pat O'Brien; **D:** Lesley Selander. NOS

Doomed Love 🎬🎬½ 1983 Love is hell, especially when the object of your affection happens to be deceased. A professor of literature in the throes of unrequited love decides to reunite himself with his lost love. Won awards when released in Berlin. **75m/C VHS.** Bill Rice; **D:** Andrew Horn. MWF, FCT

Doomed to Die 🎬🎬 1940 Cargo of stolen bonds leads to a tong war and the murder of a shipping millionaire. Part of Mr. Wong series. Worth a look if only for Karloff's performance. **67m/B VHS, Beta.** Boris Karloff, Marjorie Reynolds, Grant Withers; **D:** William Nigh. NOS, MRV, SNC

Doomsday 🎬🎬½ 1928 Vidor marries for wealth instead of love and, in classic fashion, finds that money doesn't buy happiness. **73m/B VHS.** Florence Vidor, Gary Cooper, Lawrence Grant; **D:** Rowland V. Lee. GPV

The Doomsday Flight 🎬🎬 1966 Uneven made-for-television thriller. O'Brien plants an altitude-triggered bomb on a jet in an effort to blackmail the airline. Search for the bomb provides some suspenseful and well-acted moments. **100m/C VHS, Beta.** Jack Lord, Edmond O'Brien, Van Johnson, John Saxon, Katherine Crawford, Michael Sarrazin, Ed Asner, Greg Morris, Richard Carlson, Don Stewart; **D:** William A. Graham; **W:** Rod Serling. USH

Doomsday Gun 🎬🎬½ 1994 Fact-based thriller about arms manufacturer Gerald Bull (Langella), who dreams of building the world's biggest gun—a behemoth with a range of 1000 miles. Only problem is Bull's willingness to sell the weapon to the highest bidder, who happens to be Saddam Hussein. This doesn't sit well with Israeli Mossad agent Yossi (Arkin). Made for cable TV. **110m/C VHS.** Frank Langella, Alan Arkin, Kevin Spacey, Tony Goldwyn, James Fox, Michael Kitchen, Francesca Annis, Marianne Denicourt; **D:** Robert M. Young; **W:** Lionel Chetwynd, Walter Bernstein; **C:** Ian Wilson. HBO

Doomwatch 🎬🎬½ 1972 A scientist discovers a chemical company is dumping poison into local waters, deforming the inhabitants of an isolated island when they eat the catch of the day. Unsurprising. **89m/C VHS, Beta.** GB Ian Bannen, Judy Geeson, John Paul, Simon Oates, George Sanders; **D:** Peter Sasdy. MON

Door to Door 🎬🎬 1984 A made-for-cable comedy about two door-to-door salesmen who race to stay one step ahead of the law and their own company. Pretty lightweight, but it has its moments. **93m/C VHS, Beta.** Ron Leibman, Jane Kaczmarek, Arliss Howard, Alan Austin; **D:** Patrick Bailey.

Door to Door Maniac 🎬½ *Five Minutes to Live* 1961 Criminals hold a bank president's wife hostage, unaware that the husband was looking to get rid of her in favor of another woman. Cash's screen debut. Aside from the strange cast ensemble, not particularly worth seeing. **80m/B VHS, Beta.** Johnny Cash, Ron Howard, Vic Tayback, Donald Woods, Cay Forrester, Pamela Mason; **D:** Bill Karn. VDM, AOV

Door with the Seven Locks 🎬🎬½ 1962 Bizarre Edgar Wallace story of man who leaves seven keys to a treasure vault in his will. Remake of "Chamber of Horrors." **96m/C VHS.** GE Eddi Arent, Heinz Drache, Klaus Kinski, Ady Berber; **D:** Alfred Vohrer. SNC

The Doors 🎬🎬½ 1991 (R) Stone approached Jim Morrison with an early incarnation of this docudrama, but it's hard to believe even the Lizard King could play himself with any more convincing abandon than Kilmer, in a great performance. Trouble is, the story—one of drugs, abuse, and abject self-indulgence—grows tiresome, and the audience, with the exception of die-hard fans, may lose sight of any sympathy they might have had. Ryan is forgettable as Morrison's hippie-chick wife, MacLachlan sports a funny wig and dabbles on the keyboards as Ray Manszarek, and Quinlan is atypically cast as a sado-masochistic journalist paramour. Based on "Riders on the Storm" by John Densmore.**CW:** Strong language, heavy drug content, and strong sexuality. **138m/C VHS, LV, 8mm, Letterbox, Closed Caption, DVD.** Val Kilmer, Meg Ryan, Kevin Dillon, Kyle MacLachlan, Frank Whaley, Michael Madsen, Kathleen Quinlan, Crispin Glover, Josh Evans, John Densmore, William Jordan, Mimi Rogers, Paul Williams, Bill Graham, Billy Vera, William Kunstler, Wes Studi, Costas Mandylor, Billy Idol, Michael Wincott, Dennis Burkley; **D:** Oliver Stone; **W:** Oliver Stone, Ralph Thomas, Randy Johnson, J. Randall Johnson; **C:** Robert Richardson. COL, FCT, VES

The Doors: Soft Parade, a Retrospective 1969 The Doors' final TV appearance in 1969 forms the centerpiece of this concert-video tie-in to the Oliver Stone film. Fans should a-Door previously unreleased backstage interviews and a notable version of "The Unknown Soldier." **50m/C VHS, LV, Closed Caption. D:** Ray Manzarek. USH

Doppelganger: The Evil Within 🎬🎬 1990 (R) Holly Gooding (Barrymore) seems like such a nice girl—until the police suspect her of the brutal murder of her mother. Her new friend Patrick (Newbern) begins to see another side to the vulnerable Holly—a seductress capable of doing anything to get what she wants.**CW:** Language, strong violence, and sexuality. **105m/C VHS, LV, Closed Caption.** Drew Barrymore, George Newbern, Dennis Christopher, Sally Kellerman, Leslie Hope; **D:** Avi Nesher; **W:** Avi Nesher. FOX

Dorian Gray 🎬½ *The Secret of Dorian Gray; Il Dio Chiamato a Dorian; Das Bildness des Dorian Gray; The Evils of Dorian Gray* 1970 (R) Modern-day version of the famous tale by Oscar Wilde about an ageless young man whose portrait reflects the ravages of time and a life of debauchery. More sex, less acting with Berger in lead. Not nearly as good as the original version, "The Picture of Dorian Gray." **92m/C VHS.** GE IT Richard Todd, Helmut Berger, Herbert Lom, Marie Liljedahl, Margaret Lee, Maria Rohm, Beryl Cunningham, Isa Miranda, Eleanora Rossi-Drago, Renato Romano; **D:** Massimo Dallamano; **W:** Massimo Dallamano, Marcello Costa; **C:** Otello Spila. REP, FCT

Dorm That Dripped Blood woof! 1982 (R) Five college students volunteer to close the dorm during their Christmas vacation. A series of grisly and barbaric incidents eliminates the youngsters one by one. As the terror mounts, the remaining students slowly realize that they are up against a terrifyingly real psychopathic killer. Merry Christmas. **84m/C VHS, Beta.** Laura Lopinski, Stephen Sachs, Pamela Holland; **D:** Stephen Carpenter, Jeffrey Obrow; **W:** Stephen Carpenter.

Dos Cruces en Danger Pass 🎬🎬🎬 *Peau D'Ane* 1971 Charming fairy tale about a widowed king in search of a beautiful wife. Gorgeous color production. In French with English subtitles. **0090m/C VHS, Beta.** FR Catherine Deneuve, Jacques Perrin, Jean Marais, Delphine Seyrig; **D:** Jacques Demy.

Double Agents 🎬 *La Nuit Des Espions; Night Encounter* 1959 Two double agents are sent on a rendezvous to exchange vital government secrets. Dubbed in English. **81m/B VHS, Beta.** FR Marina Vlady, Robert Hossein. VYY

Double Cross 🎬🎬 1992 (R) Tank Polling (Connery), a British journalist, uses the secrets of an ex-hooker (Donohoe) to get back at a corrupt politician who ruined Polling's life five years earlier. Lots of action and a few graphic murders in this thriller.**CW:** Strong language, strong violence, and strong sexuality. **96m/C VHS.** Amanda Donohoe, Peter Wyngarde, Jason Connery; **D:** James Marcus. VTR

Double Cross 🎬🎬 1994 (R) Man has what seems to be a chance erotic encounter with a beautiful blonde. But this wouldn't be a thriller if it ended there, so there's blackmail and murder to contend with as well. **95m/C VHS, Closed Caption.** Patrick Bergin, Jennifer Tilly, Kelly Preston, Matt Craven, Kevin Tighe. **PAR**

Double-Crossed 🎬🎬½ 1991 In 1984 Barry Seal agrees to inform on Colombia's Medellin Cartel and its links to the Sandanista government of Nicaragua in exchange for leniency on drug-smuggling charges. Little does he know that the personal consequences will turn deadly when his cover is blown and the government double-crosses him. Hopper's hyped-up performance as drug smuggler turned DEA informant Seal showcases this true-crime tale. **111m/C VHS, LV, Closed Caption.** Dennis Hopper, Robert Carradine, G.W. Bailey, Adrienne Barbeau; **C:** Donald M. Morgan; **M:** Richard Bellis. **WAR**

Double Deal 🎬🎬 1939 An honest man and a gangster are rivals in love. The gangster robs a jewelry store and tries to pin the crime on the good guy. This is a movie with a moral so don't expect him to get away with it. **60m/C VHS.** Monte Hawley, Jeni Le Gon, Edward Thompson, Florence O'Brien; **D:** Arthur Dreifuss. **FCT**

Double Deal 🎬½ 1950 Murder, mayhem, and industrial espionage come into play as parties fight over an oil field. **65m/B VHS, Beta.** Marie Windsor, Richard Denning, Taylor Holmes; **D:** Abby Berlin. **DVT**

Double Deal 🎬½ 1984 Unfaithful woman and her lover plot to steal priceless opal from hubby. Lifeless and silly. **90m/C VHS, Beta.** Louis Jourdan, Angela Punch McGregor; **D:** Brian Kavanagh. **NO**

Double Double Toil and Trouble 🎬🎬½ 1994 The twins come to the financial rescue of their family when Dad's business gets into trouble and their home is threatened. But first they need to get a magic moonstone from their wicked Aunt Agatha (Leachman) and rescue kind Aunt Sophia, all before midnight on Halloween. Made for TV. **93m/C VHS, Closed Caption.** Ashley Olsen, Mary-Kate Olsen, Cloris Leachman, Meshach Taylor; **D:** Jeff Franklin; **W:** Jeff Franklin. **WAR**

Double Dragon 🎬🎬½ 1994 (PG-13) Generally harmless brain candy, based on the video-game, finds orphaned brothers Jimmy (Dacascos) and Billy (Wolf) living in the rubble of post earthquake L.A., circa 2007. They have half of a mystical dragon amulet and obsessed mogul Koga Shuko (Patrick), who possesses the other half, after them. Because he needs the entire amulet in order to control its vast power. Non-stop action should keep the kiddies amused. **CW:** Martial arts violence. **96m/C VHS, LV, Closed Caption.** Scott Wolf, Mark Dacascos, Robert Patrick, Alyssa Milano, Kristina Malandro Wagner, Julia Nickson-Soul; **D:** Jim Yukich; **W:** Michael Paul Davis, Peter Gould; **M:** Jay Michael Ferguson. **USH**

Double Dynamite 🎬½ *It's Only Money* 1951 A bank teller is at a loss when his racetrack winnings are confused with the cash lifted from his bank during a robbery. Forgettable, forgotten shambles. Originally filmed in 1948. **80m/B VHS, Beta.** Frank Sinatra, Jane Russell, Groucho Marx, Don McGuire, Howard Freeman, Harry Hayden, Nestor Paiva, Lou Nova, Joe Devlin; **D:** Irving Cummings; **W:** Melville Shavelson. **TTC**

Double Edge 🎬🎬 1992 (PG-13) The Palestinian-Israeli conflict is the focus of this drama about an ambitious reporter (Dunaway). On her first foreign assignment, New Yorker Faye Milano finds herself way out of her depth when she covers a colleague's beat in Jerusalem. Unable to remain a detached observer, Faye instead becomes an active participant, alternating between her affair with an Israeli reserves officer and her friendship with a family of Palestinian intifada leaders. Dunaway and Kollek are unfortunately stiff in their performances but the location (Israel and the West Bank) is interesting and the story

surprisingly balanced. **CW:** One violent scene. **85m/C VHS, Beta.** *IS* Faye Dunaway, Amos Kollek, Muhamad Bakri, Shmuel Shilo, Makram Khouri, Michael Schneider, Anat Atzman, Ann Belkin; **D:** Amos Kollek; **W:** Amos Kollek. **WAR**

Double Exposure 🎬🎬 1982 (R) A young photographer's violent nightmares become the next day's headlines. Unsurprising vision. **95m/C VHS, Beta.** Michael Callan, James Stacy, Joanna Pettet, Cleavon Little, Pamela Hensley, Seymour Cassel, David Young, Misty Rowe, Don Potter; **D:** William B. Hillman. **VES**

Double Exposure 🎬½ 1993 (R) A possessive husband discovers his wife's infidelity and decides to get revenge, only his plan doesn't work out as he intends. **CW:** Language, rape scene, and strong sexuality. **93m/C VHS, LV.** Ron Perlman, Ian Buchanan, Jennifer Gatti, William R. Moses, James McEachin, Dedee Pfeiffer; **D:** Claudia Hoover; **W:** Christine Colfer, Bridget Hoffman. Claudia Hoover.

Double Exposure: The Story of Margaret Bourke-White 🎬🎬½ *Margaret Bourke-White* 1989 Beautifully shot but slow biography of a woman who became a well-known professional photographer for "Life" magazine during the 1930s and 1940s, as well as the first official female photojournalist of WWII. Made for cable television. **105m/C VHS, LV.** Farrah Fawcett, Frederic Forrest, Mitchell Ryan, David Huddleston, Jay Patterson, Ken Marshall; **D:** Lawrence Schiller; **C:** Robert Elswit. **TTC**

Double Face 🎬½ 1970 A wealthy industrialist kills his lesbian wife with a car bomb, but she seems to haunt him through pornographic films. **84m/C VHS, Beta.** Klaus Kinski, Annabella Incontrera. **UNI**

Double Happiness 🎬🎬🎬 1994 (PG-13) Slice of life comedy-drama finds 20-something Chinese-Canadian Jade Li (Oh) struggling to balance her would-be acting career and new world romance with her family's traditional values. Jade wants to please her old world father (Chang) so she endures his arranged dates and puts on a pleasant demeanor for family friends. But Jade must decide who she wants to be when she gets involved with non-Asian college student Mark (Rennie). Fine performances and assured direction from Shum in her feature film debut. **CW:** One scene of sexuality; brief strong language. **87m/C VHS, LV, Closed Caption.** *CA* Sandra Oh, Stephen Chang, Alannah Ong, Frances You, Johnny Mah, Callum Keith Rennie; **D:** Mina Shum; **W:** Mina Shum; **C:** Peter Wunstorf. Genie Awards '94: Best Actress (Oh), Best Film Editing; Nominations: Genie Awards '94: Best Director (Shum), Best Film. **TTC, NLC**

Double Identity 🎬🎬½ 1989 (PG-13) Former college professor turned criminal Mancuso moves to a corn patch called New Hope in hopes of returning to the straight and narrow. He finds a good woman to stand by him, but, alas, crime, like smoking, is easier to start than to quit. Much intrigue and deceit. **95m/C VHS.** *CA FR* Nick Mancuso, Leah K. Pinsent, Patrick Bauchau, Anne LeTourneau, Jacques Godin; **D:** Yves Boisset. **NO**

Double Impact 🎬½ 1991 (R) Van Damme plays twins re-united in Hong Kong to avenge their parents' murder by local bad guys, but this lunkhead kick-em-up doesn't even take advantage of that gimmick; the basic story would have been exactly the same with just one Jean-Claude. Lots of profane dialogue and some gratuitous nudity for the kiddies. **CW:** Strong violence, strong sensuality, and strong language. **107m/C VHS, Beta, LV, 8mm, Closed Caption.** Jean-Claude Van Damme, Cory Everson, Geoffrey Lewis; **D:** Sheldon Lettich; **W:** Jean-Claude Van Damme, Sheldon Lettich. **COL, CCB**

Double Indemnity 🎬🎬🎬🎬 1944 The classic seedy story of an insurance agent seduced by a deadly woman into killing her husband so they can collect together from his company. Terrific, influential film noir, the best of its kind. Based on the James M. Cain novel. **107m/B VHS, Beta, LV.** Fred MacMurray, Barbara Stanwyck, Edward G. Robinson, Tom Powers, Porter Hall, Jean Heather, Byron Barr, Fortunio Bonanova; **D:** Billy Wilder; **W:** Raymond Chandler, Billy Wilder; **M:** Miklos Rozsa. National Film Reg-

istry '92;; Nominations: Academy Awards '44: Best Actress (Stanwyck), Best Black and White Cinematography, Best Director (Wilder), Best Picture, Best Screenplay, Best Sound, Best Original Dramatic/Comedy Score. **USH, FCT**

Double Jeopardy 🎬🎬 1992 (R) Boxleitner stars as a married man who risks his family and life when his sexy ex-lover returns to town. She easily involves him in deception—and murder. A cake-walk for Ward as the femme fatale. Made for cable television. **101m/C VHS, Beta, LV.** Bruce Boxleitner, Rachel Ward, Sela Ward, Sally Kirkland; **D:** Lawrence Schiller; **M:** Eduard Artemyev. **PMS**

A Double Life 🎬🎬🎬 1947 Colman plays a Shakespearean actor in trouble when the characters he plays begin to seep into his personal life and take over. Things begin to look really bad when he is cast in the role of the cursed Othello. Colman won an Oscar for this difficult role, and the moody musical score garnered another for Rosza. **107m/B VHS, Closed Caption.** Ronald Colman, Shelley Winters, Signe Hasso, Edmond O'Brien, Ray Collins, Millard Mitchell; **D:** George Cukor; **W:** Ruth Gordon, Garson Kanin; **C:** Milton Krasner; **M:** Miklos Rozsa. Academy Awards '47: Best Actor (Colman), Best Original Dramatic/Comedy Score; Golden Globe Awards '48: Best Actor—Drama (Colman); Nominations: Academy Awards '47: Best Director (Cukor), Best Original Screenplay. **REP, FCT, BTV**

The Double Life of Veronique 🎬🎬 *La Double Vie de Veronique* 1991 (R) They say everyone has a twin, but this is ridiculous. Two women—Polish Veronika and French Veronique—are born on the same day in different countries, share a singing talent, a cardiac ailment, and, although the two never meet, a strange awareness of each other. Jacob is unforgettable as the two women, and director Krzysztof creates some spellbinding scenes but the viewer has to be willing to forgo plot for atmosphere. **CW:** Sexuality. **96m/C VHS, Beta, LV, Closed Caption.** *FR PL* Irene Jacob, Phillipe Volter, Sandrine Dumas, Aleksander Bardini, Louis Ducreux, Claude Duneton, Halina Gryglaszewska, Kalina Jedrusik; **D:** Krzysztof Kieslowski; **W:** Krzysztof Kieslowski, Krzysztof Piesiewicz; **C:** Slawomir Idziak. Cannes Film Festival '91: Best Actress (Jacob); National Society of Film Critics Awards '91: Best Foreign Film. **PAR**

The Double McGuffin 🎬🎬 1979 (PG) A plot of international intrigue is uncovered by teenagers—a la the Hardy Boys—when a prime minister and her security guard pay a visit to a small Virginia community. They're not believed, though. Action-packed from the makers of Benji. Dogs do not figure prominently here. **100m/C VHS, Beta.** Ernest Borgnine, George Kennedy, Elke Sommer, Ed "Too Tall" Jones, Lisa Whelchel, Vincent Spano; **D:** Joe Camp; **M:** Euel Box; **V:** Orson Welles. **VES**

The Double Negative 🎬½ *Deadly Companion* 1980 A photojournalist pursues his wife's killer in a confusing story. Based on Ross MacDonald's "The Three Roads." **96m/C VHS, Beta.** *CA* Michael Sarrazin, Susan Clark, Anthony Perkins, Howard Duff, Kate Reid, Al Waxman, Elizabeth Shepherd, John Candy; **D:** George Bloomfield; **W:** Janis Allen. **BFV**

The Double O Kid 🎬🎬½ 1992 (PG-13) Lance is a 17-year-old video game master who's interning at the Agency, a covert spy organization. Ordered to rush a package to Los Angeles, Lance discovers that a madman computer virus designer and his henchwoman desperately want what he's carrying. Aided by the prerequisite pretty girl, Lance must avoid all the hazards sent his way. **CW:** Some language and some violence. **95m/C VHS, Beta, Closed Caption.** Corey Haim, Wallace Shawn, Brigitte Nielsen, Nicole Eggert, John Rhys-Davies, Basil Hoffman, Karen Black; **Cameos:** Anne Francis; **D:** Duncan McLachlan; **W:** Andrea Buck, Duncan McLachlan.

Double Obsession 🎬½ 1993 (R) College roommates Heather (Hemingway) and Claire (d'Abo) are inseparable friends—until Claire falls in love. Heather becomes possessive and, though the years pass, her obsession with Claire only grows. When Heather's affections turn deadly, can Claire stop her? **88m/C VHS.** Margaux Hemingway, Maryam D'Abo, Frederic Forrest, Scott Valentine; **D:**

Eduardo Montes; **W:** Jeffrey Delman, R.J. Marx, Eduardo Montes. *COL*

Double Play 🎬🎬½ **1996 (PG)** Updated version of "The Prince and the Pauper" finds teenaged computer genius Rudy (Jackson) inheriting his dad's successful computer company. But his evil Uncle Mike (Shatner), who's not the boy's guardian, wants the company for himself and hires some thugs to kidnap the kid and force him to sign over control of the business. But Rudy just happens to have a double—a high school baseball star who's in town for the championship game—and confusion rules when he takes his place. Jackson's brother, Richard Lee Jackson, plays his cousin in the movie. **101m/C VHS.** Jonathan Jackson, William Shatner, Richard Lee Jackson. *HMK*

Double Revenge 🎬½ **1989** Two men feel they have a score to settle after a bank heist gone sour leaves two people dead. **90m/C VHS.** Joe Dallesandro, Nancy Everhard, Leigh McCloskey, Richard Rust, Theresa Saldana; **D:** Armand Mastroianni. *REP*

Double Standard 🎬½ **1988** You'll be less concerned with the plot—a community discovers that a prominent judge has maintained two marriages for nearly 20 years—than with the possibility that such dim-witted myopes might actually have existed in the real world. This made-for-TV slice of bigamy is for fans of the oops-I-forgot-I'm-married genre only. **95m/C VHS.** Robert Foxworth, Michele Greene, Pamela Bellwood, James Kee; **D:** Louis Rudolph.

Double Suicide 🎬🎬🎬 *Shinju Ten No Amijima* **1969** From a play by Monzarmon Chikamatsu, a tragic drama about a poor salesman in 18th century Japan who falls in love with a geisha and ruins his family and himself trying to requite the hopeless passion. Stylish with Iwashita turning in a wonderful dual performance. In Japanese with subtitles. **105m/B VHS.** *JP* Kichiemon Nakamura, Shima Iwashita, Yusuke Takita, Hosei Komatsu; **D:** Masahiro Shinoda. *HMV*

Double Take 🎬🎬 **1997 (R)** Writer Connor McEwen (Sheffer) witnesses a murder and identifies the suspect from a police line-up. But when he sees a dead ringer for the alleged murderer, he becomes convinced the police have arrested the wrong guy. **86m/C VHS, LV, Closed Caption.** Craig Sheffer, Costas Mandylor, Brigitte Bako, Torri Higginson, Maurice Godin; **D:** Mark L. Lester; **W:** Ed Rugoff, Ralph Rugoff; **M:** Paul Zaza. *ART*

Double Team 🎬🎬 **1997 (R)** Counter-terrorist expert Jack Quinn (Van Damme) teams with weapons specialist Yaz (Rodman, in his film debut) to take down international terrorist Stavros (Roarke). After Jack kills Stavros's son, he is sent to a high-security superspy retirement village. When his wife and newborn son are kidnapped, Jack escapes, with Yaz's help, to finish the job and try to save his family. Van Damme teams with his third famous Hong Kong action director, Tsui Hark (the other two are John Woo and Ringo Lam) to create yet another disappointment. He's slightly more charismatic than usual (not saying much), but Rodman easily steals the flick as he gets most of the good lines, and delivers them with relish.**CW:** Non-stop action violence. **93m/C VHS, LV, Closed Caption, DVD.** Jean-Claude Van Damme, Dennis Rodman, Mickey Rourke, Natasha Lindinger, Paul Freeman, Valeria Cavalli, Jay Benedict; **D:** Tsui Hark; **W:** Paul Mones, Don Jakoby; **C:** Peter Pau; **M:** Gary Chang. Golden Raspberry Awards '97: Worst Supporting Actor (Rodman), Worst New Star (Rodman). *COL*

Double Threat 🎬🎬 **1992 (R)** An aging sex star makes her return to the screen opposite a younger actor with whom she is having an affair. When the director wants to include nude sex scenes in the film she agrees to use a younger body-double. Then the actress discovers her lover is involved in off-screen action with the double as well. This does not please her and she decides to take a deadly revenge. An unrated version is also available.**CW:** Language and strong sexuali-

ty. **94m/C VHS.** Sally Kirkland, Andrew Stevens, Lisa Shane, Richard Lynch, Anthony (Tony) Franciosa, Sherrie Rose, Chick Vennera; **D:** David A. Prior.

Double Trouble 🎬🎬 **1967** When rock star Presley falls in love with an English heiress, he winds up involved in an attempted murder. The king belts out "Long Legged Girl" while evading cops, criminals, and crying women. A B-side. Based on a story by Marc Brandell. **92m/C VHS, Beta.** Elvis Presley, Annette Day, John Williams, Yvonne Romain, Michael Murphy, Chips Rafferty; **D:** Norman Taurog; **W:** Jo Heims. *MGM*

Double Trouble 🎬 **1991 (R)** Twin brothers—one a cop, one a jewel thief—team up to crack the case of an international jewel smuggling ring headed by a wealthy and politically well-connected businessman and his righthand man.**CW:** Language and violence. **87m/C VHS, LV.** David Paul, Peter Paul, James Doohan, Roddy McDowall, Steve Kanaly, A.J. Johnson, David Carradine; **D:** John Paragon. *COL*

Double Vision 🎬🎬 **1992 (PG-13)** Suspense thriller starring Cattrall as Caroline, a medical student who goes to London to check out the strange disappearance of her twin sister, Lisa. Assuming her identity, Caroline gets deeply involved in a kinky lifestyle that may result in murder. Based on a short story by Mary Higgins Clark.**CW:** Some language, some violence, and some sex-related situations. **92m/C VHS, Closed Caption.** Kim Cattrall, Gale Hansen, Christopher Lee; **D:** Robert Knights. *REP*

Double Wedding 🎬🎬🎬 **1937** Madcap comedy starring Powell as a wacky painter who doesn't believe in working and Loy as a workaholic dress designer. Loy has chosen a fiance for her younger sister, Irene, to marry, but Irene has plans of her own. When Irene and her beau meet bohemian Powell, the fun really begins. Script suffers slightly from too much slapstick and not enough wit, although the stars (in their seventh outing as a duo) play it well. Based on the play "Great Love" by Ferenc Molnar. **86m/B VHS.** William Powell, Myrna Loy, Florence Rice, John Beal, Jessie Ralph, Edgar Kennedy, Sidney Toler, Mary Gordon; **D:** Richard Thorpe; **W:** Jo Swerling. *MGM*

Doubting Thomas 🎬🎬½ **1935** Rogers' last film, which was in theatres when he was killed in a plane crash. Silly story of a husband and his doubts about his wife and her amateur-acting career. The show goes on in spite of his doubts, her forgotten lines, and wardrobe goofs. Remake of 1922's silent film "The Torch Bearers." **78m/B VHS.** Will Rogers, Billie Burke, Alison Skipworth, Sterling Holloway; **D:** David Butler. *FOX, FCT*

Doughboys 🎬🎬½ *Forward March* **1930** Keaton's second talkie is a so-so comedy about a rich man who mistakenly enlists in the Army during WWI. He manages to bumble his way through basic training and win the heart of a pretty girl. There are a few bright moments, particularly a musical number between Keaton and "Ukulele Ike" Edwards. **80m/B VHS.** Buster Keaton, Cliff Edwards, Edward Brophy, Sally Eilers, Victor Potel, Arnold Korff, Frank Mayo; **D:** Edward Sedgwick. *MGM*

Doughnuts & Society 🎬🎬½ **1936** Two elderly ladies who run a coffee shop suddenly strike it rich and find that life among the bluebloods is not all it's cracked up to be. No sprinkles. **70m/B VHS, Beta.** Louise Fazenda, Maude Eburne, Eddie Nugent, Ann Rutherford, Hedda Hopper, Franklin Pangborn. *VYY*

The Dove 🎬🎬½ **1974 (PG-13)** The true story of a 16-year-old's adventures as he sails around the world in a 23-foot sloop. The trip took him five years and along the way he falls in love with a girl who follows him to exotic locales. Photography and scenery are magnificent. **105m/C VHS, Beta, Closed Caption.** Joseph Bottoms, Deborah Raffin, Dabney Coleman, Peter Gwynne; **D:** Charles Jarrott; **W:** Peter S. Beagle; **C:** Sven Nykvist. *PAR, BMV*

Down Among the Z Men 🎬🎬 **1952** Enlisted man helps a girl save an atomic formula from spies. Funny in spots but weighed down by musical numbers from a female entourage. From the pre-Monty Python comedy troupe "The Goons." **71m/B VHS, Beta, LV.** *GB* Peter Sellers, Spike Milligan, Harry Secombe, Michael Bentine, Carole Carr; **D:** Maclean Rogers. *NO*

Down & Dirty 🎬🎬🎬 *Brutti, Sporchi, e Cattivi* **1976** A scathing Italian satire about a modern Roman family steeped in petty crime, incest, murder, adultery, drugs, and arson. In Italian with English subtitles. **115m/C VHS, Beta, Closed Caption.** *IT* Nino Manfredi, Francesco Annibali, Maria Bosco; **D:** Ettore Scola; **W:** Ettore Scola. Cannes Film Festival '76: Best Director (Scola).

Down and Out in Beverly Hills 🎬🎬½ **1986 (R)** A modern retelling of Jean Renoir's classic "Boudu Sauve des Eaux" with some nice star turns. A spoiled wealthy couple rescue a suicidal bum from their swimming pool. He, in turn, beds the wife, the maid, and the daughter, solves the dog's identity crisis, rescues the man and his son from frustration and finds he doesn't like being a bum. A boxoffice hit. **103m/C VHS, Beta, LV.** Nick Nolte, Bette Midler, Richard Dreyfuss, Little Richard, Tracy Nelson, Elizabeth Pena, Evan Richards, Valerie Curtin, Barry Primus, Dorothy Tristan, Alexis Arquette; **D:** Paul Mazursky; **W:** Paul Mazursky, Leon Capetanos; **M:** Andy Summers. *TOU*

Down Argentine Way 🎬🎬🎬 **1940** A lovely young woman falls in love with a suave Argentinian horse breeder. First-rate Fox musical made a star of Grable and was Miranda's first American film. ♫South American Way; Down Argentina Way; Two Dreams Met; Mama Yo Quiero; Sing to Your Senorita. **90m/C VHS, Beta, LV, Closed Caption.** Don Ameche, Betty Grable, Carmen Miranda, Charlotte Greenwood, J. Carrol Naish, Henry Stephenson, Leonid Kinskey; **D:** Irving Cummings; **C:** Leon Shamroy. Nominations: Academy Awards '40: Best Color Cinematography, Best Interior Decoration, Best Song ("Down Argentine Way").*FOX, MLB*

Down by Law 🎬🎬🎬 **1986 (R)** In Jarmusch's follow-up to his successful "Stranger than Paradise," he introduces us to three men: a pimp, an out-of-work disc jockey, and an Italian tourist. When the three break out of prison, they wander through the Louisiana swampland with some regrets about their new-found freedom. Slow-moving at times, beautifully shot throughout. Poignant and hilarious, the film is true to Jarmusch form: some will love the film's offbeat flair, and others will find it bothersome. **107m/C VHS, Beta, Closed Caption.** John Lurie, Tom Waits, Roberto Benigni, Ellen Barkin, Billie Neal, Rockets Redglare, Vernel Bagneris, Nicoletta Braschi; **D:** Jim Jarmusch; **W:** Jim Jarmusch; **M:** John Lurie, Tom Waits. *FOX*

Down Came a Blackbird 🎬🎬½ **1994 (R)** Anna Lenka (Redgrave), a Holocaust survivor, runs a clinic for healing both the physical and psychological wounds of torture victims. Journalist Helen McNulty (Dern), herself a survivor, decides to write about the clinic but Anna believes Helen's covering up the pain she's never dealt with. Also at the clinic is Tomas Ramirez (Julia), a former college professor with a terrible secret, with whom Helen discovers a special rapport. Conventional script with some fine performances; Julia died shortly after principal photography was completed on the TV film, which is dedicated to his memory.**CW:** Depictions of torture, and some sexuality. **112m/C VHS, LV, Closed Caption.** Vanessa Redgrave, Laura Dern, Raul Julia, Jay O. Sanders, Cliff Gorman, Sarita Choudhury, L. Scott Caldwell, Jeffrey DeMunn; **D:** Jonathan Sanger; **W:** Kevin Droney; **C:** Kees Van Oostrum; **M:** Graeme Revell. *REP*

Down Dakota Way 🎬½ **1949** Strange coincidence between a recent murder and a fatal cow epidemic. Rogers helps some locals bring the link to light. **67m/C VHS.** Roy Rogers, Dale Evans, Pat Brady, Monte Montana, Elisabeth Risdon, Byron Barr,

James B. Cardwell, Roy Barcroft, Emmett Vogan; **D:** William Witney. *REP*

Down Mexico Way 🎬🎬 1941 Two cowboys come to the aid of a Mexican town whose residents have been hoodwinked by a phony movie company. Very exciting chase on horseback, motorcycle, and in automobiles. **78m/B VHS, Beta.** Gene Autry, Smiley Burnette, Fay McKenzie, Duncan Renaldo; **D:** Joseph Santley. *CCB*

Down, Out and Dangerous 🎬🎬
1995 (R) Expectant couple Brad (Davison) and Monica (Ettinger) Harrington find out that Tim (Thomas), the charming homeless man they've befriended, is really a psycho killer.**CW:** Scenes of violence and terror. **90m/C VHS, Beta, Closed Caption.** Richard Thomas, Bruce Davison, Cynthia Ettinger, Steve Hytner, Christine Cavanaugh, George DiCenzo, Jason Bernard, Melinda Culea, Stuart Pankin; **D:** Noel Nosseck; **W:** Carey Hayes, Chad Hayes; **C:** Paul Maibaum; **M:** Mark Snow. *PAR*

Down Periscope 🎬🎬½ 1996 (PG-13) Tom Dodge (Grammer) dreams of commanding a nuclear sub, but gets stuck with an out-of-mothballs, rusting WWII vintage tub with the usual goof-off crew. In order for Dodge to get his dream assignment, he and his losers must beat the nuclear subs of generic mean authority figure Admiral Graham (Dern), in a war game. Predictable comedy is kept afloat by amusing cast, especially Schneider as the weasely Executive Officer Pascal. Many jokes revolve around Dodge's tattoo, which is on a body part that is normally private first-class. Denied cooperation from the U.S. Navy, the shipyard scenes were filmed on three barges tied together in the San Francisco Bay area, with empty discarded frigates and destroyers belonging to the U.S. Department of Transportation playing the fleet.**CW:** Some crude language. **92m/C VHS, Closed Caption.** Kelsey Grammer, Lauren Holly, Bruce Dern, Rob Schneider, Rip Torn, Harry Dean Stanton, William H. Macy, Ken Campbell, Toby Huss, Duane Martin, Jonathan Penner, Bradford Tatum, Harland Williams; **D:** David S. Ward; **W:** Hugh Wilson, Andrew Kurtzman, Eliot Wald; **C:** Victor Hammer; **M:** Randy Edelman. *FXV*

Down Texas Way 🎬🎬 1942 One of the "Rough Riders" series. When one of the boys is accused of murdering his best friend, his two companions search for the real killer. **57m/B VHS, Beta.** Buck Jones, Tim McCoy, Raymond Hatton; **D:** Howard Bretherton. *NOS, VCN, TIM*

Down the Drain 🎬🎬 1989 (R) A broad-as-a-city-block farce about an unscrupulous criminal lawyer and his assortment of crazy clients. A fine first half but someone pulls the plug in the middle of the bath. **90m/C VHS, Beta, LV.** Andrew Stevens, John Matuszak, Teri Copley, Joseph Campanella, Don Stroud, Stella Stevens, Jerry Mathers, Benny "The Jet" Urquidez; **D:** Robert C. Hughes. *COL*

Down the Wyoming Trail 🎬 1939
Western hero Ritter battles some rustlers who are terrorizing farmers during the winter, while still managing to find time to warble some tunes. **52m/B VHS.** Tex Ritter, Horace Murphy, Mary Brodel, Bobby Lawson, Charles "Blackie" King, Bob Terry; **D:** Al(bert) Herman; **W:** Peter Dixon, Roger Merton. *MOV*

Down to Earth 🎬 1917 Ever-gallant lover Fairbanks overruns a mental hospital to save his sweetheart. Once inside, he's determined to show the patients that their illness is illusion, and reality's the cure. A quixotic gem from Fairbanks' pre-swashbuckling social comic days. Director Emerson's wife was the scenarist, and Victor Fleming, who went on to direct "The Wizard of Oz" and "Gone with the Wind" (to name a few), was the man behind the camera. **68m/B VHS, Beta.** Douglas Fairbanks Sr., Eileen Percy, Gustav von Seyffertitz, Charles P. McHugh, Charles Gerrard, William H. Keith, Ruth Allen, Fred Goodwine; **D:** John Emerson. *GPV, FCT*

Down to Earth 🎬🎬 1947 A lackluster musical and boxoffice flop with an impressive cast. Hayworth is the Greek goddess of dance sent to Earth on a mission to straighten out Broadway producer Parks and his play that ridicules the Greek gods. Anita Ellis dubs the singing of Hayworth. A parody of "Here Comes Mr. Jordan," remade in 1980 as "Xanadu." **101m/C VHS, LV.** Rita Hayworth, Larry Parks, Marc Platt, Roland Culver, James Gleason, Edward Everett Horton, Adele Jergens, George Macready, William Frawley, James Burke, Fred F. Sears, Lynn Merrick, Myron Healey; **D:** Alexander Hall; **W:** Edwin Blum; **M:** George Duning. *COL, CCB*

Down to the Sea in Ships 🎬🎬½
The Last Adventurers **1922** Bow made her movie debut in this drama about the whalers of 19th-century Massachusetts. Highlighted by exciting action scenes of an actual whale hunt. Silent with music score and original tinted footage. **83m/B VHS, Beta.** Marguerite Courtot, Raymond McKee, Clara Bow; **D:** Elmer Clifton. *NOS, CCB, GPV*

Down Twisted 🎬 1989 (R) A young woman gets involved with a thief on the run in Mexico in this "Romancing the Stone" derivative. The muddled plot deserves such a confusing title. **89m/C VHS, Beta, Closed Caption.** Carey Lowell, Charles Rocket, Trudi Dochtermann, Thom Mathews, Linda Kerridge, Courteney Cox; **D:** Albert Pyun; **W:** Albert Pyun; **C:** Walt Lloyd; **M:** Eric Allaman.

Down Under 🎬 1986 Two gold-hungry beach boys go to Australia looking for riches, and document their adventures on film. Essentially a crudely shot, tongue-in-cheek travelogue narrated by Patrick Macnee. **90m/C VHS, Beta.** Don Atkinson, Donn Dunlop, Patrick Macnee. *NO*

Downdraft 🎬🎬 1996 (R) A special forces unit has six hours to penetrate a subterranean bunker, which protects a supercomputer that's about to launch a nuclear attack. Assaulted by a variety of sophisticated weapons, the unit must also outwit the computer's android defender.**CW:** Violence, adult language. **101m/C VHS, Closed Caption.** Vincent Spano, Kate Vernon, Paul Koslo. *REP*

Downhill Racer 🎬🎬½ 1969 (PG) An undisciplined American skier locks ski-tips with his coach and his new-found love while on his way to becoming an Olympic superstar. Character study on film. Beautiful ski and mountain photography keep it from sliding downhill. **102m/C VHS, Beta, LV.** Robert Redford, Camilla Sparv, Gene Hackman, Dabney Coleman; **D:** Michael Ritchie. *PAR*

Downhill Willie 🎬½ 1996 (PG) Willie (Coogan) isn't the brightest guy around—except on skies. Now he wants to enter the Kamikaze Run, which takes place on an extreme race course, and win the half-million top prize as well as the prettiest snow bunny (Keanan) on the slopes. **90m/C VHS.** Keith Coogan, Staci Keanan, Lochlan Monroe, Estelle Harris, Fred Stoller, Lee Reherman; **D:** David Mitchell; **W:** Stephanie Cedar; **C:** David Pelletier; **M:** Norman Orenstein. *BMG*

Downtown 🎬½ 1989 (R) Urban comedy about a naive white suburban cop who gets demoted to the roughest precinct in Philadelphia, and gains a streetwise black partner. Runs a routine beat. **96m/C VHS, Beta, LV, Closed Caption.** Anthony Edwards, Forest Whitaker, Joe Pantoliano, Penelope Ann Miller; **D:** Richard Benjamin; **M:** Alan Silvestri. *FOX*

D.P. 1985 A black orphan attaches to the only other black in post-WWII Germany. From a story by Kurt Vonnegut, Jr. Made for television. **60m/C VHS.** Stan Shaw, Rosemary Leach, Julius Gordon. *MON, KAR*

Drachenfutter 🎬🎬🎬 *Dragon's Food; Dragon Chow* **1987** Powerful story dealing with a Pakistani immigrant's attempts to enter the Western world. Themes of alienation and helplessness are emphasized. Dialogues occur in 12 languages, predominantly German and Mandarin Chinese; subtitled in English. **75m/B VHS, Beta.** GE Si Bhasker, Ric Young, Buddy Uzzaman; **D:** Jan Schütte; **W:** Thomas Strittmatter; **M:** Claus Bantzer. *NYF*

Dracula 🎬🎬🎬 1931 Lugosi, in his most famous role, plays a vampire who terrorizes the countryside in his search for human blood. From Bram Stoker's novel. Although short of a masterpiece due to slow second half, deservedly rated a film classic. What would Halloween be like without this movie? Sequelled by "Dracula's Daughter." **75m/B VHS, Beta, LV.** Bela Lugosi, David Manners, Dwight Frye, Helen Chandler, Edward Van Sloan, Frances Dade, Herbert Bunston; **D:** Tod Browning; **W:** Garrett Fort; **C:** Karl Freund. *USH, TLF, HMV*

Dracula 🎬🎬½ *Bram Stoker's Dracula* 1973 Count on squinty-eyed Palance to shine as the Transylvanian vampire who must quench his thirst for human blood. A made-for-television adaptation of the Bram Stoker novel that really flies. **105m/C VHS, Beta, LV.** Jack Palance, Simon Ward, Fiona Lewis, Nigel Davenport, Pamela Brown, Penelope Horner, Murray Brown, Virginia Wetherell, Sarah Douglas, Barbara Lindley; **D:** Dan Curtis; **W:** Richard Matheson; **C:** Oswald Morris. *ART*

Dracula 🎬🎬½ 1979 (R) Langella recreates his Broadway role as the count who needs human blood for nourishment. Notable for its portrayal of Dracula as a romantic and tragic figure in history. Overlooked since the vampire spoof "Love at First Bite" came out at the same time. **109m/C VHS, Beta, LV, Letterbox.** Frank Langella, Laurence Olivier, Kate Nelligan, Donald Pleasence, Janine Duvitsky, Trevor Eve, Tony Haygarth; **D:** John Badham; **W:** W.D. Richter; **C:** Gilbert Taylor; **M:** John Williams. *USH*

Dracula A.D. 1972 🎬🎬 *Dracula Today* 1972 Lee returned to England for his sixth (and by most accounts, worst) go-round as Dracula for Hammer Films, where the creative juices seemed to be drying up. The decision was made to turn Dracula loose in the modern world. The movie actually opens in 1872 with a scene that is one of the highlights of the entire production—an action scene that features Dracula battling his nemesis Van Helsing (Cushing) atop a speeding stagecoach. When the coach is wrecked, Dracula is impaled on a wheel spoke and dies. From that point, the scene immediately jumps ahead one century. A Satanist named Johnny Alucard and a group of naive hippie teenagers revive the long-dead vampire in an abandoned church building in England. The teens and Dracula are opposed by Van Helsing's grandson (Cushing again) and his granddaughter Jessica (Beacham). Hammer's unwillingness to pay Lee to speak more than a few lines, together with a sterile plot that had Dracula essentially paralyzed by the modern world, forced the teenagers to carry the story. It appears that the idea for *Dracula A.D. 1972* came from the Count Yorga movies, which had some success in placing an Old World vampire in modern Los Angeles. However, the Yorga movies were only moderately successful and this Hammer copy did not even do that well. *Dracula A.D. 1972* was the sequel to *The Scars of Dracula* (1971) and was followed by *The Satanic Rites of Dracula* (1973). **95m/C VHS.** GB Christopher Lee, Peter Cushing, Christopher Neame, Stephanie Beacham, Michael Coles, Caroline Munro, Marsha Hunt, Philip Miller, Janet Key, William Ellis; **D:** Alan Gibson; **W:** Don Houghton; **C:** Richard Bush; **M:** Michael Vickers. *WAR*

Dracula & Son 🎬 *Dracula Pere et Fils* 1976 (PG) Dracula spoof in which the count fathers a son who prefers girls and football to blood. Poor English dubbing and choppy ending drive a stake through the heart. **88m/C VHS, Beta.** FR Christopher Lee, Bernard Menez, Marie Breillat; **D:** Edouard Molinaro; **M:** Vladimir Cosma. *GKK*

Dracula Blows His Cool 🎬 1982 (R) Three voluptuous models and their photographer restore an ancient castle and open a disco in it. The vampire lurking about the castle welcomes the party with his fangs. **91m/C VHS, Beta, LV, Closed Caption.** John Garco, Betty Verges; **D:** Carlo Ombra; **W:** Carlo Ombra.

Dracula: Dead and Loving It WOOF!
1995 (PG-13) King of the spoofs Nielsen takes on the title role as the ever-loving, if clumsy, Count who still enjoys necking—particularly with luscious damsels in distress, Lucy (Anthony) and Mina (Yasbeck). And he's still got his bug-eating minion Renfield (MacNichol) and egomaniacal vampire-hunter Van Helsing (Brooks) around. As usual, Brooks throws everything possible on the screen, hoping some schtick will stick (not very much does). *CW:* Comedic sensuality and gore. **90m/C VHS, LV, Closed Caption.** Leslie Nielsen, Mel Brooks, Peter MacNicol, Lysette Anthony, Amy Yasbeck, Steven Weber, Harvey Korman, Anne Bancroft; *D:* Mel Brooks; *W:* Mel Brooks, Rudy DeLuca, Steve Haberman; *C:* Michael D. O'Shea; *M:* Hummie Mann. COL

Dracula/Garden of Eden 🐾🐾 1928
The abridged version of the chilling vampire film "Nosferatu" is coupled with "The Garden of Eden," in which Tini Le Brun meets her Prince Charming while vacationing with her Baroness friend. Silent. **52m/B VHS, Beta.** Max Schreck, Alexander Granach, Corine Griffith, Charles Ray, Louise Dresser. CCB

Dracula Has Risen from the Grave 🐾🐾½ 1968 (G) Lee's Dracula is foiled by the local priest before he can drain the blood from innocent villagers. Effectively gory. One of the Hammer series of Dracula films followed by "Taste the Blood of Dracula." **92m/C VHS.** *GB* Christopher Lee, Rupert Davies, Veronica Carlson, Barbara Ewing, Barry Andrews, Michael Ripper, Ewan Hooper, Marion Mathie; *D:* Freddie Francis; *W:* John Elder; *C:* Arthur Grant; *M:* James Bernard. WAR

Dracula, Prince of Darkness 🐾🐾
The Bloody Scream of Dracula; Disciple of Dracula; Revenge of Dracula 1966 Sequel to 1958's "Horror of Dracula" finds the Count (Lee) extending his hospitality at Castle Dracula to four unwary tourists, one of whom is immediately killed for his blood. Then Dracula takes the dead man's wife (Shelley) and turns her into a vampire and the gruesome twosome go after the remaining couple. Standard Hammer horror. **90m/C VHS.** *GB* Christopher Lee, Barbara Shelley, Andrew Keir, Francis Matthews, Suzan Farmer, Charles Tingwell, Thorley Walters, Philip Latham; *D:* Terence Fisher; *W:* John Sansom, John Elder; *C:* Michael Reed; *M:* James Bernard. VTR

Dracula Rising 🐾🐾½ 1993 (R) A modern-day art historian (Travis) turns out to have been a witch, burned at the stake, in a past life. She was also the blood-drinking Count's lost love. Now Dracula's a monk and when he sees this reincarnated beauty is he going to be able to keep his hands—er, fangs—off her? *CW:* Vampire violence and sexuality. **?m/C VHS.** Christopher Atkins, Stacy Travis, Doug Wert, Zahari Vatahov; *D:* Fred Gallo. NHO

Dracula (Spanish Version) 🐾🐾½ 1931 Filmed at the same time as the Bela Lugosi version of "Dracula," using the same sets and the same scripts, only in Spanish. Thought to be more visually appealing and more terrifying than the English-language counterpart. The only thing it's missing is a presence like Lugosi. Based on the novel by Bram Stoker. **104m/B VHS.** Carlos Villarias, Lupita Tovar, Eduardo Arozamena, Pablo Alvarez Rubio, Barry Norton, Carmen Guerrero; *D:* George Melford; *W:* Garrett Fort. USH

Dracula Sucks 🐾 1979 (R) A soft-core edit of a hardcore sex parody about Dracula snacking on the usual bevy of screaming quasi-virgins. **90m/C VHS, Beta.** James Gillis, Reggie Nalder, Annette Haven, Kay Parker, Serena, Seka, John Leslie; *D:* Philip Marshak. UNI, OM

Dracula: Up in Harlem WOOF! 1983
When the Prince of Darkness gets together with the people of the night, the Pentagon rolls out the heavy metal. This may suck your brain out. **90m/C VHS, Beta.** NO

Dracula vs. Frankenstein 🐾 *Assignment: Terror* 1969 An alien reanimates Earth's most infamous monsters in a bid to take over the planet. Rennie's last role. **91m/C VHS.** *IT GE SP* Michael Rennie, Paul Naschy, Karin Dor, Patty Shepard; *D:* Hugo Fregonese, Tulio Demicheli; *W:* Paul Naschy. UAV

Dracula vs. Frankenstein WOOF! *Blood of Frankenstein; They're Coming to Get You; Dracula Contra Frankenstein; The Revenge of Dracula; Satan's Bloody Freaks* 1971 (R) The Count makes a deal with a shady doctor to keep him in blood. Vampire spoof that's very bad but fun. Last film for both Chaney and Naish. Features a cameo by genre maven Forrest J. Ackerman. **90m/C VHS.** *SP* J. Carrol Naish, Lon Chaney Jr., Regina Carrol, Russ Tamblyn, Jim Davis, Anthony Eisley, Zandor Vorkov, John Joe Bob Briggs Bloom, Angelo Rossitto; *Cameos:* Forrest J. Ackerman; *D:* Al Adamson; *W:* William Pugsley, Sam M. Sherman; *C:* Paul Glickman, Gary Graver. NO

Dracula's Daughter 🐾🐾🐾 1936 Count Dracula's daughter, Countess Marya Zaleska, heads to London supposedly to find the cure to a mysterious illness. Instead she finds she has a taste for human blood, especially female blood. She also finds a man, falls in love, and tries to keep him by casting a spell on him. A good script and cast keep this sequel to Bela Lugosi's "Dracula" entertaining. **71m/B VHS, Closed Caption.** Gloria Holden, Otto Kruger, Marguerite Churchill, Irving Pichel, Edward Van Sloan, Nan Grey, Hedda Hopper; *D:* Lambert Hillyer; *W:* Garrett Fort; *C:* George Robinson. USH

Dracula's Great Love WOOF! *Gran Amore del Conde Dracula; Count Dracula's Great Love; Dracula's Virgin Lovers* 1972 (R) Four travellers end up in Dracula's castle for the night, where the horny Count takes a liking to one of the women. Left out in the sun too long. **96m/C VHS, Beta.** *SP* Paul Naschy, Charo Soriano; *D:* Javier Aguirre. SNC, MPI

Dracula's Last Rites WOOF! *Last Rites* 1979 (R) Blood-curdling tale of a sheriff and a mortician in a small town who are up to no good. Technically inept: film equipment can be spotted throughout. Don't stick your neck out for this one. **86m/C VHS, Beta.** Patricia Lee Hammond, Gerald Fielding, Victor Jorge; *D:* Domonic Paris. MGM, FCT

Dracula's Widow 🐾🐾 1988 (R) Countess Dracula, missing her hubby and desperately in need of a substitute, picks innocent Raymond as her victim. His girlfriend and a cynical cop fight to save his soul from the Countess' damnation. Directed by the nephew of Frances Ford Coppola. **85m/C VHS, Beta, Closed Caption.** Sylvia Kristel, Josef Sommer, Lenny Von Dohlen, George Stover; *D:* Christopher Coppola. HBO

Dragnet 🐾🐾½ 1954 Sgt. Joe Friday and Officer Frank Smith try to solve a mob slaying but have a rough time. Alexander plays the sidekick in "Dragnet" pre-Morgan days. Just the facts: feature version of the TV show that's suspenseful and well-acted. **88m/C VHS, Beta.** Jack Webb, Ben Alexander, Richard Boone, Ann Robinson; *D:* Jack Webb. USH

Dragnet 195? Detectives Joe Friday and Frank Smith make the streets of Los Angeles safe in this police series which ran from 1951-59. Two episodes per tape. **55m/C VHS.** Jack Webb, Ben Alexander. MOV, MRV

Dragnet 🐾🐾 1987 (PG-13) Semi-parody of the vintage '60s television cop show. Sgt. Joe Friday's straight-laced nephew and his sloppy partner take on the seamy crime life of Los Angeles. Neither Aykroyd nor Hanks can save this big-budget but lackluster spoof that's full of holes. **106m/C VHS, Beta, LV, Closed Caption.** Dan Aykroyd, Tom Hanks, Christopher Plummer, Harry (Henry) Morgan, Elizabeth Ashley, Dabney Coleman, Alexandra Paul; *D:* Tom Mankiewicz; *W:* Tom Mankiewicz, Alan Zweibel, Dan Aykroyd; *M:* Ira Newborn. USH

Dragon Force 🐾½ 1982 Korean martial artists fend off Japanese invaders in the 1930s. **101m/C VHS, Beta.** Kangjo Lee; *D:* Key-Nam Nam. CNG

Dragon Fury 🐾½ 1995 Evil dictator tries to conquer what remains of America in the year 2099—a world peopled by barbarians and victims of a deadly plague. Naturally, there's a martial arts hero around to stop him. **80m/C VHS.** Robert Chapin, Richard Lynch, Chona Jason, Deborah Stamble; *D:* David Heavener. MNC

Dragon Fury 2 🐾½ 1996 Futuristic action finds a heroic female struggling alone against a violent gang who want to rule the world (with the help of a computer chip). But a scientist unthaws an ancient warrior to help her out. Of course, things don't go exactly as expected. **90m/C VHS.** Mike Norris, Robert Chapin, Cathleen Ann Gardner, Cole Andersen, Walter Cole, Kayla Murphy; *D:* Bryan Michael Stoller; *W:* Parker Bostwick. SLI

Dragon Lord 🐾 1982 Young kung-fu hero (Chan) defends his village against greedy outlaws. Comic interludes tend to slow the action. **90m/C VHS.** Jackie Chan. TAI

Dragon Princess 🐾 197? When the king of karate and his dragon princess confront the blind master of the bloody blades, sparks fly. **90m/C VHS, Beta.** Sonny Chiba, Sue Shiomi. NO

Dragon Seed 🐾🐾½ 1944 The lives of the residents of a small Chinese village are turned upside down when the Japanese invade it. Based on the Pearl S. Buck novel. Lengthy and occasionally tedious, though generally well-made with heart-felt attempts to create Oriental characters, without having Asians in the cast. **145m/B VHS, Beta.** Katharine Hepburn, Walter Huston, Agnes Moorehead, Akim Tamiroff, Hurd Hatfield, J. Carrol Naish, Henry Travers, Turhan Bey, Aline MacMahon; *D:* Jack Conway. Nominations: Academy Awards '44: Best Black and White Cinematography, Best Supporting Actress (MacMahon). MGM, FCT

Dragon: The Bruce Lee Story 🐾🐾🐾 1993 (PG-13) Entertaining, inspiring account of the life of Chinese-American martial-arts legend Bruce Lee. Jason Scott Lee (no relation) is great as the talented artist, exuding his joy of life and gentle spirit, before his mysterious brain disorder death at the age of 32. Ironically, this release coincided with son Brandon's accidental death on a movie set. The martial arts sequences in "Dragon" are extraordinary, but there's also romance as Lee meets and marries his wife (Holly, who acquits herself well). Based on the book "Bruce Lee: The Man Only I Knew" by his widow, Linda Lee Caldwell. *CW:* Martial arts violence and sensuality. **121m/C VHS, LV, Letterbox, Closed Caption, DVD.** Jason Scott Lee, Lauren Holly, Robert Wagner, Michael Learned, Nancy Kwan, Kay Tong Lim, Sterling Macer, Ric Young, Sven Ole-Thorsen; *D:* Rob Cohen; *W:* Edward Khmara, John Raffo, Rob Cohen; *C:* David Eggby; *M:* Randy Edelman. Nominations: MTV Movie Awards '94: Breakthrough Performance (Lee). USH, BTV, FCT

Dragon vs. Needles of Death 🐾 1982 It's a battle to the finish against the unstoppable deadly needles in this Kung-Fu adventure. **86m/C VHS, Beta.** Don Chien, Wong Ting. FOX

Dragonard 🐾½ 1988 (R) Slaves on a West Indies island rebel against their cruel masters. **93m/C VHS, Beta, Closed Caption.** Eartha Kitt, Oliver Reed, Annabel Schofield, Patrick Warburton; *D:* Gerard Kikoine; *W:* R.J. Marx. WAR

Dragonfight 🐾½ 1992 (R) Corporations rule the world and vie for supremacy through gladiator combat in this action-adventure saga set in the near future. Fights are to the death and when the current champ refuses a new challenger the corporate honchos decide to provoke him into battle by having the challenger mow down innocent bystanders. Several execs also decide the slaughter has to stop but they may be the next targets. *CW:* Violence. **84m/C VHS, Beta.** Robert Z'Dar, Michael Pare, Paul Coufos, Charles Napier, James Hong, Alexa Hamilton, Fawna MacLaren. WAR

Dragonfly Squadron ✔✔ 1954 Korean war drama about pilots and their romantic problems. Never gets off the ground. 82m/C VHS. John Hodiak, Barbara Britton, Bruce (Herman Brix) Bennett, Jess Barker; *D:* Lesley Selander. *NO*

Dragonheart ✔✔½ 1996 (PG-13) Okay, get past the fact that Connery's Scottish burr is coming out of the teeth-filled mouth of an 18 ft. tall, 43 ft. long dragon and you'll be well on your way to enjoying this 10th-century fantasy. Knightly Bowen (Quaid) is the one-time mentor of evil-hearted King Einon (Thewlis) and it's up to him, Draco the dragon, feisty Kara (Meyer), and some fearful peasants to band together and free themselves from the king's tyranny. There's some slow spots but Bowen and Draco make for an amusing pairing and the dragon does seem, well, real. Work on Draco took more than a year of Industrial Light & Magic's expertise. *CW:* Action/violence. 103m/C VHS, LV, Closed Caption, DVD. Dennis Quaid, David Thewlis, Pete Postlethwaite, Dina Meyer, Julie Christie, Jason Isaacs, Brian Thompson, Wolf Christian, Terry O'Neill; *D:* Rob Cohen; *W:* Charles Edward Pogue; *C:* David Eggby; *M:* Randy Edelman; *V:* Sean Connery, John Gielgud. Nominations: Academy Awards '96: Best Visual Effects. *USH*

Dragon's Claw ✔ 198? A young man's parents are murdered, and he trains in shaolin skills in order to exact revenge. 90m/C VHS, Beta. Jimmy Liu, Hwang Cheng Li; *D:* Joseph Kuo. *GEM*

Dragons Forever ✔½ 1988 A big time lawyer is persuaded to work against a chemical plant who wants to take over a site used by local fisherman. Complications arise when he falls for the beautiful cousin of the fishery's owner. A comic king-fu battle between Chan, Hung, and Biao is the rousing finale. In Cantonese with English subtitles. 88m/C VHS. *CH* Jackie Chan, Yuen Biao, Sammo Hung; *D:* Sammo Hung. *TAI, FCT*

The Dragon's Showdown ✔ 1983 After witnessing the brutal decapitations of his parents, a young man learns Kung-Fu to avenge their deaths. 90m/C VHS, Beta. Dragon Lee; *D:* Godfrey Ho. *GEM*

Dragonslayer ✔✔✔ 1981 (PG) A sorcerer's apprentice suddenly finds himself the only person who can save the kingdom from a horrible, fire-breathing dragon. Extreme violence but wonderful special effects, smart writing, and a funny performance by Richardson. 108m/C VHS, Beta, LV. Peter MacNicol, Caitlin Clarke, Ralph Richardson, John Hallam, Albert Salmi, Chloe Salaman; *D:* Matthew Robbins; *W:* Matthew Robbins, Hal Barwood; *M:* Alex North. Nominations: Academy Awards '81: Best Original Score. *PAR, COL*

Dragonworld ✔✔½ 1994 (PG) Five-year-old Johnny McGowan is sent to Scotland to live with his grandfather. A wish for a friend has Johnny mysteriously awakening a baby dragon he names Yowler. Years later, the financially strapped adult Johnny agrees to loan Yowler to an amusement park only to find out the park's owner never intends to give Yowler back. Both baby dragon and young Johnny are unbearably cute. 86m/C VHS, Beta, Closed Caption. Sam Mackenzie, Courtland Mead, Brittney Powell, John Calvin, Andrew Keir, Lila Kaye, John Woodvine; *D:* Ted Nicolaou; *W:* Ted Nicolaou, Suzanne Glazener Naha; *M:* Richard Band. *PAR*

Dragstrip Girl ✔✔ 1957 An 18-year-old girl comes of age while burning rubber at the dragstrip—the world of boys, hot rods, and horsepower. A definite "B" movie that may seem dated. 70m/B VHS. Fay Spain, Steven Terrell, John Ashley, Frank Gorshin; *D:* Edward L. Cahn. *COL*

The Drake Case ✔✔ 1929 A slight courtroom drama made during the waning days of the silent era. You'll probably recognize Brit Lloyd from her later career. 56m/B VHS, Beta. Robert Frazer, Doris Lloyd, Gladys Brockwell. *GPV, FCT*

The Draughtsman's Contract ✔✔✔ 1982 (R) A beguiling mystery begins when a wealthy woman hires an artist to make drawings of her home. Their contract is quite unusual, as is their relationship. Everything is going along at an even pace until murder is suspected, and things spiral down to darker levels. A simple story turned into a bizarre puzzle. Intense enough for any thriller fan. 103m/C VHS. *GB* Anthony Higgins, Janet Suzman, Anne Louise Lambert, Hugh Fraser; *D:* Peter Greenaway; *W:* Peter Greenaway; *C:* Sacha Vierny; *M:* Michael Nyman. MGM, FCT

Draw! ✔✔ 1981 Two has-been outlaws warm up their pistols again in this old-fashioned Western. Star power and some smart moments make it worthwhile. Made for TV. 98m/C VHS, Beta. Kirk Douglas, James Coburn, Alexandra Bastedo, Graham Jarvis; *D:* Steven Hilliard Stern.

Dreadnaught Rivals ✔ 198? A student is taught by his drunken servant how to avenge himself on the culprits who kidnapped his girlfriend. Dubbed. 90m/C VHS, Beta. Sinon Lin, Kent Ko, Louisa Monk. *MOV*

Dream a Little Dream ✔✔ 1989 (PG-13) Strange teen transformation drama about an old man and his wife trying mystically to regain their youth. When they collide bikes with the teenagers down the street, their minds are exchanged and the older couple with the now young minds are transported to a permanent dream-like state. Same old switcheroo made bearable by cast. 114m/C VHS, Beta, LV, Closed Caption. Corey Feldman, Corey Haim, Meredith Salenger, Jason Robards Jr., Piper Laurie, Harry Dean Stanton, Victoria Jackson, Alex Rocco, Billy McNamara; *D:* Marc Rocco; *W:* Marc Rocco. ART, VES, HHE

Dream a Little Dream 2 ✔✔½ 1994 (PG-13) Friends Dinger Holefield (Haim) and Bobby Keller (Feldman) receive a mysterious package containing two pairs of sunglasses, which they discover have magic powers. The wearer of one pair is driven to do the bidding of the wearer of the second pair of specs—whether for good or evil. Naturally, there are evildoers who want the glasses as well. 91m/C VHS, Closed Caption. Corey Haim, Corey Feldman, Stacie Randall, Michael Nicolosi; *D:* James Lemmo; *W:* David Weissman, Susan Forman. *COL*

Dream Chasers ✔✔ 1984 (PG) A bankrupt old codger and an 11-year-old boy stricken with cancer run away together during the Great Depression. 97m/C VHS, Beta, Closed Caption. Harold Gould, Justin Dana. *FOX*

Dream Date ✔✔½ 1993 (PG-13) Lovely teenager is wooed by hip, playful suitor until trouble ensues when goofball sidekick enters the picture. Family entertainment. *CW:* Elements of sensuality. 96m/C VHS. Tempestt Bledsoe, Clifton Davis, Kadeem Hardison, Anne-Marie Johnson, Pauly Shore, Richard Moll; *D:* Anson Williams. *TRI, PMS*

Dream Demon ✔ 1988 The appearance of Wilhoite, a visiting American, disrupts the status quo at a spooky British manor where the charming Redgrave debates her impending marriage to wealthy rogue Greenstreet. Aside from a terrific opening dream sequence, most of the scary bits have been done before. 89m/C VHS. *GB* Jemma Redgrave, Kathleen Wilhoite, Timothy Spall, Jimmy Nail, Mark Greenstreet; *D:* Harley Cokliss. *WAR*

Dream for an Insomniac ✔✔½ 1996 (R) Irritating characters put the kibbosh on this attempt at 20-something romantic comedy. Whiny would-be actress Frankie (Skye) works at her Uncle Leo's (Cassel) cafe and hangs out with assorted, equally whiny friends. Frankie seems more interested in finding the "perfect" boyfriend than a career anyway and her interest is sparked by new guy David (a sweet Astin). Lots of overacting. Debut for writer/director DeBartolo. *CW:* Language. 108m/C VHS. Ione Skye, MacKenzie Astin, Jennifer Aniston, Seymour Cassel, Michael Landes; *D:* Tiffanie DeBartolo; *W:* Tiffanie DeBartolo; *C:* Guillermo Navarro. *COL*

A Dream for Christmas ✔✔✔ 1973 Earl Hamner, Jr. (best known for writing the "The Waltons") wrote this moving story of a black minister whose church in Los Angeles is scheduled to be demolished. Made for television. 100m/C VHS. Hari Rhodes, Beah Richards, George Spell, Juanita Moore,

Joel Fluellen, Robert DoQui, Clarence Muse; *D:* Ralph Senensky. ART, WAR

Dream Lover ✔✔ 1985 (R) Terrifying nightmares after an assault lead McNichol to dream therapy. Treatment causes her tortured unconscious desires to take over her waking behavior, and she becomes a violent schizophrenic. Slow, heavy, and not very thrilling. 105m/C VHS, Beta. Kristy McNichol, Ben Masters, Paul Shenar, Justin Deas, Joseph Culp, Gayle Hunnicutt, John McMartin; *D:* Alan J. Pakula; *W:* Jon Boorstin; *C:* Sven Nykvist. MGM

Dream Lover ✔✔ 1993 (R) Divorced architect Ray (Spader) meets and marries Lena (Amick), beautiful and seemingly perfect, who nonetheless warns him that she's just your average mixed-up gal. Suspense is supposed to come into play as Ray suspects Lena's been lying to him about her past. Visually appealing (considerably helped by the attractive leads) but good looks don't make up for the lack of substance and the minimal number of surprises expected in a thriller. Directorial debut of Kazan. Also available in an unrated version. 103m/C VHS, LV. James Spader, Madchen Amick, Frederic Lehne, Bess Armstrong, Larry Miller, Kathleen York, Blair Tefkin, Scott Coffey, William Shockley, Clyde Kusatsu; *D:* Nicholas Kazan; *W:* Nicholas Kazan; *M:* Christopher Young. *PGV*

Dream Machine ✔½ 1991 (PG) A childish teen comedy, based on that old urban legend of the lucky kid given a free Porshe by the vengeful wife of a wealthy philanderer. The gimmick is that the husband's body is in the trunk; the murderer is in pursuit. The tape includes an anti-drug commerical—but nothing against reckless driving, which the picture glorifies. 88m/C VHS, LV. Corey Haim, Evan Richards, Jeremy Slate, Randall England, Tracy Fraim, Brittney Lewis, Susan Seaforth Hayes; *D:* Lyman Dayton. *ART*

Dream Man ✔✔½ 1994 (R) Kris Anderson (Kensit) is a Seattle cop with the clairvoyant ability to see crimes as they're committed. But that doesn't stop her from getting involved with the handsome murder suspect (McCarthy) she's supposed to be investigating. *CW:* Violence, sexuality, language. 94m/C VHS, LV, Closed Caption. Patsy Kensit, Andrew McCarthy, Bruce Greenwood; *D:* Rene Bonniere; *W:* Michael Alexander Miller; *M:* Graeme Coleman. *REP*

Dream No Evil ✔½ 1975 A mentally disturbed woman is forced to commit bizarre murders to protect her warped fantasy world. 93m/C VHS, Beta. Edmond O'Brien, Brooke Mills, Marc Lawrence, Arthur Franz; *D:* John Hayes.

A Dream of Kings ✔✔✔ 1969 (R) Quinn is exceptional in this Petrakis story of an immigrant working to get his dying son home to Greece. Last film appearance for Stevens before committing suicide at age 36. 107m/C VHS. Anthony Quinn, Irene Papas, Inger Stevens, Sam Levene, Val Avery; *D:* Daniel Mann; *M:* Alex North. *WAR*

A Dream of Passion ✔✔½ 1978 (R) A woman imprisoned in Greece for murdering her children becomes the object of a publicity stunt for a production of "Medea," and she and the lead actress begin to exchange personalities. Artificial gobbledygook. 105m/C VHS, Beta. *GR SI* Ellen Burstyn, Melina Mercouri, Andreas Voutsinas; *D:* Jules Dassin; *W:* Jules Dassin. *NLC*

Dream Street ✔✔ 1921 A weak morality tale of London's lower classes. Two brothers, both in love with the same dancing girl, woo her in their own way, while a Chinese gambler plans to take her by force. Silent with music score. Based on Thomas Burke's "Limehouse Nights." 138m/B VHS, Beta. Tyrone Power Sr., Carol Dempster, Ralph Graves, Charles Mack; *D:* D.W. Griffith. *VYY*

The Dream Team ✔✔½ 1989 (PG-13) On their way to a ball game, four patients from a mental hospital find themselves lost in New York City after their doctor is knocked out by murderers. Some fine moments from a cast of dependable comics. Watch for numerous nods to "One

Flew Over the Cuckoo's Nest," another Lloyd feature. Keaton fans won't want to miss this one. 113m/C VHS, Beta, LV, Closed Caption. Michael Keaton, Christopher Lloyd, Peter Boyle, Stephen Furst, Lorraine Bracco, Milo O'Shea, Dennis Boutsikaris, Philip Bosco, James Remar, Cynthia Belliveau; **D:** Howard Zieff; **W:** Jon Connolly, David Loucka; **M:** David McHugh. *USH*

Dream to Believe ✍✍ 1985 Slice of the life of your typical high school coed—mom's dying, stepdad's from hell, sports injury hurts, and, oh yeah, championship gymnastic competitions loom. Designed to make you feel oh-so-good in that MTV kind of way. Reeves is most excellent as the girl's blushing beau. 96m/C VHS, Beta. Rita Tushingham, Keanu Reeves, Olivia D'Abo; **D:** Paul Lynch. *HHE*

Dream Trap ✍½ 1990 A young man is obsessed with a girl in his dreams. When he meets a girl who really exists, fantasy louses up every opportunity for the real thing. 90m/C VHS. Kristy Swanson, Sasha Jensen, Jeanie Moore; **D:** Tom Logan, Hugh Parks; **W:** Tom Logan. *NO*

Dream with the Fishes ✍✍½ 1997 (R) Suicidal voyeur Terry (Arquette) is about to jump from a bridge when terminally ill thief Nick (Adams) strikes a strange deal with him. In exchange for funding a few of Nick's fantasies, he will kill Terry in a less messy way. After various strange escapades (including an unplanned robbery and nude bowling), the pair arrive in Nick's hometown, where he attempts to resolve old issues with an ex-girlfriend and his abusive father. As Nick's health fades, Terry reexamines his wish to die. As the story develops, the cliches of both the buddy and road movie genres fall away, letting you actually care about both of these guys. In an homage to the independent spirit of movies of the early 70s, the film stock copies their grainy look, gradually dissolving over the course of the movie to a clearer look. Debut for director Finn Taylor. **CW:** Pervasive strong language, some drug content and sexuality. 97m/C VHS, **Closed Caption.** David Arquette, Brad Hunt, Kathryn Erbe, Cathy Moriarty, Allyce Beasley, Patrick McGaw, J.E. Freeman; **D:** Finn Taylor; **W:** Finn Taylor; **C:** Barry Stone; **M:** Tito Larriva. *COL*

Dreamchild ✍✍✍ 1985 (PG) A poignant story of the autumn years of Alice Hargreaves, the model for Lewis Carroll's "Alice in Wonderland." Film follows her on a visit to New York in the 1930s, with fantasy sequences including Wonderland characters created by Jim Henson's Creature Shop invoking the obsessive Reverend Dodgson (a.k.a. Carroll). 94m/C VHS, Beta. *GB* Coral Browne, Ian Holm, Peter Gallagher, Jane Asher, Nicola Cowper, Amelia Shankley, Caris Corfman, Shane Rimmer, James Wilby; **D:** Gavin Millar; **W:** Dennis Potter; **C:** Billy Williams; **M:** Max Harris, Stanley Myers. *MGM*

The Dreamed Life of Angels ✍✍
La Vie Revee des Anges 1998 Story of an unlikely friendship between two young women occupying the fringes of society in Lille. Optimistic vagabond Isa (Bouchez) travels from town to town picking up various menial jobs. Her latest is in a garment factory where she meets sullen loner Marie (Regnier), who agrees to let Isa stay with her. They half-heartedly get involved with the wrong guys, which leads the film to a downbeat and somewhat abrupt ending. French with subtitles. 113m/C VHS. *FR* Elodie Bouchez, Natacha Regnier, Gregoire Colin, Jo Prestia, Patrick Mercado; **D:** Erick Zonca; **W:** Erick Zonca, Roger Bohbot; **C:** Agnes Godard; **M:** Yann Thiersen. Cannes Film Festival '98: Best Actress (Bouchez), Best Actress (Regnier). *NYR*

Dreamer ✍✍ 1979 (PG) The excitement of bowling is exploited for all it's worth in this "strike or die" extravaganza. One of a kind. 86m/C VHS. Tim Matheson, Susan Blakely, Jack Warden, Richard B. Shull; **D:** Noel Nosseck; **W:** Larry J. Bischof; **M:** Bill Conti. *FOX*

Dreaming Lips ✍✍½ 1937 An orchestra conductor's wife falls in love with her husband's violinist friend. Tragedy befalls the couple. Bergner outstanding in a familiar script. 70m/B VHS, **Beta.** *GB* Raymond Massey, Elisabeth Bergner, Romney Brent, Joyce Bland, Charles Carson, Felix Aylmer; **D:** Paul Czinner, Lee Garmes; **C:** Lee Garmes. *VYY, CCB*

Dreaming of Rita ✍✍ 1994 Bob (Oscarsson) named his daughter Rita after long-lost love Sabine's resemblance to Hollywood goddess, Rita Hayworth. Now an elderly widower, Bob suddenly decides to try and find Sabine, taking off across the Swedish countryside. The unhappily married Rita (Lagercrantz), leaving husband and children behind, goes after him—and meets sympathetic hitchhiker Erik (Ersgard), who's happy to offer a little romance. Swedish with subtitles. 108m/C VHS. *SW* Per Oscarsson, Marika Lagercrantz, Patrick Ersgard, Philip Zanden; **D:** Jon Lindstrom; **W:** Jon Lindstrom, Rita Holst; **C:** Kjell Lagerros. *FCT, FRF*

Dreaming Out Loud ✍✍ 1940 Screen debut of popular radio team Lum 'n Abner. The boys get involved in several capers to bring progress to their small Arkansas town. Rural wisecracks make for pleasant outing. First in film series for the duo. 65m/B VHS, Beta. Frances Langford, Phil Harris, Clara Blandick, Robert Wilcox, Chester Lauck, Norris Goff, Frank Craven, Bobs Watson, Irving Bacon; **D:** Harold Young. *NOS, DVT, VYY*

Dreams ✍✍ *Kvinn odrom; Journey into Autumn* 1955 Unfocused film about the lives and loves of two successful women. Subtitled. 86m/B VHS, Beta, LV. *SW* Harriet Andersson, Gunnar Bjornstrand, Eva Dahlbeck, Ulf Palme; **D:** Ingmar Bergman; **W:** Ingmar Bergman. *HMV, NLC*

Dreams Come True ✍ 1984 (R) Silly young comedy-romance about two young lovers who discover the trick of out-of-body travel, and have various forms of spiritual contact while their bodies are sleeping. 95m/C VHS, Beta. Michael Sanville, Stephanie Shuford; **D:** Max Kalmanowicz.

Dreams Lost, Dreams Found ✍½ 1987 A young widow journeys from the U.S. to Scotland in search of her heritage. The third "Harlequin Romance Movie," made for cable television. 102m/C VHS. Kathleen Quinlan, Betsy Brantley, Charles Gray; **D:** Willi Patterson. *PAR*

Dreamscape ✍✍½ 1984 (PG-13) When a doctor teaches a young psychic how to enter into other people's dreams in order to end their nightmares, somebody else wants to use this psychic for evil purposes. The special effects are far more convincing than the one man-saves-the-country-with-his-psychic-powers plot. 99m/C VHS, Beta, LV. Dennis Quaid, Max von Sydow, Christopher Plummer, Eddie Albert, Kate Capshaw, David Patrick Kelly, George Wendt, Jana Taylor; **D:** Joseph Ruben; **W:** Chuck Russell; **C:** Brian Tufano; **M:** Maurice Jarre. *IME*

Dress Gray ✍✍✍ 1986 Fine, exciting adaptation of the Lucian K. Truscott IV novel about a coverup at an Eastern military academy. Baldwin is cadet Slaight, an upperclassman who finds more secrets than he can handle when a younger cadet (Cassidy), with whom he had an adversarial relationship, is murdered. He's torn between investigating the death or keeping quiet—for the sake of his career if not his life. Originally a television miniseries. 192m/C VHS, Beta. Alec Baldwin, Hal Holbrook, Eddie Albert, Lloyd Bridges, Susan Hess, Timothy Van Patten, Patrick Cassidy, Alexis Smith, James B. Sikking, Lane Smith; **D:** Glenn Jordan; **W:** Gore Vidal; **M:** Billy Goldenberg. *WAR*

Dressed for Death ✍½ *Straight on Till Morning; Til Dawn Do Us Part 1974* (R) A tale of true love gone bad as a woman is chased and murdered in her castle by the psychopath she loves. 121m/C VHS, Beta. *GB* Rita Tushingham, Shane Briant, Tom Bell, Annie Ross, Katya Wyeth, James Bolam, Claire Kelly; **D:** Peter Collinson.

Dressed to Kill ✍✍½ 1946 Sherlock Holmes finds that a series of music boxes holds the key to plates stolen from the Bank of England. The plot's a bit thin, but Rathbone/Bruce, in their final Holmes adventure, are always a delight. 72m/B VHS, LV, **Closed Caption.** Basil Rathbone, Nigel Bruce, Patricia Morison, Edmund Breon, Tom Dillon; **D:** Roy William Neill. *CNG, MRV, REP*

Dressed to Kill ✍✍½ 1980 (R) Contemporary thriller merges bombastic DePalma with a tense Hitchcockian flare. Sexually unsatisfied Dickinson ends up in bed with a man who catches her eye in a museum. Then she's found brutally murdered. Her son teams up with a prostitute to track and lure the killer into their trap. Suspenseful and fast paced. Dickinson's museum scene is wonderfully photographed and edited. DePalma was repeatedly criticized for using a stand-in during the Dickinson shower scene; he titled his next film "Body Double" as a rebuttal. 105m/C VHS, Beta, LV, Letterbox. Angie Dickinson, Michael Caine, Nancy Allen, Keith Gordon, Dennis Franz, David Margulies, Brandon Maggart; **D:** Brian DePalma; **W:** Brian DePalma; **C:** Ralf Bode; **M:** Pino Donaggio. *WAR, OM*

The Dresser ✍✍✍½ 1983 (PG) Film adaptation of Harwood's play (he also wrote the screen version) about an aging English actor/manager (Finney), his dresser (Courtenay), and their theatre company touring England during WWII. Marvelous showbiz tale is lovingly told, superbly acted. 119m/C VHS, Beta, LV, **Closed Caption.** Albert Finney, Tom Courtenay, Edward Fox, Michael Gough, Zena Walker, Eileen Atkins, Cathryn Harrison; **D:** Peter Yates; **W:** Ronald Harwood; **M:** James Horner. Golden Globe Awards '84: Best Actor—Drama (Courtenay); Nominations: Academy Awards '83: Best Actor (Courtenay), Best Actor (Finney), Best Adapted Screenplay, Best Director (Yates), Best Picture. *COL*

Dressmaker ✍✍½ 1956 French comedian Fernandel stars as a man's tailor who disguises dresses in secret so as not to compete with his dressmaker wife. Lightweight but entertaining. English subtitled. 95m/B VHS, Beta, LV. *FR* Fernandel, Francoise Fabian; **D:** Jean Boyer. *NOS, GVV, DVT*

The Dressmaker ✍✍½ 1989 Two sisters in WWII Liverpool must deal with their young niece's romantic involvement with an American soldier. Plowright and Whitelaw turn in fine performances as the two siblings with very different outlooks on life. 90m/C VHS. *GB* Joan Plowright, Billie Whitelaw, Pete Postlethwaite, Jane Horrocks, Tim Ransom; **D:** Jim O'Brien; **C:** Michael Coulter; **M:** George Fenton. *CTL*

Drift Fence ✍✍½ *Texas Desperadoes* 1936 Good early oater about a Texas ranger who goes in search of the man responsible for the murder of his buddy. Routine story saved by high quality production. Based on the story "Nevada" by Zane Grey. 57m/B VHS. Buster Crabbe, Katherine DeMille, Tom George Duryea Keene, Benny Baker; **D:** Otho Lovering; **W:** Stuart Anthony, Robert Yost. *DVT, GPV*

The Drifter ✍✍ 1932 A lumberjack makes sacrifices for the love between his brother and the lumbermill owner's daughter. 56m/B VHS, Beta, LV. William Farnum, Noah Beery Sr., Phyliss Barrington. *NOS, VYY, HEG*

The Drifter ✍✍½ 1988 (R) It's psychos, psychos everywhere as a beautiful young woman learns to regret a one-night stand. A good, low-budget version of "Fatal Attraction." Director Brand plays the cop. 90m/C VHS. Kim Delaney, Timothy Bottoms, Miles O'Keeffe, Al Shannon, Thomas Wagner, Larry Brand; **D:** Larry Brand; **W:** Larry Brand; **M:** Rick Conrad. *MGM*

The Driftin' Kid ✍ 1941 Poorly produced western has Keene posing as a rancher in order to nab a bunch of cattle rusters. So bad that even the sound of the punches are seconds off from the blows. 57m/B VHS. Tom George Duryea Keene, Betty Miles, Frank Yaconelli, Slim Andrews, Stanley Price, Glenn Strange; **D:** Robert Emmett Tansey; **W:** Robert Emmett Tansey, Frances Kavanaugh. *MOV*

Driftin' River 🎬🎬½ 1946 A shipment of horses bound for the Army is hijacked and the soldiers sent to investigate the theft are murdered. Investigators Deans and Ates are sent to take care of the culprits. Routine oater. **57m/B VHS.** Eddie Dean, Roscoe Ates, Shirley Patterson, William "Bill" Fawcett, Dennis Moore, Bob Callahan, Lottie Harrison, Forrest Taylor; **D:** Robert Emmett Tansey; **W:** Frances Kavanaugh. *GPV*

Drifting 🎬🎬½ *Nagooa* 1982 A controversial Israeli film about a homosexual filmmaker surviving in modern-day Jerusalem. First such movie to be made in Israel. In Hebrew with English titles. **103m/C VHS, Beta.** *IS* Jonathan Sagalle, Ami Traub, Ben Levine, Dita Arel; **D:** Amos Guttman. *FCT*

Drifting Souls 🎬🎬 1932 In order to save her father's life, a beautiful young woman marries for money instead of love. **65m/C VHS, Beta.** Lois Wilson, Theodore von Eltz, Shirley Grey, Raymond Hatton, Gene Gowing, Bryant Washburn; **D:** Louis King. *GPV*

Drifting Weeds 🎬🎬🎬½ *Floating Weeds; The Duckweed Story; Ukigusa* 1959 A remake by Ozu of his 1934 silent film about a troupe of traveling actors whose leader visits his illegitimate son and his lover after years of separation. Classic Ozu in his first color film. In Japanese with English subtitles. **128m/B VHS, Beta, LV.** *JP* Ganjiro Nakamura, Machiko Kyo, Haruko Sugimura, Ayako Wakao; **D:** Yasujiro Ozu. *HMV, MRV, FCT*

Driller Killer woof! 1974 (R) Frustrated artist goes insane and begins to kill off Manhattan residents with a carpenter's drill. Likewise, the plot is full of holes. **78m/C VHS, Beta.** Jimmy Laine, Carolyn Marz, Bob DeFrank; **D:** Abel Ferrara; **M:** Joe Delia. *NO*

Drive 🎬🎬 1996 (R) A technologically enhanced man, running from corporate hitmen, offers a stranger $5 million to drive him from San Franscisco to L.A. **CW:** Strong violent content and language. **99m/C VHS, LV, DVD.** Mark Dacascos, Kadeem Hardison, Brittany Murphy; **D:** Steve Wang. *APX*

Drive-In woof! 1976 (PG) A low-budget bomb showing a night in the life of teenage yahoos at a Texas drive-in. **96m/C VHS, Beta.** Lisa Lemole, Glen Morshower, Gary Cavagnaro; **D:** Rod Amateau. *COL*

Drive-In Massacre woof! 1974 (R) Two police detectives investigate a bizarre series of slasher murders at the local drive-in. Honk the horn at this one. **78m/C VHS, Beta, LV.** Jake Barnes, Adam Lawrence, Austin Johnson, Douglas Gudbye, Valdesta; **D:** Stu Segall; **W:** Buck Flower, John Goff. *NO*

Driven to Kill 🎬🎬 1990 No-name cast assemble in low-rent suspenser portraying the ugly side of love: bent on revenge, a man is out to obliterate the thugs who made his life a horrible experience highlighted by misery and boredom. **?m/C VHS.** Jake Jacobs, Chip Campbell, Michele McNeil. *PMH*

The Driver 🎬½ 1978 (PG) A police detective will stop at nothing to catch "The Driver," a man who has the reputation of driving the fastest getaway car around. Chase scenes win out over plot. **131m/C VHS, Beta, Closed Caption.** Ryan O'Neal, Bruce Dern, Isabelle Adjani, Ronee Blakley, Matt Clark; **D:** Walter Hill; **W:** Walter Hill. *FOX*

Driver's Seat woof! *Psychotic; Identikit* 1973 (R) Extremely bizarre film with a cult following that was adapted from the novel by Muriel Spark. Liz stars as a deranged woman trying to keep a rendezvous with her strange lover in Rome. In the meantime she wears tacky clothes and delivers stupid lines. **101m/C VHS, Beta.** *IT* Elizabeth Taylor, Ian Bannen, Mona Washbourne, Andy Warhol; **D:** Giuseppe Patroni Griffi.

Driving Force 🎬 1988 (R) In an effort to capitalize on the popularity of the "Road Warrior" movies, features a lone trucker battling a gang of roadhogs in another post-holocaust desert. Ultimately, runs off the road. **90m/C VHS, Beta, LV.** Sam Jones, Catherine Bach, Don Swayze; **D:** A.J. Prowse; **W:** Patrick Edgeworth.

Driving Me Crazy 🎬½ 1991 (PG-13) When an East German car inventor comes to America, it's laughs in the fast lane in this all-star comedy. **88m/C VHS, LV.** Billy Dee Williams, Thomas Gottschalk, Dom DeLuise, Milton Berle, Steve Kanaly, Michelle Johnson, Richard Moll, Morton Downey Jr., George Kennedy; **D:** Jon Turteltaub. *NO*

Driving Miss Daisy 🎬🎬🎬½ 1989 (PG) Tender and sincere portrayal of a 25-year friendship between an aging Jewish woman and the black chauffeur forced upon her by her son. Humorous and thought-provoking, skillfully acted and directed, it subtly explores the effects of prejudice in the South. The development of Aykroyd as a top-notch character actor is further evidenced here. Part of the fun is watching the changes in fashion and auto design. Adapted from the play by Alfred Uhry. **99m/C VHS, Beta, LV, 8mm, Letterbox, Closed Caption.** Jessica Tandy, Morgan Freeman, Dan Aykroyd, Esther Rolle, Patti LuPone; **D:** Bruce Beresford; **W:** Alfred Uhry; **M:** Hans Zimmer. Academy Awards '89: Best Actress (Tandy), Best Adapted Screenplay, Best Makeup, Best Picture; British Academy Awards '90: Best Actress (Tandy); Golden Globe Awards '90: Best Actor—Musical/Comedy (Freeman), Best Actress—Musical/Comedy (Tandy), Best Film—Musical/Comedy; National Board of Review Awards '89: Best Actor (Freeman); Writers Guild of America '89: Best Adapted Screenplay; Nominations: Academy Awards '89: Best Actor (Freeman), Best Art Direction/Set Decoration, Best Costume Design, Best Film Editing, Best Supporting Actor (Aykroyd). *WAR, FCT, BTV*

Drop Dead Fred woof! 1991 (PG-13) As a little girl, Lizzie Cronin had a manic, imaginary friend named Fred, who protected her from her domineering mother. When her husband dumps her 20 years later, Fred returns to "help" as only he can. Although the cast is fine, incompetent writing and direction make this a truly dismal affair. Plus, gutter humor and mean-spirited pranks throw the whole "heart-warming" premise out the window. Filmed in Minneapolis. **103m/C VHS, LV, Closed Caption.** Phoebe Cates, Rik Mayall, Tim Matheson, Marsha Mason, Carrie Fisher, Daniel Gerroll, Ron Eldard; **D:** Ate De Jong; **W:** Carlos Davis, Anthony Fingleton; **M:** Randy Edelman. *ART*

Drop-Out Mother 🎬🎬 1988 A woman gives up her executive position to become a housewife and full-time mom; expected domestic turmoil follows. Standard made for television fare and sort of a sequel to "Drop-Out Father," shown in 1982. **100m/C VHS.** Valerie Harper, Wayne Rogers, Carol Kane, Kim Hunter, Danny Gerard; **D:** Charles S. Dubin.

DROP Squad 🎬🎬 1994 (R) Not quite on target social satire revolving around buppie Burford Jackson, Jr. (La Salle), a token minority ad exec who's job is to push questionable products, using gross stereotypes, to the black community. His family's appalled and Buford becomes a prime target of D.R.O.P. (Deprogramming and Restoration of Pride), a vigilante organization that kidnaps erring black bretheren and leads them back to their cultural heritage. Frequently intense performances but the script raises some serious issues it doesn't deliver on. Based on the short story "The Deprogrammer" by David Taylor. **88m/C VHS, LV, Letterbox, Closed Caption.** Eriq La Salle, Vondie Curtis-Hall, Ving Rhames, Kasi Lemmons, Vanessa Williams, Nicole Powell, Afemo Omilami; **Cameos:** Spike Lee; **D:** David Johnson; **W:** David Johnson, Butch Robinson, David Taylor; **M:** Michael Bearden. *USH*

Drop Zone 🎬🎬½ 1994 (R) Routine action-thriller finds U.S. marshal Pete Nessip (Snipes) and his brother Terry (Warner) assigned to protect drug cartel snitch Earl Leedy (Jeter). The plane they're on is skyjacked by criminal Moncrief (Busey) who parachutes off with Leedy, Terry's killed, and while Pete's on suspension he decides to go undercover into the world of sky-diving with the aid of ex-con cutie Jessie (Butler). Plot holes are big enough to pilot a plane through but the stunts are good and Snipes is never less than

professional. **CW:** Some strong language and scenes of extreme violence. **101m/C VHS, Beta, Closed Caption.** Wesley Snipes, Gary Busey, Yancy Butler, Michael Jeter, Corin "Corky" Nemec, Kyle Secor, Luca Bercovici, Malcolm Jamal Warner, Rex Linn, Grace Zabriskie, Sam Hennings, Claire Stansfield, Mickey Jones, Andy Romano; **D:** John Badham; **W:** John Bishop, Peter Barsocchini; **M:** Hans Zimmer. *PAR*

The Dropkick 🎬🎬🎬 1927 Erstwhile D.W. Griffith leading man Barthelmess stars in this pigskin whodunnit: a coach's suicide looks like murder, and the prime suspect is the team's most valuable player. Cast includes ten bona fide university football players and Hedda "nobody's interested in sweetness and light" Hopper, while The Duke makes cameo. Webb later went on to direct a musical with Eddie Cantor and Rudy Vallee ("Glorifying the American Girl"). Silent. Based on the story "Glitter" by Katherine Brush. **62m/B VHS, Beta.** Richard Barthelmess, Barbara Kent, Dorothy Revier, Eugene Strong, Alberta Vaughn, Brooks Benedict, Hedda Hopper; **Cameos:** John Wayne; **D:** Millard Webb; **W:** Winifred Dunn. *GPV, FCT*

Drowning by Numbers 🎬🎬🎬½ 1987 (R) Three generations of women, each named Cissie Colpitts, solve their marital problems by drowning their husbands and making deals with a bizarre coroner. Further strange visions from director Greenaway, complemented by stunning cinematography courtesy of Sacha Vierny. A treat for those who appreciate Greenaway's uniquely curious cinematic statements. **CW:** Language, nudity, and sensuality. **121m/C VHS, LV.** *GB* Bernard Hill, Joan Plowright, Juliet Stevenson, Joely Richardson; **D:** Peter Greenaway; **W:** Peter Greenaway; **C:** Sacha Vierny; **M:** Michael Nyman. *ART*

The Drowning Pool 🎬🎬 1975 (PG) Newman returns as detective Lew Harper (of "Harper" by Ross MacDonald) to solve a blackmail case. Uneventful script and stodgy direction, but excellent character work from all the cast members keep this watchable. Title is taken from a trap set for Newman, from which he must escape losing most of his female companion's clothing. Adapted from a character created by Ross MacDonald. **109m/C VHS, Beta.** Paul Newman, Joanne Woodward, Anthony (Tony) Franciosa, Murray Hamilton, Melanie Griffith, Richard Jaeckel; **D:** Stuart Rosenberg; **W:** Tracy Keenan Wynn, Walter Hill; **C:** Gordon Willis; **M:** Charles Fox. *WAR*

Drug Wars 2: The Cocaine Cartel 🎬🎬 1992 Muddled drama featuring crazy unpredictable DEA agents executing the downfall of Colombia's Medellin drug kingpins. Average sequel to the award-winning miniseries "Drug Wars." **200m/C VHS.** Alex McArthur, Dennis Farina, Julie Carmen, John Glover, Karen Young, Michele Placido, Gustav Vintas, Geno Silva; **D:** Paul Krasny. *USH*

Drugstore Cowboy 🎬🎬🎬½ 1989 (R) A gritty, uncompromising depiction of a pack of early 1970s drugstore-robbing junkies as they travel around looking to score. Brushes with the law and tragedy encourage them to examine other lifestyles, but the trap seems impossible to leave. A perfectly crafted piece that reflects the "me generation" era, though it tends to glamorize addiction. Dillon's best work to date. Based on a novel by prison inmate James Fogle. **100m/C VHS, Beta, LV.** Matt Dillon, Kelly Lynch, James Remar, James LeGros, Heather Graham, William S. Burroughs, Beah Richards, Grace Zabriskie, Max Perlich; **D:** Gus Van Sant; **W:** Gus Van Sant, Daniel Yost; **M:** Elliot Goldenthal. Independent Spirit Awards '90: Best Actor (Dillon), Best Cinematography, Best Screenplay, Best Supporting Actor (Perlich); Los Angeles Film Critics Association Awards '89: Best Screenplay; New York Film Critics Awards '89: Best Screenplay; National Society of Film Critics Awards '89: Best Director (Van Sant), Best Film, Best Screenplay. *ART, FCT*

Drum woof! 1976 (R) This steamy sequel to "Mandingo" deals with the sordid interracial sexual shenanigans at a Southern plantation. Bad taste at its best. **101m/C VHS, Beta.** Ken Norton, Warren Oates, Pam Grier, Yaphet Kotto, Fiona Lewis, Isela

Vega, Cheryl "Rainbeaux" Smith; **D:** Steve Carver; **C:** Lucien Ballard. ART, VES, WAR

Drum Beat 🎭🎭 1954 An unarmed Indian fighter sets out to negotiate a peace treaty with a renegade Indian leader. Bronson is especially believable as chief. Based on historical incident. **111m/C VHS, Beta.** Alan Ladd, Charles Bronson, Marisa Pavan, Robert Keith, Rodolfo Acosta, Warner Anderson, Elisha Cook Jr., Anthony Caruso; **D:** Delmer Daves. NO

Drum Taps 🎭🎭 1933 Maynard saves the day for a young girl who is being pushed off her land by a group of speculators. **55m/B VHS, Beta.** Ken Maynard, Dorothy Dix, Frank "Junior" Coghlan, Kermit Maynard; **D:** J.P. McGowan. NOS, VDM, VYY

Drums 🎭🎭½ The Drum 1938 A native prince helps to save the British army in India from being annihilated by a tyrant. Rich melodrama with interesting characterizations and locale. **96m/C VHS, Beta, LV.** GB Sabu, Raymond Massey, Valerie Hobson, Roger Livesey, David Tree; **D:** Zoltan Korda.

Drums Along the Mohawk 🎭🎭🎭½ 1939 Grand, action-filled saga about pre-Revolutionary America, detailing the trials of a colonial newlywed couple as their village in Mohawk Valley is besieged by Indians. Based on the Walter Edmonds novel, and vintage Ford. **104m/C VHS, Beta, Closed Caption.** Henry Fonda, Claudette Colbert, Edna May Oliver, Eddie Collins, John Carradine, Dorris Bowdon, Arthur Shields, Ward Bond, Jessie Ralph, Robert Lowery; **D:** John Ford; **C:** Ray Rennahan. Nominations: Academy Awards '39: Best Color Cinematography, Best Supporting Actress (Oliver). FOX

Drums in the Deep South 🎭🎭 1951 A rivalry turns ugly as two former West Point roommates wind up on opposite sides when the Civil War breaks out. Historical drama hampered by familiar premise. **87m/C VHS, Beta.** James Craig, Guy Madison, Craig Stevens, Barbara Payton, Barton MacLane; **D:** William Cameron Menzies; **W:** Philip Yordan. NOS, MRV, VCI

Drums of Fu Manchu 🎭🎭🎭 1940 Fu Manchu searches for the scepter of Genghis Khan, an artifact that would give him domination over the East. Brandon smoothly evil as the Devil Doctor. Originally a serial in 15 chapters. **150m/B VHS, Beta.** Henry Kleinbach Brandon, Robert Kellard, George Cleveland, Dwight Frye, Gloria Franklin, Tom Chatterton; **D:** William English, John English. VCN, MLB

Drums of Jeopardy 🎭 Mark of Terror 1931 A father wanders through czarist Russia and the U.S. to seek revenge on his daughter's killer. Cheap copy of "Dr. Fu Manchu." **65m/B VHS.** Warner Oland, June Collyer, Lloyd Hughes, George Fawcett, Mischa Auer; **D:** George B. Seitz. NOS, SNC, DVT

Drums O'Voodoo woof! She Devil 1934 A voodoo princess fights to eliminate the town bad guy in this all-black feature that is greatly hampered by shoddy production values. **70m/B VHS, Beta.** Laura Bowman, J. Augustus Smith, Edna Barr; **D:** Arthur Hoerl. SNC

Drunken Angel 🎭🎭🎭 1948 Alcoholic doctor gets mixed up with local gangster. Kurosawa's first major film aided by strong performances. With English subtitles. **108m/B VHS, Beta.** JP Toshiro Mifune, Takashi Shimura, Choko Iida; **D:** Akira Kurosawa. DVT, MRV

Drunks 🎭🎭 1996 (R) Ensemble story set in a church basement in Manhattan where a diverse group of people go to their Alcoholics Anonymous meetings. Recovering alcoholic Jim (Lewis) has gone on a bender after his wife's death; Rachel's (Wiest) an overworked doctor with drug and alcohol dependencies; alcoholic Becky's (Dunaway) a divorcee with problem kids; Brenda's (Hamilton) an ex-heroin addict who's HIV positive; Joseph's (Rollins) still haunted by his son's death, which he caused while driving drunk. There's more and everyone gets their chance at the spotlight. Adapted from Lennon's play "Blackout." **CW:** Mature themes, language. **88m/C VHS.** Richard Lewis, Faye Dunaway, Dianne Wiest, Lisa Gay Hamilton, Howard E. Rollins Jr., Parker Posey, Spalding Gray, Amanda Plum-

mer, Calista Flockhart, George Martin, Anna Thomson; **D:** Peter Cohn; **W:** Gary Lennon; **C:** Peter Hawkins; **M:** Joe Delia. BMG

A Dry White Season 🎭🎭🎭 1989 (R) A white Afrikaner living resignedly with apartheid confronts the system when his black gardener, an old friend, is persecuted and murdered. A well-meaning expose that, like many others, focuses on white people. **105m/C VHS, Beta, LV, Closed Caption.** Donald Sutherland, Marlon Brando, Susan Sarandon, Zakes Mokae, Janet Suzman, Juergen Prochnow, Winston Ntshona, Susannah Harker, Thoko Ntshinga, Rowan Elmes; **D:** Euzhan Palcy; **W:** Colin Welland, Euzhan Palcy; **M:** Dave Grusin. Nominations: Academy Awards '89: Best Supporting Actor (Brando). FOX, FCT

Drying Up the Streets 🎭 1976 Tepid message tale of a police drug squad out to terminate the pattern that has young women turning to a life of prostitution and drugs. **90m/C VHS, Beta.** CA Len Cariou, Don Francks, Sarah Torgov, Calvin Butler; **D:** Robin Spry. ART, VES

D2: The Mighty Ducks 🎭🎭 The Mighty Ducks 2 1994 (PG) When an injury forces Gordon (Estevez) out of the minor leagues, he is tapped by promotor Tibbles (Tucker) to coach Team U.S.A. in the Junior Goodwill Games. Upon arriving in LA, the coach's head is turned by the money to be made in endorsements, and he soon gets a lesson in character-building (hey, it's Disney). The duck redux premise is lame, but kids will want ice time to see more of the hockey action that made the first a hit. **107m/C VHS, LV, Closed Caption.** Emilio Estevez, Michael Tucker, Jan Rubes, Kathryn Erbe, Shaun Weiss, Kenan Thompson, Ty O'Neal; **Cameos:** Kristi Yamaguchi, Kareem Abdul-Jabbar, Wayne Gretzky; **D:** Sam Weisman; **W:** Steven Brill; **M:** J.A.C. Redford. DIS

D3: The Mighty Ducks 🎭🎭 1996 (PG) Estevez proves that he'll quack for a dollar in the latest redux of the Disney franchise. This time the members of the rag-tag team are drafted by an exclusive prep school where, once again, they don't fit in. Go figure! Although billed as the star, Estevez only appears briefly at the beginning and end of the movie, leaving team captain Charlie (Jackson) as the focus of the story. Facing off against the new coach and the snooty elitist varsity team, the players learn lessons about maturity, responsibility and whacking people with sticks. In all probability, Disney will not be happy with just the hat trick, so don't be surprised if you see "D4: Mighty Old to Still Be Playing Kids" in a theatre near you soon. Cameo from professional Mighty Duck and fellow Disney employee Paul Kariya. **104m/C VHS.** Emilio Estevez, Jeffrey Nordling, Joshua Jackson, David Selby, Heidi Kling, Joss Ackland, Elden Ratliff, Shaun Weiss, Matt Doherty, Michael Cudlitz, Vincent A. Larusso, Colombe Jacobsen, Aaron Lohr, Christopher Orr; **D:** Robert Lieberman; **W:** Steven Brill, Jim Burnstein; **C:** David Hennings; **M:** J.A.C. Redford. TOU

Dual Alibi 🎭🎭 1947 Identical twin trapeze artists murder a colleague for a winning lottery ticket. Lom plays the brothers in a dual role. **87m/B VHS, Beta.** GB Herbert Lom, Terence de Marney, Phyllis Dixey, Ronald Frankau, Abraham Sofaer, Harold Berens, Sebastian Cabot; **D:** Alfred Travers. NOS, SNC

Dual Flying Kicks 🎭 1982 Chinese provincial mayor allies himself to a group of bandits amid much high kicking. **95m/C VHS, Beta.** Chen Hsing, Tan Tao Liang. WVE

Dubarry 🎭🎭½ 1930 Early sound version of the romantic experiences of Madame Dubarry, the alluring French heroine of David Belasco's "DuBarry." Talmadge's last film. **81m/B VHS, Beta.** Norma Talmadge, Conrad Nagel, William Farnum, Hobart Bosworth, Alison Skipworth; **D:** Sam Taylor. NOS, DVT, HEG

DuBarry Was a Lady 🎭🎭½ 1943 Skelton is a washroom attendant who daydreams that he is King Louis XV of France. Dorsey's band gets to dress in period wigs and costumes. ♫ Du-Barry Was a Lady; Do I Love You, Do I?; Friendship; Well, Did You Evah!; Taliostro's Dance; Katie Went to Haiti; Madame, I Love Your Crepes Suz-

ettes; Thinking of You; A Cigarette, Sweet Music and You. **112m/C VHS, Beta.** Lucille Ball, Gene Kelly, Red Skelton, Virginia O'Brien, Zero Mostel, Dick Haymes, Rags Ragland, Donald Meek, George Givot, Louise Beavers; **D:** Roy Del Ruth; **W:** Irving Brecher; **C:** Karl Freund. MGM, CCB

Dubeat-E-O 🎭½ 1984 A filmmaker races against time to finish making a documentary about the Los Angeles underground hardcore punk scene, and becomes immersed in the subculture. Somewhat of a haphazard exercise in filmmaking that is best appreciated by rock fans. **84m/C VHS, Beta.** Ray Sharkey, Joan Jett, Derf Scratch, Len Lesser, Nora Gaye; **D:** Alan Sacks. MVD

The Duchess and the Dirtwater Fox 🎭½ 1976 (PG) Period western strung together with many failed attempts at humor, all about a music-hall hooker who meets a bumbling card shark on the make. **105m/C VHS, Beta, LV.** George Segal, Goldie Hawn, Conrad Janis, Thayer David; **D:** Melvin Frank; **W:** Barry Sandler; **C:** Joseph Biroc; **M:** Charles Fox. FOX

The Duchess of Duke Street 🎭🎭🎭 1978 Cockney Rosa Lewis (Jones), a clockmaker's daughter born in 1869, goes into service with the ambition to become the best cook in London. She learns from a society household's French chef, where she was a kitchen maid, and eventually won success by an unexpected opportunity to cook for Edward, the Prince of Wales. A marriage-of-convenience and a mysterious legacy allows Rosa to buy the rundown Bentinck Hotel (actually the Cavendish) and cater fashionable dinners. By unceasing hard work, Rosa turns her establishment into an exclusive and discreet haunt for aristocrats, the wealthy, and various celebrities. British series on seven cassettes. **880m/C VHS.** GB Gemma Jones, Christopher Cazenove, John Welsh, George Pravda, June Brown, Victoria Plucknett, Richard Vernon, Doreen Mantle, Elizabeth Bennett, Donald Burton, John Cater, Holly DeJong, John Rapley; **D:** Cyril Coke, Gerry Mill, Simon Langton, Bill Bain, Raymond Menmuir; **W:** Julian Bond, Julia Jones, Rosemary Anne Sisson, Maggie Wadey, Jeremy Paul, Jack Rosenthal, Bill Craig, John Hawkesworth. SIG, PBS

The Duchess of Idaho 🎭🎭½ 1950 Williams tries to help her roommate patch up a romance gone bad, but ends up falling in love herself. MGM guest stars liven up an otherwise routine production. ♫ Baby Come Out of the Clouds; You Can't Do Wrong Doin' Right; Let's Choo Choo to Idaho; Of All Things; Or Was It Spring; Warm Hands, Cold Heart; Singlefoot Serenade; You Won't Forget Me. **98m/C VHS.** Esther Williams, Van Johnson, John Lund, Paula Raymond, Amanda Blake, Eleanor Powell, Lena Horne; **D:** Robert Z. Leonard. MGM

Duck Soup 🎭🎭🎭🎭 1933 The Marx Brothers satiric masterpiece (which failed at the box office). Groucho becomes the dictator of Freedonia, and hires Chico and Harpo as spies. Jam-packed with the classic anarchic and irreverent Marx shtick; watch for the mirror scene. Zeppo plays a love-sick tenor, in this, his last film with the brothers. **70m/B VHS, Beta, LV.** Groucho Marx, Chico Marx, Harpo Marx, Zeppo Marx, Louis Calhern, Margaret Dumont, Edgar Kennedy, Raquel Torres, Leonid Kinskey, Charles Middleton; **D:** Leo McCarey; **W:** Harry Ruby, Nat Perrin, Bert Kalmar, Arthur Sheekman; **M:** Harry Ruby, Bert Kalmar. National Film Registry '90. USH, FCT

DuckTales the Movie: Treasure of the Lost Lamp 🎭🎭½ 1990 (G) Uncle Scrooge and company embark on a lost-ark quest, ala Harrison Ford, for misplaced treasure (a lamp that can make the sky rain ice cream). Based on the daily Disney cartoon of the same name, it's more like an extended-version Saturday morning sugar smacks'n'milk 'toon. See it with someone young. **74m/C VHS, Beta, LV, Closed Caption. D:** Bob Hathcock; **W:** Alan Burnett; **M:** David Newman; **V:** Alan Young, Christopher Lloyd, Rip Taylor, June Foray, Chuck McCann, Richard Libertini, Russi Taylor, Joan Gerber, Terence McGovern. DIS

Dude Bandit 🎬🎬 **1932** An unscrupulous money-lender tries to gain control of a ranch but Gibson comes to the rescue. Gibson actually plays three roles: the rancher's best friend, an aw-shucks cowpoke disguise in order to find out what's going on, and the title character used to bedevil the crooks. **68m/B VHS, Beta.** Hoot Gibson, Gloria Shea. *VYY, VCI, VCN*

Dude Ranger 🎬🎬½ **1934** Well-acted Zane Grey story about an easterner who gets caught up in a range war and cattle rustling when he takes possession of some property out west. **58m/B VHS, Beta.** Smiley Burnette, George O'Brien, Irene Hervey; *D:* Eddie Cline. *VDM*

Dudes 🎬 **1987 (R)** Three city kids head for the desert and run afoul of some rednecks. Tired grade-6 revenge story. **90m/C VHS, Beta, LV.** Jon Cryer, Catherine Mary Stewart, Daniel Roebuck, Flea, Lee Ving, Calvin Bartlett, Pete Willcox, Glenn Withrow; *D:* Penelope Spheeris; *M:* Charles Bernstein. *NO*

Duel 🎬🎬🎬 **1971 (PG)** Spielberg's first notable film, a made-for-television exercise in paranoia. A docile traveling salesman is repeatedly attacked and threatened by a huge, malevolent tractor-trailer on an open desert highway. Released theatrically in Europe. **90m/C VHS, Beta.** Dennis Weaver, Lucille Benson, Eddie Firestone, Cary Loftin; *D:* Steven Spielberg; *W:* Richard Matheson; *M:* Billy Goldenberg. *USH*

Duel at Diablo 🎬🎬🎬 **1966** An exceptionally violent film that deals with racism in the Old West. Good casting; western fans will enjoy the action. **103m/C VHS, Closed Caption.** James Garner, Sidney Poitier, Bibi Andersson, Dennis Weaver, Bill Travers; *D:* Ralph Nelson. *MGM*

Duel at Silver Creek 🎬🎬½ **1952** A group of claim jumpers murder anyone who gets in their way, including the family of the Silver Kid (Murphy), who's deputized by Sheriff Lightning (McNally) to help him get the varmints. **76m/B VHS.** Audie Murphy, Faith Domergue, Stephen McNally, Susan Cabot, Gerald Mohr, Eugene Iglesias, Kyle James, Lee Marvin; *D:* Donald Siegel; *W:* Gerald Drayson Adams; *C:* Irving Glassberg; *M:* Hans J. Salter. *USH*

Duel in the Sun 🎬🎬🎬 **1946** A lavish, lusty David O. Selznick production of a minor western novel about a vivacious half-breed Indian girl, living on a powerful dynastic ranch, who incites two brothers to conflict. Selznick's last effort at outdoing his epic success with "Gone With the Wind." **130m/C VHS, Beta.** Gregory Peck, Jennifer Jones, Joseph Cotten, Lionel Barrymore, Lillian Gish, Butterfly McQueen, Harry Carey Sr., Walter Huston, Charles Bickford, Herbert Marshall; *D:* King Vidor; *C:* Ray Rennahan. Nominations: Academy Awards '46: Best Actress (Jones), Best Supporting Actress (Gish). *FOX*

Duel of Champions 🎬 *Orazi e Curiazi* **1961** It's ancient Rome, and the prodigal gladiator has come home. Now the family must have a duel to decide who will rule. **90m/C VHS, Beta.** *IT SP* Alan Ladd, Francesca Bett; *D:* Ferdinando Baldi. *NO*

Duel of Fists 🎬 **1989** When the owner of a boxing institute dies, he instructs his son in his will to go searching for his long-lost brother in Thailand. All he can go on is an old photograph and the knowledge that his brother is a Thai boxer. **111m/C VHS, Beta.** David Chiang, Chen Hsing, Ti Lung, Tang Ti. *MOV*

Duel of Hearts 🎬🎬 **1992 (PG-13)** Beautiful Caroline falls in love with wealthy Lord Vane Brecon, who unfortunately is accused of murder. When Caroline tries to help him clear his name she discovers he's hiding a number of secrets. Based on the romance novel "Duel of Love" by Barbara Cartland. Nothing too inspiring here, although regency romance fans will appreciate the attention to detail. Originally made for cable television. **95m/C VHS, Beta, LV, Closed Caption.** *GB* Alison Doody, Michael York, Geraldine Chaplin, Benedict Taylor, Billie Whitelaw, Virginia McKenna, Richard Johnson, Jeremy Kemp, Beryl Reid, Suzanna Hamilton, Jolyon Baker, Julie Kate; *D:* John Hough. *TTC*

Duel of the Iron Fist 🎬 **1972 (R)** Master of the martial arts must do battle with a brutal gang to save his own group from extinction. **98m/C VHS, Beta.** David Chiang, Ti Lung, Wang Ping, Yu Hui. *HHT*

Duel of the Seven Tigers 🎬🎬 **1980** Nine of the world's greatest Kung Fu and Karate exponents team up in this martial arts spectacular. **80m/C VHS, Beta.** Cliff Lok, Ka Sa Fa, Chio Chi Ling, Lam Men Wei, Yang Pan Pan, Charlie Chan. *TWE*

The Duellists 🎬🎬🎬 **1977 (PG)** A beautifully photographed picture about the long-running feud between two French officers during the Napoleonic wars. Based on "The Duel" by Joseph Conrad. **101m/C VHS, Beta, LV, Letterbox.** *GB* Keith Carradine, Harvey Keitel, Albert Finney, Edward Fox, Tom Conti, Christina Raines, Diana Quick; *D:* Ridley Scott. *PAR*

Duet for One 🎬🎬 **1986 (R)** A famous concert violinist learns she is suffering from multiple sclerosis and is slowly losing her ability to play. Convinced that her life is meaningless without music, she self-destructively drifts into bitter isolation. From the play by Tom Kempinski. **108m/C VHS, Beta.** Julie Andrews, Max von Sydow, Alan Bates, Liam Neeson; *D:* Andrei Konchalovsky. *MGM*

The Duke Is Tops 🎬🎬½ **1938** In Horne's earliest existing film appearance, she's off to attempt the "big-time," while her boyfriend joins a traveling medicine show. ♫I Know You Remember. **80m/C VHS, Beta.** Ralph Cooper, Lena Horne, Marie Bryant. *NOS, MRV, VCN*

Duke of the Derby 🎬🎬 *Le Gentleman d'Epsom* **1962** A scheming racehorse handicapper bets over his head and ruins his higher-than-means lifestyle. In French with English subtitles. **83m/C VHS, Beta.** *FR* Jean Gabin; *D:* Gilles Grangier. *FCT, DVT, HEG*

Dumb & Dumber 🎬🎬½ **1994 (PG-13)** Moronic limo driver Lloyd Christmas (Carrey) and equally dense dog groomer Harry Dunne (Daniels) travel (in the hilarious "sheep dog" van) from Rhode Island to Colorado—at one point going east!—to return a briefcase full of cash to a beautiful socialite (Holly). Engaging in all sorts of gross-out bathroom, bodily function, and slapstick humor, this one will definitely not appeal to the stuffy critic or arthouse snob. It will provide plenty of laughs, however embarrassingly rendered, for everyone else. Daniels proves a convincing dimwit sidekick, while Carrey mugs shamelessly. Occasional "Seinfeld" writer Farrelly makes his directorial debut. **CW:** Off-color humor. **110m/C VHS, LV, Closed Caption, DVD.** Jim Carrey, Jeff Daniels, Lauren Holly, Teri Garr, Karen Duffy, Mike Starr, Charles Rocket, Victoria Rowell, Felton Perry, Harland Williams; *D:* Peter Farrelly; *W:* Peter Farrelly, Bennett Yellin, Bobby Farrelly; *M:* Todd Rundgren. MTV Movie Awards '95: Best Comedic Performance (Carrey), Best Kiss (Jim Carrey/Lauren Holly); Blockbuster Entertainment Awards '96: Comedy Actor, Video (Carrey); Nominations: MTV Movie Awards '95: Best On-Screen Duo (Jim Carrey/Jeff Daniels). *TTC, NLC*

Dumb Waiter 🎬 **1987** A mini-play by Harold Pinter about two hitmen awaiting instructions for a job in an empty boardinghouse, and getting comically mixed messages. Made for television. **60m/C VHS, Beta.** John Travolta, Tom Conti; *D:* Robert Altman; *W:* Harold Pinter.

Dumbo 🎬🎬🎬🎬 **1941** Animated Disney classic about a baby elephant growing up in the circus who is ridiculed for his large ears, until he discovers he can fly. The little elephant who could fly then becomes a circus star. Expressively and imaginatively animated, highlighted by the hallucinatory dancing pink elephants sequence. Endearing songs by Frank Churchill, Oliver Wallace, and Ned Washington, including "Baby Mine," "Pink Elephants on Parade," and "I See an Elephant Fly." **63m/C VHS, Beta, LV, Closed Caption.** *D:* Ben Sharpsteen; *W:* Joe Grant, Dick Huemer; *M:* Frank Churchill, Oliver Wallace; *V:* Sterling Holloway, Edward Brophy, Verna Felton, Herman Bing, Cliff Edwards. Academy Awards '41: Scoring of a Musical; Nominations: Academy Awards '41: Best Song ("Baby Mine"). *DIS, SCH*

The Dummy Talks 🎬🎬 **1943** When a ventriloquist is murdered, a midget goes undercover as a dummy to find the killer. Watch closely and you might see his lips move. **85m/B VHS, Beta.** *GB* Jack Warner, Claude Hulbert, Beryl Orde, Derna-Hazell, Ivy Benson, Manning Whiley; *D:* Oswald Mitchell. *SNC*

Dune 🎬🎬 **1984 (PG-13)** Lynch sci-fi opus based on the Frank Herbert novel boasting great set design, muddled scripting, and a good cast. The story: controlling the spice drug of Arrakis permits control of the universe in the year 10991. Paul, the heir of the Atreides family, leads the Freemen in a revolt against the evil Harkhonens who have violently seized control of Arrakis, also known as Dune, the desert planet. That's as clear as it ever gets. **137m/C VHS, Beta, LV, Closed Caption, DVD.** Kyle MacLachlan, Francesca Annis, Jose Ferrer, Sting, Max von Sydow, Juergen Prochnow, Linda Hunt, Freddie Jones, Dean Stockwell, Virginia Madsen, Brad Dourif, Kenneth McMillan, Silvana Mangano, Jack Nance, Sian Phillips, Paul Smith, Richard Jordan, Everett McGill, Sean Young; *D:* David Lynch; *W:* David Lynch; *M:* Brian Eno. Nominations: Academy Awards '84: Best Sound. *USH, FCT*

Dune Warriors 🎬½ **1991 (R)** Earth is a parched planet in the year 2040. Renegade bands cruise the desert, making short shrift of civilized people who band together in remote villages. When peaceful farmer Carradine's family falls prey to the pillagers, surely he and the most evil warlord of all must clash. Good action and stunts, if the dummy plot doesn't get you first. **CW:** Some language, graphic violence, and sensuality. **77m/C VHS, LV.** David Carradine, Richard Hill, Luke Askew, Jillian McWhirter, Blake Boyd; *D:* Cirio H. Santiago. *COL*

The Dunera Boys 🎬🎬🎬 **1985 (R)** Hoskins shines in this story about Viennese Jews who, at the onset of WWII, escape to England where they are suspected as German spies. Subsequently, the British shipped them all to an Australian prison camp, where they recreated in peace their Viennese lifestyle. **150m/C VHS, Beta, LV.** *AU* Bob Hoskins, Joe Spano, Warren Mitchell, Joseph Furst, Moshe Kedem, Dita Cobb, John Meillon, Mary-Anne Fahey, Simon Chilvers, Steven Vidler; *D:* Sam Lewin.

Dungeon of Harrow 🎬 **1964** Unbelievably cheap tale of shipwrecked comrades who encounter a maniacal family on an otherwise deserted island. Not your stranded-on-a-desert-island fantasy come true. Filmed in San Antonio; a harrowing bore. **74m/B VHS.** Russ Harvey, Helen Hogan, Bill McNulty; *D:* Pat Boyette. *SNC*

Dungeonmaster 🎬½ *Ragewar* **1983 (PG-13)** A warlord forces a computer wiz to participate in a bizarre "Dungeons and Dragons" styled game in order to save a girl held captive. Consists of seven segments, each by a different director. Save yourself the trouble. **80m/C VHS, Beta, LV.** Jeffrey Byron, Richard Moll, Leslie Wing, Danny Dick; *D:* Jonn Carl Buechler, Charles Band, David Allen, Stephen Ford, Peter Manoogian, Ted Nicolaou, Rosemarie Turko; *W:* Allen Actor; *M:* Richard Band. *ART*

Dunston Checks In 🎬🎬½ **1995 (PG)** This just in: Hollywood thinks monkeys are funny. But, as far as "stupid people learn important life lessons from a monkey who wears clothes" movies go, this one's not bad. Robert Grant (Alexander) is the manager of a five-star hotel. His Leona Helmsley-esque boss (Dunaway) is convinced that aristocratic guest Lord Rutledge (Everett) is a travel guide critic who is there to bestow an elusive sixth star on the hotel. Actually he's a jewel thief, and Dunston the orangutan is his accomplice. When Dunston flees from his abusive owner, he's adopted by Grant's two children. Together, Dunston and the kids are left to straighten out the whole mess. **88m/C VHS, LV, Closed Caption.** Jason Alexander, Faye Dunaway, Eric Lloyd, Rupert Everett, Graham Sack, Paul (Pee Wee Herman) Reubens, Glenn Shadix, Nathan Davis, Jennifer Bassey; **Cameos:** Paul (Pee Wee Herman) Reubens; *D:* Ken Kwapis; *W:* Bruce Graham, John Hopkins; *C:* Peter Collister; *M:* Miles Goodman. Nominations: Golden Raspberry Awards '96: Worst Supporting Actress (Dunaway). *FXV*

The Dunwich Horror ♂♂ 1970 Young warlock acquires a banned book of evil spells, starts trouble on the astral plane. Stockwell hammy. Loosely based on H. P. Lovecraft story. **90m/C VHS, Beta.** Sandra Dee, Dean Stockwell, Lloyd Bochner, Ed Begley Sr., Sam Jaffe, Joanna Moore, Talia Shire; **D:** Daniel Haller; **W:** Curtis Hanson, Henry Rosenbaum, Ronald Silkosky; **C:** Richard C. Glouner; **M:** Les Baxter.

Duplicates ♂♂ 1992 (PG-13) Harrison and Greist are a married couple whose young son has disappeared. When the boy is found he has no memory of his former life or parents. The couple discover he's the victim of secret experiments which transfer human memories into computer banks. Will they become the next targets? **CW:** Violence. **92m/C VHS, Beta, Closed Caption.** Gregory Harrison, Kim Greist, Cicely Tyson, Lane Smith, William Lucking, Kevin McCarthy; **D:** Sandor Stern. *PAR, PMS*

Dupont Lajoie ♂♂ *Rape of Innocence* 1974 At a tourist campground Lajoie (Carmet) accidentally kills his son's girlfriend when she resists his sexual advances. To save his life he accuses Arabs of committing the crime and begins a racist campaign of vengeance. French with subtitles. **103m/C VHS.** *FR* Jean Carmet; **D:** Yves Boisset. *FCT*

Durango Valley Raiders ♂½ 1938 Sheriff is the leader of the outlaws, and a young cowboy finds out. **55m/B VHS, Beta.** Bob Steele; **D:** Sam Newfield. *VCN, DVT*

Dust ♂♂♂ 1985 A white woman in South Africa murders her father when he shows affection for a young black servant. Controversial and intense. **87m/C VHS, Beta.** *FR BE* Jane Birkin, Trevor Howard, John Matshikiza, Nadine Uwampa, Lourdes Christina Sayo, Rene Diaz; **D:** Marion Hansel; **W:** Marion Hansel; **M:** Martin St. Pierre. *TPV*

Dust Devil ♂♂ 1993 (R) Three travelers find themselves in Namibia's vast desert: a policeman, a woman on the run, and her abusive husband. They all have the misfortune of meeting up with a supernatural being known as the "Dust Devil," who kills humans in order to steal their souls and increase his other worldly powers. **87m/C VHS, Beta, Closed Caption.** *GB* Robert John Burke, Chelsea Field, Zakes Mokae, Rufus Swart, John Matshikiza, William Hootkins, Marianne Saegebrecht; **D:** Richard Stanley; **W:** Richard Stanley; **C:** Steven Chivers; **M:** Simon Boswell. *PAR*

Dust to Dust 1985 A short mystery made for British television about an aging gentleman who answers a request for correspondence and discovers ulterior, and evil, motives. **60m/C VHS, Beta.** *GB* Patricia Hodge, Michael Jayston, Judy Campbell.

Dusty ♂♂ 1985 Touching story of a wild dingo dog raised by an Australian rancher and trained to herd sheep. Filmed in the Australian bush and based on the children's book by Frank Dalby Davison. **89m/C VHS, Beta.** *AU* Bill Kerr, Noel Trevarthen, Carol Burns, Nicholas Holland, John Stanton; **D:** John Richardson. *FCT, FHE, BTV*

Dutch ♂½ 1991 (PG-13) Working class boob attempts to pick up his girlfriend's son from boarding school. Their trip together gives them an unexpected chance to connect, if they don't kill each other first. Silly premise from the Hughes factory has little innovation and uses type-casting instead of acting. **107m/C VHS, Closed Caption.** Ed O'Neill, Ethan Randall, JoBeth Williams; **D:** Peter Faiman; **W:** John Hughes. *IME*

Dutch Girls woof! 1987 Muddled mayhem as a horny high school field hockey team travels through Holland, cavorts about, and discovers the meaning of life. **83m/C VHS, Beta.** *GB* Bill Paterson, Colin Firth, Timothy Spall; **D:** Giles Foster.

Dutch Treat ♂ 1986 (R) Two nerds con a sultry, all-girl rock band into thinking they're powerful record company execs. Nobody's buying. **95m/C VHS, Beta.** Lorin Dreyfuss, David Landsberg; **D:** Boaz Davidson. *MGM*

Dutchman ♂♂♂ 1967 Film presentation of Amiri Baraka's one act play depicting the claustrophobic reality of the black man's situation in America. Black man shares subway conversation with a white woman who questions his race and middle class aspirations. Enraged, one takes the other's life. **55m/C VHS.** *GB* Al Freeman Jr., Shirley Knight; **D:** Anthony Harvey; **M:** John Barry. Cannes Film Festival '67: Best Film. *CAL*

D.W. Griffith Triple Feature ♂♂½ 1913 A collection of three short D.W. Griffith films including "The Battle of Elderbush Gulch," "Iola's Promise," and "The Goddess of Sagebrush Gulch." **50m/B VHS, Beta.** Mae Marsh, Lillian Gish, Mary Pickford, Blanche Sweet, Charles West; **D:** D.W. Griffith. *BAR, FCT*

The Dwelling Place ♂♂½ *Catherine Cook's The Dwelling Place* 199? Sixteen-year-old Cissie (Whitwell) struggles to hold her family together after the death of her parents in 1830's England. But her situation turns tragic when she's raped and left pregnant but drunken young aristocrat Clive (Rawle-Hicks), eventually giving the baby to be raised by Clive's father (Fox). Based on a novel by Catherine Cookson. **145m/C VHS.** *GB* Tracy Whitwell, James Fox, Edward Rawle-Hicks; **D:** Gavin Millar. *VCO, FCT*

The Dybbuk ♂♂♂½ 1937 A man's bride is possessed by a restless spirit. Set in the Polish-Jewish community before WWI and based on the play by Sholom Anski. Considered a classic for its portrayal of Jewish religious and cultural mores. In Yiddish with English subtitles. **123m/B VHS, Beta.** *PL* Abraham Morewski, Isaac Samberg, Moshe Lipman, Lili Liliana, Dina Halpern; **D:** Michal Waszynski. *IHF, FCT, NCJ*

Dying Game ♂♂ 1994 Sorority girls are being stalked and murdered and the detective investigating the crimes falls for the sorority's president. Now, he has to find the killer before his girlfriend becomes the next victim. **85m/C VHS.** Michael Hughes, Mathea Webb, D.J. Boozer; **D:** Kris Hughes. *SWI*

Dying Room Only ♂♂½ 1973 Travelling through the desert, a woman's husband suddenly disappears after they stop at a secluded roadside diner. Made for television flick is a real spooker. **74m/C VHS.** Cloris Leachman, Ross Martin, Ned Beatty, Louise Latham, Dana Elcar, Dabney Coleman; **D:** Philip Leacock; **W:** Richard Matheson; **M:** Charles Fox. *ART*

Dying to Remember ♂½ 1993 (PG-13) A fashion designer (Gilbert) regresses to a past life during hypnotherapy and discovers she was murdered in 1963. She flies to San Francisco to discover more about her past but finds that someone wants to keep things secret—and is willing to kill again. Tedious and predictable. **87m/C VHS, Closed Caption.** Melissa Gilbert, Ted Shackleford, Scott Plank, Christopher Stone, Jay Robinson; **D:** Arthur Seidelman; **W:** George Schenck, Frank Cardea, Brian Ross. *PAR*

The Dying Truth ♂♂ 1991 A wrongfully accused prisoner lies dying in his cell. Trouble is, he can't die in peace until he solves the murder they say he committed. Interesting mix of the supernatural and mystery, although perhaps not one of Carradine's more memorable roles. **80m/C VHS.** David Carradine, Stephanie Beacham, Stephen Greif, Stephan Chase, Larry Carby, Lesley Dunlop; **D:** John Hough. *NO*

Dying Young ♂½ 1991 (R) Muted romance has a wealthy leukemia victim hire a spirited, unschooled beauty as his nurse. They fall in love, but the film is either too timid or too unimaginative to mine emotions denoted by the title. Nobody dies, in fact, a grim ending (faithful to the Marti Leimbach novel on which this was based) got scrapped after testing poorly with audiences. The actors try their best, photography is lovely, and Kenny G's mellow music fills the soundtrack, but this is basically overmelodramatic drivel. Scott is the late Dewhurst's son. **CW:** Language. **111m/C VHS, Closed Caption.** Julia Roberts, Campbell Scott, Vincent D'Onofrio, Colleen Dewhurst, Ellen Burstyn, David Sel-

by; Dr Joel Oahumacher, W: Richard Friedenberg; C: Juan Ruiz-Anchia. *FOX*

Dynamite ♂ 1949 Romance explodes as two young demolitions experts vie for the same girl. Stand back. **68m/B VHS, Beta.** William Gargan, Virginia Welles, Richard Crane, Irving Bacon; **D:** William H. Pine. *NOS, DVT, HEG*

Dynamite and Gold ♂♂ *Where the Hell's the Gold?* 1988 (PG) Nelson and crew embark on a search for lost gold, battling hostile Indians, the Mexican army and assorted bandits along the way. A mediocre television movie. **91m/C VHS, LV.** Willie Nelson, Delta Burke, Jack Elam, Alfonso Arau, Gregory Sierra, Michael Wren, Gerald McRaney; **D:** Burt Kennedy; **W:** Burt Kennedy.

The Dynamite Brothers ♂ 1974 (R) Two tough guys, one a Hong Kong immigrant with martial arts skills, the other a brother from the streets of the ghetto, team up to rid Los Angeles of a Chinese crimelord. **90m/C VHS.** James Hong, Aldo Ray, Alan Tang, Timothy Brown, Carolyn Ann Speed, Don Oliver; **D:** Al Adamson; **M:** Charles Earland. *RHI*

Dynamite Canyon ♂♂ 1941 Average oater has villain Price committing murder in order to keep secret the location of a lode of copper. Standard western fare. **58m/B VHS.** Tom George Duryea Keene, Evelyn Finley, Sugar Dawn, Stanley Price, Kenne Duncan; **D:** Robert Emmett Tansey; **W:** Robert Emmett Tansey, Frances Kavanaugh. *DVT*

Dynamite Chicken ♂♂ 1970 (R) Melange of skits, songs, and hippie satire is dated. Includes performances by Joan Baez, Lenny Bruce, B.B. King, and others. **75m/C VHS, Beta.** Joan Baez, Richard Pryor, Lenny Bruce, Jimi Hendrix; **D:** Ernie Pintoff. *NO*

Dynamite Dan ♂½ 1924 A man knocks out the heavyweight boxing champion after he flirts with his girlfriend and decides to give up his day job to become a championship boxer. He is a success, and in the end he has to face the champion again. Will he win? **62m/B VHS, Beta.** Kenneth McDonald, Frank Rice, Boris Karloff, Eddie Harris, Diana Alden, Harry Woods, Jack Richardson; **D:** Bruce Mitchell. *GPV, LSV*

Dynamite Pass ♂♂ 1950 Offbeat oater about disgruntled ranchers attempting to stop the construction of a new road. **61m/B VHS, Beta.** Tim Holt, Richard Martin, Regis Toomey, Lynn (Mary Hart) Roberts, Denver Pyle; **D:** Lew (Louis Friedlander) Landers.

Dynamite Ranch ♂ 1932 Ranchers fight tooth and nail to keep their rights and property in this Maynard oater. **60m/B VHS, Beta.** Ken Maynard. *NOS, VCI, DVT*

Dynasty ♂♂ 1977 A leader of the Ming Dynasty is killed by evil Imperial Court eunuch and his son the monk sets out to avenge him. In 3-D. Run-of-the-mill kung-fu stunts. **94m/C VHS, Beta.** Bobby Ming, Lin Tashing, Pai Ying, Tang Wei, Jin Gang; **D:** Zhang Meijun. *BFV*

Dynasty ♂♂ 1982 Pulitzer Prize-winning author James Michener creates the usual sweeping saga of a family torn by jealousy, deception, and rivalry in love and business as husband, wife, and brother-in-law seek their fortune in the Ohio frontier of the 1820s. **90m/C VHS, Beta.** Sarah Miles, Harris Yulin, Stacy Keach. *TLF*

Dynasty of Fear ♂½ *Fear in the Night; Honeymoon of Fear* 1972 (PG) Matters get rather sticky at a British boys' school when the headmaster's wife seduces her husband's assistant. Together they conspire to murder her husband and share his fortune. **93m/C VHS, Beta.** *GB* Peter Cushing, Joan Collins, Ralph Bates, Judy Geeson, James Cossins, John Bown, Brian Grellis, Gillian Lind; **D:** Jimmy Sangster; **W:** Jimmy Sangster, Michael Syson; **C:** Arthur Grant. *REP*

E. Nick: A Legend in His Own Mind 1984 Satire of videos and magazines designed for adults. **75m/C VHS, Beta.** Don Calfa, Cleavon Little, Andra Akers, Pat McCormick; **D:** Robert Hegyes. *ART*

Each Dawn I Die 🎬🎬½ **1939** Cagney stars as a reporter who is a fervent critic of the political system. Framed for murder and imprisoned, he is subsequently befriended by fellow inmate, Raft, a gangster. Once hardened by prison life, Cagney shuns his friend and becomes wary of the system. Despite its farfetched second half and mediocre script, the film makes interesting viewing thanks to a stellar performance from Cagney. **92m/B VHS, Beta.** James Cagney, George Raft, George Bancroft, Jane Bryan, Maxie "Slapsie" Rosenbloom, Alan Baxter, Thurston Hall, Stanley Ridges, Victor Jory; **D:** William Keighley; **W:** Norman Reilly Raine. *MGM*

The Eagle 🎬🎬🎬 **1925** In this tale of a young Cossack "Robin Hood," Valentino assumes the persona of the Eagle to avenge his father's murder. The romantic rogue encounters trouble when he falls for the beautiful Banky much to the chagrin of the scorned Czarina Dresser. Fine performances from Valentino and Dresser. Silent, based on a Alexander Pushkin story. Released on video with a new score by Davis. **77m/B VHS, Beta, LV.** Rudolph Valentino, Vilma Banky, Louise Dresser, George Nicholls Jr., James Marcus; **D:** Clarence Brown; **C:** George Barnes; **M:** Carl Davis. *NOS, HBO, VYY*

The Eagle and the Hawk 🎬🎬🎬 **1933** Americans Jerry Young (March), and Mike Richards (Oakie) volunteer for flying duty with the British Army in 1918. Jerry is a heroic pilot but becomes depressed by the horrors of war, while gung ho Henry, who's serving as his observer/gunner, also becomes his rival. On leave, Jerry briefly finds solace with a society babe (Lombard) only to discover on his return that Henry's cockiness has gotten their buddy Mike killed. He denounces the war but Henry manages to ensure Jerry's status as a hero despite his actions. **73m/B VHS, Closed Caption.** Fredric March, Cary Grant, Jack Oakie, Carole Lombard, Guy Standing, Forrester Harvey, Kenneth Howell, Leyland Hodgson; **D:** Stuart Walker; **W:** Seton I. Miller, Bogart Rogers; **C:** Harry Fischbeck. *USH*

The Eagle Has Landed 🎬🎬🎬 **1977** (PG) Duvall, portraying a Nazi colonel in this WWII spy film, commissions Sutherland's Irish, English-hating character to aid him in his mission to kill Prime Minister Winston Churchill. Adapted from the bestselling novel by Jack Higgins. A restored version is available at 134 minutes. **123m/C VHS, Beta.** Michael Caine, Donald Sutherland, Robert Duvall, Larry Hagman, Jenny Agutter, Donald Pleasence, Treat Williams, Anthony Quayle; **D:** John Sturges; **M:** Tom Mankiewicz; **M:** Lalo Schifrin. *FOX, FCT*

The Eagle Has Two Heads 🎬🎬🎬 *L'Aigle a Deux Tetes; The Eagle with Two Heads* **1948** Set during the 19th century, poet/anarchist Marais sets out to assassinate the queen, but when he sees the beautiful monarch, it's love at first sight. Adapted from Cocteau's hugely successful play. In French with English subtitles. **93m/B VHS.** *FR* Edwige Feuillere, Jean Marais; **D:** Jean Cocteau; **W:** Jean Cocteau. *WBF*

Eagles Attack at Dawn 🎬½ **1974 (PG)** After escaping from an Arab prison, an Israeli soldier vows to return with a small commando force to kill the sadistic warden. **96m/C VHS, Beta.** *IS* Rick Jason, Peter Brown, Joseph Shiloah. *NO*

Eagle's Shadow 🎬 **1984** After a poor orphan boy rescues an aged beggar, the grateful old man tutors the lad in Snake-Fist techniques. **101m/C VHS, Beta.** Jackie Chan, Juan Jan Lee, Simon Yuen, Roy Horan; **D:** Yuen Woo Ping. *WVE*

Eagle's Wing 🎬½ **1979** John Briley, screenwriter of the award-winning epic "Gandhi," attempts to weave the threads of allegory smoothly in this white man vs. red man Western from England. The mediocre story finds Native American Waterston dueling white trapper Sheen in a quest to capture an elusive, exotic white stallion. **111m/C VHS, Beta.** *GB* Martin Sheen, Sam Waterston, Harvey Keitel, Stephane Audran, Caroline Langrishe; **D:** Anthony Harvey; **W:** John Briley; **C:** Billy Williams.

Early Cinema Vol. 1 **1919** A compendium of early silent shorts, mostly predating 1920, which includes: Melies' "Conquest of the North Pole"; Linder's "Man and the Statue" and "Max's Mother In Law"; Drew's "Auntie's Portrait"; Normand's "Mabel's Dramatic Career"; Mix's "An Angelic Attitude" Sennett and Swain's "Cowboy Ambrose"; Lloyd's "Just Neighbors" and Parrott's "Take the Air." **118m/B VHS, Beta.** Mabel Normand, Harold Lloyd, Sidney Drew, Max Linder, Paul Parrott, Tom Mix, Mack Swain; **D:** Mabel Normand, Harold Lloyd, Max Linder, Georges Melies, Mack Sennett. *FCT*

Early Days 🎬🎬 **1981** A cantankerous, salty, once-powerful politician awaits death. **67m/C VHS, Beta.** Ralph Richardson. *FOX*

Early Frost 🎬½ **1984** Near suspenseful whodunit centering around a simple divorce investigation that leads to the discovery of a corpse. **95m/C VHS, Beta, LV.** Diana McLean, Jon Blake, Janet Kingsbury, David Franklin; **D:** Terry O'Connor. *NO*

An Early Frost 🎬🎬🎬½ **1985** Highly praised, surprisingly intelligent made-for-television drama following the anguish of a successful lawyer who tells his closed-minded family that he is gay and dying of AIDS. Sensitive performance by Quinn in one of the first TV films to focus on the devastating effects of HIV. Rowlands adeptly displays her acting talents as the despairing mother. **97m/C VHS, Beta, LV.** Aidan Quinn, Gena Rowlands, Ben Gazzara, John Glover, D.W. Moffett, Sylvia Sidney; **D:** John Erman. *FCT, COL*

Early Summer 🎬🎬🎬 *Bakushu* **1951** A classic from renowned Japanese director Ozu, this film chronicles family tensions in post-WWII Japan caused by newly independent women rebelling against the social conventions they are expected to fulfill. Perhaps the best example of this director's work. Winner of Japan's Film of the Year Award. In Japanese with English subtitles. **150m/B VHS, Beta.** *JP* Ichiro Sugai, Chishu Ryu, Setsuko Hara, Chikage Awashima, Chieko Higashiyama, Haruko Sugimura, Kuniko Miyake, Kan Nihon-yanagi, Shuji Sano, Toyoko Takahashi, Seiji Miyaguchi; **D:** Yasujiro Ozu. *FCT*

The Earrings of Madame De... 🎬🎬🎬🎬 *Diamond Earrings; Madame De* **1954** A simple story about a society woman who sells a pair of diamond earrings that her husband gave her, then lies about it. Transformed by Ophuls into his most opulent, overwrought masterpiece, the film displays a triumph of form over content. In French with English subtitles. **105m/C VHS.** *FR* Charles Boyer, Danielle Darrieux, Vittorio De Sica, Lea di Lea, Jean Debucourt; **D:** Max Ophuls. Nominations: Academy Awards '54: Best Costume Design (B & W). *FCT, MRV, CVC*

Earth 🎬🎬🎬🎬 *Zemlya; Soul* **1930** Classic Russian silent film with English subtitles. Problems begin in a Ukrainian village when a collective farm landowner resists handing over his land. Outstanding camera work. Kino release runs 70 minutes. **57m/B VHS, Beta.** *RU* Semyon Svashenko, Mikola Nademsy, Stephan Shkurat, Yelena Maximova; **D:** Alexander Dovzhenko. *VYY, CCB, IHF*

Earth Entranced 🎬🎬 *Terra em Transe* **1966** A complex political lamentation from Rocha, the premiere director of Brazil's own new wave cinema. Here a writer switches his allegiance from one politician to another, only to find that he (and the masses) lose either way. In Portuguese with English subtitles. **105m/C VHS.** *BR* Jose Lewgoy, Paulo Gracindo, Jardel Filho, Glauce Rocha; **D:** Glauce Rocha; **W:** Glauce Rocha. *FCT*

Earth Girls Are Easy 🎬🎬½ **1989 (PG)** Valley girl Valerie is having a bad week: first she catches her fiancee with another woman, then she breaks a nail, then furry aliens land in her swimming pool. What more could go wrong? When the aliens are temporarily stranded, she decides to make amends by giving them a head-to-toe makeover. Devoid of their excessive hairiness, the handsome trio of fun-loving extraterrestrials set out to experience the Southern Cali-

fornia lifestyle. Sometimes hilarious sci-fi/musical, featuring bouncy shtick and a gleeful dismantling of modern culture. **100m/C VHS, Beta, LV, Closed Caption.** Geena Davis, Jeff Goldblum, Charles Rocket, Julie Brown, Jim Carrey, Damon Wayans, Michael McKean, Angelyne, Larry Linville, Rick Overton; **D:** Julien Temple; **W:** Julie Brown, Charlie Coffey, Terrance McNally; **M:** Nile Rodgers. *ART, VES*

Earth vs. the Flying Saucers 🎬🎬½ *Invasion of the Flying Saucers* **1956** Extraterrestrials land on Earth and issue an ultimatum to humans concerning their constant use of bombs and missiles. Peace is threatened when the military disregards the extraterrestrials' simple warning. Superb special effects by Ray Harryhausen. **83m/B VHS, Beta, LV.** Hugh Marlowe, Joan Taylor, Donald Curtis, Morris Ankrum; **D:** Fred F. Sears; **W:** George Worthing Yates, Bernard Gordon. *COL, MLB*

Earth vs. the Spider 🎬 *The Spider* **1958** Man-eating giant mutant (teenage ninja?) tarantula makes life miserable for a small town in general and high school partyers in particular. Silly old drive-in fare is agony for many, camp treasure for a precious few. **72m/B VHS.** Edward Kemmer, June Kennedy, Gene Persson, Gene Roth, Hal Torey, Mickey Finn; **D:** Bert I. Gordon; **W:** Laszlo Gorog, George Worthing Yates; **C:** Jack Marta. *COL, MLB*

Earthling 🎬🎬½ **1980 (PG)** A terminally ill Holden helps a young Schroder survive in the Australian wilderness after the boy's parents are killed in a tragic accident. Lessons of life and the power of the human heart are passed on in this panoramic, yet mildly sentimental film. **102m/C VHS, Beta.** *AU* William Holden, Rick Schroder, Jack Thompson, Olivia Hamnett, Alwyn Kurts; **D:** Peter Collinson; **W:** Lanny Cotler. *ART, VES*

Earthquake 🎬🎬 **1974 (PG)** Less-than mediocre drama centers on a major earthquake in Los Angeles and its effect on the lives of an engineer, his spoiled wife, his mistress, his father-in-law, and a suspended policeman. Filmed in much-hyped Sensurround—a technique intended to shake up the theatre a bit, but which will have no effect on your television set. Good special effects, but not enough to compensate for lackluster script. **123m/C VHS, Beta, LV.** Charlton Heston, Ava Gardner, George Kennedy, Lorne Greene, Genevieve Bujold, Richard Roundtree, Marjoe Gortner, Barry Sullivan, Victoria Principal, Lloyd Nolan, Walter Matthau, Scott Hylands; **D:** Mark Robson; **W:** Mario Puzo; **M:** John Williams. Academy Awards '74: Best Sound, Best Visual Effects; Nominations: Academy Awards '74: Best Art Direction/Set Decoration, Best Cinematography, Best Film Editing. *USH*

Earthworm Tractors 🎬🎬½ **1936** Ambitious tractor salesman Alexander Botts will do anything to make a sale. Brown excels as the fast-talking lead. Comedy is strengthened by its supporting cast. Based on characters first appearing in the "Saturday Evening Post." **63m/B VHS.** Joe E. Brown, June Travis, Guy Kibbee, Dick Foran, Carol Hughes, Gene Lockhart, Olin Howlin; **D:** Ray Enright. *NOS, RXM, HEG*

East and West 🎬🎬🎬 **1924** Morris Brown, a worldly New York Jew, returns home to Galicia with his daughter Mollie for a traditional family wedding. She teaches the young villagers to dance and box but meets her romantic match in a young yeshiva scholar who forsakes tradition to win her heart. Picon shines as the exuberant flapper. With English and Yiddish intertitles. **85m/B VHS.** *AU* Molly Picon, Jacob Kalish, Sidney Goldin; **D:** Ivan Abramson, Sidney Goldin. *NCJ*

East L.A. Warriors 🎬½ **1989** A mobster, Hilton-Jacobs, manipulates Los Angeles gangs in this non-stop action adventure. **90m/C VHS, Beta.** Tony Bravo, Lawrence-Hilton Jacobs, Kamar Reyes, William Smith; **D:** Addison Randall. *PAR*

East of Borneo 🎬½ **1931** Tropical adventure involving a "lost" physician whose worried wife sets out to find him in the jungle. She locates her love only to discover he has a prestigious new job tending to royalty and didn't want to be found.

76m/B VHS, Beta. Charles Bickford, Rose Hobart, Georges Renavent; **D:** George Melford. SNC, DVT, CAB

East of Eden 🎬🎬🎬🎬 1954 Steinbeck's contemporary retelling of the biblical Cain and Abel story receives superior treatment from Kazan and his excellent cast. Dean, in his first starring role, gives a reading of a young man's search for love and acceptance that defines adolescent pain. Though filmed in the 1950s, this story still rivets today's viewers with its emotional message. 115m/C VHS, Beta, LV, Letterbox, Closed Caption. James Dean, Julie Harris, Richard Davalos, Raymond Massey, Jo Van Fleet, Burl Ives, Albert Dekker; **D:** Elia Kazan; **W:** Paul Osborn; **M:** Leonard Rosenman. Academy Awards '55: Best Supporting Actress (Van Fleet); Golden Globe Awards '56: Best Film—Drama; Nominations: Academy Awards '55: Best Actor (Dean), Best Director (Kazan), Best Screenplay. WAR, BTV, HMV

East of Eden 🎬🎬½ 1980 Remade into a television mini series, this Steinbeck classic tells the tale of two brothers who vie for their father's affection and the woman who comes between them. Seymour is notable as the self-serving mother who abandons her babies to lead a disreputable life. Rife with biblical symbolism and allusions. 375m/C VHS, Beta, LV. Jane Seymour, Bruce Boxleitner, Warren Oates, Lloyd Bridges, Anne Baxter, Timothy Bottoms, Soon-Teck Oh, Karen Allen, Hart Bochner, Sam Bottoms, Howard Duff, Richard Masur, Wendell Burton, Nicholas Pryor, Grace Zabriskie, M. Emmet Walsh, Matthew "Stymie" Beard; **D:** Harvey Hart. VTR, ART

East of Elephant Rock 🎬½ 1976 In 1948, a young first secretary of the British Embassy returns from leave in England to a tense atmosphere in a colony in southeast Asia. Beautiful scenery can't make up for weak plot. 93m/C VHS, Beta. GB John Hurt, Jeremy Kemp, Judi Bowker, Christopher Cazenove; **D:** Don Boyd; **W:** Don Boyd.

East of Kilimanjaro 🎬🎬 The Big Search 1957 A freelance photographer and a doctor search frantically to find the carrier of a fatal disease near the slopes of the majestic Mt. Kilimanjaro. Routine killer virus flick filmed in Africa. 75m/C VHS. Marshall Thompson, Gaby Andre, Fausto Tozzi; **D:** Arnold Belgard.

East Side Kids 🎬🎬 1940 Early East Side kids. A hoodlum wants to prevent his brother from beginning a similar life of crime. 60m/B VHS, Beta. Leon Ames, Harris Berger, Dennis Moore, Joyce Bryant; **D:** Robert F. "Bob" Hill. NOS, MRV, DVT

East Side Kids/The Lost City 1935 The first East Side Kids film introduces some soon-familiar faces. "The Lost City" is a composite of all 12 episodes of the serial; edited for brevity. 135m/B VHS, Beta. Dennis Moore, Vince Barnett, William "Stage" Boyd, Kane Richmond. AOV

East Side, West Side 🎬🎬 1949 Stanwyck and Mason try hard to make this simple-minded soaper work, with mixed results. A wealthy couple experiences marital woes, aggravated by a ambitious young woman and a softhearted man suffering from unrequited love. Based on the popular novel by Marcia Davenport. 110m/B VHS. Barbara Stanwyck, James Mason, Ava Gardner, Van Heflin, Gale Sondergaard, William Frawley, Nancy Davis; **D:** Mervyn LeRoy; **C:** Charles Rosher; **M:** Miklos Rozsa. MGM

Easter Parade 🎬🎬🎬½ 1948 A big musical star (Astaire) splits with his partner (Miller) claiming that he could mold any girl to replace her in the act. He tries and finally succeeds after much difficulty. Astaire and Garland in peak form, aided by a classic Irving Berlin score. 🎵Happy Easter; Drum Crazy; It Only Happens When I Dance With You; Everybody's Doin' It; I Want to Go Back to Michigan; Beautiful Faces Need Beautiful Clothes; A Fella With an Umbrella; I Love a Piano; Snookey Ookums. 103m/C VHS, Beta, LV. Fred Astaire, Judy Garland, Peter Lawford, Ann Miller, Jules Munshin, Joi Lansing; **D:** Charles Walters; **W:** Sidney Sheldon; **C:** Harry Stradling; **M:** Irving Berlin. Academy Awards '48: Scoring of a Musical. MGM, HMV

Eastern Condors 🎬🎬 1007 At the end of the Vietnam War, a band of Chinese convicts are recruited by the U.S. Army (and promised their freedom) if they can destroy an ammunition dump before the Viet Cong can make use of it. Considered a Hong Kong version of "The Dirty Dozen," with the requisite level of high energy and blood. Dubbed or Chinese with English subtitles. 94m/C VHS. HK Sammo Hung, Joyce Godenzi, Yuen Biao, Haing S. Ngor; **D:** Sammo Hung. TAI, FCT

Easy Come, Easy Go 🎬🎬 1967 (PG) Elvis, as a Navy frogman, gets excited when he accidentally discovers what he believes is a vast sunken treasure. Music is his only solace when he finds his treasure to be worthless copper coins. 🎵Easy Come, Easy Go; The Love Machine; Yoga is as Yoga Goes; Sing, You Children; You Gotta Stop; I'll Take Love. 96m/C VHS, Beta. Elvis Presley, Dodie Marshall, Pat Priest, Elsa Lanchester, Frank McHugh, Pat Harrington; **D:** John Rich. PAR

Easy Kill 🎬½ 1989 A man takes the law into his own hands to exact revenge on drug lords. 100m/C VHS, Beta. Jane Badler, Cameron Mitchell, Frank Stallone; **D:** Josh Spencer. NO

The Easy Life 🎬🎬🎬 1963 Haunting film about a hedonistic man from a small Italian village who takes a mild-mannered student pleasure-seeking. The ride turns sour and the playboy is ultimately destroyed by his own brutality. 105m/B VHS. IT Vittorio Gassman, Catherine Spaak, Jean-Louis Trintignant, Luciana Angiolillo; **D:** Dino Risi. FST

Easy Living 🎬🎬½ 1949 Compromised melodrama about an over-the-hill football player who must cope with his failing marriage and looming retirement. Based on an Irwin Shaw story. 77m/B VHS, Beta, LV. Victor Mature, Lucille Ball, Jack Paar, Lizabeth Scott, Sonny Tufts, Lloyd Nolan, Paul Stewart; **D:** Jacques Tourneur. TTC

Easy Money 🎬🎬 1983 (R) A basic slob has the chance to inherit $10 million if he can give up his loves: smoking, drinking, and gambling among others. Dangerfield is surprisingly restrained in this harmless, though not altogether unpleasing comedy. 95m/C VHS. Rodney Dangerfield, Joe Pesci, Geraldine Fitzgerald, Jennifer Jason Leigh, Tom Ewell, Candice Azzara, Taylor Negron; **D:** James Signorelli; **W:** Rodney Dangerfield, Dennis Blair. VES

Easy Rider 🎬🎬🎬½ 1969 (R) Slim-budget, generation-defining movie. Two young men in late 1960s undertake a motorcycle trek throughout the Southwest in search of the real essence of America. Along the way they encounter hippies, rednecks, prostitutes, drugs, Nicholson, and tragedy. One of the highest-grossing pictures of the decade, undoubtedly an influence on two generations of "youth-oriented dramas," which all tried unsuccessfully to duplicate the original accomplishment. Psychedelic scenes and a great role for Nicholson are added bonuses. Look for the graveyard dancing scene in New Orleans. Features one of the best '60s rock scores around, including "Mean Streets" and "The Wanderers." 94m/C VHS, Beta, LV, 8mm. Peter Fonda, Dennis Hopper, Jack Nicholson, Karen Black, Toni Basil, Robert Walker Jr., Luana Anders, Luke Askew, Toni Basil, Warren Finnerty, Mac Mashorian, Antonio Mendoza, Sabrina Scharf, Phil Spector; **D:** Dennis Hopper; **W:** Terry Southern, Peter Fonda, Dennis Hopper; **C:** Laszlo Kovacs. New York Film Critics Awards '69: Best Supporting Actor (Nicholson); National Society of Film Critics Awards '69: Best Supporting Actor (Nicholson); Nominations: Academy Awards '69: Best Story & Screenplay, Best Supporting Actor (Nicholson). COL, CCB

Easy Street 🎬🎬🎬 1916 Chaplin portrays a derelict who, using some hilarious methods, reforms the residents of Easy Street. Chaplin's row with the town bully is particularly amusing. Silent with musical soundtrack added. 20m/B VHS, Beta. Charlie Chaplin; **D:** Charlie Chaplin. CAB

Easy to Love 🎬🎬½ 1953 Williams is in love with her boss, but he pays her no attention until a handsome singer vies for her affections. Set at Florida's Cypress Gardens, this aquatic

musical features spectacular water ballet productions choreographed by Busby Berkeley, and the title song penned by Cole Porter. 🎵Easy to Love; Coquette; Beautiful Spring; That's What Rainy Day is For; Look Out! I'm Romantic; Didja Ever. 96m/C VHS. Esther Williams, Van Johnson, Tony Martin, John Bromfield, King Donovan, Carroll Baker; **D:** Charles Walters; **W:** William Roberts. MGM

Easy Virtue 🎬🎬½ 1927 Hitchcock directs this adaptation of a Noel Coward play as a social melodrama. Larita is an unhappy married socialite with a lover. When her husband discovers her infidelty they divorce and she is marked as a woman of loose morals. Her reputation is not enhanced by her marriage to a younger man whose family diapproves. 79m/B VHS, Beta. GB Isabel Jeans, Ian Hunter, Franklin Dyall, Eric Bransby Williams, Robin Irvine, Violet Farebrother; **D:** Alfred Hitchcock. GPV, MRV, NOS

Easy Wheels 🎬🎬½ 1989 Like most decent biker movies, "Wheels" is propelled by bad taste and a healthy dose of existentialism nihilism. But there's an unusual plot twist in this parody. A biker named She-Wolf and her gang kidnap female babies and let wolves rear the children. Their elaborate plan is to create a race of super women who will subdue the troublesome male population. But can this "noble" plan succeed? 94m/C VHS, Beta, LV. Paul LeMat, Eileen Davidson, Marjorie Bransfield, Jon Menick, Mark Holton, Karen Russell, Jami Richards, Roberta Vasquez, Barry Livingston, George Plimpton; **D:** David O'Malley; **W:** Ivan Raimi, Celia Abrams, David O'Malley; **D:** John Ross.

Eat a Bowl of Tea 🎬🎬🎬 1989 (PG-13) Endearing light drama-comedy concerning a multi-generational Chinese family. They must learn to deal with the problems of life in America and in particular, marriage, when Chinese women are finally allowed to immigrate with their husbands to the United States following WWII. Adaptation of Louis Chu's story, directed by the man who brought us "Dim Sum." A PBS "American Playhouse" presentation. 102m/C VHS, Beta, LV, Closed Caption. Cora Miao, Russell Wong, Lau Siu Ming, Eric Tsiang Chi Wai, Victor Wong, Jessica Harper, Lee Sau Kee; **D:** Wayne Wang; **W:** Judith Rascoe; **M:** Mark Adler. COL

Eat and Run 🎬 1986 (R) A bloody comedy about a 400-pound alien with a taste for Italian (people, that is). 85m/C VHS, Beta. Ron Silver, R.L. Ryan, Sharon Schlarth; **D:** Christopher Hart. VTR

Eat Drink Man Woman 🎬🎬🎬½ 1994 (R) In Taipei, widowed master chef serves weekly feast of elaborate food and familial guilt to his three grown daughters, all of whom still live at home. They spend their time sorting out professional and romantic difficulties, searching for independence, and fulfilling traditional family obligations. Each character has a lot going on, but no one's story gets lost in the mix. Lee uses irony to great effect, introducing us to the culinary artist who has lost his sense of taste and has a daughter who works at a Wendy's. Food preparation scenes (more than 100 recipes are served up) illustrate a careful attention to detail (and are guaranteed to make you hungry). Lee's follow-up to "The Wedding Banquet" is a finely observed, comic tale of generational drift, the richness of tradition, and the power of love to redeem or improve. In Chinese with subtitles or dubbed. 123m/C VHS, LV. TW Sihung Lung, Kuei-Mei Yang, Yu-Wen Wang, Chien-Lien Wu, Sylvia Chang, Winston Chao, Ah-Leh Gua, Lester Chen; **D:** Ang Lee; **W:** Ang Lee, James Schamus, Hui-Ling Wang; **C:** Jong Lin; **M:** Mader. National Board of Review Awards '94: Best Foreign Film; Nominations: Academy Awards '94: Best Foreign Language Film; Golden Globe Awards '95: Best Foreign Film; Independent Spirit Awards '95: Best Actor (Lung), Best Actress (Wu), Best Cinematography, Best Director (Lee), Best Film, Best Screenplay. HMK

Eat My Dust 🎬🎬 1976 (PG) Teenage son of a California sheriff steals the best stock cars from a race track to take the town's heartthrob for a joy ride. Subsequently he leads the town on a wild car chase. Brainless but fast-paced. **89m/C VHS, Beta.** Ron Howard, Christopher Norris, Warren Kemmerling, Rance Howard, Clint Howard, Corbin Bernsen; **D:** Charles B. Griffith.

Eat the Peach 🎬🎬½ **1986** An idiosyncratic Irish comedy about two young unemployed rebels who attempt to break free from their tiny coast town by becoming motorcycle champs after seeing the Elvis Presley film "Roustabout." Together they create the "wall of death,"—a large wooden barrel in which they can perform various biker feats. **90m/C VHS, Beta, Closed Caption.** *IR* Stephen Brennan, Eamon Morrissey, Catherine Byrne, Niall Toibin, Tony Doyle, Joe Lynch; **D:** Peter Ormrod; **W:** Peter Ormrod, John Kelleher; **M:** Donal Lunny. *FOX*

Eat the Rich 🎬 **1987 (R)** A British farce about a group of terrorists who take over the popular London restaurant, Bastard's. Led by a former, disgruntled transvestite employee, they turn diners into menu offerings. Music by Motorhead. **89m/C VHS, Beta.** *GB* Nosher Powell, Lanah Pellay, Fiona Richmond, Ronald Allen, Sandra Dorne, Angie Bowie, Sandie Shaw; **Cameos:** Paul McCartney, Linda McCartney, Bill Wyman, Koo Stark, Miranda Richardson; **D:** Peter Richardson. *COL*

Eaten Alive 🎬🎬 *Death Trap; Starlight Slaughter; Legend of the Bayou; Horror Hotel Massacre* **1976 (R)** A Southerner takes an unsuspecting group of tourists into a crocodile death trap. Director Tobe Hooper's follow-up to "The Texas Chainsaw Massacre." Englund is more recognizable with razor fingernails as Freddy Krueger of the "Nightmare on Elm Street" films.**CW:** Contains graphic violence, nudity, sexual material. **96m/C VHS, Beta.** Neville Brand, Mel Ferrer, Carolyn Jones, Marilyn Burns, Stuart Whitman, Robert Englund, William Finley, Roberta Collins, Kyle Richards; **D:** Tobe Hooper; **W:** Marti Rustam, Alvin L. Fast, Kim Henkel; **C:** Robert Caramico; **M:** Wayne Bell.

Eating 🎬🎬½ **1990 (R)** Set in Southern California, women gather to celebrate birthdays for three of their friends who are turning 30, 40 and 50. As the party commences, women from two generations discuss their attitudes towards food and men...and discover hilarious parallels.**CW:** Language. **110m/C VHS, Beta, LV, Closed Caption.** Nelly Alard, Frances Bergen, Mary Crosby, Lisa Richards, Gwen Welles, Daphna Kastner, Elizabeth Kemp, Marlena Giovi, Marina Gregory, Toni Basil; **D:** Henry Jaglom; **W:** Henry Jaglom; **C:** Hanania Baer. *PAR*

Eating Raoul 🎬🎬🎬½ **1982 (R)** The Blands are a happily married couple who share many interests: good food and wine, entrepreneurial dreams, and an aversion to sex. The problem is, they're flat broke. So, when the tasty swinger from upstairs makes a pass at Mary and Paul accidentally kills him, they discover he's got loads of money; Raoul takes a cut in the deal by disposing of—or rather recycling—the body. This may just be the way to finance that restaurant they've been wanting to open. Wonderful, offbeat, hilariously dark comedy. **83m/C VHS, Beta.** Mary Woronov, Paul Bartel, Robert Beltran, Buck Henry, Ed Begley Jr., Edie McClurg, John Paragon, Richard Blackburn, Hamilton Camp, Bill Curtis, Susan Saiger; **D:** Mary Woronov, Paul Bartel; **W:** Paul Bartel, Richard Blackburn. *FOX*

Ebbtide 🎬🎬½ **1994 (R)** Lawyer Jeff Warren (Hamlin) takes on the case of a mother who says her son's died from chemicals dumped by the Poseidon Pacific Co. Jeff got the case when the previous lawyer died mysteriously but this doesn't stop him checking out the chemical company or its beautiful president. **90m/C VHS, Closed Caption.** Harry Hamlin, Judy McIntosh, Susan Lyons, John Gregg, Frankie J. Holden; **D:** Craig Lahiff; **W:** Robert Ellis, Peter Goldsworthy. *PAR*

Ebony Dreams **1980** WWII documentary focuses on the experience of female factory workers during and after the war. Five contemporary women relate their personal endeavors and struggles to retain their jobs once the war ended. Excellent use of newsreel footage and interesting interviews with the women. **85m/C VHS.** Philomena Nowlin; **D:** Bill Brame. *NO*

Ebony Tower 🎬🎬½ **1986** Based on the John Fowles novel about a crusty old artist who lives in a French chateau with two young female companions. They are visited by a handsome young man, thereby initiating sexual tension and recognizably Fowlesian plot puzzles. Made for British television. Features some partial nudity. **80m/C Beta.** *GB* Laurence Olivier, Roger Rees, Greta Scacchi, Toyah Wilcox; **D:** Robert Knights; **M:** Richard Rodney Bennett. *NO*

Echo Murders 🎬½ **1945** A Sexton Blake mystery wherein he investigates a mine owner's mysterious death, opening up a veritable can of murdering, power-hungry worms. **75m/B VHS, Beta.** David Farrar, Dennis Price. *NOS, VYY*

Echo Park 🎬🎬½ **1986 (R)** An unsung sleeper comedy about three roommates living in Los Angeles' Echo Park: a body builder, a single-mother waitress, and an itinerant songwriter. Charts their struggles as they aim for careers in showbiz. Offbeat ensemble effort. **93m/C VHS, Beta, LV.** *AU* Tom Hulce, Susan Dey, Michael Bowen, Richard "Cheech" Marin, Christopher Walker, Shirley Jo Finney, Cassandra Peterson, Yana Nirvana, Timothy Carey; **D:** Robert Dornhelm; **W:** Michael Ventura; **M:** David Rickets. *BAR*

Echoes 🎬🎬 **1983 (R)** A young painter's life slowly comes apart as he is tormented by nightmares that his stillborn twin brother is attempting to murder him. **90m/C VHS, Beta.** Gale Sondergaard, Mercedes McCambridge, Richard Alfieri, Ruth Roman, John Spencer, Nathalie Nell; **D:** Arthur Seidelman; **W:** Richard Alfieri, Richard J. Anthony; **C:** Hanania Baer. *NO*

Echoes in the Darkness 🎬🎬½ **1987** Television mini series based on the true-life Joseph Wambaugh bestseller about the "Main Line" murder investigation in Pennsylvania in 1979. Police are baffled when a teacher is murdered and her children vanish. Suspicion falls on a charismatic coworker and the school's principal. On two tapes. **234m/C VHS.** Peter Coyote, Robert Loggia, Stockard Channing, Peter Boyle, Cindy Pickett, Gary Cole, Zeljko Ivanek, Alex Hyde-White, Treat Williams; **D:** Glenn Jordan.

Echoes of Conflict 🎬🎬 **1989** The turbulent Middle East and Arab-Israeli tensions are spotlighted in three new wave films from Israel. Includes "The Cage," "The Movie," and "Don't Get Involved." In Hebrew with English subtitles. In color and black and white. **91m/C VHS.** *IS FCT, KIV*

Echoes of Paradise 🎬½ *Shadows of Peacock* **1986 (R)** After a series of earth-shattering events, a depressed woman journeys to an island where she falls for a Balinese dancer. Soon she must choose between returning home or beginning life anew in paradise. **90m/C VHS, Beta, LV.** *AU* Wendy Hughes, John Lone, Rod Mullinar, Peta Toppano, Steve Jacobs, Gillian Jones; **D:** Phillip Noyce.

The Eclipse 🎬🎬🎬½ *L'eclisse* **1966** The last of Antonioni's trilogy (after "L'Avventura" and "La Notte"), wherein another fashionable and alienated Italian woman passes from one lover to another searching unsuccessfully for truth and love. Highly acclaimed. In Italian with subtitles. **123m/B VHS, Beta.** *IT* Monica Vitti, Alain Delon, Francesco Rabal, Louis Seigner; **D:** Michelangelo Antonioni; **W:** Michelangelo Antonioni; **C:** Carlo DiPalma. *TPV, MRV, FCT*

Eclipse 🎬½ **1994** Sexual roundelay set in Toronto shortly before a total solar eclipse, which is apparently affecting all the generally listless characters in such a way that they meet and mate in joyless abandon. First feature for Podeswa. **96m/C VHS.** *CA GE* Von Flores, John Gilbert, Pascale Montpetit, Manuel Aranguiz, Maria Del Mar, Matthew Ferguson, Earl Pastko, Greg Ellwand, Daniel MacIvor, Kirsten Johnson; **D:** Jeremy Podeswa; **W:** Jeremy Podeswa; **C:** Miroslaw Baszak; **M:** Ernie Tollar. *FCT*

Ecstasy 🎬🎬½ *Extase; Ekstase; Symphony of Love* **1933** A romantic, erotic story about a young woman married to an older man, who takes a lover. Features Lamarr, then Hedy Kiesler, before her discovery in Hollywood. Film subsequently gained notoriety for Lamarr's nude scenes. In Czech with English subtitles. **90m/B VHS, Beta, 8mm.** *CZ* Hedy Lamarr, Jaromir Rogoz; **D:** Gustav Machaty. *VYY, NOS, MRV*

Ecstasy woof! **1984 (R)** Soft core fluff about a film director's wife's erotic adventures. **82m/C VHS, Beta.** Tiffany Bolling, Franc Luz, Jack Carter, Britt Ekland, Julie Newmar. *MGM*

Ed woof! **1996 (PG)** A must see for all fans of flatulent animatronic chimpanzees who play third base. Everyone else should stay away. LeBlanc (who should've been tipped off when they couldn't even get a real chimp to appear) plays Coop, a phenom pitcher stuck on a losing team in the minor leagues. After Ed the chimpanzee is bequeathed to the team by the late Mickey Mantle, (forgive them Mick, they know not what they do) he starts playing the hot corner like Brooks Robinson. Surprise! Ed becomes a national sensation, the team goes on a winning streak and sets up the showdown game climax. Most of the humor is derived from Ed tearing things up and passing gas, while LeBlanc yells in pop-eyed exasperation. Cameo from Tommy Lasorda playing a fat major league manager. **94m/C VHS, LV, Closed Caption.** Matthew LeBlanc, Jayne Brook, Bill Cobbs, Jack Warden, Doren Fein, Charlie Schlatter, Carl Anthony Payne II, Curt Kaplan, Zack Ward, Mike McGlone, James Caviezel, Valente Rodriguez; **D:** Bill Couturie; **W:** David Mickey Evans; **C:** Alan Caso; **M:** Stephen Endelman. Nominations: Golden Raspberry Awards '96: Worst Picture, Worst Screenplay. *USH*

Ed and His Dead Mother 🎬🎬 **1993 (PG-13)** Ed's just an average guy who happens to really love his mother. So much so that when she dies Ed tries to bring her back from the dead—and succeeds. Only death has made a few changes in Mom's personality. Now she's a bug-eating, chainsaw-wielding fiend. Just what's a good son supposed to do? **93m/C VHS, LV, Closed Caption.** Ned Beatty, Steve Buscemi, John Glover, Miriam Margolyes, Sam Jenkins; **D:** Jonathan Wacks; **W:** Chuck Hughes. *FOX*

Ed Wood 🎬🎬🎬½ **1994 (R)** Leave it to Burton to bring to the screen the story of a director many consider to be the worst of all time (he's at least in the top three) and who now occupies a lofty position as a cult icon. In this hilarious and touching tribute to a Hollywood maverick with grade-Z vision, detailed homage is paid to Wood's single-mindedness and optimism in the face of repeated failure and lack of financing, even down to the black and white photography. Depp is convincing (and engaging) as Ed Wood, Jr., the cross-dressing, angora-sweater-wearing, low-budget auteur of such notoriously "bad" cult films as "Glen or Glenda" and "Plan 9 From Outer Space." Depp is supported by terrific portrayals of the motley Wood crew, led by Landau's morphine-addicted, down-on-his-luck Bela Lugosi. Burton focuses on Wood's relationship with Lugosi, whose career is over by the time Wood befriends him. Based on Rudolph Grey's book, "Nightmare of Ecstasy: The Life and Art of Edward D. Wood, Jr." **127m/B VHS, LV, Closed Caption.** Johnny Depp, Sarah Jessica Parker, Martin Landau, Bill Murray, Jim Myers, Patricia Arquette, Jeffrey Jones, Lisa Marie, Vincent D'Onofrio; **D:** Tim Burton; **W:** Scott Alexander, Larry Karaszewski; **C:** Stefan Czapsky. Academy Awards '94: Best Makeup, Best Supporting Actor (Landau); Golden Globe Awards '95: Best Supporting Actor (Landau); Los Angeles Film Critics Association Awards '94: Best Cinematography, Best Supporting Actor (Landau), Best Score; New York Film Critics Awards '94: Best Cinematography, Best Supporting Actor (Landau); National Society of Film Critics Awards '94: Best Cinematography, Best Supporting Actor (Landau); Screen Actors Guild Award '94: Best Supporting Actor (Landau); Nominations: British Academy Awards '95: Best Supporting Actor (Landau); Golden Globe Awards '95: Best Actor—Musical/Comedy (Depp); Best Film—Musical/Comedy; Writers Guild of America '94: Best Original Screenplay. *TOU*

Ed Wood: Look Back in Angora

1994 Biography of the eccentric low-budget filmmaker frequently considered the worst director in Hollywood and now a cult fave. Wood was responsible for "Plan 9 from Outer Space," among other movie disasters but his private peculiarities (including an angora fetish) rivaled his professional ones. Director Tim Burton brings Wood's life to the big screen with the theatrical release of "Ed Wood." **51m/C VHS. D:** Ted Newsom; **W:** Ted Newsom. *AVE*

Eddie ✍✍ 1996 (PG-13)

Basketball nut Edwina (Goldberg) wins a chance to be honorary coach of her beloved Knicks in a free throw contest. When some of her courtside advice works, and the other fans seem to respond to her, the publicity-seeking maverick owner (Langella) gives her the job full-time. Predictable comedy with the usual "new team member leads underdogs to contention" characters won't suprise, or particularly thrill, anyone. Goldberg's lively performance somewhat redeems standard script but reduces everyone around her, including an All-Star roster of NBA players, to window dressing. Basically the hoops version of "Little Big League."**CW:** Some language and brief sexuality. **100m/C VHS, LV, Closed Caption.** Whoopi Goldberg, Frank Langella, Dennis Farina, Richard Jenkins, Lisa Ann Walter, John Benjamin Hickey, John Salley; **D:** Steve Rash; **W:** Jon Connolly, David Loucka, Eric Champnella, Keith Mitchell, Steve Zacharias, Jeff Buhai; **C:** Victor Kemper; **M:** Stanley Clarke. Nominations: Golden Raspberry Awards '96: Worst Actress (Goldberg). *TOU*

Eddie and the Cruisers ✍✍ 1983 (PG)

In the early 1960s, rockers Eddie and the Cruisers score with one hit album. Amid their success, lead singer Pare dies mysteriously in a car accident. Years later, a reporter decides to write a feature on the defunct group, prompting a former band member to begin a search for missing tapes of the Cruisers' unreleased second album. Questions posed at the end of the movie are answered in the sequel. Enjoyable soundtrack by John Cafferty and the Beaver Brown Band. **90m/C VHS, Beta, LV, 8mm, Closed Caption.** Tom Berenger, Michael Pare, Ellen Barkin, Joe Pantoliano, Matthew Laurance, Helen Schneider, David Wilson, Michael "Tunes" Antunes, Joe Cates, John Stockwell, Barry Sand, Howard Johnson, Robin Karfo, Rufus Harley, Bruce Brown, Louis D'Esposito, Michael Toland, Bob Garrett, Joanne Collins; **D:** Martin Davidson; **W:** Martin Davidson, Arlene Davidson; **C:** Fred Murphy; **M:** John Cafferty. *MVD, NLC*

Eddie and the Cruisers 2: Eddie Lives! ✍✍½ 1989 (PG-13)

A sequel to the minor cult favorite, in which a rock star believed to be dead emerges under a new name in Montreal to lead a new band. The Beaver Brown Band again provides the music. **106m/C VHS, Beta, LV, CA** Michael Pare, Marina Orsini, Matthew Laurance, Bernie Coulson, Anthony Sherwood; **D:** Jean-Claude Lord; **W:** Charles Zev Cohen; **M:** Leon Aronson. *CCB, IME*

Eddie Macon's Run ✍✍ 1983 (PG)

Based on a true story; Eddie Macon has been unjustly jailed in Texas and plans an escape to run to Mexico. He is followed by a tough cop who is determined to catch the fugitive. Film debut of Goodman. **95m/C VHS, Beta, LV.** Kirk Douglas, John Schneider, Lee Purcell, John Goodman, Leah Ayres; **D:** Jeff Kanew; **M:** Wendy Blackstone. *USH*

Eddie Murphy: Raw ✍✍ 1987 (R)

Murphy's second stand-up performance film, featuring many of his woman-bashing observations on life. **90m/C VHS, Beta, LV, 8mm, Closed Caption.** Eddie Murphy; **D:** Robert Townsend. *PAR*

The Eddy Duchin Story ✍✍ 1956

Glossy tearjerker that profiles the tragic life of Eddy Duchin, the famous pianist/bandleader of the 30s and 40s. Features almost 30 songs, including classics by Cole Porter, George and Ira Gershwin, Hammerstein, Chopin, and several others. **123m/C VHS, LV, Letterbox, Closed Caption.** Tyrone Power, Kim Novak, Victoria Shaw, James Whitmore, Rex Thompson; **D:** George Sidney; **C:** Harry Stradling; **M:**

George Duning. Nominations: Academy Awards '56: Best Color Cinematography, Best Sound, Best Story, Scoring of a Musical. *COL, MVD, TVC*

Eden ✍✍ 1992

Eden is a luxury resort designed to cater to personal fantasies and filled with numerous intrigues. Part-owner Eve Sinclair faces a number of professional and personal complications, including the tragic death of her husband, a brother-in-law who's interested in more than business, and an old friend with uncertain motives. Lots of sex in beautiful settings. Made for cable television. **?m/C VHS.** Barbara Alyn Woods, Jack Armstrong, Steve Chase, Darcy Demoss, Jeff Griggs; **D:** Victor Lobl; **W:** Stephen Black, Henry Stern. *UND*

Eden ✍✍ 1998 (R)

Frustrated, Multiple Sclerosis-afflicted housewife Helen (Going) deals with the physical and emotional limitations of her life with dreams of astral projection. Husband Bill (Walsh) is a prep school teacher who doesn't want her to work even though she reaches one of his problem students (Flanery) more effectively than he can. First-time director Goldberg won a Sundance competition for his screenplay, but can't quite deliver on its promise. A tight budget and too many unanswered questions keep this one on the intriguing but ultimately disappointing level.**CW:** Language and a scene of sexuality. **106m/C VHS.** Joanna Going, Dylan Walsh, Sean Patrick Flanery; **D:** Howard Goldberg; **W:** Howard Goldberg; **C:** Hubert Taczanowski; **M:** Brad Fiedel. *BMG*

Eden 2 ✍✍ 1993 (R)

The continuing saga of the luxury resort Eden. Owner Eve is still having erotic dreams of late husband Grant while fending off the very real advances of his brother Josh and becoming attracted to Paul, her late husband's best friend. The guests are equally caught up in erotic dilemmas involving sexual blackmail. Made for cable television.**CW:** Language and numerous sex-related scenes. **102m/C VHS.** Barbara Alyn Woods, Jack Armstrong, Steve Chase, Darcy Demoss, Jeff Griggs; **D:** Kristine Peterson; **W:** Stephen Black, Henry Stern. *UND*

Eden 3 ✍✍ 1993 (R)

Yet another chapter in this sexy made for cable saga. Eve Sinclair risks losing her share of the tropical resort unless she remarries, which she doesn't want to do, although fitness trainer Randi would be delighted to pick up the option. Meanwhile, an heiress discovers her new bridegroom has murderous intentions.**CW:** Language and sex-related scenes. **?m/C VHS.** Barbara Alyn Woods, Jack Armstrong, Steve Chase, Darcy Demoss, Jeff Griggs, Dean Scofield; **D:** Victor Lobl. *UND*

Eden 4 ✍✍ 1993 (R)

Further adventures in the cable series. Eve, Eden's co-owner, must cope with both Josh's jealous rage and Randi's continuing scheming as she tries to keep her guests happy at the posh resort. One of the guests, a beautiful author, gets too caught up in her sexual fantasies and may find herself in danger.**CW:** Sex-related scenes. **?m/C VHS.** Barbara Alyn Woods, Jack Armstrong, Steve Chase, Darcy Demoss, Jeff Griggs, Dean Scofield; **D:** Kristine Peterson. *UND*

Eden Valley ✍✍✍ 1994

A low-key intensity marks this northeast England drama that's produced, written, and directed by an eight-member film cooperative, the Amber Production Team. Troubled Newcastle teenager Billy (Bell) is put on probation for drug and theft charges and in a last-ditch chance at turning his life around goes to live with his estranged father, Hoggy (Hogg). They haven't seen each other in 10 years and Hoggy lives on a farm in County Durham where he raises and trains horses for harness racing. Naturally, their relationship is strained and there aren't any easy solutions (kinda like in real life). **95m/C VHS.** *GB* Darren Bell, Brian Hogg, Mike Elliott, Jimmy Killeen. *HTV*

The Edge ✍✍½ Bookworm 1997 (R)

Wealthy Charles Morse (Hopkins) isn't too pleased that fashion photog Bob Greene (Baldwin) takes such an interest in his lovely fashion model wife (Macpherson) and feels the two are out to kill him.

Despite his conspiracy theory, Morse and Greene end up depending on each other for survival when their plane crashes in the Alaskan wilderness. To compound their problems, they must do battle with a stalking killer bear. Mamet screenplay dices things up a bit with cutting dialogue which leads to the mind games Mamet is so famous for. Hopkins and Baldwin give understated, intact performances, with an intensity shared only by Bart the Bear, in this small comtemporary parable on the meaning of life. The splendid Alaskan scenery is actually breathtaking aerial and ground footage in Canada.**CW:** Language and some adventure gore/violence. **120m/C VHS, Closed Caption.** Anthony Hopkins, Alec Baldwin, Elle Macpherson, Harold Perrineau Jr., L.Q. Jones; **D:** Lee Tamahori; **W:** David Mamet; **C:** Donald McAlpine; **M:** Jerry Goldsmith. *FXV*

Edge of Darkness ✍✍✍½ 1943

Compelling war-drama about the underground movement in Norway during Nazi takeover of WWII. Flynn plays a Norwegian fisherman who leads the local underground movement and Sheridan is his loyal fiancee. Although several problems occurred throughout filming, this picture earned high marks for its superb performances and excellent camerawork. Based on the novel by William Woods. **120m/B VHS, Closed Caption.** Errol Flynn, Ann Sheridan, Walter Huston, Nancy Coleman, Helmut Dantine, Judith Anderson, Ruth Gordon, John Beal; **D:** Lewis Milestone; **W:** Robert Rossen. *MGM*

Edge of Darkness ✍✍ 1986

Originally produced as a mini series for British television, this mystery involves a police detective who investigates his daughter's murder and uncovers a web of espionage and intrigue. **307m/C VHS, Beta, Closed Caption.** *GB* Bob Peck, Joe Don Baker, Jack Woodson, John Woodvine, Joanne Whalley; **D:** Martin Campbell; **M:** Eric Clapton, Michael Kamen. *FOX, TVC, VCO*

Edge of Honor ✍½ 1991 (R)

Young Eagle Scouts camping in the Pacific Northwest discover a woodland weapons cache and wage guerilla war against killer lumberjacks out to silence them. A boneheaded, politically correct action bloodbath; you don't have to like the logging industry to disapprove of the broad slurs against its men shown here.**CW:** Language and strong violence. **92m/C VHS.** Corey Feldman, Meredith Salenger, Scott Reeves, Ken Jenkins, Christopher Neame, Don Swayze; **D:** Michael Spence; **W:** David O'Malley.

Edge of Sanity ✍½ 1989 (R)

An overdone Jekyll-Hyde reprise, with cocaine serving as the villainous substance. The coke-created Hyde is posited as a prototype for Jack the Ripper. Not for the easily queazy. Available in a 90 minute, unrated version. **85m/C VHS, Beta, LV, Closed Caption.** *GB* Anthony Perkins, Glynis Barber, David Lodge, Sarah Maur-Thorp, Ben Cole, Lisa Davis, Jill Melford; **D:** Gerard Kikoine; **W:** J.P. Felix, Ron Raley; **C:** Tony Spratling. *NO*

Edge of the Axe 1989

A small town is held in the grip of terror by a demented slasher. **91m/C VHS, Beta.** Barton Faulks, Christina Marie Lane, Page Moseley, Fred Hollyday; **D:** Joseph Braunstein. *MCG*

Edge of the World ✍✍✍ 1937

Moody, stark British drama of a mini-society in its death throes, expertly photographed on a six-square-mile island in the Shetlands. A dwindling fishing community of fewer than 100 souls agonize over whether to migrate to the mainland; meanwhile the romance of a local girl with an off-islander takes a tragic course. Choral effects were provided by the Glasgow Orpheus Choir. **80m/B VHS.** *GB* Finlay Currie, Niall MacGinnis, Grant Sutherland, John Laurie, Michael Powell; **D:** Michael Powell; **W:** Michael Powell. *NOS*

Edie & Pen ✍✍½ 1995 (PG-13)

Tilly seems to be making a career of playing the ditz who's smarter than she seems as she shows here as Edie, who meets Pen (Channing) in Reno where both are looking for quickie divorces. They hit a bar to celebrate and hook up with soft-hearted Harry (Glenn), who's been dumped by his wife. Some drunken life discussions follow and then

Edie finds out that her fiance is Pen's cold-hearted, newly ex hubby (Wilson). Slight script, charming performances.**CW:** Mature themes, sexual situations, language. **97m/C VHS.** Jennifer Tilly, Stockard Channing, Scott Glenn, Stuart Wilson; **Cameos:** Beverly D'Angelo, Louise Fletcher, Joanna Gleason, Michael McKean, Martin Mull, Michael O'Keefe, Chris Sarandon, Randy Travis, Jean Smart, Victoria Tennant; **D:** Matthew Irmas; **W:** Victoria Tennant; **C:** Alicia Weber; **M:** Shawn Colvin. *PGV*

Edie in Ciao! Manhattan 🎬 *Ciao! Manhattan* 1972 (R) Real-life story of Edie Sedgwick, Warhol superstar and international fashion model, whose life in the fast lane led to ruin. **84m/C VHS, Beta.** Edie Sedgwick, Baby Jane Holzer, Roger Vadim, Paul America, Viva. *FCT, PBS*

Edison the Man 🎬🎬½ 1940 Story of Tommy Edison's early years of experimentation in the basement. The young genious eventually invents light bulbs, motion pictures, and a sound recording device. Well played by Tracy. **108m/C VHS, Beta.** Spencer Tracy, Rita Johnson, Lynne Overman, Charles Coburn, Gene Lockhart, Henry Travers, Felix Bressart; **D:** Clarence Brown. Nominations: Academy Awards '40: Best Story. *MGM*

Edith & Marcel 🎬½ 1983 A fictionalization of the love affair between chanteuse Edith Piaf and boxer Marcel Cerdan (played by his son, Marcel Cerdan, Jr.). In French, with English subtitles. **104m/C VHS, Beta.** FR Evelyne Bouix, Marcel Cerdan Jr., Charles Aznavour, Jacques Villeret; **D:** Claude Lelouch.

Ed's Next Move 🎬🎬½ 1996 (R) Genial indie NYC comedy with a Woody Allen feel is littered with whimsical one-liners. Title character Ed (Ross) moves from small-town Wisconsin to New York after a break-up with his girlfriend. Being that he's a rice geneticist, it's not a big leap to conclude that Ed's a bit uptight, so it's imperative that Ed's big city roommate, the suave Ray (Carroll), hip him up to better meet the ladies. Soon, Ed falls for boho Lee (Thorne) leader of a band called "Ed's Redeeming Qualities." Fun fantasy sequence involving Ed, his old girlfriend and two translators is a highlight. Low-budgeter, with a first time writer/director (Walsh), and it shows, but in a good-natured way. Though more could be asked visually, picture does boast good performers and well-drawn characters.**CW:** Scene of sexuality and some language. **88m/C VHS.** Matt Ross, Calliope Thorne, Kevin Carroll, Ramsey Faragallah, Nina Shevaleva, Jimmy Cummings; **D:** John Walsh; **W:** John Walsh; **C:** Peter Nelson. *ORI*

Educating Rita 🎬🎬🎬½ 1983 (PG) Walters and Caine team beautifully in this adaptation of the successful Willy Russell play which finds an uneducated hairdresser determined to improve her knowledge of literature. In so doing, she enlists the aid of a tutor: a disillusioned alcoholic, adeptly played by Caine. Together, the two find inspiration in one another's differences and experiences. Ultimately, the teacher receives a lesson in how to again appreciate his work and the classics as he observes his pupil's unique approach to her studies. Some deem this a "Pygmalion" for the '80s. **110m/C VHS, Beta, LV, 8mm, Closed Caption.** GB Michael Caine, Julie Walters, Michael Williams, Maureen Lipman; **D:** Lewis Gilbert; **W:** Willy Russell. British Academy Awards '83: Best Actor (Caine), Best Actress (Walters), Best Film; Golden Globe Awards '84: Best Actor—Musical/Comedy (Caine), Best Actress—Musical/Comedy (Walters); Nominations: Academy Awards '83: Best Actor (Caine), Best Actress (Walters), Best Adapted Screenplay. *COL*

The Education of Little Tree 🎬🎬🎬 1997 (PG) Child's eye view of a large scale epic on par with modern classics like "The Secret Garden." In 1935, poor, orphaned, and part Native American Little Tree (Ashton) is sent to live with his grandfather (Cromwell) and Native American grandmother (Cardinal) in the Smokey Mountains of Tennessee. There he learns "The Way" of his Cherokee ancestors and how to make moonshine from his Scottish/Irish grandfather. A nosy, Bible-thumping Aunt tips off authorities and soon Little Tree is shipped off to an evil state institution to cure him of his inappropriate Indian ways. There, the old-fashioned discipline runs fierce and abusive. Adapted from a children's book by Forrest Carter. Cardinal and Cromwell carve out memorable performances alongside first-rate newcomer Joseph Ashton. **112m/C VHS, Closed Caption.** James Cromwell, Tantoo Cardinal, Joseph Ashton, Graham Greene; **D:** Richard Friedenberg; **W:** Richard Friedenberg; **C:** Anastas Michos; **M:** Mark Isham. *PAR*

The Education of Sonny Carson 🎬🎬½ 1974 (R) Chilling look at the tribulations of a black youth living in a Brooklyn ghetto amid drugs, prostitution, crime, and other forms of vice. Based on Sonny Carson's autobiography. Still pertinent some 20 years after its theatrical release. **104m/C VHS, Beta.** Rony Clanton, Don Gordon, Paul Benjamin; **D:** Michael Campus.

Edvard Munch 🎬🎬 1974 Biographical portrait of the Norwegian Expressionist painter and his tormented life in the stuffy society of 19th-century Oslo. Concentrates mainly on his early years, including the deaths of his mother and younger sister, his brother's suicide, Munch's affair with a married woman, and his struggle to maintain his sanity. Based on Munch's memoirs. In German and Norwegian with English subtitles. **167m/C VHS.** NO Geir Westby, Gro Fraas, Eli Ryg; **D:** Peter Watkins; **W:** Peter Watkins. *FCT, NYF*

Edward and Mrs. Simpson 🎬🎬 1980 Made-for-television dramatic reconstruction of the years leading to the abdication of King Edward VIII, who forfeited the British throne in 1936 so that he could marry American divorcee Wallis Simpson. Originally aired on PBS. **270m/C VHS, Beta.** Edward Fox, Cynthia Harris; **D:** Waris Hussein. *HBO, TVC, VIF*

Edward Scissorhands 🎬🎬🎬 1990 (PG-13) Depp's a young man created by loony scientist Price, who dies before he can attach hands to his boy-creature. Then the boy is rescued from his lonely existence outside of suburbia by an ingratiating Avon lady. With scissors in place of hands, he has more trouble fitting into suburbia than would most new kids on the block, and he struggles with being different and lonely in a cardboard-cutout world. Visually captivating fairy tale full of splash and color, however predictable the Hollywood-prefab denouement. **100m/C VHS, Beta, LV, Closed Caption.** Johnny Depp, Winona Ryder, Dianne Wiest, Vincent Price, Anthony Michael Hall, Alan Arkin, Kathy Baker, Conchata Ferrell, Caroline Aaron, Dick Anthony Williams, Robert Oliveri, John Davidson; **D:** Tim Burton; **W:** Tim Burton, Caroline Thompson; **C:** Stefan Czapsky; **M:** Danny Elfman. Nominations: Academy Awards '90: Best Makeup. *FOX, FCT*

Edward II 🎬🎬½ 1992 (R) Jarman's controversial adaptation of Christopher Marlowe's play "The Troublesome Reign of Edward II" portrays the weak-willed monarch as neglecting his kingdom for love. Unfortunately, it's not for his queen but for his commoner male lover. His neglect of both queen and country lead to a swift and brutal downfall. Jarman's use of contemporary anachronisms, stream of conscienceness approach, and heavy symbolism may leave more than one viewer wondering what's going on.**CW:** Some language, strong violence, and strong sensuality. **91m/C VHS, LV.** GB Steven Waddington, Kevin Collins, Andrew Tiernan, John Lynch, Dudley Sutton, Tilda Swinton, Jerome Flynn, Jody Graber, Nigel Terry, Annie Lennox; **D:** Derek Jarman; **W:** Derek Jarman; **M:** Simon Fisher Turner. Venice Film Festival '92: Best Actress (Swinton). *COL*

Edward the King 🎬🎬½ 1975 British miniseries follows the long life of Prince Edward, who waited some 60 years for his overbearing mother, Queen Victoria, to die so he could ascend the throne. Bertie scandalized with his affairs and carousing but, nevertheless, proved his worth as king-in-waiting. On six cassettes. **708m/C VHS.** GB Timothy West, Annette Crosbie, John Gielgud, Francesca Annis, Robert Hardy; **D:** John Gorrie; **C:** Tony Imi. *BWE, PBS, WMI*

Eegah! woof! 1962 Another Arch Hall (Merriwether) epic in which an anachronistic Neanderthal falls in love in '60s California. Reputed to be one of the worst films of all time. **93m/C VHS, Beta.** Marilyn Manning, Richard Kiel, Arch Hall Jr., William Waters; **D:** Ray Dennis Steckler. *RHI, FCT*

The Eel 🎬🎬🎬 *Unagi* 1996 Yamashita (Yakusho) has just been paroled after spending eight years in prison for killing his adulterous wife in a jealous rage. While there, he found and cared for an eel, which became his only confidante, and which accompanies him to his new life as a barber in a small town outside Tokyo. The newcomer is soon befriended by the locals but Yamashita's life changes most when he saves the suicidal Keiko (Shimizu) from drowning. She comes to work in his shop and would obviously like a more intimate relationship but some secrets in her past and some strange incidents in the town may jepordize Yamashita's hopes for a normal life. Based on the novel "Glimmering in the Dark" by Akira Yoshimura. Japanese with subtitles. **117m/C VHS.** JP Koji Yakusho, Misa Shimizu, Mitsuko Baisho, Shou Aikawa, Fujio Tsuneta, Akira Emoto, Etsuko Ichihara, Tomoroh Taguchi, Ken Kobayashi, Sabu Kawara; **D:** Shohei Imamura; **W:** Shohei Imamura, Motofumi Tomikawa, Daisuke Tengan; **C:** Shigeru Komatsubara; **M:** Shinichiro Ikebe. Cannes Film Festival '97: Best Film. *NYR*

The Effect of Gamma Rays on Man-in-the-Moon Marigolds 🎬🎬🎬 1973 (PG) A wonderful drama based on the Pulitzer Prize winning play by Paul Zindel. The story centers around eccentric young Matilda and her depressed family. Matilda is preparing her experiment for the school science fair, determined to beat her competition. Her exhibit shows how radiation sometimes kills the helpless marigolds, but sometimes causes them to grow into even more beautiful mutations. This mirrors Matilda, who flowers even amidst the drunkenness of her mother and the dullness of her sister. **100m/C VHS.** Joanne Woodward, Nell Potts, Roberta Wallach, Judith Lowry, Richard Venture; **D:** Paul Newman. Cannes Film Festival '73: Best Actress (Woodward). *NO*

Effi Briest 🎬🎬🎬½ *Fontane Effi Briest* 1974 A 19th-century tragedy well-played by Schygulla and empowered with Fassbinder's directorial skills. Effi (Schygulla) is a 17 year-old beauty, unhappily married to a much older man. She drifts into a brief affair, which is not discovered for several years. When her husband does discover her past infidelity, the Prussian legal code permits him a chilling revenge. Based on a popular 19th-century novel by Theodor Fontane. In German with English subtitles. **135m/B VHS.** GE Hanna Schygulla, Wolfgang Schenck, Lilo Pempeit, Ulli Lommel; **D:** Rainer Werner Fassbinder; **W:** Rainer Werner Fassbinder. *NYF, PMS*

The Efficiency Expert 🎬🎬½ *Spotswood* 1992 (PG) Lighthearted Australian comedy about a dingy moccasin factory where a rigid efficiency consultant is invited to save the eccentric family-run company from bankruptcy. Predictable ending contains a nevertheless timely message about the importance of the bottom line. **97m/C VHS, Beta, Closed Caption.** AU Anthony Hopkins, Ben Mendelsohn, Alwyn Kurts, Bruno Lawrence, Angela Punch McGregor, Russell Crowe, Rebecca Rigg, Toni Collette; **D:** Mark Joffe; **W:** Andrew Knight, Max Dann; **M:** Ricky Fataar. *PAR, BTV*

Egg 🎬🎬½ 1988 Striking film from Holland chronicles the life of a quiet, middle-aged baker who answers a personal ad from a schoolteacher. After much correspondence, the teacher visits the baker in his village, and the townspeople take great interest in what happens next. In Dutch with English subtitles. **58m/C VHS, LV.** NL Johan Leysen, Marijke Vengelers; **D:** Danniel Danniel. *KIV, LUM*

Egg and I ♂♂♂ 1947 Based on the true-life adventures of best-selling humorist Betty Mac-Donald. A young urban bride agrees to help her new husband realize his life-long dream of owning a chicken farm. A dilapidated house, temperamental stove, and suicidal chickens test the bride's perseverance, as do the zany antics of her country-bumpkin neighbors, Ma and Pa Kettle, who make their screen debut. Plenty of old-fashioned laughs. **104m/B VHS, Beta, LV.** Claudette Colbert, Fred MacMurray, Marjorie Main, Percy Kilbride, Louise Allbritton, Richard Long, Billy House, Donald MacBride; **D:** Chester Erskine; **C:** Milton Krasner. Nominations: Academy Awards '47: Best Supporting Actress (Main). USH

The Egyptian ♂♂½ 1954 Based on the sword-and-sandal novel by Mika Waltari, this is a ponderous big-budget epic about a young Egyptian in Akhnaton's epoch who becomes physician to the Pharaoh. **140m/C VHS, Beta, LV, Closed Caption.** Edmund Purdom, Victor Mature, Peter Ustinov, Bella Darvi, Gene Tierney, Henry Daniell, Jean Simmons, Michael Wilding, Judith Evelyn, John Carradine, Carl Benton Reid; **D:** Michael Curtiz; **W:** Philip Dunne, Casey Robinson; **C:** Leon Shamroy. Nominations: Academy Awards '54: Best Color Cinematography. FOX, IME

The Eiger Sanction ♂♂ 1975 (R) An art teacher returns to the CII (a fictionalized version of the CIA) as an exterminator hired to assassinate the killers of an American agent. In the process, he finds himself climbing the Eiger. Beautiful Swiss Alps scenery fails to totally compensate for several dreary lapses. Based on the novel by Trevanian. **125m/C VHS, Beta, LV, Letterbox.** Clint Eastwood, George Kennedy, Vonetta McGee, Jack Cassidy, Thayer David; **D:** Clint Eastwood; **M:** John Williams. USH, TLF

8-A ♂♂ Ochoa 1992 Reconstructs the 1989 trial and execution of Cuban general Arnaldo Ochoa Sanchez, a hero of the revolution who, along with other government officials, advocated the resignation of Fidel Castro as the solution to the country's economic and political crises. At the trial Ochoa and four other officials were convicted of illegal drug trafficking and shot by a firing squad. Spanish with subtitles. **84m/C VHS.** CU **D:** Orlando Jiminez-Leal. NYF

8 1/2 ♂♂♂♂ Otto E Mezzo; Federico Fellini's 8 1/2 1963 The acclaimed Fellini self-portrait of a revered Italian film director struggling with a fated film project wanders through his intermixed life, childhood memories, and hallucinatory fantasies. Subtitled in English. **135m/B VHS, Beta, LV, Letterbox.** IT Marcello Mastroianni, Claudia Cardinale, Anouk Aimee, Sandra Milo, Barbara Steele, Rossella Falk, Eddra Gale, Mark Herron, Madeleine LeBeau, Caterina Boratto; **D:** Federico Fellini; **W:** Tullio Pinelli, Ennio Flaiano, Brunello Rondi, Federico Fellini; **M:** Nino Rota. Academy Awards '63: Best Costume Design (B & W), Best Foreign Language Film; New York Film Critics Awards '63: Best Foreign Film; Nominations: Academy Awards '63: Best Art Direction/Set Decoration (B & W), Best Director (Fellini), Best Story & Screenplay. VES, MRV, MPI

8 Heads in a Duffel Bag ♂♂ 1996 (R) Mob bag man Tommy (Pesci, in a real stretch) loses his heads, the evidence of a successful hit, to med student Charlie Pritchett (Comeau), who's headed for a Mexican vacation with his fiance's (Swanson) uptight family. Desperate, Tommy "persuades" Charlie's roommates (Spade and Louiso) to help him find some replacement noggins. Excellent premise is almost done in by a timid script that relies a little too much on slapstick. Schulman's uneven directorial debut does little to mask the problem. Newcomer Comeau tries for a "Bachelor Party" era Tom Hanks thing, but doesn't quite get there. Pesci and Spade save flick from disaster, and get most of the good lines, pitted in a generational "battle of the smartasses," but neither one strays from their previous screen personas. **CW:** Language. **95m/C VHS, Closed Caption.** Joe Pesci, David Spade, Andy Comeau, Kristy Swanson, George Hamilton,

Dyan Cannon, Todd Louiso, Frank Reman, Anthony Mangano, Joe Basile, Ernestine Mercer, Howard George; **D:** Tom Schulman; **W:** Tom Schulman; **C:** Adam Holender; **M:** Andrew Gross. ORI

800 Leagues Down the Amazon ♂½ 1993 (PG-13) A 19th-century journey down the Amazon on a raft with a planter, his daughter, and various complications. Based on a novel by Jules Verne. **100m/C VHS.** Daphne Zuniga, Barry Bostwick, Adam Baldwin, Tom Verica, E.E. Bell; **D:** Luis Llosa; **W:** Laura Schiff, Jackson Barr. NHO

Eight Men Out ♂♂♂½ 1988 (PG) Taken from Eliot Asinof's book, a moving, full-blooded account of the infamous 1919 "Black Sox" scandal, in which members of the Chicago White Sox teamed to throw the World Series for $80,000. A dirge of lost innocence, this is among Sayles' best films. Provides an interesting look at the "conspiracy" that ended "Shoeless" Joe Jackson's major-league career. The actual baseball scenes are first-rate, and Straithairn, Sweeney, and Cusack give exceptional performances. Sayles makes an appearance as Ring Lardner. Enjoyable viewing for even the non-sports fan. **121m/C VHS, Beta, LV, Closed Caption.** John Cusack, D.B. Sweeney, Perry Lang, Jace Alexander, Bill Irwin, Clifton James, Michael Rooker, Michael Lerner, Christopher Lloyd, Studs Terkel, David Strathairn, Charlie Sheen, Kevin Tighe, John Mahoney, John Sayles, Gordon Clapp, Richard Edson, James Read, Don Harvey, John Anderson, Maggie Renzi, Michael Mantell, Nancy Travis, Michael Laskin; **D:** John Sayles; **W:** John Sayles; **C:** Robert Richardson; **M:** Mason Daring. ORI, FCT

8 Million Ways to Die ♂♂ 1985 (R) An ex-cop hires himself out to rescue a pimp-bound hooker, and gets knee-deep in a mess of million-dollar drug deals, murder, and prostitution. Slow-moving but satisfying. Based on the book by Lawrence Block. **115m/C VHS, Beta, LV, Closed Caption.** Jeff Bridges, Rosanna Arquette, Andy Garcia, Alexandra Paul; **D:** Hal Ashby; **W:** Oliver Stone; **C:** Stephen Burum; **M:** James Newton Howard. FOX

Eight on the Lam ♂ 1967 (PG) Unfunny comedy features widower Henry Dimsdale (Hope) taking off with his kids and family maid Golda (Diller) when he's accused of embezzling bank funds. Jasper Lynch (Winters) is on their trail until Henry can prove who the real culprit is. **103m/C VHS, Closed Caption.** Bob Hope, Phyllis Diller, Jonathan Winters, Jill St. John, Shirley Eaton; **D:** George Marshall; **W:** Albert Lewin, Arthur Marx, Bob Fisher, Burt Styler; **C:** Alan Stenvold; **M:** George Romanis. MGM

8 Seconds ♂♂½ The Lane Frost Story 1994 (PG-13) Love, not sports, dominates the true-life story of rodeo star Lane Frost (Perry), a world champion bull rider killed in the ring at the age of 25 in 1990. A decent guy, he finds quick success on the rodeo circuit, marries (to Geary), and finds his career getting in the way of their happiness. Bull-riding sequences are genuinely stomach churning, the performances low-key. Title refers to the amount of time a rider must stay aboard his animal. **CW:** Strong language and violence. **104m/C VHS, LV, Closed Caption.** Luke Perry, Cynthia Geary, Stephen Baldwin, James Rebhorn, Carrie Snodgress, Red Mitchell, Ronnie Clair Edwards; **D:** John G. Avildsen; **W:** Monte Merrick; **M:** Bill Conti. NLC

Eight Witnesses ♂♂ 1954 Suspense thriller about a man being murdered in front of eight blind witnesses. **?m/C VHS.** Peggy Ann Garner. LOO

18 Again! ♂♂½ 1988 (PG) After a bump on the head, an 81-year-old man and his 18-year-old grandson mentally switch places, giving each a new look at his life. Lightweight romp with Burns in especially good form, but not good enough to justify redoing this tired theme. **100m/C VHS, Beta, LV, Closed Caption.** George Burns, Charlie Schlatter, Anita Morris, Jennifer Runyon, Tony Roberts, Red Buttons, Miriam Flynn, George DiCenzo; **D:** Paul Flaherty; **W:** Jonathan Prince, Josh Goldstein; **M:** Billy Goldenberg. VTR

Eighteen Jade Arhats ♂ 1984 A kung fu epic with a blind heroine who nevertheless kicks other people in the eyes. **95m/C VHS, Beta.** Chia Ling, Ou-Yang Ksiek, Sun Chia-Lin, Otae Mofo. UNI

1860 ♂♂ 1933 During the Battle of Calatafimi in May of 1860, Sicilian peasants revolted against the King of Naples' army. The story focuses on four people caught up in the fighting: the spouse of a revolutionary, a foppish intellectual, a rebel priest, and the young shepherd who is sent with a message to Genoa asking for assistance. Blasetti made great use of location filming and natural light. In Italian with English subtitles. **72m/C VHS.** IT **D:** Alessandro Blasetti. FCT, WBF

The Eighth Day ♂♂½ Le Huitieme Jour 1995 Sugary story about workaholic businessman Harry (Auteuil), whose wife Julie (Miou-Miou) has just left him, taking their daughters. Driving home, Harry finds Georges (Duquenne) by the side of the road. Georges, who has Downs syndrome, has left the institution he's been living in and, though Harry tries to take him to the nearest police station, Georges refuses to leave him. Naturally, the emotionally deprived Harry begins to loosen up and, when Georges is finally returned to his group home, all his friends decide to help with Harry's attempts to win back his family. Thick with whimsy but the lead performances are excellent. French with subtitles. **108m/C VHS, LV.** FR BE Daniel Auteuil, Pascal Duquenne, Miou-Miou, Henri Garcin, Fabienne Loriaux, Isabelle Sadoyan, Helene Roussel, Michele Maes; **D:** Jaco Van Dormael; **W:** Jaco Van Dormael; **C:** Walther Vanden Ende; **M:** Pierre Van Dormael. Cannes Film Festival '96: Best Actor (Auteuil), Best Actor (Duquenne); Nominations: Cesar Awards '97: Best Actor (Auteuil); Golden Globe Awards '97: Best Foreign Film. PGV

The Eighties ♂♂½ 1983 A comic, pseudo-documentary romp through the making of a musical. Not just another dime-a-dozen song-and-dance flick, but plays with the genre with humor and intelligence, treating us to an insider's view of a performance arranged at a shopping plaza, from the rigorous auditions to the tedium of the production of songs and routines. Treated in a light-hearted, sensitive, just on the verge of laughable manner, it concludes with 30 minutes of song and dance. In French with English subtitles. **86m/C VHS.** FR Aurore Clement, Lio, Magaly Noel, Pascale Salkin; **D:** Chantal Akerman; **W:** Chantal Akerman, Jean Gruault. WAC, FCT

84 Charing Cross Road ♂♂♂ 1986 (PG) A lonely woman in New York and a bookseller in London begin corresponding for business reasons. Over a 20-year period, their relationship grows into a friendship, and then a romance, though they communicate only by mail. Based on a true story. **100m/C VHS, Beta, LV.** Anne Bancroft, Anthony Hopkins, Judi Dench, Jean De Baer, Maurice Denham, Eleanor David, Mercedes Ruehl, Daniel Gerroll, Hugh Whitemore; **D:** David Jones; **M:** George Fenton. British Academy Awards '87: Best Actress (Bancroft). COL, TVC, HMV

84 Charlie Mopic ♂♂♂ 1989 (R) A widely acclaimed drama about the horrors of Vietnam seen through the eyes of a cameraman assigned to a special front-line unit. Filled with a cast of unknowns, this is an unsettling film that sheds new light on the subject of the Vietnam war. Powerful and energetic; music by Donovan. **89m/C VHS, Beta, LV.** Richard Brooks, Christopher Burgard, Nicholas Cascone, Jonathon Emerson, Glen Morshower, Jason Tomlins, Byron Thames; **D:** Patrick Duncan; **W:** Patrick Duncan; **C:** Alan Caso; **M:** Donovan. COL

Eijanaika ♂♂♂½ Why Not? 1981 A gripping story of a poor Japanese man who returns to his country after a visit to America in the 1860s. Memorable performances make this an above-average film. In Japanese with English subtitles. **151m/C VHS, LV.** JP Ken Ogata, Shigeru Izumiya; **D:** Shohei Imamura. KIV, FCT

El 🎬🎬 *This Strange Passion* 1952 Bizarre black-comedy finds virginal middle-aged Francisco (De Cordova) marrying a beautiful young woman (Garces) and becoming jealously paranoid when he believes she's been unfaithful. He's eventually driven to insanity and attempted murder. Spanish with subtitles. 88m/B VHS. **MX** Arturo de Cordova, Delia Garces, Luis Beristain, Aurora Walker; **D:** Luis Bunuel; **W:** Luis Bunuel, Luis Alcoriza; **C:** Gabriel Figueroa; **M:** Luis Hernandez Breton. *HTV*

El Amor Brujo 🎬🎬🎬 *Love, the Magician* 1986 An adaptation of the work of Miguel de Falla, in which flamenco dancers enact the story of a tragic romance. 100m/C VHS, Beta, LV. Antonio Gades, Christina Hoyos, Laura Del Sol; **D:** Carlos Saura. *CTH, FCT, TPV*

El Barbaro 🎬 1984 In the beginning of civilization, when evil powers rule, a barbarian has two ambitions in life: to seek revenge for his friend's death and to rescue the world from a sorcerer's power. 88m/C VHS, Beta. **SP** Andrea Occhipinti, Maria Scola, Violeta Cela, Sabrina Sellers.

El Bruto 🎬🎬½ *The Brute* 1952 A mid-Mexican-period Bunuel drama, about a brainless thug who is used as a bullying pawn in a struggle between a brutal landlord and discontented tenants. In Spanish with English titles. 83m/B VHS, Beta. **MX** Pedro Armendariz Sr., Katy Jurado, Andres Soler, Rosita Arenas; **D:** Luis Bunuel. *FCT*

El Cid 🎬🎬🎬 1961 Charts the life of Rodrigo Diaz de Bivar, known as El Cid, who was the legendary 11th-century Christian hero who freed Spain from Moorish invaders. Noted for its insanely lavish detail, this epic tale is true to its setting and features elaborate battle scenes. 184m/C VHS, Beta, LV. Charlton Heston, Sophia Loren, Raf Vallone, Hurd Hatfield, Genevieve Page; **D:** Anthony Mann; **W:** Philip Yordan; **C:** Robert Krasker; **M:** Miklos Rozsa. Nominations: Academy Awards '61: Best Art Direction/Set Decoration (Color), Best Song ("Love Theme (The Falcon and the Dove)"), Best Original Dramatic/Comedy Score. *BFV, FCT, KAR*

El Cochecito 🎬🎬🎬 *The Wheelchair* 1960 Great Spanish actor Isbert stars as the head of a large family whose closest friends are all joined together in a kind of fraternity defined by the fact that they each use a wheelchair. He feels excluded because he does not have or need one, so he goes to great lengths to gain acceptance in this "brotherhood." In Spanish with English subtitles. 90m/B VHS, Beta. **SP** Jose Isbert; **D:** Marco Ferreri. *FCT*

El Condor 🎬½ 1970 (R) Two drifters search for gold buried in a Mexican fort. 102m/C VHS. **SP** Jim Brown, Lee Van Cleef, Patrick O'Neal, Marianna Hill, Iron Eyes Cody, Elisha Cook Jr.; **D:** John Guillermin; **W:** Larry Cohen, Steven W. Carabatsos; **M:** Maurice Jarre. *WAR*

El Diablo 🎬🎬½ 1990 (PG-13) A young man finds the West more wild than he expected. He finds "help" in the shape of Gossett as he tries to free a young girl who's being held by the notorious El Diablo. Made for television. Better than average. 107m/C VHS, Closed Caption. Louis Gossett Jr., Anthony Edwards, John Glover, Robert Beltran, M.C. Gainey, Miguel Sandoval, Sarah Trigger, Joe Pantoliano; **D:** Peter Markle; **W:** John Carpenter, Bill Phillips. *WAR, HBO*

El Diablo Rides 🎬½ 1939 A fierce feud between cattlemen and sheepmen develops, with touches of comedy in between. 57m/B VHS, Beta. Bob Steele, Carleton Young, Kit Guard. *VDM, VCN, VYY*

El Diputado 🎬🎬🎬 *The Deputy* 1978 A famous politician jeopardizes his career when he has an affair with a young man. In Spanish with English subtitles. 111m/C VHS. **SP** Jose Sacristan, Maria Luisa San Jose, Jose Alonso; **D:** Eloy De La Iglesia. *FCT*

El Dorado 🎬🎬🎬 1967 A gunfighter rides into the frontier town of El Dorado to aid a reckless cattle baron in his war with farmers over land rights. Once in town, the hired gun meets up with an old friend—the sheriff—who also happens to be the town drunkard. Switching allegiances, the gunslinger helps the lawman sober up and defend the farmers. This Hawks western displays a number of similarities to the director's earlier "Rio Bravo" (1959), staring Wayne, Dean Martin, and Ricky Nelson—who charms viewers as the young sidekick "Colorado" much like Caan does as "Mississippi" in El Dorado. 126m/C VHS, Beta, LV. John Wayne, Robert Mitchum, James Caan, Charlene Holt, Ed Asner, Arthur Hunnicutt, Christopher George, R.G. Armstrong, Jim Davis, Paul Fix, Johnny Crawford, Michele Carey; **D:** Howard Hawks. *PAR, TLF*

El Mariachi 🎬🎬🎬 1993 (R) Extremely low-budget but clever mixture of humor and violence in a tale of mistaken identity set in a small Mexican border town. 24-year-old director Rodriguez makes his feature film debut with this $7000 feature, originally intended only for the Spanish-language market. Film festival awards and critical attention brought the work to wider release. In Spanish with English subtitles or dubbed. The laserdisc version includes director's commentary and Rodriguez's eight-minute film "Bedhead." **CW:** Strong violence. 81m/C VHS, Beta, LV, 8mm. **MX** Carlos Gallardo, Consuelo Gomez, Peter Marquardt, Jaime de Hoyos, Reinol Martinez, Ramiro Gomez; **D:** Robert Rodriguez; **W:** Robert Rodriguez, Carlos Gallardo; **C:** Robert Rodriguez. Independent Spirit Awards '94: Best First Feature; Sundance Film Festival '93: Audience Award; Nominations: Independent Spirit Awards '94: Best Director (Rodriguez). *COL, FCT, BTV*

El Muerto 🎬½ 1975 In 19th-century Buenos Aires, a young man flees his home after killing an enemy. Arriving in Montevideo, he becomes a member of a smuggling ring. In Spanish with English subtitles. 103m/C VHS, Beta. **SP** Thelma Biral, Juan Jose Camero, Francesco Rabal; **D:** Hector Olivera.

El Norte 🎬🎬🎬🎬 1983 (R) Gripping account of a Guatemalan brother and sister, persecuted in their homeland, who make an arduous journey north ("El Norte") to America. Their difficult saga continues as they struggle against overwhelming odds in an attempt to realize their dreams. Passionate, sobering, and powerful. In English and Spanish with English subtitles. Produced in association with the "American Playhouse" series for PBS. Produced by Anna Thomas who also co-wrote the story with Nava. 139m/C VHS, Beta. **SP** David Villalpando, Zaide Silvia Gutierrez, Ernesto Cruz, Eraclo Zepeda, Stella Quan, Alicia del Lugo, Lupe Ontiveros; **D:** Gregory Nava; **W:** Anna Thomas, Gregory Nava. National Film Registry '95; Nominations: Academy Awards '84: Best Original Screenplay. *FOX*

El Paso Stampede 🎬½ 1953 Cowboy investigates raids on cattle herds used to feed Americans fighting in the Spanish-American War. 50m/B VHS, Beta. Allan "Rocky" Lane, Eddy Waller, Phyllis Coates; **D:** Harry Keller. *VCN*

El Super 🎬🎬🎬 1979 A Cuban refugee, still homesick after many years, struggles to make a life for himself in Manhattan as an apartment superintendent. In Spanish with English subtitles; an American production shot on location in New York City. 90m/C VHS. **SP** Raymundo Hidalgo-Gato, Orlando Jiminez-Leal, Zully Montero, Raynaldo Medina, Juan Granda, Hilda Lee, Elizabeth Pena; **D:** Leon Ichaso; **W:** Leon Ichaso, Manuel Arce. *NYF*

El: This Strange Passion 🎬🎬🎬 1952 Disturbing drama in which a man, convinced he is cuckolded, slowly descends into madness. Bunuel's surreal, almost Freudian look at the Spanish male's obsession with female fidelity. In Spanish with English subtitles. 82m/B VHS. **SP** Arturo de Cordova, Delia Garces, Luis Beristain, Aurora Walker; **D:** Luis Bunuel. *HTV, FCT*

Ele, My Friend 🎬🎬½ 1993 The British Raj still rules India in the 1920s, when 10-year-old Charles comes across a herd of wild elephants living in the jungle. Charles befriends a baby elephant he names Ele but what can he do when hunters also discover the animals. Filmed on location in south India. 104m/C VHS. Jacob Paul Guzman, Gazan Khan, R.S. Shivaji, Amjad Khan, Prabhu; **D:** Dharan Mandrayar; **W:** Dharan Mandrayar; **M:** Barry Phillips. *VCI, BTV*

Eleanor & Franklin 🎬🎬🎬½ 1976 An exceptional television dramatization of the personal lives of President Franklin D. Roosevelt and his wife Eleanor. Based on Joseph Lash's book, this Emmy award-winning film features stunning performances by Alexander and Herrmann in the title roles. 208m/C VHS, Beta. Jane Alexander, Edward Herrmann, Ed Flanders, Rosemary Murphy, MacKenzie Phillips, Pamela Franklin, Anna Lee, Linda Purl, Linda Kelsey, Lindsay Crouse; **D:** Daniel Petrie; **M:** John Barry. *SIG, TLF*

Eleanor: First Lady of the World 🎬🎬½ 1982 (G) Stapleton plays the former first lady after her husband's death as she goes on to work at the United Nations and emerges as even more of an influential public figure. Made for television. 96m/C VHS. Jean Stapleton, E.G. Marshall, Coral Browne, Joyce Van Patten, Gail Strickland, Kenneth Kimmins; **D:** John Erman; **M:** John Addison. *COL*

Electra 🎬🎬 1995 Sex-bomb Lorna (Tweed) does her oedipal best with stepson Billy (Tab), who was implanted with the secret of physical regeneration by his late scientist dad. Cybervillian Roach (Erik) wants the info, which can only be obtained through intimate contact, and Lorna's the right woman for the job. Funny how Billy's just so uncooperative. Very over-the-top. 85m/C VHS. Shannon Tweed, Joe Tab, Sten Eirik; **D:** Julian Grant; **W:** Damian Lee; **C:** Gerald R. Goozie. *NHO*

Electra Glide in Blue 🎬🎬🎬 1973 (R) An Arizona motorcycle cop uses his head in a world that's coming apart at the seams. Good action scenes; lots of violence. 113m/C VHS, LV. Robert (Bobby) Blake, Billy Green Bush, Mitchell Ryan, Jeannine Riley, Elisha Cook Jr., Royal Dano; **D:** James W. Guercio; **W:** Robert Boris; **C:** Conrad Hall. *MGM*

Electric Dreams 🎬🎬½ 1984 (PG) A young man buys a computer that yearns to do more than sit on a desk. First it takes over his apartment, then it sets its sights on the man's cello-playing neighbor—the same woman his owner is courting. To win her affections, the over-eager computer tries to dazzle her with a variety of musical compositions from his unique keyboard. Cort supplies the voice of Edgar the computer in this film that integrates a rock-music video format. 95m/C VHS, Beta, LV. Lenny Von Dohlen, Virginia Madsen, Maxwell Caulfield, Bud Cort, Koo Stark; **D:** Steven Barron. *MGM*

The Electric Horseman 🎬🎬½ 1979 (PG) Journalist Fonda sets out to discover the reason behind the kidnapping of a prized horse by an ex-rodeo star. The alcoholic cowboy has taken the horse to return it to its native environment, away from the clutches of corporate greed. As Fonda investigates the story she falls in love with rebel Redford. Excellent Las Vegas and remote western settings. 120m/C VHS, Beta, LV, Letterbox. Robert Redford, Jane Fonda, John Saxon, Willie Nelson, Valerie Perrine, Wilford Brimley, Nicolas Coster, James B. Sikking; **D:** Sydney Pollack; **M:** Dave Grusin. Nominations: Academy Awards '79: Best Sound. *USH*

The Electronic Monster 🎬🎬 *Escapement; The Electric Monster* 1957 Insurance claims investigator Cameron looks into the death of a Hollywood starlet and discovers an exclusive therapy center dedicated to hypnotism. At the facility, people vacation for weeks in morgue-like body drawers, while evil Dr. Illing uses an electronic device to control the sleeper's dreams and actions. Eerie. Intriguingly, it is one of the first films to explore the possibilities of brainwashing and mind control. 72m/B VHS. **GB** Rod Cameron, Mary Murphy, Meredith Edwards, Peter Illing; **D:** Montgomery Tully. *SNC*

The Elegant Criminal 🎬🎬½ 1992 Based on the true story of France's most infamous killer, Pierre Lacenaire. The film begins with Lacenaire in prison, writing his memoirs, receiving his admirers, and awaiting his execution (in 1836). A series of flashbacks detail his life and the supposed social crime which hindered his better instincts and turned him to the criminal life. However, Auteuil has such a wonderful time playing the charming bad guy that any blame to society fails to convince. In French with English subtitles. **120m/C VHS.** *FR* Daniel Auteuil, Jean Poiret, Jacques Weber, Marie-Armelle DeGuy, Maiwenn Le Besco, Patrick Pineau; *D:* Francois Girod; *W:* George Conchon, Francois Girod. *ORI, BTV, FCT*

The Element of Crime *✶✶½* *Forbrydelsens Element* 1984 In a monochromatic, post-holocaust future, a detective tracks down a serial killer of young girls. Made in Denmark, this minor festival favorite features an impressive directional debut and awaits cult status. Filmed in Sepiatone. **104m/C VHS, Beta.** *DK* Michael Elphick, Esmond Knight, Jerold Wells, Meme Lei, Astrid Henning-Jensen, Preben Leerdorff-Rye, Gotha Andersen; *D:* Lars von Trier. *UNI, TPV*

The Elementary School *✶✶* *Obecna Skola* 1991 Screenwriter Sverak's memories of his childhood are the basis for this child's eye view of the mysteries surrounding the adult world. In 1945, 10-year-old Eda (Jakoubek) is living in a village outside Prague. His school class is so wild that the teacher quits and is replaced by the strict Igor Hnizdo (Triska), who turns out to have a weakness for young women. Czech with subtitles. **100m/C VHS.** *CZ* Jan Triska, Vaclav Jakoubek, Zdenek Sverak, Radoslav Budas, Libuse Safrankova, Rudolf Hrusinsky, Petr Cepek; *D:* Jan Sverak; *W:* Zdenek Sverak; *C:* F.A. Brabec. Nominations: Academy Awards '91: Best Foreign Language Film. *NYF*

Elena and Her Men *✶✶✶* *Paris Does Strange Things; Elena et les Hommes* 1956 The romantic entanglements and intrigues of a poor Polish princess are explored in this enjoyable French picture. Beautiful cinematography by Claude Renoir. In French with subtitles. **98m/C VHS.** *FR* Ingrid Bergman, Jean Marais, Mel Ferrer, Jean Richard, Magali Noel, Pierre Bertin, Juliette Greco; *D:* Jean Renoir; *C:* Claude Renoir. *INT, FCT, TPV*

Eleni *✶✶* 1985 (PG) The true story of "New York Times" reporter Nicholas Gage and his journey to Athens to discover the truth about his mother's execution by Communists during the Greek rebellion after WWII. Adapted by Steve Tesich from Gage's bestselling book. **117m/C VHS, Beta, LV, 8mm, Closed Caption.** John Malkovich, Kate Nelligan, Linda Hunt, Oliver Cotton, Ronald Pickup, Dimitra Arliss, Rosalie Crutchley; *D:* Peter Yates; *W:* Steve Tesich; *C:* Billy Williams; *M:* Bruce Smeaton. *COL, IGP, NLC*

Elephant Boy *✶✶✶* 1937 An Indian boy helps government conservationists locate a herd of elephants in the jungle. Sabu's first film. Available in digitally remastered stereo. **80m/B VHS, Beta, LV.** *GB* Sabu, Walter Hudd, W.E. Holloway; *D:* Robert Flaherty, Zoltan Korda. Venice Film Festival '37: Best Director (Flaherty). *HBO, WAR*

The Elephant Man *✶✶✶✶* 1980 (PG) A biography of John Merrick, a severely deformed man who, with the help of a sympathetic doctor, moved from freak shows into posh London society. Lynch's first mainstream film, shot in black and white, it presents a startlingly vivid picture of the hypocrisies evident in the social moves of the Victorian era. Moving performance from Hurt in title role. **125m/B VHS, Beta, LV.** Anthony Hopkins, John Hurt, Anne Bancroft, John Gielgud, Wendy Hiller, Freddie Jones, Kenny Baker; *D:* David Lynch; *W:* Eric Bergren, Christopher DeVore, David Lynch; *M:* John Morris, Samuel Barber. British Academy Awards '80: Best Actor (Hurt), Best Film; Cesar Awards '82: Best Foreign Film; Nominations: Academy Awards '80: Best Actor (Hurt), Best Adapted Screenplay, Best Art Direction/Set Decoration, Best Costume Design, Best Director (Lynch), Best Film Editing, Best Picture, Best Original Score. *PAR*

Elephant Walk *✶✶½* 1954 Sri Lanka's balmy jungles provide the backdrop for a torrid love triangle in this post-prime Dieterle effort. Taylor, ignored by her wealthy drunkard hubby, finds solace in the arms of her spouse's sexy right-hand man. As if keeping the affair secret weren't a

big enough task, she also braves a cholera epidemic and a pack of vengeful elephants who take an unscheduled tour of her humble home. Lethargic lead performances make this more of a sleep walk, but Sofaer and Biberman's supporting roles are worth the price of rental. Taylor replaced Vivian Leigh early in the filming after she fell ill, but footage of Leigh in faraway shots is included. **103m/C VHS, Closed Caption.** Elizabeth Taylor, Dana Andrews, Peter Finch, Abraham Sofaer, Abner Biberman; *D:* William Dieterle; *C:* Loyal Griggs. *PAR, FCT*

11 Harrowhouse *✶✶✶* *Anything for Love; Fast Fortune* 1974 (PG) The Consolidated Selling System at 11 Harrowhouse, London, controls much of the world's diamond trade. Four adventurous thieves plot a daring heist relying on a very clever cockroach. A rather successful stab at spoofing detailed "heist" films. **95m/C VHS, Beta, Closed Caption.** *GB* Charles Grodin, Candice Bergen, James Mason, Trevor Howard, John Gielgud; *D:* Aram Avakian; *W:* Jeffrey Bloom. *FOX*

Eli Eli *✶✶½* 1940 An American Yiddish film about a family forced to live apart because of their farm's failure. Lighthearted and fun. In Yiddish with English titles. **85m/B VHS, Beta.** Esther Feild, Lazar Fried, Muni Serebroff; *D:* Joseph Seiden; *M:* Sholom Secunda. *VYY, AUD, FCT*

The Eliminators *✶* 1986 (PG) A cyborgian creature endeavors to avenge himself on his evil scientist creator with help from a kung fu expert and a Mexican. The group uses time travel and other devices to achieve their mission. **95m/C VHS, Beta, Closed Caption.** Roy Dotrice, Patrick Reynolds, Denise Crosby, Andrew Prine, Conan Lee; *D:* Peter Manoogian; *W:* Danny Bilson, Paul DeMeo; *M:* Richard Band. *FOX*

Elisa *✶✶* 1994 Teenaged sexpot Marie (Paradis) has grown up in a reform school, thanks to her mother Elisa's suicide. Along with friends Solange (Courau) and Ahmed (Sall), Marie spends her time on the Paris streets shoplifting and flirting. Obsessed with finding her long-gone father, Marie discovers that Lebovitch (Depardieu), the writer of the popular song "Elisa," is daddy dearest. He's now a drunk, living on a fishing island, and Marie sets out to right the wrongs she believes drove her mother to suicide. Based on the song by Serge Gainsbourg. French with subtitles. **111m/C VHS.** *FR* Vanessa Paradis, Gerard Depardieu, Clothilde Courau, Sekkou Sall, Florence Thomassin; *D:* Jean Becker; *W:* Jean Becker, Fabrice Carazo; *C:* Etienne Becker; *M:* Zbigniew Preisner. Cesar Awards '95: Best Supporting Actress (Courau), Best Score. *NYR*

Elisa, Vida Mia *✶✶* *Elisa, My Love; Elisa, My Life* 1977 A long-estranged father and daughter are reunited when he falls ill. She stays to help him write his biography and gradually begins to see things through his perspective. The shifting narrative can confuse but worth seeing are Rey and Chaplin's subtle performances. Spanish with subtitles. **125m/C VHS.** *SP* Fernando Rey, Geraldine Chaplin, Norman Brisky, Isabel Mestres, Joaquin Hinojosa; *D:* Carlos Saura; *W:* Carlos Saura; *M:* Erik Satie. Cannes Film Festival '77: Best Actor (Rey). *FCT, CVC*

Elizabeth of Ladymead *✶✶✶* 1948 Four generations of a British family live through their experiences in the Crimean War, Boer War, WWI, and WWII. Neagle, playing the wives in all four generations, aptly explores the woman's side of war. Enjoyable performances from husband and wife team Neagle and Wilcox. **97m/C VHS, Beta.** Anna Neagle, Hugh Williams, Bernard Lee, Michael Lawrence, Nicholas Phipps, Isabel Jeans; *D:* Herbert Wilcox. *DVT, VEC*

Elizabeth R *✶✶✶* 1972 Jackson is outstanding in the title role of this TV drama focusing on the life of Elizabeth I, from 17 to 70. Constantly besieged by court intrigue and political machinations, the Virgin Queen managed to restore England to glory and power amidst private and public turmoil. Six 90-minute cassettes. **540m/C VHS.** *GB* Glenda Jackson, Rosalie Crutchley, Robin Ellis, Robert Hardy, Peter Jeffrey, Stephen Murray, Vivian Pickles, Sarah Frampton, Ronald Hines; *D:* Claude Whatham, Herbert

Wise, Roderick Graham, Richard Martin, Donald Whatham; *W:* Hugh Whitemore, John Hale, Julian Mitchell, John Prebble, Ian Rodger, Rosemary Anne Sisson. *FOX, VIF*

Elizabeth, the Queen *✶✶* *The Private Lives of Elizabeth and Essex* 1968 Historical drama recreates the struggle for power by Robert Devereaux, Earl of Essex, whom the aging Queen Elizabeth I both loved and feared, and whose downfall she finally invoked. Part of "George Schaefer's Showcase Theatre." **76m/C VHS, Beta.** Judith Anderson, Charlton Heston; *D:* George Schaefer. *FHS*

Eliza's Horoscope *✶✶½* 1970 A frail Canadian woman uses astrology in her search for love in Montreal, and experiences bizarre and surreal events. An acclaimed Canadian film. **120m/C VHS, Beta.** *CA* Tommy Lee Jones, Elizabeth Moorman; *D:* Gordon Sheppard.

Elke *✶½* *Friend of the Family* 1995 While backpacking across the U.S., Elke (O'Brien) is invited to stay in Malibu with the Stillman family—husband Jeff, wife Linda, and their 20-something children, Josh and Montana. Naturally, the sexy Elke becomes very involved with the family. **98m/C VHS.** Shauna O'Brien, C.T. Miller, Griffin Drew, Lisa Boyle. *TRI*

Ella Cinders *✶✶✶* 1926 The American mania for breaking into the movies is satirized in this look at a girl who wins a trip to Hollywood in a small-town beauty contest. Silent with original organ score. **60m/B VHS, Beta.** Colleen Moore, Harry Langdon, Lloyd Hughes, Jed Prouty, Vera Lewis; *D:* Alfred E. Green. *NOS, GPV, VYY*

Ellen Foster *✶✶½* 1997 (PG-13) Coming-of-age TV drama concerns 10-year-old Ellen (Malone), who lives with her abusive, drunken dad (Levine) and her gentle mom (O'Connor). After mom dies, Ellen is shuffled between uncaring relatives, including a nasty grandma, Leonora (Harris), while trying to draw strength from the few friends and teachers who do care about her. Based on the book by Kaye Gibbons. **CW:** Some abusive treatment of a child. **?m/C VHS.** Jena Malone, Julie Harris, Ted Levine, Glynnis O'Connor, Debra Monk, Barbara Garrick, Kate Burton, Zeljko Ivanek, Lynne Moody, Bill Nunn, Amanda Peet, Allison Jones, Timothy Olyphant; *D:* John Erman; *W:* Maria Nation, William Hanley; *C:* Brian West; *M:* John Morris. *HMK*

Ellie *✶½* 1984 (R) A murderous widow's stepdaughter tries to save her father from being added to the woman's extensive list of dearly departed husbands. **90m/C VHS, Beta.** Shelley Winters, Sheila Kennedy, Pat Paulsen, George Gobel, Edward Albert; *D:* Peter Wittman. *ART, VES*

Elmer *✶½* 1976 (G) Follows the adventures of a temporarily blinded youth and a lovable hound dog who meet in the wilderness and together set off in search of civilization. **82m/C VHS, Beta.** Elmer Swanson, Phillip Swanson; *D:* Christopher Cain. *ART*

Elmer Gantry *✶✶✶½* 1960 The classic multi-Oscar-winning adaptation of the Sinclair Lewis novel written to expose and denounce the flamboyant, small-town evangelists spreading through America at the time. In the film, Lancaster is the amoral Southern preacher who exacts wealth and power from his congregation, and takes a nun as a mistress. Jones stars as his ex-girlfriend who resorts to a life of prostitution. **146m/C VHS, Beta, LV.** Burt Lancaster, Shirley Jones, Jean Simmons, Dean Jagger, Arthur Kennedy, Patti Page, Edward Andrews, John McIntire, Hugh Marlowe, Rex Ingram; *D:* Richard Brooks; *W:* Richard Brooks; *C:* John Alton; *M:* Andre Previn. Academy Awards '60: Best Actor (Lancaster), Best Adapted Screenplay, Best Supporting Actress (Jones); Golden Globe Awards '61: Best Actor—Drama (Lancaster); National Board of Review Awards '60: Best Supporting Actress (Jones); New York Film Critics Awards '60: Best Actor (Lancaster); Nominations: Academy Awards '60: Best Picture, Best Original Dramatic/Comedy Score. *FOX, MGM, FCT*

Elmore Leonard's Gold Coast *✶✶* *Gold Coast* 1997 (R) Miami mobster Frank DiCilia (Bradford) is dead and his widow Karen (Helgenberger) is not happy. Yes, she's inherited $15 mil but Frank's will also stipulates that she has to remain faithful to him forever. Too bad Karen and smalltime con man Maguire (Caruso) are instantly attracted to one another. And too bad Frank's also left behind loathsome hit man Roland (Kober) to enforce the edict (although if Karen wants him, Roland's willing to be flexible). Cable movie based on the novel by Elmore Leonard.*CW:* Violence, sexuality and language. 109m/ C VHS, Closed Caption. David Caruso, Marg Helgenberger, Jeff Kober, Barry Primus, Richard Bradford; *D:* Peter Weller; *W:* Harley Peyton. PAR

Elsa, Elsa 1985 Satire of moviemaking life finds a scriptwriter-director distracted by the loss of his girlfriend and unable to concentrate on writing a memoir of his career as a child actor. He creates a subplot dealing with his romantic problems, and puts the film in jeopardy. Fine acting and witty dialogue. In French with English subtitles. 85m/C VHS. FR *D:* Didier Haudepin. FCT

The Elusive Corporal 𝄞𝄞𝄞½ *Le Caporal Epingle* 1962 Set in a P.O.W. camp on the day France surrendered to Germany, this is the story of the French and Germans, complete with memories of a France that is no more. 108m/B VHS, Beta, LV. Jean-Pierre Cassel, Claude Brasseur, O.E. Hasse, Claude Rich; *D:* Jean Renoir. VYY, INT

The Elusive Pimpernel 𝄞𝄞½ *The Fighting Pimpernel* 1950 Niven sparkles in otherwise undistinguished adaptation of Baroness Orczy's "The Scarlet Pimpernel." 109m/C VHS, Beta. GB David Niven, Margaret Leighton, Jack Hawkins, Cyril Cusack, Robert Coote, Edmund Audran, Danielle Godet, Patrick Macnee; *D:* Michael Powell; *W:* Michael Powell, Emeric Pressburger. HMV, FCT

Elves 𝄞 1989 (PG-13) A group of possessed, neo-Nazi elves performs serious human harm at Christmas time in this tongue-in-check thriller. 95m/C VHS, Beta. Dan Haggerty, Deanna Lund, Julie Austin, Borah Silver; *D:* Jeffrey Mandel.

Elvira Madigan 𝄞𝄞𝄞 1967 (PG) Chronicles the 19th-century Swedish romance between a young officer and a beautiful circus tight-rope walker. Based on a true incident. Exceptional direction and photography. In Swedish with English subtitles. 90m/C VHS, Beta, LV. SW Pia Degermark, Thommy Berggren, Lennart Malmer, Nina Widerberg, Cleo Jensen; *D:* Bo Widerberg; *W:* Bo Widerberg. Cannes Film Festival '67: Best Actress (Degermark). WAC, FCT, TPV

Elvira, Mistress of the Dark 𝄞𝄞 1988 (PG-13) A manic comedy based on Peterson's infamous B-movie horror-hostess character. The mega-busted terror-queen inherits a house in a conservative Massachusetts town and causes double-entendre chaos when she attempts to sell it. 96m/C VHS, Beta, LV, Closed Caption. Cassandra Peterson, Jeff Conaway, Susan Kellerman, Edie McClurg, Daniel Greene, W. Morgan Shepherd, Kurt Fuller; *D:* James Signorelli; *C:* Hanania Baer. VTR

Elvis and Me 𝄞½ 1988 A TV mini series based on Priscilla Beaulieu Presley's autobiography about her life with the Pelvis. Features many of Presley's biggest hits, sung by country star Ronnie McDowell. Film may aggravate Elvis fans, however, as the King is often depicted negatively from his ex-wife's point of view. 187m/C VHS, Beta, Closed Caption. Dale Midkiff, Susan Walters, Billy Green Bush, Linda Miller, Jon Cypher; *D:* Larry Peerce. VTR

Elvis in Hollywood 𝄞𝄞𝄞 1993 A tribute highlighting Presley's first four films, "Love Me Tender," "Loving You," "Jailhouse Rock," and "King Creole," completed prior to his reporting for active duty in the army. Features his 1956 screen test at Paramount Studios; photos from the movie sets; interviews with co-stars, directors, writers, business associates, songwriters, and friends; and home movies as well as out-take footage from "Jailhouse Rock." 65m/C VHS, LV. *D:* Frank Martin. BMG, BTV

Elvis: The Movie 𝄞𝄞½ 1979 A made-for-television biography of the legendary singer, from his high school days to his Las Vegas comeback. Russell gives a convincing performance and lip syncs effectively to the voice of the King (provided by country singer Ronnie McDowell). Also available in 150-minute version. 117m/C VHS, Beta. Kurt Russell, Season Hubley, Shelley Winters, Ed Begley Jr., Dennis Christopher, Pat Hingle, Bing Russell, Joe Mantegna; *D:* John Carpenter. ART, VES

Emanon 𝄞½ 1986 (PG-13) A coming-of-age tale about a young kid and the Christ-like vagabond, named Emanon (or "no name" if spelled in reverse), he befriends. 101m/C VHS, Beta. Stuart Paul, Cheryl Lynn, Jeremy Miller; *D:* Stuart Paul. NLC

Embassy 𝄞𝄞 *Target: Embassy* 1972 In this mediocre espionage thriller, von Sydow is a Soviet defector under asylum at the U.S. embassy in Beirut. Colonel Connors, a Russian spy, penetrates embassy security and wounds von Sydow. He is caught, escapes, is captured, escapes, and is caught again. Great cast, but script is often too wordy and contrived. 90m/C VHS. GB Richard Roundtree, Chuck Connors, Max von Sydow, Ray Milland, Broderick Crawford, Marie-Jose Nat; *D:* Gordon Hessler. WVE

Embassy 𝄞𝄞 1985 A made-for-television movie about an American family in Rome that unknowingly possesses a secret computer chip, and thus is pursued by ruthless agents. 104m/C VHS, Beta. Nick Mancuso, Blanche Baker, Eli Wallach, Sam Wanamaker, Richard Gilliland, Mimi Rogers, George Grizzard, Richard Masur, Kim Darby; *D:* Robert Lewis. NO

Embrace of the Vampire 𝄞𝄞 1995 (R) Innocent young Charlotte (Milano) must make a choice between her college boyfriend Chris (Pruett) and a new nighttime lover (Kemp) with some decidedly different habits. Seems Charlotte looks exactly like a love lost hundreds of years ago and he's not going to take no for an answer. Also available in an unrated version.*CW:* Strong sexuality; nudity; graphic violence; language. 92m/ C VHS, LV, Closed Caption. Alyssa Milano, Martin Kemp, Harrison Pruett, Charlotte Lewis, Jordan Ladd, Rachel True, Jennifer Tilly; *D:* Anne Goursaud; *W:* Halle Eaton, Nicole Coady, Rick Bitzelberger; *M:* Joseph Williams. TTC, IME

Embryo 𝄞𝄞 *Created to Kill* 1976 (PG) An average sci-fi drama about a scientist who uses raw genetic material to artificially produce a beautiful woman, with ghastly results. 108m/C VHS, Beta. Rock Hudson, Barbara Carrera, Diane Ladd, Roddy McDowall, Ann Schedeen, John Elerick, Dr. Joyce Brothers; *D:* Ralph Nelson; *C:* Fred W. Koenekamp. ART

The Emerald Forest 𝄞𝄞𝄞 1985 (R) Captivating adventure about a young boy who is kidnapped by a primitive tribe of Amazons while his family is traveling through the Brazilian jungle. Boothe is the father who searches 10 years for him. An engrossing look at tribal life in the vanishing jungle. Beautifully photographed and based upon a true story. Features the director's son as the kidnapped youth. 113m/C VHS, Beta, LV, 8mm, Closed Caption. Powers Boothe, Meg Foster, Charley Boorman, Dira Pass, Rui Polonah; *D:* John Boorman; *W:* Rospo Pallenberg; *C:* Philippe Rousselot. NLC

Emerald Jungle 𝄞½ *Eaten Alive by Cannibals; Eaten Alive; Mangiati Vivi dai Cannibali* 1980 While searching for her missing sister in the jungle, Agren encounters cannibal tribes and a colony of brainwashed cult followers. This Italian feature was cut for its U.S. release. 92m/C VHS, Beta. IT Robert Kerman, Janet Agren, Mel Ferrer, Luciano Martino, Mino Loy, Ivan Rassimov, Paola Senatore, Me Me Lay, Meg Fleming, Franco Fantasia; *D:* Umberto Lenzi; *W:* Umberto Lenzi; *C:* Frederico Zanni. NO

Emerald of Artama 𝄞 1967 Anyone viewing the most precious and sought after stone in the history of man does not live to tell about it. 93m/C VHS. Rory Calhoun. NO

The Emigrants 𝄞𝄞𝄞 *Utvandrarna* 1972 (PG) Farmer von Sydow decides to gather his wife (Ullmann) and family together and leave 19th-century Sweden for the promise of a new life in America. Film is divided into their leaving, the voyage over, and the journey to a settlement in Minnesota. Pacing is somewhat slow; notable cinematography (by director Troell). Adapted from the novels by Vilhelm Moberg. Dubbed into English. Followed by "The New Land." Also edited with the sequel for TV as "The Emigrant Saga." 151m/C VHS. SW Max von Sydow, Liv Ullmann, Allan Edwall, Eddie Axberg, Svenolof Bern, Aina Alfredsson, Monica Zetterlund, Pierre Lindstedt; *D:* Jan Troell; *W:* Jan Troell, Bengt Forslund; *C:* Jan Troell; *M:* Erik Nordgren. New York Film Critics Awards '72: Best Actress (Ullmann); Nominations: Academy Awards '72: Best Actress (Ullmann), Best Adapted Screenplay, Best Director (Troell), Best Picture. WAR, MOV

Emil and the Detectives 𝄞𝄞½ *Emil Und Die Detektive* 1964 A German ten-year-old is robbed of his grandmother's money by gangsters, and subsequently enlists the help of pre-adolescent detectives to retrieve it. Good Disney dramatization of the Erich Kastner children's novel. Remake of the 1931 German film starring Rolf Wenkhaus. 99m/C VHS, Beta. Bryan Russell, Walter Slezak, Roger Mobley; *D:* Peter Tewkesbury; *W:* A.J. Carothers. DIS

Emily woof! 1977 Returning from her exclusive Swiss finishing school, licentious young Emily discovers mama is a prostitute and deals with the scalding news by delving into a series of erotic encounters at the hands of her willing "instructors." Stark's first venture into the realm of soft porn. 87m/C VHS, Beta. Koo Stark; *D:* Henry Herbert; *C:* Jack Hildyard. MGM

Emily Bronte's Wuthering Heights 𝄞𝄞½ *Wuthering Heights* 1992 (PG) Miscast version of the tragic tale of doomed lovers Cathy (Binoche) and Heathcliff (Fiennes). While Fiennes may seem too refined for the role, he manages to be both brooding and brutal. However, the beautiful Binoche can't successfully supress her French accent enough to pass for a heedless Yorkshire lass. Good supporting cast, with O'Connor posing as writer/narrator Bronte. 107m/C VHS, Closed Caption. GB Ralph Fiennes, Juliette Binoche, Janet McTeer, Sophie Ward, Simon Shepherd, Jeremy Northam, Jason Riddington, Jonathan Firth, Paul Geoffrey, Sinead O'Connor; *D:* Peter Kosminsky; *W:* Anne Devlin; *C:* Mike Southon; *M:* Ryuichi Sakamoto. PAR

Eminent Domain 𝄞𝄞½ 1991 (PG-13) A communist party member wakes up to find himself stripped of power in a Kafkaesque purge, not knowing what he is accused of—or why. A potent premise, indifferently handled despite filming on location in Poland. Based on actual events that befell the family of scriptwriter Androej Krakowski. 102m/C VHS. Donald Sutherland, Anne Archer, Paul Freeman, Bernard Hepton, Francoise Michaud, Jodhi May; *D:* John Irvin; *W:* Andrzej Krakowski, Richard Greggson; *M:* Zbigniew Preisner. IME

Emissary 𝄞𝄞 1989 (R) An American politician and his wife are blackmailed in Africa by the Russians into revealing state secrets that could spark WWIII. 98m/C VHS, Beta, LV. SA Robert Vaughn, Ted Leplat, Terry Norton, Andre Jacobs; *D:* Jan Scholtz. NO

Emma 𝄞𝄞½ 197? BBC TV version of the Jane Austen saga with young Emma trying her matchmaking skills on all her friends and neighbors—with disastrous results. Mr. Knightly tries to provide both a voice of reason and romance, if only Emma could realize it. 257m/C VHS. GB Doran Goodwin, Vivienne Moore, John Carson, Donald Eccles, Debbie Bowen. VCO

Emma 𝄞𝄞𝄞 1996 (PG) Jane Austen's 1816 novel about wealthy, 21-year-old Emma Woodhouse (Paltrow) who makes it her goal to "fix" the lives of all her friends, while ignoring her own problems (the modern adaptation was "Clueless"). Emma focuses much of her attention on Harriet Smith (Collete), a simple young woman who Emma believes is in need of the perfect mate. Meanwhile, Emma neglects to notice the attractive, and exasperated, Mr. Knightley (Northam). McGrath's screenplay makes Emma and

Knightley more likable than in the book, but otherwise stays true. After the success of "Sense and Sensibility," Austen's name is making it in the movies in the footsteps of the likes of John Grisham. **120m/C VHS, LV, Closed Caption.** Gwyneth Paltrow, Jeremy Northam, Greta Scacchi, Toni Collette, Alan Cumming, Juliet Stevenson, Polly Walker, Ewan McGregor, James Cosmo, Sophie Thompson, Phyllida Law; **D:** Douglas McGrath; **W:** Douglas McGrath; **C:** Ian Wilson; **M:** Rachel Portman. Academy Awards '96: Best Original Score; Nominations: Academy Awards '96: Best Costume Design; Writers Guild of America '96: Best Adapted Screenplay. *TOU*

Emma 🎬🎬🎬 *Jane Austen's Emma* **1997** British TV adaptation of the Jane Austen novel featuring young, matchmaking Emma (Beckinsale) wrecking havoc amongst her friends and neighbors with her would-be romantic alliances. Screenplay is truer to the book, with slightly less likable personalities than the 1996 big-screen version. Excellent cast, and beautiful locations and costumes make this one worth seeing. A&E Network offered "Emma" after the overwhelming success of their miniseries "Pride and Prejudice," also adapted from Austen. **107m/C VHS, Closed Caption.** GB Kate Beckinsale, Mark Strong, Samantha Bond, Prunella Scales, Bernard Hepton, Raymond Coulthard, Dominic Rowan, James Hazeldine, Samantha Morton, Lucy Robinson, Olivia Williams; **D:** Diarmuid Lawrence; **W:** Andrew Davis. *AEH, WMI, VIF*

Emmanuelle 🎬🎬½ **1974** Filmed in Bangkok, a young, beautiful woman is introduced by her husband to an uninhibited world of sensuality. Above-average soft-core skin film, made with sophistication and style. Kristel maintains a vulnerability and awareness, never becoming a mannequin. **92m/C VHS, Beta.** FR Sylvia Kristel, Alain Cuny, Marika Green, Daniel Sarky; **D:** Just Jaeckin; **C:** Richard Suzuki; **M:** Pierre Bachelet. *COL*

Emmanuelle 4 🎬 **1984 (R)** Emmanuelle flees a bad relationship and undergoes plastic surgery to mask her identity. Ultimately, she becomes a beautiful young model in the form of a different actress, of course. **95m/C VHS, Beta.** FR Sylvia Kristel, Mia Nygren, Patrick Bauchau; **D:** Francis Giacobetti. *MGM*

Emmanuelle 5 🎬½ **1987 (R)** This time around sexy Emmanuelle flees aboard a convenient yacht when she's chased by adoring fans at the Cannes Film Festival. But she winds up being forced to join an Arab sheik's harem of slaves. A good example of a series that should have quit while it was ahead. **78m/C VHS.** FR Monique Gabrielle, Charles Foster; **D:** Steve Barnett, Walerian Borowczyk; **M:** Pierre Bachelet. *NHO*

Emmanuelle 6 🎬 **1992 (R)** The saga of the sexy beauty continues. This time Emmanuelle and a group of models head for the paradise of an Amazon jungle where they promptly become the prized captives of a drug lord.**CW:** Language and strong sensuality. **80m/C VHS.** *NHO*

Emmanuelle & Joanna 🎬 **1986** A mistreated newlywed bride goes to her sister's whorehouse and stumbles across lots of soft-core antics. **90m/C VHS, Beta.** FR Sherry Buchanan, Danielle Dublino.

Emmanuelle in the Country 🎬 **1978** Emmanuelle becomes a nurse in an attempt to bring comfort and other pleasures to those in need. **90m/C VHS, Beta, LV.** FR Laura Gemser. *IME*

Emmanuelle on Taboo Island 🎬½ **1976 (R)** Marooned young man discovers a beautiful woman on his island. This delights him. **95m/C VHS, Beta.** FR Laura Gemser, Paul Giusti, Arthur Kennedy. *NO*

Emmanuelle, the Joys of a Woman 🎬 **1976** The amorous exploits of a sensuous, liberated couple take them and their erotic companions to exotic Hong Kong, Bangkok, and Bali. **92m/C VHS, Beta, LV, 8mm.** FR Sylvia Kristel, Umberto Orsini, Catherine Rivet, Frederic Lagache; **D:** Francis Giacobetti. *PAR*

Emmanuelle, the Queen 🎬 **1975** Seeking revenge, Emmanuelle plots the murder of her sadistic husband. The lecherous assassin she hires tries to blackmail her, and she challenges him at his own game of deadly seduction. **90m/C VHS, Beta.** Laura Gemser. *NO*

Emmanuelle's Daughter 🎬 **1979** A Greek-made thriller in which a vapidly sensuous heroine cavorts amid episodes of murder, blackmail, and rape. **91m/C Beta.** GR Laura Gemser, Gabriele Tinti, Livia Russa, Vagelis Varton, Nadia Neri. *NO*

Emma's Shadow 🎬🎬🎬 *Skyggen af Emma* **1988** In the 1930s, a young girl fakes her own kidnapping to get away from her inattentive family and comes to befriend an ex-convict sewer worker. In Danish with English subtitles. Winner of the Prix de la Jeunesse at Cannes, it was voted 1988's Best Danish Film. **93m/C VHS.** DK Bjorje Ahlstedt, Line Kruse; **D:** Soeren Kragh-Jacobsen. *ORI, FCT, FXL*

Emperor Jones 🎬🎬½ **1933** Loosely based on Eugene O'Neill's play, film portrays the rise and fall of a railroad porter whose exploits take him from a life sentence on a chain gang to emperor of Haiti. Robeson recreates his stage role in his first screen appearance. **72m/B VHS, Beta, LV.** Paul Robeson, Dudley Digges, Frank Wilson, Fredi Washington, Ruby Elzy; **D:** Dudley Murphy. *SNC, NOS, HHT*

Emperor Jones/Paul Robeson: Tribute to an Artist **1933** A classic, rarely viewed version of the Eugene O'Neill play about a criminal who schemes his way into becoming the king of a Caribbean island. Robeson's only true dramatic film appearance. The film is accompanied by a documentary profile of Robeson, made in 1979. **102m/B VHS, Beta.** Paul Robeson, Dudley Digges, Frank Wilson; **D:** Dudley Murphy. *COL, HMV*

Emperor of the Bronx 🎬 **1989** A look at crime, sleaze, violence, and the actions of bad guys in the inner-city. **90m/C VHS, Beta.** William Smith. *HHE*

Emperor Waltz 🎬🎬½ **1948** Typical Hollywood musical finds phonograph salesman Crosby travelling to Vienna, hoping to sell his goods to the Austrian royal family of Emperor Franz Joseph. He meets up with the Emperor's snobby niece (Fontaine) and attempts to charm her into an audience with her royal uncle. Naturally the two fall in love and everything ends in a happy fade-out. ♫The Emperor's Waltz; Friendly Mountains; Get Yourself a Phonograph; The Kiss in Your Eyes; I Kiss Your Hand, Madame; The Whistler and His Dog. **106m/C VHS, Closed Caption.** Bing Crosby, Joan Fontaine, Roland Culver, Richard Haydn, Lucile Watson, Sig Rumann, Harold Vermilyea; **D:** Billy Wilder; **W:** Billy Wilder, Charles Brackett; **C:** George Barnes; **M:** Victor Young. Nominations: Academy Awards '48: Scoring of a Musical. *USH*

The Emperor's New Clothes **1984** The story of an emperor and the unusual outfit he gets from his tailor. A "Faerie Tale Theatre" presentation. **60m/C VHS, Beta, Closed Caption.** Art Carney, Alan Arkin, Dick Shawn; **D:** Peter Medak. *KUI, FOX, FCT*

The Empire of Passion 🎬🎬🎬 **1976** A peasant woman and her low-life lover kill the woman's husband, but find the future they planned with each other is not to be. The husband's ghost returns to haunt them, and destroy the passionate bond which led to the murder. Oshima's follow-up to "In the Realm of the Senses." In Japanese with English subtitles. **110m/C VHS.** JP Nagisa Oshima, Kazuko Yoshiyuki, Tatsuya Fuji, Takahiro Tamura, Takuzo Kawatani; **D:** Nagisa Oshima. Cannes Film Festival '78: Best Director (Oshima). *FCT*

Empire of the Ants 🎬½ **1977 (PG)** A group of enormous, nuclear, unfriendly ants stalk a real estate dealer and prospective buyers of undeveloped oceanfront property. Story originated by master science-fiction storyteller H. G.

Wells. 90m/C VHS, Beta, Joan Collins, Robert Lansing, John David Carson, Albert Salmi, Jacqueline Scott, Robert Pine; **D:** Bert I. Gordon; **W:** Bert I. Gordon; **C:** Reginald Morris.

Empire of the Dragon 🎬 **198?** Rip-roaring martial arts adventure featuring standard number of wide-ranging kicks. **90m/C VHS, Beta.** Chen Tien Tse, Chia Kai, Chang Shan. *NO*

Empire of the Sun 🎬🎬🎬 **1987 (PG)** Spielberg's mature, extraordinarily vivid return to real storytelling, from the best-selling J.G. Ballard novel. Yearns to be a great film, but occasional flat spots keep it slightly out of contention. Young, wealthy British Bale lives in Shanghai, but is thrust into a life of poverty and discomfort when China is invaded by Japan at the onset of WWII and he's separated from his family and interred in a prison camp. A mysterious, breathtaking work, in which Spielberg's heightened juvenile romanticism has a real, heartbreaking context. Two other 1987 releases explore the WWII memories of young boys: "Au Revoir Les Enfants" and "Hope and Glory." **153m/C VHS, Beta, LV, 8mm, Letterbox, Closed Caption.** Christian Bale, John Malkovich, Miranda Richardson, Nigel Havers, Joe Pantoliano, Leslie Phillips, Rupert Frazer, Ben Stiller, Robert Stephens, Burt Kwouk, Masato Ibu, Emily Richard; **Cameos:** J.G. Ballard; **D:** Steven Spielberg; **W:** Tom Stoppard; **C:** Allen Daviau; **M:** John Williams. National Board of Review Awards '87: Best Director (Spielberg); Nominations: Academy Awards '87: Best Art Direction/Set Decoration, Best Cinematography, Best Costume Design, Best Film Editing, Best Sound, Best Original Score.*WAR*

Empire Records 🎬🎬 **1995 (PG-13)** Well, the soundtrack's good and that's about all this frantic movie has going for it (besides a photogenic cast). Joe's (LaPaglia) the manager of an independent record store about to be taken over by a faceless conglomerate unless he and his young-and-crisis-prone staff can come up with the cash to buy the place within 24 hours.*CW:* Sexual situations, language, a drug issue. **91m/C VHS, Closed Caption.** Anthony LaPaglia, Rory Cochrane, Liv Tyler, Renee Zellweger, Johnny Whitworth, Robin Tunney, Ethan Randall, Maxwell Caulfield, Debi Mazar; **D:** Allan Moyle; **W:** Carol Heikkinen; **C:** Walt Lloyd. *WAR*

Empire State 🎬 **1987 (R)** When his friend disappears from a posh London nightclub, a young man searches for him and finds more action and intrigue than he can handle. Even so, this movie's still pretty bland. **102m/C VHS, Beta.** GB Cathryn Harrison, Martin Landau, Ray McAnally; **D:** Ron Peck. *THV*

The Empire Strikes Back 🎬🎬🎬🎬 **1980 (PG)** Second film in the epic "Star Wars" trilogy finds young Luke Skywalker and the Rebel Alliance plotting new strategies as they prepare to battle the evil Darth Vader and the forces of the Dark Side. Luke learns the ways of a Jedi knight from master Yoda, while Han and Leia find time for romance and a few adventures of their own. Introduces the charismatic Lando Calrissian, vulgar and drooling Jabba the Hut, and a mind-numbing secret from Vadar. Offers the same superb special effects and hearty plot as set by 1977's excellent "Star Wars." Followed by "Return of the Jedi" in 1983. Also available on Laserdisc with "The Making of 'Star Wars'." **124m/C VHS, Beta, LV, Letterbox, Closed Caption.** Mark Hamill, Carrie Fisher, Harrison Ford, Billy Dee Williams, Alec Guinness, David Prowse, Kenny Baker, Frank Oz, Anthony Daniels, Peter Mayhew, Clive Revill, Julian Glover, John Ratzenberger; **D:** Irvin Kershner; **W:** Leigh Brackett, Lawrence Kasdan; **C:** Peter Suschitzsky; **M:** John Williams; **V:** James Earl Jones. Academy Awards '80: Best Sound, Best Visual Effects; Nominations: Academy Awards '80: Best Art Direction/Set Decoration, Best Original Score. *FOX, FCT, RDG*

Employees' Entrance 🎬🎬🎬 **1933** William stars as a ruthless department store manager in this story about commerce and compromise during the Depression. Young gives an excellent performance as the wife of one of his employees. Outrageous, and racy, this pre-Code film was expertly directed by veteran craftsman Del Ruth. Based on a play by David Boehm. **74m/B VHS, Closed Caption.** Warren William, Loretta Young, Wallace Ford, Alice White, Allen Jenkins; **D:** Roy Del Ruth; **W:** Robert Presnell. *MGM*

The Empty Beach 🐾½ **1985** A tough private detective investigates the disappearance of a wealthy business tycoon. **87m/C VHS, Beta.** *AU* Bryan Brown, Anna Maria Monticelli; **D:** Chris Thomson. *ART*

An Empty Bed 🐾🐾🐾 **1990** Award-winning independent production depicting Bill Frayne, an older homosexual, and the challenges of his everyday life. Told mostly in flashbacks as Bill encounters people and places during the course of one day, this is a delicate drama with important statements about homosexuality, aging and honesty. **60m/C VHS.** John Wylie, Mark Clifford Smith, Conan McCarty, Dorothy Stinnette, Kevin Kelly, Thomas Hill, Harriet Bass; **D:** Mark Gasper; **W:** Mark Gasper. *FRF, FCT, YOC*

Empty Canvas 🐾½ *La Noia: L'Ennui Et Sa Diversion, L'Erotisme* **1964** A spiritually bankrupt artist becomes obsessively jealous of his mistress who refuses to marry him in the hope that someone better will come along. Based on the Alberto Moravia novel. **118m/B VHS, Beta.** *FR IT* Horst Buchholz, Catherine Spaak, Bette Davis; **D:** Damiano Damiani; **M:** Luis Bacalov. *MLB*

Enchanted April 🐾🐾½ **1992 (PG)** Two women, tired of their overbearing husbands, rent a villa in Portofino, Italy, for a month with two other very different women—a beautiful but bored socialite, and a crusty old woman with an impeccable literary pedigree. The effects of the charming villa, with plenty of wisteria and sunshine, do wonders for the women. A charming and romantic period piece. Based on the 1922 novel by Elizabeth von Arnim. **93m/C VHS, Beta, LV, Closed Caption.** *GB* Miranda Richardson, Joan Plowright, Josie Lawrence, Polly Walker, Alfred Molina, Jim Broadbent, Michael Kitchen, Adriana Fachetti; **D:** Mike Newell; **W:** Peter Barnes; **M:** Richard Rodney Bennett. Golden Globe Awards '93: Best Actress—Musical/Comedy (Richardson), Best Supporting Actress (Plowright); Nominations: Academy Awards '92: Best Adapted Screenplay, Best Costume Design, Best Supporting Actress (Plowright). *PAR, MOV, WAR*

The Enchanted Cottage 🐾🐾½ **1945** Represents Hollywood's "love conquers all" fantasy hokum, as a disfigured war vet and a homely girl retreat from the horrors of the world into a secluded cottage, where they both regain youth and beauty. A four-tissue heart-tugger. Adopted from the Arthur Pinero play. **91m/B VHS, Beta, LV.** Dorothy McGuire, Robert Young, Herbert Marshall, Mildred Natwick, Spring Byington, Hillary Brooke, Richard Gaines, Robert Clarke; **D:** John Cromwell. Nominations: Academy Awards '45: Best Original Dramatic/Comedy Score. *NOS, TTC*

The Enchanted Forest 🐾🐾½ **1945** An elderly man teaches a boy about life and the beauty of nature when the boy gets lost in a forest. **78m/C VHS, Beta, LV.** *AR* Harry Davenport, Edmund Lowe, Brenda Joyce; **D:** Lew (Louis Friedlander) Landers. *NOS, HEG, VEC*

Enchanted Island 🐾½ **1958** Sailor stops on an island to find provisions and ends up falling in love with a cannibal princess. Thinly based upon Herman Melville's "Typee." **94m/C VHS, Beta.** Jane Powell, Dana Andrews, Arthur Shields; **D:** Allan Dwan. *NO*

The Enchantress 🐾½ *I Skiachtra* **1985** A daring boy experiences his first true loves and passions when he journeys through a mystical land in order to find a beautiful fairy. In Greek with subtitles. **93m/C VHS, Beta, Closed Caption.** *GR* Alkis Kourkoulos, Sofia Aliberti, Lily Kokodi, Antogone Amanitou, Vicky Koulianou, Nicols Papacostantinou, Stratos Pachis; **D:** Manoussos Manoussakis. *FCT*

Encino Man 🐾🐾 *California Man* **1992 (PG)** Two, like, totally uncool Valley dudes dig up a 10,000-year-old caveman in the backyard. After giving him a makeover and teaching him the nec-

essities like the four basic food groups (Milk Duds in the dairy group, Sweet Tarts in the fruit group), they use the gnarly caveman as their ticket to popularity and dates to the prom. Juvenile humor appealing to teens; strictly brain candy. **88m/C VHS, Beta, Closed Caption.** Sean Astin, Brendan Fraser, Pauly Shore, Megan Ward, Robin Tunney, Rick Ducommun, Mariette Hartley, Richard Masur, Michael DeLuise; **D:** Les Mayfield; **W:** Shawn Schepps; **C:** Robert Brinkmann. Golden Raspberry Awards '92: Worst New Star (Shore). *HPH*

Encore 🐾🐾🐾 **1952** The third W. Somerset Maugham omnibus (following "Quartet" and "Trio") which includes: "Winter Cruise," "The Ant and the Grasshopper," and "Gigolo and Gigolette." **85m/B VHS, Beta.** *GB* Nigel Patrick, Kay Walsh, Roland Culver, John Laurie, Glynis Johns, Ronald Squire, Noel Purcell, Peter Graves; **D:** Pat Jackson, Anthony Pelissier, Harold French. *NO*

Encounter at Raven's Gate 🐾½ **1988 (R)** Punk rockers and extraterrestrials meet amid hard rock and gallons of gore. **85m/C VHS, Beta, LV, Closed Caption.** Eddie Cleary, Steven Vidler; **D:** Rolf de Heer. *IME*

Encounter with the Unknown 🐾🐾½ **1975** Relates three fully documented supernatural events including a death prophesy and a ghost. **90m/C VHS, Beta.** Rosie Holotik, Gene Ross; **D:** Harry Z. Thomason. *VCI*

The End 🐾🐾🐾 **1978 (R)** Reynolds plays a young man who discovers he is terminally ill. He decides not to prolonging his suffering and attempts various tried-and-true methods for committing suicide, receiving riotous help from the crazed DeLuise. **100m/C VHS, Beta, LV.** Burt Reynolds, Sally Field, Dom DeLuise, Carl Reiner, Joanne Woodward, Robby Benson, Kristy McNichol, Norman Fell, Pat O'Brien, Myrna Loy, David Steinberg; **D:** Burt Reynolds; **W:** Jerry Belson; **M:** Paul Williams. *MGM, FOX*

End of August 🐾🐾 **1982 (PG)** A spinster of New Orleans Creole aristocracy, circa 1900, breaks out of her sheltered life and experiences new sexual and romantic awareness. Adapted from "The Awakening" by Kate Chopin. **104m/C VHS, Beta.** Sally Sharp, David Marshall Grant, Paul Roebling; **D:** Bob Graham; **W:** Anna Thomas, Gregory Nava; **C:** Robert Elswit. *NLC*

End of Desire 🐾🐾 **1962** Schell discovers that her husband, Marquand, has married her for her money and is having an affair with the maid in this melodrama based on De Maupassant's story, "Une Vie." A period place that is a little on the slow side. In French with English subtitles. **86m/C VHS.** *FR* Maria Schell, Christian Marquand, Pascale Petit, Ivan Desny; **D:** Alexandre Astruc. *NO*

The End of Innocence 🐾🐾 **1990 (R)** In her attempts to please everyone in her life, a woman experiences a nervous breakdown. Released two years after Schaeffer's murder. **102m/C VHS, Beta, Closed Caption.** Dyan Cannon, John Heard, George Coe, Lola Mason, Rebecca Schaeffer, Stephen Meadows, Billie Bird, Michael Madsen, Madge Sinclair, Renee Taylor, Viveka Davis; **D:** Dyan Cannon; **W:** Dyan Cannon; **M:** Michael Convertino. *PAR, FCT*

The End of St. Petersburg 🐾🐾🐾½ **1927** A Russian peasant becomes a scab during a workers' strike in 1914. He is then forced to enlist in the army prior to the 1917 October Revolution. Fascinating, although propagandistic film commissioned by the then-new Soviet government. Silent. **75m/B VHS, Beta.** Ivan Chuvelov; **D:** Vsevolod Pudovkin. *NOS, MRV, WFV*

End of the Line 🐾🐾½ **1988 (PG)** Two old-time railroad workers steal a locomotive for a cross-country jaunt to protest the closing of the local railroad company. Produced by Steenburgen. **103m/C VHS, Beta, LV, Closed Caption.** Wilford Brimley, Levon Helm, Mary Steenburgen, Kevin Bacon, Holly Hunter, Barbara Barrie, Bob Balaban, Howard Morris, Bruce McGill, Clint Howard, Trey Wilson, Rita Jenrette; **D:** Jay Russell; **W:** John Wohlbruck; **M:** Andy Summers. *BAR, WAR*

End of the Road 🐾🐾½ **1970 (X)** Keach is a troubled college professor whose bizarre treatment by his psychologist (Jones) produces tragic results. He eventually enters into an affair with the wife of a co-worker. Fascinating, if uneven script adapted from John Barth's story. Rated X upon release for adult story and nudity. **110m/C VHS, Beta, Closed Caption.** Stacy Keach, James Earl Jones, James Coco, Harris Yulin, Dorothy Tristan; **D:** Aram Avakian; **W:** Terry Southern; **C:** Gordon Willis. *FOX*

End of the World woof! **1976 (PG)** A coffee machine explodes, sending a man through a window and into a neon sign, where he is electrocuted. A priest witnesses this and retreats to a convent where he meets his alien double and heads for more trouble with outer space invaders. Interesting premise. **88m/C VHS, Beta.** Christopher Lee, Sue Lyon, Lew Ayres, MacDonald Carey, Dean Jagger, Kirk Scott; **D:** John Hayes; **M:** Andrew Belling.

The End of Violence 🐾🐾 **1997 (R)** Slick, manipulative action-movie producer Mike Max (Pullman) evolves from his Hollywood roots to tranquility as a gardener after his own life is touched by the violence so pervasive in his pictures. There's a sinister government agent (Benzali) and a reclusive surveillance expert (Byrne) and Max gets kidnapped, only the kidnappers mysteriously wind up dead, and then he disappears. And, no, the plot doesn't really make much sense and all the characters are paranoid anyway. But it does give you something to try to figure out. Director Wenders drastically re-edited his movie after its lukewarm work-in-progress appearance at the 1997 Cannes Film Festival. **CW:** Language. **122m/C VHS, Closed Caption.** Bill Pullman, Gabriel Byrne, Andie MacDowell, Daniel Benzali, Traci Lind, Rosalind Chao, Loren Dean, Nicole Parker, Enrique Castillo; **D:** Wim Wenders; **W:** Nicholas Klein; **C:** Pascal Rabaud; **M:** Ry Cooder. Nominations: Independent Spirit Awards '98: Best Director (Wenders). *MGM*

Endangered 🐾½ **1994** Environmentalists battle bad guys for survival in the wilderness. **91m/C VHS.** Rick Aiello, Martin Kove, Sandra Hess, Tim Quill, Richard Hench, Dale Dye, Craig Alan, Kent MacLachlan, Renee Estevez; **D:** Nick Kellis; **W:** Nick Kellis.

Endangered Species 🐾🐾½ **1982 (R)** Offbeat thriller with sci-fi leanings about a retired New York cop on vacation in America's West who is drawn into a female sheriff's investigation of a mysterious series of cattle killings. Could it be UFOs? Based on a true story. **97m/C VHS, Beta.** Robert Urich, JoBeth Williams, Paul Dooley, Hoyt Axton, Peter Coyote, Harry Carey Jr., Dan Hedaya, John Considine; **D:** Alan Rudolph; **W:** Alan Rudolph, John Binder. *MGM*

Endgame 🐾 **1985** Grotesquely deformed survivors of WWIII fight their way out of radioactive New York City to seek a better life. **98m/C VHS, Beta.** Al Oliver, Moira Chen, Jack Davis, Bobby Rhodes, Jill Elliot; **D:** Steve Benson.

Endless Descent woof! *La Grieta* **1990 (R)** At least it seems endless. A group of scientist-types set out in search of a sunken sub, but somehow take a wrong turn into the rift, the deepest chasm at the bottom of the sea. There, they discover unimaginable horrors—that is, if you've never seen "Alien," or just about any other icky-monster flick. A Spanish film, shot in English, by director Simon, whose other works of art include "Pieces" and "Slugs." **79m/C VHS, Beta, LV.** *SP* Jack Scalia, R. Lee Ermey, Ray Wise, Deborah Adair, Ely Pouget; **D:** J. Piquer Simon; **W:** David Coleman. *ART*

The Endless Game 🐾🐾 **1989 (PG-13)** Cold War suspenser has British secret-agent-man Finney attempting to solve the murder of his erstwhile fellow agent-lover, much to the dismay of the government. Written by director Forbes, this made-for-cable would-be thriller is a decidedly mediocre waste of a talented cast. Also of note, it was actor-director Sir Anthony Quayle's final appearance. **123m/C VHS, Closed Caption.** *GB* Albert Finney, George Segal, Derek De Lint, Monica Guerritore, Ian

Holm, John Standing, Anthony Quayle, Kristin Scott Thomas; *M:* Ennio Morricone. *FCT*

Endless Love *ℐℐ* 1981 (R) Although only 17, David and Jade are in love. Her parents think they are too serious and demand that the two spend time apart. David attempts to win her parents' affection and approval, goes mad in the process, and commits a foolish act (he burns the house down) that threatens their love forever. Based on the novel by Scott Spencer. Of interest only to those with time on their hands or smitten by a love so bad that this movie will seem grand in comparison. Features Cruise's first film appearance. 115m/C VHS, Beta, LV. Brooke Shields, Martin Hewitt, Don Murray, Shirley Knight, Beatrice Straight, Richard Kiley, Tom Cruise, James Spader, Robert Moore, Jami Gertz; *D:* Franco Zeffirelli; *W:* Judith Rascoe; *C:* David Watkin. Nominations: Academy Awards '81: Best Song ("Endless Love"). *ART, VES*

Endless Night *ℐℐ* *Agatha Christie's Endless Night* 1971 An adaptation of an Agatha Christie tale. Focuses on a young chauffeur who wants to build a dream house, and his chance meeting with an American heiress. 95m/C VHS, Beta, LV. *GB* Hayley Mills, Hywel Bennett, Britt Ekland, George Sanders, Per Oscarsson, Peter Bowles; *D:* Sidney Gilliat. *REP*

The Endless Summer *ℐℐℐ* 1966 Classic surfing documentary about the freedom and sense of adventure that surfing symbolizes. Director Brown follows two young surfers around the world in search of the perfect wave. (They finally find it at a then-unknown break off Cape Saint Francis in South America.) Besides the excellent surfing photography, Big Kahuna Brown provides the amusing tongue-in-cheek narrative. Considered by many to be the best surf movie ever. 90m/C VHS, Beta, LV. Mike Hynson, Robert August; *D:* Bruce Brown; *W:* Bruce Brown. *FCT, HMV, PBS*

The Endless Summer 2 *ℐℐℐ* *Bruce Brown's The Endless Summer 2* 1994 (PG) You don't have to personally hang ten to get stoked about this long-awaited sequel that once again follows two surfer dudes in their quest for the perfect wave. This time out pro surfers O'Connell and Weaver circle the globe seeking adventure and the world's best waves. Traces the evolution of surfing from the lazy, golden days of the '60s to the worldwide phenomenon it is today, complete with its own pro tour circuit. Breathtaking scenery and spectacular surfing sequences highlight this look at a unique subculture. Thirty years later and it's still a great ride, though the travelogue wears thin and the sub-culture's now fairly well exploited. 107m/C VHS, LV, Closed Caption. Robert "Wingnut" Weaver, Pat O'Connell, Robert August; *D:* Bruce Brown; *W:* Bruce Brown, Dana Brown. *NLC*

Endplay *ℐℐ½* 1975 An Australian-made crime/horror drama in which two brothers cover for each other in a series of murders involving blonde hitchhikers. Based on a novel by Russell Braddon. 110m/C VHS. *AU* George Mallaby, John Waters, Ken Goodlet, Delvene Delaney, Charles Tingwell, Robert Hewett, Kevin Miles; *D:* Tim Burstall.

Enemies, a Love Story *ℐℐℐ½* 1989 (R) A wonderfully resonant, subtle tragedy based on the novel by Isaac Bashevis Singer. A post-Holocaust Jew, living in Coney Island, can't choose between three women—his current wife (who hid him during the war), his tempestuous lover, and his reappearing pre-war wife he presumed dead. A hilarious, confident tale told with grace and patience. 119m/C VHS, Beta, LV, Closed Caption. Ron Silver, Lena Olin, Anjelica Huston, Margaret Sophie Stein, Paul Mazursky, Alan King, Judith Malina, Rita Karin, Phil Leeds, Elya Baskin, Marie-Adele Lemieux; *D:* Paul Mazursky; *W:* Paul Mazursky; *C:* Fred Murphy; *M:* Maurice Jarre. New York Film Critics Awards '89: Best Director (Mazursky), Best Supporting Actress (Olin); National Society of Film Critics Awards '89: Best Supporting Actress (Huston); Nominations: Academy Awards '89: Best Adapted Screenplay, Best Supporting Actress (Huston, Olin). *VTR*

Enemy Below *ℐℐℐ* 1957 Suspenseful WWII sea epic, in which an American destroyer and a German U-Boat chase one another and square off in the South Atlantic. 98m/C VHS, Beta. Robert Mitchum, Curt Jurgens, David Hedison, Theodore Bikel, Doug McClure, Russell Collins; *D:* Dick Powell. Academy Awards '57: Best Special Effects. *FOX, FCT*

Enemy Gold *ℐ½* 1993 (R) A crime czar and a beautiful killer without a conscience go after federal agents who have stumbled across a cache of Confederate gold. Basically, a babes-with-guns blowout.*CW:* Nudity, violence, and sexuality. 92m/C VHS, Beta, LV. Bruce Penhall, Rodrigo Obregon, Mark Barriere, Suzi Simpson, Tai Collins, Julie Strain; *D:* Drew Sidaris; *W:* Wess Rahn, Christian Sidaris.

Enemy Mine *ℐℐ* 1985 (PG-13) A space fantasy in which two pilots from warring planets, one an Earthling, the other an asexual reptilian Drac, crash land on a barren planet and are forced to work together to survive. 108m/C VHS, Beta, LV, Closed Caption. Dennis Quaid, Louis Gossett Jr., Brion James, Richard Marcus, Lance Kerwin, Carolyn McCormick; *D:* Wolfgang Petersen; *W:* Edward Khmara; *M:* Maurice Jarre. *FOX*

Enemy of the Law *ℐℐ½* 1945 Texas rangers battle evil in an old frontier town. 59m/B VHS, Beta. Tex Ritter, Dave O'Brien; *D:* Harry Fraser. *NOS, VCN, DVT*

Enemy of Women *ℐ½* *The Private Life of Paul Joseph Goebbels* 1944 Chronicles the life and loves of Nazi propagandist Dr. Joseph Goebbels. 90m/B VHS, Beta. Claudia Drake, Paul Andor, Donald Woods, H.B. Warner, Sigrid Gurie, Ralph Morgan, Gloria Stuart, Charles Halton; *D:* Alfred Zeisler; *W:* Alfred Zeisler. *NOS, DVT, GLV*

Enemy Territory *ℐℐ* 1987 (R) A handful of citizens trapped in a New York City housing project after dark are stalked by a violent, murderous street gang. 89m/C VHS, Beta, Closed Caption. Ray Parker Jr., Jan-Michael Vincent, Gary Frank, Frances Foster; *D:* Peter Manoogian. *FOX*

Enemy Unseen *ℐ* 1991 (R) A bickering squad of mercenaries slog through the African jungle to find a girl abducted by crocodile-worshipping natives. Dull Jungle-Jim-style adventure, notable for the hilariously phony crocs that occasionally clamp onto the characters. 90m/C VHS. Vernon Wells, Stack Pierce, Ken Gampu, Michael McCabe, Angela O'Neill; *D:* Elmo De Witt.

The Enemy Within *ℐℐ½* 1994 Cable TV remake of the 1964 political thriller "Seven Days in May." Set in the late 1990s, President William Foster's (Waterston) approval rating is at an all-time low and his heavy defense cuts have certain government officials plotting a coup. Hero of the tale is Joint Chief of Staffs officer, Col. Mac Casey (Whitaker), whose military career is warring with his sense of ethics. The updating is fairly clunky; for true suspense stick with the original. 86m/C VHS. Forest Whitaker, Sam Waterston, Josef Sommer, Jason Robards Jr., Dana Delany, George Dzundza; *D:* Jonathan Darby; *W:* Darryl Ponicsan, Ronald Bass; *C:* Kees Van Oostrum. *HBO*

The Enforcer *ℐℐ½* *Murder, Inc* 1951 A district attorney goes after an organized gang of killers in this film noir treatment of the real-life "Murder, Inc." case. 87m/B VHS, LV. Humphrey Bogart, Zero Mostel, Ted de Corsia, Everett Sloane, Roy Roberts, Lawrence Tolan, King Donovan, Bob Steele, Adelaide Klein, Don Beddoe, Tito Vuolo, John Kellogg; *D:* Bretaigne Windust, Raoul Walsh; *W:* Martin Rackin; *C:* Robert Burks. *REP*

The Enforcer *ℐℐ½* 1976 (R) Dirty Harry takes on a female partner and a vicious terrorist group that is threatening the city of San Francisco. See how many "punks" feel lucky enough to test the hand of the tough cop. 96m/C VHS, Beta, LV. Clint Eastwood, Tyne Daly, Harry Guardino, Bradford Dillman, John Mitchum; *D:* James Fargo; *W:* Stirling Silliphant. *WAR*

Enforcer from Death Row *ℐ* 1978 An ex-con is recruited by a secret international peacekeeping organization to track down and eliminate a band of murderous spies. 87m/C VHS, Beta. Cameron Mitchell, Leo Fong, Darnell Garcia, Booker T. Anderson, John Hammond, Mariwin Roberts. *ART*

The English Patient *ℐℐℐℐ* 1996 (R) Filled with flashbacks and moral ambiguities, this adult romance is a complicated WWII saga that finds fragile French-Canadian nurse Hana (Binoche) caring for Almasy (Fiennes), an enigmatic, dying burn patient, in an abandoned monastery in Tuscany. Hana's joined by thief-turned-spy Caravaggio (Defoe), who has a private score to settle with Almasy, and two British bomb disposal experts, Kip (Andrews), a Sikh who falls in love with Hana, and Sgt. Hardy (Whately). Almasy spends his days recalling his illicit love affair with Katharine Clifton (Scott Thomas), the wife of fellow cartographer, Geoffrey (Firth), as they map the North African desert. Exquisitely photographed in a golden glow by Seale with wonderful performances by the entire cast. Based on the novel by Michael Ondaatje.*CW:* Sexuality, some violence and language. 162m/C VHS, LV, Closed Caption. Ralph Fiennes, Kristin Scott Thomas, Juliette Binoche, Willem Dafoe, Naveen Andrews, Colin Firth, Julian Wadham, Juergen Prochnow, Kevin Whately, Clive Merrison, Nino Castelnuovo; *D:* Anthony Minghella; *W:* Anthony Minghella; *C:* John Seale; *M:* Gabriel Yared. Academy Awards '96: Best Art Direction/Set Decoration, Best Cinematography, Best Costume Design, Best Director (Minghella), Best Film Editing, Best Picture, Best Sound, Best Supporting Actress (Binoche), Best Original Dramatic/Comedy Score; British Academy Awards '96: Best Adapted Screenplay, Best Cinematography, Best Film, Best Supporting Actress (Binoche), Best Score; Directors Guild of America Awards '96: Best Director (Minghella); Golden Globe Awards '97: Best Film—Drama, Best Score; Los Angeles Film Critics Association Awards '96: Best Cinematography; National Board of Review Awards '96: Best Supporting Actress (Binoche), Best Supporting Actress (Scott Thomas); Broadcast Film Critics Association Awards '96: Best Director (Minghella), Best Screenplay; Nominations: Academy Awards '96: Best Actor (Fiennes), Best Actress (Scott Thomas), Best Adapted Screenplay, Best Sound Effects Editing; British Academy Awards '96: Best Actor (Fiennes), Best Actress (Scott Thomas), Best Director (Minghella); Golden Globe Awards '97: Best Actor—Drama (Fiennes), Best Actress—Drama (Scott Thomas), Best Director (Minghella), Best Screenplay, Best Supporting Actress (Binoche); Screen Actors Guild Award '96: Best Actor (Fiennes), Best Actress (Scott Thomas), Best Supporting Actress (Binoche), Cast; Writers Guild of America '96: Best Adapted Screenplay. *MAX*

An Englishman Abroad *ℐℐℐ* 1983 During the Cold War, a British actress visits Moscow and chances to meet a notorious English defector. Behind their gossip and small talk is a tragicomic portrait of the exiled traitor/spy. He was the infamous Guy Burgess; the actress was Coral Browne, here playing herself in a pointed recreation. Made for British TV; nuances may be lost on yank viewers. Winner of several British awards. 63m/C VHS. *GB* Alan Bates, Coral Browne, Charles Gray; *D:* John Schlesinger; *W:* Alan Bennett; *M:* George Fenton. *FOX, FCT, PRV*

The Englishman Who Went Up a Hill But Came Down a Mountain *ℐℐℐ* 1995 (PG) Charming if slight tale of town pride based on writer/director Monger's family stories. In 1917 two English cartographers—pompous George (McNeice) and naive Reginald (Grant)—travel into Wales to measure the height of Ffynnon Garw (a running gag has the surveyors struggling with the Welsh language). To the proud locals it is the first mountain in Wales, and without that designation they might as well redraw the maps and be part of England—God forbid. But in order to be designated a mountain Ffynnon Garw must be 1000 feet high, and she measures only 984. Grant stammers boyishly as the Englishman who is not only captivated by the village, but by spirited local lass Betty (Fitzgerald, with whom he starred in "Sirens"). Meaney slyly shines as innkeeper Morgan the Goat, leading the townful of color characters. Wales is shown to great advantage by cinematographer Layton. **96m/C VHS, LV, Closed Caption.** *GB* Hugh Grant, Tara Fitzgerald, Colm Meaney, Ian McNeice, Ian Hart, Kenneth Griffith; *D:* Christopher Monger; *W:* Christopher Monger; *C:* Vernon Layton; *M:* Stephen Endelman. *TOU*

Enid Is Sleeping ♂♂ *Over Her Dead Body* **1990 (R)** Well-done comedy noir in the now-popular there's-a-corpse-in-the-closet subgenre. A woman in a mythical New Mexican town tries to hide the body of her sister Enid, who she's accidentally killed. Enid, it turns out, wasn't thrilled to discover her sister sleeping with her police-officer husband. Phillips and Perkins restored the film to its original state after it was ruthlessly gutted by the studio.*CW:* Language and sensuality. **105m/C VHS.** Elizabeth Perkins, Judge Reinhold, Rhea Perlman; *D:* Maurice Phillips; *W:* Maurice Phillips; *C:* Alfonso Beato. *VES, ART*

Enigma ♂♂ **1982 (PG)** Trapped behind the Iron Curtain, a double agent tries to find the key to five pending murders by locating a Russian coded microprocessor holding information that would unravel the assassination scheme. **101m/C VHS, Beta, LV.** *FR GB* Martin Sheen, Brigitte Fossey, Sam Neill, Derek Jacobi, Frank Finlay, Michael Lonsdale, Warren Clarke; *D:* Jeannot Szwarc; *W:* John Briley.

Enigma Secret ♂♂ **1979** Three Polish mathematicians use their noggins to break the Nazi secret code machine during WWII. Based on a true story; in Polish with English subtitles. **158m/C VHS.** *PL* Tadeusz Borowski, Piotr Fronczewski, Piotr Garlicki. *FCT*

Enjo ♂♂ *Conflagration; The Flame of Torment* **1958** True story of a tormented young monk, studying at the Golden Pavilion in Kyoto, who becomes disillusioned with the pervasive corruption of the temple. In desperation, he sets fire to the national shrine in an attempt to preserve the monument from further contamination. Very disturbing yet beautiful to watch. Adapted from Mishima's novel "Temple of the Golden Pavilion." Japanese with subtitles. **98m/B VHS.** *JP* Raizo Ichikawa, Ganjiro Nakamura, Tatsuya Nakadai; *D:* Kon Ichikawa; *W:* Natto Wada, Keiji Hasebe, Toshiro Mayazumi. *NYF*

Enola Gay: The Men, the Mission, the Atomic Bomb ♂♂ **1980** Based on the bestselling book by Gordon Thomas and Max Gordon Witts, this made for television drama tells the story of the airmen aboard the B-29 that dropped the first atomic bomb. Details the events during WWII leading up to the decision to bomb Hiroshima and the concerns of the crew assigned the task. **150m/C VHS, Beta.** Patrick Duffy, Billy Crystal, Kim Darby, Gary Frank, Gregory Harrison, Ed Nelson, Robert Walden, Stephen Macht, Robert Pine, James Shigeta, Henry Wilcoxon; *D:* David Lowell Rich; *M:* Maurice Jarre.

Enormous Changes ♂♂ *Enormous Changes at the Last Minute* **1983** Three stories about New York City women and their personal relationships. Based on the stories of Grace Paley. **115m/C VHS, Beta, LV.** Ellen Barkin, David Strathairn, Ron McLarty, Maria Tucci, Lynn Milgrim, Kevin Bacon; *D:* Mirra Bank; *W:* John Sayles. *THV*

Enrapture ♂½ **1990 (R)** A chauffeur is the prime suspect when a promiscuous passenger is murdered in his limousine. The driver did it? **87m/C VHS, LV.** Ona Simms, Harvey Siegel, Richard Parnes; *D:* Chuck Vincent. *ATL*

Ensign Pulver ♂♂ **1964** A continuation of the further adventures of the crew of the U.S.S. Reluctant from "Mister Roberts," which was adapted from the Broadway play. **104m/C VHS, Beta.** Walter Matthau, Robert Walker Jr., Larry Hagman, Jack Nicholson, Millie Perkins, James Coco, James Farentino, Burl Ives, Gerald S. O'Loughlin, Al Freeman Jr.; *D:* Joshua Logan. *WAR*

Entangled ♂♂ **1993 (R)** David Mirkin (Nelson) is a struggling writer living in Paris with his beautiful girlfriend Annabelle (Treil). As she becomes ever more successful as a fashion model, David becomes ever more jealous and mistrustful. So he hires a detective (Brosnan) to spy on her. And then there's the small matter of a murder. Adapted from the novel "Les Veufs" by Boileau Narcejac. **98m/C VHS, LV, Closed Caption.** Judd Nelson, Pierce Brosnan, Laurence Treil, Roy Dupuis; *D:* Max Fischer. *COL*

Enter Laughing ♂♂ **1967** Based on Reiner's semi-autobiographical novel and play, depicts the botched efforts of a Bronx-born schlump to become an actor. Worthwhile, but doesn't live up to the original. **112m/C VHS, Beta.** Reni Santoni, Jose Ferrer, Elaine May, Shelley Winters, Jack Gilford, Don Rickles, Michael J. Pollard, Janet Margolin, Rob Reiner; *D:* Carl Reiner; *W:* Carl Reiner; *C:* Joseph Biroc; *M:* Quincy Jones. *NO*

Enter the Dragon ♂♂♂ *The Deadly Three* **1973 (R)** The American film that broke Bruce Lee worldwide combines Oriental conventions with 007 thrills. Spectacular fighting sequences including Karate, Judo, Tae Kwon Do, and Tai Chi Chuan are featured as Lee is recruited by the British to search for opium smugglers in Hong Kong. **98m/C VHS, Beta, LV, Letterbox, Closed Caption.** Bruce Lee, John Saxon, Jim Kelly; *D:* Robert Clouse; *C:* Gil Hubbs; *M:* Lalo Schifrin. *WAR*

Enter the Ninja ♂♂ **1981 (R)** First and most serious of the Cannon canon of relatively well-done ninja epics (faint praise) that created original boxoffice stir for genre (mostly among adolescents needing outlet). Ninja Nero visits old friend in Philippines who's being pressured by ruthless evil guy George to give up the farm. Nero dispatches numerous thugs before indulging in ninja slugfest with Kosugi. **99m/C VHS, Beta.** Franco Nero, Susan George, Sho Kosugi, Christopher George, Alex Courtney; *D:* Menahem Golan; *W:* Judd Bernard. *MGM*

Enter the Panther ♂ **1979** Amidst, and regardless of, a double-crossing plot featuring a treacherous family and a sought-after gold mine, a young man kicks heads and punches his way to fame. **91m/C VHS, Beta.** Bruce Li, Tsai Chin, Tse Lan. *GEM*

Enter Three Dragons ♂ **1981 (R)** Kung Fu artistry abounds in this head-kicking action-adventure film. **90m/C VHS.** Dragon Lee, Bruce Lea, Yang Tsze, Samuel Walls, Chang Li, Bruce Li, Jackie Chin. *SUN*

The Entertainer ♂♂♂½ **1960** Splendid drama of a down and out vaudevillian who tries vainly to gain the fame his dying father once possessed. His blatant disregard for his alcoholic wife and his superficial sons brings his world crashing down around him, and he discovers how self-destructive his life has been. Remade in 1975 for television. Adapted from the play by John Osborne. **97m/B VHS.** *GB* Laurence Olivier, Brenda de Banzie, Roger Livesey, Joan Plowright, Daniel Massey, Alan Bates, Shirley Anne Field, Albert Finney, Thora Hird; *D:* Tony Richardson; *W:* Nigel Kneale, John Osborne; *C:* Oswald Morris; *M:* John Addison. Nominations: Academy Awards '60: Best Actor (Olivier).*FCT, TPV*

Entertaining Angels: The Dorothy Day Story ♂♂½ **1996 (PG-13)** Dorothy Day (Kelly) was a social activist who founded the left-wing publication The Catholic Worker and was dedicated to sheltering and feeding the poor, founding soup kitchens across America. A radical journalist and New York bohemian, Day converts to Catholicism in the '20s and is soon working with the city's poor and homeless. Episodic story works mainly on indignation and its heroine's compassion.*CW:* Thematic elements, some sensuality and brief language. **110m/C VHS.** Moira Kelly, Martin Sheen, Melinda Dillon, Lenny Von Dohlen, Heather Graham, Geoffrey Blake, Boyd Kestner, Allyce Beasley, Brian Keith; *D:* Michael Ray Rhodes; *W:* John Wells; *C:* Mike Fash; *M:* Bill Conti, Ashley Irwin. *WAR*

Entertaining Mr. Sloane ♂♂½ **1970** Playwright Joe Orton's masterpiece of black comedy concerning a handsome criminal who becomes the guest and love interest of a widow and her brother. **90m/C VHS, Beta.** Beryl Reid, Harry Andrews, Peter McEnery, Alan Webb; *D:* Douglas Hickox. *NO*

The Entity ♂♂ **1983 (R)** Supposedly based on a true story about an unseen entity that repeatedly rapes a woman. Hershey's victim whom nobody believes. She eventually ends up at a university for talks with parapsychologist Silver. Pseudo-science to the rescue as the over-sexed creature is frozen dead in its tracks. Exploitative violence, gore, and nudity aplenty, balanced to a degree by Hershey's strong performance. **115m/C VHS, Beta.** Barbara Hershey, Ron Silver, Alex Rocco; *D:* Sidney J. Furie; *W:* Frank de Felitta; *C:* Stephen Burum; *M:* Charles Bernstein. *FOX*

Entr'acte ♂♂ **1924** Clair's famous dada-surrealist classic short, reflecting his sense of humor, as various eccentric characters become involved in a crazy chase. Silent. **21m/B VHS, Beta.** *FR D:* Rene Clair. *MRV, GVV*

Entre-Nous ♂♂♂½ *Between Us; Coup de Foudre* **1983 (PG)** Two attractive, young French mothers find in each other the fulfillment their husbands cannot provide. One of the women was confined in a concentration camp during WWII; the other is a disaffected artist. In French with English subtitles. **112m/C VHS, Beta.** *FR* Isabelle Huppert, Miou-Miou, Guy Marchand; *D:* Diane Kurys; *W:* Diane Kurys; *M:* Luis Bacalov. Nominations: Academy Awards '83: Best Foreign Language Film. *MGM*

Epitaph ♂ **1987** An average American family's life is disrupted by the mother's habitual axe-murdering. **90m/C VHS, Beta.** *D:* Joseph Merhi. *NO*

The Equalizer: Memories of Manon ♂♂½ **1988** Feature-length episode of the popular television crime thriller about an ex-agent who uses guns and espionage tactics to help people who are being persecuted by ruthless villians on the streets of New York City. In this installment, McCall, the Equalizer, learns that he has a daughter and that her life is in peril. **96m/C VHS, Beta.** Edward Woodward, Melissa Sue Anderson, Anthony Zerbe, George DiCenzo, Jon Polito, Robert Lansing, Keith Szarabajka; *D:* Tony Wharmby. *USH*

Equalizer 2000 ♂ **1986 (R)** A warrior in a post-holocaust future plots to overthrow a dictatorship by using a high-powered gun. **85m/C VHS, Beta.** Richard Norton, Corinne Wahl, William Steis; *D:* Cirio H. Santiago. *MGM*

Equinox ♂♂♂ **1971 (PG)** Young archaeologists uncover horror in a state forest. The ranger, questing for a book of spells that the scientists have found, threatens them with wonderful special effects, including winged beasts, huge apes, and Satan. Though originally an amateur film, it is deemed a minor classic in its genre. **80m/C VHS.** Edward Connell, Barbara Hewitt, Frank Bonner, Robin Christopher, Jack Woods; *D:* Jack Woods. *NO*

Equinox ♂♂ **1993 (R)** Modine gets to try his hand (and does well) at a dual role, with his portrayal of identical twins, separated at birth and raised in completely different environs. Garage worker Henry lives in a tenement while slick brother Freddie is a gangster's chauffeur married to the materialistic Sharon (Singer). Fate brings the brothers together when a janitor discovers a letter that reveals their parentage and the fact that a fortune has been left to them. Set in the near future, in the surreal and decaying city of Empire, this is typical Rudolph with its moody stylized appearance and convoluted plot. **110m/C VHS, LV, Letterbox, Closed Caption.** Matthew Modine, Lara Flynn Boyle, Lori Singer, Marisa Tomei, Fred Ward, M. Emmet Walsh, Tyra Ferrell, Tate Donovan, Kevin J. O'Connor, Gailard Sartain; *D:* Alan Rudolph; *W:* Alan Rudolph; *C:* Elliot Davis. Nominations: Independent Spirit Awards '94: Best Actor (Modine), Best Cinematography, Best Film, Best Supporting Actress (Boyle). *COL, FCT*

Equinox Flower 🎬🎬 1958 Ozu's first color film tells the sensitive story of two teenage girls who make a pact to protect each other from the traditional prearranged marriages their parents have set up. Lovely film that focuses on the generation gap between young and old in the Japanese family. In Japanese with English subtitles. 118m/C VHS, Closed Caption. JP Shin Saburi, Kinuyo Tanaka, Ineko Arima, Miyuki Kuwano, Chishu Ryu; D: Yasujiro Ozu. NYF, FCT, ING

Equus 🎬🎬½ 1977 (R) A psychiatrist undertakes the most challenging case of his career when he tries to figure out why a stable-boy blinded horses. Based upon the successful play by Peter Shaffer, but not well transferred to film. 138m/C VHS, Beta, LV. Richard Burton, Peter Firth, Jenny Agutter, Joan Plowright, Colin Blakely, Harry Andrews; D: Sidney Lumet; W: Peter Shaffer; C: Oswald Morris; M: Richard Rodney Bennett. British Academy Awards '77: Best Supporting Actress (Agutter); Golden Globe Awards '78: Best Actor—Drama (Burton), Best Supporting Actor (Firth); Nominations: Academy Awards '77: Best Actor (Burton), Best Adapted Screenplay, Best Supporting Actor (Firth). MGM

ER 1994 TV pilot for the hit medical series about the trials and traumas of the Chicago emergency room of an urban teaching hospital. Edwards is Dr. Mark Greene, the standards-setting team leader trying to juggle professional and personal resinobilities, Douglas Ross (Clooney) is a womanizing pediatric resident, Susan Lewis (Stringfield) a workaholic second-year resident, Peter Benton (La Salle) is the perfectionist surgical resident with no people skills, which disconcerts third year medical student John Carter (Wyle) who falls under Benton's stern gaze. Fast-paced action is enough to make you dizzy. 88m/C VHS, Closed Caption. Anthony Edwards, George Clooney, Eriq La Salle, Noah Wyle, Sherry Stringfield, Julianna Margulies, Christina Harnos, William H. Macy. WAR

Era Notte a Roma 🎬🎬🎬 1960 An American, Russian, and British soldier each escape from a concentration camp in the waning days of WWII and find refuge in the home of a young woman. 145m/C VHS. IT D: Roberto Rossellini; W: Roberto Rossellini. NO

Eraser 🎬🎬½ 1996 (R) Arnold returns to familiar big-budget action territory and looks right at home. He plays elite U.S. Marshal John Kruger, who protects federal witnesses by "erasing" their previous identities. When a beautiful witness uncovers a high-level conspiracy, the two go on the run to stay alive long enough to expose the truth. Fans of the big bang Schwarzenegger of yore will not be disappointed. Rumors of production delays and budget overruns, not to mention difficulties between director Russell and producer Kopelson, brought up the spectre of "Waterworld," but the final result is more reminiscent of the success of "True Lies." CW: Violent action throughout and some language. 115m/C VHS, LV, Closed Caption, DVD. Arnold Schwarzenegger, Vanessa L(ynne) Williams, James Caan, James Coburn, Robert Pastorelli, Andy Romano, James Cromwell, Danny Nucci, Nicholas Chinlund, Mark Rolston, Gerry Becker; D: Chuck Russell; W: Walon Green, Tony Puryear; C: Adam Greenberg; M: Alan Silvestri. Nominations: MTV Movie Awards '97: Best Action Sequence. WAR

Eraserhead 🎬🎬🎬 1978 The infamous cult classic about a numb-brained everyman wandering through what amounts to a sick, ironic parody of the modern urban landscape, innocently impregnating his girlfriend and fathering a pestilent embryonic mutant. Surreal and bizarre, the film has an inner, completely unpredictable logic all its own. Lynch's first feature-length film stars Nance, who later achieved fame in Lynch's "Twin Peaks" as Pete the Logger. 90m/B VHS, Beta, LV. Jack Nance, Charlotte Stewart, Jack Fisk, Jeanne Bates; D: David Lynch; W: David Lynch; C: Frederick Elmes. COL, OM

Erendira 🎬🎬½ 1983 Based on Gabriel García-Márquez's story about a teenage girl prostituting herself to support her witch-like grandmother after accidentally torching the elder's house. The film follows the two as they travel across the desert trying out new and inventive ways to survive. Unusual ending tops off a creative, if not eclectic, movie. In Spanish with English subtitles. 103m/C VHS, Beta. FR MX GE Irene Papas, Claudia Ohana, Michael Lonsdale, Rufus, Jorge Fegan; D: Ruy Guerra. XVC

Eric 🎬🎬🎬 Made-for-television tear-jerker about a young athlete who fights for his life after he's diagnosed with leukemia. Based on the true-life account written by Eric's mother Doris Lund. 100m/C VHS, Beta. Patricia Neal, John Savage, Claude Akins, Sian Barbara Allen, Mark Hamill, Nehemiah Persoff, Tom Clancy; D: James Goldstone; M: Dave Grusin. ART

Erik 🎬🎬 1990 An ex-government agent working in Central America finds his loyalties divided when he is approached by a female activist and his old CIA friends. They want him to help expose his current boss as a drug smuggler. 90m/C VHS, Beta. Stephen McHattie, Deborah Van Valkenburgh. MGM

Erik, the Viking 🎬 1972 The Norse Warrior discovers not only the New World but traitorous subordinates among his crew, calling for drastic measures. 95m/C VHS, Beta. Giuliano Gemma, Gordon Mitchell. UNI

Erik the Viking 🎬½ 1989 (PG-13) A mediocre Monty Pythonesque farce about a Viking who grows dissatisfied with his barbaric way of life and decides to set out to find the mythical Asgaard, where Norse gods dwell. Great cast of character actors is wasted. 104m/C VHS, Beta, LV, Closed Caption. GB Tim Robbins, Terry Jones, Mickey Rooney, John Cleese, Imogen Stubbs, Anthony Sher, Gordon John Sinclair, Freddie Jones, Eartha Kitt; D: Terry Jones; W: Terry Jones. ORI

Ermo 🎬🎬 1994 Hard-working noodle-maker Ermo (Alia) supports her slothful husband, Chief (Zhijun), and their son in their northern China village. Her smitten truck-driver neighbor Blindman (Peiqi) has an equally unpleasant wife, Fat Woman (Haiyan), with whom Ermo has an ongoing rivalry. They own a color TV (the only one in the village) and Ermo becomes determined to get a bigger and better set by selling her noodles in a nearby town and compulsively saving her money. Of course, her entrepreneurship has some unexpected consequences. Mandarin Chinese with subtitles. 93m/C VHS. CH Alia, Liu Peiqi, Ge Zhijun, Zhang Haiyan; D: Zhou Xiaowen; W: Lang Yun; C: Lu Gengxin; M: Zhou Xiaowen. EVE

Ernest Goes to Africa 🎬½ 1997 (PG) Ernest P. Worrel (Varney) finds himself in a heap 'o trouble when he's accused of buying some stolen diamonds and he and would-be girlfriend Renee are kidnapped and taken to Africa where a prince wants his property returned. Lots of sight gags and low humor. 90m/C VHS. Jim Varney, Linda Kash, Jamie Bartlett; D: John Cherry; W: John Cherry; C: James Robb. MNC

Ernest Goes to Camp 🎬½ 1987 (PG) A screwball, slapstick summer camp farce starring the character Ernest P. Worrell as an inept camp counselor. When progress threatens the camp, Ernest leads the boys on a turtle-bombing, slop-shooting attack on the construction company. Followed by "Ernest Saves Christmas" and "Ernest Goes to Jail." 92m/C VHS, Beta. Jim Varney, Victoria Racimo, John Vernon, Iron Eyes Cody, Lyle Alzado, Gailard Sartain, Daniel Butler, Hakeem Abdul-Samad; D: John R. Cherry III; W: John R. Cherry III. TOU

Ernest Goes to Jail 🎬🎬 1990 (PG) The infamous loon Ernest P. Worrell winds up in the jury box and the courtroom will never be the same again. Jury duty suddenly becomes hard-time in the slammer for poor Ernest when he is mistaken for a big-wig organized crime boss. Sequel to "Ernest Goes to Camp" and "Ernest Saves Christmas." 81m/C VHS, LV, Closed Caption. Jim Varney, Gai-

lard Sartain, Randall "Tex" Cobb, Bill Byrge, Barry Scott, Charles Napier; D: John R. Cherry III; W: Charlie Cohen; M: Bruce Arntson. TOU

Ernest Goes to School 🎬🎬½ 1994 (PG) Ernest must finish high school if he wants to keep his job as school janitor. He's "aided" by two crazy science teachers who give him an experimental IQ booster. 89m/C VHS, Closed Caption. Jim Varney, Linda Kash, Bill Byrge; D: Coke Sams. MNC

The Ernest Green Story 🎬🎬½ 1993 Made-for-cable drama based on the integration of Central High in Little Rock, Arkansas by nine black students in 1957. Green was the only senior in the group and the movie follows a year of verbal and physical abuse, vandalism, and unfair academic treatment, as he struggles to withstand every difficulty in order to graduate. 92m/C VHS, Closed Caption. Morris Chestnut, CCH Pounder, Gary Grubbs, Tina Lifford, Avery Brooks, Ruby Dee, Ossie Davis; D: Eric Laneuville. DIS

Ernest in the Army 🎬½ 1997 (PG) Ernest is talked into joining the Army reserves and promptly causes all sorts of trouble when he's assigned to drive various military vehicles. 85m/C VHS. Jim Varney; D: John Cherry; C: James Robb. MNC

Ernest Rides Again 🎬🎬½ 1993 (PG) Ernest P. "KnowwhutImean?" Worrell (Varney) is back, aiding a college professor friend who has a cockamamie theory that the British crown jewels were hidden in a Revolutionary War cannon. Naturally he's right and Ernest must battle British spies and a greedy antiquities collector to get the gems back. Goofy slapstick sticks to the formula of the other films. 93m/C VHS. Jim Varney, Ron James, Duke Ernsberger, Jeffrey Pillars, Linda Kash, Tom Butler; D: John R. Cherry III; W: John R. Cherry III, William M. Akers; M: Bruce Arntson, Kirby Shelstad. MNC

Ernest Saves Christmas 🎬½ 1988 (PG) Ernest P. Worrell is back. When Santa decides that it's time to retire, Ernest must help him recruit a has-been children's show host who is a bit reluctant. For Ernest fans only, and only the most dedicated of those. Second in the series featuring the nimble-faced Varney, the first of which was "Ernest Goes to Camp," followed by "Ernest Goes to Jail." 91m/C VHS, Beta, LV. Jim Varney, Douglas Seale, Oliver Clark, Noelle Parker, Billie Bird; D: John R. Cherry III. TOU

Ernest Scared Stupid 🎬½ 1991 (PG) Pea-brained Ernest P. Worrell returns yet again in this silly comedy. When he accidentally releases a demon from a sacred tomb a 200-year-old curse threatens to destroy his hometown, unless Ernest can come to the rescue. Would you want your town depending on Ernest's heroics? Who would have thought that the annoying Ernest P. Worrell could appear in one movie, let alone four? 93m/C VHS, Beta, Closed Caption. Jim Varney, Eartha Kitt, Austin Nagler, Jonas Moscartolo, Shay Astar; D: John R. Cherry III; W: John R. Cherry III; C: Hanania Baer; M: Bruce Arntson. TOU

Ernesto 🎬🎬½ 1979 A lushly erotic Italian film depicting the troubled relationship between a young, devil-may-care gay youth and his older, coolly seducing lover. In Italian with subtitles. 98m/C VHS, Beta. IT Martin Halm, Michele Placido; D: Salvatore Samperi. FCT

Ernie Kovacs: Between the Laughter 🎬🎬 1984 A made for television version of the television comic's life and career, ending with his tragic death in a car accident in 1962. Shows the brand of humor that made Kovacs famous as well as the devastation that he suffered after the tragic kidnapping of his children by his first wife during divorce proceedings. Kovac's second wife, Edie Adams, makes a brief appearance. 95m/C VHS, Beta. Jeff Goldblum, Cloris Leachman, Melody Anderson, Madolyn Smith, John Glover; Cameos: Edie Adams; D: Lamont Johnson; M: Ralph Burns. NO

Erotic Escape 𝄽 1986 Soft-core fun about party girls taking over a small French town. Originally in French, but dubbed in English. Check your brain at the door. 86m/C VHS, Beta. **FR** Marie-Claire Davy, Pauline Larrieu.

Erotic House of Wax 𝄽½ 1997 Young woman inherits her uncle's bizarre wax museum upon his death and discovers that the museum's inhabitants have this habit of coming to life and acting out their sexual fantasies. 90m/C VHS. Jacqueline Lovell, Josie Hunter; **D:** Sybil Richards. AFE

Erotic Images woof! 1985 (R) A beautiful psychology teacher publishes her doctoral thesis on sex and becomes a best-selling author, which threatens her marriage. 93m/C VHS, Beta. Britt Ekland, Edd Byrnes, John McCann; **D:** Declan Langan. ART, VES

Erotic Touch of Hot Skin 𝄽 1965 Sex, murder, false identities, car crashes, and striptease in the Riviera. 78m/B VHS, Beta. Fabienne Dali, Sophie Hardy, Jean Valmont, Francois Dryek; **D:** Max Pecas. VDM

Erotique 𝄽𝄽 1994 Sex quartet from female filmmakers. "Let's Talk About Sex" finds struggling Latina actress Rosie (Lopez-Dawson) supporting herself by working at a phone sex agency where a caller (Cranston) wants to know about her sexual fantasies. "Taboo Parlor" finds lesbian lovers Claire (Barnes) and Julia (Soeberg) picking up boy toy Victor (Carr) and planning some s/m games. "Wonton Soup" has Australian-born Chinese Adrian (Lounibos) reuniting with his lover Ann (Man) in Hong Kong and deciding to hold her interest by practicing some ancient Chinese sexual techniques. And in "Final Call," a school teacher (Ohana) tries a sexual adventure with a stranger. 120m/C VHS, DVD. Kamala Lopez-Dawson, Bryan Cranston, Priscilla Barnes, Camilla Soeberg, Michael Carr, Tim Lounibos, Hayley Man, Claudia Ohana; **D:** Lizzie Borden, Monika Treut, Clara Law, Ana Maria Magalhaes; **W:** Lizzie Borden, Monika Treut, Susie Bright, Eddie L.C. Fong; **C:** Larry Banks, Elfi Mikesch, Arthur Wong. FXL, FCT

The Errand Boy 𝄽𝄽½ 1961 Jerry Lewis' patented babbling schnook hits Hollywood in search of a job. When he lands a position as an errand boy, Hollywood may never be the same again in this prototypical comedy; a must for Lewis fans only. 92m/B VHS, Beta, LV, Letterbox. Jerry Lewis, Brian Donlevy, Dick Wesson, Howard McNear, Felicia Atkins, Fritz Feld, Sig Rumann, Renee Taylor, Doodles Weaver, Mike Mazurki, Lorne Greene, Michael Landon, Dan Blocker, Pernell Roberts, Snub Pollard, Kathleen Freeman; **D:** Jerry Lewis; **W:** Jerry Lewis. ART

The Errors of Youth 𝄽𝄽 Wild Oats 1978 Dimitri (Zhdanko), a construction worker in Siberia, is disillusioned over a failed love affair and moves to Leningrad where he falls in with black marketeers and a marriage of convenience. Because of political problems, director Frumin left the film unfinished when he emigrated to the U.S. and it wasn't until 1989 that he returned to Leningrad to complete the project. Russian with subtitles. 87m/C VHS. **RU** Stanislav Zhdanko, Marina Neyelova, Natalia Varley, Mikhail Vaskov; **D:** Boris Frumin. FCT

Escapade 𝄽𝄽𝄽 1955 Sons thinking their parents are en route to divorce court create a scheme to achieve peace worldwide. The pacifist father's reaction juxtaposes idealistic youth with the cynicism of adulthood. Adapted from a play by Roger MacDougall. 87m/B VHS. **GB** John Mills, Yvonne Mitchell, Alastair Sim, Jeremy Spenser, Andrew Ray, Marie Lohr, Peter Asher; **D:** Philip Leacock; **W:** Donald Ogden Stewart. VYY, MOV

Escapade in Florence 𝄽𝄽 1962 As two students in Florence paint their way to immortality, an elaborate art-forging ring preys upon their talents. 81m/C VHS, Beta. Tommy Kirk, Ivan Desny; **D:** Steve Previn. DIS

Escapade in Japan 𝄽𝄽 1957 A Japanese youth helps an American boy frantically search the city of Tokyo for his parents. Shot in Japan. 93m/C VHS, Beta. Cameron Mitchell, Teresa Wright, Jon Provost, Roger Nakagawa, Philip Ober, Clint Eastwood; **D:** Arthur Lubin; **M:** Max Steiner. NO

Escape 𝄽½ 1990 (R) A woman attempts to track down her brother's killer and finds an entire town mysteriously controlled by a sadistic and powerful man. Features General Hospital's bad-boy Shriner. 100m/C VHS. Elizabeth Jeager, Kim Richards, Kin Shriner; **D:** Richard Styles. HHE

Escape 𝄽𝄽 1990 (PG) A fun-loving, care-free Irish officer is sent to oversee the toughest POW prison in Scotland. There, he becomes consumed with keeping the facility secure despite the intricate escape plans laid out by a group of rioters. 90m/C VHS. Brian Keith, Helmut Griem; **D:** Lamont Johnson. NO

The Escape Artist 𝄽𝄽𝄽 1982 (PG) Award-winning cinematographer Deschanel's first directorial effort is this quirky film about a teenage escape artist who sets out to uncover the identity of his father's killers. 96m/C VHS, Beta, LV. Griffin O'Neal, Raul Julia, Teri Garr, Joan Hackett, Desi Arnaz Sr., Gabriel Dell, Huntz Hall, Jackie Coogan; **D:** Caleb Deschanel; **W:** Melissa Mathison; **C:** Stephen Burum; **M:** Georges Delerue. ART, VES

Escape Clause 𝄽𝄽 1996 (R) Insurance exec Richard Ramsay (McCarthy) gets a call from a hitman informing him that his wife Sarah (McNeil) has hired him to kill Richard. The hitman says if Richard will pay him, the contract's off. Instead Richard tries to figure out what's going on, with some help from police detective Ferrand (Sorvino), who discovers Richard has been treated for paranoid delusions. Fast-paced cable mystery with a few too many twists. **CW:** Violence, sexuality and language. 131m/C VHS, Closed Caption. Andrew McCarthy, Paul Sorvino, Kate McNeil, Peter Donaldson, Kenneth Welsh, Connie Britton, Stan Egi, John Evans; **D:** Brian Trenchard-Smith; **W:** Danilo Bach; **M:** Ken Thorne, Rick Marvin. MGM

Escape from Alcatraz 𝄽𝄽𝄽 1979 (PG) A fascinating account of the one and only successful escape from the maximum security prison at Alcatraz in 1962. The three men were never heard from again. 112m/C VHS, Beta, LV. Clint Eastwood, Patrick McGoohan, Roberts Blossom, Fred Ward, Danny Glover; **D:** Donald Siegel; **C:** Bruce Surtees. PAR

Escape from Atlantis 𝄽𝄽½ 1997 (PG-13) Workaholic attorney and single dad, Matt Spencer (Speakman), charters a sailboat and plans a cruise to the Bahamas so he and his three teenagers can have some quality time. The sailboat heads into the Bermuda Triangle and capsizes in a hurricane; when the Spencers come to, they're in the land of Atlantis, where fantasy is reality. **CW:** Fantasy adventure violence. 93m/C VHS, LV, Closed Caption. Jeff Speakman, Brian Bloom, Tim Thomerson, Mercedes McNab, Michael Lee Goggin, Justin Burnette, Breck Wilson; **D:** Strathford Hamilton; **W:** Arne Olsen. USH

Escape from Cell Block 3 𝄽 1978 Five escaped female convicts take it on the lam for Mexico and freedom. 82m/C VHS, Beta. Carolyn Judd, Teri Guzman, Bonita Kalem.

Escape from Death Row 𝄽 1976 (R) Convicted criminal mastermind, sentenced to die, devises a brilliant and daring plan of escape on the eve of his execution. 85m/C VHS, Beta. Lee Van Cleef, James Lane, Barbara Moore, Alice Belios. NO

Escape from DS-3 𝄽𝄽 198? Bostwick and "Police Academy" alumnus Smith team up in a familiar story: framed for a serious crime, a man attempts to escape from a maximum security satellite prison. About as good as you'd expect. 88m/C VHS. Jackson Bostwick, Bubba Smith. MOV

Escape from El Diablo 𝄽 1983 (PG) Two juvenile delinquents harass guards at a Mexican prison. Being from California, they use frisbees and skateboards to help their escape. 92m/C VHS, Beta. **SP GB** Jimmy McNichol, Timothy Van Patten, John Ethan Wayne; **D:** Gordon Hessler.

Escape from Fort Bravo 𝄽𝄽½ 1953 A Civil War era western set in an Arizona stockade. Holden is the hard-bitten Union cavalry officer who ruthlessly guards his Confederate prisoners, who are led by Forsythe. Parker is a southern spy whose job is to break the rebels out of jail by seducing Holden from his duty, which she does. When Holden discovers what's happened, he recaptures his prisoners only to be beset by hostile Mescalero Indians while trying to get everyone back to the fort. It's an old story but well-executed with lots of action. 98m/C VHS, Beta, Closed Caption. William Holden, Eleanor Parker, John Forsythe, William Demarest, William Campbell, Polly Bergen, Richard Anderson, Carl Benton Reid, John Lupton, Howard McNear, Alex Montoya, Forrest Lewis, Fred Graham, William Newell; **D:** John Sturges; **W:** Frank Fenton; **C:** Robert L. Surtees. MGM, FCT

Escape from Galaxy Three 𝄽 1976 (G) A pair of space travelers fight off a bevy of evil aliens. 90m/C VHS, Beta. James Milton, Cheryl Buchanan.

Escape from Hell woof! Hellfire on Ice, Part 2: Escape from Hell 1989 Two scantily clad women escape from a jungle prison and are pursued by their sadistic warden. ?m/C VHS. Anthony Steffen, Ajita Wilson; **D:** Edward Muller. HHE

Escape from L.A. 𝄽𝄽½ John Carpenter's Escape from L.A 1996 (R) Well, Snake Plissken is back (Russell once again) and so's Carpenter, who did the original "Escape from New York" saga, and technology's advanced a lot in 15 years, so sit back and enjoy the action. In 2013, L.A.'s been turned into a gang-infested island, thanks to a 9.6 earthquake, where Snake is forced to find a doomsday weapon in just 10 hours. Seems he's been injected with a virus that will kill him unless he can complete his job and escape to get the antidote. Naturally, there's lots of bad guys who'll try to stop him. Russell not only reprises his old role but found Snake's original leathers, which still fit, and wore the outfit in some scenes of the sequel. **CW:** Violence and some language. 101m/C VHS, Beta, Closed Caption. Kurt Russell, Georges Corraface, Stacy Keach, Peter Fonda, Steve Buscemi, Pam Grier, Valeria Golino, Cliff Robertson, Michelle Forbes, Bruce Campbell, A.J. Langer; **D:** John Carpenter; **W:** Kurt Russell, John Carpenter, Debra Hill; **C:** Gary B. Kibbe; **M:** John Carpenter, Shirley Walker. PAR

Escape from New York 𝄽𝄽½ 1981 (R) The ultimate urban nightmare: a ruined, future Manhattan is an anarchic prison for America's worst felons. When convicts hold the President hostage, a disgraced war hero unwillingly attempts an impossible rescue mission. Cynical but largely unexceptional sci-fi action, putting a good cast through tight-lipped peril. 99m/C VHS, Beta, LV. Kurt Russell, Lee Van Cleef, Ernest Borgnine, Donald Pleasence, Isaac Hayes, Adrienne Barbeau, Harry Dean Stanton, Season Hubley; **D:** John Carpenter; **W:** John Carpenter, Nick Castle; **C:** Dean Cundey; **M:** John Carpenter. NLC, FUS

Escape from Planet Earth 𝄽 The Doomsday Machine 1967 A spaceship is damaged deep in space and only a few of the crew can make it back to Earth. But who will decide who lives or dies? (Unfortunately, the Earth has been totally destroyed so who cares anyway.) Lousy special effects. 91m/B VHS, Closed Caption. Grant Williams, Bobby Van, Ruta Lee, Henry Wilcoxon, Mala Powers, Casey Kasem, Mike Farrell, Harry Hope; **D:** Lee Sholem.

Escape from Safehaven woof! 1988 (R) Brutal slimeballs rule a mad, sadistic world in the post-apocalyptic future, and a family tries to escape them. In very poor taste. 87m/C VHS, Beta. Rick Gianisi, Mollie O'Mara, John Wittenbauer, Roy MacArthur, William Beckwith; **D:** Brian Thomas Jones, James McCalmont. NO

Escape from Sobibor 𝄽𝄽𝄽 1987 (PG-13) Nail-biting, true account of the largest successful escape from a Nazi prison camp, adapted from Richard Rashke's book. Made for TV. 120m/C VHS. Alan Arkin, Joanna Pacula, Rutger Hauer, Hartmut

Becker, Jack Shepherd; **D:** Jack Gold; **M:** Georges Delerue. *ART*

Escape from the Bronx ✗ 1985 (R) Invading death squads seek to level the Bronx. Local street gangs cry foul and ally to defeat the uncultured barbarians. Sequel to "1990: The Bronx Warriors." 82m/C VHS, Beta. Mark Gregory, Henry Silva, Valeria D'Obici, Timothy Brent, Andrea Coppola; **D:** Enzo G. Castellari.

Escape from the KGB woof! 1987 A CIA agent escapes from a Soviet prison, taking plans for a new space installation with him. 99m/C VHS, Beta. Thomas Hunter, Ivan Desny, Marie Versini, Walter Barns; **D:** Harald Phillipe.

Escape from the Planet of the Apes ✗✗✗ 1971 (G) Reprising their roles as intelligent, English-speaking apes, McDowall and Hunter flee their world before it's destroyed, and travel back in time to present-day America. In L.A. they become the subjects of a relentless search by the fearful population, much like humans Charlton Heston and James Franciscus were targeted for experimentation and destruction in simian society in the earlier "Planet of the Apes" and "Beneath the Planet of the Apes." Sequelled by "Conquest of the Planet of the Apes" and a television series. 98m/C VHS, Beta, LV, Letterbox, Closed Caption. Roddy McDowall, Kim Hunter, Sal Mineo, Ricardo Montalban, William Windom, Bradford Dillman, Natalie Trundy, Eric (Hans Gudegast) Braeden; **D:** Don Taylor; **C:** Joseph Biroc; **M:** Jerry Goldsmith. *FOX, FUS*

Escape Me Never ✗1/2 1947 Flynn plays a struggling composer in this sappy period piece about poverty-stricken artists in Italy at the turn of the century. Flynn falls for his brother's wealthy fiancee (Parker), although he is married to the faithful Lupino. Atypical role for Flynn and definitely not one of his best. Based on the novel "The Fool of the Family," by Margaret Kennedy and the play "Escape Me Never" by Kennedy. 101m/B VHS, Closed Caption. Errol Flynn, Ida Lupino, Eleanor Parker, Gig Young, Reginald Denny, Isobel Elsom; **D:** Peter Godfrey; **W:** Thomas Williamson. *MGM*

Escape to Athena ✗✗1/2 1979 (PG) A motley group is stuck in a German P.O.W. camp on a Greek island during WWII. 102m/C VHS, Beta. *GB* Roger Moore, Telly Savalas, David Niven, Claudia Cardinale, Richard Roundtree, Stefanie Powers, Sonny Bono, Elliott Gould, William Holden; **D:** George P. Cosmatos; **W:** Edward Anhalt; **M:** Lalo Schifrin. *FOX*

Escape to Burma ✗✗1/2 1955 A man on the run for a murder he did not commit finds refuge and romance in an isolated jungle home. 86m/C VHS, Beta. Barbara Stanwyck, Robert Ryan, Reginald Denny; **D:** Allan Dwan. *DIS, TOU*

Escape to Love ✗1/2 1982 Beautiful student helps a famous dissident escape from Poland, only to lose him to another heroic venture. 105m/C Beta. Clara Perryman, Louis Jourdan; **D:** Herbert Stein.

Escape to Paradise ✗1/2 1939 The last of Breen's films for RKO has him as a South American motorcycle-taxi driver acting as a guide for tourist Taylor. When Breen sets Taylor up with Shelton, trouble ensues. ♫ Tra-La-La; Rhythm of the Rio; Ay, Ay, Ay. 60m/B VHS. Bobby Breen, Kent Taylor, Marla Shelton, Joyce Compton, Rosina Galli, Frank Yaconelli; **D:** Erle C. Kenton. *NOS, RXM*

Escape to the Sun ✗1/2 Habricha el Hashemesh 1972 (PG) Pair of Russian university students plan to flee their homeland so they can be allowed to live and love free from oppression. 94m/C VHS, Beta. *IS* Laurence Harvey, Josephine Chaplin, John Ireland, Jack Hawkins, Lila Kedrova, Clive Revill; **D:** Menahem Golan. *NO*

Escape to Witch Mountain ✗✗✗ 1975 (G) Two young orphans with supernatural powers find themselves on the run from a greedy millionaire who wants to exploit their amazing gift. Adapted from a novel by Alexander Key. 97m/C VHS, Beta, LV. Kim Richards, Ike Eisenmann, Eddie Albert, Ray Milland, Donald Pleasence; **D:** John Hough. *DIS, BTV*

Escape 2000 woof! Turkey Shoot 1981 (R) In a future society where individuality is considered a crime, those who refuse to conform are punished by being hunted down in a jungle. Gross, twisted takeoff of Richard Connell's "The Most Dangerous Game." 80m/C VHS, Beta. *AU* Steve Railsback, Olivia Hussey, Michael Craig; **D:** Brian Trenchard-Smith; **W:** George Schenck; **M:** Brian May. *VTR*

Escapes ✗✗ 1986 In the tradition of "The Twilight Zone," Vincent Price introduces five short thrillers featuring time travel, aliens, and telepathy. Produced with computer assistance for sharper, more contrasted images. 72m/C VHS, Beta. Vincent Price, Jerry Grisham, Lee Canfield, John Mitchum, Gil Reade; **D:** David Steensland.

Escapist woof! 1983 A professional escape artist becomes involved in a perverted corporate plot and must escape to save his life and livelihood. 87m/C VHS, Beta. Bill Shirk, Peter Lupus; **D:** Eddie Beverly Jr. *ART, VES*

The Escort ✗ 1997 (R) Debra Grey runs a highly successful (and respectable) escort service and has just hired the charming Suzanne Lane. But behind Suzanne's charm lies the dreaded face of a psycho and she takes a very personal interest in Debra and her family. The unrated version is 90 minutes. **CW:** Strong sexuality, and for language and some violence. 85m/C VHS. Shauna O'Brien. *PEG*

L'Escorte ✗✗ The Escort 1996 Thirty-years-old and long-term lovers, Jean-Marc and Philippe find their relationship in crisis thanks to both the stress caused by their failing Montreal restaurant and the intrusion of a third party. Free-spirited Steve works as an escort and soon becomes an object of desire for both men as well as a catalyst for the revelation of long-held secrets. French with subtitles. 91m/C VHS. *CA* Eric Cabana, Paul-Antoine Taillefer, Robin Aubert, Marie Lefebvre; **D:** Denis Langlois; **W:** Denis Langlois, Bertrand Lachance; **C:** Yves Beaudoin; **M:** Bertrand Chenier. *CCN, FCT*

E.S.P. 1983 A young man is given the amazing power of extra-sensory perception. 96m/C VHS, Beta. Jim Stafford, George Deaton. *BFV*

Estate of Insanity ✗ 1970 An English lord and his second wife become involved in a web of death when a maniac stalks their ancient estate. 90m/C VHS, Beta. John Turner, Heather Sears, Ann Lynn; **D:** Robert Hartford-Davis. *NO*

Esther and the King ✗1/2 1960 Biblical costumer with Egan as Persian king and Collins as the Judean maiden he wants in place of the murdered queen. Long, rambling, and torturous. 109m/C VHS. *IT* Joan Collins, Richard Egan, Denis O'Dea, Sergio Fantoni; **D:** Raoul Walsh; **W:** Raoul Walsh, Michael Elkins; **M:** Angelo Francesco Lavagnino. *FXV*

Et La Tenoresse?...Bordel! ✗✗ 1984 A French comedy about a color-blind painter and his kinky fashion photographer roommate living in Paris. In French with subtitles. 100m/C VHS, Beta. *FR* **D:** Patrick Schulmann. *FCT*

E.T.: The Extra-Terrestrial ✗✗✗✗ 1982 (PG) Spielberg's famous fantasy, one of the most popular films in history, portrays a limpid-eyed alien stranded on earth and his special bonding relationship with a young boy. A modern fairy tale providing warmth, humor and sheer wonder. Held the first place spot as the highest grossing movie of all time for years until a new Spielberg hit replaced it—"Jurassic Park." Debra Winger contributed to the voice of E.T. 115m/C VHS, Beta, LV, Letterbox, Closed Caption. Henry Thomas, Dee Wallace Stone, Drew Barrymore, Robert MacNaughton, Peter Coyote, C. Thomas Howell, Sean Frye, K.C. Martel; **D:** Steven Spielberg; **W:** Melissa Mathison; **C:** Allen Daviau; **M:** John Williams; **V:** Debra Winger. Academy Awards '82: Best Visual Effects, Best Original Score; Golden Globe Awards '83: Best Film—Drama, Best Score; Los Angeles Film Critics Association Awards '82: Best Director (Spielberg), Best Film, National Film Registry '94;; National Society of Film Critics Awards '82: Best Director (Spielberg); Writers Guild of America '82: Best Original Screenplay;

Nominations: Academy Awards '82: Best Cinematography, Best Director (Spielberg), Best Film Editing, Best Original Screenplay, Best Picture, Best Sound. *USH, RDG, HMV*

Eternal Evil ✗ 1987 (R) A bored television director is taught how to have out-of-body experiences by his devil-worshipping girlfriend. He eventually realizes that when he leaves his body, it runs around killing people. 85m/C VHS, Beta, LV. Karen Black, Winston Rekert, Lois Maxwell; **D:** George Mihalka. *ART*

Eternal Return ✗✗1/2 L'Eternel Retour; Love Eternal 1943 A lush modern retelling of the Tristan/Isolde legend. Patrice (Marais) brings the beautiful Nathalie (Sologne) to his family's castle, as his uncle's (Murat) intended bride. But thanks to a love potion, it's Nathalie and Patrice who fall in love—with tragic results. In French with English subtitles. 111m/B VHS, Beta. *FR* Jean Marais, Madeleine Sologne, Jean Murat; **D:** Jean Delannoy; **W:** Jean Cocteau. *WBF, NLC, FCT*

The Eternal Waltz ✗✗ Ewiger Walzer 1954 Overly sentimental chronicle of the life of composer Johann Strauss. Only director Verhoeven's touch holds the viewer's interest, though the production values are excellent. 97m/C VHS. Bernhard Wicki, Hilde Krahl, Annemarie Duerringer, Friedl Loor, Eduard Strauss Jr., Gert Frobe, Arnulf Schroeder; **D:** Paul Verhoeven. *NOS*

Eternally Yours ✗✗1/2 1939 A witty magician's career threatens to break up his marriage. 95m/B VHS, Beta. David Niven, Loretta Young, Hugh Herbert, Broderick Crawford, Sir C. Aubrey Smith, Billie Burke, Eve Arden, ZaSu Pitts; **D:** Tay Garnett. Nominations: Academy Awards '39: Best Original Score. *NOS, MRV, HHT*

Eternity ✗ 1990 (R) While trying to uncover corrupt corporate America a television reporter falls in love with a model who works for a media king and puts his credibility on the line. He believes he and the woman shared romance in a past life. 122m/C VHS. Jon Voight, Armand Assante, Wilford Brimley, Eileen Davidson, Kaye Ballard, Lainie Kazan, Joey Villa, Steven Keats, Eugene Roche, Frankie Valli, John P. Ryan; **D:** Steven Paul.

Eternity and a Day ✗✗ Mia Eoniotita Ke Mia Mera 1997 Seriously ill writer Alexander (Ganz) is putting his affairs in order and revisiting his past, particularly moments with his beloved late wife, Anna (Renauld). But the present isn't finished with Alexander yet. He rescues a young boy (Skevis), an illegal immigrant from Albania, who says he was taken from his grandmother. Alexander decides to take the boy home and the two set out on the journey that will surely be Alexander's last. Greek with subtitles. 134m/C VHS. *GR FR* Bruno Ganz, Isabelle Renauld, Achileas Skevis; **D:** Theo Angelopoulos; **W:** Theo Angelopoulos; **C:** Yorgos Arvanitis, Andreas Sinani; **M:** Eleni Karaindrou. Cannes Film Festival '98: Best Film. *NYR*

Ethan ✗1/2 1971 A missionary in the Philippines falls in love with a woman and exiles himself for his fall from grace. 91m/C VHS, Beta. Robert Sampson, Rosa Rosal, Eddie Infante; **D:** Michael DuPont.

Ethan Frome ✗✗1/2 1992 (PG) Neeson stars as the lonely, poverty-stricken 19th-century New England farmer who has long and faithfully cared for his bitter, invalid wife. When his wife's distant young cousin comes to take over as housekeeper they both succumb to their forbidden passion with tragic results. The performers carry the burden of the film's sluggish pacing, where the bleak setting of Massachusetts in winter tends to overwhelm the events. Based on the novel by Edith Wharton. 107m/C VHS, Beta, LV, Closed Caption. Liam Neeson, Patricia Arquette, Joan Allen, Tate Donovan, Katharine Houghton, Stephen Mendillo; **D:** Jon Madden; **W:** Richard Nelson; **C:** Bobby Bukowski. *TOU, FCT*

Eubie! 1982 The popular Broadway musical revue based on the life and songs of Eubie Blake is presented in a video transfer. Some of Eubie's best known songs, performed here by members of the original cast, include "I'm Just Wild About

Harry," "Memories of You," "In Honeysuckle Time" and "The Charleston Rag." 100m/C VHS, Beta. Gregory Hines, Maurice Hines, Leslie Dockery, Alaina Reed, Lynnie Godfrey, Mel Johnson Jr., Jeffrey V. Thompson; **D:** Julianne Boyd. WAR, OM

Eureka! 🎞🎞½ 1981 (R) A bizarre, wildly symbolic slab of Roegian artifice that deals with the dream-spliced life of a rich, bored gold tycoon who becomes tortured over his daughter's marriage and his own useless wealth. Eventually he is bothered by the Mafia and led to the courtroom by business competitors. From the book by Paul Mayersberg. 130m/C VHS, Beta. GB Gene Hackman, Theresa Russell, Joe Pesci, Rutger Hauer, Mickey Rourke, Ed Lauter, Jane Lapotaire; **D:** Nicolas Roeg. MGM

Eureka Stockade 🎞🎞 Massacre Hill 1949 Four early Australian gold prospectors join forces to fight their governor and the police for the rights to dig on the continent. 103m/B VHS, Beta. AU Chips Rafferty, Peter Finch, Jane Barrett, Peter Illing; **D:** Harry Watt. NOS, DVT, HEG

Europa, Europa 🎞🎞🎞½ 1991 (R) The incredible, harrowing and borderline-absurdist true story of Solomon Perel, a young Jew who escaped the Holocaust by passing for German at an elite, Nazi-run academy. Such a sharp evocation of the era that the modern German establishment wouldn't submit it for the Academy Awards. In German and Russian with English subtitles.**CW:** Mature subject matter. 115m/C VHS. GE Marco Hofschneider, Klaus Abramowsky, Michele Gleizer, Rene Hofschneider, Nathalie Schmidt, Delphine Forest, Julie Delpy; **D:** Agnieszka Holland; **W:** Agnieszka Holland. Golden Globe Awards '92: Best Foreign Film; National Board of Review Awards '91: Best Foreign Film; New York Film Critics Awards '91: Best Foreign Film; Nominations: Academy Awards '91: Best Adapted Screenplay. ORI, BTV

Europa '51 🎞🎞½ The Greatest Love 1952 The despairing portrait of post-war malaise, as an American woman, whose son committed suicide, lives in Rome searching for some semblance of meaning, and ends up in an asylum. One of Bergman & Rossellini's least-loved films. In Italian with subtitles. 110m/B VHS, Beta. Ingrid Bergman, Alexander Knox, Ettore Giannini, Giulietta Masina; **D:** Roberto Rossellini. FCT

The Europeans 🎞🎞🎞 1979 Fine adaptation of Henry James's satiric novel. British brother and sister visit their staid American cousins in 19th-century New England in an effort to improve their prospects through fortuitous marriages. 90m/ C VHS, Beta. Lee Remick, Lisa Eichhorn, Robin Ellis, Wesley Addy, Tim Woodward; **D:** James Ivory; **W:** Ruth Prawer Jhabvala. Nominations: Academy Awards '79: Best Costume Design. CVC, LUM

Evangeline 🎞🎞½ 1929 Based on the Henry Wadsworth Longfellow poem about the struggles of Evangeline and the tragedy of lost love. 79m/B VHS. Dolores Del Rio, Roland Drew, Alec B. Francis, George F. Marion Sr.; **D:** Edwin Carewe. FCT

Eve of Destruction WOOF! 1990 (R) Hell knows no fury like a cutting-edge android-girl on the warpath. Modeled after her creator, Dr. Eve Simmons, Eve VII has android-babe good looks and a raging nuclear capability. Wouldn't you know, something goes haywire during her trial run, and debutante Eve turns into a PMS nightmare machine, blasting all the good Doctor's previous beaux. That's where military agent Hines comes in, though you wonder why. Dutch actress Soutendijk plays dual Eves in her first American film.**CW:** Strong language and strong violence. 101m/C VHS. Gregory Hines, Renee Soutendijk, Kurt Fuller, Ross Malinger, Eugene Glazer, John M. Jackson, Loren Haynes, Michael Greene; **D:** Duncan Gibbins; **W:** Duncan Gibbins, Yale Udoff; **C:** Alan Hume. COL, NLC

Evel Knievel 🎞🎞 1972 (PG) The life of motorcycle stuntman Evel Knievel is depicted in this movie, as portrayed by George Hamilton. Stunts will be appreciated by Evel Knievel fans. 90m/C VHS, Beta. George Hamilton, Bert Freed, Rod Cameron, Sue Lyon; **D:** Marvin J. Chomsky; **W:** John Milius. NO

Evelyn Prentice 🎞🎞½ 1934 Powell and Loy again team up as a married couple (after their "The Thin Man" success) but this time things aren't so rosy. He is an attorney with a wandering eye who has an affair with Russell (in her film debut). Loy finds out and turns for sympathy to Stephens but then she decides to stay with her husband after all. Only she's written some steamy letters to Stephens and he tries blackmailing her—and winds up dead. Dramatic courtroom scene straightens things out. Adapted from the novel by W.E. Woodward. Film was remade as "Stronger Than Desire" in 1939. 78m/B VHS. Myrna Loy, William Powell, Harvey Stephens, Isabel Jewell, Una Merkel, Rosalind Russell, Henry Wadsworth, Edward Brophy, Cora Sue Collins, Jessie Ralph, Sam Flint, Pat O'Malley; **D:** William K. Howard; **W:** Lenore Coffee. MGM

Even Angels Fall 🎞🎞 1990 One of heartthrob singer Humperdinck's scattered dramatic projects, a mystery thriller about a romance novelist moving into a New York brownstone whose previous inhabitant committed suicide—or was it murder? ?m/C VHS. Morgan Fairchild, Engelbert Humperdinck; **D:** Thomas Calabrese. NO

Even Cowgirls Get the Blues 🎞½ 1994 (R) '70s counterculture loses its ill-defined charm in a meandering adaptation of cult author Tom Robbins' 1976 novel. An interesting failure, but likely to alienate both Van Sant and Robbins fans. Sissy Hackshaw (Thurman) possesses enormous thumbs which she hopes will make her the greatest hitchhiker in the world. But first they take her to a NYC modeling career for The Countess (Hurt in a high camp performance), who sends her to the Rubber Rose ranch, recently liberated by female cowhands, who are happy to welcome her. Theatrical release was delayed numerous times as Van Sant recut but it doesn't matter—the only successful feature is the soundtrack. 106m/C VHS, LV. Uma Thurman, John Hurt, Rain Phoenix, Lorraine Bracco, Noriyuki "Pat" Morita, Angie Dickinson, Keanu Reeves; **Cameos:** Sean Young, Crispin Glover, Roseanne, Ed Begley Jr.; **D:** Gus Van Sant; **W:** Gus Van Sant; **C:** Eric Alan Edwards, John Campbell; **M:** k.d. lang, Ben Mink. Nominations: Golden Raspberry Awards '94: Worst Actress (Thurman). COL

The Evening Star 🎞🎞½ 1996 (PG-13) Sequel to 1983's "Terms of Endearment" starts in 1988 and finds the overbearing Aurora (MacLaine) now wreaking havoc on the lives of her three grown grandchildren (and vice versa). And Aurora's lovelife is as active as ever—old beau Hector Scott (Moffat) is hanging around, young psychiatrist Jerry Bruckner (Paxton) becomes her lover, and former astronaut flame Garrett Breedlove (Nicholson) also makes a brief appearance to cock an eyebrow at the shenanigans. Last screen role for Johnson as neighbor Arthur Cotten. Based on the novel by Larry McMurtry. Bring a hankie for the tears.**CW:** Some sexual situations and brief strong language. 128m/C VHS, Beta, Closed Caption. Shirley MacLaine, Juliette Lewis, George Newbern, MacKenzie Astin, Bill Paxton, Miranda Richardson, Marion Ross, Ben Johnson, Donald Moffat, Scott Wolf, China Kantner; **Cameos:** Jack Nicholson; **D:** Robert Harling; **W:** Robert Harling; **C:** Don Burgess; **M:** William Ross. Nominations: Golden Globe Awards '97: Best Supporting Actress (Ross). PAR

Event Horizon 🎞🎞½ 1997 (R) Cross between "Alien" and "The Shining" has Fishburne heading an ensemble cast out to rescue a prototype spaceship that's been missing for seven years. Their own ship is sabotaged by their own demons and certain extraterrestrial ones, too, that cause much mayhem on their once peaceful mission.**CW:** Strong violence and gore, language and some nudity. 97m/C VHS, Closed Caption. Laurence "Larry" Fishburne, Sam Neill, Kathleen Quinlan, Joely Richardson, Richard T. Jones, Jack Noseworthy, Sean Pertwee, Jason Isaacs; **D:** Paul Anderson; **W:** Philip Eisner; **C:** Adrian Biddle; **M:** Michael Kamen. PAR

Ever After: A Cinderella Story 1998 (PG-13) The adorable Barrymore takes on Cinderella, renamed Danielle and very capable, in this not-quite-a-fairytale version set in Renaissance-era France. Huston's the peeved stepmom, Scott's the handsome prince. Not yet reviewed.**CW:** Momentary strong language. ?m/C VHS. Drew Barrymore, Anjelica Huston, Dougray Scott; **D:** Andy Tennant. NYR

Evergreen 🎞🎞½ 1934 The daughter of a retired British music hall star is mistaken for her mother and it is thought that she has discovered the secret of eternal youth. ♫Daddy Wouldn't Buy Me a Bow-Wow; When You've Got a Little Springtime in Your Heart; If I Give in to You; Tinkle, Tinkle, Tinkle; Dear, Dear; Dancing on the Ceiling; Just by Your Example; Over My Shoulder. 91m/B VHS, Beta, LV. GB Jessie Matthews, Sonnie Hale, Betty Balfour, Barry Mackay, Ivor McLaren, Hartley Power, Patrick Ludlow, Marjorie Gaffney; **D:** Victor Saville; **W:** Emlyn Williams; **M:** Richard Rodgers, Harry Woods, Lorenz Hart, Harry Woods. VYY, HMV, THV

The Everlasting Secret Family 🎞🎞 1988 Politics and family life make strange bedfellows. A top political figure joins a secret homosexual organization in his search for power. 93m/C VHS. AU Arthur Dignam, Mark Lee, Dennis Miller, Heather Mitchell; **D:** Michael Thornhill. FCT, CCN, TPV

Eversmile New Jersey 🎞½ 1989 (PG) A dentist travels through Patagonia, offering dental care and advice to anyone in need, and a young woman, taken with the dental knight, dumps her boyfriend and stows away with him. When he discovers his admirer, he is less than ecstatic, but a chance tooth extraction on the road reveals the young woman's natural dental talents, and the two bond. From the director of "The Official Story." 88m/C VHS, Beta, LV. AR Daniel Day-Lewis, Mirjana Jokovic; **D:** Carlos Sorin; **W:** Jorge Goldenberg, Roberto Scheuer, Carlos Sorin. FXL

Every Breath 🎞🎞 1993 (R) A kinky couple's games can be deadly and now they have someone new to play with. Jimmy couldn't resist the wife's seductive allure and if he wants to survive, he'll have to beat them at their own game.**CW:** Language, some scenes of victims buried alive, and sexuality. 88m/C VHS, Closed Caption. Judd Nelson, Joanna Pacula, Patrick Bauchau; **D:** Steve Bing; **W:** Judd Nelson, Andrew Fleming, Steve Bing; **M:** Nils Lofgren. COL

Every Day's a Holiday 🎞🎞½ 1938 In the 1890s, West stars as confidence woman Peaches O'Day, who sells the Brooklyn Bridge and is run out of New York City. But she comes back, in disguise as a French singer, to expose some crooked cops. The Hays office again came down heavily on Mae's suggestive behavior, which left her with little to rely on. West's last film for Paramount. 79m/B VHS. Mae West, Edmund Lowe, Charles Butterworth, Charles Winninger, Walter Catlett, Lloyd Nolan, Herman Bing; **D:** Edward Sutherland; **W:** Mae West. USH, BTV

Every Girl Should Be Married 🎞🎞½ 1948 A shopgirl sets her sights on an eligible bachelor doctor. 84m/B VHS, Beta, LV. Cary Grant, Betsy Drake, Diana Lynn, Franchot Tone; **D:** Don Hartman. TTC

Every Girl Should Have One 🎞½ 1978 A rambunctious comedy about a chase following a million-dollar diamond theft. 90m/C VHS, Beta. Zsa Zsa Gabor, Robert Alda, Alice Faye, Sandra Vacey, John Lazar. GEM

Every Man for Himself & God Against All 🎞🎞🎞🎞 The Mystery of Kaspar Hauser; Jeder fur Sich und Gott Gegen Alle; The Enigma of Kaspar Hauser 1975 Kaspar Hauser is a young man who mysteriously appears in the town square of Nuremberg, early in the 19th century. He cannot speak or stand upright and is found to have been kept in a dungeon for the first 18 years of his life. He becomes an attraction in society with his alternate vision of the world and attempts to reconcile with reality. A lovely, though demanding film which is based on a true story. In German with English subtitles. **110m/C VHS, Beta.** *GE* Bruno S, Brigitte Mira, Walter Laderigast, Hans Musaus, Willy Semmelrogge, Michael Kroecher, Henry van Lyck; **D:** Werner Herzog; **W:** Werner Herzog; **M:** Albinoni Pachelbel, Orlando Di Lasso. *NYF, GLV, COL*

Every Man's Law 🐾½ **1935** A cowboy who poses as a hired gunman is almost lynched by ranchers who think he is a murderer. **60m/B VHS, Beta.** Johnny Mack Brown. *VCN*

Every Other Weekend 🐾🐾🐾 *Un Weekend sur Deux* **1991** Camille Valmont (Baye) is an actress who has sacrificed everything for her now-fading career. She's divorced loving husband Adrian (Manojlovic) and given him custody of their two young children—often ignoring her every other weekend visitation rights. In financial straits, Camille takes a job out of town and decides to take the kids with her, without telling Adrian. Self-centered and easily distracted, Camille tries to get close but manages to destroy what little rapport she has with her children. Camille isn't likable but Baye is such a gifted actress that you'll still feel pity. Director Garcia's debut; French with subtitles. **100m/C VHS.** *FR* Nathalie Baye, Miki Manojlovic, Joachim Serreau, Felicie Pasotti; **D:** Nicole Garcia; **W:** Nicole Garcia, Jacques Fieschi; **C:** William Lubtchansky; **M:** Oswald D'Andrea. *NYF*

Every Time We Say Goodbye 🐾🐾½ **1986 (PG-13)** In 1942, Jerusalem, an American flyboy falls in love with a young Sephardic Jewish girl, whose family resists the match. **97m/C VHS, Beta, LV.** Tom Hanks, Christina Marsillach, Benedict Taylor, Anat Atzman, Gila Almagor; **D:** Moshe Mizrahi; **W:** Moshe Mizrahi, Leah Appet; **M:** Philippe Sarde. *ART*

Every Which Way But Loose 🐾🐾 **1978 (R)** Fairly pointless Eastwood foray featuring Clint as a beer-guzzling, country-music loving truck driver earning a living as a barroom brawler. He and his orangutan travel to Colorado in pursuit of the woman he loves. Behind him are a motorcycle gang and an L.A. cop. All have been victims of his fists. Sequel is "Any Which Way You Can." **119m/C VHS, Beta, LV.** Clint Eastwood, Sondra Locke, Geoffrey Lewis, Beverly D'Angelo, Ruth Gordon; **D:** James Fargo; **M:** Stephen Dorff. *WAR*

Everybody Sing 🐾🐾 **1938** A down-on-their-luck theatrical family, including Garland (who is kicked out of boarding school for singing Mendelssohn with a swing beat) decides to put on a show in hopes of making a comeback. Dumb plot and boring songs make this one for die-hard Garland fans only. ♫Swing, Mr. Mendelssohn, Swing; The One I Love; Down on Melody Farms; The Show Must Go On; I Wanna Swing; Never Was There Such a Perfect Day; Quainty Dainty Me; Why? Because; Snooks. **80m/B VHS.** Allan Jones, Fanny Brice, Judy Garland, Reginald Owen, Billie Burke, Reginald Gardiner, Lynne Carver, Monty Woolley; **D:** Edwin L. Marin; **M:** George Bassman. *MGM, MVD*

Everybody Wins 🐾 **1990 (R)** A mystery-romance about a befuddled private eye trying to solve a murder and getting caught up with the bizarre prostitute who hired him. Arthur Miller based this screenplay on his stage drama "Some Kind of Love Story." Confused and, given its pedigree, disappointing mystery. **110m/C VHS, Beta, LV, Closed Caption.** Nick Nolte, Debra Winger, Will Patton, Jack Warden, Kathleen Wilhoite, Frank Converse, Frank Military, Judith Ivey; **D:** Karel Reisz; **W:** Arthur Miller; **C:** Ian Baker. *ORI*

Everybody's All American 🐾🐾 **1988 (R)** Shallow, sentimental melodrama about a college football star and his cheerleader wife whose lives, subsequent to their youthful glories, is a string of disappointments and tragedies. Decently acted and based on Frank Deford's novel. **127m/C VHS, Beta, LV, 8mm, Closed Caption.** Jessica Lange, Dennis Quaid, Timothy Hutton, John Goodman, Carl Lumbly, Ray Baker, Savannah Smith; **D:** Taylor Hackford; **M:** James Newton Howard. *WAR*

Everybody's Dancin' 🐾½ **1950** A ballroom proprietor's business is marred by random killings in her establishment as the bands play on. ♫Foolish Tears; Oblivious; Deep Freeze Dinah; I Shook; Rhumba Boogie. **66m/B VHS, Beta, LV.** Spade Cooley, Dick Lane, Hal Derwin, The Pioneers, Roddy McDowall; **D:** Will Jason. *NO*

Everybody's Fine 🐾🐾½ *Stanno Tutti Bene* **1990 (PG-13)** Mastroianni stars in this bittersweet story of a father on a mission to reunite his five grown children. His journey takes him all over Italy as he tries to bring them together in this touching film about enduring family love. In Italian with English subtitles. **115m/C VHS, LV, Closed Caption.** *IT* Marcello Mastroianni, Salvatore Cascio, Valeria Cavalli, Norma Martelli, Marino Cenna, Roberto Nobile, Michele Morgan, Fabio Iellini; **D:** Giuseppe Tornatore; **W:** Giuseppe Tornatore, Tonino Guerra; **M:** Ennio Morricone. *COL*

Everyone Says I Love You 🐾🐾🐾 **1996 (R)** Woody sings! Granted, he doesn't sing very well, but who else could twist a story of love among the neurotic rich with lavish production numbers from the golden age of movie musicals? The excellent cast (who weren't told that they were in a musical until after they signed) prove that as singers, they're pretty good actors. The plot centers around the wandering love lives of Steffi (Hawn), her husband Bob (Alda), her ex-husband Joe (Allen) and their assorted children; especially the preppy Skylar (Barrymore) and her fiance Holden (Norton). Some of the musical productions are shaky (Allen's duet with Julia Roberts is straight out of Tin Ear Alley), but the feeling behind them is genuine; Besides, where else are you going to hear Groucho's "Hooray for Captain Spaulding" sung in French or a chorus of pregnant women sing "Makin' Whoopee"?*CW:* One use of strong language. **105m/C VHS, LV, Closed Caption.** Woody Allen, Alan Alda, Drew Barrymore, Goldie Hawn, Gaby Hoffman, Edward Norton, Natalie Portman, Julia Roberts, Tim Roth, Natasha Lyonne, Lukas Haas, David Ogden Stiers; **D:** Woody Allen; **W:** Woody Allen; **C:** Carlo DiPalma; **M:** Dick Hyman. Los Angeles Film Critics Association Awards '96: Best Supporting Actor (Norton); National Board of Review Awards '96: Best Supporting Actor (Norton); Nominations: Golden Globe Awards '97: Best Film—Musical/Comedy. *TOU*

Everything Happens at Night 🐾🐾🐾 **1939** Rival reporters Milland and Cummings are torn between the woman they love and the story of a lifetime. One of Henie's best romantic skating vehicles due to the strong performances by the leading men. Henie does take to the ice for a couple of numbers, but this film was largely designed to expand her image as a serious actress. Although it failed to do that, it's good entertainment nonetheless. **76m/B VHS.** Sonja Henie, Ray Milland, Robert Cummings, Maurice Moscovich, Leonid Kinskey, Alan Dinehart, Fritz Feld; **D:** Irving Cummings; **W:** Art Arthur, Robert Harari. *FXV*

Everything Relative 🐾🐾½ **1996** Seven college buddies reunite and spend a weekend in the country together in this lesbian twist on "The Big Chill." A bris held by partners Katie and Sarah for their new baby brings the mostly single forty-something women together, and bring out the unfulfilled desires and regrets of the six lesbians and one straight woman. Standouts include Weber as the stunt woman mourning the loss of a lover to a car accident 15 years prior, and the relationship between Josie (McLaughlin) and Maria (Negron), the woman who left her to get married and have children, and is now divorced and losing her children in the custody battle. Low budget ($100,000) indie debut of writer/director Pollack is right on the mark emotionally and manages to keep the characters and their stories engaging, but loses something with neatly pat solutions to the intricate problems facing these women. **110m/C VHS.** Stacey Nelkin, Ellen McLaughlin, Olivia Negron, Monica Bell, Andrea Weber, Gabriella Messina, Carol Schneider; **D:** Sharon Pollack; **W:** Sharon Pollack; **C:** Rachel Othmer; **M:** Frank London. *WLF*

Everything You Always Wanted to Know about Sex (But Were Afraid to Ask) 🐾🐾🐾 **1972 (R)** Satiric comical sketches about sex includes a timid sperm cell, an oversexed court jester, a sheep folly, and a giant disembodied breast. Quite entertaining in its own jolly way. Based on the book by Dr. David Reuben. **88m/C VHS, Beta, LV.** Woody Allen, John Carradine, Lou Jacobi, Louise Lasser, Anthony Quayle, Geoffrey Holder, Lynn Redgrave, Tony Randall, Burt Reynolds, Gene Wilder, Robert Walden, Jay Robinson; **D:** Woody Allen; **W:** Woody Allen. *MGM, FOX, FCT*

Eve's Bayou 🐾🐾🐾½ **1997 (R)** Eve (newcomer Smollett) comes from the upper-middle class Batiste family that seems all too perfect on the outside, but secrets and lies slowly surface when she mistakenly catches her doctor father Louis (Jackson) doing more than a routine check-up with a female patient. With her innocence shattered by the discovery, Eve's torment soon affects her emotionally strained mother Roz (Whitfield) and adolescent tease older sister Cisely (Good). Set in Louisiana 1962, and told in flashback, film presents a mesmerizing and complex story with haunting visuals. Ghostly appearance from Carroll adds a touch of voodoo and heightens the melodramatic intensity. Jackson is solid as the charming, yet flawed womanizer and Whitfield his equal as the suspecting wife. Impressive, multi-layered directorial debut from Lemmons didn't draw much attention during theatrical run, but has gained a following since.*CW:* Sexuality and language. **109m/C VHS.** Samuel L. Jackson, Lynn Whitfield, Debbi Morgan, Diahann Carroll, Jurnee Smollett, Meagan Good, Vondie Curtis-Hall, Lisa Nicole Carson; **D:** Kasi Lemmons; **W:** Kasi Lemmons; **C:** Amy Vincent; **M:** Terence Blanchard; **V:** Tamara Tunie. Independent Spirit Awards '98: Best First Feature, Best Supporting Actress (Morgan). *THV*

The Evictors WOOF! **1979 (PG)** Young couple moves into an abandoned, haunted farmhouse in a small Louisiana town. Unfortunately, they don't know anything about its horrible bloody history. And the real estate agent acts kinda funny. AIP Amityville scare-a-thon. **92m/C VHS, Beta.** Vic Morrow, Michael Parks, Jessica Harper, Sue Ane Langdon, Dennis Fimple; **D:** Charles B. Pierce; **W:** Charles B. Pierce. *ART, VES*

The Evil 🐾🐾 **1978 (R)** A psychologist must destroy an evil force that is killing off the members of his research team residing at an old mansion. **80m/C VHS, Beta.** Richard Crenna, Joanna Pettet, Andrew Prine, Victor Buono, Cassie Yates, George O'Hanlon Jr., Lynne Moody, Mary Louise Weller, Milton Selzer; **D:** Gus Trikonis; **W:** Donald G. Thompson; **C:** Mario DiLeo.

Evil Altar 🐾 **1989 (R)** A man controls a small town, but only so long as he offers sacrifices to the devil! **90m/C VHS.** William Smith, Robert Z'Dar, Pepper Martin, Theresa Cooney, Ryan Rao; **D:** James R. Winburn.

The Evil Below 🐾 **1987** A couple hits the high seas in search of the lost treasure ship "El Diablo," resting on the ocean floor. In the process they trigger an evil curse and then must attempt to thwart it. **90m/C VHS, Beta.** *SA* June Chadwick, Wayne Crawford; **D:** Jean-Claude Dubois. *NO*

Evil Clutch 🐾½ **1989 (R)** A young couple vacationing in the Alps encounter several creepy locals when they find themselves in the midst of a haunted forest. The cinematography is extremely amateurish in this Italian gorefest and the English dubbing is atrocious. However, the special make-up effects are outstanding and the musical score adds a touch of class to this otherwise inept horror film. **88m/C VHS, LV, Closed Caption.** *IT* Coralina Cataldi Tassoni, Diego Riba, Elena Cantarone, Luciano Crovato, Stefano Molinari; **D:** Andreas Marfori; **W:** Andreas Marfori. *UND, RHI*

Evil Dead 🐾🐾½ **1983 (NC-17)** Five vacationing college students unwittingly resurrect demons which transform the students into evil monsters. Exuberantly gory low-budgeter followed by two sequels. **126m/C VHS, Beta, LV.** Bruce Campbell, Ellen

Sandweiss, Betsy Baker, Hal Delrich, Sarah York; **D:** Sam Raimi; **W:** Sam Raimi; **C:** Tim Philo. *NO*

Evil Dead 2: Dead by Dawn 🎬🎬½ **1987 (R)** A gory, tongue-in-cheek sequel/remake of the original festival of gag and gore, in which an ancient book of magic invokes a crowd of flesh-snacking, joke-tossing ghouls. Followed by yet a third bloodfest. **84m/C VHS, Beta, LV.** Bruce Campbell, Sarah Berry, Dan Hicks, Kassie Wesley, Theodore (Ted) Raimi, Denise Bixler, Richard Domeier; **D:** Sam Raimi; **W:** Sam Raimi, Scott Spiegel; **C:** Peter Deming; **M:** Joseph LoDuca. *VTR*

Evil Ed 🎬½ **1996 (R)** Formerly mild-mannered film editor Ed (Ruebeck) becomes obsessed with the horror series he's working on, goes off the deep end, and begins a series of killings that mimic the ones from the films. Lots of splatter.**CW:** Sadistic violence and gore, language and some sexuality in a horror comedy. **90m/C VHS.** *SW* Johan Ruebeck, Olof Rhodin, Pete Lofbergh; **D:** Anders Jacobsson. *APX*

Evil Has a Face 🎬🎬½ **1996 (R)** Chicago police sketch artist Gwen McGarrell (Young) travels to rural Minnesota to help investigator Tom Sawyer (Moses) locate a child molester. But the face she draws turns out to be that of her abusive stepfather (Ross), who's been presumed dead. Made for cable.**CW:** Some violence and terror. **92m/C VHS, Closed Caption.** Sean Young, William R. Moses, Joe Guzaldo, Chelcie Ross, Brighton Hertford, Dick Cusack; **D:** Robert M. Fresco; **W:** Robert M. Fresco; **C:** Stephen Lighthill; **M:** Joseph Vitarelli. *USH*

Evil Judgement 🎬½ **1985** A young girl investigates a series of murders and finds the culprit is a psychopathic judge. **93m/C VHS, Beta.** Pamela Collyer, Jack Langedijk, Nanette Workman; **D:** Claude Castravelli.

Evil Laugh woof! **1986 (R)** Medical students and their girlfriends party at an abandoned orphanage, until a serial killer decides to join them. **90m/C VHS.** Tony Griffin, Kim McKamy, Jody Gibson, Dominick Brascia; **D:** Dominick Brascia. *CEL*

The Evil Mind 🎬🎬½ *The Clairvoyant* **1934** A fraudulent mind reader predicts many disasters that start coming true. **80m/B VHS, Beta.** *GB* Claude Rains, Fay Wray, Jane Baxter, Felix Aylmer; **D:** Maurice Elvey; **W:** Charles Bennett. *SNC, FCT, BAR*

Evil Obsession 🎬 **1996** Disturbed young man becomes obsessed with a supermodel and later becomes a suspect in the murders of 12 other models. **93m/C VHS.** Corey Feldman, Kimberly Stevens, Mark Derwin, Brion James; **D:** Richard W. Munchkin. *PRE*

The Evil of Frankenstein 🎬🎬 **1964** The third of the Hammer Frankenstein films, with the mad doctor once again finding his creature preserved in ice and thawing him out. Preceded by "The Revenge of Frankenstein" and followed by "Frankenstein Created Woman." **84m/C VHS, Beta.** *GB* Peter Cushing, Duncan Lamont, Peter Woodthorpe, Sandor Eles, Kiwi Kingston, Katy Wild; **D:** Freddie Francis; **W:** Anthony John Elder Hinds; **C:** John Wilcox; **M:** Don Banks. *USH, MLB*

Evil Spawn 🎬 *Deadly Sting; Alive by Night; Alien Within* **1987** A fading movie queen takes an experimental drug to restore her youthful beauty, but it only turns her into a giant silverfish. Releases under several alternate titles, and with varying running times. **70m/C VHS, Beta.** Bobbie Bresee, John Carradine, Drew Godderis, John Terrance, Dawn Wildsmith, Jerry Fox, Pamela Gilbert, Forrest J. Ackerman; **D:** Kenneth J. Hall; **W:** Kenneth J. Hall; **C:** Christopher Condon. *NO*

Evil Spirits 🎬½ **1991 (R)** Boardinghouse tenants are murdered while the crazy landlady cashes their social security checks. This seedy horror cheapie doesn't take itself seriously, and like-minded genre buffs may enjoy the cult-film cast.**CW:** Graphic violence and one sensual scene. **95m/C VHS, Beta, LV.** Karen Black, Arte Johnson, Virginia Mayo, Michael Berryman, Martine Beswick, Bert Remsen, Yvette Vickers, Robert Quarry, Mikel Angel, Debra Lamb; **D:** Gary Graver; **W:** Mikel Angel.

The Evil That Men Do 🎬🎬 **1984 (R)** A hitman comes out of retirement to break up a Central American government's political torture ring and, in the process, brings a friend's killer to justice. Based on the novel by R. Lance Hill. **90m/C VHS, Beta, LV, 8mm, Closed Caption.** Charles Bronson, Theresa Saldana, Joseph Maher, Jose Ferrer, Rene Enriquez, John Glover, Raymond St. Jacques, Antoinette Bower, Enrique Lucero, Jorge Luke; **D:** J. Lee Thompson; **W:** John Crowther. *COL*

Evil Toons 🎬½ **1990 (R)** A quartet of lovely coeds on a cleaning job venture into a deserted mansion. There they accidentally release a vulgar, lustful, animated demon who proceeds to cause their clothes to fall off. Can the girls escape the haunted mansion with their sanity, virtue and wardrobes intact?**CW:** Some language, nudity, and comic sex-related violence. **86m/C VHS, Beta.** David Carradine, Dick Miller, Monique Gabrielle, Suzanne Ager, Stacy Nix, Madison Stone, Don Dowe, Arte Johnson, Michelle (McClellan) Bauer; **D:** Fred Olen Ray.

Evil Town 🎬 **1987 (R)** In this poorly made movie a wandering guy discovers a town overrun with zombies created by a mad doctor. **88m/C VHS, Beta.** Dean Jagger, James Keach, Robert Walker Jr., Doria Cook, Michele Marsh; **D:** Edward Collins. *TWE, HHE*

Evil under the Sun 🎬🎬 **1982 (PG)** An opulent beach resort is the setting as Hercule Poirot attempts to unravel a murder mystery. Based on the Agatha Christie novel. **112m/C VHS, Beta, LV.** *GB* Peter Ustinov, Jane Birkin, Maggie Smith, Colin Blakely, Roddy McDowall, Diana Rigg, Sylvia Miles, James Mason, Nicholas Clay; **D:** Guy Hamilton; **W:** Anthony Shaffer. *REP*

The Evil Within woof! *Baby Blood* **1994 (R)** Parasitic beast, with an unquenchable thirst for blood, slithers from the center of the earth into the convenient womb of a young woman. She takes to murdering everyone within reach while preparing to give birth. As disgusting as it sounds. **88m/C VHS.** Emmanuelle Escourrou, Jean-Francois Guillotte; **D:** Alain Robak; **W:** Alain Robak, Serge Cukier. *APX*

Evil's Commandment 🎬🎬½ **1956** Original vampire film which started the classic Italian horror cycle. A gorgeous Countess needs blood to stay young, otherwise she reverts to a 200-year-old vampire. **?m/B VHS.** *IT* Gianna Maria Canale; **D:** Riccardo (Robert Hampton) Freda. *SMW*

Evils of the Night 🎬 **1985** Teenage campers are abducted by sex-crazed alien vampires. Bloody naked mayhem follows. **85m/C VHS, Beta.** John Carradine, Julie Newmar, Tina Louise, Neville Brand, Aldo Ray, Karrie Emerson, Bridget Hollman; **D:** Marti Rustam; **W:** Marti Rustam, Phillip D. Connors. *ART*

Evilspeak woof! **1982 (R)** Bumbling misfit enrolled at a military school is mistreated by the other cadets. With the help of his computer, he retaliates with satanic power. Bits, bytes, and gore. **89m/C VHS, Beta.** Clint Howard, Don Stark, Lou Gravance, Lauren Lester, R.G. Armstrong, Joe Cortese, Claude Earl Jones, Haywood Nelson; **D:** Eric Weston. *FOX*

Evita 🎬🎬½ **1996 (PG)** Webber/Rice rock opera about the life and death of Eva Peron finally comes to the big screen with all its extravaganza intact. Madonna's in the title role (in fine voice, lavishly costumed but unflatteringly lit) about an ambitious poor girl willing to do anything to make her mark—in this version by sleeping her way up the ladder of power to Argentine strongman Juan Peron (Pryce as wax dummy). Evita becomes a would-be champion of the people, even as the government ruthlessly suppresses their freedoms. The surprisingly strong-voiced Banderas (perhaps his emphatic enunciation is to make his English as clear as possible) is everyman narrator Che (changed from the stage version's revolutionary Che Guevera). The highlight is still Madonna's balcony scene, singing "Don't Cry for Me, Argentina," but some of the other songs are drowned by loud orchestration. Director Parker has a cameo as a frustrated film director trying to work with Evita. **133m/C VHS, LV, Closed Caption.** Madonna, Antonio Banderas, Jonathan Pryce, Jimmy Nail, Victoria Sus,

Julian Littman, Olga Meediz, Laura Pallas, Julia Worsley; **Cameos:** Alan Parker; **D:** Alan Parker; **W:** Oliver Stone, Alan Parker; **C:** Darius Khondji; **M:** Andrew Lloyd Webber, Tim Rice. Academy Awards '96: Best Song ("You Must Love Me"); Golden Globe Awards '97: Best Actress—Musical/Comedy (Madonna), Best Film—Musical/Comedy, Best Song ("You Must Love Me"); Nominations: Academy Awards '96: Best Art Direction/Set Decoration, Best Cinematography, Best Film Editing, Best Sound; British Academy Awards '97: Best Adapted Screenplay; Golden Globe Awards '97: Best Actor—Musical/Comedy (Banderas), Best Director (Parker); MTV Movie Awards '97: Best Female Performance (Madonna), Best Song ("Don't Cry for Me Argentina"). *TOU*

Evolver 🎬½ **1994 (R)** Teenager Kyle Baxter (Randall) wins a robot patterned after a video arcade game but the robot has a secret military weapon's program built into its brain, causing it to evolve into a killing machine.**CW:** Violence; language; some nudity. **90m/C VHS, LV, Closed Caption.** Ethan Randall, John de Lancie, Cassidy Rae, Cindy Pickett, Paul Dooley; **D:** Mark Rosman; **W:** Mark Rosman; **C:** Jacques Haitkin; **V:** William H. Macy. *THV*

The Ewok Adventure 🎬🎬½ **1984 (G)** Those adorable, friendly and funny characters from "Return of the Jedi" make the jump from film to television in a new adventure from George Lucas. In this installment, the Ewoks save a miraculous child from harm with the help of a young human. This fun-filled adventure has Lucas's thumbprint all over it and great special effects. Followed by "Ewoks: The Battle for Endor." **96m/C VHS, Beta, LV, Closed Caption.** Warwick Davis, Eric Walker, Aubree Miller, Fionnula Flanagan; **D:** John Korty; **M:** Elmer Bernstein, Peter Bernstein. *MGM, FCT*

The Ewoks: Battle for Endor 🎬🎬½ **1985** A television movie based on the furry creatures from "Return of the Jedi," detailing their battle against an evil queen to retain their forest home. Preceded by "The Ewok Adventure." **98m/C VHS, Beta, LV, Closed Caption.** Wilford Brimley, Warwick Davis, Aubree Miller, Sian Phillips, Paul Gleason, Eric Walker, Carel Struycken, Niki Botholo; **D:** Jim Wheat, Ken Wheat; **M:** Peter Bernstein. *MGM, FCT*

The Ex 🎬🎬 **1996 (R)** Architect David Kenyon (Mancuso) has a new life, with a sweet second wife (Amis) and a five-year-old son. Then the ex, Deirdre (Butler), comes sauntering back and it seems she and David had a very kinky relationship. Now Deirdre decides it's time to get revenge. Familiar plotline is given a high gloss and some chills.**CW:** Sex, violence, nudity. **87m/C VHS, LV.** Yancy Butler, Nick Mancuso, Suzy Amis; **D:** Mark L. Lester; **W:** John Lutz, Larry Cohen; **C:** Richard Letterman; **M:** Paul Zaza. *ART*

Ex-Cop 🎬🎬 **1993** Pete Danberg is a cop with a drinking problem. He's fired from the force but not before he puts away the "Las Vegas Slasher." Unfortunately for Pete the Slasher makes parole and is out for revenge—using Pete's kidnapped daughter as bait. **97m/C VHS.** Rick Savage, Sandy Hackett, Joan Chamberlain, Douglas Terry, Angi Davidson, Richard Cornell, Jim Williams; **D:** Patrick Kerby; **W:** Daniel S. Sample.

Ex-Lady 🎬🎬 **1933** Davis stars as a liberated woman who loves advertising writer Raymond, but doesn't want to marry him. However, she believes living together is the most suitable arrangement. The two open up an ad agency and complications ensue. Remake of "Illicit," which was filmed only two years earlier with Barbara Stanwyck in the lead role. **65m/B VHS, Closed Caption.** Bette Davis, Gene Raymond, Frank McHugh, Claire Dodd, Monroe Owsley, Ferdinand Gottschalk; **D:** Robert Florey. *MGM*

Ex-Mrs. Bradford 🎬🎬🎬 **1936** Amateur sleuth Dr. Bradford teams up with his ex-wife to solve a series of murders at the race track. Sophisticated comedy-mystery; witty dialogue. **80m/B VHS, Beta, LV.** William Powell, Jean Arthur, James Gleason, Eric Blore, Robert Armstrong; **D:** Stephen Roberts. *NOS*

Excalibur ✗✗✗½ **1981 (R)** A sweeping, visionary retelling of the life of King Arthur, from his conception, to the sword in the stone, to the search for the Holy Grail and the final battle with Mordred. An imperfect, sensationalized version, but still the best yet filmed. **140m/C VHS, Beta, LV, Letterbox.** Nigel Terry, Nicol Williamson, Nicholas Clay, Helen Mirren, Cherie Lunghi, Paul Geoffrey, Gabriel Byrne, Liam Neeson, Patrick Stewart, Charley Boorman, Corin Redgrave; **D:** John Boorman; **W:** John Boorman, Rospo Pallenberg; **M:** Trevor Jones. Nominations: Academy Awards '81: Best Cinematography. **WAR, TVC**

Excess Baggage ✗½ **1996 (PG-13)** Attention-seeking rich girl Emily (Silverstone) fakes her own kidnapping to get back at dear old dad, involving car thief Vincent Roche (del Toro) in the crime. Things get out of control when her creepy "Uncle" Ray (Walken), who's an ex-CIA assassin, is hired by Emily's father to get her back. Silverstone's character is alternately whiny and pouting, you'll wonder why dad would want her back and why Vincent hangs on at all. First picture in Silverstone's pricey production deal with Columbia went through the rumor mill (for supposed clashes between Silverstone and director Brambilla) and was originally scheduled for release in the fall of '96.**CW:** Violence, drinking and sex-related dialogue. **101m/C VHS, LV, Closed Caption, DVD.** Alicia Silverstone, Benicio Del Toro, Christopher Walken, Harry Connick Jr., Jack Thompson, Christopher Walken, Michael Bowen, Leland Orser, Robert Wisden, Sally Kirkland; **D:** Marco Brambilla; **W:** Mikhaila Max Adams, Dick Clement, Ian LaFrenais; **C:** Jean-Yves Escoffier; **M:** John Lurie. Nominations: Golden Raspberry Awards '97: Worst Actress (Silverstone). **COL**

Excessive Force ✗½ **1993 (R)** Routine actioner lives up to its title by offering lots of violence, but little else. Gang leader Young seeks revenge on the cops who he believes ruined a $3 million drug deal. Loner cop Griffith is the only one to survive the grudge killings and goes after Young himself. Talented cast underachieves. Limited theatrical release sent this one almost straight to video.**CW:** Strong language, strong violence and drug use, and sexuality. **87m/C VHS, LV, Closed Caption.** Thomas Ian Griffith, Lance Henriksen, James Earl Jones, Charlotte Lewis, Tony Todd, Burt Young, W. Earl Brown; **D:** Jon Hess; **W:** Thomas Ian Griffith; **C:** Donald M. Morgan; **M:** Charles Bernstein. **NLC, IME**

Excessive Force 2: Force on Force ✗½ **1995 (R)** Special agent Harly Cordell (Randall) volunteers to hunt down an assassination squad that is turning L.A. into murder central. Seems her former lover Francis Lydell (Gauthier) is head killer and Harly's got a score to settle. Lots of action and nifty weapons. **88m/C VHS, LV, Closed Caption.** Stacie Randall, Dan Gauthier, Jay Patterson, John Mese; **D:** Jonathan Winfrey; **W:** Mark Sevi; **C:** Russ Brandt; **M:** Kevin Kiner. **NLC, IME**

The Execution ✗½ **1985** A made-for-television movie about five female friends who discover that the Nazi doctor who brutalized them in a concentration camp during WWII is now living a normal life in California. Together they plot his undoing. **92m/C VHS, Beta.** Loretta Swit, Valerie Harper, Sandy Dennis, Jessica Walter, Rip Torn, Barbara Barrie, Robert Hooks, Michael Lerner; **D:** Paul Wendkos; **M:** Georges Delerue.

The Execution of Private Slovik ✗✗✗½ **1974** This quiet powerhouse of a TV movie recounts in straightforward terms the case of Eddie Slovik, a WWII misfit who became the only American soldier executed for desertion since the Civil War. The Levinson/Link screenplay (based on the book by William Bradford Huie) ends up deifying Slovik, which some might find hard to take. But there's no arguing the impact of the drama, or of Sheen's unaffected lead performance. **122m/C VHS.** Martin Sheen, Mariclare Costello, Ned Beatty, Gary Busey, Matt Clark, Ben Hammer, Warren Kemmerling; **D:** Lamont Johnson; **W:** Richard Levinson, William Link; **C:** Bill Butler. **USH**

Execution of Raymond Graham ✗✗½ **1985** The lawyers and family of Raymond Graham struggle to keep him from being executed for murder. Based on a true story; made for television. **104m/C VHS, Beta.** Morgan Freeman, Jeff Fahey, Kate Reid, Laurie Metcalf, Josef Sommer; **D:** Daniel Petrie. **NO**

The Executioner ✗✗ **1970 (PG)** A thriller wherein a British spy must prove that his former colleague is a double agent. Elements of back-stabbing, betrayal, and espionage abound. **107m/C VHS, Beta.** **GB** Judy Geeson, Oscar Homolka, Charles Gray, Nigel Patrick, George Peppard, Joan Collins, Keith Michell; **D:** Sam Wanamaker. **COL, GKK**

The Executioner ✗ **Like Father, Like Son; Massacre Mafia Style 1978 (R)** A very cheap, very "Godfather"-like tale of a mafia family gone awry. **84m/C VHS, Beta.** Duke Mitchell, Vic Caesar, Dominic Micelli, John Strong, Jim Williams, Lorenzo Dodo; **D:** Duke Mitchell; **W:** Duke Mitchell. **GEM, MRV**

Executioner of Venice ✗ **1963** Marauding pirates with time on hands swarm in from the Adriatic Sea and attempt to rob the Venetians blind. The Doge and his godson come to the rescue. **90m/C VHS, Beta.** Guy Madison, Lex Barker, Alessandra Panaro; **D:** Louis Capauno. **NO**

The Executioner, Part 2: Frozen Scream ✗ **1984 (R)** Brutal feud rocks the Mafia, and a crime kingpin's passionate son seeks revenge on his father's slayers. Not a sequel to any other films bearing similar titles. Strange thing is, no "Executioner, Part I" was ever made. Pretty laughable. **150m/C VHS, Beta.** Chris Mitchum, Aldo Ray, Antoine John Mottet, Renee Harmon; **D:** James Bryant. **GEM**

The Executioners ✗½ **1993** When a nuclear explosion contaminates most of the city's drinking water, the remainder falls under the harsh control of the Black Knight. Now, it's up to the Heroic Trio to defeat their nemesis. Sequel to "The Executioners"; Chinese with subtitles. **100m/C VHS, LV.** **HK** Anita Mui, Michelle Yeoh, Maggie Cheung; **D:** Ching Siu Tung. **TAI**

The Executioner's Song ✗✗½ **1982** European version of the television movie based on Norman Mailer's Pulitzer Prize-winner, recounting the life and death of convicted murderer Gary Gilmore. Features adult-minded footage not seen in the U.S. version. **157m/C VHS, Beta.** Tommy Lee Jones, Rosanna Arquette, Eli Wallach, Christine Lahti, Jenny Wright, Jordan Clark, Steven Keats; **D:** Lawrence Schiller. **ART**

Executive Action ✗✗½ **1973 (PG)** Political thriller providing a different look at the events leading to the assassination of JFK. In this speculation, a millionaire pays a professional spy to organize a secret conspiracy to kill President Kennedy. Ryan's final film. Adapted by Dalton Trumbo from Mark Lane's "Rush to Judgement." **91m/C VHS, Beta, LV.** Burt Lancaster, Robert Ryan, Will Geer, Gilbert Green, John Anderson; **D:** David Miller; **C:** Robert Steadman; **M:** Randy Edelman. **WAR**

Executive Decision ✗✗ **1996 (R)** Those wacky terrorists are at it again. You would think that after getting their butts kicked in almost every action picture since 1980 that they would learn. But here they are, hijacking a 747, cutting off communications, and affixing a nerve gas bomb to the plane. This time a group of high tech commandos, led by Russell and (briefly) Seagal, must sneak onto the plane and generally mess up the bad guys' plans. Brave stewardess Berry helps tango with the central casting mad dog terrorists. The title refers to the President's decision on whether or not to blow the plane up in order to avert disaster. Or maybe "Die Hard: Ad Nauseum" wasn't available.**CW:** Violence and brief language. **132m/C VHS, LV, Closed Caption, DVD.** Kurt Russell, Halle Berry, Oliver Platt, John Leguizamo, Steven Seagal, Joe Morton, David Suchet, B.D. Wong, Len Cariou, Whip Hubley, J.T. Walsh; **D:** Stuart Baird; **W:** Jim Thomas, John Thomas; **C:** Alex Thomson; **M:** Jerry Goldsmith. Nominations: Golden Raspberry Awards '96: Worst Supporting Actor (Seagal). **WAR**

Executive Suite ✗✗✗ **1954** One of the first dog-eat-dog dramas about high finance and big business. The plot centers on the question of a replacement for the freshly buried owner of a gigantic furniture company. **104m/B VHS, Beta, Closed Caption.** William Holden, June Allyson, Barbara Stanwyck, Fredric March, Walter Pidgeon, Louis Calhern, Shelley Winters, Paul Douglas, Nina Foch, Dean Jagger; **D:** Robert Wise; **W:** Ernest Lehman. Nominations: Academy Awards '54: Best Art Direction/Set Decoration (B & W), Best Black and White Cinematography, Best Costume Design (B & W), Best Supporting Actress (Foch). **MGM**

Executive Target ✗✗ **1997 (R)** Stunt-car driver Nick James (Madsen) is grabbed by a gang of mercenaries who want him as their getaway man when they attempt to kidnap the president (Scheider) and overthrow the U.S. government. He agrees because the gang have also taken his wife as a hostage. Lots of action sequences show where the money went.**CW:** Violence, language and a scene of sexuality. **96m/C VHS.** Michael Madsen, Keith David, Angie Everhart, Roy Scheider, Dayton Callie, Kathy Christopherson; **D:** Joseph Merhi. **PMH**

Exiled in America ✗✗ **1990** A Central American freedom fighter (Albert) flees his country for the United States, settling in a small town with his wife. She gets a waitressing job at a local diner, telling the owner her husband died in an accident, and the owner's son winds up falling in love with her. Things get complicated when the death squad, led by a corrupt CIA agent, follows Albert to his hiding place, and the local sheriff threatens to blow his cover. **84m/C VHS.** Maxwell Caulfield, Edward Albert, Viveca Lindfors, Kamala Lopez, Stella Stevens, Wings Hauser; **D:** Paul Leder; **W:** Paul Leder.

Exiled to Shanghai ✗✗½ **1937** A couple of newsreel men invent a television device that revolutionizes the business. **65m/B VHS.** Wallace Ford, June Travis, Dean Jagger, William "Billy" Bakewell, Arthur Lake, Jonathan Hale, William Harrigan, Sarah Padden; **D:** Nick Grinde. **NOS, DVT, HEG**

Exit ✗½ **1995 (R)** Gang of criminals, lead by pscho Charles (Bradley), take a strip club's dancers as hostages when their robbery attempt goes bad. Exotic dancer Diane (Whirry) manages to escape and hook up with ex-ATF agent Alex (Bucci) to stop the creeps. Lame action, silly dialogue, very attractive Whirry.**CW:** Violence, language and some strong sexuality. **90m/C VHS, Closed Caption.** Shannon Whirry, David Bradley, Larry Manetti, Joe Bucci; **D:** Ric Roman Waugh; **W:** Joe Augustyn, Brent Friedman, David Robinson; **C:** David B. Nowell; **M:** Kevin Kiner. **REP**

Exit in Red ✗½ **1997 (R)** Beverly Hills psychiatrist Ed Altman (Rourke) is hiding out after the suicide of one of his patients lead to professional misconduct charges. But he just can't leave the women alone and gets involved with unhappily married Ally (Schofield). When her husband turns up dead, Ed's charged with murder. It's a frame but just how's he going to prove it.**CW:** Sex, violence, language. **96m/C VHS.** Mickey Rourke, Annabel Schofield, Anthony Michael Hall, Carre Otis; **D:** Yurek Bogayevicz; **W:** David Womack; **C:** Ericson Core; **M:** Michael Lorenc. **PAR**

Exit to Eden ✗½ **1994 (R)** Anne Rampling's (AKA Anne Rice) novel focused on fulfilling S&M sexual fantasies, but director Marshall goes for laughs with a buddy cops-out-of-water sitcom subplot, as undercover cops Aykroyd and O'Donnell track a suspected jewel thief to the fantasy resort of Eden, run by dominatrix Delany. (What was the pitch for this one? Think "Another Stakeout" meets "Tie Me Up, Tie Me Down." It'll be great. Really.) Neither plot works, resulting in a kinky movie with no kink, and a comedy with few laughs. O'Donnell holds up her end, providing what few yuks there are. Everyone else, especially Aykroyd and Delany, seem to be sleepwalking. Lucky for them.**CW:** Nudity and sex-related scenes. 113m/C VHS, **Closed Caption.** Dan Aykroyd, Rosie O'Donnell, Dana Delany, Paul Mercurio, Hector Elizondo, Stuart Wilson, Iman, Sandi Korn; **D:** Garry Marshall; **W:** Deborah Amelon, Bob Brunner; **M:** Patrick Doyle. Golden Raspberry Awards '94: Worst Supporting Actress (O'Donnell). *HBO*

Exodus 🐾🐾🐾 1960 Chronicles the post-WWII partition of Palestine into a homeland for Jews; the anguish of refugees from Nazi concentration camps held on ships in the Mediterranean; the struggle of the tiny nation with forces dividing it from within and destroying it from the outside; and the heroic men and women who saw a job to be done and did it. Based on the novel by Leon Uris; filmed in Cyprus and Israel. Preminger battled the Israeli government, the studio, and the novel's author to complete this epic. Cost more than $4 million, a phenomenal amount at the time. 208m/C VHS, Beta, LV, **Closed Caption.** Paul Newman, Eva Marie Saint, Lee J. Cobb, Sal Mineo, Ralph Richardson, Hugh Griffith, Gregory Ratoff, Felix Aylmer, Peter Lawford, Jill Haworth, John Derek, David Opatoshu, Marius Goring, Alexandra Stewart, Michael Wager, Martin Benson, Paul Stevens, George Maharis; **D:** Otto Preminger; **W:** Dalton Trumbo; **M:** Ernest Gold. Academy Awards '60: Best Original Dramatic/Comedy Score; Golden Globe Awards '61: Best Supporting Actor (Mineo); Nominations: Academy Awards '60: Best Color Cinematography, Best Supporting Actor (Mineo). *FOX, SWC*

Exorcism 🐾½ 1974 A satanic cult in a small English village commits a series of gruesome crimes that have the authorities baffled. 90m/C VHS, Beta. Paul Naschy, Maria Perschy; **D:** Juan Bosch. *HHE*

Exorcism's Daughter 🐾 *House of Insane Women* 1974 (R) While running an insane asylum, a man discovers that a woman has lost her mind because as a child, she witnessed her mother's death during an exorcism. Pretty grim but interesting for genre fans. A natural double feature with "House of Psychotic Women." 93m/C VHS. *SP* Amelia Gade, Francesco Rabal, Espartaco Santoni; **D:** Rafael Morena Alba. *SNC*

The Exorcist 🐾🐾🐾½ 1973 (R) Truly terrifying story of a young girl who is possessed by a malevolent spirit. Brilliantly directed by Friedkin, with underlying themes of the workings and nature of fate. Impeccable casting and unforgettable, thought-provoking performances. A rare film that remains startling and engrossing with every viewing, it spawned countless imitations and changed the way horror films were made. Based on the bestseller by Blatty, who also wrote the screenplay. Not for the squeamish. When first released, the film created mass hysteria in theatres, with people fainting and paramedics on the scene. 120m/C VHS, Beta, LV, DVD. Ellen Burstyn, Linda Blair, Jason Miller, Max von Sydow, Jack MacGowran, Lee J. Cobb, Kitty Winn; **D:** William Friedkin; **W:** William Peter Blatty; **C:** Owen Roizman; **M:** Jack Nitzsche; **V:** Mercedes McCambridge. Academy Awards '73: Best Adapted Screenplay, Best Sound; Golden Globe Awards '74: Best Director (Friedkin), Best Film—Drama, Best Screenplay, Best Supporting Actress (Blair); Nominations: Academy Awards '73: Best Actress (Burstyn), Best Art Direction/Set Decoration, Best Cinematography, Best Director (Friedkin), Best Film Editing, Best Picture, Best Supporting Actor (Miller), Best Supporting Actress (Blair). *WAR*

The Exorcist 2: The Heretic 🐾🐾 1977 (R) Unnecessary sequel to the 1973 hit "The Exorcist" which featured extensive recutting by Boorman. After four years, Blair is still under psychiatric care, suffering from the effects of being possessed by the devil. Meanwhile, a priest investigates the first exorcist's work as he tries to help the high-spinning lass. Decent special effects. 118m/C VHS, Beta. Richard Burton, Linda Blair, Louise Fletcher, Kitty Winn, James Earl Jones, Ned Beatty, Max von Sydow, Paul Henreid; **D:** John Boorman; **W:** William Goodhart; **C:** William A. Fraker; **M:** Ennio Morricone. *NO*

Exorcist 3: Legion 🐾🐾 1990 (R) Apparently subscribing to the two wrongs make a right school of sequels, this time novelist Blatty is the director. The result is slightly better than the first sequel, but still a far cry from the original. Fifteen years later, Detective Kinderman (Scott) is faced with a series of really gross murders bearing the mark of a serial killer who was flambeed in the electric chair on the same night as the exorcism of the pea-soup expectorating devil of the original. With the aid of priests Flanders and Dourif, the detective stalks the transmigratory terror—without the help of Linda Blair, who was at the time spoofing "The Exorcist" in "Repossessed." 105m/C VHS, Beta, LV, **Closed Caption.** George C. Scott, Ed Flanders, Jason Miller, Nicol Williamson, Scott Wilson, Brad Dourif, Nancy Fish, George DiCenzo, Viveca Lindfors, Patrick Ewing, Fabio; **D:** William Peter Blatty; **W:** William Peter Blatty; **C:** Gerry Fisher. *FOX, CCB*

Exotica 🐾🐾🐾 1994 (R) Daunting look at eroticism, secrecy, and despair. Christina (Kirshner) is at the center of some complicated relationships. She dresses as a schoolgirl while working at the Exotica strip club in Toronto, where her former lover Eric (Koteas) is the creepily suggestive DJ. Christina's also the obsession of seemingly mild-mannered tax man Francis (Greenwood), who has turned her table dancing into a strange private ritual. Lest this seem to make sense be assured that director Egoyan has much, much more going on—not all of it clear and most of it disturbing.**CW:** Some sexuality and language. 104m/C VHS, LV, **Closed Caption.** *CA* Mia Kirshner, Elias Koteas, Bruce Greenwood, Don McKellar, Victor Garber, Arsinee Khanjian, Sarah Polley, Calvin Green, David Hemblen; **D:** Atom Egoyan; **W:** Atom Egoyan; **C:** Paul Sarossy; **M:** Mychael Danna. Genie Awards '94: Best Art Direction/Set Decoration, Best Cinematography, Best Costume Design, Best Director (Egoyan), Best Film, Best Original Screenplay, Best Supporting Actor (McKellar), Best Score; Toronto-City Award '94: Best Canadian Feature Film; Nominations: Genie Awards '94: Best Actor (Greenwood), Best Actor (Koteas); Independent Spirit Awards '96: Best Foreign Film. *MAX*

Expect No Mercy 🐾 1995 (R) Government agent must rescue a fellow agent being held in a virtual reality center that trains assassins to commit murder.**CW:** Martial arts violence and shootings. 91m/C VHS. Billy Blanks, Jalal Merhi. *AVE*

The Expendables 🐾½ 1989 (R) A rugged captain turns a platoon of criminals and misfits into a tough fighting unit for a particularly dangerous mission from which they might not return. See the "Dirty Dozen" instead. 89m/C VHS, Beta, LV. Anthony Finetti, Peter Nelson, Loren Haynes, Kevin Duffis; **D:** Cirio H. Santiago; **W:** Phillip Alderton.

Experience Preferred... But Not Essential 🐾🐾½ 1983 (PG) An English schoolgirl gets her first job at a resort where she learns about life. Made for British television. 77m/C VHS, Beta. *GB* Elizabeth Edmonds, Sue Wallace, Geraldine Griffith, Karen Meagher, Ron Bain, Alun Lewis, Robert Blythe; **D:** Peter Duffell; **W:** June Roberts; **C:** Phil Meheux. *MGM*

Experiment in Terror 🐾🐾🐾 1962 A psychopath kidnaps a girl in order to blackmail her sister, a bank teller, into embezzling $100,000. 123m/B VHS, Beta, LV. Lee Remick, Glenn Ford, Stefanie Powers, Ross Martin; **D:** Blake Edwards; **M:** Henry Mancini. *COL, IME*

Experiment Perilous 🐾🐾🐾 1945 A psychologist and a recently widowed woman band together to find her husband's murderer. An atmospheric vintage mystery. 91m/B VHS, Beta. Hedy Lamarr, Paul Lukas, George Brent, Albert Dekker; **D:** Jacques Tourneur. Nominations: Academy Awards '45: Best Interior Decoration.

The Expert 🐾🐾 1995 (R) Special operations expert John Lomax (Speakman) helps catch the creep who murdered his sister. But the killer gets a slap-on-the-wrist sentence, ticking Lomax off mightily. Now, the duo prepare for a deadly last confrontation.**CW:** Brutal violence; some lan-

guage. 92m/C VHS, **Closed Caption.** Jeff Speakman, James Brolin, Michael Shaner, Alex Datcher, Wolfgang Bodison, Elizabeth Gracen, Red West, Jim Varney; **D:** Rick Avery; **W:** Max Allan Collins; **C:** Levie Isaacks; **M:** Ashley Irwin. *ORI*

Expert Weapon 🐾½ 1993 It's a low-budget, male version of "La Femme Nikita" with an imprisoned cop killer recruited as an assassin by a secret government org (are there any other kind in these flicks). He even falls in love and then wants out. Fat chance. 90m/C VHS. Ian Jacklin, Sam Jones, Mel Novak, Judy Landers, Joe Estevez; **D:** Steve Austin. *SCP*

The Experts 🐾🐾 1989 (PG-13) When the KGB needs real Americans for their spies to study, they kidnap two out-of-work New Yorkers who mistakenly believe that they have been hired to open a nightclub in Nebraska. Shot on location in Canada. Sometimes funny and directed by former Second City TV MacKenzie Brother, Dave Thomas. 94m/C VHS, Beta, LV, 8mm, **Closed Caption.** John Travolta, Arye Gross, Charles Martin Smith, Kelly Preston, James Keach, Deborah Foreman, Brian Doyle-Murray; **D:** Dave Thomas; **W:** Nick Thiel, Eric Alter; **M:** Marvin Hamlisch. *PAR*

Explorers 🐾🐾½ 1985 (PG) Intelligent family fare involving three young boys who use a contraption from their makeshift laboratory to travel to outer space. From the director of "Gremlins," displaying Dante's characteristic surreal wit and sense of irony. 107m/C VHS, Beta, LV, **Closed Caption.** Ethan Hawke, River Phoenix, Jason Presson, Amanda Peterson, Mary Kay Place, Dick Miller, Robert Picardo, Dana Ivey, Meshach Taylor, Brooke Bundy; **D:** Joe Dante; **W:** Eric Luke; **M:** Jerry Goldsmith. *PAR*

Explosion 🐾½ 1969 (R) Distraught and disturbed young man evades the draft after losing a brother in Vietnam. Arriving in Canada, he meets another draft-dodger with whom he embarks on a murderous rampage. 96m/C VHS, Beta. Don Stroud, Gordon Thomson, Michele Chicione, Richard Conte; **D:** Jules Bricken. *TWE*

Expose woof! 1997 Congressman's daughter Tiffany gets mistaken for a call girl and propositioned by one of dad's colleagues. When the geezer pays her off to keep quiet, Tiff decides extortion is a viable career option. 78m/C VHS. Tracy Tutor, Kevin E. West, Daneen Boone, Libby George; **D:** B.A. Rudnick. *NHO*

Exposed 🐾🐾 1983 (R) High fashion model Kinski falls in with a terrorist gang through a connection with violinist Nureyev. Weak plotting undermines the end of this political thriller. However, Kinski is brilliant, stripping the barrier between performance and audience. 100m/C VHS, Beta. Nastassia Kinski, Rudolf Nureyev, Harvey Keitel, Ian McShane, Bibi Andersson; **D:** James Toback; **W:** James Toback; **C:** Henri Decae; **M:** Georges Delerue. *MGM*

Exposure 🐾 1991 (R) A rugged American photographer (Coyote) on assignment in Rio turns vigilante to locate the vicious killer of a young prostitute. Coyote and his girlfriend (Pays) get caught up in the deadly underworld of international arms trading and drug running as they search for the murderer.**CW:** Language, strong graphic violence, and sensuality. 99m/C VHS, **Closed Caption.** Peter Coyote, Amanda Pays, Tcheky Karyo; **M:** Todd Boekelheide. *HBO*

Express to Terror 🐾½ 1979 Passengers aboard an atomic-powered train en route to Los Angeles attempt to kill a sleazy theatrical agent. Pilot for the "Supertrain" series. 120m/C VHS, Beta. Steve Lawrence, George Hamilton, Vic Morrow, Broderick Crawford, Robert Alda, Don Stroud, Fred Williamson, Stella Stevens, Don Meredith; **D:** Dan Curtis.

Expresso Bongo 🐾🐾½ 1959 Soho singer/bongo player (Richards) is "discovered" by seedy talent agent Johnny Jackson (Harvey) who manages the young man into a teen idol with a 50-50 contract. But women come between the duo and Johnny finds himself without a star. 111m/

B VHS, Letterbox. *GB* Laurence Harvey, Sylvia Syms, Yolande Donlan, Cliff Richard; *D:* Val Guest. *KIV*

Exquisite Corpses 🎬½ 1988 An Oklahoma hayseed charges to New York with a new, slick image. He meets the wife of a wealthy man, and together they organize a murderous operation. 95m/C VHS, LV. Zoe Tamerlaine Lund, Gary Knox, Daniel Chapman, Ruth Collins; *D:* Temistocles Lopez. *NO*

The Exterminating Angel 🎬🎬🎬½ 1962 A fierce, funny surreal nightmare, wherein dinner guests find they cannot, for any definable reason, leave the dining room; full of dream imagery and characteristically scatological satire. One of Bunuel's best, in Spanish with English subtitles. 95m/B&W SP Film. MX Silvia Pinal, Enrique Rambal, Jacqueline Andere, Jose Baviera, Augusto Benedico, Luis Beristain; *D:* Luis Bunuel. *HTV, FCT*

Exterminator 🎬 1980 (R) Vietnam veteran hunts down the gang that assaulted his friend and becomes the target of the police, the CIA and the underworld in this bloody banal tale of murder and intrigue. Followed by creatively titled "Exterminator II." 101m/C VHS, Beta, LV. Christopher George, Samantha Eggar, Robert Ginty; *D:* James Glickenhaus. *NLC*

Exterminator 2 🎬 1984 (R) The Exterminator battles the denizens of New York's underworld after his girlfriend is crippled, then murdered by the ruthless Mr. X. Violence galore. 88m/C VHS, Beta. Robert Ginty, Mario Van Peebles, Deborah Geffner, Frankie Faison; *D:* Mark Buntzman; *W:* Mark Buntzman. *MGM*

Exterminators in the Year 3000 woof! 1983 (R) The Exterminator and his mercenary girlfriend battle with nuclear mutants over the last remaining tanks of purified water on Earth. Low-budget Road Warrior rip-off. 91m/C VHS. IT SP Robert Jannucci, Alicia Moro, Alan Collins, Fred Harris; *D:* Jules Harrison. *NLC*

Extra Girl 🎬🎬 1923 A silent melodrama/farce about a farm girl, brilliantly played by Normand, who travels to Hollywood to be a star. Once in the glamour capital, she gets used and abused for her trouble. 87m/B&W VHS, Beta, LV, 8mm. Mabel Normand, Ralph Graves, Vernon Dent; *D:* F. Richard Jones; *W:* Mack Sennett. *VYY, GPV*

Extramuros 🎬🎬 1985 A nun (Maura), living in a convent during the Spanish Inquisition, tries to repress her lesbian desires while the convent vies for fame and money through faked visions. Spanish with subtitles. 120m/C VHS. SP Carmen Maura; *D:* Miguel Picazo. *FCT*

The Extraordinary Adventures of Mr. West in the Land of the Bolsheviks 🎬🎬 1924 The first achievement from the Kuleshov workshop, a wacky satire on American insularity depicting a naive and prejudiced American visiting Russia and being taken advantage of. Silent. 55m/B&W VHS, Beta. Vsevolod Pudovkin, Boris Barnet; *D:* Lev Kuleshov. *FCT*

Extreme Justice 🎬🎬½ 1993 (R) A violent expose of the Special Investigations Section of the Los Angeles Police Department, an elite, undercover squad which specialized in catching violent repeat offenders. But their tactics left something to be desired. They were accused of stalking their prey until they committed a crime and then dealing with the criminal by shooting them in the act. Lots of gunplay. Originally a theatrical film that was pulled for release in the wake of the Rodney King verdict. 96m/C VHS, LV, Closed Caption. Lou Diamond Phillips, Scott Glenn, Yaphet Kotto, Ed Lauter, Chelsea Field; *W:* Robert Boris. *THV*

Extreme Measures 🎬🎬½ 1996 (R) Dr. Grant, Action Guy! Cast against type, Grant takes on action-suspense in this urbane medical thriller, and it works. Plot is pretty standard for the genre—doctor Luthan (Grant) suspects foul play when homeless people are turning up with mysterious symptoms before expiring in his ward. Seeking to expose what he believes is a medical conspiracy, his "darn meddling" gets him in all kinds of trouble. Enter Dr. Lawrence Myrick (Hackman), a genius neurologist who reeks of suspicion. Luthan must get by him to uncover the dangerous human experimentation that's been going on. Producer and real-life love Hurley may have had something to do with the fact that Grant pulls off a mostly convincing turn, where his normally comic persona is used to humanize an otherwise cardboard hero. Adapted from a book by Michael Palmer. *CW:* Violence, language, some nudity and graphic ER activity. 118m/C VHS, LV, Closed Caption. Hugh Grant, Gene Hackman, Sarah Jessica Parker, David Cronenberg, Bill Nunn, Debra Monk, John Toles-Bey, Paul Guilfoyle, Andre De Shields, Shaun Austin-Olsen, Peter Appel; *D:* Michael Apted; *W:* Tony Gilroy; *C:* John Bailey; *M:* Danny Elfman. *COL*

Extreme Prejudice 🎬🎬 1987 (R) A redneck Texas Ranger fights a powerful drug kingpin along the U.S.-Mexican border. Once best friends, they now fight for justice and the heart of the woman they both love. 104m/C VHS, Beta, LV. Nick Nolte, Powers Boothe, Maria Conchita Alonso, Michael Ironside, Rip Torn; *D:* Walter Hill; *W:* Deric Washburn; *M:* Jerry Goldsmith. *ART*

Extreme Vengeance 🎬🎬 1993 Police officer David puts mafia crime boss Mario Blanco away for ten years, then exposes police corruption and goes into hiding. When Blanco gets out, he seeks revenge on David's family, forcing David out of hiding to protect what is his. Available in Spanish subtitles. 97m/C VHS, LV. *NHO*

Extremities 🎬🎬 1986 (R) An adaptation of the topical William Mastrosimone play about an intended rape victim who turns on her attacker, captures him, and plots to kill him. Violent and exploitive. 83m/C VHS, Beta, LV, 8mm, Closed Caption. Farrah Fawcett, Diana Scarwid, James Russo, Alfre Woodard; *D:* Robert M. Young; *W:* William Mastrosimone. *PAR*

The Eye Creatures 🎬 1965 Alien creatures in the form of eyeballs are fought off by a teenager and his girlfriend. A low-budget, gory, science fiction feature. 80m/B&W VHS. John Ashley, Cynthia Hull, Warren Hammack, Chet Davis, Bill Peck; *D:* Larry Buchanan. *NOS, SNC*

An Eye for an Eye 🎬🎬 1981 (R) A story of pursuit and revenge with Norris as an undercover cop pitted against San Francisco's underworld and high society. 106m/C VHS, Beta. Chuck Norris, Christopher Lee, Richard Roundtree, Matt Clark, Mako, Maggie Cooper; *D:* Steve Carver; *W:* James Bruner; *M:* William Goldstein. *NLC*

An Eye for an Eye 🎬 1995 (R) A made-for-TV script that ended up on the feature film pile (and we do mean pile). Manipulative story has Karen McCann (Field) listening on the phone as her daughter is raped and killed by a scuzzball drifter (Sutherland). He's caught, but released on a technicality, driving Mom to join a vigilante group and plot revenge. Not a great career move for the director or surprisingly distinguished cast, who are given nothing but cardboard characters and push-button emotional cliches to work with. Shamelessly plays on middle class fears of crime and doubts about the judicial system. Based on the novel by Erika Holzer. *CW:* Language and disturbing violence, which includes rape. 102m/C VHS, Beta, Closed Caption. Sally Field, Ed Harris, Kiefer Sutherland, Beverly D'Angelo, Joe Mantegna, Keith David; *D:* John Schlesinger; *W:* Amanda Silver, Rick Jaffa; *C:* Amir M. Mokri; *M:* James Newton Howard. *PAR*

Eye of God 🎬🎬🎬 1997 (R) Darkly dramatic story of lonely small-town waitress Ainsley (Plimpton), who marries newly released, born-again ex-con Jack (Anderson) with whom she has been corresponding. Movie kicks off when veteran sherrif (Holbrook) questions a shaken up youth, Tommy (Stahl), who is mysteriously covered in blood but rendered mute by the experience. It soon becomes apparent in the deluge of frequent flashbacks and fast forwards that no good will come of this unlikely union, although the mere fate of the hapless Ainsley is not the point. First time director Nelson's spare narrative seeks to explore deeper issues like faith and violence in the Bible Belt locale. Performances are universally powerful, especially Plimpton's lovable dim-bulb and Anderson's maniacal Jack, giving credence to the clever but sometimes overly-flashy cinematic style. *CW:* Violence, language and depiction of abortion. 88m/C VHS. Martha Plimpton, Kevin Anderson, Hal Holbrook, Nick Stahl, Richard Jenkins, Margo Martindale, Maggie Moore, Mary Kay Place; *D:* Tim Blake Nelson; *W:* Tim Blake Nelson; *C:* Russell Fine; *M:* David Van Tiegham. *PEG*

Eye of the Demon 🎬 1987 A couple moves to a small town in Massachusetts and discovers that the area had once been a haven for witchcraft. To their horror, they soon find that old habits die hard, and the spellcasting continues in a nearby graveyard. Made for cable television. 92m/C VHS. Tim Matheson, Pamela Sue Martin, Woody Harrelson, Barbara Billingsley, Susan Ruttan; *D:* Carl Schenkel. *THV*

Eye of the Eagle 🎬½ 1987 (R) A special task force is given a dangerous assignment during the Vietnam war. 84m/C VHS, Beta. Brett Clark, Ed Crick, Robert Patrick, William Steis, Cec Verrell; *D:* Cirio H. Santiago. *MGM*

Eye of the Eagle 2 🎬 1989 (R) When his platoon is betrayed and killed in Vietnam, a surviving soldier joins with a beautiful girl and seeks revenge. 79m/C VHS, Beta. Todd Field, Andy Wood, Ken Jacobson, Ronald Lawrence; *D:* Carl Franklin. *MGM*

Eye of the Eagle 3 🎬½ 1991 (R) Filipino-made Vietnam-War shoot-em-up, rack-em-up, shoot-em-up again, with U.S. forces pinned down against seemingly overwhelming odds. Violent. 90m/C VHS. Steve Kanaly, Ken Wright, Peter Nelson, Carl Franklin; *D:* Cirio H. Santiago; *W:* Carl Franklin. *NHO*

Eye of the Needle 🎬🎬½ 1981 (R) Based on Ken Follett's novel about a German spy posing as a shipwrecked sailor on a deserted English island during WWII. Lonely, sad, yet capable of terrible violence, he is stranded on an isolated island while en route to report to his Nazi commander. He becomes involved with an English woman living on the island, and begins to contemplate his role in the war. 112m/C VHS, Beta. Donald Sutherland, Kate Nelligan, Ian Bannen, Christopher Cazenove, Philip Brown, Stephen MacKenna, Faith Brook, Colin Rix, Alex McCrindle, John Bennett, Sam Kydd, Rik Mayall, Bill Fraser; *D:* Richard Marquand; *W:* Stanley Mann; *M:* Miklos Rozsa. *MGM, FOX*

Eye of the Storm 🎬🎬½ 1991 (R) At the highway gas station/motel/diner where they live, two young brothers witness their parent's murder. Their younger brother is blinded in the same incident. Ten years later both brothers are still there and the tragedy may have turned one of them psychotic. When the abusive Gladstone and his young and sexy wife are stranded at the gas station it brings out the worst in everyone, with a violent climax during an equally violent thunderstorm. *CW:* Language and strong violence. 98m/C VHS. Craig Sheffer, Bradley Gregg, Lara Flynn Boyle, Dennis Hopper, Leon Rippy; *D:* Yuri Zeltser. *NLC*

Eye of the Stranger 🎬½ 1993 (R) Suspenser about a nameless stranger who sets out to solve the mystery of a small western town and its corrupt mayor. *CW:* Brutal violence and scene of strong sexuality. 96m/C VHS. David Heavener, Sally Kirkland, Martin Landau, Don Swayze, Stella Stevens, John Pleshette, Joe Estevez, Thomas F. Duffy; *D:* David Heavener; *W:* David Heavener; *M:* Robert Garrett. *MNC*

Eye of the Tiger 🎬🎬 1986 (R) A righteous ex-con battles a crazed, crack-dealing motorcycle gang that terrorized and murdered his wife, and is moving on to infest his town. 90m/C VHS, Beta. Gary Busey, Yaphet Kotto, Seymour Cassel, Bert Remsen, William Smith; *D:* Richard Sarafian; *C:* Peter Collister. *ART*

Eye of the Wolf ✒✒½ 1995 (PG-13) Zoologist (Fahey) brings a wild wolf into civilization and then must fight to save the animal from execution. Kazan (a wolf-dog mix) is the true star—and rightly so.**CW:** Elements of violence. **96m/C VHS.** Jeff Fahey, Sophie Duez. THV

Eye on the Sparrow ✒✒½ 1991 (PG) A couple (Winningham and Carradine) desperately want to raise a child of their own, but the system classifies them as unfit parents since they are both blind. Together they successfully fight the system in this inspiring made for television movie that was based on a true story. **94m/C VHS, Closed Caption.** Mare Winningham, Keith Carradine, Conchata Ferrell, Sandy McPeak, Karen Lee, Bianca Rose; **D:** John Korty. REP

Eye Witness ✒✒½ Your Witness 1949 An American attorney goes abroad to free a friend from the British legal system. A book of poems becomes the necessary device in deducing the whereabouts of the witness crucial to his friend's alibi. **104m/B VHS.** GB Robert Montgomery, Felix Aylmer, Leslie Banks, Michael Ripper, Patricia Wayne; **D:** Robert Montgomery; **W:** Malcolm Arnold. NOS, SNC, RXM

Eyeball woof! Gatto Rossi In Un Labirinto Do Vetro 1978 (R) An intrepid policeman is stumped by a madman who is removing eyeballs from his victims. At least they won't have to watch this movie. **87m/C VHS, Beta.** IT John Richardson, Martine Brochard; **D:** Umberto Lenzi.

Eyes Behind the Stars ✒ 1972 A news photographer accidentally gets a few pictures of invading aliens, but nobody takes him seriously, particularly the government. **95m/C VHS, Beta.** IT Martin Balsam, Robert Hoffman, Nathalie Delon, Sherry Buchanan; **D:** Roy Garrett. NO

Eyes of a Stranger woof! 1981 (R) Terrifying maniac stalks his female prey by watching their every move. Tewes is cast as a journalist, the stronger of the two sisters in this exploitative slasher. **85m/C VHS, Beta.** Lauren Tewes, John Disanti, Jennifer Jason Leigh; **D:** Ken Wiederhorn; **W:** Eric L. Bloom; **M:** Richard Einhorn. WAR

Eyes of a Witness ✒✒½ 1994 American businessman Roy Baxter (Travanti) travels to Kenya to rescue his daughter (Grey) from danger in the African bush. But Roy is falsely charged with murdering a government official and must take on the police to prove his innocence. **90m/C VHS, LV.** Daniel J. Travanti, Jennifer Grey, Carl Lumbly. NLC, IME

Eyes of an Angel ✒✒½ 1991 (PG-13) A widower (Travolta), who's heavily involved in gambling, is forced to go on the run with his young daughter (Raab) when a deal goes sour. She must abandon the family dog, who manages to follow them from Chicago to California anyway. Talk about loyalty!**CW:** Mature themes. **91m/C VHS, LV, Closed Caption.** John Travolta, Elie Raab, Jeffrey DeMunn; **D:** Robert Harmon. ART

Eyes of Fire ✒ 1984 (R) In early rural America, a group of pioneers set up camp in the wilderness and are besieged during the night by Indian witchcraft. **86m/C VHS, Beta, LV.** Dennis Lipscomb, Rebecca Stanley, Fran Ryan, Rob Paulsen, Guy Boyd, Karlene Crockett; **D:** Avery Crounse; **W:** Avery Crounse; **M:** Brad Fiedel. VES

Eyes of Julia Deep ✒✒ 1918 Rare silent film featuring the ill-fated Minter as Julia, a woman who prevents Terry (Forrest) from killing himself. Piano scored. **54m/B VHS, Closed Caption.** Mary Miles Minter, Alan Forrest, Alice Wilson, George Periolat; **D:** Lloyd Ingraham. GPV

Eyes of Laura Mars ✒✒½ 1978 (R) A photographer exhibits strange powers—she can foresee a murder before it happens through her snapshots. In time she realizes that the person responsible for a series of killings is tracking her. Title song performed by Barbra Streisand. **104m/C VHS, Beta, LV, Closed Caption.** Faye Dunaway, Tommy Lee Jones, Brad Dourif, Rene Auberjonois, Raul Julia, Dar-

ianne Fluegel, Michael Tucker; **D:** Irvin Kershner; **W:** John Carpenter, David Zelag Goodman. NO

Eyes of Texas ✒½ 1948 Bryant, a lawyer who uses a pack of killer dogs to get the land she wants, is pursued by a U.S Marshal played decently by Rogers. **54m/B VHS, Beta.** Roy Rogers, Lynn (Mary Hart) Roberts, Andy Devine, Nana Bryant, Roy Barcroft; **D:** William Witney. NOS, VCN, TIM

The Eyes of the Amaryllis ✒½ 1982 (R) A young girl becomes involved in a mysterious game when she arrives in Nantucket to care for her insane, invalid grandmother. Based on the story by Natalie Babbitt and filmed on location on Nantucket Island. **94m/C VHS, Beta.** Martha Byrne, Ruth Ford, Guy Boyd, Jonathan Bolt, Katharine Houghton; **D:** Frederick King Keller. ART, VES

Eyes of the Beholder ✒✒ 1992 (R) Janice is a psychopathic serial killer who suffered brain damage from a botched surgical attempt to reverse his insanity. Now he's escaped from the state mental institution, heading straight for the secluded home of the doctor who made him crazier than ever. During a raging storm, Janice stalks the doctor, his wife, and their two hapless dinner guests in a sadistic game of cat-and-mouse.**CW:** Violence and sexuality. **89m/C VHS, LV, Closed Caption.** Lenny Von Dohlen, Joanna Pacula, Matt McCoy, George Lazenby, Kylie Travis, Charles Napier; **D:** Lawrence L. Simeone; **W:** Lawrence L. Simeone; **M:** Greg Turner. COL

Eyes of the Panther 1990 One of Shelley Duvall's "Nightmare Classics" series, this adaptation of an Ambrose Bierce story concerns a pioneer girl haunted for years by the animal urges of a wild cat. **60m/C VHS, Beta, LV.** Daphne Zuniga, C. Thomas Howell, John Stockwell; **D:** Noel Black. NO

Eyes of Turpin Are Upon You! ✒✒ 1921 Two early Turpin silent comedies: "Idle Eyes" and "A Small Town Idol." **56m/B VHS, Beta.** Ben Turpin, Ramon Novarro, Marie Prevost, James Finlayson. VYY

The Eyes of Youth ✒✒ 1919 A young woman searches her soul for answers: to marry or not to marry is the question. A little foresight, in the form of a glimpse into the hypothetical future, helps her make the right choice. Very early Valentino fare in which the sheik plays a cad. **78m/B VHS, Beta.** Clara Kimball Young, Edmund Lowe, Rudolph Valentino. VYY, FCT, VYY

Eyes Right! ✒✒ 1926 Based on a story by Ernest Grayman, this portrayal of life in a military prep school has its main character experience struggle, recognition, love, jealousy, and triumph. Silent. **46m/B VHS, Beta.** Francis X. Bushman. VYY, GPV

The Eyes, the Mouth ✒✒ 1983 (R) A young man has an affair with his dead twin brother's fiancee. Happiness eludes them as they are haunted by the deceased's memory and the family's grief. In Italian with English subtitles. **100m/C VHS, Beta.** FR Lou Castel, Angela Molina; **D:** Marco Bellocchio; **W:** Marco Bellocchio. COL

Eyewitness ✒✒½ The Janitor 1981 (R) When a murder occurs in the office building of a starstruck janitor, he fabricates a tale in order to initiate a relationship with the television reporter covering the story. Unfortunately the killers think he's telling the truth, which plunges the janitor and reporter into a dangerous and complicated position, pursued by both police and foreign agents. Somewhat contrived, but Hurt and Weaver are always interesting. Woods turns in a wonderful performance as Hurt's somewhat-psychotic best friend. **102m/C VHS, Beta, LV.** William Hurt, Sigourney Weaver, Christopher Plummer, James Woods, Kenneth McMillan, Pamela Reed, Irene Worth, Steven Hill, Morgan Freeman; **D:** Peter Yates; **W:** Steve Tesich. FOX

Eyewitness to Murder ✒½ 1993 Stevens plays a cop who is assigned to protect beautiful artist Wolter. They both have their tragic flaws: he is a grieving widower and she is being blinded by an unknown attacker. Their flaws may draw them together. Somewhat more engaging

than a television police action drama. **75m/C VHS.** Andrew Stevens, Adrian Zmed, Sherilyn Wolter, Carl Strano, Robin Drue; **D:** Jag Mundhra. NHO

F. Scott Fitzgerald in Hollywood ✒✒ 1976 Dramatization begins in the late 1930s when Fitzgerald was lured to Hollywood to work in the burgeoning film industry. It covers the period when, with his wife in a mental institution, he lived with Sheila Graham and struggled against alcoholism. Interesting story made dull and depressing by Miller's uninspired performance, but it's almost saved by Weld's portrayal of Zelda. Made for television. **98m/C VHS, Beta.** Jason Miller, Tuesday Weld, Julia Foster, Dolores Sutton, Michael Lerner, James Woods; **D:** Anthony Page. NO

F/X ✒✒✒ 1986 (R) A Hollywood special effects expert is contracted by the government to fake an assassination to protect a mob informer. After completing the assignment, he learns that he's become involved in a real crime and is forced to reach into his bag of F/X tricks to survive. Twists and turns abound in this fast-paced story that was the sleeper hit of the year. Followed by a sequel. **109m/C VHS, Beta, LV, Closed Caption.** Bryan Brown, Cliff DeYoung, Diane Venora, Brian Dennehy, Jerry Orbach, Mason Adams, Joe Grifasi, Martha Gehman, Angela Bassett; **D:** Robert Mandel; **W:** Robert T. Megginson, Gregory Fleeman; **M:** Bill Conti. FCT

F/X 2: The Deadly Art of Illusion ✒✒ 1991 (PG-13) Weak follow-up finds the special-effects specialist set to pull off just one more illusion for the police. Once again, corrupt cops use him as a chump for their scheme, an over-complicated business involving a stolen Vatican treasure. **107m/C VHS, LV, Closed Caption.** Bryan Brown, Brian Dennehy, Rachel Ticotin, Philip Bosco, Joanna Gleason; **D:** Richard Franklin; **W:** Bill Condon; **M:** Michael Boddicker, Lalo Schifrin. ORI, IME

Fabiola ✒✒✒ 1948 The first of the big Italian spectacle movies, this one opened the door for a flood of low-budget imitators. Fabiola, the daughter of a Roman senator, becomes a Christian when her father's Christian servants are accused of murdering him. In the meantime, the Emperor Constantine speeds toward Rome to convert it to Christian status. You can bet plenty of Christians will lose their heads, be thrown to the lions and generally burn at the stake before he does. **96m/C VHS.** IT Michel Simon, Henri Vidal, Gino Cervi; **D:** Alessandro Blasetti. SNC, FCT

The Fable of the Beautiful Pigeon Fancier ✒✒½ Fabula de la Bella Palomera 1988 A powerful man who has always gotten what he wanted spies a beautiful young married woman and sets out to make her his own. Based on the Gabriel Gracia Marquez novel "Love in the Time of Cholera." In Spanish with English subtitles. **73m/C VHS, LV.** SP Ney Latorraca, Claudia Ohana, Tonia Carrero, Dina Stat, Chico Diaz; **D:** Ruy Guerra. FXL, FCT

Fabulous Adventures of Baron Munchausen ✒✒ 1961 The legendary Baron Munchausen, known for his tall tales, relates the story of his trek to the strange and beautiful land of Trukesban in a mixture of live action and animation. Wonderful special effects but a boring storyline. In German with English subtitles. **84m/C VHS, Beta.** GE Milos Kopecky, Jana Brejchova, Rudolph Jelinek, Jan Werich; **D:** Karel Zeman. ART, VES, TPV

The Fabulous Baker Boys ✒✒✒ 1989 (R) Two brothers have been performing a tired act as nightclub pianists for 15 years. When they hire a sultry vocalist to revitalize the routine, she inadvertently triggers long-suppressed hostility between the "boys." The story may be a bit uneven, but fine performances by the three leading actors, the steamy 1940s atmosphere, and Pfeiffer's classic rendition of "Makin' Whoopee," are worth the price of the rental. **116m/C VHS, Beta, LV, 8mm.** Michelle Pfeiffer, Jeff Bridges, Beau Bridges, Elie Raab, Jennifer Tilly; **D:** Steven Kloves; **W:** Steven Kloves; **C:** Michael Ballhaus; **M:** Dave Grusin. Golden Globe

Awards '90: Best Actress—Drama (Pfeiffer); Los Angeles Film Critics Association Awards '89: Best Actress (Pfeiffer), Best Cinematography; National Board of Review Awards '89: Best Actress (Pfeiffer); New York Film Critics Awards '89: Best Actress (Pfeiffer); National Society of Film Critics Awards '89: Best Actress (Pfeiffer), Best Cinematography, Best Supporting Actor (Bridges); Nominations: Academy Awards '89: Best Actress (Pfeiffer), Best Cinematography, Best Film Editing, Best Original Score. *ART, FCT*

The Fabulous Dorseys 🐾🐾 1947
The musical lives of big band leaders Tommy and Jimmy Dorsey are portrayed in this less than fabulous biography that's strong on song but weak on plot. Guest stars include Art Tatum, Charlie Barnet, Ziggy Elman, Bob Eberly and Helen O'Connell. Highlights are the tunes. 🎵At Sundown; I'll Never Say Never Again; To Me; Green Eyes; Dorsey Concerto; Art's Blues; Everybody's Doin' It; The Object of My Affection; Runnin' Wild. **91m/B VHS, LV.** Tommy Dorsey, Jimmy Dorsey, Janet Blair, Paul Whiteman, Sara Allgood, Arthur Shields; **D:** Alfred E. Green. *NOS, MRV, HHT*

Fabulous Joe 🐾🐾 1947
A talking dog named Joe gets involved in the life of a henpecked husband. **54m/C VHS, Beta.** Walter Abel, Donald Meek, Margot Grahame, Marie Wilson; **D:** Harve Foster. *NOS*

The Face at the Window 🐾🐾 1939
Melodramatic crime story of a pair of ne'er-do-well brothers who terrorize Paris to conceal their bank robberies. **65m/B VHS.** Tod Slaughter, Marjorie Taylor, John Warwick, Robert Adair, Harry Terry; **D:** George King. *NOS, MRV, HEG*

Face Down 🐾🐾 1997 (R)
You've got your standard wisecracking New York ex-cop-turned-PI Bob Signorelli (Mantegna), who has a one-nighter with your blonde bombshell type client Merre (Maroney), who has ties to a mystery man (Ant). There's a murder, there's Bob's ex-partner Lt. Cooper (Riegert), who's no friend, investigating the murder, and there's Bob trying to find the killer first. And you've certainly seen it all before. *CW:* Strong sexuality, violence and language. **107m/C VHS, Closed Caption.** Joe Mantegna, Peter Riegert, Kelli Maroney, Adam Ant; **D:** Thom Eberhardt. *PAR*

A Face in the Crowd 🐾🐾🐾½ 1957
Journalist (Neal) discovers a down-home philosopher (Griffith) and puts him on her television show. His aw-shucks personality soon wins him a large following and increasing influence—even political clout. Off the air he reveals his true nature to be insulting, vengeful, and power-hungry—all of which Neal decides to expose. Marks Griffith's spectacular film debut as a thoroughly despicable character and debut of Remick as the pretty cheerleader in whom he takes an interest. Schulburg wrote the screenplay from his short story "The Arkansas Traveler." And he and director Kazan collaborated equally well in "On the Waterfront." **126m/B VHS, Beta.** Andy Griffith, Patricia Neal, Lee Remick, Walter Matthau, Anthony (Tony) Franciosa; **D:** Elia Kazan; **W:** Budd Schulberg; **M:** Harry Stradling. *WAR, FCT*

A Face in the Fog 🐾🐾 1936
Two newspaper reporters set out to solve a number of murders that have plagued the cast of a play. Also interested is the playwright. Good low-budget thriller. **66m/B VHS, Beta.** June Collyer, Lloyd Hughes, Lawrence Gray, Al "Fuzzy" St. John, Jack Mulhall, Jack Cowell, John Elliott, Sam Flint, Forrest Taylor, Edward Cassidy; **D:** Robert F. "Bob" Hill. *NOS, SNC*

Face of Another 🐾🐾 1966
A severely burned man gets a second chance when a plastic surgeon makes a mask to hide the disfigurement. Unfortunately this face leads to him alienation, rape, infidelity, and murder. In Japanese with English subtitles. **124m/B VHS, Beta.** JP Tatsuya Nakadai, Machiko Kyo; **D:** Hiroshi Teshigahara. *NO*

Face of the Screaming Werewolf 🐾½
La Casa Del Terror; House of Terror 1959 Originally a Mexican horror/comedy that was bought for U.S. distribution by Jerry Warren,

who earned his spot in the horror hall of fame with "The Incredible Petrified World" and "Teenage Zombies." A scientist brings a mummy back to life, but when he removes the bandages (gasp), the subject turns out to be of the canine persuasion. Suffers from comic evisceration; not much to scream about. **60m/B VHS.** MX Lon Chaney Jr., Landa Varle, Raymond Gaylord; **D:** Gilberto Martinez Solares, Jerry Warren. *SNC, MRV*

Face/Off 🐾🐾🐾½ 1997 (R)
Woo returns to his blood-soaked, violence-as-poetry-in-motion roots with the story of a fed who assumes the identity of the presumed-dead terrorist who killed his son. When the master criminal wakes up, he "steals" the cop's identity. Travolta's back for another wild ride, eating up the scenery when he takes on the bad-guy role. Cage, fresh from action hits in "The Rock" and "Con Air" gets to study the nature of good and evil (another Woo specialty) while he learns the nuances of the "leap across the room with two pistols blazing" move. Woo's Hong Kong efforts have always explored the blurry line between the good guys and the bad guys, and with Cage and Travolta, he has the perfect actors to display his findings. Woo cultists will welcome the return to the old style, while those only familiar with his stateside work will understand what all the fuss was about. *CW:* Intense sequences of strong violence, and for strong language. **140m/C VHS, Beta, Closed Caption.** John Travolta, Nicolas Cage, Joan Allen, Alessandro Nivola, Gina Gershon, Nick Cassavetes, Dominique Swain, Harve Presnell, Margaret Cho, CCH Pounder, Colm Feore, John Carroll Lynch, Matt Ross, John Joe Bob Briggs Bloom; **D:** John Woo; **W:** Mike Werb, Michael Colleary; **C:** Oliver Wood; **M:** John Powell. MTV Movie Awards '98: Best On-Screen Duo (John Travolta/Nicolas Cage), Best Action Sequence; Nominations: Academy Awards '97: Best Sound Effects Editing; MTV Movie Awards '98: Best Film, Best Male Performance (Cage, Travolta), Best Villain (John Travolta/Nicolas Cage). *PAR*

Face the Evil 🐾½ 1997 (R)
TV star Tweed gets taken hostage in an art gallery by a gang of thieves. But that's not the real problem—seems their leader, Henriksen, wants to retrieve a shipment of nerve gas that's been hidden in some art work. *CW:* Language, violence. **92m/C VHS.** Shannon Tweed, Lance Henriksen, Bruce Payne, Jayne Heitmeyer; **D:** Paul Lynch. *APX*

Face the Music 🐾½ 1992 (PG-13)
Ringwald and Dempsey were once stormily married and pursuing successful, collaborative careers as singer/songwriters for the movies. But they've abandoned the work, along with the marriage, until a movie producer makes them a very lucrative offer for a new song. Only Dempsey's new girlfriend has some voracious objections. *CW:* Drug-related content and sensuality. **93m/C VHS.** Patrick Dempsey, Molly Ringwald, Lysette Anthony. *ART*

Face to Face 🐾🐾½ 1952
Dramatic adaptation of two short stories, "The Secret Sharer," by Joseph Conrad, and Stephen Crane's "The Bride Comes to Yellow Sky." The Conrad story features Mason as a sea captain who discovers a fugitive stowaway aboard his ships. The Crane story features Preston as a sheriff threatened by an old-time gunfighter. **92m/B VHS.** Bretaigne Windust, James Mason, Michael Pate, Robert Preston, Marjorie Steele, Gene Lockhart, Minor Watson; **D:** John Brahm. *NO*

Face to Face 🐾🐾🐾 Ansikte mot Ansikte 1976
Bergman's harrowing tale of a mental breakdown. Ullmann has a bravura role as a psychiatrist deciding to vacation at her grandparent's house in the country. Once there she begins to experience depression and hallucinations tied to her past with both her mother and grandmother. Her deeply repressed feelings eventually lead to a suicide attempt, which brings some much needed help. Originally a four-hour series made for Swedish television. In Swedish with English subtitles. **136m/C VHS.** SW Liv Ullmann, Erland Josephson, Gunnar Bjornstrand, Aino Taube-Henrikson, Sven Lindberg, Kary Sylway, Sif Ruud; **D:** Ingmar Bergman; **W:** Ingmar Berg-

man, **C:** Sven Nykvist. Golden Globe Awards '77: Best Foreign Film; Los Angeles Film Critics Association Awards '76: Best Actress (Ullmann), Best Foreign Film; National Board of Review Awards '76: Best Actress (Ullmann); New York Film Critics Awards '76: Best Actress (Ullmann); Nominations: Academy Awards '76: Best Actress (Ullmann), Best Director (Bergman). *PAR*

Faces 🐾🐾🐾½ 1968 (R)
Cassavetes' first independent film to find mainstream success portrays the breakup of the 14-year marriage of middle-aged Richard (Marley) and Maria (Carlin) Forst. Both seek at least momentary comfort with others—Richard with prostitute Jeannie (Rowlands) and Maria with aging hippie Chet (Cassel). The director's usual improvisational and documentary style can either be viewed as compelling or tedious but the performances are first-rate. *CW:* Adult themes. **129m/B VHS.** John Marley, Lynn Carlin, Gena Rowlands, Seymour Cassel, Val Avery, Dorothy Gulliver, Joanne Moore Jordan, Fred Draper, Darlene Conley; **D:** John Cassavetes; **W:** John Cassavetes; **C:** Al Ruban; **M:** Jack Ackerman. National Society of Film Critics Awards '68: Best Screenplay, Best Supporting Actor (Cassel); Nominations: Academy Awards '68: Best Story & Screenplay, Best Supporting Actor (Cassel), Best Supporting Actress (Carlin). *FXL*

Faces of Women 🐾🐾 1985
Two stories about women in contemporary Africa. In the first, an unhappy young woman is married to a very jealous man. When her brother-in-law visits, she decides to give her husband something to worry about. The second story finds a businesswoman running into problems when she tries to open a restaurant—problems that her daughter helps to solve. French and indigenous languages with English subtitles. **103m/C VHS.** Eugenie Cisse Roland, Sidiki Bakaba, Albertine N'Guessan; **D:** Desire Ecare. *NYF*

The Facts of Life 🐾🐾½ 1960 (PG-13)
Risque bedroom comedy finds Larry Gilbert (Hope) and Kitty Weaver (Ball) running off from boredom in suburbia and their respective spouses (Hussey and DeFore) to have a little interlude together. **103m/B VHS, Closed Caption.** Bob Hope, Lucille Ball, Ruth Hussey, Don DeFore, Louis Nye, Philip Ober; **D:** Melvin Frank; **W:** Melvin Frank, Norman Panama; **C:** Charles Lang Jr.; **M:** Leigh Harline. Academy Awards '60: Best Costume Design (B & W); Nominations: Academy Awards '60: Best Art Direction/Set Decoration (B & W), Best Black and White Cinematography, Best Song ("The Facts of Life"), Best Story & Screenplay. *MGM*

Fade to Black woof! 1980 (R)
Young man obsessed with movies loses his grip on reality and adopts the personalities of cinematic characters (Hopalong Cassidy and Dracula among them) to seek revenge on people who have wronged him. Thoroughly unpleasant, highlighted by clips from old flicks. **100m/C VHS, Beta.** Dennis Christopher, Tim Thomerson, Linda Kerridge, Mickey Rourke, Melinda Fee, Gwynne Gilford, Norman Burton, Morgan Paull, James Luisi, John Steadman, Marcie Barkin, Eve Brent Ashe; **D:** Vernon Zimmerman; **W:** Vernon Zimmerman; **C:** Alex Phillips Jr. *MLB*

Fade to Black 🐾🐾 1993 (R)
Busfield stars as a college professor with voyeuristic tendencies and a handy camcorder. After viewing his latest tape, he realizes he's filmed his neighbor's murder and that he can recognize the killer. Before he can warn the killer's girlfriend, she disappears and our nosy prof is framed for the death. *CW:* Violence. **84m/C VHS, Beta, Closed Caption.** Timothy Busfield, Heather Locklear, Michael Beck, Louis Giambalvo, Cloris Leachman, David Byron; **D:** John McPherson; **W:** Douglas Barr. *PAR*

Fahrenheit 451 🐾🐾🐾 1966
Chilling adaptation of the Ray Bradbury novel about a futuristic society that has banned all reading material and the firemen whose job it is to keep the fires at 451 degrees: the temperature at which paper burns. Werner is a fireman who begins to question the rightness of his actions when he meets the book-loving Christie—who also plays the dual role of Werner's TV-absorbed wife. Truffaut's first color and English-language film. **112m/C VHS, Beta, LV.**

FR Oskar Werner, Julie Christie, Cyril Cusack, Anton Diffring; *D:* Francois Truffaut. *USH, MLB*

Fail-Safe 🐾🐾½ **1964** A nail-biting nuclear age nightmare, in which American planes have been erroneously sent to bomb the USSR, with no way to recall them. An all-star cast impels this bitterly serious thriller, the straight-faced flipside of "Dr. Strangelove." 111m/B VHS, Beta, LV, Closed Caption. Henry Fonda, Dan O'Herlihy, Walter Matthau, Larry Hagman, Fritz Weaver, Dom DeLuise; *D:* Sidney Lumet; *W:* Walter Bernstein. *COL*

Fair Game woof! **1982 (R)** Three young women decide to ditch their private school for a weekend of fun but find out the resort town they've chosen is run by sociopaths who get their kicks by stalking our chicks. 90m/C VHS, Beta. *AU* Kim Trengove, Kerry Mack, Marie O'Loughlina, Karen West; *D:* Christopher Fitchett. *IMP*

Fair Game woof! **1985** In the Australian outback, three loathesome excuses for human beings come across a beautiful woman alone on a remote farm. Naturally, they try to do despicable things but she fights back. 83m/C VHS. *AU* Cassandra Delaney, Peter Ford, David Sandford, Gary Who; *D:* Mario Andreacchio. *ORI*

Fair Game woof! **1989 (R)** A psychotic but imaginative ex-boyfriend locks his former girlfriend in her apartment with a lethal giant Mamba snake. Understandably uninterested in its serpentine attention, the young woman must trespass against the Hollywood code and keep her wits in the face of danger. Guaranteed not to charm you. 81m/C VHS, LV. Greg Henry, Trudie Styler, Bill Moseley; *D:* Mario Orfini. *THV*

Fair Game 🐾🐾½ **1995 (R)** Miami police detective Max (Baldwin) defies orders so he can protect family attorney Kate (Crawford, in her big-screen debut) from high-tech assassins. Nice work if you can get it. Generic action plot provides Crawford and first-time director Sipes with relatively safe proving ground. Cindy wears the "Die Hard" dirty white tank top look fetchingly enough (and showers when the action slackens), while Baldwin is no slouch in the babe department (male division) either. Based on Paula Gosling's 1978 novel "Fair Game," which was previously filmed as 1986's "Cobra."*CW:* Intermittent strong violence, language, and a scene of sexuality. 91m/C VHS, LV, Closed Caption. William Baldwin, Cindy Crawford, Miguel Sandoval, Christopher McDonald, Johann Carlo, Salma Hayek, John Bedford Lloyd, Jenette Goldstein; *D:* Andrew Sipes; *W:* Charlie Fletcher; *C:* Richard Bowen; *M:* Mark Mancina. Nominations: Golden Raspberry Awards '95: Worst New Star (Crawford). *WAR*

Fairy Tales 🐾 *Fairytales* **1976 (R)** A ribald musical fantasy follows the equally risque "Cinderella." In order to save the kingdom, the prince must produce an heir. The problem is that only the girl in the painting of "Princess Beauty" can "interest" the prince and she must be found. Good-natured smut. 83m/C VHS, Beta. Don Sparks, Prof. Irwin Corey, Brenda Fogarty, Sy Richardson, Nai Bonet, Martha Reeves; *D:* Harry Tampa.

Fairytale: A True Story 🐾🐾½ *Illumination* **1997 (PG)** Discovery of hope and fantasy in bleak reality when two girls in 1917 war-torn England claim to have photographed fairies in their garden. Skeptical debunker Harry Houdini (Keitel) and spiritual believer Sir Arthur Conan Doyle (O'Toole) show up to investigate the photos of cousins Elsie (Hoath) and Frances (Earl). The issues of science and spiritualism are profusely debated between the two men, getting a little in the way of the girls and their story. Tries to appeal to both adults and children, which may leave both feeling a bit unsatisfied. Perky pixies flitting about throughout picture, courtesy of special f/x wizard Tim Webber, are bound to delight even hardened audience skeptics. Don't blink for Mel Gibson's cameo as Frances' father. This same true story, known as the Cottingley Fairies, is also part of the plotline in the surreal British film "Photographing Fairies." 99m/C VHS, Beta, Closed Caption. Harvey Keitel, Peter O'Toole, Florence Hoath, Elizabeth Earl, Paul McGann, Phoebe Nicholls, Bill Nighy, Bob Peck, Tim McInnery; *Cameos:* Mel Gibson; *D:* Charles Sturridge; *W:* Ernie Contreras; *C:* Michael Coulter; *M:* Zbigniew Preisner. *PAR*

Faith 🐾 **1992 (R)** When young dancer Faith's parents are killed in an accident she winds up in a frightening foster home. Running away, she meets a gentlemanly mobster who helps her attain her dance dreams. Laughably implausible.*CW:* Language and violence. 104m/C VHS, LV, Closed Caption. Sylvia Seidel, Ami Dolenz, Richard Maldone. *THV*

Faithful 🐾🐾½ **1995 (R)** Black comedy about depressed, rich housewife Margaret (Cher) who is rudely interrupted by Tony the hitman (Palminteri) while trying to commit suicide on her 20th wedding anniversary. Unfaithful hubby Jack (O'Neal), who has put the contract out on Margaret, is conveniently away on business. As Margaret sits tied to a chair and Tony waits for a call to confirm the hit, the two connect and decide to turn the tables. Director Mazursky succeeds in bringing Palminteri's three-character play to the screen, even if it does suffer at times from too much stage talk and not enough action. First film for Cher since 1990's "Mermaids" and the first for O'Neal since 1989's "Chances Are." Big rift between Mazursky and the film's producers over final cut led him to threaten to pull his name from the credits. Mazursky cameos as the hitman's therapist.*CW:* Language and sex-related dialogue. 91m/C VHS, LV, Closed Caption. Cher, Ryan O'Neal, Chazz Palminteri; *Cameos:* Paul Mazursky; *D:* Paul Mazursky; *W:* Chazz Palminteri; *C:* Fred Murphy. *NLC*

Fake Out 🐾 *Nevada Heat* **1982** Nightclub singer is caught between the mob and the police who want her to testify against her gangland lover. Typical vanity outing for Zadora. 89m/C VHS, Beta. Pia Zadora, Telly Savalas, Desi Arnaz Jr.; *D:* Matt Cimber. *CNG*

Falcon 🐾 **1974** Brave knight battles for the honor of a beautiful maiden; with or without the Falcon's help. 105m/C VHS, Beta. Franco Nero. *TWE*

The Falcon and the Snowman 🐾🐾🐾 **1985 (R)** True story of Daulton Lee and Christopher Boyce, two childhood friends who, almost accidentally, sell American intelligence secrets to the KGB in 1977. Hutton and Penn are excellent, creating a relationship we care about and strong characterizations. 110m/C VHS, Beta, LV, Closed Caption. Sean Penn, Timothy Hutton, Lori Singer, Pat Hingle, Dorian Harewood, Richard Dysart, David Suchet, Jennifer Runyon, Priscilla Pointer, Nicholas Pryor, Joyce Van Patten, Mady Kaplan, Michael Ironside; *D:* John Schlesinger; *W:* Steven Zaillian; *C:* Allen Daviau; *M:* Lyle Mays, Pat Metheny. *ART, VES*

The Falcon in Hollywood 🐾🐾½ **1944** The falcon gets caught up with the murder of an actor who was part of a Tinseltown love triangle. The film takes place on RKO's back lot for a behind-the-scenes view of Hollywood. Part of the popular "Falcon" series from the 1940s. 67m/B VHS. Tom Conway, Barbara Hale, Veda Ann Borg, Sheldon Leonard, Frank Jenks, Rita (Paula) Corday, John Abbott; *D:* Gordon Douglas.

The Falcon in Mexico 🐾½ **1944** When paintings from a supposedly dead artist turn up for sale in New York City, the Falcon and the artist's daughter wind up journeying to Mexico to solve the mystery. Part of "The Falcon" series. 70m/B VHS, Beta. Tom Conway, Mona Maris, Nestor Paiva; *D:* William (Lester Williams) Berke.

The Falcon Takes Over/Strange Bargain 🐾🐾 **1949** A mystery double feature. In "The Falcon Takes Over," The Falcon becomes involved in a series of murder and an ex-con's last love, and in "Strange Bargain," an underpaid bookkeeper gets in on an insurance swindle. 131m/B VHS, Beta. George Sanders, Ward Bond, Allen Jenkins, Martha Scott, Harry (Henry) Morgan, James Gleason, Anne Revere, Hans Conried, Turhan Bey; *D:* Irving Reis. *TTC*

The Falcon's Adventure/Armored Car Robbery 🐾½ **1950** A mystery double feature: The Falcon uncovers a vicious plot to steal a formula for synthetic diamonds in "The Falcon's Adventure," and four participants in an armored car robbery flee after slaying a policeman in "Armored Car Robbery." 122m/B VHS, Beta. Tom Conway, Madge Meredith, William Talman, Charles McGraw, Adele Jergens; *D:* William (Lester Williams) Berke. *TTC*

The Falcon's Brother 🐾🐾 **1942** Enemy agents intent on killing a South American diplomat are foiled by the Falcon's brothers at a steep personal cost. The plot enabled Sanders' real-life brother Conway to take over the title role in "The Falcon" mystery series, a role which he played nine more times. 64m/B VHS, Beta. Tom Conway, George Sanders, Keye Luke, Jane Randolph; *D:* Stanley Logan.

Fall 🐾🐾 **1997** Brainy supermodel falls for literary cabbie in this portrait of life in the Big Apple. Within minutes of a chance encounter in a cab, married fare Sarah Easton (DeCadenet) is whiling the hours that her gorgeous, rich, doting husband is away, listening to romantic hack Michael's poetry and writhing seductively while feasting on carry-out like it's "9 1/2 Weeks." Schaeffer places himself opposite yet another gorgeous model and egotistically pens his character as a super-sensitive writer (who does this guy think he is, Woody Allen?) faced with overwhelming acclaim after his first novel, who decides to chuck it all and drive a cab. Although nicely acted and not bad to look at, the main characters and both their dilemmas are just a little hard to relate to. 92m/C VHS, Closed Caption. Eric Schaeffer, Amanda DeCadenet, Francie Swift, Lisa Vidal, Rudolph Martin; *D:* Eric Schaeffer; *W:* Eric Schaeffer; *C:* Joe DeSalvo; *M:* Amanda Kravat. *ORI*

Fall and Rise of Reginald Perrin 1 🐾🐾🐾 **1978** Starring Leonard Rossiter, this BBC show has Reginald getting out of the rat race. 107m/C VHS. *GB* Leonard Rossiter. *VCO, HMV, FUS*

Fall and Rise of Reginald Perrin 2 🐾🐾🐾 **1978** After part one's escape from the rat race, this time Reginald is back in suburbia. 120m/C VHS. *GB* Leonard Rossiter. *VCO, HMV, FUS*

Fall from Grace 🐾🐾½ **1994** American and British intelligence officers take deadly risks in 1943 Europe in an effort to convince Hitler to end the war. 180m/C VHS. *GB* James Fox, Michael York, Patsy Kensit, Gary Cole; *D:* Waris Hussein. *AVE, FCT*

Fall from Innocence 🐾½ **1988** A girl is driven to a life of prostitution and drugs by the sexual abuse inflicted upon her by her father. 81m/C VHS. Isabelle Mejias, Thom Haverstock, Amanda Smith, Rob McEwan; *D:* Carey Connor. *NO*

The Fall of the House of Usher 🐾 **1949** Lord Roderick Usher is haunted by his sister's ghost in this poor adaptation of the Poe classic. 70m/B VHS. *GB* Kay Tendeter, Gwen Watford, Irving Steen, Lucy Pavey; *D:* Ivan Barnett. *SNC, FCT*

The Fall of the House of Usher 🐾🐾🐾 *House of Usher* **1960** The moody Roger Corman/Vincent Price interpretation, the first of their eight Poe adaptations, depicting the collapse of the famous estate due to madness and revenge. Terrific sets and solid direction as well as Price's inimitable presence. 85m/C VHS, Beta. Vincent Price, Myrna Fahey, Mark Damon, Harry Ellerbe; *D:* Roger Corman; *W:* Richard Matheson; *C:* Floyd Crosby; *M:* Les Baxter. *WAR, OM*

The Fall of the House of Usher 🐾½ **1980 (PG)** Another version of Edgar Allan Poe's classic tale of a family doomed to destruction. Stray to the Roger Corman/Vincent Price version to see how it should have been done. 101m/C VHS, Beta. Martin Landau, Robert Hays, Charlene Tilton, Ray Walston; *D:* James L. Conway. *NO*

The Fall of the Roman Empire 🎬🎬🎬 1964
An all-star, big budget extravaganza set in ancient Rome praised for its action sequences. The licentious son of Marcus Aurelius arranges for his father's murder and takes over as emperor while Barbarians gather at the gate. Great sets, fine acting, and thundering battle scenes. 187m/C VHS, Beta, LV, Letterbox. Sophia Loren, Alec Guinness, James Mason, Stephen Boyd, Christopher Plummer, John Ireland, Anthony Quayle, Eric Porter, Mel Ferrer, Omar Sharif; **D:** Anthony Mann; **W:** Philip Yordan; **C:** Robert Krasker. Golden Globe Awards '65: Best Score; Nominations: Academy Awards '64: Best Original Score. *BFV, KAR, FCT*

Fall Time 🎬🎬 *Falltime* 1994 (R)
Crime drama set in small-town Minnesota, circa 1957. Three high schoolers set in motion a prank that turns bad when they pull up in front of the local bank. David (Arquette), Joe (Blechman), and Tim (London) intend to stage a mock robbery—but a real robbery is going down and the teens wind up the terrified hostages of creepy criminals Florence (Rourke) and Leon (Baldwin). Promising premise derailed by narrative inadequacies. **CW:** Scenes of brutality and violence; strong language; scene of sexuality. 88m/C VHS, LV, **Closed Caption.** Mickey Rourke, Stephen Baldwin, Jason London, David Arquette, Jonah Blechman, Sheryl Lee; **D:** Paul Warner; **W:** Steve Alden, Paul Skemp; **C:** Mark J. Gordon. *ART*

Fallen 🎬🎬 1997 (R)
Take a police-story suspense thriller, add the occult and a big dose of the supernatural, stir in a heaping helping of philosophy, a dash of a wrong-man subplot, shake vigorously, and out pours the bitter "Fallen." After the execution of serial killer Edgar Reese (Koteas), crack cop Hobbes (Washington) is soon chasing down copycat killings springing up everywhere. The real culprit is not Reese, but a fallen angel who inhabits body after body, creating new killers with each new host. Washington manages to hold his own as the pic gets messy and overly complicated. Goodman's character provides needed earthbound common sense when the banter gets a bit too lofty, debating things like the meaning of life, existence of God, and other issues that don't belong here. Hoblit's second feature tries to take on way too much in it's already lengthy span. With a mish-mash of conflicting film styles and dicey dialogue, film manages to land on the careers of an otherwise talented cast and crew. **CW:** Violence and language. 124m/C VHS. Denzel Washington, Donald Sutherland, John Goodman, Elias Koteas, Embeth Davidtz, James Gandolfini; **D:** Gregory Hoblit; **C:** Newton Thomas Sigel; **M:** Tan Dun. *WAR*

Fallen Angel 🎬🎬½ 1981
Television movie about a child pornographer and a particular young girl he finds easily exploitable because of her unbalanced home situation. Fine cast, solid direction. 100m/C Beta. Dana Hill, Richard Masur, Melinda Dillon, Ronny Cox; **D:** Robert Lewis; **M:** Richard Bellis. *COL*

Fallen Angels 1 🎬🎬🎬 1993
Trilogy of hard-boiled, film noirish tales set in Los Angeles. "The Frightening Frammis" concerns a grifter (Gallagher) who meets his match in a mystery woman (Rossellini) in this adaptation of a Jim Thompson story. Cruise's directorial debut. "Murder, Obliquely" finds a plain Jane (Dern) falling for a heel (Rickman) who may have murdered his previous girl in a Cornell Woolrich tale. "Since I Don't Have You" has Buzz Meeks (Busey) hired to find a dame sought by both Howard Hughes (Matheson) and gangster Mickey Cohen (Woods). From a story by James Elroy. Made for cable television. 90m/C VHS, **Closed Caption.** Peter Gallagher, Isabella Rossellini, Nancy Travis, John C. Reilly, Bill Erwin, Laura Dern, Alan Rickman, Diane Lane, Robin Bartlett, Gary Busey, Tim Matheson, James Woods, Aimee Graham, Dick Miller, Ken Lerner; **D:** Tom Cruise, Alfonso Cuaron, Jonathan Kaplan; **W:** Jon Robin Baitz, Howard A. Rodman, Amanda Silver, Steven Katz; **M:** Elmer Bernstein. *PGV*

Fallen Angels 2 🎬🎬🎬 1993
Three more film noir stories set in L.A. "Dead End for Delia" finds a police detective (Oldman) arriving at a murder scene to find his estranged wife (Anwar) the victim. Based on a short story by William Campbell Gault. "I'll Be Waiting" has Kirby as a hapless hotel detective who falls for a beautiful guest (Helgenberger) and winds up a mob pawn. Adaptation of a Raymond Chandler tale. "The Quiet Room" has Bedelia and Mantegna as a pair of corrupt cops who find their shakedown schemes going very wrong. From a story by Jonathan Craig. Made for cable television. 90m/C VHS, **Closed Caption.** Gary Oldman, Gabrielle Anwar, Meg Tilly, Patrick Masset, Vondie Curtis-Hall, Paul Guilfoyle, Dan Hedaya, John Putch, Wayne Knight, Bruno Kirby, Marg Helgenberger, Jon Polito, Peter Scolari, Dick Miller, Joe Mantegna, Bonnie Bedelia, Vinessa Shaw, J.E. Freeman, Peter Gallagher, Patrick Breen, Genia Michaela, Wayne Grace; *Cameos:* Tom Hanks; **D:** Phil Joanou, Tom Hanks, Steven Soderbergh; **W:** Scott Frank, C. Gaby Mitchell, Howard A. Rodman. *PGV*

Fallen Champ: The Untold Story of Mike Tyson 🎬🎬🎬 1993
Director Kopple's provocative documentary on the boxing champ, from his roots in a Brooklyn ghetto to his conviction for rape in 1991. Tyson is shown as pathetic, vulnerable, and violent—psychologically unprepared for both acclaim and responsibility, as well as easily manipulated by promoters and opportunists. A mixture of ring footage and interviews with sportswriters, promoters, trainers, and others as well as media coverage of Tyson. Made for television. 93m/C VHS, **Closed Caption.** **D:** Barbara Kopple. *COL, BTV*

The Fallen Idol 🎬🎬🎬 *The Lost Illusion* 1949
A young boy wrongly believes that a servant he admires is guilty of murdering his wife. Unwittingly, the child influences the police investigation of the crime so that the servant becomes the prime suspect. Richardson as the accused and Henrey as the boy are notable. Screenplay adapted by Greene from his short story, "The Basement Room." 92m/B VHS, Beta, LV. **GB** Ralph Richardson, Bobby Henrey, Michele Morgan, Sonia Dresdel, Jack Hawkins, Bernard Lee, Denis O'Dea, Dora Bryan, Walter Fitzgerald, Karel Stepanek, Geoffrey Keen, James Hayter, Dandy Nichols, George Woodbridge, John Ruddock, Joan Young, Gerard Heinz; **D:** Carol Reed; **W:** Graham Greene, Lesley Storm, William Templeton; **C:** Georges Perinal. British Academy Awards '48: Best Film; National Board of Review Awards '49: Best Actor (Richardson); New York Film Critics Awards '49: Best Director (Reed); Nominations: Academy Awards '49: Best Director (Reed), Best Screenplay. *NOS, MRV, HHT*

The Fallen Sparrow 🎬🎬🎬 1943
Garfield is superb as a half-mad veteran of the Spanish Civil War. Captured and brutalized, he never revealed the whereabouts of a valuable possession. His return to the U.S. continues his torture as Nazi agent Slezak uses the woman Garfield loves to set a trap and finish the job. Solid performances and good plot are highlights. 94m/B VHS, Beta. John Garfield, Maureen O'Hara, Walter Slezak, Patricia Morison, Martha O'Driscoll, Bruce Edwards, John Miljan, John Banner, Hugh Beaumont; **D:** Richard Wallace. Nominations: Academy Awards '43: Best Original Dramatic/Comedy Score. *IME*

Falling Down 🎬🎬 1993 (R)
Douglas is "D-FENS" (taken from his license plate), a normally law-abiding white-collar geek who snaps while stuck in a traffic jam on a hot day in LA. Like Charles Bronson in "Death Wish," he decides to take matters into his own hands. Unlike Bronson, he is not avenging an attack by a specific criminal, but raging against whomever gets in his way. Duvall is a detective on his last day before retirement, Hershey has the thankless role of Douglas' ex. Essentially a revenge fantasy that was vilified by some for catering to the baser emotions. **CW:** Strong language and violence. 112m/C VHS, LV, **Letterbox, Closed Caption.** Michael Douglas, Robert Duvall, Barbara Hershey, Rachel Ticotin, Tuesday Weld, Frederic Forrest, Lois Smith, D.W. Moffett, Dedee Pfeiffer, Vondie Curtis Hall, Michael Paul Chan, Raymond J. Barry, Jack Kehoe, John Diehl; **D:** Joel Schumacher; **W:** Ebbe Roe Smith; **C:** Andrzej Bartkowiak; **M:** James Newton Howard. *WAR, FCT*

Falling from Grace 🎬🎬½ 1992 (PG-13)
Bud Parks (Mellencamp) is a successful country singer who, accompanied by his wife and daughter, returns to his small Indiana hometown to celebrate his grandfather's 80th birthday. He's tired of both his career and his marriage and finds himself taking up once again with an old girlfriend (Lenz), who is not only married to Bud's brother but is also having an affair with his father. Bud believes he's better off staying in his old hometown but the problems caused by his return may change his mind. Surprisingly sedate, although literate, family drama with good ensemble performances. Actor-director debut for Mellencamp. 100m/C VHS, LV, **Closed Caption.** John Cougar Mellencamp, Mariel Hemingway, Kay Lenz, Claude Akins, Dub Taylor, Brent Huff, Deirdre O'Connell, Larry Crane; **D:** John Cougar Mellencamp; **W:** Larry McMurtry. *COL, FCT*

Falling in Love 🎬🎬½ 1984 (PG-13)
Two married New Yorkers unexpectedly fall in love after a coincidental meeting at the Rizzoli Book Store. Weak but gracefully performed reworking of "Brief Encounter," where no one seems to ever complete a sentence. An unfortunate re-teaming for Streep and De Niro after their wonderful work in "The Deer Hunter." 106m/C VHS, Beta, LV, **Closed Caption.** Robert De Niro, Meryl Streep, Harvey Keitel, Dianne Wiest, George Martin, Jane Kaczmarek, David Clennon; **D:** Ulu Grosbard; **W:** Michael Cristofer; **M:** Dave Grusin. *PAR*

Falling in Love Again 🎬½ *In Love* 1980 (PG)
Romantic comedy about middle-aged dreamer Gould and realistic wife York. They travel from Los Angeles to their hometown of New York for his high school reunion, where Gould is suddenly attacked by nostalgia vibes for his youth, seen in countless flashbacks, and prominently featuring Pfeiffer, notable in her film debut. Like watching a home movie about people you don't care about. 103m/C VHS, LV. Elliott Gould, Susannah York, Michelle Pfeiffer; **D:** Steven Paul; **W:** Ted Allan. *APX*

False Arrest 🎬🎬½ 1992
A woman is falsely accused of killing her husband's business partner and winds up in prison where she continues to fight to prove her innocence. Mills does well in this less-than-glamorous role. Based on a true story. Made for television. 102m/C VHS, Beta, **Closed Caption.** Donna Mills, Steven Bauer, James Handy, Lane Smith, Lewis Van Bergen, Dennis Christopher, Robert Wagner; **D:** Bill W.L. Norton. *TTC, PMS*

False Colors 🎬 1943
Hopalong Cassidy unmasks a crook posing as a ranch heir. This was the 49th Hopalong Cassidy feature. 54m/B VHS, Beta. William Boyd, Robert Mitchum, Andy Clyde, Jimmy Rogers; **D:** George Archainbaud. *NOS, MRV, VYY*

False Faces 🎬🎬½ 1918
Secret agent known as The Lone Wolf is working in France for the Allies when he learns a German master spy is headed for the U.S. to cause trouble. So he heads for New York to stop him. Lots of thrills. 65m/B VHS. Henry B. Walthall, Lon Chaney Sr., Mary Anderson, Milton Ross; **D:** Irvin Willat. *FCT*

False Faces 🎬½ 1932
A ruthless, money-hungry quack is hounded by the law and the victims of his unscrupulous plastic surgery. 80m/B VHS, Beta. Lowell Sherman, Peggy Shannon, Lila Lee, Joyce Compton, Berton Churchill, David Landau, Eddie Anderson, Ken Maynard, Veda Ann Borg; **D:** Lowell Sherman. *VYY*

False Identity 🎬½ 1990 (PG-13)
A radio psychologist buys a Purple Heart medal at a garage sale and then tries to find out about the original recipient. But her questions are making a number of folks uneasy, including a potentially dangerous stranger. 97m/C VHS, Beta, LV. Genevieve Bujold, Stacy Keach, Veronica Cartwright, Tobin Bell, Mimi Maynard; **D:** James Keach; **W:** Sandra K. Bailey. *PAR*

False Witness 🎬🎬½ **1989** A New Orleans district attorney and her lover, a private investigator, find themselves working the same rape-murder case. When their methods disagree both find themselves in danger. Adapted from a novel by Dorothy Uhnak. Made for television. **96m/C VHS.** Phylicia Rashad, Philip Michael Thomas, Terri Austin, George Grizzard; **D:** Arthur Seidelman; **M:** Charles Fox. *VTR*

Fame 🎬🎬🎬 **1980 (R)** Follows eight talented teenagers from their freshmen year through graduation from New York's High School of Performing Arts. Insightful and absorbing, director Parker allows the kids to mature on screen, revealing the pressures of constantly trying to prove themselves. A faultless parallel is drawn between these "special" kids and the pressures felt by high schoolers everywhere. Great dance and music sequences. The basis for the television series. 🎵Fame; Red Light; I Sing the Body Electric; Dogs in the Yard; Hot Lunch Jam; Out Here On My Own; Is It OK If I Call You Mine?. **133m/C VHS, Beta, LV.** Irene Cara, Barry Miller, Paul McCrane, Anne Meara, Joanna Merlin, Richard Belzer, Maureen Teefy; **D:** Alan Parker; **M:** Michael Gore. Academy Awards '80: Best Song ("Fame"); Golden Globe Awards '81: Best Song ("Fame"); Nominations: Academy Awards '80: Best Film Editing, Best Original Screenplay, Best Song ("Out Here on My Own"), Best Sound. *MGM, FCT*

Fame Is the Spur 🎬🎬½ **1947** A lengthy but interesting look at the way power corrupts, plus an insight into the Conservative versus Labor dynamics of British government. Redgrave is a poor, idealistic worker who decides to help his fellow workers by running for Parliament. There, he falls prey to the trappings of office with surprising consequences. Look hard for Tomlinson, who went on to star in "Mary Poppins" and "Bedknobs and Broomsticks" for Disney. **116m/B VHS.** GB Michael Redgrave, Rosamund John, Bernard Miles, Hugh Burden, Guy Verney, Carla Lehmann, Seymour Hicks, David Tomlinson; **D:** Roy Boulting. *NOS, VEC*

The Family 🎬½ **1973** As a New Orleans hit-man who resists joining the mob, Bronson initiates an all-out war on the syndicate and its boss, played by Savalas. A poorly dubbed Italian action film. **94m/C VHS, Beta.** IT Charles Bronson, Jill Ireland, Telly Savalas; **D:** Sergio Sollima. *MPI*

The Family 🎬🎬🎬 *La Famiglia* **1987** An 80-year-old patriarch prepares for his birthday celebration reminiscing about his family's past triumphs, tragedies and enduring love. The charming flashbacks, convincingly played, all take place in the family's grand old Roman apartment. In Italian with English subtitles or dubbed. **128m/C VHS, Beta, LV.** IT Vittorio Gassman, Fanny Ardant, Philippe Noiret, Stefania Sandrelli, Andrea Occhipinti, Jo Ciampa; **D:** Ettore Scola; **W:** Ettore Scola, Ruggero Maccari, Furio Scarpelli; **M:** Armando Trovajoli. Nominations: Academy Awards '87: Best Foreign Language Film. *ART, VES, TPV*

Family Business 🎬🎬½ **1989 (R)** A bright Ivy Leaguer, impressed by the exploits and vitality of his criminal grandfather, recruits him and his ex-con dad to pull off a high-tech robbery, which goes awry. Caper film, with its interest in family relationships and being true to one's nature. Casting Connery, Hoffman, and Broderick as the three leaves a big believability problem in the family department. **114m/C VHS, Beta, LV, 8mm, Closed Caption.** Sean Connery, Dustin Hoffman, Matthew Broderick, Rosana De Soto, Janet Carroll, Victoria Jackson, Bill McCutcheon, Deborah Rush, Marilyn Cooper, Salem Ludwig, Rex Everhart, James Tolkan; **D:** Sidney Lumet; **W:** Vincent Patrick; **C:** Andrzej Bartkowiak; **M:** Cy Coleman. *COL, FCT*

Family Dog: Complete Series 1992 Ten episodes from the animated television series executive produced by Tim Burton and Steven Spielberg. This put-upon pup is property of the Binfords family and succeeds in getting himself involved in all sorts of unhappy situations. **235m/C VHS, LV, Closed Caption. D:** Chris Buck; **W:** Dennis Klein;

V: Daniel Mann, Martin Mull, Molly Cheek, Zak Huxtable Epstein, Cassie Cole. *USH*

Family Enforcer 🎬 *Death Collector* **1976 (R)** A small-time hoodlum is bent on becoming the best enforcer in an underworld society. **82m/C VHS, Beta.** Joe Cortese, Lou Criscuola, Joe Pesci, Anne Johns, Keith Davis; **D:** Ralph De Vito. *VCI, VTR*

The Family Game 🎬🎬🎬 **1983** An obsessive satire about a poor, belligerent college student hired by a wealthy contemporary Japanese family to tutor their spoiled teenage son. Provides an all-out cultural assault on the Japanese bourgeoisie. From an original story by Yohei Honma. In Japanese with English subtitles. **107m/C VHS, Beta.** JP Junichi Tsujita, Yusaku Matsuda, Juzo Itami, Saori Yuki, Ichirota Miyagawa; **D:** Yoshimitsu Morita; **W:** Yoshimitsu Morita. *FCT*

Family Jewels 🎬🎬 **1965** A spoiled child-heiress has to choose among her six uncles to decide which should be her new father. If you like Jerry Lewis, you can't miss this! In addition to playing all six uncles, Lewis plays the chauffeur, as well as serving as producer, director, and coauthor of the script. **100m/C VHS.** Jerry Lewis, Donna Butterworth, Sebastian Cabot, Robert Strauss; **D:** Jerry Lewis; **W:** Jerry Lewis. *PAR*

Family Life 🎬🎬 *Zycie Rodzinne* **1971** Melancholy mood piece finds an engineer reluctantly returning to his family's delapidated country mansion after six years in Warsaw. He must confront his own life as well as his alcoholic father and slightly mad sister. Polish with subtitles. **93m/C VHS.** PL Daniel Olbrychski, Jan Nowicki, Jan Kreczmar, Maja Komorowska, Halina Mikolajska; **D:** Krzysztof Zanussi; **W:** Krzysztof Zanussi; **M:** Wojciech Kilar. *FCT*

Family Life 🎬🎬½ *Wednesday's Child* **1971** A portrait of 19-year-old Janice Baldwin, who's forced to get an abortion by her parents and battles them constantly to establish her own identity. She is eventually sent to a mental institution for depression, where she is subjected to increasingly vigorous psychological interventions, including electro-shock. Documentary-style effort originally made for British television. **108m/C VHS.** GB Sandy Ratcliff, Bill Dean, Grace Cave; **D:** Ken Loach. *FXL*

The Family Man 🎬🎬½ **1979** A brief encounter-between a married Manhattanite (Asner) and a much younger single woman (Baxter Birney) is sensitively handled in this film which explores their passionate affair. Made-for-television. **98m/C VHS, Beta.** Ed Asner, Meredith Baxter, Paul Clemens, Mary Joan Negro, Anne Jackson, Martin Short, Michael Ironside; **D:** Glenn Jordan; **M:** Billy Goldenberg. *TLF*

A Family Matter 🎬🎬 *Vendetta: Secrets of a Mafia Bride* **1991 (R)** A Mafia chieftain adopts a child whose father was killed by hit men. She grows into a beautiful woman bent on revenge. Melodramatic Italian-American co-production, made for TV. **CW:** Gangster violence and sensuality. **100m/C VHS, LV.** Eric Roberts, Carol Alt, Eli Wallach, Burt Young. *THV*

Family of Cops 🎬🎬½ **1995 (PG-13)** Trouble comes calling on Inspector Paul Fein's (Bronson) close-knit Milwaukee family when his party girl daughter Jackie (Featherstone) comes home to visit. She's soon accused of murdering a wealthy businessman she picked up in a drunken stupor and her cop family gets deeply involved in the investigation. Made for TV. **CW:** Violence and some sexuality. **90m/C VHS.** Charles Bronson, Daniel Baldwin, Angela Featherstone, Sebastian Spence, Lesley-Anne Down, Barbara Williams, Simon MacCorkindale; **D:** Ted Kotcheff; **W:** Joel Basergo. *THV*

Family of Cops 2: Breach of Faith 🎬🎬½ *Breach of Faith: A Family of Cops 2* **1997 (PG-13)** The investigation of a priest's murder makes Inspector Paul Fein (Bronson) and his cop family the target of Russian mobsters. TV movie once again filmed in Toronto, which substitutes for Milwaukee. **CW:** Violence and brief sensuality. **90m/C VHS.** Charles Bronson, Joe Penny, Diane Ladd, Sebastian Spence, Angela Featherstone, Barbara Williams,

Andrew Jackson, Matt Birman, Kim Weeks, David Hemblen, Mimi Kuzyk, Real Andrews; **D:** David Greene; **W:** Joel Basberg; **C:** Ronald Orieux; **M:** Peter Manning Robinson. *THV*

Family Pictures 🎬🎬🎬 **1993** A photographer remembers growing up in the '50s with her autistic brother, the mother who lavished her attention on him almost to the exclusion of her five other children, and the father who blamed his wife for their son's deficiencies. Interesting portrait of an American family, which eventually cracks under pressure and splits up. Adapted from the novel by Sue Miller (no relation to screenwriter Jennifer). **240m/C VHS.** Anjelica Huston, Sam Neill, Kyra Sedgwick, Dermot Mulroney, Gemma Barry, Tara Charendoff, Torri Higginson, Jamie Harold; **D:** Philip Saville; **W:** Jennifer Miller. *NYR*

Family Plot 🎬🎬½ **1976 (PG)** Alfred Hitchcock's last film focuses on the search for a missing heir which is undertaken by a phony psychic and her private-eye boyfriend, with all becoming involved in a diamond theft. Campy, lightweight mystery that stales with time and doesn't fit well into Hitchcock's genre. **120m/C VHS, Beta, LV.** Karen Black, Bruce Dern, Barbara Harris, William Devane, Ed Lauter, Katherine Helmond; **D:** Alfred Hitchcock; **W:** Ernest Lehman; **M:** John Williams. *USH*

Family Prayers 🎬🎬½ **1991 (PG)** Coming-of-age drama, set in 1969 Los Angeles, about 13-year-old Andrew and his family troubles. His father Martin (Mantegna) is a compulsive gambler which causes wife Rita (Archer) untold anxiety and constant friction between the two. Tension is heightened by Nan (LuPone), Rita's opinionated older sister who has bailed the family out of their money problems more than once. Meanwhile, Andrew tries to look out for his younger sister and prepare for his bar-mitzvah. A little too much of a nostalgic golden glow surrounds what is essentially a family tragedy. **109m/C VHS.** Tzvi Ratner-Stauber, Joe Mantegna, Anne Archer, Patti LuPone, Paul Reiser, Allen (Goorwitz) Garfield, Conchata Ferrell, David Margulies; **D:** Scott Rosenfelt; **W:** Steven Ginsburg. *COL*

Family Reunion 🎬½ **1988** A young man brings a pretty hitchhiker to his family reunion where they mistake her for his fiancee (who recently dumped him). **97m/C VHS, Beta.** David Eisner, Rebecca Jenkins, Henry Beckman, Linda Sorensen; **D:** Dick Sarin. *NO*

Family Secrets 🎬🎬½ **1984** A made-for-television drama about a daughter, mother, and grandmother overprotecting and manipulating each other during a weekend together. **96m/C Beta.** Maureen Stapleton, Stefanie Powers, Melissa Gilbert, James Spader; **D:** Jack Hofsiss. *NO*

Family Sins 🎬🎬 **1987** A television movie about a domineering father who dotes on his sports-oriented son while willfully neglecting the other. Eventually this leads to calamity. **93m/C VHS.** James Farentino, Jill Eikenberry, Andrew Bendarski, Mimi Kuzyk, Brent Spiner, Michael Durrell, Tom Bower; **D:** Jerrold Freedman. *REP*

A Family Thing 🎬🎬🎬 **1996 (PG-13)** Racial issues are addressed in this character-driven story of two brothers. Southerner Earl Pilcher (Duvall) learns his biological mother was black and that she died during his birth. In a letter written by the recently deceased woman who raised him, Earl discovers he also has a half brother, Ray (Jones), who is black and living in Chicago. He drives to Chicago, and seeks out Ray, who to Earl's surprise knows about him already, and is not exactly thrilled about the family ties, either. As the two brothers, expertly played by Duvall and Jones, slowly find common ground, Hall steals the show as the irascible Aunt T. **CW:** Some strong language, brief violence and a childbirth scene. **109m/C VHS, LV, Closed Caption.** Robert Duvall, James Earl Jones, Irma P. Hall, Michael Beach, Grace Zabriskie, Regina Taylor, Mary Jackson, Paula Marshall, Jim Harrell; **D:** Richard Pearce; **W:** Billy Bob Thornton, Tom Epperson; **C:** Fred Murphy. *MGM*

Family Upside Down ✓✓✓ 1078 An aging couple fight their separation after the husband has a heart attack and is put into a nursing home. The fine cast received several Emmy nominations, with Astaire the winner. Made-for-television. 100m/C VHS, Beta. Helen Hayes, Fred Astaire, Efrem Zimbalist Jr., Patty Duke; **D:** David Lowell Rich; **M:** Henry Mancini. COL

Family Viewing ✓✓✓ 1987 Surrealistic depiction of a family—obsessed with television and video—whose existence is a textbook model of home sweet dysfunctional home. An early, experimental film from Canada's Egoyan, it won considerable praise for its social commentary. 92m/C VHS, LV. **CA** David Hemblen, Adian Tierney, Gabrielle Rose, Arsinee Khanjian; **D:** Atom Egoyan; **W:** Atom Egoyan; **M:** Mychael Danna. Toronto-City Award '87: Best Canadian Feature Film. FXL, FCT

Famous Five Get into Trouble ✓✓ 1987 Four precocious youngsters and a dog get involved with a criminal plot and cutely wile their way out of it. Scandinavian; dubbed in English. 90m/C VHS, Beta. Astrid Villaume, Ove Sprogoe, Lily Broberg; **D:** Trine Hedman. TWE

The Fan ✓✓ 1981 (R) A Broadway star is threatened and her immediate circle cut down when a lovestruck fan feels he has been rejected by his idol. The stellar cast makes this bloody and familiar tale seem better than it is. 95m/C VHS, Beta, LV. Lauren Bacall, Maureen Stapleton, James Garner, Hector Elizondo, Michael Biehn, Griffin Dunne; **D:** Edward Bianchi; **W:** Priscilla Chapman; **M:** Pino Donaggio. PAR

The Fan ✓✓½ 1996 (R) Obsessed baseball fan Gil Renard (De Niro, who owns the copyright on playing deranged) stalks favorite player Bobby Rayburn (Snipes) who just signed a big contract with the hometown team. When Rayburn goes into a slump, Renard figures he can help his idol—by any means necessary. As an added bonus, Gil's a knife salesman. De Niro does the psycho thing with his usual aplomb, while Snipes successfully returns to the diamond. Scott keeps the familiar storyline from becoming tedious. Based on the book by Peter Abrahams. **CW:** Strong language throughout and some intense violence. 117m/C VHS, LV, 8mm, Closed Caption, DVD. Robert De Niro, Wesley Snipes, Ellen Barkin, John Leguizamo, Benicio Del Toro, Patti D'Arbanville; **D:** Tony Scott; **W:** Phoef Sutton; **M:** Hans Zimmer. Nominations: MTV Movie Awards '97: Best Villain (De Niro). COL

Fanci's Persuasion ✓½ 1995 San Francisco-set gay feature features lesbian Fanci (Patton) 24 hours away from marrying lover Loretta (Boa) and in panic mode. Her parents refuse to come to the ceremony and there are numerous and inexplicable complications to deal with. Deliberately over-the-top performances and contrived dialogue and situations can't really take the strain despite the pic's good looks. 78m/C VHS. Jessica Patton, Boa, Justin Bond, Robert Coffman, Charles Herman-Wurmfeld; **D:** Charles Herman-Wurmfeld; **W:** Charles Herman-Wurmfeld; **C:** David Rush Morrison. WBF

Fancy Pants ✓✓½ 1950 Remake of "Ruggles of Red Gap" features Hope, a British actor posing as a butler. Also featuring Ball, an amusing contrast. Fine performances all around. ♫Fancy Pants; Home Cookin'. 92m/C VHS, Beta, LV, Closed Caption. Bob Hope, Lucille Ball, Bruce Cabot, Jack Kirkwood, Lea Penman, Eric Blore, John Alexander, Norma Varden; **D:** George Marshall; **C:** Charles B(ryant) Lang. PAR

Fandango ✓✓½ 1985 (PG) Five college friends take a wild weekend drive across the Texas Badlands for one last fling before graduation and the prospect of military service. Expanded by Reynolds with assistance from Steven Spielberg, from his student film. Provides a view at college and life during the Vietnam crisis. 91m/C VHS, Beta. Judd Nelson, Kevin Costner, Sam Robards, Chuck Bush, Brian Cesak, Elizabeth Daily, Suzy Amis, Glenne Headly, Pepe Serna, Marvin J. McIntyre; **D:** Kevin Reynolds; **W:** Kevin Reynolds; **M:** Alan Silvestri. WAR

Fanfan la Tulipe ✓✓✓ *Fanfan the Tulip; Fearless Little Soldier* 1951 Fanfan (Philipe) escapes an unwanted marriage by joining the army of Louis XV (Herrand), after being promised an illustrious career and a royal marriage. And after many heroics, it all comes true. Amusing satire of swashbucklers and historical romance movies. French with subtitles. 98m/B VHS. **FR** Gerard Philipe, Gina Lollobrigida, Marcel Herrand, Sylvia Pelayo, Genevieve Page, Noel Roquevort; **D:** Christian-Jaque; **W:** Rene Wheeler, Jean Fallet, Christian-Jaque; **M:** Georges Van Parys, Maurice Thiriet. Cannes Film Festival '52: Best Director. FCT

Fangs ✓½ 1975 (R) Unfriendly reptile-stomping villagers take the life of Mr. Snakey's favorite serpent. He sends his slithering pets on a vengeful and poisonous spree. 90m/C VHS, Beta. Les Tremayne, Janet Wood, Bebe Kelly, Marvin Kaplan, Alice Nunn; **D:** Vittorio Schiraldi. GEM, MRV

Fangs of Fate ✓½ 1925 A gang of bad guys battles the town's new marshal. 67m/B VHS, Beta, 8mm. Bill Patton, Dorothy Donald. GPV, VYY

Fangs of the Living Dead ✓½ *Malenka, the Vampire; La Nipote del Vampiro; The Niece of the Vampire; The Vampire's Niece* 1968 When a young woman inherits a castle, her uncle, who happens to be a vampire, tries to persuade her to remain among the undead. 80m/C VHS. **SP IT** Anita Ekberg, Rossana Yanni, Diana Lorys, Fernando Bilbao, Paul Muller, Julian Ugarte, Adriana Ambesi; **D:** Armando de Ossorio; **W:** Armando de Ossorio. SNC

Fangs of the Wild ✓✓ *Follow the Hunter* 1954 When a young boy witnesses a murder at his father's hunting lodge, no one but the killer believes him. When the killer decides to get rid of the boy, Buck the Wonder Dog gets involved. 72m/B VHS. Charles Chaplin Jr., Onslow Stevens, Margia Dean, Freddy Ridgeway, Phil Tead, Robert Stevenson; **D:** William Claxton. NOS, DVT, HEG

Fanny ✓✓✓✓ 1932 Second part of Marcel Pagnol's trilogy depicting the lives of the people of Provence, France. The poignant tale of Fanny, a young woman who marries an older man when Marius, her young lover, leaves her pregnant when he goes to sea. Remade several times but the original holds its own very well. "Marius" was first in the trilogy; "Cesar" was third. 128m/B VHS, Beta, LV. **FR** Raimu, Charpin, Orane Demazis, Pierre Fresnay, Alida Rauffe; **D:** Marc Allegret; **W:** Marcel Pagnol; **M:** Vincent Scotto. INT, MRV, HHT

Fanny ✓✓✓ 1961 Young girl falls in love with an adventurous sailor, and finds herself pregnant after he returns to the sea. With the help of the sailor's parents, she finds, marries, and eventually grows to love a much older man, who in turn cares for her and adores her son as if he were his own. When the sailor returns, all involved must confront their pasts and define their futures. Beautifully made, with fine performances and a plot which defies age or nationality. Part of the "A Night at the Movies" series, this tape simulates a 1961 movie evening, with a Tweety Pie cartoon, a newsreel and coming attractions for "Splendor in the Grass" and "The Roman Spring of Mrs. Stone." 148m/C VHS, Beta. **FR** Leslie Caron, Maurice Chevalier, Charles Boyer, Horst Buchholz, Lionel Jeffries; **D:** Joshua Logan; **W:** Julius J. Epstein, Philip C. Epstein; **C:** Jack Cardiff. Nominations: Academy Awards '61: Best Actor (Boyer), Best Color Cinematography, Best Film Editing, Best Picture, Best Original Dramatic/Comedy Score. NOS, WAR

Fanny and Alexander ✓✓✓✓ *Fanny Och Alexander* 1983 (R) The culmination of Bergman's career, this autobiographical film is set in a rural Swedish town in 1907. It tells the story of one year in the lives of the Ekdahl family, as seen by the young children, Fanny and Alexander. Magic and religion, love and death, reconciliation and estrangement are skillfully captured in this carefully detailed, lovingly photographed film. In Swedish with English subtitles or dubbed. 197m/C VHS, Beta, LV, Closed Caption. **SW** Pernilla Allwin, Bertil Guve, Gunn Walgren, Allan Edwall, Ewa Froling, Erland

Josephson, Harriet Andersson, Jarl Kulle, Jan Malmsjo; **D:** Ingmar Bergman; **W:** Ingmar Bergman; **C:** Sven Nykvist; **M:** Daniel Bell. Academy Awards '83: Best Art Direction/Set Decoration, Best Cinematography, Best Costume Design, Best Foreign Language Film; Cesar Awards '84: Best Foreign Film; Golden Globe Awards '84: Best Foreign Film; Los Angeles Film Critics Association Awards '83: Best Cinematography, Best Foreign Film; New York Film Critics Awards '83: Best Director (Bergman), Best Foreign Film; Nominations: Academy Awards '83: Best Director (Bergman), Best Original Screenplay. COL, NLC

Fanny Hill ✓✓ 1983 (R) A softcore adaptation of the racy Victorian classic. 80m/C VHS, Beta. **GB** Lisa Raines, Shelley Winters, Wilfrid Hyde-White, Oliver Reed. MGM

Fanny Hill: Memoirs of a Woman of Pleasure woof! 1964 Sexual exploits of an innocent in bawdy 18th-century London, as directed by notorious "Super Vixen" Meyer (though by Meyer standards, proceedings are fairly innocuous, if inept). Based on the novel. 105m/B VHS, Beta. Miriam Hopkins, Walter Giller, Alexander D'Arcy, Leticia Roman; **D:** Russ Meyer. NO

Fantasia ✓✓✓✓ 1940 Disney's most personal animation feature first bombed at the box office and irked purists who couldn't take the plotless, experimental mix of classical music and cartoons. It became a cult movie, embraced by more liberal generations of moviegoers. Reissue of the original version, painstakingly restored, ceased because of a planned remake. ♫Toccata & Fugue in D; The Nutcracker Suite; The Sorcerer's Apprentice; The Rite of Spring; Pastoral Symphony; Dance of the Hours; Night on Bald Mountain; Ave Maria; The Cossack Dance. 116m/C VHS, LV, Closed Caption. National Film Registry '90. DIS, FCT, RDG

Fantasies woof! *And Once Upon a Love* 1973 (R) Teenage lovers Derek and Hooten return to their Greek island home and decide to improve their village by turning it into a tourist haven. First collaboration of the Dereks is a loser, lacking plot, direction, and decent acting. Bo shows no talent but the obvious one and is actually credited as Kathleen Collins. 81m/C VHS, Beta. Bo Derek, Peter Hooten, Anna Alexiades; **D:** John Derek. FOX

The Fantasist ✓ 1989 (R) Sex crime thriller features a deranged killer who makes obscene, yet seductive phone calls to young ladies before murdering them. 98m/C VHS. Timothy Bottoms, Christopher Cazenove; **D:** Robin Hardy. REP

Fantastic Balloon Voyage ✓ 198? (G) Three men embark on a journey across the equator in a balloon, experiencing myriad adventures along the way. Much hot air. 100m/C VHS, Beta. Hugo Stiglitz, Jeff Cooper. GEM

Fantastic Planet ✓✓✓ *La Planete Sauvage* 1973 (PG) A critically acclaimed French, animated, sci-fi epic based on the drawings of Roland Topor. A race of small humanoids are enslaved and exploited by a race of giants on a savage planet, until one of the small creatures manages to unite his people and fight for equality. 68m/C VHS, Beta. **FR D:** Rene Laloux; **W:** Rene Laloux; **V:** Barry Bostwick. VYY, MRV, SNC

Fantastic Seven ✓½ 1982 The Fantastic Seven is a daredevil team sent to rescue a Hollywood sex symbol who has been kidnapped and held for ransom while shooting on location off the coast of Miami. 96m/C VHS, Beta. Elke Sommer, Christopher Connelly. TLF

Fantastic Voyage ✓✓✓ *Microscopia; Strange Journey* 1966 An important scientist, rescued from behind the Iron Curtain, is so severely wounded by enemy agents that traditional surgery is impossible. After being shrunk to microscopic size, a medical team journeys inside his body where they find themselves threatened by the patient's natural defenses. Great action, award-winning special effects. 100m/C VHS, Beta, LV, Letterbox. Stephen Boyd, Edmond O'Brien, Raquel Welch, Arthur Kennedy, Donald Pleasence, Arthur O'Connell, William Redfield, James Brolin; **D:** Richard Fleischer; **C:** Ernest Laszlo. Academy Awards '66: Best Art Direction/Set Decoration (Color), Best Visual Effects; Nominations: Academy Awards '66: Best Color Cinematography, Best Film Editing. *FOX, CCB*

The Fantastic World of D.C. Collins 🎬🎬 1984
Gary Coleman plays a day-dreaming teenager who thinks he is being pursued by mysterious strangers seeking a videotape that was unknowingly slipped to him. Made for television. 100m/C VHS. Gary Coleman, Bernie Casey, Shelley Smith, Fred Dryer, Marilyn McCoo, Philip Abbott, George Gobel, Michael Ansara; **D:** Leslie Martinson. *VTR*

Fantasy Island 🎬 1976
Three people fly ("De plane, boss!") to an island paradise and get to live out their fantasies for a price. Made for television; the basis for the TV series. 100m/C VHS, **Beta.** Ricardo Montalban, Bill Bixby, Sandra Dee, Peter Lawford, Carol Lynley, Hugh O'Brian, Eleanor Parker, Dick Sargent, Victoria Principal; **D:** Richard Lang.

Fantasy Man 🎬🎬½ 1984
A restless middle-aged man tries to relieve his mid-life crisis with the help of three women. 100m/C VHS, **Beta.** AU Harold Hopkins, Jeanie Drynan, Kerry Mack, Kate Fitzpatrick; **D:** John Meagher; **W:** John Meagher. *VCD*

Far and Away 🎬🎬½ 1992 (PG-13)
Meandering old-fashioned epic about immigrants, romance, and settling the American West. In the 1890s, Joseph Donelly (Cruise) is forced to flee his Irish homeland after threatening the life of his landlord, and emigrates to America in the company of the landlord's daughter, feisty Shannon Christie (Kidman). Particularly brutal scenes of Cruise earning his living as a bare-knuckled boxer contrast with the expansiveness of the land rush ending. Slow, spotty, and a little too slick for its own good, though real-life couple Cruise and Kidman are an attractive pair. Filmed in 70-mm Panavision on location in Ireland and Montana. Also available in a letterboxed version. 140m/C VHS, Beta, LV, Letterbox, Closed Caption, DVD. Tom Cruise, Nicole Kidman, Thomas Gibson, Robert Prosky, Barbara Babcock, Colm Meaney, Eileen Pollock, Michelle Johnson, Cyril Cusack, Clint Howard, Rance Howard; **D:** Ron Howard; **W:** Bob Dolman; **C:** Mikael Salomon; **M:** John Williams. *USH*

Far Away and Long Ago 🎬🎬½ 1974
Based on the autobiographical novel by Guillermo Hudson which details the memories which haunted his childhood—the Argentinian pampas, its gauchos, witchcraft, and women. In Spanish with English subtitles. 91m/C VHS. AR Juan Jose Camero, Leonor Manso; **D:** Manuel Antin. *FCT*

Far Country 🎬🎬🎬 1955
Cattlemen must battle the elements and frontier lawlessness in this classic. Stewart leads his herd to the Yukon in hopes of large profits, but ends up having to kidnap it back from the crooked sheriff and avenging the deaths of his friends. Entertaining and the Yukon setting takes it out of the usual Western arena. 97m/C VHS, Beta. James Stewart, Ruth Roman, Walter Brennan, Harry (Henry) Morgan, Corinne Calvet, Jay C. Flippen, John McIntire; **D:** Anthony Mann; **C:** William H. Daniels; **M:** Henry Mancini. *BAR*

Far Cry from Home 🎬 197?
A battered wife attempts to escape from her domineering husband before it's too late. 87m/C VHS, Beta. Mary Ann McDonald, Richard Monette. *TWE*

Far East 🎬🎬½ 1985
Two ex-lovers meet in Southeast Asia and join forces to find the woman's missing husband, a reporter. 105m/C VHS, Beta. Bryan Brown, Helen Morse; **D:** John Duigan. *ORI, VTR*

Far from Home 🎬🎬 1989 (R)
Drew Barrymore is the seductive teen being scoped by a psychotic killer while on vacation with her father. Lots of over-the-top performances by the familiar cast. 86m/C VHS, LV. Matt Frewer, Drew Barrymore, Richard Masur, Karen Austin, Susan Tyrrell, Anthony Rapp, Jennifer Tilly, Andras Jones, Dick Miller; **D:** Meiert Avis; **C:** Paul Elliott; **M:** Jonathan Elias. *ART, VES*

Far from Home: The Adventures of Yellow Dog 🎬🎬 1994 (PG)
Stalwart lad Angus (Bradford) and his faithful pooch Yellow (Dakotah) battle the elements, wild animals and fatigue as they try to get back home after being shipwrecked on a remote island in British Columbia. Good thing Dad (Davidson) gave them all those cool survival tips before they left, or else they never would've known that you can eat bugs. (Okay, the dog probably knew that already.) Mom (Rogers) does her bit by making sure the search mission stays focused. You usually can't go wrong with a kid and his dog lost in the wilderness, but this one is really short—on time and drama. Nice scenery, though. 81m/C VHS, LV, Closed Caption. Jesse Bradford, Bruce Davison, Mimi Rogers, Tom Bower; **D:** Phillip Borsos; **W:** Phillip Borsos. *FXV*

Far from the Madding Crowd 🎬🎬🎬 1967 (PG)
A lavish, long adaptation of Thomas Hardy's 19th-century classic about the beautiful Bathsheba and the three very different men who love her. Her first love is a handsome and wayward soldier (Stamp), her second the local noble lord (Finch), and her third the ever-loving and long-patient farmer (Bates). Christie is well cast as the much-desired beauty. Gorgeous cinematography by Nicolas Roeg. 165m/C VHS, Beta, LV, Letterbox. GB Julie Christie, Terence Stamp, Peter Finch, Alan Bates, Prunella Ransome; **D:** John Schlesinger; **W:** Frederic Raphael; **C:** Nicolas Roeg; **M:** Richard Rodney Bennett. National Board of Review Awards '67: Best Actor (Finch); Nominations: Academy Awards '67: Best Original Score. *MGM*

Far from the Madding Crowd 🎬🎬🎬 1997
TV version of the Thomas Hardy novel (filmed for the big screen in 1967) that follows the adventures of young Bathsheba (Baeza), who's the object of desire for three very different men in 19th-century rural England. Independent-minded Bathsheba Everdene inherits a farm and insists on managing it herself. She's aided by steadfast head man Gabriel Oak (Parker), who loves her but doesn't feel he can offer her anything; wealthy older neighbor William Boldwood (Terry), whose love for Bathsheba becomes an obsession; and rakish Sgt. Frank Troy (Firth), who captivates Bathsheba but proves to be a scoundrel. 200m/C VHS. GB Paloma Baeza, Nigel Terry, Nathaniel Parker, Jonathan Firth; **D:** Nicholas Renton; **W:** Philomena McDonagh. *WGB*

Far Frontier 🎬🎬 1948
Roy Rogers saves the day by thwarting a band of outlaws who are being smuggled across the border in soybean oil cans. Includes musical numbers and horse tricks. 60m/B VHS. Roy Rogers, Andy Devine, Clayton Moore. *NOS, TIM, REP*

Far North 🎬🎬½ 1988 (PG-13)
Quirky comedy about a woman who returns to her rural family homestead after her father is seriously injured by a horse, and tries to deal with her eccentric family's travails. Fine cast never reaches its potential. Shepard's directing debut. 96m/C VHS, Beta, LV, 8mm, Closed Caption. Jessica Lange, Charles Durning, Tess Harper, Donald Moffat, Ann Wedgeworth, Patricia Arquette, Nina Draxton; **D:** Sam Shepard; **W:** Sam Shepard; **C:** Robbie Greenberg. *NLC*

A Far Off Place 🎬🎬 1993 (PG-13)
Adolescent boy, adolescent girl, adolescent bushperson, and mature dog set out across the African desert to escape elephant poachers who want to kill them. The boy and girl find romance in the sand, bushperson finds water by listening, and dog gets very nice walk. Strong performances by the youthful leads lend charm to this Disney/Amblin flick, particularly Bok as the bushperson. Unusually violent film for studios involved (animals and people bite sand), though care is taken to edit actual blood shed on screen. Filmed in Zimbabwe and Namibia and based on the books "A Story Like the Wind" and "A Far Off Place" by Laurens van der Post. **CW:** Mild language and violence. 107m/C VHS, Beta, LV, Letterbox, Closed Caption.

Reese Witherspoon, Ethan Randall, Sarel Bok, Jack Thompson, Maximilian Schell, Robert John Burke, Patricia Kalember, Daniel Gerroll, Miles Anderson; **D:** Mikael Salomon; **W:** Robert Caswell, Jonathan Hensleigh, Sally Robinson; **C:** Juan Ruiz-Anchia; **M:** James Horner. *DIS*

Far Out Man woof! 1989 (R)
An unalterable middle-aged hippie is sent by his worried family and his psychiatrist on a cross-country journey to rediscover himself. The script makes no sense and has very few laughs. 105m/C VHS, Beta, LV. Thomas Chong, Rae Dawn Chong, C. Thomas Howell, Shelby Chong, Martin Mull, Paris Chong, Paul Bartel, Judd Nelson, Michael Winslow, Richard "Cheech" Marin; **D:** Thomas Chong; **W:** Thomas Chong. *COL*

The Far Pavilions 🎬🎬½ Blade of Steel 1984
A British officer falls in love with an Indian princess during the second Afghan War. Cross is appropriately noble and stiff-upper-lipped but Irving is miscast as his ethnic love. Based on the romantic bestseller by M.M. Kaye, this lavish production was made for cable television. 108m/C VHS, Beta. Ben Cross, Amy Irving, Omar Sharif, Benedict Taylor, Rossano Brazzi, Christopher Lee; **D:** Peter Duffell; **C:** Jack Cardiff; **M:** Carl Davis. *KAR*

Faraway, So Close! 🎬🎬 In Weiter Ferne, So Nah! 1993 (PG-13)
Wenders' erratic follow-up to his magnificent "Wings of Desire." Cassiel (Sander), the angel left behind when Damiel (Ganz) chose to become human, once again surveys Berlin, noticing the changes (not necessarily for the better). Angelic companion Raphaela (Kinski) watches events passively, including an old man's (Ruhamnn) reflections on life and the philosophical musings of Emit Flesti (Dafoe, Time Itself, get it?), even as Cassiel impulsively chooses humanity over his heavenly world. Falk makes a return appearance to little effect. Overlong and underdeveloped. **CW:** Language. 146m/C VHS, LV, Closed Caption. GE Otto Sander, Peter Falk, Horst Buchholz, Nastassia Kinski, Heinz Ruhmann, Bruno Ganz, Solveig Dommartin, Ruediger Vogler, Willem Dafoe, Lou Reed; **D:** Wim Wenders; **W:** Ulrich Zieger, Richard Reitinger, Wim Wenders; **M:** Laurent Petitgrand. Cannes Film Festival '93: Grand Jury Prize; Nominations: Golden Globe Awards '94: Best Song ("Stay"). *COL*

Farewell My Concubine 🎬🎬 Bawang Bie Ji 1993 (R)
Exotic film covers 50 years of sexual, social, and political Chinese history wrapped around the story of two male Peking Opera stars. Deposited as boys at the Opera's training school Douzi and Shitou become fast friends in their hermetically sealed world, but their friendship is tested during the chaos of Communism and the cultural revolution. Sumptuous and well-acted, but the sheer length and emotional detachment prove to be drawbacks. Adapted from a novel by Lee, who based the work on a 2000-year-old Chinese opera about an imperial concubine. Filmed on location in Beijing. In Mandarin Chinese with subtitles.**CW:** Language/strong thematic material. 157m/C VHS, LV. HK Leslie Cheung, Zhang Fengyi, Gong Li, Lu Qi, Ying Da, Ge You; **D:** Chen Kaige; **W:** Lilian Lee, Lu Wei; **C:** Gu Changwei; **M:** Zhao Jiping. British Academy Awards '93: Best Foreign Film; Cannes Film Festival '93: Best Film; Golden Globe Awards '94: Best Foreign Film; Los Angeles Film Critics Association Awards '93: Best Foreign Film; National Board of Review Awards '93: Best Foreign Film; New York Film Critics Awards '93: Best Foreign Film, Best Supporting Actress (Li); Nominations: Academy Awards '93: Best Cinematography, Best Foreign Language Film. *TOU*

Farewell, My Lovely 🎬🎬🎬 1975 (R)
A remake of the 1944 Raymond Chandler mystery, "Murder, My Sweet," featuring private eye Phillip Marlowe hunting for an ex-convict's lost sweetheart in 1941 Los Angeles. Perhaps the most accurate of Chandler adaptations, but far from the best, this film offers a nicely detailed production. Mitchum is a bit too world-weary as the seen-it-all detective. 95m/C VHS, Beta. GB Robert Mitchum, Charlotte Rampling, Sylvia Miles, John Ireland, Anthony Zerbe, Jack O'Halloran, Harry Dean Stanton, Sylvester Stallone, Cheryl "Rainbeaux" Smith; **D:** Dick Richards; **W:** David Zelag Goodman; **C:** John A. Alonzo; **M:** David Shire. Nomina-

tions: Academy Awards '75: Best Supporting Actress (Miles).

A Farewell to Arms ✹✹✹ 1932 The original film version of Ernest Hemingway's novel about the tragic love affair between an American ambulance driver and an English nurse during the Italian campaign of WWI. The novelist disavowed the ambiguous ending, but the public loved the film. Fine performances and cinematography. **85m/B VHS, Beta, LV.** Helen Hayes, Gary Cooper, Adolphe Menjou, Mary Philips, Jack LaRue, Blanche Frederici; **D:** Frank Borzage; **C:** Charles B(ryant) Lang. Academy Awards '33: Best Cinematography, Best Sound; Nominations: Academy Awards '33: Best Interior Decoration, Best Picture. *CNG, MRV, NOS*

Farewell to the King ✹✹½ 1989 (PG-13) During WWII, a ship-wrecked American deserter becomes the chief of a tribe of Borneo headhunters until his jungle kingdom is caught between the forces of the U.S. and Japanese. With the help of a British officer he helps them defend themselves when the Japanese invade. An old-fashioned war epic with a beautiful location and solid if uninspired-performances by the leads. Based on Pierre Schoendoerffer's novel "L'Adieu Au Roi." **114m/C VHS, Beta, LV, Closed Caption.** Nick Nolte, Nigel Havers, Marius Weyers, Frank McRae, Marilyn Tokuda, Elan Oberon, William Wise, James Fox, Aki Aleong; **D:** John Milius; **W:** John Milius; **M:** Basil Poledouris. *ORI*

Fargo ✹✹✹ 1996 (R) Another malicious, extra-dark comedy from the Coen brothers. Car salesman Jerry Lundegaard (Macy) hires a couple of losers to kidnap his wife so he can swindle the ransom money out of his father-in-law. Naturally, the scheme begins to unravel and the very pregnant police chief Marge Gunderson (McDormand) treks through the frozen tundra of Minnesota to put the pieces of the puzzle together. McDormand's performance as the chatty competent chief is first rate. Needling the flat-accented Midwesterners of their youth, the Coens have also returned to their filmmaking roots after the disappointing big-budget "Hudsucker Proxy." Because Minneapolis was having its warmest, driest winter in 100 years, the Coens were forced to shoot most of the exteriors in wintery North Dakota. *CW:* Strong violence, language and sexuality. **97m/C VHS, LV, Closed Caption, DVD.** William H. Macy, Frances McDormand, Steve Buscemi, Peter Stormare, Harve Presnell, Steve Reevis, John Carroll Lynch, Kristin Rudrud, Steve Park; *Cameos:* Jose Feliciano; **D:** Joel Coen; **W:** Ethan Coen, Joel Coen; **C:** Roger Deakins; **M:** Carter Burwell. Academy Awards '96: Best Actress (McDormand), Best Original Screenplay; Australian Film Institute '96: Best Foreign Film; British Academy Awards '96: Best Director (Coen); Cannes Film Festival '96: Best Director (Coen); Independent Spirit Awards '97: Best Actor (Macy), Best Actress (McDormand), Best Cinematography, Best Director (Coen), Best Film, Best Screenplay; National Board of Review Awards '96: Best Actress (McDormand), Best Director (Coen); New York Film Critics Awards '96: Best Film; Screen Actors Guild Award '96: Best Actress (McDormand); Writers Guild of America '96: Best Original Screenplay; Broadcast Film Critics Association Awards '96: Best Actress (McDormand), Best Film; Nominations: Academy Awards '96: Best Cinematography, Best Director (Coen), Best Film Editing, Best Picture, Best Supporting Actor (Macy); British Academy Awards '96: Best Actress (McDormand), Best Film, Best Original Screenplay; Cesar Awards '97: Best Foreign Film; Directors Guild of America Awards '96: Best Director (Coen); Golden Globe Awards '97: Best Actress—Musical/Comedy (McDormand), Best Director (Coen), Best Film—Musical/Comedy, Best Screenplay; MTV Movie Awards '97: Best On-Screen Duo (Peter Stormare/Steve Buscemi); Screen Actors Guild Award '96: Best Supporting Actor (Macy). *PGV*

Fargo Express ✹½ 1932 When the kid brother of Maynard's true love is falsely accused of robbing a stagecoach, Maynard works to clear his name. Routine stuff. **60m/B VHS, Beta.** Ken Maynard, Helen Mack, Paul Fix; **D:** Alan James. *NOS, VCN, DVT*

Farinelli ✹✹ *Farinelli the Castrato, Farinelli Il Castrato* 1994 (R) A movie to make men cringe. Floridly depicts the complex professional and personal ties of 18th-century opera composer Riccardo Broschi (Lo Verso) and his younger brother Carlo (Dionisi), a celebrated castrato singer under the stage name "Farinelli." In part, because of an early church prohibition against women singing in public, boys were castrated before puberty to preserve their pure soprano voices while vocal power and agility grew as they became men. Castrati were the rock stars of their day and Farinelli lived a flamboyant life before retiring to the Spanish court of Philip V. The castrato voice heard in the movie is an electronic mixture of counter-tenor Derek Lee Ragin and soprano Ewa Mallas Godlewska. French and Italian with subtitles. *CW:* Depiction of adult themes and sexuality. **110m/C VHS, LV.** *FR IT BE* Stefano Dionisi, Enrico Lo Verso, Jeroen Krabbe, Elsa Zylberstein, Caroline Cellier, Omero Antonutti, Jacques Boudet; **D:** Gerard Corbiau; **W:** Gerard Corbiau, Andree Corbiau, Marcel Beaulieu; **C:** Walther Vanden Ende; **M:** Christopher Rousset. Cesar Awards '95: Best Art Direction/Set Decoration, Best Sound; Golden Globe Awards '95: Best Foreign Film; Nominations: Academy Awards '94: Best Foreign Language Film. *COL*

Farmer & Chase ✹✹ 1996 (R) It's always nice to see an old pro like Gazzara but it's a shame it couldn't have been in something less predictable. Farmer's (Gazzara) a hold-up man who's been working with partner Ollie (Jones) for 20 years. But when Ollie's killed, Farmer, who wants to pull one last job before retiring, makes the mistake of teaming up with his pacifist son Chase (Field). And then Chase involves his new gal pal Hillary (Boyle) in on the scheme. Dumb move, dumb movie. *CW:* Violence, a scene of sexuality and pervasive strong language. **97m/C VHS.** Ben Gazzara, Todd Field, Lara Flynn Boyle, Steven Anthony Jones, Ron Kaell, David Booth; **D:** Michael Seitzman; **W:** Michael Seitzman; **C:** Michael Maley; **M:** Tony Saunders. *AVI*

The Farmer Takes a Wife ✹✹½ 1935 Henry Fonda's first film, recreating his stage role, as a mid-19th century farmer at odds with the Erie canal builders and struggling to court the woman he loves. Remade as a musical in 1953. **91m/B VHS.** Janet Gaynor, Henry Fonda, Charles Bickford, Slim Summerville, Jane Withers; **D:** Victor Fleming. *FXL*

The Farmer Takes a Wife ✹✹ 1953 Poor musical remake of the 1935 drama, about the trials of a struggling 1850s farmer and the Erie canal boat cook he loves. Contains no memorable music and Robertson can't compete with Henry Fonda's original role as the farmer. ♫We're in Business; On the Erie Canal; We're Doing it for the Natives in Jamaica; When I Close My Door; Today I Love Everybody; Somethin' Real Special; With The Sun Warm Upon Me; Can You Spell Schenectady?. **81m/C VHS, Beta, LV, Closed Caption.** Betty Grable, Dale Robertson, Thelma Ritter, John Carroll, Eddie Foy Jr.; **D:** Henry Levin. *FOX*

The Farmer's Daughter ✹✹✹ 1947 Young portrays Katrin Holmstrom, a Swedish farm girl who becomes a maid to Congressman Cotten and winds up running for office herself (not neglecting to find romance as well). The outspoken and multi-talented character charmed audiences and was the basis of a television series in the 1960s. **97m/B VHS, Beta.** Loretta Young, Joseph Cotten, Ethel Barrymore, Charles Bickford, Harry Davenport, Lex Barker, James Arness, Rose Hobart; **D:** H.C. Potter; **C:** Milton Krasner. Academy Awards '47: Best Actress (Young); Nominations: Academy Awards '47: Best Supporting Actor (Bickford). *FOX, BTV*

The Farmer's Other Daughter ✹✹ *Farm Girl* 1965 A rural comedy about Farmer Brown whose lovely daughter is eyed by all the farmhands. He also has to contend with dastardly Mr. Barksnapper who wants to take his farm away from him until one of his daughter's beaus comes to the rescue. **84m/C VHS.** Ernest Ashworth, Judy Pennebaker, Bill Michael; **D:** John Patrick Hayes. *COL*

The Farmer's Wife ♫♫½ 1928 Silent British comedy about a recently widowed farmer searching for a new wife. Meanwhile, his lovely housekeeper would be the perfect candidate. Based on Eden Philpott's play. **97m/B VHS.** Jameson Thomas, Lillian Hall-Davis, Gordon Harker; **D:** Alfred Hitchcock; **W:** Alfred Hitchcock. *REP, SNC, MLB*

Fashions of 1934 ✹✹ *Fashions* 1934 A typical, lightweight '30s musical with impressive choreography by Busby Berkeley. Powell plays a disreputable clothing designer who goes to Paris to steal the latest fashion designs and winds up costuming a musical and falls in love. ♫Spin a Little Web of Dreams; Broken Melody. **78m/B VHS, Beta.** Bette Davis, William Powell, Frank McHugh, Hugh Herbert, Reginald Owen, Busby Berkeley; **D:** William Dieterle. *VDM*

Fass Black ✹✹ 1977 (R) Yet another man against the mob flick straight out of Bartlett's familiar plot lines. Amidst gratuitous music and violence, a disco owner locks horns with the syndicate after they try to take over his place. There's a good reason disco is dead. **105m/C VHS.** John Poole, Jeanne Bell, Cal Wilson, Harold Nicholas, Nicholas Lewis; **D:** D'Urville Martin. *XVC*

The Fast and the Furious ✹✹ 1954 On the lam after being falsely charged with murder, Ireland picks up a fast car and a loose woman (or is it a loose car and a fast woman?) and makes a run for the border by entering the Pebble Beach race. **73m/B VHS.** John Ireland, Dorothy Malone, Bruce Carlisle, Iris Adrian; **D:** John Ireland, Edwards Sampson. *NOS*

Fast Break ✹✹½ 1979 (PG) New York deli clerk who is a compulsive basketball fan talks his way into a college coaching job. He takes a team of street players with him, with predictable results on and off the court. Kaplan's screen debut. **107m/C VHS, Beta.** Gabe Kaplan, Harold Sylvester, Randee Heller; **D:** Jack Smight; **M:** David Shire. *GKK*

Fast Bullets ✹½ 1944 Texas Rangers fight a gang of smugglers and rescue a kidnap victim in this typical western. **52m/B VHS, Beta.** Tom Tyler, Rex Lease. *NOS, VCN, DVT*

Fast, Cheap & Out of Control ✹✹✹½ 1997 (PG) Director Morris' use of odd camera angles, unusual editing, and dark humor increases with each outing but always seems to enhance interest in the subject matter rather than detract from it. While his previous films have focused on just one subject, this one features four: a wild-animal trainer, a topiary gardener, a scientist who creates robotic insects, and a man who studies mole rats. Through inter-cutting and the overlapping of the subjects (at times audio from one is played over the visuals of another), Morris gives the impression that they are all linked together. Old movie footage is used to add an unreal quality, and the score by Caleb Sampson of the Alloy Orchestra hypnotically completes the surrealism. This is the story of four obsessed men, but none as obsessed as director Morris himself, with his need to show that truth is stranger than fiction. **82m/C VHS, LV, Closed Caption.** **D:** Errol Morris; **C:** Robert Richardson; **M:** Caleb Sampson. National Board of Review Awards '97: Best Feature Documentary; New York Film Critics Awards '97: Best Feature Documentary; National Society of Film Critics Awards '97: Best Feature Documentary. *COL*

Fast Company ✹✹ 1978 The life story of champion race car driver Lonnie Johnson including women, money, and the drag racing sponsors. **90m/C VHS, Beta.** William Smith, John Saxon, Claudia Jennings, Nicholas Campbell, Don Francks; **D:** David Cronenberg; **M:** David Cronenberg. *AOV*

Fast Food ✹ 1989 A super-cheap, strangulated attempt at low comedy, wherein an entrepreneurial hamburger peddler invents a secret aphrodisiac sauce. Look for former porn-star Traci Lords. **90m/C VHS, Beta, LV.** Clark Brandon, Tracy Griffith, Randal Patrick, Traci Lords, Kevin McCarthy, Michael J. Pollard, Jim Varney; *D:* Michael A. Simpson; *W:* Clark Brandon.

Fast Forward 🎬½ **1984 (PG)** A group of eight teenagers from Ohio learn how to deal with success and failure when they enter a national dance contest in New York City. A break-dancing variation on the old show business chestnut. 🎵Fast Forward; How Do You Do; As Long As We Believe; Pretty Girl; Mystery; Curves; Showdown; Do You Want It Right Now?; Hardrock. **110m/C VHS, Beta, LV, Closed Caption.** John Scott Clough, Don Franklin, Tracy Silver, Cindy McGee; *D:* Sidney Poitier; *W:* Richard Wesley; *M:* Tom Bahler. *COL*

Fast Getaway 🎬🎬 **1991 (PG)** Chases scenes proliferate when a teen criminal mastermind plots bank heists for his outlaw father. Relatively painless adolescent action-comedy, cleverly acted, quickly forgotten. **91m/C VHS, Beta, LV, 8mm.** Corey Haim, Cynthia Rothrock, Leo Rossi, Ken Lerner, Marcia Strassman; *D:* Spiro Razatos. *COL*

Fast Getaway 2 🎬🎬½ **1994 (PG-13)** Ex-bank robber Nelson (Haim) has given up a life of crime to open a business with gal pal Patrice (Buxton) while waiting for his partner/dad Sam (Rossi) to get out of jail. Then Nelson gets set up by Lily (Rothrock) and finds himself trying to convince an FBI agent of his innocence. Innocuous. **90m/C VHS.** Corey Haim, Sarah Buxton, Leo Rossi, Cynthia Rothrock, Peter Paul Liapis; *D:* Oley Sassone; *W:* Mark Sevi; *M:* David Robbins. *ART*

Fast Gun 🎬½ **1993 (R)** Weapons-loving ex-CIA spook decides to take over a town—with your basic one lone hero to stop him. **90m/C VHS.** Richard Hill, Kaz Garas, Robert Dryer, Brenda Bakke, Cirio H. Santiago. *NHO*

Fast Kill 🎬 **1973** A terrorist plot begins to fall apart when the conspirators fight among themselves. **94m/C VHS, Beta.** Tom Adams, Susie Hampton, Michael Culver, Peter Halliday; *D:* Lindsay Shonteff. *GEM*

Fast Money 🎬½ **1983** Three pals can't resist the temptation of big bucks from flying drugs in from Mexico, but they find danger along the way. **92m/C VHS, Beta.** Sammy Allred, Sonny Carl Davis; *D:* Doug Holloway. *ART*

Fast Money 🎬🎬 **1996 (R)** Car thief Francesca Marsh (Butler) and journalist Jack Martin (McCoy) go on the lam from the mob (and everyone else) with a briefcase containing $2.7 million.*CW:* Violence and language. **93m/C VHS.** Yancy Butler, Matt McCoy, John Ashton, Trevor Goddard, Andy Romano, Carole Cook, Patrika Darbo; *D:* Alexander Wright; *W:* Alexander Wright; *C:* Thomas Jewett; *M:* Tony Riparetti. *ORI*

Fast Talking 🎬🎬 **1986** The story of a quick-talking, incorrigible, 15-year-old Australian boy's humorous though tragic criminal schemes. The young protagonist slides his way through a life marked by a degenerate home life, a brother who forces him to sell drugs, and a future that holds no promise. **93m/C VHS, Beta.** *AU* Steve Bisley, Tracey Mann, Dennis Moore, Rod Zuanic, Toni Allaylis, Chris Truswell; *D:* Ken Cameron; *W:* Ken Cameron. *NLC*

Fast Times at Ridgemont High 🎬🎬🎬 **1982 (R)** Teens at a Southern California high school revel in sex, drugs, and rock 'n' roll. A full complement of student types meet at the Mall—that great suburban microcosm percolating with angst-ridden teen trials—to contemplate losing their virginity, plot skipping homeroom, and move inexorably closer to the end of their adolescence. The talented young cast became household names: Sean Penn is most excellent as the California surfer dude who antagonizes teacher, Walston, aka "Aloha Mr. Hand." Based on the best-selling book by Cameron Crowe, it's one of the best of this genre. **91m/C VHS, Beta, LV.** Sean Penn, Jennifer Jason Leigh, Judge Reinhold, Robert Romanus, Brian Backer, Phoebe Cates, Ray Walston, Scott Thomson, Vincent Schiavelli, Amanda Wyss, Forest Whitaker, Kelli Maroney, Eric Stoltz, Pamela Springsteen,

James Russo, Martin Brest, Anthony Edwards; *D:* Amy Heckerling; *W:* Cameron Crowe. *USH*

Fast Walking 🎬🎬 **1982 (R)** A prison guard is offered 50 thousand dollars to help a militant black leader escape from jail, the same man his cousin has contracted to kill. **116m/C VHS, Beta.** James Woods, Kay Lenz, M. Emmet Walsh, Robert Hooks, Tim McIntire, Timothy Carey, Susan Tyrrell; *D:* James B. Harris. *FOX, HHE*

Faster Pussycat! Kill! Kill! 🎬🎬 **1966** It doesn't get any better than this! Three sexy go-go dancers get their after-work kicks by hot-rodding in the California desert. They soon find themselves enveloped in murder, kidnapping, lust and robbery after a particular race gets out of hand. Easily the most watchable, fun and funny production to spring from the mind of Russ Meyer. Those who haven't seen this cannot truly be called "cool." **83m/B VHS.** Tura Satana, Haji, Lori Williams, Susan Bernard, Stuart Lancaster, Paul Trinka, Dennis Busch, Ray Barlow, Mickey Foxx; *D:* Russ Meyer; *W:* Jack Moran, Russ Meyer. *RMF, FCT, TPV*

Fastest Guitar Alive 🎬½ **1968** Debut of the legendary Orbison is strictly for inveterate fans only. Rebel operative/crooner during the Civil War, whose rhythm is good but timing is bad, steals a Union gold supply, but the war ends before he makes it back to the land of Dixie. Seems that makes him a common thief. **88m/C VHS, Beta.** Roy Orbison, Sammy Jackson, Margaret Pierce, Joan Freeman; *D:* Michael Moore; *M:* Fred Karger. *MGM, MVD*

Fastest Gun Alive 🎬🎬🎬 **1956** Suspenseful western with ex-gunfighter Ford challenged to a showdown by Crawford. **89m/C VHS, Closed Caption.** Glenn Ford, Jeanne Crain, Broderick Crawford, Russ Tamblyn, Allyn Joslyn, Leif Erickson, John Dehner, Noah Beery Jr., J.M. Kerrigan, Rhys Williams; *D:* Russel Rouse; *W:* Russel Rouse, Frank D. Gilroy; *M:* Andre Previn. *MGM*

Fat and the Lean 🎬🎬🎬 **1961** An early short film from Roman Polanski that satirizes government tyranny and absurdity. **16m/C VHS, Beta.** *D:* Roman Polanski. *IHF, HMV, GVV*

Fat City 🎬🎬🎬½ **1972 (PG)** One of Huston's later triumphs, a seedy, street-level drama based on the Leonard Gardner novel about an aging alcoholic boxer trying to make a comeback and his young worshipful protege. Highly acclaimed. Tyrrell earned an Oscar nomination as the boxer's world-weary lover. **93m/C VHS, Beta.** Stacy Keach, Jeff Bridges, Susan Tyrrell, Candy Clark, Nicholas Colasanto; *D:* John Huston; *C:* Conrad Hall; *M:* Marvin Hamlisch. Nominations: Academy Awards '72: Best Supporting Actress (Tyrrell). *COL*

Fat Guy Goes Nutzoid woof! *Zeisters* **1986** A crude farce about an obese mental patient who escapes from the mental hospital and joins two teenagers on a wild trip to New York City. **85m/C VHS, Beta.** Tibor Feldman, Peter Linari, John MacKay, Joan Allen; *D:* John Golden. *TTV*

Fat Man and Little Boy 🎬🎬½ **1989 (PG-13)** A lavish, semi-fictional account of the creation of the first atomic bomb, and the tensions between J. Robert Oppenheimer and his military employer, Gen. Leslie Groves. Overlong but interesting. Cusack, whose character never existed, is especially worthwhile as an idealistic scientist. **127m/C VHS, LV, 8mm, Closed Caption.** Paul Newman, Dwight Schultz, Bonnie Bedelia, John Cusack, Laura Dern, John C. McGinley, Natasha Richardson, Ron Frazier; *D:* Roland Joffe; *W:* Bruce Robinson, Tony Garnett, Roland Joffe; *M:* Ennio Morricone. *PAR, FCT, HMV*

Fatal Attraction 🎬🎬 *Head On* **1980 (R)** Couple meet after an auto accident. They begin an affair which turns dark and bizarre. Fine cast doesn't get far with this peculiar premise, although every one tries hard. **90m/C VHS, Beta.** *CA* Sally Kellerman, Stephen Lack, John Huston, Lawrence Dane; *D:* Michael Grant. *VES*

Fatal Attraction 🎬🎬🎬 **1987 (R)** When a very married New York lawyer is seduced by a beautiful blonde associate, the one-night stand leads to terror as she continues to pursue the relationship. She begins to threaten his family and home with possessive, violent acts. An expertly made, manipulative thriller; one of the most hotly discussed films of the 1980s. A successful change of role for Close as the sexy, scorned, and deadly other woman. Also available in a special "director's series" edition, featuring Lyne's original, controversial ending. **120m/C VHS, Beta, LV, 8mm, Letterbox, Closed Caption.** Michael Douglas, Glenn Close, Anne Archer, Stuart Pankin, Ellen Hamilton-Latzen, Ellen Foley, Fred Gwynne, Meg Mundy, J.J. Johnston; *D:* Adrian Lyne; *W:* James Dearden; *C:* Howard Atherton; *M:* Maurice Jarre. Nominations: Academy Awards '87: Best Actress (Close), Best Adapted Screenplay, Best Director (Lyne), Best Film Editing, Best Picture, Best Supporting Actress (Archer). *PAR, FCT, CCB*

Fatal Beauty 🎬½ **1987 (R)** A female undercover cop in Los Angeles tracks down a drug dealer selling cocaine (from which the title is taken). Elliott is the mob bodyguard who helps her out. Violent and sensational, the film tries to capitalize on the success of "Beverly Hills Cop" and fails miserably. Goldberg is wasted in this effort and the picture tiptoes around the interracial romance aspects that are implied. **104m/C VHS, Beta, LV, Closed Caption.** Whoopi Goldberg, Sam Elliott, Ruben Blades, Harris Yulin, Richard "Cheech" Marin, Brad Dourif; *D:* Tom Holland; *M:* Harold Faltermeyer. *MGM*

Fatal Bond 🎬½ **1991 (R)** Blair plays a small-town hairdresser caught in an obsessive love affair with a drifter. When she suspects her boyfriend is committing a string of rape-murders, will she turn him in or protect him? Or is she next?*CW:* Language, violence, and sexuality. **89m/C VHS.** Linda Blair, Jerome Elhers, Stephen Leeder, Donal Gibson, Caz Lederman, Tao Gerbert, Penny Pederson, Joe Bugner; *D:* Vincent Monton; *W:* Phillip Avalon. *COL*

Fatal Charm 🎬🎬 **1992 (R)** There's a serial killer at work in a small town. So far six women have been raped and murdered. But cute-teen Valerie can't believe it when the townspeople accuse that sweet guy Adam, especially since he's the one boy Valerie is so very attracted to.*CW:* Violence and sexuality. **90m/C VHS, Closed Caption.** Christopher Atkins, Amanda Peterson, Mary Frann, James Remar, Andrew (Andy) Robinson, Peggy Lipton; *D:* Alan Smithee; *W:* Nicholas Niciphor.

Fatal Chase 🎬🎬 *Nowhere to Hide* **1977** Van Cleef is a U.S. Marshal assigned to protect ex-hitman Musante from his vengeful former employers. And you thought you didn't get along with your boss. Typical made-for-TV fodder written by Anhalt, who usually manages to be a trifle more entertaining. **78m/C VHS.** Lee Van Cleef, Tony Musante, Charles Robinson, Lelia Goldoni, Noel Fournier, Russell Johnson, Edward Anhalt; *D:* Jack Starrett; *W:* Edward Anhalt. *SIM*

Fatal Chase 🎬½ **1992** Police investigation Marcus Lee and undercover cop Robin investigate drug dealer Dion. Robin and fellow officer Cynthia apprehend Dion in Hong Kong and bring him back to face charges in the Philippines. But Dion escapes and the duo are forced to deal with local officer Philip in order to get Dion back. Dubbed into English. **96m/C VHS.** *HK* Robin Shou, Yukari Oshima, Waise Lee; *D:* Ki Yee Chik. *TAI*

Fatal Combat 🎬½ **1996 (R)** Reclusive billionaire Houston Armstrong (Fitzpatrick) privately broadcasts a program called "No Exit" that features combat-to-the-death. (Live on TV!) But Armstrong tends to run out of combatants so when he hears about John Stoneman (Wincott), a master martial artist, he has his minions kidnap him along with Stoneman's pupil, Jason (Demambro). Now, it's fight or die. **93m/C VHS, Closed Caption.** Jeff Wincott, Richard Fitzpatrick, Joe Demambro, Sven-Ole Thorsen; *D:* Damian Lee; *W:* Damian Lee, John Howard Lawson. *COL*

Fatal Confinement ♂♂½ 1964 Wrenching drama finds Crawford, having lived 15 years in seclusion with her young daughter, forced to sell her land to a giant corporation bent on expansion. Interesting also for the similarities to Crawford's real-life "Mommie Dearest" lifestyle. 70m/C VHS. GB Joan Crawford, Paul Burke, Charles Bickford; D: Robert Guest. FCT, MOV, TPV

Fatal Error ♂½ Outsider in Amsterdam; The Outsider; Grijpstra and de Gier 1983 Dutch police thriller about the investigation of a cop killing. Based on the mystery series by Janwillem van de Wetering. Dubbed. 85m/C VHS, Beta. NL Rutger Hauer, Rijk de Gooyer, Willeke Van Ammelrooy, Donald M. Jones; D: Wim Verstappen; M: Ennio Morricone. NO

Fatal Exposure ♂♂ 1990 The insatiably sanguinary Jack the Ripper lives on in the form of his great grandson, who avails himself of modern technology to capture those magic moments on videotape. Just goes to show home movies don't have to be bland. ?m/C VHS. Blake Bahner, Ena Henderson, Julie Austin, Dan Schmale, Renee Cline, Gary Wise, Joy Ovington. HHE

Fatal Exposure ♂♂ 1991 (PG-13) A divorcee on vacation with her young sons accidentally picks up the wrong snapshots at the developers'. It turns out she has her hands on some incriminating photos, and the subject will resort to anything, even murder, to keep her quiet. Originally made for television. 89m/C VHS, Beta, LV, Closed Caption. Mare Winningham, Nick Mancuso, Christopher McDonald, Geoffrey Blake, Christopher Pettiet; D: Alan Metzger. PAR

Fatal Fix ♂½ 198? A French film expose of urban heroin addiction. Music by the Pretenders. 90m/C VHS, Beta. FR Helmut Berger, Corinne Clery; D: Massimo Pirri. NO

Fatal Games ♂½ 1984 Young female athletes are mysteriously disappearing at the Falcon Academy of Athletics and a crazed killer is responsible. 88m/C VHS, Beta. Sally Kirkland, Lynn Banashek, Sean Masterson.

The Fatal Glass of Beer 1933 Fields' son returns to his home in the north woods after serving a jail term in this slapstick comedy short. 18m/B VHS, Beta. W.C. Fields, Rosemary Theby, George Chandler, Richard Cramer. CCB, GVV

The Fatal Hour ♂½ 1940 Karloff is enlisted to aid police in solving the murder of a detective. As Karloff is rounding up suspects, three more murders take place. Feeble. 68m/B VHS, Beta, 8mm. Boris Karloff, Marjorie Reynolds, Grant Withers, Charles Trowbridge, John Hamilton, Frank Puglia, Jason Robards Sr.; D: William Nigh. VYY, SNC

The Fatal Image ♂♂½ 1990 A mother and daughter on vacation in Paris inadvertently videotape an international mob hit, making them the target of ruthless assassins. Filmed on location in Paris. Made for television. 96m/C VHS. Michele Lee, Justine Bateman, Francois Dunoyer, Jean-Pierre Cassel, Sonia Petrovna; D: Thomas J. Wright. WOV

Fatal Images ♂ 1982 A camera mysteriously causes all the models who pose for it to die, prompting the photographer to investigate. 90m/C VHS, Beta. Lane Coyle; D: Dennis Devine.

Fatal Instinct ♂½ 1992 (R) A tough-guy cop trying to solve a murder instead finds himself a victim of sexual obsession in this erotic thriller. Also available in an unrated version. Not to be confused with (but doesn't everything sound familiar) "Basic Instinct." 93m/C VHS. Michael Madsen, Laura Johnson, Tony Hamilton; D: John Dirlam. NLC, COL

Fatal Instinct ♂♂ 1993 (PG-13) Spoof on erotic thrillers such as "Fatal Attraction" and "Basic Instinct." Suave Assante plays a guy with dual careers—he's both cop and attorney, defending the criminals he's arrested. Young plays a love-lorn psycho who's lost her panties. Plot is worth mentioning only in passing, since the point is to mercilessly skewer the entire film noir tradition. The gags occasionally hit deep-chuckle level, though for every good joke there's at least three

that misfire. Clemmons of "E Street Band" fame wanders around with sax for background music purposes, typical of the acute self-consciousness of the film. CW: Language, violence, and sexuality. 90m/C VHS, LV, Closed Caption. Armand Assante, Sean Young, Sherilyn Fenn, Kate Nelligan, Christopher McDonald, James Remar, Tony Randall; Cameos: Clarence Clemmons, Doc Severinsen; D: Carl Reiner; W: David O'Malley; M: Richard Gibbs. MGM

A Fatal Inversion ♂♂½ 1992 When 19-year-old Hodge inherits a remote English estate from his great-uncle, he invites best friend Northam to spend a carefree summer, after both have told their parents they're vacationing in Greece. The boys are soon joined by Todd, Ford, and Warnecke in an informal commune but several disasters cause them to break off all contact for 12 years—until the remains of two bodies are discovered on the grounds and a police investigation is started. Made for British TV; based on the psychological thriller by Ruth Rendell (writing as Barbara Vine). 150m/C VHS. GB Douglas Hodge, Jeremy Northam, Saira Todd, Julia Ford, Gordon Warnecke, Nicholas Woodeson, Peter Attard, Rachel Joyce, Nicholas Le Prevost, Ben Chaplin; D: Tim Fywell; W: Sandy Welch; C: Barry McCann; M: David Ferguson. FOX

Fatal Justice ♂ 199? Mars is a topnotch assassin who's been in the business too long and knows too much so the agency he works for decides to kill him off. They send young and beautiful professional Diana to do the job but will she be able to when she discovers Mars is actually her father? 90m/C VHS. Joe Estevez.

Fatal Mission ♂ 1989 (R) A Vietnam soldier captures a female Chinese guerilla and uses her as his hostage and guide through the jungle. 84m/C VHS, Beta, LV, Closed Caption. Peter Fonda, Mako, Tia Carrere, Ted Markland, Jim Mitchum; D: George Rowe; C: Phil Parmet. VTR

Fatal Passion ♂♂ 1994 Two sisters escape the city after an accidental murder but run straight into the middle of a sacrificial backwoods cult. 90m/C VHS. Lisa Hayland, Joe Pilato. SWI

Fatal Past ♂♂ 1994 (R) Bodyguard gets up close and personal with his client—who happens to be a mobster's mistress. As if this weren't trouble enough their pasts provide doom and gloom as well. CW: Language, violence, and strong sexuality. 85m/C VHS, Beta, Closed Caption. Costas Mandylor, Kaisa Figura; D: Clive Fleury; W: Richard Ryan. PAR

Fatal Pulse woof! 1988 Sorority girls are being killed off in grisly ways. Basic slasher/gore. 90m/C VHS, Beta. Michelle McCormick, Ken Roberts, Joe Phelan, Alex Courtney. CEL

Fatal Skies ♂ 1990 An evil schemer plots to dump toxic waste in a small town's water supply until a group of teens comes to the rescue. 88m/C VHS, Beta. Timothy Leary.

Fatal Vision ♂♂½ 1984 The television film version of Joe McGinniss' controversial book about the murder trial of Dr. Jeffrey MacDonald, the former Green Berets physician accused of murdering his whole family and blaming the killings on crazed hippies. McGinniss first believed MacDonald may have been innocent but his subsequent investigation, and his book, proved otherwise. The starring debut for Cole. MacDonald still protests his innocence. 192m/C VHS, Beta, LV. Gary Cole, Karl Malden, Eva Marie Saint, Andy Griffith, Barry Newman; D: David Greene. COL

Fatally Yours ♂♂ 1995 Real-estate agent Danny (Rossovich) decides to restore a long-vacant house where a mob massacre occurred in 1928. While in the house, he's "contacted" by the ghostly Sara (MacDonnell), whose husband and gangster father were among the dead. Sara tells him about a hidden treasure of jewels, which leads some present-day gangsters to take an interest in Danny's new property. 90m/C VHS. Rick Rossovich, George Lazenby, Roddy McDowall, Sage Stallone, Sarah MacDonnell; D: Tim Everitt; C: Tim Everitt. MNC

Fate ♂♂½ 1990 (PG-13) Sweet comedy. A young man plans his love-affair carefully, but his biggest problem is meeting the girl of his dreams. Cheerful acting from Lynn and Paul. Stylish and charming. 115m/C VHS. Cheryl Lynn, Stuart Paul, Kaye Ballard, Susannah York; D: Stuart Paul.

Father ♂♂♂ Apa 1967 After WWII, a Hungarian youth makes up stories about his dead father's heroism that enhance his own position. Eventually he becomes obsessed with the facts surrounding his father's death at the hands of the enemy, and learning the truth, lays the past to rest. In Hungarian with English subtitles. 96m/B VHS, Beta, LV. HU Andras Balint, Miklos Gabor; D: Istvan Szabo; W: Istvan Szabo. VYY, DVT, HEG

Father ♂♂ 1990 (PG-13) A woman receives an anonymous telephone call telling her to watch a television news program and learn the truth about her beloved father. What she sees is her father's face superimposed over that of a young Nazi soldier and an aging, unstable woman accusing her father of war crimes. The daughter fiercely believes her father to be a victim of mistaken identity but questions keep nagging at her. Very similiar in plot to "Music Box" and just as pedestrian in spite of some good performances. CW: Some language and thematic elements. 106m/C VHS. AU Max von Sydow, Carol Drinkwater, Julia Blake, Steve Jacobs; D: John Power. Australian Film Institute '90: Best Actor (von Sydow), Best Actress (Blake). MNC

Father and Scout ♂♂½ 1994 (PG) Would-be Eagle Scout Michael (Bonsall) has a problem when he takes his city-bred, whiny, basically incompetent, dad Spenser (Saget) on a camping trip. Made for TV. 92m/C VHS, LV, Closed Caption. Bob Saget, Brian Bonsall, Heidi Swedberg, Stuart Pankin, David Graf, Troy Evans; D: Richard Michaels; M: David Kitay. TTC

The Father Clements Story ♂♂½ 1987 The true story of a black priest in Chicago who battled the Roman Catholic hierarchy in order to adopt a troubled teenager. Made for television. 100m/C VHS. Louis Gossett Jr., Malcolm Jamal Warner, Carroll O'Connor, Leon Robinson, Rosetta LeNoire, Ron McClarty; D: Edwin Sherin. ART

Father Figure ♂½ 1980 When a divorced man attends his ex-wife's funeral, he discovers that he must take care of his estranged sons. Based on young adult writer Richard Peck's novel; a well-done made-for-television movie. 94m/C VHS, Beta. Hal Linden, Timothy Hutton, Cassie Yates, Martha Scott, Jeremy Licht; D: Jerry London; M: Billy Goldenberg. NO

Father Goose ♂♂½ 1964 During WWII, a liquor-loving plane-spotter stationed on a remote Pacific isle finds himself stuck with a group of French refugee schoolgirls and their teacher. Some predictable gags, romance, and heroism fill out the running time pleasantly. Scriptwriters Stone and Tarloff, who were competitors, not collaborators on the project, shared an Oscar. 116m/C VHS, Closed Caption. Cary Grant, Leslie Caron, Trevor Howard; D: Ralph Nelson; W: Peter Stone, Frank Tarloff; C: Charles B(ryant) Lang; M: Cy Coleman. Academy Awards '64: Best Story & Screenplay; Nominations: Academy Awards '64: Best Film Editing, Best Sound. REP

Father Hood ♂ 1993 (PG-13) Family drama has Swayze playing a small-time criminal whose daughter tracks him down after leaving the foster-care shelter where she and her brother are being abused. The family takes to the road, running from both the police and a journalist (Berry) who wants to expose the corrupt foster-care system. The children are obnoxious, Swayze is miscast, and the entire film is a misfire. CW: Thematic material/threatened kids. 94m/C VHS, LV, Closed Caption. Patrick Swayze, Halle Berry, Sabrina Lloyd, Brian Bonsall, Diane Ladd, Michael Ironside, Bob Gunton; D: Darrell Roodt; W: Scott Spencer. TOU

Father of the Bride 🎭🎭🎭½ 1950 A classic, quietly hilarious comedy about the tribulations of a father preparing for his only daughter's wedding. Tracy is suitably overwhelmed as the loving father and Taylor radiant as the bride. A warm vision of American family life, accompanied by the 1940 MGM short "Wedding Bells." Also available in a colorized version. Followed by "Father's Little Dividend" and later a television series. Remade in 1991. **106m/C VHS, Beta, LV, Closed Caption.** Spencer Tracy, Elizabeth Taylor, Joan Bennett, Billie Burke, Leo G. Carroll, Russ Tamblyn, Don Taylor, Moroni Olsen; *D:* Vincente Minnelli; *W:* Frances Goodrich, Albert Hackett; *C:* John Alton. Nominations: Academy Awards '50: Best Actor (Tracy), Best Picture, Best Screenplay. *MGM*

Father of the Bride 🎭🎭½ 1991 (PG) Remake of the 1950 comedy classic portrays one of the most overextravagant weddings in recent film history, but falls short of the original. Predictable plot and characters don't hide any surprises, but nothing detracts from the purpose of the film: to be a nice, charming movie. Martin is fine as the reluctant dad but Keaton is little more than window dressing as the bride's mom; Short is annoying as a pretentious wedding coordinator. Williams pulls off a nice film debut—and was almost immediately cast in a TV ad as a young-bride-to-be calling her dad long distance to tell him she's engaged. Adapted from a novel by Edward Streeter. **105m/C VHS, Beta, LV, Letterbox, Closed Caption.** Steve Martin, Diane Keaton, Kimberly Williams, Kieran Culkin, George Newbern, Martin Short, B.D. Wong, Peter Michael Goetz, Kate McGregor Stewart, Martha Gehman; *Cameos:* Eugene Levy; *D:* Charles Shyer; *W:* Charles Shyer, Nancy Meyers; *C:* John Lindley; *M:* Alan Silvestri. *TOU*

Father of the Bride Part II 🎭🎭½ 1995 (PG) Sweetly sentimental update of the 1951 film "Father's Little Dividend" finds George Banks (Martin) once again thrown for a loop—first by his beloved daughter Annie's (Williams) pregnancy and then by wife Nina's (the radiant Keaton) announcement that they are about to become parents themselves. George does deal very well with either situation but, aided by fey party planner Franck (Short), he manages to get through the predictable chaos. Martin's physical expressiveness and sly charm are a big plus. **106m/C VHS, LV, Closed Caption.** Steve Martin, Diane Keaton, Kimberly Williams, Martin Short, George Newbern, Kieran Culkin, Peter Michael Goetz, Kate McGregor Stewart, Eugene Levy, B.D. Wong, Jane Adams; *D:* Charles Shyer; *W:* Nancy Myers, Charles Shyer; *C:* William A. Fraker; *M:* Alan Silvestri. Nominations: Golden Globe Awards '96: Best Actor—Musical/Comedy (Martin). *TOU*

Father Was a Fullback 🎭🎭½ 1949 College football coach (MacMurray) has a losing team, problems with the administration and alumni, and two daughters with growing pains at home. Wife O'Hara supplies the sympathetic shoulder. **99m/B VHS.** Fred MacMurray, Maureen O'Hara, Betty Lynn, Rudy Vallee, Thelma Ritter, Natalie Wood, Jim Backus; *D:* John M. Stahl. *FCT*

Fatherland 🎭🎭½ 1994 It's 1964 and 20 years earlier Hitler has won WWII in this what-if TV movie. The Nazi leader is about to sign a historic alliance with the U.S. President in Berlin when a series of murders of high-ranking Third Reich officers begins. SS detective Xavier March (Hauer) investigates, along with visiting American journalist Charlie Maguire (Richardson), leading the two to the Gestapo coverup of the Holocaust. If the secret gets out it could ruin the summit, so guess who's in big danger? Intriguing premise but the thriller fails to sustain tension. Based on the novel by Robert Harris. Filmed in Prague, Czech Republic. **106m/C VHS, Closed Caption.** Rutger Hauer, Miranda Richardson, Peter Vaughan, Jean Marsh, Michael Kitchen, John Woodvine, John Shrapnel, Clare Higgins; *D:* Christopher Menaul; *W:* Stanley Weiser, Ron Hutchinson; *C:* Peter Sova; *M:* Gary Chang. *WAR*

Fathers and Sons 🎭½ 1992 (R) Max is a brooding, former bad-boy movie director living on the Jersey Shore. His wife's death causes him to rethink his life and deal with his drinking problem. He also tries to get to know his equally brooding teenage son, Ed. Turns out addiction may run in the family as Ed experiments with drugs. Ill-fitting subplot deals a serial killer stalking the community. Goldblum brings an uneasy gentleness to the father's role in an otherwise slow, talky, and obviously symbolic flick. *CW:* Language, some violence and drug content, and sensuality. **100m/C VHS, LV.** Jeff Goldblum, Rory Cochrane, Mitchell Marchand, Famke Janssen, Natasha Gregson Wagner, Ellen Greene, Samuel L. Jackson, Joie Lee, Rosanna Arquette, Michael Disend; *D:* Paul Mones; *W:* Paul Mones; *C:* Ron Fortunato; *M:* Mason Daring. *COL*

Father's Day 🎭🎭½ 1996 (PG-13) The comedy team of Williams and Crystal makes its feature film debut in this affable take on fatherhood. Freelance writer Putley (Williams) unites with attorney Lawrence (Crystal) to help their mutual ex-girlfriend Kinski search for her runaway son (she's led each man to believe he's the boy's father). Their quest leads to some inevitable sticky situations, but the erratic, adolescent Williams is wonderfully balanced by the calm, upstanding Crystal. Who needs a son when you have to deal with Williams? Together, they're fun to watch and almost make you forget the contrived plot. Almost. Remake of the 1984 French film "Les Comperes." *CW:* Some sex-related humor and drug references. **98m/C VHS.** Robin Williams, Billy Crystal, Nastassia Kinski, Julia Louis-Dreyfus, Charlie Hofheimer, Bruce Greenwood, Jared Harris; *D:* Ivan Reitman; *W:* Lowell Ganz, Babaloo Mandel; *C:* Stephen Burum; *M:* James Newton Howard. Nominations: Golden Raspberry Awards '97: Worst Supporting Actress (Louis-Dreyfus). *WAR*

Father's Little Dividend 🎭🎭🎭 1951 Tracy expects a little peace and quiet now that he's successfully married off Taylor in this charming sequel to "Father of the Bride." However, he's quickly disillusioned by the news he'll soon be a grandfather—a prospect that causes nothing but dismay. Reunited the stars, director, writers, and producer from the successful first film. **82m/B VHS, Beta, LV.** Spencer Tracy, Joan Bennett, Elizabeth Taylor, Don Taylor, Billie Burke, Russ Tamblyn, Moroni Olsen; *D:* Vincente Minnelli; *W:* Frances Goodrich, Albert Hackett. *CNG, MRV, NOS*

A Father's Revenge 🎭🎭½ 1988 (R) Dennehy is the only reason to bother with this average hostage drama. He's the father of a stewardess who's one of a group being held by terrorists. They're scheduled to die in 72 hours unless Dennehy can find a way to rescue them. Made for television. *CW:* Terrorist violence. **93m/C VHS, LV.** Brian Dennehy, Joanna Cassidy, Ron Silver; *D:* John Herzfeld; *M:* Klaus Doldinger. *THV*

Fatso 🎭½ 1980 (PG) After the shocking death of his obese cousin, an obsessive overeater struggles to overcome his neurosis with the aid of his sister and a self-help group called "Chubby Checkers." Bancroft's first work as both writer and director. **93m/C VHS, Beta, Closed Caption.** Dom DeLuise, Anne Bancroft, Ron Carey, Candice Azzara; *D:* Anne Bancroft; *W:* Anne Bancroft. *FOX*

Fatty and Mabel Adrift/Mabel, Fatty and the Law 1916 Fatty and Mabel have problems enjoying their wedded bliss in these two silent shorts, which have a newly recorded orchestral score on the soundtrack. **40m/B VHS, Beta.** Fatty Arbuckle, Mabel Normand, Al "Fuzzy" St. John, Minta Durfee. *CCB, GVV*

Fatty Finn 🎭½ 1984 A children's gagfest about young kids and bullies during the Depression, based on Syd Nicholls' comic strip. **91m/C VHS, Beta.** *AU* Ben Oxenbould, Bart Newton; *D:* Maurice Murphy. *NO*

Faust 🎭🎭🎭½ 1926 The classic German silent based upon the legend of Faust, who sells his soul to the devil in exchange for youth. Based on Goethe's poem, and directed by Murnau as a classic example of Germanic expressionism. Remade as "All That Money Can Buy" in 1941. **117m/B VHS, Beta.** *GE* Emil Jannings, Warner Fuetterer, Gosta Ekman, Camilla Horn; *D:* F.W. Murnau. *GPV, MRV, NOS*

The Favor 🎭🎭½ 1992 (R) Lighthearted romance rife with comic confusion, vivid fantasies, secrets, and the all-important favor. Kathy (Kozak) seeks to relieve the boredom of her marriage through best friend Emily's (McGovern) tryst with Kathy's old beau, Tom. Or so she thinks, until Em spills all the juicy details. In a change of pace, the males take a back seat to the women. Good comic performances from Kozak and McGovern and witty dialogue help overcome the plot's sheer silliness. Damian Elwes (actor Cary's brother) provided Pitt's paintings. Theatrical release was delayed three years due to financial crisis at Orion Pictures. *CW:* Adult situations. **97m/C VHS, LV, Closed Caption.** Harley Jane Kozak, Elizabeth McGovern, Bill Pullman, Brad Pitt, Ken Wahl, Larry Miller, Holland Taylor; *D:* Donald Petrie; *W:* Josann McGibbon, Sara Parriott; *M:* Thomas Newman. *ORI*

The Favor, the Watch, & the Very Big Fish 🎭🎭 1992 (R) Set in a fairytale version of Paris. Hoskins is a photographer of religious subjects searching for a man to pose as Jesus. He discovers his subject in the hirsute Goldblum, a mad bar pianist who actually thinks he's the savior. Richardson plays the object of Hoskin's shy affections, an actress who does dubbing work by providing the moaning and groaning for porno flicks. Messy attempt at screwball-comedy with some brief humorous moments. *CW:* Language and sensuality. **89m/C VHS, LV, Closed Caption.** *GB FR* Bob Hoskins, Jeff Goldblum, Natasha Richardson, Michel Blanc, Jacques Villeret, Angela Pleasence, Jean-Pierre Cassel, Bruce Altman; *D:* Ben Lewin; *W:* Ben Lewin; *M:* Vladimir Cosma. *THV, FCT*

The Favorite Son 🎭🎭🎭 *Le Fils Prefere* 1994 Troubled family history is examined between three adult French brothers and their Italian immigrant father. A dutiful son, hotel manager Jean-Paul (Lanvin) regularly visits elderly father Raphael (Herlitzka). But Jean-Paul has problems. Desperate for cash to pay his loan shark, he approaches estranged younger brother Philippe (Barr), a wealthy lawyer, who is loath to help, while older schoolteacher brother Francis (Giraudeau) has little spare cash. Jean-Paul decides to take out a life insurance policy on dad—who promptly disappears—leaving the brothers to reluctantly come to terms in order to find him. French with subtitles. **100m/C VHS.** *FR* Gerard Lanvin, Jean-Marc Barr, Bernard Giraudeau, Roberto Herlitzka, Margherita Buy; *D:* Nicole Garcia; *W:* Nicole Garcia; *C:* Eric Gautier; *M:* Philippe Sarde. Cesar Awards '95: Best Actor (Lanvin); Nominations: Cesar Awards '95: Best Director (Garcia), Best Film. *NYR*

Fawlty Towers 1977 Cleese stars as the most obnoxious and inept hotel proprietor on earth in these three comedy episodes from the BBC series: "A Touch of Class," "Hotel Inspectors," and "The Germans," (which features Cleese's extraordinary goose-stepping). Additional episodes available. **90m/C VHS, Closed Caption.** *GB* John Cleese, Prunella Scales, Connie Booth, Andrew Sachs; *W:* John Cleese, Connie Booth. *FOX, MOV, SIG*

FBI Girl 🎭🎭 1952 An FBI clerk is used as bait to trap a murderer and break up a gang. Burr, pre-Perry Mason, plays a bad guy. **74m/B VHS, Beta, LV.** Cesar Romero, George Brent, Audrey Totter, Raymond Burr, Tom Drake; *D:* William (Lester Williams) Berke. *RXM*

The FBI Story 🎭🎭🎭 1959 Mr. Stewart goes to Washington in this anatomy of the Federal Bureau of Investigation. If you're a fan of the gangster genre (LeRoy earlier directed "Little Caesar"), and not especially persnickety about fidelity to the facts, this actioner offers a pseudo-factual (read fictional) glimpse—based on actual cases from the 1920s through the 1950s—into the life of a fictitious agent-family man. **149m/C VHS, LV, Closed Caption.** James Stewart, Vera Miles, Nick Adams, Murray Hamilton, Larry Pennell; *D:* Mervyn LeRoy; *C:* Joseph Biroc; *M:* Max Steiner. WAR, FCT, CCB

Fear 🎬🎬 **1946** An impoverished medical student murders the professor he believes is tormenting him and his life suddenly gets better. He falls in love and gets a scholarship but the police are closing in on his crime. Except...did any of it really happen? Or is he suffering from hallucinations. Low-budget psycho-drama with some good paranoid moments. **68m/B VHS.** Peter Cookson, Warren William, Anne Gwynne, James B. Cardwell, Nestor Paiva; *D:* Alfred Zeisler. VES

Fear 🎬 **1988 (R)** A vacationing family is plagued by a murderous Vietnam vet and other psychotic cons. **96m/C VHS, Beta, LV.** Frank Stallone, Cliff DeYoung, Kay Lenz, Robert Factor; *D:* Robert A. Ferretti. NO

Fear 🎬🎬½ **1990 (R)** A young psychic (Sheedy) delves into the minds of serial killers and writes novels about her experiences. But what happens when the next killer is also a psychic and decides to play mind-games with her? Above average suspense sustains this made-for-cable thriller. **98m/C VHS.** Ally Sheedy, Lauren Hutton, Michael O'Keefe, Stan Shaw, Dina Merrill, John Agar, Marta DuBois; *D:* Rockne S. O'Bannon; *M:* Henry Mancini. VES

The Fear 🎬½ **1994 (R)** Student psychologist (Bowz) takes a group to a remote cabin to explore their fears as part of his research project. Then, they begin to die horribly and gradually figure out that the cabin's wooden mascot, Morty (Weiss), is coming to life and doing them in. *CW:* Strong sexuality and language; some terror and violence. **98m/C VHS.** Eddie Bowz, Darin Heames, Anna Karin, Leland Hayward, Monique Mannen, Heather Medway, Antonia Todd, Erick Weiss, Vince Edwards, Ann Turkel; *Cameos:* Wes Craven; *D:* Vincent Robert; *W:* Ron Ford; *C:* Bernd Heinl; *M:* Robert O. Ragland. APX

Fear 🎬½ *No Fear* **1996 (R)** Wahlberg (the former Marky Mark) is a parents' worse nightmare: the violent, obsessed boyfriend of a 16-year-old girl (Witherspoon) as "Fatal Attraction" goes to the prom. Some cleverness, but ultimately follows a familiar, cliched path littered with one-dimensional characters and predictable plot twists. Gory, unconvincing climax kills any credibility that was left. The one standout is Petersen as the girl's protective father. *CW:* Profanity, violence and sexual situations. **96m/C VHS, LV, Letterbox, Closed Caption.** Reese Witherspoon, Mark Wahlberg, William L. Petersen, Amy Brenneman, Alyssa Milano, Tracy Fraim, Christopher Gray, Todd Caldecott; *D:* James Foley; *W:* Christopher Crowe; *C:* Thomas Kloss; *M:* Carter Burwell. MTV Movie Awards '97: Best Song ("Machinehead"); Nominations: MTV Movie Awards '97: Best Villain (Wahlberg). USH

Fear and Loathing in Las Vegas 🎬🎬 **1998 (R)** Hunter S. Thompson's 1971 cult memoir arrives on the big screen about 20 years too late to have any meaning or much entertainment value. Director Gilliam, never one to shy away from weirdness, overdoes everything in trying to capture the wretched excess of the book. Thompson's screen alter-ego Duke (Depp) packs his Caddy with illicit drugs and his equally wasted lawyer (Del Toro), and heads for his next writing assignment—to cover a drug enforcement conference in Vegas. Depp does a great job of impersonating the completely wasted and unlikable Thompson, while Del Toro passes out and pukes a lot in the sidekick role. It's most definitely a one-of-a-kind trip, but not one that most people will be willing to take. *CW:* Pervasive extreme drug use and related bizarre behavior, strong language, and brief nudity. **119m/C VHS.** Johnny Depp, Benicio Del Toro, Christina Ricci, Gary Busey, Craig Bierko, Ellen Barkin, Cameron Diaz, Flea, Mark Harmon, Katherine Helmond, Michael Jeter, Penn Jillette, Lyle Lovett, Tobey Maguire, Harry Dean Stanton, Tim Thomerson; *D:* Terry

Gilliam, *W:* Terry Gilliam, Alex Cox, Tony Grisoni, Tod Davies; *C:* Nicola Pecorini. NYR

Fear, Anxiety and Depression 🎬½ **1989 (R)** A neurotic aspiring playwright in New York has various problems with his love life. Sub-Woody Allen comedy attempt, with a few bright spots. The dregs of New York, with all the violence and degradation, are brought to the screen here. **84m/C VHS, Beta, Closed Caption.** Todd Solondz, Stanley Tucci; *D:* Todd Solondz; *W:* Todd Solondz. NO

The Fear Chamber WOOF! *Torture Zone; Chamber of Fear; La Camara del Terror; Torture Chamber* **1968** Hardly a Karloff vehicle. Boris shot the footage for this and three other Mexican "horror" films in LA, an unfortunate swan song to his career, though he was fortunate to be quickly written out of this story. The near plot concerns a mutant rock that thrives on human fear. Doctor Karloff and his assistants make sure the rock is rolling in sacrificial victims (women, of course). A prodigious devaluation of the "B"-grade horror flick, it's so bad it's just bad. **88m/C VHS.** MX Boris Karloff, Yerye Beirut, Julissa, Carlos East, Sandra Chavez, Eva Muller, Pamela Rosas, Santanon, Isela Vega; *D:* Juan Ibanez, Jack Hill; *W:* Jack Hill, Luis Enrique Vergara; *C:* Austin McKinney, Raul Dominguez. SNC, MPI

Fear City 🎬½ **1985 (R)** Two partners who own a talent agency are after the psychopath who is killing off their prized strippers with the aid of a local cop. Sleazy look at Manhattan low life. **93m/C VHS, Beta, LV.** Billy Dee Williams, Tom Berenger, Jack Scalia, Melanie Griffith, Rae Dawn Chong, Joe Santos, Maria Conchita Alonso, Rossano Brazzi; *D:* Abel Ferrara; *W:* Nicholas St. John. NO

Fear in the City 🎬 **1981** The Sicilian Mafia and a black crime gang battle for control of the streets. **90m/C VHS, Beta.** IT Michael Constantine, Fred Williamson, Gianni Manera; *D:* Gianni Manera. NO

Fear in the Night 🎬🎬🎬 **1947** Suspenseful tale of a murder committed by a man under hypnosis. Fearing his nightmares are real Kelley talks his detective friend into investigating his "crime," which leads them to a mansion, a mirrored room, and a plot that takes some clever and unexpected twists. Remade in 1956 as "Nightmare." **72m/B VHS.** Paul Kelly, DeForest Kelley, Ann Doran, Kay Scott, Robert Emmett Keane; *D:* Maxwell Shane. SNC

The Fear Inside 🎬🎬½ **1992 (R)** Lahti plays a woman suffering from agoraphobia who, because of her fear, has not left her home in more than a year. To help out, Lahti invites a seemingly charming college student to live with her. When the young woman's equally charming "brother" comes to visit, Lahti discovers the two aren't so charming after all. A standard woman-in-terror film with a better-than-average cast. Made for cable television. *CW:* Language, violence, and sexuality. **100m/C VHS, Beta, LV, Closed Caption.** Christine Lahti, Jennifer Rubin, Dylan McDermott, David Ackroyd, Thomas Ian Nicholas, Paul Linke, Leon Ichaso; *D:* Leon Ichaso; *W:* David Birke; *C:* Bojan Bazelli. FXV, VTR

Fear No Evil 🎬🎬 **1980 (R)** A teenager who is the human embodiment of the demon Lucifer commits acts of demonic murder and destruction. His powers are challenged by an 18-year-old girl, who is the embodiment of the archangel Gabriel. First feature from La Loggia is better than it sounds. **90m/C VHS, Beta.** Stefan Arngrim, Kathleen Rowe McAllen, Elizabeth Hoffman; *D:* Frank Laloggia; *W:* Frank Laloggia. COL

Fear of a Black Hat 🎬🎬 **1994 (R)** Think "Spinal Tap" as gangsta rap and you've the plot of this good-natured imitator. The dim-witted Ice Cold (Cundilieff), Tone-Def (Lawrence), and Tasty-Taste (Scott), the trio known as NWH (Niggaz With Hats), are touring in support of their album and trying to convince filmmaker Nina Blackburn (Lemmons) of their street credibility. Like Taps metalheads, the more they explain themselves, the less sense they make. *CW:* Considerable profanity; comic violence; nudity. **87m/C VHS,**

Closed Caption. Larry B. Scott, Mark Christopher Lawrence, Rusty Cundieff, Kasi Lemmons, Rusty Cundieff; *D:* Rusty Cundieff; *W:* Rusty Cundieff; *C:* John L. Demps Jr. FXV

Fear Strikes Out 🎬🎬🎬 **1957** Perkins plays Jimmy Piersall, star outfielder for the Boston Red Sox, and Malden, his demanding father, in the true story of the baseball star's battle for sanity. One of Perkins' best screen performances. **100m/B VHS, Beta, LV, Closed Caption.** Anthony Perkins, Karl Malden, Norma Moore, Adam Williams, Perry Wilson; *D:* Robert Mulligan; *W:* Raphael David Blau; *M:* Elmer Bernstein. PAR

Fearless 🎬 **1978** An Italian detective has found a Viennese banker's daughter, but continues to pursue the unanswered questions of the case, embroiling himself in a web of intrigue and plotting. **89m/C VHS, Beta.** Joan Collins, Maurizio Merli, Franz Antel.

Fearless 🎬🎬🎬 **1993 (R)** Two plane crash survivors reach out to each other as they try and cope with everday life. Bridges is riveting as the transformed Max, and Perez compelling as the sorrowful Carla. Hulce provides dead-on amusement as a casualty lawyer who knows he's slime but can't help himself. Opening sequences of smoke in the corn fields are haunting as are flashbacks of the crash itself. Weir provides an engrossing look at facing death, both psychological and spiritual, but the ending is something of a letdown in its sappiness. Based on the novel by Yglesias. *CW:* Language and airplane crash realism. **122m/C VHS, Beta, LV, Letterbox, Closed Caption.** Jeff Bridges, Isabella Rossellini, Rosie Perez, Tom Hulce, John Turturro, Benicio Del Toro, Deirdre O'Connell, John de Lancie; *D:* Peter Weir; *W:* Rafael Yglesias; *C:* Allen Daviau; *M:* Maurice Jarre. Los Angeles Film Critics Association Awards '93: Best Supporting Actress (Perez); Nominations: Academy Awards '93: Best Supporting Actress (Perez); Golden Globe Awards '94: Best Supporting Actress (Perez). WAR

Fearless Tiger 🎬½ **1994 (R)** Martial arts action flick includes the usual combination of fierce swordplay, hand-to-hand showdowns, and the intrigue of exotic locations. *CW:* Language and martial arts violence; drug content. **?m/C VHS, LV, Closed Caption.** Bolo Yeung, Monika Schnarre, Jamie Farr, Jalal Merhi; *D:* Ron Hulme; *W:* Ron Hulme; *M:* Varouje. IMP

The Fearless Vampire Killers 🎬🎬🎬 *Pardon Me, Your Teeth Are in My Neck; Dance of the Vampires* **1967** Underrated, off-the-beat and deliberately campy spoof of vampire films in which Tate is kidnapped by some fangy villains. Vampire trackers MacGowran and Polanski pursue the villains to the haunted castle and attempt the rescue. Only vampire movie with a Jewish bloodsucker ("Boy, have you got the wrong vampire," he proclaims to a maiden thrusting a crucifix at him). Inside the castle, Polanski is chased by the count's gay vampire son. Highlight is the vampire ball with a wonderful mirror scene. Many other amusing moments. **98m/C VHS, Beta, LV, Letterbox.** GB Jack MacGowran, Roman Polanski, Alfie Bass, Jessie Robbins, Sharon Tate, Ferdinand "Ferdy" Mayne, Iain Quarrier, Terry Downes, Fiona Lewis, Ronald Lacey; *D:* Roman Polanski; *W:* Gerard Brach, Roman Polanski; *C:* Douglas Slocombe. MGM

Fearmaker *House of Fear; Violent Rage* **1989 (PG)** After the mysterious death of her father, the heiress to his fortune is tangled in a web of treachery created by other potential inheritors. **90m/C VHS, Beta.** MX Katy Jurado, Paul Picerni, Sonia Amelio, Carlos East; *D:* Anthony Carras.

Feast for the Devil 🎬½ **197?** A woman searches for her missing sister in a mysterious coastal village, only to fall under the occult spell of a mad doctor. **90m/C VHS, Beta.** Krista Nell, Teresa Gimpera. NO

Feast of July 🎬🎬 **1995 (R)** Victorian-era drama, adapted from an H. E. Bates novel, has young Bella (Vidtz) pregnant and abandoned by super-cad Arch (Wise) whom she sets out to find. After a miscarriage, she is taken in by the

Wainwright family where she becomes the object of the affections of the three grown sons. Predictably, she falls for and weds the troubled loafer, Con (Chaplin). Naturally (this being Victorian England) tragedy results. Well-crafted, a given considering the producers, but ultimately a familiar telling of an average story. Feature film debut for director Menaul, after an award-winning career in British television.**CW:** Brief violence and sexuality; childbirth scene. 116m/C VHS, LV, **Closed Caption.** Embeth Davidtz, Ben Chaplin, Tom Bell, Gemma Jones, James Purefoy, Kenneth Anderson, Greg Wise; **D:** Christopher Menaul; **W:** Christopher Neame; **C:** Peter Sova; **M:** Zbigniew Preisner. *TOU*

Federal Agent 🎬🎬 1936 Lots of cliches fill this crime film about a federal agent chasing foreign spys who are looking for a new explosive. 53m/B VHS, Beta. William Boyd, Charles A. Browne, Irene Ware, George Cooper, Lentia Lace, Dan Alvarado; **D:** Sam Newfield. *GPV*

Federal Agents vs. Underworld, Inc. *Golden Hands of Kurigal* 1949 Super G-Man Dave Worth goes up against Nila, a greedy villainess bent on finding the golden hands of Kurigal so she may rule the world. A 12-episode serial edited onto two cassettes. 167m/B VHS. Kirk Alyn, Rosemary La Planche, Roy Barcroft, Carol Forman, James Dale, Bruce Edwards; **D:** Fred Brannon. *REP, MLB*

Federal Hill 🎬🎬 1994 (R) Familiar plot and characters are still well-handled by cast and first time writer/director Corrente. Federal Hill is a working-class, Little Italy section of Providence, Rhode Island. Five buddies, mostly losers, hang out together at a weekly card game. Nicky's (De Sando) a small-time dealer who meets his uptown Brown University sweetie, Wendy (Langdon), when he sells her cocaine. His friends try to warn him, especially short-fused burglar Ralphie (Turturro). And, of course, things go very wrong for practically everyone. The video is available colorized or in the director's version in B&W.**CW:** Strong language; some sexuality and drug content. 100m/B VHS, LV, **Closed Caption.** Anthony De Sando, Nicholas Turturro, Libby Langdon, Michael Raynor, Jason Andrews, Frank Vincent, Robert Turano, Michael Corrente; **D:** Michael Corrente; **W:** Michael Corrente; **C:** Richard Crudo; **M:** Bob Held, David Bravo. Nominations: Independent Spirit Awards '95: Best Supporting Actor (Turturro). *THV*

Federal Operator 99 🎬🎬½ 1945 A fortune in stolen jewels, a chemical plant, and a priceless violin all figure in this 12 chapter serial. And it's up to Jerry Blake, Federal Operator 99, to save the day. Part of "The Cliffhanger Serials" series. 169m/B VHS. Marten Lamont, Helen Talbot, George Lewis. *REP, MOV*

Feds 🎬½ 1988 (PG-13) Two women enter the FBI Academy and take on the system's inherent sexism with feebly comic results. 82m/C VHS, Beta, LV, **Closed Caption.** Rebecca DeMornay, Mary Gross, Ken Marshall, Fred Dalton Thompson, Larry Cedar, James Luisi, Raymond Singer; **D:** Dan Goldberg; **W:** Dan Goldberg, Len Blum; **M:** Randy Edelman. *WAR*

Feel My Pulse 🎬🎬 1928 Silent comedy about a rich fanatic who leaves everything in his will to his young niece on the stipulation that she lead a germ-free life; when she reaches 21, she moves into the sanitarium she's inherited, not knowing it has become a base for prohibition-era rum runners. 86m/B VHS, Beta. Bebe Daniels, Richard Arlen, William Powell; **D:** Gregory La Cava. *VYY*

Feel the Motion 🎬 1986 A female auto-mechanic wants to make it big in the music biz. She sees her chance when she slips her demo tape onto a hit TV-music show. 98m/C VHS, Beta. Sissy Kelling, Frank Meyer-Brockman, Ingold Locke, Falco, Meat Loaf. *THV*

Feelin' Screwy 🎬 1990 A couple of misfit dweebs attempt to rid their town of the local drug dealer in order to impress a couple of babes in this limp coming-of-ager. 90m/C VHS. Quincy Reynolds, Larry Gamal, Darin McBride, Hassan Jamal, Marsha Carter, Brooks Morales, Anna Fuentes; **D:** Riffat A. Khan; **W:** Riffat A. Khan. *NO*

Feelin' Up woof! 1976 (R) A young man sells all his possessions to come to New York in search of erotic adventures. 84m/C VHS, Beta. Malcolm Groome, Kathleen Seward, Rhonda Hansome, Tony Collado, Charles Douglass; **D:** David Secter. *ART, VES*

Feeling Minnesota 🎬 1996 (R) A truly stupid movie about truly stupid, mostly nasty people. Petty criminal Jjaks (Reeves) shows up at sleazy older brother Sam's (D'Onofrio) wedding and promptly falls for beautiful-but-unhappy bride Freddie (Diaz), who's being forced into the marriage by local crime boss Red (Lindo). Manipulative Freddie easily convinces Jjaks to run away to Vegas with her but Sam isn't willing to let his bride go so easily. The only character who comes off with any dignity is the diner waitress played by Love. A very lame first effort from Baigelman. Title's from a Soundgarden song about "looking California and feeling Minnesota."**CW:** Violence, sexuality and language. 96m/C VHS, LV, **Closed Caption.** Keanu Reeves, Cameron Diaz, Vincent D'Onofrio, Delroy Lindo, Dan Akroyd, Courtney Love, Tuesday Weld, Levon Helm; **D:** Steven Baigelman; **C:** Walt Lloyd. *NLC*

Feet First 🎬🎬½ 1930 A shoe salesman puts on "upper crust" airs as he begins a shipboard romance with a girl who thinks he's wealthy. Lloyd's second sound film shows him grappling with technique and has scenes that recall highlights of his silent hits. 85m/B VHS, Beta. Harold Lloyd, Barbara Kent, Robert McWade; **D:** Clyde Bruckman. *TLF*

Feet Foremost 🎬½ 1985 A made-for-British-television horror story about an industrialist haunted by the spirit of a teenage girl. 60m/C VHS, Beta. *GB* Jeremy Kemp.

Felix the Cat: The Movie 🎬½ 1991 Classic cartoon creation Felix returns in a trite feature. The feline and his bag of tricks enter a dimension filled with He-Man/Mutant Ninja Turtles leftovers; new-age princess, comic reptiles, robots and a Darth Vader clone who's defeated with ridiculous ease. Strictly for undemanding kids. 83m/C VHS, Beta, **Closed Caption. D:** Tibor Hernadi; **V:** Chris Phillips, Alice Playten, Maureen O'Connell. *TOU, FCT*

Fellini Satyricon 🎬🎬🎬 *Satyricon* 1969 (R) Fellini's famous, garish, indulgent pastiche vision of ancient Rome, based on the novel "Satyricon" by Petronius, follows the adventures of two young men through the decadences of Nero's reign. Actually an exposition on the excesses of the 1960s, with the actors having little to do other than look good and react to any number of sexual situations. Crammed with excesses of every variety. In Italian with English subtitles. Also available on laserdisc with additional footage and letterboxing. 129m/C VHS, Beta, LV, Letterbox. *IT* Martin Potter, Capucine, Hiram Keller, Salvo Randone, Max Born; **D:** Federico Fellini; **W:** Federico Fellini; **C:** Giuseppe Rotunno; **M:** Nino Rota. Nominations: Academy Awards '70: Best Director (Fellini). *MGM, FCT, TVC*

Fellini's Roma 🎬🎬½ *Roma* 1972 (R) Fellini reviews his youth in this stream-of-consciousness homage to Rome and Italy. Best left for fervent Fellini fans. 128m/C VHS, Beta, LV, Letterbox. *FR IT* Peter Gonzales, Britta Barnes, Pia de Doses, Fiona Florence, Marne Maitland, Renato Giovannoli; **D:** Federico Fellini; **W:** Federico Fellini; **M:** Nino Rota; **V:** Federico Fellini. *MGM, FCT*

Fellow Traveler 🎬🎬🎬 1989 Two old friends, an actor and a screenwriter, both successful, get blacklisted for reputed Communist leanings in 1950s Hollywood. Good performances and a literate script. Made for cable television. 97m/C VHS, Beta. Ron Silver, Hart Bochner, Daniel J. Travanti, Imogen Stubbs, Katherine Borowitz, Jonathan Hyde; **D:** Philip Saville; **M:** Colin Towns. *PAR*

Felony 🎬½ 1995 (R) Police seek revenge when 12 cops are murdered. Turns out the culprit is a rogue CIA agent, whose spree was captured on video by a tabloid-show cameraman.**CW:** Violence and some sexuality. 90m/C VHS, **Closed Caption.** Lance Henriksen, Leo Rossi, Joe Don Baker, Charles Napier, Ashley Laurence, Cory Everson; **D:** David A. Prior; **W:** David A. Prior; **M:** Jan A.P. Kaczmarek. *NLC*

Female 🎬🎬½ 1933 Feminist look at life in the '30s stars Chatterton as the wealthy president of an auto factory who wines and dines the office men and then gives them the strictly business line the next day. However, she finally meets her match when Brent walks through the door. (The two stars were a real-life married couple at the time.) Funny, role-reversal story directed by Curtiz of "Casablanca" fame. Based on a story by Donald Henderson Clark. 60m/B VHS, **Closed Caption.** Ruth Chatterton, George Brent, Philip Reed, Ruth Donnelly, Johnny Mack Brown, Lois Wilson, Gavin Gordon, Ferdinand Gottschalk; **D:** Michael Curtiz, William Dieterle; **W:** Gene Markey, Kathryn Scola. *MGM*

The Female Bunch woof! 1969 (R) The man-free world of an all-woman settlement is shattered by the arrival of a handsome stranger. Some of this garbage was filmed on location at the notorious Charles Manson ranch, and that's the least of its flaws. 86m/C VHS. Jennifer Bishop, Russ Tamblyn, Lon Chaney Jr., Nesa Renet, Geoffrey Land, Regina Carrol; **D:** Al Adamson, John Cardos. *SNC*

The Female Jungle 🎬 *The Hangover* 1956 Below-average whocares whodunnit directed by Roger Corman stock-company actor Ve Sota. Police sergeant Tierney is caught between a rock and a hard place. The prime suspect in a murder case, Tierney discovers a series of clues that implicate his friend Carradine. Interesting only for the screen debut of the nympho-typecast Miss Jayne—of whom Bette Davis said "Dramatic art in her opinion is knowing how to fill a sweater." 56m/B VHS. Lawrence Tierney, John Carradine, Jayne Mansfield, Burt Kaiser, Kathleen Crowley, James Kodl, Rex Thorson, Jack Hill; **D:** Bruno Ve Sota. *COL, FCT*

Female Perversions 🎬🎬 1996 (R) Psycho-sexual story of Los Angeles attorney Eve Stephens (Swinton), who, because of bizarre dreams and fantasies, leads a dual life. Successful Eve is being considered for appointment as a judge, but her enormous insecurity and neuroses only increase, landing her in kinky relationships with both sexes. During an unlikely reunion with her sister, Madelyn (Madigan), a kleptomaniac with a Ph.D., Eve is forced to spend time with Madelyn's motley roommates—her landlady and the landlady's odd daughter and sister. This semi-reunion brings about some self-realization on the part of both sisters about their dysfunctional behavior. Filled with detailed symbolism, powerful imagery, and dream sequences. Rife with Freudian psychology, movie is based on Louise J. Kaplan's feminist study on female behavior and sexuality, "Female Perversions: The Temptations of Emma Bovary." Extremely glossy visuals and rich production design brings life to this rather heavy story.**CW:** Intense depictions of psychoerotic themes, scenes of strong sexuality and strong language. 110m/C VHS, **Closed Caption.** Tilda Swinton, Amy Madigan, Karen Sillas, Laila Robins, Clancy Brown, Frances Fisher, Paulina Porizkova, Lisa Jane Persky, Dale Shuger; **D:** Susan Streitfeld; **W:** Susan Streitfeld, Julie Hebert; **C:** Teresa Medina; **M:** Debbie Wiseman. *THV*

Female Trouble 🎬🎬½ 1974 (R) Divine leads a troublesome existence in this $25,000 picture. She turns to a life of crime and decadence, seeking to live out her philosophy: "Crime is beauty." Look closely at the Divine rape scene where she plays both rapist and victim. Climax of her deviant ways comes with her unusual night club act, for which the law shows no mercy. Trashy, campy; for die-hard Waters fans. 95m/C VHS, Beta. Divine, David Lochary, Mary Vivian Pearce, Mink Stole, Edith Massey, Danny Mills, Cookie Mueller, Susan Walsh; **D:** John Waters; **W:** John Waters. *NO*

Femalien 🎬 1996 (R) Advanced alien beings, composed of pure light energy, travel to earth to assume corporal form so they can once again experience sexual pleasure.**CW:** Sexuality and nudity. **90m/C VHS, LV.** Vanessa Taylor, Jacqueline Lovell, Matt Schue; *D:* Cybil Richards; *W:* Cybil Richards. *AFE*

Femme Fatale 🐾🐾½ *Fatal Woman* 1990 (R) When a man's new bride disappears he teams up with an artist pal to track her down. Their search reveals her secret double life and takes them to L.A.'s avant-garde art scene—and deeper into deception and mystery. Billy Zane (Elijah) and Lisa Zane are brother and sister. *CW:* Language, violence, and sensuality. **96m/C VHS, LV, Closed Caption.** Colin Firth, Lisa Zane, Billy Zane, Scott Wilson, Lisa Blount; *D:* Andre Guttfreund; *W:* John Brancato. *REP*

Femme Fontaine: Killer Babe for the C.I.A. woof! 1995 (R) Beautiful assassin Drew "Killer Babe" Fontaine (Hope) gets help from CIA-agent-turned-monk Master Sun (Hong) in order to avenge her father's death. Fishnet-clad women with big guns are always a Troma treat. *CW:* Sexuality, violence, and language. **93m/C VHS.** Margot Hope, James Hong, Arthur Roberts, Catherine Dao, David Shark, Kevin Fry, Harry Mok; *D:* Margot Hope; *W:* Margot Hope; *C:* Gary Graver; *M:* Gardner Cole. *TTV*

Femmes de Paris 🐾🐾 1953 A funny and risque French musical comedy about the comings and goings of the cast of a naughty nightclub shows. In French with English subtitles. **79m/C VHS, Beta.** *FR* Robert Dhery, Collette Brosset, Louis de Funes. *VDM, TPV*

The Fence 🐾🐾½ 1994 Interesting presentation of standard bad boy grows up, attempts to go straight. Terry Griff (Wirth) has been bounced from juvenile detention to prison since he was 15. On the streets for the first time in 14 years, Terry wants to lead a clean life with potential girlfriend Jackie (Gimp). But when Terry gets on the wrong side of his dishonest parole officer, the harsh world of the streets pulls him back. Bleak urban drama with sincere performances. **90m/C VHS.** Billy Wirth, Erica Gimpel, Marc Alaimo, Paul Benjamin, Lorenzo Clemons; *D:* Peter Pistor; *W:* Peter Fedorenko; *M:* Jeff Beal. *TRI*

The Fencing Master 🐾🐾½ 1992 The fencing master is the aristocratic Don Jaime de Astarloa (Antonutti) who secretly takes on female pupil, Adela de Otero (Serna), with whom he begins to fall in love. But when another pupil is murdered by de Astarloa's signature thrust to the throat, Don Jaime finds himself caught up in a bewildering world of political intrigue. Adapted from the novel by Antonio Perez Reverte. Spanish with subtitles. **88m/C VHS.** *SP* Assumpta Serna, Omero Antonutti, Joaquim de Almeida; *D:* Pedro Olea; *W:* Pedro Olea; *C:* Alfredo Mayo. *NYF*

Fer-De-Lance 🐾½ *Operation Serpent* 1974 A stricken submarine is trapped at the bottom of the sea, with a nest of deadly snakes crawling through the ship. Made for television. **120m/C VHS, Beta.** David Janssen, Hope Lange, Ivan Dixon, Jason Evers; *D:* Russ Mayberry. *WOV*

Fergie & Andrew: Behind Palace Doors 🐾🐾 1993 More soap-opera from the British royals in this tale of feisty redhead, Sarah Ferguson, and the neglectful Prince Andrew. He's away a lot, she's bored by all the palace propriety and causes too many scandals, and their marriage falls apart. Made for television. **92m/C VHS, Beta, Closed Caption.** Pippa Hinchley, Sam Miller, Peter Cellier, Harold Innocent, Edita Brychta; *D:* Michael Switzer. *TTC*

Fernandel the Dressmaker 🐾🐾½ 1957 Fernandel dreams of designing exquisite dresses, but when the opportunity arises, he finds his cheating partners get in the way. In French with English subtitles. **95m/B VHS, Beta, 8mm.** *FR* Fernandel, Suzy Delair, Francoise Fabian, Georges Chamarat; *D:* Jean Boyer. *VYY, FCT*

Ferngully: The Last Rain Forest 🐾🐾½ 1992 (G) Animated eco-musical follows the adventures of independent-minded flying sprite Crysta, who lives in a rain forest beset by pollution. She discovers the outside world and becomes smitten with the human Zak, who is helping to cut down the forest. Crysta decides to reduce him to her size and show him the error of his ways. She's aided by fellow sprite, Pips, and a crazy bat (Batty Koda with a voice provided by the lively Williams). So-so script with politically pristine environmental message may grow tiresome for both adults and children, though decent animation and brilliant coloring enlivens the tale. **72m/C VHS.** *D:* Bill Kroyer; *W:* Jim Cox; *M:* Alan Silvestri; *V:* Samantha Mathis, Christian Slater, Robin Williams, Tim Curry, Jonathan Ward, Grace Zabriskie, Richard "Cheech" Marin, Thomas Chong, Tone Loc, Jim Cox. *FXV, MLT*

Ferocious Female Freedom Fighters 🐾 1988 A typical foreign-made action flick with female wrestlers is spoofed by the L.A. Connection comedy troupe which did the totally ridiculous dubbed dialog. **90m/C VHS, Beta, LV.** Eva Arnaz, Barry Prima. *IME*

Ferris Bueller's Day Off 🐾🐾🐾 1986 (PG-13) It's almost graduation and if Ferris can get away with just one more sick day—it had better be a good one. He sweet talks his best friend into borrowing his dad's antique Ferrari and sneaks his girlfriend out of school to spend a day in Chicago. Their escapades lead to fun, adventure, and almost getting caught. Broderick is charismatic as the notorious Bueller with Grey amusing as his tattle-tale sister doing everything she can to see him get caught. Early Sheen appearance as a juvenile delinquent who pesters Grey. Led to TV series. One of Hughes' more solid efforts. **103m/C VHS, Beta, LV, 8mm, Closed Caption.** Matthew Broderick, Mia Sara, Alan Ruck, Jeffrey Jones, Jennifer Grey, Cindy Pickett, Edie McClurg, Charlie Sheen, Del Close, Virginia Capers, Max Perlich, Louis Anderson, Richard Edson, Lyman Ward, Kristy Swanson, Larry "Flash" Jenkins, Ben Stein; *D:* John Hughes; *W:* John Hughes; *C:* Tak Fujimoto; *M:* Ira Newborn. *PAR, TLF*

Ferry to Hong Kong 🐾½ 1959 World-weary, heavy drinking traveler comes aboard the "Fat Annie," a ship skippered by the pompous Captain Hart. The two men clash, until an act of heroism brings them together. Embarrassingly hammy performance by Welles as the ferry skipper. **103m/C VHS, Beta.** Curt Jurgens, Orson Welles, Sylvia Syms; *D:* Lewis Gilbert.

The Feud 🐾🐾 1990 (R) Wacky comedy about the ultimate "family feud." The Bullards of Millville and the Bealers of Hornbeck engage in a battle of the witless, and no one in either town is safe. A silly, irreverent comedy of the slapstick variety. Based on a novel by Thomas Berger. **87m/C VHS.** Rene Auberjonois, Ron McLarty, Joe Grifasi, David Strathairn, Gale Mayron; *D:* Bill D'Elia; *W:* Bill D'Elia. *THV*

Feud Maker 🐾½ 1938 Steele rides to the rescue in this range war between the bad guys and the cowmen. Hackett plays a schemer who falsely befriends both sides, plotting to buy up cheap land when the participants have killed each other off. Based on a story by Harry F. Olmsted. **55m/B VHS.** Bob Steele, Marion Weldon, Karl Hackett, Frank Ball, Budd Buster, Lew Meehan, Roger Williams; *D:* Sam Newfield; *W:* George Plympton. *MOV*

Feud of the Trail 🐾 1937 A cowboy saves a range family's gold and falls in love with their daughter in the process. Tyler plays both the hero and the villain here. **56m/B VHS, Beta.** Tom Tyler, Harlin Wood, Guinn "Big Boy" Williams; *D:* Robert F. "Bob" Hill. *NOS, DVT*

Feud of the West 🐾½ 1935 Old West disagreements settled with guns in this outing for cowboy star Gibson, here portraying a rodeo performer. **60m/B VHS, Beta.** Hoot Gibson, Buzz Barton, Robert F. (Bob) Kortman, Edward Cassidy, Joan Barclay, Nelson McDowell, Reed Howes, Lew Meehan; *D:* Harry Fraser. *NOS, VCI, VCN*

Fever 🐾🐾🐾 1981 Controversial Polish film based on Andrzej Strug's novel "The Story of One Bomb." Focusing on a period in Polish history marked by anarchy, violence, resistance, and revolution, it was banned before it won eventual acclaim at the Gdansk Film Festival. In Polish with English subtitles. **115m/C VHS.** *PL D:* Agnieszka Holland. *FCT*

Fever 🐾 1988 (R) A once-honest cop trades his good life in for a shot at dealing drugs. Meanwhile, his wife's lover wants to murder him. **83m/C VHS, Beta, LV.** Bill Hunter, Gary Sweet, Mary Regan, Jim Holt; *D:* Craig Lahiff.

Fever 🐾🐾 1991 (R) An ex-con and a high-powered lawyer join forces to rescue the woman both of them love from a vicious killer. Made for cable television. Available in Spanish. *CW:* Language, violence and drug content, and sensuality. **99m/C VHS, Closed Caption.** Armand Assante, Sam Neill, Marcia Gay Harden, Joe Spano; *D:* Larry Elikann; *W:* Larry Brothers. *HBO*

Fever Mounts at El Pao 🐾🐾½ *Los Ambiciosos* 1959 A minor effort from director Bunuel about the regime of a dictator in an imaginary South American country. In Spanish with English subtitles. **97m/B VHS, Beta.** *MX* Gerard Philipe, Jean Servais; *D:* Luis Bunuel. *NOS, FCT, FST*

Fever Pitch woof! 1985 (R) Sordid story of a sports writer (O'Neal) who becomes addicted to gambling. Very poor script. **95m/C VHS, Beta, Closed Caption.** Ryan O'Neal, Catherine Hicks, Giancarlo Giannini, Bridgette Andersen, Chad Everett, John Saxon, William Smith, Patrick Cassidy, Chad McQueen; *D:* Richard Brooks; *W:* Richard Brooks; *M:* Thomas Dolby. *FOX*

A Few Good Men 🐾🐾🐾 1992 (R) Strong performances by Cruise and Nicholson carry this story of a peacetime military coverup. Cruise is a smart aleck Navy lawyer sleepwalking through his comfortable career in DC. He's ready to write off two soldiers pinned for the murder of their cohort until he interviews their commanding officer, Nicholson. Cruise smells a rat, but Nicholson practically dares him to prove it. Moore is another military lawyer assigned to the case, though her function seems to be holding Kaffee's hand (there's no actual romance between the two). Incredible fireworks between Cruise and Nicholson in the courtroom. Based on the play by Sorkin, who also wrote the screenplay. *CW:* Language. **138m/C VHS, Beta, LV, Letterbox, Closed Caption, DVD.** Tom Cruise, Jack Nicholson, Demi Moore, Kevin Bacon, Kevin Pollak, Kiefer Sutherland, James Marshall, J.T. Walsh, Christopher Guest, J.A. Preston, Matt Craven, Wolfgang Bodison, Xander Berkeley, Cuba Gooding Jr.; *D:* Rob Reiner; *W:* Aaron Sorkin; *C:* Robert Richardson; *M:* Marc Shaiman. MTV Movie Awards '93: Best Film; National Board of Review Awards '92: Best Supporting Actor (Nicholson); Nominations: Academy Awards '92: Best Film Editing, Best Picture, Best Sound, Best Supporting Actor (Nicholson). *COL, CRC, MOV*

A Few Moments with Buster Keaton and Laurel and Hardy 🐾🐾🐾 1963 Three short appearances: "The Tree in a Test Tube," a government film with Stan & Ollie about wood's role in the war effort; an episode of "The Ed Sullivan Show," with the duo, and a commercial for Simon Pure Beer featuring Keaton. **17m/B VHS, Beta, 8mm.** Stan Laurel, Oliver Hardy, Buster Keaton, Ed Sullivan, Pete Smith. *VYY*

ffolkes 🐾🐾 *Assault Force; North Sea Hijack* 1980 (PG) Rufus Excalibur Ffolkes is an eccentric underwater expert who is called upon to stop a madman (Perkins, indulging himself) from blowing up an oil rig in the North Sea. Entertaining farce with Moore playing the opposite of his usual suave James Bond character. **99m/C VHS, Beta.** Roger Moore, James Mason, Anthony Perkins, David Hedison, Michael Parks; *D:* Andrew V. McLaglen. *USH*

The Fiance 🐾🐾 1996 (R) Faith (Anthony) suspects husband Richard (Cassidy)of being unfaithful and confides her suspicions to the friendly Walter (Moses). Only the unbalanced guy then becomes unhealthily involved in Faith's life. *CW:* Sexual situations, language, violence. **94m/C VHS, Closed Caption.** William R. Moses, Lysette Anthony, Patrick Cassidy, Alina Thompson, Wanda Acuna, Gordon Thomson; *D:* Martin Kitrosser; *W:* Greg Walker, Frank Rehwaldt; *C:* M. David Mullen; *M:* Richard Bowers. *ART*

Fiances 🎬🎬 *The Engagement; I Fidanzati* **1963**
Young man from Milan takes a welding job in Sicily that will separate him from his fiancee for 18 months. He thinks the separation will be good for them but loneliness and the strange environment makes him long for her. Non-professional leads provide strength. Italian with subtitles. **84m/B VHS.** *IT* Carlo Carbrini, Anna Canzi; *D:* Ermanno Olmi; *W:* Ermanno Olmi; *C:* Lamberto Caimi; *M:* Gianni Ferrio. *FCT*

Fiction Makers 🎬🎬 **1967** Roger Moore stars as Simon Templar, also known as "The Saint," a sophisticated detective who is hired to help Amos Klein. Klein turns out to be an alias for a beautiful novelist who is being threatened by the underworld crime ring. Based on the Leslie Chateris' character. **102m/C VHS, Beta.** Roger Moore, Sylvia Syms. *FOX*

Fictitious Marriage 1988 Eldad Ilan, a high school teacher experiencing a mid-life crisis, travels to Israel to get away from his family in order to consider his life's direction. In Hebrew with English subtitles. **90m/C VHS.** Shlomo Bar-Aba, Irit Sheleg, Ofra Veingarten; *D:* Haim Bouzaglo. *ERG*

Fiddler on the Roof 🎬🎬🎬½ **1971 (G)** Based on the long-running Broadway musical. The poignant story of Tevye, a poor Jewish milkman, at the turn of the century in a small Ukrainian village, and his five dowry-less daughters, his lame horse, his wife, and his companionable relationship with God. Topol, an Israeli who played the role in London, is charming, if not quite as wonderful as Zero Mostel, the Broadway star. Finely detailed set decoration and choreography, strong performances from the entire cast create a sense of intimacy in spite of near epic proportions of the production. Play was based on the Yiddish stories of Tevye the Dairyman, written by Sholem Aleichem. 🎵 Tradition; Matchmaker, Matchmaker; If I Were a Rich Man; Sabbath Prayer; To Life; Miracle of Miracles; Tevye's Dream; Sunrise, Sunset; Wedding Celebration. **184m/C VHS, Beta, LV, Letterbox, Closed Caption.** Chaim Topol, Norma Crane, Leonard Frey, Molly Picon; *D:* Norman Jewison; *C:* Oswald Morris; *M:* John Williams. Academy Awards '71: Best Cinematography, Best Sound, Original Song Score and/or Adaptation; Golden Globe Awards '72: Best Actor—Musical/Comedy (Topol), Best Film—Musical/Comedy; Nominations: Academy Awards '71: Best Actor (Topol), Best Art Direction/Set Decoration, Best Director (Jewison), Best Picture, Best Supporting Actor (Frey). *FOX, MGM, TLF*

The Fiddlin' Buckaroo 🎬🎬½ **1933** Maynard plays a government agent who disguises himself as a musical ventriloquist to capture Kohler and his band of outlaws. Everybody sings a lot. **63m/B VHS.** Ken Maynard, Gloria Shea, Fred Kohler Sr., Frank Rice, Jack Mower, Charles "Slim" Whitaker, Robert F. (Bob) Kortman, Hank Bell, Jack Rockwell; *D:* Ken Maynard; *W:* Nate Gatzert. *GPV*

The Field 🎬🎬🎬½ **1990 (PG-13)** After an absence from the big screen, intense and nearly over the top Harris won acclaim as an iron-willed peasant fighting to retain a patch of Irish land he's tended all his life, now offered for sale to a wealthy American. His uncompromising stand divides the community in this glowing adaptation of John B. Keane's classic play, an allegory of Ireland's internal conflicts. **113m/C VHS, LV.** *GB* Richard Harris, Tom Berenger, John Hurt, Sean Bean, Brenda Fricker, Frances Tomelty, Sean McGinley, Jenny Conroy; *D:* Jim Sheridan; *W:* Jim Sheridan. Nominations: Academy Awards '90: Best Actor (Harris). *ART, TVC*

Field of Dreams 🎬🎬🎬½ **1989 (PG)** Uplifting mythic fantasy based on W.P. Kinsella's novel "Shoeless Joe." Iowa corn farmer heeds a mysterious voice that instructs "If you build it, he will come" and cuts a baseball diamond in his corn field. Soon the ball field is inhabited by the spirit of Joe Jackson and others who were disgraced in the notorious 1919 "Black Sox" baseball scandal. Jones, as a character based on reclusive author J.D. Salinger, is reluctantly pulled into the mystery. It's all about chasing a dream, maintaining innocence, finding redemption, reconciling the child with the adult, and celebrating the mythic lure of baseball. Costner and Madigan are strong, believable characters. **106m/C VHS, Beta, LV, Letterbox, Closed Caption, DVD.** Kevin Costner, Amy Madigan, James Earl Jones, Burt Lancaster, Ray Liotta, Timothy Busfield, Frank Whaley, Gaby Hoffman, Dwier Brown; *D:* Phil Alden Robinson; *W:* Phil Alden Robinson; *C:* John Lindley; *M:* James Horner. Nominations: Academy Awards '89: Best Adapted Screenplay, Best Picture, Best Original Score. *USH, FCT, HMV*

Field of Fire 🎬🎬 **1992 (R)** One of America's top military experts has been taken hostage and it's up to a top general to rescue him. But the rescue doesn't come off as planned and all must fight their way through the Cambodian jungle to safety. *CW:* Language, nudity, and war violence. **96m/C VHS, LV, Closed Caption.** David Carradine; *D:* Cirio H. Santiago; *W:* Thomas McKelvey Cleaver. *HBO*

Field of Honor 🎬🎬½ **1986 (R)** A look at the harrowing experience of jungle combat through the eyes of a Dutch infantryman in Korea. **93m/C VHS, Beta, LV.** Everett McGill, Ron Bradsteder, Hey Young Lee; *D:* Hans Scheepmaker. *MGM*

Field of Honor 🎬🎬½ *Champ d'Honneur* **1987 (PG)** A quiet French anti-war drama set during the Franco-Prussian war in 1869 in which a peasant boy volunteers to fight in place of a rich man's son. He is befriended behind enemy lines by a young boy and both try to avoid capture. In French with English subtitles. **87m/C VHS, Beta.** *FR* Cris Campion, Eric Wapler, Pascale Rocard, Frederic Mayer; *D:* Jean-Pierre Denis. Cesar Awards '88: Best Score. *ORI*

The Fiend 🎬 **1971 (R)** A religious cultist, already unbalanced, grabs a knife and starts hacking away Jack-the-Ripper style. **87m/C VHS.** *GB* Ann Todd, Patrick Magee, Tony Beckley, Madeline Hinde, Suzanna Leigh, Percy Herbert; *D:* Robert Hartford-Davis. *NO*

Fiend woof! **1983** Glowing supernatural thing flits around graveyard before animating dead guy who needs to kill in order to go on living. Murderous dead guy becomes a small-town music teacher feeding parasitically on his students to satisfy his supernatural hunger. His neighbor suspects some discord. Low-budget time waster. **93m/C VHS, Beta.** Don Leifert, Richard Nelson, Elaine White, George Stover; *D:* Donald M. Dohler.

Fiend Without a Face 🎬🎬 **1958** An isolated air base in Canada is the site for a scientist using atomic power in an experiment to make a person's thoughts materialize. Only his thoughts are evil and reveal themselves as flying brains with spinal cords that suck human brains right out of the skull. Tons of fun for '50s SF fans and anyone who appreciates the sheer silliness of it all. **77m/B VHS, LV.** Marshall Thompson, Kim Parker, Terence Kilburn, Michael Balfour, Gil Winfield, Shane Cordell; *D:* Arthur Crabtree. *CCB, REP, MLB*

The Fiendish Plot of Dr. Fu Manchu woof! **1980 (PG)** A sad farewell from Sellers, who in his last film portrays Dr. Fu, in his desperate quest for the necessary ingredients for his secret life-preserving formula. Sellers portrays both Dr. Fu and the Scotland Yard detective on his trail, but it's not enough to save this picture, flawed by poor script and lack of direction. **100m/C VHS, Beta, LV.** *GB* Peter Sellers, David Tomlinson, Sid Caesar, Helen Mirren; *D:* Piers Haggard. *WAR, FCT*

Fierce Creatures 🎬🎬 **1996 (PG-13)** This not-really-a-sequel features the same cast as "A Fish Called Wanda" and was jokingly known as "Death Fish II" until a more appropriate title was thought of. A failing London zoo gets a new lease on life, and officious new manager Rollo Lee (Cleese) by stocking only man-eating predators. This plan has kindly, insect house manager Bugsy (Palin) tongue-tied at the thought of destroying the zoo's cuddly current occupants. Kline is again in fine form with his dastardly dual role of zoo's Aussie owner Rod McCain and his idiot son, Vince. Curtis displays her obvious talents as Willa Weston, Vince's more sympathetic partner. Despite inspired moments, flick's not as tightly told or as wickedly funny as "Fish," (an admittedly tough act to follow). A family-friendlier attitude has effectively declawed this "Creature." Many scenes were reshot after unfavorable advance screenings, necessitating a new director and the recall of the actors from far and wide. *CW:* Sexual innuendo and language. **93m/C VHS, LV, Closed Caption, DVD.** John Cleese, Jamie Lee Curtis, Kevin Kline, Michael Palin, Ronnie Corbett, Robert Lindsay, Carey Lowell, Bille Brown, Derek Griffiths, Cynthia Cleese; *D:* Robert M. Young, Fred Schepisi; *W:* John Cleese, Iain Johnstone; *C:* Adrian Biddle, Ian Baker; *M:* Jerry Goldsmith. *USH*

Fiesta 🎬🎬 **1947** A girl comes from Mexico City to her father's hacienda where her old boyfriend awaits her return with a proposal of marriage. Full of authentic Mexican dances and music. 🎵 Fantasia Mexican; La Bamba; La Luna Enamorada; Miriano; Romeria Vasca. **44m/C VHS, Beta.** Ann Ayars, George Negrete, Armida; *D:* Richard Thorpe; *C:* Charles Rosher. Nominations: Academy Awards '47: Best Original Dramatic/Comedy Score. *VYY, DVT*

Fiesta 🎬🎬½ **1995** Young, idealistic Spanish aristocrat Rafael (Colin) has been studying in France during the years since the Spanish Republic was declared. Now, it's 1936 and he has been summoned home to fight against the Communists under the command of Col. Masagual (Trintignant). Masagual assigns Rafael to the firing squad to toughen him up but Rafael eventually rediscovers his convictions and double-crosses his mentor. Based on an autobiographical novel by Jose Luis de Vilallonga. French with subtitles. **108m/C VHS.** *FR* Jean-Louis Trintignant, Gregoire Colin, Dayle Haddon, Marc Lavoine, Jean-Philippe Ecoffey, Laurent Terzieff; *D:* Pierre Boutron; *W:* Pierre Boutron; *C:* Javier Aguirresarobe; *M:* Wim Mertens. Nominations: Cesar Awards '96: Best Actor (Trintignant). *NYR*

The Fifteen Streets 🎬🎬½ **1990** Kind-hearted dock laborer John O'Brien (Teale) is the quiet one in a boozing, brawling Irish family living in near poverty in late-Victorian England. He meets well-bred schoolteacher Mary Llewellyn (Holman) and the two fall in love but bigotry, scandal, and tragedy challenge their chances at happiness. Based on a novel by Catherine Cookson. **108m/C VHS.** *GB* Owen Teale, Clare Holman, Sean Bean, Billie Whitelaw, Ian Bannen, Jane Horrocks, Anny Tobin, Leslie Schofield; *D:* David Wheatley; *W:* Rob Bettinson. *VCO*

Fifth Avenue Girl 🎬½ **1939** An unhappy millionaire brings home a poor young woman to pose as his mistress to make his family realize how they've neglected him. As this below-par social comedy drones toward its romantic conclusion, the rich folks see the error of their ways and love conquers all. **83m/B VHS, Beta, LV.** Ginger Rogers, Walter Connolly, Tim Holt, James Ellison, Franklin Pangborn; *D:* Gregory La Cava. *IME, TTC*

Fifth Day of Peace 🎬🎬 **1972 (PG)** In the aftermath of the WWI armistice, two German soldiers are tried and executed for desertion by their commander, even though the Allies forbade German military trials. An interesting plot that is marred by too obvious plot twists. Based on a true story. **95m/C VHS, Beta.** *IT* Richard Johnson, Franco Nero, Larry Aubrey, Helmut Schneider; *D:* Guiliano Montaldo.

The Fifth Element 🎬🎬½ **1997 (PG-13)** Besson's view of the future is colorful, loud and fashionable. Dressed in costumes by Jean Paul Gaultier, Willis (in a blonde dye job) is New York City cab driver turned unwilling hero Korban Dallas, who must save earth from destruction at the hands of evil arms dealer Zorg (Oldman). Bruce is up to the old heroics that made him a household name, and takes time to romance orange-haired nymph Jovovich, who holds the key to all the madness going on. Oldman is over-the-top as the icy villain with a distinct southern accent, which makes him more of a bad gag than a bad guy. Jumbled story fortunately takes a backseat to weird aliens and stunning visuals which makes this an eye-catching (albeit confusing) sci-fi trip. *CW:* Intense sci-fi violence, some sexuality and brief nudity. **125m/C VHS, LV, Closed Caption.** Bruce Willis, Gary Oldman, Ian Holm, Milla Jovovich, Luke Perry, Lee Evans, Chris Tucker; *D:* Luc Besson; *W:* Luc Besson; *C:* Thierry Arbogast; *M:* Eric Serra. British Academy Awards '97: Best Visual Effects; Cesar Awards '98: Best Art Direction/Set Decoration, Best Cinematography, Best Director (Besson); Nominations: Academy Awards '97: Best Sound Effects Editing; MTV Movie Awards '98: Best Fight (Milla Jovovich/aliens); Golden Raspberry Awards '97: Worst Supporting Actress (Jovovich), Worst New Star (Tucker). COL

The Fifth Floor WOOF! 1980 (R) College disco dancer overdoses on drugs and winds up in an insane asylum, complete with menacing attendant Hopkins and apathetic doctor Ferrer. Pathetic, exploitative trash. **90m/C VHS, Beta.** Bo Hopkins, Dianne Hull, Patti D'Arbanville, Mel Ferrer; *D:* Howard (Hikmet) Avedis; *W:* Howard (Hikmet) Avedis.

The Fifth Monkey 🎬½ 1990 (PG-13) A man embarks on a journey to sell four monkeys in order to fill a dowry for his bride, but along the way he encounters all sorts of obstacles and adventures. Filmed on location in Brazil **93m/C VHS, LV.** Ben Kingsley; *D:* Eric Rochant; *W:* Eric Rochant. COL, FCT

The Fifth Musketeer 🎬🎬 *Behind the Iron Mask* 1979 (PG) A campy adaptation of Dumas's "The Man in the Iron Mask," wherein a monarch's evil twin impersonates him while imprisoning the true king. A good cast and rich production shot in Austria make for a fairly entertaining swashbuckler. **90m/C Beta.** GB Beau Bridges, Sylvia Kristel, Ursula Andress, Cornel Wilde, Ian McShane, Alan Hale Jr., Helmut Dantine, Olivia de Havilland, Jose Ferrer, Rex Harrison, Helmut Dantine; *D:* Ken Annakin; *W:* David Ambrose; *C:* Jack Cardiff. COL

The Fifth Seal 🎬🎬 1976 A group of friends are arrested when one makes a casual remark that offends a commandant. This leads to a series of tasks that test their commitment to their moral ideals. Set at the close of WWII in Hungary. In Hungarian with English subtitles. **116m/C VHS.** HU *D:* Zoltan Fabri. FCT

Fifty/Fifty 🎬🎬 1993 (R) Jake and Frenchie are a couple of mercenaries forced by the CIA not only to work together but with a bunch of incompetent guerillas to overthrow a Southeast Asian dictator. Weller handles the violence, Hays handles the comedy, and both get chased a lot. *CW:* Language and violence. **101m/C VHS, LV, Closed Caption.** Robert Hays, Peter Weller, Ramona Rahman, Charles Martin Smith; *D:* Charles Martin Smith; *W:* Dennis Shryack, Michael Butler; *C:* David Connell; *M:* Peter Bernstein. WAR

$50,000 Reward 🎬½ 1925 Maynard's first western finds him being victimized by an unscrupulous banker who wants Maynard's land deeds for property on which a new dam is being built. **49m/B VHS, Beta.** Ken Maynard, Esther Ralston. GPV, CCB, HEG

52 Pick-Up 🎬🎬½ 1986 (R) After a fling, a wealthy industrialist is blackmailed by a trio of repulsive criminals and determines to save himself. First he becomes deeply caught in their web of murder. Based on an Elmore Leonard novel with lots of gruesome violence and good performances. **111m/C VHS, Beta, LV, Closed Caption.** Roy Scheider, Ann-Margret, Vanity, John Glover, Doug McClure, Clarence Williams III, Kelly Preston, Robert Trebor, Lonny Chapman; *D:* John Frankenheimer; *W:* John Steppling, Elmore Leonard; *M:* Gary Chang. VTR

54 1998 The days of '70s disco, drugs, and hedonism rear their heads in this look back at New York's infamous Studio 54. Myers takes the drama route as druggie club co-owner Steve Rubell, while Phillippe starts off as an innocent New Jersey boy who gets a job as a bartender and is soon taking the low road to debauchery. Others hitting the dance floor include trendy socialite Ward, pouty soap star Campbell, coat-check girl Hayek,

and her busboy hubby Meyer. The club was rebuilt to 80% scale in Toronto. Not yet reviewed. **?m/C VHS.** Mike Myers, Ryan Phillippe, Breckin Meyer, Salma Hayek, Neve Campbell, Sela Ward, Sherry Stringfield, Lauren Hutton, Heather Matarazzo, Michael York; *D:* Mark Christopher; *W:* Mark Christopher. NYR

55 Days at Peking 🎬🎬🎬 1963 A costume epic depicting the Chinese Boxer Rebellion and the fate of military Britishers caught in the midst of the chaos. Standard fare superbly handled by director Ray and an all-star cast. **150m/C VHS, Beta, LV, Letterbox.** Charlton Heston, Ava Gardner, David Niven, John Ireland, Flora Robson, Paul Lukas, Jacques Sernas; *D:* Nicholas Ray; *W:* Philip Yordan; *C:* Jack Hildyard. Nominations: Academy Awards '63: Best Song ("So Little Time"), Best Original Score. BFV, KAR

The Fig Tree 1987 After her mother passes away, Miranda becomes tormented by the fear of death. Now her aunt must help her cope with this difficult part of life. Adapted from the short story by Katherine Anne Porter. Aired on PBS as part of the "Wonderworks" family movie series. **58m/C VHS, Closed Caption.** Olivia Cole, William Converse-Roberts, Doris Roberts, Teresa Wright, Karron Graves; *D:* Calvin Skaggs. HMV, FCT, BTV

Fight for Gold 🎬 1986 In the frozen wastes of the North, a man becomes embroiled in a violent quest for gold. **107m/C VHS.** Doug McClure, Harald Leipnitz, Heinz Reinl, Roberto Bianco, Angelica Ott, Kristina Nel; *D:* Harald Reinl.

A Fight for Jenny 🎬🎬 1990 (PG) Miami Viceroy Thomas and Warren play an interracial couple who fight for custody of the wife's child from a previous marriage. Standard made-for-TV meaningful drama (bite-sized issues served with a modicum of melodrama). **95m/C VHS.** Philip Michael Thomas, Lesley Ann Warren, Jean Smart, Lynne Moody, William Atherton; *D:* Gilbert Moses.

Fight for Survival 🎬½ 1977 (R) Young female aspirant of kung fu must recover sacred books that were stolen by disguised kung fu masters. **101m/C VHS, Beta.** Shangkuan Ling-Feng. FOX

Fight for the Title 🎬🎬 1957 Benny Leonard's reign as the lightweight boxing champ has just begun when WWII is declared. Against his manager's wishes, Benny decides to enlist. **30m/C VHS.** Michael Landon, George Brenlin; *D:* Eric Kenton. FCT, RHI

Fight for Us 🎬½ *L'Insoumis* 1989 (R) A social activist, recently released from prison, takes on the death squads terrorizing the countryside in post-Marcos Philippines. In Spanish with English subtitles. **92m/C VHS, Beta, LV.** Phillip Salvador, Dina Bonnevie, Gina Alajar, Benbol Roco. NO

Fight for Your Life 🎬 1979 Three escaped convicts—a white bigot, an Asian, and a Chicano—take a black minister's family hostage. After suffering all manner of vicious torture, the family exacts an equally brutal revenge. Shades of "The Desperate Hours" and "Extremities," but with much more graphic violence and a racial twist. **89m/C VHS, Beta.** CA William Sanderson, Robert Judd, Lela Small. NO

Fight to the Death 🎬 1983 An evil businessman hires a group of deadly assassins to assist with the Japanese invasion of China at the start of WWII. Includes self-defense tips segment. **100m/C VHS.** Chang Li, Ron Van Cliff. NO

The Fighter 🎬🎬🎬 *The First Time* 1952 A Mexican patriot, involved in a struggle to overthrow a dictator, falls for a co-revolutionist. Flashbacks show the destruction of his family and village, and his pugilistic expertise, which he uses to fight for a huge purse to help the cause. Adapted from Jack London's "The Mexican." **78m/B VHS.** Richard Conte, Vanessa Brown, Lee J. Cobb, Frank Silvera, Roberta Haynes, Hugh Sanders, Claire Carleton, Martin Garralaga; *D:* Herbert Kline. DVT, HEG

The Fighter 🎬½ 1995 (R) French soldier Charlemont (Gruner) gets involved with desperate farmers opposing a greedy landlord (Ermey) and is forced to compete against former rival Ziegfeld

(Ginger). Strange western/kickboxing hybrid that does have lots of action. *CW:* Martial arts and western violence. **91m/C VHS.** Olivier Gruner, Marc Singer, R. Lee Ermey, Ian Ziering, James Brolin, Ashley Laurence; *D:* Isaac Florentine. APX

Fighter Attack 🎬🎬 1953 Story of a WWII pilot, based in Corsica, who is shot down during a mission to destroy a Nazi supply station. He meets with a woman of the Italian underground, and succeeds in destroying his target with her help. **80m/C VHS.** Sterling Hayden, J. Carrol Naish, Joy Page; *D:* Lesley Selander. REP

Fightin' Ranch 🎬🎬 1930 A famous lawman saves his reputation, previously tainted. A Maynard classic. **60m/B VHS, Beta.** Ken Maynard. NO

The Fighting American 🎬🎬 1924 A frat boy proposes to a girl on a brotherly dare, and, unflattered by the fraternal proposal, the girl flees to the Far East to return to the bosom of her family. But it turns out the boy really does love the girl, by golly, and he's got just enough of that fighting American spirit to prove it. Predates Oland's Charlie Chan career by seven years. **65m/B VHS, Beta.** Pat O'Malley, Mary Astor, Raymond Hatton, Warner Oland; *D:* Tom Forman. GPV, FCT

Fighting Back 🎬🎬 *Death Vengeance* 1982 (R) Reactionary tale of an angry resident in a crime-ridden Philadelphia neighborhood who organizes a patrol of armed civilian vigilantes. The police attempt to head off a racial confrontation in this effective drama graced with some fine performances. **96m/C VHS, Beta.** Tom Skerritt, Patti LuPone, Michael Sarrazin, Yaphet Kotto; *D:* Lewis Teague; *W:* David Zelag Goodman; *C:* Franco Di Giacomo. PAR

Fighting Black Kings 🎬 1976 (PG) Martial arts and karate masters appear in this tale of action. **90m/C VHS, Beta.** William Oliver, Charles Martin, Willie Williams, Mas Oyama. WAR, OM

Fighting Caballero 🎬 1935 Lease and his pals effectively handle a gang of mine-harassing outlaws. **60m/B VHS, Beta.** Rex Lease; *D:* Elmer Clifton. NO

Fighting Caravans 🎬🎬 *Blazing Arrows* 1931 In this early big-budget western, based on a story by Zane Grey, a wagon train sets out west from Missouri. Cooper emerges as the hero after warding off an Indian attack that takes the lives of the original leaders. **80m/B VHS, Beta.** Gary Cooper, Ernest Torrence, Tully Marshall, Fred Kohler Sr., Lili Damita; *D:* Otto Brower, David Burton. NOS, MRV, VYY

Fighting Champ 🎬 1933 Cowpunching gives way to boxing as Steele steps into the ring and takes on all comers. Poor combination of riding and boxing makes for a disappointing Western. **57m/B VHS.** Bob Steele, Arletta Duncan, George "Gabby" Hayes, Charles "Blackie" King, Lafe McKee, Kit Guard, George Chesebro; *D:* John P. McCarthy; *W:* Wellyn Totman. MOV

Fighting Cowboy 🎬 1933 Bill settles a tungsten mine dispute with a greedy miner and some outlaws. **50m/B VHS, Beta, LV.** Buffalo Bill Jr.; *D:* Victor Adamson. NO

Fighting Devil Dogs 1938 Two Marine lieutenants are assigned the task of obtaining a deadly secret weapon controlled by crooks. A serial in 12 chapters. **195m/B VHS.** Lee Powell, Bruce (Herman Brix) Bennett; *D:* John English, William Witney. REP, VCN, MLB

Fighting Father Dunne 🎬🎬 1948 Mega-hokey Hollywood steamroller about a tough priest caring for St. Louis newsboys in the early 1900s. Based on a true story. **92m/B VHS, Beta.** Pat O'Brien, Darryl Hickman, Charles Kemper, Una O'Connor, Arthur Shields, Harry Shannon, Joseph Sawyer, Anna Q. Nilsson, Donn Gift, Myrna Dell; *D:* Ted Tetzlaff. TTC

Fighting Fists of Shanghai Joe 🎬 1965 Fearsome fighting man from the Far East engages a vile American land baron in a battle of honor. **94m/C VHS, Beta.** Klaus Kinski, Gordon Mitchell, Carla Romanelli, Robert Hundar, Chen Lee; *D:* Mario Ciano. TWE

Fighting Fool ⚔ 1932 Average oater has McCoy as a sheriff constantly in pursuit of an outlaw named "The Shadow." Of course, romance blossoms between McCoy and Day, too. The real identity of "The Shadow" turns out to be quite a surprise for McCoy. **57m/B VHS.** Tim McCoy, Marceline Day, Robert Ellis, Arthur Rankin, Dorothy Granger; **D:** Lambert Hillyer. *MOV*

Fighting Jack ⚔⚔ 1926 After he saves a girl from a watery death, a man is accused of horse stealing and trespassing. **52m/B VHS, Beta.** Bill Bailey, Hazel Deane, Frona Hale, John Byron, Sailor Sharkey, Herma Cordova; **D:** Louis Chaudet. *GPV*

The Fighting Kentuckian ⚔⚔½ 1949 Homeward bound from the Battle of New Orleans in 1814, a Kentucky rifleman lingers in a French settlement in Alabama. His romance with the daughter of a French general is blocked by the father until the American saves the community from an assault by land grabbers. Hardy as a frontiersman is well worth the view. An action-packed, well-photographed hit. **100m/B VHS, Closed Caption.** John Wayne, Oliver Hardy, Vera Ralston, Marie Windsor, Philip Dorn, John Howard, Hugo Haas, Grant Withers; **D:** George Waggner. *REP*

The Fighting Legion ⚔⚔ 1930 Maynard shows his foresight here, making this one of the first westerns to fully exploit sound by adding music and singing. Standard plot has Maynard going after the villain who murdered his brother. **69m/B VHS.** Ken Maynard, Dorothy Dwan, Ernie Adams, Stanley Blystone, Frank Rice; **D:** Harry Joe Brown. *GPV, DVT, HEG*

Fighting Mad ⚔½ 1939 A singing Mountie tangles with border-crossing robbers and saves the reputation of a woman they exploit. One of the "Renfrew of the Mounties" series. **57m/B VHS, Beta.** James Newill, Milburn Stone, Sally Blane; **D:** Sam Newfield. *VDM*

Fighting Mad ⚔⚔½ 1976 (R) A peaceful land owner is driven to violence when he discovers that the business men who want his property are planning to murder two of his family members in order to get it. The local sheriff's apathy forces the man to take the law into his own hands. Unlike other Fonda films of the time which consist of chaotic violence and car crashes, this story is a well performed character study. **90m/C VHS.** Peter Fonda, Lynn Lowry, John Doucette, Phil Carey, Scott Glenn, Kathleen Miller; **D:** Jonathan Demme; **W:** Jonathan Demme. *NO*

Fighting Mad ⚔½ *Fierce* 1977 (R) Soldiers leave their buddy for dead in wartime Vietnam. He is alive, but captured by Japanese soldiers who believe they are still fighting in WWII. **96m/C VHS.** James Iglehart, Jayne Kennedy, Leon Isaac Kennedy; **D:** Cirio H. Santiago. *NO*

Fighting Marines ⚔½ 1936 U.S. Marines are trying to establish an air base on Halfway Island in the Pacific, but are thwarted by the "Tiger Shark," a modern-day pirate. First appeared as a serial. **69m/B VHS, Beta.** Jason Robards Sr., Grant Withers, Ann Rutherford, Pat O'Malley; **D:** Joseph Kane, B. Reeves Eason. *VYY, VCN, VDM*

The Fighting Marshal ⚔⚔ 1932 After serving time for a crime he didn't commit, McCoy assumes the identity of a dead sheriff and tries to find the felons who done him wrong. **58m/B VHS.** Tim McCoy, Dorothy Gulliver, Mary Carr, Matthew Betz, Pat O'Malley; **D:** David Ross Lederman. *MOV*

Fighting Parson ⚔ 1935 In order to infiltrate a lawless town Gibson, a gunsliging cowboy, dresses as a revivalist preacher. **65m/B VHS, Beta.** Hoot Gibson, Marceline Day, Robert Frazer, Stanley Blystone, Skeeter Bill Robbins, Charles "Blackie" King; **D:** Harry Fraser. *VCI, GPV*

Fighting Pilot 1935 Talmadge is a real fighter in this classic talkie. His assignment is to rescue the plans for a secret aircraft from ill fate. **62m/B VHS, Beta.** Richard Talmadge, Victor Mace, Gertrude Messinger, Eddie Davis, Robert Frazer; **D:** Noel Mason Smith. *NOS, DVT, GPV*

The Fighting Prince of Donegal ⚔⚔½ 1966 An Irish prince battles the invading British in 16th Century Ireland. Escaping their clutches, he leads his clan in rescuing his mother and his beloved in this Disney swashbuckler. Based on the novel "Red Hugh, Prince of Donegal" by Robert T. Reilly. **110m/C VHS, Beta.** Peter McEnery, Susan Hampshire, Tom Adams, Gordon Jackson, Andrew Keir; **D:** Michael O'Herlihy; **M:** George Bruns. *DIS*

The Fighting Redhead ⚔⚔ 1950 Final entry in the "Red Ryder" series has Hart as a cattle rustling murderer and Bannon as the hero, Red Ryder. Based on the comic strip, "Red Ryder." **55m/C VHS.** Jim Bannon, Don Reynolds, Emmett Lynn, Marin Sais, Peggy Stewart, John Hart, Lane Bradford; **D:** Lewis D. Collins; **W:** Paul Franklin, Jerry Thomas. *MOV*

Fighting Renegade ⚔½ 1939 The search for an Indian burial ground in Mexico prompts two murders and McCoy, disguised as a notorious bandit part of the time, is wrongly accused. Justice triumphs in the end. **60m/B VHS, Beta.** Tim McCoy; **D:** Sam Newfield. *NOS, VCN, DVT*

The Fighting Rookie ⚔½ 1934 LaRue, better known for playing hoods, is a rookie cop set up and disgraced by the mob. But he fights back to regain his honor and bring the gang to justice. **65m/B VHS, Beta, 8mm.** Jack LaRue; **D:** Spencer Gordon Bennet. *VYY*

Fighting Seabees ⚔⚔½ 1944 As a hot-tempered construction foreman who battles Navy regulations as well as the Japanese, Wayne emerges as a larger-than-life hero in this action-packed saga of the Pacific theater of WWII. Extremely popular patriotic drama depicts the founding of the Seabees, the naval construction corps, amidst the action and the would-be romance with a woman reporter. Also available colorized. **100m/B VHS, Closed Caption.** John Wayne, Susan Hayward, Dennis O'Keefe, William Frawley; **D:** Edward Ludwig. Nominations: Academy Awards '44: Best Original Dramatic/Comedy Score. *REP*

Fighting Shadows ⚔½ 1935 McCoy plays a tough lawman who rids his town of an unscrupulous bandit gang guilty of harassing the locals. Highlighted by some excellent trick riding—for which Western star McCoy was known. **58m/B VHS.** Tim McCoy, Robert Allen, Geneva Mitchell, Ward Bond, Si Jenks; **D:** David Selman; **W:** Ford Beebe. *MOV*

The Fighting Sheriff ⚔ 1931 Routine oater mixes action and romance when a sheriff is thrown together with a society debutante. **65m/B VHS.** Buck Jones, Loretta Sayers, Robert Ellis, Harlan E. Knight, Paul Fix, Lilian Worth; **D:** Louis King; **W:** Stuart Anthony. *MOV*

The Fighting 69th ⚔⚔⚔ 1940 Cornball but entertaining WWI drama with lots of action. Cagney is a Brooklyn street tough who joins the all-Irish 69th New York regiment but could care less about its famed military history. He promptly defies his superiors and barely scrapes through his training. Sent to France, the swaggering Cagney turns coward when confronted by the horrors of war but eventually redeems himself. O'Brien is the famed regimental chaplain Father Duffy, while Brent is commander "Wild Bill" Donovan, who would later found the OSS in WWII. Lots of heart-tugging emotion backed with a fine supporting cast. **90m/B VHS.** James Cagney, Pat O'Brien, George Brent, Jeffrey Lynn, Alan Hale, Frank McHugh, Dennis (Stanley Morner) Morgan, William Lundigan, Dick Foran, Guinn "Big Boy" Williams, Henry O'Neill, John Litel, George Reeves; **D:** William Keighley; **W:** Fred Niblo, Norman Reilly Raine, Dean Franklin; **C:** Gaetano Antonio "Tony" Gaudio. *MGM, FCT*

The Fighting Stallion ⚔⚔⚔ 1926 Canutt stars as a drifter hired by a rancher who's determined to capture a beautiful wild stallion (played by Boy the Wonder Horse). Silent with original organ score. **76m/B VHS, Beta, 8mm.** Yakima Canutt, Neva Gerber, Bud Osborne. *GPV, VYY*

The Fighting Sullivans ⚔⚔⚔½ *The Sullivans* 1942 The true story of five brothers killed on the Battleship Juneau at Guadalcanal during WWII. The tale tells of the fury felt by the siblings after Pearl Harbor, their enlistment to fight for their country, and their tragic fate in the heat of battle. Truly a stirring tribute to all lives lost in combat. **110m/B VHS.** Anne Baxter, Thomas Mitchell, Selena Royle, Eddie Ryan, Trudy Marshall, James B. Cardwell, Roy Roberts, Ward Bond, Mary McCarty, Bobby Driscoll, Addison Richards, Selmer Jackson, Mae Marsh, Harry Strang, Barbara Brown; **D:** Lloyd Bacon. *IVY*

Fighting Texans ⚔ 1933 An entire town invests in an oil well, on the advice of young salesman Bell, that the bankers are sure is a dud. Imagine their surprise when it turns out to be a gusler. **60m/B VHS.** Rex Bell, Luana Walters, Betty Mack, Gordon DeMain; **D:** Armand Schaefer. *NOS, DVT*

Fighting Thru ⚔ *California in 1878* 1930 Maynard fights off the bad guys and wins the girl after some nifty riding in his first all-talkie western. **60m/B VHS, Beta.** Ken Maynard, Jeanette Loff; **D:** William Nigh. *NOS, DVT*

The Fighting Trooper ⚔½ 1934 Based on the James Oliver Curwood story, "Footprints," this frontier tale presents a Mountie who goes undercover as a trapper in the Northwest. He is out to catch a murderer. **57m/B VHS, Beta.** Kermit Maynard. *NOS, VDM, DVT*

Fighting Valley ⚔⚔ 1943 Texas Rangers O'Brien, Newill, and Wilkerson ride off to break up an outlaw gang that is trying to monopolize the ore smelting business. O'Brien later went on to directing for TV and also wrote for Red Skelton. **60m/B VHS.** Dave O'Brien, James Newill, Guy Wilkerson, Patti McCarty, John Merton, Curly Dresden; **D:** Oliver Drake; **W:** Oliver Drake. *DVT, HEG*

Fighting Vigilantes ⚔⚔ 1947 A villainous food distributor is terrorizing his rivals until LaRue whips him. Holt and her father put together a committee called "The Vigilantes" to help out. Holt is the daughter of movie good guy Jack Holt. **61m/B VHS.** Lash LaRue, Al "Fuzzy" St. John, Jennifer Holt, George Chesebro, Lee Morgan, Russell Arms, Steve Clark; **D:** Ray Taylor. *NOS*

The Fighting Westerner ⚔½ *Rocky Mountain Mystery* 1935 Scott stars as a mining engineer who becomes entangled in mysterious murders. Mrs. Leslie Carter stars in a rare screen role. **54m/B VHS, Beta, 8mm.** Randolph Scott, Chic Sale, Ann Sheridan, Charles T. Barton. *VYY, MRV*

Fighting with Kit Carson 1933 Famous guide and Indian fighter lead bands of settlers westward. Action-packed. Twelve chapters. **230m/B VHS, Beta.** Johnny Mack Brown, Noah Beery Sr., Noah Beery Jr., Betsy King Ross; **D:** Armand Schaefer, Colbert Clark. *VYY, VCN, VDM*

Film House Fever ⚔ 1986 A compilation of clips from sleazy, cult-type movies, including "Blood Feast" and "Hot Night at the Go Go Lounge." **58m/C VHS, Beta.** Jamie Lee Curtis, James Keach, Lon Chaney Jr., Harvey Korman. *ART, VES*

The Final Alliance ⚔ 1989 (R) A tough loner takes on a vicious motorcycle gang that's terrorizing a small town, and realizes that they're also responsible for his family's death. **90m/C VHS, Beta, LV, Closed Caption.** David Hasselhoff, John Saxon, Bo Hopkins, Jeanie Moore; **D:** Mario Di Leo. *COL*

Final Analysis ⚔⚔½ 1992 (R) Glossy thriller starring Gere as a San Francisco psychiatrist who falls for the glamorous sister of one of his patients. Basinger plays the femme fatale and Thurman is Gere's sexually neurotic patient. Although heavily influenced by "Vertigo," this film never comes close to attaining the depth of Hitchcock's cinematic masterpiece. Roberts gives the most gripping performance in this slick suspense movie as Basinger's sleazy gangster husband. **CW:** Language, violence, and one scene of strong sensuality. **125m/C VHS, LV, Closed Caption.** Richard Gere, Kim Basinger, Uma Thurman, Eric Roberts, Paul Guilfoyle, Keith David, Robert Harper, Jolyon Baker,

Harris Yulin, Agustin Rodriguez; *D:* Phil Joanou; *W:* Wesley Strick, Robert Berger; *C:* Jordan Cronenweth; *M:* George Fenton. *WAR*

Final Appeal ✓✓½ 1993 (PG-13)
Christine Biondi (Williams) is an abused wife, living in terror of her drug-addicted doctor husband, Ed. When Christine walks in on Ed and his mistress, she's forced to kill him in self-defense. But Ed's mistress swears it was murder and Christine's on trial. Now her only chance is her hard-drinking lawyer brother Perry (Dennehy)—who doesn't believe her story. Fact-based made for TV fare. *CW:* Thematic material concerning substance abuse and domestic violence. 94m/C VHS, Closed Caption. JoBeth Williams, Brian Dennehy, Lindsay Crouse, Tom Mason, Eddie Jones, Ashley Crow, Betsy Brantley, Michael Beach; *M:* Charles Bernstein. *REP*

Final Approach ✓✓ 1991 (R)
Test pilot Jason Halsey (Sikking) crashes in the desert and awakens in the office of psychiatrist Dio Gottlieb (Elizondo). Halsey can't remember anything about his past, or his own name for that matter, but through word association games and psychological tests, he begins to remember as Gottlieb tries to pry information from his brain. Showy computer effects are excellent, but they only serve to fill holes in a story that has an unsatisfying ending. Notable as first film mde with digital sound. Also available in a letterboxed version. *CW:* Language. 100m/C VHS, LV, Letterbox, Closed Caption. James B. Sikking, Hector Elizondo, Madolyn Smith, Kevin McCarthy, Cameo Kneuer, Wayne Duvall; *D:* Eric Steven Stahl. *THV*

Final Assignment ✓ *The Moscow Chronicle*
1980 A Canadian television reporter agrees to smuggle a dissident Soviet scientist's ill granddaughter out of Russia for treatment along with a videotape documenting tragic experiments on children with steroids. She manages to evade the KGB while carrying on with a Russian press officer, and enlists the support of a Jewish fur trader. Location shooting in Canada instead of Russia is just one pitfall of this production. 101m/C VHS, Beta. *CA* Genevieve Bujold, Michael York, Burgess Meredith, Colleen Dewhurst; *D:* Paul Almond. *ART, VES*

Final Comedown ✓ 1972 (R)
A black revolutionary attempts to get white radicals behind his war against racism. He fails and starts a racial bloodbath. 84m/C VHS, Beta. Billy Dee Williams, D'Urville Martin, Celia Kaye, Raymond St. Jacques, Pamela Jones, R.G. Armstrong; *D:* Oscar Williams. *NLC, SIM*

The Final Conflict ✓½ *The Omen 3* 1981
(R) Unwelcomed third installment in the "Omen" series, concerning Satan's son Damien. Now 32, and the head of an international conglomerate, he is poised for world domination but fears another savior is born. Several monks and many babies meet gruesome deaths before he gets his comeuppance. The last theatrical release was then followed by a made-for-television movie called "Omen 4: The Awakening" (1991). 108m/C VHS, Beta, LV, Letterbox. Sam Neill, Lisa Harrow, Barnaby Holm, Rossano Brazzi, Don Gordon, Mason Adams, Robert Arden, Marc Boyle, Tommy Duggan, Richard Oldfield, Arwen Holm; *D:* Graham Baker; *W:* Andrew Birkin; *C:* Phil Meheux, Bob Paynter; *M:* Jerry Goldsmith. *FOX*

The Final Countdown ✓✓✓ 1980 (PG)
A U.S. nuclear-powered aircraft carrier, caught in a time warp, is transported back to 1941, just hours before the bombing of Pearl Harbor. The commanders face the ultimate decision—leave history intact or stop the incident and thus avoid WWII. Excellent photography and a surprise ending. 92m/C VHS, Beta, LV. Kirk Douglas, Martin Sheen, Katharine Ross, James Farentino, Charles Durning; *D:* Don Taylor; *W:* Thomas Hunter, David Ambrose. *VES*

Final Cut ✓½ 1988
While filming in a secluded swampland, a crew stumbles on a local sheriff's crooked scheme and one by one, the crew members disappear. 92m/C VHS, Beta. Carla De Lane, T.J. Kennedy, Joe Rainer, Brett Rice, Jordan Williams; *D:* Larry G. Brown. *THV*

The Final Cut ✓✓✓ 1995
Follows "House of Cards" and "To Play the King" in portraying the political adventures of Francis Urquardt (Richardson), Prime Minister. At 65, Urquardt has two goals: he wants to beat Margaret Thatcher's 11-year reign and he wants to establish a secret retirement fund (the plot involves Cyprus and could—finally—leads to Urquardt's downfall). Author Michael Dobbs objected to the adaptation and insisted his name be removed from the script. On two cassettes. 200m/C VHS. *GB* Ian Richardson, Diane Fletcher, Paul Freeman, Isla Blair, Nick Brimble, Erika Hoffman, Nickolas Grace, Julian Fellowes; *D:* Mike Vardy; *W:* Andrew Davies; *C:* Ian Punter; *M:* Jim Parker. *FOX, FCT*

The Final Cut ✓✓ 1996 (R)
John Pierce (Elliott) is a retired bomb squad specialist who's unwillingly called back to active duty to stop a bomber who's targeting Seattle. Along with ambitious officer Kathleen Hardy (Ramsay), Pierce tries to discover the bomber's next move—only to have suspicion fall upon himself. 99m/C VHS, LV, Closed Caption. Sam Elliott, Charles Martin Smith, Anne Elizabeth Ramsay, Matt Craven, Ray Baker, John Hannah, Amanda Plummer; *D:* Roger Christian; *W:* Raul Inglis; *C:* Mike Southon; *M:* Ross Vannelli. *REP*

The Final Days ✓✓½ 1989 (PG)
TV drama follows the presidency of Richard Nixon (Smith) from Watergate through his resignation. Based on the Pulitzer Prize-winning book by Bob Woodward and Carl Bernstein. 150m/C VHS, Closed Caption. Lane Smith, Richard Kiley, David Ogden Stiers, Ed Flanders, Theodore Bikel; *D:* Richard Pearce. *REP*

Final Embrace ✓½ 1992 (R)
When Laurel's famous sister is murdered she decides to do a little investigating on her own. She's aided by a young cop who just happened to be obsessed with the murdered woman. *CW:* Language, violence, and sensuality. 74m/C VHS, LV. Robert Rusler, Nancy Valen, Dick Van Patten, Linda Dona; *D:* Oley Sassone; *W:* R.J. Robertson, Jim Wynorski; *M:* Daniel Licht. *NHO*

Final Equinox ✓½ 1995
Mysterious alien artifact, which has the power to spontaneously create new life, is stolen and both the government and the mob try to be the first to find—and control—it. Cop Kove opposes them both. 90m/C VHS. Martin Kove, Joe Lara, David Warner, Gary Kasper; *D:* Serge Rodnunsky; *W:* Serge Rodnunsky. *MNC*

Final Exam WOOF! 1981 (R)
Psychotic killer stalks college students during exam week. This one's too boring to be scary. You root for the psycho to off everyone just to have the movie over. 90m/C VHS, Beta. Cecile Bagdadi, Joel Rice; *D:* Jimmy Huston. *COL*

The Final Executioner ✓ *The Last Warrior* 1983
A valiant man finds a way to stop the slaughter of innocent people in a post-nuclear world. 95m/C VHS, Beta. William Mang, Marina Costa, Harrison Muller, Woody Strode; *D:* Romolo Guerrieri. *MGM*

Final Extra ✓✓ 1927
Ambitious reporter's career gets a boost when he's assigned to investigate the murder of a rival. Silent with music score. 60m/B VHS, Beta, 8mm. Grant Withers, Marguerite de la Motte. *NOS, VYY, DVT*

The Final Goal ✓½ 1994 (R)
Evil businessman (and ex-soccer star) Paulo Ramirez (Estrada) meddles with his country's current soccer star, who's playing in the Global Cup of Soccer. He wants the player to throw the game and thinks death threats will accomplish his goal. *CW:* Language. 85m/C VHS. Erik Estrada, Steven Nijjar, Dean Butler; *D:* Jon Cassar. *AVI*

Final Impact ✓½ 1991 (R)
Nick Taylor seeks vengeance on reigning kickbox champ Jake Gerard through his prodigy, Danny Davis. Will sweet revenge for the wicked beating, suffered at the hands of Gerard years earlier, be his? *CW:* Language and kickboxing violence. 99m/C VHS. Lorenzo Lamas, Kathleen Kinmont, Mimi Lesseos, Kathrin Lautner, Jeff Langton, Mike Worth; *D:* Joseph Merhi, Stephen Smoke; *M:* John Gonzalez. *PMH*

Final Judgement ✓✓ 1992 (R)
Daniel Tyrone (Dourif) is a former gang member, now a troubled priest, who's the prime suspect in the Los Angeles murder of a beautiful stripper. Determined to find the killer Father Tyrone heads into L.A.'s underground sex industry to search for clues, which brings him face to face with evil and his own desires. 90m/C VHS. Brad Dourif, Isaac Hayes, Maria Ford, Karen Black, Orson Bean, David Ledingham; *D:* Louis Morneau; *W:* Kirk Honeycutt, Louis Morneau. *COL*

Final Justice ✓ 1984 (R)
A small-town Texan sheriff wages a war against crime and corruption that carries him to Italy and the haunts of Mafia hitmen. 90m/C VHS, Beta. Joe Don Baker, Rossano Brazzi, Patrizia Pellegrino; *D:* Greydon Clark; *M:* David Bell. *VES*

Final Mission ✓ 1984
Vengeful one-man army follows the professional hit man who slaughtered his family from L.A. to Laos. His pursuit leads to a jungle showdown. Gee, sounds like "Rambo, First Blood," though obviously less grand and glorious. 97m/C VHS, Beta. Richard Young, John Dresden, Kaz Garas, Christine Tudor; *D:* Cirio H. Santiago. *REP*

Final Mission ✓✓ 1993 (R)
Virtual reality becomes a weapon in a military conspiracy when pilots start dying. Air Force jets are supposed to be unstoppable thanks to the new technology and a general is only too willing to blame the deaths on pilot error but one fly boy is out to find the truth. 91m/C VHS, LV, Closed Caption. Billy Wirth, Corbin Bernsen, Elizabeth Gracen, Steve Railsback. *THV*

Final Notice ✓ 1989
A detective tracking a serial killer has as his only evidence a trail of shredded photos of nude women. Not released theatrically. 91m/C VHS, Beta, LV, Closed Caption. Gil Gerard, Steve Landesburg, Jackie Burroughs, Melody Anderson, Louise Fletcher, David Ogden Stiers, Kevin Hicks; *D:* Steven Hilliard Stern; *W:* John Gay; *M:* Tom Scott. *PAR*

The Final Option ✓ *Who Dares Wins* 1982
(R) An agent of England's Special Air Services team goes undercover as one of a band of antinuclear terrorists that take over the U.S. Embassy in London. Violent, but unconvincing. 125m/C VHS, Beta. *GB* Lewis Collins, Judy Davis, Richard Widmark, Robert Webber, Edward Woodward, Ingrid Pitt, Kenneth Griffith, Tony Doyle, John Duttine; *D:* Ian Sharp; *W:* Reginald Rose; *C:* Phil Meheux. *MGM*

The Final Programme ✓✓½ *The Last Days of Man on Earth* 1973
In this futuristic story, a man must rescue his sister—and the world—from their brother, who holds a microfilmed plan for global domination. Meanwhile, he must shield himself from the advances of a bisexual computer programmer who wants to make him father to a new, all-purpose human being. Based on the Michael Moorcock "Jerry Cornelius" stories, the film has gained a cult following. 85m/C VHS, Beta. *GB* Hugh Griffith, Harry Andrews, Jon Finch, Jenny Runacre, Sterling Hayden, Patrick Magee, Sarah Douglas; *D:* Robert Fuest.

Final Round ✓½ 1993 (R)
A kickboxer and his girlfriend are kidnapped by a millionaire who stages hunt the humans games for the pleasure of his gambling syndicate. Stiff but with a few good action sequences. *CW:* Language, violence, and sexuality. 90m/C VHS, Closed Caption. Lorenzo Lamas, Anthony de Longis, Kathleen Kinmont, Clark Johnson, Isabelle Jamieson; *D:* George Erschbamer; *W:* Arne Olsen; *M:* Graeme Coleman. *WOV*

Final Sanction ✓✓½ 1989
After a nuclear holocaust exhausts their military resources, the U.S. and the Soviets each send one-man armies to battle each other for final control of the world. 90m/C VHS, Beta. Robert Z'Dar, Ted Prior; *D:* David A. Prior; *W:* David A. Prior. *HHE*

Final Shot: The Hank Gathers Story ✓✓½ 1992
Inspirational story of Gathers, who rose from the ghetto to become one of America's top college basketball stars at Loyola Marymount, until tragedy strikes during a game.

92m/C VHS, Beta. Victor Love, Duane Davis, Nell Carter, George Kennedy.

The Final Terror 🎬🎬 Campsite Massacre; Bump in the Night; The Forest Primeval 1983 (R) Group of young campers is stalked by a mad killer in a desolate, backwoods area. Better-than-average stalked-teens entry is notable for the presence of some soon-to-be stars. 90m/C VHS, Beta, LV. John Friedrich, Rachel Ward, Adrian Zmed, Daryl Hannah, Joe Pantoliano, Ernest Harden, Mark Metcalf, Lewis Smith, Cindy Harrel, Akosua Busia; D: Andrew Davis. ART, VES

Final Verdict 🎬🎬½ 1991 A trial lawyer defends a man he knows is guilty, throwing his life and his family into turmoil. Made for cable television. 93m/C VHS, Beta, Closed Caption. Treat Williams, Glenn Ford, Amy Wright, Olivia Burnette; D: Paul Elliott. TTC

Final Warning 🎬🎬½ Chernobyl: The Final Warning 1990 A dramatization of actual events surrounding the 1986 melt-down of the nuclear power plant at Chernobyl. Made for television. 94m/C VHS, Closed Caption. Jon Voight, Jason Robards Jr., Sammi Davis; D: Anthony Page. TTC

Find the Lady 🎬½ Call the Cops; Kopek and Broom 1975 (R) Candy assumes a supporting role as a bumbling cop who is part of an incompetent police team trying to rescue a kidnapped socialite. 100m/C VHS, Beta. CA John Candy, Peter Cook, Mickey Rooney, Lawrence Dane, Alexandra Bastedo; D: John Trent. NO

Finders Keepers 🎬🎬 1984 (R) A wild assortment of characters on board a train en route from California to Nebraska search for five million dollars hidden in the baggage car. 96m/C VHS, Beta, Closed Caption. Michael O'Keefe, Beverly D'Angelo, Ed Lauter, Louis Gossett Jr., Pamela Stephenson, Jim Carrey, David Wayne, Brian Dennehy, John Schuck; D: Richard Lester; W: Ronny Graham. FOX

Fine Gold 🎬🎬 1988 A false charge of embezzlement leaves a man without home and family, so he decides to turn the tables on those who betrayed him. 91m/C VHS, Beta. Andrew Stevens, Ray Walston, Ted Wass, Stewart Granger, Lloyd Bochner, Jane Badler; D: J. Anthony Loma. MCG

A Fine Madness 🎬🎬🎬 1966 A near-classic comedy about a lusty, rebellious poet thrashing against the pressures of the modern world, and fending off a bevy of lobotomy-happy psychiatrists. Shot on location in New York City, based on Elliot Baker's novel. 104m/C VHS, Beta. Sean Connery, Joanne Woodward, Jean Seberg, Patrick O'Neal, Colleen Dewhurst, Clive Revill, John Fiedler; D: Irvin Kershner; M: John Addison. WAR

A Fine Mess 🎬½ 1986 (PG) Two buffoons cash in when one overhears a plan to dope a racehorse, but they are soon fleeing the plotters' slapstick pursuit. The plot is further complicated by the romantic interest of a gangster's wife. The television popularity of the two stars did not translate to the big screen; perhaps it's Edwards' fault. 100m/C VHS, Beta, LV, Closed Caption. Ted Danson, Howie Mandel, Richard Mulligan, Stuart Margolin, Maria Conchita Alonso, Paul Sorvino; D: Blake Edwards; W: Blake Edwards; C: Harry Stradling Jr.; M: Henry Mancini. COL

A Fine Romance 🎬🎬 1992 (PG-13) An improbable romance set in Paris features Andrews and Mastroianni as abandoned spouses falling in love. Andrews is the prim English Pamela who has been abandoned by her docter husband. Mastroianni is the irrepresible Cesareo, whose wife has just happened to run off with the aforementioned doctor. They meet to plan how to get their spouses back and wind up with opposites attracting. Not much story and the charm is spread thin. Based on the play "Tchin, Tchin" by Francois Billetdoux. CW: Nudity. 83m/C VHS. Julie Andrews, Marcello Mastroianni, Ian Fitzgibbon, Jean-Pierre Castaldi, Jean-Jacques Dulon, Maria Machado, Jean-Michel Cannone, Catherine Jarrett, Gene Saks; W: Ronald Harwood; M: Pino Donaggio.

Fine Things 🎬🎬½ Danielle Steel's Fine Things 1990 Bernie Fine thinks everything will be dandy now that he has a beautiful new bride and a cute stepdaughter. Then his wife dies and his stepdaughter's unreliable father wants sole custody. What's a nice guy to do? Based on the novel by Danielle Steel. Made for television. 145m/C VHS, Closed Caption. D.W. Moffett, Tracy Pollan, Judith Hoag, Cloris Leachman, Noley Thornton; D: Tom Moore; W: Peter Lefcourt. CMB, WOV

Finessing the King 🎬🎬½ 1984 Private eyes Tommy and Tuppence follow a mysterious newspaper notice to a masked ball where a murder is about to occur. Based on the Agatha Christie story. Made for British television. 60m/C VHS, Beta. GB James Warwick, Francesca Annis. TPV

The Finest Hour 🎬½ 1991 (R) Two Navy buddies have a falling out when they both fall for the same woman. But they must put aside their differences when their next mission sends them to Iraq to deal with the deadly threat of biological warfare. CW: Language and war violence. 105m/C VHS, LV, Closed Caption. Rob Lowe, Gale Hansen, Tracy Griffith, Eb Lottimer; D: Shimon Dotan; W: Shimon Dotan. COL

The Finger Man 🎬🎬½ 1955 An ex-con cooperates with the feds rather than return to jail. The deal is that he gets the dirt on an underworld crime boss. Solid performances. 82m/B VHS. Frank Lovejoy, Forrest Tucker, Peggy Castle, Timothy Carey, Glenn Gordon; D: Harold Schuster. REP

Finger on the Trigger 🎬🎬 El Dedo En El Gatillo 1965 Veterans from both sides of the Civil War are after a hidden supply of gold, but find that they must band together to fend off an Indian attack. Routine. 89m/C VHS, Beta. Rory Calhoun, James Philbrook, Todd Martin, Silvia Solar, Brad Talbot; D: Sidney Pink. NO

Fingerprints Don't Lie 🎬 1951 A fingerprint expert pins the murder of the town mayor on an innocent guy, then suspects a frame-up. 56m/B VHS, Beta, LV. Richard Travis, Sheila Ryan, Tom Neal; D: Sam Newfield. NO

Fingers 🎬🎬🎬 1978 (R) Keitel is Johnny Fingers, a mobster's son, reluctantly working as a mob debt-collector, all the while dreaming of his ambitions to be a concert pianist. The divisions between his dreams and reality cause him to crack. Toback's first film generates psychological tension and excellent performances. 89m/C VHS, Beta. Harvey Keitel, Tisa Farrow, Jim Brown, Danny Aiello, Tanya Roberts, Marian Seldes, Michael V. Gazzo, James Toback; D: James Toback; W: James Toback; C: Michael Chapman; M: George Barrie. TTC

Finian's Rainbow 🎬🎬🎬 1968 (G) A leprechaun comes to America to steal back a pot of gold taken by an Irishman and his daughter in this fanciful musical comedy based on a 1947 Broadway hit. Both the sprite and the girl find romance; the share-cropping locals are saved by the cash; a bigot learns the error of his ways; and Finian (Astaire) dances off to new adventures. The fine production and talented cast are not used to their best advantage by the director who proved much better suited for "The Godfather." Entertaining, nonetheless. ♫How Are Things in Glocca Morra?; Look To the Rainbow; That Old Devil Moon; If This Isn't Love; Something Sort of Grandish; The Be-Gat; This Time of Year; The Great Come and Get It Day; When I'm Not Near the Girl I Love. 141m/C VHS, Beta, LV, Letterbox. Fred Astaire, Petula Clark, Tommy Steele, Keenan Wynn, Al Freeman Jr., Don Francks, Susan Hancock, Dolph Sweet; D: Francis Ford Coppola. Nominations: Academy Awards '68: Best Sound, Scoring of a Musical. WAR, MVD

Finish Line 🎬🎬½ 1989 A high school track star turns to steroids to enhance his performance after being pushed by an overzealous father. The father-and-son Brolins play the pair. Made for cable. 100m/C VHS. James Brolin, Josh Brolin, Mariska Hargitay, Kristoff St. John, John Finnegan, Billy Vera, Stephen Lang; D: John Nicolella. TTC

Finishing School 🎬½ 1933 Girls' school roommates Rogers and Dee experience heartaches and loves lost while enduring disinterested parents and snobbish peers. Boxoffice bomb when released, despite a strong cast. 73m/B VHS, Beta. Ginger Rogers, Frances Dee, George Nicholls Jr., Beulah Bondi, Bruce Cabot, Billie Burke, John Halliday, Sara Haden, Jack Norton, Joan Barclay, Jane Darwell; D: George Nicholls Jr.; M: Max Steiner. TTC

The Finishing Touch 🎬🎬 1992 (R) Someone is stalking L.A.'s most gorgeous women and Detective Sam Stone (Nader) is assigned to the case. Stone discovers his prime suspect is a video artist with a taste for pornography. When Stone's investigation is cut short, his ex-wife, Detective Hannah Stone (Hack), is brought in to take over the case. Unfortunately, she finds herself falling for the suspect in this erotic thriller. CW: Language, violence, and sensuality. 82m/C VHS, Closed Caption. Michael Nader, Shelley Hack, Arnold Vosloo, Art Evans, Clark Johnson, Theodore (Ted) Raimi; D: Fred Gallo. COL

Finnegan Begin Again 🎬🎬 1984 A middle-aged schoolteacher and a grouchy, 65-year-old newspaper editor find romance despite their other obligations. Winning performances add charm to this cable TV movie. 112m/C VHS, Beta. Mary Tyler Moore, Robert Preston, Sam Waterston, Sylvia Sidney, David Huddleston; D: Joan Micklin Silver. CNG, KAR

Finnegan's Wake Passages from "Finnegans Wake"; Passages from James Joyce's "Finnegans Wake" 1963 Portions of the filmed adaptation of James Joyce's novel are shown in this program along with an interview with producer/director Mary Ellen Bute. 92m/B VHS, Beta. CMR, CAT

Fiorile 🎬🎬🎬 Wild Flower 1993 (PG-13) Covers several generations of a Tuscan clan living under a family curse which dates back to Napoleon's invasion of Italy. At that time Jean, a handsome French lieutenant, falls in love with Tuscan peasant girl Elisabetta, nicknamed Fiorile. When Jean is executed for a theft committed by her brother, the pregnant Fiorile vows revenge. Throughout sucessive generations, haunted by the past, the family's personal bad luck persists. Several of the actors play their character's ancestors, lending continuity. Attractive cast does well with the Taviani brothers' visual style and romantic narrative. In Italian with English subtitles. CW: Nudity and violence. 118m/C VHS, LV. IT Michael Vartan, Galatea Ranzi, Claudio Bigagli, Lino Capolicchio, Constanze Engelbrecht, Athina Cenci, Giovanni Guidelli, Chiara Caselli; D: Paolo Taviani, Vittorio Taviani; W: Paolo Taviani, Vittorio Taviani, Sandro Petraglia; M: Nicola Piovani. NLC

Fire 🎬½ 1977 A fire started by an escaped convict rages through Oregon timberland in this suspenseful made-for-television Irwin Allen disaster drama. 98m/C VHS, Beta. Ernest Borgnine, Vera Miles, Patty Duke, Alex Cord, Donna Mills; D: Earl Bellamy. WAR

Fire 🎬🎬½ 1996 Follows the relationship of two sisters-in-law in New Delhi—both stuck in frustrating, loveless marriages—while examining the harsh patriarchal culture of India. Radha (Azmi) is married to Ashok (Kharbanda), a video store clerk who has taken a vow of celibacy under the teachings of a scruffy swami. Sita (Das) is married to Ashok's brother Jatin (Jaaferi), who is openly having an affair with a Chinese Canadian woman. As her frustration grows, the younger Sita acts on her attraction to her sister-in-law and the two begin a lesbian affair, which is taboo in the strict Hindu culture. Dialogue is in "Hinglish," or English with occasional Hindi phrases thrown in. The attitudes portrayed must exist, because the film was banned in India. 104m/C VHS. CA Shabana Azmi, Nandita Das, Kulbashan Kharbanda, Jaaved Jaaferi, Ranjit Chowdhry, Kushal Rekhi; D: Deepa Mehta; C: Giles Nuttgens; M: A.R. Rahman. NYR

Fire Alarm ✗ 1938 A change of scene for Western star Brown as he portrays a fireman who, in-between his work, romances a career girl. 67m/B VHS, Beta, LV. Johnny Mack Brown, Noel Francis; **D:** Karl Brown. *NOS, VYY, HEG*

Fire and Ice ✗✗½ 1983 (PG) An animated adventure film that culminates in a tense battle between good and evil, surrounded by the mystical elements of the ancient past. Designed by Frank Frazetta. 81m/C VHS, Beta, LV. Randy Norton, Cynthia Leake; **D:** Ralph Bakshi; **W:** Ralph Bakshi, Willy Bogner, Gerry Conway; **V:** Susan Tyrrell, William Ostrander. *COL*

Fire and Ice ✗ 1987 (PG) A tale of love on the slopes. Two skiers realize that their feelings for each other are perhaps even stronger than their feelings about skiing. You won't care though, except for some fine ski footage. 83m/C VHS, Beta, LV, Closed Caption. Suzy Chaffee, John Eaves; **D:** Willy Bogner; **W:** George Schlatter; **M:** Harold Faltermeyer.

Fire and Rain ✗✗ 1989 Based on the real-life crash of a Delta Airlines plane in Dallas and the rescue efforts made following the disaster. Familiar cast-members turn in decent performance. Made for television. 89m/C VHS, Beta, LV, Closed Caption. Angie Dickinson, Charles Haid, Tom Bosley, David Hasselhoff, Robert Guillaume, Susan Ruttan, John Beck, Patti LaBelle, Dean Jones, Lawrence Pressman, Penny Fuller; **D:** Jerry Jameson; **W:** Gary Sherman. *PAR*

Fire and Sword ✗ 1982 A Cornish knight must choose between loyalty for king and country and the love of an Irish woman in this medieval drama. A not very inspired retelling of the Tristan and Isolde legend. 84m/C VHS, Beta. *GB* Peter Firth, Leigh Lawson, Antonia Preser, Christopher Waitz; **D:** Veith von Furstenberg. *ART*

Fire Birds ✗ *Wings of the Apache* 1990 (PG-13) Army attack helicopters and the people who fly them are used in the war on drugs in South America. Failed to match the exciting flight sequences, the romantic interest, or the boxoffice of "Top Gun." 85m/C VHS, Beta, LV, Closed Caption. Nicolas Cage, Tommy Lee Jones, Sean Young, Bryan Kestner, Dale Dye, Mary Ellen Trainor, J.A. Preston, Peter Onorati; **D:** David Green; **W:** Nick Thiel, Paul F. Edwards; **M:** David Newman. *TOU*

Fire Down Below ✗✗½ 1957 Hayworth is the been-around-the-block beauty who persuades Mitchum and Lemmon, two small-time smugglers, to take her to a safe haven, no questions asked. Both men fall for her obvious charms, causing them to have a falling out until a life or death situation puts their friendship to the test. An unoriginal melodrama indifferently acted by everyone but Lemmon. Good location work in Trinidad and Tobago. 116m/C VHS, Beta, LV. *GB* Robert Mitchum, Jack Lemmon, Rita Hayworth, Herbert Lom, Anthony Newley; **D:** Robert Parrish. *COL, COL, CCB*

Fire Down Below ✗ 1997 (R) Seagal comes armed with his trademark ponytail, martial arts expertise, big leather jackets, and environment-friendly message to the Appalachians in this hoedown showdown. As undercover (yea, he blends right in) EPA agent Jack Taggart, Seagal must stop evil industrialist Hanner (Kristofferson) from dumping toxic waste. Of course, the company town sends the usual band of thugs (thoughtfully attacking one at a time) to make him go away. He finds allies in the local outcasts (Helgenberger and Stanton) en route to the final confrontation. Not Seagal's worst, but that's not saying much. Even the usually-impressive fight scenes become tedious after a while. At least he didn't try to direct this one. Originally conceived as a Bruce Willis project at Columbia. **CW:** Violence and language. 105m/C VHS, LV, Closed Caption. Steven Seagal, Marg Helgenberger, Kris Kristofferson, Harry Dean Stanton, Stephen Lang, Levon Helm, Brad Hunt, Richard Masur, John Diehl, Randy Travis, Ed Bruce, Mark Collie, Alex Harvey; **D:** Feliz Alcala; **W:** Jeb Stuart; **C:** Tom Houghton; **M:** Nick Glennie-Smith. Nomina-

tions: Golden Raspberry Awards '97: Worst Picture, Worst Actor (Seagal), Worst Song ("Fire Down Below"). *WAR*

Fire, Ice and Dynamite ✗½ 1991 (PG) Moore is onscreen only briefly as an eccentric tycoon who fakes suicide to watch several teams of challengers scramble in a madcap wintersports contest for his millions. A German-made avalanche of crazy stunts, bad jokes, and product plugs for countless European companies, commencing with a literal parade of guests, from astronaut Buzz Aldrin to soul man Isaac Hayes. Numbing; must be seen to be believed. 105m/C VHS. Roger Moore, Shari Belafonte, Simon Shepherd, Uwe Ochsenknecht, Marjoe Gortner; **D:** Willy Bogner. *VES, ART*

Fire in the Night ✗½ 1985 In a small Southern town, a beautiful and sure-footed woman battles the limitless resources of the town's predominant dynastic family. 89m/C VHS, Beta. Graciela Casillas, John Martin. *VTR*

Fire in the Sky ✗✗ 1993 (PG-13) Mysterious disappearance of Sweeney sparks a criminal investigation, until he returns, claiming he was abducted by aliens. Though everybody doubts his story, viewers won't, since the alleged aliens have already made an appearance, shifting the focus to Sweeney as he tries to convince skeptics that his trauma is genuine. Perhaps this mirrors what director Lieberman went through while trying to convince backers the film should be made. He could have benefitted from understanding the difference between what he was telling viewers and what he was showing them. Captivating special effects are one of the few bright spots. Based on a story that might be true. **CW:** Strong language, some strong violence, and some strong sensuality. 98m/C VHS, Beta, LV, Letterbox, Closed Caption. D.B. Sweeney, Robert Patrick, Craig Sheffer, Peter Berg, James Garner, Henry Thomas; **D:** Robert Liebmann; **W:** Tracy Torme; **M:** Mark Isham. *PAR*

The Fire in the Stone ✗✗ 1985 A young boy discovers an opal mine and dreams of using the treasure to reunite his family. However, when the jewels are stolen from him, he enlists his friends to help get them back. Based on the novel by Colin Thiele. 97m/C VHS, Beta. *AU* Paul Smith, Linda Hartley, Theo Pertsinidis. *WAR*

Fire Maidens from Outer Space ✗ 1956 Fire maidens prove to be true to the space opera code that dictates that all alien women be in desperate need of male company. Astronauts on an expedition to Jupiter's 13th moon discover the lost civilization of Atlantis, which, as luck would have it, is inhabited by women only. Possibly an idea before its time, it might've been better had it been made in the '60s, when space-exploitation came into its own. 80m/B VHS. *GB* Anthony Dexter, Susan Shaw, Paul Carpenter, Harry Fowler, Jacqueline Curtiss, Sydney Tafler, Maya Koumani, Jan Holden, Kim Parker, Rodney Diak, Owen Berry; **D:** Cy Roth; **W:** Cy Roth. *CNM, MLB*

Fire Monsters Against the Son of Hercules ✗✗ 1962 The son of the muscular one does battle with a hydra-headed monster in this average sword and sandal adventure. ?m/C VHS. Reg Lewis. *SNC*

The Fire Next Time ✗✗½ 1993 In the year 2017, the United States is being ravaged by an ecological holocaust caused by a deadly combination of pollution and global warming. Nelson, Bedelia and their children are forced from their Louisiana home by a natural disaster and decide to head for better times in Canada. Their travels aren't easy. Made for television. 195m/C VHS, Closed Caption. Craig T. Nelson, Bonnie Bedelia, Juergen Prochnow, Richard Farnsworth, Justin Whalin, Charles Haid, Sal Lopez, Shawn Toovey, Ashley Jones; **Cameos:** Odetta; **D:** Tom McLoughlin; **W:** James Henerson. *CAF*

Fire Over England ✗✗✗ 1937 Young naval officer volunteers to spy at the Spanish court to learn the plans for the invasion of his native England and to identify the traitors among the English nobility. He arouses the romantic in-

terest of his queen, Elizabeth I, one of her ladies, a Spanish noblewoman who helps with his missions, and later leads the fleet to victory over the huge Spanish Armada. The first on-screen pairing of Olivier and Leigh is just one of the many virtues of this entertaining drama. 81m/B VHS. *GB* Flora Robson, Raymond Massey, Laurence Olivier, Vivien Leigh, Leslie Banks, James Mason; **D:** William K. Howard; **C:** James Wong Howe. *HMV, MRV, VYY*

Fire with Fire ✗✗ 1986 (PG-13) A boy at a juvenile detention center and a Catholic school girl fall in love. However, they find themselves on the run from the law when he escapes to be with her. Sheffer and Madsen are appealing in this otherwise unspectacular film. 103m/C VHS. Craig Sheffer, Virginia Madsen, Jon Polito, Kate Reid, Jean Smart, D.B. Sweeney; **D:** Duncan Gibbins; **W:** Bill Phillips, Paul Boorstin, Sharon Boorstin; **M:** Howard Shore. *PAR*

The Fire Within ✗✗✗ *Le Feu Follet; Fuoco Fatuo* 1964 Ronet plays an alcoholic writer recently released from a sanitorium after a breakdown. Believing his life will only continue its downward spiral, he pays a final visit to friends and calmly plots his suicide. Malle clearly and pitilessly describes a man beyond despair. Based on a novel by Pierre Drieu La Rochelle, which itself fictionalized the suicide of writer Jacques Rigaut. In French with English subtitles. 104m/B VHS. *FR* Maurice Ronet, Lena Skerla, Yvonne Clech, Hubert Deschamps, Jean-Paul Moulinot; **D:** Louis Malle; **W:** Louis Malle; **C:** Ghislan Cloquet. *NYF, PMS*

Fireback ✗½ 1978 A Vietnam vet's wife is kidnapped by the mob, causing him to take up arms and spill blood yet again. 90m/C VHS, Beta. Bruce Baron, Richard Harrison. *ART*

Fireball Forward ✗✗½ 1972 (PG) A battalion fighting in France during WWII is having a bad time until Gazzara takes over and turns them into a crack fighting team. Uses some battle footage from the movie "Patton." Made for television. 100m/C VHS. Ben Gazzara, Eddie Albert, Ricardo Montalban, Dana Elcar, L.Q. Jones, Anne Francis; **D:** Marvin J. Chomsky. *QVD*

Fireballs ✗½ 1990 Sexploitaton pic set at a firehouse, where a batch of female recruits turn up the heat for three stud hose-bearers. The title should give you some idea of the intellectual level. 89m/C VHS. Mike Shapiro, Goren Kalezik; **D:** Mike Shapiro. *ATL*

Firebird 2015 A.D. ✗ 1981 (PG) Dreary action adventure set in a 21st century society where automobile use is banned because of an extreme oil shortage. Private cars are hunted down for destruction by the Department of Vehicular Control. One over-zealous enforcer decides to make it a package deal and throws in the owners as well. Everyone connected with effort should have been cited for running stop sign. 97m/C VHS, Beta. Darren McGavin, George Touliatos, Doug McClure; **D:** David Robertson.

Firecracker ✗ 1971 Female martial arts expert retaliates against the crooks who murdered her sister. 83m/C VHS, Beta. Jillian Kesner, Darby Hinton; **D:** Cirio H. Santiago. *NO*

Firecreek ✗✗½ 1968 Fonda and his thugs terrorize a small town protected by part-time sheriff Stewart. Beautiful photography and competent cast, but meandering and long. 104m/C VHS. Henry Fonda, James Stewart, Inger Stevens, Gary Lockwood, Dean Jagger, Ed Begley Sr., Jay C. Flippen, Jack Elam, Barbara Luna; **D:** Vincent McEveety; **C:** William Clothier. *WAR, VTR, MTX*

Firefall ✗✗ *Freefall* 1994 Wildlife photog Katy Mazur (Gidley) has a brief affair with sportsman Grant Orion (Roberts) while on assignment in Africa. When they meet again, Orion tells Katy he's actually an Interpol agent who's assigned to protect her—although she has no idea why. Katy's fiance (Fahey) thinks this is strange. 95m/C VHS, LV, Closed Caption. Pamela Gidley, Eric Roberts, Jeff Fahey; **D:** John Irvin. *THV*

Firefight 🎬 **1987** After a nuclear holocaust, convicted criminals endeavor to rule the wasteland. 100m/C VHS, **Beta.** James Pfeiffer, Janice Carraher, Jack Tucker; **D:** Scott Pfeiffer. *TWE*

The Firefly 🎬🎬½ **1937** Although slow-paced and long, this adaptation of the 1912 Rudolf Friml operetta was one of MacDonald's most popular films. Co-star Jones gets to sing the best song in the film, "Donkey Serenade," while MacDonald sings most of the others. ♫Love Is Like a Firefly; English March; A Woman's Kiss; He Who Loves and Runs Away; When a Maid Comes Knocking at Your Heart; When the Wine Is Full of Fire; The Donkey Serenade; Giannina Mia; Sympathy. 140m/B VHS, Closed Caption. Jeanette MacDonald, Allan Jones, Warren William, Billy Gilbert, Henry Daniell, Douglass Dumbrille, George Zucco; **D:** Robert Z. Leonard. *MGM*

Firefox 🎬🎬½ **1982 (PG)** A retired pilot sneaks into the Soviet Union for the Pentagon to steal a top-secret, ultra-sophisticated warplane and fly it out of the country. Best for the low-altitude flight and aerial battle sequences, but too slow on character and much too slow getting started. 136m/C VHS, Beta, LV. Clint Eastwood, Freddie Jones, David Huffman, Warren Clarke, Ronald Lacey, Kenneth Colley, Nigel Hawthorne, Kai Wulff; **D:** Clint Eastwood; **C:** Bruce Surtees; **M:** Maurice Jarre. *WAR*

Firehawk 🎬🎬 **1992 (R)** Several American soldiers survive the crash of their helicopter into the jungles of Vietnam. They think their only enemy is the Vietcong but when they discover the copter has been sabotaged the hunt is on for the traitor among them.**CW:** Strong language and war violence. 92m/C VHS, LV. Martin Kove, Matt Salinger, Vic Trevino; **D:** Cirio H. Santiago; **W:** Jeff Yonis. *ART*

Firehead 🎬🎬½ **1990 (R)** A pyrokinetic Soviet defector begins using his powers to destroy American munitions in the name of peace. When a clandestine pro-war organization hears of this, they attempt to capture the man and use him for their own evil purposes. 88m/C VHS, Beta, LV. Christopher Plummer, Chris Lemmon, Martin Landau, Gretchen Becker, Brett Porter; **D:** Peter Yuval.

Firehouse 🎬🎬 **1972** Tempers ignite in a lily-white firehouse when a black rookie replaces an expired veteran. March—of "Paper Lion" renown—directed this made-for-TV emergency clone, which ran ever-so-briefly as an adventure series on TV in 1974 (with a largely different cast). 73m/C VHS. Richard Roundtree, Vince Edwards, Andrew Duggan, Richard Jaeckel, Sheila Frazier, Val Avery, Paul LeMat, Michael Lerner; **D:** Alex March. *XVC*

Firehouse 🎬 **1987 (R)** In the style of "Police Academy," three beautiful and sex-starved fire-fighting recruits klutz up an urban firehouse. A softcore frolic. 91m/C VHS, Beta. Barrett Hopkins, Shannon Murphy, Violet Brown, John Anderson; **D:** J. Christian Ingvordsen.

The Fireman 🎬🎬½ **1916** Chaplin portrays a fireman who becomes a hero. Silent with musical soundtrack added. 20m/B VHS, Beta. Eric Campbell, Edna Purviance, Charlie Chaplin; **D:** Charlie Chaplin. *CAB, GVV, VYY*

The Firemen's Ball 🎬🎬🎬 **1968** A critically acclaimed comedy about a small-town ball held for a retiring fire chief. Plans go amusingly awry as beauty contestants refuse to show themselves, raffle prizes and other items—including the gift for the guest of honor—are stolen, and the firemen are unable to prevent an old man's house from burning down. Forman's second film is sometimes interpreted as political allegory; Czech with subtitles. 73m/C VHS, Beta. *CZ* Vaclav Stockel, Josef Svet; **D:** Milos Forman. Nominations: Academy Awards '68: Best Foreign Language Film. *HMV, COL, BTV*

Firepower 🎬½ **1979 (R)** Loren blames her chemist husband's death on a rich industrialist and hires hitman Coburn to take care of the matter. Less than compelling. 104m/C VHS, Beta. Sophia Loren, James Coburn, O.J. Simpson, Christopher F. Bean;

D: Michael Winner; **W:** Michael Winner; **M:** Gato Barbieri. *FOX*

Firepower 🎬½ **1993 (R)** Two cops chase "The Swordsman" into a federally sanctioned area of legalized gambling, prostitution and crime (Las Vegas?), risking life and limb in the treacherous "Caged Ring of Death." **?m/C VHS, LV, Closed Caption.** Chad McQueen, Gary Daniels, Jim Hellwig, Joseph Ruskin, George Murdock. *PMH*

Fires on the Plain 🎬🎬🎬 *Nobi* **1959** A grueling Japanese antiwar film about an unhinged private in the Philippines during WWII who roams the war-torn countryside encountering all manner of horror and devastation. In Japanese with English subtitles. 105m/B VHS, Beta. *JP* Eiji Funakoshi, Osamu Takizawa, Mickey Curtis, Asao Suno; **D:** Kon Ichikawa. *MRV, HHT, NLC*

Fires Within 🎬🎬 **1991 (R)** A curiously flat romance with political overtones. After eight years as a political prisoner in Cuba, Nestor (Smits) is released and goes to Miami to be reunited with his wife and daughter. Once there he finds his wife has fallen in love with another man. Now Nestor must choose between his politics and the chance to win back his family. Secondary plot lines fizzle out and a talented cast is largely wasted. Scacchi is beautiful but hardly believable as the Cuban wife.**CW:** Language and sensuality. 90m/C VHS, Beta. Jimmy Smits, Greta Scacchi, Vincent D'Onofrio; **D:** Gillian Armstrong; **W:** Cynthia Cidre. *MGM*

Firestarter 🎬🎬 **1984 (R)** A C.I.A.-like organization is after a little girl who has the ability to set anything on fire in this filmed adaptation of Stephen King's bestseller. Good special effects help a silly plot. 115m/C VHS, Beta, LV, Closed Caption. David Keith, Drew Barrymore, Freddie Jones, Martin Sheen, George C. Scott, Heather Locklear, Louise Fletcher, Moses Gunn, Art Carney, Antonio Fargas, Drew Snyder; **D:** Mark L. Lester; **W:** Stanley Mann; **C:** Giuseppe Ruzzolini; **M:** Tangerine Dream. *USH*

Firestorm 🎬½ **1997 (R)** Ex-NFL tough guy Long plays Jesse Graves, a parachuting firefighter with a really square head in his first starring role. Jesse, along with "smoke jumping" mentor Wynt (Glenn), must drop into a raging Wyoming forest fire in order to save a group of trapped firemen. Except they aren't really firemen, they're convicts in disguise who have escaped through a hole in the plot. Ringleader Shaye (Forsythe) had his lawyer set the fire so that he could use the volunteer murderer/fire fighter release program to escape and find the $37 million he has hidden. Happens all the time. The smoky chain gang also stumble across beautiful bird-watcher Jennifer (Amis) and take her hostage. Jesse must foil the bad guys, save the girl and douse the fire; all the while lugging around his humongous chin and speaking in monotone. Fire effects were enhanced by computer generated graphics.**CW:** Violence and language. 89m/C VHS, LV, Closed Caption. Howie Long, Scott Glenn, William Forsythe, Suzy Amis, Christianne Hirt, Garwin Sanford, Sebastian Spence, Michael Greyeyes, Benjamin Ratner, Barry Pepper, Vladimir Kulich, Tom McBeath; **D:** Dean Semler; **W:** Chris Soth; **C:** Stephen Windon; **M:** J. Peter Robinson. *FXV*

Firestorm: 72 Hours in Oakland 🎬🎬½ **1993** Residents of an Oakland community face the threat of a big brush fire. 94m/C VHS. LeVar Burton, Jill Clayburgh, Michael Gross; **D:** Michael Tuchner.

Firewalker 🎬 **1986 (PG)** An "Indiana Jones" clone about three mercenaries endeavoring to capture a fortune in hidden gold. Paper-mache sets and a villain with an eye patch that consistently changes eyes are just some of the gaffes that make this one of the worst edited movies in history. 106m/C VHS, Beta, LV, Closed Caption. Chuck Norris, Louis Gossett Jr., Melody Anderson; **D:** J. Lee Thompson; **W:** Norman Aladjem; **M:** Gary Chang. *VTR*

Fireworks 🎬🎬 *Hana-Bi* **1997** Idiosyncratic mixture of drama, comedy, violence, and sentiment. Nishi (Kitano) is a tough detective whose wife, Miyuki (Kishimoto), is dying from leukemia. He's visiting her in the hospital when his partner Horibe (Osugi) is gunned down and paralyzed. Deciding to get justice on his own terms, Nishi quits the force and decides to settle his debts with the yakuza by robbing a bank (which also funds a last trip with his wife). Kitano (who uses his acting alias of Beat Takeshi) is the strong, silent, violent type and a very visual director. Those are Kitano's own paintings in the scenes where Horibe takes up art as his new hobby. Japanese with subtitles. 103m/C VHS. *JP* Takeshi "Beat" Kitano, Kayoko Kishimoto, Ren Osugi, Susumu Terajima, Tetsu Watanabe; **D:** Takeshi "Beat" Kitano; **W:** Takeshi "Beat" Kitano; **C:** Hideo Yamamoto; **M:** Joe Hisaishi. *NYR*

The Firing Line 🎬🎬 **1991** The Central American government hires a mercenary rebel-buster to squash insurgents. Everything's great until he finds out he agrees with the rebel cause, and he trains them to fight the government. Below average renegade-with-a-hidden-heart warpic. 93m/C VHS, LV. Reb Brown, Shannon Tweed; **D:** John Gale.

The Firm 🎬🎬🎬 **1993 (R)** Top-flight cast promises a good time—the script based on the top-selling 1991 novel by John Grisham nearly guarantees it. Ambitious, idealistic Ivy League law school grad Cruise accepts a great offer from a small but wealthy Memphis law firm. As with anything that seems too good to be true, he discovers too late that nothing in life is free. Good performances by nearly everyone involved makes up for predictability. Sorvino has an uncredited cameo as a mob boss. Book fans beware: the script is fairly faithful until the end. The movie rights were snapped up before the book was published. Placed third in the 1993 race for top boxoffice gross.**CW:** Language and some violence. 154m/C VHS, Beta, LV, CD-I, Letterbox, Closed Caption. Tom Cruise, Jeanne Tripplehorn, Gene Hackman, Hal Holbrook, Terry Kinney, Wilford Brimley, Ed Harris, Holly Hunter, David Strathairn, Gary Busey, Steven Hill, Tobin Bell, Barbara Garrick, Jerry Hardin, Karina Lombard, John Beal; **Cameos:** Paul Sorvino; **D:** Sydney Pollack; **W:** Robert Towne, David Rayfiel; **C:** John Seale; **M:** Dave Grusin. Nominations: Academy Awards '93: Best Supporting Actress (Hunter), Best Original Score; British Academy Awards '93: Best Supporting Actress (Hunter); MTV Movie Awards '94: Best Male Performance (Cruise), Most Desirable Male (Cruise). *PAR, BTV, FCT*

First Affair 🎬 **1983** A made-for-television film about a young innocent girl undergoing the pressures of freshman life at college, including her first love affair, which is with the husband of a female professor. 95m/C VHS, Beta. Loretta Swit, Melissa Sue Anderson, Joel Higgins; **D:** Gus Trikonis. *FOX*

First & Ten 🎬🎬 **1985** A failing football team emphasizes sexual, rather than athletic conquests, under the guidance of their female owner. Made for cable TV and followed by "First & Ten: The Team Scores Again." 88m/C VHS, Beta. Delta Burke, Geoffrey Scott, Reid Shelton, Ruta Lee, Fran Tarkenton; **D:** Donald Kushner. *ART, VES*

First & Ten: The Team Scores Again 🎬 **1985** A sequel to the made-for-cable-television comedy "First and Ten" about a football team's relationship with their female owner. 101m/C VHS, Beta. Delta Burke, Geoffrey Scott, Ruta Lee, Reid Shelton, Clayton Landey, Fran Tarkenton. *ART, VES*

First Blood 🎬🎬 **1982 (R)** Stallone is a former Green Beret survivor of Vietnam whose nightmares of wartime horrors are triggered by a wrongful arrest in a small town. He escapes into the mountains of the Northwest and leads his pursuers to all manner of bloody ends. Finally, the Army is summoned to crush him. Extremely violent and frequently confused, fueled on the revenge fantasy and not much concerned with the rules of plot realism. Screen debut of Caruso.

Based on David Morrell's novel. A boxoffice hit that launched the evil "Rambo" series. Followed by "Rambo: First Blood, Part 2." **96m/C VHS, Beta, LV, Letterbox.** Sylvester Stallone, Richard Crenna, Brian Dennehy, Jack Starrett, David Caruso; **D:** Ted Kotcheff; **W:** Sylvester Stallone; **M:** Jerry Goldsmith. *ART, TLF*

First Born 🐾🐾½ **1984 (PG-13)** In search of romance, divorced mother Garr finds an intriguing man, Weller. Trouble erupts when her son learns Weller is a cocaine dealer. Talented cast makes most of story. **100m/C VHS, Beta, LV, Closed Caption.** Teri Garr, Peter Weller, Christopher Collet, Corey Haim, Sarah Jessica Parker, Robert Downey Jr.; **D:** Michael Apted; **C:** Ralf Bode. *PAR*

The First Deadly Sin 🐾½ **1980 (R)** Police lieutenant Sinatra tracks down a homicidal killer in spite of wife Dunaway's illness and his impending retirement. Read Lawrence Sanders' bestselling novel; it's a lot more exciting than this. **112m/C VHS, Beta, LV.** Frank Sinatra, Faye Dunaway, David Dukes, Brenda Vaccaro, James Whitmore; **D:** Brian G. Hutton; **C:** Jack Priestley. *WAR*

First Degree 🐾½ **1995 (R)** New York City homicide detective Rick Mallory (Lowe) goes up against the mob while investigating the murder of a rich man and falling for the widow. Made for cable. **CW:** Language, violence, and some sexuality. **98m/C VHS.** CA Rob Lowe, Leslie Hope, Tom McCamus, Nadia Capone, Brett Halsey; **D:** Jeff Woolnough; **W:** Ron Base; **C:** Glen MacPherson. *PGV*

First Do No Harm 🐾🐾½ **1997 (PG-13)** Well-intentioned but routine TV movie depicts the crisis of the farming Reimuller family when the youngest child, four-year-old Robbie (Adkins), is diagnosed with epilepsy. Their health insurance won't cover Robbie's drug treatment and the bank is about to foreclose on the farm so dad Dave (Ward) takes up truck driving while mom Lori (Streep) tries to hold things together. Dismayed at Robbie's doctors, Lori also pursues an unorthodox treatment for Robbie that involves diet therapy rather than drugs. Director Abraham's own son has his epilepsy controlled by this alternative method. **CW:** Intense emotional and physical depiction of a child's illness. **94m/C VHS, LV, Closed Caption.** Meryl Streep, Fred Ward, Seth Adkins, Allison Janney, Michael Yarmush; **D:** Jim Abrahams. *TOU*

First Encounter 🐾½ **1997** Warning—when exploring space and encountering a mysteriously abandoned, apparently deserted ship—Leave It Alone! This crew decides to go sightseeing and it doesn't work out well. **88m/C VHS.** Roddy Piper, Trevor Goddard. *LEO*

First Family 🐾½ **1980 (R)** Flat satire of life in the White House. The humor is weak and silly at best, despite the excellent comedy cast. Henry's first directorial effort. **100m/C VHS, Beta.** Bob Newhart, Madeline Kahn, Gilda Radner, Richard Benjamin; **D:** Buck Henry; **W:** Buck Henry; **M:** Ralph Burns. *WAR*

First Kid 🐾🐾 **1996 (PG)** Formulaic "Home Alone Guarding Tess" does have its moments, but if you're over 14, probably not enough of them. Latest in a bevy of films to be inaugurated into the white hot "White House" genre-of-the-moment. Innocuous family comedy casts Sinbad as Sam Simms, an offbeat Secret Service agent who is given the menial job of guarding Prez's bratty son Luke (Pierce). Simms sees that Luke is merely a misunderstood misfit like himself, and helps the lad have more fun than a Presidential son is allowed. Flick's clean, inoffensive humor makes it hard to dislike. Watch for cameo from Sonny Bono. **101m/C VHS, LV, Closed Caption.** Sinbad, Brock Pierce, James Naughton, Blake Boyd, Timothy Busfield, Art LaFleur, Robert Guillaume, Lisa Eichhorn, Zachery Ty Bryan, Bill Cobbs; **D:** David Mickey Evans; **W:** Tim Kelleher; **C:** Anthony B. Richmond; **M:** Richard Gibbs. *TOU*

First Knight 🐾½ **1995 (PG-13)** King Arthur/Camelot legend comes to life again, but isn't worth the time it takes to watch. Wandering swordsman Lancelot (Gere) saves beautiful Gui-nevere (Ormond), soon to be Arthur's (Connery) queen, from evil renegade knight Malagant. They yearn, they gaze, they kiss—you gag. Written like a Harlequin romance, the dialogue (especially when uttered by Gere) is unintentionally funny, and the plot will cause much eye-rolling. Connery's regal (he knows his costume epics) and Ormond's lovely, but Gere is badly miscast. He offers a contemporary take on the flawed hero complete with American accent, an amazing feat in the 13th century. Big-scale battles, betrayals, passion, even Disneyland-like Camelot sets—the pieces for a tremendous epic are all here, it just doesn't work. **CW:** Some brutal medieval battles. **134m/C VHS, LV, 8mm, Closed Caption, DVD.** Sean Connery, Richard Gere, Julia Ormond, Ben Cross, John Gielgud, Liam Cunningham, Christopher Villiers, Valentine Pelka; **D:** Jerry Zucker; **W:** William Nicholson; **C:** Adam Greenberg; **M:** Jerry Goldsmith. *COL*

First Legion 🐾🐾½ **1951** Boyer and Addy are seminarians struggling with their faith when they are confronted with a supposed miracle. Low-key examination of religion and conflict within a religious community. **77m/B VHS, Beta.** Charles Boyer, Barbara Rush, William Demarest, Leo G. Carroll; **D:** Douglas Sirk. *ART*

First Love 🐾🐾½ **1939** Best known for Durbin's first screen kiss, this lightweight romance finds orphaned Connie Harding moving to New York to live with her wealthy Uncle James Clinton (Pallette) and his family. Connie meets handsome rich boy Ted Drake (Stack's screen debut) but her snobby debutante cousin Barbara (Parrish) already has Ted in her sights. Barbara tries to prevent Connie from going to the Drakes fancy dance but, in Cinderella fashion, the Clinton family servants help her become the belle of the ball. Durbin also does some singing. 🎵One Fine Day; Amapola; Sympathy; A Change of Heart; Deserted; Spring In My Heart; Home Sweet Home. **85m/B VHS, Closed Caption.** Deanna Durbin, Robert Stack, Eugene Pallette, Helen Parrish, Leatrice Joy, June Storey, Frank Jenks, Kathleen Howard, Charles Coleman, Mary Treen; **D:** Henry Koster; **W:** Bruce Manning, Lionel Houser; **C:** Joseph Valentine; **M:** Frank Skinner. Nominations: Academy Awards '39: Best Black and White Cinematography, Best Score. *USH*

First Love 🐾🐾½ **1970 (R)** A 16-year-old lad falls in love with a slightly older woman only to have his feelings rejected and to discover that she's his father's mistress. Actor Schell's directorial debut. **90m/C VHS, Beta.** GE SI John Moulder-Brown, Dominique Sanda, Maximilian Schell, Valentina Cortese; **D:** Maximilian Schell; **C:** Sven Nykvist. Nominations: Academy Awards '70: Best Foreign Language Film. *CNG*

First Love 🐾🐾½ **1977 (R)** A story of an idealistic college student who takes love (and especially making love) more seriously than the rest of his peers, including his girlfriend. Based on Harold Brodkey's story "Sentimental Education." Darling's directorial debut. **92m/C VHS, Beta.** William Katt, Susan Dey, John Heard, Beverly D'Angelo, Robert Loggia; **D:** Joan Darling; **M:** John Barry. *PAR*

First Man into Space 🐾🐾 *Satellite of Blood* **1959** An astronaut returns to Earth covered with strange space dust and with an organism feeding inside him (shades of "Alien"). The alien needs human blood to survive and starts killing in order to get it. **78m/B VHS, Beta.** Marshall Thompson, Marla Landi, Bill Edwards; **D:** Robert Day. *DVT, RHI, HEG*

First Men in the Moon 🐾🐾 **1964** A fun, special effects-laden adaptation of the H. G. Wells novel about an Edwardian civilian spacecraft visiting the moon and the creature found there. Visual effects by Ray Harryhausen. Finch makes a brief appearance. **103m/C VHS, Beta, LV, Letterbox.** GB Martha Hyer, Edward Judd, Lionel Jeffries, Erik Chitty, Peter Finch; **D:** Nathan (Hertz) Juran; **W:** Nigel Kneale, Jan Read. *COL, MLB*

First Monday in October 🐾🐾½ **1981 (R)** A comedy concerning the first woman appointed to the Supreme Court, a conservative, and her colleague, a crusty but benign liberal judge. Though based on a Broadway hit, it ended up seeming to foreshadow the real-life appointment of Sandra Day O'Connor, which occurred at about the time the film was released. The title refers to the date the court begins its sessions. **99m/C VHS, Beta, LV.** Walter Matthau, Jill Clayburgh, Barnard Hughes, James Stephens, Jan Sterling; **D:** Ronald Neame; **C:** Fred W. Koenekamp. *PAR*

The First Movie Cowboy **1913** Three shorts featuring the very first movie cowboy, Bronco Billy. **47m/B VHS, Beta, 8mm.** "Broncho" Billy Anderson; **D:** "Broncho" Billy Anderson. *VYY*

First Name: Carmen 🐾🐾🐾 *Prenom: Carmen* **1983** Carmen, although posing as an aspiring filmmaker, really is a bank robber and terrorist. She is also such a femme fatale that during a bank robbery one of the guards decides to run away with her. Godard cast himself as Carmen's uncle. French with subtitles. **95m/C VHS, Beta, LV.** FR Maruschka Detmers, Jacques Bonaffe, Jean-Luc Godard, Myriem Roussel, Christophe Odent; **D:** Jean-Luc Godard; **W:** Anne-Marie Mieville; **C:** Raoul Coutard. *CVC, TPV*

The First Nudie Musical 🐾🐾 **1975 (R)** A producer tries to save his studio by staging a 1930s style musical, but with a naked cast and risque lyrics. Has attained semi-cult/trash status. 🎵The First Nudie Musical; The Lights and the Smiles; Orgasm; Lesbian Butch Dyke; Dancing Dildos; Perversion; Honey, What Ya Doin' Tonight; Let 'Em Eat Cake; I Don't Have to Hide Anymore. **93m/C VHS.** Cindy Williams, Stephen Nathan, Diana Canova, Bruce Kimmel; **D:** Mark Haggard. *HHT*

The First Olympics: Athens 1896 🐾🐾½ **1984** Recounts the organization and drama surrounding the first modern-day Olympic games when the inexperienced American team shocked the games with their success. Made for television. **260m/C VHS, Beta.** Louis Jourdan, Angela Lansbury, David Ogden Stiers, Virginia McKenna, Jason Connery, Alex Hyde-White, Honor Blackman, Bill Travers; **D:** Alvin Rakoff; **M:** Bruce Broughton. *COL*

The First Power 🐾½ **1989** A detective and psychic join forces to track down a serial killer who, after being executed, uses his satanic powers to kill again. **90m/C VHS, Beta, LV, 8mm, Closed Caption.** Lou Diamond Phillips, Tracy Griffith, Jeff Kober, Mykelti Williamson, Elizabeth Arlen; **D:** Robert Resnikoff; **W:** Robert Resnikoff; **M:** Stewart Copeland. *COL, NLC*

First Spaceship on Venus 🐾🐾🐾 *Der Schweigende Stern; Milczaca Gwiazda* **1960** Eight scientists from various countries set out for Venus and find the remains of a civilization far in advance of Earth's that perished because of nuclear weapons. A sometimes compelling anti-nuclear sci-fi effort made with German and Polish backing. Originally released at 130 minutes. **78m/C VHS, Beta.** GE PL Yoko Tani, Oldrich Lukes, Ignacy Machowski, Julius Ongewe, Michal Postnikow, Kurt Rackelmann, Gunther Simon, Tang-Hua-Ta, Lucyna Winnicka; **D:** Kurt Maetzig. *NOS, MRV, SNC*

First Strike 🐾 **1985** The United States and the USSR engage in nuclear submarine warfare when the Soviets hijack a U.S. sub and aims its weapons at Arab oil fields. **90m/C VHS, Beta.** Stuart Whitman, Persis Khambatta. *VCD*

The First Time 🐾½ *You Don't Need Pajamas at Rosie's; The Beginners Three; The Beginners; They Don't Wear Pajamas at Rosie's; Doin' It* **1969 (R)** It's pre-Porky's zaniness as a vacationing youth understandably wants to spend his "first time" with Bisset. Other than her presence, this film has little to offer. **90m/C VHS.** Jacqueline Bisset, Wes Stern, Rick Kelman, Wink Roberts; **D:** James Neilson. *NO*

First Time 🐾🐾½ *Doin' It* **1982 (R)** A comedy about a college student who can't quite succeed with women, despite coaching from his roommate and counseling from a psychology professor whose assistance is part of a research project. **96m/C VHS, Beta.** Tim Choate, Krista Erickson, Marshall

Efron, Wallace Shawn, Wendie Jo Sperber, Cathryn Damon; **D:** Charles Loventhal. *NO*

First Time Felon 🎬🎬½ 1997 (R)
Based on the true story of a young Chicago drug dealer Greg Yance (Epps), who's convicted as a first-time offender and sent to a prison boot camp to straighten up. But the real challenge is when he's released and returns to his old neighborhood, with its old temptations, and tries to find an honest job.**CW:** Strong language, some violence and drug content. **106m/C VHS.** Omar Epps, William Forsythe, Rachel Ticotin, Delroy Lindo; **D:** Charles S. Dutton. *HBO*

First Turn On 🎬 1983 (R)
Not to be confused with "The Thomas Edison Story," this sex-comedy follows the adventures of several young campers who decide to die happy when an avalanche leaves them trapped in a cave. A longer unrated version is available. **84m/C VHS, Beta.** Georgia Harrell, Michael Sanville, Googy Gress, Jenny Johnson, Heide Basset, Vincent D'Onofrio, Sheila Kennedy; **D:** Michael Herz, Lloyd (Samuel Weil) Kaufman. *ART*

The First Wives Club 🎬🎬½ 1996 (PG)
As the first Mrs. Trump, who makes a most appropriate cameo, so wisely puts it, "Don't get mad, get everything." But to the three rich, middle-aged friends who are dumped by their husbands so the guys can marry younger "trophy" wives, there's just nothing like revenge. Comedy begins in 1969 with the young and idealistic Annie (Keaton), Brenda (Midler), Elise (Hawn) and Cynthia graduating college, then moves to the present with the wronged Cynthia (Channing) ledge-diving from her swanky Manhattan apartment because her husband left her. The remaining mistreated trio goes into action, using their exes' own money, businesses, power, and various mistresses against them. This film's appeal and success had Hollywood tongues wagging, predicting the dawn of new roles for older actresses. Based on the book by Olivia Goldsmith. **104m/C VHS, Beta, Closed Caption.** Goldie Hawn, Diane Keaton, Bette Midler, Sarah Jessica Parker, Heather Locklear, Marcia Gay Harden, Elizabeth Berkley, Victor Garber, Dan Hedaya, Stephen Collins, Maggie Smith, Stockard Channing, Bronson Pinchot, Jennie Dundas, Eileen Heckart, Philip Bosco, Rob Reiner, James Naughton; **D:** Hugh Wilson, Hugh Wilson; **W:** Robert Harling; **C:** Donald E. Thorin; **M:** Marc Shaiman. Nominations: Academy Awards '96: Best Original Score. *PAR*

First Yank into Tokyo 🎬🎬 *Mask of Fury*
1945 An American army pilot who grew up in Japan undergoes plastic surgery in order to infiltrate Japanese lines and get information from an American scientist. Some last minute editing to capitalize on current events made this the first American film to deal with the atomic bomb. **83m/B VHS, Beta.** Tom Neal, Richard Loo, Barbara Hale, Marc Cramer; **D:** Gordon Douglas. *TTC*

A Fish Called Wanda 🎬🎬🎬 1988 (R)
Absurd, high-speed farce about four criminals trying to retrieve $20 million they've stolen from a safety deposit box—and each other. Meanwhile, barrister Cleese falls in love with the female thief (Curtis). Some sick, but tastelessly funny, humor involves Palin's problem with stuttering and some very dead doggies. Written by Monty Python alum Cleese and director Crichton, who understand that silence is sometimes funnier than speech, and that timing is everything. Wickedly funny. **98m/C VHS, Beta, LV, Closed Caption.** John Cleese, Kevin Kline, Jamie Lee Curtis, Michael Palin, Tom Georgeson, Maria Aitken, Patricia Hayes, Geoffrey Palmer; **D:** Charles Crichton; **W:** John Cleese, Charles Crichton; **M:** John Du Prez. Academy Awards '88: Best Supporting Actor (Kline); British Academy Awards '88: Best Actor (Cleese), Best Supporting Actor (Palin); Nominations: Academy Awards '88: Best Director (Crichton), Best Original Screenplay. *MGM, BTV, FOX*

Fish Hawk 🎬½ 1979 (G)
When an alcoholic Indian, Fish Hawk, meets a young boy in the forest, they strike up a friendship and he attempts to clean up his act. Attempts to be heartwarming.

95m/C VHS, Beta. *CA* Will Sampson, Charlie Fields; **D:** Donald Shebib. *VTR*

The Fish that Saved Pittsburgh 🎬🎬 1979 (PG)
A floundering basketball team hires an astrologer to try and change their luck. She makes sure all the team members' signs are compatible with their star's Pisces sign (the fish). Produced a disco soundtrack with several Motown groups who also performed in the movie. **104m/C VHS, Beta.** Jonathan Winters, Stockard Channing, Flip Wilson, Julius Erving, Margaret Avery, Meadowlark Lemon, Nicholas Pryor, James Bond III, Kareem Abdul-Jabbar, Jack Kehoe, Debbie Allen; **D:** Gilbert Moses; **M:** Thom Bell. *ORI, WAR*

The Fisher King 🎬🎬🎬 1991 (R)
In derelict-infested Manhattan a down-and-out radio deejay meets a crazed vagabond (Williams) obsessed with medieval history and in search of the Holy Grail. At first the whimsical mix of Arthurian myth and modern urban hell seems amazingly wrongheaded. In retrospect it still does. But while this picture runs it weaves a spell that pulls you in, especially in its quiet moments. Your reaction to the silly ending depends entirely on how well you're bamboozled by a script that equates madness with enlightment and the homeless with holy fools. Filmed on the streets of New York, with many street people playing themselves.**CW:** Language and violence. **138m/C VHS, Beta, LV, 8mm, Letterbox, Closed Caption.** Robin Williams, Jeff Bridges, Amanda Plummer, Mercedes Ruehl, Michael Jeter, Harry Shearer, John de Lancie, Kathy Najimy, David Hyde Pierce; **D:** Terry Gilliam; **W:** Richard LaGravenese. Academy Awards '91: Best Supporting Actress (Ruehl); Golden Globe Awards '92: Best Actor—Musical/Comedy (Williams), Best Supporting Actress (Ruehl); Los Angeles Film Critics Association Awards '91: Best Actress (Ruehl); Nominations: Academy Awards '91: Best Actor (Williams), Best Art Direction/Set Decoration, Best Original Screenplay, Best Original Score. *COL, CCB*

Fisherman's Wharf 🎬½ 1939
Breen stars as an orphan adopted by a San Francisco fisherman who runs away when his aunt and bratty cousin come to live with them. **72m/B VHS.** Bobby Breen, Leo Carrillo, Henry Armetta, Lee Patrick, Rosina Galli, Leon Belasco; **D:** Bernard Vorhaus. *NOS*

F.I.S.T. 🎬🎬½ 1978 (R)
A young truck driver turns union organizer for idealistic reasons, but finds himself teaming with gangsters to boost his cause. His rise to the top of the union comes at the cost of his integrity, as Stallone does a character resembling Jimmy Hoffa. **145m/C VHS, Beta, LV.** Sylvester Stallone, Rod Steiger, Peter Boyle, David Huffman, Melinda Dillon, Tony LoBianco, Kevin Conway, Peter Donat, Cassie Yates, Brian Dennehy; **D:** Norman Jewison; **W:** Sylvester Stallone; **M:** Bill Conti. *MGM, FOX*

Fist 🎬 1979 (R)
Street fighter battles his way through the urban jungle seeking personal freedom and revenge. **84m/C VHS, Beta.** Richard Lawson, Annazette Chase, Dabney Coleman. *NO*

Fist Fighter 🎬½ 1988 (R)
The ups and downs of a professional bare-knuckle fighter as he avenges a friend's murder. **99m/C VHS, Beta, LV.** George Rivero, Edward Albert, Brenda Bakke, Mike Connors, Simon Andrew, Matthias Hues; **D:** Frank Zuniga; **W:** Max Bloom. *NO*

Fist of Fear, Touch of Death 🎬
1977 (R) Madison Square Garden is the scene for a high stakes martial arts face-off. Standard kung-fu film highlighted by short clips of the late Bruce Lee. **90m/C VHS, Beta.** Fred Williamson, Ron Van Cliff, Adolph Caesar, Aaron Banks, Bill Louie; **D:** Matthew Mallinson. *ART*

Fist of Glory 🎬½ 1995 (R)
In the waning days of the Vietnam War, a commando searches for the comrade who saved his life. He discovers his pal is a drug-addicted POW who's forced to fight in order to survive. **93m/C VHS.** Dale "Apollo" Cook, Maurice Smith, Robert Marius, Eric Hahn; **D:** Joe Mari Avellana. *THV*

Fist of Honor 🎬 1992 (R)
A young boxer seeks to avenge his fiance's death, a beautiful girl squares off against a bad-cop, and two mobster leaders try to take control of the same city. When a member of one family breaks a truce and begins killing rival family members, the violence escalates and old scores will be settled.**CW:** Language, violence, and sexuality. **90m/C VHS, Closed Caption.** Sam Jones, Joey House, Harry Guardino, Nicholas Worth, Frank Sivero, Abe Vigoda, Bubba Smith; **D:** Richard Pepin; **W:** Charles Kanganis. *PMH*

Fist of Legend 🎬🎬 1994 (R)
Chen Zuen (Li) is a martial arts practitioner studying abroad during WWII, who returns to his homeland to avenge his teacher's death at the hands of the invading Japanese. Homage to Bruce Lee's 1972 "Fists of Fury" AKA "Chinese Connection." Cantonese with subtitles. **CW:** Some strong martial arts violence. **92m/C VHS, Letterbox.** *HK* Jet Li, Yasuka Kurata; **D:** Corey Yuen. *FCT*

Fist of Steel 🎬½ 1993
In this futuristic martial arts film, modern day gladiators fight to the death in tournaments run by a vicious syndicate. When top gladiator Amp makes an escape bid he's hunted by henchman Mainframe, who plans to meet Amp in a fixed fight in order to become the new champion. **97m/C VHS, LV.** Dale "Apollo" Cook, Greg Douglass, Cynthia Khan, Don Nakaya Nielsen, Jim Gaines, Ned Hourani, Nick Nicholson, Kris Aguilar; **D:** Irvin Johnson; **W:** Anthony Jesu.

Fist of the North Star 🎬🎬 1995 (R)
Legendary warrior Kenshiro (Daniels) returns from the grave to avenge the death of his father (McDowell) and restore his North Star clan. He must battle evil Lord Shin (Mandylor) and his henchmen in a post-apocalyptic future. Based on the Japanese comic book series, which is also available in anime form. **90m/C VHS.** Gary Daniels, Costas Mandylor, Christopher Penn, Julie Brown, Malcolm McDowell, Melvin Van Peebles, Isako Washio; **D:** Tony Randel; **W:** Tony Randel; **C:** Jacques Haitkin. *BMG*

The Fist, the Kicks, and the Evils
1980 A young man who's father is murdered learns kung fu and sets out for revenge. **90m/C VHS, Beta.** Kao Fei, Bruce Liang. *MGI*

Fistful of Death 🎬 1967
Kinski portrays a vengefully violent and desperate cowpoke in the days of the old West. **84m/C VHS, Beta.** Klaus Kinski. *TWE*

A Fistful of Dollars 🎬🎬🎬 1964 (R)
The epitome of the "spaghetti western" pits Eastwood as "the man with no name" against two families who are feuding over land. A remake of Kurosawa's "Yojimbo," and followed by Leone's "For a Few Dollars More," and "The Good, The Bad, and The Ugly."**CW:** Violence. **101m/C VHS, Beta, LV, Letterbox, Closed Caption.** *IT* Clint Eastwood, Gian Maria Volonte, Marianne Koch; **D:** Sergio Leone; **M:** Ennio Morricone. *MGM, FCT, TLF*

A Fistful of Dynamite 🎬🎬🎬 *Duck, You Sucker; Giu la Testa* 1972 (PG)
A spaghetti western, with Leone's trademark humor and a striking score by Morricone. An Irish demolitions expert and a Mexican peasant team up to rob a bank during a revolution in Mexico. **138m/C VHS, Beta, LV, Letterbox.** *IT* James Coburn, Rod Steiger, Romolo Valli; **D:** Sergio Leone; **M:** Ennio Morricone. *MGM*

Fists of Blood 🎬½ 1987
A martial arts expert seeks revenge on the drug baron who murdered his friend and kidnapped his girl. **90m/C VHS, Beta.** *AU* Eddie Stazak; **D:** Brian Trenchard-Smith. *CEL*

Fists of Dragons 🎬 1969
Vengeful, sacrificial bloodshed abounds in this Chinese boxing extravaganza. **92m/C VHS, Beta.** Huang I Lung, Ou Ti; **D:** Yeh Yung Chu. *TWE*

Fists of Fury 🎬🎬🎬 *The Big Boss* 1973 (R)
Bruce Lee stars in this violent but charming Kung Fu action adventure in which he must break a solemn vow to avoid fighting in order to avenge the murder of his teacher by drug smugglers. **102m/C VHS, Beta.** Bruce Lee, Maria Yi; **D:** Lo Wei. *FOX*

Fists of Fury 2 *♂♂½* 1980 (R) Chen Shan must survive the Organizations' onslaughts to kill him. He escapes their perilous plots only to return to battle against them after they kill his mother for her inability to disclose Chen's hiding place. Finally Chen defeats the Evil Organization himself. **90m/C VHS, Beta.** Bruce Li, Ho Chung Do, Shum Shim Po. GEM

Fists of Iron *♂♂½* 1994 (R) Tough guy, skilled in martial arts, seeks revenge on the fighter and promoter who caused the death of his best friend. **CW:** Strong martial arts violence and some sexuality. **94m/C VHS, LV, Closed Caption.** Mike Worth, Matthias Hues, Sam Jones, Marshall Teague, Jenilee Harrison. WEA

Fit for a King *♂♂* 1937 A reporter becomes a princess' knight in shining armor when he foils an assassination plot in this screwball romance. **73m/B VHS, Beta.** Joe E. Brown, Leo Carrillo, Helen Mack, Paul Kelly, Harry Davenport; **D:** Edward Sedgwick; **C:** Paul Vogel. NOS, DVT

Fit to Kill *♂♂½* 1993 (R) Once again special agents Donna Hamilton and Nicole Justine (former Playboy centerfolds Speir and Vasquez) reteam for an adventure that matches them with an old enemy, double agents, diamonds, and revenge. Filmed on location in Hawaii. **94m/C VHS.** Dona Speir, Roberta Vasquez, R.J. Moore, Bruce Penhall, Julie Strain, Rodrigo Obregon, Cynthia Brimhall, Tony Peck; **D:** Andy Sidaris; **W:** Andy Sidaris. COL

Fitzcarraldo *♂♂♂♂* 1982 (PG) Although he failed to build a railroad across South America, Fitzcarraldo is determined to build an opera house in the middle of the Amazon jungles and have Enrico Caruso sing there. Based on a true story of a charismatic Irishman's impossible quest at the turn of the century. Of note: No special effects were used in this movie—everything you see actually occurred during filming, including hauling a large boat over a mountain. **157m/C VHS, Beta. GE** Klaus Kinski, Claudia Cardinale, Jose Lewgoy, Miguel Angel Fuentes, Paul Hittscher; **D:** Werner Herzog; **W:** Werner Herzog; **M:** Popul Vuh. Cannes Film Festival '82: Best Director (Herzog). WAR

Five Came Back *♂♂* 1939 When a plane with 12 passengers crashes in the South American jungle, only five can ride in the patched-up wreck. Since the remainder will be left to face head hunters, intense arguments ensue. Same director remade this as "Back from Eternity" in 1956. **93m/B VHS, Beta, LV.** Lucille Ball, Chester Morris, John Carradine, Wendy Barrie, Kent Taylor, Joseph Calleia, Sir C. Aubrey Smith, Patric Knowles; **D:** John Farrow. TTC

Five Card Stud *♂♂½* 1968 (PG) Five members of a lynching party are being killed one by one, and a professional gambler, who tried to prevent the lynching, attempts to ensnare the killer with the aid of a preacher with a gun. The poor script was based on a novel by Ray Gaulden. **103m/C VHS, Beta.** Robert Mitchum, Dean Martin, Inger Stevens, Roddy McDowall, Yaphet Kotto, John Anderson, Katherine Justice; **D:** Henry Hathaway; **M:** Maurice Jarre. PAR

Five Corners *♂♂♂* 1988 (R) A quixotic, dramatic comedy about the inhabitants of the 5 Corners section of the Bronx in 1964, centering around a girl being wooed by a psychotic rapist, her crippled boyfriend, and the hero-turned-racial-pacifist who cannot rescue her out of principle. **92m/C VHS, Beta.** Jodie Foster, John Turturro, Todd Graff, Tim Robbins, Elizabeth Berridge, Rose Gregorio, Gregory Rozakis, Rodney Harvey, John Seitz; **D:** Tony Bill; **W:** John Patrick Shanley; **C:** Fred Murphy; **M:** James Newton Howard. Independent Spirit Awards '89: Best Actress (Foster). MGM

5 Dark Souls *♂♂½* 1996 Three high schoolers, anxious to be part of the "in" crowd, are sent by five members of the most popular clique on a sinister woodland adventure as stars in a snuff film. **90m/C VHS.** Tina Ona Paukstelis, Mick Wynhoff, Matthew Winkler, Christopher D. Harder, Karen Dilloo, Sy Stevens, William Krekling; **D:** Jason Paul Collum. MRV

Five Days One Summer *♂♂* 1982 (PG) Set in 1932, the story of a haunting and obsessive love affair between a married Scottish doctor and a young woman who happens to be his niece. While on vacation in the Swiss Alps, the doctor must vie for her love with their handsome young mountain climbing guide. Based on a story by Kay Boyle. **108m/C VHS, Beta.** Sean Connery, Betsy Brantley, Lambert Wilson; **D:** Fred Zinnemann; **W:** Michael Austin; **M:** Elmer Bernstein. WAR

Five Easy Pieces *♂♂♂♂* 1970 (R) Nicholson's superb acting brings to life this character study of a talented musician who has given up a promising career and now works on the oil rigs. After 20 years he returns home to attempt one last communication with his dying father and perhaps, reconcile himself with his fear of failure and desire for greatness. Black, Anspach, and Bush create especially memorable characters. Nicholson ordering toast via a chicken salad sandwich is a classic. **98m/C VHS, Beta, LV, 8mm, Letterbox.** Jack Nicholson, Karen Black, Susan Anspach, Lois Smith, Billy Green Bush, Fannie Flagg, Ralph Waite, Sally Struthers, Helena Kallianiotes; **D:** Bob Rafelson; **W:** Adrien (Carole Eastman) Joyce, Bob Rafelson. Golden Globe Awards '71: Best Supporting Actress (Black); National Board of Review Awards '70: Best Supporting Actress (Black); New York Film Critics Awards '70: Best Director (Rafelson), Best Film, Best Supporting Actress (Black); National Society of Film Critics Awards '70: Best Supporting Actress (Smith); Nominations: Academy Awards '70: Best Actor (Nicholson), Best Picture, Best Story & Screenplay, Best Supporting Actress (Black). COL, WME

Five Fighters from Shaolin *♂* 197? Five high-kicking fighters endeavor to recapture their temple from an evil duke. **88m/C VHS, Beta.** Chang Nien, Lung Kwan, Dhiu Min Shien; **D:** Ko Shu-How. MPI, MOV

Five Fingers *♂♂♂½* Operation Cicero 1952 Under the alias "Cicero," Albanian valet Mason joins the espionage ring, selling highly confidential British war papers to the Germans during WWII. True story with odd real-life ending—unconvinced of document authenticity, the Nazis never acted on the information, even when they had the time and date of the European invasion! Fast-paced and absorbing. Adapted from the book "Operation Cicero" by L.C. Moyzisch. **108m/B VHS.** James Mason, Danielle Darrieux, Michael Rennie, Walter Hampden, Oscar Karlweis, Herbert Berghof, John Wengraf, Michael Pate, Ivan Triesault, Hanne Axman, David Wolfe, Nestor Paiva, Richard Loo, Keith McConnell; **D:** Joseph L. Mankiewicz; **W:** Michael Wilson; **M:** Bernard Herrmann. Golden Globe Awards '53: Best Screenplay; Nominations: Academy Awards '52: Best Director (Mankiewicz), Best Screenplay. FXV

Five for Hell *♂* 1967 The army picks five of its meanest men for a suicide mission during WWII. They must go behind German lines and find the plans for the enemy offensive. **88m/C VHS, Beta. IT** Klaus Kinski, Gianni "John" Garko, Nick Jordan, Margaret Lee; **D:** Frank Kramer. TWE, CNG

Five Giants from Texas *♂* I Cinque Della Vendetta 1966 El cheapo spaghetti western features Madison, television's former Wild Bill Hickock, as a rancher fighting off displaced Mexican peasants and outlaws. **103m/C VHS, Beta.** Guy Madison, Monica Randall; **D:** Aldo Florio. TWE

Five Golden Dragons *♂* 1967 A typical action film about an American running afoul of ruthless gold trafficking in Hong Kong. Even this stellar cast can't help the script. **92m/C VHS, Beta. GB** Robert Cummings, Christopher Lee, Brian Donlevy, Klaus Kinski, George Raft, Dan Duryea, Margaret Lee; **D:** Jeremy Summers. NO

Five Graves to Cairo *♂♂♂* 1943 Tense WWII thriller finds British soldier John Bramble (Tone) stranded in a small desert town after the defeat of the British garrison by General Rommel's (Von Stroheim) Afrika Korps. Arab hotel owner Farid (Tamiroff) agrees to let Bramble assume the identity of a dead hotel waiter, much to the dismay of French maid Moush (Baxter), whose only interest is in getting her brother out of a German POW camp. The real waiter turns out to have been a secret Nazi spy, fortunately known to Rommel only by name, so Bramble attempts to learn where the German supply depots have been hidden (the "five graves" of the title)—that is, unless Moush decides to betray him to win her brother's release. Based on the play "Hotel Imperial" by Lajos Biro. **97m/B VHS, Closed Caption.** Franchot Tone, Anne Baxter, Erich von Stroheim, Akim Tamiroff, Peter Van Eyck, Fortunio Bonanova, Miles Mander, Konstantin Shayne; **D:** Billy Wilder; **W:** Billy Wilder, Charles Brackett; **C:** John Seitz; **M:** Miklos Rozsa. Nominations: Academy Awards '43: Best Black and White Cinematography, Best Film Editing. USH

The Five Heartbeats *♂♂♂* 1991 (R) Well told story of five black singers in the 1960s, their successes and failures as a group and as individuals. Although every horror story of the music business is included, the story remains fresh and the acting excellent. Music is fine, but secondary to the people. Well written characters with few cliches. Skillfully directed by Townsend (of "Hollywood Shuffle") who did research by talking to the Dells. Less than memorable showing at the boxoffice but fun and entertaining. **CW:** Language. **122m/C VHS, Beta, LV, Closed Caption.** Robert Townsend, Tressa Thomas, Michael Wright, Harry J. Lennix, Diahann Carroll, Leon, Hawthorne James, Chuck Patterson, Roy Fegan, Tico Wells, John Canada Terrell, Harold Nicholas, Paul Benjamin, Norma Donaldson, Eugene Glazer; **D:** Robert Townsend; **W:** Robert Townsend, Keenen Ivory Wayans; **M:** Stanley Clarke. FXL

Five Miles to Midnight *♂* 1980 Brett and Danny have to depend on a photographer (Collins) for help to smuggle a gangster out of Italy. From the British "Persuaders" adventure series. Made for television. **52m/C VHS. GB** Roger Moore, Tony Curtis, Joan Collins. NO

Five Minutes to Love *♂* The Rotten Apple; It Only Take Five Minutes 1963 McClanahan (one of TV's "Golden Girls") plays a young, sleazy hussy named "Poochie, the girl from the shack." This exploitation schlocker appears to be McClanahan's first film. **85m/B VHS.** Rue McClanahan, Paul Leder, King Moody; **D:** John Hayes. SNC, TPV

The Five of Me *♂♂½* 1981 A man with five personalities finds that livin' ain't easy and seeks professional help. Made for television, based on the autobiography of Henry Hawksworth. **100m/C VHS, Beta.** David Birney, Dee Wallace Stone, Mitchell Ryan, John McLiam, James Whitmore Jr., Ben Piazza; **D:** Paul Wendkos. ART

The Five Pennies *♂♂½* 1959 Sentimental biography starring Kaye as famed jazzman Red Nichols features performances by legendary musicians Bob Crosby, Bobby Troup, Ray Anthony and Louis Armstrong. This movie marked Weld's film debut. ♫ Good Night Sleep Tight; The Five Pennies; Battle Hymn of the Republic; When the Saints Go Marching In; The Music Goes 'Round and Around; Jingle Bells; Carnival of Venice; Paradise. **117m/C VHS, Beta, Closed Caption.** Danny Kaye, Louis Armstrong, Barbara Bel Geddes, Tuesday Weld, Harry Guardino; **D:** Melville Shavelson; **W:** Melville Shavelson, Jack Rose; **C:** Daniel F. Fapp. Nominations: Academy Awards '59: Best Color Cinematography, Best Costume Design (Color), Best Song ("The Five Pennies"), Scoring of a Musical. PAR

The 5000 Fingers of Dr. T *♂♂♂* 1953 (G) In Dr. Seuss' only non-animated movie, a boy tries to evade piano lessons and runs right into the castle of the evil Dr. Terwilliger, where hundreds of boys are held captive for piano lessons. Worse yet, they're forced to wear silly beanies with "happy fingers" waving on top. Luckily, the trusted family plumber is on hand to save the day through means of an atomic bomb. Wonderful satire, horrible music, mesmerizing Seussian sets. The skating brothers (who are joined at their beards) are a treat. **88m/C VHS, Beta, LV.** Peter Lind Hayes, Mary Healy, Tommy Rettig, Hans Conried; **D:** Roy Rowland; **W:** Theodore "Dr. Seuss" Geisel, Allan Scott.

Nominations: Academy Awards '53: Scoring of a Musical. *COL, XVC, FCT*

The $5.20 an Hour Dream 🎬🎬 1980 Lavin is a divorced mother and factory worker burdened with debt and determined to get and keep a job on the higher-paying, traditionally all-male assembly line. Lesser feminist drama on the heels of "Norma Rae." Made for television. **96m/C VHS, Beta.** Linda Lavin, Richard Jaeckel, Nicholas Pryor, Pamela McMyler, Mayf Nutter, Taurean Blacque, Robert Davi, Dennis Fimple, Dana Hill, Ernie Hudson; **D:** Russ Mayberry. *TLF*

Five Weeks in a Balloon 🎬🎬 1962 (PG) This adaptation of the Jules Verne novel follows the often-comic exploits of a 19th-century British expedition that encounters many adventures on a balloon trek across Africa. Pleasant fluff with a good cast. **101m/C VHS, Beta, LV, Letterbox.** Fabian, Peter Lorre, Red Buttons, Cedric Hardwicke, Barbara Eden; **D:** Irwin Allen; **W:** Charles Bennett, Irwin Allen; **C:** Winton C. Hoch. *FCT*

The Fix 🎬 *The Agitators* 1984 A group of cocaine smugglers get their just desserts as the federal government catches them in a sting operation. **95m/C VHS, Beta.** Vince Edwards, Richard Jaeckel, Julie Hill, Charles Dierkop, Byron Cherry, Robert Tessier; **D:** Will Zens. *NO*

The Fixer 🎬🎬🎬 1968 (PG-13) Based on the true story of a Jewish handyman (Bates) in 1911 Tsarist Russia who's accused of murdering a gentile boy. Wrongly imprisoned he's tortured to confess to the crime, which he refuses to do. Bogarde is the lawyer who tries to help him. Strong direction and acting in an unrelenting drama. Adapted from Bernard Malamud's Pulitzer Prize-winning novel. **132m/C VHS.** Alan Bates, Dirk Bogarde, Georgia Brown, Hugh Griffith, Elizabeth Hartman, Ian Holm, David Opatoshu, David Warner, Carol White, Murray Melvin, Peter Jeffrey, William Hutt; **D:** John Frankenheimer; **W:** Dalton Trumbo; **M:** Maurice Jarre. Nominations: Academy Awards '68: Best Actor (Bates). *MGM*

Flambards 🎬🎬½ 19?? In the early 1900s, teenaged orphan Christine is sent to live with her tyrannical Uncle Russell and his two sons on their crumbling English estate, Flambards. Bitter rivalries and jealousies abound between arrogant, tradition-bound Mark and younger brother William, who's obsessed with the new-fangled airplane. Quarrels intensify as both young men fall in love with Christine and WWI begins, leading to sacrifice and tragedy. Based on the trilogy by K.M. Peyton. Made for British television; 12 episodes on six cassettes. **676m/C VHS.** *GB* Christine McKenna, Stephen Grives, Alan Parnaby, Edward Judd, Sebastian Abineri, Peter Settelen, Carol Leader, Frank Mills. *TVC, VCO*

The Flame & the Arrow 🎬🎬🎬 1950 Dardo the Arrow, a Robin Hood-like outlaw in medieval Italy, leads his band of mountain fighters against a mercenary warlord who has seduced his wife and kidnapped his son. Spectacular acrobatics, with Lancaster performing his own stunts, add interest to the usual swashbuckling. **88m/C VHS, Beta, LV.** Burt Lancaster, Virginia Mayo, Aline MacMahon, Nick Cravat, Robert Douglas, Frank Allenby; **D:** Jacques Tourneur; **M:** Max Steiner. Nominations: Academy Awards '50: Best Color Cinematography, Best Original Dramatic/Comedy Score. *WAR*

The Flame Is Love 🎬½ 1979 A made-for-television adaptation of one of Barbara Cartland's romantic novels. An American heiress falls tragically in love with a Parisian journalist despite her engagement to an Englishman. Takes place at the turn of the century. **98m/C VHS, Beta.** Linda Purl, Timothy Dalton, Shane Briant; **D:** Michael O'Herlihy. *ART*

Flame of Araby 🎬🎬½ 1951 When Princess Tanya's (O'Hara) father is murdered, she's threatened with an unwanted marriage and loss of the throne. But if she can win a horse race, Tanya has a chance for freedom. Now, if she can only convince handsome Bedouin chief Tamerlane (Chandler), who has the fastest black stallion in the desert, to come to her aid. **78m/C VHS.** Maureen O'Hara, Jeff Chandler, Lon Chaney Jr., Buddy Baer, Maxwell Reed, Susan Cabot, Royal Dano, Richard Egan; **D:** Charles Lamont; **W:** Gerald Drayson Adams; **C:** Russell Metty. *USH*

Flame of the Barbary Coast 🎬🎬½ 1945 A rancher from Montana vies with a gambling czar for a beautiful dance hall queen and control of the Barbary Coast district of San Francisco. The great earthquake of 1906 provides the plot with a climax. Also available colorized. **91m/B VHS.** John Wayne, Ann Dvorak, Joseph Schildkraut, William Frawley; **D:** Joseph Kane. Nominations: Academy Awards '45: Best Sound, Best Original Dramatic/Comedy Score. *REP*

Flame of the Islands 🎬🎬 1955 De Carlo plays a smoldering, passionate chanteuse who struggles with love and gangsters for possession of a Bahamian casino in this tropical heat wave. **92m/C VHS, Beta.** Yvonne De Carlo, Howard Duff, Zachary Scott, James Arness, Kurt Kasznar, Barbara O'Neil; **D:** Edward Ludwig. *NO*

Flame Over India 🎬🎬🎬 *Northwest Frontier* 1960 When Moslems lay siege to a British fortress in India, Governess Wyatt (Bacall) and Captain Scott (More) save the Maharaja's son and escape by commandeering a train. Along the way they find treason, adventure and love. **130m/C VHS.** *GB* Kenneth More, Lauren Bacall, Herbert Lom, Wilfrid Hyde-White, I.S. Johar, Ursula Jeans, Ian Hunter, Eugene Deckers, Jack Gwillim, Govind Raja Ross, Frank Olegario; **D:** J. Lee Thompson; **C:** Geoffrey Unsworth. *HEG, DVT*

Flame to the Phoenix 🎬½ 1985 A WWII drama about the Polish cavalry forces' decimation to German Panzer tanks. **80m/C VHS, Beta.** *GB* Paul Geoffrey, Ann Firbank, Frederick Treves; **D:** William Brayne. *NO*

The Flame Trees of Thika 🎬🎬🎬 1981 In 1913, a British family travels to East Africa to start a coffee plantation. Seen through the eyes of the young daughter, her childhood consists of the local Masai and Kikuyu tribes, the eccentric and sometimes unhappy English neighbors, and the wild animals that roam the plains. Based on the memoirs of writer Elspeth Huxley. Four cassettes; shown on PBS "Masterpiece Theatre." **366m/C VHS.** *GB* Hayley Mills, Holly Aird, David Robb, Ben Cross. *SIG, TVC, VIF*

Flaming Bullets 🎬🎬 1945 Last of the Texas Rangers series has solid action scenes, but little else. Ritter leads the Texas Rangers in breaking up a gang with a devious scheme: breaking men out of jail, then killing them for the cash reward. **55m/B VHS.** *MOV*

Flaming Frontiers 1938 A frontier scout matches wits against gold mine thieves. In 15 episodes. **300m/B VHS, Beta.** Johnny Mack Brown, Eleanor Hanson, Ralph Bowman; **D:** Ray Taylor. *VYY, VCN, NOS*

Flaming Lead 🎬½ 1939 A hard-drinkin' ranch owner hires a nightclub cowboy to help him get an Army horse contract. **57m/B VHS.** Ken Maynard, Eleanor Stewart, Walter Long, Tom London; **D:** Sam Newfield. *NOS, DVT, HEG*

Flaming Signal 🎬½ 1933 Featuring Flash the Wonder Labrador, this action-packed film deals with a pilot who crash-lands near a Pacific island, just as the natives, provoked by an exploitative German trader, are rising up against the whites. Both Flash and his master manage to rescue the missionary's pretty daughter. **64m/B VHS, Beta, LV.** Noah Beery Sr., Marceline Day, Carmelita Geraghty, Mischa Auer, Henry B. Walthall. *SNC, LSV, RXM*

Flaming Star 🎬🎬🎬 1960 In 1870s Texas, a family with a white father and an Indian mother is caught in the midst of an Indian uprising. The mixed-blood youth, excellently played by Presley, must choose a side with tragic results for all. A stirring, well-written drama of frontier prejudice and one of Presley's best films. **101m/C VHS, Beta.** Elvis Presley, Dolores Del Rio, Barbara Eden, Steve Forrest, John McIntire, Richard Jaeckel, L.Q. Jones; **D:** Donald Siegel. *FOX, MVD*

The Flaming Teen-Age 🎬 1956 Schlocky pseudo-documentary demonstrating the evils of drugs and alcohol. Exploitative, and the teenagers look really old. Cheaply made, and it shows. **67m/B VHS.** Noel Reyburn, Ethel Barrett, Jerry Frank, Shirley Holmes; **D:** Irvin S. Yeaworth Jr., Charles Edwards. *SNC*

The Flaming Urge 1953 A small town is plagued by mysterious fires. Could a pyromaniac be on the loose? **67m/C VHS, Beta.** Harold Lloyd Jr., Cathy Downs. *SNC*

The Flamingo Kid 🎬🎬🎬 1984 (PG-13) Brooklyn teen Dillon gets a summer job at a fancy beach club on Long Island. His father, a plumber, remembers how to dream but is also aware of how rough the world is on dreamers. Suddenly making lots of money at a mostly easy job, the kid's attracted to the high style of the local sports car dealer, and finds his father's solid life a bore. By the end of the summer, he's learned the true value of both men, and the kind of man he wants to be. Excellent performances all around, nice ensemble acting among the young men who play Dillon's buddies. Great sound track. Film debut of Jones, who seems a little old for her part as a California college sophomore. **100m/C VHS, Beta, LV, Closed Caption.** Matt Dillon, Hector Elizondo, Molly McCarthy, Martha Gehman, Richard Crenna, Jessica Walter, Carole Davis, Janet Jones, Fisher Stevens, Bronson Pinchot; **D:** Garry Marshall. *PAR, VES, ART*

Flamingo Road 🎬🎬🎬 1949 A scandalously entertaining melodrama in which Crawford portrays a carnival dancer who intrigues Scott and Brian in a small Southern town where the carnival stops. Crawford shines in a role that demands her to be both tough and sensitive in a corrupt world full of political backstabbing and sleazy characters. Remade as a TV movie and television soap-opera series in 1980. **94m/B VHS, LV, Closed Caption.** Joan Crawford, Zachary Scott, David Brian, Sydney Greenstreet, Gertrude Michael, Gladys George, Virginia Huston, Fred Clark, Alice White; **D:** Michael Curtiz; **W:** Edmund H. North, Robert Wilder; **M:** Max Steiner. *MGM*

The Flash 🎬🎬 1990 When police scientist Barry Allen is accidentally doused by chemicals and then struck by lightening the combination makes him into a new superhero. His super quickness help his quest in fighting crime in Central City where he's aided by fellow scientist Tina McGee (the only other person to know his secret). In this adventure, the Flash seeks out the violent and mesmerizing leader of a biker gang who caused the death of Barry's brother. Based on the DC comic book character, this is the pilot episode for the short-lived television series. The look is dark and stylized and not played for camp. **94m/C VHS, Beta, LV, Closed Caption.** John Wesley Shipp, Amanda Pays, Michael Nader; **M:** Danny Elfman. *WAR*

The Flash 2: Revenge of the Trickster 🎬🎬½ 1991 Every good superhero needs his nemesis—and this time around the Flash (Shipp) has that murderous mischiefmaker the Trickster (Hamill) who, along with his femme fatale sidekick Prank, is determined to outwit our hero. Can super speed and strength be enough to keep Central City safe? Based on the DC comic book character and taken from two episodes of the television series. **92m/C VHS, Beta, Closed Caption.** John Wesley Shipp, Amanda Pays, Mark Hamill, Richard Belzer. *WAR*

Flash & Firecat 🎬 1975 (PG) A beautiful blonde and a crazy thief steal and race their way across the country in a dune buggy with the police hot on their trail. **90m/C VHS, Beta.** Roger Davis, Tricia Sembera, Dub Taylor, Richard Kiel; **D:** Ferd Sebastian. *NO*

Flash Gordon 🎬🎬 1980 (PG) Camp version of the adventures of Flash Gordon in outer space. This time, Flash and Dale Arden are forced by Dr. Zarkov to accompany him on a mission to far-off Mongo, where Ming the Merciless is threatening the destruction of Earth. Music by Queen. **111m/C VHS, Beta, LV, Letterbox.** Sam Jones,

Melody Anderson, Chaim Topol, Max von Sydow, Ornella Muti, Timothy Dalton, Brian Blessed; *D:* Mike Hodges; *M:* Howard Blake. *USH*

Flash Gordon Conquers the Universe
Purple Death from Outer Space 1940 Ravaging plague strikes the earth and Flash Gordon undertakes to stop it. A serial in 12 chapters. **240m/B VHS, Beta.** Buster Crabbe, Carol Hughes, Charles Middleton, Frank Shannon. *VYY, MRV, SNC*

Flash Gordon: Mars Attacks the World
The Deadly Rays from Mars; Flash Gordon's Trip to Mars 1938 The earth is plagued by the evil Ming, but Flash Gordon steps in. From the serial. **87m/B VHS, Beta.** Buster Crabbe, Jean Rogers, Charles Middleton; *D:* Robert F. "Bob" Hill, Ford Beebe. *CAB*

Flash Gordon: Rocketship 🎬🎬½
Spaceship to the Unknown; Perils from Planet Mongo; Space Soldiers; Atomic Rocketship 1936 Re-edited from the original Flash Gordon serial in which Flash and company must prevent the planet Mongo from colliding with Earth. Good character acting and good clean fun. **97m/B VHS, Beta.** Buster Crabbe, Jean Rogers, Frank Shannon, Charles Middleton, Priscilla Lawson, Jack Lipson; *D:* Frederick Stephani. *VYY, CAB, SNC*

Flash Gordon: Vol. 1
1953 Join Flash Gordon and Dale Arden as they struggle to maintain peace in the galaxy in this pair of episodes from the series. Additional volumes available. **60m/B VHS, Beta.** Steve Holland, Irene Champlin. *DVT*

A Flash of Green 🎬🎬
1985 A crooked politician is helping a construction firm exploit valuable waterfront property. He enlists the influence of a hesitant local journalist, who then falls for the woman leading the homeowner's conservation drive against the development plan. Made for American Playhouse and produced by costar Jordon. Based on the work of John D. MacDonald. **122m/C VHS, Beta.** Ed Harris, Blair Brown, Richard Jordan, George Coe; *D:* Victor Nunez; *W:* Victor Nunez; *M:* Charles Engstrom.

Flashback 🎬🎬🎬
1989 (R) FBI agent Sutherland's assignment sounds easy: escort aging 1960s radical Hopper to prison. But Hopper is cunning and decides not to go without a fight. He uses his brain to outwit the young Sutherland and to turn him against himself. Good moments between the two leads and with Kane, as a woman who never left the '60s behind. **108m/C VHS, LV, Closed Caption.** Dennis Hopper, Kiefer Sutherland, Carol Kane, Cliff DeYoung, Paul Dooley, Michael McKean, Richard Masur; *D:* Franco Amurri; *M:* Barry Goldberg. *PAR*

Flashdance 🎬🎬
1983 (R) 18-year-old Alex wants to dance. She works all day as a welder (and has a hot affair going with her boss), dances at a local bar at night, and hopes someday to get enough courage to audition for a spot at the School of Ballet. Glossy music video redeemed somewhat by exciting choreography with Jennifer Jahan doing the dancing for Beals. Oscar-winning title song sung by Irene Cara. Inspired the torn-sweatshirt trend in fashion of the period. ♫Flashdance...What a Feeling; I Love Rock 'n Roll; Manhunt; Gloria; Lady, Lady, Lady; Seduce Me Tonight. **95m/C VHS, Beta, LV, 8mm, Closed Caption.** Jennifer Beals, Michael Nouri, Belinda Bauer, Lilia Skala, Cynthia Rhodes, Sunny Johnson, Lee Ving, Kyle T. Heffner, Ron Karabatsos, Robert Wuhl, Elizabeth Sagal; *D:* Franca Pasut. Academy Awards '83: Best Song ("Flashdance...What a Feeling"); Golden Globe Awards '84: Best Song ("Flashdance...What a Feeling"), Best Score; Nominations: Academy Awards '83: Best Cinematography, Best Film Editing, Best Song ("Maniac"). *PAR*

Flashfire 🎬🎬½
1994 (R) The torching of an apartment building and the murder of a cop seem unrelated until troubled detective Jack Flinder (Zane) becomes involved. Soon, he and murder witness Lisa (Minter) are on the run from the arsonists and crooked police.*CW:* Language, nudity, violence. **88m/C VHS.** Billy Zane, Kristin Minter, Louis Gossett Jr.; *D:* Elliot Silverstein; *W:* John Warren, Dan York; *M:* Sylvester Levay. *THV*

Flashpoint 🎬🎬
1984 (R) A pair of Texas border patrolmen discover an abandoned jeep that contains a fortune in cash, apparently from the 1960s. As they try to figure out how it got there, they become prey to those who want to keep the secret. With this cast, flick ought to be better. **95m/C VHS, Beta, LV, Closed Caption.** Treat Williams, Kris Kristofferson, Tess Harper, Rip Torn, Miguel Ferrer, Roberts Blossom; *D:* William Tannen; *W:* Michael Butler. *NO*

Flashpoint Africa 🎬🎬½
1984 When a news team follows a terrorist group's activities it winds up in a power struggle with terrifying consequences. **99m/C VHS, Beta.** Trevor Howard, Gayle Hunnicutt, James Faulkner. *NO*

Flat Top 🎬🎬½
1952 The training of Navy fighter pilots aboard "flat top" aircraft carriers during WWII provides the drama here. A strict commander is appreciated only after the war when the pilots realize his role in their survival. The film makes good use of actual combat footage; fast-paced and effective. **85m/C VHS, Beta, LV.** Sterling Hayden, Richard Carlson, Keith Larsen, John Bromfield; *D:* Lesley Selander. Nominations: Academy Awards '52: Best Film Editing. *REP, FCT*

Flatbed Annie and Sweetiepie: Lady Truckers 🎬🎬½
Flatbed Annie 1979 A couple of good ol' gals hit the road and encounter a variety of bad guys out to steal their truck. Made for television. **100m/C VHS, Beta.** Annie Potts, Kim Darby, Harry Dean Stanton, Arthur Godfrey, Rory Calhoun, Bill Carter; *D:* Robert Greenwald. *HBO, CNG*

Flatfoot 🎬🎬
The Knock-Out Cop 1978 (PG) Tough police officer will let nothing stop him from finding and arresting drug smugglers. Good for laughs as well as lots of action. **113m/C VHS, Beta.** *IT GE* Bodo, Werner Pochat, Bud Spencer, Enzo Cannavale, Dagmar Lassander, Joe Stewardson; *D:* Steno. *NO*

Flatliners 🎬🎬
1990 (R) A group of medical students begin after-hours experimentation with death and out-of-body experiences. Some standard horror film images but Roberts and Sutherland create an energy that makes it worth watching. **111m/C VHS, Beta, LV, 8mm, Letterbox, Closed Caption.** Kiefer Sutherland, Julia Roberts, William Baldwin, Oliver Platt, Kevin Bacon, Kimberly Scott, Joshua Rudoy; *D:* Joel Schumacher; *C:* Jan De Bont; *M:* James Newton Howard. *COL*

Fled 🎬🎬
1996 (R) Charles Piper (Fishburne) and Luke Dodge (Baldwin) are combative prison escapees who need to find a stash of cash and a computer disk that could save them from both the Cuban mob and the cops. Bombshell Cora (Hayek) decides to help the duo and tries to get steamy with Piper. Lots of chases, lots of violence, not much sense. The climactic battle (the film was shot around Atlanta) takes place in a sightseeing gondola at Georgia's Stone Mountain.*CW:* Strong violence and language and for some nudity. **98m/C VHS, LV, Closed Caption.** Laurence "Larry" Fishburne, Stephen Baldwin, Salma Hayek, Will Patton, Robert John Burke; *D:* Kevin Hooks; *W:* Preston A. Whitmore II; *C:* Matthew F. Leonetti; *M:* Graeme Revell. *MGM*

Flesh 🎬🎬🎬
1968 An Andy Warhol-produced seedy urban farce about a bisexual street hustler who meets a variety of drug-addicted, deformed, and sexually deviant people. Dallesandro fans will enjoy his extensive exposure (literally). **90m/C VHS, Beta.** Joe Dallesandro, Geraldine Smith, Patti D'Arbanville; *D:* Paul Morrissey. *TPV, PAR, FCT*

Flesh and Blood 🎬🎬
1922 An unjustly convicted lawyer is released from prison to find out his wife has died. He vows revenge on those who falsely imprisoned him and assumes the disguise of a crippled beggar to begin his plot. Silent with musical score. **75m/B VHS, Beta, 8mm.** Lon Chaney Sr.; *D:* Irving Cummings. *SNC, VYY, GVV*

Flesh and Blood 🎬🎬½
The Rose and the Sword 1985 (R) A rowdy group of 16th Century hellions makes off with a princess who is already spoken for and pillage and plunder their way to

revenge. Hauer leads the motley group through sword fights, raids, and the like. Dutch director Verhoeven's first English language film. Not for children; with rape scenes, nudity, and graphic sex. **126m/C VHS, Beta, LV.** Rutger Hauer, Jennifer Jason Leigh, Tom Burlinson, Susan Tyrrell, Jack Thompson, Ronald Lacey, Brion James, Bruno Kirby; *D:* Paul Verhoeven; *W:* Paul Verhoeven, Gerard Soeteman; *C:* Jan De Bont; *M:* Basil Poledouris. *ART, VES*

Flesh and Blood Show 🎬
Asylum of the Insane 1973 (R) Rehearsal turns into an execution ritual for a group of actors at a mysterious seaside theatre. Truth in titling: features blood, gore, and some sex. Shot in part in 3-D. **93m/C VHS, Beta.** *GB* Robin Askwith, Candace Glendenning, Tristan Rogers, Ray Brooks, Jenny Hanley, Luan Peters, Patrick Barr, Judy Matheson, Penny Meredith; *D:* Pete Walker; *W:* Alfred Shaughnessy; *C:* Peter Jessop. *SMW*

Flesh and Bone 🎬🎬🎬
1993 (R) Quaid is exact as a vending machine distributor with a desolate rural Texas circuit, haunted by the memory of a decades-old murder committed by his father (Caan) during a botched farm-house robbery. Alcoholic Ryan (Quaid's real-life wife) emerges from a bad marriage and helps Quaid rebuild his life, never suspecting that they may have met before. Challenging but successful role for Ryan, better known for her girlish, romantic-comedy appeal. Paltrow's unforgettable as a heartless casket robber and Caan's partner/girlfriend. Director Kloves extracts moments of earthy beauty from the bleak, humble West Texas setting. **127m/C VHS, Beta, LV, Closed Caption.** Dennis Quaid, Meg Ryan, James Caan, Gwyneth Paltrow, Scott Wilson, Christopher Rydell; *D:* Steven Kloves; *W:* Steven Kloves; *M:* Thomas Newman. *PAR*

The Flesh and the Devil 🎬🎬🎬½
1927 Classic Garbo at her seductive best as a woman who causes a feud between two friends. Gilbert is an Austrian officer, falls for the married Garbo and winds up killing her husband in a duel. Banished to the African Corps he asks his best friend (Hanson) to look after his lady love. But Hanson takes his job too seriously, falling for the lady himself. Great silent movie with surprise ending to match. The first Gilbert and Garbo pairing. **112m/B VHS.** John Gilbert, Greta Garbo, Lars Hanson, Barbara Kent, George Fawcett, Eugenie Besserer; *D:* Clarence Brown; *C:* William H. Daniels. *MGM*

Flesh and the Spur 🎬½
1957 A cowboy tracks the killer of his brother. Future Mannix Mike Connors (nicknamed 'Touch' at the time) joins the search. Unedifying western with oddball touches, notably a theme song by Chipmunks creator Ross Bagdasarian. **78m/C VHS.** John Agar, Marla English, Mike Connors, Raymond Hatton, Maria Monay, Joyce Meadows, Kenne Duncan; *D:* Edward L. Cahn. *NOS, LOO*

The Flesh Eaters 🎬½
1964 A claustrophobic low-budget thriller about a film queen and her secretary who crash-land on an island inhabited by your basic mad scientist. His latest experiment is with tiny flesh-eating sea creatures. Shock ending. **87m/C VHS, Beta.** Martin Kosleck, Rita Morley, Byron Sanders, Barbara Wilkin, Ray Tudor; *D:* Jack Curtis. *SNC*

Flesh Eating Mothers 🎬
1989 Housewives are transformed into cannibals after a mystery virus hits their town. Their kids must stop the moms from eating any more people. **90m/C VHS, Beta.** Robert Lee Oliver, Donatella Hecht, Valorie Hubbard, Neal Rosen, Terry Hayes; *D:* James Aviles Martin.

Flesh Feast
woof! 1969 (R) Classically horrendous anti-Nazi bosh, in which a mad female plastic surgeon (Lake) rejuvenates Hitler and then tortures him to death with maggots to avenge her mother's suffering. Lake's last film, and the sorriest sign-off any actress ever had. **72m/C VHS, Beta.** Veronica Lake, Phil Philbin, Heather Hughes, Martha Mischon, Yanka Mann, Dian Wilhite, Chris Martell; *D:* Brad F. Ginter. *NO*

Flesh Gordon ⚔ 1972 Soft-core spoof of the "Flash Gordon" series. Flesh takes it upon himself to save Earth from the evil Wang's sex ray; Wang, of course, being the leader of the planet Porno. Lackluster special effects and below par story dull an already ridiculous movie. Look for cameo by real-life porn starlet Candy Samples. The restored (90-minute) version also includes the theatrical trailer; a 72-minute R-rated version is also available. **90m/C VHS, LV.** Jason Williams, Suzanne Fields, Joseph Hudgins, John Hoyt, Howard Zieff, Michael Benveniste; **Cameos:** Candy Samples; **D:** Mike Light; **V:** Craig T. Nelson. *HTV, IME*

Flesh Gordon 2: Flesh Gordon Meets the Cosmic Cheerleaders ⚔ 1990 Emperor Wang (Hunt) threatens the Universe with his powerful Impotence ray. Flesh (Murdocco), along with Dale (Kelly) and Dr. Flexi Jerkoff (Travis), do battle with a belt of farting assteroids and other weirdos. Director Ziehm delivers this one on a shoestring of under $1 million, even improving technically on the original. The sex scenes are, however, more watered down in an apparent attempt to gain a wider audience. Scatological jokes are the basis for much of the humor. **98m/C VHS.** Vince Murdocco, Tony Travis, William Dennis Hunt, Robyn Kelly; **D:** Howard Ziehm. *NHO*

Fleshburn ⚔⚔ 1984 (R) An Indian Vietnam War veteran escapes from a mental institution to get revenge on the four psychiatrists who committed him. **91m/C VHS, Beta.** Steve Kanaly, Karen Carlson, Sonny Landham, Macon McCalman; **D:** George Gage.

Fleshpot on 42nd Street ⚔ 1971 Stark, realistic look at the streetwalking profession. Dusty leaves her blue collar boyfriend to move in with a transvestite and then she meets a dashing young Staten Island native (like the director). Their romance blooms until he is run over by a car, sending Dusty into a tailspin which lands her back on 42nd Street. Along the way, various rustic hookers and venerable old floozies liven up director Mulligan's version of New York. Less emphasis on the sleaze than the grittiness. **78m/C VHS.** Diana Lewis, Lynn Flanagan, Bob Walters; **D:** Andy Milligan. *SMW, TPV*

Fleshtone ⚔ 1994 (R) Artist Matthew Greco's (Kemp) work is not for the faint-hearted since he paints grisly suicides and murders. No wonder he's lonely—so lonely that he answers a phone-sex ad and is hooked up with Edna (Cutter), who becomes an obsession. Matthew even depicts her murder in one of his paintings and then she's found dead—only it turns out not to be Edna, who doesn't exist. Just what has Matthew gotten himself into? Provocative but ending is a letdown. An unrated version is also available. **CW:** Language, violence, and strong sexuality. **89m/C VHS, LV.** Martin Kemp, Lise Cutter, Tim Thomerson; **D:** Harry Hurwitz; **W:** Harry Hurwitz.

Fletch ⚔⚔ 1985 (PG) Somewhat charming comedy. When newspaper journalist Fletch goes undercover to get the scoop on the local drug scene, a wealthy young businessman enlists his help in dying. Something's rotten in Denmark when the man's doctor knows nothing of the illness and Fletch comes closer to the drug scene than he realizes. Throughout the entire film, Chevy Chase assumes a multitude of flippant comic characters to discover the truth. Based on Gregory McDonald's novel. **98m/C VHS, Beta, LV, Closed Caption.** Chevy Chase, Tim Matheson, Joe Don Baker, Dana Wheeler-Nicholson, M. Emmet Walsh, Geena Davis, Richard Libertini, George Wendt, Kareem Abdul-Jabbar, Alison La Placa, George Wyner, Tony Longo, James Avery, William Sanderson, Beau Starr, Ralph Seymour, Larry "Flash" Jenkins; **D:** Michael Ritchie; **W:** Andrew Bergman; **M:** Harold Faltermeyer. *USH*

Fletch Lives ⚔⚔ 1989 (PG) In this sequel to "Fletch," Chase is back again as the super-reporter. When Fletch learns of his inheritance of a Southern estate he is eager to claim it. During his down-home trip he becomes involved in a murder

and must use his disguise skills to solve it before he becomes the next victim. Based on the novels of Gregory MacDonald. **95m/C VHS, Beta, LV, Closed Caption.** Chevy Chase, Hal Holbrook, Julianne Phillips, Richard Libertini, R. Lee Ermey, Cleavon Little, Randall "Tex" Cobb, Richard Belzer, Geoffrey Lewis, Patricia Kalember, Phil Hartman, George Wyner; **D:** Michael Ritchie; **W:** Leon Capetanos; **M:** Harold Faltermeyer. *USH*

Flicks *Hollyweird; Loose Joints* 1985 (R) A compilation of skits parodying the tradition of Saturday afternoon matinees, including coming attractions and a cartoon. Never released theatrically. **79m/C VHS, Beta.** Martin Mull, Joan Hackett, Pamela Sue Martin, Betty Kennedy, Richard Belzer; **D:** Peter Winograd.

The Flight ⚔⚔ 1989 A non-narrative view of glider planes as they soar over the countryside and rivers of the Laurentians and Canadian Rockies. Useful in language arts classes. **96m/C VHS, Beta, LV.** Eli Danker, Sandy McPeak, Lindsay Wagner; **D:** Paul Wendkos. *VES, IME*

Flight from Glory ⚔⚔½ 1937 A group of pilots fly supplies over the Andes from their isolated base camp to even more isolated mines. Morris is their leader who watches as, one by one, the men are killed on their dangerous flights. To make a bad situation worse, Heflin arrives as a new recruit—along with his pretty wife. **66m/B VHS, Beta.** Chester Morris, Onslow Stevens, Whitney Bourne, Van Heflin; **D:** Lew (Louis Friedlander) Landers. *NO*

Flight from Singapore ⚔½ 1962 Transporting desperately needed blood to Malaysia, a flight crew is forced to crash land in the jungle. Nicely done if trite. **74m/B VHS, Beta.** *GB* Patrick Allen, Patrick Holt, William Abney, Harry Fowler; **D:** Dudley Birch; **W:** Dudley Birch. *SNC*

Flight from Vienna ⚔⚔ 1958 A high-ranking Hungarian security officer, disenchanted with communism, stages a daring escape from his country. In Vienna, he asks the British for political asylum, but is sent back to Hungary to help a scientist escape in order to prove his loyalty. Cold war drama hangs together on strength of Bikel's performance. **54m/B VHS, Beta.** Theodore Bikel, John Bentley, Donald Gray. *VYY*

Flight of Black Angel ⚔⚔½ 1991 (R) Wacked-out F-16 pilot fancies himself an angel of death, and, after annihilating a number of trainees, sets out to make Las Vegas a nuked-out ghost town. Squadron commander Strauss, however, is not pleased with his pilot's initiative. Made for cable TV script runs out of gas and heads into a nosedive. **102m/C VHS.** Peter Strauss, William O'Leary, James O'Sullivan, Michael Keys Hall; **D:** Jonathan Mostow; **W:** Henry Dominick. *THV*

Flight of Dragons ⚔⚔½ 1982 Animated tale takes place between the Age of Magic and the Age of Science, in a century when dragons ruled the skies. **96m/C VHS, Beta.** **D:** Arthur Rankin Jr., Jules Bass; **V:** John Ritter, Victor Buono, James Earl Jones, Donald E. Messick, Larry Storch. *WAR*

A Flight of Rainbirds ⚔⚔ 1981 In a dual role, Krabbe plays a biologist who dreams he must lose his virginity within a week or die and his alter ego who joins him in the search for the perfect woman. In Dutch with English subtitles. **94m/C VHS, LV.** *NL* Jeroen Krabbe; **D:** Ate De Jong. *NO*

Flight of the Eagle ⚔⚔½ 1982 Based on the actual ill-fated expedition of Salomon Andree who, with two friends, attempted to fly from Sweden to the North Pole in a hydrogen balloon in 1897. The last half of the film drags somewhat as the three struggle to survive in the frozen north after their balloon crashes. Beautifully photographed adventure. In Swedish with English subtitles. **115m/C VHS, Beta, LV.** *SW* Max von Sydow, Goran Stangertz, Clement Harari, Sverre Anker; **D:** Jan Troell. Nominations: Academy Awards '82: Best Foreign Language Film.

Flight of the Grey Wolf ⚔⚔½ 1976 A tame, innocent wolf is mistaken for a killer and must run for his life with the help of his boy-owner. **82m/C VHS, Beta.** Bill Williams, Barbara Hale, Jeff East. *DIS*

Flight of the Innocent ⚔⚔½ 1993 (R) The innocent 10-year-old Vito comes from a family who make their living as kidnappers. He is the only witness (and the only survivor) when his family is massacred by a rival gang. Vito flees the carnage and sets off to find his cousin who lives in Rome. But his journey truly ends when he is taken in by a wealthy industrialist family whose own son has been kidnapped. Directorial debut of Carlei who tends to rely on striking visuals rather than his characters. In Italian with English subtitles. **CW:** Violence. **105m/C VHS, LV.** *IT* Manuel Colao, Francesca Neri, Jacques Perrin, Frederico Pacifici, Sal Borgese; **D:** Carlo Carlei; **W:** Carlo Carlei, Gualtiero Rosella. Nominations: Golden Globe Awards '94: Best Foreign Film. *MGM*

Flight of the Intruder ⚔⚔½ 1990 (PG-13) Vietnam naval pilots aboard an aircraft carrier don't like the way the war is being handled, so they go rogue and decide to go on a mission to bomb an enemy air base in Hanoi. Loads of male bonding. **115m/C VHS, Beta, LV, Letterbox, Closed Caption.** Danny Glover, Willem Dafoe, Brad Johnson, Rosanna Arquette, Tom Sizemore, Ving Rhames, David Schwimmer; **D:** John Milius; **W:** Robert Dillon; **C:** Fred W. Koenekamp; **M:** Basil Poledouris. *PAR*

Flight of the Navigator ⚔⚔½ 1986 (PG) A boy boards an alien spacecraft and embarks on a series of time-travel adventures with a crew of wisecracking extraterrestrial creatures. When he returns home eight years later, a NASA investigation ensues. Paul Reubens, better known as Pee Wee Herman, provides the voice of the robot. **90m/C VHS, Beta, LV.** Joey Cramer, Veronica Cartwright, Cliff DeYoung, Sarah Jessica Parker, Matt Adler, Howard Hesseman; **D:** Randal Kleiser; **W:** Michael Burton, Matt MacManus; **M:** Alan Silvestri; **V:** Paul (Pee Wee Herman) Reubens. *DIS*

The Flight of the Phoenix ⚔⚔⚔ 1965 A group of men stranded in the Arabian desert after a plane crash attempt to rebuild their plane in order to escape before succumbing to the elements. Big budget, all-star survival drama based on the novel by Elleston Trevor. **147m/C VHS, Beta, LV, Closed Caption.** James Stewart, Richard Attenborough, Peter Finch, Hardy Kruger, Dan Duryea, George Kennedy, Ernest Borgnine, Ian Bannen; **D:** Robert Aldrich; **C:** Joseph Biroc. Nominations: Academy Awards '65: Best Film Editing, Best Supporting Actor (Bannen). *FOX*

Flight to Fury ⚔½ 1966 A cheap independent adventure film, featuring the novice Hellman-Nicholson team, about a few assorted mercenaries searching for a horde of diamonds when their plane crashes in the wilderness of the Philippines. Based on a story by director/producer Hellman. **73m/B VHS, Beta.** Jack Nicholson, Dewey Martin, Fay Spain, Vic Diaz, Jacqueline Hellman; **D:** Monte Hellman; **W:** Jack Nicholson.

Flight to Mars ⚔⚔ 1952 An expedition crash lands on the red planet and discovers an advanced underground society that wants to invade earth using the U.S. spacecraft. Includes previews of coming attractions from classic science fiction films. First movie of this genre to be shot in color. **72m/C VHS, LV.** Cameron Mitchell, Marguerite Chapman, Arthur Franz; **D:** Lesley Selander. *EEL, IME*

Flight to Nowhere woof! 1946 An FBI agent tracks down a stolen map of atomic bomb source material with the help of a charter pilot and a dizzy blonde. Muddled plot and no discernable acting. **74m/B VHS, Beta, LV.** Alan Curtis, Evelyn Ankers, Jack Holt; **D:** William Rowland. *SNC, VYY*

Flim-Flam Man *One Born Every Minute* 1967 A con man teams up with an army deserter to teach him the fine art of flim-flamming as they travel through small southern towns. Love may lead the young man back to the straight and narrow, but not his reprobate mentor. Scott is wonderful; and the slapstick episodes move at a good pace. **104m/C VHS, Beta, Closed Caption.** George C. Scott, Michael Sarrazin, Slim Pickens, Sue Lyon, Jack Albertson, Harry (Henry) Morgan; *D:* Irvin Kershner; *C:* Charles B(ryant) Lang; *M:* Jerry Goldsmith. *FOX*

Flinch ♦♦ **1994 (R)** Two models, who work as live mannequins, witness a murder and wonder if they'll be the next victims. *CW:* Rated R for some nudity and violence. **90m/C VHS, Closed Caption.** Judd Nelson, Nick Mancuso, Gina Gershon; *D:* George Erschbamer. *PAR*

The Flintstones 1960 The foibles of the two Stone Age families, the Flintstones and the Rubbles, are chronicled in these two animated episodes of the classic series. **50m/C VHS, Beta. V:** Alan Reed, Mel Blanc, Jean Vander Pyl, Bea Benadaret. *TTC*

The Flintstones ♦♦½ **1994 (PG)** Preceded by massive hype, popular '60s cartoon comes to life thanks to a huge budget and creative sets and props. Seems that Fred's being set up by evil corporate types MacLachlan and Barry to take the fall for their embezzling scheme. Soon he gives up dining at RocDonald's for Cavern on the Green and cans best buddy Barney (Moranis). Forget the lame plot (32 writers took a shot at it) and sit back and enjoy the spectacle. Goodman's an amazingly true-to-type Fred, O'Donnell has Betty's giggle down pat, and Perkins looks a lot like Wilma. Wilma's original voice, VanderPyl, has a cameo; listen for Korman's voice as the Dictabird. Add half a bone if you're under 12. **92m/C VHS, LV, Closed Caption, DVD.** John Goodman, Rick Moranis, Elizabeth Perkins, Rosie O'Donnell, Elizabeth Taylor, Kyle MacLachlan, Halle Berry, Jonathan Winters, Richard Moll, Irwin Keyes, Dann Florek; *Cameos:* Laraine Newman, Jean VanDerPyl, Jay Leno; *D:* Brian Levant; *W:* Tom S. Parker, Jim Jennewein, Steven E. de Souza; *C:* Dean Cundey; *M:* David Newman; *V:* Harvey Korman. Golden Raspberry Awards '94: Worst Supporting Actress (O'Donnell), Worst Screenplay; Nominations: MTV Movie Awards '95: Most Desirable Female (Berry); Golden Raspberry Awards '94: Worst Remake/Sequel, Worst Supporting Actress (Taylor). *USH*

Flipper ♦♦♦ **1963** A fisherman's son befriends an injured dolphin, is persuaded to return him to the wild, and earns the animal's gratitude. Prime kids' fare, as its sequels and television series attest. **87m/C VHS, Beta, Closed Caption.** Chuck Connors, Luke Halpin, Kathleen Maguire, Connie Scott; *D:* James B. Clark. *MVD, MGM*

Flipper 1964 Widower Porter Ricks (Kelly) is the chief ranger at Coral Key Park, Florida, who lives with sons, 15-year-old Sandy (Halpin) and 10-year-old Bud (Norden), and their pet dolphin Flipper. Adventures usually involved Flipper rescuing his trouble-prone charges from assorted acquatic dangers. The series ran from 1964-68; two episodes are included per tape. Oh yes, Flipper was played by a girl dolphin named Suzy. **60m/C VHS, Closed Caption.** Brian Kelly, Luke Halpin, Tommy Norden. *HMK*

Flipper ♦♦♦ **1996 (PG)** They still call him Flipper! Flipper, who in some scenes is played by a robot dolphin, reappears in a feature film for the first time since 1966. Sullen 14-year-old city boy Sandy Ricks (Wood) must spend the summer with crusty bachelor uncle Porter (Hogan), who would rather fish than look after his troublesome nephew. The duo witness the heartless killing of Flipper's family and are adopted by him. In addition to causing their seafood bill to skyrocket, the dolphin helps them uncover an illegal toxic waste dumper, who happens to be the same guy who made Flipper's mama sleep with the fishes. Updated along with the story is the soundtrack, which features a version of the famous theme song by Matthew Sweet. **97m/C VHS, LV, Closed Caption.** Elijah Wood, Paul Hogan, Chelsea Field, Isaac Hayes, Jonathan Banks, Luke Halpin; *D:* Alan Shapiro; *W:* Alan Shapiro; *C:* Bill Butler; *M:* Joel McNeely. *USH*

Flipper's New Adventure ♦♦♦ *Flipper and the Pirates* **1964** Believing they are to be separated, Flipper and Sandy travel to a remote island. Little do they know, a British family is being held for ransom on the island they have chosen. It's up to the duo to save the day. An enjoyable, nicely done family adventure. **103m/C VHS, Beta.** Luke Halpin, Pamela Franklin, Tom Helmore, Francesca Annis, Brian Kelly, Joe Higgins, Ricou Browning; *D:* Leon Benson. *MGM, FCT*

Flipper's Odyssey ♦♦ **1966** Flipper has disappeared and his adopted family goes looking for him, but when one of the boys gets trapped in a cave, Flipper is his only hope. **77m/C VHS, Beta.** Luke Halpin, Brian Kelly, Tommy Norden; *D:* Paul Landres. *CNG*

Flipping ♦♦ **1996 (R)** Quartet of none-too-bright wiseguy wannabes serve as debt collectors for gangster Leo Richards (David). Turns out gay undercover cop Billy (Proval) has infiltrated the gang—only to fall for ambitious hoodlum Michael (Amos)—and violent double-crosses abound. Debut for writer/director Mitchell. *CW:* Strong violence and language. **102m/C VHS, Closed Caption.** David Amos, David Proval, Gene Mitchell, Keith David, Shant Benjamin, Barry Primus, Mike Starr, Tony Burton, Paul Klar; *D:* Gene Mitchell; *W:* Gene Mitchell; *C:* Phil Parmet. *PAR*

Flirt ♦♦½ **1995 (R)** Three variations on the same theme: love, jealousy, and the problems of committing are what comprise this interesting portrait of modern romance in three countries. One character in each of the three stories is faced with an ultimatum to commit and is given a 90-minute deadline. Each are already involved in various other romantic entanglements. The best scenes show the confused flirts receiving very amusing advice from strangers. First episode is the best, as the pace subsequently slows. *CW:* Language and nudity. **84m/C VHS, Closed Caption.** *GE JP* William Sage, Parker Posey, Martin Donovan, Dwight Ewell, Dominik Bender, Geno Lechner, Miho Nikaido, Toshizo Fujisawa; *D:* Hal Hartley; *W:* Hal Hartley; *C:* Michael Spiller; *M:* Ned Rifle. *COL*

Flirtation Walk ♦♦½ **1934** West point musical that has cadet Powell falling in love with the general's daughter (Keeler), who is already engaged to lieutenant Eldredge. Some fairly good numbers, including "Mr. and Mrs. Is The Name," and "Flirtation Walk." In an attempt to change her image, Keeler hardly dances at all, which is too bad for the viewer. Based on a story by Lou Edelman and Delmer Daves. **98m/B VHS.** Dick Powell, Ruby Keeler, Pat O'Brien, Ross Alexander; *D:* Frank Borzage; *W:* Delmer Daves. Nominations: Academy Awards '34: Best Picture. *MGM*

Flirting ♦♦♦ **1989 (R)** Set in an Australian boarding school in 1965, a charming story following the misadventures of the adolescent Danny Embling, who has the misfortune to be both bright and sensitive, putting him seriously at odds with his masculine peers. He finds love with an outcast at the neighboring girls boarding school, the daughter of a diplomat from Uganda. Kidman has a supporting role as a snobbish older boarding school girl, not quite as bad as she seems. Tender and amusing. The second of director Duigan's coming-of-age trilogy, preceded by "The Year My Voice Broke" (the third film isn't yet completed). *CW:* Teen sexuality. **100m/C VHS, LV, Closed Caption.** *AU* Noah Taylor, Thandie Newton, Nicole Kidman, Bartholomew Rose, Felix Nobis, Josh Picker, Kiri Paramore, Marc Gray, Joshua Marshall, David Wieland, Craig Black, Leslie Hill; *D:* John Duigan; *W:* John Duigan. Australian Film Institute '90: Best Film. *THV, BTV*

Flirting with Disaster ♦♦♦ **1995 (R)** Mel Coplin (Stiller) is your average neurotic New York entomologist searching for his birth parents so he can finally name his 4-month-old child and make love to his wife. Tagging along on his bumpy ride are his wife Nancy (Arquette), a beautiful quirky adoption agency shrink (Leoni), and a pair of bisexual FBI agents. The excellent cast also features Moore as Mel's bra baring adoptive mother, Segal as his weirdly paranoid adoptive father, and Alda and Tomlin as hilarious send-ups of ex-hippie mentality. As events spin madly out of control, every type of relationship is satired, and every character is left in their underwear. This is director Russell's first big budget movie, and is close to a vintage screwball comedy as you'll see in the 90s. *CW:* Language, sexuality, and a comic drug scene. **92m/C VHS, LV, Closed Caption.** Ben Stiller, Patricia Arquette, Tea Leoni, Alan Alda, Mary Tyler Moore, George Segal, Lily Tomlin, Josh Brolin, Richard Jenkins, Celia Weston, Glenn Fitzgerald, Beth Ostrosky, Cynthia Lamontagne, David Patrick Kelly, John Ford Noonan, Charles Oberly; *D:* David O. Russell; *W:* David O. Russell; *C:* Eric Alan Edwards; *M:* Stephen Endelman. Nominations: Independent Spirit Awards '97: Best Director (Russell), Best Screenplay, Best Supporting Actor (Jenkins), Best Supporting Actress (Tomlin). *TOU*

Flirting with Fate ♦♦♦ **1916** Early Fairbanks-cum-acrobat vehicle. Having hired a hitman to rub himself out, a young man decides he doesn't want to die, after all. Seems there's a girl involved... **51m/B VHS, Beta.** Douglas Fairbanks Sr., Jewel Carmen, Howard Gaye, William E. Lawrence, George Beranger, Dorothy Hadel, Lillian Langdon; *D:* Christy Cabanne. *NOS, GPV, FCT*

Floating Life ♦♦ **1995** The Chans have decided to emigrate from Hong Kong before the mainland China takeover and join daughter Bing (Yip) and her family in Sydney. High-strung Bing's determined to assimilate as much as possible into Australian society and bullies her newly arrived family, who are naturally disoriented. The arrival of laggard son Gar Ming (Wong) and easy-going daughter Yen (Shun-Wah), who's been living in Germany, only provide further complications for a family completely adrift in their new world. Cantonese, German, and English dialogue. **95m/C VHS.** *AU* Annie Yip, Annette Shun-Wah, Anthony Wong, Edwin Pang, Cecilia Fong Sing Lee, Toby Wong, Toby Chan, Bruce Poon; *D:* Clara Law; *W:* Clara Law, Eddie L.C. Fong; *C:* Dion Beebe; *M:* Davood A. Tabrizi. Nominations: Australian Film Institute '96: Best Director (Law), Best Supporting Actress (Shun-Wah). *NYR*

Flood! ♦♦ **1976** Irwin Allen's first made-for-television disaster film. A dam bursts and devastates a small town, so a helicopter pilot must save the day. Good cast is swept along in a current of disaster-genre cliches. **98m/C VHS, Beta.** Robert Culp, Martin Milner, Barbara Hershey, Richard Basehart, Carol Lynley, Roddy McDowall, Cameron Mitchell, Teresa Wright, Francine York; *D:* Earl Bellamy. *WAR*

Flood: A River's Rampage ♦♦½ **1997 (PG-13)** Community struggles to rebuild after a devastating flood. *CW:* Mild flood related peril. **92m/C VHS, Closed Caption.** Richard Thomas, Kate Vernon, Jan Rubes; *D:* Bruce Pittman. *HMK, ART*

The Floorwalker ♦♦♦ **1917** Chaplin becomes involved with a dishonest floorwalker in a department store. Silent. **20m/B VHS, Beta.** Charlie Chaplin; *D:* Charlie Chaplin. *CAB, GVV*

The Floorwalker/By the Sea ♦♦♦ **1915** Two early Chaplin short comedies, featuring a hilarious scene on an escalator in the first film. Silent. **51m/B VHS, Beta, 8mm.** Charlie Chaplin, Edna Purviance, Eric Campbell; *D:* Charlie Chaplin. *VYY*

Flor Silvestre ♦ *Wild Flower* **1958** The son of a rich rancher romances a young woman against the background of the Mexican Revolution. **90m/B VHS, Beta.** *MX* Dolores Del Rio, Pedro Armendariz Sr.; *D:* Emilio Fernandez. *MAD*

The Florida Connection ♦ **1974** An action thriller set in the Florida Swamps a collection of villains and a vague plot about smuggling. **90m/C VHS, Beta.** Dan Pastorini, June Wilkinson. *UNI*

Florida Straits ♦♦ **1987 (PG-13)** A recently released Cuban prisoner hires a few losers and their boat to return to the island, supposedly to find the girl he loves. The real quest is for gold buried during the Bay-of-Pigs invasion in this none-too-original made-for-cable movie that at least offers a good cast. **98m/C VHS, Beta, LV, Closed Caption.** Raul Julia, Fred Ward, Daniel H. Jenkins, Antonio Fargas; **D:** Mike Hodges; **W:** Stephen Metcalfe; **M:** Michel Colombier. ORI

Floundering 🎬½ **1994 (R)** Misguided satire uses the 1992 L.A. riots as a backdrop to tell the saga of unemployed James Boyz (LeGros), whose life is a walking disaster. He owes the IRS, his unemployment compensation has run out, his brother (Hawke) has fled from a drug rehab clinic, and he finds his girlfriend (Zane) in bed with another man. John drags himself among the city's downtrodden as he fantasizes about life. Drag pretty much sums up the film despite good performances by LeGros and Hawke. **CW:** Strong language, sexuality and drug use and for some violence. **97m/C VHS.** James LeGros, Ethan Hawke, Steve Buscemi, John Cusack, Lisa Zane, Sy Richardson; **D:** Peter McCarthy; **W:** Peter McCarthy. APX

Flower Drum Song 🎬🎬 **1961** The Rodgers and Hammerstein musical played better on Broadway than in this overblown adaptation of life in San Francisco's Chinatown. Umeki plays the young girl who arrives from Hong Kong for an arranged marriage. Her intended (Soo) is a fast-living nightclub owner already enjoying the love of singer Kwan. Meanwhile Umeki falls for the handsome Shigeta. Naturally, everything comes together in a happy ending. 🎵I Enjoy Being A Girl; Don't Marry Me; Grant Avenue; You Are Beautiful; A Hundred Million Miracles; Fan Tan Fanny; Chop Suey; The Other Generation; I Am Going to Like It Here. **133m/C VHS, Beta, LV.** Nancy Kwan, Jack Soo, James Shigeta, Miyoshi Umeki, Juanita Hall; **D:** Henry Koster; **C:** Russell Metty; **M:** Richard Rodgers, Oscar Hammerstein. Nominations: Academy Awards '61: Best Art Direction/Set Decoration (Color), Best Color Cinematography, Best Costume Design (Color), Best Sound, Scoring of a Musical. USH, FCT

The Flower of My Secret 🎬🎬🎬 La Flor de My Secreto **1995 (R)** Emotional yet restrained story about middle-aged Leo (Paredes), whose longtime marriage is fast ending (and it's not her idea). Leo writes hugely popular romance novels under a pseudonym but her current work is so bleak it's unpublishable. So, Leo gets a job at a newspaper where editor Angel (Echanove) immediately falls for her, and indeed, lives up to his name as her guardian. Willfully myopic about her own life, Leo undergoes further trials until she slowly realizes the mess she's in and becomes willing to change. Surprisingly subdued given Almodovar's usual flamboyance but it's a welcome change of pace. Spanish with subtitles. **CW:** Language and brief sexuality. **107m/C VHS, LV, Closed Caption.** SP FR Marisa Paredes, Juan Echanove, Imanol Arias, Carmen Elias, Rossy de Palma, Chus Lampreave, Joaquin Cortes, Manuela Vargas; **D:** Pedro Almodovar; **W:** Pedro Almodovar; **C:** Alfonso Beato; **M:** Alberto Iglesias. COL

Flowers in the Attic 🎬½ **1987 (PG-13)** Based on the V.C. Andrews bestseller, a would-be thriller about four young siblings locked for years in their family's old mansion by their grandmother with their mother's selfish acquiescence. A chicken-hearted, clumsy flop that skimps on the novel's trashier themes. **93m/C VHS, Beta, LV, Closed Caption.** Victoria Tennant, Kristy Swanson, Louise Fletcher, Jeb Stuart Adams; **D:** Jeffrey Bloom; **W:** Jeffrey Bloom; **C:** Gil Hubbs. VTR

Flowers of Reverie 🎬🎬 **1984** A former soldier is imprisoned for his work in the resistance during the Hungarian Revolution (1848-9), leading to tragedy. In Hungarian with English subtitles. **106m/C VHS.** HU **D:** Laszlo Lugossy. FCT

The Flowers of St. Francis 🎬🎬🎬 **1950** Rossellini's presentation of St. Francis and his friars' attainment of spiritual harmony. In Italian with English subtitles. This is the British release version, 10-15 minutes longer than the U.S. version. **75m/B VHS, Beta.** IT Federico Fellini; **D:** Roberto Rossellini. FCT

Flubber 🎬🎬 **1997 (PG)** Bland remake of Disney's "The Absent-Minded Professor" with Williams as the befuddled, yet brilliant Prof. Brainard. Putting his wedding on the back Bunsen burner, much to the dismay of his fiancee Sara Jean (Harden), Brainard invents a bouncy, flying green slime named "flubber." As the substance becomes the cure-all for romantic turmoil and fledging school basketball teams, it also attracts the attention of a corrupt businessman and his moronic henchmen. Due to the dull subplots, kids and adults will be disappointed that the main attraction (the cute green goo) doesn't have much screen time. Williams, oddly enough, seems comfortable playing second banana to a substance that could describe his comedic skills. **93m/C VHS, Closed Caption.** Robin Williams, Marcia Gay Harden, Christopher McDonald, Raymond J. Barry, Clancy Brown, Ted Levine, Wil Wheaton, Edie McClurg; **D:** Les Mayfield; **W:** John Hughes; **C:** Dean Cundey; **M:** Danny Elfman. TOU

Fluke 🎬🎬 **1995 (PG)** "Ghost" meets "Oh, Heavenly Dog" as Tom (Modine) dies in a suspicious car accident and is reincarnated as a dog who remembers his past life. He returns to his former family (Travis and Pomeranc) to protect them from his former business partner (Stoltz), battling such puppy perils as cosmetic testing labs and dogcatchers along the way. While there's plenty of squishy sentimentality to go around, some of the scenes involving animal abuse may be a little much for the target audience of pre-teen kids. Jackson and Stoltz trade "Pulp Fiction" for pup fiction, but this dog won't hunt. Based on the novel by James Herbert. **96m/C VHS, LV, Closed Caption.** Matthew Modine, Nancy Travis, Eric Stoltz, Max Pomeranc, Ron Perlman, Jon Polito, Bill Cobbs, Frederico Pacifici, Collin Wilcox Paxton; **D:** Carlo Carlei; **W:** James Carrington, Carlo Carlei; **C:** Raffaele Mertes; **M:** Carlo Siliotto; **V:** Samuel L. Jackson. MGM

Flush 🎬🎬 **1981** Unorthodox comedy involving funny noises. **90m/C VHS.** William Calloway, William Bronder, Jeannie Linero; **D:** Andrew J. Kuehn. NO

The Flustered Comedy of Leon Errol 🎬🎬 **1939** The popular Depression-era comedian Errol is showcased in three shorts: "Crime Rave," "Man-I-Cured," and "A Panic in the Parlor." **56m/B VHS, Beta, 8mm.** Leon Errol, Vivian Tobin, Dorothy Granger, Frank Faylen, Virginia Vale. VYY

The Fly 🎬🎬🎬 **1958** The historic, chillingly original '50s sci-fi tale about a hapless scientist experimenting with teleportation who accidentally gets anatomically confused with a housefly. Campy required viewing; two sequels followed, and a 1986 remake which itself has spawned one sequel. **94m/C VHS, Beta, LV.** Vincent Price, David Hedison, Herbert Marshall, Patricia Owens; **D:** Kurt Neumann; **W:** James Clavell; **C:** Karl Struss. FOX

The Fly 🎬🎬🎬 **1986 (R)** A sensitive, humanistic remake of the 1958 horror film about a scientist whose flesh is genetically intermixed with a housefly via his experimental transportation device. A thoughtful, shocking horror film, with fine performances from Goldblum and Davis and a brutally emotional conclusion. Followed by "The Fly II" in 1989. **96m/C VHS, Beta, LV, Closed Caption.** Jeff Goldblum, Geena Davis, John Getz, Joy Boushel, Les Carlson; **D:** David Cronenberg; **W:** David Cronenberg, Charles Edward Pogue; **C:** Mark Irwin; **M:** Howard Shore. Academy Awards '86: Best Makeup. FOX

The Fly 2 🎬½ **1989 (R)** Inferior sequel to Cronenberg's opus, in which the offspring of Seth Brundle achieves full genius maturity in three years, falls in love, and discovers the evil truth behind his father's teleportation device and corporate auspices that backed it. **105m/C VHS, Beta, LV.** Eric Stoltz, Daphne Zuniga, Lee Richardson, John Getz, Harley Cross; **D:** Chris Walas; **W:** Mick Garris, Jim Wheat, Ken Wheat, Frank Darabont. FOX, CCB

Fly Away Home 🎬🎬🎬 Father Goose; Flying Wild **1996 (PG)** Does for geese what "Babe" did for pigs. Young Amy (Paquin) withdraws when she loses her mother in a car crash and is forced to live with her estranged father, Thomas (Daniels), a scruffy sculptor/inventor, in rural Ontario. Still dealing with her own mother's death, Amy suddenly becomes a mother herself to a tiny gaggle of goslings when she happens upon a nest of uprooted eggs. Extraordinary technical achievements make up for some unnecessary melodrama in the second half as the geese head South, led by Amy, in a glider built by her father. Touching but unsentimental, mostly well scripted and acted, and extraordinarily shot. Based on the true story of inventor Bill Lishman, who led domesticated geese on a winter migration from Toronto, Canada to North Carolina, leading the formation in his motor-powered glider. **107m/C VHS, LV, Closed Caption, DVD.** Jeff Daniels, Anna Paquin, Dana Delany, Terry Kinney, Jeremy Ratchford; **D:** Carroll Ballard; **W:** Robert Rodat, Vince McKewin; **C:** Caleb Deschanel; **M:** Mark Isham. Nominations: Academy Awards '96: Best Cinematography. COL

Fly by Night 🎬🎬 **1993 (PG-13)** Mismatched New York rappers Rich and I join forces to make it big as hard-core gangstas. When they're propelled to the top of the charts, forces both personal and professional work to tear them apart. **93m/C VHS, Closed Caption.** Jeffrey D. Sams, Ron Brice, Darryl (Chill) Mitchell, Todd Graff, Leo Burmester, Soulfood Jed, Lawrence Gilliard, Omar Carter, Maura Tierney, Yul Vazquez, M.C. Lyte, Christopher-Michael Gerrard, Ebony Jo-Ann; **D:** Steve Gomer; **W:** Todd Graff; **C:** Larry Banks; **M:** Kris Parker, Sidney Mills, Dwayne Sumal. Sundance Film Festival '93: Filmmakers Trophy. COL

Fly with the Hawk 🎬🎬 **19??** A troubled teenager gets lost in the wilderness for a year, and learns some important things from nature to take back to civilization. **90m/C VHS.** Peter Ferri, Peter Snook, Shelley Lynne Speigel; **D:** Robert Tanos. NO

Flying Blind 🎬½ **1941** Foreign agents are thwarted in their attempt to steal a vital air defense secret. Unconvincing espionage plot cobbled into a story about a Los Angeles-Las Vegas puddle jumper. **69m/B VHS, Beta.** Richard Arlen, Jean Parker, Marie Wilson. NOS, DVT

The Flying Deuces 🎬🎬🎬 Flying Aces **1939** Ollie's broken heart lands Laurel and Hardy in the Foreign Legion. The comic pair escape a firing squad only to suffer a plane crash that results in Hardy's reincarnation as a horse. A musical interlude with a Laurel soft shoe while Hardy sings "Shine On, Harvest Moon" is one of the film's highlights. **65m/B VHS, Beta, LV.** Stan Laurel, Oliver Hardy, Jean Parker, Reginald Gardiner, James Finlayson; **D:** Edward Sutherland. CNG, MRV, NOS

Flying Down to Rio 🎬🎬½ **1933** The first Astaire-Rogers musical, although they are relegated to supporting status behind Del Rio and Raymond. Still, it was enough to make them stars and a team that epitomizes the height of American musical films. The slim story revolves around singer Del Rio's two suitors and receives a splendid, art deco production. Showgirls dancing on plane wings in flight provide another memorable moment. 🎵Music Makes Me; The Carioca; Orchids in the Moonlight; Flying Down to Rio. **89m/B VHS, Beta.** Fred Astaire, Ginger Rogers, Dolores Del Rio, Eric Blore, Gene Raymond, Franklin Pangborn; **D:** Thornton Freeland; **M:** Vincent Youmans, Max Steiner. Nominations: Academy Awards '34: Best Song ("Carioca"). TTC

The Flying Fool 🎬🎬 **1929** Ace pilot Bill returns from the war to find his younger brother has fallen for a singer. When Bill meets the lady, he also notices her charms and the two brothers have a duel in the skies to see who'll get the girl. **75m/B VHS, Beta.** William Boyd, Marie Prevost, Russell Gleason; **D:** Tay Garnett; **W:** James Gleason. VYY, RXM, GPV

Flying from the Hawk 🎬½ **1986** A 12-year-old boy sees something he shouldn't and soon finds that his friends and relatives are mysteriously vanishing. **110m/C VHS, Beta.** John Ireland, Diane McBain. NO

Flying Leathernecks ♂♂♂ 1951 Tough squadron leader Wayne fights with his follow officer Hyan in Guadalcanal when their leadership styles clash. But when the real fighting begins all is forgotten as Wayne leads his men into victorious battle, winning the admiration and devotion of his fliers. Memorable WWII film deals with war in human terms. 102m/C VHS, Beta, LV. John Wayne, Robert Ryan, Janis Carter; **D:** Nicholas Ray. *TLF, TTC*

The Flying Saucer ♂♂½ 1950 U.S. and Russian scientists clash over their search for a huge flying saucer that is hidden under a glacier. The first movie to deal with flying saucers. The cassette includes animated opening and closing sequences plus previews of coming attractions. 71m/B VHS. Mikel Conrad, Pat Garrison, Hanz von Teuffen; **D:** Mikel Conrad. *EEL, SNC*

Flying Saucers Over Hollywood: The Plan 9 Companion 1993 This documentary looks at what many consider to be the worst film of all time, "Plan 9 from Outer Space," released in 1959. The cult classic, directed by the equally bizarre Edward D. Wood, Jr., is revealed in all its absurdity, including interviews with cast, crew, and fans. 111m/C VHS. **W:** Mark Patrick Carducci. *ATM*

The Flying Scotsman ♂♂½ 1929 A fired railroad worker tries to wreck an express train on the engineer's last journey. The daughter of the intended victim saves the day. Silent, with sound added. 60m/B VHS, Beta. Ray Milland, Pauline Johnson, Moore Marriott; **D:** Castleton Knight. *NOS, DVT, HEG*

Flying Tigers ♂♂½ 1942 Salutes the All-American Volunteer Group which flew for China under General Claire Chennault against the Japanese before the U.S. entered WWII. A squadron leader and a brash new recruit both vie for the affections of a pretty nurse in-between their flying missions. Romance and a few comic touches take a back seat to graphic scenes of aerial battles and dramatization of heroic sacrifice in this rousing war film. 101m/B VHS, LV, Closed Caption. John Wayne, Paul Kelly, John Carroll, Anna Lee, Mae Clarke, Gordon Jones; **D:** David Miller. Nominations: Academy Awards '42: Best Sound, Best Original Dramatic/Comedy Score. *REP*

Flying Wild ♂½ 1941 A gang of saboteurs is out to steal top-secret airplane blueprints. Who else but the Bowery Boys could conceivably stop them? 62m/B VHS. Leo Gorcey, Bobby Jordan, Donald Haines, Joan Barclay, David Gorcey, Bobby Stone, Sammy Morrison; **D:** William West. *NOS, LOO*

FM ♂♂ *Citizen's Band* 1978 (PG-13) The disc jockeys at an L.A. radio station rebel in the name of rock'n'roll. Despite the promising cast and setting (Mull makes his movie debut as a memorable space case), this is just disjointed and surprisingly unhip; one producer took his name off it due to creative difficulties. The decent soundtrack includes concert footage of Jimmy Buffet and Linda Ronstadt. ♫FM; Do It Again; FM Reprise; Livingston Saturday Night; The Key To My Kingdom; Green Grass and High Tides; Life In The Fast Lane; Bad Man; Poor, Poor, Pitiful Me. 104m/C VHS, LV, Letterbox. Eileen Brennan, Alex Karras, Cleavon Little, Martin Mull, Cassie Yates, Linda Ronstadt, Jimmy Buffett; **D:** Lamont Johnson. *USH*

The Fog ♂♂ 1978 (R) John Carpenter's blustery follow-up to his success with "Halloween." An evil fog containing murderous, vengeful ghosts envelops a sleepy seaside town and subjects the residents to terror and mayhem. 91m/C VHS, Beta, LV, 8mm. Hal Holbrook, Adrienne Barbeau, Jamie Lee Curtis, Janet Leigh, John Houseman, Tom Atkins; **D:** John Carpenter; **C:** John Carpenter, Debra Hill; **M:** John Carpenter. *COL*

Fog Island ♂♂½ 1945 Murder and terror lurk after a greedy inventor, who was framed for fraud by his business partner, is released from prison. He plots revenge by inviting his foes to his island home. 72m/B VHS, Beta. George Zucco, Lionel Atwill,

Terry Morse, Jerome Cowan, Veda Ann Borg; **D:** Terry Morse. *NOS, ONO, VCN*

Folks! ♂ 1992 (PG-13) Selleck is a Chicago stockbroker whose wife and kids have left him, the FBI is after him, and, worst of all, his parents have moved in with him. His parents don't want to be a burden, so Selleck decides that the best way to solve his financial woes is to help his parents commit suicide so he can collect on their insurance policies. Tasteless comedy that makes fun of aging and Alzheimer's Disease. Selleck is too sweet and cuddly for his role, but Ameche is good as the senile father, and Ebersole is great as Selleck's unpleasant sister. 109m/C VHS, Closed Caption. Tom Selleck, Don Ameche, Anne Jackson, Christine Ebersole, Wendy Crewson, Robert Pastorelli, Michael Murphy, Kevin Timothy Chevalia, Margaret Murphy; **D:** Ted Kotcheff; **M:** Michel Colombier. *FXV*

Follies Girl ♂♂ 1943 There's folly in expecting that this wartime tuner would hold up today. An army private romances a dress designer and a musical show somehow results. ♫Keep the Flag A-Flying; No Man In The House; Someone to Love; I Told A Lie; Shall We Gather at the Rhythm?; Fascination; I Knew Your Father's Son; Thoity Poiple Boids. 74m/B VHS. Wendy Barrie, Doris Nolan, Gordon Oliver, Anne Barrett, Arthur Pierson; **D:** William Rowland. *NOS, LOO*

Follies in Concert 1985 A filmed record of the famed Stephen Sondheim musical play, performed at Lincoln Center in New York with an all-star cast. Songs include "I'm Still Here," "Losing My Mind," "Broadway Baby" and "The Ladies Who Lunch." 90m/C VHS, Beta, LV. Carol Burnett, Lee Remick, Betty Comden, Andre Gregory, Adolph Green, Mandy Patinkin, Phyllis Newman, Elaine Stritch, Jim Walton, Licia Albanese. *MVD*

Follow Me ♂♂ 1969 (G) Round-the-world odyssey of three moon doggies searching for adventure—and the perfect wave. Spectacular surfing scenes are complemented by songs performed by Dino, Desi, and Billy. 90m/C VHS. Claude Codgen, Mary Lou McGinnis, Bob Purvey; **D:** Gene McCabe. *NO*

Follow Me, Boys! ♂♂♂ 1966 A Disney film about a simple man who decides to put down roots and enjoy the quiet life, after one year too many on the road with a ramshackle jazz band. That life is soon interrupted when he volunteers to lead a high-spirited boy scout troop. 120m/C VHS, Beta. Fred MacMurray, Vera Miles, Lillian Gish, Charlie Ruggles, Elliott Reid, Kurt Russell, Luana Patten, Ken Murray; **D:** Norman Tokar; **M:** George Bruns. *DIS*

Follow Me Quietly ♂♂♂ 1949 Serial strangler who only kills in the rain is stalked by Lundigan. Very good little thriller which packs a punch in less than an hour. 59m/B VHS, Beta. William Lundigan, Dorothy Patrick, Jeff Corey, Nestor Paiva, Charles D. Brown, Paul Guilfoyle; **D:** Richard Fleischer. *TTC, MLB, RXM*

Follow That Camel ♂½ *Carry On Follow That Camel* 1967 Foreign Legion sergeant who invents acts of heroism finally gets a chance to really help out a friend in need. Part of the "Carry On" series. 95m/C VHS, Beta. **GB** Phil Silvers, Kenneth Williams, Anita Harris, Jim Dale; **D:** Gerald Thomas. *NO*

Follow That Car ♂ 1980 (PG) Three southern kids become FBI agents and begin a thigh-slappin', rip-snortin' down-home escapade. 96m/C VHS, Beta. Dirk Benedict, Tanya Tucker, Teri Nunn; **D:** Daniel Haller. *NLC*

Follow That Dream ♂♂ 1961 (G) Elvis plays a musical hillbilly whose family is trying to homestead on government land along the sunny Florida coast. Based on Richard C. Powell's novel "Pioneer Go Home." The songs—the only reason to see this movie—include "Angel," "What a Wonderful Life," and the title track. 111m/C VHS, Beta, LV, Letterbox. Elvis Presley, Arthur O'Connell, Anne Helm, Simon Oakland, Jack Kruschen, Joanna Moore, Howard McNear; **D:** Gordon Douglas. *MGM*

Follow That Rainbow ♪ 1966 Believing that her long-lost father is a popular touring singer, a young lass pursues him from Switzerland to South Africa. 90m/C VHS, Beta. Joe Stewardson, Memory Jane, Joan Bickhill. *NO*

Follow the Boys ♂♂♂ 1944 Vaudeville performer Tony West (Raft) heads out to California to try his luck and gets a double break when he's noticed by leading lady Gloria Vance (Zorina). Not only does he become a star but he marries Gloria as well. When WWII breaks out Tony's turned down for military service, so he organizes camp shows for the soldiers. They're a big success but misunderstandings have put his marriage in jeopardy. Plot's merely an excuse to have haute Hollywood (including Marlene Dietrich, Orson Welles, Jeanette MacDonald, and W.C. Fields) sing, dance, and tell jokes. ♫Beyond the Blue Horizon; I'll See You In My Dreams; The Bigger the Army and the Navy; Some of These Days; I'll Get By; I'll Walk Alone; Mad About Him Blues; The House I Live In. 111m/B VHS. George Raft, Vera Zorina, Grace McDonald, Charles Butterworth, Martha O'Driscoll, Charley Grapewin, Elizabeth Patterson; **D:** Edward Sutherland; **W:** Lou Breslow, Gertrude Purcell. Nominations: Academy Awards '44: Best Song ("I'll Walk Alone"). *USH*

Follow the Fleet ♂♂♂ 1936 A song-and-dance man joins the Navy and meets two sisters in need of help in this Rogers/Astaire bon-bon featuring a classic Berlin score. Look for Betty Grable, Lucille Ball, and Tony Martin in minor roles. Hilliard went on to be best known as the wife of Ozzie Nelson in TV's "The Adventures of Ozzie and Harriet." ♫Let's Face the Music and Dance; We Saw the Sea; I'm Putting All My Eggs In One Basket; Get Thee Behind Me, Satan; But Where Are You?; I'd Rather Lead a Band; Let Yourself Go. 110m/B VHS, Beta, LV. Fred Astaire, Ginger Rogers, Randolph Scott, Harriet Hilliard Nelson, Betty Grable, Lucille Ball; **D:** Mark Sandrich; **M:** Irving Berlin, Max Steiner. *TTC, IME, MLB*

Follow the Leader ♂♂ *East of the Bowery* 1944 On leave from the Army, Hall and Gorcey discover that one of the gang has been jailed on a trumped-up charge and set about finding the real culprit. 65m/B VHS. Leo Gorcey, Huntz Hall, Gabriel Dell, Jack LaRue, Joan Marsh, Billy Benedict, Mary Gordon, Sammy Morrison; **D:** William Beaudine; **M:** Gene Austin. *NOS*

Follow the River ♂♂½ 1995 (PG) It's 1775 and Mary Ingles (Lee) is living with her husband and family on a frontier farm in the Blue Ridge Mountains. The community is raided by the Shawnee, lead by Wildcat (Schweig), who take Mary and several other settlers miles away to their home camp. Once there, Mary befriends another captive, the older Gretl (Burstyn), proves her courage to the smitten Wildcat, and plots to escape and find her way home. Based on the 1981 novel by James Alexander Thom; filmed in North Carolina. 93m/C VHS. Sheryl Lee, Eric Schweig, Ellen Burstyn, Tim Guinee, Renee O'Connor; **D:** Martin Davidson. *HMK*

Food of the Gods woof! 1976 (PG) On a secluded island giant rats, chickens, and other creatures crave human flesh, blood, bones, etc. This cheap, updated version of the H. G. Wells novel suffers from lousy performances and a lack of imagination. 88m/C VHS, Beta. Marjoe Gortner, Pamela Franklin, Ralph Meeker, Ida Lupino, Jon Cypher; **D:** Bert I. Gordon. *ART, VES*

Food of the Gods: Part 2 woof! *Gnaw: Food of the Gods 2* 1988 (R) The killer beasts and animals of the first film (and of H.G. Wells' classic novel) strike again; gigantic rats maim young girls. Easily as bad as the original. 93m/C VHS, Beta, LV. Paul Coufos, Lisa Schrage; **D:** Damian Lee; **W:** E. Kim Brewster. *NO*

A Fool and His Money 🎬🎬½ 1988 (R) Adman Morris Codman (Penner) decides to market a shady new religion based on greed but, naturally, finds the true road. Bullock is skeptical girlfriend Debby. **84m/C VHS.** Jonathan Penner, Sandra Bullock, Gerald Orange, George Plimpton; **D:** Daniel Adams; **W:** Daniel Adams. *THV*

Fool for Love 🎬🎬 1986 (R) Explores the mysterious relationship between a modern-day drifter and his long-time lover, who may or may not be his half-sister, as they confront each other in a seedy New Mexico motel. Adapted by Shepard from his play. **108m/C VHS.** Sam Shepard, Kim Basinger, Randy Quaid, Harry Dean Stanton; **D:** Robert Altman; **W:** Sam Shepard; **M:** George Burt. *MGM*

The Fool Killer 🎬🎬½ *Violent Journey* 1965 In the post-Civil War south, a 12 year-old boy learns that a terrifying legend about an axe-murderer may be all too real. Offbeat film with striking visuals and photography. Debut film for Albert and another choice psycho role for Perkins. **100m/B VHS.** Anthony Perkins, Edward Albert, Dana Elcar, Henry Hull, Salome Jens, Arnold Moss; **D:** Servando Gonzalez. *REP*

A Fool There Was 🎬🎬½ 1914 The rocket that blasted Theda Bara to stardom and launched the vamp film genre. One of the few extant Bara films, it tells the now familiar story of a good man whom crumbles from the heights of moral rectitude thanks to the inescapable influence of an unredeemable vamp. Bette Davis described Bara as "divinely, hysterically, insanely malevolent." Much heavy emoting; subtitled (notoriously) "Kiss Me, My Fool!" Based on Rudyard Kipling's "The Vampire." **70m/B VHS, Beta.** Theda Bara, Edward Jose, Runa Hodges, Clifford Bruce; **D:** Frank Powell. *VYY, FCT, GVV*

Foolin' Around 🎬🎬½ 1980 (PG) An innocent Oklahoma farm boy arrives at college and falls in love with a beautiful heiress. He will stop at nothing to win her over, including crashing her lavish wedding ceremony. **101m/C VHS, Beta.** Gary Busey, Annette O'Toole, Eddie Albert, Tony Randall, Cloris Leachman; **D:** Richard T. Heffron; **W:** Michael Kane; **M:** Charles Bernstein.

Foolish Wives 🎬🎬🎬½ 1922 A remake of Von Stroheim's classic depicting the confused milieu of post-war Europe as reflected through the actions of a bogus count and his seductive, corrupt ways. Comes as close as possible to the original film. **107m/B VHS, Beta, LV.** Erich von Stroheim, Mae Busch, Maude George, Cesare Gravina, Harrison Ford; **D:** Erich von Stroheim. *KIV, CCB, HHT*

Fools 🎬 1970 (PG) Two lonely people—he an aging horror film actor and she a young woman estranged from her husband—start a warm romance when they meet in San Francisco. The husband reacts violently. Good cast seems lost. **93m/C VHS, Beta.** Jason Robards Jr., Katharine Ross, Scott Hylands; **D:** Tom Gries.

Fools of Fortune 🎬🎬½ 1990 (PG-13) Adaptation of William Trevor's novel depicting Willie Clinton's childhood and adult experiences of family dramatics played against the backdrop of post-WWI Ireland. During the Irish war for independence, a family is attacked by British soldiers, creating emotional havoc for the survivors. Though well-acted and poignant, it's a rather disjointed and straying shamrock opera. **104m/C VHS, LV.** *GB* Mary Elizabeth Mastrantonio, Iain Glen, Julie Christie, Michael Kitchen, Sean McClory, Frankie McCafferty; **D:** Pat O'Connor; **W:** Michael Hirst; **M:** Hans Zimmer. *COL, FCT*

Fools Rush In 🎬🎬 1997 (PG-13) Uptight eastern yuppie Alex Whitman (Perry) meets cute in Vegas with beautiful Latina casino worker Isabel Fuentes (Hayek) and the duo spend the night together. Three months later, Isabel shows up at Alex's New York door to announce her pregnancy and say she's keeping the baby. Movie cliches collide with movie stereotypes when they decide to marry but find the relationship suffers over their vast ethnic and cultural differences. At least the leads are attractive. Perry's real-life dad plays his character's father. *CW:* Sensuality and brief language. **110m/C VHS, LV, Closed Caption, DVD.** Matthew Perry, Salma Hayek, Jon Tenney, Carlos Gomez, Tomas Milian, John Bennett Perry, Jill Clayburgh, Stanley DeSantis, Anne Betancourt; **D:** Andy Tennant; **W:** Katherine Reback; **C:** Robbie Greenberg; **M:** Alan Silvestri. *COL*

Footlight Frenzy 🎬🎬 1984 The Law Moan Spectacular comedy troupe are at it again as they perform a benefit play where everything goes wrong. **110m/C VHS, Beta.** *GB* Alan Shearman, Diz White, Ron House, Frances Tomelty, Michael Aldridge, Ron Pember. *NO*

Footlight Parade 🎬🎬🎬 1933 Broadway producer Cagney is out of work. Sound films have scared off his backers until his idea for staging live musical numbers before the cinema features lures them back. Lots of authentic backstage action precedes three spectacular Busby Berkeley-choreographed numbers that climax the film, including the giant water ballet featuring more than 100 performers. ♫ Ah, the Moon is Here; Sittin' on a Backyard Fence; Honeymoon Hotel; By A Waterfall; Shanghai Lil. **104m/B Beta, LV.** James Cagney, Joan Blondell, Dick Powell, Ruby Keeler, Guy Kibbee, Ruth Donnelly; **D:** Lloyd Bacon; **C:** George Barnes. National Film Registry '92. *MGM, FOX*

Footlight Serenade 🎬🎬½ 1942 A boxer falls for a beautiful dancer with whom he's costarring in a Broadway play. Unfortunately, she's secretly married to another of the actors and her husband is becoming jealous of the boxer's intentions. Light, fun musical. One of a series of Grable movies made to boost morale during WWII. ♫ Are You Kidding?; I'm Still Crazy About You; I Hear the Birdies Sing; Living High; I'll Be Marching to a Love Song; Land On Your Feet; I'm Stepping Out With a Memory Tonight. **80m/B VHS, Beta, Closed Caption.** Betty Grable, Victor Mature, John Payne, Jane Wyman, Phil Silvers, James Gleason, Mantan Moreland; **D:** Gregory Ratoff; **C:** Lee Garmes. *FOX*

Footloose 🎬🎬½ 1984 (PG) When a city boy moves to a small Midwestern town, he discovers some disappointing news: rock music and dancing have been forbidden by the local government. Determined to bring some '80s-style life into the town, he sets about changing the rules and eventually enlists the help of the daughter of the man responsible for the law. Rousing music, talented young cast, and plenty of trouble make this an entertaining musical-drama. ♫ Footloose; Let's Hear it for the Boy; The Girl Gets Around; Dancing in the Sheets; Somebody's Eyes; Almost Paradise; I'm Free; Never; Holding Out for a Hero. **107m/C VHS, Beta, LV, 8mm, Closed Caption.** Kevin Bacon, Lori Singer, Christopher Penn, John Lithgow, Dianne Wiest, John Laughlin, Sarah Jessica Parker; **D:** Herbert Ross; **M:** Miles Goodman. Nominations: Academy Awards '84: Best Song ("Footloose"), Best Song ("Let's Hear It for the Boy"). *PAR*

Footsteps in the Dark 🎬🎬½ 1941 Fairly amusing comedy-mystery with investment counselor Flynn doubling as detective. Based on the play "Blondie White" by Ladislaus Fodor, Bernard Merivale, and Jeffrey Dell. **96m/B VHS.** Errol Flynn, Brenda Marshall, Ralph Bellamy, Alan Hale, Lee Patrick, Allen Jenkins, Lucile Watson, William Frawley, Roscoe Karns, Grant Mitchell, Maris Wrixon, Noel Madison, Jack LaRue, Turhan Bey; **D:** Lloyd Bacon, Hugh MacMullen; **W:** Lester Cole, John Wexley. *MGM*

For a Few Dollars More 🎬🎬½ 1965 (PG) The Man With No Name returns as a bounty hunter who teams up with a gunslinger/rival to track down the sadistic leader of a gang of bandits. Violent. Sequel to "A Fistful of Dollars" (1964) and followed by "The Good, The Bad, and The Ugly." Letterboxed laserdisc edition features the original movie trailer. **127m/C VHS, Beta, LV, Letterbox, Closed Caption.** *IT* Clint Eastwood, Lee Van Cleef, Klaus Kinski, Gian Marie Volonte; **D:** Sergio Leone; **M:** Ennio Morricone. *FOX, MGM, FCT*

For a Lost Soldier 🎬🎬 1993 Middle-aged Dutch choreographer Jeroen (Krabbe), working on a piece about the Allied liberation, recalls his relationship with a Canadian soldier more than 40 years before. During WWII, the 13-year-old Jeroen (Smit) is sent from Amsterdam to live in the country with a foster family. With the first twinges of puberty and sexuality he longs for a special friend, whom he finds in Walt (Kelley), a young gay Canadian soldier who is part of the Allied liberation forces. Very provocative subject, delicately handled, without any implication of child abuse. In English and Dutch with subtitles. **92m/C VHS.** *NL* Marten Smit, Andrew Kelley, Jeroen Krabbe, Feark Smink, Elsje de Wijn, Derk-Jan Kroon; **D:** Roeland Kerbosch; **W:** Roeland Kerbosch; **M:** Joop Stokkermans. *FXL, ORI*

For Auld Lang Syne: The Marx Brothers 1932 Four classic comedy shorts: "Monkey Business Special," "Gai Dimanche," "Hooks and Jabs," and "For Auld Lang Syne." **46m/B VHS, Beta.** Chico Marx, Groucho Marx, Alan Marx, Harpo Marx. *VYY*

For Better and For Worse 🎬🎬½ 1992 (PG) A nice young couple is planning to have your average nice wedding when one of their friends gets hold of an invitation and decides to jokingly invite the Pope to attend. But the joke is on them when the Pope accepts. Talk about upstaging the bride! **94m/C VHS, LV.** Patrick Dempsey, Kelly Lynch. *ART*

For Better or Worse 🎬🎬 1995 (PG-13) Pathetic loser Michael Makeshift (Alexander, also making his directorial debut) falls in love with his new sister-in-law Valerie (Davidovich) even as he gets entangled in his brother Reggie's (Woods) business scams. Made for cable TV. *CW:* Language; some crude humor. **95m/C VHS.** Jason Alexander, Lolita Davidovich, James Woods, Joe Mantegna, Jay Mohr, Beatrice Arthur, Robert Costanzo, John Amos, Eda Reiss Merin; *Cameos:* Rob Reiner, Rip Torn; **D:** Jason Alexander; **W:** Jeff Nathanson; **C:** Wayne Keenan; **M:** Miles Goodman. *TTC*

For Heaven's Sake 🎬🎬🎬 1926 Lloyd's first film for Paramount has him making an accidental donation to a skid row mission, then marrying the preacher's daughter and converting all the neighborhood tough guys. **60m/B VHS.** Harold Lloyd, Jobyna Ralston, Noah Young, James Mason, Paul Weigel; **D:** Sam Taylor. *NO*

For Heaven's Sake 🎬½ 1979 A bumbling basketball team is lent some heavenly assistance in the form of a meddling angel. But can he hit the jumper? Made for television. **90m/C VHS.** Ray Bolger, Kent McCord. *ART*

For Keeps 🎬½ 1988 (PG-13) Two high school sweethearts on the verge of graduating get married after the girl becomes pregnant, and suffer all the trials of teenage parenthood. Tends toward the unrealistic and trite. **98m/C VHS, Beta, LV.** Molly Ringwald, Randall Batinkoff, Kenneth Mars; **D:** John G. Avildsen; **W:** Tim Kazurinsky, Denise DeClue; **M:** Bill Conti. *COL*

For Ladies Only 🎬🎬 1981 A struggling actor takes a job as a male stripper to pay the rent. Among the leering ladies is Davis, daughter of former President Reagan. Made for television. **100m/C VHS, Beta.** Gregory Harrison, Patricia Davis, Dinah Manoff, Louise Lasser, Lee Grant, Marc Singer, Viveca Lindfors, Steven Keats; **D:** Mel Damski. *NO*

For Love Alone 🎬🎬 1986 A young Australian college co-ed in the 1930s falls in love with a handsome, controversial teacher and follows him to London, only to discover he's not her Mr. Right after all. **102m/C VHS, Beta.** *AU* Helen Buday, Sam Neill, Hugo Weaving; **D:** Stephen Wallace. *ART*

For Love of Ivy 🎬🎬 1968 (PG) Poitier is a trucking executive who has a gambling operation on the side. Ivy is the Black maid of a rich white family who is about to leave her job to look for romance. The two are brought together but the road to true love doesn't run smooth. Based on a story by Poitier. 102m/C **VHS, Beta.** Sidney Poitier, Abbey Lincoln, Beau Bridges, Carroll O'Connor, Nan Martin; **D:** Daniel Mann; **M:** Quincy Jones. Nominations: Academy Awards '68: Best Song ("For Love of Ivy"). FOX

For Love or Money 🐾🐾 1963 A super-rich hotel owner wants her lawyer to find her three beautiful daughters. However, she doesn't trust him enough not to meddle in the search. Lavish production and a good cast can't overcome the mediocrity of the script and direction. 108m/C **VHS.** Kirk Douglas, Mitzi Gaynor, Thelma Ritter, William Bendix, Julie Newmar, Gig Young, Leslie Parrish, William Windom, Dick Sargent; **D:** Michael Gordon. NO

For Love or Money 🐾½ 1984 Made-for-television fare about game-show contestants finding money and romance. 91m/C **VHS, Beta.** Jamie Farr, Suzanne Pleshette, Gil Gerard, Ray Walston, Lawrence Pressman, Mary Kay Place; **D:** Terry Hughes; **M:** Billy Goldenberg. IME

For Love or Money 🐾🐾 1988 (PG) A real estate man with Career on the mind has to choose between the woman in his life and the condo development that stands firmly between them and happily-ever-afterdom. **?m/C VHS.** Timothy Daly, Haviland Morris, Kevin McCarthy. NO

For Love or Money 🐾🐾½ 1993 (PG) Struggling hotel concierge with a heart of gold finds himself doing little "favors" for a slimy entrepreneur who holds the key to his dreams—the cash to open an elegant hotel of his own. Romantic comedy is reminiscent of the classic screwball comedies of the '30s and '40s, but lacks the trademark tight writing and impeccable timing. Fox is appealing and likable as the wheeling and dealing concierge, a role undermined by a mediocre script offering too few laughs. 89m/C **VHS, LV, Closed Caption.** Michael J. Fox, Gabrielle Anwar, Isaac Mizrahi, Anthony Higgins, Michael Tucker, Bobby Short, Dan Hedaya, Bob Balaban, Udo Kier, Patrick Breen, Paula Laurence; **D:** Barry Sonnenfeld; **W:** Mark Rosenthal, Larry Konner; **M:** Bruce Broughton. USH

For Me and My Gal 🐾🐾½ 1942 In his film debut, Kelly plays an opportunistic song-and-dance man who lures a young vaudevillian (Garland) away from her current partners. WWI interrupts both their career and romance, but you can count on them being reunited. Loaded with vintage tunes. 🎵For Me and My Gal; They Go Wild, Simply Wild Over Me; The Doll Shop; Oh, Johnny, Oh; Oh, You Beautiful Doll; When You Wore A Tulip; Don't Leave Me Daddy; Do I Love You; By The Beautiful Sea. 104m/B **VHS, Beta, LV, Closed Caption.** Gene Kelly, Judy Garland, George Murphy, Martha Eggerth, Ben Blue, Richard Quine, Keenan Wynn, Stephen McNally; **D:** Busby Berkeley; **M:** George Bassman. Nominations: Academy Awards '42: Scoring of a Musical. MGM

For Pete's Sake 🐾🐾 July Pork Bellies 1974 (PG) Topsy-turvy comedy about a woman whose efforts to get together enough money to put her husband through school involve her with loan sharks, a madame, and even cattle rustling in New York City. Not one of Streisand's best. 90m/C **VHS, Beta.** Barbra Streisand, Michael Sarrazin, Estelle Parsons, William Redfield, Molly Picon; **D:** Peter Yates; **M:** Artie Butler. COL

For Richer, For Poorer 🐾½ Father, Son and the Mistress 1992 (PG) A very rich, successful businessman notices his son is happy just to sit back and let dad earn all the dough while he waits for his share. In order to teach his son a lesson, Dad decides to give all his money away. But the plan backfires when both realize that earning a second fortune may not be as easy as they assumed. Below average made for cable fare. 90m/C **VHS, Closed Caption.** Jack Lemmon, Talia Shire, Joanna Gleason, Jonathan Silverman, Madeline Kahn, George Wyner; **D:** Jay Sandrich; **W:** Stan Daniels. HBO

For Richer or Poorer 🐾 1997 (PG-13) Definitely poorer. Don't pity the Amish because they can't defend themselves against movies like this, envy them because they don't have to see it. Shallow New York real-estate hustler Brad (Allen)

is supposed to be divorcing socialite wife Caroline (Alley). Their inept accountant (Knight), however, has cooked the books, causing them to head for the Pennsylvania hills. They hide out with a community of Amish people, rediscovering their love along with a bunch of manure jokes. Proves once again the inherent unfunniness of butter churns and barn raisings. **CW:** Some sexual innuendo and one use of strong language. 122m/C **VHS, Closed Caption, DVD.** Tim Allen, Kirstie Alley, Wayne Knight, Larry Miller, Jay O. Sanders, Michael Lerner, Miguel Nunez, Megan Cavanagh, John Pyper-Ferguson, June Claman, Katie Moore; **D:** Bryan Spicer; **W:** Jana Howington, Steve Lukanic; **C:** Buzz Feitshans IV; **M:** Randy Edelman. UPI

For Roseanna 🐾🐾½ Roseanna's Grave 1996 (PG-13) Romantic comedy (despite the subject matter) about Marcello (Reno), the owner of a trattoria in an Italian village and his ailing wife Cecilia (Ruehl), whose dream is to be buried next to their daughter in one of the three remaining plots in their ancient local cemetery. Marcello goes to great lengths to ensure the health of the town's more at-risk citizens to save his wife's spot. Pleasant enough comedy boasts a fine job by an excellent cast, and the Italian scenery is beautiful. Overlooked at the time of its theatrical release, but worth a look for the sentimentally-inclined. **CW:** Sexuality and brief language. 99m/C **VHS, LV, Closed Caption.** Jean Reno, Mercedes Ruehl, Polly Walker, Mark Frankel, Trevor Peacock, Fay Ripley, Giuseppe Cederna, Luigi Diberti, Renato Scarpa, George Rossi, Roberto Della Casa, Romano Ghini; **D:** Paul Weiland; **W:** Saul Turteltaub; **C:** Henry Braham; **M:** Trevor Jones. NLC

For the Boys 🐾🐾 1991 (R) Midler stars as Dixie Leonard, a gutsy singer-comedian who hooks up with Eddie Sparks (Caan) to become one of America's favorite USO singing, dancing, and comedy teams. The movie spans 50 years and three wars—including Korea and Vietnam—and raises such issues as the blacklist and the role of politics in showbiz. Glitzy Hollywood entertainment falters despite Midler's strong performance. 🎵Billy-A-Dick; Come Rain or Come Shine; In My Life; Stuff Like That There. **CW:** Language. 120m/C **VHS, Closed Caption.** Bette Midler, James Caan, George Segal, Patrick O'Neal, Christopher Rydell, Arye Gross, Norman Fell, Rosemary Murphy, Dori Brenner, Bud Yorkin, Jack Sheldon, Melissa Manchester, Brandon Call; **Cameos:** Arliss Howard; **D:** Mark Rydell; **W:** Marshall Brickman, Neal Jimenez, Lindy Laub; **M:** Dave Grusin. Golden Globe Awards '92: Best Actress—Musical/Comedy (Midler); Nominations: Academy Awards '91: Best Actress (Midler). FXV

For the First Time 🐾🐾½ 1959 In his last film, Lanza plays an opera singer who tours European cities to raise money for his deaf girlfriend's medical treatment. 🎵Oh Mon Amour; Bavarian Drinking Song; Ave Maria; Vesti La Giubba; La Donna e Mobile; Niun Mi Tema; Grand March; O Solo Mio; Ich Liebe Dich. 97m/C **VHS, Closed Caption.** Mario Lanza, Zsa Zsa Gabor, Johanna von Koczian, Kurt Kasznar, Hans Sohnker, Peter Capell, Renzo Cesana, Sandro Giglio; **D:** Rudolph Mate; **W:** Andrew Solt. MGM

For the Love of Angela 🐾½ 1986 Pretty and young shop clerk involves herself with both the shopkeeper and his son. 90m/C **Beta.** Louis Jourdan.

For the Love of Benji 🐾🐾 1977 (G) In this second "Benji" film, the adorable little dog accompanies his human family on a Greek vacation. He is kidnapped to be used as a messenger for a secret code, but escapes, to have a series of comic adventures in this entertaining family fare. 85m/C **VHS, Beta.** Benji, Patsy Garrett, Cynthia Smith, Allen Finzat, Ed Nelson; **D:** Joe Camp; **W:** Joe Camp; **M:** Euel Box. FCT, BFV, HMV

For the Love of It 🐾½ 1980 Television stars galore try to hold together this farce about car chases in California, stolen secret documents, and (of course) true love. Outstandingly medio-

cre. Made for television. 100m/C **VHS, Beta.** Deborah Raffin, Jeff Conaway, Tom Bosley, Norman Fell, Don Rickles, Henry Gibson, Noriyuki "Pat" Morita, William Christopher, Lawrence-Hilton Jacobs, Adrian Zmed, Barbi Benton, Adam West; **D:** Hal Kanter.

For the Love of Mary 🐾🐾½ 1948 Durbin retired after this fluff romantic comedy (with some musical numbers) in which she played White House switchboard operator Mary Peppertree. Mary has three potential suitors and juggling her romances causes job-related problems. Includes a second ending and song, which runs an additional eight minutes. 🎵Moonlight Bay; Let Me Call You Sweetheart; I'll Take You Home Again, Kathleen; On the Wings of a Song; Largo al Factotum. 91m/B **VHS, Closed Caption.** Deanna Durbin, Edmond O'Brien, Don Taylor, Jeffrey Lynn, Harry Davenport, Ray Collins, Hugo Haas; **D:** Fred de Cordova; **W:** Oscar Brodney; **C:** William H. Daniels. USH

For the Moment 🐾🐾½ 1994 (PG-13) Aussie aviator Lachlan (Crowe) has joined the British Commonwealth Training Plan in 1942, a crash course for fighter pilots that drew men from several countries to bases across Canada. Stationed with best buddy Johnny (Outerbridge) in Manitoba, Lachlan falls for the married Lill (Hirt), sister of Johnny's honey Kate (McMillan), whose husband is away fighting. The emotional stakes are high for all concerned since they know the fliers will soon be sent off to combat. Old-fashioned (and sometimes slow-moving) romance with excellent performances and some gorgeous scenery. **CW:** Sexual situations, language and a poignant death. 120m/C **VHS, Closed Caption.** CA Russell Crowe, Christianne Hirt, Peter Outerbridge, Sara McMillan, Wanda Cannon, Scott Kraft; **D:** Aaron Kim Johnston; **W:** Aaron Kim Johnston; **C:** Ian Elkin; **M:** Victor Davies. FXV

For Those About to Rock: Monsters in Moscow 🐾🐾½ 1991 (R) A tribute to the young people who defended Russia's new freedom during 1991's attempted coup. The first open-air festival-style concert ever to take place in Russia features the music of AC/DC, Metallica, The Black Crowes, Pantera, and Russia's Electro Shock Therapy. **CW:** Language. 84m/C **VHS, Beta, LV.** D: Wayne Isham. WAR, MVD, PMS

For Us, the Living 🐾🐾🐾 1988 The life and assassination of civil rights activist Medgar Evers are dramatically presented in this production of "American Playhouse" for PBS. Provides insight into Evers' character, not just a recording of the events surrounding his life. Adapted from the biography written by Evers' widow. 84m/C **VHS, Beta.** Howard E. Rollins Jr., Rocky Aoki, Paul Winfield, Irene Cara, Margaret Avery, Roscoe Lee Browne, Laurence "Larry" Fishburne, Janet MacLachlan, Dick Anthony Williams; **D:** Michael A. Schultz. FCT

For Whom the Bell Tolls 🐾🐾🐾½ 1943 Hemingway novel, gorgeously translated to the big screen, features a star-crossed romantic tale of derring-do. American schoolteacher Robert Jordan (Cooper) decides to join the Spanish Civil War and fight the fascists. He's ordered to rendezvous with peasant guerillas, to aid in blowing up a bridge, and in the rebel camp Jordan meets the beautiful Maria (Bergman). Lots of heroics (and some romance under the stars). Both leads were personally selected by the author. Originally released at 170 minutes. 130m/C **VHS.** Gary Cooper, Ingrid Bergman, Akim Tamiroff, Katina Paxinou, Arturo de Cordova, Vladimir Sokoloff, Mikhail Rasumny, Fortunio Bonanova, Victor Varconi; **D:** Sam Wood; **W:** Dudley Nichols; **C:** Ray Rennahan; **M:** Victor Young. Academy Awards '43: Best Supporting Actress (Paxinou); Nominations: Academy Awards '43: Best Actor (Cooper), Best Actress (Bergman), Best Color Cinematography, Best Film Editing, Best Interior Decoration, Best Picture, Best Supporting Actor (Tamiroff), Best Original Dramatic/Comedy Score. USH

For Your Eyes Only 🐾🐾🐾 1981 (PG) In this James Bond adventure, 007 must keep the Soviets from getting hold of a valuable instrument aboard a sunken British spy ship. Sheds the gadgetry of its more recent predecessors in the series in favor of some spectacular stunt work and the usual beautiful girl and exotic locale. Glen's first outing as director, though he handled second units on previous Bond films. Sheena Easton sang the hit title tune. **136m/C VHS, Beta, LV, Letterbox, Closed Caption.** *GB* Roger Moore, Carole Bouquet, Chaim Topol, Lynn-Holly Johnson, Julian Glover, Cassandra Harris, Jill Bennett, Michael Gothard, John Wyman, Jack Hedley, Lois Maxwell, Desmond Llewelyn, Geoffrey Keen, Walter Gotell, Charles Dance; *D:* John Glen; *W:* Michael G. Wilson; *M:* Bill Conti. Nominations: Academy Awards '81: Best Song ("For Your Eyes Only"). *MGM, FOX, TLF*

For Your Love Only 🎬🎬 1979
A beautiful young student falls in love with her teacher and is blackmailed, leading her to murder her tormentor. Soap opera made for German television. Dubbed in English. **90m/C VHS, Beta.** *GE* Nastassia Kinski, Christian Quadflieg, Judy Winter, Klaus Schwarzkopf; *D:* Wolfgang Petersen. *GLV*

Forbidden 🎬🎬½ 1985
In Nazi Germany, a German countess has an affair with a Jewish intellectual, and she winds up hiding him from the S.S. Based on the novel "The Last Jews of Berlin" by Leonard Gross. Slow made-for-cable movie. **116m/C VHS, Beta, Closed Caption.** Jacqueline Bisset, Juergen Prochnow, Irene Worth, Peter Vaughan, Amanda Cannings, Avis Bunnage; *D:* Anthony Page; *W:* Leonard Gross. *SWC*

Forbidden Choices 🎬🎬 *The Beans of Egypt, Maine* 1994 (R)
Problems and attractions of the white trash Bean family as observed by enthralled neighbor girl Earlene (Plimpton). Hot-tempered Reuben Bean (Hauer) has just landed a long prison term, leaving his brood of nine in the care of lover Roberta (Lynch), who's also involved with Bean nephew Beal (McGaw). Downtrodden Earlene is only too eager to give in to handsome Beal's charms, leading to more heartbreak. Based on Carolyn Chute's novel "The Beans of Egypt, Maine." Directorial debut of Warren. *CW:* Language; nudity; strong sexuality. **109m/C VHS, LV, Closed Caption.** Martha Plimpton, Kelly Lynch, Rutger Hauer, Patrick McGaw, Richard Sanders; *D:* Jennifer Warren; *W:* Bill Phillips; *C:* Steven Larner; *M:* Peter Manning Rob. Nominations: Independent Spirit Awards '95: Best Cinematography, Best Supporting Actress (Lynch). *WEA*

The Forbidden Christ 🎬🎬 *Il Cristo Proibito* 1950
Bruno (Vallone) returns from the war to his Tuscan village after years as a POW, only to learn his younger brother, a Resistance fighter, was killed by the Nazis after being betrayed by someone in the town. Bruno wants revenge but when no one will help him find the truth, his rage leads him to kill the wrong man. The only film made by writer Malaparte, which was inspired by actual events, was a boxoffice disaster and caused him to abandon future film plans. Italian with subtitles. **98m/B VHS.** *IT* Raf Vallone, Gino Cervi, Alain Cuny, Elena Varzi; *D:* Curzio Malaparte; *W:* Curzio Malaparte; *C:* Gabor Pogany; *M:* Curzio Malaparte. *HTV*

The Forbidden City 🎬🎬½ 1918
San San is a young Chinese maiden who has the misfortune to fall in love with a Western diplomat. After he is sent away on business San San keeps secret the fact she has born her lover a child but her actions are unforgiven by her father, a deposed mandarin. **72m/B VHS, Beta.** Norma Talmadge, Thomas Meighan; *D:* Sidney Franklin. *VYY, GVV, GPV*

The Forbidden Dance woof! 1990
(PG-13) The first of several quickies released in 1990 applying hackneyed plots to the short-lived Lambada dance craze. The nonsensible plot has a Brazilian princess coming to the U.S. in order to stop further destruction of the rain forest. Instead, she winds up falling for a guy, teaching him to Lambada, and going on TV for a dance contest. Features an appearance by Kid Creole and the Coconuts. **90m/C VHS, Beta, LV, Closed Caption.** Laura Herring, Jeff James, Sid Haig, Richard Lynch; *D:* Greydon Clark. *COL*

Forbidden Fruit 🎬🎬🎬 *Le Fruit Defendu* 1952
Widowed country doctor (Fernandel), who lives with his domineering mother (Sylvie), marries an equally demanding woman (Nollier) and then finds himself involved with a compliant young prostitute (Arnoul). Comic Fernandel does very well with his change of pace role as a man whose illusions of middle-class respectibility are destroyed. Based on "Letter a Mon Juge" by Georges Simenon. French with subtitles. **103m/B VHS.** *FR* Fernandel, Francoise Arnoul, Claude Nollier, Sylvie, Jacques Castelot; *D:* Henri Verneuil; *W:* Jacques Companeez, Jean Manse, Henri Verneuil; *C:* Henri Alekan; *M:* Paul Durand. *FCT*

Forbidden Games 🎬🎬🎬🎬 *Les Jeux Interdits* 1952
Famous anti-war drama about two French children play-acting the dramas of war amid the carnage of WWII. Young refugee Fossey sees her parents and dog killed. She meets a slightly older boy whose family takes the girl in. The children decide to bury the animals they have seen killed in the same way that people are buried—even stealing crosses from the cemetery to use over the animal graves. Eventually they are discovered and Fossey is again separated from her newfound home. Acclaimed; available in both dubbed and English-subtitled versions. **90m/B VHS, Beta, LV.** *FR* Brigitte Fossey, Georges Poujouly, Amedee, Louis Herbert, Suzanne Courtal; Jacques Marin, Laurence Badie, Andre Wasley, Louis Sainteve; *D:* Rene Clement; *W:* Rene Clement, Jean Aurenche, Pierre Bost, Francois Boyer; *M:* Narciso Yepes. Academy Awards '52: Best Foreign Language Film; British Academy Awards '53: Best Film; New York Film Critics Awards '52: Best Foreign Film; Venice Film Festival '52: Best Film; Nominations: Academy Awards '54: Best Story. *NOS, NLC*

Forbidden Love 🎬 1982
A man in his early 20s falls in love with a woman twice his age, much to the chagrin of her daughters. Made for television. **96m/C VHS, Beta.** Andrew Stevens, Yvette Mimieux, Dana Elcar, Lisa Lucas, Jerry Hauser, Randi Brooks, Lynn Carlin, Hildy Brooks, John Considine; *D:* Steven Hilliard Stern; *M:* Hagood Hardy. *CNG*

Forbidden Passion: The Oscar Wilde Movie 🎬🎬½ 1987
A British-made look at Wilde's later years, emphasizing his homosexuality and the Victorian repression that accompanied it. **120m/C VHS, Beta.** *GB* Michael Gambon, Robin Lermitte. *THV*

Forbidden Planet 🎬🎬🎬½ 1956
In 2200 A.D., a space cruiser visits the planet Altair-4 to uncover the fate of a previous mission of space colonists. They are greeted by Robby the Robot and discover the only survivors of the Earth colony which has been preyed upon by a terrible space monster. A classic science fiction version of the Shakespearean classic "The Tempest." Laserdisc features formerly "cut" scenes, production and publicity photos, the original screen treatment, and special effects outtakes. **98m/C VHS, Beta, LV, Letterbox, DVD.** Walter Pidgeon, Anne Francis, Leslie Nielsen, Warren Stevens, Jack Kelly, Richard Anderson, Earl Holliman, George Wallace; *D:* Fred M. Wilcox; *M:* Bebe Barron, Louis Barron. *MGM, CRC*

The Forbidden Quest 🎬🎬 1993
In 1941, a journalist (Ward) tracks down the only survivor of the Hollandia's 1905 expedition to Antarctica, ship's carpenter Sullivan (O'Conor), to find out about the tragic journey. Director Delpeut mixes archival footage of actual turn-of-the-century voyages to reveal the Hollandia's murderous secrets. **75m/C VHS.** *NL* Joseph O'Conor, Roy Ward; *D:* Peter Delpeut; *W:* Peter Delpeut. *KIV*

Forbidden Sun 🎬 1989 (R)
An Olympic gymnastics coach and her dozen beautiful students go to Crete to train. When one of them is brutally raped, vengeance is meted out by the girls. **88m/C VHS, Beta, LV.** Lauren Hutton, Cliff DeYoung, Renee Estevez; *D:* Zelda Barron.

Forbidden Trails 🎬½ 1941
Rough Riders adventure has Silver the horse saving his owner from the vengeance of two outlaws. Two more heroes go under cover to bring the bad guys to justice. **60m/B VHS, Beta.** Buck Jones, Tim McCoy, Raymond Hatton; *D:* Robert North Bradbury. *NOS, VCN, DVT*

Forbidden World woof! *Mutant* 1982 (R)
Lives of a genetic research team become threatened by the very life form they helped to create: a man-eating organism capable of changing its genetic structure as it grows and matures. Corman-produced quickie follow-up to "Galaxy of Terror" is a graphically violent rip-off of "Alien." **82m/C VHS, Beta, LV.** Jesse Vint, Dawn Dunlap, June Chadwick, Linden Chiles; *D:* Allan Holzman; *W:* Jim Wynorski, R.J. Robertson, Tim Curnen.

Forbidden Zone 🎬½ 1980 (R)
A sixth dimension kingdom is ruled by the midget, King Fausto, and inhabited by dancing frogs, bikini-clad tootsies, robot boxers, and degraded beings of all kinds. Original music by Oingo Boingo, and directed by founding member Elfman. **75m/B VHS, Beta.** Herve Villechaize, Susan Tyrrell, Viva; *D:* Richard Elfman; *W:* Matthew Bright, Richard Elfman; *M:* Danny Elfman.

Forbidden Zone: Alien Abduction 🎬 1996 (R)
Three babes sharing a sauna also share sexual confidences and discover they've each had an encounter with the same unusual man. Then one of the girls figures out they've had an alien encounter of the very close kind. *CW:* Sexual situations, nudity, and language. **90m/C VHS.** Darcy Demoss, Pia Reyes, Dumitri Bogmaz, Carmen Lacatus, Alina Chivulescu, Florin Chiriac, Meredyth Holmes; *D:* Lucian S. Diamonde; *W:* Vernon Lumley; *C:* Adolfo Bartoli; *M:* Reg Powell. *AFE*

The Force 🎬🎬 1994 (R)
Rookie LAPD cop Cal Warner (Gedrick) crosses paths with maverick homicide detective Des Flynn (Hudson), who's on the trail of a brutal killer. But when Flynn dies mysteriously, it's Cal who's haunted by bizarre dreams—and finding the truth could be equally deadly. **94m/C VHS, LV, Closed Caption.** Jason Gedrick, Gary Hudson, Cyndi Pass, Kim Delaney. *REP*

Force Five 🎬🎬 1975
A group of ex-cons form an anti-crime undercover force turning their skills toward justice. Nothing new in this made for television pilot. **78m/C VHS, Beta.** Gerald Gordon, Nicholas Pryor, James Hampton, David Spielberg, Leif Erickson, Bradford Dillman; *D:* Walter Grauman.

Force: Five 🎬 1981 (R)
Mercenary gathers a group of like-minded action groupies together to rescue the daughter of a powerful man from a religious cult. All action and no brains. **95m/C VHS, Beta.** Joe Lewis, Pam Huntington, Master Bong Soo Han; *D:* Robert Clouse; *W:* Robert Clouse; *M:* William Goldstein.

Force of Evil 🎬🎬🎬 1949
A cynical attorney who works for a mob boss and for Wall Street tries to save his brother from the gangster's takeover of the numbers operation. The honorable, though criminal, brother refuses the help of the amoral lawyer, and he is finally forced to confront his conscience. Garfield's sizzling performance and the atmospheric photography have made this a film noir classic. **82m/B VHS, LV, Closed Caption.** John Garfield, Thomas Gomez, Marie Windsor, Sheldon Leonard, Roy Roberts; *D:* Abraham Polonsky; *W:* Abraham Polonsky; *C:* George Barnes. National Film Registry '94. *REP*

Force of Evil 🎬 1977
A paroled murderer returns to his hometown to brutalize the family that refused to fabricate an alibi for him. Made for television. **100m/C VHS, Beta, LV.** Lloyd Bridges, Eve Plumb, William Watson, Pat Crowley; *D:* Richard Lang. *WOV, GKK*

Force of Impulse 🎬🎬 1960
J.D. schlocker featuring an impressive cast involved with everything from hot rods to robbery to parental problems. **?m/C VHS.** J. Carrol Naish, Robert Alda, Tony Anthony, Christina Crawford, Jody McCrea, Lionel Hampton. *SNC*

Force of One 🎬🎬 **1979 (PG)** A team of undercover narcotics agents is being eliminated mysteriously, and karate expert Norris saves the day in this sequel to "Good Guys Wear Black." 91m/C VHS, Beta. Chuck Norris, Bill Wallace, Jennifer O'Neill, Clu Gulager; **D:** Paul Aaron.

Force of the Ninja **1997** When Kazuko Tokugawa (Ball), the daughter of a member of Japan's imperial family, is kidnapped and two of her friends are killed, Kenji (Ivan) is forced to take action. A U.S. agent studying the art of the ninja, he learns that the kidnapping is part of an international arms deal lead by a mercenary named Ryan (Williams). Now Kenji must return home and save the situation using his new warrior skills. m/C VHS. Douglas Ivan, Robert B. Williams, Patricia Ball, Brook Lynne, Lee Thomas. MTH

Force on Thunder Mountain 🎬 **1977** A father and son go camping and encounter ancient Indian lore and flying saucers. 93m/C VHS, Beta. Christopher Cain, Todd Dutson. VCI

Force 10 from Navarone 🎬🎬 **1978 (PG)** So-so sequel to Alistair MacLean's "The Guns of Navarone," follows a group of saboteurs whose aim is to blow up a bridge vital to the Nazi's in Yugoslavia. Keep an eye out for Ford, Nero, and Bach. Lots of double-crosses and action sequences, but doesn't quite hang together. 118m/C VHS, Beta, LV. Robert Shaw, Harrison Ford, Barbara Bach, Edward Fox, Carl Weathers, Richard Kiel, Franco Nero; **D:** Guy Hamilton; **W:** Robin Chapman. WAR, OM

Forced Entry 🎬 *The Last Victim* **1975 (R)** Psychopathic killer-rapist hesitates over one of his victims, and she murders him instead. 92m/C VHS, Beta. Tanya Roberts, Ron Max, Nancy Allen; **D:** Jim Sotos. NO

Forced March 🎬🎬½ **1990** On location in Hungary, an actor portrays a poet who fought in WWII and became a victim of the Holocaust. However, the deeper he gets into his role, the thinner the line between illusion and reality becomes. Flat drama. 104m/C VHS, Beta, LV. Chris Sarandon, Renee Soutendijk, Josef Sommer, John Seitz; **D:** Rick King. SGE, MOV, IME

Forced to Kill 🎬½ **1993 (R)** A repo man is on his way to deliver a Jaguar when he's captured by a bizarre family and forced to fight in an illegal bare-fist tournament run by the local lunatic sheriff. Professional stuntman Eubanks has his work cut out for him in this actioner.**CW:** Language, strong violence, and sexuality. 91m/C VHS, LV. Corey Michael Eubanks, Michael Ironside, Rance Howard, Don Swayze, Clint Howard, Brian Avery, Kari Whitman, Mickey Jones, Carl Ciarfalio, Cynthia J. Blessington, Alan Gelfant; **D:** Russell Solberg; **W:** Corey Michael Eubanks; **M:** Martin D. Bolin. PMH

Forced Vengeance 🎬🎬 **1982 (R)** Vietnam vet pits himself against the underworld in Hong Kong. With Norris in the lead, you can take it for granted there will be plenty of martial arts action. 103m/C VHS, Beta. Chuck Norris, Mary Louise Weller; **D:** James Fargo; **M:** William Goldstein. MGM

Ford: The Man & the Machine 🎬½ **1987** Episodic biography of ruthless auto magnate Henry Ford I from the building of his empire to his personal tragedies. The cast lacks spark and Robertson (Ford) is positively gloomy. The only one appearing to have any fun is Thomas (Ford's mistress). Based on the biography by Robert Lacey. 200m/C VHS. Cliff Robertson, Hope Lange, Heather Thomas, Michael Ironside, Chris Wiggins, R.H. Thomson; **D:** Allan Eastman; **C:** Thomas Burstyn. CAF

Foreign Affairs 🎬🎬🎬 **1993** Vinnie Miller (Woodward) is a prim New England college teacher off to London on a research sabbatical. On the flight Vinnie's seatmate is boisterous good-ole-boy Chuck Mumpson (Dennehy), with whom she appears to have nothing in common. Naturally the two middle-aged romantics find a funny, though bittersweet, love together. A rather distracting subplot find's Vinnie's young colleague Fred (Stolz) involved in an affair with an older,

eccentric British actress (Beacham). Based on the novel by Allison Lurie. Made for cable television. 100m/C VHS, LV. Joanne Woodward, Brian Dennehy, Eric Stoltz, Stephanie Beacham, Ian Richardson, Robert Hardy; **D:** Jim O'Brien; **W:** Chris Bryant; **C:** Michael Coulter. TTC

Foreign Body 🎬🎬½ **1986 (PG-13)** An Indian (played by "Passage to India" star, Banerjee) visiting London pretends to be a doctor and finds women flocking to him. Excellent overlooked British comedy. Based on the novel by Roderick Mann. 108m/C VHS. **GB** Victor Banerjee, Warren Mitchell, Trevor Howard, Geraldine McEwan, Amanda Donohoe, Denis Quilley, Eve Ferret, Anna Massey; **D:** Ronald Neame; **W:** Celine La Freniere; **M:** Ken Howard. HBO

Foreign Correspondent 🎬🎬🎬🎬 **1940** A classic Hitchcock tale of espionage and derring-do. A reporter is sent to Europe during WWII to cover a pacifist conference in London, where he becomes romantically involved with the daughter of the group's founder and befriends an elderly diplomat. When the diplomat is kidnapped, the reporter uncovers a Nazi spy-ring headed by his future father-in-law. 120m/B VHS, Beta, LV, **Closed Caption.** Joel McCrea, Laraine Day, Herbert Marshall, George Sanders, Herbert Benchley, Albert Basserman, Edmund Gwenn, Eduardo Ciannelli, Harry Davenport, Martin Kosleck, Charles Halton; **D:** Alfred Hitchcock; **W:** Robert Benchley, Charles Bennett, Joan Harrison, James Hilton; **M:** Alfred Newman. Nominations: Academy Awards '40: Best Black and White Cinematography, Best Interior Decoration, Best Original Screenplay, Best Picture, Best Supporting Actor (Basserman).WAR

A Foreign Field 🎬🎬½ **1993** Comedy/drama focuses on several WW2 veterans returning to the Normandy beaches in honor of the 50th anniversary of the invasion. Blustery British Cyril (McKern) and equally demanding Yank Waldo (Randolph) also must deal with their 50-year rivalry over their wartime love, the cheerfully vulgar Angelique (Moreau). Veteran performers get the chance to show their stuff but film descends into pathos. 90m/C VHS, **Closed Caption. GB** Leo McKern, John Randolph, Jeanne Moreau, Lauren Bacall, Alec Guinness, Edward Herrmann, Geraldine Chaplin; **D:** Charles Sturridge; **W:** Roy Clarke; **M:** Geoffrey Burgon. FOX

Foreign Student 🎬🎬½ **1994 (R)** In 1956 Philippe (Hofschneider) is a French exchange student at a tradition-bound Virginia college. At a professor's home he meets part-time housekeeper April (Givens), who wants to practice her schoolbook French (among other things). They begin a romance but, since April is black, there's trouble. Hofschneider is charming though Givens appears too glamorous and self-aware. Dutton and Battle are notable in their small roles as blues musicians Howlin' Wolf and Sonny Boy Williamson. Directorial debut for Sereny. Based on the novel "The Foreign Student" by Philippe Labro.**CW:** Rough language; brief nudity; sex scene. 96m/C VHS. Marco Hofschneider, Robin Givens, Jack Coleman, Edward Herrmann, Rick Johnson, Charlotte Ross, Charles S. Dutton, Hinton Battle; **D:** Eva Sereny; **W:** Menno Meyjes; **C:** Franco Di Giacomo; **M:** Jean-Claude Petit. USH

The Foreigner 🎬 **1978** Secret agent who comes to New York City to meet his contact becomes entrapped in a series of mysterious events revolving around the underground club scene. 90m/B VHS, Beta. Eric Mitchell, Patti Astor, Deborah Harry; **D:** Amos Poe; **W:** Amos Poe. FCT

The Foreman Went to France 🎬½ *Somewhere in France* **1942** Industrial engineer travels to France during WWII to help prevent secret machinery from falling into the hands of the Nazis and their allies. 88m/B VHS, Beta. **GB** Clifford Evans, Constance Cummings, Robert Morley; **D:** Charles Frend. NOS, MRV, DVT

Foreplay woof! *The President's Women* **1975** Inane trilogy of comedy segments involving characters with White House connections. Stories are introduced by former President Mostel discussing

his downfall in a television interview. Lame rather than risque, wasting talents of all involved. Each segment was scripted and directed by a different team. 100m/C VHS, Beta. Pat Paulsen, Jerry Orbach, Estelle Parsons, Zero Mostel; **D:** Bruce Malmuth, John G. Avildsen; **C:** Ralf Bode. ART, VES

The Forest 🎬 **1983** Spooks and a cannibalistic killer terrorize a group of campers. Nothing that hasn't been done countless times before. 90m/C VHS, Beta. **D:** Donald M. Jones.

Forest of Little Bear 🎬🎬 **1979** A man returns to his impoverished family in 1928 and decides to seek the reward put on the head of a one-eared man-eating bear. He kills the bear but faces a dilemma when he sees the bear left a helpless cub behind. In Japanese with English subtitles. 124m/C VHS. **JP D:** Toshio Goto. FCT

Forest Warrior 🎬🎬 **1995 (PG)** Children fight to save the local forests of Tanglewood Mountain from greedy developer Kiser with the help of ghostly mountain man John McKenna (Norris), who was murdered in the same woods a century before. Mild adventure with good ecology theme. 98m/C VHS. Chuck Norris, Terry Kiser, Max Gail, Roscoe Lee Browne, William Sanderson; **D:** Aaron Norris; **W:** Ron Swanson; **C:** Joao Fernandes. TTC

Forever 🎬🎬½ **1978** A teenage girl experiences true love for the first time and struggles with its meaning. Made for television adaptation of Judy Blume's novel. 100m/C VHS. Stephanie Zimbalist, Dean Butler, John Friedrich, Beth Raines, Diana Scarwid; **D:** John Korty. GEM

Forever: A Ghost of a Love Story 🎬🎬½ **1992 (R)** Coogan is a hot-shot music video director who moves into a haunted house and soon meets the resident ghost, who just happens to be a beautiful woman. He falls for the ghostly presence but his all-too-real female agent is also making her moves.**CW:** Sexuality. 93m/C VHS, Beta. Keith Coogan, Sean Young, Diane Ladd, Sally Kirkland, Terence Knox, Nicholas Guest, Renee Taylor, Steve Railsback; **D:** Thomas Palmer Jr.; **W:** Thomas Palmer Jr.

Forever Amber 🎬🎬½ **1947** Seventeenth century rags to riches story features Darnell as the poverty stricken girl who uses sex to gain wealth and status. She makes it to the bed of King Charles II, only to lose the one man she ever really loved (Wilde). The censorship of the 1940s hindered the film's erotic potential. Adapted from the best-selling novel by Kathleen Winsor. 140m/C VHS, **Closed Caption.** Linda Darnell, Cornel Wilde, Richard Greene, George Sanders, Richard Haydn, Jessica Tandy, Anne Revere, John Russell, Leo G. Carroll, Robert Coote, Margaret Wycherly, Alma Kruger, Edmund Breon, Alan Napier, Bill Ward, Richard Bailey, Skelton Knaggs, Norma Varden, Edith Evanson, Ellen Corby; **D:** Otto Preminger; **W:** Philip Dunne, Ring Lardner Jr.; **C:** Leon Shamroy; **M:** David Raksin. Nominations: Academy Awards '47: Best Original Dramatic/Comedy Score.FXV

Forever and a Day 🎬🎬🎬🎬 **1943** Tremendous salute to British history centers around a London manor originally built by an English admiral during the Napoleonic era and the exploits of succeeding generations. The house even manages to survive the blitz of WWII showing English courage during wartime. Once-in-a-lifetime casting and directing. 104m/B VHS. Brian Aherne, Robert Cummings, Ida Lupino, Charles Laughton, Herbert Marshall, Ray Milland, Anna Neagle, Merle Oberon, Claude Rains, Victor McLaglen, Buster Keaton, Jessie Matthews, Roland Young, Sir C. Aubrey Smith, Edward Everett Horton, Elsa Lanchester, Edmund Gwenn; **D:** Rene Clair, Edmund Goulding, Cedric Hardwicke, Frank Lloyd, Victor Saville, Robert Stevenson, Herbert Wilcox, Kent Smith; **W:** Charles Bennett, Michael Hogan, Peter Godfrey, Christopher Isherwood, Gene Lockhart, Donald Ogden Stewart. HTV, MLB, TPV

Forever Darling 🎬🎬 **1956** Mixed effort from the reliable comedy duo sees Desi playing a dedicated chemist who neglects his wife while pursuing the next great pesticide. Lucy calls on her guardian angel (Mason) to help her rekindle her marriage. He advises her to go with Desi when he tests his new bug killer, and a series of hilarious, woodsy calamities occur. Lucy and Desi are always fun to watch, but '60s TV sitcom fans will enjoy the fact that Mrs. Howell (Schaefer) and Jane Hathaway (Kulp) appear in the same picture. **91m/C VHS, Beta.** Lucille Ball, Desi Arnaz Sr., James Mason, Louis Calhern, John Emery, John Hoyt, Natalie Schafer, Nancy Kulp; *D:* Alexander Hall. *MGM, CCB*

Forever Emmanuelle *♂* 1982 (R) Sensual young woman finds love and the ultimate erotic experience in the wilds of the South Pacific in this sequel to the porn-with-production-values "Emmanuelle." **89m/C VHS, Beta, LV.** Annie Belle, Emmanuelle Arsan, Al Cliver. *ART, VES*

Forever Evil *♂* 1987 The vacationing denizens of a secluded cabin are almost killed off by the cult followers of a mythic god. **107m/C VHS, Beta.** Red Mitchell, Tracey Huffman, Charles Trotter, Howard Jacobsen, Kent Johnson. *VCI*

Forever Female *♂♂♂* 1953 Bright comedy about show business, egos, and love. Holden is a young playwright whose first play is accepted by stage producer Douglas on the condition that the lead role, featuring a 19-year-old heroine, be rewritten for his ex-wife Rogers. She's an aging leading lady smitten by Holden's charms—as is the ingenue Crowley, who would be perfect for the role as written. Complications and manipulations abound as the play makes its way to production. Adaptation of the Sir James Barrie play "Rosalind." **93m/B VHS, Closed Caption.** Ginger Rogers, William Holden, Paul Douglas, Pat Crowley, James Gleason, Jesse White, George Reeves, Marjorie Rambeau, King Donovan, Vic Perrin, Marion Ross; *D:* Irving Rapper; *W:* Julius J. Epstein, Philip C. Epstein. *PAR*

Forever James Dean 1988 A profile of the legendary actor/cult hero, examining his life, short career and remaining legacy. Also includes the original previews of his three feature films. A must for serious Dean fans. **69m/C VHS, Beta, Closed Caption.** James Dean, Julie Harris, William Bast, Kenneth Kendall; *D:* Ara Chekmayan. *WAR, FCT*

Forever, Lulu *♂* *Crazy Streets* 1987 (R) A down-on-her-luck novelist winds up involved with the mob and a gangster's girlfriend. Completely laughless comedy with amateurish direction. **86m/C VHS, Beta, LV.** Hanna Schygulla, Deborah Harry, Alec Baldwin, Annie Golden, Paul Gleason, Dr. Ruth Westheimer; *D:* Amos Kollek. *COL*

Forever Mary *♂♂♂* *Mery per Sempre* 1989 A teacher tries to better the lives of the boys sentenced to a reformatory in Palermo, Sicily, when a teenage transvestite prostitute (the title character) is admitted to the school. In Italian with English subtitles. **100m/C VHS.** *IT* Michele Placido, Alesandro DiSanzo, Francesco Benigno; *D:* Marco Risi; *W:* Sandro Petraglia. *CCN*

Forever Young *♂♂* 1985 A young boy immerses himself in Catholicism. Admiring a priest, he is unaware that the priest's friend is involved with his mother. Tangled, but delicate handling of the coming-of-age story. Made originally for British television. **85m/C VHS, Beta, LV.** *GB* James Aubrey, Nicholas Gecks, Alec McCowen; *D:* David Drury; *W:* Ray Connelly. *MGM*

Forever Young *♂♂½* 1992 (PG) When test pilot Gibson's girlfriend is hit by a car and goes into a coma, he volunteers to be cryogenically frozen for one year. Oops!—he's left frozen for 50 years, until he is accidentally thawed out by a couple of kids. Predictable, designed to be a tear jerker, though it serves mostly as a star vehicle for Gibson who bumbles with '90s technology, finds his true love, and escapes from government heavies, adorable as ever. Through all the schmaltz, the relationship Gibson develops with the young Wood turns out to be the most authentic and endearing love in the film. **102m/C VHS, LV, 8mm, Letterbox, Closed Caption, DVD.** Mel Gibson, Jamie Lee Curtis, Elijah Wood, Isabel Glasser, George Wendt, Joe Morton, Nicolas Surovy, David Marshall Grant, Art LaFl-

eur; *D:* Steve Miner; *W:* Jeffrey Abrams; *C:* Russell Boyd; *M:* Jerry Goldsmith. *WAR, BTV*

Forger of London *♂♂* 1961 Edgar Wallace tale in which Scotland Yard investigates a counterfeit ring connected to a prime suspect, an amnesiac playboy. **91m/C VHS.** *GE* Eddi Arent, Karin Dor, Viktor de Kowa, Hellmut Lange, Robert Graf; *D:* Harald Reinl. *SNC*

Forget Mozart *♂♂* *Zabudnite na Mozarta* 1985 On the day of Mozart's death, the head of the secret police gathers a group together for questioning. They include the composer's wife, his lyricist, the head of a Masonic lodge, and Salieri, Mozart's rival. Each has a different story to tell to the investigator about the composer's life and death. The film makes use of a number of sets and costumes from "Amadeus" and was also filmed on location in Prague. In German with English subtitles. **93m/C VHS.** *GE* Armin Mueller-Stahl, Catarina Raacke; *D:* Salvo Luther. *WBF*

Forget Paris *♂♂½* 1995 (PG-13) Pro basketball referee Mickey (Crystal) and airline executive Ellen (Winger) meet in Paris, fall in love and get married. But once the honeymoon is over, the marital bliss unravels due to conflicting work schedules and the lack of romantic scenery. This look at yuppie love and courtship finds Crystal in pre-"City Slickers 2" form, launching three-point one-liners and "When Harry Met Sally" sentiment. Bland direction and an obligation to be cute intensify the "been-there-seen-that" feeling. Winger's presence may hint of miscasting, but she has one of the films funniest scenes involving a stray pet and a pigeon. *CW:* Language, including fertility clinic scene. **101m/C VHS, LV, Closed Caption.** Billy Crystal, Debra Winger, Joe Mantegna, Cynthia Stevenson, Richard Masur, Julie Kavner, William Hickey, Cathy Moriarty, John Spencer; *D:* Billy Crystal; *W:* Billy Crystal, Lowell Ganz, Babaloo Mandel; *C:* Don Burgess; *M:* Marc Shaiman. *COL*

The Forgotten *♂♂* 1989 After 17 years as POWs, six Green Berets are freed, only to face a treacherous government conspiracy aimed at eliminating them. Made for television. **96m/C VHS, Beta, LV, Closed Caption.** Keith Carradine, Steve Railsback, Stacy Keach, Pepe Serna, Don Opper, Richard Lawson; *D:* James Keach; *W:* Keith Carradine, Steve Railsback, James Keach. *PAR*

The Forgotten One *♂½* 1989 (R) An uninspired author and a female reporter become mixed up in a century-old murder and the restless ghost it spawned. **89m/C VHS, Beta, LV.** Kristy McNichol, Terry O'Quinn, Blair Parker, Elisabeth Brooks; *D:* Phillip Badger; *W:* Phillip Badger; *C:* James Mathers.

Forgotten Prisoners *♂♂* *Forgotten Prisoners: The Amnesty Files* 1990 (R) Celluloid proof that conviction and true grit do not always entertainment make. Greenwald—whose credits range from "Xanadu" to "The Burning Bed"—directed this righteous but stationary drama about an Amnesty International official (Silver) who's assigned to look into the incarceration and egregious mistreatment of Turkish citizens. Made for cable TV. **92m/C VHS, Beta, Closed Caption.** Ron Silver, Roger Daltrey, Hector Elizondo; *D:* Robert Greenwald; *M:* Brad Fiedel. *TTC, FCT*

Forgotten Silver 1996 Jackson's mockumentary finds the director and co-director Botes "discovering" the lost films of Colin McKenzie, a pioneering New Zealand filmmaker of the early 1900s. These include McKenzie's epic film "Salome" which the duo decide to restore. The entire 'escapade is a fiction, including the silent film footage that's shown. The tape also includes the short film "Signing Off" about the final show for a radio DJ and the special request he has trouble fulfilling. **70m/C VHS.** *NZ* Costa Botes, Sam Neill, Leonard Maltin, Harvey Weinstein, John O'Shea, Hannah McKenzie, Lindsay Shelton, Johnny Morris, Marguerite Hurst; *D:* Peter Jackson, Costa Botes, Robert Sarkies; *W:* Peter Jackson, Costa Botes. *FRF*

A Forgotten Tune for the Flute *♂♂♂* 1988 A delightful, Glasnost-era romantic comedy. A bureaucrat caught up in a dull, stuffy existence has a heart attack and winds up falling in love with his nurse. He then must decide between his comfortable, cared-for life or the love which beckons him. In Russian with English subtitles. **131m/C VHS, Beta, LV.** *RU* Leonid Filatov, Tatiana Dogileva, Irina Kupchenko; *D:* Edgar Ryazanov.

Forgotten Warrior *♂½* 1986 (R) Vengeance is the name of the game as a Vietnam vet tracks down the fellow officer who tried to kill him and shot his commander. **79m/C VHS, Beta.** Quincy Frazer, Sam T. Lapuzz, Ron Marchini, Joe Meyer; *D:* Nick Cacas, Charlie Ordonez. *NO*

Forlorn River *♂½* 1937 Nevada and Weary, two law-abiding men, seek to return their hometown to peace by eliminating a gang of outlaws. Based on a novel by Zane Grey. **62m/B VHS.** Buster Crabbe, June Martel, John D. Patterson, Harvey Stephens, Chester Conklin, Lew Kelly, Syd Saylor; *D:* Charles T. Barton. *NOS, DVT, RXM*

The Formula *♂½* 1980 (R) Convoluted story about a secret formula for synthetic fuel that meanders it's way from the end of WWII to the present. A U.S. soldier waylays, and then joins forces with, a German general entrusted with the formula. Years later, after the American is murdered, his friend, a hard-nosed L.A. cop, starts investigating, meeting up with spies and a reclusive oil billionaire. Scott and Brando have one good confrontation scene but the rest of the movie is just hot air. From the novel by Steve Shagan. **117m/C VHS, Beta.** Marlon Brando, George C. Scott, Marthe Keller, G.D. Spradlin, Beatrice Straight, John Gielgud, Richard Lynch; *D:* John G. Avildsen; *M:* Bill Conti. Nominations: Academy Awards '80: Best Cinematography. *MGM*

Formula for a Murder *♂* 1985 A very rich but paralyzed woman marries a scheming con artist who plots to kill her and inherit everything. **89m/C VHS, Beta.** Christina Nagy, David Warbeck, Rossano Brazzi. *ART*

Forrest Gump *♂♂♂½* 1994 (PG-13) Grandly ambitious and slightly flawed, amounting to a wonderful bit of movie magic. As the intelligence-impaired Gump with a heart of gold and more than enough character and dignity, Hanks supplies another career highlight. Field contributes a nice turn as his dedicated mama (they were last together in "Punchline"), while Sinise is particularly effective as a handicapped Vietnam veteran with a bad attitude. Incredible special effects put Gump in the middle of historic events over a four decade period, but the real story is the life-affirming, non-judgmental power of Gump to transform the lives of those around him. From the novel by Winston Groom. **142m/C VHS, Beta, Closed Caption.** Tom Hanks, Robin Wright Penn, Sally Field, Gary Sinise, Mykelti Williamson; *D:* Robert Zemeckis; *W:* Eric Roth; *C:* Don Burgess. Academy Awards '94: Best Actor (Hanks), Best Adapted Screenplay, Best Director (Zemeckis), Best Film Editing, Best Picture, Best Visual Effects; Directors Guild of America Awards '94: Best Director (Zemeckis); Golden Globe Awards '95: Best Actor—Drama (Hanks), Best Director (Zemeckis), Best Film—Drama; National Board of Review Awards '94: Best Actor (Hanks), Best Film, Best Supporting Actor (Sinise); Screen Actors Guild Award '94: Best Actor (Hanks); Writers Guild of America '94: Best Adapted Screenplay; Blockbuster Entertainment Awards '95: Movie, Theatrical, Drama Actor, Theatrical (Hanks); Blockbuster Entertainment Awards '96: Drama Actor, Video (Hanks); Nominations: Academy Awards '94: Best Art Direction/Set Decoration, Best Cinematography, Best Makeup, Best Sound, Best Supporting Actor (Sinise), Best Original Score; Golden Globe Awards '95: Best Screenplay, Best Supporting Actor (Sinise), Best Supporting Actress (Wright Penn), Best Score; MTV Movie Awards '95: Best Film, Best Male Performance (Hanks), Breakthrough Performance (Williamson); Screen Actors Guild Award '94: Best Supporting Actor (Sinise), Best Supporting Actress (Field, Wright Penn). *PAR*

Forsaking All Others 🎬🎬½ **1935**
Screwball comedy featuring several MGM superstars. Friends since childhood, Gable has been in love with Crawford for 20 years, but she never realizes it and plans to marry Montgomery. Crawford is very funny in this delightful story of a wacky romantic triangle. **84m/B VHS, Closed Caption.** Joan Crawford, Clark Gable, Robert Montgomery, Charles Butterworth, Billie Burke, Rosalind Russell, Frances Drake; **D:** Woodbridge S. Van Dyke; **W:** Joseph L. Mankiewicz. *MGM*

Fort Apache 🎬🎬🎬½ **1948** The first of director Ford's celebrated cavalry trilogy, in which a fanatical colonel (Fonda) leads his reluctant men to an eventual slaughter, recalling George Custer at Little Big Horn. In residence: Ford hallmarks of spectacular landscapes and stirring action, as well as many vignettes of life at a remote outpost. Don't forget to catch "She Wore a Yellow Ribbon" and "Rio Grande," the next films in the series. Also available in a colorized version. **125m/B VHS, Beta, LV.** John Wayne, Henry Fonda, Shirley Temple, John Agar, Pedro Armendariz Sr., Victor McLaglen, Ward Bond, Anna Lee; **D:** John Ford; **C:** Archie Stout. *TTC, TLF*

Fort Apache, the Bronx 🎬🎬🎬 **1981**
(R) A police drama set in the beleaguered South Bronx of New York City, based on the real-life experiences of two former New York cops who served there. Newman is a decent cop who goes against every kind of criminal and crazy and against his superiors in trying to bring law and justice to a downtrodden community. **123m/C VHS, Beta, LV, Letterbox.** Paul Newman, Ed Asner, Ken Wahl, Danny Aiello, Rachel Ticotin, Pam Grier, Kathleen Beller; **D:** Daniel Petrie; **W:** Heywood Gould. *WAR, VES, CCB*

Fort Saganne 🎬🎬 **1984** Charles Saganne (Depardieu), a soldier from a peasant background, is posted to the French Sahara, where he becomes a natural leader. He gains fame and fortune, marries, and then WWI begins. Good, if cliched, adventure saga. Based on the novel by Louis Gardel. French with subtitles. **180m/C VHS.** **FR** Gerard Depardieu, Catherine Deneuve, Philippe Noiret, Sophie Marceau, Michael Duchaussoy; **D:** Alain Corneau; **W:** Alain Corneau, Louis Gardel; **M:** Philippe Sarde. *CVC*

Fortress 🎬 **1985 (R)** A teacher and her class are kidnapped from their one-room schoolhouse in the Australian outback. They must use their ingenuity and wits to save their lives in this violent made-for-cable-television suspense drama. **CW:** Strong language, strong violence, and sexuality. **90m/C VHS, Beta.** **AU** Rachel Ward, Sean Garlick, Rebecca Rigg; **D:** Arch Nicholson; **M:** Danny Beckerman. *CNG, HBO*

Fortress 🎬🎬 **1993 (R)** How come the future is never a place you'd want to be? Thanks to overpopulation a woman is only allowed one pregnancy. When John and Karen Brennick are caught trying to have a second child they are shipped to the Fortress, an underground prison in the middle of the desert. Discipline is enforced with numerous sadistic toys, including the intestinator, so-called because it's implanted in the stomach of each prisoner and infractions result in excruciating laser-activated pain. Lambert does well with his action hero but it's character actor Smith as the warden, a techno-human with some sick fantasies, who has the real fun in this horrific depiction of the future. **CW:** Torture and bloody violence. **91m/C VHS, LV, Closed Caption.** Christopher Lambert, Kurtwood Smith, Loryn Locklin, Lincoln Kilpatrick; **D:** Stuart Gordon; **W:** Steve Feinberg, Troy Neighbors, Terry Curtis Fox; **C:** David Eggby. *ART*

Fortress of Amerikka 🎬½ **1989** In the not-too-distant future, mercenaries get their hands on a secret weapon that could allow them to take over the USA. **?m/C VHS.** Gene Le Brock, Kellee Bradley. *IMP*

Fortune and Men's Eyes 🎬🎬 **1971 (R)**
Exploitative and depressing drama about life in a Canadian prison. A naive young man is sent to prison for marijuana possession and has to make a difficult choice—be regularly sodomized by a man who will protect him or be raped by everyone else. Based on the play by John Herbert. **102m/C VHS** Wendell Burton, Michael Greer, Zooey Hall, Danny Freedman; **D:** Harvey Hart; **W:** John Herbert. *MGM*

The Fortune Cookie 🎬🎬🎬 *Meet Whiplash Willie* **1966** After receiving a minor injury during a football game, a TV cameraman is convinced by his seedy lawyer brother-in-law to exaggerate his injury and start an expensive lawsuit. A classic, biting comedy by Wilder. First of several Lemmon-Matthau comedies. The letterbox laserdisc version contains the original theatrical trailer. **125m/B VHS, Beta, LV, Letterbox.** Jack Lemmon, Walter Matthau, Ron Rich, Cliff Osmond, Judi West, Lurene Tuttle; **D:** Billy Wilder; **W:** Billy Wilder, I.A.L. Diamond; **C:** Joseph LaShelle; **M:** Andre Previn. Academy Awards '66: Best Supporting Actor (Matthau); Nominations: Academy Awards '66: Best Art Direction/Set Decoration (B & W), Best Black and White Cinematography, Best Story & Screenplay. *FOX, MGM, FCT*

Fortune Dane 🎬½ **1986 (PG)** Police detective Fortune Dane goes undercover to clear his name after he is framed for murder. **83m/C VHS, Beta.** Carl Weathers, Adolph Caesar; **D:** Nicholas Sgarro; **W:** Charles Correll. *THV*

Fortune's Fool 🎬🎬 **1921** A beef king and profiteer marries a younger woman and soon discovers the problems that ambition can cause. Silent. **60m/B VHS, Beta.** **GE** Emil Jannings, Daguey Servaes, Reinhold Schunzel; **D:** Reinhold Schunzel. *NOS, MRV, VYY*

Fortunes of War 🎬🎬🎬 **1987** British professor Guy Pringle arrives with his bride, Harriet, to take up a teaching post in the Balkans in 1939. The idealistic Guy soon becomes enmeshed in anti-fascist politics and involved with the local members of the British embassy. When threatened by war they travel to Athens and then Cairo, where Guy's increasing involvement in the political situation, and his neglect of Harriet, causes a crisis in their marriage. Slow-moving drama with some self-centered characters is redeemed by the acting skills of those involved. Based on the autobiographial novels of Olivia Manning. Originally shown on "Masterpiece Theater" on PBS. **160m/C VHS.** **GB** Kenneth Branagh, Emma Thompson, Rupert Graves, Ronald Pickup, Robert Stephens, Charles Kay, James Villiers, Harry Burton, Ciaran Madden, Diana Hardcastle, Greg Hicks, Alan Bennett, Jeremy Brundell, Jeremy Sinden; **D:** James Cellan Jones; **W:** Alan Plater. *FOX, FCT, TVC*

Fortunes of War 🎬🎬 **1994 (R)** Peter Kernan (Salinger) is a burned-out relief worker in Thailand. Desperate for money, he agrees to smuggle a rare medicine across the Cambodian border to a rural war lord. Travelling with refugee Khoy Thoun (Ngor) and French Red Cross worker, Johanna (Jenkins), Peter begins to realize his need to do the right thing, even if the cost is high. Filmed on location in Manila. **CW:** Language; violence; drug use. **107m/C VHS, LV, Closed Caption.** Matt Salinger, Michael Ironside, Haing S. Ngor, Sam Jenkins, Martin Sheen, Michael Nouri; **D:** Thierry Notz; **W:** Mark Lee. *COL*

Forty Carats 🎬🎬½ **1973 (PG)** Ullmann plays the just-turned 40 divorcee who has a brief fling with the half-her-age Albert while on vacation in Greece. She figures she'll never see him again but, back in New York, he turns up on the arm of her beautiful daughter (Raffin). Except he's still interested in mom. The rest of the movie is spent trying to convince Ullmann that love can conquer all. Ullmann's very attractive but not well-suited for the part; Raffin's screen debut. Based on the Broadway hit. **110m/C VHS, Beta.** Liv Ullmann, Edward Albert, Gene Kelly, Binnie Barnes, Deborah Raffin, Nancy Walker; **D:** Milton Katselas; **W:** Jay Presson Allen; **C:** Charles B(ryant) Lang. *COL*

Forty Days of Musa Dagh 🎬🎬 **1985**
Based on the true story of Armenia's fight for freedom against Turkey in the 1914 uprising and the dreadful cost. From the novel by Franz Werfel.

120m/C VHS, Beta. Michael Constantine, David Opatoshu. *VCD*

The Forty-Niners 🎬 **1932** A forgettable oater about the hysteria surrounding the finding of gold in California. **59m/B VHS.** Tom Tyler, Betty Mack, Alan Bridge, Fern Emmett, Gordon Wood, Frank Ball; **D:** John P. McCarthy. *DVT, HEG, GPV*

The Forty-Ninth Parallel 🎬🎬🎬 *The Invaders* **1941** Six Nazi servicemen, seeking to reach neutral American land, are trapped and their U-boat sunk by Royal Canadian Air Force bombers, forcing them into Canada on foot, where they run into an array of stalwart patriots. Dated wartime propaganda made prior to the U.S. entering the war; riddled with entertaining star turns. **90m/B VHS, Beta, LV.** **GB** Laurence Olivier, Leslie Howard, Eric Portman, Raymond Massey, Glynis Johns, Finlay Currie, Anton Walbrook; **D:** Michael Powell; **W:** Emeric Pressburger, Rodney Ackland. Academy Awards '42: Best Story; Nominations: Academy Awards '42: Best Screenplay. *NO*

40 Pounds of Trouble 🎬🎬½ **1962**
Lake Tahoe casino/hotel manager Steve McCluskey (Curtis) likes to avoid complications in his life. But first he's charmed by his boss' niece Chris (Pleshette), the hotel's new headliner, and then he becomes a surrogate father to five-year-old Penny (Wilcox), abandoned by her debt-ridden dad. So what does Steve decide to do? Why take them to Disneyland, of course! Director Jewison's feature film debut. **106m/C VHS, Closed Caption.** Tony Curtis, Suzanne Pleshette, Claire Wilcox, Phil Silvers, Larry Storch, Howard Morris, Stubby Kaye, Edward Andrews, Mary Murphy, Kevin McCarthy, Sharon Farrell; **D:** Norman Jewison; **W:** Marion Hargrove; **M:** Mort Lindsay. *USH*

Forty Thousand Horsemen 🎬🎬½
1941 The story of the ANZACS of Australia, created to fight Germany in the Middle East during WWII. This Australian war drama is full of cavalry charges, brave young lads, and "Waltzing Matilda." **86m/B VHS, Beta.** **AU** Chips Rafferty, Grant Taylor, Betty Bryant, Pat Twohill. *VYY, FCT*

42nd Street 🎬🎬🎬🎬 **1933** A Broadway musical producer faces numerous problems in his efforts to reach a successful opening night. Choreography by Busby Berkeley. A colorized version of the film is also available. ♪You're Getting to Be a Habit With Me; Shuffle Off to Buffalo; Young and Healthy; Forty-Second Street; It Must Be June. **89m/B VHS, Beta, LV.** Warner Baxter, Ruby Keeler, Bebe Daniels, George Brent, Dick Powell, Guy Kibbee, Ginger Rogers, Una Merkel, Busby Berkeley, Ned Sparks, George E. Stone; **D:** Lloyd Bacon; **W:** Rian James, James Seymour; **M:** Harry Warren, Al Dubin. Nominations: Academy Awards '33: Best Picture, Best Sound. *MGM, FOX, HMV*

47 Ronin, Part 1 🎬🎬🎬 *The Loyal 47 Ronin; 47 Samurai* **1942** Turn of the 18th-century epic chronicling the samurai legend. The warriors of Lord Asano set out to avenge their leader, tricked into committing a forced seppuku, or hara-kiri. The photography is generously laden with views of 18th century gardens as well as panoramic vistas. This is the largest and most popular film of the Kabuki version of the story by Seika Mayama. In Japanese with English subtitles. **111m/C VHS.** **JP** **D:** Kenji Mizoguchi. *FCT*

47 Ronin, Part 2 🎬🎬🎬 **1942** Second half of the film in which the famous Japanese folklore tale of Lord Asano and his warriors is told. The film follows Asano's samurai as they commit themselves to avenging their leader in 1703. In Japanese with English subtitles. **108m/C VHS.** **JP** **D:** Kenji Mizoguchi. *FCT*

48 Hrs. 🎬🎬🎬 **1982 (R)** An experienced San Francisco cop (Nolte) springs a convict (Murphy) from jail for 48 hours to find a vicious murdering escaped con. Murphy's film debut is great and Nolte is perfect as his gruff foil. **97m/C VHS, Beta, LV, Closed Caption.** Nick Nolte, Eddie Murphy, James Remar, Annette O'Toole, David Patrick Kelly, Sonny Landham, Brion James, Denise Crosby; **D:** Walter Hill; **W:** Walter Hill, Larry Gross, Steven E. de Souza, Roger Spottiswoode; **M:** James Horner. *PAR*

48 Hours to Live 🎬 *Man in the Middle* 1960 A reporter travels to a nuclear scientist's secluded island only to find the scientist held hostage by nuclear weapon-seeking terrorists. 86m/B **VHS, Beta.** Anthony Steel, Ingemar Johannson, Marlies Behrens. *NO*

Foul Play 🎬🎬 1976 Bearing no similarity to the Goldie Hawn vehicle of the same name, this Polish crimer is based on a true story, and stars two of Poland's Olympic boxers. A young man, accused of theft, is coerced by the Warsaw police to go undercover in return for having the charges against him dropped. With English subtitles. 98m/C **VHS.** PL Marek Powowski, Jan Szcepanski, Jerzy Kulej. *FCT*

Foul Play 🎬🎬🎬 1978 (PG) Hawn is a librarian who picks up a hitchhiker which leads to nothing but trouble. She becomes involved with San Francisco detective Chase in an effort to expose a plot to kill the Pope during his visit to the city. Also involved is Moore as an English orchestra conductor with some kinky sexual leanings. Chase is charming (no mugging here) and Hawn both bubbly and brave. A big winner at the boxoffice; features Barry Manilow's hit tune "Ready to Take a Chance Again." 116m/C **VHS, Beta, LV, 8mm.** Goldie Hawn, Chevy Chase, Dudley Moore, Burgess Meredith, Billy Barty, Rachel Roberts, Eugene Roche, Brian Dennehy, Chuck McCann, Bruce Solomon; **D:** Colin Higgins; **M:** Charles Fox. Nominations: Academy Awards '78: Best Song ("Ready to Take a Chance Again"). *PAR*

Found Alive 🎬 1934 After a painful divorce, a woman kidnaps her son and steals away into the Mexican jungle, with only the help of her faithful butler. 65m/B **VHS, Beta.** Barbara Bedford, Maurice Murphy, Robert Frazer, Edwin Cross; **D:** Charles Hutchinson. *SNC*

The Fountainhead 🎬🎬🎬 1949 Cooper is an idealistic, uncompromising architect who refuses to change his designs. When he finds out his plans for a public housing project have been radically altered he blows up the building and winds up in court defending his actions. Neal is the subplot love interest. Based on the novel by Ayn Rand. 113m/C **VHS, Beta.** Gary Cooper, Patricia Neal, Raymond Massey, Ray Collins, Henry Hull; **D:** King Vidor; **C:** Robert Burks; **M:** Max Steiner. *MGM, FOX*

Four Adventures of Reinette and Mirabelle 🎬🎬🎬 1989 Small but touching Rohmer tale of the friendship between two women—one a naive country girl (Miquel, as Reinette), the other a sophisticated Parisian (Forde, as Mirabelle)—who share an apartment and a number of experiences, but who have a very different manner of inhabiting those experiences. A thoroughly French human comedy, one of Rohmer's better studies. In French with English subtitles. 95m/C **VHS.** FR Joelle Miquel, Jessica Forde, Philippe Laudenbach, Marie Riviere, Beatrice Romand, Yasmine Haury; **D:** Eric Rohmer; **W:** Eric Rohmer. *NYF, FCT*

Four Bags Full 🎬🎬½ 1956 A bitter comedy about two smugglers during WWII who try to get a slaughtered pig to the black market under the Nazis' noses. In French with English subtitles. 82m/C **VHS, Beta.** FR Jean Gabin, Louis de Funes, Bourvil, Jeanette Batti; **D:** Claude Autant-Lara. *VDM, FCT*

Four Daughters 🎬🎬🎬 1938 Classic, three-hankie outing in which four talented daughters of music professor Rains fall in love and marry. Garfield shines, in a role tailor-made for him, as the world-weary suitor driven to extremes in the name of love. Great performances from all. Based on the novel "Sister Act" by Fannie Hurst. 90m/B **VHS.** Claude Rains, John Garfield, May Robson, Priscilla Lane, Lola Lane, Rosemary Lane, Gale Page, Dick Foran, Jeffrey Lynn; **D:** Michael Curtiz; **M:** Max Steiner. Nominations: Academy Awards '38: Best Director (Curtiz), Best Picture, Best Screenplay, Best Sound, Best Supporting Actor (Garfield). *MGM, CCB*

Four Days in July 🎬🎬 1985 Two couples from Belfast, one Catholic and one Protestant, find they have something in common when they meet in the maternity ward as both couples become first-time parents. Script and dialog were mainly improvised, which provides both dull stretches and the film's charm. Made for British television. 99m/c **VHS.** GB Des McAleer, Brid Brennan, Charles Lawson, Paula Hamilton, Shane Connaughton, Eileen Pollock, Stephen Rea; **D:** Mike Leigh. *WBF, BTV*

Four Days in September 🎬🎬 1997 (R) Based on the true story of Charles Burke Elbrick (Arkin), the American ambassador to Brazil who, in 1969, was kidnapped by four idealistic students, part of a Marxist revolutionary group protesting their government's military dictatorship. Their leader, Fernando Gabeira (Cardoso), wants the release of political prisoners and gives the government four days to meet his terms. Adapted from the book "What's Up, Comrade?" by Gabeira. **CW:** Some language and violence. 105m/C **VHS.** BR Alan Arkin, Pedro Cardoso, Marco Ricca, Fernanda Torres; **D:** Bruno Barreto; **W:** Leopoldo Serran; **C:** Felix Monti; **M:** Stewart Copeland. Nominations: Academy Awards '97: Best Foreign Language Film. *TOU*

Four Deuces 🎬½ 1975 Gang war is underway between the Chico Hamilton mob and Vic Morano and the Four Deuces during the Depression. Comedy and action combine with elements of strong language, strong sex, and strong violence. 87m/C **VHS, Beta.** Jack Palance, Carol Lynley, Warren Berlinger, Adam Roarke; **D:** William H. Bushnell Jr. *VTR*

Four Eyes and Six Guns 🎬🎬½ 1993 In 1882 a New York optometrist, who's a fan of the popular dime-store western novels, moves to Tombstone, Arizona in search of adventure. He's just in time too because Sheriff Wyatt Earp is trying to rid the town of those pesky Doom Brothers but is having a problem with his eyesight (causing his gunshots to go astray). Now if the greenhorn can just get Earp to wear his new glasses. Silly but harmless fluff. Made for cable television. 92m/C **VHS, Beta, Closed Caption.** Judge Reinhold, Patricia Clarkson, Dan Hedaya, M. Emmet Walsh, Austin Pendleton, Fred Ward; **D:** Piers Haggard; **W:** Leon Prochnik. *TTC*

Four Faces West 🎬🎬½ *They Passed This Way* 1948 McCrea is an honest rancher who nevertheless robs the local bank in order to save his father's ranch from foreclosure. His humanity in helping a diphtheria-ridden family leads to his capture, but the sheriff promises a light sentence, since he is not a typical bad guy. Fine performances strengthen this low-key western. 90m/B **VHS.** Joel McCrea, Frances Dee, Charles Bickford; **D:** Alfred E. Green. *REP*

The Four Feathers 🎬🎬🎬🎬 1939 A grand adventure from a story by A.E.W. Mason. After resigning from the British Army a young man is branded a coward and given four white feathers as symbols by three of his friends and his lady love. Determined to prove them wrong he joins the Sudan campaign of 1898 and rescues each of the men from certain death. They then take back their feathers as does his girl upon learning of his true courage. Excellent performances by Smith and Richardson. 99m/C **VHS, Beta, LV.** GB John Clements, Ralph Richardson, Sir C. Aubrey Smith, June Duprez, Donald Gray, Jack Allen, Clive Barker, Allan Jeayes; **D:** Zoltan Korda; **W:** R.C. Sherriff; **C:** Georges Perinal; **M:** Miklos Rozsa. Nominations: Academy Awards '39: Best Color Cinematography. *FCT, HMV*

The Four Feathers 🎬🎬 1978 Determined to return the symbols of cowardice, four feathers, to his friends and fiancee, a man courageously saves his friends' lives during the British Sudan campaign and regains the love of his lady. Made-for-television movie is the fifth remake. 95m/C **VHS, Beta.** Beau Bridges, Jane Seymour, Simon Ward, Harry Andrews, Richard Johnson, Robert Powell; **D:** Don Sharp. *REP*

Four for Texas 🎬 1963 Perhaps Aldrich's later success with "The Dirty Dozen" can be attributed, in part, to this exercise in how not to make a comic western; poorly made, over long, and far too dependant on the feminine charisma of Ekberg and Andress. Slow-moving Sinatra-Martin vehicle tells the tale of con men in the Old West who battle bandits and bad bankers for a stash of loot. 124m/C **VHS, Beta, LV, Closed Caption.** Frank Sinatra, Dean Martin, Anita Ekberg, Ursula Andress, Charles Bronson, Victor Buono, Jack Elam; **D:** Robert Aldrich; **C:** Ernest Laszlo. *WAR, FCT*

Four Friends 🎬🎬🎬 *Georgia's Friends* 1981 (R) The magical good and bad dream of the 1960s is remembered in this story of four friends. A young woman and the three men in love with her first come together in high school and then separate, learning from college, war and drug abuse, and each other in this ambitious movie from Steve Tesich, the writer of "Breaking Away." Good performances by all. 114m/C **VHS, Beta.** James Leo Herlihy, Craig Wasson, Jodi Thelen, Michael Huddleston, Jim Metzler, Reed Birney; **D:** Arthur Penn; **W:** Steve Tesich; **C:** Ghislan Cloquet. *WAR, OM*

The Four Horsemen of the Apocalypse 🎬🎬🎬½ 1921 Silent classic and star maker for Valentino concerning an Argentine family torn apart by the outbreak of WWI. Valentino is a painter who moves from his native Argentina to France and is persuaded to enlist by a recruiter who invokes the image of the Biblical riders. His excellence as a soldier, however, proves to be his undoing. The 1962 remake can't hold a candle to original, adapted from a novel by Vicente Blasco-Ibanez. 110m/B **VHS.** Rudolph Valentino, Alice Terry, Pomeroy Cannon, Josef Swickard, Alan Hale, Mabel van Buren, Nigel de Brulier, Bowditch Turner, Wallace Beery; **D:** Rex Ingram. National Film Registry '95. *NO*

The Four Horsemen of the Apocalypse 🎬🎬½ 1962 The members of a German family find themselves fighting on opposite sides during WWII. This remake of the vintage Valentino silent failed at the boxoffice, with complaints about its length, disjointed script, and uninspired performances. The title refers to the horrors of conquest, pestilence, war, and death. Adapted from the book by Vicente Blasco-Ibanez. 153m/C **VHS, Beta.** Glenn Ford, Charles Boyer, Lee J. Cobb, Paul Henreid, Yvette Mimieux; **D:** Vincente Minnelli; **W:** John Gay; **C:** Milton Krasner; **M:** Andre Previn. *MGM*

The 400 Blows 🎬🎬🎬🎬 *Les Quartre Cents Coups* 1959 The classic, ground-breaking semi-autobiography that initiated Truffaut's career and catapulted him to international acclaim, about the trials and rebellions of a 12-year-old French schoolboy. One of the greatest and most influential of films, and the first of Truffaut's career-long Antoine Doinel series. With English subtitles. 97m/B **VHS, Beta, LV, Letterbox, DVD.** FR Francois Truffaut, Jean-Pierre Leaud, Claire Maurier, Albert Remy, Guy Decomble, Georges Flament, Patrick Auffay, Jeanne Moreau, Jean-Claude Brialy, Jacques Demy, Robert Beauvais; **D:** Francois Truffaut; **W:** Francois Truffaut, Marcel Moussey; **C:** Henri Decae; **M:** Jean Constantin. Cannes Film Festival '59: Best Director (Truffaut); New York Film Critics Awards '59: Best Foreign Film; Nominations: Academy Awards '59: Best Story & Screenplay. *HMV, MRV, FOX*

Four in a Jeep 🎬🎬½ 1951 In Vienna in 1945, soldiers from different countries are serving as an international military police force. They clash as a result of political demands and their love for the same woman. Shot on location in Austria. 83m/B **VHS, Beta.** Ralph Meeker, Viveca Lindfors, Joseph Yadin, Michael Medwin; **D:** Leopold Lindtberg. *NOS*

Four Jacks and a Jill 🎬🎬 1941 Four musicians are left in the lurch when their band singer leaves them for her gangster boyfriend and they must frantically search for a replacement. Not completely uninteresting, but rather bland and old now. Earlier versions of the story were released as "Street Girl" and "That Girl from Paris."

♪I'm in Good Shape For the Shape I'm In; You Go Your Way and I'll Go Crazy; I Haven't A Thing to Wear; Wherever You Are; Boogie Woogie Conga. 68m/B VHS, Beta. Anne Shirley, Ray Bolger, Desi Arnaz Sr., Jack Durant, June Havoc, Eddie Foy Jr., Fritz Feld; **D:** Jack Hively. *TTC*

The Four Minute Mile *🐾🐾* 1992 Four athletes become determined to break the record of running the mile in under four minutes. 186m/C VHS. *GB* Richard Huw, Nique Needles, John Philbin, Lewis Fitz-gerald, Michael York. *WOV*

The Four Musketeers *🐾🐾🐾* *The Revenge of Milady* 1975 (PG) A fun-loving continuation of "The Three Musketeers," reportedly filmed simultaneously. Lavish swashbuckler jaunts between France, England, and Italy, in following the adventures of D'Artagnan and his cohorts. Pictures give an amusing depiction of Lester-interpreted 17th-century Europe, with fine performances especially by Dunaway as an evil countess seeking revenge on our heroes and Welch as the scatterbrained object of York's affections. Followed, in 1989, by "The Return of the Musketeers." 108m/C VHS, Beta. Michael York, Oliver Reed, Richard Chamberlain, Frank Finlay, Raquel Welch, Christopher Lee, Faye Dunaway, Jean-Pierre Cassel, Geraldine Chaplin, Simon Ward, Charlton Heston, Roy Kinnear, Nicole Calfan; **D:** Richard Lester; **M:** Lalo Schifrin. Nominations: Academy Awards '75: Best Costume Design. *FXL*

Four Robbers *🐾* 197? The ruthless Ma initiates his series of crimes throughout the Far East, somehow staying ahead of the cops. When the final showdown occurs, it's an all out kung fu massacre. 90m/C VHS, Beta. Lau Chun, Shek Hon, Kong Seng, Lee Wing Shan. *MGI*

Four Rode Out *🐾* 1969 A Mexican outlaw is pursued by his girlfriend, one-time partner, and the law. Brutal, inferior western. 99m/C VHS. Pernell Roberts, Sue Lyon, Leslie Nielsen, Julian Mateos; **D:** John Peyser. *NO*

Four Rooms *🐾🐾* 1995 (R) Four stories by four hot indie filmers set in the same L.A. hotel on New Year's Eve are tied together by bellboy Roth, stumbling around in a Jerry/Carrey-like stupor. Leading off is Anders's roomful of witches trying to resurrect spirit of '50s stripper DeCadenet. After this disappointing start is Rockwell's bland look at infidelity, with wife Beals tied and gagged by her husband (Proval) over an alleged fling with Roth. Bandaras heads the best seg as a mobster who leaves his demonic children in Roth's hands. Tarantino is the anchor man with his take on Hitchcock, dealing with a macabre bet involving the removal of body parts. Altogether disjointed and uninspired.**CW:** Pervasive strong language, sexuality, and some drug use. 98m/C VHS, LV, Closed Caption. Tim Roth, Antonio Banderas, Jennifer Beals, Paul Calderone, Sammi Davis, Valeria Golino, Madonna, Ione Skye, Marisa Tomei, Tamlyn Tomita, Bruce Willis, David Proval, Lili Taylor, Alicia Witt, Amanda DeCadenet, Danny Verduzco, Lana McKissack, Quentin Tarantino; **Cameos:** Salma Hayek; **D:** Quentin Tarantino, Alexandre Rockwell, Robert Rodriguez, Allison Anders; **W:** Quentin Tarantino, Alexandre Rockwell, Robert Rodriguez, Allison Anders; **C:** Phil Parmet, Guillermo Navarro, Andrzej Sekula, Rodrigo Garcia; **M:** Combustible Edison, Esquivel. Golden Raspberry Awards '95: Worst Supporting Actress (Madonna). *TOU*

The Four Seasons *🐾🐾½* 1981 (PG) Three upper-middle-class New York couples share their vacations together, as well as their friendship, their frustrations and their jealousies. Alda's first outing as a film director is pleasant and easy on the eyes. 108m/C VHS, Beta, LV. Alan Alda, Carol Burnett, Sandy Dennis, Len Cariou, Jack Weston, Rita Moreno, Bess Armstrong; **D:** Alan Alda; **W:** Alan Alda. *USH*

Four Sided Triangle *🐾* 1953 Two mad scientists find their friendship threatened when they discover that they are both in love with the same woman. So they do what anyone would do in this situation—they invent a machine and duplicate her. 81m/B VHS. *GB* James Hayter, Barbara Payton,

Stephen Murray, John Van Eyssen, Percy Marmont; **D:** Terence Fisher, **M:** Malcolm Arnold. *NOS, SNC, MLB*

Four Ways Out *🐾🐾½* 1957 Four average guys are fed up by their lot in life and stage a boxoffice robbery of their local soccer stadium. They don't get to enjoy their ill-gotten gains. In Italian with subtitles or dubbed. 77m/B VHS. *IT* Gina Lollobrigida, Renato Baldini, Paul Muller; **D:** Pietro Germi. *SNC, VYY*

Four Weddings and a Funeral *🐾🐾🐾* 1994 (R) Refreshing, intelligent adult comedy brimming with stiff upper-lip wit and sophistication. Thirtyish Brit bachelor Charles (Grant) spends his time attending the weddings of his friends, but manages to avoid taking the plunge himself. Then he falls for Carrie (MacDowell), who's about to wed another. Great beginning offers loads of laughs as the first two weddings unfold, then becomes decidedly bittersweet. While Grant makes this a star turn as the romantic bumbler, MacDowell charms without seeming particularly needed. Supporting characters are superb, especially Coleman as the "flirty" Scarlett and Atkinson as a new minister. Surprising boxoffice hit found a broad audience.**CW:** Profanity, brief nudity, and sexual situations. 118m/C VHS, LV, Letterbox, DVD. *GB* Hugh Grant, Andie MacDowell, Simon Callow, Kristin Scott Thomas, James Fleet, John Hannah, Charlotte Coleman, David Bower, Corin Redgrave, Rowan Atkinson, Rosalie Crutchley, Kenneth Griffith, Jeremy Kemp, Sophie Thompson; **D:** Mike Newell; **W:** Richard Curtis; **C:** Michael Coulter; **M:** Richard Rodney Bennett. Australian Film Institute '94: Best Foreign Film; British Academy Awards '94: Best Actor (Grant), Best Director (Newell), Best Film, Best Supporting Actress (Scott Thomas); Golden Globe Awards '95: Best Actor—Musical/Comedy (Grant); Writers Guild of America '94: Best Original Screenplay; Nominations: Academy Awards '94: Best Original Screenplay, Best Picture; Directors Guild of America Awards '94: Best Director (Newell); Golden Globe Awards '95: Best Actress—Musical/Comedy (MacDowell), Best Film—Musical/Comedy, Best Screenplay; MTV Movie Awards '95: Breakthrough Performance (Grant). *PGV*

The 4D Man *🐾🐾½* 1959 A physicist makes two fateful discoveries while working on a special project that gets out of control, leaving him able to pass through matter and see around corners. He also finds that his touch brings instant death. Cheap but effective sci-fier. Young Duke has a small part. 85m/C VHS, Beta, LV. Robert Lansing, Lee Meriwether, James Congdon, Guy Raymond, Robert Strauss, Patty Duke; **D:** Irvin S. Yeaworth Jr. *MLB*

1492: Conquest of Paradise *🐾🐾½* 1992 (PG-13) Large-scale Hollywood production striving for political correctness is a drawn-out account of Columbus's (Depardieu) discovery and subsequent exploitation of the "New World." Skillful directing by Ridley Scott and impressive scenery add interest, yet don't make up for a script which chronicles events but tends towards trite dialogue and characterization. Available in both pan-and-scan and letterbox formats.**CW:** Historical violence and brutality. 142m/C VHS, Beta, LV, Letterbox, Closed Caption. Gerard Depardieu, Sigourney Weaver, Armand Assante, Frank Langella, Loren Dean, Angela Molina, Fernando Rey, Michael Wincott, Steven Waddington, Tcheky Karyo, Kario Salem; **D:** Ridley Scott; **W:** Roselyne Bosch; **M:** Vangelis. *PAR, BTV*

The 4th Man *🐾🐾🐾½* *Blunt* 1979 Steeped in saturated colors and jet black comedy, with an atmospheric score, Verhoeven's nouveau noir mystery enjoyed considerable art-house success but was not released in the US until 1984. The story is decidedly non-linear, the look stylish and symbolic. Krabbe is an alcoholic bisexual Catholic writer who inadvertently becomes the hypotenuse of a love triangle involving Herman, a young man he encounters at a railway station, and his lover Christine, who owns the Sphinx beauty parlor and whose three husbands shall we say, mysteriously. In Dutch with English subtitles. 104m/C VHS, Beta, LV. *NL* Jeroen Krabbe, Renee Soutendijk, Thom Hoffman, Jon DeVries, Geert De Jong; **D:** Paul Verhoeven; **C:**

Jan De Bont; **M:** Loek Dikker. Los Angeles Film Critics Association Awards '84: Best Foreign Film. *XVC*

The Fourth Protocol *🐾🐾🐾* 1987 (R) Well-made thriller based on the Frederick Forsyth bestseller about a British secret agent trying to stop a young KGB agent from destroying NATO and putting the world in nuclear jeopardy. Brosnan, as the totally dedicated Russkie, gives his best performance to date while Caine, as usual, is totally believable as he goes about the business of tracking down the bad guys. 119m/C VHS, Beta, LV. *GB* Michael Caine, Pierce Brosnan, Ned Beatty, Joanna Cassidy, Julian Glover, Ray McAnally, Michael Gough, Ian Richardson, Betsy Brantley, Matt Frewer, Peter Cartwright, David Conville; **D:** John MacKenzie; **W:** Frederick Forsyth, Richard Burridge, George Axelrod; **C:** Phil Meheux; **M:** Lalo Schifrin, Francis Shaw. *ORI, WAR*

Fourth Story *🐾🐾🐾* 1990 (PG-13) A misfit detective is hired by a beautiful woman to find her missing husband. The investigation reveals some unseemly facts about the gentleman. Characterizations and plot twists keep this made-for-cable mystery interesting. 91m/C VHS, Beta, LV. Mark Harmon, Mimi Rogers, Cliff DeYoung, Paul Gleason, M. Emmet Walsh; **D:** Ivan Passer; **W:** Andrew Guerdat. *IME, VTR*

The Fourth War *🐾🐾* 1990 (R) Schneider and Prochnow are American and Russian colonels, respectively, assigned to guard the West German-Czechoslovakian border against each other. With the end of the cold war looming, these two frustrated warriors begin to taunt each other with sallies into the other's territory, threatening to touch off a major superpower conflict. 109m/C VHS, Beta, LV, Closed Caption. Roy Scheider, Juergen Prochnow, Tim Reid, Lara Harris, Harry Dean Stanton; **D:** John Frankenheimer; **M:** Bill Conti. *HBO*

Fourth Wise Man *🐾🐾* 1985 A Biblical Easter story about a rich physician searching for Christ in Persia. 72m/C VHS, Beta. Martin Sheen, Lance Kerwin, Alan Arkin, Harold Gould, Eileen Brennan, Ralph Bellamy, Adam Arkin, Richard Libertini. *ART, VES, IGP*

Fourth Wish *🐾🐾* 1975 When a single father learns that his son is dying, he vows to make his son's last months as fulfilling as possible. Bring lots of hankies. 107m/C VHS, Beta. John Meillon, Robert Bettles, Robyn Nevin; **D:** Don Chaffey; **C:** Geoff Burton. Australian Film Institute '75: Best Actor (Meillon). *NO*

Fowl Play woof! 1983 An unlikely threesome encounter various hardships and mishaps on their way to the first cock-fighting Olympics. Let's hope it's the last cock-fighting Olympics. 90m/C VHS, Beta. Nancy Kwan. *NO*

Fox and His Friends *🐾🐾🐾½* *Faustrecht der Freiheit; Fist Right of Freedom* 1975 Fassbinder's breakthrough tragi-drama, about a lowly gay carnival barker who wins the lottery, thus attracting a devious, exploiting lover, who takes him for everything he has. In German with English subtitles. 123m/C VHS, Beta. *GE* Rainer Werner Fassbinder, Peter Chatel, Karl-Heinz Boehm, Adrian Hoven, Harry Baer, Ulla Jacobsson, Kurt Raab; **D:** Rainer Werner Fassbinder; **C:** Michael Ballhaus. *FCT, NYF*

The Fox and the Hound *🐾🐾🐾* 1981 (G) Sweet story of the friendship shared by a fox and hound. Young and naive, the animals become friends and swear their allegiance to one another when they are separated for a season. Upon return, the hound has become his master's best hunting dog and warns his friend the fox to stay clear of their hunting grounds, for the master is determined to catch the docile fox. Saddened, the fox retreats but soon finds himself boldly standing his ground against a bear that attacks the hound, and the hound inevitably protects the fox from the mean-spirited hunter. Very good animation, but not in the same class as other Disney favorites like "Beauty and the Beast." 83m/C VHS, Beta, Closed Caption. **D:** Art Stevens, Ted Berman, Richard Rich; **W:** Art Stevens, Peter Young, Steve Hulett, Earl Kress, Vance Gerry, Larry Clemmons, Dave Michener, Burny Mattinson; **M:** Buddy Baker; **V:** Mickey Rooney, Kurt Russell, Pearl Bailey, Jack Albertson, Sandy Duncan, Jeanette Nolan, Pat Buttram, John Fiedler, John McIntire, Richard Bakalayan, Paul Winchell, Keith Mitchell, Corey Feldman. *DIS, OM*

Foxes 🐾🐾 1980 (R) Four young California girls grow up with little supervision from parents still trying to grow up themselves. They rely on each other in a world where they have to make adult choices, yet are not considered grown-up. They look for no more than a good time and no tragic mistakes. 106m/C VHS, Beta, Closed Caption. Jodie Foster, Cherie Currie, Marilyn Kagan, Scott Baio, Sally Kellerman, Randy Quaid, Laura Dern; *D:* Adrian Lyne; *W:* Gerald Ayres. *MGM, FOX*

Foxfire 🐾🐾🐾 1987 (PG) In the role that won her Tony and Emmy awards, Tandy stars as Annie Nations, a woman who has lived her entire life in the Blue Ridge Mountains. Widowed, all she has left are the memories of her beloved husband, with whom she regularly communes. Her son tries to convince her to move, and it becomes a clash of the wills as Annie tries to decide to stay in her past or change her future. Made for television. 118m/C VHS, Closed Caption. Jessica Tandy, Hume Cronyn, John Denver, Gary Grubbs, Harriet Hall; *D:* Jud Taylor; *C:* Thomas Burstyn. *REP*

Foxfire 🐾🐾 1996 (R) Not much more than "The Craft" without the hocus-pocus. Lusty Legs Sadovsky (Jolie) is a liberated drifter who empowers a quartet of abused teens to take action against their molester, who happens to be their biology teacher. Based on the book by Joyce Carol Oates originally written in the 1950s, modern adaptation suffers from time warp, most notably when the girls expose their teacher's behavior to their principal and he promptly suspends them without further ado. After some bonding and tattooing in an abandoned house, flick descends into the more masculine and mundane territory of car chases, kidnapping and gunplay. Filmmakers rather timidly back off of leather-clad Legs' obvious lesbianism and her relationship with the adoring Maddy (Burress). Decent acting by most would've benefitted from a more cohesive screenplay. *CW:* Teen nudity, drug use, strong language and some violent situations. 102m/C VHS, LV, Closed Caption. Angelina Jolie, John Diehl, Jenny Lewis, Cathy Moriarty, Richard Beymer, Hedy Burress, Jenny Shimizu, Sarah Rosenberg, Peter Facinelli; *D:* Annette Haywood-Carter; *W:* Elizabeth White; *C:* Newton Thomas Sigel; *M:* Michel Colombier. *COL*

Foxfire Light 🐾 1982 (PG) A young woman vacationing in the Ozarks is drawn into a romance with a cowboy. But her mother's social ambitions and her own indecision may tear them apart. 102m/C VHS, Beta. Tippi Hedren, Lara Parker, Leslie Nielsen, Barry Van Dyke; *D:* Allen Baron; *C:* Thomas Ackerman.

Foxstyle 🐾½ 1973 A wealthy nightclub owner struggles with his country roots and his city sophistication. 84m/C VHS, Beta. Juanita Moore, Richard Lawson, John Taylor, Jovita Bush; *D:* Clyde Houston. *MOV*

Foxtrap 🐾 1985 An L.A. courier is hired to find a runaway girl and, upon finding her in Europe, discovers he's been led into a trap. A low budget Italian co-production. 89m/C VHS, Beta. *IT* Fred Williamson, Christopher Connelly, Arlene Golonka; *D:* Fred Williamson. *FCT, VES*

Foxtrot 🐾🐾 *The Other Side of Paradise* 1976 (R) A wealthy count isolates himself, his wife, and their two servants, on an island but cannot escape his past or the horrors of WWII. Even the good cast can't save the pretentious script and inadequate production. 91m/C VHS, Beta. *SI MX* Peter O'Toole, Charlotte Rampling, Max von Sydow, Jorge Luke; *D:* Arturo Ripstein. *NLC*

Foxy Brown 🐾 1974 (R) A bitter woman poses as a prostitute to avenge the mob-backed deaths of her drug dealer brother and undercover cop boyfriend. Extremely violent black exploitation flick. 92m/C VHS, Beta. Pam Grier, Terry Carter, Antonio Fargas, Kathryn Loder; *D:* Jack Hill. *ORI, FCT*

F.P. 1 🐾🐾 1933 An artifical island (Floating Platform 1) in the Atlantic is threatened by treason. This slow-moving 1930s technothriller is the English-language version of the German "F.P. 1 Antwortet Nicht" ("F.P. 1 Doesn't Answer"). Both were directed at the same time by Hartl, using different casts. 74m/B VHS. *GE* Leslie Fenton, Conrad Veidt, Jill Esmond. *NOS*

F.P. 1 Doesn't Answer 🐾🐾 *F.P. 1 Antwortet Nicht* 1933 A mid-Atlantic refueling station (Floating Platform 1) is threatened by treason and a pilot sets out to put things right. Features pre-Hollywood vintage Lorre; Albers was Germany's number one boxoffice draw at the time. In German. 74m/B VHS. *GE* Hans Albers, Sybille Schmitz, Paul Hartmann, Peter Lorre, Hermann Speelmanns; *D:* Karl Hartl. *SNC, LSV*

Frame by Frame 🐾🐾½ 1995 (R) Cop partners Ekberg (Helgenberger) and Stash (Biehn), who share a passion on and off the job, become implicated in the mob-style murder of Stash's wife. Cable thriller. *CW:* Violence, some strong sexuality and language. 97m/C VHS, Closed Caption. Michael Biehn, Marg Helgenberger, Ron White, Dan Lett, Von Flores; *D:* Douglas Barr; *W:* Douglas Barr; *C:* Rodney Charters; *M:* Mark Snow. *REP*

Frame Up 🐾🐾 1991 (R) A small town sheriff is trying to investigate a murder tied to a fraternity's initiation. However, he runs into opposition from the most powerful man in town. *CW:* Strong language, violence, and sensuality. 90m/C VHS, LV, Closed Caption. Wings Hauser, Bobby DiCicco, Frances Fisher, Dick Sargent, Robert Picardo; *D:* Paul Leder. *REP*

Framed 🐾🐾 1975 (R) A nightclub owner is framed for murder, which understandably irks him. He's determined to get paroled and then seek revenge on the crooked cops responsible for his incarceration. This action melodrama features the writer, director and star of "Walking Tall." 106m/C VHS, Beta. Joe Don Baker, Gabriel Dell, Brock Peters, Conny Van Dyke, John Marley; *D:* Phil Karlson; *W:* Mort Briskin. *PAR*

Framed 🐾🐾 1990 An art forger gets tripped up by a beautiful con artist. However, when they meet again he is willingly drawn into her latest swindle. 87m/C VHS, Closed Caption. Jeff Goldblum, Kristin Scott Thomas, Todd Graff; *D:* Dean Parisot. *HBO*

Fran 🐾🐾 1985 A young woman is torn between her desperate need for a male companion and the care of her children. Well made, albeit depressing, Australian production. 92m/C VHS, Beta. *AU* Noni Hazlehurst, Annie Byron, Alan Fletcher; *D:* Glenda Hambly. Australian Film Institute '85: Best Actress (Hazlehurst). *NO*

France/Tour/Detour/Deux/ Enfants 🐾🐾🐾 1978 A 12-part television series made for French television in which Godard and Mieville chronicle, in their characteristically reflexive fashion, the lives of two French schoolchildren and how their everyday growth is informed by television and the media. In French with English subtitles. 26m/C VHS, Beta. *FR D:* Jean-Luc Godard, Anne-Marie Mieville.

Frances 🐾🐾🐾 1982 The tragic story of Frances Farmer, the beautiful and talented screen actress of the '30s and early '40s, who was driven to a mental breakdown by bad luck, drug and alcohol abuse, a neurotic, domineering mother, despicable mental health care, and her own stubbornness. After being in and out of mental hospitals, she is finally reduced to a shadow by a lobotomy. Not nearly as bleak as it sounds, this film works because Lange understands this character from the inside out, and never lets her become melodramatic or weak. 134m/C VHS, Beta, LV. Jessica Lange, Kim Stanley, Sam Shepard; *D:* Graeme Clifford; *W:* Christopher DeVore, Nicholas Kazan, Eric Bergren; *M:* John Barry. Nominations: Academy Awards '82: Best Actress (Lange), Best Supporting Actress (Stanley). *REP*

Francesco 🐾🐾 1993 (PG-13) Set in 13th-century Italy and depicting the life of St. Francis of Assisi. Follows the pleasure-loving son of a wealthy merchant through his religious awakening, and the founding of the Franciscan order of monks. Rourke, in a definite change-of-pace role, is actually believable, while Bonham Carter offers fine support as a devoted disciple. *CW:* Nudity. 119m/C VHS, LV. Mickey Rourke, Helena Bonham Carter, Paolo Bonacelli, Andrea Ferreol, Hanns Zischler, Peter Berling; *D:* Liliana Cavani; *W:* Liliana Cavani.

The Franchise Affair 🐾🐾 1952 A teenage girl in need of an alibi accuses two reclusive women of kidnapping and abusing her. It's up to a lawyer to sort out the truth. Based on the novel by Josephine Tey. 149m/C VHS. *GB* Michael Denison, Dulcie Gray, Anthony Nicholls, Marjorie Fielding, Athene Seyler, Ann Stephens, Patrick Troughton; *D:* Lawrence Huntington. *FCT*

The Franchise Affair 🐾🐾½ 19?? A scandal is about to overtake the sleepy village of Milford in 1947. An elderly lady and her daughter, the owners of a forbidding country house, are accused of kidnapping and beating a teenaged girl until she agreed to work as their servant. A British TV production based on the novel by Josephine Tey and previously filmed for the big screen in 1952. 155m/C VHS. *GB* Patrick Malahide, Rosalie Crutchley, Joanna McCallum. *VCO*

Francis Covers the Big Town 🐾🐾½ 1953 The fourth in the series finds Peter Stirling (O'Connor) trying to become an ace reporter with a New York newspaper. Thanks to Francis he gets some big scoops but then runs afoul of the mob and is accused of murder. And it's up to his smarter pal to come to the rescue. 86m/B VHS, Closed Caption. Donald O'Connor, Yvette Dugay, Gene Lockhart, Nancy Guild, Larry Gates, Gale Gordon; *D:* Arthur Lubin; *W:* Oscar Brodney; *C:* Carl Guthrie; *M:* Joseph Gershenson; *V:* Chill Wills. *USH*

Francis Gary Powers: The True Story of the U-2 Spy 🐾🐾½ 1976 A television dramatization of the true experiences of Gary Powers, a CIA spy pilot whose plane was shot down over the Soviet Union in 1960. His capture, trial, and conviction are all portrayed in detail, taken from Power's own reminiscences. 120m/C VHS, Beta. Lee Majors, Noah Beery Jr., Nehemiah Persoff, Lew Ayres, Brooke Bundy; *D:* Delbert Mann. *WOV*

Francis Goes to the Races 🐾🐾½ 1951 The second in the talking-mule series finds O'Connor and Francis taking up residence on Kellaway's failing horse ranch. When mobsters seize control of the property to pay off a debt, Francis decides to check with the horses at the Santa Anita race track and find a sure winner to bet on. 88m/B VHS. Donald O'Connor, Piper Laurie, Cecil Kellaway, Jesse White, Barry Kelley, Hayden Rorke, Vaughn Taylor, Larry Keating; *D:* Arthur Lubin; *W:* Oscar Brodney; *M:* Frank Skinner; *V:* Chill Wills. *USH*

Francis Goes to West Point 🐾🐾½ 1952 Peter (O'Connor) and Francis get into West Point where the unfortunate freshman winds up last in his class. But thanks to Francis, Peter makes it past school hazing, grades, and other campus hijicks. Look for Leonard Nimoy in the bit role of a football player. Third in the series. 81m/B VHS, Closed Caption. Donald O'Connor, Lori Nelson, William Reynolds, Gregg Palmer, Alice Kelley, Les Tremayne, David Janssen, Paul Burke; *D:* Arthur Lubin; *W:* Oscar Brodney; *C:* Carl Guthrie; *M:* Joseph Gershenson; *V:* Chill Wills. *USH*

Francis in the Haunted House 🐾½ 1956 The sixth and last entry in the series finds star Donald O'Connor, director Arthur Lubin, and even Chill Wills (the voice of Francis) all abandoning the sinking series. So, it's left to Rooney (as hapless David Prescott) to get himself into trouble (trapped in a haunted house with thieves) and for Francis to get him out. Ho-hum. 80m/B VHS, Closed Caption. Mickey Rooney, Virginia Welles, James Flavin, Paul Cavanagh, David Janssen, Richard Deacon; *D:*

Charles Lamont; **W:** Herbert Margolis, William Raynor; **C:** George Robinson; **M:** Joseph Gershenson; **V:** Paul Frees. *USH*

Francis in the Navy 🐴🐴 1955
The precocious talking mule, Francis, is drafted, and his buddy, played by O'Connor, comes to the rescue. The loquacious beast proves he has the superior grey matter however, and ends up doing all the thinking. Look for Clint Eastwood in his second minor role. **80m/b VHS.** Donald O'Connor, Martha Hyer, Jim Backus, Paul Burke, David Janssen, Clint Eastwood, Martin Milner; **D:** Arthur Lubin. *USH*

Francis Joins the WACs 🐴🐴½ 1954
The fifth entry in the series finds O'Connor working as a bank clerk when he is mistakenly drafted back into the military—and sent to a WAC base. Francis tries to keep him out of trouble with the ladies. Wills, the voice of Francis, also turns up as a general. **94m/b VHS.** Donald O'Connor, Julie Adams, Chill Wills, Mamie Van Doren, Lynn Bari, ZaSu Pitts, Joan Shawlee, Mara Corday, Allison Hayes; **D:** Arthur Lubin; **V:** Chill Wills. *USH*

Francis the Talking Mule 🐴🐴🐴 Francis 1949
The first of the silly but funny series about, what else, a talking mule. Peter Stirling (O'Connor) is the dim-bulb G.I. who hooks up with Francis while fighting in Burma. Francis helps Peter become a war hero but of course everyone thinks he's crazy when Peter insists the mule can talk. The joke is that Francis is smarter than any of the humans. O'Connor starred in six of the films, with Mickey Rooney taking over the final adventure. Director Lubin went on to create the television series "Mr. Ed," about a talking horse. Watch for Tony Curtis in a small role. **91m/b VHS, LV.** Donald O'Connor, Patricia Medina, ZaSu Pitts, Ray Collins, John McIntire, Eduard Franz, Howland Chamberlin, Frank Faylen, Tony Curtis; **D:** Arthur Lubin; **M:** Frank Skinner; **V:** Chill Wills. *USH*

Frank and Jesse 🐴🐴½ 1994 (R)
Another revisionist western finds outlaw Jesse James (Lowe) brooding about his violent existence while brother Frank (Paxton) keeps the gang together and they all try to avoid capture by a vengeful Alan Pinkerton (Atherton) and his detective agency. **106m/C VHS, LV, Closed Caption.** Rob Lowe, Bill Paxton, Randy Travis, William Atherton, Alexis Arquette; **D:** Robert Boris; **W:** Robert Boris; **C:** Walt Lloyd; **M:** Mark McKenzie. *THV*

Frank and Ollie 🐴🐴🐴 1995 (PG)
If you have children, chances are you have a collection including "Cinderella," "Snow White and the Seven Dwarfs," or "Bambi." Look closely at any of the opening credits and you'll see that two of those names, part of Disney's famed "Nine Old Men," are 80-something animators Frank Thomas and Ollie Johnston. Documentary, from Thomas's son Theodore, highlights the 60-plus year friendship and storied careers of these two pioneers, who are still well-known thanks to the recent animation craze. Seven years from conception to release, the film has many great pencil drawings and scenes from the movies, but focuses as much on the men's longtime friendship. **89m/C VHS.** *D:* Theodore Thomas; **W:** Theodore Thomas; **C:** Erik Daarstad; **M:** James Stemple. *NYR*

Frankenhooker 🐴½ 1990 (R)
Jeffrey Franken is a nice guy; he didn't mean to mow his fiancee down on the front lawn. But sometimes bad things just happen to good people. Luckily Jeff thought to save her head and decides to pair it up with the body of some sexy streetwalkers. Voila! You have Frankenhooker: the girlfriend with more than a heart. The posters say it best, "A Terrifying Tale of Sluts and Bolts." **CW:** Language, gore and drugs, and sensuality. **90m/C VHS, LV, Closed Caption.** James Lorinz, Patty Mullen, Charlotte J. Helmkamp, Louise Lasser, Shirley Stoler; **D:** Frank Henenlotter. *SGE, FCT*

Frankenstein 🐴🐴🐴🐴 1931
The definitive expressionistic Gothic horror classic that set the mold. Adapted from the Mary Shelley novel about Dr. Henry Frankenstein, the scientist who creates a terrifying, yet strangely sympathetic monster. Great performance by Karloff as the creation, which made him a monster star. Several powerful scenes, excised from the original version, have been restored. Side two of the laserdisc version contains the original theatrical trailer, plus a collection of photos and scenes replayed for study purposes. **71m/b VHS, Beta, LV.** Boris Karloff, Colin Clive, Mae Clarke, John Boles, Dwight Frye, Edward Van Sloan, Frederick Kerr, Lionel Belman; **D:** James Whale; **W:** Francis Edwards Faragoh, Garrett Fort, John Balderston, Robert Florey; **C:** Arthur Edeson; **M:** David Broeckman. National Film Registry '91. *USH, TLF, HMV*

Frankenstein 🐴🐴½ 1973
A brilliant scientist plays God, unleashing a living monster from the remains of the dead. A TV movie version of the legendary horror story. Good atmosphere provided by producer Dan "Dark Shadows" Curtis. **130m/C VHS, Beta.** Robert Foxworth, Bo Svenson, Willie Aames, Susan Strasberg; **D:** Glenn Jordan. *MPI*

Frankenstein 🐴🐴½ 1982
A remake of the horror classic, closely following the original story, wherein the creature speaks (and waxes philosophical), the doctor sees him as his dark subconscious, and the two die in an arctic confrontation. **81m/C VHS, Beta.** Robert Powell, Carrie Fisher, David Warner, John Gielgud; **D:** James Ormerod. *ART*

Frankenstein 🐴🐴½ 1993
Yet another remake of Mary Shelley's 1818 novel. Bergin stars as Dr. Victor Frankenstein, fanatically believing in the power of science to solve all mankind's ills. This leads him to prove his theories on the "secret of life" with his creation of the monster (Quaid), which Frankenstein finds he cannot ultimately control. Slow-moving story but while the monster isn't really terrifying, he's vengeful and intelligent enough to be a good enemy. Made for cable television. **117m/C VHS, Closed Caption.** Patrick Bergin, Randy Quaid, John Mills, Lambert Wilson, Fiona Gilles, Jacinta Mulcahy, Timothy Stark; **D:** David Wickes; **W:** David Wickes. *TTC, BTV*

Frankenstein: A Cinematic Scrapbook 1991
A behind the scenes look at the world's most infamous monster, featuring interviews with Boris Karloff, Bela Lugosi and Lon Chaney, Jr. Also included are original movie trailers. In color and B&W. **60m/C VHS, Beta.** **D:** Ted Newsom; **W:** Ted Newsom. *RHI, FCT*

Frankenstein and Me 🐴🐴½ 1996 (PG)
Monster-mad 12-year-old Earl Williams (Boulanger) lives in a small Mojave desert town and dreams about bringing Frankenstein's creature back to life. On Halloween, Earl and his friends visit a traveling carnival that claims to have the "authentic" monster, which happens to fall off the truck when the show leaves. Earl finds the dummy and makes numerous attempts to bring the creature back to life. Lots of fantasy sequences and the picture's fun without being too scary. **91m/C VHS.** **CA** Jamieson Boulanger, Ricky Mabse, Louise Fletcher, Burt Reynolds, Myriam Cyr; **D:** Robert Tinnell; **W:** David Sherman, Richard Goudreau; **C:** Roxanne Di Santo; **M:** Normand Corbeil. *THV*

Frankenstein and the Monster from Hell 🐴🐴 1974 (R)
A young doctor is discovered conducting experiments with human bodies and thrown into a mental asylum run by none other than Dr. Frankenstein himself. They continue their gruesome work together, creating a monster who develops a taste for human flesh. This really lame film was the last of the Hammer Frankenstein series. **93m/C VHS, Closed Caption.** **GB** Peter Cushing, Shane Briant, Madeleine Smith, David Prowse, John Stratton, Bernard Lee, Patrick Troughton, Sydney Bromley; **D:** Terence Fisher; **W:** Anthony John Elder Hinds; **C:** Brian Probyn; **M:** James Bernard. *PAR*

Frankenstein '00 woof! 1979
Guy named Frankenstein pieces together a monster who goes on a killing spree. Bottom of the barrel Italian production with funky music and lots of gore. **88m/C VHS, Beta.** **IT GE** John Richardson, Gordon Mitchell, Leila Parker, Dada Gallotti, Marisa Travers; **D:** Mario Mancini. *NO*

Frankenstein General Hospital woof! 1988
A completely laughless horror spoof wherein the 12th grandson of the infamous scientist duplicates his experiments in the basement of a modern hospital. A must see for Frankenstein fans; considered by some the worst Frankenstein movie ever made. **90m/C VHS, Beta, LV.** Mark Blankfield, Kathy Shower, Leslie Jordan, Irwin Keyes; **D:** Deborah Roberts. *NO*

Frankenstein Island woof! 1981 (PG)
Four balloonists get pulled down in a storm and end up on a mysterious island. They are greeted by one Sheila Frankenstein and encounter monsters, amazons, and other obstacles. Completely inept; Carradine "appears" in a visionary sequence wearing his pajamas. **97m/C VHS, Beta.** Cameron Mitchell, Andrew Duggan, John Carradine; **D:** Jerry Warren. *NO*

Frankenstein Meets the Space Monster woof! Mars Invades Puerto Rico; Frankenstein Meets the Spacemen; Duel of the Space Monsters 1965
A classic grade-Z epic about a space robot gone berserk among Puerto Rican disco dancers. **80m/b VHS, Beta.** James Karen, Nancy Marshall, Marilyn Hanold, David Kerman, Robert Reilly, Lou Cutell; **D:** Robert Gaffney; **W:** George Garret; **C:** Saul Midwall.

Frankenstein Meets the Wolfman 🐴🐴🐴 1942
The two famous Universal monsters meet and battle it out in this typical grade-B entry, the fifth from the series. The Werewolf wants Dr. Frankenstein to cure him, but only his monster (played by Lugosi) remains. **73m/C VHS, Beta, LV.** Lon Chaney Jr., Bela Lugosi, Patric Knowles, Lionel Atwill, Maria Ouspenskaya, Ilona Massey, Dwight Frye; **D:** Roy William Neill; **W:** Curt Siodmak; **C:** George Robinson. *USH, MLB*

Frankenstein Must Be Destroyed 🐴🐴½ 1969
Evil Dr. Frankenstein (Cushing) gets interested in brain transplants but discovers the expert, Dr. Pravda, he hoped to work with has gone mad and is in an asylum. He forces a young medical couple to help him free Pravda but the man is accidentally killed. Nevertheless, Frankenstein transplants Pravda's brain into the body of an asylum inmate that Frankenstein has murdered. These things never work out as intended. Followed by "The Horror of Frankenstein." **97m/C VHS.** **GB** Peter Cushing, Veronica Carlson, Freddie Jones, Maxine Audley, Simon Ward, Thorley Walters, George Pravda, Colette O'Neil; **D:** Terence Fisher; **W:** Bert Batt; **C:** Arthur Grant. *WAR*

Frankenstein Sings...The Movie 🐴½ 1995 (PG)
Musical horror spoof finds young couple seeking shelter in a creepy mansion that happens to belong to Dr. Frankenstein. Also visiting (it just happens to be Halloween) are Mr. and Mrs. Dracula, the Wolfman and his mother, and the mummified remains of Elvis and his agent. Some amusing one-liners and mediocre music; adapted from a stage musical. **83m/C VHS, LV.** Candace Cameron, Ian Bohen, Jimmie Walker, Anthony Crivello; **D:** Joel Cohen, Alec Sokolow. *TTC*

Frankenstein Unbound 🐴🐴🐴 Roger Corman's Frankenstein Unbound 1990 (R)
Corman returns after nearly 20 years with a better than ever B movie. Hurt plays a nuclear physicist time traveler who goes back to the 1800s and runs into Lord Byron, Percy and Mary Shelley and their neighbor Dr. Frankenstein and his monster. Great acting, fun special effects, intelligent and subtle message, with a little sex to keep things going. **86m/C VHS, Beta, LV, Closed Caption.** John Hurt, Raul Julia, Bridget Fonda, Jason Patric, Michael Hutchence, Catherine Rabett, Nick Brimble, Catherine Corman, Mickey

Knox; **D:** Roger Corman; **W:** Roger Corman, F.X. Feeney; **M:** Carl Davis; **V:** Terri Treas. *FOX*

Frankenstein's Daughter ✗ *She Monster of the Night* **1958** Demented descendant of Dr. Frankenstein sets a den of gruesome monsters loose, including the corpse of a teenaged girl he revitalizes, as he continues the mad experiments of his forefathers. **85m/B VHS, Beta.** John Ashley, Sandra Knight; **D:** Richard Cunha. *NOS, MRV, RHI*

Frankenstein's Great Aunt Tillie WOOF! **1983** An excruciatingly bad send up of the Frankenstein saga with the good doctor about to be evicted from his estate because of back taxes. Gabor appears for a few seconds in a flashback. **99m/C VHS, Beta.** Donald Pleasence, Yvonne Furneaux, Aldo Ray, June Wilkinson, Zsa Zsa Gabor; **D:** Myron G. Gold; **W:** Myron G. Gold. *VCD*

Frankenweenie ✗✗½ **1984 (PG)** "Frankenweenie" is the tale of a lovable spunky dog named Sparky and his owner, Victor Frankenstein. When Sparky is hit by a car, Victor brings him back to life through the use of electric shock. This affectionate parody of "Frankenstein" launched renowned director Burton's career. **27m/B VHS, Beta, Closed Caption.** Shelley Duvall, Daniel Stern, Barret Oliver, Paul Bartel; **D:** Tim Burton; **W:** Tim Burton; **C:** Thomas Ackerman. *TOU*

Frankie and Johnny ✗ **1936** Based on the song of the same name, famed torch singer Morgan portrays a singer in a bordello who shoots her unfaithful lover. Release was delayed two years by the Hays Office's intervention in how a house of prostitution could be portrayed on screen. Too bad they reached an agreement. Not even Morgan's rendition of the title song redeems this. **68m/B VHS, Beta.** Helen Morgan, Chester Morris; **D:** Chester Erskine. *CCB*

Frankie and Johnny ✗✗½ **1965** Elvis is a riverboat gambler/singer with lousy luck until Kovack changes the odds. This upsets his girlfriend Douglas who shoots him (but not fatally). Elvis wears period costumes, but this is otherwise similar to his contemporary films. ♫When the Saints Go Marching In; Look Out Broadway; Shout It Out; Frankie and Johnny; Chesay; Come Along; Petunia; The Gardner's Daughter; Beginner's Luck. **88m/C VHS, Beta.** Elvis Presley, Donna Douglas, Harry (Henry) Morgan, Audrey Christie, Anthony Eisley, Sue Ane Langdon, Robert Strauss, Nancy Kovack; **D:** Fred de Cordova. *MGM*

Frankie and Johnny ✗✗✗ **1991 (R)** Ex-con gets a job as a short-order cook and falls for a world-weary waitress. She doesn't believe in romance, but finally gives into his pleas for a chance and finds out he may not be such a bad guy after all. Nothing can make Pfeiffer dowdy enough for this role, but she and Pacino are charming together. In a change of pace role, Nelligan has fun as a fellow waitress who loves men. Based on the play "Frankie and Johnny in the Clair de Lune" by McNally who also wrote the screenplay. **CW:** Language and sensuality. **117m/C VHS, LV, Letterbox, Closed Caption.** Al Pacino, Michelle Pfeiffer, Hector Elizondo, Nathan Lane, Kate Nelligan, Jane Morris, Greg Lewis, Al Fann, K. Callan, Phil Leeds, Tracy Reiner, Dey Young; **D:** Garry Marshall; **W:** Terrance McNally; **C:** Dante Spinotti; **M:** Marvin Hamlisch. British Academy Awards '91: Best Supporting Actress (Nelligan); National Board of Review Awards '91: Best Supporting Actress (Nelligan). *PAR, CCB*

Frankie Starlight ✗✗½ **1995 (R)** Bernadette (Parillaud) leaves France after WWII, smuggled aboard an American troop ship. By the time the ship reaches Ireland, she's pregnant and gives birth to her dwarf son, Frankie, in Dublin. She's taken in by the family of customs officer Jack Kelly (Byrne), who instills in the boy a lifelong love of the stars. The adult Frankie (Walker) becomes a celebrity when he writes a novel combining his obsession with the cosmos and his mother's erotic history. Raymo adapts from his 1993 novel "The Dork of Cork." Great perfor-

mances by both Pentony and Walker as the child and adult Frankies. **CW:** Language and some sexuality. **100m/C VHS, LV, Closed Caption.** IR Corban Walker, Alan Pentony, Gabriel Byrne, Anne Parillaud, Matt Dillon, Georgina Cates, Darbnia Molloy, Niall Toibin, Rudi Davies; **D:** Michael Lindsay-Hogg; **W:** Chet Raymo, Ronan O'Leary; **C:** Paul Laufer; **M:** Elmer Bernstein. *NLC*

Frantic ✗✗✗ *Elevator to the Gallows; Ascenseur pour L'Echafaud* **1958** From Louis Malle comes one of the first French New Wave film noir dramas. A man kills his boss with the connivance of the employer's wife, his lover, and makes it look like suicide. Meanwhile, teenagers have used his car and gun in the murder of a tourist couple and he is indicted for that crime. Their perfectly planned murder begins to unravel into a panic-stricken nightmare. A suspenseful and captivating drama. Director Malle's first feature film. Musical score by jazz legend Miles Davis. **92m/B VHS, Beta, 8mm.** FR Maurice Ronet, Jeanne Moreau, Georges Poujouly; **D:** Louis Malle; **M:** Miles Davis. *SNC, NOS, VYY*

Frantic ✗✗✗ **1988 (R)** While in Paris, an American surgeon's wife is kidnapped when she inadvertently picks up the wrong suitcase. Her kidnappers want their hidden tresure returned, which forces the husband into the criminal underground and into unexpected heroism when he seeks to rescue her. Contrived ending weakens on the whole, but Polanski is still master of the dark film thriller. **120m/C VHS, Beta, LV, Closed Caption.** Harrison Ford, Betty Buckley, John Mahoney, Emmanuelle Seigner, Jimmie Ray Weeks, Yorgo Voyagis, David Huddleston, Gerard Klein; **D:** Roman Polanski; **W:** Gerard Brach, Roman Polanski; **M:** Ennio Morricone. *WAR, FCT*

Franz ✗ **1972** A French mercenary and an insecure woman struggle with a doomed love affair. In French with English subtitles. **90m/C VHS, Beta.** FR Jacques Brel; **D:** Jacques Brel. *BAR*

Frasier the Sensuous Lion ✗✗ *Frasier the Lovable Lion* **1973 (PG)** A zoology professor is able to converse with Frasier, a lion known for his sexual stamina and whose potency is coveted by a billionaire (shadow of monkey glands rejuvenation therapy). A fairly typical, if slightly risque, talking critter film. **97m/C VHS, Beta.** Michael Callan, Katherine Justice, Frank De Kova, Malachi Throne, Victor Jory, Peter Lorre Jr., Marc Lawrence; **D:** Pat Shields.

Fraternity Vacation ✗ **1985 (R)** Two college fraternity men show a nerd the greatest time of his life while he's on vacation in Palm Springs. **95m/C VHS, Beta, LV, Closed Caption.** Stephen Geoffreys, Sheree J. Wilson, Cameron Dye, Leigh McCloskey, Tim Robbins, Matt McCoy, Amanda Bearse, John Vernon, Nita Talbot, Barbara Crampton, Kathleen Kinmont, Max Wright, Julie Payne, Franklin Ajaye, Charles Rocket, Britt Ekland; **D:** James Frawley; **M:** Brad Fiedel. *VTR*

Frauds ✗½ **1993 (R)** Collins is an immoral insurance investigator who blasts his victims for everything he can. Then he meets a couple who are out to beat him at his own game. **CW:** Terror/violence. **94m/C VHS, LV.** Phil Collins, Hugo Weaving, Josephine Byrnes. *ART*

Freaked ✗✗ **1993 (PG-13)** Bizarre little black comedy throws everything at the screen, hoping some of the gross-out humor will prove amusing (and some does). Greedy TV star Ricky Coogin (Winter) agrees to be the spokesman for E.E.S. Corporation, which markets a toxic green slime fertilizer to the third world. He's sent to South America to promote the product and is captured by the mad scientist proprietor (Quaid) of a mysterious sideshow, who douses him with the fertilizer. Before you know it he's an oozing half-man, half-beast, perfect to join other freaks as the latest attraction. Lots of yucky makeup. Reeves has an uncredited cameo as the Dog Boy. **80m/C VHS, LV.** Alex Winter, Randy Quaid, Megan Ward, Michael Stoyanov, Brooke Shields, William Sadler, Derek McGrath, Alex Zuckerman, Karyn Malchus, Mr. T, Morgan Fairchild; *Cameos:* Keanu Reeves, Tom Stern; **D:** Alex Winter, Tom Stern; **W:** Alex Winter, Tom Stern, Tim Burns; **M:** Kevin Kiner; **V:** Bob(cat) Goldthwait. *FOX*

The Freakmaker ✗✗ *Mutations; The Mutation* **1973 (R)** Mad professor attempts to breed plants with humans in his lab and has the usual bizarre results. Experiments that fail go to Dunn, a dwarf who runs a freak show. Shamelessly includes real freaks as if plot was not strange enough. **90m/C VHS, Beta.** GB Donald Pleasence, Tom Baker, Brad Harris, Julie Ege, Michael Dunn, Jill Haworth; **D:** Jack Cardiff. *VDC*

Freaks ✗✗✗½ *Nature's Mistakes; Forbidden Love; The Monster Show* **1932** The infamous, controversial, cult-horror classic about a band of circus freaks that exact revenge upon a beautiful aerialist and her strongman lover after enduring humiliation and exploitation. Based on Ted Robbins story "Spurs." It was meant to out-horror "Frankenstein" but was so successful that it was repeatedly banned. Browning's film may be a shocker but it is never intended to be exploitative since the "Freaks" are the only compassionate, loyal, and loving people around. **66m/B VHS, Beta, LV.** Wallace Ford, Olga Baclanova, Leila Hyams, Roscoe Ates, Harry Earles, Henry Victor, Daisy Earles, Rose Dione, Daisy Hilton, Violet Hilton; **D:** Tod Browning; **W:** Al Boasberg, Willis Goldbeck, Leon Gordon, Edgar Allen Woolf; **C:** Merritt B. Gerstad. National Film Registry '94. *MGM*

Freakshow ✗✗ **1995 (R)** Two teens wander into the sideshow at a local carnival and meet the Freakmaster (Hansen), whose grisly exhibits have equally grisly stories to tell. Campy horror with routine special effects. **CW:** Horror violence and gore, language and some sexuality. **102m/C VHS.** Gunnar Hansen, Veronica Carlson, Brian D. Kelly, Shannon Michelle Parsons; **D:** William Cooke, Paul Talbot. *AVI*

Freaky Friday ✗✗½ **1976 (G)** A housewife and her teenage daughter inadvertently switch bodies and each then tries to carry on the other's normal routine. Mary Rodgers' popular book is brought to the screen with great charm in this above average Disney film. **95m/C VHS, Beta, Closed Caption.** Barbara Harris, Jodie Foster, Patsy Kelly, John Astin, Dick Van Patten, Ruth Buzzi, Kaye Ballard, Charlene Tilton, James Van Patten; **D:** Gary Nelson; **W:** Mary Rodgers. *DIS*

Freddie the Frog ✗✗½ *Freddie as F.R.O.7.* **1992 (G)** Prince Frederick's life is shattered when his father is killed by his evil Aunt Messina, who wants to rule the kingdom. She even changes Frederick into a frog—but he manages to escape her with the help of friendly sea monster Nessie. But Freddie discovers that he has also been given super-frog powers, just in time to save Britain's landmarks, which are disappearing thanks to Aunt Messina's spells. **72m/C VHS, Closed Caption.** GB **D:** Jon Acevski; **W:** Jon Acevski, David Ashton; **V:** Ben Kingsley, Nigel Hawthorne, Jenny Agutter, John Sessions, Brian Blessed, Billie Whitelaw, Jonathan Pryce, Phyllis Logan, Michael Hordern. *USH*

Freddy's Dead: The Final Nightmare ✗✗ *Nightmare on Elm Street 6: Freddy's Dead* **1991 (R)** Freddy's daughter journeys to Springwood, Ohio, to put a stop to her father's evil ways. Will she be able to destroy this maniac, or is a new reign of terror just beginning? The sixth film in the "Nightmare" series; followed by "Wes Craven's New Nightmare." **CW:** Language and horror violence and drug content. **96m/C VHS, LV, Closed Caption.** Robert Englund, Lisa Zane, Shon Greenblatt, Leslie Deane, Ricky Dean Logan, Breckin Majer, Yaphet Kotto, Elinor Donahue, Roseanne, Johnny Depp, Alice Cooper, Tom Arnold; **D:** Rachel Talalay; **W:** Michael De Luca; **C:** Declan Quinn. *COL, NLC*

Free Amerika Broadcasting **1989** A drama about an alternate reality in which Richard Nixon was assassinated, leaving Spiro Agnew president. As a result, the country turns to violent revolution. **80m/C VHS.** Brian Kincaid; **D:** Dean Wilson. *NO*

Free and Easy 🎬🎬½ *Easy Go* 1930 Keaton plays the incompetent manager of a beauty contest winner (Page) from Gopher City, Kansas. Page and her overbearing mother, accompanied by Keaton, go to Hollywood to make the girl a star. They gate-crash the MGM studio where all cause havoc and it turns out Keaton is the one who lands in front of the cameras (Page has to settle for romancing Montgomery). Provides a behind-the-scenes look at the MGM studio, with a number of MGM stars making cameo appearances. 92m/B VHS. Buster Keaton, Anita Page, Robert Montgomery, Trixie Friganza, Fred Niblo; *Cameos:* Cecil B. DeMille, Jackie Coogan, Lionel Barrymore, William Haines; *D:* Edward Sedgwick. MGM

Free Grass 🎬 *Scream Free!* 1969 A gang of thoughtless hippie drug smugglers and abusers escape from the police, drink acid-spiked wine, shoot each other, and have love-ins. 82m/C VHS, Beta, LV. Russ Tamblyn, Richard Beymer, Casey Kasem, Lana Wood, Warren Finnerty. NO

Free Ride 🎬 1986 (R) A kooky kid steals a sportscar to impress a girl, and gets involved with local hoods. They chase each other around. 92m/C VHS, Beta, LV. Gary Hershberger, Reed Rudy, Dawn Schneider, Peter DeLuise, Brian MacGregor; *W:* Robert Bell. ART

A Free Soul 🎬🎬½ 1931 Tippling litigator Barrymore helps low-life mobster Gable beat a murder rap, only to discover the hood has stolen his daughter's heart. Bargaining with his ditzy daughter, he vows to eschew the bottle if she'll stay away from good-for-nothing Gable. Directed by Brown, best known for his work with Garbo, and based on the memoirs of Adela Rogers St. John. The final courtroom scene—a cloak-and-gavel classic—cinched Barrymore's Oscar. Remade with Liz Taylor as "The Girl Who Had Everything" (although, ironically, the earlier version is the racier of the two). 94m/B VHS. Norma Shearer, Leslie Howard, Lionel Barrymore, Clark Gable, James Gleason, Lucy Beaumont; *D:* Clarence Brown; *C:* William H. Daniels. Academy Awards '31: Best Actor (Barrymore); Nominations: Academy Awards '31: Best Actress (Shearer), Best Director (Brown). MGM, FCT, BTV

Free to Love 🎬🎬 1925 Screen idol Bow plays a young woman, fresh out of prison, who is taken in by a kindly, affluent patron. But, as the silent drama axiom would have it, there's no escaping the past, and she's forced to defend her former life when her guardian is murdered. 61m/B VHS, Beta. Clara Bow, Donald Keith, Raymond McKee; *D:* Frank O'Connor. GPV, FCT

Free, White, and 21 🎬🎬 1962 A black motel owner is accused of raping a white civil rights worker. Produced in a "pseudo-documentary" form which sometimes drags. 104m/B VHS. Frederick O'Neal, Annalena Lund, George Edgely, John Hicks, Hugh Crenshaw, George Russell; *D:* Larry Buchanan. NO

Free Willy 🎬🎬½ 1993 (PG) Sentimental story about a 12-year-old runaway (Richter) who befriends a whale. Should appeal to children for its heartwarming story and delightful sea acrobatics. An electronically operated stand-in whale was used for far-off shots; a domesticated performing whale named Keiko for the close-ups. Director Wincer was known to grumble about the temperamental Keiko during shooting. Suggested viewing for students of animal behavior. Proof that family films can make money, "Free Willy" placed tenth for total boxoffice receipts in 1993. 112m/C VHS, LV, 8mm, Letterbox, Closed Caption. Jason James Richter, Lori Petty, Jayne Atkinson, August Schellenberg, Michael Madsen; *D:* Simon Wincer; *W:* Keith A. Walker, Corey Blechman; *C:* Robbie Greenberg; *M:* Basil Poledouris. MTV Movie Awards '94: Best Song ("Will You Be There"); Nominations: MTV Movie Awards '94: Breakthrough Performance (Richter), Best Kiss (Jason James Richter/Willy). WAR, BTV

Free Willy 2: The Adventure Home 🎬🎬½ 1995 (PG) While camping in the Pacific Northwest, Jesse is reunited with his orca-pal Willy, who has found a new home along with his whale siblings. But an offshore oil spill separates Willy from his family and threatens their lives, so his human friends must once again come to the rescue. All the principal characters are back, except for Willy (real name Keiko), who is recuperating from a skin virus in Mexico. Animatronics and Gump-like digital effects were used to replicate the real Willy. 98m/C VHS, LV, Closed Caption. Jason James Richter, Michael Madsen, Jayne Atkinson, August Schellenberg, Jon Tenney, Elizabeth Pena; *D:* Dwight Little; *W:* Corey Blechman, John Mattson; *C:* Laszlo Kovacs; *M:* Basil Poledouris. WAR

Free Willy 3: The Rescue 🎬🎬½ 1997 (PG) Isn't this poor whale ever going to be left in peace? This time around an illegal whaling operation threatens Willie and his orca pod. But 17-year-old Jesse (Richter), who has a summer job as a whale tracker on a research vessel, is determined to rescue his friend, aided by 10-year-old Max (Berry), who's horrified to discover his commercial fisherman father (Kilpatrick) is one of the whalers. 86m/C VHS. Jason James Richter, Vincent Berry, August Schellenberg, Annie Corley, Patrick Kilpatrick; *D:* Sam Pillsbury; *W:* John Mattson; *C:* Tobias Schliessler; *M:* Cliff Eidelman. WAR

Freebie & the Bean 🎬½ 1974 (R) Two San Francisco cops nearly ruin the city in their pursuit of a numbers-running mobster. Top-flight car chases and wild humor combine. Watch for Valerie Harper's appearance as Arkin's wife. Followed by a flash-in-the-pan television series. 113m/C VHS, Beta, LV, Letterbox. Alan Arkin, James Caan, Loretta Swit, Valerie Harper, Jack Kruschen, Mike Kellin; *D:* Richard Rush. WAR

Freedom 🎬½ 1981 A young man finds the price of freedom to be very high when he tries to escape from Australian society in a silver Porsche. 102m/C VHS, Beta. Jon Blake, Candy Raymond, Jad Capelja, Reg Lye, John Clayton. NO

Freedom Is Paradise 🎬🎬🎬 1989 With his mother dead and his father missing, 13-year-old Sasha is growing up in a bleak reform school. Every time he runs away he is caught and severely beaten upon his return. When Sasha learns of his father's whereabouts he sets out on a 1,000 mile journey to the gulag-style prison where is father is being held. Bodrov's directorial debut. In Russian with English subtitles. 75m/C VHS. RU *D:* Sergei Bodrov. Montreal World Film Festival '89: Best Film. FCT

Freedom Road 🎬🎬 1979 A made for television drama about a Reconstruction Era exslave, portrayed by heavyweight champion Ali, who is elected to the U.S. Senate and subsequently killed while trying to obtain total freedom for his race. Based on a novel by Howard Fast. 186m/C VHS, Beta. Ron O'Neal, Edward Herrmann, John McLiam, Ernest Dixon, Alfre Woodard, Kris Kristofferson, Muhammad Ali; *D:* Jan Kadar. WOV, FCT

Freejack 🎬🎬 1992 (R) Futuristic thriller set in the year 2009, where pollution, the hole in the ozone layer, and the financial gap between the social classes have grown to such horrific proportions that the rich must pillage the past to find young bodies to replace their own. Estevez is a young race car driver whose sudden death makes him an ideal candidate for this bizarre type of surgery. Once transported to the future, he becomes a "Freejack" who must run for his life. Good cast including Jagger and Hopkins brings this one up slightly. Adapted from the novel "Immortality Inc." by Robert Sheckley. *CW:* Language and violence. 110m/C VHS, Beta, LV, Letterbox. Emilio Estevez, Mick Jagger, Rene Russo, Anthony Hopkins, Jonathan Banks, David Johansen, Amanda Plummer, Grand Bush, Frankie Faison, Esai Morales, John Shea; *D:* Geoff Murphy; *W:* Dan Gilroy, Ronald Shusett, Steven Pressfield; *M:* Trevor Jones, Michael Boddicker. INT

Freeway 🎬🎬 1988 (R) A nurse attempts to find the obsessive killer who shot her husband. The murderer phones a radio psychiatrist from his car, using Biblical quotes, while cruising for new victims. Okay thriller, based on the L.A. freeway shootings. 91m/C VHS, Beta, LV, Closed Caption. Darlanne Fluegel, James Russo, Billy Drago, Richard Belzer, Michael Callan, Steve Franken, Kenneth Tobey, Clint Howard; *D:* Francis Delia; *W:* Larry Ketron, Darrell Fetty, Francis Delia; *M:* Joe Delia. VTR

Freeway 🎬½ 1995 (R) Grubby modern retelling of "Little Red Riding Hood" finds surly 16-year-old Vanessa (Witherspoon) escaping from her parole officer to avoid foster care when the cops arrest her mom and stepdad. She takes the family car and heads off to grandma's but car trouble on the freeway leads to a ride from the big bad wolf—Bob Wolverton (Sutherland)—a serial killer preying on young women. Lots of lurid unpleasantness. *CW:* Explicit sexual dialogue, some lurid violence, some sexual situations, drug content. 102m/C VHS, Closed Caption. Reese Witherspoon, Kiefer Sutherland, Brooke Shields, Wolfgang Bodison, Dan Hedaya, Amanda Plummer, Bokeem Woodbine, Brittany Murphy; *D:* Matthew Bright; *W:* Matthew Bright; *C:* John Thomas; *M:* Danny Elfman. REP

The Freeway Maniac 🎬 1988 (R) A low budget thriller about an escaped convict who ends up on a movie set where he continues his former career: murder. Music by former "Doors" guitarist Robby Krieger. 94m/C VHS, Beta. Loren Winters, James Courtney, Shepard Sanders, Donald Hotton; *D:* Paul Winters; *M:* Robby Krieger.

Freeze-Die-Come to Life 🎬🎬🎬½ *Zamri Oumi Voskresni* 1990 First feature film from Kanevski, who spent eight years in a labor camp before glasnost. The story of two children who overcome the crushing poverty and bleakness of life in a remote mining community with friendship and humor. Beautifully filmed images, fine acting, touching but never overly sentimental story. The title comes from a children's game of tag. In Russian with English subtitles. 105m/B VHS. RU Pavel Nazarov, Dinara Drukarova; *D:* Vitaly Kanevski. FXL, BST, ING

Freeze Frame 🎬🎬½ 1992 Doherty is a high school TV reporter who's determined to capture a biotech conspiracy on video in this funny, fast-paced action flick. Nothing objectionable here. 78m/C VHS, LV, Closed Caption. Shannen Doherty, Charles Haid, Robyn Douglass, Seth Michaels; *D:* William Bindley; *W:* William Bindley. COL, NLC

French Can-Can 🎬🎬🎬 *Only the French Can!* 1955 Dramatically sparse but visually stunning depiction of the can-can's revival in Parisian nightclubs. Gabin plays the theatre impressario who discovers laundress Arnoul and decides to turn her into the dancing star of his new revue at the Moulin Rouge. In French with English subtitles. 93m/C VHS, Beta, LV. FR Jean Gabin, Francoise Arnoul, Maria Felix, Jean-Roger Caussimon, Edith Piaf, Patachou; *D:* Jean Renoir. INT

The French Connection 🎬🎬🎬½ 1971 (R) Two NY hard-nosed narcotics detectives stumble onto what turns out to be one of the biggest narcotics rings of all time. Cat-and-mouse thriller will keep you on the edge of your seat; contains one of the most exciting chase scenes ever filmed. Hackman's portrayal of Popeye Doyle is exact and the teamwork with Scheider special. Won multiple awards. Based on a true story from the book by Robin Moore. Followed in 1975 by "French Connection 2." 102m/C VHS, Beta, LV. Gene Hackman, Roy Scheider, Fernando Rey, Tony LoBianco, Eddie Egan, Sonny Grosso, Marcel Bozzuffi; *D:* William Friedkin; *C:* Owen Roizman. Academy Awards '71: Best Actor (Hackman), Best Adapted Screenplay, Best Director (Friedkin), Best Film Editing, Best Picture; British Academy Awards '72: Best Actor (Hackman); Directors Guild of America Awards '71: Best Director (Friedkin); Golden Globe Awards '72: Best Actor—Drama (Hackman), Best Director (Friedkin), Best Film—Drama; National Board of Review Awards '71: Best Actor (Hackman); New York Film Critics Awards '71: Best Actor (Hackman); Writers Guild of America '71: Best Adapted Screenplay; Nominations: Academy Awards '71: Best Cinematography, Best Sound, Best Supporting Actor (Scheider). FOX

French Connection 2 🦴🦴🦴 1975 (R)
New York policeman "Popeye" Doyle goes to Marseilles to crack a heroin ring headed by his arch nemesis, Frog One, who he failed to stop in the United States. Dour, super-gritty sequel to the 1971 blockbuster, and featuring one of Hackman's most uncompromising performances. 118m/C VHS, Beta, LV, Closed Caption. Gene Hackman, Fernando Rey, Bernard Fresson; **D:** John Frankenheimer; **W:** Robert Dillon. *FOX*

The French Detective 🦴🦴🦴 1975 Two detectives, one an old-time tough guy and the other a young cynic, are after a ruthless politician and his pet hood. Grim but entertaining. 90m/C VHS, Beta. *FR* Lino Ventura, Patrick Dewaere, Victor Lanoux; **D:** Pierre Granier-Deferre. *COL*

French Exit 🦴🦴 1997 (R) Another "meet cute" Hollywood romantic comedy. Neophyte screenwriters David Lake (Silverman) and Zina Hart (Amick) have a fender bender in an L.A. intersection. Flirtatious sparks fly amid their bickering but later they discover they're vying for the same big break script job. So will professional rivalry destroy the romantic fire? What do you think. **CW:** Language and a scene of drug use. 88m/C VHS, Closed Caption. Jonathan Silverman, Madchen Amick, Molly Hagen; **D:** Daphna Kastner; **W:** Daphna Kastner, Michael Alan Lerner. *COL*

French Fried Vacation 1979 Zany antics erupt when a group of unattached and consenting adults vacation in Africa. French with English subtitles. 90m/C VHS. Josiane Balasko, Michel Blanc, Mariann Chazel; **D:** Patrice Leconte. *FRA*

French Intrigue 🦴🦴 19?? (R) International agents track drug lords from the U.S. to France in a so-so spy thriller. 90m/C VHS, Beta. Jane Birkin, Curt Jurgens. *BFV*

French Kiss 🦴🦴½ 1995 (PG-13) Ultra cute Kate (Ryan) has a fear of flying but she's more afraid of losing her fiance (Hutton) to a newly met French babe. She jets off to Paris and on the way meets a dashing, but disheveled, French rogue (Kline). What happens next is predictable, but amusing just the same. Plot drags a bit in the middle, but the scenery and banter between Ryan and Kline are a pleasant enough diversion. Kline is at his charming best, while Ryan is typically perky. Watch for Spielvogel's stereotypically rude French hotel concierge. He's a hoot. **CW:** Some sexuality, language, and drug references. 111m/C VHS, LV, Closed Caption. Meg Ryan, Kevin Kline, Timothy Hutton, Jean Reno, Francois Cluzet, Renee Humphrey, Michael Riley, Susan Anbeh, Laurent Spielvogel; **D:** Lawrence Kasdan; **W:** Adam Brooks; **C:** Owen Roizman; **M:** James Newton Howard. *FXV*

The French Lesson 🦴🦴½ *The Frog Prince* 1986 (PG) A romantic British farce from a screenplay by cartoonist Simmonds, dealing with an English girl who goes to school in Paris and finds love. 90m/C VHS, Beta, Closed Caption. *GB* Alexandre Sterling, Jane Snowdon; **D:** Brian Gilbert; **W:** Posy S. Simmonds. *WAR*

The French Lieutenant's Woman 🦴🦴🦴½ 1981 (R) Romantic love and tragedy in the form of two parallel stories, that of an 19th-century woman who keeps her mysterious past from the scientist who loves her, and the lead actor and actress in the film of the same story managing an illicit affair on the set. Extraordinary performances and beautifully shot. Based on the John Fowles novel. 124m/C VHS, Beta, LV. Meryl Streep, Jeremy Irons, Leo McKern, Lynsey Baxter; **D:** Karel Reisz; **W:** Harold Pinter; **M:** Carl Davis. British Academy Awards '81: Best Actress (Streep); Golden Globe Awards '82: Best Actress—Drama (Streep); Los Angeles Film Critics Association Awards '81: Best Actress (Streep); Nominations: Academy Awards '81: Best Actress (Streep), Best Adapted Screenplay, Best Art Direction/Set Decoration, Best Costume Design, Best Film Editing. *MGM, FOX*

The French Line 🦴🦴 1954 A millionairess beauty travels incognito while trying to sort out which men are after her money, and which ones aren't. The 3-D presentation of Russell's physique in skimpy costumes earned this the condemnation of the Catholic Legion of Decency, which pumped the boxoffice even higher. Lacks the charm of "Gentlemen Prefer Blonds," which it imitates. 🎵Comment Allez-Vous; Well, I'll Be Switched; Any Gal From Texas; What Is This That I Feel?; With A Kiss; By Madame Fuelle; Wait Till You See Paris; Poor Andre; The French Line. 102m/C VHS, Beta. Jane Russell, Gilbert Roland, Craig Stevens, Kim Novak, Arthur Hunnicutt, Joi Lansing; **D:** Lloyd Bacon. *CCB, TTC*

French Postcards 🦴🦴 1979 (PG) Three American students study all aspects of French culture when they spend their junior year of college at the Institute of French Studies in Paris. By the same writers who penned "American Graffiti" a few years earlier. 95m/C VHS, Beta. Miles Chapin, Blanche Baker, Valerie Quennessen, Debra Winger, Mandy Patinkin, Marie-France Pisier; **D:** Willard Huyck; **W:** Gloria Katz, Willard Huyck. *PAR*

French Quarter 🦴🦴½ 1978 (R) A dual story about a young girl in the modern-day French Quarter of New Orleans who is also the reincarnation of a turn-of-the-century prostitute. Everyone gets to play two roles but this film is more curiosity than anything else. 101m/C VHS, Beta. Bruce Davison, Virginia Mayo, Lindsay Bloom, Alisha Fontaine, Lance LeGault, Anne Michelle; **D:** Dennis Kane. *NO*

French Quarter Undercover 🦴 1985 (R) Two undercover cops in New Orleans thwart a terrorist plot aimed at the World's Fair. 84m/C VHS, Beta. Michael Parks, Bill Holiday; **D:** Joe Catalanotto. *ART*

French Silk 🦴🦴½ 1994 (PG-13) Homicide detective (Horsley) falls for a lingerie designer (Lucci) who's a murder suspect. Filmed on location in New Orleans. Made for TV production with additional footage. "R" rating is for nudity (not Lucci's). Based on the novel by Sandra Brown. **CW:** Some sensuality. 90m/C VHS, LV. Susan Lucci, Lee Horsley, Shari Belafonte, R. Lee Ermey, Sarah Marshall, Bobby Hosea, Jim Metzler, Joe Warfield, Paul Rosenberg; **D:** Noel Nosseck. *APX*

The French Touch 🦴🦴½ 1954 Fernandel stars in this French farce about a shepherd who decides to open his own clip joint as a hairdresser and finds himself a hit among the Parisiennes. Fair to middling comedy. 84m/B VHS. *FR* Fernandel, Renee Devillers, Georges Chamarat; **D:** Jean Boyer. *NOS*

French Twist 🦴🦴½ *Bushwhacked; Gazon Maudit* 1995 (R) Romantic comedy about housewife Loli (Abril), tiredly coping with her realtor/husband Laurent (Chabat) and their two sons. Then Loli meets appealing stranger Marijo (Balasko), a very matter-of-fact lesbian, and when she discovers her hubby is a chronic philanderer, Loli gets revenge by inviting Marijo to move in with them. Laurent realizes he loves his wife but she's having too much fun and there's finally an interesting showdown between Laurent and Marijo over Loli. The French title, which translates literally to "Cursed Lawn," is an old slang term for lesbian. French with subtitles. **CW:** Sexuality, nudity and language. 100m/C VHS, LV, Closed Caption. *FR* Victoria Abril, Alain Chabat, Josiane Balasko, Ticky Holgado; **D:** Josiane Balasko; **W:** Josiane Balasko, Telsche Boorman; **C:** Gerard de Battista; **M:** Manuel Malou. Cesar Awards '96: Best Writing; Nominations: Cesar Awards '96: Best Actor (Chabat), Best Director (Balasko), Best Film, Best Supporting Actor (Holgado); Golden Globe Awards '96: Best Foreign Film. *TOU*

The French Way 🦴🦴½ 1940 One of the legendary Baker's few films, in which she portrays a Parisian nightclub owner playing matchmaker for a young couple. In French with English subtitles. 72m/B VHS, Beta. *FR* Josephine Baker, Micheline Presle, Georges Marchal; **D:** Jacques de Baroncelli. *VDM, FCT*

The French Woman 🦴 1979 (R) Softcore story of blackmail, murder, and sex involving French cabinet ministers mixing passion and politics. From the director of "Emmanuelle." 97m/C VHS, Beta. Francoise Fabian, Klaus Kinski; **D:** Just Jaeckin; **M:** Serge Gainsbourg. *NO*

Frenchman's Farm 🦴½ 1987 (R) A young woman witnesses a killing at a deserted farmhouse. When she tells the police, they tell her that the murder happened 40 years before. Average thriller that probably won't keep you on the edge of your seat. 90m/C VHS, Beta. *AU* Tracey Tanish, David Reyne, John Meillon, Norman Kaye, Tui Bow; **D:** Ron Way. *NO*

Frenzy 🦴🦴½ *Latin Quarter* 1946 A sculptor, pushed over the brink of sanity when he discovers that his wife is having an affair, turns to his art for solace...and seals his wife's corpse in a statue. Creepy. 75m/B VHS. *GB* Derrick DeMarney, Frederick Valk, Joan Greenwood, Joan Seton, Valentine Dyall, Martin Miller; **D:** Vernon Sewell; **W:** Vernon Sewell. *SNC*

Frenzy 🦴🦴🦴 1972 (R) The only film in which Hitchcock was allowed to totally vent the violence and perverse sexuality of his distinctive vision, in a story about a strangler stalking London women in the late '60s. Finch plays the convicted killer-only he's innocent and must escape prison to find the real killer. McGowen is wonderful as the put-upon police inspector. A bit dated, but still ferociously hostile and cunningly executed. 116m/C VHS, Beta, LV. *GB* Jon Finch, Barry Foster, Barbara Leigh-Hunt, Anna Massey, Alec McCowen, Vivien Merchant, Billie Whitelaw, Jean Marsh; **D:** Alfred Hitchcock; **W:** Anthony Shaffer. *USH*

Fresh 🦴🦴½ 1994 (R) Intelligent 12-year-old boy runs heroin in the morning and sells crack after school in a tough Brooklyn neighborhood. Enterprising young man draws life lessons from chess-hustler father Jackson and heroin-dealing mentor Esposito, so he looks for a way out of the dead-end business. First time director Yakin plays it straight, foregoing the usual Hollywood-style rap and automatic weapons approach to convey the message that circumstances can kill innocence just as effectively as a bullet. Startling but subdued atmosphere allows the plot and characters to become more complicated than first suspected. Excellent performance by newcomer Nelson as the kid. 114m/C VHS, Beta, LV, Closed Caption. *FR* Samuel L. Jackson, Giancarlo Esposito, Sean Nelson, N'Bushe Wright, Ron Brice, Jean LaMarre, Luis Lantigua, Yul Vazquez, Cheryl Freeman; **D:** Boaz Yakin; **W:** Boaz Yakin; **C:** Adam Holender. Independent Spirit Awards '95: Debut Performance (Nelson); Sundance Film Festival '94: Special Jury Prize, Filmmakers Trophy; Nominations: Independent Spirit Awards '95: Best Supporting Actor (Esposito). *MAX*

Fresh Horses 🦴🦴 1988 (PG-13) A wrong-side-of-the-tracks Depression-era romance. McCarthy is the engaged college boy who falls for backwoods girl Ringwald, who turns out to have a destructive secret. 92m/C VHS, Beta, LV, Closed Caption. Molly Ringwald, Andrew McCarthy, Patti D'Arbanville, Ben Stiller; **D:** David Anspaugh; **M:** David Foster. *COL*

Fresh Kill 🦴 1987 A young guy from Chicago goes to Hollywood, and gets mixed up in drugs and murder. Made for video. 90m/C VHS, Beta. Flint Keller, Patricia Parks; **D:** Joseph Merhi. *NO*

The Freshman 🦴🦴🦴🦴 1925 Country boy Lloyd goes to college and, after many comic tribulations, saves the day with the winning touchdown at the big game and wins the girl of his dreams. This was one of the comedian's most popular films. 75m/B VHS, Beta. Harold Lloyd, Jobyna Ralston, Brooks Benedict, James Anderson, Hazel Keener; **D:** Fred Newmeyer, Sam Taylor; **W:** Sam Taylor. National Film Registry '90. *TLF*

The Freshman 🦴🦴½ 1990 (PG) Brando, in an incredible parody of his Don Corleone character, makes this work. Broderick is a college student in need of fast cash, and innocent enough to believe that any work is honest. A good supporting cast and a twisty plot keep things interesting. Sometimes heavy handed with its sight gags, but Broderick and Brando push the movie to hilarious conclusion. Don't miss Burt Parks' musical extravaganza. 102m/C VHS, Beta, LV, 8mm, Letterbox, Closed Caption. Marlon Brando, Matthew Broderick, Penelope Ann Miller, Maximilian Schell, Bruno Kirby, Frank Whaley, Jon Polito, Paul Benedict, Richard Gant, B.D. Wong, Bert Parks; D: Andrew Bergman; W: Andrew Bergman; M: David Newman. COL, FCT

Freud Leaving Home 🎬🎬 1991 Freud (Roor) is the nickname of 25-year-old Angelique, who lives with her Jewish family in Stockholm. Problems erupt when her sister and brother return home for their mother's 60th birthday and all learn of her fatal illness. The siblings are forced to confront themselves and their relationships with each other and their mother. Swedish with subtitles. 100m/C VHS. SW Gunilla Roor, Ghita Norby, Philip Zanden, Jessica Zanden; D: Suzanne Bier. FRF

Frida 🎬🎬½ 1984 The life of controversial Mexican painter Frido Kahlo is told via deathbed flashbacks using the artist's paintings to set the scenes. In Spanish with English subtitles. 108m/C VHS, Beta, LV. SP Ofelia Medina, Juan Jose Gurrola, Max Kerlow; D: Paul Leduc. CVC, IME, TPV

Friday 🎬🎬½ 1995 (R) It's "Boyz N' the Hood" meets "Good Times." Ice Cube wrote and stars as Craig in this humorous look into life in the 'hood. Craig's just lost his job and spends his time sitting on the porch with his pot smoking sidekick Smokey (Tucker), with the two getting mixed up in a variety of crazy antics involving their kooky neighbors. The laughs come at the expense of overworn cliches and sterotypical characters, but there's originality in the movie's energy and boldness (i.e. the local dope dealer is also the neighborhood ice cream man). To some, this "Friday" could be something to look forward to. CW Pervasive strong language and drug use, and for a brutal fight. 91m/C VHS, LV, Closed Caption. Ice Cube, Chris Tucker, Bernie Mac, John Witherspoon, Regina King, Nia Long, Tommy (Tiny) Lister; D: F. Gary Gray; W: Ice Cube, DJ Pooh; C: Gerry Lively; M: Frank Fitzpatrick. Nominations: MTV Movie Awards '96: Breakthrough Performance (Tucker), Best On-Screen Duo (Chris Tucker/Ice Cube), Best Comedic Performance (Tucker). NLC, TTC

Friday Foster 🎬½ 1975 (R) A beautiful, young photographer investigates an assassination attempt and uncovers a conspiracy against black politicians. Based on the Chicago Tribune comic strip. 90m/C VHS, Beta. Pam Grier, Yaphet Kotto, Thalmus Rasulala, Carl Weathers, Godfrey Cambridge; D: Arthur Marks. ORI, FCT

Friday the 13th 🎬🎬 1980 (R) Notable as among the first in a very long series of slasher flicks, with effects by Tom Savini. A New Jersey camp reopens after it's been closed for 20 years after a history of "accidental" deaths. And the horror begins again. Six would-be counselors arrive to get the place ready. Each is progressively murdered: knifed, speared, and axed. Followed by numerous, equally gory sequels. 95m/C VHS, Beta, LV, Closed Caption. Betsy Palmer, Adrienne King, Harry Crosby, Laurie Bartram, Mark Nelson, Kevin Bacon, Jeannine Taylor, Robbi Morgan, Peter Brouwer, Walt Gorney; D: Sean S. Cunningham; W: Victor Miller; C: Barry Abrams. PAR

Friday the 13th, Part 2 woof! 1981 (R) New group of teen camp counselors are gruesomely executed by the still undead Jason. Equally as graphic as the first installment; followed by several more gorefests. 87m/C VHS, Beta, LV. Amy Steel, John Furey, Adrienne King, Betsy Palmer, Kirsten Baker, Stu Charno, Warrington Gillette, Walt Gorney, Marta Kober, Bill Randolph, Jack Marks; D: Steve Miner; W: Ron Kurz; C: Peter Stein. PAR

Friday the 13th, Part 3 woof! 1982 (R) Yet another group of naive counselors at Camp Crystal Lake fall victim to the maniacal Jason. The 3-D effects actually helped lessen the gory effects, but this is still awful. Followed by more

disgusting sequels. 96m/C VHS, Beta, LV, Dana Kimmell, Paul Kratka, Richard Brooker, Catherine Parks, Jeffrey Rogers, Tracie Savage, Larry Zerner; D: Steve Miner; W: Martin Kitrosser, Carol Watson; C: Gerald Feil. PAR

Friday the 13th, Part 4: The Final Chapter woof! 1984 (R) Jason escapes from the morgue to once again slaughter and annihilate teenagers at a lakeside cottage. Preceded by three earlier "Friday the 13th" films, equally as graphic. The title's also a lie since there's several more sequels to look forward to. 90m/C VHS, Beta, LV, Closed Caption. Erich Anderson, Judie Aronson, Kimberly Beck, Peter Barton, Tom Everett, Corey Feldman, Crispin Glover, Richard Brooker; D: Joseph Zito; W: Barney Cohen; C: Joao Fernandes. PAR

Friday the 13th, Part 5: A New Beginning woof! 1985 (R) Jason rises from the dead to slice up the residents of a secluded halfway house. The sequels, and the sameness, never stop. See Part 6... 92m/C VHS, Beta, LV, Closed Caption. John Shepherd, Melanie Kinnaman, Shavar Ross, Richard Young, Juliette Cummins, Corey Feldman, Carol Lacatell, Vernon Washington; D: Danny Steinmann; W: Danny Steinmann, David M. Cohen; C: Stephen Posey. PAR

Friday the 13th, Part 6: Jason Lives woof! 1986 (R) One of the few youths not butchered by Jason digs him up and discovers he's not (and never will be) dead. Carnage ensues...and the sequels continue. 87m/C VHS, Beta, LV, Closed Caption. Thom Mathews, Jennifer Cooke, David Kagen, Kerry Noonan, Renee Jones, Tom Fridley, C.J. Graham, Darcy Demoss; D: Tom McLoughlin; W: Tom McLoughlin; C: Jon Kranhouse. PAR

Friday the 13th, Part 7: The New Blood woof! 1988 (R) A young camper with telekinetic powers accidentally unchains Jason from his underwater lair with the now-familiar results. There's still another bloody sequel to go. 90m/C VHS, Beta, LV, Closed Caption. Lar Park Lincoln, Kevin Blair, Susan Blu, Terry Kiser, Kane Hodder, Elizabeth Kaitan, John Otrin, Heidi Kozak; D: John Carl Buechler; W: Daryl Haney; C: Paul Elliott. PAR

Friday the 13th, Part 8: Jason Takes Manhattan 🎬 1989 (R) Yet another sequel, with the hockey-masked walking slaughterhouse transported to New York. Most of the previous action in the movie takes place on a cruise ship. This one is less gruesome than others in the series. Followed by "Jason Goes to Hell: The Final Friday." 96m/C VHS, Beta, LV, Closed Caption. Jensen Daggett, Scott Reeves, Peter Mark Richman, Barbara Bingham, Kane Hodder, Martin Cummins, Sharlene Martin, Vincent Craig Dupree; D: Rob Hedden; W: Rob Hedden; C: Bryan England. PAR

Fridays of Eternity 🎬🎬 1981 A romantic comedy about loyalty, fidelity, love, and lovers all with a tinge of the supernatural. In Spanish with English subtitles. 89m/C VHS. AR Thelma Biral, Hector Alterio; D: Hector Olivera. NO

Fried Green Tomatoes 🎬🎬🎬 1991 (PG-13) Two stories about four women, love, friendship, Southern charm, and eccentricity are untidily held together by wonderful performances. Unhappy, middle-aged Evelyn (Bates), meets the talkative 83-year-old Ninny Threadgoode (Tandy). Ninny reminisces about her Depression-era life in the town of Whistle Stop, Alabama and the two women, Idgie (Masterson) and Ruth (Parker), who ran the local cafe. Back-and-forth narrative as it tracks multiple storylines is occasionally confusing, though strong character development holds interest. Surprising box office hit adapted by Fannie Flagg from her novel "Fried Green Tomatoes at the Whistle Stop Cafe." 130m/C VHS, Beta, LV, Closed Caption. Kathy Bates, Jessica Tandy, Mary Stuart Masterson, Mary-Louise Parker, Cicely Tyson, Chris O'Donnell, Stan Shaw, Gailard Sartain, Timothy Scott, Gary Basaraba, Lois Smith, Grace Zabriskie; D: Jon Avnet; W: Fannie Flagg, Carol Sobieski; M: Thomas Newman. Nominations: Academy Awards '91: Best Adapted Screenplay, Best Supporting Actress (Tandy). USH

Frieda 🎬🎬½ 1947 An RAF officer brings his German wife home after the war and she is naturally distrusted by his family and neighbors. An interesting look at post-war bigotry. 97m/B VHS. GB David Farrar, Glynis Johns, Mai Zetterling, Flora Robson, Albert Lieven; D: Basil Dearden. NOS, VYY, VEC

Friend of the Family 2 🎬 1996 (R) Disturbed young woman decides to get revenge on the man who used and abandoned her by becoming his family's nanny. Also available in an unrated version. 90m/C VHS, LV. Shauna O'Brien, Paul Michael Robinson, Jenna Bodnar, Jeff Rector; D: Nicholas Medina; W: Henry Krinkle; C: Gary Graver. TRI, ORI

Friendly Fire 🎬🎬🎬 1979 Based on a true story of an American family in 1970 whose soldier son is killed by "friendly fire" in Vietnam, and their efforts to uncover the circumstances of the tragedy. Touching and powerful, with an excellent dramatic performance by Burnett. Made for television. 146m/C VHS, Beta, Closed Caption. Carol Burnett, Ned Beatty, Sam Waterston, Timothy Hutton; D: David Greene. FOX

Friendly Persuasion 🎬🎬🎬 Except For Me and Thee 1956 Earnest, solidly acted tale about a peaceful Quaker family struggling to remain true to its ideals in spite of the Civil War which touches their farm life in southern Indiana. Cooper and McGuire are excellent as the parents with Perkins fine as the son worried he's using his religion to hide his cowardice. Based on a novel by Jessamyn West. 140m/C VHS, Beta, LV, Closed Caption. Gary Cooper, Dorothy McGuire, Anthony Perkins, Marjorie Main, Charles Halton; D: William Wyler; W: Michael Wilson; C: Ellsworth Fredericks; M: Dimitri Tiomkin. Cannes Film Festival '57: Best Film; Nominations: Academy Awards '56: Best Adapted Screenplay, Best Director (Wyler), Best Picture, Best Song ("Friendly Persuasion (Thee I Love)"), Best Sound, Best Supporting Actor (Perkins). FOX

Friends 🎬 1971 (R) Ho-hum drama about an orphaned French girl and an unloved English boy who meet, become friends, and decide to run away together, setting up house in a deserted beach cottage. They even have a baby before they're discovered. Provides no insight into the teenagers dilemmas. Followed by "Paul and Michelle." 101m/C VHS, Closed Caption. GB Sean Bury, Anicee Alvina, Pascale Roberts, Sady Rebbot, Ronald Lewis; D: Lewis Gilbert; M: Elton John. FOX

Friends 🎬🎬 1995 Story of three South African women sharing an apartment in Johannesburg. Fox is a white political activist, Burgers, an Afrikaner archaeologist, and Kente, a black teacher. When Fox plants a bomb that takes two innocent lives, their loyalties are tested. Debut for director Proctor. 109m/C VHS. Kerry Fox, Michele Burgers, Dambisa Kente; D: Elaine Proctor; W: Elaine Proctor. FRF

Friends Forever 🎬🎬🎬 1986 Conformity, sexuality, and friendship are explored in this coming-of-age drama. Kristian is a shy, conformist 16-year-old, starting off at a new school. He finds himself drawn to two different young men who equally dominate his class. Henrik's androgynous sexual charm is equaled by his independence while the moody Patrick is the leader of a band of troublemakers. Kristian gains in self-confidence by their friendship but is tested when he learns Patrick is gay. 95m/C VHS. DK D: Stefan Christian Henszelman. FCT

Friends, Lovers & Lunatics 🎬½ Crazy Horse; She Drives Me Crazy 1989 A weekend turns into a romantic nightmare/laugh-fest when a man visits his ex-girlfriend and her new "friend," and winds up in a new romance himself. 87m/C VHS, Beta, LV. CA Daniel Stern, Deborah Foreman, Sheila McCarthy, Page Fletcher, Elias Koteas; D: Stephen Withrow. IME

A Friendship in Vienna 🎬🎬½ 1988 The friendship of two young teenage girls, one Jewish, and the other the daughter of a Nazi collaborator, is tested as WWII looms over Europe and the Nazis begin their persecution of Austrian

Jews. Adapted from the book "Devil in Vienna" by Doris Orgel. Made for cable television. **100m/C VHS, Closed Caption.** Jenny Lewis, Ed Asner, Jane Alexander, Stephen Macht, Rosemary Forsyth, Ferdinand "Ferdy" Mayne, Kamie Harper; **D:** Arthur Seidelman; **W:** Richard Alfieri. DIS

Fright 🎬 *Spell of the Hypnotist* 1956 A woman—convinced that she died in 1889 as part of a suicide pact with Prince Rudolph of Austria—seeks help from a psychiatrist who promptly falls in love with her (didn't Freud say it was supposed to be the other way around?). **?m/B VHS.** Nancy Malone, Eric Fleming, Frank Marth, Humphrey Davis, Ned Glass, Norman Burton; **D:** W. Lee Wilder. SNC

Fright 🎬🎬 *Night Legs* 1971 (PG) A baby-sitter is menaced by a mental hospital escapee. He turns out to be the father of the boy she is watching. Tense but violent thriller. **84m/C VHS.** *GB* Susan George, Honor Blackman, Ian Bannen, John Gregson, George Cole, Dennis Waterman, Tara Collinson, Maurice Kaufman, Michael Brennan, Roger Lloyd Pack; **D:** Peter Collinson; **W:** Tudor Gates; **C:** Ian Wilson; **M:** Harry Robinson. REP, MOV

Fright House 🎬 1989 (R) Two stories of terror. "Fright House" features witches preparing an old mansion for a visit from the Devil. "Abandon" explains the prolonged youth of a teacher to her young student. **110m/C VHS, Beta.** Al Lewis, Duane Jones; **D:** Len Anthony. NO

Fright Night 🎬🎬½ 1985 (R) It's Dracula-versus-the-teens time when Charley suspects that his new neighbor descends from Count Vlad's line. He calls in the host of "Fright Night," the local, late-night, horror-flick series, to help deghoul the neighborhood. But they have a problem when the vampire discovers their plans (and nobody belives them anyway). Sarandon is properly seductive as the bloodsucker. Followed by sequel. **106m/C VHS, Beta, LV, Closed Caption.** William Ragsdale, Chris Sarandon, Amanda Bearse, Roddy McDowall, Stephen Geoffreys, Jonathan Stark, Dorothy Fielding, Art Evans; **D:** Tom Holland; **W:** Tom Holland; **C:** Jan Kiesser; **M:** Brad Fiedel. COL

Fright Night 2 🎬🎬 1988 (R) The sequel to the 1985 release "Fright Night," in which the harassed guy from the original film learns slowly that the vampire's sister and her entourage have come to roost around his college. Not quite as good as the original but the special effects are worth a look. **108m/C VHS, Beta, LV.** Roddy McDowall, William Ragsdale, Traci Lind, Julie Carmen, Jonathan Gries, Russ Clark, Brian Thompson; **D:** Tommy Lee Wallace; **W:** Tommy Lee Wallace, Tim Metcalfe, Miguel Tejada-Flores; **C:** Mark Irwin; **M:** Brad Fiedel. ART

The Frightened City 🎬🎬½ 1961 Waldo Zhernikov (Lom) decides to unite all six of London's crime syndicates into one conglomerate that would control the city. But when he gets power-mad, rival gangster Harry Foulcher (Marks) breaks away and forms his own organization. Naturally, there's a war between the factions. Paddy Damion (Connery in an early role), one of Waldo's gunsels, is sent to get rid of Foulcher. **91m/B VHS, Closed Caption.** *GB* Herbert Lom, Alfred Marks, Sean Connery, John Gregson, Yvonne Romain, Kenneth Griffith; **D:** John Lemont; **W:** Leigh Vance; **C:** Desmond Dickinson; **M:** Norrie Paramor. REP, FCT

The Frightened Woman 🎬🎬 1971 Wealthy Sayer (Leroy) likes to get his sexual kicks by playing master and slave in his villa outside Rome. When his usual hired call girl isn't available, he decides to lure a lovely journalist (Lassander) into his domination games. Dubbed into English. **90m/C VHS.** *IT* Phillippe LeRoy, Dagmar Lassander; **D:** Piero Schivazappa; **W:** Piero Schivazappa. FRF

The Frighteners 🎬🎬½ 1996 (R) Con man Frank Bannister (Fox) has a unique scam—he works with a group of ghosts who haunt a home until Frank comes along to drive them out, for the right price. But the small town of Fairwater is plagued by a serial killer's evil spirit and Frank and his spiritual cronies face the challenge of get-

ting rid of the ghost before the police decide to get rid of Frank. Interesting horror-comedy takes a lot of twists and turns to get where its going, but the payoff in gore and humor is worth it for fans of the genre. New Zealand helmer Jackson makes his American directorial debut. **CW:** Terror/violence. **106m/C VHS, LV, Letterbox, Closed Caption.** Michael J. Fox, Trini Alvarado, Peter Dobson, Dee Wallace Stone, John Astin, Jeffrey Combs, Troy Evans, Chi McBride, Jake Busey, R. Lee Ermey, Jim Fyfe; **D:** Peter Jackson; **W:** Peter Jackson, Frances Walsh; **C:** Alun Bollinger, John Blick; **M:** Danny Elfman. USH

Frightmare 🎬🎬½ *Frightmare 2* 1974 (R) A seemingly quiet British couple do indulge in one strange habit—they're cannibals. Released on video as "Frightmare 2" to avoid confusion with the 1981 film. **86m/C VHS, Beta.** *GB* Deborah Fairfax, Kim Butcher, Rupert Davies, Sheila Keith; **D:** Pete Walker.

Frightmare 🎬 1981 (R) Great horror star dies, but he refuses to give up his need for adoration and revenge. **84m/C VHS, Beta.** Ferdinand "Ferdy" Mayne, Luca Bercovici, Nita Talbot, Peter Kastner; **D:** Norman Thaddeus Vane. VES

The Fringe Dwellers 🎬🎬½ 1986 (PG) An Aborigine family leave their shantytown and move to the white, middle-class suburbs of Australia, encountering prejudice and other difficulties. Well acted and interesting but the ending's a letdown. **98m/C VHS.** *AU* Kristina Nehm, Justine Saunders, Bob Maza, Kylie Belling, Denis Walker, Ernie Dingo; **D:** Bruce Beresford; **W:** Bruce Beresford, Rhoisin Beresford; **M:** George Dreyfus. VES

The Frisco Kid 🎬🎬 *No Knife* 1979 (R) An innocent orthodox rabbi (Wilder) from Poland is sent to the wilds of San Francisco during the 1850s gold rush to lead a new congregation. He lands in Philadelphia, joins a wagon train and is promptly robbed and abandoned. He eventually meets up with a not-too-bright robber (Ford) who finds himself unexpectly befriending the man and undergoing various tribulations in order to get them both safely to their destination. This isn't a laugh riot and some scenes fall distinctly flat but Wilder is sweetness personified and lends the movie its charm. **119m/C VHS, Beta.** Gene Wilder, Harrison Ford, Ramon Bieri, Val Bisoglio, George DiCenzo, Penny Peyser, William Smith; **D:** Robert Aldrich; **W:** Michael Elias; **C:** Robert B. Hauser. WAR

Frisk 🎬🎬 1995 Disturbing depictions of sex/murder fantasies come courtesy of letters written by Dennis (Gunther), a part of the L.A. S&M scene, to his former boyfriend, Julian (Laplante). Just exactly how far Dennis has gone with some of his like-minded sexual partners is the question. Has he become the killer he claims to be? Adapted from Dennis Cooper's 1991 novel. **87m/C VHS.** Michael Gunther, Jaie Laplante, Craig Chester, Parker Posey, James Lyons, Alexis Arquette, Raoul O'Connell, Michael Stock; **D:** Todd Verow; **W:** Todd Verow, Jim Dwyer, George LaVoo; **C:** Greg Watkins. FCT

Fritz the Cat 🎬🎬🎬 1972 Ralph Bakshi's animated tale for adults about a cat's adventures as he gets into group sex, college radicalism, and other hazards of life in the '60s. Loosely based on the underground comics character by Robert Crumb. Originally X-rated. **77m/C VHS, Beta. D:** Ralph Bakshi; **W:** Ralph Bakshi; **M:** Ed Bogas. WAR, OM

Frog 1989 A boy adds a frog to his reptile collection but gets the surprise of his life when he finds it's really an enchanted Prince! Followed by "Frogs!" Part of the "Wonderworks" series. **55m/C VHS, Beta, LV, Closed Caption.** Paul Williams, Scott Grimes, Shelley Duvall, Elliott Gould, David Grossman. ORI, IME

Frogs 🎬🎬½ 1972 (PG) An environmental photographer working on a small island in Florida interrupts the birthday celebration of a patriarch. He and the folks at the party soon realize that various amphibians animals in the surrounding area are going berserk and attacking humans. One of the first environmentally motivated animal-vengeance films, and one of the best to come out of

the '70s. **91m/C VHS, Beta.** Ray Milland, Sam Elliott, Joan Van Ark, Adam Roarke, Judy Pace, Lynn Borden, Mae Mercer, David Gilliam, George Skaff, Holly Irving; **D:** George McCowan; **W:** Robert Blees, Robert Hutchison; **C:** Mario Tosi; **M:** Les Baxter. WAR, OM

Frogs! 199? Arlo is almost the most popular boy in school and is hoping to be crowned the king of his school's Spring Fling dance—until he and his friend Gus are turned into frogs by a witch. When Arlo and Gus discover their frog pond is being poisoned, they turn to the geeky Hannah for help. A sequel to "Frog." A viewers' guide is included. Part of the "Wonderworks" series. **55m/C VHS.** Shelley Duvall, Elliott Gould, Paul Williams, Scott Grimes, Judith Ivey. HMV, BTV, FCT

Frolics on Ice 🎬🎬 1940 Pleasant comedy-musical about a family man saving to buy the barber shop he works at. Irene Dare is featured in several ice skating production numbers. **65m/B VHS, Beta.** Roscoe Karns, Lynn (Mary Hart) Roberts, Irene Dare, Edgar Kennedy. VYY

From a Far Country: Pope John Paul II 🎬🎬 1981 TV biography of Polish Pope John Paul II begins in 1926 as Karol Wojtila celebrates Christmas with his father and continues through the important highlights of his life. **120m/C VHS.** *PL GB* Sam Neill, Christopher Cazenove, Warren Clarke, Kathleen Byron, Maurice Denham, Lisa Harrow, Michael Jayston; **D:** Krzysztof Zanussi; **C:** Slawomir Idziak; **M:** Wojciech Kilar. BWE

From Beyond 🎬🎬🎬 1986 (R) A gruesome, tongue-in-cheek adaptation of the ghoulish H.P. Lovecraft story. Scientists discover another dimension through experiments with the pineal gland. From the makers of "Re-Animator," and just as funny. **90m/C VHS, Beta, LV, Closed Caption.** Jeffrey Combs, Barbara Crampton, Ted Sorel, Ken Foree, Carolyn Purdy-Gordon, Bunny Summers, Bruce McGuire; **D:** Stuart Gordon; **W:** Dennis Paoli, Brian Yuzna; **C:** Mac Ahlberg; **M:** Richard Band. ART, VES

From Beyond the Grave 🎬🎬 *Creatures* 1973 (PG) This horror compendium revolves around a mysterious antique shop whose customers experience various supernatural phenomena, especially when they try to cheat the shop's equally mysterious owner. **98m/C VHS, Beta.** *GB* Peter Cushing, David Warner, Ian Bannen, Donald Pleasence, Margaret Leighton, Lesley-Anne Down, Diana Dors, Ian Ogilvy; **D:** Kevin Connor. WAR

From Dusk Till Dawn 🎬🎬½ 1995 (R) Escaped cons Seth and Richie Gecko (Clooney and Tarantino) pick up an ex-preacher (Keitel) and his two kids (Lewis and Liu) as hostages en route to their Mexican rendezvous spot, a raunchy biker joint run (unbenownst to them) by vampires. Feels like two movies in one, as Rodriguez's and Tarantino's styles don't necessarily mesh as much as they coexist. The first half features Tarantino's gift for snappy dialogue and somewhat sympathetic scumbags while the barroom finale shows off Rodriguez's mastery of the go-for-broke action set piece. Clooney proves the jump from TV to movies can be made successfully. Penned by Tarantino in 1990 during his video store days, he used the fee to get "Reservoir Dogs" off the ground. **CW:** Strong violence and gore, language and nudity. **108m/C VHS, LV, Closed Caption.** George Clooney, Quentin Tarantino, Harvey Keitel, Juliette Lewis, Ernest Liu, Fred Williamson, Richard "Cheech" Marin, Salma Hayek, Michael Parks, Tom Savini, Kelly Preston, John Saxon, Danny Trejo; **D:** Robert Rodriguez; **W:** Quentin Tarantino; **C:** Guillermo Navarro; **M:** Graeme Revell. MTV Movie Awards '96: Breakthrough Performance (Clooney); Nominations: Golden Raspberry Awards '96: Worst Supporting Actor (Tarantino). TOU

From Hell to Borneo 🎬½ 1964 (PG) A mercenary must defend his secluded island from pirates and gangsters. **90m/C VHS, Beta.** George Montgomery, Torin Thatcher, Julie Gregg, Lisa Moreno; **D:** George Montgomery. NO

From Hell to Victory 🎬🎬 1979 (PG) Group of friends of different nationalities vow to meet each year in Paris on the same date but WWII interrupts their lives and friendships. Director Lenzi used the alias Hank Milestone. Good battle scenes but nothing special. 100m/C VHS, Beta. *SP FR* George Peppard, George Hamilton, Horst Buchholz, Jean-Pierre Cassel, Capucine, Sam Wanamaker, Anny Duperey, Ray Lovelock; *D:* Umberto Lenzi. HHE, VTR

From Here to Eternity 🎬🎬🎬🎬 1953 Complex, hard-hitting look at the on and off-duty life of soldiers at the Army base in Honolulu in the days before the Pearl Harbor attack. There's sensitive Pvt. Pruitt (Clift), his always in trouble best friend Maggio (Sinatra), and their good-guy top sergeant (Lancaster) who just happens to be having a torrid affair with the commander's wife (Kerr). Pruitt, meanwhile, is introduced to a club "hostess" (Reed) who is a lot more vulnerable than she's willing to admit. A movie filled with great performances. Still has the best waves-on-the-beach love scene in filmdom. Based on the novel by James Jones, which was toned down by the censors. 118m/B VHS, Beta, LV, 8mm. Burt Lancaster, Montgomery Clift, Frank Sinatra, Deborah Kerr, Donna Reed, Ernest Borgnine, Philip Ober, Jack Warden, Mickey Shaughnessy, George Reeves, Claude Akins; *D:* Fred Zinnemann; *W:* Daniel Taradash; *C:* Burnett Guffey; *M:* George Duning. Academy Awards '53: Best Black and White Cinematography, Best Director (Zinnemann), Best Film Editing, Best Picture, Best Sound, Best Supporting Actor (Sinatra), Best Supporting Actress (Reed); Directors Guild of America Awards '53: Best Director (Zinnemann); Golden Globe Awards '54: Best Supporting Actor (Sinatra); New York Film Critics Awards '53: Best Actor (Lancaster), Best Director (Zinnemann), Best Film; Nominations: Academy Awards '53: Best Actor (Clift), Best Actor (Lancaster), Best Actress (Kerr), Best Costume Design (B & W), Best Original Dramatic/Comedy Score; Golden Globe Awards '54: Best Director (Zinnemann).COL, BTV

From Here to Eternity 🎬🎬½ 1979 (PG-13) From here to eternity...and back on the silver screen. Remake of the 1953 classic is based on James Jones' novel about life on a Hawaiian military base just before WWII. Decent actioner, but no Oscar-winner this time around. Made for television. 110m/C VHS, Beta, LV. Natalie Wood, Kim Basinger, William Devane, Steve Railsback, Peter Boyle, Will Sampson, Andy Griffith, Roy Thinnes, Barbara Hershey; *D:* Buzz Kulik. THV, FCT

From Here to Maternity 🎬🎬½ 1985 A made-for-television soap opera-based spoof about modern maternity. Three women want to be pregnant but their significant others aren't interested in paternity. 40m/C VHS, Beta. Carrie Fisher, Arleen Sorkin, Lauren Hutton, Griffin Dunne, Paul Reiser. ART, VES

From Hollywood to Deadwood 🎬🎬 1989 (R) A beautiful starlet is kidnapped and the private eye searching for her discovers blackmail and danger. 90m/C VHS, Beta, LV, Closed Caption. Scott Paulin, Jim Haynie, Barbara Schock; *D:* Rex Pickett; *W:* Rex Pickett. FCT, IME, VTR

From Noon Till Three 🎬🎬½ 1976 (PG) A change of pace role for Bronson as a two-bit gunfighter in a spoof of western legends. Bronson has a brief romance with Ireland who, believing him dead, fictionalizes their relationship in a series of books and builds the mediocre Dorsey into a western hero. When he turns up alive no one, including Ireland, believes that he is the real Dorsey and he's gradually driven crazy. Good script, weak direction but Bronson is likeable. 99m/C VHS. Charles Bronson, Jill Ireland, Douglas Fowley, Stan Haze, Damon Douglas; *D:* Frank D. Gilroy; *W:* Frank D. Gilroy; *C:* Lucien Ballard; *M:* Elmer Bernstein. MGM

From Russia with Love 🎬🎬🎬½ 1963 (PG) Bond is back and on the loose in exotic Istanbul looking for a super-secret coding machine. He's involved with a beautiful Russian spy and has the SPECTRE organization after him, including villainess Rosa Klebb (she of the killer shoe). Lots of exciting escapes but not an over-reliance on the gadgetry of the later films. The second Bond feature, thought by many to be the best. The laserdisc edition includes interviews with director Terence Young and others on the creative staff. The musical score and special effects can be separated from the actors' dialogue. Also features publicity shots, American and British trailers, on-location photos, and movie posters. 125m/C VHS, Beta, LV, Letterbox, Closed Caption. *GB* Sean Connery, Daniela Bianchi, Pedro Armendariz Sr., Lotte Lenya, Robert Shaw, Eunice Gayson, Walter Gotell, Lois Maxwell, Bernard Lee, Desmond Llewelyn, Nadja Regin, Alizia Gur, Martine Beswick, Leila; *D:* Terence Young; *C:* Ted Moore; *M:* John Barry. MGM, CRC, TLF

From "Star Wars" to "Jedi": The Making of a Saga 🎬🎬 1983 Using copious amounts of actual footage from the films, this movie follows the production of all three "Star Wars" sagas, concentrating on the special effects involved. 65m/C VHS, Beta, Closed Caption. David Prowse, Harrison Ford, Carrie Fisher, Billy Dee Williams, Alec Guinness; *D:* George Lucas. FOX, HMV

From the Dead of Night 🎬🎬🎬 1989 A spooky chiller about a near-death experience. Fashion designer Wagner narrowly escapes death but gets close enough to the other side that six of the dead feel cheated that she didn't join them. They decide to rectify the mistake and Wagner is pursued by the shadowy figures. Based on the novel "Walkers" by Gary Bradner. Made for television. 192m/C VHS. Lindsay Wagner, Bruce Boxleitner, Diahann Carroll, Robert Prosky, Robin Thomas, Merritt Butrick, Joanne Linville; *D:* Paul Wendkos.

From the Earth to the Moon 🎬🎬 1958 A mad scientist invents a new energy source and builds a rocket which takes him, his daughter, and two other men for some adventures on the moon. Based on the novel by Jules Verne. 100m/C VHS, Beta, LV. George Sanders, Joseph Cotten, Debra Paget, Don Dubbins; *D:* Byron Haskin; *W:* Robert Blees. NO

From the Hip 🎬🎬 1986 (PG) A young lawyer (Nelson) gets the chance of a lifetime when his office assigns a murder case to him. The only problem is that he suspects his client is very guilty indeed and must discover the truth without breaking his code of ethics. Nelson's courtroom theatrics are a bit out of hand, as he flares his nostrils at every opportunity. The movie is encumbered by a weak script and plot as well as a mid-story switch from comedy to drama. 112m/C VHS, Beta, LV, Closed Caption. Judd Nelson, Elizabeth Perkins, John Hurt, Ray Walston; *D:* Bob (Benjamin) Clark; *W:* Bob (Benjamin) Clark, David Kelly. ORI, WAR

From the Journals of Jean Seberg 🎬🎬 1995 An imaginary look at the life of the ill-fated actress, who began her career as a 17-year-old, miscast in Otto Preminger's "Saint Joan," achieved fame in Godard's "Breathless," and became a suicide at age 40 in 1979. Seberg (Hurt) dispassionately narrates her life story as she views film clips, from small-town Iowa teenager to would-be star, through abusive relationships, drugs and drinking, political activism, and FBI harassment. 97m/C VHS. *D:* Mark Rappaport; *W:* Mark Rappaport; *C:* Mark Daniels. WBF, PPI

From the Life of the Marionettes 🎬🎬🎬 1980 (R) A repressed man in a crumbling marriage rapes and kills a young prostitute. Another look at the powers behind individual motivations from Bergman, who uses black and white and color to relate details of the incident. 104m/C VHS, Beta, LV. *SW* Robert Atzorn, Christine Buchegger, Martin Benrath, Rita Russek, Lola Muethel, Walter Schmidinger, Heinz Bennent; *D:* Ingmar Bergman; *W:* Ingmar Bergman; *C:* Sven Nykvist. HMV

From the Manger to the Cross 🎬🎬 1915 This version of the Passion play was the first film to be done on location in Palestine. Re-enacts the Nativity, the flight into Egypt, and the crucifixion. Color-tinted. 71m/C VHS. R. Henderson-Bland, Alice Hollister, Gene Gauthier; *D:* Sidney Olcott; *W:* Gene Gauthier, Sidney Olcott. KIV

From the Mixed-Up Files of Mrs. Basil E. Frankweiler 🎬🎬½ 1995 (PG) Runaway siblings (Barnwell and Lee) secretly hide out in a New York art museum. They get caught up in trying to determine the authenticity of a sculpture (could it be the work of Michelangelo?) and turn to the statue's last owner, elusive art patron Mrs. Basil E. Frankweiler (Bacall). Based on the Newbery Award-winning novel by E.L. Konigsburg. Made for TV. 92m/C VHS. Lauren Bacall, Jean Marie Barnwell, Jesse Lee; *D:* Marcus Cole. HMK

From the Terrace 🎬🎬½ 1960 Newman is a wealthy Pennsylvania boy who goes to New York and marries into even more money and social position when he weds Woodward. He gets a job with her family's investment company and neglects his wife for business. She turns to another man and when he goes home for a visit he also finds a new romance which leads to some emotional soul searching. The explicitness of O'Hara's very long novel was diluted by the censors and Newman's performance is a stilted disappointment. Loy, as Newman's alcoholic mother, earned the best reviews. 144m/C VHS, Beta, LV. Paul Newman, Joanne Woodward, Myrna Loy, Ina Balin, Felix Aylmer, Leon Ames, George Grizzard, Patrick O'Neal, Barbara Eden, Mae Marsh; *D:* Mark Robson; *W:* Ernest Lehman; *M:* Elmer Bernstein. FOX

The Front 🎬🎬🎬 1976 (PG) Woody is the bookmaker who becomes a "front" for blacklisted writers during the communist witch hunts of the 1950s in this satire comedy. The scriptwriter and several of the performers suffered blacklisting themselves during the Cold War. Based more or less on a true story. 95m/C VHS, Beta, LV. Woody Allen, Zero Mostel, Herschel Bernardi, Michael Murphy, Danny Aiello, Andrea Marcovicci; *D:* Martin Ritt; *W:* Walter Bernstein; *C:* Michael Chapman; *M:* Dave Grusin. Nominations: Academy Awards '76: Best Original Screenplay. COL

The Front Page 🎬🎬🎬½ 1931 The original screen version of the Hecht-MacArthur play about the shenanigans of a battling newspaper reporter and his editor in Chicago. O'Brien's film debut here is one of several hilarious performances in this breathless pursuit of an exclusive with an escaped death row inmate. 101m/B VHS, Beta. Adolphe Menjou, Pat O'Brien, Edward Everett Horton, Mae Clarke, Walter Catlett; *D:* Lewis Milestone; *C:* Hal Mohr. Nominations: Academy Awards '31: Best Actor (Menjou), Best Director (Milestone), Best Picture. NOS, MRV, HHT

The Front Page 🎬🎬½ 1974 (PG) A remake of the Hecht-MacArthur play about the managing editor of a 1920s Chicago newspaper who finds out his ace reporter wants to quit the business and get married. But first an escaped convicted killer offers the reporter an exclusive interview. 105m/C VHS, LV. Jack Lemmon, Walter Matthau, Carol Burnett, Austin Pendleton, Vincent Gardenia, Charles Durning, Susan Sarandon; *D:* Billy Wilder; *W:* Billy Wilder, I.A.L. Diamond; *C:* Jordan Cronenweth. USH

Frontier Days 🎬½ 1934 Cody goes undercover to capture the leader of a gang of stagecoach robbers. He also manages to capture a killer along the way. 60m/B VHS, Beta. Bill Cody, Ada Ince, Wheeler Oakman; *D:* Sam Newfield. NOS, DVT

Frontier Fugitives 🎬½ 1945 When a trapper is murdered—allegedly by Indians—the Texas Rangers ride in to investigate. 58m/B VHS. Tex Ritter, Dave O'Brien, Guy Wilkerson, Lorraine Miller, I. Stanford Jolley, Jack Ingram; *D:* Harry Fraser. NOS

Frontier Horizon 🎬🎬 1939 Wayne and the Three Mesquiteers help out ranchers whose land is being bought up by crooked speculators. 55m/B VHS, Beta. John Wayne, Jennifer Jones, Ray Corrigan, Raymond Hatton; *D:* George Sherman. REP, CAB

Frontier Justice 🎬🎬 1935 Gibson is the foolish son of a cattle owner who has been forced into an insane asylum because of a battle over water rights. Naturally, he must take on responsibility and rescue his father. 56m/B VHS, Beta. Hoot

Gibson, Richard Cramer; **D:** Robert McGowan. *NOS, VCN, DVT*

Frontier Law 🎬½ 1943 Hayden and the boys ride into town to clean out the bad guys and clear a friend wrongly accused of murder. **55m/B VHS.** Russell Hayden, Jennifer Holt, Dennis Moore, Fuzzy Knight, Jack Ingram, Hal Taliaferro; **D:** Elmer Clifton; **W:** Elmer Clifton. *MOV*

Frontier Outlaws 🎬🎬 1944 A gang of villains is selling stolen cattle, and Crabbe poses as an interested buyer to catch them in the act. Laughs are provided by Lynn as a judge, and "Fuzzy" St. John as Crabbe's sidekick. **58m/B VHS.** Buster Crabbe, Al "Fuzzy" St. John, Frances Gladwin, Marin Sais, Charles "Blackie" King, Jack Ingram, Kermit Maynard, Edward Cassidy, Emmett Lynn, Budd Buster; **D:** Sam Newfield. *GPV, MRV, NOS*

Frontier Pony Express 🎬🎬 1939 Roy and Trigger do their best to help the Pony Express riders who are being attacked by marauding gangs in California during the time of the Civil War. Plenty of action here. **54m/B VHS, Beta.** Roy Rogers; **D:** Joseph Kane. *NOS, DVT*

Frontier Scout 🎬🎬 1938 Action-packed western has Wild Bill Hickock, portrayed by former opera singer Houston, forcing Lee's surrender in the Civil War before pursuing cattle rustlers out West. **60m/B VHS, Beta.** George Houston, Mantan Moreland; **D:** Sam Newfield. *NOS, DVT, RXM*

Frontier Uprising 🎬½ 1961 Stunning cinematography makes up for weak narrative in this otherwise routine oater. Davis stars as a frontier scout battling hordes of Mexicans and Indians while trying to gain control of California for the U.S. Based on the short story "Kit Carson" by George Bruce. **68m/B VHS.** Jim Davis, Nancy Hadley, Ken Mayer, Nestor Paiva, Don O'Kelly; **D:** Edward L. Cahn; **W:** Owen Harris. *DVT*

Frontier Vengeance 🎬½ 1940 Barry is falsely accused of murder and works to clear his name while at the same time romancing a stagecoach driver who's trying to win a race with a rival stagecoach line. **54m/B VHS, Beta.** Donald (Don "Red") Barry, Nate Watt. *RXM*

The Frontiersmen 🎬🎬 1938 Things plod along at the little red schoolhouse until Hoppy and the guys have to take off after some rustlers. Features the members of the St. Brendan Boys Choir as the schoolboys. Unusual for its lack of gunplay until near the end. **71m/B VHS.** William Boyd, George "Gabby" Hayes, Russell Hayden, Evelyn Venable, Clara Kimball Young, Charles Hughes, Dick Jones, Roy Barcroft, Emily Fitzroy; **D:** Lesley Selander. *NOS*

Frostbiter: Wrath of the Wendigo 🎬 1994 (R) Disappointing Troma entry takes itself a bit too seriously. It wants to be an "Evil Dead on Ice" (we even see a movie poster for same in the flick); the plot involves hunters trapped in the frozen woods of Northern Michigan by the evil spirit "Wendigo." It's short on original horror and the laff-factor is not up to usual Troma standards (although the killer chili was a nice touch). The only saving grace is the quirky soundtrack, including said chili's theme song by Randall and Allan Lynch, "March of the Undead" by the 3-D Invisibles, and "I'm a Hellbilly" by Elvis Hitler. Based on the comic book character of the same name. **CW:** Horror violence and gore, and for some brief nudity and language. **90m/C VHS.** Ron Asheton, Lori Baker, Patrick Butler, Devlin Burton; **D:** Tom Chaney; **C:** Tom Chaney. *TTV*

Frozen Alive 🎬 1964 A scientist experiments with suspended animation but, wouldn't you know, someone murders his wife while he's on ice. Apparently being frozen stiff does not an alibi make, and he becomes the prime suspect. Much unanimated suspense. **80m/B VHS.** *GB GE* Mark Stevens, Marianne Koch, Delphi Lawrence, Joachim Hansen, Walter Rilla, Wolfgang Lukschy; **D:** Bernard Knowles. *MOV*

Frozen Assets 🎬 1992 (PG-13) Pathetic attempt at comedy from Long and Bernsen. He's an ambitious executive who finds the "bank" of his corporation's latest acquisition deals in sperm and not cash. Still, he expects this acquisition to be a success and comes up with a number of tacky ways, much to the horror of the facility's administrator, to make that profit margin grow. **CW:** Sex-related elements. **93m/C VHS, Closed Caption.** Corbin Bernsen, Shelley Long, Larry Miller, Dody Goodman, Gerrit Graham, Paul Sand, Teri Copley, Matt Clark; **D:** George Miller; **W:** Don Klein, Tom Kartozian. *FXV*

Frozen Terror 🎬 1980 (R) A madman resembling both Jack Frost and Jack the Ripper claims victims at random. **93m/C VHS, Beta.** Bernice Stegers; **D:** Lamberto Bava. *ART, VES*

Fu Manchu 1956 Villainous arch-criminal Fu Manchu plots to enslave the world in "The Golden God" and "The Master Plan," two episodes from the television series. **60m/B VHS, Beta.** Glenn Gordon, Laurette Luez, Clark Howat, Lee Matthews. *DVT*

The Fugitive 🎬🎬🎬🎬 1948 Fonda is a priest devoted to God and the peasants under his care when he finds himself on the run after religion is outlawed in this nameless South-of-the-border dictatorship. Despite the danger of capture, he continues to minister to his flock. His eventual martyrdom unites the villagers in prayer. Considered Fonda's best performance; Ford's favorite film. Shot on location in Mexico. Excellent supporting performances. Based on the Graham Greene novel "The Power and the Glory" although considerably dumbed up for the big screen—Greene's priest had lost virtually all of his faith and moral code. Here the priest is a genuine Ford hero. A gem. **99m/B VHS, Beta, LV, Closed Caption.** Henry Fonda, Dolores Del Rio, Pedro Armendariz Sr., J. Carrol Naish, Leo Carrillo, Ward Bond, Robert Armstrong, John Qualen; **D:** John Ford; **W:** Dudley Nichols. *TTC*

The Fugitive 🎬🎬🎬½ 1993 (PG-13) Exciting big-screen version of the '60s TV series with the same basic storyline: Dr. Richard Kimble's wife is murdered and he's implicated, so he goes on the lam to find the real killer, the mysterious one-armed man. Lots of mystery and action, particularly a spectacular train/bus crash sequence, keeps the tension high. Due to illness, Richard Jordan was replaced by Krabbe after production had begun. Alec Baldwin was originally slated to star as Kimble, but backed out and Ford was cast. Sound familiar? Ford also replaced Baldwin as Jack Ryan in "Patriot Games." The second highest grossing movie of 1993. **127m/C VHS, LV, Closed Caption, DVD.** Harrison Ford, Tommy Lee Jones, Jeroen Krabbe, Julianne Moore, Sela Ward, Joe Pantoliano, Andreas Katsulas, Daniel Roebuck; **D:** Andrew Davis; **W:** David N. Twohy, Jeb Stuart; **C:** Michael Chapman; **M:** James Newton Howard. Academy Awards '93: Best Supporting Actor (Jones); Golden Globe Awards '94: Best Supporting Actor (Jones); Los Angeles Film Critics Association Awards '93: Best Supporting Actor (Jones); MTV Movie Awards '94: Best On-Screen Duo (Harrison Ford/Tommy Lee Jones), Best Action Sequence; Blockbuster Entertainment Awards '95: Action Actor, Video (Ford); Nominations: Academy Awards '93: Best Cinematography, Best Film Editing, Best Picture, Best Sound, Best Sound Effects Editing, Best Original Score; British Academy Awards '93: Best Supporting Actor (Jones); Directors Guild of America Awards '93: Best Director (Davis); Golden Globe Awards '94: Best Actor—Drama (Ford), Best Director (Davis); MTV Movie Awards '94: Best Film, Best Male Performance (Ford); Writers Guild of America '93: Best Adapted Screenplay. *WAR*

Fugitive Among Us 🎬🎬 1992 Dedicated cop is determined to return an escaped rapist to a life behind bars and he's aided by a victim who would really rather forget the whole thing. Made for TV. **97m/C VHS, Closed Caption.** Peter Strauss, Eric Roberts, Elizabeth Pena, Lauren Holly. *PAR*

The Fugitive Kind 🎬🎬½ 1960 A young drifter walks into a sleepy Mississippi town and attracts the attention of three of its women with tragic results. Based upon the Tennessee Williams' play "Orpheus Descending." good perfor-

mances but the writing never hangs well-enough together for coherence. **122m/B VHS, Beta.** Marlon Brando, Anna Magnani, Joanne Woodward, Victor Jory, R.G. Armstrong, Maureen Stapleton; **D:** Sidney Lumet; **C:** Boris Kaufman. *MGM, FOX*

The Fugitive: Premiere Episode 1963 In this introductory episode to the television series, Janssen plays Dr. Richard Kimble, who's wrongly convicted of murdering his wife. After a train taking him to prison derails, he makes his escape and begins his search for the real culprit, the mysterious one-armed man. But Kimble's pursued by the relentless Lt. Gerard. Additional episodes available. **45m/B VHS.** David Janssen, Barry Morse, Vera Miles, Brian Keith. *MOV, GKK*

Fugitive Rage 🎬🎬 1996 (R) Tara McCormick (Schumacher) winds up behind bars when she shoots the mobster who was acquitted for murdering her sister. She teams up with her cellmate Josie (O'Brien) to fight back against the mob who's put a bounty on her head and a covert government agency also out to use her. Prerequisite prison shower sequences, tough babes, and lots of action. **CW:** Strong sexuality, some violence and brief language. **90m/C VHS.** Wendy Schumacher, Shauna O'Brien, Jay Richardson; **D:** Fred Olen Ray. *APX*

Fugitive Road 🎬🎬 1934 The great von Stroheim stars as a crusty but soft-hearted border guard who arbitrarily detains people at the crossing. **69m/B VHS.** Erich von Stroheim, Wera Engels, Leslie Fenton, Harry Holman; **D:** Frank Strayer. *NOS*

The Fugitive: Taking of Luke McVane 🎬🎬 1915 An early silent western in which Hart upholds the cowboy code of honor. **28m/B VHS, Beta.** William S. Hart, Enid Markey. *VYY*

The Fugitive: The Final Episode 1967 The final episode of the acclaimed series, aired on August 29, 1967, in which Dr. Richard Kimble meets up with the one-armed man who murdered his wife and tries to bring him to justice before Lt. Gerard can bring Kimble in. Episode was the most watched television program up to that time. **78m/C VHS.** David Janssen, Barry Morse, Bill Raisch, Diane Baker, Joseph Campanella, Michael Constantine. *MOV*

Fugitive Valley 🎬½ 1941 Muddled plot has villains-turned-heroes on the trail of some outlaws and stolen money. Terhune shows off some of his vaudeville skills, and King sings some songs. **61m/B VHS.** Ray Corrigan, John "Dusty" King, Max Terhune, Julie Duncan, Glenn Strange, Robert F. (Bob) Kortman, Tom London, Reed Howes; **D:** S. Roy Luby. *NOS, HEG*

Fugitive X 🎬½ 1996 Advertising exec gets to be the prey for a group of thrill-seeking hunters. He's got a handgun, a small head start, and the slime taking bets on how long he'll last. You've seen this before. **97m/C VHS.** David Heavener, Richard Norton, Lynn-Holly Johnson, William Windom, Chris Mitchum, Robert Z'Dar; **D:** David Heavener; **W:** David Heavener. *SLI*

Fulfillment 🎬🎬½ *The Fulfillment of Mary Gray* 1989 (PG-13) Ladd stars as Mary Gray, a turn-of-the-century woman comfortably married to good but unexciting farmer, Jonathan (Levine). He's unable to give his wife the child they both desperately want and when his younger brother, Aaron (Smith), visits, the hope is Aaron can be persuaded to help out. The naturally volatile situation is heightened by the fact Mary is very drawn to the handsome Aaron anyway, and the feeling is mutual. Based on the novel "The Fulfillment" by LaVyrle Spencer. Made for television. **CW:** Mature subject matter. **96m/C VHS, Closed Caption.** Cheryl Ladd, Ted Levine, Lewis Smith; **D:** Piers Haggard. *REP*

Full Body Massage 🎬🎬 1995 (R) Wealthy art gallery owner Nina (Rogers) spends much of her time alone at her California dream home—except for a weekly appointment with young masseur Douglas (Burgard). But one week, the older Fitch (Brown) comes instead and begins discussing life and personal spirituality while he massages away the self-indulgent cares of the world-weary Nina. Good work by the leads in a chatty cable movie. **CW:** Nudity and some sexuality. **93m/C VHS, Closed Caption.** Mimi Rogers, Bryan Brown, Christopher Burgard, Elizabeth Barondes; **D:** Nicolas Roeg; **W:** Dan Gurskis; **C:** Anthony B. Richmond; **M:** Harry Gregson-Williams. *PAR*

Full Circle 🐾🐾 *The Haunting of Julia* **1977 (R)** Peter Straub wrote this eerie tale about a grief-stricken young woman whose child has recently died. To overcome her loss, she moves into a new house—which is haunted by the ghost of a long-dead child. **96m/C VHS, Beta.** *CA GB* Mia Farrow, Keir Dullea, Tom Conti, Jill Bennett, Robin Gammell; **D:** Richard Loncraine; **M:** Colin Towns.

Full Contact 🐾🐾 **1992** Nightclub bouncer Jeff helps his friend Sam escape from a loan shark. But Sam has doublecrossed him and now thinks that Jeff is dead in an arranged explosion. But Jeff's survived and plans to seek a suitable revenge. Cantonese with subtitles. **99m/C VHS, Letterbox.** *HK* Chow Yung Fat, Anthony Wong; **D:** Ringo Lam. *TAI, FCT*

Full Contact 🐾🐾 **1993 (R)** Farmhand Luke Powers heads for the decadence of Los Angeles to find his older brother. When three thugs make the mistake of trying to rob him, Luke shows off his martial arts skills. When Luke finds out his brother has been murdered by gamblers involved in an illegal back alley kickboxing circuit, he vows to get revenge. **97m/C VHS.** Jerry Trimble, Howard Jackson, Alvin Prouder, Gerry Blanck, Denise Buick; **D:** Rick Jacobson; **W:** Beverly Gray. *COL*

Full Eclipse 🐾🐾 **1993 (R)** Max Dire (Van Peebles) is seduced by the fetching Casey (Kensit) into joining a fierce elite group of underground cops whose mission is to wipe out crime. However, Max soon learns that the secret of their power is a serum which turns them into werewolves. Max is now faced with a decision: join forces with them, or expose them. Either way, blood will flow. Interesting special effects. Unrated version also available. **CW:** Language, brief nudity, and strong violence. **97m/C VHS, LV.** Mario Van Peebles, Patsy Kensit, Bruce Payne, Anthony John Denison; **D:** Anthony Hickox. *HBO*

Full Exposure: The Sex Tape Scandals 🐾½ **1989 (R)** Sleazy drama about a murdered call girl who was blackmailing her clients with sex videos. A cop and his inexperienced female partner are assigned to catch the killer. Made for television. **95m/C VHS, Closed Caption.** Jennifer O'Neill, Lisa Hartman Black, Vanessa L(ynne) Williams, Anthony John Denison, Peter Jurasik; **D:** Noel Nosseck; **W:** Stephen Zito; **M:** Dana Kaproff. *WOV*

Full Fathom Five 🐾½ **1990 (PG)** Central American militants, angered by America's invasion of Panama, hijack a submarine and threaten a nuclear assault on Houston. Boring and dumb. **81m/C VHS, Beta.** Michael Moriarty, Maria Rangel, Michael Cavanaugh, John Lafayette, Todd Field, Daniel Faraldo; **D:** Carl Franklin; **W:** Bart Davis. *MGM*

Full Hearts & Empty Pockets 🐾½ **1963** Follows the happy-go-lucky adventures of a young, handsome, impoverished gentleman on the loose in Rome. Dubbed in English. **88m/B VHS, Beta.** *IT GE* Linda Christian, Gino Cervi, Senta Berger; **D:** Camillo Mastrocinque. *VYY*

Full Metal Jacket 🐾🐾🐾½ **1987 (R)** A three-act Vietnam War epic, about a single Everyman impetuously passing through basic training then working in the field as a Marine Corps photojournalist and fighting at the onset of the Tet offensive. First half of the film is the most realistic bootcamp sequence ever done. Unfocused but powerful. Based on the novel by Hasford, who also co-scripted. **116m/C VHS, Beta, LV, 8mm, Closed Caption.** Matthew Modine, R. Lee Ermey, Vincent D'Onofrio, Adam Baldwin, Dorian Harewood, Arliss Howard, Kevyn Major Howard, Ed O'Ross, John Terry, Jon Stafford, Marcus D'Amico; **D:** Stanley Kubrick; **W:** Stanley Kubrick, Michael Herr, Gustav Hasford; **C:** Doug Milsome; **M:** Abigail

Mead. Nominations: Academy Awards '87: Best Adapted Screenplay. *WAR, FCT*

Full Metal Ninja 🐾 **1989** When his family is kidnapped, a trained martial artist trails their abductors and swears revenge. **90m/C VHS, Beta.** Patrick Allen, Pierre Kirby, Sean Odell, Jean Paul, Renato Sala; **D:** Charles Lee. *IMP*

The Full Monty 🐾🐾🐾 **1996 (R)** A group of laid off Yorkshire mill workers come up with a unique way to earn some money in this amusing Britcom. When exuberant Gaz (Carlyle) notices the local women lining up to see the Chippendale dancers, he persuades his mates to launch a striptease act themselves. But these guys are hardly cover boy material—they're variously overweight, middle-aged, depressed, and shy. Nevertheless, they turn out to be an unexpected success despite numerous mishaps and misunderstandings. Title refers to the fact that they strip down to their birthday suits. The film audience merely gets the moon view. **CW:** Language and some nudity. **90m/C VHS.** *GB* Robert Carlyle, Tom Wilkinson, Mark Addy, Steve Huison, William Snape, Steve Huison, Paul Barber; **D:** Peter Cattaneo; **W:** Simon Beaufoy; **C:** John de Borman; **M:** Anne Dudley. Academy Awards '97: Best Original Musical/Comedy Score; British Academy Awards '97: Best Actor (Carlyle), Best Film, Best Supporting Actor (Wilkinson); Screen Actors Guild Award '97: Cast; Nominations: Academy Awards '97: Best Director (Cattaneo), Best Original Screenplay, Best Picture; British Academy Awards '97: Best Director (Cattaneo), Best Film Editing, Best Original Screenplay, Best Sound, Best Supporting Actor (Addy), Best Supporting Actress (Sharp), Best Score; Golden Globe Awards '98: Best Film—Musical/Comedy; MTV Movie Awards '98: Best Dance Sequence (Cast); Writers Guild of America '97: Best Original Screenplay. *FOX*

Full Moon in Blue Water 🐾🐾½ **1988 (R)** His wife's been dead a year, he owes back taxes on his bar, his father has Alzheimer's, and his only form of entertainment is watching old home movies of his wife. Floyd has problems. Enter Louise, a lonely spinster who feels that it is her personal duty to change his life. If she doesn't do it, the bizarre things that happen after her arrival will. **96m/C VHS, Beta, LV.** Gene Hackman, Teri Garr, Burgess Meredith, Elias Koteas, Kevin Cooney, David Doty; **D:** Peter Masterson; **W:** Bill Bozzone; **M:** Phil Marshall. *VTR*

Full Moon in Paris 🐾🐾½ *Les Nuits De La Pleine* **1984 (R)** A young woman in Paris moves out on her architect lover in order to experience freedom. Through a couple of random relationships, she soon finds that what she hoped for is not what she really wanted. **101m/C VHS, Beta.** *FR* Pascale Ogier, Tcheky Karyo, Fabrice Luchini; **D:** Eric Rohmer; **W:** Eric Rohmer; **C:** Renato Berta. Venice Film Festival '84: Best Actress (Ogier). *XVC*

Full of Life 🐾🐾½ **1956** Holliday stars in this domestic comedy about a non-religious young woman who had married, in a civil ceremony, into a strict, Italian-Catholic family. Although Emily is now eight months pregnant the family still wants her and husband Nick (Conte) to have a church wedding. Holliday is a winning personality and the humor is lightly handled. Fante adapts from his own novel. **91m/B VHS.** Judy Holliday, Richard Conte, Salvatore Baccaloni, Esther Minciotti; **D:** Richard Quine; **W:** John Fante. *COL, FCT*

The Fuller Brush Girl 🐾🐾½ **1950** Lots of slapstick with Ball as a door-to-door saleswoman unexpectedly involved in a murder. She and dim-bulb boyfriend Albert are chased by cops, murderers, and smugglers in this frantic farce. Sequel to Red Skelton's (who has a cameo) 1948 film "The Fuller Brush Man." **84m/B VHS.** Lucille Ball, Eddie Albert, Carl Benton Reid, Gale Robbins, Jeff Donnell, John Litel, Fred Graham, Lee Patrick; **Cameos:** Red Skelton; **D:** Lloyd Bacon; **W:** Frank Tashlin. *COL*

The Fuller Brush Man 🐾🐾½ *That Man Mr. Jones* **1948** A newly hired Fuller Brush man becomes involved in murder and romance as he tries to win the heart of his girlfriend. A slapstick delight for Skelton fans. **93m/B VHS, Beta, LV.** Red

Skelton, Janet Blair, Don McGuire, Adele Jergens, D: Frank Tashlin. *COL*

Fun 🐾🐾 **1994** Another in the thrill kill genre. 14-year-old Bonnie (Witt) and 15-year-old Hillary (Humphrey) are best friends (and possibly lovers) who have stabbed to death an old woman—seemingly for kicks and to cement their loyalty to each other. (Can you say Leopold and Loeb?) Convicted and in a reformatory, they're documenting their actions, separately (in black & white sequences), to counselor Jane (Hope) and tabloid journalist John (Moses). Bleak dysfunction adapted by Bosley from his play. **95m/C VHS.** Alicia Witt, Renee Humphrey, Leslie Hope, William R. Moses, Ania Suli; **D:** Rafal Zielinksi; **W:** James Bosley; **C:** Jens Sturup; **M:** Marc Tschantz. Nominations: Independent Spirit Awards '95: Debut Performance (Witt). *GRE, SPC*

Fun & Fancy Free 🐾🐾🐾 **1947 (G)** Part-animated, part-live-action Disney feature is split into two segments: "Bongo" with Dinah Shore narrating the story of a happy-go-lucky circus bear looking for love; and "Mickey and the Beanstalk"—a "new" version of an old fairy tale. Disney's last performance as the voice of Mickey and the only film to star Mickey, Donald Duck, Jiminy Cricket and Goofy. **73m/C VHS.** **V:** Walt Disney. *DIS*

Fun Down There woof! **1988** This small-town boy-comes-to-the-big city is so bad, it's—bad. A naive—and unsympathetic—gay man from upstate New York moves to Greenwich Village and has fun down there (and they don't mean Australia). **110m/C VHS.** Michael Waite, Nickolas Nagurney, Gretschen Somerville, Martin Goldin, Kevin Och; **D:** Roger Stigliano; **W:** Michael Waite, Roger Stigliano. *WBF, FCT*

Fun in Acapulco 🐾🐾 **1963 (PG)** Former trapeze artist Elvis romances two beauties and acts as a part-time lifeguard and night club entertainer. He must conquer his fear of heights for a climactic dive from the Acapulco cliffs. Features ten musical numbers. ♫Fun in Acapulco; Vino, Dinero y Amor; Mexico; The Bullfighter Was A Lady; El Toro; Marguerita; (There's) No Room To Rhumba (In A Sports Car); I Think I'm Going To Like It Here; You Can't Say No In Acapulco. **97m/C VHS, Beta.** Elvis Presley, Ursula Andress, Elsa Cardenas, Paul Lukas, Alejandro Rey, Larry Domasin, Howard McNear; **D:** Richard Thorpe; **C:** Daniel F. Fapp. *FOX, MVD*

Fun with Dick and Jane 🐾🐾 **1977 (PG)** An upper-middle class couple turn to armed robbery to support themselves when the husband is fired from his job. Though it has good performances, the film never develops its intended bite. **104m/C VHS, Beta.** George Segal, Jane Fonda, Ed McMahon; **D:** Ted Kotcheff; **W:** Jerry Belson, David Giler, Mordecai Richler; **C:** Fred W. Koenekamp; **M:** Ernest Gold. *COL*

The Funeral 🐾🐾🐾½ **1984** A sharp satire of the clash of modern Japanese culture with the old. The hypocrisies, rivalries and corruption in an average family are displayed at the funeral of its patriarch who also happened to own a house of ill repute. Itami's breakthrough film; Japanese with subtitles. **112m/C VHS.** *JP* Tsutomu Yamazaki, Nobuko Miyamoto, Kin Sugai, Ichiro Zaitsu, Nekohachi Edoya, Shoji Otake; **D:** Juzo Itami. *REP, FCT*

The Funeral 🐾🐾🐾 **1996 (R)** Ferrara fuels fantastic performances from his famous thesps in this fatalistic tale of a family of gangsters in 1930s New York. Flashbacks from the opening funeral scene show a complex and troubled family of Italian brothers (Walken, Penn, and Gallo), from their formative years through their quest for justice after youngest brother Johnny is murdered. Not just another mob movie; characters are multi-dimensional with interesting quirks and Penn, especially, sprints into his role. More subtle than "Bad Lieutenant" and less pretentious than "The Addiction," this Ferrara flick is the one to see. **CW:** Strong crude sex scenes, strong violence and language. **96m/C VHS.** Christopher Walken, Benicio Del Toro, Vincent Gallo, Christopher Penn, Isabella Rossellini, Annabella Sciorra, John Ventimiglia, Paul Hipp, Gretchen

Mol; **D:** Abel Ferrara; **W:** Nicholas St. John; **C:** Ken Kelsch; **M:** Joe Delia. Nominations: Independent Spirit Awards '97: Best Actor (Penn), Best Cinematography, Best Director (Ferrara), Best Film, Best Screenplay. *HMK*

Funeral for an Assassin 🐾½ 1977 (PG) A professional assassin seeks revenge for his imprisonment by the government of South Africa, a former client. Planning to kill all of the country's leading politicians, he masquerades as a black man, a cover which is designed to fool the apartheid establishment. 92m/C VHS, Beta. Vic Morrow, Peter Van Dissel; **D:** Ivan Hall. *GEM, MRV, VTR*

Funeral Home 🐾½ *2 Cries in the Night* 1982 Terrified teen spends her summer vacation at her grandmother's tourist home, a former funeral parlor. Rip-off of "Psycho." 90m/C VHS, Beta. *CA* Lesleh Donaldson, Kay Hawtry; **D:** William Fruet. *NO*

Funeral in Berlin 🐾🐾🐾 1966 Second of the Caine/Harry Palmer espionage films (following up "Ipcress File"), in which the deadpan British secret serviceman arranges the questionable defection of a Russian colonel. Good look at the spy biz and postwar Berlin. "Billion Dollar Brain" continues the series. 102m/C VHS, Beta, LV. Michael Caine, Eva Renzi, Oscar Homolka; **D:** Guy Hamilton; **W:** Evan Jones. *PAR*

The Funhouse 🐾½ 1981 (R) Four teenagers spend the night at a carnival funhouse, witness a murder, and become next on the list of victims. From the director of cult favorite "The Texas Chainsaw Massacre," but nothing that hasn't been seen before. 96m/C VHS, Beta, LV, Letterbox. Elizabeth Berridge, Shawn Carson, Cooper Huckabee, Largo Woodruff, Sylvia Miles, Miles Chapin, Kevin Conway, William Finley, Wayne Doba; **D:** Tobe Hooper; **W:** Larry Block; **C:** Andrew Laszlo; **M:** John Beal. *USH*

Funland 🐾 1989 (PG-13) In the world's weirdest amusement park a clown goes nuts over the new corporate owners' plans for the place and decides to seek revenge. 86m/C VHS, LV. David Lander, William Windom, Bruce Mahler, Michael McManus; **D:** Michael A. Simpson. *ART, IME, VES*

Funny About Love 🐾½ 1990 (PG-13) Fairly absurd tale with dashes of inappropriate black humor about a fellow with a ticking biological clock. Nimoy sheds his Spock ears to direct a star-studded cast in this lame tale of middle-aged cartoonist Wilder who strays from wife Lahti after having problems on the conception end into the welcoming arms of fertile college co-ed Masterson in his quest to contribute to the population count. 107m/C VHS, Beta, LV, 8mm, Closed Caption. Gene Wilder, Christine Lahti, Mary Stuart Masterson, Robert Prosky, Stephen Tobolowsky, Anne Jackson, Susan Ruttan, David Margulies; **D:** Leonard Nimoy; **W:** Norman Steinberg, David Frankel. *PAR*

Funny Bones 🐾🐾🐾 1994 (R) Struggling comedian Tommy Fawkes (Platt) bombs in Vegas big-time while his Mr. Showbiz father George (Lewis) easily overshadows him at every turn. So Tommy decides to head back to his childhood home in Blackpool, England and figure out his life. What he discovers are the Parkers, a family of British vaudevillians, and the fact that his father stole their routines and, briefly, Mrs. Parker (Caron), resulting in half-brother Jack (Evans) who has all the natural talent Tommy can only dream about. Serious, funny, and hostile with notable performances from Platt and Evans.**CW:** Some language; scene of tragic violence. 128m/C VHS, LV, Closed Caption. Oliver Platt, Lee Evans, Leslie Caron, Jerry Lewis, Oliver Reed, Ian McNeice, Ruta Lee, Richard Griffith, George Carl, Freddie Davies; **D:** Peter Chelsom; **W:** Peter Chelsom, Peter Flannery; **C:** Eduardo Berra; **M:** John Altman. *TOU*

Funny, Dirty Little War 🐾🐾½ *No Hambra mas Penas ni Olvido; Funny Little Dirty War* 1983 An Argentinian farce about the petty rivalries in a small village erupting into a violent, mini-civil war. Based on the novel by Osvaldo Soriano. In Spanish with English subtitles. 80m/C VHS. *AR* Federico

Luppi, Julio de Grazia, Miguel Angel Sola; **D:** Hector Olivera. *NYF, XVC*

Funny Face 🐾🐾🐾 1957 A musical satire on beatniks and the fashion scene also features the May-December romance between Astaire and the ever-lovely Hepburn. He is a high-fashion photographer (based on Richard Avedon); she is a Greenwich Village bookseller fond of shapeless, drab clothing. He decides to take her to Paris and show her what modeling's all about. The elegant musical score features classic Gershwin. The laserdisc includes the original theatrical trailer and is available in widescreen. ♫Let's Kiss and Make Up; He Loves and She Loves; Funny Face; How Long Has This Been Going On?; Clap Yo' Hands; S'Wonderful; Bonjour Paris; On How To Be Lovely; Marche Funebre. 103m/C VHS, Beta, LV, 8mm, Letterbox. Fred Astaire, Audrey Hepburn, Kay Thompson, Suzy Parker; **D:** Stanley Donen; **M:** George Gershwin, Ira Gershwin. Nominations: Academy Awards '57: Best Art Direction/Set Decoration, Best Cinematography, Best Costume Design, Best Story & Screenplay. *PAR, FCT*

The Funny Farm 🐾½ 1982 Comedy about a group of ambitious young comics striving to make it in the crazy world of comedy at Los Angeles' famous comedy club, The Funny Farm. 90m/C VHS, Beta, Closed Caption. *CA* Miles Chapin, Eileen Brennan, Peter Aykroyd; **D:** Ron Clark; **W:** Ron Clark. *VTR*

Funny Farm 🐾🐾 1988 (PG) Chevy Chase as a New York sportswriter finds that life in the country is not quite what he envisioned. The comedy is uneven throughout, with the best scenes coming at the end. 101m/C VHS, LV, Closed Caption. Chevy Chase, Madolyn Smith, Joseph Maher, Jack Gilpin, Brad Sullivan, MacIntyre Dixon; **D:** George Roy Hill; **W:** Jeffrey Boam; **M:** Elmer Bernstein. *WAR*

Funny Girl 🐾🐾🐾 1968 (G) Follows the early career of comedian Fanny Brice, her rise to stardom with the Ziegfeld Follies and her stormy romance with gambler Nick Arnstein in a fun and funny look at back stage music hall life in the early 1900s. Streisand's film debut followed this auspicious performance of the role on Broadway. Score was augmented by several tunes sung by Brice during her performances. Excellent performances from everyone, captured beautifully by Wyler in his musical film debut. Followed by "Funny Lady." ♫My Man; Second Hand Rose; I'd Rather Be Blue Over You; People; Don't Rain On My Parade; I'm The Greatest Star; Sadie, Sadie; His Love Makes Me Beautiful; You Are Woman, I Am Man. 151m/C VHS, Beta, LV, Letterbox. Barbra Streisand, Omar Sharif, Walter Pidgeon, Kay Medford, Anne Francis; **D:** William Wyler; **C:** Harry Stradling. Academy Awards '68: Best Actress (Streisand); Golden Globe Awards '69: Best Actress—Musical/Comedy (Streisand); Nominations: Academy Awards '68: Best Cinematography, Best Film Editing, Best Picture, Best Song ("Funny Girl"), Best Sound, Best Supporting Actress (Medford), Scoring of a Musical. *COL, BTV*

Funny Lady 🐾🐾½ 1975 (PG) A continuation of "Funny Girl," recounting Fanny Brice's tumultuous marriage to showman Billy Rose in the 1930s and her lingering affection for first husband Nick Arnstein. One of the rare sequels which are just as good, or at least almost, as the original. ♫How Lucky Can You Get?; Great Day; More Than You Know; Blind Date; So Long, Honey Lamb; Isn't This Better; Let's Hear It For Me; I Like Him/I Like Her; It's Only a Paper Moon. 137m/C VHS, Beta, LV, Letterbox. Barbra Streisand, Omar Sharif, James Caan, Roddy McDowall, Ben Vereen, Carole Wells, Larry Gates, Heidi O'Rourke; **D:** Herbert Ross; **W:** Jay Presson Allen, Arnold Schulman; **C:** James Wong Howe. Nominations: Academy Awards '75: Best Cinematography, Best Costume Design, Best Song ("How Lucky Can You Get"), Best Sound, Original Song Score and/or Adaptation.*COL, FCT*

Funny Money 🐾 1982 Pointed, satirical look at the British habit of financing life with the almighty credit card. Sometimes uneven comedy. 92m/C VHS, Beta. *GB* Greg Henry, Elizabeth Daily, Gareth

Hunt, Derren Nesbitt, Annie Ross; **D:** James Kenelm Clarke. *ART*

A Funny Thing Happened on the Way to the Forum 🐾🐾🐾 1966 A bawdy Broadway farce set in ancient Rome where a conniving, slave plots his way to freedom by aiding in the romantic escapades of his master's inept son. Terrific performances by Mostel and Gilford. Keaton's second-to-last film role. The Oscar-winning score includes such highlights as "Comedy Tonight," "Lovely," and "Everybody Ought to Have a Maid." 100m/C VHS, Beta, LV. Zero Mostel, Phil Silvers, Jack Gilford, Buster Keaton, Michael Hordern, Michael Crawford, Annette Andre; **D:** Richard Lester; **M:** Ken Thorne. Academy Awards '66: Best Adapted Score. *FOX, FCT*

Funnyman 🐾🐾 1994 (R) Cartoon splatter courtesy of a demon dressed in classic British jester regalia. Rock 'n' roll mogul Young obtains Lee's creepy ancestral home in a card game but when he visits with his family, everyone but Young is killed by the Funnyman, who uses his victims own weaknesses to dispatch them. A second set of likely candidates arrive when Young's brother Devitt shows up with a motley collection of hangers-on, including psychic Black, who's the only one to realize something's seriously off.**CW:** Horror violence, language and drug content. 89m/C VHS. Tim James, Benny Young, Matthew Devitt, Pauline Black, Ingrid Lacey; **Cameos:** Christopher Lee; **D:** Simon Sprackling; **W:** Simon Sprackling. *AVI*

Furious 🐾 1983 (PG) The sister of a young martial arts apprentice is killed by the master, with a great deal of action and special effects. 85m/C VHS, Beta. Simon Rhee, Howard Jackson, Arlene Montano. *VHE*

The Furious Avenger 🐾 1976 A released convict, on his way to avenging his family's murder, stops a rape and takes on one opponent after another in this rousing kickfest. Dubbed. 84m/C VHS, Beta. Hsiung Fei, Fan Ling, Chen Pei Ling, Tien Yeh, Wang Mo Chou. *UNI*

The Further Adventures of Tennessee Buck 🐾 1988 (R) Mercenary adventurer travels through tropical jungles acting as a guide to a dizzy couple. Along the way, they encounter cannibals, headhunters, and other bizarre jungle things in this lame take on "Indiana Jones." Shot on location in Sri Lanka. 90m/C VHS, Beta, LV. David Keith, Kathy Shower, Brant Van Hoffman; **D:** David Keith; **M:** John Debney. *VTR*

Further Adventures of the Wilderness Family, Part 2 🐾🐾½ *Wilderness Family, Part 2* 1977 (G) Depicts the Robinson family who left civilization for the freedom of the Colorado wild. Predictable retread, but more good family adventure drama from the makers of "Adventures of the Wilderness Family." 104m/C VHS, Beta. Heather Rattray, Ham Larsen, George Flower, Robert F. Logan, Susan Damante Shaw; **D:** Frank Zuniga. *VTR*

Fury 🐾🐾🐾½ 1936 Tracy gives an excellent performance as an innocent young man framed for kidnapping and then nearly murdered by a lynch mob. His plans for revenge are thwarted by his girlfriend, who fears that he will turn into the murderer he has been accused of being. Powerful anti-violence message is well-made, with strong ensemble acting. Lang's favorite of his American-made films. 96m/B VHS, Beta. Spencer Tracy, Sylvia Sidney, Walter Abel, Bruce Cabot, Edward Ellis, Walter Brennan, Frank Albertson; **D:** Joseph Ruttenberg. National Film Registry '95;; Nominations: Academy Awards '36: Best Story. *MGM*

The Fury 🐾🐾🐾 1978 (R) The head of a government institute for psychic research finds that his own son is snatched by supposed terrorists who wish to use his lethal powers. The father tries to use another young woman with psychic power to locate him, with bloody results. A real chiller. 117m/C VHS, Beta. Kirk Douglas, John Cassavetes, Carrie Snodgress, Andrew Stevens, Amy Irving, Charles Durning, Carol Rossen, Rutanya Alda, William Finley, Jane Lambert,

Joyce Easton, Daryl Hannah, Dennis Franz, James Belushi; *D:* Brian DePalma; *W:* John Farris; *C:* Richard Kline; *M:* John Williams. *FOX*

Fury 🎬 198? A man and woman meet in the Amazonian jungle and the sparks begin to fly. 75m/C VHS, Beta. Stuart Whitman, Laura Gemser. *NO*

Fury Is a Woman 🎬🎬🎬½ 1961 A Polish version of Shakespeare's Macbeth which ranks with the greatest film translations of his work. In Czarist Russia the passionate wife of a plantation owner begins an affair with a farm hand, and poisons her father-in-law when he finds them out. As her madness grows, she plots the murder of the husband. Letterbox format. In Serbian with English subtitles. 93m/B VHS, Letterbox. *RU* Olivera Markovic, Ljuba Tadic, Kapitalina Eric; *D:* Andrzej Wajda. *HTV*

The Fury of Hercules 🎬½ *La Furia Di Ercole; Fury of Samson* 1961 It's up to the mighty son of Zeus to free an enslaved group of people from an oppressive, evil ruler. Surely all who stand in his way will be destroyed. Another Italian muscleman film. 95m/C VHS. *IT* Brad Harris, Brigitte Corey, Mara Berni, Carlo Tamberlani, Serge Gainsbourg, Elke Arendt, Alan Steel; *D:* Gianfranco Parolini. *GKK, SNC*

The Fury of the Wolfman 🎬 1970 A murdering werewolf is captured by a female scientist who tries to cure his lycanthropy with drugs and brain implants. Pretty slow going, but hang in there for the wolfman versus werewoman climax. 80m/C VHS, Beta. *SP* Paul Naschy, Perla Cristal; *D:* Jose Maria Zabalza; *W:* Paul Naschy. *UNI, NLC, LOO*

Fury on Wheels 🎬 1971 (PG) Tale of men who race cars and wreak havoc and vice versa. 89m/C VHS, Beta. Judd Hirsch, Tom Ligon, Paul Sorvino, Logan Ramsey, Collin Wilcox-Horne. *NO*

Fury to Freedom: The Life Story of Raul Ries 🎬🎬 1985 A young man raised in the volatile world of abusive and alcoholic parents grows into an abusive and violent adult. One night, however, he meets something he can't beat up, and it changes his life. 78m/C VHS. Gil Gerard, John Quade, Tom Silardi. *VCI*

Future Cop 🎬🎬 *Trancers* 1976 A hard-nosed, old-fashioned cop is forced to team with the ultimate enforcer—a robot. Silly made-for-TV movie, but likable leads. 78m/C VHS, Closed Caption. Ernest Borgnine, Michael J. Shannon, John Amos, John Larch, Herbert Nelson, Ronnie Clair Edwards; *D:* Jud Taylor; *W:* Danny Bilson, Paul DeMeo. *PAR*

Future Fear 🎬½ 1997 (R) Genetic scientist Dr. John Denniel (Fahey) has to find a solution for a flesh-eating virus that threatens mankind. Along with wife Anna (Ford), John tries combining human DNA with that of other species. But it turns out the virus was engineered by maniacal General Wallace (Keach) as a form of human cleansing—and he's not happy when he hears about a potential cure. *CW:* Some strong sexuality, and for violence and language. 82m/C VHS. Jeff Wincott, Maria Ford, Stacy Keach; *D:* Lewis Baumander. *ART*

Future Force 🎬 1989 (R) In the crime-filled future cops can't maintain order. They rely on a group of civilian mercenaries to clean up the streets. 90m/C VHS, Beta. David Carradine, Robert Tessier, Anna Rapagna, William Zipp.

Future Hunters 🎬 1988 In the holocaust-blitzed future, a young couple searches for a religious artifact that may decide the future of the planet. 96m/C VHS, Beta, LV. Robert Patrick, Linda Carol, Ed Crick, Bob Schott; *D:* Cirio H. Santiago. *ART, VES*

Future Kill 🎬 1985 (R) Anti-nuclear activists battle fraternity brothers in this grim futuristic world. Shaky political alliances form between revenge-seeking factions on both sides. 83m/C VHS, Beta, LV. Edwin Neal, Marilyn Burns, Doug Davis; *D:* Ronald W. Moore; *W:* Ronald W. Moore. *ART, VES*

Future Shock 🎬 1993 (PG-13) Dr. Russell Langdon is a psychiatrist who has been experimenting with virtual reality technology. Unbeknownst to three of his patients he decides to use

them as guinea pigs in his work. But confronting their deepest fears only leads to new terrors. Also available in an unrated version. *CW:* Violence and threat. 93m/C VHS. Bill Paxton, Vivian Schilling, Brion James, Martin Kove; *D:* Eric Parkinson, Matt Reeves, Oley Sassone; *W:* Vivian Schilling.

Future Zone 🎬🎬 1990 (R) In an attempt to save his father from being murdered, a young man travels backwards in time. 88m/C VHS, LV. David Carradine, Charles Napier, Ted Prior; *D:* David A. Prior.

Futurekick 🎬½ 1991 (R) In the not so distant future, a kickboxer with an attitude and cyborg capabilities must use every ounce of strength in a battle against evil. 80m/C VHS. Don "The Dragon" Wilson, Meg Foster, Christopher Penn, Eb Lottimer; *D:* Damian Klaus; *W:* Damian Klaus. *NHO*

Futureworld 🎬🎬 1976 (PG) In the sequel to "Westworld," two reporters junket to the new "Futureworld" theme park, where they first support a scheme to clone and control world leaders. Includes footage shot at NASA locations. 107m/C VHS, Beta, LV. Peter Fonda, Blythe Danner, Arthur Hill, Yul Brynner, Stuart Margolin; *D:* Richard T. Heffron; *W:* George Schenck. *WAR, OM*

Futz 🎬½ 1969 Story from off-Broadway is of a man who loves his pig and the world that can't understand the attraction. Better in original stage production. 90m/C VHS. John Pakos, Victor Lipari, Sally Kirkland; *D:* Tom O'Horgan. *IVY*

Fuzz 🎬🎬½ 1972 (PG) Reynolds in the Boston cop on the track of a bomber killing policemen, punks setting winos on fire, and some amorous fellow officers. Combines fast action and some sharp-edged humor. 92m/C VHS, Beta. Burt Reynolds, Tom Skerritt, Yul Brynner, Raquel Welch, Jack Weston, Charles Martin Smith; *D:* Richard A. Colla; *M:* Dave Grusin. *MGM, FOX*

Fyre 🎬½ 1978 (R) Young beautiful girl moves from the Midwest to Los Angeles and becomes a prostitute. 90m/C VHS, Beta. Allen (Goorwitz) Garfield, Lynn Theel, Tom Baker, Cal Haynes, Donna Wilkes, Bruce Kirby; *D:* Richard Grand.

"G" Men 🎬🎬🎬½ 1935 Powerful story based loosely on actual events that occurred during FBI operations in the early 1930s, with Cagney on the right side of the law, though still given to unreasonable fits of anger. Raised and educated by a well-known crime kingpin, a young man becomes an attorney. When his friend the FBI agent is killed in the line of duty, he joins the FBI to seek vengeance on the mob. But his mob history haunts him, forcing him to constantly prove to his superiors that he is not under its influence. Tense and thrilling classic. 86m/B VHS, Beta. James Cagney, Barton MacLane, Ann Dvorak, Margaret Lindsay, Robert Armstrong, Lloyd Nolan, William Harrigan, Regis Toomey; *D:* William Keighley. *MGM, CCB*

G-Men Never Forget *Code 645* 1948 Moore, former stunt-man and future Lone Ranger, stars in this 12-part serial about FBI agents battling the bad guys. Lots of action. On two cassettes. 167m/B VHS. Clayton Moore, Roy Barcroft, Ramsay Ames, Drew Allen, Tommy Steele, Eddie Acuff; *D:* Fred Brannon, Yakima Canutt. *REP, MLB*

G-Men vs. the Black Dragon 1943 Reedited serial of "Black Dragon of Manzanar" stars Cameron as Fed who battles Asian Axis agents during WWII. Action-packed. 244m/B VHS, LV. Rod Cameron, Roland Got, Constance Worth, Nino Pipitone, Noel Cravat; *D:* William Witney. *REP, MLB*

G. Whilliker! 🎬🎬 1993 Brothers have decided a guy named Gus Whilliker is the perfect match for their older sister/guardian. Too bad she's already dating someone. 93m/C VHS. Dan Brook, Robin Brooks, Matthew-Tompkins, Jay Michael Ferguson, William Ryan Tilk, Chris Lloyd, Jody Miller; *D:* David McClendon; *W:* Brenda Brown-Canary, Michael Helderman; *M:* Drew F. Barlow. *FFC*

Gabriel Over the White House 🎬🎬 1933 Part political satire, part fantasy, and completely fascinating. Huston is a venal politician, completely in thrall to his crooked

cohorts, who manages to get elected President. While recuperating from an auto accident Huston thinks he's sees a vision of the Archangel Gabriel, who essentially tells him to change his crooked ways. From bought man Huston changes to righteous do-gooder, much to the dismay of his criminal companions, who'll stop at nothing to get rid of the man they think has simply gone insane. Huston gives a powerful performance in this decidedly oddball film. 86m/B VHS. Walter Huston, Karen Morley, Arthur Byron, Franchot Tone, Dickie Moore, C. Henry Gordon, David Landau, Samuel S. Hinds, Jean Parker; *D:* Gregory La Cava. *MGM, MOV, BTV*

Gabriela 🎬🎬 1984 (R) A sultry romance develops between a Brazilian tavern keeper and the new cook he's just hired. Derived from Jorge Amado's novel. In Portuguese with English subtitles. 102m/C VHS, Beta. *BR* Sonia Braga, Marcello Mastroianni, Nelson Xavier, Antonio Cantafora; *D:* Bruno Barreto; *W:* Bruno Barreto; *C:* Carlo DiPalma; *M:* Antonio Carlos. *MGM*

Gaby: A True Story 🎬🎬🎬 1987 (R) The story of a woman with congenital cerebral palsy who triumphs over her condition with the help of family and loved ones, and ends up a college graduate and acclaimed author. Based on a true story. 115m/C VHS, Beta, LV. Rachel Levin, Liv Ullmann, Norma Aleandro, Robert Loggia, Lawrence Monoson, Robert Beltran, Tony Goldwyn; *D:* Luis Mandoki; *W:* Martin Salinas, Michael James Love; *C:* Lajos Koltai; *M:* Maurice Jarre. Nominations: Academy Awards '87: Best Supporting Actress (Aleandro). *COL*

Gal Young 'Un 🎬🎬🎬 1979 Set during the Prohibition era, a rich, middle-aged woman living on her property in the Florida backwoods finds herself courted by a much younger man. She discovers she is being used to help him set up a moonshining business. Unsentimental story of a strong woman. Based on a Marjorie Kinnan Rawlings story. 105m/C VHS, Beta. Dana Preu, David Peck, J. Smith; *D:* Victor Nunez. Sundance Film Festival '81: Grand Jury Prize. *ICA*

Galactic Gigolo woof! 1987 (R) An alien broccoli (yes, the vegetable) descends to earth on vacation, and discovers he's irresistible to Connecticut women. Must be something in the water. Amateurish effort intended as science-fiction satire, but there's more sleaze than humor. 80m/C Beta. Carmine Capobianco, Debi Thibeault, Ruth Collins, Angela Nicholas, Frank Stewart; *D:* Gorman Bechard. *AFE*

Galaxies Are Colliding 🎬🎬½ *Planet of Love* 1992 (R) Adam (Brown) is so afraid of tying the knot that he abandons his bride at the altar and takes off on a journey of enlightenment, accompanied by best friend Peter (Grammer). They naturally meet any number of eccentrics along the way. *CW:* Language. 97m/C VHS. Dwier Brown, Kelsey Grammer, Susan Walters, Karen Medak; *D:* John Ryman; *W:* John Ryman; *C:* Philip Lee; *M:* Stephen Barber. *PAR*

Galaxina 🎬½ 1980 (R) In the 31st century, a beautiful robot woman capable of human feelings is created. Stumbling parody of superspace fantasies features murdered Playmate Stratten in one of few film appearances. 95m/C VHS, Beta, LV. Dorothy Stratten, Avery Schreiber, Stephen Macht; *D:* William Sachs; *C:* Dean Cundey. *USH*

Galaxis 🎬½ 1995 (R) The physically impressive Nielsen stars as space- and time-traveling freedom fighter Landera, who beams down to Earth to battle your basic evil, intergalatic villain Kyla (Moll) who has the power source that could save her civilization. 91m/C VHS. Brigitte Nielsen, Richard Moll, Craig Fairbrass; *D:* William Mesa. *TTC*

Galaxy Invader 🎬 1985 (PG) Chaos erupts when an alien explorer crash lands his spacecraft in a backwoods area of the United States. 90m/C VHS, Beta. Richard Ruxton, Faye Tilles, Don Leifert. *NO*

Galaxy of Terror 🎬½ *Mindwarp: An Infinity of Terror; Planet of Horrors* 1981 (R) Astronauts sent to rescue a stranded spaceship get killed by vicious aliens. Big first: Moran (Joanie on "Happy Days") explodes. Inferior Corman-produced "Alien" imitation still manages to shock and displays generous gore. Followed by "Forbidden World." **85m/C VHS, Beta, LV.** Erin Moran, Edward Albert, Ray Walston, Grace Zabriskie, Zalman King, Taaffe O'Connell, Robert Englund; *D:* B.D. Clark; *W:* B.D. Clark, Mark Siegler; *C:* Jacques Haitkin.

Galgameth 🐾🐾½ *The Adventures of Galgameth* **1996 (PG)** Old-fashioned tale of a boy-hero and a friendly monster. 14-year-old Prince Davin (Oatway) accidentally injures his father during a joust and blames himself when the king suddenly dies. But his majesty's actually been poisoned by knight El El (Macht), who declares himself regent and terrorizes the kingdom. Davin's only hope to restore peace is a magical statue called Galgameth that the prince is able to bring to life. Romanian location provides proper storybook castles and medieval villages. **99m/C VHS.** Devin Oatway, Stephen Macht, Sean McNamara, Johna Stewart, Tom Dugan; *D:* Sean McNamara; *W:* James Angeli; *C:* Christian Sebaldt; *M:* Rick Marvin. *THV*

Gallagher's Travels 🐾 **1987** A screwball male/female reporting team chase an animal smuggling ring through the wilds of Australia. **94m/ C VHS, Beta.** *AU* Ivar Kants, Joanne Samuel, Stuart Campbell, Jennifer Hagan; *D:* Michael Caulfield. *TWE*

The Gallant Fool 🐾½ **1933** A man is wrongly accused of murder and tries to clear his name while eluding the law. **57m/B VHS.** Bob Steele, Arletta Duncan, George "Gabby" Hayes, John Elliott; *D:* Robert North Bradbury; *W:* Robert North Bradbury. *GPV*

The Gallant Hours 🐾🐾🐾 **1960** Biography of Admiral "Bull" Halsey (Cagney) covers five weeks, October 18 through December 1, 1942, in the WWII battle of Guadalcanal in the South Pacific. Director Montgomery forgoes battle scenes to focus on the human elements in a war and what makes a great leader. Fine performance by Cagney. **115m/B VHS.** James Cagney, Dennis Weaver, Ward Costello, Richard Jaeckel, Les Tremayne, Robert Burton, Raymond Bailey, Karl Swenson, Harry Landers, James T. Goto; *D:* Robert Montgomery; *W:* Frank D. Gilroy. *MGM*

Gallipoli 🐾🐾🐾🐾 **1981 (PG)** History blends with the destiny of two friends as they become part of the legendary WWI confrontation between Australia and the German-allied Turks. A superbly filmed, gripping commentary on the wastes of war. Haunting score; excellent performances by Lee and a then-unknown Gibson. Remake of a lesser 1931 effort "Battle of Gallipoli." **111m/C VHS, Beta, LV.** *AU* Mel Gibson, Mark Lee, Bill Kerr, David Argue, Tim McKenzie, Robert Grubb; *D:* Peter Weir; *W:* David Williamson, Peter Weir; *C:* Russell Boyd. Australian Film Institute '81: Best Actor (Gibson), Best Film. *PAR*

Galloping Dynamite 🐾½ **1937** Early western based on a James Oliver Curwood story. A ranger avenges the death of his brother killed for gold. **58m/B VHS, Beta.** Kermit Maynard; *D:* Harry Fraser. *VDM*

The Galloping Ghost 🐾🐾½ **1931** A 12-chapter serial starring football great "Red" Grange about big games, gambling, and underworld gangs. Grange is ousted from football when he's accused of throwing a game and he sets out to prove his innocence. **226m/B VHS, Beta.** Harold "Red" Grange, Dorothy Gulliver, Walter Miller, Tom Dugan; *D:* B. Reeves Eason. *VYY, JNM, NOS*

Galloping Romeo 🐾½ **1933** Steele stars as a heartthrob on horseback in this romantic Western. Steele had a hard time pulling off the light comedy he was asked to do, so clips from his previous films were used to pad the movie. **59m/B VHS.** Bob Steele, Doris Hill, George "Gabby" Hayes, Frank Ball, Ernie Adams; *D:* Robert North Bradbury; *W:* Harry Fraser. *GPV, MOV*

Gallowglass 🐾🐾🐾 **1995** A "gallowglass" is an ancient Gaelic term for a servant willing to sacrifice his life for his master. In this moody TV mystery that is dim Joe (Sheen), whose life was saved by manipulative, handsome Sandor (Rhys), who now demands his absolute loyalty. Sandor needs his help in kidnapping Nina (Whitely), an unhappy

ex-model who was the victim of a kidnapping years before in Italy and now lives with her husband in wealthy seclusion in the country. There, Nina is under the protection of bodyguard/chauffeur Paul (McArdle), and their mutual attraction leads to unexpected complications. Based on the thriller by Ruth Rendell (writing as Barbara Vine). **150m/C VHS.** *GB* Paul Rhys, Michael Sheen, Arkie Whiteley, John McArdle, Claire Hackett, Gary Waldhorn; *D:* Tim Fywell. *FOX*

Galyon 🐾 **1977 (PG)** Soldier of fortune is recruited by an oil tycoon to find his daughter and son-in-law who have been kidnapped by terrorists in South America. **92m/C VHS, Beta.** Stan Brock, Lloyd Nolan, Ina Balin. *NO*

Gambit 🐾🐾½ **1966** Caine's first Hollywood film casts him as a burglar who develops a "Topkapi"-style scheme to steal a valuable statue with MacLaine as the lure and Lom as the equally devious owner. Once Caine's careful plan is put into operation, however, everything begins to unravel. **109m/C VHS, Beta.** Shirley MacLaine, Michael Caine, Herbert Lom, Roger C. Carmel; *D:* Ronald Neame; *W:* Alvin Sargent, Jack Davies; *M:* Maurice Jarre. Nominations: Academy Awards '66: Best Art Direction/Set Decoration (Color), Best Costume Design (Color), Best Sound. *USH*

The Gamble 🐾🐾 **1988 (R)** A young man (Modine) seeks to rescue his father from gambling debts by wagering himself against a lustful countess (Dunaway). When he loses the bet, however, he flees and joins up with a runaway (Beals) with the countess and her henchmen in close pursuit. **108m/C VHS, Beta, LV, Closed Caption.** Matthew Modine, Jennifer Beals, Faye Dunaway; *D:* Carlo Vanzina.

Gamble on Love 🐾 **1986** Woman returns to her father's Las Vegas casino and falls for the man who manages the gaming room. **90m/C Beta.** Beverly Garland; *D:* Jim Balden.

The Gambler 🐾🐾🐾 **1974 (R)** College professor Axel Freed has a gambling problem so vast that it nearly gets him killed by his bookies. He goes to Las Vegas to recoup his losses and wins big, only to blow the money on stupid sports bets that get him deeper into trouble. Excellent character study of a compulsive loser on a downward spiral. **111m/C VHS, Beta, LV.** James Caan, Lauren Hutton, Paul Sorvino, Burt Young, James Woods; *D:* Karel Reisz; *W:* James Toback. *PAR*

The Gambler & the Lady 🐾½ **1952** A successful London-based gambler and casino owner endeavors to climb the social ladder by having an affair with a member of the British aristocracy. He not only has to contend with his jilted nightclub singer girlfriend but also with the gangsters who would like to take over his clubs. Dull direction and a mediocre script. **72m/B VHS, Beta, LV.** *GB* Dane Clark, Naomi Chance, Kathleen Byron; *D:* Patrick Jenkins. *NO*

The Gambler Returns: The Luck of the Draw 🐾🐾½ **1993** You'll see lots of familiar western television stars as Rogers returns yet again as debonair gambler Brady Hawkes. This time he's on a cross country trip to San Francisco and the biggest card game around—only some varmints are out to stop him playing his first hand. **180m/C VHS, Closed Caption.** Kenny Rogers, Reba McEntire, Rick Rossovich, Chuck Connors, Patrick Macnee, Linda Evans, James Drury, Mickey Rooney, Jere Burns, Clint Walker, Claude Akins, Gene Barry, Doug McClure, Hugh O'Brian, Brian Keith, Park Overall, Jack Kelly, David Carradine, Johnny Crawford, Marianne Rogers; *D:* Dick Lowry. *CAF*

Gambler's Choice 🐾🐾 **1944** A police lieutenant and his boyhood friend find themselves on opposite sides of the law in this crime drama. Even though both men are romantically involved with the same woman, their friendship remains intact. **66m/B VHS.** Chester Morris, Nancy Kelly, Russell Hayden, Sheldon Leonard, Lee Patrick, Lloyd Corrigan, Tom Dugan, Lyle Talbot, Charles Arnt; *D:* Frank McDonald. *NOS*

The Gambling Man 🐾🐾½ **19??** Rent collector Rory O'Connor is ambitious to escape his humble past and his talent at gambling leads him to winning a fortune. But a lie and tragedy return to haunt him. Based on a book by Catherine Cookson. **150m/C VHS.** *GB* Robson Green, Sylvestria Le Touzel, Bernard Hill, Stephanie Putson, Anne Kent. *VCO*

The Gambling Samurai 🐾🐾 *Kunisada Chuji* **1960** A samurai returns to his village to find it besieged by a ruthless government. Instead of attacking, he bides his time and works to undermine the government—finally achieving his revenge. In Japanese with English subtitles. **101m/C VHS, Beta.** *JP* Toshiro Mifune, Michiyo Aratama; *D:* Senkichi Taniguhi. *VDA*

The Gambling Terror 🐾🐾 **1937** A cowboy goes after a mobster selling protection to hapless ranchers. **53m/B VHS, Beta.** Johnny Mack Brown, Charles "Blackie" King; *D:* Sam Newfield. *NOS, VCN, HEG*

The Game 🐾 **1989** Three friends arrange a puzzle-murder-mystery for a selected group of guilty people, with $1 million as the prize—and death for the losers. **91m/C VHS, Beta, LV.** Tom Blair, Debbie Martin; *D:* Curtis Brown; *W:* Curtis Brown. *TWE*

The Game 🐾🐾🐾 **1997 (R)** Investment banker Nicholas Van Orton (Douglas) is an uptight corporate control freak. He receives a dangerous birthday present from his blacksheep younger brother Conrad (Penn). It's a subscription to Consumer Recreation Services, a real life-and-death version of a role-paying game that is designed to tap the hidden emotional and physical resources of the client. His life is overrun with an escalating series of traps and terrors, with the game reaching into every facet of his life. Excellent portrayal by Douglas as a man stuck in a Hitchcockian nightmare. *CW:* Language, and for some violence and sexuality. **128m/C VHS, LV, Closed Caption, DVD.** Michael Douglas, Sean Penn, Deborah Kara Unger, Armin Mueller-Stahl, James Rebhorn, Peter Donat, Carroll Baker, Anna Katarina; *D:* David Fincher; *W:* John Brancato, Michael Ferris; *C:* Harris Savides; *M:* Howard Shore. *PGV*

Game for Vultures 🐾½ **1986 (R)** Racial unrest in Rhodesia is the backdrop for this tale of a black revolutionary who fights racist sanctions. The noble topic suffers from stereotypes and oversimplification. **113m/C VHS, Beta.** *GB* Richard Harris, Richard Roundtree, Joan Collins, Ray Milland; *D:* James Fargo. *TWE*

The Game Is Over 🐾🐾½ **1966 (R)** A wealthy neglected wife falls in love with her grown stepson, causing her to divorce her husband and shatter her life. A good performance by Fonda, then Vadim's wife. Modern version of Zola's "La Curee." **96m/C VHS, Beta.** *FR* Jane Fonda, Peter McEnery, Michel Piccoli; *D:* Roger Vadim; *M:* Jean Bouchety.

A Game of Crime 🐾🐾 **1960** Intriguing murder story with strong horror overtones. **?m/C VHS.** John Blythe Barrymore Jr., Luisa Rivelli. *LOO*

Game of Death 🐾 *Goodbye Bruce Lee: His Last Game of Death; Bruce Lee's Game of Death* **1979 (R)** Bruce Lee's final kung fu thriller about a young martial arts movie star who gets involved with the syndicate. Lee died halfway through the filming of this movie and it was finished with out-takes and a double. **100m/C VHS, Beta, LV, Letterbox.** Bruce Lee, Dean Jagger, Kareem Abdul-Jabbar, Colleen Camp, Chuck Norris; *D:* Robert Clouse; *M:* John Barry. *FOX*

The Game of Love 🐾🐾 **1990 (PG)** Olin presides over Henry's bar, the lost and found of lonely hearts and lust, where people go to quench that deep thirst for love. **94m/C VHS, LV.** Ed Marinaro, Belinda Bauer, Ken Olin, Robert Rusler, Tracy Nelson, Max Gail, Janet Margolin, Brynn Thayer; *D:* Bobby Roth.

Game of Seduction 🐾 **1986** A murdering, womanizing playboy pursues a married woman and gets caught up in a treacherous cat-and-mouse game. Dubbed. **81m/C VHS, Beta.** Sylvia Kristel, Jon Finch, Nathalie Delon; *D:* Roger Vadim. *NO*

Game of Survival ◊ **1989** A young rebel warrior from another planet is sent to earth to battle six of the galaxy's most brutal warriors. **85m/C VHS, Beta.** Nikki Hill, Cindy Coatman, Roosevelt Miller Jr.; **D:** Armand Gazarian. **NO**

Gamera, the Invincible ◊½ *Gamera; Gammera; Daikaiju Gamera* **1966** This Japanese monster flick features the ultimate nuclear super-turtle who flies around destroying cities and causing panic. First in the series of notoriously bad films, this one is cool in black and white and has some impressive special effects. Dubbed in English. **86m/B VHS, LV.** *JP* Brian Donlevy, Albert Dekker, Diane Findlay, John Baragrey, Dick O'Neill, Eiji Funakoshi; **D:** Noriaki Yuasa. **JFK, SNC**

Gamera vs. Barugon ◊½ *Gamera Tai Barugon; Gambara vs. Barugon; The War of the Monsters* **1966** The monstrous turtle returns to Earth from his outer space prison, now equipped with his famous leg-jets. He soon wishes he had stayed airborne, however, when he is forced to do battle with 130-foot lizard Barugon and his rainbow-melting ray. Tokyo and Osaka get melted in the process. **101m/C VHS, Beta.** *JP* Kojiro Hongo, Kyoko Enami; **D:** Shigeo Tanaka. **JFK**

Gamera vs. Gaos ◊½ *The Return of the Giant Monsters; Gamera vs. Gyaos; Boyichi and the Supermonster; Gamera Tai Gaos* **1967** Now fully the good guy, Gamera slugs it out with a bat-like critter named Gaos. Suspense rules the day when Gaos tries to put out the super-turtle's jets with his built-in fire extinguisher but luckily for Earth, Gamera has a few tricks of his own up his shell. **87m/C VHS, Beta, LV.** *JP* Kojiro Hongo, Kichijiro Ueda, Naoyuki Abe; **D:** Noriaki Yuasa. **JFK**

Gamera vs. Guiron ◊ *Attack of the Monsters; Gamera Tai Guiron* **1969** Gamera risks it all to take on an evil, spear-headed monster on a distant planet. Highlight is the sexy, leotard clad aliens who want to eat the little Earth kids' brains. **88m/C VHS, Beta.** *JP* Nobuhiro Kashima, Christopher Murphy, Miyuki Akiyama, Yuko Hamada, Eiji Funakoshi; **D:** Noriaki Yuasa. **JFK**

Gamera vs. Zigra ◊ *Gamera Tai Shinkai Kaiju Jigara; Gamera vs. the Deep Sea Monster Zigra* **1971** Gamera the flying turtle chose an ecological theme for this, his final movie. It seems that the alien Zigrans have come to Earth to wrest the planet from the hands of the pollutive humans who have nearly destroyed it. The aliens kill the staunch turtle, but the love and prayers of children revive him that he may defend Earth once more. **91m/C VHS, Beta, LV.** *JP* Reiko Kasahara, Mikiko Tsubouchi, Koji Fujiyama, Arlene Zoellner, Gloria Zoellner; **D:** Noriaki Yuasa. **JFK**

Games Girls Play ◊½ *The Bunny Caper; Sex Play* **1975** The daughter of an American diplomat organizes a contest at a British boarding school to see which of her classmates can seduce important dignitaries. **90m/C VHS, Beta.** Christina Hart, Jane Anthony, Jill Damas, Drina Pavlovic; **D:** Jack Arnold. **NO**

The Gamma People woof! **1956** A journalist discovers a Balkan doctor shooting children with gamma rays, creating an army of brainless zombies. Cult-renowned grade-Z tripe. **83m/B VHS, Beta.** *GB* Walter Rilla, Paul Douglas, Eva Bartok; **D:** John Gilling; **C:** Ted Moore. **NO**

Gandhi ◊◊◊½ **1982 (PG)** The biography of Mahatma Gandhi from the prejudice he encounters as a young attorney in South Africa, to his role as spiritual leader to the people of India and his use of passive resistance against the country's British rulers, and his eventual assassination. Kingsley is a marvel in his Academy Award-winning role and the picture is a generally riveting epic worthy of its eight Oscars. **188m/C VHS, Beta, LV, Letterbox.** *GB* Ben Kingsley, Candice Bergen, Edward Fox, John Gielgud, John Mills, Saeed Jaffrey, Trevor Howard, Ian Charleson, Roshan Seth, Athol Fugard, Martin Sheen, Daniel Day-Lewis, Rohini Hattangady; **D:** Richard Attenborough; **W:** John Briley; **C:** Billy Williams; **M:** George

Fenton. Academy Awards '82: Best Actor (Kingsley), Best Art Direction/Set Decoration, Best Cinematography, Best Costume Design, Best Director (Attenborough), Best Film Editing, Best Original Screenplay, Best Picture, Best Sound; British Academy Awards '82: Best Actor (Kingsley), Best Director (Attenborough), Best Film, Best Supporting Actress (Hattangady); Directors Guild of America Awards '82: Best Director (Attenborough); Golden Globe Awards '83: Best Actor—Drama (Kingsley), Best Director (Attenborough), Best Foreign Film, Best Screenplay; Los Angeles Film Critics Association Awards '82: Best Actor (Kingsley); National Board of Review Awards '82: Best Actor (Kingsley); New York Film Critics Awards '82: Best Actor (Kingsley), Best Film; Nominations: Academy Awards '82: Best Makeup, Best Original Score. **COL, BTV, HMV**

Gang Boys ◊½ **1997** When a young man is brutally beaten by an L.A. street gang, mom Blair does not take things lying down. She contacts her estranged, ex-cop husband Hauser and he organizes a group of local victims to fight back. This time it's the gang members who should watch out. **87m/C VHS.** Wings Hauser, Linda Blair, Cole Hauser, Daryl Roach, Carmen Zapata, Ernest Harden Jr., Talbert Morton, Dave Buzzotta; **D:** Wings Hauser; **W:** Maria Dylan, Wings Hauser; **C:** Francis Grumman; **M:** Geoff Levin, Chris Many. **SPC**

Gang Bullets ◊ **1938** Mobster tries to continue his dirty systems in a new town, but finds the legal force incorruptible. **62m/B VHS, Beta.** Anne Nagel, Robert Kent, Charles Trowbridge, Morgan Wallace, J. Farrell MacDonald, Arthur Loft, John Merton; **D:** Lambert Hillyer. **SNC**

Gang Busters ◊½ **1955** Prisoners plan a breakout. Slow and uninteresting adaptation of the successful radio series. Filmed in Oregon. **78m/B VHS.** Myron Healey, Sam Edwards, Frank Gerstle; **D:** Bill Karn. **NOS, SNC**

Gang in Blue ◊◊½ **1996 (R)** Black officer Michael Rhoades (Van Peebles) is secretly investigating a white supremacist group of cops, called the Phantoms, within the LAPD. Marine Corp vet and police rookie Keith DeBruler (Brolin) becomes Rhoades' new partner and his racial comments make him a likely initiate for the Phantoms. So can he be trusted to be Rhoades' inside man and help Michael expose the corruption within the ranks? Made for cable.**CW:** Strong violence and language, and for some sexuality. **99m/C VHS.** Mario Van Peebles, Josh Brolin, Melvin Van Peebles, J.T. Walsh, Cynda Williams, Stephen Lang, Sean McCann; **D:** Mario Van Peebles, Melvin Van Peebles; **W:** David Fuller, Rick Natkin; **C:** Rhett Morita; **M:** Larry Brown. **HMK**

Gang Justice ◊ **1994** Low-budget melodrama finds sensitive Asian student Paul (Kim) battling racists at school and his crippled alcoholic father at home. Some martial arts fight scenes but this is amateur time. **92m/C VHS, LV.** Joon Kim, Jonathan Gorman, Erik Estrada, Angel Dashek; **D:** Richard W. Park.

Gang Related ◊½ **1996 (R)** Rodriguez (Shakur) and Divinci (Belushi) are a couple of scuzzball homicide cops who set up drug deals with impounded dope, then kill the customers. They keep the dope and the money, and call the murders "gang-related." Their plan unravels when they whack an undercover DEA agent posing as a dealer. They try to play a game of "pin the crime on the wino" with a derelict (Quaid) who the duo thinks is easy prey. As their scheming spins out of control, Rodriguez tries to hold things together, while Divinci rips them apart. Shakur rises above the average material as the most likable of the entirely distasteful cast of characters.**CW:** Strong language, some violence and a scene with nudity. **109m/C VHS, Closed Caption.** James Belushi, Tupac Shakur, Dennis Quaid, Lela Rochon, James Earl Jones, David Paymer, Wendy Crewson, Gary Cole, Terrence "T.C." Carson, Brad Greenquist, James Handy, Victor Love, Robert LaSardo, Gregory Scott Cummins; **D:** Jim Kouf; **W:** Jim Kouf; **C:** Brian Reynolds; **M:** Mickey Hart. **ORI**

Gang War ◊ **1940** Low-budget gangster film with an all-black cast about two gangs fighting for control of the city's jukebox business. **60m/B VHS.** Ralph Cooper, Gladys Snyder, Reggie Fenderson, Lawrence Criner, Monte Hawley, Jesse C. Brooks, Maceo B. Sheffield; **D:** Leo Popkin. **NOS, RXM**

Gang Wars ◊ *Devil's Express* **1975 (R)** There's a riot going on as Puerto Rican, Black, and Chinese gangs fight it out for control of the city. **82m/C VHS.** Warhawk Tanzania, Larry Fleishman, Sam DeFazio, Wilfred Roldan, Elsie Roman, Sarah Nyrick; **D:** Barry Rosen. **SUN**

Gangbusters ◊◊ **1938** Men battle crime in the city in this serial in 13 episodes based on the popular radio series of the same name. **253m/B VHS, Beta.** Kent Taylor, Irene Hervey, Robert Armstrong. **NOS, CAB, VCN**

The Gang's All Here ◊◊½ **1940** Darro joins a trucking firm whose rigs are being run off the road and hijacked by a competitor. Features "Charlie Chan" regulars Luke and Moreland. **63m/B VHS.** Frankie Darro, Marcia Mae Jones, Jackie Moran, Mantan Moreland, Keye Luke; **D:** Jean Yarbrough. **NOS, RXM, MOG**

Gangs, Inc. ◊◊ *Crimes, Inc.; Paper Bullets* **1941** A woman is sent to prison for a hit-and-run accident, actually the fault of a wealthy playboy. When she learns his identity she vows revenge and turns to crime to achieve her evil ends. Okay thriller suffers from plot problems. Ladd has a minor role filmed before he became a star. **72m/B VHS, Beta.** Joan Woodbury, Lash LaRue, Linda Ware, John Archer, Vince Barnett, Alan Ladd; **D:** Phil Rosen. **NOS, MRV, DVT**

The Gangster ◊◊½ **1947** Sullivan plays a small-time slum-bred hood who climbs to the top of the underworld, only to lose his gang because he allows his fears to get the better of him. (There's nothing to fear except when someone knows you're afeared.) Noir crimer with an interesting psychological perspective, though a bit sluggish at times. **84m/B VHS.** Barry Sullivan, Joan Lorring, Akim Tamiroff, Harry (Henry) Morgan, John Ireland, Fifi d'Orsay, Shelley Winters; **D:** Gordon Wiles. **FOX, FCT**

Gangster Wars ◊◊ **1981** A specially edited-for-video version of the television mini-series "The Gangster Chronicles." Based on fact, it deals with the growth of organized crime in America from the early days of this century, through the eyes of three ghetto kids who grow up to become powerful mobsters. **121m/C VHS, Beta.** Michael Nouri, Joe Penny, Brian Benben, Kathleen Lloyd, Madeleine Stowe, Robert Davi; **D:** Richard Sarafian. **USH**

Gangsters ◊ **1979** City is ruled by the mob and nothing can stop their bloody grip except "The Special Squad." **90m/C VHS, Beta.** *IT* Michael V. Gazzo, Tony Page, Vicki Sue Robinson, Nai Bonet; **D:** Mac Ahlberg. **VCD, HHE, MTX**

Gangster's Den ◊ **1945** A gang of renegades scare a woman out of buying a gold-laden piece of land and Billy the Kid comes to her rescue. **56m/B VHS, Beta.** Buster Crabbe, Kermit Maynard, Al "Fuzzy" St. John, Charles "Blackie" King; **D:** Sam Newfield. **VDM**

Gangster's Law woof! **1986** A look at a seedy gangster's downfall. Filmed on location in Italy. Dubbed. **89m/C VHS, Beta.** Klaus Kinski, Maurice Poli, Susy Anderson, Max Delys; **D:** Siro Marcellini. **TWE**

Gangsters of the Frontier ◊ **1944** The people of Red Rock are forced to work in the town mines by two prison escapees until Ritter and his friends ride to the rescue. Part of the "Texas Ranger" series. **56m/B VHS, Beta.** Tex Ritter, Dave O'Brien; **D:** Elmer Clifton; **W:** Elmer Clifton. **NOS, DVT, RXM**

Gangway ◊½ **1937** Pat Wayne (Matthews), a London newspaper reporter, is mistaken for a jewel thief and kidnapped by gangsters aboard a New York-bound ocean liner. In the meantime, the real thief is aboard posing as a Hollywood actress (Blakeney), and it's up to Scotland Yard inspector Bob Deering (Mackay) to solve the crime. Matthews was considered by many to be the English equivalent of America's Eleanor Powell. Based on an original story by Dwight Taylor. **90m/B VHS. GB** Jessie Matthews, Barry Mackay, Olive Blakeney, Liane Ordeyne, Patrick Ludlow, Nat Pendleton, Noel Madison, Alastair Sim, Doris Rogers, Laurence Anderson, Bennie Dorn; **D:** Sonnie Hale; **W:** Sonnie Hale, Lesser Samuels. *HEG*

Ganjasaurus Rex 🎬 **1987 (R)** Monster spoof about a giant green dinosaur emerging from the pot-laden hills of California. Maybe it's all in your head, man. **100m/C VHS, Beta.** Paul Bassis, Dave Fresh, Rosie Jones; **D:** Ursi Reynolds. *RHI*

Gappa the Trifibian Monster 🎬½ *Daikyoju Gappa; Monster from a Prehistoric Planet* **1967 (PG)** Researchers visiting a tropical island find a giant egg and take it back to Tokyo with them, dismaying the egg's giant monster parents. Dubbed. **90m/C VHS, Beta.** *JP ORI*

The Garbage Pail Kids Movie woof! **1987 (PG)** The disgusting youngsters, stars of bubblegum cards, make their first and last film appearance in this live action dud. The garbage is where it should be thrown. **100m/C VHS, Beta, LV.** Anthony Newley, MacKenzie Astin, Katie Barberi; **D:** Rod Amateau; **W:** Rod Amateau. *PAR, BAR, IME*

The Garbage-Picking, Field Goal-Kicking Philadelphia Phenomenon 🎬🎬½ **1998** Sports recruiters discover the natural kicking talents of sanitation engineer Barney Gorman (Danza) and turn his life upside down by giving him the chance to be the new place-kicker for the Philadelphia Eagles. TV movie. **85m/C VHS, Closed Caption.** Tony Danza, Jessica Tuck, Art LaFleur, Al Ruscio, Ray Wise, Chris Berman; **D:** Tom Kelleher. *TOU*

Garbo Talks 🎬🎬 **1984 (PG-13)** A dying eccentric's last request is to meet the reclusive screen legend Greta Garbo. Bancroft amusingly plays the dying woman whose son goes to extreme lengths in order to fulfill his mother's last wish. **104m/C VHS, Beta, Closed Caption.** Anne Bancroft, Ron Silver, Carrie Fisher, Catherine Hicks, Steven Hill, Howard da Silva, Dorothy Loudon, Harvey Fierstein, Hermione Gingold; **D:** Sidney Lumet; **C:** Andrzej Bartkowiak; **M:** Cy Coleman. *MGM, FOX*

The Garden 🎬🎬 **1990** Eternally provocative director Jarman does another take on sex and religion. He examines the role of the Church in the persecution of homosexuality by recreating the story of the Passion and replacing the figure of Christ in some sequences with two male lovers, who are arrested, humiliated, and tortured. **90m/C VHS. GB** Tilda Swinton, Johnny Mills, Philip MacDonald, Roger Cook, Kevin Collins, Pete Lee-Wilson, Spencer Lee, Jody Graber; **D:** Derek Jarman; **W:** Derek Jarman; **M:** Simon Fisher Turner. *FXL, FCT*

The Garden of Allah 🎬🎬🎬 **1936** Dietrich finds hyper-romantic encounters in the Algerian desert with Boyer, but his terrible secret may doom them both. This early Technicolor production, though flawed, is an absolute must for Dietrich fans. Yuma, Arizona substituted for the exotic locale. **85m/C VHS, Beta.** Marlene Dietrich, Charles Boyer, Basil Rathbone, Sir C. Aubrey Smith, Tilly Losch, Joseph Schildkraut, Henry Kleinbach Brandon, John Carradine; **D:** Richard Boleslawski; **C:** William Howard Greene; **M:** Max Steiner. Nominations: Academy Awards '36: Best Score. *FOX*

The Garden of Delights 🎬🎬🎬 **1970** A wicked black comedy about a millionaire, paralyzed and suffering from amnesia after a car accident. His horrendously greedy family tries to get him to remember and reveal his Swiss bank account number. Acclaimed; in Spanish with English subtitles. **95m/C VHS, Beta. SP** Jose Luis Lopez Vasquez, Lina Canelajas, Luchy Soto, Francisco Pierra, Charo Soriano; **D:** Carlos Saura. *HMV, CVC, FCT*

The Garden of Eden 🎬🎬🎬 **1928** Milestone—whose "Two Arabian Nights" had won an Academy Award the previous year, and who went on to direct "All Quiet on the Western Front" and

"Of Mice and Men"—directed this sophisticated ersatz Lubitsch sex comedy. Griffith, the so-called "Orchid Lady," is a young girl who dreams of diva-dom but falls deep into the underbelly of the seedy side of Budapest. With the aid of a fallen baroness, however, she finds her way to Monte Carlo and has her turn in the limelight. A handsome production designed by William Cameron Menzies, art director for "Gone With the Wind." **115m/B VHS, Beta, 8mm.** Corine Griffith, Louise Dresser, Charles Ray, Lowell Sherman; **D:** Lewis Milestone. *NOS, VYY*

The Garden of Redemption 🎬🎬½ **1997 (PG-13)** Italian priest Don Paolo (LaPaglia) has his faith tested when his Tuscan village is occupied in 1944 by German troops and he has to decide whether to overcome his fears and join with the partisan resistance movement. That village beauty Adriana (Davidtz) is eager to help him with the decision only complicates matters more. **CW:** Violence, language. **99m/C VHS, Closed Caption.** Anthony LaPaglia, Embeth Davidtz, Dan Hedaya, Peter Firth, David Neal, Jorge Sanz, James Acheson; **D:** Thomas Michael Donnelly; **W:** Thomas Michael Donnelly; **C:** Jacek Laskus; **M:** John Altman. *PAR*

The Garden of the Finzi-Continis 🎬🎬🎬 *Il Giardino Del Finzi-Contini* **1971 (R)** Acclaimed film by De Sica about an aristocratic Jewish family living in Italy under increasing Fascist oppression on the eve of WWII. The garden wall symbolizes the distance between the Finzi-Continis and the Nazi reality about to engulf them. Flawless acting and well-defined direction. Based on the novel by Giorgio Bassani, who collaborated on the script but later repudiated the film. Music by De Sica's son, Manuel. In Italian with English subtitles or dubbed. **94m/C VHS, Beta, LV. IT** Dominique Sanda, Helmut Berger, Lino Capolicchio, Fabio Testi, Romolo Valli; **D:** Vittorio De Sica; **W:** Cesare Zavattini; **M:** Manuel De Sica. Academy Awards '71: Best Foreign Language Film; Berlin International Film Festival '71: Golden Berlin Bear; Nominations: Academy Awards '71: Best Adapted Screenplay. *COL, IME, WAR*

Gardens of Stone 🎬🎬 **1987 (R)** A zealous young cadet during the Vietnam War is assigned to the Old Guard patrol at Arlington Cemetery, and clashes with the patrol's older officers and various pacifist civilians. Falls short of the mark, although Jones turns in an excellent performance. **112m/C VHS, Beta, LV, Closed Caption.** James Caan, James Earl Jones, D.B. Sweeney, Anjelica Huston, Dean Stockwell, Lonette McKee, Mary Stuart Masterson, Bill Graham, Sam Bottoms, Casey Siemaszko, Laurence "Larry" Fishburne; **D:** Francis Ford Coppola; **W:** Ronald Bass; **C:** Jordan Cronenweth; **M:** Carmine Coppola. *FOX*

Gargoyles, The Movie: The Heroes Awaken 🎬🎬½ **1994 (G)** Mythical crimefighting creatures, trapped in stone by day thanks to a sorcerer's spell but released to live at night, are displaced in time from their medieval Scottish home, winding up in modern-day New York City. But they discover they still have old enemies to fight. First aired as a five-episode part of the animated TV series. **80m/C VHS, Closed Caption. V:** Ed Asner, Keith David, Jonathon Frakes, Marina Sirtis, Bill Fagerbakke, Salli Richardson, Frank Welker, Thom Adcox, Jeff Bennett. *TOU*

Garringo 🎬🎬 **1969** Lawmen attempt to bring to justice a man who is intent on killing the soldiers responsible for his father's death. **95m/C VHS, Beta. IT SP** Anthony Steffen, Peter Lee Lawrence, Jose Bodalo; **D:** Rafael Romero Marchent. *MAD*

Gas woof! **1981 (R)** This dog has tycoon Hayden buying up all the gas stations in town to create a crisis that will make him richer. Everyone in the cast wastes their time, especially Sutherland as a hip DJ reporting on the gas shortage. **94m/C VHS, Beta. CA** Donald Sutherland, Susan Anspach, Sterling Hayden, Peter Aykroyd, Howie Mandel, Helen Shaver; **D:** Les Rose; **W:** Dick Wolf. *PAR*

Gas Food Lodging 🎬🎬🎬 **1992 (R)** Saga casts Adams as Nora, a weary waitress in Laramie, New Mexico, trying her best to raise two teenaged daughters on her own. The daughters, Skye and Balk, are disillusioned about love and family. Balk's special friend is Darius, an eccentric window dresser, played by Leitch, Skye's brother. Nothing works out quite as intended but multi-dimensional characters, poignant situtations, and enormous emotional appeal highlight the directorial debut of Anders. Based on the Richard Peck novel "Don't Look and It Won't Hurt." **CW:** Language and sensuality. **100m/C VHS, LV, Letterbox, Closed Caption.** Brooke Adams, Ione Skye, Fairuza Balk, James Brolin, Rob Knepper, Donovan Leitch, David Lansbury, Jacob Vargas, Chris Mulkey, Tiffany Anders; **D:** Allison Anders; **W:** Allison Anders; **C:** Dean Lent; **M:** J. Mascis, Barry Adamson. Independent Spirit Awards '93: Best Actress (Balk). *COL*

Gas Pump Girls 🎬½ **1979 (R)** Comedy about five lovely ladies who manage a gas station and use their feminine wiles to win the battle against a shady oil sheik. **102m/C VHS, Beta, LV.** Kirsten Baker, Dennis Bowen, Huntz Hall, Steve Bond, Leslie King, Linda Lawrence; **D:** Joel Bender. *VES*

Gas-s-s-s! 🎬🎬½ *Gas-s-s-s... or, It May Become Necessary to Destroy the World in Order to Save It* **1970 (PG)** A gas main leak in an Alaskan defense plant kills everyone beyond 30-something and the post-apocalyptic pre-boomer survivors are left to muddle their way through the brume. Trouble is, AIP edited the heck out of the movie, much to Corman's chagrin, and the result is a truncated comedy; Corman was so displeased, in fact, he left to create New World studios. **79m/C VHS, Beta.** Robert Corff, Elaine Giftos, Pat Patterson, George Armitage, Alex Wilson, Ben Vereen, Cindy Williams, Bud Cort, Talia Shire; **D:** Roger Corman; **W:** George Armitage. *NO*

Gaslight 🎬🎬🎬 *Angel Street* **1940** A forgotten British classic that fell victim to the American production of the same title and theme that was filmed only five years later. Set in late Victorian London, Wynyard is the rich innocent married to the calculating Walbrook, who slowly tries driving his bride insane in order to discover some hidden family jewels. She comes under the protection of a Scotland Yard detective (Pettingell) who suspects Walbrook has already murdered once. An outstandingly eerie psychological thriller. Based on the play "Angel Street" by Patrick Hamilton. **88m/C VHS. GB** Anton Walbrook, Diana Wynyard, Frank Pettingell, Cathleen Cordell, Robert Newton, Jimmy Hanley, Minnie Rayner, Mary Hinton, Marie Wright, Jack Barty, Moyna MacGill, Darmora Ballet; **D:** Thorold Dickinson; **W:** A.H. Rawlinson, Bridget Boland; **C:** Bernard Knowles; **M:** Richard Addinsell. *FCT*

Gaslight 🎬🎬🎬½ *The Murder in Thorton Square* **1944** Lavish remake of the 1939 film, based on the Patrick Hamilton play "Angel Street." A man tries to drive his beautiful wife insane while searching for priceless jewels. Her only clue to his evil acts is the frequent dimming of their gaslights. A suspenseful Victorian era mystery. Lansbury's film debut, as the tarty maid. **114m/B VHS, Beta, LV.** Charles Boyer, Ingrid Bergman, Joseph Cotten, Angela Lansbury, Terry Moore, May Whitty, Barbara Everest, Emil Rameau, Edmund Breon, Halliwell Hobbes, Tom Stevenson; **D:** George Cukor; **C:** Joseph Ruttenberg. Academy Awards '44: Best Actress (Bergman), Best Interior Decoration; Golden Globe Awards '45: Best Actress—Drama (Bergman); Nominations: Academy Awards '44: Best Actor (Boyer), Best Black and White Cinematography, Best Picture, Best Screenplay, Best Supporting Actress (Lansbury). *MGM, BTV, VEC*

The Gate 🎬🎬 **1987 (PG-13)** Kids generally like to explore and Dorff and Tripp are no exception. When a large hole is exposed in their backyard, it would be a childhood sin not to see what's in it, right? What they don't know is that this hole is actually a gateway to and from Hell. The terror they unleash includes more than just run-of-the-mill demons. Good special effects. Followed by "Gate 2." **85m/C VHS, Beta, LV.** Christa Denton, Stephen Dorff, Louis Tripp, Kelly Rowan, Jennifer Irwin; **D:** Tibor Takacs; **W:** Michael Nankin; **C:** Thomas Vamos. *AAT, VES*

Gate 2 🎬½ 1992 **(R)** Tripp returns in his role as Terry, a young student of demonology in this lame sequel to "The Gate." Terry and a few of his teen buddies call up a group of demons that have been confined behind a gate for billions of years. The demons are used to grant modest wishes, but the wishes end up having very evil effects. Incredibly weak plot saved only by the special monster effects, which include live action and puppetry. **CW:** Drug use. **90m/C VHS, LV, Closed Caption.** Louis Tripp, Simon Reynolds, Pamela Segall, James Villemaire, Neil Munro, James Kidnie, Andrea Ladanyi; **D:** Tibor Takacs; **W:** Michael Nankin; **C:** Bryan England; **M:** George Blondheim. *COL*

Gate of Hell 🎬🎬🎬½ *Jigokumen* 1954 Set in 12th-century Japan. A warlord desires a beautiful married woman and seeks to kill her husband to have her. However, he accidentally kills her instead. Filled with shame and remorse, the warlord abandons his life to seek solace as a monk. Heavily awarded and critically acclaimed; the first Japanese film to use color photography. In Japanese with English subtitles. **89m/C VHS, Beta, 8mm.** *JP* Kazuo Hasegawa, Machiko Kyo; **D:** Teinosuke Kinugasa. Academy Awards '54: Best Costume Design (Color), Best Foreign Language Film; Cannes Film Festival '54: Best Film. *VYY, DVT, VDM*

Gates of Hell woof! *Paura Nella Citta Dei Morti Viventi; City of the Living Dead; The Fear; Twilight of the Dead; Fear in the City of the Living Dead* 1983 Salem, Massachusetts, must battle the risen dead in this gorefest that tried to disguise itself under many other titles. **90m/C VHS, Beta.** Christopher George, Janet Agren, Katherine MacColl, Robert Sampson; **D:** Lucio Fulci. *IGP*

Gates of Hell 2: Dead Awakening 🎬 1996 Occultists performing an initiation rite reopen the portal to hell and a creature from its depths reawakens to cause the usual unholy terror. **87m/C VHS.** Tom Campitelli, Tamara Hext, Randy Strickland; **D:** G.D. Marcum. *TPV*

The Gathering 🎬🎬½ 1977 A dying man seeks out the wife and family he has alienated for a final Christmas gathering. James Poe authored this well-acted holiday tearjerker that won the 1977-78 Emmy for outstanding TV drama special. **94m/C VHS, Beta.** Ed Asner, Maureen Stapleton, Lawrence Pressman, Stephanie Zimbalist, Bruce Davison, Gregory Harrison, Veronica Hamel, Gail Strickland; **D:** Randal Kleiser; **M:** John Barry. *WOV*

A Gathering of Eagles 🎬🎬½ 1963 Hudson portrays a hard-nosed Air Force colonel during peacetime whose British wife must adjust to being a military spouse. **115m/C VHS.** Rock Hudson, Rod Taylor, Mary Peach, Barry Sullivan, Kevin McCarthy, Henry Silva, Leif Erickson; **D:** Delbert Mann; **M:** Jerry Goldsmith. *MGM*

The Gathering: Part 2 🎬🎬 1979 Sequel in which a widow has a Christmas reunion with her family, but conflict arises when she introduces a new man in her life. Not as effective as the original, also made for TV. **98m/C VHS.** Maureen Stapleton, Efrem Zimbalist Jr., Jameson Parker, Bruce Davison, Lawrence Pressman, Gail Strickland, Veronica Hamel; **D:** Charles S. Dubin. *TTC*

The Gathering Storm 🎬🎬 1974 Based on the first book of memoirs from Sir Winston Churchill, this drama examines the pre-WWII years. **72m/C Beta.** Richard Burton, Virginia McKenna, Ian Bannen; **D:** Herbert Wise.

The Gatling Gun 🎬½ *King Gun* 1972 **(PG)** Poor tale of the Cavalry, Apache Indians, and renegades all after the title weapon. **93m/C VHS.** Guy Stockwell, Woody Strode, Patrick Wayne, Robert Fuller, Barbara Luna, John Carradine, Pat Buttram, Phil Harris; **D:** Robert Gordon. *HHE*

Gator 🎬🎬 1976 **(PG)** Sequel to "White Lightning" (1973) follows the adventures of Gator (Reynolds), who is recruited to gather evidence to convict a corrupt political boss who also happens to be his friend. Reynolds in his good ole' boy role with lots of chase scenes. Talk show host Michael Douglas made his film debut in the role of the governor. First film Reynolds directed. **116m/C VHS, Beta.** Burt Reynolds, Jerry Reed, Lauren Hutton, Jack Weston, Alice Ghostley, Dub Taylor; **D:** Burt Reynolds; **W:** William W. Norton Sr.; **M:** Charles Bernstein. *MGM, FOX*

Gator Bait 🎬½ 1973 **(R)** The Louisiana swamp is home to the beautiful Desiree, and woe be unto any man who threatens her family. Aims to please fans of the raunchy and violent. Followed by an equally vile sequel. **91m/C VHS, Beta, LV.** Claudia Jennings, Clyde Ventura, Bill Thurman, Janet Baldwin; **D:** Ferd Sebastian, Beverly Sebastian; **W:** Ferd Sebastian, Beverly Sebastian. *PAR*

Gator Bait 2: Cajun Justice 🎬 1988 **(R)** A city girl comes to the Louisiana swamp and turns violent in an effort to exact revenge on the men who have been tormenting her. **94m/C VHS, Beta, LV, Closed Caption.** Jan MacKenzie, Tray Loren, Paul Muzzcat, Brad Kepnick, Jerry Armstrong, Ben Sebastian; **D:** Ferd Sebastian, Beverly Sebastian; **W:** Ferd Sebastian, Beverly Sebastian. *PAR*

Gattaca 🎬🎬🎬 1997 **(PG-13)** It's a future world where genetic tinkering allows parents to tweak their children's DNA before birth and a caste system of "perfect" humans exists. Vincent (Hawke) dreams of employment with the aerospace corporation Gattaca, so he assumes the identity of the genetically superior Jerome (Law). Soon Vincent is falling for icy co-worker Thurman and getting involved in a murder investigation, which could uncover his true identity. Thinking man's sci-fi (read: no spaceships or explosions) along the lines of George Lucas' "THX-1138." **CW:** Brief violent images, language and some sexuality. **112m/C VHS, Closed Caption, DVD.** Ethan Hawke, Uma Thurman, Jude Law, Gore Vidal, Alan Arkin, Loren Dean, Jayne Brook, Elias Koteas, Tony Shalhoub, Ernest Borgnine; **D:** Andrew Niccol; **W:** Andrew Niccol; **C:** Slawomir Idziak; **M:** Michael Nyman. Nominations: Academy Awards '97: Best Art Direction/Set Decoration; Golden Globe Awards '98: Best Original Score. *COL*

The Gaucho 🎬🎬🎬 1927 Fairbanks stars as the title character, an immoral swashbuckler who lusts after a virginal religious (Greear) before undergoing a change of heart (but not before dancing a red-hot tango with the less-than-virginal Velez). **?m/B VHS.** Douglas Fairbanks Sr., Lupe Velez, Geraine Greear, Gustav von Seyffertitz; **D:** F. Richard Jones; **W:** Lotta Woods; **C:** Gaetano Antonio "Tony" Gaudio. *KIV*

The Gauntlet 🎬🎬 1977 **(R)** A cop is ordered to Las Vegas to bring back a key witness for an important trial—but the witness turns out to be a beautiful prostitute being hunted by killers. Violence-packed action. **111m/C VHS, Beta, LV, Closed Caption.** Clint Eastwood, Sondra Locke, Pat Hingle, Bill McKinney; **D:** Clint Eastwood; **W:** Michael Butler. *WAR, TLF*

The Gay Divorcee 🎬🎬🎬 *The Gay Divorce* 1934 Astaire pursues Rogers to an English seaside resort, where she mistakes him for the hired correspondent in her divorce case. Based on the musical play "The Gay Divorce" by Dwight Taylor and Cole Porter. The title was slightly changed for the movie because of protests from the Hays Office. ♫ Don't Let It Bother You; A Needle in a Haystack; Let's K-nock K-nees; Night and Day; The Continental. **107m/B VHS, Beta, LV.** Fred Astaire, Ginger Rogers, Edward Everett Horton, Eric Blore, Alice Brady, Erik Rhodes, Betty Grable; **D:** Mark Sandrich; **M:** Max Steiner. Academy Awards '34: Best Song ("The Continental"); Nominations: Academy Awards '34: Best Interior Decoration, Best Picture, Best Sound, Best Score. *TTC*

The Gay Lady 🎬🎬½ *Trottie True* 1949 Light romantic comedy set in the 1890s about an actress who climbs to stardom in London theatre and winds up marrying into the aristocracy. Look for Christopher Lee and Roger Moore in early bit parts. **95m/C VHS.** *GB* Jean Kent, James Donald, Hugh Sinclair, Lana Morris, Bill Owen, Michael Medwin, Andrew Crawford; **D:** Brian Desmond Hurst. *MOV, UNI*

Gay Purr-ee 🎬🎬 1962 Delightful tale of feline romance in the City of Lights. For all ages. **85m/C VHS, LV, Closed Caption. D:** Abe Levitow; **W:** Chuck Jones; **M:** Harold Arlen; **V:** Judy Garland, Robert Goulet, Red Buttons, Hermione Gingold, Mel Blanc. *WAR, FCT*

The Gay Ranchero 🎬🎬 1942 Rogers, without Dale Evans, in an average tale of old west meets new crooks. Rogers is the sheriff who foils gangsters trying to take over an airport. The action doesn't stop him from singing a duet with leading lady Frazee on "Wait'll I Get My Sunshine in the Moonlight." **55m/B VHS, Beta.** Roy Rogers, Andy Devine, Tito Guizar, Jane Frazee, Estelita Rodriguez; **D:** William Witney. *NOS, VCN, CAB*

The Gazebo 🎬🎬🎬 1959 Wacky comedy about a TV writer who is being blackmailed by someone who has nude photos of his Broadway star wife. He decides murder is the only solution to this problem. Reynolds sings "Something Called Love." Based on a play by Alec Coppel from a story by Myra and Alec Coppel. **102m/B VHS.** Glenn Ford, Debbie Reynolds, Carl Reiner, John McGiver, Doro Merande, Bert Freed, Martin Landau; **D:** George Marshall; **W:** George Wells. Nominations: Academy Awards '59: Best Black and White Cinematography. *MGM*

Geek Maggot Bingo 🎬 *The Freak From Suckweasel Mountain* 1983 It's too bad director Zed waited until mid-"Bingo" to post a sign warning "Leave Now, It Isn't Going Get Any Better!" Conceived by the New York underground's don of the "Cinema of Transgression" to be an off-the-rack cult classic, this horror spoof is too long on in-jokes and short on substance to earn its number in the cult hall of fame. It does, however, boast Death as Scumbalina the vampire queen and Hell as a punk cowboy crooner (before alternative country hit the airwaves). TV horror-meister Zacherle narrates. **70m/C VHS.** Richard Hell, Donna Death, John Zacherle; **D:** Nick Zedd. *MWF, MOV*

Geheimakte WB1 🎬🎬 *Secret Paper WB1* 1942 Historical drama centering on the invention of the U-boat by Sergeant Wilhelm Bauer during Denmark's WWII blockade of the ports of Schleswig-Holstein. In German with no subtitles. **91m/B VHS, Beta.** *GE* Alexander Golling; **D:** Herbert Selpin. *IHF*

A Geisha 🎬🎬 *Gion Bayashi; Gion Festival Music* 1953 Miyoharu (Kogure) is a passive elderly geisha who agrees to train the naive young Eiko (Wakao) in her new role. But Eiko discovers her romantic notions of the geisha life are far from it's modern reality. Poignant look at the changing status of the geisha in Japan after WWII and the country's social upheavals. In Japanese with English subtitles. **86m/B VHS.** *JP* Michiyo Kogure, Ayako Wakao, Seizaburo Kawazu, Chieko Naniwa, Eitaro Shindo; **D:** Kenji Mizoguchi; **W:** Yoshikata Yoda; **M:** Ichiro Saito. *NYF, FCT, BTV*

The Geisha Boy 🎬🎬 1958 Jerry is a floundering magician who joins the USO and tours the Far East. His slapstick confrontations with the troupe leader and an officer who dreams of attending his own funeral provide hearty laughs, plus Lewis finds romance with a Japanese widow after her son claims him as a father. Pleshette's film debut, with an appearance by the Los Angeles Dodgers. **98m/C VHS, Closed Caption.** Jerry Lewis, Marie McDonald, Sessue Hayakawa, Barton MacLane, Suzanne Pleshette, Nobu McCarthy; **D:** Frank Tashlin. *PAR*

Geisha Girl 🎬½ 1952 Forgotten sci-fi film about a mad scientist and his Japanese cohorts who develop small explosive pills that are more powerful than nuclear bombs. Their plans of world conquest are thwarted when the pills inadvertently fall into the hands of two American G.I.s. **67m/C VHS.** Martha Hyer, William Andrews, Archer MacDonald, Kekao Yokoo, Teddy Nakamura; **D:** George Breakston, C. Ray Stahl; **W:** C. Ray Stahl. *SNC*

Gemini Affair ⚌ 198? Two women go to Hollywood to become rich and famous but end up being very disappointed. 88m/C VHS, Beta. Marta Kristen, Kathy Kersh, Anne Seymour. UNI

Gene Autry Matinee Double Feature #1 1953 Includes "Blue Canadian Rockies" (1952), where Autry must investigate a series of murders, and "Last of the Pony Riders" (1953), in which the final days of the pony express yield a sinister conspiracy. 117m/C VHS. Gene Autry; D: George Archainbaud. NO

Gene Autry Matinee Double Feature #2 1953 An exciting western double feature: A cowboy goes after the man who stole his rodeo winnings in "Melody Trail" and a territorial ranger investigates a series of Indian raids in "Winning of the West." 117m/b VHS, Beta. Gene Autry, Smiley Burnette, Alan Bridge; D: George Archainbaud, Joseph Kane. NO

Gene Autry Matinee Double Feature #3 1953 Gene stars in "Prairie Moon," in which he teaches some tough kids a lesson about life, and "On Top of Old Smokey," which sees a young woman trying to save her small town. 113m/b VHS, Beta. Gene Autry, Smiley Burnette; D: George Archainbaud, Ralph Staub. NO

The Gene Krupa Story ⚌⚌½ 1959 The story of the famous jazz drummer and his career plunge after a drug conviction. Krupa recorded the soundtrack, mimed by Mineo, who was too young for a convincing portrayal. Gavin McLeod (of "Love Boat" fame) has a small part as Mineo's dad. 101m/b VHS, Beta. Sal Mineo, James Darren, Susan Kohner, Susan Oliver, Anita O'Day, Red Nichols; D: Don Weis. COL, FCT

The General ⚌⚌⚌⚌ 1926 Keaton's masterpiece and arguably the most formally perfect and funniest of silent comedies. Concerns a plucky Confederate soldier who single-handedly retrieves a pivotal train from Northern territory. Full of eloquent man-vs-machinery images and outrageous sight gags. Remade as "The Great Locomotive Chase" in 1956 with Fess Parker. 78m/b VHS, Beta, LV, 8mm. Buster Keaton, Marion Mack, Glen Cavender, Jim Farley, Joe Keaton; D: Buster Keaton, Clyde Bruckman. National Film Registry '89. VYY, HHT, NOS

The General ⚌⚌⚌ 1998 Biopic of maverick Dublin crime lord Martin Cahill (Gleeson), nicknamed "The General" for his planning abilities. Film is one long flashback as it begins in 1994 with Cahill's assassination. Cahill supports his family through various burglaries, making a mockery of the local cops, including Ned Kenny (Voight). But Cahill's rise from petty criminal to local mobster is noted by the IRA and when he refuses to cut them in on his profits, things turn very dicey for the cocky, ruthless Cahill. 123m/b VHS. IR GB Brendan Gleeson, Adrian Dunbar, Sean McGinley, Jon Voight, Maria Doyle Doyle Kennedy, Angeline Ball, Ciaran Fitzgerald, Eamonn Owens; D: John Boorman; W: John Boorman; C: Seamus Deasy; M: Richie Buckley. Cannes Film Festival '98: Best Director (Boorman). NYR

The General Died at Dawn ⚌⚌⚌ 1936 A clever, atmospheric suspense film about an American mercenary in Shanghai falling in love with a beautiful spy as he battles a fierce Chinese warlord who wants to take over the country. Playwright-to-be Odets' first screenplay; he, O'Hara and '30s gossip hound Skolsky have cameos as reporters. 93m/b VHS, Beta. Gary Cooper, Madeleine Carroll, Akim Tamiroff, Dudley Digges, Porter Hall, William Frawley, Philip Ahn; Cameos: John O'Hara, Clifford Odets, Sidney Skolsky; D: Lewis Milestone; W: Clifford Odets; C: Victor Milner. Nominations: Academy Awards '36: Best Cinematography, Best Supporting Actor (Tamiroff), Best Score. USH

The General Line ⚌⚌⚌⚌ The Old and the New 1929 Eisenstein's classic pro-Soviet semi-documentary about a poor farm woman who persuades her village to form a cooperative. Transgresses its party-line instructional purpose by vivid filmmaking. The director's last silent film. 90m/B VHS, Beta. RU Marfa Lapkina; D: Sergei Eisenstein. NOS, MRV, DVT

General Spanky ⚌⚌ 1936 The only feature "Our Gang" comedy goofed by transplanting them to a Civil War milieu popular at the time. Confederate kids Spanky and Alfalfa play soldier, ultimately outsmarting Union troops. The rascals are still funny sometimes, but Buckwheat's role as an eager slave is disturbing today. 73m/B VHS, LV. George "Spanky" McFarland, Phillips Holmes, Ralph Morgan, Irving Pichel, Rosina Lawrence, Billie "Buckwheat" Thomas, Carl "Alfalfa" Switzer, Louise Beavers; D: Fred Newmeyer. Nominations: Academy Awards '36: Best Sound. MGM, FCT

Generale Della Rovere ⚌⚌⚌½ ll Generale Della-Rovere 1960 A WWII black marketeer is forced by the Nazis to go undercover in a local prison. To find out who the resistance leaders are, he poses as a general. But when prisoners begin to look to him for guidance, he finds the line between his assumed role and real identity diminished, leading to a tragic conclusion. Acclaimed film featuring a bravura lead performance by veteran director De Sica. In Italian with English subtitles. 139m/B VHS, Beta. IT Vittorio De Sica, Otto Messmer, Sandra Milo; D: Roberto Rossellini. NOS, CVC, HHT

A Generation ⚌⚌⚌ 1954 During WWII, a young man escapes from the Warsaw Ghetto and finds his way to the Polish Resistance. He falls in love with the leader of the local group and finds the courage to fight for his freedom. Strong directorial debut from Wajda. Part 1 of his "War Trilogy," followed by "Kanal" and "Ashes and Diamonds." Scripted by Czeszko from his novel "Pokolenie." Polish with subtitles. 90m/B VHS. PL Tadeusz Lomnicki, Ursula Modrzynska, Zbigniew Cybulski, Roman Polanski; D: Andrzej Wajda; W: Bohdan Czeszko. FCT, HMV, ING

Generation ⚌⚌ A Time For Caring 1969 A very pregnant bride informs everyone she'll give birth at home without doctors, and creates a panic. Based on the Broadway play by William Goodhart. 109m/C VHS, Beta. David Janssen, Kim Darby, Carl Reiner, Peter Duel, Andrew Prine, James Coco, Sam Waterston; D: George Schaefer; W: William Goodhart; C: Lionel Lindon; M: Dave Grusin.

Generations: Mind Control-From the Future ⚌ 1980 Max Lang has lost all self-control and is being driven by evil forces beyond time, forced to kill while fleeing total extinction. 54m/C VHS, Beta. NO

Genevieve ⚌⚌⚌ 1953 A 1904 Darracq roadster is the title star of this picture which spoofs "classic car" owners and their annual rally from London to Brighton. Two married couples challenge each other to a friendly race which becomes increasingly intense as they near the finish line. 86m/C VHS, Beta. GB John Gregson, Dinah Sheridan, Kenneth More, Kay Kendall, Geoffrey Keen, Reginald Beckwith, Arthur Wontner, Joyce Grenfell, Leslie Mitchell, Michael Medwin, Michael Balfour, Edie Martin, Harold Siddons; D: Henry Cornelius; W: William Rose; M: Larry Adler. British Academy Awards '53: Best Film; Golden Globe Awards '55: Best Foreign Film; Nominations: Academy Awards '54: Best Story & Screenplay, Best Original Dramatic/Comedy Score. BFA

Genghis Cohn ⚌⚌½ 1993 Black comedy follows the misadventures of a former Nazi concentration camp commander (Lindsay) who has settled in a small Bavarian town and taken on the position of police chief. But his quiet life is rocked by a series of murders, an affair with a kinky Baroness (Rigg), and by the ghost of Jewish comedian Genghis Cohn (Sher), a victim of the camps whose haunting presence exacts a particularly appropriate revenge. Adapted from Romain Gary's novel "The Dance of Genghis Cohn." Made for British TV. 100m/C VHS. GB Robert Lindsay, Diana Rigg, Anthony Sher; D: Elijah Moshinsky; W: Stanley Price. AEH

Genie of Darkness ⚌ 1960 The ashes of Nostradamus himself are retrieved in a bid to destroy his vampiric descendent. Edited from a Mexican serial; if you were able to sit through this one, look for "Curse of Nostradamus" and "The Monster Demolisher." ?m/B VHS. MX German Robles; D: Frederick Curiel. SNC, NOS, LOO

Gentle Giant ⚌⚌ 1967 An orphaned bear is taken in by a boy and his family and grows to be a 750 pound giant who must be returned to the wild. "Gentle Ben" TV series was derived from this feature. 93m/C VHS. Dennis Weaver, Vera Miles, Ralph Meeker, Clint Howard, Huntz Hall; D: James Neilson. REP

Gentle Savage ⚌⚌½ Camper John 1973 (R) When an Indian is wrongly accused of raping and beating a white woman, the white community seeks revenge. The vengeful mob, led by the victim's step-father, is unaware that it's really their ringleader who is responsible for the crime. When the accused's brother is slain, the Indian community retaliates. Violent but well-crafted. 85m/C VHS. William Smith, Gene Evans, Barbara Luna, Joe Flynn; D: Sean McGregor. ART

A Gentle Woman ⚌⚌ A Gentle Creature; Une Femme Douce 1969 Adaptation of Dostoevsky's short story about a young married woman who kills herself. Sanda marries pawnbroker Frangin, is miserable in her marriage, toys with killing her husband, and commits suicide instead, leaving the bewildered Frangin to try to figure out why. Several theories are offered but nothing is ever made clear: Debut of Sanda; Bressons' first film in color. French with subtitles. 89m/C VHS. FR Dominique Sanda, Guy Frangin, Jane Lobre; D: Robert Bresson; W: Robert Bresson; C: Ghislan Cloquet; M: Jean Wiener. NYF, FCT

Gentleman Bandit ⚌⚌ 1981 So-so drama about Father Bernard Pagano, a Boston priest mistakenly arrested as a stickup artist. Based on a true story. Made for television. 96m/C VHS, Beta. Ralph Waite, Julie Bovasso, Jerry Zaks, Joe Grifasi, Estelle Parsons, Tom Aldredge; D: Jonathan Kaplan. BFA

The Gentleman from California ⚌ The Californian 1937 The dashing son of a Mexican landowner returns home and finds his people's land stolen from them by greedy tax collectors. 56m/B VHS, Beta, 8mm. Ricardo Cortez, Marjorie Weaver, Katherine DeMille; D: Gus Meins. VYY

Gentleman from Dixie ⚌⚌ 1941 After LaRue is released from prison, he looks to change his life by joining his brother on a farm and seeking revenge on the man who put him in the pokey. 61m/b VHS. Jack LaRue, Marian Marsh, Clarence Muse, Mary Ruth, Robert Kellard, John Holland, Herbert Rawlinson; D: Al(bert) Herman. MOV

Gentleman from Texas ⚌ 1946 Ropin', ridin', and romance figure in this less than dramatic oater. 55m/B VHS. Johnny Mack Brown, Raymond Hatton, Claudia Drake, Reno Blair, Christine McIntyre; D: Lambert Hillyer. NOS, DVT

Gentleman Jim ⚌⚌⚌½ 1942 A colorful version of the life of old-time heavyweight boxing great Jim Corbett, transformed from a typical Warner Bros. bio-pic by director Walsh into a fun-loving, anything-for-laughs donnybrook. Climaxes with Corbett's fight for the championship against the great John L. Sullivan. One of Flynn's most riotous performances. 104m/B VHS, Beta, LV, Closed Caption. Errol Flynn, Alan Hale, Alexis Smith, Jack Carson, Ward Bond, Arthur Shields, William Frawley; D: Raoul Walsh. MGM, FOX

The Gentleman Killer ⚌ 1978 A man-with-no-name clears a ravaged border town of murdering bandits. 95m/C VHS, Beta. Anthony Steffen, Silvia Solar. UNI

Gentleman's Agreement ⚌⚌⚌ 1947 A magazine writer (Peck) looks for a new angle for an article on anti-Semitism by pretending to be Jewish. His new identity pervades his life in unexpected ways, almost destroys his relationships, but contributes to the success of his magazine series. This movie was Hollywood's first major attack on anti-Semitism. Controversial in its day, yet still timely. **118m/B VHS, LV.** Gregory Peck, Dorothy McGuire, John Garfield, Celeste Holm, Anne Revere, June Havoc, Albert Dekker, Jane Wyatt, Dean Stockwell, Nicholas Joy; **D:** Elia Kazan; **W:** Moss Hart; **C:** Arthur C. Miller. Academy Awards '47: Best Director (Kazan), Best Picture, Best Supporting Actress (Holm); Golden Globe Awards '48: Best Director (Kazan), Best Film—Drama, Best Supporting Actress (Holm); New York Film Critics Awards '47: Best Director (Kazan), Best Film; Nominations: Academy Awards '47: Best Actor (Peck), Best Director (McGuire), Best Film Editing, Best Screenplay, Best Supporting Actress (Revere). *FXV, BTV*

Gentlemen Prefer Blondes 🎬🎬🎬
1953 Amusing satire involving two show-business girls from Little Rock trying to make it big in Paris. Seeking rich husbands or diamonds, their capers land them in police court. Monroe plays Lorelei Lee, Russell is her sidekick. Despite an occasionally slow plot, the music, comedy, and performances are great fun. Film version of a Broadway adaption of a story by Anita Loos. Followed by (but without Monroe) "Gentlemen Marry Brunettes." ♫A (Two) Little Girl(s) From Little Rock; Bye, Bye Baby; Ain't There Anyone Here For Love?; When Love Goes Wrong; Diamonds Are A Girl's Best Friend. **91m/C VHS, Beta, LV.** Marilyn Monroe, Jane Russell, Charles Coburn, Elliott Reid, Tommy Noonan, George Winslow; **D:** Howard Hawks. *FOX*

Genuine Risk 🎬½
1989 (R) Gorgeous young woman turns off her crime boss boyfriend bigtime when she seduces his bodyguard. Genuine tripe. **89m/C VHS, LV.** Terence Stamp, Michelle Johnson, Peter Berg, M.K. Harris; **D:** Kurt Voss; **W:** Kurt Voss. *COL*

George! 🎬½
1970 (G) A carefree bachelor takes his girlfriend and his 250-pound St. Bernard on a trip to the Swiss Alps where he proves that a dog is not always man's best friend. **87m/C VHS, Beta.** Marshall Thompson, Jack Mullaney, Inge Schoner; **D:** Wallace C. Bennett; **W:** Wallace C. Bennett. *VCI*

George Balanchine's The Nutcracker 🎬🎬½
The Nutcracker 1993 (G) Pas de deux redeux. Tchaikovsky's classic ballet about the magic of Christmas and a little girl (Cohen) who dreams on Christmas Eve that she is in an enchanted kingdom. Culkin lamely grins through his wooden performance as the Nutcracker Prince, but the talent of the Sugarplum Fairy (Kistler) and the other dancers is such that conventional camera techniques sometimes fail to keep up with their exacting moves. Adapted from the 1816 book by E.T.A. Hoffmann. **93m/C VHS, LV, 8mm, Closed Caption.** Macaulay Culkin, Jessica Lynn Cohen, Bart Robinson Cook, Darci Kistler, Damian Woetzel, Kyra Nichols, Wendy Whelan, Gen Horiuchi, Margaret Tracey; **D:** Emile Ardolino; **W:** Susan Cooper; **C:** Ralf Bode. *WAR*

The George McKenna Story 🎬🎬½
1986 Washington stars as the newly appointed principal of George Washington High in Los Angeles. The school is located in South Central, a gang and drug-infested war zone where the students are armed for their own protection. The situation appears hopeless but McKenna refuses to give up. Based on a true story. Made for television. **95m/C VHS.** Denzel Washington, Lynn Whitfield, Akosua Busia, Richard Masur; **D:** Eric Laneuville; **W:** Charles Eric Johnson; **M:** Herbie Hancock.

George of the Jungle 🎬🎬🎬
1997 (PG) The '60s cartoon hero goes big screen and live-action with Fraser starring as the clumsy jungle hero. While on safari, socialite Ursula (Mann) falls in love with George and takes him back to San Francisco, leaving behind obnoxious fiancee Lyle (Church). But when poachers capture George's "brother" Ape (voiced by Cleese), he returns to save the day (aided by various jungle companions). Fraser is an appealing lead, and the script is sweetly funny while retaining creator Ward's smart, subversive edge. The stunts are more impressive than you'd usually expect from a cartoon

adaptation. Hollywood's recycling project is still in overdrive, but this one actually works. **91m/C VHS, Closed Caption, DVD.** Brendan Fraser, Leslie Mann, Thomas Haden Church, Holland Taylor, Richard Roundtree, Greg Cruttwell, Abraham Benrubi, John Bennett Perry, Kelly Miller; **D:** Sam Weisman; **W:** Dana Olsen, Audrey Wells; **V:** John Cleese. *TOU*

George Wallace 🎬🎬½
1997 Follows 20 years (1955-1975) in the life of politician George Wallace (Sinise) from his career as a state circuit judge, his four terms as Alabama's hard-line segregationist governor, to the first years after he was paralyzed by a would-be assassin while campaigning for the presidency. Some elements are disturbingly dramatised, including Archie (Williams), the fictional black manservant who serves as Wallace's conscience. Based on the book "Wallace" by co-scripter Frady. **?m/C VHS.** Gary Sinise, Mare Winningham, Clarence Williams III, Joe Don Baker, Angelina Jolie, Terry Kinney, William Sanderson, Mark Rolston; **D:** John Frankenheimer; **W:** Paul Monash, Marshall Frady; **C:** Alan Caso; **M:** Gary Chang. *WAR*

George Washington 🎬🎬½
1984 Bostwick stars as the father of our country in this made for television adaptation of James Thomas Flexner's biography. The destitute young Washington develops a close friendship with the wealthy Will Fairfax (Dukes), who provides him with the support to pursue his dreams, even though Washington has secretly fallen in love with Sally (Smith), Will's flirtatious wife. George himself has married the widowed Martha (Duke) and begins his military career, leading the American colonies against the Brits in the Revolutionary War. On three cassettes. **398m/C VHS, Beta, Closed Caption.** Barry Bostwick, David Dukes, Jaclyn Smith, Patty Duke, Hal Holbrook, Lloyd Bridges, Jose Ferrer, Trevor Howard, Richard Kiley, James Mason, Clive Revill, Robert Stack; **W:** Richard Fielder. *WAR*

George Washington Slept Here 🎬🎬🎬
1942 Hilarious side-splitter about a couple who moves from their Manhattan apartment to an old, broken-down country home in Connecticut. It's one catastrophe after another as the couple tries to renovate their home and deal with a greedy neighbor. Based on the play by George S. Kaufman and Moss Hart. **93m/B VHS.** Jack Benny, Ann Sheridan, Charles Coburn, Percy Kilbride, Hattie McDaniel, William Tracy; **D:** William Keighley. Nominations: Academy Awards '42: Best Interior Decoration. *MGM*

George Washington: The Forging of a Nation 🎬🎬½
1986 Sequel to the "George Washington" miniseries finds Bostwick and Duke reprising their roles as George and Martha. Unfortunately, the later part of Washington's life isn't nearly as exciting. **208m/C VHS, Closed Caption.** Barry Bostwick, Patty Duke, Penny Fuller, Jeffrey Jones, Richard Bekins; **D:** William A. Graham; **M:** Bruce Broughton. *MGM*

George White's Scandals 🎬🎬
1945 A lightweight musical comedy look at the show biz world and why the show must go on. Based on White's Broadway extravaganzas. Jazz numbers by Gene Krupa and his band. Preceded by "George White's Scandals" of 1934 and 1935. ♫Bolero in the Jungle; E.H.S.; Leave Us Leap; I Want to be a Drummer in the Band; How Did You Get Out of My Dreams?; I Wake Up in the Morning; Who Killed Vaudeville?; Scandals; Liza. **95m/B VHS, Beta.** Joan Davis, Jack Haley, Jane Greer, Phillip Terry, Margaret Hamilton, Martha Holliday; **D:** Felix Feist. *CCB*

George's Island 🎬🎬🎬
1991 (PG) When young George is placed with the worst foster parents in the world, his eccentric grandfather helps him escape. They wind up on Oak's Island, where, legend has it, Captain Kidd's ghost and buried treasure reside. They soon find out the legends are true! **89m/C VHS, LV.** Ian Bannen, Sheila McCarthy, Maury Chaykin, Nathaniel Moreau, Vicki Ridler, Brian Downey, Gary Reineke; **D:** Paul Donovan; **W:** J. William Ritchie; **M:** Marty Simon. *COL, NLC*

Georgia 🎵🎵
1987 Tough lawyer Nina Bailey (Davis) explores her past when she begins a search for information on her biological mother, Georgia White, a photographer who drowned herself years before. Only Nina has no idea about the Pandora's box of secrets she's about to unleash. Frequent flashbacks to Georgia's mysterious life and death (Davis well plays both roles). **90m/C VHS.** **AU** Judy Davis, Julia Blake, John Bach; **D:** Ben Lewin. *ORI, FXL*

Georgia 🎬🎬🎬
1995 (R) Character study about sibling rivalry, self-destruction, and the Seattle music scene. Struggling rock singer Sadie (Leigh), who relies on booze, drugs, and men to help her make it through the night, returns to Seattle to crash with big-sister Georgia (Winningham). Settled, with loving husband and kids, the much more talented Georgia is also a popular folk icon and has the type of personal/career success angry and ambitious Sadie can only dream about. Fine performances—particularly from the chameonlike Leigh; both leads do their own singing. Screenwriter Turner is Leigh's mother. **CW:** Substance abuse, language, and a sex scene. **117m/C VHS, LV, Closed Caption.** Jennifer Jason Leigh, Mare Winningham, Ted Levine, Max Perlich, John Doe, John C. Reilly, Jimmy Witherspoon; **D:** Ulu Grosbard; **W:** Barbara Turner; **C:** Jan Kiesser. Independent Spirit Awards '96: Best Supporting Actress (Winningham); Montreal World Film Festival '95: Best Actress (Leigh), Best Film; New York Film Critics Awards '95: Best Actress (Leigh); Nominations: Academy Awards '95: Best Supporting Actress (Winningham); Independent Spirit Awards '96: Best Actress (Leigh), Best Director (Grosbard), Best Supporting Actor (Perlich); Screen Actors Guild Award '95: Best Supporting Actress (Winningham). *TOU*

Georgia, Georgia 🎬½
1972 (R) Sands is a black entertainer on tour in Sweden who falls for a white photographer. Her traveling companion, who hates whites, takes drastic action to separate the lovers. Poor acting, script, and direction. Based on a book by Maya Angelou. **91m/C VHS, Beta.** Diana Sands, Dirk Benedict, Minnie Gentry; **D:** Stig Bjorkman; **W:** Maya Angelou.

Georgy Girl 🎬🎬🎬
1966 Redgrave finely plays the overweight ugly-duckling Georgy who shares a flat with the beautiful and promiscuous Meredith (Rampling). Georgy is, however, desired by the wealthy and aging Mason and soon by Meredith's lover (Bates) who recognizes her good heart. When Meredith becomes pregnant, Georgy persuades her to let her raise the baby, leaving Georgy with the dilemma of marrying the irresponsible Bates (the baby's father) or the settled Mason. The film and title song (sung by the Seekers) were both huge hits. Based on the novel by Margaret Foster who also co-wrote the screenplay. **100m/B VHS, Beta, LV.** **GB** Lynn Redgrave, James Mason, Charlotte Rampling, Alan Bates, Bill Owen, Claire Kelly, Rachel Kempson; **D:** Silvio Narizzano. Golden Globe Awards '67: Best Actress—Musical/Comedy (Redgrave); New York Film Critics Awards '66: Best Actress (Redgrave); Nominations: Academy Awards '66: Best Actress (Redgrave), Best Black and White Cinematography, Best Song ("Georgy Girl"), Best Supporting Actor (Mason). *FCT, COL*

Germany in Autumn 🎬🎬
Deutschland im Herbst **1978** Twelve West German filmmakers offer political statements and artistic commentary on the political situation in their country after the kidnapping and murder of industrialist Hans Martin Schleyer. In German with English subtitles. **124m/C VHS.** **GE D:** Volker Schlondorff, Rainer Werner Fassbinder, Alf Brustellin, Alexander Kluge, Maximiliane Mainka, Edgar Reitz, Katja Rupe, Hans Peter Cloos, Bernhard Sinkel, Beate Mainka-Jellinghaus, Peter Schubert, Heinrich Boll; **W:** Heinrich Boll. *WAC, FCT*

Germicide 🎬
1974 Scientist tries to warn the world of the threat posed by a horrifying bacterial weapon. Terrorists and his mistress hatch plots against him. **90m/C Beta.** Rod Taylor, Bibi Andersson.

Germinal 🎬🎬🎬 **1993 (R)** Recounts the struggle of working-class coal miners in France, led by Depardieu and wife Miou-Miou, to stave off poverty. While greedy investors debate how far they should lower miners' wages, the Maheu family, spurred on by newly arrived Marxist and off-camera French pop star Renaud, lead a strike. Minor themes revolving around management's adulterous adventures provide some momentary relief to relieve short attention spans. Seems so self-consciously an epic drama, however, that the overall effect is ponderous. Adaptation of the 19th century novel by Zola. In French with English subtitles. **CW:** Violence; language; brief nudity. **158m/C VHS, LV. FR** Gerard Depardieu, Miou-Miou, Bernard Fresson, Jean Carmet, Laurent Terzieff, Anny Duperey, Renaud, Jacques Dacqmine; **D:** Claude Berri; **W:** Claude Berri, Arlette Langmann; **C:** Yves Angelo; **M:** Jean-Louis Roques. Cesar Awards '94: Best Cinematography, Best Costume Design. **COL**

Geronimo 🎬🎬½ **1962** In typical Hollywood casting Connors stars as the Indian leader on the warpath against the cavalry over broken treaties. Lots of action and the Indians are actually the good guys. **101m/C VHS, LV, Letterbox.** Chuck Connors, Ross Martin, Pat Conway, Kamala Devi, Adam West, Lawrence Dobkin, Denver Pyle, Enid Jaynes, Armando Silvestre, John Anderson; **D:** Arnold Laven. **MGM**

Geronimo 🎬🎬🎬 **1993** Not to be confused with the big screen version, this made for cable television drama uses three actors to portray the legendary Apache warrior (1829-1909) at various stages of his life. The intrepid teenager who leads attacks on Mexican troops, the adult fighting the duplicitous bluecoats, and the aged man witnessing the destruction of his way of life. The true story is told from the point of view of Native American culture and historical records. Somewhat overly earnest. **120m/C VHS.** Joseph Runningfox, Jimmy Herman, Ryan Black, Nick Ramus, Michelle St. John, Michael Greyeyes, Tailinh Forest Flower, Kimberly Norris, August Schellenberg, Geno Silva, Harrison Lowe; **D:** Roger Young; **W:** J.T. Allen; **M:** Patrick Williams. **TTC**

Geronimo: An American Legend 🎬🎬½ **1993 (PG-13)** Well-intentioned bio-actioner about the legendary Apache leader who fought the U.S. Army over forcing Native Americans onto reservations. Narrator is young Army officer Gatewood (Patric), whose division is to round up the renegades led by Geronimo (Studi), whom he naturally comes to admire. Hackman and Duvall (as a General and a scout respectively) steal any scene they're in although the leads manage to hold their own. Too noble for its own good and somewhat plodding. Great location filming around Moab, Utah. **115m/C VHS, LV, 8mm, Closed Caption.** Wes Studi, Jason Patric, Robert Duvall, Gene Hackman, Matt Damon, Rodney Grant, Kevin Tighe, Carlos Palomino, Stephen McHattie; **D:** Walter Hill; **W:** John Milius, Larry Gross; **C:** Lloyd Ahern; **M:** Ry Cooder. Nominations: Academy Awards '93: Best Sound. **COL**

Geronimo's Revenge 🎬½ **1960** When Geronimo starts a battle with the settlers, a rancher he has befriended finds himself caught in the middle. The fourth soggy Disney TV oater from the "Tales of Texas John Slaughter" series. **77m/C VHS, Beta.** Tom Tryon, Darryl Hickman; **D:** Harry Keller. **NO**

Gertrud 🎬🎬🎬½ **1964** The simple story of an independent Danish woman rejecting her husband and lovers in favor of isolation. Cold, dry, minimalistic techniques make up Dreyer's final film. In Danish with subtitles. **116m/B VHS, Beta. DK** Nina Pens Rode, Bendt Rothe, Ebbe Rode; **D:** Carl Theodor Dreyer; **W:** Carl Theodor Dreyer. **FCT, DVT, HEG**

Gervaise 🎬🎬🎬 **1956** The best of several films of Emile Zola's "L'Assommoir." A 19th-century middle-class family is destroyed by the father's plunge into alcoholism despite a mother's attempts to save them. Well acted but overwhelmingly depressing. In French with English subtitles. **89m/B VHS, Beta. FR** Maria Schell, Francois Perier, Suzy Delair, Armand Mestral; **D:** Rene Clement; **M:** Georges Au-

ric. British Academy Awards '56: Best Actor (Perier), Best Film; New York Film Critics Awards '57: Best Foreign Film; Venice Film Festival '56: Best Actress (Schell); Nominations: Academy Awards '56: Best Foreign Language Film. **DVT, FST, WFV**

Get Christie Love! 🎬🎬 **1974** Vintage blaxploitation from the genre's halcyon days, when going undercover meant a carte blanche for skimpy outfits. Based on Dorothy Uhnak's detective novel, the eponymous policewoman goes undercover to bring a thriving drug empire to its knees. The outcome: a TV series. Graves previously appeared on television as one of the "Laugh-In" party girls. **95m/C VHS.** Teresa Graves, Harry Guardino, Louise Sorel, Paul Stevens, Andy Romano, Debbie Dozier; **D:** William A. Graham. **XVC**

Get Crazy 🎬🎬½ **1983** The owner of the Saturn Theatre is attempting to stage the biggest rock-and-roll concert of all time on New Year's Eve 1983, and everything is going wrong in this hilarious, off-beat film. **90m/C VHS, Beta, LV.** Malcolm McDowell, Allen (Goorwitz) Garfield, Daniel Stern, Gail Edwards, Ed Begley Jr., Lou Reed, Bill Henderson; **D:** Allan Arkush; **M:** Michael Boddicker. **NLC**

Get On the Bus 🎬🎬🎬 **1996 (R)** Lee looks at the personal side of the Million Man March through a fictional group of men who board a bus in south central L.A. and head for Washington, D.C. Practically ignoring the event itself, Lee and writer Bythewood focus on the the men who participated, their reasons, and their interaction with each other. Standouts in the melting pot of characters include Dutton as the attentive bus driver, a brash young actor (Braugher), a likable old man (Davis), an absentee father (Byrd) and his potentially delinquent son (Bonds), and a cop (Smith). Despite low budget (2.4 mil) and tight shooting schedule (21 days), Lee manages to drive the story home with fine dialogue and characterization that (for the most part) avoids stereotypes. **CW:** Language. **122m/C VHS, LV, Closed Caption.** Andre Braugher, Ossie Davis, Charles S. Dutton, De'Aundre Bonds, Gabriel Casseus, Albert Hall, Hill Harper, Harry J. Lennix, Bernie Mac, Wendell Pierce, Roger Guenveur Smith, Isaiah Washington, Steve White, Thomas Jefferson Byrd, Richard Belzer, Randy Quaid; **D:** Spike Lee; **W:** Reggie Rock Bythewood; **C:** Elliot Davis; **M:** Terence Blanchard. **COL**

Get Out Your Handkerchiefs 🎬🎬🎬½ *Preparez Vous Mouchoirs* **1978 (R)** Unconventional comedy about a husband desperately attempting to make his sexually frustrated wife happy. Determined to go to any lengths, he asks a Mozart-loving teacher to become her lover. She is now, however, bored by both men. Only when she meets a 13-year-old genius at the summer camp where the three adults are counselors does she come out of her funk and find her sexual happiness. Laure is a beautiful character, but Depardieu and Dewaere are wonderful as the bewildered would-be lovers. Academy Award winner for best foreign film. In French with English subtitles. **109m/C VHS, Beta, LV. FR** Gerard Depardieu, Patrick Dewaere, Carole Laure; **D:** Bertrand Blier; **M:** Georges Delerue. Academy Awards '78: Best Foreign Language Film; Cesar Awards '79: Best Score; National Society of Film Critics Awards '78: Best Film. **WAR, INT**

Get Rita 🎬🎬 *Gun Moll; Poopsie; Oopsie Poopsie; La Puppa del Gangster* **1975** Italian prostitute sets up her gangster boyfriend for a murder she committed and she winds up as mob boss. **90m/C VHS, Beta.** Sophia Loren, Marcello Mastroianni; **D:** Tom Rowe. **CTC**

Get Shorty 🎬🎬🎬 **1995 (R)** Low-level Miami loan shark and film buff Chili Palmer (Travolta) heads to Hollywood via Las Vegas, looking for a deadbeat drycleaner (Paymer) and a grade-Z movie producer (Hackman) who owes Vegas $150,000. Aided by B-movie scream-queen (Russo), Palmer is pitted against a variety of shady Hollywood-types, including egomaniacal star (DeVito) while trying to get into showbiz himself.

Snappy scripting and performances finally do screen justice to an Elmore Leonard novel. DeVito, with the smaller title role, was originally cast as Chili Palmer, a role Travolta twice turned down until the ubiquitous Quentin Tarantino advised him to take it. **CW:** Language and some violence. **105m/C VHS, LV, Closed Caption, DVD.** John Travolta, Gene Hackman, Danny DeVito, Rene Russo, Dennis Farina, Delroy Lindo, David Paymer, James Gandolfini; **Cameos:** Bette Midler, Harvey Keitel, Penny Marshall; **D:** Barry Sonnenfeld; **W:** Scott Frank; **C:** Don Peterman; **M:** John Lurie. Golden Globe Awards '96: Best Actor—Musical/Comedy (Travolta); Nominations: Golden Globe Awards '96: Best Film—Musical/Comedy, Best Screenplay; Screen Actors Guild Award '95: Cast; Writers Guild of America '95: Best Adapted Screenplay. **MGM**

Get Smart, Again! 🎬🎬½ **1989** Would you believe Maxwell Smart is back again as CONTROL's most incompetent agent? How about Agent 99 as his sidekick? Hymie the robot and those no-good-niks at KAOS? Well, it's all true. This second reunion movie (following "The Nude Bomb") from the '60s TV show highlights all the wacky gadgetry, including the shoe phone, but fails to find the show's original outlandishness. Made for television. **93m/C VHS, Closed Caption.** Don Adams, Barbara Feldon, Dick Gautier, Bernie Kopell, Kenneth Mars, Harold Gould, Roger Price, Fritz Feld, Robert Karvelas, King Moody; **D:** Gary Nelson. **WOV**

Get That Girl 🎬 **1932** Minor western action pic marred by former silent-screen player Talmadge's heavy German accent which soon lead to him giving up acting for a directing career. **54m/B VHS.** Richard Talmadge, Shirley Grey, Carl Stockdale; **D:** George Crone. **GPV**

Get That Man 🎬🎬 **1935** When a cabby is mistaken for the murdered heir to a vast fortune, his life suddenly becomes complex. **57m/B VHS, Beta, LV.** Wallace Ford, Leon Ames, Lillian Miles, E. Alyn Warren; **D:** Spencer Gordon Bennet. **NOS**

The Getaway 🎬🎬 **1972 (PG)** McQueen plays a thief released on a parole arranged by his wife (McGraw) only to find out a corrupt politician wants him to rob a bank. After the successful holdup, McQueen finds out his cohorts are in the politician's pocket and trying to doublecross him. McQueen and McGraw are forced into a feverish chase across Texas to the Mexican border, pursued by the politician's henchmen and the state police. Completely amoral depiction of crime and violence with McQueen taciturn as always and McGraw again showing a complete lack of acting skills. Based on a novel by Jim Thompson. McQueen and McGraw had a romance during filming and later married. Remade in 1993. **123m/C VHS, Beta.** Steve McQueen, Ali MacGraw, Ben Johnson, Sally Struthers, Al Lettieri, Slim Pickens, Jack Dodson, Dub Taylor, Bo Hopkins; **D:** Sam Peckinpah; **W:** Walter Hill; **C:** Lucien Ballard; **M:** Quincy Jones. **FCT**

The Getaway 🎬½ **1993 (R)** It was a bad movie in 1972 and the remake hasn't improved the situation. Doc and Carol are husband and wife crooks (played by marrieds Basinger and Baldwin). Doc gets double-crossed and winds up in a Mexican jail; Carol gets a well-connected crook (Woods) to spring her hubby—by sleeping with him and promising Doc will pull off another heist. The robbery's botched, there are double-crosses galore, and the couple go on the run. The stars are pretty but everything's predictable. An unrated version is also available. **CW:** Language, violence, and sexuality. **110m/C VHS, LV, Closed Caption, DVD.** Alec Baldwin, Kim Basinger, James Woods, Michael Madsen, Jennifer Tilly, David Morse; **D:** Roger Donaldson; **W:** Walter Hill, Amy Holden Jones; **C:** Peter Menzies Jr.; **M:** Mark Isham. Nominations: MTV Movie Awards '94: Most Desirable Female (Basinger). **USH**

Getting Away With Murder woof! **1996 (R)** An utterly distasteful bomb that proves the Holocaust just isn't as funny as it used to be. College professor Aykroyd takes matters into his own hands when he learns that his kindly neighbor (Lemmon) is a Nazi war criminal. After finding out he may have been a wee bit hasty, he marries the coot's daughter as penance. Writer-director Miller tries to squeeze gags out of such topics as Nazi death camps and Holocaust denial. Definitely career lows for everyone involved. (What were they thinking?) One of the last films released (with no advance warning and no advance screenings) by Savoy pictures.*CW:* Some sexual situations. **92m/C VHS.** Dan Aykroyd, Lily Tomlin, Jack Lemmon, Bonnie Hunt, Brian Kerwin; *D:* Harvey Miller; *W:* Harvey Miller; *C:* Frank Tidy; *M:* John Debney. HBO

Getting Even 🐾½ *Hostage: Dallas* 1986 (R) A maniac threatens to poison the entire population of Texas with a deadly gas unless he gets $50 million. An adventurous businessman sets out to stop him. **90m/C VHS, Beta.** Edward Albert, Joe Don Baker, Audrey Landers; *D:* Dwight Little; *C:* Peter Collister. ART, VES

Getting Even 🐾🐾 1992 (R) Dundee and Evans served together in Vietnam. Fifteen years later they're reunited by the FBI to track a former Marine, who once betrayed Evans to the enemy. Seems he's now a drug traffiker and arms dealer who also gets his sadistic pleasures by killing women. The two ex-Marines find they have one last battle to finish. *CW:* Language, violence, and sexuality. **93m/C VHS.** Richard Roundtree, Michael J. Aronin; *D:* Leandro Lucchetti. COL

Getting Even with Dad 🐾½ 1994 (PG) Crook Danson can't find the money he stole in his last heist. Why? because his precocious son has hidden it with the intention of blackmailing dear old dad into going straight and acting like a real father. Title is unintentionally funny in light of Mac's domineering dad Kit, who makes everybody in Hollywood want to go hide when he appears. Fairly bland family film squanders charm of Danson and Culkin, running formulaic plot into ground. Headly is likewise wasted as district attorney who prosecutes and then falls for Pops. And hey, Macaulay's precocious days are down to a precious few. **108m/C VHS, LV, Closed Caption.** Macaulay Culkin, Ted Danson, Glenne Headly, Hector Elizondo, Saul Rubinek, Gailard Sartain, Kathleen Wilhoite, Sam McMurray; *D:* Howard Deutch; *W:* Tom S. Parker, Jim Jennewein. Nominations: Golden Raspberry Awards '94: Worst Actor (Culkin). MGM

Getting Gotti 🐾🐾½ 1994 (R) Story of the seven year investigation and six-month trial by U.S. Attorney's Office prosecutor Diane Giacalone (Bracco) against reputed mobster "Teflon Don" John Gotti. (She lost.) Made for television.*CW:* Violence. **93m/C VHS.** Lorraine Bracco, Anthony John Denison, Kathleen Lasky, August Schellenberg, Kenneth Welsh, Ellen Burstyn, Lawrence Bayne; *D:* Roger Young; *W:* James Henerson; *M:* Patrick Williams.

Getting In 🐾½ *Student Body* 1994 (R) Pressured by the family tradition of attending Johns Hopkins Medical School, Gabriel Higgs (Mailer) decides to bribe the rivals ahead of him on the waiting list. But one of them (McCarthy) decides the easiest thing to do is murder the other candidates and frame Gabe.*CW:* Mild violence; brief nudity; language. **94m/C VHS, LV, Closed Caption.** Steven Mailer, Kristy Swanson, Andrew McCarthy, Dave Chappelle; *D:* Doug Liman; *W:* P.J. Posner, Joel Posner, Jonathan Lewin. THV

Getting It On 🐾 1983 (R) High school student uses his new-found video equipment for voyeuristic activity. **100m/C VHS, Beta.** Martin Yost, Heather Kennedy, Jeff Edmond, Kathy Rockmeier, Mark Alan Ferri; *D:* William Olsen. ART, VES

Getting It Right 🐾🐾½ 1989 (R) A sweet-natured British comedy about an inexperienced, shy adult male who is quite suddenly pursued by a middle-aged socialite, a pregnant, unstable rich girl, and a modest single mother. Novel and screenplay by Elizabeth Jane Howard. **101m/C VHS, Beta, LV.** *GB* Jesse Birdsall, Helena Bonham Carter, Lynn Redgrave, Peter Cook, John Gielgud, Jane Horrocks, Richard Huw, Shirley Anne Field, Pat Haywood, Judy Parfitt, Bryan Pringle; *D:* Randal Kleiser; *W:* Elizabeth Jane Howard; *M:* Colin Towns, Steve Tyrell. VTR

The Getting of Wisdom 🐾🐾½ 1977 A 13-year-old girl from the Australian outback tries to establish her identity, and her individuality, within the restricting confines of a Victorian girl's boarding school. Based on the novel by Henry Handel Richardson. **100m/C VHS, Beta.** *AU* Susannah Fowle, Hilary Ryan, Alix Longman, Sheila Helpmann, Patricia Kennedy, Barry Humphries, John Waters; *D:* Bruce Beresford. FCT, FOX

Getting Out 🐾🐾½ 1994 Arlie (DeMornay) is an ex-con on her way home to Georgia after an eight year prison stint and what she hopes will be a reunion with the son she bore in jail. She thinks he's in a foster home but instead her mother (Burstyn) had the child adopted and if she interferes, Arlie's parole is to be revoked. Arlie's trying desperately to rehabilitate herself but the system and old contacts are close to dragging her back down. TV movie adapted from Marsha Norman's 1977 play. **92m/C VHS, LV, Closed Caption.** Rebecca DeMornay, Ellen Burstyn, Rob Knepper, Richard Jenkins, Carol Mitchell-Leon, Tandy Cronyn, Norman Skaggs; *D:* John Korty; *W:* Eugene Corr, Ruth Shapiro; *M:* Mason Daring. HMK

Getting Over 🐾 1981 A black promoter is hired as a figurehead by a bigoted record company president and proceeds to try to run the company his own way. He develops an all-girl group called "The Love Machine" and gets involved in a singer's kidnapping and a record company run by gangsters. Filled with cliches and stereotypes. **108m/C VHS, Beta.** John Daniels, Gwen Brisco, Mary Hopkins, John Goff, Andrew "Buzz" Cooper; *D:* Bernie Rollins; *W:* Bernie Rollins. UNI

Getting Physical 🐾½ 1984 After being mugged, a secretary decides to get in shape and enters the world of female body building. Crammed with workout scenes and disco music. Made for television. **95m/C VHS, Beta, Closed Caption.** Alexandra Paul, Sandahl Bergman, David Naughton; *D:* Steven Hilliard Stern; *M:* William Goldstein. FOX

Getting Straight 🐾🐾 1970 (R) A returning Vietnam soldier (Gould) goes back to his alma mater to secure a teaching degree and gets involved in the lives of his fellow students and the turbulence of the end of the '60s, including campus riots. A now-dated "youth" picture somewhat watchable for Gould's performance. **124m/C VHS, Beta.** Elliott Gould, Candice Bergen, Jeff Corey, Cecil Kellaway, Jeannie Berlin, Harrison Ford, John Rubinstein, Robert F. Lyons, Max Julien; *D:* Richard Rush. COL

Getting Up and Going Home 🐾🐾½ 1992 Jack (Skerritt) is a married man with a midlife crisis. So what does he do? Get involved with not one, but two, other women. Is he asking for trouble or what? Adapted from the book by Robert Anderson. **93m/C VHS, Beta, Closed Caption.** Tom Skerritt, Blythe Danner, Roma Downey, Julianne Phillips, Bruce Kirby, Gary Frank, Dorian Harewood, Paul Sand; *D:* Steven Schachter; *W:* Peter Nelson.

Getting Wasted 🐾½ 1980 (PG) Set in 1969 at a military academy for troublesome young men, chaos ensues when the cadets meet hippies. **98m/C VHS, Beta.** Brian Kerwin, Stephen Furst, Cooper Huckabee. NO

Gettysburg 🐾🐾🐾½ 1993 (PG) Civil War buff Ted Turner (who has a cameo as a Confederate soldier) originally intended Michael Shaara's Pulitzer Prize-winning novel "The Killer Angels" to be adapted as a three-part miniseries for his "TNT" network, but the lure of the big screen prevailed, marking the first time the battle has been committed to film and the first time a film crew has been allowed to film battle scenes on the Gettysburg National Military Park battlefield. The greatest battle of the war and the bloodiest in U.S. history is realistically staged by more than 5,000 Civil War re-enactors. The all-male cast concentrates on presenting the human cost of the war, with Daniels particularly noteworthy as the scholarly Colonel Chamberlain, determined to hold Little Big Top for the Union. Last film role for Jordan,

to whom the movie is so dedicated. The full scale recreation of Pickett's Charge is believed to be the largest period scale motion-picture sequence filmed in North America since D.W. Griffith's "Birth of a Nation." **254m/C VHS, Letterbox, Closed Caption.** Jeff Daniels, Martin Sheen, Tom Berenger, Sam Elliott, Richard Jordan, Stephen Lang, Kevin Conway, C. Thomas Howell, Maxwell Caulfield, Andrew Prine, James Lancaster, Royce D. Applegate, Brian Mallon; *Cameos:* Ken Burns, Ted Turner; *D:* Ronald F. Maxwell; *W:* Ronald F. Maxwell; *M:* Randy Edelman. TTC

The Ghastly Ones woof! 1968 Three couples must stay in a haunted mansion to inherit an estate, but they're soon being violently killed off. No budget and no talent. Remade as "Legacy of Blood." **81m/C VHS, Beta.** Don Williams, Maggie Rogers, Hal Belsoe, Veronica Redburn; *D:* Andy Milligan. NO

Ghetto Blaster 🐾 1989 (R) A Vietnam vet takes on out-of-control street gangs to make his neighborhood safe. **86m/C VHS, Beta.** R.G. Armstrong, Richard Hatch, Richard Jaeckel, Harry Caesar, Rose Marie; *D:* Alan L. Stewart.

Ghetto Revenge 19?? An embittered Vietnam vet gets caught between white supremacists and black radical activists in this coming home story. He returns and tries to build a life but succumbs to the desire for vengeance and things are never the same. ?m/C VHS. Mike Sims. NO

Ghidrah the Three Headed Monster 🐾🐾½ *Ghidorah Sandai Kaiju Chikyu Saidai No Kessan; Ghidora, the Three-Headed Monster; Ghidrah; The Greatest Battle on Earth; The Biggest Fight on Earth; Monster of Monsters* 1965 When a three-headed monster from outer-space threatens the world, humans, having nowhere else to turn, appeal to the friendly Mothra, Rodan, and Godzilla. Rock'em, sock 'em giant thrashing about as Tokyo once again gets trampled. Dependable afternoon monster fare complete with usual dubious dubbing. **85m/C VHS, Beta.** *JP* Yosuke Natsuki, Yuriko Hoshi; *D:* Inoshiro Honda. HHT, VCN, VHE

The Ghost 🐾½ *Lo Spettro* 1963 A woman is driven mad by her supposedly dead husband and their evil housekeeper. Sequel to "The Horrible Dr. Hichcock." **96m/C VHS, Beta.** *IT* Barbara Steele, Peter Baldwin, Leonard Eliott, Harriet White; *D:* Riccardo (Robert Hampton) Freda. SNC

Ghost 🐾🐾🐾 1990 (PG-13) Zucker, known for overboard comedies like "Airplane!" and "Ruthless People," changed tack and directed this undemanding romantic thriller, which was the surprising top grosser of 1990. Swayze is a murdered investment consultant attempting (from somewhere near the hereafter) to protect his lover, Moore, from imminent danger when he learns he was the victim of a hit gone afoul. Goldberg is the medium who suddenly discovers that the powers she's been faking are real. A winning blend of action, special effects (from Industrial Light and Magic) and romance. **127m/C VHS, Beta, LV, 8mm, Letterbox, Closed Caption.** Patrick Swayze, Demi Moore, Whoopi Goldberg, Tony Goldwyn, Rick Aviles, Vincent Schiavelli, Gail Boggs, Armelia McQueen, Phil Leeds; *D:* Jerry Zucker; *W:* Bruce Joel Rubin; *M:* Maurice Jarre. Academy Awards '90: Best Original Screenplay, Best Supporting Actress (Goldberg); British Academy Awards '90: Best Supporting Actress (Goldberg); Golden Globe Awards '91: Best Supporting Actress (Goldberg); Nominations: Academy Awards '90: Best Film Editing, Best Picture, Best Original Score. PAR, FCT, BTV

The Ghost and Mrs. Muir 🐾🐾🐾 1947 A charming, beautifully orchestrated fantasy about a feisty widow who, with her young daughter, buys a seaside house and refuses to be intimidated by the crabby ghost of its former sea captain owner. When the widow falls into debt, the captain dictates his sea adventures, which she adapts into a successful novel. The ghost also falls in love with the beautiful lady. Tierney is exquisite and Harrison is sharp-tongued and manly. Based on R. A. Dick's novel. **104m/B VHS, Beta, LV, Closed Caption.** Gene Tierney, Rex Harrison, George Sanders, Edna Best, Anna Lee, Vanessa Brown,

Robert Coote, Natalie Wood, Isobel Elsom; **D:** Joseph L. Mankiewicz; **W:** Philip Dunne; **C:** Charles B(ryant) Lang; **M:** Bernard Herrmann. Nominations: Academy Awards '47: Best Black and White Cinematography. *FOX, HMV*

The Ghost and Mr. Chicken 🐾🐾½
1966 Fraidy cat Luther Heggs (Knotts) works for a small town newspaper and longs to be a hot-shot reporter. One night he thinks he sees a woman's corpse at the vacant Simmons mansion but of course there's no body when the cops come. The house is considered haunted and there is a 20-year-old murder scandal, so Luther is very reluctantly persuaded to spend the night and solve the sinister goings-on. **90m/C VHS, Closed Caption.** Don Knotts, Joan Staley, Dick Sargent, Liam Redmond, Skip Homeier, Reta Shaw, Lurene Tuttle, Philip Ober; **D:** Alan Rafkin; **W:** James Fritzell; **C:** William Margulies; **M:** Vic Mizzy. *USH*

The Ghost and the Darkness 🐾🐾½
1996 (R) Based on the true story of two man-eating lions who killed 130 people and nearly derailed the building of the East African railroad in 1896. Engineer John Patterson (Kilmer) is sent to build a bridge over the Tsavo river, but as African liaison Samuel (Kani) informs him, Tsavo prophetically means place of slaughter. The workers become convinced the lions, nicknamed "The Ghost" and "The Darkness" are actually demons and, try as he might, Patterson has little luck killing the beasts. Then, legendary big game hunter Remington (Douglas) is called in—but the lions still seem to have the advantage. Lots of crunching bones, slurping blood, and quick cut editing is used to depict the lions' attacks. **CW:** Some violence and gore involving animal attacks. **110m/C VHS, Beta, Closed Caption.** Val Kilmer, Michael Douglas, John Kani, Bernard Hill, Om Puri, Brian McCardie, Tom Wilkinson, Emily Mortimer, Henry Cele; **D:** Stephen Hopkins; **W:** William Goldman; **C:** Vilmos Zsigmond; **M:** Jerry Goldsmith. Academy Awards '96: Best Sound Effects Editing; Nominations: Golden Raspberry Awards '96: Worst Supporting Actor (Kilmer). *PAR*

The Ghost and the Guest 🐾🐾½
1943 Newlyweds spend their honeymoon in a house in the country only to find that gangsters are using the place as a hideout. Chases involving secret passages ensue. **59m/B VHS, Beta.** James Dunn, Florence Rice, Mabel Todd; **D:** William Nigh; **W:** Morey Amsterdam. *SNC, VYY*

The Ghost Breakers 🐾🐾🐾
1940 As a follow-up to the Hope/Goddard 1939 comedy thriller "The Cat and the Canary," this spooky comedy was even better. Lots of laughs and real chills as Hope and Goddard investigate a haunted mansion that she's inherited in Cuba. Effective horror scenes are expertly handled by director Marshall. Remade in 1953 as "Scared Stiff" with Dean Martin and Jerry Lewis. Based on the play by Paul Dickey and Charles Goddard. **83m/B VHS, LV, Closed Caption.** Bob Hope, Paulette Goddard, Richard Carlson, Paul Lukas, Willie Best, Pedro de Cordoba, Noble Johnson, Anthony Quinn; **D:** George Marshall; **W:** Walter DeLeon; **C:** Charles B(ryant) Lang. *USH, BTV*

The Ghost Brigade 🐾 *The Killing Box*
1993 (R) Civil War ghost story finds a Union general (Sheen) trying to discover who's slaughtering both Confederate and Union soldiers on the battlefield. So he sends Captain Harling (Pasdar) to investigate, with the help of rebel prisoner Strayn (Bernsen) and a slave (Williams). What they find is an evil brigade of soldiers—who already happen to be dead—and are eager for new recruits. **80m/C VHS, Closed Caption.** Adrian Pasdar, Corbin Bernsen, Martin Sheen, Cynda Williams, Ray Wise, Roger Wilson; **D:** George Hickenlooper; **W:** Matt Greenberg; **C:** Kent Wakeford. *TTC*

The Ghost Camera 🐾🐾½
1933 Slight story of a man falsely accused of murder. A photograph taken at the murder scene can prove his innocence if only the missing camera can be discovered. **68m/B VHS.** **GB** Henry Kendall, Ida Lupino, John Mills; **D:** Bernard Vorhaus. *HCV*

Ghost Chase 🐾½
1988 (PG-13) A young filmmaker desperate for funds inherits his dead relative's clock, from which issues the ghost of the deceased's butler. The ghostly retainer aids in a search for the departed's secret fortune. Neither scary nor funny. **89m/C VHS, Beta, LV.** Jason Lively, Jill Whitlow, Tim McDaniel, Paul Gleason, Chuck "Porky" Mitchell; **D:** Roland Emmerich. *NO*

Ghost Chasers 🐾🐾½
1951 The Bowery Boys become mixed up in supernatural hijinks when a seance leads to the appearance of a ghost that only Sach can see. **70m/B VHS.** Leo Gorcey, Huntz Hall, Billy Benedict, David Gorcey, Buddy Gorman, Bernard Gorcey, Jan Kayne, Philip Van Zandt, Lloyd Corrigan; **D:** William Beaudine. *WAR*

Ghost City 🐾
1932 Our hero must deal with a masked gang that is "haunting" a town. **60m/B VHS.** Bill Cody, Helen Foster, Ann Rutherford, John Shelton, Reginald Owen; **D:** Harry Fraser. *NOS, DVT, HEG*

Ghost Crazy 🐾🐾
1944 Three wild comedians and a gorilla create mayhem in a haunted house. **?m/C VHS.** Shemp Howard, Billy Gilbert, Maxie "Slapsie" Rosenbloom. *LOO*

Ghost Dad 🐾
1990 (PG) A widowed workaholic dad is prematurely killed and returns from the dead to help his children prepare for the future. Cosby walks through doors, walls, and other solid objects for the sake of comedy—only none of it is funny. **84m/C VHS, Beta, LV, Closed Caption.** Bill Cosby, Denise Nicholas, Ian Bannen, Christine Ebersole, Dana Ashbrook, Arnold Stang; **D:** Sidney Poitier; **W:** S.S. Wilson, Brent Maddock; **M:** Henry Mancini. *USH*

Ghost Dance 🐾
1983 Sacred Indian burial ground is violated, with grim results. **93m/C VHS, Beta.** Sherman Hemsley, Henry Ball, Julie Amato; **D:** Peter Bufa. *TWE*

Ghost Fever woof!
1987 (PG) Two bumbling cops try to evict the inhabitants of a haunted house and get nowhere. A bad rip-off of "Ghostbusters." Alan Smithee is a pseudonym used when a director does not want his or her name on a film—no wonder. **86m/C VHS, Beta, LV.** Sherman Hemsley, Luis Avalos; **D:** Alan Smithee; **W:** Oscar Brodney. *NLC*

The Ghost Goes West 🐾🐾🐾
1936 A brash American family buys a Scottish castle and transports the pieces to the United States along with the Scottish family ghost (Donat). Also along is the ghost's modern-day descendant (also played by Donat) who is the new castle caretaker and in love with the new owner's daughter. It turns out to be up to the ghost to get the two lovers together and find his own eternal rest. A rather lovable fantasy. Rene Clair's first English film. Available in digitally remastered stereo with original movie trailer. **90m/B VHS, Beta.** **GB** Robert Donat, Jean Parker, Eugene Pallette, Elsa Lanchester, Ralph Bunker, Patricia Hilliard, Everley Gregg, Mortan Selten, Chili Bouchier, Mark Daly, Herbert Lomas, Elliot Mason, Jack Lambert, Hay Petrie; **D:** Rene Clair; **W:** Robert Sherwood, Geoffrey Kerr; **C:** Harold Rosson. *HBO*

Ghost in the Machine 🐾½
1993 (R) Serial killer dies while undergoing an X-ray scan and somehow, because of a lightning storm and a power outage, his soul manages to infiltrate the hospital's computer and go on to terrorize more victims via their home computers and appliances. (You expect this to make sense?) Outlandish, predictable flick hovers between high-tech horror and satiric comedy and wastes some pretty decent talent. Horror buffs may get a kick out of it but be forewarned: You may never view your microwave, dishwasher, or electrical outlets in quite the same way again. **CW:** High-tech horror violence. **104m/C VHS, LV, Closed Caption.** Karen Allen, Chris Mulkey, Ted Marcoux, Jessica Walter, Rick Ducommun, Wil Horneff, Nancy Fish, Brandon Adams; **D:** Rachel Talalay; **W:** William Davies, William Osborne; **M:** Graeme Revell. *FOX*

Ghost in the Noonday Sun woof!
1974 Crew of a treasure-seeking pirate ship sets sail for high sea silliness in this slapstick adventure film. Not a theatrical release for one obvious reason—it's terrible. **90m/C VHS, Beta.** **GB** Peter Sellers, Spike Milligan, Anthony (Tony) Franciosa, Clive Revill, Rosemary Leach, Peter Boyle; **D:** Peter Medak. *NO*

Ghost in the Shell 🐾🐾
1995 Animated cyber thriller set in 2029 finds neighborhoods replaced by virtual environments and humans struggling to coexist with sentient cyborgs, known as "shells." A virtual spy, known as the Puppet Master, has caused political and economic havoc through data manipulation and now has left its database world for a physical existence. The Puppet Master is tracked by a shell team that seeks the truth while learning about "ghost" or false memories planted within their circuitry that give the illusion of a past life. Based on a series of comic books by Masamune Shirow. Dubbed. **81m/C VHS, DVD.** **JP D:** Mamoru Oshii. *CPM*

Ghost Keeper 🐾
1980 Three girls are trapped in a mansion with an old hag and various supernatural apparitions. **87m/C VHS, Beta.** Riva Spier, Murray Ord, Georgie Collins; **D:** Vernon Sewell.

The Ghost of Fletcher Ridge 198?
Two friends on a hunting trip run into some backwoodsmen and uncover their moonshining operation. When one of the men is killed, the other flees to the forest in a desperate bid for survival. **90m/C VHS.** Campbell Scott, Bernie White, Virginia Lantry, Len Lesser; **D:** Michael Bordon. *NO*

The Ghost of Frankenstein 🐾🐾½
1942 Fourth Frankenstein film in the Universal Studios series with Chaney filling in for Karloff as the monster. Not as good as its predecessors, but the cast is enjoyable, especially Lugosi as the monster's deformed sidekick, Ygor. Based on a story by Eric Taylor. **68m/B VHS, Closed Caption.** Cedric Hardwicke, Lon Chaney Jr., Lionel Atwill, Ralph Bellamy, Bela Lugosi, Evelyn Ankers, Dwight Frye; **D:** Erle C. Kenton; **W:** W. Scott Darling; **C:** Milton Krasner. *USH, FCT*

The Ghost of Rashmon Hall 🐾 *Night Comes Too Soon*
1947 Doctor tries to rid his home of the ghosts of a sailor, his wife and her lover. **52m/B VHS, Beta.** Valentine Dyall, Anne Howard, Alex Flavorsham, Howard Douglas, Beatrice Marsden, Arthur Brander. *SNC, EEL*

The Ghost of Yatsuya 🐾½
1958 Based on the Japanese legend of a man who must betray his wife to get the power he seeks. When he does, however, what follows is a horrifying revenge. In Japanese with English subtitles. **100m/C VHS, Beta.** **JP** Shigeru Amachi. *VDA, TPV*

Ghost on the Loose 🐾
1943 The Bowery Boys take on Nazi spies. **65m/C VHS.** Leo Gorcey, Huntz Hall, Bela Lugosi; **D:** William Beaudine. *GPV*

Ghost Patrol 🐾½
1936 A cowboy duo kidnaps the inventor of a ray gun in order to hijack mail planes, but they're stopped by G-Man McCoy and friends. An odd hybrid of science fiction and western, to say the least. **57m/B VHS, Beta.** Tim McCoy, Walter Miller, Wheeler Oakman; **D:** Sam Newfield. *GPV, VCI, VCN*

Ghost Rider 🐾
1935 A lawman is aided in his outlaw-nabbing efforts by the ghost of a gunfighter. **56m/B VHS, Beta.** Rex Lease, Bobby Nelson, Franklyn Farnum, Lloyd Ingraham, Ed Parker, Lafe McKee; **D:** Jack Levine. *NOS, GPV*

Ghost Rider 🐾🐾
1943 Former footballer Brown rides the range once again, this time with an element of the supernatural nipping at his heels. **58m/B VHS.** Johnny Mack Brown, Raymond Hatton, Tim Seidel, Beverly Boyd, Milburn Morante; **D:** Wallace Fox. *GPV*

Ghost Ship 🐾½
1953 Young couple is tortured by ghostly apparitions when they move into an old yacht with a dubious past. Grade-B haunting featuring the murdered wife of the ship's former owner as the poltergeist. **69m/B VHS, Beta.** **GB**

Dermot Walsh, Hazel Court, Hugh Burden, John Robinson; **D:** Vernon Sewell. *NOS, SNC*

Ghost Stories: Graveyard Thriller
1986 A compilation of stories with ghosts, vampires and other creatures of the night. 56m/C VHS, Beta. **D:** Lynn Silver. *ART, VES*

Ghost Story ✓✓ 1981 (R) Four elderly
men, members of an informal social club called the Chowder Society, share a terrible secret buried deep in their pasts—a secret that comes back to haunt them to death. Has moments where it's chilling, but unfortunately they're few. Based on the best-selling novel by Peter Straub. 110m/C VHS, Beta, LV, DVD. Fred Astaire, Melvyn Douglas, Douglas Fairbanks Jr., John Houseman, Craig Wasson, Alice Krige, Patricia Neal; **D:** John Irvin; **W:** Lawrence D. Cohen; **C:** Jack Cardiff. *USH, IME*

Ghost Town 1937 Good guy Carey
saves a mine from claim jumpers, but not before he is mistakenly incarcerated as his friend's murderer, and then proved innocent. 65m/B VHS, Beta, LV. Harry Carey Sr.; **D:** Harry Fraser. *VDM*

Ghost Town ✓✓½ 1988 (R) Fine sleeper
about a modern sheriff who follows a gal through a supernatural sandstorm and discovers a literal ghost town of bad guys. 85m/C VHS, LV. Franc Luz, Catherine Hickland, Jimmie F. Skaggs, Penelope Windust, Bruce Glover, Blake Conway, Laura Schaefer; **D:** Richard Governor; **W:** Duke Sandefur; **M:** Harvey R. Cohen.

Ghost Town Gold 1936 The Three
Mesquiteers series continues as the trio outwits bank robbers who have hidden their loot in a ghost town. 53m/B VHS, Beta. Bob Livingston, Ray Corrigan, Max Terhune; **D:** Joseph Kane. *NOS, DVT*

Ghost Town Law ✓½ 1942 The Rough
Riders step in to save the day when a group of outlaws defend their hideout by murdering anyone who approaches. 62m/B VHS, Beta. Buck Jones, Tim McCoy, Raymond Hatton; **D:** Howard Bretherton. *NOS, VCN, CAB*

Ghost Town Renegades ✓ 1947 A
pair of government agents prevent a crook from gaining control of a mining town. 57m/B VHS, Beta. Lash LaRue, Al "Fuzzy" St. John, Jennifer Holt; **D:** Ray Taylor. *COL*

Ghost Town Riders ✓½ 1938 An outlaw
gang is holed up in an abandoned town, threatening to steal Shannon's gold mine, until Baker comes to the rescue. 55m/B VHS. Bob Baker, Fay Shannon, George Cleveland, Glenn Strange, Forrest Taylor, Hank Worden, Murdock McQuarrie; **D:** George Waggner. *GPV*

The Ghost Train ✓✓ 1941 Passengers
stranded at a train station are told tales of a haunted train. Forced to stay at the station overnight, they encounter a number of comically spooky situations. 85m/B VHS, Beta. **GB** Arthur Askey, Richard Murdock, Kathleen Harrison; **D:** Walter Forde. *NOS, SNC*

Ghost Valley ✓✓½ 1932 When Keene
and Kennedy inherit land rich in unmined ore, the administrator (Harris) attempts to scare them off. To foil his plan, Keene conceals his identity and takes a job as the administrator's assistant. Based on a story by Adele Buffington. 54m/B VHS. Tom George Duryea Keene, Merna Kennedy, Mitchell Harris, Billy Franey, Harry Bowen, Kate Campbell, Ted Adams, Buck Moulton, Harry Semels, Al Taylor, Charles "Slim" Whitaker; **D:** Fred Allen. *HEG*

The Ghost Walks ✓✓ 1934 A playwright
has his new masterpiece acted out in front of an unsuspecting producer, who thinks that a real murder has taken place. But when the cast really does start disappearing, who's to blame? 69m/B VHS. John Miljan, June Collyer, Richard Carle, Spencer Charters, Johnny Arthur, Henry Kolker; **D:** Frank Strayer. *SNC, NOS, DVT*

Ghost Writer ✓ 1989 (PG) A writer discov-
ers the ghost of a movie star haunting her beach house, and together they solve the dead vamp's murder. 94m/C VHS, Beta. Audrey Landers, Judy Landers, Jeff Conaway, David Doyle, Anthony (Tony) Francio-

sa, Joey Travolta, John Matuszak, David Paul, Peter Paul; **D:** Kenneth J. Hall.

Ghostbusters ✓✓✓ 1984 (PG) After losing
their scholastic funding, a group of "para-normal" investigators decide to go into business for themselves, aiding New York citizens in the removal of ghosts, goblins and other annoying spirits. This comedy-thriller about Manhattan being overrun by ghosts, contains great special effects, zany characters, and some of the best laughs of the decade. Also available in a laserdisc version with letterboxing, analysis of all special effects, complete screenplay, and original trailer. Followed by a sequel. 103m/C VHS, Beta, LV, Letterbox, Closed Caption, DVD. Bill Murray, Dan Aykroyd, Harold Ramis, Rick Moranis, Sigourney Weaver, Annie Potts, Ernie Hudson, William Atherton, David Margulies, Steven Tash; **D:** Ivan Reitman; **W:** Dan Aykroyd, Harold Ramis; **C:** Laszlo Kovacs; **M:** Elmer Bernstein. Nominations: Academy Awards '84: Best Song ("Ghostbusters"). *COL, CRC*

Ghostbusters 2 ✓✓½ 1989 (PG) After be-
ing sued by the city for the damages they did in the original "Ghostbusters," the boys in khaki are doing kiddie shows at birthday parties. When a river of slime that is actually the physical version of evil is discovered running beneath the city, the Ghostbusters are back in action. They must do battle with a wicked spirit in a painting or the entire world will fall prey to its ravaging whims. 102m/C VHS, Beta, LV, 8mm, Letterbox, Closed Caption. Bill Murray, Dan Aykroyd, Sigourney Weaver, Harold Ramis, Rick Moranis, Ernie Hudson, Peter MacNicol, David Margulies, Wilhelm von Homburg, Harris Yulin, Annie Potts, Ben Stein, Richard "Cheech" Marin, Brian Doyle-Murray, Janet Margolin; **D:** Ivan Reitman; **W:** Dan Aykroyd, Harold Ramis; **C:** Michael Chapman; **M:** Randy Edelman. *COL*

Ghosthouse ✓ 1988 It looks like an aver-
age suburban house, but it's haunted by the ghost of a little girl—and when she comes, evil is sure to follow. 91m/C VHS, Beta. Lara Wendell, Gregg Scott; **D:** Humphrey Humbert. *IMP*

Ghostriders ✓ 1987 One hundred years af-
ter their hanging, a band of ghostly outlaws take revenge on the townfolk's descendents. 85m/C VHS, Beta. Bill Shaw, Jim Peters, Ricky Long, Cari Powell, Mike Ammons, Arland Bishop; **D:** Alan L. Stewart.

Ghosts Can Do It ✓½ 1990 The Hound
doesn't like jumping to conclusions, but is it possible this obscurity was titled to be reminiscent of the more publicized Bo Derek vehicle "Ghosts Can't Do It" comedy about a man who returns to his sexy wife despite her efforts at killing her. 88m/C VHS. Garry McDonald, Pamela Stephenson. *ATL, HHE*

Ghosts Can't Do It ✓ 1990 (R) Another
wet-shirted, Bo-dacious softcore epic, involving a young woman who would like to have the spirit of her virile, but unfortunately dead, husband return to inhabit a living body. 91m/C VHS, Beta, LV, Closed Caption. Bo Derek, Anthony Quinn, Don Murray, Leo Damian; **D:** John Derek. Golden Raspberry Awards '90: Worst Picture, Worst Actress (Derek), Worst Director (Derek). *COL, TTC*

Ghosts of Berkeley Square ✓✓½
1947 The ghosts of two retired soldiers of the early 18th century are doomed to haunt their former home, and only a visit from a reigning monarch can free them. 85m/B VHS, Beta. Wilfrid Hyde-White, Robert Morley, Felix Aylmer; **D:** Vernon Sewell. *VYY*

The Ghosts of Hanley House ✓½
1968 No-budget spooker with no-brain plot. Several unlucky guests spend an evening in a creepy mansion...sound familiar? Shot in Texas. 80m/C VHS, Beta. Barbara Chase, Wilkie De Martel, Elsie Baker, Cliff Scott. *SNC*

Ghosts of Mississippi ✓✓ *Ghosts from
the Past* 1996 (PG-13) Director Reiner attempts to tell the story of civil rights leader Medgar Evers, murdered in 1963, and the three trials of Byron De la Beckwith (Woods), who was finally convicted (after two hung juries) in 1994. Unfortunately, he filters the story through the eyes of white assistant D.A. Bobby De Laughter (Baldwin) while ignoring

Evers' accomplishments almost completely. Woods chews up the scenery as the wily old racist, bringing perhaps a little too much glee into a portrait of true evil. Goldberg sleepwalks through her role as Evers' widow, Myrlie; Evers' sons, Darrell and Van, play themselves; daughter Reena plays a juror while her character is played by Yolanda King, the daughter of slain civil rights leader Martin Luther King, Jr. Filmed on location in Jackson, Mississippi.**CW:** Strong scene of violence and for racial dialogue. 123m/C VHS, LV, Closed Caption. Alec Baldwin, Whoopi Goldberg, James Woods, Craig T. Nelson, Wayne Rogers, William H. Macy, Michael O'Keefe, Yolanda King, Susanna Thompson, Lucas Black, James Pickens Jr., Virginia Madsen, Bill Cobbs; **D:** Rob Reiner; **W:** Lewis Colick; **C:** John Seale; **M:** Marc Shaiman. Nominations: Academy Awards '96: Best Makeup, Best Supporting Actor (Woods); Golden Globe Awards '97: Best Supporting Actor (Woods). *COL*

Ghosts That Still Walk ✓ 1977
Spooky phenomena occur. The demons possessing a young lad's soul may be responsible. 92m/C VHS, Beta. Ann Nelson, Matt Boston, Jerry Jenson, Caroline Howe, Rita Crafts; **D:** James T. Flocker. *VCI, MRV*

Ghostwarrior ✓ *Swordkill* 1986 (R) A 16th
century samurai warrior's ice-packed body is revived and runs amuck in the streets of modern-day Los Angeles. 86m/C VHS, Beta. Hiroshi Fujioka, Janet Julian, Andy Wood, John Calvin; **D:** Larry Carroll; **W:** Tim Curnen; **C:** Mac Ahlberg. *VES*

Ghostwriter ✓✓ 1984 Based on Philip
Roth's best-selling novel, the story is of a writer coming to terms with his past. Roth co-wrote the screenplay. First seen on PBS. 90m/C VHS, Beta. Sam Wanamaker, Claire Bloom, Rose Arrick, MacIntyre Dixon, Cecile Mann, Joseph Wiseman, Mark Linn-Baker, Paulette Smit; **D:** Tristam Powell; **W:** Phillip J. Roth. *PBS*

The Ghoul ✓ 1934 An eccentric En-
glish Egyptologist desires a sacred jewel to be buried with him and vows to come back from the grave if the gem is stolen. When that happens, he makes good on his ghostly promise. A minor horror piece with Karloff only appearing at the beginning and end of the film. This leaves the middle very dull. 73m/B VHS. **GB** Boris Karloff, Cedric Hardwicke, Ernest Thesiger, Dorothy Hyson, Ralph Richardson, Anthony Bushell, Kathleen Harrison, Harold Huth, D. A. Clarke-Smith, Jack Raine; **D:** T. Hayes Hunter; **W:** Roland Pertwee, John Hastings Turner, Rupert Downing; **C:** Gunther Krampf. *VYY, SNC, DVT*

The Ghoul ✓✓ 1975 (R) A defrocked cler-
gyman has a cannibal son to contend with—especially after the drivers in a local auto race begin to disappear. Hurt is the lunatic family gardener. 88m/C VHS, Beta. **GB** Peter Cushing, John Hurt, Alexandra Bastedo, Don Henderson, Stewart Bevan; **D:** Freddie Francis.

Ghoul School ✓ 1990 (R) A spoof of horror
films and college flicks, with lots of scantily clad women and bloody creatures in dark hallways. 90m/C VHS. Joe Franklin, Nancy Siriani, William Friedman. *HHE*

Ghoulies ✓ 1984 (PG-13) A young man gets
more than he bargained for when he conjures up a batch of evil creatures when dabbling in the occult. Ridiculous but successful. Followed by three sequels. 81m/C VHS, Beta. Lisa Pelikan, Jack Nance, Scott Thomson, Tamara DeTreaux, Mariska Hargitay, Bobbie Bresee; **D:** Luca Bercovici; **W:** Luca Bercovici; **C:** Mac Ahlberg; **M:** Richard Band. *ART, VES, HHE*

Ghoulies 2 ✓ 1987 (R) Inept sequel to
"Ghoulies" (1985), wherein the little demons haunt a failing carnival horror house, whose revenues begin to soar. Followed by a second sequel. 89m/C VHS, Beta, LV. Damon Martin, Royal Dano, Phil Fondacaro, J. Downing, Kerry Remsen; **D:** Albert Band. *ART, VES*

Ghoulies 3: Ghoulies Go to
College woof! 1991 (R) Third in the series has the worst special effects and the worst storyline. Not satisfied with ripping off "Gremlins," this one imposes Three Stooges personae upon a trio of demons at large on a beer- and babe-soaked

campus. **94m/C VHS.** Kevin McCarthy, Griffin O'Neal, Evan Mackenzie; **D:** John Carl Buechler. *VES, ART*

Ghoulies 4 🎬½ 1993 (R) Dopey series continues with the satanic creatures roaming the streets of Los Angeles, searching for a way to return to their netherworld home. They get their chance when they meet a Satan-worshipping dominatrix out on a killing spree. **84m/C VHS.** Barbara Alyn Woods, Peter Paul Liapis; **D:** Jim Wynorski; **W:** Mark Sevi. *COL*

G.I. Blues 🎬🎬 1960 (PG) Three G.I.'s form a musical combo while stationed in Germany. Prowse is the nightclub singer Presley falls for. Presley's first film after his military service. 🎵Shopping Around; Tonight Is So Right For Love; What's She Really Like?; Frankfurt Special; Didya Ever; Big Boots; Pocketful of Rainbows; Doin' the Best I Can; Blue Suede Shoes. **104m/C VHS, Beta, LV.** Elvis Presley, Juliet Prowse, Robert Ivers, Leticia Roman, Ludwig Stossel, James Douglas, Jeremy Slate; **D:** Norman Taurog; **C:** Loyal Griggs. *FOX, MVD*

G.I. Executioner 🎬 *Wit's End; Dragon Lady* 1971 (R) An adventure set in Singapore featuring a Vietnam veteran turned executioner. **86m/C VHS, Beta.** Tom Kenna, Victoria Racimo, Angelique Pettyjohn, Janet Wood, Walter Hill; **D:** Joel M. Reed. *VES*

G.I. Jane 🎬 1951 A television producer faints when he gets his draft notice and dreams his company is stranded at a desert post with a company of WACs. **62m/B VHS, Beta, LV.** Jean Porter, Tom Neal, Iris Adrian, Jimmy Lloyd, Mara Lynn, Michael Whalen; **D:** Reginald LeBorg. Nominations: Golden Raspberry Awards '97: Worst Supporting Actress (Moore). *NO*

G.I. Jane 🎬🎬½ *In Pursuit of Honor; Navy Cross* 1997 (R) Moore is buffed, bold and bald in this modern day fable of the first female to become a Navy SEAL. As Jordan O'Neil, Moore endures grueling training exercises and sexist remarks from male colleagues that are tortuous for her, but enjoyable for those who sat through Moore's three previous films. Impressive supporting cast, including Mortensen as the vicious and misogynist master chief and Bancroft as a fiesty senator with a secret political agenda, pick things up when the story flags in the middle. The beginning holds the most interest, but the movie's length encourages improbable plot points. Scott shows he still knows how to make a movie look great, even if the writing doesn't quite measure up.**CW:** Language and combat violence. **124m/C VHS, LV, Closed Caption.** Demi Moore, Viggo Mortensen, Anne Bancroft, Jason Beghe, Scott Wilson, Morris Chestnut, Lucinda Jenney, James Caviezel; **D:** Ridley Scott; **W:** David N. Twohy, Danielle Alexandra; **C:** Hugh Johnson; **M:** Trevor Jones. Golden Raspberry Awards '97: Worst Actress (Moore); Nominations: MTV Movie Awards '98: Best Fight (Demi Moore/Viggo Mortensen). *TOU*

Gia 🎬🎬 1998 (R) Based on the life of self-destructive supermodel/drug addict Gia Carangi (Jolie), who died from AIDS at the age of 26. Gia grew up in an abusive Philadelphia family and hid her insecurities under a tough and wanton persona. Taken under the wing of New York modeling exec Wilhelmina Cooper (Dnaway), Gia's exoticness gets her noticed but the hedonistic lifestyle of the late '70s quickly leads to her downfall. Jolie goes all out for the title role. Made for cable.**CW:** Sexual sitations, strong language, and graphic depictions of drug use. **120m/C VHS.** Angelina Jolie, Mercedes Ruehl, Kylie Travis, Faye Dunaway, Elizabeth Mitchell, Eric Michael Cole, Louis Giambalvo, John Considine, Scott Cohen; **D:** Michael Cristofer; **W:** Michael Cristofer, Jay McInerney; **C:** Rodrigo Garcia; **M:** Terence Blanchard, Terence Blanchard. *HBO*

Giant 🎬🎬🎬½ 1956 Based on the Edna Ferber novel, this epic saga covers two generations of a wealthy Texas cattle baron (Hudson) who marries a strong-willed Virginia woman (Taylor) and takes her to live on his vast ranch. It explores the problems they have adjusting to life together, as well as the politics and prejudice of the time. Dean plays the resentful ranch hand (who secretly loves Taylor) who winds up striking oil and be-

ginning a fortune to rival that of his former boss. Dean's last movie—he died in a car crash shortly before filming was completed. **201m/C VHS, Beta, LV, Closed Caption.** Elizabeth Taylor, Rock Hudson, James Dean, Carroll Baker, Chill Wills, Dennis Hopper, Rod Taylor, Earl Holliman, Jane Withers, Sal Mineo, Mercedes McCambridge; **D:** George Stevens; **C:** William Mellor. Academy Awards '56: Best Director (Stevens); Directors Guild of America Awards '56: Best Director (Stevens); Nominations: Academy Awards '56: Best Actor (Dean), Best Actor (Hudson), Best Adapted Screenplay, Best Art Direction/Set Decoration (Color), Best Costume Design (Color), Best Film Editing, Best Picture, Best Supporting Actress (McCambridge), Best Original Dramatic/Comedy Score. *WAR, BTV*

The Giant Claw 🎬½ 1957 Giant, winged (and stringed) bird attacks from outer space and scientists Morrow, Corday and Ankrum attempt to pluck it. Good bad movie; Corday was Playboy's Miss October, 1958. **76m/B VHS.** Jeff Morrow, Mara Corday, Morris Ankrum, Louis D. Merrill, Edgar Barrier, Robert Shayne, Morgan Jones, Clark Howat; **D:** Fred F. Sears. *MOV*

Giant from the Unknown woof! 1958 Giant conquistador is revived after being struck by lightning and goes on a murderous rampage. Unbelievably bad. **80m/B VHS, Beta.** Edward Kemmer, Buddy Baer, Bob Steele, Sally Fraser; **D:** Richard Cunha. *NOS, SNC, EEL*

The Giant Gila Monster 🎬½ 1959 A giant lizard has the nerve to disrupt a local record hop, foolishly bringing upon it the wrath of the local teens. Rear-projection monster isn't particularly effective, but the film provides many unintentional laughs. **74m/B VHS.** Don Sullivan, Lisa Simone, Shug Fisher, Jerry Cortwright, Beverly Thurman, Don Flourney, Pat Simmons; **D:** Ray Kellogg; **W:** Jay Simms. *NOS, RHI, SNC*

The Giant of Marathon 🎬🎬 1960 Reeves shrugs off the role of Hercules to play Philippides, a marathoner (who uses a horse) trying to save Greece from invading Persian hordes. Lots of muscle on display, but not much talent. **90m/C VHS.** *IT* Steve Reeves, Mylene Demongeot, Daniela Rocca, Ivo Garrani, Alberto Lupo, Sergio Fantoni; **D:** Jacques Tourneur; **C:** Mario Bava. *SNC, MLB*

The Giant of Metropolis 🎬🎬 *Il Gigante Di Metropolis* 1961 Muscle-bound hero goes shirtless to take on the evil, sadistic ruler of Atlantis (still above water) in 10,000 B.C. Ordinary Italian adventure that includes interesting sets and bizarre torture scenes. **92m/C VHS.** *IT* Gordon Mitchell, Roldano Lupi, Bella Cortez, Liana Orfei; **D:** Umberto Scarpelli. *SNC*

The Giant Spider Invasion 🎬 1975 (PG) A meteorite carrying spider eggs crashes to Earth and soon the alien arachnids are growing to humongous proportions. Notoriously bad special effects, but the veteran "B" cast have a good time. **76m/C VHS.** Steve Brodie, Barbara Hale, Leslie Parrish, Robert Easton, Alan Hale Jr., Dianne Lee Hart, Bill Williams, Christianne Schmidtmer; **D:** Bill Rebane; **W:** Bill Rebane, Richard L. Huff, Robert Easton; **C:** Jack Willoughby. *MOV*

Giant Steps 🎬🎬 19?? Williams plays Slate Hopson, a moody jazz legend idolized by a talented young trumpet player. When the two meet Hopson clues the boy into some of life's lessons and rediscovers his own joy at making music. **94m/C VHS.** Billy Dee Williams, Michael Mahonen; **M:** Eric Leeds. *MNC*

Giants of Rome woof! 1963 Rome is in peril at the hands of a mysterious secret weapon that turns out to be a giant catapult. Ludicrous all around. **87m/C VHS, Beta, Closed Caption.** *IT* Richard Harrison, Ettore Manni. *SNC*

The Giants of Thessaly 🎬🎬 1960 Jason and Orpheus search for the Golden Fleece, encountering and defeating monsters, wizards, and a scheming witch. **86m/C VHS.** *IT* Roland Carey, Ziva Rodann, Massimo Girotti, Alberto Farnese; **D:** Riccardo (Robert Hampton) Freda. *SNC*

Gideon's Trumpet 🎬🎬½ 1980 True story of Clarence Earl Gideon, a Florida convict whose case was decided by the Supreme Court and set the precedent that everyone is entitled to defense by a lawyer, whether or not they can pay for it. Based on the book by Anthony Lewis. Made for television. **104m/C VHS, Beta.** Henry Fonda, Jose Ferrer, John Houseman, Dean Jagger, Sam Jaffe, Fay Wray; **D:** Robert Collins. *WOV*

Gidget 🎬🎬 1959 A plucky, boy-crazy teen-age girl (whose nickname means girl midget) discovers romance and wisdom on the beaches of Malibu when she becomes involved with a group of college-aged surfers. First in a series of Gidget/surfer films. Based on a novel by Frederick Kohner about his daughter. **95m/C VHS, Beta, LV.** Sandra Dee, James Darren, Cliff Robertson, Mary Laroche, Arthur O'Connell, Joby Baker; **D:** Paul Wendkos; **C:** Burnett Guffey. *COL*

Gidget Goes Hawaiian 🎬🎬 1961 Gidget is off to Hawaii with her parents and is enjoying the beach (and the boys) when she is surprised by a visit from boyfriend "Moondoggie." Sequel to "Gidget" and followed by "Gidget Goes to Rome." **102m/C VHS, Beta.** Deborah Walley, James Darren, Carl Reiner, Peggy Cass, Michael Callan, Eddie Foy Jr.; **D:** Paul Wendkos. *COL*

Gidget Goes to Rome 🎬½ 1963 Darren returns in his third outing as boyfriend "Moondoggie" to yet another actress playing "Gidget" as the two vacation in Rome and find themselves tempted by other romances. Second sequel to "Gidget." **104m/C VHS, Beta.** Cindy Carol, James Darren, Jeff Donnell, Cesare Danova, Peter Brooks, Jessie Royce Landis; **D:** Paul Wendkos; **M:** John Williams. *COL*

The Gift 🎬🎬½ 1982 (R) Story of a 55-year-old man who chooses early retirement in the hopes of changing his dull and boring life. Unbeknownst to him, his co-workers arrange the ultimate retirement gift—a woman. Silly French sexual farce. Dubbed. **105m/C VHS, Beta.** *FR* Pierre Mondy, Claudia Cardinale, Clio Goldsmith, Jacques Francois, Cecile Magnet, Remy Laurent; **D:** Michael Lang. *FCT*

The Gift Horse 🎬🎬 *Glory at Sea* 1952 A WWII British naval officer dispatches his duties with an iron hand in an attempt to overturn the legacy of a court-martial eight years earlier. Angry rumblings from his crew threaten to upset the ship's stability. Against this foreboding backdrop, the Nazis give battle. Not historically accurate, but exciting. Based on a story by Ivan Goff and Ben Roberts. **99m/B VHS, Beta.** *GB* Trevor Howard, Richard Attenborough, Sonny Tufts, Bernard Lee; **D:** Compton Bennett. *DVT*

The Gift of Love 🎬½ 1990 Saccharine, made-for-television adaption of O. Henry's Christmas romance "The Gift of the Magi." **96m/C VHS, Closed Caption.** James Woods, Marie Osmond, Timothy Bottoms, June Lockhart, David Wayne; **D:** Don Chaffey. *MON, KAR*

The Gig 🎬🎬½ 1985 In this small, independently made film, a band of middle-aged amateur jazz musicians give up their stable occupations for a once-in-a-lifetime shot at a two-week gig in the Catskills. Film succeeds on the strength of it's well fleshed-out characters. **95m/C VHS, Beta, LV, Closed Caption.** Wayne Rogers, Cleavon Little, Warren Vache, Joe Silver, Daniel Nalbach, Andrew Duncan, Jay Thomas, Jerry Matz; **D:** Frank D. Gilroy; **W:** Frank D. Gilroy. *ORI, WAR*

Gigi 🎬🎬🎬🎬 1958 Based on Colette's story of a young Parisian girl (Caron) trained to become a courtesan to the wealthy Gaston (Jourdan). But he finds out he prefers her to be his wife rather than his mistress. Chevalier is Gaston's roguish uncle, who casts an always admiring eye on the ladies. Gingold is Gigi's grandmother and former Chevalier flame, and Gabor amuses as Gaston's current, and vapid, mistress. One of the first MGM movies to be shot on location, this extravaganza features some of the best tributes to the French lifestyle ever filmed. Score includes memorable classics. ♫Gigi; Ah Yes, I Remember It Well; Thank Heaven For Little Girls; The Night They Invented Champagne; She's Not Thinking of Me; It's a Bore; Gossip; I'm Glad I'm Not Young Anymore; The Parisians. **119m/C VHS, Beta, LV, 8mm, Letterbox.** Leslie Caron, Louis Jourdan, Maurice Chevalier, Hermione Gingold, Eva Gabor, Isabel Jeans, Jacques Bergerac; **D:** Vincente Minnelli; **W:** Alan Jay Lerner; **C:** Joseph Ruttenberg; **M:** Frederick Loewe. Academy Awards '58: Best Adapted Screenplay, Best Art Direction/Set Decoration, Best Color Cinematography, Best Costume Design, Best Director (Minnelli), Best Film Editing, Best Picture, Best Song ("Gigi"), Scoring of a Musical; Directors Guild of America Awards '58: Best Director (Minnelli); Golden Globe Awards '59: Best Director (Minnelli), Best Film—Musical/Comedy, Best Supporting Actress (Gingold), National Film Registry '91. *MGM, BTV*

Gilda 🐾🐾🐾½ 1946 An evil South American gambling casino owner hires young American Ford as his trusted aide, unaware that Ford and his sultry wife Hayworth have engaged in a steamy affair. Hayworth does a striptease to "Put the Blame on Mame" in this prominently sexual film. This is the film that made Hayworth into a Hollywood sex goddess. **110m/B VHS, Beta, LV, Closed Caption.** Rita Hayworth, Glenn Ford, George Macready, Joseph Calleia, Steve Geray; **D:** Charles Vidor. *COL*

The Gilded Cage 🐾🐾 1954 Two brothers are falsely accused of art theft and must find the real crooks in order to clear their names. **77m/B VHS, Beta.** *GB* Alex Nicol, Veronica Hurst, Clifford Evans, Ursula Howells, Elwyn Brook-Jones, John Stuart; **D:** John Gilling. *SNC*

Gilligan's Island: Meet the Crew 1964 Join Gilligan and the Skipper of the S.S. Minnow and their unfortunate passengers—Ginger, Mary Ann, the Professor, and Mr. and Mrs. Thurston Howell III—as they try to survive life (and each other) on an uncharted desert isle. Three episodes per cassette from the slapstick television series. Additional episodes available. **?m/B VHS.** Bob Denver, Alan Hale Jr., Jim Backus, Natalie Schafer, Tina Louise, Russell Johnson, Dawn Wells. *CMB*

Gimme an F woof! 🐾 *T & A Academy 2* 1985 (R) The handsome cheerleading instructor at Camp Beaver View ruffles a few pom-poms when he discovers that the camp's owner is about to enter into a shady deal with some foreigners. The film certainly deserves an "F" for foolishness if nothing else. **100m/C VHS, Beta.** Stephen Shellan, Mark Keyloun, John Karlen, Jennifer Cooke; **D:** Paul Justman. *FOX*

Gimme Shelter 1970 The '60s ended as violence occurred at a December 1969 free Rolling Stones concert attended by 300,000 people in Altamont, California. This "Woodstock West" became a bitter remembrance in rock history, as Hell's Angels (hired for security) do some ultimate damage to the spectators. A provocative look at an out-of-control situation. **91m/C VHS, Beta, LV.** Mick Jagger, Keith Richards, Charlie Watts, Bill Wyman, Mick Taylor; **D:** David Maysles; **C:** Haskell Wexler. *COL, MVD*

Gin Game 🐾🐾🐾 1984 Taped London performance of the Broadway play about an aging couple who find romance in an old age home. Two-character performance won awards; touching and insightful. **82m/C VHS, Beta.** Jessica Tandy, Hume Cronyn; **D:** Mike Nichols. *NO*

Ginger 🐾 1972 Fabulous super-sleuth Ginger faces the sordid world of prostitution, blackmail and drugs. Prequel to "The Abductors" and followed eventually by "Girls Are for Loving." **90m/C VHS, Beta.** Cheri Caffaro, William Grannell; **D:** Don Schain. *MON*

Ginger Ale Afternoon 🐾 1989 A smutty comedy revolving around a triangle formed by a married couple and their sexy next-door neighbor. The film tries for fizz but only comes up flat. **88m/C VHS, Beta, LV.** Dana Anderson, John M. Jackson, Yeardley Smith; **D:** Rafal Zielinksi; **W:** Gina Wendkos; **M:** Willie Dixon. *IME*

Ginger & Fred 🐾🐾🐾 1986 (PG-13) An acclaimed story of Fellini-esque poignancy about an aging dance team. Years before they had gained success by reverently impersonating the famous dancing duo of Astaire and Rogers. Now, after 30 years, they reunite under the gaudy lights of a high-tech television special. Wonderful performances by the aging Mastroianni and the still sweet Masina. In Italian with English subtitles. **126m/C VHS, Beta.** *IT* Marcello Mastroianni, Giulietta Masina, Franco Fabrizi, Frederick Von Ledenberg, Martin Blau, Toto Mignone; **D:** Federico Fellini; **W:** Federico Fellini, Tonino Guerra, Tullio Pinelli; **C:** Tonino Delli Colli; **M:** Nicola Piovani. *MGM, FCT*

Ginger in the Morning 🐾🐾 1973 A salesman is enamored of a young hitchhiker whom he picks up on the road. This is the same year Spacek played the innocent-gone-twisted in "Badlands." **90m/C VHS, Beta.** Sissy Spacek, Slim Pickens, Monte Markham, Susan Oliver, Mark Miller; **D:** Gordon Wiles. *NO*

The Gingerbread Man 🐾🐾½ 1997 (R) Lawyer Rick Magruder (Branagh) falls for a scheming femme (Davidtz) who hires him to have her deranged, stalker father (Duvall) committed. Set in the new hot spot of filmdom, steamy Savannah, it becomes clear that nothing is clear and plot takes on noirish twists and turns of intrigue and suspense before the cigarette smoke clears. Shakespeare savant Branagh proves he can also master a Southern accent. Hannah, as Rick's mousy partner, surprises with an unusually good performance. Grisham's first original screenplay. Studio Polygram disliked Altman's original cut, replaced his editor, and recut the movie to its own specifications, angering Altman who threatened to remove his name from the film. Though not an Altman masterpiece, sly thriller doesn't fail to entice. *CW:* Some sexuality, violence and language. **114m/C VHS, LV, Closed Caption, DVD.** Kenneth Branagh, Embeth Davidtz, Robert Duvall, Tom Berenger, Daryl Hannah, Robert Downey Jr., Famke Janssen, Mae Whitman, Jesse James Jr.; **D:** Robert Altman; **W:** John Grisham, Al Hayes; **C:** Gu Changwei; **M:** Mark Isham. *PGV*

The Girl 🐾🐾🐾 1968 The first of Meszaros' trilogy, dealing with a young girl who leaves an orphanage to be reunited with her mother, a traditional country peasant. In Hungarian with English subtitles. Meszaros' first film. Followed by "Riddance" (1973) and "Adoption" (1975). **86m/B VHS, Beta.** *HU* **D:** Marta Meszaros. *KIV*

The Girl 🐾½ 1986 (R) Nero is a wealthy attorney who agrees to pay Powney 300 crowns to have his way with her. Although somewhat ambivalent because of her scandalous age, he takes her anyway. Soon he informs his wife he needs to go on a long business trip, which fits in with her own adulterous plans. A snooping reporter (Brennan) out for some dirt upsets the apple cart, eventually leading to murder. **104m/C VHS, Beta.** Franco Nero, Christopher Lee, Bernice Stegers, Clare Powney, Frank Brennan; **D:** Arne Mattson. *VTR*

The Girl 🐾🐾½ *Catherine Cookson's The Girl* 1996 Illegitimate Hannah Boyle is simply called "The Girl" by her jealous stepmother, who forces her into a disastrous marriage. But Hannah is willing to fight to regain her freedom and the man she truly loves. TV adaptation of the novel by Catherine Cookson. **156m/C VHS.** *GB* Sidhban Flynn, Malcolm Stoddard, Jonathan Cake. *WMI, PBS*

A Girl, a Guy and a Gob 🐾🐾 *The Navy Steps Out* 1941 A shy rich boy falls in love with a girl who has her sights on another. Silly but enjoyable cast. **91m/B VHS, Beta.** Lucille Ball, Edmond O'Brien, George Murphy, Franklin Pangborn, Henry Travers, Lloyd Corrigan; **D:** Richard Wallace. *TTC*

The Girl Can't Help It 🐾🐾½ 1956 Satiric rock and roll musical comedy about a retired mobster who hires a hungry talent agent to promote his girlfriend, a wannabe no-talent singer. Mansfield's first starring role. Classic performances by some of the early greats including Ed-

die Cochran, Gene Vincent, The Platters, Little Richard and Fats Domino. **99m/C VHS, Beta, LV.** Jayne Mansfield, Tom Ewell, Edmond O'Brien, Julie London, Ray Anthony; **D:** Frank Tashlin. *FOX*

Girl Crazy 🐾🐾🐾 *When the Girls Meet the Boys* 1943 A wealthy young playboy is sent to an all-boy school in Arizona to get his mind off girls. Once there, he still manages to fall for a local girl who can't stand the sight of him. The eighth film pairing for Rooney and Garland. ♫Sam and Delilah; Embraceable You; I Got Rhythm; Fascinating Rhythm; Treat Me Rough; Bronco Busters; Bidin' My Time; But Not For Me; Do. **99m/B VHS, Beta, LV.** Mickey Rooney, Judy Garland, Nancy Walker, June Allyson; **D:** Norman Taurog; **C:** William H. Daniels; **M:** George Gershwin, Ira Gershwin. *MGM, TTC, FCT*

Girl from Calgary 🐾 1932 A female rodeo champ ropes her boyfriends much like she ropes her cows, but not without a knock-down, drag-out fight between the two which forces our cowgirl to make the choice she seems to know is fated. Stock rodeo footage is intercut with the heroine riding an obviously mechanical bucking bronc. **66m/B VHS, Beta, LV.** Fifi d'Orsay, Paul Kelly; **D:** Philip H. Whitman. *VYY*

Girl from Chicago 🐾🐾 1932 In this crime melodrama a secret service agent falls in love while on assignment in Mississippi. When he's back in New York he finds a good friend of his girl's in serious trouble with the numbers racket. **69m/C VHS.** Starr Calloway, Grace Smith, Eugene Brooks, Frank Wilson; **D:** Oscar Micheaux. *FCT, BTV*

Girl from Hunan 🐾🐾 1986 Turn-of-the-century China, a 12-year-old girl is married to a two-year-old boy in a typical arranged marriage. She grows into womanhood treating her toddler husband with sibling affection, but conducts a secret love affair with a farmer. Intolerant village laws against adultery place her life in jeopardy. In Mandarin with English subtitles. **99m/C VHS.** Na Renhua, Deng Xiaotuang, Yu Zhang; **D:** Xie Fei. *NYF*

The Girl from Missouri 🐾🐾🐾 *One Hundred Percent Pure* 1934 Cute comedy in which Harlow tries to snag a millionaire without sacrificing her virtues. Lots of laughs and hilarious action, especially the scene where Harlow arrives at the yacht in Florida. Kelly is great as Harlow's wise-cracking girlfriend. Witty dialogue by Emerson and Loos, who also wrote "Gentlemen Prefer Blondes." **75m/B VHS, Closed Caption.** Jean Harlow, Lionel Barrymore, Franchot Tone, Lewis Stone, Patsy Kelly, Alan Mowbray, Clara Blandick, Russell Hopton; **D:** Jack Conway; **W:** Anita Loos, John Emerson. *MGM*

The Girl from Petrovka 🐾½ 1974 (PG) A high-spirited Russian ballerina falls in love with an American newspaper correspondent. Their romance is complicated by the suspicious KGB. Bittersweet with a bleak ending. **103m/C VHS, Beta.** Goldie Hawn, Hal Holbrook, Anthony Hopkins; **D:** Robert Ellis Miller; **W:** Chris Bryant, Allan Scott; **M:** Henry Mancini. *USH*

The Girl from Tobacco Row 🐾 1966 A Southern slut involved with a cache of stolen cash fools with both a convict and the sheriff. **90m/C VHS, Beta.** Tex Ritter, Rachel Romen, Earl Richards, Tim Ormond, Rita Faye, Ralph Emery; **D:** Ron Ormond. *NO*

Girl Happy 🐾 1965 The King's fans will find him in Fort Lauderdale, Florida this time as the leader of a rock 'n' roll group. His mission: to chaperone the daughter of a Chicago mobster who naturally falls for him. Why not? ♫Girl Happy; Cross My Heart and Hope to Die; Do Not Disturb; Spring Fever; Wolf Call; Do the Clam; Fort Lauderdale Chamber of Commerce; Puppet On a String; I've Got to Find About My Baby. **96m/C VHS, Beta.** Elvis Presley, Harold J. Stone, Shelley Fabares, Gary Crosby, Nita Talbot, Mary Ann Mobley, Jackie Coogan; **D:** Boris Sagal; **W:** Harvey Bulloch. *MGM*

Girl Hunters 🐾🐾½ 1963 That intrepid private eye, Mike Hammer (played by his creator, Spillane), is caught up with communist spies, wicked women, and a missing secretary. Hammer is his usual judge-and-jury character but the action is fast-paced. **103m/B VHS, Beta.** Mickey Spillane, Lloyd Nolan, Shirley Eaton, Hy Gardner, Scott Peters; **D:** Roy Rowland. *SNC, NOS, DVT*

A Girl in a Million 🎬🎬 1946
Williams dumps his verbose wife and seeks peace and quiet in a men-only War Department office. All is well until the arrival of a colonel and his daughter, mute from trauma. Finding her silence appealing, he marries her, but another trauma restores her speech. Sexist comedy may have played better in its day. **90m/B VHS.** *GB* Hugh Williams, Joan Greenwood, Naunton Wayne, Wylie Watson, Garry Marsh; **D:** Francis Searle. *NOS*

The Girl in a Swing 🎬½ 1989 (R)
An Englishman impulsively marries a beautiful German girl and both are subsequently haunted by phantoms from her past—are they caused by her psychic powers? Cliche-ridden silliness. Based on the Richard Adams novel. **119m/C VHS, Beta, LV.** Meg Tilly, Rupert Frazer, Elspet Gray, Lynsey Baxter, Nicholas Le Prevost, Jean Both; **D:** Gordon Hessler. *HBO*

Girl in Black 🎬🎬 1956
The shy daughter of a once wealthy household gets the chance to escape her genteel poverty when she falls in love with the young man boarding with her family. He is attracted to her but a shocking tragedy changes everything. In Greek with English subtitles. **100m/C VHS, Beta.** *GR* Ellie Lambetti; **D:** Michael Cacoyannis. *FCT*

Girl in Black Stockings 🎬🎬 1957
Beautiful women are mysteriously murdered at a remote, Utah hotel. Interesting, little known thriller similar to Hitchcock's "Psycho," but pre-dating it by three years. **75m/B VHS.** Lex Barker, Anne Bancroft, Mamie Van Doren, Ron Randell, Marie Windsor, John Dehner, John Holland, Diana Van Der Vlis; **D:** Howard W. Koch; **M:** Les Baxter. *FRG*

The Girl in Blue 🎬🎬 1974 (R)
A lawyer, ill at ease with his current romance, suddenly decides to search for a beautiful woman he saw once, and instantly fell in love with, years before. **103m/C VHS, Beta.** *CA* Maud Adams, David Selby, Gay Rowan, William Osler, Diane Dewey, Michael Kirby; **D:** George Kaczender.

A Girl in Every Port 🎬🎬½ 1952
Navy buddies acquire an ailing racehorse and try to conceal it aboard ship along with a healthy horse they plan to switch it with in an upcoming race. Groucho flies without his brothers in this zany film. **86m/B VHS, Beta, LV.** Groucho Marx, William Bendix, Marie Wilson, Don DeFore, Gene Lockhart; **D:** Chester Erskine. *CCB*

Girl in Gold Boots 🎬 1969
Aspiring starlet meets up with a draft evader and a biker on her way to Hollywood where she gets a job as a go-go dancer in a sleazy club. But things don't go smoothly when a murder and a drug theft are revealed. ♫Do You Want to Laugh or Cry?; For You; Hello, Michelle; One Good Time, One Good Place; Lonesome Man; You Gotta Come Down; Everything I Touch Turns to Gold; Cowboy Santa; Wheels of Love. **94m/C VHS, Beta.** Jody Daniels, Leslie McRae, Tom Pace, Mark Herron; **D:** Ted V. Mikels. *NO*

Girl in His Pocket 🎬🎬 *Amour de Poche; Nude in His Pocket* 1957
Mad scientist creates a potion that turns things into three-inch statues. He uses it mostly to have trysts with his lab assistant so his fiancee won't find out. Based on "The Diminishing Draft" by Waldemar Kaempfert. **82m/C VHS.** *FR* Jean Marais, Genevieve Page, Agnes Laurent; **D:** Pierre Kast; **C:** Ghislan Cloquet. *SNC*

The Girl in Lover's Lane 🎬🎬 1960
A drifter falls in love with a small town girl but becomes a murder suspect when she turns up dead. Interesting mainly for Elam's uncharacteristic portrayal of a village idiot. **78m/B VHS, Beta.** Brett Halsey, Joyce Meadows, Lowell Brown, Jack Elam; **D:** Charles R. Rondeau. *SNC*

The Girl in Room 2A woof! 1976 (R)
A young woman is trapped in a mansion with the elderly owner and her demented son. Routine horrorfest. **90m/C VHS, Beta.** Raf Vallone, Daniela Giordano; **D:** William Rose.

Girl in the Cadillac 🎬🎬½ 1994 (R)
Modern-day B-movie wannabe loosely adapted from the James M. Cain novella "The Enchanted Isle." 17-year-old freespirited Amanda (Eleniak) wants to get out of stifling small town Texas. She buys a bus ticket to find her long-gone daddy and winds up with not-too-smart cowpoke Rick (McNamara) instead. A bank robbery gone bad finds the twosome on the loose with $75 thou, a cherry red El Dorado convertible, and Rick's partners after them. Appealing lead performers can't overcome the cliches. **CW:** Language; some violence. **89m/C VHS.** Erika Eleniak, William McNamara, Michael Lerner, Bud Cort, Valerie Perrine, Ed Lauter, William Shockley; **D:** Lucas Platt; **W:** John Warren; **C:** Nancy Schreiber; **M:** Anton Sanko. *TTC*

The Girl in the Picture 🎬🎬½ 1986 (PG-13)
Sinclair stars in this light comedy as an unlucky photo clerk who discovers only too late that his ex-girlfriend may be the woman of his dreams. Typical understated but entertaining effort. **89m/C VHS, Beta.** *GB* John Gordon-Sinclair, Irina Brook, David McKay, Catherine Guthrie, Paul Young, Gregory Fisher; **D:** Cary Parker. *VES*

The Girl Most Likely 🎬🎬½ 1957
Light musical comedy about a romance-minded girl who dreams of marrying a wealthy, handsome man. She runs into a problem when she finds three prospects. Remake of 1941's "Tom, Dick and Harry" with Ginger Rogers. Choreography by great Gower Champion. ♫The Girl Most Likely; All the Colors of the Rainbow; I Don't Know What I Want; Balboa; We Gotta Keep Up With the Joneses; Crazy Horse. **98m/C VHS, Beta, LV.** Jane Powell, Cliff Robertson, Tommy Noonan, Kaye Ballard, Una Merkel; **D:** Mitchell Leisen. *NO*

Girl of the Golden West 🎬🎬 1938
A musical version of the David Belasco chestnut about a Canadian frontier girl loving a rogue. One of Eddy and MacDonald's lesser efforts but features Ebsen's song and dance talents. ♫Camptown Races; Shadows on the Moon; Soldiers of Fortune; Soldiers of Fortune Reprise; Shadows on the Moon Reprise; The Wind in the Trees; Liebestraum; Ave Maria; Senorita. **120m/B VHS, Beta.** Jeanette MacDonald, Nelson Eddy, Walter Pidgeon, Leo Carrillo, Buddy Ebsen, Leonard Penn, Priscilla Lawson, Bob Murphy, Olin Howlin, Cliff Edwards, Billy Bevan; **D:** Robert Z. Leonard. *MGM*

A Girl of the Limberlost 1990
A young Indiana farmgirl fights to bring her estranged parents back together, in spite of a meddling aunt and the unexplained phenomena that haunt her. Fine acting and beautiful scenery. Originally broadcast on public television as part of the "Wonderworks" family movie series, it's best appreciated by young teens. Adapted from Gene Stratton Porter's much-filmed novel. **120m/C VHS.** Annette O'Toole, Joanna Cassidy, Heather Fairfield. *HMV, FCT*

Girl on a Chain Gang woof! 1965
A girl on the run gets caught by police and does her time on a chain gang—an otherwise all-male chain gang. Predictable. **96m/B VHS, Beta.** William Watson, Julie Ange, R.K. Charles; **D:** Jerry Gross; **W:** Jerry Gross. *SNC*

The Girl on a Motorcycle 🎬🎬 *Naked Under Leather; La Motocyclette* 1968 (R)
Singer Faithfull is a bored housewife who dons black leather and hops on her motorcycle to meet up with her lover (Delon), all the while remembering their other erotic encounters. **92m/C VHS, Beta.** *GB* Alain Delon, Marianne Faithfull, Roger Mutton; **D:** Jack Cardiff. *MLB*

A Girl on Her Own 🎬🎬 1976
A young actress embarking on her first big role in Paris must also deal with family and political considerations in this drama set during the political up-heaval of 1935. **112m/C VHS.** *FR* Sophie Chemineau, Bruno La Brasca; **D:** Philippe Nahoun. *FCT*

Girl Rush 🎬 1944
Two bad vaudeville comics are stuck in California during the gold rush and are promised sacks of gold if they can persuade some women to come to a rowdy mining town. ♫Annabella's Bustle; Rainbow Valley; If Mother Could Only See Us Now; Walking Arm in Arm With Jim. **65m/B VHS, Beta.** Wally Brown, Alan Carney, Frances Langford, Vera Vague, Robert Mitchum, Paul Hurst, Patti Brill, Sarah Padden, Cy Kendall; **D:** Gordon Douglas. *TTC*

The Girl Said No 🎬½ *With Words and Music* 1937
A sleazy bookie poses as a theatrical producer in order to get even with a dance hall floozy who once stiffed him. **72m/B VHS, Beta.** Robert Armstrong, Irene Hervey, William Haines; **D:** Andrew L. Stone; **W:** Andrew L. Stone. Nominations: Academy Awards '37: Best Sound. *NOS, DVT, VYY*

Girl Shy 🎬🎬🎬 1924
Harold is a shy tailor's apprentice who is trying to get a collection of his romantic fantasies published. Finale features Lloyd chasing wildly after girl of his dreams. **65m/B VHS, Beta.** Harold Lloyd, Jobyna Ralston, Richard Daniels; **D:** Fred Newmeyer; **W:** Sam Taylor. *TLF*

Girl 6 🎬🎬½ 1996 (R)
Aspiring actress (Randle) takes job as a phone sex operator in order to make ends meet. After finally finding stardom in the world of titillating telecommunications, she starts to take her work home. Bound to be compared, unfairly and probably unfavorably, to Lee's debut "She's Gotta Have It." Terrific performance by Randle is hampered by the lack of a strong story and too many unresolved subplots. Features the obligatory Lee cameo, while Tarantino shows up as a young hotshot director. Prince provides old and new tunes (as well as his previous moniker, apparently) to the proceedings. **CW:** Explicit dialogue and nudity. **107m/C VHS.** Theresa Randle, Isaiah Washington, Ron Silver, John Turturro, Naomi Campbell, Halle Berry, Madonna, Quentin Tarantino, Debi Mazar, Peter Berg, Richard Belzer, Spike Lee, Jenifer Lewis, Michael Imperioli, Kristen Wilson, Dina Pearlman, Maggie Rush, Desi Moreno, Susan Batson; **D:** Spike Lee; **W:** Suzan-Lori Parks; **C:** Malik Hassan Sayeed; **M:** Prince. *FXV*

The Girl, the Body and the Pill 🎬 1967
Sexploitation pic from director Lewis has a high school instructor getting fired for her sex education lectures—so she continues them in the privacy of her own home. Meanwhile, her students take up playing musical beds and learn about "the pill." **?m/C VHS.** Bill Rogers, Nancy Lee Noble; **D:** Herschell Gordon Lewis. *MOV*

A Girl to Kill For 🎬½ 1990 (R)
A temptress lures a randy college guy into a plot of murder and betrayal. **85m/C VHS, Beta, LV.** Sasha Jensen, Karen Austin, Alex Cord, Rod McCary, Karen Medak; **D:** Richard Oliver. *COL*

Girl Under the Sheet 🎬 196?
A conman/archaeologist moves into an ancient castle and begins romancing a beautiful resident ghost. **89m/C VHS, Beta.** Chelo Alonso, Walter Chiari. *NO*

The Girl Who Had Everything 🎬🎬 1953
Good melodrama with top cast, intelligent script and smooth direction. Taylor plays the spoiled daughter of a criminal lawyer (Powell) who falls for her father's client (Lamas), a suave, underground syndicate boss. Remake of the 1931 film "A Free Soul," which starred Norma Shearer, Clark Gable, and Lionel Barrymore. Based on the novel of the same name by Adela Rogers St. John. **69m/B VHS.** Elizabeth Taylor, Fernando Lamas, William Powell, Gig Young, James Whitmore, Robert Burton; **D:** Richard Thorpe; **M:** Andre Previn. *MGM*

The Girl Who Spelled Freedom 🎬🎬🎬 1986
A young Cambodian girl, speaking little English, strives to adjust to life in Chattanooga, Tennessee. She faces her challenges by becoming a champion at the national spelling bee. Based on a true story. Made-for-

television. **90m/C VHS, Beta, Closed Caption.** Wayne Rogers, Mary Kay Place, Jade Chinn, Kieu Chinh, Kathleen Sisk; *D:* Simon Wincer. *DIS*

The Girl with a Suitcase 🎬🎬 *La Ragazza con la Valgia* **1960** Young nightclub singer Aida (Cardinale) falls for rich cad Marcello (Pani) and leaves her job to follow him to his family home in Parma. He was just stringing her along and instructs his 16-year-old brother Lorenzo (Perrin) to get rid of Aida. But instead Lorenzo decides to become her protector and the unlikely duo fall in love. Italian with subtitles; the original release was 135 minutes. **111m/B VHS.** *IT* Claudia Cardinale, Jacques Perrin, Corrado Pani, Luciana Angelillo, Romolo Valli, Gian Marie Volonte; *D:* Valerio Zurlini; *W:* Valerio Zurlini; *C:* Tito Santoni; *M:* Mario Nascimbene. *IVY, FCT*

The Girl with the Hat Box 🎬 **1927** Early Russian production about a poor working girl who's paid with a lottery ticket rather than rubles (an ironic pre-communist theme?). When she strikes it rich in the lottery, her boss gives chase and silent antics ensue. Silent with orchestral score. **67m/B VHS.** *RU* Anna Sten, Vladimar Fogel, Serafina Birman, Ivan Koval-Samborsky; *D:* Boris Barnet. *KIV, FCT*

The Girl with the Hungry Eyes 🎬🎬 **1994 (R)** In 1937, top fashion model and hotel owner Louise (Fulton) kills herself over a cheating fiancee. Except Louise doesn't die, instead she becomes a vampire and in the present-day, decides to return to her now-derelict haunts. Louise is determined to restore her hotel to its former glory and get her revenge on men in general. Filmed in Miami's South Beach. Adapted from a short story by Fritz Leiber. **84m/C VHS.** Christina Fulton, Isaac Turner, Leon Herbert, Bret Carr, Susan Rhodes; *D:* Jon Jacobs; *W:* Jon Jacobs; *M:* Paul Inder. *COL*

Girlfriend from Hell 🎬 **1989 (R)** The Devil inhabits the body of a teenage wallflower and turns her into an uncontrollable vamp. **95m/C VHS, Beta, LV.** Liane Curtis, Dana Ashbrook, Leslie Deane, James Daughton, Anthony Barrie, James Karen; *D:* Daniel M. Peterson; *W:* Daniel M. Peterson. *ART*

Girlfriends 🎬🎬🎬 **1978 (PG)** Bittersweet story of a young Jewish photographer learning to make it on her own. Directorial debut of Weill reflects her background in documentaries as the true-to-life episodes unfold. **87m/C VHS, Beta.** Melanie Mayron, Anita Skinner, Eli Wallach, Christopher Guest, Amy Wright, Viveca Lindfors, Bob Balaban, Kathryn Walker, Kristopher Tabori, Mike Kellin, Kenneth McMillan; *D:* Claudia Weill; *W:* Vicki Polon. Sundance Film Festival '78: Grand Jury Prize. *WAR, FRF*

Girls Are for Loving 🎬 **1973** Undercover agent Ginger faces real adventure when she battles it out with her counterpart, a seductive enemy agent. Her third adventure following "Ginger" (1970) and "The Abductors" (1971). **90m/C VHS, Beta.** Cheri Caffaro, Timothy Brown; *D:* Don Schain. *MON*

A Girl's Folly 🎬🎬 ½ **1917** A country girl falls in love with the leading man of a film shooting on location. She wants to become a rich actress, but fails miserably. The actor offers her all the luxuries she wants if she'll become his mistress. When she finally agrees, her mother shows up. What will our country maid do now? **66m/B VHS, Beta, 8mm.** Robert Warwick, Doris Kenyon, June Elvidge, Johnny Hines; *D:* Maurice Tourneur. *VYY, GPV*

Girls! Girls! Girls! 🎬🎬 **1962 (PG)** Poor tuna boat fisherman Elvis moonlights as a nightclub singer to get his father's boat out of hock. He falls for a rich girl pretending to be poor; and after some romantic trials, there's the usual happy ending. 🎵The Nearness of You; Never Let Me Go; Girls, Girls, Girls; Return to Sender; We're Coming in Loaded; A Boy Like Me, A Girl Like You; Song of the Shrimp; Earth Boy; The Walls Have Ears. **106m/C VHS, Beta.** Elvis Presley, Stella Stevens, Laurel Goodwin, Jeremy Slate, Benson Fong, Robert Strauss, Ginny Tiu, Guy Lee, Beulah Quo; *D:* Norman Taurog; *W:* Edward Anhalt; *C:* Loyal Griggs. *FOX, MVD*

Girls in Chains 🎬 ½ **1943** Girls in a reformatory, a teacher, a corrupt school official, and the detective trying to nail him. There's also a murder with the killer revealed at the beginning of the film. **72m/B VHS, Beta.** Arline Judge, Roger Clark, Robin Raymond, Barbara Pepper, Dorothy Burgess, Clancy Cooper, Sid Melton, Betty Blythe, Peggy Stewart, Francis Ford; *D:* Edgar G. Ulmer; *W:* Albert Beich; *C:* Ira Morgan; *M:* Erdody. *NOS, SNC, DVT*

Girls in Prison 🎬 ½ **1956** Anne Carson is sent to prison for a bank robbery she didn't commit, and although the prison chaplain believes her story, the other prisoners think she knows where the money is hidden. They plan a prison break, forcing Carson to go with them and get the money, but they soon run across the real robber, also searching for the loot. A below-average "B" prison movie, lacking the camp aspects of so many of these films. **87m/B VHS.** Richard Denning, Joan Taylor, Adele Jergens, Helen Gilbert, Lance Fuller, Jane Darwell, Raymond Hatton; *D:* Edward L. Cahn. *COL*

Girls Just Want to Have Fun 🎬 ½ **1985 (PG)** An army brat and her friends pull out all the stops and defy their parents for a chance to dance on a national television program. Based loosely upon Cyndi Lauper's song of the same name. **90m/C VHS, Beta, LV, Closed Caption.** Sarah Jessica Parker, Helen Hunt, Ed Lauter, Holly Gagnier, Morgan Woodward, Lee Montgomery, Shannen Doherty, Biff Yeager; *D:* Alan Metter; *C:* Thomas Ackerman; *M:* Thomas Newman. *VTR*

Girls Next Door 🎬 **1979 (R)** A bevy of boisterous beauties cavort and cause havoc in buffoon-cluttered suburbia. **85m/C VHS, Beta, LV.** Kirsten Baker, Perry Lang, Leslie Cederquist, Richard Singer; *D:* James Hong. *NO*

Girls Night Out 🎬 *The Scaremaker* **1983 (R)** Ex-cop must stop a killer who is murdering participants in a sorority house scavenger hunt and leaving cryptic clues on the local radio station. **96m/C VHS, Beta.** Hal Holbrook, Rutanya Alda, Julia Montgomery, James Carroll; *D:* Robert Deubel. *NO*

The Girls of Huntington House 🎬🎬 **1973** A teacher in a school for unwed mothers finds herself becoming increasingly absorbed in her students' lives. Made for television. **73m/C VHS.** Shirley Jones, Mercedes McCambridge, Sissy Spacek, William Windom, Pamela Sue Martin, Darrell Larson; *D:* Alf Kjellin. *ART*

Girls of the White Orchid 🎬 *Death Ride to Osaka* **1985** A naive American girl thinks she's getting a job singing in a Japanese nightclub, but it turns out to be a front for a prostitution ring run by the Japanese Yakuza. A made-for-television movie based on real stories, though the producers concentrate on the seamy side. **96m/C VHS, Beta.** Ann Jillian, Jennifer Jason Leigh; *D:* Jonathan Kaplan; *M:* Brad Fiedel. *ORI*

Girls on the Road 🎬 ½ **1973 (PG)** Two girls are just out for fun cruising the California coast, but that handsome hitchhiker turns out to be a deadly mistake. **91m/C VHS, Beta.** *CA* Kathleen Cody, Michael Ontkean, Dianne Hull, Ralph Waite, Rigg Kennedy; *D:* Thomas J. Schmidt. *UNI*

Girls Riot 🎬 **1988** Young, female juvenile delinquents have had enough! They decide to give their warden-like headmistress a taste of her own violence. **100m/C VHS, Beta.** Jocelyne Boisseau, Cornelia Calwer, Angelica Domrose, Ute Freight; *D:* Manfred Purzer.

Girls School Screamers 🎬 **1986 (R)** Six young women and a nun are assigned to spend the weekend checking the contents for sale in a scary mansion bequeathed to their school. Unfortunately, the psychotic killer inhabiting the place doesn't think that's a good idea. **85m/C VHS, Beta.** Mollie O'Mara, Sharon Christopher, Vera Gallagher; *D:* John P. Finegan. *TTV, ART*

Girls' Town 🎬 *The Innocent and the Damned* **1959** Typical bad girls and drag racing '50s flick has Van Doren sent to a correctional institute, run by nuns. This tough girl sees the error of her wicked ways and turns into a goody-two shoes. **90m/B VHS.** Mamie Van Doren, Mel Torme, Paul Anka, Ray Anthony, Maggie Hayes, Cathy Crosby, Elinor Donahue, Gigi Perreau, Jim Mitchum, Gloria Talbott, Harold Lloyd Jr., Charles Chaplin Jr.; *D:* Charles Haas; *W:* Robert Smith; *M:* Van Alexander. *REP*

Girls Town 🎬🎬 **1995 (R)** Tough look at the lives of three working-class high school seniors who are shattered by the suicide of Nikki (Ellis), the fourth member of their group, who killed herself from guilt over an undisclosed rape. Single mom Patti (Taylor), ambitious Emma (Grace), and strong-willed Angela (Harris) argue, commiserate, battle their foes (Patti's abusive boyfriend, Nikki's rapist), and lean on each other as they struggle to figure out themselves and their ambiguous futures. Lots of time's spent in the girls' bathroom at school (how realistic can you get?)*CW:* Pervasive strong language and for drug use. **90m/C VHS.** Lili Taylor, Anna Grace, Bruklin Harris, Aunjanue Ellis, Guillermo Diaz, John Ventimiglia; *D:* Denise Casano; *W:* Denise Casano, Jim McKay, Lili Taylor, Anna Grace, Bruklin Harris, Aunjanue Ellis; *C:* Russell Fine. Sundance Film Festival '96: Filmmakers Trophy; Nominations: Independent Spirit Awards '97: Best Supporting Actress (Taylor). *HMK*

Girly 🎬 *Mumsy, Nanny, Sonny, and Girly* **1970 (R)** An English gothic about an excessively weird family that lives in a crumbling mansion and indulges in murder, mental aberration, and sexual compulsion. **101m/C VHS, Beta.** *GB* Michael Bryant, Ursula Howells, Pat Heywood, Howard Trevor, Vanessa Howard; *D:* Freddie Francis.

Git! 🎬 ½ **1965** A young runaway and his faithful dog are taken in by a wealthy dog-breeder and trained by him into a crack hunting team. **90m/C VHS, Beta.** Jack Chaplain, Richard Webb, Heather North; *D:* Ellis Kadison. *COL, NLC*

Git Along Little Dogies 🎬 ½ **1937** It's cattle ranchers versus oil men with Autry caught in the middle of the petro/cow war. But Gene still finds a little time to romance the town banker's pretty daughter. **60m/B VHS, Beta.** Gene Autry, Judith Allen, Smiley Burnette, William Farnum; *D:* Joseph Kane. *NOS, VYY, DVT*

Give a Girl a Break 🎬🎬 ½ **1953** Three talented but unknown babes vie for the lead in a stage production headed for Broadway after the incumbent prima donna quits. After befriending one of the various men associated with the production, each starlet thinks she's a shoe-in for the part. Entertaining but undistinguished musical with appealing dance routines of Fosse and the Champions. Ira Gershwin, collaborating for the first and only time with Burton Lane, wrote the lyrics to two of the songs. 🎵Give the Girl a Break; In Our United State; It Happens Every Time; Nothing is Impossible; Applause, Applause; Challenge Dance. **84m/C VHS.** Marge Champion, Gower Champion, Debbie Reynolds, Helen Wood, Bob Fosse, Kurt Kasznar, Richard Anderson, William Ching, Larry Keating, Donna Martell; *D:* Stanley Donen; *M:* Andre Previn. *MGM, TTC, FCT*

Give 'Em Hell, Harry! **1975** James Whitmore's one-man show as Harry S. Truman filmed in performance on stage; Whitmore was nominated for a Tony. **103m/C VHS, Beta.** James Whitmore; *D:* Steve Binder. Nominations: Academy Awards '75: Best Actor (Whitmore). *WOV*

Give Me a Sailor 🎬🎬 ½ **1938** Hope and Whiting play brothers, and fellow Naval officers, who meet sisters Grable and Raye on shore leave. Naturally, there's comic romantic complications until a double wedding ends the farce. Not much of a musical except from Ralph Rainger and Leo Robin but the movie's fun. Based on a play by Anne Nichols. 🎵What Goes Here in My Heart?; A Little Kiss at Twilight; Give Me a Sailor; The US and You; It Don't Make Sense. **71m/B VHS.** Bob Hope, Martha Raye, Betty Grable, Jack Whiting, Clarence Kolb, Nana Bryant, Emerson Treacy; *D:* Elliott Nugent; *W:* Frank Butler, Doris Anderson. *USH*

Give My Regards to Broad Street 🎬🎬 **1984 (PG)** McCartney film made for McCartney fans. Film features many fine versions of the ex-Beatle's songs that accompany his otherwise lackluster portrayal of a rock star in search of his stolen master recordings. ♫Eleanor Rigby; Ballroom Dancing; Good Day, Sunshine; Silly Love Songs; No Values; No More Lonely Nights; Yesterday; Not Such a Bad Boy; The Long and Winding Road. **109m/C VHS, Beta, LV, Closed Caption.** *GB* Paul McCartney, Bryan Brown, Ringo Starr, Barbara Bach, Tracey Ullman, Ralph Richardson, Linda McCartney; *D:* Peter Webb. *MVD, FOX*

The Gladiator 🎬🎬🎬½ **1938** Brown stars as a mild-mannered collegiate who accidently ingests a serum which turns him into a real he-man. Things take a turn for the funniest when the effects wear off, just as he is to wrestle Man Mountain Dean. Chock-full of Brown's trademark physical humor. **70m/B VHS.** Joe E. Brown, Man Mountain Dean, June Travis, Dickie Moore, Lucien Littlefield, Robert Kent, Ethel Wales; *D:* Edward Sedgwick. *NOS*

The Gladiator 🎬½ **1986** An angry Los Angeles citizen turns vigilante against drunk drivers after his brother is one of their victims. Made for television. **94m/C VHS, Beta, LV, Closed Caption.** Ken Wahl, Nancy Allen, Robert Culp, Stan Shaw, Rosemary Forsyth; *D:* Abel Ferrara. *VTR, HHE*

Gladiator 🎬½ **1992 (R)** When suburban Golden Gloves boxing champion Tommy Riley (Marshall) is forced to move to the inner city because of his father's gambling debts, he becomes involved with an evil boxing promotor who thrives on pitting different ethnic races against each other in illegal boxing matches. Eventually Riley is forced to fight his black friend Lincoln (Gooding), even though Lincoln has been warned that another blow to the head could mean his life. Although this film tries to serve some moral purpose, it falls flat on the mat. *CW:* Language and violence. **98m/C VHS, LV, Closed Caption.** Cuba Gooding Jr., James Marshall, Robert Loggia, Ossie Davis, Brian Dennehy, Cara Buono, John Heard, Jon Seda, Lance Slaughter; *D:* Rowdy Herrington. *COL*

Gladiator Cop: The Swordsman 2 🎬½ **1995 (R)** A legendary sword, believed to have magic powers, is stolen and an ex-detective winds up fighting modern-day gladiators and a man who believes himself to be a reincarnation of Alexander the Great. *CW:* Strong violence, and for language and sexuality. **92m/C VHS.** Lorenzo Lamas. *MNC*

Gladiator of Rome 🎬 *Il Gladiatore Di Roma* **1963** A gladiator flexes his pecs to save a young girl from death at the hands of evil rulers. **105m/C VHS.** *IT* Gordon Scott, Wandisa Guida, Roberto Risso, Ombretta Colli, Alberto Farnese; *D:* Mario Costa. *SNC*

The Gladiators 🎬 *The Peace Game; Gladiatorerna* **1970** Televised gladiatorial bouts are designed to subdue man's violent tendencies in a futuristic society until a computer makes a fatal error. **90m/C VHS, Beta.** Arthur Pentelow, Frederick Danner; *D:* Peter Watkins. *NO*

Gladiators 7 🎬½ **1962** Sparta must be freed from the tyrannical rule of the Romans. In lieu of samurai or cowboys, who better than the Gladiators 7 to do the deed? Plenty of sword-to-sword action and scantily clad Italian babes. **92m/C VHS, Beta.** *SP IT* Richard Harrison, Loredana Nusciak, Livio Lorenzon, Gerard Tichy, Edoardo Toniolo, Joseph Marco, Barta Barry; *D:* Pedro Lazaga. *SNC*

Glass 🎬½ **1990** A normally complacent man is driven to the brink of savagery when a killer begins stalking his employees. **92m/C VHS.** Alan Lovell, Lisa Peers, Adam Stone, Natalie McCurry. *ATL*

The Glass Bottom Boat 🎬🎬½ **1966** A bubbly but transparent Doris Day comedy, in which she falls in love with her boss at an aerospace lab. Their scheme to spend time together get her mistaken for a spy. Made about the time they stopped making them like this anymore, it's innocuous slapstick romance with a remarkable

1960s cast, including a Robert Vaughn cameo as the Man From U.N.C.L.E. Doris sings "Que Sera, Sera" and a few other numbers. **110m/C VHS, Beta, LV, Letterbox.** Doris Day, Rod Taylor, Arthur Godfrey, Paul Lynde, Eric Fleming, Alice Pearce, Ellen Corby, John McGiver, Dom DeLuise, Dick Martin, Edward Andrews; *Cameos:* Robert Vaughn; *D:* Frank Tashlin; *W:* Everett Freeman; *C:* Leon Shamroy. *MGM*

The Glass Cage 🎬🎬 **1996 (R)** Ex-CIA agent Paul Yeager (Tyson) takes a bartending job in New Orleans' French Quarter in order to get back his exotic dancer girlfriend Jacqueline (Lewis) but the bar's jealous owner and dirty cop Montrachet (Roberts) have other plans in mind for the duo. *CW:* Gangster violence, strong sexuality, and some language. **96m/C VHS.** Richard Tyson, Charlotte Lewis, Eric Roberts, Stephen Nichols, Joseph Campanella, Richard Moll, Maria Ford, Lisa Marie Scott; *D:* Michael Schroeder; *W:* David Keith Miller; *C:* John Aronson. *ORI*

The Glass House 🎬🎬🎬 *Truman Capote's The Glass House* **1972** Alda stars as a middle-aged college professor, convicted on a manslaugter charge, who is sent to a maximum security prison and must learn to deal with life inside. Filmed at Utah State Prison, real-life prisoners as supporting cast add to the drama. Still has the power to chill, with Morrow particularly effective as one of the inmate leaders. Adapted from a Truman Capote story. Made for television. **92m/C VHS, Beta.** Alan Alda, Vic Morrow, Clu Gulager, Billy Dee Williams, Dean Jagger, Kristoper Tabori; *D:* Tom Gries; *M:* Billy Goldenberg. *MOV, HHT*

The Glass Jungle **1988** Will a cab driver save Los Angeles? When armed terrorists and the FBI battle it out in the sunny California city an innocent cabby seems to hold the solution to survival. **94m/C VHS, Beta.** Lee Canalito, Joe Filbeck, Diana Frank, Mark High, Frank Scala; *D:* Joseph Merhi. *HHE*

The Glass Key 🎬🎬 **1942** The second version of Dashiell Hammet's novel, a vintage mystery movie concerning a nominally corrupt politician (Donlevy) being framed for murder, and his assistant sleuthing out the real culprit. One of Ladd's first starring vehicles; Lake is the mystery woman who loves him, and Bendix a particularly vicious thug. **85m/B VHS, Beta, LV.** Alan Ladd, Veronica Lake, Brian Donlevy, William Bendix, Bonita Granville, Richard Denning, Joseph Calleia, Moroni Olsen, Dane Clark; *D:* Stuart Heisler. *USH*

The Glass Menagerie 🎬🎬🎬 **1987 (PG)** An aging Southern belle deals with her crippled daughter Laura, whose one great love is her collection of glass animals. The third film adaptation of the Tennessee Williams classic, which preserves the performances of the Broadway revival cast, is a solid-but-not-stellar adaptation of the play. All-star acting ensemble. **134m/C VHS, Beta, LV.** Joanne Woodward, Karen Allen, John Malkovich, James Naughton; *D:* Paul Newman; *W:* Tennessee Williams; *C:* Michael Ballhaus; *M:* Henry Mancini, Max Steiner. *USH*

The Glass Shield 🎬🎬½ **1995 (PG-13)** Timely look at racism and corruption in the Los Angeles sheriff's department as seen through the eyes of African American rookie J.J. Johnson (Boatman). His dream of being a police officer turns to disillusionment when he slowly realizes his own department is framing a black man (Ice Cube) for a murder he did not commit. First half grabs your attention, but the momentum is lost in murky plot twists and a rushed ending. Made on a shoestring, but has an interesting cast, including the reliably slimy Ironside as (what else) one of the bad cops and an almost unrecognizable Petty, who becomes Johnson's only ally on the force. **109m/C VHS, LV, Closed Caption.** Michael Boatman, Lori Petty, Michael Ironside, M. Emmet Walsh, Ice Cube, Richard Anderson, Elliott Gould; *D:* Charles Burnett; *W:* Charles Burnett; *C:* Elliot Davis; *M:* Stephen James Taylor. *TOU*

The Glass Slipper 🎬🎬🎬 **1955** In this version of the "Cinderella" saga, Caron plays an unglamourous girl gradually transformed into the expected beauty. Winwood is the fairy godmother

who inspires the girl to find happiness, rather then simply providing it for her magically. The film is highlighted by the stunning dance numbers, choreographed by Roland Petit and featuring the Paris ballet. **93m/C VHS, Beta.** Leslie Caron, Michael Wilding, Keenan Wynn, Estelle Winwood, Elsa Lanchester, Barry Jones, Amanda Blake, Lurene Tuttle; *D:* Charles Walters. *MGM, FCT*

Glass Tomb 🎬🎬 *The Glass Cage* **1955** At a circus, a man performs the world's longest fast inside a glass cage, and becomes the raison d'etre for murder. **59m/B VHS, Beta, LV.** John Ireland, Honor Blackman, Eric Pohlmann, Tonia Bern, Sidney James; *D:* Montgomery Tully. *NO*

The Glass Virgin 🎬🎬½ **199?** In 1859, young Annabella Lagrange (Mortimer) discovers that her spendthrift father, Edmund (Haver), has been hiding the secrets surrounding her birth. These revelations force Annabella to find her own way in a new life. Based on a novel by Catherine Cookson. **150m/C VHS.** *GB* Emily Mortimer, Nigel Havers, Brendan Coyle, Christine Kavanagh, Sylvia Syms, Samantha Glenn, Jan Graveson. *VCO*

Gleaming the Cube 🎬½ **1989 (PG-13)** A skateboarding teen investigates his brother's murder. Film impresses with its stunt footage only. For those with adolescent interests. **102m/C VHS, Beta, LV, Closed Caption.** Christian Slater, Steven Bauer, Min Luong, Art Chudabala, Le Tuan; *D:* Graeme Clifford; *W:* Michael Tolkin; *M:* Jay Michael Ferguson. *ART, VES*

Glen and Randa 🎬🎬½ **1971 (R)** Two young people experience the world after it has been destroyed by nuclear war. Early McBride, before the hired-gun success of "The Big Easy." **94m/C VHS, Beta, LV.** Steven Curry, Shelley Plimpton; *D:* Jim McBride; *W:* Rudy Wurlitzer, Jim McBride. *VCI, IME*

Glen or Glenda: Confessions of Ed Wood woof! *He or She; I Changed My Sex; I Led Two Lives; The Transvestite* **1953** An appalling, quasi-docudrama about transvestism, interspersed with meaningless stock footage, inept dream sequences and Lugosi sitting in a chair spouting incoherent prattle at the camera. Directorial debut of Wood, who, using a pseudonym, played the lead; one of the phenomenally bad films of this century. An integral part of the famous anti-auteur's canon. **70m/B VHS, Beta.** Bela Lugosi, Edward D. Wood Jr., Lyle Talbot, Donald Woods; *D:* Edward D. Wood Jr. *NOS, MRV, SNC*

Glengarry Glen Ross 🎬🎬🎬 **1992 (R)** A seven-character study chronicling 48-hours in the lives of some sleazy real estate men in danger of getting the ax from their hard-driving bosses. A standout cast includes Pacino as the glad-handing sales leader, Lemmon as the hustler fallen on dim prospects, and Baldwin, briefly venomous, as the company hatchet-man. Brutal and hard-edged with very strong language. Mamet scripted from his Tony-award winning Broadway play. *CW:* Language. **100m/C VHS, LV, Letterbox, Closed Caption.** Al Pacino, Jack Lemmon, Ed Harris, Alec Baldwin, Alan Arkin, Kevin Spacey, Jonathan Pryce, Bruce Altman, Jude Ciccolella; *D:* James Foley; *W:* David Mamet; *C:* Juan Ruiz-Anchia; *M:* James Newton Howard. National Board of Review Awards '92: Best Actor (Lemmon); Venice Film Festival '93: Best Actor (Lemmon); Nominations: Academy Awards '92: Best Supporting Actor (Pacino). *ART, MOV, BTV*

The Glenn Miller Story 🎬🎬🎬 **1954 (G)** The music of the Big Band Era lives again in this warm biography of the legendary Glenn Miller, following his life from the late '20s to his untimely death in a WWII plane crash. Stewart's likably convincing and even fakes the trombone playing well. ♫Moonlight Serenade; In the Mood; Tuxedo Junction; Little Brown Jug; Adios; String of Pearls; Pennsylvania 6-5000; Stairway to the Stars; American Patrol. **113m/C VHS, Beta, LV.** James Stewart, June Allyson, Harry (Henry) Morgan, Gene Krupa, Louis Armstrong, Ben Pollack; *D:* Anthony Mann; *W:* Oscar Brodney; *C:* William H. Daniels; *M:* Henry Mancini. Academy Awards '54: Best Sound; Nominations: Academy Awards

'54: Best Story & Screenplay, Scoring of a Musical *IISH HDG*

The Glimmer Man 🐾½ 1996 (R) When a vicious LA serial killer starts dispatching whole families, NY detective Jack Cole (Seagal) is teamed with local homicide detective Jim Campbell (Wayans). Since, however, this is a Seagal movie, things have to be a little different. Cole, for example, is an ex-CIA operative who has been convinced by a Buddhist monk to stop killing people and start wearing goofy Nehru jackets and prayer beads. Campbell is a couch potato who cries over old movies (or perhaps he was watching the dailies from this one). After Cole's ex-wife is killed, he's implicated; and then somehow the Russian Mafia and the CIA are brought into the mix. Cole uses his unique brand of non-violence to slash, chop and impale his way to justice. Predictable when it's not being unbelievable, this could have been called "Hard to Watch."**CW:** Strong violence, language and some nudity. 92m/ C VHS, LV, Closed Caption, DVD. Steven Seagal, Keenen Ivory Wayans, Michelle Johnson, Brian Cox, Bob Gunton, Stephen Tobolowsky, John Strong, Ryan Cutrona; **D:** John Gray; **W:** Kevin Brodbin; **C:** Rick Bota; **M:** Trevor Rabin. *WAR*

Glitch! 🐾½ 1988 (R) A throng of beautiful Hollywood hopefuls draw two youngsters unconnected with the film into posing as the film's director and producer in the hopes of conducting personal interviews on the casting couch. Straight to video. 88m/C VHS, Beta, LV. Julia Nickson-Soul, Will Egan, Steve Donmyer, Dan Speaker, Dallas Cole, Ji Tu Cumbuka, Dick Gautier, Ted Lange, Teri Weigel, Fernando Carzon, John Kreng, Lindsay Carr; **D:** Nico Mastorakis; **W:** Nico Mastorakis.

The Glitter Dome 🐾½ 1984 Two policemen discover the sleazier side of Hollywood when they investigate the murder of a pornographer. Based upon the novel by Joseph Wambaugh. Made for television. 90m/C VHS, Closed Caption. Stuart Margolin, John Marley, James Garner, John Lithgow, Margot Kidder, Colleen Dewhurst; **D:** Stuart Margolin. *REP*

Glitz 🐾🐾½ 1988 A Miami cop and an Atlantic City lounge singer team up to investigate a callgirl's death and wind up too close to a drug ring. Based on the novel by Elmore Leonard. Made for television. 96m/C VHS, Beta. Jimmy Smits, John Diehl, Markie Post, Ken Foree, Madison Mason, Robin Strasser; **D:** Sandor Stern. *WAR*

A Global Affair 🐾½ 1963 Hope is a department head in the United Nations who finds an abandoned baby in the building. The inept bachelor is wooed by a number of international beauties seeking to adopt the child for their various countries but he becomes increasingly attached to the little tyke. 84m/B VHS, Beta. Bob Hope, Lilo (Liselotte) Pulver, Michele Mercier, Yvonne De Carlo, Miiko Taka, Robert Sterling, Nehemiah Persoff, John McGiver, Mickey Shaughnessy; **D:** Jack Arnold; **W:** Charles Lederer, Arthur Marx, Bob Fisher; **C:** Joseph Ruttenberg. *MGM, FCT*

Gloria 🐾🐾 1980 (PG) She used to be a Mafia moll, now she's outrunning the Mob after taking in the son of a slain neighbor. He's got a book that they want, and they're willing to kill to get it. Trademark Cassavetes effort in which he has actors plumb their souls to discomfiting levels. 123m/ C VHS, Beta, LV. Gena Rowlands, John Adams, Buck Henry, Julie Carmen; **D:** John Cassavetes; **M:** Bill Conti. Venice Film Festival '80: Best Film; Golden Raspberry Awards '80: Worst Supporting Actor (Adams); Nominations: Academy Awards '80: Best Actress (Rowlands). *COL*

Glorifying the American Girl 🐾🐾 1930 Eaton's a chorus girl performing in the Ziegfeld Follies, which lends itself to numerous production numbers. The only film Ziegfeld ever produced. ♫What I Wouldn't Do For That Man; Blue Skies; I'm Just a Vagabond Lover; Baby Face; At Sundown; Beautiful Changes; Sam the Old Accordian Man; There Must Be Someone Waiting For Me. 96m/B VHS, Beta. Mary Eaton, Dan Healey, Eddie Cantor, Rudy Vallee; **D:** Millard Webb. *NOS, HHT, DVT*

Glory 🐾🐾 1988 O'Brien is a racehorse owner who tussles with her grandmother over how to keep the family farm open on a shoestring budget. Brennan enters the picture as the financial guru who lands them back on track, with enough left over to enter their prize filly in the Kentucky Derby. Lupton plays O'Brien's love interest. No surprises here. 100m/C VHS, Beta. Margaret O'Brien, Walter Brennan, Charlotte Greenwood; **D:** David Butler. *NO*

Glory 🐾🐾🐾½ 1989 (R) A rich, historical spectacle chronicling the 54th Massachusetts, the first black volunteer infantry unit in the Civil War. The film manages to artfully focus on both the 54th and their white commander, Robert Gould Shaw. Based on Shaw's letters, the film uses thousands of accurately costumed "living historians" (re-enactors) as extras in this panoramic production. A haunting, bittersweet musical score pervades what finally becomes an anti-war statement. Stunning performances throughout, with exceptional work from Freeman and Washington. 122m/C VHS, Beta, LV, 8mm, Letterbox, Closed Caption. Matthew Broderick, Morgan Freeman, Denzel Washington, Cary Elwes, Jihmi Kennedy, Andre Braugher, John Finn, Donovan Leitch, John Cullum, Bob Gunton, Jane Alexander, Raymond St. Jacques, Cliff DeYoung; **D:** Edward Zwick; **W:** Kevin Jarre; **C:** Freddie Francis; **M:** James Horner. Academy Awards '89: Best Cinematography, Best Sound, Best Supporting Actor (Washington); Golden Globe Awards '90: Best Supporting Actor (Washington); Nominations: Academy Awards '89: Best Art Direction/Set Decoration, Best Film Editing.*COL, FCT, BTV*

The Glory Boys 🐾½ 1984 A secret agent is hired to protect an Israeli scientist who is marked for assassination by the PLO and IRA. 78m/C VHS, Beta. Rod Steiger, Anthony Perkins, Gary Brown, Aaron Harris; **D:** Michael Ferguson. *VCO, VTR*

Glory Daze 🐾🐾 1996 (R) Gen-X comedy about graduation week for five Santa Cruz college friends/housemates. There's Jack (Affleck), Mickey (DeRamus), Rob (Rockwell), Josh (Hong), and Dennis (Stewart) who basically party and kvetch about their uncertain futures, with various girlfriends, professors, and parents around to nag the boys. Not much you haven't seen before, although a number of the cast have gone on to bigger and better things. 100m/C VHS, Closed Caption. Ben Affleck, Sam Rockwell, French Stewart, Vinnie DeRamus, Vien Hong, Alyssa Milano, Megan Ward, John Rhys-Davies, Elizabeth Ruscio, Spalding Gray, Mary Woronov; **Cameos:** Matthew McConaughey, Brendan Fraser, Matt Damon, Meredith Salenger; **D:** Rich Wilkes; **W:** Rich Wilkes; **C:** Christopher Taylor. *COL*

Glory Enough for All: The Discovery of Insulin 🐾🐾½ 1992 The drama behind the discovery of insulin in the 1920s focuses on the research of four men, sometimes not-so-friendly rivals, searching for a treatment for diabetes mellitus. Dr. Frederick Banting and science student Charles Best are granted permission by James Macleod, a Professor of Physiology at the University of Toronto, to conduct experiments on the pancreas. Macleod then assigns biochemist James Collip to assist them on developing a viable serum, an extract named insulin. Banting and Macleod were awarded the Nobel prize in 1923 for their discovery (though Banting felt Macleod was undeserving). Adapted from "The Discovery of Insulin" by Michael Bliss. Made for Canadian television. 196m/C VHS. CA R.H. Thomson, Robert Wisden, John Woodvine, Michael Zelniker, Martha Henry, Heather Hess; **D:** Eric Till; **W:** Grahame Woods. *CCC*

Glory! Glory! 🐾🐾🐾 1990 (R) Slashing satire about TV evangelism. Thomas as the meek son of founder of Church of the Champions of Christ brings in lewd female rock singer to save the money-making ministry from financial ruin. Rock music, sex, and MTV-like camera work make it worth seeing. Whitmore is a treat. 152m/C VHS, Beta, LV. Ellen Greene, Richard Thomas, Barry Morse, James Whitmore, Winston Reckert; **D:** Lindsay Anderson; **W:** Stan Daniels. *ORI, IME*

The Glory Stompers woof! 1967 Hopper prepares for his Easy Rider role as the leader of a motorcycle gang who battles with a rival leader over a woman. Very bad, atrocious dialogue, and a "love-in" scene that will be best appreciated by insomniacs. 85m/C VHS. Dennis Hopper, Jody McCrea, Chris Noel, Jock Mahoney, Lindsay Crosby, Robert Tessier, Casey Kasem; **D:** Anthony M. Lanza. *NO*

The Glory Trail 🐾½ 1936 *Glorious Sacrifice* A group of railroad workers and soldiers are constantly harassed by Indian attacks. 63m/B VHS. Tom George Duryea Keene, Joan Barclay, James Bush, Frank Melton, Walter Long; **D:** Lynn Shores. *GPV*

Glory Years 🐾 1987 Three old friends find themselves in charge of the scholarship fund at their 20th high school reunion. Unfortunately, they decide to increase the fund by gambling in Las Vegas and lose it all on a fixed fight! 150m/C VHS, Beta, Closed Caption. George Dzundza, Archie Hahn, Tim Thomerson, Tawny Kitaen, Donna Pescow, Donna Denton; **D:** Arthur Seidelman. *HBO*

The Glove 🐾½ *The Glove: Lethal Terminator; Blood Mad* 1978 (R) Ex-cop turned bounty hunter has his toughest assignment ever. It's his job to bring in a six-and-a-half foot, 250-pound ex-con who's been wreaking havoc with an unusual glove—it's made of leather and steel. 93m/C VHS, Beta. John Saxon, Roosevelt Grier, Joanna Cassidy, Joan Blondell, Jack Carter, Aldo Ray; **D:** Ross Hagen.

The Gnome-Mobile 🐾🐾 1967 A lumber baron and his two grandchildren attempt to reunite a pair of forest gnomes with a lost gnome colony. Brennan has a dual role as both a human and a gnome grandfather. Wynn's last film. Based on a children's novel by Upton Sinclair. 84m/C VHS, Beta. Walter Brennan, Richard Deacon, Ed Wynn, Karen Dotrice, Matthew Garber; **D:** Robert Stevenson; **C:** Edward Colman; **M:** Buddy Baker. *DIS, OM*

The Go-Between 🐾🐾🐾½ 1971 (PG) Wonderful tale of hidden love. Young boy Guard acts as a messenger between the aristocratic Christie and her former lover Bates. But tragedy befalls them all when the lovers are discovered. The story is told as the elderly messenger (now played by Redgrave) recalls his younger days as the go-between and builds to a climax when he is once again asked to be a messenger for the lady he loved long ago. Based on a story by L.P. Hartley. 116m/C VHS. GB Julie Christie, Alan Bates, Dominic Guard, Margaret Leighton, Michael Redgrave, Michael Gough, Edward Fox; **D:** Joseph Losey; **W:** Harold Pinter. British Academy Awards '71: Best Screenplay, Best Supporting Actor (Fox), Best Supporting Actress (Leighton); Cannes Film Festival '71: Best Film; Nominations: Academy Awards '71: Best Supporting Actress (Leighton). *COL*

Go Down Death 🐾½ 1941 In this early all-black film, a minister is caught in a moral dilemma literally between Heaven and Hell. Scenes of the afterlife are taken from early silent films. 63m/B VHS, Beta. Myra D. Hemmings, Samuel H. James, Eddy L. Houston, Spencer Williams Jr., Amos Droughan; **D:** Spencer Williams Jr. *VYY, DVT, TIM*

Go Fish 🐾🐾🐾 1994 (R) Low-budget girl-meets-girl romantic comedy finds Kia (McMillan) playing matchmaker for her roommate, energetic Max (Turner), by setting her up with shy Ely (Brodie). The opposites do, eventually, attract, with their friends eager for every detail. Good-natured and candid, with a welcome lack of melodrama.**CW:** Adult themes, blunt language, discreet nudity and sexuality. 87m/B VHS. Guinevere Turner, V.S. Brodie, T. Wendy McMillan, Anastasia Sharp, Migdalia Melendez; **D:** Rose Troche; **W:** Guinevere Turner, Rose Troche; **C:** Ann T. Rossetti; **M:** Brendan Dolan, Jennifer Sharpe. Nominations: Independent Spirit Awards '95: Best Supporting Actress (Brodie). *HMK, FCT*

Go for Broke! 🐾🐾½ 1951 Inexperienced officer Johnson leads a special WWII attack force which is made up of Japanese Americans. Sent to fight in Europe, they prove their bravery and loyalty to all. Good, offbeat story. 92m/B VHS, Beta. Van Johnson, Gianna Maria Canale, Warner Anderson, Lane Nakano, George Miki; **D:** Robert Pirosh; **C:** Paul Vogel.

Nominations: Academy Awards '51: Best Story & Screenplay. *NOS, MRV, VYY*

Go for It 🎬🎬 1983 (PG)
Oddball supercops go after a mad scientist—who has created a deadly "K"-bomb—and they encounter killer whales, karate busboys and malevolent Shirley Temple clones along the way. **109m/C VHS, Beta.** *IT* Bud Spencer, Terence Hill, David Huddleston; *D:* E.B. Clucher. *WAR*

Go for the Gold 🎬 1984
A young marathon runner risks his girlfriend's love when he decides to pursue fame and fortune. **98m/C VHS.** James Ryan, Cameron Mitchell, Sandra Horne. *ART*

Go-Get-'Em-Haines 1935
Newsman Boyd follows a fleeing bankrupt utilities tycoon onto an ocean liner for an interview only to end up trying to solve the tycoon's murder. **61m/C VHS.** William Boyd, Sheila Terry, Eleanor Hunt, Leroy Mason, Lloyd Ingraham, Jimmy Aubrey, Clarence Geldert, Louis Natheaux, Lee Shumway; *D:* Sam Newfield. *GPV*

The Go-Getter 🎬🎬 1954
Wild slapstick fun in the world of business. **?m/C VHS.** Hank McCune, Beverly Garland. *LOO*

Go, Johnny Go! 🎬🎬 1959
Rock promoter Alan Freed molds a young orphan into rock sensation "Johnny Melody." Musical performances include Ritchie Valens (his only film appearance), Eddie Cochran, Jackie Wilson. **75m/B VHS, Beta, LV.** Alan Freed, Sandy Stewart, Chuck Berry, Jimmy Clanton, Eddie Cochran, Jackie Wilson, Ritchie Valens; *D:* Paul Landres. *AOV, VTR, RXM*

Go Kill and Come Back 🎬 1968 (PG)
A bounty hunter tracks down a notoriously dangerous train robber. **95m/C VHS, Beta.** Gilbert Roland, George Helton, Edd Byrnes; *D:* Enzo G. Castellari. *MON*

The Go-Masters 🎬🎬🎬 *Mikan No Taikyoku*
1982 Historic co-production between Japan and China, centering on the ancient strategy board game "Go." A young competitor becomes obsessed with winning at any price. Episodic tale of the relationships between a Japanese and Chinese family spans 30 years and was critically acclaimed in both China and Japan. In Japanese and Chinese with English subtitles. **134m/C VHS, Beta.** *JP CH* Huang Zong-Ying, Du Peng, Yu Shao-Kang, Lui Xin, Yoshiko Mita, Keiko Matsuzaka, Mayumi Ogawa, Rentaro Mikuni, Sun Dao-Lin, Shen Guan-Chu, Misako Honno; *D:* Junya Sato, Duan Jishun. Montreal World Film Festival '83: Best Film. *FCT*

Go Now 🎬🎬🎬½ 1998
Regular guy Nick (Carlyle), a soccer-playing construction worker meets and falls in love with hotel management trainee Karen (Aubrey). All is going well until Nick starts experiencing physical problems—dropping things, double vision, numbness. As his condition worsens, it's confirmed that he's been stricken with Multiple Sclerosis. Nick goes through the usual stages of dealing with the disease, but Winterbottom's film doesn't go through the usual disease-of-the-week motions. Straightforward look at the effects of a debilitating disease doesn't create martyrs or heroes, opting instead for realistic characters and honest emotions and situations. First-rate performance by Carlyle. **81m/C VHS.** *GB* Robert Carlyle, Juliet Aubrey, James Nesbitt, Sophie Okonedo, Berwick Kaler; *D:* Michael Winterbottom; *W:* Jimmy McGovern, Paul Powell; *C:* Daf Hobson; *M:* Alastair Gavin. *NYR*

Go Tell It On the Mountain 🎬🎬½
1984 Young black boy tries to gain the approval of his stern stepfather in this fine adaptation of James Baldwin's semiautobiographical novel. Set in the 1930s; originally a PBS "American Playhouse" presentation. **100m/C VHS.** Paul Winfield, Olivia Cole, Ruby Dee, Alfre Woodard, James Bond III, Rosalind Cash, Linda Hopkins; *D:* Stan Lathan. *MON*

Go Tell the Spartans 🎬🎬🎬 1978 (R)
In Vietnam, 1964, a hard-boiled major is ordered to establish a garrison at Muc Wa with a platoon of burned out Americans and Vietnamese mercenaries. Blundering but politically interesting war epic pre-dating the flood of 1980s American-Vietnam

apologetics. Based on Daniel Ford's novel. **114m/C VHS, Beta, LV.** Burt Lancaster, Craig Wasson, David Clennon, Marc Singer; *D:* Ted Post; *W:* Wendell Mayes; *C:* Harry Stradling Jr. *VES*

Go West 🎬🎬½ 1940
The brothers Marx help in the making and un-making of the Old West. Weak, late Marx Bros., but always good for a few yucks. **80m/B VHS, Beta, LV.** Groucho Marx, Chico Marx, Harpo Marx, John Carroll, Diana Lewis; *D:* Edward Buzzell; *M:* George Bassman. MGM, CCB

Go West, Young Man 🎬🎬½ 1936
West is a movie star whose latest film is premiering in a small town, where she's naturally a sensation. Scott is the muscular farm boy who catches her eye and she decides to hang around in order to catch the rest of him as well. The censors again cut West's most overt sexual and satiric barbs. **80m/B VHS.** Mae West, Randolph Scott, Warren William, Alice Brady, Elizabeth Patterson, Lyle Talbot, Isabel Jewell; *D:* Henry Hathaway; *W:* Mae West; *C:* Karl Struss. *USH, BTV*

The Goalie's Anxiety at the Penalty Kick 🎬🎬🎬½ 1971
A chilling landmark film that established Wenders as one of the chief film voices to emerge from post-war Germany. The story deals with a soccer player who wanders around Vienna after being suspended, commits a random murder, and slowly passes over the brink of sanity and morality. A suspenseful, existential adaptation of the Peter Handke novel. In German with English subtitles. **101m/C VHS, Beta.** *GE* Arthur Brauss, Erika Pluhar, Kai Fischer; *D:* Wim Wenders. *FCT, GLV*

Goblin woof! 1993
Newlywed couple regret the purchase of their new home when the devilish creature once brought to life by the previous homeowner, a witchcraft performing farmer, is raised from the depths of hell to rip to pieces anyone in its view. Any movie whose promo says "You won't believe your eyes...until he rips them from their sockets" is sure to be a crowd pleaser. Enjoy. **75m/C VHS.** Bobby Westrick, Jenny Admire. *TEM*

God Bless the Child 🎬🎬🎬 1988
A young single mother loses her home and she and her seven-year-old daughter are forced to live on the streets. Harrowing made for television drama providing no easy answers to the plight of the homeless. **93m/C VHS, Closed Caption.** Mare Winningham, Dorian Harewood, Grace Johnston, Charlaine Woodard, Obba Babatunde, L. Scott Caldwell; *D:* Larry Elikann; *W:* Dennis Nemec; *M:* David Shire. *WOV*

God, Man and Devil 🎬🎬½ 1949
A wager between God and Satan begins this allegory of money versus the spirit. A poor Torah scribe, Hershele Dubrovner, has a life that glorifies God until Satan, disguised as a business partner, turns him greedy and dishonest. Dubrovner's success destroys both his religion and his community leaving only betrayal and abandonment. In Yiddish with English subtitles. **100m/B VHS.** Mikhail Mikhalesko, Gustav Berger; *D:* Joseph Seiden. *NCJ*

God Told Me To 🎬🎬½ *Demon* 1976 (R)
A religious New York cop is embroiled in occult mysteries while investigating a series of grisly murders. He investigates a religious cult that turns out to be composed of half-human, half-alien beings. A cult-fave Larry Cohen epic. **89m/C VHS, Beta, LV, Letterbox.** Tony LoBianco, Deborah Raffin, Sylvia Sidney, Sandy Dennis, Richard Lynch, Sam Levene, Andy Kaufman; *D:* Larry Cohen; *W:* Larry Cohen; *C:* Paul Glickman; *M:* Frank Cordell. *VTR, IME*

The Goddess 🎬🎬🎬 1958
Sordid story of a girl who rises to fame as a celluloid star by making her body available to anyone who can help her career. When the spotlight dims, she keeps going with drugs and alcohol to a bitter end. **105m/B VHS, Beta, LV.** Kim Stanley, Lloyd Bridges, Patty Duke; *D:* John Cromwell; *W:* Paddy Chayefsky. Nominations: Academy Awards '58: Best Story & Screenplay. *NO*

The Godfather 🎬🎬🎬🎬 1972 (R)
Coppola's award-winning adaptation of Mario Puzo's novel about a fictional Mafia family in the late 1940s. Revenge, envy, and parent-child conflict mix with the rituals of Italian mob life in America. Minutely detailed, with excellent performances by Pacino, Brando, and Caan as the violence-prone Sonny. Film debut of Coppola's daughter Sophia, the infant in the baptism scene, who returns in "Godfather III." The horrific horse scene is an instant chiller. Indisputably an instant piece of American culture. Followed by two sequels. **171m/C VHS, Beta, LV, 8mm.** Marlon Brando, Al Pacino, Robert Duvall, James Caan, Diane Keaton, John Cazale, Talia Shire, Richard Conte, Richard Castellano, Abe Vigoda, Alex Rocco, Sterling Hayden, John Marley, Al Lettieri, Sofia Coppola, Al Martino, Morgana King; *D:* Francis Ford Coppola; *W:* Mario Puzo, Francis Ford Coppola; *C:* Gordon Willis; *M:* Nino Rota. Academy Awards '72: Best Actor (Brando), Best Adapted Screenplay, Best Picture; Directors Guild of America Awards '72: Best Director (Coppola); Golden Globe Awards '73: Best Actor—Drama (Brando), Best Director (Coppola), Best Film—Drama, Best Screenplay, Best Score; National Board of Review Awards '72: Best Supporting Actor (Pacino), National Film Registry '90;; New York Film Critics Awards '72: Best Supporting Actor (Duvall); National Society of Film Critics Awards '72: Best Actor (Pacino); Writers Guild of America '72: Best Adapted Screenplay; Nominations: Academy Awards '72: Best Costume Design, Best Director (Coppola), Best Film Editing, Best Sound, Best Supporting Actor (Caan, Duvall, Pacino). *PAR, BTV*

The Godfather 1902-1959: The Complete Epic 🎬🎬🎬🎬 1981
Coppola's epic work concerning the lives of a New York crime family. Comprises the first two "Godfather" films, reedited into a chronological framework of the Corleone family history, with much previously discarded footage restored. **386m/C VHS, Beta, Closed Caption.** Marlon Brando, Al Pacino, Robert Duvall, James Caan, Richard Castellano, Diane Keaton, Robert De Niro, John Cazale, Lee Strasberg, Talia Shire, Michael V. Gazzo, Troy Donahue, Joe Spinell, Abe Vigoda, Alex Rocco, Sterling Hayden, John Marley, Richard Conte, G.D. Spradlin, Bruno Kirby, Harry Dean Stanton, Roger Corman, Al Lettieri; *D:* Francis Ford Coppola; *W:* Mario Puzo, Francis Ford Coppola; *M:* Nino Rota. *PAR, FCT*

The Godfather, Part 2 🎬🎬🎬🎬 1974 (R)
A continuation and retracing of the first film, interpolating the maintenance of the Corleone family by the aging Michael, and its founding by the young Vito (De Niro, in a terrific performance) 60 years before in New York City's Little Italy. Often considered the second half of one film, the two films stand as one of American film's greatest efforts, and as a 1970s high-water mark. Combined into one work for television presentation. Followed by a sequel. **200m/C VHS, Beta, LV, 8mm.** Al Pacino, Robert De Niro, Diane Keaton, Robert Duvall, James Caan, Danny Aiello, John Cazale, Lee Strasberg, Talia Shire, Michael V. Gazzo, Troy Donahue, Joe Spinell, Abe Vigoda, Marianna Hill, Fay Spain, G.D. Spradlin, Bruno Kirby, Harry Dean Stanton, Roger Corman, Kathleen Beller, John Aprea, Morgana King; *D:* Francis Ford Coppola; *W:* Mario Puzo, Francis Ford Coppola; *C:* Gordon Willis; *M:* Nino Rota, Carmine Coppola. Academy Awards '74: Best Adapted Screenplay, Best Art Direction/Set Decoration, Best Director (Coppola), Best Picture, Best Supporting Actor (De Niro), Best Original Dramatic/Comedy Score; Directors Guild of America Awards '74: Best Director (Coppola), National Film Registry '93;; National Society of Film Critics Awards '74: Best Director (Coppola); Writers Guild of America '74: Best Adapted Screenplay; Nominations: Academy Awards '74: Best Actor (Pacino), Best Costume Design, Best Supporting Actor (Gazzo, Strasberg), Best Supporting Actress (Shire); National Society of Film Critics Awards '74: Best Cinematography. *PAR, BTV*

The Godfather, Part 3 🎬🎬🎬 1990 (R)
Don Corleone (Pacino), now aging and guilt-ridden, determines to buy his salvation by investing in the Catholic Church, which he finds to be a more corrupt brotherhood than his own. Meanwhile, back on the homefront, his young daughter discovers her sexuality as she falls in love with her first cousin. Weakest entry of the trilogy is still a stunning and inevitable conclusion to the story;

Pacino adds exquisite finishing touches to his time worn character. Beautifully photographed in Italy by Gordon Willis. Video release contains the final director's cut featuring nine minutes of footage not included in the theatrical release. *CW:* Language and violence. **170m/C VHS, Beta, LV, 8mm, Closed Caption.** Al Pacino, Diane Keaton, Andy Garcia, Joe Mantegna, George Hamilton, Talia Shire, Sofia Coppola, Eli Wallach, Don Novello, Bridget Fonda, John Savage, Al Martino, Raf Vallone, Franc D'Ambrosio, Donal Donnelly, Richard Bright, Helmut Berger; *D:* Francis Ford Coppola; *W:* Mario Puzo, Francis Ford Coppola; *C:* Gordon Willis; *M:* Nino Rota, Carmine Coppola. Golden Raspberry Awards '90: Worst Supporting Actress (Coppola), Worst New Star (Coppola); Nominations: Academy Awards '90: Best Art Direction/Set Decoration, Best Cinematography, Best Director (Coppola), Best Film Editing, Best Picture, Best Song ("Promise Me You'll Remember"), Best Supporting Actor (Garcia). *PAR, FCT*

God's Bloody Acre WOOF! **1975 (R)** Three backwoods mountain-dwelling brothers kill construction workers in order to defend their land, and then begin preying on vacationers. **90m/C VHS, Beta.** Scott Lawrence, Jennifer Gregory, Sam Moree, Shiang Hwa Chyang; *D:* Harry Kerwin. *TWE*

God's Country ⚔⚔ **1946** A loner kills a man in self-defense and escapes the pursuing law by disappearing into California Redwood country with his dog. **62m/C VHS, Beta, LV.** Robert Lowery, Helen Gilbert, William Farnum, Buster Keaton; *D:* Robert Emmett Tansey. *NO*

God's Country and the Man ⚔⚔ **1937** Typical western adventurer about a cowboy out to nab a gunman who's been threatening the life of a dance hall girl. Plenty of two-fisted action when law-abiding Keene shows up. **56m/B VHS.** Tom George Duryea Keene, Betty Compson, Charlotte Henry, Charles "Blackie" King, Billy Bletcher, Ed Parker; *D:* Robert North Bradbury; *W:* Robert Emmett. *MOV*

God's Gun ⚔ *A Bullet from God* **1975 (R)** Preacher who was once a gunfighter seeks revenge on the men who tried to kill him. **93m/C VHS, Beta.** Richard Boone, Lee Van Cleef, Jack Palance, Sybil Danning; *D:* Frank Kramer. *CCB*

God's Little Acre ⚔⚔⚔ **1958** Delves into the unexpectedly passionate lives of Georgia farmers. One man, convinced there's buried teasure on his land, nearly brings himself and his family to ruin trying to find it. Based on the novel by Erskine Caldwell. **110m/B VHS, Beta.** Robert Ryan, Tina Louise, Michael Landon, Buddy Hackett, Vic Morrow, Jack Lord, Aldo Ray, Fay Spain; *D:* Anthony Mann; *W:* Philip Yordan; *M:* Elmer Bernstein. *VEC*

The Gods Must Be Crazy ⚔⚔⚔½ **1984 (PG)** An innocent and charming film. A peaceful Bushman travels into the civilized world to return a Coke bottle "to the gods." Along the way he meets a transplanted schoolteacher, an oafishly clumsy microbiologist and a gang of fanatical terrorists. A very popular film, disarmingly crammed with slapstick and broad humor of every sort. Followed by a weak sequel. **109m/C VHS, Beta, LV, Closed Caption.** N!xau, Marius Weyers, Sandra Prinsloo, Louw Verwey, Jamie Uys, Michael Thys, Nic de Jager; *D:* Jamie Uys; *M:* Johnny Bishop, John Boshoff. *FOX, FCT, TVC*

The Gods Must Be Crazy 2 ⚔⚔½ **1989 (PG)** A slapdash sequel to the original 1981 African chortler, featuring more ridiculous shenanigans in the bush. This time the bushman's children find themselves in civilization and N!xau must use his unique ingenuity to secure their safe return. **90m/C VHS, Beta, LV, Closed Caption.** N!xau, Lena Farugia, Hans Strydom, Eiros Nadies, Eric Bowen; *D:* Jamie Uys. *COL, FCT*

Gods of the Plague ⚔⚔⚔ *Gotter der Pest* **1969** Fassbinder goes noir—or grey with lots of sharp lighting—in this gangster-auteur tale of robbery gone awry. The requisite trappings of the crime genre (guys and dolls and cops and robbers) provide a vague backdrop (and a vague plot) for a moody story full of teutonic angst and alienation, and that certain Fassbinder feeling

(which need we say, isn't to everyone's taste). An early effort by the director, who remade the story later the same year as "The American Soldier" (Fassbinder acts in both). In German with (difficult-to-read) English subtitles. **92m/C VHS.** GE Hanna Schygulla, Harry Bear; *D:* Rainer Werner Fassbinder. *TPV*

The Godsend ⚔ **1979 (R)** "Omen" rip-off about a little girl who is thrust upon a couple. After adopting her, they lose their natural family to her evil ways. **93m/C VHS, Beta.** CA Cyd Hayman, Malcolm Stoddard, Angela Pleasence, Patrick Barr; *D:* Gabrielle Beaumont. *VES*

Godson ⚔⚔⚔ **1972** Emotionless assassin lives a barren life under the surveillance of Paris police who suspect him in a recent killing. He suddenly discovers that his boss has a contract out on his life. Delon's performance raises this to an above-average crime drama. **103m/C VHS.** FR Alain Delon, Nathalie Delon, Francois Perier; *D:* Jean-Pierre Melville. *PSV*

Godzilla ⚔⚔½ **1998 (PG-13)** Over-the-top remake of the 1954 cult classic has nuclear testing in France creating a giant mutant lizard to destroy all boats, piers, people, and buildings that happen to get in its way. Gone are the days of a man in a rubber suit menacing Tokyo, replaced by state-of-the-art special effects. Third rate storyline has wimpy biologist Niko Tatopoulos (Broderick) hired to track down and connect with the beast, only to realize that Godzilla has chosen the Big Apple as the birthing place for its huge brood. When various supporting characters (including Reno as a French secret agent out to destroy Godzilla) cross paths with the creature, what results looks amazingly similar to one hugely successful dinosaur movie and its sequel. Ending leaves door wide open for an inevitable sequel of its own. *CW:* Sci-fi monster action/violence. **138m/C VHS.** Matthew Broderick, Jean Reno, Maria Pitillo, Hank Azaria, Kevin Dunn, Michael Lerner, Harry Shearer, Arabella Field, Vicki Lewis, Doug Savant, Malcolm Danare; *D:* Roland Emmerich; *W:* Roland Emmerich, Dean Devlin; *C:* Ueli Steiger; *M:* David Arnold. *NYR*

Godzilla, King of the Monsters ⚔⚔½ *Gojira* **1956** An underwater prehistoric reptile emerges from the depths to terrorize Tokyo after he has been awakened by atomic testing. Burr's scenes are intercut in the American version, where he serves as a narrator telling the monster's tale in flashbacks. Ridiculously primitive special effects even in its own day. One of the first post-WWII Japanese films to break through commercially in the U.S. **80m/B VHS, Beta, LV.** JP Raymond Burr, Takashi Shimura; *D:* Terry Morse. *PAR, VES*

Godzilla 1985 ⚔½ **1985 (PG)** Godzilla is awakened from underwater slumber by trolling nuclear submarines belonging to the superpowers near Japan. The giant monster's newly acquired appetite for nuclear energy inadvertently precipitates an international incident. Burr is called in (as the only living American witness to Godzilla's destructive 1955 outburst) to help mediate the conflict. Film released to coincide with the 30th anniversary of the original. **91m/C VHS, Beta, LV.** JP Raymond Burr, Keiju Kobayashi, Ken Tanaka, Yasuka Sawaguchi; *D:* Kohji Hashimoto, Robert J. Kizer. *VTR*

Godzilla on Monster Island ⚔⚔ *Godzilla vs. Gigan* **1972** Even Godzilla himself cannot hope to take on both Ghidra and Gigan alone and hope to succeed. Therefore he summons his pal Angillus for help. Together, they offer Earth its only hope of survival. Though the terror may repel you, the movie is a must for Godzilla fans; it's his first speaking part. **89m/C VHS.** JP Hiroshi Ichikawa, Tomoko Umeda, Yuriko Hishimi, Minoru Takashima, Zan Fujita; *D:* Jun Fukuda. *SNC, MRV, IME*

Godzilla Raids Again ⚔⚔ *Gigantis, the Fire Monster; Godzilla's Counter Attack* **1959** Warner Bros. had a problem securing rights to Godzilla's name. Yearning for a change of pace, the King of

Monsters opts to destroy Osaka instead of Tokyo, but the spiny Angorous is out to dethrone our hero. Citizens flee in terror when the battle royale begins. The first Godzilla sequel. **78m/B VHS.** JP Hugo Grimaldi, Makayama, Minoru Chiaki. *VTR*

Godzilla vs. Biollante ⚔⚔ **1989 (PG)** Doctor Surigama's secret plant formula could free the industrialized world from oil dependency. He also runs his pet Godzilla experiment from the same laboratory. When terrorist thieves attempt to steal the plant formula, a petri dish mixup unleashes the abominable fury of Biollante. The return of the real Godzilla is the world's only hope, but not before another Japanese city is crushed in the reptilian rumble. **104m/C VHS, Closed Caption.** JP *D:* Kazuki Ohmori; *W:* Kazuki Ohmori. *NO*

Godzilla vs. King Ghidora ⚔½ **1991** Tokyo begins to panic when aliens from the 23rd century make an appearance. But these aliens supposedly come in peace—warning that Godzilla will soon reawaken and destroy Japan unless he can be destroyed first. But it turns out these beings aren't so benign and soon Godzilla is confronted by his arch-enemy—flying, three-headed King Ghidora. **89m/C VHS.** JP Richard Berger, Kinako Harada, Kent Gilbert, Shoji Kobayashi; *D:* Kazuki Ohmori; *W:* Kazuki Ohmori; *C:* Yoshinori Sekiguchi; *M:* Akira Ifukube. *COL*

Godzilla vs. Megalon ⚔½ *Gojira Tai Megaro* **1976 (G)** Godzilla's creators show their gratitude to misguided but faithful American audiences by transforming the giant monster into a good guy. This time, the world is threatened by Megalon, the giant cockroach, and Gigan, a flying metal creature, simultaneously. Fortuneately, the slippery hero's robot pal Jet Jaguar is on hand to slug it out side by side with Tokyo's ultimate defender. **80m/C VHS.** JP Katsuhiko Sasakai, Hiroyuki Kawase, Yutaka Hayashi, Robert Dunham; *D:* Jun Fukuda. *NOS, MRV, VTR*

Godzilla vs. Monster Zero ⚔⚔ *Monster Zero; Battle of the Astros; Invasion of the Astro-Monsters; Invasion of the Astros; Invasion of Planet X; Kaiju Daisenso* **1968 (G)** Novel Godzilla adventure with the big guy and Rodan in outer space. Suspicious denizens of Planet X require the help of Godzilla and Rodan to rid themselves of the menacing Ghidra, whom they refer to as Monster Zero. Will they, in return, leave Earth as promised, or is this just one big, fat double cross? **93m/C VHS, Beta.** JP Nick Adams; *D:* Inoshiro Honda. *PAR, FUS*

Godzilla vs. Mothra ⚔⚔ *Godzilla vs. the Thing; Godzilla vs. the Giant Moth; Godzilla Fights the Giant Moth; Mothra vs. Godzilla; Mosura Tai Goira* **1964** Mighty Mothra is called in to save the populace from Godzilla, who is on a rampage; and he's aided by two junior Mothras who hatch in the nick of time. The hesitant moth avoids the fire-breathing behemoth until succumbing to the pleadings of the Peanut Sisters to save humanity. Hilarious special effects inspire more laughter from derision than anything else. **88m/C VHS.** JP Akira Takarada, Yuriko Hoshi, Hiroshi Koizumi; *D:* Inoshiro Honda. *COL, FUS*

Godzilla vs. the Cosmic Monster ⚔⚔ *Godzilla Versus the Bionic Monster; Godzilla vs. Mechagodzilla; Gojira Tai Meka-Gojira* **1974 (G)** Godzilla's worst nightmares become a reality as he is forced to take on the one foe he cannot defeat—a metal clone of himself! To make matters worse, Earth is in dire peril at the hands of cosmic apes. We all need friends, and Godzilla is never more happy to see his buddy King Seeser, who gladly lends a claw. **80m/C VHS.** JP Masaki Daimon, Kazuya Aoyama, Reiko Tajima, Barbara Lynn, Akihiko Hirata; *D:* Jun Fukuda. *MRV, VYY*

Godzilla vs. the Sea Monster WOOF! *Nankai No Kai Ketto; Ebirah, Terror of the Deep; Big Duel in the North* **1966** Godzilla makes friends with former rival Mothra (a giant moth) and together they bash on Ebirah, an enormous lobster backed by an evil cadre of (human) totalitarians. The unrepentant crusteacean turns the tables on our heroes, however, by growing a new tentacle everytime one is ripped off. Meanwhile, a frenzied batch of helpless humans are trapped on an island about to explode, if they aren't drowned first in a shower of reptilian backwash. 80m/C VHS, Beta. *JP D:* Jun Fukuda. *DVT, MRV, HHT*

Godzilla vs. the Smog Monster 🎬

Gojira Tai Hedora; Godzilla vs. Hedora 1972 (G) Godzilla battles a creature borne of pollution, a 400-pound sludge blob named Hedora. Early 1970s period piece conveys interesting attitude towards pollution; it's treated as a sinister force that people are powerless to stop. Japanese teenagers marshal their dancing talents to combat the threat amid the hypnotic swirl of disco lighting. Great opening song: "Save the Earth." Dubbed in English. 87m/C VHS, Beta. *JP* Akira Yamauchi, Hiroyuki Kawase, Toshio Shibaki; *D:* Yoshimitu Banno. *ORI*

Godzilla's Revenge 🎬

Oru Kaiju Daishingeki 1969 A young boy who is having problems dreams of going to Monster Island to learn from Minya, Godzilla's son. Using the lessons in real life, the boy captures some bandits and outwits a bully. Uses footage from "Godzilla vs. the Sea Monster" and "Son of Godzilla" for battle scenes. One of the silliest Godzilla movies around. 70m/C VHS. *JP* Kenji Sahara, Tomonori Yazaki, Machiko Naka, Sachio Sakai, Chotaro Togin, Yoshibumi Tajima; *D:* Inoshiro Honda. *NO*

Goin' Coconuts 🎬

1978 (PG) Donny and Marie are miscast as Donny and Marie in this smarmy story of crooks and jewels. Seems someone covets the chanteuse's necklace, and only gratuitous crooning can spare the twosome from certain swindling. Big bore on the big island. 93m/C VHS. Donny Osmond, Marie Osmond, Herb Edelman, Kenneth Mars, Ted Cassidy, Marc Lawrence, Harold Sakata; *D:* Howard Morris. *NO*

Goin' South 🎬🎬🎬

1978 (PG) An outlaw is saved from being hanged by a young woman who agrees to marry him in exchange for his help working a secret gold mine. They try to get the loot before his old gang gets wind of it. A tongue-in-cheek western that served as Nicholson's second directorial effort. Movie debuts of Steenburgen and Belushi. 109m/C VHS, Beta, LV. Jack Nicholson, Mary Steenburgen, John Belushi, Christopher Lloyd, Veronica Cartwright, Richard Bradford, Danny DeVito, Luana Anders, Ed Begley Jr., Anne Ramsey; *D:* Jack Nicholson; *W:* Charles Shyer; *C:* Nestor Almendros; *M:* Perry Botkin. *PAR*

Goin' to Town 🎬🎬½

1935 Complicated yarn with West as a woman who inherits an oil field and becomes the wealthiest woman in the state. She falls for British engineer Cavanagh and decides to become a "lady" in order to get his attention. There's a subplot about Buenos Aires and a crooked horse race, an in-name-only marriage to a high society type, and a murder before Mae finally gets her man. 71m/B VHS. Mae West, Paul Cavanagh, Gilbert Emery, Ivan Lebedeff, Marjorie Gateson, Tito Coral, Monroe Owsley; *D:* Alexander Hall; *W:* Mae West; *C:* Karl Struss. *USH, BTV*

Going All the Way 🎬🎬½

1997 (R) Korean War vets Sonny Burns (Davies) and Gunner Casselman (Affleck) find themselves becoming best buds after returning to their Indianapolis hometown in 1954. Gunner's the self-confident stud, who vaguely wants to be an artist, while aspiring photographer Sonny's an anxious geek. The boys have mom troubles (Sonny's is a bible-thumper while Gunner's is a seductive flirt) and chase girls with varying success but the true bonding is strictly male. Davies is appropriately twitchy while Affleck gets to effectively use his natural charisma. Wakefield adapted from his 1970 novel. *CW:* Strong sexuality. 110m/C VHS. Jeremy Davies, Ben Affleck, Jill Clayburgh, Lesley Ann Warren, Rose McGowan, Rachel Weisz, Amy Locane; *D:* Mark Pellington; *W:* Dan Wakefield; *C:* Bobby Bukowski. *PGV*

Going Ape! 🎬🎬

1981 (PG) Danza inherits a bunch of orangutans. If the apes are treated well, a legacy of $5 million will follow. This is all you need to know. 87m/C VHS, Beta. Tony Danza, Jessica Walter, Danny DeVito, Art Metrano, Rick Hurst; *D:* Jeremy Joe Kronsberg; *M:* Elmer Bernstein. *PAR*

Going Back 🎬½

1983 Four friends reunite after college to relive a memorable summer they spent together after graduating from high school. 85m/C VHS, Beta. Bruce Campbell, Christopher Howe, Perry Mallette, Susan W. Yamasaki; *D:* Ron Teachworth. *ART, VES*

Going Bananas 🎬🎬

1988 (PG) Wacky adventure about a chimp who is being chased by a sinister circus owner. The monkey runs through Africa dragging along a boy, his caretaker, and a guide. The cast says it all. 95m/C VHS, Beta, Closed Caption. Dom DeLuise, Jimmie Walker, David Mendenhall, Herbert Lom; *D:* Boaz Davidson. *VTR*

Going Berserk 🎬🎬½

1983 (R) The members of SCTV's television comedy troupe are featured in this comedy which lampoons everything from religious cults to kung fu movies. Has moments of inspired lunacy, interspersed with more pedestrian fare. Includes wicked send-up of "Father Knows Best," with former cast member Donahue. 85m/C VHS, Beta. *CA* John Candy, Joe Flaherty, Eugene Levy, Paul Dooley, Pat Hingle, Richard Libertini, Ernie Hudson, Alley Mills, Dixie Carter, Murphy Dunne; *D:* David Steinberg. *USH*

Going for the Gold: The Bill Johnson Story 🎬🎬

1985 Biographical tale of the American downhill skier who went from hard-luck punk to Olympic champion in the 1984 games at Sarajevo, Yugoslavia. 100m/C VHS. Anthony Edwards, Dennis Weaver, Sarah Jessica Parker, Deborah Van Valkenburgh, Wayne Northrop; *D:* Don Taylor. *COL*

Going Hollywood 🎬🎬🎬

1933 Amusing musical/romantic fluff about a French teacher (Davies) who falls in love with a radio crooner (Crosby in his first MGM film). He's got the movie bug and heads for Hollywood, where he becomes an overnight sensation with a sultry costar (D'Orsay). Davies follows and proceeds to get Crosby out of D'Orsay's clutches and winds up replacing her rival in the film, promptly becoming a star herself. The underrated Davies was a fine light comedienne and supplied glamour to the production as well. Kelly, in her film debut, supplied the slapstick. The last Hearst-Cosmopolitan production made with MGM. ♫Temptation; We'll Make Hay While the Sun Shines; Going Hollywood; Our Big Love Scene; After Sundown; Cinderella's Fella; Beautiful Girl; Just an Echo in the Valley. 78m/B VHS. Marion Davies, Bing Crosby, Fifi d'Orsay, Stuart Erwin, Patsy Kelly, Ned Sparks; *D:* Raoul Walsh; *W:* Donald Ogden Stewart. *MGM*

Going Home 🎬🎬½

1986 During WWI, Canadian soldiers held in British camps awaiting transport back home stage a riot over the endless delays and intolerable conditions. A fact-based story of the events leading up to this tragedy. 100m/C VHS. Nicholas Campbell, Paul Maxwell, Eugene Lipinski. *NO*

Going in Style 🎬🎬🎬½

1979 (PG) Three elderly gentlemen, tired of doing nothing, decide to liven up their lives by pulling a daylight bank stick-up. They don't care about the consequences because anything is better than sitting on a park bench all day long. The real fun begins when they get away with the robbery. Great cast makes this a winner. 91m/C VHS, Beta. George Burns, Art Carney, Lee Strasberg; *D:* Martin Brest; *W:* Martin Brest. *WAR*

Going My Way 🎬🎬🎬½

1944 A musical-comedy about a progressive young priest assigned to a downtrodden parish who works to get the parish out of debt, but clashes with his elderly curate, who's set in his ways. Followed by "The Bells of St. Mary's." Fitzgerald's Oscar-winning Supporting Actor performance was also nominated in the Best Actor category. ♫The Day After

Forever; Swinging on a Star; Too-ra-loo-ra-loo-ra; Going My Way; Silent Night; Habanera; Ave Maria. 126m/B VHS, Beta, LV. Bing Crosby, Barry Fitzgerald, Rise Stevens, Frank McHugh, Gene Lockhart, Porter Hall; *D:* Leo McCarey; *W:* Frank Butler, Frank Cavett, Leo McCarey; *C:* Lionel Lindon. Academy Awards '44: Best Actor (Crosby), Best Director (McCarey), Best Picture, Best Screenplay, Best Song ("Swinging on a Star"), Best Story, Best Supporting Actor (Fitzgerald); Golden Globe Awards '45: Best Director (McCarey), Best Film—Drama, Best Supporting Actor (Fitzgerald); New York Film Critics Awards '44: Best Actor (Fitzgerald), Best Director (McCarey), Best Film; Nominations: Academy Awards '44: Best Actor (Fitzgerald), Best Black and White Cinematography, Best Film Editing. *USH, IGP, BTV*

Going Overboard 🎬

Babes Ahoy 1989 (R) Cruise ship waiter dreams of becoming a comedian and gets his big break when the ship's comic disappears. 99m/C VHS. Adam Sandler, Burt Young, Billy Zane, Peter Berg; *D:* Valerie Breiman. *THV*

Going Places 🎬🎬🎬

Les Valseuses; Making It 1974 (R) A cynical, brutal satire about two young thugs traversing the French countryside raping, looting and cavorting as they please. Moreau has a brief role as an ex-con trying to go straight. An amoral, controversial comedy that established both its director and two stars. In French with English subtitles or dubbed. 122m/C VHS, Beta, LV, Letterbox. *FR* Gerard Depardieu, Patrick Dewaere, Miou-Miou, Isabelle Huppert, Jeanne Moreau, Brigitte Fossey; *D:* Bertrand Blier; *W:* Bertrand Blier. *COL, INT*

Going to Congress/Don't Park There

1924 Two typical silent Rogers shorts. With original organ score. 57m/B VHS, Beta, 8mm. Will Rogers. *VYY*

Going to Town 🎬

1944 Radio team Lum and Abner in one of their last films, as two conmen who scheme to make money from a phony oil well. 77m/B VHS, Beta. Barbara Hale, Grady Sutton, Florence Lake. *GVV*

Going Under 🎬

1991 (PG) Subsurface military satire about the U.S.S. Sub Standard, the worst nuclear vessel in the Navy. It's so poorly constructed that the brass would rather sink than inspect it—if only they could. Interesting cast sinks with script headed for dry dock. 81m/C VHS, Beta, Closed Caption. Bill Pullman, Wendy Schaal, Ned Beatty, Robert Vaughn, Bud Cort, Michael Winslow. *WAR*

Going Undercover 🎬

1988 (PG-13) A bumbling private investigator is hired to protect a rich, beautiful, and spoiled young woman on her European vacation. Poor excuse for a comedy. 90m/C VHS, Beta, LV. Lea Thompson, Jean Simmons, Chris Lemmon; *D:* James Kenelm Clarke. *THV*

The Gold & Glory 🎬

1988 (PG-13) Two brothers, one a musician, the other an athlete, vie for the affections of the same girl by competing in a footrace for a golden purse. 102m/C VHS, Beta, LV. Colin Friels, Josephine Smulders, Grant Kenny. *ART*

Gold Diggers of 1933 🎬🎬🎬½

1933 In this famous period musical, showgirls help a songwriter save his Busby Berkeley-choreographed show. Followed by two sequels. ♫We're in the Money; Shadow Waltz; I've Got to Sing a Torch Song; Pettin' in the Park; Remember My Forgotten Man. 96m/B VHS, Beta, LV. Joan Blondell, Ruby Keeler, Aline MacMahon, Dick Powell, Guy Kibbee, Warren William, Ned Sparks, Ginger Rogers; *D:* Mervyn LeRoy. Nominations: Academy Awards '33: Best Sound. *MGM, FOX*

Gold Diggers of 1935 🎬🎬🎬

1935 The second Gold Diggers film, having something to do with a New England resort, romance, and a charity show put on at the hotel. Plenty of Berkeleian large-scale drama, especially the bizarre, mock-tragic "Lullaby on Broadway" number, which details the last days of a Broadway baby. ♫I'm Going Shopping With You; The Words Are in My Heart; Lullaby of Broadway. 95m/B VHS, Beta, LV. Dick Powell, Adolphe Menjou, Gloria Stuart, Alice Brady, Frank McHugh, Glenda Farrell, Grant Mitchell, Hugh Herbert, Wini Shaw; *D:* Busby Berkeley; *C:* George Barnes.

Academy Awards '35: Best Song ("Lullaby of Broadway"). *MGM, MLB*

Gold Diggers: The Secret of Bear Mountain
♂♂½ 1995 (PG) Thirteen-year-old Beth (Ricci) moves to the small town of Wheaton, Washington, and forms a close-knit friendship with rebellious tomboy Jody (Chlumsky). Together, the girls set out on a treasure hunt that takes them into a dangerous trek through sea-coast mountain terrain. The grownups are dumb (and the story's fairly boring) but the two heroines have real appeal. **94m/C VHS, LV, Closed Caption.** Christina Ricci, Anna Chlumsky, Polly Draper, Brian Kerwin, Diana Scarwid, David Keith; **D:** Kevin J. Dobson; **W:** Barry Glasser; **C:** Ross Berryman; **M:** Joel McNeely. *USH*

The Gold of Naples
♂♂♂ *L'Oro Di Napoli* 1954 A four-part omnibus film about life in Naples, filled with romance and family tragedies, by turns poignant, funny and pensive. Originally six tales; two were trimmed for U.S. release. In Italian with subtitles. **107m/B VHS, Beta.** *IT* Vittorio De Sica, Eduardo de Filippo, Paolo Stoppa, Sophia Loren, Silvana Mangano; **D:** Vittorio De Sica. *NOS, FCT*

Gold of the Amazon Women
♂ *Amazon Women* 1979 When two explorers set out to find gold, they stumble onto a society of man-hungry women who follow them into the urban jungle of Manhattan. Made for television. There is also a European "R" rated version. **94m/C VHS, Beta.** Bo Svenson, Anita Ekberg, Bond Gideon, Donald Pleasence; **D:** Mark L. Lester.

Gold Raiders
♂ 1951 Larry, Moe, and Shemp team up with an insurance agent to take on the bad guys in the wild west. The Stooges are long past their prime. **56m/B VHS.** George O'Brien, Moe Howard, Moe Howard, Shemp Howard, Larry Fine, Sheila Ryan, Clem Bevans, Lyle Talbot; **D:** Edward L. Bernds.

Gold Raiders
♂½ 1984 Team of secret agents are sent to the Jungles of Laos to find a plane carrying $200 million worth of gold, and nothing will get in their way. **106m/C VHS, Beta.** Robert Ginty, Sarah Langenfeld, William Steven.

The Gold Rush
♂♂♂♂ 1925 Chaplin's most critically acclaimed film. The best definition of his simple approach to film form; adept maneuvering of visual pathos. The "Little Tramp" searches for gold and romance in the Klondike in the mid-1800s. Includes the dance of the rolls, pantomime sequence of eating the shoe, and Chaplin's lovely music. **85m/B VHS, Beta, LV, 8mm.** Charlie Chaplin, Mack Swain, Tom Murray, Georgia Hale; **D:** Charlie Chaplin. National Film Registry '92. *CNG, NOS, CAB*

Gold Rush/Payday
1925 Chaplin drifts along the Arctic tundra, searching for gold and love in "The Gold Rush." In "Payday," he goes out drinking with his buddies. **92m/B VHS, Beta.** Charlie Chaplin, Georgia Hale, Mack Swain; **D:** Charlie Chaplin. *FOX*

Golden Age of Comedy
1958 The great comedians of silent cinema are seen in clips from some of their funniest films. **78m/B VHS, Beta, LV.** Ben Turpin, Harry Langdon, Will Rogers, Jean Harlow, Carole Lombard, Stan Laurel, Oliver Hardy, The Keystone Cops. *MLB*

Golden Boy
♂♂♂ 1939 Holden plays a young and gifted violinist who earns money for his musical education by working as a part-time prizefighter. Fight promoter Menjou has Stanwyck cozy up to the impressionable young man to convince him to make the fight game his prime concern. She's successful but it leads to tragedy. Holden's screen debut, with Cobb as his immigrant father and Stanwyck successfully slinky as the corrupting love interest. Classic pugilistic drama with well-staged fight scenes. Based on Clifford Odets' play with toned down finale. **99m/B VHS, Beta, LV.** William Holden, Adolphe Menjou, Barbara Stanwyck, Lee J. Cobb, Joseph Calleia, Sam Levene, Don Beddoe, Charles Halton; **D:** Rouben Mamoulian; **W:** Daniel

Taradash, Victor Heerman, Sarah Y. Mason. Nominations: Academy Awards '39: Best Original Score. *GKK*

The Golden Child
♂♂ 1986 (PG-13) When a Tibetan child with magic powers is kidnapped and transported to Los Angeles, Chandler, a professional "finder of lost children" must come to the rescue. The search takes him through Chinatown in a hunt that cliches every Oriental swashbuckler ever made. Good fun. **94m/C VHS, Beta, LV, 8mm, Closed Caption.** Eddie Murphy, Charlotte Lewis, Charles Dance, Victor Wong, Randall "Tex" Cobb, James Hong; **D:** Michael Ritchie; **M:** Michel Colombier. *PAR*

The Golden Coach
♂♂♂ *Le Carrosse D'Or* 1952 Based on a play by Prosper Merimee, the tale of an 18th-century actress in Spanish South America who takes on all comers, including the local viceroy who creates a scandal by presenting her with his official coach. Rare cinematography by Claude Renoir. **101m/C VHS, Beta, LV.** *FR* Anna Magnani, Odoardo Spadaro, Nada Fiorelli, Dante Rino, Duncan Lamont; **D:** Jean Renoir; **C:** Claude Renoir. *FCT, CRC, INT*

Golden Demon
♂♂½ *Konjiki Yasha* 1953 An acclaimed Japanese epic, from the novel by Koyo Ozaki, about the destructive powers of wealth on the lives of two star-crossed lovers in medieval Japan. In Japanese with English subtitles. **95m/C VHS, Beta.** *JP* Jun Negami, Fujiko Yamamoto; **D:** Koji Shima. *NLC*

Golden Earrings
♂♂½ 1947 Enjoyable, yet incredulous story about British agent Milland joining up with gypsy Dietrich for espionage work. Absurd film was so bad it became a camp classic overnight. Although Dietrich and Milland couldn't stand each other and battled constantly during production, the movie did quite well at the boxoffice. Based on a novel by Yolanda Foldes. **95m/B VHS, Closed Caption.** Ray Milland, Marlene Dietrich, Bruce Lester, Dennis Hoey, Quentin Reynolds, Reinhold Schunzel, Ivan Triesault, Mitchell Leisen; **W:** Abraham Polonsky, Frank Butler, Helen Deutsch; **C:** Daniel F. Fapp. *USH, FCT*

Golden Exterminators
♂ 197? Two brothers battle the forces of evil who have killed their martial arts master with the heels of their formidable feet. **86m/C VHS, Beta.** Raymond Chan. *UNI*

Golden Gate
♂♂ 1993 (R) Young Fed Dillon is thrown into the hysteria of the communist witch hunt in 1952 San Francisco. He snares Song, a Chinese labor activist, on some very dubious charges. Ten years later he finds himself getting involved with Song's daughter Marilyn (Chen), who knows nothing about her lover's involvement with her family. Then she finds out. Everchanging moods, sometimes film noir, sometimes a love story, sometimes a nostalgic look back, are confusing. Promising storyline meanders and fades as Director Madden tries to do too much in a short time. Beware of broad stereotypes in every character. **95m/C VHS, LV, Closed Caption.** Matt Dillon, Joan Chen, Bruno Kirby, Teri Polo, Tzi Ma, Stan Egi, Peter Murnik, Jack Shearer, George Giudall; **D:** John Madden; **W:** David Henry Hwang; **C:** Bobby Bukowski; **M:** Elliot Goldenthal. *TOU*

Golden Lady
♂½ 1979 Beautiful woman leads her female gang in a deadly game of international intrigue. **90m/C VHS, Beta.** Christina World, Suzanne Danielle, June Chadwick; **D:** Joseph Jose Ramon Larraz. *NO*

Golden Rendezvous
♂♂ *Nuclear Terror* 1977 A tale of treachery aboard a "gambler's paradise" luxury liner which is hijacked and held for ransom. Based on Alistair MacLean's novel. **103m/C VHS, Beta.** Richard Harris, David Janssen, John Carradine, Burgess Meredith, Ann Turkel, John Vernon; **D:** Ashley Lazarus. *VES*

The Golden Salamander
♂♂ 1951 Howard shines in otherwise lackluster adventure about archaeologist searching for ancient ruins in Tunisia who must deal with gun runners and their evil leader, while torridly romancing a beautiful

Tunisian girl. Filmed on location in Tunis. Based on the novel by Victor Canning. **96m/B VHS.** *GB* Trevor Howard, Anouk Aimee, Herbert Lom, Miles Malleson, Walter Rilla, Jacques Sernas, Wilfrid Hyde-White, Peter Copely, Eugene Deckers, Henry Edwards, Marcel Poncin, Percy Walsh, Sybilla Binder, Kathleen Boutall, Valentine Dyall; **D:** Ronald Neame; **C:** Oswald Morris. *FCT*

The Golden Seal
♂♂♂½ 1983 (PG) Tale of a small boy's innocence put in direct conflict, because of his love of a rare wild golden seal and her pup, with the failed dreams, pride and ordinary greed of adults. **94m/C VHS, Beta, LV, 8mm.** Steve Railsback, Michael Beck, Penelope Milford, Torquil Campbell; **D:** Frank Zuniga; **M:** John Barry.

The Golden Stallion
♂♂½ 1949 Trigger falls in love with a stunning mare. He sees her villainous owners abusing her and kills them. Roy takes the blame for his equine pal, but true love triumphs to save the day. **67m/B VHS.** Roy Rogers, Dale Evans, Estelita Rodriguez, Pat Brady, Douglas Evans, Frank Fenton; **D:** William Witney. *REP*

Golden Sun
♂ 198? Young Kung Fu student decides to investigate the death of his hero, Bruce Lee, and comes up against a sinister conspiracy. **90m/C VHS, Beta.** Lei Hsiao Lung, Chen Pei Ling, Ou-Yang Chung. *UNI*

The Golden Triangle
♂½ 1980 (PG) Big battle of the drug pushers set in the mountainous region surrounded by Laos, Thailand, and Burma. Rival gangs fight for control of the world's opium crop. **90m/C VHS, Beta.** Lo Lieh, Sambat Metanen, Tien Ner. *MGI*

Golden Voyage of Sinbad
♂♂½ 1973 (G) In the mysterious ancient land of Lemuria, Sinbad and his crew encounter magical and mystical creatures. A statue of Nirvana comes to life and engages in a sword fight with Sinbad. He later meets up with a one-eyed centaur and a griffin. Ray Harryhausen can once again claim credit for the unusual and wonderful mythical creatures springing to life. **105m/C VHS, Beta, LV, Closed Caption.** John Phillip Law, Caroline Munro, Tom Baker, Douglas Wilmer, Martin Shaw, John David Garfield, Gregoire Aslan; **D:** Gordon Hessler; **C:** Ted Moore; **M:** Miklos Rozsa. *COL, MLB*

Goldeneye
♂♂♂ 1995 (PG-13) Bond is back, in the long-awaited (eight years) debut of Brosnan as legendary Brit agent 007. Since we're through the Cold War, Bond has to make do with the villainy of the Russian Mafia, who are planning to sabotage global financial markets utilizing the "Goldeneye" satellite weapon. There's a spectacularly impossible stunt to start things out in familiar territory and lots more noisy (if prolonged) action pieces. Brosnan (who looks great in a tux) is slyly self-aware that his character is more myth than man and Janssen does a suitably over-the-top job as bad Bond girl Xenia Onatopp. Tina Turner sings the dreary title track. **CW:** Action/violence and some sexuality. **130m/C VHS, LV, Closed Caption, DVD.** Pierce Brosnan, Famke Janssen, Sean Bean, Izabela Scorupco, Joe Don Baker, Robbie Coltrane, Judi Dench, Tcheky Karyo, Gottfried John, Alan Cumming, Desmond Llewelyn, Michael Kitchen, Serena Gordon, Samantha Bond, Minnie Driver; **D:** Martin Campbell; **W:** Jeffrey Caine, Michael France; **C:** Phil Meheux; **M:** Eric Serra. Blockbuster Entertainment Awards '96: Action Actor, Theatrical (Brosnan). *MGM*

Goldengirl
♂♂ 1979 (PG) A neo-Nazi doctor tries to make a superwoman of his daughter who has been specially fed, exercised, and emotionally conditioned since childhood to run in the Olympics. Anton's starring debut. **107m/C VHS, Beta.** Susan Anton, James Coburn, Curt Jurgens, Robert Culp, Leslie Caron, Harry Guardino, Jessica Walter; **D:** Joseph Sargent; **M:** Bill Conti. *COL*

Goldenrod
♂½ 1977 A successful rodeo champion is forced to reevaluate his life when he sustains a crippling accident in the ring. Made for television. **100m/C VHS, Beta.** *CA* Tony LoBianco, Gloria Carlin, Donald Pleasence, Donnelly Rhodes; **D:** Harvey Hart.

Goldfinger 🐾🐾🐾 1964 **(PG)** Ian Fleming's James Bond, Agent 007, attempts to prevent international gold smuggler Goldfinger and his pilot Pussy Galore from robbing Fort Knox. Features villainous assistant Oddjob and his deadly bowler hat. The third in the series is perhaps the most popular. Shirley Bassey sings the theme song. The laserdisc edition includes audio interviews with the director, the writer, the editor, and the production designer; music and sound effects/dialogue separation; publicity stills, movie posters, trailers, and on-location photos. A treat for Bond fans. **117m/C VHS, Beta, LV, Letterbox, Closed Caption.** *GB* Sean Connery, Honor Blackman, Gert Frobe, Shirley Eaton, Tania Mallet, Harold Sakata, Cec Linder, Bernard Lee, Lois Maxwell, Desmond Llewelyn, Nadja Regin; *D:* Guy Hamilton; *C:* Ted Moore; *M:* John Barry. Academy Awards '64: Best Sound Effects Editing. *MGM, CRC, TLF*

Goldilocks & the Three Bears 1983 Entry from "Faerie Tale Theatre" tells the story of Goldilocks, who wanders through the woods and finds the home of three bears—only in this version Goldilocks is a nasty child, and it's the bears who'll get your sympathy. **60m/C VHS, Beta, LV, Closed Caption.** Tatum O'Neal, Alex Karras, Brandis Kemp, Donovan Scott, Hoyt Axton, John Lithgow, Carole King; *D:* Gilbert Cates. *KUI, FOX, FCT*

The Goldwyn Follies 🐾🐾 1938 Lavish disjointed musical comedy about Hollywood. A movie producer chooses a naive girl to give him advice on his movies. George Gershwin died during the filming. ♫ Romeo and Juliet; Water Nymph; Here, Pussy, Pussy; Serenade To a Fish; Love Walked In; Love is Here to Stay; Spring Again; I Was Doing Alright; La Serenata. **115m/C VHS, Beta, LV.** Adolphe Menjou, Vera Zorina, The Ritz Brothers, Helen Jepson, Phil Baker, Bobby Clark, Ella Logan, Andrea Leeds, Edgar Bergen; *D:* George Marshall; *C:* Gregg Toland; *M:* George Gershwin, Ira Gershwin. Nominations: Academy Awards '38: Best Interior Decoration, Best Score. *HBO*

Goldy: The Last of the Golden Bears 🐾½ 1984 Orphaned child and a lonely prospector risk their lives to save a Golden Bear from a circus owner. Followed by "Goldy 2: The Saga of the Golden Bear." **91m/C VHS, Beta.** *ART, VES*

Goldy 2: The Saga of the Golden Bear 🐾 1985 Continues the adventures in the High Sierras of an orphan girl and her friend, the Golden Bear. **96m/C VHS, Beta.** *ART, VES*

The Golem 🐾🐾🐾½ *Der Golem, wie er in die Welt kam* 1920 A huge clay figure is given life by a rabbi in hopes of saving the Jews in the ghetto of medieval Prague. Rarely seen Wegener expressionist myth-opus that heavily influenced the "Frankenstein" films of the sound era. **80m/B VHS, Beta.** *GE* Paul Wegener, Albert Steinruck, Ernst Deutsch, Lyda Salmonova, Otto Gebuehr, Max Kronert, Loni Nest, Greta Schroder, Hans Sturm; *D:* Carl Boese, Paul Wegener; *W:* Henrik Galeen, Paul Wegener; *C:* Karl Freund. *VYY, SNC, MRV*

Goliath Against the Giants 🐾½ *Goliath Contro I Giganti; Goliat Contra Los Gigantes; Goliath and the Giants* 1963 Goliath takes on Bokan, who has stolen his throne. Goliath must fight Amazons, storms, and sea monsters to save the lovely Elea. Goliath conquers all. **95m/C VHS, Beta.** *IT SP* Brad Harris, Gloria Milland, Fernando Rey, Barbara Carroll; *D:* Guido Malatesta. *SNC*

Goliath and the Barbarians 🐾🐾 *Il Terror Dei Baraberi* 1960 Goliath and his men go after the barbarians who are terrorizing and ravaging the Northern Italian countryside during the fall of the Roman Empire. A basic Reeves muscleman epic. **86m/C VHS, Beta.** *IT* Steve Reeves, Bruce Cabot; *D:* Carlo Campogalliani; *M:* Les Baxter. *MGM*

Goliath and the Dragon woof! *La Vendetta De Ercole* 1961 Even Goliath must have doubts as he is challenged by the evil and powerful King Eurystheus. A must for fans of ridiculous movies with ridiculous monsters. **90m/C VHS, Beta.** *IT FR*

Bruce Cabot, Mark Forest, Broderick Crawford, Gaby Andre, Leonora Ruffo; *D:* Vittorio Cottafavi; *M:* Les Baxter. *SNC*

Goliath and the Sins of Babylon 🐾🐾 *Maciste, L'Eroe Piu Grande Del Mondo* 1964 Well-sculpted Forest plays yet another mesomorph to the rescue in this poorly dubbed spaghetti legend. Goliath must spare 24 virgins whom the evil Crisa would submit as human sacrifice. Forest—who played the mythic Maciste in a number of films—was randomly assigned the identity of Goliath, Hercules, or Samson for U.S. viewing; go figure. **80m/C VHS.** *IT* Mark Forest, Eleanora Bianchi, Jose Greco, Giuliano Gemma, Paul Muller; *D:* Michele Lupo. *SNC*

Goliath Awaits 🐾🐾 1981 Harmon plays an oceanographer who discovers a ship that was sunk by German U-boats during WWI. Nothing much new there, except that the survivors still reside on board the vessel, some 40 years after the oceanliner was torpedoed. And get this: they're living a quasi-Utopian existence. Kind of hard to swallow. Made for TV, it originally aired in two parts. **110m/C VHS, LV.** Mark Harmon, Robert Forster, Christopher Lee, Eddie Albert, John Carradine, Alex Cord, Emma Samms, Jean Marsh; *D:* Kevin Connor; *M:* George Duning. *THV*

Goliathon woof! *The Mighty Peking Man* 1979 A ten-story-tall gorilla resides in the jungle and is sought by a group of Hong Kong businessman who want to display the creature. Johnny, the hunter hired to find the beast, discovers both the gorilla and a beautiful jungle goddess. Incredibly campy, with badly dubbed and hilariously awful dialogue. **81m/C VHS.** *HK* Lee Hassen, Evelyn Kraft. *VYY*

Gone Are the Days 🐾🐾½ *The Man From C.O.T.T.O.N., Purlie Victorious* 1963 Shaky adaptation of the play, "Purlie Victorious." A black preacher wants to cause the ruin of a white plantation owner. Alda's screen debut. **97m/B VHS, Beta.** Ossie Davis, Ruby Dee, Sorrell Booke, Godfrey Cambridge, Alan Alda, Beah Richards; *D:* Nicholas Webster; *W:* Ossie Davis; *C:* Boris Kaufman. *DIS*

Gone Are the Days 🐾🐾 1984 Government agent (Korman) is assigned to protect a family who witnessed an underworld shooting, but the family would like to get away from both the mob and the police. Made-for-cable Disney comedy is well-acted but done in by cliches. **90m/C VHS, Beta.** Harvey Korman, Susan Anspach, Robert Hogan; *D:* Gabrielle Beaumont. *DIS*

Gone Fishin' woof! 1997 **(PG)** Long delayed comedy (thanks to some on-set disasters and well founded doubts about quality) finds best friends and bassmasters of disaster Gus (Glover) and Joe (Pesci) thinking they're going on a peaceful fishing trip. Instead they meet two women (Arquette and Whitfield) who are on the trail of a dangerous British con artist (Brimble). Pesci and Glover have reeled in one stinky old shoe of a movie here. Granted, it's not entirely their fault, but they shouldn't have known better. There are no surprises (or laughs) as every joke and set piece is tipped way ahead of time, just so you won't miss it. Less fun than a fish hook in the eye. **94m/C VHS, LV, Closed Caption.** Danny Glover, Joe Pesci, Rosanna Arquette, Lynn Whitfield, Willie Nelson, Nick Brimble, Gary Grubbs, Carol Kane, Edythe Davis; *D:* Christopher Cain; *W:* Jeffrey Abrams, Jill Mazursky Cody; *C:* Dean Semler; *M:* Randy Edelman. *TOU*

Gone in 60 Seconds 🐾½ 1974 Car thief working for an insurance adjustment firm gets double-crossed by his boss and chased by the police. Forty minutes are consumed by a chase scene which destroyed more than 90 vehicles. **105m/C VHS, Beta.** H.B. Halicki, Marion Busia, George Cole, James McIntyre, Jerry Daugirda; *D:* H.B. Halicki.

Gone to Ground 🐾 1976 Mad killer terrorizes a group of vacationers who are trapped in an isolated beach house. **74m/C VHS, Beta.** Charles Tingwell, Elaine Lee, Eric Oldfield, Marion Johns, Robyn

Gibbes, Judy Lynne, Dennis Grosvenor, Alan Penney, Marcus Hale. *NO*

Gone with the West 🐾½ 1972 Little Moon and Jud McGraw seek revenge upon the man who stole their cattle. **92m/C VHS, Beta.** James Caan, Stefanie Powers, Sammy Davis Jr., Aldo Ray, Michael Conrad, Michael Walker Jr.; *D:* Bernard Giraudeau. *UNI*

Gone with the Wind 🐾🐾🐾🐾 1939 Epic Civil War drama focuses on the life of petulant southern belle Scarlett O'Hara. Starting with her idyllic lifestyle on a sprawling plantation, the film traces her survival through the tragic history of the South during the Civil War and Reconstruction, and her tangled love affairs with Ashley Wilkes and Rhett Butler. Classic Hollywood doesn't get any better than this; one great scene after another, equally effective in intimate drama and sweeping spectacle. The train depot scene, one of the more technically adroit shots in movie history, involved hundreds of extras and dummies, and much of the MGM lot was razed to simulate the burning of Atlanta. Based on Margaret Mitchell's novel, screenwriter Howard was assisted by producer Selznick and novelist F. Scott Fitzgerald. For its 50th anniversary, a 231-minute restored version was released that included the trailer for "The Making of a Legend: GWTW." The laserdisc is available in a limited, numbered edition, fully restored to Technicolor from the original negative, with an enhanced soundtrack and seven minutes of rare footage, including the original trailer. **231m/C VHS, Beta, LV, Closed Caption.** Clark Gable, Vivien Leigh, Olivia de Havilland, Leslie Howard, Thomas Mitchell, Hattie McDaniel, Butterfly McQueen, Evelyn Keyes, Harry Davenport, Jane Darwell, Ona Munson, Barbara O'Neil, William "Billy" Bakewell, Rand Brooks, Ward Bond, Laura Hope Crews, Yakima Canutt, George Reeves, Marjorie Reynolds, Ann Rutherford, Victor Jory, Carroll Nye, Paul Hurst, Isabel Jewell, Cliff Edwards, Eddie Anderson, Oscar Polk, Eric Linden, Violet Kemble-Cooper; *D:* Victor Fleming; *W:* Sidney Howard; *C:* Ray Rennahan; *M:* Max Steiner. Academy Awards '39: Best Actress (Leigh), Best Color Cinematography, Best Director (Fleming), Best Film Editing, Best Interior Decoration, Best Picture, Best Screenplay, Best Supporting Actress (McDaniel), National Film Registry '89;; New York Film Critics Awards '39: Best Actress (Leigh); Nominations: Academy Awards '39: Best Actor (Gable), Best Sound, Best Special Effects, Best Supporting Actress (de Havilland), Best Original Score. *MGM, FUS, BTV*

Gonza the Spearman 🐾🐾½ 1986 A gifted samurai lancer is accused of having an affair with the wife of the lord of his province. The lancer must leave to save the woman's honor, because to stay would mean death to them both. In Japanese with English subtitles. **126m/C VHS, LV, Letterbox.** *JP* Hiromi Goh, Shima Iwashita; *D:* Masahiro Shinoda. *KIV*

Good Burger 🐾🐾½ 1997 **(PG)** Teen actors Kel and Kenan from Nickelodeon fame make their feature film debut in this innocent, silly romp as employees trying to prevent the takeover of their fast food restaurant by the mega burger conglomerate across the street. Similar to comedy teams of the past, Kel is the dim-witted Ed and Kenan is the schemer Dexter, always looking for a quick way out of hard labor. The pre-adolescent humor of the film is as goofy as it is charming and the energetic duo of K&K serves up an entertaining meal for the kiddies. Shaquille O'Neal makes a cameo as does funk meister George Clinton. And yes, that is Abe Vigoda but that fry machine! **95m/C VHS, Beta, LV, Letterbox, Closed Caption.** Kenan Thompson, Kel Mitchell, Sinbad, Abe Vigoda, Dan Schneider, Shar Jackson, Jan Schweiterman, Ron Lester; *Cameos:* Shaquille O'Neal, George Clinton; *D:* Brian Robbins; *W:* Dan Schneider, Kevin Kopelow, Heather Seifert; *C:* Mac Ahlberg; *M:* Stewart Copeland. *PAR*

Good Day for a Hanging 🐾🐾½ 1958 Marshal Ben Cutler (MacMurray) finds unexpectedly opposition from the townspeople when he captures killer Eddie Campbell (Vaughn). The charismatic outlaw gains their sympathy and Cutler is going to have trouble when Campbell is sentenced to hang. **85m/C VHS.** Fred MacMurray, Robert Vaughn, Joan Blackman, Maggie Hayes, James Drury, Wendell Holmes, Emile Meyer, Bing Russell; **D:** Nathan (Hertz) Juran; **W:** Daniel Ullman, Maurice Zimm; **C:** Henry Freulich. COL

A Good Day to Die 🎬🎬½ Children of the Dust 1995 (R) Western made-for-TV saga, set during the 1880s land rush of the Oklahoma Territory, and adapted from the novel by Clancy Carlile. Half-black, half-Cherokee gunslinger Gypsy Smith (Poitier) reluctantly agrees to lead a wagon-train of freed slaves west to found their own community. Naturally, there's trouble with the Klan and Gypsy isn't the only one involved—young Cherokee brave White Wolf (Wirth), who has been raised among whites, has a forbidden romance with his foster sister, Rachel (Going), leading to lots of heartbreak. Fawcett has a brief role as the young Rachel's high-strung mother. Filmed in Alberta, Canada. **CW:** Areas of violence and some sexuality. **120m/C VHS.** Sidney Poitier, Michael Moriarty, Joanna Going, Billy Wirth, Regina Taylor, Hart Bochner, Shirley Knight, Robert Guillaume, Farrah Fawcett; **D:** David Greene; **W:** Joyce Eliason; **C:** Ronald Orieux; **M:** Mark Snow. THV

The Good Earth 🎬🎬🎬½ 1937 Pearl S. Buck's classic recreation of the story of a simple Chinese farm couple beset by greed and poverty. Outstanding special effects. MGM's last film produced by master Irving Thalberg and dedicated to his memory. Rainer won the second of her back-to-back Best Actress Oscars for her portrayal of the self-sacrificing O-Lan. **138m/B VHS, Beta.** Paul Muni, Luise Rainer, Charley Grapewin, Keye Luke, Walter Connolly; **D:** Sidney Franklin; **C:** Karl Freund. Academy Awards '37: Best Actress (Rainer), Best Cinematography; Nominations: Academy Awards '37: Best Director (Franklin), Best Film Editing, Best Picture. MGM, BTV, CCB

Good Evening, Mr. Wallenberg 🎬🎬½ 1993 Raoul Wallenberg was an upper-class Swede who imported luxury goods from Hungary. He was also responsible for saving thousands of Hungarian Jews from extermination by the Nazis. Using phony documents he first had small groups of Jews smuggled to safety but when he learns that the 65,0000 Jews of the Budapest ghetto are to be killed he uses a bluff to prevent the deaths. Later taken prisoner by the Soviet Army, Wallenberg's fate has never been determined. Characters are dwarfed by the immensity of the events and Wallenberg remains an enigma. In Swedish, German, and Hungarian with English subtitles. **115m/C VHS.** SW Stellan Skarsgard, Erland Josephson, Katharina Thalbach; **D:** Kjell Grede; **W:** Kjell Grede. ORI, FCT

The Good Father 🎬🎬🎬 1987 (R) An acclaimed British TV movie about a bitter divorced man trying to come to terms with his son, his ex-wife, and his own fury by supporting the courtroom divorce battle of a friend. **90m/C VHS, Beta, Closed Caption.** GB Anthony Hopkins, Jim Broadbent, Harriet Walter, Frances Viner, Joanne Whalley, Simon Callow, Michael Byrne; **D:** Mike Newell; **W:** Christopher Hampton; **C:** Michael Coulter; **M:** Richard Hartley. FOX

The Good Fight 🎬🎬½ 1992 Grace Cragin (Lahti) is a lawyer at a small firm who's asked by her son's best friend to represent him in a tough case against a powerful corporation. The young man is dying of mouth cancer and he wants to sue the tobacco company that makes the chewing tobacco he blames for his illness. Grace is wary of the high-powered litigation necessary but with the increasingly personal aid of her prominent lawyer ex-husband (O'Quinn), she is ready to battle the odds. Another fine performance by Lahti in this made for cable television drama. **91m/C VHS, Beta.** Christine Lahti, Terry O'Quinn, Kenneth Welsh, Lawrence Dane, Adam Trese, Tony Rosato, Andrea Roth, Jonathan Crombie; **D:** John David Coles; **W:** Beth Gutcheon; **M:** W.G. Snuffy Walden.

Good Girls Don't 🎬🎬½ 1995 Jeannie (Estevez) and Bettina (Parton) are framed for murder and take it on the lam in a red convertible with a half million in cash. It's a comedy. **85m/C VHS.** Renee Estevez, Julia Parton, Mary Woronov, Christopher Knight; **D:** Rick Sloane; **W:** Rick Sloane. LEO

Good Grief, Charlie Brown 1983 That lovably misunderstood Charlie Brown is featured again in this Peanuts production. **30m/C VHS.** **D:** Bill Melendez, Sam Jaimes, Phil Roman. BAR

The Good Guys and the Bad Guys 🎬🎬½ 1969 (PG) When Kennedy is abandoned by his gang of outlaws for being too old to keep up, he finds himself being hunted by lifelong marshall nemesis Mitchum. **91m/C VHS.** Robert Mitchum, George Kennedy, David Carradine, Tina Louise, Douglas Fowley, Lois Nettleton, Martin Balsam, John Carradine; **D:** Burt Kennedy; **W:** Ronald M. Cohen; **C:** Harry Stradling Jr. WAR

Good Guys Wear Black 🎬🎬 1978 (PG) A mild-mannered professor keeps his former life as leader of a Vietnam commando unit under wraps until he discovers that he's number one on the CIA hit list. Sequel is "A Force of One." **96m/C VHS, Beta, LV.** Chuck Norris, Anne Archer, James Franciscus; **D:** Ted Post; **W:** Mark Medoff. WAR, HBO, VES

Good Luck 🎬🎬½ 1996 (R) Inspirational buddy movie that manages to avoid the worst of sentimental excess. Tony Olezniak (D'Onofrio) is a football player left blind because of a game injury. He's on a downward spiral and winds up in jail, which is where paraplegic Bernard Lemley (Hines), once Tony's tutor, finds him. Bernard wants to enter a rigorous whitewater raft race held on Oregon's Rogue River and he needs Tony's strength to help him do it. The emotional payoff comes as the two bicker and bond instead of from the challenge of the raft race, which in itself is a change of pace. Lots of charm. **CW:** Partial nudity, adult language, adult situations. **95m/C VHS.** Vincent D'Onofrio, Gregory Hines, Max Gail, James Earl Jones; **D:** Richard LaBrie; **W:** Bob Comfort; **C:** Maximo Munzi; **M:** Tim Truman. APX

A Good Man in Africa 🎬🎬 1994 (R) Bumbling low-level British diplomat gets caught up in the high-level political turmoil of a newly independent African state. Confusing plot has borderline incompetent blackmailed by corrupt politician into bribing respected doctor for local land rights. Now, corrupt officials, ineffectual bureaucrats—go figure! Does to the British diplomatic corps what "A Fish Called Wanda" did to England's legal community, without the humor. Performances by Connery, Gossett and Lithgow almost make up for shortcomings in key areas such as writing and direction. Adapted from the novel by William Boyd. **95m/C VHS.** Colin Friels, Sean Connery, Louis Gossett Jr., John Lithgow, Joanne Whalley, Diana Rigg; **D:** Bruce Beresford; **W:** William Boyd; **C:** Andrzej Bartkowiak. USH

Good Morning, Babylon 🎬🎬🎬 Good Morning Babilonia 1987 (PG-13) The Taviani brothers' first American film. Two young Italian brothers skilled in cathedral restoration come to America and find success building the sets to D.W. Griffith's "Intolerance." Eventually, their fortune is shattered by the onslaught of WWI. **113m/C VHS, Beta, LV.** Vincent Spano, Joaquim de Almeida, Greta Scacchi, Charles Dance, Desiree Becker, Omero Antonutti, David Brandon; **D:** Paolo Taviani, Vittorio Taviani; **W:** Paolo Taviani, Vittorio Taviani, Tonino Guerra; **M:** Nicola Piovani. ART, VES

Good Morning, Vietnam 🎬🎬🎬 1987 (R) Based on the story of Saigon DJ Adrian Cronauer, although Williams' portrayal is reportedly a bit more extroverted than the personality of Cronauer. Williams spins great comic moments that may have been scripted but likely were not as a man with no history and for whom everything is manic radio material. The character ad-libs, swoops, and swerves, finally accepting adult responsibility. Engaging all the way with an out-

standing period soundtrack. **121m/C VHS, Beta, LV, 8mm, Closed Caption.** Robin Williams, Forest Whitaker, Bruno Kirby, Richard Edson, Robert Wuhl, J.T. Walsh, Noble Willingham, Floyd Vivino, Tung Thanh Tran, Chintara Sukapatana; **D:** Barry Levinson; **W:** Mitch Markowitz; **C:** Peter Sova; **M:** Alex North. Golden Globe Awards '88: Best Actor—Musical/Comedy (Williams); Nominations: Academy Awards '87: Best Actor (Williams). TOU

The Good Mother 🎬🎬½ 1988 (R) A divorced mother works at creating a fulfilling life for herself and her daughter, with an honest education for her daughter about every subject, including sex. But her ex-husband, unsure of how far this education is being taken, fights her for custody of their eight-year-old daughter after allegations of sexual misconduct against the mother's new lover. Based on Sue Miller's bestselling novel. Well acted, weakly edited and scripted. **104m/C VHS, Beta, LV, Closed Caption.** Diane Keaton, Liam Neeson, Jason Robards Jr., Ralph Bellamy, James Naughton, Teresa Wright, Asia Vieira, Joe Morton, Katey Sagal, Tracy Griffith, Charles Kimbrough, Matt Damon; **D:** Leonard Nimoy; **W:** Michael Bortman; **C:** David Watkin; **M:** Elmer Bernstein. TOU

Good Neighbor Sam 🎬🎬🎬 1964 A married advertising executive (Lemmon) agrees to pose as a friend's husband in order for her to collect a multimillion-dollar inheritance. Complications ensue when his biggest client mistakes the friend for his actual wife and decides they're the perfect couple to promote his wholesome product—milk. **130m/C VHS, Beta.** Jack Lemmon, Romy Schneider, Dorothy Provine, Mike Connors, Edward G. Robinson, Joyce Jameson; **D:** David Swift. GKK

Good News 🎬🎬½ 1947 A vintage Comden-Green musical about the love problems of a college football star, who will flunk out if he doesn't pass his French exams. Revamping of the 1927 Broadway smash features the unlikely sight of Lawford in a song-and-dance role. 🎵Varsity Drag; He's a Lady's Man; Good News; Tait Song; Students Are We; Just Imagine; If You're Not Kissing Me; Football; I Feel Pessimistic. **92m/C VHS, Beta, LV.** June Allyson, Peter Lawford, Joan McCracken, Mel Torme; **D:** Charles Walters; **W:** Betty Comden. Nominations: Academy Awards '47: Best Song ("Pass That Peace Pipe"). MGM, FCT

The Good Old Boys 🎬🎬½ 1995 Debuting as both director and co-writer, Jones also stars as aging cowpoke Hewey Calloway. The n'er-do-well Hewey makes a surprise visit to the hardscrabble 1906 Texas farm of brother Walter (Kinney), whose wife Eve (McDormand) is none too happy to see the wanderer. But Walter needs help, the local banker (Brimley) is about to foreclose, and Hewey is also taken with spirited schoolmarm Spring Renfro (Spacek, who also starred with Jones in "Coal-Miner's Daughter"). And even Hewey realizes that the 20th century is going to change his way of life forever. Easy-going drama with a fine cast. **118m/C VHS.** Tommy Lee Jones, Sissy Spacek, Terry Kinney, Frances McDormand, Wilford Brimley, Sam Shepard, Walter Olkewicz, Matt Damon, Bruce McGill, Park Overall; **D:** Tommy Lee Jones; **W:** Tommy Lee Jones, J.T. Allen; **C:** Alan Caso; **M:** John McEuen. TTC

Good Sam 🎬🎬 1948 An incurable "Good Samaritan" finds himself in one jam after another as he tries too hard to help people. Lots of missed opportunities for laughs with McCrarey's mediocre direction. **116m/B VHS.** Gary Cooper, Ann Sheridan, Ray Collins, Edmund Lowe, Joan Lorring, Ruth Roman; **D:** Leo McCarey. REP

The Good Son 🎬🎬 1993 (R) In a grand departure from cute, Culkin tackles evil as a 13-year-old obsessed with death and other unseemly hobbies. During a stay with his uncle, Mark (Wood) watches as his cousin (Culkin) gets creepier and creepier, and tries to alert the family. But will they listen? Nooo—they choose to ignore the little warning signs like the doll hanging by a noose in Culkin's room. And then there's the untimely death of a sibling. Hmmm. Culkin isn't as bad as expected, but doesn't quite get all the way down to bone-chilling terror either. Original star Jesse Bradford was dropped when Papa Culkin threatened to pull Mac off "Home Alone 2" if he wasn't cast in the lead. **CW:** Violence/terror involving children. **87m/C VHS, LV, Closed Caption.** Macaulay Culkin, Elijah Wood, Wendy Crewson, David Morse, Daniel Hugh-Kelly, Quinn Culkin; **D:** Joseph Ruben; **W:** Ian McEwan; **C:** John Lindley; **M:** Elmer Bernstein. Nominations: MTV Movie Awards '94: Best Villain (Culkin). **FOX**

The Good, the Bad, and Huckleberry Hound
1988 Journeying out West to begin a ranch, Huckleberry Hound winds up becoming a sheriff in the small town of Two-Bit. Huckleberry stands up against a group of bully brothers who have been terrorizing the town. **94m/C VHS, Beta. D:** Ray Patterson; **V:** Daws Butler. **TTC, IME**

The Good, the Bad and the Ugly
💿💿💿½ 1967 Leone's grandiloquent, shambling tribute to the American Western. Set during the Civil War, it follows the seemingly endless adventures of three dirtbags in search of a cache of Confederate gold buried in a nameless grave. Violent, exaggerated, beautifully crafted, it is the final and finest installment of the "Dollars" trilogy: a spaghetti Western chef d'oeuvre. **161m/C VHS, Beta, LV, Letterbox.** *IT* Clint Eastwood, Eli Wallach, Lee Van Cleef, Chelo Alonso, Luigi Pistilli; **D:** Sergio Leone; **W:** Sergio Leone; **C:** Tonino Delli Colli; **M:** Ennio Morricone. **FOX, MGM, FCT**

Good Times
💿💿½ 1967 Pop silliness as Sonny and Cher (playing themselves) are offered a movie deal by an eccentric tycoon (Sanders). Sonny thinks the script is terrible and dreams up various parts that he and Cher could play. Friedkin's directorial debut. **91m/C VHS.** Cher, Sonny Bono, George Sanders, Norman Alden; **D:** William Friedkin; **M:** Sonny Bono. **VTR**

The Good Wife
💿💿½ *The Umbrella Woman* 1986 (R) A bored and sexually frustrated wife scandalizes her small Australian town by taking up with the new hotel barman. There's no denying Ward's sexuality, but overall the movie is too predictable. **97m/C VHS, Beta, LV.** *AU* Rachel Ward, Bryan Brown, Sam Neill, Steven Vidler, Bruce Barry, Jennifer Claire; **D:** Ken Cameron; **M:** Cameron Allan. **BAR, IME**

Good Will Hunting
💿💿💿½ 1997 (R) Good, if predictable, first effort from screenwriting actors Damon and Affleck. Troubled, young Will Hunting (Damon) is a janitor at MIT who also happens to be an unsung mathematical genius. This gift is discovered by big-shot Professor Lambeau (Skarsgard), who must vouch for Will with the parole board by giving him weekly math sessions and taking him to a therapist to work on his anger. Naturally, only the equally troubled shrink Sean Maguire (Williams) is willing to help Hunting get beyond his blue-collar roots. But Will resists the help—not sure that he wants to leave his neighborhood and best friends behind. The Damon/Williams scenes are affecting but the southie Boston accents offer an unexpected challenge. **CW:** Strong language, including some sex-related dialogue. **126m/C VHS, LV, Closed Caption.** Matt Damon, Robin Williams, Ben Affleck, Stellan Skarsgard, Minnie Driver, Casey Affleck, Cole Hauser; **D:** Gus Van Sant; **W:** Matt Damon, Ben Affleck; **C:** Jean-Yves Escoffier; **M:** Danny Elfman. Academy Awards '97: Best Original Screenplay, Best Supporting Actor (Williams); Golden Globe Awards '98: Best Screenplay; Screen Actors Guild Award '97: Best Supporting Actor (Williams); Broadcast Film Critics Association Awards '97: Breakthrough Performance (Damon), Best Original Screenplay; Nominations: Academy Awards '97: Best Actor (Damon), Best Director (Van Sant), Best Film Editing, Best Picture, Best Song ("Miss Misery"), Best Supporting Actress (Driver), Best Original Score; Directors Guild of America Awards '97: Best Director (Van Sant); Golden Globe Awards '98: Best Actor (Damon), Best Film—Drama, Best Supporting Actor (Williams); MTV Movie Awards '98: Best Film, Best Male Performance (Damon), Best On-Screen Duo (Matt Damon/Ben Affleck), Best Kiss (Matt Damon/Minnie Driver); Screen Actors Guild Award '97: Best

Actor (Damon), Best Supporting Actress (Driver), Cast; Writers Guild of America '97: Best Original Screenplay. **TOU**

Goodbye Again
💿💿½ *Aimez-Vous Brahms* 1961 A romantic drama based on the novel by Francoise Sagan. Bergman is a middle-aged interior decorator whose lover, Montand, has a roaming eye. She finds herself drawn to the son (Perkins) of a client and begins an affair—flattered by the young man's attentions. Montand is outraged and vows to change his ways and marry Bergman if she will give up the young man. A bit soapy, but a must for Bergman fans. **120m/B VHS.** Jessie Royce Landis, Ingrid Bergman, Anthony Perkins, Yves Montand, Diahann Carroll; **D:** Anatole Litvak. Cannes Film Festival '61: Best Actor (Perkins). **MGM, FCT**

The Goodbye Bird
💿💿½ 1993 (G) Frank is accused by his school principal of stealing her prized talking parrot. With the aid of a kindly veterinarian Frank tries to discover who the thief really is. **91m/C VHS, Closed Caption.** Cindy Pickett, Concetta Tomei, Wayne Rogers, Christopher Pettiet; **D:** William Clark. **WOV**

Goodbye Columbus
💿💿💿 1969 (PG) Philip Roth's novel about a young Jewish librarian who has an affair with the spoiled daughter of a nouveau riche family is brought to late-'60s life, and vindicated by superb performances all around. Benjamin and McGraw's first starring roles. **105m/C VHS, Beta, LV.** Richard Benjamin, Ali MacGraw, Jack Klugman, Nan Martin, Jaclyn Smith; **D:** Larry Peerce; **M:** Charles Fox. Writers Guild of America '68: Best Adapted Screenplay; Nominations: Academy Awards '69: Best Adapted Screenplay. **PAR**

Goodbye Cruel World
💿½ 1982 (R) Black comedy about a suicidal television anchorman who decides to spend his last day filming the relatives who drove him to the brink. **90m/C VHS, Beta.** Dick Shawn, Cynthia Sikes, Chuck "Porky" Mitchell; **D:** David Irving. **ART**

Goodbye Emmanuelle
💿½ 1979 (R) Follows the further adventures of Emmanuelle in her quest for sexual freedom and the excitement of forbidden pleasures. The second sequel to "Emmanuelle." **92m/C VHS, Beta.** Sylvia Kristel. **NO**

The Goodbye Girl
💿💿💿 1977 (PG) Neil Simon's story of a former actress, her precocious nine-year-old daughter and the aspiring actor who moves in with them. The daughter serves as catalyst for the other two to fall in love. While Mason's character is fairly unsympathetic, Dreyfuss is great and Simon's dialogue witty. **110m/C VHS, Beta, LV.** Richard Dreyfuss, Marsha Mason, Quinn Cummings, Barbara Rhoades, Marilyn Sokol; **D:** Herbert Ross; **W:** Neil Simon; **M:** Dave Grusin. Academy Awards '77: Best Actor (Dreyfuss); British Academy Awards '78: Best Actor (Dreyfuss); Golden Globe Awards '78: Best Actor—Musical/Comedy (Dreyfuss), Best Actress—Musical/Comedy (Mason), Best Film—Musical/Comedy, Best Screenplay; Los Angeles Film Critics Association Awards '77: Best Actor (Dreyfuss); Nominations: Academy Awards '77: Best Actress (Mason), Best Original Screenplay, Best Picture, Best Supporting Actress (Cummings). **MGM, BTV**

Goodbye Love
💿💿 1934 Dull comedy about a group of ex-husbands who refuse to pay alimony and end up in jail. **65m/B VHS.** Charlie Ruggles, Verree Teasdale, Sidney Blackmer, Mayo Methot, Phyllis Barry, Ray Walker, John Kelly, Hale Grace, Luis Alberni; **D:** Herbert Ross. **FCT**

Goodbye, Lover
💿💿 1998 (R) Sandra (Arquette) and Ben (Johnson) are hot n' heavy lovers. Jake (Mulrony) is husband to one and brother to the other. Peggy (Parker) has eyes for Ben and works with Jake. Since this is a contemporary noir comedy, there's plot twists, betrayal, blackmail, murder, a fortune in insurance money, and two cops (DeGeneres and McKinnon) trying to piece it all together. Overshoots comedy and ultimately lands in silly territory, but looks good doing it. Johnson comes out the best, kicking pic up a notch whenever he's on screen. DeGeneres (as the jaded cop) and McKinnon (the wide-eyed newbie) plod through the odd-couple schtick. **CW:** Sexuality, language and violence. **104m/C VHS.** Don

Johnson, Patricia Arquette, Dermot Mulroney, Ellen DeGeneres, Mary-Louise Parker, Ray McKinnon, Alex Rocco, Andre Gregory, John Neville; **D:** Roland Joffe; **W:** Joel Cohen, Alec Sokolow, Ron Peer; **C:** Dante Spinotti; **M:** John Ottman. **NYR**

Goodbye, Miss 4th of July
💿💿½ 1988 Inspired by the true story of the teenage daughter of Greek immigrants living in pre-WWI West Virginia, the prejudice they encounter, the relationship that begins between the family and an aging African-American ex-boxer, and the girl's efforts in the influenza epidemic. Based on the 1985 book by her brother. **89m/C VHS, Closed Caption.** Roxana Zal, Louis Gossett Jr., Chris Sarandon, Chantal Contouri, Chynna Phillips, Mitchell Anderson, Conchata Ferrell, Ed Lauter; **D:** George Miller. **DIS**

Goodbye, Mr. Chips
💿💿💿½ 1939 An MGM classic, the sentimental rendering of the James Hilton novel about a shy Latin professor in an English school who marries the vivacious Garson only to tragically lose her. He spends the rest of his life devoting himself to his students and becoming a school legend. Multi award-winning soaper featuring Garson's first screen appearance, which was Oscar nominated. Special two-tape letterboxed laserdisc edition includes the original trailer and an extra-special production featurette. Remade in 1969 as a fairly awful musical starring Peter O'Toole. **115m/B VHS, Beta, LV, Letterbox, Closed Caption.** Robert Donat, Greer Garson, Paul Henreid, John Mills; **D:** Sam Wood; **C:** Frederick A. (Freddie) Young. Academy Awards '39: Best Actor (Donat); Nominations: Academy Awards '39: Best Actress (Garson), Best Director (Wood), Best Film Editing, Best Picture, Best Screenplay, Best Sound. **MGM, BTV, HMV**

Goodbye, Mr. Chips
💿💿 1969 Ross debuted as director with this big-budget (but inferior musical re-make) of the classic James Hilton novel about a gentle teacher at an English all-boys private school and the woman who helps him demonstrate his compassion and overcome his shyness. O'Toole, although excellent, is categorically a non-singer, while Clark, a popular singer at the time ("Downtown"), musters very little talent in front of the camera. The plot is altered unnecessarily and updated to the WWII era for little reason; the music is thoroughly forgettable. ♫Fill The World With Love; Where Did My Childhood Go; London is London; And the Sky Smiled; When I am Older; Walk Through the World; What Shall I Do with Today?; What a Lot of Flowers; Schooldays. **151m/C VHS, Beta, LV, Letterbox.** Peter O'Toole, Petula Clark, Michael Redgrave, George Baker, Sian Phillips, Michael Bryant, Jack Hedley, Herbert Ross; **D:** Herbert Ross; **C:** Oswald Morris; **M:** Leslie Bricusse, John Williams. Golden Globe Awards '70: Best Actor—Musical/Comedy (O'Toole); National Board of Review Awards '69: Best Actor (O'Toole); National Society of Film Critics Awards '69: Best Supporting Actress (Phillips); Nominations: Academy Awards '69: Best Actor (O'Toole), Scoring of a Musical. **MGM**

Goodbye, My Lady
💿💿 1956 Based on the novel by James Street, this is a tear-jerking film about a young Mississippi farmboy who finds and cares for a special dog that he comes to love but eventually must give up. **95m/B VHS, Beta, LV.** Brandon de Wilde, Walter Brennan, Sidney Poitier, Phil Harris, Louise Beavers; **D:** William A. Wellman. **WAR, FCT**

Goodbye, New York
💿💿 1985 (R) A New York yuppie on a vacation finds herself penniless and stranded in Israel. She makes the best of the situation by joining a kibbutz and falling for a part-time soldier. Well, of course. **90m/C VHS, Beta, LV.** *IS* Julie Hagerty, Amos Kollek, Shmuel Shilo; **D:** Amos Kollek; **M:** Michael Abene. **VES**

Goodbye, Norma Jean
💿💿 1975 (R) Detailed and sleazy recreation of Marilyn Monroe's early years in Hollywood. Followed by "Goodnight, Sweet Marilyn." **95m/C VHS, Beta.** Misty Rowe, Terrence Locke, Patch MacKenzie; **D:** Larry Buchanan; **M:** Joe Beck. **NO**

The Goodbye People 🎬🎬½ 1983 Balsam is an elderly man who decides to reopen his Coney Island hot dog stand that folded 22 years earlier. Hirsch and Reed help him realize his impossible dream in this sweetly sentimental film. 104m/C VHS, Beta, LV, Closed Caption. Judd Hirsch, Martin Balsam, Pamela Reed, Ron Silver; **D:** Herb Gardner; **W:** Herb Gardner. COL

Goodbye Pork Pie 🎬½ 1981 (R) With the police on their trail, two young men speed on a 1000-mile journey in a small, brand-new, yellow stolen car. Remember: journey of thousand miles always begin in stolen car. 105m/C VHS, Beta. NZ Tony Barry, Kelly Johnson; **D:** Geoff Murphy; **C:** Alun Bollinger.

Goodfellas 🎬🎬🎬🎬 1990 (R) Quintessential picture about "wiseguys," at turns both violent and funny. A young man grows up in the mob, works hard to advance himself through the ranks, and enjoys the life of the rich and violent, oblivious to the horror of which he is a part. Cocaine addiction and many wiseguy missteps ultimately unravel his climb to the top. Excellent performances (particularly Liotta and Pesci, with De Niro pitching in around the corners), with visionary cinematography and careful pacing. Watch for Scorsese's mom as Pesci's mom. Based on the life of Henry Hill, ex-mobster now in the Witness Protection Program. Adapted from the book by Nicholas Pileggi. 146m/C VHS, Beta, LV, Letterbox, Closed Caption, DVD. Robert De Niro, Ray Liotta, Joe Pesci, Paul Sorvino, Lorraine Bracco, Frank Sivero, Mike Starr, Frank Vincent, Samuel L. Jackson, Tony Darrow, Chuck Low, Frank DiLeo, Christopher Serrone, Illeana Douglas, Debi Mazar, Michael Imperioli, Peter Onorati, Beau Starr, Angela Pietropinto, Joseph D'Onofrio; **Cameos:** Jerry Vale, Henny Youngman; **D:** Martin Scorsese; **W:** Nicholas Pileggi, Martin Scorsese; **C:** Michael Ballhaus. Academy Awards '90: Best Supporting Actor (Pesci); British Academy Awards '90: Best Adapted Screenplay, Best Director (Scorsese); Los Angeles Film Critics Association Awards '90: Best Cinematography, Best Director (Scorsese), Best Film, Best Supporting Actor (Pesci), Best Supporting Actress (Bracco); National Board of Review Awards '90: Best Supporting Actor (Pesci); New York Film Critics Awards '90: Best Actor (De Niro), Best Director (Scorsese), Best Film; National Society of Film Critics Awards '90: Best Director (Scorsese), Best Film; Nominations: Academy Awards '90: Best Adapted Screenplay, Best Director (Scorsese), Best Film Editing, Best Picture, Best Supporting Actress (Bracco); Golden Globe Awards '90: Best Director (Scorsese), Best Film—Drama, Best Screenplay, Best Supporting Actor (Pesci), Best Supporting Actress (Bracco). WAR, FCT, BTV

Goodnight, Michelangelo 🎬🎬½ 1989 (R) Funny, engaging and somewhat confusing story of the life of an Italian immigrant family as seen through the eyes of its youngest member, eight-year-old Michelangelo. Winner of the 1990 Best Comedy Award at the Greater Fort Lauderdale Film Festival. **CW:** Language and sexual situations. 91m/C VHS. IT Lina Sastri, Kim Cattrall, Giancarlo Giannini, Daniel Desanto; **D:** Carlo Liconti; **W:** Carlo Liconti. NO

Goodnight, Sweet Marilyn 🎬 1989 (R) Supposed "never-before-told" story of Marilyn Monroe's tragic death. According to this, her death was the result of pre-arranged "mercy-killing." Follow-up to director Buchanan's "Goodbye, Norma Jean" (1977) with Lane as the 1960s Marilyn intercut with scenes of Rowe from the first film as young Marilyn. You'd be better off leaving "Sweet Marilyn" to rest in peace. 100m/C VHS, Beta. Paula Lane, Jeremy Slate, Misty Rowe; **D:** Larry Buchanan. NO

Goof Balls WOOF! 1987 (R) The tourist denizens of a island golf resort putt and cavort about, and golf isn't all that's on their minds. 87m/C VHS, Beta. Ben Gordon, Laura Robinson.

A Goofy Movie 🎬🎬½ 1994 (G) The dog finally gets his day. After 63 years of supporting roles, Disney's Goofy stars in his own movie along with his teenage son Max. When it comes to Goofy's attention that his rock music obsessed son is goofing off in school. Goofy decides to spend some quality time with Max via a road trip through the country. Their journey is plagued with mishaps, but through the obstacles, father and son bridge their generational gap and bond in the true Disney sense. A modest animated treat with six new songs that may induce some finger snapping and toe tapping. 78m/C VHS, Closed Caption. **D:** Kevin Lima; **W:** Jymn Magon, Brian Pimental, Chris Matheson; **V:** Bill Farmer, Jason Marsden, Jim Cummings, Kellie Martin, Rob Paulsen, Wallace Shawn, Florence Stanley, Jo Anne Worley. DIS

Goon Movie 🎬🎬 Stand Easy 1953 The cast of "The Goon Show," Britain's popular radio comedy series, perform some of their best routines in this, their only film appearance. 75m/B VHS, Beta. Peter Sellers, Spike Milligan, Harry Secombe. VDM

The Goonies 🎬🎬½ 1985 (PG) Two brothers who are about to lose their house conveniently find a treasure map. They pick up a couple of friends and head for the "X." If they can recover the treasure without getting caught by the bad guys, then all will be saved. Steven Spielberg produced this high-energy action fantasy for kids of all ages. The laserdisc edition comes in a widescreen format. 114m/C VHS, Beta, LV, Letterbox, Closed Caption. Sean Astin, Josh Brolin, Jeff B. Cohen, Corey Feldman, Martha Plimpton, John Matuszak, Robert Davi, Anne Ramsey, Mary Ellen Trainor, Jonathan Ke Quan, Kerri Green, Joe Pantoliano; **D:** Richard Donner; **W:** Chris Columbus, Steven Spielberg; **M:** Dave Grusin. WAR

Gor 🎬½ 1988 (PG) Sword and sorcery: a magic ring sends a meek college professor to "Gor," a faraway world in which survival goes to the fittest and the most brutal. Followed by "Outlaw of Gor." 95m/C VHS, Beta, Closed Caption. Urbano Barberini, Rebecca Ferratti, Jack Palance, Paul Smith, Oliver Reed; **D:** Fritz Kiersch; **W:** R.J. Marx. WAR

Gorath 🎬🎬 Yosei Gorasu 1964 The world's top scientists are racing to stop a giant meteor from destroying the Earth. 77m/C VHS, Beta. JP **D:** Inoshiro Honda. GEM

Gordon's War 🎬🎬 1973 (R) When a Vietnam vet returns to his Harlem home, he finds his wife overdosing on the drugs that have infiltrated his neighborhood. He leads a vigilante group in an attempt to clean up the area, which makes for a lot of action; however, there's also an excessive amount of violence. 89m/C VHS, Beta, Closed Caption. Paul Winfield, Carl Lee, David Downing, Tony King, Grace Jones; **D:** Ossie Davis; **M:** Angelo Badalamenti. FOX

Gordy 🎬½ 1995 (G) Perky talking porker Gordy manages to escape his fate as future bacon and find a couple of equally perky kids—motherless country-song-singing Jinnie Sue (Young) and lonely rich boy Hanky (Roescher), whom the pig manages to save from drowning. Plot scarcely matters and all the 25 piggies who performed as Gordy generally manage to outshine the humans, though country singer Stone (in his film debut) displays an easy charm. 90m/C VHS, Closed Caption. Doug Stone, Michael Roescher, Kristy Young, James Donadio, Deborah Hobart, Tom Lester, Ted Manson; **D:** Mark Lewis; **W:** Leslie Stevens; **C:** Richard Michalak; **M:** Tom Bahler; **V:** Justin Garms. TOU

The Gore-Gore Girls 🎬 1972 Splatter horror director Lewis' final film follows a detective's search for a madman who's been mutilating and killing beautiful young bar dancers. 84m/C VHS. **D:** Herschell Gordon Lewis. MOV

Gore-Met Zombie Chef From Hell WOOF! 1987 A demon/vampire opens up a seafood restaurant and slaughters his customers. Deliberately campy and extremely graphic. 90m/C VHS, Beta. Theo Depuay, Kelley Kunicki, C.W. Casey, Alan Marx, Michael O'Neill; **D:** Don Swan. NO

Gore Vidal's Billy the Kid 🎬🎬½ 1989 An unusual treatment of the William Bonney legend in which the Kid is merely a misunderstood teenager caught up in the midst of the brutal range wars. Made for cable television. 100m/C VHS. Val Kilmer, Duncan Regehr, Wilford Brimley, Julie Carmen, Michael Parks, Rene Auberjonois, Albert Salmi; **D:** William A. Graham. TTC

Gore Vidal's Lincoln 🎬🎬½ Lincoln 1988 Waterston is a low-key but sympathetic Lincoln, with Moore as his high-strung wife Mary, in this made for television adaptation of the Vidal bestseller. Follows the couple from their first day in Washington, through the Civil War, family tragedies, up to the day of the President's burial. 190m/C VHS. Sam Waterston, Mary Tyler Moore, John Houseman, Richard Mulligan, John McMartin, Ruby Dee, Cleavon Little, Jeffrey DeMunn, James Gammon, Deborah Adair, Robin Gammell; **D:** Lamont Johnson; **W:** Ernest Kinoy; **M:** Ernest Gold. AVE

The Gorgeous Hussy 🎬 1936 Crawford stars in this fictionalized biography of Peggy Eaton, Andrew Jackson's notorious belle, who disgraces herself and those around her. A star-studded cast complete with beautiful costumes isn't enough to save this overly long and dull picture. 102m/B VHS, Closed Caption. Joan Crawford, Robert Taylor, Lionel Barrymore, James Stewart, Franchot Tone, Louis Calhern; **D:** Clarence Brown. Nominations: Academy Awards '36: Best Cinematography, Best Supporting Actress (Bondi). MGM

Gorgo 🎬🎬½ 1961 An undersea explosion off the coast of Ireland brings to the surface a prehistoric sea monster, which is captured and brought to a London circus. Its irate mother appears looking for her baby, creating havoc in her wake. 76m/C VHS, Beta, LV. GB Bill Travers, William Sylvester, Vincent Winter, Bruce Seton, Christopher Rhodes; **D:** Eugene Lourie; **W:** Daniel James, Robert L. Richards; **C:** Frederick A. (Freddie) Young. NOS, MRV, VCI

The Gorgon 🎬🎬 1964 In pre-WWI Germany, the lovely assistant to a mad brain surgeon moonlights as a snake-haired gorgon, turning men to stone. A professor arrives in the village to investigate, only to become another victim. 83m/C VHS, Beta, LV. GB Peter Cushing, Christopher Lee, Richard Pasco, Barbara Shelley, Michael Goodliffe, Patrick Troughton, Jack Watson, Jeremy Longhurst, Toni Gilpin, Prudence Hyman; **D:** Terence Fisher; **W:** John Gilling; **C:** Michael Reed; **M:** James Bernard. NO

The Gorilla 🎬🎬 1939 Bumbling Ritzes are hired to protect a country gentleman receiving threats from a killer. Lugosi portrays the menacing butler. Derived from the play by Ralph Spence. 67m/B VHS, Beta, LV. The Ritz Brothers, Anita Louise, Patsy Kelly, Lionel Atwill, Bela Lugosi; **D:** Allan Dwan. NOS, SNC, MRV

Gorilla 🎬🎬 1956 A rampaging gorilla is sought by the local game warden and a journalist researching the natives. Filmed on location in the Belgian Congo. 79m/B VHS, Beta. SW Gio Petre, Georges Galley; **D:** Sven Nykvist, Lar Henrik Ottoson. FCT, VYY

Gorillas in the Mist 🎬🎬🎬 1988 (PG-13) The life of Dian Fossey, animal rights activist and world-renowned expert on the African gorilla, from her pioneering contact with mountain gorillas to her murder at the hands of poachers. Weaver is totally appropriate as the increasingly obsessed Fossey, but the character moves away from us, just as we need to see and understand more about her. Excellent special effects. 117m/C VHS, Beta, LV. Sigourney Weaver, Bryan Brown, Julie Harris, Iain Cuthbertson, John Omirah Miluwi, Constantin Alexandrov, Waigwa Wachira; **D:** Michael Apted; **W:** Anna Hamilton Phelan; **C:** John Seale; **M:** Maurice Jarre. Golden Globe Awards '88: Best Actress—Drama (Weaver); Golden Globe Awards '89: Best Score; Nominations: Academy Awards '88: Best Actress (Weaver), Best Adapted Screenplay, Best Film Editing, Best Sound, Best Original Score. USH, HMV

Gorky Park 🎬🎬🎬 1983 (R) Adaptation of Martin Cruz Smith's bestseller. Three strange, faceless corpses are found in Moscow's Gorky Park. There are no clues for the Russian police captain investigating the incident. He makes the solution to this crime his personal crusade, and finds himself caught in a web of political intrigue. Excellent police procedure yarn. 127m/C VHS, Beta,

LV. William Hurt, Lee Marvin, Brian Dennehy, Joanna Pacula; *D:* Michael Apted; *W:* Dennis Potter; *C:* Ralf Bode; *M:* James Horner. VES

Gorp woof! 1980 (R) Sex, fun, and lewd, sophomoric humor reign at a summer camp. For the bored and witless or those who aspire. **90m/C VHS, Beta.** Dennis Quaid, Rosanna Arquette, Michael Lembeck, Philip Casnoff, Frank Drescher; *D:* Joseph Ruben. HBO

Gospa 🎬🎬½ 1994 (PG) Based on the true story of Father Jozo Zovko (Sheen), who was put on trial for treason by the communist government in Yugoslavia in 1981 when he protected six Coatian children who repeatedly claimed that they saw visions of the Virgin Mary. Somewhat ponderous but well-meaning story that also suffers from a plethora of accents. "Gospa" means "Our Lady" in Croatian. **121m/C VHS.** Martin Sheen, Michael York, Morgan Fairchild, Frank Finlay; *D:* Jakov Sedlar; *W:* Ivan Aralica, Paul Gronseth; *C:* Vjekoslav Vrdoljak; *M:* Nona Hendryx. NYR

The Gospel According to St. Matthew 🎬🎬🎬🎬 *Il Vangelo Secondo Matteo; L'Evangile Selon Saint-Matthieu* 1964 Perhaps Pasolini's greatest film, retelling the story of Christ in gritty, neo-realistic tones and portraying the man less as a divine presence than as a political revolutionary. The yardstick by which all Jesus-films are to be measured. In Italian with English subtitles or dubbed. **142m/B VHS, Beta, LV, 8mm, Letterbox.** *IT* Enrique Irazoqui, Susanna Pasolini, Margherita Caruso, Marcello Morante, Mario Socrate; *D:* Pier Paolo Pasolini; *W:* Pier Paolo Pasolini; *C:* Tonino Delli Colli; *M:* Luis Bacalov. Nominations: Academy Awards '66: Best Adapted Score, Best Art Direction/Set Decoration (B & W), Best Costume Design (B & W). NOS, MRV, WBF

The Gospel According to Vic 🎬🎬 *Heavenly Pursuits* 1987 (PG-13) A Scottish comedy about a skeptical teacher at a remedial school, who, having survived miraculously from a fall, is taken for proof of the sainthood of the school's patron namesake. **92m/C VHS, Beta, Closed Caption.** GB Tom Conti, Helen Mirren; *D:* Charles Gormley; *C:* Michael Coulter. FOX

Gotcha! 🎬🎬½ 1985 (PG-13) The mock assassination game "Gotcha!" abounds on the college campus and sophomore Edwards is one of the best. What he doesn't know is that his "assassination" skills are about to take on new meaning when he meets up with a female Czech graduate student who is really an international spy. **97m/C VHS, Beta, LV, Closed Caption.** Anthony Edwards, Linda Fiorentino, Alex Rocco, Nick Corri, Marla Adams, Klaus Loewitsch, Christopher Rydell; *D:* Jeff Kanew; *W:* Dan Gordon; *M:* Bill Conti. USH

Gotham 🎬🎬🎬 1988 A wealthy financier hires private-eye Jones to track down beautiful wife Madsen. It seems that she keeps dunning her husband for money. Sounds easy enough to Jones until he learns that she has been dead for some time. Mystery ventures into the afterlife and back as it twists its way to its surprise ending. Intriguing throwback to '40s detective flicks. Made for television. **100m/C VHS, LV.** Tommy Lee Jones, Virginia Madsen, Colin Bruce, Kevin Jarre, Denise Stephenson, Frederic Forrest; *D:* Lloyd Fonvielle; *C:* Michael Chapman; *M:* George S. Clinton.

Gothic 🎬🎬🎬 1987 (R) Mary Shelley, Lord Byron, Percy Bysshe Shelley, and John Polidori spend the night in a Swiss villa telling each other ghost stories and experimenting with laudanum and sexual partner combinations. The dreams and realizations of the night will color their lives ever after. Interesting premise, well-carried out, although burdened by director Russell's typical excesses. Soundtrack by Thomas Dolby. **87m/C VHS, Beta, LV.** Julian Sands, Gabriel Byrne, Timothy Spall, Natasha Richardson, Myriam Cyr; *D:* Ken Russell; *W:* Stephen Volk; *C:* Mike Southon; *M:* Thomas Dolby. ART, VES

Gotta Dance, Gotta Sing 1984 Compilation of memorable dance routines from great Hollywood films. **53m/C VHS, Beta.** Fred Astaire, Ginger Rogers, Shirley Temple, Carmen Miranda, Betty Grable. NO

Gotti 🎬🎬½ 1996 (R) Follows the career of the New York mobster known as the "Teflon Don." Gotti's (Assante) mentor is Neil Dellacroce (Quinn), underboss to the aging head of the Gambino crime family. When Gambino (Lawrence) dies, Gotti is incensed that Paul Castellano (Sarafian) is named as family successor and eventually has him killed. He then grabs power (and lots of tabloid headlines), manages to beat his first federal racketeering rap, but is brought down with the aid of his own underboss, Sammy the Bull (Forsythe), whom the feds get into court. Made for cable. *CW:* Graphic violence, strong language and some drug content. **118m/C VHS.** Armand Assante, William Forsythe, Anthony Quinn, Richard Sarafian, Vinny Pastore, Robert Miranda, Frank Vincent, Marc Lawrence, Al Waxman, Alberta Watson, Silvio Oliviero, Nigel Bennett; *D:* Robert Harmon; *W:* Steve Shagan; *C:* Alan Kivilo; *M:* Mark Isham. HBO

Government Agents vs. Phantom Legion 1951 Agent Hal Duncan must stop an evil group who is stealing uranium shipments from under the government's nose. Edited from 12 episodes of the original serial on two cassettes. **167m/B VHS, Beta.** Walter Reed, Mary Ellen Kay, Dick Curtis, John Pickard. REP, MLB

The Grace Kelly Story 🎬🎬½ 1983 Ladd stars as the beautiful Philadelphia society girl who became an Oscar-winning actress and a seemingly fairy tale princess when she leaves Hollywood behind to marry Prince Rainier of Monaco. Standard TV bio but Ladd does look the part. **104m/C VHS, Closed Caption.** Cheryl Ladd, Diane Ladd, Lloyd Bridges, Ian McShane, Alejandro Rey, William Schallert, Marta DuBois, Salome Jens, Edith Fellows; *D:* Anthony Page; *W:* Cynthia Mandelberg. COL

Grace of My Heart 🎬🎬½ 1996 (R) Edna Buxton (Douglas), from a rich Philadelphia family, wins a song contest and winds up in New York at Manhattan's Brill Building, pop music's '60s song factory, where she's transformed into Denise Waverly and told to write the music—not sing it. She pens a lot of hits, winds up in hippie Malibu, and finally gets the courage to record her own concept album (think Carole King's "Tapestry"). Along the way there's a succession of wrong men and heartbreak before her independent triumph. Douglas does a fine job (her singing's dubbed by Kristen Vigard) but last minute melodrama turns this into typical showbiz kitsch. *CW:* Language, and for some sexuality and drug content. **116m/C VHS, LV, Letterbox, Closed Caption.** Illeana Douglas, John Turturro, Matt Dillon, Eric Stoltz, Bruce Davison, Patsy Kensit, Bridget Fonda, Jennifer Leigh Warren, Chris Isaak; *D:* Allison Anders; *W:* Allison Anders; *C:* Jean-Yves Escoffier; *M:* Larry Klein; *V:* Peter Fonda. USH

Grace Quigley 🎬½ *The Ultimate Solution of Grace Quigley* 1984 (PG) An elderly woman, tired of life, hires a hitman to kill her. Instead they go into business together, bumping off other elderly folk who decide they'd rather be dead. Notoriously inept black comedy noted for being the career embarrassment for both of its stars. **87m/C VHS, Beta.** Katharine Hepburn, Nick Nolte, Walter Abel, Chip Zien, Elizabeth Wilson, Kit Le Fever, William Duell, Jill Eikenberry; *D:* Anthony Harvey; *M:* John Addison. MGM

Grad Night 🎬 1981 (R) The anticipation for graduation in a small town high school brings surprises no one could have predicted, unless they've seen all the other typical adolescent films. **85m/C VHS, Beta.** Joey Johnson, Suzanna Fagan, Barry Stolze, Sam Whipple, Caroline Bates; *D:* John Tenorio; *C:* Arledge Armenaki. NO

The Graduate 🎬🎬🎬🎬 1967 (PG) Famous, influential slice of comic Americana stars Hoffman as Benjamin Braddock, a shy, aimless college graduate who, without any idea of responsibility or ambition, wanders from a casual liaison with a married woman (the infamous Mrs. Robinson) to pursuit of her engaged daughter. His pursuit of Elaine right to her wedding has become a film classic. Extremely popular and almost solely responsible for establishing both Hoffman and director Nichols. The career advice given to Benjamin, "plastics," became a catchword for the era. Watch for Dreyfuss in the Berkeley rooming house, Farrell in the hotel lobby, and screenwriter Henry as the desk clerk. Based on the novel by Charles Webb. Laserdisc edition includes screen tests, promotional stills, and a look at the creative process involved in making a novel into a movie. A 25th Anniversary Limited Edition is also available, presented in a widescreen format and including the original movie trailer and interviews with the cast and crew. **106m/C VHS, Beta, LV, 8mm, Letterbox, Closed Caption.** Dustin Hoffman, Anne Bancroft, Katharine Ross, Murray Hamilton, Brian Avery, Marion Lorne, Alice Ghostley, William Daniels, Elizabeth Wilson, Norman Fell, Buck Henry, Richard Dreyfuss, Mike Farrell; *D:* Mike Nichols; *W:* Buck Henry, Calder Willingham; *C:* Robert L. Surtees; *M:* Paul Simon, Art Garfunkel, Dave Grusin. Academy Awards '67: Best Director (Nichols); British Academy Awards '68: Best Director (Nichols), Best Film, Best Screenplay; Directors Guild of America Awards '67: Best Director (Nichols); Golden Globe Awards '68: Best Actress—Musical/Comedy (Bancroft), Best Director (Nichols), Best Film—Musical/Comedy, National Film Registry '96;; New York Film Critics Awards '67: Best Director (Nichols); Nominations: Academy Awards '67: Best Actor (Hoffman), Best Actress (Bancroft), Best Adapted Screenplay, Best Cinematography, Best Picture, Best Supporting Actress (Ross). NLC, CRC, BTV

Graduation Day 🎬 1981 (R) Another teen slasher about the systematic murder of members of a high school track team. Notable mainly for brief appearance by Vanna White. **85m/C VHS, Beta.** Christopher George, Patch MacKenzie, E. Danny Murphy, Vanna White; *D:* Herb Freed. COL

Graffiti Bridge 🎬½ 1990 (PG-13) Prince preaches love instead of sex and the result is boring. The Lavender One is a Minneapolis nightclub owner who battles with Day over the love of a beautiful woman. Chauvinistic attitudes toward women abound, but the females in the film don't seem to mind. Which must mean they were "acting." Visually interesting, although not as experimental as "Purple Rain." Music made Top Ten. **90m/C VHS, Beta, LV, Closed Caption.** Prince, Morris Day, Jerome Benton, Jill Jones, Mavis Staples, George Clinton, Ingrid Chavez; *D:* Prince; *W:* Prince; *C:* Bill Butler. MVD, WAR

Grain of Sand 🎬🎬🎬 1984 Based on a true story, an understated French drama about a troubled woman searching her past, and her home town in Corsica, for the man of her dreams. Directorial debut of Meffre. In French with English subtitles. **90m/C VHS, Beta.** FR Delphine Seyrig, Genevieve Fontanel, Coralie Seyrig, Michel Aumont; *D:* Pomme Meffre. FCT

Grambling's White Tiger 🎬🎬½ 1981 The true story of Jim Gregory, the first white man to play on Grambling College's all-black football team. Jenner's a little too old, but Belafonte, in his TV acting debut, is fine as legendary coach Eddie Robinson. Based on book by Bruce Behrenberg. Made for television. **98m/C VHS, Beta.** Bruce Jenner, Harry Belafonte, LeVar Burton, Ray Vitte, Byron Stewart; *D:* Georg Stanford Brown; *M:* John D'Andrea. USH

Grand Canyon 🎬🎬🎬 1991 (R) Diverse group of characters is thrown together through chance encounters while coping with urban chaos in L.A. The main focus is the growing friendship between an immigration lawyer (Kline) and a tow-truck driver (Glover) who meet when Kline's car breaks down in a crime-ridden neighborhood. First-rate performances by the cast make up for numerous moral messages thrown at viewers with the subtlety of a brick. Sometimes funny, sometimes preachy became more relevant in light of the violence that exploded in L.A. during the summer of '92. *CW:* Language. **134m/C VHS, Closed Caption.** Danny Glover, Kevin Kline, Steve Martin, Mary McDonnell, Mary-Louise Parker, Alfre Woodard, Jeremy Sisto, Tina Lifford, Patrick Malone, Mary Ellen Trainor; *D:* Lawrence Kasdan; *W:* Lawrence Kasdan, Meg Kasdan; *C:* Owen Roizman; *M:* James Newton Howard. Nominations: Academy Awards '91: Best Original Screenplay. FXV

Grand Canyon Trail 🎬½ **1948** Our hero is the owner of a played-out silver mine who is the target of an unscrupulous engineer who thinks there's silver to be found if you know where to look. The first appearance of the Riders of the Purple Sage, who replaced the Sons of the Pioneers. **68m/B VHS, Beta.** Roy Rogers, Andy Devine, Charles Coleman, Jane Frazee, Robert Livingston; **D:** William Witney. *NOS, DVT, TIM*

The Grand Duchess and the Waiter 🎬🎬🎬 **1926** Menjou is a French millionaire who disguises himself as a waiter in order to enter the service of a grand duchess with whom he has fallen in love. **70m/B VHS, Beta.** Adolphe Menjou, Florence Vidor, Lawrence Grant; **D:** Malcolm St. Clair. *GVV*

The Grand Duel 🎬🎬 **1973** More spaghetti thrills as Lee plays a mysterious gunman who also acts as protector of a young ruffian falsely accused of murder. **?m/C VHS.** Lee Van Cleef, Peter O'Brien, Jess Hahn, Horst Frank. *SNC, VTR*

Grand Hotel 🎬🎬🎬½ **1932** A star-filled cast is brought together by unusual circumstances at Berlin's Grand Hotel and their lives become hopelessly intertwined over a 24 hour period. Adapted (and given the red-carpet treatment) from a Vicki Baum novel; notable mostly for Garbo's world-weary ballerina. Time has taken its toll on the concept and treatment, but still an interesting star vehicle. **112m/B VHS, Beta, LV, Closed Caption.** Greta Garbo, John Barrymore, Joan Crawford, Lewis Stone, Wallace Beery, Jean Hersholt, Lionel Barrymore; **D:** Edmund Goulding; **C:** William H. Daniels. Academy Awards '32: Best Picture. *MGM, FCT, BTV*

Grand Illusion 🎬🎬🎬🎬 **1937** Unshakably classic anti-war film by Renoir, in which French prisoners of war attempt to escape from their German captors during WWI. An indictment of the way Old World, aristocratic nobility was brought to modern bloodshed in the Great War. Renoir's optimism remains relentless, but was easier to believe in before WWII. In French, with English subtitles. The laserdisc version includes an audio essay by Peter Crowe. **111m/B VHS, Beta, LV, DVD.** FR Jean Gabin, Erich von Stroheim, Pierre Fresnay, Marcel Dalio, Julien Carette, Gaston Modot, Jean Daste, Dita Parlo; **D:** Jean Renoir. New York Film Critics Awards '38: Best Foreign Film; Nominations: Academy Awards '38: Best Picture. *VYY, MRV, FOX*

Grand Isle 🎬🎬½ **1992** At the turn of the century Grand Isle is the place Louisiana gentry leisurely spend their summers. This is where Edna Pontellier (McGillis), the wife of a rich stockbroker, meets sensitive Creole artist Robert LeBrun (Pasdar). Robert gives Edna all the attention sorely lacking in her marriage and they fall in love. However, Edna's attempts to liberate herself from the strictures of society lead her to tragedy. Based on "The Awakening" by Kate Chopin. Made for cable television. **94m/C VHS, LV, Closed Caption.** Kelly McGillis, Adrian Pasdar, Julian Sands, Jon DeVries, Glenne Headly, Anthony De Sando, Ellen Burstyn; **D:** Mary Lambert; **W:** Hesper Anderson. *TTC*

Grand Larceny 🎬🎬 **1992** The daughter of a millionaire/thief has to prove that she can take over the family "business." Lots of action and stunts. **95m/C VHS.** Marilu Henner, Omar Sharif, Ian McShane, Louis Jourdan; **D:** Jeannot Szwarc. *CAF*

Grand Prix 🎬🎬 **1966** A big-budget look at the world of Grand Prix auto racing, as four top competitors circle the world's most famous racing circuits. Strictly for those who like cars racing round and round; nothing much happens off the track. Letterboxed screen is featured in the laserdisc format. **161m/C VHS, Beta, LV, Letterbox, Closed Caption.** James Garner, Eva Marie Saint, Yves Montand, Toshiro Mifune, Brian Bedford; **D:** John Frankenheimer; **C:** Lionel Lindon; **M:** Maurice Jarre. Academy Awards '66: Best Film Editing, Best Sound, Best Sound Effects Editing. *MGM, FCT*

Grand Theft Auto 🎬🎬 **1977 (PG)** In Howard's initial directorial effort, a young couple elopes to Las Vegas in a Rolls Royce owned by the bride's father. The father, totally against the marriage and angered by the stolen Rolls, offers a reward for their safe return and a cross-country race ensues. **84m/C VHS, Beta.** Ron Howard, Nancy Morgan, Marion Ross, Barry Cahill, Clint Howard; **D:** Ron Howard; **W:** Ron Howard. *NHO*

Grand Tour: Disaster in Time 🎬🎬 **1992 (PG-13)** Greenglen is a quiet, small Midwestern town, until it is visited by a sinister group of time traveling aliens. Daniels plays a widowed innkeeper who must save the town from destruction and save his daughter from being kidnapped by the fiends. Made for cable television. **98m/C VHS, LV, Closed Caption.** Jeff Daniels, Ariana Richards, Emilia Crow, Jim Haynie, Nicholas Guest, Marilyn Lightstone, George Murdock; **D:** David N. Twohy; **W:** David N. Twohy.

Grandes Amigos 🎬 *Great Friends* **197?** A young boy finds out the meaning of having a true friend in this comedy-drama in Spanish. **105m/C VHS, Beta.** SP Nino Del Arco. *MAD*

Grandma's House 🎬 **1988 (R)** A brother and sister discover that the house in which they live with their grandmother is chock-full of secrets and strange happenings, including madness, incest, and murder. **90m/C VHS, Beta, LV.** Eric Foster, Kim Valentine, Brinke Stevens, Ida Lee, Len Lesser; **D:** Peter Rader; **W:** Peter C. Jensen; **C:** Peter C. Jensen.

Grandview U.S.A. 🎬🎬½ **1984 (R)** A low-key look at low-rent middle America, centering on a foxy local speedway owner and the derby-obsessed boys she attracts. Pre-"Dirty Dancing" choreography from Patrick Swayze and wife Lisa Niemi. **97m/C VHS, Beta, Closed Caption.** Jamie Lee Curtis, Patrick Swayze, C. Thomas Howell, M. Emmet Walsh, Troy Donahue, William Windom, Jennifer Jason Leigh, Ramon Bieri, John Cusack, Joan Cusack, Jason Court; **D:** Randal Kleiser; **M:** Thomas Newman. *FOX*

The Granny 🎬½ **1994 (R)** Evil Granny Gargoli (Stevens) is so mean that just before she dies she swallows an ancient potion, enabling her to haunt her survivors. When Kelly (Whirry), the only one to really care for Granny, is cheated out of her inheritance, the rest of the family is in for some nasty shocks from the zombiefied oldster. Can't decide whether to be camp or horrific. **CW:** Violence and gore; crude sexuality; language. **85m/C VHS.** Shannon Whirry, Stella Stevens; **D:** Luca Bercovici; **W:** Luca Bercovici. *AVE*

The Grapes of Wrath 🎬🎬🎬½ **1940** John Steinbeck's classic American novel about the Great Depression. We follow the impoverished Joad family as they migrate from the dust bowl of Oklahoma to find work in the orchards of California and as they struggle to maintain at least a little of their dignity and pride. A sentimental but dignified, uncharacteristic Hollywood epic. **129m/B VHS, Beta, LV, Closed Caption.** Henry Fonda, Jane Darwell, John Carradine, Charley Grapewin, Zeffie Tilbury, Dorris Bowdon, Russell Simpson, John Qualen, Eddie Quillan, O.Z. Whitehead, Grant Mitchell; **D:** John Ford; **W:** Nunnally Johnson; **C:** Gregg Toland. Academy Awards '40: Best Director (Ford), Best Supporting Actress (Darwell), National Film Registry '89;; New York Film Critics Awards '40: Best Director (Ford), Best Film; Nominations: Academy Awards '40: Best Actor (Fonda), Best Film Editing, Best Picture, Best Screenplay, Best Sound, Best Original Score. *FXV, BTV, HMV*

The Grass Harp 🎬🎬½ **1995 (PG)** Rather dull retelling (with an excellent cast) of the Truman Capote novella covering the eccentricities of small town Southern life in the '30s and '40s. Teenaged Collin Fenwick (Furlong) is sent to live with his maiden aunts, artistic, impractical Dolly (Laurie) and shrewd, hard businesswoman Verena (Spacek). Charlie Cool's (Matthau) the retired judge who's sweet on Dolly, Morris Ritz (Lemmon) is a shady Chicago entrepreneur with plans for Verena's money, and there are various opinionated townspeople with stories to tell as well.

Screen nostalgia directed by Matthau's son Charles. **107m/C VHS, LV, Closed Caption.** Sissy Spacek, Piper Laurie, Edward Furlong, Walter Matthau, Nell Carter, Jack Lemmon, Mary Steenburgen, Roddy McDowall, Joe Don Baker, Charles Durning, Sean Patrick Flanery, Mia Kirshner; **D:** Charles Matthau; **W:** Stirling Silliphant; **C:** John A. Alonzo; **M:** Patrick Williams. *NLC*

The Grass Is Always Greener Over the Septic Tank 🎬🎬 **1978** Based on Erma Bombeck's best-seller. A city family's flight to the supposed peace of the suburbs turns out to be a comic compilation of complications. Made for television. **98m/C VHS, Beta.** Carol Burnett, Charles Grodin, Linda Gray, Alex Rocco, Robert Sampson, Vicki Belmonte, Craig Richard Nelson, Anrae Walterhouse, Eric Stoltz; **D:** Robert Day. *NO*

The Grass Is Greener 🎬🎬½ **1961** An American millionaire invades part of an impoverished Earl's mansion and falls in love with the lady of the house. The Earl, who wants to keep his wife, enlists the aid of an old girlfriend in a feeble attempt to make her jealous. The two couples pair off properly in the end. **105m/C VHS, LV, Letterbox.** Cary Grant, Deborah Kerr, Jean Simmons, Robert Mitchum; **D:** Stanley Donen. *REP*

The Grave 🎬🎬½ **1995 (R)** Rednecks King (Scheffer) and Tyn (Charles) escape from a North Carolina prison farm after learning about a possible fortune buried in a grave. Unfortunately, they can't keep their mouths shut and soon every other lowlife around them is hunting as well. **CW:** Violence, a sex scene and strong language. **90m/C VHS.** Craig Sheffer, Josh Charles, Gabrielle Anwar, Donal Logue, John Diehl, Anthony Michael Hall, Eric Roberts; **D:** Jonas Pate; **W:** Jonas Pate, Josh Pate; **C:** Frank Prinzi. *REP*

Grave Indiscretions 🎬🎬 *The Grotesque; Gentlemen Don't Eat Poets* **1996 (R)** Eccentric aristocrat, and amateur paleontologist, Sir Hugo Coal (Bates) is much more interested in the dinosaur skeleton he's attempting to assemble than in his crumbling estate or unsatisfied wife Harriet (Russell). Although he does take a dislike to the married servants his wife hires—sly butler Fledge (Sting) and his dipso cook/wife Doris (Styler). And then there's daughter Cleo (Headey) who's about to marry useles poet Sidney (Mackintosh) until he suddenly disappears. Which raises all sorts of questions, including just what the pigs have been eating recently. Based on McGrath's 1989 novel, "The Grotesque." **CW:** Nudity, sex and some gore. **97m/C VHS.** GB Sting, Alan Bates, Theresa Russell, Trudie Styler, Lena Headey, Steven Mackintosh, Anna Massey, Jim Carter, James Fleet, Maria Aitken; **D:** John-Paul Davidson; **W:** Patrick McGrath; **C:** Andrew Dunn; **M:** Anne Dudlem. *ART*

Grave of the Fireflies 🎬🎬🎬 **1988** In post-war Japan, in the city of Kobe's train station, a young boy lies dying. A janitor finds a metal canister lying next to the boy and when he opens it ashes fall out. As fireflies gather around, ghostly figures of the boy and his little sister appear, as the story flashes back to the orphaned, homeless Seita and his sister. The two youngsters struggle in the Japanese countryside but find they cannot escape the hardships of war and have no chance for survival. Stunning animated testimony to the human spirit. Based on the novel by Akiyuki Nosaka. In Japanese with English subtitles. **88m/C VHS, LV, Letterbox.** JP D: Isao Takahata; **W:** Isao Takahata. *CPM*

Grave of the Vampire 🎬 *Seed of Terror* **1972 (R)** A vampire rapes and impregnates a modern-day girl. Twenty years later, their son, who grows up to be a bitter bloodsucker, sets out to find his father and kill him. **95m/C VHS, Beta.** William Smith, Michael Pataki, Lyn Peters, Diane Holden, Jay Adler, Kitty Vallacher, Jay Scott, Lieux Dressler; **D:** John Hayes. *UNI*

Grave Secrets 🎬½ **1989 (R)** A professor of psychic phenomena teams up with a medium to find out who—or what—is controlling the life of a young woman. **90m/C VHS, LV.** Paul LeMat, Renee

Soutendijk, David Warner, Olivia Barash, Lee Ving; **D:** Donald P. Borchers. *SGE*

Grave Secrets: The Legacy of Hilltop Drive ♂♂ 1992
The Williams family finds out their dream house is built on the site of an old graveyard. The spirits are not only restless, they're deadly. Based on a true story. **94m/C VHS, Closed Caption.** Jonelle Allen, Patty Duke, David Selby, David Soul, Blake Clark; **D:** John D. Patterson. *WOV, PMS*

Gravesend ♂♂½ 1997 (R)
Big cajones, puny budget: mini-Scorsese Stabile delivers the goods. Tracks a night in the life of four delinquent Brooklyn buddies who find themselves with a dead body on their hands. To avoid police involvement, the boys recruit local drug dealer JoJo (Aquilino) to aid in the body's disposal. JoJo demands $500 and a finger from the victim in return. Rest of pic deals with the fellows' quest for the cash and incorporates a deluge of dark humor which, outside of the pat, in your face dialogue and action, is the picture's real draw. Nineteen at the time of shooting, film school dropout's $5,000 auspicious first picture grabbed the attention of such heavyweights as Spielberg (Stabile now has a two picture deal with his Dreamworks SKG) and Oliver Stone. **CW:** Extreme violence and profanity. **85m/C VHS.** Tony Tucci, Michael Parducci, Tom Malloy, Thomas Brandise, Macky Aquilino; **D:** Salvatore Stabile; **W:** Salvatore Stabile; **C:** Joseph Dell'Olio. *PGV*

The Graveyard ♂♂ Persecution; Terror of Sheba; Sheba 1974
A mommy spends many years torturing her little boy, David. In one blood-filled day, the fellow seeks his revenge. **90m/C VHS, Beta.** Lana Turner, Trevor Howard, Ralph Bates, Olga Georges-Picot, Suzan Farmer; **D:** Don Chaffey. *ELV*

Graveyard of Horror ♂ 1971
His wife and baby dead, a man seeking revenge discovers a horrible secret: his brother, a doctor, is stealing the heads from corpses. Dubbed. **105m/C VHS, Beta.** *SP* Bill Curran, Francisco (Frank) Brana, Beatriz Lacy; **D:** Miguel Madrid. *NO*

Graveyard Shift ♂½ 1987 (R)
A New York cabby on the night shift is actually a powerful vampire who uses his fares to build an army of vampires. Not to be confused with the 1990 Stephen King scripted film. Followed by "Understudy: Graveyard Shift II." **89m/C VHS, Beta.** Silvio Oliviero, Helen Papas, Cliff Stoker; **D:** Gerard Ciccoritti. *VTR*

Graveyard Shift ♂ Stephen King's Graveyard Shift 1990 (R)
Just because Stephen King wrote the original story doesn't mean its celluloid incarnation is guaranteed to stand your hair on end; unless that's your response to abject boredom. When a man takes over the night shift at a recently reopened textile mill, he starts to find remnants...and they aren't fabric. Seems there's a graveyard in the neighborhood. **89m/C VHS, Beta, LV, Closed Caption.** David Andrews, Kelly Wolf, Stephen Macht, Brad Dourif; **D:** Ralph S. Singleton; **W:** Stephen King, John Esposito; **M:** Brian Banks. *PAR, FCT*

Gray Lady Down ♂♂ 1977 (PG)
A nuclear submarine sinks off the coast of Cape Cod and with their oxygen running out, a risky escape in an experimental diving craft seems to be their only hope. Dull, all-semi-star suspenser. **111m/C VHS, Beta.** Charlton Heston, David Carradine, Stacy Keach, Ned Beatty, Ronny Cox, Christopher Reeve, Michael O'Keefe, Rosemary Forsyth; **D:** David Greene. *USH*

Grayeagle ♂♂ 1977 (PG)
When a frontier trapper's daughter is kidnapped by Cheyenne Indians, he launches a search for her recovery. More style than pace in this Western, but worth a look for fans of Johnson. **104m/C VHS, Beta.** Ben Johnson, Iron Eyes Cody, Lana Wood, Alex Cord, Jack Elam, Paul Fix, Cindy Butler, Charles B. Pierce; **D:** Charles B. Pierce; **W:** Charles B. Pierce. *WAR, OM*

Gray's Anatomy 1996
Yet another monologue from Gray, this time about his medical crisis involving a rare eye disease. **80m/C VHS.** Spalding Gray; **D:** Steven Soderbergh. *FXL*

Grazuole ♂♂ 1969
A nine-year-old girl is mockingly made "Beauty Queen" by her malicious playmates. **71m/B VHS, Beta. D:** Arunas Zhebrunas. *IHF*

Grease ♂♂♂ 1978 (PG)
Film version of the hit Broadway musical about summer love. Set in the 1950s, this spirited musical follows a group of high-schoolers throughout their senior year. The story offers a responsible moral: act like a tart and you'll get your guy; but, hey, it's all in fun anyway. Followed by a weak sequel. ♫Grease; Summer Nights; Hopelessly Devoted To You; You're the One That I Want; Sandy; Beauty School Dropout; Look at Me, I'm Sandra Dee; Greased Lightnin'; It's Raining on Prom Night. **110m/C VHS, Beta, LV.** John Travolta, Olivia Newton-John, Jeff Conaway, Stockard Channing, Eve Arden, Frankie Avalon, Sid Caesar; **D:** Randal Kleiser; **C:** Bill Butler. Nominations: Academy Awards '78: Best Song ("Hopelessly Devoted to You"). *PAR, FCT*

Grease 2 ♂♂ 1982 (PG)
Continuing saga of the T-Birds, the Pink Ladies, and young love at Rydell High. Newton-John and Travolta have graduated, leaving Pfeiffer to lead on love-struck book-neb Caulfield. Some okay tunes, though lame story lacks good-humor flair of the original. **115m/C VHS, Beta, LV.** Maxwell Caulfield, Michelle Pfeiffer, Adrian Zmed, Lorna Luft, Didi Conn, Eve Arden, Sid Caesar, Tab Hunter, Christopher McDonald; **D:** Patricia Birch; **M:** Artie Butler. *PAR*

Greased Lightning ♂♂½ 1977 (PG)
The story of the first black auto racing champion, Wendell Scott, who had to overcome racial prejudice to achieve his success. Slightly better-than-average Pryor comedy vehicle. **95m/C VHS, Beta, Closed Caption.** Richard Pryor, Pam Grier, Beau Bridges, Cleavon Little, Vincent Gardenia; **D:** Michael A. Schultz; **W:** Leon Capetanos, Melvin Van Peebles. *WAR*

Greaser's Palace ♂♂½ 1972
Seaweed-head Greaser, owner of the town's saloon, faces his arch-nemesis in this wide-ranging satiric Christ allegory from the director of "Putney Swope." **91m/C VHS, Beta.** Albert Henderson, Allan Arbus; **D:** Robert Downey; **M:** Jack Nitzsche. *COL, OM*

The Great Adventure ♂♂♂½ Det Stora Aventyret 1953
Two farm boys capture and attempt to train a wild otter. Unfortunately, the otter longs to once again join his kind despite the boys' efforts. Arne Sucksdorff won an Oscar for his arresting view of animal life. **73m/B VHS, Beta.** *SW* Anders Norberg, Kjell Sucksdorff, Arne Sucksdorff; **D:** Arne Sucksdorff; **W:** Arne Sucksdorff.

Great Adventure ♂♂ 1975 (PG)
In the severe environment of the gold rush days on the rugged Yukon territory, a touching tale unfolds of a young orphan boy and his eternal bond of friendship with a great northern dog. Based on a Jack London story. Paul Elliots is a pseudonym for Gianfranco Baldanello and Fred Romer is actually Fernando Romero. **90m/C VHS, Beta.** *IT SP* Jack Palance, Joan Collins, Fred Romer, Elisabetta Virgili, Remo de Angelis, Manuel de Blas; **D:** Paul Elliotts. *VTR*

The Great Alligator ♂ Il Fiume del Grande Caimano; Alligators 1981
As if you couldn't guess, this one's about a huge alligator who does what other huge alligators do...terrorizes the people at a resort. **89m/C VHS, Beta.** Barbara Bach, Mel Ferrer, Richard Johnson, Claudio Cassinelli, Romano Puppo; **D:** Sergio Martino; **W:** Sergio Martino, Ernesto Gastaldi, Luigi Montefiore, Maria Chiaretta; **C:** Giancarlo Ferrando. *MPI*

The Great American Broadcast ♂♂♂ 1941
Two WWI vets want more than anything to strike it rich. After many failed endeavors, the two try that new-fangled thing called radio. The station takes off, as does the plot. The girlfriend of one vet falls for his partner and numerous other misunderstandings and complications ensue. Charming and crazy musical with an energetic cast. ♫I've Got a Bone To Pick With You; It's All In a Lifetime; I Take to You; Long Ago Last Night; Where You Are; The Great American Broadcast; Albany Bound; Give My Regards to Broadway; If I Didn't Care. **92m/B VHS.** Alice Faye, John Payne, Jack Oakie, Cesar Romero, James Newill, Mary Beth Hughes; **D:** Archie Mayo; **C:** Leon Shamroy. *MLB*

The Great American Sex Scandal ♂♂½ Jury Duty 1994 (PG-13)
Sanford Lagelfust (Pinchot) is an meek accountant on trial for embezzlement, but when the prosecution's main witness turns out to be his sexy girlfriend Hope (Scoggins) the case turns into a courtroom sex scandal. Silly Canadian TV production. **94m/C VHS.** *CA* Bronson Pinchot, Tracy Scoggins, Heather Locklear, Stephen Baldwin, Lynn Redgrave, Alan Thicke, Madchen Amick, Barbara Bosson, Ilene Graff, Mark Blankfield, Danny Pintauro, Reginald Vel Johnson, Jacklyn Zeman; **D:** Michael A. Schultz. *APX*

Great American Traffic Jam ♂½ Gridlock 1980 (PG)
A made-for-television farce about the humorous variety of characters interacting on the interstate during a massive California traffic jam. **97m/C VHS, Beta, Closed Caption.** Ed McMahon, Vic Tayback, Howard Hesseman, Abe Vigoda, Noah Beery Jr., Desi Arnaz Jr., John Beck, Shelley Fabares, James Gregory; **D:** James Frawley. *FOX*

The Great American Western Collection: Roy Rogers 194?
Series of three Roy Rogers classics. "West of the Badlands" is an adaptation of Zane Grey's novel "Border Legion." Rogers plays an outlaw who sacrifices himself to save a pair of lovers. In "Jesse James at Bay," Rogers plays a romanticized version of James, stealing from the rich and powerful railroad to help the poor settlers keep their land. Rogers and Dale Evans star together in the singing western classic, Yellow Rose of Texas. **180m/B VHS.** Roy Rogers, George "Gabby" Hayes, Dale Evans. *BPG*

The Great Armored Car Swindle ♂♂ 1964
An anonymous English businessman becomes involved in international intrigue when he becomes a pawn in a plan to transfer money to a Middle Eastern government under communist rule. But thanks to his wife things don't go off as planned. **58m/B VHS, Beta.** Peter Reynolds, Dermot Walsh, Joanna Dunham, Lisa Gastoni, Brian Cobby; **D:** Lance Comfort. *SNC*

Great Balls of Fire ♂♂½ 1989 (PG-13)
A florid, comic-book film of the glory days of Jerry Lee Lewis, from his first band to stardom. Most of the drama is derived from his marriage to his 13-year-old cousin. Somewhat overacted but full of energy. The soundtrack features many of the "Killer's" greatest hits re-recorded by Jerry Lee Lewis for the film. **108m/C VHS, Beta, LV, Closed Caption.** Dennis Quaid, Winona Ryder, Alec Baldwin, Trey Wilson, John Doe, Lisa Blount, Steve Allen, Stephen Tobolowsky, Lisa Jane Persky, Michael St. Gerard, Peter Cook; **D:** Jim McBride; **W:** Jack Baran, Jim McBride; **C:** Alfonso Beato; **M:** Jack Baran, Jim McBride. *ORI*

Great Bank Hoax ♂♂½ The Great Georgia Bank Hoax; Shenanigans 1978 (PG)
Three bank managers decide to rob their own bank to cover up the fact that all the assets have been embezzled. **89m/C VHS, Beta, Closed Caption.** Richard Basehart, Ned Beatty, Burgess Meredith, Michael Murphy, Paul Sand, Arthur Godfrey; **D:** Joseph Jacoby; **C:** Walter Lassally. *WAR*

Great Bikini Off-Road Adventure ♂½ 1994 (R)
Duke Abbey is about to lose his jeep tour company because business is so slow that he can't pay the rent. Then Duke's niece Lori decides to get her bikini-clad friends to hire on as drivers, showing lots of sights on their desert tours. **90m/C VHS, LV, Closed Caption.** Avalon Anders, Lauren Hays, Floyd Irons, Laura Hudspeth, Dan Frank; **D:** Gary Orona. *IMP, IME*

The Great Caruso ♂♂½ 1951
The story of opera legend Enrico Caruso's rise to fame, from his childhood in Naples, Italy, to his collapse on the stage of the Metropolitan Opera House. Lanza is superb as the singer, and there are 27 musical numbers to satisfy the opera lover. ♫The Loveliest Night of the Year; Over the Waves; Vesti la Giubba; M'Appari; Celeste Aida; Numi, Pieta;

La Fatal Pietra; Sextet from Lucia di Lammermoor; La Donne a Mobile. 113m/C VHS, Beta, LV. Mario Lanza, Ann Blyth, Dorothy Kirsten; **D:** Richard Thorpe; **C:** Joseph Ruttenberg. Academy Awards '51: Best Sound; Nominations: Academy Awards '51: Best Costume Design (Color), Scoring of a Musical. *MGM*

Great Chase ♂♂½ 1963 A historical anthology of the funniest and most suspenseful classic movie chases, especially "The General." 79m/B VHS, Beta. Buster Keaton, Lillian Gish, Pearl White, Noah Beery Jr.; **M:** Larry Adler. *NLC*

The Great Commandment ♂ 1941 Young man throws himself into a revolution against the overbearing Roman Empire in 30 A.D. His brother joins him but is killed. The man, who has become influenced by the teachings of Christ, decides to give up his revolution and go off with his brother's widow. (He always loved her anyway.) 78m/B VHS. John Beal, Maurice Moscovich, Albert Dekker, Marjorie Cooley, Warren McCollum; **D:** Irving Pichel. *REP*

Great Dan Patch ♂½ 1949 The story of the great Dan Patch, the horse that went on to become the highest-earning harness racer in history. 92m/B VHS, Beta. Dennis O'Keefe, Gail Russell, Ruth Warrick; **D:** Joseph M. Newman. *VEC*

Great Day ♂½ 1946 A soap opera set around the wartime visit of first lady Eleanor Roosevelt to a small British town. It focuses mainly on the wife and daughter of a bitter, alcoholic WWI vet. 62m/B VHS, Beta. Eric Portman, Flora Robson, Sheila Sim, Isabel Jeans, Walter Fitzgerald, Philip Friend, Marjorie Rhodes, Maire O'Neill, Beatrice Varley; **D:** Lance Comfort. *TTC*

Great Day in the Morning ♂♂½ 1956 A rebel sympathizer and a Northern spy are both after Colorado gold to help finance the Civil War. But our Southern gentlemen soon find themselves equally interested in the local ladies. 92m/C VHS, Beta. Robert Stack, Ruth Roman, Raymond Burr, Virginia Mayo, Alex Nicol, Regis Toomey; **D:** Jacques Tourneur. *NO*

The Great Dictator ♂♂♂♂ 1940 Chaplin's first all-dialogue film, a searing satire on Nazism in which he has dual roles as a Jewish barber with amnesia who is mistaken for a Hitlerian dictator, Adenoid Hynkel. A classic scene involves Hynkel playing with a gigantic balloon of the world. Hitler banned the film's release to the German public due to its highly offensive portrait of him. The film also marked Chaplin's last wearing of the Little Tramp's (and Hitler's equally famous) mustache. 126m/B VHS, Beta, LV. Charlie Chaplin, Paulette Goddard, Jack Oakie, Billy Gilbert, Reginald Gardiner, Henry Daniell, Maurice Moscovich; **D:** Charlie Chaplin; **W:** Charlie Chaplin; **C:** Karl Struss. National Film Registry '97; New York Film Critics Awards '40: Best Actor (Chaplin); Nominations: Academy Awards '40: Best Actor (Chaplin), Best Original Screenplay, Best Picture, Best Supporting Actor (Oakie), Best Original Score. *FOX, HMV, GLV*

The Great Elephant Escape ♂♂½ 1995 Vacationing American teen Gordon-Levitt teams up with Kenyan M'Cormac, who works at an animal orphanage, to save a baby elephant from an unscrupulous businessman and his poacher friends. Made for TV. 90m/C VHS, Closed Caption. Joseph Gordon-Levitt, Frederick M'Cormac, Stephanie Zimbalist, Leo Burmester, Julian Sands; **D:** George Miller; **W:** John Sweet, Christopher Canaan. *CAF*

The Great Escape ♂♂♂½ 1963 During WWII, troublesome allied POWs are thrown by the Nazis into an escape-proof camp, where they join forces in a single mass break for freedom. One of the great war movies, with a superb ensemble cast and lots of excitement. The story was true, based on the novel by Paul Brickhill. McQueen performed most of the stunts himself, against the wishes of director Sturges. Laserdisc features an analysis of the true story that inspired the movie, actual photos of the camp, prisoners, and guards, commentary by director Sturges, composer Bernstein, and stuntman Bud Ekins,

excerpts from the script by novelist/screenwriter Clavell, over 250 production photos, and the original movie trailer. Followed by a made for TV movie 25 years later. 170m/C VHS, Beta, LV, Letterbox, Closed Caption. Steve McQueen, James Garner, Richard Attenborough, Charles Bronson, James Coburn, Donald Pleasence, David McCallum, James Donald, Gordon Jackson; **D:** John Sturges; **W:** James Clavell, W.R. Burnett; **C:** Daniel F. Fapp; **M:** Elmer Bernstein. Nominations: Academy Awards '63: Best Film Editing. *MGM, FOX, CRC*

The Great Escape 2: The Untold Story ♂♂ 1988 Bland actioner can't decide whether it's a remake of the original or a sequel; it pretends to be a sequel yet spends a lot of time retelling—poorly—the first great escape. Once it gets around to the sequel part, it dispenses with protocol: Pleasence, an escapee in the original, is a Nazi bad guy in this go-round. Poor casting, especially Reeves, unconvincing as a German-speaking British officer who rallies the surviving escapees in revenge against their WWII captors. Made for television and originally shown in two parts, but mercifully shortened for video. 93m/C VHS. Christopher Reeve, Judd Hirsch, Ian McShane, Donald Pleasence, Anthony Jonn Denison, Jud Taylor, Charles Haid; **D:** Michael Nader, Paul Wendkos. *THV, TLF*

Great Expectations ♂♂½ 1934 Weak Hollywood adaptation of the Dickens novel, easily dwarfed by the brilliant 1946 version. Holmes is Pip, the orphan who rises in the world thanks to a mysterious benefactor (Hull), with Wyatt as Pip's disdainful love, Estrella. 102m/B VHS, Closed Caption. Phillips Holmes, Henry Hull, Jane Wyatt, Florence Reed, Francis L. Sullivan, Alan Hale; **D:** Stuart Walker; **W:** Gladys Unger; **C:** George Robinson. *USH*

Great Expectations ♂♂♂♂ 1946 Lean's magisterial adaptation of the Dickens tome, in which a young English orphan is graced by a mysterious benefactor and becomes a well-heeled gentleman. Hailed and revered over the years; possibly the best Dickens on film. Well-acted by all, but especially notable is Hunt's slightly mad and pathetic Miss Havisham. Remake of the 1934 film. 118m/B VHS, Beta, LV. *GB* John Mills, Valerie Hobson, Anthony Wager, Alec Guinness, Finlay Currie, Jean Simmons, Bernard Miles, Francis L. Sullivan, Martita Hunt, Freda Jackson, Torin Thatcher, Hay Petrie, Eileen Erskine, George "Gabby" Hayes, Everley Gregg, O.B. Clarence; **D:** David Lean; **W:** David Lean, Ronald Neame; **C:** Guy Green. Academy Awards '47: Best Art Direction/Set Decoration (B & W), Best Black and White Cinematography; Nominations: Academy Awards '47: Best Director (Lean), Best Picture, Best Screenplay. *PAR, BFA, HMV*

Great Expectations ♂♂ 1981 A British television mini-series adaptation of the Dickens epic about Pip and his mysterious benefactor in Victorian London. On two tapes. 300m/C VHS, Beta, Closed Caption. *GB* Gerry Sundquist, Stratford Johns, Joan Hickson. *NO*

Great Expectations ♂♂♂ 1989 Dickens classic retold on three cassettes. A mysterious benefactor turns a poor orphan boy into a gentleman of means. 325m/C VHS, Beta, Closed Caption. *GB* Jean Simmons, Anthony Hopkins, John Rhys-Davies; **D:** Kevin Connor. *DIS*

Great Expectations ♂♂ 1997 (R) Expecting "Great Expectations?" The title and basic storyline are about all the filmmakers took for their contemporary updating of Dickens' story. The artistic, orphaned Finn (Hawke) is living a meager existence with his trashy sister and his "uncle" Joe in a Florida fishing town. His destiny is intertwined with an escaped convict (De Niro) he aids, the rich and loony Ms. Dinsmoor (Bancroft) and Dinsmoor's beautiful niece Estella (Paltrow). After being spurned by Estella as a teen, Finn quits painting and drawing entirely. Years later a mysterious art dealer offers him a one-man show in New York if he will move there and start creating again. Estella inevitably reappears in his life, providing more than a little inspiration. More style than substance. Although the visuals are stunning, the director should have learned that beauty

on the surface isn't all it's cracked up to be from, say...hmm... "Great Expectations" by Charles Dickens maybe? **CW:** Language and some sexuality. 112m/C VHS, LV, Closed Caption. Ethan Hawke, Robert De Niro, Gwyneth Paltrow, Hank Azaria, Anne Bancroft, Chris Cooper, Josh Mostel, Kim Dickens, Nell Campbell, Stephen Spinella; **D:** Alfonso Cuaron; **W:** Mitch Glazer; **C:** Emmanuel Lubezki; **M:** Patrick Doyle. *FXV*

Great Expectations: The Untold Story ♂♂½ 1987 Magwitch is an escaped convict, hiding out in the Victorian English countryside, who is aided by the young orphan, Pip. Captured and sent to the penal colonies in Australia, Magwitch serves his time and then discovers a fortune in gold, which he decides to use to make Pip into a gentleman. But Magwitch's enemies would like to get Pip's inheritance for themselves. Based on the Dickens classic, this three-tape miniseries is also available in a 102-minute feature length version. 287m/C VHS. John Stanton, Sigrid Thornton, Robert Coleby, Todd Boyce, Anne Louise Lambert, Ron Haddrick, Noel Ferrier; **D:** Tim Burstall. *FCT*

Great Flamarion ♂♂½ 1945 A woman-hating trick-shot artist is nevertheless duped into murdering the husband of his femme fatale assistant after he comes to believe she loves him. He's wrong. 78m/B VHS, Beta. Dan Duryea, Erich von Stroheim, Mary Beth Hughes; **D:** Anthony Mann. *SNC, NOS, DVT*

The Great Gabbo ♂♂ 1929 A ventriloquist can express himself only through his dummy, losing his own identity and going mad at the end. Von Stroheim's first talkie. May quite possibly be the first mentally-twisted-ventriloquist story ever put on film. Von Stroheim hated the movie, believing it to be analogous to his own life. When he tried to buy the rights to the film, presumably to destroy the prints, he found that the property had been already purchased by real-life ventriloquist, Edgar Bergen. Based on a story by Ben Hecht. ♫The New Step; I'm Laughing Ickey; I'm in Love With You; The Ga-Ga Bird; The Web of Love; Every Now and Then. 82m/B VHS, Beta. Erich von Stroheim, Betty Compson, Don Douglas, Marjorie Kane; **D:** James Cruze. *SNC, NOS, DVT*

The Great Gatsby ♂♂½ 1949 Follows the silent 1926 version of F. Scott Fitzgerald's Jazz Era novel. Mysterious Jay Gatsby (Ladd) is a wealthy gangster and bootlegger who tries to buy his way into fast-living New York society. He befriends well-bred but penniless Nick Carraway (Carey), who serves as Gatsby's one true friend and eyewitness to the unfolding events. Gatsby rekindles his love for decorative Daisy (Field), who married into money and society and merely toys with leaving it all behind for Gatsby. Finally, the shallowness and selfishness all about prove to be Gatsby's undoing. 92m/B VHS, Closed Caption. Alan Ladd, Betty Field, MacDonald Carey, Ruth Hussey, Barry Sullivan, Howard da Silva, Shelley Winters, Henry Hull, Ed Begley Sr., Elisha Cook Jr.; **D:** Elliott Nugent; **W:** Cyril Hume, Richard Maibaum; **C:** John Seitz; **M:** Robert Emmett Dolan. *USH*

The Great Gatsby ♂♂½ 1974 (PG) Adaptation of F. Scott Fitzgerald's novel of the idle rich in the 1920s. A mysterious millionaire crashes Long Island society, and finds his heart captured by an impetuous and emotionally impoverished girl. Skillful acting and directing captures the look and feel of this era, but the movie doesn't have the power of the book. 144m/C VHS, Beta, LV, Closed Caption. Robert Redford, Mia Farrow, Bruce Dern, Karen Black, Patsy Kensit, Sam Waterston, Howard da Silva, Edward Herrmann; **D:** Jack Clayton; **W:** Francis Ford Coppola; **M:** Nelson Riddle. Academy Awards '74: Best Costume Design, Original Song Score and/or Adaptation; Golden Globe Awards '75: Best Supporting Actress (Black). *PAR, FCT*

The Great Gildersleeve ♂♂ 1943 Throckmorton P. Gildersleeve adds another problem to his list; the sister of a local judge wants to marry him. His niece and nephew won't allow it and his attempts to juggle everyone's desires make for fine fun. Peary was also the voice for the popular radio series of the same name. **62m/B VHS.** Harold Peary, Jane Darwell, Nancy Gates, Charles Arnt, Thurston Hall; **D:** Gordon Douglas.

Great Gold Swindle 🐾🐾 1984 A dramatization of the 1982 swindling of the Perth Mint in Australia of over $650,000 worth of gold. **101m/C VHS, Beta.** John Hargreaves, Robert C. Hughes, Tony Rickards, Barbara Llewellyn. *ART*

The Great Gundown 🐾½ 1975 A violent tale set in the Old West. The peace of frontier New Mexico erupts when a half-breed Indian leads a brutal assault on an outlaw stronghold. **98m/C VHS, Beta.** Robert Padilla, Richard Rust, Milila St. Duval; **D:** Paul Hunt. *HHT*

Great Guns 🐾🐾 1941 Stan and Ollie enlist in the army to protect a spoiled millionaire's son but wind up being targets at target practice instead. Not one of their better efforts. **74m/B VHS, Beta.** Stan Laurel, Oliver Hardy, Sheila Ryan, Dick Nelson; **D:** Montague Banks. *FOX, MLB*

Great Guy 🐾½ *Pluck of the Irish* 1936 One of Cagney's lesser roles as an ex-boxer turned food inspector who wipes out graft in his town. **50m/B VHS, Beta.** James Cagney, Mae Clarke, Edward Brophy; **D:** John Blystone. *NOS, MRV, CAB*

The Great Hunter 🐾 1975 A village militia captain and his girlfriend seek to destroy the men who killed the girl's father. **91m/C VHS, Beta.** Chia Ling, Wang Yu, Hsu Feng. *UNI*

The Great Impostor 🐾🐾½ 1961 The true story of Ferdinand Waldo Demara, Jr., who during the 1950s, hoodwinked people by impersonating a surgeon, a college professor, a monk, a prison warden and a schoolteacher, with the FBI always one step behind him. **112m/C VHS, Beta.** Tony Curtis, Edmond O'Brien, Arthur O'Connell, Gary Merrill, Raymond Massey, Karl Malden, Mike Kellin, Frank Gorshin; **D:** Robert Mulligan; **C:** Robert Burks; **M:** Henry Mancini. *USH*

Great Jesse James Raid 🐾½ 1949 Jesse James comes out of retirement to carry out a mine theft. Routine. **73m/C VHS, Beta.** Willard Parker, Barbara Payton, Tom Neal, Wallace Ford; **D:** Reginald LeBorg. *RXM, MRV*

Great K & A Train Robbery 🐾🐾½ 1926 A railroad detective is hired to find and stop the bandits who have been preying on the K & A Railroad. Silent. **55m/B VHS, Beta.** Tom Mix, Dorothy Dwan, William Walling, Harry Grippe, Carl Miller; **D:** Lewis Seiler. *GPV, GVV*

The Great Land of Small 🐾🐾 1986 (G) Two children enter a fantasy world and try to save it from Evil. For kids. **94m/C VHS, Beta.** Karen Elkin, Michael Blouin, Michael Anderson Jr., Ken Roberts; **D:** Vojtech Jasny. *VTR, HHE*

Great Leaders of the Bibles 197? The inspiring stories of two Old Testament heroes, Gideon and Samson, are dramatized in this beautifully constructed film. **105m/C VHS, Beta.** Ivo Garrani, Fernando Rey, Giorgio Ceridni. *VCI*

The Great Lie 1941 A great soaper with Davis and Astor as rivals for the affections of Brent, an irresponsible flyer. Astor is the concert pianist who marries Brent and then finds out she's pregnant after he's presumed dead in a crash. The wealthy Davis offers to raise the baby so Astor can continue her career. But when Brent does return, who will it be to? Sparkling, catty fun. Astor's very short, mannish haircut became a popular trend. **107m/B VHS, Beta, LV.** Bette Davis, Mary Astor, George Brent, Lucile Watson, Hattie McDaniel, Grant Mitchell, Jerome Cowan; **D:** Edmund Goulding; **C:** Gaetano Antonio "Tony" Gaudio; **M:** Max Steiner. Academy Awards '41: Best Supporting Actress (Astor). *MGM, BTV*

The Great Locomotive Chase 🐾🐾½ *Andrews' Raiders* 1956 During the Civil War, Parker and his fellow soldiers head into Confederate territory to disrupt railroad supply lines. They take over a locomotive, but are pursued by Confederate Hunter, the conductor of another train; and soon a pursuit is underway. Based on the true story of Andrew's Raiders. **85m/C VHS, Beta.** Fess Parker, Jeffrey Hunter, Kenneth Tobey; **D:** Francis D. Lyon. *DIS*

The Great Los Angeles Earthquake 🐾½ *The Big One: The Great Los Angeles Earthquake* 1991 Made-for-TV disaster movie is the same old story; multiple soap-opera plotlines are spun around terrifying special effects, as L.A. is devastated by three major earth tremors and attendant disasters. Condensed from a two-part miniseries. **106m/C VHS, Closed Caption.** Ed Begley Jr., Joanna Kerns; **D:** Larry Elikann. *THV*

Great Love Experiment 🐾 1984 Everyone in a high school learns a valuable lesson about beauty and friendship when four popular students try to change the personality of an awkward classmate. **52m/C VHS, Beta.** Tracy Pollan, Esai Morales, Kelly Wolf, Scott Benderer. *NO*

The Great Lover 🐾🐾½ 1949 Aboard an ocean liner, a bumbler chaperoning school kids gets involved with a gambler, a duchess and a murder. Vintage Bob Hope. **80m/B VHS, Beta.** Bob Hope, Rhonda Fleming, Roland Young, Roland Culver, George Reeves, Jim Backus; **D:** Alexander Hall. *COL, FCT*

The Great Madcap 🐾🐾 1949 A wealthy man believes in lavishly indulging himself which drives his excessively conservative family crazy. Bunuel satirizes behavioral extremes, Christianity, advertising, sex, and a number of other popular absurdities. In Spanish with English subtitles. **90m/B VHS.** *MX* Fernando Soler, Rosario Granados, Ruben Rogo; **D:** Luis Bunuel. *WBF*

The Great Man Votes 🐾🐾🐾 1938 Alcoholic college professor Barrymore falls into a deep depression after his wife's death. His children then plan to create a situation wherein his vote will decide the fate of the new town mayor, thus instilling in him a newly found sense of importance for himself and his children. Satiric and funny. **72m/B VHS, Beta.** John Barrymore, Peter Holden, Virginia Weidler, Katherine Alexander, Donald MacBride, Elisabeth Risdon, Granville Bates, Luis Alberni, J.M. Kerrigan, William Demarest, Roy Gordon; **D:** Garson Kanin; **C:** Russell Metty. *TTC*

The Great Man's Lady 🐾🐾½ 1942 Stanwyck stars in a "stand by your man" story in which she supported and was responsible for the good deeds of a now past town hero. Told in flashback sequence, Stanwyck's character, 109-year-old Hanna Sampler, reveals to a young biographer the trials and tribulations of her life with Ethan Hoyt, founder of Hoyt City, who is being honored with the dedication of a statue in the opening of the film. The picture reveals their secrets and the truth about the woman behind the man. Based on the story "The Human Side" by Vina Delmar. **91m/B VHS, Closed Caption.** Barbara Stanwyck, Joel McCrea, Brian Donlevy; **D:** William A. Wellman; **W:** Seena Owen, W.L. Rivers, Adela Rogers St. John; **C:** William Mellor; **M:** Victor Young. *USH*

The Great McGinty 🐾🐾🐾½ *Down Went McGinty* 1940 Sturges' directorial debut, about the rise and fall of a small-time, bribe-happy politician is an acerbic, ultra-cynical indictment of modern politics that stands, like much of his other work, as bracingly courageous as anything that's ever snuck past the Hollywood censors. Political party boss Tamiroff chews the scenery with gusto while Donlevy, in his first starring role, is more than his equal as the not-so-dumb political hack. **82m/B VHS, Beta.** Brian Donlevy, Muriel Angelus, Akim Tamiroff, Louis Jean Heydt, Arthur Hoyt, William Demarest; **D:** Preston Sturges; **W:** Preston Sturges; **C:** William Mellor. Academy Awards '40: Best Original Screenplay.*USH*

Great McGonagall 🐾½ 1975 Tale of an unemployed Scot trying to become Britain's poet laureate. Sellers adds a semi-bright spot with his portrayal of Queen Victoria. **95m/C VHS.** *GB* Peter Sellers, Spike Milligan, Julia Foster; **D:** Joseph McGrath. *MOV, VTR*

The Great Mike 🐾🐾½ 1944 Unlikely but moving story of a young boy who convinces track management that his work horse has a chance against the touted thoroughbred. Sentimental, with little innovation, but generally well-acted. **72m/B VHS.** Stuart Erwin, Robert "Buzzy" Henry, Pierre Watkin, Gwen Kenyon, Carl "Alfalfa" Switzer, Edythe Elliott, Marion Martin; **D:** Wallace Fox. *NOS*

Great Missouri Raid 🐾🐾 1951 Follows the famous adventures of the James/Younger gang and their eventual demise. **81m/C VHS, Beta.** Wendell Corey, MacDonald Carey, Ellen Drew, Ward Bond; **D:** Gordon Douglas; **C:** Ray Rennahan. *BAR*

The Great Moment 🐾🐾 1944 Story of the Boston dentist who discovered ether's use as an anesthetic in 1845. Confusing at times, changing from comedy to drama and containing flashbacks that add little to the story. Surprisingly bland result from ordinarily solid cast and director. **87m/B VHS, Beta.** Joel McCrea, Betty Field, Harry Carey Sr., William Demarest, Franklin Pangborn, Porter Hall; **D:** Preston Sturges; **C:** Victor Milner. *USH*

The Great Mouse Detective 🐾🐾🐾 *The Adventures of the Great Mouse Detective* 1986 (G) Animated version of the book "Basil of Baker Street" by Eve Titus. Fun adventure about Sherlock-of-the-mouse-world. Not as good as some of the other Disney animated features, but kids will enjoy it nonetheless. In 1992 it was rereleased. **74m/C VHS, Beta, LV, Closed Caption. D:** John Musker, Ron Clements, Dave Michener, Burny Mattinson; **W:** Ron Clements, Dave Michener; **M:** Henry Mancini; **V:** Vincent Price, Barrie Ingham, Val Bettin, Susanne Pollatschek, Candy Candido, Eve Brenner, Alan Young, Melissa Manchester. *DIS, OM*

Great Movie Stunts & the Making of Raiders of the Lost Ark 1981 Two television specials: "Movie Stunts" demonstrates how major action sequences were designed and executed, and "Making of Raiders" captures the cast and crew as they tackle the many problems created in filming the spectacular scenes. **107m/C VHS, Beta, LV.** Harrison Ford. *PAR*

The Great Muppet Caper 🐾🐾🐾 1981 (G) A group of hapless reporters (Kermit, Fozzie Bear, and Gonzo) travel to London to follow up on a major jewel robbery. **95m/C VHS, Beta, LV.** Charles Grodin, Diana Rigg; **Cameos:** John Cleese, Robert Morley, Peter Ustinov, Peter Falk, Jack Warden; **D:** Jim Henson; **W:** Jack Rose; **C:** Oswald Morris; **V:** Frank Oz. Nominations: Academy Awards '81: Best Song ("The First Time It Happens"). *FOX*

The Great Northfield Minnesota Raid 🐾🐾½ 1972 (PG) The Younger/James gang decides to rob the biggest bank west of the Mississippi, but everything goes wrong. Uneven, offbeat western, but Duvall's portrayal of the psychotic Jesse James and Robertson's cunning Cole Younger are notable. **91m/C VHS, Beta.** Cliff Robertson, Robert Duvall, Elisha Cook Jr., Luke Askew, R.G. Armstrong, Donald Moffat, Matt Clark; **D:** Philip Kaufman; **W:** Philip Kaufman; **C:** Bruce Surtees; **M:** Dave Grusin. *USH*

The Great Outdoors 🐾🐾 1988 (PG) Good cast is mostly wasted in another John Hughes' tale of vacation gone bad. A family's peaceful summer by the lake is disturbed by their uninvited, trouble-making relatives. Aykroyd and Candy are two funny guys done in by a lame script that awkwardly examines friendship and coming of age and throws in a giant bear when things get unbearably slow. May be fun for small fry. **91m/C VHS, Beta, LV, Closed Caption, DVD.** Dan Aykroyd, John Candy, Stephanie Faracy, Annette Bening, Chris Young, Lucy Deakins; **D:** Howard Deutch; **W:** John Hughes; **M:** Thomas Newman. *USH*

The Great Race 🐾🐾 1965 A dastardly villain, a noble hero, and a spirited suffragette are among the competitors in an uproarious New York-to-Paris auto race circa 1908, complete with pie fights, saloon brawls, and a confrontation with a feisty polar bear. Overly long and only sporadically funny. **160m/C VHS, Closed Caption.** Jack Lemmon, Tony Curtis, Natalie Wood, Peter Falk, Keenan Wynn, George Macready; **D:** Blake Edwards; **M:** Henry Mancini. Academy Awards '65: Best Sound Effects Editing; Nominations: Academy Awards '65: Best Color Cinematography, Best Film Editing, Best Song ("The Sweetheart Tree"), Best Sound. *WAR, FCT*

Great Ride ✓ 1978 State police are after two dirt bikers who are riding through areas where bike riding is illegal. **90m/C VHS, Beta.** Perry Lang, Michael MacRae, Michael Sullivan; **D:** Don Hulette. *NO*

The Great Riviera Bank Robbery ✓✓½ 1979 A genius executes a bank robbery on the French Riviera netting 15 million dollars. Based on a true story, the film chronicles the unfolding of the heist. **98m/C VHS, Beta.** Ian McShane, Warren Clarke, Stephen Greif, Christopher Malcolm; **D:** Francis Megahy. *MPI*

The Great Rupert ✓✓✓ 1950 Durante and family are befriended by a helpful squirrel (a puppet) in obtaining a huge fortune. Good fun; Durante shines. **86m/B VHS, Beta.** Jimmy Durante, Terry Moore, Tom Drake, Frank Orth, Sara Haden, Queenie Smith; **D:** Irving Pichel. *DVT, HEG, VYY*

The Great St. Louis Bank Robbery ✓✓½ 1959 Three career criminals (Denton, Clarke, Dukas) and young turk McQueen are brought together for a bank heist. They don't trust each other, which proves fatal when the heist goes bad. Based on a true story and filmed in semi-documentary style. Nineteen-year-old McQueen's follow-up to "The Blob." **86m/B VHS.** Graham Denton, David Clarke, James Dukas, Steve McQueen, Molly McCarthy; **D:** Charles Guggenheim. *IVY*

The Great St. Trinian's Train Robbery ✓✓ 1966 Train robbers hide their considerable loot in an empty country mansion only to discover, upon returning years later, it has been converted into a girls' boarding school. When they try to recover the money, the thieves run up against a band of pestiferous adolescent girls, with hilarious results. Based on the cartoon by Ronald Searle. Sequel to "The Pure Hell of St. Trinian's." **90m/C VHS, Beta.** *GB* Dora Bryan, Frankie Howerd, Reg Varney, Desmond Walter Ellis; **D:** Sidney Gilliat, Frank Launder; **M:** Malcolm Arnold. *NO*

The Great Santini ✓✓✓ *Ace* 1980 (PG) Lt. Col. Bull Meechum, the "Great Santini," a Marine pilot stationed stateside, fights a war involving his frustrated career goals, repressed emotions, and family. His family becomes his company of marines, as he abuses them in the name of discipline, because he doesn't allow himself any other way to show his affection. With a standout performance by Duvall, the film successfully blends warm humor and tenderness with the harsh cruelties inherent with dysfunctional families and racism. Based on Pat Conroy's autobiographical novel, the movie was virtually undistributed when first released, but re-released due to critical acclaim. **118m/C VHS, Beta, 8mm.** Robert Duvall, Blythe Danner, Michael O'Keefe, Julie Ann Haddock, Lisa Jane Persky, David Keith; **D:** Lewis John Carlino; **W:** Lewis John Carlino; **M:** Elmer Bernstein. Montreal World Film Festival '80: Best Actor (Duvall); Nominations: Academy Awards '80: Best Actor (Duvall), Best Supporting Actor (O'Keefe). *WAR*

Great Scout & Cathouse Thursday ✓½ *Wildcat* 1976 (PG) Marvin and Reed vow to take revenge on their third partner, Culp, who made off with all their profits from a gold mine. The title refers to Marvin's May-December romance with prostitute Lenz. Already forgotten, unfunny, all-star comedy with cutesy title. **96m/C VHS, Beta.** Lee Marvin, Oliver Reed, Robert Culp, Elizabeth Ashley, Kay Lenz; **D:** Don Taylor. *ART, VES*

The Great Skycopter Rescue ✓ 1982 Ruthless businessmen hire a motorcycle gang to terrorize and scare away the inhabitants of an oil-rich town. A local teenage flying enthusiast organizes his friends into an attack force to

fight back. 96m/C VHS, Beta. William Marshall, Aldo Ray, Russell Johnson, Terry Michos, Terry Taylor; **D:** Lawrence Foldes. *MGM*

Great Smokey Roadblock ✓✓ *Last of the Cowboys* 1976 (PG) While in the hospital, a 60-year-old truck driver's rig is repossessed by the finance company. Deciding that it's time to make one last perfect cross country run, he escapes from the hospital, steals his truck, picks up six prostitutes, heads off into the night with the police on his tail, and becomes a folk hero. **84m/C VHS, Beta.** Henry Fonda, Eileen Brennan, Susan Sarandon, John Byner; **D:** John Leone.

The Great Texas Dynamite Chase ✓½ *Dynamite Women* 1976 (R) Two sexy young women drive across Texas with a carload of dynamite. They leave a trail of empty banks with the cops constantly on their trail. **90m/C VHS, Beta.** Claudia Jennings, Jocelyn Jones, Johnny Crawford, Chris Pennock, Tara Strohmeier, Miles Watkins, Bart Braverman; **D:** Michael Pressman. *WAR, OM*

The Great Train Robbery ✓✓✓ *The First Great Train Robbery* 1979 (PG) A dapper thief arranges to heist the Folkstone bullion express in 1855, the first moving train robbery. Well-designed, fast-moving costume piece based on Crichton's best-selling novel. **111m/C VHS, Beta, LV.** *GB* Sean Connery, Donald Sutherland, Lesley-Anne Down, Alan Webb; **D:** Michael Crichton; **W:** Michael Crichton; **C:** Geoffrey Unsworth; **M:** Jerry Goldsmith. *MGM, FCT, HMV*

The Great Train Robbery: Cinema Begins 1903 Three pioneering film shorts: "Billy Whiskers," a collection of Lumiere footage from their most famous shorts, and the title short. **42m/B VHS, Beta, 8mm.** "Broncho" Billy Anderson; **D:** Edwin S. Porter, Auguste Lumiere, Hans A. Spanuth. National Film Registry '90. *VYY*

Great Treasure Hunt ✓ 197? Four Western rogues help a blind man steal a wealthy crook's gold. **90m/C VHS, Beta.** Mark Damon, Stan Cooper, Luis Marin; **D:** Tonino Ricci. *TWE*

The Great Waldo Pepper ✓✓✓ 1975 (PG) Low key and (for Hill) less commercial film about a WWI pilot-turned-barnstormer who gets hired as a stuntman for the movies. Features spectacular vintage aircraft flying sequences. **107m/C VHS, Beta, LV.** Robert Redford, Susan Sarandon, Margot Kidder, Bo Svenson, Scott Newman, Geoffrey Lewis, Edward Herrmann; **D:** George Roy Hill; **W:** William Goldman; **C:** Robert L. Surtees; **M:** Henry Mancini. *USH*

A Great Wall ✓✓✓ *The Great Wall is a Great Wall* 1986 (PG) A Chinese-American family travels to mainland China to discover the country of their ancestry and to visit relatives. They experience radical culture shock. Wang's first independent feature. In English and Chinese with subtitles. **103m/C VHS, Beta, LV.** Peter Wang, Sharon Iwai, Kelvin Han Yee, Lin Qinqin, Hy Xiaoguang; **D:** Peter Wang; **W:** Peter Wang, Shirley Sun; **M:** David Liang, Ge Ganru. *FCT, IME, TPV*

The Great Wallendas ✓✓ 1978 The true story of the tragedies and triumphs of the Wallendas, a seven-person acrobatic family, who were noted for creating a pyramid on the high wire without nets below them. Made for television. **96m/C VHS, Beta.** Lloyd Bridges, Britt Ekland, Cathy Rigby; **D:** Larry Elikann. *NO*

The Great Waltz ✓✓✓ 1938 The first of two musical biographies on the life of Johann Strauss sees the musician quit his banking job to pursue his dream of becoming a successful composer. A fine, overlooked production rich with wonderful music and romantic comedy. ♫ Tales of Vienna Woods; There'll Come A Time; One Day When We Were Young; Voices of Spring; Du und Du; The Bat; I'm In Love With Vienna; Revolutionary March. **102m/B VHS, LV.** Luise Rainer, Fernand Gravet, Milza Korjus, Hugh Herbert, Lionel Atwill, Curt Bois, Leonid Kinskey, Al Shean, Minna Gombell, George Houston, Bert Roach, Herman Bing, Alma Kruger, Sig Rumann; **D:** Julien Duvivier; **C:** Joseph Ruttenberg. Academy Awards '38: Best Cinematography; Nominations: Academy Awards

'38: Best Film Editing, Best Supporting Actress (Korjus). *MGM, FOX, FCT*

The Great War ✓✓ *La Grande Guerre* 1959 Two Italian soldiers find themselves in the midst of WWI, much against their will. They try a number of schemes to get out of fighting and working, but their circumstance dictates otherwise. Slightly muddled, but generally good acting. **118m/B VHS.** *FR IT* Vittorio Gassman, Alberto Sordi, Silvana Mangano, Folco Lulli; **D:** Mario Monicelli; **M:** Nino Rota. Nominations: Academy Awards '59: Best Foreign Language Film. *FCT*

The Great White Hope ✓✓½ 1970 (PG-13) A semi-fictionalized biography of boxer Jack Johnson, played by Jones, who became the first black heavyweight world champion in 1910. Alexander makes her film debut as the boxer's white lover, as both battle the racism of the times. Two Oscar-nominated performances in what is essentially an "opened-out" version of the Broadway play. **CW:** Thematic elements, and for language including racist dialogue. **103m/C VHS, Beta, Closed Caption.** James Earl Jones, Jane Alexander, Lou Gilbert, Joel Fluellen, Chester Morris, Robert Webber, Hal Holbrook, R.G. Armstrong, Moses Gunn, Scatman Crothers; **D:** Martin Ritt; **C:** Burnett Guffey. Nominations: Academy Awards '70: Best Actor (Jones), Best Actress (Alexander). *FOX, FCT*

The Great White Hype ✓✓½ 1996 (R) Screenwriter Shelton, who penned "Bull Durham" and "White Men Can't Jump," returns to the sports arena with this satire of the sleazy world of boxing. Jackson's the Don King-esque promoter and manager of heavyweight champ Wayans. Noticing that pay-per-view revenues are slipping, he searches for a white boxer to generate interest and dollars and finds boxer-turned-musician Berg, who beat the champ in their Golden Glove days, and the publicity machine is cranked up for a veritable Lollapalooza. Jackson's performance as the flamboyant Rev. Fred Sultan fuels the entire movie. Concentrating on the shady wheeling and dealing, the boxing action is kept to a minimum. **CW:** Language and brief sexuality. **95m/C VHS, Closed Caption.** Samuel L. Jackson, Damon Wayans, Peter Berg, Jeff Goldblum, Jon Lovitz, Corbin Bernsen, Richard "Cheech" Marin, John Rhys-Davies, Salli Richardson, Rocky Carroll, Jamie Foxx, Michael Jace; **D:** Reginald Hudlin; **W:** Ron Shelton, Tony Hendra; **C:** Ron Garcia; **M:** Marcus Miller. *FXV*

The Great Ziegfeld ✓✓✓½ 1936 Big bio-pic of the famous showman; acclaimed in its time as the best musical biography ever done, still considered the textbook for how to make a musical. Look for cameo roles by many famous stars, as well as a walk-on role by future First Lady Pat Nixon. The movie would have stood up as a first-rate biography of Ziegfeld, even without the drop-dead wonderful songs. ♫ Won't You Come Play With Me?; It's Delightful to be Married; If You Knew Susie; Shine On Harvest Moon; A Pretty Girl is Like a Melody; You Gotta Pull Strings; She's a Follies Girl; You; You Never Looked So Beautiful. **179m/B VHS, Beta, LV.** William Powell, Luise Rainer, Myrna Loy, Frank Morgan, Reginald Owen, Nat Pendleton, Ray Bolger, Virginia Bruce, Harriet Hocter, Ernest Cossart, Robert Greig, Gilda Gray, Leon Errol, Dennis (Stanley Morner) Morgan, Mickey Daniels, William Demarest; *Cameos:* Fanny Brice; **D:** Robert Z. Leonard; **W:** William Anthony McGuire. Academy Awards '36: Best Actress (Rainer), Best Picture; New York Film Critics Awards '36: Best Actress (Rainer), Best Actress (Rainer); Nominations: Academy Awards '36: Best Director (Leonard), Best Film Editing, Best Interior Decoration, Best Story. *MGM, BTV*

The Greatest ✓½ 1977 (PG) Autobiography of Cassius Clay, the fighter who could float like a butterfly and sting like a bee. Ali plays himself, and George Benson's hit "The Greatest Love of All" is introduced. **100m/C VHS, Beta.** Muhammad Ali, Robert Duvall, Ernest Borgnine, James Earl Jones, John Marley, Roger E. Mosley, Dina Merrill, Paul Winfield; **D:** Tom Gries; **W:** Ring Lardner Jr.; **C:** Harry Stradling Jr. *COL*

The Greatest Question ♂♂½ 1919
Gish is a girl menaced by a married couple whom she saw commit a murder years before. A rush job by Griffith to fulfill his studio obligations but Gish's performance is fine. 80m/B VHS. Lillian Gish, Robert "Bobbie" Harron, Ralph Graves, Eugenie Besserer, George Fawcett, George Nicholls Jr., Josephine Crowell, Carl Stockdale; **D:** D.W. Griffith. GPV

The Greatest Show on Earth ♂♂♂
1952 DeMille is in all his epic glory here in a tale of a traveling circus wrought with glamour, romance, mysterious clowns, a tough ringmaster, and a train wreck. 149m/C VHS, Beta, LV. Betty Hutton, Cornel Wilde, James Stewart, Charlton Heston, Dorothy Lamour, Lawrence Tierney; **D:** Cecil B. DeMille. Academy Awards '52: Best Picture, Best Story; Golden Globe Awards '53: Best Director (DeMille), Best Film—Drama; Nominations: Academy Awards '52: Best Costume Design (Color), Best Director (DeMille), Best Film Editing. PAR, BTV

The Greatest Story Ever Told ♂♂
1965 Christ's journey from Galilee to Golgotha is portrayed here in true international-all-star-epic treatment by director Stevens. A lackluster version of Christ's life, remarkable only for Heston's out-of-control John the Baptist. 196m/C VHS, Beta, LV, Letterbox, Closed Caption. Max von Sydow, Charlton Heston, Sidney Poitier, Claude Rains, Jose Ferrer, Telly Savalas, Angela Lansbury, Dorothy McGuire, John Wayne, Donald Pleasence, Carroll Baker, Van Heflin, Robert Loggia, Shelley Winters, Ed Wynn, Roddy McDowall; **D:** George Stevens; **C:** William Mellor, Loyal Griggs. Nominations: Academy Awards '65: Best Art Direction/Set Decoration (Color), Best Color Cinematography, Best Costume Design (Color), Best Original Score. MGM, RDG, TVC

Greed ♂♂♂♂ 1924 A wife's obsession with money drives her husband to murder. Although the original version's length (eight hours) was trimmed to 140 minutes, it remains one of the greatest and most highly acclaimed silent films ever made. Effective use of Death Valley locations. Adapted from the Frank Norris novel, "McTeague." 140m/B VHS, LV. Dale Fuller, Gibson Gowland, ZaSu Pitts, Jean Hersholt, Chester Conklin; **D:** Erich von Stroheim. National Film Registry '91. MGM

The Greed of William Hart ♂♂ Horror Maniacs 1948 Reworking of the Burke and Hare legend has grave robbers providing Edinburgh medical students with the requisite cadavers. 78m/B VHS. GB Tod Slaughter, Henry Oscar, Jenny Lynn, Winifred Melville; **D:** Oswald Mitchell. SNC

Greedy ♂½ 1994 (PG-13) Money-grubbing family suck up to elderly millionaire uncle (Douglas) when they fear he'll leave his money to the sexy, young former pizza delivery girl (d'Abo) he's hired as his nurse. Fox is the long-lost nephew who comes to the rescue. Wicked comedy from veterans Ganz and Mandel should zing, but instead falls flat thanks to a descent into the maudlin. Fox bares his backside and Douglas plays up his role as the mean old miser, but check out Hartman, a riot as a snarky relative. **CW:** Profanity, very brief nudity, and sexual suggestiveness. 109m/C VHS, LV, Letterbox, Closed Caption. Kirk Douglas, Michael J. Fox, Olivia D'Abo, Phil Hartman, Nancy Travis, Ed Begley Jr., Bob Balaban, Colleen Camp, Jere Burns, Khandi Alexander; **Cameos:** Jonathan Lynn; **D:** Jonathan Lynn; **W:** Lowell Ganz, Babaloo Mandel; **M:** Randy Edelman. USH

Greedy Terror ♂ 1978 A cross-country motorcycle trip becomes a real nightmare when two young men realize they're being stalked by a maniac with a thirst for blood. 90m/C VHS, Beta. Michael MacRae, Perry Lang. NO

Greek Street ♂♂ Latin Love 1930 The owner of small cafe in London discovers a poor girl singing in the street for food. He takes her in and spotlights her songs in his cafe. 51m/B VHS, Beta. GB Sari Maritza, Arthur Ahmbling, Martin Lewis; **D:** Sinclair Hill. VYY, DVT, HEG

The Greek Tycoon ♂½ 1978 (R) Old familiar story about widow of an American president who marries a billionaire shipping magnate and finds that money cannot buy happiness. A transparent depiction of the Onassis/Kennedy mar-

riage, done to a turn. 106m/C VHS, Beta. Anthony Quinn, Jacqueline Bisset, James Franciscus, Raf Vallone, Edward Albert; **D:** J. Lee Thompson. USH

Green Archer 1940 Fifteen episodes of the famed serial, featuring a spooked castle complete with secret passages and tunnels, trapdoors, and the mysterious masked figure, the Green Archer. 283m/B VHS, Beta. Victor Jory, Iris Meredith, James Craven, Robert Fiske; **D:** James W. Horne. VYY, NOS, VCN

The Green Berets WOOF! 1968 (G)
Cliched wartime heroics co-directed by Wayne and based on Robin Moore's novel. The Duke stars as a Special Forces colonel, leading his troops against the Viet Cong. Painfully insipid prowar propaganda, notable as the only American film to come out in support of U.S. involvement in Vietnam. Truly embarrassing but did spawn the hit single "Ballad of the Green Beret" by Barry Sadler. 135m/C VHS, Beta, LV, Letterbox, Closed Caption. John Wayne, David Janssen, Jim Hutton, Aldo Ray, George Takei, Raymond St. Jacques; **D:** John Wayne; **C:** Winton C. Hoch; **M:** Miklos Rozsa. WAR, TLF

Green Card ♂♂½ 1990 (PG-13) Some marry for love, some for money, others for an apartment in the Big Apple. Refined, single MacDowell covets a rent-controlled apartment in Manhattan, but the lease stipulates that the apartment be let to a married couple. Enter brusque and burly Depardieu, who covets the elusive green card. The counterpoint between MacDowell, as a stuffy horticulturist, and Depardieu, as a French composer works well, and the two adroitly play a couple whose relationship covers the romantic continuum. Director Weir wrote the screenplay with Depardieu in mind. Depardieu's English-language debut. 107m/C VHS, Beta, LV, Closed Caption. Gerard Depardieu, Andie MacDowell, Bebe Neuwirth, Gregg Edelman, Robert Prosky, Jessie Keosian, Ann Wedgeworth, Ethan Phillips, Mary Louise Wilson, Lois Smith, Simon Jones; **D:** Peter Weir; **W:** Peter Weir; **M:** Hans Zimmer. Golden Globe Awards '91: Best Actor—Musical/Comedy (Depardieu), Best Film—Musical/Comedy; Nominations: Academy Awards '90: Best Original Screenplay; Golden Globe Awards '91: Best Actress—Musical/Comedy (MacDowell). TOU

Green Dolphin Street ♂♂½ 1947 Flimsy romantic epic set in 19th century New Zealand. A young girl marries the beau she and her sister are battling over in this Oscar-winning special effects show which features one big earthquake. Based on the Elizabeth Goudge novel, this was one of MGM's biggest hits in 1947. 161m/B VHS, Beta. Lana Turner, Van Heflin, Donna Reed, Edmund Gwenn; **D:** Victor Saville. Academy Awards '47: Best Special Effects; Nominations: Academy Awards '47: Best Black and White Cinematography, Best Film Editing, Best Sound. MGM

Green Dragon Inn ♂ 1982 When trying to escort an accused murderer to trial, a Ming court emissary finds himself battling against Kung Fu masters. 94m/C VHS, Beta. Yue Hwa, Lo Lei, Shangkuan Ling-Feng. WVE

Green Eyes ♂½ 1934 A costume party in a country mansion sets the scene for a routine murder mystery when the guests find their host stabbed to death in a closet. Based on the novel "The Murder of Stephen Kester" by H. Ashbrook. 68m/B VHS. Shirley Grey, Charles Starrett, Claude Gillingwater, John Wray, Dorothy Revier; **D:** Richard Thorpe; **W:** Melville Shyer. SNC

Green Eyes ♂♂♂½ 1976 Winfield, an ex-GI, returns to postwar Vietnam to search for his illegitimate son who he believes will have green eyes. A highly acclaimed, made-for-television drama featuring moving performances from Winfield and Jonathan Lippe. 100m/C VHS. Paul Winfield, Rita Tushingham, Jonathon Lippe, Victoria Racimo, Royce Wallace, Claudia Bryar; **D:** John Erman. ART

Green Fields ♂♂½ Grine Felder; Gruner Felder 1937 A quiet romance based on Peretz Hirschbein's legendary tale of a young scholar of the Talmud who leaves the shelter of the synagogue in order to learn about people in the real world.

The search takes him to the countryside where he finds himself in the middle of a battle between two families who both want him as a tutor and a suitor for their daughters. In Yiddish with English subtitles. 95m/B VHS, Beta. Michael Goldstein, Herschel Bernardi, Helen Beverly; **D:** Jacob Ben-Ami. ERG, NCJ

Green Fire ♂♂½ 1955 The screen sizzles when emerald miner Granger meets plantation-owner Kelly in the exotic jungles of South America. Usual plot complications muddle the story, but who cares when the stars are this attractive? 100m/C VHS. Stewart Granger, Grace Kelly, Paul Douglas, John Ericson, Murvyn Vye, Jose Torvay, Robert Tafur, Nacho Galindo; **D:** Andrew Marton; **W:** Ivan Goff, Ben Roberts; **M:** Miklos Rozsa. MGM

Green for Danger ♂♂ 1947 A detective stages a chilling mock operation to find a mad killer stalking the corridors of a British hospital during WWII. Sim's first great claim to fame (pre-"A Christmas Carol"). 91m/B VHS, Beta, LV. GB Trevor Howard, Alastair Sim, Leo Genn; **D:** Sidney Gilliat. HMV, RXM

The Green Glove ♂♂½ 1952 A jewel thief steals a beautiful relic from a tiny church. WWII makes it impossible for him to fence it and the church finds a relentless ally to track the thief. Excellent action sequences lift this standard plot slightly above the ordinary. 88m/B VHS. Glenn Ford, Geraldine Brooks, Cedric Hardwicke, George Macready, Gaby Andre, Roger Treville, Juliette Greco, Jean Bretonniere; **D:** Rudolph Mate; **W:** Charles Bennett. NOS, FCT, HEG

Green Grow the Rushes ♂♂ Brandy Ashore 1951 The English government tries to put a stop to brandy smuggling on the coast, but the townspeople drink up the evidence. A young Burton highlights this watered-down comedy. Based on a novel by co-scripter Harold Clewes. 77m/B VHS. GB Roger Livesey, Honor Blackman, Richard Burton, Frederick Leister; **D:** Derek Twist. HMV, NOS, VYY

Green Horizon ♂½ Afurika Monogatari; A Tale of Africa 1983 A bucolic old codger faces a dilemma when he must choose between his granddaughter's future and his disaster-prone natural environment. 80m/C VHS, Beta. James Stewart, Philip Sayer, Elenora Vallone. FHE

The Green Hornet 1939 The feature version of the original serial, in which the Green Hornet and Kato have a series of crime-fighting adventures. 100m/B VHS, Beta. Gordon Jones, Keye Luke, Anne Nagel, Wade Boteler, Walter McGrail, Douglas Evans, Cy Kendall. NOS, GKK, MLB

The Green House ♂♂ The Greenhouse; Le Jardin des Plantes 1996 Fernand Bonard (Rich) is the aged caretaker of the Paris zoo's botanical gardens during the waning days of WWII. His son Armand (Labarthe) is a collaborator who arrives at his father's home with eight-year-old daughter, Philippine (Stevenin), to celebrate her birthday. When Armand is suddenly killed by the Gestapo, Fernand begins an elaborate deception for his granddaughter, portraying her father as a hero of the French Resistance but his illusions take an unexpected turn. French with subtitles. 93m/C VHS. FR Claude Rich, Salomee Stevenin, Samuel Labarthe, Catherine Jacob, Rose Thiery; **D:** Philippe de Broca; **W:** Philippe de Broca, Alexandre Jardin; **C:** Janos Kende; **M:** Charles Court. FRF

Green Ice ♂½ 1981 An American electronics expert gets involved with a brutal South American government dealing with emeralds and plans a heist with his girlfriend and other cohorts. A little bit of romance, a little bit of action, a lot of nothing much. 109m/C VHS, Beta, LV, Closed Caption. GB Ryan O'Neal, Anne Archer, Omar Sharif, John Larroquette; **D:** Ernest Day; **W:** Edward Anhalt, Robert De Laurentiis. NO

Green Inferno ♂ 1987 A wealthy eccentric who lives deep in the South American jungle incites the natives to rebel. Mercenary agents are then hired to kill him. 90m/C VHS, Beta. Richard Yesteran, Didi Sherman, Caesar Burner. NO

The Green Man 🎬🎬🎬 1991 Maurice All-ington (Finney), the alcoholic and randy owner of the Green Man Inn in rural England, jokes about the spirits that supposedly haunt the inn. It's not too funny, however, when he discovers the spirits are real and he has to figure out who the spirit of a 17th-century murderer is inhabiting before he kills again. A classy ghost story based on the novel by Kingsley Amis. 150m/C VHS. **GB** Albert Finney, Sarah Berger, Linda Marlowe, Michael Hordern, Nickolas Grace, Michael Culver; **D:** Elijah Moshinsky; **W:** Malcolm Bradbury. *AEH, BTV, BST*

Green Mansions 🎬🎬 1959 Screen adaptation of W. H. Hudson's novel suffers due to miscasting of Hepburn as Rima the Bird Girl, who is not permitted to leave her sanctuary. Perkins is good as the male lead who fled to the jungle in search of wealth and instead finds a powerful love. Hepburn was married to director Ferrer at the time. 104m/C VHS. Audrey Hepburn, Anthony Perkins, Lee J. Cobb, Sessue Hayakawa, Henry Silva, Nehemiah Persoff, Michael Pate; **D:** Mel Ferrer; **W:** Dorothy Kingsley; **C:** Joseph Ruttenberg. *MGM*

Green Pastures 🎬🎬🎬 1936 An adaptation of Marc Connelly's 1930 Pulitzer Prize-winning play, which attempts to retell Biblical stories in black English vernacular of the '30s. Southern theatre owners boycotted the controversial film which had an all-Black cast. 93m/C VHS, Beta. Rex Ingram, Oscar Polk, Eddie Anderson, George Reed, Abraham Graves, Myrtle Anderson, Frank Wilson; **D:** William Keighley, Marc Connelly; **C:** Hal Mohr. *MGM, MOV, FOX*

The Green Promise 🎬🎬 *Raging Waters* 1949 A well-meaning but domineering farmer and his four motherless children face disaster as a result of the father's obstinacy. But when he is laid up, the eldest daughter takes over, tries modern methods and equipment, and makes the farm a success. 90m/B VHS, Beta. Walter Brennan, Marguerite Chapman, Robert Paige, Natalie Wood; **D:** William D. Russell. *NOS, DVT, HEG*

The Green Room 🎬🎬 *La Chambre Verte* 1978 (PG) Truffaut's haunting tale of a man who, valuing death over life, erects a shrine to all the dead he has known. Offered a chance at love, he cannot overcome his obsessions to take the risk. Based on the Henry James story "Altar of the Dead." In French with subtitles. 95m/C VHS, Beta. **FR** Francois Truffaut, Nathalie Baye, Jean Daste; **D:** Francois Truffaut; **C:** Nestor Almendros. *AEH*

The Green Slime woof! *Gamma Sango Uchu Daisakusen; Battle Beyond the Stars; Death and the Green Slime* 1968 (G) Danger and romance highlight the journey of a space ship assigned to intercept an oncoming asteroid. Little do the astronauts realize, but they have brought aboard the ship the malevolent alien creatures known as green slime (and we ain't talking jello here). Cheap, U.S./Japanese co-production will leave you feeling lousy in the morning. The title song is legendary among genre aficionados. 90m/C VHS, Beta. **JP** Robert Horton, Richard Jaeckel, Luciana Paluzzi, Bud Widom, Ted Gunther, Robert Dunham; **D:** Kinji Fukasaku. *MGM*

Green Snake 🎬🎬 1993 Combo of mysticism and action based on a Chinese fable. Green Snake (Cheung) and Son Ching (Wong) are actual reptiles who have been practicing taking human form. When self-righteous Buddhist monk Fa-Hai discovers them, he thinks it's a sin to tamper with the natural order. The snakes don't appreciate his lack of compassion and plot destruction. Cantonese with English subtitles. 102m/C VHS. **HK** Maggie Cheung, Joey Wong; **D:** Tsui Hark. *FCT*

The Green Wall 🎬🎬🎬 1970 A city-dwelling young man attempts to homestead with his family in the Amazon. A lovely and tragic film with stunning photography of the Peruvian forests. First Peruvian feature to be shown in the U.S. In Spanish with English subtitles. 110m/C VHS. **SP** Julio Aleman, Sandra Riva; **D:** Armando Robles Godoy; **W:** Armando Robles Godoy. *FCT, DVT, HEG*

Greenstone 🎬🎬 1985 (G) The green stone is a glowing rock in the forbidden forest that conveys a young boy into an exciting new world. 48m/C VHS, Beta. Joseph Corey, John Riley, Kathleen Irvine, Jack Mauck; **D:** Kevin Irvine.

Greetings 🎬🎬🎬 1968 (R) De Niro stars in this wild and crazy comedy about a man who tries to help his friend flunk his draft physical. One of DePalma's first films, and a pleasantly anarchic view of the late '60s, wrought with a light, intelligent tone. Followed by the sequel "Hi, Mom." 88m/C VHS, Beta, LV. Robert De Niro, Gerrit Graham, Allen (Goorwitz) Garfield; **D:** Brian DePalma; **W:** Brian DePalma. *THV*

Gregory's Girl 🎬🎬🎬½ 1980 Sweet, disarming comedy established Forsyth. An awkward young Scottish schoolboy falls in love with the female goalie of his soccer team. He turns to his 10-year-old sister for advice, but she's more interested in ice cream than love. His best friend is no help, either, since he has yet to fall in love. Perfect mirror of teenagers and their instantaneous, raw, and all-consuming loves. Very sweet scene with Gregory and his girl lying on their backs in an open space illustrates the simultaneous simplicity and complexity of young love. 91m/C VHS, Beta. **GB** Gordon John Sinclair, Dee Hepburn, Jake D'Arcy, Chic Murray, Alex Norton, John Bett, Clare Grogan; **D:** Bill Forsyth; **W:** Bill Forsyth; **C:** Michael Coulter. British Academy Awards '81: Best Screenplay. *TVC*

Gremlins 🎬🎬🎬 1984 (PG) Comedy horror with deft satiric edge. Produced by Spielberg. Fumbling gadget salesman Rand Peltzer is looking for something really special to get his son Billy. He finds it in a small store in Chinatown. The wise shopkeeper is reluctant to sell him the adorable "mogwai" but relents after fully warning him "Don't expose him to bright light, don't ever get him wet, and don't ever, ever feed him after midnight." Naturally, this all happens and the result is a gang of nasty gremlins who decide to tear up the town on Christmas Eve. Followed by "Gremlins 2: The New Batch" which is less black comedy, more parody, and perhaps more inventive. 106m/C VHS, Beta, LV, 8mm, Letterbox, Closed Caption. Zach Galligan, Phoebe Cates, Hoyt Axton, Polly Holliday, Frances Lee McCain, Keye Luke, Dick Miller, Corey Feldman, Judge Reinhold, Glynn Turman, Scott Brady, Jackie Joseph; **D:** Joe Dante; **W:** Chris Columbus; **C:** John Hora; **M:** Jerry Goldsmith; **V:** Howie Mandel. *WAR, TLF*

Gremlins 2: The New Batch 🎬🎬🎬½ 1990 (PG-13) The sequel to "Gremlins" is superior to the original, which was quite good. Set in a futuristic skyscraper in the Big Apple, director Dante presents a less violent but far more campy vision, paying myriad surreal tributes to scores of movies, including "The Wizard of Oz" and musical extravaganzas of the past. Also incorporates a Donald Trump parody, takes on television news, and body slams modern urban living. Great fun. 107m/C VHS, Beta, LV, 8mm, Letterbox, Closed Caption. Zach Galligan, Phoebe Cates, John Glover, Christopher Lee, Robert Prosky, Robert Picardo, Haviland Morris, Dick Miller, Jackie Joseph, Keye Luke, Belinda Balaski, Paul Bartel, Kenneth Tobey, John Astin, Henry Gibson, Leonard Maltin, Hulk Hogan; *Cameos:* Jerry Goldsmith; **D:** Joe Dante; **W:** Charles Haas; **C:** John Hora; **M:** Jerry Goldsmith; **V:** Howie Mandel, Tony Randall. *WAR, HHE*

Grendel, Grendel, Grendel 🎬🎬 1982 An utterly urbane dragon wants to be friends, but for some reason people are just terrified of Grendel. It's true, he bites a head off once in a while, but nobody's perfect! An ingenious, animated retelling of Beowulf. 90m/C VHS, Beta. **AU** Alexander Stitt; **M:** Bruce Smeaton; **V:** Peter Ustinov, Arthur Dignam, Julie McKenna, Keith Michell. *FHE*

Greta 🎬🎬🎬 1986 During WWII, a young Polish boy escapes from a detention camp. Now on the run, several bizarre twists of fate place him in the care of Greta, a young girl whose father is an officer in the S.S. In Polish with English subtitles. 60m/C VHS, Beta. **PL** Janusz Grabowski, Agnieszka Kruszewska, Eva Borowik, Tomasz Grochoczki, Andrzej Precig; **D:** Krzysztof Gruber.

The Grey Fox 🎬🎬🎬½ 1983 (PG) A gentlemanly old stagecoach robber tries to pick up his life after 30 years in prison. Unable to resist another heist, he tries train robbery, and winds up hiding out in British Columbia where he meets an attractive photographer, come to document the changing West. Farnsworth is perfect as the man who suddenly finds himself in the 20th century trying to work at the only craft he knows. Based on the true story of Canada's most colorful and celebrated outlaw, Bill Miner. 92m/C VHS, Beta, LV. **CA** Richard Farnsworth, Jackie Burroughs, Wayne Robson, Timothy Webber, Ken Pogue; **D:** Phillip Borsos; **M:** Michael Conway Baker. Genie Awards '83: Best Director (Borsos), Best Film, Best Supporting Actress (Burroughs).

Greyfriars Bobby 🎬🎬½ 1961 A true story of a Skye terrier named Bobby who, after his master dies, refuses to leave the grave. Even after being coaxed by the local children into town, he still returns to the cemetery each evening. Word of his loyalty spreads, and Bobby becomes the pet of 19th century Edinburgh. Nicely told, with fine location photography and good acting. Great for children and animal lovers. 91m/C VHS. Donald Crisp, Laurence Naismith, Kay Walsh; **D:** Don Chaffey. *NO*

Greystoke: The Legend of Tarzan, Lord of the Apes 🎬🎬 1984 (PG) The seventh Earl of Greystoke becomes a shipwrecked orphan and is raised by apes. Ruling the ape-clan in the vine-swinging persona of Tarzan, he is discovered by an anthropologist and returned to his ancestral home in Scotland, where he is immediately recognized by his grandfather. The contrast between the behavior of man and ape is interesting, and Tarzan's introduction to society is fun, but there's no melodrama or cliff-hanging action, as we've come to expect of the Tarzan genre. Due to her heavy southern accent, Andie MacDowell (as Jane) had her voice dubbed by Glenn Close. 130m/C VHS, Beta, LV, Letterbox, Closed Caption. Christopher Lambert, Ralph Richardson, Ian Holm, James Fox, Andie MacDowell, Ian Charleson, Cheryl Campbell, Nigel Davenport; **D:** Hugh Hudson; **W:** Michael Austin. New York Film Critics Awards '84: Best Supporting Actor (Richardson); Nominations: Academy Awards '84: Best Adapted Screenplay, Best Makeup, Best Supporting Actor (Richardson). *WAR*

Gridlock'd 🎬🎬🎬 1996 (R) Junkies and sometime-musicians Spoon (Shakur) and Stretch (Roth) decide to kick the habit after their singer Cookie (Newton) overdoses and slips into a coma. The hapless pair are thrown into the switches of social services programs and government offices where they shuffle endlessly but nothing happens. Think "Waiting for Godot" meets "Waiting for the Man." Meanwhile, their dealer is murdered and they're the prime suspects, pursued by the cops and the actual killers, who believe that they've stolen said dealer's stash. Shakur shows flashes of the brilliance that might have been as the more sensitive and sane of the pair, while Roth complements him perfectly as his bug-crazy short-sighted partner. Fellow actor Curtis-Hall's directorial debut.*CW:* Graphic drug use, pervasive strong language, some violence and brief nudity. 91m/C VHS, LV, Closed Caption. Tim Roth, Tupac Shakur, Thandie Newton, Charles Fleischer, Howard Hesseman, James Pickens Jr., John Sayles, Tom Towles, Eric Payne; *Cameos:* Vondie Curtis-Hall; **D:** Vondie Curtis-Hall; **W:** Vondie Curtis-Hall; **C:** Bill Pope; **M:** Stewart Copeland. *PGV*

Grief 🎬🎬 1994 Mark (Chester) is a writer on the syndicated daytime TV show "The Love Judge." Still numb from his lover's death from AIDS the previous year, Mark begins to take an interest in fellow writer Bill (Arquette), while writer Paula (Gutteridge) desires to become the show's new producer and secretary Leslie (Douglas) wants to take her place as the new writer. Present producer Jo (Beat) tries to keep her office family in line while sorting out her personal life. Writer-director Glatzer knows his territory since he spent five years writing for "Divorce Court." 86m/C VHS. Craig Chester, Alexis Arquette, Lucy Gutteridge, Illeana Douglas, Jackie Beat, Carlton Wilborn; *D:* Richard Glatzer; *W:* Richard Glatzer. *SHV*

Grievous Bodily Harm 🐾🐾 1989 (R)
Morris Martin's wife Claudine is missing. When he finds a videotape of Claudine in very compromising positions, he becomes murderously determined to find out where she has gone. 136m/C VHS, Beta. John Waters, Colin Friels, Bruno Lawrence; *D:* Mark Joffe.

Griffin and Phoenix: A Love Story 🐾🐾½ 1976
A sentimental film about the mortality of two vital people. Falk deserts his family when he learns he has terminal cancer. Clayburgh, also terminally ill, meets him for a short but meaningful affair. Good performances help overcome the tear-jerker aspects of the story. Made for television. 110m/C VHS. Peter Falk, Jill Clayburgh, Dorothy Tristan, John Lehne; *D:* Daryl Duke. *FOX*

Griffith Biograph Program 1909
Some of the best Biograph shorts are featured: "The Lonely Villa," "The Lonedale Operator," "The New York Hat," "Friends," and "The Unseen Enemy," all produced between 1909 and 1912. 50m/B VHS, Beta, LV. Mary Pickford, Blanche Sweet, Lillian Gish, Dorothy Gish; *D:* D.W. Griffith. *GVV*

The Grifters 🐾🐾🐾½ 1990 (R)
Evocative rendering of a terrifying sub-culture. Huston, Cusak, and Bening are con artists, struggling to stay on top in a world where violence, money, and lust are the prizes. Bening and Huston fight for Cusak's soul, while he's determined to decide for himself. Seamless performances and dazzling atmosphere, along with superb pacing, make for a provocative film. Based on a novel by Jim Thompson. 114m/C VHS, Beta, LV, Closed Caption. Anjelica Huston, John Cusack, Annette Bening, Pat Hingle, J.T. Walsh, Charles Napier, Henry Jones, Gailard Sartain, Jeremy Piven; *D:* Stephen Frears; *W:* Donald E. Westlake; *M:* Elmer Bernstein. Independent Spirit Awards '91: Best Actress (Huston); Best Film; Los Angeles Film Critics Association Awards '90: Best Actress (Huston); National Society of Film Critics Awards '90: Best Actress (Huston), Best Supporting Actress (Bening); Nominations: Academy Awards '90: Best Actress (Huston), Best Adapted Screenplay, Best Director (Frears), Best Supporting Actress (Bening). *USH, HBO, FCT*

Grim 🐾 1995 (R)
Lives up to its title as an extremely icky and evil subterranean creature is awakened from a long sleep by miners. Apparently not long enough, since he proceeds to rip apart anyone he comes in contact with.*CW:* Horror violence and gore, and for language. 86m/C VHS, LV. Emmanuel Xuereb, Tres Handley, Peter Tregloan; *D:* Paul Matthews; *W:* Paul Matthews. *APX*

Grim Prairie Tales 🐾🐾 1989 (R)
A city slicker and a crazed mountain man meet by a campfire in the high plains one night and pass the time sharing four tales of Western horror. Dourif and Jones are fun, the stories scary, making for an interesting twist on both the horror and the Western genres. 90m/C VHS, LV. Brad Dourif, James Earl Jones, Marc McClure, William Atherton, Scott Paulin, Lisa Eichhorn; *D:* Wayne Coe; *W:* Wayne Coe; *C:* Janusz Kaminski. *FCT*

The Grim Reaper 🐾🐾🐾 *La Commare Secca* 1962
22-year-old Bertolucci directed his first feature with this grim and brutal treatment of the investigation of the murder of a prostitute, told via flashbacks and from the disparate perspectives of three people who knew the woman. A commercial bust, the critics were no kinder than the public at the time; not until two years later, with "Before the Revolution," did Bertolucci earn his directorial spurs. The script was written by Pasolini, with whom the erstwhile poet had collaborated on "Accattone" the previous year (as assistant). In Italian with English subtitles. 100m/B VHS, LV. *IT* Fran-

cesco Rulu, Giancarlo de Rosa; *D:* Bernardo Bertolucci; *W:* Pier Paolo Pasolini. *CVC, FCT*

Grim Reaper 🐾½ 1981 (R)
Mia Farrow's sister is one of a group of American students vacationing on a Greek island. Farrow learns of the twisted cannibalistic murderer who methodically tries to avenge the tragic deaths of his family. 81m/C VHS, Beta. *IT* Tisa Farrow, George Eastman; *D:* Joe D'Amato. *NO*

Grind 🐾🐾 1996
Dysfunctional blue-collar family saga set in New Jersey. Eddie Dolan (Crudup), just out of the joint, moves in with brother Terry (Schulze) and sister-in-law Janey (Shelly). He gets a dull factory job and fixes up old cars to go drag-racing on the weekend—as well as helping out Terry, who has a sideline working with a car theft ring. Since gorgeous Eddie works nights, he and sulky stay-at-home-with-the-baby Janey get to be real close daytime buddies. Naturally their affair causes trouble for all. A paint-by-numbers plot with some decent acting. 96m/C VHS. Billy Crudup, Adrienne Shelly, Paul Schulze, Frank Vincent, Saul Stein, Amanda Peet, Steven Beach, Tim Devlin; *D:* Chris Kentis; *W:* Chris Kentis, Laura Lau; *C:* Stephen Kazmierski; *M:* Brian Kelly. *FXL*

Grisbi 🐾🐾 *Hands Off the Loot; Honour Among Thieves; Touchez Pas Au Grisbi* 1953
King of the French underworld, Gabin finds there's no honor among thieves when a gold heist goes wrong and the loot comes up missing. Moreau is the quintessential moll. Dubbed. 94m/C VHS. *FR* Jean Gabin, Jeanne Moreau, Lino Ventura, Daniel Cauchy, Gaby Basset; *D:* Jacques Becker; *W:* Jacques Becker, Maurice Griffe; *M:* Jean Wiener. Venice Film Festival '54: Best Actor (Gabin). *FCT*

The Grissom Gang 🐾🐾🐾 1971 (R)
Remake of the 1948 British film "No Orchids for Miss Blandish." Darby is a wealthy heiress kidnapped by a family of grotesques, led by a sadistic mother. The ransom gets lost in a series of bizarre events, and the heiress appears to be falling for one of her moronic captors. Director Robert Aldrich skillfully blends extreme violence with dark humor. Superb camera work, editing, and 1920s period sets. 127m/C VHS. Kim Darby, Scott Wilson, Tony Musante, Ralph Waite, Connie Stevens, Robert Lansing, Wesley Addy; *D:* Robert Aldrich; *C:* Joseph Biroc. *FOX*

Grit of the Girl Telegrapher/In the Switch Tower 1915
A pair of silent railroad dramas, which feature thrilling chase sequences, nefarious schemers and virginal heroines. Silent with piano scores. 47m/B VHS, Beta. Anna Q. Nilsson, Hal Clements, Walter Edwards, Frank Borzage; *M:* Jon Mirsalis. *CCB, PEN, GVV*

Grizzly 🐾 *Killer Grizzly* 1976 (PG)
Giant, killer grizzly terrorizes a state park in this blatant "Jaws" rip-off. From the same folks who produced "Abby," a blatant "Exorcist" rip-off. Filmed in Georgia. 92m/C VHS, Beta. Christopher George, Richard Jaeckel, Andrew Prine, Victoria (Vicki) Johnson, Charles Kissinger; *D:* William Girdler.

Grizzly Adams: The Legend Continues 🐾½ 1990
A small town is saved from three desperados by Grizzly and his huge grizzly bear pet, Martha. 90m/C VHS. Gene Edwards, Link Wyler, Red West, Tony Caruso, Acquanetta, L.Q. Jones; *D:* Ken Kennedy. *NO*

Grizzly Mountain 🐾🐾½ 1997 (G)
Dylan (Dylan Haggerty) and his sister Nicole (Lund) are camping in Oregon with their parents when they decide to explore a cave. After some mysterious rumbling and shaking, the siblings emerge in the 1870's. They meet mountain man Jeremiah (Haggerty), who promises to help them return home, but he's got problems of his own—bad guy Burt (Stephens) wants to dynamite the mountain so the railroad can come through. Pic wanders back and forth between the two time periods and the kids learn a lesson in ecology (and are reunited with their parents). Easy-going; some beautiful scenery. 96m/C VHS, Closed Caption. Dan Haggerty, Dylan Haggerty, Nicole Lund, Perry Stephens, Kim Morgan

Greene, Martin Kove, Robert Budaska, E.E. Bell, Marguerite Hickey, Don Borza; *D:* Jeremy Haft; *W:* Peter White, Jeremy Haft; *C:* Andy Parke; *M:* John McCallum. *ART*

The Groove Tube 🐾🐾½ 1972 (R)
A television series called "The Groove Tube" is the context for these skits that spoof everything on television from commercials to newscasts. Chevy Chase's movie debut. 75m/C VHS. Lane Sarasohn, Chevy Chase, Richard Belzer, Marcy Mendham, Bill Kemmill; *D:* Ken Shapiro. *HTV*

Gross Anatomy 🐾🐾½ 1989 (PG-13)
Lightweight comedy/drama centers on the trials and tribulations of medical students. Modine is the very bright, but somewhat lazy, future doctor determined not to buy into the bitter competition among his fellow students. His lack of desire inflames Lahti, a professor dying of a fatal disease who nevertheless believes in modern medicine. She pushes and inspires him to focus on his potential, and his desire to help people. Worth watching, in spite of cheap laughs. Interesting cast of up-and-comers. 107m/C VHS, Beta, LV, Closed Caption. Matthew Modine, Daphne Zuniga, Christine Lahti, John Scott Clough, Alice Carter, Robert Desiderio, Zakes Mokae, Todd Field; *D:* Thom Eberhardt; *W:* Ron Nyswaner; *M:* David Newman. *TOU*

Gross Misconduct 🐾🐾 1993 (R)
Charismatic university professor Justin Thorne (Smits) makes the nearly fatal mistake of getting involved with his student, Jennifer (Watts). Seems she's one of those obsessive types and when Thorne wants to break off the affair for the sake of his marriage, Jennifer goes over the edge. Thorne's charged with rape and unless Jennifer changes her story his life is over. Based on a true story that happened in the '50s but this version is set in the '90s.*CW:* Strong sexuality, a violent episode, and some language. 97m/C VHS, Closed Caption. *AU* Jimmy Smits, Naomi Watts, Sarah Chadwick, Adrian Wright, Alan Fletcher; *D:* George Miller; *W:* Lance Peters, Gerard Maguire; *C:* David Connell.

Grosse Fatigue 🐾🐾🐾 *Dead Tired* 1994 (R)
Diminutive comic everyman Blanc successfully takes up the challenge of a dual role of mistaken identity (as well as directing and writing chores). He first plays himself, bewildered by accusations of lechery and other escapades, who learns he has a psychopath double who's stolen his celebrity. So it's up to Michel and pal Carole (the gorgeous Bouquet) to track down the mischief-maker before Blanc's reputation is in complete tatters. French with subtitles.*CW:* Language, nudity. 85m/C VHS, LV. *FR* Michel Blanc, Carole Bouquet, Philippe Noiret, Josiane Balasko; *Cameos:* Charlotte Gainsbourg, Mathilda May, Thierry Lhermitte, Roman Polanski; *D:* Michel Blanc; *W:* Michel Blanc; *C:* Eduardo Serra; *M:* Rene Marc Bini. *TOU*

Grosse Pointe Blank 🐾🐾🐾 1997 (R)
Stressed-out Martin Q. Blank (Cusack) debates with his nervous shrink (Arkin) about whether to attend his 10-year high school reunion. He doesn't want to deal with the Debi (Driver), the girl he ditched on prom night, the incessant small talk, or the prospect of telling his classmates that he's a professional hit man. Then there's the matter of rival pro Grocer (Aykroyd), who wants to start an assassins union. Dark comedy with excellent writing, a charmingly off-center lead by Cusack, who attended his own reunion as research, and a surprising amount of action. Pasadena fills in for most of Grosse Pointe, but the Detroit shots are real.*CW:* Strong violence, language and some drug content. 107m/C VHS, LV, Closed Caption. John Cusack, Minnie Driver, Dan Aykroyd, Alan Arkin, Joan Cusack, Jeremy Piven, Mitchell Ryan, Hank Azaria, Michael Cudlitz, Benny "The Jet" Urquidez, Barbara Harris, Ann Cusack, Jenna Elfman; *D:* George Armitage; *W:* Tom Jankiewicz, D.V. DeVincentis, Steve Pink, John Cusack; *C:* Jamie Anderson; *M:* Joe Strummer. *TOU*

Grotesque woof! 1987 (R)
After slaughtering a young woman's family as they vacationed in a remote mountain cabin, a gang of bloodthirsty punks are attacked by the family secret, the de-

formed son. The title says it all. **1986 VHS, Beta, LV.** Linda Blair, Tab Hunter, Guy Stockwell, Donna Wilkes, Nels Van Patten; *D:* Joe Tornatore.

Ground Zero 🎬🎬🎬 **1988 (R)** Political thriller, set in the Australian outback in the '50s, in which a man searches for the reasons for his father's murder in the films of the British nuclear tests. **109m/C VHS, Beta, LV.** *AU* Colin Friels, Jack Thompson, Donald Pleasence, Natalie Bate, Simon Chilvers, Neil Fitzpatrick, Bob Maza, Peter Cummins; *D:* Bruce Myles, Michael Pattinson. *ART*

Ground Zero 🎬½ **1988 (R)** Ground Zero is the term used to describe the site of a nuclear explosion. San Francisco is threatened with just such a new name in this story of nuclear blackmail. Someone plants an atomic bomb on the Golden Gate Bridge. It must be defused and the culprit caught. **90m/C VHS, Beta.** Ron Casteel, Melvin Belli, Yvonne D'Angiers; *D:* James T. Flocker. *VTR*

Groundhog Day 🎬🎬🎬 **1993 (PG)** Phil (Murray), an obnoxious weatherman, is in Punxatawney, PA to cover the annual emergence of the famous rodent from its hole. After he's caught in a blizzard that he didn't predict, he finds himself trapped in a time warp, doomed to relive the same day over and over again until he gets it right. Lighthearted romantic comedy takes a funny premise and manages to carry it through to the end. Murray has fun with the role, although he did get bitten by the groundhog during the scene when they're driving. Elliott, who has been missed since his days as the man under the seats on "Late Night with David Letterman" is perfectly cast as a smart-mouthed cameraman. **103m/C VHS, LV, Closed Caption.** Bill Murray, Andie MacDowell, Chris Elliott, Stephen Tobolowsky, Brian Doyle-Murray, Marita Geraghty, Angela Paton; *D:* Harold Ramis; *W:* Harold Ramis, Daniel F. Rubin; *C:* John Bailey; *M:* George Fenton. British Academy Awards '93: Best Original Screenplay. *COL, FCT, BTV*

The Groundstar Conspiracy 🎬🎬🎬 **1972 (PG)** Spy thriller brings to life L.P. Davies' novel, "The Alien." After an explosion kills all but one space project scientist, Peppard is sent to investigate suspicions of a cover-up. Meanwhile, the surviving scientist (Sarrazin) suffers from disfigurement and amnesia. He pursues his identity while Peppard accuses him of being a spy. Splendid direction by Lamont Johnson. Sarrazin's best role. **96m/C VHS.** *CA* George Peppard, Michael Sarrazin, Christine Belford, Cliff Potts, James Olson, Tim O'Connor, James McEachin, Alan Oppenheimer; *D:* Lamont Johnson. *USH*

The Group 🎬🎬½ **1966** Based upon the novel by Mary McCarthy, the well-acted story deals with a group of graduates from a Vassarlike college as they try to adapt to life during the Great Depression. Has some provocative subject matter, including lesbianism, adultery, and mental breakdowns. Soapy, but a good cast with film debuts of Bergen, Hackett, Pettet, Widdoes, and Holbrook. **150m/C VHS, Beta.** Candice Bergen, Joanna Pettet, Shirley Knight, Joan Hackett, Elizabeth Hartman, Jessica Walter, Larry Hagman, James Broderick, Kathleen Widdoes, Hal Holbrook, Mary-Robin Redd, Richard Mulligan, Carrie Nye; *D:* Sidney Lumet; *C:* Boris Kaufman. *FOX*

Group Marriage 🎬🎬½ **1972 (R)** Six young professionals fall into a marriage of communal convenience and rapidly discover the many advantages and drawbacks of their thoroughly modern arrangement. **90m/C VHS, Beta.** Victoria Vetri, Aimee Eccles, Zack Taylor, Jeff Pomerantz, Claudia Jennings, Jayne Kennedy, Milt Kamen; *D:* Stephanie Rothman. *NO*

Growing Pains 🎬½ **1982** A young couple discover that their newly adopted son possesses extraordinary powers. **60m/C VHS, Beta.** Gary Bond, Barbara Keilermann, Norman Beaton. *ART*

Grown Ups 🎬🎬 **1980** A newly married couple move into their first home only to discover that the wife's ditzy sister expects to live with them and that their next door neighbor was their former

high school teacher. Made for British television. **95m/C VHS.** *GB* Philip Davis, Leslie Manville, Sam Kelly, Lindsay Duncan, Brenda Blethyn, Janine Duvitsky; *D:* Mike Leigh; *W:* Mike Leigh. *WBF, BTV, FCT*

Grown Ups 🎬🎬 **1986** A journalist watches his family slowly disintegrating around him in this adaptation of Jules Feiffer's play. **106m/C VHS, Beta.** Jean Stapleton, Martin Balsam, Charles Grodin, Marilu Henner, Kerry Segal; *D:* John Madden. *ORI, WAR*

Gruesome Twosome 🎬 **1967** Another guts/cannibalism/mutilation fun-fest by Lewis, about someone who's marketing the hair of some very recently deceased college coeds. **75m/C VHS, Beta.** Elizabeth Davis, Chris Martell; *D:* Herschell Gordon Lewis. *NO*

Grumpier Old Men 🎬🎬 **1995 (PG-13)** Max (Matthau) and John (Lemmon) are back at each other's throats, but with John happily married to Ariel (Ann-Margret), he's not much of an adversary. Enter Maria (Loren), who wants to turn the boys' favorite bait shop into an Italian restaurant. In a twist that should surprise no one, Max soon falls for the beautiful Maria, and she with him. Jokes are similar but more adolescent than in the first, and subplots involving John and Max's kids' wedding and Grandpa's (Meredith) romantic interests are forced. Suffers the standard sequel fate of not measuring up to the original.*CW:* Salty language and innuendos. **101m/C VHS, LV, Closed Caption.** Jack Lemmon, Walter Matthau, Ann-Margret, Sophia Loren, Kevin Pollak, Burgess Meredith, Daryl Hannah, Ann Guilbert; *D:* Howard Deutch; *W:* Mark Steven Johnson; *C:* Tak Fujimoto; *M:* Alan Silvestri. *WAR*

Grumpy Old Men 🎬🎬🎬 **1993 (PG-13)** Lemmon and Matthau team for their seventh movie, in parts that seem written just for them. Boyhood friends and retired neighbors, they have been feuding for so long that neither of them can remember why. Doesn't matter much, when it provides a reason for them to spout off at each other every morning and play nasty practical jokes every night. This, and ice-fishing, is life as they know it, until feisty younger woman Ann-Margret moves into the neighborhood and lights some long-dormant fires. 83-year-old Meredith is a special treat playing Lemmon's 90-something father. Filmed in Wabasha, Minnesota, and grumpy, in the most pleasant way.*CW:* Language. **104m/C VHS, LV, 8mm, Letterbox, Closed Caption, DVD.** Jack Lemmon, Walter Matthau, Ann-Margret, Burgess Meredith, Daryl Hannah, Kevin Pollak, Ossie Davis, Buck Henry, Christopher McDonald; *D:* Donald Petrie; *W:* Mark Steven Johnson; *M:* Alan Silvestri. *WAR*

Grunt! The Wrestling Movie woof! **1985 (R)** A spoof of documentaries about the behind-the-scenes world of wrestling. For fans only. **91m/C VHS, Beta.** Wally Greene, Steven Cepello, Dick Murdoch, John Tolos; *D:* Allan Holzman. *VTR*

Gryphon **1988** Ricky's new teacher can do all sorts of magical things. Hidden among her tricks are lessons about creativity, beauty, and imagination. Adapted from the short story by Charles Baxter. Aired on PBS as part of the "Wonderworks" family movie series. **58m/C VHS, Closed Caption.** Amanda Plummer, Sully Diaz, Alexis Cruz; *D:* Mark Cullingham. *HMV, FCT, BTV*

Guadalcanal Diary 🎬🎬½ **1943** A vintage wartime flag-waver, with a typical crew of Marines battling the "Yellow Menace" over an important base on the famous Pacific atoll. Based on Richard Tregaskis' first-hand account. **93m/B VHS, Beta, LV.** Preston Foster, Lloyd Nolan, William Bendix, Richard Conte, Anthony Quinn, Richard Jaeckel, Roy Roberts, Minor Watson, Miles Mander, Ralph Byrd, Lionel Stander, Reed Hadley; *D:* Lewis Seiler. *FOX, IME*

Guantanamera 🎬🎬🎬 **1995** A famous singer returns to her hometown of Guantanamo for the first time in 50 years, is reunited with her first sweetheart, and promptly dies. Her niece Georgina (Ibarra) comes to take her remains back to Havana, along with her husband Adolfo (Cruz), an oafish Communist Party worker who has de-

vised a bizarre relay system to transport corpses in order to save gasoline. Also in the caravan is Mariano (Perugorria), a former student of Georgina's who had a crush on her. Mariano attempts to seduce Georgina, while Adolfo attempts to get a clue. Celebrates the lives of everyday Cubans and skewers bumbling government bureaucrats. The final collaboration between directors Gutierrez Alea, who died in 1996, and Tabio. Spanish with subtitles. **101m/C VHS.** *CU* Carlos Cruz, Mirta Ibarra, Jorge Perugorria, Raul Eguren, Pedro Fernandez; *D:* Tomas Gutierrez Alea, Juan Carlos Tabio; *W:* Tomas Gutierrez Alea, Juan Carlos Tabio, Eliseo Alberto Diego; *C:* Hans Burman; *M:* Jose Nieto. *NYR*

The Guardian 🎬🎬½ **1984 (R)** Residents of a chic New York apartment building hire a security expert/ex-military man to aid them in combatting their crime problem. But one of the liberal tenants thinks their guard's methods may come at too high a cost. Made for cable television. **102m/C VHS, Beta, LV, Closed Caption.** Martin Sheen, Louis Gossett Jr., Arthur Hill; *D:* David Greene; *M:* Jonathan Goldsmith. *ART, VES*

The Guardian 🎬 **1990 (R)** A young couple unwittingly hires a human sacrificing druid witch as a babysitter for their child. Based on the book "The Nanny" by Dan Greenburg. **92m/C VHS, Beta, LV, Closed Caption.** Jenny Seagrove, Dwier Brown, Carey Lowell, Brad Hall, Miguel Ferrer, Natalija Nogulich, Pamela Brull, Gary Swanson; *D:* William Friedkin; *W:* William Friedkin, Stephen Volk, Dan Greenberg; *C:* John A. Alonzo. *USH*

Guardian Angel 🎬🎬½ *Beyond Justice* **1994 (R)** Detective Christy McKay (Rothrock) quits the force after her partner/lover is killed by icy seductress Nina (Denier), who manages to escape from jail. When McKay is hired to protect playboy Lawton Hobbs (McVicar), she finds that the threat comes from a psycho ex-girlfriend. Guess who. **97m/C VHS, Closed Caption.** Cynthia Rothrock, Lydie Denier, Daniel McVicar, Kenneth McLeod, Marshall Teague, John O'Leary, Dale Jacoby; *D:* Richard W. Munchkin. *PMH*

Guardian of the Abyss 🎬 **1982** A young couple who buy an antique mirror get more than they bargained for when they discover that it is the threshold to Hell and the devil wants to come through. **60m/C VHS, Beta.** Ray Lonnen, Rosalyn Landor, Paul Darrow, Barbara Ewing; *D:* Don Sharp. *ART*

Guarding Tess 🎬🎬 **1994 (PG-13)** Longsuffering Secret Service agent Cage is nearing the end of his three-year assignment to crotchety widowed First Lady MacLaine when the Prez extends his tour of duty. Feels like a TV movie, not surprising since writers Torokvei and Wilson have several sitcoms to their credit, including "WKRP in Cincinnati." Nice chemistry between Cage and MacLaine results in a few funny moments, but there are too many formulaic plot twists. End result: a pleasant, if somewhat slow buddy comedy.*CW:* Some profanity and slight violence. **98m/C VHS, LV, 8mm, Closed Caption, DVD.** Shirley MacLaine, Nicolas Cage, Austin Pendleton, Edward Albert, Richard Griffiths; *D:* Hugh Wilson; *W:* Peter Torokvei, Hugh Wilson; *C:* Brian Reynolds; *M:* Michael Convertino. Nominations: Golden Globe Awards '95: Best Actress—Musical/Comedy (MacLaine).*COL*

The Guardsman 🎬🎬🎬 **1931** Broadway's illustrious couple Lunt and Fontanne shine in this adaptation of the clever marital comedy by French playwright Molnar in which they also starred. This sophisticated comedy was their only starring film, although they were offered large sums of money to appear in other movies—they just couldn't tear themselves away from the stage. Remade as "The Chocolate Soldier" and "Lily in Love." **89m/B VHS, Closed Caption.** Alfred Lunt, Lynn Fontanne, Roland Young, ZaSu Pitts, Maude Eburne, Herman Bing, Ann Dvorak; *D:* Sidney Franklin. Nominations: Academy Awards '32: Best Actor (Lunt), Best Actress (Fontanne). *MGM*

Guerilla Brigade 🎬🎬½ *Riders* **1939** A rarely seen Ukrainian epic about Russian/Ukrainian solidarity during the Civil War. In Russian with English subtitles. **90m/B VHS, Beta.** *RU* Igor Savchenko. *FCT*

Guess What We Learned in School Today? woof! 1970 (R) Parents in a conservative suburban community protest sex education in the schools. Intended as a satire, but it only reinforces stereotypes. 85m/C VHS, Beta. Richard Carballo, Devin Goldenberg; **D:** John G. Avildsen. NO

Guess Who's Coming to Dinner ♂♂♂ 1967 Controversial in its time. A young white woman brings her black fiance home to meet her parents. The situation truly tests their open-mindedness and understanding. Hepburn and Tracy (in his last film appearance) are wonderful and serve as the anchors in what would otherwise have been a rather sugary film. Houghton, who portrays the independent daughter, is the real-life niece of Hepburn. 108m/C VHS, Beta, LV, Closed Caption. Katharine Hepburn, Spencer Tracy, Sidney Poitier, Katharine Houghton, Cecil Kellaway; **D:** Stanley Kramer; **W:** William Rose; **C:** Sam Leavitt. Academy Awards '67: Best Actress (Hepburn), Best Story & Screenplay; British Academy Awards '68: Best Actor (Tracy), Best Actress (Hepburn); Nominations: Academy Awards '67: Best Actor (Tracy), Best Adapted Score, Best Art Direction/Set Decoration, Best Director (Kramer), Best Film Editing, Best Picture, Best Supporting Actor (Kellaway), Best Supporting Actress (Richards). COL, FCT, COL

Guest in the House ♂♂ 1945 A seemingly friendly young female patient is invited to stay in the family home of her doctor. She skillfully attempts to dissect the family's harmony in the process. 121m/B VHS, Beta. Anne Baxter, Ralph Bellamy, Ruth Warrick, Marie McDonald, Margaret Hamilton; **D:** John Brahm; **C:** Lee Garmes. Nominations: Academy Awards '45: Best Original Dramatic/Comedy Score. NOS, CAB, VYY

Guest Wife ♂♂½ 1945 Determined to impress his sentimental boss, a quick-thinking bachelor talks his best friend's wife into posing as his own wife, but the hoax gets a bit out of hand and nearly ruins the real couple's marriage. 90m/B VHS. Claudette Colbert, Don Ameche, Dick Foran, Charles Dingle, Wilma Francis; **D:** Sam Wood; **C:** Joseph Valentine. Nominations: Academy Awards '45: Best Original Dramatic/Comedy Score. REP

A Guide for the Married Man ♂♂♂ 1967 One suburban husband instructs another in adultery, with a cast of dozens enacting various slapstick cameos. Based on Frank Tarloff's novel of the same name. Followed by "A Guide for the Married Woman." 91m/C VHS, Beta. Walter Matthau, Robert Morse, Inger Stevens, Sue Ane Langdon, Claire Kelly, Elaine Devry; **Cameos:** Lucille Ball, Sid Caesar, Jack Benny, Wally Cox, Jayne Mansfield, Louis Nye, Carl Reiner, Phil Silvers, Terry-Thomas, Sam Jaffe, Jeffrey Hunter, Polly Bergen; **D:** Gene Kelly; **W:** Frank Tarloff; **M:** John Williams. FOX

A Guide for the Married Woman ♂½ 1978 A bored housewife tries to take the romantic advice of a girlfriend to add a little spice to her life. A poor made-for-television follow-up to "A Guide for the Married Man." 96m/C VHS, Beta. Cybill Shepherd, Barbara Feldon, Eve Arden, Chuck Woolery, Peter Marshall, Charles Frank; **D:** Hy Averback. FOX

Guilty as Charged ♂½ 1992 (R) A butcher rigs his own private electric chair and captures and executes paroled killers in his personal quest for justice. But when a politician frames an innocent man for murder how far will this vigilante go? **CW:** Language and violence. 95m/C VHS, LV, Closed Caption. Rod Steiger, Lauren Hutton, Heather Graham, Isaac Hayes; **D:** Sam Irvin; **M:** Steve Bartek. COL

Guilty as Sin ♂♂ 1993 (R) Johnson is a ruthless Casanova accused of murdering his very wealthy wife and decides lawyer DeMornay is just the woman to defend him. Question is, who'll defend DeMornay from him? Johnson has fun as the menacing smoothie but DeMornay's supposedly hotshot criminal attorney is just plain dumb. It sounds like "Jagged Edge" but there's no sexual involvement between client and lawyer and no thrill in this thriller. **CW:** Language, violence, and

some sexuality. 120m/C VHS, Beta, LV, Letterbox, Closed Caption. Don Johnson, Rebecca DeMornay, Jack Warden, Stephen Lang, Dana Ivey, Ron White, Sean McCann, Luis Guzman; **D:** Sidney Lumet; **W:** Larry Cohen; **C:** Andrzej Bartkowiak. HPH, BTV, TOU

Guilty by Suspicion ♂♂½ 1991 (PG-13) Examination of the 1950s McCarthy investigations by the House Un-American Activities Committee comes off like a bland history lesson. De Niro plays a director who attended a Communist party meeting in the '30s but who otherwise doesn't have any red connections. He takes the moral high ground and refuses to incriminate his buddy (Wendt) to get off the hook and finds himself blacklisted. Characterized by average performances (excepting Wettig who goes overboard) and a lightweight script. "The Front" (1976) does a better job on this topic. Directorial debut for producer Winkler. Available in widescreen on laserdisc. 105m/C VHS, LV, 8mm, Letterbox, Closed Caption. Robert De Niro, Annette Bening, George Wendt, Patricia Wettig, Sam Wanamaker, Chris Cooper, Ben Piazza, Martin Scorsese, Barry Primus, Gailard Sartain, Stuart Margolin, Barry Tubb, Roxann Biggs-Dawson, Robin Gammell, Brad Sullivan, Luke Edwards, Adam Baldwin; **D:** Irwin Winkler; **W:** Irwin Winkler; **C:** Michael Ballhaus; **M:** James Newton Howard. WAR

Guilty of Innocence ♂♂ 1987 (PG) A young African-American man finds he's guilty until proven innocent when he runs into the law in Texas. A bold lawyer joins his fight for justice. Based on a true story and made for television. 95m/C VHS, Closed Caption. Dorian Harewood, Dabney Coleman, Hoyt Axton, Paul Winfield, Dennis Lipscomb, Debbi Morgan, Marshall Colt, Victor Love; **D:** Richard T. Heffron. THV

Guilty of Treason ♂♂½ 1950 A documentary on the life and times of Joszef Cardinal Mindszenty of Hungary, who was imprisoned by the communists as an enemy of the state for speaking out against the totalitarian regime. At the trial, it was revealed that the Cardinal's confession was obtained only by the use of drugs, hypnosis, and torture. A realistic look at the dark side of Communism. 86m/B VHS. Charles Bickford, Paul Kelly, Bonita Granville, Richard Derr, Berry Kroeger, Elisabeth Risdon, Roland Winters, John Banner; **D:** Felix Feist. NOS, MRV

The Guinea Pig ♂♂½ *The Outsider* 1948 Jack Read (Attenborough), the son of a tobacconist, is sent to a posh public school as an experiment but finds problems between his simple upbringing and the reactions of teachers and other students. 97m/B VHS. GB Richard Attenborough, Joan Hickson, Bernard Miles, Sheila Sim, Robert Flemyng, Timothy Bateson; **D:** Roy Boulting; **W:** Bernard Miles, Roy Boulting. FCT

Guitarman ♂ 1995 Modern version of "The Pied Piper of Hamlin" finds a mysterious musician saving a farming community's crops from a plague of locusts. But when the mayor reneges on paying the piper (so to speak), he takes the town's children instead. 92m/C VHS. Nicholas Campbell, Donnelly Rhodes, Andrea Martin, Shawn Ashmore, Jack Semple; **D:** Will Dixon. SDE

Gulag ♂♂½ 1985 An American sportscaster is wrongly sentenced to ten years of hard labor in a Soviet prison, and plans his escape from the cruel guards. Good suspense. Made for television. 130m/C VHS, Beta. GB David Keith, Malcolm McDowell, David Suchet, Warren Clarke, John McEnery; **D:** Roger Young; **M:** Elmer Bernstein.

Gulliver's Travels ♂♂½ 1939 The Fleischer Studio's animated version of Jonathan Swift's classic about the adventures of Gulliver, an English sailor who is washed ashore in the land of Lilliput, where everyone is about two inches tall. 74m/C VHS. **D:** Dave Fleischer; **V:** Lanny Ross, Jessica Dragonette. Nominations: Academy Awards '39: Best Song ("Faithful Forever"), Best Original Score. CAF, MRV, NOS

Gulliver's Travels ♂♂ 1977 (G) In this partially animated adventure the entire land of Lilliput has been constructed in miniature. Cartoon and real life mix in a 3-dimensional story of Dr. Lemuel Gulliver and his discovery of the small people in the East Indies. From the classic by Jonathan Swift. 80m/C VHS, Beta. GB Richard Harris, Catherine Schell; **D:** Peter Hunt. VTR, HHE, RDG

Gulliver's Travels ♂♂½ 1995 (PG) Faithful TV version of Jonathan Swift's 1726 satiric novel. Lemuel Gulliver (Danson) is confined to Bedlam, an English insane asylum, after having been lost at sea for eight years. While in the asylum he relates his very odd adventures—in the tiny land of Lilliput, among the giants of Brobdingnag, with the silly and impractical intellectuals of Laputa, and finally amidst the brutish human Yahoos, who are ruled by rational talking horses, the Houyhnhnms. Meanwhile, Gulliver's wife Mary (Steenburgen) and son Tom (Sturridge) struggle to prove his sanity and win his release. On two cassettes. 187m/C VHS, LV, Closed Caption. Ted Danson, Mary Steenburgen, Edward Fox, Thomas Sturridge, Edward Woodward, Nicholas Lyndhurst, Peter O'Toole, Phoebe Nicholls, Ned Beatty, Kate Maberly, Alfre Woodard, Geraldine Chaplin, John Gielgud, Kristin Scott Thomas, Omar Sharif, John Standing, Warwick Davis, Robert Hardy, Shashi Kapoor, Karyn Parsons, Edward Petherbridge; **D:** Charles Sturridge; **W:** Simon Moore; **C:** Howard Atherton; **M:** Trevor Jones. HMK

Gumball Rally ♂♂ 1976 (PG) An unusual assortment of people converge upon New York for a cross country car race to Long Beach, California where breaking the rules is part of the game. 107m/C VHS, Beta. Michael Sarrazin, Gary Busey, Raul Julia, Nicholas Pryor, Tim McIntire, Susan Flannery; **D:** Chuck Bail; **W:** Leon Capetanos. WAR

Gumby: The Movie ♂♂½ 1995 (G) Gumby and his musical group, the Clayboys, seek to save their neighbors' farms from foreclosure by putting on a benefit concert. And yes, pal Pokey is along to help out. But 90 minutes of our gentle clay hero stretches the patience of even the most enthusiastic fan. 90m/C VHS. **D:** Art Clokey; **W:** Art Clokey. KID

Gummo woof! 1997 (R) "Kids" scripter and first time helmer Korine shamelessly parades out the freaks and calls it entertainment. More like a series of grisly images than a cohesive narrative when nihilism pervades a group of disaffected Xenia, Ohio teens who explore every brand of atrocity for kicks. Disturbing, not only in the graphic violence of the bored juvies but also in the frightening lack of a point to this uneven and self-indulgent shock-fest. Touted as modern movie's golden-boy, 23 year-old Korine doesn't let any dark humor slip in to detract from the purely revolting scenarios, featuring leads who are actors ("Kids'" Sevigny) and nonprofessionals, such as the character Tummler (Sutton), recruited by the director from a "Sally Jesse Raphael Show" appearance. The result is a lack of performance power in a film that never goes beyond obvious surface appearance. The images that do summon up some truth about growing up in a dead-end town are far overshadowed by the collection of images as a whole. Scoring lavish praise from the uber-hip, for the unwashed masses (the Hound included) this one is definitely worth missing. Renowned French cinematographer Escoffier lends style to this lost cause. **CW:** Pervasive depiction of anti-social behavior of juveniles, including violence, substance abuse, sexuality and language. 88m/C VHS. Chloe Sevigny, Jacob Reynolds, Jacob Sewell, Nick Sutton, Carisa Bara, Darby Dougherty, Max Perlich, Linda Manz; **D:** Harmony Korine; **W:** Harmony Korine; **C:** Jean-Yves Escoffier. NLC

Gumshoe ♂♂½ 1972 (G) An homage to American hard-boiled detectives. Finney plays a small-time worker in a Liverpool nightclub who decides to become a detective like his movie heroes. He bumbles through a number of interconnecting cases, but finds his way in the end. Good

satire of film noir detectives. **85m/C VHS, Beta.** *GB* Albert Finney, Billie Whitelaw, Frank Finlay, Janice Dula, Carolyn Seymour; **D:** Stephen Frears; **C:** Chris Menges; **M:** Andrew Lloyd Webber. *NO*

The Gumshoe Kid 🎬 *The Detective Kid* **1989 (R)** A college-bound kid enters the family detective business to prevent his mother from being evicted. He gets in over his head though, trying to track the fiancee of a wealthy mobster. **98m/C VHS, Beta, LV.** Jay Underwood, Tracy Scoggins, Vince Edwards, Arlene Golonka, Stephen Young, Pamela Springsteen; **D:** Joseph Manduke.

A Gun, A Car, A Blonde 🎬🎬 **1997** Paraplegic Richard Spraggins (Metzler) escapes from his pain-filled life by imagining himself to be living in a 50's film noir world, where he takes on the persona of tough private eye Rick Stone. Naturally, as in all good noir worlds, he must save a femme fatale blonde (Thompson) from a killer. **101m/C VHS.** Jim Metzler, Billy Bob Thornton, Andrea Thompson, John Ritter, Kay Lenz; **D:** Stefani Ames. *AVA*

Gun Cargo 🎬 **1949** Muddled story about a conniving shipowner who fires his crew for demanding shore leave. He replaces them with assorted low-lifes, resulting in the usual hijinks. A terrible performance by an otherwise great cast. **49m/C VHS, Beta, 8mm.** Rex Lease, Smith Ballew, William Farnum, Gibson Gowland. *VYY*

Gun Code 🎬½ **1940** The white-hatted cowboy-hero puts a stop to small-town racketeering. **52m/B VHS, Beta.** Tim McCoy, Ina Guest; **D:** Sam Newfield. *VDM*

Gun Crazy 🎬🎬🎬 *Deadly Is the Female* **1949** Annie Laurie Starr—Annie Oakley in a Wild West show—meets gun-lovin' Bart Tare, who says a gun makes him feel good inside, "like I'm somebody." Sparks fly, and the two get married and live happily ever after—until the money runs out and fatal femme Laurie's craving for excitement and violence starts to flare up. The two become lovebirds-on-the-lam. Now a cult fave, it's based on a MacKinlay Kantor story. Ex-stuntman Russell Harlan's photography is daring; the realism of the impressive robbery scenes is owed in part to the technical consultation of former train robber Al Jennings. And watch for a young Tamblyn as the 14-year-old Bart. **87m/B VHS.** Peggy Cummins, John Dall, Berry Kroeger, Morris Carnovsky, Anabel Shaw, Nedrick Young, Trevor Bardette, Russ Tamblyn, Harry Lewis, Mickey Little, Paul Frison, Dave Bair, Stanley Prager, Virginia Farmer, Anne O'Neal, Frances Irwin, Don Beddoe, Robert Osterloh, Shimen Ruskin, Harry Hayden; **D:** Joseph H. Lewis; **W:** Dalton Trumbo; **C:** Russell Harlan; **M:** Victor Young. *FOX, FCT*

Gun Crazy 🎬🎬½ *A Talent for Loving* **1969** A gambler becomes enmeshed in an arranged marriage with a cursed Mexican family. Lightweight comedy, good cast. **110m/C VHS.** Richard Widmark, Chaim Topol, Cesar Romero, Genevieve Page, Judd Hamilton, Caroline Munro; **D:** Richard Quine. *SIM*

Gun Fight at Red Sands 🎬 *Gringo; Duello Nel Texas* **1963** Landmark western in the history of Italian cinema. Long before Leone's Eastwood trilogy, this film introduced the theme of an avenging stranger to the genre. Harrison stars as the dark, brooding hero who is out for revenge after learning that his family has been attacked by a gang of bandits. **?m/C VHS.** *IT* Richard Harrison, Giacomo "Jack" Rossi-Stuart, Sara Lezana; **M:** Ennio Morricone. *SNC*

Gun Fury 🎬🎬½ **1953** A panoramic western about a Civil War veteran pursuing the bandits who kidnapped his beautiful bride-to-be. First screened as a 3-D movie. **83m/C VHS, Beta, LV.** Rock Hudson, Donna Reed, Phil Carey, Lee Marvin; **D:** Raoul Walsh. *COL*

Gun Girls 🎬 **1956** Campy exploitation flick about a gun-toting gang of girls who rob anything or anyone. The guy who fences their goods ends up getting one of them pregnant. **?m/C VHS.** Timothy Farrell, Jean Ferguson, Jacquelyn Park, Jean Ann Lewis; **D:** Robert Deltano. *SNC*

Gun Glory 🎬🎬½ **1957** Granger plays Tom Early, a gunslinger who returns home after three years to find the town would rather not have him. He regains the town's respect when he stops a murderer from invading the town with his cattle herd. Based on the novel "Man of the West" by Philip Yordan. **88m/C VHS, Closed Caption.** Stewart Granger, Rhonda Fleming, Chill Wills, Steve Rowland, James Gregory, Jacques Aubuchon, Arch Johnson, William "Bill" Fawcett, Lane Bradford, Michael Dugan, Bud Osborne, May McAvoy, Charles Herbert, Carl Pitti; **D:** Roy Rowland; **W:** William Ludwig; **M:** Jeff Alexander. *MGM*

Gun Grit 🎬½ **1936** An FBI agent is sent west to break up a protection racket. **51m/B VHS.** Jack Perrin, Ethel Beck, David Sharpe, Roger Williams, Budd Buster; **D:** William (Lester Williams) Berke. *GPV*

The Gun in Betty Lou's Handbag 🎬🎬 **1992 (PG-13)** Shy, small town librarian with a dull marriage is looking for excitement when she stumbles across a gun used in a murder. She decides excitement will follow her (false) confession to the crime leaving her husband thunderstruck, the police confused, and the gossip line humming. She also intrigues the real bad guy, who comes looking for her. Lame silliness is redeemed somewhat by Miller, but there's some surprisingly nasty violence given the comedy label. **99m/C VHS, Beta, LV, Closed Caption.** Penelope Ann Miller, Eric Thal, Alfre Woodard, Cathy Moriarty, William Forsythe, Julianne Moore, Xander Berkeley, Michael O'Neill, Christopher John Fields; **D:** Allan Moyle; **W:** Grace Cary Bickley; **M:** Richard Gibbs. *TOU*

A Gun in the House 🎬 **1981** While being attacked in her own home, a woman shoots one of her assailants. The police find no conclusive evidence of attack and arrest the woman for murder. Exploitive drama on gun control. Made-for-television. **100m/C VHS, Beta.** Sally Struthers, David Ackroyd, Joel Bailey, Jeffrey Tambor; **D:** Ivan Nagy. *VHE, HHE*

Gun Law 🎬½ **1933** The hero tackles the Sonora Kid, an outlaw terrorizing Arizona folk. One of the few sound westerns with Hoxie, a silent-era star who hung up his spurs when his voice proved non-photogenic. **59m/B VHS, Beta.** Jack Hoxie, Paul Fix, Mary Carr, Edmund Cobb, Robert Burns; **D:** Lewis D. Collins. *GPV*

Gun Lords of Stirrup Basin 🎬🎬 **1937** A cattleman and the daughter of a homesteader are in love in the Old West, but a seedy lawyer wants to douse their flame. Bullets and fists fly as a result. **55m/B VHS.** Bob Steele, Louise Stanley, Karl Hackett, Ernie Adams, Frank LaRue, Frank Ball, Steve Clark; **D:** Sam Newfield. *NOS, DVT*

Gun Packer 🎬🎬 **1938** When an outlaw gang robs stagecoaches of their gold and uses the booty to salt barren mine shafts so the unsuspecting can be swindled out of their money on worthless gold mine certificates, hard-riding Randall is called in to save the day. **51m/B VHS.** Jack Randall, Louise Stanley, Charles "Blackie" King, Glenn Strange; **D:** Wallace Fox; **W:** Robert Emmett. *MOV*

Gun Play 🎬🎬 *Lucky Boots* **1936** Brother and sister venture west to run their father's ranch. Mexican bandits believe the ranch's property houses a revolutionary fortune, and set about recovering it. The brother defends his father's ranch along with a sidekick, who sweeps the sister off her feet. **59m/B VHS.** Guinn "Big Boy" Williams, Frank Yaconelli, Marion Shilling, Wally Wales, Charles French; **D:** Al(bert) Herman. *NOS, DVT, GPV*

The Gun Ranger 🎬½ **1934** Our hero plays a Texas Ranger who becomes fed up with soft judges and shady prosecutors and decides to take the law into his own hands. **56m/B VHS, Beta.** Bob Steele, Eleanor Stewart, John Merton, Ernie Adams, Budd Buster; **D:** Robert North Bradbury. *NOS, DVT, GPV*

Gun Riders 🎬½ *Five Bloody Graves; Five Bloody Days to Tombstone; Lonely Man* **1969** Gunman must seek out and stop a murderer of innocent people. **98m/C VHS, Beta.** Scott Brady, Jim Davis, John Carradine; **D:** Al Adamson. *CCB*

Gun Smugglers/Hot Lead 🎬 **1951** A western double feature: Tim Holt and his sidekick Chito must recover a shipment of stolen guns in "Gun Smugglers," and the duo gallop into action against a gang of train robbers in "Hot Lead." **120m/B VHS, Beta.** Tim Holt, Richard Martin, Martha Hyer. *TTC*

Gunblast 🎬 **197?** A convict is released from San Quentin and wastes no time in getting involved with mob-powered drug smuggling. **70m/C VHS, Beta.** Lloyd Allan, Christine Cardan, James Cunningham. *NO*

Guncrazy 🎬🎬 **1992 (R)** Girl from the wrong side of the tracks, abused her entire life, finds her freedom in a gun. She winds up killing the man who raped her, takes up with an equally lost ex-con, and the two armed misfits go on the run from the law. Barrymore's convincing and the movie is another well-made variation on the lovers-on-the-run theme. Film was inspired by, but is not a remake of, the 1949 movie "Gun Crazy." **CW:** Language, strong violence, and strong sensuality. **97m/C VHS, Beta, LV, Closed Caption.** Drew Barrymore, James LeGros, Billy Drago, Rodney Harvey, Ione Skye, Joe Dallesandro, Michael Ironside; **D:** Tamra Davis; **W:** Matthew Bright. *PMS*

A Gunfight 🎬🎬 **1971 (PG)** When Cash is stranded in a small Western town, he meets up with fellow old-time gunfighter Douglas. The two strike up a friendship, but discover the town folk expect a gun battle. Needing money, the two arrange a gunfight for paid admission — winner take all. Cash makes his screen debut. **90m/C Beta.** Kirk Douglas, Johnny Cash, Jane Alexander, Karen Black, Dana Elcar, Keith Carradine, Raf Vallone; **D:** Lamont Johnson; **W:** Harold Jack Bloom. *MTX*

Gunfight at Sandoval 🎬½ **1959** A Texas Ranger investigates the headquarters of a criminal gang while hunting for the bandits who killed his partner. Adapted from the "Texas John Slaughter" episodes of the Disney television series. **72m/C VHS, Beta.** Tom Tryon, Beverly Garland, Dan Duryea. *DIS*

Gunfight at the O.K. Corral 🎬🎬🎬 **1957** The story of Wyatt Earp and Doc Holliday joining forces in Dodge City to rid the town of the criminal Clanton gang. Filmed in typical Hollywood style, but redeemed by its great stars. **122m/C VHS, Beta, LV.** Burt Lancaster, Kirk Douglas, Rhonda Fleming, Jo Van Fleet, John Ireland, Kenneth Tobey, Lee Van Cleef, Frank Faylen, DeForest Kelley, Earl Holliman; **D:** John Sturges; **W:** Leon Uris; **C:** Charles B(ryant) Lang. Nominations: Academy Awards '57: Best Film Editing, Best Sound. *PAR, FCT*

The Gunfighter 🎬🎬🎬½ **1950** A mature, serious, Hollywood-western character study about an aging gunfighter searching for peace and quiet but unable to avoid his reputation and the duel-challenges it invites. One of King's best films. **85m/B VHS, Beta, LV.** Gregory Peck, Helen Westcott, Millard Mitchell, Jean Parker, Karl Malden, Skip Homeier, Mae Marsh; **D:** Henry King; **C:** Arthur C. Miller. Nominations: Academy Awards '50: Best Story. *FOX*

The Gunfighters 🎬½ **1987** Lackluster pilot of a proposed Canadian series pits three individualistic relatives against a powerful empire-builder. **100m/C VHS, LV.** *CA* Art Hindle, Reiner Schoene, Tony Addabbo, George Kennedy, Michael Kane, Lori Hallier; **D:** Clay Borris. *THV*

Gunfighter's Moon 🎬🎬½ **1996 (PG-13)** Legendary gunslinger Frank Morgan (Henriksen) is called on by former lover, Linda (Lenz), to help her sheriff husband prevent a jailbreak. Frank's tired of his constant challengers but can't seem to make another life for himself. **CW:** Gunfighting. **95m/C VHS, Closed Caption.** Lance Henriksen, Kay Lenz, David McIlwraith; **D:** Larry Ferguson; **W:** Larry Ferguson; **C:** James L. Carter; **M:** Lee Holdridge. *CAF*

Gunfire 🎬½ **1950** A Frank James look-alike cavorts, robs and loots the countryside until the real James decides to set things straight. **59m/B VHS, Beta, LV.** Donald (Don "Red") Barry, Robert Lowery,

Pamela Blake, Wally Vernon; *D:* William (Lester Williams) Berke. *HHE*

Gunfire 🎬🎬 *China 9, Liberty 37* 1978 A gunfighter is rescued from the hangman's noose by railroad tycoons who want him to kill a farmer. He doesn't kill the man, but runs off with his wife instead, and the incensed railway honchos send assassins after the double-crossing gunman. Peckinpah's part is pretty puny in this leisurely horse opera. 94m/C VHS. *IT* Fabio Testi, Warren Oates, Jenny Agutter, Sam Peckinpah; *D:* Monte Hellman; *M:* Pino Donaggio. *SIM*

Gung Ho! 🎬🎬 1943 Carlson's Raiders are a specially trained group of Marine jungle fighters determined to retake the Pacific island of Makin during WWII. 88m/B VHS, Beta. Robert Mitchum, Randolph Scott, Noah Beery Jr., Alan Curtis, Grace McDonald; *D:* Ray Enright; *C:* Milton Krasner. *REP, MRV, CNG*

Gung Ho 🎬🎬½ 1985 (PG-13) A Japanese firm takes over a small-town U.S. auto factory and causes major cultural collisions. Keaton plays the go-between for employees and management while trying to keep both groups from killing each other. From the director of "Splash" and "Night Shift." Made into a short-lived television series. 111m/C VHS, Beta, LV, 8mm, Closed Caption. Michael Keaton, Gedde Watanabe, George Wendt, Mimi Rogers, John Turturro, Clint Howard, Michelle Johnson, So Yamamura, Sab Shimono; *D:* Ron Howard; *W:* Babaloo Mandel, Lowell Ganz; *M:* Thomas Newman. *PAR*

Gunga Din 🎬🎬🎬🎬 1939 The prototypical "buddy" film. Three veteran British sergeants in India try to suppress a native uprising, but it's their water boy, the intrepid Gunga Din, who saves the day. Friendship, loyalty, and some of the best action scenes ever filmed. Based loosely on Rudyard Kipling's famous poem, the story is credited to Ben Hecht, Charles MacArthur, and William Faulkner (who is uncredited). Also available colorized. 117m/B VHS, Beta, LV. Cary Grant, Victor McLaglen, Douglas Fairbanks Jr., Sam Jaffe, Eduardo Ciannelli, Montagu Love, Joan Fontaine, Abner Biberman, Robert Coote, Lumsden Hare, Cecil Kellaway; *D:* George Stevens; *W:* Fred Guiol, Joel Sayre; *M:* Alfred Newman. Nominations: Academy Awards '39: Best Black and White Cinematography. *TTC, MLB*

Gunman from Bodie 🎬½ *Gun Man from Bodie* 1941 Second of the Rough Rider series. Jones, McCoy, and Hatton rescue a baby orphaned by rustlers and then go after the bad guys. 62m/B VHS, Beta. Tim McCoy, Buck Jones, Raymond Hatton; *D:* Spencer Gordon Bennet. *NOS, MRV, VCN*

Gunman's Walk 🎬🎬½ 1958 Rancher Lee Hackett (Heflin) gained his power through his gunslinging skill but wants his two sons to be respectable citizens. However, hot-tempered eldest son Ed (Hunter) wants to best the old man's reputation while younger son Davy (Darren) has his own problems when he falls for Sioux half-breed Clee (Grant), whose brother was murdered by Ed. As Ed gets more ruthless, his father must decide how far he's willing to go to protect him. 95m/C VHS. Van Heflin, Tab Hunter, James Darren, Kathryn Grant, Mickey Shaughnessy, Robert F. Simon, Edward Platt, Bert Convy; *D:* Phil Karlson; *W:* Frank Nugent; *C:* Charles Lawton Jr. *COL*

Gunmen 🎬🎬 1993 (R) A reluctant buddy team face down some bad guys. DEA agent Cole (Van Peebles) teams up with smuggler Dani (Lambert) to find stolen drug money also wanted by wheelchair-bound villain Loomis (Stewart) and his violence-loving henchman (Leary). Adds comedy to the mix as well as shameless action rip-offs from spaghetti westerns.*CW:* Language, violence, and sexuality. 90m/C VHS, LV. Christopher Lambert, Mario Van Peebles, Denis Leary, Patrick Stewart, Kadeem Hardison, Sally Kirkland; *Cameos:* Big Daddy Kane, Ed Lover, Eric B. Rakim, Dr. Dre; *D:* Deran Sarafian; *W:* Stephen Sommers; *M:* John Debney. *ART*

Gunners & Guns 🎬 1934 Vintage western starring King. 51m/B VHS, Beta. Black King, Edmund Cobb, Edna Asetin, Eddie Davis; *D:* Robert Hoyt. *VCN*

Gunplay 🎬½ 1951 Two cowboys befriend a boy whose father has been killed and search for the murderer. 61m/B VHS, Beta. Tim Holt, Joan Dixon, Richard Martin.

Gunpowder 🎬 1984 Two Interpol agents endeavor to stop a crime lord from causing the collapse of the world economy. 85m/C VHS, Beta. David Gilliam, Martin Potter, Gordon Jackson, Anthony Schaeffer. *ART, VES*

The Gunrunner 🎬½ 1984 (R) Costner plays a Canadian mobster, involved in liquor smuggling, who aids a Chinese rebellion in this 1920s drama. Interesting concept. Received more attention after Costner gained notoriety in later films. 92m/C VHS, LV. *CA* Kevin Costner, Sara Botsford, Paul Soles; *D:* Nardo Castillo. *VTR, HHE*

Guns 🎬🎬 1990 (R) An international gunrunner puts the moves on buxom women between hair-raising adventures. 95m/C VHS, LV. Erik Estrada, Dona Speir; *D:* Andy Sidaris; *W:* Andy Sidaris. *COL*

The Guns and the Fury 🎬½ 1983 Two American oil riggers in the Middle East, circa 1908, are forced to fight off an attack by a vicious Arab sheik and his tribe. 90m/C VHS, Beta. Peter Graves, Cameron Mitchell, Michael Ansara, Albert Salmi; *D:* Tony Zarindast. *NO*

Guns at Batasi 🎬🎬½ 1964 Attenborough plays a tough British Sergeant Major stationed in Africa during the anti-colonial 1960s. Ultimately the regiment is threatened by rebel Africans. Fine performances make this rather predictable film watchable. 103m/B VHS. *GB* Richard Attenborough, Jack Hawkins, Mia Farrow, Flora Robson, John Leyton; *D:* John Guillermin; *M:* John Addison. *FXL, RXM*

Guns Don't Argue 🎬🎬 1957 Entertaining schlocker about the rise and fall of famous criminal Dillinger. Non-stop action also features Bonnie and Clyde, Pretty Boy Floyd and Baby Face Nelson. ?m/C VHS. Myron Healey, Jim Davis, Richard Crane. *SNC*

Guns for Dollars 🎬🎬 *They Call Me Hallelujah* 1973 Mex-Western has four men, including a secret agent and a cossack, tangled up in the Mexican Revolution as they search for a fortune in smuggled jewels. 94m/C VHS. *MX* George Hilton, Charles Southwood, Agata Flory, Roberto Camardiel, Paolo Gozlino, Rick Boyd; *D:* Anthony Ascot.

Guns in the Dark 🎬 1937 A cowboy vows never to use a gun again when he believes that he accidentally shot his best friend. 60m/C VHS, Beta. Johnny Mack Brown, Claire Rochelle; *D:* Sam Newfield. *NOS, DVT, RXM*

Guns of Diablo 🎬🎬 1964 Wagon train master Bronson has to fight a gang that controls the supply depot, all the while showing his young helper (beardless boy Russell) the fascinating tricks of the trade. 91m/C VHS. Charles Bronson, Kurt Russell, Susan Oliver; *D:* Boris Sagal. *ACE, MTX, VTR*

Guns of Fury 🎬½ 1945 Cisco and Pancho solve the troubles of a small boy in this standard oater. 60m/B VHS, Beta. Duncan Renaldo. *NOS, VCI, VCN*

Guns of Justice 🎬 *Colorado Ranger* 1950 Undercover Colorado rangers stop a swindler from forcing homesteaders off their land. 60m/B VHS, Beta, LV. James Ellison, Russell Hayden, Tom Tyler, Raymond Hatton; *D:* Thomas Carr. *NO*

The Guns of Navarone 🎬🎬🎬½ 1961 During WWII, British Intelligence in the Middle East sends six men to the Aegean island of Navarone to destroy guns manned by the Germans. Consistently interesting war epic based on the Alistair MacLean novel, with a vivid cast. 159m/C VHS, Beta, LV, Letterbox. Gregory Peck, David Niven, Anthony Quinn, Richard Harris, Stanley Baker, Anthony Quayle, James Darren, Irene Papas; *D:* J. Lee Thompson; *C:* Oswald Morris. Academy Awards '61: Best Special Effects; Golden Globe Awards '62: Best Film—Drama, Best Score; Nominations: Academy Awards '61: Best Adapted Screenplay, Best Director (Thompson), Best Film Editing, Best Picture, Best Sound, Best Original Dramatic/Comedy Score. *COL*

Guns of the Law 🎬½ 1944 The Texas Rangers try to stop a shifty lawyer who attempts to swindle a family out of a potential fortune in property. 56m/B VHS. Dave O'Brien, James Newill, Guy Wilkerson, Jack Ingram, Robert F. (Bob) Kortman, Bob Barron; *D:* Elmer Clifton; *W:* Elmer Clifton. *MOV*

Guns of the Magnificent Seven 🎬🎬½ 1969 (G) The third remake of "The Seven Samurai." Action-packed western in which the seven free political prisoners and train them to kill. The war party then heads out to rescue a Mexican revolutionary being held in an impregnable fortress. 106m/C VHS. George Kennedy, Monte Markham, James Whitmore, Reni Santoni, Bernie Casey, Joe Don Baker, Scott Thomas, Michael Ansara, Fernando Rey; *D:* Paul Wendkos; *M:* Elmer Bernstein. *MGM*

The Gunslinger 🎬½ 1956 A woman marshall struggles to keep law and order in a town overrun by outlaws. Unique western with a surprise ending. 83m/C VHS. John Ireland, Beverly Garland, Allison Hayes, Jonathan Haze, Dick Miller, Bruno Ve Sota; *D:* Roger Corman; *W:* Charles B. Griffith. *MLB, TIM, SNC*

Gunslinger 🎬½ 197? Armed to the teeth with weaponry, Sartana shows a mining town's heavies how to sling a gun or two. 90m/C VHS, Beta. Gianni "John" Garko, Antonio Vilar; *D:* Anthony Ascot. *VDC*

Gunsmoke: Return to Dodge 🎬🎬½ 1987 The first of the made-for-television movies which reunited most of the cast of the classic television western. Matt Dillon returns to Dodge and Miss Kitty after 12 years only to be trailed by a ruthless adversary. 100m/C VHS. James Arness, Amanda Blake, Buck Taylor, Fran Ryan, Earl Holliman, Steve Forrest; *D:* Vincent McEveety. *FOX*

Gunsmoke Trail 🎬 1938 Cowpoke Randall saves an heiress from losing her estate to a phony uncle in low-budget Western. Also features the prolific "Fuzzy" St. John in his cowboy's sidekick stage (interestingly, St. John, a nephew of Fatty Arbuckle, later co-starred in the "Lone Rider" series with Randall's brother, Robert Livingston). 59m/C VHS. Jack Randall, Al "Fuzzy" St. John. *NOS, MRV, MOV*

Gus 🎬🎬½ 1976 (G) A Disney film about the California Atoms, a football team that has the worst record in the league until they begin winning games with the help of their field goal kicking mule of a mascot, Gus. The competition then plots a donkey-napping. Enjoyable comedy for the whole family. 96m/C VHS, Beta, LV. Ed Asner, Tim Conway, Dick Van Patten, Ronnie Schell, Bob Crane, Tom Bosley; *D:* Vincent McEveety; *W:* Arthur Alsberg; *M:* Robert F. Brunner. *COL, DIS*

GUY: Awakening of the Devil 🎬🎬 1993 Guy and Raina, two despicable intergalactic soldiers of fortune, embark on a continuous sky-raid adventure. Available in general release and uncut versions. Japanese with English subtitles. ?m/C VHS. *JP CPM*

The Guy from Harlem 🎬🎬 1977 He's mad, he's from Harlem, and he's not going to take it any more. 86m/C VHS. Loye Hawkins, Cathy Davis, Patricia Fulton, Wanda Starr; *D:* Rene Martinez Jr. *XVC*

A Guy Named Joe 🎬🎬½ 1944 A sentimental, patriotic Hollywood fantasy about the angel of a dead WWII pilot guiding another young pilot through battle and also helping him to romance his girl, who's still too devoted to his memory. Remade in 1989 as "Always." 121m/C VHS, Beta. Spencer Tracy, Irene Dunne, Van Johnson, Ward Bond, James Gleason, Lionel Barrymore, Esther Williams; *D:* Victor Fleming; *W:* Dalton Trumbo; *C:* Karl Freund. Nominations: Academy Awards '44: Best Story.*MGM*

The Guyana Tragedy: The Story of Jim Jones 🎬🎬 1980 Dramatization traces the story of the Reverend Jim Jones and the People's Temple from its beginnings in 1953 to the November 1978 mass suicide of more than 900 people. Boothe is appropriately hypnotic as the Reverend. Made for television. 240m/C VHS, Beta. Powers Boothe, Ned Beatty, Randy Quaid, Brad Dourif,

Brenda Vaccaro, LeVar Burton, Colleen Dewhurst, James Earl Jones. **D:** William A. Graham; **C:** Gil Hubbs; **M:** Elmer Bernstein. *VHE, HHE*

Guys and Dolls 🎬🎬🎬 **1955** New York gambler Sky Masterson takes a bet that he can romance a Salvation Army lady. Based on the stories of Damon Runyon with Blaine, Kaye, Pully, and Silver recreating their roles from the Broadway hit. Brando's not-always-convincing musical debut. ♫More I Cannot Wish You; My Time of Day; Guys and Dolls; Fugue for Tinhorns; Follow the Fold; Sue Me; Take Back Your Mink; If I Were a Bell; Luck Be a Lady. **150m/C VHS, Beta, LV, Closed Caption.** Marlon Brando, Jean Simmons, Frank Sinatra, Vivian Blaine, Stubby Kaye, Sheldon Leonard, Veda Ann Borg; **D:** Joseph L. Mankiewicz; **W:** Joseph L. Mankiewicz; **C:** Harry Stradling; **M:** Frank Loesser. Golden Globe Awards '56: Best Actress—Musical/Comedy (Simmons), Best Film—Musical/Comedy; Nominations: Academy Awards '55: Best Art Direction/Set Decoration (Color), Best Color Cinematography, Best Costume Design (Color), Scoring of a Musical. *HMK, FCT, FOX*

The Guyver 🎬½ **1991** A young college student is transformed into a super-human fighting machine through his discovery of an alien device, "The Guyver." A CIA agent (Hamill) must keep the secret device from falling into the hands of human mutants, the Zoanoids. Based on a Japanese comic book. **92m/C VHS.** Mark Hamill, Vivian Wu, David Gale, Jeffrey Combs, Michael Berryman; **D:** Steve Wang. *COL, NLC*

Guyver 2: Dark Hero 🎬½ **1994 (R)** The Guyver discovers an alien ship filled with weapons capable of destroying the planet. Naturally, he must battle the evil mutant Zoanoids in order to save the world. Adapted from a Japanese comic book. **CW:** Sci-fi violence and gore; language. **127m/C VHS, LV, Closed Caption.** David Hayter, Kathy Christopherson, Christopher Michael; **D:** Steve Wang; **W:** Nathan Long. *COL*

Gymkata 🎬 **1985 (R)** A gymnast (Olympian Thomas) must use his martial arts skills to conquer and secure a military state in a hostile European country. **89m/C VHS, Beta.** Kurt Thomas, Tetchie Agbayani, Richard Norton, Conan Lee; **D:** Robert Clouse; **W:** Charles Robert Carner. *MGM*

Gypsy 🎬🎬🎬 **1962** The life story of America's most famous striptease queen, Gypsy Rose Lee. Russell gives a memorable performance as the infamous Mama Rose, Gypsy's stage mother. Based on both Gypsy Rose Lee's memoirs and the hit Broadway play by Arthur Laurents. ♫Small World; All I Need is the Girl; You'll Never Get Away From Me; Let Me Entertain You; Some People; Everything's Coming Up Roses; You Gotta Have a Gimmick; Baby Jane and the Newsboys; Mr. Goldstone, I Love You. **144m/C VHS, Beta, LV, Letterbox.** Rosalind Russell, Natalie Wood, Karl Malden, Ann Jillian, Parley Baer, Paul Wallace, Betty Bruce; **D:** Mervyn LeRoy; **C:** Harry Stradling. Golden Globe Awards '63: Best Actress—Musical/Comedy (Russell); Nominations: Academy Awards '62: Best Adapted Score, Best Color Cinematography, Best Costume Design (Color). *WAR*

Gypsy 🎬🎬 **1975** A modern day gypsy-blooded Robin Hood cavorts between heists and romantic trysts. Dubbed. **90m/C VHS, Beta.** Alain Delon, Annie Girardot, Paul Meurisse; **D:** Jose Giovanni. *FCT*

Gypsy 🎬🎬½ **1993** If you like Bette brassy and larger than life, as only she can be, than this is the production for you. This television recreation of the 1959 Broadway musical stars Midler as notorious stage mother Mama Rose, who tries to realize all her frustrated ambitions by pushing her two young daughters, June and Louise, into vaudeville show biz. Her wish eventually comes true, in an unexpected fashion, when an adult Louise (Gibb) transforms herself into stripper Gypsy Rose Lee. ♫Everything's Coming Up Roses; You've Gotta Have a Gimmick; All I Need Is the Girl; Rose's Turn; Some People; Mr. Goldstone, I Love You; You'll Never Get Away From Me; Together, Wherever We Go. **150m/C VHS, LV, Closed Caption.** Bette Midler, Peter Riegert, Cynthia Gibb,

Ed Asner, Christine Ebersole, Michael Jeter, Andrea Martin, Jennifer Beck, Linda Hart, Rachel Sweet; **D:** Emile Ardolino; **W:** Arthur Laurents; **C:** Ralf Bode; **M:** Jule Styne, Stephen Sondheim. *CAF*

Gypsy Angels 🎬 **1994 (R)** A daredevil stunt pilot has a terrifying accident and develops amnesia. With the help of a stripper (who is in love with him), he tries to rebuild his life, this time with her in it. White's no actress and unless you like stunt flying (and there's a lot of it), fly by this one. (You'll note the director won't admit to this, since Smithee is a pseudonym.) **CW:** Profanity. **92m/C VHS, Closed Caption.** Vanna White, Richard Roundtree, Gene Bicknell; **D:** Alan Smithee. *THV*

Gypsy Blood 🎬🎬 **1918** One of the first screen versions of "Carmen," closer to Prosper Merrimee's story than to the opera, depicting the fated love between a dancing girl and a matador. Lubitsch's first notable film. Silent. **104m/B VHS, Beta.** Pola Negri; **D:** Ernst Lubitsch. *FCT, GPV*

Gypsy Colt 🎬🎬½ **1954 (G)** Gypsy is the horse beloved by the young Corcoran. But a drought forces her family to sell the animal to a racing stable 500 miles from their home. Gypsy is having none of this, escapes the stables, and returns home to be with Corcoran. Both horse and child actress are naturally appealing. **72m/C VHS.** Donna Corcoran, Ward Bond, Frances Dee, Lee Van Cleef, Larry Keating; **D:** Andrew Marton. *MGM, FCT*

The Gypsy Warriors 🎬🎬½ **1978** Two Army captains during WWII infiltrate Nazi-occupied France in order to prevent the distribution of a deadly toxin and are aided by a band of Gypsies. Made for television. **77m/C VHS, Beta.** Tom Selleck, James Whitmore Jr., Joseph Ruskin, Lina Raymond; **D:** Lou Antonio. *USH*

H 🎬 **1990** Two junkies try to kick their heroin addiction and face the difficult withdrawal period. Includes glimpses into their past that shed light on the reasons they turned to drugs. Contains explicit footage. **93m/C VHS.** **CA** Martin Neufeld, Pascale Montpetit; **D:** Darrell Wasyk. Genie Awards '91: Best Actress (Montpetit); Toronto-City Award '90: Best Canadian Feature Film. *NYR*

H-Bomb woof! **1971** Mitchum stars as a CIA agent who is sent to Bangkok to retrieve two stolen nuclear warheads from a terrorist. It just so happens that his ex-girlfriend's father is the terrorist he must contend with in this stupid movie. **98m/C VHS, Beta.** Olivia Hussey, Chris Mitchum, Krung Savilai; **D:** P. Chalong. *NO*

H-Man woof! *Bijo to Ekitainigen* **1959** A Japanese sci-fi woofer about a radioactive mass of slime festering under Tokyo. Extremely lame special effects get quite a few unintentional laughs. Dubbed. **79m/C VHS, Beta.** **JP** Koreya Senda, Kenji Sahara, Yumi Shirakawa, Akihiko Hirata; **D:** Inoshiro Honda. *COL*

Habit 🎬🎬 **1997** A very low-budget New York vampire tale that tweaks tradition. Wastrel Sam (Fessenden) is at loose ends when he meets intriguing Anna (Snaider). This first encounter is a bust (Sam's very drunk) but a later meeting leads to an intense sexual encounter—and Sam waking up alone in Battery Park with a prominently cut lip and some hazy memories. All their encounters are similarly intense (and in public places) but Anna refuses to reveal anything about herself. Sam is soon a confused physical wreck but when Anna's around, he just doesn't care. **112m/C VHS.** Larry Fessenden, Meredith Snaider, Aaron Beall, Heather Woodbury, Patricia Coleman; **D:** Larry Fessenden; **W:** Larry Fessenden; **C:** Frank DeMarco; **M:** Geoffrey Kidde. Nominations: Independent Spirit Awards '98: Best Cinematography, Best Director (Fessenden). *NYR*

Habitat 🎬🎬½ **1997 (R)** Nature goes wild when high school student Andreas (Getty) moves with his scientist parents, Hank (Kayro) and Clarissa (Krige), to the small Southwestern burg of Pleasanton. Hank's experiment with accelerated evolution takes some unexpected blips, with Hank turning into particles of matter, their house trans-

formed into a vegetation-covered fortress, and Clarissa becoming a very earthy earth mother. Some eerie special effects. **CW:** Sexuality, language and some violence/gore. **103m/C VHS.** Alice Krige, Balthazar Getty, Tcheky Karyo, Kenneth Welsh; **D:** Renee Daalder; **W:** Renee Daalder. *APX*

The Habitation of Dragons 🎬½ **1991** Family fueds and melodrama in 1930s West Texas. Wandering lawyer George Tolliver (Davis) argues with successful businessman brother Leonard (Forrest) while matriarch Leonora (Stapleton) presides and family skeletons rattle. Confusing hodgepodge. **94m/C VHS.** Jean Stapleton, Frederic Forrest, Brad Davis, Pat Hingle, Hallie Foote, Maureen O'Sullivan; **D:** Michael Lindsay-Hogg; **M:** David Shire. *TTC*

Hack O'Lantern 🎬 **1987** Granddad worships Satan, and gets his grandson involved; the result is much bloodshed, violence, and evil. **90m/C VHS, Beta.** **D:** Jag Mundhra. *NO*

Hackers 🎬🎬 **1995 (PG-13)** Group of teenaged computer cyber-geeks surf the 'net and become the prime suspects in an industrial conspiracy when hacker Dade (Miller) breaks into the computer at Ellingson Oil Company. It's really an inside job but just try getting anyone (read "adult") to believe him. So the techno whiz kids band together, with cops and security all wanting to shut them down. Jolie (hacker Acid Burn) is the daughter of actor Jon Voight. **CW:** Some sexuality; brief strong language. **105m/C VHS, LV, Closed Caption.** Jonny Lee Miller, Angelina Jolie, Fisher Stevens, Lorraine Bracco, Jesse Bradford, Wendell Pierce, Alberta Watson, Laurence Mason, Renoly Santiago, Matthew Lillard, Penn Jillette; **D:** Iain Softley; **W:** Rafael Moreu; **C:** Andrzej Sekula; **M:** Simon Boswell. *MGM*

Hadley's Rebellion 🎬🎬½ **1984 (PG)** A Georgia farm boy adjusts to relocation at an elitist California boarding school by flaunting his wrestling abilities. **96m/C VHS, Beta, Closed Caption.** Griffin O'Neal, Charles Durning, William Devane, Adam Baldwin, Dennis Hage, Lisa Lucas; **D:** Fred Walton; **W:** Fred Walton. *FOX*

Hail 🎬🎬 *Hail to the Chief; Washington, B.C* **1973 (PG)** A biting satire of what-might-have-been if certain key cabinet members had their way. **85m/C VHS, Beta.** Richard B. Shull, Dick O'Neill, Phil Foster, Joseph Sirola, Dan Resin, Willard Waterman, Gary Sandy; **D:** Fred Levinson. *NO*

Hail Caesar 🎬🎬½ **1994 (PG)** His job at an eraser factory is the only thing standing between Julius Caesar MacGruder (Hall) and fame and fortune as a rock 'n roll singer. **93m/C VHS, Beta, LV.** Anthony Michael Hall, Robert Downey Jr., Frank Gorshin, Samuel L. Jackson, Judd Nelson, Nicholas Pryor, Leslie Danon, Bobbie Philips; **D:** Anthony Michael Hall; **W:** Robert Mittenthal; **M:** Roger Tallman.

Hail, Hero! 🎬½ **1969 (PG)** A dated Vietnam War era drama about a confused hippie rebelling against his parents and the draft. First film for both Douglas and Strauss. Adapted from the novel by John Weston. Includes music by Gordon Lightfoot. **97m/C VHS, Beta.** Michael Douglas, Arthur Kennedy, Teresa Wright, John Larch, Charles Drake, Deborah Winters, Peter Strauss; **D:** David Miller; **C:** Robert B. Hauser. *FOX*

Hail Mary 🎬🎬½ *Je Vous Salue Marie* **1985 (R)** A modern-day virgin named Mary inexplicably becomes pregnant in this controversial film that discards notions of divinity in favor of the celebration of a lively, intellectual humanism. Godard rejects orthodox narrative structure and bourgeois prejudices. Very controversial, but not up to his breathless beginning work. In French with English subtitles. **107m/C VHS, Beta, LV.** **FR SI GB** Myriem Roussel, Thierry Rode, Philippe Lacoste, Manon Anderson, Juliette Binoche, Johan Leysen; **D:** Jean-Luc Godard; **W:** Jean-Luc Godard. *ART, VES*

Hail the Conquering Hero 🎬🎬🎬½ **1944** A slight young man is rejected by the Army. Upon returning home, he is surprised to find out they think he's a hero. Biting satire with Demarest's performance stealing the show. **101m/B VHS, Closed Caption.** Eddie Bracken, Ella Raines, William Demarest, Franklin Pangborn, Raymond Walburn; **D:** Preston Sturges. Nominations: Academy Awards '44: Best Original Screenplay. USH

Hair 🐾🐾🐾½ **1979 (PG)** Film version of the explosive 1960s Broadway musical about the carefree life of the flower children and the shadow of the Vietnam War that hangs over them. Great music, as well as wonderful choreography by Twyla Tharp help portray the surprisingly sensitive evocation of the period so long after the fact. Forman has an uncanny knack for understanding the textures of American life. Watch for a thinner Nell Carter. **122m/C VHS, Beta, LV, Letterbox.** Treat Williams, John Savage, Beverly D'Angelo, Annie Golden, Nicholas Ray; **D:** Milos Forman; **W:** Michael Weller. MGM

The Hairdresser's Husband 🐾🐾 **1992 (R)** Antoine (Rochefort) has had an odd obsession since boyhood—hairdressers—and in middle age he finds love with Mathilde (Galiena), a hairdresser he meets and proposes to as she cuts his hair. She accepts, and the two live their quiet lives in her barber shop as she cuts hair and he watches, occasionally breaking out in Arabian dances. A dark and odd yet refreshing film with fine performances by Rochefort and Galiena in this story about fetishism, obsession, and hair. In French with English subtitles. **84m/C VHS, LV, Closed Caption.** FR Jean Rochefort, Anna Galiena, Roland Bertin, Maurice Chevit, Philippe Clevenot, Jacques Mathou, Claude Aufaure; **D:** Patrice Leconte; **W:** Patrice Leconte; **M:** Michael Nyman. PAR, BTV

Hairspray 🐾🐾🐾 **1988 (PG)** Waters' first truly mainstream film, if that's even possible, and his funniest. Details the struggle among teenagers in 1962 Baltimore for the top spot in a local TV dance show. Deals with racism and stereotypes, as well as typical "teen" problems (hair-do's and don'ts). Filled with refreshingly tasteful, subtle social satire (although not without typical Waters touches that will please die-hard fans). Lake is lovable and appealing as Divine's daughter; Divine, in his last film, is likeable as an iron-toting mom. Look for Waters in a cameo and Divine as a man. Great '60s music, which Waters refers to as "the only known remedy to today's Hit Parade of Hell." **94m/C VHS, Beta, LV, Closed Caption.** Ricki Lake, Divine, Jerry Stiller, Colleen Fitzpatrick, Sonny Bono, Deborah Harry, Ruth Brown, Pia Zadora, Ric Ocasek, Michael St. Gerard, Leslie Ann Powers, Shawn Thompson; **Cameos:** John Waters; **D:** John Waters; **W:** John Waters. NLC, FCT

The Hairy Ape 🐾🐾 **1944** Screen adaptation of the Eugene O'Neill play. A beast-like coal stoker becomes obsessed with a cool and distant passenger aboard an ocean liner. **90m/B VHS.** William Bendix, Susan Hayward, John Loder, Dorothy Comingore, Roman Bohnen, Alan Napier; **D:** Alfred Santell. Nominations: Academy Awards '44: Best Original Dramatic/Comedy Score. NOS, MRV, FCT

Half a Lifetime **1986** The stakes are too high for four friends playing a game of poker. **85m/C VHS, Beta.** Keith Carradine, Gary Busey, Nick Mancuso, Saul Rubinek. HBO

Half a Loaf of Kung Fu 🐾 **1985** The worthy bodyguards of Sern Chuan are called upon to deliver a valuable jade statue. Prevented again and again by ruthless robbers, they falter. Only Chan carries on, meeting the enemy alone. Fast action, good story. **98m/C VHS, Beta.** Jackie Chan. NO

Half a Sixpence 🐾🐾 **1967** Former musician Sidney, who earlier directed "Showboat" and "Kiss Me Kate," shows a bit less verve in this production. Based on H.G. Wells' 1905 novel, "Kipps," it sports much of the original cast from its Broadway incarnation. Edwardian orphan Steele, a cloth-dealer-in-training, comes into a large sum of money and proceeds to lose it with great dispatch. Somewhere along the way he loses his girlfriend, too, but she takes him back because musicals end happily. ♫ Half a Sixpence; Flash,

Bang, Wallop!; All In The Cause Of Economy; I'm Not Talking To You; Money To Burn; The Race Is On; I Don't Believe A Word Of It; A Proper Gentleman; She's Too Far Above Me. **148m/B VHS, Closed Caption.** Tommy Steele, Julia Foster, Penelope Horner, Cyril Ritchard, Grover Dale; **D:** George Sidney; **W:** Beverley Cross; **C:** Geoffrey Unsworth. PAR, FCT

Half a Soldier 🐾🐾 **1940** A spoiled girl gets a big surprise when she steals a car and discovers the body of a gangster in the trunk. **59m/B VHS, Beta.** Heather Angel, John "Dusty" King. NOS, DVT, HEG

Half-Baked 🐾 **1997 (R)** Four seedy roommates whose problems stem from their love of marijuana float through life with loser jobs that give them just enough money to buy their next bag. When Kenny (H.Williams) is arrested for killing a diabetic police horse during a munchies run, the three remaining friends must put their resinated brains together and come up with a way to bail him out. Thurgood (Chapelle), a custodian for a pharmaceutical company, decides to steal some high-grade grass from the lab; and along with Brian (Breuer, doing a very convincing stoned) and Scarface (Diaz), he begins dealing. This puts them afoul of the law as well as local drug lord Samson Simpson (C. Williams). Just say no. Trust me, dude, this stuff is bogus and it won't get you off. **CW:** Pervasive drug content, language, nudity and sexual material. **83m/C VHS, DVD.** Harland Williams, Dave Chappelle, Jim Breuer, Guillermo Diaz, Rachel True, Clarence Williams III, Thomas Chong, Jon Stewart, Stephen Baldwin, Willie Nelson, Janeane Garofalo, Steven Wright, Laura Silverman, Snoop Doggy Dogg; **D:** Tamra Davis; **W:** Neal Brennan, Dave Chappelle; **C:** Steven Bernstein; **M:** Alf Clausen. USH

The Half-Breed 🐾🐾 **1951** Routine oater with settlers and Apaches fighting, and the obligatory half-breed stuck in the middle. **81m/B VHS, Beta.** Robert Young, Jack Buetel, Janis Carter, Barton MacLane, Reed Hadley, Porter Hall, Connie Gilchrist; **D:** Stuart Gilmore. TTC

Half Human 🐾½ **1958** Dull Japanese monster movie about an ape-human who terrorizes Northern Japan. When released in the U.S., Carradine and Morris were added. Without subtitles, just Carradine's narration. Director Honda made better movies before and after, with Godzilla and Rodan. **78m/B VHS.** JP John Carradine, Akira Takarada, Morris Ankrum; **D:** Inoshiro Honda. SNC, MLB

Half Moon Street 🐾🐾 *Escort Girl* **1986 (R)** A brilliant woman scientist supplements her paltry fellowship salary by becoming a hired escort and prostitute, which leads her into various incidents of international intrigue. Adapted from a story by Paul Theroux, "Dr. Slaughter." **90m/C VHS, Beta, LV, 8mm, Closed Caption.** Sigourney Weaver, Michael Caine, Keith Buckley, Ian MacInnes; **D:** Bob Swaim. NLC

Half of Heaven 🐾🐾🐾 *La Mitad del Cielo* **1986** A critically popular film about a young Spanish woman who begins to share certain telepathic powers with her wizened grandmother. In Spanish with English subtitles. **95m/C VHS, Beta.** SP Angela Molina, Margarita Lozano; **D:** Manuel Gutierrez Aragon. PBS, FCT, AUD

Half-Shot at Sunrise 🐾🐾 **1930** Madcap vaudeville comedians play AWOL soldiers loose in 1918 Paris. Continuous one-liners, sight gags, and slapstick nonsense. First film appearance of comedy team Wheeler and Woolsey. **78m/B VHS, Beta.** Bert Wheeler, Robert Woolsey, Dorothy Lee, Robert Rutherford, Edna May Oliver; **D:** Paul Sloane; **M:** Max Steiner. VYY, CAB, DVT

Half Slave, Half Free 🐾🐾½ *Solomon Northrup's Odyssey* **1985** The true story of a free black man in the 1840s who is kidnapped and forced into slavery for 12 years. Made for television as part of the "American Playhouse" series on PBS. Followed by "Charlotte Forten's Mission: Experiment in Freedom." **113m/C VHS, Beta.** Avery Brooks, Mason Adams, Petronia Paley, John Saxon, Joe

Seneca, Michael Tolan, Lee Bryant, Rhetta Greene, Janet League; **D:** Gordon Parks. XVC, KAR, KUI

The Halfback of Notre Dame 🐾🐾½ **1996 (G)** Star football player (and coach's son) Craig Modeau (Hogan) is a lumbering misfit, ripe for high school teasing, anywhere but on the gridiron. But French exchange student Esmeralda (Vaugier) thinks he's sweet—much to the dismay of current boyfriend, obnoxious quarterback Archie (Cutler). Then Craig decides to quit the team right before the big game when dad says no fraternizing and it's up to his French flame to get the jock to change his mind. Made for TV reworking of Victor Hugo's "The Hunchback of Notre Dame." **97m/C VHS, LV, Closed Caption.** Gabriel Hogan, Emmanuelle Vaugier, Scott Hylands, Sandra Nelson, Allen Cutler; **D:** Rene Bonniere; **W:** Richard Clark, Mark Trafficante; **C:** Maris Jansons; **M:** George Blondheim. HMK

Halfmoon 🐾🐾 *Paul Bowles: Halfmoon* **1995** Trilogy of stories by Paul Bowles. "Merkala Beach" looks at the friendship of two young Moroccan men who are both seduced by the same mysterious woman. "Call at Corazon" finds the honeymoon journey of a mismatched British couple turning into a nightmare as they sail up the Amazon on a crowded cargo boat. "Allal" is a Moroccan boy who's an outcast in his village because of his illegitimacy. He befriends an old snake dealer and steals one of his cobras in order to charm the reptile. Then Allal winds up in a magical transformation with the creature. English and Arabic with subtitles. **90m/C VHS.** GE GE Samir Guesmi, Khalid Ksouri, Sondos Belhassan, Veronica Quilligan, Sam Cox, Said Zakir, Mohammed Belfquih; **D:** Irene von Alberti, Frieder Schlaich; **W:** Irene von Alberti, Frieder Schlaich; **C:** Volker Tittel; **M:** Roman Bunka. FRF

Hallelujah! 🐾🐾🐾½ **1929** Haynes plays an innocent young man who turns to religion and becomes a charasmatic preacher after a family tragedy. He retains all his human weaknesses, however, including falling for the lovely but deceitful McKinney. Great music included traditional spirituals and songs by Berlin, such as "At the End of the Road" and "Swanee Shuffle." Shot on location in Tennessee. The first all-black feature film and the first talkie for director Vidor was given the go-ahead by MGM production chief Irving Thalberg, though he knew the film would be both controversial and get minimal release in the deep South. **90m/B VHS.** Daniel L. Haynes, Nina Mae McKinney, William Fontaine, Harry Gray, Fannie Belle DeKnight, Everett McGarrity; **D:** King Vidor; **M:** Irving Berlin. Nominations: Academy Awards '30: Best Director (Vidor). MGM, MOV, BTV

Hallelujah, I'm a Bum 🐾🐾½ *Hallelujah, I'm a Tramp; The Heart of New York; Happy Go Lucky; Lazy Bones* **1933** A happy-go-lucky hobo reforms and begins a new life for the sake of a woman. Bizarre Depression-era musical with a Rodgers and Hart score and continuously rhyming dialogue. The British version, due to the slang meaning of "bum," was retitled, substituting "tramp." ♫ You Are Too Beautiful; I'll Do It Again; I've Got To Get Back To New York; What Do You Want With Money?; Hallelujah, I'm a Bum; My Pal Bumper; Dear June; Bumper Found a Grand. **83m/B VHS, Beta.** Al Jolson, Madge Evans, Frank Morgan, Chester Conklin; **D:** Lewis Milestone; **W:** Ben Hecht, S.N. Behrman; **M:** Richard Rodgers, Lorenz Hart. BFA, MLB

The Hallelujah Trail 🐾🐾 **1965** Denver mining town in the late 1800s is about to batten down the hatches for a long winter, and there's not a drop of whiskey to be had. The U.S. Cavalry sends a shipment to the miners, but temperance leader Cora Templeton Massingale (Remick) and her bevy of ladies against liquor stand between the shipment and the would-be whistle whetters. Limp Western satire directed by Preston Sturges' brother, who fared much better when he kept a straight face (he also directed "The Great Escape"). Based on Bill Gulick's novel, "The Hallelujah Train." Two-laserdisc set includes additional footage (though it's already overlong), the original trailer and a letterboxing 166m/C VHS, LV, **Letterbox.** Burt Lancaster, Lee Remick, Jim Hutton, Pamela Tiffin, Donald Pleasence, Brian Keith, Martin Landau; **D:** John Sturges; **W:** John Gay; **C:** Robert L. Surtees; **M:** Elmer Bernstein. *MGM, FCT*

Halloween 🎬🎬🎬½ **1978 (R)** John Carpenter's horror classic has been acclaimed "the most successful independent motion picture of all time." A deranged youth returns to his hometown with murderous intent after 15 years in an asylum. Very, very scary—you feel this movie more than see it. **90m/C VHS, Beta, LV.** Jamie Lee Curtis, Donald Pleasence, Nancy Loomis, P.J. Soles, Charles Cyphers; **D:** John Carpenter; **W:** John Carpenter, Debra Hill; **C:** Dean Cundey; **M:** John Carpenter. *VTR*

Halloween 2: The Nightmare Isn't Over! 🎬½ **1981 (R)** Trying to pick up where "Halloween" left off, the sequel begins with the escape of vicious killer Michael, who continues to murder and terrorize the community of Haddonfield, Illinois. Lacking the innovative intentions of its predecessor, it relies on old-fashioned buckets of blood. No chills, just trauma. Co-scripted by Carpenter, director of the original. **92m/C VHS, Beta, LV.** Jamie Lee Curtis, Donald Pleasence, Jeffrey Kramer, Charles Cyphers, Lance Guest; **D:** Rick Rosenthal; **W:** John Carpenter, Debra Hill; **C:** Dean Cundey; **M:** John Carpenter. *USH*

Halloween 3: Season of the Witch 🎬🎬 **1982 (R)** Modern druid plans to kill 50 million children with his specially made Halloween masks. Produced by John Carpenter, this second sequel to the 1978 horror classic is not based on the events or characters of its predecessors or successors. Followed by Halloweens 4, 5, and 6. **98m/C VHS, Beta, LV.** Tom Atkins, Stacey Nelkin, Dan O'Herlihy, Ralph Strait, Michael Currie; **D:** Tommy Lee Wallace; **W:** Tommy Lee Wallace; **C:** Dean Cundey; **M:** John Carpenter. *USH*

Halloween 4: The Return of Michael Myers 🎬 **1988 (R)** The third sequel, wherein the lunatic that won't die returns home to kill his niece. **88m/C VHS, Beta, LV, Closed Caption.** Donald Pleasence, Ellie Cornell, Danielle Harris, Michael Pataki, George P. Wilbur, Beau Starr, Kathleen Kinmont, Sasha Jenson, Gene Ross; **D:** Dwight Little; **W:** Alan B. McElroy; **C:** Peter Collister. *FOX*

Halloween 5: The Revenge of Michael Myers 🎬½ **1989 (R)** Fifth in the series, this Halloween is an improvement over 2, 3, and 4, thanks to a few well directed scare scenes. Unfortunately, the plot remains the same: a psycho behemoth chases down and kills more teens. An open ending promises yet another installment. **96m/C VHS, Beta, LV, Closed Caption.** Donald Pleasence, Ellie Cornell, Danielle Harris, Don Shanks, Betty Carvalho, Beau Starr, Wendy Kaplan, Jeffrey Landman; **D:** Dominique Othenin-Girard; **W:** Dominique Othenin-Girard, Shem Bitterman, Michael Jacobs; **C:** Rob Draper. *FOX*

Halloween 6: The Curse of Michael Myers 🎬 *Halloween: The Origin of Michael Myers* **1995 (R)** First the return. Then his revenge. And now, his curse, aimed square at the viewer. Lame series entry connects Michael Meyers to an ancient Celtic ritual that drives him to murder whole families in his old stompin' grounds of Haddonfield. Before he finishes his reign of terror, Meyers has to contend with Dr. Loomis (Pleasence), the man who knows his true evil. Though still a profit-making monster (the entire franchise had a combined budget of $20 million and grossed over $200 million), Michael should probably join Freddy and Jason at the old slashers' retirement home. Film marks the final screen appearance of Pleasence, who died shortly after its completion.**CW:** Strong horror violence, and some sexuality. **88m/C VHS, LV, Closed Caption.** Donald Pleasence, Mitchell Ryan, Marianne Hagan, Leo Geter, George P. Wilbur, Kim Darby, Bradford English, Devin Gardner; **D:** Joe Chappelle; **W:** Daniel Farrands; **C:** Billy Dickson; **M:** Alan Howarth. *TOU*

Halloween Night 🎬🎬 **1990 (R)** Ancient evil rises up to destroy the perfect small town. **90m/C VHS.** Hy Pyke, Katrina Garner; **D:** Emilio P. Miraglio. *ATL*

Halloween with the Addams Family woof! **1979** A really pathetic production spawned during the "reunion" craze of the late '70s, sparked only by the lively performance of Coogan's Uncle Fester and the always lovable Lurch. Made for television. **87m/C VHS, Beta.** John Astin, Carolyn Jones, Jackie Coogan, Ted Cassidy. *GKK*

The Halls of Montezuma 🎬🎬½ **1950** Large, bombastic WWII combat epic. Depicts the Marines fighting the Japanese in the Pacific. **113m/C VHS, Beta.** Richard Widmark, Jack Palance, Reginald Gardiner, Robert Wagner, Karl Malden, Richard Boone, Richard Hylton, Skip Homeier, Jack Webb, Neville Brand, Martin Milner, Bert Freed; **D:** Lewis Milestone. *FOX*

Hallucination woof! *Hallucination Generation* **1967** Early flower-power exploiter about expatriate acid heads who murder an antique dealer under the influence of LSD and then attempt to hide at a monastery. Depicts LSD as the catalyst in bringing out the group's criminal behavior. In sepia while everyone's cool, breaking into color during the head trips. **90m/C VHS, Beta.** George Montgomery, Danny Stone; **D:** Edward Mann. *VDC*

Hallucinations of a Deranged Mind 🎬 *Delirios de Um Anormal* **1970** A compilation of all the magic moments ever censored by the Brazilian military dictatorship. Includes scenes banned from over 10 different Mojica Marins films, including his "Coffin Joe" character. In Portuguese with English subtitles. **?m/C VHS.** *BR* Jose Mojica Marins; **D:** Jose Mojica Marins. *SMW, FCT*

Hambone & Hillie 🎬🎬 **1984 (PG)** An elderly woman makes a 3000-mile trek across the United States to search for the dog she lost in an airport. **97m/C VHS, Beta.** Lillian Gish, Timothy Bottoms, Candy Clark, O.J. Simpson, Robert Walker Jr., Jack Carter, Alan Hale Jr., Anne Lockhart; **D:** Roy Watts; **W:** Sandra K. Bailey. *VTR*

Hamburger Hill 🎬🎬½ **1987 (R)** Popular war epic depicting the famous battle between Americans and Viet Cong over a useless hill in Vietnam. Made in the heyday of 1980s Vietnam backlash, and possibly the most realistic and bloodiest of the lot. **104m/C VHS, Beta, LV.** Michael Dolan, Daniel O'Shea, Dylan McDermott, Tommy Swerdlow, Courtney B. Vance, Anthony Barille, Michael Boatman, Don Cheadle, Tim Quill, Don James, Michael A. Nickles; **D:** John Irvin; **W:** Jim Carabatsos; **M:** Philip Glass. *ART, VES, FCT*

Hamburger...The Motion Picture 🎬 **1986 (R)** The life and times of students at Busterburger U., the only college devoted to hamburger franchise management. **90m/C VHS, Beta, LV, Closed Caption.** Leigh McCloskey, Dick Butkus, Randi Brooks, Sandy Hackett; **D:** Mike Marvin; **M:** Elmer Bernstein.

Hamlet 🎬🎬🎬🎬 **1948** Splendid adaptation of Shakespeare's dramatic play. Hamlet vows vengeance on the murderer of his father in this tight version of the four hour stage play. Some scenes were cut out, including all of Rosencrantz and Guildenstern. Beautifully photographed in Denmark. An Olivier triumph. Remade several times. **153m/B VHS.** *GB* Laurence Olivier, Basil Sydney, Felix Aylmer, Jean Simmons, Stanley Holloway, Peter Cushing, Christopher Lee, Eileen Herlie, John Laurie, Esmond Knight, Anthony Quayle; **D:** Laurence Olivier; **W:** Alan Dent; **M:** William Walton; **V:** John Gielgud. Academy Awards '48: Best Actor (Olivier), Best Art Direction/Set Decoration (B & W), Best Costume Design (B & W), Best Picture; British Academy Awards '48: Best Film; Golden Globe Awards '49: Best Actor—Drama (Olivier); New York Film Critics Awards '48: Best Actor (Olivier); Nominations: Academy Awards '48: Best Director (Olivier), Best Supporting Actress (Simmons), Best Original Dramatic/Comedy Score. *PAR, BTV, HMV*

Hamlet 🎬🎬½ **1969 (G)** Williamson brings to the screen his stage performance as the classic Shakespeare character. Something is lost in the process, although there are some redeeming mo-

ments including those with Faithfull as Ophelia. **114m/C VHS, Beta.** *GB* Nicol Williamson, Anthony Hopkins, Marianne Faithfull, Gordon Jackson, Judy Parfitt, Mark Dingham, Anjelica Huston; **D:** Tony Richardson. *COL*

Hamlet 🎬🎬🎬 **1990 (PG)** Zeffirelli—in his fourth attempt at Shakespeare—creates a surprisingly energetic and accessible interpretation of the Bard's moody play. Gibson brings charm, humor and a carefully calculated sense of violence, not to mention a good deal of solid flesh, to the eponymous role, and handles the language skillfully (although if you seek a poetic Dane, stick with Olivier). Exceptional work from Scofield and Bates. Close seems a tad hysterical (not to mention too young to play Gibson's mother), but brings insight and nuance to her role. Purists beware: this isn't a completely faithful adaptation. Beautifully costumed; shot on location in Northern Scotland. **135m/C VHS, Beta, LV, 8mm, Letterbox, Closed Caption.** Mel Gibson, Glenn Close, Alan Bates, Paul Scofield, Ian Holm, Helena Bonham Carter, Nathaniel Parker, Pete Postlethwaite; **D:** Franco Zeffirelli; **W:** Franco Zeffirelli, Christopher DeVore; **C:** David Watkin. Nominations: Academy Awards '90: Best Art Direction/Set Decoration, Best Costume Design. *WAR, BTV, FCT*

Hamlet 🎬🎬🎬🎬 **1996 (PG-13)** Branagh tackles Shakespeare once again with the uncut, four-hour long story of the melancholy Dane (played by you-know-who). Branagh's decision to use the complete text, and move the action ahead 600 years to the 19th century adds an interesting external political dimension to the palace intrigue and gives this sixth screen adaptation the stature of Olivier's 1948 masterpiece. Jacobi and Christie stand out among a very large and brilliant cast. Lemmon and Crystal, however, should stick to American comedy. A two and a half hour version was also prepared for those with shorter attention spans, but the uncut version is well worth the time invested.**CW:** Some violent images and sexuality. **242m/C VHS, LV, Closed Caption.** *GB* Kenneth Branagh, Kate Winslet, Julie Christie, Derek Jacobi, Richard Briers, Brian Blessed, Michael Maloney, Timothy Spall, Reece Dinsdale, Jack Lemmon, Nicholas Farrell, Charlton Heston, Rosemary Harris, Gerard Depardieu, Robin Williams, Billy Crystal, Simon Russell Beale, Michael Bryant, John Gielgud, Richard Attenborough, Rufus Sewell, Judi Dench, Ian McElhinney, John Mills; **D:** Kenneth Branagh; **W:** Kenneth Branagh; **C:** Alex Thomson; **M:** Patrick Doyle. Nominations: Academy Awards '96: Best Adapted Screenplay, Best Art Direction/Set Decoration, Best Costume Design, Best Original Dramatic/Comedy Score. *COL*

Hammersmith Is Out 🎬½ **1972 (R)** A violent lunatic cons an orderly into letting him escape. Chases, romance and craziness follow. **108m/C VHS, Beta.** Richard Burton, Elizabeth Taylor, Peter Ustinov, Beau Bridges, John Schuck; **D:** Peter Ustinov.

Hammett 🎬🎬 **1982 (PG)** After many directors and script rewrites, Wenders was assigned to this arch neo-noir what-if scenario. Depicts Dashiell Hammett solving a complex crime himself, an experience he uses in his novels. Interesting, but ultimately botched studio exercise, like many from executive producer Francis Coppola, who is said to have reshot much of the film. **98m/C VHS, Beta.** Frederic Forrest, Peter Boyle, Sylvia Sidney, Elisha Cook Jr., Marilu Henner; **D:** Wim Wenders; **C:** Joseph Biroc; **M:** John Barry. *WAR*

Hamsin 🎬🎬 **1983** A Jewish landowner and an Arab worker encounter difficulties in their relationship when the government announces plans to confiscate Arab land. In Hebrew with English subtitles. **90m/C VHS, Beta.** Shlomo Tarshish, Yasin Shawap, Hemda Levy, Ruth Geler; **D:** Daniel Wachsmann. *ERG*

Hamsun 🎬🎬 **1996** Highly-regarded Norwegian Nobel Prize-winning writer Knut Hamsun (von Sydow) stunned his countrymen when he sided with the Nazis in WWII and urged them to stop resisting the invaders of their homeland. An ardent nationalist, the elderly Hamsun apparently heard only what he wanted to about Hitler's policies and regarded Britain as the greater threat to

Europe. After the war Hamsun and his equally outspoken pro-German wife, Marie (Norby), are deemed traitors and are put on trial. Based on a book by Thorkild Hansen. Swedish, Danish, and Norwegian with subtitles. **154m/C VHS.** *NO DK SW* Max von Sydow, Ghita Norby, Sverre Anker Ousdal, Ernst Jacobi, Anette Hoff, Erik Hivju; **D:** Jan Troell; **W:** Per Olof Enquist; **C:** Jan Troell; **M:** Arvo Part. *FRF*

The Hand *♂½* **1960** During WWII, three British POWs are tortured by the Japanese. Refusing to give information, two of them have their right hands cut off. The third opts to talk, thereby keeping his hand. After the war, a series of murders occur in London where the victims have their hands amputated. Could there be a connection? **61m/B VHS, Beta.** *GB* Derek Bond, Ronald Lee Hunt, Reed de Rouen, Ray Cooney, Brian Coleman; **D:** Henry Cass. *SNC*

The Hand *♂♂♂* **1981 (R)** A gifted cartoonist's hand is severed in a car accident. Soon, the hand is on the loose with a mind of its own, seeking out victims with an obsessive vengeance. Stone's sophomore directorial outing is a unique, surreal psycho-horror pastiche underrated by most critics. **105m/C VHS, Beta.** *GB* Michael Caine, Andrea Marcovicci, Annie McEnroe, Bruce McGill, Viveca Lindfors; *Cameos:* Oliver Stone; **D:** Oliver Stone; **W:** Oliver Stone; **C:** King Baggot; **M:** James Horner. *WAR*

Hand Gun *♂♂½* **1993 (R)** Jack McCallister (Cassel) is wounded in a shoot-out with police but still manages to get away with half-a-million from a robbery. When word gets out, everybody begins looking for Jack, including his two sons—gun happy George (Williams) and small time con artist Michael (Schulze). **CW:** Rated R for shootings and beatings, strong language and some sexuality. **90m/C VHS, LV.** Seymour Cassel, Treat Williams, Paul Schulzie, Michael Rapaport; **D:** Whitney Ransick; **W:** Whitney Ransick. *TRI*

The Hand that Rocks the Cradle *♂♂½* **1992 (R)** DeMornay is Peyton Flanders, the nanny from hell, in an otherwise predictable thriller. Sciorra's role is a thankless one as pregnant and unbelievably naive Claire Bartel, who unwittingly starts a horrific chain of events when she levels charges of molestation against her obstetrician. Transparent plot preys on the worst fears of viewers, and doesn't offer anything innovative or new. See this one for DeMornay's Jekyll and Hyde performance. **CW:** Language, terror and violence, and sexual molestation. **110m/C VHS, Beta, Closed Caption.** Annabella Sciorra, Rebecca DeMornay, Matt McCoy, Ernie Hudson, Julianne Moore, Madeline Zima, John de Lancie, Mitchell Laurance; **D:** Curtis Hanson; **W:** Amanda Silver; **C:** Robert Elswit; **M:** Graeme Revell. MTV Movie Awards '92: Best Villain (DeMornay). *HPH*

A Handful of Dust *♂♂♂* **1988 (PG)** A dry, stately adaptation of the bitter Evelyn Waugh novel about a stuffy young aristocrat's wife's careless infidelity and how it sends her innocent husband to a tragic downfall. A well-meaning version that captures Waugh's cynical satire almost in spite of itself. Set in post-WWI England. **114m/C VHS, Beta.** *GB* James Wilby, Kristin Scott Thomas, Rupert Graves, Alec Guinness, Anjelica Huston, Judi Dench, Cathryn Harrison, Pip Torrens, John Junkin; **D:** Charles Sturridge; **W:** Charles Sturridge, Tim Sullivan, Derek Granger; **M:** George Fenton. British Academy Awards '88: Best Supporting Actress (Dench); Nominations: Academy Awards '88: Best Costume Design. *COL, TVC*

The Handmaid's Tale *♂♂½* **1990 (R)** A cool, shallow but nonetheless chilling nightmare based on Margaret Atwood's bestselling novel, about a woman caught in the machinations of a near-future society so sterile it enslaves the few fertile women and forces them into being childbearing "handmaids." **109m/C VHS, Beta, LV, Closed Caption.** Natasha Richardson, Robert Duvall, Faye Dunaway, Aidan Quinn, Elizabeth McGovern, Victoria Tennant, Blanche Baker, Traci Lind; **D:** Volker Schlondorff; **W:** Harold Pinter. *HBO, FCT, IME*

Hands Across the Border *♂½* **1943** A musical western in which Roy helps a woman find the men who killed her father. **72m/B VHS.** Roy Rogers, Ruth Terry, Guinn "Big Boy" Williams, Onslow Stevens, Mary Treen, Joseph Crehan; **D:** Joseph Kane. *NOS, DVT, TIM*

Hands Across the Table *♂♂♂* **1935** Regi Allen (Lombard) is a fortune-hunting manicurist in a swanky hotel barber shop. Has-been millionaire playboy Theodore Drew, III (MacMurray) falls for her but he's about to marry money (Allwyn) and Regi's got a wheelchair-bound rich man (Bellamy) just waiting for her to say "I do." Snappy dialogue and light-hearted performances. Based on the story "Bracelets" by Vina Delmar. **80m/B VHS, Closed Caption.** Carole Lombard, Fred MacMurray, Ralph Bellamy, Astrid Allwyn, Ruth Donnelly, Marie Prevost, William Demarest, Edward Gargan; **D:** Mitchell Leisen; **W:** Norman Krasna, Vincent Lawrence, Herbert Fields; **C:** Ted Tetzlaff. *USH*

Hands of a Murderer *♂♂½ Sherlock Holmes and the Prince of Crime* **1990** Sherlock Holmes (Woodward) and the faithful Dr. Watson (Hillerman) are in pursuit of the great detective's most evil nemisis—the nefarious Moriarty (Andrews). This time, the fiend has escaped the gallows and stolen government secrets from the safe of Holmes' brother Mycroft. TV movie. **100m/C VHS.** Edward Woodward, John Hillerman, Anthony Andrews, Kim Thomson, Peter Jeffrey, Warren Clarke; **D:** Stuart Orme; **W:** Charles Edward Pogue. *TVC*

Hands of a Stranger *♂♂* **1962** Another undistinguished entry in the long line of remakes of "The Hands of Orlac." A pianist who loses his hands in an accident is given the hands of a murderer, and his new hands want to do more than tickle the ivories. Kellerman has a very small role as does former "Sheena" McCalla. **95m/B VHS.** Paul Lukather, Joan Harvey, James Stapleton, Sally Kellerman, Irish McCalla; **D:** Newton Arnold. *SNC*

Hands of a Stranger *♂♂½* **1987** Policeman's wife is raped during an adulterous tryst. As the painful truth dawns on the cop, he himself dallies with a compassionate lady D.A. while hunting the attacker. About as sordid as a network TV-movie gets without toppling into sleaze; strong acting and a sober script pull it through. But the plot, from Robert Daly's novel, doesn't justify miniseries treatment; the two-cassette package is excessively long. **179m/C VHS.** Armand Assante, Beverly D'Angelo, Blair Brown, Michael Lerner, Philip Casnoff, Arliss Howard; **D:** Larry Elikann; **W:** Arthur Kopit. *WOV*

Hands of Death *♂* **1988** Thieves use their Ninja skills to stop any one in their path to evil. Action-packed, somewhat contrived. **90m/C VHS, Beta.** Richard Harrison, Mike Abbott; **D:** Godfrey Ho. *IMP*

The Hands of Orlac *♂♂* **1925** Classic silent film about a pianist whose hands are mutilated in an accident. His hands are replaced by those of a murderer, and his urge to kill becomes overwhelming. Contains restored footage. **92m/B VHS.** *AT* Conrad Veidt, Fritz Kortner, Carmen Cartellieri, Paul Adkonas, Alexandra Sorina; **D:** Robert Wiene; **W:** Ludwig Nerz. *LSV*

The Hands of Orlac *♂♂* *Hands of the Strangler; Hands of a Strangler* **1960** Third remake of Maurice Renard's classic tale. When a concert pianist's hands are mutilated in an accident, he receives a graft of a murderer's hands. Obsession sweeps the musician, as he believes his new hands are incapable of music, only violence. Bland adaptation of the original story. **95m/B VHS.** *GB FR* Mel Ferrer, Christopher Lee, Felix Aylmer, Basil Sydney, Donald Wolfit, Donald Pleasence, Danny Carrel, Lucile Saint-Simon, Peter Reynolds, Campbell Singer, David Peel; **D:** Edmond T. Greville; **W:** Edmond T. Greville, John Baines, Donald Taylor; **C:** Desmond Dickinson; **M:** Claude Bolling. *SNC*

Hands of Steel woof! **1986 (R)** A ruthless cyborg carries out a mission to find and kill an important scientist. Terrible acting, and lousy writing: an all-around woofer! **94m/C VHS, Beta.** Daniel

Greene, John Saxon, Janet Agren, Claudio Cassinelli, George Eastman; **D:** Martin Dolman. *ART*

Hands of the Ripper *♂♂½* **1971 (R)** Jack the Ripper's daughter returns to London where she works as a medium by day and stalks the streets at night. Classy Hammer horror variation on the perennial theme. **85m/C VHS, Beta.** *GB* Eric Porter, Angharad Rees, Jane Merrow, Keith Bell, Derek Godfrey, Dora Bryan, Marjorie Rhodes, Norman Bird; **D:** Peter Sasdy; **W:** L.W. Davidson; **C:** Ken Talbot; **M:** Christopher Gunning. *MLB*

Hands Up *♂♂½* **1926** Jaunty Confederate spy (played by much-overlooked American comedian Griffith) attempts, amidst much comic nonsense, to thwart Yankee gold mining during the Civil War. Silent. **50m/B VHS, Beta.** Raymond Griffith, Mack Swain, Marion Nixon, Montagu Love; **D:** Clarence Badger. *GPV*

Hands Up *♂♂♂* *Rece do Gory* **1981** Famed Polish film finished in 1967 but not released until 1981 for political reasons (prologue shot in '81 included). Doctors at a medical school reunion reflect upon the effect of Stalinist rule on their education and lives. In Polish with English subtitles. **78m/C VHS, Beta.** *PL* **D:** Jerzy Skolimowski. *FCT*

Hang 'Em High *♂♂½* **1967 (PG-13)** A cowboy is saved from a lynching and vows to hunt down the gang that nearly killed him in this American-made spaghetti western. Eastwood's first major vehicle made outside of Europe. **CW:** Western action/violence. **114m/C VHS, Beta, LV.** Clint Eastwood, Inger Stevens, Ed Begley Sr., Pat Hingle, James MacArthur; **D:** Ted Post. *MGM, TLF*

Hangar 18 *♂½* *Invasion Force* **1980 (PG)** Silly sci-fi drama about two astronauts who collide with a UFO during a shuttle flight. Later they learn that the government is hiding it in a hangar and they try to prove its existence. Shown on TV as "Invasion Force" with an entirely new ending. **97m/C VHS, Beta.** Darren McGavin, Robert Vaughn, Gary Collins, James Hampton, Philip Abbott, Pamela Bellwood, Tom Hallick, Cliff Osmond, Joseph Campanella; **D:** James L. Conway; **W:** David O'Malley. *WOV*

The Hanged Man *♂♂* **1974** Tale of a gunslinger in the Old West who mystically escapes death by hanging. Reborn, he re-evaluates the meaning of justice. Made for television. **78m/C VHS.** Steve Forrest, Cameron Mitchell, Sharon Acker, Dean Jagger, Will Geer, Barbara Luna, Rafael Campos; **D:** Michael Caffey. *NO*

Hangfire *♂♂* **1991 (R)** When a New Mexican prison is evacuated thanks to a nasty chemical explosion, several prisoners decide it's time for a furlough, and they elect the local sheriff's wife as a traveling companion. Another mediocre actioner from director Maris, it gets an extra bone for stunts kids shouldn't try at home. **CW:** Language and violence. **91m/C VHS, LV.** Brad Davis, Yaphet Kotto, Lee DeBroux, Jan-Michael Vincent, George Kennedy, Kim Delaney; **D:** Peter Maris; **W:** Brian D. Jeffries. *COL*

Hangin' with the Homeboys *♂♂♂* **1991 (R)** One night in the lives of four young men. Although the Bronx doesn't offer much for any of them, they have little interest in escaping its confines, and they are more than willing to complain. Characters are insightfully written and well portrayed, with strongest work from Serrano as a Puerto Rican who is trying to pass himself off as Italian. Lack of plot may frustrate some viewers. **CW:** Strong language and one strong sex scene. **89m/C VHS, LV, Closed Caption.** Mario Joyner, Doug E. Doug, John Leguizamo, Nestor Serrano, Kimberly Russell, Mary B. Ward; **D:** Joseph B. Vasquez; **W:** Joseph B. Vasquez. Sundance Film Festival '91: Best Screenplay.*NLC, FCT*

The Hanging Garden *♂♂* **1997 (R)** Bizarre family drama mixes the matter-of-fact and the surreal. Gay 25-year-old Sweet William (Leavins) returns to his rural Nova Scotia home and family after a 10-year absence for the marriage of his sister, Rosemary (Fox). The reunion brings up lots of painful memories and flashes back to the

15-year-old Sweet William (Veinotte), when he was emotionally and physically abused by his psycho father Whiskey Mac (MacNeill). After more crises, the teen hangs himself from a backyard tree. Oh yes, everyone in the present can still see the teen's ghost hanging there, including the adult William. You figure it out. **CW:** Strong sexuality, language, a scene of a hanging, and some teen drug use. **91m/C VHS. CA** Chris Leavins, Peter MacNeill, Kerry Fox, Seana McKenna, Troy Veinotte, Sarah Polley, Christine Dunsworth, Joel S. Keller, Joan Orenstein; **D:** Thom Fitzgerald; **W:** Thom Fitzgerald; **C:** Daniel Jobin. Genie Awards '97: Best Screenplay, Best Supporting Actor (MacNeill), Best Supporting Actress (McKenna); Toronto-City Award '97: Best Canadian Feature Film; Nominations: Genie Awards '97: Best Director (Fitzgerald), Best Film, Best Supporting Actress (Fox, Orenstein). *NYR*

Hanging on a Star 🐾 1978 (PG) A small rock band encounters many comic adventures as it climbs its way up the charts. Raffin stars as the band's persistent and competent road agent. **92m/C VHS.** Deborah Raffin, Lane Caudell, Wolfman Jack, Jason Parker, Danil Torppe; **D:** Mike MacFarland. *MGM*

The Hanging Tree 🐾🐾🐾 1959 Cooper plays a frontier doctor who rescues a thief (Piazza) from a lynch mob and nurses a temporarily blind girl (Schell). Malden is the bad guy who tries to attack Schell and Cooper shoots him. The townspeople take Cooper out to "The Hanging Tree" but this time it's Schell and Piazza who come to his rescue. Slow-paced western with good performances. Scott's screen debut. **108m/B VHS.** Gary Cooper, Maria Schell, Ben Piazza, Karl Malden, George C. Scott, Karl Swenson, Virginia Gregg, King Donovan; **D:** Delmer Daves; **W:** Wendell Mayes, Halsted Welles; **M:** Max Steiner. Nominations: Academy Awards '59: Best Song ("The Hanging Tree"). *WAR*

The Hanging Woman 🐾🐾½ *Return of the Zombies; Beyond the Living Dead; La Orgia de los Muertos; Dracula, the Terror of the Living Dead; Orgy of the Dead; House of Terror* 1972 (R) A man is summoned to the reading of a relative's will, and discovers the corpse of a young woman hanging in a cemetery. As he investigates the mystery, he uncovers a local doctor's plans to zombify the entire world. Not bad at all and quite creepy once the zombies are out in force. Euro-horror star Naschy plays the necrophiliac grave digger, Igor. **91m/C VHS, Beta.** *SP IT* Stan Cooper, Vickie Nesbitt, Marcella Wright, Catherine Gilbert, Gerard Tichy, Paul Naschy, Dianik Zurakowska, Maria Pia Conte, Carlos Quiney; **D:** Jose Luis Merino; **W:** Jose Luis Merino. *WIZ*

Hangman's Knot 🐾🐾½ 1952 Members of the Confederate Cavalry rob a Union train, not knowing that the war is over. Now facing criminal charges, they are forced to take refuge in a stagecoach stop. Well-done horse opera with a wry sense of humor. **80m/C VHS.** Randolph Scott, Donna Reed, Claude Jarman Jr., Frank Faylen, Glenn Langan, Richard Denning, Lee Marvin, Jeanette Nolan; **D:** Roy Huggins. *COL*

Hangmen woof! 1987 (R) Ex-CIA agents battle it out on the East side of New York. If you're into very violent, very badly acted films, then this one's for you. **88m/C VHS, Beta.** Jake La Motta, Rick Washburne, Doug Thomas; **D:** J. Christian Ingvordsen.

Hangmen Also Die 🐾🐾½ 1942 Lang's anti-Nazi propaganda film was inspired by the actual May, 1942 assassination of Reinhard Heydrich. Franz Svoboda (Donlevy) is the member of the Czech resistance who assassinates Heydrich. The Nazis seek revenge and begin rounding up and executing Czech citizens, aided by the traitorous Emil (Lockhart). Franz wants to give himself up to prevent further slaughter but is persuaded to turn the tables on Emil and make him appear to be the assassin. Bertolt Brecht had a hand in the original screenplay but did not receive screen credit and later said most of his work was cut out. **134m/B VHS.** Brian Donlevy, Gene Lockhart, Walter Brennan, Anna Lee, Dennis O'Keefe, Alexander Granach, Jonathan Hale, Margaret Wycherly, Hans von

Twardowski; **D:** Fritz Lang; **W:** John Wexley; **C:** James Wong Howe; **M:** Hanns Eisler. *KIV*

Hank Aaron: Chasing the Dream 🐾🐾🐾 1995 Docudrama combines archival footage, interviews, and reenactments to tell the story of the life and career of Henry Aaron. Follows Aaron's development as a Hall of Fame outfielder for the Milwaukee and Atlanta Braves and as a leader in the civil rights movement. Emphasis on personal and societal issues, as well as on-the-field accomplishments, raises this one above most sports biography documentaries. **120m/C VHS.** *TTC*

Hanky Panky 🐾½ 1982 (PG) Insipid comic thriller in which Wilder and Radner become involved in a search for top-secret plans. **107m/C VHS, Beta, LV, Closed Caption.** Gene Wilder, Gilda Radner, Richard Widmark, Kathleen Quinlan; **D:** Sidney Poitier. *COL*

Hanna K. 🐾🐾 1983 (R) Story of divided passions set in the tumultuous state of Israel. American lawyer Clayburgh tries to settle her personal and political affairs with various Middle-Eastern men. Mediocre Disappointing. Release generated controversy over pro-Palestine stance. **111m/C VHS, Beta.** **FR** Jill Clayburgh, Gabriel Byrne, Jean Yanne, Muhamad Bakri, David Clennon, Oded Kotler; **D:** Constantin Costa-Gavras. *USH*

Hannah and Her Sisters 🐾🐾🐾½ 1986 (PG) Allen's grand epic about a New York showbiz family, its three adult sisters and their various complex romantic entanglements. Excellent performances by the entire cast, especially Caine and Hershey. Classic Allen themes of life, love, death, and desire are explored in an assured and sensitive manner. Witty, ironic, and heartwarming. **103m/C VHS, Beta, LV, Closed Caption.** Mia Farrow, Barbara Hershey, Dianne Wiest, Michael Caine, Woody Allen, Maureen O'Sullivan, Lloyd Nolan, Sam Waterston, Carrie Fisher, Max von Sydow, Julie Kavner, Daniel Stern, Tony Roberts, John Turturro; **D:** Woody Allen; **W:** Woody Allen; **C:** Carlo DiPalma. Academy Awards '86: Best Original Screenplay, Best Supporting Actor (Caine), Best Supporting Actress (Wiest); British Academy Awards '86: Best Director (Allen), Best Original Screenplay; Golden Globe Awards '87: Best Film—Musical/Comedy; Los Angeles Film Critics Association Awards '86: Best Film, Best Screenplay, Best Supporting Actress (Wiest); National Board of Review Awards '86: Best Director (Allen), Best Supporting Actress (Wiest); New York Film Critics Awards '86: Best Director (Allen), Best Film, Best Supporting Actress (Wiest); National Society of Film Critics Awards '86: Best Supporting Actress (Wiest); Writers Guild of America '86: Best Original Screenplay; Nominations: Academy Awards '86: Best Art Direction/Set Decoration, Best Director (Allen), Best Film Editing, Best Picture. *BTV*

Hanna's War 🐾🐾½ 1988 (PG-13) A moving film about Hanna Senesh, a young Hungarian Jew living in Palestine, who volunteered for a suicide mission behind Nazi lines during WWII. After her capture by the Germans, she was killed, and is now considered by many to have been a martyr. Detmers is very believable as Hanna and Burstyn puts in a good performance as her mother. **148m/C VHS, Beta, LV.** Ellen Burstyn, Maruschka Detmers, Anthony Andrews, Donald Pleasence, David Warner, Denholm Elliott, Vincenzo Ricotta, Ingrid Pitt; **D:** Menahem Golan; **W:** Menahem Golan; **M:** Dov Seltzer. *CCB, SWC, VTR*

Hannie Caulder 🐾🐾 1972 (R) A woman hires a bounty hunter to avenge her husband's murder and her own rape at the hands of three bandits. Excellent casting but uneven direction. Boyd is uncredited as the preacher. **87m/C VHS, Closed Caption.** Raquel Welch, Robert Culp, Ernest Borgnine, Strother Martin, Jack Elam, Christopher Lee, Diana Dors, Stephen Boyd; **D:** Burt Kennedy; **W:** Burt Kennedy. *PAR, FCT, VTR*

Hanoi Hilton 🐾½ 1987 (R) A brutal drama about the sufferings of American POWs in Vietnamese prison camps. Non-stop torture, filth, and degradation. **126m/C VHS, Beta, LV, Closed Caption.** Michael Moriarty, Paul LeMat, Jeffrey Jones, Lawrence Pressman, Stephen Davies, David Soul, Rick Fitts, Aki

Aleong, Gloria Carlin; **D:** Lionel Chetwynd; **W:** Lionel Chetwynd. *WAR*

Hanover Street 🐾🐾 1979 (PG) An American bomber pilot and a married British nurse fall in love in war-torn Europe. Eventually the pilot must work with the husband of the woman he loves on a secret mission. A sappy, romantic tearjerker. **109m/C VHS, Beta, LV.** Harrison Ford, Lesley-Anne Down, Christopher Plummer, Alec McCowen; **D:** Peter Hyams; **W:** Peter Hyams; **C:** David Watkin; **M:** John Barry. *COL*

Hans Brinker 🐾🐾½ 1969 Young Hans Brinker and his sister participate in an ice skating race, hoping to win a pair of silver skates. A musical version of the classic tale. **103m/C VHS, Beta.** Robin Askwith, Eleanor Parker, Richard Basehart, Cyril Ritchard, John Gregson; **D:** Robert Scheerer. *WAR, OM*

Hans Christian Andersen 🐾🐾 1952 Sentimental musical story of Hans Christian Andersen, a young cobbler who has a great gift for storytelling. Digitally remastered editions available with stereo sound and original trailer. 🎵The King's New Clothes; I'm Hans Christian Andersen; Wonderful Copenhagen; Thumbelina; The Ugly Duckling; Anywhere I Wander; The Inch Worm; No Two People. **112m/C VHS.** Danny Kaye, Farley Granger, Zizi Jeanmaire, Joey Walsh; **D:** Charles Vidor; **W:** Moss Hart; **M:** Frank Loesser. Nominations: Academy Awards '52: Best Art Direction/Set Decoration (Color), Best Color Cinematography, Best Costume Design (Color), Best Song ("Thumbelina"), Best Sound, Scoring of a Musical. *HBO*

Hansel and Gretel 1982 From Shelly Duvall's "Faerie Tale Theatre" comes the story of two young children who get more than they bargained for when they eat a gingerbread house. **51m/C VHS, Beta, LV, Closed Caption.** Rick Schroder, Joan Collins, Paul Dooley, Bridgette Anderson; **D:** James Frawley. *KUI, FOX, FCT*

Hanussen 🐾🐾🐾½ 1988 (R) The third of Szabo and Brandauer's price-of-power trilogy (after "Mephisto" and "Colonel Redl"), in which a talented German magician and clairvoyant (based on a true life figure) collaborates with the Nazis during their rise to power in the 1930s, although he can foresee the outcome of their reign. In German with English subtitles. **110m/C VHS, Beta, LV.** **GE HU** Klaus Maria Brandauer, Erland Josephson, Walter Schmidinger; **D:** Istvan Szabo; **C:** Lajos Koltai. Nominations: Academy Awards '88: Best Foreign Language Film. *COL*

The Happiest Days of Your Life 🐾🐾🐾 1950 During the London Blitz, a girls academy is evacuated to the country and mistakenly billeted with a boys school. The headmaster and headmistress clash and the bewildered students all try to get along. Good cast, lots of laughs. Adapted from a play by John Dighton. **81m/B VHS.** **GB** Alastair Sim, Margaret Rutherford, Joyce Grenfell, Edward Rigby, Guy Middleton, John Bentley, Bernadette O'Farrell, Richard Wattis, Muriel Aked, Patricia Owens, John Turnbull, Arthur Howard; **D:** Frank Launder; **W:** Frank Launder, John Dighton; **M:** Mischa Spoliansky. *HMV, ING*

The Happiest Millionaire 🐾🐾 1967 A Disney film about a newly immigrated lad who finds a job as butler in the home of an eccentric millionaire. Based on the book "My Philadelphia Father," by Kyle Chrichton. 🎵What's Wrong With That?; Watch Your Footwork; Valentine Candy; Strengthen the Dwelling; I'll Always Be Irish; Bye-Yum Pum Pum; I Believe in This Country; Detroit; There Are Those. **118m/C VHS, Beta.** Fred MacMurray, Tommy Steele, Greer Garson, Geraldine Page, Lesley Ann Warren, John Davidson; **D:** Norman Tokar; **W:** A.J. Carothers; **C:** Edward Colman. Nominations: Academy Awards '67: Best Costume Design. *DIS, OM*

Happily Ever After 🐾🐾 1982 Las Vegas star-maker recruits and manipulates two green performers. Show business life in Vegas is given a truthful treatment in made-for-television drama. **95m/C VHS, Beta.** Suzanne Somers, John Rubinstein, Eric (Hans Gudegast) Braeden; **D:** Robert Scheerer. *TLF*

Happily Ever After 🎬🎬 *Alem Da Paixao* 1986 A Brazilian housewife meets a bisexual transvestite and has a passionate affair, bringing her into the depths of the criminal underworld. In Portuguese with English subtitles. Contains nudity. 106m/C VHS. *BR* Regina Duarte, Paul Castelli; *D:* Bruno Barreto; *C:* Alfonso Beato. *CTL, FCT, TPV*

Happily Ever After 🎬½ 1993 (G) Sequel to "Snow White" begins where the original ends, but isn't connected to the Walt Disney classic. Snow White and her Prince prepare for their wedding when the Wicked Queen is found dead by her brother, who vows revenge. So it's up to Snow and the Dwarfelles (Disney said no to using the Dwarfs, female cousins of the original Dwarfs, to rescue him. Interesting choices from the casting department: Diller is Mother Nature and Asner provides the voice of a rapping owl. Poorly animated drivel designed to ride in on Disney's coattails. While the kids might enjoy it, save your money for the original, finally slated for a video release. 74m/C VHS, Closed Caption. *D:* John Howley; *W:* Martha Moran, Robby London; *V:* Dom DeLuise, Phyllis Diller, Zsa Zsa Gabor, Ed Asner, Sally Kellerman, Irene Cara, Carol Channing, Tracey Ullman. *REP, WOV*

Happiness 🎬🎬 1934 Another zany comedy from the land of the hammer and sickle. Banned in Russia for 40 years, it was deemed to be risque and a bit too biting with the social satire. Silent with orchestral score. 69m/B VHS. *RU D:* Alexander Medvedkin. *KIV, FCT*

Happy Anniversary 007: 25 Years of James Bond 1987 Film clip retrospective of the dashing British spy created by Ian Fleming. Hosted by Roger Moore. 59m/C VHS, Beta, Closed Caption. Sean Connery, Roger Moore, George Lazenby, Timothy Dalton; *D:* Mel Stuart. *FOX*

Happy Birthday, Gemini 🎬½ 1980 (R) A coming-of-age comedy about a young man on his 21st birthday worrying about his sexual identity. Based on the play "Gemini" by Albert Innaurato. The closeness of the characters on stage did not translate to the screen. 107m/C VHS. Robert Viharo, Madeline Kahn, Rita Moreno, Alan Rosenberg, Sarah Holcomb, David Marshall Grant, David McIlwraith; *D:* Richard Benner; *W:* Richard Benner. *MGM*

Happy Birthday to Me 🎬½ 1981 (R) Several elite seniors at an exclusive private school are mysteriously killed by a deranged killer who has a fetish for cutlery. 108m/C VHS, Beta, LV. *CA* Melissa Sue Anderson, Glenn Ford, Tracy Bregman, Jack Blum, Matt Craven, Lawrence Dane, Lenore Zann, Sharon Acker, Frances Hyland, Earl Pennington; *D:* J. Lee Thompson; *W:* Timothy Bond, Peter Jobin, John C.W. Saxton; *C:* Miklos Lente. *COL*

The Happy Ending 🎬🎬½ 1969 (PG) Woman struggles with a modern definition of herself and her marriage, causing pain and confusion for her family. Simmons is solid as the wife and mother seeking herself. Michel LeGrand's theme song "What Are You Doing With the Rest of Your Life?" was a big hit. 112m/C VHS. Jean Simmons, John Forsythe, Lloyd Bridges, Shirley Jones, Teresa Wright, Dick Shawn, Nanette Fabray, Bobby Darin, Tina Louise; *D:* Richard Brooks; *W:* Richard Brooks; *C:* Conrad Hall. Nominations: Academy Awards '69: Best Actress (Simmons), Best Song ("What Are You Doing the Rest of Your Life?"). *NO*

Happy Gilmore woof! 1996 (PG-13) Skating-impaired hockey player Gilmore (Sandler) translates his slap shot into a 400-foot tee shot and joins the pro golf tour. His unique style brings a new, less refined breed of fan to the game and upsets the reigning tour hotshot (McDonald). Sandler improves on "Billy Madison," which isn't saying much, but there's still plenty of ammo for his many detractors. Replacing bathroom humor with abusive behavior, he swears at or beats up about 90% of the supporting cast, including Bob Barker in a charity pro-am. Unfortunately, it won't make anyone forget "Caddyshack II."*CW:* Language and some comic sexuality. 92m/C VHS, Closed Caption, DVD. Adam Sandler, Christopher McDonald, Carl

Weathers, Julie Bowen, Frances Bay, Ben Stiller, Richard Kiel, Joe Flaherty, Kevin Nealon, Alan Covert, Robert Smigel, Bob Barker, Dennis Dugan; *D:* Dennis Dugan; *W:* Adam Sandler, Tim Herlihy; *C:* Arthur Albert; *M:* Mark Mothersbaugh. MTV Movie Awards '96: Best Fight (Adam Sandler/Bob Barker); Nominations: MTV Movie Awards '96: Best Comedic Performance (Sandler); Golden Raspberry Awards '96: Worst Actor (Sandler). *USH*

Happy Go Lovely 🎬🎬 1951 An unscrupulous theatrical producer casts a chorus girl in a leading role in order to get closer to her boyfriend's fortune. Tired plot, but good performances in this lightweight musical. 🎵One-Two-Three; Would You, Could You; London Town. 95m/C VHS, Beta. Vera-Ellen, David Niven, Cesar Romero, Bobby Howes; *D:* H. Bruce Humberstone. *NOS, MRV, DVT*

The Happy Hooker 🎬🎬½ 1975 (R) Xaviera Hollander's cheeky (and bestselling) memoir of her transition from office girl to "working girl" has been brought to the screen with a sprightly (though sanitary) air of naughtiness, with Redgrave enjoyable in title role. Followed by "The Happy Hooker Goes to Washington" and "The Happy Hooker Goes Hollywood." 96m/C VHS, Beta, LV. Lynn Redgrave, Jean-Pierre Aumont, Nicholas Pryor; *D:* Nicholas Sgarro. *VES*

The Happy Hooker Goes Hollywood 🎬 1980 (R) Third film inspired by the title of Xaviera Hollander's memoirs, in which the fun-loving Xaviera comes to Hollywood with the intention of making a movie based on her book, but soon meets up with a series of scheming, would-be producers. 86m/C VHS, Beta, LV. Martine Beswick, Chris Lemmon, Adam West, Phil Silvers; *D:* Alan Roberts. *USH*

The Happy Hooker Goes to Washington 🎬½ 1977 (R) Further adventures of the world's most famous madam. Heatherton (not Redgrave) is Xaviera Hollander this time, testifying before the U.S. Senate in defense of sex. Fairly stupid attempt to milk boxoffice of original. Second in the holy trilogy of Happy Hooker pictures, which also include "The Happy Hooker" and "The Happy Hooker Goes Hollywood." 89m/C VHS, Beta. Joey Heatherton, George Hamilton, Ray Walston, Jack Carter; *D:* William A. Levey. *VES*

Happy Hour 🎬½ 1987 (R) A young brewing scientist discovers a secret formula for beer, and everyone tries to take it from him. Little turns in a good performance as a superspy. 88m/C VHS, Beta, LV. Richard Gilliland, Jamie Farr, Tawny Kitaen, Ty Henderson, Rich Little; *D:* John DeBello; *W:* John DeBello. *ART*

Happy Landing 🎬🎬½ 1938 Predictable, yet entertaining Henie vehicle about a plane that makes a forced landing in Norway near Henie's home. Romance follows with bandleader Romero and manager Ameche. 🎵Hot and Happy; Yonny and his Oompah; You Are The Music to the Words in my Heart; A Gypsy Told Me; You Appeal to Me. 102m/B VHS. Sonja Henie, Don Ameche, Jean Hersholt, Ethel Merman, Cesar Romero, Billy Gilbert, Wally Vernon, El Brendel; *D:* Roy Del Ruth; *W:* Milton Sperling, Boris Ingster. *FXV*

Happy New Year 🎬🎬🎬 *The Happy New Year Caper* 1974 Charming romantic comedy in which two thieves plan a robbery but get sidetracked by the distracting woman who works next door to the jewelry store. Available in both subtitled and dubbed versions. Remade in 1987. 114m/C VHS, Beta. *FR IT* Francoise Fabian, Lino Ventura, Andre Falcon; *D:* Claude Lelouch; *W:* Claude Lelouch.

A Happy New Year! 🎬🎬 1979 Two men and a woman, all engineers in a chemical plant, try to fight off a hangover as they deal with the comings and goings of friends throughout the day and night. In Hungarian with English subtitles. 84m/C VHS. *HU* Istvan Bujtor, Erika Bodnar, Cecilia Esztergalyos, Andras Balint; *D:* Reszo Szoreny; *W:* Peter Modos, Reszo Szoreny. *FCT*

Happy New Year 🎬🎬½ 1987 (PG) Two sophisticated thieves plan and execute an elaborate jewel heist that goes completely awry. Remake of the 1974 French film of the same name. 86m/C VHS, Beta. Peter Falk, Wendy Hughes, Tom Courtenay, Charles Durning, Joan Copeland; *D:* John G. Avildsen; *W:* Warren Lane; *M:* Bill Conti. Nominations: Academy Awards '87: Best Makeup. *COL*

Happy New Year, Charlie Brown 1982 Strife upsets the Peanuts gang as the New Year's Eve gala becomes a source of tension. 25m/C VHS, Beta. *D:* Bill Melendez, Sam Jaimes. *BAR, KAR*

Happy Since I Met You 🎬🎬🎬 1989 Comedy-drama about a scatterbrained drama teacher and a struggling young actor who become romantically involved. 55m/C VHS, Beta. *GB* Julie Walters, Duncan Preston; *Cameos:* Tracey Ullman, Jim Bowen; *D:* Baz Taylor; *W:* Victoria Wood. *BIJ, WOM*

Happy Together 🎬 1989 (PG-13) An eager freshman accidentally gets a beautiful, impulsive girl as his roommate. Together they meet the challenges of secondary education. 102m/C VHS, Beta, LV. Patrick Dempsey, Dan Schneider, Marius Weyers, Barbara Babcock; *D:* Mel Damski; *M:* Robert Folk. *ART*

Happy Together 🎬🎬 *Cheun Gwong Tsa Sit* 1996 Lovers Lai Yiu-Fai (Leung) and Ho Po-Wing (Cheung) travel to Argentina from Hong Kong looking for adventure but soon go their separate ways. Lai is working as a doorman at a tango bar when a badly beaten Ho unexpectedly re-enters his life. Lai looks after the self-destructive Ho but his restlessness causes him to desert Lai once again, even as Lai befriends young Taiwanese Chang (Chen). After Chang returns to Taipei, Lai begins to suffer from depression and serious homesickness, as well as still worrying about Ho. Edgy visuals and playful performances bely a serious nature. Chinese and Spanish with subtitles. 93m/C VHS. *HK* Leslie Cheung, Tony Leung, Chang Chen; *D:* Wong Kar-Wai; *W:* Wong Kar-Wai; *C:* Christopher Doyle. Cannes Film Festival '97: Best Director (Kar-Wai); Nominations: Independent Spirit Awards '98: Best Foreign Language Film. *NYR*

Hard-Boiled 🎬🎬½ *Lashou Shentan* 1992 Police Inspector Yuen (Woo regular Yun-fat) is investigating, with his usual excessive force, the Triads organized crime syndicate and a group of gun smugglers who killed his partner. He joins forces with Tony, an undercover cop who's working as a gangster hitman. There's lots of gunplay and betrayals among all the participants. Usual Woo way with violence and action sequences although the plot is more contrived. In Mandarin and Chinese with English subtitles. 126m/C VHS. *HK* Chow Yun-Fat, Tony Leung, Philip Chan, Anthony Wong, Teresa Mo; *D:* John Woo; *W:* Barry Wong; *M:* Michael Gibbs. *ORI, FCT*

Hard-Boiled Mahoney 🎬🎬½ 1947 Slip, Sach, and the rest of the Bowery Boys try to solve a mystery involving mysterious women and missing men. The last film in the series for Bobby Jordan, whose career was ended when he was injured in an accident involving a falling elevator. 64m/B VHS. Leo Gorcey, Huntz Hall, Bobby Jordan, Billy Benedict, David Gorcey, Gabriel Dell, Teala Loring, Dan Seymour, Bernard Gorcey, Patti Brill, Betty Compson; *D:* William Beaudine. *WAR*

Hard Bounty 🎬🎬½ 1994 (R) After five years of chasing desperadoes, bounty hunter Martin B. Kanning hangs up his guns to open a saloon—complete with frontier prostitutes. When one of his ladies is murdered, the other gals decide to chase after the killer. Naturally, Kanning can't let them go alone.*CW:* Violence, nudity, sexual situations. 90m/C VHS. Matt McCoy, Kelly Le Brock, Rochelle Swanson, Felicity Waterman, Kimberly Kelley; *D:* Jim Wynorski. *TRI*

Hard Choices 🎬🎬🎬 1984 A 15-year-old Tennessee boy is unjustly charged as an accessory to murder, until a female social worker decides to help him. From then on, nothing is predictable. Excellent work by Klenck, McCleery, and Seitz. Don't miss Sayles as an unusual drug dealer. Intelligent, surprising, and powerful. Based on a true story, this is a low profile film that deserves to be discovered. **90m/C VHS, Beta.** Margaret Klenck, Gary McCleery, John Seitz, John Sayles, Liane Curtis, J.T. Walsh, Spalding Gray; **D:** Rick King; **W:** Rick King. *BAR, ORI, WAR*

Hard Core Logo 🎬🎬 1996 (R) Mockumentary about a group of Canadian veteran punk rock musicians who, at 30-something, have reunited for one last benefit concert. The semi-legendary Vancouver band are so pleased by how well the concert goes that they decide to head back on the road (in a decrepit van) for one last shot at glory, trailed by a documentary film crew (led by director McDonald). The documentary inserts reveal the band's ups and downs and the ego trips that ultimately drove them apart. Adapted from a novel by Michael Turner. McDonald describes "Hard Core Logo" as the last of his rock 'n' roll road trilogy, following "Roadkill" and "Highway 61." **CW:** Strong language, substance abuse, some violence and sexuality. **96m/C VHS.** *CA* Hugh Dillon, Callum Keith Rennie, John Pyper-Ferguson, Bernie Coulson; **D:** Bruce McDonald; **W:** Noel S. Baker; **C:** Danny Nowak; **M:** Shaun Tozer. Genie Awards '96: Best Song ("Swamp Baby, Who the Hell Do You Think You Are?"); Nominations: Genie Awards '96: Best Adapted Screenplay, Best Director (McDonald), Best Film, Best Film Editing, Best Sound. *NYR*

Hard Country 🎬🎬½ 1981 (PG) Caught between her best friend's success as a country singer and the old values of a woman's place, a small town girl questions her love and her life style. A warm and intelligent rural drama. Basinger's debut. **104m/C VHS, LV.** Jan-Michael Vincent, Kim Basinger, Michael Parks, Gailard Sartain, Tanya Tucker, Ted Neeley, Daryl Hannah, Richard Moll; **D:** David Greene; **W:** Michael Kane; **M:** Michael Martin Murphy. *NO*

A Hard Day's Night 🎬🎬🎬½ 1964 The Beatles' first film is a joyous romp through an average "day in the life" of the Fab Four, shot in a pseudo-documentary style with great flair by Lester and noted as the first music video. Laser version includes original trailer and an interview with Lester. ♫A Hard Day's Night; Tell Me Why; I Should Have Known Better; She Loves You; I'm Happy Just To Dance With You; If I Fell; And I Love Her; This Boy; Can't Buy Me Love. **90m/B VHS, Beta, LV, CD-I, DVD.** *GB* John Lennon, Paul McCartney, George Harrison, Ringo Starr, Wilfrid Brambell, Norman Rossington, John Junkin, Victor Spinetti, Anna Quayle, Deryck Guyler, George Harrison, Lionel Blair, Eddie Malin, Robin Ray, Alison Seebohm, David Saxon; **D:** Richard Lester; **W:** Alun Owen. Nominations: Academy Awards '64: Best Adapted Score, Best Story & Screenplay (Owen). *MVD, MPI, CRC*

Hard Drive 🎬½ 1994 A high tech, interactive network shared fantasies to Will and Delilah. Then they become obsessed with making their dreams a reality. **92m/C VHS, LV.** Matt McCoy, Christina Fulton, Edward Albert, Leo Damian, Stella Stevens; **D:** James Merendino; **W:** James Merendino. *TRI*

Hard Drivin' 🎬 1960 Rowdy action featuring Southern stock car drivers with well shot race scenes from the Southern 500. **92m/C VHS, Beta.** Rory Calhoun, John Gentry, Alan Hale Jr.; **D:** Paul Helmick. *NO*

Hard Eight 🎬🎬🎬 1996 (R) Performances are the highlight of this low-key story set in Reno, Nevada. Sydney (Hall) is a professional gambler who decides to take under his wing the destitute John (Reilly) and teach him the trade. John falls for waitress/hooker Clementine (Paltrow) but there has to be some snake in this gambler's would-be paradise and it shows up in the malevolent form of the scary Jimmy (Jackson), who the dim John befriends despite Sydney's warnings.

Debut for writer/director Anderson. **101m/C VHS, LV, Closed Caption.** Philip Baker Hall, John C. Reilly, Gwyneth Paltrow, Samuel L. Jackson; **D:** Paul Thomas Anderson; **W:** Paul Thomas Anderson; **C:** Robert Elswit; **M:** Michael Penn, Jon Brion. Nominations: Independent Spirit Awards '98: Best Actor (Hall), Best Cinematography, Best First Feature, Best Supporting Actor (Jackson). *COL*

Hard Evidence 🎬🎬½ 1994 (R) Trent Turner (Harrison) winds up with major regrets when he joins his mistress (Timmins) on a business trip. Seems her "business" involves drug smuggling and he's forced to shoot a DEA agent to protect them. Some protection—now Turner and his wife (Severance) are caught up in murder, drugs, and blackmail. **CW:** Strong sexuality; some violence and language. **100m/C VHS.** Gregory Harrison, Joan Severance, Cali Timmins, Andrew Airlie, Nathaniel DeVeaux; **D:** Michael Kennedy; **W:** William Martell; **C:** Bruce Worrall; **M:** Barron Abramovitch. *AVE*

Hard Frame 🎬½ *Hunters Are For Killing* 1970 An ex-con returns home hoping all will turn to sweetness and light when he attempts to make nice-nice with his stepdad, who wouldn't stick by him during his trial. Reynolds' debut into TV moviedom; could be the hirsute actor was thinking of this one when he said his movies were the kind they show in prisons and airplanes because nobody can leave. **100m/C VHS.** Burt Reynolds, Melvyn Douglas, Suzanne Pleshette, Larry Storch, Martin Balsam, Peter Brown, Jill Banner, Donald (Don "Red") Barry, Angus Duncan, Ivor Francis; **D:** Bernard Girard. *SIM*

Hard Hombre 🎬🎬 1931 Gibson rides and shoots across the screen in one of his best western adventures. **60m/B VHS, Beta.** Hoot Gibson, Lena Basquette, Skeeter Bill Robbins, Jack Byron, Glenn Strange; **D:** Otto Brower. *GPV, VCN, VCI*

Hard Hunted 🎬½ 1992 (R) Three macho undercover agents try to avoid death at the hands of high-tech guerillas trying to steal nuclear weapons. No-brain actioner, heavy on the display of feminine charms. **CW:** Language, nudity, and sexuality. **97m/C VHS, Closed Caption.** Dona Speir, Roberta Vasquez, Cynthia Brimhall, Bruce Penhall, R.J. Moore, Tony Peck, Rodrigo Obregon, Al Leong, Michael J. Shane; **D:** Andy Sidaris; **W:** Andy Sidaris. *COL*

Hard Justice 🎬🎬 1995 (R) Bureau of Alcohol, Tobacco & Firearms agent Nick Adams (Bradley) goes undercover in prison to find his partner's killer and discovers that Warden Pike (Napier) is running an illegal gun operation. Now, who's he gonna trust? Lots of action thrills in a routine story. **CW:** Non-stop brutal violence, language. **95m/C VHS, LV, Closed Caption.** David Bradley, Charles Napier, Yuji Okumoto, Vernon Wells; **D:** Greg Yaitanes; **W:** Nicholas Amendolare, Chris Bold; **M:** Moshe Levin; **M:** Don Peake. *TTC*

Hard Knocks 🎬🎬½ 1980 An ex-con goes from one tragic situation to another, and is eventually stalked by shotgun-wielding rednecks in this grim, powerful drama. Excellent performance by Mann holds this picture together. **85m/C Beta.** *AU* Tracey Mann, John Arnold, Bill Hunter, Max Cullen, Tony Barry; **D:** Don McLennan. Australian Film Institute '80: Best Actress (Mann). *NO*

Hard Knocks 🎬 19?? A young man on the run is tormented by an aging actress and her husband. His attempt to leave a past of violence and pain creates even more havoc. **90m/C VHS, Beta.** Michael Christian, John Crawford, John Wilkes, Keenan Wynn. *NO*

Hard Knox 🎬 1983 A hard-nosed Marine pilot is dumped from the service and takes up command at a military school filled with undisciplined punks. A made-for-television movie. **96m/C VHS, Beta.** Robert Conrad, Frank Howard, Alan Ruck, Red West, Bill Erwin, Dean Hill, Joan Sweeney; **D:** Peter Werner. *BAR, ORI*

Hard Labour 🎬🎬 1973 Middle-aged housekeeper is humiliated at home by her children and tyrannical daughter-in-law. Made for British television. **70m/C VHS.** *GB* Alison Steadman, Ben Kingsley, Clifford Kershaw; **D:** Mike Leigh. *WBF, FCT*

Hard Part Begins ♫ 1982 A naive country singer gets sucked into the pratfalls of show business. **87m/C VHS, Beta.** Donnelly Rhodes, Nancy Belle Fuller, Paul Bradley. *TWE*

Hard Promises 🎬🎬 1992 (PG) Absence doesn't necessarily make the heart fonder, as Joey finds out when he's accidentally invited to his wife's wedding. He's been away from home for so long he doesn't even realize he's been divorced and hightails it home to win his sweetheart back. Average performances and script round out this innocuous domestic comedy-drama. Originally made for cable televisn. **95m/C VHS, LV, 8mm, Closed Caption.** Sissy Spacek, William L. Petersen, Brian Kerwin, Mare Winningham, Peter MacNicol, Ann Wedgeworth, Amy Wright, Lois Smith, Rip Torn; **D:** Martin Davidson; **M:** George S. Clinton. *COL*

Hard Rain 🎬🎬 *Flood* 1997 (R) Armored car guards Tom (Slater) and his uncle Charlie (Asner) are transporting three million dollars to high ground during a flood in a small Indiana town. When their truck gets stuck in the mud, a band of jet-skiin' motor boatin' thieves arrive and try to steal the money. Tom hides the dough and alerts the local sheriff (Quaid) who, being your normal American elected official, decides he wants to steal it, too. Tom forms an uneasy alliance with head bad guy Jim (Freeman) to thwart the lawman and his toadies. While all this is happening, Tom manages to find love interest Karen (Driver), who's there to protect her church restoration work and wear wet blouses. And now the weather report: floods are the least cinematic disasters. Everything just gets soggy and waterlogged (especially the action sequences). Director Salomon created the huge flooded town set inside a tank in Palmdale, California. **CW:** Violence. **96m/C VHS, Closed Caption.** Morgan Freeman, Christian Slater, Randy Quaid, Minnie Driver, Ed Asner, Richard Dysart, Betty White, Mark Rolston, Peter Murnik, Dann Florek, Wayne Duvall; **D:** Mikael Salomon; **W:** Graham Yost; **C:** Peter Menzies Jr.; **M:** Christopher Young. *PAR*

Hard Rain—The Tet 1968 1989 An American platoon stationed in Saigon must mobilize in the wake of the North Vietnamese Army's Tet offensive. An episode of television's "Tour of Duty." Other episodes are also available on tape. **89m/C VHS.** Terence Knox, Stephen Caffrey; **D:** Bill W.L. Norton.

The Hard Ride 🎬🎬½ 1971 (PG) Above average biker movie about a Vietnam vet who brings the body of a black buddy back home, then tries to persuade the dead man's white girlfriend and the leader of his motorcycle gang to attend the funeral. **93m/C VHS.** Robert Fuller, Sherry Bain, Tony Russell, Marshall Reed, Biff Elliot, William Bonner, R.L. Armstrong; **D:** Burt Topper; **W:** Burt Topper. *ORI*

Hard Rock Zombies 🎬½ 1985 (R) Four heavy metal band members die horribly on the road and are brought back from the dead as zombies. This horror/heavy metal spoof is somewhat amusing in a goofy way. **90m/C VHS, Beta.** E.J. Curcio, Sam Mann; **D:** Krishna Shah; **W:** David Ball. *ART, VES*

Hard Target 🎬🎬½ 1993 (R) Van Damme continues his action-hero ways as Chance Boudreaux, a Cajun (which explains the accent) merchant seaman, who comes to the rescue of Natasha (Butler), albeit with lots of violence. Brimley provides the humor as Chance's bayou uncle. It's another variation of "The Most Dangerous Game" story but it moves. American directorial debut of over-the-top Hong Kong action director Woo who had to tone down his usual stylistic effects and repeatedly cut some of the more violent scenes to earn an "R" rating. **97m/C VHS, LV, Letterbox, Closed Caption, DVD.** Jean-Claude Van Damme, Lance Henriksen, Yancy Butler, Arnold Vosloo, Wilford Brimley, Kasi Lemmons; **D:** John Woo; **W:** Chuck Pfarrer; **C:** Russell Carpenter; **M:** Graeme Revell. Nominations: MTV Movie Awards '94: Most Desirable Male (Van Damme), Best Action Sequence. *USH, BTV*

Hard Ticket to Hawaii 🎬 1987 (R) A shot-on-video spy thriller about an agent trying to rescue a comrade in Hawaii from a smuggling syndicate. Supporting cast includes many Playboy Playmates. 96m/C VHS, Beta. Ron Moss, Dona Speir, Hope Marie Carlton, Cynthia Brimhall; *D:* Andy Sidaris. *BAR, ORI, WAR*

Hard Times 🎬🎬🎬 1975 (PG) A Depression-era drifter becomes a bare knuckle street fighter, and a gambler decides to promote him for big stakes. One of grade-B meister Hill's first genre films. A quiet, evocative drama. 92m/C VHS, Beta, LV. Charles Bronson, James Coburn, Jill Ireland, Strother Martin; *D:* Walter Hill; *W:* Walter Hill. *GKK*

Hard to Die 🎬 *Tower of Terror* 1990 Director Wynorski's comic homage to Carol Frank's "Sorority House Massacre." Five beauties (former Playboy Playmates Harris, Taylor, Dare, Moore, and Carney) find employment moving boxes in a deserted lingerie factory. The film takes off from there as they uncover a mysterious spirit called the Sorority House Killer in an ancient "Soul Box." Desperate to extinguish the evil threat, they focus their efforts in an armed struggle involving high-powered weaponry against the building maintenance man, whom they fear is possessed by the spirit. Accompanied by a lovely, touching group shower scene. 77m/C VHS. Robin Harris, Melissa Moore, Debra Dare, Lindsay Taylor, Bridget Carney, Forrest J. Ackerman, Orville Ketchum; *D:* Jim Wynorski. *NHO*

Hard to Hold 🎬½ 1984 (PG) Rockin' Rick's lukewarm film debut where he falls in love with a children's counselor after an automobile accident. Springfield sings "Love Somebody" with music by Peter Gabriel. 93m/C VHS, Beta, LV, Closed Caption. Rick Springfield, Janet Eilber, Patti Hansen, Albert Salmi, Monique Gabrielle; *D:* Larry Peerce. *USH*

Hard to Kill 🎬🎬 1989 (R) Policeman Seagal is shot and left for dead in his bedroom, but survives against the odds, though his wife does not. After seven years, he is well enough to consider evening the score with his assailants. He hides while training in martial arts for the final battle. Strong outing from Seagal, with good supporting cast. 96m/C VHS, Beta, LV, 8mm, Closed Caption. Steven Seagal, Le Brock, William Sadler, Frederick Coffin, Bonnie Burroughs, Zachary Rosencrantz, Dean Norris; *D:* Bruce Malmuth; *M:* Charles Fox. *WAR*

Hard Traveling 🎬 1985 (PG) An unemployed Depression-era farmworker is accused of murder. He must fight a hostile court system to maintain his dignity and salvage the love and respect of his wife. Based on a novel by Alvah Bessie. 99m/C VHS, Beta. J.E. Freeman, Ellen Geer, Barry Corbin, James Gammon, Jim Haynie; *D:* Dan Bessie; *W:* Dan Bessie. *VTR*

The Hard Truth 🎬🎬½ 1994 (R) By-the-book actioner finds suspended cop Jonah (Rooker) suspended for having an itchy trigger finger. His gal Lisa (Anthony) knows her sleazy boss has lots of mob money handy and proposes they grab it. But then Lisa gets a cat to Chandler (Roberts), the electronic whiz blackmailed to assist in the heist, and the triangle leads to trouble. *CW:* Language; violence; nudity; sexual situations. 100m/C VHS. Michael Rooker, Eric Roberts, Lysette Anthony, Ray Baker, Don Yesso; *D:* Kristine Peterson; *W:* Jonathan Tydor; *C:* Ross Berryman. *ART*

Hard Vice 🎬½ 1994 (R) Vice cops Joe Owens (Jones) and Andrea Thompson (Tweed) have their work cut out for them on their Las Vegas beat. When the bodies start piling up, the prime suspects turn out to be a group of high-priced hookers. *CW:* Language, violence, and strong sexuality. 86m/C VHS, LV. Shannon Tweed, Sam Jones, James Gammon, Rebecca Ferratti; *D:* Joey Travolta; *W:* Joey Travolta. *APX*

Hard Way 🎬🎬 1980 A world-weary assassin is pressured by his boss to perform one last assignment. A surprise awaits him if he accepts. 88m/C VHS, Beta. Patrick McGoohan, Lee Van Cleef, Donal McCann, Edna O'Brien; *D:* Mihael Dryhurst. *TWE*

The Hard Way 🎬🎬🎬 1991 (R) Hollywood superstar Fox is assigned to hardened NYC cop Woods to learn the ropes as he trains for a role. Nothing special in the way of script or direction, but Woods and Fox bring such intensity and good humor to their roles that the package works. Fox pokes fun at the LA lifestyle as the annoying, self-absorbed actor, and Marshall has an entertaining appearance as his agent. Woods is on familiar over-the-edge turf as the brittle but dedicated detective. Silly finale almost destroys the film, but other small vignettes are terrific. *CW:* Strong language and some violence. 91m/C VHS, Beta, LV, Letterbox, Closed Caption. James Woods, Michael J. Fox, Annabella Sciorra, Stephen Lang, L.L. Cool J., John Capodice, Christina Ricci, Karen Gorney, Luis Guzman; *Cameos:* Penny Marshall; *D:* John Badham; *W:* Daniel Pyne, Lem Dobbs; *C:* Robert Primes; *M:* Arthur B. Rubinstein. *USH*

Hard Way Out: Bloodfist 8 🎬 *Bloodfist 8* 1996 Widowed teacher Rick Cowan (Wilson) turns out to have a lurid past when he and teen son Chris (White) are targeted for death. Dull dad is ex-CIA and someone is afraid their dirty secrets will get out if he's not eliminated. 78m/C VHS. Don "The Dragon" Wilson, John Patrick White, Warren Burton, Richard Farrell; *D:* Barry Samson; *W:* Alex Simon; *C:* John Aronson; *M:* John Faulkner. *NHO*

Hardbodies 🎬 1984 (R) Three middle-aged men hit the beaches of Southern California in search of luscious young girls. They find them. Mid-life crisis done stupidly. Followed by a sequel. 88m/C VHS, Beta, LV, Closed Caption. Grant Cramer, Teal Roberts, Gary Wood, Michael Rapport, Sorrels Pickard, Roberta Collins, Cindy Silver, Courtney Gains, Kristi Somers, Crystal Shaw, Kathleen Kinmont, Joyce Jameson; *D:* Mark Griffiths; *W:* Eric Alter. *COL*

Hardbodies 2 WOOF! 1986 (R) A sequel to the original comedy hit, dealing with film crew in Greece that is distracted by hordes of nude natives. Sophomoric humor dependent on nudity and profanity for laughs. 89m/C VHS, Beta, LV. Brad Zutaut, Brenda Bakke, Fabiana Udenio, James Karen; *D:* Mark Griffiths; *W:* Eric Alter; *M:* Eddie Arkin. *COL*

Hardcase and Fist 🎬🎬 1989 (R) A framed cop leaves prison with his mind on revenge. The godfather who used him is just his first target. 92m/C VHS, Beta. Maureen Lavette, Ted Prior; *D:* Tony Zarindast. *MCG*

Hardcore 🎬🎬½ *The Hardcore Life* 1979 (R) A Midwestern businessman who is raising a strict Christian family learns of his daughter's disappearance while she is on a church trip. After hiring a streetwise investigator, he learns that his daughter has become an actress in pornographic films out in California. Strong performance by Scott and glimpse into the hardcore pornography industry prove to be convincing points of this film, though it exploits what it condemns. 106m/C VHS, Beta, LV. George C. Scott, Season Hubley, Peter Boyle, Dick Sargent; *D:* Paul Schrader; *W:* Paul Schrader; *C:* Michael Chapman; *M:* Jack Nitzsche. *COL*

The Harder They Come 🎬🎬½ 1972 (R) A poor Jamaican youth becomes a success with a hit reggae record after he has turned to a life of crime out of desperation. Songs, which are blended nicely into the framework of the film, include "You Can Get It If You Really Want it" and "Sitting In Limbo." 93m/C VHS, Beta, LV, Letterbox. Jimmy Cliff, Janet Barkley, Carl Bradshaw; *D:* Perry Henzell. *CRC, FCT*

The Harder They Fall 🎬🎬🎬 1956 A cold-eyed appraisal of the scum-infested boxing world. An unemployed reporter (Bogart in his last role) promotes a fighter for the syndicate, while doing an expose on the fight racket. Bogart became increasingly debilitated during filming and died soon afterward. Based on Budd Schulberg's novel. 109m/B VHS, Beta. Humphrey Bogart, Rod Steiger, Jan Sterling, Mike Lane, Max Baer Sr.; *D:* Mark Robson; *W:* Philip Yordan; *C:* Burnett Guffey. Nominations: Academy Awards '56: Best Black and White Cinematography. *CCB, COL*

Hardhat & Legs 🎬🎬 1980 Comic complications arise when a New York construction worker falls in love with the woman who's teaching the modern sexuality course in which he's enrolled. Made for television. 96m/C VHS, Beta. Sharon Gless, Kevin Dobson, Raymond Serra, Elva Josephson, Bobby Short, Jacqueline Brookes, W.T. Martin; *D:* Lee Philips; *W:* Ruth Gordon; *M:* Brad Fiedel. *NO*

Hardly Working 🎬 1981 (PG) A circus clown finds it difficult to adjust to real life as he fumbles about from one job to another. Lewis's last attempt at resuscitating his directorial career. His fans will love it, but others need not bother. 90m/C VHS, Beta. Jerry Lewis, Susan Oliver, Roger C. Carmel, Gary Lewis, Deanna Lund; *D:* Jerry Lewis; *W:* Jerry Lewis. *FOX*

Hardware 🎬½ 1990 (R) Rag-tag ripoff in which McDermott is a post-apocalyptic garbage picker who gives girlfriend Travis some robot remains he collected (ours is not to ask why), oblivious to the fact that the tidy android was a government-spawned population controller programmed to destroy warm bodies. Seems old habits die hard, and that spells danger, danger, Will Robinson. Much violence excised to avoid x-rating. 94m/C VHS, Beta, LV, Closed Caption. Dylan McDermott, Stacy Travis, John Lynch, Iggy Pop; *D:* Richard Stanley; *M:* Simon Boswell. *HBO, WAR*

Hardware Wars & Other Film Farces 1981 (G) A collection of four award-winning spoofs of big-budget film epics, featuring "Hardware Wars," "Porklips Now," "Bambi Meets Godzilla," and "Closet Cases of the Nerd Kind." Some black-and-white segments. 48m/C VHS, Beta. *WAR, OM*

Harem 🎬 1985 A beautiful stockbroker gets kidnapped by a wealthy OPEC oil minister and becomes part of his harem. Kingsley stars as the lonely sheik who longs for the love of a modern woman. 107m/C VHS, Beta, LV. *FR* Ben Kingsley, Nastassia Kinski; *D:* Arthur Joffe. *ART, VES*

Harem 🎬🎬 1986 In the early 1900s, a dastardly Turkish sultan kidnaps an American beauty to add to his harem—mightily displeasing his jealous first wife. Lots of overwrought romance and drama until she is finally rescued. Made for television. 200m/C VHS. Omar Sharif, Nancy Travis, Ava Gardner, Julian Sands, Art Malik, Sarah Miles, Yaphet Kotto, Cherie Lunghi; *D:* Billy Hale. *VTR*

Harlan County, U.S.A. 1976 (PG) The emotions of 180 coal mining families are seen up close in this classic documentary about their struggle to win a United Mine Workers contract in Kentucky. Award-winning documentary. 103m/C VHS, Beta. *D:* Barbara Kopple; *C:* Phil Parmet. Academy Awards '76: Best Feature Documentary, National Film Registry '90. *COL, FRF*

Harlem Nights 🎬🎬 1989 (R) Two Harlem nightclub owners in the 1930s battle comically against efforts by the Mob and crooked cops to take over their territory. High-grossing, although somewhat disappointing effort from Murphy, who directed, wrote, produced, and starred in this film. 118m/C VHS, Beta, LV, Letterbox, Closed Caption. Eddie Murphy, Richard Pryor, Redd Foxx, Danny Aiello, Jasmine Guy, Michael Lerner, Arsenio Hall, Della Reese, Eugene Glazer; *D:* Eddie Murphy; *M:* Herbie Hancock. Golden Raspberry Awards '89: Worst Screenplay; Nominations: Academy Awards '89: Best Costume Design. *PAR*

Harlem on the Prairie 🎬 *Bad Man of Harlem* 1938 This first-ever western with an all-black cast has Jeffries helping a young lady find hidden gold and foiling a villain. Even though the technical standards and acting are below par, this is worth watching for the singing and a comedy routine done by a well-known contemporary black team. ♫ Harlem On The Prairie; Romance In The Rain. 54m/B VHS. Herbert Jeffries, Mantan Moreland, F.E. Miller, Connie Harris, Maceo B. Sheffield, William Spencer Jr.; *D:* Sam Newfield. *NOS*

Harlem Rides the Range 🐾½ 1939
Jeffries must outsmart villainous Brooks, who means to swindle a radium mine away from its rightful owner. Early oater of interest only because of its atypical all-black cast and crew. 58m/B VHS. Herbert Jeffries, Lucius Brooks, Artie Young, F.E. Miller, Spencer Williams Jr., Clarence Brooks, Tom Southern, Wade Dumas, Leonard Christmas; **D:** Richard C. Kahn; **W:** F.E. Miller, Spencer Williams Jr. *NOS, MRV, TPV*

Harley 🐾🐾 1990 (PG) Diamond is Harley, an L.A. thug-on-a-hog, who's on his way to an extended stay at one of the state's luxury institutions when he's sent to a Texas rehabilitation community. There, he bonds with an ex-biker, and may just find his way back down the straight and narrow. And the local longhorn rednecks applaud his efforts...not. 80m/C VHS. Lou Diamond Phillips, Eli Cummins, DeWitt Jan, Valentine Kim; **D:** Fred Holmes; **W:** Frank Kuntz, Sandy Kuntz. *THV*

Harley Davidson and the Marlboro Man 🐾 1991 (R) An awful rehash of "Butch Cassidy and the Sundance Kid" with blatant vulgarity and pointless sci-fi themes. The title duo are near-future outlaws who rob a bank to save their favorite bar, then find they've stolen mob money. Some action, but it's mostly talk: lewd, meant-to-be-whimsical soul-probing chats between H.D. and M.M. that would bore even the biker crowd—and did. **CW:** Language, violence, and sensuality. 98m/C VHS, Beta, LV, 8mm, Closed Caption. Mickey Rourke, Don Johnson, Chelsea Field, Tom Sizemore, Vanessa Williams, Robert Ginty, Daniel Baldwin; **D:** Simon Wincer; **C:** David Eggby. *MGM*

Harlow 🐾🐾½ 1965 The more lavish of the two Harlow biographies made in 1965, both with the same title. A sensationalized "scandal sheet" version of Jean Harlow's rise to fame that bears little resemblance to the facts of her life. 125m/C VHS, Beta. Carroll Baker, Martin Balsam, Red Buttons, Mike Connors, Angela Lansbury, Peter Lawford, Raf Vallone, Leslie Nielsen; **D:** Gordon Douglas; **W:** John Michael Hayes; **C:** Joseph Ruttenberg. *PAR*

Harmagedon 🐾🐾 1983 When Princess Luna's jetliner explodes she is thrown into a psychic plane where she must battle Genma, an eternal being who has destroyed half the universe. Luna gathers together the heroic Psyonic Warriors and the cyborg Vega to aid in her battle. Animated; in Japanese with English subtitles. 131m/C VHS, LV. *JP CPM*

Harmon of Michigan 🐾🐾½ 1941 College football hero Harmon starred in this loosely adapted story of his life in and out of the pros and his career at Michigan. 65m/B VHS. Tom Harmon, Anita Louise, Forest Evashevski, Oscar O'Shea, Warren Ashe, Stanley Crown, Ken Christy, Tim Ryan, Lloyd Bridges, William Hall, Chester Conklin, Larry Parks; **D:** Charles T. Barton; **W:** Howard J. Green. *GPV*

Harmony Lane 🐾🐾 1935 Highly romanticised rendition of the life of American composer, Stephen Collins Foster (1826-1864). Montgomery, as Foster, manages to lend a hint of credibility to the syrupy, melodramatic script. Very little attention is given to historical fact and almost every scene is orchestrated to showcase the composer's songs. The music steals the show. ♫Beautiful Dreamer; Old Folks at Home; Swanee River; Oh! Susanna; De Camptown Races. 84m/B VHS. Douglass Montgomery, Evelyn Venable, Adrienne Ames, Joseph Cawthorn, William Frawley, Florence Roberts, Smiley Burnette, Hattie McDaniel; **D:** Joseph Santley. *DVT, NOS, VYY*

Harmony Trail 🐾½ 1944 Maynard stars in another rip-roaring western adventure. 60m/B VHS, Beta. Ken Maynard. *NOS, VCN, DVT*

Harnessing Peacocks 🐾🐾½ 1992 Hebe (Scott Thomas) has a one-night stand with a mystery man during carnival time in Venice, gets pregnant, and winds up living a very independent life with her son in a British seaside community. She supports herself as both a chef and as an expensive mistress, with a very select

group of admirers, but always dreams of reuniting with her son's father. Based on the novel by Mary Wesley. 108m/C VHS. GB Serena Scott Thomas, Peter Davison, Renee Asherson. *VTR, CCB*

Harold and Maude 🐾🐾🐾🐾 1971 (PG) Cult classic pairs Cort as a dead-pan disillusioned 20-year-old obsessed with suicide (his staged attempts are a highlight) and a loveable Gordon as a fun-loving 80-year-old eccentric. They meet at a funeral (a mutual hobby), and develop a taboo romantic relationship, in which they explore the tired theme of the meaning of life with a fresh perspective. The script was originally the 20-minute long graduate thesis of UCLA student Higgins, who showed it to his landlady, wife of film producer Lewis. Features music by the pre-Islamic Cat Stevens. 92m/C VHS, Beta, LV, 8mm. Ruth Gordon, Bud Cort, Cyril Cusack, Vivian Pickles, Charles Tyner, Ellen Geer; **D:** Hal Ashby; **W:** Colin Higgins; **C:** John A. Alonzo; **M:** Cat Stevens. National Film Registry '97. *PAR*

Harper 🐾🐾🐾 *The Moving Target* 1966 A tight, fast-moving genre piece about cynical LA private eye Newman investigating the disappearence of Bacall's wealthy brother. From a Ross McDonald novel, adapted by William Golding. Later sequelled in "The Drowning Pool." 121m/C VHS, Beta, LV, Letterbox. Paul Newman, Shelley Winters, Lauren Bacall, Julie Harris, Robert Wagner, Janet Leigh, Arthur Hill, Pamela Tiffin; **D:** Jack Smight; **C:** Conrad Hall. *WAR*

Harper Valley P.T.A. 🐾🐾 1978 (PG) Eden raises hell in Harper Valley after the PTA questions her parental capabilities. Brain candy was adapted from a hit song; TV series followed. 93m/C VHS, Beta. Barbara Eden, Nanette Fabray, Louis Nye, Pat Paulsen, Ronny Cox, Ron Masak, Audrey Christie, John Fiedler, Bob Hastings; **D:** Richard Bennett; **W:** Barry Schneider. *VES*

Harrad Experiment 🐾½ 1973 (R) Adaptation of Robert Rimmer's love-power bestseller in which an experiment-minded college establishes a campus policy of sexual freedom. Famous for the Hedren/Johnson relationship, shortly before Johnson married Hedren's real-life daughter Melanie Griffith. Followed by "The Harrad Summer." 98m/C VHS, Beta. James Whitmore, Tippi Hedren, Don Johnson, Bruno Kirby, Laurie Walters, Victoria Thompson, Elliot Street, Sharon Taggart, Robert Middleton, Billy Sands, Melanie Griffith; **D:** Ted Post; **M:** Artie Butler. *VES*

Harrad Summer 🐾🐾 1974 (R) Sequel to "The Harrad Experiment." College coeds take their sex-education to the bedroom where they can apply their knowledge by more intensive means. 103m/C VHS. Richard Doran, Victoria Thompson, Laurie Walters, Robert Reiser, Bill Dana, Marty Allen; **D:** Steven Hilliard Stern. *NO*

Harriet Craig 🐾🐾🐾 1950 Tailor-made Crawford role finds her as seemingly perfect wife Harriet Craig. In reality, she's a domineering shrew, who's also a bully and a clean freak. Harriet squelches husband Walter's (Corey) promotion because it means he'll be travelling abroad, ruins his relationship with best friend Billy (Joslyn), and manages to sabotage her young cousin Clare's (Stevens) romance before anybody stands up to her. Third film adaptation of George Kelly's 1925 play "Craig's Wife." 94m/B VHS. Joan Crawford, Wendell Corey, Allyn Joslyn, William Bishop, K.T. Stevens, Lucile Watson, Raymond Greenleaf, Ellen Corby; **D:** Vincent Sherman; **W:** James Gunn; **C:** Joseph Walker; **M:** George Duning. *COL*

Harriet the Spy 🐾🐾½ 1996 (PG) Sixth-grade, 11-year-old tomboy Harriet M. Welsch (Trachtenberg) spies on everyone around her and, encouraged by her nanny Ole Golly (O'Donnell), writes down everything going on in her secret notebook, because she's determined to become a great writer. Unfortunately, Harriet's imagination sometimes gets the best of her and when her notebook is found, her friends and family are not too happy about its contents. Based on the award-winning novel by Louise Fitzhugh. Lovers of the book may not be enthusiastic about

some of the changes but generally it's enjoyable fare. 102m/C VHS, Closed Caption. Michelle Trachtenberg, Rosie O'Donnell, Vanessa Lee Chester, Gregory Edward Smith, Robert Joy, Eartha Kitt, J. Smith-Cameron; **D:** Bronwen Hughes; **W:** Douglas Petrie, Theresa Rebeck; **C:** Francis Kenny; **M:** Jamshield Shariffi. *PAR*

Harry & Son 🐾🐾 1984 (PG) A widowed construction worker faces the problems of raising his son. Newman is miscast as the old man and we've all seen Benson play the young role too many times. 117m/C VHS, Beta, LV. Paul Newman, Robby Benson, Ellen Barkin, Wilford Brimley, Judith Ivey, Ossie Davis, Morgan Freeman, Joanne Woodward; **D:** Paul Newman; **M:** Henry Mancini. *VES*

Harry and the Hendersons 🐾🐾½ 1987 (PG) Ordinary American family vacationing in the Northwest has a collision with Bigfoot. Thinking that the big guy is dead, they throw him on top of the car and head home. Lo and behold, he revives and starts wrecking the furniture and in the process, endears himself to the at-first frightened family. Nice little tale efficiently told, with Lithgow fine as the frustrated dad trying to hold his Bigfoot-invaded home together. Basis for the television series. 111m/C VHS, Beta, LV, Closed Caption. John Lithgow, Melinda Dillon, Don Ameche, David Suchet, Margaret Langrick, Joshua Rudoy, Kevin Peter Hall, Lainie Kazan, M. Emmet Walsh; **D:** William Dear; **W:** William Dear, William E. Martin, Ezra D. Rappaport; **C:** Allen Daviau; **M:** Bruce Broughton. Academy Awards '87: Best Makeup. *USH*

Harry and Tonto 🐾🐾🐾 1974 A gentle comedy about an energetic septuagenarian who takes a cross-country trip with his cat, Tonto. Never in a hurry, still capable of feeling surprise and joy, he makes new friends and visits old lovers. Carney deserved his Oscar. Mazursky has seldom been better. 115m/C VHS, Beta, Closed Caption. Art Carney, Ellen Burstyn, Larry Hagman, Geraldine Fitzgerald, Chief Dan George, Arthur Hunnicutt, Josh Mostel; **D:** Paul Mazursky; **W:** Paul Mazursky; **M:** Bill Conti. Academy Awards '74: Best Actor (Carney); Golden Globe Awards '75: Best Actor—Musical/Comedy (Carney); Nominations: Academy Awards '74: Best Original Screenplay. *FOX, FCT, BTV*

Harry & Walter Go to New York 🐾🐾 1976 (PG) At the turn of the century, two vaudeville performers are hired by a crooked British entrepreneur for a wild crime scheme. The cast and crew try their hardest, but it's not enough to save this boring comedy. The vaudeville team of Caan and Gould perhaps served as a model for Beatty and Hoffman in "Ishtar." 111m/C VHS, Beta, LV. James Caan, Elliott Gould, Michael Caine, Diane Keaton, Burt Young, Jack Gilford, Charles Durning, Lesley Ann Warren, Carol Kane; **D:** Mark Rydell; **W:** John Byrum; **M:** David Shire. *COL*

Harry Black and the Tiger 🐾🐾 *Harry Black* 1958 Jungle adventure involving a one-legged hunter and a man-eating tiger. The hunter initally teams up with the old war buddy who cost him his leg. The motivation grows with each failure to catch the beast and to make matters worse, the friend's wife and son are lost somewhere in the perilous jungle. Filmed in India. 107m/C VHS. GB Stewart Granger, Barbara Rush, Anthony Steel; **D:** Hugo Fregonese. *FXL*

Harry Tracy 🐾🐾½ *Harry Tracy—Desperado* 1983 (PG) Whimsical tale of the legendary outlaw whose escapades made him both a wanted criminal and an exalted folk hero. 111m/C VHS, Beta. CA Bruce Dern, Gordon Lightfoot, Helen Shaver, Michael C. Gwynne; **D:** William A. Graham; **C:** Allen Daviau. *VES*

Harry's War 🐾🐾 1984 (PG) A middle-class, middle-aged American declares military war on the IRS in this overdone comedy. 98m/C VHS, Beta. Edward Herrmann, Geraldine Page, Karen Grassle, David Ogden Stiers; **D:** Keith Merrill. *TPI*

Harum Scarum 🐾🐾 *Harem Holiday* 1965 Elvis tune-fest time! When a movie star (Presley) travels through the Middle East, he becomes involved in an attempted assassination of the king and falls in love with his daughter. He also sings at the drop of a veil: "Shake That Tambourine,"

"Harem Holiday," and seven others. **95m/C VHS, Beta.** Elvis Presley, Mary Ann Mobley, Fran Jeffries, Michael Ansara, Billy Barty, Theo Marcuse, Jay Novello; **D:** Gene Nelson. *MGM*

Harvest 🎬🎬🎬🎬 **1937** A classically Pagnolian rural pageant-of-life melodrama, wherein a pair of loners link up together in an abandoned French town and completely revitalize it and the land around it. From the novel by Jean Giono. In French with English subtitles. **128m/B VHS, Beta.** *FR* Fernandel, Gabriel Gabrio, Orane Demazis, Edouard Delmont, Henri Poupon; **D:** Marcel Pagnol; **W:** Marcel Pagnol; **M:** Arthur Honegger. New York Film Critics Awards '39: Best Foreign Film. *INT, MRV, FCT*

The Harvest 🎬🎬½ **1992 (R)** Sultry temptress Leilani sends Miguel's internal thermometer into convulsions with her preference for ice during lovemaking. However, their tryst turns sour (for him) when she takes Miguel to the beach where mystery thugs beat him unconscious and swipe his kidney. Bizarre story sure to ignite a small cult following.**CW:** Language, violence, and strong sexuality. **97m/C VHS, LV, Closed Caption.** Miguel Ferrer, Leilani Sarelle Ferrer, Harvey Fierstein, Anthony John Denison, Tim Thomerson, Matt Clark, Henry Silva; **D:** David Marconi; **W:** David Marconi; **M:** Dave Allen, Rick Boston. *COL*

Harvest Melody 🎬🎬 **1943** Singing star Gilda Parker travels to farm country for a mere publicity stunt but decides to stay. Corny in more ways than one. 🎵You Could Have Knocked Me Over With A Feather; Put It In Reverse; Let's Drive Out To The Drive-In; Tenderly. **70m/B VHS.** Rosemary Lane, Johnny Downs, Sheldon Leonard, Charlotte Wynters, Luis Alberni, Claire Rochelle, Syd Saylor; **D:** Sam Newfield. *NOS, LOO*

Harvest of Fire 🎬🎬½ **1995 (PG)** A close-knit Amish farming community in Iowa has been the target of a series of barn burnings, which come under the investigation of FBI agent Sally Russell (Davidovich). But the community doesn't want an outsider around and Sally needs some help, which she finds with Amish widow Annie Beiler (Duke). And gradually the disparate duo find some common ground. A Hallmark Hall of Frame presentation. **90m/C VHS, Closed Caption.** Patty Duke, Lolita Davidovich, J.A. Preston, Jean Louisa Kelly, Tom Aldredge, James Read, Craig Wasson; **D:** Arthur Allan Seidelman; **W:** Richard Alfieri; **C:** Neil Roach; **M:** Lee Holdridge. *HMK*

Harvey 🎬🎬🎬½ **1950** Straightforward version of the Mary Chase play about a friendly drunk with an imaginary six-foot rabbit friend named Harvey, and a sister who tries to have him committed. A fondly remembered, charming comedy. Hull is a standout, well deserving her Oscar. **104m/B VHS, Beta, LV.** James Stewart, Josephine Hull, Victoria Horne, Peggy Dow, Cecil Kellaway, Charles Drake, Jesse White, Wallace Ford, Nana Bryant; **D:** Henry Koster; **W:** Oscar Brodney; **C:** William H. Daniels. Academy Awards '50: Best Supporting Actress (Hull); Golden Globe Awards '51: Best Supporting Actress (Hull); Nominations: Academy Awards '50: Best Actor (Stewart). *USH, BTV, RDG*

The Harvey Girls 🎬🎬🎬 **1946** Lightweight musical about a restaurant chain that sends its waitresses to work in the Old West. 🎵In the Valley Where the Evening Sun Goes Down; Wait and See; On the Atchison, Topeka and Santa Fe; It's a Great Big World; The Wild Wild West. **102m/C VHS, Beta, LV.** Judy Garland, Ray Bolger, John Hodiak, Preston Foster, Angela Lansbury, Virginia O'Brien, Marjorie Main, Chill Wills, Kenny L. Baker, Selena Royle, Cyd Charisse; **D:** George Sidney; **M:** Harry Warren, Johnny Mercer. Academy Awards '46: Best Song ("On the Atchison, Topeka and Santa Fe"); Nominations: Academy Awards '46: Scoring of a Musical. *MGM, FCT*

A Hash House Fraud/The Sultan's Wife **1915** "A Hash House Fraud" (1915) features a frenetic Keystone chase. "The Sultan's Wife" (1917) concerns a woman who attracts the unwanted attention of a sultan. **33m/B VHS, Beta.** Louise Fazenda, Hugh Fay, Chester Conklin, Gloria Swanson, Bobby Vernon. *CCB*

The Hasty Heart 🎬🎬 **1986** A rowdy, terminally ill Scotsman brings problems and friendships to a makeshift war-time hospital built in the jungles of Burma. Remake of 1949 flick with Richard Todd and Ronald Reagan in leading roles. **100m/C VHS, Beta.** Gregory Harrison, Cheryl Ladd, Perry King; **D:** Martin Speer. *BAR, ORI, WAR*

Hat Box Mystery 🎬🎬 **1947** A detective's secretary is tricked into shooting a woman and private eye Neal is determined to save her from prison. Although not outstanding, it's worth seeing as perhaps the shortest detective film (a mere 44 min.) to ever make it as a feature. **44m/B VHS, Beta, LV.** Tom Neal, Pamela Blake, Allen Jenkins; **D:** Lambert Hillyer. *SNC, VYY*

Hatari! 🎬🎬🎬 **1962** An adventure-loving team of professional big game hunters ventures to East Africa to round up animals for zoos around the world. Led by Wayne, they get into a couple of scuffs along the way, including one with lady photographer Martinelli who is doing a story on the expedition. Extraordinary footage of Africa and the animals brought to life by a fantastic musical score. **158m/C VHS, Beta, LV.** John Wayne, Elsa Martinelli, Red Buttons, Hardy Kruger, Gerard Blain, Bruce Cabot; **D:** Howard Hawks; **M:** Henry Mancini. Nominations: Academy Awards '62: Best Color Cinematography. *PAR*

Hatchet for the Honeymoon 🎬 *Blood Brides; Una Hacha para la Luna de Miel; Il Rosso Segmo della Follia; An Axe for the Honeymoon; The Red Sign of Madness* **1970** A rather disturbed young man goes around hacking young brides to death as he tries to find out who murdered his wife. Typical sick Bava horror flick; confusing plot, but strong on vivid imagery. **90m/C VHS, Beta.** *SP IT* Stephen Forsyth, Dagmar Lassander, Laura Betti, Gerard Tichy, Femi Benussi, Luciano Pigozzi, Jesus Puente; **D:** Mario Bava; **W:** Mario Bava, Santiago Moncada, Mario Musy; **C:** Mario Bava. *HEG, FCT*

Hate 🎬🎬🎬 *La Haine; Hatred* **1995** Twenty-hours in the lives of young, disenfranchised Said (Taghmaoui), Vinz (Cassel), and Hubert (Kounde), who are living in a housing project outside Paris. A riot breaks out, thanks to police brutality of an Arab resident, and Vinz finds a gun the cops lost. A Paris sojourn leads to a police interrogation of Hubert and Said, a fight with some skinheads, a return to their home turf, and an unexpected conclusion. Intelligent look at the idiocy engendered by societal oppression and a buildup of hatred. French with subtitles. **95m/B VHS.** *FR* Vincent Cassel, Hubert Kounde, Said Taghmaoui, Francois Levantal; **D:** Mathieu Kassovitz; **W:** Mathieu Kassovitz; **C:** Pierre Aim, Georges Diane. Cannes Film Festival '95: Best Director (Kassovitz); Cesar Awards '96: Best Film, Best Film Editing; Nominations: Cesar Awards '96: Best Actor (Cassel), Best Cinematography, Best Director (Kassovitz), Best Sound, Best Writing. *PGV*

The Hatfields & the McCoys 🎬🎬 **1975** A made-for-television re-telling of the most famous feud in American history—the legendary mountain war between the Hatfields and the McCoys. **90m/C VHS, Beta.** Jack Palance, Steve Forrest, Richard Hatch, Karen Lamm; **D:** Clyde Ware. *WOV*

Hats Off 🎬 **1937** Clarke and Payne star as opposing press agents in this tedious musical. The only bright spot is the finale, which features white-robed girls on a cloud-covered carousel. 🎵Where Have You Been All My Life?; Little Old Rhythm; Twinkle, Twinkle, Little Star; Let's Have Another; Zilch's Hats; Hats Off. **65m/B VHS.** Mae Clarke, John Payne, Helen Lynd, Luis Alberni, Richard "Skeets" Gallagher, Franklin Pangborn; **D:** Boris L. Petroff. *NOS, MLB*

The Haunted 🎬 **1979** The ancient curse of an Indian woman haunts a present day family by possessing the body of a beautiful girl. Through the girl, a horrible vengeance is carried out. **81m/C VHS, Beta.** Aldo Ray, Virginia Mayo, Ann Michelle, Jim Negele; **D:** Michael de Gaetano. *VHE, HHE*

Haunted 🎬🎬½ **1995 (R)** At their Sussex home, David Ash watches helplessly as his younger sister Juliet drowns. Flash-forward to 1925 and the grownup David (Quinn) returns to teach a university course debunking the supernatural. Still, he's drawn to a supposedly haunted mansion, inhabited by artist Robert Mariell (Andrews), his sister Christina (Beckinsale), brother Simon (Lowe), and their elderly nanny (Massey). David starts drawn to visions of his dead sister, while mysterious fires and other unexplained manifestations occur—all of which seem tied to the unholy Mariell trio. Based on a novel by James Herbert.**CW:** Sexuality and nudity. **108m/C VHS.** *GB* Aidan Quinn, Kate Beckinsale, Anthony Andrews, Alex Lowe, Anna Massey, Geraldine Somerville, Victoria Shalet; **Cameos:** John Gielgud; **D:** Lewis Gilbert; **W:** Lewis Gilbert, Bob Kellett, Tim Prager; **C:** Tony Pierce-Roberts; **M:** Debbie Wiseman. *HMK*

The Haunted Castle 🎬🎬🎬 *Schloss Vogelod* **1921** One of Murnau's first films, and a vintage, if crusty, example of German expressionism. A nobleman entertains guests at his country mansion when strange things start to occur. Silent, with English titles. **56m/B VHS, Beta.** Arnold Korff, Lulu Keyser-Korff; **D:** F.W. Murnau. *SNC, NOS, VYY*

Haunted Gold 🎬🎬 **1932** A young Wayne, in his first Western for Warners, battles gold-hungry desperadoes and a mysterious cloaked phantom. Remake of "The Phantom City." **57m/B VHS, Closed Caption.** John Wayne, Sheila Terry, Harry Woods; **D:** Mack V. Wright; **W:** Adele Buffington. *MGM, GPV*

Haunted Harbor 🎬🎬½ *Pirate's Harbor* **1944** A high-seas financier has been murderd by a crooked crony and Captain Jim Marsden's alibi is all wet. He's got to find the gold, the girl, and avoid the goons. Part of "The Cliffhanger Serials" series. **243m/B VHS.** Kane Richmond, Kay Aldridge, Roy Barcroft. *REP, MOV*

Haunted Honeymoon 🎬 **1986 (PG)** Arthritic comedy about a haunted house and a couple trapped there. Sad times for the Mel Brooks alumni participating in this lame horror spoof. **82m/C VHS, Beta, LV.** Gene Wilder, Gilda Radner, Dom DeLuise, Jonathan Pryce, Paul Smith, Peter Vaughan, Bryan Pringle, Roger Ashton-Griffiths, Jim Carter, Eve Ferret; **D:** Gene Wilder; **W:** Terence Marsh, Gene Wilder; **C:** Fred Schuler. *ORI*

The Haunted Palace 🎬🎬½ **1963** Price plays both a 17th-century warlock burned at the stake and a descendant who returns to the family dungeon and gets possessed by the mutant-breeding forebearer. The movie has its own identity crisis, with title and ambience from Poe but story from H.P. Lovecraft's "The Case of Charles Dexter Ward." Respectable but rootless chills, also available with the quasi-Lovecraft "Curse of the Crimson Altar" on laserdisc. **87m/C VHS, Beta, LV.** Vincent Price, Debra Paget, Lon Chaney Jr., Frank Maxwell, Leo Gordon, Elisha Cook Jr., John Dierkes; **D:** Roger Corman. *HBO, MLB*

Haunted Ranch 🎬½ **1943** Reno Red has been murdered and a shipment of gold bullion is missing. A gang on the lookout for the gold tries to convince people that Red's ranch is haunted by his ghost. **56m/B VHS, Beta.** John "Dusty" King, David Sharpe, Max Terhune, Rex Lease, Julie Duncan; **D:** Robert Emmett Tansey. *NOS, DVT, VYY*

The Haunted Sea 🎬🎬 **1997 (R)** The crew of the Patna discovered an abandoned ship that's filled with Aztec treasure. But when the Patna's crew members begin disappearing, those remaining must discover what's guarding the treasure.**CW:** Violence/gore, nudity and language. **74m/C VHS.** James Brolin, Joanna Pacula, Krista Allen, Don Stroud; **D:** Dan Golden. *NHO*

The Haunted Strangler 🎬🎬½ *The Grip of the Strangler* **1958** Boris Karloff is a writer investigating a 20-year-old murder who begins copying some of the killer's acts. **78m/B VHS, Beta.** *GB* Boris Karloff, Anthony Dawson, Elizabeth Allan, Timothy Turner, Diane Aubrey, Dorothy Gordon, Jean Kent, Vera Day; **D:**

Robert Day; **W:** John C. Cooper, Jan Read; **C:** Lionel Banes. *MPI*

Haunted Summer 🎞🎞 1988 (R)
Soft-focus, sex-and-drugs period piece of the bacchanalian summer of 1816 spent by free spirits Lord Byron, Percy Shelley, Mary Shelley, and John Polidori and others that led Mary Shelley to write "Frankenstein." Based on the novel of the same name by Anne Edwards. **106m/C VHS, Beta, LV.** Alice Krige, Eric Stoltz, Philip Anglim, Laura Dern, Alex Winter; **D:** Ivan Passer; **W:** Lewis John Carlino.

Haunted Symphony 🎞🎞 *Blood Song*
1994 (R) In the 18th century, a deranged composer (Wert) is obsessed creating a symphony for the devil and killed by a mob. Years later, his niece Gabrielle (Burns) discovers the unfinished symphony hidden in an old piano and hires choir master Marius (Cross) to complete the score. But when he tries, demonic things begin to occur. **CW:** Nudity; sexual situations. **85m/C VHS.** Jennifer Burns, Ben Cross, Doug Wert, Beverly Garland; **D:** David Tausik. *NHO*

Haunted: The Ferryman 🎞🎞 1974
Adapted by Julian Bond from a Kingsley Amis story, the film deals with a novelist who is mysteriously confronted with various events and macabre set-pieces from his own novel, including a dead ferryman rising from the grave. **50m/C VHS, Beta.** *GB* Jeremy Brett, Nastasha Parry, Lesley Dunlop; **D:** John Irvin.

HauntedWeen 🎞½ 1991
All trick, no treat, as a guy nailed by a frat house prank 20 years ago comes-back-for-revenge. **?m/C VHS.** Brette Blakely, Blake Pickett, Brad Hanks, Bart White, Leslee Lacey, Ethan Adler; **D:** Doug Robertson.

The Haunting 🎞🎞🎞½ 1963
A subtle, bloodless horror film about a weekend spent in a monstrously haunted mansion by a parapsychologist, the mansion's skeptic heir, and two mediums. A chilling adaptation of Shirley Jackson's "The Haunting of Hill House," in which the psychology of the heroine is forever in question. **113m/B VHS, Beta, LV.** Julie Harris, Claire Bloom, Russ Tamblyn, Richard Johnson, Fay Compton, Rosalie Crutchley, Lois Maxwell, Valentine Dyall, Diane Clare; **D:** Robert Wise; **W:** Nelson Gidding; **C:** David Boulton. *MGM, FCT*

Haunting Fear 🎞 1991
Poe's "The Premature Burial" inspired this pale cheapie about a wife with a fear of early interment. After lengthy nightmares and graphic sex, her greedy husband uses her phobia in a murder plot. **88m/C VHS.** Jan-Michael Vincent, Karen Black, Brinke Stevens, Michael Berryman; **D:** Fred Olen Ray; **W:** Sherman Scott. *RHI*

The Haunting of Barney Palmer
199? Barney Palmer is sure he has inherited the family magic powers because he is haunted by the ghost of his great uncle. To destroy the curse, he must conquer his fears. Based on the book "The Haunting" by Margaret Mahy. Includes a viewers' guide. Part of the "Wonderworks" series. **58m/C VHS.** Ned Beatty, Alexis Banas, Eleanor Gibson. *HMV, FCT, BTV*

Haunting of Harrington House 🎞
1982 A tame teenage haunted house film originally produced for television. **50m/C VHS, Beta.** Dominique Dunne, Roscoe Lee Browne, Edie Adams, Phil Leeds; **D:** Murray Golden. *GEM*

The Haunting of Morella 🎞 1991 (R)
Poe-inspired cheapjack exploitation about a an executed witch living again in the nubile body of her teen daughter. Ritual murders result, in between lesbian baths and nude swims. Producer Roger Corman did the same story with more class and less skin in his earlier anthology "Tales of Terror." **82m/C VHS, LV.** David McCallum, Nicole Eggert, Maria Ford, Lana Clarkson; **D:** Jim Wynorski; **W:** Jim Wynorski, R.J. Robertson. *NHO*

Haunting of Sarah Hardy 🎞🎞 1989
Ward, as a recently wed heiress, returns to the scene of her unhappy childhood home. In a standard plot, Ward is torn between an apparent haunting and the question of her own sanity.

Made for TV film is redeemed by the creditable acting. **92m/C VHS, Beta, LV, Closed Caption.** Sela Ward, Michael Woods, Roscoe Born, Polly Bergen, Morgan Fairchild; **D:** Jerry London; **C:** Bojan Bazelli. *PAR*

The Haunting of Seacliff Inn 🎞🎞½
1994 (PG-13) Susan and Mark Enright struggle to start a bed-and-breakfast in their newly acquired Mendocino Victorian manse. But psychic Susie senses something—seems the former owner died violently, and, a hundred years ago, an owner was accused of murdering his wife in the house. Not-too-frightening ghost story but good cast work. Made for cable TV. **CW:** Ghostly terror and sensuality. **94m/C VHS, LV, Closed Caption.** Ally Sheedy, William R. Moses, Louise Fletcher, Lucinda Weist, Maxine Stuart, Tom McCleister, James Horan; **D:** Walter Klenhard; **W:** Walter Klenhard, Tom Walla. *USH*

The Haunting Passion 🎞🎞½ 1983
Newlywed Seymour moves into a haunted house only to be seduced by the ghost of the former occupant's dead lover. Effective and erotic presentation. Made for Television. **100m/C VHS, Beta.** Jane Seymour, Gerald McRaney, Millie Perkins, Ruth Nelson, Paul Rossilli, Ivan Bonar; **D:** John Korty. *ART*

Haunts 🎞½ *The Veil* 1977 (PG)
Tormented woman has difficulty distinguishing between fantasy and reality after a series of brutal slayings lead police to the stunning conclusion that dead people have been committing the crimes. **97m/C VHS, Beta.** Cameron Mitchell, Aldo Ray, May Britt, William Gray Espy, Susan Nohr; **D:** Herb Freed; **M:** Pino Donaggio.

Haunts of the Very Rich 🎞🎞½ 1972
A loose remake of "Outward Bound" in which a group of spoiled people on a vacation find themselves spiritually dead. Made for TV. **72m/C VHS, Beta.** Lloyd Bridges, Anne Francis, Donna Mills, Tony Bill, Robert Reed, Moses Gunn, Cloris Leachman, Ed Asner; **D:** Paul Wendkos. *THV*

Havana 🎞🎞½ 1990 (R)
During the waning days of the Batista regime, a gambler travels to Havana in search of big winnings. Instead, he meets the beautiful wife of a communist revolutionary. Unable to resist their mutual physical attraction, the lovers become drawn into a destiny which is far greater than themselves. Reminiscent of "Casablanca." **CW:** Strong language and sensuality. **145m/C VHS, Beta, LV, Closed Caption.** Robert Redford, Lena Olin, Alan Arkin, Raul Julia, Tomas Milian, Tony Plana, Betsy Brantley, Lise Cutter, Richard Farnsworth, Mark Rydell, Daniel Davis; **D:** Sydney Pollack; **W:** Judith Rascoe, David Rayfiel; **C:** Owen Roizman; **M:** Dave Grusin. Nominations: Academy Awards '90: Best Original Score. *USH, FCT, MOV*

Have Rocket Will Travel 🎞🎞½ 1959
Three janitors (guess who) help a scientist who is about to lose her job if she can't send a rocket to Venus. They accidently initiate the launch while still on board and introduce their brand of slapstick to a whole new planet. First of the late '50s-early '60s feature films to capitalize on the renewed popularity of the Three Stooges. **76m/B VHS.** Moe Howard, Larry Fine, Joe DeRita, Anna-Lisa, Jerome Cowan, Bob Colbert; **D:** David Lowell Rich; **W:** Raphael Hayes. *COL*

Having It All 🎞🎞 1982
A wry television comedy about a love triangle. Dyan Cannon stars as a successful business woman with a husband on each coast, who finds dividing her time is more than she bargained for. **100m/C VHS, Beta, LV.** Dyan Cannon, Barry Newman, Hart Bochner, Melanie Chartoff, Sylvia Sidney; **D:** Edward Zwick; **M:** Miles Goodman. *ART*

Having Wonderful Crime 🎞🎞½ 1945
Madcap comedy-thriller about a newly married couple who combine sleuthing with a honeymoon. With their criminal lawyer friend along, the trio winds up searching for a magician who has vanished. Fast-paced action and quick dialogue. **70m/B VHS, LV.** Pat O'Brien, George Murphy, Carole Landis, Lenore Aubert, George Zucco; **D:** Edward Sutherland. *TTC, FCT, IME*

Having Wonderful Time 🎞½ 1938
A young girl tries to find culture and romance on her summer vacation at a resort in the Catskills. Film debut of comic Red Skelton, who wasn't always as old as the hills. Based on a Broadway hit by Arthur Kober. **71m/B VHS, Beta.** Ginger Rogers, Lucille Ball, Eve Arden, Red Skelton, Douglas Fairbanks Jr.; **D:** Alfred Santell. *NO*

Having Wonderful Time/Carnival Boat 🎞🎞½ 1938
A Ginger Rogers double feature: "Having Wonderful Time" (1938)-fun and frolic at an adult summer camp in the Catskills; and "Carnival Boat" (1932)-the lives and loves of rugged loggers in the Pacific Northwest. **134m/B VHS, Beta.** Ginger Rogers, Douglas Fairbanks Jr., Lucille Ball, Ann Miller, Red Skelton, William Boyd. *TTC*

Hawaii 🎞🎞🎞 1966
James Michener's novel about a New England farm boy who decides in 1820 that the Lord has commanded him to the island of Hawaii for the purpose of "Christianizing" the natives. Filmed on location. Also available in a 181 minute version with restored footage. Available in director's cut version with an additional 20 minutes. **161m/C VHS, Beta, LV, Letterbox.** Max von Sydow, Julie Andrews, Richard Harris, Carroll O'Connor, Bette Midler, Gene Hackman, Jocelyn Lagarde; **D:** George Roy Hill; **W:** Daniel Taradash, Dalton Trumbo; **M:** Elmer Bernstein. Golden Globe Awards '67: Best Supporting Actress (Lagarde), Best Score; Nominations: Academy Awards '66: Best Color Cinematography, Best Costume Design (Color), Best Song ("My Wishing Doll"), Best Sound, Best Supporting Actress (Lagarde), Best Original Score. *FOX*

Hawaii Calls 🎞🎞 1938
Two young stowaways on a cruise ship are allowed to stay on after one of them (Breen) struts his stuff as a singer. The two then turn sleuth to catch a gang of spies. More ham than a can of Spam, but still enjoyable. ♫That's The Hawaiian In Me; Hawaii Calls; Down Where The Trade Winds Blow; Macushia; Aloha Oe. **72m/C VHS.** Bobby Breen, Ned Sparks, Irvin S. Cobb, Warren Hull, Gloria Holden, Pua Lani, Raymond Paige, Philip Ahn, Ward Bond; **D:** Eddie Cline. *DVT, NOS, HEG*

Hawaiian Buckaroo 🎞 1938
A couple of cowboys fight to save their pineapple plantation from a sneaky foreman. **62m/B VHS.** Smith Ballew, Evalyn Knapp, Benny Burt, Harry Woods, Pat O'Brien; **D:** Ray Taylor. *NOS, DVT, GPV*

The Hawk 🎞🎞½ 1993 (R)
Okay thriller about suburban housewife Annie (Mirren) who suspects that her husband Stephen (Costigan) is a serial killer known as the Hawk. Since Annie has a history of depression and her husband is a known louse, her suspicions are dismissed as delusional. Some surprise twists help the weak story along. Contains some graphic views of corpses. Based on the novel by Ransley. **CW:** Language and terror. **84m/C VHS.** *GB* Helen Mirren, George Costigan, Owen Teale, Rosemary Leach; **D:** David Hayman; **W:** Peter Ransley; **M:** Nick Bicat.

Hawk and Castile 19??
Bandits murder, pillage, and terrorize the nobility in Medieval Europe until the Hawk comes onto the scene. **95m/C VHS, Beta.** Tom Griffith, Jerry Cobb, Nurla Forway, Mari Real. *NO*

The Hawk of Powder River 🎞 1948
Cheapie western has Dean getting involved with a beautiful outlaw gang leader with a murderous streak. A large part of this film was lifted from earlier Dean oaters, as are all the tunes. **54m/B VHS.** Eddie Dean, Roscoe Ates, Jennifer Holt, June Carlson, Terry Frost, Lane Bradford; **D:** Ray Taylor. *MOV*

Hawk of the Wilderness *Lost Island of Kioga* 1938
A man, shipwrecked as an infant and reared on a remote island by native Indians, battles modern day pirates after an explorer finds a cache of treasure. Serial in 12 episodes. **213m/B VHS.** Bruce (Herman Brix) Bennett, Mala, William Boyle; **D:** William Witney. *REP, MLB, VCN*

Hawk the Slayer 🗡½ 1981 A comic book fantasy. A good warrior struggles against his villainous brother to possess a magical sword that bestows upon its holder great powers of destruction. Violent battle scenes; Palance makes a great villain. **93m/C VHS, Beta, LV.** Jack Palance, John Terry, Harry Andrews, Roy Kinnear, Ferdinand "Ferdy" Mayne; **D:** Terry Marcel. **ART**

Hawken's Breed 🗡🗡 1987 **(R)** Drifter meets American Indian beauty and hears her tale of woe; the two fall for each other and set out together to avenge the murder of the woman's husband and son. Nothing much to crow about. **93m/C VHS, Beta,** Serene Hedin, Jack Elam; **D:** Charles B. Pierce. **THV, IME**

Hawkeye 🗡½ 1988 After his best friend is murdered by gangsters in a seedy drug deal, Hawkeye, a rough and tumble Texas cop, and his slick new partner hit the streets of Las Vegas with a vengeance. **90m/C VHS, Beta.** Troy Donahue, Chuck Jeffreys, George Chung, Stan Wertlieb; **D:** Leo Fong. **NO**

Hawkeye: Premiere Episode 1995 Frontier scout Hawkeye (Horsley) and best friend Chingachgook (Grant) come to the aid of Elizabeth Shields (Carter), whose trading post owner husband has been captured during the French and Indian war. **82m/C VHS.** Lee Horsley, Rodney Grant, Lynda Carter. **MOV**

Hawks 🗡½ 1989 **(R)** Somewhere on the road to black-comedy this film gets waylaid by triviality. Two terminally ill men break out of the hospital, determined to make their way to Amsterdam for some last-minute fun. Mediocre at best. **105m/C VHS, Beta, LV, 8mm, Closed Caption.** **GB** Anthony Edwards, Timothy Dalton, Janet McTeer, Jill Bennett, Sheila Hancock, Connie Booth, Camille Coduri; **D:** Robert Ellis Miller; **W:** Roy Clarke. **PAR**

The Hawks & the Sparrows 🗡🗡 Uccellacci e Uccellini 1967 Shortly after "Mr. Ed" came Pasolini's garrulous crow, which follows a father and son's travels through Italy spouting pithy bits of politics. A comic Pasolinian allegory-fest full of then-topical political allusions, the story comes off a bit wooden. Worth watching to see Toto, the Italian comic, in his element. **91m/B VHS, LV, Letterbox.** **IT** Toto, Ninetto Davoli, Femi Benussi; **D:** Pier Paolo Pasolini; **W:** Pier Paolo Pasolini; **M:** Ennio Morricone. **WBF**

Hawk's Vengeance 🗡🗡 1996 **(R)** While investigating his police detective stepbrother's murder British Royal Marine Lt. Eric "Hawk" Kelly (Daniels) discovers a bizarre connection between a skinhead gang called the Death Skulls, a martial arts master crime boss (Magda), and the black market organ trade. **96m/C VHS, LV, Closed Caption.** Gary Daniels, Cass Magda. **TOU**

Hawmps! woof! 1976 **(G)** Idiotic comedy about a Civil War lieutenant who trains his men to use camels. When the soldiers and animals begin to grow fond of each other, Congress orders the camels to be set free. Hard to believe this was based on a real life incident. **98m/C VHS, Beta.** James Hampton, Christopher Connelly, Slim Pickens, Denver Pyle; **D:** Joe Camp; **W:** William Bickley; **M:** Euel Box. **VES**

Hawthorne of the USA 🗡🗡½ 1919 Reid stars as Anthony Hamilton Hawthorne, American extraordinaire. After gambling a fortune away in Monte Carlo, Hawthorne heads to mainland Europe for rest and revelry. Instead, he finds the love of a princess and a Communist coup in the making. Silent with orchestral score. **55m/B VHS, Beta.** Wallace Reid, Harrison Ford, Lila Lee, Tully Marshall; **D:** James Cruze. **GPV**

Hazel's People 🗡½ 1975 **(G)** Bitter and hostile college student attends his friend's funeral in Mennonite country. He discovers not only a way of life he never knew existed, but a personal faith in a living Christ. From the Merle Good novel, "Happy as the Grass Was Green." **105m/C VHS, Beta.** Geraldine Page, Pat Hingle, Graham Beckel, Charles Davis. **VCI**

He Got Game 🗡🗡½ 1998 **(R)** Lee hops all over the place with this basketball drama that reveals more of his love for the game than cohesive filmmaking. Actually two movies in one: High school basketball great Jesus Shuttlesworth (newcomer and Milwaukee Bucks player Allen) must decide between college or a lucrative NBA contract. Then up pops his incarcerated pops, Jake, (a haggard Washington) to pressure him to chose his warden's alma mater, which turns the film into a shallow look at a strained father-son relationship. Washington is dynamic as the embittered father and Allen is evenly effective. Yet, the reunion is never fully developed and sometimes abandoned, while Lee scores visually by beautifully photographing the glorious hoop moves. Extraneous, stereotypical characters and raunchy sex sequences drag the film further from its dramatic resonance. **CW:** Pervasive language, strong sexuality, some drug content and violence. **134m/C VHS.** Denzel Washington, Ray Allen, Milla Jovovich, Rosario Dawson, Hill Harper, Zelda Harris, Jim Brown, Ned Beatty, Lonette McKee, John Turturro, Michele Shay, Thomas Jefferson Byrd; **D:** Spike Lee; **W:** Spike Lee; **C:** Malik Hassan Sayeed; **M:** Aaron Copland. **NYR**

He Is My Brother 🗡½ 1975 **(G)** Two boys survive a shipwreck, landing on an island that houses a leper colony. **90m/C VHS, Beta.** Keenan Wynn, Bobby Sherman, Robbie Rist; **D:** Edward Dmytryk. **NO**

He Kills Night After Night After Night 🗡½ 1970 British police are baffled as they seek the man who has been killing women in the style of Jack the Ripper. And he keeps doing it. **88m/C VHS, Beta.** Jack May, Linda Marlowe, Justine Lord. **NO**

He Knows You're Alone 🗡 1980 **(R)** Lame horror flick that focuses on a psychotic killer terrorizing a bride-to-be and her bridal party in his search for a suitable bride of his own. **94m/C VHS, Beta.** Don Scardino, Caitlin Kathleen Heaney O'Heaney, Tom Rolfing, Paul Gleason, Elizabeth Kemp, Tom Hanks, Patsy Pease, Lewis Arlt, James Rebhorn, Joseph Leon, James Carroll; **D:** Armand Mastroianni; **W:** Scott Parker; **C:** Gerald Feil. **MGM**

He Lives: The Search for the Evil One 🗡 1988 A man who was imprisoned by Nazis as a child attempts to keep Hitler, now living in Buenos Aires, from starting a 4th Reich. **90m/C VHS, Beta.** Lee Patterson. **NO**

He Said, She Said 🗡🗡½ 1991 **(R)** Romance is the topic, but this isn't a typical dating film, instead a couple's relationship unfolds from differing points of view: first, the guy's (by Kwapis) and then the girl's (by Silver). Bacon and Perkins, Baltimore journalists and professional rivals, tell how their romance wound up on the rocks, and why (or so they say). The end result is overlong and lacks the zing of other war between the sexes movies, but real-life couple Silver and Kwapis do humorously highlight the fact that men and women often view the same incidents very differently. Bacon overacts, Perkins overreacts, and Stone shines as Bacon's ex-girl. **115m/C VHS, LV, Letterbox, Closed Caption.** Elizabeth Perkins, Kevin Bacon, Sharon Stone, Nathan Lane, Anthony LaPaglia, Stanley Anderson, Charlaine Woodard, Danton Stone, Phil Leeds, Rita Karin; **D:** Marisa Silver, Ken Kwapis; **W:** Brian Hohlfield; **C:** Stephen Burum; **M:** Miles Goodman. **PAR, CCB**

He Walked by Night 🗡🗡🗡½ 1948 Los Angeles homicide investigators track down cop killer Ray Morgan (Basehart) in this excellent drama. The final confrontation takes place in the L.A. County Flood Control System, consisting of some 700 miles of underground tunnels. Based on a true story from the files of the Los Angeles police, this first rate production reportedly inspired Webb to create "Dragnet." **80m/B VHS.** Richard Basehart, Scott Brady, Roy Roberts, Jack Webb, Whit Bissell; **D:** Alfred Werker, Anthony Mann; **C:** John Alton. **KIV, NOS, BAR**

He Who Gets Slapped 🗡🗡🗡 1924 Chaney portrays a brilliant scientist whose personal and professional humiliations cause him to join a travelling French circus as a masochistic clown (hence the title). There he falls in love with a beautiful circus performer and plans a spectacular revenge. Brilliant use of lighting and Expressionist devices by director Sjostrom (who used the Americanized version of his name-Seastrom-in the credits). Adapted from the Russian play "He, The One Who Gets Slapped" by Leonid Andreyev. **85m/B VHS.** Lon Chaney Sr., Norma Shearer, John Gilbert, Tully Marshall, Ford Sterling, Marc McDermott; **D:** Victor Sjostrom; **W:** Carey Wilson, Victor Sjostrom. **FCT**

He Who Walks Alone 1978 Made-for-television film documents the life of Thomas E. Gilmore, who became the South's first elected black sheriff in the 1960s. **74m/C VHS, Beta.** Louis Gossett Jr., Clu Gulager, Mary Alice, James McEachin, Barton Heyman, Barry Brown, Lonny Chapman; **D:** Jerrold Freedman. **NO**

The Head 🗡🗡 1959 A scientist comes up with a serum that can keep the severed head of a dog alive. Before too long, he tries the stuff out on a woman, transferring the head from her own hunchbacked body to that of a beautiful stripper. Weird German epic sports poor special effects and unintentional laughs, but is interesting nonetheless. **92m/B VHS.** **GE** Horst Frank, Michel Simon, Paul Dahlke, Karin Kernke, Helmut Schmidt; **D:** Victor Trivas; **W:** Victor Trivas. **SNC**

Head 🗡🗡🗡 1968 **(G)** Infamously plotless musical comedy starring the television fab four of the '60s, the Monkees, in their only film appearance. A number of guest stars appear and a collection of old movie clips are also included. ♫ Circle Sky; Can You Dig It; Long Title: Do I Have To Do This All Over Again; Daddy's Song; As We Go Along; The Porpoise Song. **86m/C VHS, Beta, LV.** Peter Tork, Mickey Dolenz, Davy Jones, Michael Nesmith, Frank Zappa, Annette Funicello, Teri Garr; **D:** Bob Rafelson; **W:** Jack Nicholson, Bob Rafelson. **RHI, COL, MVD**

Head Above Water 🗡🗡 1996 **(PG-13)** Remake of same-titled 1993 Norwegian black comedy is now set on an island off the Maine coast where marrieds Nathalie (Diaz) and George (Keitel) are vacationing at her family's cottage. George goes off on an overnight fishing trip, but Nathalie isn't alone for long—former boyfriend Kent (Zane) shows up, the duo get drunk catching up on old times, and Nathalie wakes up the next morning with Kent's corpse. The unstable Nathalie hides the body, which is quickly found by George, who discards the corpse in a more permanent manner involving cement. Then Natalie suddenly decides George must have murdered Kent and is now after her. Plot doesn't hang together well and Keitel is frequently too low-key but Diaz is watchable. **CW:** Thematic elements and some moments of strong violence. **92m/C VHS, LV, Closed Caption.** Cameron Diaz, Harvey Keitel, Craig Sheffer, Billy Zane; **D:** Jim Wilson; **W:** Theresa Marie; **C:** Richard Bowen; **M:** Christopher Young. **NLC**

Head of the Family 🗡🗡½ 1971 **(PG)** After a woman sacrifices her political ideals and career goals for her role as a family matriarch, she eventually falls apart. **105m/C VHS, Beta.** **IT FR** Nino Manfredi, Leslie Caron, Ugo Tognazzi, Claudine Auger; **D:** Nanni Loy; **W:** Nanni Loy. **GEM**

Head of the Family 🗡½ 1996 **(R)** Lance (Bailey) moves to Nob Hollow and discovers the Stackpool family's dreadful secrets—they're telepathic quadruplets under the control of brother Myron (Perra), who just happens to be a giant head that gets around in a wheelchair. Lance decides to use the whacko family to get rid of babe girlfriend Loretta's (Lovell) inconvenient husband. **CW:** Language, nudity, violence, sexual situations. **82m/C VHS.** Blake Bailey, Jacqueline Lovell, Bob Schott, J.W. Perra; **D:** Robert Talbot; **W:** Benjamin Carr; **C:** Adolfo Bartoli; **M:** Richard Band. **AFE**

Head Office 🎬🎬 1986 (PG-13) A light comedy revolving around the competition between corporate management and the lower echelon for the available position of chairman. 90m/C VHS, Beta. Danny DeVito, Eddie Albert, Judge Reinhold, Rick Moranis, Jane Seymour; **D:** Ken Finkleman; **M:** James Newton Howard. NO

Head Over Heels 🎬🎬🎬 1967 A model married to an older man has an affair with a younger one and cannot decide between them. In French with subtitles. 89m/C VHS, Beta. FR Brigitte Bardot, Laurent Terzieff, Michael Sarne; **D:** Serge Bourguignon. FCT

Head Winds 🎬🎬 1925 Silent romance in which Mr. Right spares helpless girl against her will from marrying Mr. Wrong. 52m/B VHS, Beta. House Peters Sr., Patsy Ruth Miller. GPV

Headhunter 🎬½ 1989 Voodoo-esque killers are leaving headless bodies all around Miami. Plenty of prosthetic make-up. 92m/C VHS, Beta, LV. Kay Lenz, Wayne Crawford, John Fatooh, Steve Kanaly, June Chadwick, Sam Williams; **D:** Francis Schaeffer. IME

Headin' for the Rio Grande 🎬 1936 A cowboy and his sheriff brother drive off cattle-rustlers in this Western saga. Ritter's film debut. Songs include "Campfire Love Song," "Jailhouse Lament," and "Night Herding Song." 60m/B VHS, Beta. Tex Ritter, Eleanor Stewart, Syd Saylor, Warner Richmond, Charles "Blackie" King; **D:** Robert North Bradbury. NOS, DVT

Heading for Heaven 🎬🎬 1947 A mistaken medical report leaves a frazzled realtor believing he has only three months to live, and when he disappears the family suspects the worst. A minor comedy based on a play by Charles Webb. 65m/B VHS. Stuart Erwin, Glenda Farrell, Russ Vincent, Irene Ryan, Milburn Stone, George O'Hanlon; **D:** Lewis D. Collins. NOS

Heading Home 🎬🎬½ 1924 A very early version of the Babe Ruth story—starring none other than the Babe himself. A fair print, this film is orchestra scored. 56m/B VHS, Beta. Babe Ruth. GPV

Headless Body in Topless Bar 🎬🎬½ 1996 Based on a famous New York Post headline and the crime that inspired it, this black comedy contains more than its lurid title lets on. Except for street footage at the opening and closing, the entire movie is set in a seedy strip club. After shooting the bartender in a robbery attempt, a crazed ex-con holds the patrons and employees hostage. He forces them to play a mind game called "Nazi truth," revealing the distasteful truth about the captives. Director Bruce and screenwriter Koper first worked together filming re-creations for "America's Most Wanted." The cast worked for "hostage scale," meaning if those playing captives stole the gun from the robber (a plot point), they got his pay for the day. If not, then he got their wages. 105m/C VHS. Raymond J. Barry, Jennifer MacDonald, David Selby, Taylor Nichols, Paul Williams, Biff Yeager, Rustam Branaman, April Grace; **D:** James Bruce; **W:** Peter Koper; **C:** Kevin Morrisey; **M:** Charles T. Barnett. NYR

Headless Eyes 🎬½ 1983 Gory entry into the psycho-artist category. An artist is miffed when mistaken by a woman as a burglar he loses an eye. Not one to forgive and forget, he becomes quite the eyeball fetishist, culling donations from unsuspecting women. An eye for an eye ad finitum. 78m/C VHS. Bo Brundin, Gordon Raman, Mary Jane Early; **D:** Kent Bateman; **W:** Kent Bateman. NO

Headline Woman 🎬🎬 1935 An ongoing feud between a police commissioner and a newspaper's city editor causes a reporter to make a deal with a policeman in exchange for news. A good cast makes this otherwise tired story tolerable. 75m/B VHS, Beta. Heather Angel, Roger Pryor, Jack LaRue, Ford Sterling, Conway Tearle; **D:** William Nigh. NOS, DVT, HEG

Heads 🎬🎬½ 1993 (R) Unassuming conv-reader Guy Franklin (Cryer) gets promoted to reporter and his first assignment is a doozy. He's to cover a series of decapitation murders in a small town. Can he do the job without become the next victim—or being accused of the crimes? Made for cable TV; filmed in Manitoba, Canada. 102m/C VHS, Closed Caption. CA Jon Cryer, Jennifer Tilly, Ed Asner, Roddy McDowall; **D:** Paul Shapiro; **W:** Adam Brooks; **M:** Jonathan Goldsmith. REP

Healer 🎬½ Little Pal 1936 A doctor forgets his pledge to help the lame and becomes a fashionable physician. A young crippled lad helps him eventually remember his original purpose was to serve others. 80m/B VHS, Beta. Mickey Rooney, Ralph Bellamy, Karen Morley, Judith Allen, Robert McWade; **D:** Reginald Barker. DVT

Hear My Song 🎬🎬🎬½ 1991 (R) Mickey O'Neill (Dunbar) is an unscrupulous club promoter, who books singers with names like Franc Cinatra, while trying to revive his failing nightclub in this charming, hilarious comedy. He hires the mysterious Mr. X, who claims he is really the legendary exiled singer Josef Locke, only to find out he is an imposter. To redeem himself with his fiancee and her mother, he goes to Ireland to find the real Locke (Beatty) and bring him to Liverpool to sing. Dunbar is appealing in his role, and Beatty is magnificent as the legendary Locke—so much so that he was nominated for a Golden Globe for Best Supporting Actor. **CW:** Language and one sensual scene. 104m/C VHS, Beta, Closed Caption. GB Ned Beatty, Adrian Dunbar, Shirley Anne Field, Tara Fitzgerald, William Hootkins, David McCallum; **D:** Peter Chelsom; **W:** Peter Chelsom; **M:** John Altman. PAR

Hear No Evil 🎬½ 1993 (R) Below average thriller with a deaf victim (Matlin) involved in a game of cat-and-mouse with a corrupt cop (Sheen) who's looking for a valuable coin. Weak script plays up the woman in jeopardy theme but lacks the crucial element of suspense. A waste of an otherwise talented cast. **CW:** Profanity, brief nudity, violence, and sex. 98m/C VHS, LV, Closed Caption. Marlee Matlin, D.B. Sweeney, Martin Sheen, John C. McGinley, Christina Carlisi, Greg Elam, Charley Lang; **D:** Robert Greenwald; **W:** Randall Badat, Kathleen Rowell; **M:** Graeme Revell. FOX

Hearing Voices 🎬½ 1990 Joyless Erica is a commercial model who suffers from a form of scoliosis. If she capitalized on her infirmity by advertising medical aids, she could make a lot of money but she firmly refuses her lover's pleas to do this. When her doctor suggests reconstructive surgery, she storms out of his office but not before attracting the attention of Lee, his gay lover. Erica and Lee begin a complex emotional relationship, upsetting to everyone around them. Uninvolving characters, inert direction, and amateurish acting work against Greytak's feature film debut. 87m/C VHS. Erika Nagy, Stephen Gatta, Tim Ahearn, Michael Davenport; **D:** Sharon Greytak; **W:** Sharon Greytak. WAC, FCT

The Hearse woof! 1980 (PG) Incredibly boring horror film in which a young school teacher moves into a mansion left to her by her late aunt and finds her life threatened by a sinister black hearse. 97m/C VHS, Beta. Trish Van Devere, Joseph Cotten; **D:** George Bowers; **W:** William Bleich.

The Hearst and Davies Affair 🎬🎬½ 1985 Married, middle-aged newspaper tycoon William Randolph Hearst falls for teenage Ziegfeld girl Marion Davies and tries to turn her into a Hollywood star. Davies was generally thought to be talented as a comedienne but Hearst insisted on choosing ill-suited dramatic roles for the blonde and her career was problematic. Their lavish lifestyle was enhanced when Hearst built San Simeon for Davies and their scandalous affair lasted 35 years. Made for television. 97m/C VHS, Beta. Robert Mitchum, Virginia Madsen, Fritz Weaver; **D:** David Lowell Rich.

Heart 🎬½ 1987 (R) A down-and-out small-time boxer is given a chance to make a comeback, and makes the Rocky-like most of it. 93m/C VHS, Beta. Brad Davis, Jesse Doran, Sam Gray, Steve Buscemi, Frances Fisher; **D:** James Lemmo. VTR

Heart and Souls 🎬🎬½ 1993 (PG-13) Reincarnation comedy casts Downey, Jr., as a mortal whose body is inhabited by four lost souls who died on the night he was born. Now an adult, he must finish what they could not, no matter how outrageous it may be. Talented cast wears plot that's old hat. Downey Jr. must be looking to do a trilogy of tired reincarnated soul roles—this is his second, "Chances Are" was his first. **CW:** Sensuality. 104m/C VHS, LV, Letterbox, Closed Caption. Robert Downey Jr., Charles Grodin, Tom Sizemore, Alfre Woodard, Kyra Sedgwick, Elisabeth Shue, David Paymer; **D:** Ron Underwood; **W:** Brent Maddock, S.S. Wilson, Gregory Hansen, Erik Hansen; **M:** Marc Shaiman. USH, BTV

Heart Beat 🎬🎬½ 1980 (R) The fictionalized story of Jack Kerouac (author of "On the Road"), his friend and inspiration Neal Cassady, and the woman they shared, Carolyn Cassady. Based on Carolyn Cassady's memoirs. Strong performances, with Nolte as Cassady and Spacek as his wife, overcome the sometimes shaky narrative. 105m/C VHS, Beta. Nick Nolte, John Heard, Sissy Spacek, Ann Dusenberry, Ray Sharkey, Tony Bill, Steve Allen, John Larroquette; **D:** John Byrum; **W:** John Byrum; **M:** Jack Nitzsche. WAR

Heart Condition 🎬🎬½ 1990 (R) A deceased black lawyer's heart is donated to a bigoted Los Angeles cop who was stalking the lawyer when he was alive. Soon afterwards the lawyer's ghost returns to haunt the police officer, hoping the officer will help to avenge his murder. Both Hoskins and Washington display fine performances given the unlikely script. 95m/C VHS, Beta, LV. Bob Hoskins, Denzel Washington, Chloe Webb, Ray Baker, Ja'net DuBois, Alan Rachins, Roger E. Mosley, Jeffrey Meek; **D:** James D. Parriott; **C:** Arthur Albert. NLC

The Heart Is a Lonely Hunter 🎬🎬🎬 1968 (G) Set in the South, Carson McCuller's tale of angst and ignorance, loneliness and beauty comes to the screen with the film debuts of Keach and Locke. Arkin gives an instinctive, gentle performance as the deaf mute; Locke's screen debut. 124m/C VHS, Beta, Closed Caption. Alan Arkin, Cicely Tyson, Sondra Locke, Stacy Keach, Chuck McCann, Laurinda Barrett; **D:** Robert Ellis Miller; **J:** James Wong Howe; **M:** Dave Grusin. New York Film Critics Awards '68: Best Actor (Arkin); Nominations: Academy Awards '68: Best Actor (Arkin), Best Supporting Actress (Locke). WAR

Heart Like a Wheel 🎬🎬½ 1983 (PG) The story of Shirley Muldowney, who rose from the daughter of a country-western singer to the leading lady in drag racing. The film follows her battles of sexism and choosing whether to have a career or a family. Bedelia's perfomance is outstanding. Fine showings from Bridges and Axton in supporting roles. 113m/C VHS, Beta, LV, Closed Caption. Bonnie Bedelia, Beau Bridges, Bill McKinney, Leo Rossi, Hoyt Axton, Dick Miller, Anthony Edwards; **D:** Jonathan Kaplan; **W:** Ken Friedman. Nominations: Academy Awards '83: Best Costume Design. FOX

Heart of a Champion: The Ray Mancini Story 🎬🎬 1985 Made-for-TV movie based on the life of Ray "Boom Boom" Mancini, former lightweight boxing champion. Inspired by the career his father never had due to WWII, Mancini fought his way to the top. Sylvester Stallone staged the fight sequences. 94m/C VHS, Beta. Robert (Bobby) Blake, Doug McKeon, Mariclare Costello; **D:** Richard Michaels. FOX

Heart of a Nation 🎬🎬🎬 Untel Pere et Fils 1943 Saga of the Montmarte family and their life during three wars, beginning with the Franco-Prussian War and ending with the Nazi occupation in France. Although ordered to be destroyed by the Nazis, this film was saved, along with many others, by the French "Cinema Resistance." In French with English subtitles. 111m/B VHS. FR Louis

Jouvet, Raimu, Suzy Prim, Michele Morgan, Renee Devillers; **D:** Julien Duvivier. *NOS, DVT, HEG*

Heart of Darkness 🎬🎬 **1993** Joseph Conrad's 1902 menacing novella set in the Belgian Congo is told through flashbacks by Marlow (Roth), whose employers, a Belgian trading company, hire him to find Kurtz (Malkovich), head of a remote trading station, who is rumored to be hoarding a huge cache of ivory. Marlow's journey up the river is beset by obstacles and Kurtz is rumored to be either insane or a prophet in his jungle kingdom. Filmed in Belize; made for television. Francis Ford Coppola's updated adaptation became "Apocalypse Now." **120m/C VHS, LV, Closed Caption.** Tim Roth, John Malkovich, James Fox, Isaach de Bankole, Patrick Ryecart, Geoffrey Hutchings, Peter Vaughan, Phoebe Nicholls, Allan Corduner, Alan Scarfe, Iman, Timothy Bateson; **D:** Nicolas Roeg; **W:** Benedict Fitzgerald; **M:** Stanley Myers. *TTC*

The Heart of Dixie 🎬🎬 **1989 (PG)** Three college co-eds at a southern university in the 1950s see their lives and values change with the influence of the civil rights movement. College newspaper reporter Sheedy takes up the cause of a black man victimized by racial violence. Lightweight social-conscience fare. **96m/C VHS, Beta, LV, Closed Caption.** Virginia Madsen, Ally Sheedy, Phoebe Cates, Treat Williams, Kyle Secor, Francesca Roberts, Barbara Babcock, Don Michael Paul, Kurtwood Smith, Richard Bradford; **D:** Martin Davidson; **C:** Robert Elswit. *ORI*

Heart of Dragon 🎬🎬 **1985** Police officer Chan takes care of his mentally challenged brother Hung, who gets mistaken for a robbery suspect. So Chan has to track down the real crooks. Features a 20-minute fight finale. Chinese with subtitles or dubbed. **85m/C VHS, LV.** *HK* Jackie Chan, Sammo Hung, Emily Chu; **D:** Sammo Hung. *TAI*

Heart of Glass 🎬🎬🎬 **1974** A pre-industrial Bavarian village becomes deeply troubled when their glassblower dies without imparting the secret of making his unique Ruby glass. The townspeople go to extremes, from madness to murder to magic, to discover the ingredients. From German director Herzog (who hypnotized his cast daily), this somewhat apocalyptic tale is based on legend. The colors are incredible in their intensity. In German with English subtitles. **93m/C VHS.** *GE* Josef Bierbichler, Stefan Autter, Scheitz Clemens, Volker Prechtel, Sonia Skiba; **D:** Werner Herzog. *NYF, FCT*

Heart of Humanity **1918** An intense drama of love, patriotism, and sacrifice just before the war in a small Canadian village. A traveler who is really a Prussian army lieutenant finds his way to the house of a young man who is about to wed. He ends up falling in love with his fiancee and war is declared just before the wedding. A silent film with music score. **133m/B VHS, Beta, 8mm.** Dorothy Phillips, Erich von Stroheim; **D:** Allen Holubar. *GPV, VYY, GVV*

Heart of Midnight 🎬🎬½ **1989 (R)** An emotionally unstable young woman inherits a seedy massage parlor. She works hard to turn it, and herself, into something better. Nice performance by Leigh. **93m/C VHS, Beta, LV.** Jennifer Jason Leigh, Brenda Vaccaro, Frank Stallone, Peter Coyote, Gale Mayron, Sam Schacht, Denise Dumont; **D:** Matthew Chapman; **W:** Matthew Chapman; **M:** Yanni. *NO*

Heart of Texas Ryan 🎬½ **1916** Flamboyant cowboy star fights with kidnappers and wins in this silent film. **50m/B VHS, Beta.** Tom Mix. *GPV, NOS, DVT*

Heart of the Golden West 🎬🎬 **1942** Roy protects ranchers of Cherokee City from unjust shipping charges. **65m/B VHS, Beta.** Roy Rogers, Smiley Burnette, George "Gabby" Hayes, Bob Nolan, Ruth Terry; **D:** Joseph Kane. *NOS, VYY, VCN*

Heart of the Rio Grande 🎬½ **1942** Spoiled young rich girl tries to trick her father into coming to her "rescue" at a western dude ranch. **70m/B VHS, Beta.** Gene Autry, Smiley Burnette, Fay McKenzie, Edith Fellows, Joseph Stauch Jr.; **D:** William M. Morgan. *CCB, VCN*

Heart of the Rockies 🎬½ **1937** The Three Mesquiteers stop a mountain family's rustling and illegal game trappers. **54m/B VHS, Beta.** Bob Livingston, Ray Corrigan, Max Terhune, Lynn (Mary Hart) Roberts, Yakima Canutt, J.P. McGowan; **D:** Joseph Kane. *NOS, VCN, VYY*

Heart of the Rockies 🎬½ **1951** Roy, along with his trusty horse and dog, takes care of a highway construction project. **67m/B VHS.** Roy Rogers, Penny Edwards, Gordon Jones, Ralph Morgan, Fred Graham, Mira McKinney; **D:** William Witney. *NOS, DVT, TIM*

Heart of the Stag 🎬🎬½ **1984 (R)** On an isolated sheep ranch in the New Zealand outback, a father and daughter suffer the repercussions of an incestuous relationship when she becomes enamored with a hired hand. **94m/C VHS, Beta, LV.** *NZ* Bruno Lawrence, Mary Regan, Terence Cooper; **D:** Michael Firth. *VTR*

Heartaches 🎬🎬 **1947** A reporter tries to track down a murderer who has killed twice. **71m/B VHS, Beta.** Chill Wills, Sheila Ryan, Edward Norris, James Seay. *NOS, DVT, HEG*

Heartaches 🎬🎬🎬 **1982** A young pregnant woman (Potts) meets up with a crazy girlfriend (Kidder) in this touching film about love and friendship. Although a study in contrasts, the two end up sharing an apartment together in Toronto. Fine performances from Potts and Kidder give life to this romantic comedy. **90m/C VHS, Beta, LV.** *CA* Margot Kidder, Annie Potts, Robert Carradine, Winston Rekert; **D:** Donald Shebib. *ART, VES* Genie Awards '82: Best Actress (Kidder).

Heartbeat 🎬🎬½ **1946** If you thought pointless Hollywood remakes of French films were a new phenomenon (see "Pure Luck," for example), then note this lighthearted remake of a 1940 Gallic farce. Rogers becomes the best student in a Parisian school for pickpockets, but when she tries out her skills on a dashing diplomat they fall in love instead. **100m/B VHS.** Ginger Rogers, Jean-Pierre Aumont, Adolphe Menjou, Basil Rathbone, Melville Cooper, Mona Maris, Henry Stephenson, Eduardo Ciannelli; **D:** Sam Wood; **C:** Joseph Valentine. *NOS, HEG*

Heartbeeps 🎬🎬 **1981 (PG)** In 1995, two domestic robot servants fall in love and run off together. On a beach they encounter the Energizer Bunny. No, that's not right. Young kids may enjoy the romantic robotic duo of Kaufman and Peters. **79m/C VHS, Beta.** Andy Kaufman, Bernadette Peters, Randy Quaid, Kenneth McMillan, Christopher Guest, Melanie Mayron, Jack Carter; **D:** Allan Arkush; **M:** John Williams. Nominations: Academy Awards '81: Best Makeup. *USH*

Heartbreak Hotel 🎬🎬½ **1988 (PG-13)** Johnny Wolfe kidnaps Elvis Presley from his show in Cleveland and drives him home to his mother, a die-hard Elvis fan. Completely unbelievable, utterly ridiculous, and still a lot of fun. **101m/C VHS, Beta, LV, Closed Caption.** David Keith, Tuesday Weld, Charlie Schlatter, Angela Goethals, Jacque Lynn Colton, Chris Mulkey, Karen Landry, Tudor Sherrard, Paul Harkins; **D:** Chris Columbus; **W:** Chris Columbus; **M:** Georges Delerue. *TOU*

Heartbreak House 🎬🎬½ **1986** A production of George Bernard Shaw's classic play about a captain and his daughter who invite an odd assortment of people into their home for a few days. In the course of their visit, each person shares his ambitions, hopes, and fears. From the "American Playhouse" television series. **118m/C VHS, Beta.** Rex Harrison, Rosemary Harris, Amy Irving; **D:** Anthony Page. *PBS*

The Heartbreak Kid 🎬🎬🎬 **1972 (PG)** Director May's comic examination of love and hypocrisy. Grodin embroils himself in a triangle with his new bride and a woman he can't have, an absolutely gorgeous and totally unloving woman he shouldn't want. Walks the fence between tragedy and comedy, with an exceptional performance from Berlin. Based on Bruce Jay Friedman's story. **106m/C VHS, Beta, LV.** Charles Grodin, Cybill Shepherd, Eddie Albert, Jeannie Berlin, Audra Lindley, Art Metrano; **D:** Elaine May; **W:** Neil Simon; **C:** Owen

Roizman. New York Film Critics Awards '72: Best Supporting Actress (Berlin); National Society of Film Critics Awards '72: Best Supporting Actor (Albert), Best Supporting Actress (Berlin); Nominations: Academy Awards '72: Best Supporting Actor (Albert), Best Supporting Actress (Berlin). *VTR*

Heartbreak Ridge 🎬🎬🎬 **1986 (R)** An aging Marine recon sergeant is put in command of a young platoon to whip them into shape to prepare for combat in the invasion of Grenada. Eastwood whips this old story into shape too, with a fine performance of a man who's given everything to the Marines. The invasion of Grenada, though, is not epic material. (Also available in English with Spanish subtitles.) **130m/C VHS, Beta, LV, 8mm, Closed Caption.** Clint Eastwood, Marsha Mason, Everett McGill, Arlen Dean Snyder, Bo Svenson, Moses Gunn, Eileen Heckart, Boyd Gaines, Mario Van Peebles; **D:** Clint Eastwood; **W:** Jim Carabatsos; **C:** Jack N. Green; **M:** Lennie Niehaus. Nominations: Academy Awards '86: Best Sound. *WAR, TLF*

Heartbreaker 🎬½ **1983 (R)** Eastern Los Angeles explodes with vicious turf wars when Beto and Hector battle for the affection of Kim, the neighborhood's newest heartbreaker. **90m/C VHS, Beta, LV.** Fernando Allende, Dawn Dunlap, Michael D. Roberts, Robert Dryer, Apollonia; **D:** Frank Zuniga.

Heartbreakers 🎬🎬🎬 **1984 (R)** Two male best friends find themselves in the throes of drastic changes in their careers and romantic encounters. On target acting makes this old story new, with a fine performance by Wayne, in her last film before her death. **98m/C VHS, Beta.** Peter Coyote, Nick Mancuso, Carole Laure, Max Gail, James Laurenson, Carol Wayne, Jamie Rose, Kathryn Harrold; **D:** Bobby Roth; **W:** Bobby Roth; **C:** Michael Ballhaus; **M:** Tangerine Dream. *VES*

Heartburn 🎬🎬🎬 **1986 (R)** Based on Nora Ephron's own semi-autobiographical novel about her marital travails with writer Carl Bernstein, this is a tepid, bitter modern romance between writers already shell-shocked from previous marriages. **109m/C VHS, Beta, LV, 8mm, Closed Caption.** Meryl Streep, Jack Nicholson, Steven Hill, Richard Masur, Stockard Channing, Jeff Daniels, Milos Forman, Catherine O'Hara, Maureen Stapleton, Karen Akers, Joanna Gleason, Mercedes Ruehl, Caroline Aaron, Yakov Smirnoff, Anna Maria Horsford, Wilfrid Hyde-White; **D:** Mike Nichols; **W:** Nora Ephron; **C:** Nestor Almendros; **M:** Carly Simon. *PAR*

Heartland 🎬🎬🎬½ **1981 (PG)** Set in 1910, this film chronicles the story of one woman's life on the Wyoming Frontier, the hazards she faces, and her courage and spirit. Stunningly realistic and without cliche. Based on the diaries of Elinore Randall Stewart. **95m/C VHS, Beta.** Conchata Ferrell, Rip Torn, Barry Primus, Lilia Skala, Megan Folson; **D:** Richard Pearce. Sundance Film Festival '81: Grand Jury Prize. *NO*

Hearts & Armour 🎬🎬 **1983** A holy war between Christians and Moors erupts when a Moorish princess is kidnapped. Based on Ludovico Ariosto's "Orlando Furioso." **101m/C VHS, Beta.** *IT* Tanya Roberts, Leigh McCloskey, Ron Moss, Rick Edwards, Giovanni Visentin; **D:** Giacomo Battiato. *WAR*

Heart's Desire 🎬½ **1937** Opera great Tauber stars in this musical of an unknown Viennese singer who falls in love with an English girl. **79m/B VHS, Beta.** *GB* Richard Tauber, Lenora Corbett, Kathleen Kelly, Paul Graetz; **D:** Paul Stein. *NO*

Heart's Haven 🎬🎬½ **1922** An insensitive wife (Adams), who doesn't appreciate how wonderful her husband is, winds up running away with another man. **61m/B VHS, Beta.** Claire Adams, Robert McKim, Carl Gantvoort, Jean Hersholt; **D:** Benjamin B. Hampton. *GPV, FCT*

Hearts of Darkness: A Filmmaker's Apocalypse 🎬🎬🎬🎬 **1991 (R)** This riveting, critically acclaimed documentary about the making of Francis Ford Coppola's masterpiece "Apocalypse Now" is based largely on original footage shot and directed by his wife Eleanor. Also included are recent interviews with cast and crew members including Coppola, Martin Sheen, Robert Duvall, Frederic Forrest and Dennis Hopper. **CW:**

Language. **96m/C VHS, Beta, Closed Caption.** Sam Bottoms, Eleanor Coppola, Francis Ford Coppola, Robert Duvall, Laurence "Larry" Fishburne, Frederic Forrest, Albert Hall, Dennis Hopper, George Lucas, John Milius, Martin Sheen; *D:* Fax Bahr, George Hickenlooper; *W:* Fax Bahr, George Hickenlooper; *M:* Todd Boekelheide. National Board of Review Awards '91: Best Feature Documentary. *PAR*

Hearts of Fire 🎬 **1987** A trio of successful rock 'n' roll stars work out their confused romantic entanglements. Barely released at all, and not even in the U.S. Sad outing for the cast, especially legendary Dylan. **90m/C VHS, Beta, LV, Closed Caption.** Bob Dylan, Fiona, Rupert Everett, Julian Glover; *D:* Richard Marquand; *W:* Joe Eszterhas; *M:* John Barry. *ORI, WAR*

Hearts of Humanity 🎬🎬 **1932** Mawkish melodrama concerning a Jewish antique dealer and his relationship with the son of an Irish cop. An early "Chico and the Man" variant. **56m/B VHS.** Jean Hersholt, Jackie Searl, J. Farrell MacDonald, Claudia Dell, Charles Delaney, Lucille LaVerne, George Humbert; *D:* Christy Cabanne. *NOS, HEG*

Hearts of the West 🎬🎬🎬½ *Hollywood Cowboy* **1975 (PG)** A fantasy-filled farm boy travels to Hollywood in the 1930s and seeks a writing career. Instead, he finds himself an ill-suited western movie star in this small offbeat comedy-drama that's sure to charm. **103m/C VHS, Beta.** Jeff Bridges, Andy Griffith, Donald Pleasence, Alan Arkin, Blythe Danner; *D:* Howard Zieff; *W:* Rob Thompson. New York Film Critics Awards '75: Best Supporting Actor (Arkin). *MGM*

Hearts of the World 🎬🎬🎬 **1918** A vintage Griffith epic about a young boy who goes off to WWI and the tribulations endured by both him and his family on the homefront. Overly sentimental but powerfully made melodrama, from Griffith's waning years. Silent with music score. **152m/B VHS, Beta, LV, 8mm.** Lillian Gish, Robert "Bobbie" Harron, Dorothy Gish, Erich von Stroheim, Ben Alexander, Josephine Crowell, Noel Coward, Mary Gish; *D:* D.W. Griffith. *GPV, REP, GVV*

Heartstopper 🎬 **1992** Benjamin Latham, an innocent physician in Pittsburgh, was accused of being a vampire in colonial times and hung. 200 years later, he emerges from the grave, unscathed. While trying to figure out what has happened, he falls in love with a photojournalist, who helps him find his own descendent, Matthew Latham. Unfortunately, his deep freeze has left him with the compulsion to kill, but only evil members of society. **96m/B VHS.** Moon Zappa, Tom Savini, Kevin Kindlan. *TEM, MOV*

Heartstrings 🎬🎬 **1995** Melissa wants everything in her life to be perfect, including having the perfect man, which she thinks is New York gallery owner Peter. But will Melissa's heart compromise her ambitions? **94m/C VHS.** Michelle Little, Phyllis Diller. *SWI*

Heat 🎬🎬🎬 **1972** Another Andy Warhol-produced journey into drug-addled urban seediness. Features a former child actor/junkie and a has-been movie star barely surviving in a run-down motel. This is one of Warhol's better film productions; even non-fans may enjoy it. **102m/C VHS, Beta.** Joe Dallesandro, Sylvia Miles, Pat Ast; *D:* Paul Morrissey. *TPV, PAR, FCT*

Heat 🎬½ **1987 (R)** A Las Vegas bodyguard avenges the beating of an old flame by a mobster's son, and incites mob retaliation. Based on the William Goldman novel. **103m/C VHS, Beta, LV, Closed Caption.** Burt Reynolds, Karen Young, Peter MacNicol, Howard Hesseman; *D:* R.M. Richards; *W:* William Goldman; *M:* Michael Gibbs. *PAR*

Heat 🎬🎬🎬½ **1995 (R)** Pacino and De Niro in the same scene. Together. Finally. Obsessive master thief McCauley (De Niro) leads a crack crew on various military-style heists across L.A. while equally obsessive detective Hanna (Pacino) tracks him. Each man recognizes and respects the other's ability and dedication, even as they express the willingness to kill each other, if neces-

sary. Excellent script with all the fireworks you'd expect, as well as a surprising look into emotional and personal sacrifice. Beautiful cinematography shows industrial landscape to great effect. Writer-director Mann held onto the screenplay for 12 years. *CW:* Violence and language. **171m/C VHS, LV, Closed Caption.** Robert De Niro, Al Pacino, Val Kilmer, Jon Voight, Diane Venora, Ashley Judd, Mykelti Williamson, Amy Brenneman, Ted Levine, Dennis Haysbert, William Fichtner, Natalie Portman, Hank Azaria, Henry Rollins, Kevin Gage; *Cameos:* Tone Loc, Bud Cort, Jeremy Piven; *D:* Michael Mann; *W:* Michael Mann; *C:* Dante Spinotti; *M:* Elliot Goldenthal. *WAR*

Heat and Dust 🎬🎬🎬 **1982 (R)** A young bride joins her husband at his post in India and is inexorably drawn to the country and its prince of state. Years later her great niece journeys to modern day India in search of the truth about her scandalous and mysterious relative. More than the story of two romances, this is the tale of women rebelling against an unseen caste system which keeps them second-class citizens. Ruth Jhabvala wrote the novel and screenplay. **130m/C VHS, Beta.** *GB* Julie Christie, Greta Scacchi, Shashi Kapoor, Christopher Cazenove, Nickolas Grace, Julian Glover, Susan Fleetwood, Patrick Godfrey, Jennifer Kendal, Madhur Jaffrey, Barry Foster, Amanda Walker, Sudha Chopra, Sajid Khan, Zakir Hussain, Ratna Pathak, Charles McCaughan, Parveen Paul; *D:* James Ivory; *W:* Ruth Prawer Jhabvala, Saeed Jaffrey, Harish Khare; *C:* Walter Lassally; *M:* Richard Robbins. British Academy Awards '83: Best Adapted Screenplay. *USH*

Heat and Sunlight 🎬½ **1987** A photographer becomes obsessively jealous of his lover as their relationship comes to an end. Director Nilsson again used a unique improvisational, video-to-film technique, as he did with his previous film, "Signal 7." **98m/B VHS, Beta, LV.** Rob Nilsson, Consuelo Faust, Bill Bailey, Don Bajema, Ernie Fosselius; *D:* Rob Nilsson; *W:* Rob Nilsson; *M:* Mark Adler. Sundance Film Festival '88: Grand Jury Prize. *CVC*

Heat of Desire 🎬🎬 *Plein Sud* **1984 (R)** A philosophy professor abandons everything (including his wife) for a woman he barely knows and is conned by her "relatives." With English subtitles. **90m/C VHS, Beta, LV.** *FR* Clio Goldsmith, Patrick Dewaere, Jeanne Moreau, Guy Marchand; *D:* Luc Beraud. *COL*

The Heat of the Day 🎬🎬½ **1991** A British officer is accused of treason. As he attempts to find those who framed him, he meets a lovely woman all too willing to help. But whose side is she really on? Set in WWII. Tense and well-acted; made for TV. **120m/C VHS, Closed Caption.** Michael York, Patricia Hodge, Peggy Ashcroft, Anna Carteret, Michael Gambon; *W:* Harold Pinter. *VTR, PBS, FCT*

Heat of the Flame 🎬 **1982** A vicious woodsman captures and rapes a beautiful girl. Psychological games, eroticism and exploitive nudity ensue. **88m/C VHS, Beta.** Tony Ferrandis, Ellie MacLure, Raymond Young, Anthony Mayans. *VCD*

Heat Street 🎬 **1987** Two thugs exact revenge on street gangs for the murders of loved ones. Made for video. **90m/C VHS, Beta.** Quincy Adams, Deborah Gibson, Wendy MacDonald, Del Zamora; *D:* Joseph Merhi. *HHE*

Heat Wave 🎬½ **1954** A writer gets involved with a "femme fatale" who kills her wealthy husband for the love of a young pianist. **60m/B VHS, Beta, LV.** *GB* Alex Nicol, Hillary Brooke, Sidney James, Susan Stephen, Paul Carpenter; *D:* Ken Hughes; *W:* Ken Hughes. *NO*

Heat Wave 🎬🎬🎬 **1990 (R)** The Watts ghetto uprising of 1965 is a proving ground for a young black journalist. Excellent cast and fine script portrays the anger and frustration of blacks in Los Angeles and the U.S. in the 1960s and the fear of change felt by blacks and whites when civil rights reform began. Strong drama with minimal emotionalism. Made for cable TV. **92m/C VHS, Beta, Closed Caption.** Blair Underwood, Cicely Tyson, James Earl Jones, Sally Kirkland, Margaret Avery, David Strath-

aim, Robert Hooks, Adam Arkin, Paris Vaughan, Charlie Korsmo. *TTC*

Heated Vengeance 🎬 **1987 (R)** A Vietnam vet returns to the jungle to find the woman he left behind, and runs into some old enemies. **91m/C VHS, Beta.** Richard Hatch, Michael J. Pollard, Mills Watson, Cameron Dye; *D:* Edward Murphy.

Heathers 🎬🎬🎬½ **1989 (R)** Clique of stuck-up girls named Heather rule the high school social scene until the newest member (not a Heather) decides that enough is enough. She and her outlaw boyfriend embark (accidentally on her part, intentionally on his) on a murder spree disguised as a rash of teen suicides. Dense, take-no-prisoners black comedy with buckets of potent slang, satire and unforgiving hostility. Humor this dark is rare; sharply observed and acted, though the end is out of place. Slater does his best Nicholson impression. **102m/C VHS, Beta, LV, Closed Caption.** Winona Ryder, Christian Slater, Kim Walker, Shannen Doherty, Lisanne Falk, Penelope Milford, Glenn Shadix, Lance Fenton, Patrick Laborteaux, Jeremy Applegate, Renee Estevez; *D:* Michael Lehmann; *W:* Daniel Waters; *C:* Francis Kenny; *M:* David Newman. Independent Spirit Awards '90: Best First Feature. *VTR, FCT*

The Heat's On 🎬 *Tropicana* **1943** Gaxton is a broadway producer with a failing musical and an unhappy star in West. He cranks up the publicity machine and gets the show declared immoral by the Legion of Purity which results in its closing (not what he expected). Gaxton then runs a scam to become the producer of West's new show, which just happens to be financed by some Legion members. Very uneven plot and performances with thrown-in musical numbers. West wrote her own dialogue but unlike her early films she had little control over the production and it showed. West didn't make another movie for 27 years (the appalling "Myra Breckenridge"). 🎵 Just a Stranger in Town; Hello, Mi Amigo; The White Keys and the Black Keys; There Goes That Guitar; Antonio; The Caissons Go Rolling Along; There Goes My Heart. **79m/B VHS.** Mae West, William Gaxton, Victor Moore, Almira Sessions, Lester Allen, Mary Roche, Alan Dinehart, Lloyd Bridges; *D:* Gregory Ratoff; *W:* Fitzroy Davis, George S. George, Fred Schiller. *FCT*

Heatseeker 🎬🎬 **1995 (R)** Corporations use mechanical fighters to participate in brutal kickboxing contests in 2019 New America. Human Chance (Cooke) must battle cyborg opponent Xao if he wants to save his kidnapped trainer. Lots of action and even some intentional humor. *CW:* Martial arts violence; some sexuality and language. **91m/C VHS.** Keith Cooke, Gary Daniels, Norbert Weisser, Thom Mathews; *D:* Albert Pyun. *THV*

Heatwave 🎬🎬🎬 **1983 (R)** Local residents oppose a multi-million dollar residential complex in Australia. Davis portrays a liberal activist, who wages war with the developers, and, in return, becomes involved with a possible murder case. **92m/C VHS, Beta.** *AU* Judy Davis, Richard Moir, Chris Haywood, Bill Hunter, John Gregg, Anna Jemison; *D:* Phillip Noyce. *NO*

Heaven 🎬🎬 **1987 (PG-13)** An exploration of "heaven" including the idea, the place, and people's views about it. Questions such as "How do you get there?" and "What goes on up there?" are discussed. Offbeat interviews mixed with a collage of celestial images. **80m/C VHS, Beta, LV.** *D:* Diane Keaton; *M:* Howard Shore. *LTY, FCT*

Heaven & Earth 🎬🎬🎬 **1990 (PG-13)** A samurai epic covering the battle for the future of Japan between two feuding warlords. The overwhelming battle scenes were actually filmed on location in Canada. In Japanese with English subtitles. **104m/C VHS, LV.** *JP* Masahiko Tsugawa, Takaai Enoki, Atsuko Asano, Tsunehiko Watase, Naomi Zaizen, Binpachi Ito. *ART*

Heaven and Earth 🎬🎬 **1993 (R)** Conclusion of Stone's Vietnam trilogy (after "Platoon" and "Born on the Fourth of July") focuses on Vietnamese woman (film debut of Le) and her life under the French and American occupations. Jones is the American soldier who marries her and eventually brings her to the U.S. Not one for subtleties, Stone chases melodramatic excess with finesse of lumberjack, sawing away at guilt and remorse from a "woman's point of view." Cranky Tommy Lee shows up too late to save flick and is saddled with a perplexing I.D. to boot. Flawed, ambitious, and interesting if a student of Stone. Based on the two autobiographies of Le Ly Haslip, "When Heaven and Earth Changed Places" and "Child of War, Woman of Peace." Filmed on location in Thailand.**CW:** Language, violence, and sexuality. **142m/C VHS, LV, Letterbox, Closed Caption.** Hiep Thi Le, Tommy Lee Jones, Joan Chen, Haing S. Ngor, Debbie Reynolds, Conchata Ferrell, Dustin Nguyen, Liem Whatley, Dale Dye; **D:** Oliver Stone; **W:** Oliver Stone; **C:** Robert Richardson; **M:** Kitaro. Golden Globe Awards '94: Best Score. *WAR*

Heaven Before I Die 🎞🎞 1996 **(PG)** Sheltered Jacob (Velasquez) travels from the Middle East to Toronto and is taken under the questionable wing of a small-time thief (Giannini) and a beautiful waitress (Pacula). But when Jacob finds a measure of success as a Charlie Chaplin impersonator, his innocence gets a dose of culture shock. **98m/C VHS, Closed Caption.** *CA* Andy Velasquez, Giancarlo Giannini, Catherine Oxenberg; *Cameos:* Joanna Pacula, Omar Sharif, Burt Young, Joseph Bologna; **D:** Izidore K. Musallam. *PMH*

Heaven Can Wait 🎞🎞🎞 1943 Social satire in which a rogue tries to convince the Devil to admit him to Hell by relating the story of his philandering life and discovers that he was a more valuable human being than he thought. A witty Lubitsch treat based on the play "Birthdays." **112m/C VHS, Beta, LV, Closed Caption.** Don Ameche, Gene Tierney, Laird Cregar, Charles Coburn, Marjorie Main, Eugene Pallette, Allyn Joslyn, Spring Byington, Signe Hasso, Louis Calhern, Dickie Moore, Florence Bates, Scotty Beckett, Charles Halton; **D:** Ernst Lubitsch. Nominations: Academy Awards '43: Best Color Cinematography, Best Director (Lubitsch), Best Picture. *FOX, FCT*

Heaven Can Wait 🎞🎞🎞 1978 **(PG)** A remake of 1941's "Here Comes Mr. Jordan," about a football player who is mistakenly summoned to heaven before his time. When the mistake is realized, he is returned to Earth in the body of a corrupt executive about to be murdered by his wife. Not to be confused with the 1943 film of the same name. **101m/C VHS, Beta, LV.** Warren Beatty, Julie Christie, Charles Grodin, Dyan Cannon, James Mason, Jack Warden; **D:** Buck Henry; **W:** Warren Beatty, Elaine May; **C:** William A. Fraker; **M:** Dave Grusin. Academy Awards '78: Best Art Direction/Set Decoration; Golden Globe Awards '79: Best Actor—Musical/Comedy (Beatty), Best Film—Musical/Comedy, Best Supporting Actress (Cannon); Writers Guild of America '78: Best Adapted Screenplay; Nominations: Academy Awards '78: Best Actor (Beatty), Best Adapted Screenplay, Best Cinematography, Best Director (Beatty, Henry), Best Picture, Best Supporting Actor (Warden), Best Supporting Actress (Cannon), Best Original Score. *PAR, FOX, HMV*

Heaven Help Us 🎞🎞½ *Catholic Boys* 1985 **(R)** Three mischievous boys find themselves continually in trouble with the priests running their Brooklyn Catholic high school during the mid-1960s. Realistic and humorous look at adolescent life. **102m/C VHS, Beta, LV.** Andrew McCarthy, Mary Stuart Masterson, Kevin Dillon, Malcolm Danare, Jennie Dundas, Kate Reid, Wallace Shawn, Jay Patterson, John Heard, Donald Sutherland, Yeardley Smith, Sherry Steiner, Calvert Deforest, Philip Bosco, Patrick Dempsey, Christopher Durang; **D:** Michael Dinner; **W:** Charles Purpura; **M:** James Horner. *NO*

Heaven Is a Playground 🎞🎞½ 1991 **(R)** On Chicago's South Side an inner city basketball coach and an idealistic young lawyer are determined to change the fate of a group of high school boys. The men use the incentive of athletic scholarships to keep their team in school and away from drugs and gangs.**CW:** Language and drug content. **104m/C VHS, LV, Closed Caption.** D.B.

Sweeney, Michael Warren, Richard Jordan, Victor Love; **D:** Randall Fried; **W:** Randall Fried. *COL*

Heaven Knows, Mr. Allison 🎞🎞🎞 1957 Terrific two-character WWII drama finds tough (but tender-hearted) Marine sergeant Allison (Mitchum) stranded with Irish nun, Sister Angela (Kerr), on a Pacific island overrun by Japanese troops. The duo hide out during the day and forage for food by night, gradually revealing their pasts to each other. He falls hard while she resists his advances and they struggle to stay alive until U.S. forces invade the island. Lots of action and good performances. Based on the novel by Charles Shaw. **106m/C VHS, Closed Caption.** Robert Mitchum, Deborah Kerr; **D:** John Huston; **W:** John Huston, John Lee Mahin; **C:** Oswald Morris; **M:** Georges Auric. Nominations: Academy Awards '57: Best Actress (Kerr), Best Adapted Screenplay. *FOX*

Heaven on Earth 🎞🎞½ 1989 The story of two orphaned British children who, along with thousands of orphans shipped from England to Canada between 1867 and 1914, try to make new lives in the Canadian wilderness. **101m/C VHS, Beta.** *CA* R.H. Thomson, Sian Leisa Davies, Torquil Campbell, Fiona Reid; **D:** Allen Kroeker; **W:** Margaret Atwood. *NO*

Heaven Tonight 🎞🎞½ 1993 **(R)** Ex-rock star dad copes with midlife crisis by trying for his big comeback, this time with his son.**CW:** Language and violence. **97m/C VHS.** *AU* John Waters, Rebecca Gilling, Guy Pearce, Kim Gyngell; **D:** Pino Amenta; **C:** David Connell.

Heavenly Bodies woof! 1984 **(R)** A young woman who dreams of owning a health club will stop at nothing to accomplish her goals. When a rival tries to put her out of business, a "dance-down" takes place in this lame low-budget aerobics musical. **99m/C VHS, Beta.** *CA* Cynthia Dale, Richard Rebrere, Laura Henry, Stuart Stone, Walter George Alton, Cec Linder; **D:** Lawrence Dane; **W:** Lawrence Dane, Ron Base; **C:** Thomas Burstyn. *FOX*

Heavenly Creatures 🎞🎞🎞½ 1994 **(R)** Haunting and surreal drama chronicles the true-life case of two young schoolgirls, Pauline and Juliet, who were charged with clubbing to death Pauline's mother in Christchurch, New Zealand, in 1954. Opens two years before the murder, and follows the friendship as the two teens become obsessed with each other, retreating into a rich fantasy life. They create an elaborate, medieval kingdom where they escape to their dream lovers and romantic alter egos. Elaborate morphing and animation effects vividly express the shared inner fantasy world, while innovative camerawork creates the sensations of hysteria and excitement that the girls experience as their infatuation becomes uncontrollable. Leads Lynsky and Winslet are convincing as the awkward, quiet Pauline and the pretty, intelligent, upper class Juliet. Bizarre crime story is stylish and eerily compelling, and made more so by real life events: after the film was released, mystery writer Anne Perry was revealed as Juliet Hulme.**CW:** Chilling murder; brief sexual situations. **110m/C VHS, LV, Closed Caption.** *NZ* Melanie Lynskey, Kate Winslet, Sarah Pierse, Diana Kent, Clive Merrison, Simon O'Connor; **D:** Peter Jackson; **W:** Peter Jackson, Frances Walsh; **C:** Alun Bollinger. Nominations: Academy Awards '94: Best Original Screenplay; Australian Film Institute '95: Best Foreign Film; Writers Guild of America '94: Best Original Screenplay. *TOU*

The Heavenly Kid 🎞🎞 1985 **(PG-13)** Leather-jacketed "cool" guy who died in a '60s hot rod crash finally receives an offer to exit limbo and enter heaven. The deal requires that he educate his dull earthly son on more hip and worldly ways. A big problem is that the soundtrack and wardrobe are 1955, whereas the cocky cool greaser supposedly died 17 years ago in 1968. Mildly entertaining. **92m/C VHS, Beta.** Lewis Smith, Jane Kaczmarek, Jason Gedrick, Richard Mulligan; **D:** Cary Medoway; **W:** Cary Medoway, Martin Copeland. *NO*

Heaven's a Drag 🎞🎞½ *To Die For* 1994 Low-budget British cross between a tearjerker and a supernatural comedy. HIV-positive London drag performer Mark (Williams) lives with Simon (Arklie), a TV repairman who keeps his sexuality a secret from his co-workers and his emotional distance from his stricken lover. When Mark dies, Simon is quick to get on with his life—too quick for Mark, who's ghostly presence puts a damper on Simon's dating possibilities and brings up some old resentments. **96m/C VHS.** *GB* Thomas Arklie, Ian Williams, Dilly Keane, Tony Slattery, Jean Boht, John Altman; **D:** Peter MacKenzie Litten; **W:** Johnny Byrne; **C:** John Ward. *FRF*

Heavens Above 🎞🎞🎞 1963 A sharp, biting satire on cleric life in England. Sellers stars as the quiet, down-to-earth reverend who is appointed to a new post in space. **113m/B VHS, Beta.** *GB* Peter Sellers, Cecil Parker, Isabel Jeans, Eric Sykes, Ian Carmichael; **D:** John Boulting, Roy Boulting; **M:** Richard Rodney Bennett. *FCT*

Heaven's Burning 🎞🎞 1997 **(R)** Fast-paced road movie with some unexpected twists. Midori (Kudoh) is a young Japanese woman who is honeymooning in Sydney with new hubby Yukio (Isomura). But Midori fakes her own kidnapping to wait for her lover to arrive (who doesn't show). Yukio and the cops quickly discover her plotting but, in the meantime, Midori's been caught up in the midst of a bank robbery. When the robbery goes wrong, she becomes the quai-hostage of driver Colin (Crowe), who takes off across Australia, pursued by the cops, his ex-partners, and the humiliated husband who wants revenge. Midori and Colin bond and things get increasingly stranger.**CW:** Violence, language and a scene of sexuality. **96m/C VHS.** *AU* Youki Kudoh, Russell Crowe, Kenji Isomura, Ray Barrett, Robert Mammone, Petru Gheorghiu, Matthew Dyktynski, Anthony Phelan, Colin Hay, Susan Prior, Norman Kaye; **D:** Craig Lahiff; **W:** Louis Nowra; **C:** Brian J. Breheny; **M:** Michael Atkinson. *THV*

Heaven's Gate 🎞🎞 1981 **(R)** The uncut version of Cimino's notorious folly. A fascinating, plotless, and exaggerated account of the Johnson County cattle war of the 1880s. Ravishingly photographed, the film's production almost single-handedly put United Artists out of business. **220m/C VHS, Beta, LV, Letterbox.** Kris Kristofferson, Christopher Walken, Isabelle Huppert, John Hurt, Richard Masur, Mickey Rourke, Brad Dourif, Joseph Cotten, Jeff Bridges, Sam Waterston, Terry O'Quinn, Geoffrey Lewis; **D:** Michael Cimino; **W:** Michael Cimino; **C:** Vilmos Zsigmond. Golden Raspberry Awards '81: Worst Director (Cimino); Nominations: Academy Awards '81: Best Art Direction/Set Decoration. *MGM, FCT*

Heaven's Heroes 1987 Dennis Hill, a dedicated policeman, was killed in the line of duty on August 27, 1977. This film recalls his life and deep faith in Jesus. **72m/C VHS, Beta.** David Ralphe, Heidi Vaughn, James O'Hagen; **D:** Donald W. Thompson. *RDF*

Heaven's Prisoners 🎞🎞½ 1995 **(R)** Dave Robicheaux (Baldwin) is an ex-New Orleans homicide detective and recovering alcoholic, living a quiet life on a bayou with patient wife Annie (Lynch). They witness a plane crash and Dave rescues the only survivor, a young Salvadoran girl, whom they adopt. But the crash wasn't an accident and Dave's snooping around involves him with drug runners and local crime bosses, including old high school buddy, Bubba Rocque (Roberts), and his sirenish wife, Claudette (Hatcher). Convoluted plot with some moody touches but Baldwin scores as the flawed hero. Based on the mystery series by James Lee Burke.**CW:** Strong violence and language; some nudity. **135m/C VHS, LV, Closed Caption.** Alec Baldwin, Kelly Lynch, Mary Stuart Masterson, Eric Roberts, Teri Hatcher, Vondie Curtis-Hall, Badja Djola, Joe Viterelli, Hawthorne James; **D:** Phil Joanou; **W:** Scott Frank, Harley Peyton; **C:** Harris Savides; **M:** George Fenton. Nominations: Golden Raspberry Awards '96: Worst Supporting Actress (Hatcher). *NLC*

Heavy 🎬🎬🎬 1994 (R) Sensitive character study supported by an excellent ensemble, led by Vince as Victor, an obese, painfully withdrawn, 30-ish cook. He lives with his domineering mother (a subdued Winters) and helps her run their roadside diner, along with veteran waitress Delores (Harry). Then beautiful teenager Callie (Tyler) is hired and Victor develops a suitably massive crush. Tyler is all pout and promise as Callie, making it clear why a guy like Victor could fall hard for her. Harry brings a rich cynical and sexual edge to Delores. Director Mangold's feature debut is both eloquent and economical, though at times paced to a near stand-still. **104m/C VHS, Closed Caption.** Pruitt Taylor Vince, Shelley Winters, Liv Tyler, Deborah Harry, Evan Dando, Joe Grifasi; **D:** James Mangold; **W:** James Mangold; **C:** Michael Barrow; **M:** Thurston Moore. Sundance Film Festival '95: Special Jury Prize. COL

Heavy Metal 🎬🎬🎬 1981 (R) Yes, the animated cult flick is now legally available on video, its copyright disputes finally resolved. A collection of science fiction and fantasy stories, inspired by the same-titled magazine and offered in a variety of graphic styles, that all encompass the theme of good versus evil. And don't always bet on the good. Features a soundtrack complied from the work of many top metal artists of the time as well as Bernstein's score with the London Philharmonic Orchestra. A three-minute transitional segment, called "Neverwhere Land," that was cut from the original version has been restored as an epilogue. **90m/C VHS, LV.** CA **D:** Gerald Potterton; **W:** Dan Goldberg, Len Blum; **M:** Elmer Bernstein; **V:** John Candy, Joe Flaherty, Don Francks, Eugene Levy. COL

Heavy Petting 🎬🎬½ 1989 A hilarious compilation of "love scene" footage from feature films of the silent era to the '60s, newsreels, news reports, educational films, old TV shows, and home movies. **75m/C VHS, Beta, LV.** David Byrne, Josh Mostel, Sandra Bernhard, Allen Ginsberg, Ann Magnuson, Spalding Gray, Laurie Anderson, John Oates, Abbie Hoffman, Jacki Ochs; **D:** Obie Benz. FXL

Heavy Traffic 🎬🎬🎬 1973 Ralph Bakshi's animated fantasy portrait of the hard-edged underside of city life. A young cartoonist draws the people, places, and paranoia of his environment. **76m/C VHS, Beta. D:** Ralph Bakshi; **W:** Ralph Bakshi; **M:** Ed Bogas. WAR, OM

Heavyweights 🎬 1994 (PG) A product of Disney's sometimes assembly line approach to family entertainment (think "Mighty Ducks"). Nothing new saga of overweight youngsters sent to a fat camp run by tyrannical fitness guru Tony Perkis (Stiller). His methods cause the kids to band together and overthrow him and his "evil" tactics. Oh, by the way, there's a baseball competition with the more athletic camp kids on the other side of the lake. Guess who wins. Stiller as the fame obsessed fitness fanatic, sporting a David Copperfield make-over, is the only highlight in this exercise of excess fluff. Directorial debut of Brill. **98m/C VHS, LV, Closed Caption.** Jeffrey Tambor, Ben Stiller, Jerry Stiller, Anne Meara, Shaun Weiss, Kenan Thompson; **D:** Steven Brill; **W:** Judd Apatow, Steven Brill; **C:** Victor Hammer; **M:** J.A.C. Redford. DIS

Heck's Way Home 🎬🎬½ 1995 Heck is the Neufeld family dog and best friend of 11-year-old Luke (Krowchuk). The family is moving from Winnipeg to Australia and have a three-day layover in Vancouver. Heck is supposed to come along but instead, unbeknownst to the family, he gets captured by the local dogcatcher (Arkin) and the family are forced to leave without him. Naturally, Heck escapes and starts off on a 2000-mile journey to find his family before they fly away forever. Made for cable. **92m/C VHS.** Chad Krowchuk, Alan Arkin, Michael Riley, Shannon Lawson; **D:** Michael Scott; **C:** Maris Jansons. HMK

Hector's Bunyip 1986 What's a bunyip? People think it's just Hector's scaly imaginary friend. It therefore comes as quite a surprise when Hector gets kidnapped—by his supposed imaginary friend! Aired on PBS as part of the "Wonderworks" series. **58m/C VHS, Closed Caption.** Scott Bartle, Robert Coleby, Barbara Stephens, Tushka Hose; **D:** Mark Callan. HMV, FCT, BTV

Hedd Wyn 🎬🎬 1992 True story of talented young poet Ellis Evans (Garmon), writing under the pseudonym Hedd Wyn, who dreams of winning a coveted literary prize. His hopes are put on hold when he's forced to fight in WWI, although he submits his antiwar poem "The Hero" to the competition. Welsh with subtitles. **123m/C VHS.** GB Huw Garmon, Catrin Fychan, Ceri Cunnington, Llio Silyn; **D:** Paul Turner; **W:** Alan Llwyd; **C:** Ray Orton; **M:** John E.R. Hardy. Nominations: Academy Awards '93: Best Foreign Language Film. FXL

Hedda 🎬🎬½ 1975 A dramatization of the Henrik Ibsen play, "Hedda Gabler," about a middle-class pregnant woman. The story finds her frustrated with her life and manipulating those around her with tragic results. **102m/C VHS, Beta.** GB Glenda Jackson, Peter Eyre, Timothy West, Jennie Linden, Patrick Stewart; **D:** Trevor Nunn. Nominations: Academy Awards '75: Best Actress (Jackson).

Hedda Hopper's Hollywood 1942 Newsreel version of the gossip-hound's column, featuring scoops on Ball, Cooper, Minelli and many more. **58m/B VHS.** Hedda Hopper, Gary Cooper, Lucille Ball, Gloria Swanson, Liza Minnelli. REP

Heidi 🎬🎬½ 1937 Johanna Spyri's classic tale puts Shirley Temple in the hands of a mean governess and the loving arms of her Swiss grandfather. Also available colorized. Remade in 1967. Also available with "Poor Little Rich Girl" on laserdisc. **88m/B VHS, Beta, Closed Caption.** Shirley Temple, Jean Hersholt, Helen Westley, Arthur Treacher; **D:** Allan Dwan; **C:** Arthur C. Miller. HMV, MLT

Heidi 🎬🎬½ 1952 The Swiss do their own version of the children's classic by Johanna Spyri. A precocious little girl enjoys life in the Swiss Alps with her grandfather, until her stern aunt takes her away to live in the village in the valley. **98m/B VHS.** SI Elsbeth Sigmund, Heinrich Gretler, Thomas Klameth, Elsie Attenolf; **D:** Luigi Comencini. CNG, MRV, KAR

Heidi 🎬🎬 1965 The classic story from Johanna Spyri's novel is filmed beautifully in the Swiss Alps in Eastmancolor. Heidi is kidnapped by her mean aunt and forced to work as a slave for a rich family. Her kindly old grandfather comes to her rescue. Family entertainment for all, dubbed in English. **95m/C VHS.** AT GE Eva Maria Singhammer, Gustav Knuth, Lotte Ledl; **D:** Werner Jacobs. NO

Heidi 🎬🎬 1967 The second American adaptation of the classic Johanna Spyri novel tells the story of an orphaned girl who goes to the Swiss Alps to live with her grandfather. Made for television. **100m/C VHS, Beta.** Maximilian Schell, Jennifer Edwards, Michael Redgrave, Jean Simmons; **D:** Delbert Mann; **M:** John Williams. ART, VES, GLV

Heidi 🎬🎬🎬 1993 (G) Yet another version of the children's classic, from German writer Johanna Spyri's 1881 novel. Thornton is charming as the orphan shuttled from relative to relative until she happily ends up with her crotchety grandfather (Robards) in his mountain cabin. Then her cousin comes along and whisks her off to the city to be a companion to the invalid Klara (Randall). Seymour is the snobbish, scowling governess. This "Heidi" is spunky enough to keep the sugar level tolerable. Filmed on location in Austria. Made for television. **167m/C VHS, LV, Closed Caption.** Noley Thornton, Jason Robards Jr., Jane Seymour, Lexi Randall, Sian Phillips, Patricia Neal, Benjamin Brazier, Michael Simkins, Andrew Bicknell, Jane Hazlegrove; **D:** Michael Rhodes; **W:** Jeanne Rosenberg; **M:** Lee Holdridge. DIS

The Heidi Chronicles 🎬🎬½ 1995 Some 25 years of boomer angst and friendship are covered in this cable adaptation of Wasserstein's 1988 Pulitzer Prize-winning play. Heidi Holland (Seymour) goes from prep school to Vassar to an art history career while searching for self-fulfillment, feminist ideals, and some romance along the way. The romance is on-and-off, thanks to caddish journalist Scoop (Friedman), but Heidi can always depend on soul mate, gay pediatrician Peter (Hulce), and Susan (Cattrall), her follow-the-fads confidante. Heidi's sometimes too morose for her own good but you won't mind spending a couple of hours in her company. **94m/C VHS.** Jamie Lee Curtis, Tom Hulce, Kim Cattrall, Peter Friedman, Eve Gordon, Shari Belafonte, Sharon Lawrence, Julie White, Debra Eisenstadt, Roma Maffia; **D:** Paul Bogart; **W:** Wendy Wasserstein; **C:** Isidore Mankofsky; **M:** David Shire. TTC

Heimat 1 1984 Sixteen-hour series follows the lives, loves, and tragedies of the German Simon family from the end of WWI to 1982. Based on Reitz's own family and his childhood. Shot over two years, the series has 28 lead performances and more than 140 speaking roles. German with subtitles; boxed 9-tape set. **924m/C VHS.** GE **D:** Edgar Reitz. FCT

Heimat 2 198? The continuation of the saga is composed of 25 half-hour segments and follows Hermann Simon's life in Munich from 1960 to 1970. A modernist musician and composer, Hermann falls in with a group of students, artists, and rebels. German with subtitles. **750m/C VHS.** GE **D:** Edgar Reitz. FCT

The Heiress 🎬🎬🎬½ 1949 Based on the Henry James novel "Washington Square," about a wealthy plain Jane, her tyrannical father, and the handsome fortune-seeking scoundrel who seeks to marry her. **115m/B VHS, Beta, LV.** Olivia de Havilland, Montgomery Clift, Ralph Richardson, Miriam Hopkins; **D:** William Wyler; **M:** Aaron Copland. Academy Awards '49: Best Actress (de Havilland), Best Art Direction/Set Decoration (B & W), Best Costume Design (B & W), Best Original Dramatic/Comedy Score; Golden Globe Awards '50: Best Actress—Drama (de Havilland); National Board of Review Awards '49: Best Actor (Richardson), National Film Registry '96;; New York Film Critics Awards '49: Best Actress (de Havilland); Nominations: Academy Awards '49: Best Black and White Cinematography, Best Director (Wyler), Best Picture, Best Supporting Actor (Richardson). USH, MLB, BTV

The Heist 🎬🎬 1988 (R) An explosive crime thriller. **93m/C VHS.** Lee Van Cleef, Karen Black, Edward Albert, Lionel Stander, Robert Alda. NO

The Heist 🎬🎬 1989 A made-for-cable-television film about an ex-con who, upon regaining his freedom, sets out to rip off the crook who framed him. Entertaining enough story with a first-rate cast. **97m/C VHS, Beta.** Pierce Brosnan, Tom Skerritt, Wendy Hughes; **D:** Stuart Orme. HBO, HHE

The Heist 🎬🎬 1997 Con artist plots the hijacking of a transport company's fleet and starts out by taking the firm's employees hostage. But one of the workers is an ex-cop who failed once to stop a robbery and is not about to fail again. **99m/C VHS.** Andrew McCarthy, Cynthia Geary, Wolf Larson; **D:** Michael Kennedy. AVA

Helas pour Moi 🎬🎬 Oh Woe is Me 1994 Perplexing, contemplative film on faith and love—and maybe a miracle. Told in flashback, publisher Alexander Klimt (Verley) travels to a Swiss lakeside town where it's rumored that the beautiful Rachel Donnadieu (Masliah) has been "visited" by God, who wishes to experience the pleasures of love, in the form of her own husband, simple fisherman Simon (Depardieu). Story is derived from the Greek myth concerning Zeus, who seduced Alcmene in the shape of her husband Amphitryon. French with subtitles. **84m/C VHS.** FR SI Gerard Depardieu, Laurence Masliah, Bernard Verley; **D:** Jean-Luc Godard; **W:** Jean-Luc Godard; **C:** Caroline Champtier. FCT

Held for Murder 🎬 Her Mad Night 1932 When a vacationing daughter is accused of murder, her mom lovingly takes the blame. Will the daughter come back to clear her mom, or will she let her fry in the electric chair? **67m/B VHS, Beta.** Irene Rich, Conway Tearle, Mary Carlisle, Kenneth Thomson, William B. Davidson; **D:** E. Mason Hopper. SNC

Held Hostage 🎬🎬 1991 The true story of Jerry Levin, a reporter kidnapped by terrorists while on assignment in Beirut, and his wife, Sis, who struggled with the State Department for his release. Made for television. 95m/C VHS. Marlo Thomas, David Dukes, G.W. Bailey, Ed Winter, Robert Harper, William Schallert; *D:* Roger Young. *SDE*

Helen of Troy 🎬½ 1956 Mythological fantasy finds Helen (Podesta), the beautiful daughter of Zeus, falling in love with Trojan prince Paris (Sernas)—an event that leads to the siege of Troy. Ignores script for lavish effects. Video includes behind-the-scenes footage. 135m/C VHS, LV, Closed Caption. Rossana Podesta, Jacques Sernas, Cedric Hardwicke, Stanley Baker, Niall MacGinnis, Nora Swinburne, Robert Douglas, Torin Thatcher, Harry Andrews, Janette Scott, Ronald Lewis, Brigitte Bardot; *D:* Robert Wise; *W:* John Twist, N. Richard Nash; *C:* Harry Stradling; *M:* Max Steiner. *WAR, MOV*

Hell Comes to Frogtown 🎬 1988 (R) In a post-nuclear holocaust land run by giant frogs, a renegade who is one of the few non-sterile men left on earth must rescue some fertile women and impregnate them. Sci-fi spoof is extremely low-budget, but fun. Stars "Rowdy" Roddy Piper of wrestling fame. 88m/C VHS, Beta, LV. Roddy Piper, Sandahl Bergman, Rory Calhoun, Donald G. Jackson; *D:* Robert J. Kizer. *VTR*

Hell Commandos 🎬½ 1969 Soldiers in WWII struggle to prevent the Nazis from releasing a deadly bacteria that will kill millions. Dubbed. 92m/C VHS, Beta. *IT* Guy Madison, Stan Cooper; *D:* J.L. Merino. *NO*

Hell Fire Austin 🎬½ 1932 Maynard finds himself mixed up with outlaws in the Old West. 60m/B VHS, Beta. Ken Maynard, Nat Pendleton, Jack Perrin; *D:* Forrest Sheldon. *NOS, VCN, DVT*

Hell Harbor 🎬🎬 1930 Caribbean love, murder and greed combine to make this early talkie. Exterior shots were filmed on the west coast of Florida and the beauty of the Tampa area in the 1930s is definitely something to see. 65m/B VHS, Beta. Lupe Velez, Gibson Gowland, Jean Hersholt, John Holland; *D:* Henry King. *GVV*

Hell High 🎬 1986 (R) Four high schoolers plan a night of torture and humiliation for an annoying teacher, only to find she has some deadly secrets of her own. Dumber than it sounds. 84m/C VHS, Beta. Christopher Stryker, Christopher Cousins, Millie Prezioso, Jason Brill; *D:* Douglas Grossman.

Hell Hounds of Alaska 🎬 1973 (G) The Yukon, Yugoslav-style. European co-production goes back to the Gold Rush days for an adventure about a frontiersman tracking down a stolen shipment of the precious ore while trying to save the life of an injured boy. 90m/C VHS, Beta. Doug McClure, Harald Leipnitz, Angelica Ott; *D:* Harald Reinl. *NO*

Hell Hunters 🎬 1987 Nazi-hunters foil the plot of an old German doctor to poison the population of L.A. Meanwhile, a daughter avenges the death of her mother by blowing up the doctor's jungle compound. 98m/C VHS, Beta. Stewart Granger, Maud Adams, George Lazenby, Candice Daly, Romulo Arantes, William Berger. *NO*

Hell in the Pacific 🎬🎬🎬 1969 (PG) A marvelously photographed (by Conrad Hall) psycho/macho allegory, about an American and a Japanese soldier stranded together on a tiny island and the mini-war they fight all by themselves. Overly obvious anti-war statement done with style. 101m/C VHS, Beta, LV. Lee Marvin, Toshiro Mifune; *D:* John Boorman; *C:* Conrad Hall; *M:* Lalo Schifrin. *FOX*

Hell Is for Heroes 🎬🎬🎬½ 1962 McQueen stars as the bitter leader of a small infantry squad outmanned by the Germans in this tight WWII drama. A strong cast and riveting climax make this a must for action fans. 90m/B VHS, Beta, LV, Closed Caption. Steve McQueen, Bobby Darin, Fess Parker, Harry Guardino, James Coburn, Mike Kellin, Nick Adams, Bob Newhart; *D:* Donald Siegel; *W:* Robert Pirosh, Richard Carr. *PAR*

Hell Night woof! 1981 (R) Several young people must spend the night in a mysterious mansion as part of their initiation into Alpha Sigma Rho fraternity in this extremely dull low-budget horror flick. 100m/C VHS, Beta. Linda Blair, Vincent Van Patten, Kevin Brophy, Peter Barton, Jenny Neumann; *D:* Tom De Simone; *W:* Randy Feldman; *C:* Mac Ahlberg.

Hell on Frisco Bay 🎬🎬½ 1955 An ex-waterfront cop, falsely imprisoned for manslaughter, sets out to clear his name. His quest finds him taking on the Mob, in this '30s-style gangster film. Good performances all around, especially Robinson, who steals every scene he's in. 93m/C VHS, Beta. Alan Ladd, Edward G. Robinson, Joanne Dru, Fay Wray, William Demarest, Jayne Mansfield; *D:* Frank Tuttle; *M:* Max Steiner. *NO*

Hell on the Battleground 🎬½ 1988 (R) Group of inexperienced recruits are led into combat by two battle-hardened veterans. Their only hope for survival is a counterattack by U.S. tanks. 91m/C VHS, Beta. William Smith, Ted Prior, Fritz Matthews; *D:* David A. Prior; *W:* David A. Prior.

Hell on Wheels 🎬 1967 Two successful brothers in the racing industry are torn apart by the same girl. Brotherly love diminishes into a hatred so deep that murder becomes the sole purpose of both. 96m/C VHS, Beta. Marty Robbins, Jennifer Ashley, John Ashley, Gigi Perreau, Robert Dornan, Connie Smith, Frank Gerstle; *D:* Will Zens.

Hell Raiders 🎬½ 1968 A force invades a supposedly defenseless Pacific island, and finds itself fiercely attacked. 90m/C VHS, Beta. John Agar, Richard Webb, Joan Huntington; *D:* Larry Buchanan. *JEF*

Hell River 🎬🎬 1975 (PG) In 1941 Yugoslavia, Yugoslav partisans and Nazis battle it out at a place called Hell River. 100m/C VHS, Beta. Rod Taylor, Adam West; *D:* Stole Jankovic. *VCD*

Hell-Ship Morgan 🎬🎬 1936 Bancroft is a womanizing tuna boat captain who falls for and marries Sothern. When they set up married life on the boat, she starts eyeing first mate Jory. And Bancroft finds out. 65m/B VHS. George Bancroft, Ann Sothern, Victor Jory, George Regas, Howard Hickman, Ralph Byrd; *D:* David Ross Lederman. *GPV*

Hell Ship Mutiny 🎬½ 1957 Man comes to the aid of a lovely island princess, whose people have been forced to hand over their pearls to a pair of ruthless smugglers. Excellent cast in an unfortunately tepid production. 66m/B VHS, Beta. Jon Hall, John Carradine, Peter Lorre, Roberta Haynes, Mike Mazurki, Stanley Adams; *D:* Lee Sholem, Elmo Williams. *SNC, HEG*

Hell Squad 🎬½ 1958 Lost in North Africa during WWII, five American GIs wander through the desert. They find numerous pitfalls and unexpected help. Overall, dismal and disappointing. 64m/B VHS. Wally Campo, Brandon Carroll; *D:* Burt Topper. *NOS*

Hell Squad 🎬 1985 (R) Unable to release his son from the Middle Eastern terrorists who kidnapped him, a U.S. ambassador turns to the services of nine Las Vegas showgirls. These gals moonlight as vicious commandos in this low-budget action film with skin. 88m/C VHS, Beta. Bainbridge Scott, Glen Hartford, Tina Lederman; *D:* Kenneth Hartford; *W:* Kenneth Hartford; *M:* Charles P. Barnett. *MGM*

Hell to Eternity 🎬🎬½ 1960 The true story of how WWII hero Guy Gabaldon persuaded 2,000 Japanese soldiers to surrender. Features several spectacular scenes. 132m/B VHS, Beta. Jeffrey Hunter, Sessue Hayakawa, David Janssen, Vic Damone, Patricia Owens; *D:* Phil Karlson. *FOX*

Hell Up in Harlem woof! 1973 (R) A black crime lord recuperates from an assassination attempt and tries to regain his power. Poor sequel to the decent film "Black Caesar." 98m/C VHS, Beta. Fred Williamson, Julius W. Harris, Margaret Avery, Gerald Gordon, Gloria Hendry; *D:* Larry Cohen; *W:* Larry Cohen. *ORI*

Hellbenders 🎬½ *Il Crudeli; Los Despiadados* 1967 (PG) A confederate veteran robs a Union train and must fight through acres of Civil War adversity. Dubbed. Poorly directed and acted. 92m/C VHS, Beta. *IT SP* Joseph Cotten, Norman Bengell, Julian Mateos; *D:* Sergio Corbucci; *M:* Ennio Morricone. *COL*

Hellbent 1990 A crazed musician and a revenge-obsessed housewife embark on an unusual adventure that challenges their very sanity. 90m/C VHS, Beta. Phil Ward, Lynn Levand, Cheryl Slean, David Marciano; *D:* Richard Casey; *W:* Richard Casey. *NO*

Hellbound 🎬🎬½ 1994 (R) Prosatanos (Neame), a powerful 12th-century wizard, is imprisoned and the source of his power (a scepter) is supposedly destroyed. Fast-forward several hundred years when Prosatanos manages to free himself and seek out the pieces of his scepter. Which happens to lead him to Chicago and a couple of unsuspecting cops (Norris, Levels).*CW:* Violence, language, gore. 95m/C VHS, Closed Caption. Chuck Norris, Christopher Neame, Calvin Levels, Sheree J. Wilson; *D:* Aaron Norris. *WAR*

Hellbound: Hellraiser 2 🎬🎬 *Hellraiser 2* 1988 (R) In this, the first sequel to Clive Barker's inter-dimensional nightmare, the traumatized daughter from the first film is pulled into the Cenobites' universe. Gore and weird imagery abound. An uncut, unrated version is also available. 96m/C VHS, Beta, LV, Closed Caption. *GB* Ashley Laurence, Clare Higgins, Kenneth Cranham, Imogen Boorman, William Hope, Oliver Smith, Sean Chapman, Doug Bradley; *D:* Tony Randel; *W:* Peter Atkins; *C:* Robin Vidgeon. *VTR*

Hellcats woof! 1968 (R) A mob of sleazy, leather-clad female bikers terrorize small Midwestern towns in this violent girl-gang thriller. Even biker movie fans might find this one unworthy. 90m/C VHS, Beta. Ross Hagen, Dee Duffy, Sharyn Kinzie, Sonny West, Bob Slatzer; *D:* Bob Slatzer.

Hellcats of the Navy 🎬½ 1957 Soggy true saga of the WWII mission to sever the vital link between mainland Asia and Japan. The only film that Ronald and Nancy Davis Reagan starred in together and the beginning of their grand romance. 82m/B VHS, Beta. Ronald Reagan, Nancy Davis, Arthur Franz, Robert Arthur; *D:* Nathan (Hertz) Juran; *W:* Bernard Gordon, David Lang. *GKK*

Helldorado 🎬🎬 *Heldorado* 1946 A lively western starring the singing cowboy, Roy Rogers. 54m/B VHS, Beta. Roy Rogers, George "Gabby" Hayes, Dale Evans, Paul Harvey; *D:* William Witney. *NOS, VCN, CAB*

Heller in Pink Tights 🎬🎬 1960 The Louis L'Amour story follows the adventures of a colorful theatrical troupe that visits the 1880s West. Performing amid Indians, bill collectors, and thieves, they are often just one step ahead of the law themselves in this offbeat western. 100m/C VHS, Beta, Closed Caption. Sophia Loren, Anthony Quinn, Margaret O'Brien, Steve Forrest, Edmund Lowe, Ramon Novarro; *D:* George Cukor; *W:* Walter Bernstein. *BAR, PAR, FCT*

Hellfighters 🎬🎬 1968 (G) Texas oil well fire fighters experience trouble between themselves and the women they love. 121m/C VHS, Beta, LV, Letterbox. John Wayne, Katharine Ross, Jim Hutton, Vera Miles, Bruce Cabot, Jay C. Flippen; *D:* Andrew V. McLaglen; *C:* William Clothier. *USH*

Hellfire 🎬🎬 1948 A gambler promises to build a church and follow the precepts of the Bible after a minister sacrifices his life for him. 90m/B VHS. William Elliott, Marie Windsor, Forrest Tucker, Jim Davis; *D:* R.G. Springsteen. *REP*

The Hellfire Club 🎬🎬 1961 In 18th-century Britain, a young man reaches adulthood and attempts to claim the estate of his father. No ordinary dad, his led the infamous Hellfire Club, an organization specializing in debauchery and depravity. His cousin challenges his claim and kidnaps his fiancee. Historical hokum, complete with swordplay. 88m/C VHS, Beta. *GB* Keith Michell, Kai Fischer, Adrienne Corri, Peter Arne, David Lodge, Bill Owen, Peter Cushing, Francis Matthews, Desmond Walter

Ellis; **D:** Robert S. Baker, Monty Berman; **W:** Jimmy Sangster. *SNC*

Hellgate woof! 1989 (R) A woman hitchhiking turns out to be one of the living dead. Her benefactor lives to regret picking her up. 96m/C VHS, LV. Abigail Wolcott, Ron Palillo, Carel Trichardt, Petrea Curran, Evan J. Klisser, Joanne Ward; **D:** William A. Levey; **W:** Michael O'Rourke; **C:** Peter Palmer. *THV*

Hellhole ✷ 1985 (R) A young woman who witnesses her mother's murder is sent to a sanitarium where the doctors are perfecting chemical lobotomies. Extremely weak script and poor acting make this a suspenseless thriller. 95m/C VHS, Beta, LV, Closed Caption. Judy Landers, Ray Sharkey, Mary Woronov, Marjoe Gortner, Edy Williams, Terry Moore, Dyanne Thorne; **D:** Pierre De Moro. *COL*

Hellmaster ✷ 1992 Your basic sicko mad scientist experiments on some unsuspecting college students by injecting them with an addictive drug. The drug also causes some horrifying mutations and makes its victims superhuman (but also super-ugly). Lots of gore. Creative special effects and make-up will appeal to fans of horror. 92m/C VHS. John Saxon, David Emge, Amy Raasch; **D:** Douglas Schulze; **W:** Douglas Schulze.

Hello Again ✷✷ 1987 (PG) The wife of a successful plastic surgeon chokes to death on a piece of chicken. A year later she returns to life, with comical consequences, but soon discovers that life won't be the same. 96m/C VHS, Beta, LV, Closed Caption. Shelley Long, Corbin Bernsen, Judith Ivey, Gabriel Byrne, Sela Ward, Austin Pendleton, Carrie Nye, Robert Lewis, Madeleine Potter; **D:** Frank Perry; **M:** William Goldstein. *TOU*

Hello, Dolly! ✷✷ 1969 (G) Widow Dolly Levi, while matchmaking for her friends, finds a match for herself. Based on the hugely successful Broadway musical adapted from Thornton Wilder's play "Matchmaker." Lightweight story needs better actors with stronger characterizations. Original Broadway score helps. ♫Hello Dolly; Just Leave Everything to Me; Love is Only Love; Dancing; Walter's Gavotte; It Only Takes a Moment; Ribbons Down My Back; Elegance; It Takes a Woman. 146m/C VHS, Beta, LV, Closed Caption. Barbra Streisand, Walter Matthau, Michael Crawford, Louis Armstrong, E.J. Peaker, Marianne McAndrew, Tommy Tune; **D:** Gene Kelly; **W:** Ernest Lehman; **C:** Harry Stradling; **M:** Jerry Herman. Academy Awards '69: Best Art Direction/Set Decoration, Best Sound, Scoring of a Musical; Nominations: Academy Awards '69: Best Cinematography, Best Costume Design, Best Film Editing, Best Picture. *FOX, FCT*

Hello, Frisco, Hello ✷✷½ 1943 San Francisco's wild Barbary Coast is the setting for this romantic musical. Smoothie Payne opens up a saloon that features Faye, who's in love with him, as the star singing attraction. Unfortunately, Payne is involved with a society snob and Faye heads off to European success. When she returns, it's to a sadder and wiser man. ♫Hello, Frisco, Hello; You'll Never Know; San Francisco; Ragtime Cowboy Joe; Sweet Cider Time; Has Anybody Here Seen Kelly; King Chanticleer; When You Wore a Tulip; Strike Up the Band, Here Comes a Sailor. 98m/C VHS. Alice Faye, John Payne, Jack Oakie, Lynn Bari, Laird Cregar, June Havoc, Ward Bond, Aubrey Mather, John Archer; **D:** H. Bruce Humberstone; **W:** Robert Ellis, Helen Logan. Academy Awards '43: Best Song ("You'll Never Know"); Nominations: Academy Awards '43: Best Color Cinematography. *FXV*

Hello Mary Lou: Prom Night 2 ✷½ *The Haunting of Hamilton High; Prom Night 2* 1987 (R) A sequel to the successful slasher flick, wherein a dead-for-30-years prom queen relegates the current queen to purgatory and comes back to life in order to avenge herself. Wild special effects. 97m/C VHS, Beta, LV, Closed Caption. CA Michael Ironside, Wendy Lyon, Justin Louis, Lisa Schrage, Richard Monette; **D:** Bruce Pittman; **W:** Ron Oliver; **C:** John Herzog. *NO*

Hello Trouble 1932 A Texas Ranger accidentally kills his friend, who was a former Ranger turned bandit, causing him to hang up his guns. 63m/C VHS. Buck Jones, Lena Basquette, Wallace MacDonald, "Spec" O'Donnell, Ward Bond, Frank Rice, Ruth Warren; **D:** Lambert Hillyer. *GPV*

Hellraiser ✷✷½ 1987 (R) A graphic, horror fantasy about a woman who is manipulated by the monstrous spirit of her husband's dead brother. In order for the man who was also her lover to be brought back to life, she must lure and kill human prey for his sustenance. Grisly and inventive scenes keep the action fast-paced; not for the faint-hearted. 94m/C Beta, LV, Closed Caption. GB Andrew (Andy) Robinson, Clare Higgins, Ashley Laurence, Sean Chapman, Oliver Smith, Robert Hines, Doug Bradley, Nicholas Vince; **D:** Clive Barker; **W:** Clive Barker; **C:** Robin Vidgeon; **M:** Christopher Young. *VTR*

Hellraiser 3: Hell on Earth ✷✷ 1992 (R) Pinhead is back in this film based on characters created by horrormeister Clive Barker. A strange black box holds the key to sending Pinhead back to Hell and is sought by the heroine, a TV newswoman (Farrell). But Pinhead's human henchman, a nasty nightclub owner, isn't going to make things easy. Imaginative special effects and Bradley's commanding presence as Pinhead aid this shocker, which becomes unfortunately mired in excessive gore. An unrated version at 97 minutes is also available.*CW:* Language, strong violence, and strong sexuality. 91m/C VHS, LV, Closed Caption. Doug Bradley, Terry Farrell, Kevin Bernhardt, Paula Marshall, Ken Carpenter, Peter Boynton, Ashley Laurence; **D:** Anthony Hickox; **W:** Peter Atkins; **C:** Gerry Lively. *PAR*

Hellraiser 4: Bloodline ✷ 1995 (R) You can't keep a bad Pinhead in Hell, as this unfortunate sequel demonstrates. Bradley reprises his role as the big bad S&M pincushion in the latest and supposedly last installment of Clive Barker's blood drenched series. Tracing the origin of the infernal Rubik's Cube that releases Pinhead, the plot jumps between 18th century France, present day New York, and a 22nd century space station. Along the way, the Pointy One gets to flay, skewer, and impale to his evil heart's content. Special f/x guru Kevin Yeagher was so embarrassed by this outing that he took his director's credit off of the picture. Bad acting, bad plot, bad complexion.*CW:* Strong horror violence and gore, and for some sexuality and language. 81m/C VHS, LV, Closed Caption. Bruce Ramsey, Valentina Vargas, Doug Bradley, Kim Myers, Christa Harnos, Charlotte Chatton, Paul Perri, Mickey Cotrell; **D:** Alan Smithee, Kevin Yagher; **W:** Peter Atkins; **C:** Gerry Lively; **M:** Daniel Licht. *PAR*

Hellriders woof! 1984 (R) A motorcycle gang rides into a small town and subjects its residents to a reign of terror. 90m/C VHS, Beta. Adam West, Tina Louise. *TWE*

Hell's Angels ✷✷✷ 1930 Classic WWI aviation movie is sappy and a bit lumbering, but still an extravagant spectacle with awesome air scenes. Studio owner Hughes fired directors Howard Hawks and Luther Reed, spent an unprecedented $3.8 million, and was ultimately credited as director (although Whale also spent some time in the director's chair). Three years in the making, the venture cost three pilots their lives and lost a bundle. Harlow replaced Swedish Greta Nissen when sound was added and was catapulted into blond bombshelldom as a two-timing dame. And the tinted and two-color scenes—restored in 1989—came well before Ted Turner ever wielded a crayola. 135m/B VHS. Jean Harlow, Ben Lyon, James Hall, John Darrow, Lucien Prival; **D:** Howard Hughes; **W:** Harry Behn, Howard Estabrook, Joseph Moncure March. Nominations: Academy Awards '30: Best Cinematography. *USH, MRV*

Hell's Angels Forever 1983 (R) A revealing ride into the world of honor, violence, and undying passion for motorcycles on the road. Documentary was filmed with cooperation of the Angels. Features appearances by Willie Nelson, Jerry Garcia, Bo Diddley, Kevin Keating and Johnny Paycheck. 93m/C VHS, Beta. Willie Nelson, Jerry Garcia, Johnny Paycheck, Bo Diddley; **D:** Richard Chase.

Hell's Angels on Wheels ✷✷½ 1967 Low-budget, two-wheeled Nicholson vehicle that casts him as a gas station attendant who joins up with the Angels for a cross country trip. Laszlo Kovacs is responsible for the photography. One of the better 1960s biker films. 95m/C VHS, Beta. Jack Nicholson, Adam Roarke, Sabrina Scharf, Jana Taylor, John Garwood; **D:** Richard Rush. *THV*

Hell's Angels '69 ✷✷ 1969 (PG) Figuring on robbing Caesar's Palace for the thrill, two wealthy brothers plot a deadly game by infiltrating the ranks of the Hell's Angels. Upon figuring out that they've been duped, the Angels seek revenge. Average biker epic filmed in Nevada features Hell's Angels Oakland chapter. 97m/C VHS, Beta. Tom Stern, Jeremy Slate, Conny Van Dyke; **D:** Lee Madden; **W:** Tom Stern, Jeremy Slate.

Hell's Belles ✷½ *Girl in the Leather Suit* 1969 Biker has his ride stolen by a rival, who leaves a chick as payment. The two team up to get revenge, chasing the gang across the Arizona desert and picking them off one by one. 95m/C VHS. Jeremy Slate, Adam Roarke, Jocelyn Lane, Angelique Pettyjohn, Michael Walker, William Lucking; **D:** Maury Dexter; **W:** James Gordon White, Robert McMullen; **M:** Les Baxter. *ORI*

Hell's Belles woof! 1995 (R) The Devil's bored so he leaves hell for some mortal fun but in order to stay he and his henchmen must sacrifice five ladies. 90m/C VHS. Terence Cooper, Nadine Kalmes, K.C. Kelly, Eric Liddy, Martin Howeller, Robert Mansbridge, Jeffrey Richardson; **D:** Ed Hansen; **W:** Ed Hansen, Buck Flower, Simon Hartwell; **C:** Rick Lamb.

Hell's Brigade: The Final Assault woof! 1980 (PG) Low-budget, poorly acted film in which a small band of American commandos is ordered on the most dangerous and important mission of WWII. 99m/C VHS, Beta. Jack Palance, John Douglas, Carlos Estrada; **D:** Henry Mankiewirk. *MPI*

Hell's Headquarters ✷ 1932 A startling tale of murder and greed involving a hunt for a fortune in African ivory. 59m/B VHS. Jack Mulhall, Barbara Weeks, Frank Mayo; **D:** Andrew L. Stone. *SNC, NOS, DVT*

Hell's Hinges ✷✷ 1916 The next to last Hart western, typifying his good/bad cowboy character. This time he's a gunslinger who falls for the new preacher's sister, while the minister himself is led astray by a saloon gal. Perhaps Hart's best film. 65m/B VHS. William S. Hart, Clara Williams, Jack Standing, Robert McKim; **D:** William S. Hart. National Film Registry '94. *GPV, VYY, GVV*

Hell's House ✷ 1932 After his mother dies, young lad Durkin goes to the city to live with relatives, gets mixed up with moll Davis and her bootleg boyfriend O'Brien, and is sent to a brutal reform school. Interesting primarily for early appearances by Davis and O'Brien (before he was typecast as the indefatigable good-guy). 80m/B VHS, Beta. Junior Durkin, Pat O'Brien, Bette Davis, Frank "Junior" Coghlan, Charley Grapewin, Emma Dunn; **D:** Howard Higgin. *NOS, MRV, CNG*

Hell's Wind Staff ✷ 1982 Two boys uncover a plot to sell their townsmen as slaves to other South East Asian countries. 95m/C VHS, Beta. Hwang Jang Lee, Mang Yuen Man, Mang Hai. *WVE*

The Hellstrom Chronicle ✷✷✷ 1971 (G) A powerful quasi-documentary about insects, their formidable capacity for survival, and the conjectured battle man will have with them in the future. 90m/C VHS, Beta. Lawrence Pressman; **D:** Walon Green; **W:** David Seltzer. Academy Awards '71: Best Feature Documentary. *COL, OM*

Helltown ✷½ 1938 A western programmer based on Zane Grey's novel in which Wayne tracks down a cattle rustler. 60m/B VHS, Beta. John Wayne; **D:** Charles T. Barton. *NOS, DVT, VCN*

Help! 🎵🎵🎵 **1965 (G)** Ringo's ruby ring is the object of a search by an Arab cult who chase the Fab Four all over the globe in order to acquire the bauble. The laserdisc version includes a wealth of Beatles memorabilia, rare footage behind the scenes at the film's premiere, and extensive publicity material. 🎵Help!; You're Gonna Lose That Girl; You've Got To Hide Your Love Away; The Night Before; Another Girl; Ticket To Ride; I Need You. **90m/C VHS, Beta, LV, DVD.** John Lennon, Paul McCartney, Ringo Starr, George Harrison, Leo McKern, Eleanor Bron; **D:** Richard Lester; **W:** Charles Wood, Marc Behm; **C:** David Watkin. *MPI, MVD, CRC*

Help Wanted Female 🎵 **1968** Jo Jo, a prostitute with kung fu skills who likes to rob traveling salesmen, is in a quandary over her lesbian roommate's acid dropping friends, including Mr. Gregory, who has a penchant for murder. After recounting a previous trip in which he murdered an acquaintance, he succeeds in alienating his current companions, who must fight for their life to escape him. **71m/B VHS.** Sebastian Gregory, Inga Olsen; **D:** Harold Perkins. *SMW, TPV*

Help Wanted: Male 🎵½ **1982** When a magazine publisher discovers that her fiance cannot have children, she looks for someone else who can do the job right. Made for television. **97m/C VHS, Beta.** Suzanne Pleshette, Gil Gerard, Bert Convy, Dana Elcar, Harold Gould, Caren Kaye; **D:** William Wiard. *WOV*

Helter Skelter 🎵🎵½ **1976** The harrowing story of the murder of actress Sharon Tate and four others at the hands of Charles Manson and his psychotic "family." Based on the book by prosecutor Vincent Bugliosi, adapted by J.P. Miller. Features an outstanding performance by Railsback as Manson. A TV mini-series. **194m/C VHS, Beta, Closed Caption.** Steve Railsback, Nancy Wolfe, George DiCenzo, Marilyn Burns; **D:** Tom Gries; **M:** Billy Goldenberg. *FOX*

Helter Skelter Murders woof! **1971 (R)** An independently made version of the Charles Manson story, with sequences filmed at Spawn Ranch. Includes Manson's own recording of his songs "Mechanical Man" and "Garbage Dump" on the soundtrack. **CW:** Graphic violence and nudity. **83m/B VHS.** Brian Klinknett, Debbie Duff, Phyllis Estes; **D:** Frank Howard; **W:** J.J. Wilkie, Duke Howze; **C:** Frank Howard. *EEL*

The Henderson Monster 🎵🎵½ **1980** Experiments of a genetic scientist are questioned by a community and its mayor. A potentially controversial television drama turns into typical romantic fluff. **105m/C VHS, Beta.** Jason Miller, Christine Lahti, Stephen Collins, David Spielberg, Nehemiah Persoff, Larry Gates; **D:** Waris Hussein. *ART*

Hennessy 🎵🎵½ **1975 (PG)** An IRA man plots revenge on the Royal family and Parliament after his family is violently killed. Tense political drama, but slightly far-fetched. **103m/C VHS.** *GB* Rod Steiger, Lee Remick, Richard Johnson, Trevor Howard, Peter Egan, Eric Porter; **D:** Don Sharp; **W:** John Gay. *NO*

Henry IV 🎵🎵½ **1985** The adaptation of the Luigi Pirandello farce about a modern-day recluse who shields himself from the horrors of the real world by pretending to be mad and acting out the fantasy of being the medieval German emperor Henry IV. In Italian with English subtitles. **94m/C VHS, Beta.** *IT* Marcello Mastroianni, Claudia Cardinale, Leopoldo Trieste, Paolo Bonacelli, Luciano Bartoli, Latou Chardons; **D:** Marco Bellocchio; **W:** Tonino Guerra, Marco Bellocchio, Astor Piazzolla.

Henry V 🎵🎵🎵🎵 **1944** Classic, epic adaptation of the Shakespeare play, and Olivier's first and most successful directorial effort, dealing with the medieval British monarch that defeated the French at Agincourt. Distinguished by Olivier's brilliant formal experiment of beginning the drama as a 16th Century performance of the play in the Globe Theatre, and having the stage eventually transform into realistic historical settings of storybook color. Filmed at the height of WWII suffering

in Britain (and meant as a parallel to the British fighting the Nazis), the film was not released in the U.S. until 1946. **136m/C VHS, Beta.** *GB* Laurence Olivier, Robert Newton, Leslie Banks, Esmond Knight, Renee Asherson, Leo Genn, George Robey, Ernest Thesiger, Felix Aylmer, Ralph Truman; **D:** Laurence Olivier; **W:** Laurence Olivier, Alan Dent; **C:** Robert Krasker; **M:** William Walton. National Board of Review Awards '46: Best Actor (Olivier); New York Film Critics Awards '46: Best Actor (Olivier); Nominations: Academy Awards '46: Best Actor (Olivier), Best Interior Decoration, Best Picture, Best Original Dramatic/Comedy Score. *PAR, HMV*

Henry V 🎵🎵🎵🎵 **1989** Stirring, expansive retelling of Shakespeare's drama about the warrior-king of England. Branagh stars as Henry, leading his troops and uniting his kingdom against France. Very impressive production rivals Olivier's 1945 rendering but differs by stressing the high cost of war—showing the ego-mania, doubts, and subterfuge that underlie conflicts. Marvelous film-directorial debut for Branagh (who also adapted the screenplay). Wonderful supporting cast includes some of Britain's finest actors. **138m/C VHS, LV, Letterbox, Closed Caption.** *GB* Kenneth Branagh, Derek Jacobi, Brian Blessed, Alec McCowen, Ian Holm, Richard Briers, Robert Stephens, Robbie Coltrane, Christian Bale, Judi Dench, Paul Scofield, Michael Maloney, Emma Thompson; **D:** Kenneth Branagh; **W:** Kenneth Branagh; **M:** Patrick Doyle. Academy Awards '89: Best Costume Design; British Academy Awards '89: Best Director (Branagh); National Board of Review Awards '89: Best Director (Branagh); Nominations: Academy Awards '89: Best Actor (Branagh), Best Director (Branagh). *FOX, SIG, TVC*

Henry & June 🎵🎵🎵½ **1990 (NC-17)** Based on the diaries of writer Anais Nin which chronicled her triangular relationship with author Henry Miller and his wife June, a relationship that provided the erotic backdrop to Miller's "Tropic of Capricorn." Set in Paris in the early '30s, the setting moves between the impecunious expatriate's cheap room on the Left bank—filled with artists, circus performers, prostitutes, and gypsies—to the conservative, well-appointed home of Nin and her husband. Captures the heady atmosphere of Miller's gay Paris; no one plays an American better than Ward (who replaced Alec Baldwin). Notable for having prompted the creation of an NC-17 rating because of its adult theme. **136m/C VHS, LV, Letterbox, Closed Caption.** Fred Ward, Uma Thurman, Maria De Medeiros, Richard E. Grant, Kevin Spacey; **D:** Philip Kaufman; **W:** Philip Kaufman; **C:** Philippe Rousselot. Nominations: Academy Awards '90: Best Cinematography. *USH, FCT*

Henry & Verlin 🎵🎵 **1994** Verlin (Macintosh) is a nine-year-old who doesn't talk. He lives in rural Ontario (during the Depression) with his overprotective mother Minnie (Beatty) and indifferent father Ferris (Joy), as well as Ferris' childlike brother Henry (Farmer) who befriends Verlin. The misfit duo develop a strong bond that includes disabled retired prostitute Mabel (Kidder)—much to the resentment of some of the less-enlightened townsfolk. There's some melodramatic events but the performances skirt maudlin excess. **87m/C VHS.** *CA* Gary Farmer, Keegan Macintosh, Nancy Beatty, Robert Joy, Margot Kidder, Eric Peterson; **Cameos:** David Cronenberg; **D:** Gary Ledbetter; **W:** Gary Ledbetter. Nominations: Genie Awards '94: Best Actor (Farmer), Best Actress (Beatty). *NYR*

Henry: Portrait of a Serial Killer 🎵🎵🎵🎵 **1990 (X)** Based on the horrific life and times of serial killer Henry Lee Lucas, this film has received wide praise for its straight-forward and uncompromising look into the minds of madmen. The film follows Henry and his roommate Otis as they set out on mindless murder sprees (one of which they videotape). Extremely disturbing and graphic film. Unwary viewers should be aware of the grisly scenes and use their own discretion when viewing this otherwise genuinely moving film. **90m/C VHS, Beta, LV.** Michael Rooker, Tom Towles, Tracy Arnold; **D:** John McNaughton;

W: John McNaughton, Richard Fire; **C:** Charlie Lieberman. *MPI*

Henry: Portrait of a Serial Killer 2: Mask of Sanity 🎵 **1996 (R)** Michael Rooker gave a chilling performance as serial killer Henry in part 1 but Giuntoli is merely dull. A sullen drifter, Henry manages to get a job and fellow worker Kai (Komenich) invites him to crash at his place. Turns out Kai is a part-time arsonist for hire and Henry helps him out—also introducing Kai to the pleasures of casual murder. The gore is actually limited to a few bloody scenes (usually more is heard than shown) but the whole project is boring. **CW:** Strong grisly murders and violence, sex, language and some drug use. **84m/C VHS.** Neil Giuntoli, Rich Komenich, Katherine Walsh, Carri Levinson, Penelope Milford; **D:** Chuck Parello; **W:** Chuck Parello; **C:** Michael Kohnhurst; **M:** Robert F. McNaughton. *NYR*

Her Alibi 🎵🎵 **1988 (PG)** When successful murder-mystery novelist Phil Blackwood runs out of ideas for good books, he seeks inspiration in the criminal courtroom. There he discovers a beautiful Romanian immigrant named Nina who is accused of murder. He goes to see her in jail and offers to provide her with an alibi. Narrated by Blackwood in the tone of one of his thriller novels. Uneven comedy, with appealing cast and arbitrary plot. **95m/C VHS, Beta, LV, 8mm, Closed Caption.** Tom Selleck, Paulina Porizkova, William Daniels, James Farentino, Hurd Hatfield, Patrick Wayne, Tess Harper, Joan Copeland; **D:** Bruce Beresford; **W:** Charlie Peters; **M:** Georges Delerue. *WAR*

Her and She and Him 🎵🎵 *Claude et Greta* **1969** Young Swedish beauty Greta arrives in Paris with only her guitar. Penniless, she takes up with another woman but soon feels she's only a sexual prisoner. So Greta seduces a young painter who is having an obsessive affair with a gay artist. Dubbed into English. **90m/C VHS.** *FR* Astrid Frank, Yves Vincent; **D:** Max Pecas; **C:** Robert Lefebvre. *FRF*

Her First Romance 🎵🎵½ *The Right Man* **1940** Mixed-up romance with Fellows and Wells as sisters, Linden their cousin, and Ladd her fiance. The sisters fall for Evans and use Ladd in their schemes, causing him to believe Evans is actually after Linden. Eventually, everyone pairs up properly. **77m/B VHS.** Edith Fellows, Jacqueline Wells, Alan Ladd, Judith Linden, Wilbur Evans, Roger Daniel; **D:** Edward Dmytryk; **W:** Adele Comandini. *FCT*

Her Husband's Affairs 🎵 **1947** Tone is an advertising wonder and Ball is his loving wife who always gets credit for his work. Tone does the advertising for an inventor who is searching for the perfect embalming fluid in this rather lifeless comedy. **83m/B VHS.** Lucille Ball, Franchot Tone, Edward Everett Horton, Gene Lockhart, Larry Parks; **D:** Sylvan Simon; **M:** George Duning. *GKK*

Her Life as a Man 🎵½ **1983** A female reporter is refused a job as a sportswriter because of her gender. She makes herself up as a man, gets the job, and creates havoc when she has to deal with lustful women on the job. A made-for-television movie. **93m/C VHS, Beta.** Robyn Douglass, Joan Collins, Robert Culp, Marc Singer, Laraine Newman; **D:** Robert Ellis Miller. *ORI*

Her Silent Sacrifice 🎵½ **1918** A silent melodrama about a French girl torn between material wealth and true love. **42m/B VHS, Beta.** Alice Brady, Henry Clive. *VYY*

Herbie Goes Bananas 🎵½ **1980 (G)** While Herbie the VW is racing in Rio de Janeiro, he is bothered by the syndicate, a pickpocket, and a raging bull. The fourth and final entry in the Disney "Love Bug" movies, but Herbie later made his way to a television series. **93m/C VHS, Beta.** Cloris Leachman, Charles Martin Smith, Harvey Korman, John Vernon, Alex Rocco, Richard Jaeckel, Fritz Feld; **D:** Vincent McEveety. *DIS*

Herbie Goes to Monte Carlo 🎬🎬
1077 (G) While participating in a Paris-to-Monte-Carlo race, Herbie the VW takes a detour and falls in love with a Lancia. Third in the Disney "Love Bug" series. 104m/C VHS, Beta. Dean Jones, Don Knotts, Julie Sommars, Roy Kinnear; **D:** Vincent McEveety; **W:** Arthur Alsberg. *DIS*

Herbie Rides Again 🎬🎬½ 1974 (G) In this "Love Bug" sequel, Herbie comes to the aid of an elderly woman who is trying to stop a ruthless tycoon from raising a skyscraper on her property. Humorous Disney fare. Two other sequels followed. 88m/C VHS, Beta, LV. Helen Hayes, Ken Berry, Stefanie Powers, John McIntire, Keenan Wynn; **D:** Robert Stevenson; **M:** George Bruns. *DIS*

Hercules 🎬🎬½ *La Tatiche de Ercole* 1958 The one that started it all. Reeves is perfect as the mythical hero Hercules who encounters many dangerous situations while trying to win over his true love. Dubbed in English. 107m/C VHS, Beta, LV, Letterbox. *IT* Steve Reeves, Sylva Koscina, Fabrizio Mioni, Gianna Maria Canale, Arturo Dominici; **D:** Pietro Francisci; **C:** Mario Bava. *MRV, IME, VDM*

Hercules 🎬 1983 Lackluster remake of 1957 original finds legendary muscle guy Hercules in the person of Ferrigno's Hulkster fighting against the evil King Minos for his own survival and the love of Cassiopeia, a rival king's daughter. 100m/C VHS, Beta, LV, Closed Caption. *IT* Lou Ferrigno, Sybil Danning, Ingrid Anderson; **D:** Lewis (Luigi Cozzi) Coates; **W:** Lewis (Luigi Cozzi) Coates; **M:** Pino Donaggio. Golden Raspberry Awards '83: Worst Supporting Actress (Danning), Worst New Star (Ferrigno). *MGM, IME*

Hercules 🎬🎬🎬½ 1997 (G) After a couple of animated downers, Disney's latest adventure goes for a happy heroic tone by taking on Greek myths. Baby Herc is the son of Zeus, who rules on Mt. Olympus. Hades, Lord of the Underworld, plans a takeover and learns that only Hercules' strength will stand in his way. Hades manages to kidnap the tyke and turn him mortal but when the teenaged Herc learns his true origins, he also discovers that if he proves himself to be a hero he can regain his immortality and return to Mt. Olympus. He's aided by his flying horse Pegasus, a satyr-like trainer Phil, and smart gal Meg, while Hades has his less-than-bright minions Pain and Panic. Lots of fun and lots of merchandising (even the movie makes fun of the inevitable tie-ins). ♫The Gospel Truth; Go the Distance; One Last Hope; I Won't Say; Zero to Hero. 92m/C VHS, Closed Caption. **D:** John Musker, Ron Clements; **W:** John Musker, Ron Clements, Bob Shaw, Donald McEnery, Irene Mecchi; **M:** Alan Menken, David Zippel; **V:** Tate Donovan, James Woods, Danny DeVito, Matt Frewer, Bob(cat) Goldthwait, Susan Egan, Rip Torn, Samantha Eggar, Paul Shaffer, Barbara Barrie, Hal Holbrook, Amanda Plummer, Carol Shelley. Nominations: Academy Awards '97: Best Song ("Go the Distance"); Golden Globe Awards '98: Best Song ("Go the Distance"). *TOU*

Hercules 2 🎬 *The Adventures of Hercules* 1985 (PG) The muscle-bound demi-god returns to do battle with more evil foes amidst the same stunningly cheap special effects. 90m/C VHS. *IT* Lou Ferrigno, Claudio Cassinelli, Milly Carlucci, Sonia Viviani, William Berger, Carlotta Green; **D:** Lewis (Luigi Cozzi) Coates; **M:** Pino Donaggio. *MGM*

Hercules Against the Moon Men 🎬 *Maciste la Regina di Samar* 1964 It's no holds barred for the mighty son of Zeus when evil moon men start killing off humans in a desperate bid to revive their dead queen. 88m/C VHS, Beta. *IT FR* Alan Steel, Jany Clair, Anna Maria Polani; **D:** Giacomo Gentilomo. *SNC, MRV*

Hercules and the Captive Women 🎬🎬 *Hercules and the Haunted Women; Hercules and the Conquest of Atlantis; Ercole Alla Conquista di Atlantide* 1963 Hercules' son is kidnapped by the Queen of Atlantis, and the bare-chested warrior goes on an all-out rampage to save the boy. Directed by sometimes-lauded Cottafavi. 93m/C

VHS, Beta. *IT* Reg Park, Fay Spain, Ettore Manni; **D:** Vittorio Cottafavi. *RHI, MRV, CCB*

Hercules and the Princess of Troy 🎬🎬½ 1965 Hercules is up to his pecs in trouble as he battles a hungry sea monster in order to save a beautiful maiden. Originally a pilot for a prospective TV series, and shot in English, not Italian, with Hercules played by erstwhile Tarzan Scott. Highlights are special effects and color cinematography. ?m/C VHS, Beta. *IT* Gordon Scott, Diana Hyland, Paul Stevens, Everett Sloane. *SNC, MLB*

Hercules in New York 🎬½ *Hercules: The Movie; Hercules Goes Bananas* 1970 (G) Motion picture debut of Schwarzenegger (his voice is dubbed) as a Herculean mass of muscle sent by dad Zeus to Manhattan, where he behaves likes a geek out of water and eventually becomes a professional wrestling superstar. 250 pounds of stupid, lighthearted fun. 93m/C VHS, Beta. Arnold Schwarzenegger, Arnold Stang, Deborah Loomis, James Karen, Ernest Graves; **D:** Arthur Seidelman. *MPI*

Hercules in the Haunted World 🎬🎬½ *Ercole al Centro Della Terra* 1964 Long before the days of 24-hour pharmacies, Hercules—played yet again by Reeves-clone Park—must journey to the depths of Hell in order to find a plant that will cure a poisoned princess. Better than most muscle operas, thanks to Bava. 91m/C VHS, Beta. *IT* Reg Park, Leonora Ruffo, Christopher Lee, George Ardisson; **D:** Mario Bava. *CCB, RHI, MRV*

Hercules, Prisoner of Evil 🎬 1964 Spaghetti myth-opera in which Hercules battles a witch who is turning men into werewolves. Made for Italian television by director Dawson (the nom-de-cinema of Antonio Margheriti). ?m/C VHS. *IT* Reg Park; **D:** Anthony (Antonio Margheriti) Dawson. *SNC*

Hercules the Legendary Journeys, Vol. 1: And the Amazon Women 🎬🎬½ 1994 Half-man, half-god Hercules (Sorbo) and his friend Ioleus (Hurst) are summoned to a village to kill the beasts stealing livestock. Turns out those responsible are the village's women, who are mad at their husbands and have formed a band of Amazons, lead by Hippolyta (Downey), who happens to be working for Hercules' immortal enemy, the goddess Hera. Now it's up to Herc to convince Hippolyta that men and women can work together and outsmart Hera at the same time. 91m/C VHS, Closed Caption. Kevin Sorbo, Michael Hurst, Roma Downey, Anthony Quinn, Lucy Lawless; **D:** Bill W.L. Norton; **M:** Joseph LoDuca. *USH*

Hercules the Legendary Journeys, Vol. 2: The Lost Kingdom 🎬🎬½ 1994 Hera has hidden the kingdom of Troy and only a magic compass can point Hercules (Sorbo) in the right direction. He rescues a sacrificial virgin (O'Connor) and the duo manage to find the compass and get into Troy where she learns her father was once its king. Turns out dad sent his daughter away so he wouldn't have to sacrifice her to Hera and lost his kingdom instead. Now she wants her kingdom back and Hera still wants her sacrifice—especially if it's Hercules. 91m/C VHS, Closed Caption. Kevin Sorbo, Michael Hurst, Anthony Quinn, Renee O'Connor, Robert Trebor; **D:** Harley Cokliss; **M:** Joseph LoDuca. *USH*

Hercules the Legendary Journeys, Vol. 3: The Circle of Fire 🎬🎬½ 1994 Hera's stolen fire from mankind, which is slowly freezing to death, keeping one eternal torch for herself. A villager named Deianeira (Kitaen) enlists Hercules (Sorbo) to search for Prometheus (Ferguson), the god of fire, but Hera's stolen his flame as well. When Herc finds the torch it's encircled in a ring of fire, which Hera knows can destroy Hercules' immortality. 92m/C VHS, Closed Caption. Kevin Sorbo, Michael Hurst, Anthony Quinn, Tawny Kitaen, Mark Ferguson; **D:** Doug Lefler; **M:** Joseph LoDuca. *USH*

Hercules the Legendary Journeys, Vol. 4: In the Underworld 🎬🎬½ 1994 Having married Deianeira (Kitaen), Herc's a pretty happy guy until a mysterious maiden, Iole, comes to him for help. Seems a deadly crack has opened up in the earth and is swallowing villagers. But Iole has actually been sent by Hera to destroy Hercules and when Deianeira discovers her treachery she goes to warn her husband. Only Hera manages to trick her into walking off a cliff and falling to her death. Hercules must go into the underworld to save the world from Hera but when he learns Deianeira's fate, he accepts an impossible challenge from Hades (Ferguson) to bring his wife back to life. 91m/C VHS, Closed Caption. Kevin Sorbo, Michael Hurst, Anthony Quinn, Tawny Kitaen, Mark Ferguson; **D:** Bill W.L. Norton; **M:** Joseph LoDuca. *USH*

Hercules Unchained 🎬🎬 *Ercole e la Regina de Lidia* 1959 Sequel to "Hercules" finds superhero Reeves must use all his strength to save the city of Thebes and the woman he loves from the giant Antaeus. 101m/C VHS, Beta, LV. *IT* Steve Reeves, Sylva Koscina, Silvia Lopel, Primo Carnera; **D:** Pietro Francisci. *VDM, MRV, SNC*

Here and Elsewhere *Ici et Ailleurs* 197? Godard, Gorin, and Mieville contrast the story of a French family with a look at the Palestine revolution as seen through the media of television, books, and pictures. The film was originally titled "Until Victory" and commissioned by the Palestinians to examine life in the Palestinian camps. After the defeat of the Palestinian army in the Six Day War, Godard and his cohorts transformed the film with their French family ("Here") and their impressions of Palestine ("Elsewhere"). In French with English subtitles. ?m/C VHS. *FR* Anne-Marie Mieville; **D:** Jean-Pierre Gorin, Jean-Luc Godard. *FCT*

Here Come the Co-Eds 🎬🎬½ 1945 Bud & Lou are the caretakers of an all-girl college which is about to go bankrupt unless the boys can find a way to pay off the mortgage. And come to the rescue they do, including Bud getting into the wrestling ring with the "Masked Marvel" (Chaney, Jr. as the villain). There's also a classic silent scene with Lou served a bowl of oyster stew containing a live oyster, which promptly grabs his tie, bites his fingers, and squirts in his face. 90m/B VHS. Bud Abbott, Lou Costello, Lon Chaney Jr., Peggy Ryan, Martha O'Driscoll, June Vincent, Donald Cook, Charles Dingle; **D:** Jean Yarbrough; **W:** Arthur T. Horman, John Grant. *USH, FCT*

Here Come the Girls 🎬½ 1953 An unfunny musical-comedy about a chorus boy (Hope) fired for incompetence and then rehired to set a trap when the new singer (Martin) is stalked by a killer. Weak script, weak songs. ♫Girls Are Here To Stay; Never So Beautiful; You Got Class; Desire; When You Love Someone; Ali Baba Be' My Baby; Heavenly Days; See the Circus; Peace. 100m/C VHS, Closed Caption. Bob Hope, Tony Martin, Arlene Dahl, Rosemary Clooney, Millard Mitchell, William Demarest, Fred Clark, Robert Strauss; **D:** Claude Binyon; **W:** Hal Kanter. *PAR*

Here Come the Littles: The Movie 🎬½ 1985 A 12-year-old boy finds many new adventures when he meets The Littles—tiny folks who reside within the walls of people's houses. Adapted from the books and TV series. 76m/C VHS, Beta, Closed Caption. **D:** Bernard Deyries. *FOX*

Here Come the Marines 🎬🎬 *Tell It To the Marines* 1952 The Bowery Boys accidentally join the marines and wind up breaking up a gambling ring. 66m/B VHS. Leo Gorcey, Huntz Hall, Tim Ryan; **D:** William Beaudine. *NOS*

Here Come the Nelsons 🎬🎬½ 1952 In between the radio show, "The Adventures of Ozzie and Harriet," and the TV series came this feature film. Ad man Ozzie is trying to develop a campaign for a women's wear company while the town's centennial celebration is causing problems on the homefront. Seems Harriet's houseguest for the festivities is Rock Hudson! **76m/B VHS, Closed Caption.** Ozzie Nelson, Harriet Hilliard Nelson, David Nelson, Ricky Nelson, Rock Hudson, Barbara Lawrence, Sheldon Leonard, Jim Backus; **D:** Fred de Cordova; **W:** Don Nelson, Ozzie Nelson. *USH*

Here Come the Waves 🎬🎬🎬 1945
Easy-going wartime musical finds Der Bingle as a singing idol drafted into the Navy, assigned to direct WAVE shows. The crooner meets identical twins (both played by Hutton) and falls hard. Only problem is he can't tell the gals apart—and one twin can't stand him. Amusing romantic complications mix well with some spoofing of a star's life. ♫Ac-cent-tchu-ate the Positive; I Promise You; Let's Take the Long Way Home; That Old Black Magic; There's a Fellow Waiting in Poughkeepsie; Here Come the Waves; My Mama Thinks I'm a Star; Join the Navy. **99m/B VHS, Closed Caption.** Bing Crosby, Betty Hutton, Sonny Tufts, Ann Doran, Noel Neill, Mae Clarke, Gwen Crawford, Catherine Craig; **D:** Mark Sandrich; **W:** Zion Myers. Nominations: Academy Awards '45: Best Song ("Accentuate the Positive"). *USH*

Here Comes Cookie 🎬🎬½ 1935
Amusing farce finds Gracie (Allen) the daughter of wealthy Harrison Allen (Barbier), who's afraid of the fortune hunters eyeing other daughter Phyllis (Furness). So he temporarily turns over the family fortune to Gracie, who promptly turns their Park Avenue mansion into a home for down-on-their-luck vaudevillians. Lots of specialty acts and Burns is around as straight man. **65m/B VHS, Closed Caption.** Gracie Allen, George Burns, George Barbier, Betty Furness; **D:** Norman Z. McLeod; **W:** Don Hartman, Sam Mintz; **C:** Gilbert Warrenton. *USH*

Here Comes Kelly 🎬½ 1943
Controlling his temper and hanging on to his job is more than our hero can handle. **63m/C VHS, Beta.** Eddie Quillan, Joan Woodbury, Maxie "Slapsie" Rosenbloom; **D:** William Beaudine. *GPV*

Here Comes Mr. Jordan 🎬🎬🎬🎬
1941 Montgomery is the young prizefighter killed in a plane crash because of a mix-up in heaven. He returns to life in the body of a soon-to-be murdered millionaire. Rains is the indulgent and advising guardian angel. A lovely fantasy/romance remade in 1978 as "Heaven Can Wait." Laserdisc edition includes actress Elizabeth Montgomery talking about her father Robert Montgomery as well as her television show "Bewitched." **94m/B VHS, Beta, LV.** Robert Montgomery, Claude Rains, James Gleason, Evelyn Keyes, Edward Everett Horton, Rita Johnson, John Emery; **D:** Alexander Hall; **W:** Sidney Buchman, Seton I. Miller; **M:** Friedrich Hollander. Academy Awards '41: Best Screenplay, Best Story; Nominations: Academy Awards '41: Best Actor (Montgomery), Best Black and White Cinematography, Best Director (Hall), Best Picture, Best Supporting Actor (Gleason). *COL, CRC, FCT*

Here Comes Santa Claus 🎬½ 1984
A young boy and girl travel to the North Pole to deliver a very special wish to Santa Claus. **78m/C VHS, Beta.** Karen Cheryl, Armand Meffre; **D:** Christian Gion. *VTR*

Here Comes the Groom 🎬🎬 1951
Late, stale Capra-corn, involving a rogue journalist who tries to keep his girlfriend from marrying a millionaire by becoming a charity worker. Includes a number of cameos. ♫In the Cool, Cool, Cool of the Evening; Bonne Nuit, Good Night; Misto Cristofo Columbo; Your Own Little House. **114m/B VHS, Beta, LV, Closed Caption.** Bing Crosby, Jane Wyman, Franchot Tone, Alexis Smith, James Barton, Connie Gilchrist, Robert Keith, Anna Maria Alberghetti, Charles Halton; **Cameos:** Dorothy Lamour, Phil Harris, Louis Armstrong; **D:** Frank Capra. Academy Awards '51: Best Song ("In the Cool, Cool, Cool of the Evening"); Nominations: Academy Awards '51: Best Story. *PAR*

Here We Go Again! 🎬🎬 1942
Fibber McGee and Molly are planning a cross-country trip for their 20th anniversary celebration, but complications abound. Based on the popular NBC radio series. **76m/B VHS, Beta.** Marian Jordan, Jim Jordan, Harold Peary, Gale Gordon, Edgar Bergen, Ray Noble; **D:** Allan Dwan. *CCB*

Here's Looking at You, Warner Bros. 🎬🎬🎬 1993
The 90-year history of Warner Bros. studios is profiled from the silent-era to its current success. Highlights cover the creation of Warners' gangster films, Busby Berkeley musicals, and "Looney Tunes" as well as bloopers and early screen tests by Marlo Brando, Paul Newman, Lana Turner, and Orson Welles. Includes interviews with stars, directors, and producers and numerous film clips. **108m/C VHS, LV. D:** Robert Guenette; **W:** Robert Guenette. *WAR*

Heritage of the Desert 🎬½ 1933
One of the earlier westerns made by the rugged Scott. **62m/B VHS, Beta.** Randolph Scott, Sally Blane, Guinn "Big Boy" Williams; **D:** Henry Hathaway. *DVT, TIM*

The Hero 🎬½ *Bloomfield* 1971 (PG)
A popular soccer player agrees to throw a game for big cash, and then worries about losing the respect of a young boy who idolizes him. Nothing new in this overly sentimental sports drama. **97m/C VHS, Beta.** Richard Harris, Romy Schneider, Kim Burfield, Maurice Kaufman; **D:** Richard Harris.

Hero 🎬🎬🎬 1992 (PG-13)
Interesting twist on Cinderella fable and modern media satire has television reporter Davis looking for the man who saved her life, expecting a genuine hero, and accepting without question the one who fits her vision. Critically considered disappointing, but wait—Garcia and Hoffman make a great team, and Davis is fetching as the vulnerable media person. Strong language and dark edges may keep away some of the kids, but otherwise this is a fine fable.**CW:** Strong language. **116m/C VHS, LV, 8mm, Letterbox, Closed Caption.** Geena Davis, Dustin Hoffman, Andy Garcia, Joan Cusack, Kevin J. O'Connor, Chevy Chase, Maury Chaykin, Stephen Tobolowsky, Christian Clemenson, Tom Arnold, Warren Berlinger, Susie Cusack, James Madio, Richard Riehle, Don Yesso, Darrell Larson; **D:** Stephen Frears; **W:** David Peoples; **M:** George Fenton. *COL*

A Hero Ain't Nothin' But a Sandwich 🎬🎬½ 1978 (PG)
A young urban black teenager gets involved in drugs and is eventually saved from ruin. Slow-moving, over-directed and talky. However, Scott turns in a fine performance. Based on Alice Childress' novel. **107m/C VHS, Beta, Closed Caption.** Cicely Tyson, Paul Winfield, Larry B. Scott, Helen Martin, Glynn Turman, David Groh; **D:** Ralph Nelson. *PAR, FCT*

Hero and the Terror 🎬½ 1988 (R)
Perennial karate guy Norris plays a sensitive policeman who conquers his fear of a not-so-sensitive maniac who's trying to kill him. Plenty of action and a cheesy subplot to boot. **96m/C VHS, Beta, LV, Closed Caption.** Chuck Norris, Brynn Thayer, Steve James, Jack O'Halloran, Ron O'Neal, Billy Drago; **D:** William Tannen; **W:** Michael Blodgett. *VTR*

Hero at Large 🎬🎬½ 1980 (PG)
An unemployed actor foils a robbery while dressed in a promotional "Captain Avenger" suit, and instant celebrity follows. Lightweight, yet enjoyable. **98m/ C VHS, Beta.** John Ritter, Anne Archer, Bert Convy, Kevin McCarthy, Kevin Bacon; **D:** Martin Davidson; **W:** A.J. Carothers. *MGM*

Hero Bunker 🎬🎬 1971
Hero bunk about a platoon of heroic Greek soldiers who attempt, at the expense of their personal longevity, to defend an important bunker from enemy invasion. **93m/C VHS, Beta.** John Miller, Maria Xenia; **D:** George Andrews. *ART*

Hero of Rome 1963
Rome has many who could be called "hero," but one stands biceps and pecs above the rest. **?m/C VHS, Beta.** *IT* Gordon Scott, Gabriella Pallotti. *SNC*

Hero of the Year 🎬🎬 1985
The characters from Falk's "Top Dog" return in this story of a Polish television personality who loses his job and is forced to face unemployment and job-seeking. **115m/C VHS.** *PL* **D:** Feliks Falk. *FCT*

Herod the Great 🎬 1960
Biblical epic of the downfall of Herod, the ruler of ancient Judea. Scantily clad women abound. Dubbed. **93m/C VHS.** *IT* Edmund Purdom, Sandra Milo, Alberto Lupo; **D:** Arnaldo Genoino. *SNC*

Heroes 🎬🎬 1977 (PG)
An institutionalized Vietnam vet (Winkler) escapes, hoping to establish a worm farm which will support all his crazy buddies. On the way to the home of a friend he hopes will help him, he encounters Field. Funny situations don't always mix with serious underlying themes of mental illness and post-war adjustment. **97m/C VHS, Beta.** Henry Winkler, Sally Field, Harrison Ford; **D:** Jeremy Paul Kagan; **W:** Jim Carabatsos; **M:** Jack Nitzsche. *USH*

Heroes Die Young 🎬½ 1960
A cheap independent feature depicting an American command mission with orders to sabotage German oil fields during WWII. **76m/B VHS, Beta.** Krika Peters, Scott Borland, Robert Getz, James Strother. *FOX, FCT*

Heroes for Sale 🎬🎬🎬 1933
Fascinating melodrama about a WWI veteran who returns home and manages to survive one disaster after another. Barthelmess is great in his performance as an American Everyman who must deal with everything from morphine addiction to finding work during the Depression. Fast-paced, patriotic film is helped by ambitious script and the expert direction of Wellman. **72m/B VHS, Closed Caption.** Richard Barthelmess, Loretta Young, Aline MacMahon, Robert Barrat, Grant Mitchell, Douglass Dumbrille, Charley Grapewin, Ward Bond; **D:** William A. Wellman; **W:** Robert Lord, Wilson Mizner. *MGM*

Heroes in Blue 🎬🎬 1939
Two brothers join the police force, but one goes astray and hooks up with gangsters. Plenty of action distracts from the cliched story. **60m/B VHS, Beta.** Dick Purcell, Charles Quigley, Bernadene Hayes, Edward Keane; **D:** William Watson. *SNC*

Heroes in Hell 🎬½ 1967
Two escaped WWII POWs join the Allied underground in an espionage conspiracy against the Third Reich. **90m/C VHS, Beta.** Klaus Kinski, Ettore Manni. *NO*

The Heroes of Desert Storm 🎬🎬
1991 The human spirit of the people who fought in the high-tech Persian Gulf War is captured in this film that also features real war footage from ABC News. **93m/C VHS, Beta.** Daniel Baldwin, Angela Bassett, Marshall Bell, Michael Alan Brooks, William Bumiller, Michael Champion, Maria Diaz; **D:** Don Ohlmeyer; **W:** Lionel Chetwynd.

The Heroes of Telemark 🎬🎬½ 1965
In 1942, Norway is under Nazi occupation and Nazi scientists are dangerously close to producing an essential element for making an atomic bomb in a secret factory. Underground leader Knut Straud (Harris) enlists the help of Norwegian scientist Rolf Pedersen (Douglas) and a group of saboteurs to destroy the factory. But their raid only provides a short delay and our heroes must now prevent shipment of the component from ever reaching Germany. Filmed on location in Norway, with former members of the underground serving as technical advisors for director Mann. **130m/C VHS.** *GB* Richard Harris, Kirk Douglas, Michael Redgrave, Ulla Jacobsson, David Weston, Sebastian Breaks, Alan Howard, Roy Dotrice, Patrick Jordan, Anton Diffring, Eric Porter, Ralph Michael; **D:** Anthony Mann; **W:** Ben Barzman; **C:** Robert Krasker; **M:** Malcolm Arnold. *COL*

Heroes of the Alamo 🎬½ 1937
Remember the Alamo...but forget this movie. Dull, threadbare dramatization of the battle that was scorned even back in '37. **75m/B VHS, Beta.** Rex Lease, Lane Chandler, Roger Williams, Earle Hodgins, Julian Rivero; **D:** Harry Fraser. *GPV*

Heroes of the Heart 🎬🎬½ 1994
Residents ofa West Viriginia trailer park are devastated when their homes are destroyed in a flood. But then Basquette claims she was visited by God, who's directed her to bring the poor community together so that each can be granted their most secret wish. Nicely eccentric characters, serious

theme with some whimsical touches and a country-music soundtrack. 102m/C VHS. Lena Basquette, Larry Groce, Dusty Rhodes, Webb Wilder, John McIntire, Jennifer Gurney, Johnny Paycheck; **D:** Daniel Boyd; **W:** Daniel Boyd; **C:** Larry Kopelman; **M:** Michael Lipton. *SLI*

Heroes of the Hills 🎬½ **1938** The Three Mesquiteers back up a plan that would allow trusted prisoners to work for neighboring ranchers. Part of "The Three Mesquiteers" series. 54m/B VHS, Beta. Bob Livingston, Ray Corrigan, Max Terhune. *VCN, MLB*

Heroes of the West 🎬½ **1932** Early sound action western serial. 70m/B VHS, Beta. Noah Beery Jr. *VCN, MLB*

Heroes Shed No Tears 🎬🎬 *Ying Xiong Wei Lei; The Sunset Warrior* **1986** Chinese mercenaries are hired by the Thai government to capture a drug lord from the Golden Triangle. Cantonese with subtitles. 93m/C VHS. HK Eddy Ko, Ching-Ying Lam, Chen Yue Sang, Kuo Sheng; **D:** John Woo; **W:** John Woo. *TAI*

Heroes Stand Alone 🎬 **1989 (R)** When a U.S. spy plane is downed in Central America, a special force is sent in to rescue the crew. Another "Rambo" rip-off. 84m/C VHS, Beta. Bradford Dillman, Chad Everett, Wayne Grace, Rick Dean; **D:** Mark Griffiths; **W:** Thomas McKelvey Cleaver. *MGM*

Heroes Three 🎬🎬 **1984** When his crewmate is murdered while on leave in in the Far East, a Navy officer enlists the aid of a Chinese detective to track down the killer. 90m/C VHS, Beta. Rowena Cortes, Mike Kelly, Laurens C. Postma, Lawrence Tan; **D:** S.H. Lau. *IMP*

The Heroic Trio 🎬🎬½ **1993** Three superheroines battle the Lord of the Underground to prevent him from stealing any more human babies. Lots of martial arts and supernatural action. Chinese with subtitles or dubbed. 87m/C VHS, LV. HK Michelle Yeoh, Maggie Cheung, Anita Mui, Anthony Wong; **D:** Ching Siu Tung, Johnny To. *TAI*

He's My Girl 🎬½ **1987 (PG-13)** When a rock singer wins a trip for two to Hollywood, he convinces his agent to dress up as a woman so they can use the free tickets. 104m/C VHS, Beta. David Hallyday, T.K. Carter, Misha McK, Jennifer Tilly; **D:** Gabrielle Beaumont; **W:** Terence H. Winkless, Taylor Ames, Charles F. Bohl; **C:** Peter Collister. *ART*

He's Your Dog, Charlie Brown! **1968** An animated Peanuts adventure wherein Charlie Brown decides to send Snoopy back to the Daisy Hill Puppy Farm for obedience lessons. 30m/C VHS, Beta,, Closed Caption.

Hester Street 🎬🎬🎬½ **1975** Set at the turn of the century, the film tells the story of a young Jewish immigrant who ventures to New York City to be with her husband. As she re-acquaints herself with her husband, she finds that he has abandoned his Old World ideals. The film speaks not only to preserving the heritage of the Jews, but to cherishing all heritages and cultures. Highly regarded upon release, unfortunately forgotten today. 92m/B VHS, Beta. Carol Kane, Doris Roberts, Steven Keats, Mel Howard, Dorrie Kavanaugh, Stephen Strimpell; **D:** Joan Micklin Silver; **M:** William Bolcom. Nominations: Academy Awards '75: Best Actress (Kane). *FRF, VES*

Hexed 🎬½ **1993** Walter Mitty lives in the person of bellboy Matthew Welsh, who enjoys masquerading as a debonair bon vivant. He finagles his way into the life of Hexina, a beautiful psychotic model who has checked into the hotel where Matthew works in order to murder her blackmailer. She tries to kill Matthew, apparently getting in a little practice, but he'll still follow her anywhere. Inane, charmless comedy that intends to satirize "Fatal Attraction" and similar films. **CW:** Language and sexuality. 93m/C VHS, LV, Closed Caption. Arye Gross, Claudia Christian, Adrienne Shelly, R. Lee Ermey, Norman Fell, Michael E. Knight; **D:** Alan Spencer; **W:** Alan Spencer. *COL*

Hey, Babu Riba 🎬🎬½ **1988 (R)** A popular Yugoslavian fit of nostalgia about four men convening at the funeral of a young girl they all loved years before, and their happy, Americana-

bathed memories therein. In Serbo-Croatian with English subtitles. 109m/C VHS, Beta, LV. YU Gala Videnovic, Nebojsa Bakocevic, Dragan Bjelogrlic, Marko Todorovic, Goran Radakovic, Relja Basic, Milos Zutic; **D:** Jovan Acin; **W:** Jovan Acin. *ORI*

Hey Good Lookin' **1982** Ralph Bakshi's irreverent look at growing up in the 1950s bears the trademark qualities that distinguish his other adult animated features, "Fritz the Cat" and "Heavy Traffic." 87m/C VHS, Beta. **D:** Ralph Bakshi; **W:** Ralph Bakshi. *WAR*

Hey There, It's Yogi Bear 🎬🎬 **1964** When Yogi Bear comes out of winter hibernation to search for food, he travels to the Chizzling Brothers Circus. The first feature-length cartoon to come from the H-B Studios. 98m/C VHS, Beta, LV, Closed Caption. **D:** William Hanna; **V:** Daws Butler, James Darren, Mel Blanc, J. Pat O'Malley, Julie Bennett. *WOV, IME*

Hi-De-Ho 🎬🎬½ **1935** The great Cab Calloway and his red hot jazz are featured in this film, which has the band caught between rival gangsters. The plot is incidental to the music, anyway. ♫Hi-De-Ho; I Got A Gal Named Nettie; Little Old Lady From Baltimore; A Rainy Sunday. 60m/B VHS, Beta. Cab Calloway, Ida James; **D:** Josh Binney. *MVD, NOS, DVT*

Hi-Di-Hi **1988** A British television comedy about the shenanigans that inevitably follow when a stuffy Cambridge professor becomes the entertainment manager for a holiday camp. 91m/C VHS, Beta. GB Simon Cadell, Ruth Madoc, Paul Shane, Jeffrey Holland, Leslie Dwyer. *FOX*

Hi Diddle Diddle 🎬🎬½ *Diamonds and Crime; Try and Find It* **1943** Topsy-turvy comedy features young lovers who long for conventional happiness. Instead they are cursed with con-artist parents who delight in crossing that law-abiding line. 72m/B VHS, Beta. Adolphe Menjou, Martha Scott, Dennis O'Keefe, Pola Negri; **D:** Andrew L. Stone. Nominations: Academy Awards '43: Best Original Dramatic/Comedy Score. *NOS, DVT, HEG*

Hi-Jacked 🎬 **1950** When a parolee trucker's cargo is stolen, he inevitably becomes a suspect and must set out to find the true culprits. 66m/B VHS, Beta, LV. Jim Davis, Paul Cavanagh, Marsha Jones. *RXM*

Hi, Mom! 🎬🎬🎬 *Confessions of A Peeping John; Blue Manhattan* **1970 (R)** DePalma's follow-up to "Greetings" finds amateur pornographer/movie maker De Niro being advised by a professional in the field (Garfield) of sleazy filmmaking. De Niro films the residents of his apartment building and eventually marries one of his starlets. One of De Palma's earlier and better efforts with De Niro playing a crazy as only he can. 87m/C VHS. Robert De Niro, Charles Durnham, Allen (Goorwitz) Garfield, Lara Parker, Jennifer Salt, Gerrit Graham; **D:** Brian DePalma; **W:** Brian DePalma. *FCT, HHE*

Hi-Riders 🎬 **1977 (R)** A revenge-based tale about large, mag-wheeled trucks and their drivers. 90m/C VHS, Beta. Mel Ferrer, Stephen McNally, Neville Brand, Ralph Meeker; **D:** Greydon Clark. *VCI*

The Hidden 🎬🎬🎬 **1987 (R)** A seasoned cop (Nouri) and a benign alien posing as an FBI agent (MacLachlan) team up to track down and destroy a hyper-violent alien who survives by invading the bodies of humans, causing them to go on murderous rampages. Much acclaimed, high velocity action film with state-of-the-art special effects. 98m/C VHS, Beta, LV, Closed Caption. Kyle MacLachlan, Michael Nouri, Clu Gulager, Ed O'Ross, Claudia Christian, Clarence Felder, Richard Brooks, William Boyett; **D:** Jack Sholder; **W:** Bob Hunt; **M:** Michael Convertino. *CDV, VTR*

The Hidden 2 🎬🎬½ **1994 (R)** The hyper-violent alien of the 1987 movie returns. With its love of fast cars, high-caliber weapons, and heavy metal music, this body-possessing creature appears to be unstoppable. 91m/C VHS, LV, Closed Caption. Raphael Sbarge, Kate Hodge, Michael Nouri; **D:**

Jeff Pinsker, **W:** Seth Pinsker; **M:** David McHugh. *NLC, IME*

Hidden Agenda 🎬🎬½ **1990 (R)** A human rights activist and an American lawyer uncover brutality and corruption among the British forces in Northern Ireland. Slow-paced but strong performances. The Northern Irish dialect is sometimes difficult to understand as are the machinations on the British police system. Generally worthwhile. 108m/C VHS, LV, Closed Caption. Frances McDormand, Brian Cox, Brad Dourif, Mai Zetterling, John Benfield, Des McAleer, Jim Norton, Maurice Roeves; **D:** Ken Loach; **W:** Jim Allen; **M:** Stewart Copeland. Cannes Film Festival '90: Special Jury Prize. *HBO, FCT*

Hidden Assassin 🎬 *The Shooter* **1994 (R)** French hit woman Simone (Detmers) supposedly shoots the Cuban ambassador to the U.N. and escapes back to her home base in Prague, followed by Czech-born U.S. Marshal Mickey Dane (Lundgren). Mickey starts to doubt that Simone is the killer (she claims she's long retired and is being set up) and the duo try to find the truth amid lots of double-crosses. Doesn't make much sense in any case.**CW:** Strong violence, language and brief nudity. 89m/C VHS, LV, Closed Caption. Dolph Lundgren, Maruschka Detmers, Assumpta Serna, Gavan O'Herlihy, John Ashton, Simon Andreu; **D:** Ted Kotcheff; **W:** Meg Thayer, Billy Ray, Yves Andre Martin; **C:** Fernando Arguelles; **M:** Stefano Mainetti. *TOU*

Hidden City 🎬🎬 **1987** A film archivist and a statistician become drawn into a conspiracy when a piece of revealing film is spliced onto the end of an innocuous government tape. 112m/C VHS, Beta. Charles Stuart, Cassie Stuart, Alex Norton, Tusse Silberg, Bill Paterson; **D:** Stephen Pollakoff. *NO*

Hidden Enemy 🎬½ **1940** During WWII, a scientist develops a new metal alloy that is stronger than steel yet lighter than aluminum. His nephew must protect his scientist/uncle from spies who would steal the formula to use against the Allies. 63m/B VHS, Beta. Warren Hull, Kay Linaker, William von Brinken, George Cleveland; **D:** Howard Bretherton. *SNC, RXM*

Hidden Fears 🎬🎬½ **1993** Maureen Dietz (Foster) carries the gruesome memories of her husband's murder with her. Years later she goes to the police with new evidence to reopen her husband's case. Only the killers find out and return to finish off the eyewitnesses, and she's next! Based on the novel "Exercise in Terror" by Kaminsky, who also wrote the screenplay. 90m/C VHS, Beta. Meg Foster, Frederic Forrest, Wally Taylor, Bever-Leigh Banfield, Marc Macaulay, Patrick Cherry, Scott Hayes; **D:** Jean Bodon; **W:** Stuart Kaminsky. *FCT*

The Hidden Fortress 🎬🎬🎬½ *Kakushi Toride No San Akunin; Three Rascals in the Hidden Fortress; Three Bad Men in the Hidden Fortress* **1958** Kurosawa's tale of a warrior who protects a princess from warring feudal lords. An inspiration for George Lucas' "Star Wars" series and deserving of its excellent reputation. In Japanese with English subtitles. The laserdisc edition is letterboxed to retain the film's original integrity. 139m/B VHS, Beta, LV, Letterbox. JP Toshiro Mifune, Misa Vehara, Minoru Chiaki; **D:** Akira Kurosawa. Berlin International Film Festival '59: Best Director (Kurosawa). *HMV, FCT, CRC*

Hidden Gold 🎬½ **1933** Routine western for Mix, which has him going undercover to win the confidence of three outlaws and discover where they have hidden their loot. 57m/B VHS, Beta. Tom Mix, Judith Barrie, Raymond Hatton; **D:** Arthur Rosson. *GPV, VCN, DVT*

Hidden Guns 🎬🎬🎬 **1956** Above-average tale of father-and-son lawmen out to reform a town and put the bad guys away. When dad is killed, son goes up against the villain alone. A Greek chorus adds an interesting twist to the action. Erich von Stroheim, Jr. is listed as assistant director. 66m/B VHS. Bruce (Herman Brix) Bennett, Richard Arlen, John Carradine, Faron Young, Angie Dickinson, Guinn "Big Boy" Williams; **D:** Albert C. Gannaway. *NOS*

Hidden in America 🎬🎬½ 1996 (PG-13)
Bill Januson (Bridges) has lost his auto-plant job because of downsizing and his wife to cancer. His savings exhausted and his prospects bleak, Januson struggles to put food on the table for his two kids. Cable movie produced in conjunction with the End Hunger Network, whose co-founder, Jeff Bridges, has a cameo. **CW:** Disturbing plot material. **100m/C VHS.** Beau Bridges, Bruce Davison, Jena Malone, Shelton Dane, Alice Krige, Josef Sommer, Frances McDormand; **Cameos:** Jeff Bridges; **D:** Martin Bell; **W:** Peter Silverman, Michael deGuzman; **C:** James R. Bagdonas; **M:** Mason Daring. *EVE*

Hidden Obsession 🎬½ 1992 (R) Newscaster Ellen is taking a much needed vacation at an isolated cabin when she learns that a serial killer has escaped from a nearby prison. Luckily, she has a hunky police officer neighbor for protection. But though the escaped killer is captured, the killings go on—with Ellen as the next target. **92m/C VHS, LV, Closed Caption.** Heather Thomas, Jan-Michael Vincent, Nicholas Celozzi; **D:** John Stewart; **W:** David Reskin. *USH*

The Hidden Room 🎬🎬🎬 *Obsession* 1949
A doctor finds out about his wife's affair and decides to get revenge on her lover. He kidnaps him, imprisons him in a cellar, and decides to kill him—slowly. Tense melodrama. **98m/B VHS, Beta.** *GB* Robert Newton, Sally Gray, Naunton Wayne, Phil Brown, Olga Lindo, Russell Waters, James Harcourt, Allan Jeayes, Stanley Baker; **D:** Edward Dmytryk; **W:** Alec Coppel; **M:** Nino Rota. *NOS, SNC, RXM*

Hidden Valley 🎬🎬 1932 Early Steele western in which everyone is fighting over a map that leads to hidden treasure in the valley. **60m/B VHS.** Bob Steele, Gertrude Messinger, Francis McDonald; **D:** Robert North Bradbury. *GPV*

Hide and Go Shriek 🎬 1987 (R) Several high school seniors are murdered one by one during a graduation party. Also available in an unrated, gorier version. **90m/C VHS, Beta, LV.** Annette Sinclair, Brittain Frye, Rebunkah Jones; **D:** Skip Schoolnik. *NO*

Hide and Seek 🎬 1977 When a high school hacker converts his computer into a nuclear weapon, he finds that it has developed a mind of its own. **60m/C VHS, Beta.** Bob Martin, Ingrid Veninger, David Patrick. *ORI*

Hide and Seek 🎬 1980 A study of children living in the land that would soon become Israel. Although they play as normal children, life is particularly difficult. This adversity will lay the foundation for their Israeli citizenry. In Hebrew with English subtitles. **90m/C VHS, Beta.** Gila Almagor, Doron Tavori, Chaim Hadaya; **D:** Dan Wolman. *ERG, TPV*

Hide in Plain Sight 🎬🎬🎬 1980 (PG) A distraught blue-collar worker searches for his children who disappeared when his ex-wife and her mobster husband are given new identities by federal agents. Caan's fine directorial debut is based on a true story. **96m/C VHS, Beta.** James Caan, Jill Eikenberry, Robert Viharo, Kenneth McMillan, Josef Sommer, Danny Aiello; **D:** James Caan. *MGM*

Hide-Out 🎬🎬½ 1934 A man running from the law winds up at a small farm, falls in love, and becomes reformed by the good family that takes him in. Good supporting cast includes a very young Rooney. **83m/B VHS.** Robert Montgomery, Maureen O'Sullivan, Edward Arnold, Elizabeth Patterson, Mickey Rooney, Edward Brophy; **D:** Woodbridge S. Van Dyke. Nominations: Academy Awards '34: Best Story. *MGM*

Hideaway 🎬🎬 1994 (R) Hodge podge movie finds Hatch Harrison (Goldblum) brought back from the other side after suffering injuries from a near-fatal car accident. He returns with the ability to psychically connect with Vassago (Sisto), a sadistic serial killer of young girls. Coincidentally, Harrison has a teenage daughter, Regina (Silverstone), and Vassago has her lined up as his next victim. The visual effects of spirits floating down a cosmic vortex are entertaining, but plot originality must have been hidden away to make room for the nifty special effects. Based on a novel by

Dean R. Koontz. **CW:** Terror violence; language; scene of sexuality. **103m/C VHS, LV, Closed Caption.** Jeff Goldblum, Christine Lahti, Alicia Silverstone, Jeremy Sisto, Rae Dawn Chong; **D:** Brett Leonard; **W:** Andrew Kevin Walker, Neal Jimenez; **C:** Gale Tattersall; **M:** Trevor Jones. *COL*

The Hideaways 🎬🎬½ *From the Mixed-Up Files of Mrs. Basil E. Frankweiler* 1973 (G) A 12-year-old girl and her younger brother run away and hide in the Metropolitan Museum of Art. The girl becomes enamored of a piece of sculpture and sets out to discover its creator. Based on the children's novel by E.L. Konigsburg. **105m/C VHS, Beta.** Richard Mulligan, George Rose, Ingrid Bergman, Sally Prager, Johnny Doran, Madeline Kahn; **D:** Fielder Cook. *WAR, VHE, FCT*

Hideous 🎬½ 1997 (R) Eccentric collector's greatest prize is a seemingly petrified toxic waste mutant that's not so petrified afterall. It manages to come to life and even spawn little mutants to go on a killing spree. **82m/C VHS.** Jacqueline Lovell, Michael Citrinti, Rhonda Griffin, Mel Johnson Jr., Traci May, Jerry O'Donnell; **D:** Charles Band; **W:** Benjamin Carr; **M:** Richard Band. *AFE*

Hideous Sun Demon 🎬½ *Blood on His Lips; Terror from the Sun; The Sun Demon* 1959 A physicist exposed to radiation must stay out of sunlight or he will turn into a scaly, lizard-like creature. Includes previews of coming attractions from classic sci-fi films. **75m/B VHS.** Robert Clarke, Patricia Manning, Nan Peterson, Patrick Whyte, Peter Similuk, Fred La Porta, Robert Garry; **D:** Robert Clarke; **W:** Doane R. Hoag, E. S. Seeley Jr.; **C:** Vilis Lapenieks, John Morrill, Stan Follis. *RHI, MRV, EEL*

Hider in the House 🎬🎬½ 1990 (R) In a peaceful neighborhood a family is about to spend an evening of terror when they discover a psychopath is hiding in the attic of their home. **109m/C VHS, Beta, LV.** Michael McKean, Gary Busey, Mimi Rogers, Kurt Christopher Kinder, Candy Hutson, Elizabeth Ruscio, Bruce Glover; **D:** Michael Patrick. *VES, ART*

Hiding Out 🎬🎬 1987 (PG-13) A young stockbroker testifies against the Mafia and must find a place to hide in order to avoid being killed. He winds up at his cousin's high school in Delaware, but can he really go through all these teenage troubles once again? **99m/C VHS, Beta, Closed Caption.** Jon Cryer, Keith Coogan, Gretchen Cryer, Annabeth Gish, Tim Quill; **D:** Bob Giraldi; **M:** Anne Dudley. *HBO*

The Hiding Place 🎬🎬 1975 True story of two Dutch Christian sisters sent to a concentration camp for hiding Jews during WWII. Film is uneven but good cast pulls it through. Based on the Corrie Ten Boom book and produced by Billy Graham's Evangelistic Association. **145m/C VHS.** Julie Harris, Eileen Heckart, Arthur O'Connell, Jeanette Clift; **D:** James F. Collier. *VBL, REP*

High & Low 🎬🎬🎬½ *Tengoku To Jigoku* 1962 (R) Fine Japanese film noir about a wealthy businessman who is being blackmailed by kidnappers who claim to have his son. When he discovers that they have mistakenly taken his chauffeur's son he must decide whether to face financial ruin or risk the life of a young boy. Based on an Ed McBain novel. In Japanese with English subtitles. **143m/B VHS, Beta, LV, Letterbox.** *JP* Toshiro Mifune, Tatsuya Mihashi, Tatsuya Nakadai; **D:** Akira Kurosawa. *IME, TPV*

High Anxiety 🎬🎬 1977 (PG) Brooks tries hard to please in this low-brow parody of Hitchcock films employing dozens of references to films like "Psycho," "Spellbound," "The Birds," and "Vertigo." Tells the tale of a height-fearing psychiatrist caught up in a murder mystery. The title song performed a la Sinatra by Brooks is one of the film's high moments. Brooks also has a lot of fun with Hitchcockian camera movements. Uneven (What? Brooks?) but amusing tribute. **92m/C VHS, Beta, LV, Closed Caption.** Mel Brooks, Madeline Kahn, Cloris Leachman, Harvey Korman, Ron Carey, Howard Morris, Dick Van Patten; **D:** Mel Brooks; **W:** Mel Brooks, Ron Clark, Barry Levinson, Rudy DeLuca. *FOX*

High Art 🎬🎬 1998 (R) A trio of women play romantic games in New York's art community. Ambitious magazine editor-in-training Syd (Mitchell) has a boyfriend, James (Mann), but feels something's missing. Noticing a leak in her apartment ceiling, Syd heads upstairs to confront her neighbor and meets Lucy Berliner (Sheedy), a once-celebrated, now-retired photographer with a heroin problem and an equally hooked girlfriend, Greta (Clarkson). Syd and Lucy begin a friendship that leads to an affair, while Syd also wants to revitalize Lucy's career. Ex-Brat Packer Sheedy's the real revelation with her standout performance. **CW:** Strong sexuality, pervasive drug use and language. **102m/C VHS.** Radha Mitchell, Ally Sheedy, Patricia Clarkson, Tammy Grimes, Gabriel Mann, William Sage, David Thornton; **D:** Lisa Cholodenko; **W:** Lisa Cholodenko; **C:** Tami Reiker. Sundance Film Festival '98: Best Screenplay. *NYR*

High Ballin' 🎬🎬 1978 (PG) Truckers Fonda and Reed team up with lady trucker Shaver to take on the gang trying to crush the independent drivers. **100m/C VHS, Beta.** *CA* Peter Fonda, Jerry Reed, Helen Shaver; **D:** Peter Carter; **W:** Paul F. Edwards. *ART, VES*

High Command 🎬🎬½ 1937 To save his daughter from an ugly scandal, the British general of an isolated Colonial African outpost traps a blackmailer's killer. **84m/B VHS, Beta.** *GB* Lionel Atwill, Lucie Mannheim, James Mason; **D:** Thorold Dickinson. *NOS, MRV, VYY*

High Country 🎬🎬½ *The First Hello* 1981 (PG) Two misfits, one handicapped, the other an excon, on the run from society learn mutual trust as they travel through the Canadian Rockies. **101m/C VHS, Beta.** *CA* Timothy Bottoms, Linda Purl, George Sims, Jim Lawrence, Bill Berry; **D:** Harvey Hart. *VES*

High Crime 🎬🎬 1973 A "French Connection"-style suspense story about the heroin trade. Features high-speed chases and a police commissioner obsessed with capturing the criminals. **91m/C VHS, Beta.** James Whitmore, Franco Nero, Fernando Rey; **D:** Enzo G. Castellari.

The High Crusade 🎬½ 1992 (PG-13) A group of 13th-century English crusaders are heading for the Holy Land when they're interrupted on their journey by an alien spacecraft. They overpower the space guys and take over the vessel, hoping to use the spacecraft's on autopilot, the knights wind up heading for the aliens' home planet instead. **?m/C VHS.** *GB GE* John Rhys-Davies, Michael Des Barres, Rick Overton; **D:** Holger Neuhauser. *RVN*

High Desert Kill 🎬🎬 1990 (PG) A science-fiction tale will keep you guessing. Aliens landing in the New Mexican desert want something totally unexpected, and a trio of friends will be the first to find out what it is. Written for cable by Cook ("The China Syndrome"). **93m/C VHS, Beta.** Chuck Connors, Marc Singer, Anthony Geary, Micah Grant; **D:** Harry Falk; **W:** T.S. Cook. *USH*

High Frequency 🎬🎬 1988 Two young men monitoring a satellite relay station witness the murder of a woman. Believing they know who the killer's next victim will be, they set out to warn her. Lack of development mars what could have been a tidy little thriller. **105m/C VHS, LV.** *IT* Oliver Benny, Vincent Spano, Isabelle Pasco, Anne Canovos; **D:** Faliero Rosati. *MCG*

High Gear 🎬 1933 Heartstring-tugger about a race car driver, his girlfriend and the orphan son of a driver killed in a crash. Try to guess the outcome. **65m/B VHS.** James Murray, Joan Marsh, Jackie Searl, Theodore von Eltz, Lee Moran, Gordon DeMain; **D:** Leigh Jason. *NOS, RXM*

High Heels 🎬🎬 *Docteur Popaul; Scoundrel in White* 1972 A black comedy about a doctor who believes beauty is only skin deep and marries a plain woman. However, when he meets her beautiful sister, he begins to wonder. In French with English subtitles. **100m/C VHS, Beta.** *FR* Laura Antonelli, Jean-Paul Belmondo, Mia Farrow, Daniel Ivernel; **D:** Claude Chabrol. *NO*

High Heels 🌂🌂🌂 *Tacones Lejanos* 1991 (R) An outrageous combination murder-melodrama-comedy from Almodovar. Rebecca is a TV anchorwoman in Madrid whose flamboyant singer/actress mother has returned to the city for a concert. Rebecca happens to be married to one of her mother's not-so-ex-flames. When her husband winds up dead, Rebecca confesses to his murder during her newscast—but is she telling the truth or just covering up for mom? Mix in a drag queen/judge, a dancing chorus of women prison inmates, and a peculiar police detective, and see if the plot convolutions make sense. In Spanish with English subtitles. **CW:** Language and strong sensuality. **113m/C VHS, Beta, Closed Caption.** *SP* Victoria Abril, Marisa Paredes, Miguel Bose, Feodor Atkine, Bibi Andersen, Rocio Munoz; **D:** Pedro Almodovar; **W:** Pedro Almodovar; **M:** Ryuichi Sakamoto. Cesar Awards '93: Best Foreign Film. *PAR*

High Hopes 🌂🌂🌂 1988 A moving yet nasty satiric comedy about a pair of ex-hippies maintaining their counterculture lifestyle in Margaret Thatcher's England, as they watch the signs of conservative "progress" overtake them and their geriatric, embittered Mum. Hilarious and mature. **110m/C VHS, Beta.** *GB* Philip Davis, Ruth Sheen, Edna Dore, Philip Jackson, Heather Tobias, Leslie Manville, David Bamber; **D:** Mike Leigh; **W:** Mike Leigh; **M:** Andrew Dixon.

High Ice 🌂½ 1980 Forest ranger and a lieutenant colonel are involved in a clash of wills over a rescue mission high in the snow-capped Washington state peaks. **97m/C VHS, Beta.** David Janssen, Tony Musante; **D:** Eugene S. Jones. *VES*

High Lonesome 🌂🌂½ 1950 Barrymore is a drifter in Big Bend country, suspected in a series of mysterious murders. While he is being held captive, the real killers—thought dead—return to exact revenge on those they hold responsible for the range war in which they were wounded. This was LeMay's only stint as a director. **80m/C VHS.** John Blythe Barrymore Jr., Chill Wills, John Archer, Lois Butler, Kristine Miller, Basil Ruysdael, Jack Elam; **D:** Alan LeMay; **W:** Alan LeMay. *NOS*

High Noon 🌂🌂🌂🌂 1952 Landmark Western about Hadeyville town marshal Will Kane (Cooper) who faces four professional killers alone, after being abandoned to his fate by the gutless townspeople who profess to admire him. Cooper is the ultimate hero figure, his sheer presence overwhelming. Note the continuing use of the ballad written by Dimitri Tiomkin, "Do Not Forsake Me, Oh My Darlin'" (sung by Tex Ritter) to heighten the tension and action. Laserdisc includes the original trailer, an essay by Howard Suber on audio 2, a photo essay of production stills, Carl Foreman's original notes of the film and the complete text of "The Tin Star," the story on which the film is based. 🎵High Noon (Do Not Forsake Me, Oh My Darlin'). **85m/B VHS, LV, Closed Caption.** Gary Cooper, Grace Kelly, Lloyd Bridges, Lon Chaney Jr., Thomas Mitchell, Otto Kruger, Katy Jurado, Lee Van Cleef, Harry (Henry) Morgan, Robert J. Wilke, Sheb Wooley; **D:** Fred Zinnemann; **W:** Carl Foreman; **C:** Floyd Crosby; **M:** Dimitri Tiomkin. Academy Awards '52: Best Actor (Cooper), Best Film Editing, Best Song ("High Noon (Do Not Forsake Me, Oh My Darlin')"), Best Original Dramatic/Comedy Score; Golden Globe Awards '53: Best Actor—Drama (Cooper), Best Supporting Actress (Jurado), Best Score, National Film Registry '89;; New York Film Critics Awards '52: Best Director (Zinnemann), Best Film; Nominations: Academy Awards '52: Best Director (Zinnemann), Best Picture, Best Screenplay. *REP, TLF, BTV*

High Noon: Part 2 🌂 1980 Majors attempts to fill Gary Cooper's shoes, as Marshal Kane returns a year after the events of the original "High Noon" to remove the corrupt marshal who replaced him. Subtitled "The Return of Will Kane." Made for television. **96m/C VHS, Beta.** Lee Majors, David Carradine, Pernell Roberts, Kathy Cannon; **D:** Jerry Jameson. *VTR*

High Plains Drifter 🌂🌂½ 1973 (R) A surreal, violent western focusing on a drifter who defends a town from gunmen intent on meting out death. One of Eastwood's most stylistic directorial efforts, indebted to his "Man with No Name" days with Sergio Leone. Laser format is letterboxed and includes chapter stops and the original theatrical trailer. **105m/C VHS, Beta, LV, Letterbox, DVD.** Verna Bloom, Mitchell Ryan, Marianna Hill, Clint Eastwood; **D:** Clint Eastwood; **M:** Dee Barton. *USH, TLF*

High Risk 🌂½ 1976 (R) Improbable action-adventure of four unemployed Americans who battle foreign armies, unscrupulous gunrunners, and jungle bandits in a harrowing attempt to steal five million dollars from an expatriate American drug dealer living in the peaceful splendor of his Columbian villa. Interesting in its own run-on way. **94m/C VHS, Beta.** James Brolin, Anthony Quinn, Lindsay Wagner, James Coburn, Ernest Borgnine, Bruce Davison, Cleavon Little; **D:** Stewart Raffill. *VTR*

High Road to China 🌂🌂 1983 (PG) A hard-drinking former WWI air ace is recruited by a young heiress who must find her father before his ex-partner takes over his business. Post-"Raiders of the Lost Ark" thrills and romance, but without that tale's panache. **105m/C VHS, Beta, LV.** Bess Armstrong, Tom Selleck, Jack Weston, Robert Morley, Wilford Brimley, Brian Blessed; **D:** Brian G. Hutton; **M:** John Barry. *WAR*

High Rolling in a Hot Corvette 🌂 *High Rolling* 1977 (PG) Two carnival workers leave their jobs and hit the road in search of adventure and excitement, eventually turning to crime. **82m/C VHS, Beta.** *AU* Joseph Bottoms, Greg Taylor, Judy Davis, Wendy Hughes; **D:** Igor Auzins. *VES*

High School Caesar 🌂 1956 A seedy teenage exploitation flick about a rich teenager, with no parental supervision, who starts his own gang to run his high school. **75m/B VHS, Beta.** John Ashley; **D:** O'Dale Ireland. *RHI, SNC*

High School Confidential 🌂🌂 *Young Hellions* 1958 Teen punk Tamblyn transfers to Santo Bello high school from Chicago and causes havoc among the locals. He soon involves himself in the school drug scene and looks to be the top dog in dealing, but what no one knows is that he's really a narc! A must for midnight movie fans thanks to high camp values, "hep cat" dialogue and the gorgeous Van Doren as Tamblyn's sexcrazed "aunt." **85m/B VHS, Beta.** Russ Tamblyn, Jan Sterling, John Blythe Barrymore Jr., Mamie Van Doren, Diane Jergens, Jerry Lee Lewis, Ray Anthony, Jackie Coogan, Charles Chaplin Jr., Burt Douglas, Michael Landon, Jody Fair, Phillipa Fallon, Robin Raymond, James Todd, Lyle Talbot, William Wellman Jr.; **D:** Jack Arnold. *REP*

High School High 🌂🌂½ 1996 (PG-13) Idealistic teacher Richard Clark (Lovitz) leaves the private school world for notorious inner city Marion Barry High. This school is so bad it has its own cemetery (it's a parody, folks), but Clark is determined to get through to the kids. "Clockers" star Phifer shows up as a helpful student. Penned by David Zucker of "Airplane!" fame, so don't expect a "Mr. Holland's Opus." **CW:** Crude sexual humor, partial nudity and some drug references. **86m/C VHS, LV, Closed Caption, DVD.** Jon Lovitz, Tia Carrere, Mekhi Phifer, Louise Fletcher, Malinda Williams; **D:** Hart Bochner; **W:** David Zucker, Robert Locash, Pat Proft. *COL*

High School USA 🌂½ 1984 A high-school class clown confronts the king of the prep-jock-bullies. Antics ensue in this made-for-television flick which features many stars from '50s and '60s sitcoms. **96m/C VHS, Beta.** Michael J. Fox, Nancy McKeon, Bob Denver, Angela Cartwright, Elinor Donahue, Dwayne Hickman, Lauri Hendler, Dana Plato, Tony Dow, David Nelson; **D:** Rod Amateau; **M:** Miles Goodman. *ORI, WAR*

High Season 🌂🌂½ 1988 (R) A satire about a beautiful English photographer (Bisset) stranded on an idyllic Greek island with neither money nor inspiration, and the motley assembly of char-

actors who surround her during the tourist season. **95m/C VHS, Beta, LV, 8mm.** *GB* Jacqueline Bisset, James Fox, Irene Papas, Sebastian Shaw, Kenneth Branagh, Robert Stephens, Leslie Manville; **D:** Clare Peploe; **W:** Mark Peploe, Clare Peploe; **C:** Chris Menges; **M:** Jason Osborn. *FCT, NLC*

High Sierra 🌂🌂🌂 1941 Bogart is Roy "Mad Dog" Earle, an aging gangster whose last job backfires, so he's hiding out from the police in the High Sierras. Bogart's first starring role. Based on the novel by W.R. Burnett. Remade in 1955 as "I Died A Thousand Times." Also available colorized. **96m/B VHS, Beta, LV.** Humphrey Bogart, Ida Lupino, Arthur Kennedy, Joan Leslie, Cornel Wilde, Henry Travers, Henry Hull; **D:** Raoul Walsh; **W:** John Huston, W.R. Burnett; **C:** Gaetano Antonio "Tony" Gaudio. *FOX*

High Society 🌂🌂🌂 1956 A wealthy man attempts to win back his ex-wife who's about to be remarried in this enjoyable remake of "The Philadelphia Story." Letterboxed laserdisc format also includes the original movie trailer. 🎵High Society Calypso; Little One; Who Wants to Be a Millionaire?; True Love; You're Sensational; I Love You, Samantha; Now You Has Jazz; Well, Did You Evah?; Mind if I Make Love to You?. **107m/C VHS, Beta, LV, 8mm, Letterbox.** Frank Sinatra, Bing Crosby, Grace Kelly, Louis Armstrong, Celeste Holm, Sidney Blackmer, Louis Calhern; **D:** Charles Walters; **C:** Paul Vogel; **M:** Cole Porter. Nominations: Academy Awards '56: Best Song ("True Love"), Best Story, Scoring of a Musical. *MGM*

High Spirits 🌂🌂 1988 (PG-13) An American inherits an Irish castle and a sexy 200-year-old ghost. A painful, clumsy comedy by the fine British director that was apparently butchered by the studio before its release. **99m/C VHS, Beta, LV, Closed Caption.** Daryl Hannah, Peter O'Toole, Steve Guttenberg, Beverly D'Angelo, Liam Neeson, Martin Ferrero, Peter Gallagher, Jennifer Tilly; **D:** Neil Jordan; **W:** Neil Jordan; **M:** George Fenton. *VTR*

High Stakes 🌂🌂 *Melanie Rose* 1989 (R) Kirkland stars as a prostitute who's battling the Mob and falling in love. Limited release in theatres but another fine performance from Kirkland. **102m/C VHS, LV.** Sally Kirkland, Robert LuPone, Richard Lynch, Sarah Gellar, Kathy Bates, W.T. Martin; **D:** Amos Kollek. *THV*

High Strung 🌂½ 1991 (PG) Writer Thane Furrows (Oedekerk) thinks his life can't get any worse since he's plagued by a nagging mom, pressuring boss, and an insurance salesman. Then mysterious voices and images (played by Carrey) tell him he'll die that night. Naturally, Thane tries to think of a way out of his predicament. You'll hope he dies sooner since the movie is so lame. Beware, Carrey has very little screen time in spite of the advertising. **96m/C VHS, Closed Caption.** Steve Oedekerk, Thomas F. Wilson, Fred Willard, Jim Carrey. *PAR*

High Tide 🌂🌂🌂 1987 (PG-13) A strong and strange drama once again coupling the star and director of "My Brilliant Career." A small-time rock 'n' roll singer who is stranded in a small, beach town fortuitously meets up with her previously abandoned teenage daughter. Acclaimed. **120m/C VHS, Beta, LV, 8mm.** *AU* Judy Davis, Jan Adele, Claudia Karvan, Colin Friels, John Clayton, Mark Hembrow, Frankie J. Holden, Monica Trapaga; **D:** Gillian Armstrong; **W:** Laura Jones; **C:** Russell Boyd; **M:** Peter Best, Ricky Fataar, Mark Moffatt. Australian Film Institute '87: Best Actress (Davis); National Society of Film Critics Awards '88: Best Actress (Davis). *FCT, NLC*

High Velocity 🌂½ 1976 (PG) Lame adventure about two mercenaries involved in the challenge of a lifetime—rescuing a kidnapped executive from Asian terrorists. Filmed in Manila. **105m/C VHS, Beta.** Ben Gazzara, Paul Winfield, Britt Ekland, Keenan Wynn; **D:** Remi Kramer; **M:** Jerry Goldsmith.

High Voltage 🌂🌂 1929 A fast-moving comedy adventure set in the High Sierras. **62m/B VHS, Beta.** Carole Lombard, William Boyd, Gwen Moore, Billy Bevan; **D:** Howard Higgin. *NOS, MRV, BAR*

Higher and Higher 🎬🎬 **1944** Bankrupt aristocrat conspires with servants to regain his fortune, and tries to marry his daughter into money. Sinatra's first big-screen role. ♪You Belong in a Love Song; A Most Important Affair; The Music Stopped; Today I'm A Debutante; A Lovely Way To Spend An Evening; I Couldn't Sleep a Wink Last Night; You're On Your Own; I Saw You First; Disgustingly Rich. **90m/B VHS, Beta, LV.** Frank Sinatra, Leon Errol, Michele Morgan, Jack Haley, Mary McGuire; **D:** Tim Whelan. Nominations: Academy Awards '44: Best Song ("I Couldn't Sleep A Wink Last Night"), Best Original Dramatic/Comedy Score.**CCB, IME, TTC**

Higher Education 🎬🎬 **1988 (R)** Andy leaves his small town for a big city college and falls head over heels for a student and a teacher. He didn't know college could be so much fun. **83m/C VHS.** Kevin Hicks, Isabelle Mejias, Lori Hallier, Maury Chaykin, Richard Monette; **D:** John Sheppard. **VTR**

Higher Learning 🎬🎬 **1994 (R)** Racism, idealism, and the struggle for identity converge in this stylistically shot but rarely enlightening commentary on campus life and strife, focusing on three very different freshmen at fictional Columbus University—a bright track star (Ebbs) who questions the exploitation of black student athletes; a sheltered, sexually confused beauty from the 'burbs (Swanson); and a goony, paranoid loner who falls in with a group of skinheads (Rapaport). Singleton's honorable intention—to make a movie that makes a difference—is marred by cardboard supporting characters, a penchant for in-your-face irony, and a predictable, simplistic conclusion.**CW:** Scenes of violence and sexuality; strong language. **127m/C VHS, LV, Closed Caption.** Omar Epps, Kristy Swanson, Michael Rapaport, Laurence "Larry" Fishburne, Jennifer Connelly, Ice Cube, Tyra Banks, Jason Wiles, Cole Hauser, Regina King; **D:** John Singleton; **W:** John Singleton; **C:** Peter Collister. **COL**

The Highest Honor 🎬🎬½ **1984 (R)** True story set during WWII of a friendship between an Australian army officer, captured while attempting to infiltrate Singapore, and a Japanese security officer. Too long, but gripping. **99m/C VHS, Beta, LV.** AU John Howard, Atsuo Nakamura, Stuart Wilson, Michael Aitkens, Steve Bisley; **D:** Peter Maxwell. **VTR**

Highlander 🎬🎬🎬 **1986 (R)** A strange tale about an immortal 16th-century Scottish warrior who has had to battle his evil immortal enemy through the centuries. The feud comes to blows in modern-day Manhattan. Connery makes a memorable appearance as the good warrior's mentor. Spectacular battle and death scenes. A cult favorite which spawned a weak sequel and a television series. Based on a story by Gregory Widen. **110m/C VHS, Beta, LV, Closed Caption.** Christopher Lambert, Sean Connery, Clancy Brown, Roxanne Hart, Beatie Edney, Alan North, Sheila Gish, Jon Polito; **D:** Russell Mulcahy; **W:** Gregory Widen, Peter Bellwood, Larry Ferguson; **M:** Michael Kamen. **REP**

Highlander 2: The Quickening 🎬½ Highlander 2: Renegade Version **1991 (R)** The saga of Connor MacLeod and Juan Villa-Lobos continues in this sequel set in the year 2024. An energy shield designed to block out the sun's harmful ultraviolet rays has left planet Earth in perpetual darkness, but there is evidence that the ozone layer has repaired itself. An environmental terrorist and her group begin a sabotage effort and are joined by MacLeod and Villa-Lobos in their quest to save Earth. Stunning visual effects don't make up for the lack of substance. The Renegade version is a director's cut, which has been reedited and contains some 19 additional minutes of footage.**CW:** Some language and strong violence. **90m/C VHS, LV, 8mm, Closed Caption.** Christopher Lambert, Sean Connery, Virginia Madsen, Michael Ironside, John C. McGinley; **D:** Russell Mulcahy; **W:** Peter Bellwood; **C:** Phil Meheux; **M:** Stewart Copeland. **REP**

Highlander: The Final Dimension 🎬½ Highlander 3: The Magician; Highlander 3: The Sorcerer **1994 (R)** Immortal Conner MacLeod (Lambert) battles master illusionist

Kane (Van Peebles), who seeks to rule the world. Aiding MacLeod is Alex Smith (Unger), a research scientist who discovers Kane was once buried beneath a mystical mountain along with three other immortal warriors some 300 years before. MacLeod returns to his old Scottish stomping grounds to prepare for battle. Lots of action and special effects, really dumb storyline and overacting—even for a fantasy film. Original theatrical release was PG-13 and 94 minutes; the director's cut has been re-edited and footage added.**CW:** Strong adventure violence; language; some strong sexuality. **99m/C VHS, LV, Closed Caption.** Christopher Lambert, Mario Van Peebles, Deborah Kara Unger, Mako; **D:** Andrew Morahan; **W:** Paul Ohl; **M:** J. Peter Robinson. **TOU**

Highlander: The Gathering 🎬🎬½ **1992 (PG-13)** Re-edited episodes from the syndicated TV series finds good immortals Connor MacLeod (Lambert) and distant relative Duncan (Paul) battling against an evil immortal (Moll is a particularly nasty villain) and a misguided human (Vanity). Lots of sword-play and a little bit of romance (courtesy of Vandernoot).**CW:** Swordfight violence and sex scene. **98m/C VHS.** Christopher Lambert, Adrian Paul, Richard Moll, Vanity, Alexandra Vandernoot, Stan Kirsch; **D:** Thomas J. Wright, Ray Austin; **W:** Lorain Despres, Dan Gordon.

Highpoint 🎬 **1980 (PG)** When an unemployed man becomes the chauffeur of a wealthy family, he finds himself in the middle of a mysterious murder and part of an international CIA plot. Hard to figure what's happening in this one. **91m/C VHS, Beta, LV.** CA Richard Harris, Christopher Plummer, Beverly D'Angelo, Kate Reid, Saul Rubinek; **D:** Peter Carter. **VTR**

Highway Patrolman 🎬🎬 El Patrullero **1991** Young Pedro Rojas (Sosa) has just graduated from the National Highway Patrol Academy and he and best friend Anibal (Bichir) have been assigned to the isolated roads of northern Durango. He quickly learns that most of the people he stops for minor violations are too poor to pay for licenses and fines. What Pedro does get is a wife, Griselda (Gutierrez), who's soon complaining about Pedro's meager wages. Pedro's resistance to bribery begins to weaken and he becomes more depressed as his ideals are destroyed and his rage increases. Spanish with subtitles. **104m/C VHS.** MX Roberto Sosa, Zaide Silvia Gutierrez, Bruno Bichir, Vanessa Bauche; **D:** Alex Cox; **W:** Lorenzo O'Brien; **C:** Miguel Garzon; **M:** Zander Schloss. **NYF**

Highway 61 🎬🎬 **1991 (R)** Shy barber Pokey Jones lives in the small Canadian town of Pickerel Falls and becomes a celebrity when he discovers the frozen corpse of an unknown young man in his backyard. Jackie Bangs, a rock roadie who's stolen her band's stash of drugs, finds herself stranded in the same small town. So begins a wild road trip. Lackluster direction undercuts much of the first-rate acting and amusing story quirks.**CW:** Language and one sensual scene. **110m/C VHS.** Valerie Buhagiar, Don McKellar, Earl Pastko, Peter Breck, Art Bergmann; **D:** Bruce McDonald; **W:** Don McKellar. **PAR, FCT**

Highway 13 🎬½ **1948** When a trucker witnesses an "accidental" death at the loading warehouse, he falls under suspicion. He then sets out to clear his name. **60m/B VHS, Beta, LV.** Robert Lowery, Pamela Blake, Lyle Talbot, Michael Whalen, Maris Wrixon, Clem Bevans; **D:** William (Lester Williams) Berke. **NO**

Highway to Hell 🎬🎬 **1992 (R)** Bergen plays the devil in a horror-comedy about going to hell—even if you're not dead yet. Lowe and Swanson are newlyweds on their way to Las Vegas when they're stopped by a "hellcop," who kidnaps the bride and takes her to the netherworld to be the devil's new plaything. Her human hubby doesn't take kindly to this and goes to hell to rescue his bride. Campy flick is played for laughs and has some good special effects.**CW:**

Nudity and bizarre fantasy violence. **93m/C VHS, Closed Caption.** Patrick Bergin, Adam Storke, Chad Lowe, Kristy Swanson, Richard Farnsworth, C.J. Graham, Lita Ford, Kevin Peter Hall, Pamela Gidley, Brian Helgeland; **Cameos:** Gilbert Gottfried; **D:** Ate De Jong. **HBO**

Hijacking Hollywood 🎬 **1997** Modest Hollywood satire finds naive Kevin Conroy (Thomas) using family ties to land a menial job with distant relative Michael Lawrence (Metcalf), a tyrannical producer. Kevin's supervisor is the petty Russell (Thompson), who enjoys sending the kid on useless errands. Kevin's one important task is to pick up film rushes at the airport and he tells hustling roommate Tad (Mandt) that if someone took the dailies, a production could be held hostage. Naturally, Tad is all for the idea. **91m/C VHS.** Henry Thomas, Scott Thompson, Mark Metcalf, Paul Hewitt, Art LaFleur, Neil Mandt; **D:** Neil Mandt; **W:** Jim Rossow, Neil Mandt; **C:** Anton Floquet. **NYR**

Hijazo de Mi Vidaza 🎬 Son of My Life **197?** The history of a family as told by a mother to her son. In Spanish. **90m/C VHS, Beta.** Enrique Cuenca, Eduardo Manzano, Maria Fernanda, Fernando Casanova. **MAD**

Hill Number One **1951** A dramatization of the story of Easter, featuring Dean in one of his first major roles as John the Baptist. Made for television. **57m/B VHS, Beta.** James Dean, Michael Ansara, Leif Erickson, Ruth Hussey, Roddy McDowall. RHI, FCT, HEG

Hill Street Blues, Vol. 1: Hill Street Station **1981** Landmark police drama which effectively combined a large cast of characters with plots filled with humor and tragedy. Set in an urban ghetto of a large (unnamed) American city, the precinct was run by Capt. Frank Furillo (Travanti) and staffed with "let's be careful out there!" Sgt. Phil Esterhaus (Conrad), as well as a host of offbeat detectives and beat cops. The pilot episode introduced the characters and the characteristic mayhem. Additional episodes available. **50m/C VHS.** Daniel J. Travanti, Veronica Hamel, Michael Conrad, Bruce Weitz, James B. Sikking, Joe Spano, Taurean Blacque, Kiel Martin, Rene Enriquez, Michael Warren, Charles Haid, Betty Thomas, Ed Marinaro, Barbara Babcock. MOV, MTM

Hill 24 Doesn't Answer 🎬🎬🎬 **1955** Four Zionist soldiers defend a strategic entrance to Jerusalem. While at their posts, they reflect on their lives and devotion to the cause. Made in Israel, in English. The first Israeli feature film. **101m/B VHS, Beta.** IS Edward Mulhare, Haya Harareet, Michael Wager; **D:** Thorold Dickinson. **ERG**

Hillbillies in a Haunted House woof! **1967** Two country and western singers en route to the Nashville jamboree encounter a group of foreign spies "haunting" a house. Features Rathbone's last film performance. Sequel to "Las Vegas Hillbillies" (1966). Giant step down for everyone involved. **88m/C VHS, Beta.** Ferlin Husky, Joi Lansing, Don Bowman, John Carradine, Lon Chaney Jr., Basil Rathbone; **D:** Jean Yarbrough. VCI, AOV

Hillbilly Blitzkrieg 🎬 Enemy Round-Up **1942** Two soldiers are sent to the boonies to guard a top-secret missile site from enemy agents. Come-to-life comic strip characters Snuffy Smith, Barney Google and Spark Plug join in the antics. **63m/B VHS.** Bud Duncan, Cliff Nazarro, Edgar Kennedy, Doris Linden, Lucien Littlefield, Alan Baldwin; **D:** Roy Mack. NOS, RXM

The Hills Have Eyes woof! **1977 (R)** Desperate family battles for survival and vengeance against a brutal band of inbred hillbilly cannibals. Craven gore-fest followed by Hills II. **83m/C VHS, Beta, LV.** Susan Lanier, Robert Houston, Martin Speer, Dee Wallace Stone, Russ Grieve, John Steadman, James Whitworth, Michael Berryman, Virginia Vincent, Janus Blythe; **D:** Wes Craven; **W:** Wes Craven; **C:** Eric Saarinen. NO

The Hills Have Eyes, Part 2 🐾 1984 Craven reprises Hills with Eyes number one to ill effect. Ignorant teens disregard warnings of a "Hills Have Eyes" refugee, and go stomping into the grim reaper's proving grounds. Predictably bad things happen. **86m/C VHS, Beta.** Michael Berryman, Kevin Blair, John Joe Bob Briggs Bloom, Janus Blythe, John Laughlin, Tamara Stafford, Peter Frechette; **D:** Wes Craven; **W:** Wes Craven; **C:** David Lewis. *REP*

The Hills of Home 🐾🐾🐾 *Master of Lassie* 1948 (G) Warm sentimental tale about a Scottish doctor and his beloved pet collie. One of the better films in the "Lassie" series. **97m/C VHS.** Edmund Gwenn, Donald Crisp, Tom Drake, Janet Leigh; **D:** Fred M. Wilcox; **W:** William Ludwig. *MGM, FCT*

Hills of Oklahoma 🐾🐾 1950 Allen stars as the leader of a cattlemen's association who decides not to deal with dishonest meatpacker Keane, so he drives his herd across the desert to a slaughterhouse run by an honest businesswoman. Based on an original story by Cooper. **67m/B VHS.** Rex Allen, Elisabeth Fraser, Elisabeth Risdon, Fuzzy Knight, Roscoe Ates, Robert Emmett Keane, Trevor Bardette; **D:** R.G. Springsteen; **W:** Olive Cooper, Victor Arthur. *MOV*

Hills of Utah 🐾½ 1951 Autry finds himself in the middle of a feud between the local mine operator and a group of cattlemen, while searching for his father's murderer. **70m/B VHS, Beta.** Gene Autry, Pat Buttram, Denver Pyle; **D:** John English. *CCB*

The Hillside Strangler 🐾½ *The Case of the Hillside Stranglers* 1989 Made-for-television, crime-of-the-week drama about the investigation to apprehend the serial killer responsible for 10 deaths in 1977-78. **91m/C VHS, Beta.** Richard Crenna, Dennis Farina, Billy Zane, Tony Plana, James Tolkan, Tasia Valenza; **D:** Steven Gethers.

Himatsuri 🐾🐾🐾 *Fire Festival* 1985 An acclaimed film detailing the conflicts between man and nature, as a lumberjack in a Japanese forest believes he's the protector of the mountains through his divine relationship with the ancient gods. Outraged by the destruction, pollution, and commercial exploitation of the land he turns to violence. In Japanese with English subtitles. **120m/C VHS, Beta.** *JP* Kinya Kitaoji, Kwako Taichi, Ryota Nakamoto, Norihei Miki; **D:** Mitsuo Yanagimachi; **W:** Kenji Nakagami; **M:** Toru Takemitsu. *ORI, WAR, AUD*

The Hindenburg 🐾🐾 1975 (PG) A dramatization of what might have happened on the fateful night the Hindenburg exploded. Scott plays an investigator who is aware that something is up, and has numerous suspects to interrogate. The laser edition features widescreen format, digital Stereo Surround, the original trailer, and chapter stops. **126m/C VHS, Beta, LV, Letterbox, Closed Caption.** George C. Scott, Anne Bancroft, William Atherton, Roy Thinnes, Gig Young, Burgess Meredith, Charles Durning, Richard Dysart; **D:** Robert Wise; **C:** Robert L. Surtees; **M:** David Shire. Academy Awards '75: Best Sound Effects Editing; Nominations: Academy Awards '75: Best Art Direction/Set Decoration, Best Cinematography, Best Sound. *USH*

Hindsight 🐾 1997 Ah, Hollywood. Joanne (Shower), the bored wife of studio exec Vincent (Law), is having an affair with younger, not-too-bright, aspiring actor Jason (Steadman). Joanne's finally agreed to run off when Jason happens to meet party girl Cassandra (Pass). Thanks to her studio connections, Jason soon has an important agent (Forster) and a studio deal that leaves Joanne in the back lot. But Cassandra is a wild woman with an agenda that doesn't bode well for our selfish himbo. **93m/C VHS.** Ken Steadman, Cyndi Pass, Kathy Shower, John Phillip Law, Robert Forster; **D:** John Bowen; **W:** Steve Tymon; **C:** Keith Holland; **M:** Jimmy Hodges. *PEG*

Hips, Hips, Hooray 🐾🐾½ 1934 Two supposed "hot shot" salesmen are hired by a cosmetic company to sell flavored lipstick. This lavish musical comedy is one of Wheeler and Woolsey's best vehicles. 🎵Tired of It All; Keep Romance Alive; Keep On Doin' What You're Doin'. **68m/B VHS, Beta, LV.** Robert Woolsey, Bert Wheeler, Ruth Etting, Thelma Todd, Dorothy Lee; **D:** Mark Sandrich. *CCB*

Hired Hand 🐾🐾½ 1971 Two drifters settle on a farm belonging to one of their wives, only to leave again seeking to avenge the murder of a friend. TV prints include Larry Hagman in a cameo role. **93m/C VHS, Beta.** Peter Fonda, Warren Oates, Verna Bloom, Severn Darden, Robert Pratt; **Cameos:** Larry Hagman; **D:** Peter Fonda. *BAR*

Hired to Kill 🐾½ *The Italian Connection* 1973 (R) A pair of Mafia hoods plot against each other over a $6 million drug shipment. **90m/C Beta.** Henry Silva, Woody Strode, Adolfo Celi, Mario Adorf. *NO*

Hired to Kill 🐾½ 1991 (R) The granite-hewn Thompson plays a male-chauvinist commando grudgingly leading a squad of beautiful mercenary-ettes on an international rescue mission. Not as bad as it sounds (mainly because the ladies aren't complete bimbos), but between senseless plotting, gratuitous catfights, and a love scene indistinguishable from rape, the Hound found plenty to dislike. **91m/C VHS, Beta, Closed Caption.** Brian Thompson, George Kennedy, Jose Ferrer, Oliver Reed, Penelope Reed, Michelle Moffett, Barbara Lee Alexander, Jordanna Capra; **D:** Nico Mastorakis, Peter Rader; **W:** Nico Mastorakis. *PAR*

Hiroshima 🐾🐾🐾 1995 (PG) Haunting depiction recreates the circumstances surrounding the dropping of the first atomic bomb in 1945. Juxtaposes scenes between the U.S., Japan, and their leaders—President Truman (Welsh) and Emperor Hirohito (Umewaka)—with the development of the Manhattan Project, the bombing itself, and its consequences. Filmed primarily in B&W, with newsreel and contemporary witness interviews in color; Japanese sequences are subtitled in English. Filmed on location in Montreal, PQ, and Tokyo, Japan; made for cable TV. **180m/C VHS.** *JP CA* Kenneth Welsh, Naohiko Umewaka, Wesley Addy, Richard Masur, Hisashi Igawa, Ken Jenkins, Jeffrey DeMunn, Leon Pownall, Saul Rubinek, Timothy West, Koji Takahashi, Kazuo Kato; **D:** Roger Spottiswoode, Koreyoshi Kurahara; **W:** John Hopkins, Toshiro Ishido; **C:** Pierre Mignot, Shohei Ando. *HMK*

Hiroshima Maiden 1988 An American family gains new perspective when they meet a young survivor of the atomic bomb. Based on true stories of Japanese women who stayed with Americans while undergoing surgery to minimize their scars. Originally aired on PBS as part of the "Wonderworks" family movie series. **58m/C VHS.** Susan Blakely, Richard Masur, Tamlyn Tomita; **D:** Joan Darling. *WNE, HMV, FCT*

Hiroshima, Mon Amour 🐾🐾🐾🐾 1959 A profoundly moving drama exploring the shadow of history over the personal lives of a lonely French actress living in Tokyo and a Japanese architect with whom she's having an affair. Presented in a complex network of flashbacks. Highly influential; adapted by Marguerite Duras from her book. In Japanese with English subtitles. **88m/B VHS.** *JP FR* Emmanuelle Riva, Eiji Okada, Bernard Fresson, Stella Dassas, Pierre Barbaud; **D:** Alain Resnais; **W:** Marguerite Duras; **C:** Sacha Vierny; **M:** Georges Delerue, Giovanni Fusco. New York Film Critics Awards '60: Best Foreign Film; Nominations: Academy Awards '60: Best Story & Screenplay. *HMV, MRV, HHT*

Hiroshima: Out of the Ashes 🐾🐾🐾 1990 (PG) The terrible aftermath of the bombing of Hiroshima, August, 1945, as seen through the eyes of American and Japanese soldiers, the Japanese people, and a priest. Carefully detailed and realistic, creates an amazing emotional response. Don't miss the scene in which Nelson and his buddy find themselves surrounded by Japanese—the enemy—only to realize that their "captors" have been blinded by the blast. Created as an homage for the 45th anniversary of the bombing. **98m/C VHS.** Max von Sydow, Judd Nelson, Mako, Tamlyn Tomita, Stan Egi, Sab Shimono, Noriyuki "Pat" Morita, Kim Miyori; **D:** Peter Werner. *THV*

His Brother's Ghost 🐾🐾 1945 When Fuzzy is rubbed out by bandits, Billy Carson (no longer called Billy the Kid thanks to mothers' protestations) convinces his twin brother to impersonate him in order to make the bandits believe they are the victims of hocus pocus from the otherworld. Crabbe—who dressed noir before it was chic—made this during his post sci-fi western period, when he slugged it through some 50 low-rent oaters (usually under the direction of Newfield at PRC studios). **54m/C VHS.** Buster Crabbe, Al "Fuzzy" St. John, Charles "Blackie" King, Bud Osborne, Karl Hackett, Archie Hall; **D:** Sam Newfield. *NOS, MRV, HEG*

His Butler's Sister 🐾🐾 1944 Bachelor composer Charles Gerard (Tone) lives a sybarite's life in his Manhattan penthouse, which is run by his butler Martin Murphy (O'Brien). When Murphy's stepsister Ann Carter (Durbin) arrives unexpectedly, she's delighted to hear who Murphy works for because she's a singer and wants an audition—an absolute taboo in Gerard's household. So she fools him into thinking she's the new maid until she can get her big break. Nothing new but Durbin does get to work her pretty pipes. 🎵Nessun Dorma; In the Spirit of the Moment; When You're Away; Is It True What They Say About Dixie?. **87m/B VHS, Closed Caption.** Deanna Durbin, Franchot Tone, Pat O'Brien, Evelyn Ankers, Akim Tamiroff, Alan Mowbray, Frank Jenks, Walter Catlett, Hans Conried, Florence Bates, Roscoe Karns, Franklin Pangborn; **D:** Frank Borzage; **W:** Samuel Hoffenstein, Bety Reinhardt; **C:** Woody Bredell; **M:** Hans J. Salter. Nominations: Academy Awards '44: Best Sound. *USH*

His Double Life 🐾🐾½ 1933 When a shy gentleman's valet dies, his master assumes the dead man's identity and has a grand time. From the play "Buried Alive" by Arnold Bennett. Remade in 1943 as "Holy Matrimony." **67m/B VHS, Beta.** Roland Young, Lillian Gish, Montagu Love; **D:** Arthur Hopkins. *NOS, MRV, BAR*

His Fighting Blood 🐾½ 1935 Northwest Mounties in action. Based on a James Oliver Curwood story. **63m/B VHS, Beta.** Kermit Maynard. *VDM*

His First Command 🐾½ 1929 An early talkie wherein a playboy falls in love with the daughter of a cavalry officer, and enlists in order to win her affections. **60m/B VHS, Beta, 8mm.** William Boyd, Dorothy Sebastian, Gavin Gordon; **D:** Gregory La Cava. *VYY*

His First Flame 🐾🐾🐾 1926 A classic Langdon silent romantic comedy. **62m/B VHS, Beta.** Harry Langdon, Vernon Dent, Natalie Kingston; **W:** Frank Capra. *NOS, VYY, GPV*

His Girl Friday 🐾🐾🐾🐾 1940 Classic, unrelentingly hilarious war-between-the-sexes comedy in which a reporter and her ex-husband editor help a condemned man escape the law—while at the same time furthering their own ends as they try to get the big scoop on political corruption in the town. One of Hawks' most furious and inventive screen combats in which women are given uniquely equal (for Hollywood) footing, with staccato dialogue and wonderful performances. Based on the Hecht-MacArthur play "The Front Page," which was originally filmed in 1931. Remade again in 1974 as "The Front Page," and in 1988 as "Switching Channels." Also available colorized. **92m/B VHS, Beta.** Cary Grant, Rosalind Russell, Ralph Bellamy, Gene Lockhart, John Qualen, Porter Hall, Roscoe Karns, Abner Biberman, Cliff Edwards, Billy Gilbert, Helen Mack, Ernest Truex, Clarence Kolb, Frank Jenks; **D:** Howard Hawks; **W:** Charles Lederer; **M:** Morris Stoloff. National Film Registry '93. *CNG, MRV, NOS*

His Kind of Woman 🐾🐾🐾 1951 A fall guy, being used to bring a racketeer back to the U.S. from Mexico, discovers the plan and tries to halt it. **120m/B VHS, Beta.** Robert Mitchum, Jane Russell, Vincent Price, Tim Holt, Charles McGraw, Raymond Burr, Jim Backus; **D:** John Farrow. *NO*

His Majesty O'Keefe ⚅⚅½ 1953 Lancaster stars as a South Seas swashbuckler dealing in the lucrative coconut-oil trade of the mid-1800s. The natives see him as a god and allow him to marry a beautiful maiden. When his reign is threatened by unscrupulous traders, Lancaster springs into action to safeguard his kingdom. Based on a real-life American adventurer, this was the first movie ever filmed in the Fiji Islands. 92m/C VHS, Beta, LV. Burt Lancaster, Joan Rice, Benson Fong, Philip Ahn, Grant Taylor; D: Byron Haskin. WAR

His Majesty, the American ⚅⚅½ 1919 William Brooks (Fairbanks) is a young man whose heritage is unknown to him. It turns out he's an heir to a small European kingdom. When Brooks arrives in Alaine he discovers the war minister is trying to overthrow the present king. With his usual dash, our hero saves the day and also wins the hand of a beautiful princess. First picture released by United Artists studios, formed by Fairbanks, Mary Pickford, Charles Chaplin, and D.W. Griffith. 100m/B VHS. Douglas Fairbanks Sr., Marjorie Daw, Lillian Langdon, Frank Campeau; D: Joseph Henabery. GPV, GVV

His Majesty, the Scarecrow of Oz/ The Magic Cloak of Oz ⚅⚅½ 1914 The creator of the Oz stories, L. Frank Baum, wrote, produced and directed these two stories himself, with all the characters from his best-selling children's books. 80m/B VHS, Beta. D: L. Frank Baum. GVV

His Name was King woof! 1985 A man goes after the gang who murdered his brother and raped his young wife in the old West. 90m/C VHS, Beta. IT Richard Harrison, Klaus Kinski, Anne Puskin; D: Don Reynolds. NO

His Picture in the Papers ⚅⚅ 1916 An early silent comedy wherein the robust, red-meat-eating son of a health food tycoon must get his father's permission to marry by getting his picture favorably in the paper for advertising's sake. 68m/B VHS, Beta, 8mm. Douglas Fairbanks Sr., Clarence Handysides, Rene Boucicault, Jean Temple, Charles Butler, Homer Hunt, Loretta Blake, Helena Ruppert; D: John Emerson; W: John Emerson, Anita Loos. NOS, VYY, GPV

His Prehistoric Past/The Bank 1915 Two of Chaplin's classic early shorts. 54m/B VHS, Beta. Charlie Chaplin, Mack Swain, Edna Purviance; D: Charlie Chaplin. VYY, GVV

His Private Secretary ⚅½ 1933 Wayne plays the jet-setting son of a wealthy businessman who wants his boy to settle down. And he does—after he meets the minister's beautiful daughter. 68m/B VHS, Beta. John Wayne, Evalyn Knapp, Alec B. Francis, Reginald Barlow, Natalie Kingston, Arthur Hoyt, Al "Fuzzy" St. John; D: Philip H. Whitman. DVT, HEG

His Royal Slyness/Haunted Spooks 1920 Two Harold Lloyd shorts. "His Royal Slyness" (1919) offers Harold impersonating the king of a small kingdom, while in "Haunted Spooks" (1920), Harold gets suckered into living in a haunted mansion. Both films include music score. 52m/B VHS, Beta. Harold Lloyd; D: Harold Lloyd. VYY, CCB, GVV

His Wife's Lover ⚅⚅⚅ Zayn Vaybs Lubovnik 1931 An actor disguised as an old man wins the heart of a lovely young woman. He decides to test her fidelity by reverting to his handsome young self and attempting to seduce her. An enchanting comedy in Yiddish with English subtitles. 77m/B VHS, Beta. Ludwig Satz, Michael Rosenberg, Isadore Cashier, Lucy Levine; D: Sidney Goldin. ERG, FCT

History Is Made at Night ⚅⚅⚅ 1937 A wife seeks a divorce from a jealous husband while on an Atlantic cruise; she ends up finding both true love and heartbreak in this story of a love triangle at sea. 98m/B VHS, Beta, LV. Charles Boyer, Jean Arthur, Leo Carrillo, Colin Clive; D: Frank Borzage; C: Gregg Toland. WAR, FCT

History of the World: Part 1 ⚅⚅ 1981 (R) More misses than hits in this Brooks' parody of historic epics. A bluntly satiric vision of human evolution, from the Dawn of Man to the French Revolution told in an episodic fashion. Good for a few laughs. 90m/C VHS, Beta, LV, Letterbox, Closed Caption. Mel Brooks, Dom DeLuise, Madeline Kahn, Harvey Korman, Cloris Leachman, Gregory Hines, Pamela Stephenson, Paul Mazursky, Beatrice Arthur, Fritz Feld, John Hurt, Jack Carter, John Hillerman, John Gavin, Barry Levinson, Ron Carey, Howard Morris, Sid Caesar, Jackie Mason; D: Mel Brooks; W: Mel Brooks. FOX

The History of White People in America 1985 A pseudo-documentary look at the complicated life of a white midwestern family. Succeeds in making hilarious fun of many traditional prejudices. Originally made for cable television. 48m/C VHS, Beta. Martin Mull, Fred Willard, Mary Kay Place, Teri Garr, Bob Eubanks; D: Harry Shearer. USH

The History of White People in America: Vol. 2 1985 Mull's television-special comedy satirizing WASP society in America. 40m/C VHS, Beta. Martin Mull; D: Harry Shearer. USH

Hit! ⚅⚅ 1973 (R) When the 15-year-old daughter of a government agent dies of a drug overdose, he deals his revenge to top French heroin traffickers. 135m/C VHS, Beta, Closed Caption. Billy Dee Williams, Richard Pryor, Gwen Welles, Paul Hampton, Warren Kemmerling, Sid Melton; D: Sidney J. Furie; W: Alan R. Trustman, David M. Wolf; M: Lalo Schifrin. PAR

The Hit ⚅⚅½ 1985 (R) A feisty young hooker gets mixed-up with two strong-armed hired killers as they escort an unusual stool-pigeon from his exile in Spain to their angry mob bosses. Minor cult-noir from the director of "My Beautiful Launderette" and "Dangerous Liaisons." 105m/C VHS, Beta, LV. GB Terence Stamp, John Hurt, Laura Del Sol, Tim Roth, Fernando Rey, Bill Hunter; D: Stephen Frears; W: Peter Prince; C: John A. Alonzo; M: Eric Clapton. NLC

Hit & Run ⚅ Revenge Squad 1982 David Marks, a Manhattan cab driver, is haunted by recurring flashbacks of a freak hit-and-run accident in which his wife was struck down on a city street. 96m/C VHS, Beta. Paul Perri, Claudia Cron; D: Charles Braverman; M: Brad Fiedel. NO

Hit Lady ⚅⚅ 1974 An elegant cultured woman becomes a hit lady for the syndicate in this predictable, yet slick gangster movie. Made for television. 74m/C VHS, Beta. Yvette Mimieux, Dack Rambo, Clu Gulager, Keenan Wynn; D: Tracy Keenan Wynn.

The Hit List ⚅⚅ 1988 (R) A regular guy fights back brutally when his wife and child are mistakenly kidnapped by the Mafia. Fast-paced action makes up for thin plot. 87m/C VHS, Beta, LV. Jan-Michael Vincent, Leo Rossi, Lance Henriksen, Charles Napier, Rip Torn; D: William Lustig; W: Peter Brosnan. COL

The Hit List ⚅⚅½ 1993 (R) Charles Pike (Fahey) is a professional hitman working for attorney Peter Mayhew (Coburn) to wipe out drug lords. Then Mayhew gives Pike a new assignment. He introduces him to sexy widow Jordan Henning (Butler), who wants Pike to kill the man who murdered her husband. Pike finds himself mixing business with pleasure in a deadly combination that sees him dodging crooked cops and trained assassins. 97m/C VHS, LV, Closed Caption. Jeff Fahey, Yancy Butler, James Coburn; D: William Webb; W: Reed Steiner. COL

The Hit Man ⚅⚅ Il Sicario 1961 A crime drama that profiles the crisis of a man unfit to commit murder but who does for a price. 100m/B VHS, Beta. CIG

Hit Men ⚅½ 1973 Double crosses and gun battles highlight this tale of inner-city crime. 90m/C VHS, Beta. Henry Silva, Mario Adorf, Woody Strode, Adolfo Celi. VDC

Hit the Deck ⚅½ 1955 Second-rate studio musical about sailors on leave and looking for romance. Based on the 1927 Broadway musical. ♫Sometimes I'm Happy; Hallelujah; Why, Oh Why; Keeping Myself For You; More Than You Know; I Know That You Know; Lucky Bird. 112m/C VHS, Beta, LV, Letterbox. Jane Powell, Tony Martin, Debbie Reynolds, Walter Pidgeon, Vic Damone, Gene Raymond, Ann Miller, Russ Tamblyn, J. Carrol Naish, Kay Armen, Richard Anderson; D: Roy Rowland; M: Vincent Youmans. MGM

Hit the Dutchman ⚅⚅ 1992 (R) Routine gangster flick about Dutch Schultz trying to rise to the top of the New York crime community—with or without the help of underworld pals Legs Diamond and Lucky Luciano. An unrated version is also available. CW: Language, gangster violence, and sexuality. 116m/C VHS, Closed Caption. Bruce Nozick, Sally Kirkland, Will Kempe; D: Menahem Golan. THV

Hit the Ice ⚅⚅ 1943 Newspaper photographers Bud and Lou are mistaken as gangsters in Chicago and the usual complications ensue. Includes an appearance by Johnny Long & His Orchestra. ♫I'm Like A Fish Out Of Water; Happiness Bound; I'd Like to Set You to Music; Slap Polka. 89m/C VHS, Beta. Bud Abbott, Lou Costello, Patric Knowles, Elyse Knox, Ginny Simms; D: Charles Lamont. USH

Hit the Saddle ⚅⚅ 1937 The Three Mesquiteers track down a gang involved in capturing wild horses in protected areas although one of three is more interested in the charms of a dance hall girl (played by starlet Rita Cansino who would soon become Rita Hayworth). 54m/B VHS, Beta. Bob Livingston, Ray Corrigan, Max Terhune, J.P. McGowan, Yakima Canutt, Rita Hayworth; D: Mack V. Wright. NOS, VCN, REP

Hit Woman: The Double Edge ⚅⚅½ 1993 (R) Lucci plays a dual role as an FBI agent and the look-alike killer-for-hire that she's tracking. Originally made for television, the video version contains additional footage that earned the "R" rating. 92m/C VHS. Susan Lucci, Robert Urich, Michael Woods, Robert Prosky. APX

The Hitch-Hiker ⚅⚅⚅ 1953 Two young men off on the vacation of their dreams pick up a psychopathic hitchhiker with a right eye that never closes, even when he sleeps. Taut suspense makes this flick worth seeing. 71m/B VHS. Edmond O'Brien, Frank Lovejoy, William Talman, Jose Torvay; D: Ida Lupino. EEL, SNC

The Hitcher ⚅⚅½ 1986 (R) A young man picks up a hitchhiker on a deserted stretch of California highway only to be tormented by the man's repeated appearances: is he real or a figment of his imagination? Ferociously funny, sadomasochistic comedy with graphic violence. 98m/C VHS, Beta, LV, Closed Caption. Rutger Hauer, C. Thomas Howell, Jennifer Jason Leigh, Jeffrey DeMunn, John M. Jackson, Billy Green Bush; D: Robert Harmon; W: Eric Red; C: John Seale; M: Mark Isham. HBO, OM

The Hitchhiker 1985 HBO's chilling horror anthology series contains a trio of terrifying tales. Additional episodes are available. In this first collection, Hamlin stars in "The Curse," about Yuppie occult vengeance; "W.G.O.D.," finds Busey and Page caught up in radio religion; and "Hired Help," finds Black with a less than human handyman. 90m/C VHS, Beta, LV. Harry Hamlin, Gary Busey, Geraldine Page, Karen Black. WAR, MOV

Hitchhiker 2 1985 Three more episodes from HBO's horror series: "Dead Man's Curve," "Nightshift," and "Last Scene." 90m/C VHS, Beta, LV. Peter Coyote, Margot Kidder, Darren McGavin, Susan Anspach. WAR

Hitchhiker 3 1987 Three episodes from the anthology mystery series: "Ghost Writer," "And If We Dream," and "True Believer." Made-for-cable television. 90m/C VHS, Beta, LV. Ornella Muti, Willem Dafoe, Barry Bostwick, Daggy Haddon, Stephen Collins, Robert Weiss, Tom Skerritt. ORI, WAR

Hitchhiker 4 1987 Three episodes of the cable-television suspense series: "Man's Best Friend," about a lonely man whose pet dog tears his enemies to bits. "Face to Face," about the revenge exacted upon a drug-abusing cosmetic surgeon after he mucks up an operation; and "Videodate," about a guy being lured into a sinister video performance piece via his use of video dating services. **90m/C VHS, Beta, LV.** Michael O'Keefe, Sybil Danning, Sonja Smits, Robert Vaughn, Shannon Tweed, Greg Henry. *ORI, WAR*

Hitchhikers woof! **1972 (R)** Trash film about a bunch of scantily clad female hitchhikers who rob the motorists who stop to pick them up. Keep right on going when you spot this roadkill. **90m/C VHS, Beta.** Misty Rowe, Norman Klar, Linda Avery; *D:* Ferd Sebastian. *NO*

The Hitchhiker's Guide to the Galaxy **1981** The six episode BBC television adaptation of Douglas Adams' hilarious science-fiction books. Features the intergalactic Ford Prefect, sent to Earth to update its planetary listing in the Hitchhiker's Guide; hapless hero Arthur Dent, a typical Englishman caught up in space mayhem; and an odd assortment of aliens, including Marvin the Paranoid Android. The show's sheer cheesiness is part of the charm. Available in both single-cassette and double-cassette versions, the latter includes a copy of the book and a dedication from Adams. **194m/C VHS, LV.** *GB* Simon Jones, David Dixon, Sandra Dickinson, Mark Wing-Davey; *D:* Alan Bell. *FOX, MOV, FUS*

Hitler 🎬🎬½ *Women of Nazi Germany* **1962** The true story of the infamous Nazi dictator's rise to power and his historic downfall. **103m/B VHS, Beta.** Richard Basehart, Maria Emo, Cordula Trantow; *D:* Stuart Heisler. *FOX*

Hitler: Dead or Alive 🎬🎬 **1943** Three ex-cons devise a scheme to gain a million-dollar reward for capturing Adolf Hitler in this low-budget production. **64m/B VHS, Beta.** Ward Bond, Dorothy Tree, Bruce Edwards, Warren Hymer, Paul Fix, Russell Hicks, Bobby Watson; *D:* Nick Grinde. *NOS, MRV, DVT*

Hitler: The Last Ten Days 🎬🎬 **1973 (PG)** Based on an eyewitness account, the story of Hitler's last days in an underground bunker gives insight to his madness. **106m/C VHS, Beta.** Alec Guinness, Simon Ward, Adolfo Celi, Phyllida Law; *D:* Ennio de Concini. *PAR, GLV*

Hitler's Children 🎬🎬🎬 **1943** Two young people, a German boy and an American girl, are caught in the horror of Nazi Germany. He's attracted to Hitler's rant, she's repelled. Exploitative yet engrossing. **83m/B VHS, Beta.** Tim Holt, Bonita Granville, Otto Kruger, H.B. Warner, Irving Reis, Hans Conried, Lloyd Corrigan; *D:* Edward Dmytryk. *IHF*

Hitler's Daughter 🎬 **1990 (R)** Made for TV movie following the trials and tribulations of the illegitimate daughter of Adolf Hitler. She's all grown up now...and wants to rule the United States. She secures a position of power during an election and now Nazi-hunters must figure out her identity before she takes over the world! **88m/C VHS, Beta, Closed Caption.** Kay Lenz, Veronica Cartwright, Melody Anderson, Patrick Cassidy, Carolyn Dunn, Lindsay Merrithew, George R. Robertson; *D:* James A. Contner. *PAR*

The Hitman 🎬🎬 **1991 (R)** Norris plays a cop undercover as a syndicate hit man in Seattle, where he cleans up crime by triggering a three-way mob bloodbath between beastly Italian mafiosi, snooty French-Canadian hoods, and fanatical Iranian scum. But he teaches a black kid martial arts, so you know he's politically correct. Action addicts will give this a passing grade; all others need not apply.*CW:* Language and strong gangster violence. **95m/C VHS, LV, 8mm, Closed Caption.** Chuck Norris, Michael Parks, Al Waxman, Alberta Watson, Salim Grant, Ken Pogue, Marcel Sabourin, Bruno Gerussi, Frank Ferrucci; *D:* Aaron Norris; *C:* Joao Fernandes. *WAR*

The Hitter 🎬🎬 **1979 (R)** A former prizefighter, his girlfriend, and a washed-up promoter are all on the run in this adventure tale. **94m/C VHS.** Ron O'Neal, Adolph Caesar, Sheila Frazier; *D:* Christopher Leitch. *NO*

Hittin' the Trail 🎬 **1937** The Good Cowboy is mistaken for a murdering varmint, and must prove his innocence. **57m/B VHS, Beta.** Tex Ritter, Charles "Blackie" King, Ray Whitley, The Range Ramblers; *D:* Robert North Bradbury. *NOS, VDM*

Hitz 🎬½ **1992 (R)** In a Los Angeles barrio, Musico, a Loco gang member, kills two rival gang members. Arrested and convicted when a young boy named Pepe is coerced into testifying against him, Musico is killed in the courtroom. But the violence doesn't stop. The judge, who wants to reform the juvenile court system, tries to protect Pepe, and both are targeted for death by the Loco gang. **90m/C VHS, Closed Caption.** Elliott Gould, Emilia Crow, Karen Black, Cuba Gooding Jr. *THV*

The Hobbit 🎬🎬🎬 **1978** An animated interpretation of J.R.R. Tolkien's novel of the same name. The story follows Bilbo Baggins and his journeys in Middle Earth and encounters with the creatures who inhabit it. He joins comrades to battle against evil beings and creatures. Made for television. **76m/C VHS, Beta, 8mm.** *D:* Arthur Rankin Jr., Jules Bass; *V:* Orson Bean, John Huston, Otto Preminger, Richard Boone. *WAR, CHI, FCT*

Hobgoblins 🎬 **198?** Little creatures escape from a studio vault and wreak havoc. **92m/C VHS, Beta.** Jeffrey Culver, Tom Bartlett; *D:* Rick Sloane. *TWE*

The Hoboken Chicken Emergency **1984** Arthur's supposed to pick up a turkey for the family Thanksgiving dinner. Instead he returns with a 266-pound live chicken named Henrietta. Originally aired on PBS as part of the "Wonderworks" series. **55m/C VHS.** Dick Van Patten, Peter Billingsley, Gabe Kaplan, Arlene Golonka; *D:* Peter Baldwin. *HMV, FCT, BTV*

Hobo's Christmas 🎬🎬 **1987** A man who left his family to become a hobo comes home for Christmas 25 years later. Hughes turns in a delightful performance as the hobo in this made for television special. **94m/C VHS, Beta.** Barnard Hughes, William Hickey, Gerald McRaney, Wendy Crewson; *D:* Will MacKenzie. *NO*

Hobson's Choice 🎬🎬🎬 **1953** A prosperous businessman in the 1890s tries to keep his daughter from marrying, but the strong-willed daughter has other ideas. Remade for television in 1983. **107m/B VHS, Beta, LV.** *GB* Charles Laughton, John Mills, Brenda de Banzie; *D:* David Lean; *C:* Jack Hildyard; *M:* Malcolm Arnold. British Academy Awards '54: Best Film. *ING, NLC, HMV*

Hobson's Choice 🎬🎬 **1983** Made-for-television remake of the old family comedy about a crusty, penny-pinching businessman whose headstrong daughter proves to him she'll not become an old maid. Instead she marries one of his employees. Not bad, but not as good as the original. **95m/C VHS, Beta, Closed Caption.** Jack Warden, Sharon Gless, Richard Thomas, Lillian Gish; *D:* Gilbert Cates. *FOX*

Hockey Night 🎬🎬½ **1984** A movie for pre- and early teens in which a girl goalie makes the boys' hockey team. **77m/C VHS, Beta.** *CA* Megan Follows, Rick Moranis, Gail Youngs, Martin Harburg, Henry Ramer; *D:* Paul Shapiro. *FHE*

Hocus Pocus 🎬🎬½ **1993 (PG)** The divine Miss M is back, but this time she's not so sweet. Midler, Najimy, and Parker are 17th century witches accidentally conjured up in the 20th century, appropriately enough on Halloween in Salem, Massachusetts. Seems they were hung 300 years back and they take their revenge in some surprisingly gruesome ways, given the Disney label. They rant, they rave, they sing (only once), they fly. See this one for the three stars who make up for the lack of substance with their comedic talents. **95m/C VHS, Beta, LV, Closed Caption.** Bette Midler, Kathy Najimy, Sarah Jessica Parker, Thora Birch, Doug Jones, Omri Katz, Vinessa Shaw, Stephanie Faracy, Charles Rocket; *Cameos:* Penny Marshall, Garry Marshall; *D:* Kenny Ortega; *W:* Neil Cuthbert, Mick Garris; *M:* John Debney. *DIS, BTV*

Hoffa 🎬🎬🎬🎬 **1992 (R)** The story of union organizer James R. Hoffa, who oversaw the rise of the Teamsters, a labor union composed mostly of truck drivers, from its fledgling infancy during the Great Depression to a membership of 2 million by the 1970s. Powerful performances by Nicholson in the title role and DeVito, who plays a union aide, a fictitious composite of several men who actually served Hoffa. This almost affectionate biographical treatment stands out in contrast from a career bristling with tension and violence. Proceeds through a series of flashbacks from the day Hoffa disappeared, July 30, 1975.*CW:* Strong language and violence. **140m/C VHS, LV, Letterbox, Closed Caption.** Jack Nicholson, Danny DeVito, Armand Assante, J.T. Walsh, Frank Whaley, Kevin Anderson, John P. Ryan, Robert Prosky, Natalija Nogulich, Nicholas Pryor, John C. Reilly, Karen Young, Cliff Gorman; *D:* Danny DeVito; *W:* David Mamet; *C:* Stephen Burum; *M:* David Newman. Nominations: Academy Awards '92: Best Cinematography, Best Makeup. *FOX*

Hog Wild 🎬½ **1980 (PG)** A clique of high school nerds exact revenge on bullies from the local mean motorcycle gang, and a girl is torn between the two factions. **97m/C VHS, Beta.** *CA* Patti D'Arbanville, Tony Rosato, Michael Biehn; *D:* Les Rose. *NLC*

The Holcroft Covenant 🎬🎬 **1985 (R)** Based upon the complex Robert Ludlum novel. Details the efforts of a man trying to release a secret fund that his Nazi father humanistically set up to relieve the future sufferings of Holocaust survivors. Confusing, and slow, but interesting, nonetheless. **112m/C VHS, Beta, LV, Closed Caption.** *GB* Michael Caine, Victoria Tennant, Anthony Andrews, Lilli Palmer, Mario Adorf, Michael Lonsdale; *D:* John Frankenheimer; *W:* Edward Anhalt, John Hopkins, George Axelrod. *MGM*

Hold 'Em Jail 🎬🎬½ **1932** Some good laughs with Wheeler and Woolsey starting a competitive football team at Kennedy's Bidemore Prison. **65m/B VHS, Beta.** Bert Wheeler, Robert Woolsey, Edgar Kennedy, Betty Grable, Edna May Oliver; *D:* Norman Taurog. *CCB*

Hold Me, Thrill Me, Kiss Me 🎬🎬½ **1993 (R)** "Offbeat" barely begins to describe this comedy about a hapless loser who finds true love. Eli (Parrish) has escaped marriage to a rich girl named Twinkle (Young), unfortunately it took a little shooting to do it and now Eli's hiding out in a tacky pink trailer park where Sabra (Naschak), an insatiable stripper with a fondness for sex toys, immediately goes after Eli's bod. But he falls for her naive (and virginal) sister, Dannie (Shelly). Hershman manages to keep all the free-wheeling goings on under control. Film debut of former model Parrish; directorial debut feature of Hershman.*CW:* Strong language and strong sexuality. **92m/C VHS.** Max Parrish, Adrienne Shelly, Andrea Naschak, Sean Young, Diane Ladd, Bela Lehoczky, Ania Suli; *Cameos:* Timothy Leary; *D:* Joel Hershman; *W:* Joel Hershman. *ART*

Hold That Ghost 🎬🎬🎬 *Oh, Charlie* **1941** Abbott and Costello inherit an abandoned roadhouse where the illicit loot of its former owner, a "rubbed out" mobster, is supposedly hidden. **86m/B VHS, Beta.** Bud Abbott, Lou Costello, Joan Davis, Richard Carlson, Mischa Auer, The Andrews Sisters; *D:* Arthur Lubin. *USH*

Hold the Dream 🎬 **1985** A made-for-television mini-series sequel to Barbara Taylor Bradford's "A Woman of Substance." **195m/C VHS, Beta.** Jenny Seagrove, Stephen Collins, Deborah Kerr, James Brolin; *D:* Don Sharp. *NO*

Hold Your Man 🎬🎬🎬 **1933** Great star vehicle that turns from comedy to drama with Harlow falling for hustler Gable. Harlow and Gable are at their best in this unlikely story of a crooked couple. Direction drags at times, but snappy dialogue and the stars' personalities more than make up for it. **86m/B VHS, Closed Caption.** Jean Harlow, Clark Gable, Stuart Erwin, Dorothy Burgess, Garry Owen,

Paul Hurst, Elizabeth Patterson, Laura La Plante; **D:** Sam Wood; **W:** Anita Loos, Howard Emmett Rogers. *MGM*

A Hole in the Head 🎬🎬½ **1959** A comedy-drama about a shiftless but charming lout who tries to raise money to save his hotel from foreclosure and learn to be responsible for his young son. Notable for the introduction of the song "High Hopes." ♫High Hopes; All My Tomorrows. **120m/C VHS, Beta, LV, Letterbox.** Frank Sinatra, Edward G. Robinson, Thelma Ritter, Carolyn Jones, Eleanor Parker, Eddie Hodges, Keenan Wynn, Joi Lansing; **D:** Frank Capra; **W:** Arnold Schulman; **C:** William H. Daniels. Academy Awards '59: Best Song ("High Hopes"). *MGM*

Hole in the Sky 🎬🎬½ *The Ranger, the Cook and a Hole in the Sky* **1995 (PG)** Teenaged Mac (O'Connell) is working for the Montana forestry service in the summer of 1919 under the tutelage of taciturn legend Bill Bell (a mustache-less Elliott). Mac learns some lessons about growing up, first love, card-playing—and never to rile the camp cook. Based on an autobiographical story by Norman MacLean. Made for TV; filmed on location in British Columbia. **94m/C VHS.** Sam Elliott, Jerry O'Connell, Ricky Jay, Molly Parker; **D:** John Kent Harrison; **W:** Robert W. Lenski. *HMK*

The Holes 🎬🎬½ *Les Gaspards* **1972 (PG)** A Parisian book shop owner's daughter vanishes along with other local citizens and American tourists, and he decides to investigate when the police won't. In French with subtitles. **92m/C VHS, Beta.** *FR* Philippe Noiret, Charles Denner, Michael Serrault, Gerard Depardieu. *FHE, FCT*

Holiday 🎬🎬🎬 *Free to Live; Unconventional Linda* **1938** The classically genteel screwball comedy about a rich girl who steals her sister's fiance. A yardstick in years to come for sophisticated, urbane Hollywood romanticism. Based on the play by Philip Barry who later wrote "The Philadelphia Story." **93m/B VHS, Beta, LV.** Cary Grant, Katharine Hepburn, Doris Nolan, Edward Everett Horton, Ruth Donnelly, Lew Ayres, Binnie Barnes; **D:** George Cukor; **W:** Donald Ogden Stewart, Sidney Buchman. Nominations: Academy Awards '36: Best Interior Decoration. *COL*

Holiday Affair 🎬🎬½ **1949** Hollywood yuletide charmer about a pretty widow being courted by two very different men. **86m/B VHS, Beta, LV.** Robert Mitchum, Janet Leigh, Griff Barnett, Wendell Corey, Esther Dale, Henry O'Neill, Harry (Henry) Morgan, Larry J. Blake; **D:** Don Hartman. *TTC*

Holiday Affair 🎬🎬½ **1996** Cable remake of the 1949 film finds Manhattan department store clerk Steve Mason (Elliott) intrigued by widowed mom Jodie Ennis (Gibb), who's just purchased a train set to use as a commercial prop. Jodie has a regular guy boyfriend in Paul (Irwin) and he's anxious to get married. But Jodie's more cautious and Steve's certainly interested. **93m/C VHS.** David James Elliott, Cynthia Gibb, Tom Irwin, Al Waxman, Patricia Hamilton, Victor Ertmanis, Pam Hyatt; **D:** Alan Myerson; **M:** Lee Holdridge. *BWE*

Holiday Hotel 🎬🎬 **1977 (R)** A group of wild French vacationers let loose at their favorite little resort hotel along the Brittany coast. Available in French with English subtitles or dubbed into English. **109m/C VHS, Beta.** *FR* Sophie Barjae, Daniel Ceccaldi; **D:** Michael Lang.

Holiday in Havana 🎬🎬 **1949** Desi Arnaz is back in Cuba winning hearts and dance contests. Watch only for Desi's presence. ♫Holiday in Havana; The Arnaz Jam; Straw Hat Song; Rhumba Rumbero; Copacobana; Made For Each Other; I'll Take Romance. **73m/B VHS.** Desi Arnaz Sr., Lolita Valdez, Mary Hatcher, Ann Doran; **D:** Jean Yarbrough. *GKK*

Holiday in Mexico 🎬🎬½ **1946** Pidgeon plays the U.S. ambassador to Mexico whose teenage daughter (Powell) tries to run his life along with his household. He falls for a singer while she develops a crush on an older, respected pianist (Iturbi playing himself). Lots of lively production numbers featuring Xavier Cugat and his orchestra. ♫I Think Of You; Walter Winchell

Rhumba; Yo Te Amo Mucho—And That's That; And Dreams Remain; Holiday in Mexico; Ave Maria; Les Filles de Cadiz; Italian Street Song; Polonaise in A Flat Major. **127m/C VHS.** Walter Pidgeon, Jane Powell, Ilona Massey, Jose Iturbi, Roddy McDowall, Xavier Cugat, Hugo Haas; **D:** George Sidney; **W:** Isobel Lennart; **C:** Harry Stradling; **M:** Georgie Stoll. *MGM*

Holiday Inn 🎬🎬🎬 **1942** Fred Astaire and Bing Crosby are rival song-and-dance men who decide to work together to turn a Connecticut farm into an inn, open only on holidays. Remade in 1954 as "White Christmas." ♫White Christmas; Be Careful, It's My Heart; Plenty to Be Thankful For; Abraham, Abraham; Let's Say It With Firecrackers; I Gotta Say I Love You Cause I Can't Tell A Lie; Let's Start the New Year Right; Happy Holidays; Song of Freedom. **101m/B VHS, Beta, LV.** Bing Crosby, Fred Astaire, Marjorie Reynolds, Walter Abel, Virginia Dale; **D:** Mark Sandrich. Academy Awards '42: Best Song ("White Christmas"); Nominations: Academy Awards '42: Best Story, Scoring of a Musical. *USH*

Holiday Rhythm 🎬½ **1950** A television promoter is knocked out and dreams of a worldwide trip full of entertainment, comedy, and insanity. **61m/B VHS, Beta, LV.** Mary Beth Hughes, Tex Ritter, David Street, Donald MacBride. *NO*

Hollow Gate **1988** Trick or Treat?? Four kids find out when they run into a guy with hungry dogs. **90m/C VHS, Beta.** Addison Randall. *NO*

Hollow Point 🎬🎬 **1995 (R)** After FBI agent Diane Norwood (Carrere) and DEA agent Max Perish (Griffith) get in each other's way, they reluctantly team up to bring down crime kingpin Oleg Krezinsky (Hemblen). Only Krezinsky and his partner Livingston (Lithgrow) learns she's a fed and hire assassin Lawton (Sutherland) to teach her a lesson. **CW:** Violence and language. **103m/C VHS.** Thomas Ian Griffith, Tia Carrere, John Lithgow, Donald Sutherland, David Hemblen; **D:** Sidney J. Furie; **C:** David Franco; **M:** Brahm Wenger. *THV*

Hollow Reed 🎬🎬🎬 *Believe Me* **1995** Heartwrenching, though not maudlin, drama revolves around nine-year-old Oliver Wyatt (Bould). His parents, Martyn (Donovan) and Hannah (Richardson), have bitterly divorced after Martyn finally acknowledges his homosexuality and moves in with his lover, Tom (Hart). Hannah's new live-in boyfriend Frank (Flemyng) turns out to be abusive towards Oliver, who's reluctant to say anything to destroy his mother's new happiness. But when Martyn discovers what's happening, he instigates a custody battle for his son that has everyone at each other's throats, with the terrified Oliver caught in the crossfire. Compelling performances. **105m/C VHS, Closed Caption.** *GB* Martin Donovan, Joely Richardson, Ian Hart, Jason Flemyng, Sam Bould; **D:** Angela Pope; **W:** Paula Milne; **C:** Remi Adefarasin; **M:** Anne Dudley. *COL*

Hollywood After Dark 🎬 **1965** McClanahan plays a young starlet trying to make it big in Hollywood. Pure exploitation schlock. Not released theatrically until 1968. **?m/C VHS.** Rue McClanahan. *SNC, TPV*

Hollywood Bloopers 🎬🎬½ **195?** Hilarious outtakes from some of Hollywood's finest movies, featuring stars such as Bette Davis, James Cagney, Humphrey Bogart, Rosalind Russell, Errol Flynn, Kirk Douglas, and many more. **85m/B VHS, Beta.** Lauren Bacall, Ronald Reagan, James Stewart, Joan Blondell, Rosalind Russell, Errol Flynn, Kirk Douglas, Barbara Stanwyck. *VDM*

Hollywood Boulevard 🎬🎬½ **1976 (R)** Behind-the-scenes glimpse of shoestring-budget movie making offers comical sex, violence, sight gags, one-liners, comedy bits, and mock-documentary footage. Commander Cody and His Lost Planet Airmen are featured. **93m/C VHS, Beta.** Candice Rialson, Mary Woronov, Rita George, Jonathan Kaplan, Jeffrey Kramer, Dick Miller, Paul Bartel; **D:** Joe Dante, Allan Arkush; **C:** Jamie Anderson. *WAR, OM*

Hollywood Boulevard 2 🎬 **1989 (R)** A "B" movie studio finds its top actresses being killed off and terror reigns supreme as the mystery grows more intense. Could that psycho-bimbo from outer space have something to do with it? **82m/C VHS, Beta, Closed Caption.** Ginger Lynn Allen, Kelly Monteith, Eddie Deezen, Ken Wright, Steve Vinovich; **D:** Steve Barnett. *MGM*

Hollywood Canteen 🎬🎬🎬🎬 **1944** Star-studded extravaganza with just about every Warner Bros. lot actor in this tribute to love and nationalism. Lovesick G.I. Hutton falls for Leslie, wins a date with her in a phony raffle set up at the Hollywood Canteen, and the sparks fly right away. But he thinks she tricked him as he boards his train and she's not there to see him off. Lame story is redeemed by the talented cast and wonderful musical numbers which make this picture fly with charm and style. Before production began there were arguments over "unpatriotic" actors—labeled as such due to their lack of participation in this, and other similar movies produced at the time. ♫Don't Fence Me In; Sweet Dreams, Sweetheart; You Can Always Tell A Yank; We're Having a Baby; What Are You Doin' the Rest of Your Life; The General Jumped At Dawn; Gettin' Corns For My Country; Voodoo Moon; Tumblin' Tumbleweeds. **124m/B VHS.** Robert Hutton, Dane Clark, Janis Paige, Jonathan Hale, Barbara Brown, James Flavin, Eddie Marr, Ray Teal, Bette Davis, Joan Leslie, Jack Benny, Jimmy Dorsey, Joan Crawford, John Garfield, Barbara Stanwyck, Ida Lupino, Eddie Cantor, Jack Carson, Eleanor Parker, Alexis Smith, S.Z. Sakall, Peter Lorre, Sydney Greenstreet, Helmut Dantine; **D:** Delmer Daves; **W:** Delmer Daves. Nominations: Academy Awards '44: Best Song ("Sweet Dreams Sweetheart"), Best Sound, Scoring of a Musical. *FOX, FCT*

Hollywood Chainsaw Hookers 🎬🎬 **1988 (R)** A campy, sexy, very bloody parody about attractive prostitutes who dismember their unsuspecting customers. **90m/C VHS, Beta.** Linnea Quigley, Gunnar Hansen, Jay Richardson, Michelle (McClellan) Bauer; **D:** Fred Olen Ray. *NO*

Hollywood Chaos 🎬½ **1989** Director Ballantine's stars quit his production before it even starts, so he gets the next best thing—star look-alikes. However, his problems are just beginning. One of his new "stars" is kidnapped, and his reclusive stage manager is hunted as the object of desire for a female motorcycle gang. **90m/C VHS.** Carl Ballantine, Tricia Leigh Fisher, Kathleen Freeman; **D:** Sean McNamara. *WLA*

Hollywood Confidential 🎬🎬 **1997 (R)** TV movie stars Olmos as former LAPD cop Stan Navarro, who now runs a struggling detective agency specializing in the seamier sides of Hollywood. His latest cases involve getting dirt on a studio acting coach, seeing if a bartender at the newest hotspot is skimming the receipts, and "persuading" the mistress of a well-known director to take a hike. **CW:** Sexual content and some violence. **90m/C VHS, Beta, Closed Caption.** Edward James Olmos, Anthony Yerkovich, Rick Aiello, Richard T. Jones, Charlize Theron, Angela Alvarado, Christina Harnos; **D:** Ray Villalobos; **W:** Anthony Yerkovich; **M:** Marc Bonilla. *PAR*

Hollywood Cop 🎬½ **1987 (R)** A tough cop in Hollywood goes up against the mob for the sake of a kidnapped boy. **101m/C VHS, Beta.** Jim Mitchum, David Goss, Cameron Mitchell, Troy Donahue, Aldo Ray; **D:** Amir Shervan. *CEL*

The Hollywood Detective 🎬🎬 **1989 (PG)** An average TV movie that spoofs "Kojak." A TV detective tries it out for real, and gets into troubles for which he can't pause "for a message from our sponsor." **88m/C VHS, Beta.** Telly Savalas, Helene Udy, George Coe, Joe Dallesandro, Tom Reese; **D:** Kevin Connor. *USH*

Hollywood Dreams 🎬½ **1994 (R)** Starlet on the Hollywood casting couch saga of a midwestern gal that comes to California with dreams of making it big. **CW:** Strong sexuality. **90m/C VHS.**

Kelly Cook, Danny Smith, Debra Beatty; **D:** Ralph Portillo. CEL

Hollywood Goes to War 1954 Five shorts produced for the entertainment of G.I.'s overseas or for home front bond drives: "The All-Star Bond Rally" features Hope, Crosby, Harry James and His Orchestra, Sinatra, Grable, Marx, and the Talking Pin-Ups; "Hollywood Canteen Overseas Special" features Shore, Cantor, Durante, and Skelton; "Mail Call (Strictly G.I.)" is a filmed "Mail Call" radio program; "G.I. Movie Weekly—Sing with the Stars" features Miranda and her fruit-basket hat and a Portuguese follow-the-bouncing-ball sing-along; and "Invaders in Greasepaint," the story of the North African USO tour of the "Four Jills in a Jeep." Also includes the Jill's memorable rendition of the wartime classic "Snafu," banned from the airwaves for its racy lyrics. 41m/B VHS, Beta. Bob Hope, Bing Crosby, Frank Sinatra, Betty Grable, Harpo Marx, Jimmy Durante, Eddie Cantor, Red Skelton, Bud Abbott, Lou Costello, Dinah Shore, Dorothy Lamour, Carmen Miranda. NO

Hollywood Harry 🎬 *Harry's Machine* 1986 (PG-13) A private-eye mystery/parody, about an inept detective who searches for a missing porn actress. 99m/C VHS, Beta. Robert Forster, Kathrine Forster, Joe Spinell, Shannon Wilcox; **D:** Robert Forster; **W:** Curt Allen.

Hollywood Heartbreak 🎬🎬 1989 It's heartbreak in tinseltown for a young writer who's trying to pitch his movie script but winds up defending himself from slimy agents and persistent starlets. Another entry for Bartlett's familiar plotlines. 90m/C VHS. Mark Moses, Carol Mayo Jenkins, Ron Karabatsos, Richard Romanus, James LeGros; **D:** Lance Dickson. VTR

Hollywood High 🎬 1977 (R) Four attractive teen couples converge on the mansion of an eccentric silent-film star for an unusual vacation experience in this teenage skin flick. Followed by a sequel. 81m/C VHS, Beta. Marcy Albrecht, Sherry Hardin, Rae Sperling, Susanne Kevin Mead; **D:** Patrick Wright. ART, VES

Hollywood High, Part 2 🎬 1981 (R) Ignored by their boyfriends for the lure of sun and surf, three comely high school students try their best to regain their interest. 86m/C VHS, Beta. April May, Donna Lynn, Camille Warner, Lee Thomburg; **D:** Caruth C. Byrd. ART, VES

Hollywood Hot Tubs 🎬 1984 (R) Teen sex romp has adolescent picking up some extra cash and a lot of fun repairing the hot tubs of the rich and famous. 103m/C VHS, Beta. Donna McDaniel, Michael Andrew, Katt Shea Ruben, Paul Gunning, Edy Williams, Jewel Shepard; **D:** Chuck Vincent. ART, VES, VTR

Hollywood Hot Tubs 2: Educating Crystal 🎬 1989 (R) A softcore comedy about a well-tanned ingenue learning about business in Hollywood during numerous hot tub trysts. 103m/C VHS, Beta, LV. Jewel Shepard, Patrick Day, Remy O'Neill, David Tiefen, Bart Braverman; **D:** Ken Raich.

Hollywood in Trouble 🎬 1987 A bumbling middle-aged fool decides to break into the wacky movie-making business. 90m/C VHS. Vic Vallard, Jean Levine, Jerry Tiffe, Pamela Dixon, Jerry Cleary. NO

Hollywood Man 🎬🎬 1976 (R) A Hollywood actor wants to make his own film but when his financial support comes from the mob there's trouble ahead. 90m/C VHS, Beta. William Smith, Don Stroud, Jennifer Billingsley, Mary Woronov; **D:** Jack Starrett. NO

Hollywood Mystery 🎬½ *Hollywood Hoodlum* 1934 A publicity agent stops at nothing to promote his would-be starlet girlfriend. 53m/B VHS. June Clyde, Frank Albertson, Joe Crespo; **D:** B. Reeves Eason. NOS, LOO

Hollywood or Bust 🎬🎬½ 1956 The zany duo take their act on the road as they head for Tinsel Town in order to meet Lewis' dream girl Ekberg. This was the last film for the Martin & Lewis team and it's not the swan song their fans

would have hoped for. 95m/C VHS. Dean Martin, Jerry Lewis, Anita Ekberg, Pat Crowley, Maxie "Slapsie" Rosenbloom, Willard Waterman; **D:** Frank Tashlin. PAR, CCB

Hollywood Outtakes & Rare Footage 1983 A collection of rare and unusual film clips and excerpts that feature dozens of Hollywood stars in screen tests, promotional shorts, home movies, outtakes, television appearances and WWII propaganda shorts. Some segments in black and white. 85m/C VHS, Beta, LV. Marilyn Monroe, James Dean, Joan Crawford, Humphrey Bogart, Ronald Reagan, Bette Davis, Vivien Leigh, Carole Lombard. COL, RXM

Hollywood Party 🎬🎬½ 1934 Durante plays a film star who decides to throw a Hollywood bash. Any plot is incidental as it is mainly an excuse to have numerous stars of the day appear in brief comic bits or musical numbers. Mickey Mouse and the Big Bad Wolf of Disney fame also appear in color animated footage combined with live action. Numerous MGM directors worked on parts of the film but Dwan was given the task of trying to pull the various scenes together (he is uncredited onscreen). 🎵Hollywood Party; Hello; Reincarnation; I've Had My Moments; Feeling High; Hot Chocolate Soldiers. 72m/B VHS. Jimmy Durante, Stan Laurel, Oliver Hardy, Lupe Velez, Ted Healy, Moe Howard, Curly Howard, Larry Fine, Robert Young, Charles Butterworth, Polly Moran, George Givot, Tom Kennedy; **D:** Allan Dwan; **V:** Walt Disney, Billy Bletcher. MGM

Hollywood Scandals and Tragedies 1988 A look at the skeletons-in-the-closet surrounding the deaths and private turmoils of James Dean, Rock Hudson, Vivien Leigh, Frances Farmer, Sal Mineo, Sharon Tate, Jayne Mansfield, and others. 90m/C VHS, Beta. MPI

Hollywood Shuffle 🎬🎬½ 1987 (R) Townsend's autobiographical comedy about a struggling black actor in Hollywood trying to find work and getting nothing but stereotypical roles. Written, directed, financed by Townsend, who created this often clever and appealing film on a $100,000 budget. 81m/C VHS, Beta, LV. Robert Townsend, Anne-Marie Johnson, Starletta DuPois, Helen Martin, Keenen Ivory Wayans, Damon Wayans, Craigus R. Johnson, Eugene Glazer; **D:** Robert Townsend; **W:** Robert Townsend, Keenen Ivory Wayans; **M:** Patrice Rushen, Udi Harpaz. NO

Hollywood Stadium Mystery 🎬🎬 1938 A boxer turns up dead before a big match and a D.A. investigates. Performances hold this one up, especially by Hamilton who later played Commissioner Gordon on TV's "Batman." 66m/B VHS, Beta. Neil Hamilton, Evelyn Venable, Jimmy Wallington, Barbara Pepper, Lucien Littlefield, Lynn (Mary Hart) Roberts, Charles Williams, James Spottswood, Reed Hadley, Smiley Burnette; **D:** David Howard. SNC

The Hollywood Strangler Meets the Skid Row Slasher woof! *The Model Killer* 1979 (R) Voiced-over narration, canned music and an unfathomable plot are but a few of this would-be fright fest's finer points. Uninhibited by any narrative connection, two terrors strike fear in the heart of Tinseltown. While a psycho photographer cruises L.A. taking pictures of models he subsequently strangles, a woman working in a bare-bums magazine store takes a stab (with a knife) at lowering the city's derelict population. There's a word for this sort of dribble, and it isn't versimilitude. Steckler used an alias (not surprisingly) for this one—Wolfgang Schmidt. 72m/C VHS. Pierre Agostino, Carolyn Brandt, Forrest Duke, Chuck Alford; **D:** Ray Dennis Steckler. NO

Hollywood Uncensored 1987 A history of Hollywood censorship, including long-suppressed scenes from "King Kong," "The Outlaw," "Carnal Knowledge," "Baby Doll," "Easy Rider," "Woodstock," and more. 75m/C VHS, Beta. ART, FCT

Hollywood Vice Sqaud 🎬 1986 (R) Explores the lives of Hollywood police officers and the crimes they investigate. Contains three different story lines involving prostitution, child pornography, and organized crime. The film can't decide

to be a comedy send-up of crime stories or a drama and is also crippled by a poor script. Written by the real-life chief of the Hollywood Vice Squad. 100m/C VHS, LV. Trish Van Devere, Ronny Cox, Frank Gorshin, Leon Isaac Kennedy, Carrie Fisher, Ben Frank, Robin Wright Penn; **D:** Penelope Spheeris; **M:** Michael Convertino. VTR, HHE, MTX

Hollywood Zap woof! 1986 (R) Two losers, one a Southern orphan, the other a video game nut, hit Hollywood and engage in antics that are meant to be funny, but are actually tasteless. **CW:** Language and sexuality. 85m/C VHS, Beta. Ben Frank, Ivan E. Roth, De Waldron, Annie Gaybis, Chuck "Porky" Mitchell; **D:** David M. Cohen; **W:** David M. Cohen.

Hollywood's New Blood 🎬 1988 Young actors making a movie are haunted by a film crew from hell. 90m/C VHS, Beta. Bobby Johnson, Francine Lapensee; **D:** James Shyman. VTR

Holocaust 🎬🎬🎬½ 1978 The war years of 1935 to 1945 are relived in this account of the Nazi atrocities, focusing on the Jewish Weiss family, destroyed by the monstrous crimes, and the Dorf family, Germans who thrived under the Nazi regime. Highly acclaimed riveting made-for-television mini-series with an exceptional cast. Won eight Emmys. 475m/C VHS, Beta. Michael Moriarty, Fritz Weaver, Meryl Streep, James Woods, Joseph Bottoms, Tovah Feldshuh, David Warner, Ian Holm, Michael Beck, Marius Goring; **D:** Marvin J. Chomsky. REP, SWC, WOV

Holocaust Survivors...Remembrance of Love 🎬🎬 *Remembrance of Love* 1983 A concentration camp survivor and his daughter attend the 1981 World Gathering of Holocaust Survivors in Tel-Aviv and both find romance. Made for television. 100m/C VHS, Beta. Kirk Douglas, Pam Dawber, Chana Eden, Yoram Gal, Robert Clary; **D:** Jack Smight; **M:** William Goldstein. THV

Hologram Man 🎬🎬 1995 (R) Futuristic thriller finds psycho/terrorist Slash Gallagher (Lurie) captured by rookie cop Kurt Decoda (Lara). His prison term is to be served in Holographic Stasis, which means his mind is stored on a computer. Slash's gang manges to break his mind out of the computer but since his body is destroyed, Slash roams as a powerful electro-magnetic hologram. And it's up to cop Decoda to get Slash back. **CW:** Violence; nudity; language. 96m/C VHS, LV, Closed Caption. Joe Lara, Evan Lurie, William Sanderson, Tommy (Tiny) Lister, Michael Nouri, John Amos; **D:** Richard Pepin; **W:** Evan Lurie; **M:** John Gonzalez. PMH

Holt of the Secret Service 1942 Secret service agent runs afoul of saboteurs and fifth-columnists in this 15-episode serial. 290m/B VHS. Jack Holt, Evelyn Brent, Montague Shaw, Tristram Coffin, John Ward, George Chesebro; **D:** James W. Horne. VYY, DVT, NOS

The Holy Innocents 🎬🎬🎬 *Los Santos Inocentes* 1984 (PG) A peasant family is torn asunder by their feudal obligations to their patrons. Set in the 1960s in Franco's Spain. In Spanish with English subtitles. 108m/C VHS, Beta. SP Alfredo Landa, Francesco Rabal; **D:** Mario Camus. Cannes Film Festival '84: Best Actor (Landa), Best Actor (Rabal). ORI

Holy Matrimony 🎬🎬½ 1994 (PG-13) Mild-mannered and pleasant comedy in spite of its potentially salacious plot. Thieves Peter (Donovan) and Havana (Arquette) take off to Canada to hide out in the Hutterite religious community where Peter grew up and where he's welcomed as the prodigal son. Peter hides their stolen loot but neglects to pass the word on before he's killed in an accident. Wanting to stay and search for the money, Havana uses the colony's reliance on biblical law to marry Peter's brother, Zeke (Gordon-Levitt). Only problem is Zeke is 12 and doesn't even like girls. Strictly brother-sister affection develops between the two. Amusing performances by both. 93m/C VHS, LV, Closed Caption. Patricia Arquette, Joseph Gordon-Levitt, Armin Mueller-Stahl, Tate Donovan,

John Schuck, Lois Smith, Courtney B. Vance, Jeffrey Nordling, Richard Riehle; **D:** Leonard Nimoy; **W:** David Weisberg, Douglas S. Cook; **C:** Bobby Bukowski; **M:** Bruce Broughton. *TOU*

Holy Terror 🎞🎞 **1965** The story of Florence Nightingale, who shocked Victorian society by organizing a nursing staff to aid British soldiers in the Crimean War, is told in this presentation from "George Schaefer's Showcase Theatre." 76m/C VHS, Beta. Julie Harris, Denholm Elliott, Torin Thatcher, Kate Reid; **D:** George Schaefer. *FHS*

Homage 🎞🎞 **1995 (R)** Archie's (Whaley) an emotionally disturbed mathematical nerd who needs a break from academia and persuades widowed ex-teacher Katherine Samuel (Danner) to hire him as caretaker for her New Mexico ranch. The duo achieve a strange serenity that shatters when Katherine's TV star daughter, self-absorbed Lucy (Lee), arrives seeking shelter because of her drug and drinking problems. A nasty triangle ensues as Lucy makes the mistake of sexually enticing, then rejecting, the needy Archie. In fact, the mistake's fatal. Based on Medoff's play "The Homage That Follows."**CW:** Brief strong sexuality, language and an act of violence. 100m/C VHS. Frank Whaley, Blythe Danner, Sheryl Lee, Bruce Davison, Danny Nucci; **D:** Ross Kagen Marks; **W:** Mark Medoff; **C:** Tom Richmond; **M:** W.G. Snuffy Walden. *AVI*

Hombre 🎞🎞🎞 **1967** A white man in the 1880s, raised by a band of Arizona Apaches, is forced into a showdown. In helping a stagecoach full of settlers across treacherous country, he not only faces traditional bad guys, but prejudice as well. Based on a story by Elmore Leonard. 111m/C VHS, Beta, LV, Letterbox. Paul Newman, Fredric March, Richard Boone, Diane Cilento, Cameron Mitchell, Barbara Rush, Martin Balsam; **D:** Martin Ritt; **W:** Harriet Frank Jr., Irving Ravetch; **C:** James Wong Howe. *FOX*

Hombres Armados 🎞🎞🎞 *Men with Guns* **1997 (R)** Fiercely independent filmmaker John Sayles' men with guns are not characters; they're an inevitable force like time or the weather that the characters have learned to accept. Set in a fictional Latin American country, story follows a well-to-do physician (Luppi) who trains doctors to work in the countryside among the local Mayan Indians. What he doesn't realize is that a civil war is engulfing his country, the Indians are practically enslaved, and his students have been murdered by the government that trained them. He picks up a ragged bunch of stragglers whose lives have been shattered by ever-present soldiers from either side of the war. Together they trudge through the jungle, searching for a place devoid of war or politics. Sayles based his idea on the 36-year-long civil war in Guatemala, which began in 1960. Spanish with subtitles.**CW:** Language and some violent images. 128m/C VHS. Federico Luppi, Damian Delgado, Dan Rivera Gonzalez, Tania Cruz, Damian Alcazar, Iguandili Lopez, Nandi Luna Ramirez, Rafael De Quevedo, Mandy Patinkin, Kathryn Grody, Roberto Sosa; **D:** John Sayles; **W:** John Sayles; **C:** Slawomir Idziak; **M:** Mason Daring. *NYR*

Home Alone 🎞🎞🎞 **1990 (PG)** Eight-year-old Kevin is accidentally left behind when his entire (and large) family makes a frantic rush for the airport. That's the plausible part. Alone and besieged by burglars, Culkin turns into a pint-sized Rambo defending his suburban castle with the wile and resources of a boy genius with perfect timing and unlimited wherewithal. That's the implausible part. Pesci and Stern, the targets of Macauley's wrath, enact painful slapstick with considerable vigor, while Candy has a small but funny part as the leader of a polka band traveling cross-country with mom O'Hara. The highest-grossing picture of 1990, surpassing "Ghost" and "Jaws." 105m/C VHS, Beta, LV, Letterbox, Closed Caption. Macaulay Culkin, Catherine O'Hara, Joe Pesci, Daniel Stern, John Heard, Roberts Blossom, John Candy, Catherine O'Hara, Billie Bird, Angela Goethals, Devin Ratray, Kieran Culkin; **D:** Chris Columbus; **W:** John Hughes; **M:** John Williams. Nominations: Academy Awards '90: Best

Song ("Somewhere in My Memory"), Best Original Score. *FXV, IME, RDG*

Home Alone 2: Lost in New York 🎞🎞½ **1992 (PG)** In an almost exact duplication of the original blockbuster, the hare-brained McCallister family leaves Kevin behind in the shuffle to start their Florida vacation. Boarding the wrong plane, Kevin lands in NYC, where wonder of wonders, he meets crooks Pesci and Stern, prison escapees who somehow survived the torture meted out in the first film. And they want revenge. Loaded with cartoon violence and shameless gag replicas from HA1, mega-hit still produces genuine laughs and manages to incorporate fresh material. Culkin is as adorable as ever, with supporting cast all delivering fine performances. Filmed in New York City. 120m/C VHS, LV, Closed Caption. Macaulay Culkin, Joe Pesci, Daniel Stern, Catherine O'Hara, John Heard, Tim Curry, Brenda Fricker, Devin Ratray, Hillary Wolf, Eddie Bracken, Dana Ivey, Rob Schneider, Kieran Culkin, Gerry Bamman; *Cameos:* Donald Trump; **D:** Chris Columbus; **W:** John Hughes; **M:** John Williams. *FXV, BTV*

Home Alone 3 🎞 **1997 (PG)** Regardless of the new faces, the story and cartoon violence seems all too familar. Linz (taking over for the teenaged Culkin) is stricken with the chicken pox but able to booby trap his suburban house with to foil the plans of international criminals trying to recover a microchip stashed in a toy car. Film fails to carry the charm of its predecessors and sends the wrong messages: it's okay for parents to leave underaged kids home by themselves and electrocuting people is fun. Writer Hughes should be left home alone to rethink his skills as a screenwriter. 102m/C VHS, LV, Closed Caption. Alex D. Linz, Kevin Kilner, Olek Krupa, Rya Kihlstedt, Lenny Von Dohlen, David Thornton, Haviland Morris, Marian Seldes, Scarlett Johansson, Christopher Curry, Baxter Harris, Seth Smith; **D:** Raja Gosnell; **W:** John Hughes; **C:** Julio Macat; **M:** Nick Glennie-Smith. Nominations: Golden Raspberry Awards '97: Worst Remake/Sequel. *FXV*

The Home and the World 🎞🎞🎞½ *Ghare Baire* **1984** Another masterpiece from India's Ray, this film deals with a sheltered Indian woman who falls in love with her husband's friend and becomes politically committed in the turmoil of 1907-08. Based on Rabindranath Tagore's novel. In Bengali with English subtitles. 130m/C VHS, Beta. **IN** Victor Banerjee, Soumitra Chatterjee; **D:** Satyajit Ray. *COL*

Home at Last **1988** An orphan in turn of the century New York finds himself shipped to Nebraska on an orphan train. There he works on the farm of his adopted family, whose own son has died. The boy finds that he must adjust to a new lifestyle as well as strive to be accepted as someone other than a replacement for the couple's son. From the "Wonderworks" series. 58m/C VHS. Adrien Brody, Frank Converse, Caroline Lagerfelt, Sascha Radetsky. *HMV, FCT*

Home Before Midnight 🎞½ **1984** A young songwriter falls in love with a 14-year-old, is discovered, and is subsequently charged with statutory rape. 115m/C VHS, Beta. James Aubrey, Alison Elliott; **D:** Pete Walker. *ORI, WAR*

Home for Christmas 🎞🎞½ **1990** An elderly homeless man, with the love of a young girl, teaches a wealthy family the spirit of Christmas. 96m/C VHS. Mickey Rooney, Joel Kaiser; **D:** Peter McCubbin. *RHI*

Home for the Holidays 🎞🎞 *Deadly Desires* **1972** Four daughters are called home on Christmas by their father who is convinced that his second wife is trying to poison him. Made for television. 74m/C VHS, Beta. Eleanor Parker, Walter Brennan, Sally Field, Jessica Walter, Julie Harris; **D:** John Llewellyn Moxey. *THV*

Home for the Holidays 🎞🎞½ **1995 (PG-13)** Frantic dysfunctional family saga finds eldest daughter Claudia Larson (Hunter) on her way to Baltimore to spend Thanksgiving with her

family. Frazzled Claudia must deal with badly bewigged mom Adele (Bancroft), genial dad Henry (Durning), and her siblings—frenzied gay brother Tommy (Downey, Jr.) and self-righteous sister Joanne (Stevenson), as well as screwy Aunt Glady (Chaplin) and Tommy's handsome friend Leo Fish (McDermott). Yes, there are moments of deja vu about your very own family holidays but the film seems badly paced and ultimately irritating. Adapted from a short story by Chris Radant.**CW:** Thematic material, language and brief drug use. 103m/C VHS, LV, Closed Caption. Holly Hunter, Anne Bancroft, Charles Durning, Robert Downey Jr., Dylan McDermott, Cynthia Stevenson, Geraldine Chaplin, Steve Guttenberg, Claire Danes; *Cameos:* David Strathairn, Austin Pendleton; **D:** Jodie Foster; **W:** W.D. Richter; **C:** Lajos Koltai; **M:** Mark Isham. *PGV*

Home Free All 🎞🎞½ **1984** A Vietnam vet turned revolutionary, turned writer, tries to reacquaint himself with childhood friends only to find one has joined the mob and another is settled in suburbia and none of them are dealing well with adulthood. 92m/C VHS, Beta. Allan Nicholls, Roland Caccavo, Maura Ellyn, Shelley Wyant, Lucille Rivim; **D:** Stuart Bird. *ART, VES*

Home from the Hill 🎞🎞🎞 **1960** A solemn, brooding drama about a southern landowner and his troubled sons, one of whom is illegitimate. This one triumphs because of casting. 150m/C VHS, Beta, LV, Letterbox. Robert Mitchum, George Peppard, George Hamilton, Eleanor Parker, Everett Sloane, Luana Parker, Constance Ford; **D:** Vincente Minnelli; **W:** Harriet Frank Jr., Irving Ravetch; **C:** Milton Krasner. National Board of Review Awards '60: Best Actor (Mitchum). *MGM*

Home in Oklahoma 🎞🎞 **1947** A boy will be swindled out of his inheritance and a killer will escape justice until Roy comes to the rescue. Standard series fare. 72m/B VHS, Beta. Roy Rogers, Dale Evans, George "Gabby" Hayes, Carol Hughes; **D:** William Witney. *NOS, TIM, CAB*

Home Is Where the Hart Is 🎞🎞 **1988 (PG-13)** A rich 103-year-old is kidnapped by a nurse wanting to marry him and become heir to his estate. It's up to his sons, all in their 70s, to rescue him. 94m/C VHS, Beta, LV. Martin Mull, Leslie Nielsen, Valri Bromfield, Stephen E. Miller, Eric Christmas, Ted Stidder; **D:** Rex Bromfield; **W:** Rex Bromfield. *PAR, IME*

Home Movies 🎞½ **1979 (PG)** Brian DePalma and his film students at Sarah Lawrence College devised this loose, sloppy comedy which hearkens back to DePalma's early films. Tells the story of a nebbish who seeks therapy to gain control of his absurdly chaotic life. 89m/C VHS, Beta, LV. Kirk Douglas, Nancy Allen, Keith Gordon, Gerrit Graham, Vincent Gardenia, Mary Davenport; **D:** Brian DePalma; **W:** Brian DePalma; **C:** James L. Carter; **M:** Pino Donaggio. *ART, VES, IME*

Home of Angels 🎞🎞½ **1994** Billy sneaks his granddad out of his nursing home in Philadelphia and together the twosome begin a perilous journey back to Billy's home in Long Island, New York so they can have a family Christmas. They're aided by a homeless man when they run into trouble with a street gang. 90m/C VHS. Lance Robinson, Abe Vigoda, Sherman Hemsley, Joe Frazier; **D:** Nick Stagliano. *SDE*

A Home of Our Own **1975** An American priest sets up a home in Mexico for orphan boys and changes their lives for the better. A true story of Father William Wasson. 100m/C VHS, Beta. Jason Miller. *WOV*

A Home of Our Own 🎞🎞½ **1993 (PG-13)** Semi-autobiographical tearjerker based on screenwriter Duncan's childhood. Widowed and poor mother of six (Bates) is fired from her job at a Los Angeles potato chip factory, packs up the tribe and heads for a better life and a home to call their own. They end up in Idaho, in a ramshackle house owned by lonely Mr. Moon (Oh) and what follows is a winter of discontent. Bates provides an intense performance as a poor but proud woman with a tough exterior. Furlong provides the story's narration as the eldest son. A story of spiritual triumph, this one is sure to make your heart weep. **CW:** Mild language and mild violence. 104m/C VHS, LV, **Closed Caption.** Kathy Bates, Edward Furlong, Soon-Teck Oh, Amy Sakasitz, Tony Campisi; **D:** Tony Bill; **W:** Patrick Duncan. *PGV*

Home of the Brave 🌑🌑🌑 1949 A black soldier is sent on a top secret mission in the South Pacific, but finds that he must battle with his white comrades as he is subjected to subordinate treatment and constant racial slurs. Hollywood's first outstanding statement against racial prejudice. 86m/B VHS, Beta, LV. Lloyd Bridges, James Edwards, Frank Lovejoy, Jeff Corey; **D:** Mark Robson. *REP, FCT*

Home Remedy 🌑🌑 1988 An introverted New Jersey bachelor's isolated lifestyle is invaded by a flirtatious housewife and her jealous husband. 92m/C VHS, Beta. Seth Barrish, Maxine Albert; **D:** Maggie Greenwald. *NO*

Home Sweet Home 🌑🌑½ 1914 Suggested by the life of John Howard Payne (actor, poet, dramatist, critic, and world-wanderer) who wrote the title song amid the bitterness of his sad life. Silent with musical score. 62m/B VHS, Beta. Lillian Gish, Dorothy Gish, Henry B. Walthall, Mae Marsh, Blanche Sweet, Donald Crisp, Robert "Bobbie" Harron; **D:** D.W. Griffith. *VYY, KIV, GPV*

Home Sweet Home 🌑½ *Slasher in the House* 1980 A murdering psychopath escapes from the local asylum, and rampages through a family's Thanksgiving dinner. 84m/C VHS, Beta. Jake Steinfeld, Sallee Elyse, Peter de Paula; **D:** Nettie Pena.

Home Sweet Home 🌑🌑 1982 Postman Stan fancies himself a ladies man, but his wife has left him. So Stan decides to assuage his loneliness by seducing his co-workers wives. Black comedy look at British social classism. Made for British television. 90m/C VHS. **GB** Eric Richard, Timothy Spall, Tim Barker, Su Elliot, Frances Barber, Kay Stonham; **D:** Mike Leigh; **W:** Mike Leigh. *WBF, FCT*

Home to Stay 🌑🌑 1979 A farmer who has suffered a stroke is fighting off repeated lapses into senility. His son and daughter have conflicting interests as to whether he should be committed to a nursing home. Made for television. 74m/C VHS. Henry Fonda, Frances Hyland, Michael McGuire; **D:** Delbert Mann; **M:** Hagood Hardy. *TLF*

Home Town Story 🌑🌑 1951 A politician is convinced big business is behind his election loss. Fair drama. Watch for Monroe in a bit part. 61m/B VHS. Jeffrey Lynn, Donald Crisp, Marjorie Reynolds, Alan Hale Jr., Marilyn Monroe, Barbara Brown, Melinda Plowman; **D:** Arthur Pierson. *NOS, TPV*

Homebodies 🌑🌑 1974 (PG) Six senior citizens, disgusted when they learn that they will be callously tossed out of their home, become violent murderers in their shocking attempt to solve their problem. An odd little film made in Cincinnati. 96m/C VHS, Beta. Ruth McDevitt, Linda Marsh, William Hansen, Peter Brocco, Frances Fuller; **D:** Larry Yust.

Homeboy 🌑🌑 1988 (R) A small-time club boxer who dreams of becoming middleweight champ is offered his big break, but the opportunity is jeopardized by his dishonest manager's dealings. Never released theatrically. 118m/C VHS, Beta, LV. Mickey Rourke, Christopher Walken, Debra Feuer, Kevin Conway, Antony Alda, Ruben Blades; **D:** Michael Seresin; **M:** Eric Clapton, Michael Kamen. *NO*

Homeboy 🌑½ 198? A Black boxer owes his career to the mob. When he tries to break free his wife is murdered—and he seeks revenge. 93m/C VHS. Dabney Coleman, Philip Michael Thomas. *NO*

Homeboys 🌑 1992 Two East L.A. brothers find themselves on opposite sides of the law in this quickie designed to cash in on gang violence and ghetto dramas. 91m/C VHS, LV. Todd Bridges, David Garrison, Ron Odriozola, Ken Michaels; **D:** Lindsay Norgard.

Homecoming 🌑🌑🌑 1928 Two German prisoners if nur escape from a Siberian lead mine. One reaches home first and has an affair with his comrade's wife. Silent. 74m/B VHS, Beta. GE Dita Parlo, Lars Hanson, Gustav Froehlich; **D:** Joe May. *GLV*

Homecoming 🌑🌑 1948 Average soap opera starring Gable and Turner set amidst the trenches of WW II. Gable plays a selfish doctor who leaves behind his wife and colleague to enlist in the Medical Corps as a major. Turner is the battlefield nurse who forever changes his life. Film is hindered by a story which is far below the talents of the excellent cast. Although voted by the New York Critics as one of the ten worst movies of 1948, the public loved it. Based on the story "The Homecoming of Ulysses" by Sidney Kingsley. 113m/B VHS. Clark Gable, Lana Turner, Anne Baxter, John Hodiak, Ray Collins, Gladys Cooper, Cameron Mitchell, Art Baker, Lurene Tuttle; **D:** Mervyn LeRoy; **W:** Paul Osborn, Jan Lustig. *MGM*

Homecoming 🌑🌑½ 1996 (PG) Mentally ill mother abandons her four children at a Connecticut shopping mall in the care of 13-year-old eldest daughter Dicey (Peterson). The children slowly make their way to a relative's (Bedelia) home in Bridgeport, but when she proves equally uncaring Dicey decides to continue the family trek to their maternal grandmother Ab's (Bancroft) house in Chrisfield, Maryland. No surprise when crazy grandma doesn't want them either but this time Dicey is determined to make them all a home. Based on the Newbery Medal-winning children's novel by Cynthia Voight. Made for cable TV. **?m/C VHS.** Anne Bancroft, Kimberlee Peterson, Bonnie Bedelia, Trever O'Brien, Hanna Hall, William Greenblatt. *HMK*

Homecoming: A Christmas Story 🌑🌑½ 1971 Made-for-television heart-tugger that inspired the television series "The Waltons." A depression-era Virginia mountain family struggles to celebrate Christmas although the whereabouts and safety of their father are unknown. Adapted from the autobiographical novel by Earl Hamner, Jr. 98m/C VHS, Beta, **Closed Caption.** Richard Thomas, Patricia Neal, Edgar Bergen, Cleavon Little, Ellen Corby; **D:** Fielder Cook. *FOX*

Homegrown 🌑🌑½ 1997 (R) Engaging comedy-noir has three dense Norther California pot growers (Thornton, Azaria, Phillippe) witness their Boss's (Lithgow) murder. Seeing this as a bad omen, they take off, with the crop, to the operation's packaging department (Lynch) and decide to carry on as if the boss is still alive. Amid many cameos (Danson, Curtis) they set up a big deal with a seemingly laid-back wholesaler (Bon Jovi). **CW:** Pervasive drug content and language, and for some violence and sexuality. 101m/C VHS. Billy Bob Thornton, Hank Azaria, Ryan Phillippe, Kelly Lynch, Jon Bon Jovi, John Lithgow, Jon Tenney, Matt Clark; **Cameos:** Ted Danson, Jamie Lee Curtis, Judge Reinhold; **D:** Stephen Gyllenhaal; **W:** Stephen Gyllenhaal, Nicholas Kazan; **C:** Greg Gardiner; **M:** Trevor Rabin. *NYR*

Homer and Eddie 🌑 1989 (R) A witless road comedy with Goldberg as a dying sociopath and a mentally retarded Belushi. They take off cross-country to make a little trouble, learn a little about life, and create a less than entertaining movie. 100m/C VHS, Beta, LV. Whoopi Goldberg, James Belushi, Karen Black; **D:** Andrei Konchalovsky; **W:** Patrick Cirillo; **C:** Lajos Koltai; **M:** Eduard Artemyev. *HBO*

Homer Comes Home 🌑🌑 1920 A homely and diligent inventor finds nothing but failure, but sticks it out in hopes of turning his luck around. Silent comedy starring down-home Ray. 55m/B VHS, Beta. Charles Ray. *GPV*

Homesteaders of Paradise Valley 🌑½ 1947 The Hume brothers oppose Red Ryder and a group of settlers building a dam in Paradise Valley. 54m/B VHS, Beta. Allan "Rocky" Lane, Robert (Bobby) Blake. *NOS, VCN, CAB*

Hometown Boy Makes Good 🌑🌑½ 1993 (R) Smalltown boy Boyd Geary moved to the big city to go to medical school. But what he never told his proud mom was that he dropped out and doesn't have the successful psychiatry practice she thinks he has, instead he's a barely surviving waiter. But when Boyd travels back home to confess to mom, the local mayor makes him an offer to set up his own practice and won't take no for an answer. **CW:** Language. 88m/C VHS, LV, **Closed Caption.** Anthony Edwards, Grace Zabriskie, Cynthia Bain; **D:** David Burton Morris; **W:** Allen Rucker; **M:** Barry Goldberg. *IMP, IME*

Hometown U.S.A. WOOF! 1979 (R) Set in Los Angeles in the late 50s' this teenage cruising movie is the brainchild of director Baer who is better known as Jethro from that madcap television series "The Beverly Hillbillies." 97m/C VHS, Beta. Brian Kerwin, Gary Springer, David Wilson, Cindy Fisher, Sally Kirkland; **D:** Max Baer Jr. *ART, VES*

Homeward Bound 🌑 1980 (G) A dying teenager tries to reunite his long-estranged father and grandfather. Made for television. 96m/C VHS, Beta. David Soul, Moosie Drier, Barnard Hughes; **D:** Richard Michaels. *HMV*

Homeward Bound 2: Lost in San Francisco 🌑🌑½ 1996 (G) House pets Chance, the feisty bulldog (Fox), Sassy the sophisticated feline (Field), and Shadow the sage golden retriever (Waite) find themselves on the loose again, this time in the tough streets of San Francisco. The animals escape from the airport as the family departs for a Canadian holiday, and on their way back home, encounter some tough mutts—a gang of streetwise dogs, (most notably comedian Sinbad as Riley) and, of course, some dog nappers. Chance even finds romance along the way with Delilah (Gugino). Not too scary for the little ones, flick carries the same charm of the first adventure. 88m/C VHS, **Closed Caption.** Robert Hays, Kim Greist, Veronica Lauren, Kevin Timothy Chevalia, Michael Rispoli, Max Perlich; **D:** David R. Ellis; **W:** Julie Hickson, Chris Hauty; **V:** Michael J. Fox, Sally Field, Ralph Waite, Al Michaels, Tommy Lasorda, Bob Uecker, Jon Polito, Adam Goldberg, Sinbad, Carla Gugino. *TOU*

Homeward Bound: The Incredible Journey 🌑🌑🌑 1993 (G) Successful remake of the 1963 Disney release "The Incredible Journey." Two dogs and a cat once again try to find their way home after their family relocates, armed with greater depth of character than the original. Hard not to shed a tear for the brave animal trio who develop a trusting bond through assorted misadventures. Based on the novel by Sheila Burnford. Superior family fare. 85m/C VHS, LV, Letterbox. Robert Hays, Kim Greist, Jean Smart, Benj Thall, Veronica Lauren, Kevin Timothy Chevalia; **D:** Duwayne Dunham; **W:** Linda Woolverton, Carolyn Thompson; **M:** Bruce Broughton; **V:** Don Ameche, Michael J. Fox, Sally Field. *DIS, BTV*

Homework 🌑 1982 (R) Young man's after-school lessons with a teacher are definitely not part of the curriculum. Yawning sexploitation. 90m/C VHS, Beta, LV. Joan Collins, Michael Morgan, Betty Thomas, Shell Kepler, Wings Hauser, Lee Purcell; **D:** James Beshears. *USH*

Homewrecker 🌑🌑 1992 (PG-13) Benson stars as a scientist who invents a computer, with a female voice, as the ultimate domestic worker. Only the computer turns possessive and against Benson's estranged wife. **CW:** Elements of terror and violence. 88m/C VHS, Beta, **Closed Caption.** Robby Benson, Sydney Walsh, Sarah Rose Karr; **D:** Fred Walton; **W:** Eric Harlacher; **V:** Kate Jackson. *PAR*

Homicidal Impulse 🌑½ 1992 (R) When Assistant D.A. Tim Casey has an affair with his boss' ambitious niece he doesn't realize the danger he's in. His lover decides to kill her uncle so boyfriend Tim will get his job. Some women will do anything for love. Also available in an unrated version. 84m/C VHS. Scott Valentine, Vanessa Angel. *ART*

Homicide ✇✇✇½ **1991 (R)** Terrific police thriller with as much thought as action; a driven detective faces his submerged Jewish identity while probing an anti-Semitic murder and a secret society. Playwright/filmmaker Mamet creates nail-biting suspense and shattering epiphanies without resorting to Hollywood glitz. Rich (often profane) dialogue includes a classic soliloquy mystically comparing a lawman's badge with a Star of David. **CW:** Language and violence. **100m/C VHS, LV, 8mm, Closed Caption.** Joe Mantegna, William H. Macy, Natalija Nogulich, Ving Rhames, Rebecca Pidgeon; **D:** David Mamet; **W:** David Mamet; **C:** Roger Deakins. COL, BTV

Homo Eroticus/Man of the Year ✇ 1971 Handsome servant finds it difficult to satisfy the desires of Bergamo, Italy's socialite. **93m/C VHS, Beta.** IT Lando Buzzanca, Rossana Podesta. NO

Hondo ✇✇✇ **1953** In 1874, whites have broken their treaty with the Apache nation who are now preparing for war. Calvary dispatch rider Hondo Lane (Wayne) encounters Angie (Page) and her young son at an isolated ranch and warns her of the danger but she refuses to leave. After various Indian attacks, Hondo persuades Angie (they've fallen in love) to leave for California with him. Based on the story "The Gift of Cochise" by Louis L'Amour. **84m/C VHS.** John Wayne, Geraldine Page, Ward Bond, Michael Pate, James Arness, Rodolfo Acosta, Leo Gordon, Lee Aaker, Paul Fix; **D:** John Farrow; **W:** James Edward Grant; **C:** Robert Burks, Archie Stout. Nominations: Academy Awards '53: Best Story. MPI

Honey ✇½ **1981** Attractive writer pays an unusual visit to the home of a distinguished publisher. Brandishing a pistol, she demands that he read aloud from her manuscript. As he reads, a unique fantasy unfolds, a dreamlike erotic tale that may be the writer's own sexual awakening. Or maybe not. **89m/C VHS, Beta.** IT SP Clio Goldsmith, Fernando Rey, Catherine Spaak; **D:** Gianfranco Angelucci. VES

Honey, I Blew Up the Kid ✇✇½ **1992 (PG)** Screwball suburban inventor Moranis reverses his shrinking process and this time manages to enlarge his two-year-old into a 112-foot giant who gets bigger every time he comes in contact with electricity. Yikes! Loaded with great special effects, this is a charming and funny film that's fit for the whole family. Sequel to "Honey I Shrunk the Kids." **89m/C VHS, Beta, LV, Letterbox, Closed Caption.** Rick Moranis, Marcia Strassman, Robert Oliveri, Daniel Shalikar, Joshua Shalikar, Lloyd Bridges, John Shea, Keri Russell, Gregory Sierra, Julia Sweeney, Kenneth Tobey, Peter Elbling; **D:** Randal Kleiser; **W:** Thom Eberhardt, Garry Goodrow; **M:** Bruce Broughton. DIS

Honey, I Shrunk the Kids ✇✇½ **1989 (G)** The popular Disney fantasy about a suburban inventor. His shrinking device accidentally reduces his kids to 1/4 inch tall, and he subsequently throws them out with the garbage. Now they must journey back to the house through the jungle that was once the back lawn. Accompanied by "Tummy Trouble," the first of a projected series of Roger Rabbit Maroon Cartoons. Followed by "Honey, I Blew Up the Kid." **101m/C VHS, Beta, LV, Closed Caption.** Rick Moranis, Matt Frewer, Marcia Strassman, Kristine Sutherland, Thomas Wilson Brown, Jared Rushton, Amy O'Neill, Robert Oliveri; **D:** Joe Johnston, Rob Minkoff; **W:** Ed Naha, Tom Schulman, Stuart Gordon; **M:** James Horner; **V:** Charles Fleischer, Kathleen Turner, Lou Hirsch, April Winchell. DIS, MOV, RDG

The Honey Pot ✇✇½ It Comes Up Murder; Anyone for Venice?; Mr. Fox of Venice **1967** A millionaire feigns death to see the reaction of three of his former lovers. Amusing black comedy with fine performances from all. Based on Moliere's "Volpone." **131m/C VHS.** Rex Harrison, Susan Hayward, Cliff Robertson, Capucine, Edie Adams, Maggie Smith, Adolfo Celi; **D:** Joseph L. Mankiewicz; **W:** Joseph L. Mankiewicz; **M:** John Addison. MGM

Honey, We Shrunk Ourselves ✇✇½ **1997 (PG)** Scientist Wayne Szalinsky (Moranis) manages to shrink himself, his wife, his brother, and his sister-in-law. The kids just think their parents are out of town for the weekend (so they go nuts). The third in the "Honey" series, this one was released directly to video. Though adults may find it dull, it was made with the kids in mind. **76m/C VHS, Closed Caption.** Rick Moranis, Stuart Pankin, Robin Bartlett, Eve Gordon, Bug Hall; **D:** Dean Cundey; **W:** Karey Kirkpatrick, Nell Scovell, Joel Hodgson; **C:** Raymond N. Stella. TOU

Honeybaby ✇✇ **1974 (PG)** A smooth international soldier of fortune and a bright, sexy American interpreter are entangled in Middle-Eastern turbulence when they must rescue a politician kidnapped by terrorists. **94m/C VHS.** Calvin Lockhart, Diana Sands; **D:** Michael A. Schultz. GEM, MRV, CNG

Honeyboy ✇½ **1982** Estrada tries to win fame, fortune, and a ticket out of the barrio as an up-and-coming boxer. Outstanding fight scenes, but little else in this made for television drama of the boxing scene. **100m/C VHS, Beta.** Erik Estrada, Morgan Fairchild, James McEachin, Robert Costanzo, Yvonne Wilder; **D:** John Berry. ART

Honeymoon ✇ **1987** A young French woman visiting New York learns she will be deported when her boyfriend is arrested for drug-smuggling. To stay, she is set up in a marriage of convenience and told her new husband will never see or bother her. But hubby has other plans! **96m/C VHS, Beta.** John Shea, Nathalie Baye, Richard Berry, Peter Donat; **D:** Patrick Jamain; **W:** Phillip Setbon. ORI, WAR

Honeymoon Academy ✇✇ For Better or For Worse **1990 (PG-13)** Newly married man has lots to learn in this comic outing. His new wife never told him about her unusual line of business—as an undercover agent! **94m/C VHS, LV, Closed Caption.** Robert Hays, Kim Cattrall, Leigh Taylor-Young; **D:** Gene Quintano; **W:** Gene Quintano; **M:** Robert Folk. HBO, IME

Honeymoon Horror ✇ **197?** Stranded on an island, three honeymooning couples soon realize their romantic retreat is a nightmare. A crazy man with an axe is tracking them down. Minimally effective. **90m/C VHS, Beta.** Cheryl Black, William F. Pecchi, Bob Wagner. NO

Honeymoon in Vegas ✇✇½ **1992 (PG-13)** Romantic comedy turns frantic after Cage loses his fiancee to Caan in a high stakes Vegas poker game. Cage displays lots of talent for manic comedy as the distraught young groom-to-be who encounters numerous obstacles on his way to the altar. Lightweight and funny, featuring a bevy of Elvis impersonators in every size, shape, and color and new versions of favorite Elvis tunes. Look for former Las Vegas U basketball coach Jerry Tarkanian as one of Caan's gambling buddies. **95m/C VHS, LV, Closed Caption.** James Caan, Nicolas Cage, Sarah Jessica Parker, Noriyuki "Pat" Morita, John Capodice, Robert Costanzo, Anne Bancroft, Peter Boyle, Seymour Cassel, Tony Shalhoub, Ben Stein, Angela Pietropinto; **D:** Andrew Bergman; **W:** Andrew Bergman; **C:** William A. Fraker; **M:** David Newman. COL, NLC, IME

Honeymoon Killers ✇✇✇ The Lonely Hearts Killers **1970 (R)** A grim, creepy filmization of a true multiple-murder case wherein an overweight woman and slimy gigolo living on Long Island seduce and murder one lonely woman after another. Independently made and frankly despairing. **103m/C VHS, Beta, LV.** Tony LoBianco, Shirley Stoler, Mary Jane Higby, Dortha Duckworth, Doris Roberts, Marilyn Chris, Kip McArdle, Mary Breen, Barbara Cason, Ann Harris, Guy Sorel; **D:** Leonard Kastle. ART, VES

The Honeymoon Machine ✇✇½ **1961** A lightweight comedy about two American sailors and a computer scam. McQueen and Mullaney hook up with computer expert Hutton to use their ship's computer to beat the gambling odds at an Italian casino. Their commander misinterprets the signals and thinks the ship is being attacked. Fast paced and the computer angle was new territory in '61. **87m/C VHS.** Steve McQueen, Jack Mullaney, Jim Hutton, Dean Jagger, Paula Prentiss, Brigid Bazlen, Jack Weston; **D:** Richard Thorpe. MGM, MOV

The Honeymooners "Classic 39": TV or Not TV/Honeymooners Highlights 1955 Captain Video and his video rangers are a Kramden household name after Ralph and Ed pool their resources to buy a television. Also includes clips from each of the remaining 38 episodes in "The Honeymooners" series. Video cover illustration by C.F. Payne. This 20 volumes series contains two episodes per tape. **60m/C VHS.** FOX

Honeymooners Hidden Episodes, Vol. 1 The Honeymooners: The Lost Episodes **1953** Three recently retrieved episodes of the Honeymooners sketches, which were initially aired live as part of the "Jackie Gleason Show." In "Letter to the Boss," Jackie sends some nasty correspondence to his employer when he mistakenly believes that he has been canned. In "Suspense," Ralph fears that Alice is planning his murder when he eavesdrops on her acting practice. In "Dinner Guest," Ralph's plans to suck up to his supervisor meet with hilarious disaster. This "Honeymooners" series contains 28 volumes, which are available separately for purchase. **53m/ B VHS, Beta, Closed Caption.** Jackie Gleason, Audrey Meadows, Art Carney, Joyce Randolph. MPI, FOX, MOV

Honeysuckle Rose ✇✇½ On the Road Again **1980 (PG)** A road-touring country-Western singer whose life is a series of one night stands, falls in love with an adoring young guitar player who has just joined his band. This nearly costs him his marriage when his wife, who while waiting patiently for him at home, decides she's had enough. Easygoing performance by Nelson, essentially playing himself. **120m/C VHS, Beta, LV.** Willie Nelson, Dyan Cannon, Amy Irving, Slim Pickens, Joey Floyd, Charles Levin, Priscilla Pointer; **D:** Jerry Schatzberg; **W:** William D. Wittliff, John Binder, Carol Sobieski; **M:** Willie Nelson, Richard Baskin. Golden Raspberry Awards '80: Worst Supporting Actress (Irving); Nominations: Academy Awards '80: Best Song ("On the Road Again"). WAR, MVD

Hong Kong Nights ✇✇½ **1935** Two agents attempt to break up a Chinese smuggling ring run by an unscrupulous madman. Good, action-packed low-budget film. **59m/B VHS, Beta.** Tom George Duryea Keene, Wera Engels, Warren Hymer, Tetsu Komai, Cornelius Keefe; **D:** E. Mason Hopper. SNC

Hong Kong '97 ✇✇ **1994 (R)** On the eve of China's takeover of Hong Kong from Great Britain, special agent Reg Cameron (Patrick) murders a Chinese general. With a $10 million bounty on his head, Cameron tries to escape with his partners and girlfriend in tow. Lots of action, good use of Hong Kong setting. **CW:** Language; nudity; violence. **91m/C VHS, LV, Closed Caption.** Robert Patrick, Ming-Na Wen, Brion James, Tim Thomerson; **D:** Albert Pyun. THV

Honky ✇½ **1971 (R)** An innocent friendship between a black woman and a white man develops into a passionate romance that has the whole town talking. **92m/C VHS, Beta.** Brenda Sykes, John Nielson, Maria Donzinger; **D:** William A. Graham; **M:** Quincy Jones. UNI

Honky Tonk ✇✇✇ **1941** A western soap opera in which ne'er do well Clark marries Lana and tries to live a respectable life. In this, the first of several MGM teamings between Gable and Turner, the chemistry between the two is evident. So much so in fact that Gable's then wife Carole Lombard let studio head Louis B. Mayer know that she was not at all thrilled. The public was pleased however, and made the film a hit. **106m/B VHS, Beta.** Clark Gable, Lana Turner, Frank Morgan, Claire Trevor, Marjorie Main, Albert Dekker, Chill Wills, Henry O'Neill, John Maxwell, Morgan Wallace, Betty Blythe, Francis X. Bushman, Veda Ann Borg; **D:** Jack Conway. MGM, CCB

Honky Tonk Freeway 🎬 1981 (PG) An odd assortment of people become involved in a small town Mayor's scheme to turn a dying hamlet into a tourist wonderland. You can find better things to do with your evening than watch this accident. 107m/C VHS, Beta. Teri Garr, Howard Hesseman, Beau Bridges, Hume Cronyn, William Devane, Beverly D'Angelo, Geraldine Page; **D:** John Schlesinger; **W:** Edward Clinton; **C:** John Bailey; **M:** Elmer Bernstein, Stephen Dorff. *NO*

Honky Tonk Girl 🎬 *Highway Hell* 1937 Hilarious exploitation film about a hitch-hiking prostitution ring. ?m/C VHS. Mary Chauning. *SNC*

Honkytonk Man 🎬 1982 (PG) Unsuccessful change-of-pace Eastwood vehicle set during the Depression. Aging alcoholic country singer tries one last time to make it to Nashville, hoping to perform at the Grand Ole Opry. This time he takes his nephew (played by Eastwoood's real-life son) with him. 123m/C VHS, Beta, LV. Clint Eastwood, Kyle Eastwood, John McIntire, Alexa Kenin, Verna Bloom; **D:** Clint Eastwood; **W:** Clancy Carlile; **C:** Bruce Surtees; **M:** Franz Waxman. *WAR*

Honkytonk Nights 🎬 197? (R) A honkytonkin' romp through an evening in a country/western bar, featuring legendary topless dancer Carol Doda, Georgina ("Devil in Mrs. Jones") Spelvin, and the music of The Hot Licks (minus front man Dan Hicks). 90m/C VHS, Beta. Carol Doda, Georgina Spelvin, Ramblin' Jack Elliot. *TPV*

Honolulu 🎬🎬½ 1939 A screwball comedy with Powell providing the musical numbers. Young takes on the dual role of a Hollywood star who meets his exact double, a Hawaii plantation owner. They decide to switch identities to give their lives a little oomph. The star sails to Hawaii, falling for fellow passenger Powell, only to discover he's expected to get married upon his arrival in Honolulu. Anderson and Burns and Allen provide the comic relief. ♫The Leader Doesn't Like Music; This Night Was Made For Dreaming; Honolulu; Hymn To The Sun. 83m/B VHS. Robert Young, Eleanor Powell, George Burns, Gracie Allen, Rita Johnson, Eddie Anderson, Clarence Kolb; **D:** Edward Buzzell; **W:** Frank Partos, Herbert Fields; **M:** Franz Waxman. *MGM*

Honor Among Thieves 🎬½ *Farewell, Friend* 1968 (R) Two former mercenaries reteam for a robbery that doesn't come off as planned. Not as fast paced as others in Bronson canon. 115m/C VHS, Beta. **FR** **IT** Charles Bronson, Alain Delon, Brigitte Fossey, Olga Georges-Picot, Bernard Fresson; **D:** Jean Herman. *CCB, MPI, VTR*

Honor and Glory 🎬🎬 1992 (R) Tracy Pride, an FBI agent and martial arts expert, teams up with an Interpol agent, who doubles as a TV anchorwoman, to stop an international banker from getting his greedy hands on the key to a nuclear arsenal. These fighting gals are up against a team of assassins but they can more than handle themselves.*CW:* Martial arts violence. 90m/C VHS, LV, Closed Caption. Cynthia Rothrock, Donna Jason, Chuck Jeffreys, Gerald Klein, Robin Shou, Raymond Yuen; **D:** Godfrey Hall; **W:** Herb Borkland. *IMP*

Honor of the Range 🎬🎬 1934 The good sheriff's lady is whisked away by his evil twin brother and the sheriff must go undercover to get her back. Odd plot twists for a seemingly normal western. 60m/B VHS. Ken Maynard, Cecilia Parker, Fred Kohler Sr.; **D:** Ken Maynard. *NOS, DVT, HEG*

Honor Thy Father 🎬🎬 1973 The everyday life of a real-life Mafia family as seen through the eyes of Bill Bonanno, the son of mob chieftain Joe Bonanno. Adapted from the book by Gay Talese. Made for television. 97m/C Beta. Raf Vallone, Richard Castellano, Brenda Vaccaro, Joseph Bologna; **D:** Paul Wendkos; **M:** George Duning.

Honor Thy Father and Mother: The True Story of the Menendez Brothers 🎬🎬½ 1994 First Amy Fisher won the true-sleaze-on-TV award and now its the turn of Lyle and Erik Menendez. Accused of the grue-

some 1989 shotgun murders of their wealthy parents, the trial provided numerous sordid details, including alledged sexual abuse of the brothers by both parents. (Both Menendez trials ended in hung juries and will be retried). Composite characters and compressed time sequences play fast and loose with the facts of the case. Based on public records and on the book "Blood Brothers," by reporters John Johnson and Ronald L. Soble. Made for television. 90m/C VHS. Billy Warlock, David Beron, Jill Clayburgh, James Farentino, Susan Blakely, Erin Gray, Elaine Joyce, John Beck, John David Conti, Stanley Kamel; **D:** Paul Schneider; **W:** Michael J. Murray. *AVE*

Hooch 🎬½ 1976 (PG) Comedy about three members of the New York Mafia who get some unexpected southern hospitality when they try to muscle in on a southern family's moonshine operation. 96m/C VHS, Beta. Gil Gerard, Erika Fox, Melody Rogers, Danny Aiello, Mike Allen, Raymond Serra; **D:** Edward Mann.

The Hooded Terror 1938 A merciless group of murderers take on a G-man. 70m/B VHS. Tod Slaughter, Greta Gynt. *NOS, HEG*

The Hoodlum 1951 A criminal does his best to rehabilitate and, with a little help from his brother, is able to hold a steady job. However the crime bug dies hard and when he spots an armored car, he just can't resist the temptation. Tierney's real brother, Edward, plays his screen brother. 61m/B VHS, Beta. Lawrence Tierney, Allene Roberts, Marjorie Riordan, Lisa Golm, Edward Tierney; **D:** Max Nosseck. *SNC*

Hoodlum 🎬🎬½ *Gangster; Hoods* 1996 (R) Highly fictionalized tale of '30s gangster "Bumpy" Johnson (Fishburne, reprising his role from "The Cotton Club"), who refuses to allow Dutch Schultz (Roth) and Lucky Luciano (Garcia) to muscle into the Harlem numbers rackets. Duke makes the proceedings nice to look at, and does well by the eclectic cast, but the uneven screenplay occasionally lets everybody down, especially during the cheesy time-passage montage (complete with Tommy Gun fire and flipping calendar pages). Roth is ruthless as ever and Garcia is smooth as ever. But it's definitely Fishburne's show, as he explores Johnson's professional triumphs and the personal toll they take. Fishburne previously worked with director Duke on "Deep Cover." Singer Michael McCary from Boyz II Men makes his film debut as an explosives expert.*CW:* Graphic gangster violence, strong language, a scene of sexuality and some nudity. 130m/C VHS, LV, Closed Caption. Laurence "Larry" Fishburne, Tim Roth, Andy Garcia, Vanessa Williams, Cicely Tyson, Clarence Williams III, William Atherton, Chi McBride, Richard Bradford, Loretta Devine, Queen Latifah, Paul Benjamin, Mike Starr, Beau Starr, Joe Guzaldo, Ed O'Ross, Stacey Dash, Jamie Kennedy, Michael McCary; **D:** Bill Duke; **W:** Chris Brancato; **C:** Frank Tidy; **M:** Elmer Bernstein. *WAR*

Hoodlum Empire 🎬🎬 1952 A senator enlists the aid of a former gangster, now a war hero, in his battle against the syndicate. Loosely based on the Kefauver investigations of 1950-51. 98m/B VHS. Brian Donlevy, Claire Trevor, Forrest Tucker, Vera Ralston, Luther Adler, John Russell, Gene Lockhart, Grant Withers, Taylor Holmes, Roy Barcroft, Richard Jaeckel; **D:** Joseph Kane. *REP*

The Hoodlum Priest 🎬🎬🎬 1961 Biography of the Rev. Charles Dismas Clark (Murray), a Jesuit priest who dedicated his life to working with juvenile delinquents and ex-cons in St. Louis. Dullea made his screen debut as Billy Lee Jackson, a thief who finds the straight and narrow is a hard road with more detours than he can handle. Fine performances with Murray co-scripting under the pseudonym Don Deer. 101m/B VHS, Beta. Don Murray, Keir Dullea, Larry Gates, Logan Ramsey, Cindi Wood; **D:** Irvin Kershner; **W:** Don Murray, Joseph Landon; **C:** Haskell Wexler. *MGM, FCT*

Hoodoo Ann 🎬🎬 1916 The story of Hoodoo Ann, from her days in the orphanage to her happy marriage. Silent. 27m/B VHS, Beta. Mae Marsh, Robert "Bobbie" Harron. *CCB*

Hook 🎬🎬 1991 (PG) Although he said he was never gonna to do it, Peter Pan has grown up. Uptight Peter Banning places work before family and has forgotten all about Neverland and the evil Captain Hook, until Hook kidnaps the Banning kids and takes them to Neverland. With the help of Tinkerbell, her magic pixie dust, and happy thoughts, Peter rescues his kids and rediscovers his youth while visiting with the Lost Boys. The sets and special effects are spectacular; the direction less so. Big-budget fantasy lacks the charm it needs to really fly. Still, kids seem to love it. You'll have to look hard to spot pirates Crosby and Close. Futurizes the J.M. Barrie classic. 142m/C VHS, Beta, LV, 8mm, Closed Caption. Dustin Hoffman, Robin Williams, Julia Roberts, Bob Hoskins, Maggie Smith, Charlie Korsmo, Caroline Goodall, Amber Scott, Phil Collins, Arthur Malet, Dante Basco, Gwyneth Paltrow; **Cameos:** Glenn Close, David Crosby; **D:** Steven Spielberg; **W:** Nick Castle; **C:** Dean Cundey; **M:** John Williams. Nominations: Academy Awards '91: Best Art Direction/Set Decoration, Best Costume Design, Best Makeup, Best Song ("When You're Alone"), Best Visual Effects. *COL*

Hook, Line and Sinker 🎬🎬 1930 A couple of insurance investigators try to help a young woman restore a hotel, and they find romance and run-ins with crooks. Directed by Cline, who later directed W.C. Fields in "The Bank Dick," "My Little Chickadee," and "Never Give a Sucker an Even Break." 75m/B VHS, LV. Bert Wheeler, Robert Woolsey, Dorothy Lee, Jobyna Howland, Ralf Harolde, Natalie Moorhead, George F. Marion Sr., Hugh Herbert; **D:** Eddie Cline; **W:** Rod Amateau. *NOS, TTC, FCT*

The Hooked Generation 🎬 1969 (R) A group of drug pushers kidnap defenseless victims, rape innocent girls, and even murder their own Cuban drug contacts (and all without the aid of a cohesive plot). Many gory events precede their untimely deaths; few will be entertained. 92m/C VHS. Jeremy Slate, Steve Alaimo. *NO*

Hoop Dreams 🎬🎬🎬🎬 1994 (PG-13) Exceptional documentary follows two inner-city basketball phenoms' lives through high school as they chase their dreams of playing in the NBA. We meet Arthur Agee and William Gates as they prepare to enter St. Joseph, a predominantly white Catholic school that has offered them partial athletic scholarships. The coach tabs Gates as the "next Isiah Thomas," alluding to the school's most famous alum. There's plenty of game footage, but the more telling and fascinating parts of the film deal with the kids' families and home life. Both players encounter dramatic reversals of fortune on and off the court, demonstrating the incredibly long odds they face. 169m/C VHS, LV. Arthur Agee, William Gates; **D:** Steve James; **C:** Peter Gilbert. Directors Guild of America Awards '95: Best Feature Documentary (James); Los Angeles Film Critics Association Awards '94: Best Feature Documentary; MTV Movie Awards '95: Best New Filmmaker Award (James); National Board of Review Awards '94: Best Feature Documentary; New York Film Critics Awards '94: Best Feature Documentary; National Society of Film Critics Awards '94: Best Feature Documentary; Sundance Film Festival '94: Audience Award; Nominations: Academy Awards '94: Best Film Editing.*NLC*

Hooper 🎬🎬½ 1978 (PG) Lightweight behind-the-scenes satire about the world of movie stuntmen. Reynolds is a top stuntman who becomes involved in a rivalry with an up-and-coming young man out to surpass him. Dated good-ole-boy shenanigans. 94m/C VHS, Beta, LV, Closed Caption. Burt Reynolds, Jan-Michael Vincent, Robert Klein, Sally Field, Brian Keith, John Marley, Adam West; **D:** Hal Needham. Nominations: Academy Awards '78: Best Sound. *WAR*

Hoosiers 🎬🎬🎬 1986 (PG) In Indiana, where basketball is the sport of the gods, a small town high school basketball team gets a new, but surprisingly experienced coach. He makes the team, and each person in it, better than they thought possible. Classic plot rings true because of Hackman's complex and sensitive performance coupled with Hopper's touching portrait of an alcoholic basketball fanatic. **115m/C VHS, Beta, LV, Closed Caption.** Gene Hackman, Barbara Hershey, Dennis Hopper, David Neidorf, Sheb Wooley, Fern Parsons, Brad Boyle, Steve Hollar, Brad Long; **D:** David Anspaugh; **W:** Angelo Pizzo; **C:** Fred Murphy; **M:** Jerry Goldsmith. Los Angeles Film Critics Association Awards '86: Best Supporting (Hopper); Nominations: Academy Awards '86: Best Supporting Actor (Hopper), Best Original Score. *ART*

Hootch Country Boys 🐾 *Redneck County; The Great Lester Boggs* 1975 **(PG)** A film packed with moonshine, sheriffs, busty country girls, and chases. **90m/C VHS, Beta.** Alex Karras, Scott MacKenzsie, Dean Jagger, Willie Jones, Bob Ridgely, Susan Denbo, Bob Ginnaven, David Haney; **D:** Harry Z. Thomason.

Hopalong Cassidy 🐾🐾🐾 *Hopalong Cassidy Enters* 1935 In this first of a long series of "Hopalong Cassidy" films, Hoppy and his pals intervene in a brewing range war. A gang of rustlers is helped by a two-timing foreman who's playing both sides off each other. After a career in silent films, Boyd was pretty much washed up before taking on the role of Cassidy. He was originally asked to play the villain and declined, but agreed to be the good guy if the character was cleaned up. "Gabby" Hayes' stock character was killed off in this episode, but was brought back for later installments. **60m/B VHS.** William Boyd, James Ellison, Paula Stone, Robert Warwick, Charles Middleton, Frank McGlynn, Kenneth Thomson, George "Gabby" Hayes, James Mason, Franklyn Farnum; **D:** Howard Bretherton. *NOS, MRV*

Hopalong Cassidy: Borrowed Trouble 🐾½ 1948 Hoppy must save a righteous teacher from the clutches of kidnappers who plan to place a saloon right next to the school. **61m/B VHS.** William Boyd, Andy Clyde, Rand Brooks, Elaine Riley, John Kellogg, Helen Chapman; **D:** George Archainbaud. *NO*

Hopalong Cassidy: Dangerous Venture 🐾🐾 1948 "Dangerous Venture" was one of Hoppy's last ventures, produced the final year of the series' 13-year tenure. Hoppy and the gang hunt for Aztec ruins in the great Southwest, and have to deal with renegade Indians and a band of treacherous looters along the way. **55m/B VHS, Beta.** William Boyd, Andy Clyde, Rand Brooks. *NO*

Hopalong Cassidy: False Paradise 🐾🐾 1948 Another late Hopalong has the noir-clad cowboy rushing to the aid of a girl and her dad when control of their ranch is threatened by swindlers with false mining claims. **59m/B VHS, Beta.** William Boyd, Andy Clyde, Rand Brooks; **D:** George Archainbaud. *NO*

Hopalong Cassidy: Hoppy's Holiday 🐾🐾 1947 Boyd—the only celluloid incarnation of Clarence Mulford's pulp hero—plays the Hopster yet again. This time, the non-drinking, non-smoking (what does he go for kicks?) hero and a passel of Bar-20 cowboys visit Mesa City for some well-earned R and R, but find themselves caught in a web of corruption. **60m/B VHS, Beta.** William Boyd, Andy Clyde, Rand Brooks, Jeff Corey; **D:** George Archainbaud. *NO*

Hopalong Cassidy: Renegade Trail 🐾🐾 1939 Hoppy comes to the aid of both a small town sheriff and a widow. **61m/B VHS, Beta.** William Boyd, George "Gabby" Hayes, Russell Hayden, Charlotte Wynters, Russell Hopton, Sonny Bupp, Jack Rockwell, Roy Barcroft, John Merton, Robert F. (Bob) Kortman; **D:** Lesley Selander. *HEG*

Hopalong Cassidy: Riders of the Deadline 🐾🐾 1943 Hoppy turns into a baddie in this episode in order to infiltrate a treacherous gang and apprehend their leader. **70m/B VHS, Beta.** William Boyd, Andy Clyde, Jimmy Rogers, Robert Mitchum; **D:** Lesley Selander. *NO*

Hopalong Cassidy: Silent Conflict 🐾🐾 1948 Lucky is tricked and hypnotized by a traveling medicine man who commands him to rob and kill Hoppy. **61m/B VHS, Beta.** William Boyd, Andy Clyde, Rand Brooks; **D:** George Archainbaud. *NO*

Hopalong Cassidy: Sinister Journey 🐾🐾 1948 Mysterious accidents are plaguing a railroad where an old friend of Hoppy's works, so Hoppy, California, and Lucky take railroad jobs to find out what gives. **58m/B VHS, Beta.** William Boyd, Andy Clyde, Rand Brooks; **D:** George Archainbaud. *NO*

Hopalong Cassidy: The Dead Don't Dream 🐾🐾 1948 Hoppy's sidekick Lucky decides to get married, but happily-ever-afterdom is threatened when the father of Mrs. Lucky-to-be is murdered. When Hoppy sets out to find the killer, he finds himself suspected of the dastardly deed. **55m/B VHS, Beta.** William Boyd, Andy Clyde, Rand Brooks, John Parrish; **D:** George Archainbaud. *NO*

Hopalong Cassidy: The Devil's Playground 🐾🐾 1946 Strange things are afoot in a peaceful valley adjacent to a desolate, forbidding wasteland. When Hoppy and a young woman set out across the wasteland to make a gold delivery, they encounter a band of desperados and begin to unravel the secrets of a dishonest political ring. **65m/B VHS, Beta.** William Boyd, Andy Clyde, Rand Brooks, Elaine Riley; **D:** George Archainbaud. *NO*

Hopalong Cassidy: The Marauders 🐾🐾 1947 After seeking shelter in an abandoned church one rainy night, Hoppy and the boys must defend the kirk when it is threatened by a marauder and his gang. **64m/B VHS, Beta.** William Boyd, Andy Clyde, Rand Brooks; **D:** George Archainbaud. *NO*

Hopalong Cassidy: Unexpected Guest 🐾🐾½ 1947 When a small fortune is left to a California family, the head count starts to dwindle, and Hoppy aims to find out why. **59m/B VHS, Beta.** William Boyd, Andy Clyde, Rand Brooks, Una O'Connor; **D:** George Archainbaud. *NO*

Hope 🐾🐾½ 1997 Thirteen-year-old Lily Kate Burns (Malone) is living in the small southern town of Hope in 1962. Her mother's had a severe stroke and the only family she has to turn to are racist Uncle Ray (Walsh) and fragile Aunt Emma (Lahti). Amidst the town's segregation and fears about the Cuban Missile Crisis, Lily Kate is also more open to befriending new town residents than her elders, including visiting black preacher Jediah (Sams). Hawn's directorial debut. **100m/C VHS.** Christine Lahti, Jena Malone, J.T. Walsh, Jeffrey D. Sams, Catherine O'Hara; **D:** Goldie Hawn; **W:** Kerry Kennedy. *WAR*

Hope and Glory 🐾🐾🐾½ 1987 **(PG-13)** Boorman turns his memories of WWII London into a complex and sensitive film. Father volunteers, and mother must deal with the awakening sexuality of her teenage daughter, keep her son in line, balance the ration books, and try to make it to the bomb shelter in the middle of the night. Seen through the boy's eyes, war creates a playground of shrapnel to collect and wild imaginings come true. Nice companion film to "Empire of the Sun" and "Au Revoir Les Enfants," two more 1987 releases that explore WWII from the recollections of young boys. **97m/C VHS, Beta, LV, 8mm, Closed Caption.** GB Sebastian Rice Edwards, Geraldine Muir, Sarah Miles, Sammi Davis, David Hayman, Derrick O'Connor, Susan Wooldridge, Jean-Marc Barr, Ian Bannen, Jill Baker, Charley Boorman, Annie Leon, Katrine Boorman, Gerald James; **D:** John Boorman; **W:** John Boorman; **C:** Philippe Rousselot. British Academy Awards '87: Best Film, Best Supporting Actress (Wooldridge); Golden Globe Awards '88: Best Film—Musical/Comedy; Los Angeles Film Critics Association Awards '87: Best Director (Boorman), Best Film, Best Screenplay; National Society of Film Critics Awards '87: Best Cinematography, Best Director (Boorman), Best Film, Best Screenplay; Nominations: Academy Awards '87: Best Art Direction/Set Decoration, Best Cinematography, Best Director (Boorman), Best Original Screenplay, Best Picture. *FCT, HMV, NLC*

Hope Floats 🐾🐾½ 1998 **(PG-13)** Former small town Texas beauty queen Birdee Pruitt (Bullock) finds out her husband Bill (Pare) is having an affair with her best friend (Arquette) live on

TV, thanks to a tabloid talk show expose. Completely humiliated, she takes her daughter Bernice (Whitman) and heads home to her own rather spaced-out mom Ramona (Rowlands). She's trying to gain some perspective on her life—and maybe, slowly, find a new love with the help of handsome cowpoke Justin (Connick, Jr.) Movie is sweet, sentimental, obvious, and has an appealing cast and a happy ending. Perfect girlfriend fare. **CW:** Thematic elements. **114m/C VHS.** Sandra Bullock, Harry Connick Jr., Gena Rowlands, Mae Whitman, Cameron Finley, Michael Pare, Rosanna Arquette, Kathy Najimy, Bill Cobbs; **D:** Forest Whitaker; **W:** Steve Rogers; **C:** Caleb Deschanel; **M:** Dave Grusin. *NYR*

Hoppity Goes to Town *Mr. Bug Goes to Town* 1941 Full-length animated feature from the Max Fleischer studios tells the story of the inhabitants of Bugville, who live in a weed patch in New York City. **77m/C VHS, LV.** **D:** Dave Fleischer; **M:** Frank Loesser, Hoagy Carmichael. *REP, MRV, FCT*

Hoppy Serves a Writ 🐾🐾 1943 In this last of the series to be based on the writings of the original author, Texas sheriff Cassidy tries to bring a gang of outlaws to justice. Look for a young Robert Mitchum as one of the villains. **67m/B VHS.** William Boyd, Andy Clyde, Jay Kirby, Victor Jory, George Reeves, Hal Taliaferro, Robert Mitchum, Byron Foulger, Earle Hodgins, Roy Barcroft; **D:** George Archainbaud. *NOS, MRV*

Hopscotch 🐾🐾🐾 1980 **(R)** A C.I.A. agent drops out when his overly zealous chief demotes him to a desk job. When he writes a book designed to expose the dirty deeds of the CIA, he leads his boss and KGB pal on a merry chase. Amiable comedy well-suited for Matthau's rumpled talents. **107m/C VHS, Beta, LV.** Walter Matthau, Glenda Jackson, Ned Beatty, Sam Waterston, Herbert Lom; **D:** Ronald Neame. *COL*

Horizons West 🐾🐾½ 1952 Two brothers go their separate ways after the Civil War. One leads a peaceful life as a rancher but the other, corrupted by the war, engages in a violent campaign to build his own empire. Ryan's outstanding performance eclipses that of the young Hudson. **81m/C VHS.** Robert Ryan, Julie Adams, Rock Hudson, Raymond Burr, James Arness, John McIntire, Dennis Weaver, Frances Bavier; **D:** Budd Boetticher; **M:** Henry Mancini. *USH*

The Horizontal Lieutenant 🐾🐾½ 1962 Hutton and Prentiss team up again in this moderately funny romantic-comedy about an officer's escapades during WWII. Based on the novel "The Bottleup Affair" by Gordon Cotler. **90m/C VHS.** Jim Hutton, Paula Prentiss, Jack Carter, Jim Backus, Charles McGraw, Miyoshi Umeki; **D:** Richard Thorpe; **W:** George Wells. *MGM*

The Horn Blows at Midnight 🐾🐾🐾 1945 A band trumpeter falls asleep and dreams he's a bumbling archangel, on Earth to blow the note bringing the end of the world. But a pretty girl distracts him, and...A wild, high-gloss, well-cast fantasy farce, uniquely subversive in its lighthearted approach to biblical Doomsday. Benny made the film notorious by acting ashamed of it in his later broadcast routines. **78m/B VHS.** Jack Benny, Alexis Smith, Dolores Moran, Allyn Joslyn, Reginald Gardiner, Guy Kibbee, John Alexander, Margaret Dumont; **D:** Raoul Walsh. *MGM, FCT*

Hornet's Nest 🐾🐾½ 1970 Captain Turner (Hudson) is the lone survivor of an Army commando unit which parachuted into the Italian countryside in an effort to blow up a dam being held by the Nazis. He's rescued by a group of boys, the survivors of a German massacre of their nearby town. Turner wants the boys to help him blow up the dam—and they want his help in getting revenge on the Nazis who have occupied their homes. **110m/C VHS.** Rock Hudson, Sylva Koscina, Sergio Fantoni, Jacques Sernas, Giacomo "Jack" Rossi-Stuart, Andrea Bosic, Gerard Herter, Tom Felleghi; **D:** Phil Karlson; **W:** S.S. Schweitzer. *MGM*

The Horrible Dr. Hitchcock *♂♂½*
L'Orribile Segreto Del Dr. Hichcock 1962 A sicko doctor, who accidentally killed his first wife while engaged in sexual antics, remarries to bring the first missus back from the dead using his new wife's blood. Genuinely creepy. Sequelled by "The Ghost." **76m/C VHS.** *IT* Robert Flemyng, Barbara Steele; *D:* Riccardo (Robert Hampton) Freda. *SNC*

The Horror Chamber of Dr. Faustus *♂♂♂½ Eyes without a Face; Les Yeux sans Visage; Occhi Senza Volto* 1959 A wickedly intelligent, inventive piece of Grand Guignol about a mad doctor who kills young girls so he may graft their skin onto the face of his accidentally mutilated daughter. In French with English subtitles. **84m/B VHS, Beta, LV.** *FR* Alida Valli, Pierre Brasseur, Edith Scob, Francois Guerin; *D:* Georges Franju; *C:* Eugene (Eugen Shufftan) Shuftan; *M:* Maurice Jarre. *INT, TPV*

Horror Express *♂♂½ Panic on the Trans-Siberian Express; Panico en el Transiberiano; Panic in Trans-Siberian Train* 1972 (R) A creature from prehistoric times, was removed from its tomb, is transported on the Trans-Siberian railroad. Passengers suddenly discover strange things happening—such as having their souls sucked out of them. **88m/C VHS, Beta.** *SP GB* Christopher Lee, Peter Cushing, Telly Savalas, Alberto De Mendoza, Sylvia Tortosa, Julio Pena, Angel Del Pozo, Helga Line, Jorge Rigaud, Jose Jaspe; *D:* Gene Martin; *W:* Julian Zimet, Arnaud d'Usseau; *C:* Alejandro Ulloa. *VTR, MRV, SNC*

Horror Hospital *♂ Computer Killers; Doctor Blood Bath* 1973 (R) Patients are turned into zombies by a mad doctor in this hospital where no anesthesia is used. Those who try to escape are taken care of by the doctor's guards. **91m/C VHS, Beta.** *GB* Michael Gough, Robin Askwith, Vanessa Shaw, Ellen Pollock, Skip Martin, Dennis Price; *D:* Antony Balch. *GRG*

Horror Hotel *♂♂½ The City of the Dead* 1960 A young witchcraft student visits a small Massachusetts town which has historic ties to witch burnings and discovers a new, and deadly, coven is now active. Well done and atmospheric. **76m/B VHS, LV.** *GB* Christopher Lee, Patricia Jessel, Betta St. John, Dennis Lotis, Venetia Stevenson, Valentine Dyall; *D:* John Llewellyn Moxey; *W:* George L. Baxt; *C:* Desmond Dickinson. *VTR*

Horror House on Highway 5 woof!
1986 Someone in a Nixon mask kills people in this extremely cheap dud. **90m/C VHS, Beta.** *D:* Richard Casey; *W:* Richard Casey. *NO*

The Horror of Dracula *♂♂♂½ Dracula* 1958 The first Hammer Dracula film, in which the infamous vampire is given a new, elegant and ruthless persona, as he battles Prof. Van Helsing after coming to England. Possibly the finest, most inspired version of Bram Stoker's macabre chestnut, and one that single-handedly revived the horror genre. **82m/C VHS, Beta, LV.** *GB* Peter Cushing, Christopher Lee, Michael Gough, Melissa Stribling, Carol Marsh, John Van Eyssen, Valerie Gaunt, Charles Lloyd Pack, Miles Malleson; *D:* Terence Fisher; *C:* Jack Asher; *M:* James Bernard. *WAR, FCT, MLB*

The Horror of Frankenstein *♂♂*
1970 Spoof of the standard Frankenstein story features philandering ex-med student Baron Frankenstein, whose interest in a weird and esoteric branch of science provides a shocking and up-to-date rendition of the age-old plot. Preceded by "Frankenstein Must Be Destroyed" and followed by "Frankenstein and the Monster from Hell." **93m/C VHS, Beta.** *GB* Ralph Bates, Kate O'Mara, Dennis Price, David Prowse, Veronica Carlson, Joan Rice, Bernard Archard, Graham James; *D:* Jimmy Sangster; *W:* Jimmy Sangster, Jeremy Burnham; *C:* Moray Grant. *MLB*

Horror of Party Beach woof! *Invasion of the Zombies* 1964 Considered to be one of the all-time worst films. Features a mob of radioactive seaweed creatures who eat a slew of nubile, surf-minded teenagers. ♫Zombie Stomp. **71m/C VHS, Beta.** John Scott, Alice Lyon, Allen Laurel; *D:* Del Tenney.

Horror of the Blood Monsters Woof! *Vampire Men of the Lost Planet; Horror Creatures of the Prehistoric Planet; Creatures of the Prehistoric Planet; Creatures of the Red Planet; Flesh Creatures of the Red Planet; The Flesh Creatures; Space Mission of the Lost Planet* 1970 (PG) John Carradine made a career out of being in bad movies, and this one competes as one of the worst. This is an editor's nightmare, made up of black & white film spliced together and colorized. Vampires from outer space threaten to suck all the blood from the people of Earth. **85m/C VHS, Beta.** *PH* John Carradine, Robert Dix, Vicki Volante, Jennifer Bishop; *D:* Al Adamson, George Joseph. *REP*

Horror of the Zombies *♂ El Buque Maldito* 1974 (R) Bikinied models are pursued by hooded zombies on board a pleasure yacht...the horror. Effete final installment in the "blind dead" trilogy; see also "Tombs of the Blind Dead" and "Return of the Evil Dead." **90m/C VHS.** *SP* Maria Perschy, Jack Taylor; *D:* Armando de Ossorio; *W:* Armando de Ossorio. *NO*

Horror Planet woof! *Inseminoid* 1980 (R) Alien creature needs a chance to breed before moving on to spread its horror. When a group of explorers disturbs it, the years of waiting are over, and the unlucky mother-to-be will never be the same. Graphic and sensationalistic, capitalizing on the popularity of "Aliens." **93m/C VHS, Beta, LV.** *GB* Robin Clarke, Jennifer Ashley, Stephanie Beacham, Judy Geeson, Stephen Grives, Victoria Tennant; *D:* Norman J. Warren; *W:* Gloria Maley, Nick Maley.

Horror Rises from the Tomb *♂♂*
1972 A 15th century knight and his assistant are beheaded for practicing witchcraft. Five hundred years later, they return to possess a group of vacationers and generally cause havoc. **89m/C VHS, Beta.** *SP* Paul Naschy, Vic Winner, Emma Cohen, Helga Line; *D:* Carlos Aured. *FCT, NLC, LOO*

The Horror Show *♂ House 3* 1989 (R) Serial killer fries in electric chair, an event that really steams him. So he goes after the cop who brought him in. Standard dead guy who won't die and wants revenge flick. **95m/C VHS, Beta.** Brion James, Lance Henriksen, Rita Taggart, Dedee Pfeiffer, Aron Eisenberg, Matt Clark, Thom Bray; *D:* James Isaac; *W:* Alan Smithee, Leslie Bohem; *C:* Mac Ahlberg. *MGM*

Horrors of Burke & Hare *♂* 1971 A gory tale about the exploits of a bunch of 19th-century grave robbers. **94m/C VHS, Beta, LV.** Derren Nesbitt, Harry Andrews, Yootha Joyce; *D:* Vernon Sewell.

Horrors of Spider Island *♂ It's Hot in Paradise; In Toter Hing im Netz; A Corpse Hangs in the Web* 1959 D'Arcy is a Hollywood talent scout who sniffs a goldmine in a team of young female dancers whom he schedules to perform for him in Singapore. Their transport plane crashes in the Pacific Ocean and he and the girls are forced to take refuge on an uncharted isle. Upon landing there they discover it is infested with giant crab-sized spiders. Lots of potential for both shock and arousal, which was probably why it was originally released in both "horror" and "girlie" versions. D'Arcy later admitted to taking over for director Bottger and adding all the horror sequences himself. Dubbed from the German. **77m/C VHS.** *GE* Alexander D'Arcy, Ursula Lederstger; *D:* Fritz Bottger. *SMW, TPV*

Horrors of the Red Planet *♂ The Wizard of Mars* 1964 Cheapo epic sees astronauts crash on Mars, meet its Wizard, and stumble into a few Oz-like creatures. Technically advised by Forrest J. Ackerman. **81m/C VHS, Beta.** John Carradine, Roger Gentry, Vic McGee; *D:* David L. Hewitt. *MRV, REP*

The Horse *♂♂♂½ Horse, My Horse* 1982 A moving, mature Turkish film about a father and son trying to overcome socioeconomic obstacles and their own frailties in order to make enough money to send the boy to school. In Turkish with English subtitles. **116m/C VHS, Beta.** *TU D:* Ali Ozgenturk. *KIV*

Horse Feathers *♂♂♂½* 1932 Huxley College has to beef up its football team to win the championship game, and the corrupt new college president knows just how to do it. Features some of the brothers' classic routines, and the songs "Whatever It Is, I'm Against It" and "Everyone Says I Love You." **67m/B VHS, Beta, LV.** Groucho Marx, Chico Marx, Harpo Marx, Zeppo Marx, Thelma Todd, David Landau, Nat Pendleton; *D:* Norman Z. McLeod. *USH*

A Horse for Danny *♂♂½* 1995 (G) Horse trainer Eddie (Urich), dogged by bad luck, and his 11-year-old niece Danny (Sobieski), come across a thoroughbred named Tom Thumb, who may be their chance at racing's winners circle. TV movie. **92m/C VHS.** Robert Urich, Leelee Sobieski, Ron Brice, Karen Carlson, Gary Basaraba; *D:* Dick Lowry; *C:* Steven Fierberg. *HMK*

The Horse in the Gray Flannel Suit *♂♂½* 1968 (G) Disney comedy portrays an advertising executive who links his daughter's devotion to horses with a client's new ad campaign. **114m/C VHS, Beta.** Dean Jones, Ellen Janov, Fred Clark, Diane Baker, Lloyd Bochner, Kurt Russell; *D:* Norman Tokar; *M:* George Bruns. *DIS, OM*

The Horse of Pride *♂♂½ Le Cheval D'Orgeuil* 1980 Chabrol takes a telling look at the everyday life of the peasants of Breton—both their pleasures and their sorrows. In French with English subtitles. French script booklet available. **118m/C VHS, Beta.** *FR* Jacques Dufilho, Francois Cluzet; *D:* Claude Chabrol. *INT, AUD*

The Horse Soldiers *♂♂½* 1959 An 1863 Union cavalry officer is sent 300 miles into Confederate territory to destroy a railroad junction and is accompanied by a fellow officer who is also a pacifist doctor. Based on a true Civil War incident. **114m/C VHS, Beta, Closed Caption.** John Wayne, William Holden, Hoot Gibson, Anna Lee, Russell Simpson, Strother Martin; *D:* John Ford; *C:* William Clothier. *MGM, FOX*

The Horse Thief *♂♂♂ Daoma Zei* 1987 Noted as the first movie from the People's Republic of China to be released on video, this epic tells the tale of Norbu, a man who, exiled from his people for horse thievery, is forced to wander the Tibetan countryside with his family in search of work. His son dies while he is in exile, and he, a devout Buddhist, is ultimately forced to accept tribal work in a ritual exorcism, after which he pleads to be accepted back into his clan. Beautiful and image-driven, offering a rare glimpse into the Tibet you won't see in travel brochures. Filmed on location with locals as actors. In Mandarin with English subtitles. **88m/C VHS.** *CH D:* Tian Zhuangzhuang. *KIV, FCT*

The Horse Whisperer *♂♂½* 1997 (PG-13) After her teenaged daughter Grace (Johansson) is injured in a riding accident, determined mom Annie (Thomas), believing that the girl's recovery is tied to the horse's, takes child and horse to Montana to seek the help of horse healer Tom (Redford) in the big-screen adaptation of the Nicholas Evans novel. While there, chilly New York editor Annie warms up to Tom and the possibility of love. Like "The Bridges of Madison County," this adaptation removes the overwrought syrupy melodrama of its source novel to concentrate on mature themes like fidelity, trust, and fate. Fine performances by all (although Redford could be seen as a bit self-indulgent at times) and the beautiful Montana backdrop make up for the lack of sustained dramatic impact, which is probably due to the almost three-hour run time and some dramatic changes from the book. **CW:** A disturbing accident scene. **168m/C VHS.** Robert Redford, Kristin Scott Thomas, Scarlett Johansson, Sam Neill, Chris Cooper, Dianne Wiest, Cherry Jones, Jeanette Nolan, Don Edwards, Ty Hillman, Catherine Bosworth, Steve Frye; *D:* Robert Redford; *W:* Eric Roth, Richard LaGravenese; *C:* Robert Richardson; *M:* Thomas Newman. *NYR*

The Horse Without a Head 🎬🎬½ **1963** Stolen loot has been hidden in a discarded toy horse which is now the property of a group of poor children. The thieves, however, have different plans. Good family fare originally shown on the Disney television show. **89m/C VHS, Beta.** Jean-Pierre Aumont, Herbert Lom, Leo McKern, Pamela Franklin, Vincent Winter; **D:** Don Chaffey. *DIS*

The Horseman on the Roof 🎬🎬½ *Le Hussard sur le Toit* **1995 (R)** Lavish costume drama set in Provence in the 1830s, during a cholera epidemic. Italian officer/revolutionary Angelo (Martinez) is on the run and eventually meets up with beautiful Pauline de Theus (Binoche), who hides him in a quarantined French village. Pauline's in search of her husband and Angelo reluctantly agrees to help her. Together they manage to escape a military cordon and travel to another plague town. There's lots of riding through the countryside and hiding out and not much actually happens. Nice scenery, attractive stars. Based on the 1951 novel by Jean Giono. French with subtitles; originally released at 135 minutes. **CW:** A scene of nudity. **119m/C VHS, LV.** *FR* Olivier Martinez, Juliette Binoche, Francois Cluzet, Isabelle Carre, Jean Yanne, Claudio Amendola, Pierre Arditti; **D:** Jean-Paul Rappeneau; **W:** Jean-Paul Rappeneau, Jean-Claude Carriere, Nina Companeez; **C:** Thierry Arbogast; **M:** Jean-Claude Petit. Cesar Awards '96: Best Cinematography, Best Sound; Nominations: Cesar Awards '96: Best Actress (Binoche), Best Art Direction/Set Decoration, Best Costume Design, Best Director (Rappeneau), Best Film, Best Film Editing, Best Score. *MAX*

Horsemasters 🎬🎬 **1961** A group of young riders enter a special training program in England to achieve the ultimate equestrian title of horsemaster, with Annette having to overcome her fear of jumping. Originally a two-part Disney television show, and released as a feature film in Europe. **85m/C VHS, Beta.** Tommy Kirk, Annette Funicello, Janet Munro, Tony Britton, Donald Pleasence, Jean Marsh, John Fraser, Millicent Martin; **D:** William Fairchild. *DIS*

The Horsemen 🎬½ **1970 (PG)** An Afghani youth enters the brutal buzkashi horse tournament to please his macho-minded father. Beautifully shot in Afghanistan and Spain by Claude Renoir. **109m/C VHS, Beta.** Omar Sharif, Leigh Taylor-Young, Jack Palance, David De, Peter Jeffrey; **D:** John Frankenheimer; **W:** Dalton Trumbo; **M:** Georges Delerue. *COL*

The Horseplayer 🎬½ **1991 (R)** A loner is drawn into a mysterious triangle of decadence and desire in this riveting psychothriller. **?m/C VHS, LV, Closed Caption.** Brad Dourif, Sammi Davis, M.K. Harris, Vic Tayback; **D:** Kurt Voss. *REP*

The Horse's Mouth 🎬🎬🎬 *The Oracle* **1958** An obsessive painter discovers that he must rely upon his wits to survive in London. A hilarious adaptation of the Joyce Cary novel. The laserdisc version is accompanied by an episode of the British documentary series "The Art of Film" profiling Guinness and his screen career. **93m/C VHS, Beta, LV.** *GB* Alec Guinness, Kay Walsh, Robert Coote, Renee Houston, Michael Gough; **D:** Ronald Neame. National Board of Review Awards '58: Best Supporting Actress (Walsh); Nominations: Academy Awards '58: Best Adapted Screenplay. *HMV, ING, NLC*

The Hospital 🎬🎬🎬½ **1971 (PG)** Cult favorite providing savage, unrelentingly sarcastic look at the workings of a chaotic metropolitan hospital beset by murders, witchdoctors, madness, and plain ineptitude. **101m/C VHS, Beta, Closed Caption.** George C. Scott, Diana Rigg, Barnard Hughes, Stockard Channing, Nancy Marchand, Richard Dysart; **D:** Arthur Hiller; **W:** Paddy Chayefsky. Academy Awards '71: Best Story & Screenplay; Berlin International Film Festival '72: Silver Prize; British Academy Awards '72: Best Screenplay; Golden Globe Awards '72: Best Screenplay, National Film Registry '95;; Writers Guild of America Awards '71: Best Original Screenplay; Nominations: Academy Awards '71: Best Actor (Scott). *MGM, FOX*

Hospital Massacre woof! *X-Ray; Ward 13; Be My Valentine, Or Else* **1981 (R)** Psychopathic killer is loose in a hospital. Seems he holds a grudge against the woman who laughed at his valentine when they were children 20 years earlier, and too bad for her that she just checked in as a patient. Former "Playboy" and Hefner playmate Benton frolics in dangerous health care situation presented by the Cannon organization. **89m/C VHS, Beta.** Barbi Benton, Jon Van Ness, Chip Lucio; **D:** Boaz Davidson; **W:** Marc Behm. *MGM*

Hospital of Terror 🎬🎬 *Nurse Sherri; Terror Hospital; Beyond the Living* **1978 (R)** A transmigratory religious fanatic who died on the operating table manages to possess a nurse (Jacobson) before he kicks the bucket, and once in his candystripe incarnation, vents his spleen on the doctors who botched his operation. It's got a little more plasma than Adamson's "AstroZombies," considered by many to be a world-class boner. **88m/C VHS.** Jill Jacobson, Geoffrey Land, Marilyn Joi, Mary Kay Pass, Prentiss Moulden, Clayton Foster; **D:** Al Adamson. *NO*

The Hostage 🎬🎬½ **1967 (PG)** A young teenager is witness to a gruesome and clandestine burial. The two murderers responsible take it upon themselves to see that their secret is never told. **84m/C VHS.** Don O'Kelly, Harry Dean Stanton, John Carradine, Danny Martins; **D:** Russell S. Doughten Jr. *NO*

Hostage 🎬½ **1987 (R)** Arab terrorists hijack a plane and the passengers start to fight back. Filmed in South Africa. **94m/C VHS, Beta.** Karen Black, Kevin McCarthy, Wings Hauser; **D:** Hanro Mohr; **M:** Brad Fiedel. *COL*

Hostage 🎬🎬 **1992 (R)** British Secret Service agent John Rennie is fed up after a difficult mission in Argentina. He thinks he can walk away clean but his superiors beg to differ. He's marked for murder but Rennie has a dangerous plan that could guarantee his safety—only if he returns to Argentina to set things in motion. Based on the novel "No Place to Hide" by Ted Allbeury. **CW:** Language, violence, and sexuality. **100m/C VHS, Beta, Closed Caption.** Sam Neill, Talisa Soto, James Fox; **D:** Robert W. Young. *PAR, PMS*

Hostage for a Day 🎬🎬½ **1994** Married to a shrew, toiling for an overbearing father-in-law, and suffering a midlife crisis, Wendt decides to fake his own kidnapping, take the ransom money, and head off for a better life. A series of comedic complications abound. Candy's directorial debut. Made for TV. **92m/C VHS, LV.** George Wendt, John Vernon, Robin Duke, Peter Torokvei, Don Lake, Frank Moore, John Hemphill, Christopher Templeton; **Cameos:** John Candy; **D:** John Candy; **W:** Peter Torokvei, Robert Crane, Kari Hildebrand; **M:** Ian Thomas. *THV*

The Hostage Tower 🎬🎬 **1980 (PG)** In France, a group of international crime figures capture the visiting U.S. president's mother, hold her hostage in the Eiffel Tower and demand $30 million in ransom. Made for television. **97m/C VHS, Beta, LV.** Peter Fonda, Maud Adams, Britt Ekland, Billy Dee Williams, Keir Dullea, Douglas Fairbanks Jr., Rachel Roberts, Celia Johnson; **D:** Claudio Guzman.

Hostage Train 🎬½ **1997 (R)** Cop Jack Wild (Reinhold) discovers that the train carrying his girlfriend, financial analyst Dana Townsend (Alt), and several of her wealthy clients has been hijacked by terrorists. The train is trapped by an explosion in a tunnel in the Rockies and Jack must rescue the passengers before the rest of the terrorists' plan goes into motion. **CW:** Violence, and for language and a sex scene. **98m/C VHS.** Judge Reinhold, Carol Alt, Michael Sarrazin, Robert Lee. *REP*

Hostages 🎬 **1979** A gang of criminals kidnap a family on vacation at a Caribbean island. **93m/C VHS, Beta.** Stuart Whitman, Marisa Mell. *NO*

Hostages 🎬🎬🎬 **1993 (R)** Harrowing docudrama about the Beirut hostage crisis combines acutal news footage with scenes of the prisoners and their families. Under desperate conditions hostages John McCarthy, Brian Keenan, Terry Anderson, Thomas Sutherland, Frank Reed, and Terry Waite try to hold on to their sanity and humanity as their families struggle for their release. Filmed on location in England, Israel, and Lebanon. Made for cable TV. **CW:** Strong language. **90m/C VHS, Closed Caption.** Colin Firth, Ciaran Hinds, Jay O. Sanders, Josef Sommer, Harry Dean Stanton, Kathy Bates, Natasha Richardson, Conrad Asquith; **D:** David Wheatley; **W:** Bernard MacLaverty. *IMP*

Hostile Guns 🎬🎬½ **1967** A law man discovers a woman he once loved is now an inmate he is transporting across the Texas badlands. Routine with the exception of cameos by veteran actors. Based on a story by Sloan Nibley and James Edward Grant. **91m/C VHS, LV, Closed Caption.** George Montgomery, Yvonne De Carlo, Tab Hunter, John Russell; **Cameos:** Brian Donlevy, Richard Arlen, Fuzzy Knight, Donald (Don "Red") Barry; **D:** R.G. Springsteen; **W:** Steve Fisher, Sloan Nibley. *PAR*

Hostile Intent 🎬🎬 **1997 (R)** The designers of a new computer chip become the targets of government agents when they find their friendly wargames weekend has turned deadly. **90m/C VHS, Closed Caption.** Rob Lowe, John Savage, Sofia Shinas, James Kidnie; **D:** Jonathan Heap; **W:** Manny Coto; **C:** Gerald R. Goozie; **M:** Christophe Beck. *CAF*

Hostile Intentions 🎬🎬 **1994 (R)** Three girlfriends head for a weekend of fun in the sun in Tijuana and find themselves turned into fugitives through a series of misunderstandings. In order to get home, they must risk a night border crossing with a group of illegal immigrants. **CW:** Language, violence, sexual situations. **90m/C VHS, Closed Caption.** Tia Carrere, Lisa Dean Ryan, Tricia Leigh Fisher, Carlos Gomez, Rigg Kennedy; **D:** Catherine Cyran; **W:** Catherine Cyran; **C:** Azusa Ohno; **M:** Marcos Loya. *AVE*

Hostile Takeover 🎬½ *Office Party* **1988 (R)** A mild-mannered accountant finally cracks and takes his co-workers hostage. He faces the police in a tense showdown. **93m/C VHS, Beta, LV.** David Warner, Michael Ironside, Kate Vernon, Jayne Eastwood; **D:** George Mihalka. *ART*

Hostile Waters 🎬🎬½ **1997 (PG)** Based on Soviet accounts of an October 1986 incident that nearly set off a nuclear holocaust. A Russian and a U.S. sub play a game of cat-and-mouse 500 miles east of Bermuda. There's a collision and a fire aboard the Soviet sub threatens their cargo of thermonuclear missiles. Soviet captain Igor Britanov (Hauer) tries to control the situation while the U.S. skipper (Sheen) tries to figure out just what's going on. **?m/C VHS.** Rutger Hauer, Martin Sheen, Colm Feore, Rob Campbell, Harris Yulin, Max von Sydow, Regina Taylor, John Rothman; **D:** David Drury; **W:** Troy Kennedy Martin; **C:** Alec Curtis; **M:** David Ferguson. *HBO*

Hot Blood **1989** Two bank robbers take an innocent woman hostage and thrust her in the midst of a huge family battle. Another lukewarm entry from the director of "The Arrogant." **89m/C VHS, Beta.** Sylvia Kristel, Alicia Moro, Aldo Sambrel, Gaspar Cano; **D:** Philippe Blot.

Hot Box woof! **1972 (R)** A Filipino-shot, low budget woofer. Prison flick about women who break out and foment a revolution. **85m/C VHS, Beta.** Andrea Cagan, Margaret Markov, Rickey Richardson, Laurie Rose; **D:** Joe Viola; **W:** Joe Viola, Jonathan Demme.

Hot Bubblegum 🎬 **1981 (R)** Three teenagers discover sex, the beach, rock 'n' roll, sex, drag racing, and sex. **94m/C VHS, Beta.** Jonathan Segall, Zachi Noy, Yftach Katzur. *NO*

Hot Child in the City 🎬 **1987** A country girl goes to Los Angeles and searches through the city's fleshpots for her sister's killer. Music by Nick Glider, Lou Reed, Billy Idol, and Fun Boy Three. **85m/C VHS, Beta.** Leah Ayres Hendrix, Shari Shattuck, Geof Pryssir; **D:** John Florea. *PAR*

Hot Chocolate 🎬🎬 **1992 (PG-13)** Derek is a sultry Texas tycoon who wants to buy out the French chocolate factory run by Hays. After getting a look at her, work isn't all that's on his mind. **93m/C VHS, LV.** Bo Derek, Robert Hays. *ART*

Hot Dog...The Movie! ✶✶½ 1983 (R)
There's an intense rivalry going on between an Austrian ski champ and his California challenger during the World Cup Freestyle competition in Squaw Valley. Snow movie strictly for teens or their equivalent. 96m/C VHS, Beta, Closed Caption. David Naughton, Patrick Houser, Shannon Tweed, Tracy N. Smith; **D:** Peter Markle; **M:** Peter Bernstein. MGM, FOX

Hot Foot/A Happy Married Couple 1920 Two silent comedies: "Hot Foot" (1920), is about Dunn's hobo character in the Chaplin mold; "A Happy Married Couple" (1916), is about a young married couple whose puppy, as described in a letter, is mistaken for a baby by their parents. 51m/B VHS, Beta, 8mm. Bobbie Dunn, Neal Burns, Betty Compson. VYY

Hot Lead ✶✶ 1951 Typical Holt oater which has the cowpoke and his sidekick Martin trying to avenge the death of a close friend who was killed by a gang of train robbers. 60m/B VHS. Tim Holt, Joan Dixon, Ross Elliott, John Dehner; **D:** Stuart Gilmore. MOV

Hot Lead & Cold Feet ✶✶ 1978 (G)
Twin brothers (one a gunfighter, the other meek and mild) compete in a train race where the winner will take ownership of a small western town. Dale not only plays both brothers, but also their tough father. Standard Disney fare. 89m/C VHS, Beta. Jim Dale, Don Knotts, Karen Valentine; **D:** Robert Butler; **W:** Arthur Alsberg; **M:** Buddy Baker. DIS

The Hot Line ✶✶½ The Day the Hot Line Got Hot; Le Rouble a Deux Faces; El Rublo de las dos Caras 1969 The world's two superpowers become befuddled when the hot line connecting Washington and Moscow breaks down. Taylor's final film. 87m/C VHS. Robert Taylor, Charles Boyer, George Chakiris, Dominique Fabre, Gerard Tichy; **D:** Etienne Perier. REP

Hot Millions ✶✶✶ 1968 Hysterical comedy about high-class swindling operation with Ustinov as a refined embezzler. Excellent cast and sharp script. Although it didn't do well at the box-office, this amusing romp became one of the biggest sleepers of the year. 106m/C VHS, Closed Caption. GB Peter Ustinov, Maggie Smith, Karl Malden, Bob Newhart, Robert Morley, Cesar Romero, Melinda May, Ann Lancaster, Margaret Courtenay, Lynda Baron, Billy Milton, Peter Jones, Raymond Huntley, Kynaston Reeves; **D:** Eric Till; **W:** Ira Wallach, Peter Ustinov. Nominations: Academy Awards '68: Best Story & Screenplay. MGM

Hot Money ✶ 1979 A small-town drama about an ex-con who poses as an assistant sheriff and plots a million-dollar robbery during the town's 4th of July parade. Made shortly before Welles's death, and kept on the shelf for more than five years. 78m/C VHS, Beta. Orson Welles, Michael Murphy, Bobby Pickett, Michelle Finney. THV

Hot Moves ✶ 1984 (R) Four high school boys make a pact to lose their virginity before the end of the summer. 89m/C VHS, Beta. Michael Zorek, Adam Silbar, Jill Schoelen, Deborah Richter, Monique Gabrielle, Tami Holbrook, Virgil Frye; **D:** Jim Sotos. VES

Hot Potato ✶ 1976 (PG) Black Belt Jones rescues a senator's daughter from a megalomaniacal general by using skull-thwacking footwork. 87m/C VHS, Beta. Jim Kelly, George Memmoli, Geoffrey Binney; **D:** Oscar Williams. WAR

Hot Pursuit ✶✶½ 1984 (PG) A woman who has been framed for murder runs from the law and a relentless hitman. 94m/C VHS, Beta. Mike Preston, Dina Merrill, Kerrie Keane. THV

Hot Pursuit ✶✶½ 1987 (PG-13) A prep-school bookworm resorts to Rambo-like tactics in tracking down his girlfriend and her family after being left behind for a trip to the tropics. 93m/C VHS, Beta, LV. John Cusack, Robert Loggia, Jerry Stiller, Wendy Gazelle; **D:** Steven Lisberger; **W:** Steven W. Carabatsos. PAR

Hot Resort ✶✶½ 1985 (R) Young American lads mix work and play when they sign on as summer help at an island resort. Typical teen sex fantasy. 92m/C VHS, Beta. Bronson Pinchot, Tom Parsekian, Michael Berz, Linda Kenton, Frank Gorshin; **D:** John Robins; **W:** Boaz Davidson, John Robins. MGM

The Hot Rock ✶✶✶ How to Steal a Diamond in Four Easy Lessons 1970 (PG) A motley crew of bumbling thieves conspire to steal a huge, priceless diamond; a witty, gritty comedy that makes no moral excuses for its characters and plays like an early-'70s crime thriller gone awry. Adapted from the novel by Donald E. Westlake. The sequel, 1974's "Bank Shot," stars George C. Scott in the role created by Redford. 97m/C VHS, Beta, LV, Letterbox. Robert Redford, George Segal, Ron Leibman, Zero Mostel, Moses Gunn, William Redfield, Charlotte Rae, Topo Swope; **M:** Quincy Jones. Nominations: Academy Awards '72: Best Film Editing. FOX

Hot Rod ✶ Rebel of the Road 1979 A young California hotrodder battles the evil sponsor of a drag race championship. 97m/C VHS, Beta. Greg Henry, Robert Culp, Pernell Roberts, Robin Mattson, Grant Goodeve; **D:** George Armitage. NLC

Hot Rod Girl ✶ Hot Car Girl 1956 A concerned police officer (Conners) organizes supervised drag racing after illegal drag racing gets out of hand in his community. 75m/B VHS. Lori Nelson, Chuck Connors, John W. Smith; **D:** Leslie Martinson; **W:** John McGreevey. SNC, NOS, MRV

Hot Shot ✶✶½ 1986 (PG) An inspirational tale involving a young soccer player who goes to great lengths to take training from a soccer star, played—of course—by Pele. 90m/C VHS, Beta. Pele, Jim Youngs, Billy Warlock, Weyman Thompson, Mario Van Peebles, David Groh; **D:** Rick King. WAR, MVD

Hot Shots! ✶✶✶ 1991 (PG-13) Another entry from "The Naked Gun" team of master movie parodists, this has lots of clever sight gags but the verbal humor often plummets to the ground. Spoofs "Top Gun" and similar gung-ho air corps adventures but doesn't forget other popular films including "Dances with Wolves" and "The Fabulous Baker Boys." Sheen is very funny as ace fighter pilot Sean "Topper" Harley who's to avenge the family honor. Great when you're in the mood for laughs that don't require thought. 83m/C VHS, Closed Caption. Charlie Sheen, Cary Elwes, Valeria Golino, Lloyd Bridges, Kevin Dunn, Jon Cryer, William O'Leary, Kristy Swanson, Efrem Zimbalist Jr., Bill Irwin, Heidi Swedberg, Judith Kahan, Pat Proft; **Cameos:** Charles Barkley, Bill Laimbeer; **D:** Jim Abrahams; **W:** Pat Proft, Jim Abrahams; **C:** Bill Butler; **M:** Sylvester Levay. FOX

Hot Shots! Part Deux ✶✶½ 1993 (PG-13) Second "Hot Shots" outing doesn't live up to the first, but it's not bad either. Admiral Tug Benson (Bridges) is elected President (yes, of the U.S.) and calls on Sheen's newly pumped-up Topper to take on Saddam Hussein Rambo-style. Love interest Ramada (Golino), returns but this time she's competing with Michelle (Bakke), a sexy CIA agent. Crenna spoofs his role in the "Rambo" films as Sheen's mentor; look for real-life dad Martin in a take-off of "Apocalypse Now." Shtick flies as fast and furious as the bodies, with Bridges getting a chance to reprise his glory days of "Sea Hunt." Don't miss the credits. **CW:** Language and sexual spoofs. 89m/C VHS, LV, Closed Caption. Charlie Sheen, Lloyd Bridges, Valeria Golino, Brenda Bakke, Richard Crenna, Miguel Ferrer, Rowan Atkinson, Jerry Haleva, Mitchell Ryan, Gregory Sierra, Ryan Stiles, Michael Colyar; **Cameos:** Martin Sheen, Bob Vila; **D:** Jim Abrahams; **W:** Pat Proft, Jim Abrahams; **M:** Basil Poledouris. FOX, BTV

Hot Spell ✶✶½ 1958 In an attempt to repair her marriage and unify her family, a mother plans a reunion-birthday party for her husband. Despair reigns in this sultry, Southern melodrama. 86m/B VHS, Beta. Shirley Booth, Anthony Quinn, Shirley MacLaine, Earl Holliman, Eileen Heckart; **D:** Daniel Mann; **C:** Loyal Griggs; **M:** Alex North. BAR

The Hot Spot ✶✶✶½ 1990 (R) An amoral drifter arrives in a small Texas town and engages in affairs with two women, including his boss's over-sexed wife and a young woman with her own secrets. Things begin to heat up when he decides to plot a bank robbery. Based on Charles Williams' 1952 novel "Hell Hath No Fury." 120m/C VHS, LV, Closed Caption. Don Johnson, Virginia Madsen,

Jennifer Connelly, Charles Martin Smith, William Sadler, Jerry Hardin, Barry Corbin, Leon Rippy, Jack Nance; **D:** Dennis Hopper; **W:** Charles Williams, Nona Tyson; **M:** Jack Nitzsche. ORI, FCT

Hot Stuff ✶ 1980 (PG) Officers on a burglary task force decide the best way to obtain convictions is to go into the fencing business themselves. 91m/C VHS, Beta, LV. Dom DeLuise, Jerry Reed, Suzanne Pleshette, Ossie Davis; **D:** Dom DeLuise; **W:** Donald E. Westlake, Michael Kane. COL

Hot Summer in Barefoot County ✶✶ 1974 (R) A state law enforcement officer on the search for illegal moonshiners finds more than he bargained for. 90m/C VHS, Beta. Sherry Robinson, Tonia Bryan, Dick Smith; **D:** Will Zens. NO

Hot T-Shirts woof! 1979 (R) A small town bar owner needs a boost for business, finding the answer in wet T-shirt contests. Softcore trash. 86m/C VHS, Beta. Ray Holland, Stephanie Lawlor, Pauline Rose, Corinne Alphen; **D:** Chuck Vincent. USH

Hot Target ✶ 1985 (R) An ideal mother becomes obsessed with the stranger who seduced her, even after she finds out he's a thief planning to rob her home. 93m/C VHS, Beta, LV. NZ Simone Griffeth, Steve Marachuk; **D:** Denis Lewiston. ART, VES

The Hot, the Cool, and the Vicious 198? A quiet town turns into a bloody, martial arts playground when three hombres trade blows in a tavern. ?m/C VHS. Wang Tao, Tommy Lee, Sun Chia-Lin. MGI

Hot Times ✶ 1974 (R) Low-budget comedy about a high school boy who, after striking out with the high school girls, decides to go to New York and have the time of his life. 80m/C VHS, Beta. Gail Lorber, Amy Farber, Henry Cory; **D:** Jim McBride; **W:** Jim McBride. MON

Hot to Trot! ✶ 1988 (PG) A babbling idiot links up with a talking horse in an updated version of the "Francis, the Talking Mule" comedies, by way of Mr. Ed. The equine voice is provided by Candy. Some real funny guys are wasted here. 90m/C VHS, Beta, LV, Closed Caption. Bob(cat) Goldthwait, Dabney Coleman, Virginia Madsen, Jim Metzler, Cindy Pickett, Tim Kazurinsky, Santos Morales, Barbara Whinnery, Garry Kluger; **D:** Michael Dinner; **W:** Charlie Peters; **M:** Danny Elfman; **V:** John Candy. WAR

Hot Touch woof! 198? An art forger with a large heist is besieged by a slashing maniac, and must discover the culprit. 92m/C VHS, Beta. Wayne Rogers, Samantha Eggar, Marie-France Pisier, Melvyn Douglas. TWE, HHE

Hot Under the Collar ✶✶½ 1991 (R) Jerry is a weasel who tries to seduce the luscious Monica by using hypnosis. But his plans backfire and instead Monica enters a convent and takes a vow of chastity. This isn't going to stop Jerry, he tries posing as a priest and even dressing as a nun in order to get her out. Things get even more complicated when a mobster, looking for a fortune in stolen diamonds, sneaks into the convent. **CW:** Sensuality. 87m/C VHS. Richard Gabai, Angela Visser, Daniel Friedman, Mindy Clarke, Tane McClure; **D:** Richard Gabai. HBO

Hot Water/Safety Last 1924 Two classic Harold Lloyd silent comedies, "Hot Water" (1924) and "Safety Last" (1923). "Safety Last" features one of Lloyd's most famous stunt scenes, where he is hanging from the hands of a giant clock on the side of a building, high above the city. 81m/B VHS, Beta. Harold Lloyd. TLF

Hot Wire ✶✶½ 197? Tired comedy about the unscrupulous side of the car repossession racket. 92m/C VHS, Beta. George Kennedy, Strother Martin. NO

Hotel ✶✶½ 1967 (PG) A pale rehash of the "Grand Hotel" formula about an array of rich characters interacting in a New Orleans hotel. From the Arthur Hailey potboiler; the basis for the television series. 125m/C VHS, Beta. Rod Taylor, Catherine Spaak, Karl Malden, Melvyn Douglas, Merle Oberon, Michael Rennie, Richard Conte, Kevin McCarthy; **D:** Richard Quine; **W:** Wendell Mayes; **C:** Charles B(ryant) Lang. WAR

Hotel Colonial ⟋½ 1988 (R) A young Italian idealist ventures to Columbia to retrieve the body of his brother, who reportedly killed himself. Once there, he finds the dead man is not his brother, and decides to investigate. 103m/C VHS, Beta, LV, 8mm. *IT* Robert Duvall, John Savage, Rachel Ward, Massimo Troisi; *D:* Cinzia Torrini; *W:* Ira Barmak, Enzo Monteleone; *M:* Pino Donaggio. *NLC*

Hotel de Love ⟋⟋½ 1996 (R) Seventeen-year-old fraternal twin brothers Rick (Young) and Stephen Dunne (Bossell) both fall for beautiful Melissa (Burrows) and she has a short-lived romance with the more-aggressive Rick. Ten years later, mopey stockbroker Stephen shows up at the tacky theme honeymoon hotel Rick now manages and who should show up (besides the twins bickering parents) but Melissa and her fiance Norman (O'Brien). So the twins renew their competition while Melissa decides if Norman is the right guy for her, Mrs. Dunne gets mash notes from a secret admirer, and fortuneteller Alison (Grandison), who happens to be Rick's ex-girlfriend, offers romantic advice to Stephen.*CW:* Sexuality. 93m/C VHS, LV, Closed Caption. *AU* Aden Young, Simon Bossell, Saffron Burrows, Julia Blake, Ray Barrett, Pippa Grandison, Alan Hopgood, Peter O'Brien; *D:* Craig Rosenberg; *W:* Craig Rosenberg; *C:* Stephen Windon; *M:* Brett Rosenberg. *ART*

Hotel du Lac ⟋⟋ 1986 A made-for-British-television adaptation of the Anita Brookner novel about a woman writer languishing at a Swiss lakefront hotel. 75m/C VHS, Beta. *GB* Anna Massey, Denholm Elliott, Googie Withers; *D:* Giles Foster; *M:* Carl Davis. *FOX, TVC, VCO*

Hotel Imperial ⟋⟋ 1927 Set in 1917 Budapest, six Hungarian soldiers ride into a frontier town and find it occupied by Russians. Hall plays Lieutenant Almasy, who takes refuge in the Hotel Imperial. Orchestra scored. 84m/B VHS, Closed Caption. Pola Negri, James Hall, George Siegmann, Max Davidson; *D:* Mauritz Stiller. *GPV*

The Hotel New Hampshire ⟋⟋ 1984 (R) The witless, amoral adaptation of John Irving's novel about a very strange family's adventures in New Hampshire, Vienna and New York City, which include gang rape, incest, and Kinski in a bear suit. 110m/C VHS, Beta, LV. Jodie Foster, Rob Lowe, Beau Bridges, Nastassia Kinski, Wallace Shawn, Wilford Brimley, Amanda Plummer, Anita Morris, Matthew Modine, Lisa Banes, Seth Green; *D:* Tony Richardson; *W:* Tony Richardson; *C:* David Watkin. *VES*

Hotel Paradiso ⟋⟋½ 1966 Slightly amusing bedroom farce has timid Guinness trying to carry on affair with Italian sexpot Lollibrigida. Guinness fans won't be disappointed, although it's not a top-rate production. Based on the play "L'Hotel du Libre Echange" by Georges Feydeau and Maurice Desvalliers. 100m/C VHS. *GB* Alec Guinness, Gina Lollobrigida, Akim Tamiroff, Marie Bell, Derek Fowlds; *D:* Peter Glenville; *W:* Peter Glenville, Jean-Claude Carriere. *MGM*

Hotel Reserve ⟋⟋⟋ 1944 A Nazi spy is reportedly afoot in a French resort during WWII, and tension mounts as the guests attempt to flush him out. Critical response to this film is wildly split; some find it obvious, while others call it well-done and suspenseful. Based on the novel "Epitaph for a Spy" by Eric Ambler. 79m/B VHS, Beta. *GB* James Mason, Lucie Mannheim, Raymond Lovell, Julien Mitchell, Martin Miller, Herbert Lom, Frederick Valk, Valentine Dyall, Patricia Medina; *D:* Victor Hanbury, Lance Comfort, Max Greene. *TTC, RXM*

Hotel Room ⟋⟋½ *David Lynch's Hotel Room* 1993 A trilogy of stories set in the same drab New York hotel room in three different time periods. "Getting Rid of Robert," set in 1992, has three girlfriends swilling champagne and discussing Sasha's slick, drug exec boyfriend whom she wants to dump. "Tricks," set in 1969, features Darlene, a bored, druggy prostitute; her client, Moe; and the sudden appearance of Moe's talkative friend, Lou. "Blackout" is set in 1936 and features a young husband trying to cope with the madness of his beautiful wife. Unfortunately, all three stories are rambling and lacking in energy. Made for cable television. 100m/C VHS, Closed Caption. Deborah Kara Unger, Mariska Hargitay, Chelsea Field, Griffin Dunne, Glenne Headly, Harry Dean Stanton, Freddie Jones, Crispin Glover, Alicia Witt, Clark Heathcliffe Brolly, Camilla Overbye Roos; *D:* James Signorelli, David Lynch; *W:* Barry Gifford, Jay McInerney; *M:* Angelo Badalamenti. *WOV, FCT*

Hothead ⟋ *Coup de Tete* 1978 A heedless, impulsive soccer player's behavior gets him cut from the team, fired from his mill job, and booted out of his favorite bar. In French with English subtitles or dubbed. 98m/C VHS, Beta. *FR* Patrick Dewaere, Jean Bouise, Michel Aumont, France Dougnac; *D:* Jean-Jacques Annaud; *W:* Francis Veber. Cesar Awards '80: Best Supporting Actor (Bouise). *COL*

Hotline ⟋⟋ 1982 After taking a job answering phones at a crisis center, a woman becomes the next target of a psychotic killer. Made for television. 96m/C VHS. Lynda Carter, Steve Forrest, Granville Van Dusen, Monte Markham, James Booth; *D:* Jerry Jameson. *NO*

H.O.T.S. ⟋ *T & A Academy* 1979 (R) A sex-filled sorority rivalry film, starring a slew of ex-Playboy Playmates in wet shirts. Screenplay co-written by exploitation star Caffaro. 95m/C VHS, Beta. Susan Kiger, Lisa London, Kimberly Cameron, Danny Bonaduce, Steve Bond; *D:* Gerald Seth Sindell; *W:* Cheri Caffaro. *ART, VES*

Houdini ⟋⟋½ 1953 Historically inaccurate but entertaining biopic of the infamous magician and escapologist. Chronicles his rise to stardom, his efforts to contact his dearly departed mother through mediums (a prequel to "Ghost"?), and his heart-stopping logic-defying escapes. First screen teaming of Leigh and Curtis, who had already been married for two years. 107m/C VHS, Closed Caption. Tony Curtis, Janet Leigh, Torin Thatcher, Angela Clark, Stefan Schnabel, Ian Wolfe, Sig Rumann, Michael Pate, Connie Gilchrist, Mary Murphy, Tor Johnson; *D:* George Marshall; *W:* Philip Yordan. *PAR, FCT*

The Hound of London ⟋⟋½ *Sherlock Holmes in The Hound of London* 1993 Inspector Lestrade brings Sherlock Holmes (Macnee) his latest case, a double murder that has taken place at the Strand Theatre. And among the suspects is the only woman Holmes has ever admired, the lovely Irene Adler. Eccentric characters, a sword duel, backstage mischief, and Holmes and Watson together once more. Based on the play by Craig Bowlsby. 72m/C VHS. *CA* Patrick Macnee, John Scott-Paget, Colin Skinner, Jack McCreath, Carolyn Wilkinson, Sophia Thornley, Drew Kemp, Ned Lemley, Craig Bowlsby; *D:* Gil Letourneau, Peter Reynolds-Long; *W:* Craig Bowlsby. *IPI*

The Hound of the Baskervilles ⟋⟋⟋ 1939 The curse of a demonic hound threatens descendants of an English noble family until Holmes and Watson solve the mystery. Also available with "Sherlock Holmes Faces Death" on laserdisc. 80m/B VHS, Beta, Closed Caption. *GB* Basil Rathbone, Nigel Bruce, Richard Greene, John Carradine, Wendy Barrie, Lionel Atwill, E.E. Clive; *D:* Sidney Lanfield. *FOX*

The Hound of the Baskervilles ⟋⟋½ 1959 Cushing's not half bad as Sherlock Holmes as he investigates the mystery of a supernatural hound threatening the life of a Dartmoor baronet. Dark and moody. 86m/C VHS, Beta, LV, Closed Caption. *GB* Peter Cushing, Christopher Lee, Andre Morell; *D:* Terence Fisher; *M:* James Bernard. *MGM, MLB, FOX*

The Hound of the Baskervilles woof! 1977 Awful spoof of the Sherlock Holmes classic with Cook as Holmes and Moore as Watson (and Holmes' mother). Even the cast can't save it. 84m/C VHS. Dudley Moore, Peter Cook, Denholm Elliott, Joan Greenwood, Spike Milligan, Jessie Matthews, Roy Kinnear; *D:* Paul Morrissey; *W:* Dudley Moore, Peter Cook, Paul Morrissey; *M:* Dudley Moore. *NO*

The Hound of the Baskervilles ⟋⟋ 1983 Another remake of the Sherlock Holmes story which finds the great detective investigating the murder of Sir Charles Baskerville and a mysterious haunted moor. 100m/C VHS, Beta, Closed Caption. *GB* Ian Richardson, Donald Churchill, Martin Shaw, Nicholas Clay, Denholm Elliott, Brian Blessed, Ronald Lacey; *D:* Douglas Hickox. *PAR*

Hour of Decision ⟋½ 1957 When a newspaper columnist turns up dead, a reporter investigates the murder. Things get hairy when he finds the prime suspect is his own wife. 81m/B VHS, Beta. *GB* Jeff Morrow, Hazel Court, Lionel Jeffries, Anthony Dawson, Mary Laura Wood; *D:* C.M. Pennington-Richards. *SNC*

Hour of the Assassin ⟋½ 1986 (R) A mercenary is hired to assassinate a South American ruler, and a CIA operative is sent to stop him. Shot in Peru. 96m/C VHS, Beta. Erik Estrada, Robert Vaughn; *D:* Luis Llosa. *MGM*

Hour of the Gun ⟋⟋ 1967 Western saga chronicles what happens after the gunfight at the OK Corral. Garner plays the grim Wyatt Earp on the trail of vengeance after his brothers are killed. Robards is excellent as the crusty Doc Holliday. 100m/C VHS. James Garner, Jason Robards Jr., Robert Ryan, Albert Salmi, Charles Aidman, Steve Ihnat, Jon Voight; *D:* John Sturges; *W:* Edward Anhalt; *M:* Jerry Goldsmith. *MGM*

The Hour of the Star ⟋⟋⟋½ *A Hora Da Estrela* 1985 The poignant, highly acclaimed feature debut by Amaral, about an innocent young woman moving to the city of Sao Paulo from the impoverished countryside of Brazil, and finding happiness despite her socioeconomic failures. Based on Clarice Lispector's novel. In Portuguese with English subtitles. 96m/C VHS, Beta. *BR* Marcelia Cartaxo; *D:* Suzana Amaral. Berlin International Film Festival '85: Best Actress (Cartaxo). *KIV, FCT*

Hour of the Wolf ⟋⟋⟋½ *Vargtimmen* 1968 An acclaimed, surreal view into the tormented inner life of a painter as he and his wife are isolated on a small northern island. In Swedish with English subtitles. 89m/B VHS, Beta. *SW* Max von Sydow, Liv Ullmann, Ingrid Thulin, Erland Josephson, Gertrud Fridh, Gudrun Brost, Georg Rydeberg, Naima Wifstrand, Bertil Anderberg, Ulf Johansson; *D:* Ingmar Bergman; *W:* Ingmar Bergman; *C:* Sven Nykvist. National Board of Review Awards '68: Best Actress (Ullmann); National Society of Film Critics Awards '68: Best Director (Bergman). *MGM, FCT, BTV*

Hourglass ⟋⟋ 1995 (R) Fashion industry honcho Michael Jardine (Howell) risks his reputation and his life when he becomes involved with deadly, revenge-minded seductress Dara (Shinas), who blames the Jardines for her father's suicide. Another in a long line of be careful who you sleep with movies.*CW:* Strong sexuality, and for violence, language and drug use. 91m/C VHS, LV, Closed Caption. C. Thomas Howell, Sofia Shinas, Ed Begley Jr., Timothy Bottoms, Anthony Clark; *D:* C. Thomas Howell; *W:* C. Thomas Howell, Darren Dalton; *C:* John Lambert; *M:* Chris Saranec. *ART*

The Hours and Times ⟋⟋⟋ 1992 A concise drama based on one point of fact used to quietly evoke differences in class, talent, sexual orientation, and unrequited love. The fact is that in the spring of 1963 Brian Epstein, the Beatles brilliant homosexual manager, shared a four-day Barcelona vacation with John Lennon. Director Munch speculates that the sophisticated Epstein was hopelessly in love with the younger, working-class Lennon who is friendly but unresponsive to the courtship. A tender and rueful depiction of friendship longing to be something more. 60m/B VHS. David Angus, Ian Hart, Stephanie Pack, Robin McDonald, Sergio Moreno, Unity Grimwood; *D:* Christopher Munch; *W:* Christopher Munch. Sundance Film Festival '92: Special Jury Prize. *FXL, BTV*

House ⟋ 1986 (R) A horror novelist moves into his dead aunt's supposedly haunted house only to find that the monsters don't necessarily stay in the closets. His worst nightmares come to life as he writes about his Vietnam experiences and is forced to relive the tragic events, but these aren't the only visions that start springing to life. It sounds depressing, but is actually a funny, intelligent "horror" flick. Followed by several lesser sequels. **93m/C VHS, Beta, LV, Closed Caption.** William Katt, George Wendt, Richard Moll, Kay Lenz, Michael Ensign, Mary Stavin, Susan French; *D:* Steve Miner; *W:* Ethan Wiley; *C:* Mac Ahlberg; *M:* Harry Manfredini. *VTR*

House 2: The Second Story ♂ 1987 **(PG-13)** The flaccid sequel to the haunted-house horror flick concerns two innocent guys who move into the family mansion and discover Aztec ghosts. Has none of the humor which helped the first movie along. **88m/C VHS, Beta, LV, Closed Caption.** John Ratzenberger, Arye Gross, Royal Dano, Bill Maher, Jonathan Stark, Lar Park Lincoln, Amy Yasbeck, Devin Devasquez; *D:* Ethan Wiley; *W:* Ethan Wiley; *C:* Mac Ahlberg. *VTR*

House 4: Home Deadly Home ♂½ 1991 **(R)** Another bad real estate epic on a par with the other unusually inept "House" efforts. When her husband (Katt) is killed in an auto accident, a young woman and her daughter move into a mysterious old house. Terror begins to confront them at every turn, threatening to destroy them both. We can only hope. *CW:* Language and fantasy/horror violence. **91m/C VHS, LV, Closed Caption.** Terri Treas, Scott Burkholder, Melissa Clayton, William Katt, Ned Romero; *D:* Lewis Abernathy. *COL, NLC*

House Across the Bay ♂♂½ 1940 Raft, an imprisoned nightclub owner, finds that he is being duped by his attorney who's eager to get his hooks into the lingerie-clad prisoner's wife. But prison isn't going to stop the bitter husband from getting his revenge. **88m/B VHS, Beta.** George Raft, Walter Pidgeon, Joan Bennett, Lloyd Nolan, Gladys George; *D:* Archie Mayo. *NO*

House Arrest ♂½ 1996 **(PG)** Another tired kids-think-they-know-best formula film. When Grover Beindorf (Howard) and his younger sister learn that their constantly fighting parents (Curtis and Pollak) are separating, they lock them in the basement where they'll be forced to sort things out. Word gets around and some school pals kidnap their problem parents and stash them in the basement with the Beindorfs. Most of the movie was actually shot in a basement; watch for Curtis hanging upside down in a laundry chute "True Lies" style. **107m/C VHS, Closed Caption.** Jamie Lee Curtis, Kevin Pollak, Christopher McDonald, Jennifer Tilly, Caroline Aaron, Wallace Shawn, Sheila McCarthy, Ray Walston, Kyle Howard, Jennifer Love Hewitt; *D:* Harry Winer; *W:* Michael Hitchcock; *C:* Ueli Steiger; *M:* Bruce Broughton. *HBO*

The House by the Cemetery ♂ *Quella Villa Accanto Al Cimitero* 1983 **(R)** When a family moves into a house close to a cemetery, strange things start to happen to them. **84m/C VHS, Beta.** *IT* Katherine MacColl, Paolo Malco; *D:* Lucio Fulci. *ART, VES*

House Calls ♂♂♂ 1978 **(PG)** A widowed surgeon turns into a swinging bachelor until he meets a witty but staid English divorcee. Wonderful dialogue. Jackson is exceptional. Made into a short-lived TV series. **98m/C VHS, Beta, LV.** Walter Matthau, Glenda Jackson, Art Carney, Richard Benjamin, Candice Azzara; *D:* Howard Zieff; *W:* Charles Shyer; *M:* Henry Mancini. *USH*

The House in Marsh Road ♂♂ 1960 A faithless husband decides to rid himself of She Who Must Be Obeyed, but his wife's ghost-friend intervenes. **70m/B VHS.** *GB* Tony Wright, Patricia Dainton, Sandra Dorne, Derek Aylward, Sam Kydd; *D:* Montgomery Tully. *SNC*

A House in the Hills ♂♂ 1993 **(R)** A struggling actress is housesitting at a luxurious estate and innocently lets in the exterminator. Except he's an ex-con looking for revenge on the home's current occupant (whom the actress is pretending to be) and may just exterminate her instead. **91m/C VHS, LV, Closed Caption.** Helen Slater, Michael Madsen, Jeffrey Tambor, James Laurenson, Elyssa

Davalos, Toni Barry; *D:* Ken Wiederhorn; *W:* Ken Wiederhorn, J. Josep Civit, M: Richard Einhorn. *ART*

House of Angels ♂♂ *Anglagard; Colin Nutley's House of Angels* 1992 **(R)** Charming comedy, with some serious overtones, about what happens to the gossipy inhabitants of a small Swedish village when two free-spirited newcomers come to stay. Fanny and her friend Zac, who are cabaret performers, show up at the funeral of eccentric Erik, who turns out to be the grandfather Fanny never knew. With her outrageous clothes and attitude, Fanny has most of the neighbors scandalized but what the generous Fanny wants is some information about her past, including who her father might be. What the neighbors want is for Fanny and Zac to leave as quickly as possible. In Swedish with English subtitles. **119m/C VHS.** *SW* Helena Bergstrom, Rikard Wolff, Sven Wollter, Jakob Eklund, Viveka Seldahl, Ernst Gunter, Reine Brynolfsson, Per Oscarsson; *D:* Colin Nutley; *W:* Susanne Falck. *COL, FCT*

House of Cards ♂♂♂ 1990 Depicts the political machinations of Machiavellian Tory whip Francis Urquhart (Richardson), who schemes to bring down the present government so that he can become the next Prime Minister. And there's absolutely nothing "F.U." (as he's appropriately known) won't do to achieve power. Followed by "To Play the King" and "The Final Cut"; based on the novel Michael Dobbs. On two cassettes. **200m/C VHS, Closed Caption.** *GB* Ian Richardson, Susannah Harker. *FOX, TVC*

House of Cards ♂♂½ 1992 **(PG-13)** Precocious six-year-old Sally (Menina) suddenly stops talking after her father is killed in an accident at an archeological site in Mexico. Mom Ruth (Turner) fights to bring her daughter out of her fantasy world and seeks medical advice from a psychiatrist (a sympathetic Jones) but ignores it when it clashes with her own theories. The ethereal Menina, in her acting debut, gives the best performance in this weakly plotted and confusing family saga. *CW:* Mild profanity. **109m/C VHS, LV, Closed Caption.** Kathleen Turner, Asha Menina, Tommy Lee Jones, Shiloh Strong, Esther Rolle, Park Overall, Michael Horse, Anne Pitoniak; *D:* Michael Lessac; *W:* Michael Lessac. *ART, BTV, FCT*

House of Dark Shadows ♂♂ 1970 **(PG)** A 150-year-old vampire, accidentally released by a handyman, wreaks havoc on the inhabitants of the Collinswood mansion. Based on the TV daytime soap. **97m/C VHS, Beta.** Jonathan Frid, Joan Bennett, Grayson Hall, Kathryn Leigh Scott, Roger Davis, Nancy Barrett, John Karlen, Thayer David, Louis Edmonds; *D:* Dan Curtis; *W:* Sam Hall, Gordon Russell; *C:* Arthur Ornitz. *MGM, FUS*

House of Death ♂ 1982 **(R)** The ex-Playmate of the Year runs in hysterical fear from a knife-wielding lunatic. **88m/C VHS, Beta.** Susan Kiger, William T. Hicks, Jody Kay, Martin Tucker, Jennifer Chase. *GEM*

The House of Dies Drear 1988 A modern-day African American family moves into an old house that turns out to be haunted by the ghost of a long dead abolitionist. The family is transported back to the days of slavery as they interact with the ghost. Based on the story by Virginia Hamilton. Aired on PBS as part of the "Wonderworks" family movie series. **107m/C VHS.** Howard E. Rollins Jr., Moses Gunn, Shavar Ross, Gloria Foster, Clarence Williams III; *D:* Allan Goldstein. *HMV, FCT*

House of Dracula ♂ 1945 Sequel to "House of Frankenstein" features several of the Universal monsters. Overly ambitious story gets a bit hokey, but it's entertaining nonetheless. **67m/B VHS, LV, Closed Caption.** Lon Chaney Jr., Martha O'Driscoll, John Carradine, Lionel Atwill, Onslow Stevens, Glenn Strange, Jane Adams, Ludwig Stossel; *D:* Erle C. Kenton; *W:* Edward T. Lowe; *C:* George Robinson. *USH, FCT*

House of Dreams ♂ 1964 Berry is a blocked writer coping with domestic difficulties whose dreams reveal a disturbing future. Contains a bit part for Goodnow, now a CNN talking head. **80m/B VHS.** Robert Berry, Pauline Elliott, Charlene Bradley, Lance Bird, David Goodnow; *D:* Robert Berry. *LSV*

The House of Eliott 1992 BBC miniseries set in 1920s London finds the orphaned Beatrice and Evangeline Eliott struggling to begin their fashion business as couturiers to the rich and influential, which eventually leads to their founding of the House of Eliott. Lots of romance and intrigue along the way. Boxed set of six cassettes. **600m/C VHS.** *GB* Stella Gonet, Louise Lombard, Aden Gillett, Richard Lintern. *SIG, AEH, VCO*

House of Errors ♂½ 1942 Two delivery-men pose as reporters to safeguard a prototype machine gun from the bad guys. Contrived plot consisting of outdated comic routines. This was Marsh's last film. **63m/B VHS.** Harry Langdon, Marian Marsh, Ray Walker, Betty Blythe, John Holland; *D:* Bernard B. Ray. *NOS*

House of Fear ♂♂½ 1945 Holmes and Watson investigate the murders of several members of the Good Comrades Club, men who were neither good nor comradely. **69m/B VHS, Beta, Closed Caption.** Basil Rathbone, Nigel Bruce, Dennis Hoey, Aubrey Mather, Paul Cavanagh, Gavin Muir; *D:* Roy William Neill. *FOX*

House of Frankenstein ♂♂½ 1944 An evil scientist (Karloff) escapes from prison, and, along with his hunchback manservant, revives Dracula, Frankenstein's monster, and the Wolfman to carry out his dastardly deeds. An all-star cast helps this horror fest along. **71m/B VHS, LV.** Boris Karloff, J. Carrol Naish, Lon Chaney Jr., John Carradine, Elena Verdugo, Anne Gwynne, Lionel Atwill, Peter Coe, George Zucco, Glenn Strange, Sig Rumann; *D:* Erle C. Kenton; *W:* Edward T. Lowe; *C:* George Robinson. *USH*

House of Games ♂♂♂ 1987 **(R)** The directorial debut of playwright Mamet is a tale about an uptight female psychiatrist who investigates the secret underworld of con-artistry and becomes increasingly involved in an elaborate con game. She's led along her crooked path by smooth-talking con-master Mantegna. A taut, well plotted psychological suspense film with many twists and turns. Stylishly shot, with dialogue which has that marked Mamet cadence. Most of the leads are from Mamet's theatre throng (including his wife, Crouse). **102m/C VHS, Beta, LV.** Joe Mantegna, Lindsay Crouse, Lilia Skala, J.T. Walsh, Meshach Taylor, Ricky Jay, Mike Nussbaum, Willo Hausman; *D:* David Mamet; *W:* David Mamet; *C:* Juan Ruiz-Anchia; *M:* Alaric Jans. *HBO, FCT*

House of Horrors ♂♂½ 1946 Deformed murderer "The Creeper" (Hatton) is used by a mad sculptor in a twisted revenge plot. Marcel De Lange (Kosleck) believes his work has been vilely abused by art critics so he uses his friend's homicidal urges to get rid of anyone who stands in his way. **76m/B VHS, Closed Caption.** Martin Kosleck, Rondo Hatton, Robert Lowery, Virginia Grey, Bill Goodwin, Alan Napier, Joan Shawlee, Howard Freeman; *D:* Jean Yarbrough; *W:* George Bricker. *USH*

The House of Lurking Death ♂½ 1984 Detectives Tommy and Tuppence find a box of chocolates laced with arsenic at the home of Lois Hargreaves, and the mad old maid is the prime suspect. Based on the Agatha Christie story. Made for British television. **60m/C VHS, Beta.** *GB* James Warwick, Francesca Annis. *TPV*

House of Mystery ♂♂ 1934 For a shot at some priceless jewels stolen by the host from a Hindu princess, several guests gather for a weekend in a spine-tingling mansion. A creepy curse keeps them looking over their shoulders. **62m/C VHS.** Ed Lowry, Verna Hillie, Brandon Hurst, George "Gabby" Hayes; *D:* William Nigh. *SNC, DVT, MLB*

House of Mystery 🎬🎬½ *At the Villa Rose* 1941 Splendid British remake of 1934 film in which the detective does some true sleuthing to catch the culprits. An old widow is killed for her jewels, but the murderers can't locate the goods. After they try a series of fiendish plans to retrieve them, the detective must work to stop the crooks. **61m/B VHS.** *GB* Keneth Kent, Judy Kelly, Peter Murray Hill, Walter Rilla, Ruth Maitland; *D:* Walter Summers. *NOS, DVT*

The House of 1000 Dolls 🎬 *Haus Der Tausend Freuden* 1967 Doleful, not dollful, exploitation thriller as magician Price drugs young girls and sells them to slavery rings. An international production set in Tangiers; dialogue is dubbed. **79m/C VHS, Beta.** *GE SP GB* Vincent Price, Martha Hyer, George Nader, Ann Smyrner, Maria Rohm; *D:* Jeremy Summers. *HBO*

House of Psychotic Women woof! *Los Ojos Azules de la Muneca Rota* 1973 (R) Naschy, Spain's premier horror movie star, plays a studly drifter who winds up in the home of three sisters, one with an artifical arm, one confined to a wheelchair and the other a nymphomaniac. No problemo thinks the hirsute Spaniard, until a series of bizarre murders—in which the victims eyes are ripped out—spoils his fun. Naschy, who usually sprouts fur and fangs, actually doesn't turn into a werewolf. Catchy but inappropriate score. A must for Naschy/bad movie fans. **87m/C VHS, Beta.** *SP* Paul Naschy, Maria Perschy, Diana Lorys, Eva Leon, Ines Morales, Tony Pica; *D:* Carlos Aured; *W:* Paul Naschy. *NO*

The House of Secrets 🎬🎬 1937 A Yank travels to Britain to collect an inheritance and stays in a dusty old mansion filled with an odd assortment of characters. **70m/B VHS, Beta.** Leslie Fenton, Muriel Evans, Noel Madison, Sidney Blackmer, Morgan Wallace, Holmes Herbert; *D:* Roland D. Reed. *SNC*

The House of Seven Corpses 🎬🎬 1973 (PG) A crew attempts to film a horror movie in a Victorian manor where seven people died in a variety of gruesome manners. Things take a turn for the ghoulish when a crew member becomes possesed by the house's evil spirits. Good, low budget fun with a competent "B" cast. Filmed in what was the Utah governor's mansion. **90m/C VHS.** John Ireland, Faith Domergue, John Carradine, Carole Wells; *D:* Paul Harrison. *GEM, MRV, CNG*

House of Shadows 🎬½ 1983 A 20-year-old murder comes back to haunt the victim's friends in this tale of mystery and terror. **90m/C VHS, Beta.** John Gavin, Yvonne De Carlo, Leonor Manso; *D:* Richard Wulicher.

House of Strangers 🎬🎬🎬½ 1949 Conte, in a superb performance, swears vengeance on his brothers, whom he blames for his father's death. Robinson, in a smaller part than you'd expect from his billing, is nevertheless excellent as the ruthless banker father who sadly reaps a reward he didn't count on. Based on Philip Yordan's "I'll Never Go There Again." **101m/B VHS, Closed Caption.** Edward G. Robinson, Susan Hayward, Richard Conte, Luther Adler, Efrem Zimbalist Jr., Debra Paget; *D:* Joseph L. Mankiewicz; *W:* Philip Yordan; *C:* Milton Krasner. Cannes Film Festival '49: Best Actor (Robinson). *FOX, FCT*

House of Terror 🎬 1987 A woman and her boyfriend plot to kill her rich boss, while they too are being stalked by some undefined horror. **91m/C VHS, Beta.** Jennifer Bishop, Arell Blanton, Jacquelyn Hyde. *TWE*

The House of the Arrow 🎬🎬🎬 1953 Investigating the murder of a French widow, who was killed by a poisoned arrow, a detective must sort through a grab bag of potential suspects. Superior adaptation of the A.E.W. Mason thriller. **73m/B VHS, Beta.** *GB* Oscar Homolka, Yvonne Furneaux, Robert Urquhart; *D:* Michael Anderson Sr. *NOS, SNC*

House of the Black Death 🎬½ *Blood of the Man Devil; Night of the Beast* 1965 Horror titans Chaney and Carradine manage to co-star in this as warring warlocks, yet they share no scenes together! Chaney is the evil warlock (the horns

---

are a giveaway) holding people hostage in the title edifice. **89m/B VHS.** Lon Chaney Jr., John Carradine, Katherine Victor, Tom Drake, Andrea King; *D:* Harold Daniels, Reginald LeBorg. *NOS, LOO*

House of the Damned 🎬½ 1971 A young woman, a mental hospital, a murdered father, a priceless gold statue—mix together and you get a mystery horror movie. A woman tries to solve her father's murder. **89m/C VHS, Beta.** Donald Pleasence, Michael Dunn; *D:* Gonzolo Suarez. *NO*

House of the Dead 🎬 1980 Man is trapped inside a haunted house. Scary. **100m/C VHS.** John Ericson, Charles Aidman, Bernard Fox, Ivor Francis. *NO*

House of the Living Dead 🎬 *Doctor Maniac* 1973 (PG) Brattling Manor harbors a murderous and flesh-eating secret ready to lure the unsuspecting. Don't you be one. **87m/C VHS, Beta.** *SA* Mark Burns, Shirley Anne Field, David Oxley; *D:* Ray Austin. *VCI, HHE*

House of the Long Shadows 🎬½ 1982 (PG) Comedy mixes with gore, as four of the horror screen's best leading men team up for the first time, although they have only minor roles. Might have been a contender, but Arnaz is miscast as author who stays in spooky house on a bet with Todd. Some wit but not enough. Based on the play "Seven Keys to Baldpate" by George M. Cohan (and novel by Earl Derr Biggers). **96m/C VHS, Beta.** *GB* Vincent Price, Christopher Lee, Peter Cushing, John Carradine, Desi Arnaz Jr., Sheila Keith, Richard Todd; *D:* Pete Walker; *W:* Michael Armstrong; *C:* Norman G. Langley. *MGM*

House of the Rising Sun 🎬½ 1987 A Los Angeles reporter goes under cover for a story on an exclusive brothel only to discover the owner is a psychopath who has very permanent ways of dealing with troublesome employees. **86m/C VHS, Beta.** John York, Bud Davis, Deborah Wakeham, Frank Annese; *D:* Greg Gold; *M:* Tina Turner, Bryan Ferry. *PAR*

The House of the Seven Gables 🎬🎬½ 1940 Nathaniel Hawthorne's brooding novel about greed and a family curse. Jaffrey Pyncheon (Sanders) frames his brother Clifford (Price) for the murder of their father so that he can search in peace for the fortune Jaffrey believes is hidden somewhere in the family mansion, Seven Gables. But, eventually, Clifford gets out of prison and returns to claim his birthright. The studio built an exact duplicate of the original Salem house. **89m/B VHS, Closed Caption.** George Sanders, Vincent Price, Margaret Lindsay, Dick Foran, Nan Grey, Cecil Kellaway, Alan Napier; *D:* Joe May; *W:* Harold Greene; *C:* Milton Krasner. *USH*

The House of the Spirits 🎬🎬 1993 (R) Star-studded adaptation of the novel by Isabel Allende is a multi-generational saga following the fortunes of the powerful Trueba family. The ambitious Esteban (Irons) marries the clairvoyant Clara (Streep), exploits the peasants on his property, and becomes a conservative senator. Their rebellious daughter Blanca (Ryder) falls for rabble-rousing peasant Pedro (Banderas), and the country undergoes a bloody revolution. Magical realism of the novel is lost in screen melodrama, with the international cast ill-served by tepid direction. The child Clara is played by Streep's daughter, Mary Willa (listed in the credits as Jane Gray). *CW:* Brief nudity, graphic and disturbing violence, and strong sexuality. **109m/C VHS, LV, Letterbox, Closed Caption.** Meryl Streep, Jeremy Irons, Glenn Close, Winona Ryder, Antonio Banderas, Armin Mueller-Stahl, Vanessa Redgrave, Sarita Choudhury, Maria Conchita Alonso, Vincent Gallo, Miriam Colon, Jan Niklas, Teri Polo, Jane Gray; *D:* Bille August; *W:* Bille August; *M:* Hans Zimmer. *ART*

House of the Yellow Carpet 🎬½ 1984 A couple try to sell an ancient Persian carpet heirloom, and in doing so transgress some unwritten mystical law. Havoc ensues. **90m/C VHS, Beta.** Roland Josephson, Beatrice Romand; *D:* Carlo Lizzani. *ART*

The House of Usher 🎬 *Edgar Allen Poe's House of Usher; The Fall of the House of Usher* 1988 (R) Some serious overacting by Reed (as Roderick) and Pleasence (as his balmy brother) almost elevate this Poe retread to "so bad it's good" status, and there are a few admirably grisly moments. But, without other camp virtues, it's merely dreary. Adapted by Michael J. Murray and filmed in South Africa. **92m/C VHS, LV.** *SA* Oliver Reed, Donald Pleasence, Romy Windsor, Rufus Swart, Norman Coombes, Anne Stradi; *D:* Alan Birkinshaw; *W:* Michael J. Murray; *M:* Gary Chang. *COL*

House of Wax 🎬🎬🎬 1953 (PG) A deranged sculptor (Price, who else?) builds a sinister wax museum which showcases creations that were once alive. A remake of the early horror flick "Mystery of the Wax Museum," and one of the 50s' most popular 3-D films. This one still has the power to give the viewer the creeps, thanks to another chilling performance by Price. Look for a very young Charles Bronson, as well as Carolyn "Morticia Addams" Jones as a victim. **88m/C VHS, Beta, LV.** Vincent Price, Frank Lovejoy, Carolyn Jones, Phyllis Kirk, Paul Cavanagh, Charles Bronson, Paul Picerni; *D:* Andre de Toth; *W:* Crane Wilbur; *C:* Bert Glennon. *WAR, MLB*

House of Whipcord woof! 1975 Beautiful young women are kidnapped and tortured in this British gore-o-rama. Awful and degrading. **102m/C VHS, Beta.** *GB* Barbara Markham, Patrick Barr, Ray Brooks, Penny Irving, Anne Michelle; *D:* Pete Walker. *MON, ART*

The House of Yes 🎬🎬 1997 (R) Thanksgiving certainly brings out the worst in families although the Pascal clan is dysfunction personified. Marty (Hamilton) brings home fiancee Lesley (Spelling) to meet his eccentric mom (Bujold) and siblings. Younger brother Anthony's (Prinze) a dropout with no direction and Marty's twin sister Jackie-O (Parker) is bonkers. She's recreated herself as Jackie Kennedy Onassis and has had a very intimate relationship with Marty that Lesley probably doesn't know about. *CW:* Language, perverse sex-related situations, and an image of violence. **90m/C VHS, LV, Closed Caption.** Parker Posey, Josh Hamilton, Tori Spelling, Freddie Prinze Jr., Genevieve Bujold, Rachel Leigh Cook; *D:* Mark Waters; *W:* Mark Waters; *C:* Michael Spiller; *M:* Jeff Rona. Nominations: Golden Raspberry Awards '97: Worst New Star (Spelling). *TOU*

The House on Carroll Street 🎬½ 1988 (PG) New York 1951, the middle of the McCarthy era. A young woman overhears a plot to smuggle Nazi war criminals into the U.S. She's already lost her job because of accusations of subversion, and it's not easy persuading FBI agent Daniels that she knows what she's talking about. Contrived plot and melodramatic finale help sink this period piece. **111m/C VHS, Beta, LV, Closed Caption.** Kelly McGillis, Jeff Daniels, Mandy Patinkin, Jessica Tandy; *D:* Peter Yates; *W:* Walter Bernstein; *C:* Michael Ballhaus; *M:* Georges Delerue. *HBO*

The House on Chelouche Street 🎬🎬½ 1973 In Tel-Aviv, during the summer of 1946, 15-year-old Sami, an Egyptian immigrant, tries to help support his mother and family during the upheavals of Palestine under the British mandate. A well thought-out story detailing the struggles of a North African Jewish family before the creation of the country of Israel. In Hebrew with English subtitles. **111m/C VHS, Beta.** *IS* Gila Almagor, Michal Bat-Adam, Shai K. Ophir; *D:* Moshe Mizrahi. Nominations: Academy Awards '73: Best Foreign Language Film. *VYY, NCJ, AUD*

The House on Garibaldi Street 🎬🎬½ 1979 Spy drama about the capture of Nazi war criminal Adolph Eichmann in Argentina and his extradition to Israel for trial. Based on the book by Isser Harel. Made for television. **96m/C VHS, Beta.** Chaim Topol, Nick Mancuso, Martin Balsam, Janet Suzman, Leo McKern, Charles Gray, Alfred Burke; *D:* Peter Collinson; *M:* Charles Bernstein. *SWC*

House on Haunted Hill 🎬🎬½ 1958 A wealthy man throws a haunted house party and offers ten thousand dollars to anyone who can survive the night there. Vintage cheap horror from the master of the macabre Castle. Remembered for Castle's in-theatre gimmick of dangling a skeleton over the audiences' heads in the film's initial release. Also available with "Attack of the 50-Foot Woman" on laserdisc. **75m/B VHS, Beta, LV, Closed Caption.** Vincent Price, Carol Ohmart, Richard Long, Alan Marshal, Carolyn Craig, Elisha Cook Jr.; **D:** William Castle; **W:** Robb White; **C:** Carl Guthrie. FOX, FCT, MLB

House on 92nd Street 🎬🎬🎬 1945 Documentary-style thriller finds federal investigator George Briggs (Nolan) contacted by German-American student Bill Dietrich (Eythe), who's been sought out by Nazi spies. Briggs encourages Dietrich to play along and report their nefarious activities to the feds. What Dietrich discovers is that a scientist, working on the atomic bomb project, is actually a Nazi agent. Lots of atmosphere and action, with director Hathaway incorporating newsreel footage to highlight the true-to-life feel. Title refers the house where the head of the Nazi spies resides. **89m/B VHS, Closed Caption.** William Eythe, Lloyd Nolan, Signe Hasso, Gene Lockhart, Leo G. Carroll, William Post Jr., Harry Bellaver; **D:** Henry Hathaway; **W:** Barre Lyndon, John Monks Jr., Charles G. Booth; **C:** Norbert Brodine; **M:** David Buttolph. Academy Awards '45: Best Story. FXV

The House on Skull Mountain 🎬½ 1974 (PG) The four surviving relatives of a deceased voodoo priestess are in for a bumpy night as they gather at the House on Skull Mountain for the reading of her will. **85m/C VHS, Beta, Closed Caption.** Victor French, Janee Michelle, Mike Evans, Jean Durand; **D:** Ron Honthaner. FOX

The House on Sorority Row 🎬½ *House of Evil; Seven Sisters* 1983 Less-than-harrowing story of what happens when seven sorority sisters have a last fling and get back at their housemother at the same time. **90m/C VHS, Beta, LV.** Eileen Davidson, Kate McNeil, Robin Meloy, Lois Kelso Hunt, Christopher Lawrence, Janis Zido; **D:** Mark Rosman; **W:** Mark Rosman; **C:** Tim Suhrstedt; **M:** Richard Band. VES

The House on Straw Hill 🎬½ *Expose; Trauma* 1976 (R) A successful novelist is intrigued by an attractive woman who lives in an isolated farmhouse. Her presence inspires gory hallucinations, lust, and violence. **84m/C VHS, Beta.** GB Udo Kier, Linda Hayden, Fiona Richmond, Karl Howman, Patsy Smart; **D:** James Kenelm Clarke; **W:** James Kenelm Clarke; **C:** Denis Lewiston.

House on the Edge of the Park woof! *La Casa Nel Parco* 1984 A frustrated would-be womanizer takes revenge on a parade of women during an all-night party. **91m/C VHS, Beta.** IT David Hess, Annie Belle, Lorraine De Selle; **D:** Ruggero Deodato. ART, VES

The House on Todville Road 🎬 1995 (R) Fact-based story about a dangerous cult and its followers. **94m/C VHS.** David Harrod, Terri Harrel, Lisa Marie Newmeyer. TCE

The House on Tombstone Hill 🎬½ 1992 An old, abandoned mansion seems like a good investment to a group of friends. Wrong! The original owner is still around and doesn't like strangers coming to visit. **95m/C VHS.** Doug Gibson, John Cerna, Sarah Newhouse; **D:** J. Riffel; **W:** J. Riffel.

House Party 🎬🎬🎬 1990 (R) Light-hearted, black hip-hop version of a '50s teen comedy with rap duo Kid 'n' Play. After his father grounds him for fighting, a high-schooler attempts all sorts of wacky schemes to get to his friend's party. Sleeper hit features real-life music rappers and some dynamite dance numbers. **100m/C VHS, Beta, LV.** Christopher Reid, Christopher Martin, Martin Lawrence, Tisha Campbell, Paul Anthony, A.J. Johnson, Robin Harris; **D:** Reginald Hudlin; **W:** Reginald Hudlin; **M:** Marcus Miller. Sundance Film Festival '90: Best Cinematography. NLC, FCT

House Party 2: The Pajama Jam 🎬🎬½ 1991 (R) Rap stars Kid 'N' Play are back in this hip-hop sequel to the original hit. At Harris University Kid 'N' Play hustle up overdue tuition by holding a campus "jammie jam jam." A stellar cast shines in this rap-powered pajama bash. **CW:** Language and sensuality. **94m/C VHS, LV, Closed Caption.** Christopher Reid, Christopher Martin, Tisha Campbell, Iman, Queen Latifah, Georg Stanford Brown, Martin Lawrence, Eugene Allen, George Anthony Bell, Kamron, Tony Burton, Helen Martin, William Schallert; **D:** Doug McHenry, George Jackson; **W:** Rusty Cundieff, Daryl G. Nickens; **M:** Vassal Benford. NLC

House Party 3 🎬 1994 (R) Kid is engaged to be married and Play tries to set up a blowout bachelor party. The duo are also working on their record producer careers by trying to sign a feisty female rap group (real life TLC). Strikes out early for easy profanity while never coming within spitting distance of first two flicks. **CW:** Strong language and sexual suggestiveness. **93m/C VHS, LV, Closed Caption.** Christopher Reid, Christopher Martin, Angela Means, Tisha Campbell, Bernie Mac, Barbara Edwards, Michael Colyar, David Edwards, Betty Lester, Chris Tucker; **D:** Eric Meza; **W:** Takashi Bufford; **M:** David Allen Jones. COL, IME

The House that Bled to Death 🎬 1981 Strange things happen to a family when they move into a run-down house where a murder occurred years before. **60m/C VHS, Beta.** Nicholas Ball, Rachel Davies, Brian Croucher, Pat Maynard, Emma Ridley. ART

The House that Dripped Blood 🎬🎬½ 1971 (PG) A Scotland Yard inspector discovers the history of an English country house while investigating an actor's disappearance. Four horror tales comprise the body of this omnibus creeper, following the successful "Tales from the Crypt" mold. Duffell's debut as director. **101m/C VHS, Beta.** GB Christopher Lee, Peter Cushing, Jon Pertwee, Denholm Elliott, Ingrid Pitt, John Bennett, Tom Adams, Joss Ackland, Chloe Franks; **D:** Peter Duffell; **W:** Robert Bloch.

The House that Vanished 🎬 *Scream and Die; Psycho Sex Fiend* 1973 (R) Semi-exploitative fare about a beautiful young model who witnesses a murder in a house but later can't find the place. Her boyfriend is skeptical. **84m/C VHS, Beta.** GB Andrea Allan, Karl Lanchbury, Judy Matheson, Maggie Walker, Alex Leppard; **D:** Joseph Jose Ramon Larraz. ART

House Where Evil Dwells 🎬½ 1982 (R) An American family is subjected to a reign of terror when they move into an old Japanese house possessed by three deadly samurai ghosts. The setting doesn't upgrade the creepiness of the plot. Based on a novel by James Hardiman. **88m/C VHS, Beta.** Edward Albert, Susan George, Doug McClure, Amy Barett, Mako Hattori, Toshiya Maruyama, Henry Mitowa, Tsuyako Okajima, Tsuiyuki Sasaki; **D:** Kevin Connor; **W:** Robert Subotsky; **C:** Jacques Haitkin. MGM

A House Without a Christmas Tree 🎬🎬½ 1972 A frustrated middle-aged man denies his young daughter her one desire—a Christmas tree. Charming made for cable television holiday fare. **90m/C VHS, Beta.** Jason Robards Jr., Lisa Lucas, Mildred Natwick; **D:** Paul Bogart. FCT

Houseboat 🎬🎬½ 1958 Widower Grant with three precocious kids takes up residence on a houseboat with Italian maid Loren who is actually a socialite, incognito. Naturally, they fall in love. Light, fun Hollywood froth. **110m/C Beta, LV.** Cary Grant, Sophia Loren, Martha Hyer, Eduardo Ciannelli, Murray Hamilton, Harry Guardino; **D:** Melville Shavelson; **W:** Melville Shavelson, Jack Rose; **M:** George Duning. Nominations: Academy Awards '58: Best Song ("Almost in Your Arms (Love Song from Houseboat)"), Best Story & Screenplay. PAR

Houseguest 🎬🎬 1994 (PG) Dumb comedy about mistaken identity finds hard luck dreamer Kevin Franklin (Sinbad) on the run from loan sharks. Fortunately, while trying to make a getaway at the airport, he's mistaken for the childhood buddy (who's also an eminent dentist prompting some hygiene humor) of family guy/lawyer Gary Young (Hartman), who opens his suburban home to his long lost pal. Street smart Kevin naturally manages to solve every dysfunctional family problem that arises while avoiding some inept Mafia thugs. Everyone is oh-so-good-natured but there's nothing new to hold much interest. **109m/C VHS, LV, Closed Caption.** Sinbad, Phil Hartman, Jeffrey Jones, Kim Greist, Stan Shaw, Tony Longo, Mason Adams, Paul Ben-Victor, Chauncey Leopardi, Ron Glass, Talia Seider, Kim Murphy; **D:** Randall Miller; **W:** Michael J. Di Gaetano, Laurence Gay; **C:** Jerzy Zielinski; **M:** John Debney. TOU

Household Saints 🎬🎬🎬 1993 (R) Chronicling one family from post-WWII Little Italy through the 1970s, this is a quirky little story about sausage, religion, women, and families (not necessarily in that order). Joseph (D'Onofrio) wins his bride (Ullman) in a pinochle game, much to his superstitious Catholic mother's (Malina) chagrin. The product of that union is a slightly obsessive girl (Taylor), who sees visions and wants to be a saint. Interesting study of Italian-American families, and the roles religion and food play in the culture of Little Italy. **124m/C VHS, Closed Caption.** Tracey Ullman, Vincent D'Onofrio, Lili Taylor, Judith Malina, Michael Rispoli, Victor Argo, Michael Imperioli, Rachael Bella, Illeana Douglas, Joe Grifasi, Sebastien Roche; **D:** Nancy Savoca; **W:** Nancy Savoca, Richard Guay; **C:** Bobby Bukowski; **M:** Stephen Endelman. Independent Spirit Awards '94: Best Supporting Actress (Taylor); Nominations: Independent Spirit Awards '94: Best Actor (D'Onofrio), Best Screenplay. COL

The Householder 🎬🎬 *Gharbar* 1963 An early Merchant-Ivory collaboration featuring a young Indian schoolteacher whose widowed mother arranges his marriage to a woman he doesn't know. The immature couple find their adjustment to marriage fraught with, sometimes amusing, complications. **101m/B VHS, LV.** IN Shashi Kapoor, Leela Naidu, Durga Khote; **D:** James Ivory; **W:** Ruth Prawer Jhabvala. CVC

The Housekeeper 🎬🎬 *A Judgement in Stone* 1986 (R) Tushingham's portrayal of a deranged housekeeper brings this movie to life even as she kills off her employers. **97m/C VHS, Beta, LV, Closed Caption.** CA Rita Tushingham, Ross Petty, Jackie Burroughs, Tom Kneebone, Shelly Peterson, Jessica Stern, Jonathan Crombie; **D:** Ousama Rawi. WAR

Housekeeping 🎬🎬🎬 1987 (PG) A quiet but bizarre comedy by Forsyth (his first American film). A pair of orphaned sisters are cared for by their newly arrived eccentric, free-spirited aunt in a small and small-minded community in Oregon in the 1950s. Conventional townspeople attempt to intervene, but the sisters' relationship with their offbeat aunt has become strong enough to withstand the coercion of the townspeople. May move too slowly for some viewers. Based on novel by Marilynne Robinson. **117m/C VHS, Beta, Closed Caption.** Christine Lahti, Sarah Walker, Andrea Burchill; **D:** Bill Forsyth; **W:** Bill Forsyth; **C:** Michael Coulter; **M:** Michael Gibbs. COL

Housemaster 🎬🎬½ 1938 In a British boys' school the housemaster is kind and understanding of his sometimes-unruly charges. The stern new headmaster is not, and the students conspire against him. An okay but dated comedy, featuring characters with names like Bimbo and Button. Based on "Bachelor Born" by Ian Hay, a London stage hit at the time. **95m/B VHS.** Otto Kruger, Diana Churchill, Phillips Holmes, Rene Ray, Walter Hudd, George L. Baxt, Cecil Parker, Michael Shepley, Jimmy Hanley, Rosamund Barnes; **D:** Herbert Brenon. NOS, MLB

Housesitter 🎬🎬½ 1992 (PG) Newton Davis (Martin), an architect/dreamer, builds his high school sweetheart (Delany) a beautiful house and surprises her with a marriage proposal. Delany says no, he has a one-night stand with Gwen (Hawn), and Hawn moves into his empty house and assumes the position of Davis's wife, unbeknownst to him. Gwen spins whoppers of lies and soon has the entire town, including Davis's parents and ex-girlfriend, believing her wacky stories. This romantic screwball comedy is a delight, not only because of Martin and Hawn, but also because of the array of other characters who complicate the stories they spin. **102m/C VHS, Beta, LV, Closed Caption, DVD.** Steve Martin, Goldie Hawn, Dana Delany, Julie Harris, Donald Moffat, Peter MacNicol, Richard B. Shull, Laurel Cronin, Christopher Durang; *D:* Frank Oz; *W:* Mark Stein, Brian Grazer; *C:* John A. Alonzo; *M:* Miles Goodman. *USH, PMS, BTV*

Housewife *♂♂* 1972 (R) A vengeful black man who unhappily married Beverly Hills couple hostage in their home. **96m/C VHS, Beta.** Yaphet Kotto, Andrew Duggan, Joyce Van Patten, Jeannie Berlin; *D:* Larry Cohen.

How Come Nobody's On Our Side? *♂* 1973 (PG) Two out-of-work stuntmen try astrology to find the best time to make some easy money smuggling marijuana out of Mexico. **84m/C VHS, Beta.** Adam Roarke, Larry Bishop, Alexandra Hay, Rob Reiner, Penny Marshall; *W:* Leigh Chapman. *NO*

How Funny Can Sex Be? *♂* 1976 (R) Eight risque sketches about love and marriage Italian style. **97m/C VHS, Beta.** *IT* Giancarlo Giannini, Laura Antonelli, Dulio Del Prete; *D:* Dino Risi. *FOX*

How Green Was My Valley *♂♂♂♂* 1941 Compelling story of the trials and tribulations of a Welsh mining family, from the youthful perspective of the youngest child (played by a 13-year-old McDowall). Spans 50 years, from the turn of the century, when coal mining was a difficult but fair-paying way of life, and ends, after unionization, strikes, deaths, and child abuse, with the demise of a town and its culture. Considered by many to be director Ford's finest work. When WWII prevented shooting on location, producer Zanuck built a facsimile Welsh valley in California (although Ford, born Sean Aloysius O'Fearna, was said to have been thinking of his story as taking place in Ireland rather than Wales). Based on the novel by Richard Llewellyn. **118m/C VHS, Beta.** Walter Pidgeon, Maureen O'Hara, Donald Crisp, Anna Lee, Roddy McDowall, John Loder, Sara Allgood, Barry Fitzgerald, Patric Knowles, Rhys Williams, Arthur Shields, Ann Todd, Mae Marsh; *D:* John Ford; *W:* Philip Dunne; *C:* Arthur C. Miller; *M:* Alfred Newman. Academy Awards '41: Best Black and White Cinematography, Best Director (Ford), Best Interior Decoration, Best Picture, Best Supporting Actor (Crisp), National Film Registry '90;; New York Film Critics Awards '41: Best Director (Ford); Nominations: Academy Awards '41: Best Film Editing, Best Screenplay, Best Sound, Best Supporting Actress (Allgood), Best Original Dramatic/Comedy Score. *FOX, FUS, BTV*

How I Got into College *♂♂* 1989 (PG-13) A slack, uninspired satire about a high school senior who barely manages to get into a local college so he may pursue the girl of his dreams. **87m/C VHS, Beta, LV, Closed Caption.** Corey Parker, Lara Flynn Boyle, Christopher Rydell, Anthony Edwards, Phil Hartman, Brian Doyle-Murray, Nora Dunn, Finn Carter, Charles Rocket; *D:* Steve Holland; *W:* Terrel Seltzer; *C:* Robert Elswit. *FOX*

How I Learned to Love Women *♂* 196? A British comedy of errors involving a car-loving youth who learns about women and love. **95m/C VHS, Beta.** *GB* Anita Ekberg. *NO*

How I Won the War *♂♂* 1967 (PG) An inept officer must lead his battalion out of England into the Egyptian desert to conquer a cricket field. Indulgent, scarcely amusing Richard Lester comedy; Lennon, in a bit part, provides the brightest moments. **111m/C VHS, Beta, LV.** *GB* John Lennon, Michael Crawford, Michael Hordern; *D:* Richard Lester; *W:* Charles Wood; *C:* David Watkin. *MGM*

How Many Miles to Babylon? *♂♂* 1982 During WWI, two young men become friends despite their different backgrounds. But one is court-martialed for desertion, and the other is supposed to oversee his execution. Made for British television. **106m/C VHS, Beta.** *GB* Daniel Day-Lewis, Christopher Fairbank; *D:* Moira Armstrong. *FOX, TVC, FUS*

How Sweet It Is! *♂* 1968 Typical American family takes a zany European vacation. Looks like a TV sitcom and is about as entertaining. National Lampoon's version is a lot more fun. **99m/C VHS.** James Garner, Debbie Reynolds, Maurice Ronet, Paul Lynde, Erin Moran, Marcel Dalio, Terry-Thomas; *D:* Jerry Paris; *W:* Jerry Belson; *C:* Lucien Ballard. *WAR*

How Tasty Was My Little Frenchman *♂♂* *Como Era Gostoso O Meu Frances* 1971 French explorer is captured by a cannibal tribe in the jungles of Brazil. He's treated very well and attempts to learn tribal customs to avoid his fate—he's going to be the main course in a ceremonial dinner. French and Tupi with subtitles. **80m/C VHS.** *BR* Arduino Colasanti, Ana Maria Magalhaes, Ital Natur, Eduardo Embassahy; *D:* Nelson Pereira dos Santos. *NYF*

How the Grinch Stole Christmas *♂♂♂* 1965 Classic television Christmas special from the Dr. Seuss book about a Christmas-hating grinch who steals Christmas from the town of Whoville. Fun for the whole family. **26m/C VHS, Beta.** *V:* Boris Karloff. *MGM, KUI, TVC*

How the West was Fun *♂♂½* 1995 The Olsen gals are visiting great godmother Natty's dude ranch, which is in financial difficulty, and must outsmart her greedy son Bart (Mull), a land grabber who wants to turn the ranch into an environmentally unfriendly western theme park. Made for TV. **93m/C VHS, Closed Caption.** Mary-Kate Olsen, Ashley Olsen, Martin Mull, Michele Greene, Patrick Cassidy, Leon Pownall, Peg Phillips; *D:* Stuart Margolin; *M:* Richard Bellis. *WAR*

How the West Was Won *♂♂♂* 1963 (G) A panoramic view of the American West, focusing on the trials, tribulations and travels of three generations of one family, set against the background of wars and historical events. Particularly notable for its impressive cast list and expansive western settings. **165m/C VHS, Beta, LV, Letterbox.** John Wayne, Carroll Baker, Lee J. Cobb, Spencer Tracy, Gregory Peck, Karl Malden, Robert Preston, Eli Wallach, Henry Fonda, George Peppard, Debbie Reynolds, Carolyn Jones, Richard Widmark, James Stewart, Walter Brennan, Andy Devine, Raymond Massey, Agnes Moorehead, Harry (Henry) Morgan, Thelma Ritter, Russ Tamblyn; *D:* John Ford, Henry Hathaway, George Marshall; *W:* James R. Webb; *C:* Milton Krasner, Charles B(ryant) Lang. Academy Awards '63: Best Film Editing, Best Sound, Best Story & Screenplay, National Film Registry '97;; Nominations: Academy Awards '63: Best Art Direction/Set Decoration (Color), Best Color Cinematography, Best Costume Design (Color), Best Picture, Best Original Score. *MGM*

How to Be a Perfect Person in Just Three Days 1984 Fun comedy for the whole family shows the efforts of a kid striving for perfection before realizing that individuality is more fun. Based on the book by Stephen Mane. Aired on PBS as part of the "Wonderworks" series. **58m/C VHS, Closed Caption.** Wallace Shawn, Ilan Mitchell-Smith, Hermione Gingold, Joan Micklin Silver. *FCT, HMV*

How to Beat the High Cost of Living *♂½* 1980 (PG) Three suburban housewives decide to beat inflation by taking up robbery, and they start by planning a heist at the local shopping mall. Comedic talent can't salvage whipped script and direction. **105m/C VHS, Beta.** Jessica Lange, Susan St. James, Jane Curtin, Richard Benjamin, Eddie Albert, Dabney Coleman, Fred Willard, Cathryn Damon, Art Metrano; *D:* Robert Scheerer. *ART, VES*

How to Break Up a Happy Divorce *♂♂* 1976 A divorced woman starts a vigorous campaign to win her ex-husband back by dating another man to make him jealous. Lightweight made-for-television comedy. **74m/C VHS, Beta.** Barbara Eden, Hal Linden, Peter Bonerz, Marcia Rodd, Harold Gould; *D:* Jerry Paris. *WOV*

How to Commit Marriage *♂½* 1969 (PG) Hope and Wyman have been married for 20 years when they decide to divorce—just when their daughter (Cameron) decides to marry her

college boyfriend (Matheson). His father (Gleason) tries to stop the wedding, fails, but sticks around to cause more trouble. Subplots involve the divorced duo's new loves and the fact that they're about to become grandparents but the comedy is completely uninspired. **96m/C VHS.** Bob Hope, Jane Wyman, Jackie Gleason, Joanna Cameron, Tim Matheson, Beatrice Arthur, Leslie Nielsen, Tina Louise, Paul Stewart, Prof. Irwin Corey; *D:* Norman Panama; *W:* Ben Starr, Michael Kanin; *M:* Joseph J. Lilley. *COL*

How to Frame a Figg *♂½* 1971 (G) Bookkeeper Hollis A. Figg (Knotts) is working at Dalton's corrupt city hall where he's setup to be the patsy in the fradulent doings of the mayor and city council. But his best friends Prentiss (Welker) and Ema Letha (Joyce) set out to prove the bumbler's innocence. **103m/C VHS.** Don Knotts, Elaine Joyce, Frank Welker, Joe Flynn, Edward Andrews, Yvonne Craig, Parker Fennelly, Fay DeWitt; *D:* Alan Rafkin; *W:* George Tibbles; *C:* William Margulies; *M:* Vic Mizzy. *USH*

How to Get Ahead in Advertising *♂♂♂* 1989 (R) A cynical, energetic satire about a manic advertising idea man who becomes so disgusted with trying to sell a pimple cream that he quits the business. Ultimately he grows a pimple of his own that talks and begins to take over his life. Acerbic and hilarious. **95m/C VHS, Beta, LV.** *GB* Richard E. Grant, Rachel Ward, Susan Wooldridge, Mick Ford, Richard Wilson, John Shrapnel, Jacqueline Tong; *D:* Bruce Robinson; *W:* Bruce Robinson; *M:* David Dundas, Rick Wentworth. *FCT, VTR, CRC*

How to Kill 400 Duponts *♂* 1965 Bumbling Scotland Yard detective is off to France to stop a master criminal from trying to kill off the rich Dupont family. Why? So he'll be the only one left with any claim to the remaining family fortune. **98m/C VHS, Beta.** Terry-Thomas, Johnny Dorelli, Margaret Lee. *VCD*

How to Make a Doll *♂* 1968 Lewis' sex farce about an extremely shy professor whose ineptness with women inspires him to invent android females to satisfy his sexual needs. **?m/C VHS.** Robert Wood, Jim Vance, Pamela Rhea; *D:* Herschell Gordon Lewis. *MOV, TPV*

How to Make a Monster *♂♂* 1958 In-joke from the creators of youth-oriented '50s AIP monster flicks; a mad makeup man's homebrew greasepaint brainwashes the actors. Disguised as famous monsters, they kill horror-hating movie execs. Mild fun if—and only if—you treasure the genre. Conway repeats his role as Teenage Frankenstein, but the studio couldn't get Michael Landon for the Teenage Werewolf. **73m/B VHS.** Robert Harris, Paul Brinegar, Gary Conway, Gary Clarke, Malcolm Atterbury, Dennis Cross, John Ashley, Morris Ankrum, Walter Reed, Heather Ames; *D:* Herbert L. Strock. *COL, MLB*

How to Make an American Quilt *♂♂½* 1995 (PG-13) Slow-moving take on female friendship and marriage revolves around perennial grad student Finn (the mopey Ryder), who is frantic to both finish her third attempted thesis and to answer a marriage proposal from practically perfect beau Sam (Mulroney). She takes a summer refuge with her grandmother (Burstyn), where a variety of family friends work on her wedding quilt as they tell stories of loves lost and won. Lots of (somewhat overextended) flashbacks and with so many characters, naturally some get the short end of the script. Based on the novel by Whitney Otto. *CW:* Scene of drug use, some sensuality and nudity. **109m/C VHS, LV, Closed Caption.** Winona Ryder, Ellen Burstyn, Anne Bancroft, Lois Smith, Jean Simmons, Kate Nelligan, Maya Angelou, Alfre Woodard, Dermot Mulroney, Kate Capshaw, Rip Torn, Derrick O'Connor, Loren Dean, Samantha Mathis, Joanna Going, Tim Guinee, Johnathon Schaech, Claire Danes, Jared Leto, Esther Rolle, Melinda Dillon, Alicia (Lecy) Goranson, Maria Celedonio, Mykelti Williamson; *D:* Jocelyn Moorhouse; *W:* Jane Anderson; *C:* Janusz Kaminski; *M:* Thomas Newman. Nominations: MTV Movie Awards '96: Best Kiss (Winona Ryder/Dermot Mulroney); Screen Actors Guild Award '95: Cast. *USH*

How to Marry a Millionaire 🐾🐾¼

1953 Three models pool their money and rent a lavish apartment in a campaign to trap millionaire husbands. Clever performances by three lead women salvage a vehicle intended primarily to bolster Monroe's career. The opening street scene, with the accompanying theme music, was a state-of-the-art achievement of screen and sound in the first movie to be filmed in Cinema-Scope. Remake of "The Greeks Had a Word for Them." **96m/C VHS, Beta, LV.** Lauren Bacall, Marilyn Monroe, Betty Grable, William Powell, David Wayne, Cameron Mitchell; **D:** Jean Negulesco; **W:** Nunnally Johnson; **M:** Alfred Newman. Nominations: Academy Awards '53: Best Costume Design (Color). *FOX*

How to Murder Your Wife 🐾🐾🐾

1964 While drunk, a cartoonist marries an unknown woman and then frantically tries to think of ways to get rid of her — even contemplating murder. Frantic comedy is tailored for Lemmon. **118m/C VHS, Beta, LV, Closed Caption.** Jack Lemmon, Terry-Thomas, Virna Lisi, Eddie Mayehoff, Sidney Blackmer, Claire Trevor, Mary Wickes, Jack Albertson; **D:** Richard Quine; **W:** George Axelrod; **C:** Harry Stradling. *MGM*

How to Pick Up Girls 🐾🐾 **1978** Comic

tale based on Eric Weber's bestseller follows the exploits of a small-town boy who moves to New York City and finds the secret to picking up women. Made for television. **93m/C VHS, Beta.** Desi Arnaz Jr., Bess Armstrong, Fred McCarren, Polly Bergen, Richard Dawson, Alan King, Abe Vigoda, Deborah Raffin; **D:** Bill Persky. *TWE*

How to Seduce a Woman woof!

1974 A playboy attempts to bed five supposedly unattainable women. **108m/C VHS, Beta.** Angus Duncan, Marty Ingels, Lillian Randolph.

How to Steal a Million 🐾🐾🐾 *How to Steal a Million Dollars and Live Happily Ever After* **1966**

Sophisticated comedy-crime caper involving a million-dollar heist of a sculpture in a Paris art museum. Hepburn and O'Toole are perfectly cast as partners in crime and Griffith gives a good performance as Hepburn's art-forging father. A charming, lightweight script and various Parisian locales combine for fun, above-average fluff. Based on the story "Venus Rising" by George Bradshaw. **127m/C VHS, Closed Caption.** Audrey Hepburn, Peter O'Toole, Eli Wallach, Hugh Griffith, Charles Boyer, Fernand Gravet, Marcel Dalio, Jacques Marin; **D:** William Wyler; **W:** Harry Kurnitz; **C:** Charles B(ryant) Lang; **M:** John Williams. *TVC*

How to Stuff a Wild Bikini 🐾🐾 **1965**

Tired next to last feature in the overlong tradition of Frankie and Annette doing the beach thing, featuring a pregnant Funicello (though this is hidden and not part of the plot). Avalon actually has only a small role as the jealous boyfriend trying to see if Annette will remain faithful while he's away on military duty. Keaton is the witch doctor who helps Frankie keep Annette true. "Playboy" playmates wander about in small swimsuits, garage band extraordinare "The Kingsmen" play themselves, and Brian Wilson of the "Beach Boys" drops by. Followed by "Ghost in the Invisible Bikini," the only movie in the series that isn't on video. ♫After the Party; Better Be Ready; Follow Your Leader; Give Her Lovin'; How About Us?; How to Stuff a Wild Bikini; I'm the Boy Next Door; Madison Avenue; The Perfect Boy. **90m/C VHS, Beta.** Annette Funicello, Dwayne Hickman, Frankie Avalon, Beverly Adams, Buster Keaton, Harvey Lembeck, Mickey Rooney, Brian Donlevy, Jody McCrea, John Ashley, Marianne Gaba, Len Lesser, Irene Tsu, Bobbi Shaw, Luree Holmes; **D:** William Asher; **W:** William Asher, Leo Townsend; **C:** Floyd Crosby; **M:** Les Baxter. *NO*

How to Succeed in Business without Really Trying 🐾🐾🐾½ **1967**

Classic musical comedy about a window-washer who charms his way to the top of a major company. Robert Morse repeats his Tony winning Broadway role. Loosely based on a non-fiction book of the same title by Shepherd Mead, whose book Morse purchases on his first day of work.

Excellent transfer of stage to film, with choreography by Moreda expanding Bob Fosse's original plan. Dynamite from start to finish. ♫I Believe In You; The Company Way; Coffee Break; The Brotherhood of Man; A Secretary Is Not A Toy; Grand Old Ivy; Been A Long Day; Rosemary; Finch's Frolic. **121m/C VHS, LV, Letterbox.** Robert Morse, Michele Lee, Rudy Vallee, Anthony Teague, George Fenneman, Maureen Arthur; **D:** David Swift; **W:** David Swift, Abe Burrows; **C:** Burnett Guffey; **M:** Frank Loesser. *MGM*

How to Succeed with Girls 🐾 **1964**

Marginally funny comedy about pious wax salesman (Leder) with a secret fantasy life who unwittingly enlists the aid of his wife's lover (Schrier) to help him overcome his shyness. Several fantasy sequences (in color; the rest of the film is black and white) include an Arabian harem, an old West saloon, and a science laboratory. Brubaker's secretary (Mathes) was Playboy's Miss June 1962. Pete's girlfriend (McClanahan of television's Golden Girls) is credited as either Patty Leigh or Helen Goodman. **83m/C VHS.** Marissa Mathes, Rue McClanahan, Paul Leder, Leon Schrier; **D:** Edward A. Biery. *SMW, TPV*

How U Like Me Now? 🐾🐾🐾 **1992 (R)**

Comedy set on Chicago's south side focuses on Thomas, an attractive but unmotivated guy with low earning potential, and his girl Valerie, a pretentious overachiever who wants much more than he's able to offer. Robert's second directorial effort offers a fresh look at African Americans on film with plenty of lively supporting characters and witty dialogue. Filmed on a $600,000 budget.**CW:** Strong language and sexuality. **109m/C VHS, LV, Closed Caption.** Darnell Williams, Salli Richardson, Daniel Gardner, Raymond Whitefield, Debra Crable, Jonelle Kennedy, Byron Stewart, Charnele Brown, Daryll Roberts; **D:** Daryll Roberts; **W:** Daryll Roberts; **M:** Kahil El Zabar, Chuck Webb. *USH*

Howard the Duck 🐾 **1986 (PG)** Big-bud-

get Lucasfilm adaptation of the short-lived Marvel comic book about an alien, resembling a cigar-chomping duck, who gets sucked into a vortex, lands on Earth and saves it from the Dark Overlords. While he's at it, he befriends a nice young lady in a punk rock band and starts to fall in love. A notorious boxoffice bomb and one of the '80s' worst major films, although it seems to work well with children, given the simple story line and good special effects. **111m/C VHS, Beta, LV, Closed Caption.** Lea Thompson, Jeffrey Jones, Tim Robbins; **D:** Willard Huyck; **W:** Willard Huyck, Gloria Katz; **M:** Sylvester Levay, John Barry. Golden Raspberry Awards '86: Worst Picture, Worst Screenplay.*USH*

Howard's End 🐾🐾🐾🐾 **1992 (PG)** E.M.

Forster's 1910 novel about property, privilege, class differences, and Edwardian society is brought to enchanting life by the Merchant Ivory team. A tragic series of events occurs after two impulsive sisters become involved with a working class couple and a wealthy family. Tragedy aside, this is a visually beautiful effort with subtle performances where a glance or a gesture says as much as any dialog. The winner of numerous awards and wide critical acclaim. Thompson is especially notable as the compassionate Margaret, while Hopkins plays the repressed English gentleman brilliantly. **143m/C VHS, LV, 8mm, Letterbox, Closed Caption.** *GB* Anthony Hopkins, Emma Thompson, Helena Bonham Carter, Vanessa Redgrave, James Wilby, Sam West, Jemma Redgrave, Nicola Duffett, Prunella Scales, Joseph Bennett; **Cameos:** Simon Callow; **D:** James Ivory; **W:** Ruth Prawer Jhabvala; **C:** Tony Pierce-Roberts. Academy Awards '92: Best Actress (Thompson), Best Adapted Screenplay, Best Art Direction/Set Decoration; British Academy Awards '92: Best Actress (Thompson); Golden Globe Awards '93: Best Actress—Drama (Thompson); Los Angeles Film Critics Association Awards '92: Best Actress (Thompson); National Board of Review Awards '92: Best Director (Ivory), Best Film; New York Film Critics Awards '92: Best Actress (Thompson); National Society of Film Critics Awards '92: Best Actress (Thompson); Nominations: Academy Awards '92: Best Cinematography, Best Costume Design, Best Di-

rector (Ivory), Best Picture, Best Supporting Actress (Redgrave), Best Original Score. *COL, CRC, MOV*

The Howards of Virginia 🐾🐾½ *Tree of Liberty* **1940** A lavish Hollywood historical epic,

detailing the adventures of a backwoodsman and the rich Virginia girl he marries as their families become involved in the Revolutionary War. **117m/ B VHS, Beta.** Cary Grant, Martha Scott, Cedric Hardwicke, Alan Marshal, Richard Carlson, Paul Kelly, Irving Bacon, Tom Drake, Anne Revere, Ralph Byrd, Alan Ladd; **D:** Frank Lloyd. Nominations: Academy Awards '40: Best Sound, Best Original Score. *COL*

The Howling 🐾🐾🐾 **1981 (R)** A pretty tele-

vision reporter takes a rest at a clinic and discovers slowly that its denizens are actually werewolves. Crammed with inside jokes, this horror comedy pioneered the use of the body-altering prosthetic make-up (by Rob Bottin) now essential for on-screen man-to-wolf transformations. At last count, followed by five sequels. **91m/C VHS, Beta, LV.** Dee Wallace Stone, Patrick Macnee, Dennis Dugan, Christopher Stone, Belinda Balaski, Kevin McCarthy, John Carradine, Slim Pickens, Elisabeth Brooks, Robert Picardo, Dick Miller, Kenneth Tobey; **Cameos:** John Sayles, Roger Corman; **D:** Joe Dante; **W:** John Sayles, Terence H. Winkless; **C:** John Hora; **M:** Pino Donaggio. *COL*

Howling 2: Your Sister Is a Werewolf 🐾 *Howling 2: Stirba—Werewolf Bitch*

1985 (R) A policeman (the brother of one of the first film's victims) investigates a Transylvanian werewolf-ridden castle and gets mangled for his trouble. Followed by four more sequels. **91m/C VHS, Beta, LV.** *FR IT* Sybil Danning, Christopher Lee, Annie McEnroe, Marsha Hunt, Reb Brown, Ferdinand "Ferdy" Mayne, Judd Omen, Jimmy Nail; **D:** Philippe Mora; **W:** Gary Brandner, Robert Sarner; **C:** Geoffrey Stephenson. *REP*

Howling 3: The Marsupials 🐾🐾

1987 (PG-13) Australians discover a pouch-laden form of lycanthrope. Third "Howling" (surprise), second from Mora and better than his first. **94m/C VHS, Beta, LV.** *AU* Barry Otto, Imogen Annesley, Dasha Blahova, Max Fairchild, Ralph Cotterill, Leigh Biolos, Frank Thring Jr., Michael Pate; **D:** Philippe Mora. *ART*

Howling 4: The Original Nightmare 🐾 **1988 (R)** A woman novelist

hears the call of the wild while taking a rest cure in the country. This werewolf tale has nothing to do with the other sequels. **94m/C VHS, Beta, LV.** Romy Windsor, Michael T. Weiss, Antony Hamilton, Susanne Severed, Lamya Derval, Dennis Folbigge; **D:** John Hough. *ART*

Howling 5: The Rebirth 🐾 **1989 (R)**

The fifth in the disconnected horror series, in which a varied group of people stranded in a European castle are individually hunted down by evil. **99m/C VHS, Beta, LV.** Philip Davis, Victoria Catlin, Elizabeth She, Ben Cole, William Shockley; **D:** Neal Sundstrom; **C:** Arledge Armenaki. *ART*

Howling 6: The Freaks 🐾½ **1990 (R)**

Hideous werewolf suffers from multiple sequels, battles with vampire at freak show, and discovers that series won't die. Next up: "Howling 7: The Nightmare that Won't Go Away."**CW:** Graphic horror violence. **102m/C VHS, LV.** Brendan Hughes, Michelle Matheson, Sean Gregory Sullivan, Antonio Fargas, Carol Lynley, Jered Barclay, Bruce Martyn Payne; **D:** Hope Perello. *ART, IME*

The Howling: New Moon Rising 🐾½ *Howling 7* **1995 (R)** Small desert

town is plagued by a series of terrifying murders believed to be the work of a werewolf, whose victims then join his vicious pack. **92m/C VHS, LV, Closed Caption.** Clive Turner, John Ramsden, Ernest Kester, Elizabeth She, Jacqueline Armitage, Romy Windsor; **D:** Clive Turner; **W:** Clive Turner. *NLC*

H.P. Lovecraft's Necronomicon: Book of the Dead 🐾🐾 *Necronomicon*

1993 (R) Trilogy of stories: Payne encounters a demon who resurrects his late wife and son in "The Drowning"; "The Cold" finds a reporter investigating a series of murders and uncovers crazed doctor Warner, who's discovered the secret to immortality; and a female cop discovers a subterranean alien in "Whispers." Combs serves as narrator, Lovecraft. **96m/C VHS, LV, Closed Caption.** Bruce Payne, Belinda Bauer, Bess Meyer, David Warner, Signy Coleman, Richard Lynch, Dennis Christopher, Jeffrey Combs, Maria Ford, Don Calfa; **D:** Brian Yuzna, Shusuke Kaneko, Christophe Gans; **W:** Brian Yuzna, Christophe Gans, Brent Friedman, Kazunori Ito; **C:** Gerry Lively, Russ Brandt; **M:** Joseph LoDuca, Daniel Light. *NLC*

Huck and the King of Hearts 🎬🎬½
1993 (PG) When a cardshark and his young friend Huck travel the country searching for Huck's long-lost grandfather, they find adventure everywhere from Hannibal, Missouri to L.A. to Vegas. Loose, contemporary adaptation of Mark Twain's "The Adventures of Huckleberry Finn." **103m/C VHS, Beta, LV.** Chauncey Leopardi, Graham Greene, Dee Wallace Stone, Joe Piscopo, John Astin, Gretchen Becker; **D:** Michael Keusch; **W:** Christopher Sturgeon; **M:** Chris Saranec.

Huckleberry Finn 🎬🎬 1974 (G)
The musical version of the Mark Twain story about the adventures a young boy and a runaway slave encounter along the Mississippi River. **114m/C VHS, Beta, LV, Letterbox, Closed Caption.** Jeff East, Paul Winfield, Harvey Korman, David Wayne, Arthur O'Connell, Gary Merrill, Natalie Trundy, Lucille Benson; **D:** J. Lee Thompson. *MGM, FOX, FCT*

Huckleberry Finn 🎬🎬½ 1975 (G)
Whitewashed version of the Twain classic features post Opie Howard as the incredible Huck and Dano as the sharp witted short storyist. Stars four members of the Howard clan. Made for TV. **74m/C VHS, Beta.** Ron Howard, Donny Most, Royal Dano, Antonio Fargas, Jack Elam, Merle Haggard, Rance Howard, Jean Howard, Clint Howard, Shug Fisher, Sarah Selby, Bill Erwin; **D:** Robert Totten. *KUI, FCT*

Huckleberry Finn 🎬½ 1981
A version of the classic Mark Twain novel about the adventures a young boy and a runaway slave encounter as they travel down the Mississippi River. **72m/C VHS, Beta.** *ART*

The Hucksters 🎬🎬🎬 1947
Account of a man looking for honesty and integrity in the radio advertising world and finding little to work with. All performances are excellent; but Greenstreet, as the tyrannical head of a soap company, is a stand out. Deborah Kerr's American debut. **115m/B VHS, Beta, Closed Caption.** Clark Gable, Deborah Kerr, Sydney Greenstreet, Adolphe Menjou, Ava Gardner, Keenan Wynn, Edward Arnold; **D:** Jack Conway. *MGM, FCT*

Hud 🎬🎬🎬🎬 1963
Newman is a hard-driving, hard-drinking, woman-chasing young man whose life is a revolt against the principles of stern father Douglas. Neal is outstanding as the family housekeeper. Excellent photography. Based on the Larry McMurtry novel "Horseman, Pass By." **112m/B VHS, Beta, LV.** Paul Newman, Melvyn Douglas, Patricia Neal, Brandon de Wilde, John Ashley; **D:** Martin Ritt; **W:** Irving Ravetch, Harriet Frank Jr.; **C:** James Wong Howe; **M:** Elmer Bernstein. Academy Awards '63: Best Actress (Neal), Best Black and White Cinematography, Best Supporting Actor (Douglas); British Academy Awards '63: Best Actress (Neal); National Board of Review Awards '63: Best Actress (Neal), Best Supporting Actor (Douglas); New York Film Critics Awards '63: Best Actress (Neal), Best Screenplay; Nominations: Academy Awards '63: Best Actor (Newman), Best Adapted Screenplay, Best Art Direction/Set Decoration (B & W), Best Director (Ritt). *PAR, BTV*

Hudson Hawk 🎬 1991 (R)
A big-budget star vehicle with little else going for it. Willis plays a master burglar released from prison, only to find himself trapped by the CIA into one last theft. Everyone in the cast tries to be extra funny, resulting in a disjointed situation where no one is. Weakly plotted, poorly paced. **CW:** Language. **95m/C VHS, Beta, LV, 8mm, Closed Caption.** Bruce Willis, Danny Aiello, Andie MacDowell, James Coburn, Sandra Bernhard, Richard E. Grant, Frank Stallone; **D:** Michael Lehmann; **W:** Steven E. de Souza, Daniel Waters. Golden Raspberry Awards '91: Worst Picture, Worst Director (Lehmann), Worst Screenplay. *COL*

The Hudsucker Proxy 🎬🎬🎬 1993 (PG)
In an effort to scare off would-be investors in a public stock offering dim bulb mailboy Robbins is installed as the Prez of Hudsucker Industries (in 1958) by Board Director Newman after corporate magnate Hudsucker (Durning) takes a swan dive from the 44th floor. First truly mainstream effort from the maverick Coen brothers is peppered with obscure references to numerous points on the historical map of cinematic style, and trots out an equally old but instantly recognizable story. Will delight Coen fans, but may be too dark for others. Destined to keep art history profs busy for decades. **115m/C VHS, LV, Letterbox, Closed Caption.** Tim Robbins, Paul Newman, Jennifer Jason Leigh, Charles Durning, John Mahoney, Jim True, Bill Cobbs, Bruce Campbell, Steve Buscemi; **Cameos:** Peter Gallagher; **D:** Joel Coen; **W:** Ethan Coen, Joel Coen, Sam Raimi; **C:** Roger Deakins; **M:** Carter Burwell. *WAR*

Hue and Cry 🎬🎬🎬 1947
Nobody believes a young boy when he discovers crooks are sending coded messages in a weekly children's magazine. A detective writer finally believes his story and they set off to capture the crooks. **82m/B VHS.** *GB* Alastair Sim, Jack Warner, Frederick Piper, Jack Lambert, Joan Dowling; **D:** Charles Crichton. *SNC, NOS, FCT*

Hugh Hefner: Once Upon a Time
1992 (R) Fascinating look at the "Bunny" king and Playboy Enterprises. His celebrated life of isolation and excess at the Playboy mansions is portrayed as is the founding of "Playboy" magazine in 1953 and the Playboy clubs (with their notorious Bunnies). Includes interviews, home movies, and photographs. Admiring yet not without a few sharp edges. **CW:** Language and nudity. **91m/C VHS, LV.** Hugh Hefner; **D:** Robert Heath. *UND, BTV*

Hughes & Harlow: Angels in Hell 🎬 1977 (R)
The story of the romance that occurred between Howard Hughes and Jean Harlow during the filming of "Hell's Angels" in 1930. **94m/C VHS, Beta.** Lindsay Bloom, Victor Holchak, David McLean, Royal Dano, Adam Roarke, Linda Cristal; **D:** Larry Buchanan. *NO*

Hugo Pool 🎬🎬½ 1997 (R)
Pool cleaner Hugo Dugay (Milano) has to clean the pools of 44 backyard eccentrics truck in water from the Colorado river to fill the pool of mobster Chick Chicalini (Lewis). Reluctantly, she must enlist the aid of her gambler mom (Moriarty) and drug addict father (McDowell). Bizarre characters abound, including Downey Jr. overacting as Hungarian film director Franz Mazur, whose accent changes with each line. Most interesting is Dempsey as ALS-afflicted Floyd Galen. The romance between Floyd and Hugo supplies the most sensitive and well-acted sequences. Disappointing, long-anticipated outing from director Downey Sr. (this is his first directorial effort in six years) who shared writing duties with wife Laura, who died of ALS in 1994. **CW:** Language and sex-related material. **93m/C VHS, LV.** Alyssa Milano, Patrick Dempsey, Robert Downey Jr., Malcolm McDowell, Cathy Moriarty, Sean Penn, Richard Lewis; **D:** Robert Downey; **W:** Laura Downey; **C:** Joe Montgomery; **M:** Danilo Perez. *BMG*

Hugo the Hippo 🎬🎬 1976 (G)
Animated musical about a forlorn baby hippo who struggles to survive in the human jungle of old Zanzibar. **90m/C VHS, Beta.** **W:** Thomas Baum; **V:** Paul Lynde, Burl Ives, Robert Morley, Marie Osmond. *FOX*

Hula 🎬½ 1928
Unflappable flapper Bow and her gang frolic on a Pacific island. **64m/B VHS, Beta.** Clara Bow, Clive Brook, Patricia Dupont, Arnold Kent, Agaslino Borgato; **D:** Victor Fleming. *GPV, FCT, DVT*

Hullabaloo Over Georgie & Bonnie's Pictures 🎬🎬 1978
A young maharajah has inherited a priceless collection of Indian miniature paintings he doesn't appreciate and which his greedy sister is anxious for him to sell. They're besieged by art dealers and collectors who learn about the treasure trove and will do anything to possess it. Among them are the British Ashcroft, who wants the art for the British Museum, and competing American collector Pine. Made for British television. **85m/C VHS, Beta.** *GB* Victor Banerjee, Aparna Sen, Larry Pine, Saeed Jaffrey, Peggy Ashcroft; **D:** James Ivory; **W:** Ruth Prawer Jhabvala; **C:** Walter Lassally. *NLC*

Human Beasts 🎬 1980
Jewel robbers face a tribe of hungry cannibals. **90m/C VHS, Beta.** *SP JP* Paul Naschy, Eiko Nagashima; **D:** Paul Naschy; **W:** Paul Naschy. *NO*

Human Bomb 🎬🎬½ 1997 (PG-13)
After her husband dies, Marcia Weller (Kensit) moves to Germany to be near her mother. Marcia's only been at her new teaching job a few days when she and her class of third-graders are taken hostage by a masked gunman. Captain Gerhardt (Prochnow) is brought in to resolve the crisis, but the terrorist won't negotiate, so Gerhardt must come up with a rescue plan before the bomber decides to carry out his threats. **CW:** Some violence and cruelty. **93m/C VHS, Closed Caption.** Patsy Kensit, Juergen Prochnow, Dorian Healy, Richard Moore; **D:** Anthony Page. *PAR*

The Human Comedy 🎬🎬🎬½ 1943
A small-town boy experiences love and loss and learns the meaning of true faith during WWII. Straight, unapologetically sentimental version of the William Saroyan novel. **117m/B VHS, Beta, LV.** Mickey Rooney, Frank Morgan, James Craig, Fay Bainter, Ray Collins, Donna Reed, Van Johnson, Barry Nelson, Robert Mitchum, Jackie "Butch" Jenkins; **D:** Clarence Brown; **W:** William Saroyan; **C:** Harry Stradling. Academy Awards '43: Best Story; Nominations: Academy Awards '43: Best Actor (Rooney), Best Black and White Cinematography, Best Director (Brown), Best Picture. *MGM*

The Human Condition: A Soldier's Prayer 🎬🎬🎬 1961
A Japanese pacifist escapes from his commanders and allows himself to be captured by Russian troops, hoping for better treatment as a P.O.W. The final part of the trilogy preceded by "The Human Condition: No Greater Love" and "The Human Condition: Road to Eternity." In Japanese with English subtitles. **190m/B VHS, Beta.** *JP* Tatsuya Nakadai, Michiyo Aratama, Yusuke Kawazu, Tamao Nakamura, Chishu Ryu, Taketoshi Naito, Reiko Hitomi, Kyoko Kishida, Keijiro Morozumi, Koji Kiyomura, Nobuo Kaneko, Fujio Suga; **D:** Masaki Kobayashi. *NO*

The Human Condition: No Greater Love 🎬🎬🎬 1958
First of a three-part series of films. A pacifist is called into military service and subsequently sent to a run a military mining camp. A gripping look at one man's attempt to retain his humanity in the face of war. Followed by "The Human Condition: Road to Eternity" and "The Human Condition: A Soldier's Prayer." In Japanese with English subtitles. **200m/B VHS, Beta.** *JP* Tatsuya Nakadai, Michiyo Aratama, So Yamamura, Eitaro Ozawa, Akira Ishihama, Chikage Awashima, Ineko Arima, Keiji Sada, Shinji Nambara, Seiji Miyaguchi, Toru Abe, Masao Mishima, Eijiro Tono, Yasushi Nagata, Yoshio Kosugi; **D:** Masaki Kobayashi. *NO*

The Human Condition: Road to Eternity 🎬🎬🎬 1959
No Greater Love; Ningen No Joken A Japanese pacifist is on punishment duty in Manchuria where he is beaten by sadistic officers who try to destroy his humanity. The second part of the trilogy, preceded by "The Human Condition: No Greater Love" and followed by "The Human Condition: A Soldier's Prayer." In Japanese with English subtitles. **180m/B VHS, Beta.** *JP* Tatsuya Nakadai, Michiyo Aratama, Kokinji Katsura, Jun Tatara, Michio Minami, Keiji Sada, Minoru Chiaki, Ryohei Uchida, Kan Yanagidani, Kenjiro Uemura, Yusuke Kawazu, Susumu Fujita; **D:** Masaki Kobayashi. *NO*

Human Desire 🎬🎬½ 1954
Femme fatale Grahame and jealous husband Crawford turn out the lights on Crawford's boss (seems there's some confusion about how Miss Gloria managed to convince the guy to let her hubby have his job back). Ford's wise to them but plays see no evil because he's gone crackers for Grahame, who by now has decided she'd like a little help to rid her-

self of an unwanted husband. Bleak, melodramatic, full of big heat, its Lang through and through. Based on the Emile Zola novel "La Bete Humaine," which inspired Renoir's 1938 telling as well. **90m/B VHS.** Glenn Ford, Gloria Grahame, Broderick Crawford, Edgar Buchanan, Kathleen Case; *D:* Fritz Lang; *C:* Burnett Guffey. *GKK*

Human Desires ✗✗ 1997 (R) A lingerie beauty contest provides a bevy of beauties for P.I. Dean Thomas (Noble) to investigate when one of them turns up dead. The death is ruled a suicide but a fellow contestant thinks it was murder and Thomas is around to check things out—very closely. **95m/C VHS, Closed Caption.** Shannon Tweed, Christian Noble; *D:* Ellen Earnshaw; *W:* Todd Smith. *COL*

The Human Duplicators ✗✗½ 1964 Kiel is an alien who has come to Earth to make androids out of important folk, thus allowing the "galaxy beings" to take over. Cheap stuff, but earnest performances make this more fun than it should be. **82m/C VHS, Beta.** George Nader, Barbara Nichols, George Macready, Dolores Faith, Hugh Beaumont, Richard Kiel, Richard Arlen; *D:* Hugo Grimaldi. *ART*

Human Experiments ✗ 1979 (R) Psychiatrist in a women's prison conducts a group of experiments in which he destroys the "criminal instinct" in the inmates through brute fear. **82m/C VHS, Beta.** Linda Haynes, Jackie Coogan, Aldo Ray; *D:* Gregory Goodell. *NO*

The Human Factor ✗✗½ 1975 (R) Kennedy stars as a computer expert who tracks down his family's murderers using technology. Bloody and violent. **96m/C VHS, Beta.** *GB IT* George Kennedy, John Mills, Raf Vallone, Rita Tushingham, Barry Sullivan, Arthur Franz; *D:* Edward Dmytryk; *M:* Ennio Morricone. *ART*

The Human Factor ✗✗½ 1979 (R) Unexciting spy caper has a British Secret Service agent (Williamson) betraying his country in order to aid a friend. As a result of his actions an innocent man is killed and Williamson is forced to defect to the Soviet Union. Based on a novel by Graham Greene. **115m/C VHS.** *GB* Nicol Williamson, Richard Attenborough, John Gielgud, Derek Jacobi, Robert Morley, Ann Todd, Richard Vernon, Iman; *D:* Otto Preminger; *W:* Tom Stoppard. *MGM*

Human Gorilla ✗ *Behind Locked Doors* 1948 A thriller involving a mad scientist, an insane asylum, a reporter, and various other mysterious trappings. **58m/B VHS, Beta.** Richard Carlson, Lucille Bremer, Tor Johnson. *NO*

Human Hearts ✗✗ 1922 A creaky old silent starring "Phantom of the Opera" leading lady Philbin. A family is torn apart by a con man and his femme fatale. **99m/B VHS, Beta, 8mm.** House Peters Sr., Russell Simpson, Mary Philbin. *VYY*

The Human Monster ✗✗½ *Dark Eyes of London* 1939 Scotland Yard inspector investigates five drownings of the blind patients a phony Dr. Orloff (Lugosi) is exploiting for insurance money. Superior Lugosi effort that's modestly violent and tasteless. Based on the Edgar Wallace novel. **73m/B VHS, Beta.** *GB* Bela Lugosi, Hugh Williams, Greta Gynt; *D:* Walter Summers; *W:* Walter Summers. *NOS, MRV, SNC*

The Human Shield ✗✗ 1992 (R) A man risks his life on a mission to save his brother during the Persian Gulf War. *CW:* War violence. **88m/C VHS, LV, Closed Caption.** Michael Dudikoff, Tommy Hinkley, Steve Inwood; *D:* Ted Post. *WAR*

The Human Vapor ✗✗ *Gasu Ningen Daiichigo* 1968 A normal human being has the ability to vaporize himself at will and use it to terrorize Tokyo. **81m/C VHS, Beta.** *JP GEM, CNG*

Humanoid Defender ✗✗ 1985 A made-for-television film about a scientist and an android rebelling against the government that wants to use the android as a warfare prototype. **94m/C VHS, Beta.** Terence Knox, Gary Kasper, Aimee Eccles, William Lucking; *D:* William Lucking. *USH*

Humanoids from the Deep woof! *Monster* 1980 (R) Mutated salmon-like monsters rise from the depths of the ocean and decide to chomp on some bikinied babes. Violent and bloody. **81m/C VHS, Beta.** Doug McClure, Ann Turkel, Vic Morrow, Cindy Weintraub, Anthony Penya, Denise Balik; *D:* Barbara Peeters; *W:* Frank Arnold, Frederick James; *C:* Daniel Lacambre; *M:* James Horner. *NHO*

Humanoids from the Deep ✗✗ *Roger Corman Presents: Humanoids from the Deep* 1996 (R) Cable remake of the 1980 Corman culter finds Carradine and Samms dealing with a coastal town's battle against serial killers whose DNA has been genetically combined with that of fish. When the fish monsters escape the lab, their mutations are further altered by toxic waste and they go on a rampage. *CW:* Violence/gore, nudity and language. **90m/C VHS.** Robert Carradine, Emma Samms, Mark Rolston; *D:* Jeff Yonis. *NHO*

Humongous woof! 1982 (R) Brain-dead bevy of teens shipwreck on an island where they encounter a deranged mutant giant who must kill to survive. You'll be rooting for the monster. **93m/C VHS, Beta.** *CA* Janet Julian, David Wallace, Janet Baldwin, Joy Boushel, Page Fletcher; *D:* Paul Lynch; *W:* William Gray; *C:* Brian R.R. Hebb. *NLC*

Humoresque ✗✗✗½ 1946 A talented but struggling young musician finds a patron in the married, wealthy, and older Crawford. His appreciation is not as romantic as she hoped. Stunning performance from Crawford, with excellent supporting cast, including a young Robert Blake. Fine music sequences (Isaac Stern dubbed the violin), and lush production values. Laserdisc version features the original movie trailer. **123m/B VHS, LV.** Joan Crawford, John Garfield, Oscar Levant, J. Carrol Naish, Joan Chandler, Tom D'Andrea, Peggy Knudsen, Ruth Nelson, Craig Stevens, Paul Cavanagh, Richard Gaines, John Abbott, Robert (Bobby) Blake; *D:* Jean Negulesco. Nominations: Academy Awards '46: Best Original Dramatic/Comedy Score. *MGM, BTV, FCT*

The Hunchback ✗✗½ 1997 Cable version of Victor Hugo's ever-popular "The Hunchback of Notre Dame." In 15th-century Paris, hunchbanked Notre Dame bell-ringer Quasimodo (Patinkin) loves spirited and kind gypsy Esmeralda (Hayek), who's the lustful obsession of evil archdeacon Frollo (Harris). Properly melodramatic, with Harris stealing the film as the cold cleric. **98m/C VHS, Closed Caption.** Mandy Patinkin, Richard Harris, Salma Hayek, Jim Dale, Edward Atterton; *D:* Peter Medak; *W:* John Fasano; *C:* Elemer Ragaly; *M:* Ed Shearmur. *TTC*

The Hunchback of Notre Dame ✗✗✗ 1923 The first film version of Victor Hugo's novel about the tortured hunchback bellringer of Notre Dame Cathedral, famous for the contortions of Lon Chaney's self-transformations via improvised makeup. Also available at 68 minutes. **100m/B VHS, LV.** Lon Chaney Sr., Patsy Ruth Miller, Norman Kerry, Ernest Torrence, Kate Lester, Brandon Hurst; *D:* Wallace Worsley; *W:* Edward T. Lowe; *C:* Tony Kornman, Robert S. Newhard. *KIV, MRV, NOS*

The Hunchback of Notre Dame ✗✗✗✗ 1939 Best Hollywood version of the Victor Hugo classic, infused with sweep, sadness, and an attempt at capturing a degree of spirited, Hugoesque detail. Laughton is Quasimodo, a deformed Parisian bellringer, who provides sanctuary to a young gypsy woman accused by church officials of being a witch. The final scene of the townspeople storming the cathedral remains a Hollywood classic. Great performances all around; the huge facade of the Notre Dame cathedral was constructed on a Hollywood set for this film. Remake of several earlier films, including 1923's Lon Chaney silent. Remade in 1957 and later for television. **117m/B VHS, Beta, LV.** Charles Laughton, Maureen O'Hara, Edmond O'Brien, Cedric Hardwicke, Thomas Mitchell, George Zucco, Alan Marshal, Walter Hampden, Harry Davenport, Curt Bois, George Tobias, Rod La Rocque; *D:* William Dieterle; *W:* Sonya Levien, Bruno Frank; *C:* Joseph August; *M:* Alfred Newman. Nomina-

tions: Academy Awards '39: Best Sound, Best Score. *TTC, CCB, VCN*

The Hunchback of Notre Dame ✗✗½ *Notre Dame de Paris* 1957 (PG) Slow retelling of the Victor Hugo novel, filmed entirely in France in CinemaScope. Quinn's the tragic Quasimodo with bombshell Lollobrigida appropriatley hotblooded as gypsy Esmeralda. **104m/C VHS, LV, Closed Caption.** *FR* Anthony Quinn, Gina Lollobrigida, Alain Cuny, Jean Danet, Robert Hirsch, Jean Tissier; *D:* Jean Delannoy; *W:* Jacques Prevert, Jean Aurenche; *C:* Michel Kelber; *M:* Georges Auric. *TOU*

The Hunchback of Notre Dame ✗✗✗ *Hunchback* 1982 (PG) It's not often that a classic novel is remade into a classic movie that's remade into a made-for-TV reprise, and survives its multiple renderings. But it's not often a cast so rich in stage trained actors is assembled on the small screen. Hopkins gives a textured, pre-Hannibal Lecter interpretation of Quasimodo, the Hunchback in Hugo's eponymous novel. Impressive model of the cathedral by production designer John Stoll. **102m/C VHS.** Anthony Hopkins, Derek Jacobi, Lesley-Anne Down, John Gielgud, Tim Pigott-Smith, Rosalie Crutchley, Robert Powell; *D:* Michael Tuchner. *THV*

The Hunchback of Notre Dame ✗✗✗ 1996 (G) Animated/musical version of Victor Hugo's story about deformed bell-ringer Quasimodo (Hulce) and his love for the beautiful gypsy Esmerelda (Moore). The original isn't exactly fun fare but you expect Disney to find a way to leave everybody humming (and happy). The sweeping music was provided by "Pocahontas" tunesmiths Menken and Schwartz. Comic relief is supplied by three gargoyles, companions to Quasimodo, who are voiced wonderfully by Alexander, Kimbrough and Wickes. Wickes, 85, died six weeks after voicing her role. Looks like another boatload of boxoffice, merchandising, and video sale cash is making its way into old Walt's vaults. **91m/C VHS, Closed Caption.** *D:* Kirk Wise, Gary Trousdale; *M:* Stephen Schwartz, Alan Menken; *V:* Tom Hulce, Demi Moore, Kevin Kline, Tony Jay, Charles Kimbrough, Jason Alexander, Mary Wickes, David Ogden Stiers. Nominations: Academy Awards '96: Best Original Score; Golden Globe Awards '97: Best Score. *TOU*

Hundra ✗ 1985 A warrior queen vows revenge when her all-female tribe is slain by men. Nothing can stop her fierce vendetta—except love. **96m/C VHS, Beta.** *IT* Laurene Landon, John Gaffari, Ramiro Oliveros, Marissa Casel; *D:* Matt Cimber; *M:* Ennio Morricone.

A Hungarian Fairy Tale ✗✗✗ *Hol Volt, Hol Nem Volt* 1987 Political satire meets fantasy in a magical tale of a fatherless young boy searching for a surrogate dad. Unusual characters as well as an homage to Mozart's "The Magic Flute." In Hungarian with English subtitles. **97m/B VHS.** *HU* Arpad Vermes, Maria Varga, Frantisek Husak, Eszter Csakanyi, Szilvia Toth, Judith Pogany, Geza Balkay; *D:* Gyula Gazdag. *FXL*

Hungarian Rhapsody ✗✗✗ 1978 In 1911, a Hungarian nobleman joins the ranks of the rebelling peasants in order to oppose his brother, who represents aristocratic repression. One of Jancso's clearest political films, and one that continues the filmmaker's experiments with long, uncut sequences and dynamic mise-en-scene. In Hungarian with English subtitles. **101m/C VHS, Beta.** *HU* Gyorgy Cserhalmi, Lajos Balaszovits, Gabor Koncz, Bertalan Solti; *D:* Miklos Jancso. *FCT, AUD*

Hunger ✗ *Sult* 1966 In the late 1800s, a starving Norwegian writer, unable to sell his work, rejects charity out of pride, and retains his faith in his talent. Based on a novel "Sult" by Knut Hamsun. In Danish with English subtitles. **115m/B VHS.** *DK* Per Oscarsson, Gunnel Lindblom; *D:* Henning Carlsen; *W:* Henning Carlsen. Cannes Film Festival '66: Best Actor (Oscarsson); National Society of Film Critics Awards '68: Best Actor (Oscarsson). *FCT, CVC*

The Hunger ♂♂ 1983 (R) A beautiful 2000-year-old vampire needs new blood when she realizes that her current lover, Bowie, is aging fast. Visually sumptuous but sleepwalking modern vampire tale, complete with soft-focus lesbian love scenes between Deneuve and Sarandon. Features a letterboxed screen and original movie trailer on the laserdisc format. 100m/C VHS, Beta, LV, Letterbox. Catherine Deneuve, David Bowie, Susan Sarandon, Cliff DeYoung, Ann Magnuson, Dan Hedaya, Willem Dafoe, Beth Ehlers, Suzanne Bertish, Rufus Collins, James Aubrey; D: Tony Scott; W: Michael Thomas, Ian Davis; C: Stephen Goldblatt, Tom Mangravite. MGM

Hunk ♂♂ 1987 (PG) A computer nerd sells his soul to the devil for a muscular, beach-blonde physique. Answers the question, "Was it worth it?" 102m/C VHS, Beta, LV. John Allen Nelson, Steve Levitt, Deborah Shelton, Rebecca Bush, James Coco, Avery Schreiber; D: Lawrence Bassoff; W: Lawrence Bassoff; C: Bryan England. COL

The Hunt ♂♂♂ La Caza 1965 A teenage boy accompanies three Spanish Civil War veterans on what is supposed to be a friendly rabbit hunt. Things turn violent, however, when old rivalries and tensions begin to surface. In Spanish with English subtitles. 87m/B VHS. SP Alfredo Mayo, Ismael Merlo, Jose Maria Prada, Emilio Gutierrez-Caba, Fernando Sanchez Polack; D: Carlos Saura. TPV, CVC, FCT

The Hunt for Red October 1990 (PG) Based on Tom Clancy's blockbuster novel, a high-tech Cold War yarn about a Soviet nuclear sub turning rogue and heading straight for U.S. waters, as both the U.S. and the U.S.S.R. try to stop it. Complicated, ill-plotted potboiler that succeeds breathlessly due to the cast and McTiernan's tommy-gun direction. Introduces the character of CIA analyst Jack Ryan who returns in "Patriot Games," though in the guise of Harrison Ford. 137m/C VHS, Beta, LV, 8mm, Letterbox, Closed Caption. Sean Connery, Alec Baldwin, Richard Jordan, Scott Glenn, Joss Ackland, Sam Neill, James Earl Jones, Peter Firth, Tim Curry, Courtney B. Vance, Jeffrey Jones, Fred Dalton Thompson; D: John McTiernan; W: Larry Ferguson, Donald Stewart; C: Jan De Bont; M: Basil Poledouris. Academy Awards '90: Best Sound Effects Editing; Nominations: Academy Awards '90: Best Film Editing, Best Sound. PAR

The Hunt for the Night Stalker ♂♂ Manhunt: The Search for the Night Stalker 1991 (PG-13) Another one of those True-Detective quickies so beloved by network TV, following two hardworking L.A. cops who tracked down satanic serial killer Richard Ramirez in the mid-1980s. It originally aired (under the title "Manhunt: The Search for the Night Stalker") on the date of the killer's death-sentence verdict; the videotape lacks that particular timely sparkle. 95m/C VHS, LV. Richard Jordan, A. Martinez, Lisa Eilbacher, Julie Carmen, Alan Feinstein; D: Bruce Seth Green.

Hunt the Man Down ♂♂½ 1950 An innocent man is charged with murder, and a public defender must find the real killer before time runs out. 68m/B VHS, Beta. Gig Young, Lynn (Mary Hart) Roberts, Gerald Mohr; D: George Archainbaud. NO

Hunt the Man Down/Smashing the Rackets ♂♂½ 1950 A double feature: In "Hunt the Man Down" (1950) a public defender tries to clear a captured fugitive's name, and in "Smashing the Rackets" (1938) a special prosecutor takes on the gangsters who have corrupted a big city. 137m/B VHS, Beta. Gig Young, Lynn (Mary Hart) Roberts, Chester Morris, Frances Mercer, Willard Parker, Gerald Mohr, Paul Frees; D: George Archainbaud. NO

Hunted ♂♂ 1988 (PG) WWII prisoner attempts to escape from demented officer who seems to enjoy bugging him. Hunted by the MPs, he relies on unorthodox guide to sustain feature length footage. 75m/C VHS. Andrew Buckland, Richard Carlson, Ron Smerczak, Mercia Van Wyk; D: David Lister.

The Hunted ♂½ 1994 (R) American businessman in Japan meets, beds, and witnesses the assassination of a mysterious woman and is forced on the run by the modern-day ninja clan that committed the crime. Only a notch above the low-budget, badly dubbed martial arts flicks of the '70s, this shameless bloodfest features unintentionally campy performances by Lambert and Lone and lots of silly dialogue. Beware, the cliches pile up as quickly as the bodies. CW: Bloody ninja violence; some sexuality. 110m/C VHS. Christopher Lambert, John Lone, Joan Chen, Yoshio Harada, Yoko Shimada, Maria Natsuki, Tak Kubota; D: Jonathan Lawton; W: Jonathan Lawton; C: Jack Conroy; M: Motofumi Yamaguchi. USH

The Hunted Lady ♂½ 1977 In this television pilot, Mills is an undercover policewoman who is framed by the mob. Tired and predictable. 100m/C VHS. Donna Mills, Robert Reed, Lawrence Casey, Andrew Duggan, Will Sampson, Alan Feinstein; D: Richard Lang. WOV

Hunter ♂♂½ 1973 Pilot for a television series that never emerged. A government agent uncovers an enemy brainwashing scam. 90m/C VHS. John Vernon, Steve Ihnat, Fritz Weaver, Edward Binns, Sabrina Scharf, Barbara Rhoades; D: Leonard Horn. ORI

Hunter ♂ 1977 An attorney is falsely accused of a crime and imprisoned. Released after eight years, he sets out to even the score with the mysterious millionaire who set him up. Made for television. 120m/C VHS, Beta. James Franciscus, Linda Evans, Broderick Crawford. ORI, WAR

The Hunter ♂♂½ 1980 (PG) Action drama based on the real life adventures of Ralph (Papa) Thorson, a modern day bounty hunter who makes his living by finding fugitives who have jumped bail. McQueen's last. 97m/C VHS, Beta, LV. Steve McQueen, Eli Wallach, Kathryn Harrold, LeVar Burton; D: Buzz Kulik; W: Peter Hyams; C: Fred W. Koenekamp; M: Charles Bernstein. PAR

Hunter in the Dark ♂♂ 1980 Set in 18th-century Japan, where power, betrayal, and corruption are the dark side of the samurai world. Tanuma is a powerful shogunate minister who becomes involved with Gomyo, the leader of a secret underworld organization of thieves and murderers with a violent honor code. In Japanese with English subtitles. 138m/C VHS, LV, Letterbox. JP Tatsuya Nakadai, Tetsuro Tamba, Sonny Chiba; D: Hideo Gosha. NO

The Hunters ♂♂½ 1958 A motley crew of pilots learn about each other and themselves in this melodrama set during Korean war. Incredible aerial photography sets this apart from other films of the genre. 108m/C VHS. Robert Mitchum, Robert Wagner, Richard Egan, May Britt, Lee Philips; D: Dick Powell; W: Wendell Mayes. NO

Hunter's Blood ♂½ 1987 (R) Five urbanites plunge into the Southern wilderness to hunt deer, and are stalked by maniacal hillbillies. 102m/C VHS, Beta, LV, Closed Caption. Sam Bottoms, Kim Delaney, Clu Gulager, Mayf Nutter, Eugene Glazer; D: Robert C. Hughes; W: Emmett Alston. NLC

Hunters of the Golden Cobra ♂ 1982 (R) Two American soldiers plot to recover the priceless golden cobra from the Japanese general who stole the prized relic during the last days of WWII. 95m/C VHS, Beta. David Warbeck, Almanta Suska, Alan Collins, John Steiner; D: Anthony (Antonio Margheriti) Dawson. ART, VES

The Hunting ♂♂ 1992 (R) A married woman falls for a ruthless businessman and is drawn into a web of blackmail and murder in this low-budget erotic thriller. CW: Language, violence and drug use, and strong sensuality. 97m/C VHS, Beta. John Savage, Kerry Armstrong, Guy Pearce, Rebecca Rigg; D: Frank Howson; W: Frank Howson. PAR

The Hurricane ♂♂♂ 1937 A couple on the run from the law are aided by a hurricane and are able to build a new life for themselves on an idyllic island. Filmed two years before the Academy's "special effects" award came into being, but displaying some of the best effects of the decade. Boringly remade in 1979. 102m/B VHS, Beta, LV. Jon Hall, Dorothy Lamour, Mary Astor, Sir C. Aubrey Smith, Raymond Massey, Thomas Mitchell, John Carradine; D: John Ford. Academy Awards '37: Best Sound; Nominations: Academy Awards '37: Best Supporting Actor (Mitchell), Best Score.

Hurricane ♂ 1974 Television's answer to the disaster movie craze of the early 1970s. Realistic hurricane footage and an adequate cast cannot save this catastrophe. 78m/C VHS. Larry Hagman, Martin Milner, Jessica Walter, Barry Sullivan, Will Geer, Frank Sutton; D: Jerry Jameson. NO

Hurricane woof! Forbidden Paradise 1979 (PG) And the wind cried, "turkey." Robards is the governor of a tropical island beset with environmental and personal concerns. Virginal daughter Farrow falls for hunky native, standard colonial power/indigenous people complications ensue, vital explanatory footage is cut, and overacting reaches epidemic heights. Then too late the big wind blows in, leveling the place. Expensive (most of the $22 million must have gone to catering) and essentially misdirected remake of the 1937 semiclassic. 120m/C VHS, Beta. Mia Farrow, Jason Robards Jr., Trevor Howard, Max von Sydow, Timothy Bottoms, James Keach; D: Jan Troell; C: Sven Nykvist; M: Nino Rota. PAR

Hurricane Express 1932 Twelve episodes of the vintage serial, in which the Duke pits his courage against an unknown, powerful individual out to sabotage a railroad. 223m/B VHS, Beta. John Wayne, Joseph Girard, Conway Tearle, Shirley Grey; D: J.P. McGowan, Armand Schaefer. SNC, NOS, RHI

Hurricane Smith ♂♂ 1992 (R) Weathers stars as a roughneck Texan who travels to Australia's Gold Coast in search of his missing sister. While in the land of Oz, he gets entangled in a Mafia-style drug and prostitution ring around the "Surfer's Paradise" section of the Gold Coast. Packed with mind-blowing stunts and a good performance from Weathers, this fast-paced action thriller won't disappoint fans of this genre. CW: Language, action violence, and sensuality. 86m/C VHS, Closed Caption. Carl Weathers, Juergen Prochnow, Tony Bonner, Cassandra Delaney; D: Colin Budds. WAR

Hurricane Streets ♂♂½ Hurricane 1996 Freeman's directorial debut centers on a group of young teenagers getting into trouble in lower Manhattan. 15-year-old Marcus (Sexton) is on the edge—his dad is dead, his mother's in jail, he's being ineffectually looked after by his working grandma, and the authorities are already eyeing this petty thief. He hangs with three buddies, one of whom, Chip (Frank), wants to start them stealing cars. Meanwhile, Marcus falls for 14-year-old Melena (Vega), whose father is both possessive and abusive, and tries to plan an escape for them both. 89m/C VHS. Brendan Sexton III, Isidra Vega, David Roland Frank, L.M. Kit Carson, Jose Zuniga, Lynn Cohen, Edie Falco, Shawn Elliot, Heather Matarazzo; D: Morgan J. Freeman; W: Morgan J. Freeman; C: Enrique Chediak. Sundance Film Festival '97: Best Cinematography, Best Director (Freeman), Audience Award. NYR

Hurricane Sword ♂½ 197? Thriller sets savage sword play against a background of murder, betrayal, prostitution, and reunion. 86m/C VHS, Beta. Chen Sau Kei, Li Tai Shing. NO

Hurry, Charlie, Hurry 1941 Husband gets in trouble when he bows out of a trip with his social-climber wife when he tells her he must travel to Washington to see the Vice President. 65m/B VHS, Beta. Leon Errol. MLB

Hurry Up or I'll Be Thirty ♂♂ 1973 A Brooklyn bachelor celebrates his 30th birthday by becoming morose, depressed, and enraged. His friends try to help; they fail, but he finds love anyway. For those seeking a better life through celluloid. 87m/C VHS, Beta. Danny DeVito, John Lefkowitz, Steve Inwood, Linda DeCoff, Ronald Anton, Maureen Byrnes, Francis Gallagher; D: Joseph Jacoby. ART, VES

Husband Hunting 🎬 196? Working girls hit the beach in search of husbands, and find that love isn't easy to find or hold on to. **90m/C VHS, Beta.** IT Walter Chiari. NO

Husbands and Lovers 🎬🎬 1991 (R) Controversial and confusing film focuses on a couple's untraditional marriage. Stephen (Sands) and Alina (Pacula) have agreed to be totally honest with each other and when Alina decides to take a lover, Stephen agrees on the condition that she report back to him every intimate detail of her affair. In the confusion and excitement of this kinky love triangle, everyone starts losing control as sexual boundaries are pushed to the limit. Also available in an unrated version. **CW:** Language and strong sensuality. **91m/C VHS, Closed Caption.** Julian Sands, Joanna Pacula, Tcheky Karyo; **D:** Mauro Bolognini; **W:** Sergio Bazzini; **M:** Ennio Morricone. COL

Husbands and Wives 🎬🎬🎬½ 1992 (R) Art imitates life as Allen/Farrow relationship dissolves onscreen (and off) and Woody becomes involved with young student. Mature, penetrating look at modern pair bonding and loneliness offers more painful honesty and sadness than outright laughs, though still retains essential Allen charm. Stylistically burdened by experiment with pseudo-documentary telling of tale and spasmodic hand-held cameras that annoy more than entertain. Excellent, intriguing cast, notably Davis as the overwhelming, overbearing wife/friend. Trailers became unintentionally funny in light of the highly publicized personal problems of Allen and Farrow. **CW:** Language and one sexual scene. **107m/C VHS, LV, Letterbox, Closed Caption.** Woody Allen, Mia Farrow, Judy Davis, Sydney Pollack, Liam Neeson, Juliette Lewis, Lysette Anthony, Blythe Danner; **D:** Woody Allen; **W:** Woody Allen; **C:** Carlo DiPalma. British Academy Awards '92: Best Original Screenplay; Los Angeles Film Critics Association Awards '92: Best Supporting Actress (Davis); National Board of Review Awards '92: Best Supporting Actress (Davis); National Society of Film Critics Awards '92: Best Supporting Actress (Davis); Nominations: Academy Awards '92: Best Original Screenplay, Best Supporting Actress (Davis). COL, MOV

Husbands, Wives, Money, and Murder 🎬 1986 A couple is pushed over the edge by a nosey census taker and then must dispose of the consequences. **92m/C VHS, Beta.** Garrett Morris, Greg Mullavey, Meredith MacRae, Timothy Bottoms; **D:** Bruce Cook Jr. TWE, HHE

Hush 🎬½ Kilronan; Bloodline 1998 (PG-13) Stinky thriller stars Paltrow as a working-class gal who marries wealthy dreamboat Jackson (Schaech) and moves to his family's Kentucky estate, Kilronan. There, smother-in-law Lange camps it up (albeit unknowingly) as she turns psycho on the pregnant bride while coming on to her dim-witted son who doesn't have a clue. Apparently, neither did filmmaker Darby, whose film was held from release pending two years of pasting Band-Aids on this gaping wound of a movie. Foch's crusty grandmother is the sole highlight of this horror of a film. **CW:** Some violence, sensuality and brief strong language. **100m/C VHS.** Gwyneth Paltrow, Jessica Lange, Johnathon Schaech, Nina Foch, Debi Mazar, Kaiulani Lee, David Thornton, Hal Holbrook; **D:** Jonathan Darby; **W:** Jonathan Darby, Jane Rusconi; **C:** Andrew Dunn; **M:** Christopher Young. NYR

Hush, Hush, Sweet Charlotte 🎬🎬🎬 1965 A fading southern belle finds out the truth about her married lover's murder when the case is reopened 37 years later by her cousin in an elaborate plot to drive her crazy. Grisly, superbly entertaining Southern Gothic horror tale, with vivid performances from the aging leads. **134m/B VHS, Beta, LV, Closed Caption.** Bette Davis, Olivia de Havilland, Joseph Cotten, Agnes Moorehead, Mary Astor, Bruce Dern, Cecil Kellaway, Victor Buono; **D:** Robert Aldrich; **W:** Lukas Heller, Henry Farrell; **C:** Joseph Biroc. Golden Globe Awards '65: Best Supporting Actress (Moorehead); Nominations: Academy Awards '64: Best Art Direction/Set Decoration (B & W), Best Black and White Cinematography, Best Costume Design (B & W), Best Film Editing,

Best Song ("Hush, Hush, Sweet Charlotte"), Best Supporting Actress (Moorehead), Best Original Score. FOX

Hush Little Baby, Don't You Cry 🎬 1986 A made-for-television drama about a seemingly normal middle-aged family man who is in actuality a child abuser/murderer. **110m/C VHS, Beta.** Emery L. Kedocia, Gary Giem, Tony Grant, Burt Douglas; **D:** Don Hawks.

Hussy 🎬 1980 (R) Hooker and her boyfriend find themselves trapped in a web of gangsters and drugs. **95m/C VHS, Beta, LV.** GB Helen Mirren, John Shea, Jenny Runacre; **D:** Matthew Chapman; **W:** Matthew Chapman; **M:** George Fenton. VES

The Hustle 🎬🎬 1975 (R) Gritty urban adventure with Reynolds as an L.A. detective investigating a young call girl's death. He becomes romantically entangled with high-priced call girl Deneuve. **120m/C VHS, Beta.** Burt Reynolds, Catherine Deneuve; **D:** Robert Aldrich; **C:** Joseph Biroc. PAR

The Hustler 🎬🎬🎬🎬 1961 The original story of Fast Eddie Felsen and his adventures in the seedy world of professional pool. Newman plays the naive, talented and self-destructive Felsen perfectly, Laurie is oustanding as his lover, and Gleason epitomizes the pool great Minnesota Fats. Rivetingly atmospheric, and exquisitely photographed. Parent to the reprise "The Color of Money," made 25 years later. **134m/B VHS, Beta, LV, Closed Caption.** Paul Newman, Jackie Gleason, Piper Laurie, George C. Scott, Myron McCormick, Murray Hamilton, Michael Constantine, Jake La Motta, Vincent Gardenia; **D:** Robert Rossen; **W:** Robert Rossen; **C:** Eugene (Eugen Shufftan) Shuftan. Academy Awards '61: Best Art Direction/Set Decoration (B & W), Best Black and White Cinematography; British Academy Awards '61: Best Actor (Newman), Best Film; National Board of Review Awards '61: Best Supporting Actor (Gleason), National Film Registry '97;; New York Film Critics Awards '61: Best Director (Rossen); Nominations: Academy Awards '61: Best Actor (Newman), Best Actress (Laurie), Best Adapted Screenplay, Best Director (Rossen), Best Picture, Best Supporting Actor (Gleason, Scott). FOX, FCT

Hustler Squad 🎬 1976 (R) U.S. Army major and Philippine guerrilla leader stage a major operation to help rid the Philippines of Japanese Occupation forces: they have four combat-trained prostitutes infiltrate a brothel patronized by top Japanese officers. Verrrrry clever. **98m/C VHS, Beta.** John Ericson, Karen Ericson, Lynda Sinclaire, Nory Wright; **D:** Ted V. Mikels. VCI, MRV

Hustler White 🎬🎬 1996 Outrageous underground actor/filmmaker LaBruce stars as pretentious German writer Jurgen Anger, who comes to Hollywood to research the gay scene for a book. Cruising Santa Monica Boulevard he becomes obsessively intrigued by local hustler Montgomery Ward (Ward), who serves as a tour guide to the city's sexual kinks. Yes, it's racy, but it's also not as hardcore as the subject matter might imply. **80m/C VHS.** Tony Ward, Bruce La Bruce; **D:** Rick Castro, Bruce La Bruce; **W:** Rick Castro, Bruce La Bruce; **C:** James Carman. FCT

Hustling 🎬🎬🎬 1975 A reporter writing a series of articles on prostitution in New York City takes an incisive look at their unusual and sometimes brutal world. Notable performance by Remick as the reporter and Clayburgh as a victimized hooker. Made for TV and based on a novel by Gail Sheehy. **96m/C VHS, Beta.** Jill Clayburgh, Lee Remick, Alex Rocco, Monte Markham; **D:** Joseph Sargent. WOV

Hybrid 🎬½ 1997 (R) Another bleak apocalyptic future flick, which finds a handful of survivors stumbling across a remote desert lab where they decide to take shelter. Big mistake since the lab still houses a living alien hybrid that's bent on reproduction and destruction. **CW:** Strong sexuality, and for violence/gore and language. **87m/C VHS.** Brinke Stevens, Tim Abell, John Barrymore III. PEG

Hyena of London 🎬🎬 1960 A doctor steals the hyena of London's corpse and injects the rabid protoplasm into his own brain with deadly results. **?m/C VHS.** Diana Martin, Bernard Price. LOO

Hyper-Sapien: People from Another Star 🎬½ 1986 (PG) Two cuddly aliens run away from home, are befriended by a lonely farmboy, and are chased all over the wilds of Wyoming. **93m/C VHS, Beta, LV.** Sydney Penny, Keenan Wynn, Gail Strickland, Ricky Paull Goldin, Peter Jason, Christopher Blue; **D:** Peter Hunt; **W:** Richard Adcock, Christopher Blue. WAR

Hyper Space 🎬½ 1997 Six people awaken from cryogenic sleep to discover that their spaceship has become marooned lightyears from earth and only a single passenger shuttle is available to get someone home. Naturally, everyone wants that one chance. **90m/C VHS.** Richard Norton, Don Stroud, Lynn-Holly Johnson, James Van Patten, Ron O'Neal, Rebecca Cruz; **D:** David Huey; **W:** Richard Dominguez; **C:** Roger Olkowski. SCP

The Hypothesis of the Stolen Painting 🎬🎬 L'Hypothese du Tableau Vole 1978 An art collector guides an interviewer around six paintings by Frederic Tonnerre, an academic 19th century painter, in an attempt to solve the mysterious disappearance of a seventh painting. The film presents the paintings as tableaux vivants in which the actors hold poses as they are examined. Based on the novel "Baphomet" by Pierre Klossowski. In French with English subtitles. **87m/B VHS.** D: Raul Ruiz; **W:** Raul Ruiz. WAC

Hysteria 🎬½ 1964 (PG) When an American becomes involved in an accident and has amnesia, a mysterious benefactor pays all his bills and gives the man a house to live in. But a series of murders could mean he's the murderer—or the next victim. **85m/B VHS, Beta.** GB Robert Webber, Sue Lloyd, Maurice Denham; **D:** Freddie Francis; **W:** Jimmy Sangster; **M:** Don Banks. MGM, MLB

Hysterical 🎬🎬 1983 (PG) Odd little attempt at a horror flick parody features the Hudson Brothers and involves a haunted lighthouse occupied by the vengeful spirit of a spurned woman. Late-night fun. **86m/C VHS, Beta, LV.** Brett Hudson, William Hudson, Mark Hudson, Cindy Pickett, Richard Kiel, Julie Newmar, Bud Cort; **D:** Chris Bearde; **M:** Robert Alcivar. NO

I, A Woman 🎬🎬 Jag, en Kvinna 1966 Siv (Persson) is a seductive young nurse who likes to have sex with every man she meets—and then leave them after they fall in love with her. Based on the novel by the pseudononomous Siv Holm. Dubbed. **90m/B VHS.** SW Essy Persson, Jorgen Reenberg, Preben Mahrt; **D:** Mac Ahlberg; **C:** Mac Ahlberg. FRF

I Accuse My Parents 🎬½ 1945 Juvenile delinquent tries to blame a murder and his involvement in a gang of thieves on his mom and dad's failure to raise him properly. **70m/B VHS, Beta.** Mary Beth Hughes, Robert Lowell, John Miljan. SNC, NOS, DVT

I Am a Camera 🎬🎬🎬 1955 A young English writer develops a relationship with a reckless young English girl in Berlin during the 1930s. Based on the Berlin stories by Christopher Isherwood, later musicalized as "Cabaret." **99m/B VHS, Beta.** GB Julie Harris, Shelley Winters, Laurence Harvey, Patrick McGoohan; **D:** Henry Cornelius; **C:** Guy Green; **M:** Malcolm Arnold. MON

I Am a Fugitive from a Chain Gang 🎬🎬🎬🎬 I Am a Fugitive From the Chain Gang 1932 WWI veteran Muni returns home with dreams of traveling across America. After a brief stint as a clerk, he strikes out on his own. Near penniless, Muni meets up with a tramp who takes him to get a hamburger. He becomes an unwilling accomplice when the bum suddenly robs the place. Convicted and sentenced to a Georgia chain gang, he's brutalized and degraded, though he eventually escapes and lives the life of a criminal on the run. Based on the autobiography by Robert E. Burns. Brutal docu-details combine with powerhouse performances to create a classic. Timeless and thought-provoking. **93m/B VHS, Beta.** Paul Muni, Glenda Farrell, Helen Vinson, Preston Foster, Edward Ellis, Allen Jenkins; **D:** Mervyn LeRoy; **W:** Howard J. Green. National Film Registry '91;; Nominations: Academy Awards '33: Best Actor (Muni), Best Picture, Best Sound. *MGM, FOX, CCB*

I Am Cuba 🌑🌑 1964 Agitprop Russian-Cuban co-production illustrates different aspects of the Cuban revolution from the toppling of Batista's decadent Havana to idealistic soldiers and student revolutionaries. Lots of oratory and deliberate artificiality combined with cinematographer Urusevsky's stunning high-contrast photography. Spanish and Russian with subtitles. **141m/B VHS.** *CU RU* Luz Maria Collazo, Jose Gallardo, Sergio Corrieri, Jean Bouise, Raul Garcia, Celia Rodriguez; **D:** Mikhail Kalatozov; **W:** Yevgeny Yevtushenko, Enrique Pineda Barnet; **C:** Sergei Urusevsky; **M:** Carlos Farinas. Nominations: Independent Spirit Awards '96: Best Foreign Film. *MIL, FCT*

I Am Curious (Yellow) 🌑🌑½ 1967 A woman sociologist is conducting a sexual survey on Swedish society, which leads her to have numerous sexual encounters in all sorts of places. Very controversial upon its U.S. release because of the nudity and sexual content but tame by today's standards. Followed by "I Am Curious (Blue)" which was filmed at the same time. In Swedish with English subtitles. **95m/B VHS.** *SW* Lena Nyman, Peter Lindgren; **D:** Vilgot Sjoman. *HTV*

I Am the Cheese 🌑🌑 1983 An institutionalized boy undergoes psychiatric treatment; with the aid of his therapist (Wagner) he relives his traumatic childhood and finds out the truth about the death of his parents. A bit muddled, but with its moments. Adapted from a Robert Cormier teen novel. **95m/C VHS, Beta.** Robert MacNaughton, Hope Lange, Don Murray, Robert Wagner, Sudie Bond; **D:** Robert Jiras. *ART, VES*

I Am the Law 🌑🌑🌑 1938 Robinson is given the task of stopping gangster activity in the city. Although regularly a law professor, he is made special prosecutor and starts canvassing for people to testify. His witnesses become murder victims as an enemy on the inside attempts to thwart the game plan. Robinson is dismissed from the case but continues to pursue justice in streetclothes. Fine performances but somewhat predictable. **83m/B VHS, Beta, LV.** Edward G. Robinson, Otto Kruger, John Beal, Barbara O'Neil, Wendy Barrie, Arthur Loft, Marc Lawrence, Charles Halton; **D:** Alexander Hall; **W:** Jo Swerling. *COL*

I Beheld His Glory 1953 Story based on the experience of Cornelius, the Roman centurion who guarded Christ's tomb. **53m/C VHS.** George Macready, Robert Wilson, Virginia Wave. *REP, MVC*

I Bombed Pearl Harbor 🌑🌑 1960 Mifune stars in this epic that shows events of WWII through Japanese eyes. Dramatic battle scenes boast the most ships destroyed per minute of film. Dubbed from Japanese. **98m/C VHS.** *JP* Toshiro Mifune; **D:** Shue Matsubayashi. *IVY, FCT*

I Bury the Living 🌑🌑🌑 1958 A cemetery manager sticks pins in his map of a graveyard and people mysteriously start to die. Well-done suspense film. **76m/B VHS.** Richard Boone, Theodore Bikel, Peggy Maurer; **D:** Albert Band. *SNC, MRV*

I Can't Escape 🌑🌑 1934 A man attempts to piece his life back together after serving time for a crime he didn't commit. To prove himself to his girlfriend, he tries to break up an illegal stock scam. **60m/B VHS, Beta.** Onslow Stevens, Lila Lee, Russell Gleason, Otis Harlan, Hooper Atchley, Clara Kimball Young; **D:** Otto Brower. *SNC*

I Can't Sleep 🌑🌑 *J'ai Pas Sommeil* 1993 Serial killers, French style. Gay, black Camille (Courcet), an immigrant from Martinique, and his white lover Raphael (Dupont) live in a Paris hotel and murder elderly women. Though they also rob them, the motive for their horrific crimes is vague (seemingly even to themselves). Not much actually happens—Camille visits his brother, who

longs to return home, and their status as outsiders is juxtaposed against another immigrant, Daiga (Golubeva) from Lithuania, who takes little interest in the crimes but unwittingly crosses paths with Camille. Atmospheric if nothing else. Based on the 1987 "Granny Killer" slayings of 20 women. French with subtitles. **110m/C VHS.** *FR* Richard Courcet, Vincent Dupont, Katerina Golubeva, Alex Descas, Beatrice Dalle, Laurent Grevill; **D:** Claire Denis; **W:** Claire Denis, Jean-Pol Fargeau; **C:** Agnes Godard. *NYF*

I, Claudius, Vol. 1: A Touch of Murder/Family Affairs 1991 Award-winning Masterpiece Theatre series tells the true story of the Roman Empire and the people determined to rule it. In these first two episodes, Augustus tries to control his conniving second wife, the beautiful Livia, who is determined that her son Tiberius will be the next Roman ruler. Her manipulations lead to bloody mayhem. Brilliant acting. Based on the books by Robert Graves. Also available as a seven-volume set. Made for television. **120m/C VHS.** *GB* Sian Phillips, Brian Blessed, Derek Jacobi; **D:** Herbert Wise. *PBS, FCT, SIG*

I, Claudius, Vol. 2: Waiting in the Wings/What Shall We Do With Claudius? 1980 Continuation of the Masterpiece Theatre series portraying the true story of the Roman Empire and its rulers. In the third and fourth episodes, Tiberius and his mother Livia attempt to capture the throne with a series of brutal manipulations. Young cousin Claudius, considered an ugly dimwit, watches from afar. Based on the books of Robert Graves. Also available as a seven-volume set. Made for television. **120m/C VHS.** Derek Jacobi, Sian Phillips, Brian Blessed; **D:** Herbert Wise. *PBS, FCT, SIG*

I, Claudius, Vol. 3: Poison Is Queen/Some Justice 1980 Episodes 5 and 6 see Emperor Augustus murdered and Tiberius on the throne he's coveted for so long. But how long can he stay, hiding the treachery that brought him there? Good question. Agrippina, wife of his latest victim, is determined to see him punished, and the Roman masses, not so stupid after all, have begun to see a pattern in the deaths of their best and brightest. Based on the books of Robert Graves. Also available as a seven-volume set. Made for television. **120m/C VHS.** Derek Jacobi, Sian Phillips, Brian Blessed; **D:** Herbert Wise. *PBS, FCT, SIG*

I, Claudius, Vol. 4: Queen of Heaven/Reign of Terror 1980 In episodes 7 and 8, Caligula begins his evil manipulation of Tiberius, involving him in a wide variety of amoral activities and creating a trail of blood. Based on the books of Robert Graves. Also available as a seven-volume set. Made for television. **120m/C VHS.** Derek Jacobi, Sian Phillips. *PBS, FCT, SIG*

I, Claudius, Vol. 5: Zeus, By Jove!/Hail Who? 1980 Caligula's schemes result in his rise to the throne after Tiberius. Debauchery rules and murder is a standard procedure that returns to remove the emperor. At last, patient Claudius, the only remaining heir, thought too foolish to be dangerous, ascends the throne. Award-winning Masterpiece Theatre production created by the BBC. Based on the books of Robert Graves. The first episode on this cassette contains the graphic scene of Caligula's evisceration of his sister, as he enacts the life of Zeus in demented belief that he is the god—be forewarned. Also available as a seven-volume set. Made for television. **120m/C VHS.** Derek Jacobi, John Hurt; **D:** Herbert Wise. *PBS, FCT, SIG*

I, Claudius, Vol. 6: Fool's Luck/A God in Colchester 1980 Episodes 11 and 12 see Emperor Claudius wise in the ways of statesmanship, but foolish in the ways of love. His young wife Messalina creates a furor when her sexual practices become known. In spite of his love, the emperor must punish her. Award-winning BBC production, shown in U.S. on Master-

piece Theatre. Based on the books of Robert Graves. Also available as a seven-volume set. **120m/C VHS.** Derek Jacobi; **D:** Herbert Wise. *PBS, FCT, SIG*

I, Claudius, Vol. 7: Old King Log 1980 Claudius, aging and sad, resigns himself to his destiny, as his wife makes plans for his death. Claudius wants only the time to complete the journal of his life. Brilliant acting from Jacobi in this BBC production shown in the U.S. on Masterpiece Theatre. Based on the books of Robert Graves. Also available as a seven-volume set. **60m/C VHS.** Derek Jacobi; **D:** Herbert Wise. *PBS, FCT, SIG*

I Come in Peace 🌑🌑 *Dark Angel* 1990 (R) A tough, maverick Texas cop embarks on a one-way ride to Noseblead City when he attempts to track down a malevolent alien drug czar who kills his victims by sucking their brains. Mindless thrills. **92m/C VHS, Beta, LV, Closed Caption.** Dolph Lundgren, Brian Benben, Betsy Brantley, Jesse Vint, Michael J. Pollard; **D:** Craig R. Baxley; **M:** Jan Hammer. *VTR*

I Confess 🌑🌑½ 1953 When a priest (Clift) hears a murderer's confession, the circumstances seem to point to him as the prime suspect. Tepid, overly serious and occasionally interesting midcareer Hitchcock. Adapted from Paul Anthelme's 1902 play. **95m/B VHS, Beta, LV.** Montgomery Clift, Anne Baxter, Karl Malden, Brian Aherne; **D:** Alfred Hitchcock; **C:** Robert Burks. *WAR, FCT, MLB*

I Conquer the Sea 🌑½ 1936 Two brothers, who works as whalers, cast their affection on the same woman. Drowns in its own melodrama. **68m/B VHS, 8mm.** Steffi Duna, Dennis (Stanley Morner) Morgan, Douglas Walton, George Cleveland, Johnny Pirrone; **D:** Victor Halperin. *VYY*

I Could Go on Singing 🌑🌑½ 1963 An aging American songstress, on a tour in Britain, becomes reacquainted with her illegitimate son and his British father, but eventually goes back to the footlights. Garland's last film. Songs include "By Myself" and "It Never Was You." A must for Garland fans. Letterboxed. **99m/C VHS, Beta, LV, Letterbox.** Judy Garland, Dirk Bogarde, Jack Klugman, Aline MacMahon; **D:** Ronald Neame. *MGM*

I Cover the Waterfront 🌑🌑½ 1933 A reporter is assigned to write about a boatman involved in a fishy scheme to smuggle Chinese immigrants into the country wrapped in shark skins. While trying to get the story, the journalist falls in love with the fisherman's daughter. Torrance passed away before its release. **70m/B VHS, Beta.** Claudette Colbert, Ben Lyon, Ernest Torrence, Hobart Cavanaugh; **D:** James Cruze. *NOS, MRV, VYY*

I Died a Thousand Times 🌑🌑 1955 Aging gangster Mad Dog Earle (pushup prince Palance) plans one last death-defying heist while hiding from police in the mountains. Meanwhile, the hard boiled gangster softens a bit thanks to surgery-needing girlfriend, but moll Winters doesn't seem to think that three's company. A low rent "High Sierra." From the novel by W.R. Burnett. **109m/C VHS, LV, Letterbox, Closed Caption.** Jack Palance, Shelley Winters, Lori Nelson, Lee Marvin, Earl Holliman, Lon Chaney Jr., Howard St. John; **D:** Stuart Heisler; **W:** W.R. Burnett. *WAR, FCT*

I Dismember Mama woof! *Poor Albert and Little Annie* 1974 (R) Classless story of an asylum inmate who escapes to kill his mother. Although he hates women, he likes little girls as evidenced by his nine-year-old love interest. Notably lacking in bloody scenes. **81m/C VHS, Beta.** Zooey Hall, Joanne Moore Jordan, Greg Mullavey, Marlene Tracy, Geri Reischl; **D:** Paul Leder; **W:** William W. Norton Sr.; **C:** William Swenning. *GEM*

I Do! I Do! 1984 This Los Angeles production of the Broadway musical covers 50 years of a marriage, beginning just before the turn of the century. **116m/C VHS, Beta.** Lee Remick, Hal Linden. *TTC*

I Don't Buy Kisses Anymore 🎬🎬½ 1992 (PG) Heartwarming story starring Alexander and Peeples as two mismatched lovers who end up realizing that they're made for each other. Alexander plays Bernie Fishbine, an overweight Jewish shoe store owner who falls for a psychology graduate student (Peeples). Little does he know, but Peeples is studying him for her term paper, appropriately titled "The Psychological Study of an Obese Male." Alexander gives a great performance, as do Kazan and Jacobi who play Bernie's parents. 112m/C VHS, Beta, **Closed Caption.** Jason Alexander, Nia Peeples, Lainie Kazan, Lou Jacobi, Eileen Brennan, Larry Storch, Arleen Sorkin; **D:** Robert Marcarelli; **W:** Jonnie Lindsell; **C:** Michael Ferris; **M:** Cobb Bussinger. PAR

I Don't Give a Damn 🎬🎬 1988 (R) An embittered wounded soldier returns home to his loved ones, rejects them, and becomes more and more uninterested in life itself. Subtitled. 94m/C VHS, Beta. IS Ika Sohar, Anat Waxman; **D:** Shmuel Imberman. TWE

I Don't Want to Be Born 🎬 The Devil Within Her 1975 (R) It's got all the right ingredients for overnight camp: a spurned dwarf, a large, howling baby-thing, slice and dice murder and mayhem, and Collins. It could've been so bad. Instead, this "Rosemary's Baby" rehash is just stupid bad. 90m/C VHS. GB Joan Collins, Eileen Atkins, Donald Pleasence, Ralph Bates, Caroline Munro; **D:** Peter Sasdy. NO

I Don't Want to Talk About It 🎬🎬½ De Eso No Se Habla 1994 Fable set in a small South American town in the '30s. The widowed Leonor (Brando) is the community leader, a woman determined to see that her daughter Charlotte (Podesta) be as happy and accomplished as possible. Leonor refuses to acknowledge Charlotte is a dwarf and size is never permitted to be mentioned in her presence. Her zealous protectiveness is challenged by worldly and charming newcomer Ludovico (Mastroianni) who becomes entranced by Charlotte. Mastroianni is masterly as always but the moody film proves slight. Based on story by Julio Llinas. Spanish with subtitles. 102m/C VHS, LV. AR Marcello Mastroianni, Luisina Brando, Alejandra Podesta; **D:** Maria-Luisa Bemberg; **W:** Maria-Luisa Bemberg, Jorge Goldenberg. COL

I Dood It 🎬🎬 By Hook or By Crook 1943 Young tailor's assistant Skelton falls hard for young actress Powell working near his shop. She agrees to date, and eventually marry him, but only to spite her boyfriend who has just run off with another woman. All's well however, when Skelton stumbles across a spy ring, is hailed a hero and helps Powell realize she really loves him. ♫Star Eyes; Taking a Chance on Love; Jericho; One O'Clock Jump; So Long Sarah Jane; Hola E Pae; Swing the Jinx Away. 102m/B VHS. Red Skelton, Eleanor Powell, Richard Ainley, Patricia Dane, Sam Levene, Thurston Hall, Lena Horne, Butterfly McQueen; **D:** Vincente Minnelli. MGM, CCB

I Dream of Jeannie 🎬 1952 The third and worst bio of Stephen Foster has Foster as a bookkeeper-cum-songwriter alternating between writing tunes and chasing Lawrence. When she dumps him, he goes into a funk. Will he be able to complete the title song? The suspense will kill you. Lots of singing, but not much else. 90m/C VHS. Ray Middleton, Bill Shirley, Muriel Lawrence, Lynn Bari, Rex Allen; **D:** Allan Dwan. NOS, VEC

I Dream Too Much 🎬🎬 1935 A musical vehicle for opera star Pons, as a French singer who marries an American composer played by Fonda. Songwriter falls into wife's shadow after pushing her into a singing career; she then raises his spirits a couple of octaves by helping him sell a musical comedy. Went into production after a rival company, Columbia, launched opera singer Grace Moore's acting career. Ball later bought this studio, where she was given her second starring role. ♫The Jockey on the Carousel; I'm the

Echo; I Got Love; I Dream Too Much; Bell Song; Ouro Nome. 95m/B VHS, Beta. Lily Pons, Henry Fonda, Eric Blore, Lucille Ball, Mischa Auer, Scotty Beckett; **D:** John Cromwell; **M:** Max Steiner. Nominations: Academy Awards '35: Best Sound. HHT, TTC

I Drink Your Blood 🎬½ 1971 (R) Hippie satanists looking for kicks spike an old man's drink with LSD. To get revenge, the old codger's grandson sells the nasty flower children meat pies injected with the blood of a rabid dog. The hippies then turn into cannibalistic maniacs, infecting anyone they bite. From the man responsible for "I Spit on Your Grave"; originally played on a double bill with "I Eat Your Skin." 83m/C VHS. Bhasker, Jadine Wong, Ronda Fultz, Elizabeth Marner-Brooks, George Patterson, Riley Mills, Iris Brooks, John Damon; **D:** David E. Durston. FRG, TPV

I Eat Your Skin woof! Zombies; Voodoo Blood Bath; Zombie 1964 Cannibalistic zombies terrorize a novelist and his girlfriend on a Caribbean island. Blood and guts, usually shown on a gourmet double bill with "I Drink Your Blood." 82m/C VHS. William Joyce, Heather Hewitt, Betty H. Lindon; **D:** Del Tenney. RHI, SNC, FCT

I Got the Hook-Up 🎬½ 1998 (R) Inner-city hustlers Black (Master P) and Blue (Johnson) have their own "department store" in a vacant lot where they sell various goods of dubious quality and origin. When a truckload of cell phones is mistakenly delivered to them, it ushers them into a new business venture. All hell breaks loose when a thug (Lister) has a money pick-up go bad because of the defective phones. Sporadically amusing comedy plays gang violence and misogyny for laughs, while the leads do nothing to make their characters interesting or even likable. **CW:** Pervasive strong language, crude sexual humor, nudity, drug content and some violence. 93m/C VHS. Master P, A.J. Johnson, Gretchen Palmer, Frantz Turner, Tommy (Tiny) Lister, Helen Martin, John Witherspoon, Harrison White, Ice Cube, Anthony Boswell, Lola Mae; **D:** Michael Martin; **W:** Master P; **C:** Antonio Calvache; **M:** Tommy Coster, Brad Fairman. NYR

I Hate Blondes 🎬🎬½ Odio le Bionde 1983 A group of criminals use a ghostwriter's burglaring stories as instructional manuals. The writer becomes involved with the gang. Relies heavily on visual humor. Notably among the comedy scenes is the author's search for jewels at a get-together. 90m/C VHS, Beta. IT **D:** Giorgio Capitani, Giorgio Capitani. NO

I Heard the Owl Call My Name 🎬🎬½ 1973 Poignant story of an Anglican priest who is relocated to an Indian fishing village on the ouskirts of Vancouver, British Columbia. Made for television and based on a Margaret Craven book. 74m/C Beta. Tom Courtenay, Dean Jagger, Paul Stanley; **D:** Daryl Duke.

I Killed Rasputin 🎬½ 1967 The "Mad Monk" who rose to power before the Russian Revolution lost his life in a bizarre assassination by Felix Youssoupoff. Film deals with the friendship between the men that ended in betrayal. Well-intentioned, but overwrought. Dubbed. 95m/C VHS, Beta. FR IT Geraldine Chaplin, Gert Frobe, Peter McEnery; **D:** Robert Hossein; **M:** Don Banks. NO

I Killed That Man 🎬🎬½ 1942 A prisoner scheduled to die in the electric chair is given an early ticket out when he is found poisoned. Evidence points to an unusual group of suspects. Effective low-budget thriller offers a few unexpected surprises. 72m/B VHS, Beta. Ricardo Cortez, Joan Woodbury, Iris Adrian, George Pembroke, Herbert Rawlinson, Pat Gleason, Ralf Harolde, Jack Mulhall, Vince Barnett, Gavin Gordon, John Hamilton; **D:** Phil Rosen. SNC

I Know What You Did Last Summer 🎬🎬🎬 1997 (R) Four teens get involved in a fatal hit-and-run accident and think they've managed to keep it a secret. Good girl Julie (Hewitt), beauty queen Helen (Gellar), arrogant jock Barry (Cox) and regular guy Ray (Prinze) make a pact to take the secret to their

graves, which may be sooner than they thought. One year later, the quartet receive letters which give the movie its title and set them against each other. After a few youngsters are made into bait on rather large fishing hooks, they band together to stop the bloodthirsty killer. Hint: it's not Mrs. Paul. Another quality slasher throwback written by Kevin Williamson, the man who made you "Scream." **CW:** Strong horror violence and language. 100m/C VHS, LV, **Closed Caption, DVD.** Jennifer Love Hewitt, Sarah Michelle Gellar, Ryan Phillippe, Freddie Prinze Jr., Muse Watson, Anne Heche, Bridgette Wilson, Johnny Galecki, Dan Albright; **D:** Jim Gillespie; **W:** Kevin Williamson; **C:** Denis Crossan; **M:** John Debney. Nominations: MTV Movie Awards '98: Breakthrough Performance (Gellar). COL

I Know Where I'm Going 🎬🎬🎬 1945 A young woman (Hiller), who believes that money brings happiness, is on the verge of marrying a rich old man, until she meets a handsome naval officer (Livesey) and finds a happy, simple life. Early on the female lead appears in a dream sequence filmed in the mode of surrealist painter Salvador Dali and avant garde director Luis Bunuel. Scottish setting and folk songs give a unique flavor. Brown provides a fine performance as a native Scot. 91m/B VHS, Beta, LV. GB Roger Livesey, Wendy Hiller, Finlay Currie, Pamela Brown; **D:** Michael Powell. HMV, BFA

I Know Why the Caged Bird Sings 🎬🎬🎬 1979 A black writer's memories of growing up in the rural South during the 1930s. Strong performances from Rolle and Good. Made-for-television film is based on the book by Maya Angelou. 100m/C VHS, Beta. Diahann Carroll, Ruby Dee, Esther Rolle, Roger E. Mosley, Paul Benjamin, Constance Good; **D:** Fielder Cook. KUI, ART

I Like Bats 1985 Can a psychiatrist help a vampire become a human? Polish dialogue with English subtitles. 90m/C VHS. **D:** Grzegorz Warchol. FCT

I Like It Like That 🎬🎬🎬 1994 (R) Chaotic family life and loves in the Bronx are the setting for this tale of a Cinderella in the record industry. Strong-willed black-Latina Lisette (Velez) has been married for 10 years to macho Latin, Chino (Seda), who has a wandering eye. When Chino is jailed for looting during a blackout, Lisette, needing to support their three kids, talks her way into a job with WASP record promoter Stephen Price (Dunne). When local gossips make it seem Lisette is having an affair, the newly sprung Chino retaliates by turning to lusty Magdalena (Vidal). Lisette, meanwhile, gathers support from her transvestite brother and proves to have inner resources previously unnoticed. Great Latino soundtrack illuminates the complications. Modest-budget sleeper quickly exited the theatre but proves to be a strong debut for director/writer Martin, reputed to be the first African-American woman to be given the reins by a major studio. **CW:** Brief, graphic sexual activity; scattered profanity; slight violence. 106m/C VHS, LV, **Closed Caption.** Lauren Velez, Jon Seda, Lisa Vidal, Jesse Borrego, Griffin Dunne, Rita Moreno, Tomas Melly, Desiree Casado, Isaiah Garcia; **D:** Darnell Martin; **W:** Darnell Martin; **C:** Alexander Grusynski; **M:** Sergio George. Nominations: Independent Spirit Awards '95: Best Actor (Seda), Best Actress (Velez), Best Cinematography, Best First Feature. COL

I Like to Play Games 🎬½ 1995 (R) Michael is looking for a woman who enjoys playing sexual games—and he seems to have the perfect partner in Suzanne. But just how far will their kinks take them? Also available unrated. 95m/C VHS, LV. Lisa Boyle, Ken Steadman; **D:** Moctezuma Lobato. APX

I Live in Fear 🎬🎬🎬 Record of a Living Being; Kimono No Kiroku 1955 Nakajima, an elderly, wealthy owner of a foundry, becomes increasingly fearful of atomic war and the threats to his family's safety. He tries to persuade them to leave Japan and move with him to Brazil but they fear the family will be ruined financially. Nakajima then burns down his foundry to force his children to move but instead they go to court and have him declared mentally incompetent. He is placed in an institution where he finds peace in the delusion that he has escaped to another planet and that the Earth has indeed suffered a nuclear holocaust. Provocative look at the fear of atomic warfare and radiation. In Japanese with English subtitles. 105m/C **VHS.** *JP* Toshiro Mifune, Takashi Shimura, Eiko Miyoshi, Haruko Togo; **D:** Akira Kurosawa. *FCT*

I Live in Grosvenor Square 🎬🎬 *A Yank In London* **1946** An American soldier in Great Britain falls in love with a major's fiancee. Entertaining if a bit drawn out. 106m/B **VHS.** *GB* Anna Neagle, Rex Harrison, Dean Jagger, Robert Morley, Jane Darwell; **D:** Herbert Wilcox. *NOS, DVT*

I Live My Life 🎬½ **1935** Stylish glossy flick with Crawford playing a bored New York debutante who travels to Greece and meets a dedicated archaeologist (Aherne). A love/hate relationship ensues in this typical Crawford vehicle where she is witty and parades around in sophisticated fashions, but there is little substance here. 92m/B **VHS, Closed Caption.** Joan Crawford, Brian Aherne, Frank Morgan, Aline MacMahon, Eric Blore, Fred Keating, Jessie Ralph, Arthur Treacher, Frank Conroy, Sterling Holloway, Vince Barnett, Hedda Hopper, Lionel Stander; **D:** Woodbridge S. Van Dyke; **W:** Joseph L. Mankiewicz, Gottfried Reinhardt, Ethel B. Borden. *MGM*

I Live with Me Dad 🎬½ **1986** A vagrant drunk and his son fight the authorities for the right to be together. 86m/C **VHS, Beta, Closed Caption.** *AU* Peter Hehir, Haydon Samuels; **D:** Paul Maloney. *FOX*

I Love All of You 🎬🎬½ **1983** Deneuve relives experiences with three former lovers—a composer, a well-intentioned nobody, and a rock star—as she enters into a relationship with a widower. 103m/C **VHS, Beta.** *FR* Catherine Deneuve, Jean-Louis Trintignant, Gerard Depardieu, Serge Gainsbourg; **D:** Claude Berri. *NO*

I Love Lucy **1952** Everyone's favorite redhead in scrape after scrape, along with her Cuban bandleader husband, Ricky Ricardo, and their neighbors Fred and Ethel Mertz. Episodes on this tape are "Lucy Does a TV Commercial" and "Lucy's Italian Movie." Other episodes available. 51m/B **VHS, LV.** Lucille Ball, Desi Arnaz Sr., Vivian Vance, William Frawley. *FOX, MOV*

I Love Melvin 🎬🎬½ **1953** Reynolds wants to be a Tinseltown goddess, and O'Connor just wants Reynolds; so he passes himself off as chief lenseman for a famous magazine and promises her a shot at the cover of "Look." Seems he has a little trouble on the follow through. Choreographed by Robert Alton, it's got a best ever football ballet (with Reynolds as pigskin). 🎵A Lady Loves; Saturday Afternoon Before The Game; I Wanna Wander; We Have Never Met As Of Yet; Life Has Its Funny Little Ups And Downs; Where Did You Learn To Dance?; And There You Are. 77m/C **VHS.** Donald O'Connor, Debbie Reynolds, Una Merkel, Richard Anderson, Jim Backus, Allyn Joslyn, Les Tremayne, Noreen Corcoran, Robert Taylor, Howard Keel; **D:** Don Weis. *MGM, TTC, FCT*

I Love My...Wife 🎬🎬 **1970 (R)** A medical student plays doctor with hospital nurses when he and his wife stop having sex during her pregnancy. The marriage becomes more strained when their son is born and his mother-in-law moves in. A comedy without the proper dosage of laughs. 98m/C **VHS, Beta.** Elliott Gould, Brenda Vaccaro, Angel Tompkins; **D:** Mel Stuart. *USH*

I Love N.Y. 🎬 **1987** A young metropolitan couple struggles to find true love amidst disapproving parents and doubting friends. Choppy direction and poor writing contribute to its failure. 100m/C **VHS, Beta, LV.** Scott Baio, Kelley Van Der Velden, Christopher Plummer, Jennifer O'Neill, Jerry Orbach, Virna Lisi; **D:** Alan Smithee; **M:** Bill Conti. *NO*

I Love Trouble 🎬🎬½ **1994 (PG)** Veteran reporter Peter Brackett (sexy veteran Nolte) and ambitious cub reporter Sabrina Petersen (young and sexy Roberts) are competitors working for rival Chicago newspapers. When they begin to secretly exchange information on a big story, they find their lives threatened and their rivalry turning to romance. Some action, simplistic retro script, one big star, one sorta big star, and you've got the perfect movie package for the Prozac decade. Written, produced and directed by husband/wife team Meyers and Shyer. 123m/C **VHS, LV, Closed Caption.** Julia Roberts, Nick Nolte, Saul Rubinek, Robert Loggia, James Rebhorn; **D:** Charles Shyer; **W:** Nancy Myers, Charles Shyer; **C:** John Lindley. *TOU*

I Love You 🎬½ **1981 (R)** Man down on his luck mistakenly assumes that a woman he meets is a hooker. She plays along, only to find that they are becoming emotionally involved. Pretentious cat-and-mouse game. 104m/C **VHS, Beta.** *BR* Sonia Braga, Paulo Cesar Pereio, Vera Fischer, Tarcisio Meria; **D:** Arnaldo Jabor. *MGM*

I Love You Again 🎬🎬🎬½ **1940** A classic screwball comedy with Powell and Loy working together (wonderfully) in something other than their "Thin Man" series. Powell is a gloomy businessman who's about to be divorced by Loy. But after an accident it turns out Powell had been suffering from amnesia and has now regained his memory (which he keeps a secret). It seems Mr. Respectable used to be a con man and he decides to revert to his criminal ways. He also doesn't remember Loy but falls instantly in love with her and must decide what kind of life he wants. Witty dialog, amusing situations, fine direction. 97m/B **VHS, LV.** William Powell, Myrna Loy, Frank McHugh, Edmund Lowe; **D:** Woodbridge S. Van Dyke. *MGM*

I Love You, Alice B. Toklas! 🎬🎬½ *Kiss My Butterfly* **1968** A straight uptight lawyer decides to join the peace and love generation in this somewhat maniacal satire of the hippie culture. Authored by Paul Mazursky and Larry Tucker. Incidentally, the title's Alice B. Toklas was actually the lifemate of "Lost Generation" author Gertrude Stein. 94m/C **VHS, Beta, LV.** Peter Sellers, Jo Van Fleet, Leigh Taylor-Young, Joyce Van Patten; **D:** Hy Averback; **W:** Paul Mazursky; **M:** Elmer Bernstein. *WAR, FCT*

I Love You ... Goodbye 🎬🎬 **1973** A frustrated housewife, fed up with the constant role of wife and mother, leaves her family in an effort to find a more challenging and fulfilling life. A good performance by Lange compensates for some of its muddledness. 74m/C **VHS, Beta.** Hope Lange, Earl Holliman. *BFA*

I Love You, I Love You Not 🎬🎬½ **1997** The Holocaust becomes a metaphor for one teen's survival of her first painful romance. Daisy (Danes) is a Jewish student at an anti-Semitic and snobby Manhattan prep school, where she falls in love with the ultimate gentile, Ethan (Law) in a "Kids" meets "The Way We Were" spin. Moreau is Nana, Daisy's grandmother and a Holocaust survivor who Daisy visits every weekend. The two share their painful stories (Danes also plays Nana as a young girl). Danes does what she does best as a misunderstood teen coming-of-age, Moreau shines in her role as the beloved grandmother. What misfires is the trite handling of the serious subject matter as Daisy's romance scores far more screen time than Nana's suffering. Hopkins, an established casting director, makes his feature debut. 92m/C **VHS.** *FR GE GB* Claire Danes, Jeanne Moreau, Jude Law, James Van Der Beek, Robert Sean Leonard, Kris Park, Lauren Fox, Emily Burkes-Nossiter, Carrie Slaza; **D:** Billy Hopkins; **W:** Wendy Kesselman; **C:** Maryse Alberti; **M:** Gil Goldstein. *NYR*

I Love You Rosa 🎬🎬½ **1972** Rosa, a young Jewish widow, wrestles big time with old world values. Required by custom to marry her dearly departed's eldest brother, she's not enamored with her newly betrothed. Not that he's a

nice guy; he seems to plan to take his marital duties very seriously. It's just that he's a tad youthful (11 years old, to be exact). Much rabbi consulting and soul searching. 90m/C **VHS.** Michal Bat-Adam, Gabi Oterman, Joseph Shiloah; **D:** Moshe Mizrahi; **W:** Moshe Mizrahi. Nominations: Academy Awards '72: Best Foreign Language Film. *FCT, NCJ*

I Love You to Death 🎬🎬½ **1990 (R)** Dry comedy based on a true story, concerns a woman who tries to kill off her cheating husband. Lots of stars, but they never shine. Hurt and Reeves are somewhat amusing as drugged up hit men who struggle with the lyrics to the National Anthem. Watch for director Kasdan as Devo's lawyer. Cates, Kline's real-life wife, has an un-billed part as one of his one-night stands. 110m/C **VHS, Beta, LV, Letterbox, Closed Caption.** Kevin Kline, Tracey Ullman, Joan Plowright, River Phoenix, William Hurt, Keanu Reeves, James Gammon, Victoria Jackson, Miriam Margolyes, Heather Graham; **Cameos:** Phoebe Cates; **D:** Lawrence Kasdan; **W:** John Kostmayer; **C:** Owen Roizman; **M:** James Horner. *COL*

I, Madman 🎬🎬 **1989 (R)** A novel-loving horror actress is stalked by the same mutilating madman that appears in the book she's presently reading. We call that bad luck. 90m/C **VHS, Beta, LV.** Jenny Wright, Clayton Rohner, William Cook; **D:** Tibor Takacs; **W:** David Chaskin; **C:** Bryan England.

I Married a Centerfold 🎬🎬 **1984** Television movie fluff about a young man's amorous pursuit of a model. 100m/C **VHS, Beta, LV.** Teri Copley, Timothy Daly, Diane Ladd, Bert Remsen, Anson Williams; **D:** Peter Werner. *NO*

I Married a Monster from Outer Space 🎬🎬½ **1958** The vintage thriller about a race of monster-like aliens from another planet who try to conquer earth. Despite its head-shaking title, an effective '50s sci-fi creeper. 78m/B **VHS, Beta.** Tom Tryon, Gloria Talbott, Maxie "Slapsie" Rosenbloom, Mary Treen, Ty Hardin, Ken Lynch, John Eldridge; **D:** Gene Fowler Jr. *PAR, MLB*

I Married a Vampire 🎬🎬 **1987** A country girl in the city is romanced and wed by a dashing vampire. Troma-produced hyper-camp. 85m/C **VHS, Beta.** Rachel Gordon, Brendan Hickey; **D:** Jay Raskin.

I Married a Witch 🎬🎬🎬 **1942** A witch burned at the stake during the Salem witch trials comes back to haunt the descendants of her accusers and gets romantic with one of them. Wonderfully played fantasy/comedy. 77m/B **VHS, Beta, LV.** Veronica Lake, Fredric March, Susan Hayward, Robert Benchley, Cecil Kellaway, Elizabeth Patterson, Robert Warwick, Eily Malyon, Mary Field, Nora Cecil, Emory Parnell, Helen St. Rayer, Aldrich Bowker, Emma Dunn, Harry Tyler, Ralph Peters, Ann Carter; **D:** Rene Clair; **W:** Robert Pirosh, Marc Connelly; **C:** Ted Tetzlaff; **M:** Roy Webb. Nominations: Academy Awards '42: Best Original Dramatic/Comedy Score. *MLB, WAR*

I Married a Woman 🎬🎬 **1956** Advertising executive marries beautiful blonde woman, but finds it very difficult to balance his career and marriage. Low on laughs. Shot in black and white, but includes a fantasy scene in color that features John Wayne. Pay attention to see young Angie Dickinson. 84m/B **VHS, Beta, LV.** George Gobel, Diana Dors, Adolphe Menjou, Nita Talbot; **D:** Hal Kanter. *NO*

I Married an Angel 🎬½ **1942** The last MacDonald/Eddy film. A playboy is lured away from his usual interests by a beautiful angel. Adapted from Rodgers and Hart Broadway play. Strange and less than compelling. 🎵I Married An Angel; I'll Tell the Man in the Street; Spring is Here; Tira Lira La; A Twinkle in Your Eye; Aloha Oe; Caprice Viennoise; Chanson Boheme; Anges Purs. 84m/C **VHS, Beta.** Jeanette MacDonald, Nelson Eddy, Binnie Barnes, Edward Everett Horton, Reginald Owen, Mona Maris, Janis Carter, Inez Cooper, Douglass Dumbrille, Leonid Kinskey, Marion Rosamond, Anne Jeffreys, Marek Windheim, Veda Ann Borg; **D:** Woodbridge S. Van Dyke; **W:** Anita Loos; **M:** Richard Rodgers, Lorenz Hart. *MGM, MVD*

I Met a Murderer 🎬🎬½ 1939 A man kills his nagging wife after a bitter argument and flees from her vengeful brother. Fine fugitive drama with a number of interesting twists. 79m/B VHS. James Mason, Pamela Kellino, Sylvia Coleridge, William Devlin, Esma Cannon, James Harcourt; **D:** Roy Kellino. SNC, NOS, DVT

I, Mobster 🎬🎬½ 1958 Cochran tells a Senate Sub-Committee of his rise in the ranks of the Underworld—from his humble beginning as a bet collector for a bookie to his position as kingpin of the crime syndicate. 80m/B VHS. Steve Cochran, Lita Milan, Robert Strauss, Celia Lovsky; **D:** Roger Corman; **C:** Floyd Crosby. NO

I Never Promised You a Rose Garden 🎬🎬🎬 1977 (R) A disturbed 16-year-old girl spirals down into madness and despair while a hospital psychiatrist struggles to bring her back to life. Based on the Joanne Greenberg bestseller. Compelling and unyielding exploration of the clinical treatment of schizophrenia. 90m/C VHS, Beta. Kathleen Quinlan, Bibi Andersson, Sylvia Sidney, Diane Varsi; **D:** Anthony Page; **W:** Gavin Lambert, Lewis John Carlino. Nominations: Academy Awards '77: Best Adapted Screenplay. WAR, OM

I Never Sang For My Father 🎬🎬🎬½ 1970 (PG) A devoted son must choose between caring for his cantankerous but well-meaning father, and moving out West to marry the divorced doctor whom he loves. While his mother wants him to stay near home, his sister, who fell out of her father's favor by marrying out of the family faith, argues that he should do what he wants. An introspective, stirring story based on the Robert Anderson play. 90m/C VHS, Beta, LV. Gene Hackman, Melvyn Douglas, Estelle Parsons, Dorothy Stickney; **D:** Gilbert Cates; **W:** Robert Anderson. Writers Guild of America '70: Best Adapted Screenplay; Nominations: Academy Awards '70: Best Actor (Douglas), Best Adapted Screenplay, Best Supporting Actor (Hackman). COL

I Only Want You to Love Me 🎬🎬 *Ich Will Doch Nur, Dass Ihr Mich Liebt* 1976 Peter's (Zeplichal) been denigrated by his family his entire life, so he decides to move with his wife (Aberle) to Munich and show them he can make something of himself. But his desires become compulsions and he falters under the strain of work and marriage, leading to a terrifying crackup. A true story, based on the book "Life Sentence" by Klaus Antes and Christine Eberhardt. Originally produced for TV; German with subtitles. 104m/C VHS. GE Vitus Zeplichal, Elke Aberle, Ernie Mangold, Joanna Hofe, Alexander Allerson; **D:** Rainer Werner Fassbinder; **W:** Rainer Werner Fassbinder; **C:** Michael Ballhaus; **M:** Peer Raben. WBF

I Ought to Be in Pictures 🎬🎬 1982 (PG) After hitchhiking from New York to Hollywood to break into the movies, a teenage actress finds her father, a screenwriter turned alcoholic-gambler. Late, desperately unfunny Neil Simon outing, adapted from a Simon play. 104m/C VHS, Beta. Walter Matthau, Ann-Margret, Dinah Manoff, Lance Guest, Michael Dudikoff; **D:** Herbert Ross; **W:** Neil Simon; **M:** Marvin Hamlisch. FOX

I Posed for Playboy 🎬🎬 1991 (R) Three women—one a college co-ed, one a stockbroker, and one a 37-year-old mother—quench their private passions by posing for Playboy Magazine. Made for television with additional footage added to give it an "R" rating. **CW:** Nudity and sexual scene. 98m/C VHS, LV, Closed Caption. Lynda Carter, Michele Greene, Amanda Peterson, Brittany York; **D:** Stephen Stafford. REP

I Remember Mama 🎬🎬🎬½ 1948 A true Hollywood heart tugger chronicling the life of a Norwegian immigrant family living in San Francisco during the early 1900s. Dunne triumphs as the mother, with a perfect Norwegian accent, and provides her family with wisdom and inspiration. A kindly father and four children round out the nuclear family. A host of oddball characters regularly pop in on the household—three high-strung aunts and an eccentric doctor who treats a live-in uncle. Adapted from John Van Druten's stage play, based on Kathryn Forbes memoirs, "Mama's Bank Account"; a TV series came later. 95m/B VHS, Beta, LV. Irene Dunne, Barbara Bel Geddes, Oscar Homolka, Ellen Corby, Cedric Hardwicke, Edgar Bergen, Rudy Vallee, Barbara O'Neil, Florence Bates; **D:** George Stevens. Golden Globe Awards '49: Best Supporting Actress (Corby); Nominations: Academy Awards '48: Best Actress (Dunne), Best Black and White Cinematography, Best Supporting Actor (Homolka), Best Supporting Actress (Corby, Bel Geddes). CCB, TTC

I See a Dark Stranger 🎬🎬🎬 *The Adventuress* 1946 Cynical yet whimsical postwar British spy thriller about an angry Irish lass who agrees to steal war plans for the Nazis in order to battle her native enemies, the British—then she falls in love with a British officer. A sharply performed, decidedly jaded view of nationalism and wartime "heroism." 112m/B VHS, Beta. GB Deborah Kerr, Trevor Howard, Raymond Huntley; **D:** Frank Launder. NO

I Sent a Letter to My Love 🎬🎬🎬 1981 An aging spinster, faced with the lonely prospect of the death of her paralyzed brother, places a personal ad for a companion in a local newspaper, using a different name. Unknown to her, the brother is the one who answers it, and they begin a romantic correspondence. Well-acted, touching account of relationships that change lives, but it takes its time in telling the story. 102m/C VHS, Beta. FR Simone Signoret, Jean Rochefort, Delphine Seyrig; **D:** Moshe Mizrahi; **W:** Moshe Mizrahi, Gerard Brach; **C:** Ghislan Cloquet. NO

I Shot a Man in Vegas 🎬½ 1996 (R) Low-budget variation of "Rashomon." Drinking buddies Johnny (Cubitt) and Grant (Stockwell) wind up in a back alley brawl and Johnny takes a bullet, supposedly shot dead by Grant. Only their friends, Gale (Garofalo), Martin (Drillinger), and Amy (Lippman), who witnessed the fight all saw it differently. So they decide to stash the corpse in their car trunk and head out across the desert to California. There's a last-minute revelation and a big finale but the strain shows. **CW:** Pervasive strong language, violence and a scene of sexuality. 84m/C VHS. John Stockwell, Janeane Garofalo, Brian Drillinger, Noelle Lippman, David Cubitt; **D:** Keoni Waxman; **W:** Keoni Waxman; **C:** Steven Firestone. AVI

I Shot Andy Warhol 🎬🎬🎬 1996 (R) Based on a true story, this black comedy focuses on the 15 minutes of fame achieved by Valerie Solanas, the woman who shot pop artist Andy Warhol for ignoring her in 1968. Taylor manages to recreate the more unpleasant aspects of Solanas without making her completely unsympathetic. Writer/director Harron, making her feature film debut, does a wonderful job of recreating the drugged-out world Warhol and his cohorts inhabited. Her script succeeds by attempting to understand Solanas's actions, while not excusing or sensationalizing them. Features music by former Velvet Underground member, John Cale. **CW:** Strong sexual content, language, drug use and brief violence. 100m/C VHS. Lili Taylor, Jared Harris, Stephen Dorff, Martha Plimpton, Donovan Leitch, Tahnee Welch, Michael Imperioli, Lothaire Bluteau, Anna Thompson, Peter Friedman, Jill Hennessey, Craig Chester, James Lyons, Reginald Rodgers, Jamie Harrold, Edoardo Ballerini, Lynn Cohen, Myriam Cyr, Isabel Gillies, Eric Mabius; **D:** Mary Harron; **W:** Mary Harron, Daniel Minahan; **C:** Ellen Kuras; **M:** John Cale. Nominations: Independent Spirit Awards '97: Best First Feature. HMK

I Shot Billy the Kid 🎬½ 1950 Billy the Kid decides to turn over a new leaf and live a decent life. The cards are stacked against him though: He's killed a man for nearly every year of his life, and old habits are hard to break. 58m/B VHS, Beta, LV. Donald (Don "Red") Barry, Robert Lowery, Tom Neal, Jack Perrin; **D:** William (Lester Williams) Berke. NO

I Shot Jesse James 🎬🎬🎬 1949 In his first film, director Fuller breathes characteristically feverish, maddened fire into the story of Bob Ford (Ireland) after he killed the notorious outlaw. An essential moment in Fuller's unique, America-as-tabloid-nightmare canon, and one of the best anti-westerns ever made. 83m/B VHS, Beta. John Ireland, Barbara Britton, Preston Foster, Reed Hadley; **D:** Samuel Fuller; **W:** Samuel Fuller. RXM

I Spit on Your Corpse woof! *Girls For Rent* 1974 (R) A vicious female hired killer engages in a series of terrorist activities. Stars Spelvin in a non-pornographic role. 90m/C VHS, Beta. Georgina Spelvin, Susan McIver, Kent Taylor; **D:** Al Adamson. REP

I Spit on Your Grave woof! *Day of the Woman* 1977 (R) Woman vacationing at a Connecticut lake house (on the Housatonic River) is brutally attacked and raped by four men. Left for dead, she recovers and seeks revenge. Not to be confused with the 1962 film of the same title, this one is worth zero as a film; lots of violent terror and gory death, totally irresponsibly portrayed. Also available in a 102-minute version. 98m/C VHS, Beta, LV. Camille Keaton, Eron Tabor, Richard Pace, Anthony Nichols, Gunter Kleeman; **D:** Mier Zarchi; **W:** Mier Zarchi; **C:** Yuri Haviv. VES

I Stand Condemned 🎬🎬½ *Moscow Nights* 1936 A Russian officer is tricked into borrowing money from a spy and is condemned for treason. He's saved when a girl who loves him gives herself to a profiteer. Worth seeing only for young Olivier's performance. 90m/B VHS, Beta, 8mm. GB Laurence Olivier, Penelope Dudley Ward, Robert Cochran; **D:** Anthony Asquith. NOS, MRV, VYY

I Take This Oath 🎬 1940 A cop is shocked to discover that his uncle is a wanted mobster, responsible for the death of a man. Hackneyed plot. 64m/B VHS, Beta. Gordon Jones, Joyce Compton, Craig Reynolds, J. Farrell MacDonald, Robert E. Homans, Veda Ann Borg; **D:** Sam Newfield. SNC

I, the Jury 🎬🎬 1982 (R) A remake of the 1953 Mike Hammer mystery in which the famed PI investigates the murder of his best friend. Assante mopes around as Hammer and looks out of place in this slowed-down version. 111m/C VHS, Beta. Armand Assante, Barbara Carrera, Laurene Landon, Alan King, Geoffrey Lewis, Paul Sorvino, Jessica James, Leigh Anne Harris, Lynette Harris; **D:** Richard T. Heffron; **W:** Larry Cohen; **M:** Bill Conti. FOX

I, the Worst of All 🎬🎬 *Yo, la Peor de Todas* 1990 Portrayal of 17th-century Mexican poet, Sister Juana Ines del la Cruz (Serna). She develops a passionate but chaste friendship with Maria Luisa (Sanda), the wife of the Spanish viceroy in Mexico, and writes love poems to her. However, the newly appointed archbishop (Murua) is a religious fanatic who condemns Juana's work, burns her books, and proceeds to persecute her. Adapted from the novel, "The Traps of Faith," by Octavio Paz. Spanish with subtitles. 105m/C VHS. SP Assumpta Serna, Dominique Sanda, Lautaro Murua, Hector Alterio; **D:** Maria-Luisa Bemberg; **W:** Maria-Luisa Bemberg, Antonio Larreta; **C:** Felix Monti; **M:** Luis Maria Serra. FRF

I Vitelloni 🎬🎬🎬½ *The Young and the Passionate; Vitelloni; Spivs* 1953 Fellini's semi-autobiographical drama, argued by some to be his finest work. Five young men grow up in a small Italian town. As they mature, four of them remain in Romini and limit their opportunities by roping themselves off from the rest of the world. The characters are multi-dimensional, including a loafer who is supported by his sister and a young stud who impregnates a local woman. The script has some brilliant insights into youth, adulthood and what's in between. 104m/B VHS, LV. IT Alberto Sordi, Franco Interlenghi, Franco Fabrizi, Leopoldo Trieste; **D:** Federico Fellini; **W:** Federico Fellini, Ennio Flaiano; **M:** Nino Rota. Nominations: Academy Awards '57: Best Story & Screenplay. MOV

I Wake Up Screaming 🎬🎬🎬 *Hot Spot* 1941 An actress' promoter is accused of her murder. Entertaining mystery with a surprise ending. Remade as "Vicki." 82m/B VHS, Beta, Closed

Caption. Betty Grable, Victor Mature, Carole Landis, Laird Cregar, William Gargan, Alan Mowbray, Allyn Joslyn; *D:* H. Bruce Humberstone. *FOX*

I Walked with a Zombie 🎬🎬🎬½ **1943** The definitive and eeriest of the famous Val Lewton/Jacques Tourneur horror films. Dee, a young American nurse, comes to Haiti to care for the catatonic matriarch of a troubled family. Local legends bring themselves to bear when the nurse takes the ill woman to a local voodoo ceremony for "healing." Superb, startling images and atmosphere create a unique context for this serious "Jane Eyre"-like story; its reputation has grown through the years. **69m/B VHS, Beta, LV.** Frances Dee, Tom Conway, James Ellison, Christine Gordon, Edith Barrett, Darby Jones, Sir Lancelot; *D:* Jacques Tourneur; *W:* Curt Siodmak, Ardel Wray; *C:* J. Roy Hunt. *TTC, FCT, MLB*

I Wanna Be a Beauty Queen **1985** Divine hosts the "Alternative Miss World" pageant featuring all sorts of bizarre contestants. **81m/C VHS, Beta.** Divine, Little Nell, Andrew Logan. *FCT, HHE*

I Wanna Hold Your Hand 🎬🎬½ **1978 (PG)** Teenagers try to crash the Beatles' appearance on the Ed Sullivan show. **104m/C VHS, Beta, LV, Closed Caption.** Nancy Allen, Bobby DiCicco, Wendie Jo Sperber, Marc McClure, Susan Kendall Newman, Theresa Saldana, Eddie Deezen, William Jordan; *D:* Robert Zemeckis; *W:* Robert Zemeckis. *WAR, FCT*

I Want to Live! 🎬🎬🎬 **1958** Based on a scandalous true story, Hayward gives a riveting, Oscar-winning performance as a prostitute framed for the murder of an elderly woman and sentenced to death in the gas chamber. Producer Walter Wanger's seething indictment of capital punishment. **120m/B VHS, Beta, LV.** Susan Hayward, Simon Oakland, Theodore Bikel; *D:* Robert Wise; *M:* Lionel Lindon; *M:* Johnny Mandel. Academy Awards '58: Best Actress (Hayward); Golden Globe Awards '59: Best Actress—Drama (Hayward); New York Film Critics Awards '58: Best Actress (Hayward); Nominations: Academy Awards '58: Best Adapted Screenplay, Best Black and White Cinematography, Best Director (Wise), Best Film Editing, Best Sound. *MGM, BTV, CCB*

I Want What I Want 🎬🎬 **1972 (R)** A young Englishman wants a sex-change, lives as a woman, falls in love, complications ensue. Not as shocking to watch as it might seem, but more a melodramatic gender-bender. **91m/C VHS, Beta.** *GB* Anne Heywood, Harry Andrews, Jill Bennett; *D:* John Dexter.

I Want You 🎬🎬½ **1951** Small-town life in Greenhill is disturbed for various citizens by the gathering storm of the Korean War. WWII vet Martin Greer (Andrews) is uncertain about re-enlisting while his wife Nancy (McGuire) is totally against the idea. Young Jack (Granger) doesn't want to leave his girl and family while his dad (Keith) tries to instill some patriotic fervor in his son, while George's (Milner) father (Baldwin) doesn't want to let him go. Dated but not unaffecting. **102m/B VHS.** Dana Andrews, Dorothy McGuire, Farley Granger, Peggy Dow, Robert Keith, Mildred Dunnock, Martin Milner, Walter Baldwin, Jim Backus, Ray Collins; *D:* Mark Robson; *W:* Irwin Shaw; *C:* Harry Stradling; *M:* Leigh Harline. *HBO*

I Was a Male War Bride 🎬🎬🎬 **1949** Hilarious WWII comedy. French officer Grant falls in love with and marries WAC lieutenant Sheridan in occupied Europe. Planning to leave the continent and settle down in the U.S., the couple hits a roadblock of red tape and Grant must cross-dress in order to accompany his bride on the troop ship taking her home. Worth watching for Grant's performance alone. Based on the novel by Henri Rochard. **105m/B VHS.** Cary Grant, Ann Sheridan, Randy Stuart, Kenneth Tobey, William Neff, Marion Marshall; *D:* Howard Hawks; *W:* Charles Lederer, Leonard Spigelgass, William Neff; *M:* Cyril Mockridge. *FXV*

I Was a Teenage TV Terrorist woof! *Amateur Hour* **1987** Two teenagers pull on-the-air pranks at the local cable television, blaming it all on an imaginary terrorist group. Poorly acted, cheaply made, and poin-

tless. **85m/C VHS, Beta.** Adam Nathan, Julie Hanlon; *D:* Stanford Singer; *W:* Kevin McDonough. *ART*

I Was a Teenage Werewolf 🎬🎬½ **1957** "Rebel Without a Cause" meets "The Curse of the Werewolf" in this drive-in rock 'n' roll horror. A troubled young man (pre-Bonanza Landon, in his first feature film appearance) suffers from teen angst and low production values, and falls victim to shrink Bissel. The good doctor turns out to be a bad hypnotist, and Landon's regression therapy takes him beyond childhood into his, gasp, primal past, where he sprouts a premature beard and knuckle hair. Misconstrued and full of terrible longings, the hairy highschooler is understood only by girlfriend Lime and misunderstood hair-sprouting teen viewers. Directorial debut of Fowler. **70m/B VHS.** Michael Landon, Yvonne Lime, Whit Bissell, Tony Marshall, Dawn Richard, Barney Phillips, Ken Miller, Cindy Robbins, Michael Rougas, Robert Griffin, Joseph Mell, Malcolm Atterbury, Eddie Marr, Vladimir Sokoloff, Louise Lewis, S. John Launer, Guy Williams, Dorothy Crehan; *D:* Gene Fowler Jr.; *W:* Ralph Thornton; *C:* Joseph LaShelle. *COL, OM*

I Was a Teenage Zombie 🎬 **1987** Spoof of high school horror films features a good zombie against a drug-pushing zombie. Forget the story and listen to the music by Los Lobos, the Fleshtones, the Waitresses, Dream Syndicate, and Violent Femmes. **92m/C VHS, Beta, LV.** Michael Rubin, Steve McCoy, Cassie Madden, Allen Rickman; *D:* John E. Michalakis. *NLC*

I Was a Zombie for the FBI 🎬½ **1982** Intelligence agency toughens its hiring criteria. Much McCarthyian mirth. **105m/B VHS, Beta.** James Raspberry, Larry Raspberry, John Gillick, Christina Wellford, Anthony Isbell, Laurence Hall, Rick Crowe; *D:* Maurice Penczner; *C:* Rick Dupree. *NO*

I Will Fight No More Forever 🎬🎬🎬 **1975** A vivid recounting of the epic true story of the legendary Chief Joseph who led the Nez Perce tribe on a 1,600-mile trek to Canada in 1877. Disturbing and powerful. Made for television. **100m/C VHS, Beta.** James Whitmore, Ned Romero, Sam Elliott; *D:* Richard T. Heffron. *CNG, MRV, GEM*

I Will, I Will for Now 🎬🎬 **1976 (R)** Tacky sex clinic comedy with Keaton and Gould trying to save their marriage through kinky therapy. **109m/C VHS, Beta.** Diane Keaton, Elliott Gould, Paul Sorvino, Victoria Principal, Robert Alda, Warren Bellinger; *D:* Norman Panama; *W:* Norman Panama; *C:* John A. Alonzo.

I Wonder Who's Killing Her Now? 🎬🎬 **1976** Husband pays to have his wife murdered, then changes his mind. On-again, off-again comedy. **87m/C VHS.** Bob Dishy, Joanna Barnes, Bill Dana, Vito Scotti; *D:* Steven Hilliard Stern. *ART*

Ice 🎬🎬½ **1993 (R)** Charley and Ellen Reed are thieves whose latest heist is $60 million in diamonds from mob boss Vito Malta. There's trouble when they try to fence the goods and Ellen is left with the merchandise and on the run from Malta's henchmen. *CW:* Language, gangster violence, and scene of sexuality. **91m/C VHS, LV, Closed Caption.** Traci Lords, Phillip Troy, Zach Galligan, Jorge Rivero, Michael Bailey Smith, Jamie Alba, Jean Pfleiger, Floyd Levine; *D:* Brook Yeaton; *W:* Sean Dash. *PMH*

Ice Castles 🎬🎬 **1979 (PG)** A young figure skater's Olympic dreams are dimmed when she is blinded in an accident, but her boyfriend gives her the strength, encouragement, and love necessary to perform a small miracle. Way too schmaltzy. **110m/C VHS, Beta.** Robby Benson, Lynn-Holly Johnson, Tom Skerritt, Colleen Dewhurst, Jennifer Warren, David Huffman; *D:* Donald Wrye; *W:* Donald Wrye, Gary L. Bain; *C:* Bill Butler; *M:* Marvin Hamlisch. Nominations: Academy Awards '79: Best Song ("Theme from Ice Castles—Through the Eyes of Love"). *COL*

Ice Cream Man 🎬 **1995 (R)** Quite disgusting horror tale of a dweeby, demented ice cream man who delivers gore and death along with his frozen treats. *CW:* Strong horror/terror and gore. **96m/C VHS.** Clint Howard, Sandahl Bergman, Olivia Hus-

sey, Lee Majors II, David Naughton, Jan-Michael Vincent, David Warner, Steve Garvey; *D:* Norman Apstein. *APX*

The Ice Flood 🎬🎬 **1926** Silent family type comedy of a son who proves to the old man that he wrote the book on life, wagering the successful supervision of dad's lumberjacks. **63m/B VHS, Beta.** Kenneth Harlan, Viola Dana; *D:* George B. Seitz. *GPV*

Ice House 🎬🎬 **1989** A sophisticated young lady flees Texas for Hollywood, searching for a better life. When her ex-lover shows up and wants her to go back, the lackless turmoil begins. Pairs real-life couple Gilbert and Brinkman. **81m/C VHS, Beta.** Melissa Gilbert, Bo Brinkman, Andreas Manolikakis, Buddy Quaid; *D:* Bo Brinkman, Eagle Pennell; *W:* Bo Brinkman. *NO*

The Ice House 🎬🎬🎬 **1997** Chilling TV adaptation of Minette Walters' first mystery. Ten years ago Phoebe Maybury's (Downie) abusive husband David disappeared. Locally condemned as a murderess, she and her friends Diana (Barber) and Anne (Aldridge) have been shunned by their small-minded community. Now a body has been discovered in an ice house located on Maybury property. Is it David? Inspector Walsh (Redgrave), who couldn't prove anything against Phoebe before, certainly thinks so, but his on-the-edge associate Sgt. McLoughlin (Craig) isn't so certain. **180m/C VHS.** *GB* Daniel Craig, Penny Downie, Corin Redgrave, Kitty Aldridge, Frances Barber; *D:* Tim Fywell; *W:* Lizzie Mickery. *VTR, WGB*

Ice Palace 🎬🎬 **1960** Two rugged adventurers maintain a lifelong rivalry in the primitive Alaskan wilderness, their relationship dramatizing the development of the 49th state. Silly but entertaining. Based on Edna Ferber's novel. **143m/C VHS, Beta.** Richard Burton, Robert Ryan, Carolyn Jones, Shirley Knight, Martha Hyer, Jim Backus, George Takei; *D:* Vincent Sherman; *C:* Joseph Biroc; *M:* Max Steiner. *WAR*

Ice Pawn 🎬🎬 **1992** Alex Dalton may finally get to realize his dream of becoming a gold medal ice skater if he can beat Misha, his Russian rival. He soon finds out that Misha isn't his only problem, as he unknowingly becomes a pawn in a game of corruption and greed that could totally ruin his career. **102m/C VHS.** Paul Cross, Dan Haggerty, Robert Budaska, Chris Thomas; *D:* Barry Samson; *W:* Paul Cross. *NO*

Ice Pirates 🎬½ **1984 (PG)** Space pirates in the far future steal blocks of ice to fill the needs of a thirsty galaxy. Cool plot has its moments. **91m/C VHS, Beta, LV.** Robert Urich, Mary Crosby, Michael D. Roberts, John Matuszak, Anjelica Huston, Ron Perlman, John Carradine, Robert Symonds; *D:* Stewart Raffill; *W:* Stewart Raffill; *M:* Bruce Broughton. *MGM*

The Ice Runner 🎬🎬½ **1993 (R)** Low-key Cold War thriller, filmed in 1991, about a U.S. spy who escapes from the Soviet gulag. Jeffrey West (Albert) gets caught in a botched payoff to a Soviet minister and when the diplomats wash their hands of him a rigged trial has West sentenced to 12 years hard labor. A convenient train wreck lets him assume a different prisoner's name which gets him to a minimum security camp under the eyes of a suspicious commander. Now West needs to escape and cross 39 miles of icy tundra separating his Russian prison from American freedom. *CW:* Violence and scene of sexuality. **116m/C VHS.** Edward Albert, Eugene Lazarev, Olga Kabo, Victor Wong, Alexander Kuznitsov, Basil Hoffman, Bill Bordy, Sergei Ruban; *D:* Barry Samson; *W:* Joyce Warren, Clifford Coleman, Joshua Stallings. *MNC*

Ice Station Zebra 🎬🎬½ **1968 (G)** A nuclear submarine races Soviet seamen to find a downed Russian satellite under a polar ice cap. Suspenseful Cold War adventure based on the novel by Alistair MacLean. **148m/C VHS, Beta, LV, Letterbox.** Rock Hudson, Ernest Borgnine, Patrick McGoohan, Jim Brown, Lloyd Nolan, Tony Bill; *D:* John Sturges; *C:* Daniel F. Fapp; *M:* Michel Legrand. Nominations: Academy Awards '68: Best Cinematography. *MGM*

The Ice Storm 🎬🎬🎬½ 1997 (R) Excellent family drama/period piece (the 1970s) directed by Ang Lee and based on the book by Rick Moody. Kline plays a husband and father too self-absorbed to notice his marriage (to Allen) unraveling into crisis, and his children (Maguire and Ricci) mimicking the sordid behavior that surrounds them. Skillfully fuses together a frank, unsympathetic look at family psychology, while also making a comment on the social situation of the early 1970s. Flirts with being overpoweringly negative and moody, but is elevated by Lee's insight and direction. Excellent job by the entire cast, especially Weaver, frighteningly dead-on as an emotionally reckless wife and mother, and Hann-Byrd and Wood as her eerie sons. **CW:** Sexuality and drug use, including scenes involving children, and for language. 113m/C VHS, LV, Closed Caption. Kevin Kline, Sigourney Weaver, Joan Allen, Christina Ricci, Tobey Maguire, Elijah Wood, Katie Holmes, Henry Czerny, Adam Hann-Byrd, David Krumholtz, Jamey Sheridan, Maia Danzinger; **D:** Ang Lee; **W:** James Schamus; **C:** Frederick Elmes; **M:** Mychael Danna. British Academy Awards '97: Best Supporting Actress (Weaver); Nominations: British Academy Awards '97: Best Adapted Screenplay; Golden Globe Awards '98: Best Supporting Actress (Weaver); Writers Guild of America '97: Best Adapted Screenplay. FXV

Icebox Murders woof! 1987 A crazed, motiveless, faceless killer hangs his victims in a walk-in freezer. Store this one. 90m/C VHS, Beta. Jack Taylor, Mirta Miller. NO

Iced 🎬 1988 Wild fun turns to horror on a ski trip as a group of college friends are hunted by a maniac on the loose. It's all downhill. 86m/C VHS, Beta. Debra Deliso, Doug Stevenson, Ron Kologie, Elizabeth Gorcey, Alan Johnson; **D:** Jeff Kwitny.

Iceland 🎬🎬 1942 Labored romance of an Iceland girl and a Marine with plenty of skating thrown in for good measure. Skating and singing interludes are the best part of an otherwise average film. ♪You Can't Say No to a Soldier; There Will Never Be Another You; Lover's Knot; Let's Bring New Glory to Old Glory; I Like a Military Tune. 79m/B VHS. Sonja Henie, John Payne, Jack Oakie, Felix Bressart, Osa Massen, Fritz Feld; **D:** H. Bruce Humberstone; **W:** Robert Ellis, Helen Logan. FXV

Iceman 🎬🎬🎬 1984 (PG) A frozen prehistoric man is brought back to life, after which several culture shock takes hold. Underwritten but nicely acted, especially by Lone as the primal man. 101m/C VHS, Beta, LV, Letterbox. Timothy Hutton, Lindsay Crouse, John Lone, David Strathairn, Josef Sommer, Danny Glover; **D:** Fred Schepisi; **W:** Chip Proser; **C:** Ian Baker; **M:** Bruce Smeaton. USH

The Icicle Thief 🎬🎬🎬 Ladri di Saponette 1989 "The Naked Gun" for the art-house crowd. As a stark, black-and-white neo-realist tragedy airs on TV, bright color commercials disrupt the narrative. Soon ads invade the the movie itself, and the film's director jumps into his picture to fix the damage. Study up on your postwar Italian cinema and this'll seem hilarious; otherwise the real fun doesn't kick in until the halfway point. In Italian with English subtitles. 93m/C VHS. IT Maurizio Nichetti, Caterina Sylos Labini, Claudio G. Fava, Renato Scarpa, Heidi Komarek; **D:** Maurizio Nichetti. FXL, FCT

Icy Breasts 🎬🎬🎬 1975 A French psychiatrist tries to prevent his beautiful but psychotic patient from continuing her murdering spree. Dubbed. 105m/C VHS, Beta. FR Alain Delon, Mireille Darc; **D:** Georges Lautner. FCT

I'd Climb the Highest Mountain 🎬🎬🎬 1951 Sincere, sentimental piece of Americana about a country preacher (Lundigan) and his city wife (Hayward) as they adjust to life in a small town in Southern hill country. Filmed on location in Georgia. Film was a big hit, especially in the South. Based on the novel by Corra Harris. 88m/C VHS. Susan Hayward, William Lundigan, Rory Calhoun, Gene Lockhart, Ruth Donnelly, Barbara Bates, Lynn Bari, Alexander Knox; **D:** Henry King; **W:** Lamar Trotti. FXV

I'd Give My Life 🎬½ 1936 A gangster's ex-wife is presently married to the governor. He tries to use their honest but framed son to blackmail her. 73m/B VHS, Beta. Guy Standing, Frances Drake, Tom Brown, Janet Beecher; **D:** Edwin L. Marin. VYY

Idaho 🎬½ 1943 On a mission to close down houses of ill repute, Rodgers teams up with Autry's old sidekick Burnette. 70m/B VHS, Beta. Roy Rogers, Harry Shannon, Virginia Grey, Smiley Burnette, Ona Munson; **D:** Joseph Kane. NOS, VDM, VCN

Idaho Transfer woof! Deranged 1973 (PG) Fonda's second directorial effort; Carradine's first screen appearance. An obnoxious group of teens travel through time to Idaho in the year 2044. Environmental wasteland story is dull and confused. 90m/C VHS, Beta. Keith Carradine, Kelley Bohanan; **D:** Peter Fonda. MPI, FCT

Identity Crisis 🎬 1990 (R) Campy fashion maven and flamboyant rapper switch identities causing much tedious overacting. Lifeless murder comedy from father and son Van Peebles. **CW:** Language and some sensuality. 98m/C VHS, LV. Mario Van Peebles, Ilan Mitchell-Smith, Nicholas Kepros, Shelly Burch, Richard Clarke; **D:** Melvin Van Peebles.

Identity Unknown 🎬🎬½ 1945 Shell-shocked veteran goes AWOL to discover who he is, meeting grieving relatives along the way. Interesting premise is sometimes moving. 70m/B VHS, Beta, 8mm. Richard Arlen, Cheryl Walker, Roger Pryor, Bobby Driscoll; **D:** Walter Colmes. VYY

The Idiot 🎬🎬🎬🎬 1951 Dostoevski's Russian novel is transported by Kurosawa across two centuries to post-war Japan, where the madness and jealousy continue to rage. In Japanese with English subtitles. 166m/B VHS. Toshiro Mifune, Masayuki Mori, Setsuko Hara, Yoshiko Kuga, Takashi Shimura; **D:** Akira Kurosawa. NYF

Idiot Box 🎬🎬 1997 Crazy youth comedy about lazy, brainless Kev (Mendelsohn) and Mick (Sims) who spend most of their unemployed time watching violent cop shows on TV and drinking beer. It's from the "idiot box" that the dim duo get the idea that they've learned enough to rob a bank, but it just so happens that a pair of crooks, who wear clown masks, are already on a bank crime spree. Naturally, both sets of robbers choose the same bank as their target and the cops just happen to be waiting. 83m/C VHS. AU Ben Mendelsohn, Jeremy Sims, John Polson, Robyn Loau, Graeme Blundell, Deborah Kennedy, Stephen Rae, Andrew S. Gilbert, Amanda Muggleton, Paul Gleeson, Susie Porter; **D:** David Caesar; **W:** David Caesar; **C:** Joseph Pickering; **M:** Tim Rogers, Nick Launay. Nominations: Australian Film Institute '97: Best Actor (Sims), Best Art Direction/Set Decoration, Best Director (Caesar), Best Film Editing, Best Sound, Best Score. NYR

Idiot's Delight 🎬🎬🎬 1939 At an Alpine hotel, a song and dance man meets a gorgeous Russian countess who reminds him of a former lover. Incredibly, Gable sings and dances through "Puttin' on the Ritz," the film's big highlight. Based on the Pulitzer Prize-winning play by Robert Sherwood. 107m/B VHS, Beta, LV. Clark Gable, Norma Shearer, Burgess Meredith, Edward Arnold, Charles Coburn, Joseph Schildkraut; **D:** Clarence Brown; **C:** William H. Daniels. CCB, MGM

The Idol Dancer 🎬🎬½ 1920 Romance and adventure in the South Seas with a drunken American beachcomber inspired by love to change his ways. There's also a native uprising for added excitement. Minor Griffith but nice Nassau scenery. 93m/B VHS. Richard Barthelmess, Clarine Seymour, Creighton Hale, George MacQuarrie, Kate Bruce, Anders Randolf, Walter James, Thomas Carr; **D:** D.W. Griffith. GPV, GVV

Idolmaker 🎬🎬½ 1980 (PG) A conniving agent can make a rock star out of anyone. Well-acted fluff with Sharkey taking a strong lead. The first film by hack-meister Hackford and somewhat based on true-life teen fab Fabian. 119m/C VHS, Beta, LV. Ray Sharkey, Tovah Feldshuh, Peter Gallagher, Paul Land, Joe Pantoliano, Maureen McCormick, John

Anrea, Richard Bright, Olympia Dukakis, Steven Apostlee Peck; **D:** Taylor Hackford; **C:** Adam Holender; **M:** Jeff Barry. Golden Globe Awards '81: Best Actor—Musical/Comedy (Sharkey). MGM

If... 🎬🎬🎬🎬 1969 (R) Three unruly seniors at a British boarding school refuse to conform. A popular, anarchic indictment of staid British society, using the same milieu as Vigo's "Zero de Conduite," with considerably more violence. The first of Anderson and McDowell's trilogy, culminating with "O Lucky Man!" and "Britannia Hospital." In color and black and white. 111m/C VHS, Beta, LV. GB Malcolm McDowell, David Wood, Christine Noonan, Richard Warwick, Robert Swann, Arthur Lowe, Mona Washbourne, Graham Crowden, Hugh Thomas, Guy Ross, Peter Jeffrey, Geoffrey Chater, Mary MacLeod, Anthony Nicholls, Ben Aris, Charles Lloyd Pack, Rupert Webster, Brian Pettifer, Sean Bury, Michael Cadman; **D:** Lindsay Anderson; **W:** David Sherwin; **C:** Miroslav Ondricek; **M:** Marc Wilkinson. Cannes Film Festival '69: Best Film. PAR

If Ever I See You Again 🎬 1978 (PG) The creator of "You Light Up My Life" stars in the sentimental melodrama. Two adolescent lovers meet again years later and try to rekindle old passions. Done with as much skill as "Light" minus a hit song. 105m/C VHS, Beta. Joseph Brooks, Shelley Hack, Jerry Keller, Jimmy Breslin; **D:** Joseph Brooks; **W:** Joseph Brooks; **M:** Joseph Brooks. COL

If I Were Rich 🎬🎬 Cash; For Love or Money 1933 Gwenn is arranging a meeting at his home for a group of financiers he hopes will back a scheme to save his ailing business. Meanwhile he has to dodge bill collectors and others determined to ruin his plans. 63m/B VHS, Beta. GB Edmund Gwenn, Wendy Barrie, Robert Donat, Clifford Heatherly; **D:** Zoltan Korda. VYY, FCT, NOS

If It's a Man, Hang Up 🎬½ 1975 A model is terrified by harrowing telephone calls from a stranger. 71m/C VHS, Beta. Carol Lynley, Gerald Harper. ART

If It's Tuesday, This Must Be Belgium 🎬🎬🎬 1969 (G) A fast-paced, frantic, and funny look at a group of Americans on a whirlwind European tour. The group does a nine-country, 18-day bus tour with clashing, comic personalities and lots of romantic possibilities. Remade as a 1987 television movie. 99m/C VHS, LV. Suzanne Pleshette, Ian McShane, Mildred Natwick, Norman Fell, Michael Constantine, Peggy Cass, Murray Hamilton, Marty Ingels, Sandy Baron, Pamela Britton, Luke Halpin; **D:** Mel Stuart. MGM, MOV

If Looks Could Kill 🎬🎬 1986 (R) Would-be hitman film noir about a man spying on a female embezzler and falling in love. 90m/C VHS. Alan Fisler, Tim Gail, Kim Lambert, Jeanne Marie; **D:** Chuck Vincent. REP

If Looks Could Kill 🎬🎬½ 1991 (PG-13) TV stud Grieco makes film debut as a high school class cutup who travels to France with his class to parlez vous for extra credit. Mistaken for a CIA agent, he stumbles into a plot to take over all the money in the whole wide world, and much implausible action and eyelash batting follows. Extra kibbles for supporting characterizations. Oh, and don't be put off by the fact that the Parisian scenes were shot in Montreal. 89m/C VHS, Beta, LV, 8mm, Closed Caption. Richard Grieco, Linda Hunt, Roger Rees, Robin Bartlett, Gabrielle Anwar, Roger Daltrey, Geraldine James, Carole Davis; **D:** William Dear; **W:** Fred Dekker; **M:** David Foster. WAR

If Lucy Fell 🎬🎬 1995 (R) Schaeffer serves as writer/director/star of this predictable 90s-style romantic comedy. Ludicrous premise has psychotherapist Lucy (Parker) bent on realizing a 10-year-old pact with longtime friend Joe (Schaeffer) that stipulates they both jump off the Brooklyn Bridge if neither one has found true love by age 30. With the big birthday approaching, Lucy takes a desperate shot with eccentric painter Bwick (Stiller), while Joe finally goes for the object of his desire, asking beautiful neighbor Jane (MacPherson) to a showing of his paintings. Highlights come in the casting, with Parker a solid and energetic neurotic and MacPherson showing that there's something beyond her more obvious talents.*CW:* Language and some sexuality. **92m/C VHS, LV, Closed Caption.** Sarah Jessica Parker, Eric Schaeffer, Ben Stiller, Elle Macpherson, James Rebhorn, Dominic Luchese; *D:* Eric Schaeffer; *W:* Eric Schaeffer, Tony Spiridakis; *C:* Ron Fortunato; *M:* Amanda Kravat, Charles Pettis. *COL*

If These Walls Could Talk 🐾🐾½
1996 (R) Cable movie covers four decades, from the '50s to the present, in telling the stories of three women and the different ways they deal with unexpected pregnancies. "1952" finds recently widowed nurse Claire (Moore) discovering she's pregnant—and it's not her late husband's. In some graphic scenes she tries to end the pregnancy herself with a knitting needle and later through a back-alley abortion. Happily married Barbara (Spacek) already has four children in "1974" and has just returned to college. Then she discovers she's pregnant again. Abortion's an option but does Barbara want one? Finally, college student Christine (Heche) gets pregnant by her married professor in "1996" and reluctantly opts for an abortion at a family planning clinic, which is besieged by pro-lifers and on the edge of some violent confrontations.*CW:* Realistic depiction of abortions, a graphic shooting and some language. **109m/C VHS, Closed Caption.** Demi Moore, Catherine Keener, Jason London, Shirley Knight, Kevin Cooney, CCH Pounder, Robin Gammell, Sissy Spacek, Xander Berkeley, Joanna Gleason, Harris Yulin, Anne Heche, Jada Pinkett Smith, Cher, Diana Scarwid, Lindsay Crouse, Lorraine Toussaint, Rita Wilson, Eileen Brennan, Craig T. Nelson; *D:* Cher, Nancy Savoca; *W:* Nancy Savoca, Susan Manus, I. Marlene King; *C:* Ellen Kuras, Bobby Bukowski, John Stanier; *M:* Cliff Eidelman. *HBO*

If Things Were Different 🐾½ 1979
Feisty woman struggles to hold her family together after her husband is hospitalized with a nervous breakdown. **96m/C VHS, Beta.** Suzanne Pleshette, Tony Roberts, Arte Johnson, Chuck McCann, Don Murray; *D:* Robert Lewis. *WOV*

If You Could See What I Hear 🐾½
1982 (PG) Irritatingly upbeat true-life story of blind singer-musician, Tom Sullivan. Covers his life from college days to marriage. Sophomoric comedy centers around the hero's irresponsible, and often life-endangering, behavior. **103m/C VHS, Beta, LV.** *CA* Marc Singer, R.H. Thomson, Sarah Torgov, Shari Belafonte; *D:* Eric Till. Genie Awards '83: Best Supporting Actor (Thomson). *VES*

If You Don't Stop It...You'll Go Blind 🐾½ 1977 (R) A series of gauche and tasteless vignettes from various little-known comedians. **80m/C VHS, Beta.** Pat McCormick, George Spencer, Patrick Wright; *D:* I. Robert Levy, Keefe Brasselle.

If You Knew Susie 🐾🐾 1948 Two retired vaudeville actors find a letter from George Washington which establishes them as descendants of a colonial patriot and the heirs to a seven billion dollar fortune. ♫If You Knew Susie; My Brooklyn Love Song; What Do I Want With Money?; We're Living the Life We Love; My, How the Time Goes By. **90m/B VHS, Beta.** Eddie Cantor, Joan Davis, Allyn Joslyn, Charles Dingle, Charles Halton; *D:* Gordon Douglas. *CCB*

Igor & the Lunatics 🐾 1985 (R) Tasteless tale of a cannibal cult leader released from prison who picks up where he left off. **79m/C VHS, Beta.** Joseph Eero, Joe Niola, T.J. Michaels; *D:* Billy Parolini. *ART*

Iguana 🐾🐾 1989 The videocassette box art makes this look like a horror movie, but it's really a stiff, solemn period drama about a deformed sailor with lizardlike features. After a life of mistreatment he reigns mercilessly over a handful of island castaways. An international coproduction with mostly English dialogue, some Spanish and Portuguese with subtitles. **?m/C VHS.** Everett McGill; *D:* Monte Hellman. *IMP*

Ike 🐾🐾½ *Ike: The War Years* 1979 Duvall is top brass in this made-for television epic biography tracing Eisenhower's career during WWII. Previously a six-hour mini-series. **291m/C VHS, Beta, LV.** Robert Duvall, Lee Remick, Darren McGavin, Dana Andrews, Laurence Luckinbill; *D:* Melville Shavelson. *THV*

Ikiru 🐾🐾🐾🐾 *To Live* 1952 When a clerk finds out he is dying of cancer, he decides to build a children's playground and give something of himself back to the world. Highly acclaimed, heartbreaking drama from the unusually restrained Kurosawa; possibly his most "eastern" film. In Japanese with English subtitles. **134m/B VHS, Beta, LV.** *JP* Takashi Shimura, Nobuo Kaneko, Kyoko Seki, Miki Odagari, Yunosuke Ito; *D:* Akira Kurosawa. *HMV, CRC, FCT*

Il Bell'Antonio 🐾🐾½ 1960 The boastful Antonio has a reputation as a womanizer but when he finally marries, to a lovely young woman, he faces the loss of his libido. Satire of machismo, marriage, and Catholicism. In Italian with English subtitles. **115m/C VHS.** *IT* Marcello Mastroianni, Claudia Cardinale, Pierre Brasseur; *D:* Mauro Bolognini; *W:* Pier Paolo Pasolini, Gino Vissentini. *KIV, FCT*

Il Grido 🐾🐾 *The Cry; The Outcry* 1957 A jilted husband takes his young daughter from village to village in search of the woman who deserted them for another man. Set in the desolate Po Valley of director Antonioni's childhood. In Italian with English subtitles. **116m/B VHS.** *IT* Steve Cochran, Alida Valli, Dorian Gray, Betsy Blair, Gabriella Pallotti; *D:* Michelangelo Antonioni; *W:* Michelangelo Antonioni, Ennio de Concini; *M:* Giovanni Fusco. *KIV, FCT*

Il Sorpasso 🐾🐾½ 1963 A braggart, who has failed at everything, spends all his time traveling around Italy in his sportscar. He takes a repressed law student under his wing and decides to teach him how to have fun. In Italian with English subtitles. **116m/B VHS.** *IT* Vittorio Gassman, Jean-Louis Trintignant; *D:* Dino Risi. *NO*

I'll Cry Tomorrow 🐾🐾🐾 1955 Hayward brilliantly portrays actress Lillian Roth as she descends into alcoholism and then tries to overcome her addiction. Based on Roth's memoirs. ♫Sing You Sinners; When The Red Red Robin Comes Bob Bob Bobbin' Along; Happiness Is Just a Thing Called Joe; Vagabond King Waltz. **119m/B VHS, Beta, LV.** Susan Hayward, Richard Conte, Eddie Albert, Jo Van Fleet, Margo, Don Taylor, Ray Danton, Veda Ann Borg; *D:* Daniel Mann; *M:* Alex North. Academy Awards '55: Best Costume Design (B & W); Cannes Film Festival '56: Best Actress (Hayward); Nominations: Academy Awards '55: Best Actress (Hayward), Best Art Direction/Set Decoration (B & W), Best Black and White Cinematography.*MGM*

I'll Do Anything 🐾🐾½ 1993 (PG-13) Hollywood satire finds unemployed actor Matt (Nolte) suddenly forced to care for his six-year-old daughter Jeannie (Wright), whom he hasn't seen in three years, Matt also finally gets a job—as a chauffeur to an obnoxious producer (well played by Brooks) whose company winds up making the manipulative demon Jeannie into a hot child star. Great work by Kavner as the owner of a test-screening service who romances Brooks. Originally intended as a musical, the test screenings were so disastrous that the numbers were axed. What's left is less jerky than expected; Brooks reportedly based his character in part on megamogul Joel Silver.*CW:* Sexual language and sexual situations. **115m/C VHS, LV, 8mm, Closed Caption.** Nick Nolte, Albert Brooks, Julie Kavner, Whittni Wright, Joely Richardson, Tracey Ullman; *D:* James L. Brooks; *W:* James L. Brooks; *C:* Michael Ballhaus; *M:* Hans Zimmer. *COL*

I'll Get You 🐾🐾 *Escape Route* 1953 An FBI agent goes to England on the trail of a kidnapping ring. **79m/B VHS, Beta, LV.** George Raft, Sally Gray, Clifford Evans; *D:* Seymour Friedman. *RXM*

I'll Name the Murderer 🐾🐾 1936 Suspense film in which a gossip columnist starts his own investigation into the murder of a club singer. **?m/C VHS.** Ralph Forbes, Marion Shilling; *D:* Raymond K. Johnson. *SNC*

I'll See You in My Dreams 🐾🐾½
1951 Hokey but fun musical biography of songwriter Gus Kahn (Thomas) and his wife Grace LeBoy (Day). Kahn gets his start in Ziegfeld shows but loses both his career and wife after the 1929 crash. However, she soon returns and everything ends happily ever after. ♫Ain't We Got Fun; Ukelele Lady; The One I Love Belongs To Somebody Else; I'll See You In My Dreams; It Had To Be You; Swingin' Down the Lane; My Buddy; Makin' Whoopee!; Yes Sir, That's My Baby. **109m/B VHS.** Danny Thomas, Doris Day, Frank Lovejoy, Patrice Wymore, James Gleason, Mary Wickes, Jim Backus, Minna Gombell, William Forrest; *D:* Michael Curtiz; *W:* Melville Shavelson, Jack Rose. *WAR, MVD*

I'll Take Sweden 🐾🐾½ 1965 Overprotective father Hope disapproves of teenaged daughter Weld's guitar-playing boyfriend (Avalon). So to keep her out of harm's way he finagles a company transfer to Sweden. Dad falls for an interior decorator (Merrill) while Weld gets involved with a Swedish playboy (Slate). Deciding Avalon is the lesser of two evils, Hope schemes to get the two back together. **96m/C VHS, Beta, Closed Caption.** Bob Hope, Tuesday Weld, Frankie Avalon, Dina Merrill, Jeremy Slate, Walter Sande, John Qualen, Roy Roberts, Maudie Prickett; *D:* Fred de Cordova; *W:* Arthur Marx, Bob Fisher, Nat Perrin; *C:* Daniel F. Fapp. *MGM, FCT*

Illegal 🐾🐾½ 1955 Crime melodrama stars Robinson as an attorney who risks all to acquit his assistant of murder. Early Mansfield appearance. Remake of "The Mouthpiece." **88m/B VHS.** Edward G. Robinson, Nina Foch, Hugh Marlowe, Jayne Mansfield, Albert Dekker, Ellen Corby, DeForest Kelley, Howard St. John; *D:* Lewis Allen. *NO*

Illegal Entry: Formula for Fear 🐾½
1993 Tracie's scientist father has invented a formula that could change the world. When he's murdered the formula falls into her unsuspecting hands. Tracie might not know what she has but that doesn't stop some very ruthless efforts to get the information others want. **88m/C VHS.** Sabryn Gene't, Barbara Lee Alexander, Arthur Roberts, Carol Hoyt; *D:* Henri Charr; *W:* John B. Pfeifer. *PMH*

Illegal in Blue 🐾🐾 1995 (R) Chris (Gauthier) the cop falls for sultry blues singer Kari (Dash) and then realizes she could be a suspect in the murder he's investigating. Will libido win out over loyalty to the job? Also available unrated.*CW:* Sexual content, violence, and language. **94m/C VHS, LV.** Dan Gauthier, Stacey Dash, Louis Giambalvo, Michael Durrell, David Groh; *D:* Stu Segall; *W:* Noel Hynd; *M:* Steve Edwards. *ORI*

Illegally Yours 🐾 1987 (PG) Miscast comedy about a college student serving on the jury in trial of old girlfriend. Bring down the gavel on this one. **94m/C VHS, Beta, Closed Caption.** Rob Lowe, Colleen Camp, Kenneth Mars; *D:* Peter Bogdanovich. *MGM*

Illicit 🐾🐾 1931 In love, Stanwyck fears that marrying Rennie will only ruin their wonderful relationship. Two years after their marriage her fears are realized when each searches for happiness with a past lover. A melodramatic performance that doesn't quite hit its mark. Remade two years later as "Ex-Lady" with Bette Davis in the lead. Based on the play by Edith Fitzgerald and Robert Riskin. **76m/B VHS.** Barbara Stanwyck, Ricardo Cortez, Natalie Moorhead, Charles Butterworth, Joan Blondell, Claude Gillingwater; *D:* Archie Mayo; *W:* Harvey Thew. *MGM*

Illicit Behavior 🐾🐾½ 1991 (R) A dangerous manipulative woman (Severance) is out to claim a $2 million inheritance in this intricate and seductive police thriller. Included among her victims are her husband, a Hollywood vice cop suspended for use of excessive force; his partner;

her husband's internal affairs adversary; and her own psychiatrist. Also available in an uncut, unrated version. **CW:** Language, violence, and strong sensuality. **101m/C VHS, Closed Caption.** Joan Severance, Robert Davi, James Russo, Jack Scalia, Kent McCord; **D:** Worth Keeter.

Illicit Dreams 🎬½ **1994** A lonely housewife fantasizes about a dream lover who then becomes real. Too bad her possessive and vicious tycoon hubby would rather kill than lose her. **93m/C VHS, Closed Caption.** Shannon Tweed, Andrew Stevens. *REP*

Illtown 🎬🎬½ **1996** A happy trio of yuppy-ish Florida drug dealers, led by Rapaport's Dante, land in their own inferno when Dante's former business partner Gabriel (Trese), emerges from jail hell-bent on revenge. Danza plays the evil, effeminate underworld boss while Hayes takes the high road as the saintly detective. Abundance of metaphors aside and amid all the violence, the sluggish narrative style, with everything thrown in from dream sequences and flashbacks to dissolves and slow motion, is more effective at setting a mood than telling a story. Effective score and powerful performances, beautifully filmed by Denault, make a stylish pic that sacrifices substance. **103m/C VHS, LV, Closed Caption.** Michael Rapaport, Lili Taylor, Adam Trese, Kevin Corrigan, Paul Schulze, Angela Featherstone, Saul Stein, Tony Danza, Isaac Hayes; **D:** Nick Gomez; **W:** Nick Gomez; **C:** Jim Denault; **M:** Brian Keane. *ART*

Illumination 🎬🎬 *Illuminacja* **1973** Cryptic drama about a young scientist who believes that rational analysis can solve every crisis. Until he must confront the accidental death of a close friend and his problematic affair with an older woman. Intercutting of documentary material can prove disconcerting. Polish with subtitles. **91m/C VHS.** **PL** Stanislaw Latallo, Monika Denisiewicz-Olbrzychska, Malgorzata Pritulak, Edward Zebrowski; **D:** Krzysztof Zanussi; **W:** Krzysztof Zanussi; **C:** Edward Klosinski; **M:** Wojciech Kilar. *FCT*

The Illusion Travels by Streetcar 🎬🎬🎬 *La Illusion Viaja en Tranvia* **1953** Odd but enchanting story of two men who restore a streetcar, only to find that it will not be used by the city. In a gesture of defiance, they steal the streetcar and take it for one last ride, picking up an interesting assortment of characters along the way. In Spanish with English subtitles. Not released in the U.S. until 1977. **90m/B VHS.** **MX** Lilia Prado, Carlos Navarro, Domingo Soler, Fernando Soto, Agustin Isunza, Miguel Manzano; **D:** Luis Bunuel. *CVC, FCT*

Illusions 🎬🎬 **1991 (R)** Jan (Locklear) is trying to recover from a nervous breakdown and improve her crumbling marriage when her husband's sexy sister arrives and things start to heat up. Jan thinks her husband and sister-in-law are just a little too close, but when she lets her landlord in on her suspicions, he reacts quite strangely. Will Jan have another nervous breakdown? Mysterious with lots of plot twists. Based on Colley's play "I'll Be Back Before Midnight." **CW:** Language and sexuality. **95m/C VHS, Beta, Closed Caption.** Robert Carradine, Heather Locklear, Emma Samms, Ned Beatty; **D:** Victor Kulle; **W:** Peter Colley.

The Illustrated Man 🎬🎬🎬 **1969 (PG)** A young drifter meets a tattooed man. Each tattoo causes a fantastic story to unfold. A strange, interesting, but finally limited attempt at literary sci-fi. Based on the story collection by Ray Bradbury. **103m/C VHS, Beta.** Rod Steiger, Claire Bloom, Robert Drivas, Don Dubbins; **D:** Jack Smight; **M:** Jerry Goldsmith. *WAR, FCT, MLB*

Ilsa, Harem Keeper of the Oil Sheiks woof! **1976 (R)** The naughty Ilsa works for an Arab sheik in the slave trade. More graphic violence and nudity. Plot makes an appearance. **45m/C VHS, LV.** Dyanne Thorne, Michael Thayer. *CIC*

Ilsa, She-Wolf of the SS woof! **1974 (R)** The torture-loving Ilsa runs a medical camp for the Nazis. Plot is incidental to nudity and violence. **45m/C VHS, LV.** Dyanne Thorne, Greg Knoph; **D:** Don Edmunds. *CIC*

Ilsa, the Tigress of Siberia woof! **1979** Everyone's favorite torturer has been working her wiles on political prisoners in Russia. After escaping to Canada, her past threatens to catch up with her. As usual, no plot, violence. **85m/C VHS.** Dyanne Thorne, Michel Morin, Tony Angelo, Terry Coady, Howard Mauer; **D:** Jean LaFleur. *NO*

Ilsa, the Wicked Warden woof! *Ilsa, the Absolute Power; Greta the Mad Butcher* **1978 (R)** Ilsa is now a warden of a woman's prison in South America, behaving just as badly as she always has, until the prisoners stage an uprising. Lots of skin, no violence, no acting. Also: no plot. **90m/C VHS, LV.** Dyanne Thorne, Lina Romay, Jess (Jesus) Franco; **D:** Jess (Jesus) Franco. *CIC*

I'm All Right Jack 🎬🎬🎬 **1959** Sellers plays a pompous communist union leader in this hilarious satire of worker-management relations. Based on Alan Hackney's novel "Private Life." **101m/B VHS, Beta.** Peter Sellers, Ian Carmichael, Terry-Thomas, Victor Maddern; **D:** John Boulting. British Academy Awards '59: Best Actor (Sellers), Best Screenplay. *FCT*

I'm Dancing as Fast as I Can 🎬🎬 **1982 (R)** A successful television producer hopelessly dependent on tranquilizers tries to stop cold turkey. Good story could be better; based on Barbara Gordon's memoirs. **107m/C VHS, Beta, LV.** Jill Clayburgh, Nicol Williamson, Dianne West, Joe Pesci, Geraldine Page, John Lithgow, Daniel Stern; **D:** Jack Hofsiss; **W:** David Rabe; **C:** Jan De Bont. *PAR*

I'm Dangerous Tonight 🎬½ **1990 (R)** Wallflower Amick (Shelley the Waitress in "Twin Peaks") turns into party monster when she dons red dress made from evil ancient Aztec cloak. Many dead soldiers when this girl parties. Based on a Cornell Woolrich short story, it's another in a series of ever more disappointing entries from Hooper, whose cult fave "The Texas Chainsaw Massacre" had low as they come production values, but far better scares. Originally cable fare. **CW:** Violence. **92m/C VHS.** Madchen Amick, Corey Parker, R. Lee Ermey, Mary Frann, Dee Wallace Stone, Anthony Perkins, Natalie Schafer, William Berger; **D:** Tobe Hooper; **W:** Alice Wilson. *USH*

I'm from Arkansas 🎬 **1944** The little town of Pitchfork, Arkansas, goes nuts when a pig gives birth to ten piglets. **68m/B VHS, Beta.** El Brendel, Slim Summerville, Iris Adrian, Harry Harvey, Bruce (Herman Brix) Bennett; **D:** Lew (Louis Friedlander) Landers. *NOS, MRV, DVT*

I'm Gonna Git You Sucka 🎬🎬🎬 **1988 (R)** Parody of "blaxploitation" films popular during the '60s and '70s. Funny and laced with out-right bellylaughs. A number of stars who made "blaxploitation" films, including Jim Brown, take part in the gags. **89m/C VHS, Beta, LV.** Keenen Ivory Wayans, Bernie Casey, Steve James, Isaac Hayes, Jim Brown, Ja'net DuBois, Anne-Marie Johnson, Antonio Fargas, Eve Plumb, John Vernon, Clu Gulager, Kadeem Hardison, Damon Wayans, Gary Owens, Clarence Williams III, David Alan Grier, Kim Wayans, Robin Harris, Chris Rock, Dawnn Lewis, Jester Hairston, Eugene Glazer; *Cameos:* Robert Townsend; **D:** Keenen Ivory Wayans; **W:** Keenen Ivory Wayans; **M:** David Michael Frank. *MGM*

I'm No Angel 🎬🎬🎬 **1933** "Beulah, peel me a grape." Well, you'd be hungry too if you spent your time eyeing playboy Grant as West does. She's a circus floozy who's prone to extorting money from her men (after hashing over their shortcomings with her seen-it-all-maid, the aforementioned Beulah). However, after wooing Grant, she sues for breach of promise. This leads to a comic courtroom scene with Grant bringing in all West's ex-lovers as witnesses. Grant's second film with West, following "She Done Him Wrong." **88m/B VHS.** Mae West, Cary Grant, Gregory Ratoff, Edward Arnold, Ralf Harolde, Kent Taylor, Gertrude Michael, Russell Hopton, Dorothy Peterson, William B. Davidson,

Gertrude Howard; **D:** Wesley Ruggles; **W:** Mae West. *USH, BTV*

I'm Not Rappaport 🎬🎬 **1996 (PG-13)** Matthau does some comic grump schtick as irascible, unrepentent 81-year-old New York Jewish radical Nat. He likes to vent his considerable opinions in Central Park and carries on a grumbling friendship with fellow octogenarian Midge (Davis), who stills works as a building superintendent, tending an equally ancient boiler. But Nat's fed-up daughter Clara (Irving) is threatening to put him in a home and Midge seems likely to lose his job when the boiler is scheduled for replacement. Gardner's 1986 stage play tends to show its weaknesses on the big screen. **CW:** Drug content and momentary violence. **135m/C VHS, LV, Closed Caption.** Walter Matthau, Ossie Davis, Amy Irving, Martha Plimpton, Craig T. Nelson, Boyd Gaines, Guillermo Diaz, Elina Lowensohn, Ron Rifkin; **D:** Herb Gardner; **W:** Herb Gardner; **C:** Adam Holender; **M:** Gerry Mulligan. *USH*

I'm on My Way/The Non-Stop Kid **1918** Two classic shorts: "I'm on My Way" (1919), in which Lloyd's dreams of an idyllic marriage are shattered; and "The Non-Stop Kid" (1918), in which Lloyd must contend with a rival for the affection of his beloved. **30m/B VHS, Beta.** Harold Lloyd, Snub Pollard, Bebe Daniels; **D:** Harold Lloyd. *CCB, GVV*

I'm the Girl He Wants to Kill 🎬½ **1974** A woman sees a murder committed, and the murderer sees her. Now he's after her. **71m/C VHS, Beta.** Julie Sommars, Anthony Steel. *NO*

I'm the One You're Looking For 🎬🎬½ **1988** A famous model obsessively combs Barcelona for the man who raped her. Suspenseful thriller based on a short story by Gabriel Garcia Marquez. In Spanish with English subtitles. **85m/C VHS, LV.** **SP** Patricia Adriani, Chus Lampreave, Ricard Borras, Toni Canto, Angel Alcazar, Marta Fedz, Frank Muro, Miriam DeMaeztu; **D:** Jaime Chavarri. *FXL, FCT, IME*

The Image 🎬🎬½ **1989** Anchorman Finney, the unscrupulous czar of infotainment, does a little soul delving when a man he wrongly implicated in a savings and loan debacle decides to check into the hereafter ahead of schedule. Seems the newsmonger's cut a few corners en route to the bigtime, and his public is mad as hell and...oops, wrong movie (need we say there are not a few echoes of "Network"?). Finney's great. Made for cable. **91m/C VHS.** Albert Finney, John Mahoney, Kathy Baker, Swoosie Kurtz, Marsha Mason, Spalding Gray; **D:** Peter Werner; **M:** James Newton Howard. *HBO*

Image of Bruce Lee 🎬 **197? (G)** Martial arts fight scenes prevail in this story about a jeweler who is swindled out of $1 million worth of diamonds. **88m/C VHS, Beta.** Bruce Li, Chang Wu Lang, Chang Lei, Dana.

Image of Death 🎬 **1977** Woman plots to take the life of an old school chum, assume her identity, and then blow up the Capitol. **83m/C VHS, Beta.** Cathy Paine, Cheryl Waters, Tony Banner, Barry Pierce, Sheila Helpmann, Pennie Hackforth-Jones; **D:** Kevin J. Dobson. *NO*

Image of Passion 🎬 **1986** Weak account of male stripper/lovely advertising executive romance. **90m/C Beta.** James Horan, Susan Damante Shaw, Edward Bell; **D:** Susan Orlikoff-Simon.

Imagemaker 🎬½ **1986 (R)** Uneven story of a presidential media consultant who bucks the system and exposes corruption. **93m/C VHS, Beta, LV.** Michael Nouri, Jerry Orbach, Jessica Harper, Farley Granger; **D:** Hal Wiener. *ART, VES*

Imaginary Crimes 🎬🎬 **1994 (PG)** Ray Weiler (Keitel) is a well-meaning salesman with dreams much bigger than his reach. After the death of his wife (Lynch), Ray tries to raise his two daughters, Sonya (Balk) and Greta (Moss). But gifted high school senior (in 1962) Sonya is resentful of being her sister's maternal anchor and having her father's schemes to come to nothing even as she acknowledges how much Ray cares and how he wants to improve their lives. Remarkable performances by Keitel and Balk. From the novel by Sheila Ballantyne. **106m/C VHS, LV, Closed Caption.** Harvey Keitel, Fairuza Balk, Kelly Lynch, Vincent D'Onofrio, Elissabeth Moss, Diane Baker, Christopher Penn, Seymour Cassel, Annette O'Toole; **D:** Tony Drazan; **W:** Kristine Johnson, Davia Nelson; **M:** Stephen Endelman. *WAR*

Imitation of Life 🎬🎬🎬 1959 Remake of the successful 1939 Claudette Colbert outing of the same title, and based on Fanny Hurst's novel, with a few plot changes. Turner is a single mother, more determined to achieve acting fame and fortune than function as a parent. Her black maid, Moore, is devoted to her own daughter (Kohner), but loses her when the girl discovers she can pass for white. When Turner discovers that she and her daughter are in love with the same man, she realizes how little she knows her daughter, and how much the two of them have missed by not having a stronger relationship. Highly successful at the boxoffice. **124m/C VHS, Beta.** Lana Turner, John Gavin, Troy Donahue, Sandra Dee, Juanita Moore, Susan Kohner; **D:** Douglas Sirk; **C:** Russell Metty. Golden Globe Awards '60: Best Supporting Actress (Kohner); Nominations: Academy Awards '59: Best Supporting Actress (Kohner), Best Supporting Actress (Moore). *USH, FCT*

Immediate Family 🎬🎬½ 1989 (PG-13) Childless couple contact a pregnant, unmarried girl and her boyfriend in hopes of adoption. As the pregnancy advances, the mother has doubts about giving up her baby. A bit sugar-coated in an effort to woo family trade. **112m/C VHS, Beta, LV, Closed Caption.** Glenn Close, James Woods, Kevin Dillon, Mary Stuart Masterson, Kevin Dillon, Linda Darlow, Jane Greer, Jessica James, Mimi Kennedy; **D:** Jonathan Kaplan; **W:** Barbara Benedek; **M:** Brad Fiedel. National Board of Review Awards '89: Best Supporting Actress (Masterson). *COL*

The Immigrant 🎬🎬🎬½ 1917 Chaplin portrays a newly arrived immigrant who falls in love with the first girl he meets. Silent with musical soundtrack added. **20m/B VHS, Beta.** Charlie Chaplin; **D:** Charlie Chaplin. *CAB, GVV*

Immortal Bachelor 🎬½ 1980 (PG) Good cast can't overcome the silliness of this one. A juror daydreams about the dead husband of a cleaning woman on trial for killing her adulterous spouse. She decides the dead man seems a lot more exciting than her own dull and tiresome husband. **94m/C VHS, Beta.** *IT* Giancarlo Giannini, Monica Vitti, Claudia Cardinale, Vittorio Gassman; **D:** Marcello Fondato; **C:** Pasquale De Santis. *NO*

Immortal Battalion 🎬🎬🎬 *The Way Ahead* 1944 Entertaining wartime psuedo-documentary follows newly recruited soldiers as they are molded from an ordinary group of carping civilians into a hardened battalion of fighting men by Niven. Some prints run to 116 minutes. **89m/B VHS, Beta.** David Niven, Stanley Holloway, Reginald Tate, Raymond Huntley, William Hartnell, James Donald, Peter Ustinov; **D:** Carol Reed; **W:** Peter Ustinov, Eric Ambler; **C:** Guy Green. *NOS, MRV, VYY*

Immortal Beloved 🎬🎬 1994 (R) The death of Ludwig van Beethoven prompts his loyal secretary to seek the identity of a mystery love to whom the composer has bequeathed his estate. While Beethoven's genius is awesome and his music breathtaking, his lovelife is neither, and the ensuing confessions of the maestro's former loves only get in the way of flashbacks that hint at his torment and triumph. Oldman is darkly intense, and a scene in which the aged Beethoven remembers his terrifying childhood amid the strains of "Ode to Joy" is simply stunning, but an unfocused script undoes what might have been a fine tribute to the master. The London Symphony Orchestra and soloists Murray Perahia, Emanuel Ax, and Yo Yo Ma contributed to the splendid soundtrack. **CW:** Sexual situations, rape. **121m/C VHS, LV, Closed Caption.** Gary Oldman, Jeroen Krabbe, Isabella Rossellini, Johanna Ter Steege, Marco Hofschneider, Miriam Margolyes, Barry Humphries, Valeria Golino,

Christopher Fulford; **D:** Bernard Rose; **W:** Bernard Rose. *COL*

Immortal Combat 🎬½ 1994 (R) An army of men trained in ninja and guerilla warfare have seemingly immortal powers. Can our two violent heroes find an equally destructive way to stop the killing? **109m/C VHS, LV.** Roddy Piper, Sonny Chiba, Tommy (Tiny) Lister, Meg Foster; **D:** Daniel Neira. *APX*

Immortal Sergeant 🎬🎬½ 1943 After the battle death of the squad leader, an inexperienced corporal takes command of North African troops during WWII. Fonda gives a strong performance. Based on a novel by John Brody. **91m/B VHS, Beta, Closed Caption.** Henry Fonda, Thomas Mitchell, Maureen O'Hara, Allyn Joslyn, Reginald Gardiner, Melville Cooper, Morton Lowry; **D:** John M. Stahl; **W:** Lamar Trotti; **C:** Clyde De Vinna. *FOX*

Immortal Sins 🎬 1991 (R) Michael and Susan inherited an old Spanish Castle, complete with its own curse, which comes in the form of a seductive women that has haunted families for centuries. **CW:** Horror violence and strong sensuality. **80m/C VHS.** Cliff DeYoung, Maryam D'Abo; **W:** Thomas McKelvey Cleaver. *NO*

The Immortalizer 🎬 1989 (R) A mad doctor transfers people's brains into young bodies for a price, although it's not as simple as it sounds. **85m/C VHS, Beta, LV.** Ron Kay, Chris Crone, Melody Patterson, Clarke Lindsley, Bekki Armstrong; **D:** Joel Bender. *COL*

The Immortals 🎬🎬 1995 (R) Nightclub owner Jack (Roberts) recruits eight terminally ill criminals in an elaborate heist that calls for simultaneously hitting targets citywide. But when they compare notes, the team fear a doublecross. **CW:** Strong bloody violence, strong language, nudity, and some drug use. **92m/C VHS, Closed Caption.** Eric Roberts, Tia Carrere, William Forsythe, Joe Pantoliano, Clarence Williams III, Tony Curtis, Chris Rock, Kieran Mulroney, Kevin Bernhardt; **D:** Brian Grant; **W:** Kevin Bernhardt; **C:** Anthony B. Richmond. *HMK*

Impact 🎬🎬🎬 1949 A woman and her lover plan the murder of her rich industrialist husband, but the plan backfires. More twists and turns than a carnival ride. **111m/B VHS.** Brian Donlevy, Ella Raines, Charles Coburn, Helen Walker, Anna May Wong, Philip Ahn, Art Baker, Tony Barrett, Harry Cheshire, Lucius Cooke, Sheilah Graham, Tom Greenway, Hans Herbert, Linda Johnson, Joe Kirk, Clarence Kolb, Mary Landa, Mae Marsh; **D:** Arthur Lubin; **W:** Dorothy Reid, Jay Dratler; **C:** Ernest Laszlo; **M:** Michel Michelet. *EEL, MRV, NOS*

The Imperial Japanese Empire 🎬🎬 1985 Epic of the WWII Pacific seen through Japanese eyes. **130m/C VHS, Beta.** *JP* Tetsuro Tamba, Tomokazu Miura, Teruhiko Saigo, Teruhiko Aoi, Saburo Shinoda, Keiko Sekine, Masako Natsume, Akiko Kana. *VCD*

Imperial Navy 🎬🎬 198? A WWII epic as seen from the Japanese perspective, concentrating on their great navy and its suicide squadrons. Dubbed. **145m/C VHS, Beta.** *JP D:* Paul Aaron. *MOV*

Imperial Venus 🎬🎬 1971 (PG) Biography of Napoleon's sister, Paolina Boneparte—with particular focus on her many loves, lusts and tribulations. **121m/C VHS, Beta.** Gina Lollobrigida, Stephen Boyd, Raymond Pellegrin; **D:** Jean Delannoy. *NO*

Importance of Being Earnest 🎬🎬🎬 1952 Fine production of classic Oscar Wilde comedy-of-manners. Cast couldn't be better or the story funnier. **95m/C VHS, Beta.** Michael Redgrave, Edith Evans, Margaret Rutherford, Michael Denison, Joan Greenwood; **D:** Anthony Asquith. *PAR, HMV*

The Imported Bridegroom 🎬🎬 1989 A comedy set at the turn of the century about a man who returns to Poland in order to find his daughter a proper husband. **93m/C VHS.** Eugene Trooback, Avi Hoffman, Greta Cowan, Annette Miller; **D:** Pamela Berger; **W:** Pamela Berger. *ERG*

The Impossible Spy 🎬🎬🎬 1987 True story of Elie Cohen, an unassuming Israeli who doubled as a top level spy in Syria during the 1960s. Cohen became so close to Syria's president that he was nominated to become the Depu-

ty Minister of Defense before his double life was exposed. Well-acted spy thriller made for cable and is worth a look for espionage fans. **96m/C VHS.** *GB* John Shea, Eli Wallach, Michal Bat-Adam, Rami Danon, Sasson Gabray, Chaim Girafi; **D:** Jim Goddard. *NCJ, FCT*

The Impossible Years 🎬 1968 Unattractive, leering sex farce about psychiatrist Nivens who has problems with his own young daughter. Dismal adaptation of the hit Broadway play by Bob Fisher and Arthur Marx. **97m/C VHS.** David Niven, Lola Albright, Chad Everett, Ozzie Nelson, Christina Ferrare, Jeff Cooper, John Harding; **D:** Michael Gordon; **W:** George Wells. *MGM*

The Imposter 🎬½ 1984 Improbable tale of a con artist/ex-con who impersonates a high school principal in order to regain his estranged girlfriend, who works as a teacher. Complications ensue when he tackles the school's drug problems. Made for television. **95m/C VHS, Beta.** Anthony Geary, Billy Dee Williams, Lorna Patterson; **D:** Michael Pressman.

Imposters 🎬🎬 1984 A comedy centering on the romantic problems between a self-indulgent young man and the woman who cheats on him. **110m/C VHS, Beta.** Ellen McElduff, Charles Ludlam, Lisa Todd, Peter Evans. *NO*

Impromptu 🎬🎬🎬 1990 (PG-13) A smart, sassy, romantic comedy set in 1830s Europe among the era's artistic greats—here depicted as scalawags, parasites and early beatniks. The film's ace is Davis in a lusty, dynamic role as mannish authoress George Sand, obsessively in love with the dismayed composer Chopin. Though he's too pallid a character for her attraction to be credible, a great cast and abundant wit make this a treat. Beautiful score featuring Chopin and Liszt. Film debut of stage director Lapine; screenplay written by his wife, Sarah Kernochan. **108m/C VHS, LV.** Judy Davis, Hugh Grant, Mandy Patinkin, Bernadette Peters, Julian Sands, Ralph Brown, Georges Corraface, Anton Rodgers, Emma Thompson, Anna Massey, John Savident, Elizabeth Spriggs; **D:** James Lapine; **W:** Sarah Kernochan; **C:** Bruno de Keyzer. Independent Spirit Awards '92: Best Actress (Davis). *TVC, MOV*

Improper Channels 🎬🎬 1982 (PG) Mediocre comedy about a couple trying to recover their daughter after being accused of child abuse. **91m/C VHS, Beta, LV.** Monica Parker, Alan Arkin, Mariette Hartley; **D:** Eric Till; **W:** Adam Arkin. *VES*

Improper Conduct 🎬🎬 1994 (R) Ad agency employee is sexually harassed by her boss but loses her court case. Her sister decides to get revenge by getting hired and setting the slimeball up for a fall. **CW:** Strong sexuality; violence and language. **95m/C VHS.** Steven Bauer, Lee Ann Beaman, John Laughlin, Kathy Shower, Tahnee Welch, Nia Peeples, Stuart Whitman, Adrian Zmed, Patsy Pease; **D:** Jag Mundhra; **W:** Carl Austin. *MNC*

Impulse 🎬½ 1955 When his wife leaves for a visit with her mother, a young man is thrust into cahoots with gangsters, and wrapped up in an affair with another woman. **81m/B VHS.** *GB* Arthur Kennedy, Constance Smith, Joy Shelton; **D:** Charles De Latour. *FCT*

Impulse woof! *Want a Ride, Little Girl?; I Love to Kill* 1974 (PG) Shatner, a crazed killer, is released from prison and starts to kill again in this low-budget, predictable, critically debased film about child-molesting. **85m/C VHS, Beta.** William Shatner, Ruth Roman, Harold Sakata, Kim Nicholas, Jennifer Bishop, James Dobson; **D:** William Grefe. *ART*

Impulse 🎬🎬 1984 (R) Small town residents can't control their impulses, all because of government toxic waste in their milk. A woman worried about her mother's mental health returns to town with her doctor boyfriend to discover most of the inhabitants are quite mad. Starts strong but... **95m/C VHS, Beta, LV.** Tim Matheson, Meg Tilly, Hume Cronyn, John Karlen, Bill Paxton, Amy Stryker, Claude Earl Jones, Sherri Stoner; **D:** Graham Baker; **W:** Bart Davis. *PAR*

Impulse 🎬🎬½ 1990 (R) A beautiful undercover vice cop poses as a prostitute, and gives in to base desires. Russell gives a fine performance in this underrated sleeper. **109m/C VHS, Beta, LV, Closed Caption.** Theresa Russell, Nicholas Mele, Eli Danker, Charles McCaughan, Jeff Fahey, George Dzundza, Alan Rosenberg, Lynne Thigpen, Shawn Elliott; **D:** Sondra Locke; **W:** John DeMarco, Leigh Chapman; **M:** Michel Colombier. *WAR*

Impure Thoughts 🎬🎬 1986 (PG) Four friends meet in the afterlife and discuss their Catholic school days. Odd premise never catches fire. **87m/C VHS, Beta.** Brad Dourif, Lane Davies, John Putch, Terry Beaver; **D:** Michael A. Simpson. *NLC*

In a Glass Cage 🎬🎬½ *Tras el Cristal* 1986 A young boy who was tortured and sexually molested by a Nazi official seeks revenge. Years after the war, he shows up at the Nazi's residence in Spain and is immediately befriended by his tormentor's family. Confined to an iron lung, the official is at the mercy of the young man who tortuously acts out the incidents detailed in the Nazi's journal. Suspenseful and extremely graphic, it's well crafted and meaningful but may be just too horrible to watch. Sexual and violent acts place it in the same league as Pasolini's infamous "Salo, or The 120 Days in Sodom." Definitely not for the faint of heart. In Spanish with English subtitles. **110m/C VHS.** *SP* Gunter Meisner, David Sust, Marisa Paredes, Gisela Echevarria; **D:** Agustin Villaronga; **W:** Agustin Villaronga. *CCN, FCT, TPV*

In a Lonely Place 🎬🎬🎬½ 1950 Bogart is outstanding as a volatile Hollywood screenwriter who has an affair with starlet Grahame while under suspicion of murder. Offbeat, yet superb film noir entry became one of the most memorable of the genre. Expertly directed by Ray. Based on the novel by Dorothy B. Hughes and an adaptation by Edmund H. North. **93m/B VHS, Beta.** Humphrey Bogart, Gloria Grahame, Frank Lovejoy, Carl Benton Reid, Art Smith, Jeff Donnell; **D:** Nicholas Ray; **W:** Andrew Solt; **C:** Burnett Guffey. *COL*

In a Moment of Passion 🎬½ 1993 (R) A two-bit actor wants to be a star—in the worst way possible. So he kills off the lead actor of a new film, takes his place, and proceeds to eliminate any obstacle that gets in his way. The problem comes in when an aspiring actress falls for the actor and then figures out what's going on. **CW:** Language, some violence, and sexuality. **100m/C VHS, Closed Caption.** Maxwell Caulfield, Chase Masterson, Vivian Schilling, Julie Araskog, Joe Estevez, Robert Z'Dar, Zbigniew Kaminski; **Cameos:** Jeff Conaway; **W:** Charles Haigh.

In a Shallow Grave 🎬🎬 1988 (R) Shallow treatment of James Purdy's novel about a WWII veteran, badly disfigured in combat at Guadalcanal, who returns to Virginia in an attempt to return to the life he once had with the woman he still loves. Handsome Biehn plays the disfigured vet, Mueller's his ex-fiancee, and Dempsey's the drifter who adds a bisexual hypotenuse to the love triangle. Pokey American Playhouse coproduction. **92m/C VHS.** Michael Biehn, Maureen Mueller, Patrick Dempsey, Michael Beach, Thomas Boyd Mason; **D:** Kenneth Bowser; **W:** Kenneth Bowser. *WAR*

In a Stranger's Hand 🎬🎬½ 1992 Urich stars as a respected businessman who happens to find a doll which belongs to a kidnapped young girl. The police have their suspicions but Urich teams up with the child's mother to find the girl and winds up uncovering a child-selling ring. Made for television. **93m/C VHS, Closed Caption.** Robert Urich, Megan Gallagher, Brett Cullen, Vondie Curtis-Hall, Dakin Matthews, Alan Rosenberg, Maria O'Brien; **D:** David Greene. *TTC*

In a Year of 13 Moons 🎬🎬 *In a Year with 13 Moons; In Einem Jahr Mit 13 Monden* 1978 Notorious Fassbinder tale of Erwin who becomes Elvira and is subjected to a series of humiliating relationships with men. Finally, with the aid of his/her ex-wife and a prostitute, Elvira looks into the past in an effort to resolve the present. Alternatingly depressing and pretentious. German with subtitles. **119m/C VHS.** *GE* Volker Spengler, Ingrid Caven, Gottfried John, Elisabeth Trissenaar, Eva Mattes; **D:** Rainer Werner Fassbinder; **W:** Rainer Werner Fassbinder; **M:** Peer Raben. *NYF*

In an Old Manor House 🎬🎬½ 1984 Residents of an old house are tormented by the vindictive ghost of a murdered adultress whose husband didn't approve of the, uh, affection she showed his son from a previous marriage. Based on the play by Stanislaw Witkiewicz. In Polish with English subtitles. **90m/C VHS.** *PL* **D:** Jerzy Kotkowski. *FCT*

In and Out 🎬🎬🎬 1997 (PG-13) See what an Oscar can do? When Tom Hanks thanked, and inadvertently outed, his high school drama teacher during his Academy Awards speech (for "Philadelphia"), it lead to this feature. Popular high school English teacher Howard Brackett (Kline) has his sexuality come into question on the eve of his wedding thanks to a former-student-turned-movie-star (Dillon). As a media circus converges on the small town, Howard is forced to examine his sexuality by openly gay reporter Selleck (out to prove Howard's gay), his mother Reynolds (who wants the wedding to go on regardless of his orientation) and his tightly-wound fiancee Cusack (who wants to put a serious hurtin' on Barbra Streisand). All-around excellent performances, especially by Kline and Cusack.**CW:** Sexual content and some strong language. **92m/C VHS, Beta, Closed Caption.** Kevin Kline, Joan Cusack, Matt Dillon, Debbie Reynolds, Wilford Brimley, Bob Newhart, Tom Selleck, Deborah Rush, Lewis J. Stadlen, J. Smith-Cameron, Zak Orth, Gregory Jbara, Shalom Harlow, Kate McGregor-Stewart, Shawn Hatosy, Lauren Ambrose, Alexandra Holden; **D:** Frank Oz; **W:** Paul Rudnick; **C:** Rob Hahn; **M:** Marc Shaiman. New York Film Critics Awards '97: Best Supporting Actress (Cusack); Broadcast Film Critics Association Awards '97: Best Supporting Actress (Cusack); Nominations: Academy Awards '97: Best Supporting Actress (Cusack); Golden Globe Awards '98: Best Actor—Musical/Comedy (Kline), Best Supporting Actress (Cusack); MTV Movie Awards '98: Best Kiss (Kevin Kline/Tom Selleck). *PAR*

In Between 🎬🎬½ 1992 (PG-13) When Margo, Jack, and Amy wake up they expect it to be another average day. Instead, these three strangers find themselves together in a peculiar house. An angel informs them that the house is a way station between life and the hereafter. The three must look at their pasts, imagine their futures, and decide whether to return to their old lives or accept death and go on to an afterlife.**CW:** Mature subject matter. **92m/C VHS.** Wings Hauser, Robin Mattson, Alexandra Paul, Robert Forster. *NO*

In Celebration 🎬🎬🎬 1975 (PG) Three successful brothers return to the old homestead for their parents' 40th wedding celebration. Intense drama but somewhat claustrophobic. Based on a play by David Storey. **131m/C VHS.** *GB CA* Alan Bates, James Bolam, Brian Cox, Constance Chapman, Gabrielle Daye, Bill Owen; **D:** Lindsay Anderson; **C:** Dick Bush. *NO*

In Cold Blood 🎬🎬🎬½ 1967 Truman Capote's supposedly factual novel provided the basis for this hard-hitting docu-drama about two ex-cons who ruthlessly murder a Kansas family in 1959 in order to steal their non-existent stash of money. Blake is riveting as one of the killers. **133m/B VHS, LV.** Robert (Bobby) Blake, Scott Wilson, John Forsythe; **D:** Richard Brooks; **W:** Richard Brooks; **C:** Conrad Hall; **M:** Quincy Jones. National Board of Review Awards '67: Best Director (Brooks); Nominations: Academy Awards '67: Best Director (Brooks), Best Adapted Screenplay, Best Cinematography, Best Original Score. *COL*

In Cold Blood 🎬🎬 1996 Tv miniseries version of the Truman Capote true crime classic, which follows the 1959 murders of the four members of the Clutter family in Holcomb, Kansas by ex-cons Dick Hickock (Edwards) and Perry Smith (Roberts). The TV version covers more of the background of both the killers and the subsequent relentless hunt by Al Dewey (Neill) of the Kansas Bureau of Investigation, and the duo's time on death row. **180m/C VHS, Closed Caption.** Anthony Edwards, Eric Roberts, Sam Neill, Kevin Tighe, Gillian Barber, Robbie Bowen, Margot Finley, Bethel Leslie, Gwen Verdon, Stella Stevens, L.Q. Jones, Louise Latham, Campbell Lane, Leo Rossi; **D:** Jonathan Kaplan; **W:** Benedict Fitzgerald. *CAF*

In Country 🎬🎬½ 1989 (R) Based on Bobbie Ann Mason's celebrated novel, the story of a young Kentuckian high schooler (perfectly played by Lloyd) and her search for her father, killed in Vietnam. Willis plays her uncle, a veteran still struggling to accept his own survival, and crippled with memories. Moving scene at the Vietnam Veterans Memorial. **116m/C VHS, Beta, LV, 8mm.** Bruce Willis, Emily Lloyd, Joan Allen, Kevin Anderson, Richard Hamilton, Judith Ivey, Peggy Rea, John Terry, Patricia Richardson, Jim Beaver; **D:** Norman Jewison; **W:** Frank Pierson, Cynthia Cidre; **C:** Russell Boyd; **M:** James Horner. *WAR, MVD*

The In Crowd 🎬🎬 1988 (PG) A bright high school student gets involved with a local television dance show circa 1965, and must choose between uncertain fame and an Ivy League college. A fair nostalgic look at the period. Leitch is the son of psychedelic folk singer Donovan. **96m/C VHS, Beta, Closed Caption.** Donovan Leitch, Jennifer Runyon, Scott Plank, Joe Pantoliano; **D:** Mark Rosenthal; **W:** Mark Rosenthal. *ORI*

In Custody 🎬🎬 *Hifazaat* 1994 (PG) Producer Merchant makes his feature directorial debut with this dreamy tale of small-town teacher Deven (Puri) who's urged by a publishing friend to interview Nur (Kapoor), the greatest living poet in the disappearing Urdu language. The worshipful Deven is dismayed to find his idol a wreck, surrounded by sycophants and a shrewish second wife who's plagiarizing her husband's work, and soon finds himself hopelessly entangled in the writer's life. Unabashedly literary (the poetry recited is by Faiz Ahmed Faiz) with a star cast. Based on the 1987 novel by Anita Desai. Urdu with subtitles. **123m/C VHS.** *IN* Shashi Kapoor, Om Puri, Shabana Azmi, Sushma Seth, Neena Gupta, Ajay Sahni, Tinnu Anand; **D:** Ismail Merchant; **W:** Anita Desai, Shahrukh Husain; **C:** Larry Pizer; **M:** Zakir Hussain, Ustad Sultan Khan. *COL*

In Dangerous Company 🎬 1988 (R) Beautiful babe balances beaux and battles abound. A brow lowering experience. **92m/C VHS.** Tracy Scoggins, Cliff DeYoung, Chris Mulkey, Henry Darrow, Steven Keats, Richard Portnow; **D:** Ruben Preuss; **W:** Mitch Brown; **C:** James L. Carter. *NO*

In Dark Places 🎬🎬 1997 (R) Seductive artist Chapelle (Severance) visits long-estranged brother Chazz (Kestner) with more than familial feelings on her mind. As things between them heat up, Chazz loses his girl, best friend, and job before discovering his sister's true agenda. This one actually has a story to go along with the eroticism.**CW:** Strong sexuality, and for violence and language. **96m/C VHS.** Joan Severance, Bryan Kestner, John Vargas, Suzanne Turner; **D:** James Burke. *THV*

In Deadly Heat 🎬 1987 Crime, revenge, murder, and urban warfare are done once again. **98m/C VHS, Beta.** William Dame, Catherine Dee, M.R. Murphy; **D:** Don Nardo. *JEF*

In Desert and Wilderness 🎬🎬½ 1973 Two kidnapped children escape and are thrust into the wilds of Africa, where they must survive with wits and courage. Based on a novel by Nobel prize-winning author Henyk Sienkiewicz. In Polish with English subtitles. **144m/C VHS.** *PL* **D:** Wladyslaw Slesicki. *FCT*

In for Treatment 🎬🎬🎬 1982 A terminally ill cancer patient, lost in the bureaucracy of the hospital, fights to rediscover the joy of life. Strong and disturbing story. In Dutch with English subtitles. **92m/C VHS, Beta.** *NL* Helmut Woudenberg, Frank Groothof, Hans Man Int Veld; **D:** Eric Van Zuylen, Marja Kok. *NO*

In God's Hands 🎬🎬 1998 **(PG-13)** Dude! Check it out! Three surfers (Dorian, George, and Liu) travel the world looking for (what else?) the perfect wave. Disjointed, plot-deprived, but beautifully shot flick has the trio busting out of prison (why they're there is never explained) to begin their quest. Moving from Madagascar to Bali to Hawaii, one finds love with a girl from Ipanema (!), another contracts malaria, and the other succumbs to the surf. What happens to whom doesn't really matter, because as actors, they're really great surfers. Besides, the "story" is just connective tissue for the killer surfing scenes. Gnarly.**CW:** Brief strong language. **96m/C VHS.** Patrick Shane Dorian, Matt George, Matty Liu, Brion James, Shaun Thompson, Maylin Pultar, Bret Michaels, Brian L. Keaulana, Darrick Doerner; **D:** Zalman King; **W:** Zalman King, Matt George; **C:** John Aronson. *NYR*

In Gold We Trust 🎬🎬½ 1991 Vincent leads an elite battalion of fighters against a group of rogue American MIAs (!) laying waste to the Vietnemese countryside. **89m/C VHS.** Jan-Michael Vincent, Sam Jones; **D:** P. Chalong; **M:** Hummie Mann.

In Harm's Way 🎬🎬 1965 Overdone story about two naval officers and their response to the Japanese attack at Pearl Harbor. Even the superb cast members (and there are plenty of them) can't overcome the incredible length and overly intricate plot. **165m/B VHS, Beta, LV, Closed Caption.** John Wayne, Kirk Douglas, Tom Tryon, Patricia Neal, Paula Prentiss, Brandon de Wilde, Burgess Meredith, Stanley Holloway, Henry Fonda, Dana Andrews, Franchot Tone, Jill Haworth, George Kennedy, Carroll O'Connor, Patrick O'Neal, Slim Pickens, Bruce Cabot, Larry Hagman, Hugh O'Brian, Jim Mitchum, Barbara Bouchet; **D:** Otto Preminger; **W:** Wendell Mayes; **C:** Loyal Griggs; **M:** Jerry Goldsmith. British Academy Awards '65: Best Actress (Neal); Nominations: Academy Awards '65: Best Black and White Cinematography. *PAR*

In His Father's Shoes 🎬🎬½ 1997 **(PG)** After his father (Gossett) dies, 15-year-old Clay (Ri'chard) takes a literal journey of self-discovery. Slipping on a pair of his dad's old wingtips, the teen is transported back to the '60s to revisit his father's past, and then further back to his grandfather's (Gossett again) day. Clay learns his granddad was a hard-working man who gave up his own dreams to support his family, which later caused a generational rift. Touching cable drama. **105m/C VHS, Closed Caption.** Louis Gossett Jr., Robert Ri'chard; **D:** Vic Sarin; **W:** Gary Gelt; **C:** Michael Storey; **M:** John Welsman. *HMK*

In Hot Pursuit 🎬½ 1982 Convicted for drug smuggling, two young men stage a daring but not too exciting escape from a southern prison. **90m/C VHS, Beta.** Bob Watson, Don Watson, Debbie Washington. *NO*

The In-Laws 🎬🎬🎬 1979 **(PG)** A wild comedy with Falk, who claims to be a CIA agent, and Arkin, a dentist whose daughter is marrying Falk's son. The fathers foil a South American dictator's counterfeiting scheme in a delightfully convoluted plot. **103m/C VHS, Beta, LV.** Peter Falk, Alan Arkin, Richard Libertini, Nancy Dussault, Penny Peyser, Arlene Golonka, Michael Lembeck, Ed Begley Jr., Rosana De Soto, Art Evans; **D:** Arthur Hiller; **W:** Andrew Bergman; **M:** John Morris. *WAR*

In Like Flint 🎬🎬½ 1967 Sequel to "Our Man Flint" sees our dapper spy confronting an organization of women endeavoring to take over the world. Spy spoofery at its low-level best. **107m/C VHS, Beta, LV, Letterbox.** James Coburn, Lee J. Cobb, Anna Lee, Andrew Duggan, Jean Hale; **D:** Gordon Douglas; **C:** William H. Daniels; **M:** Jerry Goldsmith. *FOX*

In Love and War 🎬½ 1991 **(R)** Woods plays Navy pilot Jim Stockdale, whose plane was grounded over hostile territory and who endured nearly eight years of torture as a POW. Meanwhile, wife Sybil is an organizer of POW wives back in the States. Low octane rendering of the US Navy Commander's true story. Aaron earlier directed "The Miracle Worker," and you may recognize Ngor from "The Killing Fields." **96m/C VHS,** LV. James Woods, Jane Alexander, Haing S. Ngor, Concetta Tomei, Richard McKenzie, James Pax; **D:** Paul Aaron; **W:** Carol Schreder. *THV*

In Love and War 🎬½ 1996 **(PG-13)** Tells the story of 19-year-old Ernest Hemingway's (O'Donnell) romance with 27-year-old Red Cross nurse Agnes (Bullock) while both were stationed in Italy during WWI. This romance later served as the basis for Hemingway's novel "A Farewell to Arms." Here's a thought. Read the book instead. The boyish O'Donnell is so miscast as testosterone-junkie Hemingway, the only analogy would be having Sylvester Stallone play Truman Capote. The lack of passion and chemistry between the two stars is unsettling, and the action is just plain clunky. Bullock looks great in a nurse's uniform, though. Adapted from "Hemingway in Love and War: The Lost Diary of Agnes Von Kurowsky" by Henry Villard and James Nagel.**CW:** Graphic war injuries and some sensuality. **115m/C VHS, LV, Closed Caption.** Chris O'Donnell, Sandra Bullock, MacKenzie Astin, Ingrid Lacey, Emilio Bonucci, Margot Steinberg, Colin Stinton, Ian Kelly; **D:** Richard Attenborough; **W:** Clancy Sigal, Dimitri Villard, Allan Scott, Anna Hamilton Phelan; **C:** Roger Pratt; **M:** George Fenton. *NLC*

In Love with an Older Woman 🎬🎬 1982 Ritter takes fewer pratfalls than usual in this film; after all, it's a romantic comedy. Adapted from "Six Months with an Older Woman," the novel by David Kaufelt. Made for television. **100m/C VHS, Beta.** John Ritter, Karen Carlson, Jamie Rose, Robert Mandan, Jeff Altman, George Murdock; **D:** Jack Bender.

In Memoriam 🎬🎬½ 1976 Tragic and gripping drama about one man's ability, albeit too late, to cope with his unforgettable past. Based on a story by Adolfo Bioy Casares. In Spanish with English subtitles. **96m/C VHS.** *SP* Geraldine Chaplin, Jose Luis Gomez; **D:** Enrique Braso. *FCT*

In 'n Out 🎬½ 1986 An American loser ventures to Mexico to recover a long-lost inheritance, meeting with mildly comic obstacles along the way. **85m/C VHS, Beta.** Sam Bottoms, Pat Hingle. *VTR*

In Name Only 🎬🎬½ 1939 Somber drama about a heartless woman who marries for wealth and prestige and holds her husband to a loveless marriage. Based on "Memory of Love" by Bessie Brewer. **102m/B VHS, Beta, LV.** Carole Lombard, Cary Grant, Kay Francis; **D:** John Cromwell. *CCB, MLB, TTC*

In Old Caliente 🎬½ 1939 Rogers battles the bad guys in the frontier town of Caliente. **60m/B VHS, Beta.** Roy Rogers, Lynn (Mary Hart) Roberts, George "Gabby" Hayes. *NOS, VCN, DVT*

In Old California 🎬🎬½ 1942 Plucky story of a young Boston pharmacist who searches for success in the California gold rush and runs into the local crime boss. Also available colorized. **88m/B VHS.** John Wayne, Patsy Kelly, Binnie Barnes, Albert Dekker, Charles Halton; **D:** William McGann. *REP*

In Old Cheyenne 🎬½ 1941 Bank holdups, cattle rustling, fist fights, and even car crashes mix with some good ol' guitar plunking in this western. **60m/B VHS, Beta.** Roy Rogers, George "Gabby" Hayes. *NOS, CAB, TIM*

In Old Chicago 🎬🎬🎬 1937 The O'Leary family travels to Chicago to seek their fortune, with mom working as a washerwoman to support her sons. Brothers Power and Ameche become power-broking rivals and when mom comes to break up a brawl between the two, she neglects to properly restrain the family cow. This leads to the great Chicago fire of 1871, supposedly started when the cow kicks over a latern and sets the barn ablaze. The city burns down in a spectacular 20-minute sequence. Based on the story "We the O'Learys" by Niven Busch. **115m/B VHS.** Tyrone Power, Alice Faye, Don Ameche, Alice Brady, Andy Devine, Brian Donlevy, Phyllis Brooks, Tom Brown, Sidney Blackmer, Gene Reynolds, Berton Churchill, Bobs Watson; **D:** Henry King; **W:** Lamar Trotti, Sonya Levien. Academy Awards '37: Best Supporting Actress (Brady); Nominations: Academy Awards '37: Best Picture, Best Sound, Best Story, Best Score. *FXV*

In Old Colorado 🎬🎬½ 1941 Ankrum and his cronies try to stir up trouble over water rights, but Boyd and his pals ride to the rescue. **67m/B VHS.** William Boyd, Russell Hayden, Andy Clyde, Margaret Hayes, Morris Ankrum, Sarah Padden, Cliff Nazarro, Stanley Andrews, James Seay, Morgan Wallace; **D:** Howard Bretherton. *NOS*

In Old Montana 🎬 1939 A Cavalry lieutenant tries to settle a cattleman vs. sheep-herding war. **60m/B VHS, Beta.** Fred Scott, Jeanne Carmen, Harry Harvey, John Merton; **D:** Raymond K. Johnson. *VDM, GPV*

In Old New Mexico 🎬 1945 The Cisco Kid and Pancho reveal the murderer of an old woman—a mysterious doctor who was after an inheritance. **60m/B VHS, Beta.** Duncan Renaldo, Martin Garralaga, Gwen Kenyon, Pedro de Cordoba. *NOS, VCI, VYY*

In Old Santa Fe 🎬🎬½ 1934 Cowboy star Maynard's best western, and the first film ever with Autry and Burnette. Maynard is framed for murder and his pals save him. **60m/B VHS, Beta.** Ken Maynard, Gene Autry, Smiley Burnette, Evalyn Knapp, George "Gabby" Hayes, Kenneth Thomson, Wheeler Oakman, George Chesebro; **D:** David Howard, Joseph Kane. *NOS, VCN, DVT*

In Person 🎬🎬½ 1935 Spry comedy about a movie star who disguises herself to take a vacation incognito and falls in love with a country doctor who is unaware of her identity. ♫Don't Mention Love To Me; Out of Sight, Out of Mind; Got a New Lease on Life. **87m/B VHS, Beta, LV.** Ginger Rogers, George Brent, Alan Mowbray, Grant Mitchell; **D:** William A. Seiter; **M:** Oscar Levant. *TTC*

In Praise of Older Women 🎬🎬 1978 Berenger is just right as a young Hungarian who is corrupted by WWII and a large number of older women. Based on a novel by Stephen Vizinczey. **110m/C VHS, Beta, LV.** *CA* Karen Black, Tom Berenger, Susan Strasberg, Helen Shaver, Alexandra Stewart; **D:** George Kaczender. *FOX*

In Pursuit of Honor 🎬🎬½ 1995 **(PG-13)** Based on the true story of five American cavalry soldiers who find themselves being phased out in the 1935 Army. Ordered by General Douglas MacArthur to destroy their horses, they instead try to outrun an elite tank division to get some 400 horses to safety in Canada. Rugged performances and the violence towards the horses is aptly disturbing. Filmed on location in Australia and New Zealand; made for cable TV.**CW:** Depiction of violence against animals. **?m/C VHS.** Don Johnson, Craig Sheffer, Gabrielle Anwar, Bob Gunton, Rod Steiger, James B. Sikking, John Dennis Johnston, Robert Coleby; **D:** Ken Olin; **W:** Dennis Lynton Clark; **C:** Stephen Windon; **M:** John Debney. *HBO*

In Search of a Golden Sky 🎬🎬 1984 **(PG)** Following their mother's death, a motley group of children move in with their secluded cabin-dwelling uncle, much to the righteous chagrin of the welfare department. **94m/C VHS, Beta, Closed Caption.** Charles Napier, George Flower, Cliff Osmond; **D:** Jefferson Richard. *FOX*

In Search of Anna woof! 1979 When a convict is released from jail, he hits the road with a flighty model in search of the girlfriend who corresponded with him in prison. There auto be a law. **90m/C VHS, Beta.** *AU* Judy Morris, Richard Moir, Chris Hayward, Bill Hunter; **D:** Esben Storm.

In Search of the Castaways 🎬🎬🎬 1962 Stirring adventure tale of a teenage girl and her younger brother searching for their father, a ship's captain lost at sea years earlier. Powerful special effects and strong cast make this a winning Disney effort. Based on a story by Jules Verne. **98m/C VHS, Beta, Closed Caption.** *GB* Hayley Mills, Maurice Chevalier, George Sanders, Wilfrid Hyde-White, Michael Anderson Jr.; **D:** Robert Stevenson. *DIS*

In Self Defense ⚔️½ 1993 (PG) Purl is supposed to be protected from the killer she testified against but it doesn't quite work out that way. 94m/C VHS, Closed Caption. Linda Purl, Yaphet Kotto, Billy Drago; **D:** Bruce Seth Green; **M:** Patrick Gleeson. TTC

In Society ⚔️⚔️½ 1944 The duo play dimwitted plumbers who are mistakenly invited to a high society party, where they promptly create catastrophe. 84m/B VHS. Bud Abbott, Lou Costello, Marion Hutton, Kirby Grant, Ann Gillis, Arthur Treacher, Thomas Gomez, Steve Geray, Margaret Irving, Thurston Hall; **Cameos:** Sid Fields; **D:** Jean Yarbrough; **W:** Sid Fields, Hal Fimberg, Edmund Hartmann, John Grant. USH, FCT

In the Aftermath: Angels Never Sleep ⚔️½ 1987 Mix of animation and live-action in this post-nuclear wasteland tale never quite works. 85m/C VHS, Beta. Tony Markes, Rainbow Dolan; **D:** Carl Colpaert. VTR

In the Army Now ⚔️ 1994 (PG) Pauly dude gets his head shaved, man. Service comedy about a slacker who joins the Army hoping to cash in on military benefits but who winds up in combat instead. Shore drops the Valley Guy shtick and ventures into the land of action when he gets sent on a mission to the Sahara. Strictly for Shore's fans. 92m/C VHS, LV, Closed Caption. Pauly Shore, Esai Morales, Lori Petty, David Alan Grier, Ernie Hudson, Andy Dick; **D:** Dan Petrie Jr.; **W:** Dan Petrie Jr., Ken Kaufman, Fax Bahr, Stu Krieger, Adam Small; **M:** Robert Folk. HPH

In the Cold of the Night ⚔️ 1989 (R) Another drowsy entry into the "to sleep perchance to have a nightmare genre." A photographer with a vivid imagination dreams he murders a woman he doesn't know, and when said dream girl rides into his life on the back of a Harley, Mr. Foto's faced with an etiquette quandary: haven't they met before? Cast includes Hedren (Hitchcock's Marnie and Melanie Griffith's mother). 112m/C VHS, LV, Closed Caption. Jeff Lester, Adrienne Sachs, Shannon Tweed, David Soul, John Beck, Tippi Hedren, Marc Singer; **D:** Nico Mastorakis. REP

In the Company of Men ⚔️⚔️ 1996 (R) A couple of dissatisfied Yuppies, Chad (Eckhart) and Howard (Malloy) are sent on a six-week job out of town by their home office. Grumbling about the lack of control in their lives (and blaming it on women), Chad formulates a nasty plan (to which Howard eventually agrees)—they'll deliberately get involved with the same girl, secretary Christine (Edwards), string her along, and then abandon her when their job is done. But Chad actually has his own agenda and bigger corporate ideas in mind. Think misogynistic satire. **CW:** Language and emotional abuse. 93m/C VHS, Closed Caption, DVD. Matt Malloy, Aaron Eckhart, Stacy Edwards, Mark Rector; **D:** Neil LaBute; **W:** Neil LaBute; **C:** Anthony P. Hettinger. Independent Spirit Awards '98: Debut Performance (Eckhart); Sundance Film Festival '97: Filmmakers Trophy; Nominations: Independent Spirit Awards '98: Best Actress (Edwards), Best First Feature. COL

In the Custody of Strangers ⚔️⚔️⚔️ 1982 A teenager's parents refuse to help when he is arrested for being drunk and he ends up spending the night in jail. Realistic handling of a serious subject. Sheen and Estevez play the father and son, mimicking their real-life relationship. Made for television. 100m/C VHS. Martin Sheen, Jane Alexander, Emilio Estevez, Kenneth McMillan, Ed Lauter, Matt Clark, John Hancock; **D:** Robert Greenwald. MOV

In the Days of the Thundering Herd & the Law & the Outlaw 1914 In the first feature, a pony express rider sacrifices his job to accompany his sweetheart on a westward trek to meet her father. In the second show, a fugitive falls in love with a rancher's daughter and risks recognition. 76m/B VHS, Beta. Tom Mix, Myrtle Stedman; **D:** Colin Campbell. CCB, GPV

In the Deep Woods ⚔️ 1991 Children's author Joanna Warren (Arquette) gets too close to mayhem when a childhood friend is murdered by the Deep Woods Killer. A mysterious private detective (Perkins) is on the killer's trail but when Joanna comes into the picture will she be a suspect or a victim? Based on the book by Nicholas Conde. ?m/C VHS. Rosanna Arquette, Anthony Perkins, Will Patton, D.W. Moffett, Christopher Rydell, Harold Sylvester, Kimberly Beck; **D:** Charles Correll; **W:** Robert Nathan, Robert Rosenbaum; **C:** James Glennon.

In the Gloaming ⚔️⚔️⚔️ 1997 (PG) Twentysomething Danny (Leonard) bitterly returns home to his suburban, wealthy, emotionally cold family because he is dying of AIDS. He and mother Janet (Close) renew their strained family ties but his businessman dad (Strathairn) doesn't know how to cope except with distance, and his sullen sister Anne (Fonda) is resentful. Wrenching story with fine work by all, including Goldberg in the small role of live-in nurse, Myrna. Based on a short story by Alice Elliot Dark. Made for cable TV; Reeve's directorial debut. 60m/C VHS. Robert Sean Leonard, Glenn Close, David Strathairn, Bridget Fonda, Whoopi Goldberg; **D:** Christopher Reeve; **W:** Will Scheffer; **C:** Frederick Elmes; **M:** Dave Grusin. HBO

In the Good Old Summertime ⚔️⚔️⚔️ 1949 This pleasant musical version of "The Shop Around the Corner" tells the story of two bickering co-workers who are also anonymous lovelorn pen pals. Minnelli made her second screen appearance at 18 months in the final scene. ♫I Don't Care; Meet Me Tonight In Dreamland; Play That Barbershop Chord; In the Good Old Summertime; Put Your Arms Around Me Honey; Wait Till the Sun Shines Nellie; Chicago; Merry Christmas. 104m/C VHS, Beta, LV. Judy Garland, Van Johnson, S.Z. Sakall, Buster Keaton, Spring Byington, Liza Minnelli, Clinton Sundberg; **D:** Robert Z. Leonard; **C:** Harry Stradling. MGM

In the Heat of Passion ⚔️½ 1991 (R) A low-budget ripoff of "Body Heat" and "Fatal Attraction" starring Kirkland as a married woman who involves a much younger man in a very steamy affair that leads to murder. This movie wants to be a thriller, but is little more than a softcore sex flick. Also available in an unrated version that contains explicit footage. **CW:** Language, violence, and sensuality. 84m/C VHS, LV. Sally Kirkland, Nick Corri, Jack Carter, Michael Greene; **D:** Rodman Flender; **W:** Rodman Flender. COL

In the Heat of Passion 2: Unfaithful ⚔️½ 1994 (R) Philip Donovan (Bostwick) is having an affair with his stepdaughter Casey (Hill) and the duo murder hapless wife/mother (Down) to get her money. But it seems someone else knows about their crime. **CW:** Some language and violence; strong sexuality. 88m/C VHS, LV. Barry Bostwick, Teresa Hill, Lesley-Anne Down, Michael Gross; **D:** Catherine Cyran. NHO

In the Heat of the Night ⚔️⚔️⚔️½ 1967 A wealthy industrialist in a small Mississippi town is murdered. A black homicide expert is asked to help solve the murder, despite resentment on the part of the town's chief of police. Powerful script with underlying theme of racial prejudice is served well by taut direction and powerhouse performances. Poitier's memorable character Virgil Tibbs appeared in two more pictures, "They Call Me Mister Tibbs" and "The Organization." 109m/C VHS, Beta, LV. Sidney Poitier, Rod Steiger, Warren Oates, Lee Grant; **D:** Norman Jewison; **W:** Stirling Silliphant; **C:** Haskell Wexler; **M:** Quincy Jones. Academy Awards '67: Best Actor (Steiger), Best Adapted Screenplay, Best Film Editing, Best Picture, Best Sound; British Academy Awards '67: Best Actor (Steiger); Golden Globe Awards '68: Best Actor—Drama (Steiger), Best Film—Drama, Best Screenplay; New York Film Critics Awards '67: Best Actor (Steiger), Best Director (Nichols), Best Film; National Society of Film Critics Awards '67: Best Actor (Steiger), Best Cinematography; Nominations: Academy Awards '67: Best Director (Jewison). MGM, FOX, BTV

In the King of Prussia ⚔️½ 1983 Recreation of the trial of the "Plowshares Eight" radicals who were jailed for sabotaging two nuclear missiles at an electric plant in Pennsylvania. 92m/

C VHS, Beta. Martin Sheen, Rev. Daniel Berrigan, MPI, BUL

In the Kingdom of the Blind the Man with One Eye Is King ⚔️⚔️ 1994 (R) The title doesn't seem to mean anything and you may feel the same way about this standard crime drama, despite a strong cast. Mobster Tony (Petersen) gets police assistance from detective Al (Vallelonga) in discovering who murdered a mob boss' brother. **CW:** Language, violence, brief nudity. 99m/C VHS. Nick Vallelonga, William L. Petersen, Michael Biehn, Paul Winfield, James Quarter; **D:** Nick Vallelonga; **W:** Nick Vallelonga. AVI

In the Land of the Owl Turds 1987 The story of a decidedly eccentric young man who drives a dada art gallery on wheels while searching for love. Blank's senior thesis film. 30m/C VHS, Beta. **D:** Harrod Blank. FFM

In the Line of Duty: A Cop for the Killing ⚔️⚔️ A Cop for the Killing 1990 (R) Undercover L.A. narcotics squad is about to bust the city's biggest drug lord when their sting operation goes bad and one of the team is brutally murdered. So, squad leader Ray Wiltern (Farentino) decides to get even. One in a series of TV movies under the "In the Line of Duty" banner. 95m/C VHS. James Farentino, Steven Weber, Charles Haid, Tony Crane, Harold Sylvester, Dan Lauria, Tony Plana; **D:** Dick Lowry; **W:** Philip Rosenberg; **C:** Frank Beasoechea; **M:** Mark Snow. NHO

In the Line of Duty: Ambush in Waco ⚔️⚔️½ Ambush in Waco 1993 (R) Insta-television movie made by NBC even before the fire which engulfed the Texas compound and ended the standoff between self-proclaimed "prophet" David Koresh and the federal government. Daly does well as the manipulative, charasmatic Branch Davidian cult leader whose stockpiling of illegal weapons lead to an investigation by the Bureau of Alcohool, Tobacco and Firearms and a botched raid which caused the ultimately fatal siege. Filmed on location outside Tulsa, Oklahoma. **CW:** Graphic depiction of a shootout. 93m/C VHS, Closed Caption. Timothy Daly, Dan Lauria, William O'Leary; **D:** Dick Lowry; **W:** Phil Penningroth. REP

In the Line of Duty: The FBI Murders ⚔️⚔️⚔️ The FBI Murders 1988 A fact-based chiller about the bloody 1986 shootout between Miami FBI agents and a pair of violent killers (Soul and Gross playing against type). 95m/C VHS, Closed Caption. David Soul, Michael Gross, Ronny Cox, Bruce Greenwood, Doug Sheehan, Teri Copley; **D:** Dick Lowry; **W:** Tracy Keenan Wynn. CAF

In the Line of Fire ⚔️⚔️⚔️½ 1993 (R) Aging Secret Service agent meets his match in a spooky caller who threatens his honor and the president in an exciting, fast-paced cat and mouse game. Terrific performance by Eastwood includes lots of dry humor and an unscripted emotional moment, but is nearly overshadowed by Malkovich's menacing bad guy. Eerie special effects add to the mood. The Secret Service cooperated and most scenes are believable, with a few Hollywood exceptions; the end result clearly pays homage to the agents who protect our presidents. Intriguing trailer showed the number "6" in "1963" slowly turning to "9" to become "1993." The seventh highest grossing movie of 1993. **CW:** Language and violence. 128m/C VHS, LV, 8mm, Letterbox, Closed Caption, DVD. Clint Eastwood, John Malkovich, Rene Russo, Dylan McDermott, Gary Cole, Fred Dalton Thompson, John Mahoney, Gregory Alan Williams; **D:** Wolfgang Petersen; **W:** Jeff Maguire; **C:** John Bailey; **M:** Ennio Morricone. Nominations: Academy Awards '93: Best Film Editing, Best Original Screenplay, Best Supporting Actor (Malkovich); British Academy Awards '93: Best Original Screenplay, Best Supporting Actor (Malkovich); Golden Globe Awards '94: Best Supporting Actor (Malkovich); MTV Movie Awards '94: Best Villain (Malkovich); Writers Guild of America '93: Best Original Screenplay. COL, BTV

In the Money ⚐ 1934 Veteran vaudevillian "Skeets" Gallagher introduces a muddled mass of acts, including a poor imitator of boxing great Gene Tunney, a mad scientist who talks to rabbits and writes rubber checks, and a limp-wristed lisper. 66m/B VHS. Lois Wilson, Warren Hymer, Arthur Hoyt, Frank "Junior" Coghlan, Louise Beavers; *D:* Frank Strayer. *NOS*

In the Mood ⚐⚐½ 1987 (PG-13) Based on fact, this is the story of teenager Sonny Wisecarver, nicknamed "The Woo Woo Kid," who in 1944, seduced two older women and eventually landed in jail after marrying one of them. Look for Wisecarver in a cameo role as a mailman in the film. 98m/C VHS, Beta, LV, Closed Caption. Patrick Dempsey, Beverly D'Angelo, Talia Balsam, Michael Constantine, Betty Jinnette, Kathleen Freeman, Peter Hobbs, Edith Fellows; *Cameos:* Ellsworth Wisecarver; *D:* Phil Alden Robinson; *W:* Phil Alden Robinson; *M:* Ralph Burns. *WAR, ORI, BAR*

In the Mouth of Madness ⚐⚐ 1995 (R) Standard horror flick pays homage to or pokes fun at Stephen King (you decide) with story of successful horror novelist whose fans become a bit too engrossed in his stories—seems his readers tend to slip into dementia and carry out the grisly acts depicted within the pages. Neill plays an insurance investigator who must track down the missing author while combating the psychotic, axe-wielding residents of the seemingly quiet east coast hamlet where the author resides. Worth a look for the above-average special effects and makeup provided by Industrial Light and Magic (ILM). 95m/C VHS, LV, Closed Caption. Sam Neill, Juergen Prochnow, Julie Carmen, Charlton Heston, David Warner, John Glover, Bernie Casey, Peter Jason, Frances Bay; *D:* John Carpenter; *W:* Michael De Luca; *M:* John Carpenter, Jim Lang. *TTC, NLC*

In the Name of the Father ⚐⚐⚐½ 1993 (R) Compelling true story of Gerry Conlon and the Guildford Four, illegally imprisoned in 1974 by British officials after a tragic IRA bombing near London. The British judicial system receives a black eye, but so does the horror and cruelty of IRA terrorism. Politics and family life in a prison cell share the focus, as Sheridan captures superior performances from Day-Lewis and Postlethwaite (beware the thick Belfast brogue). Thompson was accused of pro-IRA sympathies in the British press for her role as the lawyer who believed in Conlon's innocence. Adapted from "Proved Innocent," Conlon's prison memoirs; reunites Sheridan and Day-Lewis after "My Left Foot." Includes original songs by U2's Bono, with a haunting theme sung by Sinead O'Connor.*CW:* Language and politically-generated violence. 127m/C VHS, LV, Letterbox, Closed Caption, DVD. *GB IR* Daniel Day-Lewis, Pete Postlethwaite, Emma Thompson, John Lynch, Corin Redgrave, Beatie Edney, John Benfield, Paterson Joseph, Marie Jones, Gerard McSorley, Frank Harper, Mark Sheppard, Don Baker, Britta Smith, Aidan Grennell, Daniel Massey, Bosco Hogan, Daniel Massey; *D:* Jim Sheridan; *W:* Jim Sheridan, Terry George; *C:* Peter Biziou; *M:* Trevor Jones, Bono, Sinead O'Connor. Berlin International Film Festival '94: Golden Berlin Bear; Nominations: Academy Awards '93: Best Actor (Day-Lewis), Best Adapted Screenplay, Best Director (Sheridan), Best Film Editing, Best Picture, Best Supporting Actor (Postlethwaite), Best Supporting Actress (Thompson); British Academy Awards '93: Best Actor (Day-Lewis), Best Adapted Screenplay; Golden Globe Awards '94: Best Actor—Drama (Day-Lewis), Best Film—Drama, Best Song ("(You Made Me the) Thief of Your Heart"), Best Supporting Actress (Thompson); Writers Guild of America '93: Best Adapted Screenplay.*USH*

In the Name of the Pope-King ⚐⚐⚐ 1985 An acclaimed historical epic about the politics and warfare raging around the 1867 Italian wars that made the Pope the sole ruler in Rome. In Italian with English subtitles. 115m/C VHS, Beta. Nino Manfredi, Danilo Mattei, Carmen Scarpitta, Giovannella Grifea, Carlo Bagno; *D:* Luigi Magni. *WBF, TPV, FCT*

In the Navy ⚐⚐½ *Abbott and Costello in the Navy* 1941 Abbott and Costello join the Navy in one of four military-service comedies they cranked out in 1941 alone. The token narrative involves about a singing star (Powell) in uniform to escape his female fans, but that's just an excuse for classic A & C routines. With the Andrews Sisters. ♫*Starlight, Starbright; You're Off To See The World; Hula Ba Lua; Gimme Some Skin; A Sailor's Life For Me; We're In The Navy; Anchors Aweigh* (instrumental); *You're A Lucky Fellow, Mr. Smith* (instrumental). 85m/B VHS, LV, Letterbox, Closed Caption. Lou Costello, Bud Abbott, Dick Powell, The Andrews Sisters; *D:* Arthur Lubin; *C:* Joseph Valentine. *USH*

In the Presence of Mine Enemies ⚐⚐½ 1997 (PG-13) Cable remake of Rod Serling's 1960 script for "Playhouse 90." Rabbi Adam Heller (Mueller-Stahl) and his daughter Rachel (Lowensohn) are living in the Warsaw ghetto in 1942, trying to deal with Nazi oppression. But the Rabbi's faith is put the test when his son Paul (McKellar), who's escaped from the Treblinka labor camp, returns for vengeance and Rachel becomes the sexual victim of a vicious German officer (Dance).*CW:* Thematic elements and some scenes of violence. 100m/C VHS. Armin Mueller-Stahl, Elina Lowensohn, Don McKellar, Charles Dance, Chad Lowe; *D:* Joan Micklin Silver; *W:* Rod Serling. *EVE*

In the Realm of Passion ⚐⚐ *Empire of Passion* 1980 (R) A wife and her lover murder her husband and dump the body in an abandoned well. Guilt over their actions drive the lovers to return to the scene where they are greeted by the vengeful ghost of the betrayed husband—or is it only their consciences torturing them? In Japanese with English subtitles. 108m/C VHS. Kazuko Yoshiyuki, Takahiro Tamura, Tatsuya Fuji; *D:* Nagisa Oshima. *FXL*

In the Realm of the Senses ⚐⚐⚐ 1976 (NC-17) Taboo-breaking story of a woman and man who turn their backs on the militaristic rule of Japan in the mid-1930s by plunging into an erotic and sensual world all their own. Striking, graphic work that was seized by U.S. customs when it first entered the country. Violent with explicit sex, and considered by some critics as pretentious, while others call it Oshima's masterpiece. In Japanese with English subtitles.*CW:* Sexually explicit. 105m/C VHS. *JP FR* Tatsuya Fuji, Eiko Matsuda, Aio Nakajima, Meika Seri; *D:* Nagisa Oshima. *FXL, CVC*

In the Region of Ice ⚐⚐⚐ 1976 Award-winning short reveals the complexities of the relationship between a nun and a disturbed student. 38m/B VHS, Beta. Fionnula Flanagan, Peter Lempert; *D:* Peter Werner. *BFA*

In the Secret State ⚐⚐ 19?? Inspector Strange finds himself faced with the apparent suicide of a colleague on the day of his own retirement from the force. His private investigation into the case finds him mired in murder and espionage. 107m/C VHS. Frank Finlay, Matthew Marsh, Thorley Walters. *MOV*

In the Shadow of Kilimanjaro woof! 1986 (R) A pack of hungry baboons attacks innocent people in the wilderness of Kenya. Based on a true story but the characters are contrived and just plain stupid at times. Quite gory as well. Filmed on location in Kenya. 105m/C VHS, Beta. *GB* John Rhys-Davies, Timothy Bottoms, Michele Carey, Irene Miracle, Calvin Jung, Donald Blakely; *D:* Raju Patel. *ART*

In the Soup ⚐⚐½ 1992 (R) Adolpho is a naive New York filmmaker barely scraping by. He decides to sell his script in a classified ad which is answered by the fast-talking Joe, a would-be film producer who's true profession is as a con artist. The two then try numerous (and humorous) ways to raise the money to begin filming. Also available colorized.*CW:* Language. 93m/B VHS, LV, Closed Caption. Steve Buscemi, Seymour Cassel, Jennifer Beals, Will Patton, Pat Moya, Stanley Tucci, Sully Boyar, Rockets

Redglare, Elizabeth Bracco, Ruth Maleczech, Debi Mazar, Steven Randazzo, Francesco Messina; *Cameos:* Jim Jarmusch, Carol Kane; *D:* Alexandre Rockwell; *W:* Tim Kissell, Alexandre Rockwell; *C:* Phil Parmet; *M:* Mader. Sundance Film Festival '92: Grand Jury Prize.

In the Spirit ⚐⚐½ 1990 (R) New Age couple move from Beverly Hills to New York, where they meet an air-headed mystic and are forced to hide from a murderer. Falk gives solid performance in sometimes rocky production. Berlin is the real-life daughter of May. 94m/C VHS, Beta. Elaine May, Marlo Thomas, Jeannie Berlin, Peter Falk, Melanie Griffith, Olympia Dukakis, Chad Burton, Thurn Hoffman, Michael Emil, Christopher Durang, Laurie Jones; *D:* Sandra Seacat; *W:* Jeannie Berlin, Laurie Jones; *M:* Patrick Williams.

In the Steps of a Dead Man ⚐½ 1974 A family grieving for a fallen soldier is earmarked for evil by a young man who bears an uncanny resemblance to the dead man. A friend of the family has her suspicions and must find out the truth before something terrible happens. 71m/C VHS, Beta. Skye Aubrey, John Nolan. *NO*

In the White City ⚐⚐⚐ *Dans la Ville Blanche* 1983 A sailor jumps ship in Lisbon and uses a movie camera to record himself and his search through the twisted streets and alleys of the city for something or someone to connect to. In French, Portuguese, and German with English subtitles. 108m/C VHS. *PT SI* Bruno Ganz, Teresa Madruga; *D:* Alain Tanner. *NYF*

In This House of Brede ⚐⚐⚐ 1975 A sophisticated London widow turns her back on her worldly life to become a cloistered Benedictine nun. Rigg is outstanding as the woman struggling to deal with the discipline of faith. Made for television and based on the novel by Rumer Godden. 105m/C VHS, Beta. Diana Rigg; *D:* George Schaefer. *BFA, OM*

In This Our Life ⚐⚐½ 1942 Histrionic melodrama handled effectively by Huston about a nutsy woman who steals her sister's husband, rejects him, manipulates her whole family and eventually leads herself to ruin. Vintage star vehicle for Davis, who chews scenery and fellow actors alike. Adapted by Howard Koch from the Ellen Glasgon novel. 101m/B VHS, Beta. Bette Davis, Olivia de Havilland, Charles Coburn, Frank Craven, George Brent, Dennis (Stanley Morner) Morgan, Billie Burke, Hattie McDaniel, Lee Patrick, Walter Huston, Ernest Anderson; *D:* John Huston; *M:* Max Steiner. *MGM*

In Too Deep ⚐½ 1990 (R) A rock star and a beautiful woman are physically drawn to one another in spite of the fact that any contact between them could have disasterous results.*CW:* Strong language, some violence, and strong sensuality. 106m/C VHS, Beta. Hugo Race, Santha Press, Rebekah Elmaloglou, John Flaus, Dominic Sweeney; *D:* Colin South. *PAR*

In Trouble woof! 1967 Hard-to-follow and frequently aimless story of a pregnant girl who invents a fake rape story that her dull-witted brothers take seriously, embarking on a cross-country search for the culprit. 82m/C VHS, Beta. *CA* Julie LaChapelle, Katherine Mousseau, Daniel Pilon; *D:* Gilles Carle.

In Which We Serve ⚐⚐⚐½ 1943 Much stiff upper-lipping in this classic that captures the spirit of the British Navy during WWII. The sinking of the destroyer HMS Torrin during the Battle of Crete is told via flashbacks, with an emphasis on realism that was unusual in wartime flag-wavers. Features the film debuts of Johnson and Attenborough, and the first Lean directorial effort. Coward received a special Oscar for his "outstanding production achievement," having scripted, scored, codirected and costarred. 114m/B VHS, Beta. *GB* Noel Coward, John Mills, Bernard Miles, Celia Johnson, Kay Walsh, James Donald, Richard Attenborough; *D:* Noel Coward, David Lean; *W:* Noel Coward; *M:* Noel Coward. New York Film Critics Awards '42: Best Film; Nominations: Academy Awards '43: Best Original Screenplay, Best Picture. *NOS*

In Your Face 🐾½ *Abar, the First Black Superman* 1977 **(R)** Little known blaxploitation film about a black family harrassed in a white suburb. A black motorcycle gang comes to their rescue. **90m/C VHS.** J. Walter Smith, Tobar Mayo, Roxie Young, Tina James; **D:** Frank Packard. *XVC, HHE*

The Incident 🐾🐾½ 1967 A gritty, controversial (at-the-time) drama about two abusive thugs who take over a New York subway car late at night, humiliating and terrorizing each passenger in turn. Film debut for Sheen and Musante as the thugs. **99m/B VHS, Beta, LV.** Martin Sheen, Tony Musante, Beau Bridges, Ruby Dee, Jack Gilford, Thelma Ritter, Brock Peters, Ed McMahon, Gary Merrill, Donna Mills, Jan Sterling, Mike Kellin, Bob Bannard, Diana Van Der Vlis, Victor Arnold, Robert Fields; **D:** Larry Peerce; **W:** Charles Fox, Nicholas E. Baehr; **M:** Charles Fox. *FOX*

The Incident 🐾🐾🐾 1989 Political thriller set during WWII in Lincoln Bluff, Colorado. Matthau is excellent in his TV debut as a small-town lawyer who must defend a German prisoner of war accused of murder at nearby Camp Bremen. An all-star cast lends powerful performances to this riveting made for TV drama. **95m/C VHS, Closed Caption.** Walter Matthau, Susan Blakely, Harry (Henry) Morgan, Robert Carradine, Barnard Hughes, Peter Firth, William Schallert; **D:** Joseph Sargent. *CAF*

Incident at Channel Q 🐾½ 1986 A heavy-metal rock musical about a suburban neighborhood declaring war on a chain-and-leather deejay. **85m/C VHS, Beta, LV.** Al Corley. *MVD, BMG*

Incident at Deception Ridge 🐾🐾½ 1994 **(R)** After five years in prison, Jack Bolder (O'Keefe) is finally a free man, and headed for Seattle by bus. Unfortunately, also aboard is weasely bank manager Jack Davis (Begley, Jr.) who's bolted with the ransom money for his kidnapped wife, Helen (Purl). Now Helen is left at the mercy of her kidnappers, who've discovered where their money is and decide to go after it—no matter who gets in their way. Filmed in Vancouver, British Columbia. Made for cable. **CW:** Some violence. **94m/C VHS, LV, Closed Caption.** Michael O'Keefe, Ed Begley Jr., Linda Purl, Miguel Ferrer, Colleen Flynn, Michelle Johnson, Ian Tracey; **D:** John McPherson, John McPherson; **W:** Ken Hixon, Randy Kornfield; **C:** David Geddes. *USH*

Incident at Oglala: The Leonard Peltier Story 🐾🐾🐾 1992 **(PG)** Offers a detailed account of the violent events leading to the murder of two FBI agents in Oglala, South Dakota in 1975. American Indian activist Leonard Peltier was convicted of the murders and is presently serving two consecutive life sentences, but he's cited as a political prisoner by Amnesty International. The documentary examines the highly controversial trial and the tensions between the government and the Oglala Nation stemming back to the Indian occupation of Wounded Knee in 1973. Director Apted is sympathetic to Peltier and offers reasons why he should be allowed a retrial; he examined similar incidents in his film "Thunderheart." **90m/C VHS.** **D:** Michael Apted; **M:** John Trudell, Jackson Browne. *ART, FCT*

An Inconvenient Woman 🐾🐾 1991 When an older married man has an affair with a young seductress, there's suicide, murder, a nasty gossip columnist, a reporter, a knowing society wife, and a lot of cover-ups among the rich and famous. From the novel by Dominick Dunne and based on the Alfred Bloomingdale scandal. Originally a made for television mini-series. **126m/C VHS, Beta, Closed Caption.** Rebecca DeMornay, Jason Robards Jr., Jill Eikenberry, Peter Gallagher, Roddy McDowall, Chad Lowe.

The Incredible Hulk 🐾🐾½ 1977 Bixby is a scientist who achieves superhuman strength after he is exposed to a massive dose of gamma rays. But his personal life suffers, as does his wardrobe. Ferrigno is the Hulkster. The pilot for the television series is based on the Marvel Comics character. **94m/C VHS, Beta, LV.** Bill Bixby, Susan Sullivan, Lou Ferrigno, Jack Colvin; **D:** Kenneth Johnson. *USH*

The Incredible Hulk Returns 🐾½ 1988 The beefy green mutant is back and this time he wages war against a Viking named Thor. Very little substance in this made for television flick, so be prepared to park your brain at the door. Followed by "The Trial of the Incredible Hulk." **100m/C VHS, LV.** Bill Bixby, Lou Ferrigno, Jack Colvin, Lee Purcell, Charles Napier, Steve Levitt; **D:** Nick Corea. *VTR*

The Incredible Journey 🐾🐾½ 1963 A labrador retriever, bull terrier and Siamese cat mistake their caretaker's intentions when he leaves for a hunting trip, believing he will never return. The three set out on a 250 mile adventure-filled trek across Canada's rugged terrain. Entertaining family adventure from Disney taken from Sheila Burnford's book. **80m/C VHS, Beta, LV. D:** Fletcher Markle. *DIS*

The Incredible Journey of Dr. Meg Laurel 🐾🐾🐾 1979 A young doctor returns to her roots to bring modern medicine to the Appalachian mountain people during the 1930s. Made for television featuring Wagner in a strong performance. **143m/C VHS, Beta.** Lindsay Wagner, Jane Wyman, Dorothy Maguire, James Woods, Gary Lockwood; **D:** Guy Green. *COL*

Incredible Master Beggars 🐾 1982 **(R)** Against all odds, the Beggars challenge the Great Iron Master, using "Tam Leg" tactics versus the "Iron Cloth" fighting style. **88m/C VHS, Beta.** Tan Tao Liang, Ku Feng, Han Kuo Tsai, Li Tang Ming, Li Hai Sheng, Lui I. Fan, Pan Yao Kun. *GEM*

Incredible Melting Man woof! 1977 **(R)** Two transformations change an astronaut's life after his return to earth. First, his skin starts to melt, then he displays cannibalistic tendencies. Hard to swallow. Special effects by Rick Baker. Look for director Jonathan Demme in a bit part. Gross-out remake of 1958's "First Man Into Space." **85m/C VHS, Beta.** Alex Rebar, Burr de Benning, Cheryl "Rainbeaux" Smith; **Cameos:** Jonathan Demme; **D:** William Sachs. *ART, VES*

The Incredible Mr. Limpet 🐾🐾 1964 Limp comedy about a nebbish bookkeeper who's transformed into a fish, fulfilling his aquatic dreams. Eventually he falls in love with another fish, and helps the U.S. Navy find Nazi subs during WWII. Partially animated, beloved by some, particularly those under the age of seven. Based on Theodore Pratt's novel. **99m/C VHS, Beta, LV, Closed Caption.** Don Knotts, Jack Weston, Carole Cook, Andrew Duggan, Larry Keating, Elizabeth McRae; **D:** Arthur Lubin; **W:** Jameson Brewer. *WAR*

The Incredible Petrified World woof! 1958 Divers are trapped in an underwater cave when volcanic eruptions begin. Suffocating nonsense. **78m/B VHS.** John Carradine, Allen Windsor, Phyllis Coates, Lloyd Nelson, George Skaff; **D:** Jerry Warren. *NOS, SNC*

The Incredible Rocky Mountain Race 🐾🐾 1977 The townspeople of St. Joseph, fed up with Mark Twain's destructive feud with a neighbor, devise a shrewd scheme to rid the town of the troublemakers by sending them on a road race through the West. Made for television comedy starring the F-Troop. **97m/C VHS, Beta.** Christopher Connelly, Forrest Tucker, Larry Storch, Mike Mazurki; **D:** James L. Conway. *VTR*

The Incredible Sarah 🐾🐾 1976 **(PG)** A limp adapted stage biography from "Reader's Digest" of the great actress Sarah Bernhardt. Jackson chews scenery to no avail. **105m/C VHS, Beta, LV.** Glenda Jackson, Daniel Massey, Yvonne Mitchell, Douglas Wilmer; **D:** Richard Fleischer; **M:** Elmer Bernstein. Nominations: Academy Awards '76: Best Art Direction/Set Decoration, Best Costume Design. *IME*

The Incredible Shrinking Man 🐾🐾½ 1957 Adapted by Richard Matheson from his own novel, the sci-fi classic is a philosophical thriller about a man who is doused with radioactive mist and begins to slowly shrink. His new size means that everyday objects take on sinister meaning and he must fight for his life in an increasingly hostile, absurd environment. A surreal, suspenseful allegory with impressive special effects. Endowed with the tension usually reserved for Hitchcock films. **81m/B VHS, Beta, LV.** Grant Williams, Randy Stuart, April Kent, Paul Langton, Raymond Bailey, William Schallert, Frank Scannell, Billy Curtis; **D:** Jack Arnold; **W:** Richard Matheson; **C:** Ellis W. Carter. *USH, MLB*

The Incredible Shrinking Woman 🐾🐾½ 1981 **(PG)** "...Shrinking Man" spoof and inoffensive social satire finds household cleaners producing some strange side effects on model homemaker Tomlin, slowly shrinking her to doll-house size. She then encounters everyday happenings as big tasks and not so menial. Her advertising exec husband has a hand in the down-sizing. Sight gags abound but the cuteness wears thin by the end. **89m/C VHS, Beta, LV.** Lily Tomlin, Charles Grodin, Ned Beatty, Henry Gibson; **D:** Joel Schumacher; **W:** Jane Wagner. *USH*

The Incredible Two-Headed Transplant woof! 1971 **(PG)** Mad scientist Dern has a criminal head transplanted on to the shoulder of big John Bloom and the critter runs amuck. Low-budget special effects guaranteed to give you a headache or two. Watch for Pat "Marilyn Munster" Priest in a bikini. **88m/C VHS.** Bruce Dern, Pat Priest, Casey Kasem, Albert Cole, John Joe Bob Briggs Bloom, Berry Kroeger; **D:** Anthony M. Lanza; **M:** John Barber. *NO*

Incredibly Strange Creatures Who Stopped Living and Became Mixed-Up Zombies woof! *The Teenage Psycho Meets Bloody Mary; The Incredibly Strange Creatures* 1963 The infamous, super-cheap horror spoof that established Sheckler (for whom Cash Flagg is a pseudonym), about a carny side show riddled with ghouls and bad rock bands. Assistant cinematographers include the young Laszlo Kovacs and Vilmos Zsigmond. A must-see for connoisseurs of cult and camp. **90m/C VHS, Beta.** Cash Flagg, Carolyn Brandt, Brett O'Hara, Atlas King, Sharon Walsh, Toni Camel, Erina Enyo; **D:** Ray Dennis Steckler; **W:** Gene Pollock, Robert Silliphant; **C:** Laszlo Kovacs, Vilmos Zsigmond, Joseph Mascelli. *NO*

The Incredibly True Adventure of Two Girls in Love 🐾🐾½ 1995 **(R)** Gentle low-budget romantic comedy about first love between two high school girls. Tomboyish working-class Randy (Holloman) lives with her lesbian aunt and works part-time at the local gas station where she spots the rich and beautiful Evie (Parker), one of the popular girls in school. Some sparks fly but Evie's confused, though she's willing to be wooed and, later, defend her new relationship. The issue of race (Randy's white, Evie's black) is only briefly alluded to—more is made of the differences between the girls' social classes and their vulnerability. Directorial debut for Maggenti. **CW:** Strong sex scene involving teen girls; language; some drug use. **95m/C VHS.** Laurel Holloman, Nicole Parker, Kate Stafford, Stephanie Berry; **D:** Maria Maggenti; **W:** Maria Maggenti. *NLC*

Incubus woof! 1982 **(R)** A doctor and his teenaged daughter settle in a quiet New England community, only to encounter the incubus, a terrifying, supernatural demon who enjoys sex murders. Offensive trash. **90m/C VHS, Beta, LV.** CA John Cassavetes, Kerrie Keane, Helen Hughes, Erin Flannery, John Ireland, Duncan McIntosh; **D:** John Hough; **W:** George Franklin; **C:** Conrad Hall, Albert J. Dunk; **M:** Stanley Myers. *VES*

Indecency 🐾🐾 1992 **(PG-13)** Ellie (Beals) is still recovering from a mental breakdown when she goes to work for Marie (Clarkson) at her ad agency. There Ellie must deal with manipulative associate Nia (Davis) and Marie's charming, estranged husband Mick (Remar), who draws the fragile Ellie into an affair. Then Marie commits suicide—or maybe it was murder. **CW:** Violence and sensual scenes. **88m/C VHS, LV, Closed Caption.** Jennifer Beals, James Remar, Sammi Davis, Barbara Williams, Christopher John Fields, Ray McKinnon; **D:** Marisa Silver; **W:** Amy Holden Jones, Holly Goldberg Sloan, Alan Ormsby. *USH*

Indecent Behavior 🎬🎬 1993 (R)
Tweed is a sex therapist who's accused of murder when one of her clients overdose's on the latest designer drug. Hudson, who plays the genre's hard-boiled cop figure, gets very personally involved investigating the allegations, which really upsets Tweed's hubby, Vincent. Also available in an unrated version.**CW:** Strong language, some violence, and strong sexuality. **93m/C VHS.** Shannon Tweed, Gary Hudson, Jan-Michael Vincent, Michelle Moffett, Lawrence-Hilton Jacobs, Penny Peyser; **D:** Lawrence Lanoff. *AVE*

Indecent Behavior 2 🎬½ 1994 (R)
Sex therapist Rebecca is targeted for blackmail as she finds out all sorts of unhealthy things about her patients. Meanwhile, she's practicing her technique with a fellow therapist. Also available unrated.**CW:** Strong sexuality; violence; language. **96m/C VHS.** Shannon Tweed, James Brolin, Chad McQueen, Elizabeth Sandifer, Craig Stepp, Rochelle Swanson; **D:** Carlo Gustaff. *AVE*

Indecent Behavior 3 🎬 1995 (R)
Sex therapist becomes the obsessed object of desire for a decidedly bad client. Also available unrated.**CW:** Strong sexuality, and for language and violence. **90m/C VHS.** Shannon Tweed, Sam Hennings, Colleen Coffey, Doug Jeffrey, Beau Billingslea, Laura Rogers; **D:** Kelley Cauthen; **W:** Hel Styverson. *AVE*

An Indecent Obsession 🎬🎬½ 1985
Colleen McCullough's bestseller about WWII Australian soldiers recuperating in a field hospital mental ward. Hughes plays the nurse everyone's in love with. **100m/C VHS, Beta.** *AU* Wendy Hughes, Gary Sweet, Richard Moir, Jonathan Hyde, Bill Hunter, Bruno Lawrence; **D:** Lex Marinos; **W:** Denise Morgan. *NO*

Indecent Proposal 🎬🎬½ 1993 (R)
High-gloss movie that had couples everywhere discussing the big question: Would you let your wife sleep with a billionaire in exchange for a million bucks? Probably, if all were as goodlooking as the weathered, yet ever gorgeous Redford. Moore and Harrelson are the financially down on their luck, but happy, couple who venture to Vegas on a last-ditch gambling effort. Surreally slick direction from Lyne, but an ultimately empty film that explores the values of marriage in a terribly angst-ridden fashion. Based on the novel by Jack Engelhard. Proof that average movies can make a killing at the boxoffice, landing in sixth place for 1993.**CW:** Language and sexuality. **119m/C VHS, Beta, CD-I, Closed Caption.** Robert Redford, Demi Moore, Woody Harrelson, Seymour Cassel, Oliver Platt, Billy Bob Thornton, Rip Taylor, Billy Connolly, Joel Brooks; **Cameos:** Sheena Easton, Herbie Hancock; **D:** Adrian Lyne; **W:** Amy Holden Jones; **C:** Howard Atherton; **M:** John Barry. MTV Movie Awards '94: Best Kiss (Demi Moore/Woody Harrelson); Golden Raspberry Awards '93: Worst Picture, Worst Supporting Actor (Harrelson), Worst Screenplay; Nominations: MTV Movie Awards '94: Best Female Performance (Moore), Most Desirable Female (Moore). *PAR*

Independence Day 🎬🎬 *Follow Your Dreams* 1983 (R)
Uneven romantic drama about a small-town photographer, yearning for the big city, who falls in love with a racing car enthusiast, whose sister is a battered wife. Strong cast, particularly Wiest as the abused wife, is left occasionally stranded by a script reaching too hard for social significance. **110m/C VHS, Beta.** Kathleen Quinlan, David Keith, Frances Sternhagen, Dianne Wiest, Cliff DeYoung, Richard Farnsworth, Josef Sommer, Cheryl "Rainbeaux" Smith; **D:** Robert Mandel; **M:** Charles Bernstein. *WAR, CCB*

Independence Day 🎬🎬🎬 1996 (PG-13)
The biggest of the new wave of disaster flicks paying tribute to the Irwin Allen celebrity-fests of the '70s finds an alien armada descending on Earth to create some fireworks on the July 4th weekend. The fate of the world rests in the hands of an unlikely band of Earthlings led by President Whitmore (Pullman), a computer expert (Goldblum), and a Marine fighter pilot (Smith). Special effects, despite forgoing some of the more expensive newer technology, don't disappoint. Strong (if not A-list) cast and plenty of action. Devlin and Emmerich wrote the script while promoting "Stargate," after a reporter asked Emmerich if he believed in aliens.**CW:** Sci-fi destruction and violence. **135m/C VHS, Closed Caption.** Bill Pullman, Will Smith, Jeff Goldblum, Judd Hirsch, Margaret Colin, Randy Quaid, Mary McDonnell, Robert Loggia, Brent Spiner, James Rebhorn, Vivica A. Fox, James Duval, Harry Connick Jr., Harvey Fierstein; **D:** Roland Emmerich; **W:** Dean Devlin, Roland Emmerich; **C:** Karl Walter Lindenlaub; **M:** David Arnold. Academy Awards '96: Best Visual Effects; MTV Movie Awards '97: Best Kiss (Vivica A. Fox/Will Smith); Nominations: Academy Awards '96: Best Sound; MTV Movie Awards '97: Best Film, Best Male Performance (Smith), Breakthrough Performance (Fox), Best Action Sequence. *FXV*

The Indestructible Man 🎬 1956
Chaney, electrocuted for murder and bank robbery, is brought back to life by a scientist. Naturally, he seeks revenge on those who sentenced him to death. Chaney does the best he can with the material. **70m/B VHS.** Lon Chaney Jr., Marian Carr, Max Casey Adams Showalter; **D:** Jack Pollexfen. *NOS, MRV, SNC*

The Indian Fighter 🎬🎬🎬 1955
Exciting actioner has Douglas as a scout hired to lead a wagon train to Oregon in 1870. The train must past through dangerous Sioux territory and Douglas tries to make peace with the Sioux leader but a secret Indian gold mine and romance cause friction and keep things lively. **88m/C VHS.** Kirk Douglas, Elsa Martinelli, Walter Abel, Walter Matthau, Diana Douglas, Lon Chaney Jr., Eduard Franz, Alan Hale Jr., Elisha Cook Jr., Harry Landers; **D:** Andre de Toth; **W:** Ben Hecht. *MGM*

The Indian in the Cupboard 🎬🎬½ 1995 (PG)
On his ninth birthday, Omri receives a three-inch plastic indian named Little Bear and an old wooden medicine cabinet. (Guess they were out of Power Rangers.) When placed in the cabinet, Little Bear magically comes to life, taking Omri on adventures and teaching him important lessons. Blue screen techniques allow them appear together on-screen although they were actually shot together only once. Based on the bestselling children's book by Lynne Reid Banks. **97m/C VHS, LV, 8mm, Closed Caption.** Hal Scardino, Litefoot, Lindsay Crouse, Richard Jenkins, Rishi Bhat; **D:** Frank Oz; **W:** Melissa Mathison; **C:** Russell Carpenter; **M:** Miles Goodman. *COL*

Indian Paint 🎬🎬 1964
A pleasant children's film about an Indian boy's love for his horse and his rite of passage. Silverheels was Tonto on television's "The Lone Ranger," while Crawford was the "Rifleman's" son. **90m/C VHS, Beta.** Jay Silverheels, Johnny Crawford, Pat Hogan, Robert Crawford Jr., George Lewis; **D:** Norman Foster. *NO*

The Indian Runner 🎬🎬 1991 (R)
In Penn's debut as a writer-director, he brings us the story of two brothers in Nebraska during the late '60s, who are forced to change their lives with the loss of their family farm. Joe is a good cop and family man who can't deal with the rage of his brother Frank, who has just returned from Vietnam and is turning to a life of crime. Penn does a decent job of representing the struggle between the responsible versus the rebellious side of human nature. Based on the song "Highway Patrolman" by Bruce Springsteen.**CW:** Language and violence and drug use. **127m/C VHS, LV, Letterbox, Closed Caption.** David Morse, Viggo Mortensen, Sandy Dennis, Charles Bronson, Valeria Golino, Patricia Arquette, Dennis Hopper; **D:** Sean Penn; **W:** Sean Penn. *MGM*

The Indian Scarf 🎬🎬 1963
Heirs to a dead man's fortune are being strangled one by one at the benefactor's country estate. An Edgar Wallace suspense tale. **85m/C VHS.** *GE* Heinz Drache, Gisela Uhlen, Klaus Kinski; **D:** Alfred Vohrer. *SNC*

Indian Summer 🎬🎬 1993 (PG-13)
Yet another addition to the growing 30-something nostalgia genre. Delete the big house, add a crusty camp director (Arkin), change the characters' names (but not necessarily their lives) and you feel like you're experiencing deja vu. This time seven friends and the requisite outsider reconvene at Camp Tamakwa, the real-life summer camp to writer/director Binder. The former campers talk. They yearn. They save Camp Tamakwa and experience personal growth. A must see for those who appreciate listening to situational jokes that are followed by "I guess you had to be there."**CW:** Some language, some drug content, and some sensuality. **108m/C VHS, Beta, LV, Closed Caption.** Alan Arkin, Matt Craven, Diane Lane, Bill Paxton, Elizabeth Perkins, Kevin Pollak, Sam Raimi, Vincent Spano, Julie Warner, Kimberly Williams, Richard Chevolleau; **D:** Mike Binder; **W:** Mike Binder; **M:** Miles Goodman. *TOU, FCT*

Indian Uprising 🎬🎬 1951
An army captain tries to keep local settlers from causing trouble with Geronimo and his people when gold is discovered on their territory. **75m/C VHS, Beta.** George Montgomery, Audrey Long, Carl Benton Reid, John Baer, Joseph Sawyer; **D:** Ray Nazarro. *GKK*

Indiana Jones and the Last Crusade 🎬🎬🎬 1989 (PG)
In this, the third and last (?) Indiana Jones adventure, the fearless archaeologist is once again up against the Nazis in a race to find the Holy Grail. Connery is perfectly cast as Indy's father; opening sequence features Phoenix as a teenage Indy and explains his fear of snakes and the origins of the infamous fedora. Returns to the look and feel of the original with more adventures, exotic places, dastardly villains, and daring escapes than ever before; a must for Indy fans. **126m/C VHS, Beta, LV, 8mm, Letterbox, Closed Caption.** Harrison Ford, Sean Connery, Denholm Elliott, Alison Doody, Julian Glover, John Rhys-Davies, River Phoenix, Michael Byrne, Alex Hyde-White; **D:** Steven Spielberg; **W:** Jeffrey Boam; **M:** John Williams. Nominations: Academy Awards '89: Best Sound, Best Original Score. *PAR, TLF*

Indiana Jones and the Temple of Doom 🎬🎬🎬 1984 (PG)
Daredevil archaeologist Indiana Jones is back. This time he's on the trail of the legendary Ankara Stone and a ruthless cult that has enslaved hundreds of children. More gore and violence than the original; Capshaw's whining character is an irritant, lacking the fresh quality that Karen Allen added to the original. Enough action for ten movies, special effects galore, and the usual booming Williams score make it a cinematic roller coaster ride, but with less regard for plot and pacing than the original. Though second in the series, it's actually a prequel to "Raiders of the Lost Ark." Followed by "Indiana Jones and the Last Crusade." **118m/C VHS, Beta, LV, 8mm, Closed Caption.** Harrison Ford, Kate Capshaw, Ke Huy Quan, Amrish Puri; **D:** Steven Spielberg; **W:** Willard Huyck, Gloria Katz; **M:** John Williams. Academy Awards '84: Best Visual Effects; Nominations: Academy Awards '84: Best Original Score. *PAR*

Indictment: The McMartin Trial 🎬🎬🎬 1995 (R)
Woods stars as attorney Danny Davis, who has the unenviable task of providing a defense in the notorious McMartin child molestation trial. In 1983, Manhattan Beach, California was rocked by reports that some 60 preschoolers had been abused at a day-care center. Seven defendants were accused thanks to lurid videotaped interviews with the children. The trial lasted six years (the longest and most expensive on record) and all charges were eventually dismissed. It's clear from this telepic that public hysteria and media hype lead to a grave miscarriage of justice that put the legal system on trial as well.**CW:** Nudity; strong language. **132m/C VHS, LV, Closed Caption.** James Woods, Henry Thomas, Mercedes Ruehl, Shirley Knight, Sada Thompson, Mark Blum, Alison Elliott, Chelsea Field, Richard Bradford, Lolita Davidovich;

D: Mick Jackson; **W:** Abby Mann, Myra Mann; **C:** Rodrigo Garcia; **M:** Peter Melnick. *HBO*

Indio 🐾 1990 (R) A Marine-trained half-breed takes it on himself to save the Amazon rain forest. Not a peaceful demonstrator, his tactics are violent ones. 94m/C VHS, Beta, LV, Closed Caption. Marvin Hagler, Francesco Quinn, Brian Dennehy; **D:** Anthony (Antonio Margheriti) Dawson. *VTR*

Indio 2: The Revolt 🐾 1992 (R) Greedy developers are cutting a highway into the Amazon jungle, destroying everything in their path. All is not lost though, because U.S. Marine Sgt. Iron is on top of things, continuing his struggle to unite the Amazon tribes and save the rainforest, no matter what it takes.**CW:** Language and violence. 104m/C VHS. Marvin Hagler, Charles Napier; **M:** Pino Donaggio. *ART*

Indiscreet 🐾½ 1931 Empty-headed romantic comedy about a fashion designer whose past catches up with her when her ex-lover starts romancing her sister. No relation to the classic 1958 film with Cary Grant and Ingrid Bergman. ♫Come To Me; If You Haven't Got Love. 81m/B VHS, Beta. Gloria Swanson, Ben Lyon, Barbara Kent; **D:** Leo McCarey. *NOS, MRV, REP*

Indiscreet 🐾🐾🐾 1958 A charming American diplomat in London falls in love with a stunning actress, but protects himself by saying he is married. Needless to say, she finds out. Stylish romp with Grant and Bergman at their sophisticated best. Adapted by Norman Krasna from his stage play "Kind Sir." 100m/C VHS, Closed Caption. Cary Grant, Ingrid Bergman, Phyllis Calvert; **D:** Stanley Donen; **C:** Frederick A. (Freddie) Young; **M:** Richard Rodney Bennett. *REP, MLB*

Indiscreet 🐾½ 1988 (PG) Indistinctive made for TV rehash of the charming 1958 Grant/Bergman romantic comedy in which a suave American falls for an English actress. Both versions derive from the play "Kind Sir" by Norman Krasna, but this one suffers by comparison. 94m/C VHS, Closed Caption. Robert Wagner, Lesley-Anne Down, Maggie Henderson, Robert McBain, Jeni Barnett; **D:** Richard Michaels. *REP*

Indiscretion of an American Wife 🐾🐾 *Indiscretion; Terminus Station; Terminal Station Indiscretion* 1954 Set almost entirely in Rome's famous Terminal Station, where an ill-fated couple say goodbye endlessly while the woman tries to decide whether to join her husband in the States. Trimmed down from 87 minutes upon U.S. release. 63m/C VHS, Beta. *IT* Jennifer Jones, Montgomery Clift, Richard Beymer; **D:** Vittorio De Sica; **W:** Truman Capote; **C:** Oswald Morris. Nominations: Academy Awards '54: Best Costume Design (B & W). *NOS, FOX, HEG*

Indochine 🐾🐾🐾 1992 (PG-13) Soapy melodrama follows the fortunes of Eliane (Deneuve), a Frenchwoman born and reared in Indochina, from 1930 to the communist revolution 25 years later. She contends with the changes to her country as well as her adopted daughter as she grows up and becomes independent. Deneuve's controlled performance (and unchanging beauty) is eminently watchable. Filmed on location in Vietnam with breathtaking cinematography by Francois Catonne. In French with English subtitles.**CW:** Some violence/drug-related scenes and some sensuality. 155m/C VHS, LV, 8mm, Letterbox, Closed Caption. *FR* Catherine Deneuve, Linh Dan Pham, Vincent Perez, Jean Yanne, Dominique Blanc, Henri Marteau, Carlo Brandt, Gerard Lartigau; **D:** Regis Wargnier; **W:** Erik Orsenna, Louis Gardel, Catherine Cohen, Regis Wargnier; **C:** Francois Catonne; **M:** Patrick Doyle. Academy Awards '92: Best Foreign Language Film; Cesar Awards '93: Best Actress (Deneuve), Best Art Direction/Set Decoration, Best Cinematography, Best Sound, Best Supporting Actress (Blanc); Golden Globe Awards '93: Best Foreign Film; National Board of Review Awards '92: Best Foreign Film; Nominations: Academy Awards '92: Best Actress (Deneuve); British Academy Awards '93: Best Foreign Film. *COL, FCT, BTV*

Indomitable Teddy Roosevelt 🐾🐾⅛ 1983 Entertaining mix of newsreel footage and staged scenes traces the career of the feisty president. 93m/C VHS, Beta. **D:** Harrison Engle. *CHF*

Infamous Crimes 🐾🐾 *Philo Vance Returns* 1947 Philo investigates the murders of a playboy and his girlfriends. One of the last of the series whose character was based on the S.S. Van Dine stories. 64m/B VHS, Beta, 8mm. William Wright, Terry Austin, Leon Belasco, Clara Blandick, Iris Adrian, Frank Wilcox; **D:** William Beaudine. *VYY*

The Infernal Trio 🐾🐾½ *Le Trio Infernal* 1974 An attorney comes up with a plan involving two sisters (who are his lovers) which will make them both wealthy; but it will also make them both murderers. Sophisticated black comedy based on a true story. In French with English subtitles or dubbed. 100m/C VHS. *FR* *IT* Romy Schneider, Michel Piccoli, Mascha Gonska; **D:** Francois Girod. *CVC*

Inferno 🐾🐾 1978 (R) Uneven occult horror tale about a young man who arrives in New York to investigate the mysterious circumstances surrounding his sister's death. Dubbed. 83m/C VHS, Beta. *IT* Leigh McCloskey, Elenora Giorgi, Irene Miracle, Sacha Pitoeff; **D:** Dario Argento; **W:** Dario Argento; **M:** Keith Emerson. *FOX*

Inferno in Paradise 🐾 1988 Mucho macho firefighter and bimbous gal pal photographer get hot while trailing a murderous pyromaniac. More like purgatory in the living room (that is, unless you thought Forsyth's earlier "Chesty Anderson, US Navy" was divine comedy). 115m/C VHS. Richard Young, Betty Ann Carr, Jim Davis, Andy Jarrell, Dennis Chun; **D:** Ed Forsyth.

The Infiltrator 🐾🐾½ 1995 (R) Based on the true story of Yaron Svoray (Platt), an Israeli journalist and the son of Holocaust survivors, whose latest assignment is to go to Berlin and investigate the rising Neo-Nazi movement. Eventually, Svoray manages to meet leaders of the Nationalist Front and then finds himself enmeshed in a worldwide political network. Based on the book "In Hitler's Shadow" by Yaron Svoray and Nick Taylor. Made for cable TV.**CW:** Violence, strong language, some sexuality. 102m/C VHS. Oliver Platt, Arliss Howard, Peter Riegert, Alan King, Tony Haygarth, Michael Byrne, Julian Glover, Alex Kingston; **D:** John MacKenzie; **W:** Guy Andrews; **M:** Hal Lindes. *HBO*

Infinity 🐾🐾½ 1996 (PG) Based on memoirs covering the early years of Nobel Prize-winning physicist Richard Feynman (Broderick) and his romance with aspiring artist Arline Greenbaum (Arquette). They marry despite the fact that Arline is diagnosed with tuberculosis, at this time in the '30s a contagious and incurable disease. Richard's recruited to work on the Manhattan Project at Los Alamos, New Mexico, and the narrative travels between his scientific endeavors and Arline's worsening illness in an Albuquerque hospital. Problem is it's neither a character study or a love story but a weak combo. Directing debut of Broderick; screenplay is written by his mother. 119m/C VHS. Matthew Broderick, Patricia Arquette, James LeGros, Peter Riegert, Dori Brenner, Peter Michael Goetz, Zeljko Ivanek; **D:** Matthew Broderick; **W:** Patricia Broderick; **C:** Toyomichi Kurita; **M:** Bruce Broughton. *BMG*

The Informer 🐾½ 1929 Hanson wants to flee Ireland's poverty for America, using the reward money he gets for turning in an IRA comrade. But things don't turn out as planned and instead he's haunted by the guilt of his betrayal. Based on the novel by Liam O'Flaherty and filmed to much greater effect by John Ford in 1935. 83m/B VHS. *GB* Lars Hanson, Lya de Putti, Warwick Ward, Dennis Wynham; **D:** Arthur Robison; **W:** Benn W. Levy, Rolfe E. Vanlo. *GPV*

The Informer 🐾🐾🐾🐾 1935 Based on Liam O'Flaherty's novel about the Irish Sinn Fein Rebellion of 1922, it tells the story of a hard-drinking Dublin man (McLaglen) who informs on a friend (a member of the Irish Republican Army) in

order to collect a 20 pound reward. When his "friend" is killed during capture, he goes on a drinking spree instead of using the money, as planned, for passage to America. Director Ford allowed McLaglen to improvise his lines during the trial scene in order to enhance the realism, leading to excruciating suspense. Wonderful score. 91m/B VHS, Beta, LV. Victor McLaglen, Heather Angel, Wallace Ford, Margot Grahame, Joseph Sawyer, Preston Foster, Una O'Connor, J.M. Kerrigan, Donald Meek; **D:** John Ford; **W:** Dudley Nichols; **M:** Max Steiner. Academy Awards '35: Best Actor (McLaglen), Best Director (Ford), Best Screenplay, Best Score; New York Film Critics Awards '35: Best Director (Ford), Best Film; Nominations: Academy Awards '35: Best Film Editing, Best Picture. *BTV, TTC*

Infra-Man woof! *The Super Inframan; The Infra Superman* 1976 (PG) If you're looking for a truly bad, hokey flick, this could be it. Infra-man is a superhero who must rescue the galaxy from the clutches of the evil Princess Dragon Mom and her army of prehistoric monsters. Outlandish dialogue (delivered straight) combines with horrible special effects and costumes to create what may well be one of the best camp classics to date. Poorly dubbed in English. 92m/C VHS, Beta. *HK* Li Hsiu-shen, Wang Hsieh, Yuan Man-tzu, Terry Liu, Tsen Shu-yi, Huang Chien-lung, Lu Sheng; **D:** Hua-Shan; **W:** Peter Fernandez.

Inherit the Wind 🐾🐾🐾½ 1960 Powerful courtroom drama, based on the Broadway play, is actually a fictionalized version of the infamous Scopes "Monkey Trial" of 1925. Tracy is the defense attorney for the schoolteacher on trial for teaching Darwin's Theory of Evolution to a group of students in a small town ruled by religion. March is the prosecutor seeking to put the teacher behind bars and restore religion to the schools. 128m/B VHS, Beta, LV. Spencer Tracy, Fredric March, Florence Eldridge, Gene Kelly, Dick York; **D:** Stanley Kramer; **W:** Nedrick Young, Harold Jacob Smith; **C:** Ernest Laszlo; **M:** Ernest Gold. Berlin International Film Festival '60: Best Actor (March); Nominations: Academy Awards '60: Best Actor (Tracy), Best Adapted Screenplay, Best Black and White Cinematography, Best Film Editing. *FOX, FCT*

Inheritance 🐾🐾🐾 *Uncle Silas* 1947 Victorian-era melodrama of a young heiress endangered by her guradian, who plots to murder his charge for her inheritance. Chilling and moody story based on a novel by Sheridan Le Fanu. 103m/B VHS, Beta. *GB* Jean Simmons, Katina Paxinou, Derrick DeMarney, Derek Bond; **D:** Charles Frank. *DVT*

The Inheritance 🐾🐾½ *L'Eredita Ferramonti* 1976 (R) Wealthy patriarch becomes sexually involved with scheming daughter-in-law. Tawdry tale is nonetheless engaging. 121m/C VHS, Beta. *IT* Anthony Quinn, Fabio Testi, Dominique Sanda; **D:** Mauro Bolognini; **M:** Ennio Morricone. Cannes Film Festival '76: Best Actress (Sanda). *NO*

The Inheritor 🐾🐾 1990 (R) Set in a small New England town, this mystery centers on the death of a young woman and her sister's attempts to uncover the murderer. The local celebrity, a writer, seems to be at the heart of the mystery and the sister finds herself growing interested. Keeps you guessing. 83m/C VHS. Dan Haggerty; **D:** Brian Savegar. *NO*

The Inheritors 🐾½ 1985 Not-too-subtle tale of a young German boy who becomes involved with a Nazi youth group as his home life deteriorates. Heavy-going anti-fascism creates more message than entertainment. In German with English subtitles or dubbed. 89m/C VHS, Beta. *GE* Nikolas Vogel, Roger Schauer, Klaus Novak, Johanna Tomek; **D:** Walter Bannert; **W:** Walter Bannert. *GLV, SWC*

Inhibition 🐾 1986 A beautiful heiress has lots of sex with different people in exotic locales. Softcore soap. 90m/C VHS, Beta. Claudine Beccaire, Ilona Staller.

The Initiation 🐾 1984 (R) Trying to rid herself of a troublesome nightmare, a coed finds herself face-to-face with a psycho. Gory campus slaughterfest. 97m/C VHS, Beta. Vera Miles, Clu Gulager, James Read, Daphne Zuniga; **D:** Larry Stewart. *VTR*

Initiation of Sarah ✗ 1978 College freshman joins a sorority, undergoes abusive initiation, and gains a supernatural revenge. Made-for-television "Carrie" rip-off. 100m/C VHS, Beta. Kay Lenz, Shelley Winters, Kathryn Crosby, Morgan Brittany, Tony Bill, Tisa Farrow, Robert Hays, Morgan Fairchild; **D:** Robert Day. WOV

The Inkwell ✗✗½ 1994 (R) Quiet teenager Drew Tate finds first love when his family spends their vacation with relatives on Martha's Vineyard. Drew is drawn into the party atmosphere of the Inkwell, the area where affluent black professionals have summered for decades. Meanwhile, political differences between Drew's former Black Panther father and his conservative uncle threaten family harmony. Everything about the film has a sugary aura, with conflicts handled tastefully. Rich directs broadly, leading to some overacting. Film is set in 1976. 112m/C VHS, LV, Closed Caption. Larenz Tate, Joe Morton, Phyllis Stickney, Jada Pinkett Smith; **D:** Matty Rich; **W:** Paris Qualles, Tom Ricostronza; **C:** John L. Demps Jr.; **M:** Terence Blanchard. TOU

Inn of Temptation ✗ 1986 A bunch of bowling buddies take off for Bangkok on an impulsive weekend, and meet lots of Oriental women. 72m/C VHS, Beta. Michael Jacot, Claude Martin.

Inn of the Damned ✗½ 1974 Detective looks into an inn where no one ever gets charged for an extra day; they simply die. Anderson is watchable. 92m/C VHS, Beta. AU Alex Cord, Judith Anderson, Tony Bonner, Michael Craig, John Meillon; **D:** Terry Burke. NO

The Inn of the Sixth Happiness ✗✗✗ 1958 Inspiring story of Gladys Aylward, an English missionary in 1930s' China, who leads a group of children through wartorn countryside. Donat's last film. 158m/C VHS, Beta. Ingrid Bergman, Robert Donat, Curt Jurgens; **D:** Mark Robson; **C:** Frederick A. (Freddie) Young; **M:** Malcolm Arnold. National Board of Review Awards '58: Best Actress (Bergman); Nominations: Academy Awards '58: Best Director (Robson). NO

Inn on the River ✗✗½ 1962 Scotland Yard investigates a series of murders taking place on the waterfront by the "Shark's" gang. Remake of "The Return of the Frog." 95m/C VHS. GE Klaus Kinski, Joachim Fuchsberger, Brigitte Grothum, Richard Much; **D:** Alfred Vohrer. SNC

The Inner Circle ✗½ 1946 A private detective, framed for murder by his secretary, has a limited amount of time to find the real murderer. Confusing. 57m/B VHS, Beta. Adele Mara, Warren Douglas, William Frawley, Ricardo Cortez, Virginia Christine; **D:** Philip Ford. SNC

The Inner Circle ✗✗✗ 1991 (PG-13) Ivan Sanshin is a meek, married man working as a movie projectionist for the KGB in 1935 Russia. Sanshin is taken by the KGB to the Kremlin to show movies, primarily Hollywood features, to leader Joseph Stalin, a job he cannot discuss with anyone, even his wife. Under the spell of Stalin's personality, Sanshin sees only what he's told and overlooks the oppression and persecution of the times. Based on the life of the projectionist who served from 1935 until Stalin's death in 1953. Filmed on location at the Kremlin. 122m/C VHS, LV, 8mm, Closed Caption. Tom Hulce, Lolita Davidovich, Bob Hoskins, Alexandre Zbruev, Maria Baranova, Feodor Chaliapin Jr, Bess Meyer; **D:** Andrei Konchalovsky; **W:** Andrei Konchalovsky, Anatoli Usov; **M:** Eduard Artemyev. COL

Inner Sanctum ✗ 1948 Adequate tale of a young girl accosted by a gypsy who claims that tragedy awaits her. Based on a radio show of the same name. 62m/B VHS. Chuck Russell, Mary Beth Hughes, Lee Patrick, Nana Bryant; **D:** Lew (Louis Friedlander) Landers. SNC

Inner Sanctum woof! 1991 (R) Cheating husband hires sensuous nurse to tend invalid wife. You can guess the rest; in fact, you have to because the plot ultimately makes no sense. Available in R-rated and sex-drenched unrated editions. **CW:** Language, violence, and strong sensuality. 87m/C VHS, LV, Closed Caption. Tanya Roberts, Margaux Hemingway, Joseph Bottoms, Valerie Wildman, William Butler, Brett Clark; **D:** Fred Olen Ray. COL

Inner Sanctum 2 ✗✗½ 1994 (R) Jennifer Reed (Swope) had a breakdown and killed her husband in the first film. Now under a doctor's (Warner) care, Jennifer is under siege from her brother-in-law's (Nouri) evil plot to send her over the edge again and claim her fortune. As if that's not enough, Jennifer's also being stalked by a murderer. Also available in an unrated version. 90m/C VHS, LV, Closed Caption. Michael Nouri, Tracy Brooks Swope, Sandahl Bergman, David Warner, Jennifer Ciesar, Margaux Hemingway; **D:** Fred Olen Ray; **W:** Sherman Scott; **M:** Chuck Cirino. COL

Innerspace ✗✗½ 1987 (PG) A space pilot, miniaturized for a journey through a lab rat a la "Fantastic Voyage," is accidentally injected into a nebbish supermarket clerk, and together they nab some bad guys and get the girl. Award-winning special effects support some funny moments between micro Quaid and nerdy Short, with Ryan producing the confused romantic interest. 120m/C VHS, Beta, LV, 8mm, Closed Caption. Dennis Quaid, Martin Short, Meg Ryan, Kevin McCarthy, Fiona Lewis, Henry Gibson, Robert Picardo, John Hora, Wendy Schaal, Orson Bean, Chuck Jones, William Schallert, Dick Miller, Vernon Wells, Harold Sylvester, Kevin Hooks, Kathleen Freeman, Kenneth Tobey; **D:** Joe Dante; **W:** Jeffrey Boam, Chip Proser; **M:** Jerry Goldsmith. Academy Awards '87: Best Visual Effects. WAR

Innocence Unprotected ✗✗½ 1968 A film collage that contains footage from the 1942 film "Innocence Unprotected," the story of an acrobat trying to save an orphan from her wicked stepmother, newsreels from Nazi-occupied Yugoslavia, and interviews from 1968 with people who were in the film. Confiscated by the Nazis during final production, "Innocence Unprotected" was discovered by director Makavejev, who worked it into the collage. Filmed in color and black and white; in Serbian with English subtitles. 78m/C VHS. YU Dragoljub Aleksic, Ana Milosavljevic, Vera Jovanovic; **D:** Dusan Makavejev; **W:** Dusan Makavejev. FCT

The Innocent ✗✗✗ L'Innocente 1976 (R) The setting: turn of the century Rome, ablaze with atheism and free love. The story: Giannini's a Sicilian aristocrat who ignores wife Antonelli and dallies with scheming mistress O'Neill. Discovering his wife's infidelity, he's profoundly disillusioned, and his manly notion of self disintegrates. Visconti's last film, it was an art house fave and is considered by many to be his best. Lavishly photographed, well set and costumed, and true to the Gabrielle D'Annunzio's novel. In Italian with English subtitles. 125m/C VHS, Beta. IT Laura Antonelli, Jennifer O'Neill, Giancarlo Giannini; **D:** Luchino Visconti; **C:** Pasquale De Santis. CVC, FCT, VES

The Innocent ✗✗½ 1993 (R) Cold War thriller has naive British engineer Leonard Markham (Scott) sent to Berlin in 1955 by Brits who are warily cooperating with the U.S. forces. He's turned over to CIA operator Bob Glass (Hopkins) and asked to intercept communications between East Germany and the Soviet Union. Glass continually warns Markham not to trust anyone, including Maria (Rossellini), the married German woman with whom he begins an affair. Failure to build necessary suspense and performances leads to disappointing one-note display. Based on the novel by McEwan. **CW:** Sexuality, brief language, and a sequence of violence. 97m/C VHS, LV, Closed Caption. GE GB Anthony Hopkins, Campbell Scott, Isabella Rossellini, Hart Bochner, James Grant, Jeremy Sinden, Ronald Nitschke; **D:** John Schlesinger; **W:** Ian McEwan; **M:** Gerald Gouriet. MAX

Innocent Blood ✗✗ 1992 (R) A mediocre modern-day vampire/gangster combo with the beautiful (though red-eyed) Parillaud as the woman with a taste for someone "Italian." Unfortunately, she doesn't finish off her latest meal—mobster Loggia—who finds being undead very useful to his vicious work. LaPaglia plays the bewildered, love-struck cop involved with the vamp. Parillaud appears nude in several scenes and the gore and violence are stomach-turning. **CW:** Language, vampire violence, and sexuality. 112m/C VHS, Beta, LV, Letterbox, Closed Caption. Anne Parillaud, Anthony LaPaglia, Robert Loggia, David Proval, Don Rickles, Rocco Sisto, Kim Coates, Chazz Palminteri, Angela Bassett, Tom Savini, Frank Oz, Forrest J. Ackerman, Sam Raimi, Dario Argento, Linnea Quigley; **D:** John Landis; **W:** Michael Wolk; **C:** Mac Ahlberg; **M:** Ira Newborn. WAR, PMS

Innocent Lies ✗✗½ 1995 (R) In 1938, British policeman Alan Cross (Dunbar) heads for an island off the French coast to look into the suicide of a colleague who was investigating the expatriate Graves family. There are family tensions, skeletons in the closet, and some Nazi-sympathizers all mixed together in an old-fashioned but satisfying stew. **CW:** Sexual situations, violence. 88m/C VHS. FR GB Adrian Dunbar, Stephen Dorff, Gabrielle Anwar, Joanna Lumley; **D:** Patrick Dewolf; **W:** Kerry Crabbe, Patrick Dewolf; **C:** Patrick Blossier; **M:** Alexandre Desplat. PGV

An Innocent Man ✗✗½ 1989 (R) Uneven story of Selleck, an ordinary family man and airline mechanic, framed as a drug dealer and sent to prison. 113m/C VHS, Beta, LV, Closed Caption. Tom Selleck, F. Murray Abraham, Laila Robins, David Rasche, Richard Young, Badja Djola; **D:** Peter Yates; **W:** Larry Brothers; **M:** Howard Shore. TOU

Innocent Prey ✗✗ 1988 (R) When a woman finally summons the courage to bid hasta la vista to her abusive husband, it turns out he's not so quick to say ciao. Definitely not a highlight in Balsam's career. **CW:** Violence and sensuality. 88m/C VHS, Closed Caption. AU P.J. Soles, Martin Balsam, Kit Taylor, Grigor Taylor, John Warnock, Susan Stenmark, Richard Morgan; **D:** Colin Eggleston. NO

The Innocent Sleep ✗✗½ 1995 (R) Adequate thriller that stays true to genre cliches. Homeless drunk Alan Terry (Graves) witnesses an execution (by hanging) from London's Tower Bridge, near where he's bedded down. He's spotted but manages to escape. When he tries to report the crime, Terry realizes that one of the killers is police investigator Matheson (Gambon). Terry then goes to tabloid journalist Billie Hayman (Sciorra) for help but her probing into the death leads to even more danger. **CW:** Violence and adult language. 96m/C VHS. GB Rupert Graves, Annabella Sciorra, Michael Gambon, Franco Nero, Graham Crowden, John Hannah; **D:** Scott Michell; **W:** Ray Villis; **C:** Alan Dunlop; **M:** Mark Ayres. PEG

Innocent Sorcerers ✗✗ Niewinni Czarodzieje 1960 Ironic comedy about aimless '60s Polish youth that finds a young doctor having trouble committing himself to his superficial girlfriend and coping with the problems of his cynical friends. Polish with subtitles. 86m/B VHS. PL Tadeusz Lomnicki, Zbigniew Cybulski, Roman Polanski, Krystyna Stypulkowska, Jerzy Skolimowski; **D:** Andrzej Wajda; **W:** Jerzy Skolimowski, Andrzej Wajda; **M:** Krzysztof Komeda. FCT

Innocent Victim ✗ The Tree of Hands 1990 (R) Convoluted tale of revenge and madness. Bacall plays a mad grandmother who kidnaps a boy to take the place of her dead grandson. The kidnapped boy's stepfather then is accused of murdering him, and starts murdering others to get the boy back. 100m/C VHS. Lauren Bacall, Helen Shaver, Paul McGann, Peter Firth; **D:** Giles Foster.

The Innocents ✗✗✗½ 1961 Incredibly creepy version of Henry James' "The Turn of the Screw." Minister's daughter, Miss Giddens (Kerr), is hired by Redgrave (known only as "The Uncle") as governess to young Flora (Franklin) and her brother Miles (Stephens) at his country estate. Miss Giddens begins to see the specters of a man and a woman and is told her descriptions match that of former estate manager Peter Quint and the last governess, his mistress, whose influence on the children was thought to be malevolent. Indeed. Miss Giddens believes the children are possessed by evil—but is it true or a product of her own hysteria? **85m/B VHS, Closed Caption.** *GB* Deborah Kerr, Michael Redgrave, Pamela Franklin, Martin Stephens, Peter Wyngarde, Megs Jenkins, Clytie Jessop, Isla Cameron, Eric Woodburn; *D:* Jack Clayton; *W:* Truman Capote, William Archibald, John Mortimer; *C:* Freddie Francis; *M:* Georges Auric. *FXV*

The Innocents Abroad 🐾🐾½ 1984 Entertaining adaptation of Mark Twain's novel about a group of naive Americans cruising the Mediterranean. Ensemble cast offers some surprising performances. Originally produced for PBS. **116m/C VHS.** Craig Wasson, Brooke Adams, David Ogden Stiers. *USH*

Innocents in Paris 🐾🐾½ 1953 A group of seven Britons visit Paris for the first time. A bit long but enough ooo-la-la to satisfy. **89m/B VHS, Beta.** *GB* Alastair Sim, Laurence Harvey, Jimmy Edwards, Claire Bloom, Margaret Rutherford; *D:* Gordon Parry. *NO*

The Inquiry 🐾🐾½ 1987 A new twist on the resurrection of Christ. Carradine senses a cover-up when he's sent from Rome to investigate the problem of Christ's missing corpse. He retraces Christ's final days to solve the case in this interesting, offbeat film. Dubbed. **107m/C VHS.** *IT* Keith Carradine, Harvey Keitel, Phyllis Logan, Angelo Infanti, Lina Sastri; *D:* Damiano Damiani. *NO*

Inquisition 🐾½ 1976 Naschy is a 16th century witch hunting judge who finds himself accused of witchcraft. **85m/C VHS, Beta.** *SP* Paul Naschy, Daniela Giordano, Juan Gallardo; *D:* Paul Naschy; *W:* Paul Naschy. *VCD*

Insanity 🐾 1982 A film director becomes violently obsessed with a beautiful actress. **101m/C VHS, Beta.** Terence Stamp, Fernando Rey, Corinne Clery. *NO*

The Insect Woman 🐾🐾🐾 *The Insect; Nippon Konchuki* 1963 Chronicles 45 years in the life of a woman who must work with the diligence of an ant in order to survive. Thoughtfully reflects the exploitation of women and the cruelty of human nature in Japanese society. Beautiful performance from Hidari, who ages from girlhood to middle age. In Japanese with English subtitles. **123m/B VHS.** *JP* Sachiko Hidari, Yitsuko Yoshimura, Hiroyuki Nagaes, Sumie Sasaki; *D:* Shohei Imamura. *CVC*

Inserts 🐾 1976 (R) A formerly successful director has been reduced to making porno films in this pretentious, long-winded effort set in a crumbling Hollywood mansion in the 1930s. Affected, windbaggish performances kill it. **99m/C VHS.** *GB* Richard Dreyfuss, Jessica Harper, Veronica Cartwright, Bob Hoskins; *D:* John Byrum; *W:* John Byrum. *FOX*

Inside 🐾🐾🐾 1996 (R) Harrowing anti-apartheid drama finds university professor and white Afrikaaner Peter Martin Strydom (Stoltz) being held in a Johannesburg government prison. He's being interrogated by Colonel Kruger (Hawthorne), head of the prison security force, supposedly for conspiracy against the South African regime. Tortured, Strydom's will begins to break as the drama flashes forward ten years, with Colonel Kruger now subjected to interrogation by a nameless black questioner (Gossett, Jr.) investigating human rights crimes, including Strydom's fate. Made for cable.*CW:* Political violence and torture, language and a brief sex scene. **94m/C VHS, Closed Caption.** Eric Stoltz, Nigel Hawthorne, Louis Gossett Jr.; *D:* Arthur Penn; *W:* Bima Stagg; *C:* Jan Weincke; *M:* Robert Levin. *EVE*

Inside Daisy Clover 🐾🐾½ 1965 Wood is the self-sufficient, junior delinquent waif who becomes a teenage musical star and pays the price for fame in this Hollywood saga set in the 1930s. Discovered by tyrannical studio head Plummer, Daisy is given her big break and taken under his wing for grooming as Swan Studio's newest sensation. She falls for fellow performer, matinee idol Redford, who has some secrets of his own, and eventually has a breakdown from the career pressure. Glossy melodrama is filled

with over-the-top performances but its sheer silliness makes it amusing. **128m/C VHS, LV, Letterbox.** Natalie Wood, Christopher Plummer, Robert Redford, Ruth Gordon, Roddy McDowall, Katharine Bard; *D:* Robert Mulligan; *W:* Gavin Lambert; *C:* Charles B(ryant) Lang; *M:* Andre Previn. Golden Globe Awards '66: Best Supporting Actress (Gordon); Nominations: Academy Awards '65: Best Art Direction/Set Decoration (Color), Best Costume Design (Color), Best Supporting Actress (Gordon). *WAR*

Inside Edge 🐾🐾 1992 (R) Urban crime thriller is a complex yet surprisingly uninteresting story of a police officer who falls for the girlfriend of the drug lord he is chasing. Filled with the standard genre violence.*CW:* Strong language, strong violence, and strong sexuality. **84m/C VHS.** Michael Madsen, Richard Lynch, Rosie Vela, Tony Peck, George Jenesky, Branscombe Richmond; *D:* Warren Clark; *W:* William Tannen. *ATV*

Inside Information 🐾 1934 With Tarzan's help, a cop searches out the leader of a ring of jewel thieves. **51m/B VHS, Beta, LV.** Rex Lease, Marion Shilling, Philo McCullough. *NO*

The Inside Man 🐾🐾½ 1984 Double agents struggle to find a submarine-detecting laser device. Based on true incidents in which a soviet sub ran aground in Sweden. Made in Sweden; dubbed. **90m/C VHS, Beta.** *SW* Dennis Hopper, Hardy Kruger, Gosta Ekman, David Wilson; *D:* Tom Clegg. *CEL, VTR*

Inside Monkey Zetterland 🐾🐾 1993 (R) Monkey Zetterland (Antin) is a screenwriter and former actor with an eccentric family. His actress mother is neurotically insecure and a nag; his father is an aging hippie who only shows up at Thanksgiving; his lesbian sister Grace is trying to get over a failed relationship; and his brother Brent is totally self-absorbed. Add to this menage his equally lunatic friends: Imogene, the compulsive talker and exhibitionist; his vicious girlfriend Daphne; and frightening married couple Sophie and Sasha. Meanwhile, Monkey tries to survive amidst the chaos. Interesting cast but lots of camera tricks do not a successful film make and the effort to be hip is all too apparent.*CW:* Language. **92m/C VHS, LV.** Steve Antin, Patricia Arquette, Sandra Bernhard, Sofia Coppola, Tate Donovan, Katherine Helmond, Bo Hopkins, Debi Mazar, Martha Plimpton, Rupert Everett, Ricki Lake, Lance Loud, Frances Bay, Luca Bercovici; *D:* Jefery Levy; *W:* John Boskovich, Steve Antin; *C:* Christopher Taylor; *M:* Rick Cox, Jeff Elmassian. Nominations: Independent Spirit Awards '94: Best Supporting Actor (Donovan). *FOX*

Inside Moves 🐾🐾½ 1980 (PG) A look at handicapped citizens trying to make it in everyday life, focusing on the relationship between an insecure, failed suicide and a volatile man who is only a knee operation away from a dreamed-about basketball career. **113m/C VHS, Beta, LV.** John Savage, Diana Scarwid, David Morse, Amy Wright; *D:* Richard Donner; *W:* Valerie Curtin, Barry Levinson; *M:* John Barry. Nominations: Academy Awards '80: Best Supporting Actress (Scarwid).*FOX*

Inside Out 🐾🐾½ *The Golden Heist; Hitler's Gold* 1975 (PG) An ex-GI, a jewel thief and a German POW camp commandant band together to find a stolen shipment of Nazi gold behind the Iron Curtain. To find the gold, they help a Nazi prisoner who knows the secret to break out of prison. Good action caper. **97m/C VHS, Beta.** *GB* Telly Savalas, Robert Culp, James Mason, Aldo Ray, Doris Kunstmann; *D:* Peter Duffell. *WAR*

Inside Out 🐾🐾½ 1991 (R) Hiding in his apartment from a world which terrifies him, Jimmy doesn't feel he's missing much—since he has the necessary women and bookies come to him. He soon finds he's not quite as safe as he thought, and the only way out is "out there." Fine performance from Gould, suspenseful pacing. **87m/C VHS.** Elliott Gould, Jennifer Tilly, Howard Hesseman, Beah Richards, Timothy Scott, Sandy McPeak, Dana Elcar, Meshach Taylor, Nicole Norman; *D:* Robert Taicher; *W:* Robert Taicher. *NO*

Inside the Law 🐾🐾 1942 A gang of crooks takes over a bank and must stay "inside the law" and resist their natural inclinations. Lots of comic situations. **65m/B VHS.** Wallace Ford, Frank Sully, Harry Holman, Luana Walters, Lafayette McKee, Danny Duncan, Earle Hodgins; *D:* Hamilton MacFadden. *NOS*

Inside the Lines 🐾🐾 1930 A WWI tale of espionage and counter-espionage. **73m/B VHS, Beta.** Betty Compson, Montagu Love, Mischa Auer, Ralph Forbes. *VYY*

Inside the Third Reich 🐾🐾½ 1982 A made-for-television mini-series detailing the rise to power within the Third Reich of Albert Speer, top advisor to Hitler. Based on Speer's rather self-serving memoires. **250m/C VHS, Beta, LV.** Derek Jacobi, Rutger Hauer, John Gielgud, Blythe Danner, Maria Schell, Ian Holm, Trevor Howard, Randy Quaid, Viveca Lindfors, Robert Vaughn, Stephen Collins, Elke Sommer, Renee Soutendijk; *D:* Marvin J. Chomsky. *GLV*

Insignificance 🐾🐾 1985 A film about an imaginary night spent in a New York hotel by characters who resemble Marilyn Monroe, Albert Einstein, Joe McCarthy, and Joe DiMaggio. Entertaining and often amusing as it follows the characters as they discuss theory and relativity, the Russians, and baseball among other things. **110m/C VHS, Beta, LV.** *GB* Gary Busey, Tony Curtis, Theresa Russell, Michael Emil, Will Sampson; *D:* Nicolas Roeg; *W:* Terry Johnson; *M:* Hans Zimmer. *ORI, WAR*

The Inspector General 🐾🐾🐾 *Happy Times* 1949 Classic Kaye craziness of mistaken identities with the master comic portraying a carnival medicine man who is mistaken by the villagers for their feared Inspector General. If you like Kaye's manic performance, you'll enjoy this one. ♫The Gypsy Drinking Song; Onward Onward; The Medicine Show; The Inspector General; Lonely Heart; Soliloquy For Three Heads; Happy Times; Brodny. **103m/C VHS, Beta.** Danny Kaye, Walter Slezak, Barbara Bates, Elsa Lanchester, Gene Lockhart, Walter Catlett, Alan Hale; *D:* Henry Koster. Golden Globe Awards '50: Best Score. *MGM, MRV, NOS*

The Inspector General 🐾🐾½ 1954 The filmed performance of Gogol's great play by the Moscow Art Theatre, wherein a provincial town panics when they mistake a wandering moron for the Inspector come to check up on them. In Russian with English subtitles. **128m/C VHS, Beta.** *RU D:* Vladimir Petrov. *FCT, AUD*

Inspector Hornleigh 🐾🐾½ 1939 A pair of bumbling detectives arrive on the scene when a Chancellor's fortune is stolen. Fine comedy, although the Scottish and British accents can be rather thick now and again. **76m/B VHS, Beta.** *GB* Gordon Harker, Alastair Sim, Miki Hood, Wally Patch, Steve Geray, Edward Underdown, Hugh Williams, Gibb McLaughlin; *D:* Eugene Forde. *NOS, SNC*

Instant Justice 🐾½ *Marine Issue* 1986 (R) A professional Marine jeopardizes his military career by avenging his sister's murder, vigilante style. Exclusive action. **101m/C VHS, Beta, Closed Caption.** *GB* Michael Pare, Tawny Kitaen, Charles Napier; *D:* Craig T. Rumar. *WAR*

Instant Karma 🐾½ 1990 Would be comedy pokes young man's far fetched attempts to score babewise. Ask no more what happened to erstwhile teen heart throb Cassidy: he suffers from a major bout of bad karma. **94m/C VHS, Beta, Closed Caption.** Craig Sheffer, Chelsea Noble, David Cassidy, Alan Blumenfeld, Glen Hirsch, Marty Ingels, Orson Bean; *D:* Roderick Taylor. *MGM*

Instant Kung-Fu Man 🐾 1984 Twin brothers get involved in a case of mistaken identity in this martial arts effort. **104m/C VHS, Beta.** John Liu, Hwang Jang Lee, Yeh Fei Yang. *WVE*

The Instructor 🐾 1983 The head of a karate school proves the value of his skill when threatened by the owner of a rival school. **91m/C VHS, Beta.** Don Bendell, Bob Chaney, Bob Saal, Lynday Scharnott; *D:* Don Bendell. *ART, VES*

Interceptor 🐾🐾 1992 (R) Hijackers attempt to steal a Stealth Bomber in this action-adventure saga which features virtual reality computer-generated imagery in its combat sequences. **CW:** Language and violence. 92m/C VHS, LV, **Closed Caption.** Juergen Prochnow, Andrew Divoff, Elizabeth Morehead; **D:** Michael Cohn; **W:** John Brancato. THV

Interface 🐾½ 1984 A computer game gets out of hand at a university, turning the tunnels beneath the campus into a battleground of good and evil. 88m/C VHS, Beta. John Davies, Laura Lane, Matthew Sacks. ART, VES

Interiors 🐾🐾🐾½ 1978 (R) Ultra serious, Bergmanesque drama about three neurotic adult sisters, coping with the dissolution of their family. When Father decides to leave mentally unbalanced mother for a divorcee, the daughters are shocked and bewildered. Depressing and humorless, but fine performances all the way around, supported by the elegant camera work of Gordon Willis. Original theatrical trailer available on the laserdisc format. 95m/C VHS, Beta, LV. Diane Keaton, Mary Beth Hurt, E.G. Marshall, Geraldine Page, Richard Jordan, Sam Waterston, Kristin Griffith, Maureen Stapleton; **D:** Woody Allen; **W:** Woody Allen; **C:** Gordon Willis. British Academy Awards '78: Best Supporting Actress (Page); Los Angeles Film Critics Association Awards '78: Best Supporting Actress (Stapleton); Nominations: Academy Awards '78: Best Actress (Page), Best Art Direction/Set Decoration, Best Director (Allen), Best Original Screenplay, Best Supporting Actress (Stapleton). MGM

Intermezzo 🐾🐾 Interlude 1936 Married violinist Ekman meets pianist Bergman and they fall in love. He deserts his family to tour with Bergman, but the feelings for his wife and children become too much. When Bergman sees their love won't last, she leaves him. Shakily, he returns home and as his daughter runs to greet him, she is hit by a truck and he realizes that his family is his true love. One of the great grab-your-hanky melodramas. In Swedish with English subtitles. 1939 English re-make features Bergman's American film debut. 88m/B VHS, LV. SW Gosta Ekman, Inga Tidblad, Ingrid Bergman, Bullen Berglund; **D:** Gustaf Molander. WAC, TPV, LUM

Intermezzo 🐾🐾🐾 Intermezzo: A Love Story 1939 Fine, though weepy, love story of a renowned, married violinist who has an affair with his stunningly beautiful protege (Bergman), but while on concert tour realizes that his wife and children hold his heart, and he returns to them. A re-make of the 1936 Swedish film, it's best known as Bergman's American debut. Howard's violin playing was dubbed by Jascha Heifetz. 70m/B VHS, Beta, LV. IT Ingrid Bergman, Leslie Howard, Edna Best, Ann Todd; **D:** Gregory Ratoff; **C:** Gregg Toland; **M:** Max Steiner. Nominations: Academy Awards '39: Best Black and White Cinematography, Best Score. FOX, FCT

Internal Affairs 🐾🐾½ 1990 (R) Wild, sexually charged action piece about an Internal Affairs officer for the L.A.P.D. (Garcia) who becomes obsessed with exposing a sleazy, corrupt street cop (Gere). Drama becomes illogical, but boasts excellent, strung out performances, especially Gere as the creepy degenerate you'd love to bust. 114m/C VHS, Beta, LV, 8mm, **Closed Caption.** Richard Gere, Andy Garcia, Laurie Metcalf, Ron Vawter, Marco Rodriguez, Nancy Travis, William Baldwin, Richard Bradford, Annabella Sciorra, Michael Beach; **D:** Mike Figgis; **W:** Henry Bean; **C:** John A. Alonzo; **M:** Brian Banks, Mike Figgis. PAR

International Crime 🐾🐾 1937 Radio hero The Shadow solves a tough crime in this adventure film. 62m/B VHS, Beta. Rod La Rocque, Astrid Allwyn, William von Brinken; **D:** Charles Lamont. SNC, NOS, AOV

International House 🐾🐾½ 1933 A wacky Dada-esque Hollywood farce about an incredible array of travelers quarantined in a Shanghai hotel where a mad doctor has perfected television. Essentially a burlesque compilation of skits, gags, and routines. Guest stars Rudy Vallee, Baby Rose Marie and Cab Calloway appear on the quaint "television" device, in musical sequences. ♫Tea Cup; Thank Heaven For You; My Bluebirds are Singing the Blues; Reefer Man. 72m/B VHS, Beta, LV. W.C. Fields, Peggy Hopkins Joyce, Rudy Vallee, George Burns, Cab Calloway, Sari Maritza, Gracie Allen, Bela Lugosi, Sterling Holloway, Baby Rose Marie; **D:** Edward Sutherland. USH, MLB

International Velvet 🐾🐾½ 1978 (PG) In this long overdue sequel to "National Velvet," adult Velvet, with live-in companion (Plummer), grooms her orphaned niece (O'Neal) to become an Olympic champian horsewoman. Good photography and performances by Plummer and Hopkins manage to keep the sentiment at a trot. 126m/C VHS, Beta. GB Tatum O'Neal, Anthony Hopkins, Christopher Plummer; **D:** Bryan Forbes. MGM

Internecine Project 🐾🐾½ 1973 (PG) Stylistic espionage tale with Coburn's English professor acting as the mastermind behind an unusual series of murders where industrial spies kill each other, so Coburn can garner a top government job in D.C. Unexpected ending is worth the viewing. Based on Mort Elkind's novel. 89m/C VHS, Beta, **Closed Caption.** GB James Coburn, Lee Grant, Harry Andrews, Keenan Wynn; **D:** Ken Hughes; **W:** Barry Levinson; **C:** Geoffrey Unsworth. FOX

Internes Can't Take Money 🐾🐾½ 1937 With the help of McCrea and gangster Nolan, widow Stanwyck is desperately trying to find the daughter her bank robber husband hid before he died. Young doctor McCrea must save the life of another gangster who knows the whereabouts of the toddler. The first film featuring writer Max Brand's Dr. Kildare characters, which later became part of a series starring Lew Ayres and Laraine Day. 79m/B VHS, **Closed Caption.** Barbara Stanwyck, Joel McCrea, Lloyd Nolan, Stanley Ridges, Lee Bowman, Irving Bacon; **D:** Alfred Santell; **W:** Rian James, Theodore Reeves; **C:** Theodor Sparkuhl; **M:** Gregory Stone. USH

The Interns 🐾🐾½ 1962 Finessed hospital soaper about interns on the staff of a large city hospital, whose personal lives are fraught with trauma, drugs, birth, death, and abortion. Good performances and direction keep this medical melodrama moving in a gurney-like manner. Followed by "The New Interns" and the basis for a television series. Adapted from a novel by Richard Frede. 120m/C VHS, Beta, LV. Cliff Robertson, James MacArthur, Michael Callan, Nick Adams, Stefanie Powers, Suzy Parker, Buddy Ebsen, Telly Savalas, Haya Harareet; **D:** David Swift. COL

Interpol Connection 🐾½ 1992 International drug dealer Law Tak is being pursued by Hong Kong narcotics officer Ko Pang, international police officer Cynthia, and bumbling Philippine cop KingKong. The cop trio reluctantly decide to work together to bring down the bad guy. Dubbed into English. 91m/C VHS. HK Robin Shou, Yukari Oshima. TAI

The Interrogation 🐾🐾🐾 Przesluchanie 1982 Grueling depiction of Stalin-era Poland proves that nobody makes anticommunist movies better than those who knew tyranny firsthand. A 1950s cabaret starlet is arrested on false charges and endures years of torment in custody. Banned under Polish martial law in 1982, it circulated illegally in the country until 1989. Janda won an award at Cannes for her transformation from showgirl floozy to defiant heroine. In Polish with English subtitles. 118m/C VHS. PL Krystyna Janda, Janusz Gajos, Adam Ferency, Agnieszka Holland, Anna Romantowska; **D:** Richard Bugajski. KIV, FCT

Interrupted Journey 🐾🐾½ 1949 A married man runs away to start a new life with another woman. When she is killed in a train accident, he becomes the prime suspect in her murder. Lots of action and speed, but a disappointing ending. 80m/B VHS. GB Richard Todd, Valerie Hobson; **D:** Daniel Birt. NOS, SNC

Interrupted Melody 🐾🐾🐾 1955 True story of opera diva Marjorie Lawrence's courageous battle with polio and her fight to appear once more at the Metropolitan Opera. Parker was nominated for an Oscar in her excellent portrayal of the Australian singer who continues her career despite her handicap. Vocals dubbed by opera star Eileen Farrell. Based on the book by Marjorie Lawrence. 106m/C VHS. Glenn Ford, Eleanor Parker, Roger Moore, Cecil Kellaway, Evelyn Ellis, Walter Baldwin; **D:** Curtis Bernhardt; **W:** William Ludwig, Sonya Levien; **C:** Paul Vogel. Academy Awards '55: Best Story & Screenplay; Nominations: Academy Awards '55: Best Actress (Parker), Best Costume Design (Color), Best Screenplay. MGM

Intersection 🐾½ 1993 (R) Successful architect Vincent (Gere) is torn between his aloof wife/partner, Sally (Stone), and a sexy journalist mistress, Olivia (Davidovitch). Who to choose? Since he's a completely self-involved boor, you won't care either way. Another retooling of a French film ("Les Choses de la Vie") as a Hollywood star vehicle that doesn't work. Lousy dialogue doesn't help. Does boast some nice location shots of Vancouver, BC. **CW:** Some language and some sexuality. 98m/C VHS, Beta, LV, **Closed Caption.** Richard Gere, Sharon Stone, Lolita Davidovich, Martin Landau, David Selby, Jenny Morrison; **D:** Mark Rydell; **W:** Marshall Brickman, David Rayfiel; **C:** Vilmos Zsigmond; **M:** James Newton Howard. Golden Raspberry Awards '94: Worst Actress (Stone). PAR

Interval 🐾🐾 1973 (PG) A middle-aged, globetrotting woman becomes involved with a young American painter while running from her past. Oberon, 62 at the time, produced and played in this, her last film. Filmed in Mexico. 84m/C VHS, Beta. Merle Oberon, Robert Wolders; **D:** Daniel Mann. NLC

Interview with the Vampire 🐾🐾 1994 (R) Portrayal of the elegantly decadent world of vampires and their prey, which features the perverse Lestat (Cruise) who decides to make 18th-century New Orleans aristocrat Louis (Pitt) his latest recruit. Only problem is Louis is horrified by his blood-sucking nature and whines about it for 200 years (it does get tedious). Lestat even makes a child-vampire, Claudia (Dunst), for their own very dysfunctional family but this doesn't turn out well. Director Jordan brings some much needed humor to the dark mix along with some overdone gore. The first book in Anne Rice's "The Vampire Chronicles" was a 17-year film project beset by controversy, including the casting of Cruise (who looks nothing like Rice's description of the character, although Pitt does), leading to an outcry among the cult book's fans though Rice finally came around. Slater replaced the late River Phoenix as the interviewer. **CW:** Language; sensuality; nudity; violence. 123m/C VHS, LV, **Closed Caption, DVD.** Tom Cruise, Brad Pitt, Kirsten Dunst, Christian Slater, Antonio Banderas, Stephen Rea, Domiziana Giordano; **D:** Neil Jordan; **W:** Anne Rice; **C:** Philippe Rousselot; **M:** Elliot Goldenthal. MTV Movie Awards '95: Best Male Performance (Pitt), Breakthrough Performance (Dunst), Most Desirable Male (Pitt); Nominations: Academy Awards '94: Best Art Direction/Set Decoration, Best Original Score; Golden Globe Awards '95: Best Supporting Actress (Dunst), Best Score; MTV Movie Awards '95: Best Film, Most Desirable Male (Slater, Cruise), Best On-Screen Duo (Tom Cruise/Brad Pitt), Best Villain (Cruise). WAR

Intervista 🐾🐾🐾 Federico Fellini's Intervista 1987 A pseudo-documentary look at director Fellini's love of the movies, "Intervista" is a mixture of recollection, parody, memoir, satire, self-examination and fantasy. Fellini himself is the master of ceremonies in this joyous celebration of the studio community that features actors, actresses, bit players, make-up artists, scene painters, publicity agents, technicians, and gate-crashers. The high point of the film arrives with the stars of "La Dolce Vita" re-screening the Fellini masterpiece at Ekberg's country villa. It's a special moment of fantasy vs. reality in this glorious tribute to cinema history. In Italian with English subtitles. 108m/C VHS. IT Marcello Mastroianni, Anita Ekberg, Federico Fellini, Sernio Rubini, Lara Wendell, Antonio Cantafora, Antonella Ponziani, Maurizio Mein, Paola Liguori, Nadia Ottaviani; **D:** Federico Fellini; **W:** Federico Fellini, Gianfranco Angelucci; **C:** Tonino Delli Colli; **M:** Nicola Piovani. *TRI*

Interzone 🐾½ **1988** Humans battle mutants in a post-holocaust world. 97m/C VHS, Beta. Bruce Abbott; **D:** Deran Sarafian.

Intimate Contact 🐾🐾🐾 **1987 (PG)** Top executive discovers he has AIDS after a business trip fling. Powerful drama as he and his wife try to cope. Excellent, understated performances from Massey and Bloom. Originally made for cable television. 140m/C VHS, Beta. *GB* Claire Bloom, Daniel Massey, Abigail Cruttenden, Mark Kingston, Sylvia Syms, Sally Jane Jackson; **D:** Waris Hussein; **W:** Alma Cullen. *HBO*

Intimate Deception 🐾🐾 **1996** Artist Charles Michaels is in a crumbling marriage and having dreams about a murder that took place in his past. Into his confused life comes new neighbor John and beautiful model Tina and neither meeting is a coincidence. 96m/C VHS. George Saunders, Lisa Boyle, Dan Frank, Nicole Gian; **D:** George Saunders; **W:** George Saunders. *FRF*

Intimate Power 🐾🐾½ **1989 (R)** True story of French schoolgirl sold into slavery to an Ottoman sultan who becomes the harem queen. She bears an heir and begins to teach her son about his people's rights, in the hope that he will bring about reform in Turkey where he grows up to be a sultan. Good cast supports the exotic storytelling in this made for cable drama. 104m/C VHS, Beta, LV, Closed Caption. F. Murray Abraham, Maud Adams, Amber O'Shea; **D:** Jack Smight. *HBO*

Intimate Relations 🐾🐾½ **1995 (R)** Fifties family dysfunction—British style. Harold Guppy (Graves) is an orphaned merchant marine who winds up in an English coastal town where he takes rooms with the seemingly respectable Beasleys. Stanley Beasley (Walker) is a quiet nonentity whose life is run by homemaker extraordinaire Marjorie (Walters), with 14-year-old daughter Joyce (Sadler) rounding out the family. The needy Harold fits in fine, especially to the sexually hungry Marjorie who's soon offering her boarder unexpected services. But young Joyce won't be left out and then there's a blackmailing tug of war between the threesome. Based on the true story of a crime of passion that shocked Great Britain. **CW:** Disturbing sexual situations, a scene of related violence and some language. 105m/C VHS, Closed Caption. *GB* Julie Walters, Rupert Graves, Laura Sadler, Matthew Walker, Holly Aird, Les Dennis, Liz McKechnie; **D:** Philip Goodhew; **W:** Philip Goodhew; **C:** Andres Garreton; **M:** Lawrence Shragge. Montreal World Film Festival '95: Best Actor (Graves). *FXV*

Intimate Story 🐾🐾½ **1981** Intimate story of a husband and wife trying unsuccessfully to have a baby, amid the lack of privacy in a Kibbutz. Each blames the other for the problem and tries to escape the problems by focusing on personal fantasies. In Hebrew with English subtitles. 95m/C VHS, Beta. *IS* Chava Alberstein, Alex Peleg; **D:** Israeli Nadav Levitan. *ERG, TPV*

Intimate Stranger 🐾½ **1991 (R)** Sexy, would-be rock star by day, Harry sets out in search of a steadier source of income. Rather than wait on tables all day, he chooses instead to become a phone-sex girl. This turns out to be an unwise career move, as she promptly finds herself the target of a phone-psycho who just can't take "no" for an answer. Will Debbie be able to shake this loser, or will he put a permanent end to her life-long dreams? Made for television. **CW:** Sex-related dialogue, violence, and sensuality. 96m/C VHS, Beta, LV, Closed Caption. Deborah Harry, James Russo, Tim Thomerson, Paige French, Grace Zabriskie; **D:** Allan Holzman. *PAR*

Intimate Strangers 🐾🐾½ **1977** Taut made-for-television expose on battering and its effects on the family. Weaver and Struthers outshine the material, but the finest performance

is a cameo by Douglas as Weaver's irascible aged father. 96m/C VHS, Beta. Dennis Weaver, Sally Struthers, Quinn Cummings, Tyne Daly, Larry Hagman, Rhea Perlman; **Cameos:** Melvyn Douglas; **D:** John Llewellyn Moxey. *WOV*

Into the Badlands 🐾🐾 **1992 (R)** Mild made for cable TV thriller presents three suspense tales in "Twilight Zone" fashion, linked by the appearance of a mysterious Man in Black. No, it's not Johnny Cash, but Dern as a sinister bounty hunter in the old west, who inspires strange events on the trail. **CW:** Strong violence. 89m/C VHS. Bruce Dern, Mariel Hemingway, Helen Hunt, Dylan McDermott, Lisa Pelikan, Andrew (Andy) Robinson; **D:** Sam Pillsbury; **W:** Dick Beebe, Marjorie David, Gordon Dawson. *USH*

Into the Blue 🐾🐾½ **1997** Harry Barnett (Thaw) is a bankrupt businessman now working as a caretaker at a friend's estate on the Greek isle of Rhodes. He has a one-nighter with young Englishwoman Heather Mallender (Cruttenden) and when she mysteriously disappears, Harry becomes a suspect. Then he learns she was investigating the drowning death of her sister, which involves people Harry knows, and he returns to London to try and sort out the mess he's in. 120m/C VHS. *GB* John Thaw, Abigail Cruttenden, Miles Anderson, Michael Culkin, Celia Imrie; **D:** Jack Gold. *VTR*

Into the Darkness 🐾½ **1986** In the world of fashion models, a maniacal, demented killer stalks his prey. 90m/C VHS, Beta. Donald Pleasence, Ronald Lacey. *NO*

Into the Fire 🐾 **1988 (R)** Thriller about a young drifter who, against the backdrop of a Canadian winter, happens upon a roadside lodge and diner, where he gets involved in sex and murder. Title gives a good idea of what to do with this one. 88m/C VHS, Beta, LV. *CA* Susan Anspach, Art Hindle, Olivia D'Abo, Lee Montgomery; **D:** Graeme Campbell. *ART, VES*

Into the Homeland 🐾🐾 **1987** Seasoned ex-cop (Boothe) infiltrates a white supremacist group which had kidnapped his teenage daughter. Failed "message" about neo-nazi ethics, but good confrontation between Boothe and his son (Howell) make this so-so viewing. Made for cable television. 95m/C VHS, Beta, LV. Powers Boothe, C. Thomas Howell, Paul LeMat; **D:** Leslie Linka Glatter. *BAR, ORI, WAR*

Into the Night 🐾🐾 **1985 (R)** Campy, offbeat thriller about a middle-aged, jilted deadbeat (Goldblum), who meets a beautiful woman (Pfeiffer) when she suddenly drops onto the hood of his car, with a relentless gang of Iranians pursuing. During their search through L.A. and other parts of California for the one person who can help her out of this mess, a whole crew of Hollywood directors make cameo appearances, making this a delight for film buffs, but occasionally tedious for general audiences. B.B. King sings the title song. 115m/C VHS, Beta, LV, Closed Caption. Jeff Goldblum, Michelle Pfeiffer, David Bowie, Carl Perkins, Richard Farnsworth, Dan Aykroyd, Paul Mazursky, Roger Vadim, Irene Papas, Bruce McGill, Vera Miles, Clu Gulager, Don Steel, Kathryn Harrold; **Cameos:** Jim Henson, Paul Bartel, David Cronenberg, Jack Arnold, Jonathan Demme, Lawrence Kasdan, Amy Heckerling, Donald Siegel, Richard Franklin, Colin Higgins, Andrew Marton; **D:** John Landis; **W:** Ron Koslow; **M:** Ira Newborn. *USH*

Into the Sun 🐾½ **1992 (R)** Hall plays a Hollywood star who encounters real-life danger while hanging out with an Air Force pilot (Pare) to prepare for an upcoming role. Spectacular aerial scenes steal the show, which isn't hard to do in this lackluster movie. **CW:** Language. 101m/C VHS, LV, Closed Caption. Anthony Michael Hall, Michael Pare, Terry Kiser, Deborah Maria Moore; **D:** Fritz Kiersch; **W:** John Brancato. *THV*

Into the West 🐾🐾🐾 **1992 (PG)** Enchanting horse tale set amid the mystic isle of Eire. Brooding, drunken Riley (Byrne), once the leader of a band of travelers (the Irish version of gypsies), leaves the road after his wife's death and

settles in a Dublin slum with his two boys. The boys are enraptured when their grandfather turns up with a beautiful white horse, but their happiness is shattered when the police take it away. Boys and horse eventually escape in a wild ride across Ireland and into the west. Spiritual and mythic, with an awe-inspiring performance by the horse. Fitzgerald and Conroy make a run at best performances by kids, while Byrne is convincingly sodden and sulky. Meany and Barkin shine in small parts as sibling travellers. 97m/C VHS, LV, Closed Caption. *IR* Gabriel Byrne, Ellen Barkin, Ciaran Fitzgerald, Ruaidhri Conroy, David Kelly, Colm Meaney; **D:** Mike Newell; **W:** Jim Sheridan; **M:** Patrick Doyle. *TOU*

Into Thin Air 🐾🐾🐾 **1985** A mother searches tirelessly for her college bound son who disappeared on a cross-country drive. Well-done television drama with a good performance from Burstyn. 100m/C VHS, Beta, LV. Ellen Burstyn, Robert Prosky, Sam Robards, Tate Donovan, Caroline McWilliams, Nicholas Pryor, John Dennis Johnston; **D:** Roger Young; **W:** George Rubio, Larry Cohen; **M:** Brad Fiedel. *VTR*

Intolerance 🐾🐾🐾🐾 **1916** Griffith's largest film in every aspect. An interwoven, four-story epic about human intolerance, with segments set in Babylon, ancient Judea, and Paris. One of the cinema's grandest follies, and greatest achievements. Silent with music score. Laserdisc version contains supplemental material including cuts from other Griffith works. Black and white with some restored color footage. 175m/B VHS, LV. Lillian Gish, Mae Marsh, Constance Talmadge, Bessie Love, Elmer Clifton, Erich von Stroheim, Eugene Pallette, Seena Owen, Alfred Paget; **D:** D.W. Griffith. National Film Registry '89. *GPV, MRV, KIV*

Intrigue 🐾🐾½ **1990 (PG)** Former CIA agent (Loggia) defects to the KGB, but wants to return to the US when he realizes he has a progressive illness. Underground agent and old buddy (Glenn) is recruited with orders to smuggle his former colleague out. Tension continues throughout as murder comes along with the orders. Loads of suspense and twist ending in this made for television nail-biter. 96m/C VHS, LV. Scott Glenn, Robert Loggia, William Atherton, Martin Shaw, Cherie Lunghi, Eleanor Bron; **D:** David Drury. *THV*

Intruder 🐾🐾 **1977** A man and his stepson are terrorized by a stranger in a panel truck as they travel from Rome to Paris. 98m/C VHS, Beta. Jean-Louis Trintignant, Mireille Darc, Adolfo Celi. *NO*

Intruder 🐾🐾 **1988 (R)** A psychotic killer stalks an all-night convenience store shopping for fresh meat (customers beware). Slasher movie fans should get a kick out of the plot twist at the end. 90m/C VHS, Beta, LV, Closed Caption. Elizabeth Cox, Renee Estevez, Alvy Moore; **D:** Scott Spiegel; **W:** Lawrence Bender. *PAR*

Intruder in the Dust 🐾🐾🐾½ **1949** A small southern community develops a lynch mob mentality when a black man is accused of killing a white man. Powerful, but largely ignored portrait of race relations in the South. Solid performances from the whole cast; filmed in Mississippi. Adapted from a novel by William Faulkner. 87m/B VHS. David Brian, Claude Jarman Jr., Juano Hernandez, Porter Hall, Elizabeth Patterson; **D:** Clarence Brown; **C:** Robert L. Surtees. *MGM, MOV, BTV*

Intruder Within 🐾 **1981** Half-baked thriller about crew on an isolated oil rig in Antarctica who, while drilling, unearth a nasty creature that goes around terrorizing the frost-bitten men and occasional stray woman. Made for television. 91m/C VHS, Beta. Chad Everett, Joseph Bottoms, Jennifer Warren; **D:** Peter Carter. *TWE*

Intruders 🐾🐾 **1992** Follows the story of three people who have unexplained lapses of time in their lives which they eventually believe are connected to visits by aliens. The three are brought together by a skeptical psychiatrist. The aliens are your typical bugged-eyed, white-faced spooks but part of the film is genuinely unsettling. 162m/C VHS, Closed Caption. Richard Crenna, Mare Winningham, Susan Blakely, Ben Vereen, Steven Berkoff, Daphne Ashbrook; **D:** Dan Curtis. *FXV*

Intruso 🐾🐾½ *Intruder* 1993 Gloomy story set in a coastal city in northern Spain. Luisa (Abril) spots her destitute ex-husband Angel (Arias) and persuades him to stay with her and her new family, husband Ramiro (Valero)—once Angel's good friend—and their two young children. Angel turns out to be terminally ill and decides to wreak vengeance on Ramiro by reclaiming Luisa for himself. In Spanish with English subtitles. **85m/C VHS.** *SP* Victoria Abril, Imanol Arias, Antonio Valero; **D:** Vicente Aranda; **W:** Vicente Aranda, Alvaro del Amo. *NYF*

Invader 🐾🐾 1991 (R) When a news reporter is sent to cover a mysterious massacre, he begins to realize that the culprits are vicious aliens thirsty for blood...and now they're after him! *CW:* Language and violence. **95m/C VHS, LV.** Hans Bachman, A. Thomas Smith, Rich Foucheux, John Cooke, Robert Diedermann, Allison Sheehy, Ralph Bluemke; **D:** Phillip Cook. *THV*

The Invader 🐾🐾½ 1996 Schoolteacher Annie (Young) discovers she's pregnant by a mystery man (Cross), who turns out to be an alien from a dying race—and Annie's child may be their salvation. Only her ex-cop boyfriend (Baldwin) is on their trail as he is an intergalactic bounty hunter (Mancuso). This one is on the romance rather than the action side. **97m/C VHS, LV.** Sean Young, Ben Cross, Nick Mancuso, Daniel Baldwin; **D:** Mark Rosman. *ART*

The Invaders 🐾🐾 *Erik the Conqueror; Gli Invasori; La Ruee Des Vikings; Fury of the Vikings* 1963 Two Viking brothers battle each other and the Britons. **88m/C VHS, Beta.** *FR IT* Cameron Mitchell, George Ardisson, Andrea Checchi, Francoise Christophe, Joe Robinson; **D:** Mario Bava; **M:** Les Baxter. *NO*

The Invaders 1967 The popular science fiction series created by Larry Cohen stars Thinnes, as David Vincent, who attempts to convince people he has witnessed an alien landing and that they want to take over Earth. "Beach Head" is the pilot episode. Additional episodes available. **53m/C VHS.** Roy Thinnes, Kent Smith, Diane Baker, J.D. Cannon, James Daly, John Milford, Ellen Corby, Vaughn Taylor; **D:** Joseph Sargent. *GKK, MOV*

The Invaders 🐾🐾½ 1995 TV mini is an updated continuation of the 1967 sci-fi series that finds the pollution-loving aliens gradually conquering Earth by allowing humans to destroy their own ecosystem (which we're so good at anyway). Bewildered hero Nolan Wood (Bakula) is trying to get everyone to believe in the alien invasion but since he's just gotten out of prison, it's an uphill climb. Still, the aliens (lead by effectively evil Thomas) would like to permanently shut Nolan up. Thinnes, who starred in the original series, briefly reprises his role as David Vincent. **180m/C VHS, LV, Closed Caption.** Scott Bakula, Richard Thomas, DeLane Matthews, Terence Knox, Elizabeth Pena, Raoul Trujillo, Robert Belzer, Jon Polito, Roy Thinnes, Jon Cypher, Todd Susman, Jack Kehler, Elinor Donahue; **D:** Paul Shapiro; **W:** James Dott; **C:** Alan Kivilo; **M:** Joseph Vitarelli. *REP*

Invaders from Mars 🐾🐾½ 1953 Young boy cries "martian" in this sci-fi cheapy classic. He can't convince the townspeople of this invasion because they've already been possessed by the alien beings. His parents are zapped by the little green things first, making this perhaps an allegory for the missing Eisenhower/Stepford years. Includes previews of coming attractions from classic science fiction films. Remade in 1986 by Tobe Hooper. **78m/C VHS.** Helena Carter, Arthur Franz, Jimmy Hunt, Leif Erickson; **D:** William Cameron Menzies. *EEL, MLB*

Invaders from Mars 🐾½ 1986 (PG) A high-tech remake of Menzies' 1953 semi-classic about a Martian invasion perceived only by one young boy and a sympathetic (though hysterical) school nurse, played by mother and son Black and Carson. Instant camp. **102m/C VHS, Beta, LV,**

Closed Caption. Hunter Carson, Karen Black, Louise Fletcher, Laraine Newman, Timothy Bottoms, Bud Cort; **D:** Tobe Hooper; **W:** Dan O'Bannon, Don Jakoby. *IME*

Invasion 🐾🐾½ 1965 A hospital opens its doors to an accident victim, and his attractive female visitors don't seem sympathetic to the idea of a long hospital stay. Turns out he's an escaped alien prisoner, and the alien babes, intent on intergalactic extradition, place a force field around the hospital and demand his return. Early effort of director Bridges, who later did "The Shooting Party." Interesting, creepy, atmospheric, with very cool camera moves. **82m/B VHS.** *GB* Edward Judd, Yoko Tani, Valerie Gearon, Lyndon Brook, Tsai Chin, Barrie Ingham; **D:** Alan Bridges. *MOV*

Invasion Earth: The Aliens Are Here! 🐾 1987 A cheap spoof of monster movies, as an insectoid projectionist takes over the minds of a movie audience. Clips of Godzilla, Mothra and other beasts are interpolated. **84m/C VHS, Beta, LV.** Janice Fabian, Christian Lee; **D:** George Maitland. *VTR*

Invasion Force 🐾 1990 A terrorist army parachutes into a remote region where a film crew is preparing to set up for an action movie. The moviemakers must scare away the terrorists with their smokepots and blanks. Sounds promising, but proves to be as empty as the movie props used to scare the terrorists. **93m/C VHS.** Richard Lynch, David Shark, Renee Cline, Douglas Hartier, Graham Times, Angie Synodis; **D:** David A. Prior.

The Invasion of Carol Enders 🐾½ 1974 A woman, almost killed by a prowler, awakens with an expanded consciousness, and tries to convince her near husband that her death wasn't an accident. **72m/C VHS, Beta.** Meredith Baxter, Christopher Connelly, Charles Aidman. *ART*

Invasion of Privacy 🐾🐾 1992 (R) Alex is a psycho prison inmate obsessed with high profile journalist, Hilary. When Hilary interviews Alex for a magazine cover story, his obsession only grows stronger. Then Alex gets paroled and goes to work for Hilary. When he discovers Hilary isn't interested in him, Alex turns his fantasies to her daughter, who has no notion what she's getting into. An unrated version is also available. Made for cable television. *CW:* Language, violence, and sexuality. **95m/C VHS, Closed Caption.** Robby Benson, Jennifer O'Neill, Lydie Denier, Ian Ogilvy; **D:** Kevin Meyer; **W:** Kevin Meyer.

Invasion of Privacy 🐾🐾 1996 (R) Some hot-button topics sage the thriller route. When Theresa (Avital) becomes pregnant, she discovers her boyfriend Josh (Schaech) is seriously unbalanced. She decides on an abortion but retreats for some quiet time to an isolated lakeside cabin. Mistake—the expectant dad shows up and holds her prisoner until Theresa is too far along to terminate the pregnancy. When Josh finally releases her, Theresa heads for the cops and charges him with kidnapping. He gets a hot female lawyer (Rampling), who turns the media attention into making him a cause celebre for parental rights. Once the baby is born, Josh is also detemined to gain custody—by whatever means necessary. *CW:* Language and some violence and terror. **94m/C VHS.** Johnathon Schaech, Mili Avital, Naud Keith, Charlotte Rampling, Naomi Campbell, R.G. Armstrong; **D:** Anthony Hickox; **W:** Larry Cohen; **C:** Peter Wunstorf; **M:** Angelo Badalamenti. *THV*

Invasion of the Animal People woof! *Terror in the Midnight Sun; Space Invasion of Lapland; Horror in the Midnight Sun; Space Invasion from Lapland* 1962 Hairy monster from outer space attacks Lapland. Narrated by Carradine, the only American in the cast. Pretty silly. **73m/C VHS.** *SW* Robert Burton, Barbara Wilson, John Carradine; **D:** Virgil W. Vogel, Jerry Warren. *THV, SNC, NOS*

Invasion of the Bee Girls 🐾🐾🐾 *Graveyard Tramps* 1973 California girls are mysteriously transformed into deadly nymphomaniacs in this delightful campy science fiction romp. Written

by Meyer who later directed "Star Trek II: The Wrath of Khan." **85m/C VHS.** Victoria Vetri, William Smith, Anitra Ford, Cliff Osmond, Wright King, Ben Hammer; **D:** Denis Sanders; **W:** Nicholas Meyer; **M:** Charles Bernstein.

Invasion of the Blood Farmers woof! 1972 (PG) In a small New York town, members of an ancient Druidic cult murder young women, taking their blood in the hope of finding the precise, rare blood type to keep their queen alive. A real woofer. **86m/C VHS, Beta.** Norman Kelley, Tanna Hunter, Bruce Detrick, Jack Neubeck, Cythia Fleming, Paul Craig Jennings; **D:** Ed Adlum. *NO*

Invasion of the Body Snatchers 🐾🐾🐾 1956 The one and only post-McCarthy paranoid sci-fi epic, where a small California town is infiltrated by pods from outer space that replicate and replace humans. A chilling, genuinely frightening exercise in nightmare dislocation. Based upon a novel by Jack Finney. Remade in 1978. The laserdisc version contains commentary by Maurice Yacowar, the text of an interview with Siegel, and the original theatrical trailer. The film itself is presented in its original widescreen format. **80m/B VHS, LV, Letterbox, Closed Caption.** Kevin McCarthy, Carolyn Jones, King Donovan, Larry Gates, Jean Willes, Whit Bissell, Sam Peckinpah, Donald Siegel; **D:** Donald Siegel; **W:** Daniel Mainwaring, Sam Peckinpah; **C:** Ellsworth Fredericks. National Film Registry '94. *REP, CRC, MLB*

Invasion of the Body Snatchers 🐾🐾🐾½ 1978 (PG) One of the few instances where a remake is an improvement on the original, which was itself a classic. This time, the "pod people" are infesting San Francisco, with only a small group of people aware of the invasion. A ceaselessly inventive, creepy version of the alien-takeover paradigm, with an intense and winning performance by Sutherland. Features cameos by Don Siegel and Kevin McCarthy from the original, as well as an uncredited appearance by Robert Duvall. **115m/C VHS, Beta, LV, Letterbox.** Donald Sutherland, Brooke Adams, Veronica Cartwright, Leonard Nimoy, Jeff Goldblum, Kevin McCarthy, Donald Siegel, Art Hindle, Robert Duvall; **D:** Philip Kaufman; **W:** W.D. Richter; **C:** Michael Chapman. *MGM*

Invasion of the Body Stealers woof! *Thin Air; The Body Stealers* 1969 (PG) Aliens are thought to be the captors when sky-divers begin vanishing in mid-air. Uneven sci-fi with nothing going for it. **115m/C VHS, Beta.** *GB* George Sanders, Maurice Evans, Patrick Allen; **D:** Gerry Levy. *ART*

Invasion of the Flesh Hunters woof! *Cannibals in the Streets; Savage Apocalypse; The Slaughterers; Cannibals in the City; Virus* 1982 Group of tortured Vietnam veterans returns home carrying a cannibalistic curse with them. Smorgasbord of gore and sensationalism is not for discriminating tastes. **90m/C VHS, Beta.** *IT* John Saxon, Elizabeth Turner; **D:** Anthony (Antonio Margheriti) Dawson; **W:** Anthony (Antonio Margheriti) Dawson. *ART, VES*

Invasion of the Girl Snatchers woof! 1973 Aliens from another planet, in cahoots with a cult kingpin, subdue young earth girls and force them to undergo bizarre acts that may just rob them of their dignity. Save a bit of your own dignity by staying away. Cheap look, cheap feel, cheap thrills. **90m/C VHS, Beta.** Elizabeth Rush, Ele Grigsby, David Roster; **D:** Lee Jones. *NO*

Invasion of the Saucer Men 🐾 1957 Suburban teenagers (Terrell, Castillo) are detained by a little green man at lovers lane. When they return with police to the scene, only the corpse of the town drunk (Gorshin) remains. Fortunately, the dead man's roommate (Osborn) believes them but the trio must convince authorities before the alien creatures multiply and take over the world. **69m/B VHS.** Steven Terrell, Gloria Castillo,

Frank Gorshin, Lyn Osborn, Ed Nelson, Angela Rossitto; D: Edward L. Cahn; M: Ronald Stein. COL

Invasion of the Space Preachers
1990 Hideous creatures from outer space arrive on Earth with plans for conquest. Led by the seemingly human Reverend Lash, they prey on the innocent and trusting, fleecing God-fearing folk out of their hard earned cash! 100m/C VHS, Beta. Jim Wolfe, Guy Nelson, Eliska Hahn, Gary Brown, Jesse Johnson, John Riggs; D: Daniel Boyd; W: Daniel Boyd. RHI

Invasion of the Vampires 🎬 La Invasion de Los Vampiros 1961 Burrito bat fest has Count Frankenhausen doing his vampire thing in a small, 16th century village. Atmospheric sets are highlight. Not a good substitute for No Doze. 78m/ B VHS. MX Carlos Agosti, Rafael Etienne, Bertha Moss, Tito Junco, Erna Martha Bauman, Fernando Soto, Enrique Garcia Alvarez, David Reynoso; D: Miguel Morayta; W: Miguel Morayta. SNC

Invasion of the Zombies 🎬 1961
Bare-fisted wrestler Santo faces of brace of zombies in order to prove that men with short necks can hug other men and still be mucho macho. 85m/B VHS. MX Santo; D: Benito Alazraki. SNC, HHT

Invasion U.S.A. 🎬½ 1952 Cheap Red Scare movie using tons of stock footage showing actual bombings and air battles. O'Herlihy is a stranger who visits a New York bar and convinces the patrons that the H-bomb has been unleashed on America, while Mohr romances Castle. Full of propaganda and overacting. Based on a story by Robert Smith and Franz Spencer. 73m/B VHS. Gerald Mohr, Peggy Castle, Dan O'Herlihy, Robert Bice, Tom Kennedy, Phyllis Coates; D: Alfred E. Green; W: Robert Smith. SNC

Invasion U.S.A. 🎬 1985 (R) A mercenary defends nothing less than the entire country against Russian terrorists landing in Florida and looking for condos. A record-setting amount of people killed. Count them—it's not like you'll miss anything important. Norris is a bit less animated than a wooden Indian, and the acting is more painful to endure than the violence. Glasnost saved the movie industry from additional paranoia movies of this kind. 108m/C VHS, Beta, LV. Chuck Norris, Richard Lynch, Melissa Prophet, Alex Colon, Billy Drago; D: Joseph Zito; W: James Bruner. MGM

Inventing the Abbotts 🎬🎬 1997 (R) Appealing cast populates this sleepy, bittersweet coming-of-age story set in small town Illinois in 1957. Alice (Going), Eleanor (Connelly) and Pamela (Tyler) are the lovely daughters of wealthy Lloyd Abbott (Patton) who's determined that they'll marry well despite the temptations offered by the two working-class Holt boys. Surly stud Jacey (Crudup) holds a grudge against Lloyd for possibly cheating his deceased father in a business deal and causing whispers about his schoolteacher mother Helen's (Baker) reputation, while sweet-natured younger brother Doug (Phoenix) has his romantic ideals fixed on Pamela, who loves him in return. Not memorable, but not a complete waste of time, either. Based on the story by Sue Miller. CW: Sexuality and language. 110m/ C VHS, Closed Caption. Billy Crudup, Joaquin Rafael (Leaf) Phoenix, Liv Tyler, Will Patton, Kathy Baker, Jennifer Connelly, Joanna Going, Barbara Williams; D: Pat O'Connor; W: Ken Hixon; C: Kenneth Macmillan; M: Michael Kamen. FXV

Investigation 🎬🎬½ 1979 A Frenchman plans to murder his wife so he can marry his pregnant mistress, guaranteeing an heir. Subtle study of small town people so concerned with their own welfare that the dirty deeds of the lead character might be overlooked. Fine performances and story development make this worth investigating. In French with English subtitles. 116m/C VHS, Beta. FR Victor Lanoux, Valerie Mairesse; D: Etienne Perier.

Invincible 🎬½ 1998 (R) Martial arts student must find and correct another student who has turned evil. For Bruce Lee fans, as if they haven't already memorized all the memorable lines—"hi-yaah," "ugh," "oof," etc. 93m/C VHS, Beta. Chen Sing, Ho Chung Dao. GEM

Invincible Barbarian woof! 1983 A young man leads a tribe of amazing Amazon warriors in a sneak attack against the tribe that annihilated his native village. One of those movies that presumes "primitivism" can be recreated through bad acting. 92m/C VHS, Beta. Diana Roy, David Jenkins.

The Invincible Gladiator 🎬½ Il Gladiatore Invincible 1963 A gladiator who saves the evil man ruling a land for a boy-king is given command of an army. He eventually leads the army in revolt when the evil man tries to take over the throne. Plodding with stock characters. 96m/C VHS. IT SP Richard Harrison, Isabel Corey, Livio Lorenzon; D: Frank Gregory. SNC

Invincible Gladiators woof! 1964 The sons of Hercules labor to aid a prince whose bride had been kidnapped by an evil queen. Laborious to watch. 87m/C VHS, Beta. Richard Lloyd, Claudia Lange, Tony Freeman; D: Robert Mauri. NO

Invincible Mr. Disraeli 🎬🎬½ 1963 Presentation from "George Schaefer's Showcase Theatre" deals with the life and career of Benjamin Disraeli, novelist, philosopher, first Earl of Beaconsfield, statesman, and Prime Minister. Basically a tribute. Made for television. 76m/C VHS, Beta. Trevor Howard, Greer Garson, Hurd Hatfield, Kate Reid; D: George Schaefer. FHS

The Invincible Six 🎬🎬 1968 An unlikely band of thieves running from the law winds up protecting a small village from marauding bandits. Plenty of action, as you would expect when thieves take on bandits, but with no scene-stealers or sympathetic characters the story lacks interest. Unremarkable choreography by ballet great Rudolf Nureyev. Filmed in Iran. 96m/C VHS, Beta. Stuart Whitman, Elke Sommer, Curt Jurgens, Jim Mitchum, Ian Ogilvy; D: Jean Negulesco. NO

Invisible Adversaries 🎬🎬 1977 A photographer uncovers an extra-terrestrial plot to cause excessive aggression in humans. She and her lover attempt to hold on to their crumbling humanity. Movies like this make you mad enough to tear something up. Enjoyed a meek cult following. In German with English subtitles. 112m/C VHS, Beta. GE Susanne Widl, Peter Weibel; D: Valie Export. FCT

Invisible Agent 🎬🎬 1942 Hall plays an agent using the secret formula to outwit the Nazis in this third sequel to "The Invisible Man." Especially enjoyable for the kids. Based on characters suggested in H.G. Wells' "The Invisible Man." 83m/B VHS, Closed Caption. Ilona Massey, Jon Hall, Peter Lorre, Cedric Hardwicke, J. Edward Bromberg, Albert Basserman, John Litel, Holmes Herbert; D: Edwin L. Marin; W: Curt Siodmak. USH, FCT

The Invisible Avenger 🎬🎬 Bourbon St. Shadows 1958 Based on the vintage radio character "The Shadow." A detective who can make himself invisible investigates the murder of a New Orleans jazz musician. The mysterious element successful on radio is lost on film, and only the Shadow knows why. 60m/B VHS, Beta. Richard Derr, Marc Daniels, Helen Westcott, Jeanne Neher; D: John Sledge, Ben Parker. SNC, SMW, RXM

The Invisible Boy 🎬🎬½ 1957 (G) Science fiction story about a young boy and his robot (Robby the Robot from "Forbidden Planet"). Kids will enjoy this adventure as told through the viewpoint of the child. Based on a story by Edmund Cooper. 89m/C VHS. Richard Eyer, Diane Brewster, Philip Abbott, Harold J. Stone; D: Herman Hoffman; W: Cyril Hume; M: Les Baxter. MGM, FCT

Invisible Dad 🎬🎬 1997 (PG) Doug Dully's dad invents a machine that makes him invisible and uses it to foil the evil designs of a co-worker. Unfortunately, the machine isn't perfect and Mr. Brialy tends to reappear at inopportune moments. But when Doug discovers his dad is in danger, he figures it's time to help out. 90m/C VHS, LV. Daran Noris, William Meyers, Mary Elizabeth McGlynn, Charles Dierkop, Karen Black; D: Fred Olen Ray. APX

The Invisible Dead 🎬 Orloff Against the Invisible Man 1970 So many invisible man movies, so little time. A scientist creates an invisible man, imprisons and tortures him. A bit miffed with his host, he who can't be seen escapes, and vents his invisible spleen. 90m/C VHS. IT Howard Vernon, Britt Carva; D: Jess (Jesus) Franco. NO

The Invisible Dr. Mabuse 🎬🎬🎬 The Invisible Horror; Die Unsichtbaren Krallen des Dr. Mabuse 1962 Possibly the best of the Dr. Mabuse series sees the mad scientist using an invisibility agent in an attempt to take over the world. Preiss also played the title villian in Fritz Lang's "The Thousand Eyes of Dr. Mabuse." 89m/B VHS, Beta. GE Lex Barker, Karin Dor, Siegfried Lowitz, Wolfgang Preiss, Rudolf Fernau; D: Harald Reinl. SNC

The Invisible Ghost 🎬½ 1941 A man carries out a series of grisly stranglings while under hypnosis by his insane wife. Typically bad low-budget exploiter about a fun-lovin' crazy couple bringing down property values in the neighborhood. 70m/B VHS, Beta. Bela Lugosi, Polly Ann Young, John McGuire, Clarence Muse, Betty Compson; D: Joseph H. Lewis; W: Helen Martin, Al Martin; C: Marcel Le Picard. VYY, MRV, SNC

Invisible Invaders 🎬 1959 Short, cheap, and silly aliens-try-to-take-over-the-earth flick. This time they're moonmen who use the bodies of dead earthlings (ugh) to attack the living until Agar can save the day. Carradine has a brief role as a formerly dead scientist. 67m/B VHS, Closed Caption. John Agar, Robert Hutton, Hal Torey, Jean Byron, Philip Tonge, John Carradine; D: Edward L. Cahn; W: Samuel Newman; C: Maury Gertsman. MGM

The Invisible Kid 🎬 1988 A shy teen manages to make himself invisible, a feat which ironically permits him to get people to notice him. Now he can visit places he's only dreamed of, including the girls' locker room. For those who have dreamed about girls' locker rooms. 95m/C VHS, Beta, LV. Karen Black, Jay Underwood, Chynna Phillips, Wally Ward, Brother Theodore; D: Avery Crounse; W: Avery Crounse. VTR

The Invisible Killer 🎬½ 1940 Someone is killing folks by sending poison through telephone lines. A detective and a reporter team up to find the scoundrel by setting up an answering machine that automatically plays back messages to the caller. Bad connection of events leads to a static resolution. 61m/B VHS, Beta. Grace Bradley, Roland Drew, William Newell; D: Sam Newfield. SNC, MLB

The Invisible Man 🎬🎬🎬🎬 1933 The vintage horror-fest based on H. G. Wells' novella about a scientist whose formula for invisibility slowly drives him insane. His mind definitely wandering, he plans plans to use his recipe to rule the world. Rains' first role; though his body doesn't appear until the final scene, his voice characterization is magnificent. The visual detail is excellent, setting standards that are imitated because they are difficult to surpass; with special effects by John P. Fulton. 71m/B VHS, Beta, LV. Claude Rains, Gloria Stuart, Dudley Digges, William Harrigan, Una O'Connor, E.E. Clive, Dwight Frye, Henry Travers, Holmes Herbert, John Carradine, Walter Brennan; D: James Whale; W: R.C. Sherriff; C: Arthur Edeson. USH, MLB

The Invisible Man Returns 🎬🎬🎬
1940 Price stars as the original invisible man's brother. Using the same invisibility formula, Price tries to clear himself after being charged with murder. He reappears at the worst times, and you gotta love that floating gun. Fun sequel to 1933's classic "The Invisible Man." 81m/B VHS. Cedric Hard-

wicke, Vincent Price, John Sutton, Nan Grey; **D:** Joe May; **W:** Lester Cole, Curt Siodmak; **C:** Milton Krasner. *USH, MLB*

The Invisible Maniac woof! 1990 (R) A crazy voyeur perfects a serum for invisibility and promptly gets a job as a physics teacher in a high school. There he leers at girls taking showers and slaughters students when he is caught. For voyeurs. Get outta here, you maniac. **87m/C VHS.** Noel Peters, Shannon Wilsey, Melissa Moore, Robert Ross, Rod Sweitzer, Eric Champnella, Kalei Shellabarger, Gail Lyon, Debra Lamb; **D:** Rif Adam Rifkin Coogan; **W:** Rif Adam Rifkin Coogan; **C:** James Bay; **M:** Marc David Decker. *REP*

The Invisible Man's Revenge ♫♫½ 1944 Left for dead on a safari five years before, Hall seeks revenge against Sondergaard and Matthews, aided by scientist Carradine who renders Hall invisible. Only problem is Hall doesn't stay that way. Fifth in Universal's "Invisible Man" film series. **78m/B VHS, Closed Caption.** Jon Hall, John Carradine, Gale Sondergaard, Lester Matthews, Evelyn Ankers, Alan Curtis, Leon Errol, Doris Lloyd; **D:** Ford Beebe; **W:** Bertram Millhauser; **C:** Milton Krasner. *USH*

Invisible Mom ♫♫½ 1996 (PG) Dad (Livingston) invents an invisibility potion that his 10-year-old son decides will make him popular at school. Too bad Mom (Wallace Stone) accidentally swallows the concoction instead. **82m/C VHS.** Dee Wallace Stone, Barry Livingston, Trenton Knight, Russ Tamblyn, Stella Stevens; **D:** Fred Olen Ray. *NHO*

The Invisible Monster *Slaves of the Invisible Monster* 1950 Special investigators Lane Carlson and Carol Richards battle a mad scientist ready to take over the world with his invisible army. Twelve episodes of the original serial edited onto two cassettes. **167m/B VHS.** Richard Webb, Aline Towne, Lane Bradford, Stanley Price, John Crawford, George Meeker; **D:** Fred Brannon. *REP*

The Invisible Ray ♫♫½ 1936 For a change, this horror film features Lugosi as the hero, fighting Karloff, a scientist who locates a meteor that contains a powerful substance. Karloff is poisoned and becomes a murdering megalomaniac. Watching Karloff and Lugosi interact, and the great special effects—including a hot scene where a scientist bursts into flames—helps you ignore a generally hokey script. **82m/B VHS, Beta, LV.** Boris Karloff, Bela Lugosi, Frances Drake, Frank Lawton, Beulah Bondi, Walter Kingsford; **D:** Lambert Hillyer; **W:** John Colton; **C:** George Robinson. *USH, MLB*

The Invisible Strangler ♫½ 1976 (PG) A death-row murderer can make himself invisible and rubs out witnesses who helped put him away; woman risks her life to expose him when the police fail to see the problem. Very violent collection of brutal scenes. Not released theatrically until 1984. **85m/C VHS, Beta.** Robert Foxworth, Stefanie Powers, Elke Sommer, Sue Lyon, Leslie Parrish, Marianna Hill; **D:** John Florea. *TWE*

The Invisible Terror ♫♫ 1963 A maniac steals a mad scientist's invisibility formula and uses it on a number of innocent victims. **?m/C VHS.** Herbert Stass, Ellen Scheirs. *SNC*

Invisible: The Chronicles of Benjamin Knight ♫♫½ 1993 (R) Scientist Benjamin Knight is rendered invisible during a terrible laboratory accident. His only hope of regaining his visible form is a desperate search by Knight and his fellow scientists for just the right chemical antidote. **CW:** Violence and strong sexuality. **80m/C VHS, Beta, Closed Caption.** Brian Cousins, Jennifer Nash, Michael DellaFemina, Curt Lowens, David Kaufman, Alan Oppenheimer, Aharon Ipale; **D:** Jack Ersgard; **W:** Earl Kenton. *PAR*

The Invisible Woman ♫♫♫ 1940 Above average comedy about zany professor Barrymore discovering the secret of invisibility and making luscious model Bruce transparent. Great cast makes this a very likeable movie. Based on a story by Curt Siodmak and Joe May, the same team that wrote "The Invisible Man Returns." **73m/B VHS, Closed Caption.** John Barrymore,

Virginia Bruce, John Howard, Charlie Ruggles, Oscar Homolka, Margaret Hamilton, Donald MacBride, Edward Brophy, Shemp Howard, Charles Lane, Thurston Hall; **D:** Edward Sutherland; **W:** Robert Lees, Frederic Rinaldo, Gertrude Purcell. *USH, FCT*

Invitation au Voyage ♫♫½ 1982 (R) Follows the journey of a twin who refuses to accept the death of his sister, a rock singer. The obsession is played fairly well, but it's a no-twin situation, even though the guy can't admit it. Perversity is played to the point of overkill. From the novel "Moi, Ma Soeur Images," by Jean Bany. In French with English subtitles. **90m/C VHS, Beta.** *FR* Laurent Malet, Nina Scott, Aurore Clement, Mario Adorf; **D:** Peter Del Monte. *COL*

Invitation to a Gunfighter ♫♫ 1964 Small town politics change when a paid assassin ambles into town and creates a lot of talk among the neighbors. Like a long joke in which the teller keeps forgetting the important details, the plot grows confusing though it's not complicated. Brynner is interesting as an educated, half-black/half-creole, hired gun. **92m/C VHS, Beta, Closed Caption.** Yul Brynner, George Segal, Strother Martin, William Hickey, Janice Rule, Mike Kellin, Pat Hingle; **D:** Richard Wilson. *MGM, HHE*

Invitation to Hell woof! 1984 Tormented maiden has a devil of a time discovering a secret power that can enable her to gracefully decline a satanic summoning. The cliched evil is tormenting. **100m/C VHS, Beta.** Becky Simpson, Joseph Sheahan, Colin Efford, Stephen Longhurst. *NO*

Invitation to Hell ♫½ 1984 "Faust" meets "All My Children" in celluloid suburbia. Never Emmied Lucci is the devil's dirty worker, persuading upwardly mobile suburbanites to join a really exclusive country club in exchange for a little downward mobility. Urich, a space scientist, and family are new in town, and soul searching Lucci's got her devil vixen sights set on space jock and brood. Bound to disappoint both fans of Craven's early independent work ("Last House on the Left") and his later high gloss ("Nightmare on Elm Street") formulas. Made for the small screen. **100m/C VHS, Beta.** Susan Lucci, Robert Urich, Joanna Cassidy, Kevin McCarthy, Patty McCormack, Joe Regalbuto, Soleil Moon Frye, Barret Oliver; **D:** Wes Craven. *COL, OM*

Invitation to the Dance ♫♫½ 1956 Three classic dance sequences, "Circus," "Ring Around the Rosy," and "Sinbad the Sailor." For dance lovers, featuring excellent performances by Kelly. **93m/C VHS, Beta.** Gene Kelly, Igor Youskevitch, Tamara Toumanova; **D:** Gene Kelly. Berlin International Film Festival '56: Golden Berlin Bear. *MGM, CCB*

Invitation to the Wedding ♫♫ 1973 (PG) When the best friend of a bridegroom falls in love with the bride, he stops at nothing to halt the wedding. Not exactly the Gielgud movie of the year, but there are some excellent scenes between him and Richardson. **89m/C VHS, Beta.** John Gielgud, Ralph Richardson, Paul Nicholas, Elizabeth Shepherd; **D:** Joseph Brooks; **M:** Joseph Brooks. *VES*

The Ipcress File ♫♫♫ 1965 The first of the Harry Palmer spy mysteries that made Caine a star. Based upon the bestseller by Len Deighton, it features the flabby, nearsighted spy investigating the kidnapping of notable British scientists. Solid scenes, including a scary brainwashing session, and tongue-firmly-in-British-cheek humor. Lots of camera play to emphasize Caine's myopia. Two sequels: "Funeral in Berlin" and "Billion Dollar Brain." **108m/C VHS, Beta.** *GB* Michael Caine, Nigel Green, Guy Doleman, Sue Lloyd; **D:** Sidney J. Furie; **M:** John Barry. British Academy Awards '65: Best Film. *USH*

Iphigenia ♫♫♫ 1977 Based on the classic Greek tragedy by Euripides, this story concerns the Greek leader Agamemnon, who plans to sacrifice his lovely daughter, Iphigenia, to please the gods. Mere mortals protest and start a save-the-babe movement, but Euripides' moral—you can't please 'em all—is devastatingly realized. Fine ad-

aptation that becomes visually extravagant at times, with an equally fine musical score. In Greek with English subtitles. **130m/C VHS, Beta.** *GR* Irene Papas, Costa Kazakos, Tatiana Papamoskou, Costas Carras, Christos Tsangas, Panos Michalopoulas; **D:** Michael Cacoyannis; **W:** Michael Cacoyannis; **C:** Yorgos Arvanitis; **M:** Mikis Theodorakis. Nominations: Academy Awards '77: Best Foreign Language Film. *COL, FHS*

I.Q. ♫♫½ 1994 (PG) Albert Einstein (the irascible Matthau) thinks his co-ed niece (Ryan) is in need of a little romance, so he engineers a plan to get her into the arms of Robbins, a local auto mechanic. Robbins and Ryan are comfortable in their comic roles, although they're both above the material. Matthau shines as the famous physicist. Plot gets a little farfetched with its central contrivance of making Robbins look like a brilliant scientist, which leaves second half of story flat. However, chemistry between leads is undeniable and you can't help but cheer on the inevitable. Visually pleasing with Ryan costumed in cool, elegant '50s fashions. Filmed in Princeton, New Jersey. **95m/C VHS, Beta, Closed Caption.** Tim Robbins, Meg Ryan, Walter Matthau, Lou Jacobi, Gene Saks, Joseph Maher, Stephen Fry, Tony Shalhoub, Frank Whaley; **D:** Fred Schepisi; **W:** Michael Leeson, Andy Breckman; **C:** Ian Baker; **M:** Jerry Goldsmith. *PAR*

Iran: Days of Crisis ♫♫½ 1991 An insightful made-for-cable-TV miniseries recounts America's humiliation at the hands of Iranian radicals in 1979, told from the vantage of a U.S. embassy official married to a Tehran woman. Former Carter administration aides Hamilton Jordan and Gerald Rafshoon devised the docudrama, which spares neither them nor their president in showing how bungled and shortsighted policies led to 52 Americans held hostage for over a year. **185m/C VHS.** Arliss Howard, Alice Krige, George Grizzard, Jeff Fahey, Tony Goldwyn, Ronald Guttman, Valerie Kaprisky, Daniel Gelin; **D:** Kevin Connor. *TTC*

Irezumi ♫♫♫ *Spirit of Tattoo* 1983 A Japanese woman has her body elaborately tattooed to please her lover. Things start off well enough. He's an inept lover, so she has directions tattooed, but then he discovers a "Dear John" letter on her foot just as she gives him the boot. Actually proves an interesting study in obsession and eroticism, with the tattoos drawing the lovers deeper and deeper until they get under each other's skin. In Japanese with English subtitles. **88m/C VHS, Beta, LV.** *JP NO*

Iris ♫♫ 1989 Drama follows the passionate and tragic life of New Zealand writer Iris Wilkinson, an international novelist, poet, and journalist. Wilkinson achieved a great deal of acclaim as a writer, but suffered many personal tragedies, and eventually took her own life at age 33. Well intentioned but clunky treatment of powerful subject matter. **90m/C VHS, Beta.** *NZ* Helen Morse. *WOM*

Irish Cinderella ♫♫ 1922 A silent version of the Cinderella legend set in Ireland, with thematic stress on Irish politics and patriotism. **72m/B VHS, Beta, 8mm.** Pattie MacNamara. *VYY*

Irish Luck ♫♫ 1939 A bellhop turns detective to figure out the mysterious happenings in his hotel. Becomes terminally cute by playing on a luck o' the Irish theme. **58m/B VHS.** Frankie Darro, Dick Purcell, Sheila Darcy, Grant Withers; **D:** Howard Bretherton. *NOS, DVT, HEG*

The Irishman ♫♫½ 1978 Set in 1920s Australia, the tale of a proud North Queensland family and their struggles to stay together. The Irish immigrant father is a teamster whose horse-drawn wagons are threatened by progress. His fight to preserve old ways is impressive, but gives way to sentimentality. **108m/C VHS, Beta.** *AU* Lou Brown, Michael Craig, Simon Burke, Robyn Nevin, Bryan Brown; **D:** Donald Crombie. *VES*

Irma La Douce ♫♫½ 1963 A gendarme pulls a one-man raid on a back-street Parisian joint and falls in love with one of the hookers he arrests. Lemmon is great as a well-meaning, incompetent boob, and MacLaine gives her all as the hapless hooker. A plodding pace, however, robs it of the original's zip, though it was a boxoffice smash. Broadway musical is lost without the music. 144m/C VHS, Beta, LV, Letterbox, Closed Caption. Jack Lemmon, Shirley MacLaine, Herschel Bernardi; D: Billy Wilder; W: Billy Wilder, I.A.L. Diamond; M: Andre Previn. Academy Awards '63: Best Adapted Score; Golden Globe Awards '64: Best Actress—Musical/Comedy (MacLaine); Nominations: Academy Awards '63: Best Actress (MacLaine), Best Color Cinematography. MGM, IME, FOX

Irma Vep 🐾🐾 1996 Satiric tweaking of French filmmaking begins with has-been director Rene Vidal (Leaud) hiring Hong Kong star Maggie Cheung to take the lead role of Irma Vep in a remake of the 1915 silent French classic "Les Vampires." But from the moment the actress arrives in Paris, it's one disaster after another. Cheung has trouble with the language barrier, Vidal is having a breakdown, lesbian costumer Zoe (Richard) is instantly smitten by Cheung and has her interest humiliatingly conveyed to everyone on the production. Then there's Jose Murano (Castel), a snobbish auteur who replaces Vidal and believes the Chinese actress can't play a French thief, not knowing that Cheung has become obsessed with her role and is practicing stealing from other hotel guests. English and French with subtitles. 96m/C VHS, Letterbox, DVD. FR Maggie Cheung, Jean-Pierre Leaud, Nathalie Richard, Bulle Ogier, Lou Castel, Antoine Basler, Nathalie Boutefeu, Arsinee Khanjian, Alex Descas; D: Olivier Assayas; W: Olivier Assayas; C: Eric Gautier. FXL, CVL

Iron & Silk 🐾🐾½ 1991 (PG) A young American searches for himself while he teaches English and learns martial arts in mainland China. Based on the true story of Salzman's travels. His studies of martial arts and Chinese culture provide a model for his students in their studies of American language and culture. Beautiful photography. Fine performances. 94m/C VHS, LV. Mark Saltzman, Pan Qingfu, Jeanette Lin Tsui, Vivian Wu; D: Shirley Sun; W: Mark Saltzman, Shirley Sun; M: Michael Gibbs. ART

Iron Angel 🐾½ 1964 During the Korean War a squadron sets out to silence North Korean guns. They do. Judging by their eternal bickering they must have put the enemy to sleep. 84m/B VHS. Jim Davis, Margo Woode, Donald (Don "Red") Barry, L.Q. Jones; D: Ken Kennedy; W: Ken Kennedy. NOS, LOO

Iron Cowboy 🐾🐾 1968 Actor finds romance with film editor while audience stifles yawns. Filmed on the set of "Blue," this pre-"Deliverance" Reynolds comedy never made it to the theaters. (Smithee is actually director Jud Taylor.) 86m/C VHS. Burt Reynolds, Barbara Loden, Terence Stamp, Noam Pitlik, Ricardo Montalban, Patricia Casey, Jane Hampton, Joseph Perry; D: Alan Smithee. ACE

The Iron Crown 🐾🐾 1941 A 13th-century legend inspired this sometime violent spectacle involving the title totem, a symbol of justice ignored by a powerful king at his peril. There's wonderful pagentry and a notable Tarzan imitator, but the pace is terribly slow. Italian dialogue with English subtitles. 100m/C VHS. D: Alessandro Blasetti. FST

Iron Dragon Strikes Back 🐾 1984 Man seeks out the men who murdered his martial arts instructor. 90m/C VHS, Beta. Bruce Li. TWE

The Iron Duke 🐾🐾½ 1934 Fair to middlin' historical account of the life of the Duke of Wellington, victor over Napoleon at Waterloo. 88m/B VHS, Beta. GB George Arliss, Gladys Cooper, A.E. Matthews, Emlyn Williams, Felix Aylmer; D: Victor Saville. NOS, WFV, BAR

Iron Eagle 🐾🐾½ 1986 (PG-13) A teenager teams with a renegade fighter pilot to rescue the youth's father from captivity in the Middle East. Predictable but often exciting. Followed by two sequels. 117m/C VHS, Beta, LV, Closed Caption. Louis Gossett Jr., Jason Gedrick, Tim Thomerson, David Suchet,

Larry B. Scott, Caroline Lagerfelt, Jerry Levine, Michael Bowen, Robbie Rist, Bobby Jacoby, Melora Hardin; D: Sidney J. Furie; W: Kevin Elders, Sidney J. Furie; M: Basil Poledouris. FOX

Iron Eagle 2 🐾🐾 1988 (PG) Lower-budget extended adventures of a maverick fighter pilot after he is reinstated in the Air Force. This time he links with an equally rebellious commie fighter and blasts away at nuke-happy Ivan. Yahoo fun for all overt Yankees! Followed by "Aces: Iron Eagle 3." Available in Spanish. 102m/C VHS, Beta, LV. CA IS Louis Gossett Jr., Mark Humphrey, Stuart Margolin, Alan Scarfe, Maury Chaykin, Sharon H. Brandon; D: Sidney J. Furie; W: Sidney J. Furie, Kevin Elders; C: Alan Dostie; M: Amin Bhatia. ART

Iron Eagle 4 🐾½ 1995 (PG-13) Series has gotten old and tired though Gossett, Jr. shows professionalism in his father figure role of retired Air Force General "Chappy" Sinclair. He's now running the Iron Eagle Flight School—a training center/holding cell for troubled teens—along with pilot Doug Masters (Cadieux). Masters and his would-be pilots discover suspicious activities at a local air base, leading to biological weapons and an Air Force conspiracy. CW: Military violence, brief strong language, some drug references. 95m/C VHS, LV. CA Louis Gossett Jr., Jason Cadieux, Al Waxman, Joanne Vannicola, Rachel Blanchard, Sean McCann, Ross Hill, Karen Gayle; D: Sidney J. Furie; W: Michael Stokes; C: Curtis Petersen; M: Paul Zaza. THV

Iron Horsemen 🐾 J.C 1971 (R) A motorcycle gang leader has a prophetic vision while tripping on LSD, and returns to his former town to challenge its religious establishment. 97m/C VHS, Beta. William F. McGaha, Hannibal Penny, Hannibal Penny, Burr de Benning, Slim Pickens, Pati Delaney; D: William F. McGaha. NLC

The Iron Major 🐾🐾½ 1943 Frank Cavanaugh, a famous football coach, becomes a hero in WWI. Standard flag-waving biography to increase morale back home, but fairly well-made. 85m/B VHS, Beta. Pat O'Brien, Ruth Warrick, Robert Ryan, Leon Ames, Russell Wade, Bruce Edwards; D: Ray Enright. TTC

The Iron Mask 🐾🐾½ 1929 Early swashbuckling extravaganza with a master swordsman defending the French king from a scheme involving substitution by a lookalike. Still fairly exciting, thanks largely to director Dwan's flair. Based on Alexandre Dumas' "Three Musketeers" and "The Man in the Iron Mask" with talking sequences. 87m/B VHS, Beta, LV. Douglas Fairbanks Sr., Nigel de Brulier, Marguerite de la Motte; D: Allan Dwan. Nominations: Academy Awards '29: Best Interior Decoration. KIV, CCB, DVT

Iron Maze 🐾½ 1991 (R) A fascinating notion forms the center of this dramatic scrapheap; the classic Japanese "Rashomon" plot shifted to a rusting Pennsylvania steel town. When a Tokyo businessman is found bludgeoned, witnesses and suspects (including his American-born wife) tell contradictory stories. It's too convoluted and contrived to work, with a hollow happy ending tacked on. Oliver Stone helped produce. CW: Language and sensuality. 102m/C VHS, LV. Jeff Fahey, Bridget Fonda, Hiroaki Murakami, J.T. Walsh, Gabriel Damon, John Randolph, Peter Allas; D: Hiroaki Yoshida; W: Tim Metcalfe.

Iron Thunder 🐾½ 1989 Liberty is in peril and only much kicking and pec flexing will make the world a kinder gentler place. A thundering bore. 85m/C VHS. Iron "Amp" Elmore, George M. Young, Julius Dorsey. XVC, HHE

The Iron Triangle 🐾🐾 1989 (R) A U.S. officer taken prisoner by the Viet Cong forms a bond with one of his captors. Film lends the viewer an opportunity to see things from the other sides perspective. 94m/C VHS, Beta, LV. Beau Bridges, Haing S. Ngor, Liem Whatley; D: Eric Weston; W: John Bushelman. ART

Iron Warrior 🐾 1987 (R) A barbarian hacks his way through a fantastical world to get to a beautiful princess. 82m/C VHS, Beta, Closed Caption. Miles O'Keeffe, Savina Gersak, Tim Lane; D: Al Bradley; W: Al Bradley. VTR

Iron Will 🐾🐾½ 1993 (PG) Okay Disney family movie based on a true story. Will Stoneman is a 17-year-old farm kid from South Dakota. It's 1917 and because of his father's death there's no money to send Will to college. So he decides to enter the 500 mile winner-take-all dog sled race, with its $10,000 prize. Lots of obstacles, several villains, but Will perseveres. 109m/C VHS, LV, Closed Caption. MacKenzie Astin, Kevin Spacey, David Ogden Stiers, August Schellenberg, George Gerdes, John Terry; D: Charles Haid; W: John Michael Hayes, Jeffrey Arch, Djordje Milicevic; M: Joel McNeely. DIS

Ironclads 🐾🐾½ 1990 Memorable dramatization of the five-hour naval battle between the Confederate's Merrimac and the Union's Monitor during the Civil War. The special effects are the only thing worth watching in this overlong tale that includes standard subplots of loyalty, lost loves, and death from war. 94m/C VHS, Closed Caption. Virginia Madsen, Alex Hyde-White, Reed Edward Diamond, E.G. Marshall, Fritz Weaver, Philip Casnoff; D: Delbert Mann. TTC

Ironheart 🐾½ 1992 Slimy Milverstead and his henchman meet lovely young women at dance clubs, drug them, and sell them into slavery. But the trouble really starts when they kill a cop and his former partner, John Keem (Lee), lashes out with his blazing martial arts skill to still the perpetrators. ?m/C VHS, LV, Closed Caption. Britton Lee, Bolo Yeung, Richard Norton, Karman Kruschke; D: Robert Clouse; W: Lawrence Riggins. IMP

Ironmaster 🐾 1983 When a primitive tribesman is exiled from his tribe, he discovers a mysteriously power-filled iron staff on a mountainside. 98m/C VHS, Beta. George Eastman, Pamela Field.

Ironweed 🐾🐾🐾 1987 (R) Grim and gritty drama about bums living the hard life in Depression-era Albany. Nicholson excels as a former ballplayer turned drunk bothered by visions of the past, and Streep is his equal in the lesser role of a tubercular boozer. Waits also shines. Another grim view from "Pixote" director Babenco. Kennedy scripted based on his Pulitzer Prize-winning tragedy. 135m/C VHS, Beta, LV, Closed Caption. Jack Nicholson, Meryl Streep, Tom Waits, Carroll Baker, Michael O'Keefe, Diane Venora, Margaret Whitton, Jake Dengel, Nathan Lane, James Gammon, Joe Grifasi, Bethel Leslie, Ted Levine, Frank Whaley; D: Hector Babenco; W: William Kennedy; M: John Morris. Los Angeles Film Critics Association Awards '87: Best Actor (Nicholson); New York Film Critics Awards '87: Best Actor (Nicholson); Nominations: Academy Awards '87: Best Actor (Nicholson), Best Actress (Streep). ART

Irreconcilable Differences 🐾🐾½ 1984 (PG) When her Beverly Hills parents spend more time working and fretting than giving hugs and love, a ten-year-old girl sues them for divorce on the grounds of "irreconcilable differences." The media has a field day when they hear that she would rather go live with the maid. Well cast, with well-developed characterizations. The script, by the creators of "Private Benjamin," is humanely comic rather than uproariously funny. 112m/C VHS, Beta, LV, Closed Caption. Ryan O'Neal, Shelley Long, Drew Barrymore, Sam Wanamaker, Allen (Goorwitz) Garfield, Sharon Stone, Luana Anders; D: Charles Shyer; W: Charles Shyer, Nancy Meyers. ART, VES

Irresistible Impulse 🐾🐾½ 1995 Sleazy real estate agent Jeffrey allows himself to become entangled in a wild scheme with bad girl Beaman. 107m/C VHS. Doug Jeffrey, Lee Anne Beavan; D: Jag Mundhra. YHV

Irving Berlin's America 1986 A documentary depicting Berlin's legacy of patriotic pop tunes, shown in a variety of film and performance clips, plus interviews with the stars who sang them. 83m/C Beta. Ginger Rogers, Mary Martin, Howard Keel, Kate Smith, Fred Astaire. CMR

Is Paris Burning? 🎞️🎞️🎞️ *Paris Brule-t-il?* 1966 A spectacularly star-studded but far too sprawling account of the liberation of Paris from Nazi occupation. The script, in which seven writers had a hand, is based on Larry Collins and Dominique Lapierre's best-seller. **173m/C VHS, Closed Caption.** *FR* Jean-Paul Belmondo, Charles Boyer, Leslie Caron, Jean-Pierre Cassel, George Chakiris, Claude Dauphin, Alain Delon, Kirk Douglas, Glenn Ford, Gert Frobe, Daniel Gelin, E.G. Marshall, Yves Montand, Anthony Perkins, Claude Rich, Simone Signoret, Robert Stack, Jean-Louis Trintignant, Pierre Vaneck, Orson Welles, Bruno Cremer, Suzy Delair, Michael Lonsdale; *D:* Rene Clement; *W:* Gore Vidal, Francis Ford Coppola; *M:* Maurice Jarre. Nominations: Academy Awards '66: Best Art Direction/Set Decoration (B & W), Best Black and White Cinematography. *PAR, FCT*

Is There Life Out There? 🎞️🎞️½ 1994 Wife, mother, and waitress Lily Marshall (McEntire) decides it's time to do something for herself—so she goes to work on her college degree. But there's unexpected family resentments, a breast cancer scare, and the interest of a young teaching assistant to turn her head away from her studies. Filmed in Nashville, Tennessee. Based on a song by McEntire; made for TV. **92m/C VHS.** Reba McEntire, Keith Carradine, Mitchell Anderson, Donald Moffat, Genia Michaela; *D:* David Jones; *W:* Dalene Young. *CAF*

Is There Sex After Death? 🎞️🎞️🎞️ 1971 (R) Often funny satire on the sexual revolution is constructed as a behind-the-scenes view of the porn film world. Odd cast includes Henry and Warhol superstar Woodlawn. Originally rated "X." **97m/C VHS, Beta.** Buck Henry, Alan Abel, Marshall Efron, Holly Woodlawn, Earl Doud; *D:* Alan Abel, Jeanne Abel. *FRF*

Is This Goodbye, Charlie Brown? 1983 Charlie Brown and the gang struggle to understand their loss when a friend moves away. **25m/C VHS.** *VTR*

Isadora 🎞️🎞️🎞️ *The Loves of Isadora* 1968 A loose, imaginative biography of Isadora Duncan, the cause celebre dancer in the 1920s who became famous for her scandalous performances, outrageous behavior, public love affairs, and bizarre, early death. Redgrave is exceptional in the lead, and Fox provides fine support. Restored from its original 131-minute print length by the director. **153m/C VHS, Beta.** Vanessa Redgrave, Jason Robards Jr., James Fox, Ivan Tchenko, John Fraser, Bessie Love; *D:* Karel Reisz; *W:* Melvin Bragg; *M:* Maurice Jarre. Cannes Film Festival '69: Best Actress (Redgrave); National Society of Film Critics Awards '69: Best Actress (Redgrave); Nominations: Academy Awards '68: Best Actress (Redgrave). *USH, HEG*

Ishtar 🎞️🎞️ 1987 (PG-13) Two astoundingly untalented performers have a gig in a fictional Middle Eastern country and become involved in foreign intrigue. A big-budget boxoffice bomb produced by Beatty offering few laughs, though it's not as bad as its reputation. Considering the talent involved, though, it's a disappointment, with Beatty and Hoffman laboring to create Hope and Crosby chemistry. Anyone for a slow night? **107m/C VHS, Beta, LV, Closed Caption.** Dustin Hoffman, Warren Beatty, Isabelle Adjani, Charles Grodin; *D:* Elaine May; *W:* Elaine May; *M:* Dave Grusin. Golden Raspberry Awards '87: Worst Director (May). *COL*

The Island 🎞️🎞️🎞️½ *Hadaka No Shima; Naked Island* 1961 Poetic examination of a peasant family's daily struggle for existence on a small island. No dialogue in this slow but absorbing work by one of Japan's master directors. **96m/B VHS, Beta, LV, 8mm.** *JP* Nobuko Otowa, Taiji Tonoyama, Shinji Tanaka, Masanori Horimoto; *D:* Kaneto Shindo. *IHF, VYY, HHT*

The Island woof! 1980 (R) New York reporter embarks on a Bermuda triangle investigation, only to meet with the murderous but sterile descendants of 17th century pirates on a deserted island. Caine is designated as stud service for the last remaining fertile woman. Almost surreal in its badness. Adapted by Benchley from his novel.

113m/C VHS, Beta, LV. Michael Caine, David Warner, Angela Punch McGregor, Frank Middlemass, Don Henderson; *D:* Michael Ritchie; *W:* Peter Benchley; *C:* Henri Decae; *M:* Ennio Morricone. *USH*

The Island at the Top of the World 🎞️🎞️½ 1974 (G) A rich Englishman, in search of his missing son, travels to the Arctic Circle in 1908. The rescue party includes an American archeologist, a French astronaut, and an Eskimo guide. Astonishingly, they discover an unknown, "lost" Viking kingdom. This Jules Verne-style adventure doesn't quite measure up, but kids will like it. **93m/C VHS, Beta, LV.** David Hartman, Donald Sinden, Jacques Marin, Mako, David Gwillim; *D:* Robert Stevenson; *M:* Maurice Jarre. Nominations: Academy Awards '74: Best Art Direction/Set Decoration. *DIS*

Island Claw woof! *Night of the Claw* 1980 A group of marine biologists experimenting on a tropical island discover the "Island Claw," who evolved as the result of toxic waste seeping into the ocean. A festering, oozing woofer. **91m/C VHS, Beta.** Barry Nelson, Robert Lansing; *D:* Hernan Cardenas. *ART, VES*

Island in the Sun 🎞️🎞️ 1957 Racial tension pulls apart the lives of the residents of a Caribbean island. Good cast, but a very poor adaptation of Alec Waugh's novel. Marvelous location shots. **119m/C VHS.** James Mason, Joan Fontaine, Dorothy Dandridge, John Williams, Harry Belafonte; *D:* Robert Rossen; *C:* Frederick A. (Freddie) Young; *M:* Malcolm Arnold. *FXL*

Island Monster 🎞️½ *Monster of the Island* 1953 Deals with ruthless, kidnapping drug-smugglers led by "monster" Karloff, and the efforts to bring them to justice. **87m/B VHS, Beta.** *IT* Boris Karloff, Renata Vicario, Franco Marzi; *D:* Robert Montero. *SNC, HHT, LSV*

Island of Blood 🎞️½ 1986 Buckets of blood abound on a remote island when a film crew's beset by berserk butcher. **84m/C VHS.** Jim Williams, Dean Richards. *MOV*

Island of Desire 🎞️ *Saturday Island* 1952 An Army nurse, a doctor, and a young Navy Adonis are trapped on a deserted island. Not surprisingly, a love triangle develops. **93m/C VHS, Beta.** *GB* Tab Hunter, Linda Darnell, Donald Gray; *D:* Stuart Heisler. *MLB*

The Island of Dr. Moreau 🎞️🎞️½ 1977 (PG) This remake of the "Island of the Lost Souls" (1933) is a bit disappointing but worth watching for Lancaster's solid performance as the scientist who has isolated himself on a Pacific island in order to continue his chromosome research—he can transform animals into near-humans and humans into animals. Neat-looking critters. Adaptation of the H.G. Wells novel of the same title. **99m/C VHS, Beta.** Burt Lancaster, Michael York, Nigel Davenport, Barbara Carrera, Richard Basehart, Nick Cravat; *D:* Don Taylor; *W:* John Herman Shaner, Al Ramrus; *C:* Gerry Fisher. *WAR, OM*

The Island of Dr. Moreau 🎞️½ 1996 (PG-13) What were they thinking? Not even the frightening "manimals" could prevent the unintentional laughs from this abomination of the horrifying 1896 H.G. Wells novel. Brando's enormous presence as the mad scientist Moreau walks a tight rope between puzzling and campy, especially as he explains his ghastly DNA experiments on a remote Pacific to a miscast Thewlis. A wasted Kilmer is the doctors's right-hand hybrid who often seems to be acting in a different movie. Filming hit some big rocks when "creative differences" caused original director Richard Stanley to be replaced and Rob Morrow (originally the lawyer) to ask for his release. Previously filmed under the same title in 1977 and (terrifically) as "Island of Lost Souls" in 1933. *CW:* Sci-fi violence, horror and gore involving mutant creatures. **91m/C VHS, LV, Closed Caption.** Marlon Brando, Val Kilmer, David Thewlis, Fairuza Balk, Marco Hofschneider, Temuera Morrison, Ron Perlman; *D:* John Frankenheimer; *W:* Richard Stanley, Ron Hutchinson; *C:* William A. Fraker. Nomina-

tions: Golden Raspberry Awards '96: Worst Picture, Worst Supporting Actor (Kilmer, Brando), Worst Director (Frankenheimer), Worst Screenplay. *NLC*

Island of Lost Girls woof! 1973 (R) Young women are taken to an unknown location in the Far East to be sold as part of a white slave ring. **85m/C VHS, Beta.** Brad Harris, Tony Kendall, Monica Pardo. *SNC*

Island of Lost Souls 🎞️🎞️🎞️½ 1932 Horrifying adaptation of H.G. Wells "The Island of Dr. Moreau" was initially banned in parts of the U.S. because of its disturbing contents. Laughton is a mad scientist on a remote island obsessed with making men out of jungle animals. When a shipwreck survivor gets stranded on the island, little does he know that Laughton wants to mate him with Lota, the Panther Woman, to produce the first human-animal child. As unsettling today as it was in the '30s. Burke beat out more than 60,000 young women in a nationwide search to play the Panther Woman, winning the role because of her "feline" look. Remade as "The Island of Dr. Moreau" in both 1977 and 1996. **71m/B VHS, Closed Caption.** Charles Laughton, Bela Lugosi, Richard Arlen, Leila Hyams, Kathleen Burke, Stanley Fields, Robert F. (Bob) Kortman, Arthur Hohl; *Cameos:* Alan Ladd, Randolph Scott, Buster Crabbe; *D:* Erle C. Kenton; *W:* Philip Wylie, Waldemar Young; *C:* Karl Struss. *USH, FCT, BTV*

The Island of Nevawuz 1980 A beautiful island is in trouble when J.B. Trumphorn decides to make lots of money by building factories and refineries on it. Will the Island of Nevawuz end up a polluted mess? **50m/C VHS, Beta.**

Island of Terror 🎞️🎞️🎞️ *Night of the Silicates; The Creepers* 1966 First-rate science fiction chiller about an island overrun by shell-like creatures that suck the bones out of their living prey. Good performances and interesting twists make for prickles up the spine. **90m/C VHS, Closed Caption.** *GB* Peter Cushing, Edward Judd, Carole Gray, Sam Kydd, Niall MacGinnis; *D:* Terence Fisher. *USH, SNC, MLB*

Island of the Blue Dolphins 🎞️🎞️½ 1964 Based on a popular children's book by Scott O'Dell, this is a true story of a young Native American girl who, with her brother, are stranded on a deserted island when their people accidentally leave them. When the boy is killed, the girl learns to survive by her skills and by befriending the leader of a pack of wild dogs. Good family fare. **99m/C VHS, Beta.** Celia Kaye, Larry Domasin, Ann Daniel, George Kennedy; *D:* James B. Clark. *USH*

Island of the Burning Doomed 🎞️🎞️½ *Island of the Burning Damned; Night of the Big Heat* 1967 A brutal heat wave accompanies invading aliens in this British-made outing. Lee and Cushing carry the picture. **94m/C VHS.** *GB* Christopher Lee, Peter Cushing, Patrick Allen, Sarah Lawson, Jane Merrow; *D:* Terence Fisher. *NO*

Island of the Lost 🎞️½ 1968 An anthropologist's family must fight for survival when they become shipwrecked on a mysterious island. **92m/C VHS.** Richard Greene, Luke Halpin; *D:* John Florea; *M:* George Bruns. *REP*

Island Trader 🎞️ 1971 Young lad battles pirates and a crooked tug captain who seek hidden gold that he knows about. **95m/C VHS, Beta.** John Ewart, Ruth Cracknell, Eric Oldfield; *D:* Harold Rubie. *NO*

The Islander 🎞️ 1988 Sixteen-year-old Inga comes of age among the commercial fishermen of Lake Michigan. **99m/C VHS, Beta.** Kit Wholihan, Jeff Weborg, Celia Klehr, Jacob Mills, Julie Johnson, Mary Ann McHugh, Michael Rock, Sheri Parish; *D:* Phyllis Berg-Pigorsch. *NO*

Islands 🎞️🎞️ 1987 A made-for-television drama about a middle-aged ex-hippie and a young rebellious punk who clash during a summer together on a secluded island. **55m/C VHS, Beta.** Louise Fletcher.

Islands in the Stream 🎬🎬½ 1977 (PG)
Based on Ernest Hemingway's novel, this film is actually two movies in one. An American painter/sculptor, Thomas Hudson, lives a reclusive life on the island of Bimini shortly before the outbreak of WWII. The first part is a sensitive story of a broken family and the coming of the artist's three sons to live with their father after a four-year separation. The second part is a second rate action-adventure. 105m/C VHS, Beta, LV, **Letterbox.** George C. Scott, David Hemmings, Claire Bloom, Susan Tyrrell, Gilbert Roland; **D:** Franklin J. Schaffner; **C:** Fred W. Koenekamp; **M:** Jerry Goldsmith. Nominations: Academy Awards '77: Best Cinematography. *PAR*

Isle of Forgotten Sins 🎬🎬 *Monsoon* 1943 Deep sea divers and an evil ship's captain vie for treasure. Good cast and direction but unremarkable material. 82m/B VHS, Beta, 8mm. John Carradine, Gale Sondergaard, Sidney Toler, Frank Fenton, Veda Ann Borg; **D:** Edgar G. Ulmer. *SNC, VYY*

Isle of Secret Passion 🎬 1985 A romance novel comes to video life as two lovers thrash out their problems on a Greek island. 90m/C VHS, Beta. Patch MacKenzie, Michael MacRae, Zohra Lampert.

Isle of the Dead 🎬🎬½ 1945 A Greek general is quarantined with seemingly all manner of social vermin on a plague-infested island in the early 1900s. The fear is that vampires walk among them. Characteristically spooky Val Lewton production with some original twists. 72m/B VHS, Beta, LV. Boris Karloff, Ellen Drew, Marc Cramer, Katherine Emery, Helen Thimig, Alan Napier, Jason Robards Sr.; **D:** Mark Robson; **W:** Josef Mischel, Ardel Wray; **C:** Jack MacKenzie. *TTC, FCT, IME*

Isn't Life Wonderful 🎬🎬🎬🎬 1924 Inga's (Dempster) a Polish war orphan who struggles to provide for her family in post-WWI Germany. It means giving up her dream to marry former soldier, Paul (Hamilton), but he has a secret plan to reunite them. Filmed on location. 118m/B VHS, Beta. Carol Dempster, Neil Hamilton, Lupino Lane, Hans von Schlettow; **D:** D.W. Griffith; **W:** D.W. Griffith. *KIV, GVV, GPV*

Istanbul 🎬🎬½ 1957 Adventurer Jim Brennan (Flynn) finds a fortune in smuggled diamonds, which he hides in a hotel room. Unfortunately, he's deported before he can retrieve the gems and it takes him five years to make it back to Istanbul. Then he's hounded by the original smugglers who want their gems back and discovers his lost love Stephanie (Borchers). Cole croons a couple of songs in his role as a lounge singer. Remake of 1947's "Singapore." 🎵When I Fall In Love; I Was a Little Too Lonely. 85m/C VHS, **Closed Caption.** Errol Flynn, Cornell Borchers, John Bentley, Torin Thatcher, Leif Erickson, Peggy Knudsen, Martin Benson, Nat King Cole, Werner Klemperer; **D:** Joseph Pevney; **W:** Seton I. Miller, Barbara Gray; **C:** William H. Daniels. *USH*

Istanbul 🎬 1985 (R) An American charms a Belgian student into taking part in a kidnap scheme. 90m/C VHS, Beta. FR Brad Dourif, Dominique Deruddere, Ingrid De Vos, Francois Beukelaers; **D:** Marc Didden. *NO*

Istanbul 🎬 *Istanbul, Keep Your Eyes Open* 1990 (PG-13) Believing he has stumbled upon the best story of his career, a journalist soon discovers that he has been pulled into a world of guns and violence. 88m/C VHS, Beta, LV. TU SW Robert Morley, Timothy Bottoms, Twiggy; **D:** Mats Arehn. *IME*

It 🎬🎬½ 1927 A department store clerk with plenty of sex appeal desires her rich boss. Established Bow as a prominent screen siren. Otherwise, it's not particularly interesting. Silent. Adapted by Elinor Glyn from her own story; Glyn also makes an appearance. 71m/B VHS, Beta, LV. Clara Bow, Gary Cooper, Antonio Moreno; **D:** Clarence Badger. *GPV, CRC, CCB*

It Came from Beneath the Sea 🎬🎬🎬 1955 A giant octopus arises from the depths of the sea to scour San Francisco for human food. Ray Harryhausen effects are special. 80m/B VHS, Beta, LV. Kenneth Tobey, Faith Domergue, Ian Keith, Donald Curtis; **D:** Robert Gordon. *GKK, MLB*

It Came from Hollywood 1982 (PG) A compilation of scenes from "B" horror and science fiction films of the 1950s, highlighting the funny side of these classic schlock movies. Some sequences in black and white. 87m/C VHS, Beta, LV. **D:** Malcolm Leo. *PAR*

It Came from Outer Space 🎬🎬🎬 1953 Aliens take on the form of local humans to repair their spacecraft in a small Arizona town. Good performances and outstanding direction add up to a fine science fiction film. Based on the story "The Meteor" by Ray Bradbury, who also wrote the script. Originally filmed in 3-D. 81m/B VHS, **Closed Caption.** Richard Carlson, Barbara Rush, Charles Drake, Russell Johnson; **D:** Jack Arnold; **W:** Ray Bradbury, Harry Essex; **M:** Herman Stein. *USH, MLB, GKK*

It Came from Outer Space 2 🎬½ 1995 (PG-13) Poorly updated cable version of the sci-fi film finds photographer Jack Putnam (Kerwin) heading home to his isolated desert community. A freakish blue lightning storm causes big changes amongst the desert dwellers who are sucked into a glowing ground mass and re-emerge possessed by shape-shifting aliens, who need the human bodies to rebuild their crashed space ship. Based on a story by Ray Bradbury and the 1953 screenplay by Harry Essex. **CW:** Sci-fi violence. 85m/C VHS, **Closed Caption.** Brian Kerwin, Elizabeth Pena, Bill McKinney, Jonathan Carrasco, Adrian Sparks, Howard Morris, Mickey Jones, Lauren Tewes; **D:** Roger Duchonwny; **W:** Jim Wheat, Ken Wheat; **M:** Shirley Walker. *USH*

It Came Upon a Midnight Clear 🎬½ 1984 A heavenly miracle enables a retired (and dead) New York policeman to keep a Christmas promise to his grandson. Made for television. 96m/C VHS, Beta, **Closed Caption.** Mickey Rooney, Scott Grimes, George Gaynes, Annie Potts, Lloyd Nolan, Barrie Youngfellow; **D:** Peter H. Hunt; **C:** Dean Cundey. *GKK*

It Conquered the World 🎬🎬½ 1956 Vegetable critters from Venus follow a probe satellite back to Earth and drop in on scientist Van Cleef, who'd been their intergalactic pen pal (seems he thought a Venusian invasion would improve the neighborhood). Their travelling companions, little bat creatures, turn earth dwellers into murderous zombies, and it starts to look like the Venusians are trying to make earth their planetary exurbia. Early vintage zero-budget Corman, for schlock connoisseurs. Remade for television as "Zontar, the Thing from Venus." 68m/B VHS. Peter Graves, Beverly Garland, Lee Van Cleef, Sally Fraser, Charles B. Griffith, Russ Bender, Jonathan Haze, Dick Miller, Karen Kadler, Paul Blaisdell; **D:** Roger Corman. *COL, FCT, MLB*

It Could Happen to You 🎬½ 1937 Stepbrothers raised by a gentle immigrant take different paths in life. When one ends up killing someone during a botched robbery, the other—a lawyer—defends him. Standard '30s morality play. 64m/B VHS. Alan Baxter, Andrea Leeds, Owen Davis Jr., Astrid Allwyn, Walter Kingsford, Al Shean; **D:** Phil Rosen. *NOS, BAR*

It Could Happen to You 🎬🎬 1939 A drunken advertising executive is charged with murder after a dead nightclub singer is found in his car. His wife sets out to clear him. 64m/C VHS, Beta. Stuart Erwin, Gloria Stuart, Raymond Walburn, Douglas Fowley, June Gale, Paul Hurst, Richard Lane; **D:** Alfred Werker. *NO*

It Could Happen to You 🎬🎬½ *Cop Tips Waitress $2 Million* 1994 (PG) NYC cop Charlie Lang (Cage) doesn't have any change to leave coffee shop waitress Yvonne (Fonda) a tip, so he promised to split his lottery ticket with her. When he nets four million dollars, he makes good on the promise, much to the chagrin of his upwardly mobile wife (Perez). Capra-corn for the X-crowd is pleasant dinnertime diversion as Cage and Perez shine as henpecked nice guy and the wife committed to making him miserable. Don't look for the diner on your next trip to NYC; it was specially built in TriBeCa and dismantled after the shoot. 101m/C VHS, LV, 8mm, **Closed Caption.** Bridget Fonda, Nicolas Cage, Rosie Perez, Red Buttons, Isaac Hayes, Seymour Cassel, Stanley Tucci, J.E. Freeman, Richard Jenkins, Ann Dowd, Wendell Pierce, Angela Pietropinto; **D:** Andrew Bergman; **W:** Andrew Bergman, Jane Anderson; **C:** Caleb Deschanel. *COL*

It Couldn't Happen Here 🎬 1988 (PG-13) Fans of the techno-pop duo The Pet Shop Boys can test their loyalty by enduring this feature music-video that actually played a few theatres. The dour pair journey across a surreal England, encountering a sinister blind priest, a philosophical ventriloquist's dummy, and more. Songs, sometimes presented only as muted incidental music, include the title track, "West End Girls," "It's a Sin," and "Always on My Mind." 87m/C VHS, LV. *GB* Neil Tennant, Chris Lowe, Joss Ackland, Neil Dickson, Carmen Du Sautoy, Gareth Hunt; **D:** Jack Bond. *COL, MVD*

It Happened at Nightmare Inn 🎬🎬 *A Candle for the Devil; Nightmare Hotel* 1970 Average thriller in which Geeson travels to Spanish inn and confronts two mad sisters who run the hotel. 95m/C VHS. *SP* Judy Geeson, Aurora Bautista, Esperanza Roy, Victor Alcocer, Lone Fleming; **D:** Eugenio Martin. *SNC*

It Happened at the World's Fair 🎬🎬½ 1963 Fun and light romance comedy has Elvis and a companion (O'Brien) being escorted through the Seattle World's Fair by a fetching Chinese girl. 🎵I'm Falling In Love Tonight; They Remind Me Too Much Of You; Take Me To The Fair; Relax; How Would You Like To Be; Beyond the Bend; One Broken Heart For Sale; Cotton Candy Land; A World Of Our Own. 105m/C VHS, Beta. Elvis Presley, Joan O'Brien, Gary Lockwood, Kurt Russell, Edith Atwater, Yvonne Craig; **D:** Norman Taurog. *MGM*

It Happened in Brooklyn 🎬🎬 1947 Former sailor with blue eyes bunks with janitor with big nose in Brooklyn. Sailor and cronies encounter many musical opportunities. Lots of songs and falling in love, little entertainment. 104m/B VHS. Frank Sinatra, Kathryn Grayson, Jimmy Durante, Peter Lawford, Gloria Grahame; **D:** Richard Whorf. *MGM, FCT*

It Happened in New Orleans 🎬½ *Rainbow on the River* 1936 A young boy is cared for by a former slave in post-Civil War New Orleans until his Yankee grandmother claims him and takes him to New York. The boy is resented by his family but manages to overcome their hostilities. 86m/B VHS, Beta. Bobby Breen, May Robson, Alan Mowbray, Benita Hume. *VYY*

It Happened in the Park 🎬🎬½ 1956 A rare film exercise for De Sica, wherein the patrons of the Villa Borghese parks are surveyed for a 24-hour period. In French with English dialogue. 72m/B VHS, Beta. FR **D:** Vittorio De Sica. *NOS, FCT*

It Happened One Night 🎬🎬🎬🎬 1934 Classic Capra comedy about an antagonistic couple determined to teach each other about life. Colbert is an unhappy heiress who runs away from her affluent home in search of contentment. On a bus she meets newspaper reporter Gable, who teaches her how "real" people live. She returns the favor in this first of the 1930s screwball comedies. The plot is a framework for an amusing examination of war between the sexes. Colbert and Gable are superb as affectionate foes. Remade as the musicals "Eve Knew Her Apples" and "You Can't Run Away From It." 105m/B VHS, Beta, LV, **Closed Caption.** Clark Gable, Claudette Colbert, Roscoe Karns, Walter Connolly, Alan Hale, Ward Bond; **D:** Frank Capra; **W:** Robert Riskin. Academy Awards '34: Best

Actor (Gable), Best Actress (Colbert), Best Adapted Screenplay, Best Director (Capra), Best Picture, National Film Registry '93. *COL, BTV, HMV*

It Happens Every Spring 🎬🎬🎬½ **1949** A chemistry professor, working on a bug repellant for trees, accidentally invents a potion that repels any kind of wood that it comes in contact with. Since he needs some big bucks to pop the question to his sweetie, the prof, who also loves baseball, gets a tryout as a pitcher with a major league team and uses the solution on the baseballs he pitches. Naturally, it's strikeout time and the prof becomes a pitching phenom. Now, if he can only keep his little secret. Wacky baseball footage is a highlight. **87m/B VHS.** Ray Milland, Jean Peters, Paul Douglas, Ed Begley Sr., Ted de Corsia, Ray Collins, Jessie Royce Landis, Alan Hale Jr., Gene Evans; *D:* Lloyd Bacon; *W:* Valentine Davies; *M:* Leigh Harline. Nominations: Academy Awards '49: Best Story. *FXV*

It Means That to Me 🎬 **1963** Espionage thriller in which Constantine plays a reporter who's hired by the government to transport top secret micro-film. **?m/C VHS.** *FR* Eddie Constantine, Jean-Louis Richard. *SNC*

It Rained All Night the Day I Left 🎬🎬 **1978 (R)** Two drifters find their fortunes change when they are hired by a wealthy widow. Interesting romance adventure. **100m/C VHS, Beta.** Louis Gossett Jr., Sally Kellerman, Tony Curtis; *D:* Nicolas Gessner. *NO*

It Should Happen to You 🎬🎬🎬 **1954** An aspiring model attempts to boost her career by promoting herself on a New York City billboard. The results, however, are continually surprising. Fine comedy teamwork from master thespians Holliday and Lemmon in this, the latter's first film. **87m/B VHS, Beta, LV.** Judy Holliday, Jack Lemmon, Peter Lawford; *D:* George Cukor; *W:* Ruth Gordon, Garson Kanin; *C:* Charles B(ryant) Lang. Nominations: Academy Awards '54: Best Costume Design (B & W). *GKK*

It Started in Naples 🎬🎬🎬 **1960** Good performances by both Gable and Loren in this comedy-drama about an American lawyer in Italy who, upon preparing his late brother's estate, finds that his brother's nephew is living with a stripper. A custody battle ensues, but love wins out in the end. Loren is incredible in nightclub scenes. **100m/C VHS, Closed Caption.** Clark Gable, Sophia Loren, Marietto, Vittorio De Sica, Paolo Carlini, Claudio Ermelli, Giovanni Filidoro; *D:* Melville Shavelson; *W:* Melville Shavelson, Jack Rose. Nominations: Academy Awards '60: Best Art Direction/Set Decoration (Color). *PAR*

It Started with a Kiss 🎬🎬½ **1959** Reynolds plays a showgirl who impulsively marries an Air Force sargeant (Ford). When he's transfered to Spain they try to make a go of their hasty marriage among numerous comic complications. Flimsy farce with likeable leads. **104m/C VHS.** Debbie Reynolds, Glenn Ford, Eva Gabor, Gustavo Rojo, Fred Clark, Edgar Buchanan, Robert Warwick, Harry (Henry) Morgan, Frances Bavier; *D:* George Marshall. *MGM, MOV*

It Started with Eve 🎬🎬🎬 **1941** Funny comedy about a grumpy old millionaire (Laughton) whose dying wish is to meet the young lady his son Johnny is to wed. Unfortunately, the bride-to-be is unavailable, so Johnny (Cummings) finds a replacement in hatcheck girl Durbin. Of course, Durbin steals the old man's heart and he miraculously makes a full-blown recovery, which means big trouble for Cummings. Remade in 1964 as "I'd Rather Be Rich." Based on the story "Almost An Angel" by Hans Kraly. ♫Clavelitos; Going Home. **92m/B VHS.** Deanna Durbin, Charles Laughton, Robert Cummings, Guy Kibbee, Margaret Tallichet, Catherine Doucet, Walter Catlett, Charles Coleman, Clara Blandick; *D:* Henry Koster; *W:* Norman Krasna, Leo Townsend. Nominations: Academy Awards '42: Scoring of a Musical. *USH*

It Takes a Thief 🎬🎬 *The Challenge* **1959** Tough cookie Jayne's a buxom gangstress who does the hokey pokey with her criminal minions. A former lover who's been released from the big house seems to think she's been minding the mint

for him. Au contraire. **93m/B VHS.** *GB* Jayne Mansfield, Anthony Quayle, Carl Mohner, Peter Reynolds, John Bennett; *D:* John Gilling.

It Takes Two 🎬🎬 **1988 (PG-13)** A young man spends his last ten days of bachelorhood cruising down Texas highways with a beautiful car saleswoman. Meanwhile, back at the altar, his bride waits patiently. Upbeat with some genuinely funny moments. From the director of "Pass the Ammo." **79m/C VHS, Beta, Closed Caption.** George Newbern, Leslie Hope, Kimberly Foster, Barry Corbin; *D:* David Beaird; *M:* Carter Burwell. *MGM*

It Takes Two 🎬 **1995 (PG)** Vapid sugary comedy finds the nine-year-old Olsen twins playing a duo from opposite sides of the tracks who change identities in an effort to get their respective adults (Guttenberg and Alley) together. See "The Parent Trap" instead. **100m/C VHS, LV, Closed Caption.** Ashley Olsen, Mary-Kate Olsen, Kirstie Alley, Steve Guttenberg, Philip Bosco, Jane Sibbett, Lawrence Dane, Gerard Parkes; *D:* Andy Tennant; *W:* Deborah Dean Davis; *C:* Kenneth Zunder; *M:* Sherman Foote, Ray Foote. *WAR*

It! The Terror from Beyond Space 🎬🎬½ *It! The Vampire From Beyond Space* **1958** The sole survivor of a Martian expedition is believed to have murdered his colleagues. He's arrested and brought back to Earth via space ship. En route, a vicious alien, the actual culprit, is discovered on board and begins killing the crew members. A fun science fiction thriller which, 20 years later, would provide Ridley Scott with the plot for "Alien." **68m/B VHS, Beta.** Marshall Thompson, Shawn Smith, Kim Spalding, Ann Doran, Dabbs Greer, Paul Langton, Ray Corrigan; *D:* Edward L. Cahn. *MGM, MLB*

It Was a Short Summer, Charlie Brown **1969** The Peanuts gang enjoys the summer until it's time to go back to school. **26m/C VHS.** *D:* Bill Melendez.

The Italian **1915** The story of an Italian immigrant family living in the slums of New York during the turn of the century. **78m/B VHS, Beta.** George Beban, Clara Williams, Leo Wills, J. Frank Burke, Fanny Midgley. National Film Registry '91. *GPV, GVV*

The Italian Job 🎬🎬½ **1969 (G)** Caine and Coward pair up to steal $4 million in gold by causing a major traffic jam in Turin, Italy. During the jam, the pair steals the gold from an armored car. Silliness and chases through the Swiss mountains ensue, culminating in a hilarious ending. **99m/C VHS, LV, Closed Caption.** *GB* Michael Caine, Noel Coward, Benny Hill, Raf Vallone, Tony Beckley, Rossano Brazzi, Margaret Blye; *D:* Peter Collinson; *M:* Quincy Jones. *PAR*

The Italian Stallion 🎬 **1973** Stallone plays a man with only one thing on his mind...sex! **90m/C VHS, Beta.** Sylvester Stallone, Henrietta Holm. *JEF*

Italian Straw Hat 🎬🎬🎬 *Un Chapeau de Paille d'Italie* **1927** Classic silent about the chain of errors that ensues when a man's horse eats a woman's hat. His vast, unending struggle to replace the hat is the source of continual comedy. From Eugene Labiche's play. **114m/B VHS, Beta.** *FR* Albert Prejean, Olga Tschekowa; *D:* Rene Clair. *VYY, INT, MRV*

Italianamerican/The Big Shave **19??** Two shorts by Scorsese. "Italianamerican" (1974) features dinner and conversation with his parents in their Little Italy (New York) apartment. In "The Big Shave," (1967) a young man nicks himself shaving and suddenly has a frightening religious experience. **54m/C VHS.** *D:* Martin Scorsese. *HMV*

It's a Bundyful Life **1992** The outrageous family from television's "Married with Children" does Christmas in their own inimitable fashion. This parody of "It's a Wonderful Life" features Kinison earning his wings as father Al's guardian angel. See what the family would have been like if Al had never been born...and what Al decides to do about it. Those seeking traditional family fare should look elsewhere. **47m/C VHS.** Ed O'Neill, Katey

Sagal, Christina Applegate, David Faustino, Sam Kinison, Amanda Bearse, Ted McGinley; *D:* Gerry Cohen. *COL*

It's a Date 🎬🎬 **1940** A mother and daughter, both actresses, continually get their professional and romantic lives intertwined. It begins when Durbin (the daughter) is offered Kay's (the mother) Broadway role. It continues in Hawaii where the man that Kay is in love with tries to court Durbin. As it's a comedy, of course, all is put right in the end. ♫Musetta's Waltz; Ave Maria; Loch Lomond; Love Is All; It Happened in Kaloha; Rhythm of the Islands; Hawaiian War Chant. **103m/B VHS.** Deanna Durbin, Kay Francis, Walter Pidgeon, Samuel S. Hinds, S.Z. Sakall, Henry Stephenson, Charles Lane, Leon Belasco; *D:* William A. Seiter; *W:* Norman Krasna; *C:* Joseph Valentine. *FOX, FCT, MLB*

It's a Dog's Life 🎬🎬½ *The Bar Sinister* **1955** The hero and narrator of this story is a wily bull terrier called Wildfire. Wildfire is a tough dog on the mean streets of the Bowery in turn-of-the-century New York. His master has him in dog fights in the local saloon but eventually abandons him. Wildfire is then taken in by the kindly employee of the rich and dog-hating Jagger but naturally manages to win the codger over. Based on the short story "The Bar Sinister" by Richard Harding Davis. **87m/C VHS.** Jeff Richards, Edmund Gwenn, Dean Jagger; *D:* Herman Hoffman; *W:* John Michael Hayes; *M:* Elmer Bernstein. *FCT*

It's a Gift 🎬🎬🎬½ **1934** A grocery clerk moves his family west to manage orange groves in this classic Fields comedy. Several inspired sequences. The supporting cast shines too. A real find for the discriminating comedy buff. Remake of the silent "It's the Old Army Game." **71m/B VHS, Beta, LV.** W.C. Fields, Baby LeRoy, Kathleen Howard; *D:* Norman Z. McLeod. *USH, BAR*

It's a Great Feeling 🎬🎬½ **1949** Another er Carson and Day team-up where Carson plays a camera-hogging show-off whom no one wants to direct. He's such an industry piranha that he ends up directing himself! He cons Day, a waitress and would-be actress, by promising her a part in his new film. Some executives hear her sing before she heads back home to Wisconsin, fed up with Hollywood. They make Carson track her down to star in the new picture, but when he arrives she is at the altar with her high school sweetheart. **85m/C VHS, LV.** Dennis (Stanley Morner) Morgan, Doris Day, Jack Carson, Bill Goodwin, Errol Flynn, Gary Cooper, Joan Crawford, Ronald Reagan, Sydney Greenstreet, Danny Kaye, Eleanor Parker, Edward G. Robinson, Jane Wyman; *D:* David Butler. Nominations: Academy Awards '49: Best Song ("It's a Great Feeling"). *FOX, FCT, MLB*

It's a Great Life 🎬🎬½ **1943** Blondie wants Dagwood to buy a house but instead he buys a horse. He's scheming to impress a client of Mr. Dither's by participating in a fox hunt. Blondie comes to the rescue. 13th entry in series. **75m/B VHS.** Penny Singleton, Arthur Lake, Larry Simms, Hugh Herbert, Jonathan Hale, Danny Mummert, Alan Dinehart, Irving Bacon, Douglas Leavitt, Marjorie Ann Mutchie; *D:* Frank Strayer; *W:* Karen De Wolf, Connie Lee. *MOV*

It's a Joke, Son! 🎬🎬 **1947** Follows the fictional politician, Senator Claghorn from the Fred Allen radio show, during his first run for the U.S. Senate. **67m/B VHS.** Kenny Delmar, Una Merkel; *D:* Ben Stoloff. *NOS, MRV, DVT*

It's a Mad, Mad, Mad, Mad World 🎬🎬 **1963** Overblown epic comedy with a cast of notables desperately seeking the whereabouts of stolen money. Ultimately exhausting film undone by its length and overbearing performances. Laserdisc contains 20 minutes of supplemental footage, including interviews with some of the surviving cast members. **155m/C VHS, Beta, LV, Letterbox.** Spencer Tracy, Sid Caesar, Milton Berle, Ethel Merman, Jonathan Winters, Jimmy Durante, Buddy Hackett, Mickey Rooney, Phil Silvers, Dick Shawn, Edie Adams, Dorothy Provine, Buster Keaton, Terry-Thomas, Moe Howard, Larry Fine, Joe DeRita, Jim Backus, William Demarest, Peter Falk, Leo Gorcey, Edward Everett Horton,

Joe E. Brown, Carl Reiner, ZaSu Pitts, Eddie Anderson, Jack Benny, Jerry Lewis; **D:** Stanley Kramer; **C:** Ernest Laszlo; **M:** Ernest Gold. Academy Awards '63: Best Sound Effects Editing; Nominations: Academy Awards '63: Best Color Cinematography, Best Film Editing, Best Song ("It's a Mad, Mad, Mad, Mad World"), Best Sound, Best Original Score. *MGM, FOX, FCT*

It's a Mystery, Charlie Brown 1987
Peanuts adventure in which Snoopy interrogates everyone on the disappearance of Woodstock's birdhouse. 30m/C VHS, Beta. **D:** Phil Roman. *BAR*

It's a Wonderful Life 🎞🎞🎞🎞 1946
American classic about a man saved from suicide by a considerate angel, who then shows the hero how important he's been to the lives of loved ones. Corny but inspirational and heartwarming, with an endearing performance by Travers as angel Clarence. Stewart and Reed are typically wholesome. Perfect film for people who want to feel good, joyfully teetering on the border between Hollywood schmaltz and genuine heartbreak. Also available colorized. The laserdisc version includes production and publicity stills, the theatrical trailer, and commentary by film professor Jeanine Basinger. Also available in a 160-minute Collector's Edition with original preview trailer, "The Making of 'It's a Wonderful Life,'" and a new digital transfer from the original negative. 125m/B VHS, LV, Closed Caption. James Stewart, Donna Reed, Henry Travers, Thomas Mitchell, Lionel Barrymore, Samuel S. Hinds, Frank Faylen, Gloria Grahame, H.B. Warner, Ellen Corby, Sheldon Leonard, Beulah Bondi, Ward Bond, Frank Albertson, Todd Karns, Mary Treen, Charles Halton; **D:** Frank Capra; **W:** Frances Goodrich, Albert Hackett, Jo Swerling; **M:** Dimitri Tiomkin. Golden Globe Awards '47: Best Director (Capra), National Film Registry '90;; Nominations: Academy Awards '46: Best Actor (Stewart), Best Director (Capra), Best Film Editing, Best Picture, Best Sound. *IGP, MRV, CNG*

It's Alive! 🎞 1968
Slow-moving dud about a farmer feeding passersby to the area's cave-dwelling lizard man. The ping pong ball-eyed monster puts in a belated appearance that's not worth the wait. 80m/C VHS. Tommy Kirk, Shirley Bonne, Bill Thurman; **D:** Larry Buchanan; **W:** Larry Buchanan. *NOS, LOO*

It's Alive 🎞🎞🎞 1974 (PG)
Cult film about a mutated baby, born to a normal Los Angeles couple, who escapes and goes on a bloodthirsty, murderous rampage. It's a sight to behold. Fantastic score by Bernard Herrmann makes this chilling film a memorable one. 91m/C VHS, Beta. John P. Ryan, Sharon Farrell, Andrew Duggan, Guy Stockwell, James Dixon, Michael Ansara; **D:** Larry Cohen; **W:** Larry Cohen; **C:** Fenton Hamilton; **M:** Bernard Herrmann. *WAR, FCT*

It's Alive 2: It Lives Again woof!
1978 (R) In this sequel to "It's Alive," the original hellspun baby meets up with two more of the same and all three terrorize the city, murdering everyone they can find. Truly horrendous. 91m/C VHS, Beta. Frederic Forrest, Kathleen Lloyd, John P. Ryan, Andrew Duggan, John Marley, Eddie Constantine; **D:** Larry Cohen; **W:** Larry Cohen; **C:** Fenton Hamilton. *WAR, FCT*

It's Alive 3: Island of the Alive 🎞
1987 (R) The second sequel to the tongue-in-cheek horror film, in which the infant mutant of the previous films has been left with other mutations to spawn on a desert island. 94m/C VHS, Beta. Michael Moriarty, Karen Black, Laurene Landon, Gerrit Graham, James Dixon, Neal Israel, MacDonald Carey; **D:** Larry Cohen; **W:** Larry Cohen; **C:** Daniel Pearl. *WAR*

It's All True 🎞🎞 1993 (G)
A look at auteur Welles' ill-fated WWII filmmaking project. Welles served as a special cultural ambassador to South America and, in 1942, began a documentary covering the area's complex political and social issues. Includes footage from "Four Men on a Raft," Welles' recreation about the peasant fishermen of Brazil; surviving excerpts from "The Story of Samba," a Technicolor musical about Carnaval in Rio de Janeiro; and footage from "My Friend Bonito," set against a backdrop of bullfighting in

Mexico. 85m/C VHS, LV. **D:** Richard Wilson, Bill Krohn, Myron Meise, Orson Welles; **W:** Richard Wilson, Bill Krohn, Myron Meise; **M:** Jorge Arriagada. *PAR*

It's Always Fair Weather 🎞🎞 1955
Three WWII buddies meet again at a 10-year reunion and find that they don't like each other very much. A surprisingly cynical film. Director Donen produced "Seven Brides for Seven Brothers" the previous year. ♫Stillman's Gym; March, March; Why Are We Here? (Blue Danube); Music Is Better Than Words; Once Upon A Time; The Time For Parting; I Like Myself; Baby You Knock Me Out; Thanks A Lot But No Thanks. 102m/C VHS, Beta, LV, Letterbox. Gene Kelly, Cyd Charisse, Dan Dailey, Michael Kidd; **D:** Stanley Donen; **W:** Betty Comden, Adolph Green; **M:** Betty Comden, Adolph Green, Andre Previn. Nominations: Academy Awards '55: Best Story & Screenplay, Scoring of a Musical. *MGM, FHE*

It's an Adventure, Charlie Brown!
1983 A collection of six vignettes featuring Charlie Brown and the whole Peanuts gang. 50m/C VHS, Beta. **D:** Bill Melendez. *VTR*

It's Arbor Day, Charlie Brown 1983
Tribulations aplenty for Charlie Brown as his baseball team turns his field into an Arbor Day garden. 26m/C VHS, Beta. *BAR*

It's Called Murder, Baby 🎞 1982 (R)
The famed porn star gives the viewer a lesson in English vocabulary in this tale of a blackmailed movie queen. 94m/C VHS, Beta. John Leslie, Cameron Mitchell, Lisa Trego; **D:** Sam Weston. *ART*

It's Flashbeagle, Charlie Brown/She's a Good Skate, Charlie Brown
1984 A Peanuts double header: In "It's Flashbeagle Charlie Brown," Snoopy infects the Peanuts gang with dance fever, and in "She's a Good Skate Charlie Brown," Snoopy trains Peppermint Patty to become a figure skating champion. 55m/C VHS, Beta. **D:** Bill Melendez.

It's Good to Be Alive 🎞🎞½ 1974
The true story of how Brooklyn Dodgers' catcher Roy Campanella learned to face life after an automobile accident left him a quadriplegic. Good performances in this television drama. 100m/C VHS, Beta. Paul Winfield, Ruby Dee, Louis Gossett Jr.; **D:** Michael Landon.

It's in the Bag 🎞🎞½ The Fifth Chair 1945
A shiftless flea circus owner sells chairs he has inherited, not knowing that a fortune is hidden in one of them. 87m/B VHS, LV. Fred Allen, Don Ameche, Jack Benny, William Bendix, Binnie Barnes, Robert Benchley; **D:** Richard Wallace. *REP*

It's Love Again 🎞🎞½ 1936
A streetwise chorus girl poses as a fictional socialite in a light music-hall comedy. ♫It's Love Again; Heaven In Your Arms. 83m/B VHS, Beta. *GB* Jessie Matthews, Robert Young, Sonnie Hale; **D:** Victor Saville. *NOS, DVT, HEG*

It's Magic, Charlie Brown/Charlie Brown's All Star 1981
In the first of these two stories, Snoopy, "The Great Houndini," makes Charlie Brown disappear. Problems begin when Snoopy finds it difficult conjuring his master back to reality. In the second story, Charlie Brown's baseball team has lost 999 games in a row, and prospects are bleak. New hope arrives when he gets an offer to have the team sponsored in a real league. 55m/C VHS, Beta. **D:** Phil Roman. *VTR*

It's My Party 🎞🎞½ 1995 (R)
When L.A. architect Nick Stark (Roberts) learns that he's developed untreatable brain lesions from AIDS that will essentially leave him helpless, he decides to throw himself a monumental farewell bash before taking a drug overdose. Friends and family all turn up as does, awkwardly enough, Brandon Theis (Harrison), Nick's former live-in who couldn't handle his HIV-positive diagnosis but would like a last reapproachment. Fine, sympathetic performances, espcially by the two leads, and yes, it's a weepie. Based on a true story. **CW:** Language and

brief nudity. 120m/C VHS, LV, Closed Caption. Eric Roberts, Gregory Harrison, Marlee Matlin, Lee Grant, George Segal, Bronson Pinchot, Bruce Davison, Devon Gummersall, Roddy McDowall, Margaret Cho, Paul Regina, Olivia Newton-John, Christopher Atkins, Dennis Christopher, Ron Glass, Eugene Glazer; **D:** Randal Kleiser; **W:** Randal Kleiser; **C:** Bernd Heinl; **M:** Basil Poledouris. *MGM*

It's My Turn 🎞🎞 1980 (R)
A mathematics professor (Clayburgh) struggles in her relationship with live-in lover (Grodin) who sells real-estate in Chicago. She meets retired baseball player (Douglas) and falls in love. "Ho-hum" just about describes the rest. 91m/C VHS, Beta, LV. Jill Clayburgh, Michael Douglas, Charles Grodin, Beverly Garland, Steven Hill, Dianne Wiest, Daniel Stern; **D:** Claudia Weill; **W:** Eleanor Bergstein; **C:** Bill Butler. *COL*

It's Not the Size That Counts woof!
Percy's Progress 1974 After the Earth's drinking water is contaminated, Lawson is the only man on Earth not to be struck by impotency. Limp sequel to "Percy," the British comedy about the first man to receive a penis transplant. Promising comedy doesn't deliver. 90m/C VHS. Leigh Lawson, Elke Sommer, Denholm Elliott, Vincent Price; **D:** Ralph Thomas.

It's Pat: The Movie woof! 1994 (PG-13)
This movie is so bad, let's pray it sounds the death knell to big-screen versions of "Saturday Night Live" sketch characters—who possessed little humor to begin with. For what it's worth, the androgynous Pat (Sweeney) falls for the equally gender-suspect Chris (Foley, from Canada's version of SNL, "Kids in the Hall") and all sorts of embarrassing situations arise. Pat's quest to find Pat's self is sketch material stretched see-through thin. **CW:** Bizarre gender-related humor. 78m/C VHS, Closed Caption. Julia Sweeney, Dave Foley, Charles Rocket, Kathy Griffin, Julie Haydon, Tim Meadows, Arleen Sorkin; **Cameos:** Sally Jesse Raphael, Kathy Najimy; **D:** Adam Bernstein; **W:** Julia Sweeney, Jim Emerson, Stephen Hibbert. Nominations: Golden Raspberry Awards '95: Worst Picture, Worst New Star (Sweeney). *TOU*

It's the Great Pumpkin, Charlie Brown 1988
It's Halloween, and Charlie Brown and his friends are going trick-or-treating, but Linus faithfully awaits the arrival of the Great Pumpkin. 25m/C VHS, Beta. *PAR, VTR*

It's the Old Army Game 1926
Classic Fields gags in three of his best Ziegfeld Follies sketches: "The Drug Store," "A Peaceful Morning," and "The Family Flivver." The beautiful Brooks serves as his comic foil. 75m/B VHS, Beta. W.C. Fields, Louise Brooks, Blanche Ring, William Gaxton; **D:** Edward Sutherland. *GPV*

It's Three Strikes, Charlie Brown 1986
Misfortunes abound in the baseball diamond for the Peanuts gang. 41m/C VHS, Beta. **D:** Bill Melendez, Phil Roman, Robert E. Balzer, Sam Nicholson. *BAR*

It's Your First Kiss, Charlie Brown/Someday You'll Find Her, Charlie Brown 1977
In "It's Your First Kiss, Charlie Brown," our hero has to escort the school's homecoming queen to the ball. What's worse, he actually has to kiss her in front of everyone! In "Someday You'll Find Her, Charlie Brown," Charlie Brown sees "the most beautiful girl in the world" on television and, after recruiting Linus, embarks upon a door-to-door search to find her. 55m/C VHS, Beta. **D:** Phil Roman. *VTR*

Ivan and Abraham 🎞🎞 1994
Abraham (Alexandrovitch) is a nine-year-old Jewish boy, living on a shetl in 1930s eastern Poland, with his best friend being the family's 14-year-old Christian apprentice Ivan (Iakovlev). The boys sense the increasing family tensions and escape into the nearby forest, only to find politics and prejudice sweeping over them all. In Yiddish, Russian, Polish, and Romany, with English subtitles. 105m/B VHS. Roma Aleksandrovitch, Sacha Iakovlev, Vladimir Machkov, Maria Lipkina, Rolan Bykov, Daniel Olbrychski; **D:** Yolande Zauberman; **W:** Yolande Zauberman; **C:** Jean-Marc Fabre. *NYF*

Ivan the Terrible, Part 1 🐾🐾🐾🐾

1944 Contemplative epic of Russia's first czar is a classic, innovative film from cinema genius Eisenstein. Visually stunning, with a fine performance by Cherkassov. Ivan's struggles to preserve his country is the main concern of the first half of Eisenstein's masterwork (which he originally planned as a trilogy). In Russian with English subtitles. **96m/B VHS, Beta, 8mm, Letterbox. RU** Nikolai Cherkassov, Ludmila Tselikovskaya, Serafina Birman, Piotr Kadochnikov; **D:** Sergei Eisenstein; **W:** Sergei Eisenstein; **M:** Sergei Prokofiev. NOS, MRV, WST

Ivan the Terrible, Part 2 🐾🐾🐾½

1946 Landed gentry conspire to dethrone the czar in this continuation of the innovative epic. More stunning imagery from master Eisenstein, who makes no false moves in this one. Slow going, but immensely rewarding. Russian dialogue with English subtitles; contains color sequences. **84m/B VHS, Beta, 8mm, Letterbox. RU** Nikolai Cherkassov, Ludmila Tselikovskaya, Serafina Birman, Piotr Kadochnikov; **D:** Sergei Eisenstein. NOS, MRV, WST

Ivanhoe 🐾🐾🐾

1952 Knights fight each other and woo maidens in this chivalrous romance derived from the Sir Walter Scott classic. Taylor is suitably noble, while Sanders is familiarly serpentine. Remade in 1982. **107m/C VHS, Beta.** Robert Taylor, Elizabeth Taylor, Joan Fontaine, George Sanders, Finlay Currie, Felix Aylmer; **D:** Richard Thorpe; **W:** Marguerite Roberts, Noel Langley; **C:** Frederick A. (Freddie) Young; **M:** Miklos Rozsa. Nominations: Academy Awards '52: Best Color Cinematography, Best Picture, Best Original Dramatic/Comedy Score. MGM

Ivanhoe 🐾🐾½

1982 A version of Sir Walter Scott's classic novel of chivalry and knighthood in 12th century England. Made for television. Remake of the 1953 film classic. **142m/C VHS, Beta.** Anthony Andrews, James Mason, Lysette Anthony, Sam Neill, Olivia Hussey, Michael Hordern, Julian Glover, George Innes, Ronald Pickup, John Rhys-Davies, Chloe Franks; **D:** Douglas Camfield. TVC, COL

Ivanhoe 🐾🐾🐾

1997 TV miniseries version of Sir Walter Scott's epic tale of knights, chivalry, romance, and daring. Saxon knight Wilfred of Ivanhoe (Waddington), having fought for Richard the Lionheart (Edwards) during the Crusades, returns to England to battle the scheming Prince John (Brown) and sinister Grand Master of the Templars, Lucas De Beaumanoir (Lee) in order to regain his honor. His childhood sweetheart, Saxon heiress Rowena (Smurfit), is betrothed to another but Ivanhoe's also drawn to Jewish healer Rebecca (Lynch) as is scheming Knight Templar, Sir Brian Bois-Guilbert (Hinds). Lots of action. On six cassettes. **300m/C VHS, Closed Caption. GB** Steven Waddington, Susan Lynch, Ciaran Hinds, Victoria Smurfit, Ralph Brown, Rory Edwards, Ronald Pickup, David Horovitch, Trevor Cooper, Valentine Pelka, Nick Brimble, Jimmy Chisholm, Christopher Lee, Aden Gillett, James Cosmo, Sian Phillips, Nick Brimble, Ciaran Madden; **D:** Stuart Orme; **W:** Deborah Cook; **C:** Clive Tickner; **M:** Colin Towns. AEH, VIF, PBS

I've Always Loved You 🐾🐾½

Concerto **1946** The drama of love and jealousy explored in an extravagant production filled with classical music. **117m/C VHS, LV.** Philip Dorn, Catherine McLeod; **D:** Frank Borzage; **C:** Gaetano Antonio "Tony" Gaudio. REP, FCT

I've Heard the Mermaids Singing 🐾🐾🐾

1987 Independent Canadian semi-satiric romantic comedy details the misadventures of a klutzy woman who suddenly obtains a desirable job in an art gallery run by a lesbian on whom she develops a crush. Good-natured tone helped considerably by McCarthy's winning performance. **81m/C VHS, Beta, LV. CA** Sheila McCarthy, Paule Baillargeon, Ann-Marie MacDonald, John Evans; **D:** Patricia Rozema; **M:** Mark Korven. Genie Awards '88: Best Actress (McCarthy), Best Supporting Actress (Baillargeon). NLC, FCT

The Ivory Handled Gun 🐾

1935 The Wolverine Kid wants Buck Ward (Jones) dead because the Kid's father, John Plunkett, was rejected by Buck's mother in favor of Buck's dad, Bill, who killed the interloper in a fight. Bill also happens to be in position of one of Plunkett's ivory-handed guns and the Kid wants that back as well. In chapter 2 of "Gordon of Ghost City," Gordon and Mary Gray are observed by a mysterious, threatening figure and Mary gets caught in a stampede. **81m/B VHS, Closed Caption.** Buck Jones, Charlotte Wynters, Walter Miller, Frank Rice, Carl Stockdale, Joseph Girard, Madge Bellamy; **D:** Ray Taylor. USH

Ivory Hunters 🐾🐾½

The Last Elephant **1990** Conservationists team up to thwart a massacre of elephants by poachers. Predictable made-for-cable entertainment co-produced by the National Audubon Society. **94m/C VHS, Beta, Closed Caption.** John Lithgow, Isabella Rossellini, James Earl Jones, Tony Todd, Olek Krupa; **D:** Joseph Sargent; **W:** Richard Guttman, Bill Bozzone; **M:** Charles Bernstein. TTC

Izzy & Moe 🐾🐾½

1985 Carney and The Great One are reunited for the last time on screen as former vaudevillians who become federal agents and create havoc amid speak-easies and bathtub gin during Prohibition. A made-for-television movie based on true stories. **92m/C VHS, Beta, LV.** Jackie Gleason, Art Carney, Cynthia Harris, Zohra Lampert, Drew Snyder, Dick Latessa; **D:** Jackie Cooper. THV

J. Edgar Hoover 🐾🐾

1987 Made-for-cable adaptation from "My 30 years in Hoover's FBI" by William G. Sullivan and William S. Brown. Biographical drama deals with Hoover's 55-five year career with the government. Included are his FBI days. **110m/C VHS, Beta, LV.** Treat Williams, Rip Torn, David Ogden Stiers, Andrew Duggan, Art Hindle, Louise Fletcher; **D:** Robert Collins. MCG

J-Men Forever! 🐾🐾🐾

1979 (PG) A spoof on early sci-fi/spy serials in which an alien takeover is attempted via rock-n-roll (your parents warned you). Employs an amusing technique of dubbing footage from dozens of Republic dramas intercut with new film featuring the "Firesign Theater" crew. **73m/B VHS, Beta.** Peter Bergman, Phil Proctor; **D:** Richard Patterson. VES

Jabberwalk 🐾🐾

1979 (R) A "Mondo Cane," American-style. A reckless and funny view of the bizarre in U.S. life. **110m/C VHS, Beta.** VCD

Jabberwocky 🐾🐾½

1977 (PG) Python-esque chaos prevails in the medieval cartoon kingdom of King Bruno the Questionable, who rules with cruelty, stupidity, lust and dust. Jabberwocky is the big dragon mowing everything down in its path until hero Palin decides to take it on. Uneven, but real funny at times. **104m/C VHS, Beta. GB** Michael Palin, Eric Idle, Max Wall, Deborah Fallender, Terry Jones, John Le Mesurier; **D:** Terry Gilliam; **W:** Terry Gilliam. COL

Jacare 🐾🐾

1942 First adventure thriller filmed in the Amazon jungle. **?m/C VHS.** Frank Buck; **M:** Miklos Rozsa. SNC, VYY

J'Accuse 🐾🐾🐾

I Accuse; That They May Live **1937** A Frenchman creates a device he believes will stop the war but it is confiscated by the government and used as part of the national defense. Subsequently, he goes mad. Gance (known for his 1927 "Napoleon"), remade his 1919 silent film, retelling the powerful anti-war message with great sensitivity. Banned in Nazi Germany. **125m/B VHS. FR** Victor Francen, Jean Max, Deltaire, Renee Devillers; **D:** Abel Gance. CVC, FCT, SNC

Jack 🐾🐾½

1996 (PG-13) Ten-year-old Jack Powell (Williams) suffers from a rare genetic disorder that causes him to age at four times the normal rate so he looks like a 40-year-old. His family, fearing ridicule, has kept him isolated but since Jack's so lonely, they finally agree to let him attend school. This new fourth grader isn't the only one with a lot to learn. **CW:** Some sexual references. **111m/C VHS, LV, Closed Caption.** Robin Williams, Bill Cosby, Diane Lane, Brian Kerwin, Fran Drescher, Michael McKean, Jennifer Lopez, Don Novello; **D:** Francis

Ford Coppola; **W:** James DeMonaco, Gary Nadeau; **C:** John Toll; **M:** Michael Kamen. TOU

Jack and His Friends 🐾🐾

1992 (R) Comic satire of the tribulations of Jack the shoe salesman (Garfield), who is shown the front door by his unfaithful wife. Beset by grief, he drives the streets aimlessly until he is kidnapped by a young couple (Rockwell and Reyes) on the run from the law, who force Jack to take them to his summer house where they all try to decide what to do with their lives. **93m/C VHS.** Allen (Goorwitz) Garfield, Sam Rockwell, Judy Reyes; **D:** Bruce Ornstein. FCT

Jack and Sarah 🐾🐾½

1995 (R) Widowed London lawyer (Grant) hires American waitress (Mathis), to help raise his infant daughter Sarah. Complications arise because Amy has no child rearing skills and Jack's parents and in-laws disapprove of the whole situation. Performances are nice (especially the scene-stealing infants), and there's some fine moments combining tragedy with romance, but the plot is a little thin and the whole film is slow moving (it takes more than half the movie to get the three protagonists in place). An edited version is rated PG. **CW:** Profanity. **110m/C VHS. GB** Richard E. Grant, Samantha Mathis, Ian McKellen, Judi Dench, Cherie Lunghi, Eileen Atkins, Imogen Stubbs; **D:** Tim Sullivan; **W:** Tim Sullivan; **C:** Jean-Yves Escoffier; **M:** Simon Boswell. PGV

Jack & the Beanstalk 🐾🐾

1952 While baby-sitting, Lou falls asleep and dreams he's Jack in this spoof of the classic fairy tale. **78m/C VHS, Beta, LV.** Bud Abbott, Lou Costello, Buddy Baer; **D:** Jean Yarbrough. NOS, VTR

Jack & the Beanstalk 🐾🐾

1976 An animated musical version of the familiar story of Jack, the young boy who climbs a magic beanstalk up into the clouds, where he meets a fearsome giant. **80m/C VHS, Beta. D:** Peter J. Solmo; **W:** Peter J. Solmo. COL

Jack & the Beanstalk

1983 From the "Faerie Tale Theatre" comes this classic tale of Jack, who sells his family's cow for five magic beans, climbs the huge beanstalk that sprouts from them, and encounters an unfriendly giant. **60m/C VHS, Beta, LV, Closed Caption.** Dennis Christopher, Katherine Helmond, Elliott Gould, Jean Stapleton, Mark Blankfield; **D:** Lamont Johnson. KUI, FOX, FCT

Jack Be Nimble 🐾🐾

1994 (R) Siblings Jack (Arquette) and Dora (Kennedy) were separated as children and adopted by different families. Jack's family turns out to be sadistic and he suffers much abuse, until he enacts a violent revenge; Dora begins to hear voices and soon realizes it's Jack crying out to her. The duo finally reunite but between Jack's rage and Dora's telepathic abilities, life takes on further bizarre twists. Much psychological terror rather than gore. **CW:** Disturbing violent behavior and abuse; some sexuality and language. **93m/C VHS. NZ** Alexis Arquette, Sarah Kennedy, Bruno Lawrence; **D:** Garth Maxwell; **W:** Garth Maxwell; **M:** Chris Neal. TRI

Jack Frost 🐾🐾½

1943 Moving biographical drama that follows a man from the sweat factories of London to his eventual rise to success. **89m/B VHS, Beta, 8mm.** Michael O'Shea, Susan Hayward. VYY

Jack Frost 🐾

1997 (R) Convicted serial killer Jack Frost (McDonald) mutates after accidental exposure to an experimental liquid DNA, becomes a killer snowman, and terrorizes a town preparing for the annual Snowman Festival. Snickering seasonal gore with a killer who uses icicles and a carrot nose to dispatch some of his latest victims. **CW:** Language, violence. **89m/C VHS.** Scott McDonald, Christopher Allport, F. William Parker; **D:** Michael Cooney; **W:** Michael Cooney. APX

Jack Higgins' On Dangerous Ground 🐾

On Dangerous Ground **1995 (R)** A major miscast ruins thriller writer Higgins' chances in this cable movie. Ex-IRA assassin and all-around terrorist Sean Dillon (Lowe) nows works for a British intelligence agency, headed by Brigadier Ferguson (Cranham). A secret agreement documenting a WWII deal between Lord Mountbatten and Mau Tse-tung has come to murky light and could exacerbate the tensions between China and Britain over Hong Kong. Dillon not only is expected to retrieve the document but also prevent an assassination attempt while the U.S. prez visits England. Lowe's way too lightweight for the Dillon role and manages to throw what should have been a good action yarn completely off-balance. **CW:** Violence. **105m/C VHS, Closed Caption.** *CA GB LU* Rob Lowe, Kenneth Cranham, Juergen Prochnow, Deborah Maria Moore, Ingeborga Dapkounaite, Daphne Cheung, Richard Rees, Claude Blanchard; **D:** Laurence Gordon-Clark; **W:** Christopher Wickens; **C:** Ken Westbury; **M:** Leon Aronson. *PAR*

The Jack Knife Man 🎬🎬🎬 **1920** Sentimental silent treatment of the relationship between a boy and a man. A new mother close to death hands over her bundle of joy to a kindly old river man, and the two bond in a familial way despite incessant adversity. Made the year following Vidor's debut as a feature film director. **70m/B VHS, Beta.** Fred Turner, Harry Todd, Bobby Kelso, Willis Marks, Lillian Leighton, James Corrigan; **D:** King Vidor; **W:** William Parker. *VYY, GPV, FCT*

Jack London 🎬½ *The Adventures of Jack London; The Life of Jack London* **1944** Dramatizes London's most creative years during his careers as oyster pirate, prospector, war correspondent and author. Based on "The Book of Jack London" by Charmian London. **94m/B VHS, Beta.** Michael O'Shea, Susan Hayward, Harry Davenport, Virginia Mayo, Frank Craven; **D:** Alfred Santell. Nominations: Academy Awards '44: Best Original Dramatic/Comedy Score. *NOS, MRV, DVT*

Jack London's The Call of the Wild 🎬🎬½ *The Call of the Wild: Dog of the Yukon* **1997 (PG)** Cable adaptation of Jack London's 1903 adventure story is told from the view of Buck, an intelligent St. Bernard-Labrador mix who's kidnapped from his California home. He's sold in the Yukon and eventually winds up with prospector John Thornton (Hauer) but Buck is increasingly drawn to running free. **90m/C VHS.** Rutger Hauer, Luc Morrissette, Bronwyn Booth; **D:** Peter Svatek; **W:** Graham Ludlow; **C:** Sylvain Brault; **M:** Alan Reeves. *HMK*

Jack-O 🎬½ **1995 (R)** Halloween nightmares in the small town of Oakmoor Crossing. When warlock Walter Machen (Carradine) was hung 100 years before, he invoked a demon creature to take his revenge. Now partyers, fooling around in the local cemetery, have stumbled onto horrific Jack-O's remains and manage to once again unleash the evil within. Cheesy grade-Z horror features old footage of deceased actors Carradine and Mitchell incorporated into what little plot there is. **CW:** Violence, nudity. **90m/C VHS, LV.** Linnea Quigley, Ryan Latshaw, Cameron Mitchell, John Carradine, Dawn Wildsmith, Brinke Stevens; **D:** Steve Latshaw. *TRI, IME*

Jack the Bear 🎬½ **1993 (PG-13)** Exercise in misery centers on a father and his two sons, trying to pick up the pieces after the death of wife and mother Marcovicci. Dad DeVito is the host of a late-night horror show who's cuddly as a bear—when he's not drinking. While the talent and circumstances might have been enough to create a sensitive study, the emotion is completely overwrought by contrived plot twists, including a kidnapping by the local Nazi. TV's "thirtysomething" director Herskovitz creates an effect not unlike a cement block being dropped on a card house. Point made, but so much for subtlety. Based on a novel by Dan McCall. **CW:** Thematic elements and some terror. **98m/C VHS, LV, Letterbox, Closed Caption.** Danny DeVito, Robert J. Steinmiller Jr., Miko Hughes, Gary Sinise, Art LaFleur, Andrea Marcovicci, Julia Louis-Dreyfus, Reese Witherspoon; **D:** Marshall Herskovitz; **W:** Steven Zaillian; **C:** Fred Murphy; **M:** James Horner. *FOX*

Jack the Giant Killer 🎬🎬🎬 **1962 (G)** A young farmer johns a medieval princess on a journey to a distant convent. Along the way, they combat an evil wizard, dragons, sea monsters, and other mystical creatures, and are assisted by leprechauns, a dog, and a chimp. Generally considered a blatant rip-off of "The Seventh Voyage of Sinbad," the film nonetheless delivers plenty of fun and excitement. Jim Danforth of "Gumby" fame provided the stop-motion animation. **95m/C VHS, Beta, LV.** Kerwin Mathews, Judi Meredith, Torin Thatcher, Walter Burke, Roger Mobley, Barry Kelley, Don Beddoe, Anna Lee, Robert Gist; **D:** Nathan (Hertz) Juran. *MGM, FCT*

Jack the Ripper 🎬🎬 **1960** An American detective joins Scotland Yard in tracking down the legendary and elusive Jack the Ripper. More gory than most. The last scene is in color. **88m/B VHS.** *GB* Lee Patterson, Betty McDowall, Barbara Burke, John Le Mesurier, George Rose; **D:** Monty Berman, Robert S. Baker; **M:** Stanley Black. *SNC, PAR*

Jack the Ripper 🎬🎬 *Der Dirnenmoerder von London* **1976 (R)** The inimitable Kinski assumes the role of the most heinous criminal of modern history—Jack the Ripper. **82m/C VHS, Beta.** *SI GE* Klaus Kinski, Josephine Chaplin, Herbert Fux, Ursula von Wiese, Lina Romay, Andreas Mannkopff; **D:** Jess (Jesus) Franco; **W:** Jess (Jesus) Franco; **C:** Peter Baumgartner. *VES*

Jack the Ripper 🎬🎬🎬 **1988** Another retelling of the life of the legendary serial killer. Caine is the Scotland Yard inspector who tracks down the murderer. Ending is based on recent evidence found by director/co-writer Wickes. Extremely well done made-for-television film. **200m/C VHS.** Michael Caine, Armand Assante, Ray McNally, Susan George, Jane Seymour, Lewis Collins, Ken Bones; **D:** David Wickes; **W:** David Wickes. *VES, ART*

The Jackal 🎬🎬½ **1997 (R)** The plot has more holes than Swiss cheese but thanks to a pro cast this film manages to be at least a workmanlike thriller. Willis stars as a killer-for-hire known only as "The Jackal." His latest employer, a Russian gangster, wants revenge for FBI interference in his business, and the Jackal's target is apparently the FBI's Director. Few know what the Jackal looks like and the most available is Declan Mulqueen (Gere), an IRA gunman imprisoned in the U.S. He's given a deal by good FBI guy Preston (Poitier) and the hunt is on. Unfortunately, the Jackal's elaborate preparations don't raise the tension, though they do provide some gross-out moments. The end game (in the D.C. subway) between the Jackal and Mulqueen provides a satisfying conclusion and Willis does excel as the ice-cold killer. Started off as a heavily reworked version of the 1973 assassination thriller "The Day of the Jackal" but most of the associations have been cut. **CW:** Strong violence and language. **124m/C VHS, Closed Caption, DVD.** Bruce Willis, Richard Gere, Sidney Poitier, Diane Venora, Mathilda May, Stephen Spinella, John Cunningham, J.K. Simmons, Tess Harper, Richard Lineback, Jack Black, David Hayman, Steve Bassett; **D:** Michael Caton-Jones; **W:** Chuck Pfarrer; **C:** Karl Walter Lindenlaub; **M:** Carter Burwell. *USH*

Jackie Brown 🎬🎬🎬 **1997 (R)** Tarantino finally climbs back into the director's chair with his leisurely but satisfying adaptation of Elmore Leonard's "Rum Punch." No, it's not "Pulp Fiction," but it could do for Pam Grier what "Pulp" did for John Travolta. Grier stars as out-of-luck-and-options stewardess Jackie Brown, who runs money to Mexico for ruthless arms dealer Ordell (Jackson). Busted on one of her errands, she comes up with an intricate plan to get out from under, hopefully with the money and without getting caught or killed. Slower and less bloody than Quentin fans are used to, but as usual, he gets killer performances from everybody. Cool dialogue and chronological shifts are again key ingredients, along with a hightened sense of character development. Fonda and De Niro make the most of small (but crucial) roles, but it's Forster (another '70s whatever-happened-to refugee) who provides the standout performance. The look and feel of the movie reflects the dingy world it inhabits, as well as Tarantino's love of '70s blaxploitation flicks. **CW:** Strong language, some violence, drug use and sexuality. **155m/C VHS.** Pam Grier, Robert Forster, Samuel L. Jackson, Robert De Niro, Bridget Fonda, Michael Keaton, Michael Bowen, Chris Tucker, Lisa Gay Hamilton, Tommy (Tiny) Lister, Hattie Winston, Aimee Graham; **D:** Quentin Tarantino; **W:** Quentin Tarantino; **C:** Guillermo Navarro. Nominations: Academy Awards '97: Best Supporting Actor (Forster); Golden Globe Awards '98: Best Actor—Musical/Comedy (Jackson), Best Actress—Musical/Comedy (Grier); MTV Movie Awards '98: Best Male Performance (Jackson); Screen Actors Guild Award '97: Best Actress (Grier). *TOU*

Jackie Chan's First Strike 🎬🎬🎬 *First Strike; Police Story 4* **1996 (PG-13)** Plot, schmot. The human hurricane that is Jackie Chan is once again amazing in this kung-fu comedy homage to 60s James Bond movies. Half Bruce Lee and half Charlie Chaplin, Chan reprises the role of the Hong Kong supercop named Jackie, who is this time loaned out by his superior officer "Uncle Bill" (Tung) to the CIA. He is sent to the Ukraine to spy on a beautiful young woman involved in smuggling nuclear weapons along with rogue CIA agent Tsui (Lou). He follows the villains to Australia, where he secures justice, peace and sharp blows to the head. Enough about the plot. Listen to this! He holds bad guys at bay by whirling an aluminum stepladder like it was a drum major's baton! He kicks somebody off of a second story ledge while on stilts! He sings and dances while wearing koala bear underwear! Dubbed in English. **CW:** Plentiful action/violence. **87m/C VHS, LV, Closed Caption.** *HK* Jackie Chan, Bill Tung, Jackson Lou, Chen Chun Wu, Jouri Petrov, Grishajeva Nonna; **D:** Stanley Tong; **W:** Stanley Tong, Nick Tramontane, Elliot Tong, Greg Mellott; **C:** Jingle Ma; **M:** J. Peter Robinson. Nominations: MTV Movie Awards '97: Best Fight (Jackie Chan/A ladder). *NLC*

The Jackie Robinson Story 🎬🎬🎬 **1950** Chronicles Robinson's rise from UCLA to his breakthrough as the first black man to play baseball in the major league. Robinson plays himself; the film deals honestly with the racial issues of the time. **76m/B VHS, Beta.** Jackie Robinson, Ruby Dee, Minor Watson, Louise Beavers, Richard Lane, Harry Shannon, Joel Fluellen, Ben Lessy; **D:** Alfred E. Green. *MGM, MRV, MOV*

Jacknife 🎬🎬🎬 **1989 (R)** The well-crafted story of a Vietnam veteran who visits his old war buddy and tries to piece together what's happened to their lives since their homecoming. During his visit he encounters anger and hostility from the other veteran, and tenderness from his friend's sister. A masterfully acted, small-scale drama, adapted by Stephen Metcalfe from his play. **102m/C VHS, Beta, LV, Closed Caption.** Robert De Niro, Kathy Baker, Ed Harris, Loudon Wainwright III, Charles S. Dutton; **D:** David Jones; **W:** Stephen Metcalfe; **M:** Bruce Broughton. *HBO, IME*

Jacko & Lise 🎬🎬 **1982 (R)** A French lad falls in love with a young girl, and abandons his previously decadent lifestyle to win her. Available with English subtitles or dubbed. **92m/C VHS, Beta.** *FR* Laurent Malet, Annie Girardot; **D:** Walter Bal.

The Jackpot 🎬🎬 **1950** An average Joe wins a bushel of money from a radio quiz show but can't pay the taxes. Maybe that was funny before the age of read-my-lips economics, but the all-star cast doesn't deliver on its promise. Lang, noted for mostly mediocre pictures, went on to direct "The King and I." **87m/C VHS.** James Stewart, Natalie Wood, Barbara Hale, James Gleason, Fred Clark, Patricia Medina; **D:** Walter Lang; **C:** Joseph LaShelle. *FXL*

Jack's Back 🎬🎬🎬 **1987 (R)** When a lunatic is killing Los Angeles prostitutes Jack-the-Ripper style, twin brothers get mistakenly involved (Spader in both roles). One of the brothers is accused of the murders and it is up to the other either to clear his name or to provide the final evidence of guilt. A well-thought out story with enough twists and turns for any suspense buff. **97m/C VHS, Beta, LV, Closed Caption.** James Spader, Cynthia Gibb, Rod Loomis, Rex Ryon, Robert Picardo, Jim Haynie, Chris Mulkey, Danitza Kingsley, Wendell Wright; **D:** Rowdy Herrington; **W:** Rowdy Herrington; **C:** Shelly Johnson. *PAR*

Jackson County Jail 🐾🐾½ 1976 (R)
While driving cross-country, a young woman is robbed, imprisoned, and raped by a deputy, whom she kills. Faced with a murder charge, she flees, with the law in hot pursuit. Also known by its later remade-for-television name, "Outside Chance," this is a minor cult film. **84m/C VHS, Beta.** Yvette Mimieux, Tommy Lee Jones, Robert Carradine, Severn Darden, Howard Hesseman, Mary Woronov; **D:** Michael Miller; **W:** Donald Stewart. *NHO*

The Jacksons: An American Dream 🐾🐾½ 1992
Made for television miniseries covering the career of the Jackson 5, the working-class family from Gary, Indiana which became a celebrated show business success. The series begins with the courtship of Joseph and Katherine Jackson and ends with the group's farewell tour in 1984, covering both family and career turmoils. Simplistic, glossy biography. **225m/C VHS.** Lawrence-Hilton Jacobs, Angela Bassett, Wylie Draper, Angel Vargas, Jacen Wilkerson, Terrence DaShon Howard, Jason Weaver, Jermaine Jackson II, Billy Dee Williams, Vanessa L(ynne) Williams, Holly Robinson, Margaret Avery; **D:** Karen Arthur. *PGV*

Jacob 🐾🐾½ 1994
Jacob (Modine), second son of Isaac (Ackland), tricks his father into giving him the blessing meant for eldest son Esau (Bean). Jacob is forced to run away to his Uncle Laban (Giannini), where he promptly falls in love with his cousin Rachel (Boyle). But Laban tricks Jacob into marrying eldest daughter Leah (Aubrey), before allowing his marriage to Rachel. Finally, Jacob settles on his own land with his wives and children (who will become the tribes of Israel). Dignified retelling of the Biblical story; filmed on location in Morocco. Made for cable TV. **120m/C VHS.** Matthew Modine, Lara Flynn Boyle, Sean Bean, Juliet Aubrey, Giancarlo Giannini, Joss Ackland, Irene Papas, Christoph Waltz; **D:** Peter Hall; **W:** Lionel Chetwynd; **M:** Marco Frisina. *TTC*

Jacob Have I Loved 1988
A teenage girl struggles to overcome her jealousy of her twin sister and find her own place in life as she comes of age on a Chesapeake island. Based on the book by Katherine Paterson. Part of the "Wonderworks" family movie series from PBS. **57m/C VHS.** Bridget Fonda, Jenny Robertson, John Kellogg; **D:** Victoria Hochberg. *HMV, WNE, MGH*

Jacob's Ladder 🐾🐾½ 1990 (R)
A man struggles with events he experienced while serving in Vietnam. Gradually, he becomes unable to separate reality from the strange, psychotic world into which he increasingly lapses. His friends and family try to help him before he's lost forever. Great story potential is flawed by too many flashbacks, leaving the viewer more confused than the characters. **116m/C VHS, Beta, LV, Closed Caption.** Tim Robbins, Elizabeth Pena, Danny Aiello, Matt Craven, Pruitt Taylor Vince, Jason Alexander, Patricia Kalember, Eriq La Salle, Ving Rhames, Macaulay Culkin; **D:** Adrian Lyne; **W:** Bruce Joel Rubin; **C:** Jeffrey L. Kimball; **M:** Maurice Jarre. *ART, FCT*

Jacqueline Bouvier Kennedy 🐾½ 1981
A made-for-television biography of the former First Lady, from her childhood to "Camelot," the glorious years with JFK in the White House. Smith bears a physical resemblance to Jackie, but this drama is far too glossy. **150m/C VHS, Beta.** Jaclyn Smith, James Franciscus, Rod Taylor, Donald Moffat, Dolph Sweet, Stephen Elliott; **D:** Steven Gethers; **M:** Billy Goldenberg. *THV*

Jacquot 🐾🐾 *Jacquot de Nantes* 1991 (PG)
Director Varda offers a loving tribute to her husband, filmmaker Jacques Demy. Based on the memoirs of her husband's childhood as a boy obsessed with movies, Varda re-stages scenes and also uses clips from various Demy films to illustrate her points. In French with English subtitles. **118m/C VHS.** *FR* Philippe Maron, Edouard Joubeaud, Laurent Monnier, Brigitte de Villepoix, Daniel Dublet; **D:** Agnes Varda; **W:** Agnes Varda; **C:** Patrick Blossier; **M:** Joanne Bruzdowicz. *COL*

Jade 🐾½ 1995 (R)
Sleazy whodunnit scraped from the bottom of the Eszterhas barrel (and it's a deep one) has hot-shot San Francisco Assistant D.A. David Corelli (Caruso) tracking a trail of pubic hairs across San Francisco. Seems he's caught up in the murder of a millionaire that points to his ex-lover, psychologist Katrina Gavin (Fiorentino), as the killer. Oh yeah, she's also a kinky call girl of choice to California's rich and famous, and happens to be married to Corelli's best friend (Palminteri). Psycho-thriller with little of either injects lots of lurid details (and a car chase scene that Friedkin has done much better elsewhere) in an attempt to curtail boredom; it doesn't work. Combine it with "Showgirls" for the No Self-Respect Film Festival, then go to confession. **CW:** Grisly afterviews of murder victims, violence, language, and strong scenes of aberrant sexuality. **94m/C VHS, Closed Caption.** David Caruso, Linda Fiorentino, Chazz Palminteri, Michael Biehn, Richard Crenna, Kenneth King, Angie Everhart; **D:** William Friedkin; **W:** Joe Eszterhas; **C:** Andrzej Bartkowiak; **M:** James Horner. *PAR*

The Jade Mask 🐾½ 1945
Chan discovers a murderer and his wife use puppets and masks to make it appear their victims are still alive. Another in the detective series with nothing noteworthy about it. Luke, the brother of actor Keye Luke, takes on the role of Chan's Number Four son. **66m/B VHS.** Sidney Toler, Mantan Moreland, Edwin Luke, Janet Warren, Hardie Albright, Edith Evanson; **D:** Phil Rosen. *MGM*

JAG 🐾🐾½ 1995
TV pilot episode features Navy pilot-turned-lawyer Lt. Harmon Rabb, Jr. (Elliott) assigned to investigate the case of a young female pilot who disappears from an aircraft carrier. Seems some of her fellow sailors resented having women on board so was it an accident or murder? JAG stands for the office of the Judge Advocate General, whose Navy lawyers serve as investigators, prosecutors, and defense attorneys. **94m/C VHS, Closed Caption.** David James Elliott, Andrea Parker, Terry O'Quinn, John Roselius, Katie Rich, Scott Jaeck, Patrick Labyorteaux, Cliff DeYoung, Kevin Dunn; **D:** Donald P. Bellisario; **W:** Donald P. Bellisario; **C:** Thomas Del Ruth; **M:** Bruce Broughton. *PAR*

The Jagged Edge 🐾🐾½ 1985 (R)
The beautiful wife of successful newspaper editor, Jack Forester, is killed and the police want to point the guilty finger at Jack. Attorney Teddy Barnes is brought in to defend him and accidentally falls in love. Taut murder mystery will keep you guessing "whodunit" until the very end. **108m/C VHS, Beta, LV, 8mm, Letterbox, Closed Caption.** Jeff Bridges, Glenn Close, Robert Loggia, Peter Coyote, John Dehner, Leigh Taylor-Young, Lance Henriksen, James Karen, Karen Austin, Michael Dorn, Guy Boyd, Marshall Colt, Louis Giambalvo; **D:** Richard Marquand; **W:** Joe Eszterhas; **M:** John Barry. Nominations: Academy Awards '85: Best Supporting Actor (Loggia). *COL*

Jaguar 1956
Three men leave their homes in Niger in order to find jobs in the cities. When they return to their village, they bring back with them their experiences. **93m/C VHS.** **D:** Jean Rouch; **M:** Van Alexander. *INT*

Jaguar Lives 🐾 1979 (PG)
A high-kicking secret agent tracks down bad boy drug kings around the world. **91m/C VHS, Beta.** Joe Lewis, Barbara Bach, Christopher Lee, Woody Strode, Donald Pleasence, Joseph Wiseman, John Huston, Capucine; **D:** Ernie Pintoff. *TWE*

Jail Bait 🐾½ *Hidden Face* 1954
Early Wood film about a group of small-time crooks who are always in trouble with the law; they blackmail a plastic surgeon into using his talents to help them ditch the cops. Not as "bad" as Wood's "Plan 9 From Outer Space," but still bad enough for camp fans to love (check the cheesy score leftover from an equally cheesy Mexican mad-scientist flick).

80m/B VHS, Beta. Timothy Farrell, Clancy Malone, Lyle Talbot, Steve Reeves, Herbert Rawlinson; **D:** Edward D. Wood Jr. *SNC, AOV, LSV*

Jailbait 🐾🐾 1993 (R)
A cop gets involved with an alleged murder witness, a teenaged runaway named Kyle. What they discover is an international crime syndicate that kidnaps runaways to exploit as sex slaves. Now they know too much. An unrated version is also available. **100m/C VHS, Closed Caption.** C. Thomas Howell, Renee Humphrey; **D:** Rafal Zielinksi; **W:** Robert Vincent O'Neil, Alien Castle. *PAR*

Jailbait: Betrayed By Innocence 🐾½ 1986 (R)
A man is on trial for statutory rape. Made-for-television. **90m/C VHS, Beta.** Barry Bostwick, Lee Purcell, Paul Sorvino, Cristen Kauffman, Isaac Hayes; **D:** Elliot Silverstein. *HHE*

Jailbird Rock 🐾½ 1988
We'd like to tell you that this isn't really a sweet-young-thing-in-prison musical, but it is. When Antin shoots her stepfather (he told her to turn that damn noise down?) she tries to bring down the Big House with song and dance. No kidding. **90m/C VHS, Beta.** Ronald Lacey, Rhonda Aldrich, Robin Antin; **D:** Phillip Schuman. *TWE*

Jailbird's Vacation 🐾🐾 *Les Grandes Gueules* 1965
Two ex-cons pose as lumberjacks in order to exact revenge on the bum that put them away. In French with English subtitles. **125m/C VHS, Beta.** *FR* Lino Ventura, Bourvil, Marie DuBois; **D:** Robert Enrico. *FCT, BAR*

Jailbreakin' 🐾 1972
A faded country singer and a rebellious youth team up to break out of jail. **90m/C VHS, Beta.** Erik Estrada. *GEM*

Jailhouse Rock 🐾🐾🐾 1957 (G)
While in jail for manslaughter, a teenager learns to play the guitar. After his release, he slowly develops into a top recording star. Probably the only film that captured the magnetic power of the young Elvis Presley; an absolute must for fans. Also available in a colorized version. ♫ Jailhouse Rock; Treat Me Nice; Baby, I Don't Care; Young and Beautiful; Don't Leave Me Now; I Wanna Be Free; One More Day. **96m/B VHS, Beta, LV, Letterbox.** Elvis Presley, Judy Tyler, Vaughn Taylor, Dean Jones, Mickey Shaughnessy, William Forrest, Glenn Strange; **D:** Richard Thorpe. *MGM*

Jakarta 🐾½ 1988 (R)
A love-hardened CIA operative is whisked away to Jakarta for reasons unknown, only to find his thought-to-be-dead lover still alive and caught in a deadly game of espionage. **94m/C VHS, Beta, LV.** Christopher Noth, Sue Francis Pai, Ronald Hunter; **D:** Charles Kaufman. *NO*

Jake Speed 🐾½ 1986 (PG)
Comic-book mercenary Jake and his loyal associate Remo rescue a beautiful girl from white slave traders. Supposedly a parody of the action adventure genre. **93m/C VHS, Beta, LV, Closed Caption.** Wayne Crawford, John Hurt, Karen Kopins, Dennis Christopher; **D:** Andrew Lane; **W:** Wayne Crawford. *VTR*

Jalsaghar 🐾🐾 *The Music Room* 1958
Bisambhar Roy is the last in his aristocratic line and has inherited nothing but debts. But his position in society demands a certain style and he pawns family heirlooms in order to host expensive private concerts, even after tragedy strikes his family. Bengali with subtitles. **100m/B VHS.** *IN* Chhabi Biswas; **D:** Satyajit Ray. *COL*

Jamaica Inn 🐾🐾 1939
In old Cornwall, an orphan girl becomes involved with smugglers. Remade in 1982; based on the story by Daphne Du Maurier. **98m/B VHS, Beta.** *GB* Charles Laughton, Maureen O'Hara, Leslie Banks, Robert Newton; **D:** Alfred Hitchcock; **C:** Harry Stradling. *KIV, NOS, CAB*

Jamaica Inn 🐾🐾 1982
A made-for-television mini-series based on the old Daphne Du Maurier adventure about highwaymen and moorlurking thieves in Cornwall. Remake of the 1939 Hitchcock film. **192m/C VHS, Beta.** Patrick McGoohan, Jane Seymour; **D:** Lawrence Gordon Clark. *VTR*

James and the Giant Peach 🐾🐾🐾 1996 (PG) Terrific combo of live action and stop-motion animation highlights this adaptation of Roald Dahl's 1961 children's book. Orphaned James is sent to live with his wicked aunts. When magic "crocodile tongues," given to James by a hobo, spill at the base of a peach tree, one fruit grows to such a tremendous size that James crawls inside, meets six insect friends, and goes on numerous adventures, all the while trying to face his fears. Dahl's books are colorful and since the people who brought you "Nightmare Before Christmas" are also doing "James," expect the visuals to be astonishing but too scary for the little ones. **80m/C VHS, Closed Caption.** Paul Terry, Pete Postlethwaite, Joanna Lumley, Miriam Margolyes; **D:** Henry Selick; **M:** Randy Newman; **V:** Richard Dreyfuss, Susan Sarandon, David Thewlis, Simon Callow, Jane Leeves. Nominations: Academy Awards '96: Best Original Score. TOU

James Dean 🐾🐾 The Legend 1976 Dean's friend Bast wrote this behind-the-scenes look at the short life of the enigmatic movie star. Made for television. **99m/C VHS, Beta.** Stephen McHattie, Michael Brandon, Candy Clark, Amy Irving, Brooke Adams, Dane Clark, Jayne Meadows, Meg Foster; **D:** William Bast, Robert Butler; **W:** William Bast; **M:** Billy Goldenberg.

James Dean Story 1957 An intimate portrait of James Dean presented by Robert Altman. The program includes never-before-seen out-takes from "East of Eden" and rare footage from the Hollywood premiere of "Giant" and the infamous Highway Public Safety message Dean made for television. **80m/B VHS, Beta, LV.** James Dean; **D:** George W. George. FCT, PMS, VEC

James Dean: The First American Teenager 1976 (PG) A look at the life and legend of the charismatic filmstar, with scenes from his films and comments from those who knew him best. **83m/C VHS, Beta.** James Dean, Elizabeth Taylor, Sammy Davis Jr., Rock Hudson, Sal Mineo, Natalie Wood, Julie Harris, Jack Larson, Nicholas Ray. NO

James Joyce: A Portrait of the Artist as a Young Man 1977 A moving, lyrical adaptation of the author's autobiography, told through the character of Stephen Dedalus. Joyce's characterizations, words, and scenes are beautifully translated to the medium of film. Excellent casting. **93m/C VHS.** John Gielgud, T.P. McKenna, Bosco Hogan. MFV

James Joyce's Women 🐾🐾🐾 1985 (R) Adapted from her one-woman stage show as well as produced by Flanagan, this acclaimed film features enacted portraits of three real-life Joyce associates, including his wife (Nora Barnacle) and three of his famous characters. **91m/C VHS, Beta.** Fionnula Flanagan, Timothy E. O'Grady, Chris O'Neill; **D:** Michael Pearce; **W:** Fionnula Flanagan. USH

Jamon, Jamon 🐾🐾 Ham Ham 1993 Comedic melodrama satirizing various aspects of the Spanish character, including machismo, sex, and food. A small Spanish town is dominated by two businesses—an underwear factory and a brothel—both run by strong-minded women. The brothel's Carmen and the factory's Conchita clash when Carmen's daughter, Silvia, becomes pregnant by Conchita's son, Manuel. Conchita's appalled and hires stud Raul to seduce Silvia—only to fall for him herself. Oh yes, Raul attributes his sexual prowess to a steady diet of ham and garlic. In Spanish with English subtitles. **95m/C VHS, LV.** SP Penelope Cruz, Anna Galiena, Javier Bardem, Stefania Sandrelli, Juan Diego, Jordi Molla; **D:** Bigas Luna; **W:** Bigas Luna, Cuca Canals; **M:** Nicola Piovani.

Jane & the Lost City 🐾🐾½ 1987 (PG) A British farce based on the age-old, barely dressed comic-strip character, Jane, as she stumbles on ancient cities, treasures, villains, and blond/blue-eyed heroes. Low-budget camp fun. **94m/C VHS.** GB Kristen Hughes, Maud Adams, Sam Jones; **D:** Terry Marcel; **W:** Mervyn Haisman; **M:** Harry Robertson. VTR

Jane Austen in Manhattan 🐾¼ 1980 Two acting-teachers vie to stage a long-lost play written by a youthful Jane Austen. Dreary, despite the cast. Hodiak is the real-life daughter of Baxter. **108m/C VHS, Beta.** Anne Baxter, Robert Powell, Michael Wager, Sean Young, Kurt Johnson, Katrina Hodiak; **D:** James Ivory; **W:** Ruth Prawer Jhabvala. NLC

Jane Austen's Mafia! 1998 (PG-13) Yet another Abrahams spoof, which, despite the title, is a takeoff on the "Godfather" saga. Vincenzo Cortino (Bridges) is the aging Don who must pass his power onto one of his sons—hotheaded Joey (Burke) or war hero Anthony (Mohr). Bridges' last film. Not yet reviewed. **CW:** Crude and sex-related humor, language, violence and drug content. **?m/C VHS.** Lloyd Bridges, Jay Mohr, Billy Burke, Olympia Dukakis, Christina Applegate, Pamela Gidley, Tony LoBianco, Joe Viterelli, Vinny Pastore; **D:** Jim Abrahams. NYR

Jane Doe 🐾🐾½ 1983 Valentine plays a young amnesia victim who is linked to a series of brutal slayings. Quite suspenseful for a television movie. **100m/C VHS, Beta.** Karen Valentine, William Devane, Eva Marie Saint, Stephen E. Miller, Jackson Davies; **D:** Ivan Nagy. ART

Jane Eyre 🐾🐾🐾 1934 Stiff, early version of Charlotte Bronte's classic gothic romance. English orphan grows up to become the governess of a mysterious manor. Notable as the first talkie version. Remade several times. **67m/B VHS.** Virginia Bruce, Colin Clive, Beryl Mercer, Jameson Thomas, Aileen Pringle, David Torrence; **D:** Christy Cabanne. SNC

Jane Eyre 🐾🐾🐾 1944 Excellent adaptation of the Charlotte Bronte novel about the plain governess with the noble heart and her love for the mysterious and tragic Mr. Rochester. Fontaine has the proper backbone and yearning in the title role but to accommodate Welles' emerging popularity the role of Rochester was enlarged. Excellent bleak romantic-Gothic look. Taylor, in her third film role, is seen briefly in the early orphanage scenes. **97m/B VHS.** Joan Fontaine, Orson Welles, Margaret O'Brien, Peggy Ann Garner, John Sutton, Sara Allgood, Henry Daniell, Agnes Moorehead, Aubrey Mather, Edith Barrett, Barbara Everest, Hillary Brooke, Elizabeth Taylor; **D:** Robert Stevenson; **W:** John Houseman, Aldous Huxley, Robert Stevenson; **C:** George Barnes; **M:** Bernard Herrmann. FCT, BTV

Jane Eyre 🐾🐾🐾 1983 Made-for-British-television mini-series based on the famed Charlotte Bronte novel about the maturation of a homeless English waif, her love for the tormented Rochester, and her quest for permanent peace. **239m/C VHS, Beta, LV, Closed Caption.** GB Timothy Dalton, Zelah Clarke; **D:** Julian Aymes. PBS, FOX, SIG

Jane Eyre 🐾🐾🐾 1996 (PG) Zeffirelli creates an eloquent yet spare interpretation of Charlotte Bronte's 1847 masterpiece, about a meek governess and her mysterious employer, in its fourth film incarnation. Everything about it, from the lighting to the score, is muted and somber. Still a beautiful film, it seems to lack a certain passion that earlier versions (especially the 1944 classic) brought to the screen. Strong performances all around, including Oscar-winner Paquin and French star Gainsbourg as the younger and older Jane, and Hurt as the tormented Rochester. **116m/C VHS, LV, Closed Caption.** William Hurt, Anna Paquin, Charlotte Gainsbourg, Joan Plowright, Elle Macpherson, Geraldine Chaplin, Fiona Shaw, John Wood, Amanda Root, Maria Schneider, Josephine Serre, Billie Whitelaw; **D:** Franco Zeffirelli; **W:** Franco Zeffirelli, Hugh Whitemore; **C:** David Watkin; **M:** Alessio Vlad, Claudio Capponi. TOU

Jane Eyre 🐾🐾½ 1997 Cable version of Charlotte Bronte's dark romance between meek-yet-strong-willed governess Jane (Morton) and her tormented-yet-dashing employer, Mr. Rochester (Hinds). This version dispenses quickly with many of the subplots to concentrate on the main duo. **108m/C VHS.** GB Samantha Morton, Ciaran Hinds, Gemma Jones, Abigail Cruttenden, Richard Hawley; **D:** Robert M. Young; **W:** Kay Mellor; **M:** Richard Harvey. AEH

Janis: A Film 🎵🎵½ 1974 (R) The famous biographical film about Janis Joplin, from her Texas origins to Woodstock and superstardom, featuring performances with Big Brother and the Holding Company and rare interviews. **79m/C VHS, Beta.** D: Howard Alk. MVD, USH, FCT

The January Man 🐾🐾 1989 (R) An unorthodox cop, previously exiled by a corrupt local government to the fire department, is brought back to the force in New York City to track down a serial killer. Written by the "Moonstruck" guy, Shanley, who apparently peaked with the earlier movie. **97m/C VHS, Beta, LV, Closed Caption.** Kevin Kline, Susan Sarandon, Mary Elizabeth Mastrantonio, Harvey Keitel, Rod Steiger, Alan Rickman, Danny Aiello; **D:** Pat O'Connor; **W:** John Patrick Shanley, Pat O'Connor; **M:** Marvin Hamlisch. MGM

Japanese Connection 🐾 1982 Warring crime chiefs fight furiously with deadly kung-fu action until end of movie. **96m/C VHS, Beta.** Li Chao, Yang Wei, Wu Ming-Tsai. GEM

The Jar 1984 A recluse discovers a disgusting creature in a jar. He keeps it, only to discover that it is out to kill him. **90m/C VHS, Beta.** Gary Wallace, Karen Sjoberg; **D:** Bruce Toscano; **W:** George Bradley. NO

Jason and the Argonauts 🐾🐾🐾 1963 (G) Jason, son of the King of Thessaly, sails on the Argo to the land of Colchis, where the Golden Fleece is guarded by a seven-headed hydra. Superb special effects and multitudes of mythological creatures; fun for the whole family. **104m/C VHS, Beta, LV, DVD.** GB Todd Armstrong, Nancy Kovack, Gary Raymond, Laurence Naismith, Nigel Green, Michael Gwynn, Honor Blackman; **D:** Don Chaffey; **W:** Jan Read, Beverley Cross. COL, MLB, FUS

Jason Goes to Hell: The Final Friday woof! 1993 (R) The supposed last, at least so far, in the "Friday the 13th" gore series. Only through the bodies—dead or alive—of his Vorhees kin can supernatural killer Jason be reborn, and only at their hands can he truly die. One can only hope that this is finally true. An unrated, even gorier, version is also available. **CW:** Language, strong violence and gore, and sexuality. **89m/C VHS, LV, Closed Caption.** Kane Hodder, John D. LeMay, Kari Keegan, Steven Williams, Steven Culp, Erin Gray, Richard Gant, Leslie Jordan, Billy Green Bush, Rusty Schwimmer, Allison Smith, Julie Michaels; **D:** Adam Marcus; **W:** Dean Lorey, Jay Huguely-Cass; **M:** Harry Manfredini. NLC, IME

Jason's Lyric 🐾🐾 1994 (R) A romantic triangle, sibling rivalry, family bonds, and neighborhood violence all set on the wrong side of the Houston tracks. Jason (Payne) is the responsible young man who works hard and helps out his mom; younger brother Joshua (Woodbine) has just gotten out of jail and is headed straight for more trouble. Between the two is Lyric (Pinkett), a soul-food waitress whose bad news half-brother Alonzo (Treach) is naturally one of Joshua's homies. Good-looking but ultimately empty storytelling. **CW:** Language; strong violence; drug use; sexuality. **119m/C VHS.** Allen Payne, Bokeem Woodbine, Jada Pinkett Smith, Suzanne Douglas, Forest Whitaker, Treach; **D:** Doug McHenry; **W:** Bobby Smith Jr.; **M:** Matt Noble. PGV

Java Head 🐾🐾🐾 1935 Young Chinese wife commits suicide so her husband can marry an English girl. Set in mid-1800s England. Based on the novel by Joseph Hergesheimer. **70m/B VHS, Beta, 8mm.** GB Anna May Wong, Elizabeth Allan, John Loder, Edmund Gwenn, Ralph Richardson, George Curzon; **D:** J. Walter Ruben. VYY

Jaws 🐾🐾🐾½ 1975 (PG) Early directorial effort by Spielberg from the Peter Benchley potboiler. A tight, very scary, and sometimes hilarious film about the struggle to kill a giant great white shark that is terrorizing an eastern beach community's waters. The characterizations by Dreyfuss, Scheider, and Shaw are much more endurable than the shock effects. Memorable score. Sequelled by "Jaws 2" in 1978, "Jaws 3" in 1983, and

"Jaws: The Revenge" in 1987. Look for Benchley as a TV reporter. **124m/C VHS, Beta, LV, Letterbox.** Roy Scheider, Robert Shaw, Richard Dreyfuss, Lorraine Gary, Murray Hamilton, Carl Gottlieb; *Cameos:* Peter Benchley; *D:* Steven Spielberg; *W:* Peter Benchley, Carl Gottlieb; *C:* Bill Butler; *M:* John Williams. Academy Awards '75: Best Film Editing, Best Sound, Best Original Score; Golden Globe Awards '76: Best Score; Nominations: Academy Awards '75: Best Picture. *USH*

Jaws 2 🎬🎬½ **1978 (PG)** Unsatisfactory sequel to "Jaws." It's been four years since the man-eating shark feasted on the resort town of Amity; suddenly a second shark stalks the waters and the terror returns. Scheider—who must by now wonder at his tendency to attract large aquatic carnivores with lunch on their minds— battles without his compatriots from the original. And we haven't seen the last of the mechanical dorsal fin yet; two more sequels follow. **116m/C VHS, Beta, LV, Letterbox.** Roy Scheider, Lorraine Gary, Murray Hamilton, Joseph Mascolo, Jeffrey Kramer, Collin Wilcox; *D:* Jeannot Szwarc; *W:* Carl Gottlieb, Howard Sackler; *C:* Michael C. Butler; *M:* John Williams. *USH*

Jaws 3 🎬🎬 *Jaws 3-D* **1983 (PG)** Same monster, new setting: in a Sea World-type amusement park, a great white shark escapes from its tank and proceeds to cause terror and chaos. Little connection to the previous "Jaws" sagas. Followed by one more sequel, "Jaws: The Revenge." **98m/C VHS, Beta, LV.** Dennis Quaid, Bess Armstrong, Louis Gossett Jr., Simon MacCorkindale, Lea Thompson, John Putch; *D:* Joe Alves; *W:* Richard Matheson, Carl Gottlieb; *C:* James A. Contner; *M:* John Williams. *USH*

Jaws of Death 🎬🎬 *Mako: The Jaws of Death* **1976** "Jaws"-like saga of shark terror. Jaeckel illogically strikes out to protect his "friends," the sharks. **91m/C VHS, Beta.** Richard Jaeckel, Harold Sakata, Jennifer Bishop, John Chandler, Buffy Dee; *D:* William Grefe. *NO*

Jaws of Justice 🎬½ **1933** A Canadian Mountie and his trusty German shepherd track down outlaws in the Canadian Northwest. **55m/B VHS, Beta, 8mm.** Richard Terry, Lafe McKee. *VYY*

Jaws of Satan woof! *King Cobra* **1981 (R)** Weaver is terrorized by a slimy snake who is, in actuality, the Devil. Not released for two years after it was filmed, and generally considered a bomb of the first caliber. Unfortunate work for usually worthwhile Weaver. **92m/C VHS.** Fritz Weaver, Gretchen Corbett, Jon Korkes, Norman Lloyd, Christina Applegate; *D:* Bob Claver; *C:* Dean Cundey. *NO*

Jaws: The Revenge 🎬 **1987 (PG-13)** The third sequel, in which Mrs. Brody is pursued the world over by a seemingly personally motivated Great White Shark. Includes footage not seen in the theatrical release. Each sequel in this series is progressively inferior to the original. **87m/C VHS, Beta, LV, Closed Caption.** Lorraine Gary, Lance Guest, Karen Young, Mario Van Peebles, Michael Caine, Judith Barsi, Lynn Whitfield; *D:* Joseph Sargent; *W:* Michael de-Guzman. *USH*

The Jayhawkers 🎬🎬 **1959** Chandler and Parker battle for power and women in pre-Civil War Kansas. **100m/C VHS, Closed Caption.** Jeff Chandler, Fess Parker, Nicole Maurey, Henry Silva, Herbert Rudley, Frank De Kova, Don Megowan, Leo Gordon; *D:* Melvin Frank. *PAR, FCT*

The Jayne Mansfield Story 🎬 *Jayne Mansfield: A Symbol of the '50s* **1980** Television movie recounting the blond bombshell's career from her first career exposure, through her marriage to a bodybuilder, to the famous car crash that beheaded her. **97m/C VHS, Beta.** Loni Anderson, Arnold Schwarzenegger, Raymond Buktenica, Kathleen Lloyd, G.D. Spradlin, Dave Shelley; *D:* Dick Lowry. *ART*

The Jazz Singer 🎬🎬½ **1927** A Jewish cantor's son breaks with his family to become a singer of popular music. Of historical importance as the first successful part-talkie; a very early Loy performance. With the classic line "You ain't heard nothing yet!" Remade several times.

🎵Toot, Toot, Tootsie Goodbye; Blue Skies; My Gal Sal; Waiting for the Robert E. Lee; Dirty Hands, Dirty Face; Mother, I Still Have You; Kol Nidre; Yahrzeit; My Mammy. **89m/B VHS, Beta, LV.** Al Jolson, May McAvoy, Warner Oland, William Demarest, Eugenie Besserer, Myrna Loy; *D:* Alan Crosland; *C:* Hal Mohr. National Film Registry '96;; Nominations: Academy Awards '28: Best Adapted Screenplay.*FOX, FCT, MLB*

The Jazz Singer woof! **1980 (PG)** Flat and uninteresting (if not unintentionally funny) remake of the 1927 classic about a Jewish boy who rebels against his father and family tradition to become a popular entertainer. Stick with the original, this is little more than a vehicle for Diamond to sing. 🎵America; You Baby Baby; Jerusalem; Love on the Rocks; Summer Love; On the Robert E. Lee; Louise; Songs of Life; Hello Again. **115m/C VHS, Beta, LV, 8mm.** Neil Diamond, Laurence Olivier, Lucie Arnaz, Catlin Adams, Franklin Ajaye; *D:* Richard Fleischer. Golden Raspberry Awards '80: Worst Actor (Diamond), Worst Supporting Actor (Olivier). *REP, PAR*

Jazzman 🎬🎬🎬 **1984** A comedy set in the late 1920s with a young musician forming a jazz band with two street musicians and a saxophonist who played in the czar's marching band. Their music is condemned as a product of bourgeois society but that doesn't stop them. In Russian with English subtitles. **80m/C VHS.** *RU* Igor Sklyar, Alexander Chorny; *D:* Karen Chakhnazarov. *KIV, FCT*

J.D.'s Revenge 🎬🎬½ **1976 (R)** Attorney in training Glynn Turman is possessed by the spirit of a gangster who was murdered on Bourbon Street in the early 1940s and grisly blaxploitation results. Ever so slightly better than others of the genre. Shot in New Orleans, with a soundtrack by a then-unknown Prince. **95m/C VHS.** Louis Gossett Jr., Glynn Turman; *D:* Arthur Marks; *M:* Prince. *ORI, FCT*

Je Tu Il Elle 🎬🎬½ *I You She He* **1974** A hyperactive young woman desperately seeking the answers to life gradually gains experience and maturity as she travels around France. The directorial debut of Ackerman. In French with English subtitles. **90m/B VHS.** *FR* Niels Arestrup, Claire Wauthion, Chantal Akerman; *D:* Chantal Akerman. *WAC, FCT, TPV*

Jealousy **1984** Three dramatic episodes dealing with jealousy. Made for TV. **95m/C VHS, Beta.** Angie Dickinson, Paul Michael Glaser, David Carradine, Bo Svenson; *D:* Jeffrey Bloom. *IMP*

Jean de Florette 🎬🎬🎬½ **1987 (PG)** The first of two films (with "Manon of the Spring") based on Marcel Pagnol's novel. A single spring in drought-ridden Provence, France is blocked by two scheming countrymen (Montand and Auteuil). They await the imminent failure of the farm nearby, inherited by a city-born hunchback, whose chances for survival fade without water for his crops. A devastating story with a heartrending performance by Depardieu as the hunchback. Lauded and awarded; in French with English subtitles. **122m/C VHS, Beta, LV.** *FR* Gerard Depardieu, Yves Montand, Daniel Auteuil, Elisabeth Depardieu, Ernestine Mazurowna; *D:* Claude Berri; *W:* Gerard Brach, Claude Berri. British Academy Awards '87: Best Adapted Screenplay, Best Film, Best Supporting Actor (Auteuil); Cesar Awards '87: Best Actor (Auteuil), Best Supporting Actress (Beart). *ORI, IME, FCT*

Jeeves & Wooster: Jeeves' Arrival **1991** Based on P.G. Wodehouse's spoofs of upper-crust British life in the 1920s. The bungling Bertie Wooster, a young man who just can't stay out of trouble, is taken in hand by the unflappable "gentleman's gentleman," Jeeves. Wonderful period detail and fine acting add up to a charming and funny hour. Additional episodes available. **60m/C VHS, Closed Caption.** *GB* Hugh Laurie, Stephen Fry. *MOV, TVC, PBS*

Jefferson in Paris 🎬🎬½ **1994 (PG-13)** Costume drama explores the impact Thomas Jefferson's (Nolte) five years in pre-revolutionary Paris (as American ambassador to Versailles) had on his private life. Jefferson confronts the personal and political issues of slavery in America, as well as his feelings for Sally Hemings (Newton), a Monticello slave brought to Paris by Jefferson's daughter. The Jefferson-Hemings legend may or may not be true (more likely not, according to many historians), but it seems to be the central theme here. Merchant Ivory's trademark tasteful production values and earnest characters can't camouflage the fact that they're playing fast and loose with the historical facts.*CW:* Contains mature theme, some images of violence, and a bawdy puppet show. **139m/C VHS, LV, Closed Caption.** Nick Nolte, Greta Scacchi, Gwyneth Paltrow, Thandie Newton, Jean-Pierre Aumont, Seth Gilliam, Todd Boyce, James Earl Jones; *D:* James Ivory; *W:* Ruth Prawer Jhabvala; *M:* Richard Robbins. *TOU*

Jeffrey 🎬🎬½ **1995 (R)** AIDS-fearing Jeffrey (Weber) decides to give celibacy a try until a trip to the gym brings Mr. Right into the picture. Steve (Weiss) is a hunk, but he happens to be HIV-positive, which prompts Jeffrey to do some serious soul-searching. Hence the message: AIDS sucks, but don't let it destroy life's joys. Musical fantasy numbers, phallic fireworks, and a game show are a bit crass and the high theatrics can get annoying, but wicked barbs and one-liners score lots of laughs. Scene-stealer Stewart is caustically funny as Jeffrey's flamboyantly effeminate best friend Sterling, who works as an interior decorator and dates a "Cats" chorus boy. Adapted from the Paul Rudnick play.*CW:* Strong sexuality and language. **92m/C VHS, LV, Closed Caption.** Steven Weber, Patrick Stewart, Michael T. Weiss, Bryan Batt, Sigourney Weaver, Olympia Dukakis, Kathy Najimy, Nathan Lane; *D:* Christopher Ashley; *W:* Paul Rudnick; *C:* Jeffery Tufano; *M:* Stephen Endelman. *ORI*

Jekyll and Hyde 🎬🎬½ **1990** Unmemorable remake of the Robert Louis Stevenson tale of a doctor whose scientific experiments lead to a horrifyingly violent split personality. Caine does have a good time with his dual role. Made for TV. **100m/C VHS.** Michael Caine, Cheryl Ladd, Joss Ackland, Ronald Pickup, Kim Thomson, Lionel Jeffries, Kevin McNally, Lee Montague, Diane Keen, David Schofield; *D:* David Wickes; *W:* David Wickes; *C:* Norman G. Langley. *THV*

Jekyll & Hyde...Together Again 🎬🎬 **1982 (R)** New Wave comic version of the classic story. This time, a serious young surgeon turns into a drug-crazed punk rocker after sniffing a mysterious powder. Mad scientist Blankfield fires and misfires, occasionally eliciting a snort. **87m/C VHS, Beta.** Mark Blankfield, Bess Armstrong, Krista Errickson, Tim Thomerson; *D:* Jerry Belson; *W:* Monica Johnson, Michael Leeson, Harvey Miller, Jerry Belson. *PAR*

Jennifer 🎬½ *Jennifer (The Snake Goddess)* **1978 (PG)** Elaboration of that old "Carrie" theme: a teenage girl outcast who likes snakes wreaks havoc on her catty classmates in this supernatural thriller. **90m/C VHS.** Lisa Pelikan, Bert Convy, Nina Foch, John Gavin, Wesley Eure, Jeff Corey; *W:* Kay Cousins Johnson, Steve Krantz. *ART, VES*

Jennifer 8 🎬🎬 **1992 (R)** Mix of familiar genres results in a film about a burned-out cop moving to the suburbs where he finds the eighth victim of a serial killer and falls in love with the chief witness. Garcia is John Berlin, the cop who discovers the hand of the blind female victim, which leads him to her school and Helena Robertson (Thurman), another blind woman who may have the information he needs. Dark and mysterious atmosphere is dramatic, but plot lacks logic and sense of thrill.*CW:* Language, nudity, and violence and terror. **127m/C VHS, Beta, LV, Letterbox, Closed Caption.** Andy Garcia, Uma Thurman, Lance Henriksen, Kathy Baker, Graham Beckel, Kevin Conway, John Malkovich; *D:* Bruce Robinson; *W:* Bruce Robinson. *PAR, BTV*

Jenny 🎬 **1970 (PG)** A loveless marriage of convenience between a draft-dodger and a film buff gets turned around as they fall in love despite themselves. **90m/C VHS.** Marlo Thomas, Alan Alda, Marian Hailey, Elizabeth Wilson, Vincent Gardenia, Charlotte Rae; *D:* George Bloomfield. *FOX*

Jenny Lamour 🎬🎬 *Quai des Orfevres* 1947 A dark mystery thriller about a singer accused of murdering a man he thought was stealing his woman. Acclaimed genre piece, dubbed into English. 95m/B VHS, Beta. *FR* Louis Jouvet, Suzy Delair, Bernard Blier, Simone Renant; *D:* Henri-Georges Clouzot. NOS, FCT

Jenny's War 🎬🎬½ 1985 (PG) An unbelievable WWII adventure story of an American teacher (Cannon) who outwits the Gestapo and infiltrates a Nazi POW camp in search of her missing soldier son. Actually based on a true story. From the book by Jack Stoneley. Made for television. 192m/C VHS. Dyan Cannon, Elke Sommer, Robert Hardy, Nigel Hawthorne, Christopher Cazenove, Patrick Ryecart, Hartmut Becker; *D:* Steven Gethers; *W:* Steven Gethers. COL

Jeremiah Johnson 🎬🎬🎬 1972 (PG) The story of a man who turns his back on civilization, circa 1850, and learns a new code of survival in a brutal land of isolated mountains and hostile Indians. In the process, he becomes part of the mountains and their wildlife. A notable and picturesque film. 107m/C VHS, Beta, LV. Robert Redford, Will Geer; *D:* Sydney Pollack; *W:* Edward Anhalt, John Milius. WAR, FCT

Jericho 🎬🎬 *Dark Sands* 1938 Jericho Jackson (Robeson) is a corporal in the black unit of the U.S.'s Expeditionary Forces in WWI France. After a fight which his sergeant leads to the man's accidental death, Jackson is court-martialed and sentenced to die. He manages to escape to North Africa and begin a new life but military authorities eventually discover his whereabouts. Despite the military drama, Robeson's vocal talents are still showcased. ♪My Way; Golden River; Silent Night; Deep Desert; Shortnin' Bread. 77m/B VHS. GB Paul Robeson, Henry Wilcoxon, Wallace Ford; *D:* Thornton Freeland. KIV, HHT, DVT

Jericho Fever 🎬🎬½ 1993 (PG-13) A group of terrorists assassinate Palestinian and Israeli negotiators engaged in peace talks in Mexico. Infected with a deadly disease they escape to the U.S., tracked by Israeli Mossad agents, a border patrolman, and two investigators from the Centers for Disease Control who want to stop the spread of the plague. 88m/C VHS, Beta, Closed Caption. Stephanie Zimbalist, Perry King, Branscombe Richmond, Alan Scarfe, Elyssa Davalos, Ari Barak; *D:* Sandor Stern; *W:* I.C. Rapoport; *M:* Cameron Allan. PAR

The Jericho Mile 🎬🎬 1979 A made-for-television drama about a track-obsessed convicted murderer who is given a chance at the Olympics. 97m/C VHS, Beta. Peter Strauss, Roger E. Mosley, Brian Dennehy; *D:* Michael Mann. NLC

The Jerk 🎬🎬½ 1979 (R) A jerk tells his rags-to-riches-to-rags story in comedic flashbacks, from "I was born a poor Black child," through his entrepreneurial success with his invention of the "Optigrab," to his inevitable decline. Only film in history with a dog named "Shithead." Martin's first starring role, back in his wild and crazy days; his ridiculous misadventures pay tribute to Jerry Lewis movies of the late '60s. Followed by a TV version released in 1984 as "The Jerk Too," with Mark Blankfield as the Jerk. 94m/C VHS, Beta, LV, DVD. Steve Martin, Bernadette Peters, Catlin Adams, Bill Macy, Jackie Mason; *D:* Carl Reiner; *W:* Steve Martin, Carl Gottlieb, Michael Elias. USH

The Jerky Boys WOOF! 1995 (R) Quick! Let's make a Jerky Boys movie and exploit their popularity before everyone realizes what a lame, one-joke act it is! Too late, guys. In what passes for a plot, Johnny and Kamal prank call an irritable mob boss (Arkin), pretending to be Chicago hitmen in need of a hideout. The wiseguys soon figure out the truth, but the requisite dumb cop (Sullivan) pads the film by not catching on. All these "twists" serve only one purpose—to get our heroes to the next phone. Don't accept the charges for this one.*CW:* Continuous use of strong language. 82m/C VHS, LV, Closed Caption. Johnny Brennan, Kamal Ahmed, Alan Arkin, William Hickey, Alan North, James Lorinz, Brad Sullivan, Vinny Pastore, Ozzy Osbourne, Paul Bartel, Suzanne Shepherd; *Cameos:* Tom Jones; *D:* James Melkonian; *W:* Johnny Brennan, Kamal Ahmed, Rich Wilkes, James Melkonian. TOU

Jerry Maguire 🎬🎬🎬½ 1996 (R) Romantic sports comedy focuses on the off-field action and makes an agent the good guy. Risky business in an era of strikes, lockouts, and astronomical salaries, but writer/director Crowe manages to pull it off. Cruise is well-used as the title character in the story of a shark-like sports agent who sees the error of his ways and transforms into...a more moral sports agent. Somewhat regretting his momentary twinge of honor (which gets him fired from his ultra-huge agency), he allies himself with his obnoxious and least important client Rod Tidwell (Gooding, Jr.), as well as Dorothy, an adoring young accountant (Zellweger) with a lovable young son (Lipnicki, making a strong bid for Culkin-like stardom). Famously well-researched, film sports great dialogue, talented leads, great supporting cast and a mega-star currently riding a wave of $100-million-plus films (talk about "Show me the money!"). Pop culture bonus points for coining 1996's most memorable catch phrase, which Crowe took from real life ex-Phoenix Cardinal Tim McDonald, and is now being used to sell everything from magazines to t-shirts.*CW:* Language and sexuality. 135m/C VHS, LV, Closed Caption, DVD. Tom Cruise, Cuba Gooding Jr., Renee Zellweger, Kelly Preston, Bonnie Hunt, Jerry O'Connell, Jay Mohr, Regina King, Glenn Frey, Jonathan Lipnicki, Todd Louiso, Mark Pellington; *Cameos:* Eric Stoltz; *D:* Cameron Crowe; *W:* Cameron Crowe; *C:* Janusz Kaminski; *M:* Nancy Wilson. Academy Awards '96: Best Supporting Actor (Gooding); Golden Globe Awards '97: Best Actor—Musical/Comedy (Cruise); MTV Movie Awards '97: Best Male Performance (Cruise); National Board of Review Awards '96: Best Actor (Cruise); Screen Actors Guild Award '96: Best Supporting Actor (Gooding); Broadcast Film Critics Association Awards '96: Breakthrough Performance (Zellweger); Best Supporting Actor (Gooding); Nominations: Academy Awards '96: Best Actor (Cruise), Best Film Editing, Best Original Screenplay, Best Picture; Directors Guild of America Awards '96: Best Director (Crowe); Golden Globe Awards '97: Best Actor—Musical/Comedy (Cruise), Best Film—Musical/Comedy, Best Supporting Actor (Gooding); MTV Movie Awards '97: Best Film, Breakthrough Performance (Zellweger); Screen Actors Guild Award '96: Best Actor (Cruise), Best Supporting Actress (Zellweger); Writers Guild of America '96: Best Original Screenplay. COL

Jersey Girl 🎬🎬½ 1992 (PG-13) Toby Mastellone (Gertz) is a bright single gal from the Jersey shore who wants something better in her life. Her hard-working dad (Bologna) has fixed her up with an apprentice plumber but she wants a Manhattan guy. And then Toby meets cute with Sal (McDermott), who seems just the ticket, but can you really take the Jersey out of the girl? 95m/C VHS, Closed Caption. Jami Gertz, Dylan McDermott, Joseph Bologna, Aida Turturro, Star Jasper, Sheryl Lee, Joseph Mazzello, Molly Price; *D:* David Burton Morris; *W:* Gina Wendkos; *M:* Stephen Bedell. COL

Jerusalem 🎬🎬 1996 (PG-13) Charismatic fundamentalist preacher Hellgum (Taube) travels to a small turn-of-the-century Swedish village preaching the end of the world and encouraging the people in his belief that all Christians should move to the Holy Land in order to build the new Jerusalem. He manages to convince the wealthy Karin (August) and to tempt young Gertrud (Bonnevie), whose fiance Ingmar (Friberg) is away trying to earn money so they can get married. Based on the novel by Selma Lagerlof who was inspired by Swedes who made a move to Palestine in 1900. Swedish with subtitles.*CW:* Some violence and a scene of sensuality. 166m/C VHS. SW Maria Bonnevie, Ulf Friberg, Lena Endre, Pernilla August, Olympia Dukakis, Max von Sydow; *D:* Bille August; *W:* Bille August; *C:* Jorgen Persson; *M:* Stefan Nilsson. FXL

Jesse 🎬🎬 1988 (PG) A heroic nurse ministers to remote Death Valley residents, and state bureaucats hound her for practicing medicine without a license. Although based on a true case and well-acted, this made-for-TV drama just lacks import and impact. 94m/C VHS, Closed Caption. Lee Remick, Scott Wilson, Leon Rippy, Priscilla Lopez, Albert Salmi; *D:* Glenn Jordan; *M:* David Shire. REP

Jesse James 🎬🎬🎬 1939 A Hollywood biography of the famed outlaw. One of director King's best efforts. 105m/C VHS, Beta, LV. Henry Fonda, Tyrone Power, Randolph Scott, Henry Hull, Jane Darwell, Brian Donlevy, Charles Halton; *D:* Henry King. FOX

Jesse James at Bay 🎬🎬 1941 Rogers is the do-good Jesse who's warring against some crooked railroad execs. Interesting perspective. 54m/B VHS, Beta. Roy Rogers, George "Gabby" Hayes, Sally Payne; *D:* Joseph Kane. NOS, MRV, VCN

Jesse James Meets Frankenstein's Daughter 🎬½ 1965 The gunslinger and Frankenstein's granddaughter, Maria, meet up in the Old West in this wacky combination of western and horror genres. 95m/C VHS, Beta. John Lupton, Cal Bolder, Narda Onyx, Steve Geray, Estelita, Jim Davis, William "Bill" Fawcett, Nestor Paiva; *D:* William Beaudine. NOS

Jesse James Rides Again 1947 Originally a serial, this feature depicts the further adventures of the West's most notorious outlaw. 181m/B VHS. Clayton Moore, Linda Stirling, Roy Barcroft, Tristram Coffin; *D:* Fred Brannon, Thomas Carr. REP, MLB

Jesse James Under the Black Flag 🎬½ 1921 An interesting western/pseudo biography/flashback in which Coates and James Jr. (the outlaw's son) play themselves. As Coates attempts to gather information from Jesse's decendants, a stranger appears and falls for Jesse's granddaughter, who shuns him. He proceeds to read the Coates biography and the flashback begins, in the Jesse was really a good guy forced off the straight and narrow vein. 59m/B VHS, Beta. Jesse James Jr., Franklin Coates, Diana Reed, Marguerite Hungerford; *D:* Franklin Coates. GPV, FCT

The Jesse Owens Story 🎬🎬 1984 The moving story of the four-time Olympic Gold medal winner's triumphs and misfortunes. A made-for-television movie. 174m/C VHS, Beta. Dorian Harewood, Debbi Morgan, Georg Stanford Brown, LeVar Burton, George Kennedy, Tom Bosley, Ben Vereen; *D:* Richard Irving. PAR, FCT

Jessi's Girls 🎬½ *Wanted Women* 1975 (R) In retaliation for the murder of her husband, an angry young woman frees three female prisoners, and they embark on a bloody course of revenge. Together, they track down the killers, and one by one, they fight to even the score. 86m/C VHS, Beta. Sondra Currie, Regina Carrol, Jennifer Bishop, Rigg Kennedy; *D:* Al Adamson. MON

Jesus 🎬🎬 1979 (G) A supposedly authenticated life of Christ, using real artifacts. 118m/C VHS, Beta. Brian Deacon; *D:* Peter Sykes, John Kirsh. VBL

Jesus Christ, Superstar 🎬🎬🎬 1973 (G) A rock opera that portrays, in music, the last seven days in the earthly life of Christ, as reenacted by young tourists in Israel. Outstanding musical score was the key to the success of the film. Based on the stage play by Tim Rice and Andrew Lloyd Webber, film is sometimes stirring while exhibiting the usual heavy-handed Jewison approach. ♪Jesus Christ, Superstar; I Don't Know How To Love Him; What's The Buzz?; Herod's Song; Heaven On Their Minds; Strange Thing; Mystifying; Then We Are Decided; Everything's Alright; This Jesus Must Die. 108m/C VHS, Beta, LV, Letterbox. Ted Neeley, Carl Anderson, Yvonne Elliman, Josh Mostel; *D:* Norman Jewison; *W:* Melvin Bragg. Nominations: Academy Awards '73: Original Song Score and/or Adaptation. USH

Jesus of Montreal 🎬🎬🎬½ *Jesus de Montreal* 1989 (R) A vagrant young actor (stage-trained Canadian star Bluteau) is hired by a Montreal priest to produce a fresh interpretation of an Easter passion play. Taking the good book at its word, he produces a contemporized literal telling that captivates audiences, inflames the men of the cloth, and eventually wins the players' faith. Quebecois director Arcand (keep an eye out for him as the judge) tells a compelling, acerbically satirical and haunting story that never forces its Biblical parallels. In French with English subtitles. **119m/C VHS, LV.** *FR CA* Gilles Pelletier, Lothaire Bluteau, Catherine Wilkening, Robert Lepage, Johanne-Marie Tremblay, Remy Girard, Marie-Christine Barrault; *D:* Denys Arcand; *W:* Denys Arcand. Cannes Film Festival '89: Special Jury Prize; Genie Awards '90: Best Actor (Girard), Best Director (Arcand), Best Film, Best Supporting Actor (Girard); Nominations: Academy Awards '89: Best Foreign Language Film. *ORI, FCT*

Jesus of Nazareth 🎞🎞½ **1928** A dramatic recreation of the life of Christ from the Annunciation through the Ascension. The film titles are taken from descriptive Biblical passages. **85m/B VHS, Beta, 8mm.** Philip Van Loan, Anna Lehr, Charles McCaffrey. *VYY, FCT*

Jesus of Nazareth 🎞🎞🎞 **1977** An all-star cast vividly portrays the life of Christ in this made-for-television mini-series. Wonderfully directed and sensitively acted. On three cassettes. **371m/C VHS, Beta.** Robert Powell, Anne Bancroft, Ernest Borgnine, Claudia Cardinale, James Mason, Laurence Olivier, Anthony Quinn; *D:* Franco Zeffirelli; *M:* Maurice Jarre. *ART, FOX, IGP*

The Jesus Trip 🎞½ **1971** Hunted motorcyclists take a young nun hostage in the desert. **86m/C VHS, Beta.** Robert Porter, Tippy Walker; *D:* Russ Mayberry. *UNI*

Jet Attack/Paratroop Command 🎞🎞 **1958** A double feature of "B" war movies. "Jet Attack" is a bad movie about a scientist whose plane gets shot down over Korea. He amazingly survives, only to be taken to a hospital and brainwashed. Enter a squad of soldiers leading a rescue mission who meet up with a beautiful Russian aide and some life-saving guerillas. This movie is so bad it's funny. In "Paratroop Command," a paratrooper accidentally kills a member of his squadron. In order to regain his dignity, the paratrooper sets off land mines in North Africa to prove himself. **139m/B VHS.** John Agar, Audrey Totter, Gregory Walcott, James Dobson, Richard Bakalayan, Jack Hogan, Jimmy Murphy, Ken Lynch; *D:* Edward L. Cahn, William Witney. *COL*

Jet Benny Show **1986** A Buck Rogers/Star Wars-style spoof of Jack Benny's classic TV show. **76m/C VHS, Beta.** Steve Norman, Kevin Dees, Polly MacIntyre, Ted Luedemann; *D:* Roger Evans. *NLC*

Jet Over the Atlantic 🎞½ **1959** Dangerous situation arises as a bomb is discovered aboard a plane en route from Spain to New York. **92m/B VHS, Beta.** Guy Madison, George Raft, Virginia Mayo, Brett Halsey; *D:* Byron Haskin. *NO*

Jet Pilot 🎞🎞 **1957** An American Air Force colonel (Wayne) in charge of an Alaskan Air Force base falls in love with a defecting Russian jet pilot (Leigh). They marry, but Wayne suspects Leigh is a spy planted to find out top U.S. secrets. He pretends to defect with her back to Russia to see what he can find out, but they again flee. Ludicrous plot is saved only by spectacular flying scenes, some performed by Chuck Yeager. Although this was filmed in 1950, it took seven more years to be released because producer Hughes couldn't keep his hands off it. **112m/B VHS, LV, Closed Caption.** John Wayne, Janet Leigh, Jay C. Flippen, Paul Fix, Richard Rober, Roland Winters, Hans Conried, Ivan Triesault; *D:* Josef von Sternberg; *C:* Winton C. Hoch. *USH*

The Jetsons Meet the Flintstones 1988 Trouble arises when young Elroy Jetson's time machine takes him and his family back to the 25th century B.C. There they meet the Flintstones and the Rubbles, who accidentally get transported into the future. Will either family ever get back home? **100m/C VHS, Beta, LV.** *V:* Mel Blanc, Daws Butler, Jean VanDerPyl, George O'Hanlon, Penny Singleton. *TTC, IME*

Jetsons: The Movie 🎞🎞 **1990 (G)** The famous outer space family of '60s TV is given a new silver-screened life. George gets a promotion that puts him in charge of an asteroid populated by furry creatures. Ecological concerns are expressed; while this is rare for a cartoon, the story is overall typical. **82m/C VHS, Beta, LV, Closed Caption.** *D:* William Hanna, Joseph Barbera; *M:* John Debney; *V:* George O'Hanlon, Mel Blanc, Penny Singleton, Tiffany, Patric Zimmerman, Donald E. Messick, Jean VanDerPyl, Ronnie Schell, Patti Deutsch, Dana Hill, Russi Taylor, Paul Kreppel, Rick Dees. *USH*

The Jew 🎞🎞 **1996** Portrait of 18th century playwright Antonio Jose da Silva (Pinheiro), whose family was forcibly converted from their Jewish faith by the Catholic Church. Living in Lisbon, da Silva founded a puppet theater for which he wrote comic operas. Eventually condemned for heresy, he was executed by the Inquisition in 1739. Explicit torture scenes. Portuguese with subtitles. **85m/C VHS.** *PT* Felipe Pinheiro, Dina Sfat, Mario Viegas, Edwin Luisi, Jose Neto; *D:* Jom Tob Azulay; *W:* Millor Fernandes, Billy Eckstine, Gilvan Pereira; *C:* Eduardo Serra. *FRF*

The Jewel in the Crown 1984 Epic saga of the last years of British rule in India from 1942-47 concentrating on a controversial love affair between the Indian Hari Kumar and the English Daphne Manners, which profoundly affects the lives of many. Based on "The Raj Quartet" by Paul Scott. Originally shown on British television, it aired in the United States on the PBS series "Masterpiece Theatre." An excellent mini-series that was shown in 14 segments. Available on eight cassettes. **750m/C VHS, Beta.** *GB* Charles Dance, Susan Wooldridge, Art Malik, Tim Pigott-Smith, Geraldine James, Peggy Ashcroft, Judy Parfitt; *D:* Christopher Morahan, Jim O'Brien; *M:* George Fenton. *AEH, VCO, NEW*

The Jewel of the Nile 🎞🎞½ **1985 (PG)** Sequel to "Romancing the Stone" with the same cast but new director. Romance novelist Joan thought she found her true love in Jack but finds that life doesn't always end happily ever. After they part ways, Jack realizes that she may be in trouble and endeavors to rescue her from the criminal hands of a charming North African president. Of course, he can always check out this "jewel" at the same time. Chemistry is still there, but the rest of the film isn't quite up to the "Stone's" charm. **106m/C VHS, Beta, LV, Closed Caption.** Michael Douglas, Kathleen Turner, Danny DeVito, Avner Eisenberg, The Flying Karamazov Brothers, Spiros Focas, Holland Taylor; *D:* Lewis Teague; *W:* Mark Rosenthal, Larry Konner; *C:* Jan De Bont; *M:* Jack Nitzsche. *FOX*

The Jeweller's Shop 🎞🎞 **1990** A highly spiritual tale of two married couples in Poland whose children meet and fall in love much later in Canada. Based on a play by Karol Wojtyla—who later became Pope Jean-Paul II. Adapted under strict Vatican supervision. **90m/C VHS.** Burt Lancaster, Ben Cross, Olivia Hussey. *IGP*

Jezebel 🎞🎞🎞½ **1938** Davis is a willful Southern belle who loses fiance Fonda through her selfish and spiteful ways in this pre-Civil War drama. When he becomes ill, she realizes her cruelty and rushes to nurse him back to health. Davis' role won her an Oscar for Best Actress, and certainly provided Scarlett O'Hara with a rival for most memorable female character of all time. **105m/B VHS, Beta, LV.** Bette Davis, George Brent, Henry Fonda, Margaret Lindsay, Fay Bainter, Donald Crisp, Spring Byington, Eddie Anderson; *D:* William Wyler; *M:* Max Steiner. Academy Awards '38: Best Actress (Davis), Best Supporting Actress (Bainter); Nominations: Academy Awards '38: Best Cinematography, Best Picture, Best Score. *MGM, FCT, BTV*

Jezebel's Kiss 🎞🎞 **1990 (R)** A sizzling young beauty returns to the town where she grew up and proceeds to destroy any man she pleases. **96m/C VHS, LV.** Meg Foster, Malcolm McDowell, Meredith Baxter, Everett McGill, Katherine Barrese; *D:* Harvey Keith; *W:* Harvey Keith. *COL*

JFK 🎞🎞🎞½ **1991 (R)** Highly controversial examination of President John F. Kennedy's 1963 assassination, from the viewpoint of New Orleans district attorney Jim Garrison. Hotly debated because of Stone's conspiracy theory, it sparked new calls to open the sealed government records from the 1977 House Select Committee on Assassinations investigation. Outstanding performances from all-star principal and supporting casts, stunning cinematography, and excellent editing. Even Garrison himself shows up as Chief Justice Earl Warren. Considered by some to be a cinematic masterpiece, others see it as revisionist history that should be taken with a grain of salt. Extended version adds 17 minutes. **189m/C VHS, Beta, LV, Letterbox, Closed Caption, DVD.** Kevin Costner, Sissy Spacek, Kevin Bacon, Tommy Lee Jones, Laurie Metcalf, Gary Oldman, Michael Rooker, Jay O. Sanders, Beata Pozniak, Joe Pesci, Donald Sutherland, John Candy, Jack Lemmon, Walter Matthau, Ed Asner, Vincent D'Onofrio, Sally Kirkland, Brian Doyle-Murray, Wayne Knight, Tony Plana, Tomas Milian, Sean Stone; *Cameos:* Lolita Davidovich, Frank Whaley, Jim Garrison; *D:* Oliver Stone; *W:* Oliver Stone, Zachary Sklar; *C:* Robert Richardson; *M:* John Williams. Academy Awards '91: Best Cinematography, Best Film Editing; Golden Globe Awards '92: Best Director (Stone); Nominations: Academy Awards '91: Best Adapted Screenplay, Best Director (Stone), Best Picture, Best Sound, Best Supporting Actor (Jones), Best Original Score. *WAR*

The JFK Conspiracy 1991 Did Lee Harvey Oswald act alone? Opinions of government officials, eyewitnesses, and director Oliver Stone, in addition to testimony, photographs, documents, and other evidence, address the perennial American question. Includes footage from the House Select Committee on Assassination. Made for television. **98m/C VHS, LV.** *BMG, VTR*

JFK: Reckless Youth 🎞🎞½ **1993** Glossy made for TV docudrama details the youthful exploits of Kennedy as both ladies man and emerging leader and comes perilously close to being a tacky soap. Follows the president-to-be from his party-hearty years at prep school, through his naval career (and PT-109 heroics), and his first forays into politics. Excellent portrayal by Dempsey details JFK's chronic ill health, his ambitions, and the family ties that provided both friction and support. Based on the controversial biography by Nigel Hamilton. **182m/C VHS, Closed Caption.** Patrick Dempsey, Terry Kinney, Loren Dean, Diana Scarwid, Yolanda Jilot, Robin Tunney, Andrew Lowery, Stan Cahill, James Rebhorn, Malachy McCourt; *D:* Harry Winer; *W:* William Broyles Jr.; *M:* Cameron Allan. *CAF*

Jigsaw 🎞🎞🎞 *Gun Moll* **1949** Crime drama with a smattering of cameos by Hollywood favorites. A newspaper reporter is murdered. The dead man's friend, an assistant district attorney, seeks the punks responsible. They send in a seductress to keep the D.A. busy, but she too is murdered. Action and tension in a well-made flick. Based on a story by John Roeburt. **70m/B VHS.** Franchot Tone, Jean Wallace, Myron McCormick, Marc Lawrence, Winifred Lenihan, Betty Harper, Robert Gist; *Cameos:* Marlene Dietrich, Henry Fonda, Burgess Meredith, John Garfield; *D:* Fletcher Markle. *SNC, DVT*

Jigsaw 🎞🎞 *Man on the Move* **1971** Missing persons lawman is lured into a cover-up more complex than he had bargained for. A tense drama originated as the pilot for a series. **100m/C VHS.** James Wainwright, Vera Miles, Richard Kiley, Andrew Duggan, Edmond O'Brien; *D:* William A. Graham. *ART*

Jigsaw 🎞🎞 **1990** A developer is found dead the day after his wedding. His widow and a cop team up to find out who, what, where, and why. Lukewarm Australian mystery export. **85m/C VHS.** Rebecca Gibney, Dominic Sweeney, Michael Coard. *ATL*

The Jigsaw Man 🎞🎞 **1984 (PG)** A British-Russian double agent is sent back to England to retrieve a list of Soviet agents which he hid there many years before. **90m/C VHS, Beta, LV.** *GB* Michael

Caine, Laurence Olivier, Susan George, Robert Powell, Charles Gray, David Patrick Kelly, Michael Medwin; **D:** Terence Young. *REP*

Jigsaw Murders 1989 A macho detective is out to solve a grisly murder, but the only available leads are a jigsaw puzzle and the victim's severed, tattooed lower limb. 98m/C **VHS, Beta.** Chad Everett, Michelle Johnson, Yaphet Kotto; **D:** Jag Mundhra. *MGM*

Jim Thorpe: All American 🎬🎬½ *Man of Bronze* 1951 The life story of Thorpe, a Native American athlete who gained international recognition for his excellence in many different sports. A must for sports fans. 105m/B **VHS, Beta.** Burt Lancaster, Phyllis Thaxter, Charles Bickford, Steve Cochran, Dick Wesson; **D:** Michael Curtiz; **W:** Douglas S. Morrow; **M:** Max Steiner. *WAR*

Jimmy Hollywood 🎬🎬½ 1994 (R) Wannabe Hollywood actor Pesci has never acted in his life but longs for stardom—which he gets after he accidentally becomes a community vigilante. Burned-out sidekick Slater helps create the videotapes that will bring Jimmy his 15 minutes of fame. Although appropriately desperate, Pesci's role comes off as mostly shtick; two dogs in a row for the usually talented Levinson (after "Toys"). **CW:** Language and violence. 118m/C **VHS, Beta, LV, Closed Caption.** Joe Pesci, Christian Slater, Victoria Abril; *Cameos:* Barry Levinson, Rob Weiss; **D:** Barry Levinson; **W:** Barry Levinson; **C:** Peter Sova; **M:** Robbie Robertson. *PAR*

Jimmy, the Boy Wonder 🎬½ 1966 Goremeister Lewis' attempt at a "family" film turns out just as weird as expected. A young boy goes on a magical trip to find out who stopped time and meets an absent-minded astronomer, the evil Mr. Fig, and then discovers what happens at world's end. ?m/C **VHS. D:** Herschell Gordon Lewis. *MOV, TPV*

Jimmy the Kid 🎬🎬 1982 (PG) A young boy becomes the unlikely target for an improbable gang of would-be crooks on a crazy, "fool-proof" crime caper. Kiddie comic caper. 95m/C **VHS, Beta.** Gary Coleman, Cleavon Little, Fay Hauser, Ruth Gordon, Dee Wallace Stone, Paul LeMat, Don Adams; **D:** Gary Nelson; **W:** Sam Bobrick. *NO*

Jingle All the Way 🎬🎬 1996 (PG) Producer Chris Columbus grabs the reins of the slapstick and sentiment sleigh from mentor John Hughes in this farce of holiday capitalism. Any parent who has searched frantically for that Mighty Morphin' Cabbage Elmo will understand hapless Howard Langston (Schwarzenegger), a workaholic dad who was supposed to secure the coveted Turbo Man action figure for his son Jamie (Lloyd). Unfortunately, it slips his mind until Christmas Eve and all the Turbo Men have blasted off with more mindful parents. In his panic-stricken quest for the toy, he is confronted by a crazed postman (Sinbad) hunting Turbo Man, a pack of sleazy Santas, and a vicious reindeer attack. Meanwhile, Howard's slimy neighbor Ted (Hartman) is attempting to get into his wife Liz's (Wilson) stockings with great care. Although aimed at a younger audience, there's a definite lack of kids; which leaves it too grown-up for the kids and too childish for the adults. There is some satisfaction in seeing the Mall of America torn to shreds, however. Ho ho hum. 88m/C **VHS, LV, Closed Caption.** Arnold Schwarzenegger, Phil Hartman, Sinbad, Rita Wilson, James Belushi, Robert Conrad, Martin Mull, Jake Lloyd, Harvey Korman, Laraine Newman; **D:** Brian Levant; **W:** Randy Kornfield; **C:** Victor Kemper; **M:** David Newman. Nominations: Golden Raspberry Awards '96: Worst Director (Levant). *FXV*

Jinxed 🎬🎬 1982 (R) Las Vegas nightclub singer tries to convince a gullible blackjack dealer to murder her crooked boyfriend, but the plan backfires when the gangster electrocutes himself while taking a shower. Offscreen cast disputes were probably much more interesting than onscreen comedy. 104m/C **VHS, Beta.** Bette Midler, Ken

Wahl, Rip Torn; **D:** Donald Siegel; **W:** David Newman, Frank D. Gilroy; **M:** Miles Goodman. *MGM*

Jit 🎬🎬 1994 Unpretentious romantic comedy finds the easy-going U.K., who runs errands for his uncle in a Zimbabwe town, falling in love with the beautiful Sofi, who already has a boyfriend. But U.K. won't be stopped by this or Sofi's greedy father. "Jit" refers to the infectious local music, a fusion of traditional African rhythms and reggae-pop. 98m/C **VHS.** Dominic Makuvachuma, Sibongile Nene, Faria Sevenzo, Winnie Ndemera; **D:** Michael Raeburn. *HMV*

The Jitters 🎬 1988 (R) The Chinese hopping vampire comes to America to make a bad movie on a different continent. The murdered dead turn into zombies and seek revenge on their killers. Maybe they should've sought revenge on the producers. 80m/C **VHS, Beta.** Sal Viviano, Marilyn Tokuda, James Hong, Frank Dietz; **D:** John Fasano.

Jive Junction 🎬🎬 1943 A group of patriotic teenagers convert a barn into a canteen for servicemen and name it "Jive Junction." 62m/B **VHS, Beta.** Dickie Moore, Tina Thayer, Gerra Young, Johnny Michaels, Jan Wiley, Beverly Boyd, William Halligan; **D:** Edgar G. Ulmer. *NOS, GVV*

Jive Turkey 🎬½ 1976 Cool dude busts heads. ?m/C **VHS.** Paul Harris, Frank De Kova, Serena; **D:** Bill Brame. *MOV*

Jo Jo Dancer, Your Life Is Calling 🎬🎬½ 1986 (R) Pryor directed and starred in this semi-autobiographical price-of-fame story of a comic, hospitalized for a drug-related accident, who must re-evaluate his life. A serious departure from Pryor's slapstick comedies that doesn't quite make it as a drama; Pryor nevertheless deserves credit for the honesty he demonstrates in dealing with his real-life problems. 97m/C **VHS, Beta, LV, Closed Caption.** Richard Pryor, Debbie Allen, Art Evans, Fay Hauser, Barbara Williams, Paula Kelly, Wings Hauser, Carmen McRae, Diahnne Abbott, Scoey Mitchell, Billy Eckstine, Virginia Capers, Dennis Farina; **D:** Richard Pryor; **W:** Richard Pryor, Rocco Urbisci; **C:** John A. Alonzo; **M:** Herbie Hancock. *COL*

Joan of Arc 🎬🎬 1948 A touching and devout look at the life of Joan of Arc. Perhaps unfortunately, the film is accurately based on the play by Maxwell Anderson, and adds up to too much talk and too little action. 100m/C **VHS, Beta, LV.** Ingrid Bergman, Jose Ferrer, John Ireland, Leif Erickson; **D:** Victor Fleming; **W:** Joseph Valentine. Academy Awards '48: Best Color Cinematography, Best Costume Design (Color); Nominations: Academy Awards '48: Best Actress (Bergman), Best Art Direction/Set Decoration (Color), Best Film Editing, Best Supporting Actor (Ferrer), Best Original Dramatic/Comedy Score. *IGP, HMV*

Joan of Paris 🎬🎬½ 1942 A French resistance leader dies so that Allied pilots can escape from the Nazis. A well done, but obviously dated propaganda feature. 91m/B **VHS, Beta.** Michele Morgan, Paul Henreid, Thomas Mitchell, Laird Cregar, May Robson, Alexander Granach, Alan Ladd; **D:** Robert Stevenson; **W:** Charles Bennett. Nominations: Academy Awards '42: Best Original Dramatic/Comedy Score. *TTC*

Jock Petersen 🎬 *Petersen* 1974 (R) A lighthearted story about a blonde hunk who enrolls in college, cavorting and seducing his way to questionable fame and fortune. 97m/C **VHS, Beta.** Jack Thompson, Wendy Hughes; **D:** Tim Burstall. *NLC*

Jocks 🎬½ 1987 (R) A whiz-kid tennis team competes in a pro meet in Las Vegas, and paints the town red. 90m/C **VHS, Beta.** Christopher Lee, Perry Lang, Richard Roundtree, Scott Strader; **D:** Steve Carver; **W:** Jeff Buhai. *COL*

Joe 🎬🎬½ 1970 (R) An odd friendship grows between a businessman and a blue-collar worker as they search together for the executive's runaway daughter. Thrust into the midst of the counter-culture, they react with an orgy of violence. 107m/C **VHS, Beta, LV.** Peter Boyle, Susan Sarandon, Dennis Patrick; **D:** John G. Avildsen. Nominations: Academy Awards '70: Best Story & Screenplay. *MGM, VES*

Joe Kidd 🎬🎬½ 1972 (PG) A land war breaks out in New Mexico between Mexican natives and American land barons. Eastwood, once again portraying the "mysterious stranger," must decide with whom he should side, all the while falling in love with Garcia. Lackluster direction results in a surprisingly tedious western, in spite of the cast. One of Eastwood's lowest money grossers. The laserdisc edition is letterboxed and features chapter stops, the original trailer and digital sound. 88m/C **VHS, Beta, LV, Letterbox.** Clint Eastwood, Robert Duvall, John Saxon, Don Stroud, Stella Garcia, James Wainwright, Paul Koslo, Gregory Walcott, Dick Van Patten, Lynn Marta; **D:** John Sturges; **W:** Elmore Leonard; **C:** Bruce Surtees; **M:** Lalo Schifrin. *USH*

The Joe Louis Story 🎬🎬 1953 The story of Joe Louis' rise to fame as boxing's Heavyweight Champion of the world. 88m/B **VHS, Beta.** Coley Wallace, Paul Stewart, Hilda Simms; **M:** George Bassman. *NOS, DVT, FCT*

Joe Panther 🎬🎬🎬 1976 (G) Family drama about a young Seminole Indian who stakes his claim in the Anglo world by wrestling alligators. Montalban plays a wise old chieftain who helps the youth handle the conflict between Indian and white societies. 110m/C **VHS.** Brian Keith, Ricardo Montalban, Alan Feinstein, Cliff Osmond, A. Martinez, Robert Hoffman; **D:** Paul Krasny. *WAR*

Joe Versus the Volcano 🎬🎬 1990 (PG) Expressionistic goofball comedy about a dopey guy who, after finding out he has only months to live, contracts with a millionaire to leap into a volcano alive. Imaginative farce with great "Metropolis"-pastiche visuals that eventually fizzle out. Watch for Ryan in not one, but three roles, and mysterious symbolism throughout. Special effects courtesy of Industrial Light and Magic. 106m/C **VHS, Beta, LV, 8mm, Letterbox.** Tom Hanks, Meg Ryan, Lloyd Bridges, Robert Stack, Amanda Plummer, Abe Vigoda, Dan Hedaya, Barry McGovern, Ossie Davis; **D:** John Patrick Shanley; **W:** John Patrick Shanley; **M:** Georges Delerue. *WAR*

Joe's Apartment 🎬🎬 1996 (PG-13) Fresh-from-Iowa Joe (O'Connell) comes to New York, finds a squalid apartment, and then discovers its other occupants are hordes of singing, joking cockroaches. Lucky for Joe, his unwelcome roommates are on his side, even helping out with his love life, when necessary. Gross but interesting, throw in Vaughn as a panty-wearing politician and you've got yourself a potential cult-movie favorite. Neat freaks probably won't enjoy it much. Flick took three years to finish as computer-animated roaches had to do all the dancing and singing. Feature directorial debut for writer Payson, who created the original 1992 live-action/animation MTV short. **CW:** Crude humor and a brief drug reference. 82m/C **VHS, LV, Closed Caption.** Jerry O'Connell, Megan Ward, Robert Vaughn, Jim Turner, Don Ho, Sandra "Pepa" Denton, Shiek Mahmud-Bey; **D:** John Payson; **W:** John Payson; **C:** Peter Deming; **V:** Billy West, Reginald Hudlin. *MGM*

Joe's Bed-Stuy Barbershop: We Cut Heads 🎬🎬½ 1983 Lee's first film takes place inside a neighborhood landmark, the corner barbershop. Lee displays the social awareness and urban humor that he honed in his later, bigger films. 60m/C **VHS, Beta.** Leon Errol, Morris Carnovsky, Elyse Knox, Billy House, Trudy Marshall; **D:** Spike Lee; **W:** Spike Lee. *ICA*

Joey 🎬½ 1985 (PG) Daddy, a former doo-wopper, looks back on his years of musical success as a waste of time. His son takes to the world of rock guitar with blind fervor. Their argument plays against the backdrop of the "Royal Doo-Wopp Show" at New York City's Radio Music Hall. Features multi-generational rock songs. 90m/C **VHS, Beta.** Neill Barry, James Quinn. *NO*

Joey 🎬🎬½ 1998 (PG) Young Billy (Croft) rescues a baby kangaroo (known as a joey) who was left behind when an evil hunter captures a group of kangaroos and hauls them off to Sydney for nefarious purposes. So Billy puts Joey in his backpack and heads off to the city to reunite the little family—aided by the rebellious daughter (McKenna) of the newly appointed U.S. ambassador (Begley). **96m/C VHS, Closed Caption.** *AU* Jamie Croft, Alex McKenna, Ed Begley Jr., Rebecca Gibney, Ruth Cracknell, Harold Hopkins; *D:* Ian Barry; *W:* Stuart Beattie; *C:* David Burr; *M:* Roger Mason. *MGM*

Joey Breaker 🐾🐾🐾 1993 (R)
Joey (cult-fave Edson) is a hot-shot Manhattan talent agent who's consumed by his job. A series of encounters (romantic and otherwise) expands his outlook, first among them with Cyan (Marley), a young Jamaican waitress. On his journey to possible enlightenment Joey also meets AIDS-stricken Fondren, who helps Joey see another side of life. Quirky with a reggae beat, small pic works large message with sense of humor and sincere performances. Dedicated to Fondren, who died of AIDS in 1992. Marley, daughter of late reggae superstar Bob, shares a tune on the soundtrack with brother Ziggy. Filmed in da Big Apple and St. Lucia, West Indies.*CW:* Language. **92m/C VHS, Beta, Closed Caption.** Richard Edson, Cedella Marley, Erik King, Gina Gershon, Philip S. Hoffman, Fred Fondren; *D:* Steven Starr; *W:* Steven Starr; *C:* Joe DeSalvo; *M:* Paul Aston. *PAR, FCT*

John and Julie 🐾🐾½ 1955
Sweet story about two young friends, living in the English countryside in 1953, who decide to run away to London in order to witness the coronation of Queen Elizabeth II. They're hoping John's Uncle, a Royal Escort guard, will help them but first they have to get to the city, which involves a lot of complicated travelling plans. **82m/C VHS.** *GB* Colin Gibson, Lesley Dudley, Noelle Middleton, Moira Lister, Constance Cummings, Wilfrid Hyde-White, Sidney James, Joseph Tomelty, Megs Jenkins, Patric Doonan, Peter Sellers, John Stuart, Vincent Ball, Colin Gordon, Peter Jones, Katie Johnson, Cyril Smith, Andrew Cruikshank, Winifred Shotter, Richard Dimbleby, Wynfold Vaughn Thomas; *D:* William Fairchild; *W:* William Fairchild; *C:* Arthur Grant. *FRF*

John and the Missus 🐾½ 1987 (PG)
After the discovery of a copper mine threatens to destroy a nearby town, the Canadian government begins a relocation process. However, one man refuses to give up his generations-old home. Canadian Pinsent's directorial debut, adapting his own 1973 novel. **98m/C VHS, Beta.** *CA* Gordon Pinsent, Jackie Burroughs, Randy Follet, Jessica Steen; *D:* Gordon Pinsent. Genie Awards '87: Best Actor (Pinsent). *NO*

John & Yoko: A Love Story 🐾 1985
Appalling television movie version of the rock legend's life and marriage. With original Beatles tunes. **146m/C VHS, Beta, LV.** Mark McGann, Kim Miyori, Kenneth Price, Peter Capaldi, Richard Morant, Philip Walsh; *D:* Sandor Stern. *IME*

John Carpenter's Vampires 🐾🐾½
Vampires 1997 (R) Vatican-sponsored vampire hunter Jack Crow (Woods) leads his team of mercenaries into the American Southwest to battle master bloodsucker Valek (Griffith) and his hordes. After destroying a vampire hideout, Crow and company are ambushed at a post-stake party. The only survivors are Crow, his buddy Montoya (Baldwin), and a hooker (Lee) with a psychic link to the vampires. Satisfying horror-western packs plenty of action and gore (along with just enough humor) to hold attention until the inevitable showdown. Woods does a good job of toning down from his usual bug-eyed crazy to merely borderline disturbed here. Based on the novel "Vampires" by John Steakley.*CW:* Strong vampire violence and gore, language and sexuality. **104m/C VHS.** James Woods, Thomas Ian Griffith, Sheryl Lee, Daniel Baldwin, Tim Guinee, Maximilian Schell, Cary-Hiroyuki Tagawa, Mark Boone Jr., Tom Rosales; *D:* John Carpenter; *W:* John Carpenter, Don Jacoby; *C:* Gary B. Kibbe; *M:* John Carpenter. *NYR*

John Cleese on How to Irritate People
How to Irritate People 1968 Cleese, a master at causing irritation, demonstrates how to take care of all those annoying people who irritate you, including job interviewers, bank clerks, waiters, and salesmen. Monty Python alumni Palin and Chapman also join Cleese in the "Airline Pilots" sketch about bored pilots deliberately trying to terrify their passengers. **65m/C VHS.** John Cleese, Michael Palin, Graham Chapman, Connie Booth. *WST, FUS*

John Grisham's The Rainmaker 🐾🐾½
The Rainmaker 1997 (PG-13) Yet another legal drama from the successful pen of John Grisham. Baylor (Damon) is a young lawyer whose job disappears when his firm is absorbed by a giant company. He fills his time giving legal advice to indigents and mooning over Kelly (Danes), a young abused wife. Then he takes on the case of a couple whose leukemia-stricken son was denied treatment by their insurance company, coincidentally represented by the firm that booted Baylor. Pre-"Jack," Coppola probably wouldn't have gone anywhere near such formulaic franchise fare, and if he did, he could've directed it in his sleep. As it is he creates a serviceable, if not spectacular, piece of entertainment. His main allies are Voight's insurance company mouthpiece and DeVito's ambulance chaser. Damon plays the hero with much less bravado than previous Grisham protagonists.*CW:* A strong beating and elements of domestic abuse. **137m/C VHS, Beta, Closed Caption.** Matt Damon, Claire Danes, Danny DeVito, Jon Voight, Danny Glover, Virginia Madsen, Mary Kay Place, Mickey Rourke, Johnny Whitworth, Teresa Wright, Red West, Roy Scheider, Randy Travis, Andrew Shue; *D:* Francis Ford Coppola; *W:* Francis Ford Coppola, Michael Herr; *C:* John Toll; *M:* Elmer Bernstein. Nominations: Golden Globe Awards '98: Best Supporting Actor (Voight). *PAR*

John Paul Jones 🐾🐾½ 1959
Big bio of the Revolutionary War naval hero ("I have not yet begun to fight!") who wins a lot of battles but can't convince Congress to maintain a strong navy at war's end. He's sent to win sea battles for the Empress Catherine the Great of Russia and then spends his last years in France. Great action scenes, otherwise tedious. **126m/C VHS.** Robert Stack, Charles Coburn, MacDonald Carey, Marisa Pavan, Jean-Pierre Aumont, Peter Cushing, Erin O'Brien, Bruce Cabot, David Farrar, Basil Sydney, John Crawford; *Cameos:* Bette Davis; *D:* John Farrow; *W:* John Farrow, Jesse Lasky Jr.; *M:* Max Steiner. *WAR*

John Wayne Anthology: Star Packer/Lawless Range 1934
In addition to two of Wayne's films, this program captures 40 years of the actor's career. **156m/B VHS.** John Wayne; *D:* Robert North Bradbury. *SIM*

Johnnie Gibson F.B.I. 🐾
Johnnie Mae Gibson: FBI 1987 Supposedly based on a true story, the adventures of a beautiful, black FBI agent who falls in love with a man she's investigating. **96m/C VHS, Beta.** Howard E. Rollins Jr., Lynn Whitfield, William Allen Young, Richard Lawson; *D:* Bill Duke; *M:* Billy Goldenberg. *MRC, PTB*

Johnny Angel 🐾🐾🐾 1945
Merchant Marine captain unravels mystery of his father's murder aboard a ship. Tense film noir. **79m/B VHS, Beta, LV.** George Raft, Claire Trevor, Signe Hasso, Lowell Gilmore, Hoagy Carmichael; *D:* Edwin L. Marin. *CCB, TTC*

Johnny Apollo 🐾🐾½ 1940
Upright college student Power keeps his nose clean until Dad's sent to jail for playing with numbers. Scheming to free his old man (Arnold) from the big house, he decides crime will pay for the stiff price tag of freedom. Predictable and melodramatic, but well directed. **93m/B VHS, Beta.** Tyrone Power, Dorothy Lamour, Lloyd Nolan, Edward Arnold, Charley Grapewin, Lionel Atwill; *D:* Yves Allegret; *C:* Arthur C. Miller. *FOX, FCT*

Johnny Appleseed 1986
True story of the legendary American who spent his life planting apple trees across the country. Comedy the entire family will enjoy from Shelly Duvall's "Tall Tales and Legends" series. Originally broadcast on cable television. **60m/C VHS, Closed Caption.** Martin Short, Rob Reiner, Molly Ringwald. *FOX*

Johnny Be Good 🐾 1988 (R)
A too-talented high school quarterback is torn between loyalty to his best friend and to his girlfriend amid bribery and schemings by colleges eager to sign him up. **91m/C VHS, Beta, LV, Closed Caption.** Anthony Michael Hall, Robert Downey Jr., Paul Gleason, Uma Thurman, Jim Pankow, Steve James, Seymour Cassel, Michael Greene, Marshall Bell, Deborah May; *D:* Bud Smith; *W:* Jeff Buhai; *M:* Jay Michael Ferguson. *ORI*

Johnny Belinda 🐾🐾🐾 1948
A compassionate physician cares for a young deaf mute woman and her illegitimate child. Tension builds as the baby's father returns to claim the boy. **103m/B VHS, Beta.** Jane Wyman, Lew Ayres, Charles Bickford, Agnes Moorehead; *D:* Jean Negulesco; *M:* Max Steiner. Academy Awards '48: Best Actress (Wyman); Golden Globe Awards '49: Best Actress—Drama (Wyman), Best Film—Drama; Nominations: Academy Awards '48: Best Actor (Ayres), Best Art Direction/Set Decoration (B & W), Best Black and White Cinematography, Best Director (Negulesco), Best Film Editing, Best Picture, Best Screenplay, Best Sound, Best Supporting Actor (Bickford), Best Supporting Actress (Moorehead), Best Original Dramatic/Comedy Score. *MGM, BTV, CCB*

Johnny Belinda 🐾🐾 1982
A television movie adaptation of the Elmer Harris weepie about a small town doctor who befriends an abused deaf girl. Remake of the 1948 film. **95m/C VHS, Beta.** Richard Thomas, Rosanna Arquette, Dennis Quaid, Candy Clark, Roberts Blossom, Fran Ryan; *D:* Anthony Page. *ART*

Johnny Come Lately 🐾🐾½
Johnny Vagabond 1943 An elderly editor helps out an ex-newspaperman with a police charge. The two then team up to expose political corruption despite threats from a rival newspaperman. **97m/B VHS, LV.** James Cagney, Grace George, Marjorie Main, Marjorie Lord, Hattie McDaniel, Ed McNamara; *D:* William K. Howard. Nominations: Academy Awards '43: Best Original Dramatic/Comedy Score. *REP*

Johnny Dangerously 🐾🐾 1984 (PG-13)
A gangster spoof about Johnny Dangerously, who turned to crime in order to pay his mother's medical bills. Now, Dangerously wants to go straight, but competitive crooks would rather see him dead than law-abiding and his mother requires more and more expensive operations. Crime pays in comic ways. **90m/C VHS, Beta, Closed Caption.** Michael Keaton, Joe Piscopo, Danny DeVito, Maureen Stapleton, Marilu Henner, Peter Boyle, Griffin Dunne, Glynnis O'Connor, Dom DeLuise, Richard Dimitri, Ray Walston, Dick Butkus, Alan Hale Jr., Bob Eubanks; *D:* Amy Heckerling; *W:* Norman Steinberg, Harry Colomby. *FOX*

Johnny Eager 🐾🐾🐾 1942
Glossy crime melodrama starring Taylor as an unscrupulous racketeer and Turner as the daughter of D.A. Arnold who falls for him and ends up becoming a pawn in his schemes. Heflin won an Oscar for his outstanding performance as Taylor's alcoholic confidant. Excellent direction by LeRoy makes this a top-rate gangster film. Based on a story by James Edward Grant. **107m/B VHS.** Robert Taylor, Lana Turner, Edward Arnold, Van Heflin, Robert Sterling, Patricia Dane, Glenda Farrell, Barry Nelson, Henry O'Neill, Charles Dingle, Cy Kendall; *D:* Mervyn LeRoy; *W:* James Edward Grant, John Lee Mahin. Academy Awards '42: Best Supporting Actor (Heflin). *MGM*

Johnny Firecloud 🐾 1975
A modern Indian goes on the warpath when the persecution of his people reawakens his sense of identity. **94m/C VHS, Beta.** Victor Mohica, Ralph Meeker, Frank De Kova, Sacheen Little Feather, David Canary, Christina Hart; *D:* William Allen Castleman.

Johnny Frenchman 🐾🐾 1946
Rival fishing groups battle it out, complicated by a romance across the water. Featured in the cast are real fishermen and villagers from Cornwall, as well as authentic Free French Resistance fighters from WWII. **104m/B VHS.** *GB* Francoise Rosay, Tom Walls, Patricia Roc, Ralph Michael, Frederick Piper, Pierre Richard, Carroll O'Connor; *D:* Charles Frend. *NOS*

Johnny Got His Gun 🦴🦴🦴 1971 (R) Dalton Trumbo's story of a young WWI veteran (Bottoms) who meets a bomb with his name on it and is rendered armless, legless, and more or less faceless, as well as deaf, dumb, and blind. Regarded as a vegetable and stuck in a lightless hospital utility room, he dreams and fantasizes about life before and after the bomb, and tries vainly to communicate with the staff. Wrenching and bleak anti-war diatribe made at the climax of the Vietnam War. 111m/C VHS, Beta, LV. Timothy Bottoms, Jason Robards Jr., Donald Sutherland, Diane Varsi, Kathy Field; **D:** Dalton Trumbo. Cannes Film Festival '71: Grand Jury Prize.

Johnny Guitar 🦴🦴🦴½ 1953 Women strap on six-guns in Nicholas Ray's unintentionally hilarious, gender-bending western. A guitar-playing loner wanders into a small town feud between lovelorn saloon owner Crawford and McCambridge, the town's resident lynch mob-leading harpy. This fascinating cult favorite has had film theorists arguing for decades: is it a parody, a political McCarthy-era allegory, or Freudian exercise? The off-screen battles of the two female stars are equally legendary. Stick around for the end credits to hear Peggy Lee sing the title song. 116m/C VHS, LV, Closed Caption. Joan Crawford, Ernest Borgnine, Sterling Hayden, Mercedes McCambridge, Scott Brady, Ward Bond, Royal Dano, John Carradine; **D:** Nicholas Ray; **W:** Philip Yordan; **C:** Harry Stradling. REP

Johnny Handsome 🦴🦴🦴 1989 (R) An ugly, deformed hood, after he's been double-crossed and sent to prison, volunteers for a reconstructive surgery experiment and is released with a new face, determined to hunt down the scum that set him up. A terrific modern B-picture based on John Godey's "The Three Worlds of Johnny Handsome." 96m/C VHS, Beta, LV, Closed Caption. Mickey Rourke, Ellen Barkin, Lance Henriksen, Elizabeth McGovern, Morgan Freeman, Forest Whitaker, Scott Wilson, Blake Clark; **D:** Walter Hill; **W:** Ken Friedman; **M:** Ry Cooder. ART

Johnny Mnemonic 🦴🦴 1995 (R) Robo-yuppie data courier Johnny (Reeves) has over extended the storage capacity in his head and must download his latest job before his brain turns to applesauce. Aided by an implant-enhanced bodyguard (Meyer), underground hacker rebels called LoTeks, and a former doctor (Rollins) battling a technology-induced epidemic, Johnny is on the run from the corporation that wants his head (literally). Freshman director Longo can't seem to get a handle on the plot and doesn't get much help from Gibson, who combined characters and scenarios from his other books. Action sequences and computer effects are appropriately spiffy, preventing a total system crash. **CW:** Strong sci-fi violence; language. 98m/C VHS, LV, 8mm, Closed Caption, DVD. Keanu Reeves, Dina Meyer, Ice-T, Takeshi, Dolph Lundgren, Henry Rollins, Udo Kier, Barbara Sukowa, Denis Akiyama; **D:** Robert Longo; **W:** William Gibson; **C:** Francois Protat; **M:** Brad Fiedel. COL

Johnny Nobody 🦴🦴½ 1961 A mysterious stranger murders a writer who has been taunting the residents of a quaint Irish town. A sleeper of a thriller, especially in the treatment of the town's reaction to this murder. 88m/B VHS, Beta. GB William Bendix, Aldo Ray, Nigel Patrick, Yvonne Mitchell, Cyril Cusack; **D:** Nigel Patrick. NO

Johnny 100 Pesos 🦴🦴 1993 Seventeen-year-old Johnny (Araiza) walks into a video store that is a front for an illegal currency exchange operation. He's the advance man for a quartet of criminals who are planning to rob the place but before they can escape with the cash, the police show up and the crooks take the store's inhabitants hostage. Now there's a standoff, with the media shamelessly broadcasting all events and the Chilean authorities struggling to control the escalating situation. Based on a true 1990 incident. Spanish with subtitles. 90m/C VHS. Armando Araiza, Patricia Rivera, Willy Semler, Sergio Hernandez.

Dr Gustavo Graef Marino; M: Gustavo Graef Marino; Gerardo Caceres; **C:** Jose Luis Arredondo; **M:** Andres Pollak. FXL

Johnny Reno 🦴½ 1966 Laughable western that has U.S. Marshal Andrews trying to save an accused killer from lynching. Of interest for star-watching only. Based on a story by Steve Fisher, A.C. Lyles, and Andrew Craddock. 83m/C VHS. Dana Andrews, Jane Russell, Lon Chaney Jr., John Agar, Lyle Bettger, Tom Drake, Richard Arlen, Robert Lowery; **D:** R.G. Springsteen; **W:** Steve Fisher. PAR

Johnny Shiloh 🦴🦴 1963 An underage youth becomes a heroic drummer during the Civil War. Originally a two-part Disney television show. 90m/C VHS, Beta. Kevin Corcoran, Brian Keith, Darryl Hickman, Skip Homeier; **D:** James Neilson. DIS

Johnny Stecchino 🦴🦴🦴 1992 (R) A breathless, charming comedy about mistaken identity, with Benigni starring as both Dante, a mild-mannered Roman bus driver, and his double, a notorious Mafioso known as "Johnny Toothpick." Dante happens to meet a lovely woman who takes exceptional interest in him, even inviting him to visit her home in Palermo. The reason she's interested is that Dante is the exact double of her husband, who has ratted on his fellow mobsters and needs a patsy to take the fall. Benigni's expressive body language and sweetness of character is well-showcased. In Italian with English subtitles. **CW:** Language and drug-related humor. 100m/C VHS, LV. IT Roberto Benigni, Nicoletta Braschi, Paolo Bonacelli, Ignazio Pappalardo, Franco Volpi; **D:** Roberto Benigni; **W:** Roberto Benigni, Vincenzo Cerami; **M:** Evan Lurie. NLC, IME, FCT

Johnny Suede 🦴🦴½ 1992 (R) Hip kid with big hair wanders the city seeking an identity via retro black suede elevator shoes. Sleepy surreal comedy walks Pitt through two romantic entanglements and a rendezvous with his own rock idol in his quest for musical talent and pop singer nirvana (not necessarily in that order). Candidate for induction into the David Lynch Movie Musuem of the Weird. **CW:** Language and sexual elements. 97m/C VHS, LV, Closed Caption. Brad Pitt, Calvin Levels, Nick Cave, Wilfredo Giovanni Clark, Alison Moir, Peter McRobbie, Tina Louise, Michael Mulheren, Catherine Keener, Samuel L. Jackson; **D:** Tom DiCillo; **W:** Tom DiCillo; **M:** Jim Farmer. PAR

Johnny Tiger 🦴🦴½ 1966 A teacher has his hands full when he arrives at the Seminole Reservation in Florida to instruct the Indian children. 100m/C VHS, Beta. Robert Taylor, Geraldine Brooks, Chad Everett, Brenda Scott; **D:** Paul Wendkos. REP

Johnny Tremain & the Sons of Liberty 🦴🦴 1958 The story of the gallant American patriots who participated in the Boston Tea Party. 85m/C VHS, Beta. Sebastian Cabot, Hal Stalmaster, Luana Patten, Richard Beymer; **D:** Robert Stevenson. DIS

Johnny We Hardly Knew Ye 🦴🦴½ 1977 Well-made biographical drama recounts John F. Kennedy's first political campaign for local office in Boston in 1946. Made for television. 90m/C VHS, Beta. Paul Rudd, Kevin Conway, William Prince, Burgess Meredith, Tom Berenger, Brian Dennehy, Kenneth McMillan; **D:** Gilbert Cates. TLF

Johnny's Girl 🦴🦴½ 1995 After her mom's death, a 16-year-old (Kirshner) moves to Anchorage, Alaska to live with her wayward dad (Williams). He's a kinda con man involved in shady deals, who tries to go legit in order to give his daughter a proper home. TV movie based on the novel by Kim Rich. 92m/C VHS. Mia Kirshner, Treat Williams, Ron White, Gloria Reuben, Shirley Douglas, Janne Mortil; **D:** John Kent Harrison. HMK

Johns 🦴🦴 1996 (R) A gritty, yet predictable tale of street hustling in L.A. redeemed by intense performances by its two lead actors. It's Christmas Eve and John (Arquette) has only one thing in mind: recover his stolen money and celebrate his birthday in style. On the way, he mentors crony Don-

nor (Haas), who's love for John blinds him to the rules of hustling, which can only lead to tragedy. Arquette's controlled performance is on target for the cynical male lead and Haas's doe-eyed look is perfect for the slightly dim-witted naivete his character revels in. Downfall comes when first-time director Silver fails to maintain actors' intensity with uneven editing and out of place symbolism. Still, not a bad first try. **CW:** Strong sexual content and language, and for some violence and drug use. 2.5m/C VHS. David Arquette, Lukas Haas, Arliss Howard, Keith David, Elliott Gould, Christopher Gartin, Joshua Schaefer, Wilson Cruz, Terrence DaShon Howard, Nicky Katt, Alanna Ubach; **D:** Scott Silver; **W:** Scott Silver; **C:** Tom Richmond; **M:** Charles D. Brown. NYR

A Joke of Destiny, Lying in Wait Around the Corner Like a Bandit 🦴🦴 A Joke of Destiny 1984 (PG) A irreverent satire about a Minister of the Interior (Tognazzi, of "La Cage aux Folles" fame) who becomes trapped in his high-tech limousine before a vital press conference. An exaggerated vision of Italian bureaucracy. With English subtitles. 105m/C VHS, Beta. IT Ugo Tognazzi, Piera Degli Esposti, Gastone Moschin, Renzo Montagnani, Valeria Golino; **D:** Lina Wertmuller; **W:** Lina Wertmuller. ORI

Jokes My Folks Never Told Me 🦴 1977 Series of blackouts and sketches featuring a bevy of beautiful women. 82m/C VHS, Beta. Sandy Johnson, Mariwin Roberts; **D:** Gerry Woolery.

The Jolly Paupers 🦴🦴½ Freylekhe Kabtsonim 1938 A pre-war comedy made in Warsaw about two small-town Jews who try to achieve fame and fortune in the face of setbacks, community quarrels, and insanity. In Yiddish with English subtitles. 62m/B VHS. Shimon Dzigan, Yisroel Shumacher, Max Bozyk, Menasha Oppenheim; **D:** Zygmund Turkow. ALD

Jolson Sings Again 🦴🦴 1949 This sequel to "The Jolson Story" brings back Larry Parks as the ebullient entertainer, with Jolson himself dubbing Parks's voice for the songs. Picking up where the other film ended, the movie chronicles Jolson's comeback in the 1940s and his tireless work with the USO overseas during WWII and the Korean War. 🎵After You've Gone; Chinatown, My Chinatown; Give My Regards to Broadway; I Only Have Eyes For You; I'm Just Wild About Harry; You Made Me Love You; I'm Looking Over a Four-Leaf Clover; Is It True What They Say About Dixie?; Ma Blushin' Rose. 96m/C VHS, Beta, LV. Larry Parks, William Demarest, Barbara Hale, Bill Goodwin; **D:** Henry Levin; **M:** George Duning. Nominations: Academy Awards '49: Best Color Cinematography, Best Story & Screenplay, Scoring of a Musical. COL

The Jolson Story 🦴🦴🦴 1946 A smash Hollywood bio of Jolson, from his childhood to super-stardom. Features dozens of vintage songs from Jolson's parade of hits. Jolson himself dubbed the vocals for Parks, rejuvenating his own career in the process. 🎵Swanee; You Made Me Love You; By the Light of the Silvery Moon; I'm Sitting On Top of the World; There's a Rainbow Round My Shoulder; My Mammy; Rock-A-Bye Your Baby With a Dixie Melody; Liza; Waiting for the Robert E. Lee. 128m/C VHS, Beta, LV. Larry Parks, Evelyn Keyes, William Demarest, Bill Goodwin, Tamara Shayne, John Alexander, Jimmy Lloyd, Ludwig Donath, Scotty Beckett; **D:** Alfred E. Green; **M:** Morris Stoloff. Academy Awards '46: Best Sound, Scoring of a Musical; Nominations: Academy Awards '46: Best Actor (Parks), Best Color Cinematography, Best Film Editing, Best Supporting Actor (Demarest). COL

Jon Jost's Frameup 🦴🦴 Frameup 1993 Cocky ex-con Ricky Lee hooks up with dizzy waitress Beth Ann and they head out on a 3000-mile nightmare road trip to California. Free-form story shot in 10 days. 91m/C VHS. Howard Swain, Nancy Carlin; **D:** Jon Jost; **W:** Jon Jost. WAC

Jonah Who Will Be 25 in the Year 2000 🎬🎬🎬½ *Jonas—Qui Aura 25 Ans en l'An 2000* **1976** A group of eight friends, former 60s radicals, try to adjust to growing older and coping with life in the 70s. The eccentric octet include a disillusioned journalist turned gambler, an unorthodox teacher, and a grocery store cashier who gives away food to the elderly. Wonderful performances highlight this social comedy. In French with English subtitles. **110m/C VHS.** *SI* Jean-Luc Bideau, Myriam Meziere, Miou-Miou, Jacques Denis, Rufus, Dominique Labourier, Roger Jendly, Miriam Boyer, Raymond Bussieres, Jonah; *D:* Alain Tanner; *W:* Alain Tanner; *C:* Renato Berta; *M:* Jean-Marie Senia. National Society of Film Critics Awards '76: Best Screenplay. *NYF*

Jonathan Livingston Seagull 🎬🎬½ **1973 (G)** Based on the best-selling novella by Richard Bach, this film quietly envisions a world of love, understanding, achievement, hope and individuality. **99m/C VHS, Beta.** James Franciscus, Juliet Mills; *D:* Hall Bartlett; *M:* Neil Diamond. Golden Globe Awards '74: Best Score; Nominations: Academy Awards '73: Best Cinematography, Best Film Editing. *PAR, WSH*

Joni 🎬🎬 **1979 (G)** An inspirational story based on the real life of Tada (playing herself) who was seriously injured in a diving accident, and her conquering of the odds. A born-again feature film based on the book by Tada. **75m/C VHS, Beta.** Joni Eareckson Tada, Bert Remsen, Katherine De Hetre, Cooper Huckabee; *D:* James F. Collier. *ART*

Jornada de Muerte 🎬 **198?** An ex-cop is hired to bring an important anti-Mob witness to trial via transcontinental train, and must fend off Mob attack squads in the process. In Spanish. **90m/C VHS, Beta.** *SP* Fred Williamson, Bernie Kuby, Heidi Dobbs. *UNI*

Jory 🎬🎬 **1972 (PG)** A young man's father is killed in a saloon fight, and he must grow up quickly to survive. **96m/C VHS, Beta.** Robby Benson, B.J. Thomas, John Marley; *D:* Jorge Fons. *COL*

Joseph 🎬🎬½ **1995** Following "Abraham" and "Jacob" comes the Old Testament story of young Joseph (Mercurio), beloved son of Jacob, who's sold into slavery by his envious older brothers. Joseph is bought by the Pharoah's chief steward, Potiphar (Kingsley), and, after a long series of tribulations, rises to become a power in Egypt, which unexpectedly leads Joseph to hold the fate of his long-lost family in his hands. Filmed in Morocco. **240m/C VHS, Closed Caption.** Paul Mercurio, Ben Kingsley, Martin Landau, Lesley Ann Warren, Warren Clarke, Alice Krige, Dominique Sanda, Stefano Dionisi, Valeria Cavalli, Peter Eyre, Timothy Bateson, Jamie Glover, Mike Attwell; *D:* Roger Young; *W:* Lionel Chetwynd, James Carrington; *C:* Raffaele Mertes; *M:* Marco Frisina. *TTC*

Joseph & His Brethren 🎬 *The Story of Joseph and His Brethren; Joseph Sold by His Brothers* **1960** A full-length dramatization of the Old Testament story. **103m/C VHS, Beta.** Geoffrey Horne, Robert Morley; *D:* Irving Rapper. *KEP*

Joseph Andrews 🎬🎬 **1977 (R)** This adaptation of a 1742 Henry Fielding novel chronicles the rise of Joseph Andrews from servant to personal footman (and fancy) of Lady Booby. **98m/C VHS, Beta.** *GB* Ann-Margret, Peter Firth, Jim Dale, Michael Hordern, Beryl Reid; *D:* Tony Richardson; *W:* Chris Bryant, Allan Scott; *C:* David Watkin; *M:* John Addison. *PAR*

Josepha 🎬🎬🎬 **1982 (R)** A husband and wife, both actors, are forced to re-examine their relationship when the wife finds a new love while on a film location. In French with English subtitles. **114m/C VHS, Beta.** *FR* Miou-Miou, Claude Brasseur, Bruno Cremer; *D:* Christopher Frank. *COL*

The Josephine Baker Story 🎬🎬🎬 **1990 (R)** Made-for-cable bio of exotic entertainer/activist Josephine Baker, an Afro-American woman from St. Louis who found superstardom in pre-WWII Europe, but repeated racism and rejection in the U.S. at times tinite treatment turns her eventful life into a standard rise-and-fall showbiz tale, but a great cast and lavish scope pull it through. Whitfield recreates Baker's (sometimes topless) dance routines; Carol Dennis dubs her singing. Filmed on location in Budapest. *CW:* Sensuality. **129m/C VHS, Closed Caption.** Lynn Whitfield, Ruben Blades, David Dukes, Craig T. Nelson, Louis Gossett Jr., Kene Holliday, Vivian Bonnell; *D:* Brian Gibson; *M:* Ralph Burns. *HBO, FCT*

Josh and S.A.M. 🎬🎬 **1993 (PG-13)** Road movie for youngsters with a twist: the driver can barely see over the dashboard. Josh and Sam are brothers whose parents are splitting. They cope by taking off on their own. Sam, meanwhile has been convinced by Josh that he's not a real boy at all, but rather a S.A.M.: Strategically Altered Mutant. Weber's directorial debut will appeal to young kids, but adults will see over the dashboard and through the transparent plot. *CW:* Kids in jeopardy. **97m/C VHS, LV, Closed Caption.** Jacob Tierney, Noah Fleiss, Martha Plimpton, Joan Allen, Christopher Penn, Stephen Tobolowsky, Ronald Guttman; *D:* Billy Weber; *W:* Frank Deese; *C:* Don Burgess; *M:* Thomas Newman. *NLC*

Josh Kirby...Time Warrior: Chapter 1, Planet of the Dino-Knights 🎬🎬½ **1995 (PG)** Time-traveling 14-year-old Josh Kirby is accidently zapped to the 25th-century where fierce warriors ride dinosaurs and a madman is out to destroy the universe. The first tale in a fantasy series designed as an old-fashioned movie serial, complete with cliff-hanger ending. **88m/C VHS, Beta, Closed Caption.** Corbin Allred, Jennifer Burns, Derek Webster, John De Mita; *D:* Ernest Farino; *W:* Ethan Reiff, Cyrus Voris, Paul Callisi. *PAR*

Josh Kirby...Time Warrior: Chapter 2, The Human Pets 🎬🎬 **1995 (PG)** Josh and his friends now find themselves in the year 70,370—held hostage by the enormous Fatlings, who regard their human minds as pet-like action toys. **90m/C VHS, Beta, Closed Caption.** Corbin Allred, Jennifer Burns; *D:* Frank Arnold; *W:* Ethan Reiff, Cyrus Voris, Paul Callisi. *PAR*

Josh Kirby...Time Warrior: Chapter 3, Trapped on Toyworld 🎬🎬½ **1995 (PG)** Josh is stranded away from his friends on the strange planet of Toyworld and must rely on the lifelike creations of a toy magnate to defend himself from the villainous Dr. Zoetrope. **90m/C VHS, Beta, Closed Caption.** Corbin Allred, Jennifer Burns, Derek Webster, Sharon Lee Jones, Buck Kartalian, Barrie Ingham; *D:* Frank Arnold; *W:* Nick Paine. *PAR*

Josh Kirby...Time Warrior: Chapter 4, Eggs from 70 Million B.C. 🎬🎬½ **1995 (PG)** Josh and his pals finds themselves in a military compound that is under attack and encounter some very hungry alien worms. **93m/C VHS, Beta, Closed Caption.** Corbin Allred, Jennifer Burns, Derek Webster, Gary Kasper, Barrie Ingham; *D:* Mark Manos. *PAR*

Josh Kirby...Time Warrior: Chapter 5, Journey to the Magic Cavern 🎬🎬½ **1996 (PG)** Josh and pals find themselves in the center of a planet where they are befriended by the weird Mushroom People who are under siege by a monster known as "the Muncher." **93m/C VHS, Beta, Closed Caption.** Corbin Allred, Jennifer Burns, Derek Webster, Michael Hagiwara, Barrie Ingham; *D:* Ernest Farino; *W:* Ethan Reiff, Cyrus Voris. *PAR*

Josh Kirby...Time Warrior: Chapter 6, Last Battle for the Universe 🎬🎬½ **1996 (PG)** Josh is ready to get back to his own time but first he must survive a battle between long-feuding rivals of the time-belt. **90m/C VHS, Beta, Closed Caption.** Corbin Allred, Jennifer Burns, Derek Webster, Barrie Ingham; *D:* Frank Arnold; *W:* Ethan Reiff, Cyrus Voris. *PAR*

Joshua 🎬 *Black Rider* **1976 (R)** Western drama about a vigilante who tracks down the group of outlaws that killed his mother. **75m/C VHS.** Fred Williamson, Isela Vega; *D:* Larry Spangler. *NO*

Joshua Then and Now 🎬🎬🎬 **1985 (R)** When a Jewish-Canadian novelist (Woods) is threatened by the breakup of his marriage to his WASPy wife, compounded by a gay scandal, he re-examines his picaresque history, including his life with his gangster father (Arkin). A stirring story that is enhanced by a strong performance by Woods, as well as a picturesque Canadian backdrop. Adapted by Mordecai Richler from his own novel. **102m/C VHS, Beta, Closed Caption.** *CA* James Woods, Gabrielle Lazure, Alan Arkin, Michael Sarrazin, Chuck Shamata, Linda Sorensen, Alan Scarfe, Alexander Knox, Robert Joy, Ken Campbell; *D:* Ted Kotcheff; *W:* Mordecai Richler; *M:* Philippe Sarde. Genie Awards '86: Best Supporting Actor (Arkin), Best Supporting Actress (Sorensen). *FOX*

Jour de Fete 🎬🎬🎬½ *The Big Day; Holiday* **1948** Tati's first film, dealing with a French postman's accelerated efforts at efficiency after viewing a motivational film of the American post service. Wonderful slapstick moments. In French with English subtitles. **79m/B VHS, Beta, LV.** *FR* Jacques Tati, Guy Decomble, Paul Fankeur; *D:* Jacques Tati. *VDM, CRC, NLC*

Journey 🎬 **1977 (PG)** Violent story of a girl who is rescued from the Saguenay River and falls in love with her rescuer. Choosing to remain in the remote pioneer community of this "hero," she brings everyone bad luck and misery. **87m/C VHS, Beta.** *CA* Genevieve Bujold, John Vernon; *D:* Paul Almond. *NO*

Journey 🎬🎬½ **1995 (PG)** Eleven-year-old Journey (Pomeranc) and his teenaged sister Cat (Dushku) are abandoned by their unhappy, restless mother Min (Tilly) at the home of her parents, Marcus (Robards) and Lottie (Fricker). Marcus is an amatuer photographer and Journey searches through the family photo albums to find reasons for his mother's leaving as he and his grandfather slowly build their relationship. Based on the book by Patricia MacLachlan. **98m/C VHS.** Max Pomeranc, Jason Robards Jr., Brenda Fricker, Eliza Dushku, Meg Tilly; *D:* Tom McLoughlin; *W:* Patricia MacLachlan; *C:* Kees Van Oostrum. *HMK*

Journey Back to Oz **1971** Animated special features Dorothy and Toto returning to visit their friends in the magical land of Oz. **90m/C VHS, Beta.** *V:* Liza Minnelli, Ethel Merman, Paul Lynde, Milton Berle, Mickey Rooney, Danny Thomas. *FHE, KAR, HHE*

Journey Beneath the Desert 🎬🎬 *Antinea, l'Amante Della Citta Sepolta* **1961** Three engineers discover the lost-but-always-found-in-the-movies kingdom of Atlantis when their helicopter's forced down in the sunny Sahara. A poor hostess with a rotten disposition, the mean sub-saharan queen doesn't roll out the welcome mat for her grounded guests, so a beautiful slave babe helps them make a hasty exit. Dawdling Euro production with adequate visuals. **105m/C VHS, Beta.** *FR IT* Haya Harareet, Jean-Louis Trintignant, Brad Fulton, Amedeo Nazzari, George Riviere, Giulia Rubini, Gabriele Tinti, Gian Marie Volonte; *D:* Edgar G. Ulmer, Giuseppe Masini, Frank Borzage. *SNC*

Journey for Margaret 🎬🎬🎬 **1942** Young and Day star as an expectant American couple living in London during WWII so Young can cover the war for a newspaper back home. After she loses her baby during an air raid, Day heads back to the States. Young stays in London where he meets two young orphans and takes them under his wing. He decides to take them back to the United States and adopt them, but problems arise. A real tearjerker and a good story that shows the war through the eyes of children. O'Brien's first film. Based on the book by William L. White. **81m/B VHS.** Robert Young, Laraine Day, Fay Bainter, Signe Hasso, Margaret O'Brien, Nigel Bruce, G.P. Huntley Jr., William Severn, Doris Lloyd, Halliwell Hobbes, Jill Esmond; *D:* Woodbridge S. Van Dyke. *MGM, FCT*

Journey into Fear 🐾🐾🐾 1919 During WWII, an American armaments expert is smuggled out of Istanbul, but Axis agents are close behind. From the novel by Eric Ambler; remade for television in 1974. **71m/B VHS, Beta, LV.** Joseph Cotten, Dolores Del Rio, Orson Welles, Agnes Moorehead, Norman Foster; **D:** Norman Foster; **C:** Karl Struss. *RXM, TTC*

Journey into Fear 🐾½ *Burn Out* 1974 A remake of the 1942 Orson Welles classic about a geologist ensnared in Turkish intrigue and murder. **96m/C VHS, Beta.** *CA* Sam Waterston, Vincent Price, Shelley Winters, Donald Pleasence, Zero Mostel, Yvette Mimieux, Ian McShane; **D:** Daniel Mann; **M:** Alex North. *ART*

The Journey of August King 🐾🐾½ 1995 (PG-13) Adapted by Ehle from his own 1971 novel, set in 1815, about a runaway slave (Newton) protected by a lonely farmer against the landowner and posse tracking her down. August King (Patric), a widower on his way home from town, comes upon Annalees (Newton), prize possession of powerful slaveowner Olaf Singletary (Drake). August, a highly principled man, resists helping her at first, for fear of breaking the law and losing his farm and only remaining possessions. But he rises to higher moral ground, deciding to help her find freedom, whatever the consequences. Director Duigan ("Sirens") crafts a thoughtful, but not particularly suspenseful, period piece of early American history. Patric/Newton relationship reflects the gradual feel of the film. Drake booms as slaveowner. Includes brief brutal scene of slave torture. **CW:** Scene of shocking violence. **91m/C VHS, LV, Closed Caption.** Jason Patric, Thandie Newton, Larry Drake, Sam Waterston; **D:** John Duigan; **W:** John Ehle; **C:** Slawomir Idziak; **M:** Stephen Endelman. *TOU*

Journey of Honor 🐾🐾½ 1991 (PG-13) During a civil war in 17th century Japan, a nearly defeated Shogun sends his son, Lord Mayeda, to Spain to buy guns from King Phillip III. Along the way he must fight shipboard spies and fierce storms, and once Mayeda arrives in Spain, he is confronted by the evil Duke Don Pedro. In defeating Don Pedro, Mayeda saves King Phillip, gets his guns, and wins the love of Lady Cecilia. To get revenge, Don Pedro plots to capture the Japanese ship and enslave everyone on board. Lots of action and fine acting. Based on a story by martial artist Sho Kosugi. **107m/C VHS, Beta, LV, Letterbox, Closed Caption.** Sho Kosugi, David Essex, Kane Kosugi, Christopher Lee, Norman Lloyd, Ronald Pickup, John Rhys-Davies, Dylan Kussman, Toshiro Mifune; **D:** Gordon Hessler. *USH*

Journey of Hope 🐾🐾🐾½ 1990 (PG) Powerful drama about Kurdish family that sells its material possessions in hopes of emigrating legally to Switzerland, where life will surely be better. During the perilous journey, smugglers take their money and the family must attempt crossing the formidable slopes of the Swiss Mountains on foot. Based on a true story. In Turkish with English subtitles. **111m/C VHS; LV.** *SI* Necmettin Cobanoglu, Nur Surer, Emin Sivas, Yaman Okay, Mathias Gnaedinger, Dietmar Schoenherr; **D:** Xavier Koller; **W:** Xavier Koller. Academy Awards '90: Best Foreign Language Film. *WAR, HBO*

The Journey of Natty Gann 🐾🐾🐾½ 1985 (PG) With the help of a wolf (brilliantly portrayed by a dog) and a drifter, a 14-year-old girl travels across the country in search of her father in this warm and touching film. Excellent Disney representation of life during the Great Depression. **101m/C VHS, Beta, LV.** Meredith Salenger, John Cusack, Ray Wise, Scatman Crothers, Lainie Kazan, Verna Bloom; **D:** Jeremy Paul Kagan; **W:** Jeanne Rosenberg; **M:** James Horner. Nominations: Academy Awards '85: Best Costume Design. *DIS*

Journey Through Rosebud 1972 A reenactment of the 1970s protest at Wounded Knee by Native Americans. **93m/C VHS, Beta.** Robert Forster, Eddie Little Sky; **D:** Tom Giles. *NLC*

Journey to Spirit Island 🐾🐾½ 1992 (PG) A young Native American girl dreams of her ancestors who are buried on Spirit Island, an ancient burial ground. However, the island is now scheduled to be developed into a resort. With the help of three friends the girl tries to protect the land. Filmed in the Pacific Northwest. **93m/C VHS, Beta.** Brandon Douglas, Gabriel Damon, Tony Acierto, Nick Ramus, Marie Antoinette Rodgers, Tarek McCarthy; **D:** Laszlo Pal.

Journey to the Center of the Earth 🐾🐾🐾 1959 A scientist and student undergo a hazardous journey to find the center of the earth and along the way they find the lost city of Atlantis. Based upon the Jules Verne novel. **132m/C VHS, Beta, LV, Closed Caption.** James Mason, Pat Boone, Arlene Dahl, Diane Baker, Thayer David, Alan Napier, Peter Ronson; **D:** Henry Levin. Nominations: Academy Awards '59: Best Art Direction/Set Decoration (Color), Best Sound.*FCT, FUS*

Journey to the Center of the Earth 1976 An animated version of the Jules Verne classic about a scientist's quest to reach the earth's core. **50m/C VHS, Beta.** *MGM*

Journey to the Center of the Earth 1988 (PG) A young nanny and two teenage boys discover Atlantis while exploring a volcano. **83m/C VHS, Beta, LV.** Nicola Cowper, Paul Carafotes, Ilan Mitchell-Smith; **D:** Rusty Lemorande; **W:** Rusty Lemorande, Kitty Chalmers.

Journey to the Center of Time 🐾½ 1967 A scientist and his crew are hurled into a time trap when a giant reactor explodes. **83m/C VHS, Beta.** Lyle Waggoner, Scott Brady, Gigi Perreau, Anthony Eisley; **D:** David L. Hewitt.

Journey to the Far Side of the Sun 🐾🐾🐾 *Doppelganger* 1969 (G) Chaos erupts in the Earth's scientific community when it is discovered that a second, identical Earth is on the other side of the Sun. Both planets end up sending out identical exploratory missions. The denouement is worth the journey. **92m/C VHS, Beta, LV, Letterbox.** *GB* Roy Thinnes, Ian Hendry, Lynn Loring, Patrick Wymark, Loni von Friedl, Herbert Lom, Ed Bishop; **D:** Robert Parrish; **W:** Gerry Anderson. *USH*

Journey to the Lost City 🐾½ *Tiger of Bengal* 1958 Architect living in India happens upon a lost city, the rulership of which is being contested by two brothers. In the midst of fighting snakes and tigers, he falls in love with Paget, a beautiful dancer. This feature is actually a poorly edited hybrid of two Lang German adventures, "Der Tiger von Eschnapur" and "Das Indische Grabmal" merged for U.S. release. **95m/C VHS, Beta.** *FR IT GE* Debra Paget, Paul Christian, Walter Reyer, Claus Holm, Sabine Bethmann, Valeri Inkizhinov, Rene Deltgen, Luciana Paluzzi; **D:** Fritz Lang. *SNC*

Journeys from Berlin/1971 🐾🐾½ 1984 This is the true story about a woman who tries to find a solution to her own problems in life. **125m/C VHS, Beta.** *NO*

Joy House 🐾🐾 *The Love Cage; Les Felins* 1964 An American woman befriends a handsome French playboy when her husband sends gangsters to kill him. **98m/B VHS, Beta.** Jane Fonda, Alain Delon, Lola Albright; **D:** Rene Clement; **W:** Rene Clement. *NO*

The Joy Luck Club 🐾🐾🐾 1993 (R) Universal themes in mother/daughter relationships are explored in a clever Hollywood first rejected as too narrow, but which proved to be a modest sleeper hit. Tan skillfully weaves the plot of her 1989 best-seller into a screenplay which centers around young June's going-away party. Slowly the stories of four Chinese women, who meet weekly to play mah-jongg, are unraveled. Each vignette reveals life in China for the four women and the tragedies they survived, before reaching into the present to capture the relationships between the mothers and their daughters. Powerful, relevant, and moving.**CW:** Strong thematic material. **136m/C VHS, LV, Letterbox, Closed Caption.** Tsai

Chin, Kieu Chinh, France Nuyen, Rosalind Chao, Tamlyn Tomita, Lisa Lu, Lauren Tom, Ming-Na Wen, Michael Paul Chan, Andrew McCarthy, Christopher Rich, Russell Wong, Victor Wong, Vivian Wu, Jack Ford, Diane Baker; **D:** Wayne Wang; **W:** Amy Tan, Ronald Bass. Nominations: Writers Guild of America '93: Best Adapted Screenplay. *TOU, HPH*

The Joy of Knowledge 🐾½ *Le Gai Savoir* 1965 Godard's experimental use of language and image in a plotless narrative. Berto and Leaud sit together on a bare sound stage and are exposed to popular culture through images, word association, and conversation. In French with English subtitles. **96m/C VHS.** *FR* Juliet Berto, Jean-Pierre Leaud; **D:** Jean-Luc Godard; **W:** Jean-Luc Godard. *FCT*

Joy of Living 🐾🐾🐾 1938 Vintage screwball farce about a randy playboy trying to win over a pragmatic songstress. ♫You Couldn't Be Cuter; A Heavenly Party; What's Good About Goodnight; Just Let Me Look At You. **90m/B VHS, Beta, LV.** Irene Dunne, Douglas Fairbanks Jr., Alice Brady, Guy Kibbee, Jean Dixon, Eric Blore, Lucille Ball, Warren Hymer, Billy Gilbert, Frank Milan; **D:** Tay Garnett; **M:** Jerome Kern, Dorothy Fields. *TTC*

Joy of Sex 🐾 1984 (R) An undercover narcotics agent is sent to Southern California's Richard M. Nixon High School to investigate the school's extracurricular activities. Typical teen sex flick; no relation to the book. **93m/C VHS, Beta.** Cameron Dye, Michelle Meyrink, Colleen Camp, Christopher Lloyd, Ernie Hudson, Lisa Langlois; **D:** Martha Coolidge; **W:** Kathleen Rowell. *PAR*

Joy Ride to Nowhere 🐾 1978 (PG) Two young women steal a Cadillac with two million dollars in the trunk and ride away with the owner hot on their tail. **86m/C VHS, Beta.** Leslie Ackerman, Sandy Serrano, Len Lesser, Mel Welles, Ron Ross, Speed Stearns. *NO*

Joy Sticks WOOF! 1983 (R) Joy sticks in question are down at the arcade. Businessman wants to shut down local video game palace. Inhabitants just say no. **88m/C VHS, Beta, LV.** Joe Don Baker, Leif Green, Jim Greenleaf, Scott McGinnis, Jonathan Gries; **D:** Greydon Clark. *VES*

Joyful Laughter 🐾🐾 1954 The dreary life of an Italian movie bit player draws strength from Magnani's powerful emotions as she repeatedly comes near to success only to find disappointment. Set in Rome. With English subtitles. **106m/C VHS.** *IT* **D:** Mario Monicelli. *FST*

Joyless Street 🐾🐾🐾½ *Street of Sorrow; Die Freudlose Gasse* 1925 Silent film focuses on the dismal life of the middle class in Austria during an economic crisis. Lovely piano score accompanies the film. **96m/B VHS, Beta, LV.** *GE* Greta Garbo, Werner Krauss, Asta Nielsen, Jaro Furth, Loni Nest, Max Kohlhase, Silva Torf, Karl Ettlinger, Ilka Gruning, Agnes Esterhazy, Alexander Musky, Valeska Gert; **D:** G.W. Pabst; **W:** Willi Haas; **C:** Guido Seeber, Curt Oertel, Walter Robert Lach. *VYY, MRV, FST*

Joyride 🐾½ 1977 (R) Mistreated by a union official, three friends steal a car for a joy ride and plummet into a life of crime. **91m/C VHS, Beta.** Desi Arnaz Jr., Robert Carradine, Melanie Griffith, Anne Lockhart; **D:** Joseph Ruben. *ART, VES*

Joyride 🐾½ 1997 (R) Three friends make the mistake of stealing a car that belongs to a beautiful blonde assassin, who'll stop at nothing to get her wheels back (her latest victim is stashed in the trunk).**CW:** Violence, sexuality and strong language. **92m/C VHS, LV, Closed Caption.** Tobey Maguire, Wilson Cruz, Amy Hathaway, Chrisstina Naify, James Karen, Adam West; **D:** Quinton Peeples; **W:** Quinton Peeples; **C:** S. Douglas Smith. *ART*

Ju Dou 🐾🐾🐾🐾 1990 (PG-13) Breath-taking story of an aging factory owner in search of an heir. He takes a third wife, but she finds caring in the arms of another man, when her husband's brutality proves too much. Beautiful color cinematography, excellent acting, and epic story. Oscar nominee for Best Foreign Film. In Chinese with English subtitles. **98m/C VHS, LV.** *CH* Gong Li, Li Bao-Tian, Li Wei, Zhang Yi, Zheng Jian; **D:** Zhang Yimou; **C:** Gu

Changwei. Nominations: Academy Awards '90: Best Foreign Language Film. *ART, BTV*

Juarez ♂♂ 1939 A revolutionary leader overthrows the Mexican government and then becomes President of the country. Based on the true story of Benito Pablo Juarez. **132m/B VHS, Beta.** Paul Muni, John Garfield, Bette Davis, Claude Rains, Gale Sondergaard, Charles Halton; *D:* William Dieterle; *C:* Gaetano Antonio "Tony" Gaudio. Nominations: Academy Awards '39: Best Black and White Cinematography, Best Supporting Actor (Aherne). *MGM, FCT*

Jubal ♂♂ 1956 A rancher (Borgnine) seeks advice from a cowhand (Ford) about pleasing his wife, but another cowhand (Steiger) implies that Ford is "advising" Borgnine's wife, as well. A western take on "Othello." **101m/C VHS, Beta, LV.** Glenn Ford, Rod Steiger, Ernest Borgnine, Felicia Farr, Charles Bronson, Valerie French, Noah Beery Jr.; *D:* Delmer Daves. *IME*

Jubilee Trail ♂♂½ 1954 Wagon trail western follows the lives of a group of pioneers from New Orleans to California. A woman goes through a marriage, a baby, and her husband's death. Ralston has some good tunes in this lush picture. **103m/C VHS.** Vera Ralston, Joan Leslie, Forrest Tucker, John Russell, Ray Middleton, Pat O'Brien; *D:* Joseph Kane. *REP*

Jud ♂½ 1971 (PG) Society's refusal to understand a young soldier returning from the Vietnam conflict leads to violence and tragedy. Jennings' first film; music by Phillips of Creedence Clearwater Revival. **80m/C VHS, Beta.** Joseph Kaufmann, Robert Deman, Alix Wyeth, Norman Burton, Claudia Jennings, Maurice Sherbanee, Vic Dunlop, Bonnie Bittner; *D:* Gunther Collins; *M:* Stu Phillips.

Jud Suess ♂♂♂ 1940 Classic, scandalous Nazi anti-Semitic tract about a Jew who rises to power under the duchy of Wuerttemberg by stepping on, abusing, and raping Aryans. A film that caused riots at its screenings and tragedy for its cast and crew, and the Third Reich's most notorious fictional expression of policy. In German with English subtitles. **100m/B VHS, Beta.** *GE* Ferdinand Marian, Werner Krauss, Heinrich George, Kristina Soderbaum, Eugene Klopfer; *D:* Veit Harlan. *NOS, VCD, IHF*

The Judas Project: The Ultimate Encounter ♂½ 1994 (PG-13) Religious fantasy finds Jesse battling corruption and pseudo-religious figures in a fight to save a violent and decaying world. But Jesse's destroyed by his own disciple, Jude. Sound familiar? (There's even a cruxifixion scene.) **98m/C VHS.** John O'Bannion, Ramy Zada, Richard Herd; *D:* James H. Barden; *C:* Bryan England.

Jude ♂♂♂ *Jude the Obscure* 1996 (R) Engrossing retelling of Thomas Hardy's depressing 1896 novel "Jude the Obscure," set in his fictional Wessex. Country stonemason Jude (Eccleston) hopes to improve his impoverished lot in life by becoming a student at Christminister University. But first he's distracted into an unwise marriage with lively Arabella (Griffiths), who soon leaves him, and then into an ill-fated romance with his capricious cousin Sue Brideshead (Winslet). Class and societal barriers prove impossible for the couple to overcome and lead to a shocking tragedy. Hardy's book was so badly received by critics that he never wrote another novel and stuck to poetry for the rest of his life. *CW:* Strong sexuality and intense depictions of death and birth. **123m/C VHS.** *GB* Christopher Eccleston, Kate Winslet, Liam Cunningham, Rachel Griffiths; *D:* Michael Winterbottom; *W:* Hossein Amini; *C:* Eduardo Serra; *M:* Adrian Johnston. *PGV*

Jude the Obscure ♂♂½ 1971 Thomas Hardy's last novel is a tragic, bleak story of mismatched lovers and blighted ambitions. Jude is a poor stonemason whose dream is to get a proper education and marry his beloved cousin. Failing to get into Oxford he is seduced by a farm girl, whom he marries and fathers a child by (a gnome-like creature named "Father Time").

Meanwhile, his cousin marries a schoolteacher who disgusts her. Finally, the two thwarted lovers marry, only to find themselves living in poverty and hopelessness. After this novel (said to be Hardy's favorite), he devoted the rest of his long life to poetry. On three cassettes. **262m/C VHS.** *GB* Robert Powell, Daphne Heard, Alex Marshall, John Franklyn-Robbins, Fiona Walker; *D:* Hugh David; *W:* Harry Green. *FOX, FCT, VCO*

Judex ♂♂½ 1964 Judex, a sensitive cloaked hero-avenger, fights master criminal gangs. In French with English subtitles. Remake of the silent French serial. **103m/B VHS, Beta.** *FR IT* Channing Pollock, Francine Berge, Jacques Jouanneau; *D:* Georges Franju; *M:* Maurice Jarre. *NOS, SNC, HHT*

The Judge ♂½ 1949 A courtroom crime-drama about the consequences of infidelity. A lawyer sends an acquitted hit man to kill his wife and her lover. Things go amiss and the lawyer winds up dead. **69m/B VHS.** Milburn Stone, Katherine DeMille, Paul Guilfoyle, Jonathan Hale; *D:* Elmer Clifton. *SNC*

Judge & Jury ♂½ 1996 (R) Convicted killer Joseph Miller (Keith) dies in the electric chair but then manages to return from the dead to get revenge. So how do you kill someone who's already dead? Well, Michael Silvano (Kove) will have to find a way to send Miller back where he belongs. *CW:* Continuous strong violence and language. **98m/C VHS, LV.** David Keith, Martin Kove, Laura Johnson, Thomas Ian Nichols, Paul Koslo; *D:* John Eyres; *W:* John Eyres, John Cianetti, Amanda I. Kirpaul; *C:* Bob Paone; *M:* Johnathon Flood. *APX*

The Judge and the Assassin ♂♂♂½ *Le Juge et L'assassin* 1975 Intriguing courtroom drama. A prejudiced judge has his values challenged when he must decide if a child-killer is insane or not. The relationship that develops between the judge and the killer is the film's focus. Excellent direction by Tavernier. In French with English subtitles. **130m/C VHS, Beta, LV, Letterbox.** *FR* Philippe Noiret, Michel Galabru, Isabelle Huppert, Jean-Claude Brialy; *D:* Bertrand Tavernier; *W:* Bertrand Tavernier. Cesar Awards '77: Best Writing, Best Score. *CVC, IME, TPV*

Judge Dredd ♂½ 1995 (R) Futuristic lawman Dredd (Stallone), who acts as cop, judge, jury, and executioner, is framed for murder by his "brother" Rico (Assante), a renegade misfit. With the help of a female Judge (Lane) and an ex-con (Schneider), Dredd fights to clear his name and save the people of Mega City One. Big names, big bangs, big budget—big disappointment. Dialogue makes "Rambo" sound like Shakespeare, and the choppy, convoluted plot doesn't help. Schneider provides a rare bright spot while acting circles around Sly, who hoped (in vain) that the project would provide him with another profitable action franchise. The source comic book has been a cult favorite in England for 20 years. *CW:* Continuous violent action. **96m/C VHS, LV, Closed Caption.** Sylvester Stallone, Armand Assante, Diane Lane, Rob Schneider, Joan Chen, Juergen Prochnow, Max von Sydow; *D:* Danny Cannon; *W:* Steven E. de Souza, Michael De Luca, William Wisher; *M:* Alan Silvestri. Nominations: Golden Raspberry Awards '95: Worst Actor (Stallone). *TOU*

Judge Horton and the Scottsboro Boys ♂♂½ 1976 A courtroom drama focusing on a famous 1931 trial. A courageous judge must battle the South in the case of nine black men charged with gang-raping two white women. Made for television. **100m/C VHS.** Arthur Hill, Vera Miles, Ken Kercheval, Suzanne Lederer, Tom Ligon; *D:* Fielder Cook. *ART*

Judge Priest ♂♂♂ 1934 Small-town judge in the old South stirs up the place with stinging humor and common-sense observances as he tangles with prejudices and civil injustices. Funny, warm slice-of-life is occasionally defeated by racist characterizations. Ford remade it later as "The Sun Shines Bright." Taken from the Irvin S. Cobb stories. **80m/B VHS, Beta.** Will Rogers, Stepin

Fetchit, Anita Louise, Henry B. Walthall; *D:* John Ford. *NOS, MRV, HHT*

The Judge Steps Out ♂♂½ 1949 Pleasant, light comedy about a hen-pecked, Bostonian judge who decides he's had enough and heads for balmy California. There he finds a job in a restaurant and, more importantly, a sympathetic friend in its female owner. He soon finds himself falling for the woman, and realizes he faces an important decision. **91m/B VHS.** Alexander Knox, Ann Sothern, George Tobias, Sharyn Moffett, Florence Bates, Frieda Inescort, Myrna Dell, Ian Wolfe, H.B. Warner; *D:* Boris Ingster. *TTC*

Judgment ♂♂♂ 1990 (PG-13) A devout Catholic couple are shocked to learn that their young son has been molested by the popular priest of their small Louisiana parish. When they find out their son is not the first victim, and other families have been coerced into silence, they vow to fight back. Tasteful treatment of a real court case. Made for cable. **89m/C VHS, Closed Caption.** Keith Carradine, Blythe Danner, Jack Warden, David Strathairn, Bob Gunton, Mitchell Ryan, Michael Faustino; *D:* Tom Topor; *W:* Tom Topor. *HBO*

Judgment at Nuremberg ♂♂♂♂ 1961 It's 1948 and a group of high-level Nazis are on trial for war crimes. Chief Justice Tracy must resist political pressures as he presides over the trials. Excellent performances throughout, especially by Dietrich and Garland. Considers to what extent an individual may be held accountable for actions committed under orders of a superior officer. Consuming account of the Holocaust and WWII; deeply moving and powerful. Based on a "Playhouse 90" television program. **178m/B VHS, Beta, LV.** Spencer Tracy, Burt Lancaster, Richard Widmark, Montgomery Clift, Maximilian Schell, Judy Garland, Marlene Dietrich, William Shatner; *D:* Stanley Kramer; *W:* Abby Mann; *C:* Ernest Laszlo; *M:* Ernest Gold. Academy Awards '61: Best Actor (Schell), Best Adapted Screenplay; Golden Globe Awards '62: Best Actor—Drama (Schell), Best Director (Kramer); New York Film Critics Awards '61: Best Actor (Schell), Best Screenplay; Nominations: Academy Awards '61: Best Actor (Tracy), Best Art Direction/Set Decoration (B & W), Best Black and White Cinematography, Best Costume Design (B & W), Best Director (Kramer), Best Film Editing, Best Picture, Best Supporting Actor (Clift), Best Supporting Actress (Garland). *MGM, FOX, BTV*

Judgment Day ♂ 1988 (PG-13) Four college buddies pick the wrong New England town for their vacation. It seems that the town made a deal with the Devil in 1689 to save themselves from the plague, and now the Dark Master is here to collect. **93m/C VHS, Beta.** Kenneth McLeod, David Anthony Smith, Monte Markham, Gloria Hayes, Peter Mark Richman, Cesar Romero; *D:* Ferde Grofe Jr. *NO*

Judgment in Berlin ♂♂½ *Escape to Freedom* 1988 (PG) East German family hijacks a U.S. airliner into West Germany, and then must stand trial in Berlin before a troubled American judge. Based on a true 1978 incident and the book by Herbert J. Stern. **92m/C VHS, Beta, LV.** Martin Sheen, Sam Wanamaker, Max Gail, Sean Penn, Heinz Hoenig, Carl Lumbly, Max Volkert Martens, Harris Yulin, Jutta Speidel, Juerger Hemrich; *D:* Leonard Penn; *W:* Joshua Sinclair; *M:* Peter Goldfoot. *COL*

Judgment Night ♂♂ 1993 (R) Four macho buddies on their way to a boxing match detour a highway traffic jam via surface streets and find themselves witnesses to a murder. The rest of their guys-night-out is spent trying to escape a gloomy ghetto and determined killer (played convincingly by Leary). All of the action takes place after dark on the streets and in the sewers and, subsequently, the scenes are extremely dark with only a burnt orange lighting. Lots of action and a little oomph. Based on a story by Lewis Colick and Jere Cunningham. *CW:* Language and strong violence and brutality. **109m/C VHS, LV, Closed Caption.** Emilio Estevez, Cuba Gooding Jr., Stephen Dorff, Denis Leary, Jeremy Piven, Peter Greene; *D:* Stephen Hopkins; *W:* Lewis Colick; *M:* Alan Silvestri. *USH*

Judicial Consent ♫♫½ 1991 Gwen War wick (Bedelia) is an accomplished criminal court judge with a bland husband (Patton) and a lot of unfulfilled desires. At least one desire is taken care of when Gwen succumbs to the charms of handsome law clerk Martin (Wirth). Then her colleague Charles (Coleman) is murdered and all the evidence points to Gwen. She knows she's been set up but can Gwen prove her innocence? Familiar plot, good performances although Patton gets stuck in an underwritten role. 101m/C VHS. Bonnie Bedelia, Dabney Coleman, Billy Wirth, Will Patton, Lisa Blount; **D:** William Bindley; **W:** William Bindley; **M:** Christopher Young. AVE

Judith of Bethulia ♫♫♫ 1914 A young widow uses her charm and wits to save her city from attack by the Assyrians. Based on the Apocrypha, this is the last film Griffith directed for Biograph. It was re-released as "Her Condoned Sin" in 1971, including two reels of Griffith's outtakes. 65m/B VHS, LV. Blanche Sweet, Henry B. Walthall, Mae Marsh, Robert "Bobbie" Harron, Lillian Gish, Dorothy Gish, Kate Bruce, Harry Carey Sr.; **D:** D.W. Griffith; **W:** D.W. Griffith. GPV, NOS, VYY

Juggernaut ♫½ 1937 Not the classic disaster film of the 1970s. A young woman hires a sinister doctor (Karloff) to murder her wealthy husband. The doctor, who happens to be insane, does away with the husband and then goes on a poisoning spree. Seems to drag on forever. 64m/B VHS, Beta, Closed Caption. Boris Karloff, Mona Goya, Arthur Margetson. NOS, SNC, VYY

Juggernaut ♫♫♫ 1974 (PG-13) Well-done drama about a doomed luxury liner. A madman plants bombs aboard a cruise ship and mocks the crew about his plan over the wireless. The countdown ensues, while the bomb experts struggle to find the explosives. Suspenseful with good direction. 109m/C VHS. *GB* Richard Harris, Omar Sharif, David Hemmings, Anthony Hopkins, Shirley Knight, Ian Holm, Roy Kinnear, Freddie Jones; **D:** Richard Lester. MGM, FOX

The Juggler of Notre Dame ♫♫½ 1984 A hobo and a street juggler embark on an unusual journey that will change the lives of the people they meet. Based on a medieval folktale about the special gift given to the Virgin Mary on Christmas morning. 110m/C VHS, Beta. Carl Carlson, Patrick Collins, Melinda Dillon, Merlin Olsen, Gene Roche. PAU

Juice ♫♫½ 1992 (R) Day-to-day street life of four Harlem youths as they try to earn respect ("juice") in their neighborhood. Q, an aspiring deejay, is talked into a robbery by his friends but everything takes a turn for the worse when one of the others, Bishop, gets hold of a gun. The gritty look and feel of the drama comes naturally to Dickerson in his directorial debut. Prior to his first film, Dickerson served as cinematographer for Spike Lee's "Do the Right Thing" and "Jungle Fever."**CW:** Some violence and strong language. 95m/C VHS, Closed Caption. Omar Epps, Jermaine Hopkins, Tupac Shakur, Khalil Kain, Cindy Herron, Vincent Laresca, Samuel L. Jackson; **W:** Ernest R. Dickerson; **W:** Gerard Brown, Ernest R. Dickerson; **C:** Larry Banks. PAR

Juke Joint ♫½ 1947 "Amos 'n Andy" star Spencer Williams acted in and directed this tale of two men who arrive in Hollywood with only 25 cents between them. Features an all-black cast and musical numbers. 60m/B VHS, Beta. Spencer Williams Jr., Judy Jones, Mantan Moreland; **D:** Spencer Williams Jr. NOS, VCN, DVT

Jules and Jim ♫♫♫♫ Jules et Jim 1962 Beautiful film with perfect casting, particularly Moreau. Spanning from 1912 to 1932, it is the story of a friendship between two men and their 20-year love for the same woman. Werner is the shy German Jew and Serre the fun-loving Frenchman, who meet as students. The two men discover and woo the bohemian, destructive Moreau, although it is Werner she marries. After WWI, the friends are reunited but the marriage of Moreau and Werner is in trouble and she has an affair

with Serre, which leads to tragedy for all three. Adapted from the novel by Henri-Pierre Roche. In French with English subtitles. 104m/B VHS, Beta, LV, Letterbox. *FR* Jeanne Moreau, Oskar Werner, Henri Serre, Marie DuBois, Vanna Urbino; **D:** Francois Truffaut; **W:** Jean Gruault; **M:** Georges Delerue. HMV, FOX

Julia ♫♫♫½ 1977 (PG) The story recounted in Lillian Hellman's fictional memoir "Pentimento." Fonda plays Hellman as she risks her life smuggling money into Germany during WWII for the sake of Julia, her beloved childhood friend (Redgrave), who is working in the Resistance. All cast members show in their performances; watch for Streep in her screen debut. 118m/C VHS, Beta, LV. Jane Fonda, Jason Robards Jr., Vanessa Redgrave, Maximilian Schell, Hal Holbrook, Rosemary Murphy, Meryl Streep, Lisa Pelikan; **D:** Fred Zinnemann; **W:** Alvin Sargent; **M:** Georges Delerue. Academy Awards '77: Best Adapted Screenplay, Best Supporting Actor (Robards), Best Supporting Actress (Redgrave); British Academy Awards '78: Best Actress (Fonda), Best Film, Best Screenplay, Best Supporting Actress (Redgrave); Golden Globe Awards '78: Best Actress—Drama (Fonda), Best Supporting Actress (Redgrave); Los Angeles Film Critics Association Awards '77: Best Cinematography, Best Supporting Actor (Robards), Best Supporting Actress (Redgrave); New York Film Critics Awards '77: Best Supporting Actor (Schell); Writers Guild of America '77: Best Adapted Screenplay; Nominations: Academy Awards '77: Best Actress (Fonda), Best Cinematography, Best Costume Design, Best Director (Zinnemann), Best Film Editing, Best Picture, Best Supporting Actor (Schell), Best Original Score. FOX, BTV

Julia and Julia ♫♫½ 1987 (R) A beautiful American woman in Trieste is tossed between two seemingly parallel dimensions, one in which her husband died six years earlier in a car crash, and the other in which he didn't. A purposefully obscure Italian-made psychological thriller, filmed in high-definition video and then transferred to film stock, it has a very different look and feel from other films of the genre. Intriguing and engaging most of the time, slow moving and confusing some of the time, it ultimately challenges but fails adequately to reward the viewer. 98m/C VHS, Beta, LV, Closed Caption. Kathleen Turner, Sting, Gabriel Byrne, Gabriele Ferzetti, Angela Goodwin; **D:** Peter Del Monte; **W:** Joe Minion, Sandro Petraglia, Silvia Napolitano, Peter Del Monte; **C:** Giuseppe Rotunno; **M:** Maurice Jarre. FOX

Julia Has Two Lovers ♫♫ 1991 (R) Minimalist comedy-drama about a woman torn between two men—her dull fiance and a mysterious phone caller. Mostly a long phone conversation; don't expect blistering action.**CW:** Sexual dialogue and sensuality. 87m/C VHS. Daphna Kastner, David Duchovny, David Charles; **D:** Bashar Shbib.

Julia Misbehaves ♫♫♫ 1948 Charming comedy that has Garson returning to ex-husband Pidgeon and daughter Taylor after an 18-year absence. Taylor is about to be married at a chateau in France and wants Garson to be there. While traveling to France from England, Garson encounters a bunch of colorful circus characters who are taking their act to Paris. Wonderful slapstick scenes give the stars a chance to have some real fun. Based on the novel "The Nutmeg Tree" by Margery Sharp. 99m/B VHS. Greer Garson, Walter Pidgeon, Peter Lawford, Cesar Romero, Elizabeth Taylor, Lucile Watson, Nigel Bruce, Mary Boland, Reginald Owen, Veda Ann Borg, Joi Lansing; **D:** Jack Conway. MGM

Julian Po ♫♫½ The Tears of Julian Po 1997 (PG-13) Nondescript bookkeeper Julian Po (Slater) has his car break down near an isolated mountain community and immediately comes under suspicion when he checks into the local boarding house, which never gets any guests. And the next day Julian's car has vanished, stranding him in nowherestown. The locals become convinced he's a hit man and demand explanations. Julian unexpectedly blurts out that the only person he's planning to kill is himself. Immediately the center of attention, Julian becomes confessor to everyone's darkest secrets and a recipient of their constant kindnesses but since he really doesn't in-

tend to off himself, he's also got some unexpected problems.**CW:** Thematic elements related to suicide, and for language and some sensuality. 82m/C VHS, LV, Closed Caption. Christian Slater, Robin Tunney, Michael Parks, Frankie Faison, Harve Presnell, Allison Janney, Cherry Jones, Latanya Richardson, Dina Spybey, Zeljko Ivanek; **D:** Alan Wade; **W:** Alan Wade; **C:** Bernd Heinl; **M:** Patrick Williams. WAR

Juliet of the Spirits ♫♫♫ Giulietta Degli Spiriti 1965 Fellini uses the sparse story of a woman (Fellini's real-life wife) deliberating over her husband's possible infidelity to create a wild, often senseless surrealistic film. With a highly symbolic internal logic and complex imagery, Fellini's fantasy ostensibly elucidates the inner life of a modern woman. In Italian with English subtitles. 142m/C VHS, Beta, LV. *IT* Giulietta Masina, Valentina Cortese, Sylva Koscina, Mario Pisu; **D:** Federico Fellini; **W:** Federico Fellini, Tullio Pinelli, Ennio Flaiano, Brunello Rondi; **M:** Nino Rota. New York Film Critics Awards '65: Best Foreign Film; Nominations: Academy Awards '66: Best Art Direction/Set Decoration (Color), Best Costume Design (Color). VYY, VDM, MRV

Julius Caesar ♫♫♫½ 1953 All-star version of the Shakespearean tragedy, heavily acclaimed and deservedly so. Working directly from the original Shakespeare, director Mankiewicz produced a lifelike, yet poetic production. 121m/B VHS, Beta, LV. James Mason, Marlon Brando, John Gielgud, Greer Garson, Deborah Kerr, Louis Calhern, Edmond O'Brien, George Macready, John Hoyt, Michael Pate; **D:** Joseph L. Mankiewicz; **W:** Joseph L. Mankiewicz; **C:** Joseph Ruttenberg; **M:** Miklos Rozsa. Academy Awards '53: Best Art Direction/Set Decoration (B & W); British Academy Awards '53: Best Actor (Brando), Best Actor (Gielgud); National Board of Review Awards '53: Best Actor (Mason); Nominations: Academy Awards '53: Best Actor (Brando), Best Black and White Cinematography, Best Picture, Best Original Dramatic/Comedy Score. MGM

Julius Caesar ♫♫ 1970 Subpar adaptation of the Shakespeare play about political greed and corruption within the Roman Empire. 116m/C VHS, Beta. *GB* Charlton Heston, John Gielgud, Jason Robards Jr., Richard Chamberlain, Robert Vaughn, Diana Rigg; **D:** Stuart Burge. NOS, REP, TVC

July Group ♫½ 197? A Quaker family's peaceful existence is threatened when kidnappers invade their home and hold them for ransom. 75m/C VHS, Beta. Nicholas Campbell, Calvin Butler, Maury Chaykin. TWE

Jumanji ♫♫½ 1995 (PG) For the past 26 years Alan Parish (Williams) has been stuck in the netherworld of Jumanji, a jungle-themed board game that sucks players into its alternate universe. When unsuspecting youngsters Judy (Dunst) and Peter (Pierce) happen upon the game and begin to play, they release Williams and a jungle full of rampaging beasts from the game and into the present. Loosely based on Chris Van Allsburg's children's book, the film version relies too heavily on cutting-edge special effects to make up for a thin story. Many of the creatures and effects are utterly too bizarre and unsettling for younger audiences. With a $65 million pricetag, Jumanji is definitely a roll of the dice. 104m/C VHS, LV, Closed Caption, DVD. Robin Williams, Kirsten Dunst, Bonnie Hunt, Bradley Michael Pierce, Bebe Neuwirth, Jonathan Hyde, David Alan Grier; **D:** Joe Johnston; **W:** Jonathan Hensleigh; **C:** Thomas Ackerman. COL

The Jumper ♫♫½ Der Todersspringer 1985 An abstract, theatrical narrative about a cast of tragicomic characters floundering through their meaningless lives. In German with English subtitles. 90m/C VHS, Beta. *GE* **D:** Benno Trachtmann. FCT, VCD, GLV

Jumpin' at the Boneyard ♫♫ 1992 (R) Gritty family drama about the trials of two dispossessed brothers, set on the streets of New York. Deeply depressed, out-of-work, divorced Manny hates his recently deceased father, adores his mother, and is estranged from his younger brother, Danny. Danny is a scared crack addict who's supported by a hooker/girlfriend. The two brothers reunite for a trip into their scarred past when Danny tries to rob his brother's apartment to get dope money. Manny starts to believe that the only way to redeem his own life is to get his brother into a rehab program. Good acting helps to overcome some script weaknesses but this is one depressing movie. **107m/C** VHS, LV. Tim Roth, Alexis Arquette, Danitra Vance, Samuel L. Jackson, Kathleen Chalfant, Luis Guzman; **D:** Jeff Stanzler; **W:** Jeff Stanzler. *FOX*

Jumpin' Jack Flash 🎬🎬½ **1986 (R)** A bank worker is humorously embroiled in international espionage when her computer terminal picks up distress signals from a British agent in Russia. Marshall's directing debut. Good performances from a fun cast and a particularly energetic effort by Goldberg are held back by an average and predictable script. **98m/C** VHS, Beta, LV, **Closed Caption.** Whoopi Goldberg, Stephen Collins, Carol Kane, Annie Potts, Jonathan Pryce, James Belushi, Jon Lovitz, John Wood; **Cameos:** Michael McKean, Tracey Ullman, Roscoe Lee Browne, Sara Botsford, Jeroen Krabbe, Phil Hartman, Tracy Reiner, Paxton Whitehead, Jamey Sheridan, Garry Marshall, Robert Montgomery, Fay Bainter, Betty Lynn, Tom Tully, Barbara Bates, Jerome Cowan, Mary Wickes; **D:** Penny Marshall; **W:** David Franzoni; **C:** Jan De Bont; **M:** Thomas Newman. *FOX, OM*

Jumping Jacks 🎬🎬 **1952** Martin and Lewis are a couple of nightclub performers who wind up in the paratroop corps instead of performing their act for the soldiers. Martin gets to sing and Lewis gets to parachute into enemy territory and capture a general. **96m/B** VHS, LV, **Closed Caption.** Dean Martin, Jerry Lewis, Mona Freeman, Don DeFore, Robert Strauss, Ray Teal; **D:** Norman Taurog; **C:** Daniel F. Fapp. *PAR*

Junction 88 🎬 **1940** Early all-black musical chock full of great dancing and hot music. **60m/B** VHS, Beta. Noble Sissle, Bob Howard. *NOS, DVT*

June Bride 🎬🎬🎬 **1948** Fast-paced and entertaining comedy in which Davis and Montgomery are teamed up as magazine writers. A hilarious battle of the sexes erupts as they're sent to Indiana to do a feature story on June brides. Look for Debbie Reynolds in her film debut. **97m/B** VHS, **Closed Caption.** Bette Davis, Robert Montgomery, Fay Bainter, Betty Lynn, Tom Tully, Barbara Bates, Jerome Cowan, Mary Wickes; **D:** Bretaigne Windust; **W:** Ranald MacDougall. *MGM*

June Night 🎬🎬 *Juninatten* **1940** A woman who was victimized by a shooting incident cannot escape the public eye due to her former promiscuous behavior. In Swedish with English subtitles. **90m/C** VHS, Beta, LV. *SW* Ingrid Bergman, Marianne Lofgren, Gunnar Sjoberg, Olaf Widgren; **D:** Per Lindberg. *WAC, TPV, LUM*

Jungle 🎬 **1952** A princess and an American adventurer lead an expedition into the Indian wilds to discover the source of recent elephant attacks. **74m/B** VHS, Beta, LV. Rod Cameron, Cesar Romero, Marie Windsor; **D:** William (Lester Williams) Berke; **C:** Clyde De Vinna. *NO*

Jungle Assault 🎬 **1989** Two Vietnam vets with nothing left to lose are called back into the bloodiest action of their lives. Their assignment is to locate and destroy a terrorist base and bring back an American general's brainwashed daughter. **86m/C** VHS, Beta. William Smith, Ted Prior, William Zipp; **D:** David A. Prior.

The Jungle Book 🎬🎬 *Rudyard Kipling's Jungle Book* **1942** A lavish version of Rudyard Kipling's stories about Mowgli, the boy raised by wolves in the jungles of India. **109m/C** VHS, LV. Sabu, Joseph Calleia, Rosemary DeCamp, Ralph Byrd, John Qualen; **D:** Zoltan Korda; **C:** Lee Garmes; **M:** Miklos Rozsa. Nominations: Academy Awards '42: Best Color Cinematography, Best Original Dramatic/Comedy Score. *CNG, MRV, REP*

The Jungle Book 🎬🎬🎬 **1967** Based on Kipling's classic, a young boy raised by wolves must choose between his jungle friends and human "civilization." Along the way he meets a variety of jungle characters including zany King Louie, kind-hearted Baloo, wise Bagherra and the evil Shere Khan. Great, classic songs including "Trust in Me," "I Wanna Be Like You," and Oscar-nominated "Bare Necessities." Last Disney feature overseen by Uncle Walt himself and a must for kids of all ages. **78m/C** VHS, Beta, LV, **Closed Caption. D:** Wolfgang Reitherman; **M:** George Bruns; **V:** Phil Harris, Sebastian Cabot, Louis Prima, George Sanders, Sterling Holloway, J. Pat O'Malley, Verna Felton, Darlene Carr. Nominations: Academy Awards '67: Best Song ("The Bare Necessities"). *TOU, FCT, RDG*

Jungle Bride 🎬🎬½ **1933** Three people are shipwrecked and one of them is a suspected murderer. **66m/B** VHS, Beta, LV. Anita Page, Charles Starrett. *SNC, NOS, VYY*

Jungle Drums of Africa *U-238 and the Witch Doctor* **1953** Jungle adventures abound as Moore and Coates encounter lions, wind tunnels, voodoo and enemy agents in deepest Africa. A 12-episode serial re-edited onto two cassettes. **167m/B** VHS. Clayton Moore, Phyllis Coates, Roy Glenn, John Cason; **D:** Fred Brannon. *REP, MLB*

Jungle Fever 🎬🎬 **1991 (R)** Married black architect's affair with his white secretary provides the backdrop for a cold look at interracial love. Focuses more on the discomfort of friends and families than with the intense world created by the lovers for themselves. Provides the quota of humor and fresh insight we expect from Lee, but none of the joyous sexuality experienced by the lovers in "She's Gotta Have It." In fact, Lee tells viewers that interracial love is unnatural, never more than skin deep, never more than a blind obsession with the allure of the opposite race. Very fine cast but if you don't agree with Lee, a real disappointment as well. **CW:** Violence and drug content and sensuality. **131m/C** VHS, Beta, LV, **Closed Caption.** Wesley Snipes, Annabella Sciorra, John Turturro, Samuel L. Jackson, Ossie Davis, Ruby Dee, Lonette McKee, Anthony Quinn, Spike Lee, Halle Berry, Tyra Ferrell, Veronica Webb, Frank Vincent, Tim Robbins, Brad Dourif, Richard Edson; **D:** Spike Lee; **W:** Spike Lee; **M:** Terence Blanchard. New York Film Critics Awards '91: Best Supporting Actor (Jackson). *USH, CCB, FCT*

Jungle Goddess 🎬½ **1949** Two mercenaries set out for the reward offered for finding a wealthy heiress last seen in the jungles of Africa. **61m/B** VHS, Beta, LV. George Reeves, Wanda McKay, Ralph Byrd, Armida; **D:** Lewis D. Collins. *NO*

Jungle Heat 🎬½ *Dance of the Dwarfs* **1984 (PG)** While searching for a pygmy tribe, an anthropologist and her pilot run into a pack of anthropoid mutants. **93m/C** VHS, Beta. Peter Fonda, Deborah Raffin; **D:** Gus Trikonis. *TWE*

Jungle Hell 🎬🎬 **1955** Sabu comes to the rescue of an Indian tribe being harassed by flying saucers, death rays and radioactive debris. **?m/B** VHS, Beta. Sabu, David Bruce, George E. Stone, K.T. Stevens; **D:** Norman A. Cerf. *SNC*

Jungle Inferno 🎬 **197?** Nature boy, a fugitive from the government, fights lions, tigers and pursuing feds in this story of escape and survival. **90m/C** VHS, Beta. Brad Harris. *NO*

Jungle Master 🎬 **1956** Noble British types hunt for Karzan, the jungle's number one guy, with the aid of a tribal priestess and a lovely photo-journalist. Must see for trash movie fans. **90m/C** VHS, Beta. John Kitzmiller, Simone Blondell, Edward Mann; **D:** Miles Deem. *NO*

Jungle Patrol 🎬½ **1948** In 1943 New Guinea, a squadron of entrapped fliers are confronted with a beautiful USO entertainer. Romance and show tunes follow. **72m/B** VHS, Beta. Kristine Miller, Arthur Franz, Richard Jaeckel, Ross Ford, Tommy Noonan, Gene Reynolds; **D:** Joseph M. Newman. *NO*

Jungle Raiders 🎬½ *Legenda Del Rudio Malese; Captain Yankee* **1985 (PG-13)** An Indiana Jones-esque mercenary searches the steamy jungles of Malaysia for a valuable jewel, the Ruby of Gloom. **102m/C** VHS, Beta. Lee Van Cleef, Christopher Connelly, Marina Costa; **D:** Anthony (Antonio Margheriti) Dawson. *MGM*

Jungle Siren 🎬🎬 **1942** Nazis in Africa try to foment rebellion amongst the black natives against the white residents. Crabbe and a white woman raised in the jungle set things right. **68m/B** VHS, Beta. Ann Corio, Buster Crabbe, Evelyn Wahl, Milton Kibbee; **D:** Sam Newfield. *SNC, MLB*

Jungle 2 Jungle 🎬🎬½ **1996 (PG)** Remake of French farce released as "Little Indian, Big City," changes little of the "wild child" premise. Workaholic Wall Streeter Michael Cromwell (Allen) decides to finalize the divorce from his long-estranged doctor wife, Patricia (Williams), who happens to have been ministering to a tribe in the Amazon rain forest for many years. He gets more than the divorce when he meets the 13-year-old son, Mimi-Siku (Huntington), he never knew he had. Although the boy speaks English, he's been raised as a tribal native, which causes quite a culture shock when he returns with Michael to the jungles of Manhattan. Of course the kid's more than a match for any situation. **105m/C** VHS, **Closed Caption.** Tim Allen, Sam Huntington, Martin Short, JoBeth Williams, Lolita Davidovich, David Ogden Stiers, Bob Dishy, Valerie Mahaffey, Leelee Sobieski, Luis Avalos, Frankie J. Galasso; **D:** John Pasquin; **W:** Bruce A. Evans, Raynold Gideon; **C:** Tony Pierce-Roberts; **M:** Michael Convertino. *DIS*

The Jungle Trap 🎬🎬 **1954** Steve Davis thought he could escape his past living in Africa. However, when the judge who wrongly sentenced his brother to death arrives, he plots revenge. **30m/B** VHS. Ronald Reagan. *RHI*

Jungle Warriors 🎬½ **1984 (R)** Seven fashion models are abducted by a Peruvian cocaine dealer. To escape him, they must become Jungle Warriors. **96m/C** VHS, Beta. *GE MX* Sybil Danning, Marjoe Gortner, Nina Van Pallandt, Paul Smith, John Vernon, Alex Cord, Woody Strode, Kai Wulff; **D:** Ernst R. von Theumer.

Jungleground 🎬½ **1995 (R)** Jungleground is a urban wasteland controlled by rival gangs. Lt. Jake Cornel (Piper) gets caught in a shoot-out when a sting operation goes bad and winds up before psychotic gang leader Odin. Odin offers him one chance—Cornel's going to be hunted in Jungleground's abandoned streets and if he can escape before dawn, he gets to live. **CW:** Strong violence; language; some drug content. **90m/C** VHS, LV. Roddy Piper, Torri Higginson, Peter Williams; **D:** Don Allan; **W:** Michael Stokes. *TRI*

Junior woof! **1986** A raving, drooling lunatic cuts up girls with a chainsaw. **80m/C** VHS, Beta. Suzanne DeLaurentis, Linda Singer, Jeremy Ruthford, Michael McKeever.

Junior 🎬🎬 **1994 (PG-13)** Out of the way women! Schwarzenegger trades the war room for the delivery room to experience the miracle of birth. As scientists, he and DeVito take a dip in the gene pool once again to test an anti-miscarriage drug. Thompson provides the egg and some surprisingly good physical comedy as the klutzy cryogenics expert who moves into their university digs. Every pregnancy cliche is explored as Schwarzenegger and DeVito bring the concept to term. Sorry, action fans...nothing blows up except Arnold. **CW:** Contains sex-related humor and some profanity. **109m/C** VHS, LV, **Closed Caption.** Arnold Schwarzenegger, Danny DeVito, Emma Thompson, Frank Langella, Pamela Reed, Judy Collins, James Eckhouse, Aida Turturro; **D:** Ivan Reitman; **W:** Kevin Wade, Chris Conrad; **M:** James Newton Howard. Nominations: Academy Awards '94: Best Song ("Look What Love Has Done"); Golden Globe Awards '95: Best Actor—Musical/Comedy (Schwarzenegger), Best Actress—Musical/Comedy (Thompson), Best Song ("Look What Love Has Done"). *USH*

Junior Bonner 🎬🎬🎬 **1972 (PG)** A rowdy modern-day western about a young drifting rodeo star who decides to raise money for his father's new ranch by challenging a formidable bull. **100m/C** VHS, Beta. Steve McQueen, Robert Preston, Ida Lupino,

Don Johnson, Joe Don Baker, Barbara Leigh, **D.** Sam Peckinpah; **C:** Lucien Ballard. *FOX*

Junior G-Men 1940 The Dead End Kids fight Fifth Columnists who are trying to sabotage America's war effort. Twelve episodes. **237m/B VHS, Beta.** Billy Halop, Huntz Hall. *VYY, VCN, NOS*

Junior G-Men of the Air ⅛½ 1942 The Dead End Kids become teenage flyboys in this 12-episode serial adventure. **215m/B VHS, Beta.** Billy Halop, Huntz Hall. *SNC, NOS, MLB*

Junior High School ⅛½ 1978 A comically, on target film detailing the romantic yearnings, petty cruelties, and claustrophobia of 8th grade existence. **60m/C VHS, Beta.** Paula Abdul. *PIC*

The Juniper Tree ⅛½ 1987 Based on a tale by the Brothers Grimm, this Icelandic curio finds sisters Margit (Bjork) and Katla (Bragadottir) fleeing across the medieval countryside after their mother is burned at the stake for witchcraft. The sisters have their own special powers, which they turn on each other when they become romantic rivals over a young widower (Flygenring). **78m/B VHS.** *IC* Bjork, Bryndis Petra Bragadottir, Vladimar Orn Flygenring; **D:** Nietzchka Keene. *RHI*

Junk Mail ⅛½ Budbringeren 1997 Grimy Oslo postman Roy (Skjaerstad) enjoys reading other people's mail, stalking Line, a deaf girl (Saether) on his route, and not washing. One day the girl leaves her keys in the mailbox, so Roy decides to have a look around, later saving her from a suicide attempt. During another of his "visits," Roy learns that Line is involved in a violent crime, along with a thug named Georg (Aske). Through a series of mistaken identities and coicidences, he becomes deeply involved in the proceedings. Sletaune's promising debut is quirky and painstaking in its attention to detail. Skjaerstad does a fine job as the slovenly, slothful, though ultimately sympathetic, mailman. **83m/C VHS.** *NO* Robert Skjaerstad, Andrine Saether, Per Egil Aske, Eli Anne Linnestad; **D:** Pal Sletaune; **W:** Pal Sletaune, Jonny Halberg; **C:** Kjell Vassdal; **M:** Joachim Holbek. *NYR*

The Junkman ⅛½ 1982 (R) Movie maker whose new film is about to be premiered is being chased by a mysterious killer. Promoted as "the ultimate car chase film" since the production used and destroyed over 150 automobiles. From the makers of "Gone in 60 Seconds." **97m/C VHS, Beta.** H.B. Halicki, Christopher Stone, Susan Shaw, Hoyt Axton, Lynda Day George; **D:** H.B. Halicki. *TWE*

Juno and the Paycock ⅛½½ 1930 Perhaps if Hitchcock hadn't been so faithful to O'Casey this early effort would have been less stagey and more entertaining. In Dublin during the civil uprising, a poor family is torn apart when they receive news of an imminent fortune. Hitchcock's reported to have said that "drama is life with the dull bits left out," though here too many dull bits remain. **96m/B VHS.** Sara Allgood, Edward Chapman, John Longden, John Laurie, Maire O'Neill; **D:** Alfred Hitchcock; **W:** Alfred Hitchcock. *NOS, VEC, HHT*

Jupiter's Darling ⅛½ 1955 This spoof of Hannibal (Keel) and Amytis (Williams) gravely misses the mark in making funny world of the Roman Empire. Amytis has the job of distracting Hannibal from attacking the Eternal City, and does so through musical interludes and unfunny jokes. ♫I Have A Dream; If This Be Slav'ry; I Never Trust A Woman; Hannibal's Victory March; Don't Let This Night Get Away; The Life Of An Elephant; Horatio's Narration. **96m/C LV, Letterbox.** Esther Williams, Howard Keel, George Sanders, Gower Champion, Marge Champion, Norma Varden, Richard Haydn, William Demarest, Douglass Dumbrille, Michael Ansara, Martha Wentworth, Chris Alcaide, William Tannen; **D:** George Sidney; **C:** Charles Rosher. *MGM*

Jupiter's Thigh ⅛½½ 1981 A madcap married pair of treasure-hunters honeymoon in Greece in search of an ancient statue's lost thigh. Available in French with English subtitles, or dubbed into English. **96m/C VHS, Beta.** *FR* Annie Girardot, Philippe Noiret; **D:** Philippe de Broca. *FCT*

Jurassic Park ⅛⅛⅛½ 1993 (PG-13) Crichton's spine-tingling thriller translates well (but not faithfully) due to its main attraction: realistic, rampaging dinosaurs. Genetically cloned from prehistoric DNA, all is well until they escape from their pens—smarter and less predictable than expected. Contrived plot and thin characters (except Goldblum), but who cares? The true stars are the dinos, an incredible combination of models and computer animation. Violent, suspenseful, and realistic with gory attack scenes. Not for small kids, though much of the marketing is aimed at them. Spielberg knocked his own "E.T." out of first place as "JP" became the highest grossing movie of all time. Also available in a letterbox version. **CW:** Intense science fiction violence. **127m/C VHS, LV, Closed Caption, DVD.** Sam Neill, Laura Dern, Jeff Goldblum, Richard Attenborough, Bob Peck, Martin Ferrero, B.D. Wong, Joseph Mazzello, Ariana Richards, Samuel L. Jackson, Wayne Knight; **D:** Steven Spielberg; **W:** David Koepp, Michael Crichton; **C:** Dean Cundey; **M:** John Williams; **V:** Richard Kiley. Academy Awards '93: Best Sound, Best Sound Effects Editing, Best Visual Effects; Nominations: MTV Movie Awards '94: Best Film, Best Villain (T-Rex), Best Action Sequence. *USH*

The Juror ⅛½ 1996 (R) Plucky single mom (Moore) ends up on the jury in the trial of a powerful mobster and draws the attention of the smooth enforcer (Baldwin) who muscles her into providing a certain verdict. The usual good-vs.-evil, family-in-danger action ensues. Despite boasting a fine cast and impressive attention to detail, flick is guilty of ludicrous situations, a mechanical plot and a dopey ending. Based on the novel by George Dawes Green. **CW:** Violence, profanity, nudity and sexual situations. **107m/C VHS, LV, 8mm, Closed Caption.** Demi Moore, Alec Baldwin, Joseph Gordon-Levitt, Anne Heche, James Gandolfini, Lindsay Crouse, Tony LoBianco, Michael Constantine, Matt Craven; **D:** Brian Gibson; **W:** Ted Tally; **C:** Jamie Anderson; **M:** James Newton Howard. Nominations: Golden Raspberry Awards '96: Worst Actress (Moore). *COL*

Jury Duty ⅛ 1995 (PG-13) Mama's boy loser Tommy Collins (Shore) gets jury duty on a serial-killer case and tries to keep what seems to be an open-and-shut case going so he can continue to get free room and board. He falls for babe juror Monica (Carrere) and really drags the trial (and the film) out in a pathetic attempt to woo her. Shore is even more annoying and unfunny than ever. Low-rent bastardization of "Twelve Angry Men" tries to pass off lame O.J. references and Shore falling out of chairs as humor. Creates reasonable doubt as to Shore's talent and movie execs' judgment. **CW:** Crude sex-related humor. **88m/C VHS, LV, Closed Caption.** Pauly Shore, Tia Carrere, Shelley Winters, Brian Doyle-Murray, Abe Vigoda, Stanley Tucci, Charles Napier, Richard Edson; **Cameos:** Andrew Dice Clay; **D:** John Fortenberry; **W:** Fax Bahr, Barbara Williams. Golden Raspberry Awards '95: Worst Actor (Shore). *COL*

Just a Gigolo ⅛⅛½ 1979 (R) Bowie stars in this unusual melodrama about a Prussian war vet turned male prostitute. He spends most of his time working for the sexiest of women. Splendid cast, but a bit incoherent. **105m/C VHS, LV.** *GE* David Bowie, Sydne Rome, Kim Novak, David Hemmings, Maria Schell, Curt Jurgens, Marlene Dietrich; **D:** David Hemmings. *MOV, LUM*

Just Another Girl on the I.R.T. ⅛⅛½ 1993 (R) Double debut from two African American women, writer/director Harris, and actress Johnson, captures the sass and wit of a girl from the projects. Seventeen-year-old Chantal has a plan for her life and challenges authority with assurance, even after an unexpected pregnancy puts a twist into her plan. Strong initial statement tends to become weak and cloudy as Chantal loses her focus. This doesn't dismiss the remarkable realism and raw talent portrayed in a picture filmed in just seventeen days for $130,000. Winner of a special jury prize at the Sundance Film Festival. **CW:** Language and sexually. **98m/C VHS, LV.** Ariyan Johnson, Kevin Thigpen, Ebony Jerido, Jerard Washington, Chequita Jackson, William Badget; **D:** Leslie Harris; **W:** Leslie Harris; **C:** Richard Conners. Sundance Film Festival '93: Special Jury Prize; Nominations: Independent Spirit Awards '94: Best Actress (Johnson). *ART, FCT*

Just Another Pretty Face ⅛⅛½ Be Beautiful but Shut Up 1958 An aging detective catches a gang of jewel smugglers, and gets involved with their young moll. In French with English subtitles. **110m/C VHS, Beta.** *FR* Henri Vidal, Mylene Demongeot, Isa Miranda; **D:** Henri Verneuil. *FCT*

Just Around the Corner ⅛½ 1938 (G) Temple helps her Depression-poor father get a job after she befriends a cantankerous millionaire. Temple duets with Bill "Bojangles" Robinson with the fourth time. Also available colorized. ♫This Is A Happy Little Ditty; I'm Not Myself Today; I'll Be Lucky With You; Just Around the Corner; I Love To Walk in the Rain; Brass Buttons and Epaulets. **71m/B VHS, Closed Caption.** Shirley Temple, Charles Farrell, Bert Lahr, Joan Davis, Bill Robinson, Cora Witherspoon, Franklin Pangborn; **D:** Irving Cummings. *FXV*

Just Before Dawn ⅛⅛ 1980 (R) Another murderers stalk campers story; humans resort to their animal instincts in their struggle for survival. Not to be confused with the William Castle film (1946) from the "Crime Doctor" series. **90m/C VHS, Beta.** Chris Lemmon, Deborah Benson, Greg Henry, George Kennedy; **D:** Jeff Lieberman; **M:** Brad Fiedel. *NO*

Just Between Friends ⅛⅛ 1986 (PG-13) Two women become friends, not knowing that one is having an affair with the husband of the other. Allan Burns directorial debut. **110m/C VHS, Beta.** Mary Tyler Moore, Christine Lahti, Sam Waterston, Ted Danson, Jim MacKrell, Jane Greer; **D:** Allan Burns; **W:** Allan Burns; **C:** Jordan Cronenweth. *NO*

Just Cause ⅛⅛ 1994 (R) Incoherent mystery/thriller set in the Florida Everglades. Retired attorney, Paul Armstrong, now a Harvard law professor, decides to defend Bobby Earl (Underwood), on death row for the murder of a white girl. As Armstrong investigates the case, he discovers that the arresting officer Tanny Brown, (Fishburne) is corrupt and tortured the confession out of Bobby. Starts off promising with the electricity of Connery's and Fishburne's presence and a frigthening cameo by Ed Harris as an incarcerated serial killer, but once the barrage of plot twists start, creating gator size holes in the plot, the movie drifts into a murkey swamp of absurdity. Adapted from the legal thriller by John Katzenbach. **CW:** Violence; strong language. **102m/C VHS, LV, Closed Caption.** Sean Connery, Laurence "Larry" Fishburne, Kate Capshaw, Blair Underwood, Ruby Dee, Daniel J. Travanti, Ned Beatty, Lynne Thigpen, George Plimpton, Chris Sarandon, Kevin McCarthy, Ed Harris; **D:** Arne Glimcher; **W:** Jeb Stuart, Robert Stone; **C:** Lajos Koltai; **M:** James Newton Howard. *WAR*

Just for the Hell of It woof! Destruction, Inc 1968 A quartet of teenage punks ruthlessly terrorize their suburban Miami 'hood while an innocent kid gets blamed. More exploitation from schlock king Lewis, who also wrote the theme song, "Destruction, Inc." (pic's alternate title). Essentially the same cast as the director's "She Devils on Wheels," filmed simultaneously. **85m/C VHS.** Rodney Bedell, Ray Sager, Nancy Lee Noble, Agi Gyenes, Steve White; **D:** Herschell Gordon Lewis. *NO*

Just for You ⅛⅛½ 1952 Entertaining musical about producer Crosby who doesn't have time for his kids until Wyman steps in and shows him the way. Based on Stephen Vincent Benet's novel "Famous." ♫Zing A Little Zong; He's Just Crazy For Me; The Live Oak Tree; A Flight of Fancy; I'll Si-Si Ya In Bahia; On the 10:10; Just for You. **95m/C VHS, Closed Caption.** Bing Crosby, Jane Wyman, Ethel Barrymore, Robert Arthur, Natalie Wood, Cora Witherspoon; **D:** Elliott Nugent; **W:** Robert Carson. Nominations: Academy Awards '52: Best Song ("Zing a Little Zong"). *PAR*

Just

483 | VideoHound's Golden Movie Retriever

Just Like a Woman 🎬🎬 1995 (R)

Sweet-natured film about an unlikely romance with some decided quirks. Young American Gerald (Pasdar) is working for a London bank and renting a flat from lonely older divorcee Monica (Walters). Ideal tenant Gerald is also recently divorced and a mutual attraction develops, in fact Gerald trusts Monica enough to confess his darkest secret—seems his marriage broke up over women's lingerie—the ones Gerald likes to wear when he cross-dresses in his female persona of Geraldine. Does this put Monica off? Well, she turns out to be very understanding indeed. Based on the memoir "Geraldine" by Monica Jay. **CW:** Adult sexual themes, nudity, some language. 102m/C VHS. **GB** Adrian Pasdar, Julie Walters, Paul Freeman, Susan Wooldridge, Gordon Kennedy, Ian Redford, Shelley Thompson; **D:** Christopher Monger; **W:** Nick Evans; **C:** Alan Hume; **M:** Michael Storey. HMK

Just Like Weather 🎬🎬🎬 1986

Contemporary Hong Kong and the city's looming return to control by mainland China provide the backdrop for the troubled marriage of a young couple. Couple endure abortion, arrest, and veterinarian episodes before departing for on U.S. trip with high hopes. 98m/C VHS. **HK** Christine Lee, Lee Chi-Keung, Allen Fong; **D:** Allen Fong. FCT

Just Me & You 🎬½ 1978

An "It Happened One Night" made-for-television tale of an unlikely couple who fall in love with each other when chance brings them together on a cross-country drive. 100m/C VHS, Beta. Louise Lasser, Charles Grodin; **D:** Charles Erman; **W:** Louise Lasser. NO

Just One of the Girls 🎬½ 1993 (R)

Teen star Haim transfers to a new high school where he dresses in drag in order to avoid the itinerant leader of the school's toughest gang whom he has unwittingly enraged. Palling around with Eggert becomes one of his costume's unexpected perks. Sort of a cross between "Some Like It Hot" and "90210." **CW:** Nudity. 94m/C VHS, LV. Corey Haim, Nicole Eggert, Cameron Bancroft; **D:** Michael Keusch; **M:** Amin Bhatia. THV

Just One of the Guys 🎬🎬 1985 (PG-13)

When the school newspaper refuses to accept the work of an attractive young girl, she goes undercover as a boy to prove that her work is good. She goes on to befriend the school's nerd, and even helps him grow out of his awkward stage, falling for him in the process. Very cute, but predictable. 100m/C VHS, Beta, LV, **Closed Caption.** Joyce Hyser, Clayton Rohner, Billy Jacoby, Toni Hudson, Leigh McCloskey, Sherilyn Fenn; **D:** Lisa Gottlieb. COL

Just Suppose 🎬🎬½ 1926

Prince in waiting decides he'd prefer the simple life, travels to the land of the free in search of honest work and is felled by cupid's arrow. All's well 'til duty calls, and his princely presence is expected back in the royal fold. Features beautiful boy Barthelmess, whom Lillian Gish described as having "the most beautiful face of any man who ever went before a camera." Silent. 90m/B VHS, Beta. Richard Barthelmess, Lois Moran, Geoffrey Kerr, Henry Vibart, George Spelvin; **D:** Kenneth Webb. GPV

Just Tell Me What You Want 🎬🎬½ 1980 (R)

A wealthy, self-made married man finally drives his longtime mistress away when he refuses to let her take over the operation of a failing movie studio he has acquired. After she falls for another man, the tycoon does everything he can to win her back. The department store battle between MacGraw and King is priceless. 112m/C VHS, Beta. Alan King, Ali MacGraw, Myrna Loy, Keenan Wynn, Tony Roberts; **D:** Sidney Lumet; **W:** Jay Presson Allen; **C:** Oswald Morris. WAR

Just Tell Me You Love Me 🎬 1980 (PG)

Three budding con artists plot to make easy money in this Hawaiian romp. 90m/C VHS, Beta. Robert Hegyes, Debralee Scott, Lisa Hartman Black, Ricci Martin, June Lockhart; **D:** Tony Mordente. ART, VES

Just the Way You Are 🎬 1984 (PG)

An attractive musician struggles to overcome a physical handicap and winds up falling in love while on vacation in the French Alps. 96m/C VHS, Beta, **Closed Caption.** Kristy McNichol, Robert Carradine, Kaki Hunter, Michael Ontkean, Alexandra Paul, Lance Guest, Timothy Daly, Patrick Cassidy; **D:** Edouard Molinaro; **W:** Allan Burns; **M:** Vladimir Cosma. MGM

Just William's Luck 🎬🎬 1947

A precocious English brat sneaks into an old mansion, which just happens to be the headquarters for a gang of thieves. Based on British series of children's books. 87m/B VHS, Beta. **GB** William A. Graham, Garry Marsh; **D:** Val Guest. VYY

Just Your Luck 🎬½ 1996 (R)

The New Sudka Cafe II, owned by the high strung Nick (Polito), is the setting for one wild night. An old man promptly keels over dead upon learning that his lottery ticket is a $6 million prize-winner. Customer Kim (Madsen) tries to convince Nick and her fellow diners that they should keep the ticket and split the winnings. **CW:** Strong language and some violence. 86m/C VHS. Virginia Madsen, Sean Patrick Flanery, Ernie Hudson, Jon Polito, Alanna Ubach, Jon Favreau, Mike Starr, Carroll Baker; **D:** Gary Auerbach; **W:** Gary Auerbach. PGV

Justice 🎬🎬 Flight from Fear 1955

A crusading attorney tries to keep a waterfront kangaroo court from applying its harsh justice to an admitted killer in this television crime-drama. 26m/B VHS, Beta. William Prince, Jack Klugman, Biff McGuire, Jack Warden. VYY

Justice of the West 🎬 1961

The Lone Ranger and his sidekick, Tonto, perform good deeds in the Old West, including helping to retrieve stolen gold, helping to build an Indian school, and giving a blind man a fresh perspective on life. 71m/C VHS, Beta. Clayton Moore, Jay Silverheels; **D:** Earl Bellamy. MGM

Justice Rides Again 🎬½ 193?

Mix tries to uphold law and order, but he's up against some very tough outlaws. 55m/B VHS, Beta. Tom Mix. VCN

Justin Morgan Had a Horse 🎬🎬 1981

The true story of a colonial school teacher in post-Revolutionary War Vermont who first bred the Morgan horse, the first and most versatile American breed. 91m/C VHS, Beta. Don Murray, Lana Wood, Gary Crosby; **D:** Hollingsworth Morse. DIS

Justine 🎬🎬 1969

In the 1930s, a prostitute who marries an Egyptian banker becomes involved with a variety of men and a plot to arm Palestinian Jews in their revolt against English rule. A condensed film version of Lawrence Durrell's "The Alexandria Quartet." 115m/C VHS, Beta, **Closed Caption.** **IS** Anouk Aimee, Michael York, Dirk Bogarde, Philippe Noiret, Michael Constantine, John Vernon, Jack Albertson; **D:** George Cukor; **W:** Lawrence B. Marcus; **C:** Leon Shamroy; **M:** Jerry Goldsmith. FOX, HHE

K-9 🎬🎬½ 1989 (PG-13)

After having his car destroyed by a drug dealer, "I work alone" Belushi is forced to take on a partner—a German Shepherd. Together they work to round up the bad guys and maybe chew on their shoes a little. Sometimes amusing one-joke comedy done in by a paper-thin script. Both the dog and Belushi are good, however. 111m/C VHS, Beta, LV, **Closed Caption.** James Belushi, Mel Harris, Kevin Tighe, Ed O'Neill, Cotter Smith, James Handy, Jerry Lee; **D:** Rod Daniel; **W:** Steven Siegel, Scott Myers; **M:** Miles Goodman. USH

K-9000 🎬🎬 1989

The Hound salutes the idea behind this standard sci-fi crime-fighter; a cyberdog fights the forces of evil with the aid of a cop, a lady reporter, and the usual cliches. Made For television. 96m/C VHS, **Closed Caption.** Chris Mulkey, Catherine Oxenberg; **D:** Kim Manners; **M:** Jan Hammer.

Kafka 🎬½ 1991 (PG-13)

Disappointing and gloomy Soderbergh film that serves no purpose whatsoever. Irons plays Kafka, an insurance workers by day and a writer by night. The movie exists largely without interest until Kafka uncovers an office conspiracy and makes his way to the enemy's castle headquarters. From then on, "Kafka" is nothing but a conventional horror film. Irons is wasted in a role that requires nothing but an impeccable British accent. On the plus side, the film is exquisitely shot in black and white until the castle scenes, when the cinematography is switched to color. 100m/C VHS, Beta, LV, **Letterbox, Closed Caption.** Jeremy Irons, Theresa Russell, Joel Grey, Ian Holm, Jeroen Krabbe, Armin Mueller-Stahl, Alec Guinness, Brian Glover, Robert Flemyng, Keith Allen, Simon McBurney; **D:** Steven Soderbergh; **W:** Lem Dobbs; **C:** Walt Lloyd; **M:** Cliff Martinez. Independent Spirit Awards '92: Best Cinematography. PAR, PMS

Kagemusha 🎬🎬🎬½ The Shadow Warrior; The Double 1980 (PG)

A thief is rescued from the gallows because of his striking resemblance to a warlord in 16th Century Japan. When the ambitious warlord is fatally wounded, the thief is required to pose as the warlord. In Japanese with English subtitles. 160m/C VHS, Beta, LV, **Letterbox.** **JP** Tatsuya Nakadai, Tsutomu Yamazaki, Kenichi Hagiwara; **D:** Akira Kurosawa. British Academy Awards '80: Best Director (Kurosawa); Cannes Film Festival '80: Best Film; Cesar Awards '81: Best Foreign Film; Nominations: Academy Awards '80: Best Art Direction/Set Decoration, Best Foreign Language Film. FOX

Kalifornia 🎬🎬½ 1993 (R)

"Badlands" meets the '90s in a road trip with the hitchhikers from hell. Early Grayce (Pitt) is your average slimeball who murders his landlord and hops a ride with his waifish girlfriend Adele (Lewis) from Kentucky to California with Brian (Duchovny), a yuppie writer interested in mass murderers, and his sultry photographer girlfriend Carrie (Forbes). Pitt and Lewis were still an item when they made this. Pitt reportedly wanted to play against type, and as pretty boy gone homicidal, he succeeds. Extremely violent and disturbing. Also available in an unrated version. **CW:** Nudity and graphic and disturbing violence. 117m/C VHS, LV, **Letterbox, Closed Caption.** Brad Pitt, Juliette Lewis, David Duchovny, Michelle Forbes, Sierra Pecheur, Lois Hall, Gregory Mars Martin; **D:** Dominic Sena; **W:** Tim Metcalfe; **C:** Bojan Bazelli; **M:** Carter Burwell. PGV, BTV

Kama Sutra: A Tale of Love 🎬🎬 1996

Erotic but flawed fantasy covering the sexual and political wiles of palace life in 16th-century India. Princess Tara (Choudhury) and girlhood friend/servant Maya (Varma) are close until the Princess becomes jealous of the even-more beautiful Maya. In revenge for a public humiliation, Maya seduces Tara's dissolute fiance, Raj Singh (Andrews), and is banished from the palace after the wedding. She becomes involved with handsome royal sculptor Jai Kumar (Tikaram) and later learns the sexual arts of the Kama Sutra, becoming the chief courtesan to the Raj. Messy, somewhat overwrought plot, extremely attractive cast. Also available in an R-rated version. 117m/C VHS, LV, **Closed Caption.** **IN** Indira Varma, Sarita Choudhury, Ramon Tikaram, Naveen Andrews, Devi Rekha; **D:** Mira Nair; **W:** Mira Nair, Helena Kriel; **C:** Declan Quinn; **M:** Mychael Danna. Independent Spirit Awards '98: Best Cinematography. THV

Kameradschaft 🎬🎬🎬½ 1931

A great, early German sound film about Germans struggling to free themselves and French miners trapped underground on the countries' border. In German and French with English subtitles. 80m/B VHS, Beta. **GE** Ernst Busch, Alexander Granach, Fritz Kampers; **D:** G.W. Pabst. MRV, IHF, NLC

Kamikaze '89 🎬🎬🎬 1983

German director Fassbinder has the lead acting role (his last) in this offbeat story of a police lieutenant in Berlin, circa 1989, who investigates a puzzling series of bombings. In German with English subtitles. 90m/C VHS, Beta. **GE** Rainer Werner Fassbinder, Gunther Kaufman, Boy Gobert; **D:** Wolf Gremm; **M:** Tangerine Dream. MGM, FCT, GLV

Kamikaze Hearts 🎬🎬 1991

A quasi-documentary set in the world of two lesbian-junkies (Sharon the actress and Tina the director/producer) making underground X-rated movies. 80m/C

VHS. Sharon Mitchell, Tina "Tigr" Mennett, **D:** Juliet Bashore; **W:** Tina "Tigr" Mennett. *FCT*

Kanal ☑☑☑½ *They Loved Life* 1956 Wajda's first major success, a grueling account of Warsaw patriots, upon the onset of the Nazis toward the end of the war, fleeing through the ruined city's sewers. Highly acclaimed. Part 2 of Wajda's "War Trilogy," preceded by "A Generation," and followed by "Ashes and Diamonds." In Polish with English subtitles or dubbed. 96m/B VHS, Beta. **PL** Teresa Izewska, Tadeusz Janczar; **D:** Andrzej Wajda. Cannes Film Festival '57: Grand Jury Prize. *ING, NLC, HMV*

Kandyland ☑ 1987 (R) An over-the-hill stripper takes a young innocent stripper under her wing. 94m/C VHS, Beta. Sandahl Bergman, Kimberly Evenson, Charles Laulette, Bruce Baum; **D:** Robert Allen Schnitzer; **C:** Robert Brinkmann. *VTR*

Kangaroo ☑ 1986 (R) An Australian adaptation of the semi-autobiographical D.H. Lawrence novel. A controversial English novelist and his wife move to the Outback in 1922, and are confronted with all manner of prejudice and temptation. 115m/C VHS, Beta. **AU** Judy Davis, Colin Friels, John Walton, Hugh Keays-Byrne, Julie Nihill; **D:** Tim Burstall; **W:** Evan Jones; **C:** Dan Burstall; **M:** Nathan Waks. Australian Film Institute '86: Best Actress (Davis). *USH*

The Kansan ☑☑ 1943 The marshall in a Kansas town won't rest until he's stamped out all traces of corruption. 79m/B VHS, Beta. Richard Dix, Victor Jory, Albert Dekker; **D:** George Archainbaud. Nominations: Academy Awards '43: Best Original Dramatic/Comedy Score. *NOS, MRV, HEG*

Kansas ☑ 1988 (R) Two young men, one a lawless rebel, the other a rational loner, stage a bank heist, and then go on the lam. Lame plot and very weak acting combine to make this film a dud. 111m/C VHS, Beta, LV. Matt Dillon, Andrew McCarthy, Leslie Hope, Kyra Sedgwick; **D:** David Stevens; **C:** David Eggby; **M:** Pino Donaggio.

Kansas City ☑☑☑ 1995 (R) Altman mixes music, politics, crime and the movies in this bittersweet homage to his hometown, set in the jazz-driven 1930s. Star-struck, tough-talking Blondie (Leigh) kidnaps Carolyn Stilton (Richardson), a self-sedating wife of a political shaker (Murphy), in a hair-brained scheme to save her husband from a local mobster (Belafonte). Styled to imitate the brilliant jazz scores played by the likes of Joshua Redman and James Carter, the action can become a bit convulsive and Leigh is beyond irritating with her derivative dame routine. Belafonte, however, is brilliant, relishing the part of the legendary Seldom Seen, a real-life K.C. gangster. **CW:** Language, and for some violence and drug use. 110m/C VHS, LV, Closed Caption. Jennifer Jason Leigh, Miranda Richardson, Harry Belafonte, Michael Murphy, Dermot Mulroney, Steve Buscemi, Brooke Smith, Jane Adams; **D:** Robert Altman; **W:** Frank Barhydt, Robert Altman; **C:** Oliver Stapleton; **M:** Hal Willner. New York Film Critics Awards '96: Best Supporting Actor (Belafonte). *NLC*

Kansas City Confidential ☑☑☑ 1952 An ex-cop on the wrong side of the law launches a sophisticated armored car heist. A disgruntled ex-con gets arrested for the crime on circumstantial evidence. When released, he scours the underworld for the real thieves. 98m/B VHS. John Payne, Coleen Gray, Preston Foster, Neville Brand, Lee Van Cleef, Jack Elam; **D:** Phil Karlson. *NOS, MGM, RXM*

Kansas City Massacre ☑½ 1975 A made-for-television film chronicling the efforts of Melvin Purvis, as he tracked down Depression-era hoods. First called "Melvin Purvis, G-Man." 99m/C VHS, Beta. Dale Robertson, Sally Kirkland, Bo Hopkins, Scott Brady, Lynn Loring, Matt Clark, Mills Watson, Robert Walden; **D:** Dan Curtis. *THV*

Kansas Pacific ☑ 1953 A group of Confederate sympathizers try to stop the Kansas Pacific Railroad from reaching the West Coast in the 1860s. 73m/C VHS, Beta. Sterling Hayden, Eve Miller, Barton MacLane, Reed Hadley, Douglas Hadley; **D:** Ray Nazarro. *NOS, MRV, DVT*

The Kansas Terrors ☑☑ 1939 The "Three Mesquiteers" head for the Caribbean to deliver a herd of horses and wind up in a battle against local despot. 57m/B VHS. Bob Livingston, Raymond Hatton, Duncan Renaldo, Jacqueline Wells, Yakima Canutt, Richard Alexander, Maureen McCormack; **D:** George Sherman. *NOS*

Kaos ☑☑☑ *Chaos-Kaos* 1985 (R) The Taviani brothers adaptation of four stories by Luigi Pirandello ("The Other Son," "Moonstruck," "The Jar," and "Requiem"), which look at peasant life in Sicily, ranging from the comic to the tragic. A fictional epilog, "Conversing with Mother," has Pirandello talking with the spirit of his dead mother. As with any anthology some stories are stronger than others but all possess the Taviani's great visual style and some fine acting. In Italian with English subtitles. 188m/C VHS. **IT** Margarita Lozano, Claudio Bigagli, Massimo Bonetti, Omero Antonutti, Enrica Maria Modugno, Ciccio Ingrassia, Franco Franchi, Biagio Barone, Salvatore Rossi, Franco Scaldati, Pasquale Spadola, Regina Bianchi; **D:** Paolo Taviani, Vittorio Taviani; **W:** Paolo Taviani, Vittorio Taviani, Tonino Guerra. *MGM, BTV*

Kapo ☑☑☑ 1959 A 14-year-old Jewish girl and her family are imprisoned by the Nazis in a concentration camp. There, the girl changes identities with the help of the camp doctor, and rises to the position of camp guard. She proceeds to become taken with her power until a friend commits suicide and jolts the girl back into harsh reality. An Academy Award nominee for Best Foreign Film (lost to "The Virgin Spring"). Primarily English dialogue, with subtitles for foreign language. 116m/B VHS. **IT FR YU** Susan Strasberg, Laurent Terzieff, Emmanuelle Riva, Gianni "John" Garko; **D:** Gillo Pontecorvo; **W:** Gillo Pontecorvo. Nominations: Academy Awards '60: Best Foreign Language Film. *DVT, HEG*

Karate Cop ☑½ 1993 (R) In a future without law or order John Travis (Marchini) is the last cop on earth. He saves Rachel, a beautiful scientist, from a band of scavengers and together they hunt for a hidden crystal with mysterious powers. Only first John has to defeat a gladiator in a martial arts fight to the death. ?m/C VHS, LV, Closed Caption. Ron Marchini, Carrie Chambers, David Carradine, Michael Bristow, D.W. Landingham, Michael Foley, Dana Bentley; **D:** Alan Roberts. *IMP, IME, VTR*

The Karate Kid ☑☑☑½ 1984 (PG) A teenage boy finds out that Karate involves using more than your fists when a handyman agrees to teach him martial arts. The friendship that they develop is deep and sincere; the Karate is only an afterthought. From the director of the original "Rocky," this movie is easy to like. 126m/C VHS, Beta, LV, 8mm, Closed Caption, DVD. Ralph Macchio, Noriyuki "Pat" Morita, Elisabeth Shue, Randee Heller, Martin Kove, Chad McQueen; **D:** John G. Avildsen; **W:** Robert Mark Kamen; **M:** Bill Conti. Nominations: Academy Awards '84: Best Supporting Actor (Morita). *COL*

The Karate Kid: Part 2 ☑☑½ 1986 (PG) Sequel to the first film wherein our high-kicking hero tests his mettle in real-life karate exchanges in Okinawa, and settles a long-standing score. Followed by a second sequel. 95m/C VHS, Beta, LV, 8mm, Closed Caption. Ralph Macchio, Noriyuki "Pat" Morita, Danny Kamekona, Elisabeth Shue, Martin Kove, Tamlyn Tomita, Nobu McCarthy, Yuji Okumoto; **D:** John G. Avildsen; **W:** Robert Mark Kamen; **M:** Bill Conti. Nominations: Academy Awards '86: Best Song ("Glory of Love"). *COL*

The Karate Kid: Part 3 ☑½ 1989 (PG) Second sequel takes a tired plot and doesn't do much to perk it up. Macchio again battles an evil nemesis and learns about himself, but this time Morita refuses to be a part of his training until, of course, Macchio desperately needs his help. Followed by "The Next Karate Kid," which introduces a new kid—a girl. 105m/C VHS, Beta, LV, 8mm, Letterbox, Closed Caption. Ralph Macchio, Noriyuki "Pat" Morita, John G. Avildsen, Thomas Ian Griffith, Martin Kove, Sean Kanan, Robyn Elaine; **D:** John G. Avildsen; **W:** Robert Mark Kamen; **M:** Bill Conti. *COL*

Karate Polish Style ☑ 1982 Polish painter duo paint, plaster and draw blood. A sort of "Dances with Poles" in Warsaw's Mazurian Lake District. In Polish with English subtitles. Not a Polish joke. 91m/C VHS. **PL D:** Jerzy Wojcik. *FCT*

Karate Warrior ☑½ 1988 Young martial artist is beaten and left for dead by Filipino crime syndicate. Bones mended, he prescribes a dose of their medicine. Plenty of rest and retaliation. 90m/C VHS, Beta. Jared Martin, Ken Watanabe. *IMP*

Karate Warriors ☑ 197? Chiba takes his battle against crime to the streets. 90m/C VHS, Beta. Sonny Chiba. *NO*

Karmina ☑☑ 1996 Unusual French-Canadian vampire parody finds 140-year-old vamp Karmina (Cyr) fighting with her Transylvanian parents over their insistence that she marry nerdy Vlad (Pelletier). Karmina flees her home and heads to Montreal in search of her aunt, Esmeralda (Castel), who has managed to regain her humanity and now runs a dating service. A magic potion also makes Karmina human (it's a difficult transition) and she falls in love with Philippe (Brouillette) but Vlad's not out of the picture. He also turns up in Montreal, and begins adding to the vampire population. 109m/C VHS. **CA** Isabelle Cyr, Yves Pelletier, Robert Brouillette, France Castel, Gildor Roy, Raymond Cloutier, Sylvie Potvin; **D:** Gabriel Pelletier; **W:** Gabriel Pelletier, Andree Pelletier, Ann Burke, Yves Pelletier; **C:** Eric Cayla; **M:** Patrick Bourgeois. Genie Awards '97: Best Art Direction/Set Decoration, Best Costume Design; Nominations: Genie Awards '97: Best Actress (Cyr), Best Director (Pelletier), Best Film, Best Screenplay. *NYR*

Kashmiri Run ☑☑ 1969 (R) Action adventure about trio on the lam from Chinese communists chasing them through Tibet. 101m/C VHS. **SP** Pernell Roberts, Alexandra Bastedo, Julian Mateos, Gloria Gamata; **D:** John Peyser. *ART*

Kaspar Hauser ☑☑ 1993 Historical epic based on the true story of Kaspar Hauser (Eisermann), a 16-year-old found abandoned in Nuremberg, Germany in 1828, who was unable to walk, write, or speak. Entrusted to the scientific concerns of Professor Daumer (Samel), rumors begin to circulate that the boy is actually the Crown Prince of Baden. Supposedly, Kaspar was abducted as a baby and substituted for a child who died so his Uncle Ludwig (Oscsenknecht) could become Grand Duke. Court intrigue and threats abound as Kaspar struggles to survive. German with subtitles. 137m/C VHS. **GE** Andre Eisermann, Jeremy Clyde, Katharina Thalbach, Udo Samel, Uwe Ochsenknecht; **D:** Peter Sehr; **W:** Peter Sehr; **C:** Gernot Roll; **M:** Nikos Mamangakis. *KIV*

Katherine ☑ *The Radical* 1975 A young heiress rejects her pampered lifestyle and becomes a violent revolutionary, rebelling against social injustices and the system that spawned them. Made for television. 98m/C VHS, Beta, LV. Sissy Spacek, Art Carney, Jane Wyatt, Henry Winkler, Julie Kavner, Hector Elias, Jenny Sullivan; **D:** Jeremy Paul Kagan. *VTR, IME*

Kavanagh Q.C. 1994 James Kavanagh (Thaw), Queen's Council, is a respected Manchester criminal advocate, who may act for the prosecution in some cases and for the defense in others. In this four-tape set from the TV series, Kavanagh represents a man accused of rape, a porno star, a vigilante, and a prostitute accused of murder. 330m/C VHS. **GB** John Thaw, Lisa Harrow, Alison Steadman; **D:** Peter Carter. *VCO, VIF*

Kavik the Wolf Dog ☑½ *The Courage of Kavik, the Wolf Dog* 1984 Heartwarming story of a courageous dog's love and suffering for the boy he loves. Made for television. 99m/C VHS, Beta. Ronny Cox, Linda Sorensen, Andrew Ian McMillian, Chris Wiggins, John Ireland; **D:** Peter Carter.

Kazaam ☑½ 1996 (PG) Twelve-year-old Max (Capra) is having problems—bullies are chasing him and his single mom's just found a new boyfriend. But his luck seems ready to change when a battered boombox reveals a seven-foot rappin' genie named Kazaam (O'Neal). The kid's beyond obnoxious and Shaq shouldn't plan to give up b-ball anytime soon (at least for an acting career), even though director Glaser did think up the part for the tall guy just before he met him at an NBA All-Star Game. **93m/C VHS, LV, Closed Caption.** Francis Capra, Shaquille O'Neal, Ally Walker, John Costelloe, Marshall Manesh, James Acheson; **D:** Paul Michael Glaser; **W:** Christian Ford, Roger Soffer; **C:** Charles Minsky; **M:** Christopher Tyng. *TOU*

Keaton's Cop ♂ 1990 (R) Another cheap cop comedy involving the mistaken identity of an important mob witness. **95m/C VHS, Beta, LV.** Lee Majors, Abe Vigoda, Don Rickles; **D:** Robert Burge. *MGM, OM*

The Keep ♂♂ 1983 (R) At the height of the Nazi onslaught, several German soldiers unleash an unknown power from a medieval stone fortress. Technically impressive but lacking in all other aspects. From a novel by F. Paul Wilson. **96m/C VHS, Beta, LV, Letterbox.** Scott Glenn, Alberta Watson, Juergen Prochnow, Robert Prosky, Gabriel Byrne, Ian McKellen; **D:** Michael Mann; **W:** Michael Mann, Dennis Lynton Clark; **C:** Alex Thomson; **M:** Tangerine Dream. *PAR, OM*

Keep 'Em Flying ♂♂ 1941 Bud and Lou star in the this wartime morale-booster that hasn't aged well. The duo follow their barnstorming friend into flight academy; a not-too-taxing plot includes five musical numbers and two Martha Rayes (she plays twins). ♫Pig Foot Pete; Together; I'm Looking for the Boy with the Wistful Eyes; Let's Keep 'Em Flying; I'm Getting Sentimental Over You. **86m/B VHS, LV, Closed Caption.** Bud Abbott, Lou Costello, Martha Raye; **D:** Arthur Lubin. *USH*

Keep My Grave Open ♂♂ *The House Where Hell Froze Over* 1980 (R) A woman lives in an isolated house where a series of strange murders take place. She attributes them to her brother, but does he really exist? Made cheaply, but not without style; filmed in Harrison County, Texas. **85m/C VHS, Beta.** Camilla Carr, Gene Ross, Stephen Tobolowsky, Ann Stafford, Sharon Bunn, Chelcie Ross; **D:** S.F. Brownrigg. *UNI*

Keep Punching ♂♂ 1939 A gambler/boxer is almost destroyed by life in the fast lane, as well as by a seductive woman. **80m/C VHS.** Henry Armstrong, Mae Johnson; *Cameos:* Canada Lee; **D:** John Clein. *FCT*

Keep Talking Baby ♂♂ 1961 Action-packed thriller that finds Eddie in prison after being framed for murder. He escapes and is out for revenge on the organization that put him there. **?m/C VHS.** Eddie Constantine. *SNC*

Keep the Change ♂♂ 1992 (PG-13) Joe Starling is an artist with painter's block, living in California with his girlfriend Astrid. He decides to revisit the family ranch in Deadrock, Montana, and his crackpot Uncle Smitty and saintly Aunt Lureen. The family ranch is coveted by the evil Overstreet (typecasting for Palance), whose daughter was once loved by Joe but is now married to his ex-best friend. Character more than plot rules this moody, low-key story based on a novel by Thomas McGuane. Made for cable television. **95m/C VHS, LV, Closed Caption.** William L. Petersen, Lolita Davidovich, Rachel Ticotin, Buck Henry, Jack Palance, Fred Dalton Thompson, Jeff Kober, Lois Smith; **D:** Andy Tennant. *TTC*

Keeper ♂♂ 1984 Wealthy patients at Underwood Asylum suffer unspeakable horrors while under the care of Lee. Detective Dick Driver investigates. Obscure horror spoof. **96m/C VHS, Beta.** CA Christopher Lee, Tell Schreiber, Sally Gray; **D:** Tom Drake; **W:** Tom Drake. *TWE, HHE*

The Keeper ♂♂½ 1996 Disillusioned Paul Lamott (Esposito) is a corrections officer at the King's County House of Detention in Brooklyn. Nevertheless, Paul, who's earning a law degree, is moved by the pleas of Haitian prisoner Jean Baptiste (de Bankole), who swears he's been wrongly accused of rape. Paul, who's father was Haitian, manages to help Jean make bail and then invites him home—to the strong dismay of Paul's teacher wife Angela (Taylor). However, Angela begins warming to Jean's charm—but beware the stranger. **97m/C VHS.** Giancarlo Esposito, Regina Taylor, Isaach de Bankole; **D:** Joe Brewster; **W:** Joe Brewster; **C:** Igor Sunara; **M:** John Petersen. *KIV*

Keeper of the City ♂♂½ 1992 (R) Gossett stars as a tough detective out to get a vigilante (LaPaglia) who is roaming the streets of Chicago. LaPaglia turns in a good performance as the son of a Mafia operative who wants to rid himself of the Mafia ties that have controlled him. As he pursues his deadly course of action, a newspaper journalist tags him "The Gangster Killer." Coyote plays the crusading journalist who is always interfering in Gossett's business. Good performances and an intriguing story line combine to make this action-packed thriller worthwhile, although the script isn't as good as Di Pega's novel, which he adapted himself. **CW:** Language and violence. **95m/C VHS, Beta, LV, Closed Caption.** Louis Gossett Jr., Peter Coyote, Anthony LaPaglia, Renee Soutendijk, Aeryk Egan, Tony Todd; **D:** Bobby Roth; **W:** Gerald Di Pega. *FXV, VTR*

Keeper of the Flame ♂♂½ 1942 Tracy and Hepburn manage to keep the murk of this story at bay as war correspondent Steven O'Malley (Tracy) is assigned to write about super patriot Robert V. Forrest, who's just died in an accident. Reclusive widow Christine Forrest (Hepburn) finally agrees to help O'Malley out but what our intrepid reporter discovers is that the hero was really a heel—something Christine still doesn't want known. Based on the novel by I.A.R. Wylie. **100m/B VHS.** Spencer Tracy, Katharine Hepburn, Richard Whorf, Margaret Wycherly, Donald Meek, Stephen McNally, Audrey Christie, Frank Craven, Forrest Tucker, Percy Kilbride, Howard da Silva, Darryl Hickman; **D:** George Cukor; **W:** Donald Ogden Stewart; **C:** William H. Daniels; **M:** Bronislau Kaper. *TTC*

Keeping On ♂♂½ 1981 Television movie with a pro-union stance. A preacher, who is also a millworker, teams up with an organizer to try to unionize the mill. Originally produced for the PBS "American Playhouse" series. **75m/C VHS.** Dick Anthony Williams, Carol Kane, James Broderick, Marcia Rodd, Rosalind Cash, Carl Lee, Danny Glover, Guy Boyd; **D:** Barbara Kopple. *TWE*

Keeping Track ♂ 1986 (R) Two tourists witness a murder and robbery and find the stolen $5 million on a New York-bound train. The two are relentlessly pursued by everyone, including the CIA and Russian spies. **102m/C VHS, Beta, LV, Closed Caption.** Michael Sarrazin, Margot Kidder, Alan Scarfe, Ken Pogue, Vlasta Vrana, Donald Pilon; **D:** Robin Spry. *NLC*

Keetje Tippel ♂♂ *Katie's Passion; Cathy Tippel; Hot Sweat* 1975 (R) In 1881 Amsterdam, a young Dutch prostitute works her way out of poverty and enters a world of education and wealth. A Victorian tale of exploitation with a tough and intelligent Cinderella heroine. In Dutch with English subtitles. **104m/C VHS, Beta, LV.** NL Monique Van De Ven, Rutger Hauer, Eddie Brugman, Hannah De Leeuwe, Andrea Domburg; **D:** Paul Verhoeven; **C:** Jan De Bont. *CVC, IME, TPV*

Kelly of the Secret Service ♂♂ 1936 Agent tries to find out who stole the plans for a guided missile system. Fast-pace rides over the silliness of the plot. **69m/B VHS.** Lloyd Hughes, Sheila Mannors, Fuzzy Knight, Syd Saylor, Jack Mulhall, Forrest Taylor; **D:** Robert F. "Bob" Hill; **W:** Al Martin. *SNC*

Kelly the Second ♂½ 1936 Slow-moving boxing comedy about a punch-drunk fighter trying to win again with the encouragement of his trainer and manager. **70m/B VHS.** Guinn "Big Boy" Williams, Patsy Kelly, Charley Chase, Pert Kelton, Edward Brophy, Maxie "Slapsie" Rosenbloom, Harold Huber, DeWitt Jennings, Billy Gilbert, Syd Saylor; **D:** Gus Meins. *RXM*

Kelly's Heroes ♂♂½ 1970 (PG) A misfit band of crooks are led by Eastwood on a daring mission: to steal a fortune in gold from behind enemy lines. In the process, they almost win WWII. Sutherland is superb, as is McLeod, in his pre-Love Boat days. **145m/C VHS, Beta, LV, Letterbox.** Clint Eastwood, Donald Sutherland, Telly Savalas, Gavin MacLeod, Don Rickles, Carroll O'Connor, Stuart Margolin, Harry Dean Stanton; **D:** Brian G. Hutton; **M:** Lalo Schifrin. *MGM, TLF*

Kemek ♂ 1988 (R) An eccentric chemical company owner has his mistress push a new mind-control drug on an American writer, and has them killed after discovering their subsequent affair. Unfortunately, he didn't count on the woman's ex-husband seeking revenge. **82m/C VHS, Beta.** David Hedison, Helmut Snider, Mary Woronov, Alexandra Stewart, Cal Haynes. *OM*

Kennedy ♂♂ 1983 The long television miniseries biography of JFK from his inauguration to assassination. **278m/C VHS, Beta.** Martin Sheen, Blair Brown, Vincent Gardenia, Geraldine Fitzgerald, E.G. Marshall, John Shea; **D:** Richard Hartley.

The Kennedys of Massachusetts ♂♂½ 1995 Three cassette TV miniseries chronicles six decades of Kennedy life, from Joe Kennedy's (Petersen) courtship of Rose (O'Toole) to the presidential election of JFK and all the various scandals and tragedies. Adapted from the book "The Fitzgeralds and the Kennedys" by Doris Kearns Godwin. **278m/C VHS.** William L. Petersen, Annette O'Toole, Charles Durning, Steven Weber, Tracy Pollan, Campbell Scott. *ORI*

The Kennel Murder Case ♂♂ 1933 Debonair detective Philo Vance suspects that a clear-cut case of suicide is actually murder. Fourth Vance mystery starring Powell. Remade as "Calling Philo Vance" in 1940. **73m/B VHS, Beta.** William Powell, Mary Astor, Jack LaRue, Ralph Morgan, Eugene Pallette; **D:** Michael Curtiz. *SNC, NOS, HHT*

Kenny Rogers as the Gambler ♂♂½ 1980 Rogers stars as Brady Hawkes, debonair gambler searching for a son he never knew he had. Based on the Rogers song of the same name. One of the highest rated TV movies ever. Followed by several sequels. **94m/C VHS.** Kenny Rogers, Christine Belford, Bruce Boxleitner, Harold Gould, Clu Gulager, Lance LeGault, Lee Purcell, Noble Willingham; **D:** Dick Lowry. *NO*

Kenny Rogers as the Gambler, Part 2: The Adventure Continues ♂½ 1983 The surprise success of the made-for-TV western based on the popular Kenny Rogers' song spawned this equally popular sequel. Rogers returns as Brady Hawkes, this time searching for his kidnapped son. Followed by two more sequels. **195m/C VHS, Beta, 8mm.** Kenny Rogers, Bruce Boxleitner, Linda Evans, Harold Gould, David Hedison, Clu Gulager, Johnny Crawford; **D:** Dick Lowry. *NO*

Kenny Rogers as the Gambler, Part 3: The Legend Continues ♂♂ 1987 Roger's third attempt at humanizing the gambler from his hit '70s song. This time, the Gambler gives a hand with the mediating between the warring U.S. government and the Sioux nation. Sitting Bull and Buffalo Bill add credibility to this average undertaking. Made for TV. **190m/C VHS, Beta.** Kenny Rogers, Bruce Boxleitner, Linda Gray, Melanie Chartoff, Matt Clark, George Kennedy, Dean Stockwell, Charles Durning, Jeffrey Jones, George American Horse; **D:** Dick Lowry. *NO*

Kent State ♂♂ 1981 Made-for-television drama recounts the tragic events that took place at Kent State University in 1970, when student demonstrators faced National Guardsmen. Goldstone won an Emmy for Outstanding Direction. **120m/C VHS, Beta.** Talia Balsam, Ellen Barkin, Jane Fleiss, John Getz, Keith Gordon; **D:** James Goldstone. *USH*

The Kentuckian ⫓⫓½ 1955 Burt Lancaster stars as a rugged frontiersman who leaves with his son to go to Texas. On their journey the two are harassed by fighting mountaineers. 104m/C VHS, Beta. Burt Lancaster, Walter Matthau, Diana Lynn, John McIntire, Dianne Foster, Una Merkel, John Carradine; **D:** Burt Lancaster; **C:** Ernest Laszlo. MGM

Kentucky Blue Streak ⫓½ 1935 Young jockey is framed for murder while riding at an "illegal" racetrack. Later, almost eligible for parole, he escapes from jail to ride "Blue Streak" in the Kentucky Derby. 61m/B VHS, Beta. Eddie Nugent, Frank "Junior" Coghlan, Patricia Scott, Ben Carter. VYY

Kentucky Fried Movie ⫓⫓⫓ 1977 (R) A zany potpourri of satire about movies, television, commercials, and contemporary society. Written by the Abrahams and the Zuckers, who were later known for "Airplane!" 85m/C VHS, Beta, LV. Bill Bixby, Jerry Zucker, Jim Abrahams, David Zucker, Donald Sutherland, Henry Gibson, George Lazenby; **D:** John Landis; **W:** Jerry Zucker, Jim Abrahams, David Zucker.

Kentucky Jubilee ⫓½ 1951 At the jubilee, a movie director is kidnapped and the master of ceremonies, among others, decides to find him. 67m/B VHS, Beta, LV. Jerry Colonna, Jean Porter, James Ellison, Raymond Hatton, Fritz Feld. RXM

Kentucky Kernels ⫓⫓ Triple Trouble 1934 A pair of down and out magicians ('30s comic duo Wheeler and Woolsey) happen upon a young boy (Little Rascal Spanky) who happens to be heir to a fortune. The three head for the rascal's Kentucky home, where they're welcomed with southern inhospitality. Much feuding and slapsticking. 75m/B VHS, LV. Bert Wheeler, Robert Woolsey, Mary Carlisle, George "Spanky" McFarland, Noah Beery Sr., Lucille LaVerne, Willie Best; **D:** George Stevens; **M:** Max Steiner. TTC, FCT, GVV

Kentucky Rifle ⫓½ 1955 A Comanche Indian tribe will let a group of stranded pioneers through their territory only if they agree to sell the Kentucky rifles aboard their wagon. 80m/C VHS, Beta. Chill Wills, Lance Fuller, Cathy Downs, Jess Barker, Sterling Holloway, Jeanne Cagney; **D:** Carl K. Hittleman. MON, HHE

Kept Husbands ⫓⫓ 1931 A factory worker saves two lives in an industrial accident, and the boss invites him home to dinner. When he meets the boss' daughter, romance blooms. But their different backgrounds cause difficulties. A bit dull, and dated by its chauvinism. 76m/B VHS. Dorothy Mackaill, Joel McCrea, Robert McWade, Florence Roberts, Clara Kimball Young, Mary Carr, Ned Sparks, Bryant Washburn; **D:** Lloyd Bacon; **M:** Max Steiner. NOS, HEG

The Kettles in the Ozarks ⫓⫓½ 1956 Since Kilbride retired after the seventh comedy, Hunnicutt played a new male character, Uncle Sledge, in the eighth film. Ma (Main) takes the young'uns to visit their uncle in the Ozarks and finds she must help him and fiancee Bedelia (Merkel) save the failing farm from bootleggers. 81m/B VHS, Closed Caption. Marjorie Main, Arthur Hunnicutt, Una Merkel, Ted de Corsia, Richard Eyer, Joseph Sawyer, Richard Deacon; **D:** Charles Lamont; **W:** Kay Lenard. USH

The Kettles on Old MacDonald's Farm ⫓⫓½ 1957 The ninth and last in the series finds Ma (Main in her final film) and Pa (Kennelly replacing the retired Kilbride) playing matchmakers for humble lumberman Brad (Smith). Seems he wants to marry the boss' spoiled daughter, Sally (Talbott), whom Ma decides needs a little backwoods seasoning before she'll make the proper wife. 82m/B VHS, Closed Caption. Marjorie Main, Parker Fennelly, John Smith, Gloria Talbott, Claude Akins, Roy Barcroft, Patricia Morrow, George Dunn; **D:** Virgil W. Vogel; **W:** Herbert Margolis, William Raynor. USH

The Key ⫓⫓½ 1958 A long, slow WWII drama about the key to an Italian girl's apartment that gets passed from tugboat skipper to tugboat skipper before dangerous missions. Ultimately she finds true love, or does she? Based on the novel "Stella" by Jan de Hartog. 134m/B VHS, Beta, LV, CB. William Holden, Sophia Loren, Trevor Howard, Oscar Homolka, Kieron Moore; **D:** Carol Reed; **W:** Carl Foreman; **C:** Oswald Morris; **M:** Malcolm Arnold. British Academy Awards '58: Best Actor (Howard). COL

Key Exchange ⫓⫓½ 1985 (R) Kevin Scott and Paul Kurta based this contemporary look at love and commitments on Kevin Wade's popular play. Two New York City "yuppies" have reached a point in their relationship where an exchange of apartment keys commonly occurs—but they are hesitant. 96m/C VHS, Beta, Closed Caption. Brooke Adams, Ben Masters, Daniel Stern, Tony Roberts, Danny Aiello, Annie Golden, Nancy Mette; **D:** Barnet Kellman; **W:** Kevin Scott, Paul Kurta; **M:** Jonathan Elias. FOX

Key Largo ⫓⫓⫓½ 1948 A gangster melodrama set in Key West, Florida, where hoods take over a hotel in the midst of a hurricane. Based on a play by Maxwell Anderson. 101m/B VHS, Beta, LV. Humphrey Bogart, Lauren Bacall, Edward G. Robinson, Lionel Barrymore; **D:** John Huston; **W:** Richard Brooks, John Huston; **C:** Karl Freund; **M:** Max Steiner. Academy Awards '48: Best Supporting Actress (Trevor). MGM, FOX, TLF

The Key Man ⫓½ Life at Stake 1957 A radio show host manages to get mixed up with gangsters after recreating a crime on the air. He uses his knowledge of crime to thwart the crooks. 63m/B VHS, Beta. GB Lee Patterson, Hy Hazell, Colin Gordon, Philip Leaver, Paula Byrne; **D:** Montgomery Tully; **M:** Les Baxter. NOS, SNC

The Key to Rebecca ⫓⫓½ 1985 The Nazis and the British go head-to-head in war torn North Africa. As the Germans push their way across Egypt, they find an unexpected ally in a half-German/half-Arab killer behind the British lines. Tense, well made thriller, originally a miniseries. On two cassettes. Made for television. 190m/C VHS. David Soul, Cliff Robertson, Robert Culp, Season Hubley, Lina Raymond, Anthony Quayle, David Hemmings; **D:** David Hemmings. WOV

Key to the City ⫓⫓½ 1950 Light comedy featuring Gable and Young as two small town mayors who meet and fall in love at a convention in San Francisco. Throw in some sharp lines, a little slapstick, and a bit of satire for an amusing picture. Based on the story by Albert Beich. 99m/B VHS. Clark Gable, Loretta Young, Frank Morgan, Marilyn Maxwell, Raymond Burr, James Gleason, Lewis Stone, Raymond Walburn; **D:** George Sidney; **W:** Robert Riley Crutcher. MGM

The Keys of the Kingdom ⫓⫓⫓ 1944 An earnest adaptation of A.J. Cronin's novel about a young Scottish missionary spreading God's word in 19th Century China. 137m/B VHS, Beta, LV, Closed Caption. Gregory Peck, Thomas Mitchell, Edmund Gwenn, Vincent Price, Roddy McDowall, Cedric Hardwicke, Peggy Ann Garner, James Gleason, Anne Revere, Rose Stradner, Sara Allgood, Abner Biberman, Arthur Shields; **D:** John M. Stahl; **W:** Joseph L. Mankiewicz, Nunnally Johnson; **C:** Arthur C. Miller. Nominations: Academy Awards '45: Best Actor (Peck), Best Black and White Cinematography, Best Interior Decoration, Best Original Dramatic/Comedy Score. FOX, IGP

Keys to Tulsa ⫓⫓½ 1996 (R) After losing his job as a lowly movie reviewer (gasp!), Richter Bourdreau (Stoltz), the black-sheep son of a wealthy Tulsa family, is lured into a blackmail scheme by his ex-flame Vicky (Unger) and her perpetually stoned husband Ronnie (Spader). When the tables are turned on him, Richter finally gets up off of his slacker butt for some revenge. Excellent cast includes Moore as his flinty mother and Coburn as a wealthy redneck patriarch. Stoltz's performance holds the spiraling story of class distinction, murder and deceit together, and Spader's Elvis-helmeted loser is fun to watch. Based on the novel by Brian Fair Berkey. **CW:** Strong sexuality and language, some drug use and violence. 112m/C VHS, LV. Eric Stoltz, James Spader, Mary Tyler Moore, Joanna Going, Cameron Diaz, James Coburn, Michael Rooker, Peter Strauss, Deborah Kara Unger; Dr Leslie Greif; W: Harley Peyton; C: Robert Fraisse; **M:** Stephen Endelman. PGV

The KGB: The Secret War ⫓½ Lethal 1986 (PG-13) Reheated Cold War fare. 90m/C VHS, LV. Michael Billington, Michael Ansara, Michael Billington; **W:** Sandra K. Bailey; **C:** Peter Collister. HHE

Khartoum ⫓⫓½ 1966 A sweeping but talky adventure epic detailing the last days of General "Chinese" Gordon as the title city is besieged by Arab tribes in 1884. 134m/C VHS, Beta, LV, Letterbox. Charlton Heston, Laurence Olivier, Ralph Richardson, Richard Johnson, Alexander Knox, Hugh Williams, Nigel Green, Michael Hordern, Johnny Sekka; **D:** Basil Dearden. Nominations: Academy Awards '66: Best Story & Screenplay. MGM, CCB

The Kick Fighter ⫓ 1991 Would you believe the hero has to kickbox to finance his kid sister's operation? Grungy, Bangkok-set chopsocky cheapie leaves no cliche untouched, but fights are well-staged. A strange end credit lauds real-life champ Urquidez, here a bad guy. 92m/C VHS. Richard Norton, Benny "The Jet" Urquidez, Glen Ruehland, Franco Guerrero, Erica Van Wagener, Steve Rackman; **D:** Anthony Maharaj.

Kick of Death: The Prodigal Boxer ⫓ 198? (R) A young boxer is accused of a murder he didn't commit, and fights a battle to the death to prove it. 90m/C VHS, Beta. Mang Sei, Suma Wah Lung, Pa Hung; **D:** Chai Yang Min. GEM

Kickboxer ⫓½ 1989 (R) The brother of a permanently crippled kickboxing champ trains for a revenge match. 97m/C VHS, Beta, LV. Jean-Claude Van Damme, Rochelle Ashana, Dennis Chan, Dennis Alexio; **D:** Mark DiSalle; **W:** Jean-Claude Van Damme, Mark DiSalle, Glenn A. Bruce. HBO, WAR

Kickboxer 2: The Road Back ⫓½ 1990 (R) Mitchell takes over for Van Damme in this action sequel which finds our athletic hero seeking revenge on the kickboxer who murdered his brother. 90m/C VHS, LV. Sasha Mitchell, Peter Boyle, John Diehl; **D:** Albert Pyun. WAR, MOV, HBO

Kickboxer 3: The Art of War ⫓½ 1992 (R) Mitchell returns in this second sequel. This time the American kickboxing champ flies to Rio for a big match which turns out to be fixed by a local mobster. For a little more fun our hero saves a kidnapped girl and fights a hired killer. **CW:** Some strong violence. 92m/C VHS, LV, Closed Caption. Sasha Mitchell, Dennis Chan, Richard Comar, Noah Verduzco, Althea Miranda, Ian Jacklin; **D:** Rick King. ART

Kickboxer 4: The Aggressor ⫓⫓½ 1994 (R) Martial arts expert David Sloan (Mitchell) was framed by sworn enemy Tong Po but now he's back and looking for revenge. 90m/C VHS, LV, Closed Caption. Sasha Mitchell, Kamal Krifia, Nicholas Guest, Deborah Mansy, Brad Thornton; **D:** Albert Pyun. ART

Kickboxer the Champion ⫓ 1991 The opium trade is in for a kick to the stomach when Archer challenges the big man in charge to a deathly duel. ?m/C VHS. Don Murray, Wayne Archer; **D:** Alton Cheung. WLA

Kicked in the Head ⫓⫓ 1997 (R) Redmond, a loser who dreams of the Hindenburg disaster, is newly jobless, homeless and loveless. He decides to go on a "spiritual quest," which unfortunately consists of bad poetry and worse trouble, through Manhattan's Lower East Side. His Uncle Sam (Woods) wants him to deliver a package, his buddy Stretch (Rapaport) wants him to work for his shady (and sometimes violent) beer business and stewardess Megan (Fiorentino) wants him to leave her alone. It's all settled in a hail of gunfire and car chases, because that's how things are solved in the movies. Director Harrison did more with much less in debut "Rhythm Thief." **CW:** Strong language, drug content, some sex and brief violence. 97m/C VHS. Kevin Corrigan, Linda Fiorentino, James Woods, Lili Taylor, Michael Rapaport, Burt Young, Olek Krupa; **D:** Matthew Harrison; **W:**

Kevin Corrigan, Matthew Harrison; **C:** John Thomas, Howard Krupa; **M:** Stephen Endelman. *FXV*

Kicking and Screaming 🎬🎬🎬 1995

(R) Baumbach's deft, though slightly self-conscious directorial debut examines the post-college grad angst of Grover (Hamilton) and his three other slacker roomies. In denial of their recently achieved non-student status, the four bond together in pursuit of the inane and trivial, while their various girlfriends slip more easily into adulthood. Funny and tender flashback scenes of Grover and girlfriend Jane (D'Abo) add depth without all the dialogue, well-written though it is. Hilarious highlight occurs as roommate Otis interviews for that most popular of low-budget, Gen-X movie jobs—video store clerk. **CW:** Strong language and some sexuality. **96m/C VHS.** Josh Hamilton, Olivia D'Abo, Carlos Jacott, Christopher Eigeman, Eric Stoltz, Jason Wiles, Parker Posey, Cara Buono, Elliott Gould; **D:** Noah Baumbach; **W:** Oliver Berkman, Noah Baumbach; **C:** Steven Bernstein; **M:** Phil Marshall. *THV*

Kicks 🎬½ 1985

Two well-off San Francisco professionals play high-risk games with each other, culminating in a life-or-death hunt. Made for television. **97m/C VHS, Beta.** Anthony Geary, Shelley Hack, Tom Mason, Ian Abercrombie, James Avery; **D:** William Wiard; **M:** Peter Bernstein. *NO*

The Kid 🎬🎬🎬 1921

Sensitive and sassy film about a tramp who takes home an orphan. Chaplin's first feature. Also launched Coogan as the first child superstar. **60m/B VHS.** Charlie Chaplin, Jackie Coogan, Edna Purviance; **D:** Charlie Chaplin. *FCT, MLB*

Kid 🎬🎬½ 1990 (R)

Young guy carries grudge for the murder of his parents and seeks pound of flesh. Enter mysterious beautiful woman and copious complications. Good sound FX. **94m/C VHS, Beta, LV, Closed Caption.** C. Thomas Howell, R. Lee Ermey, Brian Austin Green, Sarah Trigger; **D:** John Mark Robinson. *ART, IME*

Kid and the Killers 🎬 198? (PG)

Young orphan and a hardened criminal band together to pursue a villain. **90m/C VHS, Beta.** Jon Cypher. *NO*

The Kid Brother 🎬🎬🎬½ 1927

The shy, weak son of a tough sheriff, Harold fantasizes about being a hero like his father and big brothers, falls in love with a carnival lady, and somehow saves the day. Classic silent comedy. **84m/B VHS, Beta.** Harold Lloyd, Walter James, Jobyna Ralston; **D:** Ted Wilde. *TLF*

Kid Colter 🎬🎬½ 1985

Enjoyable family film about a city kid who goes to visit his dad in a remote wilderness area of the Pacific Northwest. While there he is abducted by two grizzly mountain men and left for dead, but survives and pursues his abductors relentlessly. Received the Film Advisory Board Award of Excellence and the Award of Merit from the Academy of Family Films. **101m/C VHS, Beta, Closed Caption.** Jim Stafford, Jeremy Shamos, Hal Terrance, Greg Ward, Jim Turner; **D:** David O'Malley; **W:** David O'Malley. *FOX*

Kid Courageous 🎬 1935

An athlete goes west, tracks ore mine thieves and prevents a hot-blooded spitfire from marrying the wrong man. **53m/B VHS.** Bob Steele. *NOS*

Kid Dynamite Queen of Broadway 1943

A Bowery Boys series episode. Gorcey is a boxer who is kidnapped to prevent his participation in a major fight. The real fighting occurs when his brother is substituted, and Gorcey is smitten. **73m/B VHS.** Leo Gorcey, Huntz Hall, Bobby Jordan, Gabriel Dell, Pamela Blake; **D:** Wallace Fox. *NOS, HEG*

A Kid for Two Farthings 🎬🎬½ 1955

An episodic, sentimental portrait of the Jewish quarter in London's East End, centered on a boy with a malformed goat he thinks is a magic unicorn capable of granting wishes and bringing happiness to his impoverished 'hood. Acclaimed adaptation of a novel by screenwriter Wolf Mankowitz, and on tape in a shorter rehash as "The Unicorn." **96m/C VHS.** Jonathan Ashmore. *HMV, FCT*

Kid from Brooklyn 🎬🎬 1946

A shy, musically inclined milkman becomes a middleweight boxer by knocking out the champ in a street brawl. Remake of "The Milky Way" by Harold Lloyd. Available with digitally remastered stereo and original movie trailer. ♫Sunflower Song; Hey, What's Your Name; You're the Cause Of It All; Welcome, Burleigh; I Love An Old-Fashioned Song; Josie. **113m/C VHS.** Danny Kaye, Virginia Mayo, Eve Arden, Fay Bainter, Walter Abel; **D:** Norman Z. McLeod; **C:** Gregg Toland. *HBO*

Kid from Gower Gulch 🎬 1947

A singing, non-horse-riding cowboy enters a rodeo through a clever ruse. **56m/B VHS, Beta, LV.** Spade Cooley. *NOS*

The Kid from Left Field 🎬🎬 1979

Bat boy for the San Diego Padres transforms the team from losers to champions when he passes on the advice of his father, a "has-been" ballplayer, to the team members. A made-for-television remake of the 1953 classic. **80m/C VHS, Beta.** Gary Coleman, Robert Guillaume, Ed McMahon, Tab Hunter; **D:** Adell Aldrich. *VES*

Kid from Not-So-Big 🎬🎬 1978 (G)

A family film that tells the story of Jenny, a young girl left to carry on her grandfather's frontier-town newspaper. When two con-men come to town, Jenny sets out to expose them. **87m/C VHS, Beta.** Jennifer McAllister, Veronica Cartwright, Robert Viharo, Paul Tulley; **D:** William Crain. *WAR, OM*

Kid from Spain 🎬🎬½ 1932

Early Busby Berkeley choreography highlights this fun, if nonsensical, musical. Thanks to the usual mixups, college boy Eddie (Cantor) witnesses a bank robbery and flees to his friend Ricardo's (Young) home in Mexico, with the crooks on his trail. Then he gets mistaken for a famous bullfighter and is even forced into the ring. Oh, and there's some romantic complications as well. ♫The College Song; Look What You've Done; In the Moonlight; What a Perfect Combination. **96m/B VHS.** Eddie Cantor, Robert Young, Lyda Roberti, Ruth Hall, John Miljan, Noah Beery Sr., J. Carrol Naish, Robert Emmett O'Connor; **D:** Leo McCarey; **W:** William Anthony McGuire, Bert Kalmar, Harry Ruby; **C:** Gregg Toland. *HBO*

Kid Galahad 🎬🎬🎬 The Battling Bellhop 1937

Well acted boxing drama with Robinson playing an honest promoter who wants to make Morris into a prize fighter. Davis plays the girl they both want. Remade as "The Wagons Roll at Night" and then made again as an Elvis Presley vehicle. Shown on television. **101m/B VHS, Closed Caption.** Edward G. Robinson, Bette Davis, Humphrey Bogart, Wayne Morris, Jane Bryan, Harry Carey Sr., Veda Ann Borg; **D:** Michael Curtiz; **W:** Seton I. Miller; **C:** Gaetano Antonio "Tony" Gaudio; **M:** Max Steiner. *MGM*

Kid Galahad 🎬🎬 1962

The King plays a young boxer who weathers the fight game, singing seven songs along the way. ♫King of the Whole Wide World; This Is Living; I Got Lucky; A Whistling Tune; Home Is Where The Heart Is; Riding the Rainbow; Love Is For Loves. **95m/C VHS, Beta, LV, Letterbox.** Elvis Presley, Lola Albright, Charles Bronson, Ned Glass, Joan Blackman, Ed Asner, Gig Young; **D:** Phil Karlson; **C:** Burnett Guffey. *MGM*

The Kid/Idle Class 🎬🎬🎬 1921

The Little Tramp adopts a homeless orphan in "The Kid," Chaplin's first feature-length film. This tape also includes "The Idle Class," a rare Chaplin short. **85m/B VHS, Beta.** Charlie Chaplin, Jackie Coogan, Edna Purviance, Chuck Reisner, Lita Grey Chaplin; **D:** Charlie Chaplin. *FOX*

A Kid in King Arthur's Court 🎬½ 1995 (PG)

Lame adaptation of Mark Twain's "A Connecticut Yankee in King Arthur's Court" finds insecure California teen Calvin Fuller (Nicholas), falling down a hole created by an earthquake and landing in Camelot. Arthur's (Ackland) a doddering old man with a cute teen daughter, Princess Katey (Baeza), who needs some help in defeating the evil Lord Belasco (Malik). Naturally, Calvin helps out and gains confidence in himself. Okay

time-waster for the kids. **91m/C VHS, Closed Caption.** Thomas Ian Nicholas, Joss Ackland, Art Malik, Paloma Baeza, Kate Winslet, Ron Moody, Daniel Craig; **D:** Michael Gottlieb; **W:** Michael Part, Robert L. Levy; **C:** Elemer Ragaly; **M:** J.A.C. Redford. *TOU*

Kid Millions 🎬🎬½ 1934

Vintage musical comedy in which a dull-witted Brooklyn boy must travel to exotic Egypt to collect an inherited fortune. The finale is filmed in early three-strip Technicolor. Lucille Ball appears as a Goldwyn Girl. ♫Your Head on My Shoulder; Ice Cream Fantasy; An Earful of Music; When My Ship Comes In; Okay Toots; I Want to be a Minstrel Man; Mandy. **90m/B VHS.** Eddie Cantor, Ethel Merman, Ann Sothern, George Murphy; **D:** Roy Del Ruth. *HBO*

Kid Monk Baroni 🎬🎬½ 1952

Street punk Baroni (Nimoy) leaves his gang behind when a good-guy priest (Rober) introduces him to boxing. The kid rises to success thanks to a cagey manager (Cabot) and despite the presence of organized crime. Typical B-movie melodrama. **80m/B VHS.** Leonard Nimoy, Bruce Cabot, Richard Rober, Kathleen Freeman; **D:** Harold Schuster. *EEL*

Kid 'n' Hollywood and Polly Tix in Washington 1933

These two "Baby Burlesks" shorts star a cast of toddlers, featuring the most famous moppet of all time, Shirley Temple, in her earliest screen appearances. **20m/B VHS, Beta.** Shirley Temple. *CCB*

Kid Ranger 🎬 1936

A ranger shoots an innocent man, but later sets things straight by bringing the real culprit to justice. **57m/B VHS, Beta.** Bob Steele, William Farnum; **D:** Robert North Bradbury. *VYY*

Kid Sister 🎬½ 1945

A young girl is determined to grab her sister's boyfriend for herself, and enlists the aid of a burglar to do it. **56m/B VHS, Beta.** Roger Pryor, Judy Clark, Frank Jenks, Constance Worth. *VYY*

Kid Vengeance 🎬½ 1975 (R)

After witnessing the brutal slaying of his family, a boy carries out a personal vendetta against the outlaws. **90m/C VHS, Beta.** Leif Garrett, Jim Brown, Lee Van Cleef, John Marley, Glynnis O'Connor; **D:** Joseph Manduke. *NO*

The Kid Who Loved Christmas 🎬🎬 1990

After his adoptive mother is killed in a car accident, a young boy is taken from his adoptive father. The boy, upset about being removed from his new family, writes to Santa Claus for help. A touching yuletide drama. This was Sammy Davis, Jr.'s last film. Made for television. **118m/C VHS, Closed Caption.** Cicely Tyson, Michael Warren, Sammy Davis Jr., Gilbert Lewis, Ken Page, Della Reese, Esther Rolle, Ben Vereen, Vanessa L(ynne) Williams, John Beal, Trent Cameron; **D:** Arthur Seidelman; **C:** Hanania Baer. *PAR*

The Kid with the Broken Halo 🎬🎬 1982

Coleman and Guillaume are paired again in this unsuccessful pilot for a TV series. A young angel, out to earn his wings, must try to help three desperate families, with the help of an experienced angel. **100m/C VHS.** Gary Coleman, Robert Guillaume, June Allyson, Mason Adams, Ray Walston, John Pleshette, Kim Fields, Georg Stanford Brown, Telma Hopkins; **D:** Leslie Martinson. *NO*

The Kid with the 200 I.Q. 🎬🎬 1983

When an earnest boy genius enters college at age 13, predictable comic situations arise that involve his attempts at impressing his idolized astronomy professor (Guillaume), as well as an equally unrequited bout of first love. Harmless comedy, one of a series of squeaky-clean made-for-TV family fare starring Coleman. **96m/C VHS, Beta.** Gary Coleman, Robert Guillaume, Harriet Hilliard Nelson, Dean Butler, Karli Michaelson, Christina Murrull, Mel Stewart; **D:** Leslie Martinson. *ART*

Kidco 🎬🎬 1983 (PG)

The true story of a money-making corporation headed and run by a group of children ranging in age from 9 to 16. **104m/C VHS, Beta, Closed Caption.** Scott Schwartz, Elizabeth Gorcey, Cinnamon Idles, Tristine Skyler; **D:** Ronald F. Maxwell. *FOX*

Kidnap Syndicate 🐾¼ 1976 (R) Kidnappers swipe two boys, releasing one—the son of a wealthy industrialist who meets their ransom demands. When they kill the other boy, a mechanic's son, the father goes on a revengeful killing spree. 105m/C VHS, Beta. *IT* James Mason, Valentina Cortese; *D:* Fernando Di Leo. *NO*

Kidnapped 🐾🐾½ 1960 A young boy is sold by his wicked uncle as a slave, and is helped by an outlaw. A Disney film based on the Robert Louis Stevenson classic. 94m/C VHS, Beta, Closed Caption. Peter Finch, James MacArthur, Peter O'Toole; *D:* Robert Stevenson. *DIS*

Kidnapped woof! 1987 (R) When a teenage girl is kidnapped by pornographers, her sister seeks help from a tough cop and together they go undercover to find her. Plot is flimsy cover for what is actually an exploitative piece. 100m/C VHS, Beta, LV. David Naughton, Barbara Crampton, Lance LeGault, Chick Vennera, Charles Napier; *D:* Howard (Hikmet) Avedis; *W:* Howard (Hikmet) Avedis. *NO*

Kidnapped 🐾🐾½ 1995 Cable TV adaptation of Robert Louis Stevenson's 1886 novel. In 1751 shanghaied young David Balfour (McCardie) and Highland patriot Aln Breck Stewart (Assante) escape from a slave ship and return to Scotland to battle the British. ?m/C VHS. Armand Assante, Brian McCardie, Michael Kitchen, Brian Blessed, Patrick Malahide; *D:* Ivan Passer; *W:* John Goldsmith. *CAF*

Kidnapping of Baby John Doe 1988 Tragedy strikes a family's newborn, and they must make the terrifying decision between life and death. A doctor and nurse, however, take matters into their own hands to save the baby. 90m/C VHS, Beta. Helen Hughes, Jayne Eastwood, Janet-Laine Green, Geoffery Boues, Peter Gerretsen. *NO*

The Kidnapping of the President 🐾🐾½ 1980 (R) The U.S. president is taken hostage by Third World terrorists. The Secret Service is on the ball trying to recover the nation's leader. Well-integrated subplot involves the vice president in a scandal. Engrossing political thriller. Based on novel by Charles Templeton. 113m/C VHS, Beta. *CA* William Shatner, Hal Holbrook, Van Johnson, Ava Gardner, Miguel Fernandez; *D:* George Mendeluk. *NO*

Kids 🐾🐾 1995 Very controversial docudrama about 24 hours in the lives of some aimless New York teenagers. The sullen Telly (Fitzpatrick) enjoys bragging about his skill in deflowering virgins but his promiscuity has lead Jennie (Sevigny) to test H.I.V. positive—something Telly is as yet unaware of. Telly'd rather hang around with best friend Casper (Pierce) anyway, out on the streets, being generally profane and obnoxious. Can either be regarded as a brutally realistic look at teen life today or a lot of fuss about nothing. Korine was 19 when he wrote the screenplay. The MPAA rated the film NC-17, after a protest the distributors chose to release it unrated. 90m/C VHS, LV, Closed Caption. Leo Fitzpatrick, Justin Pierce, Chloe Sevigny, Rosario Dawson, Sarah Henderson, Harold Hunter, Yakira Peguero, Joseph Knafelmacher; *D:* Larry Clark; *W:* Harmony Korine; *C:* Eric Alan Edwards; *M:* Louis Barlow. Independent Spirit Awards '96: Debut Performance (Pierce); Nominations: Independent Spirit Awards '96: Best First Feature, Best Supporting Actress (Sevigny). *THV*

Kid's Auto Race/Mabel's Married Life 🐾🐾 *Kid Auto Races at Venice* 1915 "Kid's Auto Race" (1914) concerns a kiddie-car contest; "Mabel's Married Life" (1915) is about flirtations in the park between married individuals. Piano and organ scores. 21m/B VHS, Beta. Charlie Chaplin, Mabel Normand, Mack Swain; *D:* Mack Sennett. *CCB, GVV*

Kids in the Hall: Brain Candy 🐾🐾 1996 (R) The Canadian Kids bring their Monty Python-meets-SCTV humor to the big screen with moderate success. Dr. Cooper (McDonald), facing corporate downsizing, allows his new, untested anti-depressant to be released to the public after it shows promise. The drug, Gleemonex, sweeps the country by forcing the user's mind to focus on a favorite memory. As befits the troupe's twisted vision, these happy memories aren't always pleasant to the "Family Values" crowd. The easily offended should be warned—there's a character named "Cancer Boy." The story wanders a bit, giving everyone a chance to show their versatility (these Kids collectively play 32 different roles). Sophomore director Makin served the same duty on many of the TV episodes. *CW:* Language and sexual humor. 88m/C VHS, Beta, Closed Caption. Dave Foley, Bruce McCulloch, Kevin McDonald, Scott Thompson, Mark McKinney, Janeane Garofalo; *D:* Kelly Makin; *W:* Bruce McCulloch, Kevin McDonald, Scott Thompson, Mark McKinney, Norm Hiscock; *C:* David Makin; *M:* Craig Northey. Nominations: Genie Awards '96: Best Costume Design, Best Song ("Some Days It's Dark"), Best Sound. *PAR*

Kid's Last Ride 🐾 1941 Three tough guys come into town to settle a feud. 55m/B VHS. Ray Corrigan, John "Dusty" King, Max Terhune, Luana Walters, Edwin Brian; *D:* S. Roy Luby. *NOS, DVT*

Kids of the Round Table 🐾🐾½ 1996 Eleven-year-old Alex (Morina) and his buddies like to have mock sword battles, pretending to be King Arthur and his knights. When their games are broken up by the local bully, Alex takes off into the woods where he discovers a sword in a stone. It's the legendary Excalibur and when Alex removes it, and Merlin (McDowell) appears, explaining the sword will give the boy special powers. Of course, Alex abuses his newfound strength until he comes to the rescue of his friends. 89m/C VHS. *CA* Johnny Morina, Michael Ironside, Malcolm McDowell, Peter Aykroyd, Rene Simard; *D:* Robert Tinnell; *W:* David Sherman; *C:* Roxanne Di Santo; *M:* Normand Corbeil. *CAF*

Kika 🐾🐾 1994 Another flamboyant comedy from Almodovar finds irrepressible beautician Kika (Forque) involved with kinky photographer Ramon (Casanovas) and his stepfather Nicholas (Coyote), a sinister American pulp novelist. There's also Andrea Scarface (Jean-Paul Gaultier-costumed Abril), the host of a vile tabloid TV show called "Today's Worst," and Kika's lesbian maid Juana (de Palma) whose brother happens to be an escaped con/porn star, leading to an outlandish rape and...well, it's all pretty nonsensical, anyway. Spanish with subtitles. 115m/C VHS. *SP* Veronica Forque, Peter Coyote, Victoria Abril, Alex Casanovas, Rossy de Palma; *D:* Pedro Almodovar; *W:* Pedro Almodovar. *THV*

The Kill 🐾🐾½ 1973 A rough, cynical, hard-boiled, womanizing detective tracks down stolen cash in downtown Macao. 81m/C VHS, Beta. Richard Jaeckel, Henry Duval, Judy Washington.

Kill Alex Kill woof! 1983 A Vietnam POW returns to find his family murdered, and uses the crime underworld to take revenge. 88m/C VHS, Beta. Tony Zarindast, Tina Bowmann, Chris Ponti. *GEM*

Kill and Go Hide 🐾 *The Child* 1976 A young girl visits her mother's grave nightly to communicate with and command the ghoul-like creatures that haunt the surrounding woods. 95m/C VHS, Beta. *NO*

Kill and Kill Again 🐾🐾½ 1981 (PG) A martial arts champion attempts to rescue a kidnapped Nobel Prize-winning chemist who has developed a high-yield synthetic fuel. Colorful, tongue-in-cheek, and fun even for those unfamiliar with the genre. 100m/C VHS, Beta. James Ryan, Anneline Kriel, Stan Schmidt, Bill Flynn, Norman Robinson, Ken Gampu, John Ramsbottom; *D:* Ivan Hall; *W:* John Crowther.

Kill, Baby, Kill 🐾🐾🐾 *Curse of the Living Dead; Operacione Paura* 1966 A small Transylvania town is haunted by the ghost of a seven-year-old witchcraft victim, and the town's suicide victims all seem to have hearts of gold (coins, that is). Lots of style and atmosphere in this Transylvanian tale from horror tongue in cheekster Bava. Considered by many genre connoisseurs to be the B man's finest, except that it bears early symptoms of the director's late onset infatuation with the zoom shot. 90m/C VHS. *IT* Erika Blanc, Giacomo "Jack" Rossi-Stuart, Fabienne Dali, Giana Vivaldi; *D:* Mario Bava. *SNC, FRG*

Kill Castro 🐾 1980 (R) Ever hear the one about the exploding cigar? Key West boat skipper is forced to carry a CIA agent to Cuba on a mission to assassinate Castro. Low-budget adventure that's deadly dull. 90m/C VHS, Beta. Sybil Danning, Albert Salmi, Michael V. Gazzo, Raymond St. Jacques, Woody Strode, Stuart Whitman, Robert Vaughn, Caren Kaye; *D:* Chuck Workman. *NO*

Kill Cruise 🐾🐾 1990 (R) The depressed and alcoholic skipper of the yacht Bella Donna gives up sailing until he meets two beautiful young women who want to sail to Bermuda for a taste of the good life. The calm of the Atlantic is disturbed when they are plagued by bad weather and fierce storms, and tensions rise as the two women's jealousies erupt. Will it set the climate for murder? *CW:* One violent scene, and sexuality. 99m/C VHS, Beta, LV, Closed Caption. Juergen Prochnow, Patsy Kensit, Elizabeth Hurley; *D:* Peter Keglevic; *W:* Peter Keglevic. *USH*

Kill Factor woof! *Death Dimension; Black Eliminator; The Freeze Bomb* 1978 (R) Something stupid about a killer bomb tht could freeze the planet. So inept your brain cells will also be frozen if you watch it. 91m/C VHS, Beta. Jim Kelly, George Lazenby, Aldo Ray, Harold Sakata, Terry Moore; *D:* Al Adamson.

Kill Line 🐾🐾 1991 (R) Kim stars as Joe, a street fighter who seeks to clear his name after serving a 10-year prison sentence for a crime he didn't commit. When he finds his brother's family has been murdered by criminals looking for the millions he supposedly stole, Joe wages a one-man martial arts war against a corrupt police force and the gang of thugs who are looking for the money. 93m/C VHS. Bobby Kim, Michael Parker, Marlene Zimmerman, H. Wayne Lowery, C.R. Valdez, Mark Williams, Ben Pfeifer; *D:* Richard H. Kim; *W:* Richard H. Kim.

Kill Me Again 🐾🐾½ 1989 (R) Director Dahl does the contemporary noir thing through the Nevada desert with Whalley-Kilmer as a beautiful femme fatale. She asks a detective (real-life husband Kilmer) to fake her death, which gets him targeted not only by the police, but also the mob and her psycho-boyfriend (Madsen). Fun and full of plot twists that will satisfy fans of the noir persuasion. 93m/C VHS, Beta, Closed Caption. Val Kilmer, Joanne Whalley, Michael Madsen, Jonathan Gries, Bibi Besch; *D:* John Dahl; *W:* John Dahl, David Warfield. *MGM*

Kill My Wife...Please! 🐾🐾 19?? Comic adventure of a despicable husband trying to bump off his wife in order to cash in on her insurance policy. 90m/C VHS. Bob Dishy, Joanna Barnes, Bill Dana; *D:* Steven Hilliard Stern. *HHE*

The Kill-Off 🐾🐾 1990 (R) Bedridden Luanne (Gross), married to janitor Ralph (Monroe), manages to cause dissension in her isolated New Jersey community with her vicious gossip. But when Luanne learns Ralph's involved with a stripper (Haase), it puts her own life in danger. Based on a story by Jim Thompson. *CW:* Mature themes, language, violence, partial nudity. 100m/C VHS. Loretta Gross, Steve Monroe, Cathy Haase, Jackson Sims; *D:* Maggie Greenwald. *XVC*

Kill or Be Killed 🐾🐾 1980 (PG) Martial arts champion is lured to a phony martial arts contest by a madman bent on revenge. 90m/C VHS, Beta. James Ryan, Charlotte Michelle, Norman Combes; *D:* Ivan Hall.

Kill or Be Killed 🐾½ 1993 Michael Julian just spent eight years in jail for saving his brother Charlie's life. He must wonder why he bothered since Charlie has stolen his girl Beth and set up a drug empire. Michael ambushes Charlie's men and steals a million dollars to use as leverage but Charlie thinks rival drug lords are out to get him and starts a street war. 97m/C VHS. David Heavener, Joseph Nuzzolo, Paulo Tocha, Lynn Levand; *D:* Joe Straw; *W:* Joseph Nuzzolo.

The Kill Reflex ✦ 1989 (R) A tough black cop and his beautiful rookie partner battle the mob and corruption. 90m/C VHS, Beta, LV. Maud Adams, Fred Williamson, Bo Svenson, Phyllis Hyman; **D:** Fred Williamson. COL

Kill Slade ✦ 1989 (PG-13) When a United Nations food-aid diversion conspiracy is uncovered by a beautiful journalist, a plan to kidnap her is put into action. Romance follows. 90m/C VHS, Beta, LV. SA Patrick Dollaghan, Lisa Brady, Anthony Fridjhon, Danny Keogh, Alfred Nowke; **D:** Bruce McFarlane. NLC

Kill Squad ✦ 1981 (R) Squad of martial arts masters follow a trail of violence and bloodshed to a vengeful, deadly battle of skills. 85m/C VHS, Beta. Jean Claude, Jeff Risk, Jerry Johnson, Bill Cambra, Cameron Mitchell. VTR

Kill the Golden Goose ✦ 1979 (R) Two martial arts masters work on opposite sides of a government corruption and corporate influence peddling case. 91m/C VHS, Beta. Brad von Beltz, Ed Parker, Master Bong Soo Han; **D:** Elliot Hong. GEM

Killcrazy ✦ 1989 (R) On the way to a weekend camping trip, five Vietnam vets released from a mental hospital are slowly massacred by a group of dangerous killers until one of the vets decides to fight back. 94m/C VHS, LV. David Heavener, Danielle Brisebois, Burt Ward, Lawrence-Hilton Jacobs, Bruce Glover, Gary Owens, Rachelle Carson; **D:** David Heavener; **W:** David Heavener. IME

Killer ✦ 197? An ex-convict sets up an ingenious bank robbery, and gets double-crossed himself. 87m/C VHS, Beta. Henry Silva. NO

The Killer ✦✦✦½ Die Xue Shuang Xiong 1990 (R) Jeffrey Chow is a gangster gunman who wants out. He's hired by his best friend to perform one last killing, but it doesn't go as smoothly as he wanted. He's almost caught by "Eagle" Lee, a detective who vows to hunt him down using Jennie, a singer blinded by Chow in crossfire. Lots of action and gunfights, but also pretty corny and sentimental. Very similar to American action movies, but using Chinese and Asian cultural conventions. A good introduction to the Chinese gangster-flick genre. Available with subtitles or dubbed in English. 110m/C VHS, Letterbox. HK Chow Yun-Fat, Sally Yeh, Danny Lee, Kenneth Tsang, Chu Kong; **D:** John Woo. FXL, BTV, FCT

Killer: A Journal of Murder ✦✦ 1995 (R) Young, idealistic Jewish guard Henry Lesser (Leonard) befriends prisoner Carl Panzram (Woods) and encourages the man to write his life story. Then he must deal with the consequences of discovering the brutality behind Panzram's murderous crimes. The leads do fine but there's nothing new here. Inspired by true events and set in the 1920s.**CW:** Strong language and brutal violence, including a rape. 91m/C VHS, LV, Closed Caption. James Woods, Robert Sean Leonard, Ellen Greene, Cara Buono, Robert John Burke, Steve Forrest, John Bedford Lloyd, Harold Gould; **D:** Tim Metcalfe; **W:** Tim Metcalfe; **C:** Ken Kelsch. REP

Killer Commandos ✦ 19?? Mercenaries go to the rescue of an oppressed African nation to overthrow the sinister white supremacy dictator. 87m/C VHS. Cameron Mitchell, Anthony Eisley. NO

Killer Dill ✦½ 1947 Also killer dull. A meek salesman is misidentified as a death-dealing gangster, and the comic mixups begin. 71m/B VHS. Stuart Erwin, Anne Gwynne, Frank Albertson, Mike Mazurki, Milburn Stone, Dorothy Granger; **D:** Lewis D. Collins. NOS, VYY

Killer Diller ✦½ 1948 All-black musical revue featuring Nat King Cole and his Trio. 70m/B VHS, Beta. Dusty Fletcher, Nat King Cole, Butterfly McQueen, Moms Mabley, George Wiltshire; **D:** Josh Binney. MVD, NOS, DVT

Killer Elephants ✦✦ 1976 A Thai man struggles to save his plantation, his wife, and his baby from the terrorists hired by a land baron to drive him away from his property. 83m/C VHS, Beta. Sung Pa, Alan Yen, Nai Yen Ne, Yu Chien. UNI

The Killer Elite ✦✦½ 1975 (PG) Straight-ahead Peckinpah fare examining friendship and betrayal. Two professional assassins begin as friends but end up stalking each other when they are double-crossed. This minor Peckinpah effort is murky and doesn't have a clear resolution, but is plenty bloody. Lots of Dobermans roam through this picture too. 120m/C VHS, Beta, LV. James Caan, Robert Duvall, Arthur Hill, Gig Young, Burt Young, Mako, Bo Hopkins, Helmut Dantine; **D:** Sam Peckinpah; **W:** Marc Norman, Stirling Silliphant. MGM

Killer Fish ✦ Deadly Treasure of the Piranha 1979 (PG) A scheme to steal and then hide a fortune in emeralds at the bottom of a tank full of piranhas backfires as the criminals find it impossible to retrieve them...as if that took a lot of foresight. Director Dawson is AKA Antonio Margheriti. Filmed in Brazil. 101m/C VHS, Beta, Closed Caption. BR GB Lee Majors, James Franciscus, Margaux Hemingway, Karen Black, Roy Brocksmith, Marisa Berenson; **D:** Anthony (Antonio Margheriti) Dawson. FOX

Killer Force ✦½ 1975 (R) Predictable adventure involving international diamond smuggling. 100m/C VHS, Beta. Telly Savalas, Peter Fonda, Maud Adams, Hugh O'Brian; **D:** Val Guest. ART, VES

Killer Image ✦ 1992 (R) A photographer unwittingly sees more than he should and becomes involved in a lethal political coverup. At the same time a wealthy senator targets him and he must fight for his life. Viewers might feel they have to fight their boredom.**CW:** Some language, violence, and sensuality. 97m/C VHS, Beta, LV, Closed Caption. John Pyper-Ferguson, Michael Ironside, M. Emmet Walsh, Krista Errickson; **D:** David Winning. PAR

A Killer in Every Corner ✦ 1974 Three psychology students visit a loony professor and succumb to his hair-raising shenanigans. 80m/C VHS, Beta. Joanna Pettet, Patrick Magee, Max Wall, Eric Flynn. ART

Killer Inside Me ✦✦ 1976 (R) The inhabitants of a small Western town are unaware that their mild-mannered deputy sheriff is actually becoming a crazed psychotic murderer. From the novel by Jim Thompson. 99m/C VHS, Beta. Stacy Keach, Susan Tyrrell, Tisha Sterling, Keenan Wynn, John Dehner, John Carradine, Don Stroud, Charles McGraw, Julie Adams, Royal Dano; **D:** Burt Kennedy; **W:** Robert Chandlee. WAR, OM

Killer Instinct ✦✦ 1992 (R) Two brothers do bloody warfare with notorious mobster kingpin in prohibition-era New York City.**CW:** Some language, violence, and some sensuality. 101m/C VHS, LV, Closed Caption. Christopher Bradley, Bruce Nozick, Rachel York; **D:** Greydon Clark, Ken Stein. THV

Killer Klowns from Outer Space ✦✦½ 1988 (PG-13) Bozo-like aliens resembling demented clowns land on earth and set up circus tents to lure Earthlings in. Visually striking, campy but slick horror flick that'll make you think twice about your next visit to the big top. Mood is heightened by a cool title tune by the Dickies. Definitely has cult potential! 90m/C VHS, Beta, LV, Closed Caption. Grant Cramer, Suzanne Snyder, John Allen Nelson, Royal Dano, John Vernon, Peter Licassi, Michael Siegel; **D:** Stephen Chiodo; **W:** Charles Chiodo, Stephen Chiodo; **M:** John Massari. CDV

Killer Likes Candy ✦ 1978 An assassin stalks the King of Kafiristan, and a CIA operative tries to stop him. 86m/C VHS, Beta. Kerwin Mathews, Marilu Tolo; **D:** Richard Owens. GEM, MRV

Killer Looks ✦½ 1994 (R) Phil likes to watch his wife Diane seduce strangers. Then they meet Mickey, a charmer with ideas of his own. Soon Diane and Phil find their kinky world threatened. Unrated version contains 13 minutes of additional footage.**CW:** Strong sexuality and language. 87m/C VHS, LV, Closed Caption. Michael Artura, Sara Suzanne Brown, Len Donato; **D:** Toby Phillips. IMP

Killer on Board ✦✦ 1977 Folks spending their holiday on a cruise ship are afflicted by a fatal virus and subsequently quarantined. Typical made-for-TV disaster flick. 100m/C VHS, Beta.

Claude Akins, Beatrice Straight, George Hamilton, Patty Duke, Frank Converse, Jane Seymour, William Daniels; **D:** Philip Leacock. ART

Killer Party woof! 1986 (R) Three coeds pledge a sorority and are subjected to a hazing that involves a haunted fraternity house. Standard horror plot; Paul Bartel ("Eating Raoul"; "Lust in the Dust") is the only significant element. 91m/C VHS, Beta. Elaine Wilkes, Sherry Willis-Burch, Joanna Johnson, Paul Bartel, Martin Hewitt, Ralph Seymour; **D:** William Fruet; **W:** Barney Cohen; **M:** John Beal. FOX

The Killer Shrews ✦✦ 1959 Lumet (Sidney's father) creates a serum that causes the humble shrew to take on killer proportions. The creatures are actually dogs in makeup. Goude was 1957's Miss Universe. 70m/B VHS. James Best, Ingrid Goude, Baruch Lumet, Ken Curtis; **D:** Ray Kellogg. SNC, MRV, HHT

Killer Tomatoes Eat France ✦½ 1991 Professor Gangrene takes his tomato fetish to France, where the giant vegetables try to take over the streets. The fourth in the killer-vegetable series. 94m/C VHS, LV. John Astin, Marc Price, Steve Lundquist; **D:** John DeBello. FXV

Killer Tomatoes Strike Back ✦✦ 1990 The third "Killer Tomatoes" movie isn't in the league of "The Naked Gun" satires, but it's still bright parody for the Mad Magazine crowd, as tomato-mad scientist Astin harnesses the powers of trash-TV in a planned vegetable invasion. Perhaps due to a 'Killer Tomatoes' cartoon series at the time, this isn't as saucy as its predecessors and is acceptable for family audiences. Followed by "Killer Tomatoes Eat France." 87m/C VHS, Closed Caption. John Astin, Rick Rockwell, Crystal Carson, Steve Lundquist, John Witherspoon; **D:** John DeBello. FOX, IME

Killer with Two Faces ✦ 1974 A woman is terrorized by the evil twin of her boyfriend. Made for television. 70m/C VHS, Beta. Donna Mills, Ian Hendry, David Lodge, Roddy McMillian. ART

Killer Workout ✦ Aerobicide 1986 (R) A murderer stalks the clients of a sweat/sex/muscle-filled gym. 89m/C VHS, Beta. David James Campbell, Ted Prior; **D:** David A. Prior.

The Killers ✦✦✦✦ 1946 Classic film noir based on a Hemingway story. Lancaster's film debut comes as an ex-boxer, "The Swede," who's murdered in a contract hit. Insurance investigator Jim Reardon (O'Brien) reconstructs the young man's life, discovering his involvement with crime boss Big Jim Colfax (Dekker) and double-crossing femme fatale Kitty Collins (Gardner). So Reardon sets out to set up Colfax and Kitty. Rosza's musical score may sound familiar—it was later used on the TV series "Dragnet." 105m/B VHS. Edmond O'Brien, Albert Dekker, Ava Gardner, Burt Lancaster, Sam Levene, William Conrad, Charles McGraw, Virginia Christine; **D:** Robert Siodmak; **W:** Anthony Veiller, John Huston; **C:** Woody Bredell; **M:** Miklos Rozsa. Nominations: Academy Awards '46: Best Director (Siodmak), Best Film Editing, Best Screenplay, Best Original Dramatic/Comedy Score. USH

The Killers ✦✦ Ernest Hemingway's the Killers 1964 After two hired assassins kill a teacher, they look into his past and try to find leads to a $1,000,000 robbery. Reagan's last film. Remake of 1946 film of the same name, which was loosely based on a short story by Ernest Hemingway. Originally intended for television, but released to theatres instead due to its violence. 95m/C VHS, Beta. Lee Marvin, Angie Dickinson, John Cassavetes, Ronald Reagan, Clu Gulager, Claude Akins, Norman Fell; **D:** Donald Siegel; **M:** John Williams. USH

Killers ✦ 1988 Remote jungles of southern Africa are the scene of a military coup. 83m/C VHS, Beta. Cameron Mitchell, Alicia Hammond, Robert Dix; **D:** Ewing Miles Brown.

The Killer's Edge ✦½ Blood Money 1990 (R) Cop is caught between rock and hard place in L.A. when he's forced to confront criminal who once saved his life in 'Nam. Plenty of gut busting and soul wrenching. **CW:** Language, violence, and sensuality. 88m/C VHS, LV. Wings Hauser, Robert Z'Dar, Karen Black. PMH

Killers from Space woof! 1954 Cheap sci-fi flick in which big-eyed men from beyond Earth bring scientist Graves back to life to assist them with their evil plan for world domination. 80m/B VHS. Peter Graves, Barbara Bestar, James Scay; **D:** W. Lee Wilder. EEL, MRV, RHI

Killer's Kiss 🎬🎬½ 1955 A boxer and a dancer set out to start a new life together when he saves the woman from an attempted rape. Gritty, second feature from Kubrick was financed by friends and family and shows signs of his budding talent. 67m/C VHS. Frank Silvera, Jamie Smith, Irene Kane, Jerry Jarret; **D:** Stanley Kubrick; **W:** Stanley Kubrick. FCT

The Killing 🎬🎬🎬 1956 The dirty, harsh, street-level big heist epic that established Kubrick and presented its genre with a new and vivid existentialist aura, as an ex-con engineers the rip-off of a racetrack with disastrous results. Displays characteristic nonsentimental sharp-edged Kubrick vision. Based on the novel "Clean Break" by Lionel White. 83m/B VHS, Beta, LV. Sterling Hayden, Marie Windsor, Elisha Cook Jr., Jay C. Flippen, Vince Edwards, Timothy Carey, Coleen Gray, Joseph Sawyer, Ted de Corsia; **D:** Stanley Kubrick; **C:** Lucien Ballard. MGM

A Killing Affair 🎬 1985 (R) Set in West Virginia, 1943, this is the story of a widow who takes in a drifter who she believes is the man who killed her husband. She begins to fall for him, but cannot be sure if she should trust him. Vague and melodramatic. From the novel "Monday, Tuesday, Wednesday" by Robert Houston. Saperstein's directorial debut. 100m/C VHS, Beta, LV. Peter Weller, Kathy Baker, John Glover, Bill Smitrovich; **D:** David Saperstein; **M:** John Barry. VTR

Killing at Hell's Gate 🎬½ 1981 A made-for-television movie about a group of whitewater rafters being picked off by snipers as they travel down river. 96m/C VHS, Beta, Closed Caption. Robert Urich, Deborah Raffin, Lee Purcell; **M:** David Bell. FOX

The Killing Beach 🎬🎬 Turtle Beach 1992 (R) Australian photojournalist Judith Wilkes (Scacchi) travels to Malaysia in the late 1970s to report on the plight of the Vietnamese boat people seeking refuge there. She befriends the wife of the Australian ambassador, a former callgirl from Saigon, who hopes to find her own children among the refugees. But the native Malays resent the foreign intrusion and are determined to stop the boat people—no matter what the cost in blood. Based on the novel "Turtle Beach" by Blanche D'Alpuget. **CW:** Language, violence, and sensuality. 105m/C VHS, Closed Caption. AU Greta Scacchi, Joan Chen, Jack Thompson, Art Malik, Norman Kaye; **D:** Stephen Wallace; **W:** Ann Turner; **C:** Russell Boyd. COL

Killing Cars 🎬½ 1985 (R) A German car designer's pet project, a car that runs without gas, is halted by the influence of an Arab conglomerate. He nevertheless tries to complete it, and is hunted down. 104m/C VHS, Beta. Juergen Prochnow, Senta Berger, William Conrad, Agnes Soral; **D:** Michael Verhoeven. THV, HHE, VTR

The Killing Device 🎬½ 1992 Two government scientists lose their funding on a covert political assassination project and decide to eliminate the government officials responsible. When two journalists attempt to solve the murders they become the next targets. 93m/C VHS. Clu Gulager, Antony Alda, Gig Rauch. VCI

The Killing Edge 🎬½ 1986 In post-nuclear holocaust Earth, a lone warrior seeks justice, and his family, in a lawless land. 85m/C VHS. Bill French, Marv Spencer; **D:** Lindsay Shonteff. VCD, HHE

Killing 'Em Softly 🎬 1985 Segal portrays a down-on-his-luck musician who accidentally murders a music manager during an argument. Cara's boyfriend is accused and to clear his

name, the singer moonlights as a detective. She and Segal end up falling in love. Disappointing. 90m/C VHS, Beta. CA George Segal, Irene Cara; **D:** Max Fischer. HHE

The Killing Fields 🎬🎬🎬½ 1984 (R) Based on the New York Times' Sydney Schanberg's account of his friendship with Cambodian interpreter Dith Pran. They separated during the fall of Saigon, when Western journalists fled, leaving behind countless assistants who were later accused of collusion with the enemy by the Khmer Rouge and killed or sent to re-education camps during the bloodbath known as "Year Zero." Schanberg searched for Pran through the Red Cross and U.S. government, while Pran struggled to survive, finally escaping and walking miles to freedom. Ngor's own experiences echoed those of his character Pran. Malkovich's debut is intense. Joffe's directorial debut shows a generally sure hand, with only a bit of melodrama at the end. 142m/C VHS, Beta, LV, Letterbox, Closed Caption. GB Sam Waterston, Haing S. Ngor, John Malkovich, Athol Fugard, Craig T. Nelson, Julian Sands, Spalding Gray, Bill Paterson; **D:** Roland Joffe; **W:** Bruce Robinson; **C:** Chris Menges. Academy Awards '84: Best Cinematography, Best Film Editing, Best Supporting Actor (Ngor); British Academy Awards '84: Best Actor (Ngor), Best Adapted Screenplay, Best Film; Golden Globe Awards '85: Best Supporting Actor (Ngor); Los Angeles Film Critics Association Awards '84: Best Cinematography; New York Film Critics Awards '84: Best Cinematography; National Society of Film Critics Awards '84: Best Cinematography; Writers Guild of America '84: Best Adapted Screenplay; Nominations: Academy Awards '84: Best Actor (Waterston), Best Adapted Screenplay, Best Director (Joffe), Best Picture. WAR, BTV, HMV

Killing Floor 🎬🎬 1985 (PG) During WWI, black sharecropper Frank Custer (Leake) travels to Chicago to get work in the stockyards and becomes a voice in the growing labor movement. The tensions in the factories lead to the bloody race riots of 1919. Made for television. 118m/C VHS, Beta, LV. Damien Leake, Alfre Woodard, Moses Gunn, Clarence Felder, Bill Duke; **D:** William Duke. KIV, COL, FCT

Killing for Love 🎬½ 1995 (R) Sleazy producer invites several couples for a weekend retreat at his mountain cabin. The unrated version is 90 minutes. **CW:** Strong sexuality; language. 81m/C VHS. Jay Demir, Alex Demir, Lisa Haslehurst, Brandy Sanders; **D:** Mike Kesey; **W:** H.M. Johnson. ORI

The Killing Game 🎬🎬½ All Weekend Lovers; Jeu de Massacre 1967 A husband-wife cartoonist team link up with an unhinged playboy and act out a murder-mystery comic they produce together. In French with subtitles. 95m/C VHS, Beta. FR Jean-Pierre Cassel, Claudine Auger, Michael Duchaussoy, Anna Gaylor; **D:** Alain Jessua. FCT

The Killing Game 🎬 1987 A slew of Californians kill and betray each other for lustful reasons. 90m/C VHS, Beta. Chad Hayward, Cynthia Killion, Geoffrey Sadwith; **D:** Joseph Merhi. NO

Killing Grandpa 🎬🎬 Matar al Abuelito 1991 Wealthy family patriarch Don Mariano Aguero (Luppi) has lost the will to live and attempted suicide, which has left him comatose. His three greedy children are anxious for their inheritance but the Don's loyal handyman enlists the aid of his half-sister Rosita (Esteves), who possesses healing powers, to give his aged employer the strength to recover. Spanish with subtitles. 114m/C VHS. SP AR Federico Luppi, Ines Estevez; **D:** Luis Cesar D'Angiolillo; **W:** Luis Cesar D'Angiolillo, Ariel Sienra; **C:** Miguel Abal. NYF

Killing Heat 🎬½ The Grass is Singing 1984 (R) An independent career woman living in South Africa decides to abandon her career to marry a struggling jungle farmer. Based on Doris Lessing's novel "The Grass is Singing." 104m/C VHS, Beta. GB SW Karen Black, John Thaw, John Kani, John Moulder-Brown; **D:** Michael Raeburn. FOX

Killing Hour 🎬🎬 The Clairvoyant 1981 (R) A psychic painter finds that the visions she paints come true in a string of grisly murders. Her ability interests a television reporter and a homicide detective. 97m/C VHS, Beta, Closed Caption. Elizabeth Kemp, Perry King, Norman Parker, Kenneth McMillan; **D:** Armand Mastroianni. FOX

A Killing in a Small Town 🎬🎬🎬 1990 (R) Candy Morrison seems like the perfect member of her small Texas community—but appearances can be deceiving, particularly after she's charged with killing a fellow church-goer by striking her 41 times with an axe (shades of Lizzie Borden)! Dennehy is her skeptical lawyer who isn't sure if it was self-defense or a peculiar sort of revenge. Good performances by Hershey and Dennehy lift this above the usual tawdry made-for-TV level. Based on a true story; originally a television miniseries. **CW:** Violence. 95m/C VHS, LV, Closed Caption. Barbara Hershey, Brian Dennehy, Hal Holbrook, Richard Gilliland, John Terry, Lee Garlington; **D:** Stephen Gyllenhaal; **C:** Robert Elswit; **M:** Richard Gibbs. THV

Killing in the Sun 🎬 19?? (R) Gripping struggle for prosperous smuggling in the Mediterranean consume mobsters from three countries. 90m/C VHS. Henry Silva, Michael Constantine. NO

The Killing Jar 🎬🎬½ 1996 (R) Michael Sanford (Cullen) has taken his pregnant wife Diane (Tomita) back to the California wine country to take over the failing family vineyard. A series of vicious murders occur in the area, one of which Michael may have witnessed. Hypnosis brings up a lot of Michael's repressed childhood memories, he begins to unravel, and becomes the prime suspect in the killings. **CW:** Graphic violence, a strong sex scene and language. 101m/C VHS, LV, Closed Caption. Brett Cullen, Tamlyn Tomita, Wes Studi, Brion James, M. Emmet Walsh, Tom Bower, Xander Berkeley; **D:** Evan Crooke; **W:** Mark Mullin; **C:** Michael G. Wojciechowski; **M:** David Williams. APX

The Killing Kind 🎬🎬½ 1973 Man released from prison is obsessed with wreaking vengeance on his daft lawyer and his accuser. His vendetta eventually draws his mother into the fray as well. Fine performance by Savage. 95m/C VHS. Ann Sothern, John Savage, Ruth Roman, Luana Anders, Cindy Williams; **D:** Curtis Harrington; **M:** Andrew Belling. NO

The Killing Man 🎬🎬 1994 Former mobster tries going legit by changing his identity and working for the government. 100m/C VHS. Jeff Wincott. APX

The Killing Mind 1990 A young girl witnesses a grisly murder that is never solved. Twenty years later she (Zimbalist) becomes a cop who specializes in trapping psychos. Haunted by her memories, she and a reporter (Bill) team up to find the killer, never suspecting that she is his next victim. Originally made for cable television. 96m/C VHS. Stephanie Zimbalist, Tony Bill, Daniel Roebuck; **D:** Michael Rhodes. WOV

Killing Obsession 🎬½ 1994 Albert (Savage) has been locked in the Parkview State Psychiatric Facility for 20 years, ever since he murdered 11-year-old Annie's mother. Annie is Albert's obsession and in his mind she's always remained a young girl. So when Albert is released, he goes looking for Annie—murdering along the way. Now that the real Annie is an adult will Albert finally accept the passage of time or will she be just another victim? 95m/C VHS, LV. John Savage, Kimberly Chase, John Saxon, Bernie White; **D:** Paul Leder; **W:** Paul Leder. TRI

The Killing of a Chinese Bookie 🎬🎬 1976 (R) Gazzara runs a Sunset Strip nightclub and is in hock to loan sharks. When he can't come up with the cash, he's offered a deal—get rid of a troublesome Chinese bookie and all debts will be forgiven. But it turns out the bookie is highly connected in the Asian mob and nothing goes as planned. Cassavette's improv technique makes for a self-indulgent and endless film. **109m/C VHS, Beta, Closed Caption.** Ben Gazzara, Jean-Pierre Cassel, Zizi Johari, Soto Joe Hugh, Robert Phillips, Timothy Carey, Morgan Woodward; **D:** John Cassavetes; **W:** John Cassavetes; **C:** Frederick Elmes. *TOU, FCT*

Killing of Angel Street 🐾🐾 **1981 (PG)** A courageous young woman unwittingly becomes the central character in an escalating nightmare about saving a community from corrupt politicians and organized crime. **101m/C VHS, Beta.** *AU* Liz Alexander, John Hargreaves; **D:** Donald Crombie; **W:** Evan Jones; **M:** Brian May. *FCT*

Killing of Randy Webster 🐾🐾½ **1981** A father attempts to prove that his son did not die as a criminal when Texas policemen shot him after transporting a stolen van across state lines. **90m/C VHS, Beta.** Hal Holbrook, Dixie Carter, Sean Penn, Jennifer Jason Leigh; **D:** Sam Wanamaker. *NO*

The Killing of Sister George 🐾🐾 **1969 (R)** Racy, sensationalized film based on the Frank Marcus black comedy/melodrama about a lesbian love triangle between a television executive and two soap opera stars. Things get a little uncomfortable when they learn one of their characters is to be written out of the show. Shot in England. **138m/C VHS, Beta.** Beryl Reid, Susannah York, Coral Browne, Ronald Fraser, Patricia Medina, Hugh Paddick, Cyril Elaine Church, Brandan Dillon; **D:** Robert Aldrich; **C:** Joseph Biroc. *FOX*

Killing Stone 🐾🐾 **1978** A freelance writer uncovers a small town sheriff's plot to cover up a scandalous homicide. Made for television. **120m/C VHS, Beta.** Gil Gerard, J.D. Cannon, Jim Davis, Nehemiah Persoff; **D:** Michael Landon; **W:** Michael Landon.

Killing Streets 🐾🐾 **1991** A commando learns that his twin brother is being held hostage in Lebanon and plans a rescue mission. A standard farfetched actioner; noteworthy for a real sense of despair over the endless carnage in the Mideast. Some dialogue in Arabic with subtitles. **109m/C VHS, Beta.** Michael Pare, Lorenzo Lamas; **D:** Stephen Cornwell; **W:** Stephen Cornwell. *VES, ART*

The Killing Time 🐾🐾 **1987 (R)** A minor, effective murder thriller about a quiet small resort town suddenly beset by a web of murder, double-crossings, blackmail, and infidelity. They seem to coincide with the appearance of a mysterious stranger posing as the town's deputy sheriff just as the new sheriff is about to take up the badge. **94m/C VHS, Beta, LV.** Kiefer Sutherland, Beau Bridges, Joe Don Baker, Wayne Rogers; **D:** Rick King; **W:** Dan Bohlinger. *VTR*

Killing Time 🐾🐾 **1997 (R)** Twisted little English thriller about a day in the life of Italian hitwoman Maria (Torgan), who's working in Northern England. Gangland boss Reilly (Leach) has killed a police officer and revenge is wanted by the cop's mate, fellow officer Bryant (Fairbass). Only Bryant can't really afford Maria so after she does the job, Bryant wants her killed by a cheaper hitman, Charlie (Thirkeld). But Reilly won't be back in town until the evening train—so Maria decides to take out a few of Reilly's henchmen to kill some time, leading to a police investigation (by Bryant), and leaving Charlie itching to carry out his part of the killing spree. **CW:** Strong violence and language, and for some sexuality. **91m/C VHS, Closed Caption.** *GB* Kendra Torgan, Craig Fairbrass, Nigel Leach, Stephen D. Thirkeld; **D:** Bharat Nalluri; **W:** Neil Marshall, Fleur Costello, Caspar Berry. *COL*

Killing Zoe 🐾🐾 **1994 (R)** American safecracker travels to Paris for a little rest, recreation, and robbery. At the request of a childhood friend, he involves himself in an ill-conceived daytime bank heist, but not before enjoying a night with a local call girl and participating in some good ol' fashioned heroin-induced debauchery with the other bank robbers on the night before the job. Surprisingly no one (except maybe the still-stoned crooks), things don't go exactly as planned. Visually impressive debut for Tarantino collaborator

Avary, who had his actors read "Beowulf" for its portrayal of Viking excess. **CW:** extreme violence, nudity, profanity, drug use **97m/C VHS, LV.** Eric Stoltz, Julie Delpy, Jean-Hugues Anglade, Gary Kemp, Bruce Ramsay, Kario Salem, Carlo Scandiuzzi; **D:** Roger Roberts Avary; **W:** Roger Roberts Avary; **C:** Tom Richmond. *ART*

The Killing Zone 🐾½ **1990** Convict nephew of onetime Drug Enforcement agent rewrites zoning ordinances to hunt for Mexican drug lord south of the border. **90m/C VHS.** Daron McBee, James Dalesandro, Melissa Moore, Armando Silvestre, Augustine Beral, Sydne Squire, Deborah Dare; **D:** Addison Randall. *PMH*

Killings at Outpost Zeta 🐾 **1980** Earthmen investigate a barren planet where previous expeditions have disappeared, and find hordes of aliens. **92m/C VHS, Beta.** Gordon Devol, Jackie Ray, James A. Watson Jr. *VCI*

Killjoy 🐾🐾½ *Who Murdered Joy Morgan?* **1981** A sleazy surgeon's daughter is the prey in this television thriller. The plot twists are led by the array of people who become involved. A clever suspense mystery. Made for television. **100m/C VHS, Beta.** Kim Basinger, Robert Culp, Stephen Macht, Nancy Marchand, John Rubinstein, Ann Dusenberry, Ann Wedgeworth; **D:** John Llewellyn Moxey; **M:** Bruce Broughton. *ART*

Killpoint 🐾½ **1984 (R)** Special task force is assembled to catch the criminals who robbed a National Guard armory for its weapons. **89m/C VHS, Beta, LV.** Leo Fong, Richard Roundtree, Cameron Mitchell; **D:** Frank Harris. *ART, VES*

Killzone 🐾 **1985** A brainwashed Vietnam vet breaks down during a training exercise and embarks on a psychotic killing spree. **86m/C VHS, Beta.** Ted Prior, David James Campbell, Richard Massery; **D:** David A. Prior. *VES*

Kilma, Queen of the Amazons woof! **1986** A shipwrecked sailor finds himself on an island populated by man-hating Amazons. When a shipload of lusty sailors arrive to rescue him, carnage ensues. **90m/C VHS, Beta.** *NO*

Kim 🐾🐾🐾 **1950** A colorful Hollywood adaptation of the Rudyard Kipling classic about an English boy disguised as a native in 19th Century India, and his various adventures. **113m/C VHS, Beta.** Errol Flynn, Dean Stockwell, Paul Lukas, Cecil Kellaway; **D:** Victor Saville; **M:** Andre Previn. *MGM*

Kim 🐾🐾½ **1984** Kim (Sheth) is a 15-year-old boy living by his wits on the streets of 1890s India. Trying to discover his true identity, Kim's befriended by a Buddhist monk who wishes the boy to be his disciple and a British spy, who trains him for a daring mission against the Russians. Rousing TV adaptation of the Rudyard Kipling novel. **135m/C VHS.** Ravi Sheth, Peter O'Toole, Bryan Brown, John Rhys-Davies, Julian Glover; **D:** John Davies. *HMV*

Kind Hearts and Coronets 🐾🐾🐾½ **1949** Black comedy in which an ambitious young man sets out to bump off eight relatives in an effort to claim a family title. Guinness is wonderful in his role as all eight of the fated relations. Based on Roy Horiman's novel. **104m/B VHS, Beta, LV.** *GB* Alec Guinness, Dennis Price, Valerie Hobson, Joan Greenwood, Audrey Fildes, Miles Malleson, Clive Morton, Cecil Ramage, John Penrose, Hugh Griffith, John Salew, Eric Messiter, Anne Valery, Arthur Lowe, Jeremy Spenser; **D:** Robert Hamer; **W:** Robert Hamer, John Dighton; **C:** Douglas Slocombe; **M:** Ernest Irving. *REP, FCT, HMV*

A Kind of Loving 🐾🐾🐾 **1962** Two North English young people marry rashly as a result of pregnancy, then find they really didn't like each other all that much, but manage to adjust. **107m/B VHS, Beta.** *GB* Alan Bates, Thora Hird, June Ritchie; **D:** John Schlesinger. *NO*

Kindergarten 🐾🐾🐾 **1984** Endearing tale based on a true story of a young Russian street violinist. During WWII, the boy meets a variety of interesting people as he travels throughout the Soviet Union. In Russian with English subtitles. **143m/C VHS.** *RU* Klaus Maria Brandauer; **D:** Yevgeny Yevtushenko. *KIV*

Kindergarten Cop 🐾🐾½ **1990 (PG-13)** Pectoral perfect cop Kimble (Schwarzenegger) stalks mama's boy/criminal Crisp (Tyson) by locating the drug lord's ex and his six-year-old son. When the pec man's female partner succumbs to a nasty bout of food poisoning, he's forced to take her place as an undercover kindergarten teacher in the drowsy Pacific northwest community where mother and son reside incognito. A cover all the bases Christmas release, it's got romance, action, comedy and cute. And boxoffice earnings to match Arnie's chest measurements. A bit violent for the milk and cookie set. **111m/C VHS, Beta, LV, Closed Caption, DVD.** Arnold Schwarzenegger, Penelope Ann Miller, Pamela Reed, Linda Hunt, Richard Tyson, Carroll Baker, Cathy Moriarty, Park Overall, Richard Portnow, Jayne Brook; **D:** Ivan Reitman; **W:** Murray Salem, Herschel Weingrod, Timothy Harris; **C:** Michael Chapman; **M:** Randy Edelman. *USH, CCB*

Kindergarten Ninja 🐾½ **1994** Football star is sentenced to community service after a drunk-driving arrest and is guided by a kung fu angel into helping a group of children. **80m/C VHS.** Dwight Clark; **D:** Anthony Chan. *KBE*

The Kindred 🐾🐾½ **1987 (R)** A young student discovers that his mother the biologist has created a hybrid creature using his body tissue. Naturally, he is horrified and begins to search for his test-tube brother; the problem is, this brother likes eating people. Not too bad; boasts some good acting. **92m/C VHS, Beta, LV.** Rod Steiger, Kim Hunter, David Allan Brooks, Timothy Gibbs, Amanda Pays, Talia Balsam, Jeffrey Obrow, Peter Frechette, Julia Montgomery; **D:** Stephen Carpenter; **W:** Stephen Carpenter, Joseph Stefano, John Penney, Earl Ghaffari, Jeffrey Obrow; **M:** David Newman. *ART*

King 🐾🐾🐾 **1978** Docudrama with terrific cast follows the life and career of one of the greatest non-violent civil rights leaders of all time, Martin Luther King. Made for television. **272m/C VHS, Beta.** Paul Winfield, Cicely Tyson, Roscoe Lee Browne, Ossie Davis, Art Evans, Ernie Banks, Howard E. Rollins Jr., William Jordan, Cliff DeYoung; **D:** Abby Mann; **W:** Abby Mann; **M:** Billy Goldenberg. *NO*

King and Country 🐾🐾🐾 **1964** Aristocratic army officer, Capt. Hargreaves (Bogarde), serves as the defense lawyer for troubled Private Arthur Hamp (Courtenay), whose wartime experiences have caused him to desert. Hargreaves at first ignores the uneducated Hamp's obvious shell-shock but soon begins to feel sympathy for his confused client. Director Losey shows the effects of war rather than the war itself and provides a sincere and bitter condemnation of military mentality. Based on the play "Hamp" by John Wilson. **86m/C VHS.** *GB* Dirk Bogarde, Tom Courtenay, Leo McKern, Barry Foster, James Villiers, Peter Copley; **D:** Joseph Losey; **W:** Evan Jones; **C:** Denys Coop; **M:** Larry Adler. *KIT*

The King and Four Queens 🐾🐾½ **1956** Gable, on the run from the law, happens upon a deserted town, deserted, that is, except for a woman and her three daughters. Clark soon discovers that the women are looking for $100,000 in gold that one of their missing husbands had stolen. True to form, conniving Clark wastes no time putting the moves on each of them to find the whereabouts of the loot. **86m/C VHS, Beta.** Clark Gable, Eleanor Parker, Jo Van Fleet, Jean Wiles, Barbara Nichols, Sara Shane, Roy Roberts, Arthur Shields, Jay C. Flippen; **D:** Raoul Walsh; **M:** Alex North. *MGM, CCB*

The King and I 🐾🐾🐾🐾 **1956** Wonderful adaptation of Rodgers and Hammerstein's Broadway play based on the novel "Anna and the King of Siam" by Margaret Landon. English governess Kerr is hired to teach the King of Siam's many children and bring them into the 20th century. She has more of a job than she realizes, for this is a king, a country, and a people who value tradition above all else. Features one of Rodgers and Hammerstein's best-loved scores. Brynner made this role his, playing it over 4,000 times on stage and screen before his death. Kerr's voice was dubbed when she sang, the voice you hear is Marni Nixon, who also dubbed the star's singing voices in "West Side Story" and "My Fair Lady." ♫Shall We Dance?; Getting To Know You; Hello, Young Lovers; We Kiss in a Shadow; I Whistle a Happy Tune; March of the Siamese Children; I Have Dreamed; A Puzzlement; Something Wonderful. 133m/C VHS, Beta, LV, Letterbox, Closed Caption. Deborah Kerr, Yul Brynner, Rita Moreno, Martin Benson, Terry Saunders, Rex Thompson, Alan Mowbray, Carlos Rivas; D: Walter Lang; W: Ernest Lehman; M: Richard Rodgers, Oscar Hammerstein, Leon Shamroy. Academy Awards '56: Best Actor (Brynner), Best Art Direction/Set Decoration (Color), Best Costume Design (Color), Best Sound, Scoring of a Musical; Golden Globe Awards '57: Best Actress—Musical/Comedy (Kerr), Best Film—Musical/Comedy; Nominations: Academy Awards '56: Best Actress (Kerr), Best Color Cinematography, Best Director (Lang), Best Picture. FOX, BTV, RDG

King Arthur, the Young Warlord 🐾🐾 1975 (PG) The struggle that was the other side of Camelot—the campaign against the Saxon hordes. The early, somewhat violent years of King Art. 90m/C VHS, Beta. Oliver Tobias, Michael Gothard, Jack Watson, Brian Blessed, Peter Firth; D: Sidney Hayers, Pat Jackson, Peter Sasdy. GEM

King Boxer 🐾 1990 A famous martial arts school is taken over by a menacing gang. When a student-to-be finds this out, he enlists himself to take on the best individual of the gang in a deadly match. 106m/C VHS. Lo Lieh, Wang Ping.

King Boxers 🐾🐾 1980 (R) Kurate stars in this tale of elephant hunts, warding off Triad Society gangs, and personal combat. Nainam is a former Thailand fists and kick boxing champion. 90m/C VHS, Beta. Yasuka Kurata, Johnny Nainam. GEM

King Creole 🐾🐾½ 1958 (PG) The King goes film noir as a teenager with a criminal record who becomes a successful pop singer in New Orleans but is threatened by his ties to crime, represented by Walter Matthau. One of the better Elvis films, based on Harold Robbins' "A Stone for Danny Fisher." Features Elvis' last film appearance before his service in the Army. ♫King Creole; Banana; New Orleans; Turtles, Berries and Gumbo; Crawfish; Don't Ask Me Why; As Long As I Have You; Trouble; Hard-Headed Woman. 115m/B VHS, Beta, LV. Elvis Presley, Carolyn Jones, Walter Matthau, Dean Jagger, Dolores Hart, Vic Morrow, Paul Stewart; D: Michael Curtiz. MVD, FOX

King David 🐾½ 1985 (PG-13) The story of David, the legendary Biblical hero whose acts of bravery paved the way for him to become king of Israel. 114m/C VHS, Beta, LV, Closed Caption. Richard Gere, Alice Krige, Cherie Lunghi, Hurd Hatfield, Edward Woodward; D: Bruce Beresford; W: Andrew Birkin, James Costigan; M: Carl Davis. PAR

King Dinosaur 🐾½ 1955 A new planet arrives in the solar system, and a scientific team checks out its giant iguana-ridden terrain. 63m/B VHS, Beta, LV. Bill Bryant, Wanda Curtis, Patti Gallagher, Douglas Henderson. MLB

A King in New York 🐾🐾 1957 Chaplin plays the deposed king of a European mini-monarchy who comes to the United States in hope of making a new life. Looks critically at 1950s-era America, including Cold War paranoia and over reliance on technology. Containing Chaplin's last starring performance, this film wasn't released in the U.S. until 1973. Uneven but interesting. 105m/B VHS, Beta. GB Charlie Chaplin, Dawn Addams, Michael Chaplin, Oliver Johnston, Maxine Audley, Harry Green; D: Charlie Chaplin; C: Georges Perinal. FOX

King Kelly of the U.S.A. 🐾 1934 Robertson carries on a forgettable romance with a princess aboard a trans-Atlantic liner. 64m/B VHS. Guy Robertson, Irene Ware, Edgar Kennedy, Franklin Pangborn, Joyce Compton, Ferdinand Gottschalk, William von Brinken, Otis Harlan; D: Leonard Fields. NOS

King Kong 🐾🐾🐾🐾 1933 The original beauty and the beast film classic tells the story of Kong, a giant ape captured in Africa and brought to New York as a sideshow attraction. Kong falls for Wray, escapes from his captors, and rampages through the city, ending up on top of the newly built Empire State Building. Moody Steiner score adds color, and Willis O'Brien's stop-motion animation still holds up well. Remade numerous times with various theme derivations. Available in a colorized version. The laserdisc, produced from a superior negative, features extensive liner notes and running commentary by film historian Ronald Haver. 105m/B VHS, Beta, LV, 8mm, Closed Caption. Fay Wray, Bruce Cabot, Robert Armstrong, Frank Reicher, Noble Johnson, Sam Hardy, James Flavin; D: Ernest B. Schoedsack, Merian C. Cooper; W: James A. Creelman, Ruth Rose, Edgar Wallace; C: Edward Linden; M: Max Steiner. National Film Registry '91. TTC, FUS, CRC

King Kong 🐾🐾 1976 (PG) Oil company official travels to a remote island to discover it inhabited by a huge gorilla. The transplanted beast suffers unrequited love in classic fashion: monkey meets girl, monkey gets girl and brandishes her while atop the World Trade Center. An updated remake of the 1933 movie classic that also marks the screen debut of Lange. Impressive sets and a believable King Kong romp around New York City in this film. Watch for Joe Piscopo, and quickly for Corbin Bernsen as a reporter. 135m/C VHS, Beta, LV, 8mm. Jeff Bridges, Charles Grodin, Jessica Lange, Rene Auberjonois, John Randolph, Ed Lauter, Jack O'Halloran, Dennis Fimple, John Agar, Rick Baker; D: John Guillermin; W: Lorenzo Semple Jr.; C: Richard Kline; M: John Barry. Academy Awards '76: Best Visual Effects; Nominations: Academy Awards '76: Best Cinematography, Best Sound. PAR, HMV

King Kong Lives 🐾 1986 (PG-13) Unnecessary sequel to the 1976 remake of "King Kong," in which two scientists get the big ape, now restored after his asphalt-upsetting fall, together with a lady ape his size and type. 105m/C VHS, Beta, LV, Closed Caption. Brian Kerwin, Linda Hamilton, John Ashton, Peter Michael Goetz; D: John Guillermin; W: Steven Pressfield, Ronald Shusett. WAR

King Kong vs. Godzilla 🐾🐾½ King Kong Tai Godzilla 1963 The planet issues a collective shudder as the two mightiest monsters slug it out for reasons known only to themselves. Humankind can only stand by and watch in impotent horror as the tide of the battle sways to and fro, until one monster stands alone and victorious. 105m/C VHS. JP Inoshiro Honda, John Keith, Tadao Takashima; D: Thomas Montgomery. GKK

King Kung Fu 🐾 1987 (G) A karate master raises a gorilla, and sends it from Asia to the U.S. There, two out-of-work reporters decide to release it from captivity and then recapture it so they can get the story and some needed recognition. The background they don't have on the gorilla is that its master taught it kung fu. 90m/C VHS. John Balee, Tom Leahy, Maxine Gray, Bill Schwartz; D: Bill Hayes. NO

King Lear 🐾🐾🐾½ 1971 Brook's version of Shakespeare tragedy. The king drives away the only decent daughter he has, and when he realizes this, it is too late. Powerful performances and interesting effort at updating the bard. 137m/B VHS. GB Paul Scofield, Irene Worth, Jack MacGowran, Alan Webb, Cyril Cusack, Patrick Magee; D: Peter Brook. NOS, DVT

King Lear 🐾½ 1987 Loosely adapted from Shakespeare's tragedy of a king who loses everything. A fragmented French existential reading with gangster undercurrent. This updated version is dark, ominous, wandering, strange, and quite unlike the other 1984 remake. Or any other remake, for that matter. 91m/C VHS. SI Peter Sellers, Burgess Meredith, Molly Ringwald, Jean-Luc Godard, Woody Allen; D: Jean-Luc Godard; W: Norman Mailer.

The King Murder 🐾🐾 1932 High society sleuth Tearle tries to solve the mysterious death of a beautiful, yet dangerous extortionist. Looks a lot like murder, although no weapon can be found. 67m/B VHS. Conway Tearle, Natalie Moorhead, Marceline Day, Dorothy Revier; D: Richard Thorpe; W: Charles Reed Jones. SNC

King of America 🐾 1980 A Greek sailor and a local labor agent battle over who will become King of America. 90m/C VHS, Beta. D: Dezso Magyar. NO

King of Comedy 🐾🐾🐾 1982 (PG) An unhinged would-be comedian haunts and eventually kidnaps a massively popular Johnny Carson-type television personality. A cold, cynical farce devised by Scorsese seemingly in reaction to John Hinckley's obsession with his film "Taxi Driver." Controlled, hard-hitting performances, especially by De Niro and Lewis. 101m/C VHS, Beta, LV. Robert De Niro, Jerry Lewis, Sandra Bernhard, Tony Randall, Diahnne Abbott, Shelley Hack, Liza Minnelli; D: Martin Scorsese. British Academy Awards '83: Best Original Screenplay; National Society of Film Critics Awards '83: Best Supporting Actress (Bernhard). COL, FCT

The King of Hearts 🐾🐾🐾 Le Roi de Coeur 1966 In WWI, a Scottish soldier finds a battle-torn French town evacuated of all occupants except a colorful collection of escaped lunatics from a nearby asylum. The lunatics want to make him their king, which is not a bad alternative to the insanity of war. Bujold is cute as ballerina wannabe; look for Serrault ("La Cage aux Folles") as, not surprisingly, a would-be effeminate hairdresser. Light-hearted comedy with a serious message; definitely worthwhile. 101m/C VHS, Beta, LV, Letterbox. FR GB Alan Bates, Genevieve Bujold, Adolfo Celi, Francoise Christophe, Micheline Presle; D: Philippe de Broca; M: Georges Delerue. MGM, TVC, HMV

King of Jazz 🐾🐾 1930 A lavish revue built around the Paul Whiteman Orchestra with comedy sketches and songs by the stars on Universal Pictures' talent roster. (Though billed as the King of Jazz, Whiteman was never as good as jazz's real royalty.) Filmed in two-color Technicolor with a cartoon segment by Walter Lantz. ♫Rhapsody in Blue; So the Bluebirds and the Blackbirds Got Together; Mississippi Mud; It Happened in Monterey; Ragamuffin Romeo; Happy Feet; Song of the Dawn; A Bench in the Park. 93m/C VHS, Beta. Paul Whiteman, John Boles, Jeanette Loff, Bing Crosby; D: John Murray Anderson. Academy Awards '30: Best Interior Decoration. USH, MLB, RXM

King of Kings 🐾🐾½ 1927 DeMille depicts the life of Jesus Christ in this highly regarded silent epic. The resurrection scene appears in color. Remade by Nicholas Ray in 1961. 115m/B VHS, Beta. H.B. Warner, Dorothy Cumming, Ernest Torrence, Joseph Schildkraut, Jacqueline Logan, Victor Varconi, William Boyd; D: Cecil B. DeMille.

The King of Kings 🐾🐾🐾 1961 The life of Christ is intelligently told, with an attractive visual sense and a memorable score. Remake of Cecil B. DeMille's silent film, released in 1927. Laserdisc format features a special letterboxed edition of this film. 170m/C VHS, Beta, LV, Letterbox. Jeffrey Hunter, Siobhan McKenna, Hurd Hatfield, Robert Ryan, Rita Gam, Viveca Lindfors, Rip Torn; D: Nicholas Ray; W: Philip Yordan; C: Milton Krasner; M: Miklos Rozsa. MGM, IGP

King of Kong Island woof! 1978 Intent on world domination, a group of mad scientists implant receptors in the brains of gorillas on Kong Island, and the monster apes run amok. 92m/C VHS, Beta. SP Brad Harris, Marc Lawrence; D: Robert Morris. NO

The King of Marvin Gardens 🐾🐾½ 1972 (R) Nicholson stars as a Midwest radio jock who prefers to reminisce about his life and family back in Atlantic City, New Jersey to playing records. When Nicholson returns for a visit he finds brother Dern, king of the get-rich-quick schemers, working for a black crime syndicate. Dern is in-

volved in another scheme which means embezzling money from his boss—not a smart idea although Nicholson can't disuade him. Talky drama also features Burstyn as Dern's neglected girlfriend. **104m/C VHS.** Jack Nicholson, Bruce Dern, Ellen Burstyn, Scatman Crothers, Julia Anne Robinson, Charles Lavine, Arnold Williams, Josh Mostel; **D:** Bob Rafelson; **W:** Jacob Brackman. COL, BTV

King of New York 🎬🎬🎬 1990 (R) Drug

czar Frank White (Walken), recently returned from a prison sabbatical, regains control of his New York drug empire with the aid of a loyal network of black dealers. How? Call it dangerous charisma, an inexplicable sympatico. Headquartered in Manhattan's chic Plaza hotel, he ruthlessly orchestrates the drug machine, while funneling the profits into a Bronx hospital for the poor. As inscrutable as White himself, Walken makes the drug czar's power tangible, believable, yet never fathomable. **106m/C VHS, LV, Closed Caption.** Christopher Walken, Laurence "Larry" Fishburne, David Caruso, Victor Argo, Wesley Snipes, Janet Julian, Joey Chin, Giancarlo Esposito, Steve Buscemi; **D:** Abel Ferrara; **W:** Nicholas St. John; **C:** Bojan Bazelli; **M:** Joe Delia. ART

King of the Airwaves 🎬🎬½ Louis 19, le

Roi des Ondes 1994 Louis (Drainville) is a dull salesman who spends his days working in an electronics store and his nights in front of the TV. This leads Louis to enter (and win) a contest sponsored by the local TV station, which promises to provide 24-hour-a-day coverage of the winner's every move. Now, ordinary Louis is a media celebrity who must deal with constant intrusion and the soap opera-ish changes wrought upon his life. **93m/C VHS.** CA FR Martin Drainville, Agathe de la Fontaine, Dominique Michel, Patricia Tulasne, Gilbert Lachance; **D:** Michel Poulette; **W:** Michael Michaud, Emile Gaudreault, Sylvie Bouchard; **M:** Jean-Marie Benoit. Nominations: Genie Awards '94: Best Actor (Drainville), Best Film. NYR

King of the Bullwhip 🎬½ 1951 Two

undercover U.S. Marshals are sent to Tioga City to stop the killing and looting of a masked bandit, whose whip is as dangerous as his gun. **59m/B VHS, Beta.** Lash LaRue, Al "Fuzzy" St. John, Anne Gwynne, Tom Neal, Jack Holt, Dennis Moore, Michael Whalen, George Lewis; **D:** Ron Ormond. NOS, VCN, DVT

King of the Congo 🎬½ 1952 Crabbe, in

his last serial, as a pilot who is frantically searching for an important piece of film. In 15 parts. **?m/B VHS.** Buster Crabbe, Gloria Dee; **D:** Spencer Gordon Bennet, Wallace Grissell. MLB

King of the Cowboys 🎬🎬 1943 Roy

fights a gang of saboteurs and saves a defense installation. **54m/B VHS.** Roy Rogers, Smiley Burnette, James Bush. NOS, VCN, DVT

King of the Damned 🎬 1936 On an

island prison Veidt leads a convict's revolt against the cruel administrator (Hallard), who gets killed. Before he dies, Hallard alerts a convenient warship, which begins shelling the island. Hallard's daughter, who has fallen for Veidt, pleads for the men and everyone is given a fair trial. Miscast and ineptly performed, although Veidt retains some dignity. **81m/B VHS.** GB Conrad Veidt, Helen Vinson, C.M. Hallard, Noah Beery Sr., Percy Walsh, Raymond Lovell, Cecil Ramage, Peter Croft; **D:** Walter Forde; **W:** Charles Bennett, Sidney Gilliat, Noel Langley. HCV

King of the Forest Rangers 1946

Ranger Steve King must stop an evil archaeologist from finding a treasure whose secret lies within an ancient Indian rug pattern. Edited from an original, 12 episode serial on two cassettes. **167m/B VHS, Beta.** Larry Thompson, Helen Talbot, Stuart Hamblen, Anthony Warde. REP, MLB

King of the Grizzlies 🎬½ 1969 (G) The

mystical relationship between a Cree Indian and a grizzly cub is put to the test when the full grown bear attacks a ranch at which the Indian is foreman. **93m/C VHS, Beta.** Chris Wiggins, John Yesno; **D:** Ron Kelly. DIS

King of the Gypsies 🎬🎬½ 1978 (R) In-

teresting drama. A young man, scornful of his gypsy heritage, runs away from the tribe and tries to make a life of his own. He is summoned home to his grandfather's deathbed where he is proclaimed the new king of the gypsies, thus incurring the wrath of his scorned father. From Peter Maas's best-selling novel. **112m/C VHS, Beta, LV.** Sterling Hayden, Eric Roberts, Susan Sarandon, Brooke Shields, Shelley Winters, Annie Potts, Annette O'Toole, Judd Hirsch, Michael V. Gazzo, Roy Brocksmith; **D:** Frank Pierson; **W:** Frank Pierson; **C:** Sven Nykvist. PAR, CCB

King of the Hill 🎬🎬🎬½ 1993 (PG-13)

Quiet depression-era drama focuses on Aaron, a 12-year-old who lives in a seedy hotel in St. Louis. The family is barely scraping by: his mother is in a tuberculosis sanitarium, his younger brother has been sent away to live with relatives, and Aaron must fend for himself when his father gets work as a traveling salesman. Aaron excels at school and his efforts there, as well as his hotel friends, manage to provide him with some semblance of a regular life. Soderbergh's third directorial effort is unsentimental but admiring of his character's resourcefulness and imagination during difficult times. Based on the book by A.E. Hochner describing his own childhood. **CW:** Thematic elements. **102m/C VHS, LV, Letterbox, Closed Caption.** Jesse Bradford, Jeroen Krabbe, Lisa Eichhorn, Karen Allen, Spalding Gray, Elizabeth McGovern, Joseph Chrest, Adrien Brody, Cameron Boyd, Chris Samples, Katherine Heigl, Amber Benson, John McConnell, Ron Vawter, John Durbin, Lauryn Hill, David Jensen; **D:** Steven Soderbergh; **W:** Steven Soderbergh; **M:** Cliff Martinez. USH

The King of the Kickboxers woof!

1991 (R) The villains make kung-fu snuff movies with unwitting actors killed on camera. Otherwise, same old junk about a karate cop back in Bangkok to get the dude who squashed his brother. Pretty racist at times. **CW:** Language, strong violence, and sensuality. **90m/C VHS, Closed Caption.** Loren Avedon, Richard Jaeckel, Billy Blanks, Don Stroud, Keith Cooke; **D:** Lucas Lowe. IMP

King of the Kongo 🎬🎬 1929 A hand-

some young man is sent by the government to Nuhalla, deep in the jungle, to break up a gang of ivory thieves. Serial was made in silent and sound versions. **213m/B VHS, Beta.** Jacqueline Logan, Boris Karloff, Richard Tucker; **D:** Richard Thorpe. VYY, NOS, MLB

King of the Mountain 🎬½ 1981 (PG)

The "Old King" and the "New King" must square off in this tale of daredevil road racers who zoom through the streets of Hollywood. Interesting cast trapped by tired script. **92m/C VHS, Beta.** Richard Cox, Harry Hamlin, Dennis Hopper, Joseph Bottoms, Deborah Van Valkenburgh, Dan Haggerty; **D:** Noel Nosseck; **W:** Roger Christian.

King of the Pecos 🎬🎬½ 1936 A young

lawyer (who's also adept at the shootin' iron) exacts revenge on his parents' killers in the courtroom. Well made early Wayne outing, with good character development, taut pacing and beautiful photography. **54m/B VHS.** John Wayne, Muriel Evans, Cy Kendall, Jack Clifford, John Beck, Yakima Canutt; **D:** Joseph Kane. REP, MLB

The King of the Roaring '20s: The Story of Arnold Rothstein 🎬🎬½ The

Big Bankroll 1961 "True" story of infamous gangster, Arnold Rothstein, a brilliant and ruthless gambler who practically ran New York in the '20s. This version of his life focuses on his rise to power, the dealings with his enemies, and his crumbling personal life. Superficial due mostly to the weak screenplay. Adapted from the book "The Big Bankroll" by Leo Katcher. **106m/B VHS, Beta.** David Janssen, Dianne Foster, Mickey Rooney, Jack Carson, Diana Dors, Dan O'Herlihy, Mickey Shaughnessy, Keenan Wynn; **D:** Joseph M. Newman. FOX, FCT

King of the Rocketmen *Lost Planet Airmen*

1949 Jeff King thwarts an attempt by traitors to steal government scientific secrets. Serial in 12 episodes. Later released as a feature titled "Lost Planet Airmen." **156m/B VHS, LV.** Tristram Coffin, Mae Clarke, I. Stanford Jolley; **D:** Fred Brannon. VCN, REP, MLB

King of the Rodeo 🎬🎬 1928 Cowpoke

Hoot wins a rodeo and catches a thief in the Windy City. Hoot's final silent ride into the sunset. **54m/B VHS, Beta.** Hoot Gibson, Kathryn Crawford, Slim Summerville, Charles French, Monte Montague, Joseph Girard; **D:** Henry MacRae. GPV

King of the Sierras 🎬½ 1938 Bosworth

tells his nephew the story of a white horse that protected his mares from a black stallion. The acting of the horses is better than that of the humans. **58m/B VHS.** Hobart Bosworth, Harry Harvey, Harry Harvey Jr., Jim Campeau; **D:** Samuel Diege; **W:** W. Scott Darling. GPV

King of the Stallions 🎬½ 1942 A dan-

gerous stallion is a menacing threat to the herd and the cowboys and Indians and other scattered wildlife. Chief Thundercloud is the only one capable of tackling the matter. Largely Indian cast, including Iron Eyes Cody, famed for the anti-litter campaign. **63m/B VHS.** Chief Thundercloud, Princess Bluebird, Chief Yowlachie, Rick Vallin, Dave O'Brien, Barbara Felker, Iron Eyes Cody; **D:** Edward Finney. NOS, DVT

King of the Texas Rangers 1941 Tom

King, Texas Ranger, finds that his father's killers are a group of saboteurs who have destroyed American oil fields. This 12-episode serial comes on two tapes. **195m/B VHS.** Sammy Baugh, Neil Hamilton; **D:** William Witney, John English. REP, MRV, MLB

King of the Wild Horses 🎬🎬🎬 1924

Engaging children's story about a wild stallion that comes to the rescue. Terrific action photography of Rex going through his paces. Look for Chase in a rare dramatic role. Silent. **50m/B VHS, Beta.** Rex, Edna Murphy, Leon Barry, Pat Hartigan, Frank Butler, Charley Chase; **D:** Fred Jackman. NO

King of the Wind 🎬🎬½ 1993 (PG) An

epic adventure featuring the true story of a legendary Arabian horse and a poor stable boy who gave the most precious gift of all: love. **101m/C VHS, Closed Caption.** Richard Harris, Glenda Jackson. FHE

King of the Zombies woof! 1941 Mad

scientist creates his own zombies without souls, to be used as the evil tools of a foreign government. Zombie nonsense. **67m/B VHS, Beta.** John Archer, Dick Purcell, Mantan Moreland, Henry Victor, Joan Woodbury; **D:** Jean Yarbrough. Nominations: Academy Awards '41: Best Original Dramatic/Comedy Score. VYY, MRV, SNC

The King on Main Street 🎬🎬½ 1925

A king on vacation in America finds romance. **?m/B VHS, Beta.** Adolphe Menjou, Bessie Love. NO

King, Queen, Knave 🎬🎬🎬 Herzbube

1972 Sexy black comedy about a shy, awkward 19-year-old boy, keenly aware that his interest in girls is not reciprocated. He has to go live with his prosperous uncle and his much younger wife when his parents are killed. Based on the Vladimir Nabokov novel. **94m/C VHS, Beta.** GE Gina Lollobrigida, David Niven, John Moulder-Brown; **D:** Jerzy Skolimowski; **W:** David Seltzer.

King Ralph 🎬🎬 1991 (PG) When the rest of

the royal family passes away in a freak accident, lounge lizard Ralph finds himself the only heir to the throne. O'Toole is the long-suffering valet who tries to train him for the job. Funny in spots and Goodman is the quintessential good sport, making the whole outing pleasant. Sometimes too forced. **96m/C VHS, Beta, LV, Closed Caption.** John Goodman, Peter O'Toole, Camille Coduri, Joely Richardson, John Hurt; **D:** David S. Ward; **W:** David S. Ward; **M:** James Newton Howard. USH, CCB

King Rat 🐾🐾🐾 1965 Drama set in a WWII Japanese prisoner-of-war camp. Focuses on the effect of captivity on the English, Australian, and American prisoners. An American officer bribes his Japanese captors to live more comfortably than the rest. Based on James Clavell's novel. **134m/B VHS, Beta.** George Segal, Tom Courtenay, James Fox, James Donald, Denholm Elliott, Patrick O'Neal, John Mills; *D:* Bryan Forbes; *M:* John Barry. Nominations: Academy Awards '65: Best Art Direction/Set Decoration (B & W), Best Black and White Cinematography. *COL*

King Richard and the Crusaders 🐾½ 1954 Laughable costume epic with Sanders as Richard the Lionheart, who survives an assassination attempt during the Crusades. Harvey is a loyal knight sworn to find the traitors with Harrison as the noble leader of the Arab forces. Mayo plays Harvey's object of affection. Even the battle scenes are boring. Based on "The Talisman" by Sir Walter Scott. **113m/C VHS.** George Sanders, Rex Harrison, Laurence Harvey, Virginia Mayo, Robert Douglas, Michael Pate, Paula Raymond, Lester Matthews; *D:* David Butler; *W:* John Twist; *M:* Max Steiner. *FCT, MOV, WAR*

King Solomon's Mines 🐾🐾🐾 1937 The search for King Solomon's Mines leads a safari through the treacherous terrain of the desert, fending off sandstorms, Zulus, and a volcanic eruption. Adapted from the novel by H. Rider Haggard and remade twice. **80m/B VHS, Beta.** Cedric Hardwicke, Paul Robeson, Roland Young, John Loder, Anna Lee; *D:* Robert Stevenson. *SNC, NOS, HMV*

King Solomon's Mines 🐾🐾🐾 1950 A lavish version of the classic H. Rider Haggard adventures about African explorers searching out a fabled diamond mine. Remake of the 1937 classic; remade again in 1985. **102m/C VHS, Beta.** Stewart Granger, Deborah Kerr, Richard Carlson, Hugo Haas, Lowell Gilmore; *C:* Robert L. Surtees. Academy Awards '50: Best Color Cinematography, Best Film Editing; Nominations: Academy Awards '50: Best Picture. *MGM*

King Solomon's Mines 🐾½ 1985 (PG-13) The third remake of the classic H. Rider Haggard novel about a safari deep into Africa in search of an explorer who disappeared while searching for the legendary diamond mines of King Solomon. Updated but lacking the style of the previous two films. Somewhat imperialistic, racist point of view. **101m/C VHS, Beta.** Richard Chamberlain, John Rhys-Davies, Sharon Stone, Herbert Lom; *D:* J. Lee Thompson; *W:* Gene Quintano; *M:* Jerry Goldsmith. *MGM*

King Solomon's Treasure 🐾 1976 The great white adventurer takes on the African jungle, hunting for hidden treasure in the Forbidden City. Ekland stars as a Phoenician Queen—need we say more?? **90m/C VHS, Beta.** *CA GB* David McCallum, Britt Ekland, Patrick Macnee, Wilfrid Hyde-White; *D:* Alvin Rakoff. *VCI*

The Kingdom 🐾🐾½ 1995 Danish director von Trier serves up what must be the first four-and-a-half-hour long hospital soap opera/ghost story/comedy/satire. Elderly Mrs. Drusse checks herself into a hospital known as the Kingdom, which is inhabited by the usual medical suspects: Pompous surgeons, incompetent bureaucrats, and quirky residents. She hears the ghostly call of a child from an elevator shaft and sticks around to investigate. Made for Danish TV but released theatrically there and in the States, film owes a great deal to "Twin Peaks" and B-movie horror flicks. Doesn't take itself too seriously, but probably can't be watched all in one sitting. Danish and Swedish with subtitles. **279m/C VHS.** *DK* Kirsten Rolffes, Ghita Norby, Udo Kier, Ernst Hugo Jarogard, Soren Pilmark, Holger Juul Hansen, Baard Owe, Birgitte Raabjerg, Peter Mygind; *D:* Lars von Trier; *W:* Lars von Trier, Tomas Gislason; *C:* Eric Kress; *M:* Joachim Holbek. *HMK*

Kingdom of the Spiders 🐾🐾½ 1977 (PG) A desert town is invaded by swarms of killer tarantulas, which begin to consume townspeople. **90m/C VHS, Beta.** William Shatner, Tiffany Bolling, Woody Strode; *D:* John Cardos; *W:* Alan Caillou, Richard Robinson; *C:* John Morrill. *NO*

Kingfish: A Story of Huey P. Long 🐾🐾½ 1995 Charismatic political kingpin of Louisiana, Huey P. Long is brought to vivid life with Goodman's swaggering portrayal. Story is told in flashback, beginning with Long's assassination in 1935. A champion of the working man, Long parlayed charm and corruption into a Depression-era political career as governor and U.S. Senator. But naturally, the hard-drinking, hard-loving Long makes a lot of enemies along the way. Long's life was also memorably recreated in Robert Penn Warren's "All the King's Men," as was that of his younger brother, Governor Earl Long, in the film "Blaze." **97m/C VHS.** John Goodman, Matt Craven, Anne Heche, Ann Dowd, Jeffery Perry, Bob Gunton, Hoyt Axton, Kirk Baltz, Bill Cobbs; *D:* Thomas Schlamme; *W:* Paul Monash; *M:* Patrick Williams. *TTC*

Kingfisher Caper 🐾🐾 1976 (PG) A power struggle between a businessman, his brother, and a divorced sister is threatening to rip a family-owned diamond empire apart. **90m/C VHS, Beta.** Hayley Mills, David McCallum; *D:* Dirk DeVilliers.

Kingfisher the Killer 🐾 198? Charles, the Raging Titan of Ninja skill, stalks the bad gang that killed his mother and hits them with nunchakos. **90m/C VHS, Beta.** Sho Kosugi. *TWE*

Kingpin 🐾🐾½ 1996 (PG-13) Bowling epic serves up social satire while showcasing some of the worst hair ever seen at the cinema. Roy Munson (a very bald Harrelson, reasonably subdued in relation to rest of cast) is a former bowling champ who, thanks to his sleazy ways, lost a hand and is reduced to selling bowling equipment while wearing a crude rubber prosthetic (on his hand). That is until he meets innocent Amish phenom Ishmael (Quaid), resplendent in a dutch boy wig, whom he persuades to hit the road to a big money tournament in Reno, where Roy can confront an old nemesis (Murray) and compare shampoos, while Ish attempts to win enough money to save the family farm. Claudia (Angel) is around as the highly decorative love interest of Roy. Co-written by "Dumb & Dumber" writers the brothers Farrelly. Look for Amish sensations Blues Traveler at the credit roll.*CW:* Crude sex-related humor and a drug scene. **107m/C VHS, LV, Closed Caption.** Woody Harrelson, Randy Quaid, Vanessa Angel, Bill Murray, Chris Elliott; *D:* Peter Farrelly, Bobby Farrelly; *W:* Bobby Farrelly, Mort Nathan; *C:* Mark Irwin; *M:* Freedy Johnston. *MGM*

Kings and Desperate Men 🐾½ 1983 Apprentice terrorists plea their case at a public forum when they take a rakish talk show host hostage. **118m/C VHS.** *GB* Patrick McGoohan, Alexis Kanner, Andrea Marcovicci, Robin Spry, Frank Moore; *D:* Alexis Kanner. *NO*

Kings Go Forth 🐾🐾½ 1958 Hormones and war rage in this love triangle set against the backdrop of WWII France. Sinatra loves Wood who loves Curtis. When Sinatra asks for her hand in marriage she refuses because she is mixed—half black, half white. He says it doesn't matter, but she still declines because she's in love with Curtis. When Sinatra tells Curtis that Wood is mixed, Curtis says that it doesn't matter to him either because he'd never planned on marrying her. Meanwhile, the war continues. Not particularly satisfying on either the war or race front. Based on a novel by Joe David Brown. **109m/B VHS, Beta.** Frank Sinatra, Tony Curtis, Natalie Wood, Leora Dana; *D:* Delmer Daves; *C:* Daniel F. Fapp; *M:* Elmer Bernstein. *MGM*

Kings of the Road—In the Course of Time 🐾🐾🐾½ 1976 A writer and a film projectionist travel by truck across Germany. The film stands out for its simple and expressive direction, and truly captures the sense of physical and ideological freedom of being on the road. A landmark Wenders epic. In German with English subtitles. **176m/B VHS, Beta.** *GE* Ruediger Vogler, Hanns Zischler, Elisabeth Kreuzer; *D:* Wim Wenders; *W:* Wim Wenders. *FCT, GLV, TPV*

Kings, Queens, Jokers 193? Package includes a foolish lover and ghosts in "Haunted Spooks," an escaped convict in "Dangerous Females," and a search for lost jewels in "Stolen Jools." **60m/B VHS, Beta.** Harold Lloyd, Marie Dressler, Polly Moran, Edward G. Robinson, Gary Cooper, Joan Crawford. *NO*

King's Ransom woof! 1991 When the Japanese Emperor's Pearl is stolen, the underworld is abuzz with excitement. But only the wealthiest individuals are invited to bid for the jewel at Cameron King's secret casino. There, untold pleasures, and dangers, await them. **?m/C VHS.** Miles O'Keeffe, Dedee Pfeiffer, Christopher Atkins; *D:* Hugh Parks. *NO*

The King's Rhapsody 🐾🐾 1955 Flynn is an heir who abdicates his throne in order to be with the woman he loves. But when the king dies, Flynn sacrifices love for honor and goes back to marry a princess. Very dated and Flynn is long past his swashbuckling-romantic days. **93m/C VHS.** *GB* Errol Flynn, Anna Neagle, Patrice Wymore, Martita Hunt, Finlay Currie, Frank Wolff, Joan Benham, Reginald Tate, Miles Malleson; *D:* Herbert Wilcox. *FCT*

Kings Row 🐾🐾🐾 1941 The Harry Bellamann best-selling Middle American potboiler comes to life. Childhood friends grow up with varying degrees of success, in a decidedly macabre town. All are continually dependent on and inspired by Parris (Cummings) a psychiatric doctor and genuine gentleman. Many cast members worked against type with unusual success. Warner held the film for a year after its completion, in concern for its dark subject matter, but it received wide acclaim. Shot completely within studio settings—excellent scenic design by William Cameron Menzies, and wonderful score. **127m/B VHS, Beta, Closed Caption.** Ann Sheridan, Robert Cummings, Ronald Reagan, Betty Field, Charles Coburn, Claude Rains, Judith Anderson, Nancy Coleman, Karen Verne, Maria Ouspenskaya, Harry Davenport, Ernest Cossart, Pat Moriarity, Scotty Beckett; *D:* Sam Wood; *C:* James Wong Howe; *M:* Erich Wolfgang Korngold. Nominations: Academy Awards '42: Best Black and White Cinematography, Best Director (Wood), Best Picture. *MGM, FOX, CCB*

The King's Thief 🐾🐾½ 1955 Costume swashbuckler with Niven as the bad guy. He's a duke at the court of 17th-century English King Charles II and is involved in a plot to steal the crown jewels. **78m/C VHS.** David Niven, Edmund Purdom, George Sanders, Ann Blyth, Roger Moore, John Dehner, Sean McClory, Melville Cooper, Alan Mowbray; *D:* Robert Z. Leonard; *W:* Christopher Knopf; *M:* Miklos Rozsa. *MGM*

The King's Whore 🐾🐾 1990 (R) Dalton stars as a 17th-century king who falls obsessively in love with the wife of one of his courtiers. His passions lead him to make a decision between the woman and the throne. Good-looking costume epic with obligatory sword fights.*CW:* Sexuality. **111m/C VHS, LV, Closed Caption.** Timothy Dalton, Valeria Golino, Feodor Chaliapin Jr, Margaret Tyzack; *W:* Daniel Vigne, Frederic Raphael. *THV*

Kinjite: Forbidden Subjects 🐾🐾 1989 (R) A cop takes on a sleazy pimp whose specialty is recruiting teenage girls, including the daughter of a Japanese business man. Slimy, standard Bronson fare. **97m/C VHS, Beta, LV.** Charles Bronson, Juan Fernandez, Peggy Lipton; *D:* J. Lee Thompson. *MGM*

A Kink in the Picasso 🐾🐾 1990 MTV personality Daddo joins a cast of criminals who chase after a Picasso artwork and a counterfeit. Artless Australian production. **84m/C VHS.** Peter O'Brien, Jon Finlayson, Jane Clifton, Andrew Daddo; *D:* Marc Gracie. *ATL*

Kino Pravda/Enthusiasm 1931 Two famous documentaries by Vertov, the first a prime example of his pioneering avant-garde newsreels that helped establish Soviet montage aesthetic, and the second the famous portrait of Don Basin coal miners, augmented by the famous use of sound editing/montage. In Russian with English titles. 120m/B VHS, Beta. *RU* D: Dziga Vertov. *FCT, FST*

Kipperbang 🎬🎬 *Ptang, Yang, Kipperbang* 1982 (PG) During the summer of 1948, a 13-year-old boy wishes he could kiss the girl of his dreams. He finally gets the chance in a school play. Not unsatisfying, but falls short of being the bittersweet coming-of-age drama it could have been. 85m/C VHS, Beta. *GB* John Albasiny, Abigail Cruttenden, Alison Steadman; D: Michael Apted. *MGM*

Kipps 🎬🎬🎬 *The Remarkable Mr. Kipps* 1941 Based on H.G. Wells's satirical novel. A young British shopkeeper inherits a fortune and tries to join high society while neglecting his working-class girlfriend. Set the stage for the musical "Half a Sixpence." 95m/B VHS, Beta. *GB* Michael Redgrave, Phyllis Calvert, Michael Wilding; D: Carol Reed. *NOS, HHT, CAB*

The Kirlian Witness 🎬 *The Plants Are Watching* 1978 (PG) A woman uses the power of telepathic communication with house plants to solve her sister's murder. 88m/C VHS, Beta. Nancy Snyder, Joel Colodner, Ted Leplat; D: Jonathan Sarno. *NO*

Kismet 🎬🎬🎬 1920 Original screen version of the much filmed lavish Arabian Nights saga (remade in '30, '44 and '55). A beggar is drawn into deception and intrigue among Bagdad upper-crusters. Glorious sets and costumes; silent with original organ score. 98m/B VHS. Otis Skinner, Elinor Fair, Herschel Mayall; D: Louis Gasnier; C: Gaetano Antonio "Tony" Gaudio. *VYY*

Kismet 🎬🎬 1955 A big budget Arabian Nights musical drama of a Baghdad street poet who manages to infiltrate himself into the Wazir's harem. The music was adapted from Borodin by Robert Wright and George Forrest. Original trailer and letterboxed screen available in special laserdisc edition. ♫Fate; Not Since Ninevah; Baubles, Bangles, and Beads; Stranger in Paradise; Bored; Night of My Nights; The Olive Tree; And This Is My Beloved; Sands of Time. 113m/C VHS, Beta, LV, **Letterbox, Closed Caption.** Howard Keel, Ann Blyth, Dolores Gray, Vic Damone; D: Vincente Minnelli; W: Charles Lederer, Luther Davis; C: Joseph Ruttenberg; M: Andre Previn. *MGM, FCT*

The Kiss 🎬🎬🎬 1929 Garbo, the married object of earnest young Ayres' lovelorn affection, innocently kisses him nighty night since a kiss is just a kiss. Or so she thought. Utterly misconstrued, the platonic peck sets the stage for disaster, and murder and courtroom anguish follow. French Feyder's direction is stylized and artsy. Garbo's last silent and Ayres' first film. 89m/B VHS. Greta Garbo, Conrad Nagel, Holmes Herbert, Lew Ayres, Anders Randolf; D: Jacques Feyder; C: William H. Daniels. *MGM, FCT*

The Kiss 🎬 1988 (R) A kind of "Auntie Mame from Hell" story in which a mysterious aunt visits her teenage niece in New York, and tries to apprentice her to the family business of sorcery, demon possession, and murder. Aunt Felicity's kiss will make you appreciate the harmless cheek-pinching of your own aunt; your evening would be better spent with her, rather than this movie. 98m/C VHS, Beta, LV. Pamela Collyer, Peter Dvorsky, Joanna Pacula, Meredith Salenger, Mimi Kuzyk, Nicholas Kilbertus, Jan Rubes; D: Pen Densham; W: Tom Ropelewski. *COL, IME*

Kiss and Be Killed 🎬½ 1991 (R) Crazy guy with knife cuts short couple's wedding night. Shortchanged widow is mighty miffed. Will she have to return the wedding gifts? *CW:* Language, violence, and sensuality. 89m/C VHS, Beta, 8mm. Caroline Ludvik, Crystal Carson, Tom Reilly, Chip Hall, Ken Norton, Jimmy Baio; D: Tom Milo. *NO*

Kiss and Kill 🎬🎬 *Blood of Fu Manchu; Against All Odds* 1968 (R) Lee returns in his fourth outing as Fu Manchu. This time the evil one has injected beautiful girls with a deadly poison that reacts upon kissing. They are then sent out to seduce world leaders. Not on par with the previous movies, but still enjoyable. Sequel to "Castle of Fu Manchu." 91m/C VHS. Christopher Lee, Richard Greene, Shirley Eaton, Tsai Chin, Maria Rohm, H. Marion Crawford; D: Jess (Jesus) Franco. *MRV*

A Kiss Before Dying 🎬🎬 1991 (R) Botched adaptation of Ira Levin's cunning thriller novel (filmed before in 1956). This flick serves up an exploded head in the first few minutes. So much for subtlety. The highlight is Dillon's chilly role as a murderous opportunist bent on marrying into a wealthy family. Young plays two roles (not very well) as lookalike sisters on his agenda. The ending was hastily reshot and it shows. *CW:* Some language, strong violence, and graphic sensuality. 93m/C VHS, Beta, LV, **Closed Caption.** Matt Dillon, Sean Young, Max von Sydow, Diane Ladd, James Russo, Martha Gehman, Ben Browder, Joy Lee, Adam Horovitz; D: James Dearden; W: James Dearden. Golden Raspberry Awards '91: Worst Actress (Young), Worst Supporting Actress (Young). *USH*

Kiss Daddy Goodbye 🎬½ *Revenge of the Zombie; The Vengeful Dead* 1981 (R) A widower keeps his two children isolated in order to protect their secret telekinetic powers. When he is killed by bikers, the kids attempt to raise him from the dead. 81m/C VHS, Beta. Fabian, Marilyn Burns, Jon Cedar, Marvin Miller; D: Patrick Regan. *MRV*

Kiss Daddy Goodnight 🎬 1987 (R) A Danish-made thriller about a beautiful young girl who seduces men, drugs them and takes their money. One man turns the tables on her, however, and decides that she will only belong to him. 89m/C VHS, Beta. *DK* Uma Thurman, Paul Dillon, Paul Richards, David Brisbin; D: P.I. Huemer; C: Bobby Bukowski.

A Kiss for Mary Pickford 🎬🎬½ 1927 A rare, hilarious cinematic oddity, a film formulated from Kuleshov montage techniques from footage of the famous American couple's visit to Russia in 1926, wherein a regular guy tries to win a girl through friendship with the stars. Fairbanks and Pickford didn't know of their role in this film, being spliced in later according to montage theory. 70m/B VHS, Beta. Mary Pickford, Douglas Fairbanks Sr., Igor Ilinsky; D: Sergei Komarov. *FCT*

A Kiss Goodnight 🎬🎬½ 1994 (R) Natalie (Trickey) has a romp in the sheets with ad exec Kurt (Corley) when regular beau Michael (Moses) ignores her for work. But when Natalie decides to break things off, Kurt won't take no for an answer. *CW:* Language; some violence; sexuality. 88m/C VHS. Paula Trickey, Al Corley, Mark Moses, Lawrence Tierney, Brett Cullen, James Karen, Robert Wuhl, Sydney Walsh; D: Daniel Raskov; W: Daniel Raskov; C: Glenn Kershaw.

Kiss Me a Killer 🎬🎬 1991 (R) The ancient thriller plot about a young wife and her lover who scheme to kill her middle-aged husband. It's set in L.A.'s Latino community, but extensive shots of salsa music and ethnic cooking hardly raise this above the mediocre. *CW:* Language, violence, and strong sensuality. 91m/C VHS, LV. Julie Carmen, Robert Beltran, Guy Boyd, Ramon Franco, Charles Boswell; D: Marcus De Leon; W: Marcus De Leon. *COL*

Kiss Me Deadly 🎬🎬🎬½ 1955 Aldrich's adaptation of Mickey Spillane's private eye tale takes pulp literature high concept. Meeker, as Mike Hammer, is a self interested rough and tumble all American dick (detective, that is). When a woman to whom he happened to give a ride is found murdered, he follows the mystery straight into a nuclear conspiracy. Aldrich, with tongue deftly in cheek, styles a message through the medium; topsy turvy camerawork and rat-a-tat-tat pacing tell volumes about Hammer, the world he orbits, and that special 50s kind of paranoia. Now a cult fave, it's considered to be the American grandaddy to French New Wave. 105m/B VHS, LV, **Closed Caption.** Ralph Meeker, Albert Dekker, Paul Stewart, Wesley Addy, Cloris Leachman, Strother Martin, Marjorie Bennett, Jack Elam, Maxine Cooper, Gaby Rodgers, Nick Dennis, Jack Lambert, Percy Helton; D: Robert Aldrich; C: Ernest Laszlo. *MGM, FCT*

Kiss Me Goodbye 🎬🎬 1982 (PG) Young widow Fields can't shake the memory of her first husband, a charismatic but philandering Broadway choreographer, who's the antithesis of her boring but devoted professor fiance. She struggles with the charming ghost of her first husband, as well as her domineering mother, attempting to understand her own true feelings. Harmless but two-dimensional remake of "Dona Flor and Her Two Husbands." 101m/C VHS, Beta. Sally Field, James Caan, Jeff Bridges, Paul Dooley, Mildred Natwick, Claire Trevor; D: Robert Mulligan; W: Charlie Peters; M: Ralph Burns. *FOX*

Kiss Me, Guido 🎬🎬½ 1997 (R) Heterosexual and handsome Frankie (Scotti) is a Bronx born and raised pizza maker and De Niro wannabe who's not too bright. Apartment-hunting in Manhattan, he thinks an ad listing "GWM" stands for "guy with money" and mistakenly moves in with gay actor Warren (Barrile). Pokes fun at both Italian-American and gay stereotypes without offending or canonizing either group. Vitale and an excellent, if largely unknown, cast inject enough energy and humor to rise above the often predictable story. Low-budget independent sex farce that offers a promising start for first-time filmmaker Vitale. *CW:* Sexuality and strong language. 90m/C VHS, **Closed Caption.** Nick Scotti, Anthony Barrile, Craig Chester, Anthony DeSando, Christopher Lawford, Molly Price; D: Tony Vitale; W: Tony Vitale; C: Claudia Raschke; M: Randall Poster. *PAR*

Kiss Me Kate 🎬🎬🎬 1953 A married couple can't separate their real lives from their stage roles in this musical-comedy screen adaptation of Shakespeare's "Taming of the Shrew," based on Cole Porter's Broadway show. Bob Fosse bursts from the screen—particularly if you see the 3-D version—when he does his dance number. ♫Out of This World; From This Moment On; Wunderbar; So In Love; I Hate Men; Were Thine That Special Face; I've Come To Wive It Wealthily In Padua; Where Is The Life That Late I Led?; Always True To You Darling In My Fashion. 110m/C VHS, Beta, LV. Kathryn Grayson, Howard Keel, Ann Miller, Tommy Rall, Bob Fosse, Bobby Van, Keenan Wynn, James Whitmore; D: George Sidney; C: Charles Rosher; M: Andre Previn. Nominations: Academy Awards '53: Scoring of a Musical. *MGM, FCT*

Kiss Me, Kill Me 🎬½ *Devil's Witch; Baba Yaga; So Sweet, So Perverse; Cosi Dolce...Cosi Perversa; Baba Yaga—Devil Witch* 1969 (R) Confused woman is on the run after she may have murdered someone. 91m/C VHS, Beta. Carroll Baker, George Eastman, Isabelle DeFunes, Ely Gallo; D: Corrado Farina; W: Corrado Farina. *NO*

Kiss Me, Stupid! 🎬🎬 1964 (PG-13) Once condemned as smut, this lesser Billy Wilder effort now seems no worse than an average TV sitcom. Martin basically plays himself as a horny Vegas crooner stranded in the boondocks. A local songwriter wants Dino to hear his tunes but knows the cad will seduce his pretty wife, so he hires a floozy to pose as the tempting spouse. It gets better as it goes along, but the whole thing suffers from staginess, being an adaptation of an Italian play "L'Ora Della Fantasia" by Anna Bonacci. *CW:* Sex-related plot material. 126m/B VHS, Beta, LV, **Letterbox.** Dean Martin, Kim Novak, Ray Walston, Felicia Farr, Cliff Osmond, Barbara Pepper, Doro Merande, Howard McNear, Henry Gibson, John Fiedler, Mel Blanc; D: Billy Wilder; W: Billy Wilder, I.A.L. Diamond; C: Joseph LaShelle; M: Andre Previn. *MGM*

KISS Meets the Phantom of the Park 🎵½ *Attack of the Phantoms* 1978 The popular '70s rock band is featured in this Dr. Jekyll-esque Halloween horror tale, interspersed with musical numbers. **96m/C VHS, Beta.** Gene Simmons, Paul Stanley, Peter Criss, Ace Frehley, Anthony Zerbe, Deborah Ryan, John Dennis Johnston; **D:** Gordon Hessler. *MVD, WOV*

Kiss My Grits 🎬 1982 (PG) A good ole boy hightails it to Mexico with his girlfriend and son, chased by mobsters and the law. **101m/C VHS, Beta.** Bruce Davison, Anthony (Tony) Franciosa, Susan George, Bruno Kirby; **D:** Jack Starrett.

Kiss of a Killer 🎬🎬½ 1993 O'Toole is a mousy miss living a dead-end life with her nagging mother. But she has a secret—she spends weekends in a hotel, dressed to entice and picking up strangers. Involved in an auto mishap she's aided by a handsome mechanic, who turns out to be a rapist. When he accidentally kills his latest victim, he realizes our mystery woman can identify him and tries to find her. Based on the novel "The Point of Murder" by Margaret Yorke. Made for television. **93m/C VHS.** Annette O'Toole, Brian Wimmer, Eva Marie Saint, Greg Henry, Vic Polizos; **D:** Larry Elikann; **W:** David Warfield.

Kiss of Death 🎬🎬🎬 1947 Paroled when he turns state's evidence, Mature must now watch his back constantly. Widmark, in his film debut, seeks to destroy him. Police chief Donlevy tries to help. Filmed on location in New York, this gripping and gritty film is a vision of the most terrifying sort of existence, one where nothing is certain, and everything is dangerous. Excellent. **98m/B VHS, Closed Caption.** Victor Mature, Richard Widmark, Anne Grey, Brian Donlevy, Karl Malden, Coleen Gray; **D:** Henry Hathaway. Nominations: Academy Awards '47: Best Story, Best Supporting Actor (Widmark). *FCT*

Kiss of Death 🎬🎬 1977 Weird comedy about a shy undertaker's assistant and his attempts at first romance. Made for British television. **80m/C VHS.** *GB* David Threlfall, John Wheatley, Kay Adshead, Angela Curran; **D:** Mike Leigh; **W:** Mike Leigh. *WBF*

Kiss of Death 🎬🎬½ 1994 (R) Very loose contemporary remake of the 1947 film noir classic of the same name. Jimmy Kilmartin (Caruso) is a paroled car thief turned informant. He soon finds himself trapped in a web of deceit involving corrupt district attorneys and ruthless hoodlums like Little Junior (Cage, pumped up and playing against type), with no one to trust. Crime drama keeps the far-fetched genre conventions in check until the end. Caruso makes the transition from TV cop on "NYPD Blue" by not straying far from his small screen persona. Cage's standout performance may not be as chilling as Widmark's unforgettable debut in the original, but he's able to convey a level of mercilessness and depth that'll make you wince.**CW:** Violence; nudity; strong language. **100m/C VHS, LV, Closed Caption.** David Caruso, Nicolas Cage, Samuel L. Jackson, Helen Hunt, Stanley Tucci, Michael Rapaport, Ving Rhames, Anthony Heald, Anne Meara; **D:** Barbet Schroeder; **W:** Richard Price; **M:** Trevor Jones. Nominations: Golden Raspberry Awards '95: Worst New Star (Caruso). *FXV*

Kiss of the Spider Woman 🎬🎬🎬 1985 (R) From the novel by Manuel Puig, an acclaimed drama concerning two cell mates in a South American prison, one a revolutionary, the other a homosexual. Literate, haunting, powerful. **119m/C VHS, Beta, LV, 8mm, Closed Caption.** *BR* William Hurt, Raul Julia, Sonia Braga, Jose Lewgoy, Milton Goncalves, Nuno Leal Maia, Denise Dumont; **D:** Hector Babenco; **M:** Leonard Schrader; **M:** John Neschling, Wally Badarou. Academy Awards '85: Best Actor (Hurt); British Academy Awards '85: Best Actor (Hurt); Cannes Film Festival '85: Best Actor (Hurt); Independent Spirit Awards '86: Best Foreign Film; Los Angeles Film Critics Association Awards '85: Best Actor (Hurt); National Board of Review Awards '85: Best Actor (Hurt), Best Actor (Julia); Nominations: Academy Awards '85: Best Adapted Screenplay, Best Director (Babenco), Best Picture. *COL, BTV, NLC*

Kiss of the Tarantula 🎬 1975 (PG) Teen girl who lives with her family in a mortuary battles inner torment and vents anxiety by releasing her deadly pet spiders on those whom she despises. Eight-legged "Carrie" rip-off. **85m/C VHS, Beta.** Eric Mason; **D:** Chris Munger; **W:** Warren Hamilton. *MPI, FCT*

Kiss of the Vampire 🎬🎬½ *Kiss of Evil* 1962 Newlywed couple is stranded in Bavaria near a villa of vampires and are invited in by its charmingly evil owner. Fortunately, hubby manages to escape and finds a knowledgeable professor who unleashes a horde of bats to rout the bloodsuckers. Properly creepy; producer Hinds used the pseudonym John Elder for his screenplay. **88m/C VHS, Closed Caption.** *GB* Clifford Evans, Noel Willman, Edward De Souza, Jennifer Daniel, Barry Warren, Jacqueline Wallis, Peter Madden, Isobel Black, Vera Cook, Olga Dickie; **D:** Don Sharp; **W:** Anthony John Elder Hinds; **C:** Alan Hume; **M:** James Bernard. *USH*

Kiss or Kill 🎬🎬 1997 (R) Thieves/con artists and lovers Nikki (O'Connor) and Al (Day) head out across the Australian desert towards Perth when one of their schemes results in death. Since they've also got a videotape showing football player Zipper Doyle (Langrishe) engaged in pedophile activity, he's on their trail as are a couple of cops. But trouble also seems to follow them—everywhere the duo spend the night a dead body appears the next morning and soon the lovers begin wondering about each other. Quirky characters and fine performances from all concerned, even if the emotional core of the film is somewhat cold.**CW:** Some graphic sexuality, violence and language. **95m/C VHS, Closed Caption.** *AU* Frances O'Connor, Matt Day, Chris Haywood, Barry Otto, Max Cullen, Andrew S. Gilbert, Barry Langrishe, Jennifer Cluff; **D:** Bill Bennett; **W:** Bill Bennett; **C:** Malcolm McCulloch. Australian Film Institute '97: Best Director (Bennett), Best Film, Best Film Editing, Best Sound, Best Supporting Actor (Gilbert); Montreal World Film Festival '97: Best Actress (O'Connor); Nominations: Australian Film Institute '97: Best Actor (Day), Best Actress (O'Connor), Best Cinematography, Best Costume Design, Best Original Screenplay, Best Supporting Actor (Haywood). *USH*

Kiss Shot 🎬🎬 1989 Goldberg is a struggling single mother who loses her job but still must make the mortgage payments. She takes a job as a waitress but realizes it isn't going to pay the bills so she tries her hand as a pool hustler. Frantz is the promoter who finances her bets and Harewood, the pool-shooting playboy whose romantic advances are destroying her concentration. **88m/C VHS, Beta, Closed Caption.** Whoopi Goldberg, Dennis Franz, Dorian Harewood, David Marciano, Teddy Wilson; **D:** Jerry London; **M:** Stephen Dorff. *MOV*

Kiss the Girls 🎬🎬 1997 (R) After his niece is abducted, forensic psychologist Alex Cross (Freeman) joins the hunt for a lunatic who's kidnapping and collecting successful young women. After doctor Kate McTiernan (Judd), who also happens to be a kickboxer, escapes the sicko's love dungeon, she helps Cross track him down. Borrowing heavily from "Silence of the Lambs" and "Seven," this psycho-killer thriller falls short of both. Adapted from the novel by James Patterson.**CW:** Terror, violence and language. **117m/C VHS, Closed Caption.** Morgan Freeman, Ashley Judd, Cary Elwes, Tony Goldwyn, Jay O. Sanders, Bill Nunn, Brian Cox, Alex McArthur, Richard T. Jones, Jeremy Piven, William Converse-Roberts, Gina Ravera, Roma Maffia; **D:** Gary Fleder; **W:** David Klass; **C:** Aaron Schneider; **M:** Mark Isham. *PAR*

Kiss the Night 1987 (R) An unfortunate hooker falls head over heels for a man she had the pleasure of doing business with. To her chagrin, it is much harder to leave the street than she thought. A dramatic and timely presentation. **99m/C VHS.** Patsy Stephens, Warwick Moss, Gary Aron Cook; **D:** James Ricketson. *MCG*

Kiss Tomorrow Goodbye 🎬🎬 1950 A brutal, murderous escaped convict rises to crime-lord status before his inevitable downfall. Based on a novel by Horace McCoy. **102m/B VHS, LV.** James Cagney, Barbara Payton, Ward Bond, Luther Adler, Helena Carter, Steve Brodie, Rhys Williams; **D:** Gordon Douglas. *REP*

Kissed 🎬🎬 1996 The subject matter (necrophilia) is sure to give one pause though debut director Stopkewich hardly dwells on the prurient. Sandra Larson (Parker) has been obsessed with death and its rituals since childhood. So as a young adult it seems natural when she gets a job in a funeral home, preparing the bodies for embalming. Only Sandra's obsession leads her to begin making love (shown through a gauzy white light) to the corpses. She does attract the attention of a very alive medical student, Matt (Outerbridge), who becomes fascinated by Sandra's fetish and determined to make himself as appealing to her as the dead. Adapted from Barbara Gowdy's short story "We So Seldom Look on Love." **78m/C VHS.** *CA* Molly Parker, Peter Outerbridge, Jay Brazeau; **C:** Gregory Middleton; **M:** Don MacDonald. Genie Awards '97: Best Actress (Parker); Nominations: Genie Awards '97: Best Actor (Outerbridge), Best Director (Stopkewich), Best Film, Best Screenplay. *NYR*

Kisses for My President 🎬🎬½ 1964 Silly comedy about the first woman elected President and her trials and tribulations. MacMurray is the husband who has to adjust to the protocol of being "First Man." Bergen is miscast, but the other performances are just fine. **113m/C VHS.** Fred MacMurray, Polly Bergen, Arlene Dahl, Edward Andrews, Eli Wallach, Donald May; **D:** Curtis Bernhardt. Nominations: Academy Awards '64: Best Costume Design (B & W). *WAR*

Kisses in the Dark 🎬🎬 1997 Four short award-winning films. "Coriolis Effect" finds two daredevil tornado-chasers falling in love. "Solly's Diner" has a vagrant becoming a hero during a diner hold-up. "Looping" finds an egotistic Italian director deciding in the middle of shooting his big-budget Mafia musical that the material isn't worthy of him. "Joe" finds solace in his daily routine in a psych ward when an interloper disturbs his refuge. **75m/C VHS.** Jennifer Rubin, James Wilder, Dana Ashbrook, Corinne Bohrer, Ronald Guttman, Katherine Wallach; **Cameos:** Quentin Tarantino; **D:** Larry Hankin, Louis Venosta, Roger Paradiso, Sasha Wolf; **W:** Louis Venosta, Roger Paradiso, Sasha Wolf. *VNG*

Kissin' Cousins 🎬½ 1964 Air Force officer on a secluded base in the South discovers a local hillbilly is his double. Presley quickie that includes country tunes such as "Smokey Mountain Boy" and "Barefoot Ballad" as well as the title song. **96m/C VHS, Beta.** Elvis Presley, Arthur O'Connell, Jack Albertson, Glenda Farrell, Pam Austin, Yvonne Craig, Cynthia Pepper, Donald Woods, Tommy Farrell, Beverly Powers; **D:** Gene Nelson. *MGM*

Kissing a Fool 🎬½ 1998 (R) Movie asks the titillating question: Who will smart, pretty Sam marry? The unctuous Schwimmer character, Max, or the sensitive writer guy Max sets up with Sam to test her fidelity? Who cares. Hunt sets up the utterly lame opening premise as Sam's boss, who is throwing her a wedding and explains to guests how Sam and her intended met while the rote triangle scenario plays out in flashback. Schwimmer, as a Chicago sportscaster with a roving eye, plays nicely (and wisely) against type while Lee's novelist Jay, a supposedly close friend of Max, occupies a less gratifying role. Avital has little to do but does is well.**CW:** Strong language. **93m/C VHS, Closed Caption, DVD.** David Schwimmer, Jason Lee, Mili Avital, Bonnie Hunt, Vanessa Angel, Kari Wuhrer, Frank Medrano, Bitty Schram, Judy Greer; **D:** Doug Ellin; **W:** Doug Ellin, James Frey; **C:** Thomas Del Ruth; **M:** Joseph Vitarelli. *USH*

The Kissing Place 1990 A woman who abducted her "son" years ago tracks the boy to New York City to prevent him from finding his biological family. **90m/C VHS, Beta, Closed Caption.**

Meredith Baxter, David Ogden Stiers; **D:** Tony Wharmby; **W:** Richard Altabef, Cynthia A. Cherbak. *PAR*

Kissinger and Nixon 🎬🎬½ 1996 Intrigue, ambition, and backbiting politics consume the 18 weeks leading up to the signing of the Vietnam peace accords in Paris in January, 1973. Egotistical Kissinger (Silver) is prepared to sacrifice South Vietnam for the sake of his own ambitions (and an end to the conflict) while a distrustful Nixon (Bridges) lurks uneasily in the background. TV docudrama offers little insight; based on Walter Isaacson's biography "Kissinger." **94m/C VHS.** Ron Silver, Beau Bridges, Matt Frewer, Ron White, George Takei, Kenneth Welsh; **D:** Daniel Petrie; **W:** Lionel Chetwynd; **M:** Jonathan Goldsmith. *TTC*

Kit Carson 🎬🎬 1940 Frontiersman Kit Carson leads a wagon train to California, fighting off marauding Indians all the way. **97m/B VHS, Beta.** Jon Hall, Dana Andrews, Ward Bond, Lynn Bari; **D:** George B. Seitz. *VTR*

The Kitchen Toto 🎬🎬🎬 1987 (PG-13) Set in 1950 Kenya as British rule was being threatened by Mau Mau terrorists. A young black boy is torn between the British for whom he works and the terrorists who want him to join them. Complex and powerful story of the Kenyan freedom crusade. **96m/C VHS, Beta, LV, Closed Caption.** *GB* Bob Peck, Phyllis Logan, Robert Urquhart, Edward Judd, Edwin Mahinda, Kirsten Hughes; **D:** Harry Hook; **W:** Harry Hook; **C:** Roger Deakins; **M:** John Keane. *WAR*

Kitty and the Bagman 🎬🎬 1982 (R) A comedy about two rival madames who ruled Australia in the 1920s. **95m/C VHS, Beta.** *AU* Liddy Clark; **D:** Donald Crombie.

Kitty Foyle 🎬🎬🎬 1940 From the novel by Christopher Morley, Rogers portrays the white-collar working girl whose involvement with a married man presents her with both romantic and social conflicts. **108m/B VHS, Beta.** Ginger Rogers, Dennis (Stanley Morner) Morgan, James Craig, Gladys Cooper, Ernest Cossart, Eduardo Ciannelli; **D:** Sam Wood. Academy Awards '40: Best Actress (Rogers); Nominations: Academy Awards '40: Best Director (Wood), Best Picture, Best Screenplay, Best Sound. *CCB, FCT, BTV*

The Klansman 🎬 *Burning Cross; KKK* 1974 (R) Race relations come out on the short end in this film about a sheriff trying to keep the lid on racial tensions in a southern town. Even the big-name cast can't save what comes off as a nighttime soaper rather than a serious drama. **112m/C VHS, Closed Caption.** Lee Marvin, Richard Burton, Cameron Mitchell, Lola Falana, Luciana Paluzzi, Linda Evans, O.J. Simpson; **D:** Terence Young; **W:** Samuel Fuller. *PAR, FCT*

Kleptomania 🎬½ 1994 (R) Socialite meets a runaway and discoers they're both kleptomaniacs. **CW:** Language; some sexuality and violence. **90m/C VHS.** Amy Irving, Patsy Kensit, Victor Garber; **D:** Don Boyd; **W:** Don Boyd. *AVE*

Klondike Annie 🎬🎬½ 1936 West stars as a woman on the lam for a murder (self-defense) who heads out for the Yukon aboard McLaglen's ship. He falls for her, finds out about her problems, and helps her with a scam to pass herself off as a missionary, only she begins to take her saving souls seriously (although in her own risque style). **77m/B VHS.** Mae West, Victor McLaglen, Philip Reed, Helen Jerome Eddy, Harry Beresford, Harold Huber, Conway Tearle, Esther Howard; **D:** Raoul Walsh; **W:** Mae West. *USH, BTV*

Klondike Fever 🎬½ *Jack London's Klondike Fever* 1979 (PG) Join the young Jack London as he travels from San Francisco to the Klondike fields during the Great Gold Rush of 1898. **118m/C VHS, Beta.** Rod Steiger, Angie Dickinson, Lorne Greene; **D:** Peter Carter; **M:** Hagood Hardy. *NO*

Klute 🎬🎬🎬½ 1971 (R) A small-town policeman (Sutherland) comes to New York in search of a missing friend and gets involved with a prostitute/would-be actress (Fonda) being stalked by a killer. Intelligent, gripping drama. **114m/C VHS, Beta, LV, Letterbox.** Jane Fonda, Donald Sutherland, Charles Cioffi, Roy Scheider, Rita Gam, Jean Stapleton; **D:** Alan J.

Pakula; **C:** Gordon Willis. Academy Awards '71: Best Actress (Fonda); Golden Globe Awards '72: Best Actress—Drama (Fonda); New York Film Critics Awards '71: Best Actress (Fonda); National Society of Film Critics Awards '71: Best Actress (Fonda); Nominations: Academy Awards '71: Best Story & Screenplay. *WAR, BTV*

The Klutz 🎬🎬 1973 A bumbling fool, on the way to visit his girlfriend, becomes accidentally embroiled in a bank robbery and other ridiculous mishaps. Light French comedy; dubbed. **87m/C VHS, Beta.** *FR* Claude Michaud, Louise Portal, Guy Provost; **D:** Pierre Rose.

The Knack 🎬🎬🎬 *The Knack...and How to Get It* 1965 Amusing, fast-paced adaptation of the play by Ann Jellicoe. Schoolteacher Crawford is baffled by his tenant Brooks' extreme luck with the ladies so Brooks decides to teach him the "knack" of picking up women. Crawford promptly falls for the first woman (Tushingham) he meets. Swinging London at its most mod. **84m/B VHS.** *GB* Michael Crawford, Ray Brooks, Rita Tushingham, Donal Donnelly; **D:** Richard Lester; **W:** Charles Wood; **C:** David Watkin; **M:** John Barry. *MGM*

Knife in the Head 🎬🎬 *Messer Im Kopf* 1978 Biogeneticist Berthold Hoffman (Ganz) is meeting his wife (Winkler) at the left-wing youth centre where she works when there's a police raid and Berthold is shot in the head. He awakens in the hospital having lost both his memory and all physical co-ordination. Determined to battle his disabilities, Berthold also becomes the pawn in a political game between the police and political dissidents. In German with English subtitles. **108m/C VHS.** *GE* Bruno Ganz, Angela Winkler, Hans Honig, Hans Brenner, Udo Samel, Carla Egerer; **D:** Reinhard Hauff; **W:** Peter Schneider. *NYF*

Knife in the Water 🎬🎬🎬🎬 *Noz w Wodzie* 1962 A journalist, his wife and a hitchhiker spend a day aboard a sailboat. Sex and violence can't be far off. Tense psychological drama. Served as director Polanski's debut. In Polish with English subtitles. **94m/B VHS, Beta, LV.** *PL* Leon Niemczyk, Jolanta Umecka, Zygmunt Malandowicz; **D:** Roman Polanski; **W:** Jerzy Skolimowski, Roman Polanski. Nominations: Academy Awards '63: Best Foreign Language Film. *HMV, FOX, BTV*

Knight Moves 🎬🎬 1993 (R) Suspenseful thriller about a series of murders which take place at an international resort where a championship chess match is underway. The prime suspect is a chess master who has an unlikely affair with a beautiful police psychologist called in to decipher the mind of the murderer. Filmed in the Pacific Northwest. **CW:** Language, strong violence, and sexuality. **105m/C VHS, LV, Closed Caption.** Christopher Lambert, Diane Lane, Tom Skerritt, Daniel Baldwin; **D:** Carl Schenkel; **W:** Brad Mirman; **M:** Anne Dudley. *REP*

Knight Without Armour 🎬🎬🎬 1937 A journalist opposed to the Russian monarchy falls in love with the daughter of a czarist minister in this classic romantic drama. **107m/B VHS, Beta.** *GB* Marlene Dietrich, Robert Donat; **D:** Jacques Feyder; **C:** Harry Stradling; **M:** Miklos Rozsa.

Knightriders 🎬🎬½ 1981 (R) The story of a troupe of motorcyclists who are members of a traveling Renaissance Fair and look and act like modern-day Knights of the Round Table. Their battles center around who is the bravest and strongest, and who deserves to be king. **145m/C VHS, Beta, LV.** Ed Harris, Gary Lahti, Tom Savini, Amy Ingersoll; **D:** George A. Romero; **W:** George A. Romero. *FUS*

Knights 🎬½ 1993 (R) In a futuristic wasteland a young martial-arts warrior (Long) and a cyborg (Kristofferson) team up to battle rebel cyborgs that have discovered a new source of fuel—human blood. **CW:** Futuristic violence. **89m/C VHS, Beta, Closed Caption.** Kathy Long, Kris Kristofferson, Lance Henriksen, Scott Paulin, Gary Daniels; **D:** Albert Pyun; **W:** Albert Pyun. *PAR*

Knights & Emeralds 🎬½ 1987 (PG) Cross-cultural rivalries and romances develop between members of two high school marching bands in a British factory town as the national band championships draw near. **90m/C VHS, Beta, Closed Caption.** *GB* Christopher Wild, Beverly Hills, Warren Mitchell; **D:** Ian Emes; **M:** Colin Towns. *WAR*

Knights of the City 🎬 1985 (R) Miami street gangs fight each other over their "turf." One leader decides to opt out, using music. 🎵Let the Music Play; Cry of the City; Jailhouse Rap; T.K. and Jessie Rap; Kurtis Blow Rap; Bounce; My Part of Town; Can You Feel It; Love Goes Up and Down. **87m/C VHS, Beta.** Nicholas Campbell, John Mengatti, Wendy Barry, Stoney Jackson, Janine Turner, Michael Ansara; **D:** Leon Isaac Kennedy, Dominic Orlando; **W:** Leon Isaac Kennedy. *VTR*

Knights of the Range 🎬½ 1940 Vintage western. **66m/B VHS, Beta.** Russell Hayden, Victor Jory, Jean Parker, Britt Wood, J. Farrell MacDonald, Eddie Dean; **D:** Lesley Selander. *VCN, MLB, GPV*

Knights of the Round Table 🎬🎬½ 1953 The story of the romantic triangle between King Arthur, Sir Lancelot, and Guinevere during the civil wars of 6th-century England. **106m/C VHS, Beta, LV, Letterbox.** Robert Taylor, Ava Gardner, Mel Ferrer, Anne Crawford, Felix Aylmer, Stanley Baker; **D:** Richard Thorpe; **C:** Frederick A. (Freddie) Young; **M:** Miklos Rozsa. Nominations: Academy Awards '53: Best Art Direction/Set Decoration (Color), Best Sound. *MGM*

Knock Off 1998 (R) CIA agent Rochon works with jeans manufacturers Van Damme and Schneider when a conspiracy to arm a terrorist organization is discovered amidst the Chinese takeover of Hong Kong. Not yet reviewed. **CW:** Continuous violence and brief language. **?m/C VHS.** Jean-Claude Van Damme, Paul Sorvino, Lela Rochon, Rob Schneider, Michael Wong; **D:** Tsui Hark; **W:** Steven De Souza; **C:** Arthur Wong. *NYR*

Knock on Any Door 🎬🎬 1949 A young hoodlum from the slums is tried for murdering a cop. He is defended by a prominent attorney who has known him from childhood. **100m/B VHS, Beta, LV.** Humphrey Bogart, John Derek, George Macready; **D:** Nicholas Ray; **W:** Daniel Taradash, John Monks Jr.; **C:** Burnett Guffey. *COL*

Knock Outs 🎬 1992 Samantha not only loses her shirt at a sorority strip poker marathon but she loses her tuition money to a gang of biker chicks. Then Samantha and a bevy of bikini-clad friends decide to pose for a swimsuit calendar to earn some cash but are secretly videotaped in the nude by some local sleaze promoters. Tired of being taken advantage of these lovelies take up martial arts and challenge their nefarious girl biker rivals to a winner-take-all wrestling match, not forgetting about the purveyors of the not-so-secret videotape. **90m/C VHS.** Chona Jackson, Cindy Rome, Brad Zutaut; **D:** John Bowen.

The Knockout/Dough and Dynamite 🎬🎬🎬 1914 Two Chaplin shorts: "The Knockout" (1914), in which Charlie referees a big fight; "Dough and Dynamite" (1914), in which a labor dispute at a bake shop leaves Charlie in charge when the regular baker walks out. **54m/B VHS, Beta.** Charlie Chaplin, Fatty Arbuckle, Mabel Normand, The Keystone Cops; **D:** Charlie Chaplin, Sydney Chaplin. *VYY*

Knute Rockne: All American 🎬🎬🎬 *A Modern Hero* 1940 Life story of Notre Dame football coach Knute Rockne, who inspired many victories with his powerful speeches. Reagan, as the dying George Gipp, utters that now-famous line, "Tell the boys to win one for the Gipper." **96m/B VHS, Beta.** Ronald Reagan, Pat O'Brien, Gale Page, Donald Crisp, John Qualen; **D:** Lloyd Bacon. National Film Registry '97. *MGM, FHE*

Kojak: The Belarus File 🎬🎬 1985 The bald-headed detective of prime-time television fame searches for a neo-Nazi who is killing Holocaust survivors in New York. Made for television. **95m/C VHS, Beta.** Telly Savalas, Suzanne Pleshette, Max von Sydow, George Savalas; *D:* Robert Markow-itz. *USU*

Kojiro ✶✶✶ 1967 A sprawling epic by prolific Japanese director Inagaki about a dashing rogue's bid for power in feudal times. With English subtitles. 152m/C VHS, Beta. *JP* Kikunosuke Onoe, Tatsuya Nakadai; *D:* Hiroshi Inagaki. *VDA*

Kolberg ✶✶ *Burning Hearts* 1945 The true story of a Prussian town heroically withstanding Napoleon. Produced by Joseph Goebbels in the last days of the Third Reich, it is best remembered as the film whose expensive production and momentous use of real German soldiers, supplies, and ammunition eventually helped to feed the Axis war machine. In German with English subtitles. 118m/C VHS, Beta. *GE* Kristina Soderbaum, Heinrich George, Horst Caspar, Paul Wegener; *D:* Veit Harlan. *FCT, IHF, GLV*

Kolya ✶✶✶ 1996 (PG-13) Set in the late '80s, just before the Velvet Revolution ended Soviet domination of Czechoslovakia, womanizing Prague cellist Louka (Sverak) agrees to marry (for money) the Russian Klara (Safrankova) who wants Czech papers. She soon clears out to join her lover in Berlin and Louka finds himself saddled with her five-year-old son, Kolya (Chaliman). Grumpy Louka isn't obvious dad material and they don't even speak the same language but the kid (who's adorable without being cloying) manages to worm his way into his new life. Czech with subtitles or dubbed. *CW:* Some sensuality. 105m/C VHS, LV, Closed Caption. *CZ* Zdenek Sverak, Andrej Chalimon, Libuse Safrankova; *D:* Jan Sverak; *W:* Zdenek Sverak; *C:* Vladimir Smutny; *M:* Ondrej Soukup. Academy Awards '96: Best Foreign Film; Golden Globe Awards '97: Best Foreign Film; Nominations: British Academy Awards '96: Best Foreign Film. *TOU*

Konrad 199? Konrad, an "instant" child made in a factory, is accidentally delivered to an eccentric woman. The factory wants him back when the mistake is discovered, but Konrad stands up against it. Includes a viewers' guide. Part of the "Wonderworks" series. 110m/C VHS. Ned Beatty, Polly Holliday, Max Wright, Huckleberry Fox; *D:* Neil Cox; *W:* Malcolm Marmorstein. *HMV, BTV, FCT*

Korczak ✶✶✶ 1990 Based on the life of Dr. Janusz Korczak, an outspoken critic of the Nazis, who ran the Jewish orphanage in Warsaw, Poland, and accompanied 200 children to to the Treblinka concentration camp. Harshly poetic film quietly details Polish resistance to the Nazi terror. Criticized for end scenes of the children romping in the countryside, implying that they were somehow freed—since the director did not want to show the children actually entering the gas chambers, he used this allegory to imply that their souls were freed. In Polish with English subtitles. 118m/C VHS. *PL* Wojtek Pszoniak, Ewa Dalkowska, Piotr Kozlowski, Marzena Trybala, Wojciech Klata, Adam Siemion; *D:* Andrzej Wajda; *W:* Agnieszka Holland. *NYF, FCT*

Koroshi ✶✶½ 1967 Secret Agent John Drake is dispatched to Hong Kong to disband a secret society who is killing off international political figures. 100m/C VHS, Beta. Patrick McGoohan, Kenneth Griffith, Yoko Tani; *D:* Michael Truman, Peter Yates. *MPI*

Kostas ✶✶ 1979 (R) A migrant Greek taxi driver romantically pursues a wealthy Australian divorcee in England. 88m/C VHS, Beta. Takis Emmanuel, Wendy Hughes; *D:* Paul Cox. *ART, VES*

Kotch ✶✶✶ 1971 (PG) An elderly man resists his children's attempts to retire him. Warm detailing of old age with a splendid performance by Matthau. Lemmon's directorial debut. 113m/C VHS. Walter Matthau, Deborah Winters, Felicia Farr; *D:* Jack Lemmon; *M:* Marvin Hamlisch. Golden Globe Awards '72: Best Song ("Life Is What You Make It"); Writers Guild of America '71: Best Adapted Screenplay; Nominations: Academy Awards '71: Best Actor (Matthau), Best Film Editing, Best Song ("Life Is What You Make It"), Best Sound. *FOX*

Kounterfeit ✶✶ 1996 (R) Hopscotch (Hawkes) finds three million in counterfeit cash and tries to get some real cash for the fake stuff with his topless-bar owner buddy Frankie (Payne)

serving as muscle. But things go bad. Bernsen has little more than a cameo role. *CW:* Language, violence, sexual situations. 87m/C VHS, LV, Closed Caption. Andrew Hawkes, Bruce Payne, Hilary Swank, Michael Gross, Mark Paul Gosselaar, Corbin Bernsen; *D:* John Mallory Asher; *W:* Jay Irwin, David Chase; *C:* Karl Herrmann. *ART*

Kowloon Assignment ✶ 1977 Comic book superhero Golgo 13 comes to life in this action film dealing with a drug war in the Hong Kong underground. 93m/C VHS, Beta. Sonny Chiba. *NO*

Koyaanisqatsi ✶✶✶✶ 1983 A mesmerizing film that takes an intense look at modern life (the movie's title is the Hopi word for "life out of balance"). Without dialogue or narration, it brings traditional background elements, landscapes and cityscapes, up front to produce a unique view of the structure and mechanics of our daily lives. Riveting and immensely powerful. A critically acclaimed score by Glass, and Reggio's cinematography prove to be the perfect match to this brilliant film. Followed by "Powaqqatsi." 87m/C VHS, Beta, LV. *D:* Godfrey Reggio; *M:* Philip Glass. Los Angeles Film Critics Association Awards '83: Best Score. *MVD, FCT, MLB*

Kramer vs. Kramer ✶✶✶½ 1979 (PG) Highly acclaimed family drama about an advertising executive husband and child left behind when their wife and mother leaves on a quest to find herself, and the subsequent courtroom battle for custody when she returns. Hoffman and Streep give exacting performances as does young Henry. Successfully moves you from tears to laughter and back again. Based on the novel by Avery Corman. 105m/C VHS, Beta, LV, Letterbox, Closed Caption. Dustin Hoffman, Meryl Streep, Jane Alexander, Justin Henry, Howard Duff, JoBeth Williams; *D:* Robert Benton; *W:* Robert Benton; *C:* Nestor Almendros. Academy Awards '79: Best Actor (Hoffman), Best Adapted Screenplay, Best Director (Benton), Best Picture, Best Supporting Actress (Streep); Directors Guild of America Awards '79: Best Director (Benton); Golden Globe Awards '80: Best Actor—Drama (Hoffman), Best Film—Drama, Best Screenplay, Best Supporting Actress (Streep); Los Angeles Film Critics Association Awards '79: Best Actor (Hoffman), Best Director (Benton), Best Film, Best Screenplay, Best Supporting Actress (Streep); National Board of Review Awards '79: Best Supporting Actress (Streep); New York Film Critics Awards '79: Best Actor (Hoffman), Best Film, Best Supporting Actress (Streep); National Society of Film Critics Awards '79: Best Actor (Hoffman), Best Director (Benton), Best Supporting Actress (Streep); Writers Guild of America '79: Best Adapted Screenplay; Nominations: Academy Awards '79: Best Cinematography, Best Film Editing, Best Supporting Actor (Henry), Best Supporting Actress (Alexander). *COL, BTV*

The Krays ✶✶✶½ 1990 (R) An account of British gangsters Reggie and Ronnie Kray, the brothers who ruled London's East End with brutality and violence, making them bizarre celebrities of the '60s. The leads are portrayed by Gary and Martin Kemp, founders of the British pop group Spandau Ballet. 119m/C VHS, LV, 8mm, Letterbox, Closed Caption. *GB* Gary Kemp, Martin Kemp, Billie Whitelaw, Steven Berkoff, Susan Fleetwood, Charlotte Cornwell, Jimmy Jewel, Avis Bunnage, Kate Hardie, Alfred Lynch, Tom Bell, Victor Spinetti, Barbara Ferris, Julia Migenes-Johnson, John McEnery, Sadie Frost, Norman Rossington, Murray Melvin; *D:* Peter Medak; *W:* Philip Ridley; *M:* Michael Kamen. *COL, FCT*

Kriemhilde's Revenge ✶✶✶✶ *Die Nibelungen* 1924 The second film, following "Siegfried," of Lang's "Die Nibelungen," a lavish silent version of the Teutonic legends Wagner's "Ring of the Nibelungen" was based upon. In this episode, Kriemhilde avenges Siegfried's death by her marriage to the Kings of the Huns, thus fulfilling a prophecy of destruction. 95m/B VHS, LV. *GE* Paul Richter, Margareta Schoen, Theodore Loos, Hanna Ralph, Rudolf Klein-Rogge; *D:* Fritz Lang. *CCB, IHF, REP*

Krippendorf's Tribe ✶✶ 1998 (PG-13) James Krippendorf (Dreyfuss), a widowed anthropology professor, returns from an expedition to New Guinea after squandering all his grant money on his kids. Since he didn't find the rare tribe he was sent there for, he makes up tribal stories based on his own kids. When skeptic Tomlin demands proof of his amazing discoveries, the Krippendorf clan and an over-eager colleague (Elfman) go native in front of the camera. Works best when at its silliest, and in fact, could have been a fun family film. Unfortunately, most of the humor is of the smutty variety, involving mating rituals, tribal sex toys, circumcision jokes, and so on. *CW:* Sexual humor. 98m/C VHS. Richard Dreyfuss, Jenna Elfman, Natasha Lyonne, Gregory Edward Smith, Stephen Root, Elaine Stritch, Tom Poston, David Ogden Stiers, Lily Tomlin, Doris Belack, Julio Mechoso, Barbara Williams, Zakes Mokae, Carl Michael Linder, Siobhan Fallon; *D:* Todd Holland; *W:* Charlie Peters; *C:* Dean Cundey; *M:* Bruce Broughton. *TOU*

Kronos ✶✶½ 1957 A giant robot from space drains the Earth of all its energy resources. A good example of this genre from the 50s. Includes previews of coming attractions from classic science fiction films. 78m/B VHS, LV, Letterbox. Jeff Morrow, Barbara Lawrence, John Emery; *D:* Kurt Neumann. *EEL, MLB*

Krull ✶✶ 1983 (PG) Likeable fantasy adventure set in a world peopled by creatures of myth and magic. A prince embarks on a quest to find the Glaive (a magical weapon) and then rescues his young bride, taken by the Beast of the Black Fortress. 121m/C VHS, Beta, LV, Closed Caption. *GB* Ken Marshall, Lysette Anthony, Freddie Jones, Francesca Annis, Liam Neeson; *D:* Peter Yates; *M:* James Horner. *GKK*

Krush Groove ✶ 1985 (R) The world of rap music is highlighted in this movie, the first all-rap musical. ♪King of Rock; Don't You Dog Me; A Love Bizarre; Pick Up the Pace; If I Ruled the World; Holly Rock; It's Like That; Feel the Spin; I Can't Live Without My Radio. 95m/C VHS, Beta, LV, Closed Caption. Blair Underwood, Eron Tabor, Kurtis Blow, Sheila E; *D:* Michael A. Schultz. *WAR*

K2: The Ultimate High ✶✶ 1992 (R) Two men, one a skirt-chasing lawyer, the other a happily married physicist, tackle the world's second largest mountain—the K-2 in Kashmir, northern Pakistan. They encounter a number of dangers, including an ascent of sheer rock face, an avalanche, and a fall down perpendicular mountain ice, but even the exciting mountain-climbing scenes can't hold up this watered down movie. The film was actually shot on Canada's Mount Waddington. Based on the play by Patrick Meyers. 104m/C VHS, Beta, Closed Caption. Michael Biehn, Matt Craven, Raymond J. Barry, Luca Bercovici, Patricia Charbonneau, Julia Nickson-Soul, Hiroshi Fujioka, Jamal Shah; *D:* Franc Roddam; *W:* Patrick Meyers, Scott Roberts. *PAR*

Kuffs ✶✶ 1992 (PG-13) Slater stars as George Kuffs, a young guy who reluctantly joins his brother's highly respected private security team in this original action comedy. After his brother is gunned down in the line of duty, George finds himself the new owner of the business. Out to avenge his brother, George pursues a crooked art dealer as he battles crime on the streets of San Francisco. Worthwhile premise is hampered by a predictable plot and mediocre acting. 102m/C VHS, Beta, LV, Closed Caption. Christian Slater, Tony Goldwyn, Milla Jovovich, Bruce Boxleitner, Troy Evans, George de la Pena, Leon Rippy; *D:* Bruce A. Evans; *W:* Bruce A. Evans, Raynold Gideon; *M:* Harold Faltermeyer. *USH*

Kull the Conqueror ✶✶½ 1997 (PG-13) Sorbo goes from TV's heroic Hercules to action-fantasy hero Kull, a slave who becomes the warrior king of a mythic land. Overthrown by a corrupt nobility, Kull begins a perilous journey to find the one weapon that will destroy the she-demon Akivasha (Carrere) and save the land of Valusia.

Lots of action, although the PG-13 rating keeps some of the mayhem less bloody than might be expected for this genre. Based on the '30s character created by pulp writer Robert E. Howard, who also originated "Conan the Barbarian." *CW:* Fantasy action violence and sensuality. **96m/C VHS, LV, Closed Caption, DVD.** Kevin Sorbo, Tia Carrere, Thomas Ian Griffith, Karina Lombard, Litefoot, Harvey Fierstein, Roy Brocksmith, Douglas Henshall; *D:* John Nicolella; *W:* Charles Edward Pogue; *C:* Rodney Charters; *M:* Joel Goldsmith. *USH*

Kundun 🎬🎬🎬 **1997 (PG-13)** Scorsese's cinematic portrait of the life of the young 14th Dalai Lama from 1937 through 1959, when he was forced to flee Chinese-occupied Tibet and live in exile in India. The incredibly detailed and sumptuous Tibetan journey begins with the discovery of the young boy as the Buddha reborn and uses different actors to portray him through young adulthood. Dramatic depiction of the Chairman Mao-ordered slaughter of Tibetan nuns and monks around the young Kundun illustrates theme of the dilemmas facing a nonviolent man in an increasingly violent world. The adult Dalai Lama's (Tsarong) meeting with cartoonishly evil incarnate Chairman Mao Zedong (Lin) mars an otherwise realistic and honest portrayal. Made with the cooperation of the 14th Dalai Lama, the story reflects the director's yen for accuracy and integrity. Scorsese's gamble on using a cast of non-professional Tibetan refugees pays off. Beautiful scenery and dreamy Philip Glass score set the proper mood. *CW:* Violent images. **134m/C VHS.** Tanzin Thuthob Tsarong, Robert Lin; *D:* Martin Scorsese; *W:* Melissa Mathison; *C:* Roger Deakins; *M:* Philip Glass. New York Film Critics Awards '97: Best Cinematography; National Society of Film Critics Awards '97: Best Cinematography; Nominations: Academy Awards '97: Best Art Direction/Set Decoration, Best Cinematography, Best Costume Design, Best Original Score; Golden Globe Awards '98: Best Original Score. *TOU*

Kung Fu 🎬🎬½ **1972** A fugitive Buddhist quasi-Asian martial arts master accused of murder in his native land, roams across the Old West fighting injustice. Served as a pilot for the successful television series and was reincarnated 14 years later in the sequel, "Kung Fu: The Movie." **75m/C VHS, Beta.** Keith Carradine, David Carradine, Barry Sullivan, Keye Luke; *D:* Jerry Thorpe. *WAR*

Kung Fu Avengers 🎬 **1985** On his way to a karate show at Madison Square Garden, our hero Li confronts the abominable Mr. Chin and his deadly henchman. Another foot-stomper. **90m/C VHS, Beta.** Bruce Li, Carl Scott, Jim James, Ku Feng.

Kung Fu Commandos 🎬 **1980 (R)** Five martial arts masters must face an evil warlord's army to rescue a captured agent. **90m/C VHS, Beta.** John Liu, Shangkuan Ling-Feng. *GEM*

Kung Fu Massacre 🎬 **1982 (R)** Farmers hire hard-handed mercenaries to fight evil war lords. **90m/C VHS, Beta.** Yangzi, Pi Li Lee. *ART*

Kung Fu Rebels 🎬½ **1980** Rebels are fearsome enough, but when they're kung fu masters, the establishment has real trouble on its hands. **90m/C VHS, Beta.** Wang Chung, Wen Ching Lung, Chang Mei. *NO*

Kung Fu: The Movie 🎬🎬½ **1986** Carradine reprises his role as Kwai Chang Caine from the television show of the '70s. In this made-for-television fare he's hunted by evil warlord Mako, who's involved in the California opium trade. Mako sends assassin Lee (son of martial-arts star Bruce) after Caine. Luke appears in flashbacks as the young Grasshopper's blind mentor, Master Po. **93m/C VHS, Beta.** David Carradine, Mako, Brandon Lee, Keye Luke, Kerrie Keane, Martin Landau, William Lucking, Luke Askew, Benson Fong; *D:* Richard Lang. *WAR*

Kuni Lemel in Tel Aviv 🎬🎬½ **1977** The bungling folk-hero of the shtetl of 100 years ago is updated to the present. Grandpa Kuni is now 80 and living in Brooklyn. Anxious to see the family line continue, he offers five million dollars to the first of his twin grandsons to marry a nice Jewish girl and settle in Israel. However, the grandsons have plans of their own which conflict with Grandpa's. In Hebrew with English subtitles. **90m/C VHS.** *IS* Mike Burstyn, Mandy Rice-Davies; *D:* Yoel Silberg. *ERG*

Kurt Vonnegut's Harrison Bergeron 🎬🎬½ *Harrison Bergeron* **1995 (R)** In the year 2053 the American government has gone to absurd lengths to ensure equality. Mediocrity is championed and everyone is forced to wear metallic headbands that stifle intellect through electronic impulses. Too bad for Harrison Bergeron (Astin), a smart young man being punished for his intelligence. But there's a secret underground elite offering Harrison the chance to think freely, though this power comes with a price. Adapted from Vonnegut's 1961 short story; made for cable TV. *CW:* Language, and for some sexuality and violence. **99m/C VHS, Closed Caption.** Sean Astin, Christopher Plummer, Miranda de Pencier, Nigel Bennett, Buck Henry, Eugene Levy, Howie Mandel, Andrea Martin; *D:* Bruce Pittman; *W:* Arthur Crimm. *REP*

Kurt Vonnegut's Monkey House 🎬🎬🎬 **199?** Dramatization of four short stories from Vonnegut's "Welcome to the Monkey House" collection, including a twist on the familiar Frankenstein tale. Made for cable television. **100m/C VHS.** Frank Langella. *PBS*

Kwaidan 🎬🎬🎬🎬 **1964** A haunting, stylized quartet of supernatural stories, each with a surprise ending. Adapted from the stories of Lafcadio Hearn, an American author who lived in Japan just before the turn of the century. The visual effects are splendid. In Japanese with English subtitles. **164m/C VHS, Beta, LV, Letterbox.** *JP* Michiyo Aratama, Rentaro Mikuni, Katsuo Nakamura, Keiko Kishi, Tatsuya Nakadai, Takashi Shimura; *D:* Masaki Kobayashi; *M:* Toru Takemitsu. Cannes Film Festival '65: Grand Jury Prize; Nominations: Academy Awards '65: Best Foreign Language Film. *VYY, NOS, SNC*

L.627 🎬🎬🎬 **1992** Melancholy police procedural about dedicated veteran narcotics cop Lulu (Bezace) who works with a small and ill-equipped Parisian drug squad prone to taking the law into their own hands. Lulu constantly finds himself thwarted by obtuse bureaucrats while his life is disturbed by an informant—a young, drug-addicted prostitute who has disappeared and whom Lulu desires to protect. Film title refers to the French anti-drug statute. French with subtitles. **145m/C VHS.** *FR* Didier Bezace, Jean-Paul Comart, Cecile Garcia-Fogel, Lara Guirao, Charlotte Kady, Jean-Roger Milo, Philippe Torreton, Nils Tavernier; *D:* Bertrand Tavernier; *W:* Bertrand Tavernier, Michel Alexandre; *M:* Philippe Sarde. *KIV*

L.A. Bad 🎬 **1985 (R)** A Puerto Rican street thug learns he has cancer, and must come to terms with his own impending death. **101m/C VHS, Beta.** Esai Morales, Janice Rule, John Phillip Law, Chuck Bail, Carrie Snodgress. *VTR*

La Balance 🎬🎬🎬 **1982 (R)** An underworld stool pigeon is recruited by the Parisian police to blow the whistle on a murderous mob. Baye, as a prostitute in love with the pimp-stoolie, is a standout. Critically acclaimed; French with subtitles. **103m/C VHS, Beta, Closed Caption.** *FR* Philippe Leotard, Nathalie Baye, Bob Swaim; *D:* Reymond LePlont; *M:* Roland Bocquet. Cesar Awards '83: Best Actor (Leotard), Best Actress (Baye), Best Film. *FOX*

La Bamba 🎬🎬🎬 **1987 (PG-13)** A romantic biography of the late 1950s pop idol Ritchie Valens, concentrating on his stormy relationship with his half-brother, his love for his WASP girlfriend, and his tragic, sudden death in the famed plane crash that also took the lives of Buddy Holly and the Big Bopper. Soundtrack features Setzer, Huntsberry, Crenshaw, and Los Lobos as, respectively, Eddie Cochran, the Big Bopper, Buddy Holly, and a Mexican bordello band. **99m/C VHS, Beta, LV, 8mm, Closed Caption.** Lou Diamond Phillips, Esai Morales, Danielle von Zerneck, Joe Pantoliano, Brian Setzer, Marshall Crenshaw, Howard Huntsberry, Rosana De Soto, Elizabeth Pena, Rick Dees; *D:* Luis Valdez; *W:* Luis Valdez; *M:* Carlos Santana, Miles Goodman. *COL*

La Belle Noiseuse 🎬🎬🎬🎬½ *Divertimento* **1990** The connections between art and life are explored in this beautiful (and long) drama. Creatively crippled, an aging painter has left unfinished a masterpiece work, entitled "La Belle Noiseuse," for ten years. When an admiring younger artist and his beautiful lover arrive for a visit, the painter is newly inspired by the young woman and makes her the model and muse for his masterwork. The film details every nuance of the work from the first to the last brushstroke and the battle of wills between artist and model over the symbiotic creative process. Based on a novella by Honore Balzac. French with subtitles. "Divertimento" is actually a recut and shortened version (126 minutes) of the original film. **240m/C VHS.** *FR* Michel Piccoli, Emmanuelle Beart, Jane Birkin, David Bursztein, Marianne Denicourt; *D:* Jacques Rivette. Cannes Film Festival '91: Grand Jury Prize; Los Angeles Film Critics Association Awards '91: Best Foreign Film. *NYF, FCT, ING*

La Bete Humaine 🎬🎬🎬½ *The Human Beast* **1938** A dark, psychological melodrama about human passion and duplicity, as an unhinged trainman plots with a married woman to kill her husband. Wonderful performances and stunning photography. Based on the Emile Zola novel. In French with English subtitles. 1954 Hollywood remake, "Human Desire," was directed by Fritz Lang. **90m/B VHS, Beta, 8mm.** *FR* Jean Gabin, Simone Simon, Julien Carette, Fernand Ledoux; *D:* Jean Renoir. *NOS, HHT, CAB*

La Boca del Lobo 🎬🎬 *The Lion's Den* **1989** Peru's civil strife inspired this sluggish drama about government troops occupying a jungle village. Tormented by unseen communist guerillas, the stressed-out soldiers reach the breaking point. Spanish with subtitles. **111m/C VHS.** *AR* Gustavo Bueno, Tono Vega, Jose Tejada; *D:* Francisco J. Lombardi. *CCN, TPV*

La Boum 🎬🎬½ **1981** A teenager's adjustment to the changes brought about by a move to Paris is compounded by her parents' marital problems. Followed by "La Boum 2." **90m/C VHS, Beta.** *FR* Sophie Marceau, Claude Brasseur, Brigitte Fossey, Denise Grey, Bernard Giraudeau; *D:* Claude Pinoteau; *M:* Vladimir Cosma. *COL*

L.A. Bounty 🎬½ **1989 (R)** A beautiful cop and a bounty hunter go after the same murderer. Hauser steals the show as a psychopath who has completely blown a gasket. **85m/C VHS, Beta, LV.** Sybil Danning, Wings Hauser, Henry Darrow, Lenore Kasdorf, Robert Hanley; *D:* Worth Keeter. *NO*

La Cage aux Folles 🎬🎬🎬½ **1978 (R)** Adaption of the popular French play. A gay nightclub owner and his transvestite lover play it straight when Tognazzi's son from a long-ago liaison brings his fiancee and her conservative parents home for dinner. Charming music and lots of fun. So successful, it was followed by two sequels, "La Cage Aux Folles II & III" and also a Broadway musical. In French with English subtitles. **91m/C VHS, Beta, LV.** *FR* Ugo Tognazzi, Michel Serrault, Michel Galabru, Claire Maurier, Remy Laurent, Benny Luke; *D:* Edouard Molinaro; *W:* Francis Veber; *M:* Ennio Morricone. Cesar Awards '79: Best Actor (Serrault); Golden Globe Awards '80: Best Foreign Film; Nominations: Academy Awards '79: Best Adapted Screenplay, Best Costume Design, Best Director (Molinaro). *MGM, FOX, CRC*

La Cage aux Folles 2 🎬🎬½ **1981 (R)** Albin sets out to prove to his companion that he still has sex appeal, and gets mixed up in some espionage antics. This sequel to the highly successful "La Cage aux Folles" loses some steam, but is still worth seeing. Followed by "La Cage Aux Folles 3: The Wedding." **101m/C VHS, Beta, LV.** *FR* Ugo Tognazzi, Michel Serrault, Marcel Bozzuffi, Michel Galabru, Benny Luke; *D:* Edouard Molinaro; *W:* Francis Veber; *M:* Ennio Morricone. *MGM, FCT, FOX*

La Cage aux Folles 3: The Wedding 🐾½ 1986 (PG-13) The flamboyant drag queen Albin must feign normalcy by marrying and fathering a child in order to collect a weighty inheritance. Final segment of the trilogy; inferior to the previous films. In French with English subtitles. 88m/C VHS, Beta, LV. FR Michel Serrault, Ugo Tognazzi, Michel Galabru, Benny Luke, Stephane Audran; D: Georges Lautner; M: Ennio Morricone. COL

La Ceremonie 🐾🐾🐾 A Judgment in Stone 1995 Sullen maid Sophie (Bonnaire) is hired by the rich Lelievre family to work at their country estate. She's befriended by independent postmistress Jeanne (Huppert), who's disliked by Sophie's employers, and who encourages Sophie into small defiant actions. Something's off about the entire situation and there's violence beneath the seemingly calm surface. Based on Ruth Rendell's chiller "Judgment in Stone." French with subtitles. 111m/C VHS. FR Sandrine Bonnaire, Isabelle Huppert, Jacqueline Bisset, Jean-Pierre Cassel; D: Claude Chabrol; W: Claude Chabrol, Caroline Eliacheff. Cesar Awards '96: Best Actress (Huppert); Los Angeles Film Critics Association Awards '96: Best Foreign Film; National Society of Film Critics Awards '96: Best Foreign Film; Nominations: Cesar Awards '96: Best Actress (Bonnaire), Best Director (Chabrol), Best Film, Best Supporting Actor (Cassel), Best Supporting Actress (Bisset), Best Writing. NYF

La Chartreuse de Parme 🐾🐾½ Charterhouse at Parma 1948 Nineteenth century period piece featuring an Archbishop willing to break his vows for the woman he loves, and the aunt who will make sure that if she can't have him only God will. French adaptation of the novel by Stendahl. Available dubbed. ?m/C VHS. FR Gerard Philipe, Maria Casares, Rene Faure. FRA, FCT

La Chevre 🐾🐾🐾½ The Goat 1981 A screwball French comedy about two policemen (Richard and Depardieu—picture Nick Nolte and Gene Wilder with accents) stumbling along the path of a missing heiress who suffers from chronic bad luck. Contains a hilarious scene with chairs used to test the luck of the investigative team; based on one partner's ability to sit on the only broken chair in a rather large collection, he is judged to be sufficiently jinxed to allow them to recreate the same outrageous misfortunes that befell the heiress in her plight. In French with English subtitles. 91m/C VHS, Beta. FR Gerard Depardieu, Pierre Richard, Corynne Charbit, Michel Robin, Pedro Armendariz Jr.; D: Francis Veber; M: Vladimir Cosma. FCT, TPV

La Chienne 🐾🐾🐾🐾 Isn't Life A Bitch?; The Bitch 1931 Dark, troubling tale of a bedraggled husband whose only excitement is his painting hobby until he becomes consumed by the ever-tempting prostitute Lulu. Director Renoir broke ground with his use of direct sound and Paris shooting locations, and the experiment was a hit. Portrays marriage with acidity; Renoir's own marriage broke up as a result of this film's casting. Mareze died shortly after the filming was complete in a car crash. Based on the novel by Georges de la Fouchardiere. Produced in 1931, but didn't reach American theatres until 1975. In French with English subtitles. Remade in 1945 as "Scarlet Street." 93m/B VHS, Beta, LV. FR Michel Simon, Janie Mareze, Georges Flament, Madeleine Berubet; D: Jean Renoir; W: Andre Girard, Jean Renoir. INT, TPV

La Chute de la Maison Usher 🐾🐾🐾½ The Fall of the House of Usher 1928 An expressionistic, abstracted adaptation of the Poe story "The Fall of the House of Usher" about an evil mansion and its ruined denizens. Epstein used slow motion, superimpressions, and weird camera angles to obtain the proper atmosphere. 48m/B VHS, Beta. FR Marguerite Gance, Jean Debucourt, Charles Lamy; D: Jean Epstein. FCT, GVV

La Cicada 🐾½ The Cricket 1983 The sparks fly when a woman and her 17-year-old daughter become rivals for the affections of the same man. 90m/C VHS, Beta. IT Clio Goldsmith, Virna Lisi, Anthony (Tony) Franciosa, Renato Salvatori; D: Alberto Lattuada.

La Collectionneuse 🐾🐾 The Gentleman Tramp 1967 The third of Rohmer's "Moral Tales" finds an artist (Bachau) and an antiques dealer (Pommereulle) vacationing in St. Tropez and sharing a villa with a young woman (Politoff) who picks a different man to sleep with each night. Both try to resist the sexual temptations of being added to her collection of lovers. French with subtitles. 88m/C VHS. FR Patrick Bauchau, Daniel Pommereulle, Haydee Politoff, Alain Jouffroy; D: Eric Rohmer; W: Eric Rohmer; C: Nestor Almendros. FXL

L.A. Confidential 🐾🐾🐾🐾 1997 (R) Hard-boiled, complex crime drama based on James Ellroy's even more complex novel. Fifties Hollywood is ripe with corruption in many forms—politics, police, business, gangsters, racial tensions, and journalistic sleaze in the persona of Sid Hudgeons (DeVito), editor of tabloid rag Hush-Hush. Sid's police contact is celebrity Sgt. Jack Vincennes (Spacey), who serves as an advisor to a TV cop show (think "Dragnet"). There's a bloodbath murder case that involves brutal-yet-tender cop Bud White (Crowe); the ruthlessly ambitious, college-educated neophyte Ed Exley (Pearce); and their veteran boss, Capt. Dudley Smith (Cromwell). There's also wealthy pimp/businessman Pierce Patchett (Strathairn) and his moviestar look-alike hookers, including world-weary Lynn (Basinger), who gets involved with Bud, who... Well, lets just say that Hanson does a masterful job tying up all the loose ends and still leaving you wanting more. CW: Strong violence and language, and for sexuality. 136m/C VHS, LV, Closed Caption, DVD. Kevin Spacey, Russell Crowe, Guy Pearce, Danny DeVito, Kim Basinger, James Cromwell, David Strathairn, Ron Rifkin, Graham Beckel, Matt McCoy, Simon Baker-Denny, Paul Guilfoyle, Amber Smith, John Mahon, Paolo Seganti, Gwenda Deacon; D: Curtis Hanson; W: Brian Helgeland; C: Dante Spinotti; M: Jerry Goldsmith. Academy Awards '97: Best Adapted Screenplay, Best Supporting Actress (Basinger); British Academy Awards '97: Best Film Editing, Best Sound; Golden Globe Awards '98: Best Supporting Actress (Basinger); Los Angeles Film Critics Association Awards '97: Best Cinematography, Best Director (Hanson), Best Film, Best Screenplay; National Board of Review Awards '97: Best Director (Hanson), Best Film; New York Film Critics Awards '97: Best Director (Hanson), Best Film, Best Screenplay; National Society of Film Critics Awards '97: Best Director (Hanson), Best Film, Best Screenplay; Screen Actors Guild Award '97: Best Supporting Actress (Basinger); Writers Guild of America '97: Best Adapted Screenplay; Broadcast Film Critics Association Awards '97: Best Adapted Screenplay, Best Film; Nominations: Academy Awards '97: Best Art Direction/Set Decoration, Best Cinematography, Best Director (Hanson), Best Film Editing, Best Picture, Best Sound, Best Original Score; British Academy Awards '97: Best Actor (Spacey), Best Actress (Basinger), Best Adapted Screenplay, Best Cinematography, Best Costume Design, Best Director (Hanson), Best Film, Best Score; Directors Guild of America Awards '97: Best Director (Hanson); Golden Globe Awards '98: Best Director (Hanson), Best Film—Drama, Best Screenplay, Best Original Score; Screen Actors Guild Award '97: Cast. WAR

L.A. Crackdown 🐾 1987 A ruthless yet compassionate policewoman goes after crack dealers and pimps who are exploiting women. Pretty trashy fare; followed by "L.A. Crackdown 2." Made for video. 90m/C VHS, Beta. Pamela Dixon, Tricia Parks, Kita Harrison, Jeffrey Olson, Michael Coon; D: Joseph Merhi. NO

L.A. Crackdown 2 🐾 1988 A woman cop goes undercover as a dancer in a dance hall to try to catch a psychotic killer who stalks hookers in this silly sequel to "L.A. Crackdown." 90m/C VHS, Beta. Pamela Dixon, Anthony Gates, Joe Vance, Cynthia Miguel, Lisa Anderson, Bo Sabato; D: Joseph Merhi. HHE

La Discrete 🐾🐾🐾 The Discreet 1990 Antoine (Luchini) is a cocky writer who is not the lothario he imagines himself to be—in fact his girlfriend has just dumped him. He and his publisher plan a sexist revenge with Antoine advertising for a young female typist whom he will seduce and abandon—all the while keeping a diary of the experience which will be published. The self possessed Catherine (Henry) answers the ad and even though Antoine protests that she is not his type he finds himself falling in love. Then Catherine discovers Antoine's original scheme. Vincent's directorial debut. In French with English subtitles. 95m/C VHS. FR Fabrice Luchini, Judith Henry, Maurice Garrel, Marie Bunel, Francois Toumarkine; D: Christian Vincent; W: Jean-Pierre Ronssin, Christian Vincent; M: Jay Gottlieb. Cesar Awards '91: Best Writing. NYF, FCT

La Dolce Vita 🐾🐾🐾🐾 1960 In this influential and popular work a successful, sensationalistic Italian journalist covers the show-biz life in Rome, and alternately covets and disdains its glitzy shallowness. The film follows his dealings with the "sweet life" over a pivotal week. A surreal, comic tableaux with award-winning costuming; one of Fellini's most acclaimed films. In this film Fellini called his hungry celebrity photographers the Paparazzo—and it is as the paparazzi they have been ever since. In Italian with English subtitles. 175m/B VHS, LV, Letterbox. IT Marcello Mastroianni, Anita Ekberg, Anouk Aimee, Alain Cuny, Lex Barker, Yvonne Furneaux, Barbara Steele, Nadia Gray, Magali Noel, Walter Santesso, Jacques Sernas, Annibale Ninchi; D: Federico Fellini; W: Tullio Pinelli, Ennio Flaiano, Brunello Rondi, Federico Fellini; M: Nino Rota. Academy Awards '61: Best Costume Design (B & W); Cannes Film Festival '60: Best Film; New York Film Critics Awards '61: Best Foreign Film; Nominations: Academy Awards '61: Best Art Direction/Set Decoration (B & W), Best Director (Fellini), Best Story & Screenplay. REP

La Femme Nikita 🐾🐾🐾 1991 (R) Stylish French noir version of Pygmalion. Having killed a cop during a drugstore theft gone awry, young French sociopath Nikita (Parillaud) is reprieved from a death sentence in order to enroll in a government finishing school, of sorts. Trained in etiquette and assasination, she's released after three years, and starts a new life with a new beau, all the while carrying out agency-mandated assassinations. Parillaud is excellent as the once-amoral street urchin transformed into a woman of depth and sensitivity—a bitterly ironic moral evolution for a contract killer. Remade as "Point of No Return." 117m/C VHS. FR Anne Parillaud, Jean-Hugues Anglade, Tcheky Karyo, Jeanne Moreau, Jean Reno, Jean Bouise; D: Luc Besson; W: Luc Besson; C: Thierry Arbogast; M: Eric Serra. Cesar Awards '91: Best Actress (Parillaud). THV, FCT, BTV

L.A. Gangs Rising 🐾🐾 1989 The streets of Los Angeles run red with blood as a gang war explodes into bloody fury. 87m/C VHS, Beta. David Kyle, Steve Bond, John Ashton; D: John Bushelman. NO

L.A. Goddess 🐾½ 1992 (R) A hard-living, and drinking, movie star and her beautiful stunt double both fall for a studio head. Both of these women know what they want and the man in the middle hasn't got a clue. Also available in an unrated version. CW: Language and strong sexuality. 92m/C VHS. Kathy Shower, Jeff Conaway, David Heavener, Wendy McDonald, Joe Estevez, James Hong; D: Jag Mundhra; W: Jerry Davis.

La Grande Bouffe 🐾🐾🐾 The Blow-Out 1973 Four middle-aged men, bored with life, meet at a secluded mansion for one last excessive fling and to literally eat themselves to death. Four very fine actors in a vulgar feast. French with subtitles. 125m/C VHS. FR Marcello Mastroianni, Philippe Noiret, Michel Piccoli, Ugo Tognazzi, Andrea Ferreol; D: Marco Ferreri; W: Marco Ferreri, Rafael Azcona; C: Mario Vulpiani; M: Philippe Sarde. WBF

La Grande Bourgeoise 🐾🐾½ The Murri Affair 1974 Historical romance about the clash of aristocratic society and the new bourgeoisie in 1897 Italy. Great cast tries to save the true tale of murder and political intrigue from film's slow pacing, but in the end it's the movie's visual polish that shines forth. In Italian with subtitles. 115m/C VHS, Beta. IT Catherine Deneuve, Giancarlo Giannini, Fernando Rey, Tina Aumont; D: Mauro Bolognini; M: Ennio Morricone. FCT

La Grande Vadrouille ✍✍✍ *Don't Look Now, We've Been Shot At* 1966 In 1943 German-occupied France, three Allied parachutists drop in on a Paris Opera conductor and a house painter. If the pair wish to find some peace, they must help the trio get to the free zone. France's number one boxoffice hit for almost 30 years. Also available dubbed. **122m/C VHS.** *FR* Louis de Funes, Bourvil, Terry-Thomas; *D:* Gerard Oury. **FRA, FCT**

L.A. Heat ✍½ 1988 When a vice cop's partner is killed, he seeks revenge on the murderers, only to find that his own department may have been involved. Followed by "L.A. Vice." **90m/C VHS, Beta.** Jim Brown, Lawrence-Hilton Jacobs; *D:* Joseph Merhi. **PAR, HHE**

L.A. Law ✍✍✍ 1986 The pilot episode of the acclaimed dramatic series, in which the staff of a Los Angeles law firm tries a variety of cases. **97m/C VHS, Beta, Closed Caption.** Michael Tucker, Jill Eikenberry, Harry Hamlin, Richard Dysart, Jimmy Smits, Alan Rachins, Susan Ruttan, Susan Dey, Corbin Bernsen; *D:* Gregory Hoblit. **FOX**

La Lectrice ✍✍½ *The Reader* 1988 (R) Artesian landscapes, Beethoven sonatas, and a Raymond Jean novel titled "La Lectrice" provide the backdrop for Constance (Miou-Miou) to read aloud to her boyfriend in bed, and from there she imagines herself the novel's heroine, who hires out her services as a reader to various odd characters. She reads from "L'Amant," "Alice," "War and Peace," and "Les Fleurs du Mal." Richly textured and not overly intellectual. In French with English subtitles. **98m/C VHS, Beta, LV.** *FR* Miou-Miou, Christian Ruche, Sylvie Laporte, Michael Raskine, Brigitte Catillon, Regis Royer, Maria Casares, Pierre Dux, Patrick Chesnais; *D:* Michel DeVille; *W:* Rosalinde DeVille, Michel DeVille. Cesar Awards '89: Best Supporting Actor (Chesnais); Montreal World Film Festival '88: Best Film. **ORI**

La Marseillaise ✍✍✍½ 1937 Sweeping epic by Renoir made before he hit his stride with "Grand Illusion." It details the events of the French Revolution in the summer of 1789 using a cast of thousands. The opulent lifestyle of the French nobility is starkly contrasted with the peasant lifestyle of poverty and despair. The focus is on two new recruits who have joined the Marseilles division of the revolutionary army as they begin their long march to Paris, the heart of France. As they travel, they adopt a stirring and passionate song that embodies the spirit and ideals of the revolution known as "La Marseillaise," now France's national anthem. In French with English subtitles. **130m/B VHS, Beta.** *FR* Pierre Renoir, Lisa Delamare, Louis Jouvet, Aime Clarimond, Andrex Andrisson, Paul Dullac; *D:* Jean Renoir; *W:* Jean Renoir; *C:* Jean Bourgoin. **NOS, INT, HHT**

La Merveilleuse Visite ✍✍½ *The Marvelous Visit* 1974 Bittersweet fantasy about an angel that falls from the sky and is found unconscious by a priest. He's nursed back to health but causes problems for his host when he wanders into the nearby village and his curiosity is misunderstood. Adapted from a short story by H.G. Wells. In French with English subtitles. **102m/C VHS.** *FR* Gilles Kohler, Deborah Berger, Jean-Pierre Castaldi; *D:* Marcel Carne; *W:* Marcel Carne. **HTV, FCT**

La Nuit de Varennes ✍✍✍ 1982 (R) This semi-historical romp is based on an actual chapter in French history when King Louis XVI and Marie Antoinette fled from revolutionary Paris to Varennes in 1791. On the way they meet an unlikely group of characters, including Cassanova and Thomas Paine. At times witty and charming, the melange of history and fiction is full of talk, sometimes profane, punctuated by sex and nudity. Director Scola's imagination stretches to light up this night. In French with English subtitles. **133m/C VHS.** *FR IT* Marcello Mastroianni, Harvey Keitel, Jean-Louis Barrault, Hanna Schygulla, Jean-Claude Brialy; *D:* Ettore Scola; *W:* Ettore Scola. **COL, IME**

La Passante ✍✍✍ *La Passante du Sans Souci; The Passerby* 1983 An otherwise peace-loving man murders the Paraguayan ambassador to France. In somewhat clumsy flashback style the murderer's orphaned childhood and other memories provide motives for the murder. Though posed more slowly than typical intrigue plots, the movie blends love and the legacy of Nazism, passion and politics in an engaging way, spiced with nudity and some violence. In her last screen appearance Schneider movingly portrays dual roles. In French with English subtitles. **106m/C VHS, Beta, LV.** *FR GE* Romy Schneider, Michel Piccoli, Helmut Griem, Gerard Klein, Matthieu Carriere, Maria Schell; *D:* Jacques Rouffio; *M:* Georges Delerue. Cesar Awards '83: Best Sound. **TPV**

La Petite Sirene ✍✍ *The Little Mermaid* 1980 Isabelle is a 14-year-old schoolgirl, obsessed with the story of the Little Mermaid, who tries to ingratiate herself to Georges, a 40-year-old garage mechanic. Seeing him as her prince charming, she persists in trying to make him a part of her life, in spite of his resistance. In French with English subtitles. **104m/C VHS.** *FR* Laura Alexis, Philippe Leotard, Evelyne Dress, Marie DuBois; *D:* Roger Andrieux; *W:* Roger Andrieux. **WAC, FCT, TPV**

La Promesse ✍✍ *The Promise* 1996 Fifteen-year-old Igor (Renier) helps his disreputable father Roger (Gourmet) run an illegal immigrant operation in the Beligan town of Liege. African immigrant Amidou (Ouedraogo) has just been joined by his wife Assita (Ouedraogo) and their baby. When Amidou dies in an accident, Roger forces Igor to help him bury the body secretly and tells the bewildered wife that her husband has left her. But Igor is caught in the middle—he'd promised the dying Amidou to look after Assita and he still has enough conscience to want to help—but it also puts Igor into a dangerous conflict with his father. French with subtitles. **93m/C VHS.** *FR BE* Jeremie Renier, Olivier Gourmet, Assita Ouedraogo, Rasmane Ouedraogo; *D:* Jean-Pierre Dardenne, Luc Dardenne; *W:* Jean-Pierre Dardenne, Luc Dardenne; *C:* Alain Marcoen; *M:* Jean-Marie Billy. Los Angeles Film Critics Association Awards '97: Best Foreign Film; National Society of Film Critics Awards '97: Best Foreign Film. **NYR**

La Puritaine ✍✍½ 1986 Before his planned reconciliation with his daughter, the artistic manager of a theatre has young actresses portray different sides of the daughter's personality. In French with English subtitles. **90m/C VHS.** Michel Piccoli, Sandrine Bonnaire; *D:* Lou Doillon. **FCT**

La Ronde ✍✍✍½ 1951 A classic comedy of manners and sharply witty tour-de-farce in which a group of people in 1900 Vienna keep changing romantic partners until things wind up where they started. Ophuls' swirling direction creates a fast-paced farce of desire and regret with wicked yet subtle style. Based on Arthur Schnitzler's play and remade as "Circle of Love." In French with English subtitles. **97m/B VHS, Beta.** *FR* Simone Signoret, Anton Walbrook, Simone Simon, Serge Reggiani, Daniel Gelin, Danielle Darrieux, Jean-Louis Barrault, Fernand Gravet, Odette Joyeux, Isa Miranda, Gerard Philipe; *D:* Max Ophuls. British Academy Awards '51: Best Film; Nominations: Academy Awards '51: Best Art Direction/Set Decoration (B & W), Best Screenplay. **NLC, HMV**

La Rupture ✍✍½ *The Breakup* 1970 Thriller about a wife trying to protect her child from her husband's unsavory family. Audran and her son are attacked by her husband (Drouot), who's high on drugs. She fights back and he winds up in the hospital. Her father-in-law (Bouquet), who wants his grandson to live with him, then hires a seedy investigator (Cassel) to spy on Audran. Based on the Charlotte Armstrong novel. In French with English subtitles. **124m/C VHS.** *FR* Stephane Audran, Jean-Claude Drouot, Michel Bouquet, Jean-Pierre Cassel, Catherine Rouvel, Jean Carmet, Annie Cordy; *D:* Claude Chabrol; *W:* Claude Chabrol; *M:* Pierre Jansen. **CVC, FCT**

La Salamandre ✍✍ *The Salamander* 1971 Non-conformist Rosemonde, suspected of shooting her guardian, is being interviewed by a novelist and a journalist trying to write a television script about the incident. The more they supposedly learn, the more they are both intimately drawn towards her. French with subtitles. **119m/B VHS.** *SI* Bulle Ogier, Jean-Luc Bideau, Jacques Denis; *D:* Alain Tanner; *W:* Alain Tanner, John Berger; *M:* Patrick Moraz. **NYF**

La Scorta ✍✍✍½ *The Bodyguards; The Escorts* 1994 Slick, fact-based political thriller focuses on four carabinieri (state police officers) who struggle to maintain some semblance of their normal lives after they are assigned to protect a judge investigating government corruption and a related murder in a Sicilian town. A crackling alternative to Americanized mobster melodrama, marked by taut direction, meaty characters, and coolly understated performances that seamlessly portray brotherhood, heroism, suspicion, and betrayal amid the battle for power between the Italian state and the Mafia. In Italian with English subtitles. **92m/C VHS.** *IT* Claudio Amendola, Enrico Lo Verso, Tony Sperandeo, Ricky Memphis, Carlo Cecchi, Leo Gullotta; *D:* Ricardo Tognazzi; *W:* Graziano Diana, Simona Izzo; *M:* Ennio Morricone. **NYF**

La Signora di Tutti ✍✍✍ 1934 An early Italian biography of Gaby Doriot, a movie star whose professional success is paired by personal misery. Prestigious director Ophuls, working in exile from his native Germany, was unable to complete many projects in the years leading up to and during WWII. This is one of the few. Watch for innovative camera work intended to underscore the film's mood. In Italian with English subtitles. **92m/B VHS, Beta.** *IT* Isa Miranda; *D:* Max Ophuls. **CVC, FCT**

La Silence de la Mer ✍✍✍ *The Silence of the Sea* 1947 An old French farmer (Robian) and his niece (Stephane) are forced to billet a German officer (Vernon) in their home during the Occupation. They've vowed never to speak to him but the German continues to pour out his thoughts on music, war, and his love of France into their silence. Melville's first feature; French with subtitles. **86m/B VHS.** *FR* Howard Vernon, Jean-Marie Robian, Nicole Stephane; *D:* Jean-Pierre Melville; *W:* Jean-Pierre Melville; *C:* Henri Decae; *M:* Edgar Bischoff. **WBF**

L.A. Story ✍✍✍ 1991 (PG-13) Livin' ain't easy in the city of angels. Harris K. Telemacher (Martin), a weatherman in a city where the weather never changes, wrestles with the meaning of life and love while consorting with beautiful people, distancing from significant other Henner, cavorting with valley girl Parker, and falling for newswoman Tennant (Martin's real life wife). Written by the comedian, the story's full of keen insights into the everyday problems and ironies of living in the Big Tangerine. (It's no wonder the script's full of so much thoughtful detail: Martin is said to have worked on it intermittently for seven years.) Charming, fault forgiving but not fault ignoring portrait. **98m/C VHS, Beta, LV, Closed Caption.** Steve Martin, Victoria Tennant, Richard E. Grant, Marilu Henner, Sarah Jessica Parker, Sam McMurray, Patrick Stewart, Iman, Kevin Pollak; *D:* Mick Jackson; *W:* Steve Martin; *M:* Peter Melnick. **ART, WAR**

La Strada ✍✍✍✍ *The Road* 1954 Simple-minded girl, played by Fellini's wife, Masina, is sold to a brutal, coarse circus strong-man and she falls in love with him despite his abuse. They tour the countryside and eventually meet up with a gentle acrobat, played by Basehart, who alters their fate. Fellini masterwork was the director's first internationally acclaimed film, and is, by turns, somber and amusing as it demonstrates the filmmaker's sensitivity to the underprivileged of the world and his belief in spiritual redemption. Subtitled in English. **107m/B VHS, Beta, LV.** *IT* Giulietta Masina, Anthony Quinn, Richard Basehart, Aldo Silvani; *D:* Federico Fellini; *W:* Ennio Flaiano, Brunello Rondi, Tullio Pinelli, Federico Fellini; *M:* Nino Rota. Academy Awards '56:

Best Foreign Language Film; New York Film Critics Awards '56: Best Foreign Film; Nominations: Academy Awards '56: Best Original Screenplay. *IMG, HMV*

La Symphonie Pastorale 🎬🎬🎬½ 1946 A Swiss pastor takes in an orphan blind girl who grows up to be beautiful. The pastor then competes for her affections with his son. Quiet drama based on the Andre Gide novel, with breathtaking mountain scenery as the backdrop for this tragedy rife with symbolism. 105m/B VHS. *FR* Pierre Blanchar, Michele Morgan, Jean Desailly, Line Noro, Andree Clement; *D:* Jean Delannoy. Cannes Film Festival '46: Best Actress (Morgan). *HMV*

La Terra Trema 🎬🎬🎬½ *Episoda Del Mare; The Earth Will Tremble* 1948 The classic example of Italian neo-realism, about a poor Sicilian fisherman, his family and their village. A spare, slow-moving, profound and ultimately lyrical tragedy, this semi-documentary explores the economic exploitation of Sicily's fishermen. Filmed on location with the villagers playing themselves; highly acclaimed though not commercially successful. In Sicilian with English subtitles. Some radically cut versions may be available, but are to be avoided. Franco Zefferelli was one of the assistant directors. 161m/B VHS, Beta. *IT* Antonio Pietrangeli; *D:* Luchino Visconti. *FCT*

La Truite 🎬🎬🎬 *The Trout* 1983 (R) A young woman leaves her family's rural trout farm and a loveless marriage to seek her fortune in high finance and corporate mayhem. The complicated plot, full of intrigue and sexual encounters, sometimes lacks focus. Slickly filmed. 80m/C VHS, Beta. *FR* Isabelle Huppert, Jean-Pierre Cassel, Daniel Olbrychski, Jeanne Moreau, Jacques Spiesser, Ruggero Raimondi, Alexis Smith, Craig Stevens; *D:* Joseph Losey. Cesar Awards '83: Best Cinematography. *COL*

La Vengeance d'une Femme 🎬🎬 A *Woman's Revenge* 1989 Refined Cecile and sultry Suzy are two sides of a love triangle whose third member, Cecile's husband, has just died. Cecile decides to get to know his mistress better, which naturally has Suzy worried. Is Cecile out for revenge or does she sincerely want to befriend the "other woman." Based on Dostoyevski's "The Eternal Husband." In French with English subtitles. 133m/C VHS. *FR* Isabelle Huppert, Beatrice Dalle; *D:* Jacques Doillon; *W:* Jean-Francois Goyet, Jacques Doillon. *FCT*

L.A. Vice 🎬½ 1989 A detective is transferred to the vice squad, where he must investigate a series of murders. Sequel to "L.A. Heat." 90m/C VHS, Beta. Jim Brown, Lawrence-Hilton Jacobs, William Smith; *D:* Joseph Merhi. *PAR*

La Vie Continue 🎬🎬½ 1982 A middle-aged woman suddenly finds herself widowed after 20 years of marriage and tries to build a new life for herself and her children. Girardot's performance can't quite dispel melodramatic suds. Loosely and more effectively remade as "Men Don't Leave." In French with English subtitles or dubbed. 93m/C VHS, Beta. *IT* Annie Girardot, Jean-Pierre Cassel, Michel Aumont, Pierre Dux, Guilia Salvatori, Emmanuel Goyet, Rivera Andres; *D:* Moshe Mizrahi; *M:* Georges Delerue. *COL*

La Vie de Boheme 🎬🎬🎬 *Bohemian Life* 1993 Comedy takes a mocking look at art and romantic love. A trio of hapless but dedicated comrades, Rodolfo (Pellonpaa) the painter, Marcel (Wilms) the poet, and Schaunard (Vaananen), must scrounge around the mealy edges of modern Paris because their art isn't filling their stomachs. Meanwhile, they experience the pangs of love like everyone else, although each is devoutly committed to his art as well. Starkly different from the lush, operatic version by Puccini, but based on the same source, a 19th century novel by Henri Mullet. French with subtitles. 100m/C VHS. Matti Pellonpaa, Andre Wilms, Kari Vaananen, Jean-Pierre Leaud, Samuel Fuller, Louis Malle, Evelyne Didi, Christine Murillo, Laika, Carlos Salgado, Alexis Nitzer, Sylvie van den

Elsen, Gilles Charmant, Dominique Marcas; *D:* Aki Kaurismaki; *W:* Aki Kaurismaki. *FXI*

La Vie est Belle 🎬🎬 *Life is Rosy* 1987 The rags to riches story of a poor rural musician from Zaire who goes to the city to break into radio and television. He uses his wit and talent to foil a greedy boss, win a beautiful wife, and make himself a singing sensation. French with subtitles. 85m/C VHS. *D:* Nagangura Mweze, Bernard Lamy. *KIV*

L.A. Wars 🎬½ 1994 (R) A Latin American drug dealer moves into the territory of an Italian mobster, causing a turf war. When a cop rescues the mobster's daughter from the scuzzball, his boss forces him to infiltrate the mobster's organization. Abundant body count, lots of T&A. *CW:* Language, gangster violence, and sexuality. 94m/C VHS. Vince Murdocco, Mary Zilba, A.J. Stevens, Rodrigo Obregon; *D:* Martin Morris, Tony Kandah. *MNC*

Laboratory 🎬 1980 Things go awry when the earthling subjects of an alien experiment revolt against their captors. 93m/C VHS, Beta. Camille Mitchell, Corinne Michaels, Garnett Smith. *VCI*

Labyrinth 🎬🎬🎬 1986 (PG) While baby-sitting her baby brother Froud, Connelly is so frustrated she asks the goblins to take him away. To answer her idle wish, she must try to rescue Froud by solving the fantastic labyrinth. If she does not find him in time, Froud will become one of the goblins forever. During her journey, Connelly is befriended by all sorts of odd creatures created by Henson, and she grows up a little along the way. A fascinating adventure movie for the whole family. 90m/C VHS, Beta, LV, 8mm, Closed Caption. David Bowie, Jennifer Connelly, Toby Froud, Shelley Thompson, Dave Goelz, Karen Prell, Steve Whitmire; *D:* Jim Henson; *W:* Jim Henson, Terry Jones; *C:* Alex Thomson; *M:* Trevor Jones, David Bowie. *NLC*

Labyrinth of Passion 🎬🎬½ *Laberinto de Pasiones* 1982 A screwball farce, directed by Almodovar, featuring a host of strange characters running around Madrid in search of sex and laughter. They find plenty of both. An early film by an influential director. In Spanish with English subtitles. 100m/C VHS, Beta, LV, Letterbox. *SP* Antonio Banderas, Imanol Arias, Cecilia Roth; *D:* Pedro Almodovar; *W:* Pedro Almodovar. *CCN, IME, TPV*

The Lacemaker 🎬🎬🎬½ *La Dentielliere* 1977 Huppert's first shot at stardom, on videodisc with digital sound and a letterboxed print. A young beautician and a university student fall in love on vacation but soon begin to realize the differences in their lives. Adapted from the novel by Pascal Laine. In French with English subtitles. 107m/C LV, Letterbox. *FR SI GE* Isabelle Huppert, Yves Beneyton, Florence Giorgetti, Anna Marie Duringer; *D:* Claude Goretta. *HMV, CRC*

L'Addition 🎬🎬½ *The Patsy; Caged Heart* 1985 (R) According to some cinematic code, the male lead always gets in lots of trouble whenever he tries to help a beautiful stranger. This time, Berry, as Bruno Windler, winds up arrested for shoplifting when he attempts to help Abril. Jailed and on the verge of parole, Windler unwittingly becomes involved in a prison break and is accused of helping a crime don mastermind the escape and of shooting a guard. That's where that gallic flair for capturing the sado-masochistic underbelly of humanity comes in, as Windler is viciously pursued by the malevolent guard. 85m/C VHS, Beta. Richard Berry, Victoria Abril, Richard Bohringer, Farid Chopel, Fabrice Eberhard; *D:* Denis Amar; *W:* Jean Curtelin; *C:* Robert Fraisse; *M:* Jean-Claude Petit. *MOR*

The Ladies Club 🎬½ 1986 (R) A group of rape victims get together and begin to victimize rapists. 86m/C VHS, Beta. Bruce Davison, Karen Austin, Diana Scarwid, Shera Danese, Beverly Todd; *D:* A.K. Allen.

The Ladies' Man 🎬🎬 1961 Piecemeal Lewis farce, with Jerry playing a clutzy handyman working at a girl's boarding house. Some riotous routines balanced by slow pacing. 106m/C VHS, Beta, LV, Closed Caption. Jerry Lewis, Helen Traubel,

Jack Kruschen, Doodles Weaver, Gloria Jean, *D:* Jerry Lewis; *W:* Jerry Lewis. *PAR*

Ladies Man 🎬🎬 1962 Spy adventure with Constantine playing super sleuth/agent, Lemmy Caution, on the French Riviera. ?m/C VHS. Eddie Constantine. *SNC*

The Ladies of the Bois de Bologne 🎬🎬 *Les Dames du Bois de Bologne; Ladies of the Park* 1944 Beware the woman scorned—as Jean (Bernard) learns. He ends his longtime relationship with Helene (Casares), although they vow to stay friends, but she secretly plots revenge and finds it in the person of Agnes (Labourdette), a former prostitute. Helene introduces Agnes to Jean, hoping they'll be attracted to one another. She are but after the wedding ceremony Helene reveals the truth about Agnes' sordid past. Updated adaptation of a story in Diderot's "Jacques Le Fatalist." French with subtitles. 83m/B VHS. *FR* Maria Casares, Paul Bernard, Elina Labourdette; *D:* Robert Bresson; *W:* Robert Bresson, Jean Cocteau. *HTV*

Ladies of the Chorus 🎬🎬 1949 Monroe stars as a burlesque chorus girl who shares the stage with her mom (Jergens) and a handful of other beauties. She meets and falls in love with a wealthy socialite (Brooks), but her mother completely disapproves of the relationship. Monroe later learns that her mother was in love with the same man several years before. Although only her second film appearance, Monroe's talents are already quite apparent in this low-budget musical romance. ♫Every Baby Nees a Da Da Daddy; Anyone Can Tell I Love You; Crazy For You; You're Never Too Old; Ladies of the Chorus. 61m/B VHS, Closed Caption. Adele Jergens, Marilyn Monroe, Rand Brooks, Nana Bryant, Steve Geray, Bill Edwards; *D:* Phil Karlson. *COL*

Ladies of the Lotus 🎬 1987 Bloodthirsty Vancouver gangsters raid Lotus, Inc., a modeling agency, and sell beautiful young women into slavery. As bad as it sounds. 120m/C VHS, Beta. *CA* Richard Dale, Angela Read, Patrick Bermel, Darcia Carnie; *D:* Lloyd A. Simanol, Douglas C. Nicolle. *NO*

Ladies on the Rocks 🎬🎬½ *Koks I Kulissen* 1983 Aspiring comediennes Micha and Laura pack up their van and take their bizarre cabaret act on the road through rural Denmark. They find their private lives disintegrating but turn each disaster into new material for their act. In Danish with English subtitles. 100m/C VHS. *DK* Helle Ryslinge, Anne Marie Helger, Flemming Quist Moller; *D:* Christian Braad Thomsen. *NYF*

Ladies They Talk About 🎬🎬½ *Women in Prison* 1933 Stanwyck stars as a tough-talking gun moll who belongs to a gang of bank robbers. They get caught and Stanwyck is sent to the female division of San Quentin. The acting is great in this pre-Code prison movie, but the film gets a bit punchy at times. Based on the true-life experiences of actress Dorothy Mackaye, who went to jail after her husband was killed in a fight with actor Paul Kelley, who was also sent to prison. Adapted from the play "Women in Prison" by Dorothy Mackaye and Carlton Miles. 69m/B VHS, Closed Caption. Barbara Stanwyck, Preston Foster, Lyle Talbot, Dorothy Burgess, Lillian Roth, Maude Eburne, Harold Huber, Ruth Donnelly; *D:* Howard Bretherton, William Keighley. *MGM*

Ladies Who Do 🎬🎬½ 1963 A group of cleaning ladies band together against the unscrupulous businessman who wants to tear down their homes in order to build an office tower. Along with a retired colonel, they use the stock market secrets gleaned from the rubbish they toss away to make a killing in the market and save the day. 90m/B VHS. *GB* Peggy Mount, Robert Morley, Harry H. Corbett, Miriam Karlin, Avril Elgar, Dandy Nichols, Jon Pertwee, Nigel Davenport; *D:* C.M. Pennington-Richards; *W:* Michael Pertwee. *FCT*

The Lady and the Highwayman 🎬🎬½ 1989 TV adaptation of the Barbara Cartland historical romance finds a rogue falling for the lady he's sworn to protect. Naturally, there's a happy ending. 100m/C VHS. *GB* Hugh Grant, Emma Samms, Oliver Reed, Michael York, Robert Morley, John Mills; *D:* John Hough. *FUS*

Lady and the Tramp 1955 (G) The animated Disney classic about two dogs who fall in love. Tramp is wild and carefree; Lady is a spoiled pedigree who runs away from home after her owners have a baby. They just don't make dog romances like this anymore. 🎵He's a Tramp; La La Lu; Siamese Cat Song; Peace on Earth; Bella Notte. 76m/C VHS, Beta, LV. *D:* Hamilton Luske; *M:* Peggy Lee, Sonny Burke; *V:* Larry Roberts, Peggy Lee, Barbara Luddy, Stan Freberg, Alan Reed, Bill Thompson, Bill Baucom, Verna Felton, George Givot, Dallas McKennon, Lee Millar. *DIS*

Lady Avenger 🎬 1989 (R) A woman is bent on getting revenge on her brother's killers. 90m/C VHS, Beta. Peggie Sanders, Michelle (McClellan) Bauer, Daniel Hirsch; *D:* David DeCoteau; *C:* Thomas Callaway. *NO*

Lady Be Good 🎬🎬½ 1941 Adapted from the 1924 Gershwin Broadway hit, the plot's been revamped, much to the critics' distaste ("Variety" called it "molasses paced"). Sothern and Young play a tunesmith duo who excel at musical harmony and marital strife. Applauded for its music (the critics loved Hammerstein's and the Gershwins' tunes), the show's Academy Award winning song was, ironically, written by Jerome Kern. And if that's not enough, levity man Skelton and hoofer Powell are thrown in for good measure. 🎵The Last Time I Saw Paris; So Am I; Oh Lady Be Good; Fascinating Rhythm; Hang On To Me; You'll Never Know; You're Words, My Music; Saudades. 111m/B VHS. Eleanor Powell, Ann Sothern, Robert Young, Lionel Barrymore, John Carroll, Red Skelton, Dan Dailey, Virginia O'Brien, Tom Conway, Phil Silvers, Doris Day; *D:* Norman Z. McLeod; *M:* Oscar Hammerstein, George Gershwin, Ira Gershwin, Jerome Kern, George Bassman. Academy Awards '41: Best Song ("The Last Time I Saw Paris"). *MGM, TTC, FCT*

Lady Beware 🎬🎬 1987 (R) A psychotic doctor becomes obsessed with a beautiful store-window dresser who specializes in steamy, erotic fantasies. When she realizes that she must stop him before he kills her. 108m/C VHS, Beta, LV. Diane Lane, Michael Woods, Cotter Smith, Viveca Lindfors, Tyra Ferrell, Peter Nevargic, Edward Penn; *D:* Karen Arthur; *W:* Charles Zev Cohen. *ART*

Lady by Choice 🎬🎬½ 1934 Lombard stars as a beautiful young fan dancer who is arrested for a lewd public performance. Taking the advice of her press agent, she hires an old bag lady to pose as her mother on Mother's Day. Robson portrays her "mother" and comes to think of Lombard as her own daughter. Robson encourages Lombard to give up fan dancing and to strive for greater things in life. She also pushes her into romance with a wealthy young man (Pryor). Robson is excellent in her role as "mother" and Lombard shows great comic talent in this charming film. 78m/C VHS, Closed Caption. Carole Lombard, May Robson, Roger Pryor, Walter Connolly, Raymond Walburn, James Burke; *D:* David Burton; *W:* Jo Swerling. *COL*

Lady Caroline Lamb 🎬🎬 1973 Lady Caroline is a passionate young lady in 19th-century England, who, although the wife of a member of Parliament, has an affair with Lord Byron and brings about her own downfall. Costume drama that never quite goes anywhere. 123m/C Beta. *GB IT* Sarah Miles, Richard Chamberlain, Jon Finch, Laurence Olivier, John Mills, Ralph Richardson; *D:* Robert Bolt; *W:* Robert Bolt; *C:* Oswald Morris; *M:* Richard Rodney Bennett.

Lady Chatterley 🎬🎬 1992 Oh my, Russell takes his provocative ways to D.H. Lawrence's scandalous novel about the adulterous affair between aristocratic Lady Connie Chatterley (Richardson) and her husband's gamekeeper,

Oliver Mellors (Bean). Also includes material taken from two early drafts of the book "The First Lady Chatterley" and "John Thomas and Lady Jane." Made for British television. 210m/C VHS. *GB* Joely Richardson, Sean Bean, James Wilby, Shirley Anne Field, Roger Hammond; *D:* Ken Russell; *W:* Ken Russell; *C:* Robin Vidgeon; *M:* Jean-Claude Petit. *WHA*

Lady Chatterley's Lover 🎬🎬½ *L'Amant de Lady Chatterley* 1955 Englishwoman has bad luck to have husband shot up during WWI and sent home paralyzed. In her quest for sexual fulfillment, she takes a new lover, the estate's earthy gamekeeper. Limp adaptation of D.H. Lawrence's novel. In French with English subtitles. 102m/B VHS, Beta, LV. *FR* Danielle Darrieux, Erno Crisa, Leo Genn; *D:* Marc Allegret. *NOS, MRV, HHT*

Lady Chatterley's Lover 🎬🎬½ 1981 (R) Remake of the 1955 film version of D.H. Lawrence's classic novel of an English lady who has an affair with the gamekeeper of her husband's estate. Basically soft-focus soft porn. 107m/C VHS, Beta, LV. *GB FR* Sylvia Kristel, Nicholas Clay, Shane Briant; *D:* Just Jaeckin; *C:* Robert Fraisse. *MGM*

Lady Cocoa 🎬½ 1975 (R) Routine story of a young woman who gets released from jail for 24 hours and sets out for Las Vegas to find the man who framed her. 93m/C VHS, Beta. Lola Falana, Joe "Mean Joe" Greene, Gene Washington, Alex Dreier; *D:* Matt Cimber. *UNI*

The Lady Confesses 🎬🎬 1945 Average mystery that involves Hughes trying to clear her boyfriend of murder. Independently produced. "Leave it to Beaver" fans will want to watch for "Ward Cleaver" Beaumont. 66m/B VHS. Mary Beth Hughes, Hugh Beaumont, Edmund MacDonald, Claudia Drake, Emmett Vogan, Barbara Slater, Edward Howard, Dewey Robinson, Carol Andrews; *D:* Sam Newfield; *W:* Helen Martin, Irwin H. Franklyn; *M:* Lee Zahler. *NOS, SNC*

Lady Dragon 🎬🎬 1992 (R) A woman and her husband are viciously attacked and only she survives. Found by an old man, she learns a number of martial arts tricks and goes out to get her revenge. **CW:** Language, strong violence, and sexuality. 89m/C VHS, LV, Closed Caption. Cynthia Rothrock, Richard Norton, Robert Ginty, Bella Esperance, Hengko Tornando; *D:* David Worth; *W:* David Worth. *IMP*

Lady Dragon 2 🎬🎬 1993 (R) Martial arts queen Rothrock returns in another saga of kickboxing vengeance. Susan Morgan seeks revenge on the three killers who terrorized her family. When she unleashes the power of the dragon they don't stand a chance. **CW:** Language and plentiful martial arts violence. ?m/C VHS, Closed Caption. Cynthia Rothrock, Billy Drago, Sam Jones, Greg Stuart, Bella Esperance, George Rudy, Adisoerya Abdi; *D:* David Worth; *W:* Clifford Mohr; *M:* Jim West.

The Lady Eve 🎬🎬🎬🎬 1941 Two con artists, out to trip up wealthy beer tycoon Fonda, instead find themselves tripped up when one falls in love with the prey. Ridiculous situations, but Sturges manages to keep them believable and funny. With a train scene that's every man's nightmare. Perhaps the best Sturges ever. Based on the story "The Faithful Heart" by Monckton Hoffe. Later remade as "The Birds and the Bees." 93m/B VHS, Beta, LV. Barbara Stanwyck, Henry Fonda, Charles Coburn, Eugene Pallette, William Demarest, Eric Blore, Melville Cooper; *D:* Preston Sturges; *W:* Preston Sturges; *C:* Victor Milner. National Film Registry '94;; Nominations: Academy Awards '41: Best Story. *USH*

Lady for a Day 🎬🎬🎬½ 1933 Delightful telling of the Damon Runyon story, "Madame La Gimp," about an apple peddler (Robson) down on her luck, who is transformed into a lady by a criminal with a heart. "Lady By Choice" is the sequel. 96m/B VHS, Beta, LV. May Robson, Warren William, Guy Kibbee, Glenda Farrell, Ned Sparks, Jean Parker, Walter Connolly; *D:* Frank Capra. Nominations: Academy Awards '33: Best Actress (Robson), Best Adapted Screenplay, Best Director (Capra), Best Picture. *CVC, CRC, MLB*

Lady for a Night 🎬🎬 1942 The female owner of a gambling riverboat does her best to break into high society, when murder threatens to spoil her plans. Cast and costumes burdened by pacing. 88m/B VHS. John Wayne, Joan Blondell, Ray Middleton, Philip Merivale, Blanche Yurka, Edith Barrett, Leonid Kinskey, Montagu Love; *D:* Leigh Jason. *REP*

Lady Frankenstein 🎬🎬½ *La Figlia di Frankenstein; The Daughter of Frankenstein; Madame Frankenstein* 1972 (R) Frankenstein's lovely daughter graduates from medical school and returns home. When she sees what her father's been up to, she gets some ideas of her own. Good fun for fans of the genre. 84m/C VHS. *IT* Joseph Cotten, Rosalba (Sara Bay) Neri, Mickey Hargitay, Paul Muller, Herbert Fux, Renate Kasche, Ada Pometti, Lorenzo Terzon, Paul Whiteman; *D:* Mel Welles; *W:* Edward Di Lorenzo; *C:* Riccardo Pallton Pallottini. *SNC, HEG*

Lady from Louisiana 🎬🎬 1942 A lawyer in old New Orleans out to rid the city of corruption falls in love with the daughter of a big-time gambler. Great storm scene. 84m/B VHS. John Wayne, Ona Munson, Dorothy Dandridge, Ray Middleton, Henry Stephenson, Helen Westley, Jack Pennick; *D:* Bernard Vorhaus. *REP*

Lady from Nowhere 🎬🎬 1936 A woman is the only witness to a gangland rub-out and is subsequently pursued by both the mob and the police. Unfortunately for her, the gangsters catch up with her first. 60m/B VHS, Beta. Mary Astor, Charles Quigley, Thurston Hall, Victor Kilian, Spencer Charters; *D:* Gordon Wiles. *SNC*

The Lady from Shanghai 🎬🎬🎬½ 1948 An unsuspecting seaman becomes involved in a web of intrigue when a woman hires him to work on her husband's yacht. Hayworth (a one-time Mrs. Orson Welles), in her only role as a villainess, plays a manipulative, sensual schemer. Wonderful and innovative cinematic techniques from Welles, as usual, including a tense scene in a hall of mirrors. Filmed on a yacht belonging to Errol Flynn. 87m/B VHS, Beta, LV. Orson Welles, Rita Hayworth, Everett Sloane, Glenn Anders, Ted de Corsia, Erskine Sanford, Gus Schilling; *D:* Orson Welles; *W:* Orson Welles. *COL, MLB*

Lady from Yesterday 🎬 1985 An American couple's life is shattered by the appearance of the husband's Vietnamese mistress and her 10-year-old son. Made for television. 87m/C VHS, Beta. Wayne Rogers, Bonnie Bedelia, Pat Hingle, Barrie Youngfellow, Blue Dedeort, Tina Chen; *D:* Robert Day. *NO*

Lady Godiva 🎬🎬½ 1955 The lovely O'Hara is wasted in the title role as a Saxon noblewoman married to Leofric (Nader). They're trying to stem Norman influence and Godiva vows to ride naked through the streets of Canterbury to prove the Saxon people's loyalty to King Edward (Franz). Cardboard costumer. Clint Eastwood has a bit as a Saxon soldier. 89m/C VHS. Maureen O'Hara, George Nader, Eduard Franz, Leslie Bradley, Victor McLaglen, Torin Thatcher, Rex Reason; *D:* Arthur Lubin; *W:* Oscar Brodney, Harry Ruskin; *C:* Carl Guthrie. *USH*

Lady Godiva Rides 1968 A bad, campy version of the story of Lady Godiva. Godiva comes to the United States with a bevy of scantily clad maidens and winds up in the Old West. When the town villain threatens to compromise her, Tom Jones comes to the rescue. The film (of course) features Godiva's naked ride on horseback through the town. 88m/C VHS. Marsha Jordan, Forman Shane; *D:* A.C. Stephen. *VDM*

Lady Grey 🎬 1982 A poor farmer's daughter rises to the top of the country music charts, but at a price. 111m/C VHS, Beta. Ginger Alden, David Allen Coe; *D:* Worth Keeter. *NO*

Lady Ice 🎬🎬 1973 (PG) Sutherland, as an insurance investigator on the trail of jewel thieves, follows them to Miami Beach and the Bahamas. After stealing a diamond he enters into partnership with a crook's daughter. Worth seeing for the cast. 93m/C VHS, Beta. Donald Sutherland, Jennifer

O'Neill, Robert Duvall, Eric (Hans Gudegast) Braeden; **D:** Tom Gries; **W:** Alan R. Trustman; **M:** Perry Botkin. *NO*

Lady in a Cage 🐾🐾🐾 **1964** A wealthy widow is trapped in her home elevator during a power failure and becomes desperate when hoodlums break in. Shocking violence ahead of its time probably plays better than when first released. Young Caan is a standout among the star-studded cast. **95m/B VHS, Beta.** Olivia de Havilland, Ann Sothern, James Caan, Jennifer Billingsley, Jeff Corey, Scatman Crothers, Rafael Campos; **D:** Walter Grauman; **W:** Luther Davis. *PAR*

Lady in Cement 🐾½ **1968 (R)** The second Tony Rome mystery, in which the seedy Miami dick finds a corpse with cement shoes while swimming. **93m/C VHS, Beta.** Frank Sinatra, Raquel Welch, Richard Conte, Martin Gabel, Lainie Kazan, Pat Henry, Steve Peck, Joe E. Lewis, Dan Blocker; **D:** Gordon Douglas; **C:** Joseph Biroc. *FOX*

Lady in Distress 🐾🐾½ *A Window in London* **1939** A British drama about an unhappily married man who witnesses an apparent murder. He discovers, however, it was actually the prank of an illusionist and his flirtatious wife. He soon finds himself becoming increasingly involved with their lives. **59m/B VHS, Beta.** *GB* Michael Redgrave, Paul Lukas, Sally Gray; **D:** Herbert Mason. *SNC, VYY, MLB*

The Lady in Question 🐾½ *It Happened in Paris* **1940** A Parisian shopkeeper, played by Aherne, sits on a jury that acquits Hayworth of murder. His interest doesn't end with the trial, however, and matters heat up when his son also becomes involved. Remake of a melodramatic French release. **81m/B VHS, Beta, LV.** Rita Hayworth, Glenn Ford, Brian Aherne, Irene Rich, Lloyd Corrigan, George Coulouris, Evelyn Keyes, Curt Bois, Edward Norris; **D:** Charles Vidor. *COL, CCB*

Lady in Red 🐾🐾 *Guns, Sin and Bathtub Gin* **1979** A story of America in the '30s, and the progress through the underworld of the woman who was Dillinger's last lover. **90m/C VHS, Beta.** Pamela Sue Martin, Louise Fletcher, Robert Conrad, Christopher Lloyd; **D:** Lewis Teague; **W:** John Sayles; **M:** James Horner. *ART, VES*

Lady in the Death House 🐾🐾 **1944** A framed woman is set to walk the last mile, as a scientist struggles to find the real killer in time. **57m/B VHS, Beta.** Jean Parker, Lionel Atwill, Marcia Mae Jones. *VYY*

Lady in the Lake 🐾🐾½ **1946** Why is it everyone wants to get artsy with pulp fiction? Actor Montgomery directs himself in this Philip Marlowe go-round, using a subjective camera style to imitate Chandler's first person narrative (that means the only time we get to see Marlowe/Montgomery's mug is in a mirror. That pretty well says it all.) Having decided to give up eyeing privately, Marlowe turns to the pen to tell the tangled tale of the lady in the lake: once upon a time, a detective was hired to find the wicked wife of a paying client...Some find the direction clever. Others consider MGM chief Louis B. Mayer, who made sure this was Montgomery's last project with MGM, to be a wise man. **103m/B VHS, Beta.** Robert Montgomery, Lloyd Nolan, Audrey Totter, Tom Tully, Leon Ames, Jayne Meadows; **D:** Robert Montgomery; **C:** Paul Vogel. *MGM, FCT*

Lady in Waiting 🐾🐾 **1994 (R)** Detective Jimmy Scavetti (Nouri) is hunting down a serial kill preying on call girls when he meets the seductive Lori (Whirry). Then he discovers his ex-wife's new hubby was the lawyer for each of the victims—only the lawyer turns up dead and Jimmy becomes a suspect. Also available in an unrated version.**CW:** Language; violence; strong sexuality. **85m/C VHS.** Michael Nouri, Shannon Whirry, William Devane, Karen Kopins, Crystal Chappell, Robert Costanzo, Meg Foster, Charles Grant; **D:** Fred Gallo. *AVE*

The Lady in White 🐾🐾🐾 **1988 (PG-13)** Small-town ghost story about murder and revenge. When young Haas is locked in school one night, he's visited by the ghost of a little girl who wants his help in discovering who murdered her. Well developed characters, interesting style, and suspenseful plot make for a sometimes slow but overall exceptional film. **92m/C VHS, Beta, LV, Letterbox, Closed Caption.** Lukas Haas, Len Cariou, Alex Rocco, Katherine Helmond, Jason Presson, Renata Vanni, Angelo Bertolini, Jared Rushton, Joelle Jacob; **D:** Frank Laloggia; **W:** Frank Laloggia; **C:** Russell Carpenter; **M:** Frank Laloggia. *NO*

The Lady Is Willing 🐾🐾½ **1942** Dietrich is a stage star who longs for a baby and when an abandoned infant comes her way she decides to keep the child. Only she hasn't a clue about any of the practical aspects. Lucky for her MacMurray is a friendly pediatrician who gives her some advice. Dietrich finds out she can't adopt as a single parent and persuades MacMurray to marry her, in name only, but since this is a romantic comedy the two eventually fall in love. **91m/B VHS.** Marlene Dietrich, Fred MacMurray, Aline MacMahon, Stanley Ridges, Arline Judge, Roger Clark, Ruth Ford, Sterling Holloway, Harvey Stephens, Harry Shannon, Elisabeth Risdon, Charles Halton; **D:** Mitchell Leisen; **W:** James Edward Grant, Albert McCleery. *FCT*

Lady Jane 🐾🐾🐾½ **1985 (PG-13)** An accurate account of the life of 15-year-old Lady Jane Grey, who secured the throne of England for nine days in 1553 as a result of political maneuvering by noblemen and the Church of England. A wonderful film even for non-history buffs. Carter's first film. **140m/C VHS, Beta, LV, Closed Caption.** *GB* Helena Bonham Carter, Cary Elwes, Sara Kestelman, Michael Hordern, Joss Ackland, Richard Johnson, Patrick Stewart; **D:** Trevor Nunn. *PAR, TVC*

Lady Killer 🐾🐾🐾 **1933** Racy, pre-Code comedy with mobster Cagney hiding out in Hollywood. He gets discovered and becomes a big star, but his old gang turns up to blackmail him. Lots of movie "in" jokes and Clarke (of "Public Enemy" fame) turns up as a wisecracking moll. Based on the story "The Finger Man" by Rosalind Keating Shaffer. **74m/B VHS, Closed Caption.** James Cagney, Mae Clarke, Leslie Fenton, Margaret Lindsay, Henry O'Neill, Raymond Hatton, George Chandler; **D:** Roy Del Ruth; **W:** Ben Markson, Lillie Hayward. *MGM*

Lady Killer 🐾🐾 *Ladykiller* **1997 (R)** A serial killer called the Piggyback Murderer is terrorizing a college campus. Police Lt. Jack Lasky is particularly anxious since his daughter Jennifer (Allman) is a student at the school. When her new boyfriend, aspiring actor Richard Darling (McArthur), keeps turning up at the murder scenes, guess who becomes dad's prime suspect.**CW:** Language, nudity, sexual situations, violence. **80m/C VHS.** Ben Gazzara, Alex McArthur, Terri Treas, Renee Allman; **D:** Terence H. Winkless. *NHO*

Lady L 🐾½ **1965** Silly turn-of-the-century farce about a sexy laundress (Loren), married to a French anarchist (Newman!), who also marries the aristocratic Niven (in name only). Elaborate sets and Paris and London backgrounds couldn't overcome the odd casting and weak script. Adapted from the novel by Romain Gary. **107m/C VHS, Beta.** *FR IT* Sophia Loren, Paul Newman, David Niven, Cecil Parker, Claude Dauphin, Marcel Dalio, Philippe Noiret, Michel Piccoli, Daniel Emilfork, Eugene Deckers; *Cameos:* Peter Ustinov; **D:** Peter Ustinov; **W:** Peter Ustinov. *MGM, FCT*

Lady Mobster 🐾 **1988 (PG-13)** When her parents are murdered a young girl is taken in by a Mafia family. She grows up to be a shrewd lawyer but winds up working in her adoptive family's crime syndicate in order to take revenge on her parents' murderers. Exaggerated and silly but watchable for its so-bad-it's-good qualities. Made for television. **94m/C VHS, Beta, LV, Closed Caption.** Susan Lucci, Michael Nader, Roscoe Born, Joseph Wiseman; **D:** John Llewellyn Moxey. *TTC*

Lady of Burlesque 🐾🐾½ *Striptease Lady* **1943** Burlesque dancer is found dead, strangled with her own G-string. Clever and amusing film based on "The G-String Murders" by Gypsy Rose Lee. **91m/B VHS, Beta.** Barbara Stanwyck, Michael

O'Shea, Janis Carter, Pinky Lee; **D:** William A. Wellman. Nominations: Academy Awards '43: Best Original Dramatic/Comedy Score. *MRV, NOS, VCN*

Lady of the Evening 🐾🐾 **1979 (PG)** A prostitute and a crook team up to seek revenge against the mob. **110m/C VHS, Beta.** *IT* Sophia Loren, Marcello Mastroianni. *NO*

Lady of the House 🐾🐾 **1978** A true story about a madame who rose from operator of a brothel to become a political force in San Francisco. **100m/C VHS, Beta.** Dyan Cannon, Susan Tyrrell, Colleen Camp, Armand Assante; **D:** Ralph Nelson.

Lady of the Lake 🐾🐾 **1928** Rare silent adventure film in which an exiled girl saves the king from outlaws in Scotland. Orchestra score. **47m/B VHS.** *GB* Percy Marmont, Benita Hume, Haddon Mason, Lawson Butt; **D:** James A. Fitzpatrick. *GPV, FCT, GVV*

Lady on a Train 🐾🐾🐾 **1945** Travelling at Christmas, wealthy young Nicky Collins (Durbin) thinks she sees a murder from her train window but when she arrives in New York she can't get anyone to believe her. But not willing to give up, Nicky turns to Wayne Morgan (Bruce), a mystery writer for help. Recognizing the victim from a newspaper photo, Nicky checks out his family and gets mistaken for a nightclub singer (so Durbin can vamp a torch song). Lots of comedy amidst the mystery and romance, and some surprizes as well. Based on a story by Leslie Charteris. ♫Gimme a Little Kiss, Will You, Huh?; Night and Day; Silent Night. **95m/B VHS, Closed Caption.** Deanna Durbin, David Bruce, Ralph Bellamy, Dan Duryea, Edward Everett Horton, Allen Jenkins, Elizabeth Patterson, William Frawley, Jacqueline DeWit, George Coulouris; **D:** Charles David; **W:** Robert O'Brien, Edmund Beloin; **C:** Woody Bredell; **M:** Miklos Rozsa. Nominations: Academy Awards '45: Best Sound. *USH*

Lady on the Bus 🐾🐾 **1978 (R)** Sexually frustrated newlywed bride rides the city buses looking for men to satisfy her. This bothers her husband. Shot in Rio de Janeiro. In Portuguese with English subtitles. **102m/C VHS, Beta, LV.** *BR* Sonia Braga; **D:** Neville D'Almedia. *ART, VES*

The Lady Refuses 🐾🐾 **1931** A stuffy Victorian father is disappointed in his wastrel son and decides a poor but honest young woman could be the making of him. Problems arise when the girl falls for the father instead. **70m/B VHS, Beta.** Betty Compson, John Darrow, Margaret Livingston, Gilbert Emery; **D:** George Archainbaud. *DVT, VYY*

The Lady Says No 🐾🐾 **1951** A photographer must photograph an attractive author who has written a book uncomplimentary toward the male sex. **80m/B VHS.** Joan Caulfield, David Niven, James Robertson Justice, Frances Bavier, Henry Jones, Jeff York, John Wood; **D:** Frank Ross. *FCT*

Lady Scarface 🐾🐾 **1941** Murderous mobster queen breaks the law, bats men around, and takes the cops on a merry chase. Cheap, fast-paced action. **66m/B VHS, Beta.** Mildred Coles, Dennis O'Keefe, Frances Neal, Judith Anderson, Eric Blore, Charles Halton; **D:** Frank Woodruff. *NO*

Lady Scarface/The Threat **1949** A crime double feature: "Lady Scarface" (1941), a clever cop is on the trail of a dangerous gunwoman; and "The Threat" (1949), a ruthless killer escapes from prison intent on murdering those who convicted him. **132m/B VHS, Beta.** Dennis O'Keefe, Judith Anderson, Robert Knapp, Eric Blore, Charles McGraw, Michael O'Shea, Virginia Grey; **D:** Frank Woodruff. *TTC*

Lady Sings the Blues 🐾🐾½ **1972 (R)** Jazz artist Billie Holiday's life becomes a musical drama depicting her struggle against racism and drug addiction in her pursuit of fame and romance. What could be a typical price-of-fame story is saved by Ross' inspired performance as the tragic singer. ♫My Man; Strange Fruit; God Bless the Child; Don't Explain; T'Ain't Nobody's Business If I Do; Lady Sings the Blues; All Of Me; The Man I Love; Our Love Is Here to Stay. **144m/C VHS, Beta, LV.** Diana Ross, Billy Dee Williams, Richard Pryor,

James Callahan, Paul Hampton, Sid Melton; **D:** Sidney J. Furie; **C:** John A. Alonzo. Nominations: Academy Awards '72: Best Actress (Ross), Best Art Direction/Set Decoration, Best Costume Design, Best Story & Screenplay, Original Song Score and/or Adaptation. *PAR, FCT*

Lady Street Fighter 🐾 1986 A well-armed female combat fighter battles an organization of assassins to avenge her sister's murder. 73m/C VHS, Beta. Renee Harmon, Joel McCrea Jr. *UNI*

Lady Takes a Chance 🐾🐾🐾 1943 A romantic comedy about a New York working girl with matrimonial ideas and a rope-shy rodeo rider who yearns for the wide open spaces. Fine fun on the range. 86m/B VHS, Beta. John Wayne, Jean Arthur, Phil Silvers, Charles Winninger; **D:** William A. Seiter. *REP*

Lady Terminator 🐾½ 1989 (R) A student on an anthropology expedition digs up more than she bargained for when she is possessed by an evil spirit and goes on a rampage. 83m/C VHS, Beta. Barbara Constable, Christopher Hart, Joseph McGlynn, Claudia Rademaker; **D:** Jalil Jackson. *HTV*

The Lady Vanishes 🐾🐾🐾🐾 1938 When a kindly old lady disappears from a fast-moving train, her young friend finds an imposter in her place and a spiraling mystery to solve. Hitchcock's first real winner, a smarmy, wit-drenched British mystery that precipitated his move to Hollywood. Along with "39 Steps," considered an early Hitchcock classic. From the novel "The Wheel Spins," by Ethel Lina White. Special edition contains short subject on Hitchcock's cameos in his films. Remade in 1979. 99m/B VHS, Beta, LV, DVD. *GB* Margaret Lockwood, Paul Lukas, Michael Redgrave, May Whitty, Googie Withers, Basil Radford, Naunton Wayne, Cecil Parker, Linden Travers, Catherine Lacey; *Cameos:* Alfred Hitchcock; **D:** Alfred Hitchcock; **W:** Sidney Gilliat, Frank Launder; **M:** Louis Levy. New York Film Critics Awards '38: Best Director (Hitchcock). *SNC, NOS, HHT*

The Lady Vanishes 🐾½ 1979 In this re-working of the '38 Alfred Hitchcock film, a woman on a Swiss bound train awakens from a nap to find that the elderly woman seated next to her was kidnapped. Falls short of the original movie due to the "screwball" nature of the main characters, Gould and Shepherd. Based on Ethel Lina White's novel "The Wheel Spins." 95m/C VHS, Beta, LV. *GB* Elliott Gould, Cybill Shepherd, Angela Lansbury, Herbert Lom; **D:** Anthony Page; **W:** George Axelrod. *MRV*

Lady Windermere's Fan 🐾🐾½ 1926 The silent, Lubitsch adaptation of the Oscar Wilde tale concerning an upper-class couple's marriage being almost destroyed by suspected adultery. 66m/B VHS, Beta, 8mm. Ronald Colman, May McAvoy, Bert Lytell; **D:** Ernst Lubitsch. *VYY, GPV, GVV*

The Lady with the Dog 🐾🐾🐾 1959 A bittersweet love story based on the Anton Chekhov story, about two married Russians who meet by chance in a park, fall in love, and realize they are fated to a haphazard, clandestine affair. In Russian with English titles. 86m/B VHS, Beta. *RU* Iya Savvina, Alexei Batalov, Ala Chostakova, N. Alisova; **D:** Yosif Heifitz. *WST, FCT, TPV*

The Lady Without Camelias 🐾🐾½ 1953 A young woman is discovered by a film producer who casts her in a successful movie and eventually marries her. Convinced that she can sustain a career as a serious actress, the producer is dismayed by the job offers that come her way, usually of a sexually exploitive nature. What follows is a tragic decline for both. 106m/C VHS, Beta. *IT CIG*

Ladybird, Ladybird 🐾🐾🐾 1993 (R) Loach's emotionally bruising look at working-class life and family in the '90s. Maggie (Rock) is a tough unmarried mother of four who's been battered by her lovers and has come under the overwatchful eye of Britain's social services. She meets Jorge (Vega), a gentle Paraguayan, and just when things are looking up, Jorge gets immigration heat, Maggie's insecurities surface, and her baby daughter is taken into care by child wel-

fare. Rock has a no-nonsense manner and acerbic wit that precludes any hand-wringing for her character, even as you hope she'll win out over circumstance. Based on a true story. **CW:** Strong language and intense depiction of domestic abuse. 102m/C VHS. *GB* Crissy Rock, Vladimir Vega, Ray Winstone, Sandie Lavelle, Mauricio Venegas, Clare Perkins, Jason Stracey, Luke Brown, Lily Farrell; **D:** Ken Loach; **W:** Rona Munro; **C:** Barry Ackroyd; **M:** George Fenton. Berlin International Film Festival '94: Best Actress (Rock); Nominations: Independent Spirit Awards '95: Best Foreign Film. *HMK*

Ladybugs 🐾½ 1992 (PG-13) Hangdog salesman Dangerfield would like to move up the corporate ladder, but must first turn the company-sponsored girl's soccer team into winners. Routine Dangerfield vehicle exploits nearly everything for laughs, including dressing an athletic boy as a girl so he can play on the team. Obvious fluff. 91m/C VHS, Beta, Closed Caption. Rodney Dangerfield, Jackee, Jonathan Brandis, Ilene Graff, Vinessa Shaw, Tom Parks, Jeanetta Arnetta, Nancy Parsons, Blake Clark, Tommy Lasorda; **D:** Sidney J. Furie; **W:** Curtis Burch; **C:** Dan Burstall; **M:** Richard Gibbs. *PAR*

Ladyhawke 🐾🐾½ 1985 (PG-13) In medieval times, a youthful pickpocket befriends a strange knight who is on a mysterious quest. This unlikely duo, accompanied by a watchful hawk, are enveloped in a magical adventure. 121m/C VHS, Beta, LV, Letterbox, Closed Caption. Matthew Broderick, Rutger Hauer, Michelle Pfeiffer, John Wood, Leo McKern, Alfred Molina, Ken Hutchison; **D:** Richard Donner; **W:** Edward Khmara, Michael Thomas, Tom Mankiewicz; **M:** Andrew Powell. Nominations: Academy Awards '85: Best Sound. *WAR*

Ladykiller 🐾🐾 1992 (R) Rogers stars as a burned-out cop who goes to a dating service to find a man who'll give her the attention she craves. When she meets wealthy professional Shea she thinks he's the one but her cop's curiosity about her lover's past may cost her her life. **CW:** Sexuality. 92m/C VHS, LV, Closed Caption. Mimi Rogers, John Shea, Alice Krige, Tom Irwin; **D:** Michael Scott; **W:** Shelley Evans. *USH*

The Ladykillers 🐾🐾🐾½ *The Lady Killers* 1955 A gang of bumbling bank robbers is foiled by a little old lady. Hilarious antics follow, especially on the part of Guinness, who plays the slightly demented-looking leader of the gang. 87m/C VHS, Beta. *GB* Alec Guinness, Cecil Parker, Katie Johnson, Herbert Lom, Peter Sellers, Danny Green, Jack Warner, Kenneth Connor, Edie Martin, Jack Melford; **D:** Alexander MacKendrick; **W:** William Rose; **C:** Otto Heller; **M:** Tristram Cary. British Academy Awards '55: Best Actress (Johnson), Best Screenplay; Nominations: Academy Awards '56: Best Original Screenplay. *REP, FCT, HMV*

Ladykillers 🐾🐾 1988 At the glitzy L.A. club Ladykillers, men strip as the women cheer. At the climax of the performance, one of the dancers is brutally murdered, live on stage. In this decadent world of glitter and sex, the women are the hunters and the men are the reward. 97m/C VHS, Beta, Closed Caption. Marilu Henner, Susan Blakely, Lesley-Anne Down, Thomas Calabro; **D:** Robert Lewis; **W:** Greg Dinallo.

The Lady's Not for Burning 🐾🐾½ 1987 Romantic comedy, set in a medieval English village, finds ex-soldier Thomas Mendip (Branagh) invading the home of querulous Mayor Hebble Tyson (Hepton), demanding to be hanged. He says he's murdered the local rag and bone merchant but the townspeople insist Jennet Jourdemayne (Lunghi), who's seeking refuge at the mayor's, has turned him into a dog. They demand she be burned as a witch (hence the title, since Thomas, unwillingly but strongly, objects to this action). Adapted by Fry from his play; made for TV. 90m/C VHS. Kenneth Branagh, Cherie Lunghi, Bernard Hepton, Tim Watson, Susannah Harker, Angela Thorne, Shaun Scott; **D:** Julian Amyes; **W:** Christopher Fry. *VCO, FUS*

Lafayette Escadrille 🐾🐾½ *Hell Bent for Glory* 1958 Action and romance in WWI via the famed flying unit manned by American volunteers. Hunter is banal in the lead role as is his romance with a reformed prostitute (Choreau). Director Wellman actually was a member of the squadron and his son plays him in the film but the director regarded the film as a failure because of studio interference. 92m/B VHS. Tab Hunter, Etchika Choureau, William Wellman Jr., Joel McCrea, Dennis Devine, Marcel Dalio, David Janssen, Paul Fix, Will Hutchins, Clint Eastwood; **D:** William A. Wellman; **W:** A.S. Fleischman; **C:** William Clothier; **M:** Leonard Rosenman. *WAR*

L'Age D'Or 🐾🐾🐾🐾 *Age of Gold* 1930 Bunuel's first full-length film and his masterpiece of sex, repression, and of course, death. A hapless man is prevented from reaching his beloved by middle-class morality, forces of the establishment, the Church, government and every bastion of modern values. Banned for years because of its anti-religious stance. Co-scripted by Dali. A mercilessly savage, surreal satire, the purest expression of Bunuel's wry misanthropy. In French with English subtitles. 62m/B VHS, Beta, LV. *FR* Gaston Modot, Lya Lys, Max Ernst, Pierre Prevert, Marie Berthe Ernst, Paul Eluard; **D:** Luis Bunuel; **W:** Salvador Dali, Luis Bunuel. *FCT, IME, GVV*

Laguna Heat 🐾🐾½ 1987 A tired LA cop investigates a series of murders that are related to an old friend of his father's. Based on a novel by T. Jefferson Parker. Made for television. 110m/C VHS, Beta, LV. Harry Hamlin, Jason Robards Jr., Catherine Hicks, Rip Torn, Anne Francis; **D:** Simon Langton. *ORI, WAR*

Lai Shi: China's Last Eunuch 1988 A starving Chinese child becomes a eunuch in order to garner wealth in the Emperor's palace. But he is castrated at a historically inopportune moment (as if there's a good time for such modification), just prior to the turbulent 1920s. In Cantonese with English subtitles. 100m/C VHS. *CH* **D:** Chan Tsi-liang. *FCT*

The Lair of the White Worm 🐾🐾🐾 1988 (R) Scottish archaeologist uncovers a strange skull, and then a bizarre religion to go with it, and then a very big worm. An unusual look at the effects of Christianity and paganism on each other, colored with sexual innuendo and, of course, giant worms. A cross between a morality play and a horror film. Adapted from Bram Stoker's last writings, done while he was going mad from Bright's disease. Everything you'd expect from Russell. 93m/C VHS, Beta, LV. *GB* Amanda Donohoe, Sammi Davis, Catherine Oxenberg, Hugh Grant, Peter Capaldi, Stratford Johns, Paul Brooke, Christopher Gable; **D:** Ken Russell; **W:** Ken Russell; **C:** Dick Bush; **M:** Stanislas Syrewicz. *VES, ART, TPV*

Lake Consequence 🐾🐾 1992 (R) Severance plays a suburban housewife who accidentally gets locked in the camper of the tree-trimmer stud (Zane) she's been eyeing while he's been working in her neighborhood. Next thing she knows they wind up at a distant lake where the bored housewife is more than willing to give into her growing sexual fantasies. An unrated version at 90 minutes is also available. 85m/C VHS, LV, Closed Caption. Joan Severance, Billy Zane, May Karasun; **D:** Rafael Eisenman; **W:** Zalman King, Melanie Finn, Henry Cobbold; **M:** George S. Clinton. *REP*

Lakota Woman: Siege at Wounded Knee 🐾🐾½ 1994 Autobiography of Mary Crow Dog (Bedard) and her coming of age during the American Indian Movement's 1973 occupation of Wounded Knee. Tangled loyalties and the battle between Native Americans and U.S. troops make for strong drama. Bedard is remarkable in her film debut. Based on the book by Mary Crow Dog and Richard Erdoes. Filmed on location in South Dakota. 113m/C VHS, Closed Caption. Irene Bedard, August Schellenberg, Joseph Runningfox, Floyd "Red Crow" Westerman, Tantoo Cardinal, Michael Horse, Lawrence Bayne, Nancy Parsons; **D:** Frank Pierson; **W:** Bill Kerby; **C:** Toyomichi Kurita; **M:** Richard Horowitz. *TTC*

The Lamb 🎬🎬½ **1915** Intent on proving to his sweetheart that he's not the coward people say he is, a guy heads west to engage in various manly activities, including fisticuffs, karate and Indian kidnapping. Fairbanks' debut on film (he was already an established Broadway star) set the mold for the American leading man: moral, cheerful, physical, and not hard to look at. A popular guy with the public, Fairbanks formed his own film company the following year. Story's based on D.W. Griffith's book, "The Man and the Test." **60m/B VHS, Beta.** Douglas Fairbanks Sr., Seena Owen, Lillian Langdon, Monroe Salisbury, Kate Toncray, Alfred Paget, William E. Lowery; **D:** Christy Cabanne. *GPV, FCT*

Lamb 🎬🎬 **1985** Troubled 10-year-old epileptic Owen Kane (Kane) has been dumped by his abusive mother at a Catholic-run institution for wayward boys in Ireland, run by self-righteous headmaster Brother Benedict (Bannen). Owen becomes Benedict's scapegoat—much to the dismay of Brother Michael Lamb (Neeson). When Lamb claims a small family inheritance, he decides to grab Owen and head to London, posing as father and son, where they live in increasingly depressed surroundings while Michael tries painfully to make them into a real family. Based on the novel by MacLaverty, who also wrote the screenplay. **110m/C VHS.** *IR* Liam Neeson, Hugh O'Conor, Ian Bannen, Frances Tomelty; **D:** Colin Gregg; **W:** Bernard MacLaverty; **C:** Mike Garfath; **M:** Van Morrison. *CTL, FCT, TPV*

Lambada 🎬 **1989 (PG)** By day, he's a high school teacher in Beverly Hills; by night, a Latin dirty dancer cum tutor of ghetto teens. The very first of several films based on the short-lived dance craze. **92m/C VHS, Beta, LV, Closed Caption.** J. Eddie Peck, Melora Hardin, Adolfo "Shabba Doo" Quinones, Ricky Paull Goldin, Basil Hoffman, Dennis Burkley; **D:** Joel Silberg. *MGM*

Lamerica 🎬🎬🎬 **1995** Two Italian hustlers, Fiore (Placido) and his younger partner Gino (Lo Verso), head for poverty-stricken Albania in 1991, the first year after the collapse of the Communist dictatorship. They intend to set up a phony corporation and scam money from government grants but they need an Albanian figurehead. The duo find simple-minded, elderly Spiro (Di Mazzarelli), who's spent most of his life in prison camps, and stash him in an orphanage for safe keeping. Only when Spiro gets away, Gino heads for the countryside to find him and discovers some secrets about Spiro's past and just how the wily Albanians have been surviving. Italian with subtitles. **116m/C VHS, Letterbox.** *IT* Enrico Lo Verso, Michele Placido, Carmelo Di Mazzarelli, Piro Milkani; **D:** Gianni Amelio; **W:** Gianni Amelio, Andrea Porporati, Alessandro Sermoneta; **C:** Luca Bigazzi; **M:** Franco Piersanti. Nominations: Independent Spirit Awards '97: Best Foreign Film. *NYF*

L'Amour en Herbe 🎬🎬 *Budding Love; Tender Love* **1977** His parents realize Pascal has something on his mind when he fails school. It turns out to be lovely Martine, whom he is then forbidden to see. But Pascal remains true—until betrayed. In French with subtitles. **100m/C VHS.** *FR* Pascal Meynier, Guilhaine Dubos, Bruno Raffaeli, Michel Galabru, Francoise Prevost, Alix Mahieux; **D:** Roger Andrieux; **W:** Roger Andrieux, Jean-Marie Benard; **C:** Ramon Suarez; **M:** Maxime Le Forestier. *FCT*

Lamp at Midnight 🎬🎬½ **1966** Presentation from "George Schaefer's Showcase Theatre" deals with three critical periods in the life of Italian astronomer Galileo Galilei, from his invention of the telescope, through his appearance at the Holy Office of the Inquisition, to the publication of his "Dialogue on the Two Systems of the World." For those in a planetary state of mind. **76m/C VHS, Beta.** Melvyn Douglas, David Wayne, Michael Hordern, Hurd Hatfield, Kim Hunter; **D:** George Schaefer. *FHS*

Lana in Love 🎬🎬 **1992** A lonely woman places an ad in the personal section in hopes of finding her Mr. Right. **90m/C VHS, Beta.** Daphna Kastner, Clark Gregg. *NO*

Lancelot of the Lake 🎬🎬 *Lancelot du Lac; The Grail; Le Graal* **1974** The Knights of the Round Table return to the court of King Arthur after a long, bloody, and fruitless search for the Holy Grail. Rivalries and jealousies debase the heroes as Lancelot struggles with his feelings for Arthur's Queen Guinevere. Austere acting but the film's rich visuals provide a sensuous air. French with subtitles. **85m/C VHS.** *FR* Luc Simon, Laura Duke Condominas, Vladimir Antolek-Oresek, Humbert Balsan, Patrick Bernard, Arthur De Montalembert; **D:** Robert Bresson; **W:** Robert Bresson; **C:** Pasquale De Santis; **M:** Philippe Sarde. *NYF*

Land and Freedom 🎬🎬🎬 **1995** Earnestly talky drama focusing on idealist Liverpudlian communist David Carr (Hart), who heads to Spain in 1937 to fight against Franco's fascists. What David learns is that the Republican forces, made up of independent militia, are bitterly divided, with much infighting and betrayal from the Stalinist forces within David's own party. He falls for socialist Blanca (Pastor) and learns how terrifying and haphazard war can be (with timeout for ideological discussions). Sympathetic characters and sweeping action help to compensate for the political polemics. **109m/C VHS.** *GB SP GE* Ian Hart, Rosana Pastor, Iciar Bollain, Tom Gilroy, Frederic Pierrot, Marc Martinez; **D:** Ken Loach; **W:** Jim Allen; **C:** Barry Ackroyd; **M:** George Fenton. Cesar Awards '96: Best Foreign Film; Nominations: British Academy Awards '95: Best Film. *PGV*

The Land Before Time 🎬🎬🎬 **1988 (G)** Lushly animated children's film about five orphaned baby dinosaurs who band together and try to find the Great Valley, a paradise where they might live safely. Works same parental separation theme as Bluth's "American Tail." Charming, coy, and shamelessly tearjerking; producers included Steven Spielberg and George Lucas. **67m/C VHS, LV, Closed Caption, DVD. D:** Don Bluth; **W:** Stu Krieger; **M:** James Horner; **V:** Pat Hingle, Helen Shaver, Gabriel Damon, Candice Houston, Burke Barnes, Judith Barsi, Will Ryan. *USH, FCT*

The Land Before Time 2: The Great Valley Adventure 🎬🎬½ **1994 (G)** Sequel to 1988's animated adventure finds dinsosaur pals Littlefoot, Cera, Ducky, Petrie, and Spike happily settled in the Great Valley. But their adventures don't stop as they chase two egg-stealing Struthiomimuses and retrieve an egg of unknown origin from the Mysterious Beyond. **75m/C VHS, LV, Closed Caption.** *USH*

The Land Before Time 3: The Time of the Great Giving 🎬🎬½ **1995 (G)** Littlefoot and his pals try to find a new source of water when the Great Valley experiences a severe water shortage. **71m/C VHS, LV, Closed Caption. D:** Roy Allen Smith. *USH*

The Land Before Time 4: Journey Through the Mists 🎬🎬½ **1996** The little dinosaurs travel through the land of the mists in search of a rejuvenation flower that can save the life of Litefoot's sick grandpa. **74m/C VHS, LV, Closed Caption. D:** Roy Allen Smith. *USH*

The Land Before Time 5: The Mysterious Island 🎬🎬½ **1997 (G)** When a swarm of insects devour all the plants in the Great Valley, the herds are forced to move. But with the adults fighting, Littlefoot and his pals go off on their own. They cross the Big Water to a mysterious island, which just happens to be the home of their old friend, the baby T-Rex, Chomper. And it's up to Chomper to protect his plant-eating friends from the island's meat-eaters, who look on the little band as dinner. **74m/C VHS, LV, Closed Caption. D:** Charles Grosvenor. *USH*

Land of Doom 🎬 **1984** An amazon and a warrior struggle for survival in a post-holocaust fantasy setting. **87m/C VHS, Beta.** Deborah Rennard, Garrick Dowhen; **D:** Peter Maris. *ART*

The Land of Faraway 🎬🎬 **1987 (G)** Λ Swedish boy is whisked off to a magical land where he does battle with evil knights and flies on winged horses. Dubbed; based on a novel by Astrid Lindgren. **95m/C VHS, Beta.** Timothy Bottoms, Christian Bale, Susannah York, Christopher Lee, Nicholas Pickard; **D:** Vladimir Grammatikov.

Land of Fury 🎬🎬 *The Seekers* **1955** British naval officer Hawkins steps on New Zealand's shore and into trouble when he accidently walks on sacred Maori burial ground. Very British, very dated colonial saga, based on the novel "The Seekers" by John Guthrie. **90m/C VHS.** *GB* Jack Hawkins, Glynis Johns, Noel Purcell, Ian Fleming; **D:** Ken Annakin. *NOS*

Land of Hunted Men 🎬 **1943** The Range Busters are on the case as they track down the hideout of terrorizing gunmen. **58m/B VHS, Beta.** Ray Corrigan, Dennis Moore, Max Terhune. *NOS, DVT*

Land of Promise 🎬🎬½ *Ziemia Obiecana* **1974** At the turn of the century three men build a textile factory in Lodz, Poland. They each represent a particular ethnic group: a Pole (Olbrychski), a German (Seweryn), and a Jew (Pszoniak). Class conflicts threaten to overwhelm as their overworked and underpaid workers plan a revolt. Based on the novel by Wladyslav Reymont. In Polish with English subtitles. **178m/C VHS.** *PL* Daniel Olbrychski, Wojciech Pszoniak, Andrzej Seweryn, Anna Nehrebecka; **D:** Andrzej Wajda; **W:** Andrzej Wajda; **M:** Wojciech Kilar. Nominations: Academy Awards '75: Best Foreign Language Film. *FCT*

Land of the Lawless 🎬 **1947** A group of outlaws rule over a barren wasteland. What's the point? **54m/B VHS.** Rachel Brown, Raymond Hatton, Christine McIntyre, Tristram Coffin; **D:** Lambert Hillyer. *NOS, DVT*

Land of the Minotaur 🎬🎬 *The Devil's Men* **1977 (PG)** Small village is the setting for horrifying ritual murders, demons, and disappearances of young terrorists. Fans of Pleasence and Cushing won't want to miss this. **88m/C VHS, Beta.** *GB* Donald Pleasence, Peter Cushing, Luan Peters; **D:** Costa Carayiannis; **M:** Brian Eno. *VCI, MRV*

Land of the Pharaohs 🎬🎬½ **1955** Epic about the building of Egypt's Great Pyramid. Hawkins is the extremely talkative pharoah and Collins plays his sugary-sweet yet villainous wife. Sort of campy, but worth watching for the great surprise ending. **106m/C VHS, LV, Letterbox, Closed Caption.** Jack Hawkins, Joan Collins, James Robertson Justice, Dewey Martin, Alexis Minotis, Sydney Chaplin; **D:** Howard Hawks; **W:** Harold Jack Bloom; **C:** Lee Garmes. *WAR*

Land Raiders 🎬🎬 **1969** Savalas plays a man who hates Apaches and wants their land, but is distracted when his brother arrives on the scene, igniting an old feud. **101m/C VHS, Beta.** Telly Savalas, George Maharis, Arlene Dahl, Janet Landgard; **D:** Nathan (Hertz) Juran. *GKK*

The Land that Time Forgot 🎬🎬 **1975 (PG)** A WWI veteran, a beautiful woman, and their German enemies are stranded in a land outside time filled with prehistoric creatures. Based on the 1918 novel by Edgar Rice Burroughs. Followed in 1977 by "The People that Time Forgot." **90m/C VHS, Beta.** *GB* Doug McClure, John McEnery, Susan Penhaligon, Keith Barren, Anthony Ainley, Godfrey James, Bobby Parr, Declan Mulholland, Colin Farrell, Ben Howard, Roy Holder, Andrew McCulloch, Ron Pember, Steve James; **D:** Kevin Connor; **W:** James Cawthorn, Michael Moorcock; **C:** Alan Hume; **M:** Douglas Gamley. *ART, VES*

The Land Unknown 🎬🎬½ **1957** A Naval helicopter is forced down in a tropical land of prehistoric terror, complete with ferocious creatures from the Mesozoic Era. While trying to make repairs, the crew discovers the sole survivor of a previous expedition who was driven to madness by life in the primordial jungle. Good performances from cast, although monsters aren't that believable. Based on a story by Charles Palmer. **78m/B VHS, Closed Caption.** Jock Mahoney, Shawn Smith, William Reynolds, Henry Kleinbach Brandon, Douglas Kennedy; **D:** Virgil W. Vogel; **W:** Laszlo Gorog; **M:** Henry Mancini. *USH*

Landlord Blues 1987 A trashy slumlord without morals or a conscience goes one step too far, and a tenant retaliates with munitions. **96m/C VHS, Beta.** Mark Boone, Raye Dowell, Richard Litt, Bill Rice, Mary Schultz, Gigi Williams; **D:** Jacob Burckhardt. *NO*

Landscape in the Mist 🎬🎬🎬 *Topio Stin Omichli* 1988 A stark Greek landscape in a rainy winter sets the scene for a tragic search by two children for their unknown father. Relies heavily on symbolism to make its point about unfulfilled desire (including the film's imaginary German-Greek border). In Greek with English subtitles. **126m/C VHS.** *GR FR IT* Tania Palaiologou, Michalis Zeke, Stratos Tzortzoglou, Eva Kotamanidou, Alika Georgouli; **D:** Theo Angelopoulos; **W:** Thanassis Valtinos, Tonino Guerra, Theo Angelopoulos. *NYF, FCT, BTV*

Landslide 🎬🎬½ 1992 (PG-13) As a geologist, suffering from memory loss, comes closer to discovering his identity his life is endangered by a sinister plot. **95m/C VHS, LV, Closed Caption.** Anthony Edwards, Tom Burlinson, Joanna Cassidy, Melody Anderson, Ronald Lacey, Ken James, Lloyd Bochner; **D:** Jean-Claude Lord. *REP*

L'Anne Sainte 🎬🎬½ *Pilgrimage to Rome* 1978 In his last film, Gabin is an escaped convict returning to his hidden loot in Rome when his plane is hijacked by international terrorists. Available dubbed. **?m/C VHS.** *FR* Jean Gabin, Jean-Claude Brialy, Paul Giusti, Danielle Darrieux. *FRA, FCT*

L'Annee des Meduses 🎬½ *The Year of the Jellyfish* 1986 (R) An 18-year-old girl tries to seduce the local Monsieur Beefcake she meets on her vacation. When he doesn't return her interest, she decides to teach him a lesson. In French with English subtitles, or dubbed. **110m/C VHS, Beta.** *FR* Valerie Kaprisky, Barnard Giradeau; **D:** Christopher Frank; **C:** Renato Berta. *FCT, TPV*

Lantern Hill 🎬🎬½ 1990 (G) During the Depression, a 12-year-old girl attempts to fan the embers between her estranged parents. Made for cable Wonderworks production, filmed partly on Canada's Prince Edward Island. Based on a story by Lucy Maud Montgomery, whose "Anne of Green Gables" is also part of the Wonderworks series. **112m/C VHS, LV, Closed Caption.** *CA* Sam Waterston, Colleen Dewhurst, Sarah Polley, Marion Bennett, Zoe Caldwell; **D:** Kevin Sullivan. *TOU, FCT*

Lap Dancing woof! 1995 (R) What hath "Showgirls" wrought? Small town gal Angie Parker moves to Hollywood to become an actress and, when the money runs out, winds up as an exotic dancer. Also available unrated.**CW:** Nudity, violence, sexual situations, language. **90m/C VHS, LV.** Lorissa McComas, Tane McClure, C.T. Miller; **D:** Mike Sedan. *TRI*

L'Appat 🎬🎬 *Fresh Bait; Live Bait; The Bait* 1994 Deglamourizing, if familiar, look at amoral teens and violence. 18-year-old salesgirl Nathalie (Gillain) supports her unemployed boyfriend Eric (Sitruk) and his dim-bulb buddy Bruno (Putzulu). The guys hang out, watch too many gangster videos, and try to be tough, deciding to get rich by dangling Nathalie as bait. She goes to a man's home (presumably for sex) but Eric and Bruno will break in and rob the mark instead. Plan goes awry when their first victim is killed. What's truly disturbing is the trio's blase attitude that crime is a viable way to obtain money or that anything would happen to them should they be caught. Based on the book by Morgan Sportes, which recounted the 1984 crime. French with subtitles. **117m/C VHS.** *FR* Marie Gillain, Olivier Sitruk, Bruno Putzulu, Philippe Duclos, Richard Berry; **D:** Bertrand Tavernier; **W:** Bertrand Tavernier, Colo Tavernier O'Hagan; **M:** Philippe Haim. Berlin International Film Festival '94: Best Film. *NYR*

Laramie Kid 🎬 1935 A vintage Tyler sagebrush saga. **60m/B VHS, Beta.** Tom Tyler, Alberta Vaughn, Al Ferguson, Murdock McQuarrie, George Chesebro; **D:** Harry S. Webb. *NOS, DVT, RXM*

L'Argent 🎬🎬 1983 When a young man's parents refuse to lend him any money a friend helps out by giving him a counterfeit 500-franc note. This sets off a chain of events, with every passing of the money leading to another lie, betrayal, and increasingly violent crime. Austere and stylized vision is not for all tastes. In French with English subtitles. **82m/C VHS.** *FR* Christian Patey, Sylvie van den Elsen, Michel Briguet, Caroline Lang; **D:** Robert Bresson; **W:** Robert Bresson; **C:** Pasquale De Santis. Cannes Film Festival '83: Best Director (Bresson); National Society of Film Critics Awards '84: Best Director (Bresson). *NYF, FCT*

Larger Than Life 🎬½ *Nickel and Dime; Large as Life* 1996 (PG) The pitch for this movie (Murray takes an elephant on a cross-country trip) must have sounded terrific. Unfortunately, the pitch was fouled off. Murray is his usual smarmy self as cut-rate motivational speaker Jack Corcoran, who inherits the pachyderm and a pile of bills after his circus clown father dies. Following the "road movie" formula, he encounters wacky characters along the way, including a speed-freak trucker (McConaughey), a sexy animal trainer (Fiorentino) and a strait-laced zookeeper (Garofalo). In a piece of brilliant casting, Tai, the star of "Operation Dumbo Drop" appears as...the elephant. **93m/C VHS, Closed Caption.** Bill Murray, Janeane Garofalo, Linda Fiorentino, Matthew McConaughey, Keith David, Pat Hingle, Jeremy Piven, Lois Smith, Anita Gillette, Maureen Mueller; **D:** Howard Franklin; **W:** Roy Blount Jr.; **C:** Elliot Davis; **M:** Miles Goodman. *MGM*

Larks on a String 🎬🎬½ 1968 Banned for 23 years, this wonderful film is Menzel's masterpiece, even better than his Oscar winning "Closely Watched Trains." Portrays the story of life in labor camps where men and women are re-educated at the whim of the government. No matter what the hardships, these people find humor, hope and love. Their individuality will not be lost, nor their humanity dissolved. Excellent performances, tellingly directed with a beautiful sense of composition and tone. Screenplay written by Menzel and Bohumil Hrabil, author of the short story on which it is based. In Czech with English subtitles. **96m/C VHS.** *CZ* Vaclav Neckar, Jitka Zelenohorska, Jaroslav Satoransky, Rudolf Hrusinsky; **D:** Jiri Menzel; **W:** Jiri Menzel. *FXL*

Larry 🎬🎬 1974 Based on the Nevada State Hospital case history of a 26-year-old man, institutionalized since infancy, who is discovered to be of normal intelligence and must learn to live the life he has always been capable of living. Made for television. **80m/C VHS, Beta.** Frederic Forrest, Tyne Daly, Katherine Helmond, Michael McGuire, Robert Walden; **D:** William A. Graham. *BFA*

Larry McMurtry's Dead Man's Walk 🎬🎬½ *Dead Man's Walk* 1996 (PG-13) McMurtry's prequel to "Lonesome Dove" focuses on the teenaged Gus McCrae (Arquette) and Woodrow Call (Miller) and their first adventures as Texas Rangers in the 1840s. They're involved in the ill-fated Texas-Santa Fe Expedition, led by parrot-owning former seafarer Caleb Cobb (Abraham), to take Santa Fe and make New Mexico part of the Texas Republic. Instead, a Mexican Army detachment led by Capt. Salazar (Olmos), captures the rag-tag group, which is then forced to march across a deadly stretch of desert that few survive. Likeable leads but the supporting actors, including Carradine and Stanton as scouts, steal the show.**CW:** Violence and thematic elements involving the frontier experience. **271m/C VHS, Closed Caption.** Jonny Lee Miller, David Arquette, Keith Carradine, Harry Dean Stanton, F. Murray Abraham, Edward James Olmos, Eric Schweig, Patricia Childress, Jennifer Garner, Haviland Morris, Brian Dennehy, Joaquim de Almeida, Ray McKinnon, Akosua Busia; **D:** Yves Simo-

neau; **W:** Larry McMurtry, Diana Ossana; **C:** Edward Pei; **M:** David Bell. *CAF*

Larry McMurtry's Streets of Laredo 🎬🎬🎬 *Streets of Laredo* 1995 Texas Ranger-turned-bounty hunter Woodrow F. Call (a splendid Garner) is hired by the railroad to track down ruthless Mexican bandit Joey Garza (Cruz), pitting an old man's skills against a young man's daring, and driving both men across Texas, deep into Mexican territory. Call's old friend Pea Eye Parker (Shepard) reluctantly comes along, with ex-prostitute Lorena (Spacek), who's Parker's wife, and Maria (Braga), Joey's tough-but-deluded mom, providing strong support. Casual cruelty and violence are the norm in the sunset days of both Call's life and that of the west itself. Third in the TV sagas, following "Return to Lonesome Dove." **227m/C VHS.** James Garner, Alexis Cruz, Sam Shepard, Sissy Spacek, Sonia Braga, Wes Studi, Randy Quaid, Charles Martin Smith, Kevin Conway, George Carlin, Ned Beatty, James Gammon, Tristan Tait, Anjanette Comer; **D:** Joseph Sargent; **W:** Larry McMurtry, Diana Ossana; **C:** Edward Pei; **M:** David Shire. *CAF, VIF*

Las Vegas Hillbillys 🎬 *Country Music* 1966 A pair of country-singing hillbillies inherit a saloon in Las Vegas and enjoy wine, moonshine, and song. These two make the Clampetts look like high society. Followed, believe it or not, by "Hillbillys in a Haunted House." 🎬Money Greases the Wheel. **85m/C VHS, Beta.** Mamie Van Doren, Jayne Mansfield, Ferlin Husky, Sonny James; **D:** Arthur C. Pierce. *NLC*

Las Vegas Lady 🎬 1976 (PG) Three shrewd casino hostesses plot a multi-million dollar heist in the nation's gambling capital. Non-captivating caper. **90m/C VHS, Beta.** Stella Stevens, Stuart Whitman, George de Cecenzo, Andrew Stevens; **D:** Noel Nosseck; **W:** Walter Dallenbach; **M:** Alan Silvestri.

Las Vegas Serial Killer woof! 1986 A serial killer, let out of prison on a technicality, starts killing again. Made for video by Camp. **90m/C VHS, Beta.** Pierre Agostino, Ron Jason, Tara MacGowran, Kathryn Downey. *NO*

The Las Vegas Story woof! 1952 Gambling, colorful sights, and a murder provide the framework for this non-compelling fictional guided-tour of the city. Save your money for the slots. **88m/B VHS, Beta.** Victor Mature, Jane Russell, Vincent Price, Hoagy Carmichael, Brad Dexter; **D:** Robert Stevenson; **W:** Paul Jarrico. *NO*

Las Vegas Weekend 🎬 1985 A computer nerd goes to Las Vegas and discovers fun. **83m/C VHS, Beta.** Barry Hickey, Macka Foley, Ray Dennis Steckler; **D:** Dale Trevillion; **W:** Dale Trevillion. *VTR*

Laser Mission 🎬🎬½ 1990 When it is discovered that the Soviets have laser weapon capabilities, an agent is given the task of destroying the weapon and kidnapping the scientist who developed it. **83m/C VHS, LV, Closed Caption.** Brandon Lee, Debi Monahan, Ernest Borgnine, Werner Pochat, Graham Clarke, Maureen Lahoud, Pierre Knoessen; **D:** Beau Davis. *TTC*

Laser Moon 🎬🎬 1992 A serial killer uses a surgical laser beam to kill his beautiful victims, and he strikes at every full moon. When he announces his next attack on a late-night radio talk show the police call in a beautiful rookie cop (Lords) to use as bait. **90m/C VHS.** Traci Lords, Crystal Shaw, Harrison Leduke, Bruce Carter; **D:** Bruce Carter.

Laserblast woof! 1978 (PG) Standard wimp-gets-revenge story in which a frustrated young man finds a powerful and deadly laser which was left near his home by aliens; upon learning of its devastating capabilities, his personality changes and he seeks revenge against all who have taken advantage of him. **87m/C VHS, Beta, LV.** Kim Milford, Cheryl "Rainbeaux" Smith, Keenan Wynn, Roddy McDowall; **D:** Michael Raeburn; **M:** Richard Band, Joel Goldsmith.

The Laserman 🎬🎬 1990 (R) Exotic black comedy about a Chinese-American scientist who, when not fending off his overbearing Jewish mother or having telepathic orgasms, is contending with a band of political terrorists. **92m/C VHS.** Mars Huyuchi, Peter Wang, Tony Leung, Sally Yeh, Maryann Urbano, Joan Copeland; **D:** Peter Wang; **W:** Peter Wang; **M:** Mason Daring. HTV

Lassie 🐾🐾½ **1994 (PG)** Everyone's favorite collie returns as the Turner family moves to Virginia's Shenandoah Valley to take up sheep ranching. However, because this is the '90s, Dad meets financial disaster, and junior can't stand his stepmom. Can Lassie meet the challenges of dysfunctional family living? "What is it girl? Call a therapist?" This Lassie is a direct descendant of Pal, the original 1943 star. **92m/C VHS, Beta, Closed Caption.** Helen Slater, Jon Tenney, Tom Guiry, Brittany Boyd, Richard Farnsworth, Frederic Forrest; **D:** Daniel Petrie; **W:** Matthew Jacobs, Gary Ross, Elizabeth Anderson. PAR

Lassie: Adventures of Neeka 1968 America's best friend joins her Native American buddy, Neeka, for a journey through a forest in the Pacific Northwest. They camp out in a deserted settlement, pull an elderly gentleman out of a frigid pond, and risk their lives to release horses from a stable during a raging wildfire. **75m/B VHS, Beta.** Jed Allan, Mark Miranda, Robert Rockwell, Lassie; **D:** Richard Moder, Jack B. Hively. NO

Lassie, Come Home 🐾🐾½ **1943 (G)** In first of the Lassie series, the famed collie is reluctantly sold and makes a treacherous cross-country journey back to her original family. **90m/C VHS, Beta, LV.** Roddy McDowall, Elizabeth Taylor, Donald Crisp, Edmund Gwenn, May Whitty, Nigel Bruce, Elsa Lanchester, J. Pat O'Malley, Lassie; **D:** Fred M. Wilcox. National Film Registry '93;; Nominations: Academy Awards '43: Best Color Cinematography. MGM

Lassie from Lancashire 🐾🐾 **1938** Not the famous Collie—but here, a Colleen. A pair of struggling lovebirds try to make it in show biz against all odds, including the girl's lunatic aunt, who locks her away before an audition. **67m/B VHS, Beta.** Marjorie Brown, Hal Thompson, Marjorie Sandford, Lassie, Mark Daly. VYY

Lassie: The Miracle 🐾 **1975** A TV-movie featuring the faithful collie saving new-born pups and befriending a mute boy. **90m/C VHS, Beta.** Lassie. MGM

Lassie: Well of Love 1990 Various installments of the classic television series featuring the heroic collie are combined to create a movie-length presentation for home video. Lassie takes two young pups under her paw and, in the process, loses her way. As she tries to get home, she brings joy back into the lives of two despondent children. Finally, the old girl faces death when she tumbles into an abandoned well and must depend on humans for rescue. **76m/C VHS, Beta.** Lassie, Mary Gregory, Robert Donner. NO

Lassie's Great Adventure 🐾🐾½ **1962** Lassie and her master Timmy are swept away from home by a runaway balloon. After they land in the Canadian wilderness, they learn to rely on each other through peril and adventure. Made for television. **104m/C VHS, Beta.** June Lockhart, Jon Provost, Hugh Reilly; **D:** William Beaudine; **W:** Charles "Blackie" O'Neal. MGM

Lassiter 🐾🐾½ **1984 (R)** Selleck plays a jewel thief who is asked to steal diamonds from the Nazis for the FBI. Supporting cast adds value to what is otherwise a fairly ordinary adventure drama. **100m/C VHS, Beta, LV.** Tom Selleck, Jane Seymour, Lauren Hutton, Bob Hoskins, Joe Regalbuto, Ed Lauter, Warren Clarke; **D:** Roger Young. WAR

Last Action Hero 🐾🐾 **1993 (PG-13)** Newcomer O'Brien finds himself in a movie starring his idol Jack Slater, the kind of guy who never loses a fight and is impervious to gunfire and explosions (and he has a really cool car and a really big gun). Disappointing action/spoof of movies within a movie (rumored to have cost $80 million) was critically maimed and never recovered. The concept isn't new and has been done better before, though Ah-nold possesses his usual self-

mocking charm, which is more than can be said for the movie. Look for lots of big stars in small roles and cameos. Cluttered with inside Hollywood gags, the script was given uncredited assistance from William Goldman.**CW:** Strong action sequences. **131m/C VHS, Beta, LV, Closed Caption, DVD.** Arnold Schwarzenegger, Austin O'Brien, Mercedes Ruehl, F. Murray Abraham, Charles Dance, Anthony Quinn, Robert Prosky, Tom Noonan, Frank McRae, Art Carney, Bridgette Wilson; **Cameos:** Sharon Stone, Hammer, Chevy Chase, Jean-Claude Van Damme, Tori Spelling, Joan Plowright, Adam Ant, James Belushi, James Cameron, Tony Curtis, Timothy Dalton, Tony Danza, Edward Furlong, Little Richard, Damon Wayans, Robert Patrick; **D:** John McTiernan; **W:** David Arnott, Shane Black; **C:** Dean Semler; **M:** Michael Kamen. COL, BTV

The Last American Hero 🐾🐾🐾 **Hard Driver 1973 (PG)** The true story of how former moonshine runner Junior Johnson became one of the fastest race car drivers in the history of the sport. Entertaining slice of life chronicling whiskey running and stock car racing, with Bridges superb in the lead. Based on a series of articles written by Tom Wolfe. **95m/C VHS, Beta.** Jeff Bridges, Valerie Perrine, Gary Busey, Art Lund, Geraldine Fitzgerald, Ned Beatty; **D:** Lamont Johnson; **W:** William Roberts; **M:** Charles Fox. FOX

Last American Virgin 🐾🐾 **1982 (R)** Usual brainless teen sex comedy about three school buddies who must deal with a plethora of problems in their search for girls who are willing. Music by Blondie, The Cars, The Police, The Waitresses, Devo, U2, Human League, and Quincy Jones. **92m/C VHS, Beta.** Lawrence Monoson, Diane Franklin, Steve Antin, Louisa Moritz; **D:** Boaz Davidson; **W:** Boaz Davidson. MGM

The Last Angry Man 🐾🐾🐾½ **1959** An old, idealistic Brooklyn doctor attracts a television producer wanting to make a documentary about his life and career, and the two conflict. Muni was Oscar-nominated for this, his last film. **100m/B VHS, Beta.** Paul Muni, David Wayne, Betsy Palmer, Luther Adler, Dan Tobin; **D:** Daniel Mann; **C:** James Wong Howe. Nominations: Academy Awards '59: Best Actor (Muni), Best Art Direction/Set Decoration (B & W). COL

The Last Bastion 🐾🐾 **1984** A WWII drama emphasizing the political struggle between Churchill, MacArthur, Roosevelt, and Australia's John Curtin. **160m/C VHS, Beta.** AU Robert Vaughn, Timothy West.

The Last Best Year 🐾🐾½ **1990 (PG)** Basic TV tearjerker has lonely psychologist Wendy (Moore) befriending patient Jane (Peters), who has a terminal illness. **88m/C VHS.** Mary Tyler Moore, Bernadette Peters, Brian Bedford, Dorothy McGuire, Kate Reid, Kenneth Welsh; **D:** John Erman; **W:** David W. Rintels. NHO

The Last Boy Scout 🐾🐾 **1991 (R)** Are you ready for some gunplay? Formula thriller stars Willis as a private eye and Wayans as an ex-quarterback teaming up against a football team owner who will stop at nothing to get political backing for a bill promoting legalized gambling on sports. Another variation of the violent buddy-picture by "Lethal Weapon" screenwriter Black.**CW:** Very strong language and graphic violence. **105m/C VHS, LV, Letterbox, Closed Caption.** Bruce Willis, Damon Wayans, Halle Berry, Chelsea Field, Noble Willingham, Taylor Negron, Danielle Harris, Chelcie Ross, Bruce McGill; **D:** Tony Scott; **W:** Shane Black. WAR

Last Breath 🐾🐾 **1996 (R)** Perry's desperate to find a transplant donor for his dying wife—even if it means seducing another woman and then killing her. **90m/C VHS.** Luke Perry, Gia Carides, Francie Swift; **D:** P.J. Posner. APX

Last Breath 🐾🐾 **1998 (R)** Martin (Perry) is obsessively devoted to his dying wife, Chrystie (Swift), who needs a double lung transplant to survive. So Martin decides to romance lovely Gail (Carides)—with murder on his mind. Twisted ending.**CW:** Sexuality, language and some violence. **90m/C VHS.** Luke Perry, Gia Carides, Francie Swift; **D:** P.J. Posner. APX

Last Bullet 🐾🐾 **1950** A young westerner chases after a band of outlaws to avenge the cold-blooded murder of his parents. **55m/B VHS, Beta, LV.** James Ellison, Russell Hayden, John Cason. NO

The Last Butterfly 🐾🐾 **1992** Quiet Holocaust movie set in Theresienstadt, the Czechoslovak ghetto city used by the Nazis to persuade the outside world of their humane treatment of the Jews. Noted French mime Antoine Moreau (Courtenay) has fallen under suspicion by the Gestapo. He's "persuaded" to give a performance in Theresienstadt for the benefit of the visiting Red Cross but decides to subvert Nazi propaganda with his own version of "Hansel and Gretel." This time the witch feeds the children into her oven. Muted performances and screenplay (adapted from the Michael Jacot novel) heightened the film's surreal calmness. **106m/C VHS, LV.** CZ Tom Courtenay, Brigitte Fossey, Freddie Jones, Ingrid Held, Linda Jablonska; **D:** Karel Kachyna; **W:** Karel Kachyna, Ota Hofman; **M:** Alex North. NLC

Last Call 🐾 **1990 (R)** Clearly, Joe Sixpack won't rent this bimbo fest for its subtle plot. Katt, a mafiosi-cheated real estate guy, decides to even the score with the assistance of gal pal/playmate of the year Tweed, who's more than willing to compromise her position. A direct to video release, it also features the talents of playboy emerita Stevens. Available in rated and unrated versions. **90m/C VHS, Beta.** William Katt, Shannon Tweed, Joseph Campanella, Stella Stevens, Matt Roe; **D:** Jag Mundhra.

The Last Chance 🐾🐾🐾 **1945** A realistic look at the efforts of three WWII Allied officers to help a group of refugees escape across the Alps from Italy to Switzerland. The officers are played by former pilots who were shot down over Switzerland. In spite of this—or perhaps because of it—the acting is superb. Watch for inspirational scene of refugees singing. **105m/B VHS.** E.G. Morrison, John Hoy, Ray Reagan, Odeardo Mosini, Sigfrit Steiner, Emil Gerber; **D:** Leopold Lindtberg. NOS

Last Chase 🐾½ **1981 (PG)** Famed race car driver becomes a vocal dissenter against the sterile society that has emerged, in this drama set in the near future. Made for television. Screenplay written by Christopher Crowe under the pseudonym C.R. O'Cristopher. **106m/C VHS, Beta.** CA Lee Majors, Burgess Meredith, Chris Makepeace, Alexandra Stewart; **D:** Martyn Burke; **W:** Christopher Crowe, Martyn Burke. VES

Last Command 🐾🐾🐾🐾 **1928** Famous powerful silent film by Sternberg about a expatriate Czarist general forging out a pitiful living as a silent Hollywood extra, where he is hired by his former adversary to reenact the revolution he just left. Next to "The Last Laugh," this is considered Jannings' most acclaimed performance. Deeply ironic, visually compelling film with a new score by Gaylord Carter. **88m/B VHS, Beta.** Emil Jannings, William Powell, Evelyn Brent, Nicholas Soussanin, Michael Visaroff, Jack Raymond, Fritz Feld; **D:** Josef von Sternberg; **W:** Warren Duff; **M:** Max Steiner, Gaylord Carter. Academy Awards '28: Best Actor (Jannings); Nominations: Academy Awards '28: Best Picture, Best Story. PAR, FCT, BTV

The Last Command 🐾🐾½ **1955** Jim Bowie and his followers sacrifice their lives in defending the Alamo. A good cast holds its own against a mediocre script; battle scenes are terrific. **110m/C VHS.** Sterling Hayden, Richard Carlson, Ernest Borgnine, J. Carrol Naish, Virginia Grey, Anna Maria Alberghetti; **D:** Frank Lloyd. REP, PAR

The Last Contract 🐾🐾 **1986 (R)** An artist who pays his bills by working as a hitman, kills the wrong man. As a result, he must fear for his life since a counterhit is inevitable. **85m/C VHS.** Jack Palance, Rod Steiger, Bo Svenson, Richard Roundtree, Ann Turkel; **D:** Allan A. Buckhantz.

Last Cry for Help 🐾½ **1979** A psychiatrist helps a 17-year-old high school coed who, fearing she has disappointed her parents, attempts suicide. Typical made-for-television melodrama that attempts to make a statement, but falls short. Definitely not the "Partridge Family." **98m/C VHS, Beta.** Linda Purl, Shirley Jones, Tony LoBianco, Murray Hamilton, Grant Goodeve; *D:* Hal Sitowitz; *M:* Miles Goodman. UNI

Last Dance 🎬½ **1991** Five scantily clad exotic dancers are ready to compete for the title of Miss Dance-TV, but trouble ensues when the dancers start turning up dead. **86m/C VHS, Beta, LV.** Cynthia Bassinet, Elaine Hendrix, Kurt T. Williams, Allison Rhea, Erica Ringston; *D:* Anthony Markes.

The Last Dance 🎬🎬 *Sista Dansen* **1993** Two couples, Claus and Tove (Brynolfsson, Bergstrom) and best friends Lennart and Liselott (Andersson, Froling), have a shared obsession with ballroom dance competitions and some secret desires. Seems Claus and Tove have a rocky marriage and think their friends have the perfect union. Instead, Lennart is tired of his overbearing wife and longs for Tove, to whom he was once engaged. Then Liselott's body is found beneath the pier after a competition. Swedish with subtitles. **109m/C VHS.** *SW* Helena Bergstrom, Reine Brynolfsson, Ewa Froling, Peter Andersson; *D:* Colin Nutley; *W:* Colin Nutley; *C:* Jens Fischer. HTV

Last Dance 🎬🎬 **1996 (R)** Following closely on the heels of "Dead Man Walking," this death-row drama suffered from bad timing and was dubbed by some as "Bad Hair Walking." Stone plays a convicted murderess condemned to die in an unnamed Southern state. Morrow's the rookie attorney for the state's clemency office assigned to her case. As a bond grows between the two, he uncovers errors in her trial that his bosses would rather have him ignore. The movie makes its big mistake by centering on Morrow's callow lawyer instead of Stone's embittered con. The clock-ticking countdown to the execution (which will amuse fans of "The Player") even fails to hold attention.*CW:* Violence, language and some drug content. **103m/C VHS, LV, Closed Caption.** Sharon Stone, Rob Morrow, Randy Quaid, Peter Gallagher, Jack Thompson, Jayne Brook, Pamela Tyson, Skeet Ulrich, Don Harvey, Diane Sellers; *D:* Bruce Beresford; *W:* Ron Koslow; *C:* Peter James; *M:* Mark Isham. TOU

Last Day of the War 🎬½ **1969 (PG)** A German scientist is chased by Americans and Germans as WWII winds to its conclusion. Filmed in Spain. **96m/C VHS, Beta.** *SP* George Maharis, Maria Perschy, James Philbrook, Gerard Herter; *D:* Juan Antonio Bardem. ART

The Last Days of Chez Nous 🎬🎬½ **1992 (R)** Armstrong's dramatic comedy about a family falling apart has Ganz as a homesick Frenchman married to controlling, successful Australian writer Harrow. Trouble starts when his wayward sister-in-law Fox returns home to live with them and his wife decides to take an extended holiday with her father. Ganz suddenly finds himself only too involved in Fox's complicated life. Self-involved characters with messy emotional lives leave viewers feeling rather distant, though cast, and particularly Ganz, strive for intimacy.*CW:* A moment of strong sexual language. **96m/C VHS, LV, Closed Caption.** *AU* Bruno Ganz, Lisa Harrow, Kerry Fox, Kiri Paramore, Bill Hunter, Miranda Otto; *D:* Gillian Armstrong; *W:* Helen Garner; *M:* Paul Grabowsky. Australian Film Institute '92: Best Actress (Harrow); Nominations: Australian Film Institute '92: Best Director (Armstrong), Best Film, Best Supporting Actor (Hunter). NLC, IME, COL

The Last Days of Disco **1998 (R)** It's the early '80s and the waning days of disco as recent college grads Alice (Sevigny) and Charlotte (Beckinsdale) get their first real jobs, a lousy apartment, and hit the Manhattan club life, hooking up with some Harvard men. Not yet reviewed.*CW:* Some elements involving sexuality and drugs. **113m/C VHS.** Chloe Sevigny, Kate Beckinsale, Christopher Eigeman, MacKenzie Astin, Robert Sean Leonard, Matt Keeslar, Tara Subkoff, Jennifer Beals; *D:* Whit Stillman; *W:* Whit Stillman. NYR

The Last Days of Dolwyn 🎬🎬½ *Woman of Dolwyn; Dolwyn* **1949** A man banned for thievery from his Welsh village returns bent upon revenge. He plans to buy the entire district when it is designated part of a water reservoir project, but finds plans thwarted by a dowager and her stepson. Burton's first film was based on a true story. **95m/B VHS.** *GB* Edith Evans, Emlyn Williams, Richard Burton, Anthony James, Barbara Couper, Alan Aynesworth, Hugh Griffith, Roddy Hughes, Tom Jones; *D:* Emlyn Williams; *W:* Emlyn Williams. FCT, DVT

Last Days of Frank & Jesse James 🎬½ **1986** A tired television-movie rehash of the well-known western legend in which the famous brothers try to be like others after their personal war against society ends. **100m/C VHS, Beta.** Johnny Cash, Kris Kristofferson, June Carter Cash, Willie Nelson, Margaret Gibson, Gail Youngs; *D:* William A. Graham. THV

The Last Days of Frankie the Fly 🎬🎬 **1996 (R)** It's gonna seem familiar because it's yet another criminal lowlife story set in L.A. but at least Hopper's presence makes this slightly more than routine. He's Frankie, a semi-pathetic petty thief with big dreams and not much talent. He works for vicious gangster Sal (Madsen) and becomes smitten with ex-junkie Margaret (Hannah), who would like to be a legit actress but is instead working in porn. When Frankie decides to impress Margaret, he naturally gets into trouble.*CW:* Language, violence, sexual references. **96m/C VHS.** Dennis Hopper, Daryl Hannah, Michael Madsen, Kiefer Sutherland, Dayton Callie, Jack McGee; *D:* Peter Markle; *W:* Dayton Callie; *C:* Phil Parmet; *M:* George S. Clinton. CAF

The Last Days of Patton 🎬½ **1986** A made-for-television movie depicting the aging general's autumn years as a controversial ex-Nazi defender and desk-bound WWII historian. Scott reprises his feature-film role. **146m/C VHS, Beta, Closed Caption.** George C. Scott, Ed Lauter, Eva Marie Saint, Richard Dysart, Murray Hamilton, Kathryn Leigh Scott; *D:* Delbert Mann. FOX

Last Days of Planet Earth woof! *Prophecies of Nostradamus; Catastrophe 1999; Nostradamus No Daiyogen* **1974** Really stinky Japanese doomsday movie about a scientist who charges that a build-up of pollution is responsible for giant mutant sea slugs and other environmental disasters. Dubbed. **88m/C VHS, Closed Caption.** *JP* Tetsuro Tamba, So Yamamura, Takashi Shimura; *D:* Toshio Masuda. PAR

Last Days of Pompeii 🎬🎬½ **1935** Vintage DeMille-style epic based on Lord Lytton's book, where the eruption of Vesuvius threatens noblemen and slaves alike. State-of-the-art special effects still look fantastic today. Remade in 1960; available colorized. **96m/B VHS, Beta, LV, Closed Caption.** Preston Foster, Alan Hale, Basil Rathbone, George L. Baxt, Louis Calhern, David Holt, Dorothy Wilson, Wryley Birch, Gloria Shea; *D:* Ernest B. Schoedsack; *C:* Jack Cardiff. TTC

The Last Days of Pompeii 🎬🎬 *Ultimi Giorni di Pompeii* **1960** Superman Reeves plays a gladiator trying to clean up the doomed town of Pompeii in this remake of the 1935 classic. Some spectacular scenes, including the explosive climax when the mountain blows its top. **105m/C VHS.** *IT* Steve Reeves, Christine Kaufmann, Barbara Carroll, Anne Marie Baumann, Mimmo Palmara; *D:* Mario Bonnard; *W:* Sergio Leone. GKK

The Last Detail 🎬🎬🎬🎬 **1973 (R)** Two hard-boiled career petty officers (Nicholson and Young) are commissioned to transfer a young sailor facing an eight-year sentence for petty theft from one brig to another. In an act of compassion, they attempt to show the prisoner a final good time. Nicholson shines in both the complexity and completeness of his character. Adapted from a Daryl Ponicsan novel. **104m/C VHS, Beta, LV.** Jack Nicholson, Otis Young, Randy Quaid, Clifton James, Michael Moriarty, Carol Kane, Nancy Allen; *Cameos:* Gilda Radner; *D:* Hal Ashby; *W:* Robert Towne; *C:* Michael Chap-

man; *M:* Johnny Mandel. British Academy Awards '74: Best Actor (Nicholson), Best Screenplay; Cannes Film Festival '74: Best Actor (Nicholson); New York Film Critics Awards '74: Best Actor (Nicholson); National Society of Film Critics Awards '74: Best Actor (Nicholson); Nominations: Academy Awards '73: Best Actor (Nicholson), Best Adapted Screenplay, Best Supporting Actor (Quaid). COL, WME

The Last Don 🎬🎬½ *Mario Puzo's The Last Don* **1997 (R)** Re-edited version of the TV miniseries finds author Puzo, of "Godfather" fame, sticking to what he knows best. The Don in question is Domenico Clericuzo (Aiello), a ruthless patriarch who wipes out the rival family his pregnant daughter Rose Marie marries into (and doesn't spare her hubby). Carrying out the Don's orders is nephew Pippi (Mantegna), an enforcer who weds Vegas showgirl Nalene (Miller) and who gets involved in the casino business. The years pass with the Don manipulating the next generation, as bloodthirsty grandchild Dante (Cochrane) fights for control with Pippi's cool-headed son Cross (Gedrick). Divided loyalties abound. A complete five-hour version of the saga is also available.*CW:* Strong violence and some sexuality/nudity. **150m/C VHS.** Danny Aiello, Joe Mantegna, Jason Gedrick, Rory Cochrane, Penelope Ann Miller, Daryl Hannah, Kirstie Alley, Michelle Rene Thomas, David Marciano, Robert Wuhl, k.d. lang, John Colicos, Cliff DeYoung, Michael Massee; *D:* Graeme Clifford; *W:* Joyce Eliason; *C:* Gordon C. Lonsdale; *M:* Angelo Badalamenti, Roger Bellon. THV

The Last Dragon 🎬½ *Berry Gordy's The Last Dragon* **1985 (PG-13)** It's time for a Motown kung fu showdown on the streets of Harlem, for there is scarcely enough room for even one dragon. **108m/C VHS, Beta, Closed Caption.** Taimak, Vanity, Christopher Murney, Julius J. Carry III, Faith Prince; *D:* Michael A. Schultz. FOX

Last Embrace 🎬🎬🎬 **1979 (R)** A feverish thriller in the Hitchcock style dealing with an ex-secret serviceman who is convinced someone is trying to kill him. **102m/C VHS, Beta.** Roy Scheider, Janet Margolin, Christopher Walken, John Glover, Charles Napier, Mandy Patinkin; *D:* Jonathan Demme; *M:* Miklos Rozsa. MGM, FOX

The Last Emperor 🎬🎬🎬🎬 **1987 (PG-13)** Deeply ironic epic detailing life of Pu Yi, crowned at the age of three as the last emperor of China before the onset of communism. Follows Pu Yi from childhood to manhood (sequestered away in the Forbidden City) to puppet-ruler to party proletariat. O'Toole portrays the sympathetic Scot tutor who educates the adult Pu Yi (Lone) in the ways of the western world after Pu Yi abdicates power in 1912. Shot on location inside the People's Republic of China with a cast of thousands; authentic costumes. Rich, visually stunning movie. The Talking Heads' David Byrne contributed to the score. **140m/C VHS, Beta, LV, 8mm, Closed Caption.** *IT* John Lone, Peter O'Toole, Joan Chen, Victor Wong, Ryuichi Sakamoto, Dennis Dun, Maggie Han, Ying Ruocheng, Ric Young; *D:* Bernardo Bertolucci; *W:* Mark Peploe, Bernardo Bertolucci; *C:* Vittorio Storaro; *M:* Ryuichi Sakamoto, David Byrne. Academy Awards '87: Best Adapted Screenplay, Best Art Direction/Set Decoration, Best Cinematography, Best Costume Design, Best Director (Bertolucci), Best Film Editing, Best Picture, Best Sound, Best Original Score; British Academy Awards '88: Best Film; Cesar Awards '88: Best Foreign Film; Directors Guild of America Awards '87: Best Director (Bertolucci); Golden Globe Awards '88: Best Director (Bertolucci), Best Film—Drama, Best Screenplay, Best Score; Los Angeles Film Critics Association Awards '87: Best Cinematography; New York Film Critics Awards '87: Best Cinematography. COL, FCT, BTV

Last Exit to Brooklyn 🎬🎬🎬½ **1990 (R)** Hubert Selby, Jr.'s shocking book comes to the screen in a vivid film. Leigh gives a stunning performance as a young Brooklyn girl caught between the Mafia, union men, and friends struggling for something better. Set in the 1950s. Fine supporting cast; excellent pacing. **102m/C VHS, LV, Letterbox.** Jennifer Jason Leigh, Burt Young, Stephen Lang, Ricki Lake, Jerry Orbach, Maia Danzinger, Stephen

Baldwin; D: Uli Edel; C: Stefan Czapsky. New York Film Critics Awards '89: Best Supporting Actress (Leigh). COL, FCT

Last Exit to Earth 🎬🎬 *Roger Corman Presents Last Exit to Earth* 1996 (R) Your basic male fantasy. Lusty alien babes from dying world travel to earth in search of fertile males, since the men of their home planet were rendered sterile by nuclear disaster. It's a dirty job but someone's got to do it. Made for cable. *CW:* Violence, language and sexuality. 80m/C VHS. Costas Mandylor, Kim Greist, David Groh, Hilary Shepard, Michael Cudlitz, Lisa Banes, Zoe Trilling; D: Katt Shea Ruben. NHO

The Last Fight 🎬½ 1982 (R) Boxer risks his life and his girlfriend for a shot at the championship title. Watch and see if he could've been a contender. 85m/C VHS, Beta. Fred Williamson, Willie Colon, Ruben Blades, Joe Spinell, Darlanne Fluegel; D: Fred Williamson. NO

The Last Five Days 🎬🎬 1982 Based on the true story of a girl and her brother who, in 1943 Munich, were arrested for distributing anti-Nazi propaganda. The film covers the five days between their capture and execution. In German with English subtitles. 112m/C VHS. GE Lena Stolze, Irm Hermann; D: Percy Adlon. CVC

The Last Flight of Noah's Ark 🎬🎬½ 1980 (G) Disney adventure concerns a high-living pilot, a prim missionary, and two stowaway orphans who must plot their way off a deserted island following the crash landing of their broken-down plane. 97m/C VHS, Beta. Elliott Gould, Genevieve Bujold, Rick Schroder, Vincent Gardenia, Tammy Lauren; D: Charles Jarrott; W: George Arthur Bloom, Steven W. Carabatsos; M: Maurice Jarre. DIS

Last Flight Out: A True Story 🎬🎬 1990 Hours before Saigon fell to the Vietcong in 1975, Vietnamese and Americans rushed to board the last commercial flight out of Vietnam. Lukewarm account of a true story. 99m/C VHS, 8mm. James Earl Jones, Richard Crenna, Haing S. Ngor, Eric Bogosian. NO

Last Flight to Hell 🎬🎬 19?? When a drug lord is kidnapped, Brown is sent to South America to rescue the slimeball. His interest in the job picks up when the drug lord's 11-on-a-scale-of-ten daughter joins him for the chase. 94m/C VHS. Reb Brown, Chuck Connors; D: Paul D. Robinson.

The Last Fling 🎬½ 1986 When Selleca has her mind set on a romantic fling, Ritter is headed for trouble. She wants love for one night, he wants it forever. Will they solve this difference of opinion? Will true love prevail? Will Ritter consent to being used as a one-night stand? Weakly plotted and poorly acted comedy. Made for television. 95m/C VHS, LV. John Ritter, Connie Selleca, Scott Bakula, Shannon Tweed, Paul Sand, John Bennett Perry; D: Corey Allen; M: Charles Bernstein.

Last Four Days 🎬🎬 1977 (PG) A chronicle of the final days of Benito Mussolini. 91m/C VHS, Beta. Rod Steiger, Henry Fonda, Franco Nero; D: Carlo Lizzani. ART

Last Frontier 🎬🎬½ 1932 Serial of 12 chapters contains shades of spectacular figures in Western history: Custer, Hickok, and others in a background of grazing buffalo, boom towns, and covered wagon trails. 216m/B VHS, Beta. Lon Chaney Jr., Yakima Canutt, Francis X. Bushman; D: Spencer Gordon Bennet, Thomas L. Story. VCN, VYY, DVT

Last Game 🎬🎬 1980 A college student is torn between his devotion to his blind father and going out for the college's football team. 107m/C VHS, Beta. Howard Segal, Ed L. Grady, Terry Alden; D: Martin Beck. NO

The Last Gasp 🎬½ 1994 (R) Contractor Patrick murders the Mexican Indian who's interfering with his project and is cursed. He turns into a wild killer who must satisfy his blood lust every 20 days. Only Pacula tries to save him. Gory and predictable. *CW:* Scenes of strong violence and sexuality; some language. 90m/C VHS. Robert Pat-

rish, Joanna Pacula, Vyto Ruginis, Mimi Craven; D: Scott McGinnis. AVE

The Last Good Time 🎬🎬½ 1994 (R) Old-world violinist Joseph Kopple (Mueller-Stahl), retired and living in a small Brooklyn apartment, has his world turned upside down when his street-smart neighbor Charlotte (d'Abo) seeks refuge from her abusive boyfriend Eddie (Pasdar). An unsentimental friendship develops between the two inspite of the differences in their ages, educations, and lifestyles. Terrific performance from Mueller-Stahl as the lonely but dignified old man. Based on the novel by Richard Bausch. *CW:* Language and some sexuality. 90m/C VHS. Armin Mueller-Stahl, Olivia D'Abo, Maureen Stapleton, Lionel Stander, Adrian Pasdar; D: Bob Balaban; W: Bob Balaban, John McLaughlin; C: Claudia Rashke. HMK

Last Gun 1964 A legendary gunman on the verge of retirement has to save his town from a reign of terror before turning his gun in. 98m/C VHS, Beta. Cameron Mitchell. NO

The Last Hit 🎬🎬½ 1993 (R) Michael Grant (Brown) is a professional assassin, working for the CIA, who's very good at his job. But now he's burned out and ready to retire to New Mexico for some peace and quiet. He buys a house from the widowed Anna (Adams), naturally falling in love with her. Then one last assignment comes along and, wouldn't you know, his target turns out to be Anna's father (Yulin). Based on the novel "The Large Kill" by Patrick Ruell. 93m/C VHS, LV, Closed Caption. Bryan Brown, Brooke Adams, Harris Yulin; D: Jan Egleson; W: Walter Klenhard, Alan Sharp; M: Gary Chang. USH

Last Holiday 🎬🎬🎬 1950 A man who is told he has a few weeks to live decides to spend them in a posh resort where people assume he is important. 89m/B VHS, Beta. GB Alec Guinness, Kay Walsh, Beatrice Campbell, Wilfrid Hyde-White, Bernard Lee; D: Henry Cass; W: J.B. Priestley. HMV, RXM, BFA

The Last Horror Film woof! *The Fanatic* 1982 (R) Beautiful queen of horror films is followed to the Cannes Film Festival by her number one fan, who, unbeknownst to her, is slowly murdering members of her entourage in a deluded and vain attempt to capture her attentions. Title refers to lack of plans for a sequel. 87m/C VHS, Beta. Caroline Munro, Joe Spinell, Judd Hamilton, Devin Goldenberg, David Winters; D: David Winters; W: Tom Klassen, Judd Hamilton, David Winters.

The Last Hour 🎬 1991 (R) A Wall Street crook crosses a Mafia punk, so the latter holds the former's wife hostage in an unfinished skyscraper. Fortunately the lady's first husband is a gung-ho cop eager to commence the DIE HARD-esque action. Undistinguished fare that gives away the climax in an opening flash-forward. *CW:* Language, graphic violence, and sensuality. 85m/C VHS, Beta, LV. Michael Pare, Shannon Tweed, Bobby DiCicco, Robert Pucci; D: William Sachs.

Last House on Dead End Street woof! *The Fun House* 1977 (R) Gore galore as actors die for their art in this splatter flick about snuff films. 90m/C VHS. Steven Morrison, Dennis Crawford, Lawrence Bornman, Janet Sorley; D: Victor Janos. SUN

Last House on the Left 🎬🎬 *Krug and Company; Sex Crime of the Century* 1972 (R) Two girls are kidnapped from a rock concert by a gang of escaped convicts; the girls' parents exact bloody revenge when the guilty parties pay an intended housecall. Controversial and grim low-budget shocker; loosely based on Bergman's "The Virgin Spring." 83m/C VHS, Beta, LV. David Hess, Lucy Grantham, Sandra Cassel, Mark Sheffler, Fred J. Lincoln, Jeramie Rain, Gaylord St. James, Cynthia Carr, Ada Washington, Martin Kove; D: Wes Craven; W: Wes Craven; C: Victor Hurwitz. ART, VES, HHE

The Last Hunt 🎬🎬½ 1956 Well-performed western starring Taylor as a seedy buffalo hunter who gains his identity from senseless acts of murder. When personalities clash, he seeks

revenge to follow buffalo hunter Granger. Shot in Custer National Park, the buffalo scenes were real-life attempts at keeping the animals controlled. Based on the novel by Milton Lott. 108m/C VHS, Closed Caption. Robert Taylor, Stewart Granger, Lloyd Nolan, Debra Paget, Russ Tamblyn, Constance Ford, Ainslie Pryor, Ralph Moody, Fred Graham, Dan White, Bill Phillips, Roy Barcroft; D: Richard Brooks; W: Richard Brooks; M: Daniele Amfitheatrof. MGM

The Last Hunter 🎬 *Hunter of the Apocalypse* 1980 (R) A soldier fights for his life behind enemy lines during the Vietnam War. 97m/C VHS, Beta. IT Tisa Farrow, David Warbeck, Tony King, Bobby Rhodes, Margit Evelyn Newton, John Steiner, Alan Collins; D: Anthony (Antonio Margheriti) Dawson. ART, VES

Last Hurrah 🎬🎬½ 1958 An aging Irish-American mayor battles corruption and political backbiting in his effort to get re-elected for the last time. Semi-acclaimed heart warmer, based on the novel by Edwin O'Connor. 121m/B VHS, Beta, LV. Spencer Tracy, Basil Rathbone, John Carradine, Jeffrey Hunter, Dianne Foster, Pat O'Brien, Edward Brophy, James Gleason, Donald Crisp, Ricardo Cortez, Wallace Ford, Frank McHugh, Jane Darwell; D: John Ford. National Board of Review Awards '58: Best Actor (Tracy), Best Director (Ford). COL

Last Hurrah for Chivalry 🎬🎬 1978 An honorable man cannot defend his family from a ruthless enemy and turns to two swordsmen-for-hire for help. Chinese with subtitles or dubbed. 108m/C VHS, LV. HK Damian Lau, Wei Pei; D: John Woo. TAI

The Last Innocent Man 🎬🎬½ 1987 An attorney who quit law due to a guilty conscience is lured into defending a suspected murderer. Things become even more complicated when he begins having an affair with his client's seductive wife. A well-acted and suspense-filled flick. Made for cable television. 113m/C VHS, Beta. Ed Harris, Roxanne Hart, Bruce McGill, Clarence Williams III, Rose Gregorio, David Suchet, Darrell Larson; D: Roger Spottiswoode; W: Dan Bronson; M: Brad Fiedel. ORI, WAR

The Last Laugh 🎬🎬🎬½ *Der Letzte Mann* 1924 An elderly man, who as the doorman of a great hotel was looked upon as a symbol of "upper class," is demoted to washroom attendant due to his age. Important due to camera technique and consuming performance by Jannings. Silent with music score. A 91-minute version is also available. 77m/B VHS, Beta. GE Emil Jannings, Maly Delshaft, Max Hiller; D: F.W. Murnau. NOS, FCT, IHF

Last Light 🎬🎬 1993 (R) A prison guard (Whitaker) on death row forms a tenuous bond with an incorrigible inmate (Sutherland) who's about to be executed. Disturbing, especially the execution scene. Filmed on location at California's Soledad Prison. Sutherland's directorial debut. Made for cable television. *CW:* Strong language, partial nudity, and violence. 95m/C VHS, LV, Closed Caption. Kiefer Sutherland, Forest Whitaker, Clancy Brown, Lynne Moody, Kathleen Quinlan, Amanda Plummer; D: Kiefer Sutherland. THV

The Last Man on Earth 🎬🎬 *L'Ultimo Uomo Della Terra* 1964 Price is the sole survivor of a plague which has turned the rest of the world into vampires, who constantly harass him. Uneven U.S./Italian production manages to convey a creepy atmosphere of dismay. 86m/B VHS. IT Vincent Price, Franca Bettoya, Giacomo "Jack" Rossi-Stuart, Emma Danieli; D: Ubaldo Ragona, Sidney Salkow. SNC, MRV

Last Man Standing 🎬 1987 (R) A cheap, gritty drama about bare-knuckle fist fighting. Wells stars as a down-on-his-luck prizefighter trying to find work that doesn't involve pugilism. 89m/C VHS, Beta. William Sanderson, Vernon Wells, Franco Columbu; D: Damian Lee.

Last Man Standing 🎬🎬 1995 (R) L.A. police officer Wincott discovers corruption after his partner Banks is murdered. *CW:* Constant violence; strong language; some sexuality. 96m/C VHS, Closed Caption. Jeff Wincott, Jillian McWhirter, Jonathan Banks, Steve Eastin, Jonathan Fuller, Michael

Greene, Ava Fabian; **D:** Joseph Merhi; **W:** Joseph Merhi; **M:** Louis Febre. *PMH*

Last Man Standing 🐾🐾½ *Welcome to Jericho* 1996 (R)
Engaging, but not terribly original gangster/western features a plot taken from Clint Eastwood's career-making "Fistful of Dollars" (in turn, an adaptation of Akira Kurosawa's "Yojimbo"). The producers and credits claim lineage directly from the Kurosawa film, but this story's been around for a while, folks. In the small 1930s border town of Jericho Texas, Willis, under the pseudonym John Smith, hires himself out to both sides of a bootlegging war in an effort to make some quick cash. Bigger roles for Walken, the flinty trigger man for Irish boss Doyle (Kelly), and Dern, the town sheriff on the mob payroll, could have perked things up a little. Willis nicely injects his smirking brand of wit into a film that may have benefitted from more of the dark "Yojimbo" humor. Hill provides his trademark visually exciting action sequences. **CW:** Pervasive strong violence and some sexuality. 101m/C VHS, LV, **Closed Caption.** Bruce Willis, Bruce Dern, Christopher Walken, Karina Lombard, William Sanderson, David Patrick Kelly, Alexandra Powers, Leslie Mann, Michael Imperioli, R.D. Call, Ken Jenkins, Ned Eisenberg; **D:** Walter Hill; **W:** Walter Hill; **C:** Lloyd Ahern; **M:** Ry Cooder. *NLC*

The Last Married Couple in America 🐾🐾 1980 (R)
A couple fight to stay happily married amidst the rampant divorce epidemic engulfing their friends. 103m/C VHS, Beta. George Segal, Natalie Wood, Richard Benjamin, Valerie Harper, Dom DeLuise, Priscilla Barnes; **D:** Gilbert Cates; **M:** Charles Fox. *USH*

Last Mercenary woof! 1984
An angry ex-soldier kills everyone who makes him mad. 90m/C VHS, Beta. Tony Marsina, Malcolm Duff, Kitty Nichols, Louis Walser. *NO*

The Last Metro 🐾🐾🐾 *Le Dernier Metro* 1980
Truffaut's alternately gripping and touching drama about a theatre company in Nazi-occupied Paris. In 1942, Lucas Steiner (Bennent) is a successful Jewish theatre director who is forced into hiding. He turns the running of the theatre over to his wife, Marion (the always exquisite Deneuve), who must contend with a pro-Nazi theatre critic (Richard) and her growing attraction to the company's leading man (Depardieu), who is secretly working with the Resistance. In French with English subtitles. 135m/C VHS, Beta, LV. *FR* Catherine Deneuve, Gerard Depardieu, Heinz Bennent, Jean-Louis Richard, Jean Poiret, Andrea Ferreol, Paulette Dubost, Sabine Haudepin; **D:** Francois Truffaut; **W:** Suzanne Schiffman; **C:** Nestor Almendros; **M:** Georges Delerue. Cesar Awards '81: Best Actor (Depardieu), Best Actress (Deneuve), Best Art Direction/Set Decoration, Best Cinematography, Best Director (Truffaut), Best Film, Best Sound, Best Writing, Best Score; Nominations: Academy Awards '80: Best Foreign Language Film. *HMV, FOX, SWC*

The Last Mile 🐾🐾 1932
The staff of a prison prepares for the execution of a celebrated murderer. 70m/B VHS, Beta. Preston Foster, Howard Phillips, George E. Stone; **D:** Sam Bischoff. *NOS, MRV, BAR*

The Last Movie 🐾½ *Chinchero* 1971 (R)
A movie stunt man stays in a small Peruvian town after his filming stint is over. Hopper's confused, pretentious follow-up to "Easy Rider," has a multitude of cameos but little else. Given an award by the Italians; nobody else understood it. Kristofferson's film debut; he also wrote the music. Based on a story by Hopper and Stern. 108m/C VHS. Dennis Hopper, Julie Adams, Peter Fonda, Kris Kristofferson, Sylvia Miles, John Phillip Law, Russ Tamblyn, Rod Cameron; **D:** Dennis Hopper; **W:** Stewart Stern; **M:** Kris Kristofferson. *NO*

Last Night at the Alamo 🐾🐾🐾 1983
Patrons fight to stop the destruction of their Houston bar, the Alamo, which is about to be razed to make room for a modern skyscraper. Insightful comedy written by the author of "The Texas Chainsaw Massacre." 80m/B VHS. Sonny Carl Davis,

Lou Perry, Steve Matilla, Tina Hubbard, Doris Hargrave; **D:** Eagle Pennell; **W:** Ken Henkel; **M:** Wayne Bell. *NO*

The Last of England 🐾🐾🐾½ 1987
A furious non-narrative film by avant-garde filmmaker Jarman, depicting the modern British landscape as a funereal, waste-filled rubble-heap—as depleted morally as it is environmentally. 87m/C VHS, Beta, LV. *GB* Tilda Swinton, Spencer Leigh; **D:** Derek Jarman. *MFV, TPV*

The Last of His Tribe 🐾🐾 1992 (PG-13)
In 1911 an anthropologist befriends an Indian and discovers that Ishi is the last surviving member of California's Yahi tribe. Ishi then becomes a media and scientific society darling, spending the remainder of his remaining life in captivity to academia. A good portrayal of the Native American plight. Based on a true story; made for cable television. 90m/C VHS, LV, **Closed Caption.** Jon Voight, Graham Greene, David Ogden Stiers, Jack Blessing, Anne Archer, Daniel Benzali; **D:** Harry Hook. *WAR*

The Last of Mrs. Cheyney 🐾🐾🐾 1937
Remake of Norma Shearer's 1929 hit, based on the play by Frederick Lonsdale, about a sophisticated jewel thief in England. Crawford stars as the jewel thief who poses as a wealthy woman to get into parties hosted by London bluebloods. Dripping with charm, she works her way into Lord Drilling's mansion where she plans a huge heist. The film is handled well, and the cast gives solid performances throughout. This chic comedy of high society proved to be one of Crawford's most popular films of the '30s. 98m/B VHS, **Closed Caption.** Joan Crawford, Robert Montgomery, William Powell, Frank Morgan, Nigel Bruce, Jessie Ralph; **D:** Richard Boleslawski, George Fitzmaurice. *MGM*

The Last of Mrs. Lincoln 🐾🐾½ 1976
Intimate made for TV portrayal of the famous first lady. Film focuses on Mary Todd Lincoln's life from the assassination of her husband, through her autumn years, and her untimely downfall. 118m/C VHS, Beta. Julie Harris, Robby Benson, Patrick Duffy. *NO*

The Last of Philip Banter 🐾½ 1987 (R)
An alcoholic writer is terrified to learn events in his life exactly match a mysterious manuscript. 105m/C VHS. Tony Curtis, Greg Henry, Irene Miracle, Scott Paulin, Kate Vernon; **D:** Herve Hachuel. *REP*

The Last of Sheila 🐾🐾½ 1973 (PG)
A movie producer invites six big-star friends for a cruise aboard his yacht, the "Sheila." He then stages an elaborate "Whodunnit" parlor game to discover which one of them murdered his wife. 119m/C VHS, Beta. Richard Benjamin, James Coburn, James Mason, Dyan Cannon, Joan Hackett, Raquel Welch, Ian McShane; **D:** Herbert Ross; **W:** Anthony Perkins, Stephen Sondheim; **M:** Billy Goldenberg. *WAR*

Last of the Clintons 🐾½ 1935
A range detective tracks an outlaw gang amid spur jinglin', sharp shootin' and cow punchin'. 64m/B VHS, Beta, LV. Harry Carey Sr. *NOS*

Last of the Comanches 🐾🐾 *The Sabre and the Arrow* 1952
Cavalry and Indians fight for water when both are dying of thirst in the desert. 85m/C VHS, Beta. Broderick Crawford, Barbara Hale, John Stewart, Lloyd Bridges, Mickey Shaughnessy, George Mathews; **D:** Andre de Toth. *GKK*

The Last of the Dogmen 🐾🐾½ 1995 (PG)
Cliched modern western with an intriguing premise and good actors. Montana bounty hunter Lewis Gates (Berenger) is recruited to nab three escaped cons but finds them dead and a Cheyenne arrow nearby. Gates does some investigating (in a library no less!) and discovers that maybe some descendants of the 1864 Sand Creek massacre are existing in the woods. He gets anthropologist Lillian Sloan (Hershey) involved, discovers a tribe of modern-day dog soldiers, and finds a very angry sheriff (Smith) on their trail. Alberta, Canada passes for Big Sky country. 117m/C VHS. Tom Berenger, Barbara Hershey, Kurtwood Smith, Steve Reevis, Andrew Miller, Gregory

Scott Cummins; **D:** Tab Murphy; **W:** Tab Murphy; **C:** Karl Walter Lindenlaub; **M:** David Arnold. *HBO*

The Last of the Finest 🐾½ *Street Legal; Blue Heat* 1990 (R)
Overzealous anti-drug task force cops break the rules in trying to put dealer-drug lords in prison; ostensibly a parallel on the Iran-Contra affair. 106m/C VHS, Beta, LV, **Closed Caption.** Brian Dennehy, Joe Pantoliano, Jeff Fahey, Bill Paxton, Deborra-Lee Furness, Guy Boyd, Henry Darrow, Lisa Jane Persky, Michael C. Gwynne; **D:** John MacKenzie; **W:** George Armitage, Jere P. Cunningham; **M:** Jack Nitzsche. *ORI*

The Last of the Mohicans 🐾🐾🐾 1920
Color tints enhance this silent version of the James Fenimore Cooper rouser. Beery is the villanious Magua, with Bedford memorable as the lovely Cora and Roscoe as the brave Uncas. Fine action sequences, including the Huron massacre at Fort Henry. Director credit was shared when Tourneur suffered an on-set injury and was off for three months. 75m/B VHS, LV. Wallace Beery, Barbara Bedford, Albert Roscoe, Lillian Hall-Davis, Henry Woodward, James Gordon, George Hackathorne, Harry Lorraine, Nelson McDowell, Theodore Lorch, Boris Karloff; **D:** Maurice Tourneur, Clarence Brown; **W:** Robert Dillon. National Film Registry '95. *LUM, FCT, MIL*

The Last of the Mohicans 1932
Serial based on James Fenimore Cooper's novel of the life-and-death struggle of the Mohican Indians during the French and Indian War. Twelve chapters, 13 minutes each. Remade as a movie in 1936 and 1992 and as a television movie in 1977. 230m/B VHS, Beta. Edwina Booth, Harry Carey Sr., Hobart Bosworth, Frank "Junior" Coghlan; **D:** Ford Beebe, B. Reeves Eason. *VYY, VCN, NOS*

The Last of the Mohicans 🐾🐾½ 1936
James Fenimore Cooper's classic about the French and Indian War in colonial America is brought to the screen. Remake of the 1932 serial was remade itself in 1977 for television. 91m/B VHS, Beta. Randolph Scott, Binnie Barnes, Bruce Cabot, Henry Wilcoxon, Heather Angel, Hugh Buckler; **D:** George B. Seitz. *ART, CCB*

The Last of the Mohicans 🐾🐾 1985
The classic novel by James Fenimore Cooper about the scout Hawkeye and his Mohican companions, Chingachgook and Uncas during the French and Indian war, comes to life in this made-for-television film. Remake of a 1932 serial and a 1936 film. 97m/C VHS, Beta. Steve Forrest, Ned Romero, Andrew Prine, Don Shanks, Robert Tessier, Jane Actman; **D:** James L. Conway. *VCI*

The Last of the Mohicans 🐾🐾🐾 1992 (R)
It's 1757, at the height of the French and English war in the American colonies, with various Native American tribes allied to each side. Hawkeye (Day-Lewis), a white frontiersman raised by the Mohicans, wants nothing to do with either "civilized" side, until he rescues the beautiful Cora (Stowe) from the revenge-minded Huron Magua (Studi in a powerful performance). Graphically violent battle scenes are realistic, but not gratuitous. The real pleasure in this adaptation, which draws from both the James Fenimore Cooper novel and the 1936 film, is in its lush look and attractive stars. Means is terrific in his film debut as Hawkeye's foster-father. Released in a letterbox format to preserve the original integrity of the film. **CW:** Violence. 114m/C VHS, LV, **Letterbox.** Daniel Day-Lewis, Madeleine Stowe, Wes Studi, Russell Means, Eric Schweig, Jodhi May, Steven Waddington, Maurice Roeves, Colm Meaney, Patrice Chereau; **D:** Michael Mann; **W:** Christopher Crowe, Michael Mann; **C:** Dante Spinotti; **M:** Trevor Jones, Randy Edelman. Academy Awards '92: Best Sound. *FXV, BTV*

Last of the Pony Riders 🐾½ 1953
When the telegraph lines linking the East and West Coasts are completed, Gene and the other Pony Express riders find themselves out of a job. Autry's final feature film. 59m/B VHS, Beta. Gene Autry, Smiley Burnette, Kathleen Case; **D:** George Archainbaud. *CCB*

Last of the Red Hot Lovers 🎞½ 1972 (PG) Not so funny adaptation of Neil Simon's Broadway hit. Middle-aged man decides to have a fling and uses his mother's apartment to seduce three very strange women. 98m/C VHS, Beta, LV. Alan Arkin, Paula Prentiss, Sally Kellerman, Renee Taylor; **D:** Gene Saks; **W:** Neil Simon. PAR

The Last of the Redmen 🎞½ 1947 An adaptation of James Fenimore Cooper's "The Last of the Mohicans" geared toward youngsters. Hall must lead three children of a British general through dangerous Indian territory. They have a number of adventures including meeting up with Uncas, the last of the Mohicans, who's a villain in this mangled version. 79m/B VHS. Jon Hall, Michael O'Shea, Evelyn Ankers, Julie Bishop, Buster Crabbe, Rick Vallin, Frederick Worlock, Guy Hedlund; **D:** George Sherman; **W:** Herbert Dalmas. COL

Last of the Warrens 🎞 1936 A cowboy returns home after WWI to discover that an unscrupulous storekeeper has stolen his property. 56m/C VHS, Beta. Bob Steele, Charles "Blackie" King, Lafe McKee, Margaret Marquis, Horace Murphy; **D:** Robert North Bradbury. NOS, DVT, GPV

Last of the Wild Horses 🎞½ 1949 Range war almost starts when ranch owner is accused of trying to force the small ranchers out of business. 86m/B VHS, Beta. Mary Beth Hughes, James Ellison, Jane Frazee. NO

The Last Outlaw 🎞🎞 1927 Action-packed western with Cooper following his success of "Wings" with Paramount. Most excellent equine stunts. 61m/B VHS, Beta. Gary Cooper, Jack Luden, Betty Jewel; **D:** Arthur Rosson. GPV, FCT

Last Outlaw 🎞🎞 1936 The last of the famous badmen of the old West is released from jail and returns home to find that times have changed. The action climaxes in an old-time blazing shoot-out. 79m/B VHS, Beta. Harry Carey Sr., Hoot Gibson, Henry B. Walthall, Tom Tyler, Russell Hopton, Alan Curtis, Harry Woods, Barbara Pepper; **D:** Christy Cabanne. VCN

The Last Outlaw 🎞🎞½ 1993 (R) Rourke stars as an ex-Confederate officer who leads a gang of outlaws until his violent excesses leave even them disgusted. The gang shoots Rourke but of course he doesn't die and then he sets out for revenge. Made for cable television. 90m/C VHS. Mickey Rourke, Dermot Mulroney, Ted Levine, John C. McGinley, Steve Buscemi, Keith David; **D:** Geoff Murphy; **W:** Eric Red. HBO, FCT

The Last Picture Show 🎞🎞🎞🎞 1971 (R) Slice of life/nostalgic farewell to an innocent age, based on Larry McMurtry's novel. Set in Archer City, a backwater Texas town, most of the story plays out at the local hangout run by ex-cowboy Sam the Lion. Bridges is hooked up with spoiled pretty girl Shepherd, while Bottoms, a sensitive guy, is having an affair with the coach's neglected wife (Leachman). Loss of innocence, disillusionment and confusion are played out against the backdrop of a town about to close its cinema. Shepherd's and Bottoms' film debut. Stunningly photographed in black and white (Bogdanovich claimed he didn't want to "prettify" the picture by shooting in color) by Robert Surtees. Available in a laserdisc special edition with 17 minutes restored. Followed by a weak sequel, "Texasville." A boxed set featuring both films is also available.**CW:** Language, nudity, and sexuality. 118m/B VHS, LV, 8mm, Letterbox, Closed Caption. Jeff Bridges, Timothy Bottoms, Ben Johnson, Cloris Leachman, Cybill Shepherd, Ellen Burstyn, Eileen Brennan, Clu Gulager, Sharon Taggart, Randy Quaid, Sam Bottoms, John Hillerman; **D:** Peter Bogdanovich; **W:** Larry McMurtry, Peter Bogdanovich; **C:** Robert L. Surtees. Academy Awards '71: Best Supporting Actor (Johnson), Best Supporting Actress (Leachman); British Academy Awards '72: Best Screenplay, Best Supporting Actor (Johnson), Best Supporting Actress (Leachman); Golden Globe Awards '72: Best Supporting Actor (Johnson); National Board of Review Awards '71: Best Supporting Actor (Johnson), Best Supporting Actress (Leachman); New York Film Critics Awards '71:

Best Screenplay, Best Supporting Actor (Johnson), Best Supporting Actress (Burstyn); National Society of Film Critics Awards '71: Best Supporting Actress (Burstyn); Nominations: Academy Awards '71: Best Adapted Screenplay, Best Cinematography, Best Director (Bogdanovich), Best Picture, Best Supporting Actor (Bridges), Best Supporting Actress (Burstyn). COL, CRC, FCT

The Last Place on Earth 1994 Saga of bitter hardship and ambition depicting the 1911 race between the British Antarctic Expedition, led by Captain Robert Falcon (Shaw), and his Norwegian rival Roald Amundsen (Ousdal) to conquer the South Pole. On seven cassettes. 385m/C VHS. **CA** Martin Shaw, Sverre Anker Ousdal, Max von Sydow, Susan Wooldridge. TVC, VCO

Last Plane Out 🎞½ 1983 (R) A Texas journalist sent on assignment to Nicaragua falls in love with a Sandanista rebel. Based on producer Jack Cox's real-life experiences as a journalist during the last days of the Samosa regime. Low-budget propaganda. 90m/C VHS, Beta, Closed Caption. Jan-Michael Vincent, Lloyd Batista, Julie Carmen, Mary Crosby, David Huffman, William Windom; **D:** David Nelson. VTR, FOX

The Last Polka 🎞🎞🎞 1984 SCTV vets Candy and Levy are Yosh and Stan Schmenge, polka kings interviewed for a "documentary" on their years in the spotlight and on the road. Hilarious spoof on Martin Scorsese's "The Last Waltz," about The Band's last concert. Several fellow Second City-ers keep the laughs coming. If you liked SCTV or "This is Spinal Tap," you'll like this. Made for cable (HBO). 54m/C VHS, Beta. John Candy, Eugene Levy, Rick Moranis, Robin Duke, Catherine O'Hara; **D:** John Blanchard. ART, VES

The Last Porno Flick 🎞 1974 (PG) A pornographic movie script winds up in the hands of a couple of goofy cab drivers. The twosome sneak the movie's private past the producers, families, and police. 90m/C VHS. Michael Pataki, Marianna Hill, Carmen Zapata, Mike Kellin, Colleen Camp, Tom Signorelli, Antony Carbone; **D:** Ray Marsh. NO

The Last Prostitute 🎞🎞 1991 (PG-13) Two teenage boys search for a legendary prostitute to initiate them into manhood, only to discover that she has retired. They hire on as laborers on her horse farm, and one of them discovers the meaning of love. Made for cable TV. 93m/C VHS. Sonia Braga, Wil Wheaton, David Kaufman, Woody Watson, Dennis Letts, Cotter Smith; **D:** Lou Antonio; **W:** Carmen Culver. USH

The Last Remake of Beau Geste 🎞🎞 1977 (PG) A slapstick parody of the familiar Foreign Legion story from the Mel Brooksish school of loud genre farce. Gary Cooper makes an appearance by way of inserted footage from the 1939 straight version. 85m/C VHS, Beta. Marty Feldman, Ann-Margret, Michael York, Peter Ustinov, James Earl Jones; **D:** Marty Feldman; **W:** Marty Feldman, Chris Allen. USH

Last Resort 🎞🎞 *She Knew No Other Way* 1986 (R) A married furniture executive unknowingly takes his family on vacation to a sex-saturated, Club Med-type holiday spot, and gets more than he anticipated.**CW:** Language, violence, and graphic sensuality. 80m/C VHS, Beta, LV. Charles Grodin, Jon Lovitz; **D:** Zane Buzby; **W:** Jeff Buhai. ART, VES

The Last Reunion 🎞½ 1980 The only witness to a brutal killing of a Japanese official and his wife during WWII seeks revenge on the guilty American platoon, 33 years later. Violent. 98m/C VHS. Cameron Mitchell, Leo Fong, Chanda Romero, Vic Silayan, Hal Bokar, Philip Baker Hall; **D:** Jay Wertz. SNC

The Last Ride 🎞 1991 Another movie probing the dark side of hitchhiking. This time our hero thumbs a ride with a truck driver who plans to bypass the next city...for hell. 84m/C VHS. Dan Ranger, Michael Hilow.

The Last Ride 🎞🎞 *F.T.W* 1994 (R) Frank T. Wells (Rourke) is out of prison after 10 years and free to try to recapture his former rodeo glory. Hellcat Scarlett Stuart's on the run from a botched bank job/murder perpetrated by her vicious brother Clem (Berg). Scarlett manages to hook up with Frank and decides to help him out financially by robbing convenience stores. Frank's not too happy when he finds out. Rourke is surprisingly subdued and Singer's properly unsympathetic but they don't seem to be working in the same movie. Nice Montana scenery though. 102m/C VHS, Closed Caption. Mickey Rourke, Lori Singer, Brion James, Peter Berg, Rodney Grant, Aaron Neville; **D:** Michael Karbelnikoff; **W:** Mari Kornhauser; **C:** James L. Carter; **M:** Gary Chang. HMK

The Last Ride of the Dalton Gang 🎞🎞 1979 A long-winded retelling of the wild adventures that made the Dalton gang legendary among outlaws. 146m/C VHS, Beta. Larry Wilcox, Jack Palance, Randy Quaid, Cliff Potts, Dale Robertson, Don Collier; **D:** Dan Curtis. WAR, OM

The Last Riders 🎞 1990 (R) Motorcycle centaur Estrada revs a few motors fleeing from cycle club cronies and crooked cops. Full throttle foolishness. 90m/C VHS, LV. Erik Estrada, William Smith, Armando Silvestre, Kathrin Lautner; **D:** Joseph Merhi. PMH, HHE

Last Rites 🎞🎞 1988 (R) A priest at St. Patrick's Cathedral in New York allows a young Mexican woman to seek sanctuary from the Mob, who soon come after both of them. 103m/C VHS, Beta, LV, Closed Caption. Tom Berenger, Daphne Zuniga, Chick Vennera, Dane Clark, Carlo Pacchi, Anne Twomey, Paul Dooley, Vassili Lambrinos; **D:** Donald P. Bellisario; **W:** Donald P. Bellisario; **C:** David Watkin; **M:** Bruce Broughton. FOX

The Last Safari 🎞🎞½ 1967 A young man on safari in Africa befriends a bitter professional guide in a drama hampered by a poor script. Granger and Garas set out to hunt the rampaging elephant which killed Granger's friend. Granger thinks killing the beast will restore his courage and help him overcome the guilt he feels. Based on the novel "Gilligan's Last Elephant" by Gerald Hanley. 111m/C VHS, Closed Caption. Stewart Granger, Kaz Garas, Gabriella Licudi, Johnny Sekka, Liam Redmond; **D:** Henry Hathaway; **W:** John Gay; **C:** Ted Moore. PAR

The Last Samurai 🎞 1990 (R) Arab arms dealer Saxon arranges a fake kidnapping by rebel military leader Cele in order to keep their weapons deal a secret. But among the other hostages is mercenary Hendricksen, who escapes and wrecks havoc on their plotting.**CW:** Violence, language, and some nudity. 94m/C VHS. Lance Henriksen, John Saxon, Henry Cele, Arabella Holzbog, John Fujioka, James Ryan, Duncan Regehr, Lisa Eilbacher; **D:** Paul Mayersberg. AVI

The Last Season woof! 1987 Shoot 'em up involving a bunch of hunters. Their aimless destruction provokes the good guy to save the forest they are demolishing. A battle ensues. 90m/C VHS. Christopher Gosch, Louise Dorsey, David Cox; **D:** Raja Zahr. NO

The Last Seduction 🎞🎞🎞🎞 1994 (R) Dahl, the master of modern noir, delivers another stylish look exploring the darker side of urban life. Fiorentino gives the performance of her life as the most evil, rotten femme fatale to ever hit the big screen. Bridget (Fiorentino) rips off the money her husband Clay (Pullman) made in a pharmaceutical drug deal and leaves Manhattan for a small town in Upstate New York. Once there, she takes nice, naive Mike (Berg) as her lover, while Clay tries to ferret her out and get his money back. Lots of dry humor and a wickedly amusing heroine make for a devilishly entertaining film.**CW:** Language; nudity; sexual situations; violence. 110m/C VHS, LV, Closed Caption. Linda Fiorentino, Peter Berg, J.T. Walsh, Bill Nunn, Bill Pullman; **D:** John Dahl; **W:** Steve Barancik; **M:** Joseph Vitarelli. Independent Spirit Awards '95: Best Actress (Fiorentino); New York Film Critics Awards '94: Best Actress (Fiorentino). PGV

The Last Slumber Party woof! **1987** A slumber party is beset by a homicidal maniac. Heavy metal soundtrack. **89m/C VHS, Beta.** Jan Jensen, Nancy Meyer. *VCI*

Last Song 🐾½ **1980 (PG)** A singer's husband discovers a plot to cover up a fatal toxic-waste accident, and is killed because of it. It's up to her to warn the authorities before becoming the next victim. **96m/C VHS, Beta, Closed Caption.** Lynda Carter, Ronny Cox, Nicholas Pryor, Paul Rudd, Jenny O'Hara; *D:* Alan J. Levi. *FOX*

Last Stand at Saber River 🐾🐾½ **1996** Cable adaptation of Elmore Leonard's 1959 western novel finds Confederate Civil War vet Paul Cable (Selleck) coming home to his wife Martha's (Amis) family in Texas, having been wounded in the fighting. However, Martha was informed he was dead, so imagine her surprise. What Cable wants to do now is return to his pre-war life—a horse ranch in Arizona—but after making the journey the family discovers their ranch has been taken over by Union sympathizer Duane Kidston (Carradine) and he's not intending to let it go. Selleck was born to ride tall in the saddle. **95m/C VHS, Closed Caption.** Tom Selleck, Suzy Amis, David Carradine, Keith Carradine, David Dukes, Tracey Needham, Rachel Duncan, Haley Joel Osment, Harry Carey Jr., Lumi Cavazos, Patrick Kilpatrick; *D:* Dick Lowry; *W:* Ronald M. Cohen; *C:* Ric Waite; *M:* David Shire. *WAR*

The Last Starfighter 🐾🐾 **1984 (PG)** A young man who becomes an expert at a video game is recruited to fight in an inter-galactic war. Listless adventure which explains where all those video games come from. Watch for O'Herlihy disguised as a lizard. **100m/C VHS, Beta, LV.** Lance Guest, Robert Preston, Barbara Bosson, Dan O'Herlihy, Catherine Mary Stewart, Cameron Dye, Kimberly Ross, Wil Wheaton; *D:* Nick Castle; *W:* Jonathan Betuel. *USH*

Last Summer 🐾🐾½ **1969 (R)** Three teenagers discover love, sex, and friendship on the white sands of Fire Island, N.Y. The summer vacation fantasy world they create shatters when a sweet but homely female teenager joins their group. Based on a novel by Evan Hunter. **97m/C VHS, Beta.** Barbara Hershey, Richard Thomas, Bruce Davison, Cathy Burns; *D:* Frank Perry. Nominations: Academy Awards '69: Best Supporting Actress (Burns). *FOX*

Last Summer In the Hamptons 🐾🐾🐾 **1996 (R)** In her last film, Lindfors stars as Helena Mora, the matriarch of a charming three generation theatrical clan that gets together one weekend a year at her spacious, slightly run-down estate to participate in drama workshops and perform plays. When Helena is forced to sell the estate, the family reunites for one last weekend of bickering and performing. Featuring fine performances from the entire ensemble (including Lindfors' son and Jaglom's wife), Jaglom's touching and engaging tribute to his family gives nepotism a good name. *CW:* Mature language. **105m/C VHS.** Victoria Foyt, Viveca Lindfors, Jon Robin Baitz, Andre Gregory, Melissa Leo, Martha Plimpton, Roddy McDowall, Nick Gregory, Savannah Smith Boucher, Roscoe Lee Browne, Ron Rifkin, Diane Salinger, Brooke Smith, Kristopher Tabori, Holland Taylor, Henry Jaglom; *D:* Henry Jaglom; *W:* Victoria Foyt, Henry Jaglom; *C:* Hanania Baer; *M:* Johnny Mercer, Harold Arlen. *ART*

The Last Supper 🐾🐾🐾 **1976** A repentant Cuban slave-owner in the 18th-century decides to cleanse his soul and convert his slaves to Christianity by having 12 of them reenact the Last Supper. Based on a true story. In Spanish with English subtitles. **110m/C VHS, Beta.** *CU* Nelson Villagra, Silvano Rey, Lamberto Garcia, Jose Antonio Rodriguez, Samuel Claxton, Mario Balmasada; *D:* Tomas Gutierrez Alea. *NYF, FCT*

The Last Supper 🐾🐾½ **1996 (R)** First-time feature director Title dishes out an extremely black comedy about a group of liberal roommates who accidentally kill a racist marine they've invited to dinner. This leads to the devious plan of inviting more right wingers over, baiting them into arguments about controversial topics, then killing and burying them in a vegetable garden. Somehow manages to avoid excessive preachiness despite taking on all political comers. Not exactly a great feast, but there's enough tasty snacks to be satisfying. Performances are good and the victims (led by Perlman's Limbaugh turn) really shine. Too bad their characters aren't on screen very long before they become tomato fertilizer. *CW:* Violence, profanity and sexual situations. **91m/C VHS, LV, Closed Caption.** Cameron Diaz, Annabeth Gish, Ron Eldard, Jonathan Penner, Courtney B. Vance, Nora Dunn; *Cameos:* Ron Perlman, Jason Alexander, Charles Durning, Mark Harmon, Bill Paxton; *D:* Stacy Title; *W:* Dan Rosen; *C:* Paul Cameron; *M:* Mark Mothersbaugh. *COL*

Last Tango in Paris 🐾🐾🐾½ **1973 (R)** Brando plays a middle-aged American who meets a French girl and tries to forget his wife's suicide with a short, extremely steamy affair. Bertolucci proves to be a master; Brando gives one of his best performances. Very controversial when made, still quite explicit. Visually stunning. The X-rated version, at 130 minutes, is also available. **126m/C VHS, Beta, LV, Letterbox.** *IT FR* Marlon Brando, Maria Schneider, Jean-Pierre Leaud; *D:* Bernardo Bertolucci; *W:* Bernardo Bertolucci; *C:* Vittorio Storaro; *M:* Gato Barbieri. New York Film Critics Awards '73: Best Actor (Brando); National Society of Film Critics Awards '73: Best Actor (Brando); Nominations: Academy Awards '73: Best Actor (Brando), Best Director (Bertolucci). *MGM, FOX*

The Last Temptation of Christ 🐾🐾🐾½ **1988 (R)** Scorsese's controversial adaptation of the Nikos Kazantzakis novel, portraying Christ in his last year as an ordinary Israelite tormented by divine doubt, human desires and the voice of God. The controversy engulfing the film, as it was heavily protested and widely banned, tended to divert attention from what is an exceptional statement of religious and artistic vision. Excellent score by Peter Gabriel. **164m/C VHS, Beta, LV.** Willem Dafoe, Harvey Keitel, Barbara Hershey, Harry Dean Stanton, Andre Gregory, David Bowie, Verna Bloom, Juliette Caton, John Lurie, Roberts Blossom, Irvin Kershner, Barry Miller, Tomas Arana, Nehemiah Persoff, Paul Herman, Illeana Douglas; *D:* Martin Scorsese; *W:* Paul Schrader; *C:* Michael Ballhaus; *M:* Peter Gabriel. Nominations: Academy Awards '88: Best Director (Scorsese). *USH, CRC*

The Last Time I Committed Suicide 🐾🐾 **1996 (R)** Based on a Beat-era letter from Neal Cassady to Jack Kerouac and set in the late '40s, this insubstantial pic follows a 20-year-old Cassady (Jane) as he drifts into Denver's bars, and a friendship with poolhall regular Harry (Reeves), in order to escape dealing with girlfriend Joan's (Forlani) attempted suicide. Joan's eventual recovery leads Neal to consider settling down but he blows a job interview thanks to a drunken Harry and decides to take off instead. No background is provided on the characters so their actions are inexplicable although Jane offers some appeal. *CW:* Mature themes, sexual situations, nudity, language. **93m/C VHS, Closed Caption.** Thomas Jane, Keanu Reeves, Tom Bower, Adrien Brody, Claire Forlani, Marg Helgenberger, Gretchen Mol; *D:* Stephen Kay; *W:* Stephen Kay; *C:* Bobby Bukowski. *USH*

The Last Time I Saw Paris 🐾🐾½ **1954** A successful writer reminisces about his love affair with a wealthy American girl in post-WWII Paris. **116m/C VHS, Beta, LV.** Elizabeth Taylor, Van Johnson, Walter Pidgeon, Roger Moore, Donna Reed, Eva Gabor; *D:* Richard Brooks; *W:* Richard Brooks, Julius J. Epstein, Philip C. Epstein; *C:* Joseph Ruttenberg. *MGM, MRV, NOS*

Last Time Out 🐾🐾½ **1994 (PG-13)** Danny Dolan (Conrad) is a hard-partying college wide receiver who gets a shock when the father who abandoned him enrolls at his school to finish a college degree. Seems Joe (Beck) had his pro quarterback career cut short by a drinking problem and he's worried his son will follow in his unsteady footsteps. *CW:* Mature themes; mild violence; drug content. **92m/C VHS, LV, Closed Caption.** John Beck, Christian Conrad, Lori Werner, Gail Strickland, Betty Buckley; *D:* Don Fox Greene. *IMP*

The Last Tomahawk 🐾 **1965** Colorful and action packed reworking of Cooper's "Last of the Mohicans." **?m/C VHS.** *GE IT* Anthony Steffen, Karin Dor, Dan Martin, Joachim Fuchsberger. *SNC*

The Last Train 🐾🐾 **1974** Romance most hopeless in the heart of France during zee beeg war. During the 1940 invasion of Paris a man and woman turn to each other for comfort when separated from their families while trying to escape the city. French, very French. **101m/C VHS.** *FR* Romy Schneider, Jean-Louis Trintignant, Maurice Biraud; *D:* Pierre Granier-Deferre. *NO*

Last Train from Gun Hill 🐾🐾🐾 **1959** An all-star cast highlights this suspenseful story of a U.S. marshall determined to catch the man who raped and murdered his wife. Excellent action packed western. **94m/C VHS.** Kirk Douglas, Anthony Quinn, Carolyn Jones, Earl Holliman, Brad Dexter, Brian Hutton, Ziva Rodann; *D:* John Sturges; *C:* Charles B(ryant) Lang. *NO*

The Last Tycoon 🐾🐾🐾 **1976 (PG)** An adaptation of the unfinished F. Scott Fitzgerald novel about the life and times of a Hollywood movie executive of the 1920s. Confusing and slow moving despite a blockbuster conglomeration of talent. Joan Collins introduces the film. **123m/C VHS, Beta, LV.** Robert De Niro, Tony Curtis, Ingrid Boulting, Jack Nicholson, Jeanne Moreau, Peter Strauss, Robert Mitchum, Theresa Russell, Donald Pleasence, Ray Milland, Dana Andrews, John Carradine, Anjelica Huston; *D:* Elia Kazan; *W:* Harold Pinter; *M:* Maurice Jarre. Nominations: Academy Awards '76: Best Art Direction/Set Decoration. *PAR, FCT*

The Last Unicorn 🐾🐾½ **1982 (G)** Peter Beagle's popular tale of a beautiful unicorn who goes in search of her lost, mythical "family." **95m/C VHS, Beta, LV, Closed Caption.** *D:* Jules Bass; *W:* Peter S. Beagle; *M:* Jim Webb; *V:* Alan Arkin, Jeff Bridges, Tammy Grimes, Angela Lansbury, Mia Farrow, Robert Klein, Christopher Lee, Keenan Wynn. *FOX, KAR, ART*

The Last Valley 🐾🐾 **1971 (PG)** A scholar tries to protect a pristine 17th century Swiss valley, untouched by the Thirty Years War, from marauding soldiers. Historical action with an intellectual twist. **128m/C VHS.** Michael Caine, Omar Sharif, Florinda Bolkan, Nigel Davenport, Per Oscarsson, Arthur O'Connell; *D:* James Clavell; *W:* James Clavell; *M:* John Barry. *NO*

The Last Voyage 🐾🐾½ **1960** Suspenseful disaster film in which Stack and Malone play a married couple in jeopardy while on an ocean cruise. To make the film more realistic, the French liner Ile de France was actually used in the sinking scenes. Although a bit farfetched, film is made watchable because of fine performances and excellent camerawork. **91m/C VHS, LV, Closed Caption.** Robert Stack, Dorothy Malone, George Sanders, Edmond O'Brien, Woody Strode, Jack Kruschen; *D:* Andrew L. Stone; *W:* Andrew L. Stone; *C:* Hal Mohr. *MGM*

The Last Waltz **1978 (PG)** Martin Scorsese filmed this rock documentary featuring the farewell performance of The Band, joined by a host of musical guests that they have been associated with over the years. Songs include: "Up On Cripple Creek," "Don't Do It," "The Night They Drove Old Dixie Down," "Stage Fright" (The Band), "Helpless" (Young), "Coyote" (Mitchell), "Caravan" (Morrison), "Further on Up the Road" (Clapton), "Who Do You Love" (Hawkins), "Mannish Boy" (Waters), "Evangeline" (Harris), "Baby, Let Me Follow You Down" (Dylan). **117m/C VHS, Beta, LV, Closed Caption.** *D:* Martin Scorsese; *C:* Michael Chapman. *MVD, MGM*

Last War 🐾 **1968** A nuclear war between the United States and Russia triggers Armageddon. **79m/C VHS, Beta.** Frankie Sakai, Nobuko Otowa, Akira Takarada, Yuriko Hoshi; *D:* Shue Matsubayashi. *GEM*

The Last Warrior 🎬½ *Coastwatcher* **1989** (R) A good-looking but exploitive "Hell in the Pacific" rip-off, as an American and a Japanese soldier battle it out alone on a remote island during WWII. **94m/C VHS, Beta, LV.** Gary Graham, Cary-Hiroyuki Tagawa, Maria Holvoe; **D:** Martin Wragge. **COL**

The Last Wave 🎬🎬🎬 **1977 (PG)** An Australian attorney takes on a murder case involving an aborigine and he finds himself becoming distracted by apocalyptic visions concerning tidal waves and drownings that seem to foretell the future. Weir's masterful creation and communication of time and place are marred by a somewhat pat ending. **109m/C VHS, Beta.** *AU* Richard Chamberlain, Olivia Hamnett, David Gulpilil, Frederick Parslow; **D:** Peter Weir; **W:** Peter Weir; **C:** Russell Boyd. **FCT, RHI**

The Last Winter 🎬🎬 **1984 (R)** An American woman fights to find her Israeli husband who has disappeared in the 1973 Yom Kippur War. Trouble is, an Israeli woman thinks the man she's looking for is really her husband too. **92m/C VHS, Beta.** *IS* Kathleen Quinlan, Yona Elian, Zipora Peled, Michael Schnider; **D:** Riki Shelach. **COL**

The Last Winter 🎬🎬½ **1989 (PG)** Ten-year-old Will (Murray) has always lived in the country and finds it hard to accept his parents' decision to move to the city. But with the help of his grandfather (Parkes), Will begins to understand about change and growing up. **103m/C VHS, Closed Caption.** *CA* Joshua Murray, Gerard Parkes, David Ferry, Wanda Cannon, Marsha Moreau, Nathaniel Moreau, Katie Murray; **D:** Aaron Kim Johnston; **W:** Aaron Kim Johnston; **C:** Ian Elkin; **M:** Victor Davies. **FXV**

The Last Winters 🎬🎬½ **1971** From Jean Charles Tacchella, writer-producer-director of "Cousin Cousine," comes his first short film about an old couple's bittersweet romance. In French with English subtitles. **23m/C VHS, Beta.** *FR* **D:** Jean-Charles Tacchella. **INT**

Last Witness 🎬 **1988** A man on the run from the government claims that he is innocent and was unjustly persecuted, but the government sees him as a dangerous threat. Nothing will stop the hunt for the escaped man, no matter what it costs. **85m/C VHS, Beta.** Jeff Henderson. *TWE*

The Last Woman on Earth woof! **1961** Two men vie for the affections of the sole surviving woman after a vague and unexplained disaster of vast proportions. Robert Towne, who appears herein under the pseudonym Edward Wain, wrote the script (his first screenwriting effort). You might want to watch this if it were the last movie on earth, although Corman fans will probably love it. **71m/C VHS.** Antony Carbone, Edward Wain, Betsy Jones-Moreland; **D:** Roger Corman; **W:** Robert Towne. *NOS, MRV, SNC*

The Last Word 🎬🎬 *Danny Travis* **1980 (PG)** Comedy drama about struggling inventor Harris fighting to protect his home, family, and neighbors from a corrupt real estate deal involving shady politicians, angry policemen, and a beautiful television reporter. **103m/C VHS, Beta.** Richard Harris, Karen Black, Martin Landau, Dennis Christopher, Bill McGuire, Christopher Guest, Penelope Milford, Michael Pataki; **W:** Michael Varhol, L.M. Kit Carson.

The Last Word 🎬🎬 **1995 (R)** Journalist Martin (Hutton) writes a newspaper column, often featuring characters based on hometown Detroit mob figures, with info supplied to him by his friend, Doc (Pantoliano), who owes the gangsters some big bucks. Doc also introduces Martin to his latest column subject—stripper Caprice (Burke)—and, thanks again to Doc, a Hollywood studio gets interested in filming her story but wants more sex and violence, which means Martin will be betraying her deepest secrets. Now, he must choose between love, success, or friendship.**CW:** Language, sexuality and some violent images. **95m/C VHS.** Timothy Hutton, Joe Pantoliano, Michelle Burke, Chazz Palminteri, Tony Goldwyn; **Cameos:** Richard Dreyfuss, Cybill Shepherd, Jimmy Smits; **D:** Tony Spiridakis. *THV*

Last Year at Marienbad 🎬🎬🎬 *L'Anno Dernière a Marienbad* **1961** A young man tries to lure a mysterious woman to run away with him from a hotel in France. Once a hit on the artsy circuit, it's most interesting for its beautiful photography. In French with English subtitles. **93m/B VHS, Beta, 8mm.** *FR IT* Delphine Seyrig, Giorgia Albertazzi, Sacha Pitoeff, Luce Garcia-Ville; **D:** Alain Resnais; **C:** Sacha Vierny. Nominations: Academy Awards '62: Best Story & Screenplay. *FXL, MRV, NOS*

L'Atalante 🎬🎬🎬½ **1934** Vigo's great masterpiece, a slight story about a husband and wife quarreling, splitting, and reuniting around which has been fashioned one of the cinema's greatest poetic films. In French with English subtitles. **82m/B VHS, Beta.** *FR* Dita Parlo, Jean Daste, Michel Simon; **D:** Jean Vigo. *NOS, HHT, PMS*

Late Bloomers 🎬🎬 **1995** Romantic comedy focuses on what happens when two Midwestern women fall in love. Math teacher/basketball coach Dinah (Nelson) is friendly with fellow teacher Rom (Carter) and his wife, Carly (Hennigan), the high school secretary. A misinterpreted note, an impulsive kiss, and Carly's soon out of door and living with Dinah, which leads to a community uproar. The two leads are likeable but the other characters and the situation are heavily cliched. **105m/C VHS.** Connie Nelson, Dee Hennigan, Gary Carter, Lisa Peterson; **D:** Julia Dyer; **W:** Gretchen Dyer; **C:** Bill Schwarz; **M:** Ted Pine. *FCT*

Late Chrysanthemums 🎬🎬 *Bangiku* **1954** A middle-aged geisha has settled into comfortable retirement as a money lender. When she hears a former lover wants to visit her, she tries to recapture her old glamour only to be disillusioned. Based on a short story by Fumiko Hayashi. In Japanese with English subtitles. **101m/B VHS.** *JP* Haruko Sugimura, Chikako Hosokawa, Sadako Sawahura; **D:** Mikio Naruse. *WAC*

Late Extra 🎬🎬 **1935** A novice reporter attempts to track down a notorious bank robber and gets some help from a savvy female journalist. Mason's first role of substance. **69m/B VHS, Beta.** *GB* Virginia Cherrill, James Mason, Alastair Sim, Ian Colin, Clifford McLaglen, Cyril Cusack, David Horne, Antoinette Cellier, Donald Wolfit, Michael Wilding; **D:** Albert Parker. *SNC*

Late for Dinner 🎬🎬 **1991 (PG)** In 1962 Willie, a young, married man, and his best friend Frank are framed by a sleazy land developer. On the run, the two decide to become guinea pigs in a cryonics experiment and wind up frozen for 29 years. It's now 1991 and Willie wants to find his family—only his wife is middle-aged and his daughter is all grown-up. Can he make a life with them again or has time indeed passed him by? **93m/C VHS, LV.** Brian Wimmer, Peter Berg, Marcia Gay Harden, Peter Gallagher, Ross Malinger; **D:** W.D. Richter; **W:** Mark Andrus. *COL, NLC*

The Late Shift 🎬🎬½ **1996 (R)** Cable adaptation of Bill Carter's book chronicling the follies surrounding NBC's "The Tonight Show" succession battle between Jay Leno (Roebuck) and Dave Letterman (Higgins). It's the behind-the-scenes dealmakers that really steal the show, however, including Jay's profane manager Helen Kushnick (Bates) and superagent Michael Ovitz (Williams), who ultimately orchestrated Dave's move to rival CBS. Both Letterman and Leno made the movie/book fodder for their opening monlogues.**CW:** Language. **96m/C VHS.** Daniel Roebuck, John Michael Higgins, Kathy Bates, Treat Williams, Bob Balaban, Ed Begley Jr., Rich Little, Sandra Bernhard, Peter Jurasik, Reni Santoni, John Kapelos, John Getz, Lawrence Pressman; **D:** Betty Thomas; **W:** Bill Carter, George Armitage; **C:** Mac Ahlberg; **M:** Ira Newborn. *HBO*

The Late Show 🎬🎬🎬 **1977 (PG)** A veteran private detective finds his world turned upside down when his ex-partner comes to visit and winds up dead, and a flaky woman whose cat is missing decides to become his sidekick. Carney and Tomlin are fun to watch in this sleeper, a tribute to the classic detective film noirs. **93m/C**

VHS, Beta, LV, Closed Caption. Art Carney, Lily Tomlin, Bill Macy, Eugene Roche, Joanna Cassidy, John Considine; **D:** Robert Benton; **W:** Robert Benton. National Society of Film Critics Awards '77: Best Actor (Carney); Nominations: Academy Awards '77: Best Original Screenplay. *WAR*

Late Spring 🎬🎬🎬🎬 **1949** An exquisite Ozu masterpiece. A young woman lives with her widowed father for years. He decides to remarry so that she can begin life for herself. Highly acclaimed, in Japanese with English subtitles. Reworked in 1960 as "Late Autumn." **107m/B VHS, Beta.** *JP* Setsuko Hara, Chishu Ryu, Jun Usami, Haruko Sugimura; **D:** Yasujiro Ozu. *NYF, FCT*

Late Summer Blues 🎬🎬 *Blues La-Cho-fesh Ha-Godol* **1987** Experience the life and death decisions of seven teenagers who have finished their finals and face now a more difficult test: serving in the Israeli Armed Forces in the Suez Canal. In Hebrew with English subtitles. **101m/C VHS.** *IS* Dor Zweigenbom, Shahar Segal, Yoav Zafir; **D:** Renen Schorr. *ERG, AUD, HMV*

Lathe of Heaven 🎬🎬½ **1980** In a late 20th century world suffocating from pollution, a young man visits a dream specialist. He then dreams of a world free from war, pestilence, and overpopulation. At times, these dreams have disastrous side effects. Based on futuristic novel by Ursula K. LeGuin; produced for PBS. **120m/C VHS, Beta.** Bruce Davison, Kevin Conway, Margaret Avery; **D:** David Loxton. *WNE*

Latin Lovers 🎬🎬½ **1953** Turner plays a wealthy heiress who can't decide if men love her for herself or her money in this festive Brazilian romp. Lund and Montalban portray the suitors vying for her affection. Although not one of MGM's best musicals, the music is good because of the Brodszky-Robin tunes. ♫Night and You; Carlotta, You Gotta Be Mine; A Little More of Your Armor; Come To My Arms; I Had To Kiss You. **104m/C VHS.** Lana Turner, Ricardo Montalban, John Lund, Louis Calhern, Jean Hagen, Eduard Franz, Beulah Bondi; **D:** Mervyn LeRoy; **W:** Isobel Lennart. *MGM*

Latino 🎬🎬½ **1985** The self-tortured adventures of a Chicano Green Beret who, while fighting a covert U.S. military action in war-torn Nicaragua, begins to rebel against the senselessness of the war. **108m/C VHS, Beta, LV, Closed Caption.** Robert Beltran, Annette Cardona, Tony Plana, James Karen, Ricardo Lopez, Luis Torrentes, Juan Carlos Ortiz, Julio Medina; **D:** Haskell Wexler; **W:** Haskell Wexler; **M:** Diane Louie. *FOX*

Lauderdale woof! **1989 (R)** Two college schmoes hit the beach looking for beer and babes. Few laughs for the sober and mature. Surf's down in this woofer. **91m/C VHS, Beta, LV.** Darrel Gilbeau, Michelle Kemp, Jeff Greenman, Lara Belmonte; **D:** Bill Milling.

Laugh with Linder! **1913** Compilation of Linder shorts, including "Max Learns to Skate" and "Max and His Dog." **70m/B VHS, Beta.** Max Linder. *GVV*

Laughfest **191?** Five classic slapstick shorts: "It's a Gift" (1923), with Snub Pollard, "Barney Oldfield's Race for a Life" (1913), "Kid Auto Races" and "Busy Day" (1914), both with Charlie Chaplin, and "Daredevil" (1923), starring Ben Turpin. **59m/B VHS, Beta.** Ben Turpin, Barney Oldfield, Mabel Normand, Charlie Chaplin, Snub Pollard. *CCB*

Laughing at Danger 🎬🎬½ **1924** Talmadge is the supposedly playboy son of a Washington politician. In reality, he's the dashing "Mr. Pep" who comes to the rescue of a scientist who has invented a death ray and is being stalked by agents of a sinister foreign power. Talmadge was a fine silent-screen action star, though his heavy German action proved a barrier with sound films. **45m/B VHS.** Richard Talmadge, Joseph Girard, Eva Novak, Joe Harrington, Stanhope Wheatcroft; **D:** James W. Horne. *GPV*

Laughing at Life ♂½ 1933 A mercenary leaves his family to fight in South America. Years later, when he is the leader of said country, he meets a man who turns out to be his son. Rehashed plot has been done better. **72m/B VHS.** Victor McLaglen, William "Stage" Boyd, Lois Wilson, Henry B. Walthall, Regis Toomey; **D:** Ford Beebe. *NOS, DVT, HEG*

The Laughing Policeman ♂♂½ *An Investigation of Murder* 1974 (R) Two antagonistic cops embark on a vengeful hunt for a mass murderer through the seamy underbelly of San Francisco. Adapted from the Swedish novel by Per Wahloo and Maj Sjowallo. **111m/C VHS, Beta, Closed Caption.** Walter Matthau, Bruce Dern, Louis Gossett Jr.; **D:** Stuart Rosenberg; **M:** Charles Fox. *FOX*

Laughing Sinners ♂♂ 1931 Society girl Crawford attempts suicide after Hamilton dumps her and is rescued by Gable—a Salvation Army worker! Predictable drama with some unintentionally funny moments. Gable and Crawford were having an off-screen romance at the time which accounts for the sparks generated on-screen. Based on the play "Torch Song" by Kenyon Nicholson. **71m/B VHS.** Joan Crawford, Neil Hamilton, Clark Gable, Marjorie Rambeau, Guy Kibbee, Cliff Edwards, Roscoe Karns; **D:** Harry Beaumont; **C:** Charles Rosher. *MGM*

Laura ♂♂♂♂ 1944 A detective assigned to the murder investigation of the late Laura Hunt finds himself falling in love with her painted portrait. Superb collaboration by excellent cast and fine director. Superior suspense yarn, enhanced by a love story. Based on the novel by Vera Caspary. Rouben Mamoulian was the original director, then Preminger finished the film. **85m/B VHS, Beta, LV.** Gene Tierney, Dana Andrews, Clifton Webb, Lane Chandler, Vincent Price, Judith Anderson, Grant Mitchell, Dorothy Adams; **D:** Otto Preminger; **C:** Joseph LaShelle; **M:** David Raksin. Academy Awards '44: Best Black and White Cinematography; Nominations: Academy Awards '44: Best Director (Preminger), Best Interior Decoration, Best Screenplay, Best Supporting Actor (Webb). *PMS, BTV*

Laurel & Hardy and the Family 1933 Four zany comedies seeing the boys in all kinds of trouble involving homelife. Includes "Brats," "Perfect Day," "Their First Mistake" and "Twice Two." **85m/B VHS.** Stan Laurel, Oliver Hardy. *VTR, FCT*

Laurel & Hardy: Another Fine Mess 1930 The boys find themselves the owners of a magnificent Beverly Hills mansion. Yeah right. Lots of physical comedy and hilarious dialogue with a "special appearance" by Laurel in drag as a maid. Based on a sketch written by Laurel's father. Colorized. **25m/C VHS.** Stan Laurel, Oliver Hardy. *CAF*

Laurel & Hardy: At Work 1932 Three short films collected here. Includes "Towed in a Hole," "Busy Bodies," and "The Music Box." **70m/B VHS.** Oliver Hardy, Stan Laurel. *VTR, FCT*

Laurel & Hardy: Be Big 1931 Stan and Ollie ditch their wives to go to a swinging stag party at their club. Of course everything goes wrong in their quest for lascivious fun. Filled with tons of sight gags. Colorized. **25m/C VHS.** Stan Laurel, Oliver Hardy. *CAF, MOV*

Laurel & Hardy: Below Zero 1930 It's the Great Depression of 1929, and Laurel and Hardy are about as depressed as you can get, working for pennies as street musicians. Their luck changes when they find a full wallet lying in the snow. But, as the saying goes, a fool and his money are soon parted. Colorized. **25m/C VHS.** Stan Laurel, Oliver Hardy. *CAF, MOV*

Laurel & Hardy: Berth Marks 1929 Laurel & Hardy take a hilarious train trip to Pottsville for a vaudeville performance. Colorized. **25m/C VHS.** Stan Laurel, Oliver Hardy. *CAF*

Laurel & Hardy: Blotto 1930 Laurel and Hardy want to get drunk, but they can't get any alcohol and their wives won't let them get away. When they finally do escape, they wind up at the swanky Rainbow Club, where they're drastically out of their element. Colorized. **25m/C VHS.** Stan Laurel, Oliver Hardy. *CAF*

Laurel & Hardy: Brats 1930 Stan and Ollie play not only themselves but also their children when their wives go away and they have to babysit. The children, of course, wreak havoc wherever they go, playing on the hilariously oversized props and sets. One of the few films in which only Laurel and Hardy appear. Colorized. **25m/C VHS.** Stan Laurel, Oliver Hardy. *CAF, MOV*

Laurel & Hardy: Chickens Come Home 1931 Ollie is running for mayor, but things go crazy when an ex-girlfriend shows up and blackmails him with a compromising photo. Stan, acting as Ollie's campaign manager, tries to help, but things just get worse. A remake of their own film "Love 'Em and Weep." Colorized. **25m/C VHS.** Stan Laurel, Oliver Hardy, James Finlayson. *CAF, MOV*

Laurel & Hardy Comedy Classics, Vol. 1 1933 A collection of four classic comedy shorts starring Laurel and Hardy: "The Music Box," which won an Academy Award for Best Short Subject, "Country Hospital," "The Live Ghost," and "Twice Two," all from 1932-33. **84m/B VHS, Beta.** Stan Laurel, Oliver Hardy, Mae Busch, May Wallace, Charlie Hall, Billy Gilbert.

Laurel & Hardy Comedy Classics, Vol. 2 1930 A collection of four Laurel and Hardy shorts from 1930 including "Blotto," "Towed in a Hole," "Brats," and "Hog Wild." **75m/B VHS, Beta.** Stan Laurel, Oliver Hardy, Billy Gilbert, Tiny Sandford, Anita Garvin.

Laurel & Hardy Comedy Classics, Vol. 3 1934 Laurel and Hardy star in four separate comedy shorts, including "Oliver the 8th," "Busy Bodies," "Their First Mistake," and "Dirty Work," all from 1933-34. **75m/B VHS, Beta.** Stan Laurel, Oliver Hardy, Billy Gilbert, Mae Busch, Tiny Sandford.

Laurel & Hardy Comedy Classics, Vol. 4 1932 Laurel and Hardy star in four of their comedy shorts from 1931-32. Included are "Another Fine Mess," "Come Clean," "Laughing Gravy," and "Any Old Part." **75m/B VHS, Beta.** Stan Laurel, Oliver Hardy, Jacqueline Wells, James Finlayson, Thelma Todd.

Laurel & Hardy Comedy Classics, Vol. 5 1931 Four classic comedy shorts starring Laurel and Hardy. Included are "Be Big," "The Perfect Day," "Night Owls," and "Help Mates," from 1929-31. **84m/B VHS, Beta.** Stan Laurel, Oliver Hardy, Edgar Kennedy, James Finlayson, Blanche Payson.

Laurel & Hardy Comedy Classics, Vol. 6 1935 Laurel and Hardy comedy shorts are presented in this package: "Our Wife," "The Fixer Uppers," "Them Thar Hills," and "Tit for Tat," from 1932-35. **75m/B VHS, Beta.** Stan Laurel, Oliver Hardy, Charlie Hall, Billy Gilbert, Ben Turpin, Mae Busch, James Finlayson.

Laurel & Hardy Comedy Classics, Vol. 7 193? Four Laurel and Hardy two-reelers are combined on this tape: "Me and My Pal" (1933), "The Midnight Patrol" (1933), "Thicker than Water" (1935), and the classic "Below Zero" (1930). **90m/B VHS, Beta.** Stan Laurel, Oliver Hardy, Mae Busch, Daphne Pollard, James Finlayson.

Laurel & Hardy Comedy Classics, Vol. 8 193? Compilation of Laurel and Hardy shorts includes: "Men O' War" (1929), "Scram" (1932), "Laurel and Hardy Murder Case" (1930) and "One Good Turn" (1931). **90m/B VHS, Beta.** Stan Laurel, Oliver Hardy, Lewis R. Foster, James W. Horne, James Parrott.

Laurel & Hardy Comedy Classics, Vol. 9 193? Includes the shorts: "Beau Hunks" (1931), "Chickens Come Home" (1931), "Going Bye-Bye" (1934), and "Berth Marks" (1929). **100m/B VHS, Beta.** Stan Laurel, Oliver Hardy.

Laurel & Hardy: Hog Wild 1930 Hilarity ensues when Laurel and Hardy try to fix the radio antenna on Hardy's roof. It may sound easy, but come on, this is Laurel and Hardy. Colorized. **25m/C VHS.** Stan Laurel, Oliver Hardy. *CAF, MOV*

Laurel & Hardy: Laughing Gravy 1931 The boys' pet dog, oddly named Laughing Gravy, gets them into trouble with their landlord who keeps trying to evict them. So funny even the mashed potatos will laugh. Colorized. **25m/C VHS.** Stan Laurel, Oliver Hardy. *CAF, MOV*

Laurel & Hardy: Men O'War 1929 Laurel & Hardy star as two sailors on shore leave trying to impress the ladies. Things go from bad to worse when they take two ladies out on a date. Features the memorable soda fountain and canoe scenes. Colorized. **25m/C VHS.** Stan Laurel, Oliver Hardy, Gloria Greer, Anne Cornwall. *CAF*

Laurel & Hardy: Night Owls 1930 When a cop needs to capture some crooks to save his job, he sets up a fake break-in and catches two bungling burglars—Laurel and Hardy. Lots of sight gags and slapstick. Colorized. **25m/C VHS.** Stan Laurel, Oliver Hardy, Edgar Kennedy. *CAF, MOV*

Laurel & Hardy On the Lam 1930 Four Laurel & Hardy classics are collected, including "Scram," "Another Fine Mess," "One Good Turn," and "Going Bye-Bye." **90m/B VHS.** Oliver Hardy, Stan Laurel. *VTR, FCT*

Laurel & Hardy: Perfect Day 1929 Laurel & Hardy plan a quiet picnic with their wives, but car trouble turns their day into a disaster. Colorized. **25m/C VHS.** Stan Laurel, Oliver Hardy, Edgar Kennedy. *CAF*

Laurel & Hardy Special ♂♂½ 19?? A unique program of Laurel and Hardy films including the first film they appeared in together-"Lucky Dog" (1918), "The Soilers," a wild Laurel spoof of The Spoilers, "Kill or Cure," "Near Dublin," "The Sleuths," "Laurel and Hardy's Trip to Britain," and "Stan Visits Ollie," a color home movie of their last visit together. **60m/B VHS, Beta.** Stan Laurel, Oliver Hardy. *GVV*

Laurel & Hardy Spooktacular 1934 Stan and Ollie scream through four spooky comedies, including "The Live Ghost," "The Laurel-Hardy Murder Case," "Oliver the Eighth" and "Dirty Work." **95m/B VHS.** *VTR, FCT*

Laurel & Hardy: Stan "Helps" Ollie 1933 Four Stan and Ollie classics including "County Hospital," "Me and My Pal," "Hog Wild" and "Helpmates." **85m/B VHS.** Stan Laurel, Oliver Hardy. *VTR, FCT*

Laurel & Hardy: The Hoose-Gow 1929 Laurel and Hardy are mistakenly picked up by the police and sent to prison to do hard labor. Hilarity ensues when they try to convince the warden that they're innocent. Colorized. **25m/C VHS.** *CAF, MOV*

Laurel Avenue ♂♂½ 1993 Looks at the life of an extended working-class black family in St. Paul, Minnesota, over a busy weekend. Large cast includes family heads Jake and Maggie who live with their basketball coach son, teenage daughter, and elderly uncle. Other children include fraternal twin Yolanda, a cop married to a white man, who knows sister Rolanda's (a recovering drug addict) son is a dealer. Their brother Marcus manages a Mafia-controlled clothing store and is involved in some shady deals while brother Woody is an aspiring musician. The four households are all united at a disasterous Sunday afternoon party. Made for cable television. **156m/C VHS, Closed Caption.** Mary Alice, Mel Winkler, Scott Lawrence, Malinda Williams, Jay Brooks, Juanita Jennings, Rhonda Stubbins White, Monte Russell, Vonte Sweet; **D:** Carl Franklin; **W:** Michael Henry Brown, Paul Aaron. *HBO*

The Lavender Hill Mob ✰✰✰½ 1951
A prim and prissy bank clerk schemes to melt the bank's gold down and re-mold it into miniature Eiffel Tower paper-weights for later resale. The foolproof plan appears to succeed, but then develops a snag. An excellent comedy that is still a delight to watch. Also available with "The Man in the White Suit" on laserdisc. 78m/B **VHS, Beta, LV.** *GB* Alec Guinness, Stanley Holloway, Sidney James, Alfie Bass, Marjorie Fielding, John Gregson; **Cameos:** Audrey Hepburn; **D:** Charles Crichton; **W:** T.E.B. Clarke. Academy Awards '52: Best Story & Screenplay; British Academy Awards '51: Best Film; Nominations: Academy Awards '52: Best Actor (Guinness). *REP, FCT, HMV*

L'Avventura ✰✰✰½ *The Adventure* 1960 A stark, dry and minimalist exercise in narrative by Antonioni, dealing with the search for a girl on an Italian island by her lethargic socialite friends who eventually forget her in favor of their own preoccupations. A highly acclaimed, innovative film; somewhat less effective now, in the wake of many film treatments of angst and amorality. Subtitled in English. Laser edition features the original trailer, commentary and a collection of still photographs from Antonioni's work. 145m/C **VHS, Beta, LV, Letterbox.** *IT* Monica Vitti, Gabriele Ferzetti, Lea Massari, Dominique Blanchar, James Addams; **D:** Michelangelo Antonioni; **W:** Tonino Guerra, Michelangelo Antonioni. Cannes Film Festival '60: Special Jury Prize. *CVC, VDM, HMV*

Law and Disorder ✰✰✰ 1974 (R) Two average Joes, fed up with the rate of rising crime, start their own auxiliary police group. Alternately funny and serious with good performances from the leads. 103m/C **VHS.** Carroll O'Connor, Ernest Borgnine, Ann Wedgeworth, Anita Dangler, Leslie Ackerman, Karen Black, Jack Kehoe; **D:** Ivan Passer; **M:** Angelo Badalamenti. *NO*

The Law and Jake Wade ✰✰½ 1958 Gripping western starring Taylor as a former bank robber turned marshal. His old partner (Widmark) turns up and forces Taylor to lead him to buried loot. 86m/C **VHS, Closed Caption.** Robert Taylor, Richard Widmark, Patricia Owens, Robert Middleton, Henry Silva, DeForest Kelley, Burt Douglas, Eddie Firestone; **D:** John Sturges. *MGM*

Law and Lawless ✰ 1933 A roving cowboy brings justice to a gang of cattle thieves in this film. 58m/B **VHS, Beta.** Jack Hoxie. *NOS, DVT*

Law and Order ✰✰ *Billy the Kid's Law and Order* 1942 Billy the Kid impersonates a Cavalry lieutenant in order to swindle his aunt out of her money. 58m/B **VHS, Beta.** Buster Crabbe, Al "Fuzzy" St. John. *VDM, MRV*

Law for Tombstone 1935 Alamo Bowie (Jones) must protect the Wells Fargo stagecoach from outlaw Twin Gun Jack. Includes chapter 1 of the serial "Gordon of Ghost City," which features Jones as retired ranch hand Buck Gordon who's on the trail of rustlers and meets a mysterious girl. 81m/B **VHS, Closed Caption.** Buck Jones, Muriel Evans, Harvey Clark, Earle Stockdale, Earle Hodgins, Madge Bellamy, Walter Miller; **D:** Ray Taylor, Buck Jones. *USH*

Law of Desire ✰✰✰½ *La Ley del Deseo* 1986 A wicked, Almodovarian attack-on-decency farce about a love-obsessed gay Madridian and his transsexual brother-sister, among others, getting hopelessly entangled in cross-gender relationships. Unlike the work of any other director; in Spanish with English subtitles. 100m/C **VHS, Beta, LV.** *SP* Carmen Maura, Eusebio Poncela, Antonio Banderas, Bibi Andersson, Miguel Molina, Manuela Valasco, Nacho Martinez; **D:** Pedro Almodovar; **W:** Pedro Almodovar. *CCN, TPV*

Law of the Jungle ✰½ 1942 A lady scientist and a fugitive team up to uncover a secret Nazi radio base in the jungle. 61m/B **VHS, Beta.** Arline Judge, John "Dusty" King, Mantan Moreland, Martin Wilkins, Arthur O'Connell; **D:** Jean Yarbrough. *SNC*

Law of the Land ✰ 1976 A made-for-television sagebrush epic with the author/artist of "Garfield" portraying an accused but innocent man searching for a murderer. 100m/C **VHS, Beta.**

Jim Davis, Don Johnson, Barbara Parkins, Charles Martin Smith. *MOV*

Law of the Lash ✰ 1947 Cowboys and rustlers battle it out. 54m/B **VHS, Beta.** Lash LaRue, Al "Fuzzy" St. John. *NOS, MRV, VCN*

Law of the Pampas ✰✰ 1939 Boyd and Hayden ride off to South America to deliver some cattle, but the bad guys intervene. This is Toler's first outing as Hoppy's sidekick, briefly replacing "Gabby" Hayes. 72m/B **VHS.** William Boyd, Russell Hayden, Steffi Duna, Sidney Toler, Sidney Blackmer, Pedro de Cordoba, Eddie Dean, Glenn Strange; **D:** Nate Watt. *NOS*

Law of the Saddle ✰½ 1945 The Lone Rider pits himself against a gang of outlaws. 60m/ B **VHS, Beta.** Bob Livingston. *VCN, MLB*

Law of the Sea ✰ 1938 A family on a sinking ship is rescued by a lecherous sea captain who makes advances on the wife and blinds the husband in a fight. Twenty years later, the husband meets him again, recognizes his laugh, and exacts revenge. 63m/B **VHS, Beta, LV.** Priscilla Dean, Sally Blane, Ralph Ince, Rex Bell, William Farnum. *VYY*

Law of the Texan ✰½ 1938 Jones goes undercover to stop Harlan and his gang from stealing a town's store of silver bullion. 54m/B **VHS.** Buck Jones, Dorothy Fay, Kenneth Harlan, Don Douglas, Matty Kemp, Robert F. (Bob) Kortman, Dave O'Brien; **D:** Elmer Clifton. *GPV*

Law of the Underworld ✰½ 1938 An innocent couple is framed for the robbery of a jewelry store which resulted in the death of a clerk. When they are arrested, their fate lies in the hands of the gangster responsible for the crime. Will he let them fry in the electric chair, or will his conscience get the better of him? 58m/B **VHS, Beta.** Chester Morris, Anne Shirley, Eduardo Ciannelli, Walter Abel, Richard Bond, Lee Patrick, Paul Guilfoyle, Frank M. Thomas Sr., Eddie Acuff, Jack Arnold; **D:** Lew (Louis Friedlander) Landers. *SNC*

Law of the Wild 1934 The search for a magnificent stallion that was hijacked by race racketeers before a big sweepstakes race is shown in this 12 chapter serial. 230m/B **VHS.** Bob Custer, Ben Turpin, Rex Lease, Lafe McKee; **D:** B. Reeves Eason, Armand Schaefer. *GPV, NOS, VCN*

The Law Rides ✰ 1936 Rush of gold claims causes an outbreak of murder and robbery. 57m/B **VHS, Beta.** Bob Steele. *DVT*

The Law Rides Again ✰ 1943 Prairie lawmen bring a cheating Indian agent to justice. 56m/B **VHS.** Ken Maynard, Hoot Gibson, Betty Miles, Jack LaRue; **D:** William Castle. *NOS, MRV, DVT*

Law West of Tombstone ✰✰½ 1938 A former outlaw moves to a dangerous frontier town in order to restore the peace. 73m/B **VHS, Beta.** Tim Holt, Harry Carey Sr., Evelyn Brent; **D:** Glenn Tryon.

The Lawless Breed ✰✰✰ 1952 Episodic saga based on the autobiography of outlaw John Wesley Hardin, published after his release from prison in 1896. Hardin's (Hudson) life of crime begins with a killing in self-defense that escalates into further bloodshed and flights from the law. Along the way Hardin marries (Adams) and has a son, whom he fears will follow in his violent footsteps. Walsh directs with plenty of brio. 83m/C **VHS, Closed Caption.** Rock Hudson, Julie Adams, John McIntire, Hugh O'Brian, Lee Van Cleef, Dennis Weaver, Glenn Strange, Michael Ansara; **D:** Raoul Walsh; **W:** Bernard Gordon; **C:** Irving Glassberg; **M:** Joseph Gershenson. *USH*

Lawless Frontier ✰½ 1935 In the early West, the Duke fights for law and order. 53m/B **VHS, Beta.** John Wayne, George "Gabby" Hayes, Sheila Terry, Earl Dwire; **D:** Robert North Bradbury. *COL, NOS, VYY*

The Lawless Land ✰✰ 1988 (R) Postholocaust America is ruled by a tyrant. Two young lovers can't take it anymore go on the lam to escape the despotic rule. 81m/C **VHS, Beta.** Leon

Berkeley, Xander Berkeley, Nick Corri, Amanda Peterson; **D:** Jon Hess; **W:** Tony Cinciripini, Larry Leahy. *MGM*

The Lawless Nineties ✰✰ 1936 Wayne plays a government agent sent to guarantee honest elections in the Wyoming territory. Hayes is exceptional as the newspaper editor who backs him up. Re-made in 1940 as "The Dark Command." 55m/B **VHS.** John Wayne, Ann Rutherford, Lane Chandler, Harry Woods, George "Gabby" Hayes, Charles "Blackie" King, Sam Flint; **D:** Joseph Kane. *REP*

Lawless Range ✰½ 1935 Wayne and the marshal's posse save the ranchers from trouble. 56m/B **VHS.** John Wayne, Sheila Mannors, Jack Curtis, Earl Dwire; **D:** Robert North Bradbury. *REP, NOS, MRV*

A Lawless Street ✰✰½ 1955 Scott portrays a sheriff who rides the Colorado Territory cleaning up lawless towns. His dedication to duty has caused his wife to leave him and she won't come back until he lays down his guns forever, which may come sooner than they think after he rides into the corrupt town of Medicine Bend. Based on the novel "Marshal of Medicine Bend" by Brad Ward. 78m/B **VHS.** Randolph Scott, Angela Lansbury, Warner Anderson, Jean Parker, Wallace Ford, John Emery, James Bell, Ruth Donnelly, Michael Pate, Don Megowan, Jeanette Nolan; **D:** Joseph H. Lewis; **W:** Kenneth Gamet; **C:** Ray Rennahan. *COL*

Lawman ✰✰✰ 1971 (PG) Brutal western about a fanatical U.S. marshall (Lancaster) who rides into town after Cobb and his six ranch hands. The cowboys have accidentally killed a man and Lancaster is determined to bring them to justice no matter what the cost. Though the entire town is against him that doesn't stop his mission. Brooding and relentless with fine performances, particularly by Ryan as the local marshall living on past glories. 95m/C **VHS.** Burt Lancaster, Robert Ryan, Lee J. Cobb, Sheree North, Joseph Wiseman, Robert Duvall, Albert Salmi, J.D. Cannon, John McGiver, Richard Jordan, John Beck, Ralph Waite, John Hillerman, Richard Bull; **D:** Michael Winner; **W:** Gerald Wilson. *MGM*

A Lawman Is Born ✰✰✰ 1937 A tough-as-nails marshal goes gunning for a pack of no-good, land-stealing varmits in this installment of the Johnny Mack Brown movie serials. Be sure to count the number of bullets each cowboy can fire from a six-shooter before being forced to reload; you may be surprised. 58m/B **VHS, Beta.** Johnny Mack Brown, Iris Meredith, Warner Richmond, Mary MacLaren, Dick Curtis, Earle Hodgins, Charles "Blackie" King, Frank LaRue; **D:** Sam Newfield. *NOS, MOV, MRV*

Lawmen ✰½ 1944 Government agents fight to enforce the law in the badlands. 55m/B **VHS, Beta.** Johnny Mack Brown, Raymond Hatton. *NOS, DVT*

The Lawnmower Man ✰✰ 1992 (R) Brosnan is a scientist who uses Fahey, a dim-witted gardener, as a guinea pig to test his experiments in "virtual reality," an artificial computer environment. With the use of drugs and high-tech equipment, Brosnan is able to increase Fahey's mental powers—but not necessarily for the better. Fantastic special effects and a memorable "virtual reality" sex scene. Available in an unrated version which contains 32 more minutes of footage. So minimally based on a short story by Stephen King that the author sued (and won) to have his name removed from the credits. **CW:** Language, violence, and sensuality. 108m/C **VHS, LV, Closed Caption.** Jeff Fahey, Pierce Brosnan, Jenny Wright, Mark Bringleson, Geoffrey Lewis, Jeremy Slate, Dean Norris, Troy Evans, John Laughlin; **D:** Brett Leonard; **W:** Brett Leonard, Gimel Everett; **C:** Russell Carpenter. *COL, FCT, MOV*

Lawnmower Man 2: Beyond Cyberspace ✰✰ *Lawnmower Man 2: Jobe's War* 1995 (PG-13) Resurrecting Jobe (the title character from number one) was easy. So was blowing off his face to explain the new actor (Frewer in for Fahey) playing him. The hard part was tring to make an original movie with a decent script and believable characters. Better luck next time. Corporate baddie Walker (Conway) enlists Jobe to (what else?) take over the world using Virtual Reality. To the rescue comes one burned-out computer expert (Bergin) and a group of VR-addicted kids living in an abandoned subway. Techno-babble abounds but nothing interesting ever happens. Mann and Frewer must've raided their old "Max Headroom" set for the dreary near-future L.A. landscape scenes. **CW:** Sci-fi action/violence and brief language. **93m/C VHS, LV, Closed Caption.** Patrick Bergin, Matt Frewer, Austin O'Brien, Kevin Conway, Ely Pouget, Camille Cooper; **D:** Farhad Mann; **W:** Farhad Mann; **C:** Ward Russell; **M:** Robert Folk. NLC

Lawrence of Arabia 🎬🎬🎬🎬 1962 (PG) Exceptional biography of T.E. Lawrence, a British military "observer" who strategically aids the Bedouins battle the Turks during WWI. Lawrence, played masterfully by O'Toole in his first major film, is a hero consumed more by a need to reject British tradition than to save the Arab population. He takes on Arab costume and a larger-than-life persona. Stunning photography of the desert in all its harsh reality. Blacklisted co-writer Wilson had his screen credit restored by the Writers Guild of America in 1995. Laser edition contains 20 minutes of restored footage and a short documentary about the making of the film. Available in letterboxed format. **221m/C VHS, Beta, LV, Letterbox, Closed Caption.** GB Peter O'Toole, Omar Sharif, Anthony Quinn, Alec Guinness, Jack Hawkins, Claude Rains, Anthony Quayle, Arthur Kennedy, Jose Ferrer; **D:** David Lean; **W:** Robert Bolt, Michael Wilson; **C:** Frederick A. (Freddie) Young; **M:** Maurice Jarre. Academy Awards '62: Best Art Direction/Set Decoration (Color), Best Color Cinematography, Best Director (Lean), Best Film Editing, Best Picture, Best Sound, Best Original Score; British Academy Awards '62: Best Actor (O'Toole), Best Film, Best Screenplay; Directors Guild of America Awards '62: Best Director (Lean); Golden Globe Awards '63: Best Director (Lean), Best Film—Drama, Best Supporting Actor (Sharif); National Board of Review Awards '62: Best Director (Lean), National Film Registry '91;; Nominations: Academy Awards '62: Best Actor (O'Toole), Best Adapted Screenplay, Best Supporting Actor (Sharif). COL, CRC, BTV

The Lawrenceville Stories 🎬🎬½ 198? Chronicles the life and times of a group of young men at the prestigious Lawrenceville prep school in 1905. Galligan plays William Hicks, alias "The Prodigious Hickey," the ringleader of their obnoxious stunts. Based on the stories of Owen Johnson, which originally ran in the Saturday Evening Post. Shown on "American Playhouse" and The Disney Channel. Tapes are available separately or as a set. **180m/C VHS.** Zach Galligan, Edward Herrmann, Nicholas Rowe, Allan Goldstein, Robert Joy, Stephen Baldwin; **D:** Robert Iscove. MON, BTV

Laws of Gravity 🎬🎬🎬 1992 (R) Critically acclaimed debut film from 29-year-old writer/director Gomez is a three day slice of life set in Brooklyn. Hotheaded Jon (Trese) and married friend Jimmy (Greene) channel violent energy into their relationships and illegal activities. Camera follows "cinema verite" style and captures urban tension as it trails them through a gun heist and subsequent arrest. **CW:** Pervasive strong language. **100m/C VHS.** Peter Greene, Edie Falco, Adam Trese, Arabella Field, Paul Schulzie; **D:** Nick Gomez; **W:** Nick Gomez; **C:** Jean De Segonzac. TRI

Lazarillo 🎬🎬 El Lazarillo de Tormes 1959 In 17th-century Castile, a fatherless boy, abandoned by his mother, finds work with a strange succession of employers, including a blind beggar, fake nobleman, and traveling band of performers. They all teach him lessons in survival as well as cunning and deception. Spanish with subtitles. **109m/B VHS.** SP Marco Paoletti, Juan Jose Menendez, Carlos Casaravilla, Margarita Lozano; **D:** Cesar Ardavin; **M:** Ruiz De Luna. Berlin International Film Festival '60: Best Film. FCT

The Lazarus Man 🎬🎬½ 1996 Pilot episode of the TV series finds the amnesiac Urich discovering he's linked to the assassination of President Lincoln. In 1865 Texas he literally claws his way out of the grave and is taken in by a

farming family. This back from the dead Lazarus may not remember who he is but a trip to town demonstrates his gunslinger skills and images from his dreams may provide clues to his past. Now, he has to stay alive long enough to figure them out. **90m/C VHS.** Robert Urich, Elizabeth Dennehy, David Marshall Grant, John Diehl, Wayne Grace, Brion James; **D:** Johnny E. Jensen; **W:** Dick Beebe; **C:** Gary Holt; **M:** John Debney. TTC

The Lazarus Syndrome 1979 Astute doctor teams up with an ex-patient of the chief of surgery in an effort to expose the chief's unethical surgical procedures. **90m/C VHS, Beta.** Louis Gossett Jr., E.G. Marshall. NO

LBJ: A Biography 1991 Produced for the PBS series "The American Experience," this four-hour revisionist look at LBJ is one of the most critically acclaimed political documentaries of our time. Divided into four segments. "Beautiful Texas" chronicles Johnson's rise to power. "My Fellow Americans" focuses on his years as an unelected president. The Great Society and and the escalation of war in Vietnam are covered in "We Shall Overcome." "The Last Believer" highlights events leading to Johnson's withdrawal from politics. **240m/C VHS.** **D:** David Grubin; **W:** David Grubin. PBS, SIG

LBJ: The Early Years 🎬🎬🎬 1988 The early years of President Lyndon Baines Johnson's political career are dramatized in this made-for-television movie. Winning performances hoist this above other biographies. **144m/C VHS, Beta.** Randy Quaid, Patti LuPone, Morgan Brittany, Pat Hingle, Kevin McCarthy, Barry Corbin, Charles Frank; **D:** Peter Werner.

Le Bal 🎬🎬🎬 1982 You won't find many films with the music of Paul McCartney and Chopin in the credits, and even fewer without dialogue. With only music and dancing the film uses a French dance hall to illustrate the changes in French society over a 50-year period. Based on a French play. ♫La Vie en Rose; In the Mood; Michelle; Top Hat White Tie and Tails; Let's Face the Music and Dance; Harlem Nocturne; Shuffle Blues; Tutti Frutti; Only You. **112m/C VHS.** IT FR D: Ettore Scola; **M:** Irving Berlin, Paul McCartney, John Lennon, Frederic Chopin, Vladimir Cosma. Cesar Awards '84: Best Director (Scola), Best Film, Best Score; Nominations: Academy Awards '83: Best Foreign Language Film. WAR, FCT

Le Beau Mariage 🎬🎬🎬 A Good Marriage; The Well-Made Marriage 1982 (R) An award-winning comedy from the great French director about a zealous woman trying to find a husband and the unsuspecting man she chooses to marry. In French with English subtitles. **97m/C VHS, Beta.** FR Beatrice Romand, Arielle Dombasle, Andre Dussollier; **D:** Eric Rohmer; **W:** Eric Rohmer. Venice Film Festival '82: Best Actress (Romand). NO

Le Beau Serge 🎬🎬🎬 Handsome Serge 1958 Young theology student Francois returns to his home village and discovers his friend Serge, in despair of ever changing his life, has become a hopeless drunk. So Francois meddles in his life (with the best of intentions) and only causes Serge further disaster. Chabrol's first film, and a major forerunner of the nouvelle vague. In French with English subtitles. **97m/B VHS.** FR Gerard Blain, Jean-Claude Brialy, Michele Meritz, Bernadette LaFont; **D:** Claude Chabrol; **W:** Claude Chabrol. HTV, FCT

Le Bonheur 🎬🎬½ Happiness 1965 A seemingly happily married carpenter (Drouot) takes a vacation with his wife and children where he meets the local postal clerk and the two begin a passionate affair. Unwilling to leave his family, Drouot believes the two women can share him but when his wife discovers his infidelity she kills herself. His grief does not cause Drouot to stop the affair, instead he moves in with his mistress. An uninvolving, unbelievable tale with a lovely Mozart score. In French with English subtitles. **87m/C VHS.** FR Jean-Claude Drouot, Claire Drouot, Marie-France Boyer; **D:** Agnes Varda; **W:** Agnes Varda. HMV, FCT

Le Bonheur Est Dans le Pre 🎬🎬 Happiness Is In the Fields; Happiness 1995 Francis (Serrault) is the harried owner of a toilet brush-making business that is about to undergo a tax audit and is threatened by a workers strike. His wife and daughter are never happy and Francis' one relief is to have lunch with his macho, easy-going friend, Gerard (Mitchell). One day, he watches a TV show about missing persons and sees that a woman is looking for her husband who disappeared 28 years before—a man who looks suspiciously like Francis. The plot's convoluted and the comedy's flat. French with subtitles. **105m/C VHS.** FR Michel Serrault, Sabine Azema, Eddy Mitchell, Carmen Maura, Alexandra London; **D:** Etienne Chatiliez; **W:** Florence Quentin; **C:** Philippe Welt; **M:** Pascal Andreacchio. Cesar Awards '95: Best Supporting Actor (Mitchell); Nominations: Cesar Awards '95: Best Actress (Azema), Best Director (Chatiliez), Best Film, Best Supporting Actress (Maura), Best Writing. NYR

Le Boucher 🎬🎬🎬 The Butcher 1969 In a provincial French town a sophisticated schoolmistress is courted by the shy local butcher—who turns out to be a sex murderer. A well-played thriller that looks at sexual frustration. French with subtitles. **94m/C VHS, LV.** FR Stephane Audran, Jean Yanne, Antonio Passallia; **D:** Claude Chabrol; **W:** Claude Chabrol. CVC

Le Cas du Dr. Laurent 🎬🎬🎬 1957 A country doctor in a small French town tries to introduce methods of natural childbirth to the native women, but meets opposition from the superstitious villagers. Fine performance by Gabin. **88m/B VHS, Beta.** FR Jean Gabin, Nicole Courcel; **D:** Jean-Paul LeChanois. NOS, VYY, DVT

Le Cavaleur 🎬🎬 Practice Makes Perfect 1978 A light hearted comedy about a philandering concert pianist. **90m/C VHS, Beta.** FR Jean Rochefort, Lila Kedrova, Nicole Garcia, Annie Girardot, Danielle Darrieux; **D:** Philippe de Broca; **M:** Georges Delerue. NO

Le Chat 🎬🎬🎬½ The Cat 1975 A middle-aged couple's marriage dissolves into a hate-filled battle of wits, centering around the husband's love for their cat. In French with English subtitles. **88m/C VHS, Beta, LV.** FR Jean Gabin, Simone Signoret, Annie Cordy, Jacques Rispal; **D:** Pierre Granier-Deferre. Berlin International Film Festival '71: Best Actor (Gabin). FCT, LUM

Le Complot 🎬🎬🎬 The Conspiracy 1973 When de Gaulle announces his intention to abandon Algeria, several army officers, feeling that their service has been in vain, stage a coup. There's suspense aplenty as the Gaulists, the leftists, and the police spy and are spied upon. In French with English subtitles. **120m/C VHS, LV, Letterbox.** FR Michel Bouquet, Jean Rochefort; **D:** Rene Gainville. CVC, FCT

Le Corbeau 🎬🎬🎬 The Raven 1943 A great, notorious drama about a small French village whose everyday serenity is ruptured by a series of poison pen letters that lead to suicide and despair. The film was made within Nazi-occupied France, sponsored by the Nazis, and has been subjected to much misdirected malice because of it. In French with English subtitles. **92m/B VHS, Beta.** FR Pierre Fresnay, Noel Roquevort, Ginette LeClerc, Pierre Larquey, Antoine Belpetre; **D:** Henri-Georges Clouzot. NOS, HHT, GVV

Le Crabe Tambour 🎬🎬🎬 1977 Rochefort plays a dying naval captain remembering his relationship with his first officer. Revealed via flashbacks, the recollections concern the adventures which transpired on a North Atlantic supply ship. Great performances from all and award-winning cinematography by Raoul Coutard. Winner of several French Cesars. A French script booklet is available. **120m/C VHS, LV, Letterbox.** FR Jean Rochefort, Claude Rich, Jacques Dufilho, Jacques Perrin, Odile Versois, Aurore Clement; **D:** Pierre Schoendoerffer; **C:** Raoul Coutard. Cesar Awards '78: Best Actor (Rochefort), Best Cinematography, Best Supporting Actor (Dufilho). INT, IME

Le Dernier Combat 🎬🎬🎬 *The Last Battle* 1984 (R) A stark film about life after a devastating nuclear war marks the directorial debut of Besson. The characters fight to survive in a now speechless world by staking territorial claims and forming new relationships with other survivors. An original and expressive film made without dialogue. 93m/B VHS, Beta. *FR* Pierre Jolivet, Fritz Wepper, Jean Reno, Jean Bouise, Christiane Kruger; *W:* Luc Besson. COL, OM

Le Doulos 🎬🎬🎬 1961 Compelling story of an ex-convict and his buddy, a man who may be a police informant. Chronicles the efforts of the snitch (the "doulos" of the title) to bring the criminal element before the law. Melville blends in several plot twists and breathes a new-French life into the cliche-ridden genre. 108m/B VHS, Beta. *FR* Serge Reggiani, Jean-Paul Belmondo, Michel Piccoli; *D:* Jean-Pierre Melville. INT, TPV

Le Gendarme de Saint-Tropez 🎬🎬½ 1967 Officer Ludovic Cruchot's plans for career advancement are on shaky ground after he is transferred to St. Tropez where his daughter has a little too much fun at the beach. Also available dubbed. ?m/C VHS. *FR* Louis de Funes, Michel Galabru, Genevieve Grad, Jean LeFevre, Christian Marin. BAR

Le Gentleman D'Epsom 🎬🎬 1962 A French comedy about a breezy con man who scams everyone around him in order to keep up his upwardly mobile appearance and to put his bets down at the racetrack. Subtitled in English. 83m/B VHS, Beta. *FR* Jean Gabin, Paul Frankeur. BAR

Le Grand Chemin 🎬🎬🎬 *The Grand Highway* 1987 A sweet, slice-of-life French film about a young boy's idyllic summer on a family friend's farm while his mother is having a baby. Hubert's son plays the boy Louis in this retelling of the director's own childhood. In French with English subtitles. Remade with an American setting in 1991 as "Paradise." 107m/C VHS, Beta, LV. *FR* Anemone, Richard Bohringer, Antoine Hubert, Vanessa Guedj, Christine Pascal, Raoul Billerey, Pascale Roberts; *D:* Jean-Loup Hubert; *W:* Jean-Loup Hubert; *M:* Georges Granier. Cesar Awards '88: Best Actor (Bohringer), Best Actress (Anemone). FCT, IME, PBS

Le Joli Mai 1962 A famous documentary that established Marker, depicting the everyday life of Paris denizens on the occasion of the end of the Algerian War, May 1962, when France was at peace for the first time since 1939. In French with English subtitles. 180m/B VHS, Beta. *FR D:* Chris Marker. FCT

Le Jour Se Leve 🎬🎬🎬½ *Daybreak* 1939 The dark, expressionist film about a sordid and destined murder/love triangle that starts with a police stand-off and evolves into a series of flashbacks. The film that put Carne and Gabin on the cinematic map. Highly acclaimed. French with English subtitles. Remade in 1947 as "The Long Night." 89m/B VHS. *FR* Jean Gabin, Jules Berry, Arletty, Jacqueline Laurent; *D:* Marcel Carne. HMV, GVV, HHT

Le Jupon Rouge 🎬🎬 *Manuela's Loves* 1987 Bacha (Valli) is a human rights activist and concentration camp survivor who is involved with younger fashion designer Manuela (Barrault). But when Manuela becomes drawn to the even younger Claude (Grobon), Bracha's overwhelmed with jealousy and Manuela is torn by her feelings for both women. French with subtitles. 90m/C VHS. *FR* Alida Valli, Marie-Christine Barrault, Guillemette Grobon; *D:* Genevieve Lefebvre. FCT

Le Magnifique 🎬🎬 *The Magnificent One* 1976 Belmondo is a master spy and novelist who mixes fantasy with reality when he chases women and solves cases. 84m/C VHS. *FR* Jean-Paul Belmondo, Jacqueline Bisset; *W:* Francis Veber; *M:* Claude Bolling.

Le Mans 🎬🎬🎬 1971 (G) The famous 24-hour sports car race sets the stage for this tale of love and speed. McQueen (who did his own driving) is the leading race driver, a man who battles competition, fear of death by accident, and emo-

tional involvement. Excellent documentary-style race footage almost makes up for weak plot and minimal acting. 106m/C VHS, LV, Letterbox, Closed Caption. Steve McQueen, Elga Andersen, Ronald Leigh-Hunt, Luc Merenda; *D:* Lee H. Katzin; *C:* Robert B. Hauser. FOX, FCT

Le Million 🎬🎬🎬½ 1931 A comedy/musical masterpiece of the early sound era which centers on an artist's adventures in searching for a winning lottery ticket throughout Paris. Highly acclaimed member of the Clair school of subtle French farce. In French with English subtitles. 89m/B VHS, Beta. *FR* Annabella, Rene Lefevre, Paul Olivier, Louis Allibert; *D:* Rene Clair. VYY, NOS, DVT

Le Petit Amour 🎬🎬 *Kung Fu Master* 1987 (R) A popular French comedy about the fateful romance between a 40-year-old divorced woman and a 15-year-old boy obsessed with a kung fu video game. In French with English subtitles. 80m/C VHS, Beta. *FR* Jane Birkin, Mathieu Demy, Charlotte Gainsbourg, Lou Doillon; *D:* Agnes Varda.

Le Plaisir 🎬🎬½ *House of Pleasure* 1952 An anthology of three Guy de Maupassant stories, "Le Masque," "Le Modele," and "La Maison Teillier," about the search for pleasure. In French with English subtitles. 97m/B VHS, Beta. *FR* Claude Dauphin, Simone Simon, Jean Gabin, Danielle Darrieux; *D:* Max Ophuls. Nominations: Academy Awards '54: Best Art Direction/Set Decoration (B & W). NOS, DVT, GVV

Le Polygraphe 🎬🎬 *The Lie Detector* 1996 Francois (Goyette) is still a suspect in the murder of his girlfriend, Marie-Claire, two years after her death. The murder has so affected her friend Judith (Descenes) that she's written a screenplay about the unsolved crime (blaming the crime on a rogue cop). Meanwhile, actress Lucie (Brassard), who auditions for the role of Marie-Claire, gets involved with mystery man Christof (Stormare). English and French with subtitles. 97m/C VHS. CA Patrick Goyette, Jose Descenes, Marie Brassard, Peter Stormare, Maria De Medeiros; *D:* Robert Lepage; *W:* Marie Brassard, Robert Lepage; *C:* Georges Dufaux. Nominations: Genie Awards '96: Best Actress (Brassard), Best Adapted Screenplay, Best Cinematography, Best Director (Lepage), Best Film, Best Sound, Best Supporting Actress (Descenes, De Medeiros). NYR

Le Repos du Guerrier 🎬🎬 *Warrior's Rest* 1962 Star vehicle for Bardot in which she plays a respectable woman who abandons societal norms to pursue an unbalanced lover. In French with English subtitles. 100m/C VHS, Beta. *FR* Brigitte Bardot, Robert Hossein, James Robertson Justice, Jean-Mark Bory; *D:* Roger Vadim. BAR

Le Samourai 🎬🎬🎬½ *The Samurai* 1967 Cold, precise professional killer Jef Costello (Delon) lives by his version of the code of the Japanese samurai. Hired to kill a nightclub owner, he establishes an alibi with the help of his lover Jane (Nathalie Delon, Alain's then-wife) and, unexpectedly, by Valerie (Rosier), the club's black pianoplayer. Jef finds Valerie's aid suspicious and begins to dig deeper, finding himself betrayed by his employers, and the subject of a police chase throughout Paris. The icy Delon was perfect for the anti-hero role and Melville's stylized filming heightens the tension and inevitable tragedy. A film much-admired, and copied, by contemporary filmmakers. French with subtitles. 95m/C VHS. *FR* Alain Delon, Francois Perier, Cathy Rosier, Nathalie Delon, Jacques Leroy, Jean-Pierre Posier; *D:* Jean-Pierre Melville; *W:* Jean-Pierre Melville; *C:* Henri Decae; *M:* Francois de Roubaix. NYF

Le Schpountz 🎬🎬 *Heartbeat* 1938 Satire on filmmaking and film-loving fans finds a small town grocer (Fernandel) in southern France becoming the victim of a practical joke when a visiting film crew promises to make him a star (signing him to a phony contract) if he'll come to Paris. Naturally, the joke's on them when the naive grocer arrives in the City of Light and becomes a successful movie comic. French with subtitles. 135m/B VHS. *FR* Fernandel, Charpin, Orane Demazis, Odette Roger,

Jean Castan, Leon Bellieres, *D:* Marcel Pagnol; *W:* Marcel Pagnol; *C:* Willy; *M:* Casimir Oberfeld. INT

Le Secret 🎬🎬🎬 1974 This classic French thriller with a shocking ending finds an escaped convict seeking shelter with a reclusive couple in the mountains. His tales of abuse and torture create tension for the pair as one believes the woeful story and the other doesn't. Dubbed in English. 103m/C VHS, Beta. *FR* Jean-Louis Trintignant, Philippe Noiret, Jean-Francois Adam; *D:* Robert Enrico; *M:* Ennio Morricone. NO

Le Sex Shop 🎬🎬🎬 1973 (R) A man turns his little book store into a porn equipment palace, to make ends meet. When his relationship with his wife gets boring, they begin to use their erotic merchandise and adopt a swinging lifestyle. 92m/C VHS, Beta. *FR* Claude Berri, Juliet Berto, Daniel Auteuil, Nathalie Delon; *D:* Claude Berri; *M:* Serge Gainsbourg. COL

Le Sexe des Etoiles 🎬🎬 *The Sex of the Stars* 1993 Curiously uninvolving film about 12-year-old Camille who discovers that the father who abandoned her is now a transsexual. Pierre walked out years before and Camille has always dreamed of his return but though they reach a tentative relationship, it's not what Camille hoped for. Title refers to Camille's obsession with astronomy because stars have no sex. Based on the novel by Proulx (who also wrote the screenplay). In French with English subtitles. 100m/C VHS. CA Marianne-Coquelicot Mercier, Denis Mercier, Tobie Pelletier, Sylvie Drapeau; *D:* Paule Baillargeon; *W:* Monique Proulx. Genie Awards '93: Best Sound. ICA

Lea 🎬🎬 1996 Lea (Vlasakova) becomes mute after witnessing her abusive father kill her mother but writes the dead woman poems and letters to express her emotions. However, Lea becomes even more withdrawn from the world when she's given in an arranged marriage to the much-older Herbert (Redl). Herbert marries Lea because she resembles his dead wife but Lea finds he has disturbing similarities to her father. German with subtitles. 100m/C VHS. GE Lenka Vlasakov, Christian Redl, Hanna Schygulla; *D:* Ivan Fila; *W:* Ivan Fila. Nominations: Golden Globe Awards '98: Best Foreign Language Film. NYR

Leader of the Band 🎬🎬 1987 (PG) An out-of-work musician tries to train the world's worst high school band. Landesberg helps this attempted comedy along. 90m/C VHS, Beta, LV. Steve Landesburg, Gailard Sartain, Mercedes Ruehl, James Martinez, Calvert Deforest; *D:* Nessa Hyams; *M:* Dick Hyman. ART

The Leading Man 🎬🎬½ 1996 (R) Bon Jovi's charming in the title role as American movie star Robin Grange. Grange has come to London to work in the prestige stage production by playwright Felix Webb (Wilson) and he's also become aware of Webb's complex romantic situation. Although married to Elena (Galiena), Felix is having an affair with young leading lady, Hilary Rule (Newton). So the studly Robin proposes that he seduce Elena, thus leaving Felix free to carry on with his own affair. Except Felix gets jealous when Robin succeeds and decides he wants the actor out of the way. *CW:* Some language and sexuality. 99m/C VHS. GB Lambert Wilson, Jon Bon Jovi, Anna Galiena, Thandie Newton, David Warner, Barry Humphries, Patricia Hodge; *D:* John Duigan; *W:* John Duigan; *C:* Jean-Francois Robin; *M:* Ed Shearmur. BMG

The League of Gentlemen 🎬🎬🎬½ 1960 An ex-Army officer plots a daring bank robbery using specially skilled military personnel and irreproachable panache. Hilarious British humor fills the screen. 115m/B VHS, Beta. GB Jack Hawkins, Nigel Patrick, Richard Attenborough, Roger Livesey, Bryan Forbes; *D:* Basil Dearden. HMV, FCT

A League of Their Own 🎬🎬🎬 1992 (PG) Charming look at sports history and the Rockford Peaches, one of the teams in the real-life All American Girls Professional Baseball League, formed in the 40s when the men were off at war. Main focus is on sibling rivalry between Davis, the beautiful, crackerjack catcher, and Petty, the younger, insecure pitcher. Boozy coach Hanks is wonderful as he reluctantly leads the team; he also gets credit for the classic "There's no crying in baseball" scene. Great cast of supporting characters, including sarcastic talent scout Lovitz, opinionated, sleazy taxi dancer Madonna, loud-mouthed O'Donnell, and shy, homely Cavanagh. Lots of baseball for the sports fan. **127m/C VHS, Beta, LV, Letterbox, Closed Caption, DVD.** Tom Hanks, Geena Davis, Madonna, Lori Petty, Jon Lovitz, David Strathairn, Garry Marshall, Bill Pullman, Rosie O'Donnell, Megan Cavanagh, Tracy Reiner, Bitty Schram, Ann Cusack, Anne Elizabeth Ramsay, Freddie Simpson, Renee Coleman; *D:* Penny Marshall; *W:* Lowell Ganz, Babaloo Mandel; *M:* Hans Zimmer. COL

Lean on Me 🎬🎬🎬 1989 (PG-13) The romanticized version of the career of Joe Clark, a tough New Jersey teacher who became the principal of the state's toughest, worst school and, through controversial hard-line tactics, turned it around. **109m/C VHS, Beta, LV, 8mm, Closed Caption.** Morgan Freeman, Robert Guillaume, Beverly Todd, Alan North, Lynne Thigpen, Robin Bartlett, Michael Beach, Ethan Phillips, Regina Taylor; *D:* John G. Avildsen; *W:* Michael Schiffer; *M:* Bill Conti. WAR, FCT

Leap of Faith 🎬🎬½ 1992 (PG-13) Jonas Nightengale (Martin) is a traveling evangelist/scam artist whose tour bus is stranded in an impoverished farm town. Nevertheless he sets up his show and goes to work, aided by the technology utilized by accomplice Winger. Both Martin and Winger begin to have a change of heart after experiencing love—Winger with local sheriff Neeson and Martin after befriending a waitress (Davidovich) and her crippled brother (Haas). Martin is in his element as the slick revivalist with the hidden heart but the film is soft-headed as well as softhearted.*CW:* Some language. **110m/C VHS, Beta, LV, Letterbox, Closed Caption.** Steve Martin, Debra Winger, Lolita Davidovich, Liam Neeson, Lukas Haas, Meat Loaf, Philip S. Hoffman, M.C. Gainey, La Chanze, Delores Hall, John Toles-Bey, Albertina Walker, Ricky Dillard; *D:* Richard Pearce; *W:* Janus Cercone; *M:* Cliff Eidelman. PAR, BTV

Leap Year 🎬🎬½ 1921 Made at the apex of the 300-pound comedian's career, "Leap Year" wasn't released in the States until the '60s. Tried for manslaughter in 1921 (with two hung juries), Fatty was forced off camera and his films were taken out of circulation (although he did return to cinema behind the camera using the pseudonym William Goodrich). **60m/B VHS, Beta.** Fatty Arbuckle. GPV, FCT

Leapin' Leprechauns 🎬🎬½ 1995 (PG) John Dennehy's dad Michael has arrived from Ireland for a visit, accompanied by some "wee folk" who are invisible to all non-believers. Seems the little leprechauns are just in time to rescue their ancestral home from a plot by John to turn their Irish land into a theme park and make believers out of a family of skeptics. **84m/C VHS, Beta, Closed Caption.** Grant Cramer, John Bluthal, Sharon Lee Jones, Gregory Edward Smith, Sylvester McCoy, James Ellis, Godfrey James, Tina Martin, Erica Nicole Hess; *D:* Ted Nicolaou; *W:* Ted Nicolaou, Michael McGann. PAR

The Learning Tree 🎬🎬 1969 (PG) A beautifully photographed adaptation of Parks' biographical novel about a 14-year-old black boy in the 1920s South, living on the verge of manhood, maturity, love, and wisdom. **107m/C VHS, Beta.** Kyle Johnson, Alex Clarke, Estelle Evans, Dana Elcar; *D:* Gordon Parks; *C:* Burnett Guffey. National Film Registry '89. WAR, FCT, AFR

Leather Boys 🎬🎬 1963 A teenaged girl marries a mechanic and then begins to look beyond the boundaries of marriage. Considered very controversial in the '60s, but less so now. **103m/C VHS, Beta.** GB Rita Tushingham, Dudley Sutton, Gladys Henson, Colin Campbell, Avice Landon, Lockwood West, Betty Marsden, Johnny Briggs, Geoffrey Dunn, Dandy Nichols; *D:* Sidney J. Furie. NO

Leather Burners 🎬🎬 1943 Hoppy goes under cover to get the goods on a suspected rustler. When his cover is blown, the bad guys frame him for murder. Look for Robert Mitchum in his third bit part in this series. **66m/B VHS.** William Boyd, Andy Clyde, Jay Kirby, Victor Jory, George Givot, Bobby Larson, George Reeves, Hal Taliaferro, Forbes Murray, Robert Mitchum; *D:* Joseph Henabery. NOS, MRV

Leather Jackets 🎬🎬 1990 (R) Sweeney plays a nice guy who lets involvement with a childhood pal destroy his life. Elwes is the friend, now gang member, in trouble with both the cops and members of a rival gang, who needs Sweeney's help to escape. Fonda plays Sweeney's girlfriend caught between the two men. Essentially a routine fugitive pic with an attractive cast.*CW:* Language, violence, and sensuality. **90m/C VHS, LV, Closed Caption.** D.B. Sweeney, Bridget Fonda, Cary Elwes, Christopher Penn, Marshall Bell, James LeGros, Jon Polito, Craig Ng, Ginger Lynn Allen; *D:* Lee Drysdale; *W:* Lee Drysdale. COL

Leatherface: The Texas Chainsaw Massacre 3 🎬 1989 (R) The human-skin-wearing cannibal is at it again in this, the second sequel to the Tobe Hooper proto-mess. This one sports a bit more humor and is worth seeing for that reason. **81m/C VHS, Beta, LV.** Kate Hodge, William Butler, Ken Foree, Tom Hudson, R.A. Mihailoff; *D:* Jeff Burr; *W:* David J. Schow; *C:* James L. Carter. COL

The Leatherneck 🎬🎬 1928 Love unrequited in a faraway place starring soon to be cowboy (Hopalong Cassidy) matinee idol Boyd and Hale, the real life dad of Gilligan Island's skipper. **65m/B VHS, Beta.** William Boyd, Alan Hale, Diane Ellis. Nominations: Academy Awards '29: Best Writing. GPV, FCT

Leave 'Em Laughing 🎬🎬 1981 Rooney plays Chicago clown Jack Thum in this based-on-real-life TV movie. Thum takes in orphans even though he cannot find steady work, and then discovers he has cancer. **103m/C VHS, Beta, Closed Caption.** Mickey Rooney, Anne Jackson, Allen (Goorwitz) Garfield, Elisha Cook Jr., William Windom, Red Buttons, Michael Le Clair; *D:* Jackie Cooper.

Leave Her to Heaven 🎬🎬🎬 1945 Beautiful neurotic Tierney takes drastic measures to keep hubby all to herself and will do anything to get what she wants. Tierney, in a departure from her usual roles, is excellent as this pathologically possessive creature. Oscar-winner Leon Shamroy's photography (in Technicolor) is breathtaking. Based on the novel by Ben Ames Williams. **110m/C VHS.** Gene Tierney, Cornel Wilde, Jeanne Crain, Vincent Price, Mary Philips, Ray Collins, Darryl Hickman, Gene Lockhart; *D:* John M. Stahl; *W:* Jo Swerling; *C:* Leon Shamroy; *M:* Alfred Newman. Academy Awards '45: Best Color Cinematography; Nominations: Academy Awards '45: Best Actress (Tierney), Best Sound. FXV

Leave It to Beaver 🎬🎬 1997 (PG) Gee, Mrs. Cleaver, that's an awful nice updating of an old TV favorite you have there. Cut the crap, Eddie. The "let's plop a lovable sitcom family into the dysfunctional 90s" bit has had its run. This time the victims are the Cleavers: wise dad Ward (McDonald), perfect mom June (Turner), popular older brother Wally (von Detten)...and newcomer Cameron Finley as the Beaver. Unlike the Bradys, the modern world has made some impact here. Beav has an African American friend while Mom wears jeans and owns a business. Gosh Wally, do you really think America was anxiously awaiting the return of the impossible-to-live-up-to clan? Don't be such a little dope. **88m/C VHS, LV, Closed Caption, DVD.** Christopher McDonald, Janine Turner, Erik von Detten, Cameron Finley, Barbara Billingsley, Ken Osmond, Adam Zolotin, Alan Rachins; *D:* Andy Cadiff; *W:* Brian Levant; *C:* Thomas Del Ruth; *M:* Randy Edelman. UPI

Leave It to the Marines 🎬½ 1951 A jerky guy wanders into a recruiting office instead of a marriage license bureau and unwittingly signs on for military service. **66m/B VHS, Beta, LV.** Sid Melton, Mara Lynn. NO

Leaves from Satan's Book 🎬🎬½ 1919 Impressionistic episodes of Satan's fiddling with man through the ages, from Christ to the Russian Revolution. An early cinematic film by Dreyer, with ample indications of his later brilliance. Silent. **165m/B VHS, Beta.** DK Helge Milsen, Halvart Hoft, Jacob Texiere; *D:* Carl Theodor Dreyer. GPV, FCT, GVV

Leaving Las Vegas 🎬🎬🎬½ 1995 (R) Ben Sanderson (Cage) is a hopeless alcoholic who goes to Vegas to drink himself to death and meets Sera (Shue), a lonely hooker who loves him enough not to stop him. Definitely as depressing as it sounds, but still manages to have both a subtle sense of humor and compassion. Cage tops his best work and Shue proves she deserves better than the lightweight roles she's had in the past. Not for everyone, but worth the effort for people who like to see honest emotion and hate Hollywood's insistence on happy endings. Based on the semi-autobiographical novel by John O'Brien, who committed suicide shortly before pre-production began.*CW:* Strong sexuality and language, violence, pervasive alcohol abuse. **120m/C VHS, LV, Closed Caption, DVD.** Nicolas Cage, Elisabeth Shue, Julian Sands, Laurie Metcalf, David Brisbin, Richard Lewis, Valeria Golino, Steven Weber, Mariska Hargitay, Julian Lennon, Carey Lowell, Lucinda Jenney, Ed Lauter, R. Lee Ermey; *D:* Mike Figgis; *W:* Mike Figgis; *C:* Declan Quinn; *M:* Mike Figgis. Academy Awards '95: Best Actor (Cage); Golden Globe Awards '96: Best Actor—Drama (Cage); Independent Spirit Awards '96: Best Actress (Shue), Best Cinematography, Best Director (Figgis), Best Film; Los Angeles Film Critics Association Awards '95: Best Actor (Cage), Best Actress (Shue), Best Director (Figgis), Best Film; National Board of Review Awards '95: Best Actor (Cage); New York Film Critics Awards '95: Best Actor (Cage), Best Film; National Society of Film Critics Awards '95: Best Actor (Cage), Best Actress (Shue), Best Director (Figgis); Screen Actors Guild Award '95: Best Actor (Cage); Nominations: Academy Awards '95: Best Actress (Shue), Best Adapted Screenplay, Best Director (Figgis); British Academy Awards '95: Best Actor (Cage), Best Actress (Shue), Best Adapted Screenplay; Directors Guild of America Awards '95: Best Director (Figgis); Golden Globe Awards '96: Best Actress—Drama (Shue), Best Director (Figgis), Best Film—Drama; Independent Spirit Awards '96: Best Actor (Cage), Best Screenplay; Screen Actors Guild Award '95: Best Actress (Shue); Writers Guild of America '95: Best Adapted Screenplay. MGM

Leaving Normal 🎬½ 1992 (R) Darly, a fed-up waitress, and Marianne, an abused housewife, meet at a bus stop in Normal, Wyoming and decide to blow town. They travel across the American West, through Canada, and up to Alaska, where Lahti's ex-boyfriend has left her a house. Because both women have made bad choices all their lives, they decide to leave their futures to chance, and end up finding their nirvana. Plot is similar to "Thelma & Louise," but "Leaving Normal" doesn't come close to the innovativeness of the former. Sappy and sentimental to the point of annoyance at times.*CW:* Language. **110m/C VHS, LV, Closed Caption.** Christine Lahti, Meg Tilly, Lenny Von Dohlen, Maury Chaykin, James Gammon, Patrika Darbo, Eve Gordon, James Eckhouse, Brett Cullen, Rutanya Alda; *D:* Edward Zwick; *W:* Edward Solomon; *C:* Ralf Bode. USH

L'Ecole Buisoniere 🎬🎬½ 1951 In a provincial French school a teacher with modern ideas inspires his students with a passion for learning until the suspicious parents are aroused. In French with English subtitles. **108m/C VHS.** FR *D:* Jean-Paul LeChanois. FCT, WBF

The Leech Woman 🎬🎬 1959 While in Africa, an older woman (Gray) discovers how to restore her youth through a tribal ritual. The only problem is it requires the pineal gland of males, which causes her to go on a killing spree to keep that youthful look. Based on a story by Ben Pivar and Francis Rosenwald. **77m/B VHS, Closed Caption.** Coleen Gray, Grant Williams, Gloria Talbot, Phillip Terry; *D:* Edward Dein; *W:* David Duncan. USH

Left for Dead 🎬½ 1978 A millionaire is accused of brutally killing his wife, and discovers in his search for an alibi that he is the victim of a conspiracy. 82m/C VHS, Beta. Elke Sommer, Donald Pilon; *D:* Murray Markowitz. *ART, VES*

The Left Hand of God 🎬🎬🎬 1955 After an American pilot escapes from a Chinese warlord in post-WWII, he disguises himself as a Catholic priest and takes refuge in a missionary hospital. Bogie is great as the flyboy/cleric. 87m/C VHS, Beta. Humphrey Bogart, E.G. Marshall, Lee J. Cobb, Agnes Moorehead, Gene Tierney; *D:* Edward Dmytryk. *FOX*

The Left-Handed Gun 🎬🎬🎬 1958 An offbeat version of the exploits of Billy the Kid, which portrays him as a 19th-century Wild West juvenile delinquent. Newman's role, which he method-acted, was originally intended for James Dean. Based on a 1955 Philco teleplay by Gore Vidal. 102m/B VHS, Beta. Paul Newman, Lita Milan, John Dehner; *D:* Arthur Penn. *WAR, TLF*

The Legacy 🎬½ *The Legacy of Maggie Walsh* 1979 (R) An American couple become privy to the dark secrets of an English family gathering in a creepy mansion to inherit an eccentric millionaire's fortune. Death and demons abound. 100m/C VHS, Beta. *GB* Katharine Ross, Sam Elliott, John Standing, Roger Daltrey, Ian Hogg; *D:* Richard Marquand. *USH*

A Legacy for Leonette woof! 1985 A girl is led into a web of murder and love in this torrid romance novel brought to video. 90m/C Beta. Loyita Chapel, Michael Anderson Jr., Dinah Anne Rogers.

Legacy of Horror woof! 1978 (R) A weekend at the family's island mansion with two unfriendly siblings sounds bad enough, but when terror, death, and a few family skeletons pop out of the closets, things go from bad to weird. All-round poor effort with substantial gore. A remake of the director's own "The Ghastly Ones." 83m/C VHS, Beta. Elaine Boies, Chris Broderick, Marilee Troncone, Jeannie Cusik; *D:* Andy Milligan. *MPI*

Legacy of Lies 🎬🎬½ 1992 (R) Zack Resnick is a serious, honest Chicago cop assigned to a murder investigation. He first discovers the killers got the wrong man and then finds out a lot of family secrets he wishes he didn't know. His cop-father is on the take to the Mob, which is really no surprise since Zack's grandfather turns out to be a retired gangland boss, all of which leaves Zack wondering where his loyalties lie. Too intricate plot hampers the story's flow but the cast performances are well worth watching. Made for cable television. *CW:* Gangster violence. 96m/C VHS, LV, Closed Caption. Michael Ontkean, Martin Landau, Eli Wallach, Joe Morton, Patricia Clarkson, Gerry Becker, Chelcie Ross, Ron Dean; *D:* Jason Meshover-Iorg; *W:* David Black. *USH*

Legacy of Rage 🎬🎬 1986 Brandon (Lee), a waiter, befriends young mobster Michael (Wong), who turns out to be in love with Brandon's fiancee, May (Kent). In fact, Michael frames Brandon on a murder charge and gets him thrown in prison in order to get the girl. And what's Brandon's first thought when he gets out of the slammer? Revenge. Lee's first feature film. Chinese with subtitles or dubbed. 86m/C VHS, LV, Letterbox. *HK* Brandon Lee, Michael Wong, Bolo Yeung, Regina Kent; *D:* Ronny Yu. *TAI*

Legal Deceit 🎬🎬½ *The Promised Land* 1995 (R) Ambitious new lawyer Sydney Banks (Rochone) is taken under the wing of corporate hotshot Todd Hunter (Morgan). Then she learns his success is based on blackmail and murder, so she and boyfriend Derek (Morris) work to save her life as well as her career. 93m/C VHS. Lela Rochon, Jeffrey Dean Morgan, Phil Morris, John Stockwell, Cheryl Francis Harrington, Jeff Marcus; *D:* Monika Harris; *W:* Monika Harris; *C:* Stan McClain; *M:* Michael Giacchino. *SPC*

Legal Eagles 🎬🎬½ 1986 (PG) An assistant D.A. faces murder, mayhem, and romance while prosecuting a girl accused of stealing a portrait painted by her father. Redford sparkles in this otherwise convoluted tale from Reitman, while Hannah lacks depth as the daffy thief. 116m/C VHS, Beta, LV, Closed Caption. Robert Redford, Debra Winger, Daryl Hannah, Brian Dennehy, Terence Stamp, Steven Hill, David Clennon, Roscoe Lee Browne, John McMartin, Jennie Dundas, Ivan Reitman; *D:* Ivan Reitman; *W:* Jim Cash, Jack Epps Jr.; *M:* Elmer Bernstein. *USH*

Legal Tender 🎬🎬½ 1990 (R) Rude talk-show host Downey as a corrupt S & L chief? Big, menacing Davi as a romantic hero? Give this often-inept thriller credit for creative casting, if little else. Roberts adds steamy sex appeal as a lovely saloon-keeper imperiled by deadly bank fraud. *CW:* Language, graphic violence and drug use, and graphic sensuality. 93m/C VHS, Beta. Robert Davi, Tanya Roberts, Morton Downey Jr.; *D:* Jag Mundhra.

Legend 🎬🎬 1986 (PG) A colorful, unabashedly Tolkien-esque fantasy about the struggle to save an innocent waif from the Prince of Darkness. Set in a land packed with unicorns, magic swamps, bumbling dwarves and rainbows. Produced in Great Britain. 89m/C VHS, Beta, LV, Closed Caption. *GB* Tom Cruise, Mia Sara, Tim Curry, David Bennett, Billy Barty, Alice Playten; *D:* Ridley Scott; *M:* Jerry Goldsmith. Nominations: Academy Awards '86: Best Makeup. *USH*

Legend of Alfred Packer 🎬½ 1980 The true story of how a guide taking five men searching for gold in Colorado managed to be the sole survivor of a blizzard. 87m/C VHS, Beta. Patrick Dray, Ron Haines, Bob Damon, Dave Ellingson; *D:* Jim Roberson. *NO*

Legend of Big Foot 🎬 1982 Facing a spree of killings, a local town mobilizes to stop the legendary beast. 92m/C VHS, Beta. Stafford Morgan, Katherine Hopkins. *NO*

Legend of Billie Jean 🎬🎬 1985 (PG-13) Billie Jean believed in justice for all. When the law and its bureaucracy landed hard on her, she took her cause to the masses and inspired a generation. 92m/C VHS, Beta, Closed Caption. Helen Slater, Peter Coyote, Keith Gordon, Christian Slater, Richard Bradford, Yeardley Smith, Dean Stockwell; *D:* Matthew Robbins; *W:* Mark Rosenthal. *FOX*

The Legend of Black Thunder Mountain 🎬½ 1979 (G) A children's adventure in the mold of "Grizzly Adams" and "The Wilderness Family." 90m/C VHS, Beta. Holly Beeman, Steve Beeman, Ron Brown, F.A. Milovich; *D:* Tom Beeman. *NO*

The Legend of Blood Castle 🎬 *The Female Butcher; Blood Ceremony; Ceremonia Sangrienta* 1972 (R) Another version of the Countess of Bathory legend, in which an evil woman bathes in the blood of virgins in an attempt to keep the wrinkles away. Released hot on the heels of Hammer's "Countess Dracula." 87m/C VHS, Beta. *IT SP* Lucia Bose, Ewa Aulin; *D:* Jorge Grau. *NO*

Legend of Boggy Creek 🎬½ 1975 (G) A dramatized version of various Arkansas Bigfoot sightings. 87m/C VHS, Beta. Willie E. Smith, John P. Nixon, John W. Gates, Jeff Crabtree, Buddy Crabtree; *D:* Charles B. Pierce; *W:* Earl E. Smith; *C:* Charles B. Pierce. *ART, MRV*

Legend of Earl Durand 🎬½ 1974 In Wyoming 1939, a man spends his life searching for freedom and justice. His Robin Hood actions cause a manhunt of massive proportions. 90m/C VHS. Martin Sheen, Peter Haskell, Keenan Wynn, Slim Pickens, Anthony Caruso; *D:* John D. Patterson. *NO*

The Legend of Frank Woods 🎬🎬 1977 Gunslinger returns to the land of the free after an extended holiday south of the border. Mistaken for an expected preacher in a small town, he poses as the padre and signs on the dotted line to take out a new lease on life. 88m/C VHS. Troy Donahue, Brad Steward, Kitty Vallacher, Michael Christian; *D:* Deno Paoli. *SIM*

Legend of Frenchie King 🎬½ *Petroleum Girls* 1971 When prospectors discover oil on disputed land, two families feud over their conflicting claims to the property. Adult western still working out the kinks has Bardot heading a band of female outlaws. 96m/C VHS, Beta. Brigitte Bardot, Claudia Cardinale, Michael J. Pollard, Micheline Presle; *D:* Christian-Jaque. *NO*

The Legend of Gator Face 🎬½ 1996 (PG) Hermit Winfield fills three youngsters in on their small community's legend of Gator Face—half-man, half-alligator. Kids being kids, they decide to wade through the swamps in search of the creature, which they find and also realize is harmless. Too bad the local folk don't believe the same thing and call out the national guard to destroy it. 100m/C VHS. Paul Winfield, John White, Dan Warry-Smith, C. David Johnson, Gordon Michael Woolvett; *D:* Vic Sarin. *HMK*

The Legend of Hell House 🎬🎬🎬 1973 (PG) A multi-millionaire hires a team of scientists and mediums to investigate his newly acquired haunted mansion. It seems that the creepy house has been the site of a number of deaths and may hold clues to the afterlife. A suspenseful, scary screamfest. Matheson wrote the screenplay from his novel "Hell House." 94m/C VHS, Beta, LV, Closed Caption. Roddy McDowall, Pamela Franklin, Clive Revill, Gayle Hunnicutt, Peter Bowles, Roland Culver, Michael Gough; *D:* John Hough; *W:* Richard Matheson; *C:* Alan Hume; *M:* Brian Hodgson, Delia Derbyshire. *FOX*

The Legend of Hillbilly John 🎬 *Who Fears the Devil; My Name is John* 1973 (G) Hillbilly John holds off the devil with a strum of his six-string. While demons plague the residents of rural America, the hayseed messiah wanders about saving the day. 86m/C VHS, Beta, LV. Severn Darden, Denver Pyle, Susan Strasberg, Hedge Capers; *D:* John Newland.

The Legend of Jedediah Carver 🎬🎬 197? A rancher battles desert elements and hostile Indians in a desperate bid for survival. 90m/C VHS. DeWitt Lee, Joshua Hoffman, Val Chapman, Richard Montgomery, David Terril; *D:* DeWitt Lee. *XVC*

Legend of Lobo 🎬½ 1962 The story of Lobo, a crafty wolf who seeks to free his mate from the clutches of greedy hunters. A Disney wildlife adventure. 67m/C VHS, Beta. *DIS*

The Legend of Sea Wolf 🎬🎬 *Wolf Larsen* 1975 (PG) A sadistic sea captain forcefully rules his crew in this weak version of Jack London's novel. 90m/C VHS, Beta. Chuck Connors, Barbara Bach, Joseph Palmer. *NO*

The Legend of Sleepy Hollow 1949 The story of Ichabod Crane and the legendary ride of the headless horseman by Washington Irving; narrated by Crosby. Also includes two classic short cartoons, "Lonesome Ghosts" (1932) with Mickey Mouse and "Trick or Treat" (1952) with Donald Duck. 45m/C VHS, Beta. *D:* Jack Kinney, Clyde Geronimi, James Nelson Algar. *DIS*

The Legend of Sleepy Hollow 🎬🎬½ 1979 (G) Washington Irving's classic tale of the Headless Horseman of Sleepy Hollow is brought to life on the screen. Made for television. 100m/C VHS, Beta, LV. Jeff Goldblum, Dick Butkus, Paul Sand, Meg Foster, James Griffith, John S. White. *NO*

The Legend of Sleepy Hollow 1986 Classic Washington Irving tale is given the Shelly Duvall treatment in her "Tall Tales and Legends" series. When a snooty teacher goes too far, the town blacksmith decides to play the ultimate Halloween trick on him. Made for cable television. 51m/C VHS, Closed Caption. Ed Begley Jr., Beverly D'Angelo, Charles Durning, Tim Thomerson. *FOX*

The Legend of Suram Fortress 🎬🎬 *Legenda Suramskoi Kreposti* 1985 Based on a Georgian folktale about a medieval fortress that collapses as soon as it is built. The village soothsayer tells a young man he must sacrifice himself, by bricking himself up alive within the fortress walls, if the building is every to stand. In Russian with English subtitles. 89m/C VHS. *RU*

Levan Outchanechvili, Zourab Kipchidze; **D:** Sergei Paradjanov. *KIV*

Legend of the Lone Ranger 🎬½
1981 (PG) The fabled Lone Ranger (whose voice is dubbed throughout the entire movie) and the story of his first meeting with his Indian companion, Tonto, are brought to life in this weak and vapid version of the famous legend. The narration by Merle Haggard leaves something to be desired as do most of the performances. 98m/C VHS, Beta. Klinton Spilsbury, Michael Horse, Jason Robards Jr., Richard Farnsworth, Christopher Lloyd, Matt Clark; **D:** William A. Fraker; **W:** William Roberts, Ivan Goff, Michael Kane; **M:** John Barry. Golden Raspberry Awards '81: Worst Actor (Spilsbury), Worst New Star (Spilsbury). *FOX*

Legend of the Lost 🎬🎬 1957
Two men vie for desert treasure and desert women. Interesting only because of Wayne, but certainly not one of his more memorable films. 109m/C VHS. John Wayne, Sophia Loren, Rossano Brazzi, Kurt Kasznar, Sonia Moser; **D:** Henry Hathaway; **C:** Jack Cardiff. *MGM*

Legend of the Lost Tomb 🎬🎬½
1997 (PG) Made for cable adventure finds Egyptologist Dr. Leonhardt (Rossovich) discovering half of an ancient papyrus that could lead to the riches of the desert tomb of pharaoh Ramses II. But Leonhardt is ambushed by his rival Dr. Bent (Keach), who demands the rest of the document, which just happens to be in the hands of Leonhardt's son (Pierce) and his archaeologist associate Karen (Peterson). 90m/C VHS. Rick Rossovich, Stacy Keach, Kimberlee Peterson, Brock Pierce; **D:** Jonathan Winfrey. *HMK*

Legend of the Northwest 🎬🎬 1978
(G) The loyalty of a dog is evidenced in the fierce revenge he has for the drunken hunter who shot and killed his master. 83m/C VHS, Beta. Denver Pyle. *VTR, GEM, HHE*

The Legend of the Sea Wolf 🎬🎬½
Wolf Larsen; Larsen, Wolf of the Seven Seas **1958** Adaptation of Jack London's dramatic adventure novel, "The Sea Wolf." A slave driving ship captain rescues a shipwreck victim and sets to abusing him along with the rest of his crew. A rebellion ensues. Superb musical score benefits the strong acting and good pace. 83m/B VHS. Barry Sullivan, Peter Graves, Gita Hall, Thayer David; **D:** Harmon Jones; **W:** Jack DeWitt. *NO*

Legend of the Werewolf 🎬🎬 1975 (R)
A child who once ran with the wolves has forgotten his past, except when the moon is full. 90m/C VHS, Beta. *GB* Peter Cushing, Hugh Griffith, Ron Moody, David Rintoul, Lynn Dalby, Stefan Gryff, Renee Houston, Norman Mitchell, Marjorie Yates, Roy Castle; **D:** Freddie Francis; **W:** Anthony John Elder Hinds. *MRV*

The Legend of the Wolf Woman 🎬🎬½ 1977 (R)
The beautiful Daniella assumes the personality of the legendary wolf-woman, leaving a trail of gruesome killings across the countryside. Genre fans will find this one surprisingly entertaining. Also on video as "Werewolf Woman." 84m/C VHS, Beta. *IT* Anne Borel, Fred Stafford, Tino Carey, Elliot Zamuto, Ollie Reynolds, Andrea Scotti, Karen Carter; **D:** Raphael D. Silver. *VIP*

Legend of Tom Dooley 🎬🎬 1959
Somber western about three Confederate soldiers who rob a Union stagecoach and kill two soldiers, not knowing that the Civil War has ended. Landon turns in a good performance as the Rebel soldier turned outlaw. Based on the hit song by the Kingston trio. 79m/B VHS. Michael Landon, Jo Morrow, Jack Hogan, Richard Rust, Dee Pollock, Ken Lynch; **D:** Ted Post; **M:** Ronald Stein. *COL*

Legend of Valentino 1975
Made-for-television docudrama traces the legendary exploits of one of the silver screen's greatest lovers, Rudolph Valentino. Typical TV-movie fare that lacks the power of the legend's life. 96m/C VHS, Beta. Franco Nero, Suzanne Pleshette, Lesley Ann Warren, Yvette Mimieux, Judd Hirsch, Milton Berle, Harold J. Stone; **D:** Melville Shavelson. *MRV, NLC*

The Legend of Valentino 1983
A biographical documentary of perhaps the world's greatest lover, beginning with his immigration to America and ending at his unexpected, sudden death. 71m/B VHS, Beta.

Legend of Walks Far Woman 🎬
1982 A made for television film about a proud Sioux woman fighting for survival and her tribe during the American-Indian Wars. Welch is miscast. From Colin Stuart's novel. 120m/C VHS, Beta. Raquel Welch, Nick Mancuso, Bradford Dillman; **D:** Mel Damski. *NO*

The Legend of Wolf Mountain 🎬🎬½ 1992 (PG)
Three children are held hostage by two prison escapees in the Utah mountains. They are aided in their escape by a Native American "wolf spirit." With the criminals on their trail will the three be able to survive in the wilderness until a search party can find them? 91m/C VHS, LV, Closed Caption. Mickey Rooney, Bo Hopkins, Don Shanks, Vivian Schilling, Robert Z'Dar, David Shark, Nicole Lund, Natalie Lund, Matthew Lewis, Jonathan Best; **D:** Craig Clyde; **W:** Craig Clyde.

Legends of the Fall 🎬🎬 1994 (R)
Sweeping, meandering, melodramatic family saga set in Montana (though filmed in Alberta, Canada). Patriarch William Ludlow (Hopkins), a retired Army colonel, is raising three sons: reserved Alfred (Quinn), idealistic Samuel (Thomas), and wild middle son Tristan (Pitt). In 1913, Samuel returns from Boston with a fiancee, the lovely and refined Susannah (Ormond). Only problem is Alfred and Tristan take one look and also desire her—a passion that will carry them through some 20 years of heartbreak. Film loses the spare toughness of the Jim Harrison novella but is a visual feast (and not just because the camera seems to drool every time Pitt appears on screen.)*CW:* Gory violence; nudity; sexual situations. 134m/C VHS, LV, 8mm, Closed Caption, DVD. Brad Pitt, Aidan Quinn, Julia Ormond, Anthony Hopkins, Henry Thomas, Gordon Tootoosis, Tantoo Cardinal, Karina Lombard, Paul Desmond, Kenneth Welsh; **D:** Edward Zwick; **W:** Susan Shilliday, William D. Wittliff; **C:** John Toll; **M:** James Horner. Academy Awards '94: Best Cinematography; Nominations: Academy Awards '94: Best Art Direction/Set Decoration, Best Sound; Golden Globe Awards '95: Best Actor—Drama (Pitt), Best Director (Zwick), Best Film—Drama, Best Score. *COL*

Legends of the North 🎬🎬½ 1995 (PG)
Crusty prospector Whip Gorman (Quaid) and partner Paul Bel Air are searching for a mythical lake of gold when Paul takes a fall off a mountain. Whip sends for Paul's son Charles so that he can translate his father's diary (it's in French) and get the clues to the gold's whereabouts. Naturally, some rival prospectors, some Indians, and even a feisty gal or two help or hinder our treasure seekers. Based on a story by Jack London. 95m/C VHS. Randy Quaid. *THV*

Legion 🎬🎬 1998 (R)
Major Agatha Doyle (Farrell) is given a group of convicts to lead on a mission to destroy The Legion, a genetically engineered killing machine. But first she has to keep them from killing each other—or her.*CW:* Language, sexual situations, violence. 97m/C VHS. Terry Farrell, Corey Feldman, Rick Springfield, Parker Stevenson, Audie England; **D:** Jon Hess. *YHV*

Legion of Iron 🎬🎬 1990 (R)
Adventures in a computer-run, neo-Roman civilization where men and women battle for supremacy. 85m/C VHS, Beta, LV. Kevin T. Walsh, Erica Nann, Regie De Morton, Camille Carrigan; **D:** Yakov Bentsvi. *COL*

Legion of Missing Men 🎬½ 1937
Professional soldiers of fortune, the French Foreign Legion, fight the evil sheik Ahmed in the Sahara. 62m/B VHS, Beta. Ralph Forbes, Ben Alexander, Hala Linda, Roy D'Arcy, Paul Hurst, Jimmy Aubrey; **D:** Hamilton MacFadden. *VYY, GPV*

Legion of the Lawless 🎬½ 1940
Group of outlaws band together in order to spread terror and confusion among the populace. 59m/B VHS, Beta. George O'Brien, Virginia Vale.

Legs 🎬🎬 1983
Backstage story of three girls who are competing for a job with Radio City Music Hall's Rockettes. Made for television. 91m/C VHS, Beta. Gwen Verdon, John Heard, Sheree North, Shanna Reed, Maureen Teefy; **D:** Jerrold Freedman; **C:** Allen Daviau.

L'Eleve 🎬🎬 *The Pupil* 1995
In 1897 Europe, an aristocratic family hires inexperienced 25-year-old Julien (Cassel) to tutor their precocious teenaged son, Morgan (Salmon). After a tentative battle for control, the two establish a strong emotional rapport and Julien learns that the family is not only in financial difficulty but is part of an empty, amoral social class only concerned with appearance. Based on a story by Henry James; French with subtitles. 92m/C VHS. *FR* Vincent Cassel, Caspar Solmon, Caroline Cellier, Jean-Pierre Marielle, Sabine Destailleur, Sandrine Le Berre; **D:** Olivier Schatzky; **W:** Eve Deboise, Olivier Schatzky; **C:** Carlo Varini; **M:** Romano Musumarra. Montreal World Film Festival '95: Best Director (Schatzky). *NYR*

The Lemon Drop Kid 🎬🎬½ 1951
Second version of the Damon Runyon chestnut about a racetrack bookie who must recover the gangster's money he lost on a bet. As the fast-talking bookie, Hope sparkles. ♫Silver Bells; It Doesn't Cost a Dime to Dream; They Obviously Want Me to Sing. 91m/B VHS, Beta, LV. Bob Hope, Lloyd Nolan, Fred Clark, Marilyn Maxwell, Jane Darwell, Andrea King, William Frawley, Jay C. Flippen, Harry Bellaver; **D:** Sidney Lanfield; **W:** Frank Tashlin, Edmund Hartmann, Robert O'Brien; **C:** Daniel F. Fapp. *COL*

The Lemon Sisters 🎬🎬 1990 (PG-13)
Three women, friends and performance partners since childhood, struggle to buy their own club. They juggle the men in their lives with less success. Great actresses like these should have done more with this interesting premise, and the excellent male cast has much more potential. 93m/C VHS, LV, Closed Caption. Diane Keaton, Carol Kane, Kathryn Grody, Elliott Gould, Ruben Blades, Aidan Quinn; **D:** Joyce Chopra. *HBO, FCT*

Lemora, Lady Dracula 🎬 *The Lady Dracula; The Legendary Curse of Lemora; Lemora: A Child's Tale of the Supernatural* **1973 (PG)** A pretty young church singer is drawn into the lair of the evil Lady Dracula, whose desires include her body as well as her blood. Horror fans will enjoy some excellent atmosphere, particularly in a scene where the girl's church bus is attacked by zombie-like creatures; Smith remains a '70s "B" movie favorite. Perhaps a double feature with "Lady Frankenstein"...? 80m/C VHS. Leslie Gilb, Cheryl "Rainbeaux" Smith, William Whitton, Steve Johnson, Hy Pyke, Maxine Ballantyne, Parker West, Richard Blackburn; **D:** Richard Blackburn; **W:** Robert Fern, Richard Blackburn; **C:** Robert Caramico. *FRG*

Lena's Holiday 🎬🎬 1990 (PG-13)
Fluffy comedy about a winsome East German girl visiting L.A. for the first time, and the culture-shock that ensues. Sharp script and performances. 97m/C VHS, Beta, LV. Felicity Waterman, Chris Lemmon, Noriyuki "Pat" Morita, Susan Anton, Michael Sarrazin, Nick Mancuso, Bill Dana, Liz Torres; **D:** Michael Keusch.

L'Enfant d'Eau 🎬🎬 *Water Child; Behind the Blue* 1995 Mentally handicapped 20-something Emile (La Haye) and precocious 12-year-old Cedrine (Monette) must learn to work together to survive after a plane crash strands them on an island in the Bahamas. Familiar story offers no surprises and the script shies away from any sexual implications, negating two excellent performances. French with subtitles. 103m/C VHS. *CA* David La Haye, Marie-France Monette; **D:** Robert Menard; **W:** Claire Wojas. Genie Awards '95: Best Actor (La Haye). *NYR*

L'Enfer 🎞🎞🎞 *Jealousy; Torment* 1993 Claustrophobic thriller chronicles the descent into madness of an unstable hotel owner (Cluzet) convinced that his beautiful wife (Beart) is having an affair. Intriguing plot points that blur appearances and reality lead to ambiguous and unsatisfying ending. Clouzot himself began filming his screenplay in 1964, but a heart attack forced him to abandon the project. In French with English subtitles. 103m/C VHS. *FR* Emmanuelle Beart, Francois Cluzet, Nathalie Cardone, Andre Wilms, Marc Lavoine; *D:* Claude Chabrol; *W:* Claude Chabrol, Henri-Georges Clouzot, Jose-Andre Lacour. *FXL*

Leningrad Cowboys Go America 🎞🎞½ 1989 (PG-13) An outlandish Finnish band, the Leningrad Cowboys, pack up their beautiful accordians and their one dead member and go on tour in America. With matching front-swept pompadours and pointy shoes, the group's appearance is the picture's best joke—and one of its only jokes, as the road trip plods in deadpan fashion that may bore viewers. It's best appreciated by fans of comic minimalist Jim Jarmusch (who has a guest role). In Finnish with English subtitles. 78m/C VHS, LV, Letterbox. *FI* Jim Jarmusch, Matti Pellonpaa, Kari Vaananen, Nicky Tesco; *D:* Aki Kaurismaki; *W:* Aki Kaurismaki. *ORI, FCT*

Lenny 🎞🎞🎞 1974 (R) Smoky nightclubs, drug abuse, and obscenities abound in Hoffman's portrayal of the controversial comedian Lenny Bruce, whose use of street language led to his eventual blacklisting. Perrine is a gem as his stripper wife. Adapted from the Julian Barry play, this is a visually compelling piece that sharply divided critics upon release. 111m/B VHS, Beta, LV, Closed Caption. Dustin Hoffman, Valerie Perrine, Jan Miner, Stanley Beck; *D:* Bob Fosse; *W:* Julian Barry; *C:* Bruce Surtees; *M:* Ralph Burns. Cannes Film Festival '75: Best Actress (Perrine); National Board of Review Awards '74: Best Supporting Actress (Perrine); New York Film Critics Awards '74: Best Supporting Actress (Perrine); Nominations: Academy Awards '74: Best Actor (Hoffman), Best Actress (Perrine), Best Adapted Screenplay, Best Cinematography, Best Director (Fosse), Best Picture. *MGM, FOX*

Lensman 1984 In the 25th century space pirates known as the Boskande are threatening the civilized universe. Young Kimall Kenison is chosen by a higher power to become a lensman—and live or die for freedom. Based on the E.E. "Doc" Smith novels, this production is a combination of animation and computer graphics. Dubbed in English. 107m/C VHS, LV. *JP STP, FUS*

Leo Tolstoy's Anna Karenina 🎞🎞½ *Leo Tolstoy's Anna Karenina* 1996 (PG-13) Well, the third film version of Tolstoy's tempestuous, tragic romance certainly looks good, even if the performances don't engender the passion the story demands. Beautiful married Anna (Marceau) leaves stuffy husband Karenin (Fox) and their son to travel to 1880 Moscow and mend the marriage of her philandering brother Stiva (Huston). But she meets dashing soldier, Count Alexei Vronsky (Bean), who immediately decides to pursue the beauty and the two begin an all-encompassing affair that leads to tragedy. This version also includes the secondary, contrasting romance between young Kitty (Kirshner) and Tolstoy's alter ego, questioning aristo Levin (Molina). Filmed on location in St. Petersburg, Russia. The classical score includes selections from Tschaikovsky, Rachmaninoff and Prokofiev, under the direction of Georg Solti. *CW:* Mature thematic elements and some sensuality/nudity. 120m/C VHS. Sophie Marceau, Sean Bean, Alfred Molina, Mia Kirshner, James Fox, Danny Huston, Fiona Shaw, Phyllida Law, David Schofield, Saskia Wickham; *D:* Bernard Rose; *W:* Bernard Rose; *C:* Daryn Okada. *WAR*

Leolo 🎞🎞🎞 1992 Deeply disturbing black comedy about one of the screen's most dysfunctional families. Leo is a 12-year-old French Canadian from Montreal who is determined to remake himself. He's decided to be a Sicilian lad named Leolo, escaping from his horrific family into his fantasies (and potential madness). "I dream, therefore I am not," he thinks. His parents are obsessed with toilet training, his cowardly brother with body-building, his sisters are demented, and his grandfather is a sadistic, dirty old man. Striking cinematography and great soundtrack, but not for the faint of heart (or stomach). In French with English subtitles. 107m/C VHS, LV. *CA* Maxime Collin, Julien Guiomar, Ginette Reno, Pierre Bourgault, Yves Montmarquette, Roland Blouin, Giuditta del Vecchio; *D:* Jean-Claude Lauzon; *W:* Jean-Claude Lauzon. Genie Awards '92: Best Costume Design, Best Film Editing, Best Original Screenplay. *NLC, ING*

Leon Morin, Priest 🎞🎞½ 1961 A young priest and a widow, who happens to be a Communist, fall in love during the WWII German occupation of France. Based on the novel by Beatrix Beck. In French with English subtitles. 118m/B VHS. *IT FR* Jean-Paul Belmondo, Emmanuelle Riva; *D:* Jean-Pierre Melville. *INT, FCT*

Leon the Pig Farmer 🎞🎞½ 1993 Dry comedic satire about identity. Leon Geller has never quite fitted into his parents' comfortable Jewish society and no wonder—Leon accidentally discovers he is the product of artificial insemination. And what's more, the lab made a mistake and Leon isn't a true Geller after all. His father is actually a genial (and Gentile) Yorkshire pig farmer named Brian Chadwick, who cheerfully welcomes Leon as his long-lost son. All four parents try to cope while Leon moves bewilderedly amongst them. Film tends to be too timid in its satire but still has its witty moments. 98m/C VHS. *GB* Mark Frankel, Janet Suzman, Brian Glover, Connie Booth, David DeKeyser, Maryam D'Abo, Gina Bellman; *D:* Vadim Jean, Gary Sinyor; *W:* Gary Sinyor, Michael Normand. *ORI, FXL*

Leonard Part 6 🎞 1987 (PG) A former secret agent comes out of retirement to save the world from a crime queen using animals to kill agents. In the meantime, he tries to patch up his collapsing personal life. Wooden and disappointing; produced and co-written by Cosby, who himself panned the film. 83m/C VHS, Beta, LV, Closed Caption. Bill Cosby, Gloria Foster, Tom Courtenay, Joe Don Baker; *D:* Paul Weiland; *W:* Bill Cosby, Jonathan Reynolds; *C:* Jan De Bont; *M:* Elmer Bernstein. Golden Raspberry Awards '87: Worst Picture, Worst Actor (Cosby), Worst Screenplay. *COL*

Leonor 🎞 1975 Idiotic medieval drivel with Ullmann rising from the dead after husband Piccoli seals her in a tomb. Directed by the son of Luis Bunuel. 90m/C VHS, Beta. *FR SP IT* Liv Ullmann, Michel Piccoli, Ornella Muti; *D:* Juan Bunuel; *M:* Ennio Morricone. *FOX*

Leopard Fist Ninja 🎞 198? A masked ninja whacks away at American hoodlums in a fit of Maoist, anti-capitalistic fury. Dubbed. 88m/C VHS, Beta. Willie Freeman, Jack Lam, Chuck Horry. *NO*

Leopard in the Snow 🎞🎞 1978 (PG) The romance between a race car driver allegedly killed in a crash and a young woman is the premise of this film. 89m/C VHS, Beta. Keir Dullea, Susan Penhaligon, Kenneth More, Billie Whitelaw; *D:* Gerry O'Hara.

The Leopard Man 🎞🎞½ 1943 An escaped leopard terrorizes a small town in New Mexico. After a search, the big cat is found dead, but the killings continue. Minor but effective Jacques Tourneur creepie. Based on Cornell Woolrich's novel "Black Alibi." Another Val Lewton Horror production. 66m/B VHS, Beta, LV. Jean Brooks, Isabel Jewell, James Bell, Margaret Landry, Dennis O'Keefe, Margo, Rita (Paula) Corday, Abner Biberman; *D:* Jacques Tourneur; *W:* Ardel Wray; *C:* Robert De Grasse.

The Leopard Son 1996 (G) Beautiful documentary follows the birth and first two years of life for a leopard cub born on Africa's Serengeti plain. Mom leopard shows him how to survive and then he's out into the harsh world on his own. Parents should be forewarned that the hunt-and-kill scenes may upset the little ones. 87m/C VHS. *D:* Hugo Van Lawick; *W:* Michael Olmert; *C:* Hugo Van Lawick, Matthew Aeberhard; *M:* Stewart Copeland. *HMK*

The Leopard Woman 🎞🎞 1920 Long before the cat lady cut her first claws, there was the leopard woman. Vamp Glaum finds much trouble to meow about on the Equator. 66m/B VHS, Beta. Louise Glaum. *GPV, FCT, GVV*

Leper 🎞🎞 *Tredowata* 1976 A melodrama of forbidden love between a wealthy nobleman and a beautiful high school teacher. The townspeople try to destroy the love between the two because of their different social classes. In Polish with English subtitles. 100m/C VHS. *PL* Elzbieta Starostecka, Leszek Teleszynski; *D:* Jerzy Hoffman. *FCT*

Lepke 🎞🎞½ 1975 (R) The life and fast times of Louis "Lepke" Buchalter from his days in reform school to his days as head of Murder, Inc. and his execution in 1944. 110m/C VHS, Beta. Tony Curtis, Milton Berle, Gianni Russo, Vic Tayback, Michael Callan; *D:* Menahem Golan. *WAR*

Leprechaun woof! 1993 (R) A sadistic 600-year-old leprechaun winds up wreaking havoc in North Dakota. If this makes no particular sense, neither does the film which is basic horror story excess. A man goes to Ireland for his mother's funeral, steals the gold belonging to the leprechaun, locks the creature up, and winds up accidentally taking the evil imp back to the States with him. When the leprechaun gets free, he wants a bloodthirsty revenge—and shoes. One of the so-called humorous bits is the leprechaun's shoe fetish. Irish eyes will not be smiling watching this mess. *CW:* Language and horror violence. 92m/C VHS, LV. Warwick Davis, Jennifer Aniston, Ken Olandt, Mark Holton, John Sanderford, Robert Gorman, Shay Duffin, John Voldstad; *D:* Mark Jones; *W:* Mark Jones; *C:* Levie Isaacks. *THV*

Leprechaun 2 🎞🎞 1994 (R) Sequel to the horror flick about a malevolent Irish gnome. It seems one of his fairy entitlements is that he can possess any woman he wants if she sneezes three times. Thwarted in his attempt to snare a comely lass one thousand years earlier, he returns to present-day California to exact revenge on her descendant Durkin. Contrary to the popular legend that leprechauns are benign kind-hearted sprites, this nasty combines the treachery of a Gestapo officer with the firepower of Rambo in his attempt to harass the unimpressed Durkin into his clutches. 85m/C VHS, LV, Closed Caption. Warwick Davis, Sandy Baron, Adam Biesk, James Lancaster, Clint Howard, Kimmy Robertson, Charlie Heath, Shevonne Durkin; *D:* Rodman Flender; *W:* Turi Meyer, Al Septien; *M:* Jonathan Elias. *THV*

Leprechaun 3 🎞 1995 (R) A student steals the nasty little beastie's gold and he's off to Las Vegas to get it back and to kill the gamblers, also after his magic money, in decidedly disgusting ways. *CW:* Some strong horror violence and gore; a scene of sexuality. 93m/C VHS, LV, Closed Caption. Warwick Davis, John Gatins, Michael Callan, Caroline Williams, Lee Armstrong; *D:* Brian Trenchard-Smith; *W:* Brian Dubos. *THV*

Leprechaun 4: In Space woof! 1996 (R) Who knows how the little imp got there but now our old friend the Leprechaun (Davis) is busy terrorizing an alien princess (Carlton) on a distant planet. He wants to marry the babe and rule the universe but its the Marines to the rescue! Yes, an Earth platoon arrives to foil his plans. *CW:* Language, horror violence and some sexuality. 98m/C VHS. Warwick Davis, Rebekah Carlton, Brent Jasmer, Debbe Dunning, Rebecca Cross, Tim Colceri; *D:* Brian Trenchard-Smith; *W:* Dennis Pratt. *THV*

Les Assassins de L'Ordre 🎞🎞 *Law Breakers* 1971 A righteous French judge faces the case of an innocent man killed by police brutality. Subtitled in English. 100m/C VHS, Beta. *FR* Jacques Brel, Catherine Rouvel, Michael Lonsdale, Charles Denner; *D:* Marcel Carne; *M:* Michel Colombier. *NO*

Les Aventuriers 🐾🐾½ *The Last Adventure* **1977** Two friends find themselves swindled in an insurance scam and set out after the perpetrator who sent them off to Africa in search of a treasure. Available dubbed. **?m/C VHS.** *FR* Alain Delon, Lino Ventura, Joanna Shimkus. *FRA, FCT*

Les Biches 🐾🐾🐾½ *The Heterosexuals* **1968** (R) An exquisite film that became a landmark in film history with its theme of bisexuality and upper class decadence. A rich socialite picks up a young artist drawing on the streets of Paris, seduces her, and then takes her to St. Tropez. Conflict arises when a suave architect shows up and threatens to come between the two lovers. In French with English subtitles. **95m/C VHS, LV.** *FR* Stephane Audran, Jean-Louis Trintignant, Jacqueline Sassard; *D:* Claude Chabrol; *W:* Claude Chabrol. *CVC, LUM*

Les Bonnes Femmes 🐾🐾🐾 *The Good Girls; The Girls* **1960** Four Paris shopgirls dream of escaping the monotony of their lives and finding romance but instead discover broken dreams and danger. Chabrol's New Wave thriller focuses more on character and irony than suspense. French with subtitles. **105m/B VHS.** *FR* Bernadette La-Font, Stephane Audran, Clothilde Joano, Lucile Saint-Si-mon; *D:* Claude Chabrol; *W:* Paul Geoauff; *C:* Henri Decae; *M:* Pierre Jansen, Paul Misraki. *FCT*

Les Bons Debarras 🐾🐾½ **1981** In French with English subtitles, this Canadian film follows a lonely 13-year-old's effort to win her mother's exclusive love. **114m/C VHS, Beta.** *CA* Marie Tifo, Charlotte Laurier, German Houde; *D:* Francis Mankiewicz. Genie Awards '81: Best Actress (Tifo), Best Director (Mankiewicz), Best Film, Best Supporting Actor (Houde). *NO*

Les Carabiniers 🐾🐾🐾 *The Soldiers* **1963** A cynical, grim anti-war tract, detailing the pathetic adventures of two young bums lured into enlisting with promises of rape, looting, torture and battle without justification. Controversial in its day, and typically elliptical and non-narrative. In French with English subtitles. **80m/B VHS, Beta.** *GB IT FR* Anna Karina, Genevieva Galea, Marino Mase; *D:* Jean-Luc Godard. *FCT*

Les Comperes 🐾🐾🐾 **1983** A woman suckers two former lovers into finding her wayward son by secretly telling each ex he is the natural father of the punk. Depardieu is a streetwise journalist who teams up with a suicidal hypochondriac/wimp (Richard) to find the little brat. Humorous story full of bumbling misadventures. In French with English subtitles. **92m/C VHS, Beta, LV.** *FR* Pierre Richard, Gerard Depardieu, Anny Duperey, Michel Aumont; *D:* Francis Veber; *W:* Francis Veber; *M:* Vladimir Cosma. *FCT*

Les Enfants Terrible 🐾🐾🐾 *The Strange Ones* **1950** The classic, lyrical treatment of adolescent deviance adapted by Cocteau from his own play, wherein a brother and sister born into extreme wealth eventually enter into casual crime, self-destruction, and incest. In French with English subtitles. **105m/B VHS, Beta.** *FR* Edouard Dermithe, Nicole Stephane; *D:* Jean-Pierre Melville; *W:* Jean Cocteau, Jean-Pierre Melville. *FCT, WBF*

Les Girls 🐾🐾½ **1957** When one member of a performing troupe writes her memoirs, the other girls sue for libel. Told through a series of flashbacks, this story traces the girls' recollections of their relationships to American dancer Kelly. Cole Porter wrote the score for this enjoyable "Rashomon"-styled musical. Laserdisc features include the original trailer and letterboxed screen. ♫*Les Girls; Flower Song; You're Just Too, Too; Ca C'est L'Amour; Ladies In Waiting; La Habanera; Why Am I So Gone (About That Gal?).* **114m/C VHS, Beta, LV, Letterbox.** Gene Kelly, Mitzi Gaynor, Kay Kendall, Taina Elg, Henry Daniell, Patrick Macnee; *D:* George Cukor; *C:* Robert L. Surtees. Academy Awards '57: Best Costume Design; Golden Globe Awards '58: Best Actress—Musical/Comedy (Kendall), Best Film—Musical/Comedy; Nominations: Academy Awards '57: Best Art Direction/Set Decoration, Best Sound. *MGM*

Les Grandes Gueules 🐾🐾½ *Jailbirds' Vacation* **1965** From the director of the classic "An Occurrence at Owl Creek Bridge," comes this comedy-drama about a sawmill owner dealing with two ex-convicts hired as lumberjacks. In French with English subtitles. **125m/C VHS, Beta.** *FR* Lino Ventura, Bourvil, Marie DuBois; *D:* Robert Enrico. *BAR*

Les Grandes Manoeuvres 🐾🐾🐾 *Summer Manoeuvres; The Grand Maneuvers* **1955** Clair's first film in color depicts the romance between a seductive soldier (Philipe) and a divorcee (Morgan) in a pre-WWI garrison town. Gentle comedy has Philipe falling in love but his reputation as a Don Juan comes between them. French with subtitles. **106m/C VHS.** *FR* Gerard Philipe, Michele Morgan, Yves Robert, Brigitte Bardot, Jean Desailly, Pierre Dux; *D:* Rene Clair; *W:* Rene Clair; *M:* Georges Van Parys. *WBF*

Les Miserables 🐾🐾🐾🐾 **1935** Victor Hugo's classic novel about small-time criminal Jean Valjean and 18th-century France. After facing poverty and prison, escape and torture, Valjean is redeemed by the kindness of a bishop. As he tries to mend his ways, he is continually hounded by the policeman Javert, who is determined to lock him away. The final act is set during a student uprising in the 1730s. This version is the best of many, finely detailed and well-paced with excellent cinematography by Gregg Toland. **108m/B VHS, Beta, LV.** Fredric March, Charles Laughton, Cedric Hardwicke, Rochelle Hudson, John Beal, Frances Drake, Florence Eldridge, John Carradine, Jessie Ralph, Leonid Kinskey; *D:* Richard Boleslawski; *W:* W.P. Lipscomb; *C:* Gregg Toland; *M:* Alfred Newman. Nominations: Academy Awards '35: Best Cinematography, Best Film Editing, Best Picture. *FOX*

Les Miserables 🐾🐾½ **1952** Hugo's classic novel done up Italian style with lavish sets and spectacle. Dubbed in English. **119m/B VHS.** *IT* Gino Cervi, Valentina Cortese; *D:* Riccardo (Robert Hampton) Freda; *C:* Joseph LaShelle; *M:* Alex North. *VYY, FCT*

Les Miserables 🐾🐾🐾 **1957** An epic French adaptation of the Victor Hugo standard about Valjean, Javert, and injustice. Although this doesn't reach the level of the 1935 classic, it is still worth watching. Dubbed in English. **210m/C VHS, Beta.** *FR GE* Jean Gabin, Daniele Delorme, Bernard Blier, Bourvil, Gianni Esposito, Serge Reggiani; *D:* Jean-Paul LeChanois. *FCT, VEC*

Les Miserables 🐾🐾🐾½ **1978** An excellent made-for-television version of the Victor Hugo classic about the criminal Valjean and the policeman Javert playing cat-and-mouse in 18th-century France. Dauphin's last film role. **150m/C VHS, Beta, LV.** Richard Jordan, Anthony Perkins, John Gielgud, Cyril Cusack, Flora Robson, Celia Johnson, Claude Dauphin; *D:* Glenn Jordan. *FOX, FCT*

Les Miserables 🐾🐾½ **1995** (R) Clever, modern rendering of the famous Victor Hugo novel, set in World War II. Humble furniture mover Fortin (Belmondo), nicknamed Valjean for displaying the same brutish strength as his Hugo counterpart, helps a Jewish family escape German occupation. The family becomes separated in the attempt, with lawyer Monsieur Ziman (Boujenah) being hidden by farmers in the country, Madame Ziman (Martines) relegated to a Polish concentration camp, and their daughter Salome (Lelouch, daughter of the director) protected by a nun at a Catholic school. Gump-like, the unusually strong but illiterate Fortin becomes involved with the French resistance and joins in D-Day. Events, though obviously updated, mirror experiences of Hugo's characters. In one sequence, the Ziman's even teach Fortin to read Hugo's "Les Miserables," with actors playing their counterparts in dramatizations. Reportedly France's most expensive film ever. *CW:* Violence, brief language, and sexuality. **174m/C VHS, LV.** *FR* Jean-Paul Belmondo, Michel Boujenah, Annie Girardot, Philippe Leotard, Clementine Celarie, Rufus, Alessandra Martines, Salome, Philippe Khorsand; *D:* Claude Lelouch; *W:* Claude Lelouch; *M:* Francis Lai. Cesar Awards '96: Best Supporting Actress (Girardot); Golden Globe Awards '96:

Best Foreign Film; Nominations: British Academy Awards '95: Best Foreign Film. *WAR*

Les Miserables 🐾🐾🐾 **1997** (PG-13) Yet another adaptation of the Victor Hugo novel. Paroled convict Jean Valjean (Neeson) gets chased by police inspector Javert (Rush) while factory worker Fantine (Thurman) turns to prostitution to survive. August chose to begin this tale after Valjean's trial and imprisonment for petty theft, and until the final third of the film, doesn't really deal with the political upheaval of the time. Not as sweeping or grand as other versions, but what this adaptation lacks in scope, it makes up for with top-notch performances (especially by Neeson and Rush) and more careful study of the characters themselves. *CW:* Violence, and for some sexual content. **131m/C VHS.** Liam Neeson, Geoffrey Rush, Uma Thurman, Claire Danes, Paris Vaughan, Reine Brynolfsson, Hans Matheson, Mimi Newman; *D:* Bille August; *W:* Rafael Yglesias; *C:* Jorgen Persson; *M:* Basil Poledouris. *NYR*

Les Mistons 🐾🐾🐾 **1957** This study of male adolescence finds five teenage boys worshiping a beautiful girl from afar, following her everywhere, spoiling her dates, and finally reaching maturity in light of their mistakes. **18m/C VHS, Beta.** *FR D:* Francois Truffaut. *HMV*

Les Nuits Fauves 🐾🐾🐾 *Savage Nights* **1992** Collard's semi-autobiographical film about the emotional and physical havoc an H.I.V.-positive filmmaker visits on the two objects of his violent affections—an innocent 18-year-old girl and a sadomasochistic 20-year-old boy. As Jean displays increasing desperation with his situation, the life around him shows an equally arbitrary violence and humor. In French with English subtitles. Collard died of AIDS shortly before his film won both best first film and best French film at the 1993 Cesars—a first in the ceremony's history. **129m/C VHS.** *FR* Cyril Collard, Romane Bohringer, Carlos Lopez, Maria Schneider; *D:* Cyril Collard; *W:* Cyril Collard. Cesar Awards '93: Best Film. *PGV*

Les Patterson Saves the World 🐾½ **1990** (R) An obnoxious ambassador to an anonymous Middle Eastern country teams up with the singularly distastefully named Dr. Herpes to stop a new killer disease about to engulf the world. **105m/C VHS.** Barry Humphries, Pamela Stephenson, Thaao Penghlis, Andrew Clarke, Joan Rivers; *D:* George Miller; *C:* David Connell.

Les Rendez-vous D'Anna 🐾🐾 *The Meetings of Anna* **1978** An independent woman travels through Europe and comes face to face with its post-war modernism. In French with English subtitles. **120m/C VHS.** *FR BE GE* Aurore Clement, Helmut Griem, Magali Noel, Hanns Zischler, Lea Massari, Jean-Pierre Cassel; *D:* Chantal Akerman; *W:* Chantal Akerman. *WAC*

Les Vampires **1915** Irma Vep (an anagram for vampire) leads a bloodthirsty gang of thieves in Paris. She and her cohorts will use kidnapping, gas, sexual domination, and murder to gain power over the city's elite. Fueillade's 10-part serial has been restored with color-tinting and title cards in English. **?m/B VHS.** *FR* Musidora, Jean Ayme, Marcel Levesque, Edouard Mathe; *D:* Louis Feuillade; *W:* Louis Feuillade. *WBF*

Les Violons du Bal 🐾🐾 **1974** Follows the story of a young Jewish boy and his family's attempted escape from Nazi-occupied France during WWII. The boy grows up to be a filmmaker obsessed with making a movie about his childhood experiences. In French with English subtitles. **110m/C VHS.** *FR* Marie-Jose Nat, Jean-Louis Trintignant; *D:* Michael Drach. Cannes Film Festival '74: Best Actress (Nat). *CVC, PMS*

Les Visiteurs du Soir 🐾🐾🐾½ *The Devil's Envoys* **1942** A beautiful, charming fairy tale about the devil's intrepid interference with a particular love affair in 15th-century France, which he cannot squelch. Purportedly a parable about Hitler's invasion of France. Interestingly, this was released after the Nazi occupation of France, so one assumes that the Germans didn't make the connection. In French with English subtitles. **120m/B VHS.** *FR* Arletty, Jules Berry, Marie Dea, Alain Cuny, Fernand Ledoux, Marcel Herrand; *D:* Marcel Carne; *W:* Jacques Prevert, Pierre Laroche. *HMV, FCT, TPV*

Les Voleurs 🎬🎬🎬 *Thieves* 1996 (R) Unexpected romantic triangle among desperate, lonely people, set against a crime backdrop and told from a variety of viewpoints. Edgy cop Alex (Auteuil) is from a family of thieves, including his older brother Ivan (Bezace) who's been murdered. Alex gets involved with sullen Juliette (Cote) without realizing, at first, that her brother Jimmy (Magimel) is a member of Ivan's gang or that she has another lover, her philosophy teacher, Marie (Deneuve). Events finally force a meeting between Marie and Alex over the unstable Juliette (the scenes between Auteuil and Deneuve being the most interesting in the film). French with subtitles.*CW:* Strong sexuality, some violent moments and language. **116m/C VHS, LV.** *FR* Catherine Deneuve, Daniel Auteuil, Laurence Cote, Benoit Magimel, Didier Bezace, Fabienne Babe, Ivan Desny, Julien Riviere; *D:* Andre Techine; *W:* Andre Techine, Gilles Taurand; *C:* Jeanne Lapoirie; *M:* Philippe Sarde. Nominations: Cesar Awards '97: Best Actress (Deneuve), Best Director (Techine), Best Film. *COL*

Less Than Zero 🎬 1987 (R) An adaptation of Bret Easton Ellis' popular, controversial novel about a group of affluent, drug-abusing youth in Los Angeles. McCarthy and Gertz play friends of Downey who try to get him off his self-destructive path—to no avail. Although it tries, the film fails to inspire any sort of sympathy for this self-absorbed and hedonistic group. Mirrors the shallowness of the characters although Downey manages to rise above this somewhat. Music by the Bangles, David Lee Roth, Poison, Roy Orbison, Aerosmith and more. **98m/C VHS, Beta, LV, Closed Caption.** Andrew McCarthy, Jami Gertz, Robert Downey Jr., James Spader; *D:* Marek Kanievska; *M:* Thomas Newman. *FOX*

Lesson in Love 🎬🎬½ *En Lektion i Karlek* 1954 A gynecologist's philandering is discovered by his wife, who then starts an affair of her own. Change of pace for Bergman as he does this modest comedy. In Swedish with English subtitles. **95m/B VHS, Beta.** *SW* Gunnar Bjornstrand, Eva Dahlbeck, Harriet Andersson; *D:* Ingmar Bergman; *W:* Ingmar Bergman. *NLC*

Let 'Em Have It 🎬🎬½ *False Faces* 1935 Exciting action saga loosely based on the newly formed FBI and its bouts with John Dillinger. Car chases and tommy guns abound in this fairly ordinary film. **90m/B VHS.** Richard Arlen, Virginia Bruce, Bruce Cabot, Harvey Stephens, Eric Linden, Joyce Compton, Gordon Jones; *D:* Sam Wood. *MGM, NOS, HEG*

Let 'er Go Gallegher 🎬🎬 1928 A youngster sees a murder, tells his newspaper buddy about it, and the guy writes an article about the crime. It's a big hit, the guy's ego starts to overinflate, and his life starts to head downwind until he decides its time for him and the little guy to rope themselves a miscreant. **57m/B VHS, Beta.** Frank "Junior" Coghlan, Elinor Fair, Wade Boteler; *D:* Elmer Clifton. *GPV, FCT*

Let Freedom Ring 🎬🎬½ 1939 Sappy, yet enjoyable patriotism that has lawyer Eddy returning to small hometown and fighting corruption. Hokey, but it works largely due to Hecht's fine script. ♫Dusty Road; Love Serenade; Home Sweet Home; When Irish Eyes Are Smiling; America; Pat Sez He; Where Else But Here; Funiculi Funicula; Ten Thousand Cattle Straying. **100m/B VHS, Closed Caption.** Nelson Eddy, Virginia Bruce, Victor McLaglen, Lionel Barrymore, Edward Arnold, Guy Kibbee, Charles Butterworth, H.B. Warner, Raymond Walburn; *D:* Jack Conway; *W:* Ben Hecht. *MGM*

Let Him Have It 🎬🎬🎬½ 1991 (R) Compelling, controversial film about a miscarriage of British justice. In 1952 Christopher Craig, 16, and Derek Bentley, 19, climbed onto the roof of a warehouse in an apparent burglary attempt. The police arrived and captured Bentley; Craig shot and wounded one policeman and killed another. According to testimony Bentley shouted "Let him have it" but did he mean shoot or give the officer the gun? Bentley, whose IQ was 66, was sentenced to death by the British courts—though he didn't commit the murder. The uproar over the sentence was reignited by this release, leading to a request for a reexamination of evidence and sentencing by the British Home Office.*CW:* Language and violence. **115m/C VHS, LV.** *GB* Christopher Eccleston, Paul Reynolds, Tom Bell, Eileen Atkins, Clare Holman, Michael Elphick, Mark McGann, Tom Courtenay, Ronald Fraser, Michael Gough, Murray Melvin, Clive Revill, Norman Rossington, James Villiers; *D:* Peter Medak. *NLC*

Let It Be 🎬🎬 1970 Documentary look at a Beatles recording session, giving glimpses of the conflicts which led to their breakup. Features appearances by Yoko Ono and Billy Preston. **80m/C VHS, Beta, LV.** John Lennon, Paul McCartney, George Harrison, Ringo Starr, Billy Preston, Yoko Ono; *D:* Michael Lindsay-Hogg; *M:* The Beatles. Academy Awards '70: Original Song Score and/or Adaptation. *FOX*

Let It Ride 🎬🎬 1989 (PG-13) Dreyfuss is a small-time gambler who finally hits it big at the track. Some funny moments but generally a lame script cripples the cast, although the horses seem unaffected. Garr is okay as his wife who slips further into alcoholism with each race. **91m/C VHS, Beta, LV, 8mm, Closed Caption.** Richard Dreyfuss, Teri Garr, David Johansen, Jennifer Tilly, Allen (Goorwitz) Garfield, Ed Walsh, Michelle Phillips, Mary Woronov, Robbie Coltrane, Richard Edson, Cynthia Nixon; *D:* Joe Pytka. *PAR*

Let It Rock 🎬 1986 A maniacal promoter makes superstars out of his new band by staging publicity stunts. Not one of Hopper's better efforts. Filmed in Germany, but Roger Corman bought the U.S. rights and added clips from other movies before it was released here. **75m/C VHS, Beta.** *GE* Dennis Hopper, David Hess; *D:* Roland Klick.

L'Etat Sauvage 🎬🎬🎬½ *The Savage State* 1978 This French political thriller finds its heart in the middle of racism. The story unfolds around a newly independent African republic and a love affair between a black cabinet minister and a white Frenchwoman. Corruption abounds in this film based on George Conchon's award-winning novel. In French with English subtitles. **111m/C VHS, Beta, LV, Letterbox.** *FR* Marie-Christine Barrault, Claude Brasseur, Jacques Dutronc, Doura Mane, Michel Piccoli; *D:* Francois Girod. Cesar Awards '79: Best Sound. *INT, TPV*

Lethal Charm 🎬🎬 1990 Two power-hungry journalists go head-to-head in the high stakes arena of Washington D.C. **92m/C VHS.** Barbara Eden, Heather Locklear. *ART*

Lethal Games 🎬🎬 1990 Stallone and Vaccaro lead a small community against a bloodthirsty band of criminals. **83m/C VHS.** Frank Stallone, Brenda Vaccaro, Dave Adams, Christopher Whalley, Heidi Paine, Karen Russell; *D:* John Bowen.

Lethal Lolita—Amy Fisher: My Story 🎬 *Amy Fisher: My Story* 1992 The only made-for-television Amy Fisher story out of three whose cast members even remotely resemble the real people—except of course actress Parker is actually pretty. Minor details aside, this account is Amy's story, purchased by NBC for an undisclosed amount, portraying her as an incest victim who gets involved with an opportunistic married jerk who drags her into prostitution, leading her to take out her frustration on his wife. If this is true, the obvious question is "why?"...to which she answers, "He loves me. We have great sex. And he fixes my car." Oh. See also: "The Amy Fisher Story" and "Casualties of Love: The 'Long Island Lolita' Story." **93m/C VHS, Closed Caption.** Noelle Par-

ker, Ed Marinaro, Kathleen Lasky, Boyd Kestner, Mary Ann Pascal, Lawrence Dane, Kate Lynch; *D:* Bradford May. *TTC*

Lethal Ninja 🎬 1993 (R) Kickboxers Joe and Pete set out to rescue Joe's wife from some third-world country overrun by ninjas. Hackneyed but lots of action for martial arts fans. **97m/C VHS, LV.** Ross Kettle, David Webb, Karyn Hill, Frank Notaro. *THV*

Lethal Obsession 🎬½ *Der Joker* 1987 (R) Two cops battle street crime and a powerful drug ring. Filmed in Germany. **100m/C VHS, Beta.** *GE* Michael York, Elliott Gould, Tahnee Welch, Peter Maffay, Armin Mueller-Stahl; *D:* Peter Patzak; *M:* Tony Carey. *THV*

Lethal Panther 🎬🎬 1990 A film where the female is indeed deadlier than the male. Japanese hit woman Ling (Miyamoto) gets involved with drug-smuggling gangsters operating out of the Philippines and is opposed by CIA agent Betty Lee (Hu). Dubbed. **120m/C VHS.** *HK* Yoko Miyamoto, Sibelle Hu, Lawrence Ng; *D:* Godfrey Ho. *TAI*

Lethal Pursuit 🎬 1988 A popular singer who returns to the town where she grew up is tormented by her ex-boyfriend, a criminal. **90m/C VHS, Beta.** Mitzi Donahue, Blake Gahner, John Wildman; *D:* Donald M. Jones.

Lethal Seduction 🎬½ 1997 Local crime boss Gus Gruman (Estevez) is rapidly losing friends and associates to a sexually oriented serial killer. And there's obsessed cop Trent Jacobson (Mitchum) who's determined to solve the crimes. The one clue is a mystery brunette seen leaving a crime scene. **90m/C VHS.** Julie Strain, Chris Mitchum, Joe Estevez; *D:* Frederick P. Watkins; *C:* Robert Dracup. *VIC*

Lethal Tender 🎬🎬 1996 (R) A tour group is held hostage by a gang of terrorists as part of a plot to steal $400 million and it's up to a lone Chicago cop to save the day. Fahey does equally well in both bad and good guy roles and here he's in hero mode.*CW:* Violence and language. **93m/C VHS, Closed Caption.** Jeff Fahey, Kim Coates, Gary Busey, Carrie-Anne Moss; *D:* John Bradshaw. *REP*

Lethal Weapon 🎬🎬🎬 1987 (R) In Los Angeles, a cop nearing retirement (Glover) unwillingly begins work with a new partner (Gibson), a suicidal, semi-crazed risk-taker who seems determined to get the duo killed. Both Vietnam vets, the pair uncover a vicious heroin smuggling ring run by ruthless ex-Special Forces personnel. Packed with plenty of action, violence, and humorous undertones. Clapton's contributions to the musical score are an added bonus. Gibson and Glover work well together and give this movie extra punch. Followed by (so far) two sequels. **110m/C VHS, Beta, LV, Letterbox, Closed Caption, DVD.** Mel Gibson, Danny Glover, Gary Busey, Mitchell Ryan, Tom Atkins, Darlene Love, Traci Wolfe, Steve Kahan; *D:* Richard Donner; *W:* Shane Black; *M:* Michael Kamen, Eric Clapton. Nominations: Academy Awards '87: Best Sound. *WAR*

Lethal Weapon 2 🎬🎬🎬 1989 (R) This sequel to the popular cop adventure finds Gibson and Glover taking on a variety of blond South African "diplomats" who try to use their diplomatic immunity status to thwart the duo's efforts to crack their smuggling ring. Gibson finally finds romance, and viewers learn the truth about his late wife's accident. Also features the introduction of obnoxious, fast-talking con artist Leo ("OK, OK") Getz, adeptly played by Pesci, who becomes a third wheel to the crime-fighting team. Followed by a second sequel. **114m/C VHS, Beta, LV, Letterbox, Closed Caption, DVD.** Mel Gibson, Danny Glover, Joe Pesci, Joss Ackland, Derrick O'Connor, Patsy Kensit, Darlene Love, Traci Wolfe, Steve Kahan, Mary Ellen Trainor; *D:* Richard Donner; *W:* Jeffrey Boam; *M:* Michael Kamen, Eric Clapton, David Sanborn. *WAR*

Lethal Weapon 3 🎬🎬½ 1992 (R) Murtaugh and Riggs return for more action in another slam-bang adventure. Murtaugh hopes his last week before retirement will be a peaceful one, but partner Riggs isn't about to let him go quietly. Not many changes from the successful formula with bickering buddies, lots of adventure, exploding buildings, a little comic relief from Pesci, and the addition of Russo as an Internal Affairs cop who proves to be more than a match for Riggs.**CW:** Language and violence. **118m/C VHS, LV, 8mm, Closed Caption.** Mel Gibson, Danny Glover, Joe Pesci, Rene Russo, Stuart Wilson, Steve Kahan, Darlene Love, Traci Wolfe, Gregory Millar, Jason Meshover-Iorg, Delores Hall; **D:** Richard Donner; **W:** Jeffrey Boam, Robert Mark Kamen; **C:** Jan De Bont; **M:** Michael Kamen, Eric Clapton,• David Sanborn. MTV Movie Awards '93: Best On-Screen Duo (Mel Gibson/Danny Glover), Best Action Sequence. *WAR, PMS*

Lethal Weapon 4 1998 It's old home week as Gibson, Glover, Pesci, and Russo all reunite for one more escapade, six years after 1992's "Lethal Weapon 3." Rock joins the veterans as junior detective Lee Butters, who's romancing Murtaugh's daughter, and all are after an Asian crimelord (Chinese action star Li) who's set up a counterfeiting operation in L.A. Russo had to do her action sequences with a prosthetic belly since her character, Lorna Cole, and Riggs are about to become parents. Not yet reviewed. **?m/C VHS.** Mel Gibson, Danny Glover, Joe Pesci, Rene Russo, Chris Rock, Jet Li; **D:** Richard Donner. *NYR*

Lethal Woman 🎞½ 1988 A group of beautiful women, all once victimized by rapes, is recruited to an island by the "Lethal Woman," who plots revenge on any man who dares to vacation on the island. **96m/C VHS, Beta, LV.** Shannon Tweed, Merete Van Kamp. *NO*

Let's Dance 🎞🎞½ 1950 A young widow tries to protect her son from his wealthy, paternal grandmother, while Fred dances his way into her heart. More obscure Astaire vehicle, but as charming as the rest. Needless to say, great dancing. 🎵Tunnel of Love; The Hyacinth; Piano Dance; Jack and the Beanstalk; Can't Stop Talking; Oh, Them Dudes; Why Fight the Feeling?. **112m/C VHS, Beta, LV, Closed Caption.** Betty Hutton, Fred Astaire, Roland Young, Ruth Warrick, Shepperd Strudwick, Lucile Watson, Barton MacLane, Gregory Moffett, Melville Cooper; **D:** Norman Z. McLeod. *PAR*

Let's Do It Again 🎞½ 1975 **(PG)** Atlanta milkman and his pal, a factory worker, milk two big-time gamblers out of a large sum of money in order to build a meeting hall for their fraternal lodge. Lesser sequel to "Uptown Saturday Night." **113m/C VHS, Beta.** Sidney Poitier, Bill Cosby, John Amos, Jimmie Walker, Ossie Davis, Denise Nicholas, Calvin Lockhart; **D:** Sidney Poitier; **W:** Richard Wesley. *WAR*

Let's Get Harry 🎞½ *The Rescue* 1987 **(R)** Americans led by mercenaries mix it up with a Columbian cocaine franchise in an attempt to rescue their friend, Harry. Never released theatrically, for good reason. **107m/C VHS, Beta, LV, Closed Caption.** Robert Duvall, Gary Busey, Michael Schoeffling, Tom Wilson, Glenn Frey, Rick Rossovich, Ben Johnson, Matt Clark, Mark Harmon, Gregory Sierra, Elpidia Carrillo; **D:** Alan Smithee; **W:** Samuel Fuller, Charles Robert Carner; **M:** Brad Fiedel. *HBO*

Let's Get Lost 1988 Absorbing documentary of Chet Baker, the prominent '50s "cool" jazz trumpeter (and occasional vocalist) who succumbed, like many of his peers, to drug addiction. Weber's black-and-white, fashion photography style well suits his subject. Downbeat, but rarely less than worthy. **125m/B VHS.** Chet Baker; **D:** Bruce Weber. Nominations: Academy Awards '88: Best Feature Documentary. *MVD, COL*

Let's Get Married 🎞 1963 A young doctor's weakness under pressure brings him to the brink of babbling idiocy when his wife goes into early labor. **90m/B VHS, Beta.** Anthony Newley, Ann Aubrey. *NO*

Let's Get Tough 🎞 1942 The East Side Kids, unable to enlist because of their age, harass local Oriental shopkeepers and eventually get involved with a murder. **52m/B VHS, Beta, 8mm.** Leo Gorcey, Bobby Jordan, Huntz Hall, Gabriel Dell, Sammy Morrison; **D:** Wallace Fox. *VYY, NOS, RXM*

Let's Go! 🎞½ 1923 The son of a cement company president sets out to prove his worth to the firm by landing a contract with the town of Hillsboro. For some unknown reason, he sets off on an amazing set of stunts. Silent with original organ music. **79m/B VHS, Beta, 8mm.** Richard Talmadge, Hal Clements, Eileen Percy, Tully Marshall; **D:** William K. Howard. *VYY, GPV, GVV*

Let's Go Collegiate 🎞½ 1941 Two college rowers promise their girlfriends that they'll win the big race, but their plans are almost frustrated when their best oarsman is drafted. Their only hope lies in replacing him with a truck driver. 🎵Look What You've Done To Me; Sweet 16; Let's Do A Little Dreaming. **62m/B VHS.** Frankie Darro, Marcia Mae Jones, Jackie Moran, Keye Luke, Mantan Moreland, Gale Storm; **D:** Jean Yarbrough. *NOS*

Let's Kill All the Lawyers 🎞🎞½ 1993 **(R)** Low-budget satire about one man's angst over whether to become a lawyer is witty, entertaining, and not just for legal eagles. Law-firm intern Foster Merkul (Frederick) is apprenticed to a sleazeball (Vezina) who teaches him that money—not justice—is the name of the game in the law biz. Growing increasingly disillusioned, Foster sets out to reform the system with the help of Satori, a beautiful and mysterious creature of his imagination. Shot at sites in and around Detroit, this independent production features lots of cameos by local media celebrities.**CW:** Sexuality and language. **?m/C VHS.** Rick Frederick, James Vezina, Michelle De Vuono, Maggie Patton, Marty Smith; **D:** Ron Senkowski; **W:** Ron Senkowski. *NYR*

Let's Make It Legal 🎞🎞½ 1951 Amusing comedy of a married couple who decide to get a divorce after 20 years of marriage. Colbert stars as the woman who decides to leave her husband, Carey, because he's a chronic gambler. They part as friends, but soon Colbert's old flame, Scott, is back in town and things get rather complicated. A solid cast serves as the main strength in this film. **77m/B VHS, Closed Caption.** Claudette Colbert, MacDonald Carey, Zachary Scott, Barbara Bates, Robert Wagner, Marilyn Monroe; **D:** Richard Sale; **W:** F. Hugh Herbert. *FXV*

Let's Make Love 🎞🎞½ 1960 An urbane millionaire discovers he is to be parodied in an off-Broadway play, and vows to stop it—until he falls in love with the star of the show. He then ends up acting in the play. 🎵My Heart Belongs to Daddy; Let's Make Love; Specialization; Incurably Romantic; Sing Me a Song That Sells; You With the Crazy Eyes; Give Me the Simple Life. **118m/C VHS, Beta.** Yves Montand, Marilyn Monroe, Tony Randall, Frankie Vaughan, Bing Crosby, Gene Kelly, Milton Berle; **D:** George Cukor; **C:** Daniel F. Fapp. Nominations: Academy Awards '60: Scoring of a Musical. *FOX*

Let's Make Up 🎞🎞 *Lilacs in the Spring* 1955 When it comes to giving her heart, Neagle can't decide between two dashing men. **94m/C VHS.** GB Errol Flynn, Anna Neagle, David Farrar, Kathleen Harrison, Peter Graves; **D:** Herbert Wilcox. *GKK, MLB, MRV*

Let's Scare Jessica to Death 🎞🎞 1971 **(PG)** A young woman who was recently released from a mental hospital is subjected to unspeakable happenings at a country home with her friends. She encounters murder, vampires, and corpses coming out of nowhere. A supernatural thriller with quite a few genuine scares. **89m/C VHS, Beta.** Zohra Lampert, Barton Heyman, Kevin J. O'Connor, Gretchen Corbett, Alan Manson; **D:** John Hancock. *PAR*

Let's Sing Again 🎞🎞 1936 Eight-year-old singing sensation Bobby Breen made his debut in this dusty musical vehicle, as a runaway orphan who becomes the pal of a washed-up old opera star in a traveling show. 🎵Let's Sing Again; Lullaby; Farmer in the Dell; La Donna e Mobile. **70m/B VHS.** Bobby Breen, Henry Armetta, George Houston, Vivienne Osborne, Grant Withers, Inez Courtney, Lucien Littlefield; **D:** Kurt Neumann. *NOS, LOO, DVT*

The Letter 🎞🎞🎞🎞 1940 When a man is shot and killed on a Malaysian plantation, the woman who committed the murder pleads self-defense. Her husband and his lawyer attempt to free her, but find more than they expected in this tightly paced film noir. Based on the novel by W. Somerset Maugham. Davis emulated the originator of her role, Jeanne Eagels, in her mannerisms and line readings, although Eagels later went mad from drug abuse and overwork. **96m/B VHS, Beta, LV.** Bette Davis, Herbert Marshall, James Stephenson, Gale Sondergaard, Bruce Lester, Cecil Kellaway, Victor Sen Yung, Frieda Inescort; **D:** William Wyler; **W:** Howard Koch; **C:** Gaetano Antonio "Tony" Gaudio; **M:** Max Steiner. Nominations: Academy Awards '40: Best Actress (Davis), Best Black and White Cinematography, Best Director (Wyler), Best Film Editing, Best Picture, Best Supporting Actor (Stephenson), Best Original Score. *FOX, MGM*

Letter from an Unknown Woman 🎞🎞🎞 1948 A woman falls in love with a concert pianist on the eve of his departure. He promises to return but never does. The story is told in flashbacks as the pianist reads a letter from the woman. A great romantic melodrama. **90m/B VHS, LV.** Joan Fontaine, Louis Jourdan, Mady Christians, Marcel Journet, Art Smith; **D:** Max Ophuls. National Film Registry '92. *REP*

Letter of Introduction 🎞🎞½ 1938 A struggling young actress learns that her father is really a well known screen star and agrees not to reveal the news to the public. **104m/B VHS, Beta.** Adolphe Menjou, Edgar Bergen, George Murphy, Eve Arden, Ann Sheridan, Andrea Leeds; **D:** John M. Stahl; **C:** Karl Freund. *NOS, MRV, HHT*

Letter to Brezhnev 🎞🎞🎞 1986 **(R)** Acclaimed independent film about two working-class Liverpool girls who fall in love with two furloughed Russian sailors. When the men eventually return to the USSR, one of the girls contacts the Russian Secretary General in an effort to rejoin her lover. Amusing tale of different relationships. **94m/C VHS, Beta, LV, Closed Caption.** GB Margi Clarke, Alexandra Pigg, Peter Firth, Ken Campbell, Tracy Lea, Alfred Molina, Angela Clarke; **D:** Chris Bernard; **W:** Frank Clarke; **M:** Alan Gill. *ORI, IME, WAR*

Letter to My Killer 🎞🎞½ 1995 **(PG-13)** Construction worker Nick Parma (Chinlund) finds an unmailed letter in a demolished building, which he and wife Judy (Winningham) discover is 30 years old. The woman letter writer is describing major fraud and when Judy learns that she was murdered, she and Nick decide to blackmail the probable suspects—a powerful business cartel. But if they killed once..... Made for cable movie.**CW:** Some violence and sexuality. **92m/C VHS, Closed Caption.** Mare Winningham, Nicholas Chinlund, Rip Torn, Josef Sommer, Eddie Jones, Dey Young; **D:** Janet Meyers; **W:** Norman Strum; **C:** Stephen M. Katz; **M:** Mason Daring. *USH*

A Letter to Three Wives 🎞🎞🎞🎞 1949 Crain, Darnell, and Sothern star as three friends who, shortly before embarking on a Hudson River boat trip, each receive a letter from Holm (who's never shown), the fourth member in their set. The letter tells them that she has run off with one of their husbands but does not specify his identity. The women spend the rest of the trip reviewing their sometimes shaky unions which provides some of the funniest and most caustic scenes, including Douglas (as Sothern's husband) ranting against the advertising business which supports his wife's radio soap opera. Sharp dialogue, moving performances. Based on the novel by John Klempner. Remade for television in 1985. **103m/B VHS, Beta, LV.** Jeanne Crain, Linda Darnell, Ann Sothern, Kirk Douglas, Paul Douglas, Jeffrey Lynn, Thelma Ritter, Barbara Lawrence, Connie Gilchrist, Florence Bates; **D:** Joseph L. Mankiewicz; **W:** Joseph L. Mankiewicz; **C:** Arthur C. Miller; **M:** Alfred Newman; **V:** Celeste Holm. Academy Awards '49: Best Director (Mankiewicz), Best Screenplay; Directors Guild of America Awards '48: Best Director (Mankiewicz); Nominations: Academy Awards '49: Best Picture. *FXL*

Letters from Alou *ⅆⅆ Las Cartas de Alou* 1990 African immigrant Alou is trying to get to Barcelona to meet up with a friend but faces much exploitation and discrimination along the way. Spanish with subtitles. **100m/C VHS. SP** Mulie Jarju, Eulalia Ramon; **D:** Montxo Armendariz; **W:** Montxo Armendariz. *CVC*

Letters from My Windmill *ⅆⅆⅆ½* 1954 A series of three short stories: "The Three Low Masses," "The Elixir of Father Gaucher," and "The Secret of Master Cornille" from respected director Pagnol. The unique format only enhances this film. In French with English subtitles. **116m/B VHS. FR** Henri Velbert, Yvonne Gamy, Robert Vattier, Roger Crouzet; **D:** Marcel Pagnol. *NOS, DVT, INT*

Letters from the Park *ⅆⅆⅆ* 1988 In Cuba, 1913, two taciturn would-be lovers hire a poet, Victor La Place, to write love letters to each other. Normal proboscis aside, the poet follows the fate of Cyrano, and finds himself the unhappy hypotenuse in a triangular romance. Based on an original story by Marquez; made for Spanish television. In Spanish with English subtitles. **85m/C VHS. CU** Victor Laplace, Ivonne Lopez, Miguel Paneque; **D:** Tomas Gutierrez Alea; **W:** Gabriel Garcia Marquez, Tomas Gutierrez Alea. *FXL, FCT*

Letters to an Unknown Lover *ⅆⅆ½ Les Louves* 1984 During WWII, a man and woman engage in sexual and emotional combat. **101m/C VHS, Beta. GB FR** Cherie Lunghi, Mathilda May, Yves Beneyton, Ralph Bates; **D:** Peter Duffell.

Letting Go *ⅆⅆ* 1985 (PG) Made for television comedy-drama about a broken-hearted career woman and a young widower who fall in love. **94m/C VHS, Beta.** John Ritter, Sharon Gless, Joe Cortese; **D:** Jack Bender.

Letting the Birds Go Free 1986 When a stranger is caught stealing from a farmer's barn, the farmer and his son decide to let the villain work off his crime. Some very interesting relationships develop from this arrangement. **60m/C VHS.** Lionel Jeffries.

Leviathan *ⅆⅆ* 1989 (R) A motley crew of ocean-floor miners are trapped when they are accidentally exposed to a failed Soviet experiment that turns humans into insatiable, regenerating fish-creatures. **98m/C VHS, Beta, LV, Letterbox, Closed Caption.** Peter Weller, Ernie Hudson, Hector Elizondo, Amanda Pays, Richard Crenna, Daniel Stern, Lisa Eilbacher, Michael Carmine, Meg Foster; **D:** George P. Cosmatos; **W:** David Peoples, Jeb Stuart; **C:** Alex Thomson; **M:** Jerry Goldsmith. *MGM*

Lewis and Clark and George *ⅆⅆ* 1997 (R) Lewis (Xuereb) is a dim-witted killer and Clark (Gunther) is a computer nerd. Both are prison escapees in possession of what is supposed to be a map to a gold mine. Lewis happens to be illiterate and needs Clark, who's afraid of Lewis's trigger-happy ways. George (McGowan) is a sexy mute thief who takes both men for quite a wild ride. Filmed in rural New Mexico. **CW:** Strong language, sexuality and some violence. **84m/C VHS.** Salvator Xuereb, Dan Gunther, Rose McGowan, Art LaFleur, Aki Aleong, James Brolin, Paul Bartel; **D:** Rod McCall; **W:** Rod McCall; **C:** Mike Mayers; **M:** Ben Vaughn. *BMG*

L'Homme Blesse *ⅆⅆⅆ The Wounded Man* 1983 A serious erotic film about 18-year-old Henri (Anglade), cloistered by an overbearing family, and his sudden awakening to his own homosexuality. Anglade's film debut. In French with English subtitles. **90m/C VHS, Beta. FR** Jean-Hugues Anglade, Roland Bertin, Vittorio Mezzogiorno; **D:** Patrice Chereau; **C:** Renato Berta. **Cesar Awards '84:** Best Writing; **Nominations: Cesar Awards '83:** Best Supporting Actor (Anglade). *TPV, CCN*

Liana, Jungle Goddess *ⅆⅆ* 1956 A variation on the Greystoke legend featuring a beautiful (and topless) jungle goddess who is discovered living in the wilds of Africa. Thinking that she may be the lost granddaughter of a wealthy English nobleman, she's brought back to London for a reunion. Will civilization prove to be as dangerous as the jungle? **?m/C VHS.** Marion Michael Hardy Kruger. *SNC*

Lianna *ⅆⅆⅆ* 1983 (R) Acclaimed screenwriter/director John Sayles wrote and directed this story of a woman's romantic involvement with another woman. Chronicles an unhappy homemaker's awakening to the feelings of love that she develops for a female professor. Sayles makes an appearance as a family friend. **110m/C VHS, Beta.** Jon DeVries, Linda Griffiths, Jane Hallaren, Jo Henderson, Jessica Wright MacDonald; **Cameos:** John Sayles; **D:** John Sayles; **W:** John Sayles; **M:** Mason Daring. *VES*

Liar Liar *ⅆⅆ½* 1996 (PG-13) Carrey takes on one of his less manic but still appealing personas as compulsive liar and attorney Fletcher Reid. A constant disappointment to his ex-wife Audrey (Tierney) and young son Max (Cooper), Fletcher is forced to tell nothing but the truth for 24 hours, thanks to his son's supernatural birthday wish. This puts a crimp in his legal practice, especially as he tries to defend brazen would-be divorcee Samantha Cole (Tilly). Gets kinda sappy but Carrey can carry almost any situation. **CW:** Sex related humor and language. **87m/C VHS, LV, Closed Caption, DVD.** Jim Carrey, Jennifer Tilly, Maura Tierney, Amanda Donohoe, Swoosie Kurtz, Justin Cooper, Jason Bernard, Mitchell Ryan, Anne Haney, Chip Mayer, Randall "Tex" Cobb, Cary Elwes; **D:** Tom Shadyac; **W:** Paul Guay, Steve Mazur; **C:** Russell Boyd; **M:** John Debney. **MTV Movie Awards '98:** Best Comedic Performance (Carrey); **Nominations: Golden Globe Awards '98:** Best Actor—Musical/Comedy (Carrey). *USH*

The Liars *ⅆⅆ* 1964 Mystery in which a Frenchman strikes it rich in Africa, then returns home to Paris in search of a wife. He advertises for a mate, but is set up by con artists instead. In French with English subtitles. **92m/C VHS.** Dawn Addams, Jean Servais; **D:** Edmond T. Greville. *FCT*

The Liar's Club *ⅆ½* 1993 (R) High-school football teammates try to cover up a rape and wind up involved in murder. **CW:** Language, violence, and sexuality. **100m/C VHS.** Wil Wheaton, Brian Krause, Soleil Moon Frye, Jennifer Burns, Michael Cudlitz, Bruce Weitz; **D:** Jeffrey Porter. *NHO*

Liar's Edge *ⅆⅆ* 1992 (R) Tweed portrays a single mother whose teenaged son, Mark, is plagued by violent fantasies. When she remarries and her new husband and sleazy brother-in-law move in, Mark's hallucinations become stronger until he believes he's witnessed a murder. The murder turns out to be a fact and his new stepfather is involved but can Mark prove it. Filmed on location in Niagra Falls. **CW:** Language, violence, and sensuality. **97m/C VHS, LV.** Shannon Tweed, Nicholas Shields, David Keith, Joseph Bottoms, Christopher Plummer; **D:** Ron Oliver; **W:** Ron Oliver. *NLC, IME*

Liar's Moon *ⅆⅆ* 1982 (PG) A local boy woos and weds the town's wealthiest young lady, only to be trapped in family intrigue. **106m/C VHS, Beta.** Cindy Fisher, Matt Dillon, Christopher Connelly, Susan Tyrrell; **D:** David Fisher. *VES*

Libeled Lady *ⅆⅆⅆ½* 1936 A fast, complicated screwball masterwork, dealing with a newspaper editor's efforts to get something on a bratty heiress with the help of his own fiancee and a reporter he recently fired. One of the era's funniest Hollywood films. Remade in 1946 as "Easy to Wed." **98m/B VHS, Beta, LV.** Myrna Loy, Spencer Tracy, Jean Harlow, William Powell, Walter Connolly, Charley Grapewin, Cora Witherspoon, E.E. Clive, Charles Trowbridge, Dennis O'Keefe, Hattie McDaniel; **D:** Jack Conway. **Nominations: Academy Awards '36:** Best Picture. *MGM*

The Liberation of L.B. Jones *ⅆⅆ* 1970 (R) A wealthy black undertaker wants a divorce from his wife, who is having an affair with a white policeman. Wyler's final film. **101m/C VHS, Beta.** Lee J. Cobb, Lola Falana, Barbara Hershey, Anthony Zerbe, Roscoe Lee Browne; **D:** William Wyler; **W:** Stirling Silliphant; **M:** Elmer Bernstein. *COL, FCT*

Liberators *ⅆ* 1977 Kinski stars as a criminal soldier battling with the American authorities, German troops, and his fugitive partner. **91m/C VHS, Beta.** Klaus Kinski. *UNI*

The Libertine *ⅆ La Matriarca* 1969 Mimi (Spaak) is a young widow who's just discovered her late husband kept a separate apartment equipped to satisfy his more unusual sexual desires. Intrigued, Mimi decides to keep the apartment and do her own sexual exploring. Dubbed. **90m/C VHS. IT** Catherine Spaak, Jean-Louis Trintignant; **D:** Pasquale Festa Campanile. *FRF*

Liberty & Bash *ⅆ* 1990 (R) Two boyhood friends who served together in Vietnam reunite to rid their neighborhood of drug pushers and save the life of a friend. **92m/C VHS, Beta, Closed Caption.** Miles O'Keeffe, Lou Ferrigno, Mitzi Kapture, Richard Eden, Cheryl Paris, Gary Conway; **D:** Myrl A. Schreibman.

License to Drive *ⅆⅆ* 1988 (PG-13) When teen Haim fails the road test for his all-important driver's license, he steals the family car for a hot date with the girl of his dreams. The evening starts out quietly enough, but things soon go awry. If Haim survives the weekend, he'll definitely be able to pass his driving test on Monday morning. Semi-funny in a demolition derby sort of way. **90m/C VHS, Beta, LV.** Corey Feldman, Corey Haim, Carol Kane, Richard Masur; **D:** Greg Beeman; **C:** Bruce Surtees; **M:** Jay Michael Ferguson. *FOX*

License to Kill *ⅆⅆ* 1964 Constantine stars as Agent Nick Carter involved with Oriental spies and a new secret weapon. **100m/C VHS. FR** Eddie Constantine, Yvonne Monlaur, Paul Frankeur; **D:** Henri Decoin. *SNC*

License to Kill *ⅆⅆ* 1984 A young girl is killed by a drunk driver, devastating both families. A made-for-television movie with a strong message against drinking and driving. **96m/C VHS, Beta, LV.** James Farentino, Don Murray, Penny Fuller, Millie Perkins, Donald Moffat, Denzel Washington, Ari Meyers; **D:** Jud Taylor. *GEM*

License to Kill *ⅆⅆⅆ* 1989 (PG-13) Dalton's second Bond effort, in which drug lords try to kill 007's best friend and former CIA agent. Disobeying orders for the first time and operating without his infamous "license to kill," Bond goes after the fiends. Fine outing for Dalton (and Bond, too). **133m/C VHS, Beta, LV, Letterbox, Closed Caption. GB** Timothy Dalton, Carey Lowell, Robert Davi, Frank McRae, Talisa Soto, David Hedison, Anthony Zerbe, Everett McGill, Wayne Newton, Benicio Del Toro, Desmond Llewelyn, Priscilla Barnes; **D:** John Glen; **W:** Michael G. Wilson, Richard Maibaum; **M:** Michael Kamen. *FOX, MGM*

The Lickerish Quartet *ⅆⅆ* 1970 (R) A bored, aristocratic couple live with their teenaged son in a secluded castle in Italy's Abruzzi mountains. Traveling to a nearby carnival, they think they recognize the female daredevil as the same actress they've just seen in a home-viewed porno film. So they invite her back to the castle for a little family fun—only she may not be the same woman at all. **90m/C VHS.** Silvana Venturelli, Frank Wolff; **D:** Radley Metzger. *FRF*

L'Idiot *ⅆ The Idiot* 1946 Smooth adaptation of Dostoevsky's novel about noble Prince Mishkin's (Philipe) attempts to bring peace to the life of tormented Nastasia Filipovna (Feuillere). First feature for Lampin; French with subtitles. **98m/B VHS. FR** Gerard Philipe, Edwige Feuillere, Lucien Coedel, Nathalie Nattier, Marguerite Moreno; **D:** Georges Lampin; **W:** Charles Spaak; **C:** Christian Matras; **M:** Maurice Thiriet. *FCT*

Lie Down with Dogs *ⅆ* 1995 (R) You will wake up with fleas if you watch this dull, very low-budget comedy about young Tommie (White), who heads out of New York for some summer fun in the gay-friendly resort of Provincetown, Massachusetts. There's lots of temporary (discreetly filmed) encounters but no lasting romance and Tommie heads back to the Big Apple at season's end satisfied but no wiser. White's debut film. **CW:** Strong sexuality and language; some drug use.

85m/C VHS. Wally White, Randy Becker, Darren Dryden; **D:** Wally White; **W:** Wally White; **C:** George Mitas. TOU

Lie Down with Lions 🐾½ 1994 Long and dull TV adaptation of the Ken Follett spy novel. American nurse Kate Neeson (Helgenberger) is aghast when she discovers her lover, Jack Carver (Dalton), is a CIA agent. She marries Czech doctor Peter Husak (Havers) on the rebound and the newlyweds travel to Azerbijan to run a clinic, where Kate has a baby. But Jack's not out of the picture since his current assignment takes him into the war-torn region—and back into Kate's life, especially when he discovers Peter is not what he seems. On three cassettes. **136m/C VHS.** Timothy Dalton, Marg Helgenberger, Nigel Havers, Omar Sharif, Kabir Bedi, Juergen Prochnow; **D:** Jim Goddard; **W:** Guy Andrews, Julian Bond; **C:** Eddy van der Enden. CCB, TVC

Liebelei 🐾🐾 1932 Fritz (Liebeneiner), a handsome lieutenant, has broken off his romance with a married baroness and fallen for young opera singer Christine (Schneider) in turn-of-the-century Vienna. However, when the jealous baron (Grundgens) learns of his wife's infidelity, he challenges Fritz to a duel. Remade as "Christine" in 1967, with Romy Schneider in her mother's role. In German with English subtitles. **82m/B VHS.** GE Magda Schneider, Wolfgang Liebeneiner, Gustav Grundgens; **D:** Max Ophuls. KIV

Liebestraum 🐾🐾 1991 (R) An architectural expert, his old college friend, and the friend's wife form a dangerous triangle of passion and lust that strangely duplicates a situation that led to a double murder 40 years earlier. The unrated version clocks in at 116 minutes. **CW:** Language and strong sensuality. **109m/C VHS, LV, Letterbox.** Kevin Anderson, Bill Pullman, Pamela Gidley, Kim Novak; **D:** Mike Figgis; **W:** Mike Figgis. MGM

Lies 🐾🐾½ 1983 (PG) Complicated mystery about a murder/thriller movie plot becoming reality as it is being filmed, revolving around a scam to collect an inheritance from a rich guy in a mental hospital. **93m/C VHS, Beta, Closed Caption.** GB Ann Dusenberry, Gail Strickland, Bruce Davison, Clu Gulager, Bert Remsen, Dick Miller; **D:** Ken Wheat, Jim Wheat. FOX

Lies Before Kisses 🐾🐾 1992 (PG-13) A woman finds out her loving husband has been spending time with a beautiful call girl. When the call girl is murdered the husband is accused. His wife decides to help him clear his name but she just may have her own type of revenge in mind. **93m/C VHS, Beta, Closed Caption.** Jaclyn Smith, Ben Gazzara, Nick Mancuso, Greg Evigan, Penny Fuller, James Karen; **D:** Lou Antonio. TTC, PMS

Lies My Father Told Me 🐾🐾🐾 1975 (PG) Simple drama about growing up in the 1920s in a Jewish ghetto. The story revolves around a young boy's relationship with his immigrant grandfather. Quiet and moving. **102m/C VHS.** CA Yossi Yadin, Len Birman, Marilyn Lightstone, Jeffery Lynas; **D:** Jan Kadar; **W:** Ted Allan. Golden Globe Awards '76: Best Foreign Film; Nominations: Academy Awards '75: Best Original Screenplay. NO

Lies of the Twins 🐾🐾 1991 A beautiful model becomes involved with her therapist and his identical, and irresponsible, twin brother. **93m/C VHS.** Isabella Rossellini, Aidan Quinn, Iman, John Pleshette; **D:** Tim Hunter. USH

Lt. Robin Crusoe, U.S.N. 🐾 1966 (G) A lighthearted navy pilot crash lands amusingly on a tropical island, falls hard for an island babe and schemes intensely against the local evil ruler. Lackluster Disney debacle. **113m/C VHS, Beta.** Dick Van Dyke, Nancy Kwan, Akim Tamiroff; **D:** Byron Paul; **M:** Robert F. Brunner. DIS, OM

Life 🐾 1995 Explores the relationships between a group of prisoners doing time in a prison unit for HIV-positive inmates and what it means to be a man. Stylized production was developed from Brumpton's 1991 play "Containment." Feature film debut for director Johnston. **?m/C VHS.** AU John Brumpton, David Tredinnick, Robert Morgan, Noel Jor-

dan, Luke Elliot, Jeff Kovski; **D:** Lawrence Johnston; **W:** John Brumpton, Lawrence Johnston. Nominations: Australian Film Institute '96: Best Actor (Brumpton), Best Film, Best Supporting Actor (Morgan). NYR

The Life and Adventures of Nicholas Nickleby 🐾🐾🐾½ Nicholas Nickleby 1981 Nine-hour production of the 1838 Dickens' tale by the Royal Shakespeare Company, featuring the work of 39 actors portraying 150 characters. Wonderful performances are characterized by frantic action and smoothly meshing intertwining plots, focusing on the trials and tribulations of the Nickleby family, amidst wealth, poverty, and injustice in Victorian England. Nine cassettes. **540m/C VHS.** GB Roger Rees, David Thewlis, Emily Richard, John Woodvine; **D:** Jim Goddard; **W:** David Edgar; **M:** Stephen Oliver. AEH, FOX, FHS

The Life and Assassination of the Kingfish 1976 Recommended by the NEA, this story of Louisiana politician Huey Long is riveting. Asner gives a profound performance. **96m/C VHS, Beta.** Ed Asner, Nicholas Pryor, Diane Kagan; **D:** Robert Collins. NO

The Life and Death of Colonel Blimp 🐾🐾🐾🐾 Colonel Blimp 1943 Chronicles the life of a British soldier who survives three wars (Boer, WWI, and WWII), falls in love with three women (all portrayed by Kerr), and dances a fine waltz. Fine direction and performance abound. **115m/C VHS, Beta, LV.** GB Roger Livesey, Deborah Kerr, Anton Walbrook, Ursula Jeans, Albert Lieven; **D:** Michael Powell, Emeric Pressburger; **C:** Georges Perinal. NO

The Life and Loves of Mozart 🐾🐾½ 1959 Despite the title, this is really about the great composer's later life at the time of the premiere of "Die Zauberfloete" ("The Magic Flute"). This is only partly saved by a stellar performance from Werner, as well as the music. Other than that, it gets bogged down in titillation about W.A.M.'s romantic life. In German with English subtitles. **87m/C VHS.** Oskar Werner, Johanna Matz, Angelika Hauff; **D:** Karl Hartl; **V:** Anton Dermota. NOS, VEC

Life and Nothing But 🐾🐾🐾½ La Vie est Rien d'Autre 1989 (PG) Two young women search for their lovers at the end of WWI. They're helped by a French officer brutalized by the war and driven to find all of France's casualties. Romantic, evocative, and saddening. In French with English subtitles. **135m/C VHS, Beta.** FR Philippe Noiret, Sabine Azema, Francoise Perrot; **D:** Bertrand Tavernier; **W:** Bertrand Tavernier; **C:** Bruno de Keyzer. British Academy Awards '89: Best Foreign Film; Cesar Awards '90: Best Actor (Noiret), Best Score; Los Angeles Film Critics Association Awards '90: Best Foreign Film. ORI, FCT

Life and Nothing More ... 🐾🐾 And Life Goes On ...; Zendegi Va Digar Hich ... 1992 Following Iran's devastating 1990 earthquake, a filmmaker and his son search for the young actors who previously worked with him to see if they've survived, meeting various villagers trying to rebuild their lives. Sequel to Kiarostami's film "Where Is My Friend's House?" and followed by "Through the Olive Trees." Farsi with subtitles. **91m/C VHS.** Farhad Kheradmand, Pooya Payvar; **D:** Abbas Kiarostami; **W:** Abbas Kiarostami; **C:** Homayun Payvar. FCT

Life & Times of Grizzly Adams 🐾🐾 1974 (G) Lightweight family adventure film based on the rugged life of legendary frontiersman, Grizzly Adams, that served as the launching pad for the TV series. Grizzly is mistakenly chased for a crime he didn't commit and along the way befriends a big bear. **93m/C VHS, Beta.** Dan Haggerty, Denver Pyle, Lisa Jones, Marjorie Harper, Don Shanks; **D:** Richard Friedenberg. NO

Life & Times of Judge Roy Bean 🐾🐾½ 1972 (PG) Based on the life of the famed Texas "hanging judge," the film features Newman as the legendary Bean who dispenses frontier justice in the days of the Wild West. Filled with gallows humor. Gardner sparkles as actress Lily Langtry. **124m/C VHS, Beta, LV, Letterbox.** Paul

Newman, Stacy Keach, Ava Gardner, Jacqueline Bisset, Anthony Perkins, Roddy McDowall, Victoria Principal; **D:** John Huston; **W:** John Milius; **M:** Maurice Jarre. Nominations: Academy Awards '72: Best Song ("Marmalade, Molasses & Honey"). WAR

The Life & Times of the Chocolate Killer 🐾½ 1988 Police turn against the hand that's helped them save property and lives, by framing a good samaritan with deeds done by the "Chocolate Killer." **75m/C VHS.** Michael Adrian, Rod Browning, Tabi Cooper. THV

Life Begins for Andy Hardy 🐾🐾🐾 1941 Andy gets a job in New York before entering college and finds the working world to be a sobering experience. Surprisingly downbeat and hardhitting for an Andy Hardy film. Garland's last appearance in the series. **100m/B VHS, Beta.** Mickey Rooney, Judy Garland, Lewis Stone, Ann Rutherford, Fay Holden, Gene Reynolds, Ralph Byrd; **D:** George B. Seitz. MGM

A Life in the Theater 🐾🐾½ 1993 Life in the theatre as a hammy stage veteran (Lemmon) shares his experiences (and his dressing room) with a callow newcomer (Broderick). Petty squabbles, missed cues, and rare candor are displayed as the two stage scenes from their various repertory. Gentle, slight Mamet play, written when he was 25. Made for television. **78m/C VHS, LV, Closed Caption.** Jack Lemmon, Matthew Broderick; **D:** Gregory Mosher; **W:** David Mamet. TTC

Life Is a Circus, Charlie Brown/ You're the Greatest, Charlie Brown 1980 Two Peanuts favorites appear on this tape. In the Emmy award-winning "Life Is a Circus, Charlie Brown," Snoopy falls in love with Fifi, a French poodle circus performer, and winds up as a member of the traveling circus. In "You're the Greatest, Charlie Brown," our hero has a chance to win a decathlon in the Junior Olympics. With Peppermint Patty coaching, anything can happen! **60m/C VHS, Beta. D:** Phil Roman. VTR

Life Is a Long Quiet River 🐾🐾🐾 La Vie Est Une Longue Fleuve Tranquille 1988 Social comedy about a nurse who, infuriated with her married doctor employer/lover, switches two babies at birth. Twelve years later, after her lover's wife has died and he still refuses to marry her, she reveals the swap. The children are returned to their rightful families causing a multitude of confusion and adjustment. Directorial debut of Chatiliez. In French with English subtitles. **89m/C VHS.** FR Benoit Magimel, Helene Vincent, Andre Wilms, Daniel Gelin, Catherine Hiegel, Christine Pignet, Patrick Bouchitey, Valerie Lalande, Tara Romer, Jerome Floch, Sylvie Cubertafon; **D:** Etienne Chatiliez; **W:** Florence Quentin, Etienne Chatiliez; **M:** Gerard Kawczynski. Cesar Awards '89: Best Supporting Actress (Vincent), Best Writing. NYF, FCT

Life Is Beautiful 🐾🐾½ 1979 A politically neutral man is arrested and tortured in pre-revolutionary Lisbon, and forced to make, and act on, a political commitment. Dubbed. **102m/C VHS, Beta.** PT Giancarlo Giannini, Ornella Muti; **D:** Grigorij Ciukhrai.

Life is Beautiful 🐾🐾 La Vita e Bella 1997 Guido (Benigni) is a country bumpkin who begins a new life in a Tuscan town in 1938 where he falls for schoolteacher Dora (Braschi). He eventually persuades her to marry him, they start a business and have a son but circumstances don't allow them to live happily ever after. In 1944, the part-Jewish Guido and his young son Giosue (Durano) are taken to a concentration camp where Guido concocts an elaborate game to protect his innocent child from the horrors surrounding them. Yes, it's intended as a comedy. Italian with subtitles. **114m/C VHS.** IT Roberto Benigni, Nicoletta Braschi, Giustino Durano, Sergio Bustric, Horst Buchholz; **D:** Roberto Benigni; **W:** Vincenzo Cerami, Roberto Benigni; **C:** Tonino Delli Colli; **M:** Nicola Piovani. Cannes Film Festival '98: Grand Jury Prize. NYR

Life Is Sweet 🎬🎬🎬½ 1990 (R) The consuming passions of food and drink feed the lives of an oddball English working-class family beset by hopeless dreams and passions. Mother is always fixing family meals—in between helping her friend open a gourmet restaurant which features such revolting dishes as pork cyst and prune quiche. Dad is a chef who buys a snack truck and dreams of life on the road. Natalie and Nicola, the grown twins, eat their meals in front of the television but Nicola is also a bulimic who binges and purges on chocolate bars behind her bedroom door. (Note the chocolate scene between Nicola and her boyfriend.) An affectionate, if sometimes unattractive, look at a chaotic family. **CW:** Language and one sensual scene. 103m/C **VHS, LV, Closed Caption.** **GB** Alison Steadman, Jane Horrocks, Jim Broadbent, Claire Skinner, Timothy Spall, Stephen Rea, David Thewlis; **D:** Mike Leigh; **W:** Mike Leigh. Los Angeles Film Critics Association Awards '91: Best Supporting Actress (Horrocks); National Society of Film Critics Awards '91: Best Actress (Steadman), Best Film, Best Supporting Actress (Horrocks). **REP, BTV**

A Life Less Ordinary 🎬🎬½ 1997 (R) Third outing from U.K. team of Boyle/Hodge/Macdonald, who made "Shallow Grave" and "Trainspotting," has hapless janitor Robert (MacGrgor) lose his job, girlfriend, and home. He reacts by kidnapping the boss's daughter Celine (Diaz), who's more upset at Robert's ineptness than anything else. Meanwhile two angels (Hunter and Lindo) are sent to make these two kids fall in love. Confused? You should be. Hodge's script looks like someone threw "It Happened One Night," "Stairway to Heaven," outtakes from a Tarantino movie, and a Road Runner cartoon into a blender and hit frappe. Some of the surreal set pieces work, and the MacGregor/Diaz chemistry clicks sporadically, but the overall effect is overkill. Producer MacDonald is the grandson of Emeric Pressberger, co-director of "Stairway to Heaven." **CW:** Violence and language. 103m/C **VHS, Closed Caption.** Ewan McGregor, Cameron Diaz, Holly Hunter, Delroy Lindo, Ian Holm, Ian McNeice, Stanley Tucci, Dan Hedaya, Tony Shalhoub, Maury Chaykin, Judith Ivey; **D:** Danny Boyle; **W:** Ian Hodge; **C:** Brian Tufano; **M:** David Arnold. Nominations: MTV Movie Awards '98: Best Song ("Deadweight"), Best Dance Sequence (Cameron Diaz/Ewan McGregor). **FXV**

The Life of Emile Zola 🎬🎬🎬½ 1937 Writer Emile Zola intervenes in the case of Alfred Dreyfus who was sent to Devil's Island for a crime he did not commit. Well-crafted production featuring a handsome performance from Muni. 117m/B **VHS, Beta, LV.** Paul Muni, Gale Sondergaard, Gloria Holden, Joseph Schildkraut; **D:** William Dieterle; **W:** Norman Reilly Raine; **C:** Gaetano Antonio "Tony" Gaudio; **M:** Max Steiner. Academy Awards '37: Best Picture, Best Screenplay, Best Supporting Actor (Schildkraut); New York Film Critics Awards '37: Best Actor (Muni), Best Film; Nominations: Academy Awards '37: Best Actor (Muni), Best Director (Dieterle), Best Interior Decoration, Best Sound, Best Score. **MGM, BTV**

A Life of Her Own 🎬🎬½ 1950 Turner stars as a farm girl who takes her dream of becoming a top model to the Big Apple. She signs with an agency and is befriended by Dvorak, an aging model, who acts as her mentor. Turner finds success and is soon the toast of the town until she gets involved with a married man (Milland) and her life starts to crumble. Average soap opera with flimsy script. Turner is good, but Dvorak steals the show in her role as an over-the-hill fashion plate. 108m/B **VHS.** Lana Turner, Ray Milland, Tom Ewell, Louis Calhern, Ann Dvorak, Barry Sullivan, Jean Hagen, Phyllis Kirk, Sara Haden; **D:** George Cukor; **W:** Isobel Lennart. **MGM**

Life of Oharu 🎬🎬🎬½ Diary of Oharu; Saikaku Ichidai Onna 1952 A near masterpiece rivaled only by "Ugetsu" in the Mizoguchi canon, this film details the slow and agonizing moral decline of a woman in feudal Japan, from wife to concubine to prostitute. A scathing portrait of social pre-desti-

nation based on a novel by Ibara Saikaku, In Japanese with English subtitles. 136m/B **VHS, Beta.** **JP** Kinuyo Tanaka, Toshiro Mifune; **D:** Kenji Mizoguchi. **HMV, TPV**

A Life of Sin 🎬🎬 1992 (R) Scandalous drama about an impoverished Caribbean girl who rises to wealth and power as a world-famous madame. Colon stars as the beautiful Isabel, who is betrayed by her childhood friend Paulo (Julia) and rejected by the Catholic bishop (Ferrer) in this tragic story of passion and greed. 112m/C **VHS, Closed Caption.** Raul Julia, Miriam Colon, Jose Ferrer; **D:** Efrain Lopez Neris; **W:** Emilio Diaz Valcarcel. **COL, PMS**

Life of Verdi 1984 Epic mini-series biography of the famous composer, with many excerpts of his music sung by Luciano Pavarotti, Renata Telbaldi, and Maria Callas. Made for television. 600m/B **VHS, Beta.** **IT** Ronald Pickup, Carla Fracci. **HMV, KUL, MVD**

Life on a String 🎬🎬 1990 Set in the distant past, this is a lyrical story of a young boy searching for a cure for his blindness. His possible cure involves a myth which requires him to devote his life to music and the breaking of 1000 strings on a banjo. Adapted from a story by Shi Tiesheng. In Chinese with English subtitles. 110m/C **VHS.** **CH** **D:** Chen Kaige; **C:** Gu Changwei. **FCT, KIV**

Life 101 🎬🎬½ 1995 Innocent freshman Haim tries to adjust to college life in the '60s, aided by his hippie roommate Coogan, who introduces Haim to the pleasures of life. Innocuous coming-of-age comedy. 95m/C **VHS.** Corey Haim, Keith Coogan, Ami Dolenz; **D:** Redge Mahaffey; **W:** Redge Mahaffey. **MNC**

Life Stinks 🎬 1991 (PG-13) So does the film. A grasping tycoon bets he can spend a month living on the street without money, resulting in cheap laughs, heavy-handed sentiment and one musical number. Those expecting the innovative, hilarious Brooks of "Young Frankenstein" or "Blazing Saddles" will be very disappointed—these jokes are stale and the timing is tedious. Those looking for a Chaplinesque tale for modern times should stick with Chaplin. 93m/C **VHS, Beta, LV, Closed Caption.** Mel Brooks, Jeffrey Tambor, Lesley Ann Warren, Stuart Pankin, Howard Morris, Teddy Wilson, Michael Ensign, Billy Barty, Carmine Caridi, Rudy DeLuca; **D:** Mel Brooks, Rudy DeLuca; **C:** Steven Poster. **MGM**

Life Upside Down 🎬🎬 La Vie a L'Envers 1964 Ordinary Paris worker (Denner) decides to withdraw from his seemingly perfect life, including his wife and friends. He ends staring at a blank wall in a mental institution. French with subtitles. 115m/B **VHS.** **FR** Charles Denner, Anna Gaylor, Jean Yanne; **D:** Alain Jessua; **W:** Alain Jessua; **C:** Jacques Robin; **M:** Jacques Loussier. **CVC**

Life with Father 🎬🎬🎬½ 1947 Based on the writings of the late Clarence Day, Jr., this is the story of his childhood in New York City during the 1880s. A delightful saga about a stern but loving father and his relationship with his knowing wife and four red-headed sons. 118m/C **VHS, Beta.** William Powell, Irene Dunne, Elizabeth Taylor, Edmund Gwenn, ZaSu Pitts, Jimmy Lydon, Martin Milner; **D:** Michael Curtiz; **M:** Max Steiner. Golden Globe Awards '48: Best Score; New York Film Critics Awards '47: Best Actor (Powell); Nominations: Academy Awards '47: Best Actor (Powell), Best Art Direction/Set Decoration (Color), Best Color Cinematography, Best Original Dramatic/Comedy Score. **CNG, MRV, NOS**

Life with Mikey 🎬🎬½ 1993 (PG-13) Michael "Mikey" Chapman (Fox) is a washed-up former child star who now half-heartedly runs a minor talent agency for other pint-sized would-be thespians. Ever mindful of his previous glory, he believes he is doomed to obscurity when a 10-year-old Brooklyn pickpocket reanimates his taste for life. Light, sweet comedy is generally predictable, a typical Fox effort. Unbilled cameo from Reuben Blades as Vidal's father. **CW:** Language and thematic elements. 92m/C **VHS, Beta, LV, Letterbox, Closed Caption.** Michael J. Fox, Christina Vi-

dal, Cyndi Lauper, Nathan Lane, David Huddleston, Victor Garber, David Krumholtz, Tony Hendra; **Cameos:** Ruben Blades; **D:** James Lapine; **W:** Marc Lawrence; **M:** Alan Menken. **TOU, BTV**

Lifeboat 🎬🎬🎬½ 1944 When a German U-boat sinks a freighter during WWII, the eight survivors seek refuge in a tiny lifeboat. Tension peaks after the drifting passengers take in a stranded Nazi. Hitchcock saw a great challenge in having the entire story take place in a lifeboat and pulled it off with his usual flourish. In 1989, the film "Dead Calm" replicated the technique. From a story by John Steinbeck. Bankhead shines. 96m/B **VHS, Beta, LV, Closed Caption.** Tallulah Bankhead, John Hodiak, William Bendix, Canada Lee, Walter Slezak, Hume Cronyn, Henry Hull, Mary Anderson; **D:** Alfred Hitchcock. New York Film Critics Awards '44: Best Actress (Bankhead); Nominations: Academy Awards '44: Best Black and White Cinematography, Best Director (Hitchcock), Best Story. **HMV, FOX**

Lifeforce 🎬🎬½ 1985 (R) A beautiful female vampire from outer space drains Londoners and before long the city is filled with disintegrating zombies in this hi-tech thriller. Sex was never stranger. Screenwriters O'Bannon and Jakoby adapted the story from Colin Wilson's novel, "The Space Vampires." 100m/C **VHS, Beta, LV.** Steve Railsback, Peter Firth, Frank Finlay, Patrick Stewart, Michael Gothard, Nicholas Ball, Aubrey Morris, Nancy Paul, Mathilda May, John Hallam; **D:** Tobe Hooper; **W:** Dan O'Bannon, Don Jakoby; **C:** Alan Hume; **M:** Henry Mancini, Michael Kamen. **MGM**

Lifeform 🎬½ 1996 (R) Human beings may believe they're tops in the universe but when a Viking spaceship suddenly returns to Earth from a mission to Mars, NASA scientists discover a lifeform that thinks differently. **CW:** Language, violence. 90m/C **VHS, Closed Caption.** Cotter Smith, Deirdre O'Connell, Ryan Phillippe, Raoul O'Connell, Leland Orser; **D:** Mark H. Baker; **W:** Mark H. Baker; **C:** James Glennon; **M:** Kevin Kiner. **ART**

Lifeguard 🎬🎬 1975 (PG) The lifeguard lives by the credo that work is for people who cannot surf. Aging, he questions whether he should give up the beach life and start selling Porsches. Made for television. 96m/C **VHS, Beta.** Sam Elliott, Anne Archer, Stephen Young, Parker Stevenson, Kathleen Quinlan; **D:** Daniel Petrie. **PAR**

Lifepod 🎬 1980 A group of intergalactic travelers is forced to evacuate a luxury space liner when a mad computer sabotages the ship. 94m/C **VHS, Beta.** Joe Penny, Jordan Michaels, Kristine DeBell. **VCI**

Lifepod 🎬🎬½ 1993 Trapped on a ship with a killer—only this time it's a space ship. In the year 2169 an interplanetary liner is sabotaged. Nine people escape in a damaged lifepod emergency craft. The survivors are perilously short of food and water and cannot contact Earth. They also face frightening evidence that the terrorist is among their group and is determined to kill the remaining survivors. Very loose adaptation of Alfred Hitchcock's 1944 film "Lifeboat." Made for television. 120m/C **VHS, LV.** Ron Silver, Robert Loggia, CCH Pounder, Stan Shaw, Adam Storke, Jessica Tuck, Kelli Williams, Ed Gate; **D:** Ron Silver; **W:** M. Jay Roach, Pen Densham. **CAF**

Lifespan 🎬 1975 A young American scientist visiting Amsterdam discovers experiments involving a drug that halts aging. 85m/C **VHS, Beta.** **GB** Klaus Kinski, Hiram Keller, Tina Aumont; **D:** Alexander Whitelaw. **VES**

The Lifetaker woof! 1989 A woman lures an unsuspecting young man into her home where she seduces him. Violence and sex ensue. 97m/C **VHS.** Lea Dregorn, Peter Duncan, Terence Morgan; **D:** Michael Papas. **NO**

The Lift 🎬 1985 (R) Unsuspecting passengers meet an unfortunate fate when they take a ride in a demonic elevator in a highrise. In this film the last stop isn't ladies' lingerie, but death. In Dutch with English subtitles. 95m/C **VHS, Beta, LV.** **NL** Huub Stapel, Willeke Van Ammelrooy; **D:** Dick Maas.

The Light Ahead ♂♂½ 1939 Lovers Fishke and Hodel dream of escaping the poverty and prejudices of their shtetl for the possibilities of big city life in Odessa. They're aided in their quest by enlightened bookseller Mendele who turns the town's superstitions to their advantage. Based on the stories of social satirist Mendele Mokher Seforim. In Yiddish with English subtitles. **94m/b VHS.** David Opatoshu, Isadore Cashier, Helen Beverly; **D:** Edgar G. Ulmer. *NCJ, ERG*

Light at the Edge of the World ♂♂ 1971 (PG) A band of pirates torments a lighthouse keeper near Cape Horn after he sees a shipwreck they caused. **126m/C VHS, Beta.** Kirk Douglas, Yul Brynner, Samantha Eggar; **D:** Kevin Billington.

The Light in the Forest ♂♂½ 1958 Disney adaptation of the classic Conrad Richter novel about a young man, kidnapped by Indians when he was young, who is forcibly returned to his white family. **92m/C VHS, Beta.** James MacArthur, Fess Parker, Carol Lynley, Wendell Corey, Joanne Dru, Jessica Tandy, Joseph Calleia, John McIntire; **D:** Herschel Daugherty; **C:** Ellsworth Fredericks. *DIS*

The Light in the Jungle ♂♂½ 1991 (PG) The biography of Nobel Peace Prize winner Dr. Albert Schweitzer. He established a hospital in Africa and had to overcome many obstacles, including tribal superstitions and European bureaucracy to make it successful and bring health care to the area. **91m/C VHS, LV.** Malcolm McDowell, Susan Strasberg, Andrew Davis; **D:** Gray Hofmeyr. *ART*

Light of Day ♂♂ 1987 (PG-13) A rock 'n' roll semi-musical about a working-class brother and sister who escape from their parents and aimless lives through their bar band. Script tends to fall flat, although both Fox and Jett are believable. Title song written by Bruce Springsteen. **107m/C VHS, Beta, LV.** Michael J. Fox, Joan Jett, Gena Rowlands, Jason Miller, Michael McKean, Michael Rooker, Michael Dolan; **D:** Paul Schrader; **W:** Paul Schrader; **C:** John Bailey; **M:** Thomas Newman. *ART, VES*

The Light of Faith ♂ 1922 A sick young woman is cured when she touches the Holy Grail, which a man stole from her former lover in order to help her. Silent. **33m/C VHS, Beta.** Lon Chaney Sr., Hope Hampton; **D:** Clarence Brown. *SNC, BFA, CNM*

The Light of Western Stars ♂♂½ 1930 Brian plays a young woman from the east who comes to claim her late brother's ranch. She meets her murdered brother's best friend (Arlen) who is a drunken cowboy, and he falls madly in love with her. Wanting to impress her, he quickly sobers up and prevents a gang from taking over the ranch. This was Paramount's first talking adaptation of a Grey novel and the third version of this particular Grey novel; silent versions were made in 1918 and 1925. **70m/B VHS.** Richard Arlen, Mary Brian, Regis Toomey, Harry Green, Syd Saylor, George Chandler; **D:** Otto Brower, Edwin H. Knopf. *GPV*

The Light of Western Stars ♂ 1940 A proper Eastern woman goes West and falls in love with a drunken lout. **67m/B VHS.** Victor Jory, Jo Ann Sayers, Russell Hayden, Morris Ankrum; **D:** Lesley Selander. *GPV, DVT, NOS*

Light Sleeper ♂♂ 1992 (R) Schrader's moody look at upscale drug dealers in New York. Dafoe is John LaTour, a 40 year-old drug courier to the club scene. Since his boss (Sarandon) is giving up the drug business for the safer world of natural cosmetics, John must look to his own future. His life becomes even more complicated when he runs into a bitter ex-flame (Delany) and finds the attraction is still overpowering. Cynical, contemplative, and menacing.**CW:** Strong language, violence and drug content, and one sensual scene. **103m/C VHS, LV.** Willem Dafoe, Susan Sarandon, Dana Delany, David Clennon, Mary Beth Hurt; **D:** Paul Schrader; **W:** Paul Schrader; **M:** Michael Been. *ART*

Light Years ♂♂½ 1988 (PG) Garish animated fantasy epic about an idyllic land suddenly beset by evil mutations and death rays. Based on the novel "Robots Against Gondohar" by Jean-Pierre Andrevan. **83m/C VHS, Beta, LV.** **D:** Harvey Weinstein; **W:** Isaac Asimov, Raphael Cluzel; **M:** Gabriel Yared; **V:** Glenn Close, Jennifer Grey, Christopher Plummer, Penn Jillette, John Shea, David Johansen, Bridget Fonda, Paul Shaffer, Terrence Mann, Teller. *THV, FUS*

Lightblast ♂ 1985 A San Francisco policeman tries to stop a deadly explosive-wielding mad scientist from blowing the city to kingdom come. **89m/C VHS, Beta.** Erik Estrada, Michael Pritchard; **D:** Enzo G. Castellari. *ART*

The Lighthorsemen ♂♂♂ 1987 (PG-13) Compelling WWI drama follows several battle-hardened men of the Australian Light-Horse mounted infantry stationed in the Middle Eastern desert and the new recruit who joins their ranks and craves acceptance. Superbly filmed, particularly the final battle scene which pits the Aussies against the Turks for control of the wells at Beersheba. Fine performance by Andrews in this epic which contains the essential elements of a good war movie—horses, guns, and more horses. Originally filmed at 140 minutes. Good companion film for another Aussie WWI saga: "Gallipoli." **110m/C VHS, Beta, Closed Caption.** AU Jon Blake, Peter Phelps, Tony Bonner, Bill Kerr, Nick Wateres, John Walton, Tim McKenzie, Sigrid Thornton, Anthony Andrews; **D:** Simon Wincer; **W:** Ian Jones; **M:** Mario Millo. *WAR*

Lightnin' Carson Rides Again ♂½ 1938 A tough frontier lawman tracks down his payroll-carrying nephew who's been accused of murder and thievery. **58m/B VHS, Beta, 8mm.** Tim McCoy, Joan Barclay, Ted Adams, Forrest Taylor; **D:** Sam Newfield. *NOS, VYY*

Lightning Bill ♂ 1935 Bill champions good in battling rustlers. **46m/B VHS, Beta, LV.** Buffalo Bill Jr. *NO*

Lightning Bill Crandall ♂½ 1937 Gunman heads south for the quiet life. Unfortunately, Arizona proves the scene of a fierce battle between various factions of cattlemen. The gunman aids the good guys, and tries to win the daughter's heart. **60m/B VHS.** Bob Steele, Lois January, Charles "Blackie" King, Frank LaRue, Ernie Adams, Earl Dwire, Dave O'Brien; **D:** Sam Newfield. *NOS, DVT*

Lightning Bolt ♂ *Operazione Goldman* 1967 Someone is stealing moon rockets from Cape Kennedy, and secret agent Harry Sennet must find out who is doing this devilish deed. It leads him to an evil madman who plots to destroy the world from his underwater hideout. Cheap and unintentionally funny. **96m/C VHS.** IT SP Anthony Eisley, Wandisa Leigh, Folco Lulli, Diana Lorys, Ursula Parker; **D:** Anthony (Antonio Margheriti) Dawson. *SNC*

The Lightning Incident ♂ 1991 (R) McKeon plays a young Santa Fe sculptor whose worst nightmares come true when her baby is kidnapped by a devil-worshipping cult. Discovering she has a powerful psychic gift, she pursues the kidnappers across the country in a race to save her baby. Almost as bad as it sounds.**CW:** Terror violence. **90m/C VHS, Beta, Closed Caption.** Nancy McKeon, Polly Bergen, Tantoo Cardinal, Elpidia Carrillo, Tim Ryan; **D:** Michael Switzer; **W:** Michael J. Murray. *PAR*

Lightning Jack ♂½ 1994 (PG-13) Western comedy about Lightning Jack Kane (Hogan), an aging second-rate outlaw who desperately wants to become a western legend. Mute store clerk Ben (Gooding) winds up as his partner in crime, while barely eluding criticisms of Stepin Fetchitism. Cliches galore, the running gags (including Kane's surreptitious use of his eyeglasses so he can see his shooting targets) fall flat.**CW:** Sexual content. **93m/C VHS, LV.** Paul Hogan, Cuba Gooding Jr., Beverly D'Angelo, Kamala Dawson, Pat Hingle, Richard Riehle, Frank McRae, Roger Daltrey, L.Q. Jones, Max Cullen; **D:** Simon Wincer; **W:** Paul Hogan; **C:** David Eggby; **M:** Bruce Rowland. *HBO*

Lightning Over Water 1980 An odd, touching documentary co-arranged by Ray and Wenders, all about Ray's last months dying of cancer in his New York loft, and his editing of his final film "We Can't Go Home Again," his film corpus and career in general. **91m/C VHS, Beta, LV.** Nicholas Ray, Wim Wenders, Ronee Blakley, Tom Farrel, Gerry Bamman; **D:** Wim Wenders; **W:** Wim Wenders; **M:** Ronee Blakley. *IME*

Lightning Raiders ♂♂ 1945 When a stage coach filled with mail gets robbed, Billy Carson (Crabbe) and Fuzzy (St. John) set off to avenge the postal system. One of the last Crabbe/St. John efforts; perhaps they should have called it quits a few films earlier. **61m/C VHS.** Buster Crabbe, Al "Fuzzy" St. John, Mady Lawrence, Henry Hall, Steve Darrell, I. Stanford Jolley, Karl Hackett, Roy Brent, Marin Sais, Al Ferguson; **D:** Sam Newfield; **W:** Elmer Clifton. *HEG*

Lightning Range ♂ 1933 Roosevelt stars as a U.S. Deputy Marshal who continually foils the nefarious plots of a gang of outlaws. **50m/B VHS, Beta.** Buddy Roosevelt, Lafe McKee. *NOS, VYY*

Lightning Strikes West ♂½ 1940 U.S. Marshal trails an escaped convict, eventually catches him, and brings him in to finish paying his debt to society. **57m/B VHS, Beta.** Ken Maynard. *VCN, VCI*

Lightning: The White Stallion ♂½ 1986 (PG) An old gambler and his two young friends enter a horse race in order to win their beloved white stallion back from thieves. **93m/C VHS, Beta, Closed Caption.** Mickey Rooney, Susan George, Isabel Lorca; **D:** William A. Levey.

Lightning Warrior 1931 Western suspense about pioneer life and the unraveling of a baffling mystery. Twelve chapters, 13 minutes each. **156m/B VHS, Beta.** George Brent, Frankie Darro; **D:** Armand Schaefer, Ben Kline. *VCN*

Lights! Camera! Murder! ♂♂ 1989 When a 12-year-old boy witnesses a filmed murder, he becomes the next target. **89m/C VHS.** John Barrett; **D:** Frans Nel. *ATL*

Lights of Old Santa Fe ♂½ 1947 A cowboy rescues a beautiful rodeo owner from bankruptcy. The original, unedited version of the film. **78m/B VHS, Beta.** Roy Rogers, Dale Evans, George "Gabby" Hayes, Bob Nolan, The Pioneers. *NOS, DVT, TIM*

The Lightship ♂♂ 1986 (PG-13) On a stationary lightship off the Carolina coast, the crew rescues three men from a disabled boat, only to find they are murderous criminals. Duvall as a flamboyant homosexual psychopath is memorable, but the tale is pretentious, overdone, and hackneyed. Based on Siegfried Lenz's story. **87m/C VHS, Beta, Closed Caption.** Robert Duvall, Klaus Maria Brandauer, Tom Bower, William Forsythe, Arliss Howard; **D:** Jerzy Skolimowski. *FOX*

Like Father, Like Son ♂ 1987 (PG-13) First and worst of a barrage of interchangeable switcheroo movies that came out in '87-'88. Moore is in top form, but the plot is contrived. **101m/C VHS, Beta, LV.** Dudley Moore, Kirk Cameron, Catherine Hicks, Margaret Colin, Sean Astin; **D:** Rod Daniel; **W:** Steven L. Bloom, Lorne Cameron; **M:** Miles Goodman. *COL*

Like It Never Was Before ♂♂ *Pensionat Oskar* 1995 Conventional, middleaged marrieds Rune (Falkman) and Gunnel (Ekblad) Runeberg travel to a seaside hotel for their annual vacation with their three children. Ordinary family man Rune, though dissatisfied, is expecting little until he meets, and falls in love with, young handyman Petrus (Norrthon), and suddenly decides to break free. Swedish with subtitles. **108m/B VHS.** SW Loa Falkman, Stina Ekblad, Simon Norrthon, Philip Zanden, Sif Ruud, Ghita Norby; **D:** Suzanne Bier; **W:** Jonas Gardell; **C:** Kjell Lagerros; **M:** Johan Soderqvist. *CCN*

Like Water for Chocolate ♂♂♂½ *Como Agua para Chocolate* 1993 (R) Magical Mexican fairytale set in the early 1900s about family, love, and the power of food. Formidable Mama Elena is left a widow with three daughters. The youngest, Tita grows up in the kitchen surrounded by all the magic Nacha, the housekeeper, can impart to her about food. Doomed by tradition to spend her days caring for her mother, Tita escapes by cooking, releasing her sorrows and longings into the food, infecting all who eat it. Wonderfully sensuous and slyly exaggerated. Based on the novel by Esquivel who also wrote the screenplay and whose husband, Arau, directed. In Spanish with English subtitles; also available dubbed. **CW:** Sexuality. 105m/C VHS, LV. *MX* Lumi Cavazos, Marco Leonardi, Regina Torne, Mario Ivan Martinez, Ada Carrasco, Yareli Arizmendi, Claudette Maille, Pilar Aranda; **D:** Alfonso Arau; **W:** Laura Esquivel; **C:** Steven Bernstein; **M:** Leo Brower. Nominations: British Academy Awards '93: Best Foreign Film; Independent Spirit Awards '94: Best Foreign Film. TOU

Li'l Abner 🐾½ *Trouble Chaser* **1940** Al Capp's famed comic strip comes somewhat to life in this low-budget comedy featuring all of the Dogpatch favorites. 78m/C VHS, Beta. Cranville Owen, Martha Driscoll, Buster Keaton; **D:** Albert Rogell. NOS, MRV, DVT

Li'l Abner 🐾🐾½ **1959** High color Dogpatch drama adapted from the Broadway play (with most of the original cast) based on the Al Capp comic strip. When Abner's berg is considered as a site for atomic bomb testing, the natives have to come up with a reason why they should be allowed to exist. Choreography by Michael Kidd and Dee Dee Wood. ♫Jubilation T. Cornpone; Don't Take That Rag Off'n the Bush; A Typical Day; If I Had My Druthers; Room Enuff for Us; Namely You; The Country's in the Very Best of Hands; Unnecessary Town; I'm Past My Prime. 114m/C VHS, Beta, Closed Caption. Peter Palmer, Leslie Parrish, Stubby Kaye, Julie Newmar, Howard St. John, Stella Stevens, Billie Hayes, Joe E. Marks; **D:** Melvin Frank; **W:** Norman Panama; **C:** Daniel F. Fapp; **M:** Johnny Mercer, Jean De Paul. Nominations: Academy Awards '59: Scoring of a Musical. PAR, FCT

Lili 🐾🐾🐾 **1953** Delightful musical romance about a 16-year-old orphan who joins a traveling carnival and falls in love with a crippled, embittered puppeteer. Heartwarming and charming, if occasionally cloying. Leslie Caron sings the film's song hit, "Hi-Lili, Hi-Lo." 81m/C VHS, Beta, Closed Caption. Leslie Caron, Jean-Pierre Aumont, Mel Ferrer, Kurt Kasznar, Zsa Zsa Gabor; **D:** Charles Walters; **M:** Bronislau Kaper. Academy Awards '53: Best Original Dramatic/Comedy Score; British Academy Awards '53: Best Actress (Caron); Golden Globe Awards '54: Best Screenplay; Nominations: Academy Awards '53: Best Actress (Caron), Best Art Direction/Set Decoration (Color), Best Color Cinematography, Best Director (Walters), Best Screenplay. MGM

Lilian's Story 🐾🐾½ **1995** Aging Lilian (Cracknell) has just been released after spending 40 years in a mental institution, placed there as an adolescent by her controlling, possessive father. The haunted Lilian is given a room at a residential hotel in Sydney's red-light district where the local prostitutes look out for her and she spends her days wandering the streets. Flashbacks reveal what lead the high-strung young Lilian (Collette) to her incarceration. Based on Kate Greville's 1984 novel, which was a fictional account of real-life Sydney eccentric Bea Miles. 94m/C VHS. *AU* Ruth Cracknell, Barry Otto, Toni Collette, John Flaus, Essie Davis, Susie Lindemann, Anne Louise Lambert, Iris Shand; **D:** Jerzy Domaradzki; **W:** Steve Wright; **C:** Slawomir Idziak; **M:** Cezary Skubiszewski. Australian Film Institute '95: Best Supporting Actress (Collette). NYR

Lilies 🐾🐾 *Les Feluettes* **1996** Strange revenge fantasy set in a northern Quebec men's prison in 1952. A bishop (Sabourin) goes to the prison to hear the confession of a dying convict and is taken hostage in the chapel by the prison's homosexual population. There, he's forced to watch a play that recreates a 40-year-old incident in his own life. As the prison walls fade away, the actor/prisoners turn into students Simon (Cadieux) and Vallier (Gilmore), who take the lovers' roles in a

pageant about the martyrdom of St. Sebastien too seriously for comfort. The female roles in the flashbacks (which include Vallier's crazy mother and Simon's would-be fiance) are played by men. Adapted from Bouchard's play "Les Feluettes out La Repetition d'un Drame Romantique." 95m/C VHS. *CA* Marcel Sabourin, Jason Cadieux, Danny Gilmore, Brent Carver, Matthew Ferguson, Alexander Chapman, Aubert Pallascio; **D:** John Greyson; **W:** Michel Marc Bouchard; **C:** Daniel Jobin; **M:** Mychael Danna. Genie Awards '96: Best Art Direction/Set Decoration, Best Costume Design, Best Film, Best Sound; Nominations: Genie Awards '96: Best Actor (Cadieux), Best Actor (Ferguson, Gilmore), Best Adapted Screenplay, Best Cinematography, Best Director (Greyson), Best Film Editing, Best Supporting Actor (Chapman), Best Score. NYR

Lilies of the Field 🐾🐾🐾 **1963** Five East German nuns enlist the aid of a free-spirited U.S. Army veteran. They persuade him to build a chapel for them and teach them English. Poitier is excellent as the itinerant laborer, holding the saccharine to an acceptable level, bringing honesty and strength to his role. Actress Skala had been struggling to make ends meet in a variety of day jobs until this opportunity. Poitier was the first African-American man to win an Oscar, and the first African-American nominated since Hattie MacDaniel in 1939. Followed by "Christmas Lilies of the Field," (1979). 94m/B VHS, Beta, Closed Caption. Sidney Poitier, Lilia Skala, Lisa Mann, Isa Crino, Stanley Adams; **D:** Ralph Nelson; **M:** Jerry Goldsmith. Academy Awards '63: Best Actor (Poitier); Berlin International Film Festival '63: Best Actor (Poitier); Golden Globe Awards '64: Best Actor—Drama (Poitier); Nominations: Academy Awards '63: Best Adapted Screenplay, Best Black and White Cinematography, Best Picture, Best Supporting Actress (Skala). MGM, FOX, BTV

Liliom 🐾🐾🐾 **1935** Boyer goes to heaven and is put on trial to see if he is deserving of his wings. Lang's first film after leaving Nazi Germany is filled with wonderful ethereal imagery, surprising coming from the man responsible for such grim visions as "Metropolis." In French only. 85m/B VHS, Beta. *FR* Charles Boyer, Madeleine Ozeray, Florelle, Roland Toutain; **D:** Fritz Lang. SNC, DVT, HEG

Lilith 🐾🐾🐾 **1964** Therapist-in-training Beatty falls in love with beautiful mental patient Seberg and approaches madness himself. A look at the doctor-patient relationship among the mentally ill and at the nature of madness and love. Doesn't always satisfy, but intrigues. Rossen's swan song. 114m/B VHS, Beta. Warren Beatty, Jean Seberg, Peter Fonda, Gene Hackman, Kim Hunter; **D:** Robert Rossen; **C:** Eugene (Eugen Shufftan) Shuftan. COL, MLB

Lillie 🐾🐾🐾 **1979** The life of Edwardian beauty Lillie Langtry, known as "The Jersey Lily," is portrayed in this British made-for-television drama. Defying the morals of the times, Lillie was the first publicly acknowledged mistress of the Prince of Wales, only one of her numerous lovers. On seven cassettes. Shown on "Masterpiece Theatre" on PBS. 690m/C VHS. *GB* Francesca Annis, Cheryl Campbell, John Castle, Dennis Lill, Peter Egan, Anton Rodgers, Ann Firbank. SIG, TVC, HMV

Lily Dale 🐾🐾½ **1996 (PG)** Nineteen-year-old Horace Robedaux (Guinee) is in Houston to visit his estranged mother Corella (Channing) and sister Lily Dale (Masterson) while his taciturn stepfather Pete Davenport (Shepard) is supposed to be away. Pete dislikes Horace and left the boy behind with relatives when he married Corella and they moved away. Self-centered Lily Dale resents Horace taking away attention from herself and matters only get worse when Pete comes home early and Horace becomes so ill that he can't leave. Set in 1910; Foote wrote the play as a memoir to his father, Horace. Made for TV. 95m/C VHS. Tim Guinee, Stockard Channing, Mary Stuart Masterson, Sam Shepard, John Slattery, Jean Stapleton; **D:** Peter Masterson; **W:** Horton Foote; **C:** Don E. Fauntleroy; **M:** Peter Melnick. HMK

Lily in Love 🐾🐾½ *Playing for Keeps; Jatszani Kell* **1985 (PG-13)** An aging stage star disguises himself as a suave Italian to star in his playwright wife's new play, and woos her to test her fidelity. Charming, warm, and sophisticated. Loosely based on Molnar's "The Guardsman." Made for television. 100m/C VHS, Beta, LV. *HU* Maggie Smith, Christopher Plummer, Elke Sommer, Adolph Green; **D:** Karoly Makk; **W:** Frank Cucci. ART, VES

Lily in Winter 🐾🐾½ **1994 (PG)** Christmas story about families and the ties that bind, set in 1957. Black nanny Lily (Cole in her film debut) works for busy showbiz New Yorkers, the Towlers (Hoffmann and Brown), looking after their neglected 10-year-old son Michael (Bonsall). But Lily thinks she's in trouble, thanks to her no-account brother Booker (Russell), and takes off to her rural Alabama roots without realizing Michael has followed her. His parents, however, think Lily has kidnapped him. Made for cable TV. 120m/C VHS. Natalie Cole, Brian Bonsall, Dwier Brown, Cecil Hoffmann, Marla Gibbs, Monte Russell, Rae'ven Kelly, Salli Richardson, James Pickens Jr., Matthew Faison; **D:** Delbert Mann; **W:** Robert Eisele; **C:** Charles Mills; **M:** David Shire. USH

Lily of Killarney 🐾🐾 *The Bride of the Lake* **1934** A musical comedy romance about a British lord who arranges to pay his debts via horseraces, arranged marriages and inheritances. 82m/B VHS, Beta, 8mm. *GB* Gina Malo, John Garrick, Stanley Holloway; **D:** Maurice Elvey. VYY

Lily Was Here 🐾½ **1989 (R)** After her fiancee is senselessly murdered, a young woman named Lily is forced to turn to a life of crime in order to survive. A series of petty thefts evolves into a huge crime wave and Lily soon finds herself the object of a massive manhunt. Lily must make the ultimate choice between freedom and motherhood in this shocking thriller. Soundtrack by Dave Stewart features hit instrumental theme "Lily was Here" by saxophonist Candy Dulfur. **CW:** Strong language and some sexuality. 110m/C VHS. Marion Van Thijn, Thom Hoffman, Adrian Brine, Dennis Rudge; **D:** Ben Verbong; **W:** Ben Verbong, Sytze Van Der Laan, Willem Jan Otten. NO

The Limbic Region 🐾🐾 **1996** Terminally ill police detective Jon Lucca (Olmos) has spent 20 years tracking a serial killer known as "The Scorekeeper," who likes to shotgun the young inhabitants of smalltown lovers' lanes. His most likely suspect is Lloyd Warden (Dzundza) and the duo engage in a deadly cat-and-mouse battle that may destroy them both. Made for cable. 96m/C VHS, Closed Caption. Edward James Olmos, George Dzundza, Gwynyth Walsh; **D:** Michael Pattinson; **W:** Patrick Ranahan, Todd Johnson; **C:** Tobias Schliessler. MGM

Limelight 🐾🐾🐾 **1952** A nearly washed-up music hall comedian is stimulated by a young ballerina to a final hour of glory. A subtle if self-indulgent portrait of Chaplin's own life, featuring an historic pairing of Chaplin and Keaton. 120m/B VHS, Beta, LV. Charlie Chaplin, Claire Bloom, Buster Keaton, Nigel Bruce, Sydney Chaplin; **D:** Charlie Chaplin; **C:** Karl Struss. FOX

Limit Up 🐾🐾 **1989 (PG-13)** An ambitious Chicago Trade Exchange employee makes a deal with the devil to corner the market in soybeans. Turgid attempt at supernatural comedy, featuring Charles as God. Catch Sally Kellerman in a cameo as a nightclub singer. 88m/C VHS, Beta, LV, Closed Caption. Nancy Allen, Dean Stockwell, Brad Hall, Danitra Vance, Ray Charles, Luana Anders; **Cameos:** Sally Kellerman; **D:** Richard Martini; **C:** Peter Collister. NO

The Limping Man 🐾🐾 **1953** Bridges returns to post-WWII London to renew a wartime romance. On the way, he gets caught up in solving a murder. Unexceptional of-its-era thriller. 76m/B VHS, Beta. *GB* Lloyd Bridges, Moira Lister, Leslie Phillips, Helene Cordet, Alan Wheatley; **D:** Charles De Latour. SNC, RXM, VYY

Linda 🎬🎬½ **1929** Linda, a young mountain girl, is forced to marry a much older man though her heart belongs to a young doctor. Her kind husband tries to make the best of the situation. **75m/B VHS.** Helen Foster, Warner Baxter, Noah Beery Sr., Mitchell Lewis, Kate Price, Alan Connor; **D:** Dorothy Davenport Reid. *GPV, FCT*

Linda **1993 (PG-13)** Madsen in her femme fatale mode as treacherous wife Linda who wants to frame her schlump husband (Thomas) for murder. Whose murder? Why the inconvenient wife (Harrington) of her boyfriend (McGinley). The two homicidal lovebirds want to take the insurance money and run—leaving hubby to face the consequences. Based on the novella "Linda" by John D. MacDonald. **88m/C VHS, Beta, Closed Caption.** Virginia Madsen, Richard Thomas, Ted McGinley, Laura Harrington; **D:** Nathaniel Gutman; **W:** Nevin Schreiner; **M:** David Michael Frank. *PAR*

The Lindbergh Kidnapping Case 🎬🎬🎬 **1976** The famous Lindbergh baby kidnapping in 1932 and the trial and execution of Bruno Hauptmann, convincingly portrayed by Hopkins. DeYoung as Lindbergh is blah, but the script is quite good. Made for TV. **150m/C VHS, Beta.** Anthony Hopkins, Joseph Cotten, Cliff DeYoung, Walter Pidgeon, Dean Jagger, Martin Balsam, Laurence Luckinbill, Tony Roberts; **D:** Buzz Kulik; **M:** Billy Goldenberg. *COL*

The Line 🎬½ **1980 (R)** Not-so-hot anti-war drama about a sit-down strike at a military installation by Vietnam veteran prison inmates. Leans heavily on recycled footage from director Siegel's own "Parade" (1971). **94m/C VHS, Beta.** Russ Thacker, David Doyle, Erik Estrada; **D:** Robert Siegel. *NO*

The Linguini Incident 🎬🎬 **1992 (R)** An inept escape artist, a pathological liar, a lingerie designer, a deaf restaurant hostess who throws out one-liners in sign language, and two sinister, yet chic, restaurant owners get together in this marginal comedy about magic and adventure. **99m/C VHS, LV, Closed Caption.** Rosanna Arquette, David Bowie, Eszter Balint, Andre Gregory, Buck Henry, Viveca Lindfors, Marlee Matlin, Lewis Arquette; **Cameos:** Julian Lennon, Iman; **D:** Richard Shepard; **W:** Richard Shepard, Tamar Brott; **M:** Thomas Newman. *IME*

Link woof! **1986 (R)** A primatologist and his nubile assistant find their experiment has gone—you guessed it—amry, and their hairy charges are running—yep, that's right—amok. Run for your life! **103m/C VHS, Beta, Closed Caption.** *GB* Elisabeth Shue, Terence Stamp, Steven Pinner, Richard Garnett; **D:** Richard Franklin; **W:** Everett DeRoche; **C:** Mike Molloy; **M:** Jerry Goldsmith. *REP*

The Lion Has Wings 🎬🎬½ **1940** The story of how Britain's Air Defense was set up to meet the challenge of Hitler's Luftwaffe during their "finest hour." Dated, now-quaint but stirring wartime period piece. "Docudrama" style was original at the time. **75m/B VHS, Beta, LV.** Merle Oberon, Ralph Richardson, Flora Robson, June Duprez; **D:** Michael Powell, Brian Desmond Hurst; **C:** Harry Stradling. *RXM*

The Lion in Winter 🎬🎬🎬🎬 **1968 (PG)** Medieval monarch Henry II and his wife, Eleanor of Aquitaine, match wits over the succession to the English throne and much else in this fast-paced film version of James Goldman's play. The family, including three grown sons, and visiting royalty are united for the Christmas holidays fraught with tension, rapidly shifting allegiances, and layers of psychological manipulation. Superb dialogue and perfectly realized characterizations. O'Toole and Hepburn are triumphant. Screen debuts for Hopkins and Dalton. Shot on location, this literate costume drama surprised the experts with its boxoffice success. **134m/C VHS, LV.** Peter O'Toole, Katharine Hepburn, Jane Merrow, Nigel Terry, Timothy Dalton, Anthony Hopkins, John Castle, Nigel Stock; **D:** Anthony Harvey; **W:** James Goldman; **M:** John Barry. Academy Awards '68: Best Actress (Hepburn), Best Adapted Screenplay, Best Original Score; Directors Guild of America Awards '68: Best Director (Harvey); Golden Globe Awards '69: Best Actor—Drama (O'Toole), Best Film—Drama; New

York Film Critics Awards '68: Best Film; Nominations: Academy Awards '68: Best Actor (O'Toole), Best Costume Design, Best Director (Harvey), Best Picture.*COL, BTV, TVC*

A Lion Is in the Streets 🎬🎬🎬 **1953** Cagney stars as a backwoods politician in a southern state who fights on the side of the share-croppers and wins their support when he exposes the corrupt practices of a powerful businessman. On his way up the political ladder, however, Cagney betrays and exploits the very people who support him. Although this is a familiar storyline, Cagney is riveting as the corrupt politician, and Hale is wonderful as his patient wife. **88m/C VHS.** James Cagney, Barbara Hale, Anne Francis, Warner Anderson, John McIntire, Jeanne Cagney, Lon Chaney Jr., Frank McHugh, Larry Keating, Onslow Stevens; **D:** Raoul Walsh. *WAR*

The Lion King 🎬🎬🎬🎬 **1994 (G)** Highest grossing film in Disney history (likely a temporary title) is a winner for kids and their folks. Like his dad Mufasa (Jones), Lion cub Simba (Taylor) is destined to be king of the beasts, until evil uncle Scar (Irons) plots against him and makes him an outcast. Growing up in the jungles of Africa, Simba (now Broderick) learns about life and responsibility, before facing his uncle once again. Supporting characters frequently steal the show, with Sabella's Pumba the warthog and Lane's Timon the meerkat heading the procession (though Chong and Goldberg as hyenas give them a run). Disney epic features heartwarming combo of crowd-pleasing songs, a story with depth, emotion, and politically correct multiculturalism, and stunning animation. The sound quality is equally spectacular; during the two and a half-minute wildebeest stampede scene, you'll swear the animals are running amuck in the house. Thirty-second Disney animated feature is the first without human characters, the first based on an original story, and the first to use the voices of a well known, ethnically diverse cast. Scenes of violence in the animal kingdom may be too much for younger viewers. ♫Can You Feel the Love Tonight; The Circle of Life; I Just Can't Wait to Be King; Be Prepared; Hakuna Matata. **88m/C VHS, Closed Caption. D:** Rob Minkoff, Roger Allers; **W:** Jonathan Roberts, Irene Mecchi; **M:** Elton John, Hans Zimmer, Tim Rice; **V:** Matthew Broderick, Jeremy Irons, James Earl Jones, Madge Sinclair, Robert Guillaume, Jonathan Taylor Thomas, Richard "Cheech" Marin, Whoopi Goldberg, Rowan Atkinson, Nathan Lane, Ernie Sabella, Niketa Calame, Moira Kelly, Jim Cummings. Academy Awards '94: Best Song ("Can You Feel the Love Tonight"), Best Original Score; Golden Globe Awards '95: Best Film—Musical/Comedy, Best Song ("Can You Feel the Love Tonight?"), Best Score; Blockbuster Entertainment Awards '95: Family Movie, Theatrical, Best Soundtrack; Nominations: Academy Awards '94: Best Song ("Circle of Life"), Best Song ("Hakuna Matata"); Golden Globe Awards '95: Best Song ("Circle of Life"); MTV Movie Awards '95: Best Villain (Irons), Best Song ("Can You Feel the Love Tonight"). *DIS*

The Lion Man 🎬🎬 **1936** Arabian tale of a boy raised by lions. **?m/B VHS.** Jon Hall, Ted Adams. *LOO*

Lion Man 🎬 **1979** Raised by wild animals, the son of King Solomon returns to his father's kingdom and roars his way to the throne. **91m/C VHS, Beta.** Steve Arkin. *BFV*

The Lion of Africa 🎬🎬 **1987** A down-to-earth woman doctor and an abrasive diamond dealer share a truck ride across Kenya. Filmed on location in East Africa. Fine lead performances in otherwise nothing-special made-for-cable adventure. **115m/C VHS, Beta.** Brian Dennehy, Brooke Adams, Joseph Shiloah; **D:** Kevin Connor; **M:** George S. Clinton. *ORI, WAR*

Lion of the Desert 🎬🎬🎬 *Omar Mukhtar* **1981 (PG)** Bedouin horse militias face-off against Mussolini's armored terror in this epic historical drama. Omar Muktar (Quinn as the "Desert Lion") and his Libyan guerrilla patriots kept the Italian troops of Mussolini (Steiger) at bay for 20 years. Outstanding performances enhanced by the des-

ert backdrop. A British-Libyan co-production. **162m/C VHS, Beta.** *GB* Anthony Quinn, Oliver Reed, Irene Papas, Rod Steiger, Raf Vallone, John Gielgud; **D:** Moustapha Akkad; **W:** H.A.L. Craig; **C:** Jack Hildyard; **M:** Maurice Jarre. *IBT*

The Lion of Thebes 🎬🎬🎬 **1964** A muscleman unhesitatingly jumps into the thick of things when Helen of Troy is kidnapped. A superior sword and sandal entry. **?m/C VHS, Beta.** *IT* Mark Forest, Yvonne Furneaux. *SNC*

Lionheart 🎬½ **1987 (PG)** A romantic portrayal of the famous English King Richard the Lionheart's early years. Meant for kids, but no Ninja turtles herein—and this is just as silly, and slow to boot. **105m/C VHS, Beta, LV, Closed Caption.** Eric Stoltz, Talia Shire, Nicola Cowper, Dexter Fletcher, Nicholas Clay, Deborah Barrymore, Gabriel Byrne; **D:** Franklin J. Schaffner; **W:** Richard Outten; **M:** Jerry Goldsmith. *WAR*

Lionheart 🎬½ *A.W.O.L.; Wrong Bet* **1990 (R)** Van Damme deserts the foreign legion and hits the streets when he learns his brother has been hassled. Many fights ensue, until you fall asleep.*CW:* Strong language and graphically violent fight scenes. **105m/C VHS, Beta, LV, Closed Caption.** Jean-Claude Van Damme, Harrison Page, Deborah Rennard, Lisa Pelikan, Brian Thompson; **D:** Sheldon Lettich; **W:** Jean-Claude Van Damme, Sheldon Lettich. *USH*

Lion's Den 🎬½ **1936** A night club performer and a detective head west to fight crime in this film. **59m/B VHS, Beta.** Tim McCoy, Dave O'Brien. *NOS, DVT*

The Lion's Share 🎬 **1979** A gang of bank robbers have their loot stolen and go after the guy who ripped them off. **105m/C VHS, Beta.** *SP* Julio de Grazia, Luisina Brando, Fernanda Mistral, Ulises Dumont, Julio Chavez. *NO*

Lip Service 🎬🎬🎬 **1988** Satirical comedy-drama about the TV news industry. An ambitious young newscaster befriends a veteran reporter. He then manipulates his way to replace him on the reporter's morning program. Dooley as the veteran and Dunne as the upstart are fun to watch in this well-done cable rip-off of "Broadcast News." **67m/C VHS, Beta.** Griffin Dunne, Paul Dooley; **D:** William H. Macy.

Lipstick woof! **1976 (R)** Fashion model Margaux seeks revenge on the man who brutally attacked and raped her, after he preys on her kid sister (real-life sis Mariel, in her debut). Exquisitely exploitative excuse for entertainment. **90m/C VHS, Beta, LV.** Margaux Hemingway, Anne Bancroft, Perry King, Chris Sarandon, Mariel Hemingway; **D:** Lamont Johnson; **W:** David Rayfiel; **C:** Bill Butler, William A. Fraker. *PAR*

Lipstick Camera 🎬🎬 **1993 (R)** Keats wants a career in television news and seeks out a successful freelance cameraman (Wimmer) to help her out. She also asks to borrow her techno-friend Feldman's mini-camera and then goes after a story on an ex-spy and his sexy companion. Only no one expects what the camera captures. Weak plot but strong cast and high-end production.*CW:* Language, violence, and sexual situations. **93m/C VHS, LV.** Ele Keats, Brian Wimmer, Corey Feldman, Sandahl Bergman, Terry O'Quinn; **D:** Mike Bonifer; **W:** Mike Bonifer. *TRI*

Lipstick On Your Collar **1994** British TV fantasy/drama set in the stuffy confines of the British War Offices during the Suez Crisis of 1956. Two army clerks fantasize about the world outside through daydreams set to original tunes. Last series for the innovative Potter; on three cassettes. **360m/C VHS.** *GB* Ewan McGregor, Giles Thomas, Louise Germaine; **D:** Renny Rye; **W:** Dennis Potter. *TVC, NEW*

Liquid Dreams 🎬🎬 **1992 (R)** In this fast-paced, futuristic thriller, Daly goes undercover as an erotic dancer in a glitzy strip joint to try and solve her sister's murder. She finds that the owner and clientele deal not only in sexual thrills, but also in a strange brain-sucking ritual that provides the ultimate rush. Also available in an unrated

Little

version. **CW:** Language, violence and drug content, and sexuality. **92m/C VHS, Beta.** Richard Steinmetz, Candice Daly, Barry Dennen, Juan Fernandez, Tracey Walter, Frankie Thorn, Paul Bartel, Mink Stole; **D:** Mark Manos; **W:** Mark Manos, Zach Davis.

Liquid Sky 🎬🎬🎬 **1983 (R)** An androgynous bisexual model living in Manhattan is the primary attraction for a UFO, which lands atop her penthouse in search of the chemical nourishment that her sexual encounters provide. Low-budget, highly creative film may not be for everyone, but the audience for which it was made will love it. Look for Carlisle also playing a gay male. **112m/C VHS, Beta, LV.** Anne Carlisle, Paula Sheppard, Bob Brady; **D:** Slava Tsukerman; **W:** Anne Carlisle; **C:** Yuri Neyman.

Lisa 🎬 **1990 (PG-13)** A young girl develops a crush on the new guy in town and arranges a meeting with him in which she pretends to be her mother. Little does she realize he's a psychotic serial killer. Lock your doors! Don't let anyone in if they have this video! **95m/C VHS, Closed Caption.** Staci Keanan, Cheryl Ladd, D.W. Moffett, Tanya Fenmore, Jeffrey Tambor, Julie Cobb; **D:** Gary Sherman; **W:** Karen Clark. *FOX*

Lisa and the Devil woof! *The House of Exorcism; La Casa Dell'Exorcismo; The Devil and the Dead; The Devil in the House of Exorcism; El Diablo se Lleva a los Muertos; Il Diavolo e i Morti; Lisa e il Diavolo* **1975 (R)** An unfortunate outing for Savalas and Sommer, about devil worship. Poor quality leaves little room for redemption. Just like on the telly, Telly's sucking on a sucker. A shortened version of the director's original 1972 release, re-edited and with additional footage added by producer Alfred Leone. **93m/C VHS.** *IT SP* Telly Savalas, Elke Sommer, Sylva Koscina, Robert Alda, Alessio Orano, Gabriele Tinti, Eduardo Fajardo, Espartaco Santoni, Alida Valli; **D:** Mario Bava; **W:** Mario Bava, Alfred Leone; **C:** Cecilio Paniagua. *VTR*

Lisbon 🎬🎬 **1956** First film directed by Milland, shot in Portugal, details the adventures of a sea captain entangled in international espionage and crime while attempting to rescue damsel O'Hara's husband from communist doings. A familiar plot told with less-than-average panache. **90m/C VHS, Beta.** Ray Milland, Claude Rains, Maureen O'Hara, Francis Lederer, Percy Marmont; **D:** Ray Milland. *NO*

Lisbon Story 🎬🎬 **1994** Director Friedrich Monroe (Bauchau) calls his friend, sound engineer Phillip Winter (Vogler), to come to Lisbon to help him finish his film on the city. By the time Winter arrives in Portugal, Monroe has vanished, leaving the unfinished silent film behind. While waiting for his friend to return, Winter starts work, wandering through the city streets in search of inspiring sounds. English, German, and Portuguese with subtitles. **100m/C VHS, Letterbox.** *GE* Ruediger Vogler, Patrick Bauchau; **D:** Wim Wenders; **W:** Wim Wenders; **C:** Lisa Renzler. *FXL, FCT*

The List of Adrian Messenger 🎬🎬🎬 **1963** A crafty murderer resorts to a variety of disguises to eliminate potential heirs to a family fortune. Solid Huston-directed thriller with a twist: you won't recognize any of the name stars. **98m/B VHS, Beta.** Kirk Douglas, George C. Scott, Robert Mitchum, Dana Wynter, Burt Lancaster, Frank Sinatra; **D:** John Huston; **M:** Jerry Goldsmith. *USH*

Listen 🎬½ **1996 (R)** Sex and violence and a faulty cordless telephone. Krista's (Buxton) suffered a nervous breakdown after her breakup with Sarah (Langton). But now they're friends again and Krista's even encouraging Sarah's new romance with weirdo boyfriend Jake (Currie) who likes phone sex. Then there's the obscene phone caller who seems to live in Sarah's apartment building and a serial killer who preys on women. Lots of nastiness and it's easy to figure out who the real killer is. **104m/C VHS, LV.** Brooke Langton, Sarah Buxton, Gordon Currie, Andy Romano, Joel Wyner; **D:** Gavin Wilding; **W:** Jonas Quastel, Michael Bafaro; **C:** Brian Pearson; **M:** David Davidson. *ORI*

Listen, Darling 🎬🎬½ **1938** Garland is appealing in her first big screen role as Pinky Wingate, who decides to find the perfect husband for her widowed mother (Astor). Pinky and her friend Buzz (Bartholomew) manage to find Pidgeon and have him become the engaging objection of everyone's affections. ♫Zing! Went the Strings of My Heart; Ten Pins in the Sky; On the Bumpy Road to Love. **70m/C VHS.** Judy Garland, Freddie Bartholomew, Mary Astor, Walter Pidgeon, Alan Hale, Scotty Beckett; **D:** Edwin L. Marin. *MGM, FCT*

Listen to Me 🎬½ **1989 (PG-13)** A small-town college debate team heads for the big time when they go to a national debate tournament. The usual mutual-distaste-turns-to-romance thing. Cheesy-as-all-get-out climactic abortion debate, in front of supposed real-life Supreme Court justices—yeah, right. And Kirk Cameron: get an accent, will ya? **109m/C VHS, Beta, LV, Closed Caption.** Kirk Cameron, Jami Gertz, Roy Scheider, Amanda Peterson, Tim Quill, Christopher Atkins; **D:** Douglas Day Stewart; **C:** Fred W. Koenekamp; **M:** David Foster. Golden Raspberry Awards '89: Worst Supporting Actor (Atkins). *COL*

Listen to Your Heart 🎬½ **1983** Office romance in the '80s! Sounds like a mediocre, forgettable made-for-TV comedy-drama—which is exactly what it is. If Jackson was the brainy one on "Charlie's Angels," why wasn't she smart enough to avoid this one? **90m/C VHS, Beta.** Tim Matheson, Kate Jackson; **D:** Don Taylor. *FOX*

Lisztomania woof! **1975 (R)** Russell's excessive vision of what it must have been like to be classical composer/musician Franz Liszt, who is depicted as the first pop star. Rock opera in the tradition of "Tommy" with none of the sense or music. **106m/C VHS, Beta, LV, Letterbox.** *GB* Roger Daltrey, Sara Kestelman, Paul Nicholas, Fiona Lewis, Ringo Starr, Veronica Quilligan, Nell Campbell, John Justin, Andrew Reilly, Anulka Dziubinska, Rick Wakeman, Rikki Howard, Felicity Devonshire, Aubrey Morris, Kenneth Colley, Ken Parry, Otto Diamont, Murray Melvin, Andrew Faulds, Oliver Reed; **D:** Ken Russell; **W:** Ken Russell; **C:** Peter Suschitzsky; **M:** Rick Wakeman. *WAR*

The Little American 🎬🎬½ **1917** German-American Karl Von Austreim leaves behind sweetheart Angela Moore, returning to Germany to fight in WWI. Angela travels to France to care for her dying aunt and discovers her aunt's chateau has been turned into a hospital. She remains in the face of a German advance and is naturally reunited with her much-changed beau. **80m/B VHS, Beta.** Mary Pickford, Jack Holt, Raymond Hatton, Walter Long, Hobart Bosworth, Ben Alexander, DeWitt Jennings. *GPV*

Little Annie Rooney 🎬🎬 **1925** A policeman's tomboy daughter spends her time mothering her father and brother while getting into mischief with street punks. Minor melodrama. Silent. **60m/B VHS, Beta, LV.** Mary Pickford, William Haines, Walter James, Gordon Griffith, Vola Vale; **D:** William Beaudine; **C:** Charles Rosher. *NOS, CCB, IME*

Little Ballerina 🎬🎬 **1947** A young dancer struggles against misfortune and jealousy to succeed in the world of ballet, under the auspices of Fonteyn. **62m/B VHS, Beta.** Margot Fonteyn, Anthony Newley, Martita Hunt, Yvonne Marsh. *VYY*

Little Big Horn 🎬🎬½ *The Fighting Seventh* **1951** Low-budget depiction of Custer et al. at Little Big Horn actually has its gripping moments; solid acting all around helps. **88m/B VHS, Beta.** Marie Windsor, John Ireland, Lloyd Bridges, Reed Hadley, Hugh O'Brian, Jim Davis; **D:** Charles Marquis Warren. *MRV*

Little Big League 🎬🎬½ **1994 (PG)** 12-year-old inherits the Minnesota Twins baseball team from his grandfather, appoints himself manager when everyone else declines, and becomes the youngest owner-manager in history. Nothing new about the premise, but kids and America's favorite pastime add up to good clean family fun. Features real-life baseball players, including the Mariners' Griffey and O'Neil from the Yankees.

Good cast features TV's Busfield at first base. Screenwriting debut from Pincus, and directorial debut from the executive producer of "Seinfeld," Scheinman. **120m/C VHS, LV, Closed Caption.** Luke Edwards, Jason Robards Jr., Kevin Dunn, Dennis Farina, John Ashton, Jonathan Silverman, Wolfgang Bodison, Timothy Busfield, Ashley Crow, Scott Patterson, Billy L. Sullivan, Miles Feulner, Kevin Elster, Leon "Bull" Durham, Brad "The Animal" Lesley; **Cameos:** Don Mattingly, Ken Griffey Jr., Paul O'Neill; **D:** Andrew Scheinman; **W:** Gregory Pincus, Adam Scheinman. *COL*

Little Big Man 🎬🎬🎬½ **1970 (PG)** Based on Thomas Berger's picaresque novel, this is the story of 121-year-old Jack Crabb and his quixotic life as gunslinger, charlatan, Indian, ally to George Custer, and the only white survivor of Little Big Horn. Told mainly through flashbacks. Hoffman provides a classic portrayal of Crabb, as fact and myth are jumbled and reshaped. **135m/C VHS, Beta, LV, Letterbox, Closed Caption.** Dustin Hoffman, Faye Dunaway, Chief Dan George, Richard Mulligan, Martin Balsam, Jeff Corey, Aimee Eccles; **D:** Arthur Penn; **W:** Calder Willingham; **C:** Harry Stradling Jr. New York Film Critics Awards '70: Best Supporting Actor (George); National Society of Film Critics Awards '70: Best Supporting Actor (George); Nominations: Academy Awards '70: Best Supporting Actor (George). *FOX, HMV*

Little Bigfoot 🎬🎬½ **1996 (PG)** The Shoemaker family are taking a camping vacation when the kids discover a baby bigfoot in the wilderness. They find out the hairy little guy and his mom are threatened by the owner of a logging company, who's hired a group of hunters to get rid of the critters. **99m/C VHS, Closed Caption.** Ross Malinger, P.J. Soles, Ken Tigar, Kelly Packard, Don Stroud, Matt McCoy; **D:** Art Camacho; **W:** Richard Preston Jr.; **C:** Ken Blakey; **M:** Louis Febre. *REP*

Little Boy Lost 🎬🎬 **1978 (G)** The true story of the disappearance of a young boy in Australia. **92m/C VHS, Beta.** *AU* John Hargreaves, Tony Barry, Lorna Lesley; **D:** Alan Spires. *NO*

Little Buddha 🎬🎬 **1993 (PG)** Tibetan Lama Norbu informs the Seattle Konrad family that their 10-year-old son Jesse may be the reincarnation of a respected monk. He wants to take the boy back to Tibet to find out and, with some apparently minor doubts, the family head off on their spiritual quest. In an effort to instruct Jesse in Buddhism, this journey is interspersed with the story of Prince Siddhartha, who will leave behind his worldly ways to follow the path towards enlightenment and become the Buddha. The two stories are an ill-fit, the acting awkward (with the exception of Ruocheng as the wise Norbu), but boy, does the film look good (from cinematographer Vittorio Storaro). Filmed on location in Nepal and Bhutan. **123m/C VHS, LV, Closed Caption.** Keanu Reeves, Alex Wiesendanger, Ying Ruocheng, Chris Isaak, Bridget Fonda; **D:** Bernardo Bertolucci; **W:** Mark Peploe, Rudy Wurlitzer; **C:** Vittorio Storaro; **M:** Ryuichi Sakamoto. *MAX*

Little Caesar 🎬🎬🎬 **1930** A small-time hood rises to become a gangland czar, but his downfall is as rapid as his rise. Still thrilling. The role of Rico made Robinson a star and typecast him as a crook for all time. **80m/B VHS, Beta.** Edward G. Robinson, Glenda Farrell, Sidney Blackmer, Douglas Fairbanks Jr.; **D:** Mervyn LeRoy; **C:** Gaetano Antonio "Tony" Gaudio. Nominations: Academy Awards '31: Best Adapted Screenplay. *FOX, FCT*

Little Church Around the Corner 🎬🎬½ **1923** Silent small town melodrama about a preacher who falls in love with a mine owner's daughter, but finds he isn't dad's favorite fella when he confronts him about poor mining conditions. When the mine caves in, the preacher man's caught between a rock and a hard place when his sweetie's family needs protection from an angry mob. **70m/B VHS, Beta.** Kenneth Harlan, Hobart Bosworth, Walter Long, Pauline Starke, Alec B. Francis, Margaret Seddon, George Cooper; **D:** William A. Seiter. *GPV*

The Little Colonel 🎬🎬🎬 1935 (PG) After the Civil War, an embittered Southern patriarch turns his back on his family, until his dimple-cheeked granddaughter softens his heart. Hokey and heartwarming. Shirley's first teaming with Bill "Bojangles" Robinson features the famous dance scene. Adapted by William Conselman from the Annie Fellows Johnston best-seller. 80m/B VHS, Beta, Closed Caption. Shirley Temple, Lionel Barrymore, Evelyn Venable, John Lodge, Hattie McDaniel, Bill Robinson, Sidney Blackmer; D: David Butler; C: Arthur C. Miller. FOX

Little Darlings woof! 1980 (R) Distasteful premise has summer campers Kristy and Tatum in a race to lose their virginity. Kristy is better (at acting, that is); but who cares? And just who is meant to be the market for this movie, anyway? 95m/C VHS, Beta, LV. Tatum O'Neal, Kristy McNichol, Matt Dillon, Armand Assante, Margaret Blye; D: Ronald F. Maxwell; M: Charles Fox. PAR

The Little Death 🎬🎬 1995 Struggling musician Nick Hannon (Fraser) is forced to work for wealthy dad Ted (Walsh), who's married to young trophy wife Kelly (Gridley). She's being stalked by weirdo Bobby (Yoakam), who kills Ted but manages to get off by claiming self-defense. Kelly's no lonely widow since she's now bedding Nick but he soon has suspicions of his former stepmom's involvement in her hubby's death. 91m/C VHS, Closed Caption. Brent Fraser, Pamela Gidley, Dwight Yoakam, J.T. Walsh, Troy Beyer, D.W. Moffett, Richard Beymer; D: Jan Verheyen; W: Nicholas Bogner, Michael Holden; C: David Phillips; M: Christopher Tyng. PGV

Little Dorrit, Film 1: Nobody's Fault 🎬🎬🎬 1988 The mammoth version of the Dickens tome, about a father and daughter trapped interminably in the dreaded Marshalsea debtors' prison, and the good samaritan who works to free them. Told in two parts (on four tapes), "Nobody's Fault," and "Little Dorrit's Story." 369m/C VHS, Beta, LV, Closed Caption. GB Alec Guinness, Derek Jacobi, Cyril Cusack, Sarah Pickering, Joan Greenwood, Max Wall, Amelda Brown, Daniel Chatto, Miriam Margolyes, Bill Fraser, Roshan Seth, Michael Elphick, Eleanor Bron, Patricia Hayes, Robert Morley, Sophie Ward; D: Christine Edzard; W: Christine Edzard; C: Bruno de Keyzer; M: Giuseppe Verdi. Los Angeles Film Critics Association Awards '88: Best Film, Best Supporting Actor (Guinness); Nominations: Academy Awards '88: Best Adapted Screenplay, Best Supporting Actor (Guinness). WAR, SIG, TVC

Little Dorrit, Film 2: Little Dorrit's Story 🎬🎬🎬 1988 The second half of the monumental adaptation of Dickens' most popular novel during his lifetime tells of Amy Dorrit's rise from debtor's prison to happiness. 369m/C VHS, Beta, LV, Closed Caption. GB Alec Guinness, Derek Jacobi, Cyril Cusack, Sarah Pickering, Joan Greenwood, Max Wall, Amelda Brown, Daniel Chatto, Miriam Margolyes, Bill Fraser, Roshan Seth, Michael Elphick, Patricia Hayes, Robert Morley, Sophie Ward, Eleanor Bron; D: Christine Edzard; W: Christine Edzard; C: Bruno de Keyzer; M: Giuseppe Verdi. Los Angeles Film Critics Association Awards '88: Best Film, Best Supporting Actor (Guinness). WAR, SIG, TVC

Little Dragons 🎬 1980 A grandfather and two young karate students rescue a family held captive by a backwoods gang. 90m/C VHS, Beta. Ann Sothern, Joe Spinell, Charles Lane, Chris Petersen, Pat Petersen, Sally Boyden, Rick Lenz, Sharon Weber, Tony Bill; D: Curtis Hanson; W: Alan Ormsby.

The Little Drummer Girl 🎬🎬🎬 1984 (R) An Israeli counterintelligence agent recruits an actress sympathetic to the Palestinian cause to trap a fanatical terrorist leader. Solid performances from Keaton as the actress and Kinski as the Israeli counter-intelligence office sustain interest through a puzzling, sometimes boring and frustrating, cinematic maze of espionage. Keaton is at or near her very best. Based on the bestselling novel by John Le Carre. 130m/C VHS, Beta, LV, Closed Caption. Diane Keaton, Klaus Kinski, Yorgo Voya-

gis, Sami Frey, Michael Cristofer, Anna Massey, Thorley Walters; D: George Roy Hill; M: Dave Grusin. WAR

The Little Foxes 🎬🎬🎬½ 1941 A vicious southern woman destroys everyone around her to satisfy her desire for wealth and power. Filled with corrupt characters who commit numerous revolting deeds. The vicious matriarch is a part made to fit for Davis, and she makes the most of it. Script by Lillian Hellman from her own play. 116m/B VHS, Beta, LV. Bette Davis, Herbert Marshall, Dan Duryea, Teresa Wright, Charles Dingle, Richard Carlson; D: William Wyler. Nominations: Academy Awards '41: Best Actress (Davis), Best Director (Wyler), Best Film Editing, Best Interior Decoration, Best Picture, Best Screenplay, Best Supporting Actress (Collinge, Wright), Best Original Dramatic/Comedy Score.

Little Fugitive 🎬🎬🎬 1953 Seven-year-old Joey (Andrusco) is convinced by his Brooklyn pals that he's murdered his brother. So the tyke takes off and winds up wandering lost around Coney Island. Independent feature made on a miniscule budget features endearing performances from non-pros. 80m/C VHS. Richie Andrusco, Ricky Brewster, Winnifred Cushing, Jay Williams; D: Morris Engel, Ruth Orkin. National Film Registry '97. KIV

Little Giant 🎬🎬½ 1946 The duo fly separately in this entry, which highlights Costello's comic talents and puts Abbott in the supporting role. Costello is a country bumpkin come to the big city to get enough money to marry his sweetheart. He's hired to sell vacuum cleaners by Abbott and becomes the butt of everyone's jokes but the joke's on them when Lou becomes the company's top-selling salesman. 92m/B VHS. Bud Abbott, Lou Costello, Brenda Joyce, Jacqueline De Wit, George Cleveland, Elena Verdugo, Mary Gordon, Pierre Watkin; D: William A. Seiter; W: Walter DeLeon. USH

Little Giants 🎬🎬½ 1994 (PG) Familiar kids/sport movie about the klutzy coach (Moranis) of an equally woeful pee-wee football team. Coach Danny is up against his overbearing big brother Kevin (O'Neill), former local football hero and the coach of the best team in town. Naturally, there's the big game between the misfit underdogs and the stars. Predictable, of course, but not without some amusing moments. 106m/C VHS, LV. Rick Moranis, Ed O'Neill, Shawna Waldron, Mary Ellen Trainor, Devon Sawa, Susanna Thompson, John Madden; D: Duwayne Dunham; W: Tommy Swerdlow, Michael Goldberg, James Ferguson, Robert Shallcross; C: Janusz Kaminski; M: John Debney. WAR

Little Girl ... Big Tease 🎬 1975 (R) Teen society girl is kidnapped and exploited (along with the viewer) by a group which includes her teacher. 86m/C VHS, Beta. Jody Ray, Rebecca Brooke; D: Roberto Mitrotti. NO

The Little Girl Who Lives Down the Lane 🎬🎬½ 1976 (PG) Engrossing, offbeat thriller about a strange 13-year-old girl whose father is never home, and who hides something—we won't say what—in her basement. Very young Foster is excellent, as are her supporters, including Sheen as the child molester who knows what she's hiding. 90m/C VHS, Beta, LV. CA Jodie Foster, Martin Sheen, Alexis Smith, Scott Jacoby; D: Nicolas Gessner. ART, VES

Little Gloria...Happy at Last 🎬🎬½ 1984 Mini series based on the best-selling book about the custody battle over child heiress Gloria Vanderbilt, and her tumultuous youth. Lansberry leads a fine cast as the poor little rich girl's aunt Gertrude, the matriarchal family power broker. Made for television. 180m/C VHS, Beta. Bette Davis, Angela Lansbury, Christopher Plummer, Maureen Stapleton, Martin Balsam, Barnard Hughes, John Hillerman; D: Waris Hussein. PAR

Little Heroes 🎬🎬½ 1991 (G) An impoverished little girl gets through hard times with the aid of her loyal dog (the Hound can relate). A low-budget family tearjerker that nonetheless works, it claims to be based on a true story. 78m/C VHS. Raeanin Simpson, Katherine Willis, Keith Christensen; D: Craig Clyde; W: Craig Clyde; M: John McCallum.

Little Heroes of Shaolin Temple 🎬 1972 The "Prince of Blood" attacks the Shaolin temple, but the Master's Ninjas await him. 90m/C VHS, Beta. Cheng Tain Syh, Hw-Luen, Li Shuen Hwa, Tang Chen Da. TWE

Little House on the Prairie 🎬🎬🎬 1974 The pilot for the television series based on the life of Laura Ingalls Wilder and her family's struggles on the American plains in the 1860s. Other episodes are also available on tape, including one in which Patricia Neal guest stars as a terminally ill widow seeking a home for her children. Neal's performance earned her a best actress Emmy in 1975. 98m/C VHS, Beta. Michael Landon, Karen Grassle, Victor French, Melissa Gilbert, Melissa Sue Anderson; D: Michael Landon. GKK, TLF

Little Indian, Big City 🎬🎬½ An Indian in the City; Un Indien dans la Ville 1995 (PG) French blockbuster dubbed over with "Americanized" English to give U.S. audiences an appetite for upcoming Disney remake. Lhermitte travels to the Amazon to finalize the divorce of a long-dead marriage, only to find he has a 12-year-old son, Mimi-Siku (Briand). Father and son bond and Dad decides to bring the jungle-bred boy to his home in Paris. Dubbing process unfortunately tomahawks this charming story as loin cloth meets Eiffel Tower, but Lhermitte, Briand and Miou-Miou (as estranged wife Patricia) shine through. Subplot of Russian mobsters who cut the fingers off their victims gives an indication of the French definition of "family fare." 90m/C VHS, Closed Caption. FR Thierry Lhermitte, Miou-Miou, Patrick Timsit, Arielle Dombasle, Ludwig Briand; D: Herve Palud; W: Thierry Lhermitte, Herve Palud, Philippe Bruneau, Igor Aptekman; C: Pierre Lorraine; M: Manu Katche. TOU

Little Johnny Jones 1980 George M. Cohan's classic musical is featured in a 1980 revival. Songs include "Yankee Doodle Dandy" and "Give My Regards to Broadway." 93m/C VHS, Beta. WAR, OM

The Little Kidnappers 🎬🎬½ 1990 (G) Embittered man (Heston) is forced to take in his Scottish grandsons when the two boys are orphaned. They settle in with gramps in Nova Scotia but when the duo decide to adopt the abandoned baby they've found, they are accused of being kidnappers. Cable remake of 1953 British film. 100m/C VHS. CA Charlton Heston, Bruce Greenwood, Leah K. Pinsent, Charles Miller, Leo Wheatley, Patricia Gage; D: Donald Shebib. AVE

Little Ladies of the Night 🎬 Diamond Alley 1977 Former pimp tries to save Purl and other teenagers from the world of prostitution. Exploitation posing as "significant drama." 96m/C VHS, Beta. Linda Purl, David Soul, Clifton Davis, Carolyn Jones, Louis Gossett Jr.; D: Marvin J. Chomsky.

Little Laura & Big John 🎬🎬 1973 The true-life exploits of the small-time Ashley Gang in the Florida everglades around the turn of the century. Fabian's comeback vehicle, for what it's worth. 82m/C VHS, Beta. Fabian, Karen Black; D: Luke Moberly. NO

Little Lord Fauntleroy 🎬🎬🎬½ 1936 The vintage Hollywood version of the Frances Hodgson Burnett story of a fatherless American boy who discovers he's heir to a British dukedom. Also available in computer-colorized version. Well cast, charming, remade for TV in 1980. Smith is loveable as the noble tyke's crusty old guardian. 102m/B VHS, Beta, Closed Caption. Freddie Bartholomew, Sir C. Aubrey Smith, Mickey Rooney, Dolores Costello, Jessie Ralph, Guy Kibbee; D: John Cromwell; C: Charles Rosher; M: Max Steiner. NOS, MRV, VEC

Little Lord Fauntleroy 🎬🎬½ 1980 A poor boy in New York suddenly finds himself the heir to his grandfather's estate in England. Lavish remake of the 1936 classic, adapted from Frances Hodgson Burnett's novel. Well-deserved Emmy winner for photography; Guinness is his usual old-pro self. Made for TV. 98m/C VHS, Beta, Closed Caption. Rick Schroder, Alec Guinness, Victoria

Tennant, Eric Porter, Colin Blakely, Connie Booth, Rachel Kempson; **D:** Jack Gold. FHE

Little Lord Fauntleroy 🎞🎞½ 1995 (G)
British TV adaptation of the Frances Hodgson Burnett classic finds Cedric Erroll's life changing forever when he's discovered to be the only heir to the Earl of Dorincourt. But the Earl turns out to be a bitter miser and it's up to the innocent child to get grandpa to enjoy life. 100m/C VHS, **Closed Caption.** GB Michael Benz, Betsy Brantley, George Baker, Bernice Stegers; **D:** Andrew Morgan. FXV

Little Man Tate 🎞🎞🎞 1991 (PG)
A seven-year-old genius is the prize in a tug of war between his mother, who wants him to lead a normal life, and a domineering school director who loves him for his intellect. An acclaimed directorial debut for Foster, with overtones of her own extraordinary life as a child prodigy. 99m/C VHS, **Closed Caption.** Jodie Foster, Dianne Wiest, Harry Connick Jr., Adam Hann-Byrd, George Plimpton, Debi Mazar, Celia Weston, David Pierce, Danitra Vance, Josh Mostel, P.J. Ochlan; **D:** Jodie Foster; **W:** Scott Frank; **M:** Mark Isham. ORI, CCB

Little Marines 1990
Three young boys journey into the wilderness for three days of fun and instead embark on an incredible adventure. 90m/C VHS. Stephen Baker, Steve Landers Jr., Noah Williams; **D:** A.J. Hixon.

The Little Match Girl 🎞🎞 1984
A musical version of the Hans Christian Andersen classic about a girl whose dying grandmother tells her of the magic in the matches she sells. 54m/C VHS, Beta. Monica McSwain, Nancy Duncan, Matt McKim, Don Hays; **D:** Mark Hoeger.

The Little Match Girl 🎞🎞 1987
The Hans Christian Andersen Yuletide classic about an orphan selling magical matches, this time set in the 1920s, with the littlest "Cosby" kid in the title role. Ain't she cute? 90m/C VHS, Beta, **Closed Caption.** GB Roger Daltrey, Twiggy, Natalie Morse; **D:** Michael Custance.

Little Men 🎞½ 1940
A modern version of the classic juvenile story by Louisa May Alcott is too cute for words. 86m/B VHS, Beta. Jack Oakie, Jimmy Lydon, Kay Francis, George Bancroft; **D:** Norman Z. McLeod. NOS, MRV, VCN

Little Men 🎞🎞½ 1998 (PG)
Louisa May Alcott's sequel to "Little Women" hits the screen with a lot less hoopla than its 1994 predecessor. Jo March (Hemingway) has grown up, married Fritz Bhaer (Sarandon), and opened an idyllic, wholesome school for troubled boys. The house is immaculate, the grounds are beautiful, and the boys are little angels. That is, until streetwise 14-year-old Dan (Cook) shows up. He soon has the boys smoking, drinking, and stealing, until they almost burn the place down. Since this is a family movie, with moral lessons to be learned, all's well by the end. Adults may find the syrupy sweetness too much to take, and the characters are barely two-dimensional, but young kids should enjoy it. 98m/C VHS. Mariel Hemingway, Chris Sarandon, Michael Caloz, Ben Cook, Michael Yarmush, Gabrielle Boni, Ricky Mabe, Julia Garland, B.J. McLellan, Tyler Hines, Kathleen Fee; **D:** Rodney Gibbons; **W:** Mark Evan Schwartz; **C:** Arch Archambault; **M:** Milan Kymlicka. WAR

The Little Mermaid 🎞🎞½ 1978 (G)
An animated version of Hans Christian Andersen's tale about a little mermaid who rescues a prince whose boat has capsized. She immediately falls in love and wishes that she could become a human girl. Not to be confused with the 1989 Disney version. 71m/C VHS, Beta. **D:** Tim Reid. VTR, GEM

The Little Mermaid 1984
From "Faerie Tale Theatre" comes an adaptation of the Hans Christian Andersen tale of a little mermaid who makes a large sacrifice to win the prince she loves. 60m/C VHS, Beta, **Closed Caption.** Karen Black, Brian Dennehy, Helen Mirren, Pam Dawber, Treat Williams; **D:** Robert Iscove. FOX, FCT

The Little Mermaid 🎞🎞🎞½ 1989 (G)
Headstrong teenage mermaid falls in love with a human prince and longs to be human too. She makes a pact with the evil Sea Witch to trade her voice for a pair of legs; based on the famous Hans Christian Andersen tale. Charming family musical, which harks back to the days of classic Disney animation, and hails a new era of superb Disney animated musicals. Sebastian the Crab nearly steals the show with his wit and showstopping number "Under the Sea." 🎵Under the Sea; Kiss the Girl; Daughters of Triton; Part of Your World; Poor Unfortunate Souls; Les Poissons. 82m/C VHS, Beta, LV, 8mm, **Closed Caption. D:** John Musker, Ron Clements; **W:** John Musker, Ron Clements; **M:** Alan Menken, Howard Ashman; **V:** Jodi Benson, Christopher Daniel Barnes, Pat Carroll, Rene Auberjonois, Samuel E. Wright, Buddy Hackett, Jason Marin, Edie McClurg, Kenneth Mars, Nancy Cartwright. Academy Awards '89: Best Song ("Under the Sea"), Best Original Score; Golden Globe Awards '90: Best Song ("Under the Sea"), Best Score; Nominations: Academy Awards '89: Best Song ("Kiss the Girl"). DIS, OM

Little Minister 🎞🎞🎞 1934
An adaptation of the James Barrie novel about a prissy Scottish pastor who falls in love with a free-spirited gypsy...he thinks she is, in fact, the local earl's daughter, played to perfection by the young Hepburn. 101m/B VHS, Beta. Katharine Hepburn, John Beal, Alan Hale, Donald Crisp; **D:** Richard Wallace; **M:** Max Steiner. TTC

Little Miss Broadway 🎞🎞 1938
Orphan Temple brings the residents of a theatrical boarding house together in hopes of getting them into show business. She and Durante give worthwhile performances. Also available in computer-colorized version. 🎵Be Optimistic; How Can I Thank You; I'll Build a Broadway For You; If All the World Were Paper; Thank You For the Use of the Hall; We Should Be Together; Swing Me an Old-Fashioned Song; When You Were Sweet Sixteen; Happy Birthday to You. 70m/B VHS, Beta, **Closed Caption.** Shirley Temple, George Murphy, Jimmy Durante, Phyllis Brooks, Edna May Oliver, George Barbier, Donald Meek, Jane Darwell; **D:** Irving Cummings; **C:** Arthur C. Miller. FOX

Little Miss Innocence 🎞 1973
Recording executive tries to survive the amorous advances of the two attractive female hitchhikers that he drove home. 79m/C VHS, Beta. John Alderman, Sandy Dempsey, Judy Medford; **D:** Chris Warfield.

Little Miss Marker 🎞🎞🎞 _Girl in Pawn_ 1934
Heartwarming story starring Temple as the title character, who is left with bookie Sorrowful Jones (Menjou) as the IOU for a gambling debt. But when her father doesn't return, it's up to Jones and his racetrack friends to make little Marky a home. Naturally, Temple steals her way into everyone's heart. Based on a story by Damon Runyon; remade three times as "Sorrowful Jones," as "40 Pounds of Trouble," and in 1980 with the original title. 88m/B VHS, **Closed Caption.** Adolphe Menjou, Shirley Temple, Dorothy Dell, Charles Bickford, Lynne Overman; **D:** Alexander Hall. USH

Little Miss Marker 🎞½ 1980 (PG)
Mediocre remake of the often retold story of a bookie who accepts a little girl as a security marker for a $10 bet. Disappointing performance from Curtis adds to an already dull film. 103m/C VHS, Beta. Walter Matthau, Julie Andrews, Tony Curtis, Bob Newhart, Lee Grant, Sara Stimson, Brian Dennehy; **D:** Walter Bernstein; **W:** Walter Bernstein; **M:** Henry Mancini. USH

Little Miss Millions 🎞🎞½ 1993 (PG)
A 12-year-old has run away from her wicked stepmom who hires a bounty hunter to bring her back—for a half a million bucks. Only when he finds the girl stepmom doesn't want to pay up and she tells anyone who will listen that the bounty hunter actually kidnapped the girl. Bounty hunter turns to friends, including the 12-year-old who isn't a fool and knows stepmom is a lying witch, for help. 90m/C VHS, **Closed Caption.** Howard Hesseman, Anita Morris, Love Hewitt; **D:** Roger Corman. NHO

Little Monsters 🎞🎞 1989 (PG)
A young boy (Savage) discovers a monster (Mandel) under his bed and eventually befriends it. The pair embark on adventures that land them in trouble. Hardworking, talented cast hurdles the weak script, but can't save the film. 100m/C VHS, Beta, LV, **Closed Caption.** Fred Savage, Howie Mandel, Margaret Whitton, Ben Savage, Daniel Stern, Rick Ducommun, Frank Whaley; **D:** Richard Alan Greenberg; **W:** Ted Elliot, Terry Rossio; **M:** David Newman. MGM

Little Moon & Jud McGraw 🎞½ 1978
A wronged Indian woman and a framed cowpoke take their revenge on a small, corrupt town, razing it overnight. Already-weak plot is disabled by too many flashbacks. 92m/C VHS, Beta. James Caan, Sammy Davis Jr., Stefanie Powers, Aldo Ray; **D:** Bernard Girard.

Little Mother 🎞🎞 1971
Metzger's take on Argentina's Eva Peron highlights her sexual powers (of course) as it tells of Eva's climb out of poverty and into the heights of political power. Filmed in Yugoslavia. 95m/C VHS. Christiane Kruger, Ivan Desny, Anton Diffring; **D:** Radley Metzger. FRF

Little Murders 🎞🎞 1971 (PG)
Black comedy set in New York City. A woman convinces a passive photographer to marry her. Gardenia gives an excellent performance as the woman's father. A shadow of crime, depression, and strife seem to hangs over the funny parts of this film; more often depressing than anything else. Adapted by Jules Feiffer from his own play. 108m/C VHS, Beta. Elliott Gould, Marcia Rodd, Vincent Gardenia, Elizabeth Wilson, Jon Korkes, Donald Sutherland, Alan Arkin, Lou Jacobi; **D:** Alan Arkin; **W:** Jules Feiffer; **C:** Gordon Willis. FOX

Little Nellie Kelly 🎞🎞½ 1940
Garland plays both mother and daughter in a film based on a musical comedy by George M. Cohan. Garland is married to Irish cop Murphy but dies in childbirth. The film then advances 20 years to daughter Garland who is trying to make good on the stage and have a romance with a young man her father disapproves of. 🎵Nellie Kelly I Love You; Nellie is a Darling; It's a Great Day For the Irish; A Pretty Girl Milking Her Cow; Danny Boy; Singing in the Rain. 100m/B VHS. Judy Garland, George Murphy, Charles Winninger, Douglas McPhail; **D:** Norman Taurog. MGM, FCT

Little Nemo: Adventures in Slumberland 🎞🎞½ 1992 (G)
A bland animated tale of a young boy whose dreams take him to Slumberland. There, Nemo unwittingly unleashes a monster from Nightmare Land who kidnaps Slumberland's king. Nemo must then rescue the king—aided by the king's daughter, a comic squirrel sidekick, and a mischievous con-frog. Based on Winsor McCay's 1900 comic strip. Has some cute comic moments for the kiddies and, while the animation is better than Saturday-morning cartoon quality, it's not Disney. 85m/C VHS, Letterbox. **D:** William T. Hurtz, Masami Hata; **W:** Chris Columbus, Richard Outten; **M:** Tom Chase, Steve Rucker; **V:** Gabriel Damon, Mickey Rooney, Rene Auberjonois, Daniel Mann, Laura Mooney, Bernard Erhard, William E. Martin.

A Little Night Music 🎞½ 1977 (PG)
Features four interwoven, contemporary love stories adapted from the Broadway play, and based loosely on Bergman's "Smiles of a Summer Night." Taylor's pathetic rendition of "Send in the Clowns" should be banned. Filmed on location in Austria. 110m/C VHS, Beta, LV. Elizabeth Taylor, Diana Rigg, Hermione Gingold, Len Cariou, Lesley-Anne Down; **D:** Harold Prince. Academy Awards '77: Original Song Score and/or Adaptation; Nominations: Academy Awards '77: Best Costume Design. NLC

Little Nikita 🎞🎞 1988 (PG)
A California boy (Phoenix) discovers that his parents are actually Soviet spies planted as American citizens for eventual call to duty. Poitier's performance as the FBI agent tracking the spies is about the only spark in this somewhat incoherent thriller. 98m/C VHS, Beta, LV, **Closed Caption.** River Phoenix, Sidney Poitier, Richard Bradford, Richard Lynch, Caroline Kava,

Lucy Deakins; **D:** Richard Benjamin; **W:** Bo Goldman; **M:** Marvin Hamlisch. *COL*

Little Ninjas ♫♫½ 1992 Three topnotch ninja kids go up against the Sarak to rescue their friend who is being held hostage. 85m/C VHS, LV. Steven Nelson, Jon Anzaldo, Alan Godshaw; **D:** Emmett Alston. *THV*

Little Noises ♫♫ 1991 Glover stars as an artist who seeks not only fame and fortune, but also the love of his best friend (O'Neal). He finally creates a piece that his agent loves, but problems arise. 91m/C VHS, Beta. Crispin Glover, Tatum O'Neal, Rik Mayall, Tate Donovan, John C. McGinley; **D:** Jane Spencer; **W:** Jane Spencer.

Little Odessa ♫♫½ 1994 (R) Working for the stateside Russian mafia, hitman Joshua Shapira (Roth) returns to his childhood neighborhood to carry out his next assignment. Set in the Russian-Jewish emigre community of Brooklyn's Brighton Beach, Gray's directorial debut explores Joshua's relationship with his family—especially kid brother Reuben (Furlong). Not your typical mob opera, this one focuses more on characters than killing. Relationships between family members are explored to the hilt, but the audience is left with too many unanswered questions. Dimly lit and entirely too ambiguous, this family tragedy could spawn a serious case of depression.**CW:** Contains violence, profanity, nudity, and sexual situations. 98m/C VHS, LV, Closed Caption. Tim Roth, Edward Furlong, Moira Kelly, Vanessa Redgrave, Maximilian Schell, Paul Guilfoyle, Natasha Andreichenko, David Vadim, Mina Bern, Boris McGiver, Mohammed Ghaffari, Michael Khumrov, Dmitry Preyers, David Ross, Ron Brice, Jace Kent, Marianna Lead, Gene Ruffini; **D:** James Gray; **W:** James Gray; **C:** Tom Richmond; **M:** Dana Sano. Nominations: Independent Spirit Awards '96: Best Actor (Roth), Best Cinematography, Best First Feature, Best Supporting Actress (Redgrave). *ART*

Little Orphan Annie 1918 Surrounded by a group of children, poet James Whitcomb Riley narrates the story of Little Orphant Annie, who loses her mother at an early age and is sent to an orphanage where she charms the other children with her stories of ghosts and elves. 57m/B VHS. Thomas Santschi, Eugenie Besserer, Ben Alexander, Lillie Hayward, Lafayette McKee, Colleen Moore, Harry Lonsdale, Doris Baker, Lillian Wade, Billy Jacobs, James Whitcomb Riley; **D:** Colin Campbell. *GPV*

Little Orphan Annie ♫♫½ 1932 The unjustly forgotten first sound adaptation of the comic strip. Fun score adds a lot, as does the good cast. 60m/B VHS, Beta. May Robson, Buster Phelps, Mitzie Green, Edgar Kennedy; **D:** John S. Robertson; **M:** Max Steiner. *CCB*

The Little Prince ♫♫ 1974 (G) Disappointing adaptation of the classic children's story by Antoine de Saint-Exupery, about a little boy from asteroid B-612. Lousy Lerner and Loewe score underscores a general lack of magic or spontaneity. ♫It's a Hat; I Need Air; I'm On Your Side; Be Happy; You're a Child; I Never Met a Rose; Why Is the Desert (Lovely to See)?; Closer and Closer and Closer; Little Prince (From Who Knows Where). 88m/C VHS, Beta, LV. **GB** Richard Kiley, Bob Fosse, Steven Warner, Gene Wilder, Joss Ackland, Clive Revill, Victor Spinetti, Graham Crowden, Donna McKechnie; **D:** Stanley Donen; **W:** Alan Jay Lerner; **C:** Christopher Challis; **M:** Frederick Loewe, Alan Jay Lerner. Golden Globe Awards '75: Best Score; Nominations: Academy Awards '74: Best Song ("Little Prince"), Original Song Score and/or Adaptation. *PAR*

The Little Princess ♫♫♫½ 1939 (G) Based on the Frances Hodgson Burnett children's classic; perhaps the best of the moppet's films. Shirley is a young schoolgirl in Victorian London sent to a harsh boarding school when her Army officer father is posted abroad. When her father is declared missing, the penniless girl must work as a servant at the school to pay her keep, all the while haunting the hospitals, never believing her father has died. A classic tearjerker. 91m/B VHS, Beta, LV, Closed Caption. Shirley Temple, Richard

Greene, Anita Louise, Ian Hunter, Cesar Romero, Arthur Treacher, Sybil Jason, Miles Mander, Marcia Mae Jones, E.E. Clive; **D:** Walter Lang; **C:** Arthur C. Miller. *CNG, MRV, NOS*

The Little Princess 1987 A three-cassette adaptation of Frances Hodgson Burnett's book. In Victorian England, kind-hearted Sara is forced into poverty when her father suddenly dies. Can his longtime friend find her and restore her happiness? Originally aired on PBS as part of the "Wonderworks" family movie series. 180m/C VHS. **GB** Amelia Shankley, Nigel Havers, Maureen Lipman; **D:** Carol Wiseman. *FCT, SIG, TVC*

A Little Princess ♫♫♫½ 1995 (G) Compelling fantasy, based on the children's book by Frances Hodgson Burnett, and previously best known for the 1939 Shirley Temple incarnation. Sara (Matthews) has been raised in India by her widowed father (Cunningham). When he's called up to fight in WWI, Sara is taken to New York to be educated at stern Miss Michin's (Bron) school, where her money makes her a favored boarder. However, the irrepressible Sara suffers a severe reversal of fortune when her father is reported killed and Miss Michin promptly makes her a servant to pay her way. But Sara's charm has made her some true friends who become her allies under trying circumstances. Lively script, dazzling visuals, and a welcome lack of sappiness create a classic-in-the-making. 97m/C VHS, LV, Closed Caption. Liesl Matthews, Eleanor Bron, Liam Cunningham, Rusty Schwimmer, Arthur Malet, Vanessa Lee Chester, Errol Sitahal, Heather DeLoach, Taylor Fry; **D:** Alfonso Cuaron; **W:** Richard LaGravenese, Elizabeth Chandler; **C:** Emmanuel Lubezki; **M:** Patrick Doyle. Nominations: Academy Awards '95: Best Art Direction/Set Decoration, Best Cinematography. *WAR*

The Little Rascals ♫♫½ 1994 (PG) Alfalfa runs afoul of the membership requirements for the "He-Man Womun Haters Club" when he starts to fall for Darla. Charming remake of the short film series, now set in suburban L.A., from Spheeris, who also redid another television favorite, "The Beverly Hillbillies." 83m/C VHS, LV, Closed Caption. Daryl Hannah, Courtland Mead, Travis Tedford, Brittany Ashton Holmes, Bug Hall, Zachary Mabry, Kevin Jamal Woods, Ross Bagley, Sam Saletta, Blake Collins, Jordan Warkol, Blake Ewing, Juliette Brewer, Heather Karasek; *Cameos:* Whoopi Goldberg; **D:** Penelope Spheeris; **W:** Penelope Spheeris, Paul Guay, Steve Mazur; **C:** Richard Bowen; **M:** David Foster, Linda Thompson. *USH*

Little Rascals, Book 1 193? Three "Our Gang" shorts: "Railroadin'" (1929), in which the gang takes off on a runaway train; "A Lad and a Lamp" (1932), wherein they find an Aladdin's lamp; and "Beginner's Luck" (1935), in which Spanky wins a dress for a young actress. Additional volumes are available. 59m/B VHS, Beta. Farina Hoskins, Joe Cobb, Matthew "Stymie" Beard, George "Spanky" McFarland, Carl "Alfalfa" Switzer, Mary Ann Jackson. *CCB*

Little Rascals Christmas Special 1979 Spanky and the Little Rascals attempt to raise enough money to buy a winter coat for Spanky's mom and learn the true meaning of Christmas along the way. 60m/C VHS, Beta. Darla Hood, Matthew "Stymie" Beard; **D:** Fred Wolf, Charles Swenson. *FHE*

Little Rascals, Vol. 1 1929 A collection of three uncut "Little Rascals" short subjects. In "Boxing Gloves" (1929), Chubby and Joe decide two settle their differences over who should have Jean Darling's love by staging a winner-take-all boxing match. In "The Kid from Borneo" (1933), Spanky thinks he's met a crazy relative when he confuses an untamed human from Borneo for his uncle from the circus. In "Roamin' Holiday" (1936), Alfalfa and Spanky lead the gang on a journey fit for a hobo. 50m/B VHS. Darla Hood, George "Spanky" McFarland, Carl "Alfalfa" Switzer, Matthew "Stymie" Beard. *REP, CCB*

Little Rascals, Vol. 2 1930 Another uncut compilation of three classic episodes featuring the goofy gang. In "The First Seven Years" (1930), Speck and Jackie battle for the attention of a beautiful Mary Ann. In the award-winning "Bored of Education" (1936), Spanky and Alfalfa devise a plan to play hooky from school by developing very acute tooth problems. In "Rushin' Ballet" (1937), Alfalfa and Spanky establish the Secret Revengers Club and liberate Buckwheat and Porky from the bonds of tyranny. 50m/B VHS. George "Spanky" McFarland, Carl "Alfalfa" Switzer. *REP, CCB*

Little Red Riding Hood 1983 From "Faerie Tale Theatre" comes the retelling of the story about a girl (Mary Steenburgen) off to give her grandmother a picnic basket, only to get stopped by a wicked wolf McDowell. Not particularly faithful, but fun and scary. 60m/C VHS, Beta, LV, Closed Caption. Mary Steenburgen, Malcolm McDowell; **D:** Graeme Clifford. *FOX, FCT*

Little Red Schoolhouse ♫♫ 1936 A hard-nosed schoolteacher hunts for a truant lad and both of them land in jail. 64m/C VHS, Beta. Frank "Junior" Coghlan, Dickie Moore, Ann Doran. *NOS, BAR, FCT*

A Little Romance ♫♫♫ 1979 (PG) An American girl living in Paris falls in love with a French boy; eventually they run away, to seal their love with a kiss beneath a bridge. Olivier gives a wonderful, if not hammy, performance as the old pickpocket who encourages her. Gentle, agile comedy based on the novel by Patrick Cauvin. 110m/C VHS, Beta, LV, Letterbox. Laurence Olivier, Diane Lane, Thelonious Bernard, Sally Kellerman, Broderick Crawford; **D:** George Roy Hill; **W:** Allan Burns; **M:** Georges Delerue. Academy Awards '79: Best Original Score; Nominations: Academy Awards '79: Best Adapted Screenplay. *WAR*

A Little Sex ♫♫ 1982 (R) Capshaw, in her screen debut, finds herself the wife of womanizer Matheson. Harmless, but pointless, with a TV-style plot. 94m/C VHS, Beta. Tim Matheson, Kate Capshaw, Edward Herrmann, Wallace Shawn, John Glover; **D:** Bruce Paltrow; **W:** Robert De Laurentis; **C:** Ralf Bode; **M:** Georges Delerue. *USH*

Little Shop of Horrors ♫♫♫½ 1960 The landmark cheapie classic, which Roger Corman reputedly filmed in three days, about a nebbish working in a city florist shop who unknowingly cultivates an intelligent plant that demands human meat for sustenance. Notable for then-unknown Nicholson's appearance as a masochistic dental patient. Hilarious, unpretentious farce—if you liked this one, check out Corman's "Bucket of Blood" for more of the same. Inspired a musical of the same name; remade as a movie again in 1986. Available colorized. 70m/B VHS, Beta, LV. Jackie Joseph, Jonathan Haze, Mel Welles, Jack Nicholson, Dick Miller, Myrtle Vail; **D:** Roger Corman; **W:** Charles B. Griffith; **C:** Arch R. Dalzell. *VTR, HHT, VCN*

Little Shop of Horrors ♫♫♫ 1986 (PG-13) During a solar eclipse, Seymour buys an unusual plant and takes it back to the flower shop where he works. The plant, Audrey 2, becomes a town attraction as it grows at an unusual rate, but Seymour learns that he must feed Audrey fresh human blood to keep her growing. Soon, Audrey is giving the orders ("Feed me") and timid Seymour must find "deserving" victims. Martin's performance as the masochistic dentist is alone worth the price. Song, dance, gore, and more prevail in this outrageous musical comedy. Four Tops Levi Stubbs is the commanding voice of Audrey 2. Based on the Off-Broadway play, which was based on Roger Corman's 1960 horror spoof. ♫Mean Green Mother From Outer Space; Some Fun Now; Your Day Begins Tonight. 94m/C VHS, Beta, LV, Closed Caption. Rick Moranis, Ellen Greene, Vincent Gardenia, Steve Martin, James Belushi, Christopher Guest, Bill Murray, John Candy, Tisha Campbell, Tichina Arnold, Michelle Weeks; **D:** Frank Oz; **W:** Howard Ashman; **C:** Bob Paynter; **M:** Miles Goodman, Alan Menken,

Howard Ashman; **V:** Levi Stubbs Jr. Nominations: Academy Awards '86: Best Song (*Mean Green Mother from Outer Space*"). **WAR, HMV, MVD**

Little Sister ⅋½ 1992 (PG-13) Prankster Silverman, on a dare, dresses up as a girl and joins a sorority. Problems arise when he falls in love with his "big sister" (Milano) in the sorority. What will happen when she finds out the truth? Will we care? **94m/C VHS.** Jonathan Silverman, Alyssa Milano; **W:** Sergio D. Altieri. **ART**

A Little Stiff ⅋⅋ 1991 Slacker romantic comedy about the unrequited romance between filmmaker Caveh and fellow UCLA student McKim from first meeting, through angst, and grand final gestures. **85m/C VHS.** Erin McKim, Caveh Zahedi; **D:** Caveh Zahedi; **M:** Kath Bloom. **WAC**

Little Sweetheart ⅋½ 1990 (R) A reworking of "The Bad Seed," with a nine-year-old girl engaging in murder, burglary, and blackmail, ruining the adults around her. Based on "The Naughty Girls" by Arthur Wise. **93m/C VHS, Beta, LV, 8mm.** John Hurt, Karen Young, Barbara Bosson, John McMartin, Cassie Barasch; **D:** Anthony Simmons.

The Little Theatre of Jean Renoir ⅋⅋⅋ 1971 A farewell by director Jean Renoir featuring three short films. In the first, Renoir's humanist beliefs are apparent in "The Last Christmas Dinner," a Hans Christian Andersen-inspired story. Next, "The Electric Floor Waxer" is a comic opera. The third piece is called "A Tribute to Tolerance." Slight but important late statement by a great director. In French with English subtitles. **100m/C VHS, Beta, LV.** Jean Renoir, Fernand Sardou, Jean Carmet, Francoise Arnoul, Jeanne Moreau; **D:** Jean Renoir; **W:** Jean Renoir. **INT, HMV, IME**

The Little Thief ⅋⅋⅋ 1989 (PG-13) Touted as Francois Truffaut's final legacy, this trite minidrama is actually based on a story he cowrote with Claude de Givray about a post-WWII adolescent girl who reacts to the world around her by stealing and petty crime. Truffaut's hand is markedly absent, but this film is a testament to his abruptly and sadly truncated career. Director Miller was Truffaut's longtime assistant. French with subtitles. **108m/C VHS, Beta, LV.** **FR** Charlotte Gainsbourg, Simon de la Brosse, Didier Bezace, Raoul Billerey, Nathalie Cardone; **D:** Claude Miller; **W:** Annie Miller, Claude Miller; **C:** Dominique Chapuis; **M:** Alain Jomy. **HBO**

Little Tough Guys ⅋⅋ 1938 The Little Tough Guys (a.k.a. Dead End Kids) come to the rescue of Halop, a young tough guy gone bad to avenge his father's unjust imprisonment. First of the "Little Tough Guys" series for the former Dead End Kids, who later became the East Side Kids before eventually evolving into the Bowery Boys. **84m/B VHS, Beta.** Helen Parrish, Billy Halop, Leo Gorcey, Marjorie Main, Gabriel Dell, Huntz Hall; **D:** Harold Young. **NOS, MRV, VYY**

Little Treasure ⅋½ 1985 (R) A stripper heads for Mexico to search for her long-lost father, but ends up looking for treasure with an American guy. Disappointing effort of director Sharp. **95m/C VHS, Beta, LV, Closed Caption.** Burt Lancaster, Margot Kidder, Ted Danson, Joseph Hacker, Malena Doria; **D:** Alan Sharp; **W:** Alan Sharp. **COL**

The Little Valentino ⅋ 1979 One day in the aimless life of a young punk who gets by on his wits and petty theft. Jeles' directorial debut. In Hungarian with English subtitles. **102m/B VHS.** **HU** **D:** Andras Jeles. **FCT, AUD**

Little Vegas ⅋⅋½ 1990 (R) Looks like easy street for a young man who inherits a bundle from his girlfriend, but he's forced to wake up and smell the cappucino when her family and the other residents of the tiny desert berg think there's a gigolo in the woodpile. Much strife with siblings as he wages a battle for the bucks with the son while wooing the woman's daughter, with a measure of mob inflicted plot twists. Mildly amusing, cut from vein of you if you can't get rich quick and get away with it. **90m/C VHS, LV.** Michael Nouri, Jerry Stiller, John Sayles, Anthony John Denison, Catherine O'Hara, Bruce

McGill, Anne Francis, Bob(cat) Goldthwait, Jay Thomas, Perry Lang; **D:** Perry Lang; **W:** Perry Lang; **M:** Mason Daring. **COL**

Little Vera ⅋⅋⅋ *Malenkaya Vera* 1988 Extremely well-done Soviet film chronicles the life of a young working-class woman who loves rock music and who has been profoundly affected by Western civilization. Post-glasnost Soviet production gives Westerners a glimpse into the Russian way of life. A boxoffice bonanza back home. Russian with subtitles. **130m/C VHS, Beta, LV.** **RU** Natalia Negoda, Andrei Sokolov, Yuri Nazarov, Ludmila Zaisova, Alexander Niegreva; **D:** Vassili Pitchul. **FCT, LUM, WBF**

Little White Lies ⅋⅋ 1989 Jillian and Matheson meet and fall in love during an exotic vacation. But both are traveling under assumed identities—she's a policewoman tracking a jewel thief and he's an incognito doctor. When they reunite stateside they try to stick to their ruses in humdrum comedic fashion. Made for network TV. **88m/C VHS.** Ann Jillian, Tim Matheson; **D:** Anson Williams. **RHI**

Little Witches ⅋⅋ 1996 (R) Rejected group of seniors at Catholic girls' high school are transformed into a witches coven, thanks to a book of spells. A rip-off of "The Craft." **CW:** Violence, nudity, sexual situations. **91m/C VHS.** Mimi Reichmeister, Jack Nance, Jennifer Rubin, Sheeri Rappaport, Melissa Taub, Zoe Alexander, Zelda Rubinstein, Eric Pierpont; **D:** Jane Simpson; **W:** Brian DiMuccio, Dino Vindeni; **M:** Nicholas Rivera. **APX**

Little Women ⅋⅋⅋ 1933 Louisa May Alcott's Civil War story of the four March sisters—Jo, Beth, Amy, and Meg—who share their loves, their joys, and their sorrows. Everything about this classic film is wonderful, from the lavish period costumes to the excellent script, and particularly the captivating performances by the cast. A must-see for fans of Alcott and Hepburn, and others will find it enjoyable. Remade in 1949, in 1978 for television, and again in 1994. **107m/B VHS, Beta, 8mm, Closed Caption.** Katharine Hepburn, Joan Bennett, Paul Lukas, Edna May Oliver, Frances Dee, Spring Byington, Jean Parker, Douglass Montgomery; **D:** George Cukor; **W:** Victor Heerman, Sarah Y. Mason; **M:** Max Steiner, Max Steiner. Academy Awards '33: Best Adapted Screenplay; Venice Film Festival '34: Best Actress (Hepburn); Nominations: Academy Awards '33: Best Director (Cukor), Best Picture. **MGM, IGP**

Little Women ⅋⅋⅋ 1949 Stylized color remake of the George Cukor 1933 classic. Topnotch if too obvious cast portrays Louisa May Alcott's story of teenage girls growing up against the backdrop of the Civil War. Remade again, for television in 1978. **121m/C VHS, Closed Caption.** June Allyson, Peter Lawford, Margaret O'Brien, Elizabeth Taylor, Janet Leigh, Mary Astor; **D:** Mervyn LeRoy; **W:** Andrew Solt; **M:** Adolph Deutsch. Academy Awards '49: Best Art Direction/Set Decoration (Color); Nominations: Academy Awards '49: Best Color Cinematography. **MGM**

Little Women ⅋⅋ 1978 The third screen version of Louisa May Alcott's classic story. Lackluster compared to the previous attempts, particularly the sterling 1933 film, but still worthwhile. During the Civil War, four sisters share their lives as they grow up and find romance. Garson's television debut. Followed by a television series. **200m/C VHS, Closed Caption.** Meredith Baxter, Susan Dey, Ann Dusenberry, Eve Plumb, Dorothy McGuire, Robert Young, Greer Garson, Cliff Potts, William Shatner; **D:** David Lowell Rich; **M:** Elmer Bernstein. **NO**

Little Women ⅋⅋⅋⅋ 1994 (PG) Beloved story of the March women is beautifully portrayed in a solid production that blends a seamless screenplay with an excellent cast, authentic period costumes, and lovely cinematography and music. Ryder, perfectly cast as the unconventional Jo, is also the strongest of the sisters: domestically inclined Meg (Alvarado), the fragile Beth (Danes), and the youngest, mischievous Amy (the delightful Dunst) who grows up into a sedate young lady (Mathis). Charming adaptation remains faithful to the spirit of the Alcott classic

while adding contemporary touches. Fittingly brought to the big screen by producer Denise Di Novi, writer/co-producer Swicord, and director Armstrong. **118m/C VHS, LV, 8mm, Closed Caption, DVD.** Winona Ryder, Gabriel Byrne, Trini Alvarado, Samantha Mathis, Kirsten Dunst, Claire Danes, Christian Bale, Eric Stoltz, John Neville, Mary Wickes, Susan Sarandon; **D:** Gillian Armstrong; **W:** Robin Swicord; **C:** Geoffrey Simpson; **M:** Thomas Newman. Nominations: Academy Awards '94: Best Actress (Ryder), Best Costume Design, Best Original Score; Writers Guild of America '94: Best Adapted Screenplay. **COL**

Little World of Don Camillo ⅋⅋⅋ *Le Petit Monde de Don Camillo* 1951 A French-made farce based on the beloved novels of Giovanni Guareschi. Earthy priest Don Camillo clashes repeatedly with his friendly enemy, the communist mayor of a tiny Italian village. The hero talks directly to God, whose voice is provided by Orson Welles, also narrator of the English version. Charming, good-natured approach. **106m/B VHS, Beta, 8mm.** **FR IT** Fernandel, Gino Cervi, Sylvia, Vera Talqui; **D:** Julien Duvivier. **VYY, FCT**

The Littlest Angel ⅋⅋ 1969 Musical about a shepherd boy who dies falling off a cliff and wants to become an angel. He learns a valuable lesson in the spirit of giving. Made for TV. **77m/C VHS, Beta.** Johnny Whitaker, Fred Gwynne, E.G. Marshall, Cab Calloway, Connie Stevens, Tony Randall. **KAR**

The Littlest Horse Thieves ⅋⅋½ 1976 *Escape from the Dark* (G) Good Disney film about three children and their efforts to save some ponies who work in mines. The children take it upon themselves to see that the animals escape the abuse and neglect they are put through. Filmed on location in England with excellent photography. **109m/C VHS, Beta.** Alastair Sim, Peter Barkworth; **D:** Charles Jarrott. **DIS**

The Littlest Outlaw ⅋⅋½ 1954 A Mexican peasant boy steals a beautiful stallion to save it from being destroyed. Together, they ride off on a series of adventures. Disney movie filmed on location in Mexico. **73m/C VHS, Beta.** Pedro Armendariz Sr., Joseph Calleia, Andres Velasquez; **D:** Roberto Gavaldon. **DIS**

The Littlest Rebel ⅋⅋½ 1935 (PG) Temple stars in this well-done piece set during the Civil War in the Old South. She befriends a Union officer while protecting her father at the same time. She even goes to Washington to talk with President Lincoln. Nice dance sequences by Temple and Robinson. Available in computer-colored version. **70m/B VHS, Beta, Closed Caption.** Shirley Temple, John Boles, Jack Holt, Bill Robinson, Karen Morley, Willie Best; **D:** David Butler. **FOX**

The Littlest Viking ⅋⅋½ 1994 (PG) Twelve-year-old Sigurd finds archery practice and mock battles an exciting way to learn to be a Viking. But when his older brother is killed in battle, Sigurd's father expects him to avenge the death, and Sigurd must decide just what being a Viking prince means. Scenic Scandinavian settings; obvious dubbing. **85m/C VHS, LV.** Kristian Tonby, Per Jansen, Terje Stromdahl; **D:** Knut W. Jorfald, Lars Rasmussen, Paul Trevor Bale.

Live a Little, Love a Little ⅋⅋ 1968 (PG) Itinerant photographer Elvis juggles two different jobs by running around a lot. Sexually more frank than earlier King vehicles. ♫ Almost in Love; A Little Less Conversation; Edge of Reality; Wonderful World. **90m/C VHS, Beta.** Elvis Presley, Michele Carey, Rudy Vallee, Don Porter, Dick Sargent, Sterling Holloway, Eddie Hodges; **D:** Norman Taurog. **MGM**

Live and Let Die ⅋⅋ 1973 (PG) Agent 007 is out to thwart the villainous Dr. Kananga, a black mastermind who plans to control western powers with voodoo and hard drugs. Moore's first appearance as Bond. Can't we have the real Bond back? Title song by Paul McCartney. **131m/C VHS, Beta, LV, Letterbox.** **GB** Roger Moore, Jane Seymour, Yaphet Kotto, Clifton James, Julius W. Harris, Geoffrey

Holder, David Hedison, Gloria Hendry, Bernard Lee, Lois Maxwell, Madeleine Smith; **D:** Guy Hamilton; **W:** Tom Mankiewicz; **C:** Ted Moore; **M:** George Martin. Nominations: Academy Awards '73: Best Song ("Live and Let Die"). *MGM, FOX, TLF*

Live Bait 🎬🎬½ 1995 Canadian-flavored Gen-X comedy features suburban 23-year-old virgin Trevor MacIntosh (Scholte) trying for a little romance (or at least sex) but seemingly doomed to failure. At least until he meets much older artist Charlotte (Maunsell). Sweeney handles his debut writing, directing, and producing skills with equal aplomb. 84m/B VHS. *CA* Tom Scholte, Micki Maunsell, Kevin McNulty, Babz Chula, David Lovgren, Laara Sadiq, Michelle Beaudoin, Kelly Aisenstat; **D:** Bruce Sweeney; **W:** Bruce Sweeney; **C:** David Pelletier. Toronto-City Award '95: Best Canadian Feature Film. *NYR*

Live Flesh 🎬🎬🎬½ *Carne Tremula* 1997 (R) The courses of five lives in Madrid are forever altered when naive, young Victor (Rabal) accidentally shoots cop David (Bardem) and is sent to prison after an argument with Elena (Neri), a one-night stand he falls for. When he gets out he discovers Elena has transformed from junkie to model wife who runs a home for children and has married David, now a paraplegic. Still, Victor both wants and resents Elena, who he blames for the accident. While apparently stalking Elena, Victor enters into a relationship with Clara, the wife of David's former partner, Sancho (Sancho) which dramatically draws all five back together. Complex, noirish drama shows a new, more serious side for director Almadovar, who still manages some of his patented brand of humor. Highly original plot and unexpected twists delivered by a talented and attractive cast. Adapted from a British novel by Ruth Rendell. **CW:** Strong sexuality, language and some drug content. 100m/C VHS. *FR SP* Javier Bardem, Francesca Neri, Angela Molina, Liberto Rabal, Jose Sancho, Penelope Cruz, Pilar Bardem, Alex Angula; **D:** Pedro Almodovar; **W:** Pedro Almodovar, Ray Loriga, Jorge Guerricaechevarria; **C:** Alfonso Beato; **M:** Alberto Iglesias. *ORI*

Live! From Death Row 🎬🎬 1992 Cassidy plays a tabloid TV host who'll do anything to get ratings. She's set to do a live interview with a condemned serial killer (Davison) shortly before his execution. But Davison and his fellow death-row inmates take Cassidy and her crew hostage as he decides to use the show for his own media message. 94m/C VHS. Joanna Cassidy, Bruce Davison, Art LaFleur, Calvin Levels, Michael D. Roberts; **D:** Patrick Duncan; **W:** Patrick Duncan.

Live Nude Girls 🎬🎬 1995 (R) Group of 30-something girlfriends get together to throw a bachelorette party for one of their number and sit around gossiping about sex, relationships, family, and friends. Not much plot but nice ensemble work. **CW:** Graphic sexual dialogue and scenes of sexuality. 92m/C VHS, LV, Closed Caption. Dana Delany, Kim Cattrall, Cynthia Stevenson, Laila Robins, Olivia D'Abo, Lora Zane, Glenn Quinn, Tim Choate; **D:** Julianna Lavin; **W:** Julianna Lavin; **C:** Christopher Taylor; **M:** Anton Sanko. *REP*

The Live Wire 🎬🎬 1934 Stunt-ridden action fare featuring Talmadge at his most daring. This adventure is complete with desert island, lost treasure, stowaways, evil-doers, and a race against the clock. 57m/B VHS, Beta. Richard Talmadge, George Walsh, Charles French, Alberta Vaughn; **D:** Harry S. Webb. *NOS, DVT, GPV*

Live Wire 🎬🎬½ 1992 (R) Brosnan is an FBI bomb expert who needs a new line of work. He's up against a terrorist psychopath who has his greedy hands on a new type of explosive. It's liquid, undetectable, looks as innocent as a glass of water, and is capable of blowing up Washington, D.C. Made for cable television. Also available in an unrated version. **CW:** Language, strong violence, and strong sensuality. 85m/C VHS, Closed Caption. Pierce Brosnan, Ben Cross, Ron Silver, Lisa Eilbacher; **D:** Christian Duguay; **W:** Bart Baker. *COL, NLC*

Live Wire: Human Timebomb 🎬½ 1995 (R) FBI agent Jim Parker is captured by a Cuban general who implants a computer chip into his neck—turning Parker into a human timebomb. **CW:** Language, violence. 98m/C VHS, Closed Caption. Bryan Genesse, Joe Lara, Frantz Dobrowsky, J. Cynthia Brooks; **D:** Mark Roper; **W:** Jeff Albert; **C:** Rod Stewart; **M:** Itai Haber. *TTC*

The Lives of a Bengal Lancer 🎬🎬🎬 1935 One of Hollywood's greatest rousing adventures. Three British Lancers, of varying experience, encounter a vicious revolution against colonial rule. Rivaled only by "Gunga Din" as the ultimate 1930s swashbuckler. Swell plot, lotsa action, great comraderie. Based on the novel by Major Francis Yeats-Brown, and remade in 1939 as "Geronimo." 110m/B VHS, Beta. Gary Cooper, Franchot Tone, Richard Cromwell, Guy Standing, Sir C. Aubrey Smith, Monte Blue, Kathleen Burke, Noble Johnson, Lumsden Hare, Akim Tamiroff, J. Carrol Naish, Douglass Dumbrille; **D:** Henry Hathaway; **W:** Waldemar Young, John Balderston; **C:** Charles B(ryant) Lang; **M:** Milan Roder. Nominations: Academy Awards '35: Best Director (Hathaway), Best Film Editing, Best Interior Decoration, Best Picture, Best Screenplay, Best Sound. *USH*

Livin' Large 🎬🎬 1991 (R) An African-American delivery boy gets the break of his life when a nearby newscaster is shot dead. Grabbing the microphone and continuing the story, he soon finds himself hired by an Atlanta news station as an anchorman, fulfilling a life-long dream. But problems arise when he finds himself losing touch with his friends, his old neighborhood and his roots. Comedy "deals" with the compelling issue of blacks finding success in a white world by trivializing the issue at every turn and resorting to racial stereotypes. **CW:** Language. 96m/C VHS, Closed Caption. Terrence "T.C." Carson, Lisa Arrindell, Blanche Baker, Nathaniel "Afrika" Hall, Julia Campbell; **D:** Michael A. Schultz; **C:** Peter Collister; **M:** Herbie Hancock. *HBO*

The Living Coffin 🎬½ *El Grito de la Muerte* 1958 Woman has alarm rigged on her coffin in case she's buried alive. And they called her paranoid. Loosely based on Poe's "Premature Burial." 72m/C VHS. *MX* Gaston Santos, Maria Duval, Pedro de Aguillon; **D:** Fernando Mendez. *SNC*

The Living Daylights 🎬🎬🎬 1987 (PG) After being used as a pawn in a fake Russian defector plot, our intrepid spy tracks down an international arms and opium smuggling ring. Fine debut by Dalton as 007 in a rousing, refreshing cosmopolitan shoot-em-up. Let's be frank: we were all getting a little fatigued by Roger Moore. 130m/C VHS, Beta, LV, Letterbox, Closed Caption. Timothy Dalton, Maryam D'Abo, Jeroen Krabbe, John Rhys-Davies, Robert Brown, Joe Don Baker, Desmond Llewelyn, Art Malik, Geoffrey Keen, Walter Gotell, Andreas Wisniewski; **D:** John Glen; **W:** Richard Maibaum, Michael G. Wilson; **M:** John Barry. *MGM, TLF, FOX*

The Living Dead 🎬🎬 *The Scotland Yard Mystery* 1936 An English film about a mad, re-animating scientist. 76m/B VHS, Beta. *GB* Gerald du Maurier, George Curzon. *NOS, SNC, DVT*

The Living End 🎬🎬 1992 Director Araki's radical lovers-on-the-lam story concerns freelance L.A. writer Jon (Gilmore) who has just learned he is H.I.V.-positive. He meets a handsome, violent, hustler named Luke (Dytri) and the two begin a desperate road trip along the California coast which can only end in tragedy. Araki not only wrote and directed the film but also served as cinematographer and editor—all on a $23,000 budget. Stylish, tragic, and filled with black humor and frank homoeroticism. 92m/C VHS. Craig Gilmore, Mike Dytri, Darcy Marta; **D:** Gregg Araki; **W:** Gregg Araki; **C:** Gregg Araki.

Living Free 🎬🎬½ 1972 (G) Sequel to "Born Free," based on the nonfictional books by Joy Adamson. Recounts the travails of Elsa the lioness, who is now dying, with three young cubs that need care. Nice and pleasant, but could you

pick up the pace? 91m/C VHS, Beta, LV. Susan Hampshire, Nigel Davenport; **D:** Jack Couffer. *COL, GKK*

The Living Head 🎬🎬½ *La Cabeza Viviente* 1959 Archaeologists discover the ancient sepulcher of the great Aztec warrior, Acatl. Ignoring a curse, they steal his severed head and incur the fury of Xitsliapoli. They should have known better. Dubbed in English. 75m/B VHS, Beta. *MX* Mauricio Garces, Ana Luisa Peluffo, German Robles, Abel Salazar; **D:** Chano Urueto. *VYY, SNC*

Living in Oblivion 🎬🎬🎬 1994 (R) Humorous tri-part story is an insiders joke on the problems of low-budget filmmaking, including talent, libido, ego, and pervasive chaos. First, director Nick Reve (Buscemi) tries to film an emotional scene with leading lady Nicole (Keener) only to have everything go wrong; then star Chad (LeGros), a dimwit but a "name," arrives to throw his weight around (and seduce Nicole); and finally the leading lady must deal with an overly sensitive dwarf and Nick's mother. A sleeper. **CW:** Strong language. 92m/C VHS, LV, Closed Caption. Steve Buscemi, Catherine Keener, James LeGros, Dermot Mulroney, Danielle von Zerneck, Robert Wightman, Rica Martens, Hilary Gilford, Peter Dinklage, Kevin Corrigan, Matthew Grace, Michael Griffiths, Ryna Bowker, Francesca DiMauro; **D:** Tom DiCillo; **W:** Tom DiCillo; **C:** Frank Prinzi; **M:** Jim Farmer. Sundance Film Festival '95: Best Screenplay; Nominations: Independent Spirit Awards '96: Best Film, Best Screenplay, Best Supporting Actor (LeGros). *COL*

Living in Peril 🎬🎬 1997 (R) Ambitious architect Walter Woods (Lowe) is in L.A. to design a mansion for an eccentric client (Belushi). But a series of accidents threaten to ruin his reputation, if not provoke something more deadly. **CW:** Language, violence and some sexuality. 95m/C VHS, LV, Closed Caption. Rob Lowe, James Belushi, Dean Stockwell, Dana Wheeler-Nicholson, Richard Moll, Alex Meneses, Patrick Ersgard; **D:** Jack Ersgard; **W:** Patrick Ersgard. *NLC*

Living on Tokyo Time 🎬🎬½ 1987 Interesting but often dull, low budget independent comedy about a young Japanese woman who hitches up with a boorish Japanese-American man in order to stay in the United States. An Asian view of Asian-America, filmed on location in San Francisco. 83m/C VHS, Beta. Minako Ohashi, Ken Nakagawa, Kate Connell, Mitzi Abe, Bill Bonham, Brenda Aoki; **D:** Steven Okazaki; **W:** Steven Okazaki, John McCormick. *NLC*

Living Proof: The Hank Williams Jr. Story 🎬🎬½ 1983 TV biopic focusing on the country singer's hell-raising ways as he seeks to get out from under the shadow of his famous father and into the spotlight on his own right. Based on Williams, Jr.'s autobiography; includes 10 songs by Sr. and Jr. 97m/C VHS, Closed Caption. Richard Thomas, Clu Gulager, Allyn Ann McLerie, Naomi Judd, Christian Slater; **D:** Dick Lowry; **W:** I.C. Rapoport, Stephen Kandel. *WAR*

Living to Die 🎬½ 1991 (R) Vegas gumshoe is assigned to investigate a blackmailed official, and discovers a woman believed to be dead is alive and beautiful and living incognito. This mystifies him. 84m/C VHS. Wings Hauser, Darcy Demoss, Asher Brauner, Arnold Vosloo, Jim Williams; **D:** Wings Hauser. *PMH, HHE*

The Lizzies of Mack Sennett 1915 Three quick-paced, hilarious Sennett "Tin Lizzie" comedies: "Lizzies of the Field," "Leading Lizzie Astray" and "Love, Speed and Thrills." Plenty of signature slapstick from the master. 51m/C VHS, Beta. Billy Bevan, Fatty Arbuckle, Mack Swain, Chester Conklin; **D:** Mack Sennett. *VYY*

Lloyds of London 🎬🎬🎬 1936 If you wonder how the story of a British insurance company can be exciting, just watch this lavish spectacular (which, of course, lacks historical accuracy). Jonathan Blake (Power) has risen in the ranks of the firm, thanks in part to his lifelong friendship with Lord Horatio Nelson (Burton), much to the disgust of haughty Lord Everett Stacy (an ever-supercilious Sanders). As Bonaparte comes to power, Blake travels to France to rescue some friends and saves Elizabeth (Carroll), who turns out to be Stacy's wife. Stacy is also spreading rumors about Lloyds' solvency and Nelson's heroics at Trafalgar and his machinations lead to further trouble with Blake. 115m/B VHS, Letterbox, Closed Caption. Tyrone Power, George Sanders, Madeleine Carroll, John Burton, Guy Standing, Sir C. Aubrey Smith, Freddie Bartholomew, Virginia Field, Montagu Love, Una O'Connor; **D:** Henry King; **W:** Ernest Pascal, Walter Ferris; **C:** Bert Glennon. Nominations: Academy Awards '36: Best Film Editing. FXV

Loaded ✽✽ *Bloody Weekend* 1994 (R) Writer-director Campion (sister of director Jane) follows a group of teens to an abandoned English mansion as they try to film an amateur horror movie. While there, the group decides to have some fun, with the help of LSD. This leads to some therapeutic and angst-ridden discussions about each of their problems, as well as a tragic accident, which changes the lives of all involved. There's some nice character sketches, unfortunately they're more interesting than the loose plot, which leaves too many questions unanswered. Retitled and re-cut since its original '94 release.**CW:** Profanity, sexual situations and partial nudity. 95m/C VHS, LV, Closed Caption. *Catherine McCormack, Oliver Milburn, Nick Patrick, Danny Cunningham, Mathew Eggleton, Biddy Hodson; **D:** Anna Campion; **W:** Anna Campion; **C:** Alan Almond; **M:** Simon Fisher Turner. MAX

Loaded Guns woof! 1975 Airline stewardess-cum-double agent must totally immobilize a top drug trafficking ring. Pathetic spy tale with plenty of unintended laughs. 90m/C VHS, Beta. *Ursula Andress, Woody Strode; **D:** Fernando Di Leo. ART

Loaded Pistols ✽ 1948 Story set in the old West starring Gene Autry. 80m/B VHS, Beta. *Gene Autry, Jack Holt, Barbara Britton; **D:** John English. NOS, VCN, DVT

Loan Shark ✽✽ 1952 An ex-convict gets a job at a tire company, working undercover to expose a loan shark ring. Hackneyed plot moves quickly. 79m/B VHS, Beta, LV. *George Raft, John Hoyt; **D:** Seymour Friedman. NO

Lobster for Breakfast ✽✽½ 1982 (R) An Italian gag-fest about a toilet salesman infiltrating his friend's confused marital existence just to make a sale. With English subtitles; also available in a dubbed version. 96m/C VHS, Beta. IT *Enrico Montesano, Claude Brasseur, Claudine Auger; **D:** Giorgio Capitani.

Lobster Man from Mars ✽✽ 1989 (PG) When rich movie producer (Curtis) learns from his accountant that he must produce a flop or be taken to the cleaners by the IRS, he buys a homemade horror movie from a young filmmaker. The film is an ultra-low budget production featuring a kooky lobster man and a screaming damsel. The premise peters out about halfway through, but there are enough yuks to keep you going. 84m/C VHS, Beta, LV. *Tony Curtis, Deborah Foreman, Patrick Macnee, Tommy Sledge, Billy Barty, Phil Proctor; **D:** Stanley Shiff. ART

Local Badman ✽ 1932 A dim-witted cowhand saves the day in this rip-roaring tale of the old west. 60m/B VHS, Beta. *Hoot Gibson. NOS, VCI, RXM

Local Hero ✽✽✽✽ 1983 (PG) Riegert is a yuppie representative of a huge oil company who endeavors to buy a sleepy Scottish fishing village for excavation, and finds himself hypnotized by the place and its crusty denizens. Back in Texas at company headquarters, tycoon Lancaster deals with a psycho therapist and gazes at the stars looking for clues. A low-key, charmingly offbeat Scottish comedy with its own sense of logic and quiet humor, poetic landscapes, and unique characters, epitomizing Forsyth's original style. 112m/C VHS, Beta, LV, Closed Caption. GB *Peter Riegert, Denis Lawson, Burt Lancaster, Fulton Mackay, Jenny

Seagrove, Peter Capaldi, Norman Chancer; **D:** Bill Forsyth; **W:** Bill Forsyth; **C:** Chris Menges; **M:** Mark Knopfler. British Academy Awards '83: Best Director (Forsyth); New York Film Critics Awards '83: Best Screenplay; National Society of Film Critics Awards '83: Best Screenplay. WAR

Loch Ness ✽✽½ 1995 (PG) American zoologist Jonathan Dempsey (Danson) specializes in hunting legendary animals and his latest assignment is to head for the Scottish highlands and take on the Nessie legend. He gets an assistant (Frain), a potential romance with single mom Laura (Richardson), and a lot of grief from some hostile locals before Laura's young daughter Isabel (Graham) decides to help him out. Jim Henson's Creature Shop takes care of the monster's animatronics. 101m/C VHS. GB *Ted Danson, Ian Holm, Joely Richardson, Kirsty Graham, James Frain, Harris Yulin, Keith Allen, Nick Brimble; **D:** John Henderson; **W:** John Fusco; **C:** Clive Tickner; **M:** Trevor Jones. PGV

The Loch Ness Horror woof! 1982 The famed monster surfaces and chomps on the local poachers—and with good reason. Would that it had munched this movie's producer in, say, 1981. 93m/C VHS, Beta. *Barry Buchanan, Miki McKenzie, Sandy Kenyon; **D:** Larry Buchanan. NO

Lock 'n' Load ✽✽ 1990 (R) Why are all the soldiers in the 82nd Airborne stealing vast sums, then committing suicide? One of the guys involved wants to know. ?m/C VHS, LV. *Jack Vogel; **D:** David A. Prior.

Lock Up ✽½ 1989 (R) Peaceful con Stallone, with only six months to go, is harassed and tortured by vicious prison warden Sutherland in retribution for an unexplained past conflict. Lackluster and moronic; semi-color; surely Sutherland can find better roles. 115m/C VHS, Beta, Closed Caption. *Sylvester Stallone, Donald Sutherland, Sonny Landham, John Amos, Darlanne Fluegel, Frank McRae; **D:** John Flynn; **W:** Jeb Stuart; **M:** Bill Conti. ART

Lockdown ✽½ 1990 Charged with his partner's murder, a detective is forced to ponder the perennial puzzle of life. Not a pretty sight. 90m/C VHS. *Joe Estevez, Mike Farrell, Richard Lynch. THV

The Locusts ✽½ 1997 (R) Backwater beefcake Clay Hewitt (Vaughn) swaggers into a small Kansas town where everyone has a lit cigarette and a secret and no one is safe from hopeless cliches and corny dialogue. Clay's sweaty, sleeveless t-shirts and choir-boy face soon have the women swarming, but he's only interested in helping a mentally and emotionally challenged kid named Flyboy (Davies) get out from under his emasculating and abusive mother Delilah (Capshaw), also Clay's boss and overly-ardent admirer. Judd is barely used as Clay's spunky squeeze in this slow-paced, small-town drama by first-time director Kelley. Any high school freshman with an English lit class under his belt won't miss the not-so-subtle metaphors at play—Delilah has workers castrating bulls a lot.**CW:** Sexuality. 123m/C VHS, Closed Caption. *Kate Capshaw, Jeremy Davies, Vince Vaughn, Ashley Judd, Paul Rudd, Daniel Meyer, Jessica Capshaw; **D:** John Patrick Kelley; **W:** John Patrick Kelley; **C:** Phedon Papamichael; **M:** Carter Burwell. ART

L'Odeur des Fauves ✽ 1966 One of a cynical reporter's scandalous stories gets an innocent man killed, compelling the reporter somehow to make restitution. Subtitled in English. 86m/C VHS, Beta. FR *Maurice Ronet, Josephine Chaplin, Vittorio De Sica; **D:** Richard Balducci. BAR

The Lodger ✽✽✽ *The Case of Jonathan Drew; The Lodger: A Case of London Fog* 1926 A mysterious lodger is thought to be a rampaging mass murderer of young women. First Hitchcock film to explore the themes and ideas that would become his trademarks. Silent. Climactic chase is memorable. Remade three times. Look closely for the Master in his first cameo. 91m/B VHS, Beta. GB *Ivor Novello, Marie Ault, Arthur Chesney, Malcolm Keen, June; *Cameos:* Alfred Hitchcock; **D:** Alfred Hitchcock; **W:** Alfred Hitchcock, Eliot Stannard. VYY, NOS, VDM

Logan's Run ✽✽½ 1976 In the 23rd century, a hedonistic society exists in a huge bubble and people are only allowed to live to the age of 30. Intriguing concepts and great futuristic sets prevail here. Based on the novel by William Nolan and George Clayton Johnson. 120m/C VHS, Beta, LV, Letterbox. *Michael York, Jenny Agutter, Richard Jordan, Roscoe Lee Browne, Farrah Fawcett, Peter Ustinov, Camilla Carr, Ann Ford; **D:** Michael Anderson Sr.; **W:** David Zelag Goodman; **C:** Ernest Laszlo; **M:** Jerry Goldsmith. Academy Awards '76: Best Visual Effects; Nominations: Academy Awards '76: Best Art Direction/Set Decoration, Best Cinematography. MGM

Lois Gibbs and the Love Canal ✽✽ 1982 Mason's television movie debut as Lois Gibbs, a housewife turned activist, fighting the authorities over chemical-dumping in the Love Canal area of Niagara Falls, New York. The script doesn't convey the seriousness of developments in that region. 100m/C VHS. *Marsha Mason, Bob Gunton, Penny Fuller, Roberta Maxwell, Jeremy Licht, Louise Latham; **D:** Glenn Jordan. NO

Lola ✽✽✽ 1961 A wonderful tale of a nightclub dancer and her amorous adventures. Innovative film that marked the beginning of French New Wave. In French with English subtitles. 90m/B VHS. FR *Anouk Aimee, Marc Michel, Elina Labourdette, Jacques Harden; **D:** Jacques Demy. INT, TPV

Lola ✽½ *The Statutory Affair; Twinky* 1969 (PG) A teenaged girl links up romantically with a considerably older writer of pornographic books. One would expect more from such a good cast, but the film never follows through. British release was originally 98 minutes. 88m/C VHS, Beta. GB IT *Charles Bronson, Susan George, Trevor Howard, Michael Craig, Honor Blackman, Lionel Jeffries, Robert Morley, Jack Hawkins, Orson Bean, Kay Medford, Paul Ford; **D:** Richard Donner. FCT, MRV

Lola Montes ✽✽✽✽ 1955 Ophuls' final masterpiece recounts the life and sins of the famous courtesan, mistress of Franz Liszt and the King of Bavaria. Ignored upon release, but hailed later by the French as a cinematic landmark. Presented in its original widescreen format; in French with English subtitles. Also available in a 110-minute version. Adapted from an unpublished novel by Cecil Saint-Laurent. 140m/C Beta, LV, Letterbox. FR *Martine Carol, Peter Ustinov, Anton Walbrook, Ivan Desny, Oskar Werner; **D:** Max Ophuls; **W:** Max Ophuls; **M:** Georges Auric. CRC, NLC

Lolita ✽✽✽ 1962 A middle-aged professor is consumed by his lust for a teenage nymphet in this strange film considered daring in its time. Based on Vladimir Nabokov's novel. Watch for Winters' terrific portrayal as Lolita's sex-starved mother. 152m/B VHS, Beta, LV, Letterbox. GB *James Mason, Shelley Winters, Peter Sellers, Sue Lyon, Gary Cockrell, Jerry Stovin, Diana Decker, Lois Maxwell, Cec Linder, Bill Greene, Shirley Douglas, Marianne Stone, Marion Mathie, James Dyrenforth, C. Denier Warren, Terence Kilburn, John Harrison; **D:** Stanley Kubrick; **C:** Oswald Morris; **M:** Nelson Riddle. Nominations: Academy Awards '62: Best Adapted Screenplay. MGM, CRC

Lolita 2000 ✽½ 1997 In the future all sexual activity is prohibited (bummer). Lolita's working for an organization that destroys sexual material but three particular stories arouse feelings in her that she just has to act on. 90m/C VHS. *Jacqueline Lovell, Gabriella Hall, Eric Acsell; **D:** Sybil Richards. AFE

London Kills Me ✽✽ 1991 (R) A slice-of-life story London-style. Set at the end of the Thatcher era, Clint is a homeless drifter dealing drugs to get by. He's trying to get enough money for a new pair of shoes which will enable him to get a job in a fancy restaurant and away from his aimless life. His friend Muffdiver leads the group of drug pushers and is obsessed with money and power. Sylvie is the sultry junkie who drifts between Clint, Muffdiver, and her drug needs. The directorial debut of Kureishi is more a collection of characters and situations than a complete film but there are moments of disturbing intensity and odd sweetness.**CW:** Language, nudity, and drug use.

105m/C VHS, LV, Closed Caption. *GB* Justin Chadwick, Steven Mackintosh, Emer McCourt, Roshan Seth, Fiona Shaw, Brad Dourif, Gordon Warnecke; *D:* Hanif Kureishi; *W:* Hanif Kureishi. *ART, PMS*

London Melody 🐾½ *Girl in the Street* 1937 Neagle is a spirited Cockney busker who meets a kindly Italian diplomat who decides to finance her musical education. He promptly also falls in love with her. **71m/B VHS, Beta, 8mm.** *GB* Anna Neagle, Tullio Carminati, Robert Douglas, Horace Hodgers; *D:* Herbert Wilcox. *VYY*

The Lone Avenger 🐾🐾 1933 Average oater centers around a bank panic, with two-gun Maynard clearing up the trouble. **60m/B VHS, Beta.** Ken Maynard, Muriel Gordon, James Marcus. *NOS, VCN, CAB*

Lone Bandit 🐾½ 1933 Vintage western starring Chandler. **57m/B VHS, Beta.** Lane Chandler, Doris Brook, Wally Wales; *D:* J.P. McGowan. *VCN*

The Lone Defender 1932 A dozen episodes of the western serial starring the canine crusader, Rin Tin Tin. **235m/B VHS, Beta.** Walter Miller, June Marlowe, Buzz Barton, Josef Swickard, Frank Lanning, Robert F. (Bob) Kortman; *D:* Richard Thorpe. *VDM, GPV, MLB*

Lone Justice 🐾🐾½ 1993 (R) Cowboy Ned Blessing has seen and done it all (from outlaw to sheriff) but his wild ways have caught up with him. Now, he's relating his exploits from a jail cell as he awaits his fate at the end of a rope. Beware—this looks like the first chapter of a series and there's no real ending.*CW:* Western violence. **94m/C VHS, LV, Closed Caption.** Daniel Baldwin, Luis Avalos, Chris Cooper, Sean Baca, Taylor Fry, Julia Campbell, Rene Auberjonois, Timothy Scott, Bob Gunton, Miguel Sandoval, Jeff Kober; *D:* Peter Werner; *W:* William D. Wittliff; *M:* Basil Poledouris.

Lone Justice 2 🐾🐾½ *Ned Blessing: The Story of My Life and Times* 1993 (PG-13) Laconic hero Ned Blessing (Johnson), along with Mexican sidekick Crecencio (Avalos), return to Blessing's hometown after a six-year absence and find it ruled by six-shooters and fists. The despicable Borgers clan has murdered the local sheriff (who happens to be Blessing's daddy) and rules by intimidation—until Ned gets involved. Cliched but amusing TV movie.*CW:* Some violence. **93m/C VHS.** Brad Johnson, Luis Avalos, Wes Studi, Bill McKinney, Brenda Bakke, Julius Tennon, Richard Riehle, Gregory Scott Cummins, Rob Campbell, Rusty Schwimmer; *D:* Jack Bender; *W:* William D. Wittliff. *TRI*

Lone Justice 3: Showdown at Plum Creek 🐾🐾½ 1996 (PG) Ex-outlaw-turned-sheriff Ned Blessing (Johnson) discovers the body of the previous sheriff has disappeared from its grave, Big Emma has taken over the saloon and wants Blessing out of the way, and Oscar Wilde comes to town. Three re-edited stories from the TV miniseries. **94m/C VHS.** Brad Johnson, Wes Studi, Brenda Bakke, William Sanderson, Luis Avalos, Rusty Schwimmer, Stephen Fry; *D:* Jack Bender, Dan Lerner, David Hemmings; *W:* Stephen Harrigan; *C:* Neil Roach. *TRI*

The Lone Ranger 1938 Western serial about the masked man and his faithful Indian sidekick. From a long-sought print found in Mexico, this program is burdened by a noisy sound track, two completely missing chapters, an abridged episode #15, and Spanish subtitles. **234m/B VHS, Beta.** Lee Powell; *D:* William Witney, John English. *VYY, NOS, VCN*

Lone Ranger 1956 Tonto and that strange masked man must prevent a war between ranchers and Indians in the first of the "Lone Ranger" series. "Hi-ho Silver!" **87m/C VHS, Beta.** Clayton Moore, Jay Silverheels, Lyle Bettger, Bonita Granville; *D:* Stuart Heisler. *MGM*

Lone Ranger and the Lost City of Gold 🐾🐾 1958 Three Indian men are found dead, and the Lone Ranger and Tonto set out to discover the killers. **80m/C VHS.** Clayton Moore, Jay

Silverheels, Douglas Kennedy; *D:* Lesley Selander; *M:* Les Baxter. *NO*

The Lone Rider in Cheyenne 🐾½ 1942 One of the last in the "Lone Rider" series. The Lone Rider is out to clear the name of an innocent man accused of murder. **59m/B VHS.** George Houston, Al "Fuzzy" St. John; *D:* Sam Newfield. *NOS, DVT, HEG*

The Lone Rider in Ghost Town 🐾½ 1941 Outlaws "haunt" a ghost town to protect their hidden mine and the Lone Rider and his pal, Fuzzy, are out to solve the mystery. Installment in the short-lived "Lone Rider" series. **64m/B VHS.** George Houston, Al "Fuzzy" St. John, Budd Buster; *D:* Sam Newfield. *NOS, DVT, HEG*

The Lone Runner woof! 1988 (PG) An adventurer rescues a beautiful heiress from Arab kidnappers in this dud. **90m/C VHS, Beta, LV.** Miles O'Keeffe, Ronald Lacey, Michael J. Aronin, John Steiner, Al Yamanouchi; *D:* Ruggero Deodato.

Lone Star 🐾🐾 1952 Big stars, big budget western in which Texas fights for independence as good guy Gable and badman Crawford fight each other. Gardner plays a fiery newspaper editor as well as Gable's love interest. Script is chock full of holes, but great action scenes make up for it. Based on the story by Borden Chase. **94m/B VHS.** Clark Gable, Ava Gardner, Broderick Crawford, Lionel Barrymore, Beulah Bondi, Ed Begley Sr., William Farnum, Lowell Gilmore; *D:* Vincent Sherman; *W:* Howard Estabrook, Borden Chase. *MGM*

Lone Star 🐾🐾🐾½ 1995 (R) Terrific contemporary western set in the border town Frontera, Texas. Sheriff Sam Deeds (Cooper) is still dealing with the legacy of his father, legendary lawman Buddy Deeds (McConaughey) who, 40 years before, wrestled control of the town from his racist, corrupt predecessor Charlie Wade (Kristofferson) and supposedly sent him packing. But when skeletal remains and a sheriff's badge turn up on an abandoned Army rifle range, guess whose bones they turn out to be. Buddy's friends would like Sam to just leave the past lie but he can't and learns some hard home truths. This is only one of the town's stories that Sayles gracefully tells and, as always, his ensemble cast all offer outstanding performances.*CW:* Brief language, sex, and violence. **137m/C VHS, LV, Closed Caption.** Chris Cooper, Matthew McConaughey, Kris Kristofferson, Elizabeth Pena, Joe Morton, Ron Canada, Clifton James, Miriam Colon, Frances McDormand; *D:* John Sayles; *W:* John Sayles; *C:* Stuart Dryburgh; *M:* Mason Daring. Independent Spirit Awards '97: Best Supporting Actress (Pena); Nominations: Academy Awards '96: Best Original Screenplay; British Academy Awards '96: Best Original Screenplay; Golden Globe Awards '97: Best Screenplay; Independent Spirit Awards '97: Best Actor (Cooper), Best Film, Best Screenplay; Writers Guild of America '96: Best Original Screenplay. *COL*

Lone Star Kid 1988 11-year-old Brian Zimmerman lives in Crabb, Texas—population 400. After he witnesses a car accident death because there's no adequate emergency service, he decides to run for mayor and help modernize the town. Based on a true story. Includes a viewers' guide. Presented as part of the "Wonderworks" series. **55m/C VHS.** James Earl Jones, Chad Sheets; *M:* Charlie Daniels. *HMV, BTV, FCT*

Lone Star Law Men 🐾 1942 A U.S. marshal has his hands full in a border town overrun with bandits. Keene stars as the deputy marshall who goes undercover and joins the gang in an attempt to foil their crooked plans. **58m/B VHS.** Tom George Duryea Keene, Frank Yaconelli, Sugar Dawn, Betty Miles; *D:* Robert Emmett Tansey. *NOS, DVT*

The Lone Star Ranger 🐾½ 1930 Former outlaw O'Brien is trying to go straight by helping to bring a gang of rustlers to justice. Interesting plot twist in the link between his girlfriend and the head of the gang. **64m/B VHS.** George O'Brien, Sue Carol, Walter McGrail, Warren Hymer, Russell Simpson; *D:* A.F. Erickson. *DVT, HEG*

Lone Wolf 🐾 1988 A werewolf terrorizes a high school, and a few computerniks track it down. **97m/C VHS, Beta.** Dyann Brown, Kevin Hart, Jamie Newcomb, Ann Douglas; *D:* John Callas.

Lone Wolf McQuade 🐾🐾½ 1983 Martial arts action abounds in this modern-day Western which pits unorthodox Texas Ranger Norris against a band of gun-running mercenaries led by Carradine. Oh, and there's a conflict-ridden love interest as well. Violent (and not particularly literary) but worthy entry in chop-socky genre. **107m/C VHS, Beta, LV.** Chuck Norris, Leon Isaac Kennedy, David Carradine, L.Q. Jones, Barbara Carrera; *D:* Steve Carver; *W:* H. Kaye Dyal. *VES*

The Loneliest Runner 🐾🐾 1976 Based on the true story of an Olympic track star who, as a teenager, suffered humiliation as a bed-wetter. The real-life experiences of producer-director Landon are presented in a touching and sensitive manner. Made for television. **74m/C VHS, Beta.** Michael Landon, Lance Kerwin, DeAnn Mears, Brian Keith, Melissa Sue Anderson; *D:* Michael Landon. *WAR, OM*

The Loneliness of the Long Distance Runner 🐾🐾🐾 *Rebel with a Cause* 1962 Courtenay, in his film debut, turns in a powerful performance as an angry young man infected by the poverty and hopelessness of the British slums. His first attempt at crime is a bust and lands him in a boys reformatory where he is recruited for the running team. While training for the big event with a rival school, Redgrave's obsession with winning the race and Courtenay's continued indifference to the outcome lock the two in an intriguing, seemingly one-sided power struggle. Though widely overlooked when first released, it has since been praised as one of the finest teenage angst films of the '60s. Riveting depiction on a boy's rite of passage into manhood. **104m/B VHS, Beta.** *GB* Tom Courtenay, Michael Redgrave, Avis Bunnage, Peter Madden, James Bolam, Julia Foster, Topsy Jane, Frank Finlay; *D:* Tony Richardson; *C:* Walter Lassally; *M:* John Addison. *WAR, SNC*

Lonely Are the Brave 🐾🐾🐾 1962 A free-spirited cowboy out of sync with the modern age tries to rescue a buddy from a local jail, and in his eventual escape is tracked relentlessly by modern law enforcement. A compelling, sorrowful essay on civilized progress and exploitation of nature. Adapted from the novel "Brave Cowboy" by Edward Abbey. **107m/B VHS, Beta, LV.** Kirk Douglas, Walter Matthau, Gena Rowlands, Carroll O'Connor, George Kennedy; *D:* David Miller; *M:* Jerry Goldsmith. *USH*

The Lonely Guy 🐾🐾½ 1984 (R) Romantic comedy with Martin as a jilted writer who writes a best-selling book about being a lonely guy and finds stardom does have its rewards. Based on "The Lonely Guy's Book of Life" by Bruce Jay Friedman. **91m/C VHS, Beta, LV.** Steve Martin, Charles Grodin, Judith Ivey, Steve Lawrence, Robyn Douglass, Merv Griffin, Dr. Joyce Brothers; *D:* Arthur Hiller; *W:* Stan Daniels; *M:* Jerry Goldsmith. *USH*

Lonely Hearts 🐾🐾🐾 1982 (R) An endearing Australian romantic comedy about a piano tuner, who at 50 finds himself alone after years of caring for his mother, and a sexually insecure spinster, whom he meets through a dating service. Wonderful performances and a good script make this a delightful film that touches the human heart. **95m/C VHS, Beta.** *AU* Wendy Hughes, Norman Kaye, Jon Finlayson, Julia Blake, Jonathon Hardy; *D:* Paul Cox; *W:* John Clarke, Paul Cox. Australian Film Institute '82: Best Film.

Lonely Hearts 🐾½ 1991 (R) A handsome con man works his wiles on a lonely woman in this erotic thriller. Standard plot wastes a good cast.*CW:* Language, violence, and sensuality. **109m/C VHS.** Eric Roberts, Beverly D'Angelo, Joanna Cassidy; *W:* R.E. Daniels. *ART*

Lonely in America 🐾🐾½ 1990 Charming romantic comedy of a newcomer in New York City. Arun (Chowdhry) has just arrived from India and has quite a few things to learn about life in the

Big Apple. **96m/C VHS, Closed Caption.** Ranjit Chowdhry, Adelaide Miller, Robert Kessler, Melissa Christopher, David Toney, Tiruk Malik, D. Barry Brown; **W:** Barry Brown, Satyajit Joy Smith.

The Lonely Lady woof! 1983 (R) Young writer comes to Hollywood with dreams of success, gets involved with the seamy side of moviemaking, and is driven to a nervous breakdown. Pia needs acting lessons, yet it probably wouldn't have helped this trash. Adapted from the novel by Harold Robbins. **92m/C VHS, Beta, LV.** Pia Zadora, Lloyd Bochner, Bibi Besch, Joseph Cali, Ray Liotta; **D:** Peter Sasdy. Golden Raspberry Awards '83: Worst Picture, Worst Actress (Zadora), Worst Director (Sasdy), Worst Screenplay, Worst Song ("The Way You Do It"). USH

Lonely Man 🎬🎬½ 1957 A gunfighter tries to end his career, but is urged into one last battle. Strong performances and tight direction make up for weak plot. **87m/B VHS, Beta.** Jack Palance, Anthony Perkins, Neville Brand, Elaine Aiken; **D:** Henry Levin; **C:** Lionel Lindon. PAR, BAR

The Lonely Passion of Judith Hearne 🎬🎬🎬 1987 (R) A self-effacing Dublin spinster meets a man who gives her his attention, but she must overcome her own self-doubt and crisis of faith. Adapted from Brian Moore's 1955 novel. Excellent performances from both Hoskins and Smith. **116m/C VHS.** GB Maggie Smith, Bob Hoskins, Wendy Hiller, Marie Kean, Ian McNeice, Alan Devlin, Rudi Davies, Prunella Scales; **D:** Jack Clayton; **W:** Peter Nelson; **M:** Georges Delerue. British Academy Awards '88: Best Actress (Smith). VTR

The Lonely Sex 🎬½ 1959 Creepy and bizarre film in which a maniac kidnaps a young girl and is then harassed by her psychotic housemate. **?m/C VHS.** Jean Evans, Karl Light, Mary Gonzales. SNC, TPV

Lonely Trail/Three Texas Steers 1939 Double your pleasure with two early Duke operas. In "Lonely Trail," Wayne dukes it out with dastardly carpetbaggers after the Civil War, while "Three Texas Steers," part of the "Three Mesquiteers" series, has Wayne and company spare a gal rancher/major babe from certain peril. **112m/B VHS.** John Wayne, George "Gabby" Hayes, Ray Corrigan, Raymond Hatton; **D:** George Sherman. REP

Lonely Wives 🎬🎬 1931 A lawyer hires an entertainer to serve as his double because of his marital problems. **86m/B VHS, Beta.** Edward Everett Horton, Patsy Ruth Miller, Laura La Plante, Esther Ralston; **D:** Russell Mack. NOS, VYY

Lonelyhearts 🎬🎬½ 1958 Clift plays a reporter who is assigned the lovelorn column of his paper and gets too immersed in the problems of his readers. Given the superior cast and excellent material, this is a somewhat disappointing adaptation of the brilliant Nathanael West novel "Miss Lonelyhearts." Film debuts of both Stapleton and director Donehue. **101m/B VHS.** Montgomery Clift, Robert Ryan, Myrna Loy, Dolores Hart, Maureen Stapleton, Frank Maxwell, Jackie Coogan, Mike Kellin; **D:** Vincent J. Donehue. Nominations: Academy Awards '58: Best Supporting Actress (Stapleton). MGM

Loners 🎬🎬 1972 (R) Three teenagers run from the Southwest police after they are accused of murdering a highway patrolman. **80m/C VHS, Beta.** Dean Stockwell, Gloria Grahame, Scott Brady, Alex Dreier, Pat Stich; **D:** Sutton Roley; **W:** Barry Sandler. NO

Lonesome Dove 🎬🎬🎬½ 1989 Classic western saga with Duvall and Jones in outstanding roles as two aging ex-Texas Rangers who decide to leave their quiet lives for a last adventure—a cattle drive from Texas to Montana. Along the way they encounter a new love (Lane), a lost love (Huston), and a savage renegade Indian (well-played by Forrest). Based on Larry McMurtry's Pulitzer Prize winning novel, this handsome television miniseries is a finely detailed evocation of the Old West, with a wonderful cast and an equally fine production. Available in a four volume boxed set. Followed by "Return to Lonesome Dove." **480m/C VHS, LV, Closed Caption.** Robert Duvall,

Tommy Lee Jones, Anjelica Huston, Danny Glover, Diane Lane, Rick Schroder, Robert Urich, D.B. Sweeney, Frederic Forrest; **D:** Simon Windsor; **W:** William D. Wittliff; **M:** Basil Poledouris. CAF, TVC, IME

Lonesome Trail 🎬½ 1955 Routine Western that differs from the average oater by having the good guys use bows and arrows to fight their battles. **73m/B VHS, Beta.** Jimmy Wakely, Lee White, Lorraine Miller, John James; **D:** Richard Bartlett. NO

Long Ago Tomorrow 🎬🎬 *The Raging Moon* 1971 (PG) A paralyzed athlete enters a church-run home for the disabled rather than return to his family as the object of their pity. A love affair with a woman, who shares the same disability, helps the embittered athlete. **90m/C VHS, Beta.** GB Malcolm McDowell, Nanette Newman, Bernard Lee, Georgia Brown, Gerald Sim; **D:** Bryan Forbes. COL

The Long Dark Hall 🎬🎬½ 1951 Courtroom drama in which an innocent man is brought to trial when his showgirl mistress is found dead. **86m/B VHS, Beta.** GB Rex Harrison, Lilli Palmer, Denis O'Dea, Raymond Huntley, Patricia Wayne, Anthony Dawson; **D:** Anthony Bushell, Reginald Beck. SNC

The Long Day Closes 🎬🎬🎬 1992 (PG) It's 1956 Liverpool and 11-year-old Bud (McCormack) is part of a working-class Catholic family who longs to escape from his humdrum life. And how? By going to the movies of course and filling his head with pop songs. Nostalgic view of family life filled with sweet, small everyday moments set in a dreary postwar England. Sequel to Davies's also autobiographical film "Distant Voices, Still Lives." **84m/C VHS, Closed Caption.** GB Leigh McCormack, Marjorie Yates, Anthony Watson, Ayse Owens; **D:** Terence Davies; **W:** Terence Davies; **C:** Michael Coulter. COL

Long Day's Journey into Night 🎬🎬🎬🎬 1962 A brooding, devastating film based on Eugene O'Neill's most powerful and autobiographical play. Depicts a day in the life of a family deteriorating under drug addiction, alcoholism, and imminent death. Hepburn's performance is outstanding. In 1988, the Broadway version was taped and released on video. **174m/B VHS, LV.** Ralph Richardson, Katharine Hepburn, Dean Stockwell, Jeanne Barr, Jason Robards Jr.; **D:** Sidney Lumet; **W:** Eugene O'Neill; **C:** Boris Kaufman; **M:** Andre Previn. Cannes Film Festival '62: Best Actress (Hepburn); National Board of Review Awards '62: Best Supporting Actor (Robards); Nominations: Academy Awards '62: Best Actress (Hepburn). REP

Long Day's Journey into Night 🎬🎬 1988 A taped version of the Broadway production of the epic Eugene O'Neill play about a Southern family deteriorating under the weight of terminal illness, alcoholism and drug abuse. In 1962 a movie adaptation of the play was released with outstanding performances from its cast. **169m/C VHS, Beta.** Jack Lemmon, Bethel Leslie, Peter Gallagher, Kevin Spacey, Jodie Lynne McLintock; **D:** Jonathan Miller. ART, VES

Long Day's Journey Into Night 🎬🎬🎬 1996 Eugene O'Neill's autobiographical play about his family is adapted from Canada's Stratford Festival production. The Tyrones are a troubled Irish-American family: bullying James (Hutt) was a once-great Shakespearean actor who has been typecast in a popular stage potboiler; wife Mary (Henry) is a morphine addict; elder son James, Jr. (Donaldson) is an alcoholic; and O'Neill's alter-ego is Edmund (McCamus), an overly sensitive, consumptive writer. Fine performances, excellent production. **174m/C VHS.** CA William Hutt, Martha Henry, Tom McCamus, Peter Donaldson, Martha Burns; **D:** David Wellington; **W:** Eugene O'Neill; **C:** Paul Franco; **M:** Ron Sures. Genie Awards '96: Best Actor (Hutt), Best Actress (Henry), Best Supporting Actor (Donaldson), Best Supporting Actress (Burns); Toronto-City Award '96: Best Canadian Feature Film; Nominations: Genie Awards '96: Best Actor (McCamus), Best Film, Best Film Editing. NYR

The Long Days of Summer 🎬🎬 1980 Set in pre-WWII America, this film portrays a Jewish attorney's struggle against the prejudices of the New England town where he lives. Sequel to "When Every Day Is the Fourth of July." Made for television. **105m/C VHS.** Dean Jones, Joan Hackett, Louanne, Donald Moffat, Andrew Duggan, Michael McGuire; **D:** Dan Curtis. ART

Long Gone 🎬🎬½ 1987 In the '50s, an over-the-hill minor-league player/manager is given a last lease on life and the pennant with two talented rookies and a sexy baseball groupie. Made for cable television. **113m/C VHS, Beta, LV.** William L. Petersen, Henry Gibson, Katy Boyer, Virginia Madsen; **D:** Martin Davidson. ORI, WAR

The Long Good Friday 🎬🎬🎬½ 1980 Set in London's dockland, this is a violent story of a crime boss who meets his match. Hoskin's world crumbles over an Easter weekend when his buildings are bombed and his men murdered. He thinks its the work of rival gangsters only to discover an even deadlier threat is behind his troubles. One of the best of the crime genre, with an exquisitely charismatic performance by Hoskins. **109m/C VHS, Beta.** GB Bob Hoskins, Helen Mirren, Dave King, Bryan Marshall, George Coulouris, Pierce Brosnan, Derek Thompson, Eddie Constantine, Brian Hall, Stephen Davies, P. H. Moriarty, Paul Freeman, Charles Cork, Paul Barber, Patti Love, Ruby Head, Dexter Fletcher, Roy Alon; **D:** John MacKenzie; **W:** Barrie Keefe; **C:** Phil Meheux; **M:** Francis Monkman. VTR

The Long Goodbye 🎬🎬🎬 1973 (R) Raymond Chandler's penultimate novel with the unmistakable Altman touch—which is to say that some of the changes to the story have pushed purist noses out of joint. Gould is cast as an insouciant anti-Marlowe, the film noir atmosphere has been transmuted into a Hollywood film neon, genre jibing abounds, and the ending has been rewritten. But the revamping serves a purpose, which is to make Marlowe a viable character in a contemporary world. Handsomely photographed by Vilmos Zsigmond. Don't miss bulky boy Arnold's cameo (his second film appearance). **112m/C VHS, Beta, LV, Letterbox.** Elliott Gould, Nina Van Pallandt, Sterling Hayden, Henry Gibson, Mark Rydell, David Arkin, Warren Berlinger; *Cameos:* Arnold Schwarzenegger, David Carradine; **D:** Robert Altman; **W:** Leigh Brackett; **C:** Vilmos Zsigmond; **M:** John Williams. National Society of Film Critics Awards '73: Best Cinematography. MGM, FCT

The Long Gray Line 🎬🎬🎬 1955 Power gives an outstanding performance as Marty Maher, a humble Irish immigrant who became an institution at West Point. This is the inspiring story of his rise from an unruly cadet to one of the academy's most beloved instructors. O'Hara does a fine job of playing his wife, who like her husband, adopts the young cadets as her own. Director Ford gracefully captures the spirit and honor associated with West Point in this affectionate drama. **138m/C VHS, Closed Caption.** Tyrone Power, Maureen O'Hara, Robert Francis, Donald Crisp, Ward Bond, Betsy Palmer, Phil Carey; **D:** John Ford. COL

The Long Haul 🎬🎬 1957 A truck driver becomes involved with crooks as his marriage sours. **88m/C VHS.** Victor Mature, Diana Dors, Patrick Allen, Gene Anderson; **D:** Ken Hughes. GKK

The Long, Hot Summer 🎬🎬🎬½ 1958 A tense, well-played adaptation of the William Faulkner story about a wanderer latching himself onto a tyrannical Mississippi family. The first on-screen pairing of Newman and Woodward, and one of the best. Remade for television in 1986. **117m/C VHS, Beta.** Paul Newman, Orson Welles, Joanne Woodward, Lee Remick, Anthony (Tony) Franciosa, Angela Lansbury, Richard Anderson; **D:** Martin Ritt; **W:** Harriet Frank Jr., Irving Ravetch; **C:** Joseph LaShelle; **M:** Alex North. Cannes Film Festival '58: Best Actor (Newman). FOX

The Long, Hot Summer 🎬🎬🎬½ 1986 A made-for-television version of the William Faulkner story, "The Hamlet," about a drifter taken under a Southern patriarch's wing. He's bribed into courting the man's unmarried daughter. Wonderful performances from the entire cast, especially Ivey and surprisingly, Johnson. Remake of the 1958 film with Paul Newman and Joanne Woodward that is on par with the original. **172m/C VHS, Beta, Closed Caption.** Don Johnson, Cybill Shepherd, Judith Ivey, Jason Robards Jr., Ava Gardner, William Russ, Wings Hauser, William Forsythe, Albert Hall; **D:** Stuart Cooper; **M:** Charles Bernstein. *FOX*

The Long Island Four 🎟️🎟️½ 1980
Four Nazi saboteurs are smitten by the decadent nightlife of the Big Apple in 1942. The late Grafstrom's Super-8 film, based on a true story, was an underground hit. **100m/C VHS. D:** Anders Grafstrom. *MWF*

Long John Silver 🎟️½
Long John Silver Returns to Treasure Island 1953 Famed pirate John Silver plans a return trip to Treasure Island to search for the elusive treasure; unofficial sequel to "Treasure Island" by Disney. **106m/C VHS, Beta.** *AU* Robert Newton, Connie Gilchrist, Kit Taylor, Grant Taylor, Rod Taylor; **D:** Byron Haskin. *GEM, MRV, CAB*

Long Journey Back 🎟️🎟️ 1978
The biographical story of a young woman's rehabilitation after her injury in a school bus accident. Produced for television. **100m/C VHS.** Mike Connors, Cloris Leachman, Stephanie Zimbalist, Katy Kurtzman; **D:** Mel Damski. *ART*

The Long Kiss Goodnight 🎟️🎟️½
1996 (R) Audience-pleasing, blood-soaked, foul-mouthed, and action-packed. Davis obviously has a career as a '90s action star (female division), displaying the proper bravado, and muscles, necessary for her dual role. As mild-mannered, brown-haired Samantha Caine, she's a schoolteacher with an eight-year-old daughter, Caitlin (Zima), a nice boyfriend, Hal (Amandes), and amnesia. Sam begins having flashbacks to her past—and what a past it turns out to be. With the help of seedy PI Mitch Henessey (Jackson), she discovers her name is Charly Baltimore and she's a highly trained and very deadly CIA assassin. And the now bleached-blonde, beyond-tough Charly must match her quickly regained lethal abilities with ruthless former nemesis Timothy (Bierko). The body count's high, the blood flows freely, and there's some spectacular stunts. If you're not squeamish it's a guaranteed wild ride. Black got $4 million for his script. **CW:** Substantial amount of strong bloody violence, and for strong language. **120m/C VHS, LV, Closed Caption.** Geena Davis, Samuel L. Jackson, Craig Bierko, Patrick Malahide, Brian Cox, David Morse, Yvonne Zima, Tom Amandes, Melina Kanakaredes, G.D. Spradlin; **D:** Renny Harlin; **W:** Shane Black; **C:** Guillermo Navarro; **M:** Alan Silvestri. *NLC*

The Long, Long Trailer 🎟️🎟️🎟️½ 1954
A couple on their honeymoon find that trailer life is more than they bargained for. Lots of fun with charming direction from Minelli, and Ball's incredible slapstick style. **97m/C VHS, LV, Closed Caption.** Desi Arnaz Sr., Lucille Ball, Marjorie Main, Keenan Wynn; **D:** Vincente Minnelli. *MGM, FCT, BTV*

Long Pants 🎟️🎟️🎟️ 1927
Langdon, in a typical man/child role, plays a naive young man who gets his first pair of long pants, which officially ushers him into adulthood. He immediately falls for the wrong gal (Bonner), a drug runner who winds up in jail. So he breaks her out and they go on the lam. **58m/B VHS.** Harry Langdon, Priscilla Bonner, Alma Bennett; **D:** Frank Capra. *KIV*

The Long Riders 🎟️🎟️🎟️ 1980 (R)
Excellent mythic western in which the Jesse James and Cole Younger gangs raid banks, trains, and stagecoaches in post-Civil War Missouri. Stylish, meticulous and a violent look back, with one of the better slow-motion shootouts in Hollywood history. Notable for the portrayal of four sets of brothers by four Hollywood brother sets. Complimented by excellent Cooder score. **100m/C VHS, Beta, LV.** Stacy Keach, James Keach, Randy Quaid, Dennis Quaid, David Carradine, Keith Carradine, Robert Carradine, Christopher Guest, Nicholas Guest, Pamela Reed, Savannah Smith, James Whitmore Jr., Harry Carey Jr.; **D:**

Walter Hill; **W:** Stacy Keach, James Keach, Bill Bryden; **M:** Ry Cooder. *MGM*

Long Road Home 🎟️🎟️½ 1991 (PG)
Migrant family must decide between working under inhumane conditions or risk losing everything by joining the labor movement during the depression. TV movie. **88m/C VHS.** Mark Harmon, John Evans, Adam Horovitz, Lee Purcell, Leon Russom, Donald Sutherland, Morgan Weisser; **D:** John Korty; **C:** Kees Van Oostrum. *NHO*

Long Shadows 🎟️½ 1986
An analysis of how the resonating effects of the Civil War can still be felt on society, via interviews with a number of noted writers, historians, civil rights activists and politicians. **88m/C VHS, Beta.** Robert Penn Warren, Studs Terkel, Jimmy Carter, Robert Coles, Tom Wicker. *JAF*

The Long Ships 🎟️ 1964
Silly Viking saga finds brothers Rolfe (Widmark) and Orm (Tamblyn) stealing a ship and heading off in search of a solid-gold bell. Among their trials are a mutinous crew and battling Moorish Prince El Mansuh (Poitier). Something to be left off the resume. **125m/C VHS.** Richard Widmark, Russ Tamblyn, Sidney Poitier, Oscar Homolka, Rosanna Schiaffino, Beba Loncar, Lionel Jeffries, Edward Judd; **D:** Jack Cardiff; **W:** Beverley Cross, Berkely Mather; **C:** Christopher Challis; **M:** Dusan Radic. *COL*

Long Shot 1981
Two foosball enthusiasts work their way through local tournaments to make enough money to make it to the World Championships in Tahoe. **100m/C VHS, Beta.** Ian Giatti. *NO*

Long Time Gone 🎟️ 1986
An over-the-hill detective tries to solve a murder while dealing with his bratty, alienated 11-year-old son. Made for television. **97m/C VHS, Beta.** Paul LeMat, Wil Wheaton, Ann Dusenberry, Barbara Stock; **D:** Robert Butler. *NO*

The Long Voyage Home 🎟️🎟️🎟️½
1940 A talented cast performs this must-see screen adaptation of Eugene O'Neill's play about crew members aboard a merchant steamer in 1939. Wayne plays a young lad from Sweden who is trying to get home and stay out of trouble as he and the other seaman get shore leave. **105m/B VHS, Beta, LV.** John Wayne, Thomas Mitchell, Ian Hunter, Barry Fitzgerald, Mildred Natwick, John Qualen; **D:** John Ford; **C:** Gregg Toland. New York Film Critics Awards '40: Best Director (Ford); Nominations: Academy Awards '40: Best Black and White Cinematography, Best Film Editing, Best Picture, Best Screenplay, Best Original Score. *WAR*

The Long Walk Home 🎟️🎟️🎟️ 1989 (PG)
In Montgomery Alabama, in the mid 1950s, sometime after Rosa Parks refused to sit in the black-designated back of the bus, Martin Luther King Jr. led a bus boycott. Spacek is the affluent wife of a narrow-minded businessman while Goldberg is their struggling maid. When Spacek discovers that Goldberg is supporting the boycott by walking the nine-mile trek to work, she sympathizes and tries to help, antagonizing her husband. The plot marches inevitably toward a white-on-white showdown on racism while quietly exploring gender equality between the women. Outstanding performances by Spacek and Goldberg, and a great 50s feel. **95m/C VHS, LV, Closed Caption.** Sissy Spacek, Whoopi Goldberg, Dwight Schultz, Ving Rhames, Dylan Baker; **D:** Richard Pearce; **W:** John Cork; **C:** Roger Deakins; **M:** George Fenton. *ART, IME, FCT*

A Long Way Home 🎟️🎟️ 1981
A television movie about a grown man searching for his long-lost siblings, after the three of them were given up for adoption after birth. **97m/C VHS, Beta.** Timothy Hutton, Brenda Vaccaro, Rosanna Arquette, Paul Regina, George Dzundza, John Lehne, Bonnie Bartlett; **D:** Robert Markowitz; **C:** Ralf Bode; **M:** William Goldstein. *ART*

The Long Weekend 🎟️ 1986
When a vacationing couple goes camping and carelessly destroys a forest, Mother Nature turns her powers of retribution on them. **95m/C VHS, Beta.** *AU TWE*

The Longest Day 🎟️🎟️🎟️½ 1962
The complete story of the D-Day landings at Normandy on June 6, 1944, as seen through the eyes of American, French, British, and German participants. Exhaustively accurate details and extremely talented cast make this one of the all-time great Hollywood epic productions. The first of the big budget, all-star war productions; based on the book by Cornelius Ryan. Three directors share credit. Also available in a colorized version. **179m/C VHS, Beta, LV, Letterbox.** John Wayne, Richard Burton, Red Buttons, Robert Mitchum, Henry Fonda, Robert Ryan, Paul Anka, Mel Ferrer, Edmond O'Brien, Fabian, Sean Connery, Roddy McDowall, Arletty, Curt Jurgens, Rod Steiger, Jean-Louis Barrault, Peter Lawford, Robert Wagner, Sal Mineo, Leo Genn, Richard Beymer, Jeffrey Hunter, Stuart Whitman, Eddie Albert, Tom Tryon, Alexander Knox, Ray Danton, Kenneth More, Richard Todd, Gert Frobe, Christopher Lee; **D:** Ken Annakin; **W:** Bernhard Wicki; **M:** Maurice Jarre. Academy Awards '62: Best Black and White Cinematography, Best Special Effects; Nominations: Academy Awards '62: Best Art Direction/Set Decoration (B & W), Best Film Editing, Best Picture. *TLF, HMV*

The Longest Drive 🎟️🎟️ *The Quest* 1976
Two brothers comb the wildest parts of the West for their sister, whom they believe is living with Indians. A made-for-television movie originally titled "The Quest," which became a brief television series. Highlights include colorful performances from the veteran actors and a unique horse/camel race. A continuation of the series is available on video as "The Captive: The Longest Drive 2." **92m/C VHS, LV.** Kurt Russell, Tim Matheson, Brian Keith, Keenan Wynn, Neville Brand, Cameron Mitchell, Morgan Woodward, Iron Eyes Cody, Luke Askew; **D:** Lee H. Katzin. *THV*

The Longest Yard 🎟️🎟️½ 1974 (R)
A one-time pro football quarterback, now an inmate, organizes his fellow convicts into a football team to play against the prison guards. Filmed on location at Georgia State Prison. **121m/C VHS, Beta, LV.** Burt Reynolds, Eddie Albert, Bernadette Peters, Ed Lauter, Richard Kiel; **D:** Robert Aldrich; **W:** Tracy Keenan Wynn; **C:** Joseph Biroc. Golden Globe Awards '75: Best Film—Musical/Comedy; Nominations: Academy Awards '74: Best Film Editing. *PAR*

The Longshot woof! 1986 (PG-13)
Four bumblers try to raise cash to put on a sure-bet racetrack tip in this sorry comedy. Mike Nichols is the executive producer. **89m/C VHS, Beta.** Tim Conway, Harvey Korman, Jack Weston, Ted Wass, Jonathan Winters, Stella Stevens, Anne Meara; **D:** Paul Bartel; **W:** Tim Conway, John Myhers; **M:** Charles Fox. *CNG*

Longtime Companion 🎟️🎟️🎟️½ 1990 (R)
Critically acclaimed film follows a group of gay men and their friends during the 1980s. The closely knit group monitors the progression of the AIDS virus from early news reports until it finally hits home and begins to take the lives of their loved ones. One of the first films to look at the situation in an intelligent and touching manner. Produced by PBS "American Playhouse" company. **100m/C VHS.** Stephen Caffrey, Patrick Cassidy, Brian Cousins, Bruce Davison, John Dossett, Mark Lamos, Dermot Mulroney, Mary-Louise Parker, Michael Schoeffling, Campbell Scott, Robert Joy, Brad O'Hara; **D:** Norman Rene; **W:** Craig Lucas; **C:** Tony Jennelli. Golden Globe Awards '91: Best Supporting Actor (Davison); Independent Spirit Awards '91: Best Supporting Actor (Davison); New York Film Critics Awards '90: Best Supporting Actor (Davison); National Society of Film Critics Awards '90: Best Supporting Actor (Davison); Sundance Film Festival '90: Audience Award; Nominations: Academy Awards '90: Best Supporting Actor (Davison). *THV, FCT, BTV*

Look Back in Anger 🎟️🎟️🎟️½ 1958
Based on John Osbourne's famous play, the first British "angry young man" film, in which a squalor-living lad takes out his anger on the world by seducing his friend's wife. **99m/B VHS, Beta, LV.** *GB* Richard Burton, Claire Bloom, Mary Ure, Edith Evans, Gary Raymond; **D:** Tony Richardson; **W:** John Osborne; **C:** Oswald Morris; **M:** John Addison.

Look Back in Anger 🎬🎬 1980 A working class man angered by society's hypocrisy lashes out at his upper class wife, his mistress, and the world. Inferior remake of 1958 film version starring Richard Burton, based on '50s stage hit. **100m/C VHS, Beta.** Malcolm McDowell, Lisa Banes, Fran Brill, Raymond Hardie, Lindsay Anderson. *WAR, OM*

Look Back in Anger 🎬🎬🎬 1989 There's something about John Osborne's play that brings out the angry young man in British leads. Richard Burton played Osborne's irascible guy in 1958, Malcom McDowell looked back angrily in '80, and now Branagh convincingly vents his spleen on wife and mistress in this made for British TV production. Director Jones earlier filmed "84 Charing Cross Road" and "Jacknife." **114m/C VHS. GB** Kenneth Branagh, Emma Thompson, Gerard Horan, Siobhan Redmond; **D:** David Jones. *HBO*

Look for the Silver Lining 🎬🎬½ 1949 Insipid musical biography of Broadway star Marilyn Miller (Haver). Bolger is the highlight as Miller's mentor from vaudeville to the Great White Way. 🎵Look for the Silver Lining; Whip-Poor-Will; A Kiss in the Dark; Pirouette; Just a Memory; Time On My Hands; Wild Rose; Shine On Harvest Moon; Back, Back, Back to Baltimore. **100m/C VHS, Beta.** June Haver, Ray Bolger, Gordon MacRae, Charlie Ruggles, Rosemary DeCamp, S.Z. Sakall; **D:** David Butler; **W:** Phoebe Ephron, Henry Ephron, Marian Spitzer. Nominations: Academy Awards '49: Scoring of a Musical.*MGM, FCT, BTV*

Look Out Sister 🎬🎬🎬 1948 Jordan and an all-black cast star in this musical satire of westerns. "Two Gun" Jordan saves a dude ranch from foreclosure and wins the girl. Lots of black culture, slang and music from the '40s. Broad but enjoyable humor. 🎵Caldonia; Don't Burn the Candle at Both Ends. **64m/B VHS.** Louis Jordan, Suzette Harbin, Monte Hawley, Maceo B. Sheffield; **D:** Bud Pollard. *NOS*

Look Who's Laughing 🎬🎬 1941 Bergen's plane lands in a town conveniently populated by radio stars. Not much plot here, but it might be worth a look to fans of the stars including Jim and Marion Jordan, better known as Fibber McGee and Molly. **79m/B VHS, Beta, LV.** Edgar Bergen, Jim Jordan, Marian Jordan, Lucille Ball, Harold Peary, Lee Bonnell, Charles Halton; **D:** Allan Dwan. *TTC, MLB*

Look Who's Talking 🎬🎬🎬 1989 (PG-13) When Alley bears the child of a married, and quite fickle man, she sets her sights elsewhere in search of the perfect father; Travolta is the cabbie with more on his mind than driving Alley around and babysitting. All the while, the baby gives us his views via the voice of Bruce Willis. A very light comedy with laughs for the whole family. **90m/C VHS, Beta, LV, Closed Caption, DVD.** John Travolta, Kirstie Alley, Olympia Dukakis, George Segal, Abe Vigoda; **D:** Amy Heckerling; **W:** Amy Heckerling; **M:** David Kitay; **V:** Bruce Willis. *COL, RDG*

Look Who's Talking Now 🎬½ 1993 (PG-13) Continuing to wring revenue from a tired premise, the family dogs throw in their two cents in the second sequel to "Look Who's Talking." For anyone who thinks Diane Keaton's hair makes her look a little like a hound dog, here's a chance to visualize her as a similarly long-eared poodle with an attitude. DeVito is also cast in character as the voice of a rough street-smart mutt, who happens to get thrown into the same household as the bosses' pure-bred poodle. Sparks, Alpo, and butt jokes fly as the dogs mark their territory. Meanwhile, dimwit wife Alley is worried that husband Travolta is having an affair, and is determined to get him back.**CW:** Off-color dialogue. **95m/C VHS, LV, 8mm, Closed Caption.** John Travolta, Kirstie Alley, Olympia Dukakis, George Segal, Lysette Anthony; **D:** Tom Ropelewski; **W:** Tom Ropelewski, Leslie Dixon; **M:** William Ross; **V:** Diane Keaton, Danny DeVito. *COL*

Look Who's Talking, Too 🎬 1990 (PG-13) If Academy Awards for Stupidest Sequel and Lamest Dialogue existed, this diaper drama would have cleaned up. The second go-round throws the now married accountant-cabbie duo into a marital tailspin when Alley's babysitting brother moves in and the Saturday Night dancer moves out. Meanwhile, Willis cum baby smartasses incessantly. A once-clever gimmick now unencumbered by plot; not advised for linear thinkers. The voice of Arnold, though, is a guarantee you'll get one laugh for your rental. **81m/C VHS, LV, 8mm, Closed Caption.** Kirstie Alley, John Travolta, Olympia Dukakis, Elias Koteas; **D:** Amy Heckerling; **V:** Bruce Willis, Mel Brooks, Damon Wayans, Roseanne. *COL*

The Lookalike 🎬🎬 1990 (PG-13) A made for cable adaptation of Kate Wilhelm's novel. Bereaved mother Gilbert questions her sanity when she thinks she sees her daughter after she was killed in an automobile accident. Could this girl provide answers to questions about her past? **88m/C VHS, Closed Caption.** Melissa Gilbert, Diane Ladd, Frances Lee McCain, Jason Scott Lee, Thaao Penghlis; **D:** Gary Nelson; **W:** Linda J. Bergman. *USH*

Looker 🎬🎬½ 1981 (PG) Stunning models are made even more beautiful by a plastic surgeon, but one by one they begin to die. Finney plays the Beverly Hills surgeon who decides to investigate when he starts losing all his clients. **94m/C VHS, Beta, LV, Closed Caption.** Albert Finney, James Coburn, Susan Dey, Leigh Taylor-Young; **D:** Michael Crichton; **W:** Michael Crichton. *WAR*

Lookin' to Get Out 🎬🎬½ 1982 (R) Comedy about two gamblers running from their debts. They wind up at the MGM Grand in Las Vegas trying to get out of a mess. **70m/C VHS, Beta.** Ann-Margret, Jon Voight, Burt Young; **D:** Hal Ashby; **M:** John Beal, Miles Goodman. *FOX*

Looking for Miracles 🎬🎬½ 1990 (G) Two brothers, separated during the Depression because of poverty, get a chance to cultivate brotherly love when they're reunited in 1935. A Wonderworks production based on the A.E. Hochner novel. **104m/C VHS, Beta, LV, Closed Caption.** Zachary Bennett, Greg Spottiswood, Joe Flaherty. *TOU, DIS, FCT*

Looking for Mr. Goodbar 🎬🎬 1977 (R) Young teacher Keaton seeks companionship and love by frequenting single's bars and furthers her self-destruction by her aimless intake of drugs and alcohol. In need of a father figure, she makes herself available to numerous men and eventually regrets her hedonistic behavior. Unpleasant, aimless characters do little for this dreary film, whose sexual theme sparked a bit of public conversation when first released. Based on the bestselling novel by Judith Rossner. Oscar nominations for supporting actress Weld, and cinematography. **136m/C VHS, Beta, LV.** Diane Keaton, Tuesday Weld, Richard Gere, Tom Berenger, William Atherton, Richard Kiley; **D:** Richard Brooks; **W:** Richard Brooks; **C:** William A. Fraker. Nominations: Academy Awards '77: Best Cinematography, Best Supporting Actress (Weld). *PAR*

Looking for Richard 🎬🎬🎬 1996 (PG-13) A Shakespearean "Vanya on 42nd Street," "Richard" is the first semi-documentary addition to the barrage of Bard adaptations. Pacino's protracted pic dwells on a filmmaker's struggles to understand the play. Punctuated with comic relief, Pacino makes a pilgrimage to the Globe Theatre, taps Brit theatre heavyweights Gielgud and Redgrave for thoughts on interpreting Shakespeare, and combs New York for candid "man in the street" impressions in a quest to bring his subject to a wider public. Over the course of four years, Pacino, in various stages of facial hair growth, plays the deformed usurper with a cast of worthy Americans (Spacey, Kline, Ryder, Baldwin, and Quinn), illustrating key scenes of the play.**CW:** Brief strong language and some scenes of violence. **108m/C VHS, Closed Caption.** Alec Baldwin, Winona Ryder, Kevin Spacey, Aidan Quinn, F. Murray Abraham, Kenneth Branagh, Kevin Conway, John Gielgud, James Earl

Jones, Kevin Kline, Estelle Parsons, Vanessa Redgrave, Harris Yulin, Penelope Allen, Al Pacino; **D:** Al Pacino; **C:** Robert Leacock; **M:** Howard Shore. Directors Guild of America Awards '96: Best Feature Documentary (Pacino). *FXV*

Looking for Trouble 🎬 1996 (PG) Lame kid-friendly movie finds young Jaime (Butler) befriending a baby circus elephant she names Trouble, who has an abusive owner. When the circus leaves town, worried Jaime follows along. **73m/C VHS.** Holly Butler, Shawn McAllister, Art Turk; **D:** Peter Tors, Jay Aubrey; **W:** Peter Tors, Jay Aubrey. *NHO*

The Looking Glass War 🎬🎬 1969 (PG) Polish defector is sent behind the Iron Curtain on a final mission to photograph a rocket in East Berlin. He's guided by frustrated British security officers Rogers and Richardson, who both offer sly turns. An otherwise slow-moving adaptation of John Le Carre's bestselling spy novel. **108m/C VHS, Beta. GB** Christopher Jones, Ralph Richardson, Pia Degermark, Anthony Hopkins, Susan George; **D:** Frank Pierson; **W:** Frank Pierson. *COL, MLB*

Looney Looney Looney Bugs Bunny Movie 🎬🎬🎬 *Friz Freleng's Looney Looney Looney Bugs Bunny Movie* 1981 (G) A feature-length compilation of classic Warner Bros. cartoons tied together with new animation. Cartoon stars featured include Bugs Bunny, Elmer Fudd, Porky Pig, Yosemite Sam, Duffy Duck, and Foghorn Leghorn. **80m/C VHS, Beta. D:** Isadore "Friz" Freleng, Chuck Jones, Bob Clampett; **V:** Mel Blanc, June Foray. *WAR, FCT*

Loophole 🎬🎬 *Break In* 1983 An out-of-work architect, hard pressed for money, joins forces with an elite team of expert criminals, in a scheme to make off with millions from the most established holding bank's vault. **105m/C VHS, Beta. GB** Albert Finney, Martin Sheen, Susannah York, Robert Morley, Colin Blakely, Jonathan Pryce; **D:** John Quested. *HHE, MTX*

Loose Cannons 🎬 1990 (R) Yet another mismatched-cop-partner comedy, wherein a mystery is ostensibly solved by a veteran cop and a schizophrenic detective. **95m/C VHS, Beta, LV, Closed Caption.** Gene Hackman, Dan Aykroyd, Dom DeLuise, Ronny Cox, Nancy Travis, David Alan Grier; **D:** Bob (Benjamin) Clark; **W:** Bob (Benjamin) Clark, Richard Matheson. *COL*

Loose Connections 🎬🎬 1987 A feminist driving to a convention in Europe advertises for a travelmate, and gets a hopeless chauvinist who is masquerading as a gay man in this offbeat cult comedy. **90m/C VHS, Beta. GB** Lindsay Duncan, Stephen Rea, Robbie Coltrane; **D:** Richard Eyre. *TPV*

Loose in New York 🎬🎬 198? Much to her surprise, a cynical socialite begins to fall for her computer-arranged mate. **91m/C VHS, Beta.** Rita Tushingham, Aldo Maccione; **D:** Gian Polidoro. *NO*

Loose Screws 🎬 1985 (R) Four perverted teenagers are sent to a restrictive academy where they continue their lewd ways in this stupid sequel to "Screwballs." **75m/C VHS, Beta. CA** Bryan Genesse, Karen Wood, Alan Deveau, Jason Warren; **D:** Rafal Zielinski; **M:** Michael Cory. *ART*

Loose Shoes 🎬 *Coming Attractions* 1980 (R) A collection of vignettes that satirize movie trailers, teasers and special announcements. Murray's film debut. **84m/C VHS, Beta.** Bill Murray, Howard Hesseman, Jaye P. Morgan, Buddy Hackett, Misty Rowe, Susan Tyrrell; **D:** Ira Miller. *FOX*

Loot ... Give Me Money, Honey! 🎬🎬½ 1970 Black comedy about a motley crew of greed-driven golddiggers who chase after a heisted fortune in jewels, which is hidden in a coffin belonging to one of the thieves' mother. From Joe Orton's play. **101m/C VHS, Beta. GB** Richard Attenborough, Lee Remick, Hywel Bennett, Milo O'Shea, Roy Holder; **D:** Silvio Narizzano. *NO*

Lord Jim 🎬🎬🎬 1965 A ship officer (O'Toole) commits an act of cowardice that results in his dismissal and disgrace, which leads him to the Far East in search of self-respect. Excellent supporting cast. Based on Joseph Conrad's novel. **154m/C VHS, Beta.** Peter O'Toole, James Mason, Curt Jurgens, Eli Wallach, Jack Hawkins, Paul Lukas, Akim Tamiroff, Daliah Lavi, Andrew Keir, Jack MacGowran, Walter Gotell; **D:** Richard Brooks; **W:** Richard Brooks; **C:** Frederick A. (Freddie) Young. *COL, TVC*

Lord of Illusions 🎞🎞½ *Clive Barker's Lord of Illusions* 1995 (R) New York P.I. Harry D'Amour (Bakula), who has an affinity for the occult, becomes involved with Dorothea (Janssen), the supposed widow of magician Philip Swann (O'Connor). As Harry investigates he discovers some terrifying secrets, including resurrected cult leader Nix (Von Bargen). Gruesome effects rather than excessive gore but you'll feel like you've been dropped in the middle of a plot without a clear idea what's happening. Bakula's Harry obviously has more stories to tell but Janssen's Dorothea, while attractive, is just around to cower. Barker directs from his own short story "The Last Illusion." The unrated director's cut clocks in at 120 minutes.**CW:** Strong violence and gore; language; sexuality. **109m/C VHS, LV, Closed Caption.** Scott Bakula, Famke Janssen, Kevin J. O'Connor, Daniel von Bargen, Joel Swetow, Barry Sherman, Jordan Marder, Joseph Latimore, Vincent Schiavelli; **D:** Clive Barker; **W:** Clive Barker; **C:** Ronn Schmidt. *MGM*

Lord of the Flies 🎞🎞½ 1963 Proper English schoolboys stranded on a desert island during a nuclear war are transformed into savages. A study in greed, power, and the innate animalistic/survivalistic instincts of human nature. Based on William Golding's novel, which he described as a "journey to the darkness of the human heart." The laserdisc version contains outtakes, the film trailer, and additional material. **91m/B VHS, Beta, LV.** *GB* James Aubrey, Tom Chapin, Hugh Edwards, Roger Elwin, Tom Gamen; **D:** Peter Brook; **W:** Peter Brook. *HMV, FUS*

Lord of the Flies 🎞🎞 1990 (R) Inferior second filming of the famed William Golding novel about schoolboys marooned on a desert island who gradually degenerate into savages. Lushly photographed, yet redundant and poorly acted. **90m/C VHS, Beta, LV, 8mm, Closed Caption.** Balthazar Getty, Danuel Pipoly, Chris Furrh, Badgett Dale, Edward Taft, Andrew Taft; **D:** Harry Hook. *COL, TVC, NLC*

The Lord of the Rings 🎞🎞 1978 (PG) An animated interpretation of Tolkien's classic tale of the hobbits, wizards, elves, and dwarfs who inhabit Middle Earth. Animator Ralph Bakshi used live motion animation (roto-scoping) to give his characters more life-like and human motion. Well done in spite of the difficulty of adapting from Tolkien's highly detailed and lengthy works. **128m/C VHS, Beta. D:** Ralph Bakshi; **W:** Peter S. Beagle, J.C. (Chris) Conkling; **V:** Christopher Guard, John Hurt. *REP, FCT*

The Lords of Discipline 🎞🎞½ 1983 (R) A military academy cadet is given the unenviable task of protecting a black freshman from racist factions at a southern school circa 1964. Based on Pat Conroy's autobiographical novel. **103m/C VHS, Beta, LV.** David Keith, Robert Prosky, Barbara Babcock, Judge Reinhold, G.D. Spradlin, Rick Rossovich, Michael Biehn, Bill Paxton, Matt Frewer; **D:** Franc Roddam; **C:** Brian Tufano; **M:** Howard Blake. *PAR*

The Lords of Flatbush 🎞🎞½ 1974 (PG) Four street toughs battle against their own maturation and responsibilities in 1950s Brooklyn. Winkler introduces the leather-clad hood he's made a career of and Stallone introduces a character not unlike Rocky. Interesting slice of life. **88m/C VHS, Beta, LV.** Sylvester Stallone, Perry King, Henry Winkler, Susan Blakely, Armand Assante, Paul Mace; **D:** Stephen Verona, Martin Davidson; **M:** Joseph Brooks. *COL*

Lords of Magick 🎞 1988 (PG-13) Two warriors chase an evil sorcerer and the princess he's kidnapped across some time to the 20th century. **98m/C VHS, Beta.** Jarrett Parker, Matt Gauthier, Brendan Dillon Jr.; **D:** David Marsh.

Lords of the Deep WOOF! 1989 (PG-13) A Roger Corman cheapie about underwater technicians trapped on the ocean floor with a race of aliens. A film rushed out to capitalize on the undersea sci-fi subgenre highlighted by "The Abyss." **95m/C VHS, Beta.** Bradford Dillman, Priscilla Barnes, Melody Ryane, Eb Lottimer, Daryl Haney; **D:** Mary Ann Fisher; **W:** Daryl Haney, Howard R. Cohen. *MGM*

Lorenzo's Oil 🎞🎞🎞 1992 (PG-13) Based on the true story of Augusto and Michaela Odone's efforts to find a cure for their five-year-old, Lorenzo, diagnosed with the rare and incurable disease ALD (Adrenoleukodystrophy). Confronted by a slow-moving and clinically cold medical community, the Odones embark on their own quest for a cure. Sarandon delivers an outstanding and emotionally charged performance as Lorenzo's determined mother. Nolte is his equally devoted Italian father, complete with black hair and hand gestures. They are a powerful presence in a film which could have easily degenerated into a made-for-TV movie, but is instead a tribute to what love and hope can accomplish.**CW:** Thematic elements. **135m/C VHS, Beta, LV, Letterbox, Closed Caption.** Nick Nolte, Susan Sarandon, Zach O'Malley-Greenberg, Peter Ustinov, Kathleen Wilhoite, Gerry Bamman, Margo Martindale, James Rebhorn, Ann Hearn; **D:** George Miller; **W:** Nick Enright, George Miller; **C:** John Seale. Nominations: Academy Awards '92: Best Actress (Sarandon), Best Original Screenplay. *USH, MOV, BTV*

The Loretta Young Show 1954 Two enchanting episodes of the popular '50s series "The Loretta Young Show," entitled "Somebody Else's Dream" and "So Bright the Light." Other episodes are also available, two per tape. **60m/C VHS, Beta.** Loretta Young. *MVC*

Lorna Doone 🎞🎞½ 1922 A young girl of royal descent is kidnapped and raised by the bandit Doone family in the highlands of Scotland. Adapted from the novel by R.D. Blackmore. **79m/B VHS.** Madge Bellamy, John Bowers; **D:** Maurice Tourneur. *GPV*

Lorna Doone 🎞🎞½ 1934 Early version of the R.D. Blackmore novel about an English farmer who falls in love with the daughter of an outlaw family. Set in rural England in the 1600s; remade in 1951 and 1990. **90m/B VHS.** *GB* Victoria Hopper, John Loder, Margaret Lockwood, Roy Emerton, Mary Clare, Edward Rigby, Roger Livesey; **D:** Basil Dean; **W:** Miles Malleson. *FCT*

Lorna Doone 🎞🎞½ 1990 (PG) Classic romance set in 17th-century England and based on the novel by R.D. Blackmore. John Ridd (Bean) vows to destroy the land-grabbing Doone family, whom he blames for the death of his parents. Then he meets, and immediately falls in love with, the beautiful and innocent Lorna Doone (Walker). Made for British television. **90m/C VHS, Beta, Closed Caption.** *GB* Sean Bean, Polly Walker, Clive Owen, Billie Whitelaw; **D:** Andrew Grieve; **W:** Matthew Jacobs. *PAR*

Los Locos Posse 🎞🎞 1997 (R) Uneven would-be sequel to 1993's "Posse." Chance (Van Peebles) is a black military scout who is found, injured, by one of the unhinged denizens of a nearby mission. The Mother Superior enlists Chance to lead the nuns and their "Los Locos" charges to another mission some hundred miles away. The trip doesn't go smoothly and their arrival only leads to more problems. First English-language feature for Montreal director Vallee.**CW:** Violence, sexuality and language. **100m/C VHS, LV.** Mario Van Peebles, Rene Auberjonois, Paul Lazar, Danny Trejo, Melora Walters, Rusty Schwimmer; **D:** Jean-Marc Vallee; **W:** Mario Van Peebles; **C:** Pierre Gill; **M:** Lesley Barber. *PGV*

Los Olvidados 🎞🎞🎞½ *The Young and the Damned* 1950 From surrealist Bunuel, a powerful story of the poverty and violence of young people's lives in Mexico's slums. In Spanish with English subtitles. **88m/B VHS, Beta.** *MX* Alfonso Mejias, Roberto Cobo; **D:** Luis Bunuel. Cannes Film Festival '51: Best Director (Bunuel), Best Film. *HHT, DVT, NOS*

Loser 🎞½ 1997 Very low-budget street drama concerns young small-time drug dealer James Dean Ray (Harris) and his self-destruction slide towards oblivion. **85m/C VHS.** Kirk Harris, Jonathon Chaus, Peta Wilson, Norman Salect, Jack Rubio; **D:** Kirk Harris; **W:** Kirk Harris; **C:** Kent Wakeford. *TPV*

The Losers 🎞½ 1970 (R) Four motorcyclists are hired by the U.S. Army to rescue a presidential advisor who is being held captive by Asian bad guys. **96m/C VHS, Beta.** William Smith, Bernie Hamilton, Adam Roarke, Houston Savage, Brad Johnson, Vernon Wells; **D:** Jack Starrett.

Losin' It 🎞🎞 1982 (R) Four teens travel across the Mexican border to Tijuana on a journey to lose their virginity. Cruise meets a married woman who says she is in town for a divorce, while the others become caught up in frenzied undertakings of their own. **104m/C VHS, Beta, LV.** Tom Cruise, John Stockwell, Shelley Long, Jackie Earle Haley; **D:** Curtis Hanson. *NLC*

Losing Chase 🎞🎞½ 1996 (R) Bacon makes his directorial debut in this cable drama that features wife Sedgwick as Elizabeth, mother's helper to Chase (Mirren) and Richard Philips (Bridges) at their summer home on Martha's Vineyard. Chase is still recovering from a mental breakdown, having spent several months in an institution, and she resents Elizabeth's presence, constantly criticizing her. But when the two women are alone together a confusing and emotional bond gradually begins to form between them.**CW:** Brief language. **95m/C VHS, Closed Caption.** Helen Mirren, Kyra Sedgwick, Beau Bridges; **D:** Kevin Bacon; **W:** Anne Meredith; **C:** Dick Quinlan; **M:** Michael Bacon. *EVE*

Losing Isaiah 🎞🎞🎞 1994 (R) "Kramer vs. Kramer" meets the movie-of-the-week in this controversial and emotionally moving story of a social worker (Lange) who adopts the title character, an African American baby abandoned by his drug-addicted mother (Berry). Courtroom battle ensues when four years later mom, now clean and sober, discovers Isaiah is alive. She enlists the aid of a lawyer (Jackson) known for his high-profile, racially charged cases. Lange and Berry lead the parade of fine performances. Taking on some volatile issues, director Gyllenhaal manages (for the most part) to refrain from melodrama. Based on the novel by Seth Margolis.**CW:** Drug related material; brief strong language. **108m/C VHS, Beta, Closed Caption.** Jessica Lange, Halle Berry, David Strathairn, Samuel L. Jackson, Cuba Gooding Jr., Latanya Richardson; **D:** Stephen Gyllenhaal; **W:** Naomi Foner; **C:** Andrzej Bartkowiak; **M:** Mark Isham. *PAR*

Lost 🎞½ 1983 A young girl runs away into the wilderness because of the resentment she feels toward her new stepfather. **92m/C VHS, Beta.** Sandra Dee, Don Stewart, Ken Curtis, Jack Elam, Sheila Newhouse.

Lost 🎞🎞 1986 When their boat capsizes in the Pacific, three sailors desperately cling to life, drifting aimlessly for 74 days. Based on a true story, this film is adult-fare. **93m/C VHS, Beta.** *CA* Michael Hogan, Helen Shaver, Kenneth Welsh; **D:** Peter Rowe. *HHE, BMV*

Lost and Found 🎞🎞½ 1979 (PG) An American professor of English and an English film production secretary fall in love on a skiing vacation. Good cast but Segal and Jackson did romance better in "A Touch of Class." **104m/C VHS, Beta.** George Segal, Glenda Jackson, Maureen Stapleton, Hollis McLaren, John Cunningham, Paul Sorvino, John Candy, Martin Short; **D:** Melvin Frank; **W:** Jack Rose. *GKK*

Lost Angels 🎞🎞½ 1989 (R) A glossy "Rebel Without a Cause" '80s reprise providing a no-holds-barred portrait of life in the fast lane. A wealthy, disaffected San Fernando Valley youth immerses himself in sex, drugs and rock 'n' roll. Ultimately he is arrested and sent by his parents to a youth home, where a dedicated therapist assists his torturous road back to reality. **116m/C VHS, Beta, LV, Closed Caption.** Donald Sutherland, Adam Horovitz, Amy Locane, Kevin Tighe, John C. McGinley, Graham Beckel, Park Overall, Don Bloomfield, Celia Weston; **D:** Hugh Hudson; **W:** Michael Weller; **M:** Philippe Sarde. *ORI*

Lost Boundaries ⅊⅊½ **1949** Respected physician Scott Carter (debut role for Ferrer) and his family live and work in a small New Hampshire town, hiding the fact that they are black, passing for white, in their segregated society. But then the truth becomes known. Strong, if slow-moving, and based on a true story; the use of white leads for black roles was common casting. **99m/B VHS.** Mel Ferrer, Beatrice Pearson, Richard Hylton, Susan Douglas, Canada Lee, Carleton Carpenter, Seth Arnold, Wendell Holmes; **D:** Alfred Werker; **W:** Virginia Shaler, Eugene Ling, Charles A. Palmer, Furland de Kay; **C:** William J. Miller; **M:** Louis Applebaum. *WAR*

The Lost Boys ⅊⅊ **1987 (R)** Santa Cruz seems like a dull town when Michael, his younger brother, and their divorced mom move into their eccentric grandfather's home. But when Michael falls for a pretty girl with some hard-living friends he takes on more than he imagines—these partying teens are actually a group of vampires. Some humor, some bloodletting violence, and an attractive cast help out this updated vampire tale. Rock-filled soundtrack. **97m/C VHS, Beta, LV, 8mm, Letterbox, Closed Caption.** Jason Patric, Kiefer Sutherland, Corey Haim, Jami Gertz, Dianne Wiest, Corey Feldman, Barnard Hughes, Edward Herrmann, Billy Wirth, Jamison Newlander, Brooke McCarter, Alex Winter; **D:** Joel Schumacher; **W:** Jeffrey Boam, Janice Fischer, James Jeremias; **C:** Michael Chapman; **M:** Thomas Newman. *WAR, FUS*

Lost Canyon ⅊⅊ **1943** Hoppy tries to help a fugitive who's been framed for bank robbery. This is the second installment distributed by United Artists. The song "Jingle, Jangle, Jingle" is sung by the Sportsman Quartet. **61m/B VHS.** William Boyd, Jay Kirby, Andy Clyde, Lola Lane, Douglas Fowley, Herbert Rawlinson; **D:** Lesley Selander. *NOS*

The Lost Capone ⅊⅊⅊ **1990 (PG-13)** Made for cable TV version of the story of Al Capone's youngest brother, a clean living small town sheriff who struggles with his sibling's reputation at every turn. **93m/C VHS, Beta, Closed Caption.** Ally Sheedy, Eric Roberts, Adrian Pasdar, Titus Welliver, Jimmie F. Skaggs, Maria Pitillo, Anthony Crivello; **D:** John Gray; **W:** John Gray; **C:** Paul Elliott. *TTC*

The Lost City ⅊⅊ **1934** A feature version of the rollicking vintage movie serial about a lost jungle city, adventurers and mad scientists. **74m/B VHS, Beta.** William "Stage" Boyd, Kane Richmond, George "Gabby" Hayes, Claudia Dell; **D:** Harry Revier. *NOS, SNC, DVT*

Lost City of the Jungle 1945 13-chapter serial focusing on a crazed Atwill, in his last screen role, believing that he can rule the world from the heart of a deep, dark jungle by utilizing a special mineral. The final Universal serial. **169m/B VHS, Beta.** Russell Hayden, Lionel Atwill, Jane Adams; **D:** Ray Taylor, Lewis D. Collins. *NOS, GPV, DVT*

The Lost Command ⅊⅊½ **1966** A French colonel, relieved of his command, endeavors to regain power by battling a powerful Arab terrorist with his own specially trained platoon of soldiers. Crisp adventure set in post-WWII North Africa. Based on "The Centurions" by Jean Larteguy. **129m/C Beta.** Anthony Quinn, Michele Morgan, George Segal, Alain Delon, Maurice Ronet, Claudia Cardinale; **D:** Mark Robson; **C:** Robert L. Surtees. *COL*

The Lost Continent ⅊½ **1951** An expedition searching for a lost rocket on a jungle island discovers dinosaurs and other extinct creatures. **82m/B VHS, Beta, LV.** Cesar Romero, Hillary Brooke, Chick Chandler, John Hoyt, Acquanetta, Sid Melton, Whit Bissell, Hugh Beaumont; **D:** Sam Newfield. *VTR, MRV, MLB*

Lost Diamond ⅊ **1974** Bumbling spies search for a smuggled gem. **83m/C VHS, Beta.** Juan Ramon, Sonia Rivas, Ricardo Bauleo.

The Lost Empire ⅊ **1983 (R)** Three bountiful and powerful women team up to battle the evil Dr. Syn Do. **86m/C VHS, Beta.** Melanie Vincz, Raven De La Croix, Angela Aames, Paul Coufos, Robert Tessier, Angus Scrimm, Angelique Pettyjohn, Kenneth Tobey; **D:** Jim Wynorski; **W:** Jim Wynorski. *ART*

Lost Highway ⅊⅊ **1996 (R)** Welcome once again to Lynch-world—that parallel universe understood only by master David. Jazz musician Fred Madison (Pullman) is on Death Row—supposedly for the murder of his wife Renee (Arquette). Only why does young mechanic Pete Dayton (Getty) wind up in Fred's cell (with Fred missing)? Oh, and why does gangster Mr. Eddy (Loggia) have a girlfriend named Alice (Arquette again) who looks just like Renee? And is she real—or did Fred conjure her up? Who's the Mystery Man (Blake), who literally looks like death warmed over. And.....well, you get the idea. Or maybe you're not supposed to. **CW:** Bizarre violent and exual content, and for strong language. **135m/C VHS, LV, Closed Caption.** Bill Pullman, Patricia Arquette, Balthazar Getty, Robert Loggia, Robert (Bobby) Blake, Gary Busey, Jack Nance, Richard Pryor, Natasha Gregson Wagner, Lisa Boyle, Michael Massee, Jack Kehler, Henry Rollins, Gene Ross, Scott Coffey; **D:** David Lynch; **W:** David Lynch, Barry Gifford; **C:** Peter Deming; **M:** Angelo Badalamenti. *PGV*

Lost Honeymoon ⅊⅊ **1947** Monkeyshines abound as a soldier marries a girl while in a state of amnesia, and then wakes up to find twin daughters. **70m/B VHS, Beta.** Franchot Tone, Ann Richards; **D:** Leigh Jason. *NOS, DVT, HEG*

The Lost Honor of Katharina Blum ⅊⅊⅊ *Die Verlorene Ehre Der Katharina Blum* **1975 (R)** A woman becomes involved with a man who's under police surveillance and finds her life open to public scrutiny and abuse from the media and the government. Based on Heinrich Boll's prize-winning novel. In German with English subtitles. Remade for television as "The Lost Honor of Kathryn Beck." **97m/C VHS, Beta.** **GE** Angela Winkler, Mario Adorf, Dieter Laser, Juergen Prochnow; **D:** Volker Schlondorff, Margarethe von Trotta. *GLV*

Lost Horizon ⅊⅊⅊⅊ **1937** A group of strangers fleeing revolution in China are lost in the Tibetan Himalayas and stumble across the valley of Shangri La. The inhabitants of this Utopian community have lived for hundreds of years in kindness and peace—but what will the intrusion of these strangers bring? The classic romantic role for Colman. Capra's directorial style meshed perfectly with the pacifist theme of James Hilton's classic novel, resulting in one of the most memorable films of the 1930s. This version restores more than 20 minutes of footage which had been cut from the movie through the years. **132m/B VHS, Beta, LV, Letterbox.** Ronald Colman, Jane Wyatt, H.B. Warner, Sam Jaffe, Thomas Mitchell, Edward Everett Horton, Isabel Jewell, John Howard, Margo; **D:** Frank Capra; **W:** Robert Riskin; **M:** Dimitri Tiomkin. Academy Awards '37: Best Film Editing, Best Interior Decoration; Nominations: Academy Awards '37: Best Picture, Best Sound, Best Supporting Actor (Warner), Best Score. *COL, RDG*

The Lost Idol/Shock Troop 198? In "The Lost Idol," a lone soldier raids a sacred temple in order to retrieve a golden idol. "Shock Troop" tells of top secret mission to destroy a powerful computer that lies behind enemy lines. **219m/C VHS.** Danny Aiello, Lyle Alzado, Erik Estrada. *NO*

Lost in a Harem ⅊⅊½ **1944** Abbott & Costello play magicians in a theatrical troupe stranded in a desert kingdom ruled by an evil sheik. The sheik's nephew (and rightful heir) hires the two to steal some magic rings and the pretty Maxwell to play footsie with his susceptible uncle in an attempt to regain his kingdom. Average comedy with musical numbers by Jimmy Dorsey and His Orchestra. **89m/B VHS.** Bud Abbott, Lou Costello, Marilyn Maxwell, John Conte, Douglass Dumbrille, Lottie Harrison; **D:** Charles Riesner. *MGM*

Lost in Alaska ⅊⅊⅓ **1952** Up in the Alaskan wilderness, Abbott & Costello save Ewell from a greedy saloon owner and his cohorts who are trying to get their hands on Ewell's fortune. **87m/B VHS.** Bud Abbott, Lou Costello, Tom Ewell, Mitzie Green, Bruce Cabot, Emory Parnell, Jack Ingram, Rex Lease; **D:** Jean Yarbrough; **W:** Martin Ragaway, Leonard Stern; **M:** Henry Mancini. *USH, FCT*

Lost in America ⅊⅊⅊ **1985 (R)** After deciding that he can't "find himself" at his current job, advertising executive David Howard and his wife sell everything they own and buy a Winnebago to travel across the country. This Albert Brooks comedy is a must-see for everyone who thinks that there is more in life than pushing papers at your desk and sitting on "Mercedes leather." Available in widescreen on laserdisc. **91m/C VHS, Beta, LV, Letterbox, Closed Caption.** Albert Brooks, Julie Hagerty, Michael Greene, Tom Tarpey, Garry Marshall, Art Frankel; **D:** Albert Brooks; **W:** Albert Brooks, Monica Johnson; **M:** Arthur B. Rubinstein. National Society of Film Critics Awards '85: Best Screenplay. *WAR*

Lost in Space ⅊⅊½ **1998 (PG-13)** Big-screen remake of the cheesy late 60s sci-fi TV show retains the basic plot and premise, but jettisons the camp. in 2058, the Robinsons and pilot Don West (LeBlanc) are chosen to pioneer the colonization of a far-off world because Earth has become nearly uninhabitable. The evil Dr. Smith (Oldman) sabotages the mission but gets stuck on board. Once the family is appropriately lost, the story veers into familiar sci-fi territory of apparently-deserted spaceships, marauding aliens, and time warps. It's visually impressive, but writer Goldsman can't resist turning the Robinsons into an annoying collection of 1990s dysfunction. The plot pretty much hinges on Dad's lousy parenting skills, and the kids are disaffected and resentful. Eye-candy effects, the occasionally witty inside joke for fans of the show, and Oldman's deliciously oily Smith provide plenty of fun, but where's the giant carrot? **CW:** Some intense sci-fi action. **131m/C VHS.** William Hurt, Mimi Rogers, Gary Oldman, Heather Graham, Matthew LeBlanc, Lacey Chabert, Jack Johnson, Lennie James, Jared Harris, Mark Goddard, Edward Fox, Adam Sims; **Cameos:** June Lockhart, Marta Kristen, Angela Cartwright; **D:** Stephen Hopkins; **W:** Akiva Goldsman; **C:** Peter Levy; **M:** Bruce Broughton; **V:** Dick Tufeld. *NYR*

Lost in the Barrens ⅊⅊ **1991** Two young boys, one a Canadian Indian and the other a rich white boy, get lost in the wilderness of the Canadian north. Out of necessity and common need they become close and form a lifelong friendship. Based on the book by Farley Mowat. **95m/C VHS.** **CA** Graham Greene, Nicholas Shields. *NO*

Lost in Yonkers ⅊⅊½ **1993 (PG)** *Neil Simon's Lost in Yonkers* Arty and Jay are two teenage brothers who, while their widowed father looks for work, are sent to live with their stern grandmother, small-time gangster uncle, and childlike aunt in 1942 New York. Ruehl reprises her Tony award-winning performance as Aunt Bella, who loses herself in the movies while trying to find a love of her own, out from under the oppressive thumb of her domineering mother (Worth). Performances by the adults are more theatrical than necessary but the teenagers do well in their observer roles. Based on the play by Neil Simon, which again chronicles his boyhood. **114m/C VHS, LV, 8mm, Letterbox, Closed Caption.** Mercedes Ruehl, Irene Worth, Richard Dreyfuss, Brad Stoll, Mike Damus, David Strathairn, Robert Miranda, Jack Laufer, Susan Merson; **D:** Martha Coolidge; **W:** Neil Simon; **M:** Elmer Bernstein. *COL, FCT*

The Lost Jungle 1934 Circus legend Beatty searches for his girl and her dad in the jungle. Animal stunts keep it interesting. Serial in 12 chapters, 13 minutes each. **156m/B VHS, Beta.** Clyde Beatty, Cecilia Parker, Syd Saylor, Warner Richmond, Wheeler Oakman; **D:** Armand Schaefer, David Howard. *NOS, VCN, VDM*

The Lost Language of Cranes
🎥🎥🎥 1992 David Leavitt's novel is transported from New York to present-day London but the wrenching emotional drama remains the same. A family is in crisis as long-hidden secrets concerning homosexuality and infidelity are finally revealed. The title refers to one character's social worker's thesis on a young boy from a dysfunctional family who imitates the movements of the building cranes he sees. Fine performances by all. Adult sexual situations. **90m/C VHS.** *GB* Brian Cox, Eileen Atkins, Angus McFadyen, Corey Parker, Cathy Tyson; *Cameos:* John Schlesinger, Rene Auberjonois; *D:* Nigel Finch; *C:* Remi Adefarasin. *FOX, BTV*

Lost Legacy: A Girl Called Hatter Fox
🎥🎥½ 1977 Tradition and technology are at odds in the life of a young Indian girl. Strong cast makes this work. Made for television and better than average. **100m/C VHS.** Ronny Cox, Joanelle Romero, Conchata Ferrell; *D:* George Schaefer. *GEM*

Lost, Lonely, and Vicious
🎥 1959 Clayton is a suicidal Hollywood actor who spends much of his time indulging his penchant for women, figuring he may as well enjoy what little time he has left. Then he meets Wilson, a drugstore clerk who moves him to reconsider his self-destructive ways. **73m/B VHS.** Ken Clayton, Barbara Wilson, Lilyan Chauvin, Richard Gilden, Carole Nugent, Sandra Giles, Allen Fife, Frank Stallworth, Johnny Erben, Clint Quigley, T. Earl Johnson; *D:* Frank Myers; *W:* Norman Graham. *SMW, TPV*

The Lost Man
🎥🎥½ 1969 (PG-13) Odd, updated remake of 1947's "Odd Man Out," which was based on the novel by F.L. Green. Jason (Poitier) leads a group of black militants in robbing a factory in order to provide money for some civil rights organizations. Two are killed during the crime, which leads to various police shootouts. Meanwhile, Jason enlists the help of white social worker Cathy (Shimkus) to help him escape the country. *CW:* Some violence. **122m/C VHS.** Sidney Poitier, Joanna Shimkus, Al Freeman Jr., Michael Tolan, Richard Dysart, Paul Winfield, Bernie Hamilton, Dolph Sweet, David Steinberg; *D:* Robert Arthur; *W:* Robert Arthur; *C:* Gerald Perry Finnerman; *M:* Quincy Jones. *USH*

The Lost Missile
🎥🎥 1958 A lost, alien missile circles the Earth, causing overheating and destruction on the planet's surface. A scientist works to find a way to save the planet before it explodes into a gigantic fireball. Director Burke's last film. **70m/B VHS.** Robert Loggia, Ellen Parker, Larry Kerr, Phillip Pine, Marilee Earle; *D:* William (Lester Williams) Berke. *FRG*

Lost Moment
🎥🎥 1947 A publisher travels to Italy to search for a valuable collection of a celebrated author's love letters, but finds a neurotic woman in his way. Based on Henry James' "Aspern Papers." **89m/B VHS.** Robert Cummings, Agnes Moorehead, Susan Hayward; *D:* Martin Gabel; *C:* Hal Mohr. *REP*

The Lost One
🎥🎥 *Der Verlone* 1951 A German scientist's lover is suspected of selling his findings to England during WWII. Based on a true story; Lorre's only directorial outing. **97m/B VHS.** *GE* Peter Lorre, Karl John, Renate Mannhardt; *D:* Peter Lorre. *NO*

The Lost Patrol
🎥🎥🎥½ 1934 WWI British soldiers lost in the desert are shot down one by one by Arab marauders as Karloff portrays a religious soldier convinced he's going to die. The usual spiffy Ford exteriors peopled by great characters with a stirring score. Based on the story, "Patrol" by Philip MacDonald. **66m/B VHS, Beta, LV.** Victor McLaglen, Boris Karloff, Reginald Denny, Wallace Ford, Alan Hale; *D:* John Ford; *M:* Max Steiner. Nominations: Academy Awards '34: Best Score. *CCB, RXM*

Lost Planet Airmen
🎥½ 1949 A feature-length condensation of the 12-part sci-fi serial "King of the Rocket Men." Rocket Man is pitted against the sinister Dr. Vulcan in this intergalactic battle of good and evil. **65m/B VHS, Beta.** Tristram Coffin, Mae Clarke, Dale Van Sickel; *D:* Fred Brannon. *AOV, DVT, RXM*

The Lost Platoon
1989 (R) A troop of soldiers are transformed into vampires. **120m/C VHS, Beta, LV.** David Parry, William Knight, Sean Heyman; *D:* David A. Prior.

Lost Squadron
🎥🎥½ 1932 A look at the dangers stuntmen go through in movie-making. **79m/B VHS, Beta, LV.** Richard Dix, Erich von Stroheim; *D:* George Archainbaud; *M:* Max Steiner. *RXM*

The Lost Stooges
1933 From the trio's one year at MGM, rare clips of them performing their famous slapstick gags. In black and white and color. **68m/B VHS, Beta.** Moe Howard, Curly Howard, Larry Fine, Clark Gable, Joan Crawford, Jimmy Durante, Robert Montgomery. *TTC*

The Lost Tribe
🎥 1989 A man takes his wife on a trek through the jungle to find his lost brother. **96m/C VHS, Beta.** John Bach, Darien Teakle; *D:* John Laing.

The Lost Weekend
🎥🎥🎥🎥 1945 The heartrending Hollywood masterpiece about alcoholism, depicting a single weekend in the life of a writer, who cannot believe he's addicted. Except for its pat ending, it is an uncompromising, startlingly harsh treatment, with Milland giving one of the industry's bravest lead performances ever. Acclaimed then and now. **100m/B VHS, Beta, LV.** Ray Milland, Jane Wyman, Phillip Terry, Howard da Silva, Doris Dowling, Frank Faylen, Mary Young; *D:* Billy Wilder; *W:* Charles Brackett, Billy Wilder; *M:* Miklos Rozsa. Academy Awards '45: Best Actor (Milland), Best Director (Wilder), Best Picture, Best Screenplay; Cannes Film Festival '46: Best Actor (Milland), Best Film; Golden Globe Awards '45: Best Actor—Drama (Milland), Best Director (Wilder), Best Film—Drama; National Board of Review Awards '45: Best Actor (Milland); New York Film Critics Awards '45: Best Actor (Milland), Best Director (Wilder), Best Film; Nominations: Academy Awards '45: Best Black and White Cinematography, Best Film Editing, Best Original Dramatic/Comedy Score. *USH, PAR, BTV*

The Lost World
🎥🎥½ 1925 A zoology professor leads a group on a South American expedition in search of the "lost world," where dinosaurs roam in this silent film. Based on a story by Sir Arthur Conan Doyle. A 90-minute version includes the film's original trailer and a recreation of some of the missing footage (the film was released at 108 minutes). **62m/B VHS, Beta, LV, DVD.** Wallace Beery, Lewis Stone, Bessie Love, Lloyd Hughes; *D:* Harry Hoyt. *NOS, MIL, VYY*

The Lost World
🎥🎥½ 1992 "Land of the Lost"/"Jurassic Park" themes, based on the story by Sir Arthur Conan Doyle. A scientific team ventures deep into uncharted African jungles where they find themselves confronted by dinosaurs and other dangers. **99m/C VHS, Closed Caption.** John Rhys-Davies, David Warner; *D:* Timothy Bond. *WOV*

The Lost World: Jurassic Park 2
🎥🎥½ *Jurassic Park 2* 1997 (PG-13) Sequel to "Jurassic Park," proves only that Spielberg has tapped this well one too many times. It's four years after the first adventure and the surviving dinos have peacefully set up house on a deserted island near Costa Rica. Mathematician Ian Malcolm (Goldblum, reprising his role) reluctantly becomes part of an expedition to monitor the beasts, only because his paleontologist girlfriend (Moore) is so gung-ho. Other characters exist, but are reduced to the role of entrees. More dinos (two T-Rexs, a clan of Raptors, and bite-sized newcomers Compsognathus), thrilling special effects, and more gore make up for thin subplots involving a rich businessman who wants to use the dinosaurs for a new zoo and another who hunts them for sport. Ironically, Spielberg's predictablity owes much to better films such as "King Kong," "Aliens" and "Godzilla." Still, T-Rex and buddies, the true stars, rise to the occasion to entertain in an otherwise lackluster sequel. Based on Michael Crichton's book. *CW:* Intense sci-fi terror and violence. **129m/C VHS, LV, Letterbox, Closed Caption, DVD.** Jeff Goldblum, Julianne Moore, Vince Vaughn, Arliss Howard, Pete Postlethwaite, Peter Stormare, Vanessa Lee Chester, Richard Schiff; *D:* Steven Spielberg; *W:* David Koepp; *C:* Janusz Kaminski; *M:* John Williams. Nominations: Academy Awards '97: Best Visual Effects; MTV Movie Awards '98: Best Action Sequence; Golden Raspberry Awards '97: Worst Remake/Sequel, Worst Screenplay. *USH*

Lost Zeppelin
🎥🎥 1929 A dirigible becomes lost in the wastes of Antarctica, forcing its passengers to combat the elements. Impressive special effects and miniatures for its time. **73m/B VHS, Beta.** Virginia Valli, Ricardo Cortez, Duke Martin, Kathryn McGuire; *D:* Edward Sloman. *SNC, GPV*

Lotna
🎥🎥½ 1964 Wadja's first color film serves as a tribute to the Polish calvary who fought against the Germans in WWII. The story is told through the trials of a horse that passes to various military officials until it breaks a leg and must be shot. Wadja himself is the son of a cavalryman killed in the war. Polish with subtitles. **89m/C VHS.** *PL* Bozena Kurowska, Jerzy Pichelski, Jerzy Moes, Adam Pawlikowski; *D:* Andrzej Wajda; *W:* Andrzej Wajda, Wojciech Zukrowski; *C:* Jerzy Lipman; *M:* Tadeusz Baird. *FCT*

Lots of Luck
🎥🎥 1985 A knee-slapping comedy about a family that wins the million-dollar lottery and sees that money doesn't solve all problems. Disney made for cable. **88m/C VHS, Beta.** Martin Mull, Annette Funicello, Fred Willard, Polly Holliday, Hamilton Camp, Vincent Schiavelli; *D:* Peter Baldwin; *M:* William Goldstein. *DIS*

Lottery Bride
🎥🎥½ 1930 In this charming musical, Jeanette MacDonald is the lottery bride who is won by the brother of the man she really loves. A fine outing for all involved, particularly the supporting cast. ♫You're an Angel; My Northern Lights; Come Drink to the Girl That You Love; Yubla; Round She Whirls; Shoulder to Shoulder; High and Low; Napoli; Two Strong Men. **85m/B VHS, Beta.** Jeanette MacDonald, Joe E. Brown, ZaSu Pitts, John Garrick, Carroll Nye; *D:* Paul Stein. *NO*

Lotto Land
🎥🎥½ 1995 Looks at the lives of black and Hispanic characters from the same Brooklyn neighborhood. Ambitious high school grad Hank (Gilliard, Jr.) works stocking shelves at the local liquor store for manager Flo (Costallos), who's raised Hank's girlfriend, the college-bound Joy (Gonzalez). The neighborhood's abuzz when someone in their area holds the winning ticket for a $27 million lottery, which was sold from Flo's store, but just who it is and what happens when the money is claimed leads to a dramatic twist. Debut for Rubino, who shows real affection for his characters. **90m/C VHS.** Larry Gilliard Jr., Barbara Gonzalez, Suzanne Costallos, Wendell Holmes, Jamie Tirelli, Luis Guzman, Paul Calderone; *D:* John Rubino; *W:* John Rubino; *C:* Rufus Standefer. *BMG*

The Lotus Eaters
🎥🎥 1993 (PG-13) Sensitive family drama set in British Columbia in the 1960s about a wife who discovers her husband has fallen in love with their childrens' new teacher. Domestic angst done with naturalism and not without humor. *CW:* Nudity; children exposed to parental infidelities. **100m/C VHS.** *CA* Sheila McCarthy, R.H. Thomson, Michelle-Barbara Pelletier, Frances Hyland, Paul Soles; *D:* Paul Shapiro; *W:* Peggy Thompson. Genie Awards '93: Best Actress (McCarthy), Best Original Screenplay, Best Sound. *SDE, FCT*

Louisiana
🎥 1987 A belle of the Old South tries to get back the family plantation by romancing the new owner, even though she loves someone else. Oh, and then the Civil War breaks out. Made for television. **130m/C VHS.** Ian Charleson, Margot Kidder, Victor Lanoux, Len Cariou, Lloyd Bochner; *D:* Philippe de Broca.

Louisiana Purchase
🎥🎥½ 1941 Successful screen adaptation of the Broadway musical features several performers from the original cast, lavish costumes, and great musical numbers. As usual, Hope's comedy is extremely funny, especially his famous filibuster scene in Congress. Based on the stage musical by Morrie

Ryskind and B. G. DeSylva. **95m/C VHS.** Bob Hope, Vera Zorina, Victor Moore, Dona Drake, Irene Dardoni, Ruy mond Walburn, Maxie "Slapsie" Rosenbloom, Frank Albertson, Barbara Britton; **D:** Irving Cummings. Nominations: Academy Awards '41: Best Color Cinematography, Best Interior Decoration. *USH, BTV*

Louisiana Story 🐾🐾🐾 1948 The final effort by the master filmmaker, depicting the effects of oil industrialization on the southern Bayou country as seen through the eyes of a young boy. One of Flaherty's greatest, widely considered a premiere achievement. **77m/B VHS, Beta. D:** Robert Flaherty; **M:** Virgil Thomson. National Film Registry '94;; Nominations: Academy Awards '48: Best Story. *HMV, VYY, DVT*

Loulou 🐾🐾🐾½ 1980 (R) A woman leaves her middle-class husband for a leather-clad, uneducated jock who is more attentive. Romantic and erotic. In French with English subtitles. **110m/C VHS, Beta.** *FR* Isabelle Huppert, Gerard Depardieu, Guy Marchand; **D:** Maurice Pialat. *NYF*

The Lovable Cheat 🐾🐾 1949 Pretty lame adapatation of Balzac's play "Mercadet Le Falseur," about a father who cons money from his friends in order to line up a marriage suitable for his daughter. **75m/B VHS.** Charlie Ruggles, Peggy Ann Garner, Richard Ney, Alan Mowbray, Iris Adrian, Ludwig Donath, Fritz Feld; **D:** Richard Oswald. *FCT*

Love 🐾🐾🐾½ *Szerelem* 1971 Torocsik, touted as Hungary's leading actress in the '70s, plays a young woman whose husband has been imprisoned for political crimes. Living in a cramped apartment with her mother-in-law, she keeps the news from the aged and dying woman (Darvas) by reading letters she's fabricated to keep alive the woman's belief that her son is a successful movie director in America. The story is punctuated by the older woman's dreamy remembrances of things past. Exceptional performances by both women, it was Darvas' final film. Based on two novellas by Tibor Dery. Hungarian with subtitles. **92m/B VHS, LV.** *HU* Lili Darvas, Mari Torocsik, Ivan Darvas; **D:** Karoly Makk. *CVC, IME, HMV*

Love Affair 🐾🐾🐾½ 1939 Multi-kleenex weepie inspired countless romantic dreams of true love atop the Empire State Building. Dunn and Boyer fall in love on a ship bound for NYC, but they're both involved. They agree to meet later at, guess where, to see if their feelings hold true, but tragedy intevenes. Excellent comedydrama is witty at first, more subdued later, with plenty of romance and melodrama. Remade in 1957 (by McCarey) as "An Affair to Remember," a lesser version whose popularity overshadows the original. Look for fleeting glimpses of Leslie, Beckett, and Mohr. Ignore the public domain video, which replaces the original music. Remade again in 1994 as "Love Affair." **87m/B VHS.** Irene Dunne, Charles Boyer, Maria Ouspenskaya, Lee Bowman, Astrid Allwyn, Maurice Moscovich, Scotty Beckett, Joan Leslie, Gerald Mohr, Dell Henderson, Carol Hughes; **D:** Leo McCarey; **W:** Delmer Daves, Leo McCarey, Donald Ogden Stewart. Nominations: Academy Awards '39: Best Actress (Dunne), Best Interior Decoration, Best Picture, Best Song ("Wishing"), Best Story, Best Supporting Actress (Ouspenskaya). *NOS, MRV, TTC*

Love Affair 🐾🐾 1994 (PG-13) Second remake of the timeless classic has a contemporary look and feel but doesn't justify a new version. The photogenic leads may meet on a plane, but never fear, the Empire State Building and a tragedy are still the main plot devices. The problem is viewers never feel drawn into their lives. Hepburn has a small but moving role as Beatty's aunt. Superb cinematography makes it easy on the eyes and Morricone's lush romantic score makes it easy on the ears, but ultimately, it's all gloss with little substance. Watch this one, but then set aside time to see the superior original (made in 1939) or the better known 1957 attempt "An Affair to Remember." *CW:* Mild language. **108m/C VHS, LV, Closed Caption.** Warren Beatty, Annette Bening, Katharine Hepburn, Garry Shandling, Chloe Webb, Pierce Bros-

nan, Kate Capshaw, Paul Mazursky, Brenda Vaccaro, Glenn Shadix, Barry Miller, Harold Ramis; **D:** Glenn Gordon Caron; **W:** Warren Beatty, Robert Towne; **M:** Ennio Morricone. *WAR*

The Love Affair, or The Case of the Missing Switchboard Operator 🐾🐾🐾 *Switchboard Operator; Case of the Missing Switchboard Operator; Ljubarni Slucaj; An Affair of the Heart* 1967 Makavejev's second film, a dissertation on the relationship between sex and politics, involving an affair between a switchboard operator and a middle-aged ex-revolutionary, is told in the director's unique, farcically disjointed manner. In Serbian with English subtitles. **73m/B VHS, Beta.** *YU* Eva Ras, Slobodan Aligrudic, Ruzica Sokic; **D:** Dusan Makavejev; **W:** Dusan Makavejev. *FCT*

Love Affair: The Eleanor & Lou Gehrig Story 🐾🐾🐾 1977 The true story, told from Mrs. Gehrig's point of view, of the love affair between baseball great Lou Gehrig and his wife Eleanor from his glory days as a New York Yankee, to his battle with an incurable disease. A television drama that is supported by Herrmann and Danner's convincing portrayals. **96m/C VHS, Beta.** Blythe Danner, Edward Herrmann, Patricia Neal, Ramon Bieri, Lainie Kazan; **D:** Fielder Cook. *WOV*

Love After Love 🐾🐾 *Apres l'Amour* 1994 A look at sex and relationships among 30-something professionals in Paris. Lola (Huppert), a successful romance novelist, is suffering a crisis in both her career and, ironically, her love life. She is involved with two men who, in turn, are involved with different women who happen to have borne them children. The movie starts off with so much mate switching and secret sexual rendezvous, that by the second half, you really don't care who Lola ends up with. French with English subtitles. **104m/C VHS.** *FR* Isabelle Huppert, Hippolyte Girardot, Lio; **D:** Diane Kurys; **W:** Diane Kurys, Antoine Lacomblez; **C:** Fabio Conversi; **M:** Yves Simon, Serge Perathone, Jannick Top. *ORI*

Love Among the Ruins 🐾🐾🐾 1975 A made-for-television romance about an aging, wealthy widow who, after being scandalously sued for breach of promise by her very young lover, turns for aid to an old lawyer friend who has loved her silently for more than 40 years. **100m/C VHS, Beta, LV, Closed Caption.** Laurence Olivier, Katharine Hepburn, Leigh Lawson, Colin Blakely; **D:** George Cukor; **M:** John Barry. *FOX*

Love and a.45 🐾🐾 1994 (R) Satirical and violent road movie finds petty career criminal Watty Watts (Bellows) living in a Texas trailer park with gal Starlene (Zellweger), for whom he's just purchased an expensive engagement ring. But he's borrowed the money from some crazed gangster types who want the loan repaid in a timely fashion. Soon, the dippy duo are on the run to Mexico with a trail of dead bodies behind them and the media just delighted to make them the next tabloid darlings. *CW:* Ugly, graphic violence; sexual situations. **101m/C VHS, LV, Closed Caption.** Gil Bellows, Renee Zellweger, Rory Cochrane, Ann Wedgeworth, Peter Fonda, Jeffrey Combs, Jace Alexander; **D:** C.M. Talkington; **W:** C.M. Talkington; **M:** Tom Verlaine. Nominations: Independent Spirit Awards '95: Debut Performance (Zellweger). *THV*

Love and Anarchy 🐾🐾🐾 *Film d'Amore et d'Anarchia* 1973 An oppressed peasant vows to assassinate Mussolini after a close friend is murdered. Powerful drama about the rise of Italian facism. In Italian with English subtitles. **108m/C VHS, Beta, LV.** *IT* Giancarlo Giannini, Mariangela Melato; **D:** Lina Wertmuller; **W:** Lina Wertmuller; **M:** Nino Rota. Cannes Film Festival '73: Best Actor (Giannini). *COL*

Love and Bullets 🐾½ 1979 (PG) An Arizona homicide detective is sent on a special assignment to Switzerland to bring a mobster's girlfriend back to the United States to testify against him in court. **95m/C VHS, Beta, Closed Caption.** *GB* Charles Bronson, Jill Ireland, Rod Steiger, Strother Martin, Bradford Dillman, Henry Silva, Michael V. Gazzo; **D:** Stuart

Rosenberg; **W:** Wendell Mayes; **C:** Fred W. Koenekamp; **M:** Lalo Schifrin. *FOX*

Love and Death 🐾🐾🐾 1975 (PG) In 1812 Russia, a condemned man reviews the follies of his life. Woody Allen's satire on "War and Peace," and every other major Russian novel. **89m/C VHS, Beta, LV.** Woody Allen, Diane Keaton, Georges Adel, Despo Diamantidou, Frank Adu, Harold Gould; **D:** Woody Allen; **W:** Woody Allen; **C:** Ghislan Cloquet. *MGM, FOX*

Love & Death on Long Island 🐾🐾½ 1997 (PG-13) Stuffy English author Giles De'Ath (Hurt), barely on speaking terms with the 20th century, wanders into the wrong theater, encounters a teen exploitation flick and becomes obsessed with Ronnie Bostock (Priestley), one of the movie's "stars." De'Ath's obsession leads to his discovery of fan magazines, TV, and video, which provide some moments of amusement as he comes to grips with the technology. It also leads Giles to seek out Bostock at his home on Long Island, where Hurt shines as Giles tries to reconcile his dignity and increasingly irrational behavior. Priestley does a fine job lampooning his own image (while not exactly dispelling it), and the supporting characters (especially Chaykin's diner owner) are appropriately quirky. Subtle reworking of "Death in Venice," based on a novel by Gilbert Adair, has its moments, but is probably best enjoyed by the same type of people who would like De'Ath's books.*CW:* Brief strong language, thematic elements and some sexual content. **93m/C VHS.** John Hurt, Jason Priestley, Fiona Loewi, Sheila Hancock, Maury Chaykin, Gawn Grainger, Elizabeth Quinn; **D:** Richard Kwietniowski; **W:** Richard Kwietniowski; **C:** Oliver Curtis; **M:** Richard Grassby-Lewis. *NYR*

Love and Faith 🐾🐾🐾 1978 Two lovers are torn between their love for each other and their faiths during 16th-century Japan. English subtitles. **154m/C VHS, Beta.** *JP* Toshiro Mifune, Takashi Shimura, Yoshiko Nakana; **D:** Kei Kumai. *VDA*

Love and Hate: A Marriage Made in Hell 🐾🐾½ *Love and Hate: The Story of Colin and Joanne Thatcher* 1990 Marital murder mystery based on a true Canadian case. Joanne (Nelligan), the wife of wealthy rancher-politico Colin (Walsh), leaves her publicly charismatic and privately abusive husband with two thirds of their brood. A bitter battle for custody is waged, and Joanne is soon found savagely slain. The number one suspect: philandering ex-spouse Colin. Based on Maggie Siggins' "A Canadian Tragedy," the faux biography originally aired in two parts on Canadian TV. **156m/C VHS, Beta, LV.** Kate Nelligan, Ken Walsh, Leon Pownall, John Colicos, Noam Zylberman, Victoria Snow, Cedric Smith, R.H. Thomson, Victoria Wauchope, Doris Petrie, Duncan Ollenenshaw; **D:** Francis Mankiewicz; **W:** Suzette Couture. *PAR*

Love and Human Remains 🐾🐾🐾 1993 (R) Director Arcand's first English-language film features a group of late 20ish urbanites trying to come to grips with their place in the world (and their sexuality). David (Gibson) is an amoral Lothario who doesn't believe in love and can only manage casual gay relationships. He hangs out with a variety of friends, all of whom are trying to cope with their varying sexual natures. Melodramatic framing story about a serial murderer who may, or may not, be one of the principal characters proves somewhat of a distraction. Lots of caustically witty dialogue and some fine performances (particularly Gibson's); filmed in Montreal. Adaptation of the play "Unidentified Human Remains and the True Nature of Love" by Fraser, who also did the screenplay.*CW:* Strong sexual content; language; violence; some drug use. **100m/C VHS, LV.** *CA* Thomas Gibson, Ruth Marshall, Cameron Bancroft, Mia Kirshner, Joanne Vannicola, Matthew Ferguson, Rick Roberts; **D:** Denys Arcand; **W:** Brad Fraser; **C:** Paul Sarossy. Genie Awards '94: Best Adapted Screenplay. *COL*

Love & Murder ♂♂½ 1991 (R) Poorly developed tale of a photographer and his bevy of with beautiful models involved with murder and love, not necessarily in that order. *CW:* Language. 87m/C VHS. Todd Waring, Kathleen Lasky, Ron White, Wayne Robson; *D:* Steven Hilliard Stern.

Love and Other Catastrophes ♂♂ 1995 (R) Short, low-budget first feature from 23-year-old Croghan engagingly focuses on 24 hours in the lives of five confused college students. Film students Alice (Garner) and Mia (O'Connor) need a third roommate for their new apartment. Danni (Mitchell), Mia's girlfriend, is upset that Mia doesn't want them living together, while Alice is eyeing potential boyfriends, including shy med student Michael (Day) and womanizing Ari (Dyktynski). Meanwhile, both Alice and Mia try to cope with various academic frustrations. *CW:* Sexuality, language, and some drug use. 76m/C VHS, Closed Caption. *AU* Frances O'Connor, Alice Garner, Matt Day, Radha Mitchell, Matthew Dyktynski, Suzi Dougherty, Kim Gyngell; *D:* Emma-Kate Croghan; *W:* Emma-Kate Croghan, Yael Bergman, Helen Bandis; *C:* Justin Brickle; *M:* Oleh Witer. Nominations: Australian Film Institute '96: Best Actress (O'Connor), Best Film, Best Supporting Actress (Garner). *FXV*

Love and the Frenchwoman ♂♂♂ *La Francaise et L'Amour* 1960 A French tale tracing the nature of love through stages. Deals with a story about where babies come from, puppy love, saving sex for marriage, and the way some men treat women. 135m/B VHS, Beta. *FR* Jean-Paul Belmondo, Pierre-Jean Vaillard, Marie-Jose Nat, Annie Girardot; *D:* Jean Delannoy; *M:* Georges Delerue. *DVT, MRV, HEG*

Love at First Bite ♂♂½ 1979 (PG) Intentionally campy spoof of the vampire film. Dracula is forced to leave his Transylvanian home as the Rumanian government has designated his castle a training center for young gymnasts. Once in New York, the Count takes in the night life and falls in love with a woman whose boyfriend embarks on a campaign to warn the city of Dracula's presence. Hamilton of the never-fading tan is appropriately tongue-in-cheek in a role which resurrected his career. 93m/C VHS, Beta, LV. George Hamilton, Susan St. James, Richard Benjamin, Dick Shawn, Arte Johnson, Sherman Hemsley, Isabel Sanford, Barry Gordon, Michael Pataki, Basil Hoffman, Eric Laneuville; *D:* Stan Dragoti; *W:* Robert Kaufman; *M:* Charles Bernstein. *ORI, WAR*

Love at First Sight ♂ *Love is Blind; At First Sight* 1976 A pre-"Saturday Night Live" hack job for Aykroyd, playing a blind man who falls in love with a girl he bumps into. ♫Love at First Sight. 86m/C VHS, Beta. Dan Aykroyd, Mary Ann McDonald, George Murray, Barry Morse; *D:* Rex Bromfield. *NO*

Love at Large ♂♂♂ 1989 (R) Hired by a beautiful woman, a private detective accidentally follows the wrong man and winds up being followed himself. He vies with a female detective in solving this case of mistaken identity. 90m/C VHS, Beta, LV, Closed Caption. Tom Berenger, Elizabeth Perkins, Anne Archer, Ann Magnuson, Annette O'Toole, Kate Capshaw, Ted Levine, Kevin J. O'Connor, Ruby Dee, Neil Young, Barry Miller; *D:* Alan Rudolph; *W:* Alan Rudolph; *C:* Elliot Davis. *ORI, FCT*

Love at Stake ♂♂½ 1987 (R) It's condo owners versus the witches in this charming parody that features a hilarious cameo by Dr. Joyce Brothers and a very sexy performance from Carrera. 83m/C VHS, LV. Patrick Cassidy, Kelly Preston, Bud Cort, Barbara Carrera, Stuart Pankin, Dave Thomas, Georgia Brown, Annie Golden; *Cameos:* Dr. Joyce Brothers; *D:* John Moffitt; *M:* Charles Fox. *NLC*

Love at the Top ♂♂½ 1986 Ladies' foundation designer falls in love with her boss's son-in-law, jeopardizing her career. 90m/C Beta. Janis Paige, Richard Young, Jim MacKrell; *D:* John Bowab.

The Love Boat 197? All aboard! Love's waiting for you in this special movie presentation of the immensely popular television series. Captain Stuebing, Julie, Gopher, Isaac (your bartender) and a whole host of celebrities at the end of

their careers, fall in and out of love as they sail back and forth between expensive resorts. ?m/C VHS. Gavin MacLeod, Bernie Kopell, Ted Lange, Lauren Tewes. *GKK*

The Love Bug ♂♂½ 1968 (G) A race car driver (Jones) is followed home by Herbie, a white Volkswagen with a mind of its own. Eventually, Jones follows the "Love Bug" to a life of madcap fun. Followed by several sequels. 110m/C VHS, Beta, LV, Closed Caption. Dean Jones, Michele Lee, Hope Lange, Robert Reed, Bert Convy; *D:* Robert Stevenson; *C:* Edward Colman; *M:* George Bruns. *DIS*

Love Butcher 1982 (R) A crippled old gardener kills his female employers with his garden tools and cleans up neatly afterward. 84m/C VHS, Beta. Erik Stern, Kay Neer, Robin Sherwood; *D:* Mikel Angel, Donald M. Jones. *NO*

Love by Appointment ♂ 1976 An unlikely romantic comedy with a very unlikely cast has two businessmen meeting up with European prostitutes. Made for television. 96m/C VHS, Beta. Ernest Borgnine, Robert Alda, Francoise Fabian, Corinne Clery. *NLC*

Love Camp ♂ 1976 A woman is invited to a swinger's holiday camp, frolics for a while, then is told she can never leave. Suspenseful hijinks ensue. 100m/C VHS, Beta. Laura Gemser, Christian Anders, Gabriele Tinti.

Love, Cheat & Steal ♂♂ 1993 (R) Convicted murderer Reno Adams (Roberts) breaks out of prison when he hears that his luscious ex (Amick) has just married another man (Lithgow). He turns up on her door, threatening to destroy her new life, but things aren't exactly what they seem. Faux noir. 95m/C VHS, Closed Caption. Eric Roberts, Madchen Amick, John Lithgow, Richard Edson, Donald Moffat, David Ackroyd, Dan O'Herlihy; *D:* William Curran; *W:* William Curran. *COL*

Love Child ♂♂ 1982 (R) The story of a young woman in prison who becomes pregnant by a guard and fights to have and keep her baby. 97m/C VHS, Beta. Amy Madigan, Beau Bridges, MacKenzie Phillips, Albert Salmi; *D:* Larry Peerce; *M:* Charles Fox. *WAR*

Love Crazy ♂♂♂½ 1941 Powell and Loy team once again for a non-"Thin Man" romp through a married-people farce. Via a nosy mother-in-law and a series of misunderstandings, Powell and Loy squabble almost to the point of divorce. Not the wry wit the team was known for, but zany, high-action comedy at its best. 99m/B VHS. William Powell, Myrna Loy, Gail Patrick, Jack Carson, Florence Bates, Sidney Blackmer, Sig Rumann; *D:* Jack Conway. *MGM*

Love Crimes ♂ 1992 (R) A con man (Bergin) poses as a photographer who sexually intimidates women while playing on their erotic fantasies. Young is the Atlanta district attorney who sets out to nail him when none of his victims will testify against him, only she may be enjoying her undercover work more than she realizes. Implausible and sleazy. Also available in an unrated version. *CW:* Language and strong sensuality. 84m/C VHS, LV. Sean Young, Patrick Bergin, Arnetia Walker, James Read; *D:* Lizzie Borden; *C:* Phedon Papamichael; *M:* Graeme Revell. *HBO*

Love Desperados ♂ 1986 Cowboys and ranchers' wives mix it up in a lot of softcore hay. 99m/C VHS, Beta. Virginia Gordon, James Arena.

Love 'Em and Leave 'Em ♂♂♂ 1926 Two sisters, with opposite personalities, are department store sales clerks. Brent is the "good" girl and Brooks the "bad" flirt who, under the influence of Perkins, bets the store's welfare benefit money on the horses and loses it all. Brent manages to make things right, while keeping boyfriend Gray from her sister's clutches. Brooks' baby vamp (the actress was 19) stole the picture. Introduced the "Black Bottom" shimmy dance to the screen. Remade in 1929 as "The Saturday Night Kid" with Clara Bow and Jean Arthur. 70m/B VHS,

Beta. Louise Brooks, Evelyn Brent, Lawrence Gray, Osgood Perkins; *D:* Frank Tuttle. *GPV*

The Love Factor ♂ *Zeta One* 1969 A secret agent tries to foil the plans of a race of topless female aliens in this sleazy softcore sci-fi film. ?m/C VHS. *GB* Robin Hawdon, James Robertson Justice, Yutte Stensgaard. *SNC*

Love Field ♂♂½ 1991 (PG-13) Pfeiffer is a Jackie Kennedy-obsessed hairdresser who decides to travel by bus to D.C. when she hears about President Kennedy's assassination. Along the way she gets involved in an interracial friendship with the secretive Haysbert, who's traveling with his young daughter. Pfeiffer's Lurene is basically a sweet dim bulb and Haysbert has an unfortunately written one-note character (mainly exasperation). The six-year-old McFadden (in her debut) makes the most impact. 104m/C VHS, LV, Closed Caption. Michelle Pfeiffer, Dennis Haysbert, Stephanie McFadden, Brian Kerwin, Louise Latham, Peggy Rea, Beth Grant, Cooper Huckabee, Mark Miller, Johnny Rae McGhee; *D:* Jonathan Kaplan; *W:* Don Roos; *C:* Ralf Bode; *M:* Jerry Goldsmith. Nominations: Academy Awards '92: Best Actress (Pfeiffer). *ORI, MOV*

Love Film ♂♂ 1970 A train trip from Budapest, Hungary to Lyon, France leads a young man to recall his past as he journeys to visit a childhood sweetheart. Jancsi and Kata's friendship has been disrupted by the 1956 uprising and Jancsi wonders if the love once developing between them has been broken by distance and time. In Hungarian with English subtitles. 130m/C VHS. *HU* Andras Balint, Judit Halasz; *D:* Istvan Szabo. *TPV*

Love Finds Andy Hardy ♂♂♂ 1938 Young Andy Hardy finds himself torn between three girls before returning to the girl next door. Garland's first appearance in the acclaimed Andy Hardy series features her singing "In Between" and "Meet the Best of my Heart." Also available with "Andy Hardy Meets Debutante" on laserdisc. 90m/B VHS, Beta, LV, Closed Caption. Mickey Rooney, Judy Garland, Lana Turner, Ann Rutherford, Fay Holden, Lewis Stone, Marie Blake, Cecilia Parker, Gene Reynolds; *D:* George B. Seitz. *MGM*

The Love Flower ♂♂½ 1920 A man kills his second wife's lover and escapes with his daughter to a tropical island, pursued by a detective and a young adventurer. Interesting ending wraps things up nicely. Silent. 70m/B VHS, Beta. Carol Dempster, Richard Barthelmess, George MacQuarrie, Anders Randolf, Florence Short; *D:* D.W. Griffith; *W:* D.W. Griffith. *NO*

Love for Lydia ♂♂♂ 1979 Made for British television miniseries following wayward beauty Lydia, orphaned heiress to a manufacturing fortune, through the high-spirited 1920s. Set in the industrial Midlands and farming communities of England, Lydia dazzles every man she meets, often to an unhappy end. Based on the novel by H.E. Bates. Available as a seven cassette boxed set. 657m/C VHS. *GB* Mel Martin, Christopher Blake, Peter Davison, Jeremy Irons, Michael Aldridge, Rachel Kempson, Beatrix Lehmann. *FCT, SIG, VIF*

Love from a Stranger ♂♂ 1937 Thriller about a working woman who wins a lottery. Soon she is charmed by and marries a man whom she later suspects may be trying to kill her. Remade in 1947. 90m/B VHS. *GB* Ann Harding, Basil Rathbone, Binnie Hale, Bruce Seton, Bryan Powley, Jean Cadell; *D:* Rowland V. Lee. *NOS, SNC*

Love from a Stranger ♂♂½ *A Stranger Walked In* 1947 In this remake of the 1937 film, a young newlywed bride fears that the honeymoon is over when she suspects that her husband is a notorious killer and that she will be his next victim. 81m/B VHS, Beta, LV. Sylvia Sidney, John Hodiak, John Howard, Ann Richards, Isobel Elsom, Ernest Cossart; *D:* Richard Whorf.

The Love God? ♂♂½ 1970 (PG-13) Very silly comedy finds mild-mannered Abner Peacock (Knotts) trying on Hugh Hefner's mantle. With his bird-watcher's magazine in financial trouble, Abner takes on a couple of shifty partners who change it into a different kind of bird watching magazine (the nude female kind) that gets Abner charged with pornography and finds him becoming a (very) unlikely sex symbol. 103m/C VHS, **Closed Caption.** Don Knotts, Edmond O'Brien, Anne Francis, Maureen Arthur, James Gregory, Margaret (Maggie) Peterson, Marjorie Bennett; **D:** Nat Hiken; **W:** Nat Hiken; **C:** William Margulies; **M:** Vic Mizzy. USH

The Love Goddesses 1965 A 60-year examination of some of the most beautiful women on the silver screen, reflecting with extraordinary accuracy the customs, manners and mores of the times. Released theatrically in 1972. 83m/B VHS, **Beta, LV.** Marlene Dietrich, Greta Garbo, Jean Harlow, Gloria Swanson, Mae West, Betty Grable, Rita Hayworth, Elizabeth Taylor, Marilyn Monroe, Theda Bara, Claudette Colbert, Dorothy Lamour; **D:** Saul J. Turell. COL

Love Happy 🐾🐾½ 1950 A group of impoverished actors accidentally gain possession of valuable diamonds. Unfortunately for them, detective Groucho is assigned to recover them! 85m/B VHS, LV. Groucho Marx, Harpo Marx, Chico Marx, Vera-Ellen, Ilona Massey, Marion Hutton, Raymond Burr, Marilyn Monroe; **D:** David Miller; **C:** William Mellor. REP

Love Has Many Faces 🐾½ 1965 Judith Crist was too kind when she said this was for connoisseurs of truly awful movies. Playgal Turner marries beachboy Robertson and many faces come between them. Much melodrama. Filmed on location. 104m/C VHS, Beta. Lana Turner, Cliff Robertson, Hugh O'Brian, Ruth Roman, Stefanie Powers, Virginia Grey, Ron Husmann; **D:** Alexander Singer. GKK

Love Hurts 🐾🐾 1991 (R) A guy looking for romance finds his hands full with a number of beautiful women. Will he find the love he craves, or will the pain be too much to bear? 110m/C VHS, **Closed Caption.** Jeff Daniels, Judith Ivey, John Mahoney, Cynthia Sikes, Amy Wright; **D:** Bud Yorkin; **W:** Ron Nyswaner. ART, VES

Love in Bloom 🐾🐾 1935 Predictable romance, with Burns and Allen providing some much-needed comic relief. Carnival gal Violet Downey (Lee) falls for struggling songwriter Larry Deane (Morrison) but thinks her tawdry background will ruin his chances and takes off. After Larry becomes successful he searches for Violet, still determined to marry her. 75m/B VHS, **Closed Caption.** George Burns, Gracie Allen, Joe Morrison, Dixie Lee, Lee Kohlmar, Richard Carle; **D:** Elliott Nugent; **W:** J.P. McEvoy, Keene Thompson; **C:** Leo Tover. USH

A Love in Germany 🐾🐾½ 1984 (R) *Un Amour En Allemagne; Eine Liebe in Deutschland* A tragic love affair develops between a German shopkeeper's wife and a Polish prisoner-of-war in a small German village during WWII. In German with English subtitles. 110m/C VHS, Beta, **Closed Caption.** FR GE Hanna Schygulla, Piotr Lysak, Elisabeth Trissenaar, Armin Mueller-Stahl; **D:** Andrzej Wajda; **W:** Andrzej Wajda, Agnieszka Holland, Boleslaw Michalek. COL, GLV

Love in the Afternoon 🐾🐾½ 1957 A Parisian private eye's daughter (Hepburn) decides to investigate a philandering American millionaire (Cooper) and winds up falling in love with him. Cooper's a little old for the Casanova role but Hepburn is always enchanting. 126m/B VHS, Beta, **Closed Caption.** Gary Cooper, Audrey Hepburn, John McGiver, Maurice Chevalier; **D:** Billy Wilder; **W:** Billy Wilder, I.A.L. Diamond; **C:** William Mellor. FOX, IME

Love in the City 🐾🐾🐾 1953 Five stories of life, love and tears in Rome. In Italian with English subtitles and narration. 90m/B VHS, Beta. IT Ugo Tognazzi, Maresa Gallo, Caterina Rigogolioso, Silvia Lillo; **D:** Michelangelo Antonioni, Federico Fellini, Dino Risi, Carlo Lizzani, Alberto Lattuada, Francesco Maselli, Cesare Zavattini; **W:** Federico Fellini. NOS, FCT, AUD

Love in the Present Tense 🐾 1985 A woman's romantic novel on video, dealing with an affair that reawakens the torpid, tragic life of a beautiful ex-model. 90m/C VHS, Beta.

Love Is a Gun 🐾½ 1994 (R) A police photographer (Roberts) begins having violent and erotic hallucinations that begin to affect his fiancee (Garrett). Things get even weirder when a femme fatale model (Preston) enters the picture. CW: Sexual situations; language; violence. 92m/C VHS, LV, **Closed Caption.** Eric Roberts, Kelly Preston, Eliza Garrett, R. Lee Ermey; **D:** David Hartwell. THV

Love Is a Many-Splendored Thing 🐾🐾½ 1955 A married American war correspondent and a beautiful Eurasian doctor fall in love in post-WWII Hong Kong. They struggle with racism and unhappiness, until he's sent to Korea to observe the Army's activities there. Based on the novel by Han Suyin. The extensive LA Asian acting community got some work out of this film, although the leads are played by Caucasians. Oscar winning song was a very big popular hit. ♫Love is a Many-Splendored Thing. 102m/C VHS, Beta, LV, **Closed Caption.** William Holden, Jennifer Jones, Torin Thatcher, Isobel Elsom, Jorja Curtright, Virginia Gregg, Richard Loo; **D:** Henry King; **C:** Leon Shamroy; **M:** Alfred Newman. Academy Awards '55: Best Costume Design (Color), Best Song ("Love Is a Many-Splendored Thing"), Best Original Dramatic/Comedy Score; Nominations: Academy Awards '55: Best Actress (Jones), Best Art Direction/Set Decoration (Color), Best Color Cinematography, Best Picture, Best Sound. BTV

Love Is All There Is 🐾🐾½ 1996 (R) It's a kind of comedic (happy-ending) version of "Romeo and Juliet," set in the Bronx, about rival restaurant families. Beautiful Gina's (Jolie) a finishing-school grad and Rosario's (Marston) the local boy too handsome for his own good. Both sets of parents are crazy. Oddly enough, Sorvino also plays the heroine's dad in the '96 "William Shakespeare's Romeo & Juliet." 98m/C VHS. Angelina Jolie, Nathaniel Marston, Paul Sorvino, Renee Taylor, Joseph Bologna, Lainie Kazan, Barbara Carrera, William Hickey, Abe Vigoda, Dick Van Patten, Connie Stevens; **D:** Renee Taylor, Joseph Bologna; **W:** Renee Taylor, Joseph Bologna; **C:** Alan Jones; **M:** Jeff Beal. EVE

Love Is Better Than Ever 🐾🐾½ *The Light Fantastic* 1952 Lightweight romantic-comedy casts Taylor as a dancing instructor who travels to the Big Apple for a convention. Once there, she meets and falls for talent agent Parks. Carefree, bachelor Parks is too busy to be bothered by small town Taylor, but Liz is determined to land her man. Release of this picture was held back because of Parks' blacklisting by the McCarthy committee. 81m/B VHS. Larry Parks, Elizabeth Taylor, Josephine Hutchinson, Tom Tully, Ann Doran, Elinor Donahue, Kathleen Freeman; **Cameos:** Gene Kelly; **D:** Stanley Donen; **W:** Ruth Brooks Flippen. MGM

Love Jones 🐾🐾🐾 1996 (R) A contemporary Chicago nightclub, the Sanctuary, is the gathering spot for middle-class black urbanites looking for romance. Would-be writer/poet Darius (Tate) spouts provocative verse to beautiful photographer Nina (Long), who's not too happy with men at the moment (she's just been dumped). But they make a connection, with both protesting a little too much that it's just a "sex thing." Funny what happens when love clearly enters the picture. Witcher's directorial debut features fine lead performances. CW: Language and sexuality. 105m/C VHS, LV, **Closed Caption.** Larenz Tate, Nia Long, Isaiah Washington, Lisa Nicole Carson, Khalil Kain, Bill Bellamy, Leonard Roberts, Bernardette L. Clarke; **D:** Theodore Witcher; **W:** Theodore Witcher; **C:** Ernest Holzman; **M:** Darryl Jones. Sundance Film Festival '97: Audience Award. NLC

Love Kills 🐾🐾 1991 (PG-13) Is the man a beautiful heiress falls in love with actually an assassin hired by her husband to kill her? Find out in this steamy suspenser. 92m/C VHS, Beta, LV, **Closed Caption.** Virginia Madsen, Lenny Von Dohlen, Erich Anderson, Kate Hodge, Jim Metzler; **D:** Brian Grant. PAR

Love Laughs at Andy Hardy 🐾🐾 1946 Andy Hardy, college boy, is in love and in trouble. Financial and romantic problems come to a head when Andy is paired with a six-foot tall blind date. One in the series. 93m/B VHS, Beta. Mickey Rooney, Lewis Stone, Sara Haden, Lina Romay, Bonita Granville, Fay Holden; **D:** Willis Goldbeck. NOS, MRV, HHT

Love Leads the Way 🐾🐾 1984 The true story of how Morris Frank established the seeing-eye dog system in the 1930s. 99m/C VHS, Beta. Timothy Bottoms, Eva Marie Saint, Arthur Hill, Susan Dey, Ralph Bellamy, Ernest Borgnine, Patricia Neal; **D:** Delbert Mann. DIS

Love Letters 🐾🐾½ 1945 Typical forties weepie finds Victoria (Jones) marrying soldier Roger Morland (Sully) because of the beautiful letters he wrote her. Only he didn't write them, his best bud Alan Quinton (Cotten) did. Roger's actually a wife-beater and winds up dead. Victoria becomes an amnesiac from the shock but when Alan comes to check out the situation he falls immediately in love with her anyway. Based on the novel "Pity My Simplicity" by Chris Massie. 101m/B VHS. Jennifer Jones, Joseph Cotten, Robert Sully, Ann Richards, Anita Louise, Cecil Kellaway, Gladys Cooper, Byron Barr, Reginald Denny; **D:** William Dieterle; **W:** Ayn Rand; **C:** Lee Garmes; **M:** Victor Young. USH

Love Letters 🐾🐾🐾 *Passion Play; My Love Letters* 1983 (R) A young disc jockey falls under the spell of a box of love letters that her mother left behind which detailed her double life. She, in turn, begins an affair with a married man. Thoughtful treatment of the psychology of infidelity. 102m/C VHS, Beta, LV. Jamie Lee Curtis, Amy Madigan, Bud Cort, Matt Clark, Bonnie Bartlett, Sally Kirkland, James Keach; **D:** Amy Holden Jones. ART, VES, IMF

Love, Lies and Murder 🐾🐾½ 1991 (PG-13) Shocking psychological thriller in which a businessman convinces his daughter and sister-in-law to murder his wife and then sends his daughter to prison for the crime. The "perfect murder" is not so perfect, however, when the daughter learns that her father has remarried and is now living an insurance-rich lifestyle. She decides to fight back in this true made-for-television story of bizarre murder and deception. CW: Mature themes and one violent scene. 190m/C VHS, LV, **Closed Caption.** Clancy Brown, John Ashton, Sheryl Lee, Moira Kelly, Ramon Bieri, Ken Walsh, Tom Bower, John M. Jackson; **D:** Robert Markowitz. REP

The Love Machine 🐾½ 1971 (R) A power-hungry newscaster climbs the corporate ladder by sleeping with many, including the president's wife. An adaptation of Jacqueline Susann's novel. 108m/C VHS, Beta. John Phillip Law, Dyan Cannon, Robert Ryan, Jackie Cooper, David Hemmings, Jodi Wexler, William Roerick, Maureen Arthur, Shecky Greene, Clinton Greyn, Sharon Farrell, Alexandra Hay, Eve Bruce, Greg Mullavey, Edith Atwater, Gene Baylos, Claudia Jennings, Mary Collinson, Madeleine Collinson, Ann Ford, Gayle Hunnicutt; **D:** Jack Haley Jr.; **C:** Charles B(ryant) Lang; **M:** Artie Butler. COL, MLB

Love Matters 🐾🐾 1993 (R) Tom and Julie's fast-track marriage is hovering on the brink when Tom's best friend Geoff, who's also married, shows up on their doorstep with his sexy mistress and announces he's getting a divorce. Reluctantly, Tom and Julie allow the X-rated lovebirds to stay the night but all that heat only shows up the flaws in their own marriage even more. An unrated version at 103 minutes is also available. 97m/C VHS, LV, **Closed Caption.** Griffin Dunne, Tony Goldwyn, Annette O'Toole, Gina Gershon, Kate Burton; **D:** Eb Lottimer; **W:** Eb Lottimer; **M:** Simon Boswell. REP

Love Me Deadly 🐾 1976 (R) A young woman tries to get her husband interested in her new hobby—necrophilia. 95m/C VHS, Beta. Mary Wilcox, Lyle Waggoner, Christopher Stone, Timothy Scott. GEM

Love Me or Leave Me 🐾🐾🐾 1955 A hard-hitting biography of '20s torch singer Ruth Etting and her rise and fall at the hand of her abusive, gangster husband, a part just made for

Cagney. Day emotes and sings expressively in one of the best performances of her career. ♫I'll Never Stop Loving You; Never Look Back; Shaking the Blues Away; Mean to Me; Love Me or Leave Me; Sam, the Old Accordian Man; At Sundown; Everybody Loves My Baby; Five Foot Two. **122m/C VHS, Beta, LV, Letterbox, Closed Caption.** Doris Day, James Cagney, Cameron Mitchell, Robert Keith, Tom Tully, Veda Ann Borg; **D:** Charles Vidor. Academy Awards '55: Best Story; Nominations: Academy Awards '55: Best Actor (Cagney), Best Screenplay, Best Song ("I'll Never Stop Loving You"), Best Sound, Scoring of a Musical. *MGM*

Love Me Tender 🐾🐾 1956 A Civil War-torn family is divided by in-fighting between two brothers who both seek the affections of the same woman. Presley's first film. Songs include "Poor Boy," "We're Gonna Move," and the title tune. **89m/B VHS, Beta.** Elvis Presley, Richard Egan, Debra Paget, Neville Brand, Mildred Dunnock, James Drury, Barry Coe; **D:** Robert D. Webb. *MVD, FOX*

Love Meetings *Comizi d'Amore* 1964 Pasolini acts as director and interviewer to query a wide-range of individuals on their experiences at love, including homosexuality, prostitution, marital and non-marital interludes. In Italian with English subtitles. **90m/B VHS, LV, Letterbox.** *IT* **D:** Pier Paolo Pasolini. *WBF*

Love Nest 🐾🐾 1951 Lundigan stars as Jim Scott, the landlord of an apartment building brimming with wacky tenants, including Monroe, Paar, and Fay. He dreams of becoming a famous writer, but his time is always filled with fixing up the building and trying to pay the mortgage. When one of the tenants ends up in jail because he was living off wealthy widows, Scott's luck changes. This moderately funny film is a good look at the early careers of Monroe and Paar. **84m/B VHS.** William Lundigan, June Haver, Frank Fay, Marilyn Monroe, Jack Paar; **D:** Joseph M. Newman. *FXV*

Love Notes 1988 Three short vignettes of soft core fantasy, in the life of an ordinary guy. **60m/C VHS, Beta.** Jeff Daniels, Christine Veronica.

The Love of Three Queens 🐾½ 1954 The loves, on and off stage, of a beautiful actress in a European traveling theatre group. **80m/C VHS, Beta.** Gerard Oury, Massimo Serato, Robert Beatty, Cathy O'Donnell, Terence Morgan, Hedy Lamarr; **D:** Marc Allegret. *FCT, VDM*

Love on the Dole 🐾🐾🐾 1941 In a gloomy industrial section of England during the early '30s a family struggles to survive and maintain dignity. Grim Depression drama salvaged by great acting. **89m/B VHS, Beta.** *GB* Deborah Kerr, Clifford Evans, George Carney; **D:** John Baxter. *NOS, VYY*

Love on the Run 🐾🐾½ 1936 Enjoyable romantic comedy starring Crawford as a rich American heiress and Gable and Tone (Crawford's real husband at the time) as journalists stationed in Europe. Gable and Tone are assigned to cover an international aviator, who turns out to be an evil spy, as well as the upcoming wedding of flighty Crawford. When Crawford asks for help in getting out of her marriage, Gable and Tone steal a plane and the trio are chased across Europe by spies. Wild and farfetched plot, but the stars make it worthwhile. Based on the story "Beauty and the Beast" by Alan Green and Julian Brodie. **80m/B VHS.** Joan Crawford, Clark Gable, Franchot Tone, Reginald Owen, Mona Maris, Ivan Lebedeff, Charles Judels, William Demarest; **D:** Woodbridge S. Van Dyke; **W:** John Lee Mahin, Manuel Seff, Gladys Hurlbut. *MGM*

Love on the Run 🐾🐾🐾 *L'Amour en Fuite* 1978 The further amorous adventures of Antoine Doinel, hero of "The 400 Blows," "Stolen Kisses," and "Bed and Board." Doinel is now in his 30s and newly divorced. He renews affairs with several women from his past but, after his mother's death, must contend with his emotional immaturity and his inability to sustain a relationship. In French with English subtitles. **95m/C VHS, Beta.** *FR* Jean-Pierre Leaud, Marie-France Pisier, Claude Jade; **D:**

Francois Truffaut; **C:** Nestor Almendros; **M:** Georges Delerue. Cesar Awards '80: Best Score. *HMV, WAR*

Love on the Run 🐾½ 1985 A beautiful lawyer helps a wrongly accused convict escape from prison, then they both evade the law. Made for television. **102m/C VHS, Beta.** Stephanie Zimbalist, Alec Baldwin, Constance McCashin, Howard Duff; **D:** Gus Trikonis; **M:** Billy Goldenberg. *COL*

Love or Money? 🐾½ 1988 (PG-13) A small comedy about a yuppie who must choose between a woman and a real estate deal. **90m/C VHS, Beta, LV, Closed Caption.** Timothy Daly, Haviland Morris, Kevin McCarthy, Shelley Fabares, David Doyle, Allen Havey; **D:** Todd Hallowell; **W:** Bart Davis.

Love Play 🐾🐾 *Playtime; La Recreation* 1960 Debut film for Moreuil, who was married to leading lady Seberg at the time, is a bland drama based on a story by Francoise Sagan (who also wrote the much better "Bonjour Tristesse" that Seberg starred in). Young American Kate Hudson (Seberg), enrolled in a Paris school, becomes obsessed with her next-door neighbors—sculptor Philippe (Marquand) and his wealthy older mistress and patron (Prevost). Soon Kate's involved in a triangle that's even more complicated than it first appears. **87m/B VHS.** *FR* Jean Seberg, Christian Marquand, Francoise Prevost, Evelyne Ker; **D:** Francois Moreuil; **W:** Francois Moreuil, Daniel Boulanger; **C:** Jean Penzer; **M:** Georges Delerue. *FRF*

Love Potion #9 🐾½ 1992 (PG-13) Two nerdy biochemists procure a love potion that they test on animals. Meeting with success they agree to test it on themselves. Predictably, the scientists are transformed and fall in love with each other. Features a talented young cast, with an amusing cameo by Bancroft, but the script is a real disappointment because of its shallow characters and lame gags. Inspired by the song by Jerry Leiber and Mike Stoller. **96m/C VHS, LV, Closed Caption.** Tate Donovan, Sandra Bullock, Mary Mara, Dale Midkiff, Hillary Bailey Smith, Dylan Baker; **Cameos:** Anne Bancroft; **D:** Dale Launer; **W:** Dale Launer. *FXV*

Love Serenade 🐾🐾 1996 (R) Former big-time Brisbane DJ and 70s refugee Ken Sherry (Shevtsov) arrives in a sleepy Australian backwater town, setting off a rivalry between two bored sisters, Dimity (Otto) and Vicki-Ann (Frith). Fishing is one of his hobbies and metaphorically, Ken is the big fish in a very little pond. To them, his pretentious disco-era schmooze comes off as sophistication, mostly because he uses Barry White lyrics and his pillow-talk DJ voice to sell it. Critically speaking, director/writer Barrett's debut demonstrates a keen ear for dialogue and comic timing. To the average viewer though, this one's a dog, boring and very strange. If you're looking for a good Aussie comedy rent "Strictly Ballroom" or "Muriel's Wedding" instead. **CW:** Some sexuality. **101m/C VHS, LV, Closed Caption.** *AU* Miranda Otto, Rebecca Frith, George Shevtsov, John Alansu, Jessica Napier; **D:** Shirley Barrett; **W:** Shirley Barrett; **C:** Mandy Walker. *TOU*

Love Songs 🐾🐾 1985 (R) A mother of two is confronted with her husband's abandonment and a subsequent romance with a younger man. In French with English subtitles or dubbed. ♫Leave It to Me; Psychic Flash; I Am With You Now; Human Race; We Can Dance; One More Moment; From the Heart; This Must Be Heaven. **107m/C VHS, Beta.** *FR CA* Catherine Deneuve, Christopher Lambert; **D:** Elie Chouraqui; **C:** Robert Alazraki. *ART, VES*

Love Story 🐾🐾🐾 1970 (PG) Melodrama had enormous popular appeal. O'Neal is the son of Boston's upper crust at Harvard; McGraw's the daughter of a poor Italian on scholarship to study music at Radcliffe. They find happiness, but only for a brief period. Timeless story, simply told, with artful direction from Hiller pulling exceptional performances from the young duo (who have never done as well since). The end result is perhaps better than Segal's simplistic novel, which was

produced after he sold the screenplay and became a best-seller before the picture's release—great publicity for any film. Remember: "Love means never having to say you're sorry." **100m/C VHS, Beta, LV.** Ryan O'Neal, Ali MacGraw, Ray Milland, John Marley, Tommy Lee Jones; **D:** Arthur Hiller; **W:** Erich Segal. Academy Awards '70: Best Original Score; Golden Globe Awards '71: Best Actress—Drama (MacGraw), Best Director (Hiller), Best Film—Drama, Best Screenplay, Best Score; Nominations: Academy Awards '70: Best Actor (O'Neal), Best Actress (MacGraw), Best Director (Hiller), Best Picture, Best Story & Screenplay, Best Supporting Actor (Marley). *PAR*

Love Strange Love 🐾½ 1982 A young boy develops a bizarre relationship with his mother who works in a luxurious bordello. Also available in an unedited 120-minute version. **97m/C VHS, Beta.** Vera Fischer, Mauro Mendonca. *ART, VES*

Love Streams 🐾🐾½ 1984 (PG-13) A quirky character drama about a writer and his sister who struggle to find love despite their personal problems. **122m/C VHS, Beta.** Gena Rowlands, John Cassavetes, Diahnne Abbott, Seymour Cassel; **D:** John Cassavetes; **W:** Ted Allan. Berlin International Film Festival '84: Golden Berlin Bear. *MGM*

Love Thrill Murders woof! 1971 (R) A film about a Mansonesque lunatic who is worshipped and obeyed by a mob of runaways and dropouts. **89m/C VHS, Beta.** Troy Donahue. *ART, VES*

Love to Kill 🐾🐾 *The Girl Gets Moe* 1997 (R) Moe (Danza) is a low-level arms dealer who falls for Elizabeth (Barondes), a gal who happens to like guns. But things go wrong thanks to dead bodies, double-crosses, and dirty cops. **102m/C VHS.** Tony Danza, Michael Madsen, James Russo, Elizabeth Barondes, Louise Fletcher, Amy Locane; **D:** James Bruce. *APX*

Love Under Pressure 🐾🐾 198? Man and woman's marriage starts to evaporate when they realize their son is seriously disturbed. **92m/C VHS.** Karen Black, Keir Dullea.

Love! Valour! Compassion! 🐾🐾½ 1996 (R) Follows eight gay men, longtime friends, who spend summer holiday weekends together at a beach house. Excellent cast features Alexander as Buzz, who has a severe show tune fixation, and Glover playing a pair of twins with very different personalities (and they're actually named Jeckyll). Together they wander through the turmoil of AIDS, infidelity, rage and impromptu ballet practice. Excellent cast only occasionally swerves from humor and genuine pathos into maudlin. Intermittent periods of stagy claustrophobia betray pic's Broadway origin. Based on the play by Terrence McNally. **CW:** Graphic nudity, some sexuality and brief violence. **120m/C VHS, LV, Closed Caption.** Jason Alexander, John Glover, Randy Becker, John Benjamin Hickey, Stephen Bogardus, Stephen Spinella, Justin Kirk; **D:** Joe Mantello; **W:** Terrance McNally; **C:** Alik Sakharov; **M:** Harold Wheeler. *NLC*

Love Walked In 🐾🐾 1997 (R) Hardly an original story but this B-movie has a standout performance from the edgy Leary. He's Jack Hanaway, a lounge piano player with a sultry singer/wife, Vicky (Sanchez-Gijon). Jack's old P.I. friend Eddie (Badalucco) shows up with a scheme to make them all rich. He's been hired by a wealthy woman (Dusay) who suspects her husband Fred (Stamp) of infidelity. Fred's faithful (he likes his wife's money) but he's a patron of Jack's and is naturally appreciative of Vicky's charms. So they try to set Fred up. Scenes of would-be writer Jack's pulp novel intrude into the action and provide an unneeded distraction. Adapted from the novel by Jose Pable Feinmann. **CW:** Sexuality, language and some violence. **90m/C VHS, Closed Caption.** Denis Leary, Aitana Sanchez-Gijon, Terence Stamp, Michael Badalucco, Marj Dusay, Danny Nucci, Moira Kelly, Neal Huff; **D:** Juan J. Campanella; **W:** Larry Golin, Juan J. Campanella; **C:** Daniel Shulman; **M:** Wendy Blackstone. *COL*

Love with a Perfect Stranger 1986 This Harlequin Romance takes place in Italy where a young widow meets a dashing Englishman. He changes her life forever. 102m/C VHS, Beta. Marilu Henner, Daniel Massey; **M:** John Du Prez. *PAR*

Love with the Proper Stranger 🎬🎬🎬 1963 A quiet, gritty romance about an itinerant musician and a young working girl in Manhattan awkwardly living through the consequences of their one-night stand. Moved Wood well into the realm of adult roles, after years playing teenagers and innocents. Although the story is about an Italian neighborhood and family, an exceptional number of the cast members were Jewish, as was the screenwriter. Story does not conclude strongly, although this did not hamper the boxoffice returns. 102m/B VHS, Beta, LV, Closed Caption. Natalie Wood, Steve McQueen, Edie Adams, Herschel Bernardi, Tom Bosley, Harvey Lembeck, Penny Santon, Virginia Vincent, Nick Alexander, Augusta Ciolli; **D:** Robert Mulligan; **W:** Arnold Schulman; **C:** Milton Krasner; **M:** Elmer Bernstein. Nominations: Academy Awards '63: Best Actress (Wood), Best Art Direction/Set Decoration (B & W), Best Black and White Cinematography, Best Costume Design (B & W), Best Story & Screenplay. *PAR*

Love Without Fear 1990 A dramatic, heart-rendering look at children with AIDS. Story focuses on the lives of three women from completely different backgrounds who adopt babies with AIDS and develop a special love for these children. Also shows their confrontations with a society which fears the disease and the women's strength to reach out and make a difference. ?m/C VHS. *NO*

Love Without Pity 🎬🎬½ 1991 Rochant's theatrical debut is a modern romance, with more distance and alienation than joy. A lovely, successful grad student loses her heart to a jobless, unambitious layabout who wants total commitment from her. Untypical, sardonic love story may be too cynical for sentimental types. In French with English subtitles. 95m/C VHS. **FR** Hippolyte Girardot, Mireille Perrier, Jean Marie Rollin; **D:** Eric Rochant; **W:** Eric Rochant; **M:** Gerard Torikian. *ORI*

Love Your Mama 🎬🎬½ 1989 (PG-13) An urban black drama about the strong Dorothy whose faith helps her cope with her many family complications, including her drunken husband, car thief son, and pregnant teenage daughter. Believable role models and good performances help out this amatuer filmmaking effort. 93m/C VHS. Audrey Morgan, Carol E. Hall, Andre Robinson, Ernest Rayford, Kearo Johnson, Jacqueline Williams; **D:** Ruby L. Oliver; **W:** Ruby L. Oliver. *BTV, FCT*

Loved 🎬🎬 1997 (PG-13) Hedda's (Wright Penn) obsessively and destructively in love with the nameless ex-boyfriend (Lucero) who left her scarred after a suspicious fall out a window. The loser's being arraigned for the murder of his latest girlfriend and prosecutor Dietrickson (Hurt) wants Hedda to testify. But what no one counts on, and what no one can understand, is Hedda's justification for her ex's abuse. Pic and performances are vague. **CW:** Intense thematic elements, brief disturbing images, language and nudity. 109m/C VHS. Robin Wright Penn, William Hurt, Amy Madigan, Anthony Lucero, Lucinda Jenney, Joanna Cassidy, Paul Dooley, Jennifer Rubin; **Cameos:** Sean Penn; **D:** Eric Dignam; **W:** Eric Dignam; **C:** Reynaldo Villalobos; **M:** David Baerwald. Nominations: Independent Spirit Awards '98: Best Actress (Wright Penn), Best Film, Best Supporting Actress (Madigan). *NYR*

The Loved One 🎬🎬🎬 1965 A famously outlandish, death-mocking farce based on Evelyn Waugh's satire about a particularly horrendous California funeral parlor/cemetery and how its denizens do business. A shrill, protracted spearing of American capitalism. 118m/B VHS, Beta, LV. Robert Morse, John Gielgud, Rod Steiger, Liberace, Anjanette Comer, Jonathan Winters, James Coburn, Dana Andrews, Milton Berle, Tab Hunter, Robert Morley, Lionel Stander, Margaret Leighton, Roddy McDowall, Bernie Ko-

pell, Alan Napier; **D:** Tony Richardson; **W:** Terry Southern, Christopher Isherwood; **C:** Haskell Wexler; **M:** John Addison. *MGM*

Loveless 🎬🎬 1983 (R) A menacing glance into the exploits of an outcast motorcycle gang. In the 50s, a group of bikers on their way to the Florida Cycle Races stop for lunch in a small-town diner. While repairs are being made on their motorcycles, they decide to take full advantage of their situation. 85m/C VHS, Beta. Robert Gordon, Willem Dafoe, J. Don Ferguson; **D:** Kathryn Bigelow; **W:** Kathryn Bigelow.

Lovelife 🎬🎬½ 1997 (R) Yet another romantic saga about a group of disenchanted boomer friends who can't seem to make that love connection work. Maybe they should stop serial dating within their same small circle and take advantage of the outside world. **CW:** Language and drug content. 97m/C VHS. Sherilyn Fenn, Bruce Davison, Saffron Burrows, Jon Tenney, Carla Gugino; **D:** John Harmon Feldman. *THV*

Lovelines 🎬 1984 (R) Two rock singers from rival high schools meet and fall in love during a panty raid. Laughs uncounted ensue. 93m/C VHS, Beta, Closed Caption. Greg Bradford, Michael Winslow, Mary Beth Evans, Don Michael Paul, Tammy Taylor, Stacey Toten, Miguel Ferrer, Shecky Greene, Aimee Eccles, Sherri Stoner; **D:** Rod Amateau. *ART, VES*

Lovely ... But Deadly 🎬½ 1982 (R) Young girl wages a war against the drug dealers in her school after her brother dies of an overdose. 95m/C VHS, Beta. Lucinda Dooling, John Randolph, Richard Herd, Susan Mechsner, Mel Novak; **D:** David Sheldon. *ART, VES*

Lovely to Look At 🎬🎬🎬 1952 Three wanna-be Broadway producers (Skelton, Keel, Champion) go to gay Paree to peddle Skelton's half interest in Madame Roberta's, a chi chi dress shop. There, they meet the shop's other half interest, two sisters (Champion and Miller), and together they stage a fashion show to finance the floundering hospice of haute couture. Lavish production, light plot. Filmed in Technicolor based on Kern's 1933 Broadway hit (inspired by Alice Duer Miller's "Gowns by Roberta"). Vincent Minelli staged the fashion show, with gowns by Adrian (watch for cop-beater Zsa Zsa as a model). Laserdisc format features the original motion picture trailer. ♬Opening Night; Smoke Gets in Your Eyes; Lovely to Look At; The Touch of Your Hand; Yesterdays; I Won't Dance; You're Devastating; The Most Exciting Night; I'll Be Hard to Handle. 105m/C VHS, LV. Kathryn Grayson, Red Skelton, Howard Keel, Gower Champion, Marge Champion, Ann Miller, Zsa Zsa Gabor, Kurt Kasznar, Marcel Dalio, Diane Cassidy; **D:** Mervyn LeRoy; **M:** Jerome Kern. *MGM, TTC, FCT*

The Lover 🎬🎬 *L'Amant* 1992 (R) Portrays the sexual awakening of a French teenager and her older Chinese lover in Indochina in 1929. The characters, who remain nameless, meet on a ferry where the man is smitten by the girl's beauty. Detached, determined, and unromantic (the opposite of her indolent lover), she allows herself to be seduced for the experience, and money, he offers. The film is equally detached, including the beautifully photographed but uninvolving sex scenes. Moreau narrates as an adult looking back on her life. March's debut; filmed on location in Vietnam. Based on the semi-autobiographical novel by Marguerite Duras who reputiated director Annuad's film when it was released in France. Also available in an unrated, letterbox version at 115 minutes. 103m/C VHS, Beta, LV, Letterbox, Closed Caption. **FR** Jane March, Tony Leung, Frederique Meininger, Arnaud Giovanietti, Melvil Poupaud, Lisa Faulkner, Xiem Mang; **D:** Jean-Jacques Annaud; **W:** Gerard Brach, Jean-Jacques Annaud; **C:** Robert Fraisse. Cesar Awards '93: Best Score; Nominations: Academy Awards '92: Best Cinematography. *MGM, BTV*

Lover Come Back 🎬🎬½ 1961 More Day-Hudson antics in which an advertising executive falls in love with his competitor but that doesn't stop him from stealing his clients. Is there

no shame? 107m/C VHS, Beta. Rock Hudson, Doris Day, Tony Randall, Edie Adams, Joe Flynn, Ann B. Davis, Jack Oakie, Jack Albertson, Jack Kruschen, Howard St. John; **D:** Delbert Mann. Nominations: Academy Awards '61: Best Story & Screenplay. *USH, MOV*

Loverboy 🎬 1989 (PG-13) A college schnook takes a summer job as a Beverly Hills pizza delivery boy and is preyed upon by many rich and sex-hungry housewives. 105m/C VHS, Beta, LV, Closed Caption. Patrick Dempsey, Kate Jackson, Barbara Carrera, Kirstie Alley, Carrie Fisher, Robert Ginty; **W:** Tom Ropelewski, Leslie Dixon; **M:** Michel Colombier. *COL*

The Lovers 🎬🎬🎬 1959 Chic tale of French adultery with Moreau starring as a provincial wife whose shallow life changes overnight when she meets a young man. Had a controversial American debut because of the film's tender eroticism and innocent view of adultery. In French with English subtitles. 90m/B VHS. **FR** Jeanne Moreau, Alain Cuny, Jose-Luis De Villalonga, Jean-Mark Bory; **D:** Louis Malle; **W:** Louis Malle. Venice Film Festival '59: Special Jury Prize. *NYF, FCT, ING*

Lovers: A True Story 🎬🎬🎬 1990 (R) Erotic love triangle in 1950s Madrid, while Spain is under the suffocating dictatorship of Franco. Naive, young Paco has a virginal, hardworking fiancee named Trini. Things would seem to be headed for an average life until Paco rents a room from young widow Luisa and they embark on a sexual affair bordering on obsession. When Trini discovers what's going on she turns out to have a more passionate, and violent, nature than even Paco could imagine. Steamy and highly dramatic with excellent performances. Based on a true story. In Spanish with English subtitles. An unrated version is also available. **CW:** Language and sexuality. 105m/C VHS. **SP** Victoria Abril, Jorge Sanz, Maribel Verdu; **D:** Vicente Aranda. Berlin International Film Festival '91: Best Actress (Abril). *REP*

Lovers and Liars 🎬🎬 *Travels with Anita; A Trip with Anita* 1981 (R) A romantic adventure in Rome turns into a symphony of zany mishaps when the man forgets to tell the woman that he is married!! 93m/C VHS, Beta. **IT** Goldie Hawn, Giancarlo Giannini, Laura Betti; **D:** Mario Monicelli; **M:** Ennio Morricone.

Lovers and Other Strangers 🎬🎬🎬 1970 (R) Two young people decide to marry after living together for a year and a half. Various tensions surface between them and among their families as the wedding day approaches. Good comedy features some charming performances. Keaton's first film. ♬For All We Know. 106m/C VHS. Gig Young, Beatrice Arthur, Bonnie Bedelia, Anne Jackson, Harry Guardino, Michael Brandon, Richard Castellano, Bob Dishy, Marian Hailey, Cloris Leachman, Anne Meara, Diane Keaton; **D:** Cy Howard; **W:** Renee Taylor, Joseph Bologna, David Zelag Goodman. Academy Awards '70: Best Song ("For All We Know"); Nominations: Academy Awards '70: Best Adapted Screenplay, Best Supporting Actor (Castellano). *FOX*

Lover's Knot 🎬🎬½ 1996 (R) Cutesy romantic comedy has Curry as an angel whose heavenly mission is to get the proper romantic couples together. His current pair are poetic college English prof Steve (Campbell) and practical pediatrician Megan (Grey). Steve's imaginative courtship wins Megan but day-to-day living takes its toll and the duo separate, leaving their angelic guide to get them back together. **CW:** Sexuality. 82m/C VHS, Closed Caption. Bill Campbell, Jennifer Grey, Tim Curry, Adam Baldwin; **Cameos:** Adam Ant, Anne Francis; **D:** Peter Shaner; **W:** Peter Shaner; **C:** Garett Griffin; **M:** Laura Karpman. *CAF*

Lovers Like Us 🎬🎬½ *Le Sauvage; The Savage* 1975 Two people each leave their spouses, meet one another, and fall in love. 103m/C VHS, Beta. **FR** Catherine Deneuve, Yves Montand, Luigi Vannucchi, Tony Roberts, Dana Wynter; **D:** Jean-Paul Rappeneau; **W:** Jean-Paul Rappeneau. *NO*

Lovers' Lovers ✶✶½ **1994** All sorts of bizarre and erotic adventures ensue when Blaire the jilted narcissist meets Michael, who doesn't want to commit to girlfriend Teri. Michael plans an affair with Blaire without realizing that Teri is already having a fling with Ray, Blaire's ex. Some funny situations but too many talky scenes stop the film cold. **90m/C VHS, LV.** Serge Rodnunsky, Jennifer Ciesar, Cindy Parker, Ray Bennett; **D:** Serge Rodnunsky; **W:** Serge Rodnunsky; **M:** Pierre Rodnunsky. TRI

Lovers of Their Time ✶ **1985** A romantic novel on tape, about forbidden love and other problems. **60m/C Beta.** Edward Petherbridge, Cheryl Prime, Lynn Farleigh; **D:** Robert Knights.

Loves & Times of Scaramouche ✶✶½ Scaramouche **1976** Eighteenth-century rogue becomes involved in a plot to assassinate Napoleon and winds up seducing Josephine in the process. Dubbed. **92m/C VHS, Beta.** IT Michael Sarrazin, Ursula Andress, Aldo Maccione; **D:** Enzo G. Castellari. COL

Loves of a Blonde ✶✶✶½ A Blonde in Love; Lasky Jedne Plavovlasky **1965** A shy teenage factory girl falls in love with a visiting piano player when the reservist army comes to her small town. But when she goes to visit his family, she discovers things aren't as she imagined. Touching look at the complications of love and our expectations. Czech with subtitles. **88m/B VHS, Beta.** CZ Jana Brejchova, Josef Sebanek, Vladimir Pucholt; **D:** Milos Forman. Nominations: Academy Awards '66: Best Foreign Language Film. HMV, COL

The Loves of Carmen ✶✶½ **1948** Film version of the classic Prosper Merrimee novel about a tempestuous Spanish gypsy and the soldier who loves her. Hayworth is great to look at and the film's main selling point. **98m/C VHS, Beta.** Rita Hayworth, Glenn Ford, Ron Randell, Victor Jory, Arnold Moss, Luther Adler, Joseph Buloff; **D:** Charles Vidor. Nominations: Academy Awards '48: Best Color Cinematography. COL

The Loves of Edgar Allen Poe ✶✶ **1942** A bland biographical drama about young Poe's adoption, his treatment at the hands of his foster father, his rejection by a woman for a more well-off man, his marriage to his first cousin, and his early death from alcoholism. **67m/B VHS.** Linda Darnell, Shepperd Strudwick, Virginia Gilmore, Jane Darwell, Mary Howard; **D:** Harry Lachman. FXL

The Loves of Hercules woof! Hercules and the Hydra **1960** The mythic mesomorph finds a mate with equiponderant chest measurements, and must save her from an evil queen. Somehow it eludes him that both queen and maiden are Miss Jayne in red and black wigs. Kudos for worst dubbing and special effects; a must see for connoisseurs of kitsch. **94m/C VHS.** IT FR Jayne Mansfield, Mickey Hargitay; **D:** Carlo L. Bragaglia. SNC, VDM

The Loves of Irina ✶ Erotikill **198?** Franco's dreamy, sanguine, produced-on-a-dime tale of a vampiress. She cruises the Riviera, seducing and nibbling on a variety of men and women. Not for most tastes. **95m/C VHS, Beta.** Lina Romay, Monica Swin, Jack Taylor, Alice Arno; **D:** Jess (Jesus) Franco.

Love's Savage Fury woof! **1979** Two escapees from a Union prison camp seek out a hidden treasure that could determine the outcome of the Civil War. A bad made-for-television "Gone With the Wind" rip-off. **100m/C VHS, Beta.** Jennifer O'Neill, Perry King, Robert Reed, Raymond Burr, Connie Stevens, Ed Lauter; **D:** Joseph Hardy; **M:** John Addison.

Lovesick ✶✶ **1983 (PG)** A very-married New York psychiatrist goes against his own best judgment when he falls in love with one of his patients. **98m/C VHS, Beta, LV.** Dudley Moore, Elizabeth McGovern, Alec Guinness, John Huston, Ron Silver; **D:** Marshall Brickman; **W:** Marshall Brickman. WAR

Lovespell ✶ Tristan and Isolde **1979** A retelling of the legend of Isolde and Tristan. Stilted direction and writing, but another chance to reminisce on Richard Burton. **91m/C VHS.** Richard Burton, Kate Mulgrew, Nicholas Clay, Cyril Cusack, Geraldine Fitzgerald,

Niall Toibin, Diana Van Der Vlis, Niall O'Brien; **D:** Tom Donovan. NO

Lovey: A Circle of Children 2 ✶✶ **1982** Teacher for special children takes in a terrified girl diagnosed as brain damaged or schizophrenic, and discovers love and intelligence in the girl as well as finding some important insights into her own life. **120m/C VHS, Beta.** Jane Alexander, Kris McKeon, Karen Allen; **D:** Jud Taylor. TLF

Loving ✶✶½ **1984** The full-length, shot-on-video pilot for the daytime television soap opera, with various guest stars. Exteriors shot at C.W. Post Center on Long Island. **120m/C VHS, Beta.** Lloyd Bridges, Geraldine Page. NO

Loving Couples ✶✶ **1980 (PG)** Two happily married couples meet at a weekend resort...and switch partners. Tired and predictable but it has its moments. **120m/C VHS, Beta.** Shirley MacLaine, James Coburn, Susan Sarandon, Stephen Collins, Sally Kellerman; **D:** Jack Smight. VES

Loving You ✶✶ **1957** A small town boy with a musical style all his own becomes a big success thanks to the help of a female press agent. Features many early Elvis hits. ♫Loving You; Teddy Bear; Lonesome Cowboy; Got a Lot of Livin' To Do; Party; Mean Woman Blues; Hot Dog. **101m/C VHS, Beta, LV.** Elvis Presley, Wendell Corey, Lizabeth Scott, Dolores Hart, James Gleason; **D:** Hal Kanter; **W:** Hal Kanter. WAR, OM

Low Blow ✶ **1985** A kung fu expert tracks down a mind-bending cult. **90m/C VHS, Beta.** Cameron Mitchell, Leo Fong; **D:** Frank Harris. ART, VES

A Low Down Dirty Shame ✶✶ **1994 (R)** Shame (Wayans) is a down-on-his-luck private eye, with the obligatory wisecracking secretary, Peaches (Pinkett), who's hired by an old friend to find a vicious drug lord, a sultry ex-girlfriend, and $20 million. Lots of fun stunts and one liners can't make up for major plot holes. **CW:** Violence; strong lanugage; brief sexuality. **100m/C VHS, LV, Closed Caption.** Keenen Ivory Wayans, Jada Pinkett Smith, Salli Richardson, Charles S. Dutton, Andrew Divoff, Corwin Hawkins; **D:** Keenen Ivory Wayans; **W:** Keenen Ivory Wayans. TOU

The Low Life ✶✶½ **1995 (R)** A "day in the life" sort of story about aspiring writer John (Cochrane) who comes to L.A. with high hopes but instead gets stuck in the low life of awful temp jobs, a lousy landlord (LeGros), and now, his newly arrived loser cousin Andrew (Astin). He tries to cozy up to looker Sedgwick but she doesn't seem too interested—so what's a would-be cool guy to do? **CW:** Language, sexuality and some drug use. **96m/C VHS, Closed Caption.** Rory Cochrane, Kyra Sedgwick, Sean Astin, James LeGros, Christian Meoli, Shawnee Smith, J.T. Walsh, Renee Zellweger; **D:** George Hickenlooper; **W:** George Hickenlooper, John Enbom; **C:** Richard Crudo; **M:** Bill Boll. CAF

The Lower Depths ✶✶✶½ Les Bas Fonds; Underground **1936** Renoir's adaptation of the Maxim Gorky play about a thief and a financially ruined baron learning about life from one another. In French with English subtitles. **92m/B VHS, Beta.** FR Jean Gabin, Louis Jouvet, Vladimir Sokoloff, Robert Le Vigan, Suzy Prim; **D:** Jean Renoir. FCT, DVT, GVV

The Lower Depths ✶✶✶½ **1957** Kurosawa sets the Maxim Gorky play in Edo during the final Tokugawa period, using Noh theatre elements in depicting the lowly denizens of a low-rent hovel. In Japanese with English subtitles. **125m/B VHS.** JP Toshiro Mifune, Isuzu Yamada, Ganjiro Nakamura, Kyoko Kagawa, Bokuzen Hidari; **D:** Akira Kurosawa. HMV, FCT, COL

Lower Level ✶ **1991 (R)** While working late, an attractive business woman becomes trapped in an office building by her psychotic secret admirer. **CW:** Language, violence and sensuality. **88m/C VHS, LV, Closed Caption.** David Bradley, Elizabeth Gracen, Jeff Yagher; **D:** Kristine Peterson. REP

Loyalties ✶✶½ **1986 (R)** A strong treatment of the issue of sexual abuse of girls by men, and of an upper-class woman's willingness to establish a true friendship with a woman of a so-called lower economic class. **98m/C VHS.** CA Kenneth Welsh, Tantoo Cardinal, Susan Wooldridge, Vera Martin, Christopher Barrington-Leigh; **D:** Anne Wheeler; **W:** Sharon Riis; **M:** Michael Conway Baker. NO

Loyola, the Soldier Saint **1952** A biography of the founder of the Jesuits from his years as a page in the Spanish court to his daring exploits on the battle field and, finally, his spiritual awakening at the University of Paris. Narrated by Father Alfred J. Barrett. **93m/B VHS.** Rafael Duran, Maria Rosa Jiminez; **D:** Jose Diaz Morales. IVY, KEP

Lucas ✶✶✶ **1986 (PG-13)** A high school brain falls in love with the new girl in town, and tries to win her by trying out for the football team. Genuine film about the perils of coming of age. Thoughtful, non-condescending, and humorous. **100m/C VHS, Beta, Closed Caption.** Corey Haim, Kerri Green, Charlie Sheen, Winona Ryder, Courtney Thorne-Smith, Thomas E. Hodges; **D:** David Seltzer; **W:** David Seltzer; **M:** Dave Grusin. FOX

The Lucifer Complex ✶ **1978** Nazi doctors are cloning exact duplicates of such world leaders as the Pope and the President of the United States on a remote South American island in the year 1996. **91m/C VHS, Beta.** Robert Vaughn, Merrie Lynn Ross, Keenan Wynn, Aldo Ray; **D:** David L. Hewitt, Kenneth Hartford. VCI

Lucky Cisco Kid ✶✶½ **1940** Romero takes over from Warner Baxter in the fourth entry in the series, with Martin as his loyal sidekick. This time a rustler and his gang are stealing cattle and using the Kid's name to place the blame. Fast-paced with Romero appropriately debonair. Andrews screen debut. **67m/B VHS.** Cesar Romero, Chris-Pin Martin, Mary Beth Hughes, Dana Andrews, Evelyn Venable, Joseph Sawyer, Francis Ford; **D:** H. Bruce Humberstone; **W:** Robert Ellis, Helen Logan. GPV

Lucky Devil ✶✶½ **1925** Lucky devil wins car and motors around the country to the tune of organ music. **63m/B VHS, Beta.** Richard Dix, Esther Ralston, Edna May Oliver, Tom Findley; **D:** Frank Tuttle. GPV, FCT

Lucky Jim ✶✶½ **1958** A junior lecturer in history at a small university tries to get himself in good graces with the head of his department, but is doomed from the start by doing the wrong things at the worst possible times. Minus the social satire of the Kingsley Amis novel on which it was based; what's left is a cheerful comedy. **91m/B VHS.** GB Ian Carmichael, Terry-Thomas, Hugh Griffith, Sharon Acker, Jean Anderson, Maureen Connell, Clive Morton, John Welsh, Reginald Beckwith, Kenneth Griffith, Jeremy Hawk, Harry Fowler; **D:** John Boulting; **W:** Jeffrey Dell, Patrick Campbell; **M:** John Addison. NO

Lucky Luciano ✶✶ A Proposito Luciano; RE: Lucky Luciano **1974 (R)** A violent depiction of the final years of Lucky Luciano, gangster kingpin. **108m/C VHS, Beta.** IT FR Edmond O'Brien, Rod Steiger, Vincent Gardenia, Gian Marie Volonte; **D:** Francesco Rosi; **C:** Pasquale De Santis. NLC

Lucky Luke ✶✶½ **1994 (PG)** Fastest gun in the west brings the law to Daisy Town, aided by his horse, Jolly Jumper—who can talk. Not exactly John Wayne material but amusing. **91m/C VHS.** Terence Hill, Nancy Morgan, Ron Carey; **D:** Terence Hill; **V:** Roger Miller. APX

Lucky Luke: The Ballad of the Daltons **1978** Easygoing cowboy hero Lucky Luke gets involved in a wild feud with the bumbling Dalton Brothers gang in this animated feature. **82m/C VHS, Beta, LV.** **D:** Rene Goscinny. DIS

Lucky Me ✶✶ **1954** A group of theatre entertainers are stranded in Miami and are forced to work in a hotel kitchen. They soon acquire the support of a wealthy oilman (Goodwin) who invests in their show, but not before his spoiled daughter tries to thwart all plans. ♫Lucky Me; Superstition Song; I Speak to the Stars; Take a

Memo to the Moon; Love You Dearly; Bluebells of Broadway; Parisian Pretties; Wanna Sing Like an Angel; High Hopes. 100m/C VHS, LV, Letterbox. Doris Day, Robert Cummings, Phil Silvers, Eddie Foy Jr., Nancy Walker, Martha Hyer, Bill Goodwin, Marcel Dalio, James Burke, Jack Shea, William "Billy" Bakewell, Charles Cane, Ray Teal, Tom Powers, Angie Dickinson, Dolores Dorn; **D:** Jack Donohue. WAR, CCB, MVD

Lucky Partners 🎬🎬 1940 When an artist and an errand girl share a winning lottery ticket, funny complications arise as they embark on a fantasy honeymoon. Although Rogers' innocence and Coleman's savoir faire provide an interesting contrast, the script isn't equal to the status of its stars. 101m/B VHS, Beta. Ronald Colman, Ginger Rogers, Jack Carson, Spring Byington, Harry Davenport; **D:** Lewis Milestone. TTC

Lucky Stiff 🎬🎬 1988 (PG) A fat, unpopular dweeb has the shock of his life when a radiant woman falls in love with him, the strangeness of which becomes evident when he meets her very weird family. 93m/C VHS, Beta, LV. Donna Dixon, Joe Alaskey, Jeff Kober, Elizabeth Arlen, Charles Frank, Barbara Howard; **D:** Anthony Perkins; **W:** Pat Proft. COL

Lucky Terror 🎬 1936 Routine Hoot cowboy drama. 60m/B VHS, Beta. Hoot Gibson, Lona Andre, Charles "Blackie" King; **D:** Alan James. NOS, GPV, VCN

Lucky Texan 🎬½ 1934 Wayne plays a tough easterner who goes West and finds himself involved with miners and claim jumpers. 61m/B VHS, Beta. John Wayne, George "Gabby" Hayes, Yakima Canutt; **D:** Robert North Bradbury. COL, REP, MRV

Lucy and Desi: Before the Laughter 🎬🎬½ 1991 (PG-13) The meeting and early married life of actress/comedian Lucille Ball and Cuban bandleader Desi Arnaz is depicted in this routine biopic. Film depicts Desi's womanizing, their struggles with fame, and their efforts to get their television show on the air. Fisher does well as television's favorite redhead but this made-for-television effort is melodramatic. Daughter Lucy Arnaz vehemently opposed this depiction of her parents life.**CW:** Language and sensuality. 95m/C VHS, LV, Closed Caption. Frances Fisher, Maurice Benard, John Wheeler, Robin Pearson Rose; **D:** Charles Jarrott; **W:** William Luce. REP, PMS

L'Udienza 🎬🎬½ 1971 A bizarre black comedy about a guy who does anything he can, at any criminal cost, to obtain an audience with the Pope. In Italian with subtitles. 111m/C VHS, Beta. IT Claudia Cardinale, Ugo Tognazzi; **D:** Marco Ferreri. FCT

Ludwig 🎬🎬 1972 (PG) Lavish-but-slow epic bio of Bavaria's mad monarch, Ludwig II (Berger), who built extravagant fantasy castles and sponsored composer Richard Wagner (Howard), whom the king became obsessed with. Italian with subtitles. 231m/C VHS, Letterbox. IT GE Helmut Berger, Trevor Howard, Romy Schneider, Silvana Mangano, Helmut Griem, Gert Frobe; **D:** Luchino Visconti; **W:** Luchino Visconti; **C:** Armando Nannuzzi. FCT, FXL

Luggage of the Gods 🎬🎬 1987 (G) A lost tribe of cave people are confronted with civilization when suitcases fall from an airplane. Low-budget comedy reminiscent of "The Gods Must Be Crazy." 78m/C VHS, Beta. Mark Stolzenberg, Gabriel Barre, Gwen Ellison; **D:** David Kendall.

Lullaby of Broadway 🎬🎬½ 1951 Many songs highlight this flimsy musical about a girl (Day) who ventures from England to the Big Apple in search of an acting career. She soon discovers that her mom has become a has-been actress now performing in a Greenwich Village dive. Day struggles to gain her own success while coping with her mother's downfall. 🎵Lullaby of Broadway; You're Getting to Be a Habit With Me; Just One of Those Things; Somebody Loves Me; I Love the Way You Say Goodnight; Fine and Dandy; Please Don't Talk About Me When I'm Gone; A Shanty in Old Shanty Town; We'd Like to Go On A Trip. 92m/C VHS. Doris Day, Gene Nelson, S.Z. Sakall, Billy DeWolfe, Gladys George, Florence Bates; **D:** David Butler. WAR, CCB, MVD

Lumiere 🎬🎬½ 1976 (R) An acclaimed drama about four actresses who, during the course of one night together, make pivotal decisions about their lives and relationships. Moreau's first directorial effort; dubbed. 101m/C VHS, Beta. FR Jeanne Moreau, Lucia Bose, Francine Racette, Caroline Cartier, Keith Carradine, Francois Simon, Francis Huster, Bruno Ganz, Rene Feret, Niels Arestrup, Jerome Lapperrousaz; **D:** Jeanne Moreau; **W:** Jeanne Moreau; **C:** Ricardo Aronvich; **M:** Astor Piazzolla.

Luna e L'Altra 🎬🎬 1996 Dizzy schoolteacher Luna (Forte) is the butt of practical jokes by her students and ignored by the other faculty. Dutiful and self-effacing, she's also the secret crush of school custodian Angelo (Nichetti). But Luna has a hidden side that comes to the surface thanks to magician Igor's magic latern and it turns out to be a sexy one. Italian with subtitles. 92m/C VHS. IT Iaia Forte, Maurizio Nichetti, Aurelio Fierro, Luigi Burruano; **D:** Maurizio Nichetti; **W:** Maurizio Nichetti; **C:** Luca Bigazzi; **M:** Carlo Siliotto. Nominations: Golden Globe Awards '97: Best Foreign Language Film. NYR

Luna Park 🎬🎬 1991 In contemporary Russia, Andrei (Goutine) is the leader of a gang of body-builder, right-wing skinheads who beat up Jews, foreigners, and anyone else they dislike. Then the anti-Semitic Andrei learns his father is Jewish and he frantically searches through Moscow to find him and discover his past. In Russian with subtitles. 105m/C VHS. RU Oleg Borisov, Andrei Goutine, Natalya Yegorova; **D:** Pavel Lounguine; **W:** Pavel Lounguine. NYF

Lunatic 🎬 1991 "Some minds should be wasted" according to the film promo and if you're in the mood for an amateur mind (and time) waster, this is for you. High schoolers in the woods encounter mayhem in the best horror tradition as the innocents are slaughtered by an escapee from the local lunatic asylum. 90m/C VHS. Rocky Tucker, Ondrea Tucker, Brian D'Lawrence, Keith Vallot, Bronwyn St. John, Cameron Derrick, Ernest Jackson, Rookie Macpherson, Susan Spain; **D:** James Tucker; **W:** James Tucker. CTC

The Lunatic 🎬🎬 1992 (R) A robust, over-sexed, and scheming German tourist travels to Jamaica where she meets the village idiot, a man who regularly holds conversations with the local plants. The two hook up with a butcher, and the three live happily in the hills, that is until the money is gone. The Jamaican scenery, a few bawdy laughs, and a great reggae soundtrack make this one worthwhile.**CW:** Sensuality. 93m/C VHS, Beta. GB Julie Wallace, Paul Campbell, Reggie Carter, Carl Bradshaw; **D:** Lol Creme; **M:** Wally Badarou.

Lunatics: A Love Story 🎬🎬🎬 1992 (PG-13) Hank (Raimi) is an ex-mental patient poet suffering from hallucinations and afraid to leave his Los Angeles apartment. For companionship he dials a party-line until, one day, he misdials and insteads gets the number of a local pay telephone, which is answered by a naive woman dumped by her boyfriend. When Nancy (Foreman) decides to visit Hank you learn she's as crazy as he is—so it only makes sense that they would fall in love. A well-acted fable of how love fragilely connects even the most unlikely of people. 87m/C VHS, LV. Theodore (Ted) Raimi, Deborah Foreman, Bruce Campbell, Brian McCree, Eddie Rosmaya, Michele Stacey; **D:** Josh Becker; **W:** Josh Becker; **M:** Joseph LoDuca. NO

Lunatics & Lovers 🎬½ 1976 (PG) Musician meets a bizarre nobleman who is in love with an imaginary woman. 92m/C VHS, Beta. IT Marcello Mastroianni, Lino Toffalo; **D:** Flavio Mogherini. FOX

Lunch Wagon 🎬🎬 Come 'n' Get It; Lunch Wagon Girls 1981 (R) Two co-eds are given a restaurant to manage during summer vacation and wind up involved in a hilarious diamond chase and sex romp. 88m/C VHS, Beta. Rick Podell, Candy Moore, Pamela Bryant, Rosanne Katon; **D:** Ernie Pintoff.

Lupo 🎬🎬 1970 (G) When threatened with the loss of his home and the separation of his family, an exuberant Greek man challenges the modern world. 99m/C VHS, Beta. Yuda Barkan, Gabi Armoni, Esther Greenberg; **D:** Menahem Golan. MGM

Lure of the Islands 🎬 1942 Federal agents track wanted criminals to an island retreat in this highly predictable low-budget thriller. 61m/B VHS, Beta. Margie Hart, Robert Lowery, Guinn "Big Boy" Williams, Warren Hymer, Gale Storm; **D:** Jean Yarbrough. NOS, SNC

Lure of the Sila 🎬🎬½ 1949 Italian melodrama about a young peasant girl infiltrating a landowner's home in order to avenge the death of her brother and mother. Dubbed and more interesting than it sounds. 72m/B VHS, Beta, 8mm. IT Silvana Mangano, Amedeo Nazzari, Vittorio Gassman; **D:** Duilio Coletti. VYY

Lurkers woof! 1988 (R) An unappealing metaphysical morass about a woman who has been haunted throughout her life by...something. 90m/C VHS. Christine Moore, Gary Warner, Marina Taylor, Carissa Channing, Tom Billett; **D:** Roberta Findlay; **W:** Ed Kelleher, Hariette Vidal; **C:** Roberta Findlay.

Lurking Fear 🎬🎬 1994 (R) The town of Lefferts Corner has suffered from generations of horror thanks to man-eating ghouls that dwell beneath the local graveyard and arise whenever a storm breaks out. The inhabitants prepare to fight back but their plan is hindered by the arrival of a group of criminals who are after a fortune supposedly hidden in one of the graves. Based on a story by H.P. Lovecraft.**CW:** Language and violence. 78m/C VHS, Beta, LV. Jon Finch, Blake Bailey, Ashley Lauren, Jeffrey Combs, Paul Mantee, Allison Mackie, Joe Leavengood, Vincent Schiavelli; **D:** C. Courtney Joyner; **W:** C. Courtney Joyner; **M:** Jim Manzie. PAR

Lush Life 🎬🎬🎬 1994 (R) New York jazz session musicians Al (Goldblum) and Buddy (Whitaker) roam the city's musical scene until dawn, on the prowl for food, women, and ever more music. When trumpeter Buddy is diagnosed with an inoperable brain tumor, saxophonist Al decides on a grand final gesture—a Park Avenue farewell bash, though no one is to know just how final the farewell is to be. Great jazz soundtrack, fine acting, and atmospheric use of the Big Apple. And it avoids overt tearjerking. Made for cable.**CW:** Strong language. 96m/C VHS, Closed Caption. Jeff Goldblum, Forest Whitaker, Kathy Baker, Lois Chiles, Don Cheadle; **D:** Michael Elias; **W:** Michael Elias. COL

Lust and Revenge 🎬🎬 1995 When wealthy George Oliphant (Haywood) needs a tax break, he commissions a statue (to be donated to the National Gallery) and gets daughter Georgina (Karvan) to choose the subject and artist. Flirty Georgina hires lesbian sculptress Lily (Eagger) and decides on the depiction of a male nude, for which Karl-Heinz Applebaum (Hope) is hired to pose. Applebaum's religious wife Cecilia (Dobrowolska) is not pleased, especially when hubby begins an affair. But she's also not above plotting a suitable revenge. Last role for Hargreaves (a cameo as a gallery habitue) while Hughes, who also worked for director Cox in "My First Wife," plays a male financial adviser. 95m/C VHS. AU Claudia Karvan, Chris Haywood, Nicholas Hope, Gosia Dobrowolska, Victoria Eagger, Norman Kaye; **Cameos:** Wendy Hughes, John Hargreaves; **D:** Paul Cox; **W:** Paul Cox, John Clarke; **C:** Nino Martinetti; **M:** Paul Grabowsky. Nominations: Australian Film Institute '96: Best Director (Cox). NYR

Lust for a Vampire 🎬🎬 To Love a Vampire 1971 (R) The sanguine tale of a deadly vampire who indiscriminately preys on pupils and teachers when she enrolls at a British finishing school. Moody and erotically charged, with an impressive ending. Quasi-sequel to "The Vampire Lovers." 95m/C VHS, Beta, LV. GB Ralph Bates, Barbara Jefford, Suzanna Leigh, Michael Johnson, Yutte Stensgaard, Pippa Steele, Helen Christie, David Healy, Mike Raven; **D:** Jimmy Sangster; **W:** Tudor Gates; **C:** David Muir. MLB

Lust for Freedom 🎬 **1987** An undercover cop decides to hit the road after she sees her partner gunned down. She winds up near the California-Mexico border, where she is wrongly imprisoned with a number of other young women in a white slavery business. This low-budget film includes lots of steamy women-behind-bars sex scenes. **92m/C VHS.** Melanie Coll, William J. Kulzer; **D:** Eric Louzil. *MOV*

Lust for Gold 🎬🎬 **1949** Ford battles against greedy former lover Lupino and her husband for control of the Lost Dutchman gold mine. **90m/B VHS, Beta.** Ida Lupino, Glenn Ford, Gig Young, William Prince, Edgar Buchanan, Will Geer, Paul Ford, Jay Silverheels; **D:** Sylvan Simon; **M:** George Duning. *GKK*

Lust for Life 🎬🎬🎬½ **1956** Absorbing, serious biography of Vincent Van Gogh, from his first paintings to his death. Remarkable for Douglas' furiously convincing portrayal. Featuring dozens of actual Van Gogh works from private collections. Based on an Irving Stone novel, produced by John Houseman. **122m/C VHS, Beta, LV, Letterbox.** Kirk Douglas, Anthony Quinn, James Donald, Pamela Brown, Everett Sloane, Henry Daniell, Niall MacGinnis, Noel Purcell, Lionel Jeffries, Jill Bennett; **D:** Vincente Minnelli; **M:** Miklos Rozsa. Academy Awards '56: Best Supporting Actor (Quinn); Golden Globe Awards '57: Best Actor—Drama (Douglas); New York Film Critics Awards '56: Best Actor (Douglas); Nominations: Academy Awards '56: Best Actor (Douglas), Best Adapted Screenplay, Best Art Direction/Set Decoration (Color). *MGM, BTV*

Lust in the Dust 🎬🎬 **1985 (R)** When part of a treasure map is found on the derriere of none other than Divine, the hunt is on for the other half. This comedy western travels to a sleepy town called Chile Verde (green chili for those who don't speak Spanish) and the utterly ridiculous turns comically corrupt. Deliciously distasteful fun. Features Divine singing a bawdy love song in his/her break from John Waters. **85m/C VHS, Beta, LV, Closed Caption.** Tab Hunter, Divine, Lainie Kazan, Geoffrey Lewis, Henry Silva, Cesar Romero, Gina Gallego, Courtney Gains, Woody Strode, Pedro Gonzalez-Gonzalez; **D:** Paul Bartel; **W:** Philip John Taylor; **M:** Peter Matz. *VTR, HHE*

The Lusty Men 🎬🎬🎬 **1952** Two rival rodeo champions, both in love with the same woman, work the rodeo circuit until a tragic accident occurs. Mitchum turns in a fine performance as the has-been rodeo star trying to make it big again. **113m/B VHS, Beta, LV.** Robert Mitchum, Susan Hayward, Arthur Kennedy, Arthur Hunnicutt; **D:** Nicholas Ray; **C:** Lee Garmes. *NO*

Luther 🎬🎬½ **1974 (G)** A well-acted characterization of Martin Luther's development from a young seminarian to his leadership of the Reformation Movement. **112m/C VHS.** Stacy Keach, Patrick Magee, Hugh Griffith, Robert Stephens, Alan Badel, Julian Clover, Judi Dench, Leonard Rossiter, Maurice Denham, Peter Cellier, Thomas Heathcote, Malcolm Stoddard, Bruce Carstairs; **D:** Guy Green; **W:** Edward Anhalt, John Osborne; **C:** Frederick A. (Freddie) Young; **M:** John Addison. *NO*

Luther the Geek woof! **1990** Little Luther's visit to the circus is dramatically changed when he sees the geek, a sideshow freak. Since then Luther has taken to biting off chicken's heads and drinking their blood in his small Illinois town; the town will never be the same. (And neither will you if you watch this stupid film.) **90m/C VHS.** Edward Terry, Joan Roth, J. Jerome Clarke, Tom Mills, Stacy Haiduk; **D:** Carlton J. Albright; **W:** Whitey Styles; **C:** David Knox. *DAP*

Luv 🎬½ **1967 (PG)** Although good cast tries hard, they can't do much with this comic farce. Three intellectuals, including one that's suicidal, discuss the trials and tribulations of their middle-class New York existence. **95m/C VHS, Beta, LV.** Jack Lemmon, Peter Falk, Elaine May; **D:** Clive Donner; **W:** Murray Schisgal; **C:** Ernest Laszlo. *GKK*

Luzia 🎬🎬½ **1988** Ohana stars as a tough and sexy Brazilian cowgirl who is caught in the middle of a class struggle where the personal is definitely political. Her horseriding skills and beauty give her options in both lifestyles. Will she choose to side with the squatters or the wealthy landowners? In Portuguese with English subtitles. **112m/C VHS.** *BR* Claudia Ohana, Thales Pan Chacon, Jose de Abreu, Luiza Falcao; **D:** Fabio Barreto. *FXL, FCT*

Lydia 🎬🎬🎬 **1941** Sentimental drama in which an elderly lady (Oberon) gets to relive her romantic past when she has a reunion with four of her lost loves. Well acted and directed, Oberon gives one of her best performances ever. Adapted from the highly regarded French film "Un Carnet de Bal." **98m/B VHS, Beta, LV.** Merle Oberon, Joseph Cotten, Alan Marshal, George Reeves; **D:** Julien Duvivier; **C:** Lee Garmes; **M:** Miklos Rozsa. Nominations: Academy Awards '41: Best Original Dramatic/Comedy Score.

Lying Lips 🎬½ **1939** All-black detective mystery about a young nightclub singer framed for murder. Her boyfriend then turns detective to clear her name. **60m/B VHS, Beta.** Edna Mae Harris, Carmen Newsome, Earl Jones, Amanda Randolph; **D:** Oscar Micheaux. *FCT, VCN, DVT*

M 🎬🎬🎬🎬 **1931** The great Lang dissection of criminal deviance, following the tortured last days of a child murderer, and the efforts of both the police and the underground to bring him to justice. Poetic, compassionate, and chilling. Inspired by real-life serial killer Peter Kurten, known as "Vampire of Dusseldorf," Lang also borrowed story elements from Jack the Ripper's killing spree. Lorre's screen debut. Lang's personal favorite among his own films. In German with English subtitles. Remade in 1951. **111m/B VHS.** *GE* Peter Lorre, Ellen Widmann, Inge Landgut, Gustav Grundgens, Otto Wernicke, Ernest Stahl-Nachbaur, Franz Stein, Theodore Loos, Fritz Gnass, Fritz Odemar, Paul Kemp, Theo Lingen, Georg John, Karl Platen, Rosa Valetti, Hertha von Walther, Rudolf Blumner; **D:** Fritz Lang; **W:** Fritz Lang, Thea von Harbou; **C:** Fritz Arno Wagner, Gustav Rathje; **M:** Edvard Grieg. *HMV, NOS, HHT*

M. Butterfly 🎬🎬 **1993 (R)** Disappointing adaptation of Hwang's award-winning play, which was based on a true story. Irons is Rene Gallimard, a minor French diplomat sent to China in 1964. Taken in by the exoticism of the mysterious east, he falls for a Chinese opera performer, Song Liling (Lone). Only she's no lady and the oblivious diplomat turns out to be a patsy as Song Liling uses him to gather information. The story only works if the passion, however deceptive, between Gallimard and Song Liling is believable, passion which is noticeably lacking between Irons and Lone. Irons comes across as too intelligent to be gullible and the usually excellent Lone does not make his role believable. **CW:** Brief bloody sequence and sexuality. **101m/C VHS, Beta, LV, Letterbox, Closed Caption.** Jeremy Irons, John Lone, Ian Richardson, Barbara Sukowa, Vernon Dobtcheff, Annabel Leventon, Shizuko Hoshi, Richard McMillan; **D:** David Cronenberg; **W:** David Henry Hwang; **M:** Howard Shore. *WAR*

Ma and Pa Kettle 🎬🎬½ *The Further Adventures of Ma and Pa Kettle* **1949** The hillbilly couple were supporting characters in "The Egg and I" but their popularity found them spun off into their own cornpone series. This first feature finds the couple and their 15 children about to be evicted only to have Pa win a tobacco slogan contest. The prize is a brand-new fully automated house whose futuristic contraptions get the better of Pa. **76m/B VHS, Closed Caption.** Marjorie Main, Percy Kilbride, Richard Long, Meg Randall, Esther Dale, Barry Kelley, Patricia Alphin; **D:** Charles Lamont; **W:** Al Lewis, Herbert Margolis, Louis Morheim. *USH*

Ma and Pa Kettle at Home 🎬🎬½ **1954** Elwin, one of the Kettle's 15 children, is a finalist in an essay contest that could win him a college scholarship. Then Pa Kettle hears the two judges plan to visit each of the finalists' homes so he tries to spruce-up the family's tumbled-down farm. **80m/B VHS, Closed Caption.** Marjorie Main, Percy Kilbride, Alan Mowbray, Ross Elliott, Brett Halsey, Mary Wickes, Irving Bacon, Emory Parnell; **D:** Charles Lamont; **W:** Kay Lenard. *USH*

Ma and Pa Kettle at the Fair 🎬🎬½ **1952** The Kettle's eldest daughter Rosie wants to go to college so Ma enters the county fair baking contest to win some money and Pa buys a decrepit old nag to enter in the fair's horse race. Somehow things just have a way of working out for the Kettles. **79m/B VHS, Closed Caption.** Marjorie Main, Percy Kilbride, Lori Nelson, James Best, Esther Dale, Russell Simpson, Emory Parnell; **D:** Charles T. Barton; **W:** John Grant, Richard Morris. *USH*

Ma and Pa Kettle at Waikiki 🎬🎬½ **1955** Ma (Main) and Pa (Kilbride), as well as oldest daughter Rosie (Nelson), head for Hawaii to help out cousin Rodney's (Smith) pineapple factory. Seems he's ill and about to go bankrupt and he thinks Pa is some kind of financial whiz who can bail him out. Pa accidentally does help the business and then gets kidnapped by some sleazy competitors. But it's Ma to the rescue (and the bad guys don't stand a chance). Kilbride retired after his seventh take as Pa in the comedy series. **79m/B VHS, Closed Caption.** Marjorie Main, Percy Kilbride, Lori Nelson, Loring Smith, Russell Johnson, Byron Palmer, Mabel Albertson, Hilo Hattie, Fay Roope, Oliver Blake, Lowell Gilmore, Teddy Hart; **D:** Lee Sholem; **W:** Jack Henley, Harry Clork, Elwood Ullman. *USH*

Ma and Pa Kettle Back On the Farm 🎬🎬½ **1951** First-time grandparents, the Kettles have to deal with their daughter-in-law's snobby Bostonian parents and their parenting ideas. The family's also moved back to their ramshackle farm where Pa thinks he's found uranium, leading to all sorts of problems. **81m/B VHS, Closed Caption.** Marjorie Main, Percy Kilbride, Richard Long, Meg Randall, Ray Collins, Barbara Brown, Emory Parnell; **D:** Edward Sedgwick; **W:** Jack Henley. *USH*

Ma and Pa Kettle Go to Town 🎬🎬½ **1950** Ma and Pa head off for New York City when Pa wins a jingle-writing contest, unknowingly leaving their brood in the care of on the lam mobster Mike, who asks the Kettles to deliver a package to his brother. This gets both the crooks and the cops trailing the hillbilly couple, whose backwoods ways are more than a match for any city slicker. **80m/B VHS, Closed Caption.** Marjorie Main, Percy Kilbride, Richard Long, Meg Randall, Charles McGraw, Ray Collins, Esther Dale, Ellen Corby, Barbara Brown; **D:** Charles Lamont; **W:** Martin Ragaway, Leonard Stern. *USH*

Ma and Pa Kettle on Vacation 🎬🎬½ *Ma and Pa Kettle Go to Paris* **1953** Ma and Pa visit Paris as guests of their son's wealthy in-laws and Pa unwittingly gets involved with spies and shady ladies. **79m/B VHS, Closed Caption.** Marjorie Main, Percy Kilbride, Ray Collins, Sig Rumann, Bodil Miller, Barbara Brown, Peter Brocco, Jay Novello; **D:** Charles Lamont; **W:** Jack Henley. *USH*

Ma Barker's Killer Brood 🎬🎬 **1960** Biography of the infamous American criminal and her four sons, edited together from a television serial. The shoot-em-up scenes and Tuttle's performance keep the pace from slackening. **82m/B VHS, Beta.** Lurene Tuttle, Tristram Coffin, Paul Dubov, Nelson Leigh, Myrna Dell, Vic Lundin, Donald Spruance; **D:** Bill Karn. *SNC, DVT, HEG*

Ma Saison Preferee 🎬🎬🎬 *My Favorite Season* **1993** Focuses on the intense relationship between a middleaged brother (Auteuil) and sister (Deneuve). When the elderly Berthe (Villalonga) collapses, she goes to stay with daughter Emilie and her family, which provides Emilie with an excuse to invite her estranged brother Antoine for Christmas. It's a disaster with numerous family fights, that leads Emilie to declare her marriage over and to an eventual reapproachmont with Antoine. Film is divided into four parts, to coincide with the four seasons, beginning with autumn and ending with summer. French with subtitles. Deneuve and Auteuil reteamed for Techine's "Les Voleurs." **124m/C VHS, Letterbox.** *FR* Daniel Auteuil, Catherine Deneuve, Marthe Villalonga, Jean-Pierre Bouvier, Chiara Mastroianni, Anthony Prada, Carmen Chaplin; **D:**

Andre Techine; W: Andre Techine; C: Thierry Arbogast; M: Philippe Sarde. FXL

Ma Vie en Rose 🎬🎬🎬 *My Life In Pink*
1997 (R) Berliner's debut portrays seven-year-old misfit Ludovic (du Fresne), who is convinced he's really a girl and likes to dress in girls' clothes. His close-knit family merely regards this as a childhood eccentricity Ludovic will grow out of. But when the child decides he's going to marry Jerome (Rivere), the boy next door, and stages a mock wedding ceremony, things get a bit dicey. Jerome's father is the straitlaced Albert (Hanssens), who happens to be the boss of Ludovic's father, Pierre (Ecoffey), and he's not nearly so understanding (neither are the other neighbors in the conservative Parisian suburb). Poignant and funny look at a child's search for identity. Convincing turn by pre-pubescent performer du Fresne.*CW:* Brief strong language. **90m/C VHS.** BE FR GB Georges DuFresne, Jean-Philippe Ecoffey, Michele Laroque, Daniel Hanssens, Julien Riviere, Helene Vincent, Helene Vincent; *D:* Alain Berliner; *W:* Alain Berliner, Chris Vander Stappen; *C:* Yves Cape; *M:* Dominique Dalcan. Golden Globe Awards '98: Best Foreign Film; Nominations: British Academy Awards '97: Best Foreign Film. COL

Mabel & Fatty 🎬🎬
1916 Three silent shorts featuring the two stars, made with Mack Sennett: "He Did and He Didn't," "Mabel and Fatty Viewing The World's Fair at San Francisco" (with scenes of the actual 1914 World's Fair) and "Mabel's Blunder." **61m/B VHS, Beta, 8mm.** Mabel Normand, Fatty Arbuckle, Al "Fuzzy" St. John. VYY

Maborosi 🎬🎬🎬 *Mirage; Maboroshi no Hikari*
1995 Yumiko (Esumi) has a contented life in Osaka with her husband Ikuo (Asano) and their newborn son. Yet, inexplicably, her husband commits suicide one night. Later, a neighbor of Yumiko's helps her with an arranged marriage to prosperous widower Tamio (Naitoh), who lives in a remote fishing village, and once again things seem to be happy. But her first husband's death still haunts her and Yumiko seeks an explanation that will allow her to have some peace in her life. Adapted from a story by Teru Miyamoto. Japanese with subtitles. **110m/C VHS, Letterbox.** JP Makiko Esumi, Takashi Naitoh, Tadanobu Asano, Gohki Kashiyama; *D:* Hirokazu Kore-eda; *W:* Yoshihisa Ogita; *C:* Masao Nakabori; *M:* Chen Ming-Chang. NYF

Mac 🎬🎬🎬
1993 (R) It's a family affair. Immigrant carpenter's funeral is the starting point for the story of his three sons, construction workers who live in Queens, New York in the 1950s. The passionate bros battle, bitch, and build, with Turturro as the eldest summing up the prevailing philosophy: "It's the doing, that's the thing." Turturro's directorial debut is a labor of love and a tribute to his own dad. Filmed on location in New York City. Fine performances from newcomers Badalucco and Capotorto are complemented by smaller roles from Amos, Barkin, and Turturro's real-life wife Borowitz and brother Nick.*CW:* Strong language and some sexuality. **118m/C VHS, LV, Letterbox, Closed Caption.** John Turturro, Carl Capotorto, Michael Badalucco, Katherine Borowitz, John Amos, Olek Krupa, Ellen Barkin, Joe Paparone, Nicholas Turturro, Dennis Farina, Steven Randazzo; *D:* John Turturro; *W:* Brandon Cole, John Turturro; *C:* Ron Fortunato; *M:* Richard Termini, Vin Tese. Nominations: Independent Spirit Awards '94: Best Director (Turturro), Best First Feature. COL, FCT

Mac and Me 🎬
1988 (PG) Lost E.T.-like alien stranded on Earth befriends a wheelchair-bound boy. Aimed at young kids, it's full of continual product plugs, most notably for McDonald's. Make the kids laugh and stick to the real thing. **94m/C VHS, Beta, LV, Closed Caption.** Christine Ebersole, Jonathan Ward, Katrina Caspary, Lauren Stanley, Jade Calegory; *D:* Stewart Raffill; *W:* Stewart Raffill; *M:* Alan Silvestri. Golden Raspberry Awards '88: Worst Director (Raffill). ORI

Macabre 🎬🎬
1977 A beautiful woman, lustful and precocious, kills her husband and his twin brother. **89m/C VHS, Beta.** Larry Ward, Teresa Gimpera, Giacomo "Jack" Rossi-Stuart. NO

Macao 🎬🎬🎬
1952 On the lam for a crime he didn't commit, an adventurer sails to the exotic Far East, meets a buxom cafe singer, and helps Interpol catch a notorious crime boss. A strong film noir entry. Russell sneers, Mitchum wise cracks. Director von Sternberg's last film for RKO. **81m/B VHS, Beta, LV.** Robert Mitchum, Jane Russell, William Bendix, Gloria Grahame; *D:* Josef von Sternberg.

Macaroni 🎬½ *Maccheroni*
1985 (PG) An uptight American businessman returns to Naples 40 years after being stationed there in WWII. Comedic situations abound when he is reunited with his Italian war buddy, brother of his lover. Pleasant acting can't save irritating script. **104m/C VHS, Beta, LV, Closed Caption.** IT Jack Lemmon, Marcello Mastroianni, Daria Nicolodi, Isa Danieli; *D:* Ettore Scola; *W:* Ettore Scola. PAR

MacArthur 🎬🎬
1977 (PG) General Douglas MacArthur's life from Corregidor in 1942 to his dismissal a decade later in the midst of the Korean conflict. Episodic saga with forceful Peck but weak supporting characters. Fourteen minutes were cut from the original version; intended to be Peck's "Patton," it falls short of the mark. **130m/C VHS, Beta, LV.** Gregory Peck, Ivan Bonar, Ward Costello, Nicolas Coster, Dan O'Herlihy; *D:* Joseph Sargent; *W:* Matthew Robbins, Hal Barwood; *M:* Jerry Goldsmith. USH, TLF

MacArthur's Children 🎬🎬🎬
1985 A poignant evocation of life in a Japanese fishing village as it faces the end of WWII and American occupation. Not as good as some of the other Japanese films, but it is an interesting look at the changes in culture caused by their defeat in the war. In Japanese with English subtitles. **115m/C VHS, Beta, LV.** JP Masako Natsume, Shima Iwashita, Hiromi Go, Takaya Yamamauchi, Shiori Sakura, Ken Watanabe, Juzo Itami, Yoshiyuka Omori; *D:* Masahiro Shinoda; *W:* Takeshi Tamura. FCT, TPV

Macbeth 🎬🎬🎬½
1948 Shakespeare's classic tragedy is performed with a celebrated lead performance by Welles, who plays the tragic king as a demonic leader of a barbaric society. A low budget adaptation with cheap sets, a three-week shooting schedule, lots of mood, and an attempt at Scottish accents. After making this film, Welles took a 10-year break from Hollywood. **111m/B VHS, LV.** Orson Welles, Jeanette Nolan, Dan O'Herlihy, Roddy McDowall, Robert Coote; *D:* Orson Welles. REP, TVC

Macbeth 🎬🎬🎬
1971 (R) Polanski's notorious adaptation of the Shakespearean classic, marked by realistic design, unflinching violence, and fatalistic atmosphere. Contains stunning fight scenes and fine acting. Polanski's first film following the grisly murder of his pregnant wife, actress Sharon Tate, was torn apart by critics. It is in fact a worthy continuation of his work in the horror genre. Very well made. First film made by Playboy Enterprises. Originally rated X. **139m/C VHS, Beta, LV.** Jon Finch, Nicholas Selby, Martin Shaw, Francesca Annis, Terence Baylor; *D:* Roman Polanski; *W:* Roman Polanski, Kenneth Tynan. COL, HMV

Macbeth 🎬🎬🎬
1976 An extraordinary version of Shakespeare's "Macbeth" in which all the fire, ambition and doom of his text come brilliantly to life. **137m/C VHS.** Eric Porter, Janet Suzman. TLF

Macbeth 🎬🎬🎬
1990 Another production of the classic tragedy by Shakespeare. Produced as part of HBO's Thames Collection. **110m/C VHS, Beta.** Michael Jayston, Leigh Hunt. HBO

The Machine 🎬🎬
1996 Psychiatrist and inventor Marc Lacroix (Depardieu) is obsessed with the brain. He develops a brain transfer machine and decides to test it on himself (naturally) by fusing his psyche with that of his patient, cold-blooded killer Michael Zyto (does this sound like a good idea to you?). Naturally, the experiment causes terrifying consequences for Lacroix and his family. **96m/C VHS.** Gerard Depardieu, Nathalie Baye, Didier Boundon, Natalia Woerner, Erwan Baynaud; *D:* Francois Dupeyron; *W:* Francois Dupeyron; *C:* Dietrich Lohmann; *M:* Michel Portal. PGV

Machine Gun Blues 🎬🎬 *Black Rose of Harlem*
1995 (R) 1930s jazz singer Georgia (Williams) sings at a black-owned club that mobster Constanza (Viterelli) wants to take over. Right-hand man Johnny Verona (Cassavettes) is sent to help things along and makes the mistake of falling for the chanteuse amidst a scene of moonshine, gunrunning and racketeering.*CW:* Violence, sexuality and language. **80m/C VHS.** Cynda Williams, Nick Cassavetes, Joe Viterelli, Maria Ford, Lawrence Monoson, Garrett Morris, Richard Brooks; *D:* Fred Gallo; *W:* Charles Philip Moore; *C:* John Aronson; *M:* David Wurst, Eric Wurst. NHO

Machine Gun Kelly 🎬🎬½
1958 Corman found Euro-appeal with this '30s style gangster bio. Bronson, who was just gaining a reputation as an action lead, stars as criminal Kelly, who's convinced by his moll to give up bank robbery for kidnapping. Amsterdam, the wisecracking writer from "The Dick Van Dyke Show," is the fink who turns him in. **80m/B VHS.** Charles Bronson, Susan Cabot, Morey Amsterdam, Barboura Morris, Frank De Kova, Jack Lambert, Wally Campo; *D:* Roger Corman; *W:* Mike Werb; *C:* Floyd Crosby. COL, FCT

Machine to Kill Bad People 🎬🎬 *La Macchina Ammazzacattivi*
1948 In a small Italian village, a photographer receives a magical camera that has the power to terrify and kill anyone it photographs. The photographer decides to get rid of all the village's evil people but soon learns the difficulty of distinguishing between the grey areas of good and bad. Italian with subtitles. **80m/B VHS.** IT Gennaro Pisano, Giovanni Amato, Marilyn Buferd; *D:* Roberto Rossellini; *W:* Roberto Rossellini. FCT

Macho Callahan 🎬🎬
1970 (R) A Civil War convict escapes from a frontier jail bent on tracking down the man who imprisoned him. (The escaped prisoner bit is a recurring theme in Janssen's oeuvre.) Confused script even has a one-armed Carradine! **99m/C VHS, Beta.** David Janssen, Jean Seberg, David Carradine, Lee J. Cobb; *D:* Bernard L. Kowalski. COL, NLC

Machoman 🎬
197? The matchless, peerless, Machoman knows all the best killing methods including: Lizard Fists, Crane Kung Fu, and the Drunken Fist. **94m/C VHS, Beta.** Araujo, Enyaw Liew, Jerry Rages. NO

Maciste in Hell 🎬½ *Witch's Curse*
1960 Inexplicably living in 17th century Scotland, Italian hero Maciste pursues a witch into the depths of Hell. She's placed a curse on the world and he wants her to remove it. **78m/C VHS.** IT Kirk Morris, Helene Chanel, Vira Silenti, Andrea Bosic, Angelo Zanolli, John Karlsen; *D:* Riccardo (Robert Hampton) Freda. UNI, SNC

The Mack 🎬½
1973 (R) The Mack is a pimp who comes out of retirement to reclaim a piece of the action in Oakland, California. Violent blaxploitation flick was boxoffice dynamite at time of release. Early Pryor appearance. **110m/C VHS, Beta.** Max Julien, Richard Pryor, Don Gordon, Roger E. Mosley, Carol Speed; *D:* Michael Campus. NLC

Mack & Carole
1928 Lombard began her screen career, in earnest, as a Mack Sennett comedienne. These three shorts represent her earliest screen work. **60m/B VHS, Beta.** Carole Lombard. GVV

Mack Sennett Comedies: Vol. 1
1921 Four Sennett films are included: "The Eyes Have It," "The Cannon Ball," "The Desperate Scoundrel," and "Pride of Pikeville." Ben Turpin and the Keystone Cops at their manic best. **85m/B VHS.** Ben Turpin, Chester Conklin, Ford Sterling, Minta Durfee; *D:* Mack Sennett. REP

Mack Sennett Comedies: Vol. 2
1916 Four more Sennett shorts are featured: "Mabel and Fatty Adrift," "Mabel, Fatty, and the Law," "Fatty's Tin-Type Tangle," and "Our Congressman." The last film features Will Rogers in a lampoon of Capitol Hill. **84m/B VHS.** Fatty Arbuckle, Mabel Normand, Will Rogers, Madge Hunt; *D:* Mack Sennett. REP

Mack the Knife woof! *The Threepenny Opera* 1989 (PG-13) Terrible adaptation of Brecht and Weill's "Threepenny Opera," detailing the adventures of a master thief in love with an innocent girl. Too much music, too much dancing, too much emoting. 121m/C VHS, Beta, LV. Raul Julia, Roger Daltrey, Richard Harris, Julie Walters, Clive Revill, Erin Donovan, Rachel Robertson, Julia Migenes-Johnson; **D:** Menahem Golan. COL

MacKenna's Gold 🐾🐾½ 1969 (PG) Grim desperados trek through Apache territory to uncover legendary cache of gold in this somewhat inflated epic. Subdued stars Peck and Shariff vie for attention here with such overactors as Cobb, Meredith, and Wallach. Meanwhile, Newmar (Catwoman of TV's Batman) swims nude. A must for all earthquake buffs. 128m/C VHS, Beta, LV. Gregory Peck, Omar Sharif, Telly Savalas, Julie Newmar, Edward G. Robinson, Keenan Wynn, Ted Cassidy, Eduardo Ciannelli, Eli Wallach, Raymond Massey, Lee J. Cobb, Burgess Meredith, Anthony Quayle, John David Garfield; **D:** J. Lee Thompson; **M:** Quincy Jones. GKK

Mackintosh Man 🐾🐾½ 1973 (PG) An intelligence agent must undo a communist who has infiltrated the free world's network in this solid but somewhat subdued thriller. Good cast keeps narrative rolling, but don't look here for nudity-profanity-violence fix. 100m/C VHS, Beta. Paul Newman, Dominique Sanda, James Mason, Ian Bannen, Nigel Patrick, Harry Andrews, Leo Genn, Peter Vaughan, Michael Hordern; **D:** John Huston; **W:** Walter Hill; **M:** Maurice Jarre. WAR

Macon County Line 🐾🐾½ 1974 (R) A series of deadly mistakes and misfortunes lead to a sudden turn-around in the lives of three young people when they enter a small Georgia town and find themselves accused of brutally slaying the sheriff's wife. Sequelled by "Return to Macon County" in 1975, starring Don Johnson and Nick Nolte. 89m/C VHS, Beta. Alan Vint, Jesse Vint, Cheryl Waters, Geoffrey Lewis, Joan Blackman, Max Baer Jr.; **D:** Richard Compton.

Macumba Love 🐾 1960 An author journeys to Brazil to prove a connection between mysterious murders and voodoo. A tedious suspense exploitation travelogue with generous servings of cheesecake and calypso music. 86m/C VHS. Walter Reed, Ziva Rodann, William Wellman Jr., June Wilkinson, Ruth de Souza; **D:** Douglas Fowley. NO

Mad About Money 🐾🐾 *He Loved an Actress; Stardust* 1937 Comedy about a bespectacled mild-mannered fellow who runs up against a Mexican spitfire. ♫Oh So Beautiful; Perpetual Motion; Little Lost Tune; Dustin' The Stars. 80m/B VHS, Beta. GB Lupe Velez, Wallace Ford, Ben Lyon, Harry Langdon, Jean Colin; **D:** Melville Brown. NOS, DVT

Mad About Music 🐾🐾🐾 1938 On the advice of her publicist, film star Gwen Taylor (Patrick) sends her teenaged daughter Gloria (Durbin) off to a Swiss boarding school and keeps her identity a secret. So Gloria invents an exciting world-traveler father that envious schoolmate Felice (Parrish) insists upon meeting. Gloria manages to persuade a complete stranger, composer Richard Todd (Marshall), into playing the role (he's charmed by her singing). Naturally, there's lots of confusion, especially when mother and "father" finally meet. ♫I Love to Whistle; Chapel Bells; Serenade to the Stars; There Isn't a Day Goes By. 92m/B VHS, Closed Caption. Deanna Durbin, Herbert Marshall, Gail Patrick, Arthur Treacher, Helen Parrish, William Frawley, Marcia Mae Jones, Jackie Moran; **D:** Norman Taurog; **W:** Bruce Manning, Felix Jackson; **C:** Joseph Valentine. Nominations: Academy Awards '38: Best Cinematography, Best Story, Best Score.USH

Mad About You woof! 1990 (PG) Millionaire helps his daughter measure prospective suitors. Adam West is not the fourth man in the Montgomery Clift-James Dean-Marlon Brando chain of American acting greats. 92m/C VHS, Beta, LV. Claudia Christian, Joseph Gian, Adam West, Shari Shattuck; **D:** Lorenzo Doumani.

Mad at the Moon 🐾🐾 1992 (R) Western thriller in which a young bride (Masterson) discovers that the man she married is less than human with the rising of the full moon. The only one who can protect her is her husband's half-brother played by Bochner. Masterson gives a great performance as a woman torn apart by a terrifying family secret out on the American plains.*CW:* Sexuality. 98m/C VHS, LV, Closed Caption. Mary Stuart Masterson, Hart Bochner, Fionnula Flanagan, Cec Verrell, Stephen Blake; **D:** Martin Donovan; **W:** Martin Donovan, Richard Pelusi. REP

The Mad Bomber woof! *Police Connection; Detective Geronimo* 1972 Grim lawman Edwards tracks deranged bomber Connors, who is determined to blow up anyone who ever offended him. A must for all connoisseurs of acting that is simultaneously overblown and flat. 80m/C VHS, Beta. Vince Edwards, Chuck Connors, Neville Brand; **D:** Bert I. Gordon. MRV

Mad Bull 🐾 1977 Sensitive wrestler finds meaning in life when he falls in love. If you ever cared about Karras, then you probably already saw this. If you never cared about Karras, then you probably never heard of this. If you ever cared about Anspach, rent "Five Easy Pieces" instead. 96m/C VHS, Beta. Alex Karras, Susan Anspach, Nicholas Colasanto, Tracey Walter; **D:** Walter Doniger. NO

The Mad Butcher 🐾 1972 Typically unhinged mental patient seeks teenage flesh for his various instruments of torture and death. Buono has never been more imposing. 90m/C VHS, Beta. IT Victor Buono, Karin Field, Brad Harris; **D:** John Zuru. MRV

Mad City 🐾🐾½ 1997 (PG-13) Out-of-work security guard Sam Baily (Travolta) goes postal, taking hostages in a museum while has-been journalist Max Brackett (Hoffman) manages to exploit Baily and hype the situation into a massive broadcast news event. The media circus that ensues provides social commentary on the questionable state of journalism. Drawing from famously explored material in numerous older films ("Network" and "All the President's Men") the subject is also enjoying a revival in current films ("Primary Colors" and "Wag the Dog"). Relationship between Max and Sam carries most interest in Costa-Gravas' intense drama, while uneven tone and script inadequacies hold back satisfying story development. Talented supporting cast (Alda, Danner, Kirshner, Prosky) have little to do.*CW:* Depiction of a hostage situation, including violence and brief language. 114m/C VHS, Closed Caption. John Travolta, Dustin Hoffman, Mia Kirshner, Alan Alda, Blythe Danner, Robert Prosky, William Atherton, Ted Levine; **D:** Constantin Costa-Gavras; **W:** Tom Matthews; **C:** Patrick Blossier; **M:** Thomas Newman. WAR

Mad Death 🐾🐾 1985 The British Isles take extreme steps to quarantine themselves against rabies from the European continent. This condensed TV miniseries preys on fears of the worst, as an outbreak of the virus spreads from dogs and other pets to humans, and special commandos are mobilized. 120m/C VHS. GB FCT, VCO

Mad Doctor of Blood Island woof! *Tomb of the Living Dead; Blood Doctor* 1969 Dull band of travelers arrive on mysterious tropical island and encounter bloodthirsty creature. Warning: This film is not recognized for outstanding achievements in acting, dialogue, or cinematography. 110m/C VHS, Beta. PH John Ashley, Ronald Remy, Alicia Alonzo, Alfonso Carvajal; **D:** Gerardo (Gerry) De Leon, Eddie Romero; **C:** Justo Paulino. NO

Mad Dog woof! 1984 An escaped convict seeks revenge on the cop responsible for his imprisonment. 90m/C VHS, Beta. Helmut Berger, Marisa Mell; **D:** Sergio Grieco. VDC

Mad Dog and Glory 🐾🐾🐾 1993 (R) Cast against type, Murray and De Niro play each other's straight man in this dark romantic comedy. Meek "Mad Dog" (De Niro) is an off-duty police photographer who happens upon a convenience store robbery and manages to save the life of Frank (Murray), obnoxious gangster by day, obnoxious stand-up comic by night. To settle up, Frank offers him Glory (Thurman), for a week. Eventually, Frank wants Glory back, forcing wimpy Mad Dog to either confront or surrender. Directed by McNaughton, who established himself with "Henry: Portrait of a Serial Killer." Uneven and not of the knee-slapper ilk, but the performances are tight, including "NYPD Blue" Caruso as a cop buddy of De Niro's.*CW:* Language, violence and drug content, and sexuality. 97m/C VHS, LV, Letterbox, Closed Caption. Robert De Niro, Uma Thurman, Bill Murray, David Caruso, Mike Starr, Tom Towles, Kathy Baker, Derek Anunciation, J.J. Johnston, Richard Belzer; **D:** John McNaughton; **W:** Richard Price; **M:** Elmer Bernstein. USH, FCT

Mad Dog Morgan 🐾🐾½ *Mad Dog* 1976 (R) Hopper delivers an engaging outlaw roaming outlands of 19th-century Australia. Quirky and violent G'day man. Based on a true story. 93m/C VHS, Beta. AU Dennis Hopper, David Gulpilil; **D:** Philippe Mora. SIM

The Mad Executioners 🐾🐾 *Der Henker Von London* 1965 Scotland Yard inspector searches for a sex maniac who decapitates women. In the meantime, a group of vigilantes capture criminals and sentence them without a trial. Confusing film with a predictable ending. Based on the book "White Carpet" by Bryan Edgar Wallace. 92m/B VHS. GE Hansjorg Felmy, Maria Perschy, Dieter Borsche, Rudolph Forster, Chris Howland, Wolfgang Preiss; **D:** Edwin Zbonek. SNC

The Mad Ghoul 🐾🐾½ 1943 Mad scientist (is there any other kind?) Dr. Morris (Zucco) is researching an ancient Egyptian gas that causes paralysis, turning victims into obedient zombies. Morris exposes his innocent assistant Ted (Bruce) to the gas, making Ted dependent on the antidote serum made from newly dead hearts. Poor Ted's fiance Isabel (Ankers) just can't understand what's the matter. 66m/B VHS, Closed Caption. George Zucco, David Bruce, Evelyn Ankers, Turhan Bey, Robert Armstrong, Milburn Stone, Charles McGraw, Rose Hobart; **D:** James Hogan; **W:** Brenda Weisberg, Paul Gangelin. USH

Mad Love 🐾🐾🐾 *The Hands of Orlac* 1935 A brilliant surgeon (Lorre) falls madly in love with an actress, but she rebuffs him. When her pianist husband's hands are cut off in a train accident, Lorre agrees to attach new hands, using those of a recently executed murderer. Lorre then kills the man's stepfather, and to drive him crazy uses psychological terror to make the pianist think he killed him. There's also an appearance by the supposedly executed murderer who shows up to reclaim his hands. A real chiller about obsessive love and psychological fear. The only downfall to this one is the unnecessary comic relief by Healy. Lorre's first American film. 70m/B VHS. Peter Lorre, Colin Clive, Frances Drake, Ted Healy, Edward Brophy, Sara Haden, Henry Kolker; **D:** Karl Freund; **W:** P.J. Wolfson, John L. Balderston, Guy Endore; **C:** Gregg Toland, Chester Lyons. MGM

Mad Love 🐾½ 1995 (PG-13) Teen love has rarely been so insipid. Impulsive, fragile, and annoyingly melodramatic Casey (Barrymore) bewitches responsible, straightlaced Matt (O'Donnell) with her kewpie-doll charm and penchant for mischief. When Casey's bipolar ways land her in a mental hospital, Matt breaks her out and the two unconvincing duo hit the road, where their supposedly free-spirited, passion-filled escapades grow increasingly inconsistent and silly, eventually halted by Casey's clinical crash. Slightly redeemed by a cool soundtrack and decent acting, but otherwise dull and insignificant, with an ending that may induce involuntary eyerolling. You've been warned.*CW:* Brief strong language; issues of an emotionally disturbed teen, including risk-taking situations and sexuality. 95m/C VHS, LV, Closed Caption. Chris O'Donnell, Drew Barrymore, Joan Allen,

Kevin Dunn, Jude Ciccolella, Amy Sakasitz, T.J. Lowther; **D:** Antonia Bird; **W:** Paula Milne; **C:** Fred Tammes. TOU

Mad Max 🐾🐾🐾½ 1980 (R) Set on the stark highways of the post-nuclear future, an ex-cop seeks personal revenge against a rovin' band of vicious outlaw bikers who killed his wife and child. Futuristic scenery and excellent stunt work make for an exceptionally entertaining action-packed adventure. Followed by "The Road Warrior" (also known as "Mad Max 2") in 1981 and "Mad Max Beyond Thunderdome" in 1985. **93m/C VHS, Beta, LV.** Mel Gibson, Joanne Samuel, Hugh Keays-Byrne, Steve Bisley, Tim Burns, Roger Ward; **D:** George Miller; **W:** George Miller; **C:** David Eggby; **M:** Brian May. ART, VES

Mad Max: Beyond Thunderdome 🐾🐾½ 1985 (PG-13) Max drifts into evil town ruled by Turner and becomes gladiator, then gets dumped in desert and is rescued by band of feral orphans. Third in a bleak, extremely violent, often exhilirating series. **107m/C VHS, Beta, LV, Letterbox, Closed Caption, DVD.** AU Mel Gibson, Tina Turner, Helen Buday, Frank Thring Jr., Bruce Spence, Robert Grubb, Angelo Rossitto, Angry Anderson, George Spartels, Rod Zuanic; **D:** George Miller, George Ogilvie; **W:** George Miller, Terry Hayes; **M:** Maurice Jarre. WAR

Mad Miss Manton 🐾🐾 1938 A socialite turns detective to solve murder. Pleasant comedy-mystery provides occasional laughs and suspense. **80m/B VHS, Beta, LV.** Barbara Stanwyck, Henry Fonda, Hattie McDaniel, Sam Levene, Miles Mander, Charles Lane; **D:** Leigh Jason. TTC

Mad Mission 3 🐾½ 1984 Chinese man vacationing in Paris becomes involved in plot to recover precious jewels stolen from England's royal crown. Has there already been "Mad Mission" and "Mad Mission 2"? **81m/C VHS, Beta.** Richard Kiel, Sam Kui, Karl Muka, Sylvia Chang, Tsuneharu Sugiyama. NO

The Mad Monster 🐾½ 1942 This "Wolf Man"-inspired cheapie looks like a misty relic today. A mad scientist furthers the war effort by injecting wolf's blood into a handyman, who becomes hairy and anti-social. **77m/B VHS.** Johnny Downs, George Zucco, Anne Nagel, Sarah Padden, Glenn Strange, Gordon DeMain, Mae Busch; **D:** Sam Newfield. NOS, LOO, VCN

Mad Monster Party 🐾🐾½ 1968 Frankenstein is getting older and wants to retire from the responsibilities of being senior monster, so he calls a convention of creepy creatures to decide who should take his place—The Wolfman, Dracula, the Mummy, the Creature, It, the Invisible Man, or Dr. Jekyll and Mr. Hyde. Animated feature using the process of "Animagic." **94m/C VHS, Beta. D:** Jules Bass; **V:** Boris Karloff, Ethel Ennis, Phyllis Diller. COL

Mad Wax: The Surf Movie 🐾 1990 A flimsy plot about a window-cleaner who discovers a magical surfing wax serves as a framework for lots and lots of scenes of surfin' dudes. **45m/C VHS, Beta.** Richard Cram, Marvin Foster, Aaron Napolean, Tom Carroll, Bryce Andrews, Ross Clarke-Jones; **D:** Michael Hohensee. FCT

The Mad Whirl 🐾½ 1925 The Roarin' '20s are a mad mad whirl in this silent silent period piece. **80m/B VHS, Beta.** Myrtle Stedman, Barbara Bedford, Alec B. Francis, George Fawcett, Joseph Singleton. GPV, FCT

Mad Youth woof! 1940 A teenage girl falls in love with a man whom her slutty, alcoholic mother had been chasing. Bottom of the barrel production provides many unintentional laughs. Extraneous South American dance sequences included as character development. **61m/B VHS, Beta.** Mary Ainslee, Betty Atkinson, Willy Castello, Betty Compson, Tommy Wonder; **D:** Melville Shyer; **W:** Willis Kent. SNC

Madagascar Skin 🐾🐾 1995 (R) Harry (Hannah) is a young gay man who's disfigured by a large port-wine birthmark on one side of his face (in the shape of Madagascar). Suicidally depressed he drives to a deserted beach on the Welsh coast but before making any final decisions, he picks up an overturned bucket lying on the sand. To his shock, it's covering the head of the very much alive middle-aged Flint (Hill), who's been buried up to his neck in sand and left to drown by some fellow crooks. Flint knows of a deserted beach shack, the oddly matched duo move in, and Harry falls in love. Deliberately dreamlike in some respects, the leads provide a bittersweet, adult romance. **95m/C VHS.** GB John Hannah, Bernard Hill; **D:** Chris Newby; **W:** Chris Newby; **C:** Oliver Curtis. NYR

Madam Satan 🐾🐾½ 1930 Extremely bizarre DeMille film highlighted by lavish musical numbers and outrageous costumes. Wealthy socialite realizes she's losing her husband to a young showgirl, so she disguises herself as a sultry French tramp and entices her husband at a masquerade party aboard a zeppelin—surely one of the wildest party scenes ever captured on film. Chorus girls perform several exotic dance numbers inside the airship that are nothing short of fantastic. A storm breaks out and the floating dirigible is struck by lightning—leading viewers to wonder if the mad party-goers will make it to safety or crash and burn like this pic did at the boxoffice. **115m/B VHS, Closed Caption.** Kay Johnson, Reginald Denny, Lillian Roth, Roland Young, Boyd Irwin, Elsa Peterson; **D:** Cecil B. DeMille. MGM

Madame Bovary 🐾🐾🐾 1934 A young adultress with delusions of romantic love finds only despair in this offbeat adaptation of Flaubert's masterpiece. In French with English subtitles. **102m/B VHS, Beta.** FR Pierre Renoir, Valentine Tessier, Max Dearly; **D:** Jean Renoir. HTV

Madame Bovary 🐾🐾🐾 1949 Young adultress with delusions of romantic love finds only despair, even in this Hollywood version of Flaubert's classic. Mason/Flaubert is put on trial for indecency following publication of the novel, with the story told from the witness stand. While this device occasionally slows the narrative, astute direction helps the plot along. Minnelli's handling of the celebrated ball sequence is superb. **115m/B VHS, Beta.** Jennifer Jones, Van Heflin, Louis Jourdan, James Mason, Gene Lockhart, Gladys Cooper, George Zucco; **D:** Vincente Minnelli; **M:** Miklos Rozsa. Nominations: Academy Awards '49: Best Art Direction/Set Decoration (B & W). MGM, CCB

Madame Bovary 🐾🐾🐾½ 1991 (PG-13) Provincial 19th century France is the setting for the tragedy of a romantic woman. Emma Bovary is bored by her marriage to an unsuccessful country doctor and longs for passion and excitement. She allows herself to be seduced (and abandoned) by a local aristocrat and herself seduces a young banker. She also struggles with an increasing burden of debt as she continues her quest for luxury. Realizing she will never find the passion she desires, Emma takes drastic, and tragic, measures. Sumptuous-looking film, with an extraordinary performance by Huppert. In French with English subtitles. Based on the novel by Gustave Flaubert. **130m/C VHS, LV.** FR Isabelle Huppert, Jean-Francois Balmer, Christophe MaLavoy, Jean Yanne; **D:** Claude Chabrol; **W:** Claude Chabrol; **M:** Matthieu Chabrol. Nominations: Academy Awards '91: Best Costume Design.REP, BTV

Madame Butterfly 🐾🐾 1995 A French production, filmed in Tunisia, with a Chinese soprano, and Italian subtitles. Mitterrand takes on Puccini's opera, setting it in 1904 Nagasaki, but playing most of the story straight (he adds some documentary footage of old Japan between the acts). 15-year-old Butterfly (Huang) is a geisha who makes the mistake of falling in love and marrying deceitful American naval officer Pinkerton (Troxell). She's disowned by her family, he eventually sails away, and when he does return, it's with an American bride. Tragedy ensues. Newcomer Huang's fine but the handsome Troxell's a little stiff. **129m/C VHS.** FR Ying Huang, Richard Troxell,

Ning Liang, Richard Cowan, Dr Frederic Mitterrand; **W:** Frederic Mitterrand; **C:** Philippe Welt. COL

Madame Curie 🐾🐾🐾 1943 The film biography of Madame Marie Curie, the woman who discovered Radium. A deft portrayal by Garson, who is reteamed with her "Mrs. Miniver" co-star, Pidgeon. Certainly better than most biographies from this time period and more truthful as well. **124m/B VHS, LV.** Greer Garson, Walter Pidgeon, Robert Walker, May Whitty, Henry Travers, Sir C. Aubrey Smith, Albert Basserman, Victor Francen, Reginald Owen, Van Johnson; **D:** Mervyn LeRoy; **C:** Joseph Ruttenberg. Nominations: Academy Awards '43: Best Actor (Pidgeon), Best Actress (Garson), Best Black and White Cinematography, Best Interior Decoration, Best Picture, Best Sound, Best Original Dramatic/Comedy Score. MGM, CCB

Madame Rosa 🐾🐾🐾 La Vie Devant Soi 1977 (PG) An aging Jewish prostitute tends prostitutes' offspring in this warmhearted work. A survivor of the Holocaust, the old woman finds her spirit revived by one of her charges—an abandoned Arab boy. In French with English subtitles. **105m/C VHS, Beta.** FR IS Simone Signoret, Claude Dauphin; **D:** Moshe Mizrahi; **C:** Nestor Almendros. Academy Awards '77: Best Foreign Language Film; Cesar Awards '78: Best Actress (Signoret); Los Angeles Film Critics Association Awards '78: Best Foreign Film. HTV, VES

Madame Sin 🐾🐾½ 1971 Aspiring world dominator enlists former CIA agent in scheme to obtain nuclear submarine. Davis is appealing as evil personified, in her first television movie. **91m/C VHS, Beta.** Bette Davis, Robert Wagner; **D:** David Greene; **M:** Michael Gibbs. CCB, FOX

Madame Sousatzka 🐾🐾🐾 1988 (PG-13) Eccentric, extroverted piano teacher helps students develop spiritually as well as musically. When she engages a teenage Indian student, however, she finds herself considerably challenged. MacLaine is perfectly cast in this powerful, winning film. **113m/C VHS, Beta, LV.** Shirley MacLaine, Peggy Ashcroft, Shabana Azmi, Twiggy, Leigh Lawson, Geoffrey Bayldon, Navin Chowdhry, Lee Montague; **D:** John Schlesinger; **W:** Ruth Prawer Jhabvala, John Schlesinger; **M:** Gerald Gouriet. Golden Globe Awards '89: Best Actress—Drama (MacLaine); Venice Film Festival '88: Best Actress (MacLaine). USH

Madame X 🐾🐾½ 1937 Fourth version of this classic tearjerker finds diplomat's wife George having a fling with a playboy. There's a murder and she turns to her nasty mother-in-law for aid. She arranges for daughter-in-law-dearest's "death" in order to prevent a scandal. Then George is on the slippery path to alcoholism and prostitution. Adapted from the play by Alexandre Bisson. Run-of-the-mill; Lana Turner's 1966 version is still the one to watch. **96m/B VHS.** Gladys George, John Beal, Warren William, Reginald Owen, William Henry, Henry Daniell, Philip Reed, Lynne Carver, Emma Dunn, Ruth Hussey; **D:** Sam Wood; **W:** John Meehan. MGM

Madame X 🐾🐾 Absinthe 1966 Turner is perfectly cast in this oft-filmed melodrama about a social outcast who is tried for murder and defended by her unknowing son, who believes her long dead. Bennett's last film. **100m/C VHS, Beta.** Lana Turner, John Forsythe, Ricardo Montalban, Burgess Meredith, Virginia Grey, Constance Bennett, Keir Dullea; **D:** David Lowell Rich; **C:** Russell Metty. USH

M.A.D.D.: Mothers Against Drunk Driving 🐾🐾½ 1983 Emotionally gripping television movie recounts the story of Candy Lightner, who, after her daughter was killed in a drunk driving accident, founded M.A.D.D. and built it into a nationwide organization. Similar to "License to Kill," which dramatized the effect that a drunk driving accident can have on the families of those involved. **97m/C VHS, Beta.** Mariette Hartley, Paula Prentiss, Bert Remsen; **D:** William A. Graham; **C:** Dean Cundey; **M:** Bruce Broughton. USH

The Maddening 🐾½ 1995 (R) When their car breaks down in a remote area, Cassie (Sara) and daughter Samantha find refuge at the home of Roy Scudder (Reynolds) and his wife Georgina

(Dickinson). At least Cassie thought it was a refuge—until she realizes the Scudders are crazy killers. **CW:** Violence and terror; some language. 97m/C VHS, LV, **Closed Caption.** Burt Reynolds, Angie Dickinson, Mia Sara, Brian Wimmer, Josh Mostel, William Hickey; **D:** Danny Huston; **W:** Leslie Greif. *THV*

Made for Each Other 🎬🎬🎬 1939
Newlyweds must overcome meddlesome in-laws, poverty, and even serious illness in this classic melodrama. Dated but appealing. 85m/B VHS, Beta, **Closed Caption.** James Stewart, Carole Lombard, Charles Coburn, Lucile Watson; **D:** John Cromwell; **C:** Leon Shamroy. *CNG, MRV, NOS*

Made for Love 🎬½ 1926
Couple journeys romantically in Egypt until disaster strikes: they fall into a tomb and can't get out. 65m/B VHS, Beta. Leatrice Joy, Edmund Burns, Ethel Wales, Brandon Hurst, Frank Butler; **D:** Paul Sloane. *GPV, FCT*

Made in America 🎬🎬 1993 (PG-13)
High-energy, lightweight comedy stars Whoopi as a single mom whose daughter Long discovers her birth was the result of artifical insemination. More surprising is her biological dad: white, obnoxious, country-western car dealer Danson. Overwrought with obvious gags, basically a one-joke movie. Nonetheless, Goldberg and Danson chemically connect onscreen (and for a short time offscreen as well) while supporting actor Smith grabs comedic attention as Teacake, Long's best friend. Both Goldberg and Danson deserve better material. **CW:** Language and sexual situations. 111m/C VHS, Beta, LV, Letterbox, **Closed Caption.** Whoopi Goldberg, Ted Danson, Will Smith, Nia Long, Paul Rodriguez, Jennifer Tilly, Peggy Rea, Clyde Kusatsu; **D:** Richard Benjamin; **W:** Holly Goldberg Sloan; **C:** Ralf Bode; **M:** Mark Isham. *WAR*

Made in Argentina 🎬🎬 1986
An Argentinean couple living in New York decide to return for a visit. Having left for political reasons, they still harbor bitterness. 90m/C VHS, Beta. *AR* Luis Brandoni, Marta Bianchi, Leonor Manso; **D:** Juan Jose Jusid. *VES*

Made in Heaven 🎬🎬 1952
Arid comedy in which British newlyweds try to sustain honeymoon for entire year. The bride, however, eventually suspects her husband of shenanigans with the maid. If this sounds good, then you may like it. 90m/C VHS, Beta, **Closed Caption.** *GB* Petula Clark, David Tomlinson, Sonja Ziemann, A.E. Matthews; **D:** John Paddy Carstairs. *HMV*

Made in Heaven 🎬🎬½ 1987 (PG)
Two souls in heaven fall in love and must find each other after being reborn on Earth if they are to remain eternal lovers. Contains ethereal interpretations of heaven and several cameo appearances by famous actors and musicians. 105m/C VHS, Beta, LV, **Closed Caption.** Timothy Hutton, Kelly McGillis, Maureen Stapleton, Mare Winningham, Ann Wedgeworth, Don Murray, Amanda Plummer, Timothy Daly, Marj Dusay; **Cameos:** Ellen Barkin, Neil Young, Tom Petty, Ric Ocasek, Tom Robbins, Debra Winger, Gary Larsen, David Rasche; **D:** Alan Rudolph; **W:** Raynold Gideon, Bruce A. Evans; **M:** Mark Isham. *WAR, ORI*

Made in USA 🎬½ 1988 (R)
Wayward dudes engage vixen while cruising Midwest. Trouble, however, awaits. Note: This is not Godard's mid-'60s classic. 82m/C VHS, Beta, LV. Adrian Pasdar, Lori Singer, Christopher Penn; **D:** Ken Friedman; **W:** Ken Friedman. *NLC*

Madeleine 🎬🎬½
The Strange Case of Madeleine 1950 Courtroom drama of woman charged with poisoning her French lover in 1850s Scotland. Directed by the same David Lean who made "Bridge on the River Kwai" and "Lawrence of Arabia." Here, though, he was merely trying to provide a vehicle for his wife, actress Todd. Intrigued? 114m/B VHS, Beta. Ann Todd, Leslie Banks, Ivan Desny, Norman Wooland, Barbara Everest, Susan Stranks, Patricia Raine, Elizabeth Sellars, Edward Chapman, Jean Cadell, Eugene Deckers, Amy Veness, John Laurie, Henry Edwards, Ivor Barnard, Barry Jones, David Morne, Andre Morell, Douglas Barr; **D:** David Lean; **W:**

Nicholas Phipps, Stanley Haynes; **C:** Guy Green; **M:** William Alwyn. *BFA*

Madeline 1998 (PG)
Adaptation of Ludwig Bemelman's classic 1939 children's book about 12 little French orphaned schoolgirls living in Paris, the trouble-finding Madeline (Jones), and their patient teacher Miss Clavel (McDormand). ?m/C VHS. Hatty Jones, Frances McDormand, Nigel Hawthorne; **D:** Daisy von Scherler Mayer; **W:** Marc Levin, Jennifer Flacket, Chris Weitz, Paul Weitz; **M:** Michel Legrand. *NYR*

Mademoiselle 1966
Moreau is a psychotic, sexually repressed schoolteacher in a small village who manages to keep herself under control until studly woodcutter Manni and his son take up residence. The locals distrust the stranger but Moreau can't wait to get her hands on him. Suddenly, the village is battered by a rash of poisonings, fires, and floods, all of which are blamed on Manni, leading the locals to exact a terrible vengeance. In French with English subtitles. 105m/B VHS. *FR GB* Jeanne Moreau, Ettore Manni, Umberto Orsini, Keith Skinner, Jane Berretta, Mony Rey; **D:** Tony Richardson; **W:** Jean Genet. *MGM, FCT*

Mademoiselle Fifi 🎬½ 1944
Simon stars as a French laundress in 1870 France who refuses to give in to her small town's Prussian oppressors. The film title is the nickname of the most brutal of the Prussian officers, played by Kreuger. An unsuccessful attempt at political allegory for the devastation of WWII. 69m/B VHS, LV. Simone Simon, John Emery, Kurt Kreuger, Alan Napier, Jason Robards Sr.; **D:** Robert Wise. *FCT*

Mademoiselle Striptease 🎬🎬½
Please! Mr. Balzac; While Plucking the Daisy; En Effeuillant la Marguerite 1957 Bardot stars as a young woman who finds a valuable stolen book. Her attempts to disassociate herself from the actual theft are supposed to be funny. Bardot is characteristically appealing. 100m/B VHS, Beta. Brigitte Bardot, Robert Hirsch, Daniel Gelin; **D:** Marc Allegret. *STV, MRV*

Madhouse 🎬🎬 1974
A troubled horror film star tries to bring his "Dr. Death" character to television, but during production people begin dying in ways remarkably similar to the script. A strong genre cast should hold the fans' attention during this mild adaptation of Angus Hall's novel "Devilday." 92m/C VHS, Beta. *GB* Vincent Price, Peter Cushing, Robert Quarry, Adrienne Corri, Natasha Pyne, Linda Hayden, Michael Parkinson; **D:** Jim Clark. *HBO*

Madhouse 🎬🎬 1987
A woman has bizarre recollections of her twin sister whom she finally meets when she escapes from a mental hospital. Lots of violence and gore, has definite cult potential. 90m/C VHS, Beta. Trish Everly, Michael MacRae, Dennis Robertson, Morgan Hart; **D:** Ovidio G. Assonitis. *NO*

Madhouse 🎬🎬 1990 (PG-13)
New homeowners find themselves unable to expel loathsome, boorish guests. Presumably, a comedy cashing in on two of sitcom's brightest lights. 90m/C VHS, Beta, LV, **Closed Caption.** John Larroquette, Kirstie Alley, Alison La Placa, John Diehl, Jessica Lundy, Bradley Gregg, Dennis Miller, Robert Ginty; **D:** Tom Ropelewski; **W:** Tom Ropelewski; **M:** David Newman. *ORI*

Madhouse Mansion 🎬🎬½
Ghost Story 1974 (PG) A horror actor revives his career and becomes embroiled in murder. Plenty of in-jokes and clips from older movies. 86m/C VHS. *GB* Marianne Faithfull, Leigh Lawson, Anthony Bate, Larry Dann, Sally Grace, Penelope Keith, Vivian Mackerell, Murray Melvin, Barbara Shelley; **D:** Stephen Weeks; **C:** Peter Hurst. *NO*

Madigan 🎬🎬🎬 1968
Realistic and exciting and among the best of the behind-the-scenes urban police thrillers. Hardened NYC detectives (Widmark and Guardino) lose their guns to a sadistic killer and are given 72 hours to track him down. Fonda is the police chief none too pleased with their performance. Adapted by Howard Rodman, Abraham Polonsky, and Harry Kleiner from Richard Dougherty's "The Commissioner." 101m/C VHS, Beta. Richard Widmark, Henry Fonda, Inger Stevens, Harry Guardino, James Whitmore, Susan Clark, Mi-

chael Dunn, Don Stroud; **D:** Donald Siegel; **W:** Abraham Polonsky; **C:** Russell Metty. *USH*

Madigan's Millions WOOF! 1967 (G)
Incompetent Treasury agent treks to Italy to recover funds swiped from deceased gangster. This is Hoffman's first film, and is to his career what "The Last Chalice" was to Paul Newman's and "Studs and Kitty" was to Sylvester Stallone. Recommended only to the terminally foolhardy. 89m/C VHS, Beta. Dustin Hoffman, Elsa Martinelli, Cesar Romero; **D:** Stanley Prager. *RHI*

Madman 🎬 1979 (R)
Deranged Soviet Jew joins Israeli army to more effectively fulfill his desire to kill loathsome Soviets. Good date movie for those nights when you're home alone. Weaver's first starring role. 95m/C VHS, Beta. *IS* Sigourney Weaver, Michael Beck, F. Murray Abraham; **D:** Dan Cohen. *CNG*

Madman 🎬 1982 (R)
Camp leader prompts terror when he revives legend regarding ax murderer. Seems that when you call his name, he appears. Buffoon does not believe story and calls out madman's name. Madman hears the call and emerges from forest, says hi, and hacks everyone to death. Lesson learned, case closed. Filmed on Long Island. 89m/C VHS, Beta. Alexis Dubin, Tony Fish. *HHE*

The Madness of King George 🎬🎬🎬½ 1994 (R)
Poor King George is a monarch with problems—his 30 years of royal authority are being usurped by Parliament, his American colonies have been lost, and, in 1788, he's begun to periodically lose his mind. So what do you do when a ruler becomes irrational? The royal physicians are baffled, his loving Queen Charlotte (Mirren) is in despair, but the noxious Prince of Wales (Everett) can barely contain his glee at finally having a chance at the throne. A last resort is offered by Dr. Willis (Holm), a former clergyman with some unusual and sadistic ideas about treating the mentally ill (even if they do have royal blood). Brilliant performance by Hawthorne (who originated the stage role in Bennett's 1991 play "The Madness of George III"). Screen note explains that King George suffered from the metabolic disorder known as porphyria. A Tony Award-winner for his Broadway productions of "Miss Saigon" and "Carousel," Hytner makes his feature-film directing debut. **CW:** Adult themes and situations; profanity. 110m/C VHS, LV, **Closed Caption.** *GB* Nigel Hawthorne, Helen Mirren, Ian Holm, Rupert Everett, Amanda Donohoe, Rupert Graves, Julian Wadham, John Wood, Julian Rhind-Tutt; **D:** Nicholas Hytner; **W:** Alan Bennett; **M:** George Fenton. Academy Awards '94: Best Art Direction/Set Decoration; British Academy Awards '95: Best Actor (Hawthorne); Cannes Film Festival '95: Best Actress (Mirren); Nominations: Academy Awards '94: Best Actor (Hawthorne), Best Adapted Screenplay, Best Supporting Actress (Mirren); British Academy Awards '95: Best Actress (Mirren), Best Adapted Screenplay, Best Cinematography, Best Director (Hytner), Best Film, Best Supporting Actor (Holm), Best Score; Writers Guild of America '94: Best Adapted Screenplay. *HMK*

Mado 🎬🎬🎬 1976
A middle-aged businessman's life is undone when he falls for a mysterious woman. Piccoli and Schneider are, as usual, convincing. Another of underrated director Sautet's effective, low-key works. In French with subtitles. 130m/C VHS, Beta. Romy Schneider, Michel Piccoli, Charles Denner; **D:** Claude Sautet. Cesar Awards '77: Best Sound. *FCT*

Madonna: Innocence Lost 🎬½ 1995
Tacky TV movie focusing on the ambitious singer and would-be actress who made wearing underwear as outerwear almost acceptable. Tawdry gossip highlights this laughfest as the trash talker hustles her way to the top of the heap, uncaring of whom she steps on along the way. Toronto substitutes for New York City grit. 90m/C VHS, **Closed Caption.** Terumi Matthews, Wendie Malick, Jeff Yagher, Dean Stockwell, Nigel Bennett, Don Francks, Rod Wilson, Tom Melissis; **D:** Bradford May; **W:** Michael J. Murray. *FXV*

Madron 🐾½ **1970 (PG)** Road western filmed in the Israel desert, complete with menacing Apaches, wagon train massacre, a nun and a gunslinger. **93m/C VHS, Beta.** Richard Boone, Leslie Caron, Paul Smith; **D:** Jerry Hopper. Nominations: Academy Awards '70: Best Song ("Till Love Touches Your Life"). *NO*

The Madwoman of Chaillot 🐾½ **1969 (G)** Four men conspire to drill for oil which they believe lurks under Paris. Hepburn finds out about their plot and tells each man that oil is bubbling up through her basement. Before the men can arrive at her house to confirm this, she and her three cronies hold a mock trial and sentence the men to death. Features a stellar cast, but this modern-day adaptation of Jean Giraudoux's play "La Folle de Chaillot" falls flat. **142m/C VHS, LV, Letterbox.** Katharine Hepburn, Charles Boyer, Claude Dauphin, Edith Evans, John Gavin, Paul Henreid, Oscar Homolka, Margaret Leighton, Giulietta Masina, Nanette Newman, Richard Chamberlain, Yul Brynner, Donald Pleasence, Danny Kaye, Fernand Gravet; **D:** Bryan Forbes; **W:** Edward Anhalt. *WAR*

Mae West 🐾🐾½ **1984** This made-for-television film details West's life from her humble beginnings to her racy film stardom. Jillian does a good job bringing the buxom legend back to life. **97m/C VHS, Beta.** Ann Jillian, James Brolin, Piper Laurie, Roddy McDowall; **D:** Lee Philips; **M:** Brad Fiedel. *ORI*

Maedchen in Uniform 🐾🐾🐾½ *Girls in Uniform* **1931** A scandalous early German talkie about a rebellious schoolgirl who falls in love with a female teacher and commits suicide when the teacher is punished for the relationship. A controversial criticism of lesbianism and militarism that impelled the Nazis, rising to power two years later, to exile its director. It was also banned in the United States. In German with English subtitles. Remade in 1965. **90m/B VHS, Beta.** *GE* Dorothea Wieck, Ellen Schwannecke, Hertha Thiele; **D:** Leontine Sagan. *MRV, NLC*

Mafia Princess 🐾🐾 **1986** The daughter of a Mafia boss tries to discover her own identity despite her father's involvement in crime. Based on a best-selling autobiography by a real-life member of a Mob family, Antoinette Giancana. Made for television. **100m/C VHS.** Tony Curtis, Susan Lucci, Kathleen Widdoes, Chuck Shamata, Louie Dibianco; **D:** Robert Collins. *NO*

Mafia vs. Ninja 🐾½ **1984** The mob wants to control the city, but the Ninja has other ideas. **90m/C VHS, Beta.** Alexander Lou, Silvio Azzolini, Wang Hsia, Charlema Hsu, Eugene Trammel. *NO*

Magdalene 🐾½ **1988 (PG)** Somewhere in medieval Europe, a violent Baron seeks revenge on a beautiful whore that spurned him. Small-budget costumer. **89m/C VHS, Beta, LV.** Steve Bond, Nastassia Kinski, David Warner, Gunter Meisner, Ferdinand "Ferdy" Mayne, Anthony Quayle, Franco Nero, Janet Agren; **D:** Monica Teuber. *PAR, FCT*

Magee and the Lady 🐾🐾 *She'll Be Sweet* **1978 (PG)** The crusty captain of a rusty ship must warm up to a spoiled debutante or lose his ship to a foreclosure firm. Could be better. Made for TV. **92m/C VHS, Beta.** *AU* Tony LoBianco, Sally Kellerman; **D:** Gene Levitt.

Magic 🐾🐾½ **1978 (R)** Ventriloquist Hopkins and his dummy, an all-too-human counterpart, get involved with a beautiful but impressionable woman lost between reality and the irresistible world of illusion. Spine-chilling psycho-drama with a less-than-believable premise. Screenplay by Goldman from his novel. **106m/C VHS, Beta, LV.** Anthony Hopkins, Ann-Margret, Burgess Meredith, Ed Lauter, Jerry Houser, David Ogden Stiers, Lillian Randolph; **D:** Richard Attenborough; **W:** William Goldman; **C:** Victor Kemper; **M:** Jerry Goldsmith. *NO*

The Magic Bow 🐾½ **1947** Typically ridiculous musical bio—this time of violinist Nicolo Paganini (Granger). He's the talented poor boy who falls for the wealthy Jeanne (Calvert) but his one true love is for his Stradivarius. Yehudi Menuhin plays the solos. Based on the novel by Manuel Komroff. **105m/B VHS.** *GB* Stewart Granger, Phyllis Calvert, Jean Kent, Dennis Price, Cecil Parker, Felix Aylmer, Frank Cellier, Marie Lohr; **D:** Bernard Knowles; **W:** Roland Pertwee, Norman Ginsburg; **C:** Jack Asher, Jack Cox. *HMK*

The Magic Bubble 🐾🐾½ **1993 (PG-13)** On her 40th birthday, Julia Cole finds the fountain of youth...inside a bottle of enchanted bubbles. Ageless and timeless, she begins to know the meaning of true happiness. **CW:** Brief nudity and mild sensuality. **90m/C VHS.** Diane Salinger, John Calvin, Priscilla Pointer, Colleen Camp, Tony Peck, Wallace Shawn, George Clooney; **D:** Alfredo Ringel, Deborah Taper Ringel; **W:** Meredith Baer, Geof Pryssir. *MNC*

The Magic Christian 🐾🐾🐾 **1969 (PG)** A series of related skits about a rich man (Sellers) and his son (Starr) who try to prove that anyone can be bought. Raucous, now somewhat dated comedy; music by Badfinger, including Paul McCartney's "Come and Get It." **101m/C VHS, Beta, LV.** *GB* Peter Sellers, Ringo Starr, Isabel Jeans, Wilfrid Hyde-White, Graham Chapman, John Cleese, Peter Graves, John Lennon, Yoko Ono, Richard Attenborough, Leonard Frey, Laurence Harvey, Christopher Lee, Spike Milligan, Yul Brynner, Roman Polanski, Raquel Welch; **D:** Joseph McGrath; **W:** Terry Southern; **C:** Geoffrey Unsworth. *REP, MRV*

The Magic Flute 🐾🐾🐾½ **1973 (G)** Bergman's acclaimed version of Mozart's famous comic opera, universally considered one of the greatest adaptations of opera to film ever made. Staged before a live audience for Swedish television. In Swedish with English subtitles. **134m/C VHS, Beta, LV.** *SW* Josef Kostlinger, Irma Urrila, Hakan Hagegard, Elisabeth Erikson; **D:** Ingmar Bergman. Nominations: Academy Awards '75: Best Costume Design. *HMV, PAR, MVD*

The Magic Fountain 🐾🐾 **1961** Three princes search for a magic fountain whose waters will cure their ailing father. Two of them, however, take the evil course and are turned into ravens by a wicked dwarf. Based on the fairy tale "Das Wasser des Lebens" by the Brothers Grimm. **82m/C VHS.** Peter Nestler, Helmo Kinderman, Josef Marz, Catherine Hansen, Cedric Hardwicke; **D:** Allan David. *SNC*

Magic Hunter 🐾🐾 **1996** Max (Kemp) is supposed to be the best sharpshooter on the Budapest police force, but his skill deserts him and he accidentally shoots the woman he was assigned to protect. A sinister colleague gives him seven magic bullets guaranteed to hit their target but what Max doesn't realize is that he's made a bargain with the Devil, and the Devil gets to choose the seventh target. Hungarian with subtitles. **106m/C VHS.** *HU* Gary Kemp, Alexander Kaidanovsky, Sadie Frost; **D:** Ildiko Enyedi. *FRF*

Magic in the Mirror: Fowl Play 🐾🐾½ **1996 (G)** Young Mary Margaret (Smith) does an "Alice Through the Looking Glass" when she steps through an antique mirror bequeathed to her by her grandmother and discovers an enchanted kingdom run by giant ducks. But just how will MM find her way back? **86m/C VHS, Beta, Closed Caption.** Jaime Renee Smith, Kevin Wixted, Saxon Trainor, David Brooks, Godfrey James; **D:** Ted Nicolaou; **W:** Frank Dietz, Ken Carter Jr.; **C:** Adolfo Bartoli; **M:** Richard Kosinski. *PAR*

Magic in the Water 🐾½ **1995 (PG)** Divorced, obnoxious radio shrink and neglectful dad Dr. Jack Black (Harmon) takes the kiddies on a summer jaunt to a Canadian lake, where they begin to explore the legend of Orky, Canada's answer to the Loch Ness monster. Dad becomes a believer when Orky possesses his body and (New Age Alert!) releases his inner child. Harmless fun for the kids, but parents will gag at the attempt to provide a meaningful and symbolic message, which arrives with all the subtlety of an Oliver Stone history lesson. Sort of an "E.T." meets "Free Willy" with Orky shilling for the EPA. Beautiful cinematography showcasing the British Columbia landscape helps, but not enough. **100m/C VHS, Closed Caption.** Mark Harmon, Joshua Jackson, Harley Jane Kozak, Sarah Wayne, Willie Nark-Orn, Frank S.

Salsedo, **D:** Nick Stevenson; **W:** Icel Dobell Massey, Rick Stevenson; **C:** Thomas Burstyn; **M:** David Schwartz. Genie Awards '95: Best Cinematography, Best Sound. *COL*

Magic Island 🐾🐾½ **1995 (PG)** Thirteen-year-old Jack (Bryan) gets sucked into the pages of a pirate book and finds himself with Blackbeard and his scurvy crew. They're on a treasure hunt and figure Jack's book contains some missing clues. Naturally, Jack finds himself in lots of trouble. **88m/C VHS, Closed Caption.** Zachery Ty Bryan, Edward Kerr, Lee Armstrong, French Stewart, Abraham Benrubi, Jessie-Ann Friend, Oscar Dillon, Sean O'Kane, Schae Harrison, Ja'net DuBois, Andrew Divoff; **D:** Sam Irvin; **W:** Neil Ruttenberg, Brent Friedman; **C:** James Lawrence Spencer; **M:** Richard Band. *PAR*

Magic Kid 🐾🐾½ *Ninja Dragons* **1992 (PG)** Thirteen-year-old martial-arts champ Kevin and his older sister vacation in L.A., staying with their shady Uncle Bob, a second-rate talent agent. Kevin wants to meet his martial arts movie idol and his sister her favorite soap opera hunk. But they wind up being chased by the mobsters Uncle Bob owes money to. **91m/C VHS, LV, Closed Caption.** Ted Jan Roberts, Shonda Whipple, Stephen Furst, Joseph Campanella, Billy Hufsey, Sondra Kerns, Pamela Dixon, Lauren Tewes, Don "The Dragon" Wilson; **D:** Joseph Merhi; **W:** Stephen Smoke; **M:** Jim Halfpenny. *PMH*

Magic Kid 2 🐾🐾½ **1994 (PG)** The young star of a popular martial arts program wants to quit and go to high school like a normal teenager. But the studio execs have other ideas. **90m/C VHS, LV.** Ted Jan Roberts, Stephen Furst, Donald Gibb, Jennifer Savidge; **D:** Stephen Furst. *PMH*

Magic Moments 🐾🐾½ **199?** Ambitious British TV exec Melanie James (Seagrove) is about to score the coup of her career. She's persuaded charismatic American illusionist Troy Gardner (Shea) to recreate his death-defying act on TV—but only if Melanie will produce the show herself. Too bad her power-hungry boss is out to cause trouble. Made for British TV. **103m/C VHS.** *GB* Jenny Seagrove, John Shea. *VCO*

Magic of Lassie 🐾🐾 **1978 (G)** Stewart is engaging as the nice grandpa who refuses to sell his land to mean rich guy Roberts. Innocuous, pleasant remake of "Lassie Come Home." Stewart sings, as do Pat Boone and daughter Debby. **100m/C VHS, Beta.** James Stewart, Mickey Rooney, Stephanie Zimbalist, Alice Faye, Pernell Roberts, Lassie; **D:** Don Chaffey. Nominations: Academy Awards '78: Best Song ("When You're Loved"). *MGM*

The Magic of the Golden Bear: Goldy 3 🐾 *Goldy 3* **1994 (G)** Down-on-his-luck magician (Marin) tries to buy Goldy to save his failing act and Jessie (Morgan) is torn between wanting to keep the bear or return her to the wild. An animal-loving holy man (Mr. T.) tries to help her decide. **104m/C VHS, Closed Caption.** Bonnie Morgan, Richard "Cheech" Marin, Mr. T; **D:** John Quinn. *FHE*

Magic on Love Island 🐾 **1980** Romantic misadventures ensue when eight ladies go on vacation to Love Island, a tropical paradise. **96m/C VHS, Beta.** Adrienne Barbeau, Bill Daily, Howard Duff, Dody Goodman, Dominique Dunne, Lisa Hartman Black, Janis Paige; **D:** Earl Bellamy. *NO*

Magic Serpent 🐾🐾🐾 **1966** Fantasy set in medieval Japan features a grand duel in magic between a good hero and evil sorcerer who transform into a giant dragon and a giant frog to do battle. **?m/C VHS.** Hiroki Matsukata, Tomoko Ogawa, Ryutaro Otomo, Bin Amatsu; **D:** Tetsuya Yamauchi. *SMW*

The Magic Stone 🐾🐾½ *Kilian's Chronicle* **1995** Kilian is the 10th-century Irish slave of brutish Viking Ivar, who decides to sacrifice him to the Norse god Thor when the Vikings become lost while sailing off the North American coast. Kilian manages to escape and make it to shore where he's rescued by a Native American tribe and falls in love with local beauty, Turtle. But Ivar goes after Kilian to steal his magic stone, which can navigate a ship through the worst weather, and begins a Viking war with the tribe. **95m/C VHS.**

Christopher Johnson, Robert McDonough, Eva Kim, Jonah Ming Lee; **D:** Pamela Berger; **W:** John Hoover; **M:** R. Carlos Nakai, Bevan Manson. *MNC*

The Magic Sword 🐾🐾 *St. George and the Seven Curses; St. George and the Dragon* 1962 A family-oriented adventure film about a young knight who sets out to rescue a beautiful princess who is being held captive by an evil sorcerer and his dragon. 80m/C VHS, Beta. Basil Rathbone, Estelle Winwood, Gary Lockwood; **D:** Bert I. Gordon. *MGM, MRV, VYY*

Magic Town 🐾🐾½ 1947 An opinion pollster investigates a small town which exactly reflects the views of the entire nation, making his job a cinch. The publicity causes much ado in the town with ensuing laughs. Uneven but entertaining. 103m/B VHS. Jane Wyman, James Stewart, Kent Smith, Regis Toomey, Donald Meek; **D:** William A. Wellman; **C:** Joseph Biroc. *REP*

The Magic Voyage 🐾🐾½ 1993 (G) Animated tale of a friendly woodworm named Pico who voyages with Columbus to the new world and convinces him that the world is indeed round. He then comes to the aid of a magical firefly named Marilyn who helps Columbus find gold to bring back to Spain. 82m/C VHS, LV. **V:** Dom DeLuise, Mickey Rooney, Corey Feldman, Irene Cara, Dan Haggerty, Samantha Eggar.

The Magic Voyage of Sinbad 🐾🐾 *Sadko* 1952 Sinbad embarks on a fantastic journey after promising the people of his Covasian home that he will find the elusive Phoenix, the bird of happiness. Unreleased in the U.S. until 1962; rewritten for the American screen by a young Coppola. 79m/C VHS, Beta. **RU** Sergey Stolyarov, Alla Larionova, Mark Troyanovsky; **D:** Alexander Ptushko; **W:** Francis Ford Coppola. *SNC*

Magical Mystery Tour 1967 On the road with an oddball assortment of people, the Beatles experience a number of strange incidents around the English countryside. Originally made for British television. ♫Magical Mystery Tour; Blue Jay Way; Your Mother Should Know; The Fool on the Hill. 55m/C VHS, Beta, LV, DVD. **GB** John Lennon, George Harrison, Ringo Starr, Paul McCartney, Victor Spinetti. *MPI, WFV, MVD*

Magical Wonderland 1985 Join a handsome prince and his fair young maiden as they venture through such fairy tale classics as "Beauty and the Beast" and "Sleeping Beauty." 90m/C VHS, Beta. *VCI*

The Magician 🐾🐾🐾 1958 A master magician in 19th century Sweden (von Sydow) wreaks ill in this darkly comical, supernatural parable. Dark, well photographed early Bergman effort. In Swedish with English subtitles. 101m/B VHS, Beta, LV. **SW** Max von Sydow, Ingrid Thulin, Gunnar Bjornstrand, Bibi Andersson, Naima Wifstrand; **D:** Ingmar Bergman; **W:** Ingmar Bergman. Venice Film Festival '59: Special Jury Prize. *HMV, MRV, HHT*

The Magician of Lublin 🐾½ 1979 (R) Based on an unusual story by Issac Bashevis Singer. Follows the exploits of a magician/con man in turn-of-the century Poland whose personal flaws kill his career, until a chance emerges for one last trick. A good example of movie not as good as book; this rendering is superficial, badly acted and unsatisfying. Made soon after Singer won the Nobel Prize for literature in 1978. 105m/C VHS, Beta. Alan Arkin, Valerie Perrine, Louise Fletcher, Lou Jacobi, Shelley Winters; **D:** Menahem Golan; **M:** Maurice Jarre. *NO*

Magnificent Adventurer 🐾 1976 Ostensibly a biography of Benvenuto Cellini, the Florentine sculptor, with a concentration on his love life and swordplay. 94m/C VHS, Beta. Brett Halsey. *UNI*

The Magnificent Ambersons 🐾🐾🐾🐾 1942 Welles' second film. A fascinating, inventive translation of the Booth Tarkington novel about a wealthy turn of the century family collapsing under the changing currents of progress. Pure Welles, except the glaringly bad tacked-on ending that the studio

shot (under the direction of the great Robert Wise and Fred Fleck), after taking the film from him. It seems they wanted the proverbial happy ending. Also available on laserdisc, with interviews and the original story boards. 88m/B VHS, Beta, LV, Closed Caption. Joseph Cotten, Anne Baxter, Tim Holt, Richard Bennett, Dolores Costello, Erskine Sanford, Ray Collins, Agnes Moorehead; **D:** Freddie Fleck, Robert Wise, Orson Welles; **W:** Orson Welles; **M:** Bernard Herrmann, Roy Webb. National Film Registry '91;; New York Film Critics Awards '42: Best Actress (Moorehead); Nominations: Academy Awards '42: Best Black and White Cinematography, Best Interior Decoration, Best Picture, Best Supporting Actress (Moorehead). *CRC, MLB, TTC*

The Magnificent Dope 🐾🐾½ 1942 Fonda is likeable, as usual, as the hapless yokel in the big city. A trip to New York to take a course on being successful is his prize for winning a "laziest man" contest. He falls for his teacher; she uses his crush to motivate him. Funny and entertaining. 83m/B VHS. Henry Fonda, Lynn Bari, Don Ameche, Edward Everett Horton, Hobart Cavanaugh, Pierre Watkin; **D:** Walter Lang. *FXL*

The Magnificent Matador 🐾🐾½ *The Brave and the Beautiful* 1955 The story of an aging matador who faces death in the bullring to win the love of a woman. Quinn is the bullfighter on the horns of a dilemma. Lots of bull in script carried by harried bull in ring. 94m/C VHS, Beta. Anthony Quinn, Maureen O'Hara, Thomas Gomez; **D:** Budd Boetticher. *VHE*

Magnificent Obsession 🐾🐾½ 1954 A drunken playboy (Hudson) kills a man and blinds his wife in an automobile accident. Plagued by guilt, he devotes his life to studying medicine in order to restore the widow's sight. Well-acted melodrama lifted Hudson to stardom. Faithful to the 1935 original, based on a novel by Lloyd C. Douglas. 108m/C VHS, Beta. Jane Wyman, Rock Hudson, Barbara Rush, Agnes Moorehead; **D:** Douglas Sirk; **W:** Robert Blees; **C:** Russell Metty. Nominations: Academy Awards '54: Best Actress (Wyman). *USH*

The Magnificent Seven 🐾🐾🐾🐾 1960 Western remake of Akira Kurosawa's classic "The Seven Samurai." Mexican villagers hire gunmen to protect them from the bandits who are destroying their town. Most of the actors were relative unknowns, though not for long. Sequelled by "Return of the Seven" in 1966, "Guns of the Magnificent Seven" in 1969, and "The Magnificent Seven Ride" in 1972. Excellent score. Uncredited writing by Walter Newman and Walter Bernstein. 126m/C VHS, Beta, LV, Letterbox. Yul Brynner, Steve McQueen, Robert Vaughn, James Coburn, Charles Bronson, Horst Buchholz, Eli Wallach, Brad Dexter; **D:** John Sturges; **W:** William Roberts; **C:** Charles B(ryant) Lang; **M:** Elmer Bernstein. Nominations: Academy Awards '60: Best Original Dramatic/Comedy Score. *MGM, FOX, TLF*

The Magnificent Yankee 🐾🐾🐾 *The Man with Thirty Sons* 1950 Adaptation of Emmet Lavery's Broadway play on the life of Supreme Court Justice Oliver Wendell Holmes, starring Calhern (who also did the stage version). America's foremost legal mind was well-served by Calhern, with Harding as his ever-patient wife. 80m/B VHS, Beta. Louis Calhern, Ann Harding, Eduard Franz, Philip Ober, Ian Wolfe, Edith Evanson, Richard Anderson, Jimmy Lydon, Robert Sherwood, Hugh Sanders; **D:** John Sturges; **W:** Emmet Lavery. Nominations: Academy Awards '50: Best Actor (Calhern), Best Costume Design (B & W). *MGM, FCT, BTV*

Magnum Force 🐾🐾 1973 (R) Eastwood's second "Dirty Harry" movie. Harry finds a trail leading from a series of gangland killings straight back to the P.D. Less gripping than "Dirty Harry" (1971); followed by "The Enforcer" (1976), "Sudden Impact" (1983), and "The Dead Pool" (1988). Holbrook is cast intriguingly against type, and the premise is good, but little else recommends this too-violent installment. 124m/C VHS, Beta, LV. Clint Eastwood, Hal Holbrook, Mitchell Ryan, David Soul, Robert Urich, Tim Matheson, Kip Niven; **D:** Ted Post; **W:** Michael Cimino, John Milius; **M:** Lalo Schifrin. *WAR, TLF*

Magnum Killers 🐾 1976 A young man becomes involved in a web of deadly intrigue when he sets out to find who cheated him out of a small fortune during a card game. 92m/C VHS, Beta. Sombat Methance, Prichela Lee. *UNI*

Magnum P.I.: Don't Eat the Snow in Hawaii 1980 Series pilot finds Vietnam-vet-turned-private-eye Thomas Sullivan Magnum (Selleck) living in Hawaii (in the guest house of never-seen mystery writer Robin Masters) and investigating the death of a wartime buddy. Hillerman excels as autocratic major domo Higgins. 99m/C VHS. Tom Selleck, John Hillerman, Roger E. Mosley, Larry Manetti; **D:** Roger Young; **W:** Donald P. Bellisario, Glen Larson. *USH*

The Mahabharata 1989 Adapted from the myths and folklore of ancient India, the screen version of the original nine-hour stage play is the story of a devastating war between two powerful clans. Initially broadcast on public television, the six-hour movie is divided into three two-hour tapes, "The Game of Dice," "Exile in the Forest," and "The War." 318m/C VHS, LV. **GB FR** Robert Langton-Lloyd, Antonin Stahly-Vishwanadan, Bruce Myers; **D:** Peter Brook; **W:** Jean-Claude Carriere; **M:** Toshi Tsuchitori. *BTV, WSH, FCT*

Mahler 🐾🐾🐾 1974 (PG) Strange Russell effort on the life of the great composer Gustav Mahler. Imperfect script is rescued by fine acting. 110m/C VHS, Beta. Robert Powell, Georgina Hale, Richard Morant, Lee Montague, Terry O'Quinn; **D:** Ken Russell; **W:** Ken Russell. *HMV*

Mahogany 🐾½ 1975 (PG) Poor girl becomes world-famous high fashion model and designer, ditches boyfriend in the old neighborhood, gets a career boost when she daringly appears in a dress of her own creation at a Roman fashion show, and still yearns for the boy back home. Motown attempt to make mainstream hit that's glossy and predictable. 109m/C VHS, Beta, LV. Diana Ross, Billy Dee Williams, Jean-Pierre Aumont, Anthony Perkins, Nina Foch; **D:** Berry Gordy; **W:** John Byrum; **C:** David Watkin. Nominations: Academy Awards '75: Best Song ("Theme from Mahogany"). *PAR, CCB, FCT*

The Maid 🐾🐾½ 1990 (PG) An offbeat comedy romance with Sheen as the house husband to Bisset's female executive character. Nice acting; charming, if unoriginal, premise. 91m/C VHS, Beta, LV, Closed Caption. Martin Sheen, Jacqueline Bisset, Jean-Pierre Cassel, James Faulkner, Victoria Shalet; **D:** Ian Toynton. *VTR*

Maid to Order 🐾½ 1987 (PG) Rich girl Sheedy's fairy godmother puts her in her place by turning her into a maid for a snooty Malibu couple. Good-natured and well-acted if rather mindless Cinderella story. 92m/C VHS, Beta, LV. Ally Sheedy, Beverly D'Angelo, Michael Ontkean, Dick Shawn, Tom Skerritt, Valerie Perrine, Rigg Kennedy; **D:** Amy Holden Jones; **W:** Perry Howze; **M:** Georges Delerue. *ART*

Maid's Night Out 🐾🐾 1938 Pleasant, simple-minded mistaken-identity comedy. Fontaine is an heiress; rich-guy posing-as-milkman Lane thinks she is a maid. They fall in love, of course. 64m/B VHS. Joan Fontaine, Allan "Rocky" Lane, Hedda Hopper, George Irving, William Brisbane, Billy Gilbert, Cecil Kellaway; **D:** Ben Holmes. *MLB*

Maids of Wilko 🐾🐾 *The Young Ladies of Wilko; Panny z Wilka* 1979 Wajda's adaptation of Jaroslav Iwaszkiewicz's memoirs set in the late '20s. Viktor Ruben (Olbrychski) reexamines his life following the death of a friend. He returns to the home of his aunt and uncle in Wilko where he renews friendships with five sisters on a neighboring estate in an attempt to resurrect a happier past. Lots of fruitless romantic yearning. In French and Polish with English subtitles. 118m/C VHS. **PL FR** Daniel Olbrychski, Christine Pascal, Maja Komorowska, Anna Seniuk, Krystyna Zachwatowicz, Stanislawa Celinska, Zofia Jaroszewska, Tadeusz Bialoszczynski; **D:** Andrzej Wajda; **W:** Zbigniew Kaminski. Nominations: Academy Awards '79: Best Foreign Language Film. *FCT*

The Main Event 🎬🎬 1979 (PG) Streisand plays a wacky—and bankrupt—cosmetic executive who must depend on the career of washed-up boxer O'Neal to rebuild her fortune. Desperate (and more than a little smitten), she badgers and bullies him back into the ring. Lame, derivative screwball comedy desperate to suggest chemistry of Streisand and O'Neal's "What's Up, Doc?" (1972). Streisand sings the title song. 109m/C VHS, Beta. Barbra Streisand, Ryan O'Neal; *D:* Howard Zieff. *WAR*

Main Street to Broadway 🎬🎬 1953 Superficial story of a struggling playwright. Interesting mainly for abundant big-name cameos. Based on a story by Robert E. Sherwood. 102m/B VHS, Beta. Tom Morton, Mary Murphy, Agnes Moorehead, Herb Shriner, Rosemary DeCamp, Clinton Sundberg; *Cameos:* Lionel Barrymore, Ethel Barrymore, Tallulah Bankhead, Shirley Booth, Cornel Wilde, Rex Harrison, Joshua Logan, Helen Hayes, Mary Martin; *D:* Tay Garnett. *MPI, MLB*

Mainline Run 🎬½ 1998 Smalltime drug runner Taro (Speer) gets out of prison and immediately goes back to work for crime boss Mr. Fletcher (Ward). Taro sets up a deal, which goes bad, the drugs are lost, and one of his men is killed. Now Taro and his buddy Sean (Joseph) are looking to get out, but Mr. Fletcher has something else in mind. 96m/C VHS. Hugo Speer, Andrew Joseph, Nelson E. Ward, Kelly Marcel; *D:* Howard Ford; *C:* Jonathan Ford. *SPC*

Maitresse 🎬🎬½ 1976 An examination of the sexual underworld in the same vein as "Blue Velvet" and "Crimes of Passion." Director Schroeder also created "Reversal of Fortune." In French with English subtitles. 112m/C VHS. Gerard Depardieu; *D:* Barbet Schroeder; *C:* Nestor Almendros. *WAR, BTV, FCT*

The Major and the Minor 🎬🎬🎬½ 1942 Very funny comedy that marked Wilder's directorial debut. Susan Applegate (Rogers) decides she's had it with New York and wants to head home to Iowa, but she only has enough money for a child's half-price train ticket. So she passes herself off as a 12-year-old (!) and then runs into problems when Army major Kirby (Milland), who's traveling to a boys military school, decides to take the child under his protective wing. Soon he's insisting Susan stay at the school until her mother (played by Rogers' mother Lela) can collect her. Potentially risque situations never cross the line into sleaze but remain bright and breezy. 101m/B VHS. Ginger Rogers, Ray Milland, Rita Johnson, Robert Benchley, Diana Lynn, Frankie Thomas Jr.; *D:* Billy Wilder; *W:* Billy Wilder, Charles Brackett; *C:* Leo Tover; *M:* Robert Emmett Dolan. *USH*

Major Barbara 🎬🎬🎬½ 1941 A wealthy, idealistic girl joins the Salvation Army against her father's wishes. Based on the play by George Bernard Shaw. The excellent adaptation of the original and the cast make this film a winner. Deborah Kerr's film debut. 90m/B VHS, Beta. GB Wendy Hiller, Rex Harrison, Robert Morley, Sybil Thorndike, Deborah Kerr; *D:* Gabriel Pascal. *FCT, HMV*

Major Dundee 🎬🎬½ 1965 A Union army officer (Heston) chases Apaches into Mexico with a motley collection of prisoner volunteers. Too long and flawed; would have been better had Peckinpah been allowed to finish the project. Excellent cast. 124m/C VHS, Beta. Charlton Heston, Richard Harris, James Coburn, Jim Hutton, Ben Johnson, Slim Pickens; *D:* Sam Peckinpah; *C:* Sam Leavitt. *GKK*

Major League 🎬🎬½ 1989 (R) Comedy about a pathetic major league baseball team whose new owner schemes to lose the season and relocate the team to Miami. Sheen is okay as the pitcher with control problems (both on and off the field), while Bernsen seems to be gazing affectionately at "L.A. Law" from a distance. Predictable sports spoof is good for a few laughs, particularly those scenes involving Haysbert as a slugger with voodoo on his mind (and in his lock-

er) and Snipes as a base stealer whose only problem is getting on base. 107m/C VHS, Beta, LV, 8mm, Closed Caption. Tom Berenger, Charlie Sheen, Corbin Bernsen, James Gammon, Margaret Whitton, Bob Uecker, Rene Russo, Wesley Snipes, Dennis Haysbert, Charles Cyphers, Chelcie Ross; *D:* David S. Ward; *W:* David S. Ward; *C:* Reynaldo Villalobos; *M:* James Newton Howard. *PAR*

Major League 2 🎬½ 1994 (PG) It's been five years since they won the series, and this plodding sequel finds the wacky championship Cleveland Indians ruined by success and once again struggling in last place. Limited charm of original is lost; dull and filled with so many lame jokes that you won't care if they manage to make it to the top again. Cast returns, with the exception of Wesley Snipes as Willie Mays Hays (now played by Epps). 105m/C VHS, LV, Letterbox, Closed Caption. Charlie Sheen, Tom Berenger, Corbin Bernsen, James Gammon, Dennis Haysbert, Omar Epps, David Keith, Bob Uecker, Alison Doody, Michelle Burke, Margaret Whitton, Eric Bruskotter, Takaaki Ishibashi; *D:* David S. Ward; *W:* R.J. Stewart; *M:* Michel Colombier. *WAR*

Major League 3: Back to the Minors 🎬½ 1998 (PG-13) Three strikes and this franchise is out. Gus Cantrell (Bakula) is a burned-out pitcher who's offered the chance to manage the Minnesota Twins' Triple A team and finds a bunch of central casting misfits. Just when you thought they'd run out of baseball cliches, in comes a young prospect who won't take advice (Goggins), an arrogant manager (McGinley), and the "big game" showdown (twice!). We've seen this stuff done (not much better) in the first two "Major Leagues" and (very much better) elsewhere. Bakula's always solid, but it's not enough to get the save. Take an intentional pass on this one. 90m/C VHS. Scott Bakula, Corbin Bernsen, Dennis Haysbert, Takaaki Ishibashi, Jensen Daggett, Eric Bruskotter, Walton Goggins, Ted McGinley, Kenneth Johnson, Peter M. MacKenzie, Bob Uecker, Steve Yeager, Larry Brandenburg, Judson Mills, Lobo Sebastian, Thom Barry, Tim DiFilippo, Tom DiFilippo, Ted DiFilippo; *D:* John Warren; *W:* John Warren; *C:* Tim Suhrstedt; *M:* Robert Folk. *NYR*

Major Payne 🎬 1995 (PG-13) When the marines have no more use for killing-machine Major Payne (Wayans), he reluctantly agrees to train the inept junior ROTC cadets at academically challenged Madison Academy. The misfit brigade contains the usual assortment of stock loser-types who follow the predictable "outcasts get even" plot to the letter. Wayans shows flashes of comic genius, but not nearly enough to make up for the one-dimensional characters and indifferent writing. Most of the showcase jokes involve the humiliation and degradation of the kids, always a laugh-riot. Sub-moronic remake of 1955's "The Private War of Major Benson." *CW:* Some crude humor and behavior. 97m/C VHS, LV, Closed Caption. Damon Wayans, Karyn Parsons, William Hickey, Albert Hall, Steven Martini, Andrew Harrison Leeds, Scott "Bam Bam" Bigelow; *D:* Nick Castle; *W:* Damon Wayans, Dean Lorey, Gary Rosen; *C:* Richard Bowen. *USH*

The Majorettes 🎬 1987 (R) Eek! Someone is lurking around a high school murdering the majorettes with their own batons. A bare-bones plot lurks within this otherwise worthless pic. 93m/C VHS, Beta. Kevin Kindlan, Terrie Godfrey, Mark V. Jevicky, Sueanne Seamans, John Russo, Bill Hinzman, Russell Streiner; *D:* Bill Hinzman; *W:* John Russo. *ART, VES, TEM*

A Majority of One 🎬🎬½ 1956 Dated comedy about late-in-life romance and prejudice. Russell stars as Jewish Brooklyn widow Mrs. Jacoby, who tags along with her daughter and diplomat son-in-law on their shipboard trip to Japan. She meets the charming Koichi Asano (a surprisingly effective Guinness), who's with the Japanese diplomatic corp, runs into problems with her family, and decides she must give up her chance at romance. Adapted from the play by Leonard Spigelgass. 149m/C VHS. Rosalind Russell, Alec Guinness, Ray Danton, Madlyn Rhue, Mae Questel, Frank

Wilcox, Alan Mowbray; *D:* Mervyn LeRoy; *W:* Leonard Spigelgass. *WAR*

Make a Million 🎬🎬 1935 The Depression is played (successfully) for yuks in this tale of an economics professor fired from his post for advocating radical income redistribution. He doesn't get mad, he gets even: he makes a million by advertising for money. 66m/B VHS, Beta. Charles Starrett, Pauline Brooks. *VYY*

Make a Wish 🎬🎬 1937 A noted composer goes stale in this colorful musical about backstage life. The comic relief provides the films best moments. 🎵Music In My Heart; My Campfire Dreams; Make a Wish; Old Man Rip. 80m/B VHS, Beta. Basil Rathbone, Leon Errol, Bobby Breen, Ralph Forbes; *D:* Kurt Neumann; *M:* Oscar Straus. Nominations: Academy Awards '37: Best Score. *VYY*

Make Haste to Live 🎬🎬½ 1954 Good, scary thriller. A woman survives attempted murder by her husband; moves far away to raise their infant daughter. He does time, then returns for revenge. McGuire is good as the terrorized wife. 90m/B VHS. Dorothy McGuire, Stephen McNally, Edgar Buchanan, John Howard; *D:* William A. Seiter; *M:* Elmer Bernstein. *REP*

Make Me an Offer 🎬🎬 1955 Somewhat slow-moving comedy centering on an antique dealer who attempts to buy an expensive vase from an old man. From the novel by Wolf Mankowitz. 88m/C VHS. GB Peter Finch, Adrienne Corri, Rosalie Crutchley, Finlay Currie; *D:* Cyril Frankel.

Make Me an Offer 🎬½ 1980 Made-for-TV movie about selling real estate in Hollywood. Better than similar efforts. 97m/C VHS, Beta. Susan Blakely, Stella Stevens, Patrick O'Neal; *D:* Jerry Paris; *M:* Ralph Burns. *NLC*

Make Mine Mink 🎬🎬🎬 1960 Oft-hilarious British comedy about guests at an elegant but run-down mansion who become unlikely thieves, stealing furs for charity. Good cast headed by Terry-Thomas. 100m/C VHS, Beta. GB Terry-Thomas, Billie Whitelaw, Hattie Jacques; *D:* Robert Asher. *NO*

Make Room for Tomorrow 🎬🎬 1981 (R) Subtle, somewhat funny French comedy about generations in a family. A man in mid-life crisis has to cope with his father, son, and grandfather on the grandfather's 90th birthday. 106m/C VHS, Beta. FR Victor Lanoux, Jane Birkin, George Wilson; *D:* Peter Kassovitz.

Make-Up 🎬🎬 1937 A doctor turned circus clown uses his medical skills when an elephant renders a society girl unconscious. After she awakens the two become involved. The clown's daughter objects, but is soon caught up in an accusation that she murdered the lion tamer. Her father the clown tries to save the day. Predictable doctor/clown relationship. 72m/B VHS. Nils Asther, June Clyde, Judy Kelly, Kenne Duncan, John Turnbull; *D:* Alfred Zeisler. *NOS, DVT, MLB*

Making Contact 🎬½ 1986 (PG) A small boy's telekinetic powers enable him to bring to life his favorite toys. The ridicule he endures because of this leads him to set off on terrifying adventures with only his toys and a friend for company. 83m/C VHS, Beta. Joshua Morrell, Eve Kryll; *D:* Roland Emmerich. *VTR*

Making Love 🎬🎬 1982 (R) A closet homosexual risks his eight-year marriage by getting involved with a carefree writer. What could be a powerful subject gets only bland treatment. 112m/C VHS, Beta. Kate Jackson, Harry Hamlin, Michael Ontkean, Wendy Hiller, Arthur Hill, Nancy Olson, Terry Kiser, Camilla Carr, Michael Dudikoff; *D:* Arthur Hiller; *W:* Barry Sandler. *FOX*

Making Mr. Right 🎬🎬½ 1986 (PG-13) Under-rated satire about a high-powered marketing and image consultant who falls in love with the android that she's supposed to be promoting. Unbelievable comedy is shaky at times, but Magnuson and Malkovich create some magic. 95m/C VHS, Beta, LV. John Malkovich, Ann Magnuson, Glenne Headly, Ben Masters, Laurie Metcalf, Polly Bergen, Hart

Bochner, Polly Draper, Susan Anton; *D:* Susan Seidelman; *W:* Floyd Byars. HBO

Making the Grade 🎬🎬 *Preppies* 1984 (PG)
Jersey tough kid owes the mob; attends prep school in place of a rich kid who can't be bothered. Better than similar '80s teen flicks, but not by much. 105m/C VHS, Beta. Judd Nelson, Joanna Lee, Dana Olsen, Ronald Lacey, Scott McGinnis, Gordon Jump, Carey Scott, Andrew Dice Clay; *D:* Dorian Walker; *W:* Gene Quintano; *M:* Basil Poledouris. MGM

The Makioka Sisters 🎬🎬🎬 1983 Much
praised drama centering around the lives of four Japanese sisters who are heiresses to the family fortune and, hence, must be found proper husbands. The efforts of the older sisters to "match" their younger siblings are entwined with a gradual realization on the part of the elders that the quiet way of life representative of their own formative years is passing away with the advent of WWII. The movie is as visually stunning as it is poignant. In Japanese with English subtitles. 140m/C VHS, LV. *JP* Keiko Kishi, Yoshiko Sakuma, Sayuri Yoshinaga; *D:* Kon Ichikawa. FCT, TPV

Malarek 🎬🎬 1989 (R) Tough Montreal jour-
nalist Victor Malarek exposed abuse in that city's teen detention center in his book "Hey, Malarek." Compelling lead performance from Koteas in decent though not great screen adaptation. 95m/C VHS, Beta, LV. Michael Sarrazin, Elias Koteas, Al Waxman, Kerrie Keane; *D:* Roger Cardinal. COL

Malaya 🎬🎬½ *East of the Rising Sun* 1949 Hokey
adventure tale set in WWII that's based on a true story. Stewart and Tracy are hired to smuggle a huge shipment of rubber out of Malaya to waiting U.S. ships without the Japanese finding out. Greenstreet does his usual shifty role. 98m/B VHS. Spencer Tracy, James Stewart, Sydney Greenstreet, Valentina Cortese, John Hodiak, Lionel Barrymore, Gilbert Roland, Richard Loo, Roland Winters; *D:* Richard Thorpe; *W:* Frank Fenton; *M:* Bronislau Kaper. MGM

Malcolm 🎬🎬½ 1986 (PG-13) An offbeat com-
edy about a slightly retarded young man who is mechanically inclined and his unusual entry into a life of crime. Directorial debut for actress Tass, whose husband Parker wrote the screenplay (and designed the Tinkertoys). Music score performed by The Penguin Cafe Orchestra. 86m/C VHS, Beta, LV. *AU* Colin Friels, John Hargreaves, Lindy Davies, Chris Haywood, Charles Tingwell, Beverly Phillips, Judith Stratford; *D:* Nadia Tass; *W:* David Parker; *M:* Simon Jeffes. Australian Film Institute '86: Best Actor (Friels), Best Film. ART, VES

Malcolm X 🎬🎬🎬 1992 (PG-13) Stirring trib-
ute to the controversial black activist, a leader in the struggle for black liberation. Hitting bottom during his imprisonment in the '50s, he became a Black Muslim and then a leader in the Nation of Islam. His assassination in 1965 left a legacy of black nationalism, self-determination, and racial pride. Marked by strong direction from Lee and good performances (notably Freeman Jr. as Elijah Muhammad), it is Washington's convincing performance in the title role that truly brings the film alive. Based on "The Autobiography of Malcolm X" by Malcolm X and Alex Haley. *CW:* Some language and some violence and drug content. 201m/C VHS, Beta, LV, 8mm, Letterbox, Closed Caption. Denzel Washington, Angela Bassett, Albert Hall, Al Freeman Jr., Delroy Lindo, Spike Lee, Theresa Randle, Kate Vernon, Lonette McKee, Tommy Hollis, James McDaniel, Ernest Thompson, Jean LaMarre, Giancarlo Esposito, Craig Wasson, John Ottavino, David Patrick Kelly, Shirley Stoler; *Cameos:* Christopher Plummer, Karen Allen, Peter Boyle, William Kunstler, Bobby Seale, Al Sharpton; *D:* Spike Lee; *W:* Spike Lee, Arnel Perl, James Baldwin; *M:* Terence Blanchard. MTV Movie Awards '93: Best Male Performance (Washington); New York Film Critics Awards '92: Best Actor (Washington); Nominations: Academy Awards '92: Best Actor (Washington), Best Costume Design. WAR, MOV, BTV

Malcolm X: Make It Plain 1995 In-
depth portrait of the life of Malcolm X as told through the memories of many of Malcolm's close personal friends and individuals who had worked closely with him. Contains footage of Malcolm X speaking at rallies, meetings, and interviews with Maya Angelou, Ossie Davis, Alex Haley, Mike Wallace, and his family. 136m/C VHS. MPI

Male and Female 🎬🎬🎬🎬 1919 A group
of British aristocrats is shipwrecked on an island and must allow their efficient butler (Meighan) to take command for their survival. Swanson is the spoiled rich girl who falls for her social inferior. Their rescue provides a return to the rigid British class system. Based on the play "The Admirable Crichton" by James M. Barrie. 110m/B VHS, Beta. Gloria Swanson, Thomas Meighan, Lila Lee, Raymond Hatton, Bebe Daniels; *D:* Cecil B. DeMille. GPV

Malibu Beach 🎬½ 1978 (R) The California
beach scene is the setting for this movie filled with bikini clad girls, tanned young men, and instant romances. For connoisseurs of the empty-headed teen beach movie. 93m/C VHS, Beta. Kim Lankford, James Daughton; *D:* Robert J. Rosenthal; *C:* Jamie Anderson.

The Malibu Beach Vampires 1991 (R)
Three unscrupulous yuppies, Congressman Teri Upstart, Col. Ollie West and Rev. Timmy Fakker, keep beautiful mistresses in their Malibu beach house. What they don't know is, the girls are all really vampires who have injected them with a serum that compels them to tell the truth! Will our "heroes" continue to dupe the American Public, or will the sexy blood suckers cause their downfall? 90m/C VHS. Angelyne, Becky Le Beau, Joan Rudelstein, Marcus A. Frishman, Rod Sweitzer, Francis Creighton, Anet Anatelle, Yvette Buchanan, Cherie Romaors, Kelly Galindo; *D:* Francis Creighton. NO

Malibu Bikini Shop 🎬 1986 (R) Two
brothers manage a beachfront bikini shop in Malibu, and spend their time ogling the customers and arguing about running the "business." Just another excuse for parading babes in bathing suits across the naked screen. 90m/C VHS, Beta, Closed Caption. Michael David Wright, Bruce Greenwood, Barbara Horan, Debra Blee, Jay Robinson, Galyn Gorg, Ami Julius, Frank Nelson, Kathleen Freeman, Rita Jenrette; *D:* David Wechter; *W:* David Wechter. FOX

Malibu Express 🎬 1985 (R) Mystery/ad-
venture plot about a P.I. is the excuse; babes in swimsuits is the reason for this waste of time. 101m/C VHS, Beta. Darby Hinton, Sybil Danning, Art Metrano, Shelley Taylor Morgan, Niki Dantine, Barbara Edwards; *D:* Andy Sidaris. USH

Malibu High 🎬 1979 (R) The accidental
death of a young prostitute's client leads her to a new series of illegal activities of the "sex and hit" variety. Dark, sleazy, and antisocial; belies Beach Boys-esque title. 92m/C VHS, Beta. Jill Lansing, Stuart Taylor; *D:* Irvin Berwick. NO

Malibu Hot Summer 🎬 *Sizzle Beach U.S.A*
1974 (R) Three aspiring young actresses want a shot at becoming famous and travel to Los Angeles where they spend their time at the beach with little budget and no particular purchase. Re-released and renamed in 1986 when Costner (in his film debut) became more well-known. 89m/C VHS. Terry Congie, Leslie Brander, Roselyn Royce, Kevin Costner; *D:* Richard Brander. VHE, THV, VTR

Malice 🎬🎬½ 1993 (R) In a sleepy little col-
lege town, strange things sure do happen. Too bad rumpled college dean Andy Safian (Pullman) didn't see "Pacific Heights." If he did, he would know that sometimes roommates are more trouble than they're worth, even if renovation on that old Victorian is getting expensive. Routine thriller throws out an inventive twist to keep things moving, but manages to be fairly predictable anyway. *CW:* Language, some violence, and sexuality. 107m/C VHS, LV, Closed Caption. Alec Baldwin, Nicole Kidman, Bill Pullman, Bebe Neuwirth, Anne Bancroft, George C. Scott, Peter Gallagher, Josef Sommer; *D:* Harold Becker; *W:* Aaron Sorkin, Scott Frank; *C:* Gordon Willis; *M:* Jerry Goldsmith. NLC

Malicious 🎬🎬 *Malizia* 1974 (R) A house-
keeper hired for a widower and his three sons becomes the object of lusty affection of all four men. As Papa makes plans to court and marry her, his 14-year-old son plots to have her as a companion on his road to sensual maturity. Dubbed in English. 98m/C VHS, Beta. *IT* Laura Antonelli, Turi Ferro, Alessandro Momo, Tina Aumont; *D:* Salvatore Samperi. PAR

Malicious 🎬🎬 1995 (R) College athlete
Doug Gordon (McGaw) impulsively has what he thinks is a one-nighter with mystery lady, Melissa (Ringwald). Only she's not willing to give him up and his rejection sends her on the road to revenge. *CW:* Scenes of strong sexuality; language; some violence. 92m/C VHS, LV, Closed Caption. Molly Ringwald, Patrick McGaw, Sarah Lassez, John Vernon, Mimi Kuzyk, Rick Henrickson; *D:* Ian Corson; *W:* George Saunders; *C:* Michael Slovis; *M:* Graeme Coleman. REP

Mallrats 🎬🎬½ 1995 (R) Smith's better-fi-
nanced follow-up to the legendary "Clerks" (the second in the "Lord of the Rings" trilogy) follows Jersey slackers T.S. (London) and Brodie (Lee) to the mall, where they intend to wallow in food-court cookies and reclaim their girlfriends, who recently dumped them. While wandering the mall in low-key and confused pursuit of their women and self respect, they encounter the usual band of bizarre inhabitants, including Ivannah, the topless psychic, and Silent Bob (Smith) and stoner Jay (Mewes), the guys who hung out in front of the video shop during "Clerks." Dialogue and sight-gags are director/writer Smith's strong point; moving the plot forward is not high on the priority list. The ensemble cast, featuring Doherty as the boring babe who spurns Brodie, is up to the often funny sidebits and gen-x references. Ribald humor is not for young teens with virgin ears, unless mom and dad are out for the evening. Slick packaging with alternative soundtrack insures return on investment. *CW:* Strong language, including sexual dialogue, and scenes of sexuality and drug content. 95m/C VHS, LV, Closed Caption. Shannen Doherty, Jeremy London, Jason Lee, Claire Forlani, Michael Rooker, Priscilla Barnes, Renee Humphrey, Ben Affleck, Joey Lauren Adams, Jason Mewes, Brian O'Halloran, David Brinkley, Kevin Smith; *Cameos:* Stan Lee; *D:* Kevin Smith; *W:* Kevin Smith; *C:* Daniel Klein; *M:* Ira Newborn. USH

Malone 🎬½ 1987 (R) A burnt-out secret agent
stumbles into a real-estate swindle/murder plot in Oregon and sets out to stop it. Film tries hard but doesn't succeed in being believable. 92m/C VHS, Beta, LV, Closed Caption. Burt Reynolds, Lauren Hutton, Cliff Robertson, Kenneth McMillan, Scott Wilson, Cynthia Gibb; *D:* Harley Cokliss; *M:* David Newman. ORI

Malou 🎬🎬 1983 (R) A young French woman
tries to uncover the truth about her late mother's life, sifting through wildly contradictory evidence in the desire to discover her own identity and avoid her mother's mistakes. A feminist story. In German with English subtitles. 95m/C VHS, Beta. *GE* Grischa Huber, Ingrid Caven, Helmut Griem; *D:* Jeanine Meerapfel; *C:* Michael Ballhaus. GLV

Malta Story 🎬🎬½ 1953 A British WWII flier
becomes involved with the defense of Malta. 103m/B VHS, Beta. Alec Guinness, Jack Hawkins, Anthony Steel, Flora Robson, Muriel Pavlow; *D:* Brian Desmond Hurst.

The Maltese Falcon 🎬🎬🎬 *Dangerous*
Female 1931 A good first screen version of the Dashiell Hammett story about private detective Sam Spade's search for the elusive Black Bird. Remade five years later as "Satan Met a Lady" with Bette Davis. Its most famous remake, however, occurred in 1941 with Humphrey Bogart in the lead. 80m/B VHS, Beta. Bebe Daniels, Ricardo Cortez, Dudley Digges, Thelma Todd, Una Merkel, Dwight Frye, Robert Elliott; *D:* Roy Del Ruth. MLB

The Maltese Falcon 🎬🎬🎬🎬 1941 After
the death of his partner, detective Sam Spade finds himself enmeshed in a complicated, intriguing search for a priceless statuette. "It's the stuff

dreams are made of," says Bogart of the Falcon. Excellent, fast-paced film noir with outstanding performances, great dialogue, and concentrated attention to details. Director Huston's first film and Greenstreet's talky debut. First of several films by Bogart and Astor. Based on the novel by Dashiell Hammett. Also available colorized. **101m/B VHS, Beta, LV, Closed Caption.** Humphrey Bogart, Mary Astor, Peter Lorre, Sydney Greenstreet, Ward Bond, Barton MacLane, Gladys George, Lee Patrick, Elisha Cook Jr.; Jerome Cowan; **Cameos:** Walter Huston; **D:** John Huston; **W:** John Huston; **M:** Adolph Deutsch. National Film Registry '89;; Nominations: Academy Awards '41: Best Picture, Best Screenplay, Best Supporting Actor (Greenstreet).*MGM, FOX, TLF*

Mama Dracula woof! **1980** Fletcher stars in this poor satire of the horror genre. She's a vampire who needs the blood of virgins to stay young. Her son helps out—what good son wouldn't? **90m/C VHS.** *FR* Louise Fletcher, Bonnie Schneider, Maria Schneider, Marc-Henri Wajnberg, Alexander Wajnberg, Jess Hahn; **D:** Boris Szulzinger. *TWE*

Mama, There's a Man in Your Bed 🎬🎬🎬 *Romauld et Juliet* **1989 (PG)** When a powerful executive is framed for insider trading, the only witness to the crime and his only hope is an earthy cleaning woman named Juliette. Together they plot revenge and takeovers in her tiny apartment, filled with children. Soon, he regains his former position of power but realizes his life isn't complete without his co-conspirator. In French with English subtitles. **111m/C VHS, Beta, LV.** *FR* Daniel Auteuil, Firmine Richard, Pierre Vernier, Maxime LeRoux, Gilles Privat, Muriel Combeau, Catherine Salviat, Sambou Tati; **D:** Coline Serreau; **W:** Coline Serreau. *HBO, FCT*

Mama Turns a Hundred 🎬🎬🎬 **1979 (R)** A baronial family (a bizarre set of characters) is celebrating their mother's 100th birthday at her estate. One of the daughter's seduces her brother-in-law, another has a uniform fetish, a religious zealot is desperate to hang-glide, and several of them are trying to kill poor Mama. But of course she prevails, although sick and ailing. Slow-paced yet uproarious film full of inept characters who bumble along. In Spanish with English subtitles. **100m/C VHS, Beta.** *SP* Geraldine Chaplin, Fernando Gomez, Amparo Munoz; **D:** Carlos Saura. Nominations: Academy Awards '79: Best Foreign Language Film. *INT, AUD, TPV*

Mama's Dirty Girls **1974 (R)** A gangster mom's daughters take over where their mother left off and have the time of their lives. **82m/C VHS, Beta.** Gloria Grahame, Paul Lambert, Sondra Currie, Candice Rialson, Mary Stoddard; **D:** John Hayes; **M:** Don Bagley. *TWE*

Mambo 🎬🎬½ **1955** A poor young dancer inspires patronage and lust by dancing the Mambo. Although attracted to Gassman, she marries Rennie for his money. Technically weak but artistically interesting, though Rennie and Mangano have done their roles somewhat better elsewhere. **94m/B VHS.** Silvana Mangano, Michael Rennie, Vittorio Gassman, Shelley Winters, Katherine Dunham, Mary Clare, Eduardo Ciannelli; **D:** Robert Rossen; **M:** Nino Rota. *NOS, HTV*

The Mambo Kings 🎬🎬🎬 **1992 (R)** Armand and Banderas (in his first English speaking role) are Cesar and Nestor Castillo, two brothers who flee Cuba for New York City with dreams of hitting it big with their mambo music. Desi Arnaz Jr. gets to play his own dad in a funny and technical scene that leads to a climactic confrontation between the brothers. Good cast and great music make this one worthwhile. Based on the Pulitzer prizewinning novel "The Mambo Kings Play Songs of Love" by Oscar Hijuelos. **100m/C VHS, LV, 8mm, Closed Caption.** Armand Assante, Antonio Banderas, Cathy Moriarty, Maruschka Detmers, Desi Arnaz Jr., Celia Cruz, Roscoe Lee Browne, Vondie Curtis-Hall, Tito Puente, Talisa Soto; **D:** Arne Glimcher; **W:** Cynthia Cidre; **C:** Michael Ballhaus; **M:** Robert Kraft, Carlos Franzetti.

Nominations: Academy Awards '92: Best Song ("Beautiful Maria of My Soul"). *WAR, FCT, MVD*

Mame 🎬🎬 **1974 (PG)** In an adaptation of the Broadway musical "Auntie Mame" by Jerry Herman, Ball plays a dynamic woman who takes it upon herself to teach a group of eccentrics how to live life to the fullest. Arthur plays Mame's friend just as splendidly as she did in the Broadway version, but Ball in her last feature film is a lame Mame. Overly ambitious production avoids reaching goal. ♫Mame; We Need a Little Christmas; If He Walked Into My Life; Bosom Buddies; It's Today; Loving You; My Best Girl; What Do I Do Now? (Gooch's Sont); Open a New Window. **132m/C VHS, Beta, LV, Letterbox.** Lucille Ball, Beatrice Arthur, Robert Preston, Joyce Van Patten, Bruce Davison; **D:** Gene Saks. *WAR, MVD*

Mamele 🎬½ *Little Mother* **1938** Picon prematurely becomes the "mother" of her seven siblings when their mother dies. Quintessential Yiddish musical with the usual shimmering performance from Picon. In Yiddish with English subtitles. **95m/B VHS, Beta.** *PL* Molly Picon, Max Bozyk, Edmund Zayenda; **D:** Joseph Green. *ERG, TPV*

Mamma Roma 🎬🎬🎬½ **1962** Pasolini's second film is a heartbreaking story of family ties, escaping the past, and dreams of the future. The title character (Magnani) is a former prostitute who attempts respectability for herself and her teenaged son (Garofolo). But her ex-pimp (Citti) threatens her new life and Rome's big-city temptations prove to be a pathway to crime and tragedy for the boy. Magnani gives one of her finest performances. Italian with subtitles. **110m/B VHS.** *IT* Anna Magnani, Ettore Garofolo, Franco Citti, Silvana Corsini, Luisa Loiano; **D:** Pier Paolo Pasolini; **W:** Pier Paolo Pasolini; **C:** Tonino Delli Colli. *CVC*

A Man, a Woman, and a Bank 🎬🎬½ *A Very Big Weekend* **1979 (PG)** Two con-men plan to rob a bank by posing as workers during the bank's construction. An advertising agency woman snaps their picture for a billboard to show how nice the builders have been, then becomes romantically involved with one of the would-be thieves. Nice performances, but wacky touches aren't plentiful enough or well timed to sustain comedy. **100m/C VHS, Beta.** *CA* Donald Sutherland, Brooke Adams, Paul Mazursky; **D:** Noel Black; **W:** Bruce A. Evans, Raynold Gideon; **C:** Jack Cardiff; **M:** Bill Conti. *NLC*

A Man, a Woman and a Killer 🎬🎬½ **19??** Unusual film within a film shows the actual making of a movie while unfolding a story of a hired killer. A joint project from the directors of the well-received "Emerald Cities" and "Chan is Missing." **75m/C VHS.** *D:* Rick Schmidt, Wayne Wang. *FCT*

A Man About the House 🎬🎬½ **1947** Two unmarried English sisters move into the Italian villa they have inherited. There, one marries the caretaker, who secretly plans to regain the property that once belonged to his family. When the newly married sister is found dead, her sibling sets out to solve the murder. **83m/B VHS.** *GB* Kieron Moore, Margaret Johnston, Dulcie Gray, Guy Middleton, Felix Aylmer; **D:** Leslie Arliss. *NOS, SNC*

A Man Alone 🎬🎬 **1955** Man falsely accused of robbing a stagecoach hides not alone but with comely sheriff's daughter. Milland's debut behind the camera. **96m/C VHS.** Ray Milland, Ward Bond, Mary Murphy, Raymond Burr, Lee Van Cleef; **D:** Ray Milland; **C:** Lionel Lindon. *REP*

A Man and a Woman 🎬🎬🎬 *Un Homme et Une Femme* **1966** When a man and a woman, both widowed, meet and become interested in one another but experience difficulties in putting their past loves behind them. Intelligently handled emotional conflicts within a well-acted romantic drama, acclaimed for excellent visual detail. Remade in 1977 as "Another Man, Another Chance." Followed in 1986 with "A Man and A Woman: 20 Years Later." Dubbed. **102m/C VHS,**

Beta, Closed Caption. *FR* Anouk Aimee, Jean-Louis Trintignant, Pierre Barouh, Valerie Lagrange; **D:** Claude Lelouch; **W:** Claude Lelouch. Academy Awards '66: Best Foreign Language Film, Best Story & Screenplay; British Academy Awards '67: Best Actress (Aimee); Cannes Film Festival '66: Best Film; Golden Globe Awards '67: Best Actress—Drama (Aimee), Best Foreign Film; Nominations: Academy Awards '66: Best Actress (Aimee), Best Director (Lelouch). *WAR, HMV*

A Man and a Woman: 20 Years Later 🎬½ *Un Homme Et Une Femme: Vingt Ans Deja* **1986 (PG)** Slouchy sequel to the highly praised "A Man and a Woman" that catches up with a couple after a long separation. The sad romantic complications of the original are more mundane in this sequel, which is burdened by a film-within-a-film script as well as shots from the original. In French with English subtitles. **112m/C VHS, Beta.** *FR* Jean-Louis Trintignant, Anouk Aimee, Richard Berry; **D:** Claude Lelouch. *WAR*

Man & Boy 🎬🎬 *Ride a Dark Horse* **1971 (G)** A black Civil War veteran, played by Bill Cosby, encounters bigotry and prejudice when he tries to set up a homestead in Arizona. An acceptable family film, some might be disappointed that Cosby is not playing this one for laughs. **98m/C VHS, Beta.** Bill Cosby, Gloria Foster, George Spell, Henry Silva, Yaphet Kotto; **D:** E.W. Swackhamer; **M:** Quincy Jones. *COL*

The Man and the Monster 🎬½ **1965** When a concert pianist sells his soul to the devil, he fails to realize that part of the deal has him turning into a hideous beast every time he hears a certain piece of music. Maybe it was "Stairway to Heaven." **78m/B VHS.** *MX* Enrique Rambal, Abel Salazar, Martha Roth; **D:** Rafael Baledon. *SNC*

Man Bait 🎬🎬½ *The Last Page* **1952** A complex web of intrigue and mystery surrounds a blackmailed book dealer when he allows a blonde woman to catch his eye. A competently made film. **78m/B VHS, Beta, LV.** *GB* George Brent, Marguerite Chapman, Diana Dors; **D:** Terence Fisher. *RXM, MLB*

Man Beast 🎬 **1955** The abominable snowman is sought and found in this grade-Z '50s monster movie. **65m/B VHS, Beta.** Rock Madison, Virginia Maynor, George Skaff, Lloyd Nelson, Tom Maruzzi; **D:** Jerry Warren. *NOS, MRV, RHI*

Man Bites Dog 🎬🎬 **1991 (NC-17)** A pseudo-documentary about a serial killer, filled with ever-mounting violence. Ben is the killer being followed by a two-man camera/sound crew (which he's hired), who record his casual carnage without lifting a finger to stop him. Indeed his continued killing and robbing is to pay for financing the documentary about himself. This satire on film violence, as well as reality-based television shows, is both appalling and humorous in a sick way. In French with English subtitles. Also available in an unrated edited version. **95m/B VHS.** *BE* Benoit Poelvoorde, Remy Belvaux, Andre Bonzel; **D:** Benoit Poelvoorde, Remy Belvaux, Andre Bonzel; **W:** Benoit Poelvoorde, Remy Belvaux, Andre Bonzel, Vincent Tavier. *FXL, FCT*

A Man Called Adam 🎬½ **1966** A jazz musician is tortured by prejudice and the guilt created by his having accidentally killed his wife and baby years before. Davis is appropriately haunted, but the film is poorly produced. **103m/B VHS, Beta.** Sammy Davis Jr., Louis Armstrong, Ossie Davis, Cicely Tyson, Frank Sinatra Jr., Lola Falana, Mel Torme, Peter Lawford; **D:** Leonard Penn; **C:** Jack Priestley. *COL, NLC*

A Man Called Horse 🎬🎬🎬 **1970 (PG)** After a wealthy Britisher is captured and tortured by the Sioux Indians in the Dakotas, he abandons his formal ways and discovers his own strength. As he passes their torture tests, he is embraced by the tribe. In this very realistic and gripping portrayal of American Indian life, Harris provides a strong performance. Sequelled by "Return of a Man Called Horse" (1976) and "Triumphs of a Man Called Horse" (1983). **114m/C VHS, Beta, LV, Letterbox, Closed Caption.** Richard Harris, Judith Anderson, Jean Gascon, Stanford Howard, Manu Tupou, Dub

Taylor; **D:** Elliot Silverstein; **W:** Jack DeWitt; **C:** Robert B. Hauser. *FOX*

A Man Called Peter 🎬🎬🎬 1955 A biographical epic about Peter Marshall, a Scottish chaplain who served the U.S. Senate. Todd does his subject justice by sensitively showing all that was human in Marshall, and a talented supporting cast makes for a thoroughly watchable film. **119m/C VHS, Beta, Closed Caption.** Richard Todd, Jean Peters, Marjorie Rambeau, Jill Esmond, Les Tremayne, Robert Burton; **D:** Henry Koster. Nominations: Academy Awards '55: Best Color Cinematography. *FOX*

A Man Called Rage woof! 1984 Rage is the only man capable of safely escorting a group of pioneers through a nuclear wasteland infested with mutants and cannibals. **90m/C VHS, Beta.** *IT* Stelio Candelli, Conrad Nichols; **D:** Anthony Richmond. *ART*

A Man Called Sarge 🎬½ 1990 (PG-13) Sophomoric comedy about a daffy WWII sergeant leading his squad against the Germans at Tobruk. **88m/C VHS, Beta, LV.** Gary Kroeger, Marc Singer, Gretchen German, Jennifer Runyon; **D:** Stuart Gillard. *WAR, OM*

A Man Called Sledge 🎬🎬 1971 Garner fans might be surprised to see the star play a villain in this violent story of a gang of outlaws who wind up fighting each over a cache of gold. This is mainstream Western entertainment. **93m/C VHS.** James Garner, Dennis Weaver, Claude Akins, John Marley, Laura Antonelli; **D:** Vic Morrow. *COL, GKK*

A Man Escaped 🎬🎬🎬½ *Un Condamne a Mort s'est Echappe; The Wind Bloweth Where it Listeth* 1957 There's an excruciating realism about Bresson's account of a WWII Resistance fighter's escape from a Nazi prison just before he was to be executed by the Gestapo. It's the sounds and lingering camera shots, not the wham bam variety of action, that create and sustain the film's suspense. Bresson, who had been a Nazi prisoner, solicited the supervision of Andre Devigny, whose true story the film tells. Contributing to the realistic feel was the use of non professional actors. An award-wiining film that fellow director Truffaut lauded as the most crucial French film of the previous ten years. In French with English subtitles. **102m/B VHS.** Francois Leterrier; **D:** Robert Bresson. Cannes Film Festival '57: Best Director (Bresson). *NYF*

Man Facing Southeast 🎬🎬🎬½ *Hombre Mirando Al Sudeste; Man Looking Southeast* 1986 (R) The acclaimed Argentinean film about the sudden appearance of a strange man in an asylum who claims to be an extraterrestrial, and a psychologist's attempts to discover his true identity. The sense of mystery intensifies when the new patient indeed seems to have some remarkable powers. Although the pace at times lags, the story intriguingly keeps one guessing about the stranger right to the end. In Spanish, with English subtitles. **105m/C VHS, Beta, LV.** *AR* Lorenzo Quinteros, Hugo Soto, Ines Vernengo; **D:** Eliseo Subiela; **C:** Ricardo De Angelis; **M:** Pedro Aznar. *VTR, IME, HHE*

A Man for All Seasons 🎬🎬🎬🎬 1966 (G) Sterling, heavily Oscar-honored biographical drama concerning the life and subsequent martyrdom of 16th-century Chancellor of England, Sir Thomas More (Scofield). Story revolves around his personal conflict when King Henry VIII (Shaw) seeks a divorce from his wife, Catherine of Aragon, so he can wed his mistress, Anne Boleyn—events that ultimately lead the King to bolt from the Pope and declare himself head of the Church of England. Remade for television in 1988 with Charlton Heston in the lead role. **120m/C VHS, Beta, LV, Closed Caption.** *GB* Paul Scofield, Robert Shaw, Orson Welles, Wendy Hiller, Susannah York, John Hurt, Nigel Davenport, Vanessa Redgrave; **W:** Constance Willis, Robert Bolt; **C:** Ted Moore; **M:** Georges Delerue. Academy Awards '66: Best Actor (Scofield), Best Adapted Screenplay, Best Color Cinematography, Best Costume Design (Color), Best Director (Zinnemann), Best Picture; British Academy Awards '67: Best Actor (Scofield), Best Film, Best Screenplay; Directors Guild of America Awards '66: Best Director (Zinnemann); Golden Globe

Awards '67: Best Actor—Drama (Scofield), Best Director (Zinnemann), Best Film—Drama, Best Screenplay; National Board of Review Awards '66: Best Actor (Scofield), Best Director (Zinnemann), Best Supporting Actor (Shaw); New York Film Critics Awards '66: Best Actor (Scofield), Best Director (Zinnemann), Best Film, Best Screenplay; Nominations: Academy Awards '66: Best Supporting Actor (Shaw), Best Supporting Actress (Hiller).*COL, BTV, TVC*

A Man for All Seasons 🎬🎬🎬 1988 Fresh from the London stage, Heston directs and stars in this version of Robert Bolt's play depicting the conflict between Henry VIII and his chief advisor, Sir Thomas More. Strong supporting cast. Made for cable TV. **150m/C VHS, LV.** Charlton Heston, Vanessa Redgrave, John Gielgud, Richard Johnson, Roy Kinnear, Martin Chamberlain; **D:** Charlton Heston. *TTC*

Man Friday 🎬🎬 1975 (PG) Stranded on a deserted island, a man forces a native from a neighboring island to be his slave. Based on the classic story "Robinson Crusoe" by Daniel Defoe, this adaptation charts the often-brutal treatment the native receives as his captor tries to civilize him. Through his intelligence, the enslaved man regains his freedom and returns home with his former captor, who then seeks acceptance from the native's tribe. A sometimes confusing story line and excessive blood and guts detract from this message-laden effort. **115m/C VHS.** *GB* Peter O'Toole, Richard Roundtree, Peter Cellier, Christopher Cabot, Joel Fluellen; **D:** Jack Gold; **M:** Carl Davis. *FOX*

The Man from Atlantis 🎬🎬 1977 Patrick Duffy stars as the water-breathing alien who emerges from his undersea home, the Lost City of Atlantis. The made-for-TV movie led to a brief television series. **60m/C VHS, Beta.** Patrick Duffy, Belinda J. Montgomery, Victor Buono; **D:** Lee H. Katzin. *WOV*

The Man from Beyond 🎬🎬½ 1922 Frozen alive, a man returns 100 years later to try and find his lost love. Silent. **50m/B VHS, Beta.** Harry Houdini, Arthur Maude, Nita Naldi; **D:** Burton King. *SNC, VYY, DVT*

Man from Button Willow 🎬🎬 1965 (G) Classic animated adventure is the story of Justin Eagle, a man who leads a double life. He is a respected rancher and a shrewd secret agent for the government, but in 1869 he suddenly finds himself the guardian of a four-year-old Oriental girl, leading him into a whole new series of adventures. Strictly for younger audiences. **79m/C VHS, Beta. M:** George Bruns; **V:** Dale Robertson, Edgar Buchanan, Barbara Jean Wong, Howard Keel. *NO*

Man from Cairo 🎬🎬 1954 An American in Algiers is mistaken for a detective in search of gold lost during WWII and decides to play along. **82m/B VHS, Beta, LV.** *IT* George Raft, Gianna Maria Canale; **D:** Ray Enright. *NO*

Man from Cheyenne 🎬 1942 Cowboy comes home to find his town under a siege of terror from a lawless gang of cattle rustlers. He gets mad and seeks some frontier justice. **54m/B VHS, Beta.** Roy Rogers, Gale Storm, George "Gabby" Hayes, Sally Payne. *NOS, DVT, RXM*

Man from Colorado 🎬🎬½ 1949 An odd Technicolor western about two Civil War vets at odds, one an honest marshall, the other a sadistic judge. Solid Western fare with a quirky performance by Ford. **99m/C VHS, Beta.** William Holden, Glenn Ford, Ellen Drew, Ray Collins, Edgar Buchanan, Jerome Courtland, James Millican, Jim Bannon; **D:** Henry Levin; **M:** George Duning. *COL*

Man from Deep River woof! 1977 (R) A photographer is captured by a savage tribe in Thailand and forced to undergo a series of grueling initiation rites. Full of very violent and sickening tortures inflicted on both human and animal victims. **90m/C VHS, Beta.** *IT* Ivan Rassimov; **D:** Umberto Lenzi. *NO*

The Man from Gun Town 🎬½ 1936 McCoy comes to the rescue of a woman who has been framed by an evil gang for the murder of her brother. **58m/B VHS.** Tim McCoy, Billie Seward, Rex

Lease, Jack Clifford, Wheeler Oakman, Bob McKenzie; **D:** Ford Beebe. *NOS, DVT*

Man from Headquarters 🎬🎬 1928 Good silent mystery in which a U.S. agent takes on a gang of foreign operatives. **?m/B VHS.** Cornelius Keefe, Edith Roberts. *SNC*

The Man from Hell 🎬 1934 Sheriff Russell goes undercover to expose the head of a gang of outlaws. Low-budget fare. **55m/C VHS.** Reb Russell, Fred Kohler Jr., Ann Darcy, George "Gabby" Hayes, Jack Rockwell, Charles French, Charles "Slim" Whitaker, Yakima Canutt; **D:** Lewis D. Collins. *DVT, HEG, GPV*

Man from Hell's Edges 🎬½ 1932 An innocent cowpoke escapes from jail and brings the real baddy to justice. **63m/B VHS, Beta.** Bob Steele, Nancy Drexel, Julian Rivero, Robert E. Homans, George "Gabby" Hayes; **D:** Robert North Bradbury. *NOS, DVT*

The Man from Laramie 🎬🎬🎬½ 1955 Aging ranch baron Alec Waggoman (Crisp), who is going blind, worries about which of his two sons he will leave the ranch to. Into this tension-filled familial atmosphere rides Lockhart (Stewart), a cow-herder obsessed with hunting down the men who sold guns to the Indians that killed his brother. Needless to say, the tension increases. Tough, surprisingly brutal western, the best of the classic Stewart-Mann films. **104m/B VHS.** James Stewart, Arthur Kennedy, Donald Crisp, Alex Nicol, Cathy O'Donnell, Aline MacMahon, Wallace Ford, Jack Elam; **D:** Anthony Mann; **W:** Philip Yordan; **C:** Charles B(ryant) Lang. *COL*

The Man from Left Field 🎬½ 1993 Homeless man winds up coaching a little league baseball team, inspiring the kids, and turning his life around. Made for TV. **96m/C VHS, Closed Caption.** Burt Reynolds, Reba McEntire; **D:** Burt Reynolds; **M:** Bobby Goldsboro. *CAF*

Man from Mallorca 🎬🎬 *Mannen fran Mallorca* 1984 Sgts. Jarnebring (Wollter) and Johansson (von Bromssen) are in pursuit of a gunman who robbed a Stockholm post office. The robber gets away and the investigation stalls until two witnesses are murdered. The detectives begin to suspect an official cover-up and think that senior police officer Hedberg (Hellberg) has something to hide. When they're taken off the case, the duo forge ahead on their own time with some disturbing results. Swedish with subtitles. **104m/C VHS.** *SW* Sven Wollter, Tomas von Bromssen, Thomas Hellberg; **D:** Bo Widerberg; **W:** Bo Widerberg; **C:** Thomas Wahlberg. *NYF*

Man from Montana 🎬½ *Montana Justice* 1941 Brown is a sheriff who battles outlaws trying to stir up trouble between ranchers and homesteaders. **56m/B VHS.** Johnny Mack Brown, Fuzzy Knight, William Gould, Kermit Maynard, Nell O'Day, Billy Lenhart, Kenneth Brown, Murdock McQuarrie, Ray Taylor. *GPV*

Man from Monterey 🎬🎬 1933 South-of-the-border Western has U.S. Army captain Wayne trying to get Mexican landowners to register their property under Spanish land grants or lose them to public domain. Wayne's last series western for Warner Bros. **59m/B VHS, Closed Caption.** John Wayne, Ruth Hall, Luis Alberni, Francis Ford, Lafe McKee, Lillian Leighton, Charles "Slim" Whitaker; **D:** Mack V. Wright; **W:** Lesley Mason. *MGM*

The Man from Music Mountain 🎬🎬 1938 Worthless mining stock is sold in a desert mining town, but Gene and Smiley clear that up, with a little singing as well. **54m/B VHS, Beta.** Gene Autry, Smiley Burnette, Carol Hughes, Polly Jenkins. *NOS, VDM, HHT*

Man from Nowhere 🎬🎬½ 1937 A henpecked man gets the break of his life when his domineering wife and mother-in-law believe he's dead. Based on the novel by Luigi Pirandello. In French with English subtitles. **98m/B VHS, Beta.** *FR* Pierre Blanchar, Ginette LeClerc; **D:** Pierre Chenal. *FCT, AUD*

The Man from Painted Post 🎬 1917
Fairbanks plays a Cattlemen's Association detective who comes to the range to stop the cattle rustlers as well as to find the man who murdered his sister. **?m/B VHS.** Douglas Fairbanks Sr., Eileen Percy, Frank Campeau, Monte Blue; *D:* Joseph Henabery. GVV

The Man from Snowy River 🎬🎬½
1982 (PG) Stunning cinematography highlights this otherwise fairly ordinary adventure story set in 1880s Australia. A young man comes of age in the outback while taming a herd of wild horses. In a dual role, Douglas portrays battling brothers, one a rich landowner and the other a one-legged prospector. Based on the epic poem by A.B. "Banjo" Paterson and followed by "Return to Snowy River Part II." A big hit in Australia and not directed by "Mad Max's" Miller, but another Miller named George. **104m/C VHS, Beta, LV, Letterbox.** AU Kirk Douglas, Tom Burlinson, Sigrid Thornton, Terence Donovan, Tommy Dysart, Jack Thompson, Bruce Kerr; *D:* George Miller. FOX, TVC, HMV

Man from Texas 🎬🎬 1939 Singing and gun-slinging Tex defends a kid accused of horse thieving until the kid turns bad and Tex must bring him in. **55m/B VHS, Beta.** Tex Ritter, Hal Price, Charles B. Wood, Vic Demourelle Sr.; *D:* Al(bert) Herman. NOS, VDM

Man from the Alamo 🎬🎬🎬 1953 A soldier sent from the Alamo during its last hours to get help is branded as a deserter, and struggles to clear his name. Well acted, this film will satisfy those with a taste for action. **79m/C VHS, Closed Caption.** Glenn Ford, Julie Adams, Chill Wills, Victor Jory, Hugh O'Brian; *D:* Budd Boetticher. USH

The Man from the Pru 🎬🎬½ 1989 Shocking 1931 murder case follows insurance agent William Wallace (Pryce) who was sentenced to hang for the murder of his wife, Julia. Wallace insisted he was called from home on a possible insurance sale and returned home to find his wife dead. His case made British legal history when the appeals court overturned the verdict. Made for TV. **90m/C VHS.** GB Jonathan Pryce, Anna Massey, Susannah York; *D:* Rob Rohrer. TVC, AEH

Man from Thunder River 🎬🎬 1943 A group of cowboys uncover a plot to steal gold ore and wind up saving a young girl's life in the process. Standard western with lots of action. **55m/B VHS, Beta.** Wild Bill Elliott, George "Gabby" Hayes, Anne Jeffreys, Ian Keith, John James; *D:* John English. DVT

The Man from U.N.C.L.E. 1964 Vaughn and McCallum star as Napoleon Solo and Illya Kuryakin, two super-cool super-agents battling the evil forces of THRUSH. The series ran from 1964-68. Two episodes per tape; additional episodes available. On this tape: "The Project Strigas Affair" has Solo and Illya against a Balkan intelligence agent. In "The Never Never Affair" an innocent translator is captured by a ruthless THRUSH operator who's after some valuable microfilm. **110m/B VHS, Beta.** Robert Vaughn, David McCallum, Leo G. Carroll, Leonard Nimoy, William Shatner, Barbara Feldon, Cesar Romero. MGM, MOV

Man from Utah 🎬½ 1934 The Duke tangles with the crooked sponsor of some rodeo events who has killed several of the participants. Also available with "Blue Steel" on laserdisc. **55m/B VHS, Beta, LV.** John Wayne, George "Gabby" Hayes, Polly Ann Young, Yakima Canutt, Lafe McKee; *D:* Robert North Bradbury. COL, NOS, MRV

The Man I Love 🎬🎬🎬 1946 Slick drama about nightclub singer Lupino falling for no-good mobster Alda. Enjoyable and well-acted, although script doesn't make sense. Great selection of tunes. This film inspired Scorsese's "New York, New York." Based on the novel "Night Shift" by Maritta Wolff. ♫Body and Soul; Why Was I Born; Bill; The Man I Love; Liza; If I Could Be With You. **96m/B VHS, Closed Caption.** Ida Lupino, Robert Alda, Andrea King, Martha Vickers, Bruce (Herman Brix) Bennett, Alan Hale, Dolores Moran, John Ridgely, Don McGuire, Warren Douglas, Craig Stevens; *D:* Raoul Walsh, John

Maxwell; *W:* Catherine Turney, Jo Pagano; *M:* Max Steiner. MGM, FCT

The Man in Grey 🎬🎬🎬 1945 In a story of romantic intrigue set in 19th-century England, a Marquis's wife is betrayed by her vile husband and the schoolmate she once befriended who has an affair with him. Stunning costumes and fine performances compensate for the overly extravagant production values in a work that helped bring stardom to Mason. **116m/B VHS, Beta.** GB James Mason, Margaret Lockwood, Stewart Granger, Phyllis Calvert; *D:* Leslie Arliss. NO

A Man in Love 🎬🎬🎬 Un Homme Amoureux **1987 (R)** An international romantic melodrama set during the Italian filming of a biography of suicidal author Cesar Pavese. The self-important lead actor and a beautiful supporting actress (Coyote and Scacchi) become immersed in the roles and fall madly in love, oblivious to the fact that Coyote is married and Scacchi's engaged. The two make a steamy pair, to the detriment of friends, family, and the movie they're making. Kurys' first English-language film is visually appealing with a lush, romantic score, seamlessly weaving the story lines among vivid characters. **110m/C VHS, Beta, LV.** FR Peter Coyote, Greta Scacchi, Jamie Lee Curtis, Peter Riegert, Jean Pigozzi, John Berry, Claudia Cardinale, Vincent Lindon; *D:* Diane Kurys; *W:* Diane Kurys, Olivier Schatzky, Israel Horovitz; *M:* Georges Delerue. COL

The Man in the Attic 🎬½ 1994 (R) Harris certainly leaves his "Doogie Howser" past behind as he takes a grownup turn in an erotic thriller based on a true case history from the early 20th century, gathered from the book "Sex and the Criminal Mind." Teenaged Edward (Harris) has a blazing affair with married, mature Krista (Archer), who does indeed hide her young lover in the family attic when her clueless husband (Cariou) returns home at night. But such consuming passion can hardly be kept a secret for long—and takes a decidedly deadly turn. Made for cable. *CW:* Sexuality and a murder scene. **97m/C VHS, Beta, Closed Caption.** Anne Archer, Neil Patrick Harris, Len Cariou, Alex Carter; *D:* Graeme Campbell; *W:* Duane Poole, Tom Swale; *M:* Lou Natale. PAR

The Man in the Glass Booth 🎬🎬🎬 **1975 (PG)** In this adaptation of a play written by actor Robert Shaw, a successful Jewish businessman is suspected of being a Nazi war criminal. Loosely based on the life of death camp commandant Otto Adolf Eichmann, the film depicts the arrest and subsequent trial of the former Nazi by the Israelis. The film's title is derived from the fact that Eichmann sat in a glass booth during his trial. Schell's performance is outstanding. **117m/C VHS.** Maximilian Schell, Lois Nettleton, Luther Adler, Lawrence Pressman, Henry Brown, Richard Rasof; *D:* Arthur Hiller; *W:* Edward Anhalt; *C:* Sam Leavitt. Nominations: Academy Awards '75: Best Actor (Schell).NO

The Man in the Gray Flannel Suit 🎬🎬½ 1956 A very long and serious adaptation of the Sloan Wilson novel about a Madison Avenue advertising exec trying to balance his life between work and family. The Hollywood treatment falls short of the adaptation potential of the original story. **152m/C VHS, Beta, LV, Closed Caption.** Gregory Peck, Fredric March, Jennifer Jones, Ann Harding, Arthur O'Connell, Henry Daniell, Lee J. Cobb, Marisa Pavan, Gene Lockhart, Keenan Wynn, Gigi Perreau, Joseph Sweeney, Kenneth Tobey, DeForest Kelley; *D:* Nunnally Johnson. FXL

The Man in the Iron Mask 🎬🎬🎬 **1939** Swashbuckling tale about twin brothers separated at birth. One turns out to be King Louis XIV of France, and the other a carefree wanderer and friend of the Three Musketeers. Their eventual clash leads to action-packed adventure and royal revenge. Remake of the "The Iron Mask" (1929) with Douglas Fairbanks. Remade for television in 1977 with Richard Chamberlain. **110m/B VHS, Beta.** Louis Hayward, Alan Hale, Joan Bennett, Warren William, Joseph Schildkraut, Walter Kingsford, Marion Martin; *D:*

James Whale. Nominations: Academy Awards '39: Best Original Score. CCB

The Man in the Iron Mask 🎬🎬🎬 **1977** A tyrannical French king kidnaps his twin brother and imprisons him on a remote island. Chamberlain, the king of the miniseries, is excellent in a dual role in this big production swashbuckler. Adapted from the Dumas classic. Made for television. **105m/C VHS, Beta, Closed Caption.** Richard Chamberlain, Patrick McGoohan, Louis Jourdan, Jenny Agutter, Ian Holm, Ralph Richardson; *D:* Mike Newell. ART, FUS, FOX

The Man in the Iron Mask 🎬½ **1997** Low-budget, personalized version of the Dumas swashbuckler from director Richert, which he filmed at the historic Mission Inn in Riverside, CA. Prologue establishes the birth of twin royals to the French Queen (Foster) and the fate of Philippe (Richert's son Nick) as the man in the iron mask. A deathbed confession to Count Aramis (the director himself) alerts the Musketeers, who decide to set things right. Well-intentioned but not a lot of fun. **85m/C VHS.** William Richert, Edward Albert, Rex Ryon, Timothy Bottoms, Dennis Hayden, Nick Richert, Meg Foster, James Gammon, Dana Barron, Brigid Brannah, Fannie Brett; *D:* William Richert; *W:* William Richert; *C:* William Barber; *M:* Jim Ervin. MON

The Man in the Iron Mask 🎬🎬🎬 **1998 (PG-13)** Lavish retelling of Alexandre Dumas's classic story boasts a stellar cast with teen heartthrob DiCaprio in a dual role. Snotty tyrant King Louis XIV's (DiCaprio) lust for women inadvertently leads to the reunion of the retired Musketeers, bent on replacing cold Louis with his more sensitive twin brother Philippe (DiCaprio, again), an inmate of the Bastille and hidden behind a ghastly mask. Irons, Malkovich, Depardieu, and Byrne bring a welcome seriousness and style to the often-told story as the older, jaded Musketeers, while DiCaprio holds his own in the presence of such formidable company. Although first-time director Wallace doesn't balance the star power with enough swordplay, the high gloss production provides old-fashioned escapist entertainment. *CW:* Sequences of violence and some sensuality/nudity. **132m/C VHS, DVD.** Leonardo DiCaprio, Gabriel Byrne, Jeremy Irons, John Malkovich, Gerard Depardieu, Anne Parillaud, Judith Godreche, Edward Atterton, Peter Sarsgaard, Hugh Laurie; *D:* Randall Wallace; *W:* Randall Wallace; *C:* Peter Suschitzsky; *M:* Nick Glennie-Smith. MGM

The Man in the Mist 1983 Private investigators Tommy and Tuppence Beresford find themselves trying to solve a murder while on vacation in a provincial hotel. Made for British television and based upon the Agatha Christie story. **51m/C VHS, Beta.** GB Francesca Annis, James Warwick. TPV

The Man in the Moon 🎬🎬🎬½ 1991 **(PG-13)** Beautifully rendered coming-of-age tale. On a farm outside a small Louisiana town in the 1950s, 14-year-old Dani wonders if she will ever be as pretty and popular as her 17-year-old sister Maureen. This becomes especially important as Dani is beginning to notice boys, particularly Court, the 17-year-old young man she meets when swimming. Although Dani and Maureen have always been especially close, a rift develops between the sisters after Court meets Maureen. Intelligently written, excellent direction, lovely cinematography, and exceptional acting make this a particularly worthwhile and entertaining film. **100m/C VHS, Closed Caption.** Reese Witherspoon, Emily Warfield, Jason London, Tess Harper, Sam Waterston, Gail Strickland; *D:* Robert Mulligan. MGM

The Man in the Raincoat 🎬🎬 1957 French film about a bumbling clarinet player who is erroneously tracked down as a murderer. Strenuous efforts to evoke laughter usually fail. Dubbed. **97m/B VHS, Beta, 8mm.** FR Fernandel, John McGiver, Bernard Blier; *D:* Julien Duvivier. VYY

Man in the Saddle 🎬🎬½ *The Outcast* 1951 Western star Scott gets roped in a romantic triangle out on the range, leading to some exciting gunplay. As usual, justice triumphs in this above average oater. Based on the novel by Ernest Haycox. **87m/C VHS.** Randolph Scott, Joan Leslie, Ellen Drew, Alexander Knox, Richard Rober, John Russell; **D:** Andre de Toth; **W:** Kenneth Gamet. *COL*

The Man in the Santa Claus Suit 🎬🎬 1979 A costume shop owner has an effect on three people who rent Santa Claus costumes from him. Astaire plays seven different roles in this made for television film. Average holiday feel-good movie. **96m/C VHS, Beta.** Fred Astaire, Gary Burghoff, John Byner, Nanette Fabray, Bert Convy; **D:** Corey Allen.

Man in the Shadow 🎬🎬½ 1957 Sheriff Ben Sadler (Chandler) is the only man in the county willing to stand up to wealthy Texas rancher Virgil Renchler (Welles). Sadler suspects Renchler is behind the brutal death of a Mexican laborer but gets no support when he tries to find justice. **80m/C VHS, Closed Caption.** Jeff Chandler, Orson Welles, Colleen Miller, John Larch, James Gleason, Barbara Lawrence, Royal Dano, Paul Fix, William Schallert; **D:** Jack Arnold; **W:** Gene L. Coon; **C:** Arthur E. Arling; **M:** Joseph Gershenson. *USH*

Man in the Silk Hat 🎬🎬 1915 A collection of the nearly forgotten French comic's early silent comedy shorts, made in France before his resettlement in America. **96m/B VHS, Beta.** *FR* Max Linder; **D:** Maud Linder. *NO*

Man in the Silk Hat 🎬🎬🎬 1983 Gabriel-Maximilien Leuvielle, known in films as Max Linder, is now credited with developing the style of silent-movie slapstick comedy that Mack Sennett, Charlie Chaplin, and others became more famous for in their time. Here, Linder's daughter has done a fine job writing and directing a film full of historic footage of her father's work. **99m/B VHS, Beta.** Mack Sennett, Buster Keaton, Charlie Chaplin, Max Linder. *XVC*

The Man in the White Suit 🎬🎬🎬½ 1951 A humble laboratory assistant in a textile mill invents a white cloth that won't stain, tear, or wear out, and can't be dyed. The panicked garment industry sets out to destroy him and the fabric, resulting in some sublimely comic situations and a variety of inventive chases. Also available with "Lavender Hill Mob" on laserdisc. **82m/B VHS.** *GB* Alec Guinness, Joan Greenwood; **D:** Alexander MacKendrick. Nominations: Academy Awards '52: Best Screenplay. *REP, HMV*

Man in the Wilderness 🎬🎬½ 1971 (PG) Harris is part of an expedition traveling through the Northwest Territory. He's mauled by a grizzly and left for dead by leader Huston. While Harris fights for survival, he also plots revenge. Blood and violence is somewhat offset by good lead performances. **108m/C VHS.** Richard Harris, John Huston, Henry Wilcoxon, Percy Herbert, Dennis Waterman, Prunella Ransome, Norman Rossington, James Doohan; **D:** Richard Sarafian; **W:** Jack DeWitt; **M:** Johnny Harris. *WAR*

A Man in Uniform 🎬🎬 *I Love a Man in Uniform* 1993 (R) A look at the making of a sociopath. Henry (McCamus) is a quiet bank employee who moonlights as an actor. Then he gets his big break in the role of a self-righteous cop in a TV series. Only the lines between his make-believe cop and the real world begin to blur and Henry's intensity turns to violence. Fine performances lead to an unsatisfying film conclusion. **99m/C VHS.** *CA* Tom McCamus, Brigitte Bako, Kevin Tighe, David Hemblen, Alex Karzis, Graham McPherson; **D:** David Wellington; **W:** David Wellington. Genie Awards '93: Best Actor (McCamus), Best Supporting Actor (Tighe). *APX*

The Man Inside 🎬½ 1976 Undercover agent infiltrates a powerful underworld narcotics ring and finds his honesty tested when $2 million is at stake. **96m/C VHS, Beta.** *CA* James Franciscus, Stefanie Powers, Jacques Godin; **D:** Gerald Mayer. *TWE*

The Man Inside 🎬🎬 1990 (PG) Lukewarm Cold War saga based on the true story of Gunther Wallraff, a West German journalist who risked all to expose the corruption behind a large European newspaper. **93m/C VHS, LV.** *NL GE* Juergen Prochnow, Peter Coyote, Nathalie Baye, Dieter Laser, Monique Van De Ven, Sylvie Granotier; **D:** Bobby Roth; **W:** Bobby Roth. *COL*

Man Is Not a Bird 🎬🎬½ 1965 Follows the destructive love of a factory engineer and a hairdresser in a small Yugoslavian mining town. In Serbian with English subtitles. **80m/B VHS, Beta.** *YU* Eva Ras, Milena Dravic, Janez Urhovec; **D:** Dusan Makavejev; **W:** Dusan Makavejev. *FCT*

A Man Like Eva 🎬🎬🎬 *Ein Mann wie Eva* 1983 A weird, morbid homage to and portrait of Rainer Werner Fassbinder after his inevitable death, detailing his work-obsessed self-destruction. Mattes, one of Fassbinder's favorite actresses, plays him in drag, in an eerie gender-crossing transformation. In German with English subtitles. **92m/C VHS, Beta.** *GE* Eva Mattes, Elisabeth Kreuzer, Charles Regnier, Werner Stocker; **D:** Radu Gabrea. *FCT, GLV, CCN*

Man Made Monster 🎬🎬½ *Atomic Monster; The Electric Man* 1941 Chaney stars as carnival performer "Dynamo" Dan McCormick, whose act has caused Dan to build up an immunity to electrical charges. Dan falls prey to the mad Dr. Rigas (Atwill) who seeks to create a race of electro-men who'll do his bidding. Experiments on the hapless Dan turn him into a glowing monster whose very touch can kill. Chaney's first role in the horror genre led to Universal's casting him in "The Wolf Man" and "The Ghost of Frankenstein." **61m/B VHS, Closed Caption.** Lon Chaney Jr., Lionel Atwill, Anne Nagel, Frank Albertson, Samuel S. Hinds; **D:** George Waggner; **W:** Joseph West; **C:** Elwood Bredell. *USH*

Man of a Thousand Faces 🎬🎬🎬½ 1957 A tasteful and touching portrayal of Lon Chaney, from his childhood with his deaf and mute parents to his success as a screen star. Recreates some of Chaney's most famous roles, including the Phantom of the Opera and Quasimodo in "Notre Dame." Cagney is magnificent as the long-suffering film star who was a genius with makeup and mime. **122m/B VHS, LV, Letterbox.** James Cagney, Dorothy Malone, Jane Greer, Marjorie Rambeau, Jim Backus, Roger Smith, Robert Evans; **D:** Joseph Pevney; **W:** Ivan Goff; **C:** Russell Metty. Nominations: Academy Awards '57: Best Story & Screenplay. *USH*

Man of Action 🎬½ 1933 Texas Ranger McCoy is out to solve the mystery of what happened to money, recovered from a robbery, which has vanished once again. **56m/B VHS.** Tim McCoy, Wheeler Oakman, Walter Brennan, Stanley Blystone, Charles French; **D:** George Melford. *GPV*

Man of Aran 🎬🎬🎬 1934 Celebrated account of a fisherman's struggle for survival on a barren island near the west coast of Ireland, featuring amateur actors. Three years in the making, it's the last word in man against nature cinema, and a visual marvel. A former explorer, Flaherty became an influential documentarian. Having first gained fame with "Nanook of the North," he compiled an opus of documentaries made for commercial release. **132m/B VHS.** **D:** Robert Flaherty. *HMV, GVV*

Man of Destiny 🎬🎬½ 1973 Bonaparte (Keach) and a mysterious woman battle good-humoredly over a collection of love letters. From a Bernard Shaw story. Charming and well-acted. **60m/C VHS, Beta.** Stacy Keach, Samantha Eggar. *NO*

Man of Evil 🎬🎬 *Fanny by Gaslight* 1948 The hard times of the illegitimate daughter of a member of the British Parliament in the early 1900s, told with an astonishing number of plot twists and a plodding melodramtic style. Based on the novel "Fanny by Gaslight." **108m/B VHS.** *GB* Phyllis Calvert, James Mason, Wilfred Lawson, Stewart Granger, Margaretta Scott, Jean Kent, John Laurie, Stuart Lindsell, Nora Swinburne, Amy Veness, Ann Wilton, Helen Haye, Cathleen Nesbitt, Guy le Feuvre, John Turnbull, Peter Jones; **D:** Anthony Asquith. *FCT*

Man of Flowers 🎬🎬½ 1984 Because of his puritan upbringing, a reclusive art collector has trouble coping with his feelings of sexuality. He pays a woman to disrobe in front of him, but is never able to bring himself to see her naked. A moody piece with overtones of black humor, this work has limited audience appeal. **91m/C VHS, Beta, LV.** *AU* Norman Kaye, Alyson Best, Chris Haywood, Sarah Walker, Julia Blake, Bob Ellis, Werner Herzog; **D:** Paul Cox; **W:** Bob Ellis, Paul Cox. Australian Film Institute '83: Best Actor (Kaye). *ART, VES*

Man of Iron 🎬🎬🎬 *Czlowiek z Zelaza* 1981 (PG) Director Wajda's follow-up to "Man of Marble" deals with a reporter (Odania) who is expected to tow the government line when writing about the Gdansk shipyard strike of 1980. He meets the harassed laborer son (Radziwilowicz) of worker-hero Birkut, against whom Odania is expected to conduct a smear campaign, and finds his loyalties tested. In Polish with English subtitles. **116m/C VHS.** *PL* Jerzy Radziwilowicz, Marian Opania, Krystyna Janda; **D:** Andrzej Wajda; **W:** Aleksander Scibor-Rylski; **M:** Andrzej Korzynski. Cannes Film Festival '81: Best Film; Nominations: Academy Awards '81: Best Foreign Language Film. *MGM*

Man of La Mancha 🎬½ 1972 (PG) Arrested by the Inquisition and thrown into prison, Miguel de Cervantes relates the story of Don Quixote. Not nearly as good as the Broadway musical it is based on. ♫It's All the Same; The Impossible Dream; Barber's Song; Man of La Mancha; Dulcinea; I'm Only Thinking of Him; Little Bird, Little Bird; Life as It Really Is; The Dubbing. **129m/C VHS, Beta, LV.** Peter O'Toole, Sophia Loren, James Coco, Harry Andrews, John Castle, Brian Blessed; **D:** Arthur Hiller. National Board of Review Awards '72: Best Actor (O'Toole); Nominations: Academy Awards '72: Original Song Score and/or Adaptation. *FOX, FCT*

Man of Legend 🎬🎬 1971 (PG) An adventure-romance filmed in Morocco; a WWI German soldier flees to the Foreign Legion and fights with nomadic rebels, ultimately falling in love with their chief's beautiful daughter. An unoriginal desert saga. **95m/C VHS, Beta.** *IT SP* Peter Strauss, Tina Aumont, Pier Paola Capponi; **D:** Sergio Grieco. *NO*

Man of Marble 🎬🎬🎬 1976 A satire on life in post-WWII Poland. A young filmmaker sets out to tell the story of a bricklayer who, because of his exceptional skill, once gained popularity with other workers. He became a champion for worker rights, only to then find himself being persecuted by the government. The conclusion was censored by the Polish government. Highly acclaimed and followed by "Man of Iron" in 1981. In Polish with English subtitles. **160m/C VHS.** *PL* Krystyna Janda, Jerzy Radziwilowicz, Tadeusz Lomnicki, Jacek Lomnicki, Krystyna Zachwatowicz; **D:** Andrzej Wajda; **W:** Aleksander Scibor-Rylski; **M:** Andrzej Korzynski. *NYF, FCT*

A Man of No Importance 🎬🎬🎬 1994 (R) Touching and entertaining saga of lovable Alfie Byrne (Finney), a 1960s Dublin bus conductor with a passion for the work of Oscar Wilde, who successfully represses his own homosexuality. He also moonlights as director of a community theatre, where he sets out to produce Wilde's controversial play "Salome" starring fetching new bus passenger Adele (Fitzgerald), who further confuses Alfie's take on his identity. Finney is both delightful and heartbreaking in this character study of an innocent soul whose life is tested by the social code of his day. Equally affecting and charming supporting performances round out this witty but sad tale.**CW:** Contains a nude scene, some violence, and complex adult themes. **98m/C VHS, LV, Closed Caption.** *GB* Albert Finney, Brenda Fricker, Michael Gambon, Tara Fitzgerald, Rufus Sewell, Patrick Malahide, David Kelly; **D:** Suri Krishnamma; **W:** Barry Devlin; **M:** Julian Nott. *COL*

A Man of Passion ⅃⅃ 199? (R) Quinn plays an aging artist living pleasurably on a Mediterranean isle. His summer guest is his uptight grandson, a classical pianist. Naturally, Gramps is about to teach the kid to loosen up, including appreciating one of his lovely artist's models. Another variation for Quinn on his "Zorba" personality but it works. **90m/C VHS.** Anthony Quinn, Ramon Sheen, Maud Adams, Elizabeth Ashley, R.J. Williams, Ray Walston, Victoria Vera; **D:** J. Anthony Loma; **W:** J. Anthony Loma. *ATV*

Man of the Forest ⅃⅃ 1933 A cowboy goes to the aid of a damsel in distress and he winds up being framed for murder for his efforts. Based on Zane Grey's novel. **59m/B VHS.** Randolph Scott, Verna Hillie, Harry Carey Sr., Noah Beery Sr., Barton MacLane; **D:** Henry Hathaway. *NOS, DVT, MLB*

Man of the House ⅃⅃ 1995 (PG) Kids' comedy about a boy's scheme to sabotage his mother's new love interest. Ben (Thomas) concocts a plan to join the YMCA Indian Guides to discourage daddy wannabe Jack (Chase), while mom (Fawcett) stands idly by tolerating her son's bratty behavior. Subplot involves a screwy gangster theme that deteriorates into a "Home Aloneish" ending. Film attempts to play off of Chase's knack for physical comedy, but falls short. And what's with the mime? Wendt is amusing as the Indian Guide leader. Will probably appeal more to younger crowds as Thomas' scheming teen upstages Chase's deadpan dad-to-be. **97m/C VHS, LV, Closed Caption.** Chevy Chase, Farrah Fawcett, Jonathan Taylor Thomas, George Wendt, David Shiner, Art LaFleur, Richard Portnow, Richard Foronjy, Spencer Vrooman, John Disanti, Chief Leonard George, Peter Appel, George Greif, Chris Miranda, Ron Canada, Zachary Browne, Nicholas Garrett; **D:** James Orr; **W:** James Orr, Jim Cruickshank; **C:** Jamie Anderson; **M:** Mark Mancina. *DIS*

Man of the West ⅃⅃½ 1958 Reformed bad guy Cooper is asked to deliver a tidy hunk of cash to another city to recruit a school marm. Ambushed en route by his former partners in crime (who are led by his wacko uncle) he's forced to revert to his wanton ways in order to survive and save innocent hostages. There's a raging debate among Cooper fans whether this late effort has been unduly overlooked or duly ignored. A number of things conspire to give it a bad rap: Cooper does little but look mournful until the very end; there's no hiding the fact that he's older than Cobb, who plays his uncle; and the acting is in general more befitting of a B-grade slice and dicer. You be the judge. **100m/C VHS, Beta, Closed Caption.** Gary Cooper, Julie London, Lee J. Cobb, Arthur O'Connell, Jack Lord, John Dehner, Royal Dano, Guy Wilkerson, Emory Parnell; **D:** Anthony Mann; **W:** Reginald Rose. *MGM, FCT*

Man of Violence ⅃ *The Sex Racketeers* 1971 A vulgar, tasteless man spends the worthless hours of his wasted life lurking about the more wretched entrance-ways of his native land. **107m/C VHS, Beta.** Michael Latimer, Luan Peters; **D:** Pete Walker. *NO*

Man on a String ⅃⅃½ 1971 (PG) In order to bring down a Mob boss the feds first frame cop Peter King and send him to the pen. When he gets out, King uses his prison contacts to get in with the Mob and winds up pitting two rival gangs against each other in order to destroy them both. Made for television. **73m/C VHS.** Christopher George, Jack Warden, Keith Carradine, Joel Grey, William Schallert, Kitty Winn; **D:** Joseph Sargent. *COL*

Man on Fire ⅃ 1987 (R) Told via flashback, a cynical ex-CIA man is hired as a bodyguard for the daughter of a wealthy Italian couple, who is soon thereafter kidnapped by terrorists. He goes to her rescue with all the subtlety of a wrecking ball. Decent cast goes down the tubes in this botched thriller. **92m/C VHS, Beta, LV.** FR Scott Glenn, Brooke Adams, Danny Aiello, Joe Pesci, Paul Shenar, Jonathan Pryce, Jade Malle; **D:** Elie Chouraqui. *ART, VES*

The Man on the Box ⅃⅃½ 1925 Chaplin is a wealthy bachelor who takes a job as a gardener to be near his girl. He overhears a plot by the butler, who's an enemy agent, to steal the secret plans for a helicopter from his sweetie's father. In order to thwart the dastardedly scheme Chaplin dresses as a maid to infiltrate the household. **58m/B VHS.** Sydney Chaplin, David Butler, Alice Calhoun, Kathleen Calhoun, Helene Costello, Theodore Lorch; **D:** Charles F. Reisner. *GPV, GVV*

Man on the Eiffel Tower ⅃⅃⅃ 1948 Laughton plays Inspector Maigret, the detective created by novelist Georges Simenon, in a highly suspenseful and cerebral mystery about a crazed killer who defies the police to discover his identity. This is the first film Meredith directed. **82m/C VHS, Beta.** Charles Laughton, Burgess Meredith, Franchot Tone, Patricia Roc; **D:** Burgess Meredith. *NOS, MRV, GEM*

The Man on the Roof ⅃⅃ *Manen Pa Taket* 1976 A police officer, who's been accused of brutality, is murdered and Martin Beck (Lindstedt) and his colleagues are called in to investigate. Then someone climbs a roof in central Stockholm and begins killing policemen with a rifle. Turns out the cases are related and involve an ex-cop named Eriksson (Hirdwall). Based on the novel "The Abominable Man" by Maj Sjowall and Per Wahloo. Swedish with subtitles. **110m/C VHS.** SW Carl Gustav Lindstedt, Ingvar Hirdwall, Sven Wollter, Thomas Heelberg; **D:** Bo Widerberg; **W:** Bo Widerberg; **C:** Odd Geir Saether, Per Kallberg. *NYF*

Man on the Run ⅃⅃ 1949 A robbery takes place in the store where an Army deserter is trying to sell his gun, and he ends up taking the rap. It's up to a lovely lady lawyer to prove his innocence. Efficiently told "B" crime drama. **82m/B VHS, Beta.** GB Derek Farr, Joan Hopkins, Edward Chapman, Laurence Harvey, H. Marion Crawford, Alfie Bass, John Bailey, John Stuart, Edward Underdown, Leslie Perrins, Kenneth More, Martin Miller, Eleanor Summerfield; **D:** Lawrence Huntington; **W:** Lawrence Huntington. *SNC*

Man on the Run ⅃½ 1974 (R) After an unwitting involvement with a small robbery, a teenager finds himself the object of a police manhunt for a murder suspect. **90m/C VHS, Beta.** Kyle Johnson, James B. Sikking, Terry Carter; **D:** Herbert L. Strock.

Man or Gun ⅃½ 1958 Standard western yarn involving a drifter who rides into a town operated by a powerful family and liberates the cowardly townsfolk. **79m/B VHS.** MacDonald Carey, Audrey Totter, James Craig, James Gleason, Warren Stevens, Harry Shannon; **D:** Albert C. Gannaway; **W:** Vance Skarstedt, James C. Cassity. *MOV*

The Man Outside ⅃⅃ 1968 (R) After a CIA agent is fired for allegedly assisting another agent in defecting to the East, he becomes involved in further intrigue. A Russian spy is looking to defect. In the process, the ex-agent is framed for murder. Straightforward espionage tale taken from Gene Stackleborg's novel "Double Agent." **98m/C VHS.** GB Van Heflin, Heidelinde Weis, Pinkas Braun, Peter Vaughan, Charles Gray, Ronnie Barker; **D:** Samuel Gallu. *NO*

Man Outside ⅃ 1988 (PG-13) Logan is an ex-lawyer who takes to the Arkansas outback after his wife dies. Anthropologist/teacher Quinlan takes a shine to him. He seems like an okay guy, but bad guy Dillman has made it look like he's a child snatcher. Slick on the outside but empty inside independent effort. Look for former members of The Band in supporting roles. **109m/C VHS, LV.** Robert F. Logan, Kathleen Quinlan, Bradford Dillman, Rick Danko, Levon Helm; **D:** Mark Stouffer. *NO*

The Man They Could Not Hang ⅃⅃½ 1939 A good doctor tinkering with artificial hearts is caught by police while experimenting on a willing student. When the doctor is convicted and hanged for a murder, his assistant uses the heart to bring him back to life. No longer a nice guy, he vows revenge against the jurors that sentenced him. Karloff repeated the same story line in several films, and this one is representative of the type. **70m/B VHS, Beta.** Boris Karloff, Adrian Booth, Roger Pryor, Robert Wilcox; **D:** Nick Grinde. *GKK*

Man Trouble ⅃⅃ 1992 (PG-13) A divorcing opera singer (Barkin) seeks the help of a sleazy attack-dog trainer (Nicholson) when she becomes the victim of a stalker. Nicholson hits on her, first because that's one of his habits, and then because he is being paid to by a billionaire who wants him to steal the manuscript of a tell-all book about her written by Barkin's sister. Although both Nicholson and Barkin are excellent actors, they lack the electricity to make the romance credible, and the jokes are weak. Supporting cast, including D'Angelo, Stanton, and McKean, provide the funny parts in this otherwise dull film. **100m/C VHS, LV, Letterbox, Closed Caption.** Jack Nicholson, Ellen Barkin, Harry Dean Stanton, Beverly D'Angelo, Michael McKean, Saul Rubinek, Viveka Davis, Veronica Cartwright, David Clennon, John Kapelos, Paul Mazursky; **D:** Bob Rafelson; **W:** Adrien (Carole Eastman) Joyce; **C:** Stephen Burum; **M:** Georges Delerue. *FXV*

The Man Upstairs ⅃⅃½ 1993 Escaped con Moony Polaski (O'Neal) hides out in the home of crotchety spinster Victoria Brown (Hepburn). When she finds the crook in her attic, instead of turning him in, Victoria befriends the slob and soon the two are sharing dinner and secrets. Meanwhile, the manhunt for Moony is intensifying and, oh yes, Christmas is coming as well. Made for television cornpone barely saved by some professional performances. Executive producer Burt Reynolds was hoping for a part until scheduling made it impossible. **95m/C VHS, Closed Caption.** Katharine Hepburn, Ryan O'Neal, Henry Beckman, Helen Carroll, Brenda Forbes; **D:** George Schaefer; **W:** James Prideaux. *CAF*

The Man Who Broke 1,000 Chains ⅃⅃ 1987 A made-for-television movie about a man who is committed to a chain gang after WWII for a petty crime, and his efforts, after escaping, in making a new life for himself. An unimaginative plot is occasionally highlighted by a good scene or two. **113m/C VHS, Beta.** Val Kilmer, Charles Durning, Sonia Braga; **D:** Daniel Mann; **M:** Charles Bernstein. *ORI, WAR*

The Man Who Came to Dinner ⅃⅃⅃½ 1941 Based on the Moss Hart-George S. Kaufman play, this comedy is about a bitter radio celebrity (Woolley) on a lecture tour (a character based on Alexander Woolcott). He breaks his hip and must stay in a quiet suburban home for the winter. While there, he occupies his time by barking orders, being obnoxious and generally just driving the other residents nuts. Woolley reprises his Broadway role in this film that succeeds at every turn, loaded with plenty of satiric jabs at the Algonquin Hotel Roundtable regulars. **112m/B VHS, Beta, LV.** Monty Woolley, Bette Davis, Ann Sheridan, Jimmy Durante, Reginald Gardiner, Richard Travis, Billie Burke, Grant Mitchell, Mary Wickes, George Barbier, Ruth Vivian, Elisabeth Fraser; **D:** William Keighley; **W:** Julius J. Epstein, Philip C. Epstein; **C:** Gaetano Antonio "Tony" Gaudio. *MGM*

The Man Who Captured Eichmann ⅃⅃½ 1996 In 1960 Israeli Mossad agents prepare to capture Adolf Eichmann (Duvall), who organized the transport of millions of Jews to the concentration camps, from his home in Argentina. Peter Malkin (Howard), the agent responsible for the kidnapping, holds Eichmann in a Buenos Aires safe house before smuggling him into Israel as Eichmann tries to ingratiate himself with Malkin, refusing to accept responsiblity and constantly maintaining his innocence. Cable movie based on the book "Eichmann In My Hands" by Peter Z. Malkin and Harry Stein. **96m/C VHS, Closed Caption.** Robert Duvall, Arliss Howard, Jeffrey Tambor, Jack Laufer, Nicolas Surovy, Joel Brooks, Sam Robards, Michael Tucci; **D:** William A. Graham; **W:** Lionel Chetwynd; **C:** Robert Steadman; **M:** Laurence Rosenthal. *WAR*

The Man Who Could Work Miracles 🎬🎬🎬½ 1937

A mild-mannered draper's assistant becomes suddenly endowed with supernatural powers to perform any feat he wishes. Great special effects (for an early film) and fine performances result in a classic piece of science fiction. **82m/B VHS, Beta, LV.** Ralph Richardson, Joan Gardner, Roland Young; **D:** Lothar Mendes.

The Man Who Cried 🎬🎬½ 1993

Abel Mason (Hinds) is an unhappily married man with a vindictive wife (Walsh) and a young son he's desperate to provide for. When an affair with a married woman ends in murder, Mason and his son travel in search of a new life. Desperate for a home, Mason enters into a bigamous marriage with a widow—only to find himself falling in love with her sister. Based on the novel by Catherine Cookson. Set in the years between England's depression and WW2. **156m/C VHS.** GB Ciaran Hinds, Amanda Root, Kate Buffery, Angela Walsh. VCO, FCT

The Man Who Envied Women 🎬½ 1985

The non-narrative feminist story of a smug womanizer: the man "who knows almost too much about women." **125m/C VHS, Beta.** Bill Raymond, Larry Loonin, Trisha Brown; **D:** Yvonne Rainer; **W:** Yvonne Rainer. NO

The Man Who Fell to Earth 🎬🎬🎬½ 1976 (R)

Entertaining and technically adept cult classic about a man from another planet (Bowie, in a bit of typecasting) who ventures to earth in hopes of finding water to save his family and drought-stricken planet. Instead he becomes a successful inventor and businessman, along the way discovering the human vices of booze, sex, and television. Also available in a restored version at 138 minutes. Remade for television in 1987 and based on Walter Tevis' novel. **118m/C VHS, Beta, LV, Letterbox.** GB David Bowie, Candy Clark, Rip Torn, Buck Henry, Bernie Casey; **D:** Nicolas Roeg. COL

The Man Who Guards the Greenhouse 1988

Tracy must come to terms with her attraction for Jeff as well as once again trying to write a meaningful novel. **150m/C VHS.** Christopher Cazenove, Rebecca Dewey. ORI

Man Who Had Power Over Women 🎬🎬 1970 (R)

Disappointing sex farce about the exploits of a carnally insatiable (and married) talent executive (Taylor) who has an affair with every woman he meets and creates problems aplenty. Adapted from a novel by Gordon Williams. **89m/C VHS, Beta.** GB Rod Taylor, James Booth, Carol White, Penelope Horner, Clive Francis; **D:** John Krish; **W:** Chris Bryant, Allan Scott.

The Man Who Haunted Himself 🎬🎬 1970

While a man lies in critical condition on the operating table after a car accident, his alter-ego emerges and turns his ideal life into a nightmare until the man recovers and moves toward a fateful encounter. An expanded version of an episode of the television series "Alfred Hitchcock Presents," this was Moore's first movie after having starred in the TV series "The Saint," and it was Dearden's last film; he died in a car accident the following year. Appeals primarily to those fascinated by "Hitchcock" or "The Twilight Zone"—where mystery matters most. Filmed in London. **94m/C VHS, Closed Caption.** GB Roger Moore, Hildegarde Neil, Olga Georges-Picot; **D:** Basil Dearden. REP, FCT

The Man Who Knew Too Little 🎬🎬½ 1997 (PG)

Watch That Man Wallace (Murray), a video store clerk from Iowa, travels to London in order to surprise his yuppie brother James (Gallagher) on his birthday. James is hosting an important dinner party, however, so he sends his less than upper-crusty brother to the Theater of Life, where the patrons take part in scenes with actors in real-life settings. Unbeknownst to Wallace, the designated call to start the play is intended for a real hit man, and he is thrown into a plot to rekindle the Cold War. Totally oblivious to the danger he is in, he treats every threat and tense situation with a sly smile and a smart-aleck remark. Joanne Whalley is the call girl/spy who turns into the sidekick/love interest. Although it's mainly a stretched out one-joke premise, that joke is delivered by comedy maestro Bill Murray. If you like his previous work, you'll love him as he messes with snooty Europeans. If you don't, seek professional help immediately. **94m/C VHS, Closed Caption.** Bill Murray, Peter Gallagher, Joanne Whalley, Alfred Molina, Richard Wilson, Geraldine James, John Standing, Anna Chancellor, Nicholas Woodeson, Simon Chandler; **D:** Jon Amiel; **W:** Howard Franklin, Robert Harrar; **C:** Robert Stevens; **M:** Chris Young. WAR

The Man Who Knew Too Much 🎬🎬🎬 1934

Hitchcock's first international success. A British family man on vacation in Switzerland is told of an assassination plot by a dying agent. His daughter is kidnapped to force his silence. In typical Hitchcock fashion, the innocent person becomes caught in a web of intrigue; the sticky situation culminates with surprising events during the famous shootout in the final scenes. Remade by Hitchcock in 1956. **75m/B VHS, Beta.** GB Leslie Banks, Edna Best, Peter Lorre, Nova Pilbeam, Pierre Fresnay, Frank Vosper, Hugh Wakefield, Cicely Oates, D. A. Clarke-Smith, George Curzon, Henry Oscar, Wilfrid Hyde-White; **D:** Alfred Hitchcock; **W:** Emlyn Williams, Charles Bennett, A.H. Rawlinson, Edwin Greenwood, D. B. Wyndham-Lewis. SNC, NOS, MRV

The Man Who Knew Too Much 🎬🎬½ 1956 (PG)

Hitchcock's remake of his 1934 film, this time about an American doctor and his family vacationing in Marrakech. They become involved in a complicated international plot involving kidnapping and murder. While Doris tries to save the day by singing "Que Sera, Sera," Stewart tries to locate his abducted son. More lavish settings and forms of intrigue make this a less focused and, to some, inferior version. 🎵Que Sera, Sera. **120m/C VHS, Beta, LV.** James Stewart, Doris Day, Brenda de Banzie, Bernard Miles, Ralph Truman, Daniel Gelin, Alan Mowbray, Carolyn Jones, Hillary Brooke; **D:** Alfred Hitchcock; **W:** John Michael Hayes; **C:** Robert Burks. Academy Awards '56: Best Song ("Que Sera, Sera"). USH, HHE

The Man Who Laughs 🎬🎬🎬½ 1927

Veidt's sensitive performance highlights this silent classic. He plays a young man whose features are surgically altered into a permanent smile because his family are political enemies of the current ruler. The man is befriended by the owner of a sideshow who first exhibits him as a freak but later finds Veidt gaining fame as a clown. A beautiful blind girl in the show loves Veidt for who he is and the two find happiness. **110m/B VHS.** Conrad Veidt, Mary Philbin, Olga Baclanova, Josephine Crowell, George Siegmann, Brandon Hurst; **D:** Paul Leni. GPV

The Man Who Lived Again 🎬🎬½ 1936

The Man Who Changed His Mind; The Brainsnatchers; Dr. Maniac Boris strives to be a brain-switcher, and suspense builds around the question of whether or not he will change his mind. Shot in England with fine sets and a definite Anglo feel to the proceedings, with Karloff doing one of his better mad scientist routines. **61m/B VHS, Beta, 8mm.** GB Boris Karloff, Anna Lee, John Loder, Frank Cellier, Lyn Harding, Cecil Parker; **D:** Robert Stevenson. SNC, VYY, MLB

Man Who Loved Cat Dancing 🎬🎬 1973 (PG)

Reynolds is an outlaw on the run after avenging his wife's murder and robbing a safe with pals Hopkins and Warden, and Miles has recently escaped from her abusive husband. It's love on the run as Burt and Sarah are pursued by bounty hunters and their tragic pasts—coming close to making us care, but close doesn't mean as much in movies as it does in dancing. Based on Marilyn Durham's novel. **114m/C VHS, Beta.** Burt Reynolds, Sarah Miles, Jack Warden, Lee J. Cobb, Jay Silverheels, Robert Donner; **D:** Richard Sarafian; **C:** Harry Stradling Jr.; **M:** John Williams. MGM, FCT

The Man Who Loved Women 🎬🎬🎬 1977

L'Homme Qui Aimait les Femmes An intelligent, sensitive bachelor writes his memoirs and recalls the many, many, many women he has loved. Truffaut couples sophistication and lightheartedness, the thrill of the chase and, when it leads to an accidental death, the wondering what-it's-all-about in the mourning after. In French with English subtitles. Remade in 1983. **119m/C VHS, Beta, LV, Closed Caption.** FR Charles Denner, Brigitte Fossey, Leslie Caron, Nelly Borgeaud, Genevieve Fontanel, Nathalie Baye, Sabine Glaser; **D:** Francois Truffaut; **W:** Francois Truffaut, Suzanne Schiffman, Michel Fermaud; **C:** Nestor Almendros; **M:** Maurice Jaubert. MGM, BTV

The Man Who Loved Women 🎬🎬 1983 (R)

A remake of the 1977 French film, this is slower, tries to be funnier, and is less subtle than the original. Reynolds is a Los Angeles sculptor whose reputation as a playboy leads him to a psychoanalyst's couch, where a lot of talk slows the action—though Burt & Julie (the shrink) do share the couch. **110m/C VHS, Beta, Closed Caption.** Burt Reynolds, Julie Andrews, Kim Basinger, Marilu Henner, Cynthia Sikes, Jennifer Edwards; **D:** Blake Edwards; **W:** Blake Edwards; **M:** Henry Mancini. COL

The Man Who Never Was 🎬🎬🎬 1955

Tense true story (with melodramatic embroidery) from WWII shows in step-by-step detail how Britain duped the Axis by letting them find an Allied corpse bearing phony invasion plans. Based on the book by the scheme's mastermind Ewen Montagu, played by Webb; Peter Sellers provides the voice of an offscreen Winston Churchill. **102m/C VHS, Beta.** GB Clifton Webb, Gloria Grahame, Robert Flemyng, Josephine Griffin, Stephen Boyd, Andre Morell, Laurence Naismith, Geoffrey Keen, Michael Hordern; **D:** Ronald Neame; **C:** Oswald Morris. British Academy Awards '56: Best Screenplay. FOX, FCT, TVC

The Man Who Shot Liberty Valance 🎬🎬🎬½ 1962

Tough cowboy Wayne and idealistic lawyer Stewart join forces against dreaded gunfighter Liberty Valance, played leatherly by Marvin. While Stewart rides to Senatorial success on his reputation as the man who shot the villain, he suffers moral crises about the act, but is toughened up by Wayne. Wayne's use of the word "pilgrim" became a standard for his impersonators. Strong character acting, great Western scenes, and value judgments to ponder over make this last of Ford's black-and-white westerns among his best. **123m/B VHS, Beta, LV, Closed Caption.** James Stewart, John Wayne, Vera Miles, Lee Marvin, Edmond O'Brien, Andy Devine, Woody Strode, Ken Murray, Jeanette Nolan, John Qualen, Strother Martin, Lee Van Cleef, John Carradine, Carleton Young; **D:** John Ford; **C:** William Clothier. Nominations: Academy Awards '62: Best Costume Design (B & W). PAR, HMV

The Man Who Skied Down Everest 🎬🎬½ 1975 (G)

Documentary about a Japanese athlete who undertakes a demanding downhill run, and the cost (human and financial) of getting there. **86m/C VHS.** Academy Awards '75: Best Feature Documentary. NO

The Man Who Wagged His Tail 🎬🎬 An Angel Passed Over Brooklyn; Un Angelo e Sceso a Brooklyn 1957

A mean slumlord is turned into a dog as the result of a curse cast upon him. In order to return to his human form, he must be loved by someone. Despite his attempts to be loved, the dog alienates his only friend and must try to redeem himself. Played for fun, this is a mildly amusing fantasy filmed in Spain and Brooklyn. Not released in the U. S. until 1961. **91m/B VHS.** IT SP Peter Ustinov, Pablito Calvo, Aroldo Tieri, Silvia Marco; **D:** Ladislao Vajda. SNC, VYY

The Man Who Wasn't There 🎬 1983 (R)

A member of the State department receives a formula from a dying spy that can render him invisible, see? He has to use the formula to protect himself from the police and other spies, becoming a comic "Invisible Man," see? Generally chaotic tale that's bad, but not so bad that it's worth seeing, though you might want to see what invisibility looks like in 3-D. **111m/C VHS, Beta.** Steve Guttenberg, Jeffrey Tambor, Art Hindle, Lisa Langlois; **D:** Bruce Malmuth; **M:** Miles Goodman. **PAR**

The Man Who Would Be King 🐾🐾🐾🐾 1975 (PG)
A grand, old-fashioned adventure based on the classic story by Rudyard Kipling about two mercenary soldiers who travel from India to Kafiristan in order to conquer it and set themselves up as kings. Splendid characterizations by Connery and Caine, and Huston's royal directorial treatment provides it with adventure, majestic sweep, and well-developed characters. **129m/C VHS, Beta, LV, Letterbox, Closed Caption.** Sean Connery, Michael Caine, Christopher Plummer, Saeed Jaffrey, Shakira Caine; **D:** John Huston; **W:** Gladys Hill, John Huston; **C:** Oswald Morris; **M:** Maurice Jarre. Nominations: Academy Awards '75: Best Adapted Screenplay, Best Art Direction/Set Decoration, Best Costume Design, Best Film Editing. **FOX**

The Man Who Would Not Die 🐾🐾 *Target in the Sun* 1975 (PG)
During his investigation of several deaths, a man discovers that all of the deceased were actually the same man. It seems the deaths were part of a intricate scheme to cover up a million dollar heist. Two of the top three actors are killed early on; it's not very suspenseful. It's more like the mystery that would not die. From Charles Williams' novel "The Sailcloth Shroud." **83m/C VHS, Beta.** Dorothy Malone, Keenan Wynn, Aldo Ray; **D:** Robert Arkless. **WAR, OM**

Man with a Cross 🐾🐾 1943
Archaeologists of the cinema may want to unearth this early Rossellini, made by the future father of neo-realist cinema as a propaganda piece for the fascist war effort. A heroic Italian chaplain on the Russian front ministers to foe and friend alike, and even converts a few commies to Christ. Not as awful as it sounds—but never forget where this came from. **88m/B VHS.** **IT D:** Roberto Rossellini. **FST**

Man with a Gun 🐾🐾½ 1995 (R)
Hitman John Hardin (Madsen) is asked by mobster employer Jack Rushton (Busey) to kill his ex-girlfriend Rena (Tilly) and get a CD-ROM filled with info he doesn't want to get out. Rena now happens to be John's gal pal but isn't too upset since she figures they'll substitute Rena's goody two-shoes twin sister Kathy for the needed corpse. Too bad John starts to fall for the intended victim, leaving the plan to unravel. It's a connect-the-dots plot with a creditable cast. Based on the novel "The Shroud Society" by Hugh C. Rae. **CW:** Violence, language, and some sexuality. **100m/C VHS, Closed Caption.** Michael Madsen, Jennifer Tilly, Gary Busey, Robert Loggia, Ian Tracey, Bill Cobbs; **D:** David Wyles; **W:** Laurie Finstad-Knizhik; **C:** Jan Kiesser; **M:** George Blondheim. **HMK**

A Man with a Maid 🐾 *The Groove Room; What the Swedish Butler Saw* 1973
A bizarre British exploitation pic mixes spookhouse cliches and sex, as a young man finds his new bachelor pad haunted by Jack the Ripper. Originally shot in 3-D. **83m/C VHS.** Sue Longhurst, Martin Long, Diana Dors; **D:** Vernon Becker. **VDM**

The Man with a Movie Camera 🐾🐾🐾 1929
A plotless, experimental view of Moscow through the creative eye of the cameraman Dziga Vertov, founder of the Kino Eye. The editing methods and camera techniques used in this silent film were very influential and still stand up to scrutiny today. **69m/B VHS, Beta.** RU **D:** Dziga Vertov. **IHF, MRV, DVT**

The Man with Bogart's Face 🐾🐾 *Sam Marlowe, Private Eye* 1980 (PG)
Sacchi is no Bogart, but he does imitate him well. Bogart fans will enjoy this fond tribute to the late great actor, but the story uncertainly wavers between genuine detective story and detective spoof. **106m/C VHS, Beta.** Robert Sacchi, Misty Rowe, Sybil Danning, Franco Nero, Herbert Lom, Victor Buono, Olivia Hussey; **D:** Robert Day; **W:** Andrew J. Fenady; **M:** John Beal, George Duning. Golden Raspberry Awards '80: Worst Song ("The Man with Bogart's Face"). **FOX**

The Man with One Red Shoe 🐾🐾 1985 (PG)
Hanks is a lovable clod of a violinist who ensnares himself in a web of intrigue when CIA agents, both good and evil, mistake him for a contact by his wearing one red shoe. Sporadically funny remake of the French "The Tall Blond Man with One Black Shoe." **92m/C VHS, Beta, Closed Caption.** Tom Hanks, Dabney Coleman, Lori Singer, Carrie Fisher, James Belushi, Charles Durning, Edward Herrmann, Tom Noonan, Gerrit Graham, David Lander, David Ogden Stiers; **D:** Stan Dragoti; **M:** Thomas Newman. **NO**

The Man with the Golden Arm 🐾🐾🐾 1955
A gripping film version of the Nelson Algren junkie melodrama, about an ex-addict who returns to town only to get mixed up with drugs again. Considered controversial in its depiction of addiction when released. Sinatra's performance as Frankie Machine is a stand-out. **119m/B VHS, Beta.** Frank Sinatra, Kim Novak, Eleanor Parker, Arnold Stang, Darren McGavin, Robert Strauss, George Mathews, John Conte, Doro Merande; **D:** Otto Preminger; **C:** Sam Leavitt; **M:** Elmer Bernstein. Nominations: Academy Awards '55: Best Actor (Sinatra), Best Art Direction/Set Decoration (B & W), Best Original Dramatic/Comedy Score. **WAR, MRV, NOS**

The Man with the Golden Gun 🐾🐾½ 1974 (PG)
Roger Moore is the debonair secret agent 007 in this ninth James Bond flick. Assigned to recover a small piece of equipment which can be utilized to harness the sun's energy, Bond engages the usual bevy of villains and beauties. **134m/C VHS, Beta, LV, Letterbox.** GB Roger Moore, Christopher Lee, Britt Ekland, Maud Adams, Herve Villechaize, Clifton James, Soon-Teck Oh, Richard Loo, Marc Lawrence, Bernard Lee, Lois Maxwell, Desmond Llewelyn; **D:** Guy Hamilton; **W:** Tom Mankiewicz; **C:** Ted Moore; **M:** John Barry. **MGM, FOX**

The Man with the Perfect Swing 🐾🐾½ 1995
Middle-aged ex-baseball player-turned-business entrepreneur Anthony "Babe" Lombardo (Black) is deep in debt and having trouble with the IRS even as he schemes to find success with his latest endeavor—designing specialty golf equipment. But Babe's latest design is a radically new golf swing (combining putting with his baseball expertise) featured in a how-to video with a budding PGA star. Naturally, given Babe's woeful record, the money just doesn't seem to be coming his way. **94m/C VHS.** James Black, Suzanne Savoy, Marco Perella, James Belcher, Richard Bradshaw; **D:** Michael Hovis; **W:** Michael Hovis; **C:** Jim Barham; **M:** Paul English. **MNC**

The Man with Two Brains 🐾🐾🐾 1983 (R)
Did you hear the one about the brilliant neuro-surgeon who falls in love with a woman in his laboratory? He only has two problems: dealing with his covetous wife and finding a body for his cerebral lover. Plenty of laughs in this spoof of mad scientist movies that is redeemed from potential idiocy by the cast's titillating performances. Listen closely and you'll recognize the voice of Spacek as the brain-in-the-jar of Martin's dreams. **91m/C VHS, Beta, LV.** Steve Martin, Kathleen Turner, David Warner, Sissy Spacek; **D:** Carl Reiner; **W:** Steve Martin, George Gipe, Carl Reiner; **C:** Michael Chapman; **M:** Joel Goldsmith. **WAR**

Man with Two Heads 🐾 1972 (R)
Doctor Jekyll gets in touch with his innermost feelings when his muffed experiments turn him into, gasp, Mr. Blood. Another forlorn addition to the Dr. Jekyll retread collection. **80m/C VHS. D:** Andy Milligan; **W:** Andy Milligan. **NO**

The Man with Two Lives 🐾🐾½ 1942
Well done horror thriller about a wealthy young man who's killed in a car accident, then brought back to life by a mad scientist. At precisely the moment his life is restored, a murderous gangster is executed and his soul enters the young man's body. **?m/C VHS.** Edward Norris, Addison Richards, Marlo Dwyer. **SNC**

The Man Without a Face 🐾🐾½ 1993 (PG-13)
Gibson plays a badly scarred recluse in Maine who develops a mentor relationship with a lonely, fatherless boy. Chuck (Stahl) wants to go away to military school, but flunks the extrance exam, and enlists former teacher McLeod as a tutor. First foray for Gibson into the director's chair tends to be overly melodramatic. Adapted from a novel by Isabelle Holland.**CW:** Sex talk; adult themes and sexual situations. **115m/C VHS, Beta, LV, Closed Caption.** Mel Gibson, Nick Stahl, Margaret Whitton, Fay Masterson, Richard Masur, Gaby Hoffman, Geoffrey Lewis, Jack DeMave; **D:** Mel Gibson; **W:** Malcolm MacRury; **M:** James Horner. **WAR**

Man Without a Star 🐾🐾🐾 1955
A cowboy helps ranchers stop a ruthless cattle owner from taking over their land. The conflict between freedom in the wild west and the need for order and settlements is powerfully internalized in Douglas, whose fight for justice will tame the cowboy code he lives by. You'll shed a tear for the fading frontier. **89m/B VHS, Beta.** Kirk Douglas, Jeanne Crain, Claire Trevor, William Campbell; **D:** King Vidor. **USH**

Man, Woman & Child 🐾🐾 1983 (PG)
A close, upscale California family is shocked when a child from the husband's long-ago affair with a Frenchwoman appears at their door. Pure sentimentalism, as the family confronts this unexpected development. Two hankies—one each for fine performances by Sheen and Danner. Based on a sentimental novel by Erich Segal of "Love Story" fame, who co-wrote the script. **99m/C VHS, Beta.** Martin Sheen, Blythe Danner, Craig T. Nelson, David Hemmings; **D:** Dick Richards; **W:** Erich Segal; **M:** Georges Delerue. **PAR**

Managua 🐾🐾 1997 (R)
Three friends must battle a Nicaraguan drug lord and jungle terrain in order to rescue a friend.**CW:** Scene of strong sexuality, and for nudity, language and some violence. **108m/C VHS.** Louis Gossett Jr., Assumpta Serna, John Savage, Robert Beltran, Michael Moriarty, John Diehl; **D:** Michele Taverna. **CAF**

Manchurian Avenger 🐾 1984 (R)
Desperados have wrested control of a Colorado gold rush town from Joe Kim's family, but he'll put an end to that, chop chop. **87m/C VHS, Beta.** Bobby Kim, Bill Wallace; **D:** Ed Warnick. **NO**

The Manchurian Candidate 🐾🐾🐾🐾 1962
Political thriller about an American Korean War vet who suspects that he and his platoon may have been brainwashed during the war, with his highly decorated, heroic friend programmed by commies to be an operational assassin. Loaded with shocks, conspiracy, inventive visual imagery, and bitter political satire of naivete and machinations of the left and right. Excellent performances by an all-star cast, with Lansbury and Gregory particularly frightening. Based on the Richard Condon novel. Featuring a special interview with Sinatra and Frankenheimer in which Sinatra is deified. **126m/B VHS, Beta, LV, Closed Caption.** Frank Sinatra, Laurence Harvey, Angela Lansbury, Janet Leigh, James Gregory, Leslie Parrish, John McGiver, Henry Silva, Khigh Deigh; **D:** John Frankenheimer; **W:** George Axelrod, John Frankenheimer; **C:** Lionel Lindon; **M:** David Amram. Golden Globe Awards '63: Best Supporting Actress (Lansbury); National Board of Review Awards '62: Best Supporting Actress (Lansbury), National Film Registry '94;; Nominations: Academy Awards '62: Best Film Editing, Best Supporting Actress (Lansbury). **MGM**

The Mandarin Mystery 🐾½ 1937
In the process of trying to retrieve a stolen Mandarin stamp, detective Ellery Queen uncovers a counterfeiting ring. Some fine performances, but a muddled script creates a mystery as to whether or not the action is played for laughs. **65m/B VHS, Beta.** Eddie Quillan, Charlotte Henry, Rita La Roy, Wade Boteler, Franklin Pangborn, George Irving, Kay Hughes, William Newell; **D:** Ralph Staub. **NOS, SNC**

Mandela 🐾🐾🐾 1987
A gripping, powerful drama about human rights and dignity, tracing the real-life trials of Nelson and Winnie Mandela. The story focuses on the couple's early opposition to

South African apartheid, as well as the events leading up to Nelson's life-imprisonment sentencing in 1964. Excellent, restrained performances from Glover and Woodard. Made for cable television. **135m/C VHS, Beta.** Danny Glover, Alfre Woodard, John Matshikiza, Warren Clarke, Allan Corduner, Julian Glover; **D:** Philip Saville. *KUI, FCT*

Mandela and de Klerk ♪♪½ 1997 (PG)
Cable docudrama about the two men who changed South Africa. White Afrikaaner president F.W. de Klerk (Caine) declared an end to apartheid in 1992 and two years later was succeeded as the country's president by Nelson Mandela (Poitier), a black activist imprisoned on treason charges for 27 years before his release. Both men shared the Nobel Peace Prize for their efforts to unite South Africa. **114m/C VHS, Closed Caption.** Sidney Poitier, Michael Caine, Tina Lifford, Ian Roberts, Gerry Maritz, Jerry Mofokeng; **D:** Joseph Sargent; **W:** Richard Wesley; **C:** Tobias Schliessler; **M:** Cedric Gradus-Samson. *EVE*

Mandinga ♪ 1977
A plantation owner develops an obsession for one of his female slaves. Made to cash in on the already exploitive "Mandingo"; two wrongs don't make a right. **100m/C VHS, Beta.** Anthony Gismondi; **D:** Mario Pinzauti. *PAR*

Mandingo ♪ 1975 (R)
Overheated Southern-fried tale of slavery in the Deep South, circa 1840, dealing with the tangled loves and hates of a family and their slaves. Heavyweight boxer Norton made his screen debut in the title role as the slave who makes his master money with his boxing prowess. King is the wastrel son who makes Norton's wife, another slave, his mistress. Followed by 1975's "Drum." Based on the novel by Kyle Onstott. **127m/C VHS, Beta, LV.** James Mason, Susan George, Perry King, Richard Ward, Ken Norton, Ben Masters, Brenda Sykes, Paul Benedict, Ji Tu Cumbuka; **D:** Richard Fleischer; **W:** Maurice Jarre. *PAR*

Mandroid ♪½ 1993 (R)
Two scientists design a high-tech robot, Mandroid, to handle a powerful new element they've discovered. Dr. Zimmer and daughter Zanna want to use their creation to help mankind while mad scientist Dr. Drago wants the power Mandroid can give him. When a laboratory accident leaves Drago horribly disfigured it also gives him the chance to steal Mandroid and put his evil plan into action. Filmed on location in Romania. **CW:** Violence and sex scene. **81m/C VHS, Beta, Closed Caption.** Brian Cousins, Jane Caldwell, Michael DellaFemina, Curt Lowens, Patrick Ersgard, Robert Symonds; **D:** Joakim Ersgard; **W:** Jackson Barr, Earl Kenton. *PAR*

Mandy ♪♪♪ Crash of Silence 1953
Poignant drama of a deaf child and the family who must come to terms with her deafness. Well-developed plot and well performed; an intelligent treatment in all. **93m/B VHS, Beta.** GB Phyllis Calvert, Jack Hawkins, Mandy Miller; **D:** Alexander MacKendrick. *BFA*

Manfish ♪♪½ 1956
Two men venture out in a boat, the Manfish, to hunt for sunken treasure in the Caribbean. Only one survives the trip, as his greed destroys the other. The scenes off the Jamaican coast are lovely, but the story fails to take hold. Though there is a star aboard in Chaney, you'll look astern and bow out with a sinking feeling. Derived from two Edgar Allan Poe stories, "The Gold Bug" and "The Tell-Tale Heart." **76m/C VHS.** John Bromfield, Lon Chaney Jr., Victor Jory, Barbara Nichols; **D:** W. Lee Wilder. *NOS, SNC*

The Mangler ♪ 1994 (R)
Laundry machine munches workers in a small-town Maine industrial plant. Bossman Englund's only concern (besides huge workman's comp premiums) is keeping the machine well-fed. Weak attempt at horror by veteran Tobe "If it's worth doing, it's worth overdoing" Hooper ("The Texas Chainsaw Massacre") that tries to capitalize on the popularity of story originator Stephen King. Offers little in plot or scare, but fans of the gore genre will enjoy the overuse of chunky-style blood and guts spewed from the monstrous steam ironer and folder that is

apparently possesed by the devil. About 45 minutes too long for anybody to suspend their disbelief. **CW:** Language; gory horror violence, mostly mangling. **106m/C VHS, LV, Closed Caption.** Robert Englund, Ted Levine, Daniel Matmor, Vanessa Pike, Demetre Phillips, Lisa Morris, Ashley Hayden, Vera Blacker; **D:** Tobe Hooper; **W:** Tobe Hooper, Peter Welbeck, Stephen Brooks; **C:** Amnon Salomon; **M:** Barrington Pheloung. *NLC, TTC, IME*

The Mango Tree ♪♪½ 1977
A young man comes of age in a small Australian town during the 1920s. Everything is well done, if not dramatic or fascinating. **93m/C VHS, Beta.** AU Geraldine Fitzgerald, Robert Helpmann, Diane Craig, Gerald Kennedy, Christopher Pate; **D:** Kevin J. Dobson. *NO*

Manhandled ♪♪½ 1924
Department store clerk Swanson is the hit of an artist's party with her impersonations and is asked by Morgan to impersonate a Russian countess to lend some class to his store. She winds up with lots of suitors. **67m/B VHS.** Gloria Swanson, Frank Morgan, Tom Moore, Lilyan Tashman, Ian Keith, Arthur Houseman; **D:** Allan Dwan. *GPV*

The Manhandlers ♪ 1973 (R)
After the uncle of a young woman is killed by the mob, she goes after them for revenge. For your entertainment pleasure, best stick with the soup commercial of the same name. **87m/C VHS, Beta.** Cara Burgess, Judy Brown, Vince Cannon, Rosalind Miles; **D:** Lee Madden. *TWE*

Manhattan ♪♪♪♪ 1979 (R)
Successful TV writer Allen yearns to be a serious writer. He struggles through a series of ill-fated romances, including one with high school senior Hemingway, about 25 years younger, and another with Keaton, who's also having an on-again, off-again affair with Murphy, Allen's best friend. Scathingly serious and comic view of modern relationships in urban America and of the modern intellectual neuroses. Shot in black-and-white to capture the mood of Manhattan and mated with an excellent Gershwin soundtrack, the video version preserves the widescreen effect adding yet another impressive element to the overall production. **96m/B VHS, Beta, LV, Letterbox.** Woody Allen, Diane Keaton, Meryl Streep, Mariel Hemingway, Michael Murphy, Wallace Shawn, Anne Byrne, Tisa Farrow, Mark Linn-Baker, David Rasche, Karen Allen; **D:** Woody Allen; **W:** Woody Allen, Marshall Brickman; **C:** Gordon Willis; **M:** George Gershwin. British Academy Awards '79: Best Film, Best Screenplay; Cesar Awards '80: Best Foreign Film; Los Angeles Film Critics Association Awards '79: Best Supporting Actress (Streep); New York Film Critics Awards '79: Best Director (Allen), Best Supporting Actress (Streep); National Society of Film Critics Awards '79: Best Director (Allen), Best Supporting Actress (Streep); Nominations: Academy Awards '79: Best Original Screenplay, Best Supporting Actress (Hemingway). *MGM*

Manhattan Baby ♪ 1982
Unscary horror film about an archaeologist who digs up a relic that draws evil into the world and infects an American girl with powers that lead to many deaths. Advice to you that might have saved the archaelogist: don't dig this. **90m/C VHS, Beta.** IT Christopher Connelly, Martha Taylor; **D:** Lucio Fulci. *ART*

Manhattan Melodrama ♪♪½ 1934
Powell and Gable are best friends from childhood, growing up together in an orphanage. Their adult lives take different paths, however, as Powell becomes a respected prosecuting attorney while Gable becomes a notorious gambler/racketeer. Lovely Loy is Gable's girl who comes between the two. Eventually, Powell must prosecute his lifelong friend for murder in order to win the governorship. One of Gable's toughest roles; Powell's character, however, is a bit unbelievable as his ethics seem to extend beyond love and friendship. This is the first film to team Powell and Loy, who would go on to make 13 more films together, including the "Thin Man" series. **93m/B VHS, Beta, LV.** Clark Gable, William Powell, Myrna Loy, Leo Carrillo, Nat Pendleton, George Sidney, Isabel Jewell, Muriel Evans, Claudelle Kaye, Frank Conroy, Jimmy Butler, Mickey Roo-

ney, Edward Van Sloan; **D:** Woodbridge S. Van Dyke; **C:** James Wong Howe. Academy Awards '34: Best Story. *MGM, CCB*

Manhattan Merengue! ♪♪½ Rice, Beans and Ketchup 1995 (R)
Young mambo dancer Miguel (Perez) has been unable to get a visa to come to the U.S. from the Dominican Republic so he stows away and eventually makes it to New York with new friend Carmello (Leonardi), who's searching for an old girlfriend and their son. While Miguel tries for dance work on Broadway, he makes a friend in dance instructor Susan (Reed) and locates long-lost girlfriend Rosita (Cavazos). Too bad Carmello's luck isn't as good. Sweetly cornball and romantic. **CW:** Language and brief violence. **100m/C VHS.** George Perez, Lumi Cavazos, Marco Leonardi, Alyson Reed; **D:** Joseph B. Vasquez; **W:** Joseph B. Vasquez, Rue Kent Wildman; **C:** David Castillo; **M:** Lalo Schifrin. *BMG*

Manhattan Merry-Go-Round ♪♪ 1937
One of the movies where a corrupt boss—in this case a record producer—threatens a bunch of good people as a pretense for a plot when the movie simply serves as a showcase for stars. Features many singing stars of the '30s ("where have you gone Cab Calloway?") plus Joltin' Joe, who ended up having a hit-streak in another genre. ♫Mama I Wanna Make Rhythm; Manhattan Merry-Go-Round; Heaven?; I Owe You; It's Round Up Time in Reno. **89m/B VHS, Beta.** Cab Calloway, Louis Prima, Ted Lewis, Ann Dvorak, Phil Regan, Kay Thompson, Gene Autry, Joe DiMaggio; **D:** Charles Riesner. Nominations: Academy Awards '37: Best Interior Decoration. *NOS, VCN, HHT*

Manhattan Murder Mystery ♪♪♪ 1993 (PG)
Keaton and Allen team up again as two New Yorkers who get involved in a mystery when their neighbor dies under strange circumstances. Light, entertaining comedy steers clear of some of Allen's heavier themes and should keep audiences laughing till the end. Allen, writing with Brickman for the first time since "Annie Hall" and "Manhattan," makes viewers fall in love with the magic of NYC all over again. **105m/C VHS, LV, 8mm, Closed Caption.** Woody Allen, Diane Keaton, Anjelica Huston, Alan Alda, Jerry Adler, Ron Rifkin, Joy Behar, Lynn Cohen, Melanie Norris; **D:** Woody Allen; **W:** Woody Allen, Marshall Brickman; **C:** Carlo DiPalma. Nominations: Golden Globe Awards '94: Best Actress—Musical/Comedy (Keaton). *COL*

The Manhattan Project ♪♪ Manhattan Project: The Deadly Game 1986 (PG-13)
An exceptionally bright teenager decides to build a nuclear bomb for his project at the New York City science fair. He's out to prove how dangerously easy it is to build big bombs. When he steals plutonium from a local government installation, the feds attempt to nab the precocious youngster. Light moral overtones abound. Director Brickman co-wrote similarly titled "Manhattan." **112m/C VHS, Beta, LV.** John Lithgow, Christopher Collet, Cynthia Nixon, Jill Eikenberry, John Mahoney, Sully Boyer, Richard Council, Robert Schenkkan, Paul Austin; **D:** Marshall Brickman; **W:** Marshall Brickman, Thomas Baum; **C:** Billy Williams. *REP*

Manhunt ♪♪ The Italian Connection; La Mala Ordina 1973 (R)
A man marked for execution by the mob launches his own assault on the organization's headquarters. Action and Italian food, but not much else. Dubbed. **93m/C VHS, Beta.** IT Henry Silva, Mario Adorf, Woody Strode, Luciana Paluzzi; **D:** Fernando Di Leo.

The Manhunt ♪♪ 1986
A framed cowhand escapes from prison to prove his innocence. Made-for-TV movie. **89m/C VHS, Beta.** Ernest Borgnine, Bo Svenson, John Ethan Wayne; **D:** Larry Ludman.

Manhunt ♪♪½ 1995 (R)
Fugitive Jim Trudell (Wilson) rescues a woman from a gang of thugs and winds up in a net of police corruption. Now he needs to survive long enough to figure out what's going on. **95m/C VHS, LV.** Don "The Dragon" Wilson, Jillian McWhirter, Jonathan Penner; **D:** Jonathan Winfrey. *NHO*

Manhunt for Claude Dallas 🎬🎬 1986 Mountain man uses game wardens for firing practice, ticks off local sheriff Torn, is tossed behind bars, checks out ahead of schedule and becomes a legend in his own time. Mediocre made-for-TV macho man melodrama. From the novel "Outlaw" by Jeff Long. 93m/C VHS, Beta. Matt Salinger, Rip Torn, Claude Akins, Pat Hingle, Lois Nettleton, Beau Starr, Frederick Coffin; **D:** Jerry London; **W:** John Gay; **M:** Stephen Dorff.

Manhunt in the African Jungle 1954 An American undercover agent battles Nazi forces in Africa. A serial in 15 episodes. 240m/B VHS, LV. Rod Cameron, Joan Marsh, Duncan Renaldo. VCN, REP, MLB

Manhunt of Mystery Island Captain Mephisto and the Transformation Machine 1945 Serial about the super-powered Captain Mephisto. 100m/C VHS, Beta, LV. Linda Stirling, Roy Barcroft, Richard Bailey, Kenne Duncan; **D:** Spencer Gordon Bennet. MLB

Manhunter 1974 A made-for-television escapade about a WWI Marine who returns home from China in 1933 to track down a bunch of gangsters headed by his sister. 87m/B VHS, LV, Closed Caption. Ken Howard, Stefanie Powers, Gary Lockwood, Tim O'Connor, L.Q. Jones; **D:** Walter Grauman. WAR, TWE

Manhunter 🎬🎬½ 1983 A mercenary sets out to disengage organized crime from high-level politics. Produced by Owensby. 92m/C VHS, Beta. Earl Owensby, Johnny Popwell, Doug Hale, Elizabeth Upton; **D:** Earl Owensby.

Manhunter 🎬🎬🎬 Red Dragon 1986 (R) FBI forensic specialist—who retired after a harrowing pursuit of a serial killer—is called back to duty to find a psychotic family killer. His technique: to match the thought processes of serial killers and thus anticipate their moves. Intense thriller, based on the Thomas Harris novel "Red Dragon." Harris also wrote "The Silence of the Lambs," whose most notorious character Hannibal ("The Cannibal") Lecter, appears in this movie as well. Director Mann applies the slick techniques he introduced in the popular television series "Miami Vice," creating a quiet, moody intensity broken by sudden onslaughts of violence. Available in widescreen on laserdisc. 100m/C VHS, Beta, LV, Letterbox, Closed Caption. William L. Petersen, Kim Greist, Joan Allen, Brian Cox, Dennis Farina, Stephen Lang, Tom Noonan; **D:** Michael Mann; **W:** Michael Mann; **C:** Dante Spinotti. WAR

Mania 🎬🎬½ The Flesh and the Fiends; Fiendish Ghouls; Psycho Killers 1960 Fine adaptation of the Burke and Hare grave robbing legend. Cushing is the doctor who needs corpses and Pleasence and Rose provide them by any means. Highly atmospheric representation of dismal, 19th century Edinburgh. Very graphic for its time. 87m/B VHS. GB Peter Cushing, June Laverick, Donald Pleasence, George Rose, Dermot Walsh, Renee Houston, Billie Whitelaw, John Cairney, Michael Balfour; **D:** John Gilling; **M:** Stanley Black. SNC, DVT, MLB

Mania 🎬🎬 198? Four suspense/murder stories set in a sleazy urban milieu. 120m/C Beta. Deborah Grover, Stephen Hunter, Lenore Zann, Wayne Robson. NO

Maniac woof! 1934 A scientist has designs on raising the dead and searches for victims on which to experiment. Bizarre "adults only" exploitation feature was considered very risque for its time, and includes eaten eyeballs, a cat fight with syringes, and a rapist who thinks he's an orangutan. A must for genre aficionados. 67m/B VHS, Beta. Bill Woods, Horace Carpenter, Ted Edwards, Thea Ramsey, Jennie Dark, Marcel Andre, Celia McGann; **D:** Dwain Esper. VDM, SNC, MRV

Maniac 🎬 1963 An American artist living in France becomes involved with the daughter of a cafe owner, not suspecting that murder will follow. Seems that her old man is locked up in an insane asylum for torching the daughter's rapist several years earlier. 86m/B VHS, Beta. GB Kerwin Mathews,

Nadia Gray, Donald Houston, Liliane Brousse. **D:** Michael Carreras; **W:** Jimmy Sangster; **C:** Wilkie Cooper; **M:** Stanley Black. COL, MLB

Maniac 🎬 Ransom; Assault on Paradise; The Town That Cried Terror 1977 (PG) A New York cop hunts down an arrow-shooting and obviously crazed Vietnam veteran who endeavors to hold an entire Arizona town for ransom. Which is entirely appropriate, since the cast is in it only for the money. 87m/C VHS, Beta. Oliver Reed, Deborah Raffin, Stuart Whitman, Jim Mitchum, Edward Brett, John Ireland, Richard Compton, Paul Koslo; **D:** Richard Compton. ART, VES

Maniac woof! 1980 A psycho murderer slaughters and scalps his victims, adding the "trophies" to his collection. Carries a self-imposed equivalent "X" rating due to its highly graphic gore quotient. For extremely strong stomachs only. 91m/C VHS, Beta. Joe Spinell, Caroline Munro, Gail Lawrence, Kelly Piper, Tom Savini, Rita Montone, Hyla Marrow; **D:** William Lustig; **W:** C.A. Rosenberg, Joe Spinell; **C:** Robert Lindsay. VTR

Maniac Cop 🎬 1988 (R) In New York city, a cop goes beyond the realm of sanity and turns vigilante. Low-budget slasher/thriller that too often sags. 92m/C VHS, Beta. Tom Atkins, Bruce Campbell, Laurene Landon, Richard Roundtree, William Smith, Robert Z'Dar, Sheree North, Sam Raimi; **D:** William Lustig; **W:** Larry Cohen; **C:** Vincent Rabe. TWE, HHE

Maniac Cop 2 🎬 1990 (R) Everyone thought he was dead but you can't keep a bad guy down so this grossly disfigured policeman forms a one-man vigilante squad, seeking revenge (why never matters—just the body count). Blood and guts fly as any plot shortcomings are cleverly disguised by an array of violent video deaths. Sequel to "Maniac Cop." 90m/C VHS, LV, Letterbox, Closed Caption. Robert Davi, Claudia Christian, Michael Lerner, Bruce Campbell, Laurene Landon, Robert Z'Dar, Clarence Williams III, Leo Rossi; **D:** William Lustig; **W:** Larry Cohen; **C:** James Lemmo. ART

Maniac Cop 3: Badge of Silence 🎬 1993 (R) The grossly disfigured policeman returns yet again to exact gory vengeance as the good guys try to get rid of him once and for all. 85m/C VHS, Closed Caption. Robert Z'Dar, Robert Davi, Gretchen Becker, Paul Gleason, Doug Savant, Caitlin Dulany, Jackie Earle Haley, Robert Forster; **D:** William Lustig, Joel Soisson; **W:** Larry Cohen; **M:** Jerry Goldsmith.

Maniac Warriors 🎬 199? A nuclear apocalypse has caused some strange changes in the population—and not for the better. Blood-crazed mutants attack the heavily armed inhabitants of New State Idaho and there's lots of mayhem in store. 91m/C VHS. Tom Schioler, John Wood, Melanie Kilgour. MOV

The Manions of America 🎬🎬½ 1981 The long and sometimes interesting rags-to-riches tale of Rory O'Manion, a feisty Irish patriot who leaves his native land during the potato famine of 1845 to settle in America. Originally a television miniseries. 290m/C VHS, Beta. Pierce Brosnan, Kate Mulgrew, Linda Purl, David Soul, Kathleen Beller, Simon MacCorkindale; **D:** Joseph Sargent, Charles S. Dubin. WMI, PAR

Manipulator 🎬 1971 (R) A deranged ex-movie makeup man (Rooney, playing to type) kidnaps a young actress and holds her prisoner in a deserted Hollywood sound stage. 91m/C VHS, Beta. Mickey Rooney, Luana Anders, Keenan Wynn; **D:** Yabo Yablonsky. ART, VES

The Manitou 🎬🎬 1978 (PG) A San Francisco woman suffers from a rapidly growing neck tumor which eventually grows into a 400-year-old Indian witch doctor. (I hate when that happens.) Redeemed only by good special effects, especially those that kept Curtis, Strasberg, and Meredith from laughing. 104m/C VHS, Beta, LV. Susan Strasberg, Tony Curtis, Stella Stevens, Ann Sothern, Burgess Meredith, Michael Ansara, Jon Cedar, Paul Mantee, Lurene Tuttle, Jeanette Nolan; **D:** William Girdler; **W:** William Girdler, Tom Pope, Jon Cedar; **C:** Michael Hugo; **M:** Lalo Schifrin. COL, NLC

Mankilloro 🎬 1987 A group of tough female convicts are enlisted to hunt down and rub out a psycho drug dealer, all the while displaying their feminine charms. 90m/C VHS, Beta. Edd Byrnes, Gail Fisher, Edy Williams, Lynda Aldon, William Zipp, Christopher Lunde, Susanne Tegman, Marilyn Stafford, Paul Bruno, Byron Clark; **D:** David A. Prior. COL

Mannequin 🎬🎬½ 1937 Tracy and Crawford star in this romantic story of a poor girl who finds temporary happiness by marrying a wealthy man after ditching her con-artist husband. Somewhat predictable, the movie reads like a "People" magazine story on The Donald and Ivana. Tracy and Crawford keep the story afloat (in their only film together), with an able assist from Curtis. 95m/B VHS. Joan Crawford, Spencer Tracy, Alan Curtis, Ralph Morgan, Leo Gorcey, Elisabeth Risdon, Paul Fix; **D:** Frank Borzage; **W:** Lawrence Hazard. Nominations: Academy Awards '38: Best Song ("Always and Always"). MGM

Mannequin 🎬🎬 1987 (PG) A young artist creates a store window display using various mannequins, one of which contains the spirit of an ancient Egyptian woman. She comes to life when he is around, and naturally none of his co-workers believe him. Very light comedy, featuring two pretty stars and music by Jefferson Starship. 90m/C VHS, Beta, LV, Closed Caption. Andrew McCarthy, Kim Cattrall, Estelle Getty, James Spader, Meshach Taylor, Carole Davis, G.W. Bailey; **D:** Michael Gottlieb; **W:** Ed Rugoff. Nominations: Academy Awards '87: Best Song ("Nothing's Gonna Move Us Now"). CCB, VTR

Mannequin 2: On the Move woof! 1991 (PG) Less of a sequel, more of a lame rehash proving that the first "Mannequin" could have been even dumber. At this rate part three will be off the scale. Now it's a lovesick Teutonic princess frozen for 1,000 years who revives in a department store. Taylor reprises his grotesque gay role. 95m/C VHS, LV. Kristy Swanson, William Ragsdale, Meshach Taylor, Terry Kiser, Stuart Pankin; **D:** Stewart Raffill; **W:** Ed Rugoff. ART

Manny & Lo 🎬🎬🎬 1996 (R) Krueger's directorial debut features fine performances in a story about three misfits forming a unique family bond. Surly 16-year-old Lo (Palladino) and her serious 11-year-old sister Manny (Johansson) have run away from their foster homes and hit the road together. Living hand-to-mouth, it's Manny who persuades her irresponsible pregnant sister that they need a home and they settle into an isolated cabin. When the sisters visit a baby store, eccentric clerk Elaine (Place) seems such a font of wisdom that the girls kidnap her and hold her as a hostage to help with the pregnancy. But Elaine's not trying to escape and has an agenda of her own. **CW:** Mild profanity and a brief sexual situation. 90m/C VHS, LV, Closed Caption. Mary Kay Place, Scarlett Johansson, Aleksa Palladino, Paul Guilfoyle, Glenn Fitzgerald, Cameron Boyd, Novella Nelson, Angie Phillips; **D:** Lisa Krueger; **W:** Lisa Krueger; **C:** Tom Krueger; **M:** John Lurie. Nominations: Independent Spirit Awards '97: Best Actress (Johansson), Best First Feature, Best Supporting Actress (Place). COL

Manny's Orphans 🎬 Here Come the Tigers 1978 (PG) An out-of-work teacher takes on a lovable home for orphaned boys. Dull remake of "Bad News Bears." 92m/C VHS, Beta. Richard Lincoln, Malachy McCourt, Sel Skolnick; **D:** Sean S. Cunningham. ART, VES

Manon 🎬🎬 1950 Tragic tale of a French woman condemned for her affair with a Resistance fighter. They flee to Paris, where her brother forces her into prostitution. Based on the novel "Manon Lescaut" by Abbe Antoine-Francois Prevost. In French with English subtitles. 91m/B VHS. Cecile Aubry, Michel Auclair, Serge Reggiani, Henri Vilbert, Daniel Ivernel; **D:** Henri-Georges Clouzot. NOS

Manon of the Spring 🎬🎬🎬½ Manon des Sources; Jean de Florette 2 1987 (PG) In this excellent sequel to "Jean de Florette," the adult daughter of the dead hunchback, Jean, discovers who blocked up the spring on her father's land. She plots her revenge, which proves greater than she could ever imagine. Montand is astonishing. Based on a Marcel Pagnol novel. In French with English subtitles. 113m/C **VHS, Beta, LV.** *FR* Yves Montand, Daniel Auteuil, Emmanuelle Beart, Hippolyte Girardot; *D:* Claude Berri; *W:* Gerard Brach, Claude Berri. *ORI, HMV*

Manos, the Hands of Fate woof! 1966 Horrible acting and laughable special effects elevate this story of a family ensnared by a satanic cult a notch above your average bad horror film. Highlights include a Satan-like character who can't stop laughing; the dreaded "hounds of hell" (or are those mangy dogs with big ears glued on?); and Torgo the monstrous henchman, who you know is evil because he has giant kneecaps (a sure sign of the devil's work). Notable as the one of the most often requested movies on Comedy Central's satiric "Mystery Science Theatre 3000," this one is good for a laugh. 74m/C **VHS.** Tom Nayman, Diane Mahree, Hal P. Warren, John Reynolds; *D:* Hal P. Warren; *W:* Hal P. Warren. *SNC*

Man's Best Friend 🎬½ 1993 (R) A guard dog is the object of a genetic experiment that has given him the agressiveness of other creatures, including a cobra and a leopard. Since Max is an enormous Tibetan mastiff this means big trouble for everyone but the reporter (Sheedy) who rescued him—and even she better watch out. *CW:* Profanity, terror, and sexual situations. 87m/C **VHS, LV, Closed Caption.** Ally Sheedy, Lance Henriksen, Frederic Lehne, Robert Costanzo, John Cassisi, J.D. Daniels; *D:* John Lafia; *W:* John Lafia; *M:* Joel Goldsmith. *NLC*

Man's Country 🎬🎬 1938 A rip-roarin' western saga filled with the usual action and danger, as ranger Randall leads the fight against a band of nasties headed by Long, in a dual role as twin brothers. 55m/B **VHS, Beta.** Jack Randall, Ralph Peters, Marjorie Reynolds, Walter Long; *D:* Robert F. "Bob" Hill. *NOS, DVT*

Man's Favorite Sport? 🎬🎬½ 1963 A slapstick comedy about a renowned fishing expert author who actually hates fishing, but is forced to compete in a major tournament by a romantically inclined publicity agent. Very funny in spots. 121m/C **VHS, Beta.** Rock Hudson, Paula Prentiss, Charlene Holt, Maria Perschy, John McGiver; *D:* Howard Hawks; *M:* Henry Mancini. *USH, CCB*

Man's Land 🎬½ 1932 A ranch needs savin', and Hoot's the guy to do it in this formulaic Gibson epic. 65m/B **VHS, Beta.** Hoot Gibson, Marion Shilling, Skeeter Bill Robbins, Alan Bridge; *D:* Phil Rosen. *VCI*

Mansfield Park 🎬🎬½ 1985 Fanny is an impoverished young woman, snubbed by society, who earns the respect and love of her cousin in a BBC mini-series adaptation of the Jane Austen classic set in 19th century England. 261m/C **VHS, Beta, Closed Caption.** *GB* Sylvestria Le Touzel, Bernard Hepton, Anna Massey, Donald Pleasence; *D:* David Giles. *FOX, TVC, HMV*

The Manster 🎬 *The Manster—Half Man, Half Monster; The Split* 1959 Another masterpiece from the director who brought us "Monster from Green Hell." Womanizing, whiskey swilling American journalist receives mysterious injection from crazed scientist and sprouts unsightly hair and extra head. Although shot in the land of the rising sun, lips move in sync with dialogue. 72m/B **VHS.** *JP* Peter Dyneley, Jane Hylton, Satoshi Nakamura, Terri Zimmern; *D:* Kenneth Crane, George Breakston. *SNC, MRV*

Mantis in Lace 🎬½ *Lila* 1968 (R) A go-go dancer slaughters men while tripping on LSD. Watch it for the "hep" dialogue. 68m/C **VHS.** Susan Stewart, Steve Vincent, M.K. Evans, Vic Lance, Pat Barrington, Janu Wine, Stuart Lancaster, John Carrol, Judith Crane, Cheryl Trepton; *D:* William Rotsler; *C:* Laszlo Kovacs. *TPV*

Mantrap 🎬🎬½ 1926 Early silent success by Fleming, who later directed "Gone with the Wind" and "The Wizard of Oz." Fabled flapper Bow tempts a lawyer on retreat in the woods. 66m/B

VHS, Beta. Clara Bow, Ernest Torrence, Percy Marmont, Eugene Pallette, Tom Kennedy; *D:* Victor Fleming. *GPV, FCT*

The Manxman 🎬🎬½ 1929 Hitchcock's last silent film, a romantic melodrama about ambition and infidelity on the Isle of Man. 129m/B **VHS, Beta.** *GB* Carl Brisson, Anny Ondra; *D:* Alfred Hitchcock. *VYY, MRV, MLB*

The Many Adventures of Winnie the Pooh 1977 (G) Disney's 22nd animated feature offers A.A. Milne's beloved characters and their adventures in the Hundred Acre Wood. Includes a behind-the-scenes featurette with the original creators, animators, and voices. 83m/C **VHS, Closed Caption.** *TOU*

Many Faces of Sherlock Holmes 1986 A documentary look at the various incarnations of the famous sleuth from A. Conan Doyle's stories to various film portrayals. 58m/C **VHS, Beta.** Christopher Plummer, Basil Rathbone, Christopher Lee.

Map of the Human Heart 🎬🎬 1993 (R) Thirty-year saga told in flashback. Young Eskimo Avik (Lee) and his Metis love interest Albertine (Parillaud) struggle with racism in a white world. They meet and become friends as children and years later meet again in Dresden during WWII, but now Albertine is married to Avik's once close friend, denying her heritage and living in the white world that he has been fighting for so long. Mediocre movie with extraordinary Arctic scenery. Cusack has a small role as a mapmaker. *CW:* Some language and one sexual scene. 109m/C **VHS, Closed Caption.** Jason Scott Lee, Anne Parillaud, Patrick Bergin, Robert Joamie, Annie Galipeau, John Cusack, Jeanne Moreau; *D:* Vincent Ward; *W:* Vincent Ward, Louis Nowra. *HBO, FCT, BTV*

Mapp & Lucia 🎬🎬½ 1985 British TV adaptation of H.E. Benson's stories of provincial English society in the fictional village of Tilling-on-Sea in the 1920s. Miss Mapp (Scales) holds local court but finds a potential usurper when elegant widow Lucia (McEwan) comes to town. Battle lines are formed between the two women in this sharp-tongued satire. On five cassettes; followed by a second series of five episodes. 270m/C **VHS.** *GB* Prunella Scales, Geraldine McEwan, Nigel Hawthorne. *WMI, VIF*

Marat/Sade 🎬🎬🎬½ *Persecution and Assassination of Jean-Paul Marat as Performed by the Inmates of the Asylum of Charenton Under the Direction of the Marquis De Sade* 1966 (R) A theatrical production presented by patients at a mental institution is directed by the Marquis de Sade. Well directed and visually effective, featuring Jackson's first film performance. Based on a play by Peter Weiss. Some theatres were forced to add extensions to the marquee when the film was first released. 115m/C **VHS, LV.** *GB* Patrick Magee, Clifford Rose, Glenda Jackson, Ian Richardson, Brenda Kempner, Ruth Baker, Michael Williams; *D:* Peter Brook; *C:* David Watkin. *WBF, MGM, LUM*

Marathon 🎬🎬 1980 When a middle-aged jogger's ego gets a boost through the attention of a beautiful young woman, he takes up marathon running. Light comedy. Made for television. 100m/C **VHS.** Bob Newhart, Leigh Taylor-Young, Herb Edelman, Dick Gautier, Anita Gillette, John Hillerman; *D:* Jackie Cooper. *ART*

Marathon Man 🎬🎬🎬 1976 (R) Nightmarish chase-thriller in which a graduate student becomes entangled in a plot involving a murderous Nazi fugitive. As student Hoffman is preparing for the Olympic marathon, he is reunited with his secret-agent brother, setting the intricate plot in motion. Courtesy of his brother, Hoffman becomes involved with Olivier, an old crazed Nazi seeking jewels taken from concentration camp victims. Non-stop action throughout, including a torture scene sure to set your teeth on edge. Goldman adapted the screenplay from his novel. 125m/C **VHS, Beta, LV.** Dustin Hoffman, Laurence Olivier, Marthe Keller, Roy Scheider, William Devane, Fritz Weaver; *D:*

John Schlesinger; *W:* William Goldman; *C:* Conrad Hall. Golden Globe Awards '77: Best Supporting Actor (Olivier); Nominations: Academy Awards '76: Best Supporting Actor (Olivier). *PAR*

Marauder 🎬🎬 1965 The prince of Venice leads a sea-faring onslaught against ransacking pirates and enemy fleets. 90m/C **VHS, Beta.** *IT* Gordon Scott, Gianna Maria Canale, Franca Bettoya; *D:* Luigi Capuano. *NO*

Marbella 🎬½ 1985 A luxury resort in Spain is the setting for a big caper heist of three million dollars from a monarchical tycoon. 96m/C **VHS, Beta.** Rod Taylor, Britt Ekland; *D:* Miguel Hermoso. *ART*

March of the Wooden Soldiers 🎬🎬🎬 *Babes in Toyland* 1934 The classic Mother Goose tale about the secret life of Christmas toys, with Laurel and Hardy as Santa's helpers who must save Toyland from the wicked Barnaby. A Yuletide "must see." Also available in a colorized version. 73m/B **VHS, LV.** Stan Laurel, Oliver Hardy, Charlotte Henry, Henry Kleinbach Brandon, Felix Knight, Jean Darling, Johnny Downs, Marie Wilson; *D:* Charles R. Rogers, Gus Meins. *NOS, GKK, IME*

March or Die 🎬🎬½ 1977 (PG) Great potential, unrealized. An American joins the French Foreign Legion during WWI after his dismissal from West Point. Following the brutality of training, he is assigned to guard an archeological expedition in Morocco, where he pulls together a rag-tag outfit for the mission. Hackman proves once again the wide range of his acting abilities, surmounting the cliched and fairly sadistic plot. Shot on location in the Sahara Desert. 104m/C **VHS.** *GB* Gene Hackman, Terence Hill, Max von Sydow, Catherine Deneuve, Ian Holm; *D:* Dick Richards; *W:* David Zelag Goodman; *M:* Maurice Jarre. *FOX*

Marciano 🎬🎬 1979 A made-for-television version of the great boxer's life. Average fight movie. 97m/C **VHS, Beta.** Tony LoBianco, Vincent Gardenia; *D:* Bernard L. Kowalski; *M:* Ernest Gold. *NLC*

Marco 🎬🎬 1973 Entertaining musical adventure of Marco Polo's life casts Arnaz as Marco Polo and Mostel as Kublai Khan. A couple of cut-ups, right? One of the first films to combine animation with live action. Shot partially on location in the Orient. ♫By Damn; Walls; A Family Man; Spaghetti. 109m/C **VHS, Beta.** Desi Arnaz Jr., Zero Mostel, Jack Weston, Cie Cie Win; *D:* Seymour Robbie.

Marco Polo, Jr. 🎬 1972 Marco Polo, Jr., the daring descendant of the legendary explorer, travels the world in search of his destiny in this song-filled, feature-length, but poorly animated, fantasy. 82m/C **VHS, Beta.** *D:* Eric Porter; *V:* Bobby Rydell. *FHE*

Mardi Gras for the Devil 🎬🎬 *Night Trap* 1993 (R) Black magic and the occult combine as a New Orleans cop tries to catch a killer who strikes only at Mardi Gras. The cop's got his work cut out for him since the killer is no mere mortal but a demon who believes in human sacrifice. 95m/C **VHS, Beta.** Robert Davi, Michael Ironside, Lesley-Anne Down, Lydie Denier, Mike Starr, Margaret Avery, John Amos; *D:* David A. Prior; *W:* David A. Prior.

Mardi Gras Massacre woof! *Crypt of Dark Secrets* 1978 Aztec priest arrives in New Orleans during Mardi Gras to revive the blood ritual of human sacrifice to an Aztec god. A police detective relentlessly pursues him. Much gore and gut-slicing, with no redeeming social value. 92m/C **VHS, Beta.** Curt Dawson, Gwen Arment, Wayne Mack, Laura Misch; *D:* Jack Weis. *VHE*

Margaret's Museum 🎬🎬🎬½ 1995 (R) The museum of the title is the bizarre shrine Margaret (Bonham Carter) dedicates to the family members who have been killed in the coal mines that dominate her small (1940s) Cape Breton, Nova Scotia town. Both Margaret and her mother, Catherine (Nelligan), are embittered by their tragedies and when Margaret finds romance with eccentric bagpiper Neil (Russell), she makes him promise he'll never return to mine work. But with a bad economy, Neil is forced back to the pits and inevitable disaster. It's Bonham Carter's picture all the way and she shows a wide (and welcome) range of emotions and strength. Adapted from a story by Sheldon Currie. **CW:** Strong language and some sexuality. 114m/C VHS. *CA GB* Helena Bonham Carter, Clive Russell, Kate Nelligan, Kenneth Welsh, Craig Olejnik; **D:** Mort Ransen; **W:** Mort Ransen, Gerald Wexler; **C:** Vic Sarin; **M:** Milan Kymlicka. Genie Awards '95: Best Actress (Bonham Carter), Best Adapted Screenplay, Best Costume Design, Best Supporting Actor (Welsh), Best Supporting Actress (Nelligan), Best Score. **CAF**

Margin for Murder 🎞🎞 *Mickey Spillane's Margin for Murder* 1981 Mike Hammer investigates a mysterious accident that killed his best friend. Made for television. 98m/C VHS, Beta. Kevin Dobson, Cindy Pickett, Donna Dixon, Charles Hallahan; **D:** Daniel Haller.

Maria Candelaria 🎞🎞 *Portrait of Maria; Xochimilco* 1946 Society rejects a woman because people don't like her mother. (She posed nude for an artist, and the town responds by stoning her to death, proving that going against small-town morals can be lethal). Eventually, time and circumstance push daughter onto mother's path in this tragic soaper. Del Rio portrays the scorned young woman, although she was 40 years old. 96m/B VHS, Beta. *MX* Dolores Del Rio, Pedro Armendariz Sr., Margarita Cortes; **D:** Emilio Fernandez. **MAD**

Maria Chapdelaine 🎞🎞🎞 1934 An early film from the renowned French director, in which a brutish trapper and a sophisticate battle for the love of a girl in the Canadian wilderness. English subtitles. Remade in 1984. 75m/B VHS, Beta. *FR* Jean Gabin, Jean-Pierre Aumont, Madeleine Renaud; **D:** Julien Duvivier. **HHT**

Maria Chapdelaine 🎞🎞½ 1984 Around the turn of the century, a young girl in the Northern Canadian wilderness endures a year of passion, doomed love, and tragedy. In French with subtitles. Remake of a 1935 French film. 108m/C VHS, Beta. *FR CA* Nick Mancuso, Carole Laure, Claude Rich, Pierre Curzi; **D:** Gilles Carle.

Marianne and Juliane 🎞🎞🎞½ 1982 Powerful combination of relationships and politics in West Germany as experienced through the lives of two sisters—Juliane, a feminist editor, and Marianne, a political terrorist. Based on the lives of Gudrun and Christiane Ensslin. German with subtitles. 106m/C VHS. *GE* Jutta Lampe, Barbara Sukowa, Ruediger Vogler, Doris Schade, Franz Rudnick; **D:** Margarethe von Trotta. **NYF**

Maria's Child 🎞🎞½ 1993 Light comedy about a dancer who becomes pregnant and must decide whether or not to keep the baby. When her live-in boyfriend (not the father) admits he cheated on her, she kicks him out. Unable to make up her mind, she imagines a dialogue with the fetus. Second of a trilogy by British television screenwriter Malcolm McKay on the subject of forgiveness. 97m/C VHS. *GB* Yolanda Vasquez, David O'Hara, Fiona Shaw, Alec McCowen, Sophie Okenado, Linda Davidson, Rudi Davies, Nicholas Woodeson, Anita Zagaria; **D:** Malcolm McKay; **W:** Malcolm McKay; **M:** Philip Appleby. **NYR**

Maria's Day 🎞🎞🎞 1984 Chronicles the plague-riddled downfall of a formerly aristocratic and wealthy Hungarian family in the years following the failed 1849 Revolution. In Hungarian with English subtitles. 113m/C VHS, Beta. **D:** Judit Elek. **FCT, AUD**

Maria's Lovers 🎞🎞½ 1984 (R) The wife (Kinski) of an impotent WWII veteran (Savage) succumbs to the charms of a rakish lady-killer (Spano). Savage turns to the charms of an older woman, finds love again with Kinski, but is still impotent; she gets pregnant by a wandering minstrel (Carradine) and on we go to film climax. Offbeat and uneven, representing Russian director Konchalovsky's first American film and one of Kinski's better roles. 103m/C VHS, Beta. Nastassia Kinski, John Savage, Robert Mitchum, Keith Carradine, Anita Morris, Bud Cort, Karen Young, Tracy Nelson, John Goodman, Vincent Spano; **D:** Andrei Konchalovsky; **W:** Marjorie David, Andrei Konchalovsky, Gerard Brach; **C:** Juan Ruiz-Anchia MGM

Maricela 1988 Young Maricela Flores and her mother have come to the U.S. from El Salvador to escape the fighting. Living with a Southern Californian family, Maricela has a hard time adjusting to American life and, in particular, dealing with prejudice. An entry in the PBS "Wonderworks" series. 55m/C VHS. Linda Lavin, Carlina Cruz. HMV, BTV, FCT

Marie 🎞🎞🎞 1985 (PG-13) In this true story, a divorced (and battered) mother works her way through school and the system to become the first woman to head the Parole Board in Tennessee. Finding rampant corruption, she blows the whistle on her bosses, who put her life in jeopardy. Spacek gives a powerful performance, as does first-time actor Thompson, portraying himself as the abused woman's attorney. Based on the book by Peter Maas. 113m/C VHS, Beta, Closed Caption. Sissy Spacek, Jeff Daniels, Keith Szarabajka, John Cullum, Morgan Freeman, Fred Dalton Thompson, Don Hood, Lisa Banes, Vincent Irizarry; **D:** Roger Donaldson; **W:** John Briley; **C:** Chris Menges; **M:** Francis Lai. MGM

Marie Antoinette 🎞🎞½ 1938 An elephantine costume drama chronicling the French queen's life from princesshood to her final days before the Revolution. A Shearer festival all the way, and a late example of MGM's overstuffed period style and star-power. Overlong, but engrossing for the wrong reasons. Morley, in his first film, plays Louis XVI. Power's only MGM loan-out casts him as a Swedish count and Marie's romantic dalliance. Based on a book by Stephan Zweig, with script assistance from (among others) F. Scott Fitzgerald. 160m/B VHS, Beta, LV. Norma Shearer, Tyrone Power, John Barrymore, Robert Morley, Gladys George, Anita Louise, Joseph Schildkraut, Henry Stephenson, Reginald Gardiner, Peter Bull, Albert Dekker, Joseph Calleia, George Zucco, Cora Witherspoon, Barry Fitzgerald, Mae Busch, Harry Davenport, Scotty Beckett; **D:** Woodbridge S. Van Dyke; **W:** F. Scott Fitzgerald; **C:** William H. Daniels. Nominations: Academy Awards '38: Best Actress (Shearer), Best Interior Decoration, Best Supporting Actor (Morley), Best Original Score. MGM

Marie Galante 🎞🎞🎞 1934 Fine spy drama has Tracy running into Gallien in Panama (years earlier she had been left there after a kidnapping). He finds her most helpful in his attempt to thwart the bombing of the Panama Canal. It's the performances that raise this otherwise standard thriller up a few notches. 88m/B VHS, Beta. Spencer Tracy, Katie Galian, Ned Sparks, Helen Morgan, Sig Rumann, Leslie Fenton, Jay C. Flippen; **D:** Henry King. NOS, SNC, HEG

Marihuana 🎞 *Marijuana: The Devil's Weed* 1936 An unintentionally hilarious, "Reefer Madness"-type cautionary film about the exaggerated evils of pot smoking. A real dopey film favored by right-winger zealots. 58m/B VHS, Beta. Harley Wood, Hugh McArthur, Pat Carlyle; **D:** Dwain Esper. SNC, VYY, HEG

Marilyn & Bobby: Her Final Affair 🎞½ 1994 Sordid account of the alleged romance between movie star Monroe (Anderson) and Attorney General Robert Kennedy (Kelly). Culminates in a silly scene at Marilyn's home, on the night of her death, where various men all try to find her tell-all diary while keeping out of sight of each other. Made for cable TV. 95m/C VHS. Melody Anderson, James F. Kelly, Richard Dysart, Thomas Wagner, Raymond Serra, Kristopher Tabori, Jonathan Banks, Geoffrey Blake, Ian Buchanan; **D:** Bradford May. AVE

Marilyn: The Untold Story 🎞🎞🎞 1980 Nominated for an Emmy, Hicks elevates what could easily have been a dull made-for-TV movie with her remarkable performance as Marilyn Monroe. Based on the book by Norman Mailer. 156m/C VHS. Catherine Hicks, Richard Basehart, Frank Converse, John Ireland, Sheree North, Anne Ramsey, Viveca Lindfors, Jason Miller, Bill Vint; **D:** Jack Arnold, John Flynn, Lawrence Schiller; **M:** William Goldstein.

Marine Raiders 🎞🎞 1943 Marines train and then fight at Guadalcanal. A typical flag-waver, watchable but not particularly engaging. 90m/B VHS, Beta. Pat O'Brien, Robert Ryan, Ruth Hussey, Frank McHugh, Barton MacLane; **D:** Harold Schuster. TTC

Marius 🎞🎞🎞🎞 1931 This is the first of Marcel Pagnol's trilogy ("Fanny" and "Cesar" followed), about the lives and adventures of the people of Provence, France. Marius is a young man who dreams of going away to sea. When he acts on those dreams, he leaves behind his girlfriend, Fanny. Realistic dialogue and vivid characterizations. Adapted by Pagnol from his play. The musical play and film "Fanny" (1961) were adapted from this trilogy. 125m/B VHS, Beta, LV. *FR* Raimu, Pierre Fresnay, Charpin, Orane Demazis; **D:** Alexander Korda; **W:** Marcel Pagnol; **M:** Francis Gromon. NOS, MRV, INT

Marius and Jeannette 🎞🎞½ *Marius et Jeannette: Un Conte de L'Estaque* 1997 Single mother of two, Jeannette (Ascaride), works as a checkout clerk in a poor Marseilles neighborhood. Marius (Meylan) works as a security guard at a closed cement factory and meets Jeannette when he catches her stealing paint cans from the property. He offers to help her paint her apartment and the two begin a tentative romance. But something spooks Marius and he begins to drink heavily, abandoning Jeannette. Two of Jeannette's male neighbors decide to find out what Marius' problem is and get the twosome back together. Very sweet and sentimental. 101m/C VHS. *FR* Ariane Ascaride, Gerard Meylan, Pascale Roberts, Jacques Boudet, Jean-Pierre Darroussin, Frederique Bonnal; **D:** Robert Guediguian; **W:** Robert Guediguian, Jean-Louis Milesi; **C:** Bernard Cavile. Cesar Awards '98: Best Actress (Ascaride). NYR

Marjoe 1972 (PG) Documentary follows the career of rock-style evangelist Marjoe Gortner, who spent 25 years of his life touring the country as a professional preacher. Marjoe later went on to become an actor and professional fundraiser. 88m/C VHS, Beta. Marjoe Gortner; **D:** Howard Smith, Sarah Kernochan. Academy Awards '72: Best Feature Documentary. COL

Marjorie Morningstar 🎞🎞 1958 A temperate Hollywood adaptation of the Herman Wouk story of a young actress who fails to achieve stardom and settles on being a housewife. Wood slipped a bit in this story. 123m/C VHS. Natalie Wood, Gene Kelly, Martin Balsam, Claire Trevor, Ed Wynn, Everett Sloane, Carolyn Jones; **D:** Irving Rapper; **C:** Harry Stradling; **M:** Max Steiner. Nominations: Academy Awards '58: Best Song ("A Very Precious Love"). REP

The Mark 🎞🎞🎞½ 1961 Story of a convicted child molester who cannot escape his past upon his release from prison. Whitman gives a riveting performance as the convict. 127m/B VHS, Beta. *GB* Stuart Whitman, Maria Schell, Rod Steiger, Brenda de Banzie, Maurice Denham, Donald Wolfit, Paul Rogers, Donald Houston, Amanda Black, Russell Napier, Marie Devereux; **D:** Guy Green; **W:** Sidney Buchman, Raymond Stross; **M:** Richard Rodney Bennett. Nominations: Academy Awards '61: Best Actor (Whitman). NO

Mark of Cain 🎞🎞½ 1984 Twin brothers, one normal, the other a raving lunatic with murderous tendencies, confuse the authorities who imprison the nice guy, allowing the nutcase to chase after his beautiful sister-in-law. 90m/C VHS, Beta. Robin Ward, Wendy Crewson, August Schellenberg; **D:** Bruce Pittman; **W:** Peter Colley. ART, VES

Mark of the Beast 🎞 19?? Two students inadvertently videotape an assassination, and are then relentlessly pursued by the killer. 90m/C VHS. Carolyn Guillet, David Smulker; **D:** Robert Stewart. NO

Mark of the Devil 🎞 *Burn, Witch, Burn; Brenn, Hexe, Brenn; Satan; Hexen bis aufs Blut Gequaelt* 1969 (R) Witchcraft and romance don't mix, as a Medieval witch hunter and a sexy girl accused of witchery discover. Notoriously graphic torture scenes add to the mayhem but the weird part is that this is based on true stories. 96m/C VHS, Beta. *GB GE* Herbert Lom, Olivera Vuco, Udo Kier, Reggie Nalder, Herbert Fux, Michael Maien, Ingeborg

Schoener, Johannes Buzalski, Gaby Fuchs, Adrian Hoven; **D:** Michael Armstrong; **W:** Sergio Casstner, Adrian Hoven; **C:** Ernst W. Kalinke. *VTR, TPV, VDM*

Mark of the Devil 2 *🎬* 1972 (R) Sadistic witchhunters torture satan's servants and torch sisters of mercy, whilst trying to horn in on a nobleman's fortune. It's just not as gross without the vomit bags. 90m/C VHS. *GB GE* Erika Blanc, Anton Diffring, Reggie Nalder; **D:** Adrian Hoven. *VDM*

The Mark of the Hawk *🎬🎬🎬* *The Accused* 1957 A uniquely told story of African nations struggling to achieve racial equality after gaining independence. Songs include "This Man Is Mine," sung by Kitt. 83m/C VHS. *GB* Sidney Poitier, Eartha Kitt, Juano Hernandez, John McIntire; **D:** Michael Audley. *MRV*

Mark of the Spur *🎬½* 1932 The mark on an injured man's face is used to track down his attacker. 60m/B VHS, Beta. Bob Custer, Lillian Rich, Franklyn Farnum, Bud Osborne; **D:** J.P. McGowan. *NOS, DVT, GPV*

Mark of the Vampire *🎬🎬🎬* *Vampires of Prague* 1935 A murder in a small town is solved through the use of vaudeville actors who pose as vampires. Great cast, surprise ending. 61m/B VHS, Beta. Lionel Barrymore, Bela Lugosi, Elizabeth Allan, Lionel Atwill, Jean Hersholt, Donald Meek, Carroll Borland; **D:** Tod Browning; **W:** Tod Browning, Guy Endore, Bernard Schubert; **C:** James Wong Howe. *MGM, MLB*

Mark of Zorro *🎬🎬🎬* 1920 Fairbanks plays a dual role as the hapless Don Diego and his dashing counterpart, Zorro, the hero of the oppressed. Silent film. 80m/B VHS, LV. Douglas Fairbanks Sr., Marguerite de la Motte, Noah Beery Sr.; **D:** Fred Niblo. *REP, MRV, GPV*

The Mark of Zorro *🎬🎬🎬½* 1940 The dashing Power swashbuckles his way through this wonderfully acted and directed romp. He plays the foppish son of a 19th-century California aristocrat who is secretly the masked avenger of the oppressed peons. Bromberg plays the wicked governor, with the beautiful niece (Darnell) beloved by Power, and Rathbone is supremely evil as his cruel minion. Lots of swordplay with a particularly exciting duel to the death between Rathbone and Power. Based on the novel "The Curse of Capistrano" by Johnston McCulley. Remake of the 1921 silent film and followed by a number of other Zorro incarnations. 93m/B VHS. Tyrone Power, Linda Darnell, Basil Rathbone, Gale Sondergaard, Eugene Pallette, J. Edward Bromberg, Montagu Love, Janet Beecher; **D:** Rouben Mamoulian; **W:** John Taintor Foote; **C:** Arthur C. Miller; **M:** Alfred Newman. Nominations: Academy Awards '40: Best Original Score. *FOX, BTV*

Mark Twain and Me *🎬🎬½* 1991 Robards portrays the aging and irascible Mark Twain, attended by a neglected but devoted daughter, and befriended by 11-year-old Dorothy Quick, as they travel on the same ship. Based on a true story. Made for television. 93m/C VHS. Jason Robards Jr., Talia Shire, Amy Stewart, Chris Wiggins, R.H. Thomson, Fiona Reid; **D:** Daniel Petrie. *DIS, BTV*

Marked for Death *🎬½* *Screwface* 1990 (R) Having killed a prostitute, DEA agent Seagal decides it's time to roll out the white picket fence in the 'burbs with the little woman and brood. Trouble is, a bunch of guys with dreadlocks don't approve of his early retirement, and the Jamaican gangsters plan to send him and his family to the great Rasta playground in the sky. Whereupon the Stevester kicks and punches and wags his ponytail. Much blood flows, mon. Tunes by Jimmy Cliff. 93m/C VHS, LV, Closed Caption. Steven Seagal, Joanna Pacula, Basil Wallace, Keith David, Danielle Harris, Arlen Dean Snyder, Teri Weigel; **D:** Dwight Little; **W:** Mark Victor, Michael Grais. *CCB*

Marked for Murder *🎬½* 1945 Another in the Texas Ranger series. In this entry, the Rangers come to the rescue when a rancher war appears inevitable. 58m/B VHS, LV. Tex Ritter, Dave O'Brien, Guy Wilkerson; **D:** Elmer Clifton; **W:** Elmer Clifton. *THV*

Marked for Murder *🎬½* 1989 (R) Two TV station employees are framed for murder after being sent out to find a missing videocassette. Renee Estevez is part of the Sheen/Estevez dynasty. 88m/C VHS, Beta. Renee Estevez, Wings Hauser, Jim Mitchum, Ross Hagen, Ken Abraham; **D:** Rick Sloane. *THV*

Marked Man *🎬🎬* 1996 (R) After auto mechanic Frank Stanton (Piper) witnesses a murder he finds himself accused of the crime and on the run, trying to prove his innocence.**CW:** Violence and language. 94m/C VHS, LV, Closed Caption. Roddy Piper, Jane Wheeler, Alina Thompson, Miles O'Keeffe; **D:** Marc Voizard; **W:** Thomas Ritz; **C:** Stephen Reizes; **M:** Marty Simon. *ART*

Marked Money *🎬🎬* 1928 Amiable captain takes in boy who'll soon roll in the dough and swindlers show up on the scene. The captain's courageous girl and her pilot beau step in to right the rookery. 61m/B VHS, Beta. Frank "Junior" Coghlan, Tom George Duryea Keene, Tom Kennedy, Bert Woodruff, Virginia Bradford, Maurice Black, Jack Richardson; **D:** Spencer Gordon Bennet. *GPV, FCT*

Marked Trails *🎬* 1944 One clue stamps out the guilty parties in this wild west saga. 59m/B VHS, Beta. Hoot Gibson, Bob Steele, Veda Ann Borg. *NOS, DVT*

Marked Woman *🎬🎬🎬* 1937 Gangster drama about crusading District Attorney who persuades a group of clipjoint hostesses to testify against their gangster boss. A gritty studio melodrama loosely based on a true story. 97m/B VHS, Beta, LV, Closed Caption. Bette Davis, Humphrey Bogart, Eduardo Ciannelli, Isabel Jewell, Jane Bryan, Mayo Methot, Allen Jenkins, Lola Lane; **D:** Lloyd Bacon; **C:** George Barnes. Venice Film Festival '37: Best Actress (Davis). *MGM*

Marlowe *🎬🎬½* 1969 (PG) Updated telling by Stirling Silliphant of Chandler's "The Little Sister" sports retro guy Garner as Philip Marlowe, gumshoe. Hired by a mystery blonde to find her misplaced brother, rumpled sleuth Marlowe encounters kicking Bruce Lee in his first film. Slick looking, but the story's a bit slippery. 95m/C VHS, Beta. James Garner, Gayle Hunnicutt, Carroll O'Connor, Rita Moreno, Sharon Farrell, William Daniels, Bruce Lee; **D:** Paul Bogart; **W:** Stirling Silliphant; **C:** William H. Daniels. *MGM, FCT*

Marnie *🎬🎬🎬½* 1964 A lovely blonde with a mysterious past robs her employers and then changes her identity. When her current boss catches her in the act and forces her to marry him, he soon learns the puzzling aspects of Marnie's background. Criticized at the time of its release, the movie has since been accepted as a Hitchcock classic. 130m/C VHS, Beta, LV. Tippi Hedren, Sean Connery, Diane Baker, Bruce Dern, Louise Latham; **D:** Alfred Hitchcock; **W:** Jay Presson Allen; **C:** Robert Burks. *UNI*

Maroc 7 *🎬* 1967 Slow story of a secret agent after a thief suffering from a split personality. 92m/C VHS, Closed Caption. Gene Barry, Elsa Martinelli, Cyd Charisse, Leslie Phillips; **D:** Gerry O'Hara. *PAR*

Marooned *🎬½* *Space Travellers* 1969 (G) Tense thriller casts Crenna, Hackman, and Franciscus as astronauts stranded in space after a retro-rocket misfires and their craft is unable to return to earth. Amazingly inept despite an Academy Award for effects and an excellent cast. Story bears a striking resemblance to 1995's "Apollo 13." 134m/C VHS, Beta, LV. Gregory Peck, David Janssen, Richard Crenna, James Franciscus, Gene Hackman, Lee Grant; **D:** John Sturges; **C:** Daniel F. Fapp. Academy Awards '69: Best Visual Effects; Nominations: Academy Awards '69: Best Cinematography, Best Sound. *GKK*

Marquis *🎬🎬* 1990 A bizarre satire combining sex, lust, and the French Revolution, based on the writings of the Marquis de Sade. Amusing, decadent, and not for the prudish. In French with English subtitles. 88m/C VHS. *FR* **D:** Henri Xhonneux. *FRF*

Marquis de Sade *🎬½* *Dark Prince: Intimate Tales of Marquis de Sade* 1997 (R) Justine searches for her sister Juliette in 17th-century Paris and is drawn into the sexually deviant world of the Marquis de Sade. Also available unrated.**CW:** Strong perverse sexuality, some violence and brief language. 88m/C VHS. Nick Mancuso, Janet Gunn, John Rhys-Davies; **D:** Gwyneth Gibby. *NHO*

The Marriage Circle *🎬🎬🎬* 1924 A pivotal silent comedy depicting the infidelity of several married couples in Vienna. Director Lubitsch's first American comedy. Remade as a musical, "One Hour With You," in 1932. Silent. 90m/B VHS. Florence Vidor, Monte Blue, Marie Prevost, Creighton Hale, Adolphe Menjou, Harry Myers, Dale Fuller; **D:** Ernst Lubitsch. *NOS, MOV, GVV*

Marriage Is Alive and Well *🎬* 1980 A wedding photographer reflects on the institution of marriage from his unique perspective. Made for television. 100m/C VHS. Joe Namath, Jack Albertson, Melinda Dillon, Judd Hirsch, Susan Sullivan, Fred McCarren, Swoosie Kurtz; **D:** Russ Mayberry. *ART*

Marriage Italian Style *🎬🎬🎬* 1964 When an engaged man hears that his mistress is on her death bed, he goes to her side and, in an emotional gesture, promises to marry her if she survives. She does, and holds him to his promise. After they're married, however, she gives him a big surprise—three grown sons. A silly film, but DeSica's direction keeps it from being too fluffy. Lots of fun. Based on the play "Filumena Marturano" by Eduardo De Filippo. 102m/C VHS. *IT* Sophia Loren, Marcello Mastroianni, Tecla Scarano, Marilu Tolo; **D:** Vittorio De Sica. Golden Globe Awards '65: Best Foreign Film; Nominations: Academy Awards '64: Best Actress (Loren). *VTR*

The Marriage of Maria Braun *🎬🎬🎬🎬* *Die Ehe Der Maria Braun* 1979 (R) In post-WWII Germany, a young woman uses guile and sexuality to survive as the nation rebuilds itself into an industrial power. The first movie in Fassbinder's trilogy about German women in Germany during the post war years, it is considered one of the director's finest films, and an indispensable example of the New German Cinema. In German with English subtitles. 120m/C VHS, Beta. *GE* Hanna Schygulla, Klaus Lowitsch, Ivan Desny, Gottfried John, Gisela Uhlen; **D:** Rainer Werner Fassbinder; **W:** Rainer Werner Fassbinder; **C:** Michael Ballhaus; **M:** Peer Raben. Berlin International Film Festival '79: Best Actress (Schygulla). *NYF, COL, GLV*

Married? *🎬½* 1926 Couple endures 365 days of marital bliss in order to inherit big bucks. Some do it for less. 65m/B VHS, Beta. Owen Moore, Constance Bennett; **D:** George Terwilliger. *GPV, FCT*

A Married Man *🎬🎬* 1984 Story focusing on a bored British lawyer who begins cheating on his wife. Amid the affair, someone gets murdered. Made for television. 200m/C VHS, Beta. *GB* Anthony Hopkins, Ciaran Madden, Lise Hilboldt, Yvonne Coulette, John Le Mesurier, Sophie Ashton; **D:** John Davies. *ART*

Married People, Single Sex *🎬🎬½* 1993 (R) Three couples decide to spread their sexual wings. Shelly takes a new lover; Artie makes obscene phone calls; and Beth and Mike, who end their relationship, still can't keep out of bed. An unrated version is also available.**CW:** Sex-related dialogue and strong sexuality. 110m/C VHS. Chase Masterson, Joe Pilato, Darla Slavens, Shelley Michelle, Wendi Westbrook, Robert Zachar, Samuel Mongiello, Teri Thompson; **D:** Mike Sedan; **W:** Catherine Tavel. *TRI*

Married People, Single Sex 2: For Better or Worse *🎬½* 1994 (R) Three women are faced with sexual unhappiness: Carol's hubby had an affair, Valerie wants a baby but her spouse doesn't, and Karen's husband is just too darn nice (she wants some spice in her life). So, there's lots of sexual encounters to solve their problems. Also available unrated.**CW:** Language; nudity; strong sexuality. 93m/C VHS. Kathy Shower, Monique Parent, Liza Smith, Craig Stepp, Doug Jeffrey; **D:** Mike Sedan. *TRI*

Married to It ✗✗ 1993 (R) Three vastly different couples work together to plan a pageant at a private school. The oil and water group includes struggling hippie leftovers Bridges and Channing, '80s-era corporate cutthroats Shepherd and Silver, and starry-eyed newlyweds Masterson and Leonard. Contrived plot offers few humourous moments, with the main focus revolving around coping rather than comedy. And the coping is slow business, done by characters you don't really care about with problems that don't really matter. **CW:** Language and one sensual scene. 112m/C VHS, LV, **Closed Caption.** Beau Bridges, Stockard Channing, Robert Sean Leonard, Mary Stuart Masterson, Cybill Shepherd, Ron Silver; **D:** Arthur Hiller; **W:** Janet Kovalcik; **M:** Henry Mancini. ORI

Married to the Mob ✗✗✗ 1988 (R) After the murder of her husband, an attractive Mafia widow tries to escape "mob" life, but ends up fighting off amorous advances from the current mob boss while being wooed by an undercover cop. A snappy script and a spry performance by Pfeiffer pepper this easy-to-watch film. 102m/C VHS, Beta, LV, **Closed Caption.** Michelle Pfeiffer, Dean Stockwell, Alec Baldwin, Matthew Modine, Mercedes Ruehl, Anthony J. Nici, Joan Cusack, Ellen Foley, Chris Isaak, Trey Wilson, Charles Napier, Tracey Walter, Al Lewis, Nancy Travis, David Johansen, Jonathan Demme; **D:** Jonathan Demme; **W:** Mark Burns, Barry Strugatz; **C:** Tak Fujimoto; **M:** David Byrne. New York Film Critics Awards '88: Best Supporting Actor (Stockwell); National Society of Film Critics Awards '88: Best Supporting Actor (Stockwell), Best Supporting Actress (Ruehl); Nominations: Academy Awards '88: Best Supporting Actor (Stockwell). ORI

Married Too Young ✗ I Married Too Young 1962 High school honeys elope, despite disapproval from the parental units. When the boy groom trades his med school plans for a monkey wrench in order to support the little missus, he finds much trouble with the hot rod heavies. 76m/B VHS. Harold Lloyd Jr., Jana Lund, Anthony Dexter, Marianna Hill, Trudy Marshall, Brian O'Hara, Nita Loveless; **D:** George Moskov. HHT, SNC

A Married Woman ✗✗✗ La Femme Mariee 1965 Dramatizes a day in the life of a woman who has both a husband and a lover. One of Godard's more mainstream efforts. 94m/B VHS, Beta, 8mm. FR Macha Meril, Phillipe LeRoy, Bernard Noel; **D:** Jean-Luc Godard; **W:** Jean-Luc Godard. VYY, MRV, DVT

Marry Me, Marry Me ✗✗✗ Mazel Tov Ou le Mariage 1969 (R) While in Paris, a Jewish encyclopedia salesman falls in love with a pregnant Belgian woman. A sensitive story about European Jewish families. Berri wrote, produced, directed, and starred in this romantic comedy. 87m/C VHS. FR Elisabeth Wiener, Regine, Claude Berri, Louisa Colpeyn; **D:** Claude Berri; **C:** Ghislan Cloquet. NO

The Marrying Kind ✗✗½ 1952 Marrieds Florence (Holliday) and Chet (Ray) Keefer are in the chambers of Judge Carroll (Kennedy) talking about why they want a divorce. They flashback to their courtship and marriage and the bumps they've endured along the way, and then realize they still love each other. Holliday reunited with Cukor and scriptwriters Gordon and Kanin after their triumph with "Born Yesterday." 92m/B VHS. Judy Holliday, Aldo Ray, Madge Kennedy, Sheila Bond, John Alexander, Peggy Cass, Rex Williams; **D:** George Cukor; **W:** Ruth Gordon, Garson Kanin; **C:** Joseph Walker; **M:** Hugo Friedhofer. COL

The Marrying Man ✗½ 1991 (R) Young man meets his match when his buddies take him to Las Vegas for his bachelor party. He falls like a ton of bricks for the singer, not knowing she belongs to the local crime lord, who catches them together and forces them to marry. They immediately divorce, can't forget each other and eventually re-marry, again and again and again. Silly story supposedly based on the story of Harry Karl (eventual husband of Debbie Reynolds) and Marie MacDonald. Basinger and Baldwin's off-stage romance created quite a stir but their chemistry onscreen is zilch. Ineffective, not funny, poorly

paced and acted: a good example of what happens when egotistical stars get their way. **CW:** Language and sensuality. 116m/C VHS, LV, **Closed Caption.** Alec Baldwin, Kim Basinger, Robert Loggia, Armand Assante, Elisabeth Shue, Paul Reiser, Fisher Stevens, Peter Dobson, Gretchen Wyler; **D:** Jerry Rees; **W:** Neil Simon; **M:** David Newman. HPH

Mars ✗✗ 1996 Fast-paced space western finds independent lawman Caution Templar (Gruner) receiving a frantic message from his brother to return to the wild mining town of Alpha City, Mars. Only by the time he arrives his brother is dead and Templar is determined to find out what happened. 92m/C VHS. Olivier Gruner, Shari Belafonte, Scott Valentine, Amber Smith, Alex Hyde-White, Lee DeBroux; **D:** Jon Hess. AVA

Mars Attacks! ✗✗½ 1996 (PG-13) Only director Burton could make a movie based on a series of 1960s trading cards. Intentionally tacky, this huge scale epic spoof of monster, sci-fi, and disaster flicks finds moronic President Dale (Nicholson), his frigid wife (Close) and a cast of thousands battling the green-skinned invaders. Jack's back for a second role as Vegas hotel developer Art Land, who tries to cash in on the opportunities the invasion brings. Plot is relatively nonexistent and zig-zags wildly throughout, but the gist is that the aliens are bent on destroying the population, and have little trouble battling the bumbling humans. Brosnan is the hilariously deluded alien-hugger, Professor Kessler. A semi-lampoon of fellow alien flick competitor "Independence Day," this film goes all out for the camp laugh, but its big budget effects, way over-the-top style and all-star cast can't conquer the audience. **CW:** Sci-fi fantasy violence and brief sexuality. 106m/C VHS, LV, **Closed Caption, DVD.** Jack Nicholson, Glenn Close, Martin Short, Pierce Brosnan, Lukas Haas, Sarah Jessica Parker, Michael J. Fox, Natalie Portman, Rod Steiger, Paul Winfield, Annette Bening, Sylvia Sidney, Danny DeVito, Tom Jones, Pam Grier, Jim Brown, Lisa Marie; **D:** Tim Burton; **W:** Jonathan Gems; **C:** Peter Suschitzsky; **M:** Danny Elfman. Nominations: MTV Movie Awards '97: Best Fight (Jim Brown/A Martian). WAR

Mars Needs Women ✗ 1966 When the Martian singles scene starts to drag, Mars boys cross the galaxy in search of fertile earth babes to help them repopulate the planet. Seems Batgirl Craig, the go-go dancing lady scientist, is at the top of their dance cards. 80m/C VHS. Tommy Kirk, Yvonne Craig; **D:** Larry Buchanan; **W:** Larry Buchanan. SNC

Marshal Law ✗✗ 1996 (R) Highland Glen is a gated community in L.A. that seems very secure, especially to ex-Texas Marshal Jack Coleman (Smits) and his family. But an earthquake leaves the neighborhood prey to a vicious gang unless Coleman can find a way to outwit them. **CW:** Strong violence and language and for some sexuality and drug use. 96m/C VHS, **Closed Caption.** Jimmy Smits, James LeGros, Vonte Sweet, Scott Plank, Kristy Swanson, Channon Roe, Michael Cavalieri, Rodney Rowland, Tai Thai; **D:** Stephen Cornwell; **W:** Stephen Cornwell, Nick Gregory; **C:** Levie Isaacks; **M:** Tim Truman. MGM

Marshal of Cedar Rock ✗✗ 1953 Marshal Rocky Lane sets a prisoner free, thinking the guy will lead him to a stash of stolen bank funds. Seems he miscalculates, but by way of consolation, he routs a rotten railroad agent who's rooking innocent people. Features the equine talent of Black Jack. 54m/B VHS. Allan "Rocky" Lane, Phyllis Coates, Roy Barcroft, William Henry, Robert Shayne, Eddy Waller; **D:** Harry Keller. HEG, DVT, NOS

Marshal of Heldorado ✗ 1950 An outlaw-infested town needs an injection of law and order. 53m/B VHS. James Ellison, Russell Hayden, Raymond Hatton, Fuzzy Knight; **D:** Thomas Carr. NOS, DVT

The Marshal's Daughter ✗½ 1953 A father and daughter team up to outwit an outlaw. Features many cowboy songs, including the title track by Tex Ritter. 71m/B VHS. Tex Ritter, Ken Murray,

Laurie Anders, Preston Foster, Hoot Gibson; **D:** William (Lester Williams) Berke. NOS, MOV, HEG

Martha and I ✗✗✗ 1991 In 1934 Czechoslovakia, distinguished Jewish doctor Ernest Paul Fuchs (Piccoli), having divorced his unfaithful wife, impulsively marries his lower-class gentile German maid Martha (Sagebrecht). What turns out to be a true love match is witnessed through the adolescent eyes of nephew Emil (Chalupa), who comes to live with the couple. With the rise of Nazism and increased Jewish persecution the devoted Martha begins to fear for her husband and makes a futile attempt to find a safe haven. Stirring drama based on the director's childhood (he's the semi-fictionalized Emil). German with subtitles. 107m/C VHS. GE Marianne Saegebrecht, Michel Piccoli, Vaclav Chalupa, Ondrej Vetchy; **D:** Jiri Weiss; **W:** Jiri Weiss; **C:** Viktor Ruzicka; **M:** Jiri Stivin. NYR

Martial Law ✗½ 1990 (R) A film solely for martial arts fans. Two cops use their hands, feet, and other body parts to fight crime. 90m/C VHS. Chad McQueen, Cynthia Rothrock, David Carradine, Andy McCutcheon; **D:** S.E. Cohen; **W:** Richard Brandes. FOX, VTR

Martial Law 2: Undercover ✗½ 1991 (R) Two cops, martial arts experts and part of an elite police force called Martial Law, go undercover to investigate the murder of a colleague. They uncover a fast-growing crime ring headed by a bad cop and a nightclub owner. The nightclub is host to the city's rich and powerful, who are treated to a bevy of beautiful women, protected by martial arts experts, and entertained by martial arts fights to the death. Lots of high-kicking action. **CW:** Language, violence, and one sensual scene. 92m/C VHS, LV, **Closed Caption.** Jeff Wincott, Cynthia Rothrock, Paul Johansson, Evan Lurie, L. Charles Taylor, Sherrie Rose, Billy Drago; **D:** Kurt Anderson; **W:** Richard Brandes, Jiles Fitzgerald. USH

Martial Outlaw ✗✗ 1993 (R) DEA man Kevin White (Wincott) has been following a drug-dealing ex-KGB kingpin from Moscow to San Francisco. The Russian's latest move takes him to Los Angeles where Kevin meets up with his older brother Jack (Hudson), a maverick LA cop. Jack persuades Kevin to let him in on the action but Kevin begins to suspect Jack is playing both sides and their sibling rivalry could lead to death. 89m/C VHS, LV, **Closed Caption.** Jeff Wincott, Gary Hudson, Richard Jaeckel, Krista Errickson, Vladimir Skomarovsky, Liliana Komorowska, Gary Wood; **D:** Kurt Anderson; **W:** Thomas Ritz. REP

The Martian Chronicles: Part 1 1979 Series episode "The Explorers." Adapted from Ray Bradbury's critically acclaimed novel. Futuristic explorations of the planet Mars. Strange fates of the discovery teams make everything more curious. Made for television. 120m/C VHS, Beta. Rock Hudson, Bernie Casey, Nicholas Hammond, Darren McGavin; **D:** Michael Anderson Sr.

The Martian Chronicles: Part 2 ✗½ 1979 Episode following the television movie. This part is called "The Settlers." The planet Mars meets with its first colonization and the settlers watch the Earth explode. 97m/C VHS, Beta. Rock Hudson, Fritz Weaver, Roddy McDowall, Bernie Casey, Darren McGavin, Gayle Hunnicutt, Barry Morse, Bernadette Peters; **D:** Michael Anderson Sr.

The Martian Chronicles: Part 3 ✗✗½ 1979 In the final chapter of this space saga, the Martian's secrets become known and will forever change man's destiny. Adapted from Ray Bradbury's classic novel; made-for-television. 97m/C VHS, Beta. Rock Hudson, Bernadette Peters, Christopher Connelly, Fritz Weaver, Roddy McDowall, Bernie Casey, Nicholas Hammond, Darren McGavin, Gayle Hunnicutt, Barry Morse; **D:** Michael Anderson Sr.

Martians Go Home! ✗½ 1990 (PG-13) Joke-loving Martians come to earth and pester a nerdy composer. 89m/C VHS, Beta, LV. Randy Quaid, Margaret Colin, Anita Morris, John Philbin, Ronny Cox, Gerrit Graham, Barry Sobel, Vic Dunlop; **D:** David Odell. NO

Martin 🎬🎬🎬 **1977 (R)** Martin is a charming young man, though slightly mad. He freely admits of the need to drink blood. Contemporary vampire has found a new abhorrent means of killing his victims. **96m/C VHS, Beta, LV.** John Amplas, Lincoln Maazel, Christine Forrest, Elayne Nadeau, Tom Savini, Sarah Venable, George A. Romero, Fran Middleton; **D:** George A. Romero; **C:** Michael Gornick; **M:** Donald Rubinstein. *VTR*

Martin Chuzzlewit 🎬🎬½ **1994** Martin Chuzzlewit (Scofield) is a rich and elderly man with a lot of greedy relatives just waiting for him to die so they can get their hands on his money. The only exceptions being his already disinherited namesake grandson and his young orphaned nurse, Mary Graham. Adapted from the Charles Dickens novel. On three cassettes. **288m/C VHS, Closed Caption.** Paul Scofield, John Mills, Pete Postlethwaite, Tom Wilkinson, Julia Sawalha; **D:** Pedr James. *PBS, FOX, VIF*

Martin Luther 🎬½ **1953** French-made biography of the 16th century reformer who began the Protestant Reformation. **105m/B VHS, Beta.** *FR* Niall MacGinnis, John Ruddock, Pierre Leeavre, Guy Verney. Nominations: Academy Awards '53: Best Art Direction/Set Decoration (B & W), Best Black and White Cinematography. *NOS, VCI, ECU*

Martin's Day 🎬🎬 **1985 (PG)** An unusual friendship develops between an escaped convict and the young boy he kidnaps. **99m/C VHS, Beta, Closed Caption.** *CA* Richard Harris, Lindsay Wagner, James Coburn, Justin Henry, Karen Black, John Ireland; **D:** Alan Gibson; **W:** Chris Bryant, Allan Scott. *MGM, FOX*

Marty 🎬🎬🎬½ **1955** Marty is a painfully shy bachelor who feels trapped in a pointless life of family squabbles. When he finds love, he also finds the strength to break out of what he feels is a meaningless existence. A sensitive and poignant film from the writer of "Altered States." Remake of a television version that originally aired in 1953. Notable for Borgnine's sensitive portrayal, one of his last quality jobs before sinking into the B-Movie sludge pit. **91m/B VHS, Beta, LV, Closed Caption.** Ernest Borgnine, Betsy Blair, Joe De Santis, Esther Minciotti, Jerry Paris, Karen Steele; **D:** Delbert Mann; **W:** Paddy Chayefsky; **C:** Joseph LaShelle. Academy Awards '55: Best Actor (Borgnine), Best Director (Mann), Best Picture, Best Screenplay; British Academy Awards '55: Best Actor (Borgnine), Best Actress (Blair); Directors Guild of America Awards '55: Best Director (Mann); Golden Globe Awards '56: Best Actor—Drama (Borgnine); National Board of Review Awards '55: Best Actor (Borgnine), National Film Registry '94;; New York Film Critics Awards '55: Best Actor (Borgnine), Best Film; Nominations: Academy Awards '55: Best Art Direction/Set Decoration (B & W), Best Black and White Cinematography, Best Supporting Actor (Mantell), Best Supporting Actress (Blair). *MGM, FOX, BTV*

Marvelous Stunts of Kung Fu 🎬 **1983** Beautiful woman, fortune teller, and martial arts hero team up to seek vengeance against the evil empire. **86m/C VHS, Beta.** Ling Yun, Wei Ping Line, Lung Fei. *TWE*

Marvin & Tige 🎬🎬½ **1984 (PG)** A deep friendship develops between an aging alcoholic and a street-wise 11-year-old boy after they meet one night in an Atlanta park. **104m/C VHS, Beta.** John Cassavetes, Gibran Brown, Billy Dee Williams, Fay Hauser, Denise Nicholas-Hill; **D:** Eric Weston; **W:** Eric Weston, Wanda Dell.

Marvin's Room 🎬🎬½ **1996 (PG-13)** Guaranteed sobfest with a gifted set of performers. Sensitive spinster Bessie (Keaton) is living in Orlando where she's been caring for her bedridden father, Marvin (Cronyn), who's been dying for the last 20 years, and her eccentric aunt Ruth (Verdon). When she's stricken with leukemia and needs a bone marrow donor, Bessie must rely on tough, estranged sister Lee (Streep) to help out. But divorcee Lee's got her hands full with rebellious teenaged son Hank (DiCaprio) and his geeky younger bro Charlie (Scardino) and is none too eager to renew the family ties. Based on Scott McPherson's 1991 Off-Broadway play.**CW:** Thematic elements and brief language. **98m/C VHS, LV, Closed Caption.** Diane Keaton, Meryl Streep, Leonardo DiCaprio, Hume Cronyn, Gwen Verdon, Hal Scardino, Robert De Niro, Dan Hedaya, Margo Martindale, Cynthia Nixon; **D:** Jerry Zaks; **W:** Scott McPherson; **C:** Piotr Sobocinski; **M:** Rachel Portman. Nominations: Academy Awards '96: Best Actress (Keaton); Golden Globe Awards '97: Best Actress—Drama (Streep); Screen Actors Guild Award '96: Best Actress (Keaton), Best Supporting Actress (Verdon), Cast. *TOU*

The Marx Brothers in a Nutshell 🎬🎬🎬½ **1990** A tribute to the Marx Brothers, narrated by Gene Kelly. Contains clips from "Duck Soup," "Horse Feathers," "Animal Crackers," "Cocoanuts," and "Room Service." Also contains rare outakes and interviews with the brothers, plus guest appearances by Dick Cavett, Robert Klein, David Steinberg, and others. Indispensible. **100m/B VHS, LV.** Groucho Marx, Chico Marx, Harpo Marx, Zeppo Marx, Robert Klein, David Steinberg, George Fenneman, Dick Cavett. *FCT*

Mary and Joseph: A Story of Faith 🎬½ **1979** A speculative look at the experiences and courtship of Mary and Joseph before the birth of Jesus. Made for television. **100m/C VHS, Beta.** Blanche Baker, Jeff East, Colleen Dewhurst, Stephen McHattie, Lloyd Bochner, Paul Hecht; **D:** Eric Till. *ART, WAR*

Mary, Mary, Bloody Mary 🎬 **1976 (R)** Young beautiful artist ravages Mexico with her penchant for drinking blood. Turns out she's a bisexual vampire. When even her friends become victims, her father steps in to end the bloodbath. **85m/C VHS, Beta.** Christina Ferrare, David Young, Helena Rojo, John Carradine; **D:** Juan Lopez Moctezuma; **W:** Malcolm Marmorstein; **M:** Tom Bahler. *NO*

Mary, My Dearest 🎬🎬 *Maria di Mi Corazon* **1983** Maria (Rojo) persuades her smalltime crook boyfriend Hector (Bonilla) to join her in a traveling magic show. When the van breaks down while they're touring, Maria goes in search of a telephone and winds up in a mental institution. Mixture of styles—from an everyday look at the bourgeoise to magic realism and terror—may confuse. Spanish with subtitles. **100m/C VHS.** *MX* Maria Rojo, Hector Bonilla, Salvador Sanchez; **D:** Jaime Humberto Hermosillo; **W:** Gabriel Garcia Marquez, Jaime Humberto Hermosillo; **C:** Angel Goded; **M:** Joaquin Gutierrez Heras. *CVC*

Mary of Scotland 🎬🎬🎬 **1936** The historical tragedy of Mary, Queen of Scots and her cousin, Queen Elizabeth I of England is enacted in this classic film. Traces Mary's claims to the throne of England which ultimately led to her execution. Based on the Maxwell Anderson play. **123m/B VHS, Beta, LV.** Katharine Hepburn, Fredric March, Florence Eldridge, Douglas Walton, John Carradine, Robert Barrat, Gavin Muir, Ian Keith, Moroni Olsen, William Stack, Alan Mowbray; **D:** John Ford. *TTC*

Mary Poppins 🎬🎬🎬½ **1964** Magical English nanny arrives one day on the East Wind and takes over the household of a very proper London banker. She introduces her two charges to her friends and family, including Bert, the chimney sweep (Van Dyke), and eccentric Uncle Albert (Wynn). She also changes the lives of everyone in the family. From her they learn that life can always be happy and joyous if you take the proper perspective. Film debut of Andrews. Based on the books by P.L. Travers. A Disney classic that hasn't lost any of its magic. Look for the wonderful sequence where Van Dyke dances with animated penguins. ♫Chim Chim Cheree; A Spoonful of Sugar; The Perfect Nanny; Sister Suffragette; The Life I Lead; Stay Awake; Feed the Birds; Fidelity Feduciary Bank; Let's Go Fly a Kite. **139m/C VHS, Beta, LV, Letterbox, Closed Caption.** Ed Wynn, Hermione Baddeley, Julie Andrews, Dick Van Dyke, David Tomlinson, Glynis Johns; **D:** Robert Stevenson; **C:** Edward Colman. Academy Awards '64: Best Actress (Andrews), Best Film Editing, Best Song ("Chim Chim Cher-ee"), Best Visual Effects, Best Original Score; Golden Globe Awards '65: Best Actress—Musical/Comedy (Andrews); Nominations: Academy Awards '64: Best Adapted Screenplay, Best Art Direction/Set Decoration (Color), Best Color Cinematography, Best Costume Design (Color), Best Director (Stevenson), Best Picture, Best Sound, Best Original Score. *DIS, BTV, HMV*

Mary, Queen of Scots 🎬🎬½ **1971 (PG-13)** Redgrave does a spirited job in the title role as the headstrong and romantic queen who came to an unfortunate end. Mary is raised in France by her mother's Catholic family, from whom she inherits the Scottish title after her mother's death. She claims the throne much to the dismay of her Protestant half-brother James Stuart (McGoohan) and England's equally Protestant Queen Elizabeth (Jackson), who does not want her own Catholic subjects to get any ideas. Mary makes two unfortunate marriages and winds up being betrayed, eventually forcing Elizabeth to eliminate her dangerous cousin.**CW:** Some violence. **128m/C VHS.** Vanessa Redgrave, Glenda Jackson, Patrick McGoohan, Timothy Dalton, Nigel Davenport, Trevor Howard, Daniel Massey, Ian Holm; **D:** Charles Jarrott; **W:** John Hale; **C:** Christopher Challis; **M:** John Barry. Nominations: Academy Awards '71: Best Actress (Redgrave), Best Art Direction/Set Decoration, Best Costume Design, Best Sound, Best Original Dramatic/Comedy Score. *USH*

Mary Reilly 🎬🎬 **1995 (R)** Mary (Roberts) is an innocent maid whose employer happens to be the infamous Dr. Jekyll (Malkovich). They both seem to be employed by Dr. Freud in this dank, dreary psychosexual thriller. Mary is torn between the repressed affection of the doctor and the oily sexuality of his alter ego, who conjures up images of her abusive father. Reuniting the crew and some of the cast of "Dangerous Liaisons" (Glenn Close also appears as a bawdy brothel owner), they fail to reach their previous heights. Most of the gloomy sets will make you wish you were wearing galoshes. Release date was bumped several times as the ending of the film was reshot (more than once). Based on the novel by Valerie Martin.**CW:** Notable gore and some strong violence. **108m/C VHS, LV, Closed Caption.** Julia Roberts, John Malkovich, George Cole, Michael Gambon, Kathy Staff, Glenn Close, Michael Sheen, Bronagh Gallagher, Linda Bassett, Henry Goodman, Ciaran Hinds, Sasha Hanav; **D:** Stephen Frears; **W:** Christopher Hampton; **C:** Philippe Rousselot; **M:** George Fenton. Nominations: Golden Raspberry Awards '96: Worst Actress (Roberts), Worst Director (Frears). *COL*

Mary Shelley's Frankenstein 🎬🎬½ *Frankenstein* **1994 (R)** Branagh turns from Shakespeare to another form of literary classic with his operatic (and loose) adaptation of the Shelley novel. He also plays Victor, the overwrought medical student who decides that death can be vanquished and sets out to prove his theories by making a man. De Niro is sufficently grisly (though lacking in pathos) as the reanimated corpse with Bonham Carter alternately suffering and excitable as Victor's fiancee Elizabeth. Visually arresting—particularly the Creature's birth scene—pic doesn't engender audience sympathy for the characters' trials and final fates.**CW:** Horrific images; violence; gore. **123m/C VHS, LV, 8mm, Closed Caption.** Kenneth Branagh, Robert De Niro, Helena Bonham Carter, Tom Hulce, Aidan Quinn, John Cleese, Ian Holm, Richard Briers, Robert Hardy, Cherie Lunghi, Celia Imrie, Trevyn McDowell; **D:** Kenneth Branagh; **W:** Frank Darabont, Steph Lady; **M:** Patrick Doyle. Nominations: Academy Awards '94: Best Makeup. *COL*

Mary White 🎬🎬 **1977** The true story of Mary White, the 16-year-old daughter of a newspaper editor who rejects her life of wealth and sets out to find her own identity. **102m/C VHS, Beta.** Ed Flanders, Kathleen Beller, Tim Matheson, Donald Moffat, Fionnula Flanagan; **D:** Jud Taylor; **C:** Bill Butler. *PAR*

Masada 🎬🎬🎬 **1981** Based on Ernest K. Gann's novel "The Antagonists," this dramatization recreates the first-century A.D. Roman siege of the fortress Masada, headquarters for a group of Jewish freedom fighters. Abridged from the original television presentation. **131m/C VHS, Beta.** Peter O'Toole, Peter Strauss, Barbara Carrera, Anthony

Quayle, Giulia Pagano, David Warner; **D:** Boris Sagal; **M:** Jerry Goldsmith. *USH*

Masala 🐾🐾 **1991** An experiment in a variety of genres, including glitzy musical-comedy numbers, erotic fantasy sequences, and all manner of kitsch. Krishna (who both stars and directs in his feature film debut) is a violence-prone, ex-junkie still trying to recover from the deaths of his family in a plane crash as they travelled from their home in Toronto to a vacation in India. Jaffrey has multiroles as Krishna's unscrupulous uncle and cousin as well as the blue-skinned Indian deity, Lord Krishna, who appears to an Indian grandmother on her television set. Multicultural confusion. **105m/C VHS.** *CA* Srinivas Krishna, Saeed Jaffrey, Zohra Segal, Sakina Jaffrey; **D:** Srinivas Krishna; **W:** Srinivas Krishna. *FXL, FCT*

Mascara 🐾🐾 **1987 (R)** A group inspecting a transvestite's death are led into the seedy underground world of Belgian nightlife. **99m/C VHS, Beta, Closed Caption.** *BE* Derek De Lint, Charlotte Rampling, Michael Sarrazin; **D:** Patrick Conrad. *WAR*

Masculine Feminine 🐾🐾🐾½ *Masculin Feminin* **1966** A young Parisian just out of the Army engages in some anarchistic activities when he has an affair with a radical woman singer. Hailed as one of the best French New Wave films. In French with English subtitles. **103m/B VHS, Beta.** *FR* Jean-Pierre Leaud, Chantal Goya, Marlene Jobert; **D:** Jean-Luc Godard. Berlin International Film Festival '66: Best Actor (Leaud). *NYF, DVT, VDM*

M*A*S*H 🐾🐾🐾🐾 **1970 (R)** Hilarious, irreverent, and well-cast black comedy about a group of surgeons and nurses at a Mobile Army Surgical Hospital in Korea. The horror of war is set in counterpoint to their need to create havoc with episodic late-night parties, practical jokes, and sexual antics. An all-out anti-war festival, highlighted by scenes that starkly uncover the chaos and irony of war, and establish Altman's influential style. Watch for real-life football players Fran Tarkenton, Ben Davidson, and Buck Buchanan in the game. Loosely adapted from the novel by the pseudonymous Richard Hooker (Dr. H. Richard Hornberger and William Heinz). Subsequent hit TV series moved even further from the source novel. **116m/C VHS, Beta, LV, Letterbox.** Donald Sutherland, Elliott Gould, Tom Skerritt, Sally Kellerman, JoAnn Pflug, Robert Duvall, Rene Auberjonois, Roger Bowen, Gary Burghoff, Fred Williamson, John Schuck, Bud Cort, G. Wood; **D:** Robert Altman; **W:** Ring Lardner Jr.; **M:** Johnny Mandel. Academy Awards '70: Best Adapted Screenplay; Cannes Film Festival '70: Best Film; Golden Globe Awards '71: Best Film—Musical/Comedy, National Film Registry '96;; National Society of Film Critics Awards '70: Best Film; Writers Guild of America '70: Best Adapted Screenplay; Nominations: Academy Awards '70: Best Director (Altman), Best Film Editing, Best Picture, Best Supporting Actress (Kellerman). *FOX*

M*A*S*H: Goodbye, Farewell & Amen 🐾🐾🐾½ **1983** The final two-hour special episode of the television series "M*A*S*H" follows Hawkeye, B.J., Colonel Potter, Charles, Margaret, Klinger, Father Mulcahy, and the rest of the men and women of the 4077th through the last days of the Korean War, the declaration of peace, the dismantling of the camp, and the fond and tearful farewells. **120m/C VHS, Beta, LV.** Alan Alda, Mike Farrell, Harry (Henry) Morgan, David Ogden Stiers, Loretta Swit, Jamie Farr, William Christopher, Allan Arbus. *FOX, OM*

The Mask 🐾🐾 *Eyes of Hell; The Spooky Movie Show* **1961** A deservedly obscure gory horror film about a masked killer, filmed mostly in 3-D. With special 3-D packaging and limited edition 3-D glasses. **85m/B VHS, Beta, LV.** *CA* Paul Stevens, Claudette Nevins, Bill Walker, Anne Collings, Martin Lavut, Leo Leyden, Bill Bryden, Eleanor Beecroft, Steven Appleby; **D:** Julian Roffman; **W:** Slavko Vorkapich, Franklin Delessert, Sandy Haver, Frank Taubes; **C:** Herbert S. Alpert. *RHI, MLB*

Mask 🐾🐾🐾 **1985 (PG-13)** A dramatization of the true story of a young boy afflicted with craniodiaphyseal dysplasia (elephantiasis). The boy overcomes his appearance and revels in the joys of life in the California bikers' community. Well acted, particularly the performances of Stoltz and Cher. A touching film, well-directed by Bogdanovich, that only occasionally slips into maudlin territory. **120m/C VHS, Beta, LV, Closed Caption, DVD.** Cher, Sam Elliott, Eric Stoltz, Estelle Getty, Richard Dysart, Laura Dern, Harry Carey Jr., Lawrence Monoson, Marsha Warfield, Barry Tubb, Andrew (Andy) Robinson, Alexandra Powers; **D:** Peter Bogdanovich; **W:** Anna Hamilton Phelan. Academy Awards '85: Best Makeup; Cannes Film Festival '85: Best Actress (Cher). *USH*

The Mask 🐾🐾🐾 **1994 (PG-13)** Adolescent supernatural comedy with lollapalooza special effects is Carrey's follow-up to "Ace Ventura." Mild-mannered bank clerk Carrey discovers an ancient mask that has supernatural powers. Upon putting on the mask, he turns into one truly animated guy. He falls for a dame mixed up with gangsters and from there on, our hero deals not only with the incredible powers of the mask, but with hormones and bad guys as well. Based on the Dark Horse comic book series and originally conceived as a horror flick, director Russell, who gave Freddy Krueger a sense of humor, recast this one as a hellzapoppin' cartoon-action black comedy. Carrey's rubber face is an asset magnified by the breakthrough special effects courtesy of Industrial Light and Magic. **CW:** Some stylized violence. **100m/C VHS, Closed Caption.** Jim Carrey, Cameron Diaz, Peter Greene, Peter Riegert, Amy Yasbeck, Orestes Matacena, Richard Jeni, Ben Stein; **D:** Chuck Russell; **W:** Mike Werb; **C:** John R. Leonetti; **M:** Randy Edelman. Blockbuster Entertainment Awards '95: Comedy Actor (Carrey), Female Newcomer, Theatrical (Diaz); Blockbuster Entertainment Awards '96: Comedy Actor, Video (Carrey); Nominations: Academy Awards '94: Best Visual Effects; Golden Globe Awards '95: Best Actor—Musical/Comedy (Carrey); MTV Movie Awards '95: Breakthrough Performance (Diaz), Most Desirable Female (Diaz), Best Comedic Performance (Carrey), Best Dance Sequence (Jim Carrey/Cameron Diaz). *NLC*

Mask of Death 🐾🐾 **1997 (R)** Detective Dan McKenna's (Lamas) wife is killed by Frank Dallio (Dunn) during the criminal's escape from the FBI and he's shot in the face by Dallio's buddy Mason, who happens to be a ringer for McKenna and conveniently dies in a car crash. Since the FBI want Dallio, Agent Jeffries (Williams) persuades McKenna to pose as Mason, which he does in order to get revenge. **125m/C VHS, LV, Closed Caption.** Lorenzo Lamas, Billy Dee Williams, Rae Dawn Chong, Conrad Dunn. *TOU*

The Mask of Dijon 🐾🐾½ **1946** A mad magician suspects that his wife is cheating on him and tries to hypnotize her into killing her supposed paramour. The plan goes awry when the wife uses a gun loaded with blanks. Von Stroheim's performance makes it worthwhile. **73m/B VHS.** Erich von Stroheim, Jeanne Bates, William Wright, Edward Van Sloan, Denise Vernac; **D:** Lew (Louis Friedlander) Landers. *NOS*

The Mask of Fu Manchu 🐾🐾½ **1932** The evil Dr. Fu Manchu and his equally evil daughter set out to capture the scimitar and golden mask of Genghis Khan. With them, they will be able to destroy all white men and rule the world. Although a detective from Scotland Yard tries to stop them, the pair obtain the treasures and begin sadistically torturing their victims to death. Can they be stopped before they destroy the earth? One of the creepiest entries in the Fu Manchu series, and Loy's last oriental role. Based on the novel by Sam Rohmer. **72m/B VHS.** Boris Karloff, Lewis Stone, Karen Morley, Charles Starrett, Myrna Loy, Jean Hersholt, Lawrence Grant, David Torrence; **D:** Charles Brabin; **C:** Gaetano Antonio "Tony" Gaudio. *MGM*

Mask of the Dragon 🎵 **1951** A soldier's friend and girlfriend track down his killer after he delivers a golden curio to a shop in Los Angeles. **54m/B VHS, Beta, LV.** Richard Travis, Sheila Ryan, Richard Emory, Jack Reitzen. *NO*

The Mask of Zorro *Zorro* **1998** The dashing masked swordsman, who first made an appearance in a 1919 newspaper comic, returns to the big screen. Aging Zorro (Hopkins) has just been released from 20 years in prison and is looking for a younger protege to take on his swashbuckling work. He picks the already dashing bandit, Alejandro (Banderas). Elena's (Zeta Jones) a spirited beauty who was raised by Zorro's mortal enemy (Wilson) and doesn't know she's his daughter. She wields quite a mean sword herself as Alejandro learns before any romancing can begin. Not yet reviewed. **?m/C VHS.** Antonio Banderas, Anthony Hopkins, Catherine Zeta-Jones, Stuart Wilson; **D:** Martin Campbell; **W:** Ted Elliott, Terry Rossio. *NYR*

The Masked Marvel *Sakima and the Masked Marvel* **1943** The Masked Marvel saves America's war industries from sabotage. Serial in 12 episodes. **195m/B VHS.** William Forrest, Louise Currie, Johnny Arthur; **D:** Spencer Gordon Bennet. *VCN, REP, MLB*

The Masked Rider 🐾🐾½ **1941** Drifters Brown and Knight head south of the border and find themselves trying to solve crimes committed by a mysterious masked rider. Latin American dancers and singers provide a nice change of pace from the usual cowpoke musical relief. Based on a story by Sam Robins. **57m/B VHS.** Johnny Mack Brown, Fuzzy Knight, Nell O'Day, Grant Withers; **D:** Ford Beebe; **W:** Sherman Lowe, Victor McLeod. *MOV*

Masks of Death 🐾🐾 **1986** New adventure for Sherlock Holmes, as he is pulled from retirement to find the murderer of three unidentified corpses found in London's East End. **80m/C VHS, Beta, LV.** Peter Cushing, John Mills, Anne Baxter, Ray Milland; **D:** Roy Ward Baker. *ORI, IME, WAR*

Mason of the Mounted 🐾🐾 **1932** Harmless enough western in which a Canadian Mountie tracks down a murderer in the U.S. **58m/B VHS.** Bill Cody, Nancy Drexel, Art Mix, Nelson McDowell; **D:** Harry Fraser. *NOS, DVT, HEG*

Masque of the Red Death 🐾🐾🐾 **1965** An integral selection in the famous Edgar Allan Poe/Roger Corman canon, it deals with an evil prince who traffics with the devil and playfully murders any of his subjects not already dead of the plague. Remade in 1989 with Corman as producer. **88m/C VHS, Beta.** *GB* Vincent Price, Hazel Court, Jane Asher, Patrick Magee, David Weston, Nigel Green, Julian Burton, Skip Martin, Gaye Brown, John Westbrook; **D:** Roger Corman; **W:** Charles Beaumont, R. Wright Campbell; **C:** Nicolas Roeg. *ORI, MLB*

Masque of the Red Death 🐾🐾 **1989 (R)** Roger Corman's second attempt at Edgar Allan Poe's horror tale pales compared to his Vincent Price version made 25 years earlier. Underaged cast adds youth appeal but subtracts credibility from the fable of a sadistic prince and his sycophants trying to ignore the plague outside castle walls. Only late in the plot does veteran actor Macnee add proper note of doom. **90m/C VHS, Beta, LV.** Patrick Macnee, Jeffery Osterhage, Adrian Paul, Tracy Reiner, Maria Ford, Clare Hoak; **D:** Larry Brand; **W:** Larry Brand, Daryl Haney. *MGM, IME*

Masque of the Red Death 🐾½ **1990 (R)** Unrecognizable Poe mutation has guests invited to the mansion of a dying millionaire, only to be murdered by an unknown stalker. One scene features a pendulum, and that's it for literary faithfulness. **90m/C VHS, Beta, LV.** Frank Stallone, Brenda Vaccaro, Herbert Lom, Michelle McBride, Christine Lunde; **D:** Alan Birkinshaw. *COL*

Masque of the Red Death/ Premature Burial **1965** Double feature of horror classics adapted from Edgar Allan Poe's work. Price stars in "Masque of the Red Death" as a satan worshipper. Milland plays a man obsessed with the fear of catastrophe in "Premature

Burial." **175m/C VHS, LV.** Vincent Price, Hazel Court, Jane Asher, Patrick Magee, Nigel Green, Ray Milland; **D:** Roger Corman. *IME*

Masquerade 🎬🎬🎬 **1988 (R)** A lonely young heiress meets a handsome "nobody" with a mysterious background and it is love at first sight. The romance distresses everyone in the circle of the elite because they assume that he is after her money and not her love. At first it seems decidedly so, then definitely not, and then nothing is certain. A real romantic thriller, with wonderful scenes of the Hamptons. **CW:** Strong sexuality. **91m/C VHS, Beta, LV, Closed Caption.** Rob Lowe, Meg Tilly, John Glover, Kim Cattrall, Doug Savant, Dana Delany, Eric Holland; **D:** Bob Swaim; **W:** Dick Wolf; **C:** David Watkin; **M:** John Barry. *FOX*

Mass Appeal 🎬🎬 **1984 (PG)** An adaptation of the Bill C. Davis play about the ideological debate between a young seminarian and a complacent but successful parish pastor. Lemmon has had better roles and done better acting. **99m/C VHS, Beta, LV, Closed Caption.** Jack Lemmon, Zeljko Ivanek, Charles Durning, Louise Latham, James Ray, Sharee Gregory, Talia Balsam; **D:** Glenn Jordan; **W:** Bill Davis; **M:** Bill Conti. *USH*

Massacre at Central High 🎬🎬½ *Blackboard Massacre* **1976 (R)** A new student takes matters into his own hands when gang members harass other students at a local high school. Other than some silly dialogue, this low-budget production is above average. **85m/C VHS.** Derrel Maury, Andrew Stevens, Kimberly Beck, Robert Carradine, Roy Underwood, Steve Bond, Steve Sikes, Lani O'Grady, Damon Douglas, Cheryl "Rainbeaux" Smith; **D:** Renee Daalder; **W:** Renee Daalder; **C:** Bert Van Munster. *MPI*

Massacre in Dinosaur Valley 🎬½ **1985** A dashing young paleontologist and his fellow explorers go on a perilous journey down the Amazon in search of the Valley of the Dinosaur. **98m/C VHS, Beta.** Michael Sopkiw, Suzanne Carvall. *ART*

Massacre in Rome 🎬🎬½ **1973 (PG)** A priest opposes a Nazi colonel's plan to execute Italian civilians in retaliation for the deaths of 33 German soldiers. Strong drama based on a real event. **110m/C VHS, Beta.** Richard Burton, Marcello Mastroianni, Leo McKern, John Steiner, Anthony Steel; **D:** George P. Cosmatos; **W:** George P. Cosmatos; **M:** Ennio Morricone. *NO*

Masseuse 🎬 **1995 (R)** Kristy (Drew) decides to get back at cheating fiance Jack (Abell), who's out of town on a business trip, by turning their house into a massage parlor. **CW:** Language, nudity, sexual situations. **90m/C VHS.** Griffin Drew, Monique Parent, Tim Abell; **D:** Daniel Peters. *TRI*

Massive Retaliation 🎬 **1985** Hordes of pesky villagers seek refuge within the secluded safety of a family's country house as WWIII approaches. **90m/C VHS, Beta, LV.** Tom Bower, Peter Donat, Karlene Crockett, Jason Gedrick, Michael Pritchard; **D:** Thomas A. Cohen. *ART, VES*

Master Blaster 🎬½ **1985 (R)** Friendly game of survival with paintball guns goes awry when one of the contestants exchanges the play guns for deadly weapons. **94m/C VHS.** Jeff Moldovan, Donna Rosae, Joe Hess, Peter Lunblad; **D:** Glenn Wilder. *MVD*

Master Harold and the Boys 🎬🎬🎬 **1984** Stagey cable presentation of South African Athol Fugard's play about relationship between white man and two black servants. Occasionally provocative. **90m/C VHS, Beta.** Matthew Broderick; **D:** Michael Lindsay-Hogg. *ORI, WAR*

Master Key 🎬½ **1944** Federal agents battle Nazis in this action-packed 12-chapter serial. **169m/B VHS, Beta.** Jan Wiley, Milburn Stone, Lash LaRue, Dennis Moore; **D:** Ray Taylor, Lewis D. Collins. *NOS, DVT, MLB*

Master Killer 🎬 *The Thirty-Sixth Chamber* **1984 (R)** Master Killers are made, not born. Liu trains as he readies himself for an attack on the brutal Manchu assassins. **109m/C VHS, Beta.** Liu Chia Hui; **D:** Liu Chia Liang. *FXL*

Master Mind 🎬🎬 **1973** A renowned Japanese super sleuth attempts to solve the theft of a sophisticated midget android. **86m/C VHS, Beta.** Zero Mostel, Keiko Kishi, Bradford Dillman, Herbert Berghof, Frankie Sakai; **D:** Alex March. *UNI*

Master Minds 🎬½ **1949** The Bowery Boys run into trouble when Hall gets a toothache and can suddenly predict the future. He takes a job at a carnival where a mad scientist wants to transplant his brain into that of a monster ape man. **64m/B VHS.** Leo Gorcey, Huntz Hall, Glenn Strange, Gabriel Dell, Alan Napier, Billy Benedict, Bennie Bartlett, David Gorcey; **D:** Jean Yarbrough. *GPV*

Master Ninja 🎬½ *The Master* **1978** First in the continuing adventures of the Master and Max (Van Cleef and Van Patten) follow the pair across the US in their search for the Master's long-lost daughter. They're pursued by Kosugi. Originally filmed for television; each tape includes two programs. **93m/C VHS, Beta.** Lee Van Cleef, Sho Kosugi, Timothy Van Patten. *QVD, TWE*

The Master of Ballantrae 🎬🎬 **1953** Flynn plays James Durrisdear, the heir to a Scottish title, who gets involved in a rebellion with Bonnie Prince Charlie against the English crown. When the rebellion fails, Flynn heads for the West Indies where he and his partner amass quite a fortune through piracy. Flynn eventually returns to Scotland where he finds that his brother has taken over his title as well as his longtime love. Based on the novel by Robert Louis Stevenson. Flynn's riotous life had put him long past his peak swashbuckling days, as this film unfortunately demonstrates. **89m/C VHS, Beta, LV.** Errol Flynn, Roger Livesey, Anthony Steel, Beatrice Campbell, Yvonne Furneaux, Jacques Berthier, Felix Aylmer, Mervyn Johns; **D:** William Keighley; **C:** Jack Cardiff. *WAR*

Master of Dragonard Hill 🎬½ **1989** A low-rent swashbuckling romance-novel pastiche. **92m/C VHS, Beta.** Oliver Reed, Eartha Kitt; **W:** R.J. Marx.

Master of Kung Fu 🎬 **1977** A Kung Fu instructor calls upon his former teacher to help him fend off loan sharks who want to take over his school. **88m/C VHS, Beta.** Yu Chan Yuan, Chi Hsiao Fu. *FOX*

Master of the House 🎬🎬🎬 *Thou Shalt Honour Thy Wife* **1925** Story of a spoiled husband, a type extinct in this country but still in existence abroad. Silent with titles in English. **118m/B VHS, Beta. D:** Carl Theodor Dreyer. *VYY, FCT*

Master of the World 🎬🎬½ **1961** Visionary tale of a fanatical 19th century inventor who uses his wonderous flying fortress as an antiwar weapon. Adapted from "Robur, the Conqueror" and "Master of the World," both by Jules Verne. **95m/C VHS, Beta.** Vincent Price, Charles Bronson, Henry Hull; **D:** William Witney; **W:** Richard Matheson; **M:** Les Baxter. *ORI, WAR*

Master Race 🎬🎬½ **1944** Absorbing cautionary tale of a German officer who escapes retribution when the Nazis collapse, continuing to hold control over the inhabitants of a small town through intimidation. **98m/B VHS, Beta.** George Coulouris, Lloyd Bridges, Osa Massen, Nancy Gates, Stanley Ridges; **D:** Herbert Biberman; **C:** Russell Metty. *TTC*

Master Touch 🎬½ *Hearts and Minds; Un Uomo da Rispettare* **1974 (PG)** When a legendary safecracker is released from prison, he attempts one last heist at a Hamburg insurance company. **96m/C VHS, Beta.** GE IT Kirk Douglas, Florinda Bolkan, Giuliano Gemma; **D:** Michele Lupo; **M:** Ennio Morricone.

Masterminds 🎬🎬½ **1996 (PG-13)** Mildly diverting actioner has teen troublemaker Ozzie (Kartheiser) once again on the outs with his workaholic father Jake (Craven) and stepmom Helen (Hurwitch). Forced to take bratty stepsister Melissa (Stuart) to the private school he's been expelled from, Ozzie plans one more prank on officious principal Claire Maloney (Fricker). But the joke's on everyone when security analyst Ralph Bentley (Stewart) puts his plan in motion, taking control of the school and asking a ransom for a group of the wealthiest children. But the ingenious Ozzie's lurking about to get the best of the adults. **CW:** Violence included in a children hostage situation, and for language. **105m/C VHS.** Vincent Kartheiser, Patrick Stewart, Brenda Fricker, Matt Craven, Bradley Whitford, Annabelle Gurwitch, Katie Stuart, Callum Keith Rennie, Michael MacRae, Earl Pastko, Michael Simms, Jon Abrahams; **D:** Roger Christian; **W:** Floyd Byars; **C:** Nic Morris; **M:** Anthony Marinelli. *COL*

The Masters of Menace 🎬½ **1990 (PG-13)** The men in blue are mighty miffed when a bunch of bikers break parole to pay their last respects to a comrade in leather. Comic bits by Candy, Belushi, Aykroyd and Wendt provide little relief. **97m/C VHS, LV.** David Rasche, Catherine Bach, Dan Aykroyd, James Belushi, John Candy, George Wendt, Tino Insana; **D:** Daniel Raskov; **W:** Tino Insana. *COL*

Masters of the Universe 🎬🎬 **1987 (PG)** A big-budget live-action version of the cartoon character's adventures, with He-Man battling Skeletor for the sake of the universe. **109m/C VHS, Beta, LV, Closed Caption.** Dolph Lundgren, Frank Langella, Billy Barty, Courteney Cox, Meg Foster; **D:** Gary Goddard; **C:** Hanania Baer; **M:** Bill Conti. *WAR*

Masters of Venus 🎬½ **1959** Eight-part serial about spaceships, space maidens and the like. **121m/B VHS, Beta.** Ferdinand "Ferdy" Mayne. *SNC, VDM*

Master's Revenge 🎬½ **1971** When a girl is kidnapped by a violent motorcycle gang, martial artists are called in to rescue her. Originally released as "Devil Rider." **78m/C VHS.** Sharon Mahon, Ridgely Abele, Johnny Pachivas.

Mata Hari 🎬🎬🎬 **1932** During WWI, a lovely German spy steals secrets from the French through her involvement with two military officers. Lavish production and exquisite direction truly make this one of Garbo's best. Watch for her exotic pseudo-strip tease. **90m/B VHS, Beta.** Greta Garbo, Ramon Novarro, Lionel Barrymore, Lewis Stone, C. Henry Gordon, Karen Morley, Alec B. Francis; **D:** George Fitzmaurice; **C:** William H. Daniels. *MGM, FCT*

Mata Hari 🎬🎬 **1985 (R)** Racy, adventure-prone story of WWI's most notorious spy, Mata Hari, who uses her seductive beauty to seduce the leaders of Europe. Stars "Emmanuelle" Kristel. **105m/C VHS, Beta.** Sylvia Kristel, Christopher Cazenove, Oliver Tobias, Gaye Brown, Gottfried John; **D:** Curtis Cunningham. *MGM*

Matador 🎬🎬½ **1986** Bizarre, entertaining black comedy about a retired matador who finds a new way to satiate his desire to kill. He meets his match in an equally deadly woman and the two are drawn closer together by a young bullfighting student who confesses to a series of murders. Not for all tastes, but fine for those who like the outrageous. In Spanish with English subtitles. **90m/C VHS, Beta, LV, Letterbox.** SP Assumpta Serna, Antonio Banderas, Nacho Martinez, Eva Cobo, Carmen Maura, Julieta Serrano, Chus Lampreave, Eusebio Poncela; **D:** Pedro Almodovar; **W:** Pedro Almodovar, Jesus Ferrere; **M:** Bernardo Bonazzi. *CCN, TPV*

The Match Factory Girl 🎬🎬🎬 *Tulitkkutehtaan Tytto* **1990** Kaurismak's final segment of his "working class" trilogy. Iris, a plain, shy outsider shares a drab dwelling with her one-dimensional mother and stepfather, works in a match factory, and hopes desperately for romantic love. Her world is transformed when the extraordinary occurs—she spots a brightly colored party dress in a shop window, buys it, wears it to a bar, and meets the Scandinavian creep who will soon get her pregnant and dump her. Angry at the world, Iris seeks revenge, and in so doing the audience learns that she has become very real and human. Kaurismaki makes his point that beauty can exist in ugly places. In Finnish with English subtitles. **70m/C VHS.** SW FI Kati Outinen, Elina Salo, Esko Nikkari, Vesa Vierikko; **D:** Aki Kaurismaki; **W:** Aki Kaurismaki. *KIV, BTV, FCT*

The Matchmaker 🎭🎭🎭 1958 An adaptation of the Thornton Wilder play concerning two young men in search of romance in 1884 New York. Later adapted as "Hello Dolly." An amusing diversion. 101m/B VHS, Beta, LV, Closed Caption. Shirley Booth, Anthony Perkins, Shirley MacLaine, Paul Ford, Robert Morse, Perry Wilson, Wallace Ford, Russell Collins, Rex Evans, Gavin Gordon, Torben Meyer; *D:* Joseph Anthony; *W:* John Michael Hayes; *C:* Charles B(ryant) Lang. *PAR, FCT*

The Matchmaker 🎭🎭½ 1997 (R) Big city girl Marcy (Garofalo) heads to a wee quaint Ireland burgh where she finds love and humanity amid the beer-guzzling, blarney-slinging locals. Jaded aide to a politico spin doctor (Leary), Marcy is there to track down some McGlory's, the Irish relatives of an American senator, in order to help his re-election campaign but hits town during the annual matchmaking festival and becomes the target of Irish marriage broker O'Shea. O'Hara is Sean, Marcy's laconic and appealing local suitor. Entertaining enough, with Garofalo and O'Hara more than filling the bill in a romantic comedy that heavily flirts with cliche. Sweeping vistas and a soundtrack appropriately filled with Irish favorites, old and new. Filmed in the village of Roundstone, Ireland. *CW:* Language. 97m/C VHS, Closed Caption. Janeane Garofalo, Milo O'Shea, David O'Hara, Denis Leary, Jay O. Sanders, Rosaleen Linehan, Maria Doyle Doyle Kennedy, Saffron Burrows, Paul Hickey, Jimmy Keogh; *D:* Mark Joffe; *W:* Louis Nowra, Karen Janszen, Graham Linehan; *C:* Ellery Ryan; *M:* John Altman. *PGV*

Maternal Instincts 🎭🎭½ 1996 (PG-13) Tracy (Burke) is a childless woman who undergoes an emergency hysterectomy without her consent. But she badly wants a baby and decides to get revenge on anyone thwarting her plans. Made for cable. *CW:* Some violent content. 92m/C VHS, Beta, Closed Caption. Delta Burke, Beth Broderick, Garwin Sanford, Sandra Nelson, Gillian Barber, Kevin McNulty, Tom Butler, Tom Mason; *D:* George Kaczender. *PAR*

Matewan 🎭🎭🎭½ 1987 (PG-13) An acclaimed dramatization of the famous Matewan massacre in the 1920s, in which coal miners in West Virginia, reluctantly influenced by a young union organizer, rebelled against terrible working conditions. Complex and imbued with typically superb Sayles dialogue and Haskell Wexler's beautiful and poetic cinematography. Jones delivers an economical yet intense portrayal of the black leader of the miners. The director makes his usual on-screen appearance, this time as an establishment-backed reactionary minister. Partially based on the Sayles novel "Union Dues." 130m/C VHS, Beta, LV, Closed Caption. Chris Cooper, James Earl Jones, Mary McDonnell, William Oldham, Kevin Tighe, David Strathairn, Jace Alexander, Gordon Clapp, Mason Daring, Joe Grifasi, Bob Gunton, Jo Henderson, Jason Jenkins, Ken Jenkins, Nancy Mette, Josh Mostel, Michael B. Preston, Maggie Renzi, Frank Hoyt Taylor; *Cameos:* John Sayles; *D:* John Sayles; *W:* John Sayles; *C:* Haskell Wexler; *M:* Mason Daring. Independent Spirit Awards '88: Best Cinematography; Nominations: Academy Awards '87: Best Cinematography. *ORI, WAR*

Matilda 🎭🎭 1978 (PG) Family fare about a entrepreneur who decides to manage a boxing kangaroo, which nearly succeeds in defeating the world heavyweight champion. Uneven and occasionally engaging. Based on Paul Gallico's novel. 103m/C VHS, Beta. Elliott Gould, Robert Mitchum, Harry Guardino, Clive Revill; *D:* Daniel Mann. *ART, VES*

Matilda 🎭🎭🎭 1996 (PG) Intelligent child Matilda Wormwood (Wilson) is oppressed by both her monstrous parents (DeVito and Perlman) and awful school principal, Trunchbull (Ferris). However, her first grade teacher, appropriately named Miss Honey (Davidtz), believes in her, which is enough to make Matilda plot an appropriate fate for the miserable people in her life. Excellent adaptation of a typically subversive book by Roald Dahl. Director DeVito, who wanted to create the

illusion of a live-action cartoon, built among other things a "Carrot-cam" to capture the flying food of a food fight. 93m/C VHS, LV, Closed Caption, DVD. Mara Wilson, Danny DeVito, Rhea Perlman, Embeth Davidtz, Pam Ferris, Paul (Pee Wee Herman) Reubens, Tracey Walter; *D:* Danny DeVito; *W:* Robin Swicord, Nicholas Kazan; *C:* Stefan Czapsky; *M:* David Newman. *COL*

Matinee 🎭🎭½ 1992 (PG) "MANT: Half-man, Half-ant, All Terror!" screams from the movie marquee after Lawrence Woolsey, promoter extraordinare, and Ruth Corday, his leading lady, roll in to Key West circa 1962. Meanwhile, teen Gene Loomis listens to his health teacher push the benefits of red meat and his girlfriend question life, while worrying about his dad, stationed in Cuba. Builds sly parallels between real life and movie horror by juxtaposing Woolsey (modeled after B-movie king William Castle) hyping his schlock, shown in "Atomo-Vision," against JFK solemnly announcing the Russian's approach. Fun, nostalgic look at days gone by—and the matinees that died with them. 98m/C VHS, Beta, LV, Closed Caption. John Goodman, Cathy Moriarty, Simon Fenton, Omri Katz, Lisa Jakub, Kellie Martin, Jesse Lee, Lucinda Jenney, James Villemaire, Robert Picardo, Dick Miller, John Sayles, Mark McCracken, Jesse White, David Clennon, Luke Halpin; *D:* Joe Dante; *M:* Jerry Goldsmith. *USH, BTV*

The Mating Game 🎭🎭🎭 1959 A fast-paced comedy about a tax collector, a beautiful girl, and a wily farm couple. Randall is the strait-laced IRS agent who finds out that the farming Larkins have never paid taxes and use a complicated barter system to get along. Randall falls for farm daughter Reynolds, gets drunk with her Pa, and decides to help the family out of their government dilemma—to the dismay of his superiors. Randall has a terrific drunk scene among his many comedic capers and Reynolds is a highlight. 96m/C VHS. Tony Randall, Debbie Reynolds, Paul Douglas, Una Merkel, Fred Clark, Philip Ober, Charles Lane; *D:* George Marshall; *W:* William Roberts. *MGM*

Mating Season 🎭🎭½ 1981 Successful female attorney Arnaz meets good-natured laundromat owner Luckinbill at a bird-watching retreat. Romance ensues. Made for television. 96m/C VHS, Beta. Lucie Arnaz, Laurence Luckinbill; *D:* John Llewellyn Moxey. *BFA*

Matrimaniac 🎭🎭 1916 A man goes to great lengths to marry a woman against her father's wishes. Silent with music score. 48m/B VHS, Beta. Douglas Fairbanks Sr., Constance Talmadge. *VYY, GPV*

A Matter of Degrees 🎭🎭 1990 (R) Weeks before his graduation, a beatnik-type college senior finally acquires a goal: romancing a mystery girl...or maybe saving the student radio station...or not. The hero's aimlessness permeates the script, which never goes anywhere in its exploration of campus ennui. Good photography and a great stratum of alternative music groups on the soundtrack: Dream Syndicate, Pere Ubu, Schooly D, Pixies, Poi Dog Pondering, Minutemen, and Throwing Muses. *CW:* Language. 89m/C VHS, Beta. Arye Gross, Judith Hoag, Tom Sizemore, John Doe; *Cameos:* John F. Kennedy Jr., Fred Schneider, Kate Pierson; *D:* W.T. Morgan.

A Matter of Dignity 🎭🎭 1957 Young girl, forced into marriage with millionaire, eventually brings ruin to the entire family. Why? In Greek with English subtitles. 104m/B VHS, Beta. *GR* Georges Pappas, Ellie Lambetti, Athena Michaelidou, Eleni Zafirou; *D:* Michael Cacoyannis. *FCT*

A Matter of Honor 🎭🎭 1995 (PG) Rugby player is killed during match and his coach gets blamed. So, to clear his name, said coach takes up an unusual challenge with the captain of the opposing team. 95m/C VHS. Jackson Bostwick, Allen Arkus, Rebecca Gray, David Michie; *D:* Frederick P. Watkins. *AVI*

A Matter of Life and Death 🎭🎭 1981 True story follows the real-life experiences of nurse Joy Ufema who has devoted her life to helping terminally ill patients. Exceptional work

from Lavin. Made for television. 98m/C VHS. Linda Lavin, Salome Jens, Gail Strickland, Gerald S. O'Loughlin, Ramon Bieri, Tyne Daly, Larry Breeding, John Bennett Perry; *D:* Russ Mayberry. *NO*

A Matter of Love 🎭 1978 (R) Two couples indulge in spouse swapping while vacationing at the beach. 89m/C VHS, Beta. Michelle Harris, Mark Anderson, Christy Neal, Jeff Alin; *D:* Chuck Vincent. *ART, VES*

A Matter of Principle 1983 The perennial Christmas special about a Scrooge-like character's yuletide change of heart. He decides it's time to shape up when he realizes he may lose his family permanently. 60m/C VHS, Beta. Alan Arkin, Barbara Dana, Tony Arkin; *D:* Gwen Arner.

A Matter of Time woof! 1976 (PG) Maid is taught to enjoy life by an eccentric, flamboyant contessa, then finds the determination to become an aspiring actress. Often depressing and uneven, arguably Minnelli's worst directing job and his last film. Also Boyer's last appearance and first bit for Bergman's daughter Rosellini, in a small part as a nun. 97m/C VHS, Beta. Liza Minnelli, Ingrid Bergman, Charles Boyer, Tina Aumont, Spiros Andros, Anna Proclemer, Isabella Rossellini; *D:* Vincente Minnelli; *C:* Geoffrey Unsworth. *VES*

A Matter of WHO 🎭🎭 1962 A detective for the World Health Organization, or WHO, investigates the disease related deaths of several oil men. Travelling to the Middle East, he uncovers a plot by an unscrupulous businessman to control the oil industry by killing off its most powerful members. Although intended as a comedy, the subject matter is too grim to be taken lightly. 92m/B VHS, Beta. *GB* Terry-Thomas, Alex Nicol, Sonja Ziemann, Richard Briers, Clive Morton, Vincent Ball, Honor Blackman, Carol White, Martin Benson, Geoffrey Keen; *D:* Don Chaffey; *M:* Edwin Astley. *SNC*

Matters of the Heart 🎭🎭 1990 Young pianist searches for an opportunity to display his talents, much to the disapproval of his veteran father. He meets a successful but embittered musician who takes him under her wing and passion between the two soon flares. Made for cable TV and based on "The Country of the Heart" by Barbara Wershba. 94m/C VHS, Closed Caption. Jane Seymour, Christopher Gartin, James Stacy, Geoffrey Lewis, Nan Martin, Allen Rich, Clifford David, Kathy Cannon; *D:* Michael Rhodes; *W:* Linda J. Bergman. *USH*

Maurice 🎭🎭🎭 1987 (R) Based on E.M. Forster's novel about a pair of Edwardian-era Cambridge undergraduates who fall in love, but must deny their attraction and abide by British society's strict norms regarding homosexuality. Maurice finds, however, that he cannot deny his nature, and must come to a decision regarding family, friends, and social structures. A beautiful and stately film of struggle and courage. 139m/C VHS, Beta, LV, Closed Caption. *GB* James Wilby, Hugh Grant, Rupert Graves, Mark Tandy, Ben Kingsley, Denholm Elliott, Simon Callow, Judy Parfitt, Helena Bonham Carter, Billie Whitelaw, Phoebe Nicholls, Barry Foster; *D:* James Ivory; *W:* James Ivory, Kit Hesketh-Harvey; *M:* Richard Robbins. Nominations: Academy Awards '87: Best Costume Design. *ORI, IME, WAR*

Mausoleum 🎭🎭 1983 (R) Only one man can save a woman from eternal damnation. 96m/C VHS, Beta, LV. Marjoe Gortner, Bobbie Bresee, Norman Burton, LaWanda Page, Shari Mann, Julie Christy Murray, Laura Hippe, Maurice Sherbanee; *D:* Michael Dugan; *W:* Robert Madero, Robert Barich; *C:* Robert Barich.

Mauvaise Graine 🎭🎭 *Bad Seed* 1933 Wilder (in his debut) filmed this comedy-drama (along with Esway) before heading off to Hollywood. Parisian wastrel Henri Pasquier (Mingand) impulsively steals a car when his disgusted wealthy father cuts him off. This lands Henri in with a professional gang of thieves, headed by Jean (Galle), who uses his pretty teenaged sister Jeannette (Darrieux) as a decoy. Henri enjoys his new career (and Jeannette) until jealousy gets in the way. French with subtitles. 76m/B VHS. *FR* Pierre Mingand, Danielle Darrieux, Raymond Galle, Jean Wall; *D:*

Billy Wilder, Alexander Esway; **W:** Billy Wilder, Alexander Esway; **C:** Paul Cotteret, Maurice Delattre; **M:** Franz Waxman, Walter Gray. KIV

Maverick 🐾🐾½ **1994 (PG)** Entertaining remake of the popular ABC series is fresh and funny, with sharp dialogue and a good cast. Everybody looks like they're having a great time, not difficult for the charming Gibson, but a refreshing change of pace for the usually serious Foster and Greene. In a fun bit of casting, Garner, the original Maverick, shows up as Marshal Zane Cooper. Lightweight, fast-paced comedy was reportedly highly improvised, though Donner retained enough control to keep it coherent. The end is left wide open so a sequel seems likely. Keep your eyes peeled for cameos from country stars, old time Western actors, and an unbilled appearance from Glover. 127m/C VHS, LV, **Letterbox, Closed Caption, DVD.** Mel Gibson, Jodie Foster, James Garner, Graham Greene, James Coburn, Alfred Molina, Paul Smith, Geoffrey Lewis, Max Perlich; **Cameos:** Dub Taylor, Dan Hedaya, Robert Fuller, Doug McClure, Bert Remsen, Denver Pyle, Will Hutchins, Waylon Jennings, Kathy Mattea, Danny Glover, Clint Black; **D:** Richard Donner; **W:** William Goldman; **C:** Vilmos Zsigmond; **M:** Randy Newman. Blockbuster Entertainment Awards '95: Comedy Actress, Theatrical (Foster); Nominations: Academy Awards '94: Best Costume Design. WAR

The Maverick Queen 🐾🐾½ **1955** Barbara Stanwyck, owner of a gambling casino and a member of the "Wild Bunch" outlaw gang, is torn between going straight for the love of a lawman or sticking with the criminals. Stanwyck is perfectly cast in this interesting Western. 90m/C VHS. Barbara Stanwyck, Barry Sullivan, Wallace Ford, Scott Brady, Jim Davis, Mary Murphy; **D:** Joseph Kane. REP

Maverick: The Collector's Edition 195? Offbeat television western starring Garner as conniving gambler Bret Maverick. The premiere show, "War of the Silver Kings," finds Maverick falling out over the richest man in town over a card game. "Point Blank" features Connors as a conniving bank clerk. Additional episodes are available. 100m/B VHS. James Garner, Mike Connors. WAR, MOV

Max 1922 Compilation of hilarious Linder shorts plus two features, "Seven Years Bad Luck" and "The Three Must-Get-Theres" 90m/B VHS, Beta. Max Linder. GVV

Max 🐾🐾 **1979** A night watchman watches an aspiring actress who is working on her performance in a Broadway play. He tells her she would be better off marrying a doctor. 20m/C VHS, Beta. Jack Gilford, Lynn Lipton; **D:** Joseph Gilford, Jennifer Lax. NO

Max and Helen 🐾🐾½ **1990** Uneven, but sensitive and at times highly moving made for TV story of two lovers who are victims of the holocaust. Max (Williams) survives both Nazi and Stalinist camps out of both love for his fiancee and guilt for having lived while she did not. 94m/C VHS, Beta, **Closed Caption.** GB Treat Williams, Alice Krige, Martin Landau, Jodhi May, John Phillips, Adam Kotz; **D:** Philip Saville; **W:** Corey Blechman. TTC

Max Dugan Returns 🐾🐾 **1983 (PG)** A Simon comedy about an ex-con trying to make up with his daughter by showering her with presents bought with stolen money. Sweet and light, with a good cast. 98m/C VHS, Beta, LV. Jason Robards Jr., Marsha Mason, Donald Sutherland, Matthew Broderick, Kiefer Sutherland; **D:** Herbert Ross; **W:** Neil Simon; **M:** David Shire. FOX

Max Fleischer's Documentary Features 1923 Two scientific films, "Evolution" and "Einstein's Theory of Relativity," from Fleischer's early studio were made to finance their cartoons. Features animated sequences. 60m/B VHS, Beta. **D:** Max Fleischer. GVV

Max Headroom, the Original Story 🐾🐾 **1986** The computer-generated, British Channel-4 comedy personality stars in his first film, actually a shot-on-video feature about an innocent reporter who is transformed by an evil futuristic TV station into Headroom, the perfect (read: artificial) talk show host. 60m/C VHS, Beta, LV, **Closed Caption.** GB Matt Frewer, Nickolas Grace, Hilary Tindall, Amanda Pays, Rocky Morton, Annabel Jankel. ORI, WAR

Max Is Missing 🐾🐾½ **1995 (PG)** 12-year-old Max (Caudell) gets separated from his father, is given a priceless Incan artifact by a dying man, and joins with a local lad to guard it from fortune hunters. Set in the ruins of Machu Picchu in the Peruvian Andes. Made for cable. 95m/C VHS, **Closed Caption.** Toran Caudell, Victor Rojas, Matthew Sullivan, Rick Dean, Charles Napier; **D:** Mark Griffiths. HMK

Max, Mon Amour 🐾🐾 **Max, My Love 1986** A very refined British diplomat in Paris discovers his bored wife has become involved with Max, who happens to be a chimpanzee. Instead of being upset, the husband decides Max should live with them. Very strange menage a trois manages to avoid the obvious vulgarities. In French with English subtitles. 97m/C VHS. FR Anthony Higgins, Charlotte Rampling, Victoria Abril, Christopher Hovik, Anne-Marie Besse, Pierre Etaix; **D:** Nagisa Oshima; **W:** Jean-Claude Carriere; **M:** Michel Portal. CVC, ING

Maxie 🐾🐾 **1985 (PG)** Highly predictable, and forgettable, comedy where a ghost of a flamboyant flapper inhabits the body of a modern-day secretary, and her husband is both delighted and befuddled with the transformations in his spouse. Close is okay, but the film is pretty flaky. 98m/C VHS, Beta, LV. Glenn Close, Ruth Gordon, Mandy Patinkin, Barnard Hughes, Valerie Curtin, Harry Hamlin; **D:** Paul Aaron; **W:** Patricia Resnick; **M:** Georges Delerue. NO

Maxim Xul woof! **1991** A professor of the occult is forced to tangle with a beast from Hell that possesses enormous strength and an insatiable appetite for human blood. 90m/C VHS. Adam West, Jefferson Leinberger, Hal Strieb, Mary Schaeffer; **D:** Arthur Egeli. NO

Maximum Breakout 🐾½ **1991** A beautiful and wealthy girl is kidnapped, her boyfriend left for dead. But he recovers and leads a posse of mercenaries to the rescue. 93m/C VHS. Sydney Coale Phillips; **D:** Tracy Lynch Britton.

Maximum Force 🐾½ **1992 (R)** Three renegade cops join together to infiltrate the underworld and bring to justice both the city's leading crime king and their own corrupt chief of police. **CW:** Language, violence, and sexuality. 90m/C VHS, LV. Sam Jones, Sherrie Rose, Jason Lively, John Saxon, Richard Lynch, Mickey Rooney, Jeff Langton; **D:** Joseph Merhi. PMH

Maximum Overdrive 🐾 **1986 (R)** Based upon King's story "Trucks," recounts what happens when a meteor hits Earth and machines run by themselves, wanting only to kill people. Score by AC/DC. 97m/C VHS, Beta, LV. Emilio Estevez, Pat Hingle, Laura Harrington, Christopher Murney, Yeardley Smith, Stephen King; **D:** Stephen King; **W:** Stephen King; **M:** AC/DC. ORI, WAR

Maximum Risk 🐾🐾½ **1996 (R)** Like we need two of them? Van Damme, in a deja vu storyline (see "Double Impact") plays identical twins—a good French guy and a bad Russian guy—and when the bad guy gets killed, his brother takes over his life to find out whodunit. Risk and danger aside, the ruse is not all that bad, what with Henstridge as his sib's squeeze, unaware that the man she has in a lip lock is not her beloved. Has all the action you'd expect from a pic with "The Muscles from Brussels" and more guns, fists, and car chases is, of course, the major reason to invest your entertainment dollars here. Hong Kong action auteur Lam's stateside debut ensures that fast-paced chases and full-throttle combat is well done and visually appealing. 100m/C VHS, LV, **Closed Caption, DVD.** Jean-Claude Van Damme, Natasha Henstridge, Jean-Hugues Anglade, Stephane Audran, Paul Ben-Victor, Zach Grenier, Frank Senger; **D:** Ringo Lam; **W:** Larry Ferguson; **C:** Alexander Grusynski; **M:** Robert Folk. COL

Maximum Security 🐾 **1987** A small-budget prison film detailing the tribulations of a model prisoner struggling to resist mental collapse. 113m/C VHS, LV. Geoffrey Lewis, Jean Smart, Robert Desiderio; **D:** Bill Duke. VTR

Maximum Thrust woof! Waldo Warren: Private Dick Without a Brain 1988 A few white men confront a deadly Caribbean voodoo tribe. 80m/C Beta. Rick Gianisi, Joe Derrig, Jennifer Kanter, Mizan Nunes; **D:** Tim Kincaid. NO

May Fools 🐾🐾🐾 Milou en Mai; Milou in May 1990 (R) Malle portrays individuals collectively experiencing personal upheaval against the backdrop of unrelated social upheaval. An upper-crust family gathers at a country estate for the funeral of the clan's matriarch, while the May of '68 Parisian riots unfold. Few among the family members mourn the woman's passing, save her son Milou (Piccoli) who leads a pastoral existence tending grapes on the estate. Milou's daughter (Miou-Miou), like the others, is more concerned with her personal gain, suggesting, to her father's horror, that they divide the estate in three. Touching, slow, keenly observed. In French with English subtitles. **CW:** Adult situations, nudity, and sexual situations. 105m/C VHS, LV. FR Michel Piccoli, Miou-Miou, Michael Duchaussoy, Dominique Blanc, Harriet Walter, Francois Berleand, Paulette Dubost, Bruno Carette, Martine Gautier; **D:** Louis Malle; **W:** Jean-Claude Carriere, Louis Malle; **M:** Stephane Grappelli. Cesar Awards '91: Best Supporting Actress (Blanc). ORI, FXL, FCT

May Wine 🐾🐾 **1990 (R)** A sexy, romantic comedy starring "Twin Peaks" alumna, Boyle. 85m/C VHS, LV, **Closed Caption.** Guy Marchand, Lara Flynn Boyle, Joanna Cassidy. VTR

Maya 🐾½ **1966** After the death of his mother, young Terry (North) goes to join his big-game hunting father in India. After a quarrel Terry runs off and meets an Indian boy who has promised his dying father he will deliver a sacred white elephant to a jungle temple. The two lads join forces for the trek and have all sorts of adventures along the way. Basis for a short-lived television series. 91m/C VHS. Jay North, Clint Walker, Sajid Kahn, I.S. Johar; **D:** John Berry; **W:** John Fante. MGM, FCT

Maya woof! **1982** A teacher of fashion in a high school becomes the object of a student's devotion and another teacher's insane jealousy. 114m/C VHS, Beta. Berta Dominguez, Joseph D. Rosevich; **D:** Agust Agustsson. NO

Mayalunta 1986 A young artist is emotionally tortured by a dying older couple. 90m/C VHS. SP Federico Luppi, Miguel Angel Sola, Barbara Mujica. VES

Maybe I'll Be Home in the Spring 🐾🐾½ Deadly Desire 1970 (PG) Denise (Field) is estranged from her family and decides to leave home for life on a commune where she becomes involved with drugs. When she decides to return home everyone finds it hard to adjust. Made for television. 90m/C VHS. Sally Field, Jackie Cooper, Eleanor Parker, David Carradine, Lane Bradbury; **D:** Joseph Sargent. VTR

Maybe ... Maybe Not 🐾🐾 Der Bewegte Mann; The Most Desired Man 1994 (R) The German title refers to a man who moves between both sexual preferences although the film takes a straighter line. Hunky-but-dumb Axel (Schweiger) has cheated on girlfriend Dorothy (Riemann) once too often and she kicks him out. Axel winds up staying with gay pal Norbert (Krol), who would like to go from friendship to lovers, which Axel doesn't pick up on. Dorothy does, however, and wonders if Axel is really gay, but when she discovers she's pregnant, Dorothy decides to marry him anyway. Warm-hearted and campy, with some blatantly sexual dialogue. Based on two gay comic books by Ralf Koenig. German with subtitles or dubbed. **CW:** Sexuality and language, including some explicit sexual dialogue. 93m/C VHS, LV, **Closed Caption.** GE Til Schweiger, Katja Riemann, Joachim Krol, Rufus Beck; **D:** Soenke Wortmann; **W:** Soenke Wortmann; **C:** Gernot Roll; **M:** Torsten Breuer. ART

Mayerling �󠀠✓✓½ 1936 Considered one of the greatest films about doomed love. Story of the tragic and hopeless affair between Crown Prince Rudolf of Hapsburg and young Baroness Marie Vetsera. Heart wrenching and beautiful, with stupendous acting. Remade in 1968. In French with English subtitles. 95m/B VHS, Beta, LV. Charles Boyer, Danielle Darrieux; *D:* Anatole Litvak. New York Film Critics Awards '37: Best Foreign Film. *HMV, MRV, FCT*

Mayerling ✓✓½ 1968 (PG-13) Based on the tragic romance between Crown Prince Rudolf of Hapsburg (Sharif) and the teenaged Baroness Maria Vetsera (Deneuve). Set in 1888, the royal Rudolf defies his father, the Emperor Franz Josef (Mason), to take part in a student revolt for the liberation of Hungary and to fall for the common-born Maria (despite his political marriage). No doubt meant to be a sweeping combo of politics and love ala "Doctor Zhivago," it's mostly tedious; see the 1936 version instead.*CW:* Sex-related scenes. 140m/C VHS. *GB FR* Omar Sharif, Catherine Deneuve, James Mason, Ava Gardner, James Robertson Justice, Genevieve Page, Ivan Desny, Fabienne Dali; *D:* Terence Young; *W:* Terence Young; *C:* Henri Alekan; *M:* Francis Lai. *MGM*

Mayflower Madam ✓✓ 1987 (R) Fairly unsexy and uninteresting made-for-TV movie recounting the business dealings and court battles of the real-life Sydney Biddle Barrows. Barrows/Bergen is a prominent New York socialite and madam of an exclusive escort service whose clientele includes businessmen and dignitaries. 93m/C VHS, Beta. Candice Bergen, Chris Sarandon, Chita Rivera; *D:* Lou Antonio; *M:* David Shire. *THV*

Mayhem ✓ 1987 Two loners in Hollywood confront all types of urban low-life murderers, drug pushers, and child molesters. 90m/C VHS, Beta. Raymond Martino, Pamela Dixon, Robert Gallo, Wendy MacDonald. *NO*

Maytime ✓✓✓ 1937 Lovely story of an opera star (MacDonald) and penniless singer (Eddy) who fall in love in Paris, but her husband/teacher (Barrymore) interferes. One of the best films the singing duo ever made. ♫Maytime Finale; Virginia Ham and Eggs; Vive l'Opera; Student Drinking Song; Carry Me Back to Old Virginny; Reverie; Jump Jim Crow; Road to Paradise; Page's Aria. 132m/B VHS, LV. Jeanette MacDonald, Nelson Eddy, John Barrymore, Herman Bing, Tom Brown, Lynne Carver; *D:* Robert Z. Leonard; *W:* Noel Langley. Nominations: Academy Awards '37: Best Sound, Best Score. *MGM*

Maytime in Mayfair ✓✓ 1952 A dress shop owner's rival is getting all the goodies first, for which he takes the heat from his partner. When he finds out how the rival is doing it, the partners up and head for a vacation in the south of France. Overly simplistic but charming kitsch, helped along by Technicolor shots of the fashions and sets. 94m/C VHS. Anna Neagle, Michael Wilding, Peter Graves, Nicholas Phipps, Tom Walls, Tom Walls Jr.; *D:* Herbert Wilcox. *NOS*

The Maze ✓✓✓ 1985 Made-for-British-television mystery about a young girl who meets the ghost of her mother's first love in her garden estate. 60m/C VHS, Beta. *GB* Francesca Annis, James Bolam, Sky McCatskill.

Mazes and Monsters ✓✓½ *Rona Jaffe's Mazes and Monsters; Dungeons and Dragons* 1982 A group of university students becomes obsessed with playing a real life version of the fantasy role-playing game, Dungeons and Dragons (known in the film as Mazes & Monsters since D&D is trademarked). Early Hanks appearance is among the film's assets. Adapted for television from the book by Rona Jaffe. 100m/C VHS, Beta. *CA* Tom Hanks, Wendy Crewson, David Wallace, Chris Makepeace, Lloyd Bochner, Peter Donat, Murray Hamilton, Vera Miles, Louise Sorel, Susan Strasberg, Anne Francis; *D:* Steven Hilliard Stern; *M:* Hagood Hardy. *ORI, HHE, WAR*

McBain ✓✓✓ 1991 (R) In this exciting fast-paced action melodrama, HOW Robert McBain (Walken) leads a group of veterans into battle against the Columbian drug cartel. Stunning cinematography and superb performances combine to make this a riveting action film you won't soon forget.*CW:* Language and strong war violence and drug use. 104m/C VHS, **Closed Caption.** Christopher Walken, Maria Conchita Alonso, Michael Ironside, Steve James, Jay Patterson, Thomas G. Waites; *D:* James Glickenhaus; *W:* James Glickenhaus. *USH*

McCabe & Mrs. Miller ✓✓✓✓ 1971 (R) Altman's characteristically quirky take on the Western casts Beatty as a self-inflated entrepreneur who opens a brothel in the Great North. Christie is the madame who helps stabilize the haphazard operation. Unfortunately, success comes at a high price, and when gunmen arrive to enforce a business proposition, Beatty must become the man he has, presumably, merely pretended to be. A poetic, moving work, and a likely classic of the genre. Based on the novel by Edmund Naughton. 121m/C VHS, Beta, LV, **Closed Caption.** Warren Beatty, Julie Christie, William Devane, Keith Carradine, John Schuck, Rene Auberjonois, Shelley Duvall, Bert Remsen, Michael Murphy, Hugh Millais, Jack Riley; *D:* Robert Altman; *W:* Robert Altman; *C:* Vilmos Zsigmond; *M:* Leonard Cohen. Nominations: Academy Awards '71: Best Actress (Christie). *WAR*

The McConnell Story ✓✓½ *Tiger in the Sky* 1955 True story of ace flyer McConnell, his heroism during WWII and the Korean conflict, and his postwar aviation pioneer efforts. Fine acting from Allyson and Ladd, with good support from Whitmore and Faylen. 107m/C VHS, Beta, LV, **Closed Caption.** Alan Ladd, June Allyson, James Whitmore, Frank Faylen; *D:* Gordon Douglas; *M:* Max Steiner. *WAR, FCT*

The McGuffin ✓✓ 1985 A film critic's inquisitiveness about the activities of his neighbors gets him caught up in murder and a host of other problems. A takeoff of Alfred Hitchcock's 1954 classic "Rear Window." 95m/C VHS. *GB* Charles Dance, Ritza Brown, Francis Matthews, Brian Glover, Phyllis Logan, Jerry Stiller, Anna Massey; *D:* Colin Bucksey. *NO*

McHale's Navy ✓✓½ 1964 The TV sitcom came to the big screen with its silly humor intact as Lt. Commander Quinton McHale (Borgnine) and the reprobate crew of PT-73 get into debt gambling with a bunch of marines, which they try to get out of in a variety of unorthodox ways. 93m/C VHS, **Closed Caption.** Ernest Borgnine, Tim Conway, Joe Flynn, Bob Hastings, Billy Sands, Gavin MacLeod, George Kennedy; *D:* Edward Montagne; *W:* Frank Gill Jr., George Carleton Brown; *C:* William Margulies. *USH*

McHale's Navy ✓½ 1997 (PG) Yet another (unsuccessful) attempt to take a TV series and let it loose on the big screen. Retired Navy skipper McHale (Arnold) has set up his scheming ways on the Caribbean island of San Ysidro, where he can be a thorn in the side of Capt. Binghampton (Stockwell), the newly transferred commanding officer of the island's sleepy naval base. McHale's former cronies aid their leader when he's reluctantly reunited with the Navy in order to prevent the terrorist threats of his former Soviet nemesis Vladakov (Curry). A shining example of "why bother?" moviemaking. TV's original McHale, Borgnine, has a cameo (and gets a promotion to admiral). 108m/C VHS, LV, **Closed Caption.** Tom Arnold, Tim Curry, Dean Stockwell, David Alan Grier, Debra Messing, Thomas Chong, Bruce Campbell, French Stewart, Brian Haley, Danton Stone; *Cameos:* Ernest Borgnine; *W:* Peter Crabbe; *C:* Buzz Feitshans IV; *M:* Dennis McCarthy. Nominations: Golden Raspberry Awards '97: Worst Remake/Sequel. *USH*

McHale's Navy Joins the Air Force ✓✓½ 1965 McHale is conspicuously missing from this sequel (Borgnine had a contract dispute) so second banana Conway, as Ensign Charles Parker, gets to shine in slapstick gags. A drunken Parker winds up in an Air Force uniform and is mistaken for a hot-shot flier, gets involved with some Russians, and is even cited for bravery

by President Franklin D. Roosevelt. 01m/B VHS, **Closed Caption.** Tim Conway, Joe Flynn, Tom Tully, Ted Bessell, Bob Hastings, Gavin MacLeod, Billy Sands; *D:* Edward Montagne; *W:* John Fenton Murray; *C:* Lionel Lindon. *USH*

McKenzie Break ✓✓✓ 1970 Irish intelligence agent John Connor (Keith) is sent to Scotland to Camp McKenzie, a prison for German POWs during WWII. Captured U-boat commander Schluetter (Griem) is suspected of planning a mass escape and Connor is supposed to stop the action. The battle of wills between the hard-headed Connor and wily Schluetter provides taut, suspenseful drama. Adapted from "The Bowmanville Break" by Sidney Shelley. 106m/C VHS. Brian Keith, Helmut Griem, Ian Hendry, Jack Watson, Horst Janson, Patrick O'Connell; *D:* Lamont Johnson; *W:* William W. Norton Sr. *MGM*

McLintock! ✓✓✓ 1963 Rowdy western starring Wayne as a tough cattle baron whose refined wife (O'Hara) returns from the east after a two-year separation. She wants a divorce and custody of their 17-year-old daughter (Powers), who's been away at school. In the meantime, he's hired a housekeeper (De Carlo), whose teenage son (real-life son Patrick) promptly falls for Powers. It's a battle royal between the feisty wife and cantankerous husband but no one out-dukes the Duke. Other Wayne family members involved in the production include daughter Aissa (as the housekeeper's daughter) and son Michael who produced the film. 127m/C VHS, LV. John Wayne, Maureen O'Hara, Yvonne De Carlo, Patrick Wayne, Stefanie Powers, Jack Kruschen, Chill Wills, Jerry Van Dyke, Edgar Buchanan, Bruce Cabot, Perry Lopez, Michael Pate, Strother Martin, Gordon Jones; *D:* Andrew V. McLaglen; *W:* James Edward Grant; *C:* William Clothier. *MPI, GKK, ING*

The McMasters ✓✓ *The Blood Crowd; The McMasters...Tougher Than the West Itself* 1970 (PG) Set shortly after the Civil War, the film tells the story of the prejudice faced by a black soldier who returns to the southern ranch on which he was raised. Once there, the rancher gives him half of the property, but the ex-soldier has difficulty finding men who will work for him. When a group of Native Americans assist him, a band of bigoted men do their best to stop it. The movie was released in two versions with different endings: in one, prejudice prevails; in the other, bigotry is defeated. 89m/C VHS. Burl Ives, Brock Peters, David Carradine, Nancy Kwan, Jack Palance, Dane Clark, L.Q. Jones, Alan Vint, John Carradine; *D:* Alf Kjellin. *VTR, XVC*

McQ ✓✓½ 1974 (PG) After several big dope dealers kill two police officers, a lieutenant resigns to track them down. Dirty Harry done with an aging Big Duke. 116m/C VHS, Beta, LV, **Closed Caption.** John Wayne, Eddie Albert, Diana Muldaur, Clu Gulager, Colleen Dewhurst, Al Lettieri, Julie Adams, David Huddleston; *D:* John Sturges; *C:* Harry Stradling Jr.; *M:* Elmer Bernstein. *WAR*

McVicar ✓✓½ 1980 (R) A brutish and realistic depiction of crime and punishment based on the life of John McVicar, who plotted to escape from prison. From the book by McVicar. 90m/C VHS, Beta, LV. *GB* Roger Daltrey, Adam Faith, Cheryl Campbell; *D:* Tom Clegg; *W:* Tom Clegg. *VES*

Me and Him ✓½ *Ich und Er* 1989 (R) An unsuspecting New Yorker finds himself jockeying for position with his own instincts when his libido decides it wants a life of its own. 94m/C VHS, LV, **Closed Caption.** *GE* Griffin Dunne, Carey Lowell, Ellen Greene, Craig T. Nelson; *D:* Doris Dorrie; *M:* Klaus Doldinger; *V:* Mark Linn-Baker. *COL*

Me and the Colonel ✓✓½ 1958 Average satire meets Jewish refugee S.L. Jacobowsky (Kaye) trying to get out of Paris to Spain before the Nazis occupy the city. He gets stuck travelling with anti-Semitic Polish colonel Prokoszny (Jurgens), who's also not eager to fall into German hands. If the trip went smoothly, there wouldn't be a story, so naturally the men are forced to put aside their differences to survive. Adapted from Franz Werfel's play "Jacobowsky and the Colonel." **110m/B VHS.** Danny Kaye, Curt Jurgens, Akim Tamiroff, Nicole Maurey, Francoise Rosay, Martita Hunt, Alexander Scourby, Liliane Montevecchi; **D:** Peter Glenville; **W:** S.N. Behrman, George Froeschel; **C:** Burnett Guffey; **M:** George Duning. **COL**

Me and the Kid 🎬🎬½ 1993 (PG) Minor career criminals Aiello and Pantoliano try a robbery on a ruthless financier's (Dukes) home and wind up kidnapping his 10-year-old son instead. But dad doesn't want to pay the ransom and Aiello dumps his partner (who wants to kill the kid) and heads out on the road with the boy. **97m/C VHS, LV, Closed Caption.** Danny Aiello, Joe Pantoliano, Alex Zuckerman, Cathy Moriarty, David Dukes, Anita Morris; **D:** Dan Curtis. **ORI**

Me and the Mob 🎬½ *Wo Do I Gotta Kill?* 1994 (R) Writer Jimmy Corona (Lorinz) thinks the way to get some colorful stories is to join up with his mobster uncle (Darrow). But Jimmy's no tough guy and the feds coerce him into wearing a wire to bust the local godfather. Low-budget comedy is a lesson in tedium. **CW:** Profanity; sexual situations. **85m/C VHS.** James Lorinz, Tony Darrow, John Costelloe, Sandra Bullock, Anthony Michael Hall, Stephen Lee, Ted Sorel; **Cameos:** Steve Buscemi; **D:** Frank Rainone; **W:** James Lorinz, Frank Rainone. **AVI**

Me & Veronica 🎬🎬 1993 (R) Two estranged sisters try to come to terms with each other and their dead end lives. Good sister Fanny (McGovern) is a divorced waitress living in a run-down seaside town in New Jersey. One day bad sister Veronica (Wettig) shows up, announcing she's about to be sent to jail for welfare fraud. Veronica asks Fanny to look after her two kids while she's in jail and it is while visiting Veronica in prison that Fanny comes to realize her seemingly flamboyant sister is actually mentally ill and possibly suicidal. Grim little film with good lead performances. **97m/C VHS.** Elizabeth McGovern, Patricia Wettig, Michael O'Keefe, John Heard; **D:** Don Scardino; **W:** Leslie Lyles; **M:** David Mansfield. **COL**

Me, Myself & I 🎬🎬½ 1992 (R) Segal is a successful New York writer who falls in love with next-door neighbor Williams. But the road to romance is never smooth—particularly when your paranoid gal suffers from multiple personality disorder. Fun leads, dumb movie. **CW:** Strong language, some drug use, and some sexuality. **97m/C VHS.** George Segal, JoBeth Williams, Shelley Hack, Don Calfa, Bill Macy, Betsey Lynn George, Sharon McNight, Ruth Gilbert; **D:** Pablo Fero; **W:** Julian Barry. **COL**

The Meal 🎬🎬 *Deadly Encounter* 1975 (R) During a dinner party held by a wealthy woman, the rich and powerful guests divulge each others' secrets with reckless disregard for the consequences. **90m/C VHS.** Dina Merrill, Carl Betz, Leon Ames, Susan Logan, Vicki Powers, Steve Potter; **D:** R. John Hugh. **MOV**

Mean Dog Blues 🎬🎬½ 1978 (PG) A musician is convicted of hit-and-run driving after hitching a ride with an inebriated politician. **108m/C VHS, Beta.** George Kennedy, Kay Lenz, Scatman Crothers, Greg Henry, Gregory Sierra, Tina Louise, William Windom; **D:** Mel Stuart; **C:** Robert B. Hauser. **ART, VES**

Mean Frank and Crazy Tony 🎬🎬 1975 (R) A mobster and the man who idolizes him attempt a prison breakout in this fun, action-packed production. **92m/C VHS, Beta.** IT Lee Van Cleef, Tony LoBianco, Jean Rochefort, Jess Hahn; **D:** Michele Lupo. **ART**

Mean Guns 🎬🎬 1997 (R) Lots of mayhem will redeem this silly plot for the action fan. Moon (Ice-T) lures 100 assassins to an abandoned prison with the promise of $10 million for the last three men standing. Lou (Lambert) and Marcus (Halsey) are Moon's rivals. **CW:** Violence, language. **90m/C VHS, Closed Caption.** Ice-T, Christopher Lambert, Michael Halsey, Deborah Van Valkenburgh, Tina Cote, Yuji Okumoto; **D:** Albert Pyun. **THV**

Mean Johnny Barrows 🎬½ 1975 When Johnny Barrows returns to his home town after being dishonorably discharged from the Army he is offered a job as a gang hitman. **83m/C VHS, Beta.** Fred Williamson, Roddy McDowall, Stuart Whitman, Luther Adler, Jenny Sherman, Elliott Gould; **D:** Fred Williamson. **UNI**

Mean Machine 🎬🎬 1973 (R) A man and his beautiful cohort plot revenge on organized crime for the murder of his father. **89m/C VHS, Beta.** Chris Mitchum, Barbara Bouchet, Arthur Kennedy. **NO**

Mean Season 🎬🎬 1985 (R) A vicious mass murderer makes a Miami crime reporter his confidante in his quest for publicity during his killing spree. In time, the madman's intentions become clear as the tensions and headlines grow with each gruesome slaying. Then the reporter must come to terms with the idea that he is letting himself be used due to the success that the association is bringing him. Suspenseful story with a tense ending. Good performance from Russell as the reporter. Screenplay written by Christopher Crowe under the pseudonym Leon Piedmont. **106m/C VHS, Beta, LV.** Kurt Russell, Mariel Hemingway, Richard Jordan, Richard Masur, Andy Garcia, Joe Pantoliano, Richard Bradford, William Smith; **D:** Phillip Borsos; **W:** Christopher Crowe; **M:** Lalo Schifrin. **NO**

Mean Streets 🎬🎬🎬🎬 1973 (R) A grimy slice of street life in Little Italy among lower echelon Mafiosos, unbalanced punks, and petty criminals. A riveting, free-form feature film, marking the formal debut by Scorsese (five years earlier he had completed a student film, "Who's That Knocking At My Door?"). Unorthodox camera movement and gritty performances by De Niro and Keitel, with underlying Catholic guilt providing the moral conflict. Excellent early '60s soundtrack. **112m/C VHS, Beta, LV, Closed Caption.** Harvey Keitel, Robert De Niro, David Proval, Amy Robinson, Richard Romanus, David Carradine, Robert Carradine, Cesare Danova, George Memmoli; **D:** Martin Scorsese; **W:** Mardik Martin, Martin Scorsese. National Film Registry '97;; National Society of Film Critics Awards '73: Best Supporting Actor (De Niro). **WAR**

The Meanest Men in the West 🎬 1976 (PG) Two criminal half-brothers battle frontier law and each other. **92m/C VHS, Beta.** Charles Bronson, Lee Marvin, Lee J. Cobb, James Drury, Albert Salmi, Charles Grodin; **D:** Samuel Fuller; **W:** Charles S. Dubin. **USH**

Meantime 🎬🎬 1981 British TV comedy/drama about the working class finds brothers Mark (Daniels) and Colin (Roth) living with their unemployed dad in a depressing East London flat. Colin, who's looking to escape his dreary life, befriends skinhead Coxy (Oldman) to the dismay of the rest of the family. **90m/C VHS.** GB Tim Roth, Gary Oldman, Phil Daniels, Alfred Molina, Pam Ferris; **D:** Mike Leigh; **C:** Roger Pratt; **M:** Andrew Dickson. **FXL**

Meatballs 🎬🎬 1979 (PG) The Activities Director at a summer camp who is supposed to organize fun for everyone prefers his own style of "fun." If you enjoy watching Murray blow through a movie, you'll like this one even as it lapses into boxoffice sentimentality. **92m/C VHS, Beta, LV, Closed Caption.** CA Bill Murray, Harvey Atkin, Kate Lynch; **D:** Ivan Reitman; **W:** Len Blum, Harold Ramis, Janis Allen; **M:** Elmer Bernstein. Genie Awards '80: Best Actress (Lynch). **PAR**

Meatballs 2 🎬½ 1984 (PG) The future of Camp Sasquatch is in danger unless the camp's best fighter can beat Camp Patton's champ in a boxing match. The saving grace of Bill Murray is absent in this one. **87m/C VHS, Beta, LV, 8mm, Closed Caption.** Archie Hahn, John Mengatti, Tammy Taylor, Kim Richards, Ralph Seymour, Richard Mulligan, Hamilton Camp, John Larroquette, Paul (Pee Wee Herman) Reubens, Misty Rowe, Elayne Boosler; **D:** Ken Wiederhorn. **COL**

Meatballs 3 WOOF! 1987 (R) Second sequel to the teenage sex/summer camp comedy. Enough is enough! **95m/C VHS, Beta.** Sally Kellerman, Shannon Tweed, George Buza, Isabelle Mejias, Al Waxman, Patrick Dempsey; **D:** George Mendeluk. **ART**

Meatballs 4 🎬½ 1992 (R) Feldman stars as a water skier hired to serve as recreation director of Lakeside Water Ski Camp. His enemy is Monica (Douglas) of a nearby rival camp who wants to buy out Lakeside's owner and use the land for real estate development. Lame plot only serves to showcase some good water skiing stunts. **CW:** Nudity and sensual scene. **87m/C VHS, Closed Caption.** Corey Feldman, Jack Nance, Sarah Douglas, Bojesse Christopher; **D:** Bob Logan. **HBO**

The Meateater WOOF! 1979 Disgusting horror flick of a disfigured hermit who inhabits a closed-up movie house. When it is reopened he turns into a stereotypical slasher. Vegetarians beware: references throughout about eating meat. **84m/C VHS, Beta.** Arch Jaboulian, Diane Davis, Emily Spendler; **D:** Derek Savage. **NO**

The Mechanic 🎬🎬 *Killer of Killers* 1972 (R) Bronson stars as Arthur Bishop, a wealthy professional killer for a powerful organization. He has innumerable ways to kill. **100m/C VHS, Beta, LV.** Charles Bronson, Jan-Michael Vincent, Keenan Wynn, Jill Ireland, Linda Ridgeway; **D:** Michael Winner; **W:** Lewis John Carlino. **MGM, FOX**

Medea 1959 Medea, who betrayed her homeland for Jason, is becoming wary of his boredom with her. The classic story of love and revenge ensues thereafter in unbridled fury and passion. **107m/B VHS.** Colleen Dewhurst, Zoe Caldwell, Judith Anderson; **D:** Jose Quintero. **IVY, FHS**

Medea 1970 Cinema poet Pasolini directs opera diva Callas in this straightforward adaptation of Euripides's classic about a sorceress whose escapades range from assisting in the theft of the Golden Fleece to murdering her own children. Not Pasolini at his best, but still better than most if what you're looking for is something arty. In Italian with English subtitles. **118m/C VHS, Beta.** IT Maria Callas, Guiseppi Gentile, Laurent Terzieff; **D:** Pier Paolo Pasolini. **HMV, VAI**

Medicine Man 🎬½ 1930 Benny stars as a con-man who fronts a medicine show in this early talkie comedy. **57m/B VHS, Beta.** Jack Benny, Betty Bronson, E. Alyn Warren, George E. Stone, Tom Dugan; **D:** Scott Pembroke. **NOS, DVT, VYY**

Medicine Man 🎬🎬 1992 (PG-13) Connery's usual commanding presence and the beautiful scenery are the only things to recommend in this lame effort. Dr. Robert Campbell (Connery) is a biochemist working in the Amazon rain forest on a cancer cure. Bracco is Dr. Rae Crane, a fellow researcher sent by the institute sponsoring Campbell to see how things are going. Although Crane is uptight and Campbell is gruff, they fall in love (supposedly), but they're sorely lacking in chemistry. Oh, Campbell's cancer cure is made from a rare flower being eradicated by the destruction of the rain forest. This politically correct cause meets romance falls short of ever being truly entertaining. **105m/C VHS, Beta.** Sean Connery, Lorraine Bracco, Jose Wilker, Rodolfo de Alexandra, Francisco Tsirene Tsere Rereme, Elias Monteiro da Silva; **D:** John McTiernan; **M:** Jerry Goldsmith. **HPH**

Medicine River 🎬🎬½ 1994 (PG) A Native American photojournalist returns to his hometown after a 20-year absence and winds up in hot water with newfound friend Harlen Bigbear. **96m/C VHS.** Graham Greene, Tom Jackson, Sheila Tousey, Jimmy Herman, Raoul Trujillo; **D:** Stuart Margolin.

The Mediterranean in Flames 🎬½ 1972 In Nazi-occupied Greece, a small but brave resistance is formed to fight its captors. One of the women within the group is forced to seduce a Nazi officer in an attempt to learn enemy secrets. **85m/C VHS, Beta.** GR Costas Karras, Costas Precas; **D:** Dimis Dadiras. **NO**

Mediterraneo 🎬🎬🎬 1991 (R) Languid, charming comedy based on the premise that love does make the world go 'round—especially in wartime. In 1941, eight misfit Italian soldiers are stranded on a tiny Greek island and are absorbed into the life of the island, finding love and liberty in the idyllic setting. Lighthearted fun. In Italian with English subtitles. **CW:** Language, drug content, and sexuality. 90m/C VHS, Beta, LV, Closed Caption. IT Diego Abatantuono; Giuseppe Cederna, Claudio Bigalli, Vanna Barba, Claudio Bisio, Luigi Alberti, Ugo Conti, Memo Dini, Vasco Mirandola, Luigi Montini, Irene Grazioli, Antonio Catania; D: Gabriele Salvatores. Academy Awards '91: Best Foreign Language Film. TOU, IME

The Medium 🎬🎬 1951 A phony medium is done in by her own trickery in this filmed version of the Menotti opera. 80m/B VHS, Beta. Marie Powers, Anna Maria Alberghetti, Leo Coleman; D: Gian-Carlo Menotti; W: Gian-Carlo Menotti. Nominations: Academy Awards '52: Scoring of a Musical. MVD, VAI

Medium Cool 🎬🎬🎬½ 1969 Commentary on life in the '60s focuses on a television news cameraman and his growing apathy with the events around him. His involvement with a Appalachian woman and her young son reawakens his conscience, leading to the three getting caught up in the turbulence of the 1968 Chicago Democratic convention. A frightening depiction of detachment in modern society. 111m/C VHS, Beta, Closed Caption. Robert Forster, Verna Bloom, Peter Bonerz, Marianna Hill, Peter Boyle; D: Haskell Wexler; W: Haskell Wexler; C: Haskell Wexler. PAR

Medusa 🎬 Twisted 1974 A bizarre series of events occur when an abandoned yacht containing two lifeless bodies is found on the Aegean Sea. 103m/C VHS, Beta. George Hamilton, Cameron Mitchell, Luciana Paluzzi, Theodore Roubanis; D: Gordon Hessler. SNC

Medusa Against the Son of Hercules 🎬 Perseus the Invincible 1962 This time the strongman takes on the evil Medusa and her deadly army of rock men. ?m/C VHS, Beta. IT Richard Harrison. SNC

The Medusa Touch 🎬 1978 (R) A man is struck over the head and is admitted to a hospital. Meanwhile, strange disasters befall the surrounding city. It seems that despite his unconscious state, the man is using his telekinetic powers to will things to happen.... 110m/C VHS. GB Richard Burton, Lino Ventura, Lee Remick, Harry Andrews, Alan Badel, Marie-Christine Barrault, Michael Hordern, Derek Jacobi, Jeremy Brett; D: Jack Gold; W: Jack Gold, John Briley. FOX

Meet Danny Wilson 🎬🎬½ 1952 Talented New York singer Wilson (Siantra) and his pianist buddy Mike Ryan (Nicol) head out to Hollywood to try their luck. Danny meets club singer Joy Carroll (Winters) who introduces him to gangster owner Nick Driscoll (Burr). Nick manages Danny for a hefty percentage and makes him a star at his club but Danny's lovelife goes south when Joy picks Mike over him. Then Driscoll demands his money. Sinatra gets to croon some great tunes. 🎵I've Got a Crush on You; How Deep Is the Ocean; When You're Smiling; All of Me; She's Funny That Way; That Old Black Magic; You're a Sweetheart; Lonesome Man Blues; A Good Man Is Hard to Find. 88m/B VHS, Closed Caption. Frank Sinatra, Alex Nicol, Shelley Winters, Raymond Burr, Tommy Farrell, Vaughn Taylor, Jack Kruschen, Donald MacBride; D: Joseph Pevney; W: Don McGuire. USH

Meet Dr. Christian 🎬½ 1939 The good old doctor settles some problems. Part of a series. 72m/B VHS, Beta. Jean Hersholt, Robert Baldwin, Paul Harvey; D: Bernard Vorhaus. NOS, DVT, VYY

Meet John Doe 🎬🎬🎬 1941 A social commentary about an unemployed, down-and-out man selected to be the face of a political goodwill campaign. Honest and trusting, he eventually realizes that he is being used to further the careers of corrupt politicians. Available in colorized version. 123m/B VHS, LV. Gary Cooper, Barbara Stanwyck, Edward Arnold, James Gleason, Walter Brennan, Spring Byington, Gene Lockhart, Regis Toomey, Ann Doran, Rod La Rocque; D: Frank Capra; C: George Barnes. Nominations: Academy Awards '41: Best Story. NOS, MRV, BAR

Meet Me in Las Vegas 🎬🎬 1956 Compulsive gambler/cowboy Dailey betters his luck when he hooks up with hoofer girlfriend Charisse. Much frolicking and dancing and cameo appearances by a truckload of stars. A little more entertaining than a game of solitaire. 🎵The Girl With the Yaller Shoes; If You Can Dream; Hell Hath No Fury; Lucky Charm; I Refuse to Rock 'n Roll; Rehearsal Ballet; Sleeping Beauty Ballet; Frankie and Johnny. 112m/C VHS, LV, Letterbox. Dan Dailey, Cyd Charisse, Agnes Moorehead, Lili Darvas, Jim Backus, Cara Williams, Betty Lynn, Oscar Karlweis, Liliane Montevecchi, Jerry Colonna, Frankie Laine; Cameos: Debbie Reynolds, Frank Sinatra, Peter Lorre, Vic Damone, Tony Martin, Elaine Stewart; D: Roy Rowland; W: Isobel Lennart. Nominations: Academy Awards '56: Scoring of a Musical. MGM, TTC, FCT

Meet Me in St. Louis 🎬🎬🎬½ 1944 Wonderful music in this charming tale of a St. Louis family during the 1903 World's Fair. One of Garland's better musical performances. 🎵You and I; Skip to My Lou; Over the Bannister; Meet Me In St. Louis; Brighten the Corner; Summer In St. Louis; All Hallow's Eve; Ah, Love; The Horrible One. 113m/C VHS, Beta, LV, 8mm. Judy Garland, Margaret O'Brien, Mary Astor, Lucille Bremer, Tom Drake, June Lockhart, Harry Davenport; D: Vincente Minnelli. National Film Registry '94;; Nominations: Academy Awards '44: Best Color Cinematography, Best Screenplay, Best Song ("The Trolley Song"), Scoring of a Musical. MGM, TLF, HMV

Meet Sexton Blake 🎬🎬 1944 A detective is hired to find a ring and some secret papers that were stolen from the corpse of a man killed in an air raid. He discovers that the papers contained the plans for a new metal alloy to be used in planes. Entertaining for its melodramatic elements. 80m/B VHS, Beta. GB David Farrar, John Varley, Magda Kun, Gordon McLeod, Manning Whiley; D: John Harlow; W: John Harlow. SNC

Meet the Deedles 🎬½ 1998 (PG) The answer to the question, "What would happen if Bill and Ted or Wayne and Garth were even dumber?" Hard to believe? No, just hard to watch. Phil and Stew Deedle (Walker and Van Wormer) are two rich surfer airheads who just wanna have fun, dude. Facing expulsion from school, the twins are forced to attend the bogus Camp Broken Spirit by their father. The boys slip and fall on a plot device and wake up in the hospital, mistaken for rookie Yellowstone park rangers there to fight a mounting prarie dog problem. It seems that bitter ex-ranger Slater (Hopper, phoning in his patented mondo-weirdo) has enslaved the rodents and is trying to redirect the geyser Old Faithful. Features heinous dialogue and stunts lifted from Mountain Dew commercials. 90m/C VHS. Steve Van Wormer, Paul Walker, A.J. Langer, John Ashton, Dennis Hopper, Eric (Hans Gudegast) Braeden, Richard Lineback, Robert Englund, Ana Gasteyer, Megan Cavanaugh; D: Steve Boyum; W: Jim Herzfeld, Dale Pollock; C: David Hennings; M: Steve Bartek. NYR

Meet the Feebles 🎬🎬 1989 Sex and violence gorefest perpetuated by puppets—and the dementia of director Jackson. A TV variety show, populated by animal puppets and humans in costume, is the setting for backstage mayhem, including sex, drugs, and a shooting spree. Among the characters are a sleazy walrus producer, his slinky Siamese cat mistress, a junkie frog, and a manic-depressive elephant. There's also several musical production numbers, if things aren't strange enough for you already. 94m/C VHS. NZ D: Peter Jackson; W: Peter Jackson, Danny Mulheron, Frances Walsh. MTH

Meet the Hollowheads 🎬½ 1989 (PG-13) Family situation comedy set in a futuristic society. 89m/C VHS, LV, Closed Caption. John Glover, Nancy Mette, Richard Portnow, Matt Shakman, Juliette Lewis, Anne Ramsey; D: Tom Burman; W: Tom Burman. IME

Meet the Mob 🎬🎬 1942 A country spinster visits her son in the big city and is mistaken for a notorious murderess. Complications arise when she tries to keep the boy honest. Could have worked better. 62m/B VHS. ZaSu Pitts, Roger Pryor, Warren Hymer, Gwen Kenyon, Douglas Fowley, Elizabeth Russell, Tristram Coffin, Lester Dorr, Wheeler Oakman, Bud McTaggart; D: Jean Yarbrough. NOS

Meet the Navy 🎬🎬 1946 Post-war musical revue about a pianist and a dancer. 81m/B VHS, Beta. Joan Pratt, Margaret Hurst, Lionel Murton. VYY

Meet the Parents 🎬🎬 1991 A young man visits his fiance's parents and every nightmare, every tragedy that can possibly happen, does. From the minds of "National Lampoon," with an appearance by beyond-bizarre comedian Emo Phillips. ?m/C VHS. Greg Glionna, Jacqueline Cahill, Dick Galloway, Carol Wheeler, Mary Ruth Clarke, Emo Phillips; D: Greg Glionna; W: Mary Ruth Clarke. NO

Meet Wally Sparks 🎬🎬 1997 (R) No-brow "Man Who Came to Dinner." Smutty TV shock-talk host Sparks (Dangerfield) is given one week to save his failing show when producer Reynolds (with a noticeably bad rug) puts him on notice. Opportunity knocks when he is invited to a party at the governor's mansion to interview the conservative head honcho (Stiers). Once there, a freak accident with a drunken horse prevents Sparks from leaving, and the new guest makes himself right at home by turning the fancy digs into a broadcast studio. Dangerfield's machine gun spray of one liners occasionally hits, as do his sometimes lengthy and elaborately set up jokes that do little to propel the plot along but are pure Dangerfield. Not much beyond Rodney makes lackluster "Sparks" fly. **CW:** Continuous sexual humor and partial nudity. 107m/C VHS. Rodney Dangerfield, David Ogden Stiers, Burt Reynolds, Debi Mazar, Cindy Williams, Alan Rachins; D: Peter Baldwin; W: Rodney Dangerfield, Harry Basil; C: Richard Kline; M: Michel Colombier. THV

Meeting at Midnight 🎬🎬 1944 Charlie Chan is invited to a seance to solve a perplexing mystery. Chan discovers that they use mechanical figures and from there on solving the murder is easy. 67m/B VHS, Beta. Sidney Toler, Joseph Crehan, Mantan Moreland, Frances Chan, Ralph Peters, Helen Beverly; D: Phil Rosen. MGM, VCN, MRV

Meeting Venus 🎬🎬½ 1991 (PG-13) Backstage drama featuring Close as Karin Anderson, a world-famous Swedish opera diva. An international cast of characters adds to this sophisticated film of romance, rivalry and political confrontation set amidst a newly unified Europe. 121m/C VHS, Beta, LV. Glenn Close, Niels Arestrup, Erland Josephson, Johanna Ter Steege, Maria De Medeiros, Ildiko Bansagi, Macha Meril, Dorottya Udvaros, Jay O. Sanders, Victor Poletti; D: Istvan Szabo; W: Istvan Szabo, Michael Hirst; C: Lajos Koltai; V: Kiri Te Kanawa. WAR

Meetings with Remarkable Men 🎬🎬½ 1979 An acclaimed, visually awesome film version of the memoir by Gurdjieff, about his wanderings through Asia and the Middle East searching for answers and developing his own spiritual code. Mildly entertaining but only of true interest to those familiar with the subject. 108m/C VHS, Beta. Terence Stamp, Dragan Maksimovic, Mikica Dmitrijevic; D: Peter Brook. WSH

Megaforce woof! 1982 (PG) Futuristic thriller directed by stuntman Needham follows the adventures of the military task force, Megaforce, on its mission to save a small democratic nation from attack. Bostwick leads the attack. 'Nuff said. 99m/C VHS, Beta. Barry Bostwick, Persis Khambatta, Edward Mulhare, Henry Silva, Michael Beck, Ralph Wilcox; D: Hal Needham. FOX

Megaville 🎬🎬 1991 (R) Set in the not too distant future, corrupt politician Travanti struggles to corner the market on the evil technology "Dream-a-Life," which aims to control the rebellious "riff-raff" of Megaville. He does all of his dealings while up against a hitman who has a defective memory chip in his brain. 96m/C VHS. Billy Zane, Daniel J. Travanti, J.C. Quinn, Grace Zabriskie; **D:** Peter Lehner; **W:** Peter Lehner. *ART*

Mein Kampf: Hitler's Rise and Fall
1960 The rise and fall of German fascism and its impact upon the world is examined in this documentary. 120m/C VHS, Beta, LV. **D:** Erwin Leiser. *MRV, CCP, FCT*

Melanie 🐾🐾½ 1982 (PG) Drama tells the tale of one poor woman's courage, determination, and optimism, as she tries to regain her child from her ex-husband. She befriends musician Cummings (a founding member of "Guess Who" rock band) who helps. Usual cliches balanced by good performances. 109m/C VHS, Beta. **CA** Glynnis O'Connor, Paul Sorvino, Don Johnson, Burton Cummings; **D:** Rex Bromfield. *VES*

Melanie Darrow 🐾½ 1997 (PG-13) Routine cable drama finds relentless attorney Melanie Darrow (Burke) defending the younger husband of a socialite friend for the woman's murder, much to the dismay of Melanie's homicide cop brother (Bloom). **CW:** Some violence and brief sensuality. 88m/C VHS. Delta Burke, Brian Bloom, Daniel Birt, Jonathan Banks, Bruce Abbott, Shawn Ashmore, Wendel Meldrum; **D:** Gary Nelson. *PAR*

Melodie en Sous-Sol 🐾🐾 *Any Number Can Win* 1963 Two ex-convicts, one old and one young, risk their lives and freedom for one last major heist: a gambling casino. In French with English subtitles. 118m/B VHS, Beta. **FR** Jean Gabin, Alain Delon, Viviane Romance; **D:** Henri Verneuil. *BAR*

Melody 🐾🐾 1971 (G) Sensitive but slow study of a special friendship which enables two pre-teens to survive in a regimented and impersonal world. Features music by the Bee Gees. 106m/C VHS, Beta. **GB** Tracy Hyde, Jack Wild, Mark Lester, Colin Barrie, Roy Kinnear; **D:** Waris Hussein; **W:** Alan Parker.

Melody Cruise 🐾🐾 1932 Boring musical romantic comedy that can't stay with any one of those three things for more than a minute without careening into one of the other two. 🎵 I Met Her at a Party; He's Not the Marrying Kind; Isn't This a Night For Love; This is the Hour. 75m/B VHS, Beta. Phil Harris, Charlie Ruggles, Greta Nissen, Helen Mack, Chick Chandler; **D:** Mark Sandrich; **M:** Max Steiner. *TTC*

Melody for Three 🐾🐾 1941 In the tradition of matchmaker, Doctor Christian aids in the reuniting of music-teacher mother and great-conductor father, who have been divorced for years, in order to help the couple's son, a violin prodigy. 69m/B VHS, Beta, 8mm. Jean Hersholt, Fay Wray; **D:** Erle C. Kenton. *NOS, VYY, DVT*

Melody in Love 🐾 1978 A young girl visits her cousin and her swinging friends on a tropical island. Dubbed. 90m/C VHS, Beta, **Closed Caption.** Melody O'Bryan, Sasha Hehn; **D:** Hubert Frank. *FOX*

Melody Master 🐾🐾 *New Wine* 1941 Romanticized biography of composer Franz Schubert, chronicling his personal life and loves, along with performances of his compositions. If you just have to know what drove the composer of "Ave Maria" it may hold your interest, but otherwise not very compelling. 80m/B VHS, Beta. Alan Curtis, Ilona Massey, Binnie Barnes, Albert Basserman, Billy Gilbert, Sterling Holloway; **M:** Miklos Rozsa. *NOS, VYY, DVT*

Melody of the Plains 🐾 1937 Singing cowpoke teams up with a young girl for some cattle-rustlin' adventure. Substandard horse opry due to poor direction and haphazard lensing. 53m/B VHS. Fred Scott, Louise Small, Al "Fuzzy" St. John, David Sharpe, Lafe McKee, Charles "Slim" Whitaker, Hal Price, Lew Meehan; **D:** Sam Newfield; **W:** Bennett Cohen. *MOV*

Melody Ranch 🐾½ 1940 Gene returns to his home town as an honored guest and appointed sheriff. But gangster MacLane is determined to drive him out of town. 🎵 Melody Ranch; Call of the Canyon; We Never Dream the Same Dream

Twice; Vote for Autry; My Gal Sal; Torpedo Joe; What Are Cowboys Made Of?; Rodeo Rose; Back in the Saddle Again. 84m/C VHS, Beta. Gene Autry, Jimmy Durante, George "Gabby" Hayes, Ann Miller, Barton MacLane, Joseph Sawyer, Horace McMahon, Veda Ann Borg; **D:** Joseph Santley. *CCB, VCN*

Melody Time 1948 Seven animated/musical tales from the Disney studios, including "Blame It On the Samba" with Donald Duck; "Once Upon a Wintertime;" "Bumble Boogie;" "Johnny Appleseed;" "Little Toot" with musical narration provided by the Andrews Sisters; Fred Waring and the Pennsylvanians singing "Trees," the Joyce Kilmer poem; and Roy Rogers narrating the story of "Pecos Bill." 75m/C VHS, **Closed Caption.** *TOU*

Melody Trail 🐾 1935 Autry wins $1000 in a rodeo, loses the money to a gypsy, gets a job, falls for his employer's daughter...and in the end captures a kidnapper and cattle rustlers. 🎵 Hold On, Little Doggie, Hold On; On the Prairie; Lookin for the Lost Chord; The Hurdy Gurdy Man; My Prayer For Tonight; End of the Trail; I'd Love a Home in the Mountains. 60m/B VHS, Beta. Gene Autry, Smiley Burnette, Ann Rutherford; **D:** Joseph Kane. *CCB, VCN*

Melvin and Howard 🐾🐾🐾½ 1980 (R) Story of Melvin Dummar, who once gave Howard Hughes a ride. Dummar later claimed a share of Hughes's estate. Significant for Demme's direction and fine acting from Steenburgen/LeMat, and Robards in a small role as Hughes. Offbeat and very funny. 95m/C VHS, Beta, LV. Paul LeMat, Jason Robards Jr., Mary Steenburgen, Michael J. Pollard, Dabney Coleman, Elizabeth Cheshire, Pamela Reed, Cheryl "Rainbeaux" Smith; **D:** Jonathan Demme; **W:** Bo Goldman. Academy Awards '80: Best Original Screenplay, Best Supporting Actress (Steenburgen); Golden Globe Awards '81: Best Supporting Actress (Steenburgen); Los Angeles Film Critics Association Awards '80: Best Supporting Actress (Steenburgen); New York Film Critics Awards '80: Best Director (Demme), Best Screenplay, Best Supporting Actress (Steenburgen); National Society of Film Critics Awards '80: Best Film, Best Screenplay, Best Supporting Actress (Steenburgen); Writers Guild of America '80: Best Original Screenplay; Nominations: Academy Awards '80: Best Supporting Actor (Robards). *USH, BTV*

Melvin Purvis: G-Man 🐾🐾 *The Legend of Machine Gun Kelly* 1974 Mediocre action film has dedicated federal agent tracking killer Machine Gun Kelly across American Midwest during Depression. Made for television. 78m/C VHS. Dale Robertson, Harris Yulin, Margaret Blye, Matt Clark, Elliot Street, Dick Sargent, John Karlen, David Canary; **D:** Dan Curtis. *HBO*

The Member of the Wedding 🐾🐾🐾 1952 While struggling through her adolescence, a 12-year-old girl growing up in 1945 Georgia seeks solace from her family's cook. Based on Carson McCullers's play, this story of family, belonging, and growth is well acted and touching. 90m/C VHS, Beta. Ethel Waters, Julie Harris, Brandon de Wilde, Arthur Franz; **D:** Fred Zinnemann; **W:** Edward Anhalt; **C:** Hal Mohr; **M:** Alex North. Nominations: Academy Awards '52: Best Actress (Harris). *NO*

The Member of the Wedding 🐾🐾 1983 TV rehash of Carson McCuller's play about a young girl who finds she's got some growing up to do when big brother marries. No match for Zinnemann's '52 version, or for Mann's earlier "All Quiet on the Western Front" and "Marty." 90m/C VHS. Dana Hill, Pearl Bailey, Howard E. Rollins Jr.; **D:** Delbert Mann. *VHE*

The Member of the Wedding 🐾🐾½ 1997 (PG) The second TV remake of Carson's McCuller's 1946 novel follows the adolescent struggles of 12-year-old Frankie Adams (Paquin). It's the summer of 1944 in Georgia and desperate for a change, Frankie decides the wedding of her brother Jarvis (McGrath) will give her the opportunity to leave her troubles behind. Woodard is the family's gentle but no-nonsense housekeeper Berenice. 93m/C VHS, **Closed Caption.** Anna Paquin, Alfre Woodard, Matt McGrath, Corey Dunn, Anne Tremko,

Enrico Colantoni; **D:** Fielder Cook; **W:** David W. Rintels; **C:** Paul LaMastra; **M:** Laurence Rosenthal. *HMK*

Memoirs of an Invisible Man 🐾🐾½ 1992 (PG-13) Nick Halloway, a slick and shallow stock analyst, is rendered invisible by a freak accident. When he is pursued by a CIA agent-hit man who wants to exploit him, Nick turns for help to Alice, a documentary filmmaker he has just met. Naturally, they fall in love along the way. Effective sight gags, hardworking cast can't overcome pitfalls in script, which indecisively meanders between comedy and thrills. 99m/C VHS, LV, **Closed Caption.** Chevy Chase, Daryl Hannah, Sam Neill, Michael McKean, Stephen Tobolowsky, Jim Norton, Patricia Heaton, Rosalind Chao; **D:** John Carpenter; **W:** Robert Collector. *WAR*

Memorial Day 🐾🐾 1983 Good cast highlights this made-for-television outing covering a Vietnam veterans reunion. With the old memories come new problems for the men and their families. 120m/C VHS. Mike Farrell, Shelley Fabares, Keith Mitchell, Bonnie Bedelia, Robert Walden, Edward Herrmann, Danny Glover; **D:** Joseph Sargent; **M:** Billy Goldenberg. *NO*

Memorial Valley Massacre 🐾 1988 (R) When campers settle for a weekend in a new, unfinished campground, they're slaughtered in turn by a nutty hermit. 93m/C VHS, Beta, LV. Cameron Mitchell, William Smith, John Kerry, Mark Mears, Lesa Lee, John Caso; **D:** Robert C. Hughes. *NLC*

Memories of a Marriage 🐾🐾🐾 1990 A nostalgic look at a couple's many years of marriage, from the husband's point of view, as they face their most trying times. Touchingly reminiscent as it spans the youthful years of new love and marriage to the more quiet, solid years of matured love. In Danish with English subtitles. 90m/C VHS. **DK** Ghita Norby, Frits Helmuth, Rikke Bendsen, Henning Moritzen; **D:** Kaspar Rostrup. *ORI, FXL*

Memories of Hell 1987 Examines the special bonds of friendship that have been maintained among the New Mexicans who survived one of WWII's most brutal battles and subsequent prisoner experiences. 57m/C VHS, Beta. *NO*

Memories of Me 🐾🐾 1988 (PG-13) A distraught doctor travels to L.A. to see his ailing father and make up for lost time. Both the doctor and his father learn about themselves and each other. Story of child/parent relationships attempts to pull at the heartstrings but only gets as far as the liver. Co-written and co-produced by Crystal, this film never quite reaches the potential of its cast. 103m/C VHS, Beta, LV, **Closed Caption.** Billy Crystal, Alan King, JoBeth Williams, David Ackroyd, Sean Connery, Janet Carroll; **D:** Henry Winkler; **W:** Billy Crystal, Eric Roth; **M:** Georges Delerue. *FOX*

Memories of Murder 1990 A woman suffering from amnesia is stalked by a merciless killer, apparently seeking revenge. Can she regain her memory and understand why she is being hunted, before it's too late? 104m/C VHS, Beta. Vanity, Nancy Allen, Robin Thomas; **D:** Robert Lewis; **W:** John Kent Harrison, Nevin Schreiner.

Memories of Underdevelopment 🐾🐾½ 1968 Set in the early 1960s. An anti-revolutionary, Europeanized intellectual takes a stand against the new government in Cuba. In Spanish with English subtitles. 97m/B VHS. **CU** Sergio Corrieri, Daisy Granados; **D:** Tomas Gutierrez Alea; **W:** Tomas Gutierrez Alea. *NYF, FCT*

Memory of Us 🐾🐾 1974 (PG) Still-relevant story of a married, middle-aged woman who starts to question her happiness as a wife and mother. Written by its star Geer, whose father, Will, plays a bit part. 93m/C VHS. Ellen Geer, Jon Cypher, Barbara Colby, Peter Brown, Robert Hogan, Rose Marie, Will Geer; **D:** H. Kaye Dyal.

Memphis 🐾🐾½ 1991 (PG-13) In 1957 three white drifters (two men and a woman) decide to secure some easy money by kidnapping the young grandson of the richest black businessman in Memphis. They think it's an easy job since, given the prejudice of the times, the police will do little or nothing but they reckon without the resources of the black community itself. Based on the novel "September, September" by Shelby Foote. Originally made for cable. **92m/C VHS, Beta, LV, Closed Caption.** Cybill Shepherd, John Laughlin, J.E. Freeman, Richard Brooks, Moses Gunn, Vanessa Bell, Martin C. Gardner; **D:** Yves Simoneau; **W:** Cybill Shepherd, Larry McMurtry; **M:** David Bell. *TTC*

Memphis Belle 🐾🐾🐾 **1990 (PG-13)** Satisfying Hollywood version of the documentary of the same name captures the true story of the final mission of a WWII bomber crew stationed in England. The boys of the Memphis Belle were the first group of B-17 crewmen to complete a 25 mission tour—no small feat in an air war that claimed many lives. Good ensemble cast of up and coming young actors; Lithgow has a nice turn as an army PR guy determined to exploit their boyish good looks on the homefront. Caton-Jones effectively uses 1940s film techniques and some original footage, making up for a rather hokey script. Film debut of singer Connick. Produced by Catherine Wyler, whose father made the original.**CW:** Language; adult situations and violence. **107m/C VHS, Beta, LV, 8mm, Closed Caption.** Matthew Modine, John Lithgow, Eric Stoltz, Sean Astin, Harry Connick Jr., Reed Edward Diamond, Tate Donovan, D.B. Sweeney, Billy Zane, David Strathairn, Jane Horrocks, Courtney Gains, Neil Giuntoli; **D:** Michael Caton-Jones; **W:** Monte Merrick; **C:** David Watkin; **M:** George Fenton. *WAR, VYY, FCT*

Memphis Belle: A Story of a Flying Fortress 1944 The entire final mission of the B-25 bomber "Memphis Belle" and its daring daylight attack on the submarine pens at Wilhelmshaven, Germany is captured through newsreel footage. The crew was the first to complete a 25 run mission. A film version of the story was released in 1990 as "Memphis Belle." Produced by William Wyler. **43m/C VHS, Beta.** *TPV, NOS, HHT*

The Men 🐾🐾🐾½ *Battle Stripe* **1950** A paraplegic WWII veteran sinks into depression until his former girlfriend manages to bring him out of it. Marlon Brando's first film. A thoughtful story that relies on subtle acting and direction. **85m/C VHS.** Marlon Brando, Teresa Wright, Everett Sloane, Jack Webb; **D:** Fred Zinnemann. Nominations: Academy Awards '50: Best Story & Screenplay. *REP*

Men... 🐾🐾🐾½ **1985** A funny and insightful satire about a man who discovers his loving wife has been having an affair with a young artist. In a unique course of revenge, the husband ingratiates himself with the artist and gradually turns him into a carbon copy of himself. In German with English subtitles or dubbed. **96m/C VHS.** *GE* Heiner Lauterbach, Uwe Ochsenknecht, Ulrike Kriener, Janna Marangosof; **D:** Doris Dorrie. *ING, NYF*

Men Are Not Gods 🐾🐾½ **1937** Verbose film (precursor to "A Double Life") about an actor playing Othello who nearly kills his wife during Desdemona's death scene. **90m/B VHS, Beta, LV.** *GB* Rex Harrison, Miriam Hopkins, Gertrude Lawrence; **D:** Walter Reisch.

Men at Work 🐾🐾 **1990 (PG-13)** Garbage collectors Sheen and Estevez may not love their work, but at least it's consistent from day to day. That is, until they get wrapped up in a very dirty politically motivated murder. And who will clean up the mess when the politicians are through trashing each other? A semi-thrilling semi-comedy that may leave you semi-satisfied. **98m/C VHS, Beta, LV, Closed Caption.** Charlie Sheen, Emilio Estevez, Leslie Hope, Keith David; **D:** Emilio Estevez; **W:** Emilio Estevez. *COL, FOX*

Men Don't Leave 🐾🐾½ **1989 (PG-13)** A recent widow tries to raise her kids single-handedly, suffers big city life, and takes a chance at a second love. Good performances by all, especially Cusack as the sweet seducer of teenaged O'Donnell. By the director of "Risky Business." **115m/C VHS, Beta, LV, 8mm, Closed Caption.** Jessica Lange, Arliss Howard, Joan Cusack, Kathy Bates, Charlie

Korsmo, Corey Carrier, Chris O'Donnell, Tom Mason, Jim Haynie; **D:** Paul Brickman, W. Barbara Benedek, Paul Brickman; **C:** Bruce Surtees; **M:** Thomas Newman. *WAR*

Men in Black 🐾🐾🐾 *MIB* **1997 (PG-13)** Charm, wit and some outrageous insect-type aliens make a winning cosmic combination. K (Jones) and J (Smith) are top-secret government operatives, investigating alien visitations on Earth, who must stop terrorist extraterrestrial D'Onofrio from causing a galactic disaster. Excellent chemistry between deadpan Jones and hip-hop Smith is strengthened by a very funny script. Director Sonnenfeld tops it off with just enough detail and human element to keep the special effects from stealing the show, and with Rick Baker around, that's not easy to do. Boxoffice hit that should spawn a sequel or two. Adapted from the Marvel comic book.**CW:** Language and sci-fi violence. **98m/C VHS, LV, Closed Caption, DVD.** Tommy Lee Jones, Will Smith, Linda Fiorentino, Rip Torn, Vincent D'Onofrio, Tony Shalhoub, Carel Struycken, Sergio Calderon; **D:** Barry Sonnenfeld; **W:** Edward Solomon; **C:** Don Peterman; **M:** Danny Elfman. Academy Awards '97: Best Makeup; MTV Movie Awards '98: Best Song ("Men in Black"), Best Fight (Will Smith/alien); Nominations: Academy Awards '97: Best Art Direction/Set Decoration, Best Original Musical/Comedy Score; Golden Globe Awards '98: Best Film—Musical/Comedy; MTV Movie Awards '98: Best Film, Best On-Screen Duo (Tommy Lee Jones/Will Smith), Best Comedic Performance (Smith). *COL*

Men in Love 🐾🐾 **1990** A young San Franciscan travels to Hawaii with the cremated remains of his lover, who has succumbed to AIDS. There he encounters a supportive group of men who nurse him back to sexual and spiritual wholeness. **93m/C VHS.** Doug Self, Joe Tolbe, Emerald Starr, Kutira Decostered, Scott Catamas; **D:** Marc Huestis; **C:** Fawn Yacker. *WBF, FCT*

Men in War 🐾🐾½ **1957** Korean War drama about a small platoon trying to take an enemy hill by themselves. A worthwhile effort with some good action sequences. **100m/B VHS, Beta.** Robert Ryan, Robert Keith, Aldo Ray, Vic Morrow; **D:** Anthony Mann; **W:** Philip Yordan; **M:** Elmer Bernstein. *FGF, MRV, BMV*

Men of Boys Town 🐾🐾½ **1941** Sequel to 1938's "Boys Town" has the same sentimentality, even more if that's possible. Father Flanagan's reformatory faces closure, while the kids reach out to an embittered new inmate. Worth seeing for the ace cast reprising their roles. **106m/B VHS.** Spencer Tracy, Mickey Rooney, Darryl Hickman, Henry O'Neill, Lee J. Cobb, Sidney Miller; **D:** Norman Taurog. *MGM, FCT*

Men of Ireland 🐾🐾 **1938** A Dublin medical student cavorts with islanders off the Irish coast. Uninspired programmer with authentic native folk of the Blasket Islands, plus their songs and dances. **62m/B VHS, Beta, 8mm.** *IR* Cecil Ford, Eileen Curran, Brian O'Sullivan, Gabriel Fallon; **D:** Richard Bird. *VYY*

Men of Respect 🐾🐾 **1991 (R)** Shakespeare meets the mafia in this misbegotten gangster yarn. Turturro, a gangster MacBeth, is prodded by wife and psychic to butcher his way to the top o' the mob. Well acted but ill conceived, causing Bard's partial roll over in grave. **113m/C VHS, LV, 8mm, Letterbox, Closed Caption.** John Turturro, Katherine Borowitz, Peter Boyle, Dennis Farina, Chris Stein, Steven Wright, Stanley Tucci; **D:** William Reilly; **W:** William Reilly; **C:** Bobby Bukowski. *COL*

Men of Sherwood Forest 🐾🐾½ **1957** Robin Hood and his band take it to the sheriff et al in this colorful Hammer version of the timeless legend. **77m/C VHS.** *GB* Don Taylor, Reginald Beckwith, Eileen Moore, Davis King-Wood, Patrick Holt, John Van Eyssen, Douglas Wilmer; **D:** Val Guest. *NOS, SNC, DVT*

Men of Steel 🐾 **1988 (PG)** Two Canadian military officers, one French and one English, must struggle to survive when their plane crashes in the wilderness. Besides contending with the surroundings, they must deal with one another's instilled bitterness and underlying prejudices. **91m/**

C VHS, Beta. Allan Royal, Robert Lalonde, David Ferry, Mavor Moore, Yvan Ponton; **D:** Donald Shebib. *TWE*

Men of the Fighting Lady 🐾🐾🐾½ **1954** Action-adventure offers plenty of exciting battle footage. Features the stories of selected pilots stationed on a U.S. aircraft carrier in the Pacific during the Korean War. The stories, told to Calhern as writer James A. Michener, center around the lead pilot Johnson. Dramatic airflights include a scene in which Johnson helps a blinded Martin land his plane safely on the carrier deck. Gene Ruggerio's editing of the war footage was so expertly done that he was questioned by the Pentagon when they had a hard time believing the scenes were achieved by skillful editing and painted backdrops. Look for "Beaver" Mathers as one of Wynn's sons. **81m/C VHS, Beta.** Van Johnson, Walter Pidgeon, Louis Calhern, Dewey Martin, Keenan Wynn, Frank Lovejoy, Robert Horton, Bert Freed, Jerry Mathers; **D:** Andrew Marton; **M:** Miklos Rozsa. *MGM*

Men of Two Worlds 🐾🐾 *Witch Doctor; Kisenga, Man of Africa* **1946** Classical musician raised in Africa is the toast of Europe until he finds out he's got a voodoo curse, and suddenly he's got the heebie jeebies too bad to play chopsticks. **90m/C VHS, Beta.** Robert Adams, Eric Portman, Orlando Martins, Phyllis Calvert, Arnold Marle, Cathleen Nesbitt, David Horne, Cyril Raymond; **D:** Thorold Dickinson. *SNC*

Men of War 🐾½ **1994 (R)** Ex-Special Forces mercenaries decide to defend, rather than destroy, the inhabitants of an exotic island, whose land is wanted by a suspicious company interested in mining rights.**CW:** Non-stop violence; strong language; some sexuality. **102m/C VHS, LV, Closed Caption.** Dolph Lundgren, Charlotte Lewis, B.D. Wong, Anthony John Denison, Tim Guinee, Don Harvey, Tommy (Tiny) Lister, Kevin Tighe; **D:** Perry Lang; **W:** John Sayles, Ethan Reiff, Cyrus Voris; **C:** Ronn Schmidt; **M:** Gerald Gouriet. *TOU*

The Men Who Tread on the Tiger's Tail 🐾🐾 **1945** Twelfth-century Japan is the setting for this struggle of power between two brothers, one a reigning shogun, the other on the run. English subtitles. **60m/B VHS, Beta.** *JP* **D:** Akira Kurosawa. *IHF*

Menace on the Mountain 🐾🐾 **1970 (G)** Family-oriented drama about a father and son who battle carpetbagging Confederate deserters during the Civil War. **89m/C VHS, Beta.** Patricia Crowley, Albert Salmi, Charles Aidman; **D:** Vincent McEveety. *DIS*

Menace II Society 🐾🐾🐾½ **1993 (R)** Portrayal of black teens lost in inner-city hell is realistically captured by 21-year-old twin directors, in their big-screen debut. Caine (Turner) lives with his grandparents and peddles drugs for spending money, from the eve of his high school graduation to his decision to escape south-central Los Angeles for Atlanta. Bleak and haunting, with some of the most unsettling, bloodiest violence ever shown in a commercial film. Disturbing to watch, but critcally acclaimed. The Hughes' make their mark on contemporary black cinema with intensity, enhanced by an action-comics visual flair. Based on a story by the Hughes' and Tyger Williams.**CW:** Language and strong violence and drug use. **104m/C VHS, LV, Closed Caption.** Tyrin Turner, Larenz Tate, Samuel L. Jackson, Glenn Plummer, Julian Roy Doster, Bill Duke, Charles S. Dutton, Jada Pinkett Smith, Vonte Sweet, Ryan Williams; **D:** Allen Hughes, Albert Hughes; **W:** Tyger Williams; **C:** Lisa Rinzler. Independent Spirit Awards '94: Best Cinematography; MTV Movie Awards '94: Best Film; Nominations: Independent Spirit Awards '94: Best Actor (Turner), Best First Feature. *COL, NLC, IME*

Menage 🐾🐾🐾 *Tenue de Soiree* **1986** Depardieu is the homosexual crook who breaks into the home of an impoverished couple—the dominating Miou-Miou and her submissive husband, Blanc. An unrepentant thief, he begins to take over their lives, introducing them to the wonderful world of crime, among other, more kinky, pastimes. Gender-bending farce that doesn't hold up to the end but is worth watching for sheer outrageousness. In French with English subtitles. **84m/C VHS.** *FR* Gerard Depardieu, Michel Blanc, Miou-Miou, Bruno Cremer, Jean-Pierre Marielle; **D:** Bertrand Blier; **W:** Bertrand Blier; **M:** Serge Gainsbourg. Cannes Film Festival '86: Best Actor (Blanc). *TRI, FCT*

The Men's Club *♫½* 1986 (R)
Seven middle-aged buddies get together for a single night, and bare their respective souls and personal traumas, talking about women and eating and drinking. Banal. Based on novel by Leonard Michael. **100m/C VHS, Beta, LV.** Harvey Keitel, Roy Scheider, Craig Wasson, Frank Langella, David Dukes, Richard Jordan, Treat Williams, Stockard Channing, Jennifer Jason Leigh, Ann Dusenberry, Cindy Pickett, Gwen Welles; **D:** Peter Medak. *PAR*

Menschenfrauen *♫♫½* 1980
A philandering journalist is put in his place by the four women with whom he is simultaneously having relationships. In German with English subtitles. **100m/C VHS, Beta.** *GE* **D:** Valie Export. *FCT*

Mephisto *♫♫♫½* 1981
An egomaniacal actor, compellingly played by Brandauer, sides with the Nazis to further his career, with disastrous results. The first of three brilliant films by Szabo and Brandauer exploring the price of power and personal sublimation in German history. Critically hailed. In German with English subtitles. From the novel by Klaus Mann. Followed by "Colonel Redl" and "Hanussen." **144m/C VHS, Beta.** *HU* Klaus Maria Brandauer, Krystyna Janda, Ildiko Bansagi, Karin Boyd, Rolf Hoppe, Christine Harbort, Gyorgy Cserhalmi, Christiane Graskoff, Peter Andorai, Ildiko Kishonti; **D:** Istvan Szabo; **C:** Lajos Koltai. Academy Awards '81: Best Foreign Language Film. *REP, SWC, GLV*

The Mephisto Waltz *♫♫♫* 1971 (R)
Journalist gets more than a story when he is granted an interview with a dying pianist. It turns out that he is a satanist and the cult he is a part of wants the journalist. Chilling adaptation of the Fred Mustard Stewart novel features a haunting musical score. **108m/C VHS.** Alan Alda, Jacqueline Bisset, Barbara Parkins, Curt Jurgens, Bradford Dillman, William Windom, Kathleen Widdoes; **D:** Paul Wendkos; **M:** Jerry Goldsmith. *FOX*

The Mercenaries *♫½* 1965
Romantic warrior fights to save the lives and honor of his people who are under attack from mercenaries murdering and raping their way across Europe. **98m/C Beta.** Debra Paget.

The Mercenaries *♫* Cuba Crossing; Kill Castro; Assignment: Kill Castro; Key West Crossing; Sweet Dirty Tony 1980
A tough guy, given the assignment to kill Fidel Castro, encounters all sorts of adversity along the way. Key West scenery is the only thing of interest. **92m/C VHS, Beta.** Stuart Whitman, Robert Vaughn, Caren Kaye, Raymond St. Jacques, Woody Strode, Sybil Danning, Albert Salmi, Michael V. Gazzo; **D:** Chuck Workman. *JEF*

Mercenary *♫♫* 1996
Ex-Commando-turned-mercenary Alex Hawks (Gruner) is hired by wealthy businessman Jonas Ambler (Ritter) to avenge his wife's death at the hands of terrorists. Only Ambler's desk jockey doesn't want to stay on the sidelines and watch—he wants to do. So, Hawks is forced to take him along to Iraq when he goes after the bad guys. **97m/C VHS.** Olivier Gruner, John Ritter, Robert Culp, Ed Lauter, Martin Kove. *PGV*

Mercenary Fighters *♫½* 1988 (R)
An American soldier-of-fortune fights for both sides of an African revolution. Shot in South Africa. **90m/C VHS, Beta, LV.** Peter Fonda, Reb Brown, Ron O'Neal, Jim Mitchum; **D:** Riki Shelach. *VTR*

The Merchant of Four Seasons *♫♫♫* 1971
Story focuses on the depression and unfulfilled dreams of an average street merchant. Direction from Fassbinder is slow, deliberate, and mesmerizing. In German with English subtitles. **88m/C VHS, Beta.** Hans Hirschmuller, Irm Hermann, Hanna Schygulla, Andrea Schober, Gusti Kreissl; **D:** Rainer Werner Fassbinder; **W:** Rainer Werner Fassbinder. *NYF*

The Merchant of Venice *♫♫♫* 1973
Shakespeare's tragedy of prejudice, vengeance, and sacrifice stars Olivier as the persecuted money lender Shylock, who demands his payment of a pound of flesh for a defaulted loan. **131m/C VHS.** *GB* Laurence Olivier, Joan Plowright, Jeremy Brett. *FUS, FCT*

Merchants of War *♫* 1990 (R)
Sent out by the CIA on a mission, two best friends are soon the target of one of the most dangerous terrorists in the world. The fanatical Islamic terrorist soon casts his wrath upon the two men. **100m/C VHS.** Asher Brauner, Jesse Vint, Bonnie Beck; **D:** Peter M. MacKenzie. *THV*

Mercury Rising *♫♫½* 1998 (R)
Renegade FBI agent Art Jeffries (Willis) must protect an autistic child who has inadvertently cracked a secret government code. Together, they dodge bullets from evil government forces headed by Nicholas Kudrow (Baldwin), who insist on having the innocent boy killed rather than change the code. That glaring logic aside, Willis does more than grunt here, showing moments of tenderness as he bonds with the orphaned boy in between nailing bad guys and amassing an assortment of cuts and bruises. Baldwin is effective as the snake who truly believes killing a child will benefit national security. When action time isn't being sacrificed for Jeffries' paternal aspirations, film rises slightly above tepid to provide substantial thrills. **112m/C VHS.** Bruce Willis, Alec Baldwin, Miko Hughes, Kim Dickens, Chi McBride, Robert Stanton, Peter Stormare, Kevin Conway; **D:** Harold Becker; **W:** Larry Konner, Mark Rosenthal; **C:** Michael Seresin; **M:** John Barry. *NYR*

Mercy *♫♫* 1996 (R)
When New York lawyer Frank Kramer's (Rubenstein) daughter is kidnapped he comes to realize it wasn't for ransom but for revenge. **CW:** Strong language. **82m/C VHS.** John Rubinstein, Sam Rockwell, Phil Brock, Novella Nelson, Amber Kain, Jane Lanier; **D:** Richard Shepard; **W:** Richard Shepard; **C:** Sarah Cawley. *APX*

Mercy Mission *♫♫½* 1993
Young pilot Bakula runs into trouble over the Pacific with his small plane and it's upto Air New Zealand airline pilot Loggia, who risks the lives of his passengers and crew, to come to his rescue. **92m/C VHS.** Scott Bakula, Robert Loggia; **D:** Roger Young. *HMK*

Meridian: Kiss of the Beast *♫½* 1990 (R)
A beautiful heiress is courted, kidnapped and loved by a demonic man-beast. **90m/C VHS, Beta, LV, Closed Caption.** Sherilyn Fenn, Malcom Jamieson, Hilary Mason, Alex Daniels, Phil Fondacaro, Charlie Spradling; **D:** Charles Band; **W:** Dennis Paoli; **M:** Pino Donaggio. *PAR*

Merlin *♫♫½* 1992 (PG-13)
In a remote California town reporter Christy Lake is stunned to discover her ancient heritage. Turns out she's the reincarnated daughter of legendary Merlin the magician and it is her duty to protect the Sword of Power from the evil sorcerer Pendragon. And aided by a handsome warrior and an ancient sage, that's just what she intends to do. **CW:** Action/adventure violence. **112m/C VHS.** Nadia Cameron, Peter Phelps, Richard Lynch, James Hong, Ted Markland, Desmond Llewelyn; **D:** Paul Hunt; **W:** Nick McCarty.

Merlin *♫♫♫* 1998
Legend of Camelot and Arthur's mentor is brought to the small screen with fine performances and equally impressive special effects. Merlin is conceived through the magic of evil Queen Mab (Richardson) to bring Britain back to its pagan roots. But Merlin doesn't really like magic and grows up to be (in the commanding persona of Neill) a most reluctant sorcerer. Still, he mentors Arthur (Curran) and continues to battle Mab, who works with Arthur's half sister Morgan Le Fey (Bonham Carter) to destroy Camelot. Merlin also pursues a long-time romance with Nimue (Rossellini), who falls victim to Mab's treachery. **?m/C VHS.** Sam Neill, Miranda Richardson, Isabella Rossellini, Martin Short, Helena Bonham Carter, Rutger Hauer, Paul Curran, Billie Whitelaw, Lena Headey, Jason Done, Mark Jax, John McEnery, Nicholas Clay, Sebastien Roche, Jeremy Sheffield; **Cameos:** John Gielgud; **D:** Steven Barron; **W:** David Stevens, Edward Khmara; **C:** Sergei Kozlov; **M:** Trevor Jones; **V:** James Earl Jones. *HMK, ART*

Merlin and the Sword *♫* Arthur the King 1985
Poor use of a good cast in this treatment of the legend of Merlin, Arthur and Excalibur. **94m/C VHS, Beta.** Malcolm McDowell, Edward Woodward, Candice Bergen, Dyan Cannon; **D:** Clive Donner. *ART, VES*

Merlin of the Crystal Cave *♫♫½* 1991
Depicts the adventures of the young boy Merlin as he learns the ways of magic in the days before Camelot and King Arthur. Made for British television. **159m/C VHS.** *GB* *FOX*

Mermaids *♫♫♫* 1990 (PG-13)
Mrs. Flax (Cher) is the flamboyant mother of two who hightails out of town every time a relationship threatens to turn serious. Having moved some 18 times, her daughters, Charlotte (Ryder), 15, and Kate (Ricci), 8, are a little worse for the wear, psychologically speaking. One aspires to be a nun though not Catholic, and the other holds her breath under water. Now living in Massachusetts, Mrs. Flax starts having those "I got you, babe" feelings for Hoskins, a shoestore owner. Amusing, well-acted multi-generational coming of ager based on a novel by Patty Dann. **CW:** Adult situations; language and sexual situations. **110m/C VHS, Beta, LV, Closed Caption.** Cher, Winona Ryder, Bob Hoskins, Christina Ricci, Michael Schoeffling, Caroline McWilliams, Jan Miner; **D:** Richard Benjamin; **W:** June Roberts; **C:** Howard Atherton; **M:** Jack Nitzsche. National Board of Review Awards '90: Best Supporting Actress (Ryder). *ORI*

The Mermaids of Tiburon *♫* The Aqua Sex 1962
A marine biologist and a criminal travel to a remote island off Mexico in search of elusive, expensive "fire pearls." There they encounter a kingdom of lovely mermaids who promptly liven things up. Filmed in "Aquascope" for your viewing pleasure. **77m/C VHS.** Diane Webber, George Rowe, Timothy Carey, Jose Gonzalez-Gonzalez, John Mylong, Gil Baretto, Vicki Kantenwine, Nani Morrissey, Judy Edwards, Jean Carroll, Diana Cook, Karen Goodman, Nancy Burns; **D:** John Lamb; **W:** John Lamb. *FRG*

Merrill's Marauders *♫♫½* 1962
Chandler is the commander of a battle-hardened regiment fighting in the jungles of Burma in 1944. The exhausted unit gains their latest objective and expects to be relieved, only to be continuously pushed into more fighting down the line. Director Fuller excels at showing the confusion of battle; Chandler's last film role (he died before the film was released). **98m/C VHS.** Jeff Chandler, Ty Hardin, Peter Brown, Andrew Duggan, Will Hutchins, Claude Akins; **D:** Samuel Fuller; **W:** Milton Sperling, Samuel Fuller; **C:** William Clothier; **M:** Howard Jackson. *WAR*

Merry Christmas, Mr. Lawrence *♫♫♫* 1983 (R)
An often overlooked drama about a WWII Japanese POW camp. Taut psychological drama about clashing cultures and physical and emotional survival focusing on the tensions between Bowie as a British POW and camp commander Sakamoto, who also composed the outstanding score. A haunting and intense film about the horrors of war. Based on the novel by Laurens van der Post. **124m/C VHS, Beta.** *JP GB* David Bowie, Tom Conti, Ryuichi Sakamoto, Takeshi, Jack Thompson; **D:** Nagisa Oshima. National Board of Review Awards '83: Best Actor (Conti). *USH*

Merry-Go-Round *♫♫♫* 1923
A handsome Austrian count is engaged to a woman of his class when he meets the beautiful Agnes, who works as an organ grinder for the local merry-go-round. He disguises himself to woo her but finally decides to marry his fiance, although Agnes continues to love him. But the story doesn't end for the two lovers who are destined to be together. Producer Thalberg and director von Stroheim battled over the expense and length of the film until Thalberg had the director replaced. However, much of the film still shows the von Stroheim brilliance and attention to lavish detail. **110m/B VHS.**

Norman Kerry, Mary Philbin, Cesare Gravina, Edith Yorke, George Hackathorne; **D:** Rupert Julian, Erich von Stroheim. *FCT, HEG*

The Merry Widow 🎬🎬🎬½ *The Lady Dances* **1934** The first sound version of the famous Franz Lehar operetta, dealing with a playboy from a bankrupt kingdom who must woo and marry the land's wealthy widow or be tried for treason. A delightful musical comedy, with a sterling cast and patented Lubitschian gaiety. Made as a silent in 1912 and 1925; remade in color in 1952. ♫Girls, Girls, Girls; Vilia; Tonight Will Teach You to Forget; Melody of Laughter; Maxim's; The Girls at Maxim's; The Merry Widow Waltz; If Widows are Rich; Russian Dance. **99m/B VHS, Beta, LV.** Maurice Chevalier, Jeanette MacDonald, Edward Everett Horton, Una Merkel, George Barbier, Minna Gombell, Ruth Channing, Sterling Holloway, Henry Armetta, Barbara Leanard, Donald Meek, Akim Tamiroff, Herman Bing; **D:** Ernst Lubitsch; **M:** Franz Lehar, Lorenz Hart. Academy Awards '34: Best Interior Decoration. *MGM*

The Merry Widow 🎬🎬½ **1952** Rich widow Turner travels to her husband's homeland of Marshovia to dedicate a statue to his memory. The country is deeply in debt and the king would like the widow to marry a local count and remain (along with her fortune). Lamas is charming as the intended bridegroom but Turner, though lovely looking, is miscast; her singing was dubbed by Erwin. Uninspired remake of the 1934 film only benefits from being shot in color and the lavish production values. Based on the operetta by Lehar. ♫The Merry Widow Waltz; Can-Can; Girls, Girls, Girls; I'm Going to Maxim's. **105m/C VHS.** Lana Turner, Fernando Lamas, Una Merkel, Richard Haydn, Thomas Gomez, John Abbott, Marcel Dalio, King Donovan, Robert Coote, Joi Lansing; **Cameos:** Gwen Verdon; **D:** Curtis Bernhardt; **W:** Sonya Levien, William Ludwig; **C:** Robert L. Surtees; **M:** Franz Lehar; **V:** Trudy Erwin. Nominations: Academy Awards '52: Best Art Direction/Set Decoration (Color), Best Costume Design (Color). *MGM*

Merton of the Movies 🎬🎬½ **1947** Skelton stars as star-struck, small town theatre usher Merton Gill who wins a trip to Hollywood. He's befriended by stunt double Phyllis (O'Brien) who recognizes his comedic talents and works to get him that big break. Based on the play by George S. Kaufman and Marc Connelly and previously filmed in 1924 and 1932 (as "Make Me a Star"). **82m/B VHS, Closed Caption.** Red Skelton, Virginia O'Brien, Gloria Grahame, Leon Ames, Alan Mowbray, Charles D. Brown, Hugo Haas, Harry Hayden; **D:** Robert Alton; **W:** George Wells, Lou Breslow. *MGM, FCT*

Mesa of Lost Women woof! *Lost Women; Lost Women of Zarpa* **1952** Mad scientist creates brave new race of vicious women with long fingernails. So bad it's a wanna-B. Addams Family buffs will spot the Fester in Coogan. **70m/B VHS.** Jackie Coogan, Richard Travis, Allan Nixon, Mary Hill, Robert Knapp, Tandra Quinn, Lyle Talbot, Katherine Victor, Angelo Rossitto; **D:** Herbert Tevos, Ron Ormond; **W:** Herbert Tevos; **C:** Gilbert Warrenton, Karl Struss. *NOS, MRV, SNC*

Mesmerized 🎬🎬 *Shocked* **1984** Based on the work by Jerzy Skolimowski, the film is a dramatization of the Victoria Thompson murder case in 1880s New Zealand. A teenaged orphaned girl marries an older man and decides after years of abuse to kill him through hypnosis. An unengaging drama, though the lovely New Zealand landscape serves as a fitting contrast to the film's ominous tone. **90m/C VHS, Beta.** *GB NZ AU* John Lithgow, Jodie Foster, Michael Murphy, Dan Shor, Harry Andrews; **D:** Michael Laughlin. *ART, VES*

Mesquite Buckaroo 🎬 **1939** Two cowboys bet over who is the better bronco buster, but one of them gets kidnapped. **59m/B VHS, Beta.** Bob Steele, Carolyn Curtis, Frank LaRue, Juanita Fletcher, Charles "Blackie" King; **D:** Harry S. Webb. *NOS, DVT*

Messalina vs. the Son of Hercules 🎬 **1964** A Roman slave leads a rebellion against the emperor Messalina. Italian; dubbed into English. **105m/C VHS, Beta.** *IT* Richard

Harrison, Marilu Tolo, Lisa Gastoni; **D:** Umberto Lenzi. *SNC, NLC*

The Messenger 🎬 **1987 (R)** A man right out of prison sets out to avenge his wife's murder by an Italian drug syndicate. **95m/C VHS, Beta.** Fred Williamson, Sandy Cummings, Christopher Connelly, Cameron Mitchell. *FCT*

Messenger of Death 🎬🎬½ **1988 (R)** A tough detective investigates the slaughter of a Mormon family, and uncovers a conspiracy centering around oil-rich real estate. **90m/C VHS, Beta, LV, Closed Caption.** Charles Bronson, Trish Van Devere, Laurence Luckinbill, Daniel Benzali, Marilyn Hassett, Jeff Corey, John Ireland, Penny Peyser, Gene Davis; **D:** J. Lee Thompson; **W:** Paul Jarrico; **M:** Robert O. Ragland. *VTR*

The Messenger of the Blessed Virgin 🎬🎬 **1930** When his beloved niece Dorothy is tragically paralyzed Uncle John makes a trip to the shrine at Lourdes to pray for a miracle. The story of the original vision of Bernadette and the blessed virgin in 1856 is also related to Uncle John for inspiration. **105m/B VHS.** *VYY*

The Messiah 🎬🎬🎬½ **1975** Rossellini's final film, a rarely seen version of the life of Christ, completely passed over any notions of divinity to portray him as a morally perfect man. In Italian with subtitles. **145m/C VHS, Beta.** *IT* **D:** Roberto Rossellini. *FCT, MVD*

Messiah of Evil 🎬 *Dead People; Return of the Living Dead; Revenge of the Screaming Dead; The Second Coming* **1974 (R)** California coastal town is invaded by zombies. Confusing low-rent production from the writers of "American Graffiti." **90m/C VHS, Beta.** Marianna Hill, Joy Bang, Royal Dano, Elisha Cook Jr., Michael Greer; **D:** Gloria Katz, Willard Huyck; **W:** Gloria Katz, Willard Huyck. *GEM, MRV*

Messidor 🎬🎬 **1977** Bored university student Jeanne (Amouroux) and shop assistant Marie (Retore) meet while hitchhiking and decide to travel together through Europe—committing robberies when they run out of money. French with subtitles. **118m/C VHS.** *SI* Clementine Amouroux, Catherine Retore, Franziskus Abgottspon, Gerald Battiaz, Hansjorg Bedschard; **D:** Alain Tanner; **W:** Alain Tanner; **C:** Renato Berta; **M:** Arie Dzierlatka. *NYF, FCT*

Metallica 🎬 **1985** Alien warmongers endeavor to conquer Earth and scientists try to stop them. **90m/C VHS, Beta.** Anthony Newcastle, Sharon Baker; **D:** Al Bradley. *NO*

Metalstorm: The Destruction of Jared Syn 🎬 **1983 (PG)** It's the science fiction battle of the ages with giant cyclopes and intergalactic magicians on the desert planet of Lemuria. **84m/C VHS, Beta, LV.** Jeffrey Byron, Mike Preston, Tim Thomerson, Kelly Preston, Richard Moll; **D:** Charles Band; **W:** Alan J. Adler; **C:** Mac Ahlberg; **M:** Richard Band. *USH*

Metamorphosis 🎬 **1990 (R)** Novice scientist foolishly uses himself as the guinea pig for his anti-aging experiments. He quickly loses control of the project. **90m/C VHS, Beta.** Gene Le Brock, Catherine Baranov, Stephen Brown, Harry Cason, Jason Arnold; **D:** G.L. Eastman. *IMP, THV*

Metamorphosis: The Alien Factor 🎬🎬½ **1993 (R)** Gerard is a genetic engineer who is bitten by a frog injected with a mutation sample from outer space. He turns into a slimy virus that infects everything he touches. **92m/C VHS.** George Gerard, Tony Gigante, Katharine Romaine; **D:** Glen Takakjian. *THV*

Meteor woof! **1979 (PG)** American and Soviet scientists attempt to save the Earth from a fast-approaching barrage of meteors from space in this disaster dud. Destruction ravages parts of Hong Kong and the Big Apple. **107m/C VHS, Beta, LV.** Sean Connery, Natalie Wood, Karl Malden, Brian Keith, Martin Landau, Trevor Howard, Henry Fonda, Joseph Campanella, Richard Dysart; **D:** Ronald Neame. Nominations: Academy Awards '79: Best Sound. *WAR, OM*

The Meteor Man 🎬🎬½ **1993 (PG)** Townsend is a school teacher who reluctantly becomes a hero when he acquires semi-super powers after being hit by a meteor. Meteor Man flies only four feet off the ground (because he's afraid of heights) and wears costumes fashioned by his mother. Funny premise satires "superhero" movies, but is inconsistent with some hilarious gags and others that fall flat. Includes interesting cameos by Cosby, Sinbad, Vandross, and Page. **100m/C VHS, LV, Letterbox, Closed Caption.** Robert Townsend, Robert Guillaume, Marla Gibbs, James Earl Jones, Frank Gorshin; **Cameos:** Bill Cosby, Sinbad, Luther Vandross, LaWanda Page; **D:** Robert Townsend; **W:** Robert Townsend; **C:** John A. Alonzo. *MGM*

Meteor Monster woof! *Teenage Monster* **1957** A young boy is hit by a meteor and is somehow transformed into a raving, slime-covered maniac. **73m/C VHS, Beta.** Anne Gwynne, Stuart Wade, Gloria Castillo, Chuck Courtney; **D:** Jacques Marquette. *SNC*

Metro 🎬½ **1996 (R)** Murphy has now officially made this exact movie one kajillion times. He plays fast-talking, fast-shooting cop Axel Fo...er.. Scott Roper, who's forced to accept a partner that he doesn't want, played by Nick...um...Judge...oh...Michael Rapaport! When a villain kills his best friend, he vows revenge. He and his sidekick are involved in car chases, shoot-outs and a tense situation where his girlfriend is taken hostage. Any of this ring a bell? Maybe it was in that "Another 48 Beverly Hills Cop Movies." **CW:** Strong violence and language. **117m/C VHS, LV, Closed Caption.** Eddie Murphy, Michael Rapaport, Michael Wincott, Carmen Ejogo, Denis Arndt, Art Evans, Donal Logue, Paul Ben-Victor, Kim Miyori, David Michael Silverman; **D:** Thomas Carter; **W:** Randy Feldman; **C:** Fred Murphy; **M:** Steve Porcaro. *TOU*

Metropolis 🎬🎬🎬🎬 **1926** Now a classic meditation on futurist technology and mass mentality, this fantasy concerns mechanized society. Original set design and special effects made this an innovative and influential film in its day. Is now considered one of the hippest films of the sci-fi genre. Silent, with musical score. The 1984 re-release features some color tinting, reconstruction, and a digital score with songs by Pat Benatar, Bonnie Tyler, Giorgio Moroder, and Queen. **115m/B VHS, Beta, LV.** *GE* Brigitte Helm, Alfred Abel, Gustav Froehlich, Rudolf Klein-Rogge, Fritz Rasp, Heinrich George, Theodore Loos, Erwin Biswanger, Olaf Storm, Hans Leo Reich, Heinrich Gotho; **D:** Fritz Lang; **W:** Fritz Lang, Thea von Harbou; **C:** Karl Freund, Gunther Rittau, Eugene Schufftan; **M:** Gottfried Huppertz. *SNC, NOS, MRV*

Metropolitan 🎬🎬🎬 **1990 (PG-13)** The Izod set comes of age on Park Avenue during Christmas break. Tom Townsend (Clements), a member of the middle class, finds himself drawn into a circle of self-proclaimed urban haute bourgeoisie types. They're embarrassingly short on male escorts for the holiday season's parties so he stands in and gets an inside look at life with the brat pack. Intelligently written and carefully made, it transcends the flirting-with-adulthood genre. **CW:** Adult situations; profanity and substance abuse. **98m/C VHS, LV.** Carolyn Farina, Edward Clements, Taylor Nichols, Christopher Eigeman, Allison Rutledge-Parisi, Dylan Hundley, Isabel Gillies, Bryan Leder, Will Kempe, Elizabeth Thompson; **D:** Whit Stillman; **W:** Whit Stillman; **M:** Mark Suozzo. Independent Spirit Awards '91: Best First Feature; New York Film Critics Awards '90: Best Director (Stillman); Nominations: Academy Awards '90: Best Original Screenplay. *COL, FCT*

Mexican Bus Ride 🎬🎬½ *Ascent to Heaven; Subida Al Cielo* **1951** A good-natured Bunuel effort about a newlywed peasant who travels to the big city to attend to his mother's will. While en route, he encounters a diversity of people on the bus and some temptation. In Spanish with English subtitles. **85m/B VHS, Beta.** *MX* Lilia Prado, Esteban Marquez, Carmelita Gonzalez; **D:** Luis Bunuel. *FCT, AUD*

Mexican Hayride 🎬🎬 **1948** Bud heads a gang of swindlers and Lou is the fall guy. When things up north get too hot, the boys head south of the border to cool off and start a mining scam. Watch for the hilarious bullfighting scene. Believe it or not, this is based on a Cole Porter musical—minus the music. **77m/B VHS.** Bud Abbott, Lou Costello, Virginia Grey, Luba Malina, John Hubbard, Pedro de Cordoba, Fritz Feld, Tom Powers, Pat Costello, Frank Fenton; **D:** Charles T. Barton; **W:** Oscar Brodney. *USH*

Mexican Spitfire at Sea 🎬🎬½ **1942** The feisty wife from South of the Border heads for Hawaii to close a deal for her husband. He goes along to help her, impersonating nobility. The thin story line keeps it from being quite as good as the first "Mexican Spitfire" film. Most of the action takes place aboard ship. **73m/B VHS.** Lupe Velez, Leon Errol, Charles "Buddy" Rogers, ZaSu Pitts, Elisabeth Risdon, Florence Bates, Marion Martin, Eddie Dunn, Harry Holman; **D:** Leslie Goodwins. *NOS*

Mexican Spitfire/Smartest Girl in Town **1940** A comedy double feature: In "Mexican Spitfire," a man impersonates an English lord in order to save a contract for the spitfire's husband. In "The Smartest Girl in Town," a photographer's model mistakes a millionaire for a fellow magazine model. **125m/B VHS, Beta.** Lupe Velez, Leon Errol, Donald Woods, Ann Sothern, Gene Raymond. *TTC*

MGM: When the Lion Roars **1992** Three-part documentary covers the history and films of the Metro-Goldwyn-Mayer (MGM) studio from its beginnings in 1924 with the release of the studio's first film ("He Who Gets Slapped"), through its glory years, to the studio's gradual decline and ever-changing leadership. MGM brought out such films as "The Wizard of Oz," "Gone With the Wind," the Andy Hardy series, and the Thin Man films. Features clips of films and stars as well as footage of studio executives, including Louis B. Mayer and legendary studio chief and producer Irving Thalberg. Tapes are also available individually for $19.98. Originally made for cable TV. **360m/C VHS, LV.** *MGM*

MGM's The Big Parade of Comedy **1992** An anthology of more than 50 of MGM's stars and comedians in some of their funniest screen moments. Looks at Laurel & Hardy, the Marx Brothers, W.C. Fields, Clark Gable, Jean Harlow, Greta Garbo, and others. **100m/C VHS.** *MGM*

Mi Vida Loca 🎬🎬 *My Crazy Life* **1994 (R)** Looks at the lives of Latina gang members from L.A.'s Echo Park. The women talk about their romantic dreams, friendships, families, and raising children amidst the pervasive violence and despair of their tough neighborhood. Small budget and some unpolished performances don't lessen film's impact—about the stupidity of violence and how "average" the hopes and dreams of these women are. **92m/C VHS.** Angel Aviles, Jacob Vargas, Jesse Borrego, Seidy Lopez, Marlo Marron, Neilida Lopez, Bertilla Damas, Art Esquer, Christina Solis, Salma Hayek, Magali Alvarado, Julian Reyes, Panchito Gomez; **D:** Allison Anders; **W:** Allison Anders; **M:** John Taylor. *HBO*

Miami Beach Cops 🎬🎬½ **1993** Two vets return home expecting life to be routine when they become sheriff's deputies. But when bad guys murder a local merchant things heat up fast. **97m/C VHS.** Frank Maldonatti, Salvatore Rendino, William Childers, Joyce Geier, Raff Baker, Dan Preston, Deborah Daniels; **D:** James R. Winburn.

Miami Blues 🎬🎬½ **1990 (R)** Cold-blooded killer plays cat-and-mouse with bleary cop while diddling with an unflappable prostitute. Violent and cynical, with appropriate performances from three leads. Based on the novel by Charles Willeford. **CW:** Nudity, violence; drug use, and sexual situations. **97m/C VHS, Beta, LV, Closed Caption.** Fred Ward, Alec Baldwin, Jennifer Jason Leigh, Nora Dunn, Charles Napier, Jose Perez, Paul Gleason, Obba Babatunde, Martine Beswick, Shirley Stoler; **D:** George Armitage;

W: George Armitage; **M:** Gary Chang. New York Film Critics Awards '90: Best Supporting Actress (Leigh). *ORI, IME*

Miami Cops 🎬 **1989** When a cop's father is killed by a drug smuggler, he and his partner pursue the murderer over two continents. Italian-made adventure is a bit drawn-out. **103m/C VHS, Beta.** *IT* Richard Roundtree, Harrison Muller, Dawn Baker, Michael J. Aronin; **D:** Al Bradley.

Miami Horror 🎬 **1987** A Florida scientist is experimenting with bacteria from space, trying to recreate a human only to have his efforts stolen by a crook. His intentions for the use of the experiment are not exactly for the furtherance of science. **85m/C VHS, Beta.** *IT* David Warbeck, Laura Trotter, Lawrence Loddi, John Ireland; **D:** Martin Herbert. *NO*

Miami Hustle 🎬🎬½ **1995 (R)** Con artist Marsha (Ireland) is forced by a sleazy lawyer to impersonate a bar waitress (England) who's about to inherit a fortune. But when things turn sour, she gets a computer mogul (Enos) to figure out who's setting her up. Made for cable. **CW:** Erotic dance nudity. **81m/C VHS, Closed Caption.** Kathy Ireland, John Enos, Audie England, Richard Sarafian; **D:** Lawrence Lanoff. *REP*

Miami Rhapsody 🎬🎬 **1995 (PG-13)** Woody Allen-ish romantic comedy about a young, neurotic copywriter who becomes disillusioned with the idea of marriage as she discovers every member of her family is having an affair. Parker plays the newly engaged Gwyn who is not entirely sure if she wants to marry her cute, zoologist boyfriend. Most of the characters come across as annoying, self-absorbed whiners, except for Banderas, who charms as a sexy Cuban nurse. Film moves along with its light-hearted narrative, but never reaches the comic or emotional depth of Allen's work. Director/writer Frankel shows promise, but should come out from behind the Woodman's shadow. Filmed on location in Miami. **CW:** Profanity and sexual situations. **95m/C VHS, LV, Closed Caption.** Sarah Jessica Parker, Gil Bellows, Antonio Banderas, Mia Farrow, Paul Mazursky, Kevin Pollak, Barbara Garrick, Carla Gugino, Bo Eason, Naomi Campbell, Jeremy Piven, Kelly Bishop, Ben Stein; **D:** David Frankel; **W:** David Frankel; **C:** Jack Wallner; **M:** Mark Isham. *TOU*

Miami Supercops 🎬🎬½ **1985** Two goofy policemen strike out against such threats as a gang that hassles buses, the attempted kidnapping of an Orange Bowl quarterback, and a multi-million-dollar robbery. **97m/C VHS, Beta.** Terence Hill, Bud Spencer, Jack Castellano, C.V. Wood Jr.; **D:** Bruno Corbucci. *WAR*

Miami Vendetta 🎬 **1987** L.A. vice cop risks it all to avenge his friend's death at the hands of Cuban drug smugglers. **90m/C VHS, Beta.** Sandy Brooke, Frank Gargani, Maarten Goslins, Barbara Pilavin; **D:** Steven Seemayer. *NO*

Miami Vice 🎬🎬½ **1984** Pilot for the popular television series paired Crockett and Tubbs for the first time on the trail of a killer in Miami's sleazy underground. Music by Jan Hammer and other pop notables. **99m/C VHS, Beta, LV.** Don Johnson, Philip Michael Thomas, Saundra Santiago, Michael Talbott, John Diehl, Gregory Sierra; **D:** Thomas Carter. *USH*

Miami Vice 2: The Prodigal Son 🎬🎬 **1985** The second full-length television movie spawned by the popular series, following the laconic Floridians to the gritty streets of New York. **99m/C VHS, Beta, LV.** Don Johnson, Philip Michael Thomas, Edward James Olmos, Penn Jillette. *USH*

Michael 🎬🎬½ **1996 (PG)** Following up "Phenomenon" with another celestial storyline, Travolta tries on the giant, molting wings of Michael, an atypical archangel with an amazing joie de vive and an appetite for alcohol, women, and sugar. Residing in Iowa with the elderly Pansy (Stapleton), Michael is being tracked by a cynical tabloid reporter (Hurt) and an angel expert (MacDowell), so he figures he might as well play cupid. The now standard dance sequence in Travolta movies takes place in a bar to the tune of "Chain of

Fools" and is one of the movie's stand-outs. While Travolta gives another stellar performance, Hurt and MacDowell have little to do but play out their tired romantic subplot in a script that could've used some inspiration from its lead character. **105m/C VHS, LV, Closed Caption, DVD.** John Travolta, William Hurt, Andie MacDowell, Bob Hoskins, Robert Pastorelli, Jean Stapleton, Teri Garr; **D:** Nora Ephron; **W:** Nora Ephron, Delia Ephron, Pete Dexter; **C:** John Lindley; **M:** Randy Newman. *WAR*

Michael Collins 🎬🎬🎬 **1996 (R)** Collins (Neeson) was a revolutionary leader with the Irish Volunteers, a guerilla force (an early version of the IRA) dedicated to freeing Ireland from British rule by any means necessary. After a number of successful moves against British intelligence, Collins is unwillingly drawn into a statesman's role as negotiations for an Anglo-Irish Treaty begin in 1921, ultimately dividing the country in two and leading to Collins' own assassination. Controversy surrounded the film as historians, politicians, and the media took potshots at director Jordan's admittedly personal look at the complexities of Irish life and one of its equally complicated heroes. **CW:** Violence and language. **117m/C VHS, DVD.** Liam Neeson, Aidan Quinn, Alan Rickman, Stephen Rea, Julia Roberts, Ian Hart, Sean McGinley, Gerard McSorley, Stuart Graham, Brendan Gleeson, Charles Dance, Jonathan Rhys Myers; **D:** Neil Jordan; **W:** Neil Jordan; **C:** Chris Menges; **M:** Elliot Goldenthal. Los Angeles Film Critics Association Awards '96: Best Cinematography; Venice Film Festival '96: Golden Lion, Best Actor (Neeson); Nominations: Academy Awards '96: Best Cinematography, Best Original Dramatic/Comedy Score; British Academy Awards '96: Best Supporting Actor (Rickman); Golden Globe Awards '97: Best Actor—Drama (Neeson), Best Score. *WAR*

The Michigan Kid 🎬🎬 **1928** Two boys fight for the same girl in this silent love triangle set in Alaska. Film's most notable scene is of a raging forest fire, considered a classic even today. **62m/B VHS, Beta.** Conrad Nagel, Renee Adoree, Fred Esmelton, Virginia Grey, Adolph Milar, Lloyd Whitlock; **D:** Irvin Willat. *GPV*

Mickey 🎬🎬 **1917** Spoof on high society as a penniless young woman moves in with relatives and works as the family's maid. Silent film. **105m/B VHS, Beta.** Mabel Normand, Lew Cody, Minta Durfee; **D:** Mack Sennett. *NOS, VYY, DVT*

Mickey 🎬 **1948** A tomboy becomes a woman even as she plays matchmaker for her own father and sings a few songs. Not too exciting; you may fall asleep if you're slipped this "Mickey." Based on the novel "Clementine," by Peggy Goodin. **87m/C VHS.** Lois Butler, Bill Goodwin, Irene Hervey, John Sutton, Hattie McDaniel; **D:** Ralph Murphy. *NOS*

Mickey One 🎬🎬½ **1965** Nightclub comic Mickey (Beatty) gets into trouble when he can't pay his gambling debts. So he hides out in Chicago under an assumed name, working as a janitor, but can't live without the applause. His agent finds him a club job but Mickey panics, thinking the place is under mob control, and spends a lot of time running around, trying to clear his debts. Finally, returning to the club, Mickey resigns himself to a bleak fate. Beatty's jumpy character is an acquired taste—as is the film. Silent film. **93m/B LV.** Warren Beatty, Hurd Hatfield, Alexandra Stewart, Franchot Tone, Teddy Hart, Jeff Corey; **D:** Arthur Penn; **W:** Alan M. Surgal; **C:** Ghislan Cloquet; **M:** Jack Shaindlin, Eddie Sauter. *FCT*

Mickey the Great **1939** Stitched together from several late '20s Mickey McGuire shorts, starring 10-year-old Rooney. **70m/B VHS, Beta.** Billy Barty, Mickey Rooney. *VYY, DVT, NOS*

Mickey's Christmas Carol 🎬🎬🎬 **1983 (G)** Mickey Mouse returns along with all the other Disney characters in this adaptation of the Charles Dickens classic. Includes a documentary on how the featurette was made. **25m/C VHS, Beta, LV. V:** Alan Young, Hal Smith, Will Ryan, Wayne Alline, Clarence Nash, Eddie Carroll, Pat Parris, Susan Sheridan. *DIS*

Micki & Maude 🎬🎬 1984 (PG-13) When a man longs for a baby, he finds that his wife, Micki, is too busy for motherhood. Out of frustration, he has an affair with Maude that leads to her pregnancy. Still shocked by the news of his upcoming fatherhood, the man learns that his wife is also expecting. 117m/C VHS, Beta, LV, Closed Caption. Dudley Moore, Amy Irving, Ann Reinking, Richard Mulligan, Wallace Shawn, George Gaynes, Andre the Giant; **D:** Blake Edwards; **C:** Harry Stradling Jr. Golden Globe Awards '85: Best Actor—Musical/Comedy (Moore). COL

Microcosmos 🎬🎬🎬 1996 (G) Warning: Do not attempt to smash the bugs on the screen with your shoe. They're supposed to be there. This French documentary uses special cameras and sound recording devices to explore the world of insects like never before. The editing and score also add a human dimension to the creepy-crawly world under the lawn, making amorous snails and workaholic beetles seem like people you know (well, if they had an extra set of legs and a shell-like carapace). Of course, if you don't like bugs, then this is just a 77-minute gross out. Cameo appearances by some birds and frogs. 77m/C VHS. FR **D:** Claude Nuridsany, Marie Perennou; **C:** Claude Nuridsany, Marie Perennou, Hughes Ryffel, Thierry Machado; **M:** Bruno Coulais. Cesar Awards '97: Best Art Direction/Set Decoration, Best Cinematography, Best Film Editing, Best Sound, Best Score; Nominations: Cesar Awards '97: Best Film. TOU

Microwave Massacre 🎬 1983 (R) Killer kitchen appliances strike again as late lounge comic Vernon murders nagging wife and 'waves her. Overcome by that Betty Crocker feeling, he goes on a microwave murdering/feeding spree of the local ladies. Lots of Roger Corman copying. 80m/C VHS. Jackie Vernon, Loren Schein, Al Troupe; **D:** Wayne Berwick. RHI, FCT

Mid-Channel 🎬🎬½ 1920 A married couple become bored with each other and the wife seeks diversion with other men. Surprise ending. 70m/C VHS, Beta. Clara Kimball Young, J. Frank Glendon, Edward M. Kimball, Bertram Grassby, Eileen Robinson, Helen Sullivan, Katherine Griffith, Jack Livingston; **D:** Harry Garson. NOS, MRV, GPV

Mid Knight Rider 🎬 1984 Penniless actor becomes a male prostitute at the service of bored, rich women. At an all-night orgy, he suddenly goes on a rampage, nearly killing one of his customers. 76m/C VHS, Beta. Michael Christian, Keenan Wynn. TWE

The Midas Touch 🎬🎬 1989 A flea market merchant in 1956 Budapest has the ability to turn items into gold. In Hungarian with English subtitles. 100m/C VHS, Beta. HU **D:** Geza Beremenyi; **W:** Geza Beremenyi. FCT

Middle Age Crazy 🎬½ 1980 (R) Story of a Texas building contractor who takes life pretty lightly until his own father dies. Then he becomes immersed in a mid-life crisis and has an affair with a Dallas Cowboys' cheerleader. Ann-Margret plays the victim wife of the middle aged swingin' guy. 95m/C VHS. CA Bruce Dern, Ann-Margret, Graham Jarvis, Eric Christmas, Deborah Wakeham; **D:** John Trent. FOX

The Middleman 🎬🎬 Jana Aranya 1976 Recent college graduate Somnath has struggled to find a job and eventually enters the business world as a middleman, where he soons discovers that success will depend on his willingness to break the rules. Bengali with subtitles. 131m/B VHS. IN Pradip Mukherjee; **D:** Satyajit Ray. COL

Middlemarch 🎬🎬🎬 1993 Stylish British TV costume drama, adapted from George Eliot's 1872 novel, finds idealistic Dorothea Brooke (Aubrey) determined to be a helpmate to the older scholar, the Rev. Edward Casaubon (Malahide), whom she marries. Too bad that he takes so little interest in her ability (or in Dorothea herself). This leads Casaubon's distant cousin, young and handsome Will Ladislaw (Sewell), to discreetly make his interest clear. Naturally, Eliot has a number of other plots (some dealing with the impact of the Industrial Revolution on 19th-century life) and romances worked into the mix. Filmed in Stamford, England. On three cassettes. 360m/C VHS, Closed Caption. GB Juliet Aubrey, Patrick Malahide, Rufus Sewell, Douglas Hodge, Trevyn McDowell, Michael Hordern, Robert Hardy, John Savident, Jonathan Firth, Peter Jeffrey, Simon Chandler, Julian Wadham; **D:** Anthony Page; **W:** Andrew Davies, Stanley Myers; **C:** Brian Tufano. FOX, TVC

Midnight 🎬🎬½ Call It Murder 1934 A jury foreman's daughter is romantically involved with a gangster who is interested in a particular case before it appears in court. The foreman, who sentenced a girl to death, faces a dilemma when his own daughter is arrested for the same crime. An early Bogart appearance in a supporting role led to a re-release of the film as "Call it Murder" after Bogart made it big. Weak melodrama. 74m/B VHS, Beta. Humphrey Bogart, Sidney Fox, O.P. Heggie, Henry Hull, Richard Whorf, Margaret Wycherly, Lynne Overman; **D:** Chester Erskine. CCB, DVT, BAR

Midnight 🎬🎬🎬½ 1939 Struggling showgirl Colbert masquerades as Hungarian countess in sophisticated comedy of marital conflicts. Near-classic film scripted by Wilder and Brackett. Based on a story by Edwin Justus Mayer and Franz Schulz. Remade as "Masquerade in Mexico." 94m/B VHS, Closed Caption. Claudette Colbert, Don Ameche, John Barrymore, Francis Lederer, Mary Astor, Hedda Hopper, Rex O'Malley; **D:** Mitchell Leisen; **W:** Billy Wilder, Charles Brackett; **C:** Charles B(ryant) Lang. USH

Midnight 🎬 Backwoods Massacre 1981 (R) Russo, who cowrote the original "Night of the Living Dead," wrote and directed this film about a runaway girl who is driven out of her home by a lecherous stepfather and meets two young thieves and then a family of cultists. Russo adapted his own novel. He also attains some of "Night of the Living Dead's" low-budget ambience. 88m/C VHS, Beta. Lawrence Tierney, Melanie Verliin, John Hall, John Amplas; **D:** John Russo. THV

Midnight 🎬 1989 (R) Murder-thriller involving the vampirish hostess of a television horror movie showcase and a fanatical fan. 90m/C VHS, Beta, LV. Lynn Redgrave, Tony Curtis, Steve Parrish, Rita Gam, Gustav Vintas, Karen Witter, Frank Gorshin, Wolfman Jack; **D:** Norman Thaddeus Vane. VTR

Midnight 2: Sex, Death, and Videotape 🎬 1993 Sequel to "Midnight" finds the sole surviving member of the crazed family stalking a beautiful unsuspecting teller with a video camera. Only she's teamed up with a detective to solve the murder of her best friend—even if it means she's bait for a psycho. 70m/C VHS. Matthew Jason Walsh, Jo Norcia; **D:** John Russo. TEM, MOV

Midnight at the Wax Museum 🎬 Midnight at Madame Tussaud's 1936 A man attempts to spend an evening in a wax museum's chamber of horrors, only to find that he is the target of a murder plot. 66m/B VHS. Lucille Lisle, James Carew, Charles Oliver, Kim Peacock; **D:** George Pearson. NOS, DVT, SNC

Midnight Auto Supply 🎬½ Love and the Midnight Auto Supply 1978 Dealers in hot car parts, working out of the garage behind the local brothel, become persuaded to donate some of their profits to the cause of Mexican farm workers. 91m/C VHS. Michael Parks, Rory Calhoun, Scott Jacoby, Rod Cameron, Colleen Camp, Linda Cristal, John Ireland; **D:** James Polakof. NO

Midnight Blue 🎬🎬 1996 (R) Martin Blake (Chapa) is a lonely banker on a trip to Atlanta where he meets prostitute Martine (Schofield). They have a one-nighter and Martin later decides he loves her and hires a detective (Stockwell) to find her—only Martine has disappeared. After Martin has moved to L.A., he discovers his new boss' wife, Georgine, just happens to be a double for Martine. Naturally, Martin becomes obsessed and this leads to big trouble.**CW:** Nudity, language, sexual situations, violence. 98m/C VHS, LV. Damian Chapa, Annabel Schofield, Steve Kanaly, Dean Stockwell, Harry Dean Stanton, Jennifer Jostyn; **D:** Skott Snider. ORI

Midnight Cabaret woof! 1990 (R) A New York nightclub-based Satanic cult selects a child actress to bear Satan's child. 94m/C VHS, Beta, LV. Michael Des Barres, Thom Mathews, Carolyn Seymour, Leonard Termo, Norbert Weisser, Lydie Denier; **D:** Pece Dingo; **W:** Pece Dingo; **M:** Michel Colombier. WAR

A Midnight Clear 🎬🎬🎬 1992 (PG) Sensitive war drama that takes place in the Ardennes Forest, near the French-German border in December 1944. It's Christmastime and six of the remaining members of a 12-member squad are sent on a dangerous mission to an abandoned house to locate the enemy. Filmed in a dreamy surreal style, the setting is somewhat reminiscent of a fairytale, although a sense of anguish filtrates throughout the picture. A solid script, excellent direction, and a good cast make this a worthwhile film that pits the message of peace against the stupidity of war. Adapted from the novel by William Wharton. 107m/C VHS, LV, Closed Caption. Peter Berg, Kevin Dillon, Arye Gross, Ethan Hawke, Gary Sinise, Frank Whaley, John C. McGinley, Larry Joshua, Curt Lowens; **D:** Keith Gordon; **W:** Keith Gordon; **M:** Mark Isham. COL, PMS

Midnight Confessions 🎬 1995 (R) Provocative night-time DJ Vannesse (Hoyt) lures her listeners into revealing their sexual fantasies. But when an obessed fan begins killing women just how deeply is she involved?**CW:** Strong, lurid sexuality and sex-related dialogue. 98m/C VHS, LV. Carol Hoyt, Julie Strain, Monique Parent, Richard Lynch. TRI

Midnight Cop 🎬 1988 (R) A young woman gets tangled up in a web of murder, intrigue, prostitution and drugs, and she enlists the aid of a cop to help get her out of it. 100m/C VHS, Beta, LV. Michael York, Morgan Fairchild, Frank Stallone, Armin Mueller-Stahl; **D:** Peter Patzak. THV, HHE

Midnight Cowboy 🎬🎬🎬½ 1969 (R) Drama about the relationship between a naive Texan hustler and a seedy derelict, set in the underbelly of New York City. Graphic and emotional character study is brilliantly acted and engaging. Shocking and considered quite risque at the time of its release, this film now carries an "R" rating. It is the only film carrying an "X" rating ever to win the Best Picture Oscar. From James Leo Herlihy's novel. Laserdisc version features: audio commentary by director John Schlesinger and producer Jereome Hellman, behind the scenes production photos, and original movie trailer. 113m/C VHS, Beta, LV, Letterbox, DVD. Dustin Hoffman, Jon Voight, Sylvia Miles, Brenda Vaccaro, John McGiver, Bob Balaban, Barnard Hughes; **D:** John Schlesinger; **W:** Waldo Salt; **C:** Adam Holender; **M:** John Barry. Academy Awards '69: Best Adapted Screenplay, Best Director (Schlesinger), Best Picture; British Academy Awards '69: Best Actor (Hoffman), Best Director (Schlesinger), Best Film, Best Screenplay; Directors Guild of America Awards '69: Best Director (Schlesinger), National Film Registry '94;; New York Film Critics Awards '69: Best Actor (Voight); National Society of Film Critics Awards '69: Best Actor (Voight); Writers Guild of America '69: Best Adapted Screenplay; Nominations: Academy Awards '69: Best Actor (Hoffman), Best Actor (Voight), Best Film Editing, Best Supporting Actress (Miles). MGM, CRC, BTV

Midnight Crossing 🎬🎬 1987 (R) Two married couples are subjected to jealousy, betrayal and uncloseted-skeletons as their pleasure cruise on a yacht turns into a ruthless search for sunken treasure. 96m/C VHS, Beta, LV. Faye Dunaway, Daniel J. Travanti, Kim Cattrall, John Laughlin, Ned Beatty; **D:** Roger Holzberg. ART, VES

Midnight Dancer 🎬🎬 1987 A young ballerina is forced to work as an erotic dancer. 97m/C VHS, Beta. AU Deanne Jeffs, Mary Regan; **D:** Pamela Gibbons.

Midnight Dancers �så *1994* Seamy look at Manila's gay subculture and male prostitution. Sonny and his older brothers Dennis and Joel work as dancers at a sleazy club whose upstairs apartments are used for prostitution. The boys need the money to help their impoverished family survive in the slums but the emotional wear and tear (not to mention police raids and assorted brutalities) provide lots of melodrama. Filipino with subtitles. **115m/C VHS.** *PH* Alex Del Rosario, Gandong Cervantes, Laurence David, Perla Bautista, Soxy Topacio; *D:* Mel Chionglo; *W:* Ricardo Lee; *C:* George Tutanes; *M:* Nonong Buenoamino. *FRF*

Midnight Edition ✔✔ *1993 (R)* Investigative reporter Jack Travers (Patton) returns to his Georgia hometown newspaper just in time to write the story of his life. Nineteen-year-old Darryl Weston (DeLuise) massacres a local family for no apparent reason, is tried, convicted, and sentenced to die. Jack's death row interviews with Darryl become hot news but his reporter's objectivity is lost and he becomes a pawn in an escape plan. Good interplay between the charming sociopath and the self-deluded reporter in a sometimes confusing thriller. Based on the autobiography "Escape of My Dead Men" by Charles Postell. *CW:* Strong language; violence; sexual situations. **98m/C VHS, Closed Caption.** Will Patton, Michael DeLuise, Clare Wren, Nancy Moore Atchison, Sarabeth Tucek, Judson Vaughn, Ji Tu Cumbuka, Jay Bernard; *D:* Howard Libov; *W:* Howard Libov, Yuri Zeltser, Michael Stewart; *M:* Murray Attaway. *USH*

Midnight Express ✔✔✔ *1978 (R)* Gripping and powerful film based on the true story of Billy Hayes. Davis plays Hayes as a young American in Turkey who is busted trying to smuggle hashish. He is sentenced to a brutal and nightmarish prison for life. After enduring tremendous mental and physical torture, he seeks escape along the "Midnight Express." Not always easy to watch, but the overall effect is riveting and unforgettable. **120m/C VHS, Beta, LV, 8mm, Letterbox.** John Hurt, Randy Quaid, Brad Davis, Paul Smith, Bo Hopkins, Oliver Stone; *D:* Alan Parker; *W:* Oliver Stone; *M:* Giorgio Moroder. Academy Awards '78: Best Adapted Screenplay, Best Original Score; British Academy Awards '78: Best Director (Parker), Best Supporting Actor (Hurt); Golden Globe Awards '79: Best Film—Drama, Best Screenplay, Best Supporting Actor (Hurt), Best Score; Writers Guild of America '78: Best Adapted Screenplay; Nominations: Academy Awards '78: Best Director (Parker), Best Film Editing, Best Picture, Best Supporting Actor (Hurt). *COL*

Midnight Faces ✔✔ *1926* Mysterious doings abound in a house in the Florida bayous, recently inherited by Bushman. Silent, with original organ music. **72m/B VHS, Beta, 8mm.** Francis X. Bushman, Jack Perrin, Kathryn McGuire. *SNC, VYY, LSV*

Midnight Fear ✔½ *1990* When a sexually demented killer skins a woman alive, Sheriff Hanley sets out to find whodunit. He suspects two weird brothers, who turn out to be holding a woman hostage, but the situation may not be so simple. Carradine plays the good-guy sheriff in this creeper. **90m/C VHS.** David Carradine, Craig Wasson; *D:* William Crain. *RHI*

Midnight Girl ✔½ *1925* A fading opera impresario plots to steal a family's fortune. Lugosi before he became Dracula. Silent. **84m/B VHS, Beta, 8mm.** Bela Lugosi, Lila Lee. *GPV, VYY, DVT*

Midnight Heat ✔✔½ *1995 (R)* Football player is the prime suspect when his lover's husband (who happens to be the team owner) is murdered. **97m/C VHS.** Tim Matheson, Stephen Mendel, Mimi Craven; *D:* Harvey Frost. *AVE*

The Midnight Hour ✔½ *1986* A group of high schoolers stumbles upon a vintage curse that wakes up the dead. Made for television. More humor than horror. **97m/C VHS.** Shari Belafonte, LeVar Burton, Lee Montgomery, Dick Van Patten, Kevin McCarthy, Jonelle Allen, Peter DeLuise, Dedee Pfeiffer, Mark Blankfield; *D:* Jack Bender; *M:* Brad Fiedel. *THV*

Midnight in Saint Petersburg ✔✔½ *1997 (R)* Caine once again returns to his role of super spy Harry Palmer, who's after terrorists buying stolen plutonium to use in nuclear weapons. Harry's aided by Nikolai (Connery), whose girlfriend Tatiana is kidnapped, leading the men to a link between the kidnapping, the terrorists, and recent art thefts from the Hermitage Museum. Adapted from stories by Len Deighton. *CW:* Some language. **90m/C VHS, Closed Caption.** Michael Caine, Jason Connery, Michael Gambon, Michael Sarrazin, Michelle Rene Thomas. *PAR*

Midnight in the Garden of Good and Evil ✔✔ *1997 (R)* An all-star cast can't save Eastwood's grossly mishandled adaptation of John Berendt's best-selling novel on the eccentric citizens and lush scenery of Savannah. New York journalist John Kelso (Cusack) is sent on assignment to report on the glamourous Christmas parties of famed citizen and ham Jim Williams (Spacey, oozing his usual silky charm), only to be detoured by Williams shooting his male, live-in companion. Was it cold-blooded murder or self defense? With Eastwood's clumsy direction, a dragging running time, an overabundance of characters taken verbatim from the book (including drag queen Lady Chablis playing herself, unfortunately), and a dull romance between Kelso and local flower Mandy (Eastwood's daughter), the rich subject which made the book a top-seller for four years is all but lost and the answer to the above question mute. Midnight has the star power for greatness, but looks certainly are deceiving. *CW:* Language and brief violence. **155m/C VHS.** Kevin Spacey, John Cusack, Jack Thompson, Alison Eastwood, The Lady Chablis, Irma P. Hall, Paul Hipp, Jude Law, Dorothy Loudon, Anne Haney, Kim Hunter, Geoffrey Lewis; *D:* Clint Eastwood; *W:* John Lee Hancock; *M:* Lennie Niehaus. *WAR*

Midnight Kiss ✔✔½ *1993 (R)* When a woman police detective investigates a mysterious series of deaths—women whose blood has been drained—she gets more than she bargains for. She's attacked by a vampire and is herself turned into a reluctant bloodsucker. Quick moving and some gross special effects. Also available in an unrated version. **85m/C VHS.** Michelle Owens, Gregory A. Greer, Celeste Yarnall, Ken Lamplugh; *D:* Joel Bender; *W:* John Weidner, Ken Lamplugh. *NHO*

Midnight Lace ✔✔½ *1960* Acceptable thriller about a woman in London who is being harassed by a telephone creep. Day is at her frantic best, and Harrrison is suitably charming. Handsome Gavin later became American ambassador to Mexico. Adapted from the play "Matilda Shouted Fire." **108m/C VHS, Beta.** Doris Day, Rex Harrison, John Gavin, Myrna Loy, Roddy McDowall; *D:* David Miller; *W:* Ivan Goff; *C:* Russell Metty. Nominations: Academy Awards '60: Best Costume Design (Color). *USH*

Midnight Limited ✔✔ *1940* A detective sets out to thwart the criminals who would rob the "Midnight Limited" train on its route from New York to Montreal. **61m/B VHS, Beta.** John "Dusty" King, Marjorie Reynolds, George Cleveland, Edward Keane, Pat Flaherty, Monty Collins, I. Stanford Jolley; *D:* Howard Bretherton. *SNC*

Midnight Madness ✔ *1980 (PG)* Five teams of college students search the city of Los Angeles for clues leading to hundreds and thousands of dollars in buried treasure. **110m/C VHS, Beta.** David Naughton, Stephen Furst, Debra Clinger, Eddie Deezen, Michael J. Fox, Maggie Roswell; *D:* David Wechter; *W:* David Wechter. *TOU, OM*

Midnight Movie Massacre ✔✔½ *Attack from Mars 1988* Retro splatterama has really gross vampire alien land outside a Burbank movie theatre in 1956, and the really weird movie patrons try to terminate it. **86m/C VHS.** Robert Clarke, Ann Robinson; *D:* Mark Stock. *EEL*

Midnight Murders ✔✔½ *Manhunt in the Dakotas; In the Line of Duty: Manhunt in the Dakotas 1991 (R)* Steiger stars as a farmer and Posse Commitatus member whose paramilitary pretensions lead to a bloody confrontation with federal marshals. Gross is the FBI agent sent to hunt him down. Made for TV. *CW:* Language. **95m/C VHS.** Rod Steiger, Michael Gross, Gary Basaraba, Christopher Rich, Henderson Forsythe; *D:* Dick Lowry. *NHO*

The Midnight Phantom ✔✔ *1935* Incredibly rare horror film featuring a bizarre murder at a midnight lecture. **?m/B VHS.** Reginald Denny. *SNC*

Midnight Ride ✔½ *1992* Lots of silly action fails to save this slight tale of a cop (Dudikoff) chasing after his runaway wife (Gersak), who has made the mistake of picking up a psycho hitchhiker (Hamill, gleefully overacting). **95m/C VHS.** Michael Dudikoff, Mark Hamill, Savina Gersak; *Cameos:* Robert Mitchum; *D:* Robert Bralver.

Midnight Run ✔✔✔ *1988 (R)* An ex-cop, bounty hunter must bring in an ex-mob accountant who has embezzled big bucks from his former boss. After he catches up with the thief, the hunter finds that bringing his prisoner from New York to Los Angeles will be very trying, especially when it is apparent that the Mafia and FBI are out to stop them. The friction between the two leads—De Niro and Grodin—is fun to watch, while the action and comic moments are enjoyable. **125m/C VHS, Beta, LV.** Robert De Niro, Charles Grodin, Yaphet Kotto, John Ashton, Dennis Farina, Joe Pantoliano, Richard Foronjy, Wendy Phillips; *D:* Martin Brest; *W:* George Gallo; *C:* Donald E. Thorin; *M:* Danny Elfman. *USH*

Midnight Tease ✔½ *1994* Strip bar, the Club Fugazi, is having trouble with its help—the dancers keep getting murdered. Dancer Samantha (Leigh) actually dreams about the murders before they occur, so naturally she becomes the prime suspect. Leigh can actually do more than look fetching but plot is barely apparent. **87m/C VHS, LV.** Cassandra Leigh, Rachel Reed, Edmund Halley, Ashlie Rhey, Todd Joseph; *D:* Scott Levy; *W:* Daniella Purcell. *NHO*

Midnight Tease 2 ✔ *1995 (R)* Jen Brennan (Kelly) goes undercover at an L.A. strip club to find out who's been murdering the dancers, including her sister. *CW:* Pervasive sex-related material, and for violence. **93m/C VHS.** Kimberly Kelley, Tane McClure, Ross Hagen; *D:* Richard Styles; *W:* Richard Styles; *C:* Gary Graver. *NHO*

Midnight Warning ✔✔½ *1932* A woman thinks she's going off the deep-end when her brother and all records of his existence disappear. Based on an urban legend that appeared somewhere around the time of the 1893 World's Fair. Remade in 1952 as "So Long at the Fair." **63m/B VHS.** William Boyd, Claudia Dell, Henry Hall, John Harron, Hooper Atchley; *D:* Spencer Gordon Bennet. *SNC, NOS, DVT*

Midnight Warrior ✔ *1989* A reporter strikes it big when he investigates the underside of L.A. nightlife, but things go terribly wrong when he becomes wrapped up in the sleaze. **90m/C VHS, Beta.** Bernie Angel, Michelle Berger, Kevin Bernhardt, Lilly Melgar; *D:* Joseph Merhi. *PAR*

Midnight Witness ✔½ *1993 (R)* Guy finds himself on the run when after he videotapes the beating of a young drug dealer by corrupt cops. Plot bears more than a little resemblance to the Rodney King incident, but according to writer Foldy it was written before it took place. Low-budget thriller went direct to video. *CW:* Language, violence, and strong sexuality. **90m/C VHS.** Maxwell Caulfield, Jan-Michael Vincent, Paul Johansson, Karen Moncrieff, Mark Pellegrino, Virginia Mayo; *D:* Peter Foldy; *W:* Peter Foldy; *M:* Graydon Hillock.

Midnight's Child ✔½ *1993* Another Nanny-from-Hell story, only this time it's literal. D'Abo is the Nanny in question, who belongs to a Satanic cult. Her mission is to select the young daughter in her care as a bride for the devil, even if the girl's parents don't approve of the match. **89m/C**

VHS, Beta. Olivia D'Abo, Marcy Walker, Cotter Smith, Elissabeth Moss, Jim Norton, Judy Reyfin, Dermot Diggy Danson, Mary Larkin; D: Colin Bucksey; W: David Chaskin.

Midnite Spares 🐾🐾 1985 A young man's search for the men who kidnapped his father leads him into the world of car thieves and chopshops. 90m/C VHS, Beta. Bruce Spence, Gia Carides, James Laurie; C: Geoff Burton; M: Cameron Allan. NO

A Midsummer Night's Dream 🐾🐾🐾 1935 Famed Reinhardt version of the Shakespeare classic, featuring nearly every star on the Warner Bros. lot. The plot revolves around the amorous battle between the king and queen of a fairy kingdom, and the humans who are drawn into their sport. Features de Havilland's first film role. Classic credit line: Dialogue by William Shakespeare. 117m/B VHS, Beta. James Cagney, Dick Powell, Joe E. Brown, Hugh Herbert, Olivia de Havilland, Ian Hunter, Mickey Rooney, Victor Jory, Arthur Treacher, Billy Barty; D: Max Reinhardt, William Dieterle; C: Hal Mohr. Academy Awards '35: Best Cinematography, Best Film Editing; Nominations: Academy Awards '35: Best Picture. MGM, FOX, FCT

A Midsummer Night's Dream 🐾🐾½ 1968 Fine acting from the Royal Shakespeare Company cast in this filmed version of the play. Makes very little use of the Athens, Greece scenery. 124m/C VHS. GB David Warner, Diana Rigg, Ian Richardson, Judi Dench, Ian Holm, Barbara Jefford, Nicholas Selby, Helen Mirren, Michael Jayston, Derek Godfrey, Hugh Sullivan, Paul Rogers, Sebastian Shaw, Bill Travers; D: Peter Hall. WBF, WAR, BTV

A Midsummer Night's Sex Comedy 🐾🐾🐾½ 1982 (PG) Allen's homage to Shakespeare, Renoir, Chekhov, Bergman, and who knows who else is an engaging ensemble piece about hijinks among friends and acquaintances gathered at a country house at the turn of the century. Standouts include Ferrer as pompous professor and Steenburgen as Allen's sexually repressed wife. Mia's first for the Woodman. 88m/C VHS, Beta. Woody Allen, Mia Farrow, Mary Steenburgen, Tony Roberts, Julie Hagerty, Jose Ferrer; D: Woody Allen; W: Woody Allen; C: Gordon Willis. WAR

Midway 🐾🐾 1976 (PG) The epic WWII battle of Midway, the turning point in the war, is retold through Allied and Japanese viewpoints in a big all-star cast saddled with dumpy dialogue and enough weaponry to seize Hollywood on any given Wednesday. 132m/C VHS, Beta, LV, Letterbox. Charlton Heston, Henry Fonda, James Coburn, Glenn Ford, Hal Holbrook, Robert Mitchum, Cliff Robertson, Robert Wagner, Kevin Dobson, Christopher George, Toshiro Mifune, Tom Selleck; D: Jack Smight; C: Harry Stradling Jr.; M: John Williams. USH, TLF

A Midwinter's Tale 🐾🐾½ In the Bleak Midwinter 1995 (R) Branagh assembles a largely unknown cast in this low-budget backstage saga about an out-of-work thesp, Joe Harper (Maloney), who assembles a shaggy crew of actors to stage an alternative "Hamlet" in a small English country church. The diverse cast squabble, stumble, and emote their way through rehearsals, finally pulling together for the big show. Funny and interesting performances manage to show through the dense and somewhat cliched script. Maloney's Joe, who exhibits the proper frustration of being forced to deal with amateurs and Sessions as a camp queen playing the Queen (Gertrude, that is) stand out. CW: Some language. 98m/B VHS, LV, Closed Caption. GB Michael Maloney, Richard Briers, Mark Hadfield, Nicholas Farrell, Gerard Horan, John Sessions, Celia Imrie, Hetta Charnley, Julia Sawalha, Joan Collins, Jennifer Saunders; D: Kenneth Branagh; C: Roger Lanser; M: Jimmy Yuill. COL

Mighty Aphrodite 🐾🐾½ 1995 (R) Neurotic (Surprise!) New York sportswriter Lenny Weinrib (Allen) is trapped in an unhappy marriage to art dealer Amanda (Bonham-Carter), who talks him into adopting a child. Film comes alive when Lenny tracks down his son's biological mother, consummate dumb blond and hooker/porno actress Linda, played with over-the-top (in a good

way) gusto by Sorvino. Lenny attempts to reform his son's real mother while a Greek chorus (including Abraham and Dukakis) provide a running commentary on the tragedy/comedy of Lenny's predicaments. Allen's 31st film treads into familiar Woodman waters but falls short of his past comic genius. CW: Language and sex-related material. 95m/C VHS, LV, Closed Caption. Woody Allen, Helena Bonham Carter, Mira Sorvino, F. Murray Abraham, Michael Rapaport, Jack Warden, Olympia Dukakis, Peter Weller, Claire Bloom, David Ogden Stiers; D: Woody Allen; W: Woody Allen; C: Carlo DiPalma; M: Dick Hyman. Academy Awards '95: Best Supporting Actress (Sorvino); Golden Globe Awards '96: Best Supporting Actress (Sorvino); National Board of Review Awards '95: Best Supporting Actress (Sorvino); New York Film Critics Awards '95: Best Supporting Actress (Sorvino); Broadcast Film Critics Association Awards '95: Best Supporting Actress (Sorvino); Nominations: Academy Awards '95: Best Original Screenplay; British Academy Awards '95: Best Supporting Actress (Sorvino); Screen Actors Guild Award '95: Best Supporting Actress (Sorvino); Writers Guild of America '95: Best Original Screenplay. TOU

The Mighty Ducks 🐾🐾½ 1992 (PG) Bad News Bears on skates. Selfish yuppie lawyer is arrested for drunk driving and as part of his community service sentence, he is forced to coach an inner-city hockey team full of the usual misfits and underachievers. Although sarcastic and skeptical, Coach Gordon Bombay (Estevez) eventually bonds with the Ducks and learns to treat them with respect. Dual themes of teamwork and redemption are repeated constantly, and it gets a bit hokey at times, but the kids won't mind with this fun Disney film, while adults will appreciate the sarcasm. Followed by "D2: The Mighty Ducks." 114m/C VHS, Beta, LV, Closed Caption. Emilio Estevez, Joss Ackland, Lane Smith, Heidi Kling, Josef Sommer, Matt Doherty, Steven Brill, Joshua Jackson, Elden Ratliff, Shaun Weiss; D: Stephen Herek; W: Steven Brill, Brian Hohlfield; M: David Newman. TOU, BTV

Mighty Joe Young 🐾🐾½ 1949 Tongue-in-cheek King Kong variation features giant ape brought to civilization and exploited in a nightclub act, whereupon things get darned ugly. Bullied and given the key to the liquor cabinet, mild-mannered Joe goes on a drunken rampage, but eventually redeems himself by rescuing orphans from a fire. Special effects (courtesy of Willis O'Brien and the great Ray Harryhausen) are probably the film's greatest asset. Also available colorized. 94m/B VHS, Beta, LV. Terry Moore, Ben Johnson, Robert Armstrong, Frank McHugh; D: Ernest B. Schoedsack. Academy Awards '49: Best Special Effects. TTC

Mighty Jungle 🐾🐾 1964 Lost in the Amazon jungle, a hunter must fight off killer iguanas, man-eating crocodiles and bloodthirsty natives who perform human sacrifices. 90m/C VHS, Beta. Marshall Thompson, David Dalie. NO

Mighty Morphin Power Rangers: The Movie 🐾🐾 1995 (PG) From the living room onto the big screen, these six suburban teenagers with super powers battle the evil Ivan Ooze to save Earth. Offers more special effects, new Zord animals, more ooze and more growth to the retail toy industry than the small screen could provide. A child's dream come true, but a parent's nightmare. 93m/C VHS. Paul Freeman, Jason Harold Yost, Amy Jo Johnson, Jason David Frank, John Yong Bosch, Stephen Antonio Cardenas; D: Bryan Spicer; W: Arne Olsen, John Camps; C: Paul Murphy; M: Graeme Revell. FXV

The Mighty Pawns 1987 Inner-city kids turn to chess when their teacher inspires them to stay off the streets. Originally aired on PBS as part of the "Wonderworks" family movie series. 58m/C VHS, Closed Caption. Paul Winfield, Alfonso Ribeiro, Terence Knox, Rosalind Cash, Teddy Wilson; D: Eric Laneuville. HMV, FCT

The Mighty Quinn 🐾🐾 1989 (R) While investigating the local murder of a rich white guy, the black Jamaican head of police becomes convinced that the prime suspect, a childhood friend,

is innocent. As the police chief, Denzel is good in this off-beat comedy mystery. 98m/C VHS, Beta, LV. Denzel Washington, Robert Townsend, James Fox, Mimi Rogers, M. Emmet Walsh, Sheryl Lee Ralph, Esther Rolle, Art Evans, Norman Beaton, Keye Luke; D: Carl Schenkel; W: Hampton Fancher; M: Anne Dudley. MGM, FOX

The Migrants 🐾🐾🐾 1974 Adaptation of the Tennessee Williams play about the hard-scrabble world of a migrant family yearning for a better life. Made for TV. 83m/C VHS. Cloris Leachman, Ron Howard, Sissy Spacek, Cindy Williams, Ed Lauter, Lisa Lucas, Mills Watson, Claudia McNeil, Dolph Sweet; D: Tom Gries; W: Lanford Wilson. MON

Mike's Murder 🐾½ 1984 (R) Disjointed drama about a shy bank teller who falls for a slick tennis player. When he is murdered, she investigates the circumstances, placing herself in dangerously close contact with his seedy, drug-involved buddies. The twists and confused plot leave the viewer bewildered. 109m/C VHS, Beta. Debra Winger, Mark Keyloun, Paul Winfield, Darrell Larson, Dan Shor, William Ostrander; D: James Bridges; W: James Bridges; M: John Barry. WAR

Mikey 🐾½ 1992 (R) Mikey seems like such a sweet little boy—but these awful things keep happening all around him. At every foster home and every school people have such dreadful, and deadly, accidents. But innocent Mikey couldn't be to blame—or could he. 92m/C VHS, Closed Caption. Brian Bonsall, John Diehl, Lyman Ward, Josie Bissett, Ashley Laurence, Mimi Craven, Whitby Hertford; D: Dennis Dimster. IMP

Mikey & Nicky 🐾🐾½ 1976 (R) Quirky, uneven film about longtime friends dodging a hit man during one long night. Bears little evidence of time and money invested. Cassavetes and Falk, however, provide some salvation. 105m/C VHS, Beta. John Cassavetes, Peter Falk, Ned Beatty, Oliver Clark, William Hickey; D: Elaine May; W: Elaine May. FRF

The Milagro Beanfield War 🐾🐾🐾½ 1988 (R) Redford's endearing adaptation of John Nichols's novel about New Mexican townfolk opposing development. Seemingly simple tale provides plenty of insight into the human spirit. Fine cast, with especially stellar turns from Blades, Braga, and Vennera. 118m/C VHS, Beta, LV. Chick Vennera, John Heard, Ruben Blades, Sonia Braga, Daniel Stern, Julie Carmen, Christopher Walken, Richard Bradford, Carlos Riquelme, James Gammon, Melanie Griffith, Freddy Fender, M. Emmet Walsh; D: Robert Redford; W: David S. Ward; C: Robbie Greenberg; M: Dave Grusin. Academy Awards '88: Best Original Score. USH

Mildred Pierce 🐾🐾🐾½ 1945 Gripping melodrama features Crawford as hard-working divorcee rivaling daughter for man's love. Things, one might say, eventually get ugly. Adaptation of James M. Cain novel is classic of its kind. 113m/B VHS, Beta, LV, Closed Caption. Joan Crawford, Jack Carson, Zachary Scott, Eve Arden, Ann Blyth, Bruce (Herman Brix) Bennett; D: Michael Curtiz; W: Ranald MacDougall; M: Max Steiner. Academy Awards '45: Best Actress (Crawford), National Film Registry '96;; Nominations: Academy Awards '45: Best Black and White Cinematography, Best Picture, Best Screenplay, Best Supporting Actress (Arden, Blyth). MGM, FOX, BTV

Miles from Home 🐾🐾 Farm of the Year 1988 (R) Times are tough for farmers Frank and Terry Roberts. The brothers are about to have another bad harvest and the bank is threatening to foreclose. In a symbolic last ditch effort to save their pride, they decide to burn the farm and leave. On their journey, they meet strangers who recognize the pair and help them escape the police. A melodrama with many members of Chicago's Steppenwolf Theater. 113m/C VHS, Beta, LV, Closed Caption. Richard Gere, Kevin Anderson, John Malkovich, Brian Dennehy, Judith Ivey, Penelope Ann Miller, Laurie Metcalf, Laura San Giacomo, Daniel Roebuck, Helen Hunt; D: Gary Sinise; W: Chris Gerolmo; C: Elliot Davis; M: Robert Folk. WAR

Miles to Go 🎬½ **1986** A successful businesswoman tries to enjoy her last days after learning she has terminal cancer. 88m/C VHS, Beta. Mimi Kuzyk, Tom Skerritt, Jill Clayburgh; *D:* David Greene. *NO*

Miles to Go before I Sleep 🎬🎬½ **1974** A retired, lonely man and a delinquent girl distrust each other but eventually reach out in mutual need. 78m/C VHS, Beta. Martin Balsam, MacKenzie Phillips, Kitty Winn, Elizabeth Wilson; *D:* Fielder Cook. *BFA*

Milk Money 🎬½ **1994 (PG-13)** Twelve year-old Frank (Carter) talks his pals into pooling their milk money and heading to the big city so they can get a look at a naked woman. They find a prostitute (Griffith) for the job, whom Frank decides would be perfect to bring home to his widower dad (Harris). Although Griffith is generally adorable and the movie is actually less salacious than the premise might suggest, overall, it's sappy and another in the long line of cute-hooker/Cinderella fairytales.*CW:* Sexual themes involving adolescents. 110m/C VHS, Beta, Closed Caption. Michael Patrick Carter, Melanie Griffith, Ed Harris, Malcolm McDowell, Casey Siemaszko, Anne Heche, Philip Bosco; *D:* Richard Benjamin; *W:* John Mattson; *M:* Michael Convertino. *PAR*

Milky Way 🎬🎬½ **1936** Loopy comedy about milkman who finds unhappiness after accidentally knocking out champion boxer. Adequate, but not equal to Lloyd's fine silent productions. 89m/B VHS, Beta, LV. Harold Lloyd, Adolphe Menjou, Verree Teasdale, Helen Mack, William Gargan; *D:* Leo McCarey. *VYY, MRV, NOS*

The Milky Way 🎬🎬🎬 **1968** Wicked anticlerical farce. Two bums team on religious pilgrimage and encounter seemingly all manner of strangeness and sacrilege in this typically peculiar Bunuel work. Perhaps the only film in which Jesus is encouraged to shave. In French with English subtitles. 102m/C VHS, Beta, LV. *FR* Laurent Terzieff, Paul Frankeur, Delphine Seyrig, Alain Cuny, Bernard Verley, Michel Piccoli, Edith Scob; *D:* Luis Bunuel; *W:* Jean-Claude Carriere. *XVC, FCT, IME*

Mill of the Stone Women 🎬🎬½ 🎬 *Mulino Delle Donne di Pietra; Horror of the Stone Women; The Horrible Mill Women* **1960** Sculpture-studying art student encounters strange carousel with beautiful babes within her horsies, and soon finds out that the statues contain shocking secrets. Filmed in Holland, it's offbeat and creepy. 94m/C VHS. *FR IT* Pierre Brice, Scilla Gabel, Danny Carrel, Wolfgang Preiss, Herbert Boenne, Liana Orfei; *D:* Giorgio Ferroni. *SNC*

The Mill on the Floss 🎬🎬 **1937** Based on George Eliot's classic novel, this film follows the course of an ill-fated romance and family hatred in rural England. Underwhelming, considering the source. 77m/B VHS, Beta. *GB* James Mason, Geraldine Fitzgerald, Frank Lawton, Victoria Hopper, Fay Compton, Griffith Jones, Mary Clare; *D:* Tim Whelan. *NOS, MRV, DVT*

The Mill on the Floss 🎬🎬½ **1997** Maggie Tulliver (Watson) is a smart, emotional young woman painfully at odds with her conventional times. She adores her intolerant older brother Tom (Meredith) but when Maggie becomes involved with Philip Wakeum (Frain), the son of their father Edward's (Hill) greatest enemy, she reluctantly acquieses when Tom forbids the romance. When Stephen Guest (Weber-Brown), the fiance of Maggie's cousin Lucy (Whybrow), falls in love with her, his attentions bring scandal and tragedy to both Maggie and Tom. Watson is fine as the harried heroine but Meredith seems too young for his role, upsetting the sibling balance between the two. Based on the novel by George Eliot. 90m/C VHS. *GB* Emily Watson, Ifan Meredith, James Frain, Bernard Hill, James Weber-Brown, Lucy Whybrow, Nicholas Gecks, Cheryl Campbell; *D:* Graham Theakston; *W:* Hugh Stoddart; *C:* David Johnson; *M:* John Scott. *VTR*

Mille Bolle Blu 🎬🎬 **1993** Follows the lives of the inhabitants of a single block in 1961 Rome, on the eve of a solar eclipse. The neighborhood children take the opportunity to spy on their elders, including the engaged Elvira, whose old boyfriend Antonio wants her back, escaped convict Caligiuri who returns to his loving wife, and blind Guido, who's undergone an operation to restore his sight. Italian with subtitles. 83m/C VHS. *IT* Stefano Dionisi, Claudio Bigagli, Paolo Bonacelli, Nicoletta Boris; *D:* Leone Pompucci; *W:* Leone Pompucci; *M:* Franco Piersanti. *NYF*

Millenium 🎬🎬½ **1989 (PG-13)** The Earth of the future is running out of time. The people are sterile and the air is terrible. To keep the planet viable, Ladd and company must go back in time and yank people off planes that are doomed to crash. Great special effects and well-thought out script make this a ball of fun. 108m/C VHS, Beta, LV, Closed Caption. Kris Kristofferson, Cheryl Ladd, Daniel J. Travanti, Lloyd Bochner, Robert Joy, Brent Carver, Maury Chaykin, David McIlwraith, Al Waxman; *D:* Michael Anderson Sr.; *W:* John Varley; *M:* Eric N. Robertson. *CCB*

Miller's Crossing 🎬🎬🎬½ **1990 (R)** From the Coen brothers (makers of "Blood Simple" and "Raising Arizona") comes this extremely dark entry in the gangster movie sweepstakes of 1990. Jewish, Italian, and Irish mobsters spin webs of deceit, protection, and revenge over themselves and their families. Byrne is the protagonist, but no hero, being as deeply flawed as the men he battles. Harden stuns as the woman who sleeps with Byrne and his boss, Finney, in hopes of a better life and protection for her small-time crook brother. Visually exhilarating, excellently acted and perfectly paced. 115m/C VHS, Beta, LV, Closed Caption. Albert Finney, Gabriel Byrne, Marcia Gay Harden, John Turturro, Jon Polito, J.E. Freeman; *D:* Joel Coen; *W:* Ethan Coen, Joel Coen; *M:* Carter Burwell. *FCT*

Millie 🎬½ **1931** Creaky melodrama about a divorcee who wants every man but one. He pursues her teenage daughter instead, leading to tragedy and courtroom hand-wringing. Twelvetrees still stands out in this hokum, based on a Donald Henderson novel considered daring in its day. 85m/B VHS. Helen Twelvetrees, Robert Ames, Lilyan Tashman, Joan Blondell, John Halliday, James Hall, Anita Louise, Frank McHugh; *D:* John Francis Dillon. *NOS*

Million Dollar Duck 🎬½ **1971 (G)** A family duck is doused with radiation and begins to lay gold eggs. Okay Disney family fare, especially for youngsters. 92m/C VHS, Beta. Dean Jones, Sandy Duncan, Joe Flynn, Tony Roberts; *D:* Vincent McEveety; *M:* Buddy Baker. *DIS, OM*

Million Dollar Haul 🎬 **1935** Tarzan sniffs out a ring of warehouse thieves. 60m/B VHS, Beta, LV. Reed Howes, Janet Chandler, William Farnum. *NO*

Million Dollar Kid 🎬🎬 **1944** When a group of thugs wreak havoc in the neighborhood, the East Side Kids try to help a wealthy man put a stop to it. They face an even greater dilemma when they discover that the man's son is part of the gang. Part of the "Bowery Boys" series. 65m/B VHS. Leo Gorcey, Huntz Hall, Gabriel Dell, Louise Currie, Noah Beery Jr., Iris Adrian, Mary Gordon; *D:* Wallace Fox. *VYY, DVT, NOS*

Million Dollar Mermaid 🎬🎬 **1952** The prototypical Williams aquashow, with the requisite awesome Berkeley dance numbers. As a biography of swimmer Annette Kellerman it isn't much, but as an MGM extravaganza, it fits the bill. 115m/C VHS, Beta. Esther Williams, Victor Mature, Walter Pidgeon, Jesse White, David Brian, Maria Tallchief, Howard Freeman, Busby Berkeley; *D:* Mervyn LeRoy. Nominations: Academy Awards '52: Best Color Cinematography. *MGM*

Million Dollar Mystery 🎬½ **1987 (PG)** A dying man's last words indicate that several million dollars have been stashed near a diner. Chaos breaks out as nearly everyone in town tries to dig up the loot. 95m/C VHS, LV, Closed Caption. Eddie Deezen, Penny Baker, Tom Bosley, Rich Hall, Wendy

Sherman, Rick Overton, Mona Lyden; *D:* Richard Fleischer; *W:* Rudy DeLuca, Tim Metcalfe; *C:* Jack Cardiff. *HBO, CNG*

A Million to Juan 🎬🎬½ **1994 (PG)** Familiar rags-to-riches tale, this time set in a Los Angeles barrio, centers on Juan Lopez (Rodriguez), an uneducated good guy struggling to raise his son. Juan gets his lucky break when a stranger hands him a check for one million dollars, explains it's a loan, and if Juan can use the money properly for a month, he'll get a reward. Juan remains incredibly noble; the movie remains mushy. Loose adaptation of the Mark Twain story "The Million Pound Bank Note." Directorial debut for Rodriguez. 97m/C VHS, Closed Caption. Paul Rodriguez, Polly Draper, Pepe Serna, Bert Rosario, Jonathan Hernandez, Gerardo, Victor Rivers, Edward James Olmos, Paul Williams; *Cameos:* Tony Plana, Ruben Blades, Richard "Cheech" Marin, David Rasche, Liz Torres; *D:* Paul Rodriguez; *W:* Francisca Matos, Robert Grasmere.

A Million to One 🎬 **1937** An athlete trains for the Olympic decathlon, and catches the eye of an upper-class woman in the process. The lead Bennett was actually a shot-putter in the 1932 Olympic Games. 60m/B VHS. Bruce (Herman Brix) Bennett, Joan Fontaine, Monte Blue, Kenneth Harlan, Reed Howes; *D:* Lynn Shores. *VYY*

The Millionaire's Express 🎬🎬 *Shanghai Express; Fu Gui Lie Che* **1986** Hung returns to his village with a plan to derail the local train, which carries a number of wealthy passengers, in hopes of saving his poor hometown. Chinese with subtitles or dubbed. 107m/C VHS, LV. *HK* Sammo Hung, Yuen Biao, Cynthia Rothrock, Richard Norton, Yukari Oshima; *D:* Sammo Hung. *TAI*

The Millionairess 🎬🎬½ **1960** Loren is an incredibly rich woman who has ended a bad marriage, and feels that the only thing she still needs to fulfill her life is a good husband. She meets a humble doctor from India, in the person of Sellers, and finds he evades her every effort to snare him. In the process she learns that money can't buy everything. From a play by George Bernard Shaw. 90m/C VHS. *GB* Sophia Loren, Peter Sellers, Alastair Sim, Vittorio De Sica, Dennis Price; *D:* Anthony Asquith; *C:* Jack Hildyard. *FXL*

Millions 🎬½ **1990 (R)** To a family of millionaires, money is everything, and the heir to the family fortune is willing to do anything to get his hands on all that money. Even if it means sleeping with his sister-in-law and cousin! Lucky for him they happen to be beautiful models.*CW:* Some language, drug content, and sexuality. 118m/C VHS, Beta, Closed Caption. *IT* Billy Zane, Lauren Hutton, Carol Alt, Alexandra Paul, Catherine Hickland, Donald Pleasence; *D:* Carlo Vanzina.

Milo & Otis 🎬🎬½ **1989 (G)** Charming tale of a kitten named Milo and his best friend, a puppy named Otis. The two live on a farm and, when exploring the countryside, Milo is swept down a rushing river. Otis goes after to rescue his friend and the two begin a series of adventures as they try to return home. 76m/C VHS, Closed Caption. *COL*

Milo Milo 🎬🎬 **196?** Comedy about some very silly French people who propose to steal the Venus de Milo from the Louvre. 110m/C VHS, Beta. Antonio Fargas, Joe Higgins. *VCD*

The Milpitas Monster 🎬 **1975 (PG)** Creature spawned in a Milpitas, California, waste dump terrorizes the town residents. 80m/C VHS, Beta. Doug Hagdahl, Scott A. Henderson, Scott Parker; *D:* Robert L. Burrill. *VCI*

Mimi 🎬🎬 **1935** Melodrama with a down-on-his-luck playwright falling for a poor lass who provides him with the needed inspiration to be a winner. The question is, will she die before he hits the big time? Loosely based on "La Vie de Boheme" by Henri Murger. 98m/B VHS. *GB* Douglas Fairbanks Jr., Gertrude Lawrence, Diana Napier, Harold Warrender, Carol Goodner, Richard Bird, Austin Trevor, Lawrence Hanray, Paul Graetz, Martin Walker; *D:* Paul Stein. *VYY, FCT*

Mimic 🦴🦴½ **1997 (R)** Married biotech scientists Sorvino and Northam upset the balance of nature when they cure a plague only to have their concoction unleashed in the New York subways. This causes giant cockroaches to mimic, and kill, humans. Far-fetched story is forgiven with a unique script (both John Sayles and Steven Soderbergh made additions) and original kills and thrills. Plenty of gore also makes it a worthy addition to the horror genre. **CW:** Terror/violence and language. **105m/C VHS, LV, Closed Caption.** Jeremy Northam, Mira Sorvino, Josh Brolin, Charles S. Dutton, Giancarlo Giannini, F. Murray Abraham; **D:** Guillermo del Toro; **W:** John Sayles, Steven Soderbergh, Matthew Robbins; **M:** Marco Beltrami. *TOU*

Min & Bill 🦴🦴 **1930** Patchy early talkie about two houseboat dwellers fighting to preserve their waterfront lifestyle and keep their daughter from being taken to a "proper" home. **66m/B VHS, Beta.** Marie Dressler, Wallace Beery, Marjorie Rambeau, Dorothy Jordan; **D:** George Hill. Academy Awards '31: Best Actress (Dressler). *MGM, BTV, FHE*

Mina Tannenbaum 🦴🦴 **1993** Touching but unsentimental look at the 25-year friendship between two Jewish women in Paris. Mina (Bohringer) and Ethel (Zylberstein) meet as seven-year-olds and go through various childhood and teenage tramas together, including the desperate pangs of first love. Mina becomes an intense artist while flirty Ethel works as a freelance journalist. And, naturally, their friendship undergoes its own relentless changes. Pacing problems cause something of a letdown. Directorial debut for cinematographer Dugowson. French with subtitles. **128m/C VHS.** *FR* Romane Bohringer, Elsa Zylberstein, Nils Tavernier, Florence Thomassin, Jean-Philippe Ecoffey, Stephane Slima; **D:** Martine Dugowson; **W:** Martine Dugowson; **C:** Dominique Chapuis. *NYF*

Minbo—Or the Gentle Art of Japanese Extortion 🦴🦴 **1992** Satire on Japanese mobsters, known as the Yakuza, focusing on the blackmail and intimidation that gives these criminals a great deal of their power. The ill-mannered group like to congregate at a local hotel—much to the detriment of business—and hotel management finally hire a hardball-playing female lawyer to solve their problems with the thugs. Japanese with subtitles. **123m/C VHS.** *JP* Nobuko Miyamoto, Akira Takarada, Takehiro Murata, Yasuo Daichi, Hideji Otaki; **D:** Juzo Itami; **W:** Juzo Itami; **C:** Yonezo Maeda; **M:** Toshiyuki Honda. *HMV*

Mind, Body & Soul 🦴🦴 **1992 (R)** When a woman witnesses a human sacrifice performed by her boyfriend's satanic cult, she goes to the police. The cops, however, believe she is part of the cult, so she is forced to rely on the public defender to protect her from angry cult members. Pretty dull, but Hauser and Allen add some spice to this hokey thriller. **93m/C VHS.** Wings Hauser, Ginger Lynn Allen, Jay Richardson, Ken Hill, Jesse Kaye, Tami Bakke; **D:** Rick Sloane.

Mind Games 🦴½ **1989 (R)** A young couple and their ten-year-old son pick up a hitcher in their mobile home, never suspecting that he's a deranged psychology student ready to pit the family against each other as an experiment. **93m/C VHS, Beta.** Edward Albert, Shawn Weatherly, Matt Norero, Maxwell Caulfield; **D:** Bob Yari. *FOX, HHE*

Mind Snatchers 🦴🦴½ **1972 (PG)** An American G.I. becomes involved in U.S. Army experimental psychological brain operations when he is brought into a western European hospital for treatment. Also know as "The Happiness Cage." **94m/C VHS, Beta.** Christopher Walken, Ronny Cox, Ralph Meeker, Joss Ackland; **D:** Bernard Girard.

A Mind to Kill 🦴🦴 **1995** When a murdered girl is found in a small English seaside town, the crime is linked to a previous death. Police call on a university professor for help but then a new victim, with ties to the professor, is discovered and the police detective in charge finds that his own loved ones are now in danger. **95m/C VHS.**

GB Hywel Bennett, Philip Madoc, Sue Jones-Davies, Nicola Beddoe; **D:** Peter Edwards *FCT*

A Mind to Murder 🦴🦴½ *P.D. James: A Mind to Murder* **1996** Scotland Yard Commander Adam Dalgliesh (Marsden) is still depressed over the murder of a colleague some months earlier when he's discreetly called in to investigate the stabbing death of the administrator of the Steen Clinic, located in East Anglia. The exclusive psychiatric facility is home to some politically sensitive patients and Dalgliesh is under pressure to solve the crime quickly and quietly. His work would go a lot easier if people cooperated, but naturally the investigation doesn't go smoothly at all. Based on the 1963 novel by P.D. James and updated for the TV movie. **100m/C VHS.** *GB* Roy Marsden, Sean Scanlan, Robert Pugh, Mairead Carty, Frank Finlay, Cal Macaninch, Ann-Gisel Glass, Sian Thomas, Jerome Flynn, Suzanne Burden, Donald Douglas, Christopher Ravenscroft; *Cameos:* David Hemmings; **D:** Gareth Davies; **C:** Bill Broomfield. *VCO, AEH*

Mind Trap 🦴½ **1991** A beautiful movie star's family is killed due to her father's involvement with naval research. The government wants no part of her troubles so she is forced to take the law into her own hands. **90m/C VHS.** Dan Haggerty, Lyle Waggoner, Martha Kincare, Thomas Elliot, Samuel Steven; **D:** Eames Demetrios. *NO*

Mind Twister 🦴½ **1993 (R)** Erotic thriller finds a tough police detective on the trail of a sadistic killer with a twist. An unrated version is available at 94 minutes. **87m/C VHS.** Telly Savalas, Gary Hudson, Richard Roundtree, Erica Nann, Suzanne Slater; **D:** Fred Olen Ray. *VCI*

Mind Warp 🦴½ *Grey Matter; The Brain Machine* **1972** A future society exercises mental control and torture over its citizens. **92m/C VHS, Beta.** James Best, Barbara Burgess, Gil Peterson, Gerald McRaney, Marcus J. Grapes, Doug Collins, Anne Latham; **D:** Joy Houck Jr. *COL*

Mindfield 🦴½ **1989 (R)** An innocent man gets trapped by the CIA and is used by them in mind control experiments. **91m/C VHS, Beta, LV.** *CA* Michael Ironside, Lisa Langlois, Christopher Plummer, Stefan Wodoslowsky, Sean McCann; **D:** Jean-Claude Lord. *NO*

Mindkiller 🦴½ **1987** A tongue-in-cheek gore-fest about a shy young guy who develops his brain in an effort to be socially accepted. Unfortunately, he overdoes it and his brain mutates, bursts from his head, and runs around on its own. **84m/C VHS, Beta.** Joe McDonald, Christopher Wade, Shirley Ross, Kevin Hart; **D:** Michael Krueger.

Mindwalk: A Film for Passionate Thinkers 🦴🦴🦴 **1991 (PG)** A feature-length intellectual workout; a physicist, poet and politician stroll the ancient grounds of Mont St. Michel monastery in France and discuss the need to change mankind's view of the universe. Uncinematic? Perhaps, but it entertainingly conveys the epochal ideas of scientist/author Fritjof Capra (whose book was adapted for the screen by younger brother Bernt). **111m/C VHS, Beta, Closed Caption.** Liv Ullmann, Sam Waterston, John Heard, Ione Skye; **D:** Bernt Capra; **W:** Fritjof Capra, Floyd Byars; **M:** Philip Glass. *PAR, WSH*

Mindwarp 🦴🦴 **1991 (R)** After an ecological disaster, residents of Earth move to a sterile haven known as "Inworld." When survivor Judy (Alicia) seeks answers about her missing father (accidentally killing her mother in the process), she is cast from "Inworld" into Earth's wasteland, where she and human compatriot Stover (Campbell) are left to fight the elements and learn the awful truth about Judy's father. **CW:** Horror violence and gore. **91m/C VHS, LV, Closed Caption.** Marta Alicia, Bruce Campbell, Angus Scrimm, Elizabeth Kent, Mary Becker; **D:** Steve Barnett; **W:** Henry Dominick. *COL*

Mine Own Executioner 🦴🦴🦴 **1947** Determined but unstable psychologist in postwar London struggles to treat schizophrenic who suffered torture by Japanese while wartime prisoner. Strong, visually engrossing fare. **102m/B VHS.** *GB*

Burgess Meredith, Kieron Moore, Dulcie Gray, Christine Norden, Barbara White, John Laurie, Michael Shepley; **D:** Anthony Kimmins. *FCT, DVT, HHT*

Mines of Kilimanjaro 🦴½ **1987 (PG-13)** An archaeology student heads for Africa to investigate his professor's murder and comes up with a heap of trouble. **88m/C VHS, Beta.** Christopher Connelly, Tobias Hoels, Gordon Mitchell, Elena Pompei; **D:** Mino Guerrini. *IMP*

Ministry of Fear 🦴🦴🦴 **1944** Creepy noir based on the novel by Graham Greene. Stephen Neale (Milland) has just been released from two years in an insane asylum. As he waits for a train, he decides to visit a nearby carnival that turns out to be fronted by a Nazi organization, where Neale's mistaken for an agent. After finally reaching London, he's later accused of murder, escapes the police, and is aided by the sympathetic Carla (Reynolds). No one and nothing is as it seems, however, and soon the unwitting Neale is deeply involved in espionage. Since the viewer sees only what Neale does, it's just as puzzling for the audience as it is for the character. **85m/B VHS.** Ray Milland, Marjorie Reynolds, Percy Waram, Dan Duryea, Carl Esmond, Hillary Brooke, Alan Napier, Erskine Sanford; **D:** Fritz Lang; **W:** Seton I. Miller; **C:** Henry Sharp; **M:** Victor Young. *USH*

Ministry of Vengeance 🦴 **1989 (R)** A psychotic murderer who hates grapes of any kind finds the woman of his dreams—she's a psychotic murderer who hates grapes! Together they find bliss—until the plumber discovers their secret! **90m/C VHS, Beta, LV.** John Schneider, Ned Beatty, George Kennedy, Yaphet Kotto, James Tolkan, Apollonia. *ART, VTR*

The Miniver Story 🦴🦴 **1950** Weepy sequel to "Mrs. Miniver" reunites the family in post-WWII England, but clearly lacks the inspiration of the original. Garson is again Mrs. Miniver and she's secretly suffering from a never-named fatal disease. She decides to straighten out the family troubles before her time is up, including her daughter's love life and her husband's plan to move to Brazil. Depressing and glum. **104m/B VHS.** *GB* Greer Garson, Walter Pidgeon, John Hodiak, Leo Genn, Cathy O'Donnell, Reginald Owen, Anthony Bushell; **D:** H.C. Potter; **W:** Ronald Millar, George Froeschel; **C:** Joseph Ruttenberg; **M:** Miklos Rozsa. *MGM*

Minnesota Clay 🦴½ *L'Homme du Minnesota* **1965** A blind gunman, who aims by sound and smell, is marked by two rival gangs and a tempestuous tramp. **89m/C VHS, Beta, LV.** *FR IT* Cameron Mitchell, Diana Martin; **D:** Sergio Corbucci. *NO*

A Minor Miracle 🦴🦴 **1983 (G)** Tender family fare about a group of orphaned children who band together under the loving guidance of their guardian (Huston) to save St. Francis School for boys from the town planners. Warms the cockles. **100m/C VHS, Beta, LV.** John Huston, Pele, Peter Fox; **D:** Terrell Tannen. *COL*

Minsky's Follies **1983** Recreation of an old time burlesque revue complete with strippers. **60m/C VHS, Beta.** Phyllis Diller, Rip Taylor, Stubby Kaye. *NO*

A Minute to Pray, a Second to Die 🦴🦴 *Un Minuto Per Pregare, Un Istante Per Morire; Dead or Alive; Outlaw Gun* **1967** A notorious, wanted-dead-or-alive gunman retreats to the amnesty of the New Mexico Territory, but finds he cannot shake his past. **100m/C VHS, Beta.** *IT* Robert Ryan, Arthur Kennedy, Alex Cord; **D:** Franco Giraldi. *FOX*

The Miracle 🦴🦴🦴 *Ways of Love* **1948** An innocent peasant woman is seduced by a shepherd and becomes convinced that her pregnancy will produce a second Christ. Controversial, compelling film derived from a story by Federico Fellini. In Italian with English subtitles. **43m/B VHS, Beta.** *IT* Anna Magnani, Federico Fellini; **D:** Roberto Rossellini; **W:** Federico Fellini. *NOS, FCT, HEG*

The Miracle 🎬🎬½ **1991 (PG)** Irish teens, whose strong friendship is based upon their equally unhappy home lives, find both tested when a secretive American woman turns up in town. Excellent debuts from Byrne and Pilkington but tedious pacing in a dreamy script that tells too much too soon. Worth watching just for D'Angelo's smouldering rendition of "Stardust." **97m/C VHS, LV.** *GB* Beverly D'Angelo, Donal McCann, Niall Byrne, Lorraine Pilkington, J.G. Devlin; *D:* Neil Jordan; *W:* Neil Jordan; *C:* Philippe Rousselot; *M:* Anne Dudley. *ART*

Miracle at Moreaux 1986 Three Jewish children fleeing from Nazis find sanctuary with a nun and her wards. Based on Clare Huchet Bishop's book "Twenty and Ten." Originally aired on PBS as part of the "Wonderworks" family movie series. **58m/C VHS.** Loretta Swit, Marsha Moreau, Robert Joy, Ken Pogue, Robert Kosoy, Talya Rubin; *D:* Paul Shapiro; *M:* Jonathan Goldsmith. *HMV, IGP, FCT*

Miracle Beach 🎬½ **1992 (PG-13)** Scotty McKay has lost his job, his apartment, and his girl. Then he gets rejected by Dana, the super model he's secretly adored. Can things get any worse? Scotty decides to take a walk along the beach and sort things out when he stumbles across a girl genie, named Jeanie, who has been sent to Earth on a good will mission. Scotty gets Jeanie to grant his every material wish in order to dazzle model Dana. But when Jeanie falls in love with Scotty can she get him to recognize the difference between true love and fantasy? *CW:* Nudity and sexual situations. **88m/C VHS, LV.** Dean Cameron, Felicity Waterman, Ami Dolenz, Alexis Arquette, Martin Mull, Noriyuki "Pat" Morita, Vincent Schiavelli; *D:* Skott Snider. *COL*

Miracle Down Under 🎬 **1987** A family endures arduous times in 1890s Australia before a Christmas miracle changes their fortunes. Inoffensive Disney-produced drama. Australia has two directors named George Miller—one directs Mad Max movies; the other directs family fare such as "The Man from Snowy River." This Miller is the latter. **101m/C VHS, Beta, Closed Caption.** *AU* Dee Wallace Stone, John Waters, Charles Tingwell, Bill Kerr, Andrew Ferguson; *D:* George Miller. *TOU, IGP*

Miracle in Harlem 🎬🎬 **1948** A gang tries to take over a candy shop and when the gang leader is killed, the evidence points to the foster daughter of the shop owner. The script suffers from cliched dialog and less-than-believable situations, but the all-black cast turns in good performances. **69m/B VHS.** Sheila Guyse, Stepin Fetchit, Hilda Offley, Lawrence Criner, Monte Hawley; *D:* Jack Kemp. *NOS*

Miracle in Milan 🎬🎬🎬 *Miracolo a Milano* **1951** An innocent, child-like fantasy about heavenly intervention driving capitalists out of a Milanese ghetto and helping the poor to fly to a new Utopia. Happy mixture of whimsy and neo-realism. In Italian with English subtitles. **95m/B VHS, Beta, LV.** *IT* Francesco Golisano, Brunella Bova, Emma Gramatica, Paolo Stoppa; *D:* Vittorio De Sica; *W:* Cesare Zavattini. Cannes Film Festival '51: Best Film; New York Film Critics Awards '51: Best Foreign Film. *HMV, FCT*

Miracle in Rome 🎬🎬½ *Milagro en Roma* **1988** Margarito Duarte digs up his dead daughter and finds her body in perfect condition despite 12-year internment. Attempting to convince the local clergy that she's miracle material, he finds them less than eager to elect her to sainthood. Based on a story by Gabriel Garcia marquez; made for Spanish TV. In Spanish with English subtitles. **76m/C VHS, LV.** *SP* Frank Ramirez, Gerardo Arellano, Amalia Duque Garcia, Lisandro Duque, Daniel Priolett; *D:* Lisandro Duque Naranjo; *W:* Lisandro Duque Naranjo, Gabriel Garcia Marquez. *FXL, FCT*

Miracle in the Wilderness 🎬🎬½ **1991** A Christmas western based on Paul Gallico's novella, "The Snow Goose." Kristofferson stars as Jericho Adams, a former Indian fighter, who turns to farming to support his wife and child. When they are captured by a raiding party of Blackfeet, Adams discovers they have never heard the story of the Nativity. **88m/C VHS, LV.** Kris Kristofferson, Kim Cattrall, John Dennis Johnston, Joanelle Romero, Dennis Olvers, Sheldon Peters Wolfchild; *D:* Kevin J. Dobson; *W:* Jim Byrnes. *TTC, FCT*

Miracle Kid 🎬🎬 **1942** Standard story of a young boxer who'd rather be something else. His romance is interrupted when he becomes successful in the ring. **66m/B VHS.** Tom Neal, Carol Hughes, Betty Blythe, Minta Durfee, Gertrude Messinger; *D:* William Beaudine. *NOS*

Miracle Mile 🎬🎬🎬 **1989 (R)** A riveting, apocalyptic thriller about a mild-mannered misfit who, while inadvertently standing on a street corner at 2 a.m., answers a ringing pay phone. The caller is a panicked missile-silo worker who announces that the bombs have been launched for an all-out nuclear war. With about an hour left before the end, he decides to head into the city and rendezvous with his new girlfriend. A surreal, wicked farce sadly overlooked in theatrical release. Music by Tangerine Dream. **87m/C VHS, Beta, LV, Closed Caption.** Anthony Edwards, Mare Winningham, John Agar, Denise Crosby, Lou Hancock, Mykelti Williamson, Kelly Jo Minter, Kurt Fuller, Robert DoQui, Danny De La Paz, O-lan Jones, Alan Rosenberg, Claude Earl Jones; *D:* Steve DeJarnatt; *W:* Steve DeJarnatt; *M:* Tangerine Dream. *HBO*

The Miracle of Marcelino 🎬🎬½ *Marcelino, Pan y Vino; Marcelino* **1955** Marcelino (Calvo) was left at birth on a monastery doorstep and raised by the Franciscan friars. The high-spirited young boy finds a life-sized crucifix in the church attic and, believing the figure of Christ to be real, befriends the image, bringing it food and wine. Then, one day, the image of Jesus comes to life. Spanish with subtitles. **88m/B VHS.** *SP* Pablito Calvo, Fernando Rey, Rafael Rivelles; *D:* Ladislao Vajda; *W:* Ladislao Vajda; *C:* Enrique Guerner; *M:* Pablo Sarosabal. *CVC*

Miracle of Morgan's Creek 🎬🎬🎬🎬 **1944** The breakneck comedy that stands as Sturges' premier achievement. Details the misadventures of a wartime floozy who gets drunk, thinks she marries a soldier on leave, gets pregnant by him, forgets the whole thing, and then tries to evade scandal by getting a local schnook to marry her again. And she's expecting sextuplets. Hilarious, out-to-make-trouble farce that shouldn't have, by all rights, made it past the censors of the time. Sturges' most scathing assault on American values earned him an Oscar nomination for writing. Remade as "Rock-A-Bye Baby" in 1958. **98m/B VHS, Beta.** Eddie Bracken, Betty Hutton, Diana Lynn, Brian Donlevy, Akim Tamiroff, Porter Hall, Emory Parnell, Alan Bridge, Julius Tannen, Victor Potel, Almira Sessions, Chester Conklin, William Demarest, Jimmy Conlin; *D:* Preston Sturges; *W:* Preston Sturges; *M:* Leo Shuken, Charles Bradshaw. Nominations: Academy Awards '44: Best Original Screenplay. *PAR, CCB*

Miracle of Our Lady of Fatima 🎬🎬 *The Miracle of Fatima* **1952** Slick cold-war version of the supposedly true events surrounding the sighting of a holy vision by three children in Portugal during WWI. **102m/C VHS, Beta, LV.** Gilbert Roland, Susan Whitney, Sherry Jackson, Sammy Ogg, Angela Clark, Frank Silvera, Jay Novello; *D:* John Brahm; *M:* Max Steiner. Nominations: Academy Awards '52: Best Original Dramatic/Comedy Score. *WAR, IGP, KEP*

The Miracle of the Bells 🎬🎬 **1948** A miracle occurs after a dead movie star is buried in the cemetary of her modest hometown. Given the premise, the casting is all the more peculiar. Adapted by Ben Hecht from Russell Janney's novel. **120m/B VHS, Beta.** Fred MacMurray, Alida Valli, Frank Sinatra, Lee J. Cobb; *D:* Irving Pichel. *REP, IGP*

Miracle of the Heart: A Boys Town Story 🎬🎬 **1986** A television movie based on the story of Boys Town, and an old priest who sticks up for Boys Town's principles in the face of a younger priest with rigid ideas. **100m/C VHS, Beta.** Art Carney, Casey Siemaszko, Jack Bannon; *D:* Georg Stanford Brown. *COL*

The Miracle of the White Stallions 🎬½ *The Flight of the White Stallions* **1963** A disappointing Disney adventure about the director of a Viennese riding academy who guides his prized Lipizzan stallions to safety when the Nazis occupy Austria in WWII. **92m/C VHS, Beta.** Robert Taylor, Lilli Palmer, Eddie Albert, Curt Jurgens; *D:* Arthur Hiller; *W:* A.J. Carothers. *DIS*

Miracle on Ice 🎬🎬½ **1981** Occasionally stirring television film recounts the surprise triumph of the American hockey team over the touted Soviet squad during the 1980 Winter Olympics at Lake Placid. **150m/C VHS, Beta.** Karl Malden, Steve Guttenberg, Andrew Stevens, Lucinda Dooling, Jessica Walter; *D:* Steven Hilliard Stern. *NO*

Miracle on 34th Street 🎬🎬🎬🎬 *The Big Heart* **1947** The actual Kris Kringle is hired as Santa Claus for the Macy's Thanksgiving parade but finds difficulty in proving himself to the cynical parade sponsor. When the boss's daughter also refuses to acknowledge Kringle, he goes to extraordinary lengths to convince her. Holiday classic equal to "It's a Wonderful Life," with Gwenn and Wood particularly engaging. Also available colorized. **97m/B VHS, Beta, LV, Closed Caption.** Maureen O'Hara, John Payne, Edmund Gwenn, Natalie Wood, William Frawley, Porter Hall, Gene Lockhart, Thelma Ritter, Jack Albertson; *D:* George Seaton; *W:* George Seaton; *M:* Cyril Mockridge. Academy Awards '47: Best Screenplay, Best Story, Best Supporting Actor (Gwenn); Golden Globe Awards '48: Best Screenplay, Best Supporting Actor (Gwenn); Nominations: Academy Awards '47: Best Picture. *CCB, FOX, HMV*

Miracle on 34th Street 🎬🎬½ **1994 (PG)** Updated remake of the 1947 Christmas classic in which a jolly, bearded gent (Attenborough) claiming to be Santa Claus brings happiness to a doubting girl (Wilson) and her jaded mother (Perkins). Before he can prove himself to the precocious child, he must prove himself in a court of law with the help of Perkins's impossibly perfect neighbor (McDermott), a lawyer with a heart of gold (talk about your Christmas miracles!). This version can't compete with the original's "classic" status, but Attenborough and Wilson bring soul and substance to this otherwise average adaptation. **114m/C VHS.** Richard Attenborough, Elizabeth Perkins, Dylan McDermott, J.T. Walsh, Mara Wilson, Joss Ackland, James Remar, Jane Leeves, Simon Jones, Robert Prosky, William Windom; *D:* Les Mayfield; *W:* John Hughes, George Seaton; *M:* Bruce Broughton. *FXV*

The Miracle Rider 1935 A 15-chapter serial finds the bad guys trying to run the Indians off their lands in this saga of the old west. **295m/B VHS.** Tom Mix, Joan Gale, Charles Middleton, Jason Robards Sr., Pat O'Malley, Robert Frazer, Wally Wales, Tom London, George Chesebro, Lafe McKee; *D:* B. Reeves Eason, Armand Schaefer. *GPV, MRV, VCN*

The Miracle Woman 🎬🎬½ **1931** Stanwyck's particularly fine as evangelist Florence "Faith" Fallon, who becomes very successful thanks to her way with words, some fake miracles, and the talents of shady promoter Hornsby (Hardy). After blind ex-pilot John Carson (Manners) hears her on the radio, he decides Faith might be able to cure him. Florence winds up falling in love with John but Hornsby starts to worry she's going soft and will end their scam. Even Capra apparently thought this film was corny but it still works. Based on the play "Bless You Sister" by John Meehan and Robert Riskin. **90m/B VHS.** Barbara Stanwyck, David Manners, Sam Hardy, Beryl Mercer, Russell Hopton, Charles Middleton, Eddie Boland; *D:* Frank Capra; *W:* Dorothy Howell, Jo Swerling; *C:* Joseph Walker. *COL*

The Miracle Worker 🎬🎬🎬½ **1962** Depicts the unconventional methods that teacher Anne Sullivan used to help the deaf and blind Helen Keller adjust to the world around her and shows the relationship that built between the two courageous women. An intense, moving experience. William Gibson adapted his own play for the screen. **107m/B VHS, Beta.** Anne Bancroft, Patty Duke,

Victor Jory, Inga Swenson, Andrew Prine, Beah Richards; **D:** Arthur Penn. Academy Awards '62: Best Actress (Bancroft), Best Supporting Actress (Duke); British Academy Awards '62: Best Actress (Bancroft); National Board of Review Awards '62: Best Actress (Bancroft); Nominations: Academy Awards '62: Best Adapted Screenplay, Best Costume Design (B & W), Best Director (Penn). *MGM, BTV, CCB*

The Miracle Worker ✍✍✍ 1979 Remade for television story of blind, deaf and mute Helen Keller and her teacher, Annie Sullivan, whose patience and perseverance finally enable Helen to learn to communicate with the world. Duke was Keller in the 1962 original, but plays the teacher in this version. 98m/C VHS, Beta. Patty Duke, Melissa Gilbert; **D:** Paul Aaron; **M:** Billy Goldenberg. *WAR, OM*

Miracles ✍½ 1986 (PG) Comedic misfire pairs a recently divorced couple as reluctant adventurers dodging jewel thieves and peculiar tribes in South America. In a desperate move to create a plot, Mexican jewel thieves, strange tribal rites, and some outrageously unlikely coincidences reunite the family. If this sounds good, see "Romancing the Stone." 90m/C VHS, Beta, LV. Tom Conti, Teri Garr, Paul Rodriguez, Christopher Lloyd, Jorge Russek, Charles Rocket, Bob Nelson; **D:** Jim Kouf; **M:** Peter Bernstein. *IME*

Mirage ✍✍✍ 1966 An amnesiac finds himself the target of a dangerous manhunt in New York City in this offbeat thriller. Peck is particularly sympathetic in the lead, and McCarthy, Matthau, and Kennedy all shine in supporting roles. Worth it just to hear thug Kennedy grunt, "I owe this man some pain!" 108m/B VHS, Beta. Gregory Peck, Diane Baker, Walter Matthau, Jack Weston, Kevin McCarthy, Walter Abel, George Kennedy; **D:** Edward Dmytryk; **M:** Quincy Jones. *BAR, MLB*

Mirage ✍½ 1994 (R) Neo-noir with plot problems has former Palm Springs cop Matteo Juarez (Olmos) hired to protect Jennifer (Young), the wife of wealthy environmentalist Donald Gale (Williams). But Jennifer just happens to suffer from multiple personality disorder, leading a not-so-secret second life as a stripper and having trouble always on her heels.**CW:** Sexuality, language, and some shootings. 106m/C VHS. Edward James Olmos, Sean Young, James Andronica, Paul W. Williams; **D:** Paul W. Williams; **W:** James Andronica. *USH*

Mirele Efros ✍✍½ 1938 A widowed but successful businesswoman finds herself at odds with her daughter-in-law in this film set in the turn of the century. In Yiddish with English subtitles. 80m/B VHS, Beta. Berta Gersten, Michael Rosenberg, Ruth Elbaum, Albert Lipton, Sarah Krohner, Moishe Feder; **D:** Joseph Berne. *ERG*

The Mirror ✍✍✍ *Zerkalo; A White White Boy* 1975 Wonderful child's view of life in Russia during WWII. Black and white flashbacks of important events in the country's history are interspersed with scenes of day-to-day family life. In Russian with English subtitles. 106m/C VHS. *RU* Margarita Terekhova, Philip Yankovsky, Ignat Daniltsev, Oleg Yankovsky; **D:** Andrei Tarkovsky. *TPV, KIV*

The Mirror Crack'd ✍✍ 1980 (PG) While filming a movie in the English countryside, an American actress is murdered and Miss Marple must discover who the killer is. Based on the substantially better Agatha Christie novel. 105m/C VHS, Beta, LV. *GB* Elizabeth Taylor, Rock Hudson, Kim Novak, Tony Curtis, Edward Fox, Geraldine Chaplin, Charles Gray, Pierce Brosnan; **D:** Guy Hamilton; **W:** Barry Sandler. *REP*

The Mirror Has Two Faces ✍✍ 1996 (PG-13) Gregory (Bridges) is a hunky, but flustered, professor (hunky professor?) looking for romance without all that complicated sex, which shortly leads him to plain but soulful Rose (Streisand), the ugly duckling of her family. Rose's mother (Bacall) seems more happy with her much married sister (Rogers), who is headed down the aisle again with gorgeous Alex (Brosnan). Rose decides it's her turn, despite Gregory's protests,

and she weds the bow-tied (and perhaps hogtied?) educator anyway. When Gregory leaves her on a promotional book tour, frumpy Babs decides a big makeover is in order. Her newfound outer beauty, however, becomes the beast on the inside. Premise is marred by Streisand's unwillingness to look bad, and there's a too-subtle transformation between the "ugly" Rose and the updated version. Bacall gives a memorable, Oscar-nominated performance. Remake of 1959 French film. La Streisand added to her reputation for being a "difficult" perfectionist with her constant reshoots and personnel firings that extended the film's schedule.**CW:** Language, sensuality and some mature thematic material. 127m/C VHS, LV, Closed Caption. Barbra Streisand, Jeff Bridges, Pierce Brosnan, Mimi Rogers, Lauren Bacall, Brenda Vaccaro, Austin Pendleton, George Segal, Elle Macpherson; **D:** Barbra Streisand; **W:** Richard LaGravenese; **C:** Dante Spinotti, Andrzej Bartkowiak; **M:** Barbra Streisand, Marvin Hamlisch. Golden Globe Awards '97: Best Supporting Actress (Bacall); Screen Actors Guild Award '96: Best Supporting Actress (Bacall); Nominations: Academy Awards '96: Best Song ("I've Finally Found Someone"), Best Supporting Actress (Bacall); British Academy Awards '96: Best Supporting Actress (Bacall); Golden Globe Awards '97: Best Actress—Musical/Comedy (Streisand), Best Song ("I've Finally Found Someone"), Best Score. *COL*

Mirror Images ✍½ 1991 (R) Although sexy twins Kaitlin and Shauna may look alike, they couldn't have more diverse personalities. Yet the gorgeous twins find their lives thrown together in a mad tornado of passion and danger when they each encounter a handsome, mysterious stranger. Could it be that this guy has something more on his mind than love, something like... murder? Also available in an even steamier unrated version.**CW:** Drug content and strong sensuality. 94m/C VHS. Delia Sheppard, Jeff Conaway, Richard Arbolino, John O'Hurley, Korey Mall, Julie Strain, Nels Van Patten; **D:** Alexander Gregory Hippolyte.

Mirror Images 2 ✍✍ 1993 Direct-to-video erotic thriller features identical twins Carrie and Terrie (Whirry in a dual role). Carrie's Miss Goody Two-Shoes and Terrie's a murderous nympho who likes Carrie's guys. Terrie dies in a mysterious fire and Carrie sets out to investigate. Sex and nudity sells. 92m/C VHS. Shannon Whirry, Luca Bercovici, Tom Reilly; **D:** Alexander Gregory Hippolyte.

Mirror, Mirror ✍✍ 1990 (R) The prolific Ms. Black turns on the ol' black magic when her daughter's classmates decide it's open season for taunting shrinking violets. Thanks to a magical mirror on the wall, the cheerleading classmates are willed to the great pep rally in the sky. 105m/C VHS, LV. Karen Black, Rainbow Harvest, Kristin Datillo, Ricky Paull Goldin, Yvonne De Carlo, William Sanderson, Charlie Spradling, Ann Hearn, Stephen Tobolowsky; **D:** Marina Sargenti; **W:** Marina Sargenti.

Mirror, Mirror 2: Raven Dance ✍½ 1994 (R) Teenaged Marlee (Wells) and her brother are temporarily housed in a convent after the death of their parents. The mystery mirror is discovered and looking into it causes Marlee to become partially blind. Meanwhile, her inheritance is threatened and a mysterious stranger, living in the convent's basement, may be Marlee's only hope. 91m/C VHS, LV. Tracy Wells, Roddy McDowall, Sally Kellerman, Veronica Cartwright, William Sanderson, Lois Nettleton; **D:** Jimmy Lifton; **W:** Jimmy Lifton, Virginia Perfili. *ORP*

Mirror Mirror 3: The Voyeur ✍½ 1996 Artist discovers a mirror in an abandoned mansion and sees that it reflects the presence of his lost lover, who is now able to manipulate his dreams. 91m/C VHS. Billy Drago, Monique Parent, David Naughton, Mark Ruffalo, Elizabeth Baldwin, Richard Cansino; **D:** Rachel Gordon, Virginia Perfili; **W:** Steve Tymon; **C:** Nils Erickson. *MTH*

Mirror of Death ✍ 1987 A woman subject to physical abuse gets more than she bargains for when she seeks revenge by unleashing the gruesome Queen of Hell. Watch this if you dare! 85m/C

VHS, Beta, Julie Merrill, Kari Browne, John Reno, Deryn Warren. *NO*

Mirrors ✍ 1978 Woman finds that her dreams lead to death and destruction in New Orleans. 83m/C VHS, Beta. Kitty Winn, Peter Donat, William Swetland, Mary-Robin Redd, William Burns; **D:** Noel Black. *NO*

Mirrors ✍✍½ 1985 A Detroit-born ballerina goes to the Big Apple in search of fame and glory, leaving behind her journalist boyfriend. This upbeat love story features some spectacular dance routines and a behind-the-scenes look at a Broadway dancer's lifestyle. Originally made for television. 99m/C VHS, Closed Caption. Timothy Daly, Marguerite Hickey, Antony Hamilton; **D:** Harry Winer. *THV*

The Misadventures of Merlin Jones ✍½ 1963 (G) A pair of college sweethearts become embroiled in a rollicking chimp-napping scandal. Disney pap done appropriately. A sequel, "The Monkey's Uncle," followed. 90m/C VHS, Beta. Tommy Kirk, Annette Funicello, Leon Ames, Stuart Erwin, Connie Gilchrist; **D:** Robert Stevenson; **W:** Alfred Lewis Levitt, Helen Levitt; **C:** Edward Colman; **M:** Buddy Baker. *DIS*

The Misadventures of Mr. Wilt ✍✍ *Wilt* 1990 (R) Bumbling college lecturer has to convince inept inspector that he murdered a blowup doll, not his more missing wife. Based on Tom Sharpe's bestseller.**CW:** Language and cosmic sexual situations. 84m/C VHS. *GB* Griff Rhys Jones, Mel Smith, Alison Steadman, Diana Quick; **D:** Michael Tuchner; **M:** Anne Dudley. *THV*

Misbegotten ✍✍ 1998 (R) Infertile couple Paul (Mancuso) and Caitlin (Anthony) are able to have their bundle of joy thanks to artifical insemination. Only psycho donor daddy Billy Crapshoot (Dillon) finds out who they are and decides to come for his soon-to-be-born offspring.**CW:** Strong violence, and for language and a sex scene. 97m/C VHS, Closed Caption. Kevin Dillon, Nick Mancuso, Lysette Anthony; **D:** Mark L. Lester. *THV*

Misbehaving Husbands ✍½ 1941 Weak story finds store-owner Langton suspected of being untrue by wife Blythe—thanks to rumors spread by a shyster lawyer only too happy to console the lady after the divorce. 65m/B VHS. Harry Langdon, Betty Blythe, Ralph Byrd, Esther Muir, Luana Walters; **D:** William Beaudine. *GPV*

Mischief ✍✍ 1985 (R) Alienated youths form a friendship during James Dean's heydey. Warning: this film offers a fairly convincing recreation of the 1950s. 97m/C VHS, Beta, LV, Closed Caption. Doug McKeon, Catherine Mary Stewart, Kelly Preston, Chris Nash, D.W. Brown, Jami Gertz, Margaret Blye, Graham Jarvis, Terry O'Quinn; **D:** Mel Damski; **W:** Noel Black. *FOX*

Misery ✍✍✍ 1990 (R) Author Caan decides to chuck his lucrative but unfulfilling pulp novels and write seriously by finishing off his most popular character, Misery Chastain. However, fate intervenes when he crashes his car near the home of Bates, his "biggest fan ever," who saves his life, but then tortures him into resurrecting her favorite character. Bates is chillingly glib and calmly brutal—watch your ankles. Based on the novel by Stephen King.**CW:** Language and violence. 107m/C VHS, Beta, LV, Closed Caption. James Caan, Kathy Bates, Lauren Bacall, Richard Farnsworth, Frances Sternhagen, Graham Jarvis; **D:** Rob Reiner; **W:** William Goldman; **C:** Barry Sonnenfeld; **M:** Marc Shaiman. Academy Awards '90: Best Actress (Bates); Golden Globe Awards '91: Best Actress—Drama (Bates).*COL*

The Misfit Brigade ✍✍ *Wheels of Terror* 1987 (R) Variation on the "Dirty Dozen" finds German misfits recruited for warfare by desperate Nazis during WWII. 99m/C VHS, Beta. Bruce Davison, Oliver Reed, David Carradine, David Patrick Kelly, D.W. Moffett, Keith Szarabajka; **D:** Gordon Hessler. *TWE*

The Misfits ✍✍✍ 1961 A cynical floozy befriends grim cowboys in this downbeat drama. Compelling performances from leads Clift, Monroe (screenwriter Miller's wife), and Gable. Last film for the latter two performers, and nearly the end for Clift. 124m/B VHS, Beta, LV. Clark Gable, Marilyn Monroe, Montgomery Clift, Thelma Ritter, Eli Wallach, James Barton, Estelle Winwood; *D:* John Huston; *W:* Arthur Miller; *C:* Russell Metty; *M:* Alex North. *MGM, FOX, FCT*

Misfits of Science ✔ 1985 Pilot for a failed television series about a group of teens with special powers who fight to save the world. 96m/C VHS, Beta. Dean Paul Martin, Kevin Peter Hall, Mark Thomas Miller, Kenneth Mars, Courteney Cox; *D:* Philip DeGuere. *USH*

Mishima: A Life in Four Chapters ✔✔✔ 1985 (R) Somewhat detached account and indulgent portrayal of the narcissistic Japanese author (and actor, filmmaker, and militarist) alternates between stylized interpretations of his books and a straightforward account of his life. Culminates in a pseudo-military operation that, in turn, resulted in Mishima's ritualistic suicide. A U.S./Japanese production. Innovative design by Eiko Ishioka. In Japanese with English subtitles. 121m/C VHS, Beta, Closed Caption. Ken Ogata, Kenji Sawada, Yasosuke Bando; *D:* Paul Schrader; *W:* Leonard Schrader, Paul Schrader; *C:* John Bailey; *M:* Philip Glass. *WAR*

Miss A & Miss M 1986 A young girl is shocked when she realizes that two teachers she has befriended also live together. 60m/C VHS. Kika Markham, Jennifer Hilary.

Miss All-American Beauty ✔✔½ 1982 A behind-the-scenes look at a smalltime Texas beauty pageant. Lane stars as a contestant who comes to realize her self-respect is more important than winning an award. Meadow's mean pageant director adds an ironic edge that the movie as a whole lacks. Made for television. 96m/C VHS, Beta. Diane Lane, Cloris Leachman, David Dukes, Jayne Meadows, Alice Hirson, Brian Kerwin; *D:* Gus Trikonis. *ART*

Miss Annie Rooney ✔✔ 1942 (G) Intended to bill the child star in a more mature role, Temple receives her first screen kiss in this story about a poor Irish girl who falls in love with a wealthy young man. The well-worn plot is weighed down by lifeless dialogue. 86m/B VHS, Beta. Shirley Temple, Dickie Moore, William Gargan, Guy Kibbee, Peggy Ryan, June Lockhart; *D:* Edwin L. Marin. *ART*

Ms. Bear ✔✔½ 1997 (G) Logging operations in a Canadian forest have disturbed the local bear population and down-on-his-luck Barney decides to make some money by tranquilizing the animals and selling them to a zoo importer. A cub escapes and wanders into the yard of lonely, seven-year-old Emily, who befriends the cute critter. Then, with Emily's help, Barney learns the importer is actually killing the bears and only selling their paws to the overseas market. So a rescue is in order. 95m/C VHS, Closed Caption. Ed Begley Jr., Kaitlyn Burke, Shawn Johnston; *D:* Paul Ziller. *CAF*

Miss Evers' Boys ✔✔½ 1997 (PG) Wrenching cable docudrama covers a 40-year U.S. Public Health Service study in which black men suffering from syphilis were monitored but not treated for the disease. Eunice Evers (Woodard) is a nurse at Alabama's Tuskegee Hospital in 1932, assisting Dr. Brodus (Morton) in the care of the afflicted men. White Dr. Douglas (Sheffer) first has a funded government program for treatment but when the program is cut, he's offered funding only for the study of syphilitic black men and establishing whether the disease affects blacks and whites differently. Brodus and Evers both lie to their patients as each comes to realize that treatment will never be re-established and only the deaths of their patients will provide the final information for the study. Based on the play by David Feldshuh. 120m/C VHS. Alfre Woodard, Laurence "Larry" Fishburne, Joe Morton, Craig Sheffer, Obba Babatunde, Ossie Davis, E.G. Marshall; *D:* Joseph Sargent; *W:* Walter Bernstein; *C:* Donald M. Morgan; *M:* Charles Bernstein. *HBO*

Miss Firecracker ✔✔✔ 1989 (PG) Hunter, longing for love and self-respect, decides to change her promiscuous image by entering the local beauty pageant in her conservative southern hometown. The somewhat drippy premise is transformed by a super script and cast into an engaging and upbeat film. Henley's script was adapted from her own Off-Broadway play where Hunter created the role. Actress Lahti, wife of director Schlamme, makes a brief appearance. 102m/C VHS, Beta, LV, Closed Caption. Holly Hunter, Scott Glenn, Mary Steenburgen, Tim Robbins, Alfre Woodard, Trey Wilson, Bert Remsen, Ann Wedgeworth, Christine Lahti, Amy Wright; *D:* Thomas Schlamme; *W:* Beth Henley; *C:* Arthur Albert; *M:* David Mansfield. *HBO*

Ms. 45 ✔✔✔ *Angel of Vengeance* 1981 (R) Rough, bristling cult favorite about a mute girl who, in response to being raped and beaten twice in one night, goes on a man-killing murder spree. Wild ending. 84m/C VHS, Beta, LV. Zoe Tamerlis, Steve Singer, Jack Thibeau, Peter Yellen, Darlene Stuto, Editta Sherman, Albert Sinkys, Jimmy Laine; *D:* Abel Ferrara. *ART, FCT*

Miss Grant Takes Richmond ✔✔ *Innocence is Bliss* 1949 Zipperhead secretary finds herself in hot water a la Lucy when she finds out the company she's been working for is really the front for a gambling getup. Only Lucy fans need apply. 87m/B VHS. Lucille Ball, William Holden, Janis Carter, James Gleason, Gloria Henry, Frank McHugh, George Cleveland, Arthur Space, William Wright, Jimmy Lloyd; *D:* Lloyd Bacon. *COL, FCT*

Miss Julie ✔✔ 1950 Melodramatic stew adapted from from the August Strindberg play about a confused noblewoman who disgraces herself when she allows a servant to seduce her. In Swedish with English subtitles. 90m/B VHS, Beta. *SW* Anita Bjork, Ulf Palme, Anders Henrikson; *D:* Alf Sjoberg. Cannes Film Festival '51: Best Film. *HMV, COL*

Miss Mary ✔✔½ 1986 (R) A compassionate English governess in Buenos Aires conflicts with the honor-obsessed family she works for and Argentina's tumultuous history. Christie gives a wonderful performance. *CW:* Some profanity and nudity. 100m/C VHS, Beta. *AR* Julie Christie, Donald McIntire, Sofia Viruboff, Luisina Brando; *D:* Maria-Luisa Bemberg; *W:* Jorge Goldenberg, Maria-Luisa Bemberg. *VTR*

Miss Melody Jones ✔ 1973 A beautiful young black woman's dreams of stardom unravel as she is forced to pander to prurient men by disrobing publicly for financial recompense. 86m/C VHS. Philomena Nowlin, Ronald Warren, Jacqueline Dalya, Peter Jacob; *D:* Bill Brame; *W:* Bill Brame. *XVC*

Miss Right ✔ 1981 (R) A young man determines to find the ideal woman for himself and casts aside his other romantic interests. Sputtering lightweight comedy. 98m/C VHS, LV. William Tepper, Karen Black, Virna Lisi, Margot Kidder, Marie-France Pisier; *D:* Paul Williams. *IME*

Miss Rose White ✔✔✔ 1992 (PG) Sedgwick is Rose, a modern young career woman in post-WWII New York, as American as apple pie, who lives two very separate lives. Born Rayzel Weiss, a Polish Jew, she immigrated to the U.S. with her father as a very young girl, before the holocaust devastated her remaining family in Poland. After the war her older sister, thought dead, comes to America. The haunted Luisa causes Rose to question whether she can ever leave her past behind. Above average Hallmark Hall of Fame presentation has a good cast, particularly Plummer as Luisa. Based on the play "A Shayna Maidel" by Barbara Lebow. 95m/C VHS, Closed Caption. Kyra Sedgwick, Amanda Plummer, Maximilian Schell, D.B. Sweeney, Penny Fuller, Milton Selzer, Maureen Stapleton; *D:* Joseph Sargent; *W:* Anna Sandor. *REP, BTV*

Miss Sadie Thompson ✔✔✔ 1953 Based on the novel "Rain" by W. Somerset Maugham. Promiscuous tart Hayworth arrives on a Pacific island occupied by a unit of Marines and a sanctimonious preacher played by Ferrer While Hayworth parties with the Marines and becomes involved with Ray's Sgt. O'Hara, Ferrer moralizes and insists her return to the mainland to face moral charges. Quasi-musical with a scattering of dubbed songs by Hayworth includes a memorable erotic dance scene complete with tight dress and dripping sweat. Hayworth's strong performance carries the picture with Ferrer and Ray turning in cardboard versions of their Maugham characters. Originally filmed in 3-D. 91m/C VHS, Beta, LV. Rita Hayworth, Jose Ferrer, Aldo Ray, Charles Bronson; *D:* Curtis Bernhardt. Nominations: Academy Awards '53: Best Song ("Sadie Thompson's Song (Blue Pacific Blues)"). *COL*

Missile to the Moon ✔½ 1959 First expedition to the moon encounters not acres of dead rock but a race of gorgeous women in lingerie and high heels. A bad but entertaining remake of "Cat Women of the Moon," featuring a bevy of beauty contest winners from New Hampshire to Yugoslavia. Who says truth is stranger than fiction. 78m/B VHS, Beta. Gary Clarke, Cathy Downs, K.T. Stevens, Laurie Mitchell, Michael Whalen, Nina Bara, Richard Travis, Tommy Cook, Marjorie Hellen; *D:* Richard Cunha. *RHI, SNC, CNM*

Missiles of October ✔✔✔ 1974 Telling the story of the October 1962 Cuban Missile crisis, this made-for-TV drama keeps you on the edge of your seat while unfolding the sequence of events within the U.S. government. Well written, with a strong cast including Devane, who turns in a convincing performance as—guess who—J.F.K. 155m/C VHS, Beta. William Devane, Ralph Bellamy, Martin Sheen, Howard da Silva; *D:* Anthony Page. *MPI, BFA*

Missing ✔✔✔½ 1982 (PG) At the height of a military coup in Chile (never named in the movie), a young American writer (Shea) disappears. His right-wing father Lemmon tries to get to the bottom of his disappearance while bickering with Shea's wife, played by Spacek, a bohemian who is the political opposite of her father-in-law. Outstanding performances by Spacek and Lemmon along with excellent writing and direction result in a gripping and thought-provoking thriller. Based on the book by Thomas Hauser from the true story of Charles Horman. 122m/C VHS, Beta, LV. Jack Lemmon, Sissy Spacek, John Shea, Melanie Mayron, David Clennon, Charles Cioffi, Joe Regalbuto, Richard Venture, Janice Rule; *D:* Constantin Costa-Gavras; *W:* Constantin Costa-Gavras, Donald Stewart; *M:* Vangelis. Academy Awards '82: Best Adapted Screenplay; British Academy Awards '82: Best Screenplay; Cannes Film Festival '82: Best Actor (Lemmon), Best Film; Writers Guild of America '82: Best Adapted Screenplay; Nominations: Academy Awards '82: Best Actor (Lemmon), Best Actress (Spacek), Best Picture. *USH*

The Missing Corpse ✔✔ 1945 When a newspaper publisher's worst rival is murdered, he fears that he will be implicated. He decides the only thing to do is hide the body to prevent its being discovered. Enjoyable, light comedy/mystery. 62m/B VHS. J. Edward Bromberg, Eric Sinclair, Frank Jenks, Isabelle Randolph, Paul Guilfoyle, John Shay, Lorell Sheldon; *D:* Al(bert) Herman. *NOS, MRV, SNC*

Missing in Action ✔½ 1984 (R) An army colonel returns to the Vietnam jungle to settle some old scores and rescue some POWs while on an MIA fact-finding mission. Box office smash. 101m/C VHS, Beta, LV. Chuck Norris, M. Emmet Walsh; *D:* Joseph Zito; *W:* James Bruner; *C:* Joao Fernandes. *MGM, TLF*

Missing in Action 2: The Beginning ✔ 1985 (R) Set in Vietnam, this prequel to the original "Missing in Action" provides some interesting background on Norris's rocky relationship with communism. Packed with violence, bloodshed and torture. 96m/C VHS, Beta, LV. Chuck Norris, Soon-Teck Oh, Cosie Costa, Steven Williams; *D:* Lance Hool; *W:* Steve Bing. *MGM*

Missing Link ✓✓½ 1988 (PG) A strange, meditative quasi-documentary depicting the singular adventures of a humanoid silently transversing the African wilderness and confronting various natural phenomena. Beautifully photographed. Make-up by Rick Baker. 92m/C VHS, Beta. Peter Elliott, Michael Gambon; D: David Hughes. USH

Missing Pieces ✓✓½ 1983 A woman takes a job as a private investigator in order to find her journalist husband's killer. Effective made-for-television mystery taken from the novel "A Private Investigation" by Karl Alexander. 96m/C VHS. Elizabeth Montgomery, Louanne, John C. Reilly, Ron Karabatsos, Robin Gammell, Julius W. Harris; D: Mike Hodges. ART

Missing Pieces ✓✓½ 1991 (PG) Goof-ups Wuhl and Idle find out about a potential inheritance thanks to a fortune cookie. Now if they can jut figure out what the riddle means. 93m/C VHS. Eric Idle, Robert Wuhl, Lauren Hutton; D: Leonard Stern; W: Leonard Stern. HBO

The Mission ✓✓✓ 1986 (PG) Sweeping, cinematically beautiful historical drama about an 18th-century Jesuit mission in the Brazilian jungle. The missionaries struggle against the legalized slave trade of Portugal and political factions within the church. Written by Bolt (of "A Man for All Seasons" fame), its visual intensity is marred by length and so much overt symbolism that an emotional coolness surfaces when the action slows. Nonetheless, epic in ambition and nearly in quality. Magnificent musical score. 125m/C VHS, Beta, LV, 8mm, Letterbox, Closed Caption. Robert De Niro, Jeremy Irons, Ray McAnally, Philip Bosco, Aidan Quinn, Liam Neeson, Cherie Lunghi, Rev. Daniel Berrigan, Ronald Pickup; D: Roland Joffe; W: Robert Bolt; C: Chris Menges; M: Ennio Morricone. Academy Awards '86: Best Cinematography; British Academy Awards '86: Best Supporting Actor (McAnally); Cannes Film Festival '86: Best Film; Golden Globe Awards '87: Best Screenplay, Best Score; Los Angeles Film Critics Association Awards '86: Best Cinematography; Nominations: Academy Awards '86: Best Art Direction/Set Decoration, Best Costume Design, Best Director (Joffe), Best Film Editing, Best Picture, Best Original Score. WAR

Mission Batangas ✓½ 1969 Unremarkable adventure-war-heist movie tells the story of a shallow American WWII pilot (Weaver) and a missionary nurse (Miles), who team up to steal the Philippine government's entire stock of gold bullion from the Japanese who captured it. Beautiful scenery, shot in the Philippines, adds something to an otherwise vacant effort. 100m/C VHS, Beta, LV. Dennis Weaver, Vera Miles, Keith Larsen; D: Keith Larsen. VTR

Mission Corbari ✓ 197? One heavily armed and ill-tempered hombre takes on the Nazis, with indifferent results. 88m/C VHS, Beta. NO

Mission Galactica: The Cylon Attack ✓✓ 1979 Spaceship Battlestar Galactica is stranded in space without fuel and open to attack from the chrome-plated Cylons. Adama (Greene) is forced to stop Commander Cain's (Bridges) efforts to launch an attack against the Cylons, while countering the attacks of the Cylon leader. Warmed over made-for-television sci-fi. 108m/C VHS, Beta, LV. Lorne Greene, Lloyd Bridges, Richard Hatch, Dirk Benedict. USH

Mission Impossible 1966 Six-volumes (containing two episodes each) follow the adventures of a team of highly specialized government agents known as the Impossible Missions Force, under the leadership of Jim Phelps (Graves), who took on top-secret assignments. The original TV series ran from 1966-73 and was briefly revived in 1988-90. The show's distinctively jazzy theme by Lalo Schifrin was a hit single in 1968. 102m/C VHS, Beta, Closed Caption. Peter Graves, Barbara Bain, Martin Landau, Greg Morris, Peter Lupus, Steven Hill, George Takei, Pernell Roberts, Martin Sheen, Lee Meriwether. PAR

Mission: Impossible ✓✓✓ 1996 (PG-13) Cruise and director DePalma did not completely succeed or fail in their mission to create a blockbuster hit based on the popular '60s TV series. Cruise (one of the film's producers) is Ethan Hunt, pointman extraordinaire of the IMF team headed by Jim Phelps (Jon Voight). Their team is sent to recover a computer disk with devastating information from a mercenary Russian spy. Smelling a double cross, Hunt confronts his conniving agency boss Kitteridge (the perfectly cast Czerny) and creates his own team of crack agents to get to the truth, mind-boggling plot twists and crazy train rides be damned. The plotline may have self-destructed two-thirds into the movie and the absence of a truly sinister villain causes some damage, but with solid acting talent, tight pacing, alluring European locales, and tension-inducing special effects, who has time to notice? $100 million gross in the first two weeks would seem to indicate a sequel is in order. CW: Some intense action violence. 110m/C VHS. Tom Cruise, Jon Voight, Emmanuelle Beart, Ving Rhames, Henry Czerny, Emilio Estevez, Vanessa Redgrave, Jean Reno; D: Brian DePalma; W: Robert Towne, David Koepp; C: Stephen Burum; M: Danny Elfman. Nominations: MTV Movie Awards '97: Best Action Sequence. PAR

Mission in Morocco ✓ 1959 When an oilman scouting for oil fields in the Sahara is killed, his partner, Barker, hops a jet to Morocco to find the whereabouts of a microfilm that gives the location of a valuable oil deposit. The search for the secret microfilm is complicated by competing parties also interested in the black gold. Ho-hum action adventure. 79m/C VHS. Lex Barker, Juli Reding. REP

Mission Manila ✓ 1987 (R) An ex-CIA operative and Manila-based drug addict is called by his ex-lover to return to Manila to help his brother, who has gotten in much the same trouble he had. 98m/C VHS, Beta, LV. Larry Wilcox. NO

Mission Mars ✓ 1967 American astronauts McGavin and Adams, on a mission to the red planet, discover the bodies of two cosmonauts floating in space. After landing on the planet's surface, they find a third cosmonaut, this one in a state of suspended animation. While putting the viewer to sleep, they proceed to revive the third cosmonaut and have at it with the sinister alien force responsible for all the trouble. 87m/C VHS, Beta. Darren McGavin, Nick Adams, George DeVries; D: Nicholas Webster. UNI

Mission: Monte Carlo ✓✓ 1975 An episode from the television series "The Persuaders," wherein our two vacationing adventurers discover a girl's drowned body and try to solve the case. 102m/C VHS, Beta. Roger Moore, Tony Curtis, Susan George, Annette Andre, Alfred Marks, Laurence Naismith; D: Basil Dearden, Roy Ward Baker. FOX

Mission of Justice ✓✓ 1992 (R) Revel in non-stop martial arts action with this tale of a cop who goes undercover to get the goods on a corrupt female politico, who also happens to run her own ruthless private army. CW: Language and strong martial arts violence. ?m/C VHS, LV, Closed Caption. Jeff Wincott, Brigitte Nielsen, Matthias Hues, Luca Bercovici, Cyndi Pass, Billy "Sly" Williams, Tony Burton; D: Steve Barnett; W: John Bryant. REP

Mission of the Shark ✓✓✓ 1991 A top secret naval mission leads to a scandal-ridden court martial in this true WWII saga, based on the worst sea disaster in naval history. The U.S.S. Indianapolis has just completed a secret mission when it is torpedoed by enemy subs. The survivors spend five days in shark-infested waters awaiting rescue and, when the Navy points fingers, the ship's highly decorated and well-respected Captain McVay accepts responsibility for the good of the service. Contains some harrowing scenes of sailors versus sharks. Made for television. 92m/C VHS. Stacy Keach, Richard Thomas, Steve Landesburg, Carrie Snodgrass, Bob Gunton, Andrew Prine, Stacy Keach Sr., Don Harvey; D: Robert Iscove. TRI

Mission Phantom ✓ 1979 A group of spies on a mission in Russia plans to steal some diamonds and help a woman get to the United States. 90m/C VHS, Beta. Andrew Ray, Ingrid Sholder, Peter Martell; D: James Reed. NO

Mission Stardust ✓½ 1968 4...3...2...1...Morte An internationally produced but thoroughly unambitious adaptation of the once-popular Perry Rhodan sci-fi serial, in which Rhodan and his team bring ill aliens back to Earth and defend them against evil spies. Dubbed. 90m/C VHS, Beta. GE IT SP Essy Persson, Gianni Rizzo, Lang Jeffries, Pinkas Braun; D: Primo Zeglio. RHI

Mission to Death 1966 An adventure extravaganza in which a group of friends must risk their very lives. 76m/C VHS. Jim Brewer, James E. McLarty, Jim Westerbrook, Robert Stolper, Dudley Hafner, Jerry Lasater. LBD

Mission to Glory ✓✓ 1980 (PG) The Father Kino Story This dozer tells the story of Father Francisco "Kino" Kin, a tough, 17th-century priest in California who took on the Apaches and murderous Conquistadors in defense of his people. 100m/C VHS, Beta. Richard Egan, John Ireland, Cesar Romero, Ricardo Montalban, Rory Calhoun, Michael Ansara, Keenan Wynn, Aldo Ray; D: Ken Kennedy. IGP

Mission to Kill ✓½ 1985 (R) An American demolitions expert, Ginty, joins a Latin American guerrilla force in battling tyrannical junta forces. This action-packed, fast-paced thriller is big on revenge and violence but not much else. 97m/C VHS, Beta. Robert Ginty, Olivia D'Abo, Cameron Mitchell; D: David Winters.

Mission to Venice ✓✓ 1963 Flynn plays a sleuth attempting to find a missing husband when he accidentally stumbles upon a ring of spies. ?m/C VHS. Sean Flynn, Madeleine Robinson. SNC

The Missionary ✓✓½ 1982 (R) A mild-mannered English missionary returns to London from his work in Africa and is recruited into saving the souls of a group of prostitutes. Aspiring to gentle comedy status, it's often formulaic and flat, with Palin and Smith fighting gamely to stay above script level. Still, good for some laughs, particularly during the near classic walking butler sequence. 86m/C VHS, Beta. GB Michael Palin, Maggie Smith, Trevor Howard, Denholm Elliott, Michael Hordern; D: Richard Loncraine; W: Michael Palin. PAR, TVC, FCT

Mississippi Burning ✓✓✓ 1988 (R) Hard-edged social drama centers around the civil rights movement in Mississippi in 1964. When three activists turn up missing, FBI agents Hackman and Dafoe are sent to head up the investigation. Unfortunately, this is another example of a "serious" film about racial conflict in which white characters predominate and blacks provide background. 127m/C VHS, Beta, LV, Closed Caption. Gene Hackman, Willem Dafoe, Frances McDormand, Brad Dourif, R. Lee Ermey, Gailard Sartain, Stephen Tobolowsky, Michael Rooker, Pruitt Taylor Vince, Badja Djola, Kevin Dunn, Frankie Faison, Tom Mason, Park Overall; D: Alan Parker; W: Chris Gerolmo; C: Peter Biziou; M: Trevor Jones. Academy Awards '88: Best Cinematography; Berlin International Film Festival '88: Best Actor (Hackman); National Board of Review Awards '88: Best Actor (Hackman), Best Director (Parker), Best Supporting Actress (McDormand); Nominations: Academy Awards '88: Best Actor (Hackman), Best Director (Parker), Best Film Editing, Best Picture, Best Sound, Best Supporting Actress (McDormand). ORI

Mississippi Masala ✓✓✓ 1992 (R) "Masala" is an Indian seasoning blending different-colored spices, as this film is a blend of romance, comedy, and social conscience. An interracial romance sets off a cultural collision and escalates racial tensions in a small Southern town when Mina, a sheltered young Indian woman, falls in love with Demetrius, an ambitious black man with his own carpet-cleaning business. Washington and Choudhury are engaging as the lovers with Seth, as Mina's unhappy father, especially watchable.*CW:* Language and sensuality. **118m/C VHS, LV, Closed Caption.** Denzel Washington, Sarita Choudhury, Roshan Seth, Sharmila Tagore, Charles S. Dutton, Joe Seneca; *Cameos:* Mira Nair; *D:* Mira Nair; *W:* Sooni Taraporevala; *M:* L. Subramaniam. COL, FCT

Mississippi Mermaid 🐾🐾🐾 **1969 (PG)** Truffaut generally succeeds in merging his own directorial style with Hitchcockian suspense, but this is not considered one of his best. Millionaire tobacco planter Belmondo looks for a bride in the personals and finds Deneuve. Belmondo feels lucky landing this beauty until she leaves him and takes his money with her. A lookalike, also played by Deneuve, takes over his wife's role and attempts to poison Belmondo. Look for numerous references to the movies, including Bogart, Balzac and Cocteau. Based on the Cornell Woolrich novel "Waltz into Darkness." In French with English subtitles. **110m/C VHS, LV, Letterbox.** FR IT Jean-Paul Belmondo, Catherine Deneuve, Michel Bouquet, Nelly Borgeaud, Marcel Berbert, Martine Ferriere; *D:* Francois Truffaut; *W:* Francois Truffaut; *M:* Antoine Duhamel. MGM, FCT

Missouri Breaks 🐾🐾 **1976 (PG)** Thomas McGuane wrote the screenplay for this offbeat tale of Montana ranchers and rustlers fighting over land and livestock in the 1880s. Promising combination of script, cast and director unfortunately yields rather disappointing results, though both Brando and Nicholson chew up scenery to their hearts' content. **126m/C VHS, Beta.** Jack Nicholson, Marlon Brando, Randy Quaid, Kathleen Lloyd, Frederic Forrest, Harry Dean Stanton; *D:* Arthur Penn; *W:* Thomas McGuane; *M:* John Williams. FOX

Missouri Traveler 🐾🐾🐾 **1958** An orphan boy struggles to get his own farm in Missouri. Family fare based on John Buress' novel. **103m/C VHS, Beta.** Lee Marvin, Gary Merrill, Brandon de Wilde, Paul Ford. MRV

Missourians 🐾🐾½ **1950** Small-town sheriff Hale helps a Polish rancher overcome ethnic prejudice among the townspeople. The situation worsens with the arrival in town of the rancher's outlaw brother. Strong direction and engaging storyline. **60m/B VHS, Beta.** Monte Hale, Paul Hurst. DVT

Mrs. 'Arris Goes to Paris 🐾🐾½ **1992** Ada Harris (Lansbury) is a widowed charwoman, living in '50s London, whose one dream is to visit Paris and buy a Christian Dior gown at the designer's own salon. Naturally, her dream comes true—and she even finds a little romance too. Adapted from the Paul Gallico novel; made for TV. **90m/C VHS.** Angela Lansbury, Omar Sharif, Diana Rigg, Lothaire Bluteau, Lila Kaye, John Savident. TVC, CCB

Mrs. Brown 🐾🐾🐾 **1997 (PG)** Unusual drama finds Queen Victoria (Dench), bereft by the death of Prince Albert, withdrawing from public life to her Scottish retreat at Balmoral. There she's looked after by coarse highlander John Brown (Connolly), who encourages her to take an interest in life. As he rises in the Queen's esteem, the brash commoner begins to become overly protective of her; leading to whispers of an affair. The powers-that-be, including the Prince of Wales (Westhead) and the oily Prime Minister Disraeli (Sher), then must persuade Brown to withdraw from her company in order to preserve her reputation. Merely hints at what may or may not have been a sexual relationship between the two, but isn't that the Victorian way? **103m/C VHS, LV, Closed Caption.** GB Judi Dench, Billy Connolly, Geoffrey Palmer, Anthony Sher, Richard Pasco, Gerard Butler, David Westhead; *D:* John Madden; *W:* Jeremy Brock; *C:* Richard Greatrex; *M:* Stephen Warbeck. British Academy Awards '97: Best Actress (Dench), Best Costume Design; Golden Globe Awards '98: Best Actress—Drama (Dench); Nominations: Academy Awards '97: Best Actress (Dench), Best Makeup; British Academy Awards '97: Best Actor (Connolly), Best Film, Best Original Screenplay; Screen Actors Guild Award '97: Best Actress (Dench), Best Supporting Actor (Connolly). TOU

Mrs. Brown, You've Got a Lovely Daughter 🐾½ **1968 (G)** The Herman's Hermits gang inherits a greyhound and attempts to make a racer out of him while singing their songs. For the Brit group's diehard fans only. 🎵It's Nice To Be Out in the Morning; Ooh, She's Done It Again; Lemon and Lime; The World is for the Young; Holiday Inn; The Most Beautiful Thing in My Life; Daisy Chain; Mrs. Brown, You've Got a Lovely Daughter; There's a King of Hush. **95m/C VHS, Beta.** Peter Noone, Stanley Holloway, Mona Washbourne; *D:* Saul Swimmer. MGM

Mrs. Dalloway 🐾🐾 **1997 (PG-13)** Mannered retelling of the Virginia Woolf novel has a radiant performance by Redgrave in the title role. Wealthy, middle-aged, and long-married to boring politician Richard (Standing), Clarissa Dalloway is making preparations for her latest soiree in 1923 London. But the past rudely intrudes when old flame Peter Walsh (Kitchen) suddenly re-enters, causing Clarissa to reflect on her youth and the choices she's made. She's also shaken out of her social ennui by the unexpected sight of a shell-shocked WWI veteran (Graves) whose tragic plight disturbs her placid life. Director Gorris' English-language debut. **97m/C VHS.** GB Vanessa Redgrave, Michael Kitchen, John Standing, Rupert Graves, Natascha McElhone, Alan Cox, Sarah Badel, Lena Headey, Robert Portal, Amelia Bullmore, Margaret Tyzack, Robert Hardy; *D:* Marleen Gorris; *W:* Eileen Atkins; *C:* Sue Gibson; *M:* Ilona Sekacz. NYR

Mrs. Doubtfire 🐾🐾½ **1993 (PG-13)** Williams is an unemployed voiceover actor going through a messy divorce. When his wife gets custody, the distraught father decides to dress up as a woman and become a nanny to his own children. He also has to deal with the old flame who re-enters his ex-wife's life. Williams schtick extraordinaire with more than a little sugary sentimentality. Based on the British children's book "Madame Doubtfire" by Anne Fine.*CW:* Sexual references. **120m/C VHS, LV, Closed Caption.** Robin Williams, Sally Field, Pierce Brosnan, Harvey Fierstein, Robert Prosky, Mara Wilson; *D:* Chris Columbus; *W:* Randi Mayem Singer, Leslie Dixon; *M:* Howard Shore. Academy Awards '93: Best Makeup; Golden Globe Awards '94: Best Actor—Musical/Comedy (Williams), Best Film—Musical/Comedy; MTV Movie Awards '94: Best Comedic Performance (Williams); Nominations: MTV Movie Awards '94: Best Male Performance (Williams). FOX

Mrs. Miniver 🐾🐾🐾🐾 **1942** A moving tale of a courageous, gentle middle-class British family and its struggle to survive during WWII. A classic that garnered six Academy Awards, it's recognized for contributions to the Allied effort. Contains one of the most powerful orations in the film history, delivered by Wilcoxon, who portrayed the vicar. Followed by "The Miniver Story." Adapted from Jan Struther's book. **134m/B VHS, Beta, LV.** Greer Garson, Walter Pidgeon, Teresa Wright, May Whitty, Richard Ney, Henry Travers, Reginald Owen, Henry Wilcoxon, Helmut Dantine, Aubrey Mather, Rhys Williams, Tom Conway, Peter Lawford; *D:* William Wyler; *W:* George Froeschel, James Hilton, Arthur Wimperis, Claudine West; *C:* Joseph Ruttenberg; *M:* Herbert Stothart. Academy Awards '42: Best Actress (Garson), Best Black and White Cinematography, Best Director (Wyler), Best Picture, Best Screenplay, Best Supporting Actress (Wright); Nominations: Academy Awards '42: Best Actor (Pidgeon), Best Film Editing, Best Sound, Best Supporting Actor (Travers), Best Supporting Actress (Whitty). MGM, BTV

Mrs. Munck 🐾🐾 **1995 (R)** Creepy cable thriller finds widowed Rose Munck (Ladd) agreeing to care for bitter father-in-law Patrick Leary (Dern, Ladd's real-life ex-hubby), who's suffered a debilitating stroke. But they share a nasty past—seems he seduced a teenaged Rose (played by Preston), she had a child, Patrick refused any responsibilty, and the child died. So whacked-out Rose is really out for revenge. Based on a novel by Ella Leffland. Ladd's debut as writer/director.*CW:* Strong sex scene. **99m/C VHS, Closed Caption.** Diane Ladd, Bruce Dern, Kelly Preston, Shelley

Winters; *D:* Diane Ladd; *W:* Diane Ladd; *C:* James Glennon; *M:* Leonard Rosenman. REP

Mrs. Parker and the Vicious Circle 🐾🐾½ *Mrs. Parker and the Round Table* **1994 (R)** Bio of witty, suicidal writer Dorothy Parker and her equally witty friends, including theatre critics, playwrights, and novelists, who lunched together at New York's Algonquin Hotel for most of the 1920s. An irreverant band known as the Algonquin Round Table, their numerous bon mots were regularly reported in the papers. Their private lives were often less than happy with alcohol, drug addiction and depression prominent factors. Parker's downward spiral is depressing though compelling to watch, thanks to Leigh's performance (in spite of much criticism for her lockjawed accent) but many of the characters come and go so quickly they make little impression. **124m/C VHS, LV, Closed Caption.** Jennifer Jason Leigh, Matthew Broderick, Andrew McCarthy, Campbell Scott, Jennifer Beals, Tom McGowan, Nick Cassavetes, Sam Robards, Rebecca Miller, Wallace Shawn, Martha Plimpton, Gwyneth Paltrow, Peter Gallagher, Lili Taylor; *D:* Alan Rudolph; *W:* Rudolph Coburn, Randy Sue Coburn; *C:* Jan Kiesser; *M:* Mark Isham. National Society of Film Critics Awards '94: Best Actress (Leigh); Nominations: Golden Globe Awards '95: Best Actress—Drama (Leigh); Independent Spirit Awards '95: Best Actor (Scott), Best Actress (Leigh), Best Director (Rudolph), Best Film, Best Screenplay. NLC, IME

Mrs. Parkington 🐾🐾½ **1944** Overblown epic drama spanning six decades tells the story of the rise and fall of an American dynasty made on easy money. Garson plays the woman who goes from working as a maid in a boarding house to living a life of luxury when she marries a multimillionaire. This was the fifth pairing of Garson and Pidgeon and although it's not one of their best, it proved to be a big hit with audiences. Lavish costumes and good performances by Garson and Moorehead. Based on the novel by Louis Bromfield. **124m/B VHS.** Greer Garson, Walter Pidgeon, Edward Arnold, Frances Rafferty, Agnes Moorehead, Selena Royle, Gladys Cooper, Lee Patrick; *D:* Tay Garnett; *W:* Robert Thoeren, Polly James; *C:* Joseph Ruttenberg. Golden Globe Awards '45: Best Supporting Actress (Moorehead); Nominations: Academy Awards '44: Best Actress (Garson), Best Supporting Actress (Moorehead). MGM

Mrs. R's Daughter 🐾🐾 **1979** An outraged mother fights the judicial systems in order to bring her daughter's rapist to trial. Based on a true story and made for television. **97m/C VHS, Beta.** Cloris Leachman, Season Hubley, Donald Moffat, John McIntire, Stephen Elliott, Ron Rifkin; *D:* Dan Curtis. WAR, OM

Mrs. Santa Claus 🐾🐾½ **1996 (G)** Who better than Lansbury to star as the title character in this sweet TV musical set in 1910. Vivacious Mrs. C is tired of being left home during Santa's (Durning) annual trip and decides to borrow the sleigh for a test drive just before the big day. But bad weather and an injured reindeer force an emergency landing in New York City where she befriends the young sweatshop workers at villainous toy-maker A.P. Tavish's (Mann) factory and does a little matchmaking too. But Mrs. Claus still must make it back to the North Pole by Christmas Eve. 🎵Avenue A; Almost Jolly; We Don't Go Together; Suffragette March; He Needs Me. **90m/C VHS, Closed Caption.** Angela Lansbury, Charles Durning, Terrence Mann, David Norona, Debra Wiseman, Rosalind Harris, Bryan Murray, Lynsey Bartilson, Michael Jeter; *D:* Terry Hughes; *W:* Mark Saltzman; *C:* Stephen M. Katz; *M:* Jerry Herman. HMK

Mrs. Silly 🐾 **1985** Romance novel on tape, following the exploits of an aging woman who in losing material wealth, gains contentment. **60m/C Beta.** Maggie Smith, James Villiers, Cyril Luckham.

Mrs. Soffel 🐾🐾½ **1984 (PG-13)** Falling in love with a convicted murderer and helping him flee confinement occupies the time of the prison warden's wife. Effectively captures the 1901 setting, yet a dark pall fairly strangles any emotion.

Based on a true story. **110m/C VHS, Beta, LV, Letterbox, Closed Caption.** Diane Keaton, Mel Gibson, Matthew Modine, Edward Herrmann, Trini Alvarado, Terry O'Quinn, Jennie Dundas, Danny Corkill, Maury Chaykin, Dana Wheeler-Nicholson; *D:* Gillian Armstrong; *W:* Ron Nyswaner; *C:* Russell Boyd; *M:* Mark Isham. *MGM*

Mrs. Wiggs of the Cabbage Patch ✗✗½ 1942

A warm, funny, and altogether overdone story of a mother whose husband abandons her, leaving the woman to raise their four children alone. It's Thanksgiving, so the rich visit the poor household to deliver a turkey dinner, and in the end all live happily ever after. Not one of Fields' larger roles; he doesn't even make an appearance until midway through the schmaltz. **80m/B VHS.** Pauline Lord, ZaSu Pitts, W.C. Fields, Evelyn Venable, Donald Meek, Barbara Britton; *D:* Norman Taurog. *GKK*

Mrs. Winterbourne ✗✗ 1996 (PG-13)

Pregnant loser Connie Doyle (Lake) is whisked into the lap of luxury when she's assumed to be the widowed Patricia Winterbourne after a train wreck. The grieving family (who had never met the bride) take her in and accept her and her baby as part of the household. Since her life is now going well, Connie decides to keep her true identity a secret while she falls for faux-brother-in-law Bill (Fraser). MacLaine is brilliant as the spirited matriarch of the family. Retooled as a comedy, the story is actually based on the noirish novel "I Married a Dead Man" by Cornell Woolrich and a remake of the equally dark "No Man of Her Own" from 1950. *CW:* Some thematic elements and brief strong language. **106m/C VHS, LV, Closed Caption.** Ricki Lake, Brendan Fraser, Shirley MacLaine, Miguel Sandoval, Loren Dean, Susan Haskell, Paula Prentiss; *D:* Richard Benjamin; *W:* Phoef Sutton, Lisa-Marie Rodano; *C:* Alex Nepomniaschy; *M:* Patrick Doyle. *COL*

Mistaken Identity ✗½ 1936

A swank hotel is the setting for this so-so comedy about three con men who wind up conning each other as much as their supposed victims. A couple of light romances are also thrown in for good measure. **75m/B VHS.** Chick Chandler, Evalyn Knapp, Berton Churchill, Patricia Farr, Richard Carle, Bradley Page, Lew Kelly; *D:* Phil Rosen. *VYY*

Mistaken Identity ✗½ 1941

All-black mystery set against the background of a nightclub, and featuring a production number, "I'm a Bangi from Ubangi." **60m/B VHS, Beta.** Nellie Hill, George Oliver. *VCN, DVT, RXM*

Mr. Ace ✗½ 1946

A congresswoman decides to run for governor without the approval of the loyal political kingpin, Mr. Ace. **85m/B VHS, Beta, LV.** George Raft, Sylvia Sidney, Sara Haden, Stanley Ridges; *D:* Edwin L. Marin. *COL*

Mr. & Mrs. Bridge ✗✗✗✗ 1990 (PG-13)

Set in the '30s and '40s in Kansas City, Ivory's adaptation of Evan S. Connell's novels painstakingly portrays an upper middle-class family struggling to survive within an emotional vacuum. Newman and Woodward, together for the first time in many years as Walter and Ivory Bridge, bring a wealth of experience and insight to their characterizations. Many consider this to be Newman's best, most subtle and nuanced performance. **127m/C VHS, LV, Closed Caption.** Joanne Woodward, Paul Newman, Kyra Sedgwick, Blythe Danner, Simon Callow, Diane Kagan, Robert Sean Leonard, Saundra McClain, Margaret Welsh, Austin Pendleton, Gale Garnett, Remak Ramsay; *D:* James Ivory; *W:* Ruth Prawer Jhabvala; *C:* Tony Pierce-Roberts. New York Film Critics Awards '90: Best Actress (Woodward), Best Screenplay; Nominations: Academy Awards '90: Best Actress (Woodward). *FCT*

Mr. & Mrs. Loving ✗✗✗ 1996 (PG-13)

Fact-based cable movie, set in the 1960s, follows the romance, marriage, and struggle of Richard Loving (Hutton) and Mildred "Bean" Jeter (Rochon). Growing up in rural Central Point, Virginia, their interracial relationship isn't considered uncommon. But when Bean gets pregnant, they aren't allowed to marry and live together because of Virginia's racial laws. Instead, the Lovings start

a life in Washington, DC, but desperately homesick and increasingly aware of the civil rights movement, Bean writes a letter to the Attorney General's office. What results is young ACLU lawyer Bernie Cohen (Parker) taking on their case—which eventually leads to a landmark Supreme Court decision about miscegenation laws. *CW:* Some sexuality. **95m/C VHS, LV.** Timothy Hutton, Lela Rochon, Corey Parker, Ruby Dee, Isaiah Washington, Bill Nunn, Charles Gray; *D:* Richard Friedenberg; *W:* Richard Friedenberg; *C:* Kenneth Macmillan; *M:* Branford Marsalis. *HMK*

Mr. & Mrs. Smith ✗✗✗½ 1941

Hitchcock's only screwball comedy, an underrated, endearing farce about a bickering but happy modern couple who discover their marriage isn't legitimate and go through courtship all over again. Vintage of its kind, with inspired performances and crackling dialogue. **95m/B VHS, Beta, LV.** Carole Lombard, Robert Montgomery, Gene Raymond, Jack Carson, Lucile Watson, Charles Halton; *D:* Alfred Hitchcock; *W:* Norman Krasna. *TTC*

Mr. Arkadin ✗✗✗ Confidential Report 1955

Screenwriter, director, star Welles, adapting from his own novel, gave this plot a dry run on radio during early 1950s. Welles examines the life of yet another ruthless millionaire, but this one can't seem to remember the sordid source of all that cash. Investigator Arden follows the intriguing and descending trail to a surprise ending. As in "Citizen Kane," oblique camera angles and layered dialogue prevail, but this time only serve to confuse the story. Shot over two years around Europe, required seven years of post production before finding distribution in 1962. **99m/B VHS, Beta, LV.** *GB* Orson Welles, Akim Tamiroff, Michael Redgrave, Patricia Medina, Mischa Auer; *D:* Orson Welles; *C:* Jean Bourgoin. *HMV, HTV, HEG*

Mr. Baseball ✗✗ 1992 (PG-13)

Washed-up American baseball player tries to revive his career by playing in Japan and experiences cultures clashing under the ballpark lights. Semi-charmer swings and misses often enough to warrant return to minors. Film drew controversy during production when Universal was bought by the Japanese Matsushita organization and claims of both Japan- and America-bashing were thrown about. *CW:* Language and sensuality. **109m/C VHS, Beta, LV, Letterbox, Closed Caption.** Tom Selleck, Ken Takakura, Toshi Shioya, Dennis Haysbert, Aya Takanashi; *D:* Fred Schepisi; *W:* Gary Ross, Kevin Wade, Monte Merrick; *C:* Ian Baker; *M:* Jerry Goldsmith. *USH*

Mr. Billion ✗✗ 1977 (PG)

Engaging chase adventure comedy about an Italian mechanic who stands to inherit a billion dollar fortune if he can travel from Italy to San Francisco in 20 days. Of course, things get in his way. Hill made his American debut in this film. **89m/C VHS, Beta, Closed Caption.** Jackie Gleason, Terence Hill, Valerie Perrine, Slim Pickens, Chill Wills; *D:* Jonathan Kaplan; *W:* Jonathan Kaplan, Ken Friedman; *M:* Dave Grusin. *FOX*

Mr. Bill's Real Life Adventures 1986

A made-for-television live-action adventure for the "Saturday Night Live" clay star, portrayed by Scolari, who is victimized as usual by his nemesis, Mr. Sluggo. **43m/C VHS, Beta.** Peter Scolari, Valerie Mahaffey, Lenore Kasdorf, Michael McManus; *D:* Jim Drake. *PAR*

Mr. Blandings Builds His Dream House ✗✗✗½ 1948

Classic comedy features Grant as an adman who tires of city life and moves his family to the country, where his troubles really begin. Grant is at his funniest. Loy and Douglas provide strong backup. A must for all homeowners. **93m/B VHS, Beta, LV.** Cary Grant, Myrna Loy, Melvyn Douglas, Lex Barker, Reginald Denny, Louise Beavers; *D:* H.C. Potter; *W:* Norman Panama. *TTC, MLB*

Mr. Boggs Steps Out ✗½ 1938

A pencil-pusher wins a bundle and invests it in a barrel factory. Trouble arises when a slickster tries to close it down. Even with the usual romantic entanglements, the film has trouble staying interest-

ing. **68m/B VHS.** Stuart Erwin, Helen Chandler, Toby Wing, Tully Marshall, Spencer Charters, Otis Harlan, Walter Byron, Milburn Stone; *D:* Gordon Wiles. *NOS, VYY*

Mr. Corbett's Ghost ✗✗ 1990

A young man, displeased with his boss's managerial finesse, cuts a deal with a soul collector who pink slips the guy to the great unemployment line in the sky. Once a boss always a boss, and the guy's ghost stops in to say boo, while the soul collector is hot to get his hands on his part of the bargain. Huston's final film appearance. Made for television. **60m/C VHS, Closed Caption.** John Huston, Paul Scofield, Burgess Meredith. *MON, KAR*

Mr. Deeds Goes to Town ✗✗✗½ 1936

Typical Capra fare offers Cooper as philanthropic fellow who inherits $20 million and promptly donates it to the needy. He also manages to find time to fall in love with a beautiful reporter. Arthur is the hard-edged reporter determined to fathom the good guy's motivation. Superior entertainment. Based on Clarence Budington Kelland's play "Opera Hut." **118m/B VHS, Beta, LV.** Gary Cooper, Jean Arthur, Raymond Walburn, Walter Catlett, Lionel Stander, George Bancroft, H.B. Warner, Ruth Donnelly, Douglass Dumbrille, Margaret Seddon, Margaret McWade; *D:* Frank Capra; *W:* Robert Riskin. Academy Awards '36: Best Director (Capra); New York Film Critics Awards '36: Best Film; Nominations: Academy Awards '36: Best Actor (Cooper), Best Picture, Best Screenplay, Best Sound. *COL, BTV*

Mr. Destiny ✗✗ 1990 (PG-13)

Mid-level businessman Belushi has a mid-life crisis of sorts when his car dies. Wandering into an empty bar, he encounters bartender Caine who serves cocktails and acts omniscient before taking him on the ten-cent tour of life as it would've been If he hadn't struck out in a high school baseball game. Less than wonderful rehash of "It's a Wonderful Life." **110m/C VHS, Beta, LV, Closed Caption.** James Belushi, Michael Caine, Linda Hamilton, Jon Lovitz, Bill McCutcheon, Hart Bochner, Rene Russo, Jay O. Sanders, Maury Chaykin, Pat Corley, Douglas Seale, Courteney Cox, Kathy Ireland; *D:* James Orr; *W:* James Orr, Jim Cruickshank. *TOU, FCT*

Mr. Emmanuel ✗✗½ 1944

An elderly Jewish widower leaves his English home in 1935 in quest of the mother of a German refugee boy, and is subjected to shocking treatment in Germany. **97m/B VHS, Beta.** Felix Aylmer, Greta Gynt, Walter Rilla, Jean Simmons. *BFA*

Mr. Frost ✗ 1989 (R)

Goldblum feigns fascination in this lackluster tale of the devil incarnate, who is imprisoned after owning up to a series of grisly murders, and who hides his true identity until approached by a woman psychiatrist. **92m/C VHS, Closed Caption.** Jeff Goldblum, Kathy Baker, Alan Bates, Roland Giraud, Jean-Pierre Cassel; *D:* Phillip Setbon; *W:* Phillip Setbon, Brad Lynch. *FCT, IME*

Mister Halpren & Mister Johnson ✗✗ 1983

Gleason attends the funeral of a longtime friend and one time flame (Olivier). Heavyweight cast wasted on flimsy script...and away we go! **57m/C VHS, Beta.** Laurence Olivier, Jackie Gleason; *D:* Alvin Rakoff. *NO*

Mr. Hobbs Takes a Vacation ✗✗✗ 1962

Good-natured comedy in which beleaguered parents try to resolve family squabbles while the entire brood is on a seaside vacation. Stewart and O'Hara are especially fine and funny as the well-meaning parents. **116m/C VHS, Beta, Closed Caption.** James Stewart, Maureen O'Hara, Fabian, John Saxon, Marie Wilson, John McGiver, Reginald Gardiner; *D:* Henry Koster; *M:* Henry Mancini. Berlin International Film Festival '62: Best Actor (Stewart). *FOX, HMV*

Mr. Holland's Opus ✗✗✗ 1995 (PG)

Well-done Disney tearjerker begins in 1965 as musician Glenn Holland (Dreyfuss) takes a teaching job to get himself off the wedding reception circuit and help support his wife, Iris (Headley), and their deaf son. Spanning three decades, with actual newsreel footage thrown in to highlight time passing, Holland sets aside his dream of composing a great symphony and finds his true calling—mentoring and inspiring young minds. Holland's son being deaf might have proved corny, but their rocky relationship is deeply rooted to the storyline. Dreyfuss turns in his most vibrant performance in years and, while sentimental buttons are definitely pushed, director Herek avoids falling into sappiness. **142m/C VHS, LV, Closed Caption.** Richard Dreyfuss, Glenne Headly, Jay Thomas, Olympia Dukakis, William H. Macy, Alicia Witt, Jean Louisa Kelly, Anthony Natale; **D:** Stephen Herek; **W:** Patrick Sheane Duncan; **C:** Oliver Wood; **M:** Michael Kamen. Nominations: Academy Awards '95: Best Actor (Dreyfuss); Golden Globe Awards '95: Best Actor—Drama (Dreyfuss), Best Screenplay. TOU

Mr. Horn 🐾🐾 1979 Based on the William Goldman western novel, this slow-paced film about folk-hero Scott Tom Horn capturing the famous Apache warrior, Geronimo, is average at best. **200m/C VHS.** David Carradine, Richard Widmark, Karen Black, Jeremy Slate, Enrique Lucero, Jack Starrett; **D:** Jack Starrett. ART

Mr. Hulot's Holiday 🐾🐾🐾½ Les Vacances de Monsieur Hulot; Monsieur Hulot's Holiday 1953 Superior slapstick details the misadventures of a dullard's seaside holiday. Inventive French comedian Tati at his best. Light-hearted and natural, with magical mime sequences. Followed by "Mon Oncle." **86m/B VHS, Beta, LV, 8mm.** FR Jacques Tati, Natalie Pascaud, Michelle Rolia; **D:** Jacques Tati. Nominations: Academy Awards '55: Best Story & Screenplay. NOS, MRV, VYY

Mr. Inside, Mr. Outside 🐾½ 1974 A television movie about two New York City cops, one undercover, one not, trying to infiltrate a tough diamond-smuggling ring. **74m/C VHS, Beta.** Tony LoBianco, Hal Linden; **D:** William A. Graham. THV

Mister Johnson 🐾🐾🐾 1991 (PG-13) In 1923 Africa, an educated black man working for the British magistrate constantly finds himself in trouble, thanks to backfiring schemes. This highly enjoyable film from the director of "Driving Miss Daisy" suffers only from the underdevelopment of the intriguing lead character. Based on the novel by Joyce Cary. **105m/C VHS, Closed Caption.** Pierce Brosnan, Edward Woodward, Maynard Eziashi, Beatie Edney, Denis Quilley, Nick Reding; **D:** Bruce Beresford; **W:** Bruce Beresford, William Boyd; **M:** Georges Delerue. VES, ART

Mr. Jones 🐾½ 1993 (R) Psychiatrist (Olin) falls in love with her manic-depressive patient (Gere). Head case Mr. Jones (Gere) is a charmer who gets a rush from tightrope walking a high beam on a construction site, yet is prone to bad moods when he fails to remember his own name. He can't resist flirting with the seductive Dr. Bowen, who eagerly leaps past professional boundaries while trying to coax him out of his illness. Wastes the talents of its stars with Gere showy, Olin brittle, and the whole story as contrived as their prefunctory love affair. Psychiatrists are getting as bad a rep professionally as lawyers in their recent film appearances. **CW:** Language. **110m/C VHS, LV, Letterbox, Closed Caption.** Richard Gere, Lena Olin, Anne Bancroft, Tom Irwin, Delroy Lindo, Bruce Altman, Lauren Tom; **D:** Mike Figgis; **W:** Michael Cristofer, Eric Roth; **M:** Maurice Jarre. COL

Mr. Kingstreet's War 🐾🐾½ Heroes Die Hard 1971 An idealistic game warden and his wife defend the wildlife of Africa against the fighting Italian and British armies at the dawn of WWII. **92m/C VHS, Beta.** John Saxon, Tippi Hedren, Rossano Brazzi, Brian O'Shaughnessy; **D:** Percival Rubens. VCI

Mr. Klein 🐾🐾🐾 1976 (PG) Cleverly plotted script and fine direction in this dark and intense film about French-Catholic art dealer Robert Klein (Delon), who buys valuables from Jews trying to escape Nazi occupied France in 1942, paying far less than what the treasures are worth. Ironically, he is mistaken for another Robert Klein, a Jew who's wanted for anti-Nazi activities. French with subtitles. **122m/C VHS.** FR Alain Delon, Jeanne Moreau, Suzanne Flon, Michel Lonsdale, Juliet Berto, Louis Seigner,

Francine Racette, Massimo Girotti; **D:** Joseph Losey; **W:** Franco Solinas; **C:** Gerry Fisher; **M:** Egisto Macchi. Cesar Awards '77: Best Film. FRF

Mr. Love 🐾🐾½ 1986 (PG-13) A meek gardener is perceived by neighbors as a fool until he dies and numerous women arrive for his funeral. Is it his cologne? The radishes? **91m/C VHS, Beta, Closed Caption.** GB Barry Jackson, Maurice Denham, Margaret Tyzack, Linda Marlowe; **D:** Roy Battersby; **M:** Willy Russell. WAR

Mr. Lucky 🐾🐾🐾 1943 Likeable wartime drama about a gambler who hopes to swindle a philanthropic organization, but then falls in love and determines to help the group in a fundraising effort. Grant is, no surprise, excellent as the seemingly cynical con artist who actually has a heart of gold. Cliched, but nonetheless worthwhile. Later developed into a television series. **99m/B VHS, Beta, LV, Closed Caption.** Cary Grant, Laraine Day, Charles Bickford, Gladys Cooper, Paul Stewart, Henry Stephenson, Florence Bates; **D:** H.C. Potter; **C:** George Barnes. RXM, TTC

Mr. Magoo 🐾 1997 (PG) Ah Magoo, we wish you wouldn't have done it again! Live-action version of the cartoon character popular in the 50's and 60's. Elderly myopic millionaire Quincy Magoo (Nielsen) unwittingly comes into possession of a stolen gem that he gives to his bulldog Angus as a toy. Bumbling government agents and evil arch-criminals are after the gem and Magoo, but he avoids them through luck and bad plot devices. Meanwhile, Magoo is mistaking a mummy's sarcophagus for a phone booth, a riverboat paddle wheel for an escalator and...well, you get the idea. Nielsen puts a "Naked Gun" spin on Magoo, and that routine is getting a bit stale. Although criticized by some blind groups as an inaccurate portrayal of the visually challenged, after a very brief run in the theaters, no one was able to see it. Opening and closing sequences include animated Magoo bits. **87m/C VHS, LV, Closed Caption.** Leslie Nielsen, Kelly Lynch, Matt Keeslar, Nicholas Chinlund, Ernie Hudson, Malcolm McDowell, Stephen Tobolowsky, Jennifer Garner, Miguel Ferrer; **D:** Stanley Tong; **W:** Pat Proft, Tom Sherohman; **C:** Jingle Ma; **M:** Michael Tavera. TOU

Mr. Majestyk 🐾🐾½ 1974 (PG) When a Vietnam veteran's attempt to start an honest business is thwarted by Mafia hitmen and the police, he goes after them with a vengeance. **103m/C VHS, Beta.** Charles Bronson, Al Lettieri, Linda Cristal, Lee Purcell; **D:** Richard Fleischer; **W:** Elmore Leonard; **M:** Charles Bernstein. MGM

Mister Mean 🐾 1977 A man who once worked for a mafia don is now given the task of rubbing him out. For Cosa Nostra diehards and gluttons for Roman scenery. **98m/C VHS, Beta.** IT Fred Williamson; **D:** Fred Williamson. NO

Mr. Mike's Mondo Video 🐾🐾 1979 (R) A bizarre, outrageous comedy special declared too wild for television conceived by the "Saturday Night Live" alumnus Mr. Mike. **75m/C VHS, Beta.** Michael O'Donoghue, Dan Aykroyd, Jane Curtin, Carrie Fisher, Teri Garr, Joan Haskett, Deborah Harry, Margot Kidder, Bill Murray, Laraine Newman, Gilda Radner, Julius LaRosa, Paul Shaffer, Sid Vicious; **W:** Mitch Glazer. NO

Mr. Mom 🐾🐾🐾 1983 (PG) A tireless auto exec loses his job and stays home with the kids while his wife becomes the breadwinner. He's forced to cope with the rigors of housework and child care, resorting to drugs, alcohol and soap operas. Keaton's hilarious as the homebound dad chased by killer appliances and poker buddy to the ladies in the neighborhood. **92m/C VHS, Beta, LV, Closed Caption.** Michael Keaton, Teri Garr, Christopher Lloyd, Martin Mull, Ann Jillian, Jeffrey Tambor, Edie McClurg, Valri Bromfield; **D:** Stan Dragoti; **W:** John Hughes. ART, VES

Mr. Moto's Last Warning 🐾🐾🐾 1939 One of the better in the series of Mr. Moto, the wily detective! Lorre is convincing in the title role and gets good support from character villains Carradine and Sanders in this story of saboteurs converging on the Suez Canal plotting to blow up the

French Fleet. **71m/B VHS, Beta.** Peter Lorre, George Sanders, Ricardo Cortez, John Carradine, Virginia Field, Robert Coote; **D:** Norman Foster. SNC, NOS, CAB

Mr. Moto's Last Warning/Meeting at Midnight 1944 The first film finds Moto at the Suez Canal trying to save France's flotilla from a deadly conspiracy. The second feature is classic Charlie Chan fare. This time his driver, Birmingham, gets Chan caught in the midst of the occult. **130m/B VHS, Beta.** Sidney Toler, Peter Lorre, Mantan Moreland. AOV

Mr. Music 🐾🐾½ 1950 Crosby is a successful songwriter who would rather enjoy life on the golf course than pen any more tunes. He's persuaded by his secretary to help out an old-time producer who's fallen on hard times by writing a new Broadway show. Light-hearted fluff. Based on the play "Accent on Youth" by Samson Raphaelson which had been filmed in 1935. 🎵Life is So Precious; Accidents Will Happen; High on the List; Wouldn't It Be Funny; Wasn't I There?; Mr. Music; Once More the Blue and White; Milady; Then You'll Be Home. **113m/B VHS, Closed Caption.** Bing Crosby, Nancy Olson, Charles Coburn, Robert Stack, Tom Ewell, Ruth Hussey, Charles Kemper, Donald Woods, Gower Champion, Marge Champion; **Cameos:** Groucho Marx, Peggy Lee; **D:** Richard Haydn. PAR

Mr. Nanny 🐾🐾 1993 (PG) For those who fear change, this predictable plot should serve as comforting assurance that Hollywood will still sacrifice substance for the quick buck. Basic story line has the child-hating Hulkster playing nanny/bodyguard to a couple of bratty kids. Meanwhile, his arch rival (Johansen) hatches a scheme to gain world dominance by kidnapping the kids for the ransom of their father's top secret computer chip. Never fear—in this world, the good guys kick butt, naturally, and everyone learns a lesson. **85m/C VHS, Closed Caption.** Hulk Hogan, Sherman Hemsley, Austin Pendleton, Robert Gorman, Madeline Zima, Mother Love, David Johansen; **D:** Michael Gottlieb; **W:** Ed Rugoff, Michael Gottlieb; **M:** David Johansen, Brian Koonin. COL

Mr. Nice Guy 🐾 1986 (PG-13) In the near future, a hired gun strives for national recognition as the best of his now legitimate profession. Comedy with few laughs. **92m/C VHS, Beta.** Michael Macdonald, Jan Smithers, Joe Silver. VTR

Mr. Nice Guy 🐾🐾½ 1998 (PG-13) Jackie Chan brings another installment of his Bruce Lee-meets-Charlie Chaplin action adventure shenanigans to the screen. This time he plays a TV cooking show host who gets into boiling water when he saves a female reporter (Fitzpatrick) who has videotaped a drug deal. He ends up with the videotape, so reptilian bad guy Giancarlo (Norton) sends his lackeys out to chop-suey Jackie, though they turn out to be boneless chickens. The high action/low talk meter is cranked up in this outing, due to the fact that it's Chan's first movie filmed primarily in English (although it was still produced in Hong Kong). The plot seems to have been chopped up a bit while travelling over the Pacific, but Chan fans are well aware that the whirling dervish stunts are more important than a silly old story anyway. **CW:** Pervasive action violence, some sensuality and drug content. **90m/C VHS.** Jackie Chan, Richard Norton, Gabrielle Fitzpatrick, Miki Lee, Karen McLymont, Vince Poletto, Barry Otto, Sammo Hung; **D:** Sammo Hung; **W:** Edward Tang, Fibe Ma; **C:** Raymond Lam; **M:** J. Peter Robinson. NLC

Mr. North 🐾🐾½ 1988 (PG) Capra-corn fable about a charming, bright Yale graduate who encounters admiration and disdain from upper-crust Rhode Island residents when news of his miraculous "cures" spreads. Marks the directorial debut of Danny Huston, son of John Huston, who co-wrote the script and served as executive producer before dying several weeks into shooting. Set in the 1920s and adapted from Thornton Wilder's "Theophilus North." **90m/C VHS, Beta, LV, Closed Caption.** Anthony Edwards, Robert Mitchum, Lauren Bacall, Harry Dean Stanton, Anjelica Huston, Mary Stuart Masterson, Virginia Madsen, Tammy Grimes, David Warner,

Hunter Carson, Christopher Durang, Mark Metcalf, Katharine Houghton, Christopher Lawford; **D:** Danny Huston; **W:** John Huston, Janet Roach, James Costigan; **M:** David McHugh. *NO*

Mr. Peabody & the Mermaid 🎜🎜½

1948 Lightweight fish story about a middle-aged married man who hooks a beautiful mermaid while fishing in the Caribbean and eventually falls in love with her. Powell is smooth as always, though hampered by the unrestrained absurdity of it all. Based on the novel by Guy and Constance Jones. Also available colorized. **89m/B VHS.** William Powell, Ann Blyth, Irene Hervey, Andrea King, Clinton Sundberg, Art Smith; **D:** Irving Pichel; **W:** Nunnally Johnson. *REP*

Mr. Peek-A-Boo 🎜🎜½ *Garou Garou le Passe Muraille* **1950** A French clerk discovers he has the ability to walk through walls. Although friends try to coax him into a life of crime, he instead comes to the aid of an English girl who is being blackmailed. Good-natured French comedy was shot with English dialogue for the American market. **74m/B VHS, Beta.** *FR* Joan Greenwood, Bourvil, Marcel Arnold, Roger Treville; **D:** Jean Boyer. *SNC*

Mr. Reeder in Room 13 🎜🎜 **1938**
Based on the mystery stories created by Edgar Wallace, Mr. Reeder (a cultured English gentleman who fights crime) enlists the aid of a young man to get evidence on a gang of counterfeiters. **66m/B VHS, Beta.** Gibb McLaughlin. *VYY*

Mr. Reliable: A True Story 🎜🎜 **1995**
(R) A "truth is stranger than fiction" comedy about Australia's first hostage situation. During the summer of 1968, recently released car thief Wally Mellish (Friels) rents a rundown cottage in a Sydney suburb. He finds a girlfriend in Beryl Muddle (McKenzie), who moves in with her two-year-old daughter. When Wally steals some trifles to brighten up the place, the cops come 'round and Wally, who's still on probation, pulls a gun. The authorities think Beryl and the baby are hostages and are afraid to storm the cottage while the standoff becomes hot media news. Wally and Beryl are thrilled with the attention but there's increasing political pressure to put an end to the farcical situation. **CW:** Language and a sex scene involving teenagers. **112m/C VHS.** *AU* Colin Friels, Jacqueline McKenzie, Paul Sonkkila, Frank Gallacher, Barry Otto, Lisa Hensley, Ken Radley, Neil Fitzpatrick; **D:** Nadia Tass; **W:** Terry Hayes, Don Catchlove; **C:** David Parker; **M:** Phil Judd. Nominations: Australian Film Institute '96: Best Film. *PGV*

Mister Roberts 🎜🎜🎜🎜 **1955** Crew of a
Navy cargo freighter in the South Pacific during WWII relieves the boredom of duty with a series of elaborate practical jokes, mostly at the expense of their long-suffering and slightly crazy captain, who then determines that he will get even. The ship's cargo officer, Mr. Roberts, longs to be transferred to a fighting vessel and see some action. Originally a hit Broadway play (based on the novel by Thomas Heggen) which also featured Fonda in the title role. Great performance from Lemmon as Ensign Pulver. Powell's last film. Sequelled in 1964 by "Ensign Pulver," and later a short-lived TV series as well as a live TV special. Newly transferred in 1988 from a pristine stereo print. **120m/C VHS, Beta.** Henry Fonda, James Cagney, Jack Lemmon, William Powell, Betsy Palmer, Ward Bond, Harry Carey Jr., Nick Adams, Phil Carey, Ken Curtis, Martin Milner, Jack Pennick, Perry Lopez, Patrick Wayne; **D:** John Ford, Mervyn LeRoy; **W:** Frank Nugent, Joshua Logan; **C:** Winton C. Hoch; **M:** Franz Waxman. Academy Awards '55: Best Supporting Actor (Lemmon); Nominations: Academy Awards '55: Best Picture, Best Sound. *WAR, BTV*

Mr. Robinson Crusoe 🎜🎜½ **1932** Rollicking adventure in the South Seas as Fairbanks makes a bet that he can live on a desert island for a year without being left any refinements of civilization. Lucky for him, a woman arrives. Also written by Fairbanks. **76m/B VHS, Beta, LV.** Douglas Fairbanks Sr., William Farnum, Maria Alba, Earle Brown; **D:** Edward Sutherland; **W:** Douglas Fairbanks Sr.; **M:** Alfred Newman. *NOS, GPV, CCB*

Mr. Saturday Night 🎜🎜½ **1992 (R)**
Crystal, in his directorial debut, stars as Buddy Young, Jr., a self-destructive comedian whose career spans five decades. His nasty one-liners and witty jokes combine with poignancy in this satisfying comedy/drama. Paymer is excellent as Young's long-suffering, faithful brother and manager. Watch for Lewis in a cameo role. Expectations were very high and the boxoffice results were disappointing, but fans of Crystal shouldn't miss this one. The video also includes additional footage and outtakes selected and hosted by Crystal. **CW:** Language. **118m/C VHS, LV, Closed Caption.** Billy Crystal, David Paymer, Julie Warner, Helen Hunt, Mary Mara, Jerry Orbach, Ron Silver, Sage Allen, Jackie Gayle, Carl Ballantine, Slappy (Melvin) White, Conrad Janis; **Cameos:** Jerry Lewis; **D:** Billy Crystal; **W:** Billy Crystal, Babaloo Mandel, Lowell Ganz; **M:** Marc Shaiman. Nominations: Academy Awards '92: Best Supporting Actor (Paymer). *COL, IME, MOV*

Mr. Scarface 🎜½ **1977 (R)** A young man searches for the man who murdered his father years earlier in a dark alley. **85m/C VHS, Beta.** Jack Palance, Edmund Purdom, Al Cliver, Harry Baer, Gisela Hahn; **D:** Fernando Di Leo. *CNG*

Mr. Skeffington 🎜🎜 **1944** A supergrade soap opera spanning 26 years in the life of a ravishing, spoiled New York socialite. The beauty with a fondness for bedrooms marries for convenience, abuses her husband, then enjoys a highly equitable divorce settlement. Years later when diphtheria leaves her totally deformed and no man will have her, she is saved by her former husband. Based on the novel by "Elizabeth" (Mary Annette Beauchamp Russell) and adapted by "Casablanca's" Julius and Philip Epstein. **147m/B VHS, Beta, LV.** Bette Davis, Claude Rains, Walter Abel, Richard Waring, George Coulouris, John Alexander; **D:** Vincent Sherman. Nominations: Academy Awards '44: Best Actress (Davis), Best Supporting Actor (Rains). *MGM*

Mr. Skitch 🎜🎜 **1933** Weak Rogers offering.
Couple loses their farm and begins cross country jaunt with mishaps at every turn. All ends well when their daughter meets an Army cadet, but few laughs and lots of loose ends. **70m/B VHS.** Will Rogers, ZaSu Pitts, Rochelle Hudson, Charles Starrett; **D:** James Cruze. *FOX, FCT*

Mr. Smith Goes to
Washington 🎜🎜🎜🎜 **1939** Another classic from Hollywood's golden year of 1939. Jimmy Stewart is an idealistic and naive young man selected to fill in for an ailing Senator. Upon his arrival in the Capitol, he is inundated by a multitude of corrupt politicians. He takes a stand for his beliefs and tries to denounce many of those he feels are unfit for their positions, meeting with opposition from all sides. Great cast is highlighted by Stewart in one of his most endearing performances. Quintessential Capra tale sharply adapted from Lewis Foster's story. Outstanding in every regard. **130m/B VHS, Beta, LV.** James Stewart, Jean Arthur, Edward Arnold, Claude Rains, Thomas Mitchell, Beulah Bondi, Eugene Pallette, Guy Kibbee, Harry Carey Sr., H.B. Warner, Porter Hall, Jack Carson, Charles Lane; **D:** Frank Capra; **W:** Sidney Buchman; **M:** Dimitri Tiomkin. Academy Awards '39: Best Story, National Film Registry '89;; New York Film Critics Awards '39: Best Actor (Stewart); Nominations: Academy Awards '39: Best Actor (Stewart), Best Director (Capra), Best Film Editing, Best Interior Decoration, Best Picture, Best Sound, Best Supporting Actor (Rains, Carey), Best Score. *COL, HMV*

Mr. Stitch 🎜 **1995 (R)** Demented scientist
(Hauer) plays Frankenstein and makes a creature, named Lazarus (Wheaton), from the body parts of more than 80 men and women. Unfortunately, the sensitive Lazarus has retained the collective memories of all these people and becomes obsessed with finding the reason for his existence. He receives compassion from a shrink (Peeples) but his maker has less-than-honorable plans for Lazarus. **CW:** Mature themes, violence, language. **98m/C VHS.** Rutger Hauer, Wil Wheaton, Nia Peeples, Taylor Negron, Ron Perlman, Michael Harris;

Cameos: Tom Savini, Dr Roger Roberts Avary; **W:** Roger Roberts Avary. *AVE*

Mr. Superinvisible 🎜🎜 *Mr. Invisible; L'Innafferrabile Invincible* **1973 (G)** Searching to cure the common cold, a bumbling scientist invents a bizarre virus, then strives with his loyal (of course) sheepdog to keep it from falling into the wrong hands. The Disney-like plot, featuring enemy agents and invisibility, may appeal to youngsters. **90m/C VHS, Beta.** *IT GE SP* Dean Jones, Ingeborg Schoener, Gastone Moschin; **D:** Anthony (Antonio Margheriti) Dawson. *NO*

Mr. Sycamore 🎜½ **1974** A sappy mail carrier escapes his badgering wife by sprouting into a tree. A potentially whimsical piece that wilts. **90m/C VHS, Beta.** Jason Robards Jr., Jean Simmons, Sandy Dennis; **D:** Pancho Kohner; **M:** Maurice Jarre. *WOV*

Mr. Walkie Talkie 🎜🎜 **1952** Tired of a sargeant's jabber-jaws, a soldier requests to be relocated to the front lines, only to find his catty comrade has followed. Set during the Korean War and featuring some truly amusing escapades set between the lulls in the war. **65m/B VHS, Beta, LV.** William Tracy, Joseph Sawyer; **D:** Fred Guiol. *NO*

Mr. Winkle Goes to War 🎜🎜 **1944** A weak, nerdy former banker is drafted for service during WWII and proves himself a hero by bulldozing a Japanese foxhole. Bits of genuine war footage add a measure of realism to an otherwise banal flag-waving comedy that is based on a novel by Theodore Pratt. **80m/B VHS, Beta.** Edward G. Robinson, Ruth Warrick, Richard Lane, Robert Armstrong; **D:** Alfred E. Green. *COL*

Mr. Wise Guy 🎜🎜 **1942** The East Side Kids break out of reform school to clear one of the Kids' brother of a murder charge. Typical pre-Bowery Boys vehicle. **70m/B VHS, Beta.** Leo Gorcey, Huntz Hall, Billy Gilbert, Guinn "Big Boy" Williams, Benny Rubin, Douglas Fowley, Ann Doran, Jack Mulhall, Warren Hymer, David Gorcey; **D:** William Nigh. *NOS, DVT, HEG*

Mr. Wonderful 🎜🎜½ **1993 (PG-13)** Bittersweet (rather than purely romantic) look at love and romance. Divorced Con Ed worker Gus (Dillon) is hard up for cash and tries to marry off ex-wife Lee (Sciorra) so he can use her alimony to invest in a bowling alley with his buddies. Routine flick's saved by the cast, who manage to bring a small measure of believability to a transparent plot. Minghella was a hit with his first film "Truly, Madly, Deeply" but may find that fame can be fleeting with this second effort. **99m/C VHS, Beta, LV, Letterbox, Closed Caption.** Matt Dillon, Annabella Sciorra, William Hurt, Mary-Louise Parker, Luis Guzman, Dan Hedaya, Vincent D'Onofrio; **D:** Anthony Minghella; **W:** Amy Schor, Vicki Polon; **M:** Michael Gore. *WAR*

Mr. Wong, Detective 🎜🎜 **1938** The first in the Mr. Wong series, the cunning detective traps a killer who feigns guilt to throw suspicion away from himself. The plot is loaded with the usual twists and villains. However, Karloff is a standout. **69m/B VHS, Beta.** Boris Karloff, Grant Withers; **D:** William Nigh. *NOS, MRV, HHT*

Mr. Wong in Chinatown 🎜½ **1939**
Third of the Mr. Wong series finds James Lee Wong investigating the murder of a wealthy Chinese woman. She had been helping to fund the purchase of airplanes to equip China in its 1930s' struggle with Japan. **70m/B VHS.** Boris Karloff, Grant Withers, William Royle, Marjorie Reynolds, Peter George Lynn, Lotus Long, Richard Loo; **D:** William Nigh. *VYY, MRV, SNC*

Mr. Write 🎜🎜 **1992 (PG-13)** Modest advertising satire mixed with romance. Aspiring writer Charlie (Reiser) decides to make some money by acting in commercials. He falls for ad exec Nicole (Tuck) but there are some complications to be overcome first, including her dim bulb boyfriend and obnoxious father. Adapted from the play by Howard J. Morris. **89m/C VHS, LV, Closed Caption.** Paul Reiser, Jessica Tuck, Doug Davidson, Martin Mull, Wendie Jo Sperber, Eddie Barth, Darryl M. Bell, Tom Wil-

son, Jane Leeves, Calvert Deforest, Ben Stein; *D:* Charles Loventhal; *W:* Howard J. Morris; *C:* Elliot Davis. *USH*

Mr. Wrong ♂♂ 1995 (PG-13) In her feature film debut, DeGeneres plays Martha, a 30-something single woman with wacky friends who's being pressured by parents toward marriage while having little luck in the dating scene. Hmm...sounds familiar. Pullman plays Whitman, her dreamboat who quickly turns into the Titanic. Along the relationship road to ruin she is forced to deal with bad poetry, charades and...gum in her hair!! The usually entertaining DeGeneres is given little to do but react lamely to the wild events going on around her. Those that have had an experience with "the ex that would not go away" might want to rent something more calming, such as "Psycho."*CW:* Crude language, some sex related scenes and drug content. 97m/C VHS, LV, **Closed Caption.** Ellen DeGeneres, Bill Pullman, Joan Cusack, Dean Stockwell, Joan Plowright, John Livingston, Robert Goulet, Ellen Cleghorne, Brad Henke, Polly Holliday, Briant Wells; *D:* Nick Castle; *W:* Chris Matheson, Kerry Ehrin, Craig Munson; *C:* John Schwartzman; *M:* Craig Safan. Nominations: Golden Raspberry Awards '96: Worst New Star (DeGeneres). *TOU*

Mistral's Daughter ♂♂½ 1984 Frothy miniseries, based on the Judith Krantz novel, about a French artist and his relationship with three beautiful women. Formulaic TV melodrama offers sexual scenes and revealing glimpses. Produced, like other Krantz miniseries, by author's hubby, Steve. 390m/C VHS, Beta. Stefanie Powers, Lee Remick, Stacy Keach, Robert Urich, Timothy Dalton; *D:* Douglas Hickox; *M:* Vladimir Cosma. *ART*

Mistress ♂♂♂ *Wild Geese* 1953 A classic Japanese period piece about an innocent woman who believes she's married to a ruthless industrialist, only to find he is already married and she is but his mistress. Her love for a medical student unleashes tragedy. Subtly moving in a low-key way; starkly beautiful in black and white. In Japanese, with English subtitles. 106m/B VHS, Beta. *JP* Hideko Takamine, Hiroshi Akutagawa; *D:* Shiro Toyoda. *NO*

Mistress ♂½ 1987 Weepy made-for-television melodrama about a woman who makes a living as a mistress. When her lover dies, she must learn to stand on her own two feet. 96m/C VHS. Victoria Principal, Alan Rachins, Don Murray; *D:* Michael Tuchner; *M:* Michael Convertino. *REP*

Mistress ♂♂ 1991 (R) A weak script does in a formidable cast in a behind-the-scenes look at movie making. Wuhl plays Marvin Landisman, a failed director/screenwriter, who's approached by has-been producer Jack Roth (Landau) who says he's found a backer to finance a movie from one of Marvin's old scripts. It turns out Roth has three men (De Niro, Aiello, and Wallach) ready to finance the film as long as each of their mistresses, who all have acting ambitions, gets the starring role. Double-dealing at a bargain basement level sets up the rest of this lifeless comedy.*CW:* Language. 100m/C VHS, LV, **Closed Caption.** Robert Wuhl, Martin Landau, Robert De Niro, Eli Wallach, Danny Aiello, Sheryl Lee Ralph, Jean Smart, Tuesday Weld, Jace Alexander, Laurie Metcalf; *Cameos:* Christopher Walken, Ernest Borgnine; *D:* Barry Primus; *W:* J.F. Lawton, Barry Primus. *ART, PMS*

Mistress of the Apes woof! 1979 (R) A woman searches for her missing husband in Africa with a group of scientists and discovers a tribe of near-men, who may be the missing link in evolution (or perhaps, a professional football team). Into their little group she is accepted, becoming their queen. Buchanan earned his reputation as a maker of horrible films honestly. Includes the songs "Mistress of the Apes" and "Ape Lady." 88m/C VHS, Beta. Jenny Neumann, Barbara Leigh, Garth Pillsbury, Walt Robin, Stuart Lancaster, Suzy Mandel; *D:* Larry Buchanan; *W:* Larry Buchanan. *MON*

Mistress of the World ♂♂ 1959 A scientist, aided by Swedish Intelligence agent Ventura, works to protect his gravity-altering invention from Chinese agents. Partly based on a German

serial from the silent film era, but not up to director Dieterle's usual fare. A must-see for Ventura fans and Mabuse mavens. 107m/C VHS, Beta. Martha Hyer, Micheline Presle, Gino Cervi, Lino Ventura, Sabu, Wolfgang Preiss; *D:* William Dieterle. *THV*

Mistress Pamela ♂½ 1974 (R) When young Pamela goes to work in the household of handsome Lord Devonish, he sets about in wild pursuit of her virginity. Loosely based on the 1740 work "Pamela" by Samuel Richardson, considered the first modern English novel. Read the book unless you only have 95 minutes to spend finding out who gets what. 95m/C VHS, Beta. Anne Michelle, Julian Barnes, Anna Quayle, Rosemary Dunham; *D:* Jim O'Connor. *NO*

Mistrial ♂♂ 1996 (R) NYC cop Steve Donohue (Pullman) is incensed when accused cop killer Eddie Rios (Seda) is acquitted and Donohue himself is about to be charged in the wrongful deaths of the suspect's wife and brother, which occurred during his pursuit. So he takes the entire courtroom hostage. Made for cable. 90m/C VHS. Bill Pullman, Robert Loggia, Jon Seda, Blair Underwood; *D:* Heywood Gould; *W:* Heywood Gould. *HBO*

Misty ♂♂½ 1961 Ladd and Smith are two kids who capture a wild pony and teach it to run around in circles and step over things. Based on Marguerite Henry's bestselling "Misty of Chincoteague," and filmed on an island off the coast of Virginia. 92m/C VHS, **Closed Caption.** David Ladd, Arthur O'Connell, Pam Smith; *D:* James B. Clark. *PAR, WAX, FCT*

Misunderstood ♂♂½ 1984 (PG) A former black market merchant has to learn how to relate to his sons after his wife dies. The father, now a legitimate businessman, is more concerned with running his shipping business than growing closer to his boys. Fine acting can't overcome a transparent plot. 92m/C VHS, Beta. Gene Hackman, Susan Anspach, Henry Thomas, Rip Torn, Huckleberry Fox; *D:* Jerry Schatzberg; *C:* Pasquale De Santis. *MGM*

Misunderstood 1987 A father learns his lonely son is full of love and sensitivity when a tragedy reveals that it is this son who takes the blame for all the wrongs his brother commits. 101m/C VHS, Beta. Anthony Quayle, Stefano Colagrande, Simone Gianozzi, John Sharp; *D:* Luigi Comencini. *IMP*

Mitchell ♂ 1975 (R) Tough cop battles drug traffic and insipid script. Big screen release with that certain TV look. 90m/C VHS. Joe Don Baker, Linda Evans, Martin Balsam, John Saxon, Merlin Olsen, Harold J. Stone; *D:* Andrew V. McLaglen. *VTR*

Mixed Blood ♂♂½ 1984 (R) From the renowned underground film-maker, a dark comedy that examines the seedy drug subculture in New York. Violent, fast, and funny. 98m/C VHS, Beta. Marilia Pera, Richard Vlacia, Linda Kerridge, Geraldine Smith, Angel David; *D:* Paul Morrissey; *W:* Paul Morrissey.

Mixed Nuts ♂ *Lifesavers* 1994 (PG-13) Misfits man a suicide hotline on Christmas Eve in this unfunny, pathetic comedy that's a real downer. Director/writer Ephron (along with her co-writer sister Delia) try way too hard to fashion a hip, racy, madcap farce reminiscent of the screwball comedies that Hollywood churned out in the 1930s and '40s. Film never finds its style and the story line is very weak. Most of the performances are over the top, although Martin, Shandling, and Kahn are good for a few amusing scenes. Ephron and the cast are capable of doing so much better, it's a shame their talents are virtually wasted here. Adapted from the French film "Le Pere Noel Est Une Ordure."*CW:* Sex-related humor, profanity, mature themes. 97m/C VHS, LV, **Closed Caption.** Steve Martin, Madeline Kahn, Robert Klein, Anthony LaPaglia, Juliette Lewis, Rob Reiner, Adam Sandler, Rita Wilson, Garry Shandling, Liev Schreiber; *D:* Nora Ephron; *W:* Nora Ephron, Delia Ephron; *M:* George Fenton. *COL*

M'Lady's Court ♂ 198? A lawyer searching for an heiress in a convent of lusty maidens has loads of fun. None too captivating. 92m/C VHS, Beta. Sonia Jeanine, Maja Hoppe.

Mo' Better Blues ♂♂½ 1990 (R) Not one of his more cohesive or compelling works, Lee's fourth feature is on the surface a backstage jazz biopic. But all Lee features are vitally concerned with complicated racial issues, and though subtle, this is no exception. Bleek Gilliam is a handsome, accomplished jazz trumpeter who divides his limited extra-curricular time between Clarke (newcomer Williams) and Indigo (junior Lee sibling Joie). What's interesting is not so much the story of self-interested musician and ladies' man Gilliam, but the subtle racial issues his life draws into focus. The Branford Marsalis Quartet provides the music for Bleek's group, scored by Lee's dad Bill (on whose life the script is loosely based).*CW:* Adult situations; language, nudity, violence, and sexual situations. 129m/C VHS, Beta, LV, **Closed Caption.** Denzel Washington, Spike Lee, Joie Lee, Wesley Snipes, Cynda Williams, Giancarlo Esposito, Robin Harris, Bill Nunn, John Turturro, Dick Anthony Williams, Ruben Blades, Nicholas Turturro, Samuel L. Jackson, Abbey Lincoln, Tracy C. Johns, Joe Seneca; *D:* Spike Lee; *W:* Spike Lee; *M:* Branford Marsalis, Bill Lee. *USH, FCT*

Mo' Money ♂♂½ 1992 (R) Damon Wayans is a small-time con-artist who is inspired to go straight by a beautiful woman (Dash). He lands a job at the credit card company she works for, but temptation overcomes him, he swipes some plastic, and the scamming begins anew. With the help of his younger brother (played by real-life younger brother Marlon), they get involved in an even bigger, more dangerous scam being operated by the credit card company's head of security. Crude formula comedy driven by energetic, inventive performances by the brothers Wayans. Needless to say, will be especially enjoyed by fans of TV's "In Living Color."*CW:* Language and violence. 97m/C VHS, Beta, LV, 8mm, **Letterbox.** Damon Wayans, Marlon Wayans, Stacey Dash, Joe Santos, John Diehl, Harry J. Lennix, Mark Beltzman, Quincy Wong, Larry Brandenburg, Almayvonne; *D:* Peter Macdonald; *W:* Damon Wayans; *C:* Don Burgess; *M:* Jay Gruska. *COL*

Moana, a Romance of the Golden Age ♂♂♂½ 1926 An early look through American eyes at the society of the people of Samoa, in the Pacific Islands. Picturesque successor to Flaherty's "Nanook of the North." 76m/B VHS. Ta'avale, Fa'amgase, Moana; *D:* Robert Flaherty. *GPV, FCT*

Mob Boss ♂ 1990 (R) Gangster films spoof starring Hickey as the head of a successful California crime ring. When his beautiful wife conspires to have him killed, he is left just breaths away from his demise. He calls his nerdy son to his bedside to ask him to take over the family business. But this kid thinks that money laundering requires detergent! Take this one down for a walk by the river in its new cement shoes. 93m/C VHS. Eddie Deezen, Morgan Fairchild, William Hickey, Stuart Whitman; *D:* Fred Olen Ray. *THV*

Mob Story ♂½ 1990 (R) Vernon stars as a big-wig mob boss on the run from the government and a few of his "closest" friends. He plans to disappear into Canada, but if his girl (Kidder) and best friend (Waxman) find him first he'll be traveling in a body-bag. Very silly, but fun. 98m/C VHS, Beta, LV. John Vernon, Margot Kidder, Al Waxman, Kate Vernon; *D:* Gabriel Markiw, Jancarlo Markiw. *IME*

Mob War ♂½ 1988 (R) A war breaks out between the head of New York's underworld and a media genius. After deciding to become partners, the "family" tries to take over. For fun, count how many times the word "respect" pops up in the script. Tries hard but fails. 96m/C VHS, Beta. John Christian, David Henry Keller, Jake La Motta, Johnny Stumper; *D:* J. Christian Ingvordsen. *MCG*

Mobsters ♂½ 1991 (R) It sounded like a great idea, casting the hottest young actors of the '90s as youthful racketeers "Lucky" Luciano, Meyer Lansky, Bugsy Siegel, and Frank Costello. But it would take an FBI probe to straighten out the blood-choked plot, as the pals' loyalties get tested the hard way in a dismembered narrative. Sicker than the violence is a seeming endorsement of the glamorous hoods. **CW:** Language and violence. **104m/C VHS, Beta, LV, Closed Caption.** Christian Slater, Patrick Dempsey, Richard Grieco, Costas Mandylor, Anthony Quinn, F. Murray Abraham, Lara Flynn Boyle, Michael Gambon, Christopher Penn; **D:** Michael Karbelnikoff; **W:** Nicholas Kazan; **C:** Lajos Koltai. *USH, CCB*

Moby Dick 🎬🎬🎬 **1956** This adaptation of Herman Melville's high seas saga features Peck as Captain Ahab. His obsession with desire for revenge upon the great white whale, Moby Dick, isn't always believable, but the moments that click, however, make the film more than worthwhile. **116m/C VHS, Beta, LV, Closed Caption.** Gregory Peck, Richard Basehart, Orson Welles, Leo Genn, Harry Andrews, Friedrich Ledebur; **D:** John Huston; **W:** Ray Bradbury, John Huston; **C:** Oswald Morris. National Board of Review Awards '56: Best Director (Huston); New York Film Critics Awards '56: Best Director (Huston). *MGM*

Moby Dick 🎬🎬½ **1998 (PG)** TV adaptation of Herman Melville's 1851 novel, starring a mesmerizing Stewart as the obsessive peg-legged Captain Ahab. Novice seaman Ishmael (Thomas) signs aboard the whaling ship Pequod, making friends with Polynesian native, harpooner Queequeg (Waretini). Soon enough Ishmael learns about the great whale who claimed the captain's leg and Ahab's determination to seek revenge on the beast, no matter what the cost to himself, his crew, or the ship. Peck, who starred as Ahab in the 1956 movie version, takes on the role of Jonah-and-the-whale sermonizing Father Mapple. **145m/C VHS, Closed Caption.** Patrick Stewart, Henry Thomas, Ted Levine, Piripi Waretini, Gregory Peck, Bill Hunter, Hugh Keays-Byrne, Norman D. Golden II, Bruce Spence; **D:** Franc Roddam; **W:** Franc Roddam, Anton Diether; **C:** David Connell; **M:** Christopher Gordon. *HMK*

Mockery 🎬🎬½ **1927** Chaney plays a peasant working for a Russian countess. He becomes involved in a peasant revolution against the rich and threatens the countess but eventually saves her from the mob. **75m/B VHS.** Lon Chaney Sr., Barbara Bedford, Ricardo Cortez, Emily Fitzroy; **D:** Benjamin Christianson. *FCT*

The Mod Squad **1968** The ultimate '60s series features a trio of young misfits who are recruited by a gruff police captain in Southern California. Their undercover assignments take them into the counter-culture. The series was created by former L.A. police officer Bud Ruskin, and was based on his own experiences. Two episodes per tape: "Teeth of the Barracuda" explains the formation of the Mod Squad, while "Mother of Sorrow" finds a generation gap leading to murder. Additional episodes are available. **60m/C VHS.** Michael Cole, Clarence Williams III, Peggy Lipton, Tige Andrews, Lee Grant, Richard Dreyfuss. *MOV*

Model Behavior 🎬½ **1982** Fresh from college, an aspiring photographer pines for a glamorous model. **86m/C VHS, Beta.** Richard Bekins, Bruce Lyons, Cindy Harrel; **D:** Bud Gardner. *ART*

Model by Day 🎬½ **1994 (R)** When New York model Janssen's father is murdered, she takes up martial arts training and becomes the vengeful "Lady X." Then she becomes the prime suspect in a murder and finds herself falling for a plainsclothes cop. Fair amount of action, somewhat less exploitive than usual for the genre. **89m/C VHS, Beta, LV, Closed Caption.** Famke Janssen, Stephen Shellan, Shannon Tweed, Sean Young; **D:** Christian Duguay.

A Modern Affair 🎬½ **Mr. 247 1994 (R)** Single executive Grace Rhodes' (Eichorn) biological clock is ringing and without Mr. Right in sight, she decides to visit a sperm bank. Grace gets pregnant and also very curious about her anonymous donor—who of course doesn't stay anonymous. Grace even manages to fall for photographer Peter Kessler (Tucci) but how does she tell him she's carrying his baby when they haven't even had sex yet? **CW:** Language. **91m/C VHS, Closed Caption.** Lisa Eichhorn, Stanley Tucci, Caroline Aaron,

Tammy Grimes, Robert Joy, Wesley Addy, Cynthia Martells, Mary Jo Salerno; **D:** Vern Oakley; **W:** Paul Zimmerman; **C:** Rex Nicholson; **M:** Jan Hammer. *COL*

Modern Girls 🎬½ **1986 (PG-13)** Teen comedy about three bubble-headed LA rock groupies and their various wild adventures during a single night on the town. Interesting in that the three lead actresses waste their talents in this lesson in exploitation. Bruce Springsteen's younger sister portrays a drug user. **82m/C VHS, Beta, LV.** Cynthia Gibb, Daphne Zuniga, Virginia Madsen; **D:** Jerry Kramer; **W:** Laurie Craig; **M:** Eddie Arkin. *PAR*

Modern Love 🎬 **1990 (R)** An average slob realizes that marriage, fatherhood and in-law-ship isn't quite what he expected. Benson stars, directs and produces as well as co-starring with real-life wife DeVito. A plotless hodgepodge of bits that were more successful in "Look Who's Talking" and "Parenthood." **89m/C VHS, Beta, Closed Caption.** Robby Benson, Karla DeVito, Rue McClanahan, Kaye Ballard, Frankie Valli, Cliff Bemis, Louise Lasser, Burt Reynolds, Lyric Benson; **D:** Robby Benson; **W:** Robby Benson. *NO*

Modern Problems 🎬🎬 **1981 (PG)** A man involved in a nuclear accident discovers he has acquired telekinetic powers, which he uses to turn the tables on his professional and romantic rivals. A fine cast but an unsuccessful fission trip. **93m/C VHS, Beta.** Chevy Chase, Patti D'Arbanville, Mary Kay Place, Brian Doyle-Murray, Nell Carter, Dabney Coleman; **D:** Ken Shapiro. *FOX*

Modern Romance 🎬🎬🎬 **1981 (R)** The romantic misadventures of a neurotic film editor who is hopelessly in love with his girlfriend but can't seem to maintain a normal relationship with her. Smart and hilarious at times and always simmering with anxiety. Offers an honest look at relationships as well as an accurate portrait of filmmaking. **102m/C VHS, Beta, LV.** Albert Brooks, Kathryn Harrold, Bruno Kirby, George Kennedy, James L. Brooks, Bob Einstein; **D:** Albert Brooks; **W:** Albert Brooks, Monica Johnson. *COL*

Modern Times 🎬🎬🎬🎬 **1936** This "mostly" silent film finds Chaplin playing a factory worker who goes crazy from his repetitious job on an assembly line and his boss' demands for greater speed and efficiency. Ultimately encompassing the tyranny of machine over man, this cinematic masterpiece has more relevance today than ever. Chaplin wrote the musical score which incorporates the tune "Smile." Look for a young Gloria De Haven as one of Goddard's sisters; she's the real-life daughter of Chaplin's assistant director. **87m/B VHS, Beta, LV.** Charlie Chaplin, Paulette Goddard, Henry Bergman, Stanley Sandford, Gloria De Haven, Chester Conklin; **D:** Charlie Chaplin; **W:** Charlie Chaplin. National Film Registry '89. *FOX, HMV*

The Moderns 🎬🎬🎬 **1988 (R)** One of the quirkier directors around, this time Rudolph tries a comedic period piece about the avant-garde art society of 1920s Paris. Fleshed out with some familiar characters (Ernest Hemingway, Gertrude Stein) and some strange art-world types. The tone is not consistently funny but, instead, romantic as the main characters clash over art and love. **126m/C VHS, Beta, LV, 8mm.** Keith Carradine, Linda Fiorentino, John Lone, Genevieve Bujold, Geraldine Chaplin, Wallace Shawn, Kevin J. O'Connor; **D:** Alan Rudolph; **W:** Alan Rudolph; **M:** Mark Isham. Los Angeles Film Critics Association Awards '88: Best Supporting Actress (Bujold). *NLC*

Modigliani 🎬🎬½ *Montparnasse 19; The Lovers of Montparnasse; Modigliani of Montparnasse* **1958** Life of dissolute 19th-century painter Modigliani (Philipe), which tracks his affairs with British poet Beatrice Hastings (Palmer) and later mistress Jeanne (Aimee), who commits suicide shortly before his death. Female performances make up for the lackluster lead. Becker inherited the film from director Max Ophuls, who co-wrote the screenplay but who died before the start of production. In French with English subtitles. **110m/B VHS.** *FR* Gerard Philipe, Lilli Palmer, Anouk Aimee, Gerard Sety, Lino

Ventura, Lila Kedrova, Lea Padovani; **D:** Jacques Becker; **W:** Max Ophuls, Henri Jeanson, Jacques Becker. *FCT*

Mogambo 🎬🎬🎬 **1953** Remake of "Red Dust," this is the steamy story of a love triangle between an African game hunter, a proper British lady, and an American showgirl in the jungles of Kenya. **115m/C VHS, Beta.** Clark Gable, Ava Gardner, Grace Kelly; **D:** John Ford; **C:** Robert L. Surtees. Golden Globe Awards '54: Best Supporting Actress (Kelly); Nominations: Academy Awards '53: Best Actress (Gardner), Best Supporting Actress (Kelly). *MGM, FCT, CCB*

Mohammed: Messenger of God 🎬🎬 *The Message; Al-Ris-Alah* **1977 (PG)** Sprawling saga of the genesis of the religion of Islam, with Quinn portraying Mohammad's uncle, Hamza, an honored warrior. The story behind the movie might prove much more successful as a sequel than did the movie itself. The filming itself created a religious controversy. **180m/C VHS.** *GB* Damien Thomas, Anthony Quinn, Irene Papas, Michael Ansara, Johnny Sekka, Michael Forest, Neville Jason; **D:** Moustapha Akkad; **C:** Jack Hildyard; **M:** Maurice Jarre. Nominations: Academy Awards '77: Best Original Score. *NO*

Mohawk 🎬½ **1956** A cowboy and his Indian maiden try to stop a war between Indian tribes and fanatical landowners. **80m/C VHS, Beta.** Rita Gam, Neville Brand, Scott Brady, Lori Nelson; **D:** Kurt Neumann; **C:** Karl Struss. *NOS, MRV, GEM*

Mojave Moon 🎬🎬½ **1996 (R)** Middle-aged car dealer Al (Aiello) is asked by nymphet Ellie (Jolie) to drive her home—a trailer in the desert where Al meets her perky-yet-kinky mom Julie (Archer) and Julie's violent boyfriend Boyd (Biehn). A series of strange happenings finds Al tied to the trio and discovering both adventure and romance. **CW:** Language and some nudity. **95m/C VHS.** Danny Aiello, Anne Archer, Angelina Jolie, Michael Biehn, Alfred Molina; **D:** Kevin Dowling; **W:** Leonard Glasser; **C:** James Glennon. *THV*

Mole Men against the Son of Hercules 🎬 **1961** Italian muscleman Maciste battles the pale-skinned denizens of an underground city. **?m/C VHS, Beta.** *IT* Mark Forest. *SNC*

The Mole People 🎬 **1956** A really bad '50s creature feature which finds two archeologists accidentally discovering an underground civilization of albinos who shun all forms of light. They've also enslaved the local populace of half-human, half-mole creatures who decide to help the good guys escape by rising up in a revolt against their evil masters. When the weapon of choice is a flashlight you know not to expect much. **78m/B VHS, Closed Caption.** John Agar, Cynthia Patrick, Hugh Beaumont, Alan Napier, Nestor Paiva, Phil Chambers; **D:** Virgil W. Vogel; **W:** Laszlo Gorog. *USH*

Moll Flanders 🎬🎬½ **1996** Rousing, bawdy retelling of Daniel Defoe's 1722 novel about the wickedly seductive Moll (Kingston). Born in London's Newgate prison, Moll becomes a house servant, embarks on her first marriage, is soon widowed, and decides to make her own way (and fortune). She becomes a thief, a whore, marries several more times, and eventually winds up back in prison and a likely candidate for the gallows. But the ever-enterprising Moll always finds her way. TV miniseries on two cassettes. **210m/C VHS, Closed Caption.** *GB* Alex Kingston, Daniel Craig, Diana Rigg, Colin Buchanan, Christopher Fulford, James Fleet, Ian Driver, Tom Ward; **D:** David Attwood; **W:** Andrew Davies; **C:** Ivan Strasburg. *VTR, PBS, VIF*

Moll Flanders 🎬🎬½ **1996 (PG-13)** Writer/director Densham takes only the title character and the 18th-century London setting from Daniel Defoe's 1722 novel in telling of spirited heroine Moll Flanders' (Wright) life. Orphaned Moll eventually finds herself working at the brothel of greedy, scheming Mrs. Allworthy (Channing). Her life as a prostitute leads her to drink and near suicide—despite the unwavering friendship of Hibble (Freeman), Allworthy's dignified servant—until she falls for an impoverished artist (Lynch) and briefly finds happiness. Wright's heartfelt performance holds everything together (with help from a talented supporting cast) but things get dreary.**CW:** Violence, nudity and sex-related material. **120m/C VHS, LV, Closed Caption.** Robin Wright Penn, Morgan Freeman, Stockard Channing, John Lynch, Brenda Fricker, Aisling Corcoran, Geraldine James, Jim Sheridan, Jeremy Brett, Britta Smith, Ger Ryan; **D:** Pen Densham; **W:** Pen Densham; **C:** David Tattersall; **M:** Mark Mancina. *MGM*

Molly and Gina 🐾🐾 **1994 (R)** The very different lives of Molly and Gina intersect suddenly when their boyfriends are killed in the street by gunfire. They are drawn into the underworld of gun-runners and violence, as they seek justice for the men they loved.**CW:** Language, violence, and sexuality. **90m/C VHS.** Frances Fisher, Natasha Gregson Wagner, Bruce Weitz, Stella Stevens, Peter Fonda; **D:** Paul Leder; **W:** Reuben Leder; **M:** Dana Walden. *APX*

Molly & Lawless John 🐾🐾 **1972** Average western, with Miles the wife of a sadistic sheriff who helps a prisoner escape the gallows so they can run away together. Enough cliches for the whole family to enjoy. **90m/C VHS, Beta.** Sam Elliott, Vera Miles; **D:** Gary Nelson. *NO*

Molly Maguires 🐾🐾½ **1970 (PG)** Dramatization based on a true story, concerns a group of miners called the Molly Maguires who resort to using terrorist tactics in their fight for better working conditions during the Pennsylvania Irish coal mining rebellion in the 1870s. During their reign of terror, the Mollies are infiltrated by a Pinkerton detective who they mistakenly believe is a new recruit. It has its moments but never fully succeeds. Returned less than 15 percent of its initial 11 million dollar investment. **123m/C VHS, Beta.** Sean Connery, Richard Harris, Samantha Eggar, Frank Finlay; **D:** Martin Ritt; **W:** Walter Bernstein; **C:** James Wong Howe; **M:** Henry Mancini. Nominations: Academy Awards '70: Best Art Direction/Set Decoration. *PAR, CCB*

The Mollycoddle 🐾🐾 **1920** Fairbanks is a British-educated American whom everyone thinks is less-than-manly until he brings a smuggler to justice. **?m/B VHS.** Douglas Fairbanks Sr., Wallace Beery, Ruth Renick; **D:** Victor Fleming; **W:** Douglas Fairbanks Sr. *KIV*

Mom woof! **1989 (R)** When his mother is bitten by a flesh-eater, Clay Dwyer is at a loss as to what to do. How do you tell your own mother that she must be destroyed, lest she continue to devour human flesh? A campy horror/comedy. **95m/C VHS, LV, Closed Caption.** Mark Thomas Miller, Art Evans, Mary McDonough, Jeanne Bates, Brion James, Stella Stevens, Claudia Christian; **D:** Patrick Rand. *COL*

Mom & Dad 🐾🐾 **1947** An innocent young girl's one night of passion leads to an unwanted pregnancy. Stock footage of childbirth and a lecture on the evils of syphilis concludes this campy schlock that features the national anthem. Banned or denied release for years, this movie is now a cult favorite for its time-capsule glimpse at conventional 1940s sexual attitudes. **97m/B VHS, Beta.** Hardie Albright, Sarah Blake, George Eldridge, June Carlson, Jimmy Clark, Bob Lowell; **D:** William Beaudine. *VDM*

Mom and Dad Save the World 🐾½ **1992 (PG)** A suburban housewife (Garr) is transported along with her husband in the family station wagon to the planet Spengo, ruled by King Tod Spengo (Lovitz), who has fallen in love with her and wants to save her from his plans to blow up Earth. While trying to prevent the king from marrying her and killing him, Garr and Jones wind up in many goofy situations and wind up saving the Earth from its imminent doom. Uninspired comedy just isn't funny, and the excellent cast is misused, especially Idle and Shawn. Save this one for the kiddies. **87m/C VHS, LV, Closed Caption.** Teri Garr, Jeffrey Jones, Jon Lovitz, Eric Idle, Wallace Shawn, Dwier Brown, Kathy Ireland, Thalmus Rasulala; **D:** Greg Beeman; **M:** Jerry Goldsmith. *HBO*

Mom, the Wolfman and Me 🐾🐾½ **1980** An 11-year-old girl arranges and manages the love affair of her mother, an ultra-liberated photographer, and an unemployed teacher, who is also the owner of an Irish wolfhound. Charming adaptation of a novel by Norma Klein. **100m/C VHS, Beta.** Patty Duke, David Birney, Danielle Brisebois, Keenan Wynn, Viveca Lindfors, John Lithgow; **D:** Edmond Levy. *TLF*

Moment in Time 🐾 **1984** A romantic novel on tape, about a guy, a girl, and their various troubles. **60m/C Beta.** Jean Simmons.

Mommie Dearest 🐾🐾 **1981 (PG)** Film based on Christina Crawford's memoirs of her incredibly abusive and violent childhood at the hands of her adoptive mother, actress Joan Crawford. The story is controversial and sometimes trashy, but fairly well done nevertheless. **129m/C VHS, Beta, LV.** Faye Dunaway, Diana Scarwid, Steve Forrest, Mara Hobel, Rutanya Alda, Harry Goz, Howard da Silva; **D:** Frank Perry; **W:** Robert Getchell; **M:** Henry Mancini. Golden Raspberry Awards '81: Worst Picture, Worst Actress (Dunaway), Worst Supporting Actor (Forrest), Worst Supporting Actress (Scarwid), Worst Screenplay. *PAR*

Mommy 🐾🐾½ **1995** Schoolteacher is stalked by murderous mom who'll do anything for her daughter. Mommy McCormack was the original "Bad Seed" child. Filmed in Muscatine, Iowa. **89m/C VHS.** Patty McCormack, Majel Barrett, Jason Miller, Brinke Stevens, Rachel Lemieux, Mickey Spillane, Michael Cornelison, Sarah Jane Miller; **D:** Max Allan Collins; **W:** Max Allan Collins; **C:** Phillip W. Dingeldein; **M:** Richard Lowry. *MNC*

Mommy 2: Mommy's Day 🐾🐾½ **1990** Murderous Mommy (McCormack) returns as does her beloved daughter (now rebellious teenager), Jessica Ann (Lemieux). Mommy's on Death Row, awaiting execution after her murder spree but the Mommy-style killings continue. Shot on location in Iowa. **89m/C VHS.** Patty McCormack, Rachel Lemieux, Brinke Stevens, Michael Cornelison, Sarah Jane Miller, Mickey Spillane, Gary Sandy, Paul Petersen, Arlen Dean Snyder, Todd Eastland, Del Close; **D:** Max Allan Collins; **W:** Max Allan Collins; **C:** Phillip W. Dingeldein; **M:** Richard Lowry. *EAG*

Mon Amie Max 🐾🐾 **1994** Marie-Alexandrine (Max) Babant (Bujold) is a middle-aged former pianist who returns to her native Quebec City after 25 years of self-imposed exile. Pregnant at 15, Max was forced to give her son up for adoption and ran away from friends and family. Now, she's meet former best friend Catherine (Keller), who's had the concert career Max never did, who's also agreed to help Max find her son. Slow-going melodrama with little emotional impact. **107m/C VHS.** *CA FR* Genevieve Bujold, Marthe Keller, Michel Rivard, Johanne McKay; **D:** Michel Brault; **W:** Jefferson Lewis. Nominations: Genie Awards '94: Best Actress (Bujold), Best Film. *NYR*

Mon Homme 🐾🐾 **My Man 1996** Marie's (Grinberg) a very happy hooker (think male fantasy) whose kindly impulses wind up getting her into difficulty. She picks up the homeless Jeannot (Lanvin), invites him in for a meal, offers him sex, and is enthralled by his unexpected prowess. Marie decides Jeannot should become her pimp but, unfortunately for her, he takes to his new job with great zeal, seducing manicurist Sanguine (Bruni-Tedeschi) as another lover/prostitute. But when Jeannot gets arrested, his two women decide to abandon him and turn respectable. Nothing actually works out. French with subtitles. **95m/C VHS, Letterbox.** *FR* Anouk Grinberg, Gerard Lanvin, Valeria Bruni-Tedeschi, Olivier Martinez; **Cameos:** Mathieu Kassovitz, Jean-Pierre Leaud; **D:** Bertrand Blier; **W:** Bertrand Blier; **C:** Pierre Lhomme. *NYF*

Mon Oncle 🐾🐾🐾🐾 **My Uncle; My Uncle, Mr. Hulot 1958** Tati's celebrated comedy contrasts the simple life of Monsieur Hulot with the technologically complicated life of his family when he aids his nephew in war against his parents' ultramodern, push-button home. An easygoing, delightful comedy, this is the director's first piece in color.

Sequel to "Mr. Hulot's Holiday," followed by "Playtime." In French with English subtitles. **110m/C VHS, Beta, LV, 8mm.** *FR* Jacques Tati, Jean-Pierre Zola, Adrienne Serrantie, Alain Bacourt; **D:** Jacques Tati; **C:** Jean Bourgoin. Academy Awards '58: Best Foreign Language Film; Cannes Film Festival '58: Grand Jury Prize; New York Film Critics Awards '58: Best Foreign Film. *HMV, MRV, HHT*

Mon Oncle Antoine 🐾🐾🐾½ **1971** A splendid tale of young Benoit, who learns about life from a surprisingly compassionate uncle, who works as everything from undertaker to grocer in the depressed area where they live. **104m/C VHS.** *CA* Jean Duceppe, Olivette Thibault; **D:** Claude Jutra. *HMV, HMV, AUD*

Mon Oncle D'Amerique 🐾🐾🐾½ *Les Somnambules* **1980 (PG)** Three French characters are followed as they try to find success of varying kinds in Paris, interspersed with ironic lectures by Prof. Henri Laborit about the biology that impels human behavior. Their disappointments lead them to dream of a legendary American uncle, who could make their desires come true. An acclaimed, witty comedy by former Nouvelle Vague filmmaker, dubbed into English. **123m/C VHS, Beta.** *FR* Gerard Depardieu, Nicole Garcia, Roger-Pierre, Marie DuBois; **D:** Alain Resnais; **W:** Jean Gruault; **C:** Sacha Vierny. Cannes Film Festival '80: Grand Jury Prize; New York Film Critics Awards '80: Best Foreign Film; Nominations: Academy Awards '80: Best Original Screenplay.*NYF, BTV*

Mona Lisa 🐾🐾🐾½ **1986 (R)** Jordan's wonderful, sad, sensitive story of a romantic, small-time hood who gets personally involved with the welfare and bad company of the high-priced whore he's been hired to chauffeur. Hoskins is especially touching and Caine is chilling as a suave gangster. Fine film debut for Tyson. Brilliantly filmed and critically lauded. **104m/C VHS, Beta, LV.** *GB* Bob Hoskins, Cathy Tyson, Michael Caine, Clarke Peters, Kate Hardie, Robbie Coltrane, Zoe Nathenson, Sammi Davis, Rod Bedall, Joe Brown, Pauline Melville; **D:** Neil Jordan; **W:** David Leland, Neil Jordan; **M:** Michael Kamen. British Academy Awards '86: Best Actor (Hoskins); Cannes Film Festival '86: Best Actor (Hoskins); Golden Globe Awards '87: Best Actor—Drama (Hoskins); Los Angeles Film Critics Association Awards '86: Best Actor (Hoskins), Best Supporting Actress (Tyson); New York Film Critics Awards '86: Best Actor (Hoskins); National Society of Film Critics Awards '86: Best Actor (Hoskins); Nominations: Academy Awards '86: Best Actor (Hoskins). *VTR*

Monaco Forever 🐾🐾 **1983** An enigmatic American meets a mysterious Frenchwoman and they set off on a string of unusual romantic adventures. Set around the 1956 marriage of Grace Kelly to Prince Rainier of Monaco. Film debut of Van Damme. **79m/C VHS.** Charles Pitt, Martha Farris, Sydney Lassick, Jean-Claude Van Damme; **D:** William A. Levey; **W:** C. William Pitt, William A. Levey. *VHE, FCT*

Mondo Balardo 🐾 **1964** Translated as "Crazy World," this is crude sensationalism masked as a horror story. Karloff guides the viewer through a curious mixture of society's fringe elements. A loosely connected series of sketches includes portraits of a reincarnated Rudolph Valentino, practitioners of transvestism, Roman coke whores, and an Italian-Japanese rock 'n roll midget (Drago) in director Montero's unusual vision of an anti-paradise. Includes standard lesbian club scene. Volume 11 of Frank Henenlotter's Sexy Shockers. **86m/C VHS.** Franz Drago; **D:** Robert Montero; **W:** Albert T. Viola. *SMW, TPV*

Mondo Cane 🐾🐾 **1963 (R)** A documentary showcasing the eccentricities of human behavior around the world, including cannibalism, pig killing and more. Dubbed in English. Inspired a rash of "shockumentaries" over the next several years. The song "More" made its debut in this film. **105m/C VHS, Beta.** *IT* **D:** Gualtiero Jacopetti. Nominations: Academy Awards '63: Best Song ("More"). *SNC, VDC, VDM*

Mondo Cane 2 🐾 *Mondo Pazzo* **1964 (R)** More documentary-like views of the oddities of mankind and ethnic rituals around the world. Enough, already. **94m/C VHS, Beta.** *IT* **D:** Gualtiero Jacopetti. *VDC, HHE, TPV*

Mondo Magic *🎬½* 1976 A compilation of tribal rituals offering viewers a look on the darker side of matters magical. 100m/C VHS, Beta. *D:* Melvin Ashford. *NO*

Mondo Trasho woof! 1969 A major trasho film of the last day in the life of a most unfortunate woman, complete with sex and violence. First full length effort from cult filmmaker Waters, who was also writer, producer, and editor. 95m/B VHS, Beta. Divine, Mary Vivian Pearce, John Leisenring, Mink Stole, David Lochary, Chris Atkinson; *D:* John Waters; *W:* John Waters. *NO*

The Money *🎬🎬* 1975 (R) The quest for money drives a young man to kidnap the child that his girlfriend is baby-sitting. Average but Workman's direction is right on the money. 88m/C VHS. Laurence Luckinbill, Elizabeth Richards, Danny DeVito, Graham Beckel; *D:* Chuck Workman. *VTR*

Money for Nothing *🎬🎬* 1993 (R) $1.2 million falls off a truck in the warehouse district of Philadelphia where a simple-minded unemployed longshoreman (Cusack) finds the chance of a lifetime. Indiscreetly leaving behind a trail of spending, he soon has a detective (Madsen) snooping around dangerously close. But he only digs himself deeper by enlisting the assistance of the mob to help him launder the money. At this point the film disintegrates into a limp diatribe on the injustice of capitalism on society's downtrodden. Mazar plays Joey's ex-girlfriend who double-times it back to the fold after his find. Based on a true story. *CW:* Language and a scene of sexuality. 100m/C VHS, LV, Closed Caption. John Cusack, Michael Madsen, Benicio Del Toro, Michael Rapaport, Debi Mazar, Fionnula Flanagan, Maury Chaykin, James Gandolfini, Elizabeth Bracco, Ashleigh Dejon, Lenny Venito; *D:* Ramon Menendez; *W:* Ramon Menendez, Carol Sobieski, Tom Musca; *M:* Craig Safan. *TOU*

Money Madness *🎬🎬* 1947 Beaumont (Ward Cleaver) plays a taxi driver turned thief in this curiosity. ?m/C VHS. Hugh Beaumont, Frances Rafferty, Harlan Warde, Cecil Weston, Ida Moore, Danny Morton, Joel Friedkin, Lane Chandler; *D:* Peter Stewart, Sam Newfield; *W:* Al Martin; *C:* Jack Greenhalgh. *NO*

Money Movers *🎬🎬* 1978 Aussie thieves plan megabuck bank robbery but heist and plot go sour. An oft told tale based on a true story. Features early appearance from burly boy Brown. 94m/C VHS. *AU* Terence Donovan, Ed Devereaux, Tony Bonner, Lucky Grills, Charles Tingwell, Candy Raymond, Bryan Brown, Alan Cassell; *D:* Bruce Beresford; *W:* Bruce Beresford. *IMP*

The Money Pit *🎬🎬* 1986 (PG) A young yuppie couple encounter sundry problems when they attempt to renovate their newly purchased, seemingly self-destructive, Long Island home. However, the collapse of their home leads directly to the collapse of their relationship as well. Somewhat modeled after "Mr. Blandings Builds His Dream House." Hanks and Long fail to jell as partners and the many sight gags are on the predictable side. A Spielberg production. 91m/C VHS, Beta, LV, Closed Caption. Tom Hanks, Shelley Long, Alexander Godunov, Maureen Stapleton, Philip Bosco, Joe Mantegna, Josh Mostel; *D:* Richard Benjamin; *C:* Gordon Willis; *M:* Michel Colombier. *USH*

Money Talks *🎬🎬* 1997 (R) Hustler Franklin Hatchett (Tucker) is falsely accused of orchestrating a violent jail break. Ratings-hungry TV reporter James Russell (Sheen) agrees to help Franklin clear his name in return for exclusive rights to his story. The mismatched pair search for stolen jewels, dodge bullets and endure explosive escapes, but this being an action-comedy, there needs to be some laughs. These are provided (intermittently) by the frenzied comic style of Tucker, who easily eclipses Sheen's straight man demeanor (which could be mistaken for acting if you've never seen any of Sheen's previous films). Tucker shows flashes of deserving better material than he has to work with here. *CW:* Graphic violence and pervasive strong language. 92m/C VHS, LV, Letterbox, Closed Caption. Chris Tucker, Charlie Sheen, Heather Locklear, Paul Sorvino, Veronica Cartwright, Elise Neal, Paul Gleason, Larry Hankin, Daniel Roebuck, David Warner, Michael Wright, Gerard Ismael; *D:* Brett Ratner; *W:* Joel Cohen, Alec Sokolow; *C:* Russell Carpenter, Robert Primes; *M:* Lalo Schifrin. Nominations: Golden Raspberry Awards '97: Worst New Star (Tucker). *WAR, IME*

Money to Burn *🎬🎬* 1983 Aging high school counselor and two senior citizens develop a plan to steal $50 million dollars from the Federal Reserve Bank. Harmless bit of fun. 90m/C VHS, Beta. Jack Kruschen, Meegan King, David Wallace, Phillip Pine; *D:* Virginia Lively Stone. *NO*

Money to Burn *🎬½* 1994 (R) Two buddies go off on a wild spending spree when $2 million in cash falls into their laps. Only one problem—a crazy cop who's determined to stop them squandering the money. 96m/C VHS, LV. Chad McQueen, Don Swayze, Joe Estevez, Julie Strain, Sydney Lassick; *D:* John Sjogren; *W:* John Sjogren, Scott Ziehl. *NLC, COL*

Money Train *🎬½* 1995 (R) Snipes and Harrelson team up again, this time as New York City transit cops (and foster brothers) who decide to rob the money-train—a subway car that collects all the cash accrued from the transit system each day. To complicate matters, they're both in love with their new Latina partner (Lopez). Lame attempt to cash in on the Snipes and Harrelson chemistry leaves out one important ingredient—a competent script. The movie is almost over before the train actually becomes part of the plot line. Film came under criticism when it was blamed for a series of "copycat" arsons in which a New York City subway clerk was killed. *CW:* Contains strong language, violence, and a sex scene. 110m/C VHS, LV, 8mm, Closed Caption. Woody Harrelson, Wesley Snipes, Jennifer Lopez, Robert (Bobby) Blake, Chris Cooper, Joe Grifasi; *D:* Joseph Ruben; *W:* Doug Richardson, David Loughery; *C:* John Lindley; *M:* Mark Mancina. *COL*

The Moneytree *🎬½* 1993 A carefree would-be actor decides to make some money by harvesting a huge marijuana crop in the California hills, all the while fending off his girlfriend, the cops, and some wild boars. 92m/C VHS. Christopher Dienstag; *D:* Alan Dienstag. *TPV*

A Mongolian Tale *🎬🎬* Hei Ma 1994 Nai Nai has raised her granddaughter Somiya and the abandoned Bayingbulag among the Mongolian steppes. Eventually, Bayingbulag leaves to get an education but promises to return and marry Somiya. Away three years, he comes back only to discover Somiya pregnant, so he takes off, finds success as a folk singer, and doesn't return for 12 years. Somiya now has a drunken husband, four sons, and an illegitimate 12-year-old daughter who is desperate for a father. Mongolian dialogue. Adapted by Chengzhi from his story "A Song of the Grassland." 105m/C VHS. *CH HK* Narenhua, Tengger; *D:* Xie Fei; *W:* Zhang Chengzhi. Montreal World Film Festival '95: Best Director (Fei). *NYF*

The Mongols *🎬🎬½* Les Mongols 1960 Splashy Italian production has Genghis Khan's son repelling invading hordes while courting buxom princess. Pairing of Palance and Ekberg makes this one worthy of consideration. 105m/C VHS. *IT FR* Jack Palance, Anita Ekberg, Antonella Lualdi, Franco Silva, Gianni "John" Garko, Roldano Lupi, Gabriella Pallotti; *D:* Andre de Toth, Leopoldo Savona, Riccardo (Robert Hampton) Freda. *SNC*

Mongrel woof! 1983 El-cheapo kennel horror about a man who dreams he's a wild murderous mutt. His relief upon waking up is short-lived, however, when he discovers the people he killed in his dreams are really dead. Flick will make you want to gnaw on a bone. 90m/C VHS, Beta. Aldo Ray, Terry Evans; *D:* Robert Burns. *NO*

Monika *🎬🎬½* Summer with Monika 1952 Two teenagers who run away together for the summer find the winter brings more responsibility than they can handle when the girl becomes pregnant and gives birth. Lesser, early Bergman, sensitively directed, but dull. Adapted by Bergman from a Per Anders Fogelstrom novel. In Swedish with English subtitles. 96m/B VHS. *SW* Harriet Andersson, Lars Ekborg, John Harryson, Georg Skarstedt, Dagmar Ebbesen, Ake Gronberg; *D:* Ingmar Bergman; *W:* Ingmar Bergman; *M:* Les Baxter. *HMV, CVC, TPV*

Monique *🎬* 1983 A sophisticated career woman is about to unleash a terrifying secret on her new husband. 96m/C VHS, Beta. Florence Giorgetti, John Ferris. *NO*

Monkey Boy *🎬🎬½* 1990 Decent sci-fi horror from Britain, about a cunning human-ape hybrid that escapes from a genetics lab after massacring the staff. Not excessively gruesome or vulgar, and some sympathy is aroused for the killer mutant. Based on the novel "Chimera." 104m/C VHS, Beta. John Lynch, Christine Kavanagh, Kenneth Cranham; *D:* Lawrence Gordon Clark.

Monkey Business *🎬🎬🎬½* 1931 Marx Brothers run amok as stowaways on ocean liner. Fast-paced comedy provides seemingly endless amount of gags, quips, and pratfalls, including the fab four imitating Maurice Chevalier at Immigration. This film, incidentally, was the group's first to be written—by noted humorist Perelman—directly for the screen. 77m/B VHS, Beta, LV. Groucho Marx, Harpo Marx, Chico Marx, Zeppo Marx, Thelma Todd, Ruth Hall, Harry Woods; *D:* Norman Z. McLeod. *USH*

Monkey Business *🎬🎬🎬* 1952 A scientist invents a fountain-of-youth potion, a lab chimpanzee mistakenly dumps it into a water cooler, and then grown-ups start turning into adolescents. Top-flight crew occasionally labors in this screwball comedy, though comic moments shine. Monroe is the secretary sans skills, while absentminded Grant and sexy wife Rogers race hormonally as teens. 97m/B VHS, Beta, LV. Cary Grant, Ginger Rogers, Charles Coburn, Marilyn Monroe, Hugh Marlowe, Larry Keating, George Winslow; *D:* Howard Hawks; *W:* Ben Hecht, Charles Lederer, I.A.L. Diamond; *C:* Milton Krasner. *FOX*

Monkey Grip *🎬🎬🎬* 1982 An unmarried woman copes with parenthood and a drug-addicted boyfriend while working on the fringe of Australia's music business. Grim but provocative, based on Helen Graham's novel. 101m/C VHS. *AU* Noni Hazlehurst, Colin Friels, Alice Garner, Harold Hopkins, Candy Raymond; *D:* Ken Cameron; *W:* Ken Cameron. Australian Film Institute '82: Best Actress (Hazlehurst).

Monkey Hustle *🎬* 1977 (PG) Vintage blaxploitation has trouble hustling laffs. The Man plans a super freeway through the ghetto, and law abiding do gooders join forces with territorial lords of vice to fight the project. Shot in the Windy City. 90m/C VHS. Yaphet Kotto, Rudy Ray Moore, Rosalind Cash, Debbi Morgan, Thomas Carter; *D:* Arthur Marks. *ORI, FCT*

Monkey Shines *🎬🎬* Monkey Shines: An Experiment in Fear; Ella 1988 (R) Based on the novel by Michael Stuart, this is a sick, scary yarn about a quadriplegic who is given a specially trained capuchin monkey as a helpmate. However, he soon finds that the beast is assuming and acting on his subconscious rages. 108m/C VHS, Beta, LV, Closed Caption. Jason Beghe, John Pankow, Kate McNeil, Christine Forrest, Stephen Root, Joyce Van Patten, Stanley Tucci, Janine Turner; *D:* George A. Romero; *W:* George A. Romero; *C:* James A. Contner; *M:* David Shire. *ORI*

Monkey Trouble *🎬🎬½* 1994 (PG) Lonely schoolgirl Birch is feeling abandoned when mom and stepdad shower attention on her new baby brother. Then a monkey trained as a pickpocket enters her life. Keitel is the organ grinder turned bad who must answer to the mob when the monkey scampers off to suburbia. Stakes a lot of its entertainment wallop on the considerable talents of the slippery-fingered monkey, who steals the show. Birch is amusing as the youngster caught in all sorts of uncomfortable situations. Formula abounds, but the milk and cookies set won't notice; fine family fare. 95m/C VHS, LV, Closed Caption. Thora Birch, Harvey Keitel, Mimi Rogers, Christopher McDonald; *D:* Franco Amurri; *W:* Franco Amurri, Stu Krieger; *M:* Mark Mancina. *COL*

Monkeys, Go Home! 🐒½ **1966** Dumb Disney yarn about young American who inherits a badly neglected French olive farm. When he brings in four chimpanzees to pick the olives, the local townspeople go on strike. People can be so sensitive. Based on "The Monkeys" by G. K. Wilkinson. Chevalier's last film appearance. **89m/C VHS, Beta.** Dean Jones, Yvette Mimieux, Maurice Chevalier, Clement Harari, Yvonne Constant; *D:* Andrew V. McLaglen; *M:* Robert F. Brunner. *DIS*

Monkey's Uncle 🐒½ **1965** A sequel to Disney's "The Misadventures of Merlin Jones" and featuring more bizarre antics and scientific hoopla, including chimps and a flying machine. **90m/C VHS, Beta.** Tommy Kirk, Annette Funicello, Leon Ames, Arthur O'Connell; *D:* Robert Stevenson; *W:* Alfred Lewis Levitt, Helen Levitt; *C:* Edward Colman; *M:* Buddy Baker. *DIS*

The Monocle 🐒🐒 **1964** Steele plays a seductive villainess in this rare, spy/comedy thriller. **?m/C VHS.** *FR* Paul Meurisse, Barbara Steele, Marcel Dalio. *SNC*

Monolith 🐒🐒½ **1993 (R)** Tucker (Paxton) and Flynn (Frost) are unlikely partners on the LAPD. But they're teamed up on an unlikely case: a Russian scientist commits a seemingly senseless murder and is taken away by a mystery man (Hurt) before she can be interrogated. What the curious duo discover is a lethal alien force capable of possessing any living creature and whose objective is the destruction of the planet. **96m/C VHS, LV, Closed Caption.** Bill Paxton, Lindsay Frost, John Hurt, Louis Gossett Jr.; *D:* John Eyres; *W:* Stephen Lister. *USH*

The Monolith Monsters 🐒🐒 **1957** A geologist investigates a meteor shower in Arizona and discovers strange crystals. The crystals attack humans and absorb their silicone, causing them to grow into monsters. Good "B" movie fun. **76m/B VHS, Closed Caption.** Grant Williams, Lola Albright, Les Tremayne, Trevor Bardette; *D:* John Sherwood; *W:* Norman Jolley, Robert M. Fresco; *M:* Joseph Gershenson. *USH, MLB, FRG*

Monsieur Beaucaire 🐒½ **1924** The Duke of Chartres ditches France posing as a barber, and once in Britain, becomes a lawman. Not a classic Valentino vehicle. **100m/B VHS, Beta.** Rudolph Valentino, Bebe Daniels, Lois Wilson, Doris Kenyon, Lowell Sherman, John Davidson; *D:* Sidney Olcott. *GPV*

Monsieur Beaucaire 🐒🐒🐒 **1946** Entertaining Hope vehicle that casts him as a barber impersonating a French nobleman in the court of Louis XV. He's set to wed a Spanish princess in order to prevent a full-scale war from taking place. However, he really wants to marry social-climber chambermaid Caulfield. Director Marshall was at his best here. Based on the novel by Booth Tarkington. **93m/B VHS, Closed Caption.** Bob Hope, Joan Caulfield, Patric Knowles, Marjorie Reynolds, Cecil Kellaway, Joseph Schildkraut, Reginald Owen, Constance Collier; *D:* George Marshall; *W:* Melvin Frank, Norman Panama; *C:* Lionel Lindon. *USH, BTV*

Monsieur Hire 🐒🐒🐒½ *M. Hire* **1989 (PG-13)** The usual tale of sexual obsession and suspense. Mr. Hire spends much of his time trying to spy on his beautiful young neighbor woman, alternately alienated and engaged by her love affairs. The voyeur soon finds his secret desires have entangled him in a vicious intrigue. Political rally set-piece is brilliant. Excellent acting, intense pace, elegant photography. Based on "Les Fiancailles de M. Hire" by Georges Simenone and adapted by Leconte and Patrick Dewolf. In French with English subtitles. **81m/C VHS, LV.** *FR* Michel Blanc, Sandrine Bonnaire, Luc Thuillier, Eric Berenger, Andre Wilms; *D:* Patrice Leconte; *W:* Patrice Leconte. Cesar Awards '90: Best Sound. *FXL, FCT, IME*

Monsieur Verdoux 🐒🐒🐒 **1947** A thorough Chaplin effort, as he produced, directed, wrote, scored and starred. A prim and proper bank cashier in Paris marries and murders rich women in order to support his real wife and family. A mild scandal in its day, though second-thought pacifism and stale humor date it. A bomb upon release (leading Chaplin to shelve it for 17 years) and a cult item today, admired for both its flaws and complexity. Raye fearlessly chews scenery and croissants. Initially based upon a suggestion from Orson Welles. **123m/B VHS, Beta, LV.** Charlie Chaplin, Martha Raye, Isobel Elsom, Mady Correll, Marilyn Nash, Irving Bacon, William Frawley, Allison Roddan, Robert Lewis; *D:* Charlie Chaplin; *W:* Charlie Chaplin. Nominations: Academy Awards '47: Best Original Screenplay. *FOX*

Monsieur Vincent 🐒🐒🐒 **1947** True story of 17th century French priest who became St. Vincent de Paul (Fresnay). He forsakes worldly possessions and convinces members of the aristocracy to finance his charities for the less fortunate. Inspirational. French with subtitles. **112m/B VHS.** *FR* Pierre Fresnay, Lisa Delamare, Aime Clairmond, Jean Debucourt, Jean Pieux, Gabrielle Dorziat, Jean Carmet, Michel Bouquet; *D:* Maurice Cloche; *W:* Jean Anouilh, Jean-Bernard Luc; *C:* Claude Renoir; *M:* Jean Jacques Grunenwald. Academy Awards '48: Best Foreign Language Film. *INT*

Monsignor woof! **1982 (R)** Callow, ambitious priest befriends mobsters and even seduces a nun while managing Vatican's business affairs. No sparks generated by Reeve and Bujold (who appears nude in one scene), and no real conviction related by most other performers. Absurd, ludicrous melodrama best enjoyed as unintentional comedy. Based on Jack Alain Leger's book. **121m/C VHS, Beta.** Christopher Reeve, Fernando Rey, Genevieve Bujold, Jason Miller; *D:* Frank Perry; *W:* Abraham Polonsky, Wendell Mayes; *C:* Billy Williams; *M:* John Williams. *FOX*

Monsignor Quixote 🐒🐒½ **1991** A small town priest takes on the persona of his ancestor, Don Quixote, and prepares to battle the evil he sees around him. Based on the novel by Graham Greene. **118m/C VHS.** Alec Guinness, Ian Richardson, Graham Crowden, Maurice Denham, Philip Stone, Rosalie Crutchley, Valentine Pelka, Don Fellows, Leo McKern; *D:* Rodney Bennett. *FCT*

The Monster 🐒🐒🐒 **1925** This silent horror film has all the elements that would become genre standards. A mad scientist (Chaney), working in an asylum filled with lunatics, abducts strangers to use in his fiendish experiments to bring the dead back to life. There's the obligatory dungeon and even a lovely heroine that needs rescuing. Great atmosphere and Chaney's usual spine-tingling performance. **86m/B VHS.** Lon Chaney Sr., Gertrude Olmsted, Johnny Arthur, Charles Sellon; *D:* Roland West. *FCT*

Monster 🐒 **1978 (R)** Bloodthirsty alien indiscriminately preys on gaggle of teens in wilds of civilization. Performers struggle with dialogue and their own self-esteem. **98m/C VHS, Beta.** Jim Mitchum, Diane McBain, Roger Clark, John Carradine, Phil Carey, Anthony Eisley, Keenan Wynn; *D:* Herbert L. Strock. *MRV*

The Monster 🐒🐒½ *Il Mostre* **1996 (R)** Italian impresario of comedy Benigni co-wrote, directed and starred in this film that has become the highest grossing film in Italian history to date. Jaded American audiences, however, may find the broad comedy of errors all too familiar territory with Loris (Benigni) as a criminal Clouseau, an incompetent petty thief whom police mistake for a serial murderer on the loose. Cops install an attractive female detective (Braschi, Benigni's wife) in the sexually strained shyster's apartment to tempt him into striking again. Sight gags aplenty populate Benigni's highly physical performance, including: being pulled wildly around a garage attached to an out-of-control chainsaw; contending with a lit cigarette down his pants; and scores of pratfalls, all of which garner comparisons to American comedy phenom, Jim Carrey. French director and actor Blanc ("Dead Tired") is great as the loony police psychiatrist. **110m/C VHS.** *IT* Roberto Benigni, Nicoletta Braschi, Michel Blanc, Dominque Lavanant, Jean-Claude Brialy, Ivano Marescotti, Laurent Spielvogel, Massimo Girotti, Franco Mescolini; *D:* Roberto Benigni; *W:* Roberto Benigni, Vincenzo Cerami; *C:* Carlo DiPalma; *M:* Evan Lurie. *COL*

Monster a Go-Go! woof! **1965** Team of go-go dancers battle a ten-foot monster from outerspace whose mass is due to a radiation mishap. He can't dance, either. **70m/B VHS, Beta.** Phil Morton, June Travis, Bill Rebane, Sheldon Seymour; *D:* Herschell Gordon Lewis. *VCI*

The Monster and the Girl 🐒🐒½ **1941** It's the mob vs. the ape in this tale of revenge. Scott (Terry) discovers innocent sister Susan (Drew) is being lead down the path to prostitution by suave mobster Reed (Paige). But Reed manages to frame Scott for murder and he's executed, although not before donating his brain to science. Then scientist Parry (Zucco) decides to transplant the brain into the body of an ape who goes on a rampage aimed at the mobster. **65m/B VHS, Closed Caption.** Ellen Drew, Robert Paige, Phillip Terry, Paul Lukas, Joseph Calleia, Onslow Stevens, Rod Cameron, George Zucco, Marc Lawrence, Gerald Mohr; *D:* Stuart Heisler; *W:* Stuart Anthony; *C:* Victor Milner. *USH*

The Monster Club 🐒🐒 **1985** Price and Carradine star in this music-horror compilation, featuring songs by Night, B.A. Robertson, The Pretty Things and The Viewers. Soundtrack music by John Williams, UB 40 and The Expressos. **104m/C VHS, Beta, LV.** *GB* Vincent Price, Donald Pleasence, John Carradine, Stuart Whitman, Britt Ekland, Simon Ward, Patrick Magee; *D:* Roy Ward Baker. *ART*

The Monster Demolisher 🐒🐒 **1960** Nostradamus' descendent shares the family penchant for sanguine cocktails and threatens a professor who protects himself with an electronic wonder of modern technology. Edited from a sombrero serial; if you make it through this one, look up its Mexican siblings, "Curse of Nostradamus" and "Genie of Darkness." **?m/B VHS.** *MX* German Robles; *D:* Frederick Curiel. *NOS, LOO*

Monster Dog woof! **1982** A rock band is mauled, threatened, and drooled upon by an untrainable mutant canine. Rock star Cooper plays the leader of the band. No plot, but the German shepherd is worth watching. **88m/C VHS, Beta.** Alice Cooper, Victoria Vera; *D:* Clyde Anderson. *TWE*

Monster from Green Hell 🐒 **1958** An experimental rocket containing radiation-contaminated wasps crashes in Africa, making giant killer wasps that run amok. Stinging big bug horror. **71m/B VHS, Beta.** Jim Davis, Robert Griffin, Barbara Turner, Eduardo Ciannelli; *D:* Kenneth Crane. *NOS, MRV, SNC*

Monster from the Ocean Floor 🐒 *It Stalked the Ocean Floor; Monster Maker* **1954** An oceanographer in a deep-sea diving bell is threatened by a multi-tentacled creature. Roger Corman's first production. **66m/C VHS, Beta.** Anne Kimball, Stuart Wade; *D:* Wyott Ordung. *THV*

Monster High 🐒 **1989 (R)** Bloodthirsty alien indiscriminately preys on gaggle of teens in wilds of civilization. Even the people who made this one may not have seen it all the way through. **89m/C VHS, Beta, LV.** David Marriott, Dean Iandoli, Diana Frank, D.J. Kerzner; *D:* Rudiger Poe. *COL*

Monster in a Box 🐒🐒🐒 **1992 (PG-13)** Master storyteller Gray spins a wonderful tale about his life, including stories about his adventures at a Moscow film festival, a trip to Nicaragua, and his first experience with California earthquakes. Filled with wit, satire, and hilarity. Filmed before an audience, this is based on Gray's Broadway show of the same title. By the way, the monster in the box is a 1,900-page manuscript of his autobiography and the box in which he lugs it around. **88m/C VHS, LV, Closed Caption.** Spalding Gray; *D:* Nick Broomfield; *W:* Spalding Gray; *C:* Michael Coulter; *M:* Laurie Anderson. *NLC, COL, BTV*

Monster in the Closet 🐒🐒 **1986 (PG)** A gory horror spoof about a rash of San Francisco murders that all take place inside closets. A news reporter and his scientist friend decide they will be the ones to protect California from the evil but shy creatures. From the makers of "The Toxic Avenger." **07m/0 VHS, Beta, Closed Caption.** Donald Grant, Claude Akins, Denise DuBarry, Stella Stevens, Howard Duff, Henry Gibson, Jesse White, John Carradine; **D:** Bob Dahlin; **W:** Bob Dahlin. *ORI, WAR*

The Monster Maker 🎬🎬 1944 Low-budget gland fest in which deranged scientist develops serum that inflates heads, feet, and hands. He recklessly inflicts others with this potion, then must contend with deformed victims while courting a comely gal. **65m/B VHS, Beta.** J. Carrol Naish, Ralph Morgan, Wanda McKay, Terry Frost; **D:** Sam Newfield. *NOS, MRV, SNC*

The Monster of London City 🎬½
Das Ungeheuer von London City 1964 During a stage play about Jack the Ripper, murders occur paralleling those in the production. The lead actor finds himself to be the prime suspect. Lightweight horror from Germany. **87m/B VHS, Beta.** *GE* Hansjorg Felmy, Marianne Koch, Dietmar Schoenherr, Hans Nielsen; **D:** Edwin Zbonek. *SNC*

The Monster of Piedras Blancas woof! 1957 During a seaside festival, two fisherman are killed by a bloodthirsty oceanic critter with no respect for holidays. The fishing village is determined to find it and kill it. Low-budget, with amateurish effects and poor acting. **72m/B VHS.** Les Tremayne, Jeanne Carmen, Forrest Lewis, John Harmon, Don Sullivan; **D:** Irvin Berwick; **W:** H. Haile Chace; **C:** Philip Lathrop. *VDM, MRV, REP*

Monster on the Campus 🎬🎬½ 1959 Science-fiction thriller about the blood of a prehistoric monster turning college professor into murderous beast. Will the halls of Dunsfield University ever be safe again? **76m/B VHS, Closed Caption.** Arthur Franz, Joanna Moore, Judson Pratt, Nancy Walters, Troy Donahue; **D:** Jack Arnold; **W:** David Duncan. *USH*

The Monster Squad 🎬½ 1987 (PG-13) Youthful monster enthusiasts find their community inundated by Dracula, Frankenstein creature, Wolf Man, Mummy, and Gill Man(!?!), who are all searching for a life-sustaining amulet. Somewhat different, but still somewhat mediocre. **82m/C VHS, Beta, LV.** Andre Gower, Stephen Macht, Tom Noonan, Duncan Regehr; **D:** Fred Dekker; **W:** Fred Dekker, Shane Black; **M:** Bruce Broughton. *ART, VES*

The Monster That Challenged the World 🎬🎬½ 1957 Huge, ancient eggs are discovered in the Salton Sea and eventually hatch into killer, crustaceous caterpillars. Superior monster action. **83m/B VHS.** Tim Holt, Audrey Dalton, Hans Conried, Harlen Ward, Max Casey Adams Showalter, Mimi Gibson, Gordon Jones; **D:** Arnold Laven. *MGM, FRG, MLB*

The Monster Walks 🎬🎬 *The Monster Walked* 1932 A whodunit thriller, complete with stormy nights, suspicious cripples, weird servants, a screaming gorilla, and a spooky house. Not unique but entertaining. **60m/B VHS, Beta.** Rex Lease, Vera Reynolds, Mischa Auer, Willie Best; **D:** Frank Strayer. *SNC, NOS, CCB*

Monsters Crash the Pajama Party 🎬🎬 1965 Mad scientist is discovered conducting weird experiments by a group of teens who enter a supposedly haunted house. This one was much better in the theatre, because "monsters" would run through the audience and select a victim. Then the monsters and the victim would magically appear on the screen. Weird. **?m/C VHS.** Peter J. D'Noto; **D:** David L. Hewitt. *SNC*

Montana 🎬🎬½ 1990 (PG) Hoyce and Bess Guthrie are long-married and strong-willed ranchers who are at odds over the family ranch in Montana. He wants to sell the land to a power company for oil drilling but she wants to keep the land in the family. Made for cable television. **91m/C VHS, Beta, Closed Caption.** Gena Rowlands, Richard Crenna, Lea Thompson, Justin Deas, Elizabeth Berridge, Scott Coffey, Darren Dalton; **D:** William A. Graham; **W:** Larry McMurtry. *TTC, FCT*

Montana Belle 🎬🎬 1952 A buxom bandit teams with the notorious Dalton Brothers before embarking on a life of reform. In the cardgame of life, Russell is always holding a pair. **81m/C VHS, Beta.** Jane Russell, George Brent, Scott Brady, Forrest Tucker, Andy Devine, Jack Lambert, John Litel, Ray Teal; **D:** Allan Dwan. *TTC*

Monte Carlo 🎬🎬 1986 A sexy Russian woman aids the Allies by relaying important messages during WWII. Fun, made for television production featuring Collins at her seductive best. **200m/C VHS, Beta, Closed Caption.** Joan Collins, George Hamilton, Lisa Eilbacher, Lauren Hutton, Robert Carradine, Malcolm McDowell; **D:** Anthony Page. *VTR*

Monte Carlo Nights 🎬½ 1934 Wrongly convicted murderer determines to prove his innocence even as he is tracked by police. **60m/B VHS, Beta.** Mary Brian, John Darrow, Kate Campbell, Robert Frazer, Astrid Allwyn, George "Gabby" Hayes, George Cleveland; **D:** William Nigh. *SNC*

Monte Walsh 🎬🎬🎬 1970 (PG) Aging cowboy sees declining of Old West, embarks on mission to avenge best friend's death. Subdued, moving western worthy of genre greats Marvin and Palance. Cinematographer Fraker proves himself a proficient director in this, his first venture. Based on Jack Schaefer's novel. **100m/C VHS, Beta, Closed Caption.** Lee Marvin, Jack Palance, Jeanne Moreau, Jim Davis, Mitchell Ryan; **D:** William A. Fraker; **W:** David Zelag Goodman; **M:** John Barry. *FOX*

Montenegro 🎬🎬🎬½ *Montenegro—Or Pigs and Pearls* 1981 Offbeat, bawdy comedy details experiences of bored, possibly mad housewife who lands in a coarse, uninhibited ethnic community. To its credit, this film remains unpredictable to the end. And Anspach, an intriguing, resourceful—and attractive—actress, delivers what is perhaps her greatest performance. **97m/C VHS, Letterbox.** *SW* Susan Anspach, Erland Josephson; **D:** Dusan Makavejev; **W:** Dusan Makavejev. *FXL*

Monterey Pop 🎬🎬🎬½ 1968 This pre-Woodstock rock 'n' roll festival in Monterey, California, features landmark performances by some of the most popular '60s rockers. Compelling for the performances, and historically important as the first significant rock concert film. Appearances by Jefferson Airplane, Janis Joplin, Jimi Hendrix, Simon and Garfunkel, The Who, and Otis Redding. **72m/C VHS, Beta, LV, 8mm.** *MVD, COL*

A Month by the Lake 🎬🎬½ 1995 (PG) Redgrave takes the plunge into highly familiar romantic comedy of the Proper English sort and glides effortlessly through this slow-moving but often charming adaptation of an H. E. Bates short story. Set in pre-WWII northern Italy, Miss Bentley (Redgrave) sets her spinster's eye on the somewhat wooden, but gradually warming, English Major Wilshaw (Fox). Petulant American nanny Thurman arrives to provide an arresting diversion for Wilshaw, while Gassman proves an unwitting pawn for Miss Bentley's game of "get the major." Touching and lighthearted performances, especially by heavyweight Redgrave, are complemented by glorious cinematography. **92m/C VHS, LV, Closed Caption.** Vanessa Redgrave, Edward Fox, Uma Thurman, Alida Valli, Alessandro Gassman, Carlo Cartier; **D:** John Irvin; **W:** Trevor Bentham; **C:** Pasquale De Santis; **M:** Nicola Piovani. Nominations: Golden Globe Awards '96: Best Actress—Musical/Comedy (Redgrave). *TOU*

A Month in the Country 🎬🎬🎬 1987 The reverently quiet story of two British WWI veterans, one an archaeologist and the other a church painting restorer, who are working in a tiny village while trying to heal their emotional wounds. Based on the novel by J.L. Carr. **92m/C VHS, Beta, LV.** *GB* Colin Firth, Natasha Richardson, Kenneth Branagh, Patrick Malahide, Tony Haygarth, Jim Carter; **D:** Pat O'Connor; **W:** Simon Gray; **M:** Howard Blake. *ORI, WAR*

Monty Python and the Holy Grail 🎬🎬🎬½ 1975 (PG) Britain's famed comedy band assaults the Arthurian legend in a cult classic replete with a Trojan rabbit and an utterly dismembered, but inevitably pugnacious, knight. Fans of manic comedy—and graphic violence—should get more than their fill here. **90m/C VHS, Beta, LV, 8mm, Letterbox.** *GB* Graham Chapman, John Cleese, Terry Gilliam, Eric Idle, Terry Jones, Michael Palin, Carol Cleveland, Connie Booth, Neil Innes, Patsy Kensit; **D:** Terry Gilliam, Terry Jones; **W:** Graham Chapman, John Cleese, Terry Gilliam, Eric Idle, Terry Jones, Michael Palin. *COL, SIG, TVC*

Monty Python Live at the Hollywood Bowl 🎬🎬🎬 1982 The revered comedy group perform many of their most celebrated routines in this uproarious performance documentary. A must-see for all Python aficionados. **78m/C VHS, Beta, LV, Closed Caption.** *GB* Eric Idle, Michael Palin, John Cleese, Terry Gilliam, Terry Jones, Graham Chapman; **D:** Terry Hughes; **W:** John Cleese, Terry Gilliam; **M:** John Du Prez. *PAR*

Monty Python's Flying Circus 1971 The original classic irreverant BBC comedy series that introduced the gang of six comics to the world. Two episodes per tape. Four skits: "The Architect's Sketch," "The Naughty Chemist," "Ministry of Silly Walks," and "The Piranha Brothers." **60m/C VHS, Beta, LV.** *GB* Michael Palin, Graham Chapman, Eric Idle, John Cleese, Terry Jones, Terry Gilliam, Carol Cleveland, Connie Booth, Neil Innes; **D:** Ian MacNaughton. *MOV, PAR*

Monty Python's Life of Brian 🎬🎬🎬½ *Life of Brian* 1979 (R) Often riotous spoof of Christianity tracks hapless peasant mistaken for the messiah in 32 A.D. Film reels from routine to routine, and only the most pious will remain unmoved by a chorus of crucifixion victims. Probably the group's most daring, controversial venture. **94m/C VHS, Beta, LV, Letterbox, Closed Caption.** *GB* Graham Chapman, John Cleese, Terry Gilliam, Eric Idle, Michael Palin, George Harrison, Terry Jones; **D:** Terry Jones; **W:** Graham Chapman, John Cleese, Terry Gilliam, Eric Idle, Michael Palin, Terry Jones; **C:** Peter Biziou; **M:** Geoffrey Burgon. *PAR, IME, SIG*

Monty Python's Parrot Sketch Not Included 1990 To celebrate their 20th anniversary, the crazy guys of Monty Python put together this collection of some of their funniest sketches. The parrot was pretty disappointed that he wasn't included. **75m/C VHS, LV, Closed Caption.** Graham Chapman, John Cleese, Terry Gilliam, Eric Idle, Terry Jones, Michael Palin. *PAR, SIG, TVC*

Monty Python's The Meaning of Life 🎬🎬🎬 1983 (R) Funny, technically impressive film conducts various inquiries into the most profound questions confronting humanity. Notable among the sketches here are a live sex enactment performed before bored schoolboys, a student-faculty rugby game that turns quite violent, and an encounter between a physician and a reluctant, untimely organ donor. Another sketch provides a memorable portrait of a glutton prone to nausea. And at film's end, the meaning of life is actually revealed. **107m/C VHS, Beta, LV, Letterbox, DVD.** *GB* Graham Chapman, John Cleese, Terry Gilliam, Eric Idle, Terry Jones, Michael Palin, Carol Cleveland, Matt Frewer; **D:** Terry Jones; **W:** Graham Chapman, John Cleese, Terry Gilliam, Eric Idle, Terry Jones, Michael Palin; **M:** John Du Prez. Cannes Film Festival '83: Grand Jury Prize. *USH, CCB, SIG*

The Moon and Sixpence 🎬🎬🎬 1943 Stockbroker turns ambitious painter in this adaptation of W. Somerset Maugham's novel that was, in turn, inspired by the life of artist Paul Gauguin. Fine performance from Sanders. Filmed mainly in black and white, but uses color sparingly to great advantage. Compare this one to "Wolf at the Door," in which Gauguin is played by Donald Sutherland. **89m/B VHS.** George Sanders, Herbert Marshall, Steve Geray, Doris Dudley, Eric Blore, Elena Verdugo, Florence Bates, Albert Basserman, Heather Thatcher;

D: Albert Lewin. Nominations: Academy Awards '43: Best Original Dramatic/Comedy Score. **MGM, IVY**

Moon 44 *♂♂½* **1990 (R)** A space prison is overrun by thugs who terrorize their fellow inmates. Fine cast, taut pacing. Filmed in Germany. 102m/C **VHS, LV, Closed Caption. GE** Malcolm McDowell, Lisa Eichhorn, Michael Pare, Stephen Geoffreys, Roscoe Lee Browne, Brian Thompson, Dean Devlin, Mechmed Yilmaz, Leon Rippy; *D:* Roland Emmerich. **ART, IME, BTV**

Moon in Scorpio *♂½* **1986** Three Vietnam-vet buddies go sailing and are attacked by the back-from-the-dead victims of a bloody war crime. 90m/C **VHS, Beta.** John Phillip Law, Britt Ekland, William Smith; *D:* Gary Graver. **TWE**

Moon in the Gutter *♂½ La Lune Dans le Caniveau* **1983 (R)** In a ramshackle harbor town, a man searches despondently for the person who killed his sister years before. Various sexual liaisons and stevedore fights intermittently spice up the action. Nasty story that doesn't make much sense on film; adapted from a book by American pulp writer David Goodis. In French with English subtitles. 109m/C **VHS, Beta.** *IT FR* Gerard Depardieu, Nastassia Kinski, Victoria Abril, Vittorio Mezzogiorno, Dominique Pinon; *D:* Jean-Jacques Beineix; *W:* Jean-Jacques Beineix; *C:* Philippe Rousselot. Cesar Awards '84: Best Art Direction/Set Decoration. **COL**

The Moon Is Blue *♂♂½* **1953** A young woman flaunts her virginity in this stilted adaptation of F. Hugh Herbert's play. Hard to believe that this film was once considered risque. Good performances, though, from Holden and Niven. 100m/B Beta, **LV.** William Holden, David Niven, Maggie McNamara, Tom Tully; *D:* Otto Preminger; *C:* Ernest Laszlo. Golden Globe Awards '54: Best Actor—Musical/Comedy (Niven); Nominations: Academy Awards '53: Best Actress (McNamara), Best Film Editing, Best Song ("The Moon is Blue"). **WAR**

Moon of the Wolf *♂* **1972** A small town in bayou country is terrorized by a modern-day werewolf that rips its victims to shreds. Made-for-television. 74m/C **VHS, Beta.** David Janssen, Barbara Rush, Bradford Dillman, John Beradino; *D:* Daniel Petrie. **WOV, GKK**

Moon over Harlem *♂½* **1939** A musical melodrama about a widow who unwittingly marries a fast-talking gangster involved in the numbers racket. The film features 20 chorus girls, a choir, and a 60-piece orchestra. 67m/B **VHS, Beta.** Bud Harris, Cora Green, Alec Lovejoy, Sidney Bechet; *D:* Edgar G. Ulmer. **FCT, DVT, NOS**

Moon over Miami *♂♂♂* **1941** Manhunting trio meet their match in this engaging musical. A remake of 1938's "Three Blind Mice," this was later remade in 1946 as "Three Little Girls in Blue." ♫Moon Over Miami; I've Got You All To Myself; What Can I Do For You?; Kindergarten Congo; You Started Something; Oh Me Oh Mi-Am-Mi; Solitary Seminole; Is That Good?; Loveliness and Love. 91m/C **VHS, Beta, Closed Caption.** Don Ameche, Betty Grable, Robert Cummings, Carole Landis, Charlotte Greenwood, Jack Haley; *D:* Walter Lang; *W:* Mitch Glazer; *C:* Leon Shamroy. **FOX**

Moon over Parador *♂♂½* **1988 (PG-13)** An uneven comedy about a reluctant American actor who gets the role of his life when he gets the chance to pass himself off as the recently deceased dictator of a Latin American country. A political strongman wants to continue the charade until he can take over, but the actor begins to enjoy the benefits of dictatorship. Look for a cameo by director/writer Mazursky in drag. 103m/C **VHS, Beta, LV.** Richard Dreyfuss, Sonia Braga, Raul Julia, Jonathan Winters, Fernando Rey, Ed Asner, Dick Cavett, Michael Greene, Sammy Davis Jr., Polly Holliday, Charo, Marianne Saegebrecht, Dana Delany, Ike Pappas; *Cameos:* Paul Mazursky; *D:* Paul Mazursky; *W:* Leon Capetanos; *M:* Maurice Jarre. **USH**

Moon Pilot *♂♂* **1962** An astronaut on his way to the moon encounters a mysterious alien woman who claims to know his future. 98m/C **VHS, Beta.** Tom Tryon, Brian Keith, Edmond O'Brien, Dany Saval, Tommy Kirk; *D:* James Neilson. **DIS**

The Moon-Spinners *♂♂* **1964 (PG)** Lightweight Disney drama featuring Mills as a young tourist traveling through Crete who meets up with a young man, accused of being a jewel thief, and the two work together to find the real jewel thieves. Watch for silent film star Pola Negri. 118m/C **VHS, Beta.** Hayley Mills, Peter McEnery, Eli Wallach, Pola Negri; *D:* James Neilson. **DIS, OM**

The Moon Stallion *♂♂½* **1985** A charming tale of mystery and fantasy for children and adults. Professor Purwell is researching King Arthur. His blind daughter soon becomes involved with supernatural events and a white horse that appears to lead her into adventures not of this age. 95m/C **VHS.** *GB* Sarah Sutton, David Haig, James Greene, John Abineri, Caroline Goodall; *D:* Dorothea Brooking. **VCO, HMV**

Moonbase *♂♂* **1997 (R)** In the year 2045, John Russell, manager of the Moonbase Waste Disposal Plant, has his hands full with more than garbage when a group of prison escapees take over the facility. *CW:* Sci-fi violence and some sexuality. 89m/C **VHS, LV, Closed Caption.** Scott Plank, Jocelyn Seagrave, Kurt Fuller, Robert O'Reilly; *D:* Paolo Mazzucato; *W:* Brian DiMuccio, Dino Vindeni; *M:* Michael Sherwood. **ART**

Mooncussers *♂½* **1962** A children's film detailing the exploits of a precocious 12-year-old determined to exact revenge upon a band of ruthless pirates. 85m/C **VHS, Beta.** Kevin Corcoran, Rian Garrick, Oscar Homolka; *D:* James Neilson. **DIS**

Moondance *♂♂* **1995 (R)** When lovely young German tourist Anya (Brendler) comes to an Irish fishing village on a summer holiday, two young brothers, Patrick (Shaw) and Dominic (Conroy), vie for her affections causing a family rift. Adapted from the novel "The White Hare" by Francis Stuart. *CW:* Sexuality and some language. 96m/C **VHS.** *GB* Ruaidhri Conroy, Ian Shaw, Julia Brendler, Marianne Faithfull, Gerard McSorley, Kate Flynn; *D:* Dagmar Hirtz. **TOU**

Moonfleet *♂♂½* **1955** Follows the adventures of an 18th century buccaneer who tries to swindle a young lad in his charge of a valuable diamond. From J. Meade Falkner's novel. 89m/C **VHS, LV.** Stewart Granger, Jon Whiteley, George Sanders, Viveca Lindfors, Joan Greenwood, Ian Wolfe; *D:* Fritz Lang; *M:* Miklos Rozsa. **MGM**

Moonlight and Valentino *♂♂* **1995 (R)** To help her recover from the death of her husband, Rebecca turns to the comfort of flaky neighbor Sylvie (Goldberg), self-destructive sis Lucy (Paltrow), and overbearing ex-stepmother Alberta (Turner). Together they sit around and talk some of the more contrived and cliched "women talk" ("Chicken soup is the most womanly thing on the face of the planet") in recent film history. The finale, a hokey ritual in a cemetery, will have you pulling out hair rather than hankies. Rock star Bon Jovi makes his screen debut as the beefcake (discussion of his butt takes up about two-thirds of the dialogue) who puts the fire back into Rebecca's life. Not for the estrogen impaired. *CW:* Brief strong language. 104m/C **VHS, LV.** Elizabeth Perkins, Whoopi Goldberg, Gwyneth Paltrow, Kathleen Turner, Jon Bon Jovi, Jeremy Sisto, Josef Sommer, Peter Coyote; *D:* David Anspaugh; *W:* Ellen Simon; *C:* Julio Macat; *M:* Howard Shore. **PGV**

Moonlight Sonata *♂♂½* **1938** Professional concert pianist Paderewski performs his way through a confusing soap-opera of a film. Includes performances of Franz Liszt's "Second Hungarian Rhapsody" and Frederic Chopin's "Polonaise." 80m/B **VHS.** *GB* Ignace Jan Paderewski, Charles Farrell, Marie Tempest, Barbara Greene, Eric Portman; *D:* Lothar Mendes. **NOS, DVT**

Moonlighting *♂♂♂* **1982 (PG)** Compelling drama about Polish laborers illegally hired to renovate London flat. When their country falls under martial law, the foreman conceals the event and pushes workers to complete project. Unlikely casting of Irons as foreman is utterly successful.

97m/C **VHS, Beta, LV.** *PL GB* Jeremy Irons, Eugene Lipinski, Jiri Stanislav, Eugeniusz Haczkiewicz; *D:* Jerzy Skolimowski; *C:* Tony Pierce-Roberts; *M:* Hans Zimmer. **USH**

Moonlighting *♂♂½* **1985** The television-pilot for the popular detective show, where Maddie and David, the daffy pair of impetuous private eyes, meet for the first time and solve an irrationally complex case. 93m/C **VHS, Beta, Closed Caption.** Cybill Shepherd, Bruce Willis, Allyce Beasley; *D:* Robert Butler. **WAR, OM**

The Moonraker *♂♂½* **1958** Compelling action scenes highlight this tale set at the end of the English Civil War, as the Royalists attempt to sneak the king out of England and into France. 82m/C **VHS.** *GB* George Baker, Sylvia Syms, Peter Arne, Marius Goring, Clive Morton, Gary Raymond, Richard Leech, Patrick Troughton; *D:* David MacDonald. **NOS**

Moonraker *♂♂* **1979 (PG)** Uninspired Bond fare has 007 unraveling intergalactic hijinks. Bond is aided by a female CIA agent, assaulted by a giant with jaws of steel, and captured by Amazons when he sets out to protect the human race. Moore, Chiles, and Lonsdale all seem to be going through the motions only. 136m/C **VHS, Beta, LV, Letterbox, Closed Caption.** *GB* Roger Moore, Lois Chiles, Richard Kiel, Michael Lonsdale, Corinne Clery, Geoffrey Keen, Emily Bolton, Walter Gotell, Bernard Lee, Lois Maxwell, Desmond Llewelyn; *D:* Lewis Gilbert; *M:* John Barry. **MGM, TLF**

Moonrise *♂♂* **1948** A melodramatic tale about the son of an executed murderer who becomes the object of derision in the small town where he lives. One tormentor finally attacks him, and the young man must make a split-second decision that may affect his own mortality. 90m/B **VHS,** **LV.** Dane Clark, Gail Russell, Ethel Barrymore, Allyn Joslyn, Harry (Henry) Morgan, Lloyd Bridges, Selena Royle, Rex Ingram, Harry Carey Jr.; *D:* Frank Borzage. Nominations: Academy Awards '48: Best Sound. **REP**

The Moon's Our Home *♂♂½* **1936** A fast-paced, breezy, screwball comedy about an actress and adventurer impulsively marrying and then bickering through the honeymoon. Silliness at its height. Fonda and Sullavan were both married and then divorced before filming this movie. 80m/B **VHS, Beta.** Margaret Sullavan, Henry Fonda, Beulah Bondi, Charles Butterworth, Margaret Hamilton, Walter Brennan; *D:* William A. Seiter; *C:* Joseph Valentine. **BAR**

Moonshine County Express *♂½* **1977 (PG)** Three sexy daughters of a hillbilly moonshiner set out to run the still and avenge their father's murder. 95m/C **VHS, Beta.** John Saxon, Susan Howard, William Conrad, Morgan Woodward, Claudia Jennings, Jeff Corey, Dub Taylor, Maureen McCormick, Albert Salmi, Candice Rialson; *D:* Gus Trikonis. **WAR**

Moonshine Highway *♂♂* **1996 (PG-13)** Redneck alert! '50s Tennessee moonshiner Jed Muldoon (MacLachlan) clashes with Sheriff Miller (Quaid), who's not only aggrieved about Jed's illegal liquor running but is not happy that his estranged wife Ethel (Del Mar) has taken up with the miscreant. Lots of backwoods car chases. Made for cable. *CW:* Some scenes of violence. 96m/C **VHS, Beta, Closed Caption.** Kyle MacLachlan, Randy Quaid, Maria Del Mar, Gary Farmer, Jeremy Ratchford; *D:* Andy Armstrong; *W:* Andy Armstrong; *C:* Dick Quinlan. **PAR**

Moonshine Mountain woof! *White Trash on Moonshine Mountain* **1964** A country-western star travels with his girlfriend to the singer's home in backwoods Carolina. When the girl is killed by a lusting resident, all hell breaks loose. One of gore-meister Lewis' excursions into the dramatic. 90m/C **VHS, Beta.** Chuck Scott, Adam Sorg, Jeffrey Allen, Bonnie Hinson, Carmen Sotir, Ben Moore, Pat Patterson, Mark Douglas; *D:* Herschell Gordon Lewis. **SNC**

The Moonstone *♂♂♂* **1997** In the mid-19th century, the Moonstone, a sacred Hindu diamond, is stolen from a shrine in India. The jewel, which carries a curse, winds up in the hands of heiress Rachel Verinder (Hawes), thanks to her suitor Franklin Blake (Wise). But when the diamond is stolen from Rachel, police Sergeant Cuff

(Sher) investigates and uncovers deception and a variety of villains. Based on the novel by Wilkie Collins and considered the first detective story, some 20 years before Conan Doyle's Sherlock Holmes. 120m/C VHS. Greg Wise, Anthony Sher, Keeley Hawes, Patricia Hodge; **D:** Robert Bierman. VTR

Moonstruck 🎬🎬🎬½ 1987 (PG-13) Winning romantic comedy about widow engaged to one man but falling in love with his younger brother in Little Italy. Excellent performances all around, with Cher particularly fetching as attractive, hapless widow. Unlikely casting of usually dominating Aiello, as unassuming mama's boy also works well, and Cage is at his best as a tormented one-handed opera lover/baker. 103m/C VHS, Beta, LV, Letterbox, Closed Caption. Cher, Nicolas Cage, Olympia Dukakis, Danny Aiello, Vincent Gardenia, Julie Bovasso, Louis Guss, Anita Gillette, Feodor Chaliapin Jr, John Mahoney; **D:** Norman Jewison; **W:** John Patrick Shanley; **C:** David Watkin. Academy Awards '87: Best Actress (Cher), Best Original Screenplay, Best Supporting Actress (Dukakis); Berlin International Film Festival '87: Best Director (Jewison); Golden Globe Awards '88: Best Actress—Musical/Comedy (Cher), Best Supporting Actress (Dukakis); Los Angeles Film Critics Association Awards '87: Best Supporting Actress (Dukakis); National Board of Review Awards '87: Best Supporting Actress (Dukakis); Writers Guild of America '87: Best Original Screenplay; Nominations: Academy Awards '87: Best Director (Jewison), Best Picture, Best Supporting Actor (Gardenia). MGM, BTV, HMV

Moontrap 🎬🎬 1989 An astronaut discovers an alien frozen in space and returns to Earth with it. Once thawed, the creature reveals its horrible secret. 92m/C VHS, LV. Walter Koenig, Bruce Campbell, Leigh Lombardi; **D:** Robert Dyke. MOV, IME

Morals for Women 🎬½ 1931 This soap-opera's so old it almost predates soap. A secretary becomes the Kept Woman of her boss in the Big Bad City. She escapes, but not for long. 65m/B VHS. Bessie Love, Conway Tearle, John Holland, Natalie Moorhead, Emma Dunn, June Clyde; **D:** Mort Blumenstock. NOS, LOO

Moran of the Lady Letty 🎬🎬½ 1922 Seaweed saga of Ramon Laredo (Valentino), a high society guy who's kidnapped aboard a pirate barge. When the salty dogs rescue/capture Moran (a theme ahead of its time?) from a ship fuming with burning coal, Ramon is smitten in a big way with the boyish girl and battles contagiously to prevent the pirates from selling her as a slave. Excellent fight scenes with much hotstepping over gangplanks and swinging from masts, with a 60-foot death dive from above. Little known Dalton was a celluloid fave in the 'teens and twenties, and Valentino is atypically cast as a man's man. The sheik himself is said not to have like this one because it undermined his image as a ladies' man. 71m/B VHS, Beta. Dorothy Dalton, Rudolph Valentino, Charles Brinley, Walter Long, Emil Jorgenson; **D:** George Melford. GPV, FCT

More 🎬🎬½ 1969 Smells like teen angst in the '60s when a German college grad falls for an American in Paris, to the tune of sex, drugs, and Pink Floyd. Schroeder's first effort as director, it's definitely a '60s pic. In French with English subtitles. 110m/C VHS, Beta. Mimsy Farmer, Klaus Grunberg, Heinz Engelmann, Michel Chanderli; **D:** Barbet Schroeder; **C:** Nestor Almendros. WAR, BTV, FCT

More American Graffiti 🎬½ 1979 (PG) Sequel to 1973's acclaimed '50s homage "American Graffiti" charts various characters' experiences in the more radical '60s. George Lucas didn't direct, Richard Dreyfuss didn't reprise. Ron Howard doesn't direct, he acts. B.W.L. Norton doesn't direct either, though he's credited. Pass on this one and have that root canal done instead. 111m/C VHS, LV, Closed Caption. Candy Clark, Bo Hopkins, Ron Howard, Paul LeMat, MacKenzie Phillips, Charles Martin Smith, Anna Bjorn, Richard Bradford, Cindy Williams, Scott Glenn; **D:** Bill W.L. Norton; **C:** Caleb Deschanel. USH

More! Police Squad 1982 More episodes from the seminal spoof of television cop shows, episodes entitled "Revenge and Remorse," "The Butler Did It" and "Testimony of Evil." 75m/C VHS, Beta, LV. Leslie Nielsen, Alan North, Rex Hamilton, Peter Lupus. PAR

The More the Merrier 🎬🎬🎬 1943 Likeable romantic comedy in which working girl must share apartment with two bachelors in Washington, D.C., during WWII. Arthur is especially endearing as a young woman in male company. 104m/B VHS, Beta, LV. Joel McCrea, Jean Arthur, Charles Coburn, Richard Gaines, Bruce (Herman Brix) Bennett, Ann Savage, Ann Doran, Frank Tully, Grady Sutton; **D:** George Stevens. Academy Awards '43: Best Supporting Actor (Coburn); New York Film Critics Awards '43: Best Director (Stevens); Nominations: Academy Awards '43: Best Actress (Arthur), Best Director (Stevens), Best Picture, Best Screenplay, Best Story. COL, BTV

More Wild, Wild West 🎬🎬 1980 Another feature-length continuation of the satirical television western series, with Winters taking on Conrad and Martin. Made for television. 94m/C VHS, Beta, LV. Robert Conrad, Ross Martin, Jonathan Winters, Victor Buono; **D:** Burt Kennedy. FOX

Morgan! 🎬🎬½ Morgan: A Suitable Case for Treatment; A Suitable Case for Treatment 1966 Offbeat comedy in which deranged artist copes with divorce by donning ape suit. Some laughs ensue. Based on David Mercer's play. 93m/B VHS, Beta, LV. GB Vanessa Redgrave, David Warner, Robert Stephens, Irene Handl, Bernard Bresslaw, Arthur Mullard, Newton Blick, Nan Munro, Graham Crowden, John Rae, Peter Collingwood, Edward Fox; **D:** Karel Reisz; **W:** David Mercer. British Academy Awards '66: Best Screenplay; Cannes Film Festival '66: Best Actress (Redgrave); Nominations: Academy Awards '66: Best Actress (Redgrave), Best Costume Design (B & W). NO

Morgan Stewart's Coming Home 🎬 Home Front 1987 (PG-13) When Dad needs a good family image in his political race, he brings Morgan home from boarding school. Fortunately, Morgan can see how his parents are using him and he doesn't approve at all. He decides to turn his family's life upside down while pursuing the love of his life. 96m/C VHS, Beta, LV. Jon Cryer, Lynn Redgrave, Nicholas Pryor, Viveka Davis, Paul Gleason, Andrew Duncan, Savely Kramorov, John Cullum, Robert Sedgwick, Waweru Njenga, Sudhir Rad; **D:** Alan Smithee; **M:** Peter Bernstein. NO

Morgan the Pirate 🎬🎬 Capitaine Morgan; Morgan il Pirata 1960 Steve Reeves is at his finest as Morgan, an escaped slave who becomes a notorious pirate in the Caribbean and is wrongly condemned to death in this brisk, sea-going adventure. 93m/C VHS, Beta, LV. FR IT Steve Reeves, Valerie Lagrange; **D:** Andre de Toth. FCT

Morituri 🎬🎬🎬 Saboteur: Code Name Morituri; The Saboteur 1965 Gripping wartime drama in which an Allied spy tries to persuade German gunboat captain to surrender his vessel. Brando is—no surprise—excellent. 123m/C VHS, Beta, Closed Caption. Marlon Brando, Yul Brynner, Trevor Howard, Janet Margolin, Wally Cox, William Redfield; **D:** Bernhard Wicki; **W:** Daniel Taradash; **C:** Conrad Hall; **M:** Jerry Goldsmith. Nominations: Academy Awards '65: Best Black and White Cinematography, Best Costume Design (B & W). FOX

Mork & Mindy 1978 Williams struts his comedic stuff in this 1978-81 sitcom as a mixed-up alien from the planet Ork who lands in Boulder, Colorado, and manages to convince Mindy McConnell (Dawber) to let him stay with her while he studies human behavior (and tries to adapt). And a good "Nanu, nanu" to you too! Two episodes per tape. 50m/C VHS, Closed Caption. Robin Williams, Pam Dawber, Conrad Janis. PAR

A Mormon Maid 🎬½ 1917 Young woman and her family, after being saved from an Indian attack by a Mormon group, come to live among them without converting to their beliefs. Considered a shocking expose of controversial Mormon practices, including polygamy. 78m/B VHS, Beta.

Mae Murray, Frank Borzage, Hobart Bosworth, Noah Beery Sr.; **D:** Robert Z. Leonard. VYY, GVV

The Morning After 🎬🎬 1986 (R) A predictable suspense-thriller about an alcoholic actress who wakes up one morning with a corpse in bed next to her, but cannot remember anything about the night before. She evades the police, accidentally meets up with an ex-cop, and works with him to unravel an increasingly complicated mystery. 103m/C VHS, Beta, LV, Closed Caption. Jane Fonda, Jeff Bridges, Raul Julia, Diane Salinger, Richard Foronjy, Geoffrey Scott, Kathleen Wilhoite, Frances Bergen, Rick Rossovich, Kathy Bates; **D:** Sidney Lumet; **W:** James Cresson; **C:** Andrzej Bartkowiak. Nominations: Academy Awards '86: Best Actress (Fonda). ORI, WAR

Morning Glory 🎬🎬½ 1933 Small-town girl finds love and fame in the big city. Predictable fare nonetheless boasts fine performances from Hepburn and Fairbanks. Adapted from Zoe Atkins' stage play. 74m/B VHS, Beta, LV. Katharine Hepburn, Douglas Fairbanks Jr., Adolphe Menjou, Mary Duncan; **D:** Lowell Sherman; **M:** Max Steiner. Academy Awards '33: Best Actress (Hepburn). CCB, BTV, TTC

Morning Glory 🎬🎬½ 1993 (PG-13) Sappy romance, set during the Depression, about a pregnant widow (Raffin) trying to survive on her hardscrabble farm in Georgia. Elly Dinsmore advertises for a husband, not for romance but to help with the work, and is answered by Will Parker (Reeve), an ex-con trying to live down his past. When a local floozy who has been eyeing Will is killed the sheriff (Walsh) is only too happy to go after the stranger in town. Light-weight with some unbelievable plot twists. Based on the novel "Morning Glory" by LaVyrle Spencer. **CW:** Sex-related scene. 90m/C VHS. Deborah Raffin, Christopher Reeve, Lloyd Bochner, Nina Foch, Helen Shaver, J.T. Walsh; **D:** David Hillard Stern; **W:** Deborah Raffin, Charles Jarrott; **M:** Jonathan Elias.

Morocco 🎬🎬🎬½ 1930 A foreign legion soldier falls for a world-weary chanteuse along the desert sands. Cooper has never been more earnest, and Dietrich has never been more blase and exotic. In her American film debut, Dietrich sings "What Am I Bid?" A must for anyone drawn to improbable, gloriously well-done kitsch. Based on Benno Vigny's novel, "Amy Jolly." 92m/B VHS, Beta, LV. Marlene Dietrich, Gary Cooper, Adolphe Menjou, Ullrich Haupt, Francis McDonald, Eve Southern, Paul Porcasi; **D:** Josef von Sternberg; **C:** Lee Garmes. National Film Registry '92; Nominations: Academy Awards '31: Best Actress (Dietrich), Best Cinematography, Best Director (von Sternberg), Best Interior Decoration. USH, FCT

Morons from Outer Space 🎬🎬 1985 (PG) Slow-witted aliens from elsewhere in the universe crash onto Earth, but unlike other sci-fis, these morons become internationally famous, despite them acting like intergalactic stooges. Plenty of sight gags. 87m/C VHS. GB Griff Rhys Jones, Mel Smith, James B. Sikking, Dinsdale Landen, Jimmy Nail, Joanne Pearce, Paul Brown; **D:** Mike Hodges; **C:** Phil Meheux; **M:** Peter Brewis. MGM

Mortal Challenge 🎬½ 1997 (R) A corrupt police force, known as the Centurions, guard a futuristic L.A., which is divided into rich and poor sectors. When wealthy Tori is captured visiting her wrong-side-of-the-sectors boyfriend, the Centurions decide to have some fun by matching her with a cyborg in a death game. 77m/C VHS. Timothy Bottoms, David McCallum, Evan Lurie, Nick Hill; **D:** Randolph Cheveldare. NHO

Mortal Danger 🎬🎬½ Turn Your Pony Around 1994 (PG-13) Kathy and Phil are suicidal teens finding different solutions to their difficulties over the same weekend. Comes across like a TV movie but does maintain an honest message with affecting performances. **CW:** Language and drug & alcohol abuse, suicide. 86m/C VHS, LV, Closed Caption. Ami Dolenz, Noah Hathaway, Paul Coufos, Larry Gatlin, Charles Napier; **D:** Brianne Murphy. IMP, BPG

Mortal Kombat 1: The Movie 🎬🎬

1995 (PG-13) Inevitable film version of mega popular arcade game intended to cash in fast on the game's popularity. Shameless nirvana for youngin's with permanent joystick scars on their hands. Grown-ups forced to sit through it may get into some of the eye-popping special effects and nifty martial arts sequences if they can block out the contrived plot, lame acting, and Lambert's presence as Thunder God. **CW:** Martial arts combat. **101m/C VHS, Closed Caption, DVD.** Christopher Lambert, Talisa Soto, Cary-Hiroyuki Tagawa, Bridgette Wilson; **D:** Paul Anderson. *NLC*

Mortal Kombat 2: Annihilation 🎬½

1997 (PG-13) The treacherous Shao-Khan brings his evil horde of video-game villians through a portal ripped in the universe and threatens to destroy the Earth in this highly unneccesary sequel. Liu Kang and his buds are on the scene to once again do battle to save humanity. Moves from one badly staged fight scene to another with little story or acting (except for Remar in the role of Rayden, replacing Christopher Lambert in the first "Kombat"), and adults should quickly tire of the nonstop back flips and somersaulting that combine with computer graphics to give each character their own special abilities. Kids and gamers, however, should enjoy the new characters, the samesounding pulse-pounding techno music, and the non-stop, but fairly bloodless, violence. **CW:** Nonstop martial arts violence. **98m/C VHS, LV, Closed Caption.** James Remar, Robin Shou, Talisa Soto, Daron McBee, Sandra Hess, Brian Thompson, Reiner Schoene, Musetta Vander, Marjean Holden, Litefoot, Lynn Red Williams, Irina Pantaeva; **D:** John R. Leonetti; **W:** Brent Friedman, Bruce Zabel; **C:** Matthew F. Leonetti; **M:** George S. Clinton. *WAR*

Mortal Passions 🎬½

1990 (R) Another "Double Indemnity" rip-off, with a scheming tramp manipulating everyone around her with betrayal, sex, and murder. Her dead husband's brother eventually ignites old flames to steer her away from his money. **96m/C VHS, Beta, Closed Caption.** Zach Galligan, Krista Errickson, Michael Bowen, Luca Bercovici, Sheila Kelley, David Warner; **D:** Andrew Lane. *FOX*

Mortal Sins 🎬

1990 (R) A TV evangelist finds more than salvation at the altar, when bodies begin to turn up. The detective he hires is close-mouthed, but more than a little interested in the preacher's daughter. A tense psycho-sexual thriller. **85m/C VHS.** Brian Benben, Anthony LaPaglia, Debrah Farentino; **D:** Yuri Sivo. *NO*

Mortal Sins 🎬🎬

1992 (PG-13) Reeve stars as parish priest Thomas Cusack, who hears the confession of a serial killer. What's worse is that the killer is preying on the women of Cusack's parish. Since he can't break the seal of the confessional, the good Father tries to stop the killer himself before another murder takes place. **CW:** Violence. **93m/C VHS, LV, Closed Caption.** Christopher Reeve; **D:** Bradford May. *FOX*

The Mortal Storm 🎬🎬🎬½

1940 Phyllis Bottome's famous novel comes to life in this extremely well acted film about the rise of the Nazi regime. Stewart and Sullavan are young lovers who risk everything to escape the country after their families are torn apart by the Nazi takeover. Although Germany is never identified as the country, it is obvious in this story about the early days of WWII. Hitler took one look at this and promptly banned all MGM movies in Nazi Germany. **100m/B VHS.** Margaret Sullavan, James Stewart, Robert Young, Frank Morgan, Robert Stack, Bonita Granville, Irene Rich; **D:** Frank Borzage; **W:** Claudine West, George Froeschel, Anderson Ellis; **C:** William H. Daniels. *MGM*

Mortal Thoughts 🎬🎬½

1991 (R) Best friends find their relationship tested when the brutal husband of one of them is murdered. Moore and Headly are exceptional, capturing the perfect inflections and attitudes of the hard-working New Jersey beauticians sure of their friendship. Excellent pacing, fine supporting cast, with Keitel and

Willis stand-outs. **CW:** Strong language and momentary violence and drug content. **104m/C VHS, Beta, LV, 8mm, Letterbox, Closed Caption.** Demi Moore, Bruce Willis, Glenne Headly, Harvey Keitel, John Pankow, Billie Neal; **D:** Alan Rudolph; **W:** William Reilly, Claude Kerven; **C:** Elliot Davis; **M:** Mark Isham. National Society of Film Critics Awards '91: Best Supporting Actor (Keitel). *COL*

Mortuary 🎬

1981 (R) Young woman's nightmares come startlingly close to reality. **91m/C VHS, Beta.** Christopher George, Lynda Day George, Paul Smith; **D:** Howard (Hikmet) Avedis; **W:** Howard (Hikmet) Avedis. *ART, VES*

Mortuary Academy 🎬

1991 (R) To win an inheritance two brothers must attend the family mortician school, a situation paving the way for aggressively tasteless jokes on necrophilia. An attempt to recapture the successful black humor of the earlier Bartel/Woronov teaming "Eating Raoul," this one's dead on arrival. **86m/C VHS, LV.** Christopher Atkins, Perry Lang, Paul Bartel, Mary Woronov, Tracey Walter, Lynn Danielson, Cesar Romero, Wolfman Jack; **D:** Michael Schroeder. *COL*

The Mosaic Project 🎬½

1995 (R) Action junkies should be happy with the chases, explosions, and other mayhem engendered by this story of two buddies who find themselves the victims of a mad scientist. Now they have experimental computer chips implanted in their brains that make them skilled in 25 martial arts forms (and some other stuff that doesn't matter much). **CW:** Language, sexual situations, violence. **89m/C VHS.** Jon Tabler, Ben Marley, Joe Estevez; **D:** John Sjogren; **W:** John Sjogren. *MNC*

Mosby's Marauders 🎬🎬

1966 A young boy joins a Confederate raiding company during the Civil War and learns about bravery, war, and love. **79m/C VHS, Beta.** Kurt Russell, James MacArthur, Jack Ging, Peggy Lipton, Nick Adams; **D:** Michael O'Herlihy. *DIS*

Moscow Does Not Believe in Tears 🎬🎬🎬

Moscow Distrusts Tears; Moskwa Sljesam Nje Jerit **1980** Three Soviet women realize very different fates when they pursue their dreams in 1950s' Moscow. Bittersweet, moving fare that seems a somewhat surprising production from pre-Glasnost USSR. Brief nudity and violence. In Russian with English subtitles. A 150-minute version has also been released. **115m/C VHS, Beta, LV.** *RU* Vera Alentova, Irina Muravyova, Raisa Ryazanova, Natalie Vavilova, Alexei Batalov; **D:** Vladimir Menshov. Academy Awards '80: Best Foreign Language Film. *COL, IME, KIV*

Moscow on the Hudson 🎬🎬🎬

1984 (R) Good-natured comedy has Williams as Soviet defector trying to cope with new life of freedom in fast-paced, freewheeling melting pot of New York City. Williams is particularly winning as naive jazzman, though Alonso also scores as his Hispanic love interest. Be warned though, it's not just played for laughs. **115m/C VHS, Beta, LV, 8mm, Closed Caption.** Robin Williams, Maria Conchita Alonso, Cleavant Derricks, Alejandro Rey, Elya Baskin; **D:** Paul Mazursky; **W:** Leon Capetanos, Paul Mazursky. *COL*

Moscow Parade 🎬🎬

Prorva **1992** Sexy cabaret singer gets caught up in the shifting alliances caused by war. Set in Russia before the Nazi invasion. Russian with subtitles. **103m/C VHS.** *RU* Ute Lemper, Vladimir Simonov; **D:** Ivan Dykhovichny. *FRF*

Moses woof!

1976 (PG) Lancaster goes biblical as Moses, the man with the tablets. Edited from the 360-minute British television series, with no improvement obvious from the economy, except that the bad parts are shorter. Poor chatter and scattered bouts of acting are surpassed in inadequacy only by special effects. **141m/C VHS, Beta.** Burt Lancaster, Anthony Quayle, Ingrid Thulin, Irene Papas, William Lancaster; **D:** Gianfranco DeBosio; **W:** Anthony Burgess, Vittorio Bonicelli; **M:** Ennio Morricone. *FOX, ART, VES*

Moses 🎬🎬½

1996 Another entry in TNT's series of Bible stories finds a humble Moses (Kingsley), raised in the Egyptian court, finding his way to his own people, the Israelites. Chosen by God to be his messenger and lead his people out of bondage, Moses must unleash a series of plagues upon Egypt before pharaoh Mernefta (Langella) will let them go. If you want action, look to "The Ten Commandments," since this is a faithful but tedious retelling. Filmed on location in Morocco; on two cassettes. **185m/C VHS.** Ben Kingsley, Frank Langella, David Suchet, Christopher Lee, Anna Galiena, Enrico Lo Verso, Geraldine McEwan, Maurice Roeves, Anthony Higgins, Anton Lesser; **D:** Roger Young; **W:** Lionel Chetwynd; **C:** Raffaele Mertes; **M:** Marco Frisina. *TTC*

Mosiac Project 🎬

1995 (R) Two average guys are mistaken for spies who are supposed to be used in a scientific experiment. They have a computer chip implanted in their brains that turns them into super-strong super agents. **89m/C VHS.** Jon Tabler, Ben Marley, Colleen Coffey, Julie Strain, Joe Estevez, Robert Z'Dar; **D:** John Sjogren. *MNC*

Mosquito 🎬

1995 (R) Alien forces transform the annoying insects into monstrous mutants. Schlocky special effects are good for laughs. **CW:** Sci-fi violence and gore; scene of sexuality/nudity; some language. **92m/C VHS.** Gunnar Hansen, Ron Asheton, Steve Dixon, Rachel Loiselle, Tim Lovelace; **D:** Gary Jones; **W:** Gary Jones, Steve Hodge, Tom Chaney; **C:** Tom Chaney; **M:** Allen Lynch, Randall Lynch.

The Mosquito Coast 🎬🎬½

1986 (PG) Ambitious adaptation of Paul Theroux's novel about an asocial inventor who transplants his family to a rainforest to realize his utopian dream. A nightmare ensues. Ford tries hard, but supporters Mirren and Phoenix are main appeal of only intermittently successful drama. **119m/C VHS, Beta, LV, Letterbox, Closed Caption.** Harrison Ford, Helen Mirren, River Phoenix, Andre Gregory, Martha Plimpton, Conrad Roberts, Butterfly McQueen, Jadrien Steele, Hilary Gordon, Rebecca Gordon, Dick O'Neill, Jason Alexander; **D:** Peter Weir; **W:** Paul Schrader; **C:** John Seale; **M:** Maurice Jarre. *WAR*

The Most Dangerous Game 🎬🎬🎬

The Hounds of Zaroff **1932** Shipwrecked McRae washed ashore on the island of Banks' Count Zaroff, a deranged sportsman with a flair for tracking humans. Guess who becomes the mad count's next target. Oft-told tale is compellingly related in this, the first of many using Richard Connell's famous short story. If deja vu sets in, don't worry. This production uses most of the scenery, staff, and cast from its studio cousin, "King Kong." Remade in 1945 as "A Game of Death" and in 1956 as "Run for the Sun." **78m/B VHS, Beta.** Joel McCrea, Fay Wray, Leslie Banks, Robert Armstrong, Noble Johnson; **D:** Ernest B. Schoedsack, Irving Pichel; **W:** James A. Creelman; **C:** Henry W. Gerrard; **M:** Max Steiner. *VYY, SNC, NOS*

Most Wanted 🎬½

1976 A psychopath with a penchant for raping nuns and collecting crucifixes is tracked down by a special police unit in this made-for-television film. Became a TV series. **78m/C VHS, Beta.** Robert Stack, Shelly Novack, Leslie Charleson, Tom Selleck, Sheree North; **D:** Walter Grauman. *WOV*

Most Wanted 🎬🎬½

1997 (R) Marine Sgt. James Dunn (Wayans), framed for the assassination of the first lady, is on the run from the CIA, FBI, LAPD, and the covert team he was working with, which is led by Voight, the gung-ho general who set up the whole scam. Wayans, who wrote and produced, seems convinced that an action hero must be of the strong-silent-superhero mold, and appears at a loss without a joke to crack. Voight, however, is right at home in the bad-guy role, employing an overdone but effective southern drawl. Plenty of elaborate stunts, oversized fireballs, shootings, and chases provide the expected wild ride, including the film's funniest sequence as thousands of L.A. natives spontaneously become wild-in-the-street bounty hunters.*CW:* Violence and language. 99m/C VHS, LV, DVD. Keenen Ivory Wayans, Jon Voight, Jill Hennessey, Eric Roberts, Paul Sorvino, Robert Culp, Wolfgang Bodison, Simon Baker-Denny; *D:* David Hogan; *W:* Keenen Ivory Wayans; *C:* Marc Reshovsky; *M:* Paul Bruckmaster. Nominations: Golden Raspberry Awards '97: Worst Supporting Actor (Voight). *WAR*

Motel Hell 🎬½ 1980 **(R)** A completely tongue-in-cheek gore-fest about a farmer who kidnaps tourists, buries them in his garden, and reaps a human harvest to grind into his distinctive brand of smoked, preservative-free sausage. 102m/C VHS, Beta, LV. Rory Calhoun, Nancy Parsons, Paul Linke, Nina Axelrod, Wolfman Jack, Elaine Joyce, Dick Curtis, Rosanne Katon, Monique St. Pierre; *D:* Kevin Connor; *W:* Robert Jaffe, Steven-Charles Jaffe; *C:* Thomas Del Ruth. *MGM*

The Moth 🎬🎬½ *Catherine Cookson's The Moth* 1996 Robert Bradley leaves the shipyards only to work in his uncle's furniture business but soon finds himself at odds with the old man. So he becomes a servant for the destructive Thormans, and falls for the lady of the house, Sarah. But in 1913 this upstairs/downstairs romance can only lead to disaster. TV movie based on the novel by Catherine Cookson. 150m/C VHS. *GB* Jack Davenport, Juliet Aubrey, David Bradley, Justine Waddell. *VCO*

Mother 🎬🎬🎬½ 1926 Pudovkin's innovative classic about a Russian family shattered by the uprising in 1905. A masterpiece of Russian cinema that established Pudovkin, and rivaled only Eisenstein for supremacy in montage, poetic imagery, and propagandistic ideals. Based on Maxim Gorky's great novel, it's one of cinematic history's seminal works. Striking cinematography, stunning use of montage make this one important. Silent with English subtitles. 70m/B VHS, Beta. *RU* Vera Baranovskaya, Nikolai Batalov; *D:* Vsevolod Pudovkin. *NOS, IHF, DVT*

Mother 🎬🎬🎬½ *Okasan* 1952 A Japanese family is undone after the devastation of WWII. An uncharacteristically dramatic, and thus more accessible, film from one of the Japanese cinema's greatest masters. In Japanese with English subtitles. 98m/B VHS, Beta, LV. *JP* Kinuyo Tanaka, Kyoko Kagawa, Eiji Okada, Akihiko Katayama; *D:* Mikio Naruse. *FCT, IME*

Mother 🎬🎬½ 1994 **(R)** Olivia Hendrix (Ladd) is a very over-protective mom—even though son Tom (Weisser) is nineteen and anxious to untie the apron strings. But Mom thinks she knows best and she's willing to kill to made certain Tom stays home where he belongs. *CW:* Implied violence, language. 90m/C VHS, LV. Diane Ladd, Olympia Dukakis, Morgan Weisser, Ele Keats; *D:* Frank Laloggia. *TRI*

Mother 🎬🎬½ 1996 **(PG-13)** Yes, you will shake your head in recognition of that parent-child bond. Twice-divorced writer John Henderson (Brooks) decides it's all Mom's fault he has problems with women, so he decides to move back home and figure out what went wrong. Mom Beatrice (Reynolds) is exasperated and married younger brother Jeff (Morrow) winds up jealous of mom's attentions to his sibling. Reynolds' first feature film in 25 years. *CW:* Some sexual references. 104m/C VHS, Closed Caption. Albert Brooks, Debbie Reynolds, Rob Morrow, Lisa Kudrow, John C. McGinley, Isabel Glasser, Peter White; *D:* Albert Brooks; *W:* Albert Brooks, Monica Johnson; *C:* Lajos Koltai; *M:* Marc Shaiman. New York Film Critics Awards '96: Best Screenplay; National Society of Film Critics Awards '96: Best Screenplay; Nominations: Golden Globe Awards '97: Best Actress—Musical/Comedy (Reynolds). *PAR*

Mother & Daughter: A Loving War 🎬½ 1980 A made-for-television film about three women experiencing motherhood. Special appearance by Harry Chapin as himself. 96m/C VHS, Beta. Tuesday Weld, Frances Sternhagen, Kathleen Beller, Jeanne Lang, Ed Winter; *D:* Burt Brinckerhoff. *NLC*

Mother and Son 🎬🎬 1931 Melodrama finds the wayward Young shielding her son from the fact that she runs a gambling hall. He grows up to be a society lad before discovering the de-

vastating truth. 67m/B VHS. Clara Kimball Young, Dana Warren, Mildred Golden, John Elliott, Gordon Wood, Ernest Hilliard; *D:* John P. McCarthy. *GPV*

Mother Doesn't Always Know Best 🎬½ 196? A strange relationship between a young count and his widowed mother initiates a strange series of events. 95m/C VHS, Beta. Senta Berger; *D:* Alfredo Gianelli. *NO*

Mother Goose Rock 'n' Rhyme 1990 Duvall follows the success of her "Faerie Tale Theatre" series with a new comedic fable, starring some of Hollywood's top names. Great fun for the whole family. 96m/C VHS, Beta, Closed Caption. Shelley Duvall, Teri Garr, Howie Mandel, Jean Stapleton, Ben Vereen, Bobby Brown, Art Garfunkel, Dan Gilroy, Deborah Harry, Cyndi Lauper, Little Richard, Paul Simon, Harry Anderson, Elayne Boosler, Woody Harrelson, Richard "Cheech" Marin, Garry Shandling.

Mother Joan of the Angels 🎬🎬🎬 *The Devil and the Nun; Matka Joanna Od Aniolow* 1960 A priest investigating demonic possession among nuns in a 17th-century Polish convent becomes involved in a mutual attraction with the Mother Superior. A powerful allegory complemented by the stylized narrative and performances. Polish with subtitles. Based on actual events at Loudun and also the subject of a play by John Whiting, an opera by Krzysztof Penderecki, "The Devils of Loudon" novel by Aldous Huxley, and Ken Russell's movie "The Devils." 108m/B VHS. *PL* Lucyna Winnicka, Mieczyslaw Voit, Anna Ciepielewska, Maria Chwalibog; *D:* Jerzy Kawalerowicz; *W:* Jerzy Kawalerowicz, Tadeusz Konwicki; *M:* Adam Walacinski. Cannes Film Festival '61: Grand Jury Prize. *FCT*

Mother, Jugs and Speed 🎬½ 1976 **(PG)** Black comedy about the day-to-day tragedies encountered by a group of ambulance drivers. Interesting mix of stars. 95m/C VHS. Bill Cosby, Raquel Welch, Harvey Keitel, Allen (Goorwitz) Garfield, Larry Hagman, Bruce Davison, Dick Butkus, L.Q. Jones, Toni Basil; *D:* Peter Yates; *W:* Tom Mankiewicz. *FOX*

Mother Kusters Goes to Heaven 🎬🎬🎬 *Mutter Kusters Fahrt Zum Himmel* 1976 Mrs. Kusters's husband is a frustrated factory worker who goes over the edge and kills the factory owner's son and himself. Left alone, she learns that everyone is using her husband's death to further their own needs, including her daughter, who uses the publicity to enhance her singing career. A statement that you should trust no one, not even your family and friends. This film was banned from the Berlin Film Festival because of its political overtones. In German with English subtitles. 108m/C VHS. *GE* Brigitte Mira, Ingrid Caven, Armin Meier, Irm Hermann, Gottfried John, Margit Carstensen, Karl-Heinz Boehm; *D:* Rainer Werner Fassbinder; *W:* Rainer Werner Fassbinder; *C:* Michael Ballhaus. *NYF*

Mother Lode 🎬½ *Search for the Mother Lode; The Last Great Treasure* 1982 **(PG)** The violent conflict between twin brothers (played by Heston) is intensified by greed, near madness, and the all-consuming lust for gold in this action-adventure. Heston's son, Fraser Clarke Heston, wrote as well as produced the film. 101m/C VHS, Beta. Charlton Heston, Nick Mancuso, Kim Basinger; *D:* Charlton Heston. *VES*

Mother Night 🎬🎬🎬 1996 **(R)** American writer Howard Campbell (Nolte) is recruited as a spy in pre-World War II Germany in this adaptation of Kurt Vonnegut's 1962 novel. He poses as a Nazi sympathizer in broadcasts to American troops, but his anti-semitic diatribes are actually coded information crucial to the Allies. After the war, Campbell's life unravels as he loses his young wife (Lee) and the U.S. government refuses to acknowledge his efforts. He is smuggled back to the U.S., where both Israeli Nazi-hunters and twisted neo-Nazis search for him. After being captured, imprisoned in Israel, and conversing with fellow prisoner Adolf Eichmann (Gibson), Campbell realizes the moral of this dark comedy: "We are what we pretend to be." Arkin is excel-

lent as his Greenwich Village neighbor who also has some secrets. If you look closely, you can see author Vonnegut in a cameo. *CW:* Scene of sexuality. 113m/C VHS. Nick Nolte, Sheryl Lee, Alan Arkin, John Goodman, Kirsten Dunst, David Strathairn, Arye Gross, Frankie Faison, Bernard Behrens; *D:* Keith Gordon; *W:* Robert B. Weide; *C:* Tom Richmond; *M:* Michael Convertino; *V:* Henry Gibson. *NLC*

Mother of Kings 🎬🎬 1982 Livin' ain't easy for a widowed charwoman thanks to WWII and Stalinism. Innovative use of newsreel scenes. In Polish with English subtitles. 126m/C VHS. *PL* Magda Teresa Wojcik. *FCT*

Mother Teresa: In the Name of God's Poor 🎬🎬 1997 Bio of the missionary begins when the 36-year-old cloistered nun (Chaplin) starts her work in the Calcutta slums and founds the Missionaries of Charity, and culminates with her 1979 Nobel Peace Prize acceptance speech. The cable drama was unauthorized and reportedly did not receive the approval of Mother Teresa when she learned of the project. 93m/C VHS. Geraldine Chaplin, Keene Curtis, William Katt, Alan Shearman, Cornelia Hayes O'Herlihy; *D:* Kevin Connor; *W:* Dominique Lapierre, Carol Kaplan. *HMK*

Mother's Boys 🎬🎬 1994 **(R)** Estranged mother Curtis attempts to reunite with the family she abandoned only to be snubbed, inspiring in her a ruthless effort to win back the children and oust father Gallagher's new live-in girlfriend Whalley-Kilmer. With an almost psychotic devotion, she terrorizes everyone in the family, including enticing her 12-year-old son Edwards into a nude bathtub game of peek-a-boo. Film lacks the tension necessary to carry suspense. Based on the novel by Bernard Taylor. *CW:* Language and mother's sociopathic behavior. 96m/C VHS, LV, Closed Caption. Jamie Lee Curtis, Peter Gallagher, Joanne Whalley, Luke Edwards, Vanessa Redgrave, Colin Ward, Joss Ackland, Paul Guilfoyle, John C. McGinley, J.E. Freeman, Ken Lerner, Lorraine Toussaint, Joey Zimmerman, Jill Freedman; *D:* Yves Simoneau; *W:* Richard Hawley, Barry Schneider; *C:* Elliot Davis; *M:* George S. Clinton. *MAX, TOU*

Mother's Day 🎬½ 1980 Three women who were former college roommates plan a reunion together in the wilderness. All goes well until they are dragged into an isolated house by two insane boys who constantly watch television, ardently consume the products advertised, and then terrorize and torture people to please their mom. Sanitized gore with black satiric intentions. 98m/C VHS, Beta. Tiana Pierce, Nancy Hendrickson, Deborah Luee, Holden McGuire, Billy Ray McQuade, Rose Ross; *D:* Charles Kaufman; *W:* Warren Leight, Charles Kaufman.

A Mother's Prayer 🎬🎬½ 1995 **(PG-13)** Fact-based story about young mom Rosemary Holmstrom (Hamilton), who has AIDS, and is determined to find a home for her eight-year-old son T.J. (Fleiss) before she dies. Guaranteed to make the tear ducts flow, with a determined performance from Hamilton that lessens the sentimentality. Made for cable TV. Holmstrom died at the age of 36 in 1994. *CW:* Emotionally charged subject matter. 94m/C VHS, Closed Caption. Linda Hamilton, Noah Fleiss, Bruce Dern, Kate Nelligan, S. Epatha Merkerson, Corey Parker, Jenny O'Hara, RuPaul; *D:* Larry Elikann; *W:* Lee Rose; *C:* Eric Van Haren Noman; *M:* Tom Scott. *USH*

Mothra 🎬🎬🎬 1962 Classic Japanese monster shenanigans about an enraged giant caterpillar that invades Tokyo while searching for the Ailenas, a set of very tiny, twin princesses who've been kidnapped by an evil nightclub owner in the pursuit of big profits. After tiring of crushing buildings and wreaking incidental havoc, the enormous crawly thing zips up into a cocoon and emerges as Mothra, a moth distinguished by both its size and bad attitude. Mothra and the wee babes make appearances in later Godzilla epics. 101m/C VHS, Beta. *JP* Yumi Ito, Frankie Sakai, Lee Kresel, Emi Ito; *D:* Inoshiro Honda. *GKK*

Motor

Motor Patrol ⚙½ 1950 A cop poses as a racketeer to infiltrate a car-stealing ring. 66m/B VHS, Beta, LV. Don Castle, Jane Nigh, Charles Victor. *NO*

Motor Psycho woof! 1965 When a motorcycle gang rapes a woman, she and her husband pursue them into the desert to seek their brutal revenge. 73m/B VHS. Haji, Alex Rocco, Stephen Oliver, Holle K. Winters, Joseph Cellini, Thomas Scott, Coleman Francis, Sharon Lee; *D:* Russ Meyer. *RMF*

Motorama ⚙⚙ 1991 (R) A 10-year-old juvenile delinquent becomes obsessed with winning a gas station contest which involves collecting game cards. So he steals a car and hits the road where he gets his first tattoo and encounters a beautiful "older" woman (Barrymore) and lots of trouble. *CW:* Language and sensual scene. 89m/C VHS. Jordan Christopher Michael, Martha Quinn, Flea, Michael J. Pollard, Meat Loaf, Drew Barrymore, Garrett Morris, Robin Duke, Sandy Baron, Mary Woronov, Susan Tyrrell, John Laughlin, John Diehl, Robert Picardo, Jack Nance, Vince Edwards, Dick Miller, Allyce Beasley, Shelley Berman; *D:* Barry Shils; *W:* Joe Minion; *M:* Andy Summers. *COL, BTV*

Motorcycle Gang ⚙ 1957 It's the summer of '57, and Randy plans to bring home the title at the Pacific Motorcycle Championships for his club, the "Skyriders." But first his old rival Nick, who's just out of jail, turns up and challenges Randy to an illegal street race. Will Randy succumb to peer pressure and race? Lame plot + lame acting = lame movie. 78m/B VHS. Steven Terrell, John Ashley, Anne Neyland, Carl "Alfalfa" Switzer, Raymond Hatton; *D:* Edward L. Cahn; *W:* Lou Rusoff. *COL*

Motorcycle Squad ⚙½ 1937 A policeman is dishonorably discharged so he can get the "inside" dope on a gang of crooks in this 'B' thriller. ?m/C VHS. Kane Richmond, Wynne Gibson. *SNC*

Mouchette ⚙⚙⚙½ 1967 A lonely 14-year-old French girl, daughter of a drunk father and dying mother, eventually finds spiritual release by committing suicide. Typically somber, spiritual fare from unique master filmmaker Bresson. Perhaps the most complete expression of Bresson's austere, Catholic vision. In French with English subtitles. 80m/B VHS, Beta. *FR* Nadine Nortier, Maria Cardinal, Paul Hebert; *D:* Robert Bresson; *C:* Ghislan Cloquet. *FCT, TPV, HTV*

Moulin Rouge ⚙⚙⚙½ 1952 Colorful, entertaining portrait of acclaimed Impressionist painter Toulouse-Lautrec, more famous for its production stories than on-screen drama, Ferrer delivers one of his most impressive performances as the physically stunted, cynical artist who basked in the seamy Montmartre nightlife. 119m/C VHS, Beta, LV. Jose Ferrer, Zsa Zsa Gabor, Christopher Lee, Peter Cushing, Colette Marchand, Katherine Kath, Michael Balfour, Eric Pohlmann, Suzanne Flon, Claude Nollier, Muriel Smith, Mary Clare, Walter Crisham, Harold Kasket, Jim Gerald, George Lannes, Lee Montague, Maureen Swanson, Lily Lemkow, Jill Bennett, Theodore Bikel; *D:* John Huston; *W:* John Huston, Anthony Veiller; *C:* Oswald Morris. Academy Awards '52: Best Art Direction/Set Decoration (Color), Best Costume Design (Color); Nominations: Academy Awards '52: Best Actor (Ferrer), Best Director (Huston), Best Film Editing, Best Picture, Best Supporting Actress (Marchand). *MGM*

The Mountain ⚙⚙ 1956 A man and his shady younger brother set out to inspect a Paris-routed plane that crashed in the French Alps. After some harrowing experiences in climbing the peak, it becomes evident that one brother has designs to save whatever he can, while the other intends to loot it. Many real, as well as staged, climbing scenes. Based on Henri Troyat's novel. 105m/C VHS, Beta, Closed Caption. Spencer Tracy, Robert Wagner, Claire Trevor, William Demarest, Richard Arlen, E.G. Marshall; *D:* Edward Dmytryk. *PAR*

Mountain Charlie ⚙½ 1980 Mountain girl's life is destroyed by three drifters. 96m/C VHS, Beta. Denise Neilson, Dick Robinson, Rick Guinn, Lynn Seus; *D:* George Stapleford. *NO*

Mountain Family Robinson ⚙⚙ 1979 (G) An urban family, seeking escape from the hassles of city life, moves to the Rockies, determined to get back to nature. They soon find that nature may be more harsh than rush-hour traffic and nasty bosses when a bear comes calling. More "Wilderness Family"-type adventures. 102m/C VHS, Beta. Robert F. Logan, Susan Damante Shaw, Heather Rattray, Ham Larsen, William Bryant, George Flower; *D:* John Cotter. *VTR*

Mountain Justice ⚙⚙½ *Kettle Creek* 1930 Maynard's first all-talkie western finds our hero in search of his father's murderer. Good action sequences (with stunts performed by Maynard), including those aboard a moving train and a buckboard. 73m/B VHS. Ken Maynard, Otis Harlan, Kathryn Crawford, Paul Hurst; *D:* Harry Joe Brown. *GPV*

Mountain Man ⚙⚙½ *Guardian of the Wilderness* 1977 Historically accurate drama about Galen Clark's successful fight in the 1860s to save the magnificent wilderness area that is now Yosemite National Park. Together with naturalist John Muir, he fought a battle against the lumber companies who wanted the timber and won President Lincoln's support for his cause. 96m/C VHS, Beta. Denver Pyle, John Dehner, Ken Berry, Cheryl Miller, Don Shanks, Cliff Osmond, Jack Kruschen, Ford Rainey; *D:* David O'Malley; *W:* David O'Malley. *LME*

The Mountain Men ⚙½ 1980 (R) Dull adventure drama set in the American West of the 1880s. Two trappers argue about life and have trouble with Indians. 102m/C VHS, Beta, LV. Charlton Heston, Brian Keith, John Glover, Seymour Cassel, Victor Jory; *D:* Richard Lang. *COL*

The Mountain Road ⚙½ 1960 Listless drama of an American squadron stationed in China during the last days of WWII. Only Stewart makes this drab film worthwile. 102m/B VHS. James Stewart, Harry (Henry) Morgan, Glenn Corbett, Mike Kellin; *D:* Daniel Mann. *COL*

Mountains of the Moon ⚙⚙⚙½ 1990 (R) Sprawling adventure detailing the obsessive search for the source of the Nile conducted by famed Victorian rogue/explorer Sir Richard Burton and chief John Hanning Speke in the late 1800s. Spectacular scenery and images. Director Rafelson, better known for overtly personal films such as "Five Easy Pieces" and "The King of Marvin Gardens," shows considerable skill with this epic. From William Harrison's novel "Burton and Speke." 140m/C VHS, Beta, LV, Closed Caption. Patrick Bergin, Iain Glen, Fiona Shaw, Richard E. Grant, Peter Vaughan, Roger Rees, Bernard Hill, Anna Massey, Leslie Phillips, John Savident, James Villiers, Delroy Lindo, Roshan Seth; *D:* Bob Rafelson; *W:* Bob Rafelson; *C:* Roger Deakins. *ART*

Mountaintop Motel Massacre woof! 1986 (R) A resort motel's hostess is a raving lunatic who regularly slaughters her guests. 95m/C VHS, Beta. Bill Thurman, Anna Chappell, Will Mitchell; *D:* Jim McCullough. *VTR*

Mountbatten: The Last Viceroy ⚙⚙½ *Lord Mountbatten: The Last Viceroy* 1986 Originally a British TV miniseries detailing English viceroy Lord Mountbatten's (Williamson) turning over ruling power from Great Britain to India in 1947 and the birth of Pakistan. 107m/C VHS. *GB* Nicol Williamson, Janet Suzman, Sam Dastor, Nigel Davenport, Wendy Hiller, Ian Richardson, Julian Wadham; *D:* Tom Clegg; *W:* David Butler; *C:* Peter Jessop; *M:* John Scott. *BWE*

Mouse and His Child ⚙⚙ 1977 A gentle animated fantasy adventure about a toy wind-up mouse and his child who fall into the clutches of a villainous rat when they venture into the outside world. 83m/C VHS, Beta. *D:* Fred Wolf; *V:* Peter Ustinov, Cloris Leachman, Andy Devine. *COL*

Mouse Hunt ⚙⚙⚙ 1997 (PG) The Smuntz brothers (Lane and Evans) inherit a run-down mansion from their wealthy string magnate father (Hickey, in his last role). Since the boys are involved in a bitter long-standing argument over cord versus twine, they're happy to learn about an offer from a preservation society for a small fortune. The boys try to fix up the house, only to be foiled by the mouse who had been the sole occupant. There are plenty of new mouse traps and tricks thanks to the 65 trained mice (along with 3-D animation) who play the hero. The plucky rodent must also battle a psychotic cat and an obsessed exterminator (Walken, or Lord High King Psycho). If you've ever laughed at a cartoon character taking an anvil to the head, you'll like this. The cartoon-like action livens up the otherwise dismal setting of the mansion and it's surroundings. Directorial debut by Verbinski, the man who brought you the Bud frogs. 97m/C VHS, Closed Caption. Nathan Lane, Lee Evans, Christopher Walken, William Hickey, Vicki Lewis, Maury Chaykin, Eric Christmas, Michael Jeter, Debra Christofferson, Camilla Soeberg; *D:* Gore Verbinski; *W:* Adam Rifkin; *C:* Phedon Papamichael; *M:* Alan Silvestri. *USH*

The Mouse That Roared ⚙⚙⚙ 1959 With its wine export business going down the drain, a tiny, desperate country decides to declare war on the United States in hopes that the U.S., after its inevitable triumph, will revive the conquered nation. So off to New York go 20 chain-mail clad warriors armed with bow and arrow. Featured in three roles, Sellers is great as the duchess, less effective (though still funny) as the prime minister, and a military leader. A must for Sellers' fans; maintains a sharp satiric edge throughout. Based on the novel by Leonard Wibberley. 83m/C VHS, Beta. *GB* Peter Sellers, Jean Seberg, Leo McKern, David Kossoff, William Hartnell, Timothy Bateson; *D:* Jack Arnold; *W:* Roger MacDougall, Stanley Mann; *M:* Edwin Astley. *COL*

Mouth to Mouth ⚙⚙ *Boca a Boca* 1995 (R) Budding actor Victor (Bardem) is working in Madrid as a phone sex operator while waiting to hear about his big break on an American picture. Victor's regularly called by repressed gay surgeon Ricardo (Flotats) and Amanda (Sanchez-Gijon), who says she's Ricardo's wife. Naive Victor falls for Amanda—who of course isn't Ricardo's wife but seems to be involved in a plot to kill Ricardo masterminded by his real wife Angela (Barranco) and her lover David (Gutierrez Caba). The plot's a tangled but there's lots of visual gags and bedroom farce and the virile Bardem turns out to be a gifted comedian. Spanish with subtitles. *CW:* Sexuality and language. 97m/C VHS, Closed Caption. *SP* Javier Bardem, Aitana Sanchez-Gijon, Josep Maria Flotats, Maria Barranco, Emilio Gutierrez-Caba, Fernando Guillen, Myriam Meziere; *D:* Manuel Gomez Pereira; *W:* Manuel Gomez Pereira, Joaquin Oristrell, Naomi Wise, Juan Luis Iborra; *C:* Juan Amoros; *M:* Bernardo Bonazzi. Nominations: Independent Spirit Awards '98: Best Foreign Language Film. *TOU*

Mouvements du Desir ⚙⚙ *Desire in Motion* 1994 Sex-on-a-train sequences add more than a little steam to this romantic drama. Catherine (Kaprisky) is travelling with her young daughter on the Montreal to Vancouver train in order to forget a failed relationship. She meets shy Vincent (Pichette), who is supposed to be on his way to meet his lover, but somewhere on the journey the sexual sparks start igniting. There are some eccentric fellow passengers to contend with (and director Pool drops in some surreal dream sequences as well) but the heat generated by the leads is genuine enough. 94m/C VHS. *CA SI* Valerie Kaprisky, Jean-Francois Pichette, Jolianne L'Allier-Matteau, Matthew Mackay, William Jacques; *D:* Lea Pool; *W:* Lea Pool; *C:* Pierre Mignot; *M:* Zbigniew Preisner. Nominations: Genie Awards '94: Best Actress (Kaprisky), Best Director (Pool). *NYR*

Movers and Shakers ⚙½ 1985 (PG) An irreverent spoof of Hollywood depicting a filmmaker's attempt to render a best-selling sex manual into a blockbuster film. Fails to live up to its potential and wastes a star-studded cast. 100m/C VHS, Beta. Walter Matthau, Charles Grodin, Gilda Radner, Vincent Gardenia, Bill Macy, Tyne Daly, Steve Martin, Penny

Marshall, Luana Anders; **D:** William Asher; **W:** Charles Grodin. *MGM*

The Movie House Massacre ♪ 1978
A psychopath runs rampant in a theatre killing and maiming moviegoers. No refunds are given. **80m/C VHS, Beta.** Mary Woronov. *MRV*

Movie ... In Your Face ♂ 1990 Japanese mobsters want to take over a movie studio. This supposed comedy comes with a "PU-13" rating—"Stinks to anyone with an I.Q. over 13," make of that what you will and be forewarned that it's also sophomoric and tasteless. **85m/C VHS.** Tommy Sledge. *HTV*

Movie Maker ♂ *Smart Alec* 1986 A young filmmaker ineptly raises money for his next film. **87m/C VHS, Beta.** Zsa Zsa Gabor, Antony Alda, Orson Bean, Bill Henderson; **D:** Jim Wilson. *ART*

Movie, Movie ♂♂½ 1978 (PG) Acceptable spoof of 1930s films features Scott in twin-bill of black and white "Dynamite Hands," which lampoons boxing dramas, and "Baxter's Beauties," a color send-up of Busby Berkeley musicals. There's even a parody of coming attractions. Wholesome, mildly entertaining. **107m/B VHS.** Stanley Donen, George C. Scott, Trish Van Devere, Eli Wallach, Red Buttons, Barbara Harris, Barry Bostwick, Harry Hamlin, Art Carney; **D:** Stanley Donen; **W:** Larry Gelbart; **M:** Ralph Burns. Writers Guild of America '78: Best Original Screenplay. *FOX*

A Movie Star's Daughter 1979 The daughter of a famous movie star moves to a new town and school. She is afraid her popularity is due to her famous father. She must make choices and learn the real meaning of friendship. Also available in a 33-minute edited version. **46m/C VHS, Beta.** Frank Converse, Trini Alvarado; **D:** Robert Fuest. *BFA*

Movie Stuntmen ♂ *Hollywood Thrillmakers; Hollywood Stunt Man* 1953 A retired Hollywood stunt man takes a job for a dead friend so that the friend's widow can receive the fee. Good stunt work taken mostly from old Richard Talmadge movies almost makes up for poor production. **56m/B VHS.** James Gleason, William Henry; **D:** Bernard B. Ray. *NOS*

Movies Money Murder ♂♂ 1996
Ruthless actress Lee McNight (Purcell) seduces Dr. Jim (Mull) into helping her produce a movie and then invites the moviemakers, including the writer (Black), to his beach house. Too bad the doc's wife (Kazan) shows up unexpectedly and the doc kills her. And when Dr. Jim hears the plot of the movie (about a murder in a doctor's house), he figures he's being blackmailed and decides to get rid of the suspects. **?m/C VHS.** Martin Mull, Lee Purcell, Karen Black, Lainie Kazan; **D:** Arthur Webb. *MTH*

Moving ♂ 1988 (R) An engineer must relocate his family from New Jersey to Idaho in order to get his dream job. Predictable calamities ensue. Not apt to move you. **89m/C VHS, Beta, LV, 8mm, Closed Caption.** Richard Pryor, Randy Quaid, Dana Carvey, Dave Thomas, Rodney Dangerfield, Stacey Dash; **D:** Alan Metter; **W:** Andy Breckman; **M:** Howard Shore. *WAR*

Moving Out ♂♂ 1983 Adolescent migrant Italian boy finds it difficult to adjust to his new surroundings in Melbourne, Australia. **91m/C VHS, Beta.** Vince Colosimo, Sally Cooper, Maurice Devincentis, Tibor Gyapjas; **D:** Michael Pattinson. *NO*

Moving Target ♂½ 1989 (R) A young woman witnesses the brutal murder of her boyfriend by mobsters and flees to Florida. Unbeknownst to her, the thugs are still after her. Although top-billed, Blair's role is actually a supporting one. **85m/C VHS, Beta.** *IT* Linda Blair, Ernest Borgnine, Stuart Whitman, Charles Pitt, Jainine Linde, Kurt Woodruff; **D:** Marius Mattei.

Moving Target ♂♂ 1996 (R) Sonny McClean (Dudikoff) is a bounty hunter. But his latest job has him framed for murder and caught up in the middle of mob rivalries. So in order to clear his name, Sonny has to avoid getting killed by violent gangs and quick-draw cops. **106m/C VHS, LV.** Michael Dudikoff, Billy Dee Williams, Mishelle Johnson, Aaron Bess, Tom Harvey, Len Doncheff, Noam Jenkins; **D:** Damian Lee; **W:** Mark Sevi, Kevin Mcarthy; **C:** David Pelletier; **M:** David Lawrence. *APX*

Moving Targets ♂♂ 1987 A young girl and her mother find themselves tracked by a homicidal maniac. **95m/C VHS, Beta.** *AU* Michael Aitkens, Carmen Duncan, Annie Jones, Shane Briant; **D:** Chris Langman.

Moving Violation ♂♂ 1976 (PG) Crooked cops chase two young drifters who have witnessed the local sheriff commit a murder. Corman car chase epic. **91m/C VHS, Beta, LV.** Eddie Albert, Kay Lenz, Stephen McHattie, Will Geer, Lonny Chapman; **D:** Charles S. Dubin; **W:** William W. Norton Sr. *FOX*

Moving Violations ♂ 1985 (PG-13) This could be entitled "Adventures in Traffic Violations School." A wise-cracking tree planter is sent to traffic school after accumulating several moving violations issued to him by a morose traffic cop. Bill Murray's little brother in feature role. **90m/C VHS, Beta, LV, Closed Caption.** John Murray, Jennifer Tilly, James Keach, Brian Backer, Sally Kellerman, Fred Willard, Clara Peller, Wendie Jo Sperber; **D:** Neal Israel; **W:** Pat Proft; **C:** Robert Elswit; **M:** Ralph Burns. *FOX*

Mozart: A Childhood Chronicle ♂♂♂ 1976 An experimental, semi-narrative portrait of the immortal composer, from the ages of seven to twenty, filmed on authentic locations and with the original instruments of the era. Entire soundtrack is composed of Mozart's music. In German with English subtitles. **224m/B VHS, Beta, LV.** *GE* **D:** Klaus Kirschner. *KIV, IME, GLV*

The Mozart Brothers ♂♂♂ 1986 An angst-ridden Swedish opera director decides to break all the rules while doing an innovative production of Mozart's "Don Giovanni." At first he horrifies his conservative opera company but as his vision is gradually realized their resistance breaks down. A wonderful look at behind-the-scenes chaos and not just for opera aficionados. In Swedish with English subtitles. **111m/C VHS.** *SW* Etienne Glaser, Philip Zanden, Henry Bronett; **D:** Suzanne Osten. *FRF, TPV*

The Mozart Story ♂♂ 1948 After Mozart's death, music minister to the Emperor, Antonio Salieri, reflects on how his jealousy and hatred of the musical genius held the great composer back and contributed to his death. Originally filmed in Austria in 1937, scenes were added for the U.S. release in 1948. **91m/B VHS, Beta.** Hans Holt, Winnie Markus, Irene von Meyendorf, Rene Deltgen, Edward Vedder, Wilton Graff, Walther Jansson, Curt Jurgens, Paul Hoerbiger; **D:** Karl Hartl. *VYY, GLV*

Much Ado about Nothing ♂♂♂½ 1993 (PG-13) Shakespeare for the masses details romance between two sets of would-be lovers—the battling Beatrice and Benedick (Thompson and Branagh) and the ingenuous Hero and Claudio (Beckinsale and Leonard). Washington is the noble warrior leader, Reeves his evil half-dressed half-brother, and Keaton serves comic relief as the officious, bumbling Dogberry. Sunlit, lusty, and revealing about all the vagaries of love, Branagh brings passion to his quest of making Shakespeare more approachable. His second attempt after "Henry V" at breaking the stuffy Shakespearean tradition. Filmed on location in Tuscany, Italy. **CW:** Mild sexual situations. **110m/C VHS, LV, Closed Caption.** *GB* Kenneth Branagh, Emma Thompson, Robert Sean Leonard, Kate Beckinsale, Denzel Washington, Keanu Reeves, Michael Keaton, Brian Blessed, Phyllida Law, Imelda Staunton, Gerard Horan, Jimmy Yuill, Richard Clifford, Ben Elton, Richard Briers; **D:** Kenneth Branagh; **W:** Kenneth Branagh; **C:** Roger Lanser; **M:** Patrick Doyle. Nominations: Golden Globe Awards '94: Best Film—Musical/Comedy; Independent Spirit Awards '94: Best Actress (Thompson), Best Film. *COL*

Mugsy's Girls ♂ *Delta Pi* 1985 (R) A messy comedy about six sorority women, educated in the refined skills of bar mud wrestling, who wallow in a Las Vegas championship tournament. Features pop singer Laura Branigan. **87m/C VHS, Beta.** Ruth Gordon, Laura Branigan, Eddie Deezen; **D:** Kevin Brodie. *ART, VES*

Mulan 1998 (G) Disney's 36th animated tale is taken from a Chinese fable. The Emperor (Morita) sends out an order that one man from every family must become a soldier in order to repel the advances into China of Shan-Yu (Ferrer) and his army of Huns. But Mulan's (Wen) father (Oh) is ill and she's afraid he won't return, so she decides to take his place and disguises herself as a warrior. The family's ancestral spirits enlist a guardian to watch over the girl—the pint-sized dragon, Mushu (Murphy)—as Mulan goes off to war. Not yet reviewed. **?m/C VHS. D:** Barry Cook, Tony Bancroft; **M:** Matthew Wilder, David Zippel; **V:** Ming-Na Wen, Eddie Murphy, B.D. Wong, Miguel Ferrer, Soon-Teck Oh, Noriyuki "Pat" Morita, Harvey Fierstein. *NYR*

Mulholland Falls ♂♂♂½ 1995 (R) Noir meets the nuclear age in this stylish period piece from New Zealand director Tamahori. Nolte plays the leader of the Hat Squad, a vicious group of fedora-sporting detectives assigned to bust organized crime in '50s L.A. at all costs. While investigating the murder of his ex-mistress, Nolte and cohorts Madsen, Palminteri and Penn discover evidence linking the murder to a general (Malkovich) in charge of the top secret nuclear program. Although the cast is dripping with big name stars, the best performance is put in by the glossy set design of Richard Sylbert, who probably had a strong case of deja vu, having previously done "Chinatown." **CW:** Sexuality, violence and language. **107m/C VHS, LV, Closed Caption.** Nick Nolte, Melanie Griffith, Chazz Palminteri, Michael Madsen, Christopher Penn, Treat Williams, Jennifer Connelly, Andrew McCarthy, John Malkovich, Daniel Baldwin, Bruce Dern, Ed Lauter; **Cameos:** William L. Petersen, Rob Lowe; **D:** Lee Tamahori; **W:** Pete Dexter; **C:** Haskell Wexler; **M:** Dave Grusin. Golden Raspberry Awards '96: Worst Supporting Actress (Griffith). *MGM*

Multiple Maniacs ♂ 1970 Waters at his most perverse. Divine's travelling freak show, filled with disgusting side-show sex acts, is the vehicle used for robbing and killing hapless spectators. One of the best scenes of a sordid lot is Divine being raped by Lobstora, a 15-foot broiled lobster. **90m/B VHS.** Divine, David Lochary, Mary Vivian Pearce, Edith Massey, Mink Stole; **D:** John Waters. *NO*

Multiplicity ♂♂½ 1996 (PG-13) With too many business and personal responsibilities, construction supervisor Doug Kinney (Keaton) is a prime candidate for the cloning experiments of Dr. Leeds (Yulin). Since the cloning process isn't exactly perfect, each clone (Doug winds up with three) has a different dominant personality trait—a hard-charger, a "Mister Mom," and a dopey slacker. Confusion reigns as wife Laura (MacDowell) deals with separation anxiety on a grand scale. Pleasant comedy shows Keaton can still be funny given the chance. Keaton had his choice of cloning comedies and chose this one over Chris Columbus's "More." **CW:** Sexual situations. **117m/C VHS, LV, Closed Caption, DVD.** Michael Keaton, Andie MacDowell, Harris Yulin, Richard Masur, Eugene Levy, Obba Babatunde, Ann Cusack, Brian Doyle-Murray, Julie Bowen; **D:** Harold Ramis; **W:** Harold Ramis, Chris Miller, Lowell Ganz, Babaloo Mandel, Mary Hale; **C:** Laszlo Kovacs; **M:** George Fenton. *COL*

The Mummy ♂♂♂½ 1932 Eerie chills mark this classic horror tale of an Egyptian priest, buried alive nearly 4000 years earlier, who comes back to life after a 1921 archaeological dig. Eight hours of extraordinary makeup transformed Karloff into the macabre mummy, who believes the soul of the long-deceased (and probably long-decayed) lover resides in the body of a young woman. Marked the directing debut of famed German cinematographer Freund. **72m/B VHS, Beta, LV.** Boris

Karloff, Zita Johann, David Manners, Edward Van Sloan, Arthur Byron, Bramwell Fletcher, Noble Johnson, Leonard Mudie, Henry Victor; **D:** Karl Freund; **W:** John L. Balderston; **C:** Charles Stumar. *USH, TLF*

The Mummy *♂♂♂* **1959** A group of British archaeologists discover they have made a grave mistake when a mummy kills off those who have violated his princess' tomb. A summation of all the previous "mummy" films, this one has a more frightening mummy (6'4" Lee) who is on screen much of the time. Additionally, there is pathos in this monster, not merely murder and revenge. An effective remake of the 1932 classic. **88m/C VHS, Beta, LV.** *GB* Peter Cushing, Christopher Lee, Felix Aylmer, Yvonne Furneaux, Eddie Byrne, Raymond Huntley, George Pastell, Michael Ripper, John Stuart; **D:** Terence Fisher; **W:** Jimmy Sangster; **C:** Jack Asher. *WAR, MLB*

Mummy & Curse of the Jackal woof! **1967** Upon opening the tomb of female mummy, a man is cursed to roam the streets of Las Vegas as a werejackal. Impossibly inept. **86m/C VHS.** Anthony Eisley, Martina Pons, John Carradine, Saul Goldsmith; **D:** Oliver Drake.

The Mummy's Curse *♂♂* **1944** Sequel to "The Mummy's Ghost" and Chaney's last outing as Kharis. Construction by a government order causes Kharis and Ananka to be dug up in a Louisiana bayou and taken to Cajun country for study by archaeologists. The usual havoc ensues. Includes lots of stock footage from earlier mummy movies. Based on a story by Leon Abrams and Dwight V. Babcock. **61m/B VHS, Closed Caption.** Lon Chaney Jr., Peter Coe, Virginia Christine, Kay Harding, Dennis Moore, Martin Kosleck, Kurt Katch; **D:** Leslie Goodwins; **W:** Bernard Schubert; **C:** Virgil Miller. *USH, FCT*

The Mummy's Ghost *♂♂* **1944** Sequel to "The Mummy's Tomb" has Chaney, Jr. searching for the reincarnation of his ancient love, Princess Ananka. The least interesting entry in the series. Based on a story by Griffith Jay and Henry Sucher. **61m/B VHS, Closed Caption.** Lon Chaney Jr., John Carradine, Ramsay Ames, Robert Lowery, Barton MacLane, George Zucco; **D:** Reginald LeBorg; **W:** Griffin Jay, Henry Sucher, Brenda Weisberg; **C:** William Sickner. *USH, FCT*

The Mummy's Hand *♂♂½* **1940** Two archaeologists (Foran and Ford) searching for the tomb of ancient Egyptian Princess Ananka discover more than they bargained for when they find that an evil and deadly mummy is the tomb's guardian. From there the plot unravels, but the good cast and a mix of scares and comedy make this worth watching. **70m/B VHS, Closed Caption.** Dick Foran, Wallace Ford, Peggy Moran, Cecil Kellaway, George Zucco, Tom Tyler, Eduardo Ciannelli, Charles Trowbridge; **D:** Christy Cabanne; **W:** Griffin Jay, Maxwell Shane; **C:** Elwood Bredell. *USH*

The Mummy's Revenge *♂* **1973** A fanatic revives a mummy with virgin blood. The first mummy movie to feature open gore. **91m/C VHS, Beta.** *SP* Paul Naschy, Jack Taylor, Maria Silva, Helga Line; **D:** Carlos Aured; **W:** Paul Naschy. *UNI*

The Mummy's Tomb *♂♂* **1942** Chaney, Jr. in wraps for the first time in this sequel to "The Mummy's Hand." Kharis is transported to America by a crazed Egyptian high priest to kill off surviving members of the expedition. Weakened by a lame script and too much stock footage. Based on a story by Neil P. Varnick. **71m/B VHS, Closed Caption.** Lon Chaney Jr., Dick Foran, John Hubbard, Elyse Knox, George Zucco, Wallace Ford, Turhan Bey; **D:** Harold Young; **W:** Griffin Jay, Henry Sucher; **C:** George Robinson. *USH, FCT*

Munchie *♂½* **1992 (PG)** A forgotten alien critter is discovered in a mine shaft by young Gage. Munchie turns out to be a good friend, protecting Gage from bullies and granting other wishes. Frequent sight gags help keep the film moving but it's still awfully slow. Sequel to "Munchies" (1987). **80m/C VHS, Closed Caption.** Loni Anderson, Andrew Stevens, Arte Johnson, Jamie McEnnan; **D:** Jim Wynorski; **V:** Dom DeLuise. *NHO*

Munchies *♂* **1987 (PG)** "Gremlins" rip-off about tiny aliens who love beer and fast food, and invade a small town. Lewd and ribald. **83m/C VHS, Beta.** Harvey Korman, Charles Stratton, Nadine Van Der Velde; **D:** Bettina Hirsch. *MGM*

The Munsters' Revenge *♂♂* **1981** Television movie based on the continuing adventures of the 1960s comedy series characters. Herman, Lily, and Grandpa have to contend with robot replicas of themselves that were created by a flaky scientist. **96m/C VHS, Beta.** Fred Gwynne, Yvonne De Carlo, Al Lewis, Jo McDonnel, Sid Caesar, Ezra Stone, Howard Morris, Bob Hastings, K.C. Martel; **D:** Don Weis. *USH*

The Muppet Christmas Carol *♂♂½* **1992 (G)** Christmas classic features all the muppet favorites together and in Victorian garb. Storyline is more or less faithful to Dickens original, with pleasant special effects. Gonzo the Great as Dickens narrates the tale as Scrooge (Caine) takes his legendary Christmas Eve journey escorted by three (flannel) spirits. The Cratchits are led by Kermit and Miss Piggy. Directed by Brian Henson, Jim's son, the film is as heartwarming as the Cratchit's crackling fire, but doesn't quite achieve the former muppet magic. Also features some sappy songs by Williams, including "Love is Like a Heatwave" and "Island in the Sun." **120m/C VHS, Beta, Closed Caption.** Michael Caine; **D:** Brian Henson; **C:** John Fenner; **M:** Paul Williams, Miles Goodman; **V:** Dave Goelz, Steve Whitmire, Jerry Nelson, Frank Oz.

The Muppet Movie *♂♂♂½* **1979 (G)** Seeking fame and footlights, Kermit the Frog and his pal Fozzie Bear travel to Hollywood, and along the way are joined by sundry human and muppet characters, including the lovely Miss Piggy. A delightful cult favorite filled with entertaining cameos, memorable (though somewhat pedestrian) songs and crafty special effects—Kermit rides a bike and rows a boat! A success for the late Jim Henson. ♫The Rainbow Connection; Frog's Legs So Fine; Movin Right Along; Can You Picture That?; Never Before; Something Better; This Looks Familiar; I'm Going Back There Someday. **94m/C VHS, Beta, LV.** *GB* Cameos: Edgar Bergen, Milton Berle, Mel Brooks, Madeline Kahn, Steve Martin, Carol Kane, Paul Williams, Charles Durning, Bob Hope, James Coburn, Dom DeLuise, Elliott Gould, Cloris Leachman, Telly Savalas, Orson Welles; **D:** James Frawley; **W:** Jack Burns; **M:** Paul Williams; **V:** Jim Henson, Frank Oz. Nominations: Academy Awards '79: Best Song ("The Rainbow Connection"), Original Song Score and/or Adaptation. *FOX*

Muppet Treasure Island *♂♂½* **1996 (G)** Literary classic gets its first coat of felt as Kermit the Frog, Miss Piggy and the entire Muppet gang hit the high seas in an adaptation of Robert Louis Stevenson's 1883 well-worn adventure tale. Delightful settings, from an old English tavern to an exotic south sea island, frame the journey of young Jim Hawkins (flesh and blood Bishop), who along with tavern owners Rizzo the Rat (Whitmire) and the Great Gonzo (Goelz) search for buried treasure. Long John Silver is played to the hilt by Curry, master of the over-the-top villain. Helmer Henson steers a steady ship, with over 400 Muppet critters making an appearance. **99m/C VHS.** Tim Curry, Kevin Bishop, Billy Connolly, Jennifer Saunders; **D:** Brian Henson; **W:** Jerry Juhl, Jim V. Hart, Kirk R. Thatcher; **C:** John Fenner; **M:** Hans Zimmer; **V:** Steve Whitmire, Frank Oz, Dave Goelz. *TOU*

The Muppets Take Manhattan *♂♂♂* **1984 (G)** Following a smashing success with a college musical, the Muppets take their show and talents to Broadway, only to face misfortune in the form of an unscrupulous producer. A less imaginative script than the first two Muppet movies, yet an enjoyable experience with numerous major stars making cameo appearances. **94m/C VHS, Beta, LV, Closed Caption.** Cameos: Dabney Coleman, James Coco, Art Carney, Joan Rivers, Gregory Hines, Linda Lavin, Liza Minnelli, Brooke Shields, John Landis; **D:** Frank Oz; **M:** Ralph Burns; **V:** Jim Henson, Frank Oz. Nominations: Academy

Awards '84: Original Song Score and/or Adaptation. *FOX, HMV*

Murder *♂♂♂* **1930** Believing in a young woman's innocence, one jurist begins to organize the pieces of the crime in order to save her. Fine early effort by Hitchcock based on play "Enter Sir John," by Clemense Dane and Helen Simpson. **92m/B VHS, Beta.** *GB* Herbert Marshall, Nora Baring, Phyllis Konstam, Miles Mander; **D:** Alfred Hitchcock; **W:** Alfred Hitchcock. *REP, NOS, HHT*

Murder Ahoy *♂♂½* **1964** Miss Marple looks perplexed when dead bodies surface on a naval cadet training ship. Dame Marge is the dottie detective in the final, and least appealing, of her four Agatha Christie films of the '60s (although it was released in the States prior to "Murder Most Foul"). **74m/B VHS, Beta.** Margaret Rutherford, Lionel Jeffries, Charles Tingwell, William Mervyn, Francis Matthews; **D:** George Pollock. *MGM, FCT*

Murder at 45 R.P.M. *♂♂* *Meurtre en 45 Tours* **1965** A singer and her lover suspect each other of her husband's murder. Things become sticky when she receives a recorded message from her dead husband. Average. **98m/C VHS.** *FR* Danielle Darrieux, Michel Auclair, Jean Servais, Henri Guisol; **D:** Etienne Perier. *SNC*

Murder at Midnight *♂♂* **1931** The killings begin with a game of charades in which the gun wasn't supposed to be loaded, and continue as members of English high society die one by one. "Blondie" director Strayer still working on his change of pace. **69m/B VHS, Beta, 8mm.** Alice White, Leslie Fenton, Aileen Pringle, Hale Hamilton, Robert Elliott, Clara Blandick, Brandon Hurst; **D:** Frank Strayer. *SNC, NOS, DVT*

Murder at 1600 *♂♂* **1997 (R)** Jaded D.C. detective Harlan Regis (Snipes) is called to investigate the murder of Carla Town (Moore), a secretary found dead in a White House bathroom. He's reluctantly assisted by hard-boiled Secret Service agent Chance (Lane), while head of security Nick Spikings (Benzali) wants the whole matter wrapped up quickly and quietly—justice not being his main concern. Cliche-fest gives stereotypical characters a little more development than you may be used to seeing, but doesn't give them anything new or interesting to say or do. Snipes and Lane make a good team, however, and Miller fulfills his usual wise-cracking sidekick role effortlessly. **CW:** Sexuality, violence and some language. **107m/C VHS, LV, Closed Caption.** Wesley Snipes, Diane Lane, Daniel Benzali, Dennis Miller, Alan Alda, Ronny Cox, Tate Donovan, Diane Baker, Mary Moore, Harris Yulin; **D:** Dwight Little; **W:** Wayne Beach, David Hodgin; **C:** Steven Bernstein; **M:** Christopher Young. *WAR*

Murder at the Baskervilles *♂♂* *Silver Blaze* **1937** Sherlock Holmes is invited to visit Sir Henry Baskerville at his estate, but then finds that Baskerville's daughter's fiance is accused of stealing a race horse and murdering its keeper. Based on Sir Arthur Conan Doyle's story "Silver Blaze." **67m/B VHS, Beta.** *GB* Arthur Wontner, Ian Fleming, Lyn Harding; **D:** Thomas Bentley. *SNC, CCB, REP*

Murder at the Gallop *♂♂♂½* **1963** Snooping Miss Marple doesn't believe a filthy rich old-timer died of natural causes, despite the dissenting police point of view. Wheedling her way into the police investigation, she discovers the secret of the Gallop club, a place where people bounce up and down on top of horses. Much mugging between Dame Margaret and Morley. Marple's assistant, Mr. Stringer, is the real life Mr. Dame Margaret. Based on Christie's Poirot mystery "After the Funeral." **81m/B VHS, Beta.** Margaret Rutherford, Robert Morley, Flora Robson, Charles Tingwell, Duncan Lamont; **D:** George Pollock. *MGM, FCT*

Murder at the Vanities *♂♂½* **1934** Vintage murder mystery set against a musical revue format, in which a tough detective must find a killer before the Earl Carroll-based cabaret ends and he or she will escape with the exiting crowd. Also featured is a mind-boggling production number based on the song "Marijuana." ♫Marijuana; Lovely One; Where Do They Come From Now; Live and Love Tonight; Cocktails for Two; Ebony Rhapsody. **91m/B VHS, Beta.** Victor McLaglen, Kitty Carlisle Hart, Jack Oakie, Duke Ellington, Carl Brisson; **D:** Mitchell Leisen. *USH*

Murder by Death 🎬🎬½ 1976 **(PG)** Capote is an eccentric millionaire who invites the world's greatest detectives to dinner, offering one million dollars to the one who can solve the evening's murder. Entertaining and hammy spoof of Agatha Christie's "And Then There Were None" and the earlier "Ten Little Indians." **95m/C VHS, Beta, LV.** Peter Falk, Alec Guinness, David Niven, Maggie Smith, Peter Sellers, Eileen Brennan, Elsa Lanchester, Nancy Walker, Estelle Winwood, Truman Capote, James Coco; **D:** Robert Moore; **W:** Neil Simon; **M:** Dave Grusin. *COL, TVC*

Murder by Decree 🎬🎬🎬 1979 **(PG)** Realistic and convincing version of the Jack the Ripper story. Sherlock Holmes and Dr. Watson find a vast web of conspiracy when they investigate the murders of Whitechapel prostitutes. Based partially on facts, it's a highly detailed suspenser with interesting camera work and fine performances. **120m/C VHS, Beta.** **CA** Christopher Plummer, James Mason, Donald Sutherland, Genevieve Bujold, Susan Clark, David Hemmings, Frank Finlay, John Gielgud, Anthony Quayle; **D:** Bob (Benjamin) Clark; **W:** John Hopkins. Genie Awards '80: Best Actor (Plummer), Best Director (Clark), Best Supporting Actress (Bujold).*NLC*

Murder by Moonlight 🎬🎬 1991 **(PG-13)** Rival agents investigate a mysterious murder in a prosperous mining colony on the moon. Not only do they discover a dastardly trail that leads all the way back to Earth, but a strange romantic attraction for each other. Originally broadcast on British TV. **94m/C VHS, Closed Caption.** **GB** Julian Sands, Brigitte Nielsen, Gerald McRaney, Jane Lapotaire, Brian Cox; **D:** Michael Lindsay-Hogg; **M:** Trevor Jones. *THV*

Murder by Natural Causes 🎬🎬🎬 1979 A made-for-TV brain teaser in which a woman and her lover plot to kill her mind-reader husband. Lots of twists make this fun for viewers who enjoy a challenge. **96m/C VHS, Beta.** Hal Holbrook, Barry Bostwick, Katharine Ross, Richard Anderson; **D:** Robert Day. *NO*

Murder by Night 🎬🎬½ 1989 **(PG-13)** Amnesia victim Urich is found next to a dead body, the result of a gruesome murder. Urich is the only witness and thinks he may be the next victim. Others think he's the killer. Made for cable mystery with enough twists to make it worthwhile. **95m/C VHS, Beta.** Robert Urich, Kay Lenz, Jim Metzler, Richard Monette, Michael Ironside, Michael Williams; **D:** Paul Lynch. *USH*

Murder by Numbers 🎬½ 1989 **(PG-13)** Murder in the art world stumps a detective. What might have been a good suspense story is ruined by bad editing and a lack of continuity, resulting in confusion rather than suspense. **91m/C VHS, Beta, LV.** Sam Behrens, Shari Belafonte, Ronee Blakley, Stanley Kamel, Jayne Meadows, Debra Sandlund, Dick Sargent, Cleavon Little; **D:** Paul Leder; **W:** Paul Leder. *NO*

Murder by Phone 🎬🎬 1982 **(R)** *Bells; The Calling* A deranged technician has turned his phone into an instrument of electronic death. Chamberlain is the visiting professor trying to discover who's permanently disconnecting the numbers of his students. Good cast decides to test schlock meter. **79m/C VHS, Beta.** **CA** Richard Chamberlain, John Houseman, Sara Botsford; **D:** Michael Anderson Sr.; **W:** Michael Butler, John Kent Harrison; **M:** John Barry. *WAR*

Murder by Television 🎬½ *The Houghland Murder Case* 1935 Low-budget murder mystery with Lugosi in a dual role as twins—one good, one not so. When a professor and the evil twin are murdered, the instrument of death suspected is...television. Still an exotic and misunderstood invention when this was made, TV sometimes invoked fear and suspicion in the general public.

Historically interesting and Lugosi fans will appreciate seeing him in a non-vampiric role. **55m/B VHS, Beta.** Bela Lugosi, George Meeker; **D:** Clifford Sanforth. *VYY, SNC, NOS*

Murder by the Book 🎬🎬½ *Alter Ego* 1987 A mystery writer finds that his fictional character, a hard-boiled private eye, has taken control of his life. With his new macho persona the writer solves a crime and saves the obligatory dame. Based on the novel "Alter Ego" by Mel Arrighi. Made for television. **100m/C VHS, Beta.** Robert Hays, Catherine Mary Stewart, Celeste Holm, Fred Gwynne, Christopher Murney; **D:** Mel Damski. *NO*

Murder Czech Style 🎬🎬 *Vrazda Po Cesky* 1966 Chubby and boring office clerk Frantisek (Hrusinsky) is amazed when a colleague, the beautiful Alice (Fialova), agrees to marry him. He can't believe his good fortune—and he's right—Frantisek soon discovers his wife has a married lover. So, he plots to murder her in several increasingly silly fantasies. Czech with subtitles. **87m/C VHS.** **CZ** Rudolf Hrusinsky, Kveta Fialova, Vaclav Voska, Vladimir Mensik; **D:** Jiri Weiss; **W:** Jiri Weiss, Jan Otcenasek; **C:** Jan Nemecek; **M:** Zdenek Liska. *FCT*

Murder Elite 🎬½ 1986 A murdering maniac terrorizes the rural English countryside, where MacGraw has returned after losing all her money in America. Poor acting and direction make this one a dust-gatherer. **98m/C VHS, Beta.** Ali MacGraw, Billie Whitelaw, Hywel Bennett; **D:** Claude Whatham. *ART, VES*

Murder for Sale 🎬 1970 Secret Agent 117 stages an elaborate scam in order to infiltrate a ring of terrorists and criminals. Ask for Bond next time. **90m/C VHS, Beta.** John Gavin, Margaret Lee, Curt Jurgens.

Murder in Coweta County 🎬🎬½ 1983 Griffith and Cash are strong in this true-crime drama based on the book by Margaret Anne Barnes. Griffith is a Georgia businessman who thinks he's gotten away with murder; Cash is the lawman who tenaciously pursues him. Based on an actual 1948 case. Made for television. **100m/C VHS, Beta.** Johnny Cash, Andy Griffith, Earl Hindman, June Carter Cash, Cindi Knight, Ed Van Nuys; **D:** Gary Nelson; **M:** Brad Fiedel. *ART*

Murder-in-Law 🎬 1992 **(R)** Graphic slasher flick about a mother-in-law from hell who escapes from an insane asylum and terrorizes her son-in-law (Estevez) and his family in a series of gruesome killings. **CW:** Language, horror violence, and sexuality. **97m/C VHS.** Marilyn Adams, Joe Estevez, Sandy Snyder, Darrel Guilbeau; **D:** Tony Jiti Gill. *MNC*

Murder in Mind 🎬🎬½ 1997 **(R)** Caroline Walker's (Parker) accused of murdering her husband (Smits) but can't remember doing so. She tries to figure out the truth by undergoing regression therapy with a hypnotherapist (Hawthorne). But what she supposedly uncovers are a lot of ugly secrets that were better left hidden. Adapted by Cooney from his play. **89m/C VHS, LV, Closed Caption.** Nigel Hawthorne, Mary-Louise Parker, Jimmy Smits, Jason Scott Lee, Gailard Sartain; **D:** Andrew Morahan; **W:** Michael Cooney; **C:** John Aronson. *ART*

Murder in New Hampshire: The Pamela Smart Story 🎬🎬½ 1991 **(PG-13)** A sleazy true story about a young high school teacher who seduces an impressionable student into murdering her husband. Hunt's fine as the seductress but this made-for-television fare is just average. **93m/C VHS, Beta, Closed Caption.** Helen Hunt, Chad Allen, Larry Drake, Howard Hesseman, Ken Howard, Michael Learned; **D:** Joyce Chopra; **M:** Gary Chang. *TTC, PMS*

Murder in Space 🎬½ 1985 Nine multinational astronauts are stranded aboard a space station when they discover one of them is a murderer. This creates anxiety, particularly since the killer's identity is unknown. Oatmeal salesman Brimley is the earth-bound mission control chief trying desperately to finger a spaceman while the bodies pile up. Made for television. **95m/C VHS,**

Beta. Wilford Brimley, Martin Balsam, Michael Ironside, **D:** Steven Hilliard Stern. *THV*

Murder in Texas 🎬🎬🎬 1981 Made for television docudrama looks at the strange but true events surrounding the death of society woman Joan Robinson Hill, first wife of prominent plastic surgeon, Dr. John Hill, and daughter of wealthy oilman Ash Robinson. Well-crafted script and effective performances keep your interest. Griffith was Emmy nominated. From the book "Prescription Murder," written by the doctor's second wife. **200m/C VHS, Beta.** Farrah Fawcett, Katharine Ross, Andy Griffith, Sam Elliott, Craig T. Nelson, Barbara Sammeth; **D:** William Hale. *VHE, HHE*

Murder in the Doll House 🎬½ 1979 Private detective must find out who is systematically killing off the family of a Japanese toy executive. With English subtitles. **92m/C VHS, Beta.** **JP** Yusaku Matsuda, Hiroko Shino, Yoko Nosaki. *VDA*

Murder In the First 🎬🎬½ 1995 **(R)** Hours after leaving a three-year stint in solitary confinement at Alcatraz, petty thief Henri Young (Bacon) kills the inmate he thinks ratted him out. Young, eager-puppy lawyer James Stamphill (Slater) defends Young by claiming that inhumane and brutal prison treatment turned him into a murderer. Heavy-handed and uneven despite excellent performances by top-notch cast. Oldman does his usual fine job with yet another unsympathetic character, the sadistic warden. Major professional landmark for both Slater and Bacon. Loosely based on a true story that led to the closing of Alcatraz.**CW:** Contains profanity, sadistic violence, and mild sexual situations. **123m/C VHS, LV, Closed Caption.** Christian Slater, Kevin Bacon, Gary Oldman, Embeth Davidtz, Bill Macy, Stephen Tobolowsky, Brad Dourif, R. Lee Ermey, Mia Kirshner, Stefan Gierasch, Kyra Sedgwick; **D:** Marc Rocco; **W:** Dan Gordon; **C:** Fred Murphy; **M:** Christopher Young. Broadcast Film Critics Association Awards '95: Best Actor (Bacon); Nominations: Screen Actors Guild Award '95: Best Supporting Actor (Bacon). *WAR*

Murder in the Footlights 🎬🎬 1951 Murder drama involving a socialite and a vaudeville team. **?m/C VHS.** **GB** Lesley Brook, David Hutcheson. *SNC*

Murder in the Old Red Barn 🎬 *Maria Marten* 1936 Based on the real murder of an unassuming girl by a randy squire. Stiff, melodramatic performances are bad enough, but the play-style production, unfamiliar to modern viewers, is the last nail in this one's coffin. **67m/B VHS, Beta.** **GB** Tod Slaughter, Sophie Stewart, D.J. Williams, Eric Portman; **D:** Milton Rosmer. *NOS, MRV, SNC*

A Murder Is Announced 🎬🎬 *Agatha Christie's Miss Marple: A Murder Is Announced* 1987 From the critically acclaimed BBC television series. While on holiday, super-sleuth Marple encounters a murder that was advertised in the local newspaper one week prior to its occurrence. Based on the 1952 Agatha Christie novel. Hickson shines once again as Christie's detective extraordinaire. **155m/C VHS, Beta, Closed Caption.** **GB** Joan Hickson; **D:** David Giles. *FOX, HMV, VCO*

Murder Mansion 🎬½ 1970 Some decent scares ensue when a group of travelers is stranded in an old haunted mansion. **84m/C VHS, Beta.** **SP** Evelyn Stewart, Analia Gade; **D:** Francisco Lara Polop. *UNI, SNC, FCT*

Murder Most Foul 🎬🎬🎬 1965 Erstwhile school marm Dame Margaret is excellent as the only jury member to believe in the accused's innocence. Posing as a wealthy actress to insinuate herself into the local acting troupe, she sniffs out the true culprit. Based on the Poirot mystery "Mr. McGinty's Dead." **90m/B VHS, Beta.** Margaret Rutherford, Ron Moody, Charles Tingwell, Megs Jenkins, Dennis Price, Ralph Michael; **D:** George Pollock. *MGM, FCT*

Murder Motel 🎬 1974 Inept made-for-television spine-tingler about a motel keeper who makes a practice of killing his customers. There's always a vacancy at the Murder Motel, at least until the fiancee of one of his victims decides to look into the matter. **80m/C VHS, Beta.** Robyn Millan, Derek Francis, Ralph Bates, Edward Judd. *ART*

Murder, My Sweet 🐾🐾🐾½ *Farewell, My Love* 1944 Down-on-his-luck private detective Philip Marlowe (Powell) searches for an ex-convict's missing girlfriend through a dark world of murder, mayhem, and ever-twisting directions. Classic film noir screen version of Raymond Chandler's tense novel "Farewell, My Lovely," which employs flashback fashion using that crisp Chandler narrative. A breakthrough dramatically for singer Powell; Chandler's favorite version. Remade using the novel's title in 1975. **95m/B VHS, Beta, LV.** Dick Powell, Claire Trevor, Mike Mazurki, Otto Kruger, Anne Shirley, Miles Mander; *D:* Edward Dmytryk. *CCB*

Murder of a Moderate Man 🐾½ 197? An Interpol agent sets out for the Alps to apprehend an assassin gunning down political leaders. A British-made effort based on a novel by John Howlett. **165m/C VHS.** *GB* Denis Quilley, Susan Fleetwood. *FCT, MOV, VCO*

The Murder of Mary Phagan 🐾🐾🐾½ 1987 (PG) Lemmon stars as John Slaton, governor of Georgia during one of America's most notorious miscarriages of justice. In 1913, timid, Jewish factory manager Leo Frank is accused of the brutal murder of a female worker. Prejudice and a power hungry prosecuting attorney conspire to seal the man's fate at the end of the hangman's noose. Sensing the injustice, Slaton re-opens the case, causing riots in Atlanta. Top notch television drama, featuring a superb recreation of turn of the century atmosphere and a compelling, true story which was not finally resolved until the 1970s. **251m/C VHS.** Jack Lemmon, Peter Gallagher, Richard Jordan, Robert Prosky, Paul Dooley, Rebecca Miller, Kathryn Walker, Charles S. Dutton, Kevin Spacey, Wendy J. Cooke; *D:* Billy Hale; *M:* Maurice Jarre. *ORI*

Murder on Approval 🐾 *Barbados Quest* 1956 Conway is a carbon-copy Sherlock Holmes, called in to verify the authenticity of a stamp and finds himself involved in murder. Slow-paced, weak and transparent. **70m/B VHS.** Tom Conway, Delphi Lawrence, Brian Worth, Michael Balfour, John Colicos; *D:* Bernard Knowles. *NOS*

Murder on Flight 502 🐾🐾 1975 A crisis arises on a 747 flight from New York to London when a terrorist runs amuck. Big cast of TV stars and Stack as the pilot keep this stale television flick from getting lost in the ozone. **97m/C VHS, Beta.** Farrah Fawcett, Sonny Bono, Ralph Bellamy, Theodore Bikel, Dane Clark, Polly Bergen, Laraine Day, Fernando Lamas, George Maharis, Hugh O'Brian, Molly Picon, Walter Pidgeon, Robert Stack; *D:* George McCowan.

Murder on Lenox Avenue 🐾🐾½ 1941 When the leader of the Harlem Better Business Bureau is overthrown, he swears revenge. **60m/C VHS.** Alec Lovejoy. *BBE, MOV*

Murder on Line One 🐾🐾 1990 A London murderer films his crimes for his later viewing pleasure. The police arrest a suspect, but the killings continue. Both the police and viewer are soon aware that they've made a mistake. **103m/C VHS, Beta.** Emma Jacobs, Peter Blake, Simon Shepherd, Allan Surtees, Andrew Wilde, Dirkan Tulane, Neil Duncan, Brett Forrest; *D:* Anders Palm; *W:* Anders Palm. *TTC*

Murder on the Bayou 🐾🐾🐾 *A Gathering of Old Men* 1991 (PG) Down on the L'siana bayou, a white guy who thinks civil rights are color coded is murdered, and an elderly black man is accused of the crime. Made for TV, well performed, engaging. From the novel by Ernest J. Gaines. **91m/C VHS, LV.** Louis Gossett Jr., Richard Widmark, Holly Hunter, Woody Strode, Joe Seneca, Papa John Creach, Julius W. Harris, Will Patton; *D:* Volker Schlondorff. *THV*

Murder on the Campus 🐾🐾 *Out of the Shadow* 1952 A reporter investigates the apparant suicide of his brother at Cambridge University. He discovers that a number of other mysterious deaths have occurred as well. Interesting charac-

terizations hampered by predictability. **61m/B VHS, Beta.** *GB* Terence Longdon, Donald Gray, Diane Clare, Robertson Hare, Dermot Walsh; *D:* Michael Winner; *W:* Michael Winner. *NOS, MRV, SNC*

Murder on the High Seas 🐾🐾 1932 Infidelity and murder aboard a cruise ship. **?m/C VHS.** Natalie Moorhead, Jack Mulhall. *SNC*

Murder on the Midnight Express 🐾½ 1974 Made-for-television mystery about spies, thieves, honeymooners and a corpse aboard an all-night train. All aboard. **70m/C VHS, Beta.** Judy Geeson, James Smilie, Charles Gray. *ART*

Murder on the Orient Express 🐾🐾🐾 1974 (PG) An Agatha Christie mystery lavishly produced with an all-star cast. In 1934, a trainful of suspects and one murder victim make the trip from Istanbul to Calais especially interesting. Super-sleuth Hercule Poirot sets out to solve the mystery. An entertaining whodunit, ably supported by the remarkable cast. Followed by "Death on the Nile." **128m/C VHS, Beta, LV.** *GB* Albert Finney, Martin Balsam, Ingrid Bergman, Lauren Bacall, Sean Connery, Richard Widmark, Anthony Perkins, John Gielgud, Jacqueline Bisset, Jean-Pierre Cassel, Wendy Hiller, Rachel Roberts, Vanessa Redgrave, Michael York, Colin Blakely, George Coulouris, Denis Quilley, Vernon Dobtcheff, Jeremy Lloyd; *D:* Sidney Lumet; *W:* Paul Dehn; *C:* Geoffrey Unsworth; *M:* Richard Rodney Bennett. Academy Awards '74: Best Supporting Actress (Bergman); British Academy Awards '74: Best Supporting Actor (Gielgud), Best Supporting Actress (Bergman); Nominations: Academy Awards '74: Best Actor (Finney), Best Adapted Screenplay, Best Cinematography, Best Costume Design, Best Original Dramatic/Comedy Score. *PAR, BTV*

Murder on the Yukon 🐾½ 1940 An installment in the "Renfrew of the Royal Mounted" series. Newill and O'Brien's vacation plans are ruined when they find a corpse in a canoe and must investigate. Lots of action, but a somewhat threadbare production. Based on "Renfrew Rides North" by Lauri York Erskine. **57m/B VHS, Beta.** James Newill, Dave O'Brien, Polly Ann Young; *D:* Louis Gasnier. *VDM*

Murder Once Removed 🐾½ 1971 A private eye discovers that a respectable doctor has a bedside manner that women are dying for. Made for television. **74m/C VHS, Beta.** John Forsythe, Richard Kiley, Barbara Bain, Joseph Campanella; *D:* Charles S. Dubin. *ORI*

Murder One 🐾 1988 (R) Two half-brothers escape from a Maryland prison and go on a killing spree, dragging their younger brother with them. Low-budget and it shows. Based on a true story. **83m/C VHS, Beta, LV.** Henry Thomas, James Wilder, Stephen Shellan, Errol Slue; *D:* Graeme Campbell. *NLC*

Murder 101 🐾🐾 1991 (PG-13) Brosnan plays Charles Lattimore, an author and English professor who specializes in murder mysteries. He gives his students a rather unique assignment of planning the perfect murder. When a student is killed right before his eyes and a fellow teacher turns up dead, Lattimore realizes he's being framed for murder. Surprising twists abound in this stylish thriller. **93m/C VHS, Closed Caption.** Pierce Brosnan, Dey Young, Raphael Sbarge, Kim Thomson; *D:* Bill Condon; *W:* Bill Condon. *USH*

Murder or Mercy 🐾🐾½ 1974 Still timely story of a famous doctor accused of killing his terminally ill wife. Focuses on the morality of mercy killing. Made for television. **78m/C VHS.** Melvyn Douglas, Bradford Dillman, David Birney, Denver Pyle, Mildred Dunnock; *D:* Harvey Hart. *WOV*

Murder Ordained 🐾🐾½ 1987 Yet another true-crime network miniseries, this time about a Kansas minister and her lover plotting the demise of their spouses. Good acting for this sort of thing. In two-cassette package. **183m/C VHS, Closed Caption.** Keith Carradine, JoBeth Williams, Terry Kinney, Guy Boyd, Terence Knox, Darrell Larson, M. Emmet Walsh, Kathy Bates; *D:* Mike Robe.

Murder over New York 🐾🐾 1940 Episode in the Charlie Chan mystery series. Chan visits New York City and becomes involved in an investigation at the airport. With the aid of his klutzy son, he sleuths his way through a slew of suspects until the mystery is solved. Standard fare for the Chan fan. **65m/B VHS, Beta, Closed Caption.** Sidney Toler, Marjorie Weaver, Robert Lowery, Ricardo Cortez, Donald MacBride, Melville Cooper, Victor Sen Yung; *D:* Harry Lachman. *FOX*

Murder Rap 🐾 1987 An aspiring musician/sound technologist becomes involved with a mysterious woman and her plot to kill her husband. Complications galore, especially for the viewer. **90m/C VHS, Beta.** John Hawkes, Seita Kathleen Feigny; *D:* Kliff Keuhl. *VCI*

Murder She Said 🐾🐾½ *Meet Miss Marple* 1962 Dame Margaret, playing the benign Miss M for the first time, witnesses a murder on board a train, but the authorities don't seem inclined to believe her. Posing as a maid at an estate near where she thought the body was dropped, she solves the murder and lands three more Miss Marple movies. Based on Christy's "4:50 From Paddington," it features Marple-to-be Hickson as the cook. **87m/B VHS, Beta.** Margaret Rutherford, Arthur Kennedy, Muriel Pavlow, James Robertson Justice, Thorley Walters, Charles Tingwell, Conrad Phillips; *D:* George Pollock. *MGM, FCT*

Murder So Sweet 🐾🐾½ *Poisoned by Love: The Kern County Murders* 1993 Hamlin stars as a slick small-town loser, with an apparently limitless appeal to women. He marries five of them but two wives and his mother mysteriously die of poisoning. Then an ex gets suspicious and tries to make certain it'll never happen again. Based on a true story. Made for television. **94m/C VHS.** Harry Hamlin, Helen Shaver, Faith Ford, Daphne Ashbrook, Eileen Brennan, K.T. Oslin, Terence Knox, Ed Lauter.

Murder Story 🐾🐾½ 1989 (PG) An aspiring mystery writer finds himself mixed up in a real murder and winds up involving his mentor as well. An overdone story, but a reasonably enjoyable film. **90m/C VHS, Beta, LV.** Christopher Lee, Bruce Boa; *D:* Eddie Arno, Markus Innocenti; *W:* Eddie Arno. *FHS*

Murder: Ultimate Grounds for Divorce 🐾 1985 A quiet weekend of camping turns into a night of horror for two couples when one of them plans an elaborate murder scheme. **90m/C VHS, Beta.** Roger Daltrey, Toyah Wilcox, Leslie Ash, Terry Raven. *ORI, WAR*

Murder with Music 🐾🐾 1945 A musical drama featuring an all-black cast. **60m/B VHS, Beta.** Bob Howard, Noble Sissle, Nellie Hill; *D:* George P. Quigley. *NOS, DVT, VDM*

Murder without Motive 🐾🐾½ 1992 When two African American teenagers harrass an undercover cop, a struggle ensues and one teen ends up dead. Was the struggle racially motivated, or did the police act justifiably? **93m/C VHS.** Curtis McClaren, Anna Maria Horsford, Carla Gugino, Christopher Daniel Barnes, Cuba Gooding Jr., Georg Stanford Brown; *D:* Kevin Hooks. *TTC*

Murdered Innocence 🐾🐾 1994 (R) In 1972, a rookie New York cop is called to a crime scene where a woman has been stabbed to death. Her young son is hysterical and her husband is holding the knife. When the husband panics and tries to flee, the cop shoots him in the back. Now, it's 1992, the convicted killer is out of prison and out for revenge (seems the son said his mother's lover committed the crime but there was a police coverup). *CW:* Violence; language; some sexuality; drug content. **88m/C VHS, Closed Caption.** Jason Miller, Ellen Greene, Fred Carpenter; *D:* Frank Coraci; *W:* Frank Coraci, Diego Matamoros. *COL*

Murderers Among Us: The Simon Wiesenthal Story 🐾🐾 1989 Powerful re-enactment of concentration camp survivor Simon Wiesenthal's search for war criminals. Kingsley's gripping performance drives this made-for-cable film. Be prepared for disturbing death camp scenes. **157m/C VHS, Closed Caption.** Ben Kingsley, Renee Soutendijk, Craig T. Nelson, Paul Freeman, Louisa Haigh, Jack Shepherd; **D:** Brian Gibson; **W:** Abby Mann; **M:** Bill Conti. *HBO, FCT, VIF*

Murderers Are Among Us 🎬🎬 *Die Morder Sind Unter Uns* 1946 In post WWII Germany, Suzanne Wallner (Knef) returns from a concentration camp to her apartment in Berlin only to find it occupied by Dr. Hans Mertens (Borchert). Haunted by his wartime experiences, Mertens has turned to women and alcohol. Suzanne refuses to give up her claim and moves in with Hans, eventually falling in love with him. In turn, Hans decides to face his demons by going after his former superior, Colonel Otto Bruckner (Paulsen), who's living an untroubled life despite the war crimes he committed. German with subtitles. **84m/B VHS.** *GE* Hildegarde Knef, Ernst Borchert, Arno Paulsen; **D:** Wolfgang Staudte; **W:** Wolfgang Staudte; **C:** Friedl Behn-Grund, Eugen Klagemann; **M:** Ernst Roters. *KIV*

Murderer's Keep woof! 1988 Secret ingredients used in the Central Meat Market's hamburger are discovered by a young, deaf girl. Beware of filler, she learns, particularly if it's someone you know. **89m/C VHS, Beta.** Vic Tayback, Talia Shire, Robert Walden; **D:** Paulmichel Miekhe.

Murderers' Row 🎬🎬½ 1966 Daredevil bachelor and former counter-espionage agent Matt Helm is summoned from his life of leisure to ensure the safety of an important scientist. Martin's attempt as a super-spy doesn't wash, and Margret is implausible as the kidnapped scientist's daughter. Unless you want to hear Martin sing "I'm Not the Marrying Kind," don't bother. Second in the "Matt Helm" series. **108m/C VHS, Beta.** Dean Martin, Ann-Margret, Karl Malden, Beverly Adams, James Gregory; **D:** Henry Levin; **M:** Lalo Schifrin. *COL*

Murderlust woof! 1986 Employers in search of a security guard make a poor choice in offering the position to a sexually frustrated man whose hobbies include strangling prostitutes. Poor hiring decisions come into play later when he secures a job at an adolescent crisis center. **90m/C VHS, Beta.** Eli Rich, Rochelle Taylor, Dennis Gannon, Bonnie Schneider, Lisa Nichols; **D:** Donald M. Jones.

Murderous Vision 🎬🎬 1991 (R) Television fixture Boxleitner is a bored detective in this outing. But one day, while tracking a young mother in the missing persons bureau, he stumbles upon the trail of a serial killer. Enter a beautiful psychic who wants to help, add a race to catch the murderer, and Bruce suddenly has his hands full. Made for television. **93m/C VHS, LV, Closed Caption.** Bruce Boxleitner, Laura Johnson, Robert Culp; **D:** Gary Sherman. *PAR*

Murders at Lynch Cross 1985 Made-for-British-television mystery about a weird, isolated hotel on the Yorkshire moors. **60m/C VHS, Beta.** *GB* Jill Bennett, Joanna David, Barbara Jefford, Sylvia Syms.

Murders in the Rue Morgue 🎬🎬½ 1932 Lugosi stars as a deranged scientist (what a stretch) who wants to find a female companion for his pet gorilla. He kidnaps a beautiful woman and prepares to make her the gorilla's bride. Very loosely based on the story by Edgar Allan Poe, which has been remade several times. **61m/B VHS, Closed Caption.** Bela Lugosi, Sidney Fox, Leon Ames, Brandon Hurst, Arlene Francis, Noble Johnson; **D:** Robert Florey; **W:** John Huston, Tom Reed, Dale Van Every; **C:** Karl Freund. *USH*

Murders in the Rue Morgue 🎬🎬½ 1971 (PG) A young woman has frightening dreams inspired by a play that her father is producing in Paris at the turn of the century. After many people associated with the production become murder victims, the girl becomes involved with one of her father's former associates, a man who killed her mother years ago and then faked his own suicide. The fourth film based on Edgar Allan Poe's classic horror story. **87m/C VHS, Beta.** Jason Robards Jr.,

Lilli Palmer, Herbert Lom, Michael Dunn, Christine Kaufmann, Adolfo Celi; **D:** Gordon Hessler. *NO*

The Murders in the Rue Morgue 🎬🎬🎬 1986 (PG) The fifth filmed version of the Edgar Allan Poe story. Set in 19th-century Paris; actors in a mystery play find their roles coming to life. Scott is terrific, with good supporting help. Made for television. **92m/C VHS.** George C. Scott, Rebecca DeMornay, Val Kilmer, Ian McShane, Neil Dickson; **D:** Jeannot Szwarc; **C:** Bruno de Keyzer. *THV*

Murders in the Zoo 🎬🎬½ 1933 Zoologist Atwill has a reason to be insanely jealous since his wife (Burke) has been having lots of extramarital affairs. But his way of dealing with these other men is certainly unique—he feeds them to various zoo animals (after first sewing the victims' lips shut). Censors were outraged and the film underwent various edits for its theatrical release. **62m/B VHS, Closed Caption.** Lionel Atwill, Kathleen Burke, Charlie Ruggles, Randolph Scott, Gail Patrick, John Lodge, Harry Beresford; **D:** Edward Sutherland; **W:** Philip Wylie, Seton I. Miller. *USH*

Muriel 🎬🎬🎬½ *Muriel, Ou le Temps d'Un Retour; The Time of Return; Muriel, Or the Time of Return* 1963 A complex, mosaic drama about a middle-aged woman who meets an old lover at Boulogne, and her stepson who cannot forget the needless suffering he caused a young woman named Muriel while he was a soldier at war. Throughout, director Alain Resnais plumbs the essential meanings of memory, age, and the anxieties created from the tension between personal and public actions. Acclaimed; in French with subtitles. **115m/C VHS, Beta.** *FR IT* Delphine Seyrig, Jean-Pierre Kerien, Nita Klein, Jean-Baptiste Thierree; **D:** Alain Resnais; **C:** Sacha Vierny; **M:** Georges Delerue. Venice Film Festival '63: Best Actress (Seyrig). *HTV, FCT*

Muriel's Wedding 🎬🎬🎬 1994 (R) Muriel (Collette) can catch a bridal bouquet, but can she catch a husband? Her blonde, bitch-goddess friends don't think so. But dowdy, pathetic, overweight Muriel dreams of a fairy tale wedding anyway. How she fulfills her obsessive fantasy is the basis for this quirky, hilarious, and often touchingly poignant ugly duckling tale with the occasional over-the-top satiric moment. Strong cast is led by sympathetic and engaging performances from Collette (who gained 40-plus pounds for the role) and Griffiths as her best friend, Rhonda. '70s pop supergroup ABBA lends its kitschy but catchy tunes to the plot and soundtrack. Not released in the U.S. until 1995.**CW:** Contains profanity and sexual situations. **105m/C VHS, LV, Closed Caption.** *AU* Toni Collette, Bill Hunter, Rachel Griffiths, Jeanie Drynan, Gennie Nevinson Brice, Matt Day, Daniel Lapaine, Sophie Lee, Rosalind Hammond, Belinda Jarrett; **D:** P.J. Hogan; **W:** P.J. Hogan; **M:** Peter Best. Australian Film Institute '94: Best Actress (Collette), Best Film, Best Sound, Best Supporting Actress (Griffiths); Nominations: Australian Film Institute '94: Best Director (Hogan), Best Original Screenplay, Best Supporting Actor (Hunter), Best Supporting Actress (Drynan); British Academy Awards '95: Best Original Screenplay; Golden Globe Awards '96: Best Actress—Musical/Comedy (Collette); Writers Guild of America '95: Best Original Screenplay. *MAX*

Murmur of the Heart 🎬🎬🎬½ 1971 (R) Honest treatment of a 14-year-old's coming of age. After his older brothers take him to a prostitute for his first sexual experience, he comes down with scarlet fever. He then travels to a health spa with his mom to recover. There they find that their mother-son bond is stronger than most. Music by Charlie Parker is featured in the score. In French with English subtitles. **118m/C VHS, Beta, LV.** *FR* Benoit Ferreux, Daniel Gelin, Lea Massari, Corinne Kersten, Jacqueline Chauveau, Marc Wincourt, Michael Lonsdale; **D:** Louis Malle. Nominations: Academy Awards '72: Best Story & Screenplay. *ORI*

Murph the Surf 🎬🎬½ *Live a Little, Steal a Lot; You Can't Steal Love* 1975 (PG) Fact-based, engrossing story of two beach bums turned burglars who grow bored with small-time robbery and plan

a trip to New York City to steal the Star of Africa sapphire. Notable among the many action scenes is a boat chase through the inland waterways of Miami, Florida. **102m/C VHS, Beta.** Robert Conrad, Don Stroud, Donna Mills, Luther Adler, Robyn Millan, Paul Stewart; **D:** Marvin J. Chomsky. *WAR, OM*

Murphy's Fault 🎬🎬 1988 (PG-13) Dark comedy about a night watchman/writer plagued by a series of bad luck incidents. **94m/C VHS, Beta, LV.** Patrick Dollaghan, Anne Curry, Stack Pierce; **D:** Robert J. Smawley. *THV*

Murphy's Law 🎬 1986 (R) A hard-headed cop gets framed for his ex-wife's murder and embarks on a mission to find the actual killer. He is slowed down by a smart-mouthed prostitute who is handcuffed to him during his search. Casting a female in the role of a psycho-killer is unique to the genre. **101m/C VHS, Beta, LV, Closed Caption.** Charles Bronson, Carrie Snodgress, Kathleen Wilhoite, Robert F. Lyons, Richard Romanus, Angel Tompkins, Bill Henderson, James Luisi, Janet MacLachlan, Lawrence Tierney; **D:** J. Lee Thompson; **M:** Mark Donohue. *VTR*

Murphy's Romance 🎬🎬🎬 1985 (PG-13) A young divorced mother with an urge to train horses pulls up the stakes and heads for Arizona with her son. There she meets a pharmacist who may be just what the doctor ordered to help her build a new life. **107m/C VHS, Beta, LV, Closed Caption.** James Garner, Sally Field, Brian Kerwin, Corey Haim, Dennis Burkley, Charles Lane, Georgann Johnson; **D:** Martin Ritt; **W:** Harriet Frank Jr., Irving Ravetch; **M:** Carole King. Nominations: Academy Awards '85: Best Actor (Garner), Best Cinematography. *COL, HMV*

Murphy's War 🎬🎬 1971 (PG) In WWII, the Germans sink an English ship and gun down most of its crew. An Irishman, however, survives and returns to health with the help of a nurse. He then seeks revenge on those who killed his crewmates, even after he learns the war has ended. O'Toole is interesting as the revenge-minded seaman though saddled with a mediocre script. **106m/C VHS, Beta.** *GB* Peter O'Toole, Sian Phillips, Philippe Noiret; **D:** Peter Yates; **W:** Stirling Silliphant; **M:** John Barry. *PAR, CCB*

Murrow 🎬🎬½ 1986 A cable television biography of the renowed chain-smoking journalist who changed broadcasting history by fearlessly voicing his liberal ideas on the air waves. His life was more interesting though Travanti does his best to breathe some life into the script. **114m/C VHS, Beta.** Daniel J. Travanti, Dabney Coleman, Edward Herrmann, David Suchet, John McMartin, Robert Vaughn, Kathryn Leigh Scott; **D:** Jack Gold; **W:** Ernest Kinoy; **M:** Carl Davis. *FCT, ART*

Muscle Beach Party 🎬🎬 1964 Sequel to "Beach Party" finds Frankie and Annette romping in the sand again. Trouble invades teen nirvana when a new gym opens and the hardbodies try to muscle in on surfer turf. Meanwhile, Paluzzi tries to muscle in on Funicello's turf. Good clean corny fun, with the usual lack of script and plot. Lorre appeals in a cameo, his final screen appearance. Watch for "Little" Stevie Wonder in his debut. Rickles' first appearance in the "BP" series; Lupus was credited as Rock Stevens. Followed by "Bikini Beach." 🎵Muscle Beach Party; Runnin' Wild; Muscle Bustle; My First Love; Surfin' Woodie; Surfer's Holiday; Happy Street; A Girl Needs a Boy; A Boy Needs a Girl. **94m/C VHS, Beta, LV.** Frankie Avalon, Annette Funicello, Buddy Hackett, Luciana Paluzzi, Don Rickles, John Ashley, Jody McCrea, Morey Amsterdam, Peter Lupus, Candy Johnson, Dolores Wells, Stevie Wonder, Donna Loren, Amadee Chabot; **Cameos:** Peter Lorre; **D:** William Asher; **W:** William Asher, Robert Dillon; **M:** Les Baxter. *NO*

Music Box 🎬🎬½ 1989 (R) An attorney defends her father against accusations that he has committed inhumane Nazi war crimes. If she loses, her father faces deportation. As the case progresses, she must struggle to remain objective in the courtroom and come to terms with the possibility that her father is guilty. Lange's portrayal of an ethnic character is highly convincing. **126m/C**

VHS, Beta, LV, Letterbox. Jessica Lange, Frederic Forrest, Lukas Haas, Armin Mueller-Stahl, Michael Rooker, Donald Moffat, Cheryl Lynn Bruce; *D:* Constantin Costa-Gavras; *W:* Joe Eszterhas; *C:* Patrick Blossier; *M:* Philippe Sarde. Nominations: Academy Awards '89: Best Actress (Lange). *NO*

Music Box/Helpmates 1932 These two classic, award-winning comedy shorts by the dynamic duo have been color-enhanced by Colorization. *50m/B VHS, Beta.* Stan Laurel, Oliver Hardy. *VTR*

Music in My Heart ✁✁½ 1940 Two taxi cabs crash and spur the love of Martin and Hayworth. She proceeds to break off her engagement to save Martin from deportation. Hayworth's last low-budget film before becoming a Hollywood goddess. *69m/B VHS.* Rita Hayworth, Tony Martin, Edith Fellows, Alan Mowbray, Eric Blore, George Tobias, Joseph Crehan, George Humbert, Phil Tead; *D:* Joseph Santley; *M:* Robert Wright, Chet Forrest. Nominations: Academy Awards '40: Best Song ("It's a Blue World"). *COL, CCB*

The Music Lovers ✁✁½ 1971 (R) Russell's version of Tchaikovsky's tormented life and glorious achievements is a shocker, a movie that infuriates professed music lovers but, nonetheless, has introduced many a neophyte to the world of classical music via its sensationalism. Homosexual Tchaikovsky marries an admirer to appease the Russian government and his financial benefactor. Stunned when he discovers his wife is a nymphomaniac, he banishes her to a netherworld of prostitution and eventual insanity which Russell mercilessly explores. Tchaikovsky's own squalid life is hardly better, though he does enjoy success before the bottom falls out. *122m/C VHS, LV, Letterbox. GB* Richard Chamberlain, Glenda Jackson, Max Adrian, Christopher Gable, Kenneth Colley, Izabella Telezynska, Maureen Pryor; *D:* Ken Russell; *M:* Melvin Bragg. *MGM, MLB, FCT*

The Music Man ✁✁✁✁ 1962 (G) Con man in the guise of a traveling salesman gets off the train in River City, Iowa. After hearing about plans to build a pool hall, he argues it would be the gateway to hell for the young, impressionable males of the town. He then convinces the River Cityzens to look toward the future of the community and finance a wholesome children's marching band. Although the huckster plans to take their money and run before the instruments arrive, his feelings for the town librarian cause him to think twice about fleeing the Heartland. This isn't just a slice of Americana; it's a whole pie. Acting and singing are terrific "with a capital 'T' and that rhymes with 'P' and that stands for" Preston, who epitomizes the charismatic pitchman. ♫ Seventy-six Trombones; Trouble; Till There Was You; The Wells Fargo Wagon; Being in Love; Goodnight, My Someone; Rock Island; Iowa Stubborn. *151m/C VHS, Beta, LV, Letterbox, Closed Caption.* Robert Preston, Shirley Jones, Buddy Hackett, Hermione Gingold, Paul Ford, Pert Kelton, Ron Howard; *D:* Morton DaCosta; *W:* Marion Hargrove; *C:* Robert Burks. Academy Awards '62: Best Adapted Score; Golden Globe Awards '63: Best Film—Musical/Comedy; Nominations: Academy Awards '62: Best Art Direction/Set Decoration (Color), Best Costume Design (Color), Best Film Editing, Best Picture, Best Sound. *WAR, MVD, TLF*

The Music of Chance ✁✁½ 1993 (R) Convoluted story about a smalltime gambler (Spader) and a drifter (Patinkin) who wind up involved in a bizarre high stakes poker game with a Laurel and Hardyish pair (Durning and Grey) who live in an isolated mansion. When Spader and Patinkin lose, their debt forces them into an indentured servitude where they must construct a brick wall around their new masters' estate. Bloated with symbolism, this adaptation from cult fave novelist Auster (who has a small part), loses its eclectic significance in the translation to the big screen. Nonetheless, valiant effort by rookie director Haas. *98m/C VHS, LV, Closed Caption.* James Spader, Mandy Patinkin, Joel Grey, Charles Durning, M. Emmet Walsh, Samantha Mathis, Christopher Penn, Pearl Jones, Paul Auster; *D:* Philip Haas; *W:* Philip Haas, Belinda

Haas; *C:* Bernard Zitzermann; *M:* Philip Johnston. *COL, BTV*

Music Shoppe ✁✁ 1982 (G) Four teenagers form a rock band with the assistance of the local music store proprietor. Interesting cast. *93m/C VHS, Beta.* Gary Crosby, Nia Peeples, Benny Medina, Stephen Schwartz, David Jackson, Jesse White, Doug Kershaw, Giselle MacKenzie. *GEM*

The Music Teacher ✁✁½ *Le Maitre de Musique* 1988 (PG) A Belgian costume drama dealing with a famed singer who retires to devote himself to teaching two students exclusively. In time, he sees his prized pupils lured into an international competition by an old rival of his. Although the singing is sharp, the story is flat. In French with yellow English subtitles. *95m/C VHS, Beta, LV. BE* Patrick Bauchau, Sylvie Fennec, Phillipe Volter, Jose Van Dam, Johan Leysen, Anne Roussel; *D:* Gerard Corbiau. Nominations: Academy Awards '88: Best Foreign Language Film. *ORI*

Musica Proibita ✁✁½ 1943 A serious opera-spiced drama about a young romance crushed by adultery in the teenage couple's ancestry. In Italian with English subtitles. *93m/B VHS, Beta.* Tito Gobbi, Maria Mercader. *VYY*

Mussolini & I ✁✁½ *Mussolini: The Decline and Fall of II Duce* 1985 Docudramatization of the struggle for power between Italy's Benito Mussolini and his son-in-law, Galeazzo Ciano. Narrated by Sarandon in the role of II Duce's daughter. Made for cable television. *130m/C VHS, Beta.* Bob Hoskins, Anthony Hopkins, Susan Sarandon, Annie Girardot, Barbara DeRossi, Fabio Testi, Kurt Raab; *D:* Alberto Negrin. *NLC*

Mutant ✁½ *Night Shadows* 1983 (R) Another argument for the proper disposal of toxic waste. Hazardous materials transform the people of a southern town into monsters. *100m/C VHS, Beta, LV.* Wings Hauser, Bo Hopkins, Jennifer Warren, Lee Montgomery; *D:* John Cardos; *M:* Richard Band. *ART, VES*

Mutant Hunt woof! *Matt Riker* 1987 Made for video movie about a battle between robots gone haywire and an all-American hero. The detective cyborgs are set free while high on a sexual stimulant called Euphoron to wreak their technological havoc on a rampage in Manhattan. *90m/C VHS, Beta.* Rick Gianisi, Mary-Anne Fahey; *D:* Tim Kincaid; *W:* Tim Kincaid. *NO*

Mutant on the Bounty ✁½ 1989 A musician, lost in space as a beam of light for 23 years, is transported aboard a spaceship. Once he materializes, it becomes apparent that he has undergone some incredible physical changes. As if that's not enough, the crew then must flee from a couple of thugs who are trying to steal a vial of serum they have on board. A space spoof that never gets into orbit. *93m/C VHS.* John Roarke, Deborah Benson, John Furey, Victoria Catlin, John Fleck, Kyle T. Heffner; *D:* Robert Torrance.

Mutant Species ✁ *Bio-Force I* 1995 (R) Soldier is accidentally exposed to altered DNA and begins to mutate into a remorseless and terrifying killer. *CW:* Violence and language. *100m/C VHS, LV.* Leo Rossi, Ted Prior, Grant Gelt, Denise Crosby, Powers Boothe, Wilford Brimley; *D:* David A. Prior; *W:* David A. Prior, William Vigil; *C:* Carlos Gonzalez. *ART*

Mutant Video 1976 Six comedic, award-winning short-subject films from Jim Belushi and Rob Riley. Outrageous humor. *60m/B VHS, Beta.* James Belushi, Rob Riley. *ART*

Mutants In Paradise woof! 1988 Comedy about a human guinea-pig who always gets involved in some sort of mishap. *78m/C VHS, Beta.* Brad Greenquist, Robert Ingham, Anna Nicholas. *TWE*

Mutator ✁✁ *Time of the Beast* 1990 (R) A corporation makes a tiny genetic mistake and winds up creating a new life form...a demonic pussycat who preys on humans. *CW:* Language and monster violence and gore. *91m/C VHS, Beta.* Brion James, Carolyn Ann Clark, Milton Raphiel Murrill; *D:* John R. Bowey; *W:* Lynn Rose Higgins.

Mute Witness ✁✁½ 1995 (R) Low-budget British thriller, lensed in Moscow film studio, about U.S. filmers making a cheap thriller in Moscow film studio. Billy (Sudina) is the mute make-up artist of the title who, returning to the studio for a forgotten item, witnesses one of the crew shooting a snuff film with a real-life stabbing. First-timer Waller mocks both thriller genre and film biz, sometimes relying on, rather than spoofing, cliched elements. Highlight is 20-minute long chase scene with the killers pursuing Billy in the cavernous studio. Guinness makes a surprise appearance in a cameo. *CW:* Violence and a strong scene combining sex and violence. *100m/C VHS, LV, Closed Caption. GB* Marina Sudina, Fay Ripley, Evan Richards, Oleg Jankowsky, Igor Volkow, Sergei Karlenkov; *Cameos:* Alec Guinness; *D:* Anthony Waller; *W:* Anthony Waller; *C:* Egon Werdin; *M:* Wilbert Hirsch. *COL*

The Muthers ✁✁ 1976 (R) Women prisoners escape from their confinement in a South American jungle. *101m/C VHS, Beta.* Jeanne Bell, Rosanne Katon, Jayne Kennedy, Trina Parks; *D:* Cirio H. Santiago. *NO*

The Mutilator woof! *Fall Break* 1985 (R) After accidentally bumping off his mother, a young man stalks five high school students wanting to cut them up into tiny bits. An unedited version is also available. Bloody boredom. *85m/C VHS, Beta, LV.* Jack Chatham, Trace Cooper, Frances Raines, Bill Hitchcock; *D:* Buddy Cooper. *ART, VES*

Mutiny ✁✁ 1952 In the War of 1812, the crew of an American ship carrying $10 million in gold fight among themselves for a part of France's donation to the war effort. The beautiful photography doesn't make up for the predictability of the storyline. *76m/C VHS, Beta.* Mark Stevens, Gene Evans, Angela Lansbury, Patric Knowles; *D:* Edward Dmytryk; *W:* Philip Yordan. *NOS, VCI*

Mutiny in the Big House ✁✁½ 1939 A man is sent to prison for writing a bad ten dollar check and must choose between seeking salvation with the prison chaplain or toughing it out with a hardened convict. Suprisingly good low-budget programmer. *83m/B VHS, Beta.* Charles Bickford, Barton MacLane, Pat Moriarity, Dennis Moore, William Royle, Charles Foy, George Cleveland; *D:* William Nigh. *SNC*

The Mutiny of the Elsinore ✁ 1939 A writer on board an old sailing ship fights mutineers and wins back both the helm and the captain's daughter. Tedious British flotsam that made hash of an oft-filmed Jack London tale, and made news even in 1939 for its use of modern-day slang and clothing in the period setting. *74m/B VHS.* Paul Lukas, Lyn Harding, Kathleen Kelly, Clifford Evans, Ben Soutten, Jiro Soneya; *D:* Roy Lockwood. *NOS, DVT, FCT*

Mutiny on the Bounty ✁✁✁✁ 1935 Compelling adaptation of the true story of sadistic Captain Bligh, Fletcher Christian and their turbulent journey aboard the HMS Bounty and the subsequent mutiny in 1788. No gray here: Laughton's Bligh is truly a despicable character and extremely memorable in this MGM extravaganza. Remade twice, in 1962 and again in 1984 as "The Bounty." Much, much better than the 1962 remake. *132m/B VHS, Beta, LV, 8mm.* Clark Gable, Franchot Tone, Charles Laughton, Donald Crisp, Dudley Digges, Spring Byington, Henry Stephenson, Eddie Quillan, Herbert Mundin, Movita, Ian Wolfe; *D:* Frank Lloyd; *W:* Talbot Jennings, Jules Furthman, Carey Wilson; *M:* Herbert Stothart. Academy Awards '35: Best Picture; New York Film Critics Awards '35: Best Actor (Laughton); Nominations: Academy Awards '35: Best Actor (Gable), Best Actor (Tone, Laughton), Best Director (Lloyd), Best Film Editing, Best Screenplay, Best Score. *MGM, BMV, BTV*

Mutiny on the Bounty ✁✁½ 1962 Based on the novel by Charles Nordhoff and James Norman Hall, this account of the 1789 mutiny led by Fletcher Christian against Captain Bligh of the Bounty is highlighted by lavish photography and an eccentric, though interesting, portrayal of the mutiny leader by Brando. Though overshadowed by Laughton's compelling performance in the original 1935 masterpiece, Howard's Bligh is ship-shape as the cold-hearted, single-minded captain determined to reach Tahati and return with a hold full of breadfruit trees. Brando is all knickers and attitude as the peeved Mr. Christian, who finally can take no more of Bligh's social criticism. The other actors, especially Harris, join in the slightly over the top spirit of things. **177m/C VHS, Beta, LV, Letterbox.** Marlon Brando, Trevor Howard, Richard Harris, Hugh Griffith, Richard Haydn, Percy Herbert, Noel Purcell; **D:** Lewis Milestone; **W:** Charles Lederer; **C:** Robert L. Surtees. Nominations: Academy Awards '62: Best Art Direction/Set Decoration (Color), Best Color Cinematography, Best Film Editing, Best Picture, Best Song ("Love Song (Follow Me)"), Best Original Score. *MGM*

Mutual Respect ⚫½ 1977 (PG) A dying wealthy man sets out to find the son he never knew. **88m/C VHS, Beta.** Lloyd Bridges, Beau Bridges.

My African Adventure woof! 1987 Silly tale of an ambassador's son discovering a talking monkey in Africa and meeting a slew of opportunistic misfits in his travels. A comedy unfortunately short on laughs. Based on Tamar Burnstein's book. **93m/C VHS, Beta.** Dom DeLuise, Jimmie Walker; **D:** Sam Firstenberg.

My American Cousin ⚫⚫⚫ 1985 (PG) Award-winning Canadian coming-of-age comedy about a 12-year-old girl who falls for her rebellious, fun-loving 17-year-old American cousin over summer vacation. Followed by "American Boyfriends." **94m/C VHS, Beta, LV.** *CA* Margaret Langrick, John Wildman, Richard Donat, Jane Mortifee; **D:** Sandy Wilson; **W:** Sandy Wilson. Genie Awards '86: Best Actor (Wildman), Best Actress (Langrick), Best Director (Wilson), Best Film. *VTR*

My Antonia ⚫⚫½ 1994 (PG) Orphaned teenaged farm boy Jim Burden (Harris) discovers first romance with poor immigrant girl Antonia (Lowensohn) in 1886 Nebraska. They fall in love, separate, but maintain a 30-year friendship. Based on the book by Willa Cather. **92m/C VHS, Beta, Closed Caption.** Neil Patrick Harris, Jason Robards Jr., Eva Marie Saint, Elina Lowensohn, Norbert Weisser, Travis Fine, Jan Triska, Anne Tremko, Mira Furlan, Boris Krutonog; **D:** Joseph Sargent; **C:** Robert Primes. *PAR*

My Apprenticeship ⚫⚫⚫ 1939 The second film of Donskoi's trilogy on Maxim Gorky has the writer earning his living, at the age of eight, as an apprentice to a bourgeois family. Although they promise him an education, Gorky is forced to learn to read on his own and eventually sets off on a series of land and sea voyages. He recognizes that the poverty and abuse he has suffered is typical of the lives of most Russians and he encounters the beginnings of revolution. In Russian with English subtitles. Preceded by "My Childhood" and followed by "My Universities." **100m/C VHS.** *RU* **D:** Mark Donskoi. *FCT*

My Beautiful Laundrette ⚫⚫⚫ 1985 (R) Omar (Warnecke), the nephew of a Pakistani businessman, is given the opportunity to better himself by turning his uncle's run-down laundry into a profitable business. He reunites with Johnny (Day Lewis), a childhood friend and a working-class street punk, and they go into the business together. They find themselves battling the prejudice of each other's families and friends in order to succeed. An intelligent look at the sexuality, race relations and economic problems of Thatcher's London. Great performances by a relatively unknown cast (for contrast, note Day Lewis' performance in "Room with a View," released in the same year.) **93m/C VHS, Beta, LV, Closed Caption.** Gordon Warnecke, Daniel Day-Lewis, Saeed Jaffrey, Roshan Seth, Shirley Anne Field, Derrick Branche, Rita Wolf, Souad Faress, Richard Graham, Dudley Thomas, Garry Cooper, Charu Bala Choksi, Neil Cunningham, Walter Donohue, Stephen Marcus, Badi Uzzaman; **D:** Stephen Frears; **W:** Hanif Kureishi; **C:** Oliver Stapleton; **M:** Ludus Tonalis, Stanley Myers. National Board of Review Awards '86: Best Supporting Actor (Day-Lewis); New York Film Critics Awards '86: Best Screenplay, Best Supporting Actor

(Day-Lewis); National Society of Film Critics Awards '86: Best Screenplay. Nominations: Academy Awards '86: Best Original Screenplay. *ORI, WAR*

My Best Friend Is a Vampire ⚫⚫ 1988 (PG) Another teenage vampire story, about trying to cope with certain changes that adolescence and bloodsucking bring. Good supporting cast. **90m/C VHS, Closed Caption.** Robert Sean Leonard, Evan Mirand, Cheryl Pollak, Rene Auberjonois, Cecilia Peck, Fannie Flagg, Kenneth Kimmins, David Warner, Paul Wilson; **D:** Jimmy Huston; **M:** Stephen Dorff. *HBO*

My Best Friend's Girl ⚫⚫½ *La Femme De Mon Pote* 1984 Coy, sardonic French romance about a woman who slaloms between two buddies working at a ski resort. Despite fine performances from all, it never quite makes it to the top of the hill. In French with English subtitles. **99m/C VHS, Beta.** *FR* Isabelle Huppert, Thierry Lhermitte, Coluche, Francoise Perrot; **D:** Bertrand Blier; **W:** Bertrand Blier, Gerard Brach. *COL*

My Best Friend's Wedding ⚫⚫½ 1997 (PG-13) Yes, it's a romantic comedy, but like director Hogan's previous effort, "Muriel's Wedding," there's some snap among the smiles. Restaurant critic Julianne (Roberts) and sports writer Michael (Mulroney) are best friends who have a pact that they'll marry each other if neither has found someone else by the age of 28. Michael finds sweet, wealthy Kimmy (Diaz) and invites Julianne to his nuptials. Naturally, Julianne realizes she's in love with Michael and she'll stop at nothing to break up the wedding, even enlisting gay friend George (Everett) to pose as her new beau. Roberts appears as the critics prefer her (long hair and smiling) while she extends her range of physical comedy. Diaz gets to be nice, Everett gets to steal every scene he's in, and Mulroney gets to be the lucky object of two lovely women's affections. Shot on location in Chicago. **CW:** One use of strong language and brief sex-related humor. **105m/C VHS, LV, Closed Caption, DVD.** Julia Roberts, Dermot Mulroney, Cameron Diaz, Rupert Everett, Philip Bosco, M. Emmet Walsh, Rachel Griffiths, Susan Sullivan, Paul Giamatti; **D:** P.J. Hogan; **W:** Ronald Bass; **C:** Laszlo Kovács; **M:** James Newton Howard. Nominations: Academy Awards '97: Best Original Musical/Comedy Score; British Academy Awards '97: Best Supporting Actor (Everett); Golden Globe Awards '98: Best Actress—Musical/Comedy (Roberts), Best Film—Musical/Comedy, Best Supporting Actor (Everett); MTV Movie Awards '98: Best Female Performance (Roberts), Breakthrough Performance (Everett), Best Comedic Performance (Everett). *COL*

My Best Girl ⚫⚫ 1927 Mary attempts to bring her new sweetheart home for dinner, with disastrous results. A gentle satire on middle-American life in the 1920s. Includes organ score. **78m/B VHS, Beta, LV.** Mary Pickford, Charles "Buddy" Rogers; **D:** Sam Taylor; **C:** Charles Rosher; **M:** Gaylord Carter. Nominations: Academy Awards '28: Best Cinematography. *CCB*

My Bloody Valentine ⚫⚫ 1981 (R) Psychotic coal miner visits the peaceful little town of Valentine Bluffs on the night of the yearly Valentine Ball. Many of the townspeople have their hearts removed with a pick axe and sent to the sheriff in candy boxes. The bloodiest scenes were cut out to avoid an X-rating. **91m/C VHS, Beta, LV.** *CA* Paul Kelman, Lori Hallier, Neil Affleck, Keith Knight, Alf Humphreys, Cynthia Dale, Terry Waterland, Peter Cowper, Don Francks, Jack Van Evera; **D:** George Mihalka; **W:** John Beaird; **C:** Rodney Gibbons. *PAR*

My Blue Heaven ⚫⚫ 1990 (PG-13) After agreeing to rat on the Mafia, Martin is dropped into suburbia as part of the witness protection program. Moranis plays the FBI agent assigned to help the former mobster become an upstanding citizen. Adjusting to life in the slow lane isn't easy for an ex con who has grown accustomed to the big time. Not the typical role for Martin, who plays a brunette with a New York accent and is handcuffed by bad writing. **96m/C VHS, Beta, LV, Closed Caption.** Steve Martin, Rick Moranis, Joan Cusack, Melanie Mayron, Carol Kane, Bill Irwin, William Hickey, Daniel Stern;

D: Herbert Ross; **W:** Nora Ephron; **C:** John Bailey; **M:** Ira Newborn. WAR, BTV

My Bodyguard ⚫⚫⚫ 1980 (PG) An undersized high school student fends off attacking bullies by hiring a king-sized, withdrawn lad as his bodyguard. Their "business" relationship, however, develops into true friendship. An adolescent coming of age with more intelligence and sensitivity than most of its ilk, and a pack of up and coming stars as well as old stand-bys Houseman and Gordon. **96m/C VHS, Beta.** Chris Makepeace, Adam Baldwin, Martin Mull, Ruth Gordon, Matt Dillon, John Houseman, Joan Cusack, Craig Richard Nelson; **D:** Tony Bill; **W:** Alan Ormsby; **M:** Dave Grusin. *FOX*

My Boy ⚫⚫½ 1921 Coogan stars as a foreign orphan who faces deportation. Instead he escapes and follows an old man home. This rare film includes an organ score. **56m/B VHS, Beta.** Jackie Coogan, Claude Gillingwater, Mathilde Brundage; **D:** Albert Austin. *GPV*

My Boyfriend's Back ⚫ *Johnny Zombie* 1993 (PG-13) Embarrassingly dumb flick about a teenage boy who wants to take the prettiest girl in the school to the prom. The only problem is that he's become a zombie. Bits of him keep falling off (his girl thoughtfully glues them back on) and if he wants to stay "alive" long enough to get to the dance he has to munch on human flesh. Yuck. **CW:** Strong language, zombie violence, and teen sex fantasy. **85m/C VHS, LV, Closed Caption.** Andrew Lowery, Traci Lind, Edward Herrmann, Mary Beth Hurt, Danny Zorn, Austin Pendleton, Jay O. Sanders, Paul Dooley, Bob Dishy, Matthew Fox, Paxton Whitehead; **D:** Bob Balaban; **W:** Dean Lorey; **C:** Mac Ahlberg. *TOU*

My Boys Are Good Boys ⚫ 1978 (PG) A young foursome steal from an armored car and have to face the consequences. Quirky with an implausible storyline. **90m/C VHS, Beta.** Ralph Meeker, Ida Lupino, Lloyd Nolan, David Doyle; **D:** Bethel Buckalew. *NO*

My Breakfast with Blassie 1983 Kaufman and professional wrestler Blassie meet for breakfast and carry on a comical dialogue. **60m/C VHS, Beta.** Andy Kaufman, Freddie Blassie; **D:** Johnny Legend, Linda Lautrec. *RHI*

My Brilliant Career ⚫⚫⚫½ 1979 (G) A headstrong young woman spurns the social expectations of turn-of-the-century Australia and pursues opportunities to broaden her intellect and preserve her independence. Davis is wonderful as the energetic and charismatic community trendsetter. Based on an autobiographical novel by Miles Franklin which has been marvelously transferred to the screen. Armstrong deserves credit for her fine direction. **101m/C VHS, Beta.** *AU* Judy Davis, Sam Neill, Wendy Hughes; **D:** Gillian Armstrong. Australian Film Institute '79: Best Film; British Academy Awards '80: Best Actress (Davis); Nominations: Academy Awards '80: Best Costume Design. *VES*

My Brother Has Bad Dreams ⚫ 1988 Young man with sibling tosses and turns in bed. **97m/C VHS.** Nick Kleinholz, Marlena Lustic. *VCI*

My Brother's Wife ⚫⚫½ 1989 (PG) Barney (Ritter), the black sheep of a wealthy family, spends two decades pursuing Eleanor (Harris), the woman of his dreams. Unfortunately, she's already married—to the brother he despises. Adapted from the play "The Middle Ages" by A.R. Gurney. Made for television. **94m/C VHS.** John Ritter, Mel Harris, Polly Bergen, Dakin Matthews, David Byron, Lee Weaver; **D:** Jack Bender; **W:** Percy Granger. *APX, TPV*

My Champion ⚫ 1984 Chance meeting propels Mike Gorman and Miki Tsuwa into a relationship based on the strong bonds of love and athletic competition. **101m/C VHS, Beta.** Yoko Shimada, Chris Mitchum.

My Chauffeur ⚫⚫½ 1986 (R) When a wise-cracking female is hired on as a chauffeur at an all-male chauffeur service, sparks fly. And when the owner takes a definite liking to her work, things take a turn for the worse. As these sort of sexploitation flicks go, this is one of the better ones. **94m/C VHS, Beta, LV.** Deborah Foreman, Sam Jones, Howard Hesseman, E.G. Marshall, Sean McClory; **D:** David Beaird; **W:** David Beaird. *ART, VES*

My Childhood 🎬🎬🎬 1938
The first of director Donskoi's trilogy on the life of Maxim Gorky, based on Gorky's autobiographical stories. In this first film, Donskoi depicts Gorky's childhood of abuse and poverty with his grandparents in the 1870s. Eventually, Gorky is forced into the streets and he becomes a wandering beggar. In Russian with English subtitles. Followed by "My Apprenticeship" and "My Universities." **100m/C VHS.** *RU* **D:** Mark Donskoi. *FCT*

My Cousin Vinny 🎬🎬🎬 1992 (R)
Vinny Gambini (Pesci), a lawyer who took the bar exam six times before passing, goes to Wahzoo City, Alabama to get his cousin and a friend off the hook when they're accused of killing a store clerk. Leather jackets, gold chains, Brooklyn accents, and his fiancee Tomei's penchant for big hair and bold clothing don't go over well with conservative judge Gwynne, causing plenty of misunderstandings. Surprising hit with simplistic story reaches popular heights via entertaining performances by the entire cast. Tomei in particular steals every scene she's in and has an Oscar to prove it.*CW:* Language. **120m/C VHS, Closed Caption.** Joe Pesci, Ralph Macchio, Marisa Tomei, Mitchell Whitfield, Fred Gwynne, Lane Smith, Austin Pendleton, Bruce McGill; **D:** Jonathan Lynn; **W:** Dale Launer; **M:** Randy Edelman. Academy Awards '92: Best Supporting Actress (Tomei); MTV Movie Awards '93: Breakthrough Performance (Tomei). *MOV, PMS, BTV*

My Darling Clementine 🎬🎬🎬½ 1946
One of the best Hollywood westerns ever made, this recounts the precise events leading up to and including the gunfight at the O.K. Corral. Ford allegedly knew Wyatt Earp and used his stories to recount the details vividly, though not always accurately. Remake of 1939's "Frontier Marshal." **97m/B VHS, Beta, LV, Closed Caption.** Henry Fonda, Victor Mature, Walter Brennan, Linda Darnell, Tim Holt, Ward Bond, John Ireland; **D:** John Ford. National Film Registry '91. *FOX, TLF*

My Daughter's Keeper 🎬🎬 1993 (R)
The apparently perfect nanny of an unsuspecting family reveals her deadly agenda of murder, adultery, and more. **94m/C VHS.** Nicholas Guest, Jocelyn Broderick, Ana Padrao. *ART*

My Dear Secretary 🎬🎬½ 1949
After she marries her boss, a woman grows jealous of the secretary that replaces her. Comedic dialogue and antics result. **94m/B VHS.** Kirk Douglas, Laraine Day, Keenan Wynn, Rudy Vallee, Florence Bates, Alan Mowbray, Charles Martin; **D:** Charles Martin; **W:** Charles Martin. *EEL, MRV, BAR*

My Demon Lover 🎬🎬 1987 (PG-13)
This sex comedy is complicated by the hero's transformation into a demon whenever he is aroused. Saved from complete mediocrity by Family Ties's Valentine in a likable performance. **90m/C VHS, Beta, LV.** Scott Valentine, Michelle Little, Arnold Johnson, Gina Gallego; **D:** Charles Loventhal; **M:** David Newman, Ed Alton. *COL*

My Dinner with Andre 🎬🎬🎬½ 1981
Two friends talk about their lives and philosophies for two hours over dinner one night. A wonderful exploration into storytelling, the conversation juxtaposes the experiences and philosophies of nerdish, bumbling Shawn and the globe-trotting spiritual pilgrimage of Gregory, in this sometimes poignant, sometimes comic little movie that starts you thinking. **110m/C VHS, Beta, LV.** Andre Gregory, Wallace Shawn; **D:** Louis Malle. *HMV, TPV*

My Dog Shep 🎬½ 1946
An orphan and his dog run away and are pursued diligently when it is discovered that he is a wealthy heir. **71m/B VHS, Beta, LV.** Tom Neal, William Farnum, Lannie Rees; **D:** Ford Beebe. *NOS, VYY*

My Dog, the Thief 🎬 1969
A helicopter weatherman is unaware that the lovable St. Bernard he has adopted is a kleptomaniac. When the dog steals a valuable necklace from a team of professional jewel thieves, the fun begins. **88m/C VHS, Beta.** Joe Flynn, Elsa Lanchester, Roger C. Carmel, Mickey Shaughnessy, Dwayne Hickman, Mary Ann Mobley; **D:** Robert Stevenson. *DVT*

My Dream Is Yours 🎬🎬½ 1949
Day plays an up-and-coming radio star in this Warner Bros. musical comedy with a cameo from Bugs Bunny in a dream sequence. This fresh, fun remake of "Twenty Million Sweethearts" is often underrated, but is well worth a look. ♫My Dream is Yours; Some Like You; Tic, Tic, Tic; Love Finds a Way; I'll String Along with You; Canadian Capers; Freddie Get Ready; You Must Have Been a Beautiful Baby; Jeepers, Creepers. **101m/C VHS.** Jack Carson, Doris Day, Lee Bowman, Adolphe Menjou, Eve Arden, S.Z. Sakall, Selena Royle, Edgar Kennedy; **D:** Michael Curtiz. *FOX, FCT, MLB*

My Fair Lady 🎬🎬🎬½ 1964 (G)
Colorful production of Lerner and Loewe's musical version of "Pygmalion," about an ill-mannered cockney girl who is plucked from her job as a flower girl by Professor Henry Higgins. Higgins makes a bet with a colleague that he can turn this rough diamond into a "lady." Winner of eight Academy Awards. Hepburn's singing voice is dubbed by Marni Nixon, who was also responsible for the singing in "The King and I" and "West Side Story"; the dubbing may have undermined her chance at an Oscar nomination. Typecasting role for Harrison as the crusty, egocentric Higgins. A timeless classic. ♫Why Can't the English?; Wouldn't It Be Lovely?; I'm an Ordinary Man; With a Little Bit of Luck; Just You Wait, 'Enry 'Iggins; The Servant's Chorus; The Rain in Spain; I Could Have Danced all Night; Ascot Gavotte. **170m/C VHS, Beta, LV, Letterbox, Closed Caption.** Audrey Hepburn, Rex Harrison, Stanley Holloway, Wilfrid Hyde-White, Theodore Bikel, Mona Washbourne, Jeremy Brett, Robert Coote, Gladys Cooper; **D:** George Cukor; **C:** Harry Stradling; **M:** Frederick Loewe, Alan Jay Lerner. Academy Awards '64: Best Actor (Harrison), Best Adapted Score, Best Art Direction/Set Decoration (Color), Best Color Cinematography, Best Costume Design (Color), Best Director (Cukor), Best Picture, Best Sound; British Academy Awards '65: Best Film; Directors Guild of America Awards '64: Best Director (Cukor); Golden Globe Awards '65: Best Actor—Musical/Comedy (Harrison), Best Director (Cukor), Best Film—Musical/Comedy; New York Film Critics Awards '64: Best Actor (Harrison), Best Film; Nominations: Academy Awards '64: Best Adapted Screenplay, Best Film Editing, Best Supporting Actor (Holloway), Best Supporting Actress (Cooper). *FOX, FCT, BTV*

My Family 🎬🎬🎬½ *Mi Familia* 1994 (R)
Patriarch Jose Sanchez (Rojas) comes to America in the early 1900s from Mexico and soon finds that the grass is not always greener on the other side. Thus begins the multigenerational saga of the Sanchez family in L.A., which chronicles their struggles and hopes over a time span of 60 years. Overlooked in the glut of Hispanic-themed movies released, featuring soulful performances from the ensemble cast, especially Smits and Morales as troubled men from separate generations. Their deep-seated need to assimilate matched by a disdain for authority provide most of the family's heartaches. English and Spanish dialogue.*CW:* Strong language; some graphic violence; scene of sexuality. **126m/C VHS, LV, Closed Caption.** Jimmy Smits, Esai Morales, Eduardo Lopez Rojas, Jenny Gago, Elpidia Carrillo, Lupe Ontiveros, Jacob Vargas, Jennifer Lopez, Scott Bakula, Edward James Olmos, Michael De Lorenzo, Maria Canals, Leon Singer, Jonathan Hernandez, Constance Marie, Enrique Castillo, Mary Steenburgen; **D:** Gregory Nava; **W:** Gregory Nava, Anna Thomas; **C:** Edward Lachman; **M:** Pepe Avila, Mark McKenzie. Nominations: Academy Awards '95: Best Makeup; Independent Spirit Awards '96: Best Actor (Smits), Best Supporting Actress (Lopez). *NLC, TTC*

My Family Treasure 🎬🎬½ 1993
Mother tells her children about her dangerous trip into Russia to recover a family legacy—a priceless Faberge egg. **95m/C VHS.** Dee Wallace Stone, Theodore Bikel, Alex Vincent, Bitty Schram; **D:** Rolfe Kanefsky, Edward Staroselsky. *AVI*

My Father Is Coming 🎬🎬 1991
German immigrant, Vicky, is trying to get an acting career off the ground in New York. She shares her apartment with Ben, a gay man, and generally does more work as a waitress than actress. Vicky's alarmed when her father, Hans, arrives for a visit. She's told him she's married (Vicky's also gay), so Ben agrees to pose as her husband. The rest of the film details Vicky's complicated love life, unsuccessful career tryouts, and her father's increasing bewilderment. It's meant as a sort of reverse, and perverse, innocents abroad, with the two Germans adrift in zany New York but this only works fitfully. **82m/C VHS, Closed Caption.** *GE* Shelley Kastner, Alfred Edel, David Bronstein, Mary Lou Graulau, Michael Massee, Annie Sprinkle, Bruce Benderson; **D:** Monika Treut; **W:** Monika Treut. *FRF*

My Father, My Rival 🎬 1985
A high school student's crush on his teacher leads to emotional complications when his widowed father becomes romantically involved with her. **60m/C VHS, Beta.** Lance Guest. *NO*

My Father the Hero 🎬🎬 1993 (PG)
Another adaptation of a French film ("Mon Pere, Ce Heroes") finds 14-year-old Heigl on an island paradise with divorced dad Depardieu, passing him off as her boyfriend (without his knowledge) to impress a cute boy, causing obvious misunderstandings. Depardieu shows a flair for physical comedy, but his talent is wasted in a role that's vaguely disturbing; one of the few funny moments finds him unwittingly singing "Thank Heaven For Little Girls" to a horrified audience. For the preteen set only, others will probably find it a waste of time. Top notch actress Thompson's surprising (uncredited) cameo is due to her friendship with Depardieu. **90m/C VHS, LV, Closed Caption.** Gerard Depardieu, Katherine Heigl, Dalton James, Lauren Hutton, Faith Prince; **Cameos:** Emma Thompson; **D:** Steve Miner; **W:** Francis Veber, Charlie Peters; **M:** David Newman. *TOU*

My Father's Glory 🎬🎬🎬 *La Gloire de Mon Pere* 1991 (G)
Based on Marcel Pagnol's tales of his childhood, this is a sweet, beautiful memory of a young boy's favorite summer in the French countryside of the early 1900s. Not much happens, yet the film is such a perfect evocation of the milieu that one is carried swiftly into the dreams and thoughts of all the characters. One half of a duo, followed by "My Mother's Castle." In French with English subtitles. **110m/C VHS.** *FR* Julien Ciamaca, Philippe Caubere, Nathalie Roussel, Therese Liotard, Didier Pain; **D:** Yves Robert; **W:** Lucette Andrei; **C:** Robert Alazraki; **M:** Vladimir Cosma. *ORI, BTV*

My Father's House 🎬🎬 1975
Magazine editor recounts his youth while recovering from a heart attack. He measures his own quality of life against the life that his father led and begins to question his own choices with regard to his family. **96m/C VHS, Beta.** Cliff Robertson, Robert Preston, Eileen Brennan, Rosemary Forsyth. *WOV*

My Father's Nurse 🎬 1985
While father convalesces upstairs, the family frolics about the house and plots his dispatch. When his new nurse secretly cures him, he takes to a wheelchair and mounts a comedic covert counter offensive. **97m/C VHS, Beta.** *VCD, MOV*

My Favorite Blonde 🎬🎬🎬 1942
Beautiful British spy Carroll convinces Hope to aid her in carrying out a secret mission. Lots of fun as Hope and his trained penguin, along with Carroll, embark on a cross-country chase to elude the Nazis. Hope's behavior is hilarious and the pacing of the film is excellent. Based on a story by Melvin Frank and Norman Panama. **78m/B VHS, Closed Caption.** Bob Hope, Madeleine Carroll, Gale Sondergaard, George Zucco, Lionel Royce, Walter Kingsford, Victor Varconi;

Cameos: Bing Crosby; **D:** Sidney Lanfield; **W:** Frank Butler, Don Hartman; **C:** William Mellor. *USH, BTV*

My Favorite Brunette ♂♂½ 1947 Detective parody starring Hope as a photographer turned grumbling private eye. He becomes involved with a murder, a spy caper, and a dangerous brunette (Lamour). 85m/B VHS, Beta, LV. Bob Hope, Dorothy Lamour, Peter Lorre, Lon Chaney Jr., Alan Ladd, Reginald Denny, Bing Crosby; **D:** Elliott Nugent; **C:** Lionel Lindon. *CNG, MRV, NOS*

My Favorite Wife ♂♂♂ 1940 Handsome widower Grant remarries only to discover that first wife Dunne, shipwrecked seven years earlier and presumed dead, has reappeared. Eventually, a judge must decide what to do in this most unusual situation, completely lacking precedent. Farcical and hilarious story filled with a clever cast. The 1963 remake "Move Over Darling" lacks the style and wit of this presentation. Also available colorized. 88m/B VHS, Beta, LV. Irene Dunne, Cary Grant, Randolph Scott, Gail Patrick, Scotty Beckett; **D:** Garson Kanin; **W:** Samuel Spewack, Bella Spewack, Leo McCarey. Nominations: Academy Awards '40: Best Story, Best Original Score. *MLB, TTC*

My Favorite Year ♂♂♂ *My Favourite Year* 1982 (PG) A young writer on a popular live television show in the 1950s is asked to keep a watchful eye on the week's guest star—his favorite swashbuckling movie hero. Through a series of misadventures, he discovers his matinee idol is actually a drunkard and womanizer who has trouble living up to his cinematic standards. Sterling performance from O'Toole, with memorable portrayal from Bologna as the show's host, King Kaiser (a take-off of Sid Caesar from "Your Show of Shows"). 92m/C VHS, Beta, LV, Letterbox. Peter O'Toole, Mark Linn-Baker, Joseph Bologna, Jessica Harper, Lainie Kazan, Bill Macy, Anne DeSalvo, Lou Jacobi, Adolph Green, Cameron Mitchell, Gloria Stuart; **D:** Richard Benjamin; **W:** Norman Steinberg; **M:** Ralph Burns. Nominations: Academy Awards '82: Best Actor (O'Toole). *MGM*

My Fellow Americans ♂♂ 1996 (PG-13) Political "Odd Couple" pits cantankerous conservative Kramer (Lemmon) against womanizing liberal Douglas (Garner) when current President Aykroyd frames his two predecessors for a White House scandal. The age-old adversaries must set aside their differences long enough to clear their names by reaching Kramer's presidential library, where he has vindicating papers. Along the way, they encounter adventure, danger and "the people," the average Americans they used to work for. "Grumpy Old Men" veteran Lemmon is plenty cranky while Garner's charisma is a suitable foil. The ironic "charm" of course banter from the mouths of two ex-Presidents is supposed to carry much of the humor, but instead wears thin. Supporting characters (Aykroyd, Bacall) aren't as well used as the two main characters. Mainly for Lemmon, Garner, and "Grumpy" fans. **CW:** Salty language and innuendo. 96m/C VHS, LV, Closed Caption, DVD. Dan Aykroyd, James Garner, Jack Lemmon, John Heard, Sela Ward, Wilford Brimley, Everett McGill, Bradley Whitford, Lauren Bacall, James Rebhorn, Esther Rolle, Conchata Ferrell, Jack Kehler, Tom Everett, Jeff Yagher; **D:** Peter Segal; **W:** E. Jack Kaplan, Richard Chapman, Peter Tolan; **C:** Julio Macat; **M:** William Ross. *WAR*

My First Wife ♂♂½ 1984 (PG) Strong drama about a self-indulgent man's devastation when his wife abruptly leaves him after ten years of marriage. Realistic and well-acted. 95m/C VHS. *AU* John Hargreaves, Wendy Hughes, Lucy Angwin, Anna Jemison, David Cameron; **D:** Paul Cox; **W:** Paul Cox, Bob Ellis. Australian Film Institute '84: Best Actor (Hargreaves). *NO*

My Forbidden Past ♂♂½ 1951 Melodrama set in 1890 New Orleans centers on a young woman (Gardner) with an unsavory past who unexpectedly inherits a fortune and vows to break up the marriage of the man (Mitchum) she loves. His wife is murdered and he is charged with doing the deed until Gardner, exposing her past, wins his love and helps to extricate him. 81m/B

VHS, Beta. Ava Gardner, Melvyn Douglas, Robert Mitchum; **D:** Robert Stevenson.

My Friend Flicka ♂♂♂ 1943 Boy makes friends with four-legged beast. Dad thinks the horse is full of wild oats, but young Roddie trains it to be the best gosh darned horse in pre-Disney family faredom. Based on Mary O'Hara book, followed by "Thunderhead, Son of Flicka," and TV series. 89m/C VHS, Beta. Roddy McDowall, Preston Foster, Rita Johnson, James Bell, Jeff Corey; **D:** Harold Schuster. *FCT, HMV*

My Friend Irma ♂½ 1949 An adaptation of the radio series, featuring Wilson as the dumb blonde with boyfriend trouble and Lynn as her sensible pal. The film debut of Martin (singing) and Lewis (mugging) as juice-bar operators. Followed by a sequel, "My Friend Irma Goes West," and later by a television series. 103m/B VHS, Beta, Closed Caption. Marie Wilson, Diana Lynn, John Lund, Don DeFore, Dean Martin, Jerry Lewis, Hans Conried; **D:** George Marshall. *PAR*

My Friend Walter ♂♂½ 1993 Bess Throckmorten attends a family reunion in London with her Aunt Ellie and discovers one of her ancestors is Sir Walter Raleigh. Visiting the Tower of London, Bess finds Sir Walter's ghost who wants to follow her home to Devon to see how the family is doing. He finds that the Throckmorten's are about to lose the family farm but Sir Walter comes up with a plan to restore their fortunes. Shot on location in England and based on the book by Michael Morpurgo. 87m/C VHS. *GB* Polly Grant, Ronald Pickup, Prunella Scales, Louise Jameson, James Hazeldine, Lawrence Cooper, Constance Chapman; **D:** Gavin Millar. *HMV, BTV*

My Geisha ♂♂½ 1962 MacLaine and husband experience bad karma because she wants to be in his new film. In pancake makeup and funny shoes, she poses as a geisha girl and is cast as Madame Butterfly. Her husband, however, is one sharp cookie. Filmed in Japan. 120m/C VHS, Closed Caption. Shirley MacLaine, Yves Montand, Edward G. Robinson, Robert Cummings; **D:** Jack Cardiff. Nominations: Academy Awards '62: Best Costume Design (Color). *PAR, WAX, FCT*

My Giant ♂♂ 1998 (PG) Billy Crystal plays a short, annoying, Hollywood-type guy and Romanian-born NBA player Gheorghe Muresan plays a really tall Romanian guy, so you know there's not exactly an Olivier thing happening here. Crystal is the brutish showbiz agent Sammy, who accidentally stumbles onto Muresan's Max. The gentle Max is at peace in his monastery; but Sammy, being an agent, quickly finds a way to make money off of him. Max is talked into a movie career so he can be reunited with his childhood crush Lillianna (Pacula). The odd couple schtick is milked until bone dry, and then the sentimentality floodgates open when it's discovered that Max has a serious medical condition. Warning: although presented as a family film, unless you want to recreate that whole "Why did Bambi's mom have to die?" scene (with you as the parent this time), you might want to reconsider renting this movie for small children. 103m/C VHS. Billy Crystal, Gheorghe Muresan, Kathleen Quinlan, Joanna Pacula, Rider Strong, Harold Gould, Doris Roberts, Philip Sterling, Heather Thomas, Zane Carney; **Cameos:** Steven Seagal; **D:** Michael Lehmann; **W:** David Seltzer; **C:** Michael Coulter; **M:** Marc Shaiman. *NYR*

My Girl ♂♂½ 1991 (PG) Chlumsky is delightful in her film debut as an 11-year-old tomboy who must come to grips with the realities of life. Culkin plays her best friend Thomas, who understands her better than anyone else, including her father, a mortician, and his girlfriend, the makeup artist at the funeral parlor. Some reviewers questioned whether young children would be able to deal with some unhappy occurrences in the film, but most seemed to classify it as a movie the whole family would enjoy. 102m/C VHS, LV, 8mm, Closed Caption, DVD. Dan Aykroyd, Jamie Lee Curtis, Macaulay Culkin, Anna Chlumsky, Griffin Dunne, Raymond Buktenica, Richard Masur, Ann Nelson, Peter Michael

Goetz, Tom Villard; **D:** Howard Zieff; **W:** Laurice Elehwany; **C:** Paul Elliott; **M:** James Newton Howard. MTV Movie Awards '92: Best Kiss (Macaulay Culkin/Anna Chlumsky). *COL*

My Girl 2 ♂♂½ 1994 (PG) It's 1974 and Chlumsky is back as Vada (this time without Culkin, given the killer bee attack in MG1) in this innocent coming-of-ager. Portly Aykroyd and flaky Curtis return as parental window dressing who encourage Vada's search for information on her long-dead mother. She tracks down old friends of her mom's (Masur and Rose) who are having difficulties with their obnoxious adolescent son (O'Brien). Predictable, but enjoyable. Certain to fail the credibility test of nit-pickers who may wonder why the only thing Aykroyd can remember of his first wife is that she left behind a paper bag with a date scribbled on it. 99m/C VHS, LV, 8mm, Closed Caption. Anna Chlumsky, Dan Aykroyd, Jamie Lee Curtis, Austin O'Brien, Richard Masur, Christine Ebersole, Ben Stein; **D:** Howard Zieff; **W:** Janet Kovalcik; **C:** Paul Elliott; **M:** Cliff Eidelman. *COL*

My Girl Tisa ♂♂½ 1948 Chronicles the experiences of a young immigrant woman who struggles to survive in the U.S. at the turn of the century and hopes to bring her father over from their home country. Based on a play by Lucille S. Prumbs and Sara B. Smith. 95m/B VHS. Lilli Palmer, Sam Wanamaker, Akim Tamiroff, Alan Hale, Hugo Haas, Gale Robbins, Stella Adler; **D:** Elliott Nugent; **M:** Max Steiner. *REP*

My Grandpa Is a Vampire ♂½ 1992 (PG) When 12 year-old Lonny and his pal visit Grandpa Cooger in New Zealand Lonny discovers a long-hidden family secret—Grandpa's a vampire! This doesn't stop either boy from joining with Grandpa in lots of scary adventures. 90m/C VHS, Closed Caption. Al Lewis, Justin Gocke, Milan Borich, Noel Appleby; **D:** David Blyth. *REP*

My Heroes Have Always Been Cowboys ♂♂½ 1991 (PG) An aging rodeo rider returns to his hometown to recuperate and finds himself forced to confront his past. His ex-girlfriend, his dad and his sister all expect something from him. He learns how to give it, and gains the strength of purpose to get back on the bull that stomped him. Excellent rodeo footage, solid performances, but the story has been around the barn too many times to hold much interest. 106m/C VHS, Beta, LV, Closed Caption. Scott Glenn, Kate Capshaw, Ben Johnson, Balthazar Getty, Mickey Rooney, Gary Busey, Tess Harper, Clarence Williams III, Dub Taylor, Clu Gulager, Dennis Fimple; **D:** Stuart Rosenberg; **W:** Joel Don Humphreys; **M:** James Horner. *VTR, COL*

My Lady of Whims ♂ 1925 Clara Bow's dad disapproves of debutante daughter's desire to hang out with the girls who just want to have fun. 42m/B VHS, Beta. Clara Bow, Betty Baker, Carmelita Geraghty, Donald Keith, Lee Moran. *GPV, FCT*

My Left Foot ♂♂♂♂ 1989 (R) A gritty, unsentimental drama based on the life and autobiography of cerebral-palsy victim Christy Brown. Considered an imbecile by everyone but his mother (Fricker, in a stunning award-winning performance) until he teaches himself to write. He survives his impoverished Irish roots to become a painter and writer using his left foot, the only appendage over which he has control. He also falls in love and finds some heartaches along the way. Day-Lewis is astounding; the supporting cast, especially Shaw and Cusack, match him measure for measure. 103m/C VHS, Beta, LV, Closed Caption. *IR* Daniel Day-Lewis, Brenda Fricker, Ray McAnally, Cyril Cusack, Fiona Shaw, Hugh O'Conor, Adrian Dunbar, Ruth McCabe, Alison Whelan; **D:** Jim Sheridan; **W:** Shane Connaughton, Jim Sheridan; **M:** Elmer Bernstein. Academy Awards '89: Best Actor (Day-Lewis), Best Supporting Actress (Fricker); British Academy Awards '89: Best Actor (Day-Lewis), Best Supporting Actor (McAnally); Independent Spirit Awards '90: Best Foreign Film; Los Angeles Film Critics Association Awards '89: Best Actor (Day-Lewis), Best Supporting Actress (Fricker); Montreal World Film Festival '89: Best Actor (Day-Lewis); New York Film Critics

Awards '89: Best Actor (Day-Lewis), Best Film; National Society of Film Critics Awards '89: Best Actor (Day-Lewis); Nominations: Academy Awards '89: Best Adapted Screenplay, Best Director (Sheridan), Best Picture. *HBO, BTV, HMV*

My Life 🐾🐾½ 1993 (PG-13) Maudlin, sometimes depressing production preaches the power of a well-examined life. Public relations exec Keaton is diagnosed with cancer and the doctors predict he will most likely die before the birth of his first child. Film follows his transition from uncommunicative and angry to acceptance, a role to which Keaton brings a sentimental strength. Kidman is window dressing as the ever-patient, nobly suffering wife, a cardboard character notable mainly for her beauty. *CW:* Mature subject matter. 114m/C VHS, LV, 8mm, **Closed Caption.** Michael Keaton, Nicole Kidman, Haing S. Ngor, Bradley Whitford, Queen Latifah, Michael Constantine, Toni Sawyer, Rebecca Schull, Lee Garlington; *D:* Bruce Joel Rubin; *W:* Bruce Joel Rubin; *M:* John Barry. *COL*

My Life and Times with Antonin Artaud 🐾🐾🐾 *En Compagnie d'Antonin Artaud* 1993 Postwar Parisian bohemia is depicted in the obsessive friendship between ambitious young poet Jacques Prevel (Barbe) and famed intellectual/poet/impressario Antonin Artaud (Frey), who founded the Theatre of Cruelty. Artaud has returned to Paris after spending nine years in an asylum and is suffering from terminal cancer, the misery of which is partially alleviated by the opiates that Prevel can provide. Delusional and paranoid, Artaud makes his self-destruction into genius while Prevel documents Artaud's last two years in diaries, hoping to gain some measure of fame for himself. French with subtitles. Based on Prevel's "En Compagnie d'Antonin Artaud." 93m/B VHS. *FR* Sami Frey, Marc Barbe, Valerie Jeannet, Julie Jezequel; *D:* Gerard Mordillat; *W:* Gerard Mordillat, Jerome Prieur; *C:* Francois Catonne; *M:* Jean-Claude Petit. *FXL*

My Life As a Dog 🐾🐾🐾🐾 *Mitt Liv Som Hund* 1985 A troublesome boy is separated from his brother and is sent to live with relatives in the country when his mother is taken ill. Unhappy and confused, he struggles to understand sexuality and love and tries to find security and acceptance. Remarkable Swedish film available with English subtitles or dubbed. 101m/C VHS, Beta, LV. *SW* Anton Glanzelius, Tomas Van Bromssen, Anki Liden, Melinda Kinnaman, Kicki Rundgren, Ing-mari Carlsson; *D:* Lasse Hallstrom. Golden Globe Awards '88: Best Foreign Film; Independent Spirit Awards '88: Best Foreign Film; New York Film Critics Awards '87: Best Foreign Film; Nominations: Academy Awards '87: Best Adapted Screenplay, Best Director (Hallstrom). *PAR, HMV*

My Life to Live 🐾🐾🐾🐾 *Vivre Sa Vie; It's My Life* 1962 A woman turns to prostitution in this probing examination of sexual, and social, relations. Idiosyncratic Godard has never been more starstruck than in this vehicle for the endearing Karina, his wife at the time. A classic. In French with English subtitles. 85m/B VHS, Beta. *FR* Anna Karina, Sady Rebbot, Andre S. Labarthe, Guylaine Schlumberger; *D:* Jean-Luc Godard; *W:* Jean-Luc Godard; *M:* Michel Legrand. Venice Film Festival '62: Special Jury Prize. *FXL, NYF, DVT*

My Life's in Turnaround 🐾🐾 1994 (R) Amusing low-budget comedy takes a behind-the-scenes, semi-autobiographical look at the lives of two would-be filmmakers. They try for cool but manage only goofy. *CW:* Strong language and some explicit sex-related dialogue. 84m/C VHS. Eric Schaeffer, Donal Lardner Ward, Lisa Gerstein, Dana Wheeler-Nicholson, Debra Clein, Sheila Jaffe; *Cameos:* Casey Siemaszko, John Sayles, Martha Plimpton, Phoebe Cates; *D:* Eric Schaeffer, Donal Lardner Ward; *W:* Eric Schaeffer, Donal Lardner Ward; *M:* Reed Hays. *AVI*

My Little Chickadee 🐾🐾🐾 1940 Classic comedy about a gambler and a fallen woman who marry for convenience so they can respectably enter an unsuspecting town. Sparks fly in their adventures together. Fields and West are both at their best playing their larger-than-life

selves. 91m/B VHS, Beta, LV. W.C. Fields, Mae West, Joseph Calleia, Dick Foran, Margaret Hamilton, Donald Meek; *D:* Eddie Cline; *C:* Joseph Valentine. *USH, MLB, BTV*

My Little Girl 🐾🐾 1987 (R) A rich Philadelphia girl idealistically volunteers her time to help local institutionalized orphans, but meets with opposition. 118m/C VHS, Beta, LV. Mary Stuart Masterson, James Earl Jones, Geraldine Page, Anne Meara, Peter Gallagher, George Newbern; *D:* Connie Kaiserman.

My Little Pony: The Movie 🐾🐾½ 1986 Animated tale about the siege of Ponyland by malevolent witches. 87m/C VHS, Beta, **Closed Caption.** *D:* Michael Joens; *V:* Danny DeVito, Cloris Leachman, Tony Randall, Madeline Kahn.

My Love For Yours 🐾🐾½ *Honeymoon in Bali* 1939 The romantic tale of a young man hoping to win the love of a beautiful but icy girl. A tad silly in parts, but the clever dialogue moves the story along. 99m/B VHS, Beta. Fred MacMurray, Madeleine Carroll; *D:* Edward H. Griffith. *NOS, CAB*

My Lucky Star 🐾🐾½ 1938 Skating star Henie plays a department store clerk that gets sent off to college to model clothes from the store's sports line. She somehow manages to convince school officials to stage their winter ice show in the department store, where she gets to show off her stuff. Don't miss the grand finale, a performance of "Alice in Wonderland Ice Ballet." Based on the story "They Met in Chicago" by Karl Tunberg and Don Ettlinger. ♫I've Got a Date With a Dream; Could You Pass in Love; This May Be the Night; The All-American Swing; Plymouth University Song. 81m/B VHS. Sonja Henie, Richard Greene, Joan Davis, Cesar Romero, Buddy Ebsen, Arthur Treacher, George Barbier, Gypsy Rose Lee; *D:* Roy Del Ruth; *W:* Harry Tugend, Jack Yellen. *FXV*

My Magic Dog 🐾🐾½ 1997 Lucky is eight-year-old Toby's dog. Lucky happens to be invisible. Which turns out to be a good thing when evil Aunt Violet tries to steal Toby's inheritance. 98m/C VHS. Leo Millbrook, Russ Tamblyn, John Phillip Law; *D:* John Putch. *APX*

My Man Adam 🐾🐾 1986 (R) A dreamy, Mitty-esque high schooler falls in love with a girl (Daryl's auburn-haired sister, Page Hannah), and becomes ensnared in a real life crime, leaving his friend to bail him out. Typical boy-meets-girl, boy-gets-in-trouble yarn. 84m/C VHS, Beta, **Closed Caption.** Raphael Sbarge, Veronica Cartwright, Page Hannah, Larry B. Scott, Charlie Barnett, Arthur Pendleton, Dave Thomas; *D:* Roger L. Simon. *FOX*

My Man Godfrey 🐾🐾🐾🐾 1936 A spoiled rich girl picks up someone she assumes is a bum as part of a scavenger hunt and decides to keep him on as her butler. In the process, he teaches her about life, money, and happiness. Top-notch screwball comedy defines the genre. Lombard is a stunner alongside the equally charming Powell. Watch for Jane Wyman as an extra in the party scene. Remade in 1957 with June Allyson and David Niven. From the novel by Eric Hatch, who also co-scripted. 95m/B VHS, Beta. William Powell, Carole Lombard, Gail Patrick, Alice Brady, Mischa Auer, Eugene Pallette, Alan Mowbray, Franklin Pangborn, Jane Wyman; *D:* Gregory La Cava; *W:* Morrie Ryskind, Gregory La Cava. Nominations: Academy Awards '36: Best Actor (Powell), Best Actress (Lombard), Best Director (La Cava), Best Screenplay, Best Supporting Actor (Auer), Best Supporting Actress (Brady). *CNG, MRV, NOS*

My Man Godfrey 🐾🐾½ 1957 Inferior remake of the sophisticated screwball comedy of the '30s about a butler who brings a touch of the common man to the filthy rich. Niven stars as the butler and Allyson plays the rich girl, but nothing compares to the original roles created by Powell and Lombard. 92m/C VHS. June Allyson, David Niven, Martha Hyer, Jessie Royce Landis, Robert Keith, Eva Gabor, Jay Robinson, Jeff Donnell; *D:* Henry Koster; *W:* Everett Freeman, Peter Berneis, William Bowers; *C:* William H. Daniels. *USH*

My Michael 🐾🐾🐾 1975 Sensitive adaptation of Amos Oz's novel set in Jerasalem in the late 1950s. A young woman is stifled by marriage and the conventions of her bourgeois life and her fantasies begin to take over. In Hebrew with English subtitles. 90m/C VHS, Beta. *IS* Efrat Lavie, Oded Kotler; *D:* Dan Wolman. *ERG, FCT, TPV*

My Mom's a Werewolf 🐾🐾½ 1989 (PG) An average suburban mother gets involved with a dashing stranger and soon, to her terror, begins to turn into a werewolf. Her daughter and companion must come up with a plan to regain dear, sweet mom. 90m/C VHS, Beta, LV. Susan Blakely, John Saxon, John Schuck, Katrina Caspary, Ruth Buzzi, Marilyn McCoo, Marcia Wallace, Diana Barrows; *D:* Michael Fischa; *W:* Mark Pirro.

My Mother's Castle 🐾🐾🐾½ *Le Chateau de Ma Mere* 1991 (PG) The second half of the two part film series based on the autobiography of Marcel Pagnol. Picking up where "My Father's Glory" left off, the family begins a series of vacations in a beautiful country home. Dynamically acted and tenderly directed, charming and suitable for the entire family. In French with English subtitles. 98m/C VHS. *FR* Philippe Caubere, Nathalie Roussel, Didier Pain, Therese Liotard, Julien Ciamaca, Victorien Delmare; *D:* Yves Robert; *M:* Vladimir Cosma. *ORI, BTV*

My Mother's Secret Life 🐾½ 1984 Dull drama focusing on a long-forgotten daughter who suddenly appears on her mother's doorstep and discovers that mom makes a living as a high-priced hooker. 100m/C VHS, Beta. Loni Anderson, Paul Sorvino, Amanda Wyss, James Sutorius, Sandy McPeak; *D:* Robert Markowitz; *M:* Brad Fiedel.

My Name Is Ivan 🐾🐾🐾½ *Ivan's Childhood; The Youngest Spy* 1962 Tarkovsky's first feature film is a vivid, wrenching portrait of a young Soviet boy surviving as a spy behind enemy lines during WWII. Technically stunning, heralding the coming of modern cinema's greatest formalist. In Russian with English subtitles. 84m/B VHS, Beta, LV. *RU* Kolya Burlyayev, Valentin Zubkov, Ye Zharikov, S. Krylov; *D:* Andrei Tarkovsky. Venice Film Festival '62: Best Film. *FXL, FCT*

My Name is Joe 🐾🐾 1998 Set in Glasgow, the Scots accents prove a distinct challenge in this story of working-class romance. Unemployed alcoholic Joe Kavanagh (Mullan) is 10 months sober and does odd jobs to get by, while coaching the local no-hoper football team. By chance he meets community health worker Sarah (Goodall) and the two are drawn together by their similar outlooks on life and begin a cautious romance. But Joe's loyalty to his mates and his efforts to get his friend Liam (McKay) out of trouble, helps to put a strain on the relationship. 105m/C VHS. *GB* Peter Mullan, Louise Goodall, David McKay, Annemarie Kennedy, David Hayman, Gary Lewis, Lorraine McIntosh; *D:* Ken Loach; *W:* Paul Laverty; *C:* Barry Ackroyd; *M:* George Fenton. Cannes Film Festival '98: Best Actor (Mullan). *NYR*

My Name Is Nobody 🐾🐾½ *Il Mio Nome e Nessuno* 1974 (PG) Fast-paced spaghetti-western wherein a cocky, soft-hearted gunfighter is sent to kill the famous, retired outlaw he reveres, but instead they band together. 115m/C VHS, Beta. Henry Fonda, Terence Hill, R.G. Armstrong; *D:* Tonino Valerii; *M:* Ennio Morricone. *BAR, HHE*

My Neighbor Totoro 🐾🐾½ 1993 (G) Rather gooey Japanese animated movie about Satsuki and her younger sister Lucy, whose new house in the country is filled with magic, including a friendly creature named Totoro. Totoro is a cuddly, if weird, mix of bear, owl, and seal, with whiskers and a gentle roar. He can fly, has a magic bus, and can only be seen by children. Naturally, every time the two girls get into mischief Totoro is there to rescue them. Dubbed into English. 76m/C VHS, LV. *JP D:* Hayao Miyazaki; *W:* Hayao Miyazaki. *FXV*

My New Gun 🎬🎬½ 1992 (R) Uneven, restless dark comedy about Debbie and Gerald Bender, yuppified suburban couple whose lives are disrupted by a gun. When their newly engaged friends get a gun, Gerry decides they need a gun as well. Debbie is very uncomfortable about having a weapon in the house and doesn't want anything to do with it. When mysterious neighbor LeGros steals the gun, it sets off a bizarre chain of events that culminate at the wedding of their friends. Impressive first effort for writer/director Cochran. **99m/C VHS, LV, Letterbox, Closed Caption.** Diane Lane, Stephen Collins, James LeGros, Tess Harper, Bill Raymond, Bruce Altman, Maddie Corman; **D:** Stacy Cochran; **W:** Stacy Cochran; **M:** Pat Irwin. Cannes Film Festival '92: Best Film. *COL*

My New Partner 🎬🎬½ *Les Ripoux* 1984 (R) Amiable French comedy in which cynical veteran cop is saddled with straight arrow rookie partner. French Cesars for best film and best director, but remember: They like Jerry Lewis too. In French with English subtitles. **106m/C VHS, Beta, LV.** *FR* Philippe Noiret, Thierry Lhermitte, Regine, Grace de Capitani, Claude Brosset, Julien Guiomar; **D:** Claude Zidi; **W:** Claude Zidi. *IME*

My Night at Maud's 🎬🎬🎬 *My Night with Maud; Ma Nuit Chez Maud* 1969 Typically subtle Rohmer entry concerns quandary of upright fellow who finds himself drawn to comparatively carefree woman. Talky, somewhat arid film is one of director's Six Moral Tales. You'll either find it fascinating or wish you were watching "Rocky XXIV" instead. In French with English subtitles. **111m/B VHS, Beta, LV.** *FR* Jean-Louis Trintignant, Francoise Fabian, Marie-Christine Barrault, Antoine Vitez; **D:** Eric Rohmer; **W:** Eric Rohmer; **C:** Nestor Almendros. New York Film Critics Awards '70: Best Screenplay; National Society of Film Critics Awards '70: Best Cinematography, Best Screenplay; Nominations: Academy Awards '70: Best Foreign Language Film, Best Story & Screenplay. *COL*

My Old Man 🎬🎬½ 1979 Plucky teen and her seedy horsetrainer father come together over important horse race. Oates makes this one worth watching on a slow evening. A Hemingway story made for television. **102m/C VHS, Beta.** Kristy McNichol, Warren Oates, Eileen Brennan; **D:** John Erman. *CAF*

My Old Man's Place 🎬½ 1971 (R) A veteran, with two war buddies and a girl, returns to his father's run-down farm, hoping to fix it up. Sexual tensions arise and violence erupts. **93m/C VHS, Beta.** Arthur Kennedy, Michael Moriarty, Mitchell Ryan, William Devane, Topo Swope; **D:** Edwin Sherin.

My Other Husband 🎬🎬½ *Attention! Une Femme Peut en Cacher une Autre* 1985 (PG-13) A woman has two husbands and families, one in Paris and one in Trouville, who eventually meet each other. Seems silly but grows into a sensitive and sad portrait of married life. In French with English subtitles. **110m/C VHS, Beta.** *FR* Miou-Miou, Rachid Ferrache, Roger Hanin; **D:** Georges Lautner. *COL*

My Outlaw Brother 🎬🎬 *My Brother, the Outlaw* 1951 A man travelling West to visit his brother in Mexico meets a Texas Ranger on the train. The man discovers that his brother is an outlaw, and teams up with the Ranger to capture him. **82m/B VHS.** Mickey Rooney, Wanda Hendrix, Robert Preston, Robert Stack, Jose Torvay; **D:** Elliott Nugent. *MOV, MRV, VYY*

My Own Private Idaho 🎬🎬🎬 1991 (R) Director Van Sant of "Drugstore Cowboy" returns to the underworld to examine another group of outsiders, this time young, homosexual hustlers. On the streets of Seattle, narcoleptic hustler Mike meets slumming rich boy Scott, and together they begin a search for Mike's lost mother, which leads them to Idaho and Italy. Stunning visuals, an elliptical plot, and a terrific performance by Phoenix highlight this search for love, the meaning of life, and power. Van Sant couples these with scenes from Shakespeare's "Henry IV" for a sometimes inscrutable, but always memorable film. Look for director Richert's Falstaff role as an aging chickenhawk. **CW:** Language, drug use, and sensuality. **105m/C VHS, LV, Letterbox, Closed Caption.** River Phoenix, Keanu Reeves, James Russo, William Richert, Rodney Harvey, Michael Parker, Flea, Chiara Caselli, Udo Kier, Grace Zabriskie, Tom Troupe; **D:** Gus Van Sant; **W:** Gus Van Sant; **C:** John Campbell, Eric Alan Edwards. Independent Spirit Awards '92: Best Actor (Phoenix), Best Screenplay; National Society of Film Critics Awards '91: Best Actor (Phoenix).*COL, NLC*

My Pal, the King 🎬🎬½ 1932 Amusing western with Rooney as the boy king of Ruritania, who's bored with his official duties. He meets Mix, the proprietor of a traveling wild west show which just happens to be performing in the country. Good thing too because Rooney has an evil prime minister who wants the throne for himself and kidnaps the kid. Naturally, Mix and his friends arrive to save him in the nick of time. **62m/B VHS.** Tom Mix, Mickey Rooney, Stuart Holmes, Paul Hurst, Noel Francis, James Kirkwood, Jim Thorpe; **D:** Kurt Neumann. *GPV*

My Pal Trigger 🎬🎬 1946 Roy is unjustly imprisoned in this high adventure on the plains. Better than usual script and direction makes this is one of the more entertaining of the singing cowboy's films. **79m/B VHS, Beta.** Roy Rogers, George "Gabby" Hayes, Dale Evans, Jack Holt; **D:** Frank McDonald. *NOS, MRV, HHT*

My Pleasure Is My Business 1974 (R) Cinematic autobiography of Xaveria Hollander, the world's most renowned prostitute of the '70s, and the zany occurrences which abound in her profession. **85m/C VHS.** *CA* Xaviera Hollander, Henry Ramer, Colin Fox, Ken Lynch, Jayne Eastwood; **D:** Al Waxman. *NO*

My Samurai 🎬½ 1992 (R) When young Peter McCrea witnesses a gang murder he turns to his martial-arts expert friend Young Park to help him. On the run from both the gang and the police Peter learns self-defense and the courage to face his fears. **CW:** Violence. **87m/C VHS, LV, Closed Caption.** Julian Lee, Terry O'Quinn, Bubba Smith, Jim Turner, Carlos Palomino, John Kallo; **D:** Fred Dresch. *IMP*

My Science Project 🎬½ 1985 (PG) Teenager Stockwell stumbles across a crystal sphere with a funky light. Unaware that it is an alien time-travel device, he takes it to school to use as a science project in a last-ditch effort to avoid failing his class. Chaos follows and Stockwell and his chums find themselves battling gladiators, mutants, and dinosaurs. Plenty of special effects and a likeable enough, dumb teenage flick. **94m/C VHS, Beta, LV.** John Stockwell, Danielle von Zerneck, Fisher Stevens, Raphael Sbarge, Richard Masur, Barry Corbin, Ann Wedgeworth, Dennis Hopper, Candace Silvers, Beau Dremann, Pat Simmons, Pamela Springsteen; **D:** Jonathan Betuel; **W:** Jonathan Betuel; **M:** Peter Bernstein. *TOU*

My Sex Life...Or How I Got Into an Argument 🎬🎬 *Ma Vie Sexuelle...Comment Je Me Suis Dispute* 1996 Paul (Amalric) is unhappy personally and professionally. He's a bored grad student/assistant professor of philosophy and breaking up with lover of ten years, Esther (Devos). Soon Paul's romancing other women, one of whom, Sylvia (Denicourt), is already involved with Paul's best friend Nathan (Salinger). Very talky and Frenchly intellectual. French with subtitles. **178m/C VHS, Letterbox.** *FR* Mathieu Amalric, Marianne Denicourt, Emmanuelle Devos, Emmanuel Salinger, Jeanne Balibar, Michel Vuillermoz; **D:** Arnaud Desplechin; **W:** Arnaud Desplechin, Emmanuel Bourdieu; **C:** Eric Gautier; **M:** Krishna Levy. *FXL*

My Side of the Mountain 🎬🎬½ 1969 (G) A 13-year-old boy decides to emulate his idol, Henry David Thoreau, and gives up his home and his family to live in the Canadian mountains. **100m/C VHS, Beta.** *CA* Teddy Eccles, Theodore Bikel; **D:** James B. Clark. *PAR*

My Sister Eileen 🎬🎬🎬 1955 Ruth and Eileen are two small-town Ohio sisters who move to Manhattan seeking excitement. They live in a basement apartment in Greenwich Village with an assortment of oddball tenants as they pursue success and romance. Everyone is daffy and charming, as is the film. Fun, but unmemorable songs, however the terrific choreography is by Fosse, who also appears as one sister's suitor. Remake of a 1942 film which was based on a Broadway play, which was based on a series of autobiographical stories published in the New Yorker. The play was later turned into a Broadway musical known as "Wonderful Town," which has nothing to do with this version of the original stories. ♫Give Me a Band and My Baby; It's Bigger Than You and Me; There's Nothing Like Love; As Soon As They See Eileen; I'm Great; Conga; Atmosphere. **108m/C VHS.** Janet Leigh, Betty Garrett, Jack Lemmon, Bob Fosse, Kurt Kasznar, Dick York, Lucy Marlow, Tommy Rall, Barbara Brown, Horace McMahon; **D:** Richard Quine; **W:** Blake Edwards, Richard Quine; **M:** Jule Styne. *COL, MOV, MVD*

My Sister, My Love 🎬½ *The Cage; The Mafu Cage* 1978 (R) Odd tale of two sisters' incestuous relationship and what happens when one of them takes another lover. The cage of the alternate titles refers to the place where their pet apes are kept and seems to symbolize the confining nature of their life together. **102m/C VHS.** Lee Grant, Carol Kane, Will Geer, James Olson; **D:** Karen Arthur. *NO*

My Son, the Vampire 🎬½ *Old Mother Riley Meets the Vampire; The Vampire and the Robot; Vampire Over London; Mother Riley Meets the Vampire* 1952 Last of Britain's Old Mother Riley series in which Lucan plays the Irish housekeeper in drag. Lugosi is a crazed scientist who thinks he's a vampire and wants to take over the world with his giant robot. Mother Riley interferes. Theme song by Alan Sherman. **72m/B VHS.** *GB* Bela Lugosi, Arthur Lucan, Dora Bryan, Richard Wattis; **D:** John Gilling. *NOS, SNC*

My Song Goes Round the World 🎬 1934 Chronicles the romantic foibles of a singing trio and the one girl they decide they all love. **68m/B VHS.** Joseph Schmidt, John Loder, Charlotte Ander; **D:** Richard Oswald. *NOS, DVT*

My Stepmother Is an Alien 🎬🎬 1988 (PG-13) When eccentric physicist Aykroyd sends a message beam to another galaxy on a stormy night, the last thing he expects is a visit from beautiful alien Basinger. Unfortunately, he does not realize that this gorgeous blonde is an alien and he continues to court her despite her rather odd habits. Only the daughter seems to notice the strange goings on, and her dad ignores her warnings, enabling Basinger's evil sidekick to continue in its plot to take over the Earth. **108m/C VHS, Beta, LV, Closed Caption, DVD.** Dan Aykroyd, Kim Basinger, Jon Lovitz, Alyson Hannigan, Joseph Maher, Seth Green, Wesley Mann, Adrian Sparks, Juliette Lewis, Tanya Fenmore; **D:** Richard Benjamin; **W:** Jerico Weingrod, Herschel Weingrod, Timothy Harris, Jonathan Reynolds; **M:** Alan Silvestri. *COL*

My Summer Story 🎬🎬½ *It Runs in the Family* 1994 (PG) Humorist Shepherd and director Clark re-team for another period family comedy in the tradition of their first collaboration, "A Christmas Story," now a video classic. This time the Parkers find themselves battling their crazy new neighbors, the Bumpus family, Ralphie (Kieran Culkin) has troubles with a neighborhood bully and tries to bond with his dad (Grodin) while fishing, and mom (Steenburgen) goes loopy over gravy boats. Charming family fun. Based on Shepherd's novels "In God We Trust, All Others Pay Cash" and "Wanda Hickey's Night of Golden Memories and Other Disasters." **85m/C VHS, LV, Closed Caption.** Charles Grodin; Mary Steenburgen, Kieran Culkin, Chris Culkin, Al Mancini, Troy Evans, Glenn Shadix, Dick O'Neill, Wayne Grace; **D:** Bob (Benjamin) Clark; **W:** Jean Shepherd, Bob (Benjamin) Clark, Leigh Brown; **C:** Stephen M. Katz; **M:** Paul Zaza. *MGM*

My Sweet Charlie 🎬🎬½ 1970 Unwed, pregnant white woman hides out with black lawyer in backwater Texas. Better than it sounds, with nice performances by Duke and Freeman. Made for television. **97m/C VHS, Beta.** Patty Duke, Al Freeman Jr., Ford Rainey, William Hardy, Chris Wilson, Archie Moore, Noble Willingham; **D:** Lamont Johnson. *USH*

My Sweet Little Village 🎬🎬½ *Vesnicko Ma Strediskova* 1986 Gentle comedy set in a rural village and dealing with everyday events, including a romantic teenager who develops a crush on a schoolteacher, an adulterous wife and her boyfriend, the accident-prone doctor, a Laurel and Hardy duo of truck drivers, and others. Czech with subtitles. **100m/C VHS.** *CZ* Rudolf Hrusinsky, Janos Ban, Marian Labuda, Milena Dvorska, Ladislav Zupanic, Petr Cepek; **D:** Jiri Menzel; **W:** Zdenek Sverak; **C:** Jaromir Sofr; **M:** Jiri Sust. Nominations: Academy Awards '86: Best Foreign Language Film. *HTV*

My Sweet Victim 🎬🎬 1985 A young couple who recently moved to the United States from Poland try to make a go of their own business. The business fails, and so does their marriage. Will it end in murder? **92m/C VHS.** Candice Bergen, Juergen Prochnow. *QVD*

My Therapist woof! 1984 A sex therapist's boyfriend cannot bear the thought of her having intercourse with other men as part of her work. Soft core. **81m/C VHS, Beta.** Marilyn Chambers; **D:** Gary Legon. *NO*

My Tutor 🎬½ 1982 (R) When a high school student is in danger of flunking French, his parents hire a private tutor to help him learn the lessons. It becomes clear that his studies will involve many more subjects, however. Standard teen sex comedy. **97m/C VHS, Beta, LV.** Caren Kaye, Matt Lattanzi, Kevin McCarthy, Clark Brandon, Bruce Bauer, Arlene Golonka, Crispin Glover, Shelley Taylor Morgan, Francesca "Kitten" Natividad, Jewel Shepard, Marilyn Tokuda; **D:** George Bowers; **C:** Mac Ahlberg. *USH*

My Twentieth Century 🎬🎬🎬 *Az en XX. Szazadom* 1990 This quirky gem of a movie is a charming, sentimental journey through the early 1900s. Twins Dora and Lili are separated in early childhood. They reunite as grown, very different women on the Orient Express after they both (unknowingly) have sex with the same man. Dora is a sex kitten, while Lili is a radical equipped with explosives. When the two sisters come together, they both lose their destructive, dependent selves (Dora on men, Lili on politics) and become independent women. Lots of sidelights and subplots that are sure to amuse the viewer. In Hungarian with English subtitles. **104m/B VHS.** *HU* Dortha Segda, Oleg Jankowsky, Peter Andorai, Gabor Mate, Paulus Manker, Laszlo Vidovszky; **D:** Ildiko Enyedi; **W:** Ildiko Enyedi. *FXL*

My Uncle: The Alien 🎬🎬½ 1996 (PG) Kelly, President Sullivan's teenaged daughter, travels to L.A. to visit a children's shelter at Christmas. When she finds out the shelter needs money to stay open, she eludes the Secret Service and hatches a plan to raise the funds. But she does have someone watching out for her—no, not a guardian angel, a guardian alien! **90m/C VHS, Closed Caption.** Hailey Foster; **D:** Henri Charr. *PMH*

My Universities 🎬🎬🎬 1940 In the final part of Donskoi's trilogy on Maxim Gorky, Gorky is a young man at university who is introduced to radical politics by several liberal intellectuals. He makes his first attempts at writing and joins the revolution as he leaves his painful past behind. In Russian with English subtitles. Preceded by "My Childhood" and "My Apprenticeship." **100m/C VHS.** *RU* **D:** Mark Donskoi. *FCT*

My Very Best Friend 🎬🎬 1996 (PG) Former model Dana Griffin (Smith) likes the good life and seems to have latch onto the prize when a multi-millionaire (Mason) proposes marriage. But Dana has a nasty habit of lying and when things fall, she turns to her oldest friend, Barbara (Eikenberry), to help rebuild her life. But instead of re-

building her own life, Dana decides she'd just rather take over Barbara's. TV movie. **92m/C VHS, Closed Caption.** Jaclyn Smith, Jill Eikenberry, Tom Mason, Tom Irwin, Mary Kay Place, Garwin Sanford; **D:** Joyce Chopra. *PAR*

My Wicked, Wicked Ways 🎬🎬½ 1984 Cleverly cast, low-budget television drama based on the autobiography of Errol Flynn. **95m/C VHS, Beta.** Duncan Regehr, Barbara Hershey, Hal Linden, Darren McGavin; **D:** Don Taylor. *FOX*

My Wonderful Life 🎬 1990 (R) Softcore gristle about a beautiful tramp climbing the social ladder via the boudoir. **107m/C VHS, Beta, LV.** *IT* Pierre Cosso, Jean Rochefort, Massimo Venturiello, Carol Alt, Elliott Gould; **D:** Carlo Vanzina. *COL*

Myra Breckinridge woof! 1970 (R) A tasteless version of the Gore Vidal novel. An alleged satire of a film critic who undergoes a sex change operation and then plots the destruction of the American male movie star stereotype. Created an outcry from all sides, and hung out to dry by studio where it's reportedly still blowing in the wind. **94m/C VHS, Beta.** Mae West, John Huston, Raquel Welch, Rex Reed, Farrah Fawcett, Jim Backus, John Carradine, Andy Devine, Tom Selleck; **D:** Michael Sarne. *FOX*

The Mysterians 🎬🎬½ *Earth Defense Forces; Chikyu Boelgun* 1958 A race of gigantic scientific intellects from a doomed planet attempts to conquer Earth. They want to rebuild their race by reproducing with earth women. Earth fights back. From the director of "Godzilla." Dubbed in English from Japanese. **85m/C VHS, Beta.** *JP* Kenji Sahara, Yumi Shirakawa, Takashi Shimura; **D:** Inoshiro Honda. *MLB*

Mysteries 🎬½ 1984 A rich tourist becomes obsessed by a beautiful local girl. As his obsession grows, his behavior becomes stranger. Interesting and well-acted. The film is an adaptation of the famous love story by Nobel-laureate Knut Hamsun. Suffers from poor dubbing. **100m/C VHS, Beta.** Rutger Hauer, Sylvia Kristel, David Rappaport, Rita Tushingham; **D:** Paul de Lussanet. *NO*

Mysterious Desperado 🎬½ 1949 Young man, about to inherit a large estate, is framed on a murder charge by land grabbers. **61m/B VHS, Beta.** Tim Holt, Richard Martin. *NO*

Mysterious Desperado/Rider From Tucson 🎬🎬½ 1949 A western double feature. In "Mysterious Desperado," a young man is framed for a crime he did not commit. In "Rider From Tucson," evil claim jumpers will resort to murder to gain control of a gold mine. **121m/B VHS, Beta.** Tim Holt, Richard Martin. *TTC*

Mysterious Doctor Satan 🎬🎬 1940 A mad satanic scientist builds an army of mechanical robots to rob and terrorize the nation. In 15 episodes. **250m/B VHS.** Eduardo Ciannelli, Robert Wilcox, Ella Neal; **D:** William Witney. *REP, VCN, MLB*

Mysterious Island 🎬🎬🎬 1961 Exhilirating sci-fi classic adapted from Jules Verne's novel about escaping Civil War soldiers who go up in Verne balloon and come down on a Pacific island populated by giant animals. They also encounter two shipwrecked English ladies, pirates, and Captain Nemo (and his sub). Top-rate special effects by master Ray Harryhausen. **101m/C VHS, Beta, LV, Closed Caption.** *GB* Michael Craig, Joan Greenwood, Michael Callan, Gary Merrill, Herbert Lom, Beth Rogan, Percy Herbert, Dan Jackson, Nigel Green; **D:** Cy Endfield; **M:** Bernard Herrmann. *COL, MLB*

Mysterious Island of Beautiful Women 🎬 1979 A male sextet is stranded on a South Sea island, where they must endure the trials of an angry tribe of conveniently bikini-clad women. **100m/C VHS, Beta.** Jamie Lyn Bauer, Jayne Kennedy, Kathryn Davis, Deborah Shelton, Susie Coelho, Peter Lawford, Steven Keats, Clint Walker; **D:** Joseph Pevney. *ART*

Mysterious Jane 🎬 1987 Amid soft-focus nudity, a husband and his lover conspire to institutionalize his wife. **90m/C VHS, Beta.** Amber Lee, Sandy Carey.

The Mysterious Lady 🎬🎬½ 1928 Pre-Ninotchka Garbo plays Russian spy who betrays her mother country because she does not want to be alone. **99m/B VHS.** Greta Garbo, Conrad Nagel, Gustav von Seyffertitz, Richard Alexander, Albert Pollet, Edward Connelly; **C:** William H. Daniels. *MGM, FCT*

The Mysterious Magician 🎬🎬½ 1965 Entertaining suspense story of the mad murderer known as "The Wizard," who was thought by Scotland Yard to be dead, but the current murderwave in London suggests otherwise. Based on an Edgar Wallace story. **95m/C VHS.** *GE* Joachim Fuchsberger, Eddi Arent, Sophie Hardy, Karl John, Heinz Drache; **D:** Alfred Vohrer. *SNC*

Mysterious Mr. Wong 🎬½ 1935 The Thirteen Coins of Confucius put San Francisco's Chinatown in a state of terror until Mr. Wong arrives. **56m/B VHS, Beta.** Arline Judge, Wallace Ford; **D:** William Nigh. *VYY, MRV, SNC*

The Mysterious Rider 🎬🎬½ *The Fighting Phantom* 1933 A cowboy tries to prevent unscrupulous homesteaders from cheating farmers out of their land. **59m/B VHS.** Kent Taylor, Lona Andre, Gail Patrick, Warren Hymer, Berton Churchill; **D:** Fred Allen. *SNC, DVT*

The Mysterious Rider 🎬½ *Mark of the Avenger* 1938 A man framed for murder must help innocent homesteaders from being cheated out of their land. **75m/B VHS.** Douglass Dumbrille, Sidney Toler, Russell Hayden, Charlotte Field; **D:** Lesley Selander. *NOS, DVT, RXM*

The Mysterious Rider 🎬🎬 1942 Routine oater has Crabbe and St. John helping a couple of kids protect their inheritance. **56m/B VHS.** Buster Crabbe, Al "Fuzzy" St. John, Caroline Burke, John Merton, Kermit Maynard, Jack Ingram, Charles "Slim" Whitaker; **D:** Sam Newfield. *DVT, HEG*

The Mysterious Stranger 🎬🎬 1982 Printer's apprentice is given to bouts of daydreaming about a magic castle in Austria. Based on Twain tale. **89m/C VHS.** Chris Makepeace, Lance Kerwin, Fred Gwynne; **D:** Peter H. Hunt. *USH*

Mysterious Two 🎬🎬 1982 Two aliens visit the Earth in an effort to enlist converts to travel the universe with them. **100m/C VHS, Beta.** John Forsythe, Priscilla Pointer, Noah Beery Jr., Vic Tayback, James Stephens, Karen Werner, Robert Englund, Robert Pine; **D:** Gary Sherman. *ART*

Mystery at Fire Island 🎬 1981 A clever young girl and her cousin encounter some strange people as they try to find out why their fisherman friend mysteriously vanished. **52m/C VHS, Beta.** Frank Converse, Barbara Byrne, Beth Ehlers, Eric Gurry. *NO*

Mystery Date 🎬🎬 1991 (PG-13) A sort of teen version of "After Hours," in which a shy college guy gets a date with the girl of his dreams, only to be mistaken for a master criminal and pursued by gangsters, police and a crazed florist. Not terrible, but if you're old enough to drive you're probably too old to watch with amusement. **98m/C VHS, Closed Caption.** Ethan Hawke, Teri Polo, Brian McNamara, Fisher Stevens, B.D. Wong; **D:** Jonathan Wacks; **W:** Terry Runte, Parker Bennett; **M:** John Du Prez. *ORI*

Mystery in Swing 🎬🎬 1940 An all-black mystery with music, about a trumpet player who has snake venom put on his mouthpiece. **66m/B VHS, Beta.** F.E. Miller, Monte Hawley, Marguerite Whitten, Tom Moore, Ceepee Johnson; **D:** Arthur Dreifuss. *VYY*

Mystery Island 🎬🎬½ 1981 Beautifully filmed underwater scenes in this children's film about four youths who discover a deserted island which they name Mystery Island, and a retired pirate who lives there. When the children find counterfeit money and the bad guys return for it, the old pirate's clever plans keep the kids safe. **75m/C VHS, Beta.** *NO*

Mystery Liner 🎬🎬½ *The Ghost of John Holling* 1934 Dead bodies are found aboard ocean liner and passengers are concerned about it. Slow-moving sea cruise. **62m/B VHS, Beta.** Noah Beery Sr.,

Astrid Allwyn, Cornelius Keefe, Gustav von Seyffertitz, Edwin Maxwell, Boothe Howard, George "Gabby" Hayes; **D:** William Nigh. *NOS, SNC*

The Mystery Man 🐾🐾½ 1935 A Chicago reporter goes on a drinking binge and ends up in St. Louis. There he stumbles upon a mystery which may involve the paper for which he works. He teams up with a beautiful woman to try to crack the case. 65m/B VHS, Beta. Robert Armstrong, Maxine Doyle, Henry Kolker, Leroy Mason, James Burke; **D:** Ray McCarey. *SNC*

Mystery Man 🐾½ 1944 Below-average episode has rancher Hoppy being bothered by rustlers. Boyd solves things in the usual way, while Clyde provides the laughs. 58m/B VHS. William Boyd, Andy Clyde, Jimmy Rogers, Don Costello, Francis McDonald, Forrest Taylor, Eleanor Stewart; **D:** George Archainbaud. *NOS*

Mystery Mansion 🐾🐾 1983 (PG) Fortune in gold and a hundred-year-old mystery lead three children into an exciting treasure hunt. Family fare. 95m/C VHS, Beta. Dallas McKennon, Greg Wynne, Jane Ferguson.

Mystery Mountain 🐾½ 1934 Twelve episodes depict the villain known as the "Rattler" attempting to stop the construction of a railroad over Mystery Mountain. 156m/B VHS, Beta. Ken Maynard, Gene Autry, Smiley Burnette; **D:** Otto Brower, B. Reeves Eason. *NOS, VCN, CAB*

The Mystery of Alexina 🐾🐾½ *Mystere Alexina* 1986 True story of Herculine Adelaide Barbin, a 19th-century French hermaphrodite, who, after growing up a woman, fell in love with another woman and was actually revealed to be a man. Subtitled. 86m/C VHS, Beta. *FR* Vuillemin, Valeri Stroh; **D:** Rene Feret; **W:** Jean Gruault. *NLC*

The Mystery of Edwin Drood 🐾🐾½ 1935 Nicely creepy gothic atmosphere highlights this version of Charles Dickens' final novel, which was unfinished at the time of his death. English choirmaster and opium addict John Jasper (Rains) is visited by his nephew Edwin Drood (Manners), who's soon to enter into an arranged marriage with Rosa (Angel). Unbeknownst to anyone, Jasper has long desired Rosa for himself and kills his nephew in a jealous rage. Now that Drood's disappeared, will Jasper have Rosa to himself? 85m/B VHS, **Closed Caption.** Claude Rains, Heather Angel, Douglass Montgomery, Valerie Hobson, David Manners, Francis L. Sullivan, Ethel Griffies, E.E. Clive; **D:** Stuart Walker; **W:** John L. Balderston, Gladys Unger; **C:** George Robinson; **M:** Edward Ward. *USH*

The Mystery of Edwin Drood 🐾🐾½ 1993 When Edwin Drood vanishes on Christmas Eve, his disappearance leads to a terrifying mystery that unfolds amidst the slums of Victorian England. Adapted from Charles Dickens' last novel, which was left unfinished at his death. 98m/C VHS. *GB* Robert Powell, Michelle Evans, Jonathan Phillips, Finty Williams, Rupert Rainsford, Nanette Newman, Freddie Jones, Rosemary Leach, Ronald Fraser; **D:** Timothy Forder; **W:** Timothy Forder. *AEH, TVC*

Mystery of Mr. Wong 🐾½ 1939 The largest star sapphire in the world, the "Eye of the Daughter of the Moon," is stolen from a museum in its home country of China. Mr. Wong becomes involved in trying to trace its trail and the perpetrator of the murders that follow in its wake. One in the series of detective films. 67m/B VHS. Boris Karloff, Grant Withers, Dorothy Tree, Lotus Long; **D:** William Nigh. *VYY, MRV, DVT*

The Mystery of Rampo 🐾🐾🐾 1994 (R) Visually dazzling fantasy that propels mystery writer Edogawa Rampo (Takenaka) into his own stories. Set just before WWII, Rampo is despondent when his latest novel (about a woman suffocating her husband in a trunk) is censored by the government and then amazed when a newspaper story reveals a similar crime. So Rampo decides to meet the widow Shizuko (Hada) and discovers she's a double for his fictional character. He then writes a sequel, again featuring Shizuko, and

once again finds reality and fiction blending into the bizarre. Rampo was the pseudonym for renowned writer Hirai Taro, regarded as the Japanese Edgar Allan Poe. The film had its own complications when the version filmed by original director Rentaro Mayusumi was rejected by producer Okuyama, who then reshot much of the film himself. Japanese with subtitles. **CW:** Adult themes, nudity, violence. 96m/C VHS. *JP* Naoto Takenaka, Michiko Hada, Masahiro Motoki, Teruyoki Yamaguchi, Mikijiro Hira; **D:** Kazuyoshi Okuyama; **W:** Kazuyoshi Okuyama, Yuhei Enoki; **C:** Yasushi Sasakibara; **M:** Akira Senju. *HMK*

Mystery of the Hooded Horseman 🐾🐾 1937 Tex finds himself pitted against a very strange adversary. 61m/B VHS, Beta. Tex Ritter, Iris Meredith, Charles "Blackie" King, Joseph Girard, Lafe McKee; **D:** Ray Taylor. *NOS, VDM, DVT*

Mystery of the Leaping Fish/Chess Fever 🐾🐾½ 1925 Two silent shorts. The first, filmed in 1916, is a surreal comedy-mystery about a doped-up detective named Coke Ennyday and his hallucinatory, sped-up adventures. The second, made in 1925 during the Moscow Chess Tournament, is a parody of professional chess playing and the fever with which it grips a country. Pudovkin's second directorial credit. 64m/B VHS, Beta, 8mm. Douglas Fairbanks Sr., Bessie Love, Alma Rubens; **D:** John Emerson, Vsevolod Pudovkin; **W:** Tod Browning. *VYY, MRV*

The Mystery of the Mary Celeste 🐾🐾 *The Phantom Ship; The Mystery of the Marie Celeste* 1937 Tale of terror based on the bizarre case of the "Marie Celeste," an American ship found adrift off the coast of England with her sails set but minus any of her crew on December 5, 1872. 64m/B VHS, Beta. Bela Lugosi, Shirley Grey, Edmund Willard, Arthur Margetson. *NOS, MRV, VYY*

Mystery of the Million Dollar Hockey Puck 🐾½ 198? Sinister diamond smugglers learn a lesson on ice from a pair of orphan lads. Features the National Hockey League's Montreal Canadiens in one of their few film appearances. 88m/C VHS, Beta. Michael MacDonald, Angele Knight; **D:** Jean LaFleur, Peter Svatek. *NO*

Mystery of the Riverboat 🐾🐾½ 1944 Louisiana and the Mississippi River are the background for these 13 episodes of mystery and murder. 90m/B VHS, Beta. Robert Lowery, Eddie Quillan, Lyle Talbot, Francis McDonald, Arthur Hohl; **D:** Ray Taylor, Lewis D. Collins. *VCI, MLB, GPV*

Mystery of the Wax Museum 🐾🐾🐾 1933 Rarely seen, vintage horror classic about a wax-dummy maker who, after a disfiguring fire, resorts to murder and installs the wax-covered bodies of his victims in his museum. Famous for its pioneering use of two-strip Technicolor. Remade in 1953 in 3-D as "House of Wax." 77m/C VHS, Beta, LV. Lionel Atwill, Fay Wray, Glenda Farrell, Frank McHugh, Allen Vincent, Holmes Herbert; **D:** Michael Curtiz; **W:** Carl Erickson, Don Mullaly; **C:** Ray Rennahan. *MGM, MLB*

Mystery Plane 🐾½ 1939 An inventor devises a new bomb-dropping mechanism, and must evade secret agents on his way to deliver it to the government. 60m/B VHS, Beta. John Trent, Marjorie Reynolds, Milburn Stone, Peter George Lynn, Polly Ann Young; **D:** George Waggner. *NOS, DVT, HEG*

Mystery Ranch 🐾½ 1934 A cowboy finds himself in strange predicaments out on the range. 52m/B VHS, Beta. George O'Brien, Charles Middleton, Cecilia Parker; **D:** David Howard. *NOS, DVT, GPV*

Mystery Science Theater 3000: The Movie 🐾🐾½ 1996 (PG-13) Mad scientist Dr. Clayton Forrester (Beaulieu) maroons Mike Nelson on the Satellite of Love, forces him to watch bad movies, and monitors his reactions. Mike and his robotic pals, Tom Servo and Crow T. Robot, save their sanity by wisecracking their way through the movies. Today's experiment is "This Island Earth," an uncharacteristically semi-respectable flick. As regular viewers know, the

jokes and snide remarks come fast and in bunches. Not all of them work, but the ones that do will be remembered and repeated often. Audience participation is inevitable. Weekend theme-party status is virtually assured. **CW:** Some sexual humor. 73m/C VHS, LV, **Letterbox, Closed Caption.** Trace Beaulieu, James Mallon, Michael J. Nelson, Kevin Murphy, John Brady; **D:** James Mallon; **W:** Trace Beaulieu, James Mallon, Michael J. Nelson, Kevin Murphy, Mary Jo Pehl, Paul Chaplin, Bridget Jones; **C:** Jeff Stonehouse; **M:** Billy Barber. *USH*

Mystery Squadron 1933 Twelve chapters, 13 minutes each. Daredevil air action in flight against the masked pilots of the Black Ace. 240m/B VHS, Beta. Bob Steele, Guinn "Big Boy" Williams, Lucille Browne, Jack Mulhall, J. Carrol Naish, Jack Mower; **D:** Colbert Clark. *GPV, VCN, DVT*

Mystery Train 🐾🐾🐾 1989 (R) A run down hotel in Memphis is the scene for three vignettes concerning the visit of foreigners to the U.S. Themes of mythic Americana, Elvis, and life on the fringe pervade this hip and quirky film. The three vignettes all tie together in clever and funny overlaps. Waits fans should listen for his performance as a DJ. 110m/C VHS, LV, **Letterbox.** Masatoshi Nagase, Youki Kudoh, Jay Hawkins, Cinque Lee, Joe Strummer, Nicoletta Braschi, Elizabeth Bracco, Steve Buscemi, Tom Noonan, Rockets Redglare, Rick Aviles, Rufus Thomas; **D:** Jim Jarmusch; **W:** Jim Jarmusch; **M:** John Lurie; **V:** Tom Waits. *ORI*

Mystery Trooper 🐾🐾 *Trail of the Royal Mounted* 1932 Adventures in the great wilderness full of prospecting, greed, and Indians all being observed by the Royal Mounties. Ten chapters of the serial at 20 minutes each. 200m/B VHS, Beta. Robert Frazer, Buzz Barton. *GPV, NOS, CAB*

Mystic Circle Murder 🐾 *Religious Racketeers* 1939 Reporter sets out to uncover phony mediums, particularly the Great La Gagge, whose fake apparitions are so convincing that it caused one of his clients to have a heart attack. Cheaply made, and it's obvious. Watch for a cameo by Harry Houdini's wife, who talks about life after death. Based on a story by director O'Connor. 69m/B VHS. Betty Compson, Robert Fiske, Helene Le Berthon, Arthur Gardner; **D:** Frank O'Connor. *SNC*

Mystic Pizza 🐾🐾🐾 1988 (R) Intelligent coming of age drama centers on two sisters and their best friend as they struggle with their hopes, loves, and family rivalries in the small town of Mystic, Connecticut. At times predictable, there are enough unexpected moments to keep interest high; definite appeal to young women, but others may not relate. The relatively unknown Roberts got most of the attention, but is the weakest of the three leads, so watch this one for the strong performances from Gish and Taylor. 101m/C VHS, Beta, LV, **Closed Caption.** Annabeth Gish, Julia Roberts, Lili Taylor, Vincent D'Onofrio, William R. Moses, Adam Storke, Conchata Ferrell, Joanna Merlin, Matt Damon; **D:** Donald Petrie; **W:** Amy Holden Jones, Perry Howze, Alfred Uhry; **M:** David McHugh. Independent Spirit Awards '89: Best First Feature. *VTR*

The Myth of Fingerprints 🐾🐾½ 1997 (R) Four adult siblings and their various partners return to their New England home to spend Thanksgiving with their parents. As with most movie families of upper-middle class status, old resentments and issues abound. Dad (Scheider), a sullen, misanthropic near-recluse, isn't thrilled about the reunion. Younger son Warren (Wyle) hopes to reconcile with his high school sweetheart, a relationship mostly done in by his father's indiscretion. Another brother can't commit. Older sister Mia (Moore) can't think of anything nice to say about anyone, and her tomboy sister Leigh (Holloman) does the sibling rivalry dance with her. Subdued and interesting, Freundlich's debut doesn't go for a grand conclusion or startling revelation. Depending on your taste for pat endings and easy answers, that could be it's greatest asset or a reason not to bother. Excellent performances by a great cast should have a bearing on the decision. **CW:** Sexuality and language. **91m/C VHS, Closed Caption.** Blythe Danner, Roy Scheider, Julianne Moore, Noah Wyle, Michael Vartan, Laurel Holloman, Hope Davis, Brian Kerwin, James LeGros; **D:** Bart Freundlich; **W:** Bart Freundlich; **C:** Stephen Kazmierski; **M:** David Bridie, John Phillips. Nominations: Independent Spirit Awards '98: Best Supporting Actor (Scheider). *COL*

Nabonga 🐾🐾 *Gorilla; Jungle Woman* 1944 The daughter of an embezzler, whose plane crashes in the jungle, befriends a gorilla who protects her. Soon a young man comes looking for the embezzler's cash, meets the woman and the ape, and together they go on a wonderful journey. **72m/B VHS.** Buster Crabbe, Fifi d'Orsay, Barton MacLane, Julie London, Herbert Rawlinson; **D:** Sam Newfield. *SNC, NOS, MOV*

Nadia 🐾🐾½ 1984 Entertaining account of the life of Nadia Comaneci, the Romanian gymnast who earned six perfect tens with her stunning performance at the 1976 Olympic Games. Made for television. **100m/C VHS, Beta.** Talia Balsam, Jonathan Banks, Simone Blue, Johann Carlo, Carrie Snodgress; **D:** Alan Cooke. *FHE, STP*

Nadine 🐾🐾½ 1987 **(PG)** In Austin circa 1954, an almost divorced beautician witnesses a murder and goes undercover with her estranged husband to track down the murderer, before he finds her. Plenty of low-key humor. Well-paced fun; Basinger is terrific. **83m/C VHS, Beta, LV, Closed Caption.** Jeff Bridges, Kim Basinger, Rip Torn, Gwen Verdon, Glenne Headly, Jerry Stiller, Jay Patterson; **D:** Robert Benton; **W:** Robert Benton; **C:** Nestor Almendros; **M:** Howard Shore. *FOX*

Nadja 🐾🐾🐾 1995 **(R)** Fresh, modern comic take on the vampire tale is about family ties and the power of home, with the required AIDS analogy and lesbian sex scenes. Tired of nightly bloodletting, the daughter of the now-deceased Count, Nadja (Lowensohn), lives in New York's East Village, hoping to change her life. She seduces and falls in love with Lucy (Craze), whose husband is the nephew of old family nemesis Van Helsing (Fonda, in a surprisingly comedic role). Manic Fonda Van Helsing sets out to save Lucy and steal the film. Meanwhile, Nadja finds her long lost twin brother (Harris, son of Richard) and Lucy discovers sex with Nadja is draining. Innovative camera work (vampire point-of-view scenes shot with a toy Pixelvision camera and blown up to 35mm for a moody, grainy look) and a great score keep "Nadja" very watchable despite some missteps in the plot. (Director Almereyda pioneered use of the Pixel-vision camera in "Another Girl, Another Planet.") Executive producer David Lynch contributes a cameo as a guard at the morgue where Nadja claims her father's body. **CW:** Some scenes of bizarre vampire sexuality and gore, some language. **92m/B VHS.** Elina Lowensohn, Suzy Amis, Galaxy Craze, Martin Donovan, Peter Fonda, Karl Geary, Jared Harris; **Cameos:** David Lynch; **D:** Michael Almereyda; **W:** Michael Almereyda; **C:** Jim Denault; **M:** Simon Fisher Turner. Nominations: Independent Spirit Awards '96: Best Actress (Lowensohn), Best Cinematography, Best Director (Almereyda). *HMK*

Nail Gun Massacre woof! 1986 A crazed killer with a penchant for nailing bodies to just about anything goes on a hammering spree. In horrific, vivid color. **90m/C VHS, Beta.** Rocky Patterson, Ron Queen, Beau Leland, Michelle Meyer; **D:** Bill Lesley. *NO*

Nails 🐾½ 1992 **(R)** Harry "Nails" Niles (Hopper) is a tough, experienced cop whose partner has been killed by drug dealers. Harry doesn't take this well and decides to go on a violent spree for revenge. Archer is wasted as Harry's estranged wife and Hopper can sleepwalk through this type of cliched wildman role. Made for cable television. **CW:** Language, strong violence, and sexuality. **96m/C VHS, Beta, LV, Closed Caption.** Dennis Hopper, Anne Archer, Tomas Milian, Cliff DeYoung; **D:** John Flynn. *FXV, VTR*

Nairobi Affair 🐾🐾 1988 **(PG)** Savage and Heston fight poachers and each other in Kenya, when the father has an affair with his son's ex-wife. Mediocre, derivative script, but beautiful scenery. Made for television. **95m/C VHS, Beta.** Charlton Heston, John Savage, Maud Adams, John Rhys-Davies, Connie Booth; **D:** Marvin J. Chomsky. *THV*

Nais 🐾🐾🐾 1945 Vintage Pagnolian peasant drama. A hunchback sacrifices himself for the girl he loves. She escapes to another man's arms. Adapted from the Emile Zola novel "Naïs Micoulin." In French with English subtitles. **105m/B VHS, Beta, 8mm.** *FR* Fernandel; **D:** Fernand Lauterier; **W:** Marcel Pagnol. *VYY, FCT, DVT*

Naked 🐾🐾🐾 *Mike Leigh's Naked* 1993 **(R)** Existential angst in a '90s London filled with Leigh's usual eccentrics. The unemployed Johnny (Thewlis) comes to London and bunks with former girlfriend Louise (Sharp). After seducing her flatmate Sophie (Cartlidge), Johnny leaves to wander the streets, exchanging philosophical, if foul-mouthed, dialogues with a variety of odd characters. Thewlis gives an explosive performance as the calculatingly brutal and desolate Johnny. Chaotic shifts in mood from comedy to violence to love prove a challenge and the pervasive abuse of all the women characters is very disturbing. Critically acclaimed; see it as a reflection on the mess of modern England. **CW:** Vulgar & profane language, nudity, and explicit & violent sex. **131m/C VHS, LV.** *GB* David Thewlis, Lesley Sharp, Katrin Cartlidge, Greg Cruttwell, Claire Skinner, Peter Wight, Ewen Bremmer, Susan Vidler, Deborah MacLaren, Gina McKee; **D:** Mike Leigh; **W:** Mike Leigh; **C:** Dick Pope; **M:** Andrew Dickson. Cannes Film Festival '93: Best Actor (Thewlis), Best Director (Leigh); New York Film Critics Awards '93: Best Actor (Thewlis); National Society of Film Critics Awards '93: Best Actor (Thewlis); Nominations: British Academy Awards '93: Best Film; Independent Spirit Awards '94: Best Foreign Film. *COL, IME*

The Naked and the Dead 🐾🐾½ 1958 Sanitized adaptation of Norman Mailer's bestselling novel about army life in the Pacific during WWII. Resentment between officers and enlisted men proves to be almost as dangerous as the Japanese. Uneven acting and cliched characterizations make this an average outing. Don't expect to hear the profane language that sensationalized the book, because most of it was edited out of the screenplay. **131m/C VHS, Beta.** Aldo Ray, Cliff Robertson, Joey Bishop, Raymond Massey, Lili St. Cyr, James Best; **D:** Raoul Walsh; **C:** Joseph LaShelle. *NO*

The Naked Angels 🐾 1969 **(R)** Rape, mayhem, beatings, and road-hogging streetbikes highlight this biker film, acted, in part, by actual bikers, and in part by others who were actually (almost) actors. The gang war rages from Los Angeles to Las Vegas. Roger Corman was the executive producer. **83m/C VHS, Beta.** Michael Greene, Richard Rust, Felicia Guy; **D:** Bruce Clark; **W:** Bruce Clark. *CRV*

Naked Cage woof! 1986 **(R)** Brutal women's prison film that is borderline soft-core, about an innocent country woman, a horseriding fanatic, who is framed for a robbery and sent to the slammer. There, she contends with lesbian wardens and inmates. Disgusting. **97m/C VHS, Beta.** Shari Shattuck, Angel Tompkins, Lucinda Crosby, Christina Whitaker; **D:** Paul Nicholas. *COL*

The Naked City 🐾🐾🐾½ 1948 Film noir classic makes spectacular use of its NYC locations. Beautiful playgirl is murdered and police detectives Fitzgerald and Taylor are left without clues. They spend most of their time running down weak leads and interviewing various suspects and witnesses. When they finally get a break, it leads to playboy Duff. Spectacular ending on the Brooklyn Bridge between cops and killer. Producer Hellinger provided the hard-boiled narration, patterned after the tabloid newspaper stories he once wrote. Served as the impetus for the TV show of the same name, where Hellinger's film postscript also became the show's noted tag-

line: "There are eight million stories in the naked city, this has been one of them." **96m/B VHS.** Barry Fitzgerald, Don Taylor, Howard Duff, Ted de Corsia, Dorothy Hart; **D:** Jules Dassin; **C:** William H. Daniels; **M:** Miklos Rozsa. Academy Awards '48: Best Black and White Cinematography, Best Film Editing; Nominations: Academy Awards '48: Best Story. *IVY*

The Naked Civil Servant 🐾🐾🐾½ 1975 Remarkable film, based on the life of flamboyant homosexual Quentin Crisp, who came out of the closet in his native England, long before his lifestyle would be tolerated by Britains. For mature audiences. **80m/C VHS, Beta.** John Hurt; **D:** Jack Gold; **M:** Carl Davis. *HBO*

The Naked Country 🐾½ 1985 **(R)** In the untamed frontier of Australia rancher bigoted Lance Dillion and his sensual wife Mary are determined to make their way. But when Lance finds out that the neglected Mary is fooling around with a local cop, he goes on a killing spree on land sacred to the Aborigines. Plodding plot. **90m/C VHS, Closed Caption.** *AU* John Stanton, Rebecca Gilling, Ivar Kants; **D:** Tim Burstall; **C:** David Eggby; **M:** Bruce Smeaton.

The Naked Edge 🐾🐾 1961 Cooper stars as a middle-aged businessman whose wife suspects him of murder after she begins snooping into his business affairs. Cooper's last film and far from his best. Poor direction and holes in the screenplay divert from what could have been a tight thriller. **99m/C VHS, Closed Caption.** *GB* Gary Cooper, Deborah Kerr, Eric Portman, Diane Cilento, Hermione Gingold, Peter Cushing, Michael Wilding, Ronald Howard; **D:** Michael Anderson Sr.; **W:** Joseph Stefano. *MGM, MOV*

The Naked Face 🐾🐾 1984 **(R)** A psychiatrist tries to find out why his patients are being killed. He gets no help from police, who suspect he is the murderer. A dull affair featuring unusual casting of Moore, while Steiger's suspicious police captain character provides spark. From the novel by Sidney Sheldon. **105m/C VHS, Beta.** Roger Moore, Rod Steiger, Elliott Gould, Art Carney, Anne Archer, David Hedison; **D:** Bryan Forbes. *MGM*

The Naked Flame woof! 1968 **(R)** O'Keefe plays an investigator in a strange town inhabited by weird, religious fanatics. After he arrives, the womenfolk shed their clothes in this pitiful, pathetic hilarity. **?m/C VHS.** Dennis O'Keefe, Linda Bennett, Kasey Rogers. *SNC*

The Naked Gun: From the Files of Police Squad 🐾🐾🐾 1988 **(PG-13)** More hysterical satire from the creators of "Airplane!" The short-lived television cop spoof "Police Squad" moves to the big screen and has Lt. Drebin uncover a plot to assassinate Queen Elizabeth while she is visiting Los Angeles. Nearly nonstop gags and pratfalls provide lots of laughs. Nielsen is perfect as Drebin and the supporting cast is strong; cameos abound. **85m/C VHS, Beta, LV, 8mm, Closed Caption.** Leslie Nielsen, Ricardo Montalban, Priscilla Presley, George Kennedy, O.J. Simpson, Nancy Marchand, John Houseman; **Cameos:** Weird Al Yankovic, Reggie Jackson, Dr. Joyce Brothers; **D:** David Zucker; **W:** Jerry Zucker, Jim Abrahams, Pat Proft, David Zucker; **M:** Ira Newborn. *PAR*

Naked Gun 33 1/3: The Final Insult 🐾🐾 1994 **(PG-13)** Ever dumb, crass, and crude, Lt. Drebin returns to the force from retirement to lead an investigation into terrorist activities in Hollywood. Lots of current events jokes—dated as soon as they hit the screen. Sure to satisfy genre fans with a taste for bad puns. Watch for the cameos, especially at the "Oscars." **CW:** Off-color humor and sexual innuendo. **90m/C VHS, Beta, LV, Closed Caption.** Leslie Nielsen, Priscilla Presley, O.J. Simpson, Fred Ward, George Kennedy, Gary Cooper, Kathleen Freeman, Raquel Welch; **Cameos:** Pia Zadora, James Earl Jones, Weird Al Yankovic, Ann B. Davis; **D:** Peter Segal; **W:** Robert Locash, David Zucker, Pat Proft; **M:** Ira Newborn. Golden Raspberry Awards '94: Worst Supporting Actor (Simpson), Worst New Star (Smith). *PAR*

Naked Gun 2 1/2: The Smell of Fear 🐾🐾½ 1991 (PG-13) Lt. Drebin returns to rescue the world from a faulty energy policy devised by the White House and oil-lords. A notch down from the previous entry but still hilarious cop parody. Nielsen has this character down to a tee, and there's a laugh every minute. Laserdisc version is letterboxed and features dolby surround sound. 85m/C VHS, Beta, LV, 8mm, Letterbox, Closed Caption. Leslie Nielsen, Priscilla Presley, George Kennedy, O.J. Simpson, Robert Goulet, Richard Griffiths, Jacqueline Brookes, Lloyd Bochner, Tim O'Connor, Peter Mark Richman; *Cameos:* Mel Torme, Eva Gabor, Weird Al Yankovic; *D:* David Zucker; *W:* David Zucker, Pat Proft; *M:* Ira Newborn. PAR

Naked Hills 🐾½ 1956 Meandering tale about a man (Wayne) who, suffering from gold fever, searches for 40 years in 19th Century California and ends up out of luck, losing his wife and family. 72m/C VHS. David Wayne, Keenan Wynn, James Barton, Marcia Henderson, Jim Backus, Denver Pyle, Myrna Dell, Frank Fenton, Fuzzy Knight; *D:* Josef Shaftel; *W:* Josef Shaftel. NO

Naked in New York 🐾🐾½ 1993 (R) Aspiring New York playwright Jake Briggs (Stoltz) and his girlfriend Joanne (Parker), an aspiring photographer, find their relationship in jeopardy when their respective careers start to take off. Offspring from the "Annie Hall" school of neurotic romance examines a number of issues, including ambition, commitment, and the societal dynamics of theatre and art. Celebrity appearances abound, including Styron as himself and Goldberg as a tragedy mask on a wall. Directorial debut of Scorsese protege Algrant is uneven but charming. Parker is particularly strong, and Turner's a riot as a sexpot soap star on the prowl for Jake. *CW:* Language, pot use and sexuality. 89m/C VHS, LV, Closed Caption. Eric Stoltz, Mary-Louise Parker, Ralph Macchio, Jill Clayburgh, Tony Curtis, Kathleen Turner, Timothy Dalton, Lynne Thigpen, Roscoe Lee Browne; *Cameos:* Whoopi Goldberg, William Styron, Eric Bogosian, Quentin Crisp; *D:* Dan Algrant; *W:* Dan Algrant, John Warren; *M:* Angelo Badalamenti; *V:* David Johansen. COL

Naked in the Night 🐾 1958 Cheap German exploitation film about the dangers of promiscuous women. Dubbed in English. ?m/C VHS. GE Eva Bartok, Alexander Kerst. SNC, TPV

Naked in the Sun 🐾🐾 1957 The true story of events leading to the war between the Osceola and Seminole Indians and a slave trader. Somewhat slow. 95m/C VHS. James Craig, Lita Milan, Barton MacLane, Tony Hunter; *D:* R. John Hugh. REP

Naked Is Better 🐾 1973 A couple of buffoons pose as hospital workers so they can play doctor with a hospitalized actress. 93m/C VHS, Beta. Alberto Olmedo, Jorge Porcel, Jorge Barreiro, Maria Casan.

Naked Jungle 🐾🐾🐾 1954 Suspenseful, well-done jungle adventure of a plantation owner (Heston) in South America and his North American mail-order bride (Parker), who do battle with a deadly, miles-long siege of red army ants. Realistic and worth watching. Produced by George Pal, shot by Ernest Laszlo and based on the story "Leiningen vs. the Ants" by Carl Stephenson. 95m/C VHS, Beta, LV. Charlton Heston, Eleanor Parker, Abraham Sofaer, William Conrad; *D:* Byron Haskin; *W:* Philip Yordan; *C:* Ernest Laszlo. PAR

Naked Killer 🐾 1992 Kitty (Ching) turns to a female assassin to learn the art of killing so that she may avenge her father's death. When her teacher is herself unceremoniously murdered, Kitty and her policeman boyfriend (Yam) have two scores to settle. Sex and violence. Subtitled in English. 86m/C VHS, Letterbox. CN My Yau Ching, Simon Yam; *D:* Clarence Fok Yiu Leung. WVE

Naked Kiss 🐾🐾½ The Iron Kiss 1964 Fuller's most savage, hysterical film noir. A brutalized prostitute escapes her pimp and tries to enter respectable small-town society. She finds even more perversion and sickness there. 92m/B VHS,

LV, Letterbox. Constance Towers, Anthony Eisley, Michael Dante, Virginia Grey, Patsy Kelly, Betty Bronson; *D:* Samuel Fuller. HMV

Naked Lie 🐾🐾 1989 A District Attorney and a judge engage in an ultra-steamy affair and inevitably clash when she is assigned as a prosecutor on the politically explosive case over which he is presiding. 89m/C VHS. Victoria Principal, James Farentino, Glenn Withrow, William Lucking, Dakin Matthews; *D:* Richard A. Colla; *M:* Robert Alcivar. ING

Naked Lunch 🐾🐾🐾 1991 (R) Whacked-out movie based on William S. Burroughs's autobiographical account of drug abuse, homosexuality, violence, and weirdness set in the drug-inspired land called Interzone. Hallucinogenic images are carried to the extreme: typewriters metamorphose into beetles, bloblike creatures with sex organs scurry about, and characters mainline insecticide. Some of the characters are clearly based on writers of the Beat generation, including Jane and Paul Bowles, Allen Ginsberg, and Jack Kerouac. *CW:* Language, violence, and strong sensuality. 117m/C VHS, Closed Caption. Peter Weller, Judy Davis, Ian Sands, Roy Scheider, Monique Mercure, Nicholas Campbell, Michael Zelniker, Robert A. Silverman, Joseph Scorsiani; *D:* David Cronenberg; *W:* David Cronenberg; *M:* Howard Shore. Genie Awards '92: Best Adapted Screenplay, Best Art Direction/Set Decoration, Best Cinematography, Best Director (Cronenberg), Best Film, Best Sound, Best Supporting Actress (Mercure); New York Film Critics Awards '91: Best Screenplay, Best Supporting Actress (Davis); National Society of Film Critics Awards '91: Best Director (Cronenberg), Best Screenplay. FXV

The Naked Maja 🐾🐾 1959 Elaborate, yet dull drama about the tumultuous romance between a Spanish duchess and the legendary painter Francisco Goya. Even the gorgeous costumes and spectacular sets can't overcome the weak script and poor direction that plague the film. Based on a story by Oscar Saul and Talbot Jennings. 111m/C VHS, Closed Caption. Ava Gardner, Anthony (Tony) Franciosa, Amedeo Nazzari, Gino Cervi, Lea Padovani, Massimo Serato, Carlo Rizzo, Renzo Cesana; *D:* Henry Koster, Mario Russo; *W:* Norman Corwin, Giorgio Prosperi. MGM, FCT

Naked Massacre 🐾 198? A maniac kills nurses, leaving no clues for the police to follow. 90m/C VHS, Beta. Matthieu Carriere, Carol Laurie; *D:* Denis Heroux. VDC

Naked Obsession 🐾½ 1991 (R) A city councilman running for mayor is mugged in one of the seedier parts of the city. He's found by a homeless man who takes him to a kinky nightclub where the councilman is promptly seduced by a topless bar hostess with secrets of her own. Also available in an unrated version. 93m/C VHS. William Katt, Maria Ford, Rick Dean; *D:* Dan Golden. VES, MOV

Naked Paradise 1978 (R) A young woman moves in with her mother and step-sister and finds difficulty in adjusting. 86m/C VHS, Beta. Laura Gemser, Annie Belle. NO

The Naked Prey 🐾🐾🐾 1966 Unnerving African adventure which contains some unforgettably brutal scenes. A safari guide (Wilde), leading a hunting party, must watch as an indigenous tribe murders all his companions, and according to their customs, allows him to be set free, sans clothes or weapons, to be hunted by the best of the tribe. 96m/C VHS, Beta, LV. Cornel Wilde, Gertrude Van Der Berger, Ken Gampu; *D:* Cornel Wilde. Nominations: Academy Awards '66: Best Story & Screenplay. PAR

Naked Souls 🐾 1995 (R) Artist Brit Clark (Anderson) must save scientist fiance Edward (Krause) from the evil experiments of murderous scientist Longstreet (Warner). Like you'll care as long as the Anderson bod is on display. *CW:* Strong sexuality, and for language and violence. 90m/C VHS. Pamela Anderson, Brian Krause, Clayton Rohner, Justina Vail, David Warner; *Cameos:* Dean Stockwell; *D:* Lyndon Chubbuck; *W:* Frank Dietz; *C:* Eric Goldstein; *M:* Nigel Holton. WEA

The Naked Spur 🐾🐾🐾½ 1986 A compulsive bounty hunter tracks down a vicious outlaw and his beautiful girlfriend. An exciting film from the Mann-Stewart team and considered one of their best, infusing the traditional western with psychological confusion. Wonderful use of Rockies locations. 93m/C VHS, Beta. James Stewart, Robert Ryan, Janet Leigh, Millard Mitchell; *D:* Anthony Mann; *C:* William Mellor. National Film Registry '97;; Nominations: Academy Awards '53: Best Story & Screenplay. MGM, TLF

The Naked Sword of Zorro 🐾 1969 Deadly Don Luis taxes the town by day and violates the women by night, but Zorro takes a stand and saves the town. When he's not dressed as Zorro, he is Don Diego, an inept fool, but when he puts that suit on, look out. The ladies can't keep their hands off of him. There are more lusty females than villains, but there's still lots of swordplay and action. 94m/C VHS. VDM

Naked Tango 🐾🐾½ 1991 (R) A lurid recreation of the Argentinian underworld in 1924. Stephanie is a bored wife with an older husband who, while traveling with her husband on a cruise ship, pretends to fall overboard in order to establish a new identity. The problem is she becomes the supposed mail-order bride of a young man who promptly sells her into white slavery. One of her customers is a charismatic killer named Cholo who isn't interested in Stephanie for sex, he just wants to dance the tango with her. This is meant to be taken seriously but is one of the many pretensions, erotic and otherwise, that hamper the film. 90m/C VHS. Mathilda May, Vincent D'Onofrio, Esai Morales, Fernando Rey; *D:* Leonard Schrader; *W:* Leonard Schrader; *M:* Thomas Newman. NO

The Naked Truth 🐾🐾½ Your Past is Showing 1958 A greedy publisher tries to get rich quick by publishing a scandal magazine about the "lurid" lives of prominent citizens. Well-drawn characters in an appealing offbeat comedy. 92m/C VHS, Beta. GB Peter Sellers, Terry-Thomas, Shirley Eaton, Dennis Price; *D:* Mario Zampi.

Naked Vengeance woof! Satin Vengeance 1985 (R) A woman's husband is murdered, she is beaten and raped, and she becomes a vengeful, vicious killing machine. Gratuitous violence, distasteful to the max. 97m/C VHS, Beta. Deborah Tranelli, Kaz Garas, Bill McLaughlin; *D:* Cirio H. Santiago. ART

Naked Venus 🐾½ 1958 Ulmer's last film is a slow-paced tale about an American artist, married to a model who poses in the nude and belongs to a nudist camp, whose wealthy mother tries to tear the marriage apart. Discrimination and intolerance of nudist camps is explored. 80m/B VHS, Beta. Patricia Conelle; *D:* Edgar G. Ulmer. VDM, TPV

Naked Warriors 🐾🐾 The Arena 1973 (R) Ancient Romans capture beautiful women from around the world and force them to compete in gladiatorial games. New World exploitation gem featuring mostly Italian cast, including Bay, who starred in the previous year's "Lady Frankenstein." 75m/C VHS, Beta. Margaret Markov, Pam Grier, Lucretia Love, Paul Muller, Daniel Vargas, Marie Louise, Mary Count, Rosalba (Sara Bay) Neri, Vic Karis, Sid Lawrence, Peter Cester, Anna Melita; *D:* Steve Carver. MGM

The Naked Witch 🐾 The Naked Temptress 1964 College student researching witchcraft digs up the grave of a long-dead witch. She comes back to life and takes revenge on the village that killed her years earlier. The nude shots feature someone's finger over the camera lens to cover the witch's vital organs. 60m/C VHS. Beth Porter, Robert Burgos, Bryarly Lee, Lee Forbes; *D:* Andy Milligan. SNC

Naked Youth woof! Wild Youth 1959 Seedy drive-in cheapie about two punks breaking out of juvenile prison and heading south of the border on a trail filled with crime, drugs, and loose women. 80m/B VHS, Beta. Robert Hutton, John Goddard, Carol Ohmart, Jan Brooks, Robert Arthur, Steve Rowland, Clancy Cooper; *D:* John F. Schreyer. RHI, SNC

Nam Angels ✶ 1988 (R) Hell's Angels enter Southeast Asia and rescue POWs. **91m/C VHS, Beta.** Brad Johnson, Vernon Wells, Kevin Duffis; *D:* Cirio H. Santiago. *NO*

A Name for Evil ✶✶ 1970 (R) Having grown tired of city living, a couple moves to an old family estate out in the country near the Great Lakes. Strange sounds in the night are the first signs of the terror to come. **74m/C VHS, Beta.** Robert Culp, Samantha Eggar, Sheila Sullivan, Mike Lane; *D:* Bernard Girard. *NO*

The Name of the Rose ✶✶½ 1986 (R) An exhaustive, off-center adaptation of the best-selling Umberto Eco novel about violent murders in a 14th-century Italian abbey. An English monk struggles against religious fervor in his quest to uncover the truth. **128m/C VHS, Beta, LV, Closed Caption.** *IT GE FR* Sean Connery, F. Murray Abraham, Christian Slater, Ron Perlman, William Hickey, Feodor Chaliapin Jr, Elya Baskin, Michael Lonsdale; *D:* Jean-Jacques Annaud; *W:* Andrew Birkin, Gerard Brach, Howard Franklin; *C:* Tonino Delli Colli; *M:* James Horner. British Academy Awards '87: Best Actor (Connery); Cesar Awards '87: Best Foreign Film.*NLC*

Namu, the Killer Whale ✶✶½ 1966 Based on the true story of a marine biologist (Lansing) who gets the perfect opportunity to study killer whales when one is confined to a small cove. The local fisherman want to kill the creature because it feeds on the salmon they catch but they are persuaded against their baser instincts. Filmed on location in the San Juan Islands of Puget Sound. The real Namu lived at the Seattle Public Aquarium. **89m/C VHS.** Robert Lansing, John Anderson, Robin Mattson, Richard Erdman, Lee Meriwether, Joe Higgins; *D:* Laslo Benedek. *MGM, FCT*

Nana ✶✶✶ 1955 French version of Emile Zola's novel about an actress-prostitute who seduces the high society of Paris in the late 1880s, and suffers a heart-breaking downfall and death. Film has three remakes of the original 1926 version. **118m/C VHS, Beta.** *FR* Charles Boyer, Martine Carol. *NOS, DVT, HEG*

Nana ✶✶½ 1982 A lavishly photographed, graphic adaptation of the Emile Zola novel about a Parisian whore who acquires power by seducing the richest and politically formidable men. Dubbed. **92m/C VHS, Beta.** *IT* Katya Berger, Jean-Pierre Aumont; *D:* Dan Wolman; *W:* Marc Behm; *M:* Ennio Morricone. *FCT, MGM*

Nancy Astor ✶✶ 1982 A portrait of the beautiful, spirited Virginian who became a member of the British Parliament. **55m/C VHS, Beta.** *GB* Lisa Harrow, James Fox, Dan O'Herlihy, Sylvia Syms. *TLF*

Nancy Drew, Reporter ✶✶ 1939 The young sleuth gets to play reporter after winning a newspaper contest. In no time at all, she's involved in a murder mystery. **68m/B VHS, Beta.** Bonita Granville, John Litel, Frankie Thomas Jr., Mary Lee, Sheila Bromley, Betty Amann, Dick Jones, Olin Howlin, Charles Halton; *D:* William Clemens. *HTV, NOS*

Nancy Goes to Rio ✶✶½ 1950 Actresses Powell and Sothern compete for the same part in a play and for the same man. Catch is, they're mother and daughter. Zany consequences ensue. Sothern's last film for MGM. ♫Time and Time Again; Shine On Harvest Moon; Cha Bomm Pa Pa; Yipsee-I-O; Magic is the Moonlight; Musetta's Waltz; Love is Like This; Nancy Goes to Rio. **99m/C VHS.** Ann Sothern, Jane Powell, Barry Sullivan, Carmen Miranda, Louis Calhern, Scotty Beckett, Hans Conried, Glenn Anders; *D:* Robert Z. Leonard; *W:* Sidney Sheldon. *MGM, MLB, CCB*

The Nanny ✶✶½ 1965 Creepfest stars Davis as a seemingly proper nameless nanny who's been accused by her young charge Joey (Dix) of drowning his sister in the bathtub. But it's Joey who's sent away to a home for disturbed children and when he returns two years later (and just why is the nanny still around a childless home?) it's a battle of wills between the duo over who's responsible for some evil goings-on. Based

on a novel by Evelyn Piper. **93m/B VHS, Closed Caption.** *GB* Bette Davis, William Dix, Wendy Craig, Jill Bennett, James Villiers, Pamela Franklin, Jack Watling, Alfred Burke, Maurice Denham; *D:* Seth Holt; *W:* Jimmy Sangster; *C:* Henry Waxman; *M:* Richard Rodney Bennett. *FXV*

Napoleon ✶✶✶✶ 1927 A vivid, near-complete restoration of Gance's epic silent masterpiece about the famed conqueror's early years, from his youth through the Italian Campaign. An innovative, spectacular achievement with its use of multiple split screens, montage, color, and triptychs. Given a gala theatrical re-release in 1981. Remade in 1955. **235m/B VHS, Beta, LV.** *FR* Albert Dieudonne, Antonin Artaud, Pierre Batcheff, Gina Manes, Armand Bernard, Harry Krimer, Albert Bras, Abel Gance, Georges Cahuzac; *D:* Abel Gance; *M:* Carmine Coppola. *USH*

Napoleon ✶✶ 1955 Depicts life story of Napoleon from his days as a soldier in the French army to his exile on the Island of Elba. Falls short of the fantastic 1927 silent classic as it attempts to delve into Napoleon the man, as opposed to his conquests. Some might find it too slow for their tastes. **123m/C VHS, Beta, LV.** *FR* Raymond Pellegrin, Orson Welles, Maria Schell, Yves Montand, Erich von Stroheim, Jean Gabin, Jean-Pierre Aumont; *D:* Sacha Guitry. *NOS, MRV, MPI*

Napoleon ✶✶½ 1996 (G) Cute pic for young kiddies who like animals. A very curious golden retriever puppy named Muffin manages to slip into a balloon-covered basket and finds himself airborne across Australia. Deciding he likes the idea of adventuring, Muffin renames himself Napoleon because it sounds braver. He lands unexpectedly near Sydney Harbor and is befriended by Birdo, who becomes his guide when Napoleon decides he wants to meet his wild dog cousins, the dingoes. And it's off into the bush, with kangaroos, koalas, snakes, and lizards to help or hinder along the way. **81m/C VHS, Closed Caption.** *AU JP D:* Mario Andreacchio; *W:* Mario Andreacchio, Mark Saltzman; *C:* Roger Dowling; *M:* Bill Conti; *V:* Jamie Croft, Philip Quast, Carole Skinner, Anne Lambert, David Argue, Joan Rivers, Steven Vidler, Susan Lyons. *ORI*

Napoleon and Samantha ✶✶✶ 1972 Disney adventure about Napoleon, an orphan (Whitaker), who is befriended by Danny, a college student (Douglas). After the death of his grandfather, Napoleon decides to take Major, his elderly pet lion, and follow Danny, who is herding goats for the summer, across the American northwest mountains and they are joined by Samantha (Foster in her film debut). Worth watching. **91m/C VHS, Beta.** Jodie Foster, Johnny Whitaker, Michael Douglas, Will Geer, Henry Jones; *D:* Bernard McEveety; *W:* Stewart Raffill; *M:* Buddy Baker. Nominations: Academy Awards '72: Best Original Dramatic/Comedy Score.*DIS*

The Narcotics Story woof! 1958 Bad film on the same vein as "Reefer Madness." Originally intended as a police training film, this shows the evils and destruction of heroin addiction. Portrayals of drug addicts are hilarious. **75m/C VHS.** Sharon Strand, Darlene Hendricks, Herbert Crisp, Fred Marratto; *D:* Robert W. Larsen. *SNC, TPV*

The Dreaded Persuasion

The Narrow Margin ✶✶✶ 1952 Well-made, harrowing adventure about a cop who is in charge of transporting a gangster's widow to a trial where she is to testify. On the train he must try to keep her safe from the hit-men who would murder her. A real cat and mouse game—one of the best suspense movies of the '50s. **71m/B VHS.** Charles McGraw, Marie Windsor, Jacqueline White, Queenie Leonard, Gordon Gebert, Don Beddoe, Harry Harvey; *D:* Richard Fleischer. Nominations: Academy Awards '52: Best Story. *TTC, MLB, TTC*

Narrow Margin ✶✶ 1990 (R) Archer reluctantly agrees to testify against the mob after witnessing a murder, and Los Angeles D.A. Hackman is assigned to protect her on the train through the Rockies back to L.A. Bad idea, she finds out. No match for its '52 predecessor. **99m/C VHS, LV, Letterbox, Closed Caption.** Gene Hackman,

Anne Archer, James B. Sikking, J.T. Walsh, M. Emmet Walsh; *D:* Peter Hyams; *W:* Peter Hyams; *M:* Bruce Broughton. *ART*

Narrow Trail ✶✶✶½ 1917 A silent classic that still stands as one of the best Westerns ever made. A tough cowboy with a troubled past hopes a good woman can save him. But she's seen trouble, too. They meet up again in San Francisco's Barbary Coast. A horse race might hold the answer. **56m/B VHS, Beta.** William S. Hart, Sylvia Bremer, Milton Ross; *D:* William S. Hart. *NOS, GPV, CCB*

Nashville ✶✶✶✶ 1975 (R) Altman's stunning, brilliant film tapestry that follows the lives of 24 people during a political campaign/music festival in Nashville. Seemingly extemporaneous vignettes, actors playing themselves (Elliott Gould and Julie Christie), funny, touching, poignant character studies concerning affairs of the heart and despairs of the mind. Repeatedly blurs reality and fantasy. ♫I'm Easy; Two Hundred Years; Keep A'Goin'; One, I Love You; Let Me Be the One; The Day I Looked Jesus in the Eye; For the Sake of the Children; I Never Get Enough; It Don't Worry Me. **159m/C VHS, Beta, LV.** Keith Carradine, Lily Tomlin, Henry Gibson, Ronee Blakley, Keenan Wynn, David Arkin, Geraldine Chaplin, Lauren Hutton, Shelley Duvall, Barbara Harris, Allen (Goorwitz) Garfield, Karen Black, Christina Raines, Michael Murphy, Ned Beatty, Barbara Baxley, Scott Glenn, Jeff Goldblum, Gwen Welles, Bert Remsen, Robert DoQui; *Cameos:* Elliott Gould, Julie Christie; *D:* Robert Altman; *W:* Joan Tewkesbury; *M:* Richard Baskin. Academy Awards '75: Best Song ("I'm Easy"); Golden Globe Awards '76: Best Song ("I'm Easy"); National Board of Review Awards '75: Best Director (Altman), Best Supporting Actress (Blakley); National Film Registry '92;; New York Film Critics Awards '75: Best Director (Altman), Best Film, Best Supporting Actress (Tomlin); National Society of Film Critics Awards '75: Best Director (Altman), Best Film, Best Supporting Actor (Gibson), Best Supporting Actress (Tomlin); Nominations: Academy Awards '75: Best Director (Altman), Best Picture, Best Supporting Actress (Blakley, Tomlin). *PAR*

Nashville Beat ✶✶ 1989 Gang targets the citizens of Nashville, Tennessee, until two tough cops stomp the gang's delusion that Southern folk are easy marks. **110m/C VHS.** Kent McCord, Martin Milner; *D:* Bernard L. Kowalski. *NO*

Nashville Girl ✶ 1976 (R) Innocent country girl who wants to make good in the country music scene, rises to the top of the Nashville success ladder, by compromising everything and hanging out with stereotyped no-goods in the show biz world. It's as good as a yawn. **90m/C VHS, Beta.** Monica Gayle, Johnny Rodriguez; *D:* Gus Trikonis. *NLC*

Country Music Daughter; New Girl in Town

The Nasty Girl ✶✶✶½ 1990 (PG-13) A bright young German model plans to enter a national essay contest on the topic of her hometown's history during the Third Reich. While researching the paper, she's harassed and even brutalized, but refuses to cease her sleuthing. Excellent performances, tight direction, with comedic touches that charmingly imparts an important message. Based on a true story. In German with English subtitles. **93m/C VHS.** *GE* Lena Stolze, Monika Baumgartner, Michael Gahr; *D:* Michael Verhoeven; *W:* Michael Verhoeven. British Academy Awards '91: Best Foreign Film; New York Film Critics Awards '90: Best Foreign Film; Nominations: Academy Awards '90: Best Foreign Language Film. *HBO*

Nasty Habits ✶✶ 1977 (PG) Broad farce depicting a corrupt Philadelphia convent as a satiric parallel to Watergate, with nuns modeled on Nixon, Dean and Mitchell. Includes cameo appearances by various media personalities. Based on the British novel "The Abbess of Crewe" by Muriel Spark. **92m/C VHS, Beta.** *GB* Glenda Jackson, Geraldine Page, Anne Jackson, Melina Mercouri, Sandy Dennis, Susan Penhaligon, Anne Meara, Edith Evans, Rip Torn, Eli Wallach, Jerry Stiller; *Cameos:* Mike Douglas, Bill Jorgensen, Jessica Savitch, Howard K. Smith; *D:* Michael Lindsay-Hogg.

Nasty Hero *🗡½* **1989 (PG-13)** Hard-boiled ex-con comes to Miami to avenge the car thieves who framed him and got him sent to the slammer. This is car-chase scene heaven—little plot or drama. **79m/C VHS, Beta, LV.** Robert Sedgwick, Carlos Palomino, Scott Feraco, Mike Starr, Rosanna DaVon; **D:** Nick Barwood. *COL*

Nasty Rabbit *🗡* *Spies-A-Go-Go* **1964** Ridiculous spoof about Soviet spies intent on releasing a rabbit with a hideous Communist disease into the U.S. Everyone gets in on the chase: Nazi forces, cowboys and Indians, sideshow freaks, banditos—what is the point? **88m/C VHS, Beta.** Arch Hall Jr., Micha Terr, Melissa Morgan, John Akana; **D:** James Landis. *RHI*

Natas ... The Reflection *🗡* **1983 (PG)** A reporter persists in validating an Indian demon myth. **90m/C VHS, Beta.** Randy Mulkey, Pat Bolt, Craig Hensley, Kelli Kuhn. *ART*

Nate and Hayes *🗡🗡½* **1983 (PG)** Set during the mid-1800s in the South Pacific, the notorious real-life swashbuckler Captain "Bully" Hayes ("good pirate") helps young missionary Nate recapture his fiancee from a cutthroat gang of evil slave traders. Entertaining "jolly rogers" film. **100m/C VHS, Beta, LV.** *NZ* Tommy Lee Jones, Michael O'Keefe, Max Phipps, Jenny Seagrove; **D:** Ferdinand Fairfax; **M:** Trevor Jones. *PAR*

A Nation Aflame *🗡½* **1937** Anti-Klan film is based on a story by Thomas L. Dixon, the author of "The Clansman," from which D.W. Griffith made "The Birth of a Nation." In this story, a con man gains control of the state's government through an ultra-nationalistic secret society, and eventually pays for his corruption. **70m/B VHS, Beta.** Lila Lee, Noel Madison, Snub Pollard, Norma Trelvar; **D:** Victor Halperin. *SNC, NOS, GVV*

National Lampoon Goes to the Movies *🗡🗡* **1981** Parodies of popular Hollywood genres, including cop thrillers, melodramas, and inspirational biographies, done in goofy "Lampoon" style. **89m/C VHS.** Robby Benson, Candy Clark, Diane Lane, Christopher Lloyd, Peter Riegert, Richard Widmark, Henny Youngman; **D:** Henry Jaglom. *MOV*

National Lampoon's Animal House *🗡🗡½* *Animal House* **1978 (R)** Classic Belushi vehicle running amuck. Set in 1962 and responsible for launching Otis Day and the Knights and defining cinematic food fights. Every college tradition from fraternity rush week to the homecoming pageant is irreverently and relentlessly mocked in this wild comedy about Delta House, a fraternity on the edge. Climaxes with the homecoming parade from hell. Sophomoric, but very funny, with a host of young stars who went on to more serious work. Remember: "Knowledge is good." **109m/C VHS, Beta, LV, DVD.** John Belushi, Tim Matheson, John Vernon, Donald Sutherland, Peter Riegert, Stephen Furst, Bruce McGill, Mark Metcalf, Verna Bloom, Karen Allen, Tom Hulce, Mary Louise Weller, Kevin Bacon; **D:** John Landis; **W:** Harold Ramis; **M:** Elmer Bernstein. *USH*

National Lampoon's Attack of the 5 Ft. 2 Women *🗡🗡* *Attack of the 5 Ft. 2 Women* **1994 (R)** Brown parodies two of 1994's most notorious tabloid queens in "Tonya: The Battle of Wounded Knee" and "He Never Give Me Orgasm: The Lenora Babbitt Story." Made for cable TV. **CW:** Language and comic sex-related material. **82m/C VHS, Closed Caption.** Julie Brown, Sam McMurray, Adam Storke, Priscilla Barnes, Lauren Tewes, Dick Miller, Rick Overton, Stanley DeSantis, Anne DeSalvo, Liz Torres, Vicki Lawrence, Stella Stevens, Peter DeLuise; **D:** Julie Brown, Richard Wenk; **W:** Julie Brown, Charlie Coffey; **M:** Christopher Tyng. *PAR*

National Lampoon's Christmas Vacation *🗡🗡½* *Christmas Vacation* **1989 (PG-13)** The third vacation for the Griswold family finds them hosting repulsive relatives for Yuletide. The sight gags, although predictable, are sometimes on the mark. Quaid is a standout as the slovenly cousin. **93m/C VHS, Beta, LV, 8mm, Closed Caption.** Chevy Chase, Beverly D'Angelo, Randy Quaid, Diane Ladd, John Randolph, E.G. Marshall, Doris Roberts, Julia Louis-Dreyfus, Mae Questel, William Hickey, Brian Doyle-Murray, Juliette Lewis, Johnny Galecki, Nicholas Guest, Miriam Flynn; **D:** Jeremiah S. Chechik; **W:** John Hughes; **C:** Thomas Ackerman; **M:** Angelo Badalamenti. *WAR*

National Lampoon's Class of '86 *Class of '86* **1986** This is a live stage comedy show written and sponsored by the infamous adult humor magazine, featuring a new cast of comics. **86m/C VHS, Beta.** Rodger Bumpass, Veanne Cox, Annie Golden, John Michael Higgins, Tommy Koenig. *PAR*

National Lampoon's Class Reunion *woof!* *Class Reunion* **1982 (R)** Class reunion with some very wacky guests and a decided lack of plot or purpose. Things go from bad to worse when a crazed killer decides to join in on the festivities. Disappointing with very few laughs. **85m/C VHS, Beta, LV.** Shelley Smith, Gerrit Graham, Michael Lerner; **D:** Michael Miller; **W:** John Hughes; **M:** Peter Bernstein. *PAR, VES*

National Lampoon's Dad's Week Off *🗡🗡* *Dad's Week Off* **1997 (R)** Jack (Winkler) is a stressed-out salesman who decides he needs time away from both his job and his family. His wife agrees to take their kids camping while Jack spends a week peacefully at home. But before he knows it, Jack's bud (Jeni) has introduced him to kooky Cherice (d'Abo) and it's party-time at Jack's place. **CW:** Some sexual content. **92m/C VHS, Closed Caption.** Henry Winkler, Olivia D'Abo, Richard Jeni, Justin Louis, Ken Pogue, Wendel Meldrum; **D:** Neal Israel; **W:** Neal Israel; **C:** Jan Kiesser; **M:** Marc Bonilla. *PAR*

National Lampoon's European Vacation *🗡½* *European Vacation* **1985 (PG-13)** Sappy sequel to "Vacation" that has witless Chase and his family bumbling around in the land "across the pond." The Griswolds nearly redefine the term "ugly American." Stonehenge will never be the same. **94m/C VHS, Beta, LV, 8mm, Closed Caption.** Chevy Chase, Beverly D'Angelo, Dana Hill, Jason Lively, Victor Lanoux, John Astin; **D:** Amy Heckerling; **W:** John Hughes, Robert Klane, Eric Idle; **M:** Charles Fox. *WAR*

National Lampoon's Favorite Deadly Sins *🗡🗡½* **1995 (R)** Three sketches about greed, anger, and lust. In "Lust," Leary plays a security guard who spies on a neighbor; "Anger" finds Clay as an irate convenience store shopper; and Mantegna, in "Greed," stars as a sleazoid producer who helps a young woman kill her wicked stepmother and stepsisters in order to make a movie about it. **CW:** Nudity, strong language, brief violence. **99m/C VHS, Closed Caption.** Joe Mantegna, Denis Leary, Annabella Sciorra, Andrew Dice Clay, Cassidy Rae, Brian Keith, William Ragsdale, Farrah Forke, Tanya Pohlkotte; **D:** Denis Leary, David Jablin; **W:** Michael Barrie, Jim Mulholland, Lee Biondi, Ann Lembeck. *REP*

National Lampoon's Last Resort *🗡½* **1994 (PG-13)** Retired film actor finds his long-time movie nemesis can't separate screen life from the real thing anymore and is planning an invasion of the actor's private island. So, he calls on his nephew (who brings along a friend) to help him out. **91m/C VHS, LV, Closed Caption.** Corey Feldman, Corey Haim, Geoffrey Lewis, Robert Mandan; **D:** Rafal Zielinksi. *THV*

National Lampoon's Loaded Weapon 1 *🗡½* *Loaded Weapon 1* **1993 (PG-13)** Cop Jack Colt (Estevez) and partner Wes Luger (Jackson) attempt to recover a microfilm which contains a formula for turning cocaine into cookies. Essentially a sendup of the popular "Lethal Weapon" series, although other movies and themes make an appearance, well sort of. Short on plot and up on slapstick, but that's the whole point. Tired formula creates nostalgia for the granddaddy of them all, "Airplane." Lots of cameos, including one from sibling spoof star Sheen. The magazine folded while the movie was in production, an ominous sign. **83m/C VHS, LV.** Emilio Estevez, Samuel L. Jackson, Jon Lovitz, Tim Curry, Kathy Ireland, William Shatner; *Cameos:* Dr. Joyce Brothers, James Doohan, Richard Moll, F. Murray Abraham, Denis Leary, Corey Feldman, Phil Hartman, J.T. Walsh, Erik Estrada, Larry Wilcox, Allyce Beasley, Charlie Sheen; **D:** Gene Quintano; **W:** Gene Quintano, Don Holley. *COL, IME*

National Lampoon's Senior Trip *🗡* *Senior Trip* **1995 (R)** According to the promotion, "they came, they saw, they passed out." Good dumb fun is hard to come by, particularly here. Latest lesser "Lampoon" effort in a long line of lesser Lampoons is about midwestern high school seniors who take a bus trip to Washington to meet the President. Along the way they have hijinks, including manipulation by a stereotypically corrupt senator out to embarrass his politcal opponent. Frewer is the inept principal who leads the hopelessly cliched group of misfits through the dopey corridors of power. Somehow, even the Coreys avoided this one. **CW:** Continuous teenage alcohol and drug abuse; crude sexual references. **91m/C VHS, LV, Closed Caption.** Matt Frewer, Valerie Mahaffey, Lawrence Dane, Thomas Chong, Kevin McDonald; **D:** Kelly Makin; **W:** I. Marlene King, Roger Kumble. *NLC*

National Lampoon's The Don's Analyst *🗡🗡* *The Don's Analyst* **1997 (R)** Don Vito (Loggia) has lots of problems—his wife has left him, his sons are too stupid to take over the business, and his mob rival wants both his business and his wife. The Don's so upset he's thinking of going legit. Instead, his sons kidnap therapist Dr. Riceputo (Pollak) to straighten the Don out. **CW:** Language and some nudity. **103m/C VHS, Closed Caption.** Robert Loggia, Kevin Pollak, Joseph Bologna, Angie Dickinson, Sherilyn Fenn; **D:** David Jablin. *PAR*

National Lampoon's Vacation *🗡🗡🗡* *Vacation* **1983 (R)** The Clark Griswold (Chase) family of suburban Chicago embarks on a westward cross-country vacation via car to the renowned "Wally World." Ridiculous and hysterical misadventures, including a falling asleep at the wheel sequence and the untimely death of Aunt Edna. **98m/C VHS, Beta, LV, DVD.** Chevy Chase, Beverly D'Angelo, Imogene Coca, Randy Quaid, Christie Brinkley, James Keach, Anthony Michael Hall, John Candy, Eddie Bracken, Brian Doyle-Murray, Eugene Levy; **D:** Harold Ramis; **W:** John Hughes, Harold Ramis; **M:** Ralph Burns. *WAR*

National Velvet *🗡🗡🗡* **1944 (G)** A young English girl wins a horse in a raffle and is determined to train it to compete in the famed Grand National race. Taylor, only 12 at the time, is superb in her first starring role. Rooney also gives a fine performance. Filmed with a loving eye on lushly decorated sets, this is a masterpiece version of the story of affection between a girl and her pet. Based on the novel by Enid Bagnold and followed by "International Velvet" in 1978. **124m/C VHS, LV, Closed Caption.** Elizabeth Taylor, Mickey Rooney, Arthur Treacher, Donald Crisp, Anne Revere, Angela Lansbury, Reginald Owen, Norma Varden, Jackie "Butch" Jenkins, Terence Kilburn; **D:** Clarence Brown; **W:** Helen Deutsch, Theodore Reeves; **M:** Herbert Stothart. Academy Awards '45: Best Film Editing, Best Supporting Actress (Revere); Nominations: Academy Awards '45: Best Color Cinematography, Best Director (Brown). *MGM, TLF, BTV*

Native Son *🗡🗡½* **1951** A young black man from the ghettos of Chicago is hired as a chauffeur by an affluent white family. His job is to drive their head-strong daughter anywhere she wants to go. Unintentionally, he kills her, tries to hide, and is ultimately found guilty. Based on the classic novel by Richard Wright, who also stars. Remade in 1986. Unprofessional direction and low budget work against the strong story. **91m/B VHS.** Richard Wright, Jean Wallace, Nicholas Joy, Gloria Madison, Charles Cane; **D:** Pierre Chenal. *NOS, XVC, FCT*

Native Son *🗡🗡½* **1986 (R)** This second film adaptation of the classic Richard Wright novel is chock full of stars and tells the story of a poor black man who accidentally kills a white woman and then hides the body. Changes in the script soft-soap some of the novel's disturbing truths and themes—so-so drama for those who have not read the book. **111m/C VHS, Beta, LV, Closed Caption.** Geraldine Page, Oprah Winfrey, Matt Dillon, John Karlen, Elizabeth McGovern, Akosua Busia, Carroll Baker, Victor Love, John McMartin, Art Evans, Willard Pugh, David Rasche; **D:** Jerrold Freedman; **W:** Richard Wesley; **C:** Thomas Burstyn; **M:** James Mtume. *MON, KUI, ART*

Nativity *1978* Unmemorable, made-for-TV portrayal of the romance between Mary and Joseph (of the Bible story), Joseph's response to Mary's pregnancy, and the birthing of Jesus. Not exactly a Bible epic, the direction and acting are uninspired. **97m/C VHS, Beta, Closed Caption.** John Shea, Madeleine Stowe, Jane Wyatt, John Rhys-Davies, Kate O'Mara; **D:** Bernard L. Kowalski. *FOX*

The Natural 🐾🐾🐾 *1984 (PG)* A beautifully filmed movie about baseball as myth. A young man, whose gift for baseball sets him apart, finds that trouble dogs him, particularly with a woman. In time, as an aging rookie, he must fight against his past to lead his team to the World Series, and win the woman who is meant for him. From the Bernard Malamud story. **134m/C VHS, Beta, LV, Letterbox, Closed Caption.** Robert Redford, Glenn Close, Robert Duvall, Kim Basinger, Wilford Brimley, Barbara Hershey, Richard Farnsworth, Robert Prosky, Darren McGavin, Joe Don Baker, Michael Madsen; **D:** Barry Levinson; **C:** Caleb Deschanel; **M:** Randy Newman. Nominations: Academy Awards '84: Best Art Direction/Set Decoration, Best Cinematography, Best Supporting Actress (Close), Best Original Score. *COL*

Natural Born Killers 🐾🐾 *1994 (R)* An old script by (Graphic Screen Violence) Tarantino is resurrected by (Damn the Torpedoes) Stone and invested with its own unique subtle nuance and style. Controversial (natch, considering the director and writer) look at the way the media portrays criminals. Harrelson and Lewis are the lovestruck, white-trash serial killers who become tabloid-TV darlings, thanks to a sensationalistic press led by Downey, Jr. Stone's dark and manic comment on America's fascination and revulsion with violence is strictly of the love it or leave it variety. Bloodshed galore, dazzling photography, and a dynamite soundtrack (with over 75 selections) add up to sensory overload. **CW:** Strong language, extreme violence, graphic carnage, and sexuality. **119m/C VHS, LV, Closed Caption.** Woody Harrelson, Robert Downey Jr., Juliette Lewis, Tommy Lee Jones, Ashley Judd, Tom Sizemore, Rodney Dangerfield, Rachel Ticotin, Arliss Howard, Russell Means, Denis Leary, Steven Wright, Pruitt Taylor Vince; **D:** Oliver Stone; **W:** Oliver Stone; **C:** Robert Richardson; **M:** Trent Reznor. Nominations: Golden Globe Awards '95: Best Director (Stone); MTV Movie Awards '95: Best On-Screen Duo (Woody Harrelson/Juliette Lewis), Best Kiss (Woody Harrelson/Juliette Lewis). *WAR, THV*

Natural Causes 🐾½ *1994 (PG-13)* Muddled political thriller finds Dr. Jessie McCarthy (Purl) traveling to Thailand to visit her estranged mother Rachel (Paige), only to discover she's just been murdered. Then Jessie learns Rachel had a secret life aiding Vietnamese refugees and a scheme is afoot to sabotage a reconciliation treaty between the U.S. and Vietnam. However, none of this makes much sense, though the Bangkok settings provide a pleasant distraction. **90m/C VHS, Closed Caption.** Linda Purl, Cary-Hiroyuki Tagawa, Will Patton, Tim Thomerson, Janis Paige, Ali MacGraw; **D:** James Becket; **W:** Jake Raymond Needham; **C:** Denis Maloney; **M:** Nathan Wang. *COL*

Natural Enemies 🐾🐾½ *1979 (R)* A successful publisher begins to consider suicide and murder as the cure for his family's increasing alienation and despair. Dark and depressing drama. **100m/C VHS, Beta.** Hal Holbrook, Louise Fletcher, Jose Ferrer, Viveca Lindfors; **D:** Jeff Kanew; **W:** Jeff Kanew. *COL*

Natural Enemy 🐾🐾 *1996 (R)* Unsuspecting married couple become the target of a disturbed man with a big secret. Made for cable. **CW:** Violence, some strong sexuality and language. **?m/C VHS.** Donald Sutherland, William McNamara, Lesley Ann Warren, Joe Pantoliano, Tia Carrere; **D:** Douglas Jack-

son; **W:** Kevin Bernhardt; **C:** Rodney Gibbons; **M:** Alan Reeves. *PMH*

The Natural History of Parking Lots 🐾🐾 *1994* What's a rich L.A. father to do when his teenage son hot-wires antique cars for kicks? Why pay his gun-running older brother to keep an eye on him. And the whackiness is just beginning. **92m/C VHS. D:** Everet Lewis. *FCT*

Nature of the Beast 🐾🐾 *1994 (R)* A businessman and a drifter are both hiding deadly secrets as police search for both a serial killer and the million dollars missing in a Vegas casino robbery. Just which man is involved in which crime? **CW:** Hard drug use; a sex scene; strong language; some terror/violence. **91m/C VHS, LV, Closed Caption.** Eric Roberts, Lance Henriksen, Brion James; **D:** Victor Salva; **W:** Victor Salva. *NLC*

Nature's Playmates 🐾 *1962* A beautiful private eye tours Florida nudist camps in search of a missing man with a distinctive tattoo on his posterior. One of H.G. Lewis' obscure "nudie" flicks, sexually tame by modern standards, awful by any standards. **56m/B VHS.** Vicki Miles, Scott Osborne; **D:** Herschell Gordon Lewis. *VDM, TPV*

Naughty Knights 🐾 *Up the Chastity Belt* *1971 (PG)* Soft-core romp in a medieval setting. Toss it in the moat. **56m/B VHS, Beta.** Frankie Howerd, Graham Crowden, Bill Fraser, Roy Hudd, Hugh Paddick, Anna Quayle, Eartha Kitt, Dave King, Fred Emney; **D:** Bob Kellett; **M:** Carl Davis.

Naughty Marietta 🐾🐾½ *1935* A French princess switches identities with a mail-order bride to escape from her arranged marriage, and is captured by pirates. When she's saved by a dashing Indian scout, it's love at first sight. The first MacDonald-Eddy match-up and very popular in its day. ♫ Italian Street Song; Chansonette; Antoinette and Anatole; Prayer; Tramp, Tramp, Tramp; The Owl and the Bobcat; Neath the Southern Moon; Mon Ami Pierrot; Ship Ahoy. **106m/B VHS, Beta, LV.** Jeanette MacDonald, Nelson Eddy, Frank Morgan, Elsa Lanchester, Douglass Dumbrille, Cecilia Parker; **D:** Woodbridge S. Van Dyke; **C:** William H. Daniels. Academy Awards '35: Best Sound; Nominations: Academy Awards '35: Best Picture. *MGM*

The Naughty Nineties 🐾🐾 *1945* Bud and Lou help a showboat owner fend off crooks in the 1890s. Usual slapstick shenanigans, but highlighted by verbal banter. Includes the first on-screen rendition of the classic "Who's on First?" routine. ♫ Rolling Down the River; Uncle Tom's Cabin; I Can't Get You Out of My Mind; On a Sunday Afternoon; I'd Leave My Happy Home for You; Nora Malone; Ma Blushin' Rosie; The Showboat's Comin' to Town; A Blarney from Killarney. **72m/B VHS, Beta.** Bud Abbott, Lou Costello, Henry Travers, Alan Curtis, Joseph Sawyer, Rita Johnson, Joe Kirk, Lois Collier; **D:** Jean Yarbrough. *USH, MLB*

Navajo Blues 🐾🐾 *1997 (R)* Police detective Nicholas Epps is installed in the federal witness protection program after seeing a mob hit on his partner. He's sent to a Native American reservation to hide out until the trial but can't resist investigating a series of local murders. **CW:** Violence and language. **99m/C VHS.** Steven Bauer, Irene Bedard, Charlotte Lewis, Ed O'Ross, Michael Horse, Tom Fridley; **D:** Joey Travolta. *APX*

Navajo Joe 🐾½ *1967* The sole survivor of a massacre single-handedly kills each person involved in the atrocity, and aids a terrorized, though unappreciative, town in the process. Low-budget Spanish-Italian western only worth watching because of Reynolds. Filmed in Spain. **89m/C VHS. IT SP** Burt Reynolds, Aldo Sambrel, Tanya Lopert, Fernando Rey; **D:** Sergio Corbucci; **M:** Ennio Morricone. *MGM*

The Navigator 🐾🐾🐾 *1924* Ever the quick thinker, Keaton actually bought a steamer headed for the scrap heap and used it to film an almost endless string of sight gags. Rejected by a socialite, millionaire Keaton finds himself alone with her on the abandoned boat. As he saves her from

various and sundry perils, the gags and thrills abound—including one stunt that was inspired by a near-accident on the set. Too bad they don't make 'em like this anymore. Silent. **60m/B VHS.** Buster Keaton, Kathryn McGuire, Frederick Vroom, Noble Johnson, Clarence Burton, H. M. Clugston; **D:** Buster Keaton, Donald Crisp. *NO*

The Navigator 🐾🐾🐾 *1988 (PG)* A creative time-travel story of a 14th-century boy with visionary powers who leads the residents of his medieval English village away from a plague by burrowing through the earth's core and into late-20th-century New Zealand. Quite original and refreshing. **92m/C VHS. NZ** Hamish McFarlane, Bruce Lyons, Chris Haywood, Marshall Napier, Noel Appleby, Paul Livingston, Sarah Pierse; **D:** Vincent Ward; **W:** Vincent Ward. Australian Film Institute '88: Best Cinematography, Best Director (Ward), Best Film. *HTV*

Navy Blue and Gold 🐾🐾½ *1937* Three football-playing midshipmen (Young, Stewart, and Brown) at Annapolis share a friendship. Stewart has registered under a false name since his dad was unfairly cashiered from the service. When he hears some slander about his old man he stands up and tells the truth and gets suspended, just before the big game with Army. Naturally, he's reinstated just in time to make the big play and carry the team to victory. Well-done, old-fashioned hokum. **94m/B VHS.** James Stewart, Robert Young, Tom Brown, Lionel Barrymore, Florence Rice, Billie Burke, Samuel S. Hinds, Paul Kelly, Frank Albertson, Minor Watson; **D:** Sam Wood; **W:** George Bruce. *MGM, MOV*

The Navy Comes Through 🐾🐾 *1942* Salty sailors aboard a mangy freighter beat the odds and sink Nazi warships and subs with the greatest of ease. Boy meets girl subplot is added for good measure. Morale booster includes newsreel footage. **81m/B VHS.** Pat O'Brien, George Murphy, Jane Wyatt, Jackie Cooper, Carl Esmond, Max Baer Sr., Desi Arnaz Sr., Ray Collins, Lee Bonnell, Frank Jenks, Helmut Dantine; **D:** Edward Sutherland. *TTC*

Navy SEALS 🐾½ *1990 (R)* A group of macho Navy commandos, whose regular work is to rescue hostages from Middle Eastern underground organizations, finds a stash of deadly weapons. They spend the middle of the movie attempting to destroy the arsenal. Sheen chews the scenery as a crazy member of the commando team. Lots of action and violence, but simplistic good guys-bad guys philosophy and plot weaknesses keep this from being more than below average. **113m/C VHS, Beta, LV, Closed Caption.** Charlie Sheen, Michael Biehn, Joanne Whalley, Rick Rossovich, Cyril O'Reilly, Bill Paxton, Dennis Haysbert, Paul Sanchez, Ron Joseph, Nicholas Kadi; **D:** Lewis Teague; **W:** Gary Goldman; **C:** John A. Alonzo. *ORI*

Navy vs. the Night Monsters woof! *Monsters of the Night* *1966* When horrifying, acid-secreting plant monsters try to take over the world, Van Doren and the Navy must come to the rescue, with the action taking place in a tropical South Pole setting. Amazing deployment of talents. **87m/C VHS.** Mamie Van Doren, Anthony Eisley, Pamela Mason, Bobby Van, Russ Bender; **D:** Michael Hoey; **W:** Michael Hoey. *EEL*

Navy Way 🐾 *1944* Hurriedly produced war propaganda film in which a boxer gets inducted into the Navy just before his title shot. **74m/B VHS.** Robert Lowery, Jean Parker; **D:** William (Lester Williams) Berke, William C. Thomas. *NOS, DVT, HEG*

Nazarin 🐾🐾🐾 *1958* Bunuel's scathing indictment of Christianity finds its perfect vehicle in the adventures of a defrocked priest attempting to relive Christ's life. Gathering a group of disciples, he wanders into the Mexican desert as a cross between Christ and Don Quixote. Filmed in Mexico, this is Bunuel at his grimmest. Based on a novel by Benito Perez Galdos; Spanish with subtitles. **92m/B VHS, Beta, LV. MX** Francesco Rabal, Rita Macedo, Margo Lopez, Rita McLedo, Ignacio Lopez Tarso, Jesus Fernandez; **D:** Luis Bunuel. *FCT, CVC, TPV*

Nea ☑☑½ **1978 (R)** Comic drama about a young girl from a privileged home who writes a best selling pornographic novel anonymously. When her book writing talents are made public through betrayal, she gets even in a most unique way. Subtitled "A Young Emmanuelle." Kaplan also performs. Appealing and sophisticated. 101m/ C VHS, Beta. Sami Frey, Ann Zacharias, Heinz Bennent; **D:** Nelly Kaplan. COL

Near Dark ☑☑☑ **1987 (R)** A farm boy falls in unwillingly with a family of thirsty, outlaw-fringe vampires who roam the West in a van. The first mainstream effort by Bigelow, and a rollicking, blood-saturated, slaughterhouse of a movie, with enough laughs and stunning imagery to revive the genre. 95m/C VHS, Beta, LV. Adrian Pasdar, Jenny Wright, Bill Paxton, Jenette Goldstein, Lance Henriksen, Tim Thomerson, Joshua Miller; **D:** Kathryn Bigelow; **W:** Kathryn Bigelow, Eric Red; **C:** Adam Greenberg; **M:** Tangerine Dream. HBO, IME

Near Misses ☑½ **1991** Missable farce with Reinhold as a bigamist in the foreign service. To make time for a mistress he swaps identities with a young Marine in Paris, but then the KGB kidnaps the imposter. Doors slam in hallways all over the place as the performers crank up the mixups to maximum frenzy, but with little effect since you really don't care much about these fools. 93m/C VHS, Beta, LV. Judge Reinhold, Casey Siemaszko; **D:** Baz Taylor; **W:** Peter Baloff, Dave Wollert. FXV, VTR

Near the Rainbow's End ☑½ **1930** Cattle rancher Steele (in his first talking western) finds out that rustlers are aggravating the trouble between the cattlemen and the sheep herders. So he goes after the bad guys and then settles the feud by marrying a sheep herder's daughter. 57m/ B VHS. Bob Steele, Lafe McKee, Louise Lorraine, Al Ferguson, Al Hewston; **D:** J.P. McGowan. GPV

'Neath Brooklyn Bridge ☑☑ **1942** The Boys from the Bowery get tangled up in crime when they try to help a young girl whose guardian was murdered. 61m/B VHS. Leo Gorcey, Huntz Hall, Bobby Jordan, Sammy Morrison, Ann Gillis, Noah Beery Jr., Marc Lawrence, Gabriel Dell; **D:** Wallace Fox. NOS, MRV, HMV

'Neath Canadian Skies ☑ **1946** Mounted lawman who says "eh" a lot tracks murdering gang of mine looters. 41m/B VHS, Beta, LV, 8mm. CA Russell Hayden, Inez Cooper, Cliff Nazarro, Kermit Maynard, Jack Mulhall. VYY

'Neath the Arizona Skies ☑☑ **1934** Low budget oater epic about a cowhand who finds all the action he and his friends can handle as they try to rescue a young Indian girl (and oil heiress) who has been kidnapped. 'Nuff said. 54m/ B VHS. John Wayne, George "Gabby" Hayes, Sheila Terry; **D:** Harry Fraser. COL, NOS, REP

Necessary Parties **1988** Based on Barbara Dana's book that has a 15-year-old boy filing a lawsuit to stop his parents' divorce. Originally aired on PBS as part of the "Wonderworks" family movie series. 120m/C VHS. Alan Arkin, Mark Paul Gosselaar, Barbara Dana, Adam Arkin, Donald Moffat, Julie Hagerty, Geoffrey Pierson, Taylor Fry; **D:** Gwen Arner. WNE, HMV, FCT

Necessary Roughness ☑☑ **1991 (PG-13)** After losing their NCAA standing, the Texas Southern University (passing for the real Texas State) Armadillos football team looks like it's headed for disaster. The once proud football factory is now composed of assorted goofballs instead of stud players. But hope arrives in the form of a 34-year-old farmer with a golden arm, ready to recapture some lost dreams as quarterback. Can this unlikey team rise above itself and win a game, or will their hopes be squashed all over the field? 108m/C VHS, Beta, LV, Letterbox, Closed Caption. Scott Bakula, Robert Loggia, Harley Jane Kozak, Sinbad, Hector Elizondo, Kathy Ireland, Jason Bateman; **D:** Stan Dragoti; **M:** Bill Conti. PAR

Necromancer: Satan's Servant ☑☑ **1988 (R)** After a woman is brutally raped, she contacts a sorceress and makes a pact with the devil to ensure her successful revenge. Plenty of graphic violence and nudity. 90m/C VHS, Beta, LV. Elizabeth Cayton, Russ Tamblyn, Rhonda Dorton; **D:** Dusty Nelson. MCG, IME

Necropolis ☑ **1987 (R)** A witch burned at the stake 300 years ago is brought back to life as a motorcycle punkette in New York searching for a sacrificial virgin (in New York?). New wave horror should have been watchable. 77m/C VHS, Beta. Leeanne Baker, Michael Conte, Jacquie Fritz, William Reed, Paul Ruben; **D:** Tim Kincaid. ART, VES

Ned Kelly ☑☑½ Ned Kelly, Outlaw **1970 (PG)** Dramatizes the life of Australia's most notorious outlaw. Kelly (Jagger) and his family start off as horse thieves and proceed from there. A manhunt results in death and the eventual capture and execution of Kelly. The very contemporary British Jagger was miscast as a period Australian and British director Richardson seems to have lacked an empathy for the material, given his lethargic direction. 100m/C VHS. GB Mick Jagger, Allen Bickford, Geoff Gilmour, Mark McManus, Serge Lazareff, Peter Sumner, Ken Shorter, James Elliott, Diane Craig, Sue Lloyd, Clarissa Kaye; **D:** Tony Richardson; **W:** Ian Jones, Tony Richardson; **M:** Shel Silverstein. MGM

Needful Things ☑☑½ **1993 (R)** Stephen King film adaptations are becoming as prolific as his novels, though few seem to improve in the transition from page to screen. This time a scheming Maine shopkeeper (Von Sydow) sells unsuspecting small towners peculiar items that, not surprisingly, begin to cause horror and mayhem. Harris is the town sheriff who tries to warn everyone that he's the devil in disguise. Big screen directorial debut for Heston (yes, Charlton's son). 120m/C VHS, LV, Closed Caption. Ed Harris, Bonnie Bedelia, Max von Sydow, Amanda Plummer, J.T. Walsh; **D:** Fraser Heston; **W:** W.D. Richter; **M:** Patrick Doyle. COL

Nefertiti, Queen of the Nile ☑☑ **1964** Woman, married against her will, turns into Nefertiti. For fans of Italo-Biblical epics only. 97m/ C VHS. IT Jeanne Crain, Vincent Price, Edmund Purdom, Amedeo Nazzari, Liana Orfei; **D:** Fernando Cerchio. NO

Negatives ☑☑ **1968** A couple indulge in sexual fantasies to dangerous extremes, with the man first impersonating Dr. Crippen, the early 1900s murderer, and later a WWI flying ace. When a photographer friend joins the fun, the action careens off the deep end. 90m/C VHS. GB Peter McEnery, Diane Cilento, Glenda Jackson, Maurice Denham, Norman Rossington; **D:** Peter Medak. NO

The Negotiator **1998 (R)** Police officer Danny Roman (Jackson) has had his life destroyed by false accusations of theft and murder. So he decides to go after his accusers by taking hostage the chief and staff of the Chicago Internal Affairs Bureau. Hostage negotiator Chris Sabian (Spacey) is brought in to diffuse the situation but, since Roman was a hostage negotiator himself, Sabian's job is going to be very tricky indeed. Not yet reviewed.**CW:** Violence and language. ?m/C VHS. Samuel L. Jackson, Kevin Spacey, David Morse, Ron Rifkin, John Spencer, Regina Taylor, J.T. Walsh; **D:** F. Gary Gray; **W:** James De Monaco, Kevin Fox. NYR

The Neighbor ☑☑½ **1993 (R)** See nice city couple John and Mary move to small town Vermont. See their nice retired obstetrician neighbor Myron welcome them. See Mary get pregnant and Myron take an obsessional interest. See John arrested for murder. See Mary left alone—except for Myron's tender care.**CW:** Violence and terror. 93m/C VHS. Linda Kozlowski, Ron Lea, Rod Steiger, Frances Bay, Bruce Boa, Jane Wheeler; **D:** Rodney Gibbons; **W:** Kurt Wimmer.

Neighbors ☑☑ **1981 (R)** The Keeses (Belushi and Walker) live in a quiet, middle-class suburban neighborhood where life is calm and sweet. But their new neighbors, Ramona and Vic (Ay-

kroyd and Moriarty), prove to be loud, obnoxious, crazy, and freeloading. Will Earl and Enid Keese mind their manners as their neighborhood disintegrates? Some funny moments, but as the script fades, so do the laughs. Belushi's last waltz is based on Thomas Berger's novel. 90m/C VHS, Beta, LV. John Belushi, Dan Aykroyd, Kathryn Walker, Cathy Moriarty; **D:** John G. Avildsen; **W:** Larry Gelbart; **M:** Bill Conti. NO

Neil Simon's The Odd Couple 2 ☑ The Odd Couple 2 **1998 (PG-13)** In the not-too-grand tradition of "Caddyshack II," "Son of the Pink Panther," and "Blues Brothers 2000" they waited too long. And like the others, they shouldn't have even bothered. Oscar (Matthau) and Felix (Lemmon) reunite when their respective kids (Silverman as Oscar's son, Waltz as Felix's daughter) marry. Meeting at LAX, the duo immediately falls into the old routine of annoying each other and, this time out, the audience. Simon fills his script with leftover road movie cliches and vaudeville jokes, leaving Lemmon and Matthau nothing to do but mug and yell. Since almost everything these two have done together since the original has been a de facto sequel, it's a shame that the real thing falls so flat.**CW:** Brief strong language. 96m/C VHS. Jack Lemmon, Walter Matthau, Jonathan Silverman, Lisa Waltz, Christine Baranski, Jean Smart, Barnard Hughes, Doris Belack, Ellen Geer, Jay O. Sanders, Rex Linn, Mary Beth Peil, Alice Ghostley, Rebecca Schull, Florence Stanley, Lou Cutell; **D:** Howard Deutch; **W:** Neil Simon; **C:** Jamie Anderson; **M:** Alan Silvestri. NYR

Nell ☑☑½ **1994 (R)** "Wild child" story—adult version. When illiterate, barely verbal backwoods Nell (Foster) is discovered after her stroke-afflicted mother's death, she's placed in the care of a doctor (Neeson) and psychologist (Richardson) who have different ideas about how to bring her into society. Unfairly dismissed by some as self-indulgent, Foster's raw, physical performance is truly mesmerizing; dull script, unconvincingly tidy ending, and gross over-sentimentality are what disappoint. From the play "Idioglossia" by Mark Handley.**CW:** Rated PG-13 for nudity. 114m/C VHS, Closed Caption. Jodie Foster, Liam Neeson, Natasha Richardson, Richard Libertini; **D:** Michael Apted; **W:** William Nicholson. Screen Actors Guild Award '94: Best Actress (Foster); Nominations: Academy Awards '94: Best Actress (Foster); Golden Globe Awards '95: Best Actress—Drama (Foster), Best Film—Drama, Best Score; MTV Movie Awards '95: Best Female Performance (Foster). FXV

Nelly et Monsieur Arnaud ☑☑☑ Nelly and Mr. Arnaud **1995** Chatty adult May/December would-be romance between 25-year-old secretary Nelly (Beart) and Pierre Arnaud (Serrault), the mid-60s retired magistrate for whom she's working. The arrogant divorced Arnaud is intrigued by the independent Nelly, whom he finds he can't control, while she comes to appreciate their emotional ties (altogether different from the selfishness of the younger men she knows). Conclusion avoids a neat resolution to a situation beset by bad timing. French with subtitles. 105m/C VHS, Letterbox. IT GE FR Emmanuelle Beart, Michel Serrault, Jean-Hugues Anglade, Francoise Brion, Claire Nadeau, Michael Lonsdale, Charles Berling, Michele Laroque; **D:** Claude Sautet; **W:** Jacques Fieschi, Claude Sautet; **C:** Jean-Francois Robin; **M:** Philippe Sarde. Cesar Awards '96: Best Actor (Serrault), Best Director (Sautet); Nominations: British Academy Awards '96: Best Foreign Film; Cesar Awards '96: Best Actress (Beart), Best Film, Best Film Editing, Best Sound, Best Supporting Actor (Anglade, Lonsdale), Best Supporting Actress (Nadeau), Best Writing, Best Score. NYF

Nemesis ☑½ **1993 (R)** Futuristic thriller that combines cybernetics and cyborgs in post-nuclear Los Angeles. Gruner plays a human (although he's mostly composed of mechanical replacement parts) in a world overwrought with system cowboys, information terrorists, bio-enhanced gangsters, and cyborg outlaws. Film's biggest flaw is the extremely confusing script that makes no attempt at logic whatsoever. Special visual effects are good despite the obviously low f/x budget. **CW:** Strong futuristic violence. **95m/C VHS, LV, Letterbox, Closed Caption.** Olivier Gruner, Tim Thomerson, Cary-Hiroyuki Tagawa, Merele Kennedy, Yuji Okumoto, Marjorie Monaghan, Nicholas Guest, Vincent Klyn; **D:** Albert Pyun; **W:** Rebecca Charles; **M:** Michael Rubini. IMP, UND

Nemesis 2: Nebula 🎬½ **1994 (R)** Cyborg goes on a rampage across time with a superhuman in pursuit. **CW:** Sci-fi violence. **83m/C VHS.** Sue Price, Tina Cote, Earl White, Jahi JJ Zuri, Traci Davis; **D:** Albert Pyun. IMP

Nemesis 3: Time Lapse 🎬½ Nemesis 3: Prey Harder **1996 (R)** Superhuman mutant Alex is the last hope for mankind as the cyborgs once again prepare to destroy civilization. **CW:** Sci-fi violence and language. **90m/C VHS.** Sue Price, Tim Thomerson, Norbert Weisser, Xavier DeClie, Sharon Bruneau, Debbie Muggli; **D:** Albert Pyun; **W:** Albert Pyun; **C:** George Mooradian; **M:** Tony Riparetti. IMP

Nenette and Boni 🎬🎬🎬 **1996** Boni (Colin) is a 19-year-old pizza chef in Marseilles who likes to have sexual fantasies about the local baker's sensuous wife (Bruni-Tedeschi). His life is basically carefree until his pregnant, rebellious 15-year-old sister Nenette (Houri) shows up at his door, having run away from school. Nenette really doesn't want to deal with the pregnancy until Boni forces her to do so and, just to make the teens lives more complicated, their estranged small-time gangster dad (Nolot) has learned about Nenette's condition and wants to help her out. Fine performances. French with subtitles. **103m/C VHS, Letterbox.** FR Gregoire Colin, Alice Houri, Valeria Bruni-Tedeschi, Jacques Nolot, Vincent Gallo; **D:** Claire Denis; **W:** Claire Denis, Jean-Pol Fargeau; **C:** Agnes Godard. Nominations: Independent Spirit Awards '98: Best Foreign Language Film. NYF

The Neon Bible 🎬🎬 **1995** Beautifully crafted, yet thin telling of the struggles of a rural family in 1940s Georgia. The stories unfold in a series of flashbacks, as a 15-year-old boy travels alone on a train, reflecting on his dysfunctional early adolescence. An abusive father (Leary) who dies in the war, suicidal mom (Scarwid), and ex-showgirl visiting aunt (Rowlands) provide plenty of opportunities for familial angst. Starts out strong, with some stunning scenes sprinkled throughout, but director Davies never ventures far from the narrative territory he's covered thoroughly in his other films ("Distant Voices, Still Lives" and "The Long Day Closes"). Adapted from the novel by Pulitzer Prize winning author John Kennedy Toole. **92m/C VHS.** Gena Rowlands, Jacob Tierney, Diana Scarwid, Drake Bell, Denis Leary, Leo Burmester, Frances Conroy, Peter McRobbie, Joan Glover, Dana Dick, Virgil Graham Hopkins; **D:** Terence Davies; **W:** Terence Davies; **C:** Michael Coulter. FXL

Neon City 🎬🎬 **1991 (R)** Title refers to a rumored city of refuge in the year 2053, where eight misfit adventurers in an armored transport seek safety from the Earth's toxic environment and "Mad Max" cliches. **CW:** Violence. **99m/C VHS, Closed Caption.** Michael Ironside, Vanity, Lyle Alzado, Valerie Wildman, Nick Klar, Juliet Landau, Arsenio "Sonny" Trinidad, Richard Sanders; **D:** Monte Markham. THV

The Neon Empire 🎬½ **1989 (R)** Tepid tale of two gangsters battling inner mob opposition and backstabbing to build Las Vegas. Ostensibly based on the story of Bugsy Siegel and Meyer Lansky. Made for cable. **120m/C VHS, Beta, LV.** Martin Landau, Ray Sharkey, Gary Busey, Harry Guardino, Julie Carmen, Linda Fiorentino, Dylan McDermott; **D:** Larry Peerce; **W:** Pete Hamill.

Neon Maniacs woof! **1986 (R)** An even half-dozen fetish-ridden zombies stalk the streets at night, tearing their victims into teensy weensy bits. Brave teenagers try to stop the killing. Brave viewers will stop the tape. **90m/C VHS, Beta.** Allan Hayes, Leilani Sarelle Ferrer, Bo Sabato, Donna Locke, Victor Elliot Brandt; **D:** Joseph Mangine. ART, VES

Neptune Factor 🎬 The Neptune Disaster; An Underwater Odyssey **1973 (G)** Scientists board a special new deep-sea sub to search for their colleagues lost in an undersea earthquake. Diving ever deeper into the abyss that swallowed their friend's Ocean Lab II, they end up trapped themselves. The plot's many holes sink it. **94m/C VHS, Beta, Closed Caption.** Ben Gazzara, Yvette Mimieux, Walter Pidgeon, Ernest Borgnine; **D:** Daniel Petrie; **W:** Jack DeWitt. FOX

Neptune's Daughter 🎬🎬 **1949** A swim-happy bathing suit designer finds romance and deep pools of studio water to dive into. Typically lavish and ridiculous Williams aqua-parade. ♫Baby It's Cold Outside; I Love Those Men; My Heart Beats Faster. **92m/C VHS, Beta, LV, Closed Caption.** Esther Williams, Red Skelton, Ricardo Montalban, Betty Garrett, Keenan Wynn, Xavier Cugat, Ted de Corsia, Mike Mazurki, Mel Blanc, Juan Duvall, George Mann, Joi Lansing; **D:** Edward Buzzell; **C:** Charles Rosher. Academy Awards '49: Best Song ("Baby It's Cold Outside"). MGM

Nerolio 🎬🎬 **1996** Three imagined episodes depicting the final months of an unnamed poet/director (Cavicchioli), who is actually based on homosexual writer/filmmaker Pier Paolo Pasolini. The contradictory, hypocritical, aging Poet is shown buying sex, while extolling the virtues of male beauty in voiceover, and as the maker of his own doom (Pasolini was murdered in 1975). "Nerolio" is a contraction of "nero" (black) and "Petrolio" (oil), which refers to Pasolini's posthumous novel "Petrolio." Italian with subtitles. **82m/B VHS.** IT Marco Cavicchioli, Vincenzo Crivello, Salvatore Lazzaro; **D:** Aurelio Grimaldi; **W:** Aurelio Grimaldi; **C:** Maurizio Calvesi; **M:** Maria Soldatini. CCN

Nervous Ticks 🎬🎬½ **1993 (R)** Ninety minutes in the life of airline employee York Daley. All he needs to do is get off work, go home, grab his luggage, pick up his married girlfriend, and get back to the airport for a flight to Rio De Janeiro. Simple, right? Not in this movie. **95m/C VHS, Closed Caption.** Bill Pullman, Julie Brown, Peter Boyle, James LeGros, Brent Jennings; **D:** Rocky Lang; **W:** David Frankel. COL

The Nervous Wreck 🎬🎬🎬 **1926** Harrison Ford (not the one from "Indiana Jones") heads West, seeking a cure for what he believes is a terminal illness. Once there, he becomes romantically entangled with the sheriff's fiancee, uses a wrench to hold up a gas station, and gets involved in other shenanigans. And then he discovers he's going to live after all. **70m/B VHS, Beta.** Harrison Ford, Phyllis Haver, Chester Conklin, Mack Swain, Hobart Bosworth, Charles Gerrard; **D:** Scott Sidney. NO

The Nest 🎬🎬½ **1980** Tragic romance of an elderly man and a 13-year-old girl is helped along by superior script and directing. **109m/C VHS, Beta.** SP Ana Torrent, Hector Alterio, Patricia Adriani; **D:** Jaime de Arminan. Nominations: Academy Awards '80: Best Foreign Language Film.

The Nest 🎬🎬½ **1988 (R)** A small island is overcome by giant cockroaches created by, you guessed it, a scientific experiment gone wrong. Special effects make it watchable. **89m/C VHS, Beta.** Robert Lansing, Lisa Langlois, Franc Luz, Terri Treas, Stephen Davies, Diana Bellamy, Nancy Morgan; **D:** Terence H. Winkless; **W:** Robert King; **M:** Rick Conrad. MGM

The Nesting 🎬½ **1980 (R)** Too-long tale of a neurotic author who rents a haunted Victorian manor and finds herself a pawn in a ghostly plan for revenge. Features Grahame's last performance. **104m/C VHS, Beta.** Robin Groves, John Carradine, Gloria Grahame, Christopher Loomis, Michael Lally; **D:** Armand Weston; **C:** Joao Fernandes. WAR

The Net 🎬🎬½ **1995 (PG-13)** The ever-spunky Bullock gets stuck behind a computer screen rather than the wheel of a bus as reclusive computer systems analyst Angela Bennett. She's puzzled by a mysterious Internet program, which Angela finds can easily access highly classified databases. It's soon apparent that someone knows she knows because every record of her

identity has been erased and the conspirators decide to take care of one last detail by eliminating her as well. Miller's the ex who turns to for help and Northam's a seductive British hacker. Techno paranoia. **CW:** Violence, some sexuality, brief strong language. **114m/C VHS, LV, 8mm, Closed Caption, DVD.** Sandra Bullock, Jeremy Northam, Dennis Miller, Diane Baker, Ken Howard, Wendy Gazelle, Ray McKinnon; **D:** Irwin Winkler; **W:** John Brancato, Michael Ferris; **C:** Jack N. Green; **M:** Mark Isham. COL

Netherworld 🎬½ **1990 (R)** A young man investigating his mysterious, dead father travels to his ancestral plantation in the bayou. To his horror, he discovers that his father was involved in the black arts. Now two beautiful young witches are after him. Can he possibly survive this madness? **CW:** Language, strong horror violence, and strong sensuality. **87m/C VHS, LV, Closed Caption.** Michael C. Bendetti, Denise Gentile, Anjanette Comer, Holly Floria, Robert Burr, Robert Sampson; **D:** David Schmoeller; **W:** Billy Chicago; **C:** Adolfo Bartoli; **M:** Edgar Winter. FLL

Network 🎬🎬🎬½ **1976 (R)** As timely now as it was then; a scathing indictment of the television industry and its propensity towards self-prostitution. A television newscaster's mental breakdown turns him into a celebrity when the network tries to profit from his illness. The individual characters are startlingly realistic and the acting is excellent. **121m/C VHS, Beta, LV.** Faye Dunaway, Peter Finch, William Holden, Robert Duvall, Wesley Addy, Ned Beatty, Beatrice Straight; **D:** Sidney Lumet; **W:** Paddy Chayefsky; **C:** Owen Roizman. Academy Awards '76: Best Actor (Finch), Best Actress (Dunaway), Best Original Screenplay; British Academy Awards '77: Best Actor (Finch); Golden Globe Awards '77: Best Actor—Drama (Finch), Best Actress—Drama (Dunaway), Best Director (Lumet), Best Screenplay; Los·Angeles Film Critics Association Awards '76: Best Director (Lumet), Best Film; New York Film Critics Awards '76: Best Screenplay; Writers Guild of America '76: Best Original Screenplay; Nominations: Academy Awards '76: Best Actor (Holden), Best Cinematography, Best Director (Lumet), Best Film Editing, Best Picture, Best Supporting Actor (Beatty). MGM, BTV

Neurotic Cabaret 🎬½ **1990** Would-be actress dances exotically and finds more exotic ways to roll in dough. **90m/C VHS.** Edwin Neal, Tammy Stone.

Neutron and the Black Mask 🎬 **1961** Man wears mask with lightning bolts and gains comic book style powers to do deathly battle with a scientist with a neutron bomb up his sleeve. First Neutron feature. **80m/B VHS.** MX Wolf Ruvinskis, Julio Aleman, Armando Silvestre, Rosita Arenas, Claudio Brook; **D:** Frederick Curiel. SNC

Neutron vs. the Amazing Dr. Caronte 🎬 **1961** Dr. Caronte from "Neutron and the Black Mask" just won't give up that neutron bomb and let the series die. **80m/B VHS.** MX Wolf Ruvinskis, Julio Aleman, Armando Silvestre, Rosita Arenas, Rodolfo Landa; **D:** Frederick Curiel. SNC

Neutron vs. the Death Robots 🎬 **1962** Guy with a mask takes on army of killer robots and neutron bomb to protect the world from future sequels. **80m/B VHS.** MX Wolf Ruvinskis, Julio Aleman, Armando Silvestre, Rosita Arenas; **D:** Frederick Curiel. SNC

Neutron vs. the Maniac 🎬 **1962** Man in mask hunts guys who kill people. **80m/B VHS.** MX Wolf Ruvinskis. SNC

Nevada 🎬🎬½ **1927** Entertaining silent western with a great cast finds gunslinger Cooper running from the law and winding up on a ranch where he falls for Todd, the rancher's daughter. Naturally, Cooper redeems himself by going after a gang of cattle rustlers, led by Powell. Based on a novel by Zane Grey. **67m/B VHS.** Gary Cooper, Thelma Todd, William Powell, Ernie Adams, Philip Strange; **D:** John Waters. GPV

Nevada 🎬🎬½ **1944** Cowpoke Mitchum is mistaken for the killer of a homesteader and narrowly escapes the rope by finding the real killer. First leading role for Mitchum as the tough but laconic hero. Based on a story by Zane Grey. 62m/B VHS. Robert Mitchum, Anne Jeffreys, Nancy Gates, Craig Reynolds, Guinn "Big Boy" Williams, Richard Martin, Harry Woods; **D:** Edward Killy. **GPV**

Nevada City 🎬½ 1941 Roy outwits a financier who is trying to monopolize transportation in California. 54m/B VHS, Beta. Roy Rogers. **VCN**

Nevada Smith 🎬🎬 1966 The half-breed Nevada Smith (previously introduced in Harold Robbins' story "The Carpetbaggers" and film of same name) seeks the outlaws who killed his parents. Standard western plot, characters. Later remade as a TV movie. 135m/C VHS, Beta, LV. Steve McQueen, Karl Malden, Brian Keith, Arthur Kennedy, Raf Vallone, Suzanne Pleshette; **D:** Henry Hathaway; **W:** John Michael Hayes. **PAR**

The Nevadan 🎬½ *The Man From Nevada* 1950 A marshal goes in search of an outlaw's gold cache, only to be opposed by a crooked rancher. Good scenery and action, but not one of Scott's best. 81m/C VHS, Beta. Randolph Scott, Dorothy Malone, Forrest Tucker, Frank Faylen, George Macready, Charles Kemper, Jeff Corey, Tom Powers, Jock Mahoney; **D:** Gordon Douglas. **GKK**

Never a Dull Moment 🎬🎬 1950 New York songwriter falls for rodeo Romeo, moves out West, and finds welcome wagon deficient. Mediocre songs; many dull moments. 🎵Once You Find Your Guy; Sagebrush Lullaby; The Man With the Big Felt Hat. 89m/B VHS. Irene Dunne, Fred MacMurray, William Demarest, Andy Devine, Gigi Perreau, Natalie Wood, Philip Ober, Jack Kirkwood, Ann Doran, Margaret Gibson; **D:** George Marshall. **TTC, FCT**

Never a Dull Moment 🎬🎬 1968 (G) Mobsters mistake an actor for an assassin in this gag-filled adventure. They threaten the thespian into thievery, before the trouble really starts when Ace, the actual assassin, arrives. 90m/C VHS, Beta, LV. Dick Van Dyke, Edward G. Robinson, Dorothy Provine, Henry Silva, Joanna Moore, Tony Bill, Slim Pickens, Jack Elam; **D:** Jerry Paris; **W:** A.J. Carothers; **M:** Robert F. Brunner. **DIS**

Never Cry Wolf 🎬🎬🎬½ 1983 (PG) A young biologist is sent to the Arctic to study the behavior and habitation of wolves, then becomes deeply involved with their sub-society. Based on Farley Mowat's book. Beautifully photographed. 105m/C VHS, Beta, LV. Charles Martin Smith, Brian Dennehy, Samson Jorah; **D:** Carroll Ballard; **W:** Curtis Hanson, Sam Hamm. National Society of Film Critics Awards '83: Best Cinematography; Nominations: Academy Awards '83: Best Sound. **DIS**

Never Forget 🎬🎬 1991 Made-for-cable-TV true story of California resident Mel Mermelstein (played by Nimoy), a survivor of Hitler's death camps who accepted a pro-Nazi group's challenge to prove in court that the Holocaust of six million Jews really happened. A sincere, well-meaning courtroom drama that just can't surmount the uncinematic nature of the source material. 94m/C VHS, Beta, Closed Caption. Leonard Nimoy, Blythe Danner, Dabney Coleman; **D:** Joseph Sargent; **M:** Henry Mancini. **TTC**

Never Give a Sucker an Even Break 🎬🎬🎬½ *What a Man* 1941 An almost plotless comedy, based on an idea reputedly written on a napkin by Fields (he took screenplay credit as Otis Criblecoblis), and features Fields at his most unleashed. It's something of a cult favorite, but not for all tastes. Classic chase scene ends it. Fields' last role in a feature-length film. 71m/B VHS, Beta, LV. W.C. Fields, Gloria Jean, Franklin Pangborn, Leon Errol, Margaret Dumont; **D:** Eddie Cline. **USH, BAR**

Never Let Go 🎬🎬 1960 A man unwittingly tracks down the mastermind of a gang of racketeers. Sellers sheds his comedic image to play the ruthless and brutal gang boss, something he shouldn't have done. 91m/C VHS, Beta. GB Peter Sellers, Richard Todd, Elizabeth Sellars, Carol White; **D:** John Guillermin; **M:** John Barry.

Never Let Me Go 🎬🎬½ 1953 Implausible yet entertaining account of American newsman Gable trying to smuggle ballerina wife Tierney out of Russia. Hard to believe Gable as a one-man assault force infiltrating Russia, but enjoyable nonetheless. Based on the novel "Came the Dawn" by Roger Bax. 94m/B VHS. Clark Gable, Gene Tierney, Richard Haydn, Bernard Miles, Kenneth More, Karel Stepanek, Theodore Bikel; **D:** Delmer Daves; **W:** Ronald Millar, George Froeschel. **MGM**

Never Love a Stranger 🎬🎬 1958 A young man becomes a numbers runner for a mobster and ultimately winds up heading his own racket. Later he finds himself in conflict with his old boss and the district attorney. No surprises here. Based on the Harold Robbins' novel. 93m/B VHS. John Blythe Barrymore Jr., Steve McQueen, Lita Milan, Robert Bray; **D:** Robert Stevens. **REP**

Never on Sunday 🎬🎬🎬 1960 An American intellectual tries to turn a Greek prostitute into a refined woman. Fine performances and exhilarating Greek photography. Fun all around. 🎵Never on Sunday. 91m/B VHS, Beta. GR Melina Mercouri, Titos Vandis, Jules Dassin, Mitsos Liguisos; **D:** Jules Dassin; **W:** Jules Dassin; **M:** Manos Hadjidakis. Academy Awards '60: Best Song ("Never on Sunday"); Cannes Film Festival '60: Best Actress (Mercouri); Nominations: Academy Awards '60: Best Actress (Mercouri), Best Costume Design (B & W), Best Director (Dassin), Best Story & Screenplay. **MGM, HMV**

Never on Tuesday 🎬½ 1988 (R) Two jerks from Ohio head to California and find themselves stuck midway in the desert with a beautiful girl, who has plans of her own. 90m/C VHS, Beta, LV, Closed Caption. Claudia Christian, Andrew Lauer, Peter Berg; **Cameos:** Charlie Sheen, Emilio Estevez; **D:** Adam Rifkin; **W:** Adam Rifkin. **PAR**

Never Pick Up a Stranger 🎬½ *Bloodrage* 1979 When a local hooker is murdered, her cop boyfriend, who never gives up on a case, hunts her killer with a vengeance. Extremely graphic. 82m/C VHS, Beta. Ian Scott, Judith-Marie Bergan, James Johnston, Lawrence Tierney; **D:** Joseph Bigwood. **ART, BFV**

Never Say Die 🎬½ 1990 Two innocents are thrown into a web of international intrigue and acquit themselves rather well. Lots of explosions and car crashes for a film shot in New Zealand. 98m/C VHS, Beta. NZ George Wendt, Lisa Eilbacher; **D:** Geoff Murphy. **JTC**

Never Say Die 🎬🎬 1994 (R) Ex-Special Forces soldier John Blake (Zagarino), ambushed and left to die, returns to seek vengeance on the renegade commander who betrayed him. And he has the perfect opportunity when his nemesis kidnaps a general's daughter. **CW:** Violence, language. 99m/C VHS, LV, Closed Caption. Frank Zagarino, Billy Drago, Todd Jensen, Jennifer Miller, Robin Smith; **D:** Yossi Wein; **W:** Jeff Albert; **M:** Wendy Oldfield, Adrian Levy. **TTC, NLC**

Never Say Goodbye 🎬🎬 1946 Cliche-ridden story about a man trying to win back his divorce-bound wife. Flynn tries hard, but the material just isn't up to par. Based on the story "Don't Ever Leave Me" by Ben and Norma Barzman. Co-screenwriter Diamond later became famous when he teamed up with Billy Wilder to script "Some Like it Hot" and "The Apartment." 97m/B VHS. Errol Flynn, Eleanor Parker, Lucile Watson, S.Z. Sakall, Forrest Tucker, Donald Woods, Peggy Knudsen, Tom D'Andrea, Hattie McDaniel; **D:** James V. Kern; **W:** James V. Kern, I.A.L. Diamond, Lewis R. Foster. **MGM**

Never Say Never Again 🎬🎬½ 1983 (PG) James Bond matches wits with a charming but sinister tycoon who is holding the world nuclear hostage as part of a diabolical plot by SPECTRE. Connery's return to the world of Bond after 12 years is smooth in this remake of "Thunderball" hampered by an atrocious musical score. Carrera is stunning as Fatima Blush. Although Connery is back, purists will have qualms considering this part of the "official" Bond series since

longtime Bond producer, Albert "Cubby" Broccoli, had nothing to do with this endeavor. 134m/C VHS, Beta, LV, Closed Caption. Sean Connery, Klaus Maria Brandauer, Max von Sydow, Barbara Carrera, Kim Basinger, Edward Fox, Bernie Casey, Pamela Salem, Rowan Atkinson, Valerie Leon, Prunella Gee, Saskia Cohen Tanugi; **D:** Irvin Kershner. **WAR, TLF**

Never So Few 🎬🎬½ 1959 A military commander and his outnumbered troops overcome incredible odds against the Japanese. There is a lot of focus on romance, but the script and acting make a strong impression nonetheless. Based on the novel by Tom T. Chamales. 124m/C VHS, LV, Letterbox. Frank Sinatra, Gina Lollobrigida, Peter Lawford, Steve McQueen, Richard Johnson, Paul Henreid, Charles Bronson; **D:** John Sturges; **C:** William H. Daniels. **MGM**

Never Steal Anything Small 🎬½ 1959 A tough union boss pushes everyone as he battles the mob for control of the waterfront. A strange musical-drama combination that will be of interest only to the most ardent Cagney and Jones fans. Based on the Maxwell Anderson/ Rouben Mamoulian play "The Devil's Hornpipe." Largely forgettable songs. 🎵I'm Sorry, I Want a Ferrari; I Haven't Got a Thing to Wear; It Takes Love to Make a Home; Never Steal Anything Small; Helping Out Friends. 94m/C VHS, Beta. James Cagney, Shirley Jones, Cara Williams; **D:** Charles Lederer; **M:** Henry Mancini. **USH**

Never Talk to Strangers 🎬🎬 1995 (R) Sarah Taylor (DeMornay) is an uptight criminal psychologist who gets involved with handsome stranger Tony Ramirez (Banderas) while working on the case of a serial killer (Stanton). Then Sarah finds herself the target of an increasingly malevolent stalker—and she has lots of suspects to choose from. Typical woman-in-peril film with equally standard frights but the leads certainly look good (and Banderas is a fine sex object in a bit of role reversal). Filmed in Toronto. **CW:** Violence, language and some strong graphic sexuality. 86m/C VHS, LV, Closed Caption. Rebecca DeMornay, Antonio Banderas, Harry Dean Stanton, Dennis Miller, Len Cariou, Beau Starr; **D:** Peter Hall; **W:** Lewis Green, Jordan Rush; **C:** Elemer Ragaly; **M:** Pino Donaggio. **COL**

Never Too Late to Mend 🎬🎬 1937 Victorian British play about the abuses of the penal system which had, upon its initial London West End run, caused Queen Victoria to institute a sweeping program of prison reform. The movie caused considerably less stir. 67m/B VHS, Beta, 8mm. GB Tod Slaughter, Marjorie Taylor, Jack Livesey, Ian Colin; **D:** David MacDonald. **VYY, MRV, SNC**

Never Too Young to Die 🎬 1986 (R) A young man is drawn into a provocative espionage adventure by his late father's spy associates. Together they try to discover who killed the young man's father. High point may be Simmons as a crazed hermaphrodite plotting to poison L.A. 97m/C VHS, Beta, LV, Closed Caption. John Stamos, Vanity, Gene Simmons, George Lazenby; **D:** Gil Bettman; **W:** Gil Bettman; **M:** James Newton Howard, Lennie Niehaus. **COL, NLC**

Never Wave at a WAC 🎬🎬½ *The Private Wore Skirts* 1952 A Washington socialite joins the Women's Army Corps hoping for a commission that never comes. She has to tough it out as an ordinary private. A reasonably fun ancestor of "Private Benjamin," with a cameo by Gen. Omar Bradley as himself. 87m/B VHS. Rosalind Russell, Paul Douglas, Marie Wilson, William Ching, Arleen Whelan, Leif Erickson, Hillary Brooke, Regis Toomey; **Cameos:** Omar Bradley; **D:** Norman Z. McLeod; **M:** Elmer Bernstein. **NOS, DVT, HEG**

Never Weaken/Why Worry? 🎬🎬🎬 1923 Silent comedy shorts from Harold. In "Never Weaken" (1921), Lloyd hustles customers. In "Why Worry?" (1923), he plays a wealthy young man who journeys to South America for his health and gets caught in the middle of a revolution. 78m/ B VHS, Beta. Harold Lloyd. **TLF**

The NeverEnding Story 🎬🎬½ **1984**
(PG) A lonely young boy helps a warrior save the fantasy world in his book from destruction by the Nothing. A wonderful, intelligent family movie about imagination, with swell effects and a sweet but not overly sentimental script. Petersen's first English-language film, based on the novel by Michael Ende. **94m/C VHS, Beta, LV, 8mm, Letterbox, Closed Caption.** Barret Oliver, Noah Hathaway, Gerald McRaney, Moses Gunn, Tami Stronach, Patricia Hayes, Sydney Bromley; **D:** Wolfgang Petersen; **W:** Wolfgang Petersen; **M:** Klaus Doldinger, Giorgio Moroder. *WAR, GLV, HMV*

NeverEnding Story 2: The Next Chapter 🎬🎬 **1991 (PG)** Disappointing sequel to the first story that didn't end. Boy Oliver staves off life of couch potatodom reading books and escaping into fantasy land. Even the kids may wander away. But wait: contains the first Bugs Bunny theatrical cartoon in 26 years, "Box Office Bunny." **90m/C VHS, LV, 8mm, Letterbox, Closed Caption.** Jonathan Brandis, Kenny Morrison, Clarissa Burt, John Wesley Shipp, Martin Umbach; **D:** George Miller; **C:** David Connell; **M:** Robert Folk. *WAR*

The NeverEnding Story 3: Escape from Fantasia 🎬🎬 **1994 (G)** The third time was not the charm in this case. Bastian, on the edge of puberty, is being bullied by a group at school called the Nasties. He seeks refuge in the library and enters the world of Fantasia through the "Neverending Story" tome. When the book is stolen by the Nasties, it is up to Bastian to return it. Unfortunately, the story does not have the charm of the original, trying to incorporate too much reality and not enough of dreamland. **95m/C VHS, Closed Caption.** Jason James Richter, Melody Kay, Freddie Jones, Jack Black, Ryan Bollman, Tracey Ellis, Kevin McNulty; **D:** Peter Macdonald; **C:** Robin Vidgeon; **M:** Peter Wolf. *TOU*

Nevil Shute's The Far Country 🎬🎬½ *The Far Country* **1985** Carl Zlintner (York), once a doctor in Hitler's army, escapes to Australia from postwar Europe to begin a new life with a new identity. Falling in love with the beautiful Jennifer Morton (Thornton), Carl hopes he's left his past behind. But nothing is every that simple. Made-for-television adaptation of the Shute novel. **120m/C VHS, Beta.** *AU* Michael York, Sigrid Thornton; **D:** George Miller. *NO*

The New Adventures of Pippi Longstocking 🎬½ **1988 (G)** Decent cast is trapped in another musical rehashing of the Astrid Lindgren children's books about a precocious redheaded girl and her fantastic adventures with horses, criminals, and pirates. **100m/C VHS, Beta, LV, Closed Caption.** Tami Erin, Eileen Brennan, Dennis Dugan, Dianne Hull, George DiCenzo, John Schuck, Dick Van Patten; **D:** Ken Annakin; **W:** Ken Annakin. *COL, TVC*

The New Adventures of Tarzan *Tarzan and the Green Goddess* **1935** Twelve episodes, each 22 minutes long, depict the adventures of Edgar Rice Burrough's tree-swinging character—Tarzan. **260m/B VHS, Beta.** Bruce (Herman Brix) Bennett, Ula Holt, Frank Baker, Dale Walsh, Lewis Sargent; **D:** Edward Kull. *SNC, NOS, VCN*

The New Age 🎬🎬 **1994 (R)** Illusions in L.A. centering on talent agent Peter (Weller) and art designer Katherine (Davis) Witner. Katherine loses her job the same day Peter decides to quit his and suddenly the caustic duo are dependent upon each other. The trendy couple decide to open a boutique and quickly find themselves in a fiscal sinkhole and on a downhill slide. The acting is fine but the story is empty. **CW:** Sexuality; language; nudity. **106m/C VHS, LV, Closed Caption.** Peter Weller, Judy Davis, Adam West, Patrick Bauchau, Corbin Bernsen, Jonathan Hadary, Samuel L. Jackson, Patricia Heaton, Audra Lindley, Paula Marshall, Maureen Mueller, Bruce Ramsay, Sandra Seacat, Susan Traylor; **D:** Michael Tolkin; **W:** Michael Tolkin, Mark Mothersbaugh. *WAR*

The New Centurions 🎬🎬½ **1972 (R)** Rookies training for the Los Angeles Police Department get the inside info from retiring cops. Gritty and realistic drama based on the novel by former cop Joseph Wambaugh. Tends to be disjointed at times, but overall is a good adaptation of the bestseller. Scott, excellent as the retiring beat-walker, is supported well by the other performers. **103m/C VHS, Beta, LV.** George C. Scott, Stacy Keach, Jane Alexander, Scott Wilson, Erik Estrada, James B. Sikking; **D:** Richard Fleischer; **W:** Stirling Silliphant; **M:** Quincy Jones. *COL, FCT*

New Crime City: Los Angeles 2020 🎬½ **1994 (R)** Prisoner Tony Ricks (Rossovich) is executed and then revived thanks to technology. But there's a price to pay for his life and freedom—he must retrieve a biowarfare weapon from a prison gang and he only has 24 hours to do it. **CW:** Violence; language; sexuality. **95m/C VHS, LV.** Rick Rossovich, Stacy Keach, Sherrie Rose; **W:** Rick Rossovich. *NHO*

New Eden 🎬🎬 **1994 (R)** In the year 2237 wartime prisoners are condemned to a desert planet where they are preyed upon by brutal Sand Pirates. An idealistic engineer falls in love and seeks to protect his new family from a deadly confrontation. **89m/C VHS, LV, Closed Caption.** Stephen Baldwin, Lisa Bonet, Tobin Bell, Michael Bowen, Janet Hubert-Whitten; **D:** Alan Metzger; **W:** Dan Gordon. *USH*

New Faces of 1952 🎬🎬½ **1954** Based on the hit Broadway revue. The plot revolves around a Broadway show that is about to be closed down, and the performers who fight to keep it open. Lots of hit songs. Mel Brooks is credited as a writer, under the name Melvin Brooks. ♫C'est Si Bon; Santa Baby; Uskadara; Monotonous; Bal Petit Bal; Boston Beguine; I'm in Love with Miss Logan; Penny Candy; Time for Tea. **98m/C VHS, Beta.** Ronny Graham, Eartha Kitt, Robert Clary, Alice Ghostley, June Carroll, Carol Lawrence, Paul Lynde; **D:** Harry Horner. *FCT, NOS, VAI*

New Fist of Fury 🎬 **1985** During WWII, a former pickpocket becomes a martial arts whiz with the assistance of his fiancee, and fights the entire Imperial Army. **120m/C VHS, Beta.** Jackie Chan; **D:** Jackie Chan. *NO*

The New Frontier 🎬½ **1935** Wayne is a small-town sheriff whose predecessor, his father, was murdered. The local saloon-keeper and his gang do everything they can to prevent Wayne from bringing the culprit to justice. **59m/B VHS.** John Wayne, Muriel Evans, Murdock McQuarrie, Mary MacLaren, Warner Richmond; **D:** Carl Pierson. *NOS, MLB*

The New Gladiators woof! **1987** In the future, criminals try to kill each other on television for public entertainment. Two such gladiators discover that the network's computer is using the games in order to take over mankind, and they attempt to stop it. Even if the special effects were any good, they couldn't save this one. **90m/C VHS, Beta.** *IT* Jared Martin, Fred Williamson, Eleanor Gold, Howard Ross, Claudio Cassinelli; **D:** Lucio Fulci.

The New Invisible Man 🎬🎬 *H.G. Wells' New Invisible Man* **1958** A so-so Mexican adaptation of the popular H.G. Wells novel has a prisoner receiving a vanishing drug from his brother, who created it—perhaps to aid an escape attempt. **95m/B VHS.** *MX* Arturo de Cordova, Ana Luisa Peluffo, Jorge Mondragon; **D:** Alfredo B. Crevenna. *SNC*

New Jack City 🎬🎬½ **1991 (R)** Just say no ghetto-melodrama. Powerful performance by Snipes as wealthy Harlem drug lord sought by rebel cops Ice-T and Nelson. Music by Johnny Gill, 2 Live Crew, Ice-T and others. **CW:** Language; strong violence and drug content, and sensuality. **101m/C VHS, LV.** Wesley Snipes, Ice-T, Mario Van Peebles, Chris Rock, Judd Nelson, Tracy C. Johns, Allen Payne, Kim Park, Vanessa Williams, Nick Ashford, Thalmus Rasulala, Michael Michele, Bill Nunn, Russell Wong; **D:** Mario Van Peebles; **W:** Keith Critchlow, Barry Michael Cooper; **M:** Roger Bourland, Michel Colombier. *WAR, CCB*

New Jersey Drive 🎬🎬 **1995 (R)** Jason (Corley) has dreams of life outside the mean streets of Newark, but he jeopardizes his future by stealing cars and joyriding around the neighborhood with his friends. Unblinking realism, provided by credible actors (especially Corley, a former gang member), dialogue, and filming in the projects of Brooklyn and Queens, is nuetralized by stereotypical characters (especially the lilywhite, sadistically brutal cops) and lack of a sympathetic point of view. Loosely based on a series of articles by Michel Mariott, a reporter for the "New York Times." **98m/C VHS, LV, Closed Caption.** Sharron Corley, Gabriel Casseus, Saul Stein, Andre Moore, Donald A. Faison, Conrad Meertin Jr., Deven Eggleston, Gwen McGee, Koran C. Thomas, Samantha Brown, Christine Baranski, Robert Jason Jackson, Roscoe Orman, Dwight Errington Myers, Gary DeWitt Marshall; **D:** Nick Gomez; **W:** Nick Gomez, Michel Mariott; **C:** Adam Kimmel; **M:** Wendy Blackstone. Nominations: Independent Spirit Awards '96: Debut Performance (Casseus). *USH*

The New Kids 🎬🎬 **1985 (R)** An orphaned brother and sister find out the limitations of the good neighbor policy. A sadistic gang terrorizes them after their move to a relatives' home in Florida. They go after expected revenge. **90m/C VHS, Beta, LV, Closed Caption.** Shannon Presby, Lori Loughlin, James Spader, Eric Stoltz; **D:** Sean S. Cunningham; **W:** Brian Taggert, Stephen Gyllenhaal. *COL*

A New Kind of Love 🎬🎬½ **1963** Romantic fluff starring real-life couple Newman and Woodward who meet en route to Paris and end up falling in love. Newman plays a reporter and Woodward is a fashion designer in this light comedy set amidst the sights of Paris. **110m/C VHS, Beta, Closed Caption.** Paul Newman, Joanne Woodward, Thelma Ritter, Eva Gabor, Maurice Chevalier, George Tobias; **D:** Melville Shavelson; **W:** Melville Shavelson; **C:** Daniel F. Fapp. Nominations: Academy Awards '63: Best Adapted Score, Best Costume Design (Color). *PAR*

The New Land 🎬🎬🎬 *Nybyggarna* **1973 (PG)** Sequel to "The Emigrants" follows Von Sydow and his family as they struggle to make their new home in the new world. Hardships include severe weather which devastates the farm, a Sioux indian uprising, and a disastrous trek to the Southwest to search for gold. Sensitive performances and direction. Based on the novels by Vilhelm Moberg. Dubbed into English. **161m/C VHS.** *SW* Max von Sydow, Liv Ullmann, Allan Edwall, Eddie Axberg, Hans Alfredson, Halvar Bjork, Peter Lindgren, Monica Zetterlund, Pierre Lindstedt, Per Oscarsson; **D:** Jan Troell; **W:** Jan Troell, Bengt Forslund; **M:** Bengt Ernyd, George Oddner. National Board of Review Awards '73: Best Actress (Ullmann); National Society of Film Critics Awards '73: Best Actress (Ullmann). *WAR, MOV*

A New Leaf 🎬🎬½ **1971 (G)** A playboy who has depleted his financial resources tries to win the hand of a clumsy heiress. May was the first woman to write, direct and star in a movie. She was unhappy with the cuts that were made by the studio, but that didn't seem to affect its impact with the public. Even with the cuts, the film is still funny and May's performance is worth watching. **102m/C VHS.** Walter Matthau, Elaine May, Jack Weston, George Rose, William Redfield, James Coco; **D:** Elaine May; **W:** Elaine May. *PAR, CCB*

A New Life 🎬🎬½ **1988 (PG-13)** An uptight stockbroker is abandoned by his wife. The New York singles scene beckons both of them to a new chance at life. Appealing performances cannot completely mask the old story line, but it's definitely worth a look. **104m/C VHS, Beta, LV, Closed Caption.** Alan Alda, Ann-Margret, Hal Linden, Veronica Hamel, John Shea, Mary Kay Place, Cynthia Belliveau, Beatrice Alda; **D:** Alan Alda; **W:** Alan Alda; **M:** Joseph Turrin. *PAR*

New Mafia Boss 🎬½ *Crime Boss* **1972 (PG)** Italian-made plodder has Savalas taking over a huge Mafia family and all hell breaking loose. **90m/C VHS, Beta.** *IT* Telly Savalas, Lee Van Cleef, Antonio Sabato Jr., Paolo Tedesco; **D:** Alberto De Martino. *VCD*

New Moon 🎵🎵½ 1940 An adaptation of the operetta by Sigmund Romberg and Oscar Hammerstein II. A French heiress traveling on a boat that is captured by pirates falls in love with their leader. Remake of the 1930 film. Includes the 1935 Robert Benchley MGM short "How to Sleep." 🎵Dance Your Cares Away; Stranger in Paris; The Way They Do It in Paris; Lover Come Back; Shoes; Softly as in a Morning Sunrise; One Kiss; Troubles of the World; No More Weeping. **106m/B VHS, Beta.** Jeanette MacDonald, Nelson Eddy, Buster Keaton, Joe Yule, Jack Perrin, Mary Boland; **D:** Robert Z. Leonard. *MGM*

New Orleans After Dark 🎵🎵 1958 A pair of New Orleans detectives tour the city, crime-buster style, and bag a dope ring. Average crime tale, shot on location in the Big Easy. **69m/B VHS.** Stacy Harris, Louis Sirgo, Ellen Moore; **D:** John Sledge. *NOS, LOO*

New Pastures 🎵🎵½ 1962 Three ex-convicts run into some humorous situations when they go back to their small hometown. A semi-acclaimed Czech comedy, with subtitles. **92m/B VHS, Beta.** CZ **D:** Vladimir Cech. *IHF*

New Year's Day 🎵🎵🎵 1989 (R) Jaglom continues his look at modern relationships in this story of a man reclaiming his house from three female tenants. Introspective character study lightened by humor and insight. **90m/C VHS, Beta, Closed Caption.** Maggie Jakobson, Gwen Welles, Melanie Winter, Milos Forman, Michael Emil, David Duchovny, Tracy Reiner, Henry Jaglom; **D:** Henry Jaglom; **W:** Henry Jaglom. *PAR, BTV, FCT*

New Year's Evil woof! 1978 (R) Every hour during a New Year's Eve concert, a madman kills an unsuspecting victim. After each killing, the murderer informs a local disc jockey of his deed. Little does the disc jockey know that she will soon be next on his list. No suspense, bad music makes this slash and crash a holiday wrecker. **88m/C VHS, Beta.** Roz Kelly, Kip Niven, Chris Wallace, Louisa Moritz, Grant Kramer, Jed Mills; **D:** Emmett Alston; **W:** Emmett Alston.

New York Cop 🎵½ 1994 (R) Japanese martial arts expert Toshi (Nakamura) joins the NYPD and is given an undercover assignment to infiltrate a gun-running gang that supplies both drug lords and Japanese mobsters. But internal rivalries force Toshi to bond with gang leader Hawk (McQueen) and the duo to do battle together.**CW:** Gangster violence; language; some sexuality. **88m/C VHS, Closed Caption.** Toru Nakamura, Chad McQueen, Mira Sorvino; **D:** Toru Murakawa. *COL*

New York, New York 🎵🎵🎵 1977 (PG) Tragic romance evolves between a saxophonist and an aspiring singer/actress in this salute to the big-band era. A love of music isn't enough to hold them together through career rivalries and life on the road. Fine performances by De Niro and Minnelli and the supporting cast. Re-released in 1981 with the "Happy Endings" number, which was cut from the original. Look for "Big Man" Clarence Clemons on sax. 🎵New York, New York; There Goes the Ball Game; Happy Endings; But the World Goes 'Round; Night in Tunisia; Opus One; Avalon; You Brought a New Kind of Love to Me; I'm Getting Sentimental Over You. **163m/C VHS, Beta, LV, Letterbox, Closed Caption.** Robert De Niro, Liza Minnelli, Lionel Stander, Barry Primus, Mary Kay Place, Dick Miller, Diahnne Abbott; **D:** Martin Scorsese; **W:** Mardik Martin; **M:** Ralph Burns. *FOX*

New York Nights 🎵 1984 (R) The lives of nine New Yorkers intertwine in a treacherous game of passion and seduction. Liberal borrowing from plot of "La Ronde." **104m/C VHS, Beta.** Corinne Alphen, George Auyer, Bobbi Burns, Peter Matthey, Cynthia Lee, Willem Dafoe; **D:** Simon Nuchtern. *ART*

New York Ripper woof! 1982 A New York cop tracks down a rampaging murderer in this dull, mindless slasher flick. **88m/C VHS, Beta.** IT Fred Williamson; **D:** Lucio Fulci. *THV*

New York Stories 🎵🎵🎵 1989 (PG) Entertaining anthology of three separate short films by three esteemed directors, all set in New York. In "Life Lessons" by Scorsese, an impulsive artist tries to prevent his live-in girlfriend from leaving him. "Life Without Zoe" by Coppola involves a youngster's fantasy about a wealthy 12-year-old who lives mostly without her parents. Allen's "Oedipus Wrecks," generally considered the best short, is about a 50-year-old man who is tormented by the specter of his mother. **124m/C VHS, Beta, LV.** Nick Nolte, Rosanna Arquette, Woody Allen, Mia Farrow, Mae Questel, Julie Kavner, Talia Shire, Giancarlo Giannini, Don Novello, Patrick O'Neal, Peter Gabriel, Paul Herman, Deborah Harry, Steve Buscemi, Heather McComb, Chris Elliott, Carole Bouquet, Edward I. Koch; **D:** Woody Allen, Martin Scorsese, Francis Ford Coppola; **W:** Woody Allen, Francis Ford Coppola, Richard Price, Sofia Coppola; **C:** Sven Nykvist, Nestor Almendros; **M:** Carmine Coppola. *TOU*

New York's Finest 🎵 1987 (R) Three prostitutes are determined to leave their calling and marry very eligible millionaires. But becoming society ladies is more difficult than they thought. Would-be sophisticated comedy misfires. **80m/C VHS, Beta.** Ruth Collins, Jennifer Delora, Scott Thompson Baker, Heidi Paine, Jane Hamilton, Alan Naggar, John Altamura, Alan Fisler, Josey Duval; **D:** Chuck Vincent.

The Newlydeads 🎵½ 1987 An uptight, conservative, honeymoon resort owner murders one of his guests and finds out that "she" is really a he. Fifteen years later, on his wedding night, all of his guests are violently murdered by the transvestite's vengeful ghost. Oddball twist to the usual slasher nonsense. **84m/C VHS, Beta.** Scott Kaske, Jim Williams, Jean Levine, Jay Richardson; **D:** Joseph Merhi. *NO*

Newman's Law 🎵🎵 1974 (PG) A city detective is implicated in a corruption investigation. While on suspension, he continues with his own investigation of a large drug ring and finds corruption is closer than he thought. Director Heffron's first feature film. **98m/C VHS, Beta.** George Peppard, Roger Robinson, Eugene Roche, Gordon Pinsent, Louis Zorich, Abe Vigoda; **D:** Richard T. Heffron. *USH*

News at Eleven 🎵🎵 1986 A fading news anchorman is pressured by his ambitious young boss to expose a touchy local sex scandal, forcing him to consider the public's right to know versus the rights of the individual. About average for made-for-television drama. **95m/C VHS, Beta, LV.** Martin Sheen, Peter Riegert, Barbara Babcock, Sheree J. Wilson, Sydney Penny, David S. Sheiner, Christopher Allport; **D:** Mike Robe. *TTC*

News from Home 🎵🎵 1976 Scenes of life in New York are juxtaposed with voiceover from the letters of a mother to her young daughter. Plotless narrative deals with the small details of life. **85m/C VHS. D:** Chantal Akerman; **W:** Chantal Akerman. *WAC, FCT*

Newsfront 🎵🎵🎵 1978 A story about two brothers, both newsreel filmmakers, and their differing approaches to life and their craft in the 1940s and '50s. Tribute to the days of newsreel film combines real stories and fictionalized accounts with color and black and white photography. Noyce's feature film debut. **110m/C VHS, LV.** AU Bill Hunter, Gerard Kennedy, Angela Punch McGregor, Wendy Hughes, Chris Haywood, John Ewart, Bryan Brown; **D:** Phillip Noyce. Australian Film Institute '78: Best Actor (Hunter), Best Film.

Newsies 🎵½ 1992 (PG) An unfortunate attempt at an old-fashioned musical with a lot of cute kids and cardboard characters and settings. The plot, such as it is, concerns the 1899 New York newsboys strike against penny-pinching publisher Joseph Pulitzer. Bale plays the newsboy's leader and at least shows some charisma in a strictly cartoon setting. The songs are mediocre but the dancing is lively. However, none of it moves the story along. Add a bone for viewers under 12. Choreographer Ortega's feature-film directorial debut. **121m/C VHS, Beta, Closed Caption.** Christian Bale, Bill Pullman, Robert Duvall, Ann-Margret, Michael Lerner, Kevin Tighe, Charles Cioffi, Luke Edwards, Max Casella, David Moscow; **D:** Kenny Ortega; **M:** Alan Menken, Jack Feldman. Golden Raspberry Awards '92: Worst Song ("High Times, Hard Times"). *DIS*

The Newton Boys 🎵🎵½ 1997 (PG-13) Fact-based drama chronicling the careers and love lives of the bank robbing Newton brothers, who robbed their way from Texas to Toronto during the '20s and '30s. They lived and worked by a romantic credo: no killing, stealing from women or children, and no ratting each other out. McConaughey and Ulrich lead the group as Willis and Joe, respectively, and both prove likeable gangsters. Hawke and D'Onfrio do their best in less developed roles. Highlight is the great train robbery, which garnered the outlaws $3 million and eventually landed the boys in court. Though well-acted with interesting material, Linklater's departure lacks precise angle, which keeps the story from really humming. Stealing the show is the real-life footage of a 1980 "Tonight Show" where Johnny Carson interviews the personable Joe.**CW:** Violence including bloody aftermath of a shooting, and for language. **122m/C VHS.** Matthew McConaughey, Skeet Ulrich, Ethan Hawke, Vincent D'Onofrio, Julianna Margulies, Dwight Yoakam, Gail Cronauer, Chloe Webb, Charles Gunning, Becket Gremmels; **D:** Richard Linklater; **W:** Claude Stanush, Clark Lee Walker; **C:** Peter James; **M:** Edward D. Barnes. *FXV*

Next Door 🎵🎵½ 1994 (R) College professors Matt (Woods) and Karen (Capshaw) have the perfect suburban home—complete with the perfect suburban garden. Then their boorish blue-collar neighbor Lenny (Quaid) takes to enthusiastic lawn watering and ruins their flowers. One thing leads to a full-scale feud. Made for cable TV.**CW:** Strong language; some violence. **95m/C VHS.** James Woods, Randy Quaid, Kate Capshaw, Lucinda Jenney; **D:** Tony Bill; **W:** Barney Cohen; **C:** Thomas Del Ruth. *COL*

The Next Karate Kid 🎵🎵½ 1994 (PG) Fourth installment in the "Kid" series finds martial arts expert Miyagi (Morita) training Julie Pierce (Swank), the orphaned tomboy daughter of an old war buddy who saved his life 50 years earlier. He even teaches her the waltz, just in time for the prom, but she's still tough enough to scrap with a guy. A must-see for "Karate Kid" fans, if there are any left. **107m/C VHS, LV, Closed Caption.** Noriyuki "Pat" Morita, Hilary Swank; **D:** Christopher Cain; **W:** Mark Lee; **M:** Bill Conti. *COL*

Next of Kin 🎵 1982 A daughter moves into her dead mother's retirement home and discovers an unspeakable evil that lurks there. Typical horror stuff has some very creepy moments; filmed in New Zealand. **90m/C VHS, Beta, LV, 8mm.** AU Jackie Kerin, John Jarratt, Gerida Nicholson, Alex Scott; **D:** Tony Williams. *NO*

Next of Kin 🎵🎵 1984 A young man experiencing familial difficulties undergoes experimental video therapy where he views a videotape of an Armenian family who gave their son up for adoption. When he discovers the actual family he insinuates himself into their life, determined to be their long-lost son. **72m/C VHS.** CA Patrick Tierney; **D:** Atom Egoyan; **W:** Atom Egoyan. *CVC, FCT*

Next of Kin 🎵🎵 1989 (R) A Chicago cop returns to his Kentucky home to avenge his brother's brutal murder. Swayze's return to action films after his success in "Dirty Dancing" is unimpressive. **108m/C VHS, Beta, LV, 8mm, Closed Caption.** Patrick Swayze, Adam Baldwin, Bill Paxton, Helen Hunt, Andreas Katsulas, Ben Stiller, Michael J. Pollard, Liam Neeson; **D:** John Irvin; **C:** Steven Poster; **M:** Jack Nitzsche. *WAR*

Next One 🎵½ 1984 Mysterious visitor from another time winds up on an isolated Greek island as the result of a magnetic storm. The local inhabitants are amazed when the visitor displays some Christ-like characteristics. **105m/C VHS, Beta.** Keir Dullea, Adrienne Barbeau, Jeremy Licht, Peter Hobbs; **D:** Nico Mastorakis. *VES*

Next Stop, Greenwich Village 🎬🎬🎬 1976 (R) An affectionate, autobiographical look by Mazursky at a Brooklyn boy with acting aspirations, who moves to Greenwich Village in 1953. Good performances, especially by Winters as the overbearing mother. 109m/C VHS, Closed Caption. Lenny Baker, Christopher Walken, Ellen Greene, Shelley Winters, Lou Jacobi, Mike Kellin; D: Paul Mazursky; W: Paul Mazursky; M: Bill Conti. FXV

Next Summer 🎬🎬🎬 L'Ete Prochain 1984 A large, character-studded French family pursues power, love and beauty. Excellent performances. In French with English subtitles. 120m/C VHS, Beta. FR Jean-Louis Trintignant, Claudia Cardinale, Fanny Ardant, Philippe Noiret, Marie Trintignant; D: Nadine Trintignant. CTL, FCT, TPV

Next Time I Marry 🎬½ 1938 Lucy fraternizes with ditch digger Ellison because she needs to hitch a Yankee in order to inherit $20 mill. Seems she really loves a foreigner, though. Not much to bobaloo about. Director Kanin's second effort. 65m/B VHS. Lucille Ball, James Ellison, Lee Bowman, Granville Bates, Mantan Moreland, Florence Lake; D: Garson Kanin. TTC, FCT, MLB

The Next Victim 🎬 Lo Strano Vizio Della Signora Wardh 1971 (PG) The unfaithful wife of an Austrian diplomat attempts to find out who has been slicing up beautiful jet-setters. Tepid mystery. 87m/C VHS, Beta. George Hilton, Edwige French, Christina Airoldi, Ivan Rassimov; D: Sergio Martino. GEM, CNG

Next Victim 🎬 1974 A beautiful woman confined to a wheelchair is stalked by a lunatic killer. You've seen it before, and done better. 80m/C VHS, Beta. GB Carroll Baker, T.P. McKenna, Ronald Lacey, Maurice Kaufman; D: James Ormerod. ART

The Next Voice You Hear 🎬🎬½ 1950 Lives are changed forever when a group of people hear the voice of God on the radio. Interesting premise presented seriously. 84m/B VHS, Beta. James Whitmore, Nancy Davis, Gary Gray, Lillian Bronson, Art Smith, Tom D'Andrea, Jeff Corey, George Chandler; D: William A. Wellman. MGM

Next Year If All Goes Well 🎬🎬½ 1983 Two young lovers struggle to overcome insecurities while establishing a relationship. Dubbed. 95m/C VHS, Beta. FR Isabelle Adjani, Thierry Lhermitte, Mariann Chazel; D: Jean-Loup Hubert. VTR

Niagara 🎬🎬½ 1952 During their honeymoon in Niagara Falls, a scheming wife (Monroe) plans to kill her crazed war-vet husband (Cotten). Little does she know that he is plotting to double-cross her. Steamy, quasi-Hitchcockian mystery ably directed, with interesting performances. Monroes sings "Kiss." 89m/B VHS, Beta, LV. Joseph Cotten, Jean Peters, Marilyn Monroe, Max Casey Adams Showalter, Don Wilson; D: Henry Hathaway. FOX

Niagara, Niagara 🎬🎬 1997 (R) Marcy (Tunney) is a victim of Tourette's Syndrome, which causes the sufferer to twitch and unleash strings of profanity that would make a longshoreman blush. She meets shy, introverted Seth (Thomas) while they're both shoplifting, and it's love at first sight. They hit the road, supposedly for a doll that Marcy believes can be found in Toronto, but in reality because they are already outcasts at home. When Seth is injured in a botched pharmacy robbery, they're taken in by fellow oddball Walter, a tow truck driver who dotes on a pet chicken named after his dead wife. All of these lost characters are on a road to nowhere, and are pulled apart by Marcy's bourbon-fueled tics and tantrums. Compelling performance by Tunney carries the rest of this dull, flat movie on its back.CW: Violence, sexuality, substance abuse and strong language. 96m/C VHS. Robin Tunney, Henry Thomas, Michael Parks, Stephen Lang, John MacKay; D: Bob Gosse; W: Matthew Weiss; C: Michael Spiller; M: Michael Timmins, Jeff Bird. NYR

Nice Girl? 🎬🎬½ 1941 Jane (Durbin) develops a crush on visiting professor Richard Calvert (Tone), much to his embarrassment. But her steady beau Don (Stack) sticks around to provide support while Calvert seeks a way to let Jane down easy. The video includes a 3-minute alternate ending. 96m/B VHS. Deanna Durbin, Franchot Tone, Robert Stack, Robert Benchley, Walter Brennan, Ann Gillis, Helen Broderick, Anne Gwynne; D: William A. Seiter; W: Richard Connell, Gladys Lehman; C: Joseph Valentine. USH

Nice Girl Like Me 🎬🎬 1969 (PG) An orphaned young girl roams Europe, getting pregnant twice by two different men. She eventually finds love in the form of a kind caretaker. Harmless fluff. Based on Anne Piper's novel "Marry At Leisure." 91m/C VHS, Beta. GB Harry Andrews, Barbara Ferris, Gladys Cooper, Bill Hinnant, James Villiers; D: Desmond Davis. NLC

Nice Girls Don't Explode 🎬🎬 1987 (PG) A girl telekinetically starts fires when sexually aroused. This puts a bit of a damper on her relationship with O'Leary, much to her mother's delight. Matchless entertainment. 92m/C VHS, Beta. Barbara Harris, Wallace Shawn, Michelle Meyrink, William O'Leary; D: Chuck Martinez; M: Brian Banks. VTR

Nice Neighbor 🎬🎬🎬 1979 An acclaimed film about an outwardly self-sacrificing neighbor who cold-bloodedly manipulates his fellow rooming house tenants for his own ends. In Hungarian with English subtitles. 90m/C VHS, Beta. HU Laszlo Szabo, Margit Dayka, Agi Margittay; D: Zsolt Kedzi-Kovacs. FCT

Nicholas and Alexandra 🎬🎬½ 1971 (PG) Epic chronicling the final years of Tsar Nicholas II, Empress Alexandra and their children. Their lavish royal lifestyle gives way to imprisonment and eventual execution under the new Lenin government. Beautiful, but overlong costume epic that loses steam in the second half. Based on the biography by Robert Massie. Available in widescreen format on laserdisc. 183m/C VHS, Beta, LV, Letterbox. Michael Jayston, Janet Suzman, Tom Baker, Laurence Olivier, Michael Redgrave, Harry Andrews, Jack Hawkins, Alexander Knox, Curt Jurgens; D: Franklin J. Schaffner; C: Frederick A. (Freddie) Young; M: Richard Rodney Bennett. Academy Awards '71: Best Art Direction/ Set Decoration, Best Costume Design; Nominations: Academy Awards '71: Best Actress (Suzman), Best Cinematography, Best Picture, Best Original Dramatic/Comedy Score. COL, TVC

Nicholas Nickleby 🎬🎬🎬 The Life and Adventures of Nicholas Nickleby 1946 An ensemble cast works hard to bring to life Charles Dickens' novel about an impoverished family dependent on their wealthy but villainous uncle. Young Nicholas is an apprentice at a school for boys, and he and a student run away to a series of exciting adventures. An enjoyable film, though it is hard to tell the entire story in such a small amount of time. 108m/B VHS, Beta. GB Cedric Hardwicke, Stanley Holloway, Derek Bond, Alfred Drayton, Sybil Thorndike, Sally Ann Howes, Bernard Miles, Mary Merrall, Cathleen Nesbitt; D: Alberto Cavalcanti; C: Georges Perinal. MRV, DVT, HEG

Nick and Jane 🎬🎬 1996 (R) See John sleep with another woman. See Jane see John sleep with another woman. See Jane run out of the building to catch a cab. See Nick pick her up in the cab. This is just a glimpse of all the hilarious fun you'll see when New Yorker Jane (Wheeler-Nixon) gets a fake boyfriend, Nick (McCaffrey) to upset the real one, John (Dossett). Chillingly predictable romantic comedy does have something to offer in sparks between leads McCaffrey and Wheeler-Nixon, but they're buried amid the bizarre sub-plots and off-beat supports. The opening scene where Jane catches her boyfriend cheating is the lone unique and funny segment. Cost-saving camera work, devoid of close-ups and reaction shots, shows.CW: Some language. 94m/C VHS. Dana Wheeler-Nicholson, James McCaffrey, Lisa Gay Hamilton, George Coe, David Johansen, Gedde Watanabe, Saundra Santiago, Clinton Leupp; D: Rich Mauro; W: Rich Mauro, Peter Quigley, Neil Alumkal; C: Chris Norr; M: Mark Suozzo. NYR

Nick Knight 🎬🎬 198? An L.A. cop on the night beat is really a good-guy vampire, who quaffs cattle blood as he tracks down another killer who's draining humans of their plasma. A gimmicky pilot for a would-be TV series that never bit. 92m/C VHS. Rick Springfield, Michael Nader, Laura Johnson. VTR

Nick of Time 🎬½ 1995 (R) A malicious stranger (Walken) and his cohort give ordinary accountant Gene Watson (Depp) 90 minutes to assassinate the governor of California (Mason) or his little girl will be killed. Walken as an evil psycho...now there's a stretch. On the other hand, Depp as a button-down, conservative widower is a bit of a switch after his usually quirky roles of the recent past. This may be the first time Depp's picked up a gun since "21 Jump Street." Illogical scenarios (even for an action flick) and curiously uneven pacing do this one in. Shot almost entirely in L.A's Bonaventure Hotel in real time with a handheld camera.CW: Contains violence and strong language. 98m/C VHS, Beta, Closed Caption. Johnny Depp, Christopher Walken, Charles S. Dutton, Peter Strauss, Roma Maffia, Gloria Reuben, Marsha Mason, Courtney Chase, Bill Smitrovich, G.D. Spradlin; D: John Badham; W: Patrick Duncan; C: Roy Wagner; M: Arthur B. Rubinstein. PAR

Nickel & Dime 🎬🎬 1992 (PG) A con artist's luck turns bad when the IRS catches up with him, impounds all his worldly goods, and sticks him with an officious auditor. But if Jack can find the heiress to a fortune, within 48 hours, he can claim a hefty finder's fee and his money worries will be a thing of the past. 96m/C VHS. C. Thomas Howell, Wallace Shawn, Lise Cutter, Lynn Danielson, Roy Brocksmith; D: Ben Moses; W: Seth Front, Eddy Polon, Ben Moses. COL

Nickel Mountain 🎬🎬½ 1985 Heartwarming story of a suicidal 40-year-old man who finds a new reason to live when he falls in love with a pregnant 16-year-old girl who works at his diner. Langenkamp particularly appealing. Based on a John Gardner novel. 88m/C VHS, Beta. Michael Cole, Heather Langenkamp, Ed Lauter, Brian Kerwin, Patrick Cassidy, Grace Zabriskie, Don Beddoe; D: Drew Denbaum. ORI

Nico Icon 🎬🎬🎬 1995 (R) Documentary probes the life of Velvet Underground sensation and Warhol superstar Nico. A pastiche showing V.U. concert footage and movie clips from Nico's most famous film appearances: Fellini's "La Dolce Vita" and Warhol's "The Chelsea Girls." Also features interviews from Warhol's Factory inhabitants, band members, and Nico's grown son Ari. Visually as interesting as the subject herself, film manages to bring the viewer closer to the untouchable Teutonic figure without being sensational or overly flashy. Director Paul Morrissey and musician Jackson Browne make appearances. Some French and German language; subtitled. 75m/C VHS. GE D: Susanne Ofteringer; W: Susanne Ofteringer. FXL

Nicole 🎬🎬 1972 (R) The downfall of a wealthy woman who is able to buy everything she wants except love. 91m/C VHS, Beta. Leslie Caron, Catherine Bach, Ramon Bieri; D: Itsvan Ventilla.

The Night After Halloween 🎬 1983 (R) A young woman gets the shock of her life when she discovers that her boyfriend is a crazed killer. 90m/C VHS, Beta. IT Chantal Contouri, Robert Bruning, Sigrid Thornton. NO

Night After Night 🎬🎬½ 1932 West's screen debut finds her in an unaccustomed secondary role, although a prime scene-stealer. In Raft's first starring role, he's a monied low-life who opens a fancy nightclub and becomes infatuated with Park Avenue beauty Cummings. His problems are compounded by the arrival of raucous ex-flames West and Gleason. When a hatcheck girl cries "Goodness!" over West's diamonds, she replies, in suggestive West-style, "Goodness had nothing to do with it, dearie."

Adapted from the novel "Single Night" by Louis Bromfield. 76m/B VHS. George Raft, Constance Cummings, Mae West, Wynne Gibson, Alison Skipworth, Roscoe Karns, Louis Calhern; *D:* Archie Mayo; *W:* Mae West, Kathryn Scola, Vincent Lawrence. *USH*

Night Ambush 🎬🎬½ *Ill Met By Moonlight* **1957** A Nazi general is kidnapped on Crete by British agents, who embark on a dangerous trip to the coast where a ship awaits to take them to Cairo. The general tries to thwart their plans, but they outwit him at every turn. Based on a novel by W. Stanley Moss that details a similar real-life event. 100m/B VHS. *GB* Dirk Bogarde, Marius Goring, David Oxley, Cyril Cusack, Christopher Lee; *D:* Michael Powell, Emeric Pressburger. *NO*

Night and Day 🎬🎬½ **1946** Sentimental musical about the life of bon-vivant composer-extraordinaire Cole Porter. His intensity and the motivations for his music are dramatized, but this film succeeds best as a fabulous showcase for Porter's songs. ♫ Begin the Beguine; My Heart Belongs to Daddy; You're the Top; I've Got You Under My Skin; Just One of Those Things; I Get a Kick Out of You; Night and Day; What Is This Thing Called Love; Do I Love You. 128m/C VHS, Beta. Cary Grant, Alexis Smith, Jane Wyman, Eve Arden, Mary Martin, Jane Hale, Monty Woolley, Ginny Simms, Dorothy Malone; *D:* Michael Curtiz; *M:* Max Steiner. Nominations: Academy Awards '46: Scoring of a Musical. *MGM, FCT*

Night and Day 🎬🎬🎬 *Nuit et Jour* **1991** Charming adult romance about Jack and Julie, young lovers newly arrived in Paris. When Jack gets a night job driving a cab, Julie finds her evenings lonely. But not for long. She meets Joseph, a cab driver on the day shift. Soon, Julie is juggling sexual affairs with both men and everything gets increasingly complicated. Her lovers find out about each other but Julie doesn't want to fully commit to either of them. In French with English subtitles. 90m/C VHS. *FR BE SI* Guilaine Londez, Thomas Langmann, Francois Negret; *D:* Chantal Akerman; *W:* Pascal Bonitzer, Chantal Akerman; *M:* Marc Herouel. *FXL, ORI, FCT*

Night and the City 🎬🎬🎬½ **1950** A film noir classic about a hustler's money-making schemes. Widmark is Harry Fabian, a small-time promoter working for slimy nightclub owner Sullivan, whose job is to hustle the marks into the club where his girlfriend Tierney is the singer. Widmark also happens to be romancing Sullivan's wife, Withers, and wants her to back his latest con. But his schemes go awry and Fabian's on the run for his life. Widmark gives a riveting performance of a lowlife whose brains don't match his ambitions. Filmed in London with appropriate brooding tawdriness. Adapted from the novel by Gerald Kersh; remade in 1992. 95m/B VHS. *GB* Richard Widmark, Gene Tierney, Googie Withers, Francis L. Sullivan, Hugh Marlowe, Herbert Lom, Mike Mazurki, Charles Farrell; *D:* Jules Dassin; *W:* Jo Eisinger; *M:* Franz Waxman. *MOV, RXM*

Night and the City 🎬🎬🎬 **1992 (R)** Harry Fabian (De Niro), a con-artist/ambulance-chaser, concocts a scheme to make it big, and approaches an old boxing great (Warden) to come out of retirement and revive a local boxing night. Problem is, although Harry has energy and ambition, he also has a talent for making enemies out of the wrong people, like the boxer's brother (King), a neighborhood mobster. Filled with details more interesting than the plot; more about fast-living, fast-talking New Yorkers, a fine showcase for De Niro's talent. Winkler's remake of the 1950 Jules Dassin film. *CW:* Strong language. 98m/C VHS, LV, Closed Caption. Robert De Niro, Jessica Lange, Cliff Gorman, Alan King, Jack Warden, Eli Wallach, Barry Primus, Gene Kirkwood, Pedro Sanchez; *Cameos:* Regis Philbin, Joy Philbin, Richard Price; *D:* Irwin Winkler; *W:* Richard Price; *C:* Tak Fujimoto; *M:* James Newton Howard. *FXV*

The Night and the Moment 🎬½ **1994 (R)** Dull, mishmashy costume drama (set in the 17th century) about an imprisoned author (Dafoe) who became intrigued with the mystery woman who had occupied the next cell. They exchanged notes, and he vows to find her when he's released from prison. But first he spends a seductive night, exchanging stories about past conquests, at the chateau of the Marquise (Olin), who, of course, turns out to be the mystery lady. Based on the novel "La Nuit er le Moment" by Claude-Prosper de Joiyot Crebillon. *CW:* Sexuality. 89m/C VHS, Closed Caption. *GB FR IT* Willem Dafoe, Lena Olin, Miranda Richardson, Jean-Claude Carriere, Carole Richert; *D:* Anna Maria Tato; *W:* Anna Maria Tato, Jean-Claude Carriere; *C:* Giuseppe Rotunno; *M:* Ennio Morricone. *TOU*

Night Angel 🎬 **1990 (R)** A beautiful seductress lures men into a deadly trap from which only true love can free them. 90m/C VHS, Beta, LV. Isa Anderson, Linda Ashby, Debra Feuer, Helen Martin, Karen Black, Doug Jones, Gary Hudson, Sam Hennings; *D:* Dominique Othenin-Girard; *W:* Joe Augustyn.

A Night at the Opera 🎬🎬🎬🎬 **1935** The Marx Brothers get mixed up with grand opera in their first MGM-produced epic and their first without Zeppo. Jones, as a budding opera singer warbles "Alone" and "Cosi Cosa." One of their best films, blessed with a big budget—used to reach epic anarchic heights. Some scenes were tested on live audiences before inclusion, including the Groucho/Chico paper-tearing contract negotiation and the celebrated stateroom scene, in which the boys are joined in a small closet by two maids, the ship's engineer, his assistant, a manicurist, a young woman, a cleaning lady, and four food-laden waiters. Laserdisc includes letterboxing, digital sound, original trailers, production photos, memorabilia, and soundtrack commentary by film critic Leonard Maltin. 92m/B VHS, Beta, LV, Letterbox. Groucho Marx, Chico Marx, Harpo Marx, Allan Jones, Kitty Carlisle Hart, Sig Rumann, Margaret Dumont, Walter Woolf King; *D:* Sam Wood; *W:* George S. Kaufman, Morrie Ryskind, Bert Kalmar, Harry Ruby, Al Boasberg; *M:* Herbert Stothart. National Film Registry '93. *MGM, CRC, CCB*

Night Beast 🎬 **1983** Alien creature lands his spaceship near a small town and begins a bloody killing spree. 90m/C VHS, Beta. Tom Griffith, Dick Dyszel, Jaimie Zemarel; *D:* Donald M. Dohler. *NO*

Night Beat 🎬½ **1948** A labored crime drama from postwar Britain. Two army pals pursue diverging careers. One becomes a cop, the other a crook. Want to bet that they meet again? 95m/B VHS. *GB* Anne Crawford, Maxwell Reed, Ronald Howard, Christine Norden; *D:* Harold Huth. *LOO*

The Night Before 🎬🎬½ **1988 (PG-13)** Snobby high school beauty Loughlin loses a bet and has to go to the prom with the school geek Reeves. On the way, they get lost on the wrong side of the tracks, and become involved with pimps, crime, and the police. A drunken Reeves loses Loughlin as well as his father's car. Typical teen farce. 90m/C VHS, Beta, Closed Caption. Keanu Reeves, Lori Loughlin, Trinidad Silva, Michael Greene, Theresa Saldana, Suzanne Snyder, Morgan Lofting, Gwil Richards; *D:* Thom Eberhardt; *W:* Gregory Scherick, Thom Eberhardt. *HBO*

Night Birds 🎬 **1931** Early British thriller about a notorious crook named "Flash Jack," who heads a gang of top-hatted criminals that rob the wealthy. Poor production quality and Raine's standoffish screen presence contribute to this below-average film. 76m/B VHS. *GB* Jameson Thomas, Jack Raine, Muriel Angelus, Eve Gray; *D:* Richard Eichberg; *W:* Miles Malleson. *SNC*

Night Breed 🎬½ **1990 (R)** A teenager flees a chaotic past to slowly become a member of a bizarre race of demons that live in a huge, abandoned Canadian graveyard; a place where every sin is forgiven. Based on Barker's novel "Cabal," and appropriately gross, nonsensical and strange.

Good special effects almost save this one. 102m/C VHS, Beta, LV, Closed Caption. *CA* Craig Sheffer, Anne Bobby, David Cronenberg, Charles Haid; *D:* Clive Barker; *W:* Clive Barker.

The Night Brings Charlie 🎬½ **1990** A disfigured tree surgeon is the prime suspect in some grisly murders committed with a tree trimming saw. Obviously, everyone in the town fears him as a result. Not a sequel to "Roots." 90m/C VHS. Kerry Knight, Joe Fishback, Aimee Tenalia, Monica Simmons; *D:* Tom Logan. *NO*

Night Call Nurses 🎬🎬 *Young L.A. Nurses 2* **1972 (R)** Three gorgeous nurses find danger and intrigue on the night shift at a psychiatric hospital. Third in the "nurse" quintet is back on target, shrugging off the previous film's attempts at "serious" social commentary. Miller provides comic relief. Preceded by "The Student Nurses" and "Private Duty Nurses," and followed by "The Young Nurses" and "Candy Stripe Nurses." 85m/C VHS, Beta. Patricia T. Byrne, Alana Collins, Mittie Lawrence, Clinton Kimbrough, Felton Perry, Stack Pierce, Richard Young, Dennis Dugan, Dick Miller; *D:* Jonathan Kaplan; *W:* George Armitage. *NLC*

The Night Caller 🎬🎬 **1997 (R)** Radio psychologist attracts the attentions of a deranged listener. *CW:* Violence and some language. 94m/C VHS, LV, Closed Caption. Shanna Reed, Tracy Nelson, Mary Crosby, Cyndi Pass; *D:* Rob Malenfant; *W:* Frank Rehwaldt; *C:* M. David Mullen. *ART*

Night Caller from Outer Space 🎬½ *Blood Beast from Outer Space; The Night Caller* **1966** When a woman-hunting alien arrives in London, women begin to disappear. At first, incredibly, no one makes the connection, but then the horrible truth comes to light. 84m/B VHS, Beta, LV. *GB* John Saxon, Maurice Denham, Patricia Haines, Alfred Burke, Jack Watson, Aubrey Morris; *D:* John Gilling. *COL*

Night Children 🎬 **1989 (R)** Tough L.A. cop teams with a parole officer to battle a nasty gang leader. The battle is quite violent and senseless. 90m/C VHS, Beta. David Carradine, Nancy Kwan, Griffin O'Neal, Tawny Fere; *D:* Norbert Meisel. *THV*

The Night Club 🎬🎬½ **1925** Swinging single stands to gain fortune if he weds a certain girl, and, as luck would have it, he falls for her. When the usual hearts and roses don't convince her he's earnest, he tries to prove his love is true by attempting suicide and hiring a hit man. 62m/B VHS, Beta. Raymond Griffith, Vera Reynolds, Wallace Beery, Louise Fazenda; *D:* Frank Urson. *GPV*

Night Creature 🎬 *Out of the Darkness; Fear* **1979 (PG)** A tough, Hemingway-type writer is determined to destroy the man-eating black leopard which nearly killed him once before. Filmed in Thailand. 83m/C VHS, Beta. Donald Pleasence, Nancy Kwan, Ross Hagen; *D:* Lee Madden. *VCI*

Night Cries 🎬🎬½ **1978** After a woman's baby dies at birth, she has persistent dreams that he is alive and in trouble. No one will believe her when she tells them that something is wrong. Made for television. 100m/C VHS, Beta. Susan St. James, Michael Parks, William Conrad; *D:* Richard Lang. *WOV*

Night Crossing 🎬🎬½ **1981 (PG)** The fact-based story of two East German families who launch a daring escape to the West in a home-made hot air balloon. Exciting action for the whole family. 106m/C VHS, Beta. John Hurt, Jane Alexander, Glynnis O'Connor, Doug McKeon, Beau Bridges; *D:* Delbert Mann; *W:* John McGreevey; *M:* Jerry Goldsmith. *DIS*

The Night Cry 🎬🎬 **1926** Silent canine melodrama has sheep-murdering dog sentenced to death row until he saves little girl from unbelievably big bird. 65m/B VHS, Beta. John Harron, June Marlowe, Mary Louise Miller; *D:* Herman C. Raymaker. *GPV, GVV*

The Night Evelyn Came Out of the Grave 🎬½ *La Notte Che Evelyn Usca Dalla Tomba* **1971 (R)** A wealthy Italian playboy, obsessed with his dead, flame-haired wife, lures living redheads into his castle, where he tortures and kills them.

Standard '70s Euro/horror/sex stuff enlivened by the presence of the incredible Erika Blanc as a stripper who works out of a coffin. 99m/C VHS. *IT* Anthony Steffen, Marina Malfatti, Rod Murdock, Erika Blanc, Giacomo "Jack" Rossi-Stuart, Umberto Raho; *D:* Emilio P. Miraglio. *FRG*

Night Eyes *⊘* *Hidden Vision* 1990 (R) Surveillance can be a dangerous profession, especially when your boss happens to be the jealous husband of a very sexy woman. Watching turns to yearning for this professional peeper, but he may just get more than he bargained for. Roberts is worth watching. 95m/C VHS, Beta, LV. Andrew Stevens, Tanya Roberts, Warwick Sims, Cooper Huckabee; *D:* Emilio P. Miraglio; *W:* Tom Citrano.

Night Eyes 2 *⊘½* 1991 (R) A security expert assigned to protect the sultry wife of a foreign diplomat finds himself spending a little too much time eyeing her through his hidden cameras. Soon he can no longer control his desire and he makes a move on her that may have international implications. Also available in an unrated version.*CW:* Language, violence, and sensuality. 97m/C VHS, Beta, Closed Caption. Andrew Stevens, Shannon Tweed, Tim Russ, Richard Chaves, Geno Silva; *D:* Rodney McDonald.

Night Eyes 3 *⊘⊘* 1993 (R) Night Eyes Security boss Stevens' latest assignment is to protect the superstar lead (Shannon Tweed) of a top TV cop show from a stalker. They wind up in very close contact but someone is videotaping their private moments which don't stay private for long. Maybe on-screen partner Tracy (Shannon's sister) has something to do with it. Also available in an unrated version.*CW:* Language, violence, and strong sexuality. 97m/C VHS, Beta. Andrew Stevens, Shannon Tweed, Tracy Tweed, Tristan Rogers; *D:* Andrew Stevens; *W:* Andrew Stevens, Michael W. Potts.

Night Eyes 4: Fatal Passion *⊘½* 1995 (R) Beverly Hills shrink gets involved with the bodyguard hired to protect her from a stalker. Also available unrated.*CW:* Some strong sexuality. 101m/C VHS. Paula Barbieri, Jeff Trachta, Andrew Stevens; *D:* Rodney McDonald; *W:* John Eubanks, Henry Krinkle; *C:* Gary Graver; *M:* Patrick Seymour.

Night Falls on Manhattan *⊘⊘⊘* 1996 (R) One man's search for truth runs into serious problems in this adaptation of "Tainted Evidence" by Robert Daley. Former cop turned junior DA, Sean Casey (Garcia), is chosen to lead the prosecution in a sensational NY trial involving a drug dealer/cop killer, who also seriously wounded Sean's long-time cop father, Liam (Holm). He wins but allegations of police corruption dog the trial, thanks to liberal defense lawyer Vigoda (Dreyfuss), and when Sean father unexpectedly becomes the new district attorney, the issue becomes a full-blown scandal, leading the naive Sean very close to home. Veteran director Lumet knows this scandal-ridden territory very well and is aided by fine performances from his leads.*CW:* Violence and language. 114m/C VHS, Closed Caption, DVD. Andy Garcia, Ian Holm, Richard Dreyfuss, Lena Olin, James Gandolfini, Ron Leibman, Colm Feore, Shiek Mahmud-Bey; *D:* Sidney Lumet; *W:* Sidney Lumet; *C:* David Watkin; *M:* Mark Isham. *PAR*

Night Fire *⊘½* 1994 (R) Barry wants wife Lydia to try to rekindle the passion in their marriage by getting away for the weekend at their remote ranch. But they're interrupted in their leisure by the stranded Cal and Gwen. Only it turns out Barry has hired the duo, who like kinky games, to peak Lydia's interest. She's merely disgusted and Barry gets nasty. Also available unrated. 93m/C VHS. Shannon Tweed, John Laughlin, Martin Hewitt, Rochelle Swanson; *D:* Mike Sedan; *W:* Catherine Tavel, Helen Haxton. *TRI*

Night Flight from Moscow *⊘⊘½* *The Serpent* 1973 (PG) A Soviet spy defects with a fistful of secret documents that implicate every free government. Then the CIA must decide if he's telling the truth. Complex espionage thriller. 113m/C VHS,

Beta. *FR IT GE* Yul Brynner, Henry Fonda, Dirk Bogarde, Virna Lisi, Philippe Noiret, Farley Granger, Robert Alda, Marie DuBois, Elga Andersen; *D:* Henri Verneuil; *M:* Ennio Morricone. *NLC*

A Night for Crime *⊘⊘* 1942 A movie star disappears during the filming of a movie. When she turns up dead, a bumbling cop suspects everyone on the set. 75m/B VHS. Glenda Farrell, Lyle Talbot, Lena Basquette, Donald Kirke, Ralph Sanford; *D:* Alexis Thurn-Taxis. *NOS, DVT*

Night Friend *⊘* 1987 (R) A priest sets out to help a young woman caught up in a world of drug abuse and prostitution. Exploitation morality flick. 94m/C VHS. Art Carney, Chuck Shamata, Jayne Eastwood, Heather Kjollesdal; *D:* Peter Gerretsen.

A Night Full of Rain *⊘½* *End of the World (in Our Usual Bed in a Night Full of Rain)* 1978 (R) Italian communist tries unsuccessfully to seduce vacationing American feminist. They meet again in San Francisco and wedding bells chime. They argue. They argue more. They put all but rabid Wertmuller fans to sleep. The director's first English-language film. 104m/C VHS. *IT* Giancarlo Giannini, Candice Bergen, Anne Byrne, Flora Carabella; *D:* Lina Wertmuller; *W:* Lina Wertmuller. *WAR, FCT*

Night Gallery *⊘⊘⊘* 1969 Serling is the tour guide through an unusual art gallery consisting of portraits that reflect people's greed, desire and guilt. Made for television pilot for the series, which ran from 1969 to 1973. Three stories, including "Eyes," which saw novice Spielberg directing veteran Crawford. 95m/C VHS, Beta. Joan Crawford, Roddy McDowall, Tom Bosley, Barry Sullivan, Ossie Davis, Sam Jaffe, Kate Greenfield, Richard Kiley, George Macready, Norma Crane, Barry Atwater; *D:* Steven Spielberg, Boris Sagal, Boris Shear; *W:* Rod Serling. *USH*

Night Game *⊘½* 1989 (R) A cop links a string of serial killings to the night games won by the Houston Astros. Brave cast tries hard, but is retired without a hit. 95m/C VHS, Beta, LV. Roy Scheider, Karen Young, Paul Gleason, Lane Smith, Carlin Glynn; *D:* Peter Masterson; *M:* Pino Donaggio. *HBO*

Night Games *⊘* 1980 (R) Raped as a child, California girl Pickett has trouble relating to her husband. To overcome her sexual anxieties, she engages in a number of bizarre fantasies. 100m/C VHS, Beta, LV. Cindy Pickett, Joanna Cassidy, Barry Primus, Gene Davis; *D:* Roger Vadim; *W:* John Barry.

The Night God Screamed woof! *Scream* 198? (PG) A fanatical cult leader is convicted of murder and the cult goes wild. 85m/C VHS, Beta. Michael Sugich, Jeanne Crain, James B. Sikking; *D:* Lee Madden. *TWE*

The Night Has Eyes *⊘⊘½* *Terror House* 1942 Tense melodrama concerns a young teacher who disappears on the Yorkshire moors at the same spot where her girlfriend had vanished the previous year. Early film appearance for Mason. 79m/B VHS, Beta. *GB* James Mason, Joyce Howard, Wilfred Lawson, Mary Clare; *D:* Leslie Arliss. *NOS, SNC, DVT*

Night Hunter *⊘⊘* 1995 (R) Jack Cutter's (Wilson) vampire-hunting parents were killed by a group of bloodsuckers so he teams up with a tabloid reporter (Smith) to eliminate the last nine vampires who have gathered together in Los Angeles and plan to multiply.*CW:* Language, violence. 86m/C VHS. Don "The Dragon" Wilson, Melanie Smith, Nicholas Guest, Maria Ford; *D:* Rick Jacobson. *NHO*

A Night in Casablanca *⊘⊘⊘* 1946 Groucho, Harpo and Chico find themselves in the luxurious Hotel Casablanca, going after some leftover Nazis searching for treasure. One of the later Marx Brothers' films, but still loaded with the familiar wisecracks and mayhem. 85m/B VHS, Beta. Groucho Marx, Harpo Marx, Chico Marx, Charles Drake, Dan Seymour, Sig Rumann; *D:* Archie Mayo. *NO*

A Night in Heaven woof! 1983 (R) A college teacher gets involved with one of her students, who moonlights as a male stripper. Will he earn that extra credit he needs to pass? Uninspired, overly explicit. Look for Denny Terrio of

"Dance Fever" fame. 85m/C VHS, Beta, Closed Caption. Christopher Atkins, Lesley Ann Warren, Carrie Snodgress, Andy Garcia; *D:* John G. Avildsen; *W:* Joan Tewkesbury. Golden Raspberry Awards '83: Worst Actor (Atkins). *FOX*

A Night in the Life of Jimmy Reardon *⊘½* 1988 (R) A high school Casanova watches his friends leave for expensive schools while he contemplates a trip to Hawaii with his rich girlfriend, a ruse to avoid the dull business school his father has picked out. Well photographed, but acting leaves something to be desired. Based on Richert's novel "Aren't You Even Going to Kiss Me Good-bye?" 95m/C VHS, Beta, LV, Closed Caption. River Phoenix, Meredith Salenger, Matthew L. Perry, Louanne, Ione Skye, Ann Magnuson, Paul Koslo, Jane Hallaren, Jason Court; *D:* William Richert; *M:* Elmer Bernstein, Bill Conti. *FOX*

Night Is My Future *⊘⊘½* *Music in Darkness* 1947 A young musician, blinded in an accident, meets a girl who tries to bring him happiness. Usual somber Bergman, but unimportant story. In Swedish with English subtitles. 89m/B VHS, Beta. *SW* Mai Zetterling, Birger Malmsten, Naima Wifstrand, Olof Winnerstrand, Hilda Borgstrom; *D:* Ingmar Bergman. *VYY, DVT, HEG*

Night Life *⊘⊘* 1990 (R) A teenager gets the all-out, high-stakes ride of his life when four cadavers are re-animated in his uncle's mortuary. 92m/C VHS, LV. Scott Grimes, John Astin, Cheryl Pollak, Alan Blumenfeld; *D:* David Acomba; *W:* Keith Critchlow; *M:* Roger Bourland. *COL*

Night Life in Reno *⊘⊘* 1931 When a man leaves his wife, she sets out for Reno and falls in love with a married man. When her new love is killed by his jealous wife, the woman returns to her husband and they begin their marriage anew. Watchable melodrama. 58m/B VHS, Beta, LV. Jameson Thomas, Dorothy Christy, Virginia Valli, Carmelita Geraghty. *NO*

Night Master *⊘* 1987 A handful of karate students practice their homework with much higher stakes away from the classroom. For them, deadly Ninja games are the only way to study. 87m/C VHS, Beta. Tom Jennings, Nicole Kidman, Vince Martin; *D:* Mark Joffe.

Night Monster *⊘⊘½* *House of Mystery* 1942 A maniac wears artifical limbs to hunt down and murder the doctors responsible for amputating his legs. Picture was shot in 11 days. Fire scene was stock footage from "The Ghost of Frankenstein." 80m/B VHS, Closed Caption. Bela Lugosi, Ralph Morgan, Lionel Atwill, Leif Erickson, Don Porter, Irene Hervey, Nils Asther; *D:* Ford Beebe; *W:* Clarence Upson Young; *C:* Charles Van Enger. *USH*

'night, Mother *⊘⊘½* 1986 (PG-13) A depressed woman, living with her mother, announces one evening that she is going to kill herself. Her mother spends the evening reliving their lives and trying to talk her out of it, but the outcome seems inevitable. Well acted, though depressing. Based on Marsha Norman's Pulitzer Prize-winning novel. 97m/C VHS, Beta, LV, Closed Caption. Sissy Spacek, Anne Bancroft, Ed Berke, Carol Robbins, Jennifer Roosendahl; *D:* Tom Moore; *W:* Marsha Norman; *M:* David Shire. *USH*

Night Moves *⊘⊘⊘½* 1975 (R) While tracking down a missing teenager, a Hollywood detective uncovers a bizarre smuggling ring in the Florida Keys. Hackman is realistic as the detective whose own life is unraveling and in one of her early roles, Griffith plays the teenager. The dense, disjointed plot reaches a shocking end. Underrated when released and worth a view. 100m/C VHS, Beta. Gene Hackman, Susan Clark, Jennifer Warren, Melanie Griffith, Harris Yulin, Edward Binns, Kenneth Mars, James Woods, Dennis Dugan, Max Gail; *D:* Arthur Penn; *C:* Bruce Surtees. *WAR*

Night Nurse *⊘⊘⊘* 1931 Stanwyck is a nurse who uncovers a sordid plot involving the murder of two young children for an inheritance. An entertaining, overlooked crime-drama, initially notorious for Stanwyck and roommate Blondell's continual onscreen dressings and undressings. Gable is compelling in an early, villainous role. **72m/B VHS, LV.** Barbara Stanwyck, Ben Lyon, Joan Blondell, Charles Winninger, Charlotte Merriam, Eddie Nugent, Blanche Frederici, Allan "Rocky" Lane, Walter McGrail, Ralf Harolde, Clark Gable; **D:** William A. Wellman. *MGM*

Night Nurse 🐱 1977 Young nurse signs on to care for an aging, wheelchair-bound opera star, only to find that the house is haunted. **80m/C VHS, Beta.** Davina Whitehouse, Kay Taylor, Gary Day, Kate Fitzpatrick; **D:** Igor Auzins. *NO*

Night of a Thousand Cats 🐱🐱 *La Noche de los Mil Gatos; Blood Feast; Cats* 1972 (R) A reclusive playboy cruises Mexico City in his helicopter, searching for beautiful women. It seems he needs their bodies for his cats who, for some reason, eat only human flesh. He keeps the heads, for some reason, for his private collection. A really odd '70s cannibal cat entry, but it moves along nicely and features some truly groovy fashions (floppy hats, translucent blouses, etc.). Not to be confused with the 1963 film of the same name. From the director of "Night of the Bloody Apes" and "Survive!" **83m/C VHS, Beta.** *MX* Anjanette Comer, Zulma Faiad, Hugo Stiglitz, Christa Linder, Teresa Velasquez, Barbara Ange; **D:** Rene Cardona Jr. *JEF*

Night of Bloody Horror 🐱½ 1976 (R) Tale of a former mental patient who is believed to be responsible for the brutal murders of his ex-girlfriends. A night of bloody horror indeed, as the gore is liberally spread. **89m/C VHS, Beta.** Gaye Yellen, Evelyn Hendricks, Gerald McRaney. *NO*

Night of Dark Shadows woof! *Curse of Dark Shadows* 1971 (PG) An abominable film which even fans of the TV show have a hard time liking. The last of the Collins family and his new bride are sent 150 years into the past. Sequel to "House of Dark Shadows." **97m/C VHS, Beta, Closed Caption.** David Selby, Lara Parker, Kate Jackson, Grayson Hall, John Karlen, Nancy Barrett, James Storm; **D:** Dan Curtis. *MGM*

Night of Evil 🐱½ 1962 Girl is released from reform school and promptly wins a beauty contest. Her bid to win the Miss America title is blown to smithereens however, when it is discovered that she has been secretly married all along. From there she resorts to working in strip joints and attempts to pull off an armed robbery. As exploitation fare goes, a winner. **88m/B VHS, Beta.** Lisa Gaye, William Campbell; **D:** Richard Galbreath. *SNC*

Night of Horror 🐱½ 198? (R) Zombies attack four young people stranded in the wilderness. **76m/C VHS, Beta.** Steve Sandkuhler, Gae Schmitt, Rebecca Bach, Jeff Canfield. *MRV*

A Night of Love 🐱🐱½ *Manifesto* 1987 (R) Because of an assassination threat on the new king, Inspector Avanti (Molina) is charged with rounding up the town's troublemakers. Among them is a beguiling debutante (Soeberg) whose sexual appetites are matched only by her passion to kill the king. Based on a story by Emile Zola. **CW:** Nudity, sexual situations. **97m/C VHS.** Alfred Molina, Camilla Soeberg, Eric Stoltz, Gabrielle Anwar; **D:** Dusan Makavejev. *ORI, FXL*

Night of Terror 🐱½ *He Lived to Kill* 1933 A swami, a couple of Hindu servants, a pretty heroine, a reporter, and all stalked by a killer who's after a formula that can put people in a state of suspended animation. Lame chiller. **64m/B VHS.** Bela Lugosi, Sally Blane, Wallace Ford, Tully Marshall, George Meeker, Edwin Maxwell; **D:** Ben Stoloff; **C:** Joseph Valentine. *GPV*

Night of Terror 1987 A bizarre family conducts brain experiments on themselves and then begins to kill each other. Bloodshed for the whole family. **105m/C VHS.** Renee Harmon, Henry Lewis. *IME*

Night of the Assassin 🐱 1977 Priest leaves his pulpit to become a terrorist. He plans a surprise for a U.N. secretary visiting Greece that would put the U.S. and Greek governments in the palm of his hand. Hard to believe. **98m/C VHS, Beta.**

Klaus Kinski, Michael Craig, Eva Renzi; **D:** Robert McMahon. *ART*

Night of the Blood Beast 🐱½ *Creature from Galaxy 27* 1958 An astronaut comes back from space with an alien growing inside his body. The low-budget defeats a valiant attempt at a story. **65m/B VHS.** Michael Emmet, Angela Greene, John Baer, Ed Nelson; **D:** Bernard L. Kowalski. *SNC, MRV*

Night of the Bloody Apes woof! *Gomar the Human Gorilla; La Horriplante Bestia Humana* 1968 (R) When a doctor transplants an ape's heart into his dying son's body, the son goes berserk. Gory Mexican-made horror at its finest. **84m/C VHS, Beta.** *MX* Jose Elias Moreno, Armando Silvestre, Norma Lazarendo, Augustin Martinez Solares, Gina Moret, Noelia Noel, Gerard Zepeda; **D:** Rene Cardona Jr. *MPI*

Night of the Bloody Transplant woof! 1986 (R) A lunatic scientist switches hearts from one person to another in this bloody gorefest. Footage of real surgery adds authenticity, but not believeability. **90m/C VHS, Beta.** Dick Grimm; **D:** David W. Hanson. *NO*

Night of the Cobra Woman 🐱 1972 (R) A woman who can turn herself into a cobra needs constant sex and snake venom to keep her eternally young. Shot on location in the Philippines. One-time underground filmmaker Meyer co-wrote the script, for the Corman factory. **85m/C VHS, Beta.** *PH* Joy Bang, Marlene Clark, Roger Garrett, Slash Marks, Vic Diaz; **D:** Andrew Meyer; **W:** Andrew Meyer. *NLC, OM*

Night of the Comet 🐱🐱½ 1984 (PG-13) After surviving the explosion of a deadly comet, two California girls discover that they are the last people on Earth. When zombies begin to chase them, things begin to lose their charm. Cute and funny, but the script runs out before the movie does. **90m/C VHS, Beta, Closed Caption.** Catherine Mary Stewart, Kelli Maroney, Robert Beltran, Geoffrey Lewis, Mary Woronov, Sharon Farrell, Michael Bowen; **D:** Thom Eberhardt; **W:** Thom Eberhardt; **C:** Arthur Albert. *FOX*

Night of the Creeps 🐱🐱½ *Creeps; Homecoming Night* 1986 (R) In 1958 an alien organism lands on earth and infects a person who is then frozen. Thirty years later he is accidentally unfrozen and starts spreading the infection throughout a college town. B-movie homage contains every horror cliche there is. Director Dekker's first film. **89m/C VHS, Beta, LV, Closed Caption.** Jason Lively, Jill Whitlow, Tom Atkins, Steve Marshall, Wally Taylor, Bruce Solomon, Kenneth Tobey, Dick Miller; **D:** Fred Dekker; **W:** Fred Dekker; **C:** Robert New. *NO*

Night of the Cyclone 🐱🐱 1990 (R) A complex but not overly interesting thriller about a big city cop who goes to an island paradise in search of his missing daughter and finds murder. **90m/C VHS, LV, Closed Caption.** Kris Kristofferson, Jeffrey Meek, Marisa Berenson, Winston Ntshona, Gerrit Graham; **D:** David Irving. *REP*

Night of the Death Cult 🐱🐱 *Night of the Seagulls* 1975 After moving to a quiet seaside community, a young couple is plagued by cult practising human sacrifice in order to appease the Templars, a zombie-like pack of ancient clergymen who rise from the dead and torture the living. Last in a four film series about the Templars. **90m/C VHS, Beta.** *SP* Victor Petit, Julie James, Maria Kosti, Sandra Mozarowsky; **D:** Armando de Ossorio. *NO*

Night of the Demon woof! 1980 Anthropology students are attacked by the legendary Bigfoot. Later they discover that he has raped and impregnated a young woman. Gore and sex prevail. **97m/C VHS, Beta.** Jay Allen, Michael J. Cutt, Bob Collins, Jodi Lazarus; **D:** James C. Watson. *VHE*

Night of the Demons 🐱🐱 1988 (R) A gory, special-effects-laden horror farce about teenagers calling up demons in a haunted mortuary. On Halloween, of course. **92m/C VHS, LV.** Linnea Quigley, Cathy Podewell, Alvin Alexis, William Gallo, Mimi Kinkade, Lance Fenton; **D:** Kevin S. Tenney; **W:** Joe Augustyn. *REP*

Night of the Demons 2 🐱🐱 1994 (R) Some humor and reasonable special effects help this rise above the usual teen-slasher horror sequels. The demonic Angela (complete with her skull-shaped lollipops) lives on in legend, handily haunting her creepy old house where a group of dumb teens end up on Halloween (and soon wind up dead). With each casualty, a new victim also joins the ranks of the undead. Funniest parts come with heroic rescuer, yardstick-wielding Sister Gloria, who's not about to let any of Satan's helpers get the better of her. **96m/C VHS, LV, Closed Caption.** Amelia Kinkade, Jennifer Rhodes, Merele Kennedy, Bobby Jacoby, Rod McCary, Zoe Trilling, Cristi Harris, Johnny Moran, Rick Peters, Christine Taylor, Ladd York, Darin Heames; **D:** Brian Trenchard-Smith; **W:** Joe Augustyn; **M:** Jim Manzie. *REP*

Night of the Demons 3 woof! 1997 (R) Yet another bunch of moronic teenagers take refuge in Hull House funeral home on Halloween. Don't they know the mansion houses a bloodthirsty demon by now? May the demon win. **CW:** Strong violence and gore, sexuality and language. **85m/C VHS.** Amelia Kinkade, Kris Holdenried, Vlasta Vrana; **D:** Jim Kaufman. *REP*

The Night of the Following Day 🐱🐱 1969 (R) Four professional criminals kidnap a young girl at France's Orly airport, demanding a large ransom from her wealthy father. Each kidnapper turns out to be beset by personal demons, hindering their plans and leading to a bloody climax. Then, there's a final twist to the entire story. Brando and Boone are properly chilling but the plot is muddled and melodramatic. From the novel "The Snatchers" by Lionel White. **93m/C VHS, Closed Caption.** Marlon Brando, Richard Boone, Rita Moreno, Pamela Franklin, Jess Hahn, Jacques Marin, Gerard Buhr, Hughes Wanner; **D:** Hubert Cornfield; **W:** Robert Phippeny, Hubert Cornfield. *USH, FCT*

Night of the Fox 🐱🐱 1990 (R) An American officer with top secret knowledge is captured by Germans on the brink of D-day. His home team plans to kill him if he cannot be rescued before spilling the beans. On-location filming adds much. Made for cable. **95m/C VHS, LV.** Michael York, Deborah Raffin, George Peppard; **D:** Charles Jarrott. *THV*

Night of the Generals 🐱🐱🐱 *La Nuit de Generaux* 1967 (R) A Nazi intelligence officer is pursuing three Nazi generals who may be involved in the brutal murder of a Warsaw prostitute. Dark and sinister, may be too slow for some tastes. Based on Hans Helmut Kirst's novel. **148m/C VHS, Beta, LV.** Peter O'Toole, Omar Sharif, Tom Courtenay, Joanna Pettet, Donald Pleasence, Christopher Plummer, Philippe Noiret, John Gregson, Charles Gray; **D:** Anatole Litvak; **M:** Maurice Jarre. *COL, MOV*

Night of the Ghouls woof! *Revenge of the Dead* 1959 Second to last in Wood's celebrated series of inept horror films that began with "Bride of the Monster" and "Plan 9 from Outer Space." This one tells of a phony spiritualist who swindles the grieving by pretending to raise the dead. To his great surprise he actually does enliven some cadavers, who then go after him. Unreleased for over 20 years because Wood couldn't pay the film lab. Not quite as classically bad as his other films, but still a laugh riot. **69m/B VHS, Beta.** Paul Marco, Tor Johnson, Duke Moore, Kenne Duncan, John Carpenter; **D:** Edward D. Wood Jr. *RHI, SNC, FCT*

Night of the Grizzly 🐱🐱 1966 An ex-lawman's peaceful life as a rancher is threatened when a killer grizzly bear goes on a murderous rampage terrorizing the residents of the Wyoming countryside. **99m/C VHS, Beta.** Clint Walker, Martha Hyer; **D:** Joseph Pevney. *PAR*

Night of the Howling Beast 🐱 *The Werewolf and the Yeti* 1975 (R) The selling point of this one is an epic, first-time battle between a werewolf and a Yeti. Unfortunately it lasts about 15 seconds. Naschy's eighth stint as the wolfman. **87m/C VHS, Beta.** *SP* Paul Naschy, Grace Mills, Castillo Escalona, Silvia Solar, Gil Vidal; **D:** Miguel Iglesias. *REP*

The Night of the Hunter 🎬🎬🎬🎬

1955 The nightmarish story of a psychotic preacher who marries a lonely widow with two children in the hopes of finding the cache of money her thieving husband had stashed. A dark, terrifying tale, completely unique in Hollywood's history. Mitchum is terrific. From novel by Davis Grubb and, sadly, Laughton's only directorial effort. **93m/B VHS, Beta, LV.** Robert Mitchum, Shelley Winters, Lillian Gish, Don Beddoe, Evelyn Varden, Peter Graves, James Gleason, Billy Chapin, Sally Jane Bruce; **D:** Charles Laughton; **W:** James Agee. National Film Registry '92. *MGM*

The Night of the Iguana 🎬🎬🎬 **1964**

An alcoholic ex-minister acts as a tour guide in Mexico, becoming involved with a spinster and a hotel owner. Based on Tennessee Williams' play. Excellent performances from Burton and Gardner. **125m/B VHS, Beta, LV, Letterbox.** Richard Burton, Deborah Kerr, Ava Gardner, Grayson Hall, Sue Lyon; **D:** John Huston. Academy Awards '64: Best Costume Design (B & W); Nominations: Academy Awards '64: Best Art Direction/Set Decoration (B & W), Best Black and White Cinematography, Best Supporting Actress (Hall). *MGM*

Night of the Juggler 🎬🎬½ **1980 (R)** An ex-cop encounters countless obstacles in trying to track down his daughter's kidnapper in New York City. Just a tad too complicated for some tastes. **101m/C VHS, Beta.** James Brolin, Cliff Gorman, Richard Castellano, Mandy Patinkin, Julie Carmen; **D:** Robert Butler; **W:** William W. Norton Sr.

Night of the Kickfighters 🎬 **1991** A mighty band of martial artists takes on a terrorist group that has in their possession a secret weapon that could destroy the world. **87m/C VHS.** Andy Bauman, Adam West, Marcia Karr; **D:** Buddy Reyes.

Night of the Laughing Dead 🎬½

Crazy House; House in Nightmare Park **1975** Veteran British comedy cast perform unthinkable spoof. Man stands to inherit lotsa money as his family members kick the bucket one by one. **90m/C VHS, LV.** *GB* Ray Milland, Frankie Howerd, Rosalie Crutchley, Kenneth Griffith; **D:** Peter Sykes. *MGM*

Night of the Living Babes woof!

1987 Two yuppie men go looking for fun at a brothel. They get their just deserts in the form of sex-seeking female zombies. **60m/C VHS.** Michelle (McClellan) Bauer, Connie Woods, Andrew Nichols, Louie Bonanno; **D:** Jon Valentine. *NO*

Night of the Living Dead 🎬🎬🎬½ **1968** Cult favorite is low budget but powerfully frightening. Space experiments set off a high level of radiation that makes the newly dead return to life, with a taste for human flesh. Handful of holdouts find shelter in a farmhouse. Claustrophobic, terrifying, gruesome, extreme, and yes, humorous. Followed by "Dawn of the Dead" (1979) and "Day of the Dead" (1985). Romero's directorial debut. Available in a colorized version. **90m/B VHS, LV.** Judith O'Dea, Duane Jones, Karl Hardman, Marilyn Eastman, Keith Wayne, Judith Ridley, Russell Streiner, Bill "Chilly Billy" Cardille; **D:** George A. Romero; **W:** John A. Russo; **C:** George A. Romero. *VTR, NOS, HHT*

Night of the Living Dead 🎬🎬 **1990**

(R) A bunch of people are trapped in a farmhouse and attacked by ghouls with eating disorders. Remake of the '68 classic substitutes high tech blood 'n' guts for bona fide frights. **92m/C VHS, LV.** Tony Todd, Patricia Tallman, Tom Towles, William Butler, Bill Moseley, McKee Anderson, Kate Finneran; **D:** Tom Savini; **W:** George A. Romero; **C:** Frank Prinzi. *COL*

Night of the Living Dead, 25th Anniversary Documentary **1993** Features behind the scenes look at low-budget 1968 classic film about legions of dead people who stalk the earth looking for live humans to feed on. **83m/C VHS, LV.** *MTH*

Night of the Running Man 🎬½ **1994**

(R) Las Vegas cab driver McCarthy finds $1 million stolen from a casino and goes on the run from hit man Glenn, who's been hired to recover the loot. **CW:** Strong sexuality, violence and language.

93m/C VHS, LV, Closed Caption. Scott Glenn, Andrew McCarthy, John Glover; **D:** Mark L. Lester. *THV*

Night of the Scarecrow 🎬🎬½ **1995**

(R) Hundreds of years before a small town made a pact with a warlock (Lazar) to ensure prosperity. After regretting the deal, the townspeople kill him and bury the body in a field where it's eventually uncovered. Now the warlock's ghost inhabits the frame of a scarecrow and is off on a murderous rampage. Formula horror with some decent production values. Based on a comic book. **CW:** Strong horror violence; some sexuality and language. **90m/C VHS, Closed Caption.** Elizabeth Barondes, John Mese, Stephen Root, Bruce Glover, Dirk Blocker, Howard Swain, Gary Lockwood, John Lazar, John Hawkes, Martine Beswick; **D:** Jeff Burr; **W:** Reed Steiner, Dan Mazur; **C:** Thomas Callaway; **M:** Jim Manzie. *REP*

Night of the Sharks woof! **1989** Mercenaries in a downed plane go after a jewel-ridden shipwreck despite a plethora of sharks. **87m/C VHS, Beta, LV.** Treat Williams, Christopher Connelly, Antonio Fargas, Janet Agren; **D:** Anthony Richmond. *ART, VTR*

The Night of the Shooting Stars 🎬🎬🎬🎬 *The Night of San Lorenzo; La Notte di San Lorenzo* **1982 (R)** Set in an Italian village during the last days of WWII, this film highlights the schism in the village between those who support the fascists and those who sympathize with the Allies. This division comes to a head in the stunning final scene. A poignant, deeply moving film. **106m/C VHS, Beta.** *IT* Omero Antonutti, Margarita Lozano, Claudio Bigagli, Massimo Bonetti, Norma Martel; **D:** Paolo Taviani, Vittorio Taviani; **W:** Tonino Guerra, Giuliani G. De Negri, Paolo Taviani, Vittorio Taviani; **C:** Franco Di Giacomo; **M:** Nicola Piovani. Cannes Film Festival '82: Grand Jury Prize; National Society of Film Critics Awards '83: Best Director (Taviani), Best Director (Taviani), Best Film. *MGM, AUD*

Night of the Sorcerers woof! **1970** An expedition to the Congo uncovers a bizarre tribe of vampire leopard women who lure young girls to their deaths. **85m/C VHS, Beta.** Jack Taylor, Simon Andrew, Kali Hansa; **D:** Armando de Ossorio. *UNI*

Night of the Strangler 🎬🎬 **1973 (R)** A love affair between a white society girl and a young black man causes a chain of events that end with brutal murders in New Orleans. **88m/C VHS, Beta.** Mickey Dolenz, James Ralston, Susan McCullough; **D:** Joy Houck Jr. *NO*

Night of the Twisters 🎬🎬½ **1995** Teenager Dan (Sawa) and his new stepfather Jack (Schneider) must work together to protect the family when tornadoes rip through their small Nebraska town. Based on the book by Ivy Ruckman. Made for cable. **91m/C VHS.** John Schneider, Devon Sawa, Lori Hallier, Helen Hughes; **D:** Timothy Bond; **M:** Lawrence Shragge. *GKK*

Night of the Warrior 🎬 **1991 (R)** Music videos and martial arts don't mix...not here, anyway. A hunky exotic-dance-club owner pays his disco bills by fighting in illegal, underground blood matches, but not enough to make it exciting. Lamas stars with real life wife Kinmont and mom Dahl. **CW:** Language, strong violence and drug content; and sensuality. **96m/C VHS, LV.** Lorenzo Lamas, Anthony Geary, Kathleen Kinmont, Arlene Dahl. *THV*

Night of the Wilding 🎬 **1990** Very, very loosely based on the story of the female jogger who was gang-raped and left for dead in New York's Central Park. Made for television, soon after the actual incident occurred. **90m/C VHS, Beta, LV.** Erik Estrada, Kathrin Lautner; **D:** Joseph Merhi. *NO*

Night of the Zombies 🎬 *Gamma 693; Night of the Wehrmacht Zombies* **1981 (R)** WWII soldiers with eating disorders shuffle through 88 minutes of gratuitous gore, while pursued by porn star cum intelligence agent. From the director of "Bloodsucking Freaks." **88m/C VHS.** James Gillis, Ryan Hilliard, Samantha Grey, Joel M. Reed; **D:** Joel M. Reed; **W:** Joel M. Reed.

Night of the Zombies woof! *Apocalipsis Canibal; Hell of the Living Dead; Zombie Creeping Flesh* **1983** Staff of a scientific research center are killed and then resurrected as cannibals who prey on the living. The living will suffer again if trapped into watching. Mattel is pseudonym for director Vincent Dawn. Cheap, dubbed, and possessing minimal coherence. **101m/C VHS, Beta.** *IT SP* Margit Evelyn Newton, Frank Garfield, Selan Karay; **D:** Bruno Mattei. *VES*

Night on Earth 🎬🎬🎬 **1991 (R)** Jarmusch's "road" movie comprises five different stories taking place on the same night in five different cities—Los Angeles, New York, Paris, Rome, and Helsinki—between cabbies and their passengers. As with any anthology some stories work better than others but all have their moments in this ambitious film with its outstanding international cast. Subtitled in English for the three foreign segments. **CW:** Language and sensuality. **125m/C VHS, LV, Letterbox.** Winona Ryder, Gena Rowlands, Giancarlo Esposito, Armin Mueller-Stahl, Rosie Perez, Beatrice Dalle, Roberto Benigni, Paolo Bonacelli, Matti Pellonpaa, Kari Vaananen, Sakari Kuosmanen, Tomi Salmela, Lisanne Falk, Isaach de Bankole, Alan Randolph Scott, Anthony Portillo, Richard Boes, Pascal Nzonzi, Emile Abossolo-M'Bo; **D:** Jim Jarmusch; **W:** Jim Jarmusch; **C:** Frederick Elmes; **M:** Tom Waits, Kathleen Brennan. Independent Spirit Awards '93: Best Cinematography. *NLC, FAF*

Night Partners 🎬½ **1983** Bored housewives assist the police to patrol the streets after the kids have gone to bed. Originally made for television with the intention of turning it into a series, but the script doesn't hold water. **100m/C VHS, Beta.** Yvette Mimieux, Diana Canova, Arlen Dean Snyder, M. Emmet Walsh, Patricia Davis, Larry Linville; **D:** Noel Nosseck.

The Night Patrol 🎬🎬½ **1926** Talmadge is a cop who winds up arresting his girlfriend's brother for murder. Convinced the boy is innocent, Talmadge disguises himself in order to infiltrate the gang he thinks is actually responsible for the crime. Lots of derring-do and a last-minute rescue from the electric chair. **53m/B VHS.** Richard Talmadge, Mary Carr, Rose Blossom, Josef Swickard, Gardner James; **D:** Noel Mason Smith. *GPV*

Night Patrol woof! **1985 (R)** The streets of Hollywood will never be the same after the night patrol runs amuck in the town. Crude imitation of "Police Academy." **87m/C VHS, Beta, LV, Closed Caption.** Linda Blair, Pat Paulsen, Jaye P. Morgan, Jack Riley, Murray Langston, Billy Barty, Noriyuki "Pat" Morita, Sydney Lassick, Andrew Dice Clay; **D:** Jackie Kong; **C:** Hanania Baer. Golden Raspberry Awards '85: Worst Actress (Blair). *VTR*

The Night Porter 🎬🎬 *Il Portiere di Notte* **1974 (R)** Max, an ex-SS concentration camp officer, unexpectedly meets his former lover-victim at the Viennese hotel where he works as the night porter. After they get reacquainted, the couple must hide from the porter's ex-Nazi friends who want the women dead because they fear she will disclose their past. A sado-masochistic voyage not for the faint-hearted. **115m/C VHS, LV.** *IT* Dirk Bogarde, Charlotte Rampling, Phillippe LeRoy, Gabriele Ferzetti, Isa Miranda; **D:** Liliana Cavani. *HMV, GLV, NLC*

Night Rhythms 🎬½ **1992 (R)** Nick West is a radio talk show host with a sexy voice that causes his women listeners to reveal their most intimate fantasies and problems to him on the air. When one listener goes too far, it's murder, and Nick must work to prove his innocence in the crime if he intends to save his career—and his life. Also available in an unrated version. **CW:** Sex-related dialogue and strong sexuality. **?m/C VHS, LV, Closed Caption.** Martin Hewitt, Delia Sheppard, David Carradine, Terry Tweed, Sam Jones, Deborah Driggs, Julie Strain; **D:** Alexander Gregory Hippolyte. *IMP, MOV*

Night Rider ✓ 1932 A cowboy posing as a gunman ends a trail of murder and violence in a small western town. 54m/B VHS, Beta. Harry Carey Sr., George "Gabby" Hayes. NOS, DVT

Night Riders of Montana ✓ 1950 A state ranger helps a group of ranchers to fight off a band of rustlers. 60m/B VHS, Beta. Allan "Rocky" Lane. DVT

Night Ripper ✓ 1986 A psychopathic killer stalks high fashion models and kills them by carving them up. Lots of violence. 88m/C VHS, Beta. James Hansen, April Anne, Larry Thomas; D: Jeff Hathcock. NO

Night School ✓ Terror Eyes 1981 (R) A police detective must find out who has been decapitating the women attending night school at Wendell College. Ward's first film. 89m/C VHS, Beta. Leonard Mann, Rachel Ward, Drew Snyder, Joseph R. Sicari, Nicholas Cairis, Bill McCann, Margo Skinner; D: Ken Hughes; W: Ruth Avergon; C: Mark Irwin; M: Brad Fiedel. FOX

Night Screams ✓ 1987 Violent scaremonger about two escaped convicts who crash a high school house party. Kids and convicts start getting killed, one by one. 85m/C VHS, Beta. Joe Manno, Ron Thomas, Randy Lundsford, Megan Wyss; D: Allen Plone.

Night Shade ✓✓ 1997 (R) Recent widower Scott Travers (Abell) is still grieving over the death of his wife although his friends are persistent that he should get out and mingle. So he goes to a club and notices one of the dancers looks very familiar, yep, it's the missus and she really is kinda dead—she's become a vampire. CW: Strong sexuality, and for some violence and language. 90m/C VHS. Tim Abell, Tane McClure, Teresa Langley; D: Fred Olen Ray; W: Sean O'Bannon; C: James Lawrence Spencer. FRF

Night Shadow ✓ 1990 (R) A woman, returning home after being away for years, picks up a hitchhiker. Soon after her arrival, terrible serial killings begin, and only she has the nerve to track down the killer. 90m/C VHS. Brenda Vance, Dana Chan, Tom Boylan; D: Randolph Cohlan; W: Randolph Cohlan. NO

Night Shift ✓✓ 1982 (R) Two morgue attendants, dull Winkler and manic Keaton, decide to spice up their latenight shift by running a callgirl service on the side. Keaton turns in a fine performance in his film debut, and Howard's surehanded direction almost overcomes the silly premise. Watch closely for Costner in the morgue frat party scene. 106m/C VHS, Beta, LV. Henry Winkler, Michael Keaton, Shelley Long, Kevin Costner, Pat Corley, Bobby DiCicco, Nita Talbot, Richard Belzer, Shannen Doherty; D: Ron Howard; W: Babaloo Mandel, Lowell Ganz; M: Burt Bacharach. WAR

Night Siege Project: Shadowchaser 2 ✓✓½ Project Shadowchaser 2 1994 (R) Smooth actioner finds a terrorist android taking over a nuclear arsenal and threatening to make Washington, D.C. a mushroom cloud. Naturally, there's a hero (and a heroine) to take care of the evildoers. 97m/C VHS, LV, Closed Caption. Bryan Genesse, Frank Zagarino, Beth Toussaint; D: John Eyres; W: Nick Davis; M: Steve Edwards. TTC, NLC

Night Slasher ✓ 1984 A madman enjoys spilling the innards of London prostitutes with his dagger. 87m/C VHS, Beta. Jack May, Linda Marlowe. NO

Night Stage to Galveston ✓½ 1952 Autry leads his Texas Rangers on a mission to uncover corruption in the Texas State Police during the turbulent post-Civil War era. 61m/B VHS, Beta. Gene Autry, Pat Buttram, Virginia Huston, Thurston Hall; D: George Archainbaud. CCB

The Night Stalker ✓✓½ 1971 Pilot movie for the TV series finds veteran reporter Carl Kolchak (McGavin) investigating a series of murders that lead him to believe a modern-day vampire is stalking the streets of Vegas. 73m/C VHS. Darren McGavin, Carol Lynley, Simon Oakland, Ralph Meeker, Claude Akins, Kent Smith, Larry Linville, Barry At-

water; D: John Llewellyn Moxey; W: Richard Matheson. FGM, MOV

Night Stalker ✓✓ 1987 (R) A bloodthirsty serial killer is tracked by a detective through the streets in New York. The usual rigamarole of fisticuffs, gunplay, and car chases ensure. Impressive acting from Napier raises the film from the run-of-the-mill. 91m/C VHS, Beta. Charles Napier, John Goff, Robert Viharo, Robert Z'Dar, Joseph Gian, Gary Crosby, Joan Chen, Michelle Reese; D: Max Cleven; C: Don Burgess. VES

The Night Strangler ✓✓½ 1972 Still creepy sequel to 1971's "The Night Stalker" finds reporter Carl Kolchak (McGavin) investigating a series of murders with female victims. He discovers that similar crimes have been committed in Seattle every 21 years for more than a century and the killer's description is always the same. 90m/C VHS. Darren McGavin, Richard Anderson, Simon Oakland, Wally Cox, Margaret Hamilton, John Carradine, Al Lewis; D: Dan Curtis; W: Richard Matheson. VTR

Night Terror ✓ 1976 Everyone's after a hausfrau who saw a highway patrolman murdered on an expressway...including the psychotic murderer. Pretty standard fare. Made for television. 73m/C VHS, Beta. Valerie Harper, Richard Romanus, Michael Tolan, Beatrice Manley, John Quade, Quinn Cummings, Nicholas Pryor; D: E.W. Swackhamer. WOV

Night Terror ✓✓ 1989 A man wakes up from a nightmare only to find that his terrors are still present. 90m/C VHS, Beta. Lloyd B. Mote, Jeff Keel, Guy Ecker, Jon Hoffman, Michael Coopet; D: Michael Weaver, Paul Howard. NO

The Night the City Screamed ✓✓½ 1980 (PG) It's the hottest day of the year, the city experiences a massive blackout, and nighttime brings out less-than-noble emotions amongst the citizenry. Made for television. 96m/C VHS. Raymond Burr, Georg Stanford Brown, Linda Purl, Robert Culp, Clifton Davis, David Cassidy, George DiCenzo, Gary Frank, Don Meredith, Shelley Smith, Vic Tayback, Dick Anthony Williams; D: Harry Falk; W: Larry Brody. COL

The Night the Lights Went Out in Georgia ✓✓ 1981 (PG) Loosely based on the popular hit song, the film follows a brother and sister as they try to cash in on the country music scene in Nashville. McNichol is engaging. 112m/C VHS, Beta. Kristy McNichol, Dennis Quaid, Mark Hamill, Don Stroud; D: Ronald F. Maxwell; W: Bob Bonney; C: Bill Butler; M: David Shire. TWE

The Night They Raided Minsky's ✓✓✓ The Night They Invented Striptease 1969 (PG) Chaotic but interesting period comedy about a young Amish girl who leaves her tyrannical father to come to New York City in the 1920s. She winds up at Minsky's Burlesque and accidentally invents the striptease. Lahr's last performance—he died during filming. ♫The Night They Raided Minsky's; Take Ten Terrific Girls But Only 9 Costumes; How I Love Her; Perfect Gentleman; You Rat, You; Penny Arcade; Wait For Me. 97m/C VHS, Beta, Closed Caption. Jason Robards Jr., Britt Ekland, Elliott Gould, Bert Lahr, Norman Wisdom, Denholm Elliott; D: William Friedkin; W: Norman Lear, Arnold Schulman. FOX

The Night They Robbed Big Bertha's ✓ 1983 Bungling burglar attempts to knock off Big Bertha's massage parlor. 83m/C VHS, Beta. Robert Nichols. NO

The Night They Saved Christmas ✓½ 1987 A Christmas special in which Santa's North Pole headquarters are endangered by the progress of an expanding oil company. Will the attempts of three children be enough to save the day? 94m/C VHS, Beta. Art Carney, Jaclyn Smith, Paul Williams, Paul LeMat; D: Jackie Cooper. CAF

Night Tide ✓✓½ 1963 Hopper in another off the wall character study, this time as a lonely sailor. He falls for a mermaid (Lawson) who works at the dock. She may be a descendent of the man-killing Sirens. Interesting and different little

love story, sometimes advertised as horror, which it is not. 84m/B VHS. Dennis Hopper, Gavin Muir, Luana Anders, Marjorie Eaton, Tom Dillon; D: Curtis Harrington. SNC, FRG, TPV

Night Time in Nevada ✓✓½ 1948 Young woman heads West to claim $50,000 trust left by dear old dad, but his crooked lawyer and associate have their hands in the pot. Cowboy Roy rides horse and flexes dimples while helping helpless girl. 67m/B VHS, Beta, 8mm. Roy Rogers, Adele Mara, Andy Devine, Grant Withers, Joseph Crehan; D: William Witney. NOS, HEG, VYY

A Night to Remember ✓✓✓ 1942 A murder-mystery writer's wife convinces him to move to a new apartment because she thinks the change might help him finish a novel he started long ago. When they find a dead body behind their new building, they try their hands at sleuthing. A clever and witty mystery, indeed, supported by likeable performances. 91m/B VHS. Loretta Young, Brian Aherne, Sidney Toler, Gale Sondergaard, William Wright, Donald MacBride, Blanche Yurka; D: Richard Wallace. COL

A Night to Remember ✓✓✓ 1958 Gripping tale of the voyage of the Titanic with an interesting account of action in the face of danger and courage amid despair. Large cast is effectively used. Adapted by Eric Ambler from the book by Walter Lord. 119m/B VHS, Beta, LV. Kenneth More, David McCallum, Anthony Bushell, Honor Blackman, Michael Goodliffe, George Rose, Laurence Naismith, Frank Lawton, Alec McCowen, Jill Dixon, John Cairney, Joseph Tomelty, Jack Watling, Richard Clarke, Ralph Michael, Kenneth Griffith; D: Roy Ward Baker; W: Eric Ambler; C: Geoffrey Unsworth. Golden Globe Awards '59: Best Foreign Film. PAR, HMV

The Night Train to Kathmandu ✓✓ 1988 A young girl accompanies her parents on a research expedition to Nepal, where her head is turned by an exotically handsome young Sherpa. Old story without much help from actors or director. Made for cable. 102m/C VHS, Beta, LV, Closed Caption. Milla Jovovich, Pernell Roberts, Eddie Castrodad; D: Robert Wiemer. PAR

Night Train to Munich ✓✓✓ Night Train; Gestapo 1940 There's Nazi intrigue galore aboard a big train when a scientist's daughter joins allied intelligence agents in retrieving some secret documents. From the book "Report on a Fugitive" by Gordon Wellesley. 93m/B VHS, Beta. GB Margaret Lockwood, Rex Harrison, Paul Henreid, Basil Radford, Naunton Wayne, James Harcourt, Felix Aylmer, Roland Culver, Raymond Huntley, Austin Trevor, Kenneth Kent, C.V. France, Frederick Valk, Morland Graham, Wally Patch, Irene Handl, Albert Lieven, David Horne; D: Carol Reed; W: Frank Launder, Sidney Gilliat. KIV, DVT, HEG

Night Train to Terror WOOF! 1984 (R) Strange things start happening on the train where a rock band makes its last appearance. Clips from other horror flicks were pieced together to make this film that's so bad it's almost good. 98m/C VHS, Beta. John Phillip Law, Cameron Mitchell, Marc Lawrence, Charles Moll, Ferdinand "Ferdy" Mayne; D: Jay Schlossberg-Cohen.

Night Train to Venice ✓½ 1993 (R) Martin (Grant) is aboard the Orient Express on his way to Venice to deliver his book about the rise of neo-Nazism. He meets a mystery man (McDowell) and an actress (Welch) with ties to a neo-Nazi group, who also happen to be aboard the train and anxious to stop Martin from delivering his expose. Extended dream sequences and flashbacks tend to stop the story cold but Grant is a draw (and probably the only reason this mishmash has been released to video). CW: Language; sexuality; violence; drug content. 98m/C VHS, LV, Closed Caption. Hugh Grant, Malcolm McDowell, Tahnee Welch, Kristina Soderbaum; D: Carlo U. Quinterio; W: Leo Tichat, Toni Hirtreiter; M: Alexander Bubenheim. ART, WEA

Night Vision ✽ 1987 A young writer in the big city is given a video monitor by a street thief which is equipped with some remarkable features, including the ability to present scenes of future murders and demon worship. 102m/C VHS, **Beta.** Ellie Martins, Stacy Carson, Shirley Ross, Tony Carpenter; **D:** Michael Krueger.

Night Vision ✽✽ 1997 (R) Burned-out detective Dak Smith (Williamson) has been demoted to motorcycle cop on the graveyard shift. But he unexpectedly becomes involved with the case of a serial killer who likes to stalk and videotape his victims. Now Dak and his new partner Kristen O'Conner (Rothrock) are working to capture this psychopath.**CW:** Sex, violence and language. 95m/C VHS. Fred Williamson, Cynthia Rothrock, Robert Forster, Frank Pesce, Willie Gault, Amanda Welles, Nina Richardson; **D:** Gil Bettman; **W:** Michael Thomas Montgomery; **C:** Trey Smith. PEG

The Night Visitor ✽✽½ 1970 (PG) A man in a prison for the criminally insane seeks violent vengeance on those he believes have set him up. Heavily detailed, slow moving. Ullman and von Sydow can do better. 106m/C VHS, **Beta.** GB DK Max von Sydow, Liv Ullmann, Trevor Howard, Per Oscarsson, Andrew Keir; **D:** Laslo Benedek; **M:** Henry Mancini. VCI

Night Visitor ✽ Never Cry Devil 1989 (R) A retired police detective teams up with a teenage peeping tom to disclose the identity of a satanic serial killer. The killer, of course, is one of the youth's teachers. 95m/C VHS, **Beta.** Derek Rydell, Shannon Tweed, Elliott Gould, Allen (Goorwitz) Garfield, Michael J. Pollard, Richard Roundtree, Henry Gibson; **D:** Rupert Hitzig; **W:** Randal Viscovich. MGM

The Night Walker ✽✽½ 1964 Stanwyck is always worth watching and she has the best moments in this psycho-thriller which suffers from a low-budget and confused script. The basic story has Stanwyck as a rich widow with a recurring nightmare featuring a faceless lover. There's also a too-helpful lawyer (Taylor), a suspicious private detective (Bochner)—and maybe her husband isn't so dead after all. Taylor and Stanwyck, who had once been married, worked together for the first time in 27 years. 86m/B VHS, Closed Caption. Barbara Stanwyck, Robert Taylor, Lloyd Bochner, Hayden Rorke, Judith Meredith, Rochelle Hudson; **W:** Robert Bloch. USH, GPV

Night Warning ✽✽ Nightmare Maker; Butcher Baker (Nightmare Maker) 1982 (R) A slasher gorefest redeemed by Tyrrell's go-for-broke performance. She plays a sexually repressed aunt who makes up for her problems by going on murderous rampages. Hide the kitchen knives! 96m/C VHS, **Beta.** Bo Svenson, Jimmy McNichol, Susan Tyrrell, Julia Duffy; **D:** William Asher; **W:** Stephen Breimer. NO

Night Wars ✽½ 1988 Two ex-POWs who are plagued by their memories turn to dream therapy to relive their escape. Eventually, they rescue a buddy they left behind. 90m/C VHS, **Beta.** Dan Haggerty, Brian O'Connor, Cameron Smith; **D:** David A. Prior. COL

Night Watch ✽½ Le Trou; Il Buco 1972 A woman recovering from a nervous breakdown witnesses a murder, but no one will believe her. 100m/C VHS, **Beta.** GB Elizabeth Taylor, Laurence Harvey, Billie Whitelaw; **D:** Brian G. Hutton; **C:** Billy Williams.

The Night We Never Met ✽✽½ 1993 (R) Three yuppies bring different visions of romance and a case of mistaken identity to a time-share apartment in New York's Greenwich Village. Sam (Broderick) needs a quiet space to get over being dumped by a flaky performance artist (Tripplehorn). Ellen (Sciorra) is looking for space to paint away from the confines of her thick-headed spouse (Mantell). Brian, the organizer of the living arrangement, wants a space where he can be one of the boys and escape from his cloying fiancee (Bateman). Fairly predictable but enjoyable romantic comedy.**CW:** Language. 98m/C VHS. Matthew Broderick, Jeanne Tripplehorn, Kevin Anderson,

Justine Bateman, Annabella Sciorra, Christine Baranski, Doris Roberts, Dominic Chianese, Michael Mantell, Tim Guinee, Greg Germann, Dana Wheeler-Nicholson, Louise Lasser, Bill Campbell, Ranjit Chowdhry, Garry Shandling, Katharine Houghton, Brooke Smith; **D:** Warren Leight; **W:** Warren Leight; **M:** Evan Lurie. HBO

Night Zoo ✽✽ Un Zoo, La Nuit 1987 A confusing story about a father/son reconciliation and the lurid underworld of drugs and sex in Montreal. The graphic sex and violence undermines the sensitive aspects of the film. 115m/C VHS, Beta, LV. CA Gilles Maheu, Roger Le Bel, Lynne Adams, German Houde; **D:** Jean-Claude Lauzon. Genie Awards '88: Best Actor (Le Bel), Best Director (Lauzon), Best Film, Best Supporting Actor (Houde). VTR, IME

Nightbreaker ✽✽✽ 1989 Revelation of the U.S. government's deliberate exposure of servicemen to atomic bomb tests and the resulting radiation, in order to observe the effects on humans. Sheen and his son, Estevez, portray a U.S. doctor in the 1980s and the 1950s, respectively. 100m/C VHS. Martin Sheen, Emilio Estevez, Lea Thompson, Melinda Dillon, Nicholas Pryor, Joe Pantoliano; **D:** Peter Markle; **W:** T.S. Cook; **M:** Peter Bernstein. TTC

The Nightcomers ✽✽ 1972 (R) A pretend "prequel" to Henry James's "The Turn of the Screw," wherein an Irish gardener trysts with the nanny of two watchful children who believe that lovers unite in death. Don't be fooled: stick to the original. 96m/C VHS, Beta, LV. GB Marlon Brando, Stephanie Beacham, Thora Hird, Harry Andrews, Christopher Ellis, Verna Harvey, Anna Palk; **D:** Michael Winner; **W:** Michael Hastings; **C:** Bob Paynter; **M:** Jerry Fielding. COL, NLC

Nightfall ✽✽✽ 1956 Ray, accused of a crime he didn't commit, is forced to flee from both the law and the underworld. Classic example of film noir, brilliantly filmed by Tourneur. 78m/B VHS. Aldo Ray, Brian Keith, Anne Bancroft, Jocelyn Brando, James Gregory, Frank Albertson; **D:** Jacques Tourneur; **W:** Stirling Silliphant. GKK

Nightfall ✽✽ 1988 (PG-13) Television adaptation of the classic Isaac Asimov short story. A planet that has two suns (and therefore no night) experiences an eclipse and its inhabitants go mad. 87m/C VHS, Beta. David Birney, Sarah Douglas, Alexis Kanner, Andra Millian; **D:** Paul Mayersberg; **C:** Darius Wolski. MGM

Nightflyers ✽½ 1987 (R) Aboard a weathered space freighter, the crew experience a series of deadly accidents caused by an unknown evil presence. From a novella by George R.R. Martin; T.C. Blake is better known as Robert Collector. 88m/C VHS, Beta, LV. Michael Praed, Michael Des Barres, Catherine Mary Stewart, John Standing, Lisa Blount; **D:** T.C. Blake. NO

Nightforce ✽ 1986 (R) Five buddies plunge into Central American jungles to rescue a young girl held by terrorists. 82m/C VHS, Beta. Linda Blair, James Van Patten, Chad McQueen, Richard Lynch, Cameron Mitchell; **D:** Lawrence Foldes. NO

Nighthawks ✽✽ 1978 Jim (Robertson) is a geography teacher in London who lives a closeted life. His quiet daily routine is separate from his cruising of the city's gay pleasure spots until his two worlds converge when he's confronted by his students. 113m/C VHS. GB Ken Robertson; **D:** Ron Peck; **W:** Ron Peck, Paul Hallam; **C:** Johanna Davis; **M:** David Graham Ellis. WBF

Nighthawks ✽✽½ 1981 (R) New York City cops scour Manhattan to hunt down an international terrorist on the loose. They race from disco to subway to an airborne tramway. Exciting and well paced. Hauer's American film debut. 100m/C VHS, Beta, LV, Closed Caption. Sylvester Stallone, Billy Dee Williams, Rutger Hauer, Lindsay Wagner, Nigel Davenport, Persis Khambatta, Catherine Mary Stewart, Joe Spinell; **D:** Bruce Malmuth; **M:** Keith Emerson. USH

The Nightingale 1983 From "Faerie Tale Theatre" comes the story of an Emperor who discovers the value of true friendship and loyalty from his palace kitchen maid who gives him a nightingale. 60m/C VHS, Beta, LV, Closed Caption.

Mick Jagger, Barbara Hershey, Bud Cort, Mako; **D:** Ivan Passer. KUI, FOX, FCT

Nightjohn ✽✽½ 1996 (PG-13) Nightjohn (Lumbly) is the new slave purchased by Southern plantation owner Clel Walker (Bridges). He moves into the cabin shared by 12-year-old Sarny (Jones) and Delie (Toussaint). When Sarny finds out that Nightjohn can read and write (illegal for slaves), she's determined to learn from him. And with her new knowledge, Sarny looks for ways to help her fellow slaves. Based on Gary Paulsen's 1993 novel; made for cable and filmed on location at Rip Raps Plantation in Sumter, South Carolina.**CW:** Some scenes of racial oppression and abuse. 96m/C VHS. Carl Lumbly, Allison Jones, Beau Bridges, Lorraine Toussaint, Bill Cobbs, Kathleen York, Gabriel Casseus, Tom Nowicki, Monica Ford, Joel Thomas Traywick; **D:** Charles Burnett; **W:** Bill Cain; **C:** Elliot Davis; **M:** Stephen James Taylor. HMK

Nightkill ✽✽½ 1980 (R) Simple love affair turns into a deadly game of cat and mouse when a bored wife plots to do away with her wealthy, powerful husband with the aid of her attractive lover. Mitchum is the reluctant investigator pulled into the game. 104m/C VHS, Beta. Jaclyn Smith, Mike Connors, James Franciscus, Robert Mitchum, Sybil Danning; **D:** Ted Post. NLC

Nightlife ✽✽½ 1990 An ancient vampiress who rises from the dead spends her time haunting a blood clinic, where the Jewish hematologist starts to fall for her. Made for cable. 93m/C VHS, Beta, LV. Ben Cross, Maryam D'Abo, Keith Szarabajka, Jesse Corti, Oliver Clark, Glenn Shadix, Camille Saviola; **D:** Daniel Taplitz. USH

The Nightman ✽✽ 1993 (R) Ex-soldier Marcoux becomes the night manager of a failing southern resort, run by sexy, and lonely, Kerns. They begin an affair, which turns sour when Roberston, Kerns' teenaged daughter, also falls for the stud. Then mom is murdered and Marcoux goes to prison. But 18 years later Robertson's past comes back to haunt her. Just what did happen all those years ago? Made for television thriller with additional footage. 96m/C VHS, LV. Ted Marcoux, Jenny Robertson, Joanna Kerns; **D:** Charles Haid; **W:** James Poe; **M:** Gary Chang. APX

Nightmare ✽✽½ 1963 As a child, Janet sees her insane mother stab her father to death. Left in the care of two guardians, the now-grown Janet has recurring nightmares and fears she's inherited her mother's madness. Routine, with red herrings galore. 83m/B VHS, Closed Caption. GB Jennie Linden, David Knight, Moira Redmond, Brenda Bruce; **D:** Freddie Francis; **W:** Jimmy Sangster; **C:** John Wilcox; **M:** Don Banks. USH

Nightmare woof! Blood Splash 1982 (R) Boring splatterthon has a young boy hacking his father and his aggressive mistress to pieces when he discovers them in bed. He grows up to be a psycho who continues along the same lines. Humorless and dreadful, the original ads claimed Tom Savini did the special effects. He had nothing to do with it. 97m/C VHS, Beta. Baird Stafford, Sharon Smith, C.J. Cooke, Mik Cribben, Kathleen Ferguson, Danny Ronan; **D:** Romano Scavolini; **W:** Romano Scavolini. NO

Nightmare ✽✽ 1991 (PG-13) Single mom Linda Hemmings (Principal) takes matters into her own hands when her daughter Dana (Harris) is kidnapped. Though Dana escapes and her assailant, Edward Ryter (Banks), is arrested, he's soon released and threatening Dana to prevent her testifying. So mom teams up with police detective Jake Wilman (Sorvino) to get the goods on the psycho before he can do further harm.**CW:** Mature theme; element of terror. 84m/C VHS. Victoria Principal, Jonathan Banks, Paul Sorvino, Danielle Harris; **D:** John Pasquin; **W:** Rich Husky; **C:** Denis Lewiston; **M:** Dana Kaproff. NHO

Nightmare at Bittercreek ✍✍ 1991 (PG-13) Four babes and a tour guide are pursued by psycho gang in the Sierra mountains. Made for television nightmare in your living room. 92m/C VHS. Tom Skerritt, Joanna Cassidy, Lindsay Wagner, Constance McCashin, Janne Mortil; **D:** Tim Burstall. THV

Nightmare at 43 Hillcrest 1974 A family's life becomes a living hell when the police mistakenly raid their house. Based on a true story. 72m/C VHS, Beta. Jim Hutton, Mariette Hartley. NO

Nightmare at Noon ✍ 1987 (R) Watered-down thriller about a small desert town beset by violent terrorists (who are really locals gone mad from a chemical experiment dumped into the water system). Only the sheriff's small staff is there to stop them. 96m/C VHS. Wings Hauser, George Kennedy, Bo Hopkins, Brion James, Kimberly Beck, Kimberly Ross; **D:** Nico Mastorakis. REP

The Nightmare Before Christmas ✍✍✍ Tim Burton's The Nightmare Before Christmas 1993 (PG) Back when he was a animator trainee at Disney, Burton came up with this adventurous idea but couldn't get it made; subsequent directorial success brought more clout. Relies on a painstaking stop-motion technique that took more than two years to film and is justifiably amazing. The story revolves around Jack Skellington, the Pumpkin King of the dangerously weird Halloweentown. Suffering from ennui, he accidentally discovers the wonders of Christmastown and decides to kidnap Santa and rule over this peaceable holiday. Fast pace is maintained by the equally breathless score. Not cuddly, best appreciated by those with a feel for the macabre. 75m/C VHS, LV, Closed Caption. **D:** Henry Selick; **W:** Caroline Thompson, Tim Burton; **M:** Danny Elfman; **V:** Danny Elfman, Chris Sarandon, Catherine O'Hara, William Hickey, Ken Page, Ed Ivory, Paul (Pee Wee Herman) Reubens, Glenn Shadix. Nominations: Academy Awards '93: Best Visual Effects; Golden Globe Awards '94: Best Score. TOU

Nightmare Castle ✍✍ Amanti d'Oltretomba; Night of the Doomed; The Faceless Monsters; Lovers from Beyond the Tomb 1965 Jealous mad scientist murders his wife and her lover. Then he conducts a bizarre experiment using the dead couple's blood to rejuvenate an old servant. Not quite satisfied with his revenge, he then seeks to marry his late wife's sister after realizing that she has been left the inheritance. In time, the perturbed ghosts of the late lovers appear and seek revenge. A real nightmare. 90m/B VHS, Beta. IT Barbara Steele, Paul Muller, Helga Line; **D:** Allan Grunewald; **M:** Ennio Morricone. SNC, HHT

Nightmare in Badham County ✍ Nightmare 1976 Two girls get arrested on trumped-up charges in a small backwoods town. They soon discover that the prison farm is a front for a slavery ring. Made for television. 100m/C VHS, Beta. Deborah Raffin, Lynne Moody, Chuck Connors, Della Reese, Robert Reed, Ralph Bellamy, Tina Louise; **D:** John Llewellyn Moxey; **M:** Charles Bernstein. THV

Nightmare in Blood ✍½ Horror Convention 1975 Vampires lurk in San Francisco and wreak havoc on the night life. 90m/C VHS, Beta. Kerwin Mathews, Jerry Walter, Barrie Youngfellow; **D:** John Stanley. VCD

Nightmare in Wax ✍½ Crimes in the Wax Museum 1969 After suffering disfigurement in a fight with a studio boss, a former make-up man starts a wax museum. For fun, he injects movie stars with a formula that turns them into statues. 91m/C VHS, Beta. Cameron Mitchell, Anne Helm; **D:** Bud Townsend. MRV

A Nightmare on Elm Street ✍✍½ 1984 (R) Feverish, genuinely frightening horror film about Freddy Krueger (Englund), a scarred maniac in a fedora and razor-fingered gloves who kills neighborhood teens in their dreams and, subsequently, in reality. One of the children-fight-back genre, in which the lead victim (Langenkamp) ingeniously goes to great lengths to destroy Freddy. In the tradition of "Friday the 13th"'s Jason and "Halloween"'s Michael Myers, "Elm Street" spawned a "Freddy" phenomenon: seven sequels (including 1998's "Freddy Vs. Jason," linking "Elm Street, Part 8" with "Friday the 13th, Part 10"); a TV series ("Freddy's Nightmares," a horror anthology show hosted by Englund to capitalize on his character); and an army of razor-clawed trick or treaters at Halloween. 92m/C VHS, Beta, LV, Closed Caption. John Saxon, Heather Langenkamp, Ronee Blakley, Robert Englund, Amanda Wyss, Nick Corri, Johnny Depp, Charles Fleischer; **D:** Wes Craven; **W:** Wes Craven; **C:** Jacques Haitkin; **M:** Charles Bernstein. VTR, CDV, IME

A Nightmare on Elm Street 2: Freddy's Revenge ✍½ 1985 (R) Mediocre sequel to the popular horror film. Freddy, the dream-haunting psychopath with the ginsu knife hands, returns to possess a teenager's body in order to kill again. Nothing new here, however praise is due for the stunning high-tech dream sequence. 87m/C VHS, Beta, LV, Closed Caption. Mark Patton, Hope Lange, Clu Gulager, Robert Englund, Kim Myers, Robert Rusler, Marshall Bell, Sydney Walsh; **D:** Jack Sholder; **W:** David Chaskin; **C:** Jacques Haitkin. VTR, CDV, IME

A Nightmare on Elm Street 3: Dream Warriors ✍✍ 1987 (R) Chapter three in this slice and dice series. Freddy Krueger is at it again, haunting the dreams of unsuspecting suburban teens. Langenkamp, the nightmare-freaked heroine from the first film, returns to counsel the latest victims of Freddy-infested dreams. Noted for the special effects wizardry but little else, Part Three was produced on a $4.5 million shoe string and took in more than $40 million, making it one of the most successful independently produced films in Hollywood. Followed by "A Nightmare on Elm Street 4: Dream Master." 96m/C VHS, Beta, LV, Closed Caption. Patricia Arquette, Robert Englund, Heather Langenkamp, Craig Wasson, Laurence "Larry" Fishburne, Priscilla Pointer, John Saxon, Brooke Bundy, Jennifer Rubin, Rodney Eastman, Nan Martin, Dick Cavett, Zsa Zsa Gabor; **D:** Chuck Russell; **W:** Chuck Russell, Bruce Wagner, Wes Craven, Frank Darabont; **C:** Roy Wagner; **M:** Angelo Badalamenti. VTR, CDV, IME

A Nightmare on Elm Street 4: Dream Master ✍✍½ 1988 (R) Freddy Krueger is still preying on people in their dreams, but he may have met his match as he battles for supremacy with a telepathically talented girl. What Part 4 lacks in substance, it makes up for in visual verve, including scenes of a kid drowning in his waterbed, and a pizza covered with pepperoni-like faces of Freddy's previous victims. This boxoffice bonanza set a new record as the most successful opening weekend of any independently released film. Followed by "A Nightmare on Elm Street 5: Dream Child." 99m/C VHS, Beta, LV, Closed Caption. Robert Englund, Rodney Eastman, Danny Hassel, Andras Jones, Tuesday Knight, Lisa Wilcox, Ken Sagoes, Toy Newkirk, Brooke Theiss, Brooke Bundy; **D:** Renny Harlin; **W:** Brian Helgeland, Scott Pierce; **C:** Steven Fierberg; **M:** Craig Safan. VTR, CDV, IME

A Nightmare on Elm Street 5: Dream Child ✍✍ 1989 (R) The fifth installment of Freddy Krueger's never-ending adventures. Here, America's favorite knife-wielding burn victim, unable to best the Dream Master from the previous film, haunts the dreams of her unborn fetus. Gore fans may be disappointed to discover that much of the blood and guts ended up on the cutting room floor. 90m/C VHS, Beta, LV, Closed Caption. Robert Englund, Lisa Wilcox, Kelly Jo Minter, Danny Hassel, Erika Anderson, Nicholas Mele, Beatrice Boepple, Christopher Ellis; **D:** Stephen Hopkins; **W:** Leslie Bohem; **C:** Peter Levy; **M:** Jay Michael Ferguson. Golden Raspberry Awards '89: Worst Song ("Bring Your Daughter to the Slaughter"). VTR, IME

A Nightmare on the 13th Floor ✍ 1990 (PG-13) A travel writer at an old hotel glimpses murder on a supposedly non-existent floor. Nasty devil-worshippers are afoot, but the chills in this mild made-for-cable throwaway seldom dip below room temperature. 85m/C VHS, Beta, Closed Caption. Michael Greene, John Karlen, Louise Fletcher, Alan Fudge, James Brolin; **D:** Walter Grauman. PAR

Nightmare Sisters WOOF! 1987 (R) Three sorority sisters become possessed by a demon and then sexually ravage a nearby fraternity. 83m/C VHS, Beta. Brinke Stevens, Michelle (McClellan) Bauer, Linnea Quigley; **D:** David DeCoteau. TWE

Nightmare Weekend ✍ 1986 (R) A professor's evil assistant lures three young women into his lab and performs cruel and vicious experiments that transform the girls and their dates into crazed zombies. 86m/C VHS, Beta. Dale Midkiff, Debbie Laster, Debra Hunter, Lori Lewis; **D:** Henry Sala. ART

The Nightmare Years 1989 An American reporter in Nazi Germany dares to report the truth to an unbelieving world. Based on a true story. Two cassettes. 237m/C VHS, Beta. Sam Waterston, Marthe Keller, Kurtwood Smith; **D:** Anthony Page; **M:** Vladimir Cosma. TTC

Nightmares ✍✍ 1983 (PG) A less-than-thrilling horror anthology featuring four tales in which common, everyday occurrences take on the ingredients of a nightmare. In the same vein as "Twilight Zone" and "Creepshow." 99m/C VHS, Beta. Christina Raines, Emilio Estevez, Moon Zappa, Lance Henriksen, Richard Masur, Veronica Cartwright; **D:** Joseph Sargent; **W:** Jeffrey Bloom, Christopher Crowe. USH

Nights and Days ✍✍½ 1976 Adaptation of writer Maria Dabrowska's tale about a Polish family chronicles the persecution, expulsions, and land grabbing that occurred after the unsuccessful Uprising of 1864. In Polish with English subtitles. 255m/C VHS. PL Jadwiga Baranska, Jerzy Binczycki; **D:** Jerzy Antczak. Nominations: Academy Awards '76: Best Foreign Language Film. FCT

Nights in White Satin ✍½ 1987 A made-for-video Cinderella story about the growing love between a fashion photographer and a young model whose boyfriend has just been murdered. 96m/C VHS, Beta. Kenneth Gilman, Priscilla Harris; **D:** Michael Bennard. PAR

Nights of Cabiria ✍✍✍½ Le Notti de Cabiria; Cabiria 1957 Fellini classic which details the personal decline of a naive prostitute who thinks she's found true love. In Italian with English subtitles or dubbed. Basis for the musical "Sweet Charity." 111m/B VHS, Beta. IT Giulietta Masina, Amedeo Nazzari; **D:** Federico Fellini; **W:** Federico Fellini, Tullio Pinelli, Ennio Flaiano; **M:** Nino Rota. Academy Awards '57: Best Foreign Language Film; Cannes Film Festival '57: Best Actress (Masina). NOS, VYY, TPV

Nightscare ✍✍ Night Scare; Beyond Bedlam 1993 (R) When Dr. Stephanie Lyell's (Hurley) drug behavior-modification experiment goes wrong it allows serial killer Marc Gilmour (Allen) to get to his victims through their dreams. The doc tries to prove to Detective Inspector Terry Hamilton (Fairbrass) that the drug is safe by injecting them both but things get out of hand. Adapted from the novel by Harry Adam Knight. **CW:** Strong horror violence and gore, sexuality and language. 89m/C VHS, LV, Closed Caption. GB Craig Fairbrass, Elizabeth Hurley, Keith Allen, Jesse Birdsall, Craig Kelly; **D:** Vadim Jean; **W:** Vadim Jean. ART

Nightstalker WOOF! 1979 A brother and sister who were condemned to eternal death 12,000 years ago must eat virgins to keep their bodies from rotting. Trouble is, while they search for dinner, the movie decomposes. For mature audiences with no fantasies of celluloid nirvana. 90m/C VHS, Beta. Aldo Ray. ART

Nightstick ✍½ Calhoun 1987 (R) New York vigilante cop fights nasties who threaten to blow the lid off the city. Worse, they kidnap super cop's girl forcing him to save her along with the city. Lots of violence, predictable plot, and mediocre acting leave this one without much bang. 90m/C VHS, Beta. Bruce Fairbairn, Kerrie Keane, John Vernon,

Robert Vaughn, Isaac Hayes, Leslie Nielsen; **D:** Joseph L. Scanlan. **COL**

Nightwatch 🎬🎬 **1996 (R)** Law student Martin (McGregor) takes a job as a night watchman in a morgue at the same time a serial killer is killing prostitutes and gouging out their eyes. As if that weren't enough, he has to deal with a cop (Nolte) who suspects him, a sadistic best friend (Brolin) who likes to scare him on the job, and a creepy boss (Dourif) who doesn't like him. Adapted by director Bornedal from his Dutch film "Nattevagten," this one's effectively creepy, but disjointed. Excellent cast is misused, as hardly any of the characters are developed beyond simple types. If you enjoyed the murky, depressing atmosphere of "Seven," you'll probably like this.**CW:** Strong morbid violence, language, sexuality and some drug content. **101m/C VHS.** Ewan McGregor, Nick Nolte, Patricia Arquette, Josh Brolin, John C. Reilly, Brad Dourif, Lonny Chapman, Alix Koromzay, Lauren Graham; **D:** Ole Bornedal; **W:** Ole Bornedal, Steven Soderbergh; **C:** Dan Laustsen; **M:** Joachim Holbek. **NYR**

Nightwing 🎬½ **1979 (PG)** Suspense drama about three people who risk their lives to exterminate a colony of plague-carrying vampire bats in New Mexican Indian community. From the novel by Martin Cruz Smith and adapted by Smith, Steve Shagan, and Bud Shrake. O.K. viewing for those who aren't choosy about their rabid bat movies. **103m/C VHS, Beta, LV.** Nick Mancuso, David Warner, Kathryn Harrold, Strother Martin, Stephen Macht, Pat Corley, Charles Hallahan, Ben Piazza, George Clutesi; **D:** Arthur Hiller; **W:** Steve Shagan, Bud Shrake, Martin Cruz Smith; **C:** Charles Rosher Jr.; **M:** Henry Mancini. **COL**

Nightwish 🎬½ **1989 (R)** Students do more than homework when a professor leads them into their own horrifying dreams. Soon it becomes impossible to distinguish dreams from reality. **96m/C VHS, LV.** Jack Starrett, Robert Tessier, Clayton Rohner, Elizabeth Kaitan, Alisha Das, Tom Dugan, Brian Thompson, Artur Cybulski; **D:** Bruce Cook Jr.; **W:** Bruce Cook Jr. **NO**

Nijinsky 🎬🎬 **1980 (R)** An opulent biography of the famous ballet dancer. His exciting and innovative choreography gets little attention. The film concentrates on his infamous homosexual lifestyle and his relationship with impresario Sergei Diaghilev (Bates, in a tour-de-force performance). Lovely to look at, but slow and unconvincing. **125m/C VHS, Beta, Closed Caption.** Alan Bates, George de la Pena, Leslie Browne, Alan Badel, Carla Fracci, Colin Blakely, Ronald Pickup, Ronald Lacey, Vernon Dobtcheff, Jeremy Irons, Frederick Jaeger, Janet Suzman, Sian Phillips; **D:** Herbert Ross. **PAR**

Nikki, the Wild Dog of the North 🎬½ **1961 (G)** When a Malemute pup is separated from his Canadian trapper master, he teams up with a bear cub for a series of adventures. Later the pup is reunited with his former master for still more adventures. Adapted from a novel by James Oliver Curwood for Disney. **73m/C VHS, Beta.** Jean Coutu; **D:** Jack Couffer, Don Haldane. **DIS**

Nil by Mouth 🎬🎬 **1996 (R)** Oldman draws on his own dysfunctional working-class London background for his impressive writer/director debut, which casually puts you into the middle of one Cockney family's life. There's brutal Ray (Winstone), husband to Val (Burke) and brother-in-law to young addict Billy (Creed-Miles), as well as his tough mother-in-law Janet (Morse) and her mother, Kath (Dore). Billy gets kicked out of the house by Ray and struggles to survive outside his family while a drunken Ray beats the pregnant Val, prompting a display of female solidarity. Formless pic drops into characters' lives at random, showcasing family loyalty and generosity amidst the violence.**CW:** Graphic drug use, nonstop strong language, brutal domestic violence and some nudity. **128m/C VHS, Closed Caption.** GB Ray Winstone, Kathy Burke, Charlie Creed-Miles, Laila Morse, Edna Dore, Steve Sweeney, Chrissie Cotterill, Jon Morrison, Jamie Forman; **D:** Gary Oldman; **W:** Gary Oldman; **C:** Ron Fortunato; **M:** Eric Clapton. British Academy

Awards '97: Best Film, Best Original Screenplay; Cannes Film Festival '97: Best Actress (Burke); Nominations: British Academy Awards '97: Best Actor (Winstone), Best Actress (Burke). **COL**

Nina Takes a Lover 🎬🎬 **1994 (R)** Romantic comedy finds Nina (San Giacomo) deciding that the passion is gone from her three-year marriage so, while her husband is out of town, she picks up a nameless Welsh photographer (Rhys) and begins an affair. The affair is over as the movie begins but Nina tells her story to a tabloid journalist (O'Keefe) who's writing about adultery. Gimmicky, with shallow if attractive characters and an equally attractive San Francisco setting.**CW:** Language; some strong sexuality. **100m/C VHS, LV, Closed Caption.** Laura San Giacomo, Paul Rhys, Michael O'Keefe, Cristi Conaway, Fisher Stevens; **D:** Alan Jacobs; **W:** Alan Jacobs; **C:** Phil Parmet; **M:** Todd Boekelheide. **COL**

Nine Ages of Nakedness 🎬 **1969** The story of a man whose ancestors have been plagued by a strange problem: beautiful, naked women who create carnal chaos. **88m/C VHS, Beta.** Harrison Marks. **VDM, MRV**

9 1/2 Ninjas 🎬🎬½ **1990 (R)** A cautious and disciplined martial artist trains a young and flirtatious woman in the ways of the ninja. His life becomes exciting in more ways than one, when he realizes she's being followed by ninjas with more on their minds than her training—they want to assassinate her! Crazy mixture of sex, kung fu and humor make this film one surprise after another. **88m/C VHS, Beta, LV, Closed Caption.** Michael Phenicie, Andee Gray, Tommy (Tiny) Lister; **D:** Aaron Worth; **W:** Bill Crounse. **REP**

9 1/2 Weeks 🎬🎬½ **1986 (R)** Chance meeting between a Wall Street exec and an art gallery employee evolves into an experimental sexual relationship bordering on sado-masochism. Video version is more explicit than the theatrical release, but not by much. Strong characterizations by both actors prevent this from being strictly pornography. Well-written, with strength of male and female personalities nicely balanced. Intriguing, but not for all tastes. **114m/C VHS, Beta, LV, Letterbox.** Mickey Rourke, Kim Basinger, Margaret Whitton, Karen Young, David Margulies, Christine Baranski, Roderick Cook, Dwight Weist; **D:** Adrian Lyne; **W:** Patricia Louisiana Knop, Zalman King; **C:** Peter Biziou; **M:** Jack Nitzsche. **MGM**

Nine Days a Queen 🎬🎬🎬 *Lady Jane Grey; Tudor Rose* **1936** An historical drama based on the life of Lady Jane Grey, proclaimed Queen of England after the death of Henry VIII of England and summarily executed for treason by Mary Tudor after a nine-day reign. An obscure tragedy with good performances and absorbing storyline. Remade as "Lady Jane" (1985). **80m/B VHS, Beta.** GB John Mills, Cedric Hardwicke, Nova Pilbeam, Sybil Thorndike, Leslie Perrins, Felix Aylmer, Miles Malleson, Frank Cellier, Desmond Tester, Gwen Francon-Davies, Martita Hunt, John Laurie, Roy Emerton, John Turnbull, J.H. Roberts; **D:** Robert Stevenson; **W:** Robert Stevenson, Miles Malleson. **HHT, DVT**

Nine Deaths of the Ninja woof! **1985 (R)** Faceless ninja warrior Kosugi leads a team of commandos on a mission to rescue a group of political prisoners held captive in the Philippine jungles. Features Ozone-depleted plot, incongruous performances, and inane dialogue, not to mention two main villains—a neurotic Nazi in a wheelchair and a black lesbian amazon—who chew jungle and bring bad art to a new level of appreciation. Amazing in its total badness. Produced by Cannon. **93m/C VHS, Beta.** Sho Kosugi, Brent Huff, Emelia Lesniak, Regina Richardson; **D:** Emmett Alston; **W:** Emmett Alston. **MGM**

The Nine Lives of Elfego Baca 🎬🎬 **1958** Venerable Western hero Loggia faces a veritable army of gunfighters and bandits. Action-packed but not too violent; family fun. **78m/C VHS, Beta.** Robert Loggia, Robert Simon, Lisa Montell, Nestor Paiva; **D:** Norman Foster. **DIS**

Nine Lives of Fritz the Cat 🎬🎬 **1974** Fritz feels that life's too square in the '70s, so he takes off into some of his other lives for more adventure. Cleaner but still naughty sequel to the X-rated "Fritz the Cat," featuring neither the original's writer/director Ralph Bakshi nor cartoonist Robert Crumb. Tame and lame. Animated. **77m/C VHS, LV. D:** Robert Taylor. **VES**

Nine Months 🎬🎬½ **1995 (PG-13)** Happily single Samuel (Grant) gets girlfriend Rebecca (Moore) pregnant and promptly wigs out. He makes amends to the lovely Rebecca, they marry, and true to writer/director Columbus' style, live happily ever after. Bachelor pal Sean (Goldblum) and an expectant couple (Arnold and Cusack) with three kids round out the cast, with Williams offering his usual manic flair as a Russian obstetrician, improvising his scenes with glee. Grant's knack for clumsy befuddlement fits well with the warm, fuzzy style of Columbus. "Nine" doesn't go out on any limbs, but is a pleasant diversion anyway. Film may well have gotten lost in the megaboxoffice summer of '95, till Grant guaranteed publicity when his dalliance with Divine Brown threw him into jail and the headlines. His faux pas causes unintended laughs during a few key scenes. The trailer clip showing Grant during a mug shot is gone—producers claim the segment was deleted before his real-life arrest. Remake of the French film "Neuf Mois."**CW:** Language and sexual innuendo. **103m/C VHS, LV, Closed Caption.** Hugh Grant, Julianne Moore, Tom Arnold, Joan Cusack, Jeff Goldblum; **Cameos:** Robin Williams; **D:** Chris Columbus; **W:** Chris Columbus; **C:** Donald McAlpine; **M:** Hans Zimmer. **FXV**

9 to 5 🎬🎬½ **1980 (PG)** In this caricature of large corporations and women in the working world, Coleman plays the male chauvinist boss who calls the shots and keeps his employees, all female, under his thumb. Three of the office secretaries daydream of Coleman's disposal and rashly kidnap him after a silly set of occurrences threaten their jobs. While they have him under lock and key, the trio take office matters into their own hands and take a stab at running things their own way, with amusing results. The basis for a television series. **111m/C VHS, Beta, LV.** Jane Fonda, Lily Tomlin, Dolly Parton, Dabney Coleman, Sterling Hayden, Norma Donaldson; **D:** Colin Higgins; **W:** Patricia Resnick; **C:** Reynaldo Villalobos; **M:** Charles Fox. Nominations: Academy Awards '80: Best Song ("Nine to Five"). **FOX**

976-EVIL 🎬🎬 **1988 (R)** Englund (the infamous Freddy from the Nightmare on Elm Street epics) directs this horror movie where a lonely teenager dials direct to demons from hell. **102m/C VHS, LV, Closed Caption.** Stephen Geoffreys, Jim Metzler, Maria Rubell, Sandy Dennis, Robert Picardo, Leslie Deane, Pat O'Bryan, J.J. Cohen; **D:** Robert Englund; **W:** Brian Helgeland, Rhet Topham; **C:** Paul Elliott; **M:** Tom Chase, Steve Rucker. **COL**

976-EVIL 2: The Astral Factor 🎬½ **1991 (R)** Satan returns the call in this supernatural thriller that sequels the original film.**CW:** Horror violence. **93m/C VHS, Closed Caption.** Pat O'Bryan, Rene Assa, Debbie James; **D:** Jim Wynorski; **W:** Erik Anjou. **ART, VES**

984: Prisoner of the Future *The Tomorrow Man* **1984** A shocking, futuristic tale of human self-destruction. **70m/C VHS, Beta.** Don Francks, Stephen Markle; **D:** Tibor Takacs. **NO**

1900 🎬🎬🎬 *Novecento* **1976 (R)** Bertolucci's impassioned epic about two Italian families, one land-owning, the other, peasant. Shows the sweeping changes of the 20th century begun by the trauma of WWI and the onslaught of Italian socialism. Edited down from its original 360-minute length and dubbed in English from three other languages, the film suffers somewhat from editing and from its nebulous lack of commitment to any genre. **255m/C VHS, Beta, LV.** FR IT GE Robert De Niro, Gerard Depardieu, Burt Lancaster, Donald Sutherland, Dominique Sanda, Sterling Hayden, Laura Betti, Francesca Bertini, Werner Bruhns, Stefania Sandrelli, Anna Henkel,

Alida Valli; *D:* Bernardo Bertolucci; *W:* Giuseppe Bertolucci; Bernardo Bertolucci; *C:* Vittorio Storaro. *PAR*

1918 ♂♂½ 1985 An adaptation of the Horton Foote play about the effects of WWI and an influenza epidemic on a small Texas town. Slow-moving but satisfying. Score by Willie Nelson. Originally produced for PBS's "American Playhouse." Prequelled by "On Valentine's Day." **89m/C VHS, Beta, Closed Caption.** Matthew Broderick, Hallie Foote, William Converse-Roberts, Rochelle Oliver, Michael Higgins, Horton Foote Jr., William Bill McGhee, Jeannie McCarthy; *D:* Ken Harrison; *W:* Horton Foote; *M:* Willie Nelson. *FOX*

1931: Once Upon a Time in New York ♂♂ 1972 Prohibition-era gangsters war, beat each other up, make headlines, and drink bathtub gin. **90m/C VHS, Beta.** Richard Conte, Adolfo Celi, Lionel Stander, Irene Papas. *VCD*

1941 ♂♂½ 1979 (PG) Proved to be the most expensive comedy of all time with a budget exceeding $35 million. The depiction of Los Angeles in the chaotic days after the bombing of Pearl Harbor combines elements of fantasy and black humor. **120m/C VHS, Beta, LV.** John Belushi, Dan Aykroyd, Patti LuPone, Ned Beatty, Slim Pickens, Murray Hamilton, Christopher Lee, Tim Matheson, Toshiro Mifune, Warren Oates, Robert Stack, Nancy Allen, Elisha Cook Jr., Lorraine Gary, Treat Williams, Mickey Rourke, John Candy; *D:* Steven Spielberg; *W:* Robert Zemeckis, Bob Gale; *C:* William A. Fraker; *M:* John Williams. Nominations: Academy Awards '79: Best Cinematography, Best Sound. *USH, CCB*

1969 ♂♂♂½ 1989 (R) Three teenage friends during the 1960s become radicalized by the return of one of their friends from Vietnam in a coffin. Critically lambasted directorial debut for "On Golden Pond" author Ernest Thompson. **96m/C VHS, Beta, LV, Closed Caption.** Kiefer Sutherland, Robert Downey Jr., Winona Ryder, Bruce Dern, Joanna Cassidy, Mariette Hartley; *D:* Ernest Thompson.

1984 ♂♂♂½ 1984 (R) A very fine adaptation of George Orwell's infamous novel, this version differs from the overly simplistic and cautionary 1954 film because of fine casting and production design. The illegal love affair of a government official becomes his attempt to defy the crushing inhumanity and lack of simple pleasures of an omniscient government. Filmed in London, it skillfully visualizes our time's most central prophetic nightmare. **117m/C VHS, Beta, LV.** John Hurt, Richard Burton, Suzanna Hamilton, Cyril Cusack, Gregory Fisher, Andrew Wilde, Rupert Baderman; *D:* Michael Radford; *C:* Roger Deakins. *ART*

1990: The Bronx Warriors woof! *1990 I Guerrieri del Bronx; Bronx Warriors* 1983 (R) Good street gang members combat evil corporate powers in a semi-futuristic South Bronx. Lame copy of "Escape from New York." **86m/C VHS, Beta.** *IT* Vic Morrow, Christopher Connelly, Fred Williamson; *D:* Enzo G. Castellari.

1991: The Year Punk Broke 1992 Documents a grunge rock tour of European festivals in 1991 when the alternative bands were largely unknown to all but hardcore fans. Follows Sonic Youth, Nirvana, Dinosaur Jr., Babes in Toyland, Gumball, and grandaddy punk idols, The Ramones, behind-the-scenes and through their performances. **95m/C VHS.** *D:* David Markey. *MOV*

90 Days ♂♂♂ 1986 Charming independently made Canadian comedy about two young men handling their respective romantic dilemmas—one awaiting an oriental fiancee he's never met, the other who is being kicked out of his house by his wife. **99m/C VHS, Beta, Closed Caption.** *CA* Stefan Wodoslowsky, Sam Grana, Christine Pak; *D:* Giles Walker. *FOX*

92 in the Shade ♂♂♂ 1976 (R) Based upon McGuane's novel, the film deals with a bored, wealthy rogue who becomes a fishing guide in the Florida Keys, and battles against the competition of two crusty, half-mad codgers. Sloppy, irreverent comedy as only a first-time writer-turned-director can fashion. **91m/C VHS, Beta.** Peter Fonda, Warren Oates, Margot Kidder, Burgess Meredith, Harry Dean Stanton; *D:* Thomas McGuane; *W:* Thomas McGuane. *FOX*

99 & 44/100 Dead ♂ *Call Harry Crown* 1974 (PG) Frankenheimer falters with this silly gangster flick. Harris is hired to kill Dillman, by local godfather O'Brien. Originally written as a satirical look at gangster movies, but it doesn't stick to satire, and as a result is disappointing. **98m/C VHS.** Richard Harris, Chuck Connors, Edmond O'Brien, Bradford Dillman, Ann Turkel; *D:* John Frankenheimer; *W:* Robert Dillon; *M:* Henry Mancini. *FOX*

99 Women ♂♂½ *Isle of Lost Women* 1969 (R) Sympathetic prison warden attempts to investigate conditions at a women's prison camp. Thin and exploitative view of lesbianism behind bars that sensationalizes the subject. **90m/C VHS, Beta.** *GB SP GE IT* Maria Schell, Herbert Lom, Mercedes McCambridge, Luciana Paluzzi; *D:* Jess (Jesus) Franco. *NO*

Ninja 3: The Domination ♂♂ 1984 (R) Ninja master must remove the spirit of a deadly ninja assassin from a young woman intent on wreaking havoc among the Phoenix police department. Extremely silly super ninja epic utterly uninhibited by the usual plot conventions. **92m/C VHS, Beta.** Lucinda Dickey, Sho Kosugi; *D:* Sam Firstenberg; *W:* James R. Silke; *C:* Hanania Baer. *MGM*

Ninja Academy ♂♂½ 1990 (R) Seven wimps, losers, and spoiled brats come to the Ninja Academy to learn the art. Will they make it? **93m/C VHS.** Will Egan, Kelly Randall, Gerald Okomura, Michael David, Robert Factor, Jeff Robinson; *D:* Nico Mastorakis. *NO*

Ninja: American Warrior ♂½ 1990 An evil ninja takes on the U.S. Drug Enforcement Agency when the authorities threaten to shut him down. **90m/C VHS, Beta.** Joff Houston, John Wilford; *D:* Tommy Cheng. *IMP*

Ninja Brothers of Blood ♂ 1989 A guy falls for a rival gang member's girl. Neither the gang nor the guy's former girlfriend take kindly to this! **90m/C VHS, Beta, LV.** Marcus Gibson, Fonda Lynn, Brian McClave, Jonathan Soper; *D:* Raymond Woo. *IMP*

Ninja Champion woof! 198? White-clad and masked ninja heros come to the aid of some Interpol agents tracking down a sleazy diamond smuggler. Invisible storyline features very little actual ninja. Extremely unconvincing and poorly dubbed. **90m/C VHS, Beta.** HK Bruce Baron, Richard Harrison; *D:* Godfrey Ho; *W:* Godfrey Ho. *TWE*

Ninja Checkmate ♂ 1990 An evil ninja seems indestructible, but finally he meets his match. **90m/C VHS, Beta.** Simon Lee, Jack Long, Jeanie Chang. *MGI*

Ninja Commandments ♂ 1987 Everything is at stake when an evil warrior takes on the greatest fighter in the land: the winner will rule the empire! **90m/C VHS, Beta.** Richard Harrison, Dave Wheeler; *D:* Joseph Lai. *IMP*

Ninja Condors ♂ 1987 A young man grows up to avenge the murder of his father. **85m/C VHS, Beta.** Alexander Lou, Stuart Hugh; *D:* James Wu. *TWE*

Ninja Connection ♂ 1990 Ninja terrorism is employed as a scare tactic to deter a group who wants to break up an international drug ring. **90m/C VHS, Beta.** Patricia Greenford, Jane Kingsly, Joe Nelson, Louis Roth, Henry Steele, Stuart Steen; *D:* York Lam. *IMP*

Ninja Death Squad ♂ 1987 A team specializing in political assassinations is hunted down by a special agent. **89m/C VHS, Beta.** Glen Carson, Patricia Goodman, Joff Houston, Billy Jones, Wallace Jones, John Wilford; *D:* Tommy Cheng. *IMP*

Ninja Demon's Massacre ♂ 198? Ninja named Willie responds to federal investigations into his spying business by wearing a black robe and slashing feds with long swords. **89m/C VHS, Beta.** Ted Brooke, James Lear. *TWE*

Ninja Destroyer ♂ 197? (R) Ninja warriors battle over an emerald mine. **92m/C VHS, Beta.** HK Bruce Baron, Stuart Smith; *D:* Godfrey Ho; *W:* Godfrey Ho. *TWE*

Ninja Dragon ♂ 198? Two Ninjas are hired in a gang war and dazzle all those who watch by kicking their enemies to death. **92m/C VHS, Beta.** Richard Harrison. *TWE*

Ninja Exterminators woof! 1981 Low-grade kung-fu antics mascarading as ninja rib-kicking bonanza. Dubbed. **85m/C VHS, Beta.** HK Jacky Cheng, Ko Shou Liang, Tai Chen. *NO*

Ninja Fantasy woof! 1986 Ninja drug smugglers and government officials battle over a large drug shipment. Everybody go chop socky. Not much in way of ninja fantasy. Dubbed. **95m/C VHS, Beta.** HK Adam Nell, Ian Frank, Jordan Heller, Ken Ashley, Jenny Mills, Jack Rodman; *D:* Bruce Lambert; *W:* Anthony Green. *TWE*

Ninja Hunt woof! 198? This time, ninjas kick international terrorists in the head while searching for secret formula. Poorly dubbed pseudo ninja developed by Godfrey Ho. **92m/C VHS, Beta.** HK Bruce Baron, Stuart Smith; *D:* Joseph Lai; *W:* Stephen Saul. *TWE*

Ninja Massacre ♂ 1984 Gangsters covet a secret manual of kung fu techniques. Heel-splintering battles break out as a result. **87m/C VHS, Beta.** Lo Lieh, Pai Ying, Lung Jun Ehr, Tiki Shirtee. *GEM, MRV*

Ninja Masters of Death ♂ 1985 Terrorists reign supreme until the white ninja saves the city. **90m/C VHS, Beta.** Mick Jones, Chris Petersen, Daniel Wells, Richard Young; *D:* Bruce Lambert. *TWE*

Ninja Mission ♂½ 1984 (R) First Scandinavian ninja epic follows CIA agent and his group of ninja fighters as they embark on a hazardous mission to rescue two people from a Soviet prison. They use their fighting skills (Swedish ninjas favor guns more than ninjutsu) against Russian soldiers. Dubbed. **95m/C VHS, Beta.** SW Christopher Kohlberg, Curt Brober, Hanna Pola; *D:* Mats Helge.

Ninja Nightmare ♂ 1988 (R) A man seeks revenge for his family's death. **98m/C VHS, Beta.** Leo Fong.

Ninja of the Magnificence ♂½ 1989 When the ninja master is killed, factions within his group battle for control. **90m/C VHS, Beta.** Sam Baker, Patrick Frbezar, Clive Hadwen, Tim Michael, Renato Sala; *D:* Charles Lee. *IMP*

Ninja Operation: Licensed to Terminate ♂ 1987 Two warriors risk broken noses and twisted limbs to take on the Black Ninja Empire. **89m/C VHS, Beta.** Richard Harrison, Paul Marshall, Jack McPeat, Grant Temple; *D:* Joseph Lai. *IMP*

Ninja Phantom Heroes ♂ 1987 Two Vietnam vets are imprisoned for war crimes. One escapes and forms his own secret ninja society. **90m/C VHS, Beta.** Glen Carson, George Dickson, Allen Leung, Christine Wells; *D:* Bruce Lambert. *TWE*

The Ninja Pirates ♂½ 1990 In the Sung Dynasty, a group of bloodthirsty pirates are hunted down after stealing a golden treasure. **90m/C VHS, Beta.** Chi Lan, Lo Lieh, Carter Wong, Nancy Yan. *MGI*

Ninja Powerforce ♂½ 1990 Two childhood friends end up as members of rival ninja gangs in the midst of a bloody war. Usual assortment of ninja-inflicted injuries result. **90m/C VHS, Beta.** Jonathan Bould, Richard Harrison; *D:* Joseph Lai. *IMP*

Ninja Showdown ♂ 1990 A warrior must take on a number of vicious bandits in order to defend his small town. He vows revenge on anyone who threatens his people. **92m/C VHS, Beta.** Richard Harrison; *D:* Joseph Lai. *TWE*

Ninja Squad ♂ 198? Empires, families, and honor are at stake in a fierce battle of heel-to-head action. **92m/C VHS, Beta.** Dave Wheeler, Richard Harrison, Timalden. *TWE*

Ninja Strike Force 🥷½ 1988 The Black Ninjas steal the powerful "spirit sword," and go on a bloody rampage. 89m/C VHS, Beta. Richard Harrison, Gary Carter; **D:** Joseph Lai. IMP

Ninja Supremo 🥷½ 1990 A rebellious teenager studies Kung-fu, and then returns to his village as a hero after he gains expertise in his chosen field. 100m/C VHS, Beta. David Tao, Andrew Kam Yeun Wah, Sun Yueh. MGI

Ninja Swords of Death 🥷½ 1990 A noble warrior challenges a vicious assassin who uses a spur-sword. He is nearly decapitated in the process. 90m/C VHS, Beta. Chang Ying Chun, Chia Ling, Tien Pang, Kong Pun. MGI

Ninja the Battalion 🥷 1990 Agents from America, the Soviet Union, and China try to recover germ warfare secrets stolen by the Japanese secret service. 90m/C VHS, Beta, Closed Caption. Roger Crawford, Sam Huxley, Alexander Lou, Dickson Warn; **D:** Victor Sears. TWE

Ninja the Protector 🥷 198? A ninja tracks down and kicks the ninja head of a counterfeiting ring. 92m/C VHS, Beta. Richard Harrison. TWE

Ninja, the Violent Sorcerer 🥷½ 1986 Murderer, with the help of Chinese vampires, does battle with the ghost of a dead gambling lord's wife and the gambling lord's living brother. Often tedious even with above average production and incredible plot. 90m/C VHS, Beta. **D:** Bruce Lambert; **W:** Daniel Clough. TWE

Ninja Turf 🥷 L.A. Streetfighters 1986 (R) Teenage kick artists rip off a Hollywood drug dealer and are pursued by a swarm of ninja hitmen. 83m/C VHS, Beta, LV. Jun Chong, Bill Wallace, Rosanna King, James Lew, Phillip Rhee. COL

Ninja Vengeance 🥷½ 1993 (R) The corrupt sheriff of a small Texas town, who also leads the KKK, is terrorizing a young African-American local. Then our lone hero rides into town on his trusty motorcycle to save the day. Only this time instead of your average gunman, he's a ninja.**CW:** Language, violence, and sexuality. 87m/C VHS, Closed Caption. Stephen K. Hayes, Janet K. Pawlak, Craig Boyett, David Paul Lord; **D:** Karl Armstrong; **W:** Carrie Armstrong, Karl Armstrong. COL

Ninja vs. Ninja 🥷½ 1990 A scientist has found a cure for heroin addiction, but ninja drug lords won't let his discovery see the light of day! 90m/C VHS, Beta. Hui Hsiao Chiang, Callan Leong. MGI

Ninja vs. the Shaolin 🥷½ 1984 Savage fighting between priests and ninjas results in one of the bloodiest pages in history. 90m/C VHS, Beta. Alexander Lou, John Wu; **D:** Jacky Hwong. MGI

Ninja's Extreme Weapons 🥷½ 1990 Blue Ninja takes it to the streets when his brother is killed by the underworld. 90m/C VHS, Beta. James Gray, Donald Muir; **D:** Victor Sears. TWE, HHE

Ninotchka 🥷🥷🥷½ 1939 (R) Delightful romantic comedy. Garbo is a cold Russian agent sent to Paris to check up on her comrades, who are being seduced by capitalism. She inadvertently falls in love with a playboy, who melts her communist heart. Garbo talks and laughs. Satirical, energetic, and witty. Later a Broadway musical called "Silk Stockings."**CW:** Language and strong sexuality. 110m/B VHS, Beta, LV, 8mm. Greta Garbo, Melvyn Douglas, Ina Claire, Sig Rumann, Felix Bressart, Bela Lugosi; **D:** Ernst Lubitsch; **W:** Billy Wilder; **C:** William H. Daniels. National Film Registry '90;; Nominations: Academy Awards '39: Best Actress (Garbo), Best Picture, Best Story. MGM

The Ninth Configuration 🥷🥷🥷 Twinkle, Twinkle, Killer Kane 1979 (R) Based on Blatty's novel "Twinkle, Twinkle, Killer Kane" (also the film's alternate title), this is a weird and surreal tale of a mock rebellion of high-ranking military men held in a secret base hospital for the mentally ill. Keach is good as the commander who is just as insane as the patients. Available in many different lengths, this is generally considered to be the best. 115m/C VHS, Beta, LV. Stacy Keach, Scott

Wilson, Jason Miller, Ed Flanders, Neville Brand, Alejandro Rey, Robert Loggia, George DiCenzo; **D:** William Peter Blatty; **W:** William Peter Blatty. Golden Globe Awards '81: Best Screenplay.

Nitti: The Enforcer 🥷🥷 1988 (PG-13) Made-for-TV saga about Al Capone's brutal enforcer and right-hand man, Frank Nitti. Diversified cast (Moriarty in particular) do their best to keep things moving along, and the atmosphere is consistently and appropriately violent. Made to capitalize on the success of 1987's "The Untouchables." 94m/C VHS. Anthony LaPaglia, Vincent Guastaferro, Trini Alvarado, Michael Moriarty, Michael Russo, Louis Guss, Bruno Kirby; **D:** Michael Switzer.

Nixon 🥷🥷🥷 1995 (R) Stone again "interprets" historical events of the '60s and '70s with a sprawling, bold bio of Richard Nixon. Covering all the highlights of Nixon's public life, and speculating on his private one, Hopkins convincingly portrays "Tricky Dick" as an embattled, lonely political genius. Gigantic all-star cast is lead by Oscar-caliber performance of Joan Allen as Pat Nixon. Even at over three hours, there isn't nearly enough time to explore the significance of all the events covered here. As usual, Stone has taken some creative license, which lead to the Nixon daughters publicly trashing the film, and Walt Disney's daughter expressing "shame" at being affiliated with it.**CW:** Language. 192m/C VHS, LV, Letterbox, Closed Caption. Anthony Hopkins, Joan Allen, Ed Harris, Bob Hoskins, David Paymer, Paul Sorvino, J.T. Walsh, James Woods, Madeline Kahn, Brian Bedford, Mary Steenburgen, Powers Boothe, E.G. Marshall, David Hyde Pierce, Kevin Dunn, Annabeth Gish, Tony Goldwyn, Larry Hagman, Edward Herrmann, Saul Rubinek, Tony LoBianco; **D:** Oliver Stone; **W:** Christopher Wilkinson, Stephen J. Rivele, Oliver Stone; **C:** Robert Richardson; **M:** John Williams. Los Angeles Film Critics Association Awards '95: Best Supporting Actress (Allen); National Society of Film Critics Awards '95: Best Supporting Actress (Allen); Nominations: Academy Awards '95: Best Actor (Hopkins), Best Original Screenplay, Best Supporting Actress (Allen), Best Original Dramatic/Comedy Score; British Academy Awards '95: Best Supporting Actress (Allen); Golden Globe Awards '96: Best Actor—Drama (Hopkins); Screen Actors Guild Award '95: Best Actor (Hopkins), Best Actress (Allen), Cast. TOU

No Big Deal 🥷½ 1983 (PG-13) Dillon is a streetwise teenager who makes friends at his new school. Blah promise; bad acting makes this no big deal. 86m/C VHS. Kevin Dillon, Sylvia Miles, Tammy Grimes, Jane Krakowski, Christopher Gartin, Mary Joan Negro; **D:** Robert Charlton. BTV

No Comebacks 1985 Two British mysteries, made for television from stories by Frederick Forsyth: "A Careful Man," about a dying millionaire who cheats his heirs, and "Privilege," about a clever stamp dealer who exacts revenge upon a libelous gossip columnist. 60m/C VHS, Beta. GB Milo O'Shea, Cyril Cusack, Dan O'Herlihy, Gayle Hunnicutt.

No Contest 🥷🥷 1994 (R) International terrorists, lead by Oz (Clay), hold the TV host (Tweed) and contestants of the Ms. Galaxy beauty pageant hostage with a $10 million ransom demand.**CW:** Great amount of strong violence; language. 98m/C VHS, Closed Caption. Andrew Dice Clay, Shannon Tweed, Robert Davi, Roddy Piper, Nicholas Campbell; **D:** Paul Lynch; **W:** Robert Cooper. COL

No Dead Heroes 🥷 1987 Green Beret Vietnam war hero succumbs to Soviet scheming when they plant a computer chip in his brain. Unoriginal and unworthy. 86m/C VHS, Beta. Max Thayer, John Dresden, Toni Nero; **D:** J.C. Miller. NO

No Deposit, No Return 🥷🥷 Double Trouble 1976 (G) Tedious, silly, pointless Disney action comedy. Rich brats persuade bumbling crooks to kidnap them, offer them for ransom to millionaire grandfather. 115m/C VHS, Beta. David Niven, Don Knotts, Darren McGavin, Barbara Feldon, Charles Martin Smith; **D:** Norman Tokar; **W:** Arthur Alsberg; **M:** Buddy Baker. DIS

No Dessert Dad, 'Til You Mow the Lawn 🥷½ 1994 (PG) Suburban parents Ken and Carol Cochran (Robert Hays and Joanna Kerns) are harassed at home by their annoying offspring, Justin, Monica, and Tyler. When they try hypnosis tapes to quit smoking, the kids discover by doctoring the tapes, they can plant suggestions resulting in parental perks. 80m/C VHS. Robert Hays, Joanna Kerns, Joshua Schaefer, Allison Meek, Jimmy Marsden, Richard Moll, Larry Linville; **D:** Howard McCain. NHO

No Drums, No Bugles 🥷½ 1971 (G) A West Virginia farmer and conscientious objector leaves his family to live alone in a cave for three years during the Civil War. Bad direction spoils Sheen's good performance. 85m/C VHS, Beta. Martin Sheen, Davey Davidson, Denine Terry, Rod McCary; **D:** Clyde Ware. VTR

No End 🥷🥷 Bez Konca 1984 The ghost of a dead lawyer watches as his wife and young son struggle to survive without him, including the widow getting involved in her husband's last case about a worker arrested for organizing a strike. Well-acted but overly solemn and slow; set during Poland's martial law in 1982. In Polish with English subtitles. 108m/C VHS, Beta. PL Grazyna Szapolowska, Jerzy Radziwilowicz, Maria Pakulnis, Aleksander Bardini, Artur Barcis, Michal Bajor; **D:** Krzysztof Kieslowski; **W:** Krzysztof Piesiewicz, Krzysztof Kieslowski. NYF, FCT, ING

No Escape 🥷🥷½ 1994 (R) In 2022, Captain Robbins (Liotta) has been banished to a prison colony island inhabited by the most dangerous criminals. With no walls and no guards, the prisoners are left to kill each other. Then Robbins discovers a relatively peaceful community of prisoners who help each other. But this group is soon bedeviled by the evil nasties on the other side of the island. Attempts at escape define the plot, so the film is filled with superhuman feats of sheer courage, determination, and guts. Adapted from the book "The Penal Colony" by Richard Herley.**CW:** Some language and large amount of strong violence. 118m/C VHS, LV, Closed Caption. Ray Liotta, Lance Henriksen, Stuart Wilson, Kevin Dillon, Kevin J. O'Connor, Michael Lerner, Ernie Hudson, Ian McNeice, Jack Shepherd; **D:** Martin Campbell; **W:** Joel Gross; **M:** Graeme Revell. HBO

No Escape, No Return 🥷🥷½ 1993 (R) An FBI agent (Nouri) and a police captain (Saxon) force three renegade cops (Nguyen, Caulfield, and Loveday) to infiltrate a drug syndicate. But things go from bad to worse when a war breaks out between rival drug gangs, leaving a lot of bodies, and a large chunk of money gone missing. Now the trio is sought by both the cops and the crooks. 93m/C VHS, LV, Closed Caption. Maxwell Caulfield, Dustin Nguyen, Denise Loveday, John Saxon, Michael Nouri, Kevin Benton; **D:** Charles Kanganis; **W:** Charles Kanganis; **M:** Jim Halfpenny. PMH

No Fear, No Die 🥷🥷 1990 To make some quick cash two black immigrants in France train and sell birds for illegal cockfights at a roadside restaurant. Jocelyn, who trains the cocks, pays them lavish, obsessive attention. But cultural conflicts and repressed passions are just waiting to explode. In French with English subtitles. 97m/C VHS. FR Alex Descas, Isaach de Bankole, Jean-Claude Brialy, Solveig Dommartin, Christopher Buchholz; **D:** Claire Denis; **W:** Claire Denis, Jean-Pol Fargeau; **M:** Abdullah Ibrahim. FRF

No Greater Love 🥷🥷½ 1943 Capra-esque Soviet war movie. A peasant woman mobilizes her village against the Nazis to avenge her family's death. Dubbed into English by the Soviets for Western circulation during WWII. 74m/B VHS, Beta. RU Vera Maretskaya; **D:** Frederic Ermler. FCT, IHF

No Highway in the Sky 🥷🥷 1951 Eccentric scientist Theodore Honey (Stewart) works for the Royal Aircraft Establishment, which has just produced a new plane, the Reindeer. But Honey tells his boss Dennis Scott (Hawkins) that the plane has a serious defect. While flying to examine a Reindeer crash site, Honey befriends Monica (Dietrich), a musical star, and stewardess Marjorie (Johns), who support him when his company accuses him of maliciously damaging the aircraft's reputation. Dietrich steals every scene with her Christian Dior wardrobe and star attitude. Based on the novel "No Highway" by Nevil Shute. **98m/B VHS. *GB* James Stewart, Marlene Dietrich, Glynis Johns, Jack Hawkins, Ronald Squire, Niall MacGinnis, Elizabeth Allan, Kenneth More, David Hutcheson; *D:* Henry Koster; *W:* R.C. Sherriff, Oscar Millard; *M:* Malcolm Arnold. *FXV***

No Holds Barred 🐾½ 1989 (PG-13)
Cheesy, campy remake of cheesy, campy 1952 wrestling movie. Hulk Hogan on the big screen, at last. **98m/C VHS, Beta, LV, Closed Caption.** Hulk Hogan, Kurt Fuller, Joan Severance, Tommy (Tiny) Lister; *D:* Thomas J. Wright. *COL*

No Looking Back 🐾🐾 Long Time, Nothing New 1998 (R)
Small-town 30ish waitress Claudia (Holly) is about to settle for a boring life with decent-but-dull Michael (Bon Jovi) when her ne'er-do-well former boyfriend Charlie (Burns) comes home looking to relive the glory days. Burns stays with the working-class, northeastern setting, but goes for drama this time. With themes that cover economic hopelessness and a yearning to escape, Burns seems to be trying for a cinematic distillation of Bruce Springsteen's (very cinematic) music. In fact, many Springsteen songs are used to set scenes. Like Bruce, Burns knows the working class vernacular, and uses it well. But this time, all traces of subtlety are gone, and the story plays out pretty much as expected. Holly doesn't help much, barely registering in the crucial role. She also looks too damn good to be a washed-up waitress with no options. *CW:* Language. **96m/C VHS, LV, Closed Caption.** Lauren Holly, Edward Burns, Jon Bon Jovi, Blythe Danner, Connie Britton; *D:* Edward Burns; *W:* Edward Burns; *C:* Frank Prinzi; *M:* Joe Delia. *PGV*

No Love for Johnnie 🐾🐾🐾 1960
Well acted if unoriginal political drama. Finch is a British M.P. who fails in both public and private life. Based on the novel by Wilfred Fienburgh. **105m/B VHS, Beta. *GB* Peter Finch, Stanley Holloway, Donald Pleasence, Mary Peach, Mervyn Johns, Dennis Price, Oliver Reed, Billie Whitelaw; *D:* Ralph Thomas; *W:* Mordecai Richler; *M:* Malcolm Arnold. British Academy Awards '61: Best Actor (Finch). *NO***

No Man of Her Own 🐾🐾½ 1932
Gable and Lombard in their only screen pairing. Gambler Babe Stewart (Gable) marries small town librarian (Lombard) on a bet and attempts to hide his secret life from her. Neither star's best film. **81m/B VHS, Beta, LV.** Carole Lombard, Clark Gable, Grant Mitchell, Elizabeth Patterson, Dorothy Mackaill; *D:* Wesley Ruggles. *USH, BAR*

No Man's Land 🐾🐾 1987 (R)
Undercover cop Sweeney tails playboy Sheen but is seduced by wealth and glamour. Flashy surfaces, shiny cars, little substance. **107m/C VHS, Beta, LV, Closed Caption.** Charlie Sheen, D.B. Sweeney, Lara Harris, Randy Quaid; *D:* Peter Werner; *W:* Dick Wolf; *M:* Basil Poledouris. *ORI*

No Man's Law 🐾🐾½ 1927
Hardy plays the depraved villian desperate to get the goldmine owned by an old prospector and his beautiful daughter. But the mine is protected by Rex the Wonder Horse! **?m/B VHS.** Oliver Hardy, Barbara Kent, James Finlayson, Theodore von Eltz; *D:* Fred Jackman. *NO*

No Man's Range 🐾 No Man's Land 1935
Unremarkable, typical, predictable Western: good guys, bad guys, guns, bullets, horses. **56m/B VHS, Beta.** Bob Steele. *NO*

No Mercy 🐾🐾 1986 (R)
A Chicago cop (Gere) plunges into the Cajun bayou in order to avenge the murder of his partner. He falls for a beautiful girl enslaved by the killer, but that doesn't stop him from using her to flush out the powerful swamp-inhabiting crime lord. Absurd story without much plot. **108m/C VHS, Beta, LV, DVD.** Richard Gere, Kim Basinger, Jeroen Krabbe, George

Dzundza, William Atherton, Ray Sharkey, Bruce McGill; *D:* Richard Pearce; *W:* Jim Carabatsos, Al Alan Silvestri. *COL*

No Name On the Bullet 🐾🐾🐾 1959
Aloof gunman John Gant (Murphy) is seeking revenge from someone in the town of Lordsburg, only none of the inhabitants know who the intended victim is. And slowly the town's citizens begin to panic. Great final showdown. **77m/C VHS.** Audie Murphy, Charles Drake, Joan Evans, Edgar Stehli, Warren Stevens, R.G. Armstrong, Whit Bissell, Karl Swenson; *D:* Jack Arnold; *W:* Gene L. Coon; *C:* Harold Lipstein. *USH*

No, No Nanette 🐾🐾½ 1940
Lackluster filming of the Broadway production which fared better on the stage. Stock story of a young woman (Neagle) who rescues her uncle from financial ruin and finds romance in the process. **96m/B VHS.** Anna Neagle, Richard Carlson, Victor Mature, Roland Young, ZaSu Pitts, Eve Arden, Billy Gilbert, Keye Luke; *D:* Herbert Wilcox; *C:* Russell Metty. *NOS*

No One Cries Forever woof! 1985
When a prostitute breaks away from a gangster-madam after finding love, she is tracked down and disfigured. Swedish; dubbed. **96m/C Beta.** Elke Sommer, Howard Carpendale, Zoli Marks; *D:* Jans Rautenbach. *NO*

No Place to Hide 🐾🐾½ 1981
A girl's father drowns and she blames herself. Her mother and psychologist try to convince the girl that her father's spirit isn't stalking her. She doesn't believe them. Made for television. **120m/C VHS, Beta.** Keir Dullea, Mariette Hartley, Kathleen Beller, Arlen Dean Snyder, Gary Graham, John Llewellyn Moxey; *D:* John Llewellyn Moxey.

No Place to Hide 🐾🐾½ 1993 (R)
Barrymore is the target of a psycho who's already killed her sister. Kristofferson plays the hard-edged cop who's out to protect her and trap the killer. *CW:* Language, violence, and sexuality. **90m/C VHS.** Drew Barrymore, Kris Kristofferson, Martin Landau, O.J. Simpson, Dey Young, Bruce Weitz; *D:* Richard Danus; *W:* Richard Danus.

No Place to Run 🐾🐾 1972
An elderly man fights for custody of his grandson, then kidnaps him and flees with him to Canada. Made for TV. **78m/C VHS, Beta.** Herschel Bernardi, Larry Hagman, Stefanie Powers, Neville Brand; *D:* Delbert Mann. *THV*

No Prince for My Cinderella 1978
A schizophrenic girl who has turned to prostitution is sought desperately by her social worker. **100m/C VHS, Beta.** Robert Reed. *WOV*

No Problem 🐾🐾 197?
A man is pursued, shot, and drops dead in the apartment of an unsuspecting man who doesn't know what to do with the body. Dubbed in English. **94m/C VHS, Beta. *FR* Miou-Miou. *NO***

No Regrets for Our Youth 🐾🐾🐾 1946
A feminist saga depicting the spiritual growth of a foolish Japanese girl during the tumultuous years of WWII. In Japanese with English subtitles. **110m/B VHS. *JP* Setsuko Hara; *D:* Akira Kurosawa. *CVC***

No Retreat, No Surrender 🐾 1986
(PG) A young American kick-boxer battles a formidable Russian opponent and wins, quite improbably, after having been tutored by the ghost of Bruce Lee in an abandoned house. Notable as Van Damme's debut, but little else recommends this silly "Rocky" rehash. Followed by "No Retreat, No Surrender II." **85m/C VHS, Beta, LV.** Kurt McKinney, J.W. Fails, Jean-Claude Van Damme; *D:* Corey Yuen. *VTR*

No Retreat, No Surrender 2 🐾 1989
(R) With help from two karate experts, a man sets out to find his girlfriend who has been kidnapped by Soviets. Has little or nothing to do with the movie to which it is ostensibly a sequel. High level kick-boxing action sequences. **92m/C VHS, Beta.** Loren Avedon, Max Thayer, Cynthia Rothrock; *D:* Corey Yuen; *W:* Maria Elene Cellino. *MCG*

No Retreat, No Surrender 3: Blood Brothers 🐾 1991 (R)
Sibling martial arts rivals decide to bond in a manly way when CIA agent dad is most heinously slain by terrorists. Answers the burning question: "Whatever became of Joseph Campanella?" *CW:* Martial arts violence. **97m/C VHS, Closed Caption.** Keith Vitali, Loren Avedon, Joseph Campanella. *IMP*

No Room to Run 🐾½ 1978
Concert promoter's life turns into a nightmare of deadly corporate intrigue when he arrives in Australia. Luckily, he finds time to fall in love. Made for television hokum. **101m/C VHS, Beta. *AU* Richard Benjamin, Paula Prentiss, Barry Sullivan; *D:* Robert Lewis.**

No Safe Haven 🐾 1987 (R)
A government agent seeks revenge for his family's death. **92m/C VHS, Beta.** Wings Hauser, Marina Rice, Robert Tessier; *D:* Ronnie Rondell; *M:* Joel Goldsmith. *MCG*

No Secrets 🐾½ 1991 (R)
A young man on the run seeks refuge with three girls in an isolated house. His dread secret isn't so dread, leaving this mild teen-oriented thriller starved for lack of menace. **92m/C VHS, LV.** Adam Coleman Howard, Amy Locane, Heather Fairfield, Traci Lind; *D:* Dezso Magyar. *COL*

No Small Affair 🐾🐾 1984 (R)
A 16-year-old aspiring photographer becomes romantically involved with a sultry 22-year-old rock star. **102m/C VHS, Beta, LV, Closed Caption.** Jon Cryer, Demi Moore, George Wendt, Peter Frechette, Elizabeth Daily, Tim Robbins, Jennifer Tilly, Rick Ducommun, Ann Wedgeworth; *D:* Jerry Schatzberg; *C:* John A. Alonzo; *M:* Rupert Holmes. *COL*

No Surrender 🐾🐾🐾 1986 (R)
An unpredictable, darkly charming comedy about a Liverpool nightclub newly managed by Angelis. On New Year's Eve, a small drunken war is triggered when two groups of irate senior citizens are booked into the club and clash over their beliefs. The group is made up of Protestants and Catholics and the fight resembles the ongoing conflicts in modern-day Northern Ireland, although most of the action takes place in the loo. Watch for Costello as an inept magician. **100m/C VHS, Beta. *GB* Ray McAnally, Michael Angelis, Avis Bunnage, James Ellis, Tom Georgeson, Mark Mulholland, Joanne Whalley, Elvis Costello, Bernard Hill, Michael Ripper; *D:* Peter Smith; *W:* Alan Bleasdale; *C:* Michael Coulter; *M:* Daryl Runswick.**

No Survivors, Please 🐾½ Der Chef Wuenscht Keine Zeugen; The Chief Wants No Survivors 1963
Aliens from Orion take over politicians in order to rule the Earth. Bizarre, obscure, based on true story. **92m/B VHS. *GE* Maria Perschy, Uwe Friedrichsen, Robert Cunningham, Karen Blanguernon, Gustavo Rojo; *D:* Hans Albin, Peter Berneis. *MOV***

No Time for Romance 🐾🐾 1948
A sprightly musical with an all-black cast. First such film to be shot in color. **?m/C VHS.** Bill Walker. *FCT*

No Time for Sergeants 🐾🐾🐾 1958
Hilarious film version of the Broadway play by Ira Levin. Young Andy Griffith is excellent as the Georgia farm boy who gets drafted into the service and creates mayhem among his superiors and colleagues. Story also told on an earlier television special and later in a series. Note Don Knotts and Benny Baker in small roles along with Jameel Farah who went on to star in TV's M*A*S*H after changing his name to Jamie Farr. **119m/B VHS, Beta, LV, Closed Caption.** Andy Griffith, Nick Adams, Murray Hamilton, Don Knotts, Jamie Farr, Myron McCormick; *D:* Mervyn LeRoy. *WAR*

No Time to Die 🐾 1978
In Indonesia, two corporate pawns and a beautiful reporter battle for the possession of a new laser cannon. **87m/C VHS, Beta.** Chris Mitchum, John Phillip Law, Grazyna Dylong. *TWE*

No Trace 🐾🐾 1950
A writer who broadcasts his crime stories as part of a radio show is the victim of blackmail. It seems a former associate is aware that the stories are all based in fact. A Scotland Yard detective investigates when murder rears its ugly head. **76m/B VHS, Beta. *GB* Hugh**

Sinclair, Dinah Sheridan, John Laurie, Barry Morse, Michael Brennan, Dora Bryan; **D:** John Gilling. *SNC*

No Way Back 🎬🎬 1974 (R) Way. Writer, director, and producer Williamson portrays Jess Crowder, a man-for-hire who is an expert with guns, fists, and martial arts. An angry look at the white establishment. **92m/C VHS, Beta.** Fred Williamson, Charles Woolf, Tracy Reed, Virginia Gregg, Don Cornelius; **D:** Fred Williamson. *UNI*

No Way Back 🎬🎬 1996 (R) FBI agent Zack Grant (Crowe) has never dealt with the death of his wife in childbirth and his career has suffered. His last professional chance is a sting operation involving the Mafia and the Yakuza. But when the operation goes wrong, Grant has a vendetta on his hands. Mafia boss Serlano (Lerner) kidnaps Zack's young son so Zack will turn over his prisoner—Yuji (Toyokawa), a Yakuza whom Serlano believes is responsible for his own son's death. Zack's only interest is to rescue his son and he doesn't care who gets in his way, including his fellow feds and the gangsters. **92m/C VHS, Closed Caption.** Russell Crowe, Helen Slater, Michael Lerner, Etsushi Toyokawa, Ian Ziering; **D:** Frank Cappello; **W:** Frank Cappello; **C:** Richard Clabaugh; **M:** David Williams. *COL*

No Way Home 🎬🎬 1997 (R) Joey (Roth), who's mentally a little slow, returns to his tough Staten Island neighborhood after being paroled from prison. He goes to live with his low-level drug dealer older brother Tommy (Russo) and Tommy's wife, Lorrain (Unger), who's not too happy about the situation—at first. But Joey's basically a decent guy and Lorrain begins to respond to his consideration. Meanwhile, desperate Tommy's in debt to a loan shark and his behavior may once again find Joey taking the rap for his brother's misdeeds. The story's predictable but the cast definitely rises above the material. **CW:** Strong violence, sexuality and language. **101m/C VHS, LV, Closed Caption.** Tim Roth, James Russo, Deborah Kara Unger; **D:** Buddy Giovinazzo; **W:** Buddy Giovinazzo; **C:** Claudia Raschke. *ART*

No Way Out 🎬🎬½ 1950 When bigoted bad guy Roy Biddle (Widmark) and his brother George (Bellaver) are shot, they're taken to a small hospital run by Dr. Wharton (McNally), who believes in giving all his doctors a fair chance. So black doctor Luther Brooks (Poitier) works on George, who dies. Naturally, Roy blames the doctor and gets his hoodlum pals to cause some bloody confrontations. **105m/B VHS.** Sidney Poitier, Richard Widmark, Stephen McNally, Linda Darnell, Harry Bellaver, Stanley Ridges, Ruby Dee, Ossie Davis; **D:** Joseph L. Mankiewicz; **W:** Joseph L. Mankiewicz, Lesser Samuels; **C:** Milton Krasner; **M:** Alfred Newman. Nominations: Academy Awards '50: Best Story & Screenplay. *FXV*

No Way Out 🎬🎬🎬 1987 (R) Career Navy man Costner is involved with a beautiful, sexy woman who is murdered. Turns out she was also the mistress of the Secretary of Defense, Costner's boss. Assigned to investigate the murder, he suddenly finds himself the chief suspect. A tight thriller based on 1948's "The Big Clock," with a new surprise ending. **114m/C VHS, Beta, LV.** Kevin Costner, Sean Young, Gene Hackman, Will Patton, Howard Duff, George Dzundza, Iman, Chris D, Marshall Bell, Jason Bernard, Fred Dalton Thompson, David Paymer, Eugene Glazer; **D:** Roger Donaldson; **W:** Robert Garland; **M:** Maurice Jarre. *HBO*

No Way to Treat a Lady 🎬🎬🎬 1968 Steiger is a psychotic master of disguise who stalks and kills various women in this suspenseful cat-and-mouse game. Segal, as the detective assigned to the case, uncovers clues, falls in love, and discovers that his new girl may be the killer's next victim. **108m/C VHS, Beta.** Rod Steiger, Lee Remick, George Segal, Eileen Heckart, Murray Hamilton; **D:** Jack Smight; **W:** John Gay; **C:** Jack Priestley. *PAR*

Noa at Seventeen 🎬🎬🎬 1982 The political/social turmoil of Israel in 1951 is allegorically depicted by the school vs. kibbutz debate within a young girl's middle-class family. In Hebrew with English subtitles. **86m/C VHS, Beta.** *IS* Dalia Shimko, Idit Zur, Shmuel Shilo, Moshe Havazelet; **D:** Isaac Yeshurun. *ERG, FCT, TPV*

Noble House 1988 Continuation of James Clavell's Hong Kong series, following "Tai-Pan," and set in the present day. Ian Dunross (Brosnan) is the head of Struan and Company, Hong Kong's leading trading company, which is being undermined by the nefarious Quillan Gornt (Rhys-Davies) who plots to destroy his archrival. American businesswoman Casey Tcholok (the bland Raffin) serves as Dunross' love interest. Originally a four-part TV miniseries partially filmed on location. **350m/C VHS.** Pierce Brosnan, John Rhys-Davies, Deborah Raffin, Ben Masters, Julia Nickson-Soul, Khigh Deigh, Tia Carrere, Gordon Jackson. *VTR, TVC, PBS*

The Noble Ninja 🎬🎬 1990 In a fantastic prehistoric world, a ninja does battle with foes both real and supernatural. **90m/C VHS, Beta.** Tsui Fung, Lo Lieh. *MGI*

Nobody's Daughter 🎬🎬½ 1976 The tragedy of an eight-year-old orphan shuttled from one family to another, all of whom are only interested in the money the government will pay for her care. In Hungarian with English subtitles. **90m/C VHS.** *HU* Zsuzsa Czinkoczi; **D:** Lazlo Ranody.

Nobody's Fool 🎬🎬 1986 (PG-13) Another entry in the genre of quirky Americana, this romantic comedy concerns a hapless Midwestern waitress suffering from low-self esteem who falls in love with a traveling stage-hand. **107m/C VHS, Beta, LV, Closed Caption.** Rosanna Arquette, Eric Roberts, Mare Winningham, Louise Fletcher, Jim Youngs, Gwen Welles, Stephen Tobolowsky, Charlie Barnett, Lewis Arquette; **D:** Evelyn Purcell; **W:** Beth Henley; **C:** Misha Susov; **M:** James Newton Howard. *ORI, WAR*

Nobody's Fool 🎬🎬🎬½ 1994 (R) Newman shines as 60-year-old Donald "Sully" Sullivan, a construction worker who, in spite of himself, begins mending his many broken relationships over the course of the holiday season. Seemingly plotless scenario is sprinkled with enough humor, hope, and understated inspiration to become a delightfully modest celebration of a perfectly ordinary man. Character-driven story is blessed with commendable performances by supporting players—obviously inspired by Newman's brilliant portrayal. Based on the novel by Richard Russo. **CW:** Contains some nudity and mild profanity. **110m/C VHS, Beta, Closed Caption.** Paul Newman, Jessica Tandy, Bruce Willis, Melanie Griffith, Dylan Walsh, Pruitt Taylor Vince, Gene Saks, Josef Sommer, Philip S. Hoffman, Philip Bosco, Margo Martindale, Jay Patterson; **D:** Robert Benton; **W:** Robert Benton; **C:** John Bailey; **M:** John Joe Bob Briggs Bloom. Berlin International Film Festival '94: Best Actor (Newman); New York Film Critics Awards '94: Best Actor (Newman); National Society of Film Critics Awards '94: Best Actor (Newman); Nominations: Academy Awards '94: Best Actor (Newman), Best Adapted Screenplay; Golden Globe Awards '95: Best Actor—Drama (Newman); Screen Actors Guild Award '94: Best Actor (Newman). *PAR*

Nobody's Perfect 🎬 1990 (PG-13) Where "Tootsie" and "Some Like It Hot" collide (or more likely crash and burn). A lovesick teenager masquerades as a girl and joins the tennis team to be near his dream girl. Takes its title from Joe E. Brown's famous last line in "Some Like It Hot." **90m/C VHS, Beta, LV, Closed Caption.** Chad Lowe, Gail O'Grady, Patrick Breen, Kim Flowers, Robert Vaughn; **D:** Robert Kaylor; **W:** Joel Block. *VTR*

Nobody's Perfekt woof! 1979 (PG) Supposed comedy about three psychiatric patients who decide to extort $650,000 from the city of Miami when their car is wrecked. Lacks laughs and generally considered a turkey. **95m/C VHS, Beta.** Gabe Kaplan, Robert Klein, Alex Karras, Susan Clark; **D:** Peter Bonerz. *COL*

Nocturna woof! *Nocturna, Granddaughter of Dracula* 1979 (R) Hard times have fallen upon the house of Dracula. To help pay the taxes on the castle, the owners have converted it to the Hotel Transylvania. In order to increase business and the blood supply at the hotel, Nocturna books a

disco group to entertain the guests. Hard times fell on this script, too. It's no wonder that director Tampa hid behind the alias Harry Hurwitz. **82m/C VHS, Beta, LV.** Yvonne De Carlo, John Carradine, Tony Hamilton, Nai Bonet; **D:** Harry Tampa; **C:** Mac Ahlberg.

Nocturne 🎬🎬½ 1946 A police lieutenant investigates the supposed suicide of a famous composer and uncovers dark secrets that suggest murder is afoot. An overlooked RKO production shines thanks to Raft's inimitable tough guy performance and some offbeat direction. For film noir completists. **88m/B VHS, Beta, LV.** George Raft, Lynn Bari, Virginia Huston, Joseph Pevney, Myrna Dell, Edward Ashley, Walter Sande, Mabel Paige; **D:** Edwin L. Marin. *TTC*

Noir et Blanc 🎬🎬 1986 Antoine (Frappat) is a shy accountant who takes a job in a health club and begins an increasingly sado-masochistic relationship with black masseur, Jacques (Martial). The violence is inferred not actually shown but still makes for some kinky adult fare. Based on a short story by Tennessee Williams; debut film for director Devers. French with subtitles. **82m/B VHS.** *FR* Francis Frappat, Jacques Martial, Josephine Fresson, Marc Berman, Claire Rigollier; **D:** Claire Devers; **W:** Claire Devers. *CCN*

Noises Off 🎬🎬½ 1992 (PG-13) An Americanization of a British farce about a group of second-rate actors touring in a sex comedy and their convoluted private lives. Wretched rehearsals and equally disasterous preformances, backstage sniping, lovers' quarrels, and a beleaguered director all bumble along together. It worked better on stage, where it was a Broadway hit, but the actors at least have some fun with the material. Based on the play by Michael Frayn. **101m/C VHS, Beta, LV, Letterbox.** Michael Caine, Carol Burnett, Denholm Elliott, Julie Hagerty, Marilu Henner, Mark Linn-Baker, Christopher Reeve, John Ritter, Nicolette Sheridan; **D:** Peter Bogdanovich; **W:** Marty Kaplan; **M:** Phil Marshall. *TOU, PMS*

Nomad Riders 🎬 1981 A la "Mad Max," (though with an even smaller budget and a decided lack of originality) one rugged man goes after the bikers who killed his wife and daughter. **82m/C VHS, Beta.** Wayne Chema, Richard Cluck, Ron Gregg; **D:** Frank Roach. *ART, VES*

Nomads 🎬🎬½ 1986 (R) A supernatural thriller set in Los Angeles about a French anthropologist who is mysteriously killed, and the woman doctor who investigates and becomes the next target of a band of strange street people with nomadic spirits. Nomad notables include pop stars Adam Ant and Josie Cotton. **91m/C VHS, Beta, LV.** Pierce Brosnan, Lesley-Anne Down, Adam Ant, Anna Maria Monticelli, Mary Woronov, Hector Mercado; **D:** John McTiernan; **W:** John McTiernan; **C:** Stephen Ramsey; **M:** Bill Conti. *IME, PAR*

Nomads of the North 🎬½ 1920 Vintage silent melodrama set in the North Woods with the requisite young girl beset by evil villians, a climactic forest fire, and a dashing Mountie who allows a man wrongly sought by the law to be reunited with the woman he secretly loves. Also available at 75 minutes. **109m/B VHS, Beta, 8mm.** Lon Chaney Sr., Lewis Stone, Betty Blythe; **D:** David M. Hartford. *SNC, GPV, VYY*

Nomugi Pass 🎬🎬½ 1979 A young woman working in a Japanese silk mill in the early 1900s must endure hardship and abuse. English subtitles. **154m/C VHS, Beta.** *JP* Shinobu Otake, Meiko Harada, Rentaro Mikuni, Takeo Jii. *VDA*

Non-Stop New York 🎬🎬½ 1937 Mystery tale with interesting twist. A wealthy woman can give an alibi for a murder suspect, but no one will listen, and she is subsequently framed. Pays homage to Hitchcock with its photography and humor. Quick and charming. **71m/B VHS.** Anna Lee, John Loder, Francis L. Sullivan, Frank Cellier, Desmond Tester, Athene Seyler, William Dewhurst, Drusilla Wills, Jerry Verno, James Pirrie, Ellen Pollock, Arthur Goullet, James Carew, Alf Goddard, Danny Green; **D:** Robert Stevenson; **W:** Curt Siodmak, Roland Pertwee, Derek Twist, J.O.C. Orton, E.V.H. Emmett. *NOS, SNC*

None But the Brave 🐾🐾 1965 During WWII, an American bomber plane crash-lands on an island already inhabited by stranded Japanese forces. After a skirmish, the two groups initiate a fragile truce, with the understanding that fighting will resume if one or the other sends for help. The Americans repair their radio unit and must decide on their next actions. Sinatra's directorial debut is a poor effort. 105m/C VHS, Beta, LV, Closed Caption. Frank Sinatra, Clint Walker, Tommy Sands, Brad Dexter, Tony Bill, Tatsuya Mihashi, Takeshi Kato, Sammy Jackson; **D:** Frank Sinatra; **M:** John Williams. WAR, FCT

None But the Lonely Heart 🐾🐾🐾 1944 In the days before WWII, a Cockney drifter (Grant) wanders the East End of London. When his get-rich-quick schemes fail, his dying shop-keeper-mother tries to help and lands in prison. Interesting characterization of life in the slums. Odets not only directed, but wrote the screenplay. 113m/B Beta. Cary Grant, Ethel Barrymore, Barry Fitzgerald, Jane Wyatt, Dan Duryea, George Coulouris, June Duprez; **D:** Clifford Odets; **W:** Clifford Odets; **C:** George Barnes. Academy Awards '44: Best Supporting Actress (Barrymore); Nominations: Academy Awards '44: Best Actor (Grant), Best Film Editing, Best Original Dramatic/Comedy Score. BTV

Noon Sunday 🐾 1971 (PG) A cold war situation in the Pacific islands explodes into an orgy of death. 104m/C VHS, Beta. Mark Lenard, John Russell, Linda Avery, Keye Luke.

Noon Wine 🐾🐾🐾 1984 Dramatization of Katherine Anne Porter's classic story about a Swedish worker on a Texas farm who becomes the center of a family battle. Made for PBS' American Playhouse. 60m/C VHS, Beta. Fred Ward, Lise Hilboldt, Stellan Skarsgard, Jon Cryer; **D:** Michael Fields. MON, FCT, KAR

The Noose Hangs High 🐾🐾🐾 1948 This broad comedy has our heroes as window washers mistaken for gamblers and getting involved with a bunch of gangsters. Much physical and verbal shenanigans as only these two can do it. The bits may be a bit old, but they're done with a fresh twist. Some good word play with the phrase "You can't be here" runs in the same vein as their classic "Who's on first?" routine. Genuinely funny. 77m/B VHS. Bud Abbott, Lou Costello, Cathy Downs, Joseph Calleia, Leon Errol, Mike Mazurki, Jack Overman, Fritz Feld, Vera Martin, Joe Kirk, Matt Willis, Benny Rubin; **D:** Charles T. Barton. MGM, NOS

Norma Jean and Marilyn 🐾🐾½ 1995 (R) Blonde screen goddess Marilyn Monroe (Sorvino) is haunted by her past, literally, since she never escapes the legacy of ambitious Norma Jean Baker (Judd). As her relationships and career falter, Norma Jean is always there (thanks to drug-induced hallucinations) to remind Marilyn how worthless she is. Cable drama deals with Norma Jean's troubled past and how she was willing to do anything to be in the movies, although it (apparently) brought her little happiness. The dual stars work surprisingly well and director Fywell offers the proper camp flair.*CW:* Sexual situations, strong language, and violence. 133m/C VHS. Mira Sorvino, Ashley Judd, Josh Charles, Peter Dobson, Ron Rifkin, David Dukes, Taylor Nichols, Lindsay Crouse, John Rubinstein, Steven Culp, Perry Stephens, Earl Boen; **D:** Tim Fywell; **W:** Jill Isaacs; **C:** John Thomas; **M:** Christopher Young. HBO

Norma Rae 🐾🐾🐾 1979 (PG) A poor, uneducated textile worker joins forces with a New York labor organizer to unionize the reluctant workers at a Southern mill. Field was a surprise with her fully developed character's strength, beauty, and humor; her Oscar was well-deserved. Ritt's direction is top-notch. Jennifer Warnes sings the theme song, "It Goes Like It Goes," which also won an Oscar. ♫It Goes Like It Goes. 114m/C VHS, Beta, LV. Sally Field, Ron Leibman, Beau Bridges, Pat Hingle; **D:** Martin Ritt; **W:** Harriet Frank Jr., Irving Ravetch; **D:** John A. Alonzo; **M:** David Shire. Academy Awards '79: Best Actress (Field), Best Song ("It Goes Like It Goes"); Cannes Film Festival '79: Best Actress

(Field); Golden Globe Awards '80: Best Actress—Drama (Field); Los Angeles Film Critics Association Awards '79: Best Actress (Field); National Board of Review Awards '79: Best Actress (Field); New York Film Critics Awards '79: Best Actress (Field); National Society of Film Critics Awards '79: Best Actress (Field); Nominations: Academy Awards '79: Best Adapted Screenplay, Best Picture. FOX, BTV

Normal Life 🐾🐾 1996 (R) Straight-arrow, smalltown Illinois rookie cop Chris Anderson (Perry) comes to the aid of sexy, impetuous biker chick Pam (Judd) and they impulsively marry. Fast forward two years and the willfully irresponsible Pam has turned their lives into a disaster but for some reason Chris (now a security guard) sticks it out, even pulling bank jobs to afford Pam's luxuries. When she finds out what Chris has been doing, Pam insists on joining in, leading to a bitter end. Based on the true story of Jeffrey and Jill Erickson, who went on a bank robbing spree and were killed in 1991. Great lead performances though character motivation is lacking.*CW:* Scenes of violence, sexuality, drug use and language. 108m/C VHS, LV, Closed Caption. Luke Perry, Ashley Judd, Bruce A. Young, Jim True, Dawn Maxey, Penelope Milford, Tom Towles; **D:** John McNaughton; **W:** Bob Schneider, Peg Haller; **C:** Jean De Segonzac. NLC

Norman Conquest 🐾 Park Plaza 1953 Conway finds himself drugged and framed for murder in this bargain-basement thriller. Bartok is the leader of a diamond-smuggling operation who may be involved. 75m/B VHS. GB Tom Conway, Eva Bartok, Joy Shelton, Sidney James, Richard Wattis, Robert Adair, Ian Fleming; **D:** Bernard Knowles; **W:** Bernard Knowles. NOS, SNC

The Norman Conquests, Part 1: Table Manners 🐾🐾🐾 1980 Part one of playwright Alan Ayckbourn's comic trilogy of love unfulfilled, as the charmingly unreliable Norman (Conti) works his amorous wiles on three women. 108m/C VHS, Beta. GB Tom Conti, Richard Briers, Penelope Keith. TVC

The Norman Conquests, Part 2: Living Together 🐾🐾🐾 1980 Part two concerns the happenings in the living room during Norman's disastrous weekend of unsuccessful seduction. 93m/C VHS, Beta. GB Tom Conti, Penelope Keith, Richard Briers. TVC

The Norman Conquests, Part 3: Round and Round the Garden 🐾🐾🐾 1980 Part three concerns Norman's furtive appearance in the garden, which suggests that the weekend is going to misfire. 106m/C VHS, Beta. GB Tom Conti, Penelope Keith, Richard Briers. TVC

Norman, Is That You? 🐾½ 1976 Unsuccessful film adaptation based on the unsuccessful Broadway play about one family's sexual revolution. Revamped by a host of black stars, it's basically a one-joke affair when Foxx discovers his son is gay and living with his white lover. Shot on videotape and transferred to film. 91m/C VHS. Redd Foxx, Pearl Bailey, Dennis Dugan, Michael Warren, Tamara Dobson, Vernee Watson-Johnson, Jayne Meadows, George Furth; **D:** George Schlatter; **W:** George Schlatter, Ron Clark, Sam Bobrick; **M:** William Goldstein. MGM

Norman Loves Rose 🐾½ 1982 (R) A precocious 13-year-old and his married sister-in-law join forces in this substandard comedy. When Rose tries to help Norman by teaching him about sex, she learns a little too—she's pregnant. 95m/C VHS, Beta. AU Carol Kane, Tony Owen, Warren Mitchell, Myra de Groot; **D:** Henri Safran. ART, VES

Norman's Awesome Experience woof! 1988 (PG-13) Three adolescents are transported back in time to the Roman Empire. Bill and Ted, anyone? 90m/C VHS, Beta. Tom McCamus, Laurie Paton, Jaques Lussier; **D:** Paul Donovan. NO

Norseman 🐾½ 1978 (PG) Leader of a band of Norsemen sets sail for the New World in search of his missing royal father. Low-budget Viking adventure. 90m/C VHS, Beta. Lee Majors, Cornel Wilde, Mel

Ferrer, Christopher Connelly, Jack Elam; **D:** Charles B Pierce; **W:** Charles B. Pierce. ART, VES

North 🐾🐾½ 1994 (PG) Some laughs with a message in family fare from Reiner. Eleven-year-old ace kid actor Wood divorces his workaholic parents Alexander and Louis-Dreyfus and searches the world for a functional family (good luck). Willis, who's a treat in a pink bunny suit, acts as guardian angel/narrator and shows the kid what's really important. Illustrious comedic cast inhabits story based on a book by original "Saturday Night Live" screenwriter (and "Gary Shandling Show" co-creator) Zweibel, who put things in motion ten years ago when he asked Reiner to write a book jacket quote for the novel. 87m/C VHS, LV, Closed Caption. Elijah Wood, Jason Alexander, Julia Louis-Dreyfus, Bruce Willis, Jon Lovitz, Alan Arkin, Dan Aykroyd, Kathy Bates, Faith Ford, Graham Greene, Reba McEntire, John Ritter, Abe Vigoda, Kelly McGillis, Alexander Godunov, Noriyuki "Pat" Morita, Ben Stein; **D:** Rob Reiner; **W:** Andrew Scheinman, Alan Zweibel; **M:** Marc Shaiman. Nominations: Golden Raspberry Awards '94: Worst Picture, Worst Actor (Willis). NLC

North and South Book 1 🐾🐾🐾 1985 Lavish spectacle about a friendship tested by the turbulent times leading up to Civil War. Orry Main (Swayze) is a South Carolina plantation owner while his best friend George Hazard (Read) comes from a Pennsylvania industrial family. Orry is also involved in a doomed romance with the beautiful Madeline (Down), who's forced to marry the odious Justin LaMotte (Carradine). Lots of intrigue and excitement. Based on the novel by John Jakes. Filmed on location in Charleston, South Carolina. Originally broadcast as a six-part TV miniseries. Available on six cassettes. 561m/C VHS, Beta. Patrick Swayze, James Read, Lesley-Anne Down, David Carradine, Kirstie Alley, Jean Simmons, Inga Swenson, Jonathon Frakes, Genie Francis, Terri Garber, Georg Stanford Brown, Olivia Cole, David Ogden Stiers, Robert Guillaume, Hal Holbrook, Gene Kelly, Robert Mitchum, Johnny Cash, Elizabeth Taylor; **M:** Bill Conti. WAR, FUS, TVC

North and South Book 2 🐾🐾🐾 1986 Equally dramatic sequel follows the southern Main clan and the northern Hazard family into the Civil War as friendship and romance struggle to survive the fighting. Casnoff is a notable presence as the aptly named Bent, who will go to any length to settle old scores with both families. Based on the John Jakes novel "Love and War." Originally broadcast as a six-part TV miniseries; on six cassettes. The last of the Jakes trilogy, "Heaven and Hell," was finally filmed for TV in '94 but proved a major disappointment. 570m/C VHS. Patrick Swayze, James Read, Lesley-Anne Down, Terri Garber, Genie Francis, Jean Simmons, Kirstie Alley, Philip Casnoff, Hal Holbrook, Lloyd Bridges, James Stewart, Morgan Fairchild, Nancy Marchand, Parker Stevenson, Lewis Smith; **M:** Bill Conti. WAR, TVC

The North Avenue Irregulars 🐾🐾½ 1979 (G) Slapstick Disney comedy along the same lines as some of their earlier laugh-fests. A priest and three members of the local ladies' club try to bust a crime syndicate. Though the premise is silly, there are still lots of laughs in this family film. 99m/C VHS. Edward Herrmann, Barbara Harris, Susan Clark, Karen Valentine, Michael Constantine, Cloris Leachman, Melora Hardin, Alan Hale Jr., Ruth Buzzi, Patsy Kelly, Virginia Capers; **D:** Bruce Bilson; **M:** Robert F. Brunner. DIS

North by Northwest 🐾🐾🐾 1959 Self-assured Madison Avenue ad exec Grant inadvertently gets involved with international spies when they mistake him for someone else. His problems are compounded when he's framed for murder. The movie where Grant and Saint dangle from the faces of Mount Rushmore and a plane chases Grant through farm fields. Exceptional performances, particularly Grant's. Plenty of plot twists are mixed with tongue-in-cheek humor. Considered by many to be one of Hitchcock's greatest films. Laserdisc includes letterboxing, digital soundtrack, Hitchcock interview, production and publicity photos, storyboards, and the original trailer. **136m/C VHS, Beta, LV, Letterbox.** Cary Grant, Eva Marie Saint, James Mason, Leo G. Carroll, Martin Landau, Jessie Royce Landis, Philip Ober, Adam Williams, Josephine Hutchinson, Edward Platt; *D:* Alfred Hitchcock; *W:* Ernest Lehman; *C:* Robert Burks; *M:* Bernard Herrmann. National Film Registry '95;; Nominations: Academy Awards '59: Best Art Direction/Set Decoration (Color), Best Film Editing, Best Story & Screenplay. *MGM*

North Dallas Forty 🐾🐾🐾½ *1979* Based on the novel by former Dallas Cowboy Peter Gent, the film focuses on the labor abuses in pro-football. One of the best football movies ever made, it contains searing commentary and very good acting, although the plot is sometimes dropped behind the line of scrimmage. **119m/C VHS, Beta, LV.** Nick Nolte, Mac Davis, Charles Durning, Bo Svenson, Brian Dennehy, John Matuszak, Dayle Haddon, Steve Forrest, Dabney Coleman, G.D. Spradlin; *D:* Ted Kotcheff. *PAR*

North of the Border 🐾🐾½ *1946* A cowboy in Canada gets involved with back-stabbing and treachery in and around Alberta. **40m/B VHS, Beta, LV.** *CA* Russell Hayden, Lyle Talbot, Inez Cooper, Douglas Fowley, Jack Mulhall; *D:* B. Reeves Eason. *VYY*

North of the Great Divide 🐾½ *1950* Standard Rogers programmer, with Roy as a half-breed mediator between salmon fisherman and Indians. **67m/C VHS.** Roy Rogers, Penny Edwards, Gordon Jones, Roy Barcroft, Jack Lambert, Douglas Evans, Noble Johnson; *D:* William Witney. *REP*

North Shore 🐾½ *1987 (PG)* A young surfer from Arizona hits the beaches of Hawaii and discovers love, sex, and adventure. Only redeeming quality is surfing footage. **96m/C VHS, Beta.** Matt Adler, Nia Peeples, John Philbin, Gregory Harrison, Christina Raines; *D:* Will Phelps. *USH*

North Shore Fish 🐾🐾 *1997 (R)* North Shore Fish is a failing Massachusetts fish packing factory with various cynical managers and employees, including divorcee Flo (Ruehl), who just found out she's pregnant by her married boss Sal (Danza), 60ish Arlyne (Baker), who regards her co-workers as family, and Josie (Schwimmer), who's husband has left her for a younger woman. It's on this one day that they realize how uncertain all their futures are. Based on the play by Israel Horovitz.*CW:* Language. **95m/C VHS.** Mercedes Ruehl, Peter Riegert, Carroll Baker, Tony Danza, Rusty Schwimmer, Wendie Malick, Cordelia Richards; *D:* Steve Zuckerman; *W:* Israel Horovitz; *C:* Levie Isaacks. *HMK*

The North Star 🐾🐾🐾 *Armored Attack 1943* Gripping war tale of Nazis over-running an eastern Russian city, with courageous villagers fighting back. Colorized version available. **108m/B VHS, Beta.** Dana Andrews, Walter Huston, Anne Baxter, Farley Granger, Walter Brennan, Erich von Stroheim, Jack Perrin, Dean Jagger; *D:* Lewis Milestone; *M:* Aaron Copland. Nominations: Academy Awards '43: Best Black and White Cinematography, Best Interior Decoration, Best Original Screenplay, Best Sound, Best Original Dramatic/Comedy Score. *NOS, MRV, VYY*

North Star 🐾½ *1996 (R)* Formulaic actioner where no one seems very enthusiastic. Half-breed trapper Hudson Ipsehawk (Lambert) refuses to mine the gold on his Alaskan property because the land is considered sacred. This doesn't concern greedy miner Sean McLennon (Caan) who wants the property for himself. Oh yeah, there's also a babe, Sarah (McCormack), that both men are interested in. Norway substitutes for Alaska. Based on the novel by Will Henry.*CW:* Some violence and language. **89m/C VHS, Closed Caption.** Christopher Lambert, James Caan, Catherine McCormack, Burt Young; *D:* Nils Gaup; *W:* Paul Ohl, Sergio Donati, Lorenzo Donati; *C:* Bruno de Keyzer; *M:* Bruce Rowland. *WAR*

North to Alaska 🐾🐾🐾 *1960* A gold prospector encounters many problems when he agrees to pick up his partner's fiancee in Seattle to bring her home to Nome, Alaska, in the 1890s. Overly slapstick at times, but great fun nonetheless. Loosely based on Laszlo Fodor's play "The

---

Birthday Gift." **120m/C VHS, Beta, LV, Letterbox, Closed Caption.** John Wayne, Stewart Granger, Ernie Kovacs, Fabian, Capucine; *D:* Henry Hathaway; *C:* Leon Shamroy. *FOX*

Northanger Abbey 🐾🐾½ *1987* Catherine is a young woman whose head is turned by her romance readings of dark secrets, sinister castles, dashing heroes, and helpless women. When the handsome Henry Tilney invites her to visit his ancestral home, Northanger Abbey, it seems all her fancies have come to life. A somewhat tepid adaptation of Jane Austen's parody of the popular Gothic romances of her day. **90m/C VHS.** *GB* Peter Firth, Katherine Schlesinger, Googie Withers, Robert Hardy. *TVC, VCO, FUS*

Northeast of Seoul 🐾 *1972 (PG)* Three people will stop at nothing to steal a legendary jewel-encrusted sword out of Korea. **84m/C VHS, Beta.** Anita Ekberg, John Ireland, Victor Buono; *D:* David Lowell Rich. *MGM*

Northern Extremes 🐾½ *Buried on Sunday 1993 (PG)* Silly comedy about an eccentric Canadian island village whose fishing livelihood is threatened. So the town mayor captures an errant nuclear submarine and uses it as a big bargaining chip. Filmed in Nova Scotia, Canada. **80m/C VHS.** *CA* Paul Gross, Denise Virieux, Henry Czerny, Jeff Leder, Tommy Sexton, Louis Del Grande, Maury Chaykin; *D:* Paul Donovan; *W:* Bill Flemming.

Northern Lights 🐾🐾🐾 *1979* A small, black-and-white independent drama depicting the struggle of a lowly farmer combating governmental forces in the 1915 heartland. Subtitled. **85m/B VHS, Beta.** Robert Behling, Susan Lynch, Joe Spano, Rob Nilsson, Henry Martinson, Marianne Astrom-DeFina, Ray Ness, Helen Ness; *D:* Rob Nilsson, John Hanson; *W:* Rob Nilsson. *VTR*

Northern Passage 🐾🐾½ *1995 (PG-13)* Cowboy tries to protect a young Native American woman from harm in the wilderness.*CW:* Some intense violence. **97m/C VHS.** Jeff Fahey, Neve Campbell. *THV*

Northern Pursuit 🐾🐾½ *1943* A Canadian Mountie disguises himself to infiltrate a Nazi spy ring in this exciting adventure film. Based on Leslie White's "Five Thousand Trojan Horses." **94m/B VHS, Beta.** Errol Flynn, Helmut Dantine, Julie Bishop, Gene Lockhart, Tom Tully; *D:* Raoul Walsh. *MGM, MLB*

Northville Cemetery Massacre 🐾 *The Northfield Cemetery Massacre 1976 (R)* Gang of bikers comes to town and all hell breaks loose. The result is a horribly bloody war between the townsfolk and the gang. Yup, it was a massacre. **81m/C VHS, Beta.** David Hyry, Craig Collicott, Jan Sisk; *W:* William Dear. *NO*

Northwest Outpost 🐾½ *End of the Rainbow 1947* Eddy is a California cavalry officer in this lightweight operetta. He helps a young woman who is trying to free her husband from jail, and after his death they are able to pursue their relationship. Eddy's last film. ♫Weary; Raindrops on a Drum; Tell Me With Your Eyes; One More Mile to Go; Russian Easter Hymn; Love is the Time; Nearer and Dearer. **91m/B VHS.** Nelson Eddy, Ilona Massey, Hugo Haas, Elsa Lanchester, Lenore Ulric; *D:* Allan Dwan. *REP*

Northwest Passage 🐾🐾🐾 *1940* The lavish first half of a projected two-film package based on Kenneth Roberts' popular novel, depicting the troop of Rogers' Rangers fighting the wilderness and hostile Indians. Beautifully produced; the second half was never made and the passage itself is never seen. **126m/C VHS, Beta.** Spencer Tracy, Robert Young, Ruth Hussey, Walter Brennan, Nat Pendleton, Robert Barrat, Lumsden Hare; *D:* King Vidor. Nominations: Academy Awards '40: Best Color Cinematography. *MGM*

Northwest Trail 🐾🐾 *1946* Royal Canadian Mountie Steele's assignment is to escort Woodbury across the wilderness. She's carrying a large sum of money to save her uncle's business. Problem is, killers are on their trail. **75m/C**

VHS, Beta. Bob Steele, Joan Woodbury, John Litel, Raymond Hatton, Madge Bellamy, Charles Middleton; *D:* Derwin Abrahams. *NOS, HHT, VCN*

Nosferatu 🐾🐾🐾🐾 *Nosferatu, Eine Symphonie des Grauens; Nosferatu, A Symphony of Terror; Nosferatu, A Symphony of Horror; Nosferatu, the Vampire; Terror of Dracula; Die Zwolfte Stunde 1922* The first film adaptation of Bram Stoker's "Dracula" remains one of the creepiest and most atmospheric versions. Murnau knew how to add just the right touches to make this one of the best vampire films ever made. All it lacks is the name of Dracula, which was changed due to copyright problems with Stoker's widow. Filmed in Bavaria. Silent with music and English titles. Remade by Werner Herzog in 1979. **63m/B VHS, Beta, LV.** *GE* Max Schreck, Alexander Granach, Gustav von Wagenheim, Greta Schroeder, John Gottowt, Ruth Landshoff, G.H. Schnell; *D:* F.W. Murnau; *W:* Henrik Galeen; *C:* Fritz Arno Wagner. *KIV, MRV, NOS*

Nostalghia 🐾🐾 *1983* Russian academic Jankovsky comes to Tuscany to research the life of an 18th-century composer and meets the mysterious Josephson, who's convinced the end of the world is near. And soon the homesick Russian is in a search for himself. Filled with Christian iconography and some extraordinary images. Tarkovsky's first film outside his native Russia. Russian and Italian with subtitles; the Russian sequences are filmed in B&W. **126m/C VHS.** *IT* Oleg Jankowsky, Erland Josephson, Domiziana Giordano, Delia Boccardo; *D:* Andrei Tarkovsky; *W:* Andrei Tarkovsky, Tonino Guerra; *C:* Giuseppe Lanci. *FCT, FXL*

Nostradamus 🐾🐾 *1993 (R)* Historical soap opera about unconventional 16th-century French physician and astrologer Michel de Nostradame. Persecuted by the Inquisition, he comes under the protection of Queen Catherine de Medici of France, although his visions of destruction and death continue to haunt him. Nostradamus' prophecies, first published in 1555, have continued to fascinate, being used to predicate everything from the death of historical leaders to WWI. The film, however, is slow going and fails to hold much interest.*CW:* Some images of violence and strong sexuality. **118m/C VHS, LV, Closed Caption.** *FR* Tcheky Karyo, F. Murray Abraham, Julia Ormond, Rutger Hauer, Amanda Plummer, Assumpta Serna, Anthony Higgins, Diana Quick, Michael Gough; *D:* Roger Christian; *W:* Knut Boeser, Piers Ashworth. *ORI*

The Nostradamus Kid 🐾🐾 *1992 (R)* Young man, convinced the world is about to end, decides his last goal will be to make love (for the first time) with his girlfriend.*CW:* Sexuality and language. **120m/C VHS.** Noah Taylor, Miranda Otto, Arthur Dignam; *D:* Bob Ellis. *ART*

Nostromo 🐾🐾 *Joseph Conrad's Nostromo 1996* Tediously drawn-out TV adaptation of the 1904 novel by Joseph Conrad takes place in the 1890s in the fictional South American country of Costaguana. Englishman Charles Gould (Firth) is determined to reopen his family's silver mine—a plan supported by the local regime, which is, however, soon to be overthrown. Amidst the revolution is the title character Nostromo (Amendola), a contraction of "nostro uomo" or "our man," an enigmatic Italian immigrant who organizes the dockworkers and is thrust into the role of hero. Filmed on location in Cartagena, Colombia. On three cassettes. **360m/C VHS.** Colin Firth, Albert Finney, Claudio Amendola, Serena Scott Thomas, Claudia Cardinale, Brian Dennehy, Lothaire Bluteau, Ruth Gabriel, Joaquim de Almeida; *D:* Alastair Reid; *W:* John Hale; *M:* Ennio Morricone. *FOX, SIG, WMI*

Not as a Stranger 🐾🐾½ *1955* Glossy film about the medical profession and the varying degrees of dedication shown by doctors. Mitchum stars as an medical student who can't afford to pay his tuition, so he marries nurse de Havilland and continues going to school on her money, although their relationship is far from being a loving one. Producer Kramer's directorial debut. Based on the book by Morton Thompson. **135m/B VHS, Closed Caption.** Olivia de Havilland, Robert Mitchum, Frank Sinatra, Gloria Grahame, Broderick Crawford, Charles Bickford, Myron McCormick, Lon Chaney Jr.; **D:** Stanley Kramer; **W:** Edward Anhalt. Nominations: Academy Awards '55: Best Sound. *MGM*

Not for Publication ♂♂ 1984 (R) A woman working as both a tabloid reporter and a mayoral campaign worker uncovers governmental corruption with the help of a shy photographer and a midget. Meant to be on par with older screwball comedies but lacking the wit and subtlety. **87m/C VHS, Beta.** Nancy Allen, David Naughton, Richard Paul, Alice Ghostley, Laurence Luckinbill; **D:** Paul Bartel; **W:** Paul Bartel. *NO*

Not in This Town ♂♂½ 1997 (PG-13) Fact-based cable drama stars Baker as Billings, Montana housewife Tammie Schnitzer, who is shocked when white supremacists, led by Henry Whitcomb (Begley Jr.), begin harassing religious and ethnic minorities in her town. She forms the Montana Coalition for Human Rights and begins a public appeal to rally the community but soon Tammie and her family need some protection of their own.**CW:** Thematic elements, including depiction of hate crimes. **95m/C VHS, Closed Caption.** Kathy Baker, Adam Arkin, Ed Begley Jr., Bradford Tatum, Max Gail; **D:** Donald Wrye; **W:** Adam Gilad. *USH*

Not Like Us ♂½ 1996 (R) Bored Anita's (Pacula) tired of life in her small town and glad to make a new friend in Janet. But she's shocked to discover Janet may be involved in several mysterious deaths (oh yeah, and she happens to be an alien).**CW:** Sci-fi violence and gore, sexuality and language. **87m/C VHS.** Joanna Pacula, Annabelle Gurwitch, Peter Onorati, Morgan Englund, Rainer Grant; **D:** Dave Payne; **W:** Daniella Purcelli. *NHO*

Not My Kid ♂♂½ 1985 The 15-year-old daughter of a surgeon brings turmoil to her family when she becomes heavily involved in drugs. Producer Polson, along with Dr. Miller Newton, wrote the original book for this emotional story that is one of the better treatments of this important subject. Made for television. **120m/C VHS, Beta.** George Segal, Stockard Channing, Viveka Davis, Andrew (Andy) Robinson, Gary Bayer, Nancy Cartwright, Tate Donovan; **D:** Michael Tuchner; **W:** Christopher Knopf. *SVE*

Not of This Earth ♂½ 1988 (R) In a remake of the 1957 Roger Corman quickie, an alien wearing sunglasses makes an unfriendly trip to Earth. In order to save his dying planet he needs major blood donations from unsuspecting Earthlings. Not a match for the original version, some may nevertheless want to see ex-porn star Lords in her role as the nurse. **92m/C VHS, Beta.** Traci Lords, Arthur Roberts, Lenny Juliano, Rebecca Perle, Ace Mask, Roger Lodge; **D:** Jim Wynorski; **W:** Jim Wynorski, R.J. Robertson. *MGM*

Not of This Earth ♂♂ 1996 (R) Corman cable remake of his own 1957 cheapie is both camp and sexy. Sunglass-wearing mystery millionaire Paul Johnson (York) apparently suffers from a rare condition and must have constant blood transfusions, so he hires a sexy live-in nurse (Barondes) to be at his beck-and-call. Yes, he does turn out to be a vampire but of the space alien-with-telepathic-powers variety who has a particular purpose for coming to earth.**CW:** Language, extreme violence, nudity, gore. **92m/C VHS.** Michael York, Elizabeth Barondes, Richard Belzer, Parker Stevenson; **D:** Terence H. Winkless; **W:** Charles Philip Moore. *NHO*

Not Quite Human ♂♂ 1987 When Jonas Carson builds himself an android teenage son, he must keep the technology from falling into the hands of an evil toy manufacturer with plans of his own. Humorous hijinks abound. Based on the book series "Not Quite Human" by Seth McEvoy. Made for cable television; followed by two sequels. **91m/C VHS, Beta, Closed Caption.** Alan Thicke, Robin Lively, Robert Harper, Joseph Bologna, Jay Underwood; **D:** Steven Hilliard Stern. *DIS*

Not Quite Human 2 ♂♂½ 1989 In this sequel, Dr. Jonas Carson sends his cyber-son off to college where Chip meets the not-quite-human girl of his dreams. Followed by "Still Not Quite Human." Made for cable television. **91m/C VHS, Beta, Closed Caption.** Alan Thicke, Jay Underwood, Robin Lively, Greg Mullavey, Katie Barberi, Mark Arnott; **D:** Eric Luke. *DIS*

Not Quite Paradise ♂ Not Quite Jerusalem 1986 (R) A young American medical student falls in love with a young Israeli girl living on a kibbutz. **106m/C VHS, Beta.** Sam Robards, Joanna Pacula; **D:** Lewis Gilbert. *VTR*

Not Tonight Darling ♂ 1972 (R) A bored suburban housewife becomes involved with a fast-talking businessman who leads her into a web of deceit and blackmail. **70m/C VHS, Beta.** Luan Peters, Vincent Ball, Jason Twelvetrees. *GEM*

Not Without My Daughter ♂♂½ 1990 (PG-13) Overwrought drama shot in Israel about American Field, who travels with her Arab husband and their daughter to his native Iran, where (he must have forgotten to tell her) she has no rights. He decides the family will stay, using beatings and confinement to persuade his uncooperative wife, but she risks all to escape with daughter. Based on the true story of Betty Mahmoody. **116m/C VHS, Beta, LV, 8mm, Closed Caption.** Sally Field, Alfred Molina, Sheila Rosenthal, Roshan Seth, Sarah Badel, Mony Rey, Georges Corraface; **D:** Brian Gilbert. *MGM, FCT*

Notes for an African Orestes ♂♂ 1970 Director Pasolini's insight into how a filmmaker works and what motivates him, as the camera reveals his plans to film a modern day version of Aeschylus' "Orestes" in Africa. **75m/B VHS. D:** Pier Paolo Pasolini; **M:** Gato Barbieri. *MFV, CIG*

Nothing But a Man ♂♂½ 1964 Duff Anderson (Dixon) is a black laborer trying to make a life in a small Alabama town. He falls for the daughter of a minister, they marry, and he gets a job at a local sawmill. When he won't bend to his racist white employers, he's fired and labeled a troublemaker. Unsentimental depiction of the times. **95m/B VHS.** Ivan Dixon, Abbey Lincoln, Gloria Foster, Julius W. Harris, Martin Priest, Yaphet Kotto; **D:** Michael Roemer; **W:** Michael Roemer. National Film Registry '93. *NEW, BTV, AEH*

Nothing But the Night ♂½ The Devil's Undead; The Resurrection Syndicate 1972 (PG) Lee's company produced this convoluted story of orphans who are victims of a cult that uses them in their quest for immortality. **90m/C VHS. GB** Christopher Lee, Peter Cushing, Diana Dors, Georgia Brown, Keith Barron, Fulton Mackay, Gwyneth Strong; **D:** Peter Sasdy. *SNC*

Nothing But Trouble ♂♂½ 1944 Laurel & Hardy's last film for MGM is a complicated tale of two servants who wind up protecting an exiled boy king from the machinations of his power-mad uncle. **70m/B VHS.** Stan Laurel, Oliver Hardy, Henry O'Neill, Mary Boland, David Leland, John Warburton, Connie Gilchrist, Philip Merivale; **D:** Sam Taylor. *MGM*

Nothing But Trouble ♂ 1991 (PG-13) Yuppie couple out for weekend drive find themselves smoldering in small town hell thanks to a traffic ticket. Horror and humor mix like oil and water in Aykroyd's debut as director. **93m/C VHS, Beta, LV, 8mm, Closed Caption.** Dan Aykroyd, Demi Moore, Chevy Chase, John Candy, Taylor Negron, Bertila Damas, Valri Bromfield; **D:** Dan Aykroyd; **W:** Dan Aykroyd, Peter Aykroyd; **C:** Dean Cundey. Golden Raspberry Awards '91: Worst Supporting Actor (Aykroyd). *WAR*

Nothing in Common ♂♂½ 1986 (PG) In his last film, Gleason plays the abrasive, diabetic father of immature advertising agency worker Hanks. After his parents separate, Hanks learns to be more responsible and loving in caring for his father. Comedy and drama are blended well here with the help of satirical pokes at the ad business and Hanks turns in a fine performance, but the unorganized, lengthy plot may lose some viewers.

119m/C VHS, Beta, LV, Closed Caption. Tom Hanks, Jackie Gleason, Eva Marie Saint, Bess Armstrong, Hector Elizondo, Barry Corbin, Sela Ward, John Kapelos, Jane Morris, Dan Castellaneta, Tracey Reiner; **D:** Garry Marshall; **W:** Rick Podell; **C:** John A. Alonzo; **M:** Patrick Leonard. *WAR*

Nothing Personal ♂½ 1980 (PG) Confused mix of romantic comedy and environmental themes. Lawyer (?) Somers attempts to help college professor Sutherland prevent the slaughter of seals. Enter romance (hey, but what about the baby seals?). Enlivened by appearances of Canadian SCTV vets and Somers's first starring theatrical role. **96m/C VHS, Beta, LV.** Donald Sutherland, Suzanne Somers, Dabney Coleman, John Dehner, Roscoe Lee Browne, Catherine O'Hara; **D:** George Bloomfield. *ART, VES*

Nothing Personal ♂♂♂ 1995 (R) Uncompromising drama about the sectarian violence in northern Ireland that engulfs even the innocent. The IRA bombing of a Protestant pub sets a Loyalist unit, led by dedicated Kenny (Frain) and psychotic Ginger (a terrifying Hart), on an increasingly deadly 24-hour rampage through Belfast (in 1975). Catholic single father Liam Kelly (Lynch) finds himself in the wrong part of town and only wants to return to his two children but is inexorably drawn into the violence, which leads to tragedy for all. Adapted from the novel "All Our Fault" by Mornin, who wrote the screenplay.**CW:** Strong intense violence, language and a sex scene. **86m/C VHS. GB IR** Ian Hart, John Lynch, James Frain, Michael Gambon, Ruaidhri Conroy, Jeni Courtney, Gary Lydon, Maria Doyle Doyle Kennedy, Gerard McSorley, Gareth O'Hare; **D:** Thaddeus O'Sullivan; **W:** Daniel Mornin; **C:** Dick Pope; **M:** Philip Appleby. *THV*

Nothing Sacred ♂♂♂½ 1937 Slick, overzealous reporter takes advantage of a small-town girl's situation. As a publicity stunt, his newspaper brings her to the Big Apple to distract her from her supposedly imminent death in order to manipulate the public's sentiment as a means to sell more copy. Innocent young Lombard, however, is far from death's door, and deftly exploits her exploitation. Scathing indictment of the mass media and bovine mentality of the masses. Both hysterically funny and bitterly cynical; boasts Lombard's finest performance as the small-town rube who orchestrates the ruse. Remade in 1954 as "Living It Up." DVD version includes home movie footage of a Lombard-Gable hunting trip and two Mack Sennett shorts—"Campus Vamp" (1928) and "Matchmaking Mama." **75m/C VHS, LV, DVD.** Fredric March, Carole Lombard, Walter Connolly, Sig Rumann, Charles Winninger, Margaret Hamilton; **D:** William A. Wellman; **W:** Ben Hecht; **C:** William Howard Greene; **M:** Oscar Levant. *KIV, MRV, VYY*

Nothing to Lose ♂♂½ 1996 (R) Ad exec Nick Beam (Robbins) is having a very bad day. He loses his job, finds his wife is having an affair, then gets carjacked by street-wise but dim-witted thief T-Paul (Lawrence). T-Paul picked the wrong day to rob Nick, who ironically takes T-Paul hostage. The unlikely pair find they have more in common than realized. Screwball buddy comedy shows its originality in casting, and not much else. Robbins and Lawrence are an inspired pair with great comedic potential but are trapped in a mundane story. Filming was delayed due, in part, to Lawrence's constant run-ins with the law.**CW:** Pervasive strong language and a sex scene. **97m/C VHS, LV, Closed Caption.** Tim Robbins, Martin Lawrence, John C. McGinley, Giancarlo Esposito, Kelly Preston, Michael McKean, Irma P. Hall, Susan Barnes, Rebecca Gayheart, Patrick Cranshaw; **D:** Steve Oedekerk; **W:** Steve Oedekerk; **C:** Donald E. Thorin; **M:** Robert Folk. *TOU*

Nothing Underneath ♂½ 1985 An American guy goes to Rome to search for his model twin sister, who may be one of the victims of a series of scissor killings. **95m/C VHS, Beta.** Tom Schanley, Renee Simonsen, Nicola Perring, Donald Pleasence; **D:** Carlo Vanzina. *NO*

Notorious 🎬🎬🎬🎬 1946 Post-WWII story of a beautiful playgirl sent by the US government to marry a suspected spy living in Brazil. Grant is the agent assigned to watch her. Duplicity and guilt are important factors in this brooding, romantic spy thriller. Suspenseful throughout, with a surprise ending. The acting is excellent all around and Hitchcock makes certain that suspense is maintained throughout this classy and complex thriller. Laserdisc contains original trailer, publicity photos, and additional footage. 101m/B VHS, Beta, LV, Closed Caption. Cary Grant, Ingrid Bergman, Claude Rains, Louis Calhern, Madame Konstantin, Reinhold Schunzel, Moroni Olsen; D: Alfred Hitchcock; W: Ben Hecht. Nominations: Academy Awards '46: Best Original Screenplay, Best Supporting Actor (Rains). FOX, CRC, MLB

The Notorious Lady 🎬🎬½ 1927 Englishman Stone kills the man he finds in Bedford's room, believing him to be his wife's lover. He's mistaken but she lies to save him and Stone takes off for the diamond mines in Africa. Bedford hears he's dead and sets out, seeking the truth. 79m/B VHS. Lewis Stone, Barbara Bedford, Earl Metcalfe, Francis McDonald; D: King Baggot; C: Gaetano Antonio "Tony" Gaudio. FCT

Nous N'Irons Plus au Bois 🎬🎬 1969 On the outskirts of a forest held by the Germans, a small group of French resistance fighters capture a German soldier during WWII. He actually wants to join forces with them, however, after falling in love with a lovely young French girl. In French; subtitled in English. 98m/C VHS, Beta. FR Marie-France Pisier, Siegfried Rauch, Richard Leduc; D: Georges Dumoulin. NO

Nouvelle Vague 🎬🎬½ New Wave 1990 Delon is a philosopher king and Giordano a wealthy countess involved in Godard's usual sexual and political themes, which has society geared toward support of the rich. Dialogue is composed entirely of quotations. In French with English subtitles. 89m/C VHS. SI FR Alain Delon, Domiziana Giordano, Roland Amstutz, Laurence Cote, Christophe Odent; D: Jean-Luc Godard; W: Jean-Luc Godard. FCT

Novel Desires 🎬½ 1992 (R) Brian Freedman is a best-selling author who teams up with his writing rival, Vicky Chance. But it isn't just their imaginations they give free reign to, it's all their desires as well. CW: Strong sexuality. 80m/C VHS. Tyler Gains, Caroline Monteith, Mitchell Clark, Lisa Hayland; D: Lawrence Unger. CEL

November Conspiracy 🎬🎬½ 1996 (R) Journalist Jenny Baron (Turco) is covering the presidential campaign of a senator (Segal) when she uncovers a conspiracy linking a number of assassinations and murder attempts. A computer disk reveals more information but when her lover (Benedict) is murdered during an attempted political assassination, Baron goes on the run to save her own life. CW: Nudity, language, violence. 103m/C VHS, Closed Caption. Paige Turco, George Segal, Elliott Gould, Bo Hopkins, Dirk Benedict, Conrad Janis; D: Conrad Janis. MET

The November Men 🎬½ 1993 (PG) In 1992, liberal Hollywood director Arthur Gwenlyn (Williams) begins filming a thriller about an assassin after a presidential candidate. But cinematographer Elizabeth (Bevis) begins to suspect that Gwenlyn's actually serious about killing off some right-wing politicos and is using the production as a cover. Doesn't make a lot of sense. 98m/C VHS. Paul W. Williams, James Andronica, Leslie Bevis, Robert Davi; D: Paul W. Williams; W: James Andronica. TTV

Now and Forever 🎬🎬½ 1934 Penny (Temple) is the young daughter of charming widower and con man Jerry Day (Cooper). Penny's been in the care of her uncle but Jerry's decided to settle down in Paris with his lady love Toni (Lombard) and figures he can give the tyke a home. But the hard-up Jerry can't resist stealing a valuable necklace and there's much trouble ahead (and not your average happy ending). Temple steals the film from her elders. Adapted from the story "Honor Bright" by Jack Kirkland and Melville Baker. Colorized. 82m/C VHS, Closed Caption. Gary Cooper, Carole Lombard, Shirley Temple, Guy Standing, Charlotte Granville, Gilbert Emery; D: Henry Hathaway; W: Vincent Lawrence, Sylvia Thalberg; C: Harry Fischbeck. USH

Now and Forever 🎬½ 1982 (R) Young wife's life is shattered when her unfaithful husband is wrongly accused and convicted of rape. After he is sent to prison, she begins drinking and taking drugs. From the novel by Danielle Steel, it will appeal most to those who like their romances a la Harlequin. 93m/C VHS, Beta, LV. AU Cheryl Ladd, Robert Coleby, Carmen Duncan, Christine Amor, Aileen Britton; D: Adrian Carr. USH

Now and Then 🎬🎬 1995 (PG-13) Four women hold a reunion 25 years after their most eventful childhood summer to relive the good ol' days of prepubescent triumphs and tragedies. Flashback, which thankfully comprises about 85% of the movie, explores first kisses, budding breasts, death and divorce. Despite good intentions, this nostalgic coming-of-ager for the girls is a jumbled mass of borrowed formulas that just can't shake that feeling of forced sentimentality. The young actresses are talented and charming, but their less convincing adult counterparts serve mostly as big names to draw crowds and studio support. CW: Contains strong language, brief nudity, and adolescent discussions about sex. 97m/C VHS, LV, Closed Caption. Rosie O'Donnell, Melanie Griffith, Demi Moore, Rita Wilson, Christina Ricci, Thora Birch, Gaby Hoffman, Ashleigh Aston Moore, Cloris Leachman, Lolita Davidovich, Bonnie Hunt, Brendan Fraser; D: Leslie Linka Glatter; W: I. Marlene King; C: Ueli Steiger; M: Cliff Eidelman. NLC

Now, Voyager 🎬🎬🎬½ 1942 Davis plays a lonely spinster who is transformed into a vibrant young woman by therapy. She comes out of her shell to have a romantic affair with a suave European (who turns out to be married) but still utters the famous phrase "Oh, Jerry, we have the stars. Let's not ask for the moon." Definitely melodramatic, but an involving story nonetheless. Based on a novel by Olive Higgins Prouty. 117m/B VHS, Beta, LV. Bette Davis, Gladys Cooper, Claude Rains, Paul Henreid, Bonita Granville; D: Irving Rapper; M: Max Steiner. Academy Awards '42: Best Original Dramatic/Comedy Score; Nominations: Academy Awards '42: Best Actress (Davis), Best Supporting Actress (Cooper). MGM

Now You See Him, Now You Don't 🎬🎬 1972 (G) Light Disney comedy involving a gang of crooks who want to use a college student's invisibility formula to rob a local bank. Sequel to Disney's "The Computer Wore Tennis Shoes." 85m/C VHS, Beta. Kurt Russell, Joe Flynn, Cesar Romero, Jim Backus; D: Robert Butler; M: Robert F. Brunner. DIS

Nowhere 🎬🎬 1996 (R) Third in Araki's teen trilogy, following "Totally F***ed Up" and "The Doom Generation" is a basic day-in-the-life look at alienated L.A. 18-year-old Dark Smith (Duval), adrift in a world of consumerism and looking for love. He loves Mel (True) but she's torn between Dark and girlfriend Lucifer (Robertson), so Dark turns to Montgomery (Bexton). His friends have their own trials with drugs and sex (in various combos), and violence. Angst to the Nth degree, with Araki's imagination in wild disarray. CW: Scenes of strong violence, sexuality and drug use involving teens, and for strong language. 82m/C VHS. James Duval, Rachel True, Kathleen Robertson, Nathan Bexton, Guillermo Diaz, Alan Boyce, Christina Applegate, Jeremy Jordan, Chiara Mastroianni, Debi Mazar, Jordan Ladd, Thyme Lewis, Sarah Lassez, Ryan Phillippe, Heather Graham, Scott Caan; Cameos: John Ritter, Beverly D'Angelo, David Leisure, Traci Lords, Shannen Doherty; D: Gregg Araki; W: Gregg Araki; C: Arturo Smith. NLC

Nowhere to Hide 🎬🎬 1987 (R) A widow whose Marine officer husband has been assassinated is chased by some bad guys who are after a helicopter part (say what?) and she must fight for survival for herself and her six-year-old son. 91m/C VHS, Beta, Closed Caption. Amy Madigan, Daniel Hugh-Kelly, Michael Ironside; D: Mario Azzopardi; M: Brad Fiedel. ORI, HHE, WAR

Nowhere to Hide 🎬🎬 19?? A hitman is hired to kill a young boy who witnesses a brutal murder. The hitman, however, decides he's already killed too many people and wants to get out of the business. Will he become the next murder target? 80m/C VHS. Paul Winfield, Rod Taylor. QVD

Nowhere to Run 🎬 1988 (R) Slipshod version of a true story about a series of murders in Caddo, Texas in 1960. Carradine, paroled from prison, murders for revenge while six high school seniors get involved in the chase and in the seedy side of politics, police, and their own puberty. 80m/ C VHS, Beta. David Carradine, Jason Priestley, Kieran Mulroney, Henry Jones; D: Carl Franklin. MGM

Nowhere to Run 🎬½ 1993 (R) Kickboxer with heart seeks cross-over movie to establish real acting career. Unfortunately, even if such a movie existed, Van Damme wouldn't know what to do with it. Arquette plays the damsel in distress, facing eviction from the family farm with her two small children. Fortunately for Van Damme's escaped convict character, she is also a very lonely widow (nudge, nudge). He saves the day by abusing the daylights out of the big bad bankers, yet also finds time to play surrogate dad. Whatta guy. CW: Language, violence, and sexuality. 95m/ C VHS, LV, 8mm, Closed Caption. Jean-Claude Van Damme, Rosanna Arquette, Kieran Culkin, Tiffany Taubman, Joss Ackland, Ted Levine; D: Robert Harmon; W: Joe Eszterhas, Leslie Bohem, Randy Feldman; M: Mark Isham. COL

Nuclear Conspiracy 🎬½ 1985 A reporter disappears while investigating a huge nuclear waste shipment, and his wife searches for him. 115m/C VHS, Beta. Birgit Doll, Albert Fortell. THV

The Nude Bomb 🎬🎬½ The Return of Maxwell Smart 1980 (PG) Proof that old TV shows never die—they just get made into big screen movies. Maxwell Smart from "Get Smart" (would you believe?) tries to save the world from a bomb intended to destroy clothing and leave everyone in the buff. Old hat lines. Followed by the TV movie "Get Smart, Again!" 94m/C VHS, LV. Don Adams, Dana Elcar, Pamela Hensley, Sylvia Kristel, Norman Lloyd, Rhonda Fleming, Joey Forman; D: Clive Donner; W: Bill Dana; M: Lalo Schifrin. USH

Nude on the Moon woof! 1961 Lunar expedition discovers moon inhabited by people who bare skin as hobby. Groovy theme song, "I'm Mooning Over You, My Little Moon Doll." Part of Joe Bob Brigg's "Sleaziest Movies in the History of the World" series. 83m/C VHS. D: Doris Wishman. VTR

Nudity Required 🎬 1990 Two pals use the casting couch, pretending to be Hollywood producers, to seduce young women. Silly comedy with gratuitous nudity (Ms. Newmar included). Hardly a laugh to be found. 90m/C VHS. Julie Newmar, Troy Donahue, Brad Zutaut, Billy Frank, Ty Randolph, Alvin Silver, Eli Rich, Phil Hock; D: John Bown. NO

Nudo di Donna 🎬🎬🎬 Portrait of a Woman, Nude 1983 A witty comedy about a Venetian bookseller who is becoming tired of marital struggles with his sexy wife of 16 years. He wanders into a fashion photography shop, sees a backside nude photo of a model who looks like his wife, and he takes off in fiery pursuit to find the subject of the photo. Venetian location photography is quite nice. In Italian with English subtitles. 112m/C VHS, Beta, LV. IT Nino Manfredi, Jean-Pierre Cassel, George Wilson, Elenora Giorgi; D: Nino Manfredi. TPV

Nueba Yol 🎬🎬 1995 Balbuena (Marti) is a recent widower with nothing much to look forward to in his native Dominican Republic, so he's easily persuaded by fast-talking friend Fellito (Carbonell) into immigrating to New York (illegally). He has trouble finding any kind of work, is confused and intimidated by the city, and finds himself at odds with more acclimated immigrants from his home-land. Spanish with subtitles. 103m/C VHS. Luisito Marti, Caridad Ravelo, Raul Carbonell, Joel Garcia; **D:** Angel Muniz; **W:** Angel Muniz; **C:** Chris Norr. *KIT*

Nukie 🎬🎬½ **1993 (G)** Brothers from another planet crash land on Earth. The first one is subjected to a dizzying array of scientific experiments in Florida involving electric cattle prods. The other one, Nukie, lands in Africa and is befriended by twins from a remote tribal village. They join him in his quest to free his brother from the sadistic clutches of suntanned professionals who have lost all compassion. Important message for our youth about the dangers of a runaway technocracy. 99m/C VHS, LV. Glynis Johns, Steve Railsback; **D:** Sias Odendal. *THV*

Number One Fan 🎬½ **1994 (R)** Hollywood action star Zane Barry (McQueen) is stalked by Blair (Ammann), a fan with whom he had a brief romance. Zane manages to patch things up when fiancee Holly (Stewart) finds out but Blair's determined to be the only woman in his life. **CW:** Some language; strong violence; sexuality. 93m/C VHS, Closed Caption. Chad McQueen, Catherine Mary Stewart, Renee Ammann, Hoyt Axton, Paul Bartel, Eric Da Re, Charles Matthau; **D:** Jane Simpson; **W:** Anthony Laurence Greene. *ORI*

Number 1 of the Secret Service 🎬🎬 **1977 (PG)** A handsome secret agent must foil the plans of a millionaire industrialist to destroy the economy. Spy spoof that's marginally interesting. 87m/C VHS, Beta. *GB* Nicky Henson, Geoffrey Keen, Sue Lloyd, Aimi MacDonald, Richard Todd; **D:** Lindsay Shonteff. *MGM*

Number One with a Bullet 🎬🎬 **1987 (R)** Two unorthodox "odd couple" detectives are demoted after losing a key witness, but still set out on their own to unearth a drug czar. Carradine and Williams are better than this standard action material. 103m/C VHS, Beta. Robert Carradine, Billy Dee Williams, Peter Graves, Valerie Bertinelli; **D:** Jack Smight; **W:** James Belushi, Andrew Kurtzman, Rob Riley. *MGM*

No. 17 🎬🎬🎬 **1932** A humorous early thriller by the Master Hitchcock, filmed before the likes of "The 39 Steps." An unsuspecting hobo accidentally discovers a jewel thief's cache. The chase is on—superb final chase sequence involving a bus and a train. Based on the play by J. Jefferson Farjeon. 64m/B VHS, Beta, 8mm. *GB* Leon M. Lion, Anne Grey, John Stuart, Donald Calthrop; **D:** Alfred Hitchcock; **W:** Alfred Hitchcock. *REP, NOS, HHT*

Numero Deux 🎬🎬 *Number Two* **1975** Godard explores politics, sex, and the trials of the modern family. A dissatisfied wife suffers from chronic constipation, her exhausted husband is impotent, they, their children, and grandparents all try to cope with daily life. For nine-tenths of the film Godard only used small portions of the screen (the upper left and lower right corners) to manipulate his message of frustration. It's only at the end that the full-screen is used to offer some sort of relief. In French with English subtitles. 90m/C VHS. *FR* Sandrine Battistella, Pierre Oudry, Alexandre Rignault, Rachel Stefanopol; **D:** Jean-Luc Godard; **W:** Anne-Marie Mieville, Jean-Luc Godard. *FCT*

The Nun 🎬🎬½ **1966** A young woman, unable to meet financial obligations, is forced into a convent. Victimized by the mother superior and betrayed by a clergyman who befriends her, she escapes from the convent and eventually ends up in a bordello, despairing and suicidal. Not a cheery story. Banned in France for two years. In French with English subtitles. 155m/C VHS. *FR* Anna Karina, Lilo (Liselotte) Pulver, Micheline Presle, Christine Lenier, Francine Berge, Francesco Rabal, Wolfgang Reichmann, Catherine Diamant, Yori Bertin; **D:** Jacques Rivette. *INT, FCT*

Nuns on the Run 🎬🎬 **1990 (PG-13)** Idle and Coltrane are two nonviolent members of a robbery gang who double-cross their boss during a hold-up and disguise themselves as nuns while on the run from both the Mob and the police.

Catholic humor, slapstick, and much fun with habits dominate. Idle and Coltrane do their best to keep the so-so script moving with its one-joke premise. 95m/C VHS, Beta, LV. Eric Idle, Robbie Coltrane, Janet Suzman, Camille Coduri, Robert Patterson, Tom Hickey, Doris Hare, Lila Kaye; **D:** Jonathan Lynn; **W:** Jonathan Lynn. *FOX*

The Nun's Story 🎬🎬🎬½ **1959** The melancholy tale of a young nun working in the Congo and Belgium during WWII, and struggling to reconcile her free spirit with the rigors of the order. Highly acclaimed; from the Kathryn Hulme novel. 152m/C VHS, Beta, LV. Audrey Hepburn, Peter Finch, Edith Evans, Peggy Ashcroft, Mildred Dunnock, Dean Jagger, Beatrice Straight, Colleen Dewhurst; **D:** Fred Zinnemann; **W:** Robert Anderson. British Academy Awards '59: Best Actress (Hepburn); National Board of Review Awards '59: Best Director (Zinnemann), Best Supporting Actress (Evans); New York Film Critics Awards '59: Best Actress (Hepburn), Best Director (Zinnemann); Nominations: Academy Awards '59: Best Actress (Hepburn), Best Adapted Screenplay, Best Color Cinematography, Best Director (Zinnemann), Best Film Editing, Best Picture, Best Sound, Best Original Dramatic/Comedy Score. *WAR*

Nurse 🎬🎬½ **1980** A recently widowed woman resumes her career as a nurse in a large urban hospital, after her son leaves for college. Based on Peggy Anderson's book. Made for television; became a weekly series. 105m/C VHS, Beta. Michael Learned, Robert Reed, Antonio Fargas; **D:** David Lowell Rich. *ART*

The Nurse 🎬½ **1997 (R)** Nurse (Zane) seeks revenge from the man she holds responsible for her father's suicide. 94m/C VHS, LV, Closed Caption. Lisa Zane, John Stockwell, Janet Gunn, William R. Moses, Nancy Dussault, Sherrie Rose, Jay Underwood, Michael Fairman; **D:** Rob Malenfant; **W:** Richard Brandes; **C:** Feliks Parnell; **M:** Richard Bowers. *ART*

Nurse Edith Cavell 🎬🎬🎬 **1939** Fine performances in this true story of Britain's famous nurse who aided the Belgian underground during WWI, transporting wounded soldiers out of the German-occupied country. Decidedly opposes war and, ironically, was released just as WWII began to heat up in 1939. 95m/B VHS, Beta. George Sanders, Edna May Oliver, ZaSu Pitts, Robert Coote, May Robson, Anna Neagle; **D:** Herbert Wilcox. Nominations: Academy Awards '39: Best Original Score. *NOS, CAB, BAR*

Nurse Marjorie 🎬🎬 **1920** Aristocratic nurse Marjorie (Minter) falls in love and marries the leader of the Labor Party, much to her family's dismay. Based on the play by Israel Zangwill. Minter made four films with director Taylor, whose murder in 1922 has never been solved. ?m/B VHS. Mary Miles Minter, Clyde Fillmore, George Periolat, Mollie McConnell, Frank Leigh, Vera Lewis; **D:** William Desmond Taylor; **W:** Julia Crawford Ivers. *GPV*

Nurse on Call 🎬 **1988** A bevy of trampy nurses cavort throughout a big city hospital. Softcore. 80m/C VHS, Beta. Anne Tilson, Jennie Martinez, Christopher Floyd.

The Nut 🎬🎬½ **1921** Charlie Jackson (Fairbanks) is a wacky, wealthy inventor who falls for Estrell Wynn (De La Motte), a society gal dedicated to improving the lives of underprivileged children. He tries to aid her in a variety of ways—none of which work out as he expects. The usually swashbuckling Fairbanks does get to rescue the heroine. 61m/B VHS. Douglas Fairbanks Sr., Marguerite de la Motte, William E. Lowery; **D:** Theodore Reed; **W:** William Parker. *FCT, KIV*

Nutcase 🎬 **1983** A trio of young children in New Zealand attempt to thwart a group of terrorists who threaten to reactivate a large city's volcanoes unless they are given a large sum of money. Novel twist there. 49m/C VHS, Beta. *NZ* Nevan Rowe, Ian Watkin, Michael Wilson; **D:** Roger Donaldson. *NO*

The Nutcracker Prince 🎬🎬 **1991** The classic children's Christmas tale comes alive in this feature-length animated special. 75m/C VHS, LV, 8mm, Closed Caption. *CA* **D:** Paul Schibli; **V:** Kiefer Sutherland, Megan Follows, Michael MacDonald, Phyllis Diller, Peter O'Toole. *WAR*

Nutcracker Sweet 🎬 **1984** Ridiculous drama about a beautiful and powerful socialite (Collins) who runs a renowned ballet company with an iron fist. A Russian ballerina defects and infiltrates Collins's company to try out her own treacherous motives. 101m/C VHS, Beta. Joan Collins, Finola Hughes, Paul Nicholas; **D:** Anwar Kawadri. *ART, VES*

Nutcracker: The Motion Picture 🎬🎬½ **1986** A lavish, stage-bound filmization of the Tchaikovsky ballet, designed by Maurice Sendak. 82m/C VHS, Beta. **D:** Carroll Ballard. *PAR, BAR, KAR*

Nuts 🎬🎬🎬 **1987 (R)** A high-priced prostitute attempts to prove her sanity when she's accused of manslaughter. Ashamed of her lifestyle, and afraid of her reasons for it, her parents attempt to institutionalize her. A filmed version of Tom Topor's play that manages to retain its mesmerizing qualities. Fine performances, although the funnygirl goes over the top on several occasions. 116m/C VHS, Beta, LV, 8mm, Closed Caption. Barbra Streisand, Richard Dreyfuss, Maureen Stapleton, Karl Malden, James Whitmore, Robert Webber, Eli Wallach, Leslie Nielsen, William Prince, Dakin Matthews, Hayley Taylor Block; **D:** Martin Ritt; **W:** Tom Topor, Darryl Ponicsan, Alvin Sargent; **C:** Andrzej Bartkowiak; **M:** Barbra Streisand. *WAR*

Nuts in May 🎬🎬 **1976** Two smug, middle-aged, middle-class vegetarians go on a camping trip and totally alienate their cynical, working-class fellow campers. Made for British television. 84m/C VHS. *GB* Alison Steadman; **D:** Mike Leigh. *WBF, BTV*

The Nutt House 🎬½ **1995 (PG-13)** Identical twins—separated at birth—grow up to be a slimy politician and a nutcase (living up to the family name) with multiple personalities. Naturally, when the two are reunited it makes for lots of outrageous complications. **CW:** Farcical sex-related scenes. 90m/C VHS, LV. Stephen Kearney, Traci Lords, Amy Yasbeck; **Cameos:** Stella Stevens, Robert Mandan, Catherine Bach; **D:** Adam Rifkin. *TRI*

The Nutty Professor 🎬🎬🎬 **1963** A mild-mannered chemistry professor creates a potion that turns him into a suave, debonair, playboy type with an irresistible attraction to women. Lewis has repeatedly denied the slick character is a Dean Martin parody, but the evidence is quite strong. Easily Lewis's best film. 107m/C VHS, Beta, LV. Jerry Lewis, Stella Stevens, Howard Morris, Kathleen Freeman; **D:** Jerry Lewis; **W:** Jerry Lewis. *PAR*

The Nutty Professor 🎬🎬🎬 **1996 (PG-13)** Remake of the 1963 Jerry Lewis comedy stars Murphy as Professor Sherman Klump, a severely overweight but bright man whose heft gets in the way of his love life. He takes a swig of his own secret potion and is transformed into the slim and suave Buddy Love. Only the formula isn't perfect and seems to wear off at the worst possible times. After a string of bad movies, Murphy may have stumbled upon his own formula for a comeback by relinquishing creative control and concentrating on the comedy. Reminiscent of "Coming to America," Murphy plays eight different roles. The fat and fart jokes are plentiful and so are the laughs. **CW:** Crude humor and sexual references. 96m/C VHS, LV, Closed Caption, DVD. Eddie Murphy, Jada Pinkett Smith, James Coburn, Dave Chappelle; **D:** Tom Shadyac; **W:** David Sheffield, Barry W. Blaustein, Steve Oedekerk, Tom Shadyac; **C:** Julio Macat; **M:** David Newman. Academy Awards '96: Best Makeup; National Society of Film Critics Awards '96: Best Actor (Murphy); Nominations: Golden Globe Awards '97: Best Actor—Musical/Comedy (Murphy); MTV Movie Awards '97: Best Male Performance (Murphy), Best Comedic Performance (Murphy). *USH*

A Nymphoid Barbarian in Dinosaur Hell woof! **1994** Nuclear holocaust survivors, human and otherwise, vie for the affections of the last woman alive, a voluptuous nymphoid barbarian. 90m/C VHS. Linda Corwin, Paul Guzzi. *TTV*

Nyoka and the Tigermen *Nyoka and the Lost Secrets of Hippocrates; Perils of Nyoka* **1942** The adventures of the jungle queen Nyoka and her rival Vultura in their search for the lost tablets of Hippocrates. In 15 episodes. **250m/B VHS, LV.** Kay Aldridge, Clayton Moore; **D:** William Witney. *VCN, REP, MLB*

O Lucky Man! 🎬🎬🎬🎬 **1973 (R)** Surreal, black comedy following the rise and fall and eventual rebirth of a modern British coffee salesman. Several actors play multiple roles with outstanding performances throughout. Price's excellent score combines with the hilarity for an extraordinary experience. **178m/C VHS, Beta.** *GB* Malcolm McDowell, Ralph Richardson, Rachel Roberts, Arthur Lowe, Alan Price, Helen Mirren, Mona Washbourne, Warren Clarke; **D:** Lindsay Anderson; **M:** Alan Price. British Academy Awards '73: Best Supporting Actor (Lowe). *WAR*

O Pioneers! 🎬🎬½ **1991 (PG)** Lange plays Alexandra Bergson, an unmarried woman at the turn of the century, who inherits her family's Nebraska homestead because her father knows how much she loves the land. Although the family has prospered through Alexandra's smart investments, her brothers come to resent her influence. When her first love returns after 15 years and romance is rekindled, family resentments surface once again. Based on the novel by Willa Cather. A Hallmark Hall of Fame presentation. **99m/C VHS, LV, Closed Caption.** Jessica Lange, David Strathairn, Tom Aldredge, Reed Edward Diamond, Anne Heche, Heather Graham, Josh Hamilton, Leigh Lawson, Graham Beckel; **D:** Glenn Jordan; **W:** Glenn Jordan. *REP, FCT*

O Quatrilho 🎬🎬 **1995** Two young couples from Italy immigrate to southern Brazil in the 1910s, hoping to find their fortunes. Thrifty peasant Angelo (Paternost) marries romantic Teresa (Pillar) and goes into business with the equally romantic Massimo (Campos), who's married to the thrifty Pierina (Pires). The grain mill thrives but the romantic half of each couple delve into some illicit amore and decide to flee while their left-behind spouses discover their own attractions. A happy ending is had by all (this must be a fairytale). Lots of high-gloss gush. Based on the novel by Jose Clemente Pozenat. Portuguese and Italian with subtitles. **120m/C VHS.** *BR* Gloria Pires, Patricia Pillar, Bruno Campos, Alexandre Paternost; **D:** Fabio Barreto; **W:** Leopoldo Serran; **C:** Felix Monti; **M:** Caetano Veloso. Nominations: Academy Awards '95: Best Foreign Language Film. *NYR*

The Oak 🎬🎬½ **1993** Morgenstern grieves over the loss of her father until she realizes she can't get rid of the body. Her difficulties in locating adequate medical facilities reflect the nightmarish realities of pre-1990 communist Romania. Potentially farcical aspects of storyline are successfully removed by violence in following scene involving Morgenstern and a band of roaming soldiers. A tragicomic look at obstinate communist bureaucrats and the wily, willful peasants who overcome them. Based on a novel by Ion Baiesu. In Romanian with English subtitles. **105m/C VHS.** *RO* Maia Morgenstern, Razvan Vasilescu, Victor Rebengiuc, Dorel Visan, Mariana Mihut, Dan Condurache, Virgil Andriescu, Leopoldina Balanuta, Matei Alexandru, Gheorghe Visu, Magda Catone, Ionel Mahailescu; **D:** Lucian Pintilie; **W:** Lucian Pintilie. *NYF*

Oath of Vengeance 🎬½ **1944** Billy the Kid rides the West once more. **50m/B VHS, Beta.** Buster Crabbe, Al "Fuzzy" St. John, Jack Ingram, Charles "Blackie" King; **D:** Sam Newfield. *VCN, RXM*

The Object of Beauty 🎬🎬🎬 **1991 (R)** Two Americans, trapped in Europe by their love of pleasure and their lack of money, bicker over whether to sell their one object of value—a tiny Henry Moore sculpture. When it disappears, their relationship is challenged. Excellent acting and telling direction. Forces an examination of one's own value placement.**CW:** Language. **105m/C VHS, LV, Closed Caption.** Andie MacDowell, John Malkovich, Joss Ackland, Lolita Davidovich, Peter Riegert, Bill Paterson, Rudi Davies, Ricci Harnett; **D:** Michael Lindsay-Hogg;

W: Michael Lindsay-Hogg; **C:** David Watkin; **M:** Tom Bahler. *ART*

The Object of My Affection 🎬🎬½ **1998 (R)** Nina (Aniston) is a Brooklyn social worker with an overbearing boyfriend, Vince (Pankow), she doesn't really love. Unfortunately, the man she does fall for is handsome gay teacher George (Rudd), who's just broken up with his pretentious boyfriend Joley (Daly), and who winds up renting Nina's spare room. When Nina discovers she's pregnant, she decides George would make a terrific father and asks him to raise the baby with her. But both turn out to have very unrealistic expectations about friendship and romance. Mix of humor and tears, with good performances, particularly by the appealing leads. Adapted from the novel by Stephen McCauley.**CW:** Strong language and some sexuality. **112m/C VHS.** Jennifer Aniston, Paul Rudd, John Pankow, Timothy Daly, Alan Alda, Nigel Hawthorne, Allison Janney, Amo Gulinello, Steve Zahn; **D:** Nicholas Hytner; **W:** Wendy Wasserstein; **C:** Oliver Stapleton; **M:** George Fenton. *NYR*

Object of Obsession 🎬½ **1995 (R)** One wrong phone call propels divorcee Margaret into an affair with a stranger that leads to kinky psycho/sexual games and revenge.**CW:** Strong sexual content; sex-related dialogue. **91m/C VHS, LV.** Erika Anderson, Scott Valentine; **D:** Alexander Gregory Hippolyte. *APX*

Objective, Burma! 🎬🎬🎬🎬 **1945** Deemed by many to be the greatest and most moving WWII production released during the war. American paratroopers are dropped over Burma where their mission is to destroy a Japanese radar station. The Americans led by Flynn are successful in wiping out the station, but they are spotted and descended upon by Japanese forces. Impeded from returning to Allied lines, the American soldiers must try to survive enemy encounters, exhaustion, starvation, and the elements until they are rescued. Splendid performance by Flynn and exceptional direction from Walsh; excellent performances enhanced by energetic score. **142m/B VHS, Beta.** Errol Flynn, James Brown, William Prince, George Tobias, Henry Hull, Warner Anderson, Richard Erdman, Mark Stevens, Anthony Caruso, Hugh Beaumont; **D:** Raoul Walsh; **W:** Ranald MacDougall, Lester Cole; **C:** James Wong Howe; **M:** Franz Waxman. Nominations: Academy Awards '45: Best Film Editing, Best Story, Best Original Dramatic/Comedy Score. *MGM*

Oblivion 🎬🎬 **1994 (PG-13)** In this sci-fi western, set in the year 3031, its cowboys versus the aliens. A sheriff's son (Paul) returns to the town of Oblivion to avenge his father's murder and finds a reptilian extraterrestrial (Divoff) terrorizing the community.**CW:** Language; sci-fi violence; some sensuality. **94m/C VHS, Beta, Closed Caption.** Richard Joseph Paul, Andrew Divoff, Jackie Swanson, Meg Foster, Isaac Hayes, Julie Newmar, Carel Struycken, George Takei; **D:** Sam Irvin; **W:** Peter David; **M:** Pino Donaggio. *PAR*

Oblomov 🎬🎬🎬½ *A Few Days in the Life of I.I. Oblomov; Neskolko Dnei iz Zhizni I.I. Oblomov* **1981** A production of the classic Goncharov novel about a symbolically inert Russian aristocrat whose childhood friend helps him find a reason for action. Well made, with fine performances. In Russian with English subtitles. **145m/C VHS, Beta.** *RU* Oleg Tabakov, Elena Solovei; **D:** Nikita Mikhalkov. *TPV, KIV, AUD*

The Oblong Box 🎬🎬 *Edgar Allen Poe's The Oblong Box* **1969 (PG)** Coffins, blood, and live corpses fill drawn-out and lifeless adaptation of Edgar Allan Poe story. English aristocrat Price attempts to hide his disfigured brother in an old tower. Brother predictably escapes and rampages through town before being killed. **91m/C VHS, Beta.** *GB* Vincent Price, Christopher Lee, Alastair Williamson, Hilary Dwyer, Peter Arne, Harry Baird, Carl Rigg, Sally Geeson, Maxwell Shaw; **D:** Gordon Hessler; **W:** Lawrence Huntington; **C:** John Coquillon. *NO*

The Obsessed 🎬🎬 *The Late Edwina Black* **1951** Uninspiring story with Farrar suspected of murdering his wife. Competent performances, but this mystery isn't developed with any sense of style and the killer's real identity will be obvious to anyone watching. Cliches and stereotyped situations don't add anything. **77m/B VHS, LV.** *GB* David Farrar, Geraldine Fitzgerald, Roland Culver, Jean Cadell, Mary Merrall, Harcourt Williams, Charles Heslop, Ronald Adam, Sydney Monkton; **D:** Maurice Elvey; **W:** Charles Frank, David Evans. *SNC, NOS, MOV*

Obsessed 🎬½ **1988 (PG-13)** Semi-realistic tale of a woman's exhausting desire for revenge against hit-and-run driver who killed her son. Cast acceptable but lack of psychological foundation weakens plot. **100m/C VHS, Beta, LV.** Kerrie Keane, Alan Thicke, Colleen Dewhurst, Saul Rubinek, Daniel Pilon, Lynne Griffin; **D:** Robin Spry. Genie Awards '89: Best Supporting Actress (Dewhurst). *NO*

Obsession 🎬🎬½ **1976 (PG)** A rich, lonely businessman meets a mysterious young girl in Italy, the mirror image of his late wife who was killed by kidnappers. Intriguing suspense film that's not quite up to comparisons with Hitchcock thrillers. Music by Hitchcock-collaborator Herrmann. **98m/C VHS, Beta, LV.** Cliff Robertson, Genevieve Bujold, John Lithgow; **D:** Brian DePalma; **W:** Paul Schrader; **M:** Bernard Herrmann. Nominations: Academy Awards '76: Best Original Score. *COL, HHE*

Obsession: A Taste for Fear 🎬½ **1989 (R)** Diane's high fashion models are being killed and although there are plenty of suspects, she can't find the killer. **90m/C VHS, Beta.** Virginia Hey, Gerard Darmon, Carlo Mucari; **D:** Piccio Raffanini. *IMP*

Obsessive Love 🎬🎬½ **1984** A lonely, mentally unstable typist (Mimieux) becomes obsessed with her soap opera hero and decides to go to Hollywood to seduce him. She transforms herself into a sleek and stunning Hollywood temptress to woo him, and at first he goes along with her—until he realizes that she is insane. An average made-for-TV movie of the older woman/younger man genre. **97m/C VHS.** Yvette Mimieux, Simon MacCorkindale, Kin Shriner, Constance McCashin, Allan Miller, Lainie Kazan; **D:** Steven Hilliard Stern. *ART*

O.C. and Stiggs 🎬½ **1987 (R)** Two teens spend a summer harassing a neighbor and his family. Flimsy attempts at comedy fall flat. A failed adaptation of a National Lampoon short story, it was held for three years before release. **109m/C VHS, Beta, Closed Caption.** Daniel H. Jenkins, Neill Barry, Jane Curtin, Tina Louise, Jon Cryer, Dennis Hopper, Paul Dooley, Ray Walston, Louis Nye, Martin Mull, Melvin Van Peebles; **D:** Robert Altman; **W:** Donald Cantrell. *FOX*

An Occasional Hell 🎬🎬½ **1996 (R)** Ernest DeWalt (Berenger) is an ex-cop turned writer and college professor. He investigates the death of a fellow professor (Lang) at the behest of the beautiful widow (Golino) and then learns the lady is the prime suspect. Filmed in South Carolina.**CW:** Strong sexuality, violence, language and some drug content. **93m/C VHS, LV.** Tom Berenger, Valeria Golino, Kari Wuhrer, Robert Davi, Stephen Lang; **D:** Salome Breziner. *THV*

The Occultist woof! **1989** Satan worshippers do the dance of death as they skin men alive for their evil purposes. **82m/C VHS, Beta.** Rick Gianisi; **D:** Tim Kincaid; **W:** Tim Kincaid. *UNI*

An Occurrence at Owl Creek Bridge/Coup de Grace **1962** "Occurrence at Owl Creek Bridge" (1962), from a story by Ambrose Bierce documents the last moments of a man who is to be hanged for sabotage. "Coup de Grace" (1978) tells the story of a group of friends who are caught up amongst the turmoil of the Bolshevik revolution. **123m/B VHS, Beta.** Margarethe von Trotta, Matthias Habich, Rudiger Kirschstein, Matthieu Carriere, Valeska Gert; **D:** Volker Schlondorff, Robert Enrico. *NO*

Ocean Drive Weekend woof! 1985
(PG-13) Several college students congregate at "Ocean Drive" for a weekend of beer, sex, and dancing. Stereotypical characters, lack of plot, and poor versions of 1960 classics combine for boring and inane comedy. 98m/C VHS, Beta. Robert Peacock, Charles Redmond, Tony Freeman; **D:** Brian Thomas Jones. ART, VES

Ocean's 11 ♂♂½ 1960 A gang of friends plans to rob five Las Vegas casinos simultaneously. Part of the "A Night at the Movies" series, this tape simulates a 1960 movie evening, with Bugs Bunny cartoon, "Person to Bunny"; a newsreel; and coming attractions for "The Sundowners" and "Sunrise at Campobello." 148m/C VHS, Beta, LV, Letterbox. Frank Sinatra, Dean Martin, Sammy Davis Jr., Angie Dickinson, Peter Lawford; **D:** Lewis Milestone; **C:** William H. Daniels. WAR

Oceans of Fire ♂ 1986 (PG) Average rehash of the tension-filled world of oil riggers. Lives of two ex-cons are threatened when they hire on as divers for world's deepest undersea oil rig. 100m/C VHS, Beta, LV. Gregory Harrison, Billy Dee Williams, Cynthia Sikes, Lyle Alzado, Tony Burton, Ray "Boom Boom" Mancini, David Carradine, Ken Norton; **D:** Steve Carver. THV

Octagon ♂♂ 1980 (R) Norris protects a woman from threatening Ninja warriors in average kung-fu adventure. Enough action and violence for fans of the genre. 103m/C VHS, Beta, LV. Chuck Norris, Karen Carlson, Lee Van Cleef, Kim Lankford, Art Hindle, Jack Carter; **D:** Eric Karson; **W:** Paul Aaron, Leigh Chapman.

Octaman ♂½ 1971 Comical thriller featuring non-threatening octopus-man discovered by scientists in Mexico. Rip-off of director Essex's own "Creature from the Black Lagoon." Not without its curiosity factor: young Rick Baker designed the octopus man, while actress Angeli died of a drug overdose during filming. 79m/C VHS, Beta. Kerwin Mathews, Pier Angeli, Harry Guardino, David Essex, Jeff Morrow, Norman Fields; **D:** Harry Essex. GEM, CNG

Octavia ♂ 1982 (R) A contemporary fable about a blind girl who befriends a convict and learns about life and love. 90m/C VHS, Beta. Susan Curtis; **D:** David Beaird; **W:** David Beaird. NLC

The October Man ♂♂♂ 1948 When a model is found murdered, a stranger with mental problems must prove his innocence to others and himself. Strong characters make good, suspenseful mystery reminiscent of Hitchcock. 95m/B VHS. GB John Mills, Joan Greenwood, Edward Chapman, Joyce Carey, Kay Walsh, Felix Aylmer, Juliet Mills; **D:** Roy Ward Baker. FCT

Octopussy ♂♂ 1983 (PG) The Bond saga continues as Agent 007 is on a mission to prevent a crazed Russian general from launching a nuclear attack against the NATO forces in Europe. Lots of special effects and gadgets keep weak plot moving. 140m/C VHS, Beta, LV, Letterbox. GB Roger Moore, Maud Adams, Louis Jourdan, Kristina Wayborn, Kabir Bedi; **D:** John Glen; **W:** Michael G. Wilson; **M:** John Barry. MGM, FOX, TLF

The Odd Angry Shot ♂♂½ 1979 Australian soldiers fighting in Vietnam discover the conflict is not what they expected. Ironic perspective of men struggling with their feelings about the war. More of an unremarkable drama with comic overtones than a combat film, it will appeal to those who prefer good direction to bloodshed. 90m/C VHS, Beta. AU Tom Jeffrey. ART, VES

Odd Birds ♂♂½ 1985 Coming of age drama set in 1965 California. Shy 15-year-old Joy Chan is a Chinese-American dreaming of becoming an actress. Her widowed immigrant mother wants Joy to have a practical profession—like nursing. Longing for someone to understand Joy meets Brother Murphy, a math teacher at the local boys school. Murphy's been trying to reconcile his religious commitment with his unorthodox views. It isn't long before these two individualists recognize a fellow kindred spirit. 87m/C VHS. Mi-

chael Moriarty, Donna Lai Ming Lew, Nancy Lee, Bruce Gray, Karen Maruyama, Scott Crawford; **D:** Jeanne Collachia; **W:** Jeanne Collachia. WAC

The Odd Couple ♂♂♂½ 1968 (G) Two divorced men with completely opposite personalities move in together. Lemmon's obsession with neatness drives slob Matthau up the wall, and their inability to see eye-to-eye results in many hysterical escapades. A Hollywood rarity, it is actually better in some ways than Neil Simon's original Broadway version. Simon based the characters on brother Danny and his roommates. Basis for the hit television series. 106m/C VHS, Beta, LV. Jack Lemmon, Walter Matthau, Herb Edelman, John Fiedler, Monica Evans, Carol Shelley; **D:** Gene Saks; **W:** Neil Simon; **C:** Robert B. Hauser. Nominations: Academy Awards '68: Best Adapted Screenplay, Best Film Editing. PAR

The Odd Job ♂♂ 1978 Insurance salesman Chapman, depressed after his wife leaves him, hires a hit man to kill him. Chapman then has a hard time shaking his stalker after deciding he wants to live. Monty Python fans will enjoy seeing ex-troupe member Chapman again, but the comic's heart isn't in this unoriginal story. 100m/C VHS, Beta. GB Graham Chapman; **D:** Peter Medak; **M:** Howard Blake. VES

Odd Jobs ♂♂ 1985 (PG-13) When five college friends look for jobs during summer break, they wind up running their own moving business with the help of the mob. Good comic talent, but a silly slapstick script results in only a passable diversion. 89m/C VHS, Beta. Paul Reiser, Scott McGinnis, Rick Overton, Robert Townsend; **D:** Mark Story; **W:** Robert Conte; **C:** Arthur Albert, Peter Collister; **M:** Robert Folk. NO

Odd Man Out ♂♂♂½ Gang War 1947 An Irish revolutionary is injured during a robbery attempt. Suffering from gunshot wounds and closely pursued by the police, he must rely on the help of others who could betray him at any moment. A gripping tale of suspense and intrigue that will keep the proverbial seat's edge warm until the final credits. Adapted from F.L. Green's novel, previously filmed as "The Last Man." 111m/B VHS, Beta, LV. GB James Mason, Robert Newton, Dan O'Herlihy, Kathleen Ryan, Cyril Cusack; **D:** Carol Reed; **C:** Robert Krasker. British Academy Awards '47: Best Film; Nominations: Academy Awards '47: Best Film Editing. PAR

Odd Obsession ♂♂½ The Key 1960 One of Ichikawa's first films, about an elderly Japanese gentleman with a young wife whose feelings of jealousy and impotence eventually wreak havoc on the marriage. In Japanese with English subtitles. 96m/C VHS. JP Machiko Kyo, Ganjiro Nakamura; **D:** Kon Ichikawa. Golden Globe Awards '60: Best Foreign Film. HMV, COL

The Odd Squad ♂ 1986 (R) Five GIs in WWII defend a bridge from the enemy, and manage in doing so to have loads of laughs. 82m/C VHS, Beta. Johnny Dorelli, Vincent Gardenia; **D:** E.B. Clucher. VTR

Oddball Hall ♂♂ 1991 (PG) Two aging jewel thieves hide out in the African wilds, masquerading as powerful "wizards." When they head back to civilization, an African tribe beseeches the phony sorcerers to cure their long drought. 87m/C VHS. Don Ameche, Burgess Meredith; **D:** Jackson Hunsicker; **W:** Jackson Hunsicker. WAR

Oddballs woof! 1984 (PG-13) In another attempt to capitalize on the success of Bill Murray's "Meatballs," this summer camp story follows three campers and their pathetic attempts to lose their virginity. Brooks has his moments, but there is little else to recommend here. 92m/C VHS, Beta. Foster Brooks, Jason Sorokin, Wally Wodchis, Konnie Krome; **D:** Miklos Lente. ART

Odds Against Tomorrow ♂♂♂ 1959 Compulsive gambler/nightclub singer Johnny Ingram (Belafonte) owes big money to gangster Bacco (Kuluva). He hooks up with racist ex-con Earl Slater (Ryan) and former policeman Dave Burke (Begley) to rob a bank but everything goes

wrong. Ingram and Slater manage to escape to a nearby oil storage area but the racial tensions between the two are proving deadlier than the cops on their trail. Based on the novel by William P. McGivern; because of the blacklist screenwriter Polonsky was "fronted" by John O. Killens. Polonsky officially received credit for his work in 1996. 120m/B VHS, Closed Caption. Harry Belafonte, Robert Ryan, Shelley Winters, Ed Begley Sr., Gloria Grahame, Will Kuluva, Richard Bright; **D:** Robert Wise; **W:** Abraham Polonsky, Nelson Gidding; **C:** Joseph Brun; **M:** John Lewis. WAR

Odds and Evens ♂½ 1978 (PG) Italian supercops pretend they don't have badges in order to clean up illegal betting and gambling rings in sunny Miami. Odds are this spaghetti cop-o-rama won't keep Morpheus at bay. 109m/C VHS, Beta. IT Terence Hill, Bud Spencer; **D:** Sergio Corbucci. WAR

Ode to Billy Joe ♂♂ 1976 (PG) The 1967 Bobby Gentry hit song of the same title is expanded to tell why a young man jumped to his death off the Tallahatchie Bridge. The problems of growing up in the rural South and teenage romance do not match the appeal of the theme song. Benson and O'Connor, however, work well together. 106m/C VHS, Beta. Robby Benson, Glynnis O'Connor, Joan Hotchkis, Sandy McPeak, James Best; **D:** Max Baer Jr. CCB, WAR

The Odessa File ♂♂½ 1974 (PG) During 1963, a German journalist attempts to track down some SS war criminals who have formed a secret organization called ODESSA. The story, from Frederick Forsyth's novel, drags in some places, but the scene where bad guy Schell and reporter Voight finally confront each other is a high point. 128m/C VHS, Beta, LV, Closed Caption. GB GE Jon Voight, Mary Tamm, Maximilian Schell, Maria Schell, Derek Jacobi, Peter Jeffrey, Klaus Lowitsch, Kurt Meisel, Hannes Meesember, Garfield Morgan, Shmuel Rodensku, Ernst Schroder, Noel Willman, Hans Canineberg, Towje Kleiner, Gunnar Moiler; **D:** Ronald Neame; **W:** Kenneth Ross, George Markstein; **C:** Oswald Morris; **M:** Andrew Lloyd Webber. GKK

The Odyssey ♂♂½ 1997 (PG-13) Lavish TV miniseries based on Homer's 2,700-year-old epic poem, relating the adventures of King Odysseus of Ithaca. On the day his son is born to faithful wife Penelope (Scacchi), Odysseus (Assante) is commanded by the goddess Athena (Rossellini) to leave his home and travel to battle the Trojans. Little does he realize that this is the beginning of a 20-year sojourn, where additional trials include sea monsters, the Cyclops, the Kingdom of the Dead, enchantress Circe (Peters), and getting shipwrecked on the isle of Calypso (Williams), who wants to keep the hunk around. But even Odysseus realizes there's no place like home. 165m/C VHS, Closed Caption. Armand Assante, Greta Scacchi, Geraldine Chaplin, Eric Roberts, Bernadette Peters, Irene Papas, Vanessa L(ynne) Williams, Christopher Lee, Isabella Rossellini, Jeroen Krabbe, Nicholas Clay, Ron Cook, Michael J. Pollard, Paloma Baeza, Alan Cox, Heathcote Williams; **D:** Andrei Konchalovsky; **W:** Andrei Konchalovsky, Chris Solimine; **C:** Sergei Koslov; **M:** Eduard Artemyev. HMK

The Odyssey of the Pacific ♂♂½ The Emperor of Peru 1982 Three young Cambodian refugees encounter retired train engineer Rooney living in the woods where a railway station once thrived. Together they work to restore an old locomotive. The ordinary, inoffensive script will not endanger quality family time. 82m/C VHS, Beta. CA Mickey Rooney, Monique Mercure; **D:** Fernando Arrabal. USH

Oedipus Rex ♂♂♂ Edipo Re 1967 A new twist on the famous tragedy as Pasolini gives the story a modern prologue and epilogue. The classic plot has Oedipus spiraling downward into moral horror as he tries to avoid fulfilling the prophecy that he will murder his father and sleep with his mother. Cross-cultural curiosities include Japanese music and Lenin-inspired songs, some written by Pasolini, who also stars as the high priest. In Italian with English subtitles. **110m/C VHS.** *IT* Franco Citti, Silvana Mangano, Alida Valli, Julian Beck, Pier Paolo Pasolini; **D:** Pier Paolo Pasolini. *FST, FCT, WBF*

Of Cooks and Kung-Fu 🎔🎔 198? A martial arts culinary adventure. **90m/C VHS, Beta.** Jacky Cheng, Chia Kai, Lee Kuen. *MGI*

Of Human Bondage 🎔🎔🎔 1934 The first movie version of W. Somerset Maugham's classic novel in which a young, handicapped medical student falls in love with a crude cockney waitress, in a mutually destructive affair. Established Davis's role as the tough, domineering woman. Remade in 1946 and 1964. **84m/B VHS, Beta, LV.** Bette Davis, Leslie Howard, Frances Dee, Reginald Owen, Reginald Denny, Alan Hale; **D:** John Cromwell; **M:** Max Steiner. *CNG, MRV, NOS*

Of Human Bondage 🎔🎔 1964 An essentially decent man falls fatally in love with an alluring but heartless waitress, who subtly destroys him. Based on the W. Somerset Maugham novel. Miscast and least interesting of the three film versions, although Novak gives a good performance. **100m/B VHS, Beta.** *GB* Kim Novak, Laurence Harvey, Robert Morley, Roger Livesey, Siobhan McKenna; **D:** Henry Hathaway, Ken Hughes; **W:** Bryan Forbes; **C:** Oswald Morris. *MGM*

Of Human Hearts 🎔🎔½ 1938 Rural life just before the Civil War sets up this cornpone tale of family strife. Huston is a stern preacher who has his family living in near poverty as an example of sacrifice to his flock. Son Stewart wants to study medicine and Bondi, defying her husband, manages to fund his dream. Only Stewart becomes so engrossed by his ambitions that he ignores the family, even after his father dies and his mother is left poor and alone. Then Stewart joins the Civil War as a doctor where he meets President Lincoln (Carradine), who tells him he should never neglect his mother. Oy. Well, the cast is good. Adapted from the story "Benefits Forgot" by Honore Morrow. **100m/B VHS.** James Stewart, Beulah Bondi, Walter Huston, John Carradine, Guy Kibbee, Charles Coburn, Ann Rutherford, Charley Grapewin, Gene Lockhart; **D:** Clarence Brown; **W:** Bradbury Foote; **C:** Clyde De Vinna. Nominations: Academy Awards '38: Best Supporting Actress (Bondi). *MGM, MOV*

Of Love and Shadows 🎔🎔 1994 (R) Political photojournalist Francisco (Banderas) begins investigating the disappearance of a self-proclaimed saint after the bloody 1973 coup in Chile. He's aided by aristocratic Chilean Irene (Connelly), who's engaged to her Army captain cousin Gustavo (Gallardo) but can't resist Francisco's ever-smoldering charms. The intrepid duo naturally find lots of corruption. Based on the novel by Isabel Allende; shot on location in Argentina. **CW:** Scene of strong sexuality and for some violence. **103m/C VHS, Closed Caption.** Antonio Banderas, Jennifer Connelly, Stefania Sandrelli, Camillo Gallardo, Patricio Contreras; **D:** Betty Kaplan; **W:** Donald Freed; **C:** Felix Monti; **M:** Jose Nieto. *TOU*

Of Mice and Men 🎔🎔🎔🎔 1939 A powerful adaptation of the classic Steinbeck tragedy about the friendship between two itinerant Southern ranch hands during the Great Depression. Chaney is wonderful as the gentle giant and mentally retarded Lenny, cared for by migrant worker Meredith. They both get into an irreversible situation when a woman is accidentally killed. **107m/C VHS, Beta.** Lon Chaney Jr., Burgess Meredith, Betty Field, Bob Steele, Noah Beery Jr., Charles Bickford; **D:** Lewis Milestone; **M:** Aaron Copland. Nominations: Academy Awards '39: Best Picture, Best Sound, Best Original Score. *NO*

Of Mice and Men 🎔🎔🎔 1981 Made-for-television remake of the classic Steinbeck tale, casting TV's Baretta (Blake) as George and Quaid as Lenny. Worth watching. **150m/C VHS, Beta.** Robert (Bobby) Blake, Randy Quaid, Lew Ayres, Mitchell Ryan, Ted Neeley, Cassie Yates, Pat Hingle, Whitman Mayo, Dennis Fimple, Pat Corley; **D:** Reza Badiyi.

Of Mice and Men 🎔🎔🎔½ 1992 (PG-13) Set on the migratory farms of California, John Steinbeck's novel covers the friendship of the simple-minded Lenny, his protector George, and a flirtatious farm wife who doesn't know Lenny's strength. Director Sinise got permission from Steinbeck's widow to film the novel (actually the third adaptation). **CW:** Violent scenes. **110m/C VHS, LV, Closed Caption.** John Malkovich, Sherilyn Fenn, Casey Siemaszko, Joe Morton, Ray Walston, Gary Sinise, John Terry, Richard Riehle; **D:** Gary Sinise; **W:** Horton Foote. *MGM, PMS, BTV*

Of Unknown Origin 🎔🎔½ 1983 (R) Weller encounters a mutated rampaging rat in his New York townhouse while his family is away on vacation. His house becomes the battleground in a terror-tinged duel of survival. A well-done rat thriller not for those with a delicate stomach. Based on the novel "The Visitor." **88m/C VHS, Beta.** *CA* Peter Weller, Jennifer Dale, Lawrence Dane, Kenneth Welsh, Louis Del Grande, Shannon Tweed; **D:** George P. Cosmatos; **W:** Brian Taggert; **C:** Rene Verzier. *WAR*

Off and Running 🎔½ 1990 (PG-13) Struggling actress Cyd (Lauper) is working as a mermaid at a Miami hotel lounge when her horse trainer boyfriend Woody is suddenly murdered by a psycho thug (Belzer). Turns out he's after a key hidden in a necklace now in Cyd's possession. Cyd goes on the run and gets some help from failed golf pro Jack (Keith) as they try to stay one step ahead of the killer and discover what the key unlocks. **91m/C VHS.** Cyndi Lauper, David Keith, Richard Belzer, David Thornton, James Morris; **D:** Edward Bianchi; **W:** Eugene Glazer; **C:** Andrzej Bartkowiak; **M:** Mason Daring. *HBO*

Off Beat 🎔½ 1986 (PG) A shy librarian unluckily wins a spot in a police benefit dance troupe, and then falls in love with a tough police woman. With a screenplay by playwright Medoff, and a good supporting cast, it still manages to miss the mark. **92m/C VHS, Beta, LV.** Judge Reinhold, Meg Tilly, Cleavant Derricks, Fred Gwynne, John Turturro, Jacques D'Amboise, James Tolkan, Joe Mantegna, Harvey Keitel, Amy Wright, Christopher Noth; **D:** Michael Dinner; **W:** Mark Medoff; **C:** Carlo DiPalma; **M:** James Horner. *TOU*

Off Limits 🎔🎔½ 1953 When a boxing manager is drafted into the Army, he freely breaks regulations in order to train a fighter as he sees fit. Hope and Rooney, while not in peak form, make a snappy duo in this amusing romp. **89m/B VHS, Beta, LV.** Bob Hope, Mickey Rooney, Marilyn Maxwell, Marvin Miller; **D:** George Marshall. *BAR*

Off Limits 🎔½ 1987 (R) A spree of murders involving Vietnamese hookers draws two cops from the Army's Criminal Investigation Department into the sleazy backstreets of 1968 Saigon. There is little mystery as to who the killer is in this tale that seems worth more for the sake of foul language and gratuitous gunfights than actual plot. **102m/C VHS, Beta, LV, Closed Caption.** Willem Dafoe, Gregory Hines, Fred Ward, Scott Glenn, Amanda Pays, Keith David, David Alan Grier; **D:** Christopher Crowe; **W:** Christopher Crowe, Jack Thibeau; **M:** James Newton Howard. *FOX*

Off the Mark 🎔🎔 1987 (R) Neely is a young athlete suffering from a childhood affliction that causes spasms in his legs. Facing the ultimate challenge, he must overcome his handicap and defeat a talented woman athlete and a Russian student in a triathalon competition. An unremarkable effort, it had a limited one-week run in theatres. **89m/C VHS, Beta.** Mark Neely, Terry Farrell, Jon Cypher, Clarence Gilyard Jr.; **D:** Bill Berry; **C:** Arledge Armenaki.

Off the Wall 🎔 1982 (R) Two hitchhikers wind up in a southern maximum security prison after being accused of a crime they did not commit. What follows is a series of shenanigans as they try to escape. This supposed comedy falls flat in every way with the possible exception of Arquette's portrayal of the governor's daughter. **86m/C VHS, Beta.** Paul Sorvino, Rosanna Arquette, Patrick

Cassidy, Billy Hufsey, Monte Markham, Mickey Gilley; **D:** Rick Friedberg. *ART, VES*

Off Your Rocker 🎔½ 1980 Representatives of a corporate conglomerate find that the residents of Flo Adler's Mapleview Nursing Home can still muster stiff resistance to a threatened takeover. **99m/C VHS, Beta.** Milton Berle, Red Buttons, Lou Jacobi, Dorothy Malone, Helen Shaver, Sharon Acker, Helen Hughes; **D:** Morley Markson, Larry Pall. *NO*

The Offence 🎔🎔🎔 *Something Like the Truth* 1973 (R) Connery plays a London detective who beats a suspected child molester to death during a police interrogation. Turns out he's reacting to a long-buried molestation incident from his own childhood. A chilling psycho-drama highlighted by a strong lead performance by Connery. **108m/C VHS.** *GB* Sean Connery, Trevor Howard, Vivien Merchant, Ian Bannen, Derek Newark, John Hallam, Peter Bowles; **D:** Sidney Lumet; **W:** John Hopkins. *MGM*

Offerings 🎔 1989 (R) After a boy is tormented by a gang of children who cause him to fall down a well, his resulting brain injuries turn him into a psychopathic killer. Seeking revenge ten years later, he systematically murders his oppressors, offering bits of their anatomy to the one girl who treated him kindly. A typical slasher movie, the plot is only slightly better than the worst examples of the genre. **96m/C VHS, Beta.** G. Michael Smith, Loretta L. Bowman; **D:** Christopher Reynolds.

Office Killer 🎔 1997 Just when you thought it was safe to run with scissors! Kane stars as meek copy editor Dorine, who is in danger of losing her job. After helping to secure her position by accidentally electrocuting a fellow employee, Dorine begins some downsizing of her own. Pent up frustrations at home and work cause her sanity to take a personal leave of absence, and she begins to streamline her department by folding, spindling and mutilating her co-workers. She covers her trails by sending e-mail from her victims, but management is just happy they're eating less donuts. Office tramp Kim (Ringwald) suspects the truth, but no one believes her. Stab at horror-black comedy isn't very scary or very funny. First directorial effort by still photographer Cindy Sherman, who didn't adapt very well to people moving around. **83m/C VHS.** Carol Kane, Molly Ringwald, Jeanne Tripplehorn, Barbara Sukowa, Michael Imperioli, David Thornton, Alice Drummond, Mike Hodge; **D:** Cindy Sherman; **W:** Elise MacAdam, Tom Kalin, Todd Haynes; **C:** Russell Fine; **M:** Evan Lurie. *NYR*

Office Romances 🎔🎔 1986 A woman who has moved to London from the country is seduced by her employer. Because of her plain appearance, she is flattered by his attention even though he is married and has no real feelings for her. Competently made, nonetheless hard to watch because of the slow pace. **60m/C VHS, Beta.** *GB* Judy Parfitt, Ray Brooks, Suzanne Burden.

An Officer and a Gentleman 🎔🎔🎔½ 1982 (R) Young drifter Gere, who enters Navy Officer Candidate School because he doesn't know what else to do with his life, becomes a better person almost despite himself. Winger is the love interest who sets her sights on marrying Gere, and Gossett is the sergeant who whips him into shape. Strong performances by the whole cast made this a must-see in 1982 that is still appealing, despite the standard Hollywood premise. ♫Up Where We Belong; Hungry for Your Love; An Officer and a Gentleman; Treat Me Right; Tunnel of Love. **126m/C VHS, Beta, LV, 8mm.** Richard Gere, Louis Gossett Jr., David Keith, Lisa Eilbacher, Debra Winger, David Caruso, Robert Loggia, Lisa Blount; **D:** Taylor Hackford; **C:** Donald E. Thorin; **M:** Jack Nitzsche. Academy Awards '82: Best Song ("Up Where We Belong"), Best Supporting Actor (Gossett); Golden Globe Awards '83: Best Song ("Up Where We Belong"), Best Supporting Actor (Gossett); Nominations: Academy Awards '82: Best Actress (Winger), Best Film Editing, Best Original Screenplay, Best Original Score. *PAR, FCT, BTV*

Official Denial ✓✓½ 1993 A victim of an alien abduction becomes the only hope for a captured space being. Can Paul help the alien escape from a special Air Force UFO group and what secrets will he uncover if he does? Made for television. **86m/C VHS, Beta, Closed Caption.** Parker Stevenson, Erin Gray, Dirk Benedict, Chad Everett; **D:** Brian Trenchard-Smith; **W:** Bruce Zabel; **M:** Garry McDonald, Laurie Stone. PAR

The Official Story ✓✓✓½ La Historia Oficial; The Official History; The Official Version 1985 (R) A devastating drama about an Argentinian woman who realizes her young adopted daughter may be a child stolen from one of the thousands of citizens victimized by the country's repressive government. A powerful, important film. In Spanish with English subtitles or dubbed. **112m/C VHS, Beta, LV.** AR Norma Aleandro, Hector Alterio, Chunchuna Villafane, Patricio Contreras; **D:** Luis Puenzo; **W:** Luis Puenzo, Aida Bortnik. Academy Awards '85: Best Foreign Language Film; Cannes Film Festival '85: Best Actress (Aleandro); Golden Globe Awards '86: Best Foreign Film; Los Angeles Film Critics Association Awards '85: Best Foreign Film; New York Film Critics Awards '85: Best Actress (Aleandro); Nominations: Academy Awards '85: Best Original Screenplay. TPV

The Offspring ✓✓ From a Whisper to a Scream 1987 (R) In four stories of past evils Price reveals his hometown can force folks to kill. Not the usual Price material: dismemberment, cannibalism, and necrophilia clash with his presence. Strong yuk factor. **99m/C VHS, Beta, LV.** Vincent Price, Cameron Mitchell, Clu Gulager, Terry Kiser, Susan Tyrrell, Harry Caesar, Rosalind Cash, Martine Beswick, Angelo Rossitto, Lawrence Tierney; **D:** Jeff Burr; **W:** C. Courtney Joyner, Jeff Burr; **M:** John Beal. ART

Oh, Alfie ✓✓ Alfie Darling 1975 (R) In every man's life, there comes a time to settle down... but never when you're having as much fun as Alfie! Inadequate sequel to "Alfie". **99m/C VHS, Beta.** GB Joan Collins, Alan Price, Jill Townsend; **D:** Ken Hughes; **W:** Ken Hughes. HHE

Oh, Bloody Life! ✓✓½ 1988 Young actress faces deportation during the Stalin era in Hungary because of her aristocratic family ties. In Hungarian with English subtitles. **115m/C VHS.** HU Udvaros Dorottya, Szacsvay Laszlo, Kern Andras, Bezeredi Zoltan, Oze Lajos, Lukacs Margit; **D:** Peter Bacso; **W:** Peter Bacso. Montreal World Film Festival '88: Best Actress (Dorottya). TPV

Oh! Calcutta! ✓✓½ 1972 Film version of the first nude musical to play on Broadway, which caused a sensation in the late 1960s. It's really a collection of skits, some of which were written by such notables as John Lennon, Sam Shepard, and Jules Feiffer. And it's really not that funny or erotic. **105m/C VHS, Beta.** Bill Macy, Mark Dempsey, Raina Barrett, Samantha Harper, Patricia Hawkins, Mitchell McGuire; **D:** Guillaume Martin Aucion. NO

Oh Dad, Poor Dad (Momma's Hung You in the Closet & I'm Feeling So Sad) ✓✓ 1967 Cult fave black comedy about a bizarre family on a vacation in Jamaica. The domineering mother travels with a coffin containing the stuffed body of her late husband. Additional corpses abound. Based on the play by Arthur L. Kopit. **86m/C VHS, Beta.** Rosalind Russell, Robert Morse, Barbara Harris, Hugh Griffith, Lionel Jeffries, Jonathan Winters; **D:** Richard Quine. PAR

Oh, God! ✓✓✓½ 1977 (PG) God, in the person of Burns, recruits Denver as his herald in his plan to save the world. Despite initial skepticism, Denver, in his film debut, keeps faith and is rewarded. Sincere performances and optimistic end make for satisfying story. Followed by "Oh God! Book 2" and "Oh God! You Devil." **104m/C VHS, Beta, LV.** George Burns, John Denver, Paul Sorvino, Ralph Bellamy, Teri Garr, William Daniels, Donald Pleasence, Barnard Hughes, Barry Sullivan, Dinah Shore, Jeff Corey, David Ogden Stiers; **D:** Carl Reiner; **W:** Larry Gelbart. Writers Guild of America '77: Best Adapted Screenplay; Nominations: Academy Awards '77: Best Adapted Screenplay. WAR

Oh, God! Book 2 ✓ 1980 (PG) Burns returns as the "Almighty One" in strained sequel to "Oh God!" This time he enlists the help of a young girl to remind others of his existence. The slogan she concocts saves God's image, but not the movie. Followed by "Oh, God! You Devil." **94m/C VHS, Beta.** George Burns, Suzanne Pleshette, David Birney, Louanne, Conrad Janis, Wilfrid Hyde-White, Hans Conried, Howard Duff; **D:** Gilbert Cates; **M:** Charles Fox. WAR

Oh, God! You Devil ✓✓ 1984 (PG) During his third trip to earth, Burns plays both the Devil and God as he first takes a struggling musician's soul, then gives it back. A few zingers and light atmosphere save unoriginal plot. The second sequel to "Oh, God!" **96m/C VHS, Beta, LV, Closed Caption.** George Burns, Ted Wass, Roxanne Hart, Ron Silver, Eugene Roche, Robert Desiderio; **D:** Paul Bogart; **W:** Andrew Bergman; **M:** David Shire. WAR

Oh, Heavenly Dog! ✓✓ 1980 (PG) A private eye returns from the dead as a dog to solve his own murder. Man's best friend and intelligent to boot. The famous dog Benji's third film, and his acting improves with each one. Adults may find this movie slow, but kids will probably love it. **104m/C VHS, Beta, Closed Caption.** Chevy Chase, Jane Seymour, Omar Sharif, Robert Morley, Susan Kellerman; **D:** Joe Camp; **W:** Joe Camp, Rod Browning. FOX

Oh, Mr. Porter ✓✓ 1937 Billeted at an obscure railway post, the stationmaster hero renovates the place and hires a special train to transport the area soccer team. Trouble arises when the train is hijacked by gun smugglers. **85m/B VHS.** GB Will Hay, Moore Marriott, Graham Moffatt, Frederick Piper; **D:** Marcel Varnel. NOS

Oh Susannah! ✓✓ 1938 Robbed and thrown from a train, Autry and the two drifters who rescue him follow the thieves to Mineral Springs. Their journey is plagued by too many songs and the bad guys are predictably punished in the end. **59m/B VHS, Beta.** Gene Autry, Boothe Howard, Smiley Burnette, Frances Grant, Donald Kirke, Clara Kimball Young; **D:** Joseph Kane. NOS, VDM, HHT

Oh, What a Night ✓✓ 1992 (PG-13) Bittersweet coming of age tale about a lonely 17-year-old (Haim) who has moved with his father and stepmother to a chicken farm in 1955 Ontario. After struggling with the untimely death of his mother, Haim falls in love with an older woman who has a husband and two kids. Features a great '50s soundtrack and beautiful scenes of the Canadian countryside. **CW:** Elements of teen sexuality. **93m/C VHS, LV, Closed Caption.** CA Corey Haim, Barbara Williams, Keir Dullea, Genevieve Bujold, Robbie Coltrane; **D:** Eric Till. COL, NLC

O'Hara's Wife ✓✓½ 1982 Loving wife Harley continues to care for her family even after her untimely death. Only husband Asner, however, can see her ghost. Lightweight, made-for-television drama traps good cast. **87m/C VHS, Beta.** Ed Asner, Mariette Hartley, Jodie Foster, Tom Bosley, Perry Lang, Ray Walston; **D:** William S. Bartman; **W:** William S. Bartman; **M:** Artie Butler. VES

O.H.M.S. ✓✓½ 1937 Convoluted story about a New York hood (Ford) who flees to England where he joins the British Army by posing as a Canadian. He buddies up with Mills and they both fall for Lee. His regiment is sent to China, via ship, and Lee just happens to be a stowaway. In China, Ford manages to prove his worth by saving Lee from bandits. Maybe it's not supposed to make sense. **71m/B VHS.** GB Wallace Ford, John Mills, Anna Lee, Frank Cellier, Frederick Leister, Peter Croft; **D:** Raoul Walsh. HCV

Oil ✓ 1978 (PG) Seven men fight a raging oil fire that threatens to destroy an entire country. Unfortunately, the movie is unable to ignite any interest at all. **95m/C VHS, Beta.** Ray Milland, Woody Strode, Stuart Whitman, Tony Kendall, William Berger; **D:** Mircea Dragan. VCI

The O.J. Simpson Story ✓ 1994 Tacky tabloid TV movie follows incredibly exploited story about former gridiron star Simpson (Hosea) who's accused of murdering blonde babe ex-wife Nicole (Tuck). Mainly stolid performances though Weitz is slick as Simpson lawyer Robert Shapiro. Told in flashbacks, the actual murder is never depicted. Director Jerry Friedman took his name off the credits, leaving the standard Smithee pseudonym as a replacement. **90m/C VHS.** Bobby Hosea, Jessica Tuck, James Handy, Kimberly Russell, David Roberson, Bruce Weitz; **D:** Alan Smithee; **W:** Stephen Harrigan; **M:** Harald Kloser. FXV

Oklahoma! ✓✓✓½ 1955 (G) Jones's film debut; a must-see for musical fans. A cowboy and country girl fall in love, but she is tormented by another unwelcomed suitor. At over two hours, cuteness wears thin for some. Actually filmed in Arizona. Adapted from Rodgers and Hammerstein's broadway hit with original score; choreography by Agnes de Mille. ♫Oh, What a Beautiful Morning; Surrey with the Fringe on Top; I Cain't Say No; Many a New Day; People Will Say We're in Love; Poor Jud Is Dead; All 'Er Nuthin'; Everything's Up to Date in Kansas City; The Farmer and the Cowman. **145m/C VHS, Beta, LV, Letterbox, Closed Caption.** Gordon MacRae, Shirley Jones, Rod Steiger, Gloria Grahame, Eddie Albert, Charlotte Greenwood, James Whitmore, Gene Nelson, Barbara Lawrence, Jay C. Flippen; **D:** Fred Zinnemann; **W:** Sonya Levien, William Ludwig; **C:** Robert L. Surtees; **M:** Richard Rodgers, Oscar Hammerstein. Academy Awards '55: Best Sound, Scoring of a Musical; Nominations: Academy Awards '55: Best Color Cinematography, Best Film Editing. FOX, RDG, HMV

Oklahoma Annie ✓ 1951 Storekeeper Canova joins the new sheriff in booting undesirables out of town, and tries to sing her way into his heart. Amazingly, it works—not for delicate ears. **90m/C VHS, Beta.** Judy Canova, Fuzzy Knight, Grant Withers, John Russell, Denver Pyle, Allen Jenkins, Almira Sessions; **D:** R.G. Springsteen. MLB

Oklahoma Badlands ✓½ 1948 Lane and his horse outsmart a corrupt newspaper publisher trying to steal land from a female rancher. An early directorial work for veteran stuntman Canutt. **59m/B VHS, Beta.** Allan "Rocky" Lane, Mildred Coles; **D:** Yakima Canutt. DVT

Oklahoma Bound ✓ 1981 A feisty farmer tries to save his failing farm through a series of ostensibly comedic, unsuccessful schemes. **92m/C VHS, Beta.** F.E. Bowling, Dan Jones; **D:** Patrick C. Poole. NO

Oklahoma Crude ✓✓½ 1973 (PG) Sadistic oil trust rep Palence battles man-hating Dunaway for her well. Drifter Scott helps her resist on the promise of shared profits. In this 1913 setting, Dunaway tells Scott she wishes she could avoid men altogether, but later settles for him. **108m/C VHS.** George C. Scott, Faye Dunaway, John Mills, Jack Palance, Harvey Jason, Woodrow Parfrey; **D:** Stanley Kramer; **W:** Marc Norman; **C:** Robert L. Surtees; **M:** Henry Mancini. FOX

Oklahoma Cyclone ✓½ 1930 A group of bronco busters find action and adventure on the prairie. Second of eight talkies in Steele series, includes his first of few singing roles. **64m/B VHS.** Bob Steele, Al "Fuzzy" St. John, Nita Ray, Charles "Blackie" King; **D:** John P. McCarthy. NOS, GPV, DVT

Oklahoma Kid ✓½ 1939 Offbeat, hilarious western with Bogie as the villain and gunfighter Cagney seeking revenge for his father's wrongful death. Highlight is Cagney's rendition of "I Don't Want To Play In Your Yard," complete with six-shooter accompaniment. **82m/B VHS, Beta.** James Cagney, Humphrey Bogart, Rosemary Lane, Ward Bond, Donald Crisp, Charles Middleton, Harvey Stephens; **D:** Lloyd Bacon; **C:** James Wong Howe; **M:** Max Steiner. MGM, FCT

The Oklahoman ✓✓ 1956 A routine western with some trivia value. Town doc McCrea helps Indian Pate keep his land. Talbott plays Indian maiden in same year as her title role in

Daughter of Jekyll. Continuity buffs will note Hale wears the same outfit in most scenes. **80m/C VHS, Beta.** Joel McCrea, Barbara Hale, Brad Dexter, Gloria Talbott, Verna Felton, Douglas Dick, Michael Pate, Scotty Beckett; **D:** Francis D. Lyon. *FOX*

Okoge 🎬🎬 **1993** Rueful sexual comedy about a triangular friendship. Sayoko is a single young working woman living in a tiny Tokyo apartment. She meets the gay Noh and his older married lover Tochi and when they become friendly, Sayoko lets them use her apartment as their love nest—to the complications of all concerned. Title is a slang term used to refer to women who prefer the company of gay men. In Japanese with English subtitles. **120m/C VHS.** *JP* Misa Shimizu, Takehiro Murata, Takeo Nakahara, Masayuki Shionoya, Noriko Songoku, Kyozo Nagatsuka, Toshie Nogishi; **D:** Takehiro Nakajima; **W:** Takehiro Nakajima. *FCT, CCN*

Old Barn Dance 🎬½ **1938** Autry and his singing cowboys are selling horses until a crooked tractor company puts them out of business. They join a radio program, discovers that it is owned by the same company that put them out of the horse-selling business, and runs the crooks out of town. **54m/B VHS, Beta.** Gene Autry, Smiley Burnette, Roy Rogers; **D:** Joseph Kane. *NOS, VCN, DVT*

Old Boyfriends 🎬🎬 **1979 (R)** Shire is weak as a psychologist searching for old boyfriends in order to analyze her past. Strange combination of Carradine and Belushi may draw curious fans. **103m/C VHS, Beta, LV.** Talia Shire, Richard Jordan, John Belushi, Keith Carradine, John Houseman, Buck Henry; **D:** Joan Tewkesbury; **W:** Leonard Schrader, Paul Schrader; **M:** David Shire. *NLC*

Old Corral 🎬🎬 *Texas Serenade* **1936** Sheriff Autry protects his love interest, a girl fleeing the Mob. **54m/B VHS, Beta.** Gene Autry, Roy Rogers, Smiley Burnette; **D:** Joseph Kane. *NOS, MRV, VTR*

The Old Curiosity Shop 🎬🎬½ **1935** Webster and Benson are an old gambler and his daughter in this well-made film adaptation of the Dickens tale. Their miserly landlord tries to ruin their lives by evicting them and forcing them into a life of poverty. Remade as "Mr. Quilp" in 1957. **90m/B VHS.** Ben Webster, Elaine Benson, Hay Petrie, Beatrix Thompson, Gibb McLaughlin, Reginald Purdell; **D:** Thomas Bentley. *NOS*

The Old Curiosity Shop 🎬🎬 *Mr. Quilp* **1975 (G)** Flat musical version of the Charles Dickens story about an evil man who wants to take over a small antique shop run by an elderly man and his granddaughter. ♫When a Felon Needs a Friend; Somewhere; Love Has the Longest Memory; Happiness Pie; The Sport of Kings; What Shouldn't Happen to a Dog; Quilp. **118m/C VHS, Beta.** *GB* Anthony Newley, David Hemmings, David Warner, Jill Bennett, Peter Duncan, Michael Hordern; **D:** Michael Tuchner; **M:** Elmer Bernstein. *REP*

The Old Curiosity Shop 🎬🎬 **1984 (G)** An animated adaptation of the classic Dickens story about a young girl and her grandfather who are evicted from their curiosity shop by an evil man. **72m/C VHS, Beta, Closed Caption. V:** John Benton, Jason Blackwell, Wallas Easton, Pennie Hackforth-Jones, Brian Harrison. *ART*

The Old Curiosity Shop 🎬🎬½ **1994 (PG)** Another adaptation of Charles Dickens' 1840 tale about Grandfather Trent (Ustinov), an antiques dealer who has lost his fortune through gambling and makes matters worse by borrowing money from the miserable Mr. Quilp (Courtenay). Unable to repay the debt, Trent and young granddaughter Sally (Walsh) try to escape London, which turns Quilp's wrath upon them. Fine performances and a colorful production; made for cable TV. **280m/C VHS.** Peter Ustinov, Tom Courtenay, James Fox, Sally Walsh, William Mannering, Christopher Ettridge, Julia McKenzie, Anne White, Jean Marlow, Cornelia Hayes O'Herlihy, Michael Mears; **D:** Kevin Connor; **W:** John Goldsmith; **C:** Doug Milsome; **M:** Mason Daring. *HMK*

The Old Dark House 🎬🎬🎬 **1932** An atmospheric horror film, with more than a touch of comedy, well-directed by Whale. In an old haunted house live the bizarre Femm family: the 102 year-old patriarch, an atheist son, a religious fanatic daughter, and a crazed pyromaniac son, all watched over by the mute, scarred, and psychotic butler (Karloff's first starring role). Into this strange group wander five unsuspecting, stranded travelers who set all sorts of dastardly plots in motion. Based on the novel "Benighted" by J.B. Priestley. **71m/B VHS.** Boris Karloff, Melvyn Douglas, Charles Laughton, Gloria Stuart, Ernest Thesiger, Raymond Massey, Lillian Bond, Eva Moore, Brember Wills, John Dudgeon; **D:** James Whale; **W:** Benn W. Levy, R.C. Sherriff; **C:** Arthur Edeson. *KIV, FCT*

Old Enough 🎬🎬 **1984 (PG)** Slow-moving coming-of-age comedy on the rich kid-poor kid friendship theme. Silver's directing debut. **91m/C VHS, Beta.** Sarah Boyd, Rainbow Harvest, Neill Barry, Danny Aiello, Susan Kingsley, Roxanne Hart, Alyssa Milano, Fran Brill, Anne Pitoniak; **D:** Marisa Silver; **W:** Marisa Silver; **C:** Michael Ballhaus. Sundance Film Festival '84: Grand Jury Prize.

Old Explorers 🎬🎬½ **1990 (PG)** Two old friends refuse to let old age lessen their want for excitement, so they get together on a regular basis to set out on dangerous, imaginary adventures. They search for Atlantis, explore the Himalayan Mountains, and visit the Bermuda Triangle. After one of the men survives a stroke, the two set out on a real-life adventure on a tugboat cruising down the Mississippi River. Although the leads put in strong performances, they can't hide the slow-moving plot or the thin action sequences. Based on the play by James Cada and Mark Keller. **91m/C VHS, LV.** Jose Ferrer, James Whitmore, Jeffrey Gadbois, Caroline Kaiser, William Warfield, Christopher Pohlad, Storm Richardson, William M. Pohlad.

Old Gringo 🎬🎬½ **1989 (R)** Adapted from Carlos Fuentes' novelization of writer Ambrose Bierce's mysterious disappearance in Mexico during the revolution of 1913. Features Fonda in the unlikely role of a virgin schoolteacher, Smits as her revolutionary lover, and Peck as her hero. Soggy acting by all but Peck, whose presence is wasted in a sketchy character. Technical problems and cheesy sets and costumes—look for the dusk backdrop in the dance scene and Smits' silly moustache. Better to read the book. **119m/C VHS, Beta, LV, 8mm, Letterbox, Closed Caption.** Jane Fonda, Gregory Peck, Jimmy Smits, Patricio Contreras, Jenny Gago, Gabriela Roel, Jorge Calderon, Guillermo Rios, Anne Pitoniak, Pedro Armendariz Jr., Jim Metzler; **D:** Luis Puenzo; **W:** Aida Bortnik, Luis Puenzo; **M:** Lee Holdridge. *COL*

Old Gun 🎬🎬🎬 **1976** A grief-plagued doctor finds he must seek out and kill each Nazi involved in the slaughter of his wife and child to ease his pain. Excellent directing and a fully formed main character. **141m/C VHS, Beta.** Philippe Noiret, Romy Schneider, Jean Bouise; **D:** Robert Enrico.

Old Ironsides 🎬🎬🎬 **1926** Silent, black-and-white version of the big budget/important director and stars action-adventure. Merchant marines aboard the famous Old Ironsides battle 19th century Barbary pirates in rousing action scenes. Home video version features an engaging organ score by Gaylord Carter. Based on the poem "Constitution" by Oliver Wendell Holmes. **111m/B VHS, Beta.** Esther Ralston, Wallace Beery, Boris Karloff, Charles Farrell, George Bancroft; **D:** James Cruze; **M:** Gaylord Carter. *PAR*

The Old Lady Who Walked in the Sea 🎬🎬 *La Vieille qui Marchait dans la Mer* **1991** Eccentric Lady M (Moreau) and her equally aging ex-lover Pompilius (Serrault) have spend their lives conning the rich. Summering on the French Riviera, Lady M spots handsome beach boy/thief Lambert (Thuiller) and decides to groom him for their latest caper, a jewel heist. Meanwhile, Pompilius pursues the young Noemie (Danon) and brings her into their menage, where Lambert is instantly smitten. Their lust leads to some unexpected complications but the real drama in the film is watching old pros Moreau and Serrault at work. Based on the novel by San Antonio; French with subtitles. **95m/C VHS.** *FR* Jeanne Moreau, Michel Serrault, Luc Thuillier, Geraldine Danon; **D:** Laurent Heynemann; **W:** Dominique Roulet; **C:** Robert Alazraki; **M:** Philippe Sarde. *HMK*

The Old Maid 🎬🎬🎬 **1939** After her beau is killed in the Civil War, a woman allows her cousin to raise her illegitimate daughter, and therein begins a years-long struggle over the girl's affections. High grade soaper based on Zoe Adkin's stage adaptation of Edith Wharton's novel. **96m/B VHS, Beta.** Bette Davis, Miriam Hopkins, George Brent, Donald Crisp, Jane Bryan, Louise Fazenda, Henry Stephenson; **D:** Edmund Goulding; **C:** Gaetano Antonio "Tony" Gaudio; **M:** Max Steiner. *MGM*

The Old Man and the Sea 🎬🎬½ **1990** Quinn is wonderful as Hemingway's aging Cuban fisherman, Santiago, who battles a band of marauding sharks for a giant marlin in the Gulf Stream. Unfortunately, this made for TV adaptation is ordinary. **97m/C VHS.** Anthony Quinn, Gary Cole, Alexis Cruz, Patricia Clarkson, Francesco Quinn; **D:** Jud Taylor; **W:** Roger O. Hirson; **C:** James Wong Howe; **M:** Bruce Broughton. *VCO*

Old Mother Riley's Ghosts 🎬🎬 **1941** A group of spies "haunt" Mother Riley's castle home in a futile attempt to scare her out; she turns the tables. Some good scares and laughs. Part of the Old Mother Riley series. Look for similarities to later Monty Python films. **82m/B VHS, Beta.** *GB* Arthur Lucan, Kitty McShane, John Stuart; **D:** John Baxter. *NOS, SNC*

Old Spanish Custom 🎬 *The Invader* **1936** Only a Keaton fan could love this comedy, set in Spain and filmed in England. One of his rarest—and poorest—sound films. He plays a bumbling rich yachtsman smitten with Tovar, a Spanish maiden who uses him to make her lover jealous. **58m/B VHS, Beta.** *GB* Buster Keaton, Lupita Tovar, Lyn Harding, Esme Percy; **D:** Adrian Brunel. *VYY, GPV, VDM*

Old Swimmin' Hole 🎬🎬 *When Youth Conspires* **1940** Small-town friends Moran and Jones try to bring their single parents together; his mother can't afford to finance his dream to be a doctor. Dull, melodramatic ode to heartland America, reminiscent of "Our Town." **78m/B VHS, Beta.** Marcia Mae Jones, Jackie Moran, Leatrice Joy, Charles D. Brown; **D:** Robert McGowan. *VYY*

Old Yeller 🎬🎬🎬½ **1957 (G)** Disney Studios' finest and best boy-and-his-dog film. Fifteen-year-old Kirk is left in charge of the family farm while Parker is away. When his younger brother brings home a stray dog, Kirk is displeased but lets him stay. Yeller saves Kirk's life, but contracts rabies in the process. Kirk is forced to kill him. Keep tissue handy, especially for the kids. Stong acting, effective scenery—all good stuff. Based on the novel by Fred Gipson. Sequel "Savage Sam" released in 1963. **84m/C VHS, Beta, LV, Closed Caption.** Dorothy McGuire, Fess Parker, Tommy Kirk, Kevin Corcoran, Jeff York, Beverly Washburn, Chuck Connors; **D:** Robert Stevenson. *DIS*

Oldest Confederate Widow Tells All 🎬🎬🎬 **1995** TV drama starts with the recollections of 99-year-old Lucy Marsden (Bancroft), the widow of the title, as she revisits her marriage to troubled Civil War veteran Capt. William Marsden (Sutherland, sporting an impressive set of whiskers). In 1899, the teenaged Lucy (played by Lane) marries the eccentric 50-year-old, who constantly relives battlefield horrors and the loss of his boyhood friend, while she deals with family and various domestic crises. Somewhat meandering story with fine performances and subtle details. Based on Allan Gurganus' novel. **180m/C VHS, Closed Caption.** Diane Lane, Donald Sutherland, Anne Bancroft, Cicely Tyson, Blythe Danner, E.G. Marshall, Gwen Verdon, Marianne Mueller, Wil Hornoff; **D:** Ken Cameron; **W:** Joyce Eliason; **M:** Mark Snow. *CAF*

Oldest Living Graduate 🐾🐾🐾½ 1982 Fonda is memorable in his last stage role as the oldest graduate of a Texas military academy. He and his son clash when Fonda refuses to give up his land. Teleplay features strong performances from Leachman and other big-name cast members. 75m/C VHS, Beta. Cloris Leachman, Henry Fonda, John Lithgow, Timothy Hutton, Harry Dean Stanton, David Ogden Stiers, George Grizzard, Penelope Milford. VHE

Oldest Profession 🐾 Le Plus Vieux Metier du Monde 1967 A study of prostitution from prehistoric times to the future. Generally unexciting and unfunny. In six segments meant as vehicles for their directors. 97m/C VHS, Beta. FR GE IT Raquel Welch, Jeanne Moreau, Elsa Martinelli, Michele Mercier; D: Jean-Luc Godard, Philippe de Broca, Claude Autant-Lara, Franco Indovina, Mauro Bolognini, Michael Pfleghar; W: Jean-Luc Godard. IME

Oleanna 🐾½ 1994 Mamet directs the big-screen version of his controversial play about political correctness, sexual harrassment, and the gender gap. Pompous, burned-out college professor (Macy) is accused of sexual harassment by dense, shrill, academically weak student (Eisenstadt) after she misconstrues a self-important speech as a come-on. Unbalanced perspective, obvious stereotyping of unsympathetic characters, and weak performances remove any hint of the intended drama. 90m/C VHS, LV, Closed Caption. William H. Macy, Debra Eisenstadt; D: David Mamet; W: David Mamet; C: Andrzej Sekula; M: Rebecca Pidgeon. Nominations: Independent Spirit Awards '95: Best Actor (Macy). HMK

Oliver! 🐾🐾🐾½ 1968 (G) Splendid big-budget musical adaptation of Dickens' "Oliver Twist." An innocent orphan is dragged into a life of crime when he is befriended by a gang of pickpockets. ♫Food, Glorious Food; Oliver; Boy For Sale; Where Is Love?; Consider Yourself; Pick a Pocket or Two; I'd Do Anything; Be Back Soon; As Long As He Needs Me. 145m/C VHS, Beta, LV, Letterbox, Closed Caption. GB Mark Lester, Jack Wild, Ron Moody, Shani Wallis, Oliver Reed, Hugh Griffith; D: Carol Reed; C: Oswald Morris. Academy Awards '68: Best Adapted Score, Best Art Direction/Set Decoration, Best Director (Reed), Best Picture, Best Sound; Golden Globe Awards '69: Best Actor—Musical/Comedy (Moody), Best Film—Musical/Comedy; Nominations: Academy Awards '68: Best Actor (Moody), Best Adapted Screenplay, Best Cinematography, Best Costume Design, Best Film Editing, Best Supporting Actor (Wild). COL, BTV, HMV

Oliver & Company 🐾🐾½ 1988 (G) Animated animal retelling of Dicken's "Oliver Twist"—Disney style. Kitten Oliver (Lawrence) is left to fend for himself on the mean streets of New York until he's taken under the paw of Dodger (Joel) the dog. Dodger heads up a gang of doggy thieves, who help down-and-out human Fagin (DeLuise), who owes money to ruthless loan shark Sykes (Loggia). Out on his first job, Oliver's found by rich little Jenny (Gregory) and happily adopted. But his pals think he's been kidnapped and are off to rescue him. ♫Once Upon a Time in New York City; Why Should I Worry?. 72m/C VHS, Closed Caption. D: George Scribner; W: Jim Cox, James Mangold; V: Joey Lawrence, Billy Joel, Richard "Cheech" Marin, Bette Midler, Dom DeLuise, Roscoe Lee Browne, Richard Mulligan, Sheryl Lee Ralph, Robert Loggia, Taurean Blacque, Carl Weintraub, Natalie Gregory, William Glover. TOU

Oliver Twist 🐾🐾🐾 1922 Silent version of the Dickens classic is a vehicle for young Jackie Coogan. As orphan Oliver Twist, he is subjected to many frightening incidents before finding love and someone to care for him. Remade numerous times, most notably in 1933 and 1948 and as the musical "Oliver!" in 1968. 77m/B VHS, Beta. Jackie Coogan, Lon Chaney Sr., Gladys Brockwell, George Siegmann, Esther Ralston; D: Frank Lloyd. NOS, CCB, KIV

Oliver Twist 🐾🐾 1933 The first talking version of Dickens' classic about an ill-treated London orphan involved with youthful gang of pickpockets. Moore was too young—at five—to be very credible in the lead role. The 1948 version is much more believable. 70m/B VHS, Beta, Closed Caption. Dickie Moore, Irving Pichel, William "Stage" Boyd, Barbara Kent; D: William J. Cowen. NOS, MRV, HHT

Oliver Twist 🐾🐾🐾🐾 1948 Charles Dickens' immortal story of a workhouse orphan who is forced into a life of crime with a gang of pickpockets. The best of many film adaptations, with excellent portrayals by the cast. 116m/C VHS, Beta, LV. GB Robert Newton, John Howard Davies, Alec Guinness, Francis L. Sullivan, Anthony Newley, Kay Walsh, Diana Dors, Henry Stephenson; D: David Lean; W: David Lean; C: Guy Green. PAR, DVT, FHS

Oliver Twist 🐾🐾🐾 1982 Good made-for-television version of the classic Dicken's tale of a boy's rescue from a life of crime. Scott's Fagin is a treat, and period details are on the mark. 100m/C VHS, Closed Caption. George C. Scott, Tim Curry, Michael Hordern, Timothy West, Lysette Anthony, Eileen Atkins, Cherie Lunghi; D: Clive Donner; W: James Goldman; M: Nick Bicat. TVC, VES, REP

Oliver Twist 1985 A British television miniseries adaptation of the Charles Dickens classic about an orphan boy plunging into the underworld of 19th-century London. On two tapes. 333m/C VHS, Beta. GB Ben Rodska, Eric Porter, Frank Middlemass, Gillian Martell. FOX, SIG, HMV

Oliver Twist 🐾🐾½ 1997 Lavish TV version of the Dickens tale finds orphaned Oliver (Trench) escaping to 1837's London and being befriended by the wicked Fagin (Dreyfuss) and his gang of pickpocketing youngsters, including the Artful Dodger (Wood). 92m/C VHS, Closed Caption. Alex Trench, Richard Dreyfuss, Elijah Wood, David O'Hara, Antoine Byrne, Olivia Caffrey; D: Tony Bill; W: Monte Merrick; C: Keith Wilson. DIS

Oliver's Story 🐾 1978 (PG) A "not so equal" sequel to "Love Story," where widower O'Neal wallows in grief untils rich heiress Bergen comes along. He falls in love again, this time with money. 90m/C VHS, Beta. Ryan O'Neal, Candice Bergen, Ray Milland, Edward Binns, Nicola Pagett, Charles Haid; D: John Korty; W: Erich Segal. PAR

Olivia 🐾½ 1983 Abused housewife moonlights as a prostitute and begins killing her customers. She falls in love with an American businessman and flees to America when her husband finds out about the affair. Revenge and murder are the result. 90m/C VHS, Beta. Suzanna Love, Robert Walker Jr., Jeff Winchester; D: Ulli Lommel. VHE

Olivier, Olivier 🐾🐾🐾 1992 (R) Holland's directorial follow-up to "Europa, Europa" is based on a 1984 French newspaper story and evokes "The Return of Martin Guerre" and its update, "Sommersby." Beloved nine-year-old boy disappears from his home in a small French town and his dysfunctional family falls apart. Mom obsesses and falls into trances, dad escapes to North Africa, and sister Nadine develops telekinetic powers in order to cope. Six years later a detective brings an amnesiac teenager, who has been working as a hustler in Paris, to the boy's family. Is it the missing Olivier? Spooky, provocative, and emotionally resonate. In French with English subtitles. CW: Language and sexuality. 110m/C VHS, LV. FR Francois Cluzet, Brigitte Rouan, Gregoire Colin, Marina Golovine, Jean-Francois Stevenin, Emmanuel Morozof, Faye Gatteau, Frederic Quiring; D: Agnieszka Holland; W: Agnieszka Holland. Los Angeles Film Critics Association Awards '93: Best Score. COL

Ollie Hopnoodle's Haven of Bliss 🐾🐾½ 1988 Humorist Jean Shepherd (of "A Christmas Story" fame) spins another tale of frantic family life with his alter ego, Ralphie. This time the family is off on a summer vacation—with all its inherent problems. Made for cable television. 90m/C VHS, Beta, Closed Caption. James B. Sikking, Dorothy Lyman, Jerry O'Connell; D: Dick Bartlett. DIS

Olly Olly Oxen Free 🐾🐾 The Great Balloon Adventure 1978 Junkyard owner Hepburn helps two boys fix up and fly a hot-air balloon, once piloted by McKenzie's grandfather, as a surprise for the man's birthday. Beautiful airborne scenes over California and a dramatic landing to the tune of the "1812 Overture," but not enough to make the whole film interesting. 89m/C VHS, Beta. Katharine Hepburn, Kevin McKenzie, Dennis Dimster, Peter Kilman; D: Richard A. Colla; M: Robert Alcivar. TLF

Olongape: The American Dream 🐾½ 1989 A young woman works in a cheap bar while waiting for the chance to come to America. 97m/C VHS, Beta. Jacklyn Jose, Susan Africa, Chanda Romero, Joel Torre, Marilou Sadiua; D: Chito Rono. TWE

omaha (the movie) 🐾🐾 1995 Gen-Xer Simon (Walkinshaw) flees his native Nebraska and eccentric, dysfunctional family for enlightenment in Tibet. He's instructed in Buddhism and returns home but doesn't find the peace he's seeking and decides to hit the road with former girlfriend Gina (Anderson). 85m/C VHS. Hughston Walkinshaw, Jill Anderson; D: Dan Mirvish; W: Dan Mirvish; C: Oslo Anderson. WAC

Omar Khayyam 🐾🐾 1957 In medieval Persia, Omar (Wilde) becomes involved in a romance with the Shah of Persia's fiancee, while trying to fight off a faction of assassins trying to overthrow the Shah. Although this film has a great cast, the script is silly and juvenile, defeating the cast's fine efforts. 101m/C VHS, Closed Caption. Cornel Wilde, Michael Rennie, Debra Paget, Raymond Massey, John Derek, Yma Sumac, Margaret Hayes, Joan Taylor, Sebastian Cabot; D: William Dieterle. PAR

Omega Cop 🐾 John Travis, Solar Survivor 1990 (R) In a post-apocalyptic future, there's only one cop left. He uses his martial arts skills and tons of guns attempting to rescue three women, but the violence doesn't cover the poor acting and shoddy production. Fans of TV's Batman might enjoy this for West's presence. 89m/C VHS. Ron Marchini, Adam West, Stuart Whitman, Troy Donahue, Meg Thayer, Jennifer Jostyn, Chrysti Jimenez, D.W. Landingham, Chuck Katzakian; D: Paul Kyriazi.

Omega Doom 🐾🐾 1996 (PG-13) Four hundred years after an apocalyptic war the most organic thing around are the cyborgs, who exist along with androids and robots in a world where humans no longer matter. Omega Doom (Hauer) is an android developed as a fighter who has no function except to kill. In a ruined amusement park, the Roms and Droids, two rival cyborg groups, maintain an uneasy truce and when Doom wanders in they unite to destroy the intruder. But they don't know what they're up against. CW: Sci-fi violence. 84m/C VHS, Closed Caption. Rutger Hauer, Anna Katarina, Norbert Weisser, Jahi JJ Zuri, Shannon Whirry, Earl White, Tina Cote, Jill Pierce; D: Albert Pyun; W: Ed Naha. COL

Omega Man 🐾🐾½ 1971 (PG) In post-holocaust Los Angeles, Heston is immune to the effects of a biologically engineered plague and battles those who aren't—an army of albino victims bent on destroying what's left of the world. Strong suspense with considerable violence, despite the PG rating. Based on the science fiction thriller "I Am Legend" by Richard Matheson, which is also the basis for the film "The Last Man on Earth." 98m/C VHS, Beta, LV. Charlton Heston, Anthony Zerbe, Rosalind Cash, Paul Koslo, Eric Laneuville, Lincoln Kilpatrick; D: Boris Sagal; W: John W. Corrington, Joyce H. Corrington; C: Russell Metty. WAR

Omega Syndrome 🐾½ 1987 (R) Neo-Nazis kidnap Wahl's daughter. He and Vietnam buddy DiCenzo get her back. Ho hum. DiCenzo's is the best performance. Tolerable for vigilante film fans. 90m/C VHS, Beta. Ken Wahl, Ron Kuhlman, George DiCenzo, Doug McClure; D: Joseph Manduke. VTR

The Omen 🐾🐾½ *Birthmark* 1976 **(R)** American diplomat's family adopts a young boy who always seems to be around when bizarre and inexplicable deaths occur. Of course, what else would you expect of Satan's son? The shock and gore prevalent in "The Exorcist" is replaced with more suspense and believable effects. Well-done horror film doesn't insult the viewer's intelligence. Followed by three sequels: "Damien: Omen 2," "The Final Conflict," and "Omen 4." **111m/C VHS, Beta, LV, Letterbox.** Gregory Peck, Lee Remick, Harvey Stephens, Billie Whitelaw, David Warner, Holly Palance, Robert Rietty, Patrick Troughton, Martin Benson, Leo McKern, Richard Donner; **D:** Richard Donner; **W:** David Seltzer; **C:** Gilbert Taylor; **M:** Jerry Goldsmith. Academy Awards '76: Best Original Score; Nominations: Academy Awards '76: Best Song ("Ave Satani"). FOX

Omen 4: The Awakening 🐾🐾 1991 It turns out Damien of Omens past had a daughter, Delia, who takes up where dear old devilish Dad left off. Delia is adopted by your basic clueless couple and proceeds to wreak havoc wherever she goes, including getting rid of several interfering adults. She also plans to make her adoptive father, a U.S. senator, President, so that his delightful child anti-Christ can have him carry out all her evil plans. **97m/C VHS, Closed Caption.** Faye Grant, Michael Woods, Michael Lerner, Asia Vieira; **D:** Jorge Montesi, Dominique Othenin-Girard. FXV

Omoo Omoo, the Shark God 🐾 1949 A sea captain is cursed when he removes the black pearls from a stone shark god in this extremely cheap adventure. **58m/B VHS.** Ron Randell, Devera Burton, Trevor Bardette, Pedro de Cordoba, Richard Benedict, Rudy Robles, Michael Whalen, George Meeker; **D:** Leo Leonard. SNC

On a Clear Day You Can See Forever 🐾🐾 1970 **(G)** A psychiatric hypnotist helps a girl stop smoking and finds that in trances she remembers previous incarnations. He falls in love with one of the women she used to be. Alan Jay Lerner of "My Fair Lady" and "Camelot" wrote the lyrics and the book. Based on a musical by Lerner and Burton Lane. ♫On a Clear Day, You Can See Forever; Come Back to Me; What Did I Have That I Don't Have?; He Isn't You; Hurry, It's Lovely Up Here; Go To Sleep; Love with All the Trimmings; Melinda. **129m/C VHS, Beta, LV.** Barbra Streisand, Yves Montand, Bob Newhart, Jack Nicholson, Simon Oakland; **D:** Vincente Minnelli; **C:** Harry Stradling. PAR

On an Island with You 🐾🐾½ 1948 Williams plays a movie star who finds romance on location in Hawaii in this musical extravaganza. Contains many of Williams' famous water ballet scenes and a bevy of bathing beauties. ♫On an Island with You; If I Were You; Taking Miss Mary to the Ball; Dog Song; Buenas Noches, Buenos Aires; Wedding Samba; I Can Do Without Broadway, But Can Broadway Do Without Me?. **107m/C VHS.** Esther Williams, Peter Lawford, Ricardo Montalban, Jimmy Durante, Cyd Charisse, Leon Ames; **D:** Richard Thorpe. MGM

On Approval 🐾🐾🐾 1944 Hilarious British farce in which two women trade boyfriends. Lillie's performace provides plenty of laughs. Brook runs the show as leading man, co-author, director, and co-producer. Based on the play by Frederick Lonsdale. **80m/B VHS, Beta.** GB Clive Brook, Beatrice Lillie, Googie Withers, Roland Culver, O.B. Clarence, Lawrence Hanray, Elliot Mason, Hay Petrie, Marjorie Munks, Molly Munks; **D:** Clive Brook; **W:** Terence Young, Clive Brook. KIV, MRV, HHT

On Borrowed Time 🐾🐾🐾 1939 Engrossing tale of Death (Hardwicke) coming for an old man (Barrymore) who isn't ready to die so he traps him in his backyard apple tree. Performances are first rate in this good adaptation of the stage success (originally by Eugene O'Neill). Hardwicke is especially a standout; he gave up theatre for Hollywood after making this film. **99m/B VHS, Closed Caption.** Lionel Barrymore, Cedric Hard-

wicke, Beulah Bondi, Una Merkel, Bobs Watson, Henry Travers; **D:** Harold Bucquet; **C:** Joseph Ruttenberg. MGM

On Dangerous Ground 🐾🐾🐾 1951 A world-weary detective is sent to the countryside to investigate a murder. He encounters the victim's revenge-hungry father and the blind sister of the murderer. In the hateful father the detective sees a reflection of the person he has become, in the blind woman, he learns the redeeming qualities of humanity and compassion. A well-acted example of film noir that features the composer Herrman's favorite score. **82m/B VHS, Beta, LV.** Robert Ryan, Ida Lupino, Ward Bond, Ed Begley Sr., Cleo Moore, Charles Kemper; **D:** Nicholas Ray; **M:** Bernard Herrmann. TTC

On Deadly Ground woof! 1994 **(R)** Seagal nearly destroys Alaska in an effort to save it in this inane, preachy story of an oil-rig roughneck out to protect the landscape from an evil oil company's drilling habits. Directorial debut for Seagal lumbers from scene to scene. Violence is expected, as is silly dialogue—just try to keep from laughing when stonyfaced Steven intones "What does it take to change the essence of man?" A better script, for one.**CW:** Language, nudity, and strong violence. **102m/C VHS, LV, Closed Caption.** Steven Seagal, Michael Caine, Joan Chen, John C. McGinley, Billy Bob Thornton, R. Lee Ermey; **D:** Steven Seagal; **W:** Ed Horowitz; **M:** Basil Poledouris. Golden Raspberry Awards '94: Worst Director (Seagal); Nominations: Golden Raspberry Awards '94: Worst Picture. WAR

On Golden Pond 🐾🐾🐾½ 1981 **(PG)** Henry Fonda won his first, and long overdue, Oscar for his role as the curmudgeonly patriarch of the Thayer family. He and his wife have grudgingly agreed to look after a young boy while at their summer home in Maine. Through his gradually affectionate relationship with the boy, Fonda learns to allay his fears of mortality. He also gains an understanding of his semi-estranged daughter. Jane Fonda plays his daughter and Hepburn is his loving wife in this often funny adaptation of Ernest Thompson's 1978 play. Predictable but deeply moving. Henry Fonda's final screen appearance. **109m/C VHS, Beta, LV.** Henry Fonda, Jane Fonda, Katharine Hepburn, Dabney Coleman, Doug McKeon, William Lanteau; **D:** Mark Rydell; **W:** Ernest Thompson; **C:** Billy Williams; **M:** Dave Grusin. Academy Awards '81: Best Actor (Fonda), Best Actress (Hepburn), Best Adapted Screenplay; British Academy Awards '82: Best Actress (Hepburn); Golden Globe Awards '82: Best Actor—Drama (Fonda), Best Film—Drama, Best Screenplay; National Board of Review Awards '81: Best Actor (Fonda); Writers Guild of America '81: Best Adapted Screenplay; Nominations: Academy Awards '81: Best Cinematography, Best Director (Rydell), Best Film Editing, Best Picture, Best Sound, Best Supporting Actress (Fonda), Best Original Score. FHE, KAR, BTV

On Her Majesty's Secret Service 🐾🐾🐾 1969 **(PG)** In the sixth 007 adventure, Bond again confronts the infamous Blofeld, who is planning a germ-warfare assault on the entire world. Australian Lazenby took a crack at playing the super spy, with mixed results. Many feel this is the best-written of the Bond films and might have been the most famous, had Sean Connery continued with the series. Includes the song "We Have All the Time In the World," sung by Louis Armstrong. **144m/C VHS, Beta, LV, Letterbox.** GB George Lazenby, Diana Rigg, Telly Savalas, Gabriele Ferzetti, Ilse Steppat, Bernard Lee, Lois Maxwell, Desmond Llewelyn, Catherine Schell, Julie Ege, Joanna Lumley, Mona Chong, Anouska Hempel, Jenny Hanley; **D:** Peter Hunt; **M:** John Barry. MGM, FOX, TLF

On Moonlight Bay 🐾🐾½ 1951 Set in small-town Indiana in 1917 with Day as the tomboyish Marjorie who falls for college man MacRae. Her father (Ames) doesn't approve but the trouble really begins when Marjorie's younger brother gets into trouble at school. The incorrigible Wesley (Gray) blames everything on dear old dad and MacRae feels he must come to Marjorie's rescue! Gray steals the movie as the bratty brother—otherwise its business as usual. Based

on Booth Tarkington's "Penrod" stories and followed by "By the Light of the Silvery Moon." ♫Love Ya; On Moonlight Bay; Till We Meet Again; Pack Up Your Troubles In Your Old Kit Bag; I'm Forever Blowing Bubbles; Christmas Story; Tell Me Why Nights Are Lonely; Cuddle Up a Little Closer; Every Little Movement Has a Meaning All Its Own. **95m/C VHS, LV.** Doris Day, Gordon MacRae, Leon Ames, Billy Gray, Rosemary DeCamp, Mary Wickes, Ellen Corby, Esther Dale; **D:** Roy Del Ruth; **W:** Melville Shavelson, Jack Rose; **M:** Max Steiner. WAR, MVD

On My Own 🐾🐾 1992 Fifteen-year-old Simon Henderson (Ferguson) struggles to cope with his life when he's sent away to school after his mother (Davis) suffers a nervous breakdown. Just as he begins to adjust and make friends, his mother pays a disturbing visit and reveals the source of her troubles. **96m/C VHS.** CA Judy Davis, Matthew Ferguson, David McIlwraith; **D:** Antonio Tibaldi. FCT, CCN

On the Air Live with Captain Midnight 🐾½ *Captain Midnight* 1979 Socially challenged teen finds hipness as a rebel DJ operating an illegal radio station from his van. Leading actor is the son of the director/writer/producer but nepotism does not a good film make. **90m/C VHS, Beta.** Tracy Sebastian; **D:** Ferd Sebastian. NO

On the Avenue 🐾🐾🐾 1937 Broadway showman Powell opens up a new musical, starring Faye as the richest girl in the world, in this musical-comedy satirizing upper-crust society. Debutante Carroll is outraged because she realizes it's mocking her actual life. Carroll tries to get Powell to change the show, they fall in love, Faye gets her nose out of joint, and after lots of fuss everything ends happily. Fine Berlin score. ♫He Ain't Got Rhythm; You're Laughing at Me; This Year's Kisses; Slumming on Park Avenue; The Girl on the Police Gazette; I've Got My Love to Keep Me Warm. **90m/B VHS.** Dick Powell, Madeleine Carroll, Alice Faye, George Barbier, The Ritz Brothers, Alan Mowbray, Cora Witherspoon, Walter Catlett, Stepin Fetchit, Sig Rumann, Douglas Fowley, Joan Davis; **D:** Roy Del Ruth; **W:** Gene Markey; **M:** Irving Berlin. FXV

On the Beach 🐾🐾🐾½ 1959 A group of survivors attempt to live normal lives in post-apocalyptic Australia, waiting for the inevitable arrival of killer radiation. Astaire is strong in his first dramatic role. Though scientifically implausible, still a good anti-war vehicle. Based on the best-selling novel by Nevil Shute. **135m/B VHS, Beta, LV.** Gregory Peck, Anthony Perkins, Donna Anderson, Ava Gardner, Fred Astaire; **D:** Stanley Kramer; **C:** Daniel F. Fapp; **M:** Ernest Gold. Golden Globe Awards '60: Best Score; Nominations: Academy Awards '59: Best Film Editing, Best Original Dramatic/Comedy Score. FOX, FCT

On the Comet 🐾🐾🐾 *Na Komete; Hector Servadac's Ark* 1968 Zeman's fourth fantasy based on Jules Verne stories, about a chunk of the Earth's crust suddenly becoming a comet and giving its passengers a ride through the galaxy. Complete with Zeman's signature animation fantasias. In English. **76m/C VHS, Beta.** CZ Emil Horvath Jr., Magda Vasarykova, Frantisek Filipovsky; **D:** Karel Zeman. FCT, MRV

On the Edge 🐾 1982 A narcotics agent tracks down a wealthy Brazilian drug kingpin. **82m/C VHS, Beta.** Anthony Steffen. NO

On the Edge 🐾🐾½ 1986 **(PG-13)** A drama about the inevitable Rocky-esque triumph of Dern as an aging marathon runner. Simultaneous to his running endeavor, Dern is trying to make up for lost time with his father. Available in two versions, one rated, the other unrated with a racy appearance by Pam Grier as the runner's interracial lover. **86m/C VHS, Beta.** Bruce Dern, John Marley, Bill Bailey, Jim Haynie, Pam Grier; **D:** Rob Nilsson; **W:** Rob Nilsson. NO

On the Edge: The Survival of Dana
1979 Another entry from the world of low-quality made-for-TV films. A young girl moves with her family to a new town. When she falls in with the "bad" crowd, her ethical standards are challenged. A stinker that may appeal to those with campy tastes. Not for the discriminating palate. **92m/C VHS, Beta.** Melissa Sue Anderson, Robert Carradine, Marion Ross, Talia Balsam, Michael Pataki, Kevin Breslin, Judge Reinhold, Barbara Babcock; **D:** Jack Starrett. *GEM*

On the Fiddle
Operation Snafu; Operation Warhead 1961 Conniving Horace Pope (Lynch) gets his mate Pedlar Pascoe (Connery) to join the Royal Air Force with him during WWII. Horace sets up a number of rackets but, despite their larceny, they become unintentional heroes. Based on the novel "Stop at a Winner" by R.F. Delderfield. **93m/B VHS, Closed Caption.** *GB* Alfred Lynch, Sean Connery, Cecil Parker, Stanley Holloway, Wilfrid Hyde-White; **D:** Cyril Frankel; **W:** Harold Buchman; **C:** Edward Scaife; **M:** Malcolm Arnold. *REP*

On the Line
1983 Two Mexico-US border guards, one hard-bitten, the other sympathetic to the illegal immigrants' plight, battle it out over a beautiful Mexican whore. Disjointed and confusing. **SP** David Carradine, Victoria Abril, Scott Wilson, Sam Jaffe, Jesse Vint; **D:** Jose Luis Borau; **W:** Jose Luis Borau. *NLC*

On the Nickel
1980 An ex-alcoholic returns to Fifth Street in Los Angeles to save his friend from a life of despair. Waits' musical score enhances this sentimental skid row drama. Scripted, directed, and produced by "The Waltons'" Waite. **96m/C VHS, Beta.** Ralph Waite, Donald Moffat, Hal Williams, Jack Kehoe; **D:** Ralph Waite; **W:** Ralph Waite; **M:** Tom Waits. *VES*

On the Night Stage
1915 Gruff bandit (legendary Hart) loses his girl-of-questionable-values to town preacher. One of the first feature length westerns. **83m/B VHS, Beta, 8mm.** William S. Hart, Robert Edeson, Rhea Mitchell, Shorty Hamilton; **D:** Reginald Barker. *GPV, VYY*

On the Old Spanish Trail
1947 Rogers becomes a singing cowboy with a traveling tent show in order to pay off a note signed by the Sons of the Pioneers. **56m/B VHS, Beta.** Roy Rogers, Jane Frazee, Andy Devine, Tito Guizar; **D:** William Witney. *NOS, MRV, VCN*

On the Right Track
1981 (PG) Young orphan living in Chicago's Union Station has the gift of being able to pick winning race horses. May be appealing to fans of Coleman and "Different Strokes" television show, but lacks the momentum to keep most viewers from switching tracks. **98m/C VHS, Beta.** Gary Coleman, Lisa Eilbacher, Michael Lembeck, Norman Fell, Maureen Stapleton, Herb Edelman; **D:** Lee Philips. *FOX*

On the Run
1985 (R) An ex-con and his gal cut a law-defying swath through the Bayou. **96m/C VHS, Beta.** Jack Conrad, Rita George, Dub Taylor, David Huddleston. *GEM*

On the Third Day
1983 A headmaster finds a mysterious stranger in his house who turns out to be his long-lost illegitimate son. **101m/C VHS, Beta.** Richard Marant, Catherine Schell, Paul Williamson. *ORI*

On the Town
1949 Kelly's directorial debut features three sailors on a one day leave search for romance in the Big Apple. Filmed on location in New York City, with uncompromisingly authentic flavor. Based on the successful Broadway musical, with a score composed by Leonard Bernstein, Betty Comden, and Adolph Green. Additional songs by Roger Edens. Available in a deluxe collector's laserdisc edition. ♫New York, New York; I Feel Like I'm Not Out of Bed Yet; Come Up to My Place; Miss Turnstiles Ballet; Main Street; You're Awful; On the Town; You Can Count on Me; Pearl of the Persian Sea. **98m/C VHS, Beta, LV.** Gene Kelly, Frank Sinatra, Vera-Ellen, Ann Miller, Betty Garrett; **D:** Gene Kelly, Stanley Do-

nen; **W:** Betty Comden, Adolph Green. Academy Awards '49: Best Scoring of a Musical. *MGM*

On the Town
1991 Bernstein's first big Broadway success in 1944, recorded in a live performance June 1992, at London's Barbican Centre. Follows the story of three sailors on a 24-hour leave in New York City during WWII. This version includes numbers which never made it into the original Broadway show. **110m/C VHS, LV.** Frederica von Stade, Tyne Daly, Marie McLaughlin, David Garrison, Thomas Hampson, Kurt Ollman, Evelyn Lear, Samuel Ramey, Cleo Laine; **M:** Leonard Bernstein, Betty Comden, Adolph Green. *PGV, FCT*

On the Waterfront
1954 A trend-setting, gritty portrait of New York dock workers embroiled in union violence. Cobb is the gangster union boss, Steiger his crooked lawyer, and Brando, Steiger's ex-fighter brother who "could've been a contender!" Intense performances and excellent direction stand up well today. The picture was a huge financial success. **108m/B VHS, Beta, LV, Closed Caption.** Marlon Brando, Rod Steiger, Eva Marie Saint, Lee J. Cobb, Karl Malden, Pat Henning, Leif Erickson, Tony Galento, John Hamilton, Nehemiah Persoff; **D:** Elia Kazan; **W:** Budd Schulberg; **C:** Boris Kaufman; **M:** Leonard Bernstein. Academy Awards '54: Best Actor (Brando), Best Art Direction/Set Decoration (B & W), Best Black and White Cinematography, Best Director (Kazan), Best Film Editing, Best Picture, Best Story & Screenplay, Best Supporting Actress (Saint); British Academy Awards '54: Best Actor (Brando); Directors Guild of America Awards '54: Best Director (Kazan); Golden Globe Awards '55: Best Actor—Drama (Brando), Best Director (Kazan), Best Film—Drama, National Film Registry '89;; New York Film Critics Awards '54: Best Actor (Brando), Best Director (Kazan), Best Film; Nominations: Academy Awards '54: Best Supporting Actor (Cobb), Best Supporting Actor (Malden, Steiger), Best Original Dramatic/Comedy Score. *COL, BTV*

On the Yard
1979 (R) An attempt to realistically portray prison life. Focuses on a murderer who runs afoul of the leader of the prisoners and the system. A fairly typical prison drama with above average performances from Heard and Kellin. **102m/C VHS, Beta.** John Heard, Thomas G. Waites, Mike Kellin, Joe Grifasi; **D:** Raphael D. Silver; **W:** Malcolm Braly.

On Top of Old Smoky
1953 Autry and the Cass County Boys are mistaken for Texas Rangers by a gang of land poachers. **59m/B VHS, Beta.** Gene Autry, Smiley Burnette, Gail Davis, Sheila Ryan; **D:** George Archainbaud. *CCB*

On Top of the Whale
1982 Two scholars move onto the estate of strange but wealthy benefactor to conduct research on the few survivors of a disappearing clan of Indians. Two tribesmen speak bizarre dialect which utilizes only one word while others confound the researchers with stories of ghosts and graveyards. Dutch comedy subtitled in English. **93m/C VHS.** *NL* **D:** Raul Ruiz. *KIV, FCT*

On Valentine's Day
Story of a Marriage 1986 (PG) Author Horton Foote based this story loosely on his parents' lives. A wealthy Southern girl marries a poor but decent young man and finds herself ostracized from her family. A prequel to the same author's "1918." Produced with PBS for "American Playhouse." **106m/C VHS, Beta.** Hallie Foote, Matthew Broderick, Michael Higgins, Steven Hill, William Converse-Roberts, Rochelle Oliver, Richard Jenkins, Horton Foote Jr., Carol Goodheart; **D:** Ken Harrison; **W:** Horton Foote; **M:** Jonathan Sheffer. *ORI*

On Wings of Eagles
1986 During the 1979 Iranian revolution two American executives are imprisoned by Islamic radicals. Help arrives in the form of covert agents of their boss—Texas tycoon H. Ross Perot (played by Crenna). Don't expect strict historical veracity or insight from this network miniseries (based on the "nonfiction novel" by Ken Follett), an okay but lengthy "mission impossible." It came out in a two-cassette set, just in time for Perot's 1992 presidential campaign. **221m/C VHS.** Burt Lancaster, Richard Cren-

na, Paul LeMat, Esai Morales, Constance Towers, Jim Metzler, James Sutorius, Lawrence Pressman, Karen Carlson, Cyril O'Reilly; **D:** Andrew V. McLaglen. *WOV*

Onassis
The Richest Man in the World: The Story of Aristotle Onassis 1988 Romanticized biography of Greek shipping magnate Aristotle Onassis, from the poverty of his youth to his later wealth and family and romantic liaisons and tragedies. Julia is adequate as the title character but English actress Annis is badly miscast as Jackie Kennedy Onassis. However, Seymour is terrific as Onassis' lover, opera star Maria Callas. Quinn, who played Onassis in "The Greek Tycoon," plays Onassis' father in this one. Based on the novel by Peter Evans. Originally a made for television miniseries. **120m/C VHS, LV, Closed Caption.** Raul Julia, Jane Seymour, Francesca Annis, Anthony Quinn, Anthony Zerbe, Lorenzo Quinn; **D:** Waris Hussein. *TTC*

Once a Hero
1988 The dregs of society, the Cicero Gang, have taken Captain Justice's number one fan and his mother hostage. Is it really curtains for rosy cheeks, bubble gum, and apple pie? But wait, it's Captain Justice, the man, the myth, to the rescue! **74m/C VHS.** Jeff Lester, Robert Forster, Milo O'Shea; **D:** Claudia Weill. *VTR*

Once a Thief
1996 (R) A fun and action-packed TV movie finds adopted children Li Ann (Holt) and Mac (Sergei) being raised along with natural son Michael (Wong) by Hong Kong crime head Tang (Ito) and trained as daring professional thieves. A falling out finds Li Ann in Vancouver, involved with ex-cop Victor (Lea), and both of them working for a covert crime-fighting agency headed by a very tough director (Dale). Then Mac is forced to join the duo in an elaborate heist to bring down Michael and his family's criminal empire. Woo's director's cut contains additional footage. **CW:** Some strong violence. **101m/C VHS, LV.** Ivan Sergei, Sandrine Holt, Nicholas Lea, Michael Wong, Robert Ito, Jennifer Dale, Alan Scarfe; **D:** John Woo; **W:** Glenn Davis, William Laurin; **C:** Bill Wong; **M:** Amin Bhatia. *APX*

Once Around
1991 (R) 30ish, lonely Renata Bella (Hunter) meets boisterous, self-assured (read utterly obnoxious) Lithuanian salesman Sam Sharpe (Dreyfuss). He sweeps her off her feet, showers her with affection and gifts, and then tries hard—too hard—to please her close-knit Italian family. Casting doesn't get much better than the group assembled here and Hallstrom steers everyone to wonderful performances in his American directorial debut. The major flaw is the script, a light romantic comedy that sometimes swerves into heavy drama, so much so that you may need Kleenex. **115m/C VHS, Beta, LV, Closed Caption.** Richard Dreyfuss, Holly Hunter, Danny Aiello, Gena Rowlands, Laura San Giacomo, Roxanne Hart, Danton Stone, Tim Guinee, Greg Germann, Griffin Dunne; **D:** Lasse Hallstrom; **W:** Malia Scotch Marmo; **M:** James Horner. *USH, FCT*

Once Before I Die
1965 Army soldiers caught in the Philippines during WWII struggle to survive and elude the Japanese. A single woman traveling with them becomes the object of their spare time considerations. A brutal, odd, and gritty war drama. Director/actor Derek was Andress' husband at the time. **97m/C VHS.** *PH* Ursula Andress, John Derek, Richard Jaeckel, Rod Lauren, Ron Ely; **D:** John Derek. *MOV*

Once Bitten
1985 (PG-13) Centuries-old though still remarkably youthful vampiress comes to LA to stalk male virgins. That may be the wrong city, but she needs their blood to retain her young countenance. Vampire comedy theme was more effectively explored in 1979s "Love at First Bite," notable, however for the screen debut of comic Carrey who would later gain fame for TV's "In Living Color" and "Ace Ventura, Pet Detective." **94m/C VHS, Beta, LV, Closed Caption.** Lauren Hutton, Jim Carrey, Cleavon Little, Karen Kopins, Thomas Balltore, Skip Lackey; **D:** Howard Storm; **W:** Jonathan Roberts, David Hines, Jeffrey Hause; **C:** Adam Greenberg; **M:** John Du Prez. *ART*

Once in Paris... 🎬🎬½ 1979 (PG) A bittersweet romance about a scriptwriter working in Paris, the chauffeur who befriends him, and the aristocratic British woman with whom the writer falls in love. Beautiful French scenery and the engaging performance of Lenoir as the chauffeur make this film a diverting piece of entertainment. 100m/C VHS, Beta. Wayne Rogers, Gayle Hunnicutt, Jack Lenoir; *D:* Frank D. Gilroy; *W:* Frank D. Gilroy.

Once Is Not Enough 🎬½ *Jacqueline Susann's Once is Not Enough* 1975 (R) Limp trash-drama concerning the young daughter of a has-been movie producer who has a tempestuous affair with a writer who reminds her of her father. Based on the novel by Jacqueline Susann. 121m/C VHS, Beta. Kirk Douglas, Brenda Raffin, David Janssen, George Hamilton, Brenda Vaccaro, Alexis Smith, Melina Mercouri; *D:* Guy Green; *W:* Julius J. Epstein, Philip C. Epstein; *C:* John A. Alonzo; *M:* Henry Mancini. Golden Globe Awards '76: Best Supporting Actress (Vaccaro); Nominations: Academy Awards '75: Best Supporting Actress (Vaccaro). *PAR*

Once Upon a Brothers Grimm 🎬🎬 1977 An original musical fantasy in which the Brothers Grimm meet a succession of their most famous storybook characters including Hansel and Gretel, the Gingerbread Lady, Little Red Riding Hood, and Rumpelstiltskin. 102m/C VHS, Beta. Dean Jones, Paul Sand, Cleavon Little, Ruth Buzzi, Chita Rivera, Teri Garr. *VCI*

Once Upon a Crime 🎬½ 1992 (PG) Extremely disappointing comedy featuring a high profile cast set in Europe. The plot centers around Young and Lewis finding a dachshund and travelling from Rome to Monte Carlo to return the stray and collect a $5,000 reward. Upon arrival in Monte Carlo, they find the dog's owner dead and they end up getting implicated for the murder. Other prime suspects include Belushi, Candy, Hamilton, and Shepherd. Weak script is made bearable only by the comic genius of Candy. 94m/C VHS, Closed Caption. John Candy, James Belushi, Cybill Shepherd, Sean Young, Richard Lewis, Ornella Muti, Giancarlo Giannini, George Hamilton, Joss Ackland, Elsa Martinelli; *D:* Eugene Levy; *M:* Richard Gibbs. *MGM*

Once Upon a Forest 🎬🎬 1993 (G) Animated tale of three woodland creatures in a daring race against time when their young friend's life is at stake. Ecologically correct story by "American Tail" creator David Kirschner is light on humor and heavy on gloom, as little animals encounter oppressive human society and their big, bad machines. Servicable animation, though not up to Don Bluth standards (and a long, long way from Disney). Crawford, the voice of the wise old uncle, has a song, while Vereen breaks into a fervent gospel number as a marsh bird with a yen for preaching. For an evening of anti-pollution, treat the earth kindly animation, see it with "Ferngully." 80m/C VHS, LV, Closed Caption. *D:* Charles Grosvenor; *W:* Mark Young, Kelly Ward; *V:* Michael Crawford, Ben Vereen. *FOX, FUS*

Once Upon a Honeymoon 🎬🎬½ 1942 Set in 1938, Grant is an American radio broadcaster reporting on the oncoming war. Rogers is the ex-showgirl who unknowingly marries a Nazi. In this strange, uneven comedy, Grant tries to get the goods on him and also rescue Rogers. The plot is basic and uneven with Grant attempting to expose the Nazi and save Rogers. However, the slower moments are offset by some fairly surreal pieces of comedy. 116m/B VHS, Beta, LV. Ginger Rogers, Cary Grant, Walter Slezak, Albert Dekker; *D:* Leo McCarey; *C:* George Barnes. Nominations: Academy Awards '42: Best Sound. *CCB, TTC, FCT*

Once Upon a Midnight Scary 🎬🎬 1990 Price narrates a collection of three tales of terror, "The Ghost Belonged to Me," "The Legend of Sleepy Hollow," and "The House with a Clock in Its Walls." Aimed at the kiddies. 50m/C VHS. Rene Auberjonois, Severn Darden; *D:* Neil Cox. *GEM, MRV*

Once Upon a Scoundrel 🎬🎬½ 1973 (G) A ruthless Mexican land baron arranges to have a young woman's fiancee thrown in jail so he can have her all to himself. 90m/C VHS, Beta. Zero Mostel, Katy Jurado, Titos Vandis, Priscilla Garcia, A. Martinez; *D:* George Schaefer; *M:* Alex North.

Once Upon a Time 1976 (G) A pretty girl, her puppy, a charming prince, and a grinch combine for a magical, wondrous animated fantasy. 83m/C VHS, Beta. *GEM*

Once Upon a Time 1987 Two rival tribes spoil the love of a prince and princess in ancient times. Animated. 92m/C VHS, Beta.

Once Upon a Time in America 🎬🎬🎬½ 1984 (R) The uncut original version of director Leone's saga of five young men growing up in Brooklyn during the '20s who become powerful mob figures. Also available in a 143-minute version. Told from the perspective of De Niro's Noodles as an old man looking back at 50 years of crime, love, and death, told with a sweeping and violent elegance. 225m/C VHS, Beta, LV, Closed Caption. Robert De Niro, James Woods, Elizabeth McGovern, Treat Williams, Tuesday Weld, Burt Young, Joe Pesci, Danny Aiello, Darlanne Fluegel, Jennifer Connelly; *D:* Sergio Leone; *C:* Tonino Delli Colli; *M:* Ennio Morricone. *WAR*

Once Upon a Time in the West 🎬🎬🎬½ 1968 (PG) The uncut version of Leone's sprawling epic about a band of ruthless gunmen who set out to murder a mysterious woman waiting for the railroad to come through. Filmed in John Ford's Monument Valley, it's a revisionist western with some of the longest opening credits in the history of the cinema. Fonda is cast against type as an extremely cold-blooded villain. Brilliant musical score. 165m/C VHS, Beta, LV. *IT* Henry Fonda, Jason Robards Jr., Charles Bronson, Claudia Cardinale, Keenan Wynn, Lionel Stander, Woody Strode, Jack Elam; *D:* Sergio Leone; *W:* Sergio Leone, Bernardo Bertolucci, Dario Argento; *C:* Tonino Delli Colli; *M:* Ennio Morricone. *PAR*

Once Upon a Time ... When We Were Colored 🎬🎬🎬 1995 (PG) Actor Reid makes a fine directorial debut with the story of a black youngster growing up parentless in '50s Mississippi. His family faces the usual troubles of the time, including poor wages and white bigotry, but manages to provide a positive and loving home life for him. Nostalgic, sensitive, and heartwarming adaptation of Clifton Taulbert's autobiographical book. 112m/C VHS, LV, Closed Caption. Al Freeman Jr., Paula Kelly, Phylicia Rashad, Polly Bergen, Richard Roundtree, Charles Taylor, Willie Norwood, Jr., Damon Hines, Leon; *D:* Tim Reid; *W:* Paul Cooper; *C:* Johnny Simmons; *M:* Steve Tyrell. *REP*

Once Were Warriors 🎬🎬🎬 1994 (R) Violent story of the struggling Maori Heke family, who have left their rural New Zealand roots to live in the city. Feisty mom Beth (Owen) is struggling with five kids and volatile hubby Jake (Heke), who's continuously out of work, boozing, and fighting. Eldest son Nig (Arahanga) has left home and joined a street gang and the rest of the kids hate Jake for beating up on their mother. They also fall victim to his temper and his habit of bringing his brawling, drunk buddies home-leading to further tragedy. Intense drama showcases great performances, with Owen honored as best actress at the Montreal World Film Festival. Based on the novel by Alan Duff. Feature-film directorial debut of Tamahori. *CW:* Pervasive language; strong depiction of domestic abuse, including sexual violence and substance abuse. 102m/C VHS, LV, Closed Caption. *NZ* Rena Owen, Temuera Morrison, Mamaengaroa Kerr-Bell, Julian (Sonny) Arahanga, Taungaroa Emile, Rachael Morris, Joseph Kairau, Pete Smith; *D:* Lee Tamahori; *W:* Riwia Brown; *C:* Stuart Dryburgh; *M:* Murray Grindlay, Murray McNabb. Australian Film Institute '95: Best Foreign Film; Montreal World Film Festival '94: Best Actress (Owen), Best Film. *NLC*

One Against the Wind 🎬🎬🎬 1991 (PG) A true story of one woman's courage against great odds. British Mary Liddell and her children are living in Paris during the WWII Nazi occupation. Mary's secret agenda is to smuggle downed Allied pilots out of the country to safety without arousing Nazi suspicions. Great performances by Davis as the resourceful Mary and Neill as one of the pilots she rescues. A Hallmark Hall of Fame presentation. 96m/C VHS, Closed Caption. Judy Davis, Sam Neill, Denholm Elliott, Anthony Higgins, Christien Anholt, Kate Beckinsale, Frank Middlemass; *D:* Larry Elikann. *REP*

One A.M. 1916 Charlie is a drunk who must first battle a flight of stairs in order to get to bed. Silent with music track. 20m/B VHS, Beta. Charlie Chaplin. *CAB, GVV*

The One and Only 🎬🎬½ 1978 (PG) An egotistical young man is determined to make it in show business. Instead, he finds himself in the world of professional wrestling. Most of the humor comes from the wrestling scenes, with Winkler and Darby's love story only serving to dilute the film. 98m/C VHS, Beta. Henry Winkler, Kim Darby, Gene Saks, William Daniels, Harold Gould, Herve Villechaize; *D:* Carl Reiner. *PAR*

The One and Only, Genuine, Original Family Band 🎬🎬🎬 1968 (G) A harmonious musical family becomes divided when various members take sides in the presidential battle between Benjamin Harrison and Grover Cleveland, a political era that has been since overlooked. 110m/C VHS, Beta, LV. Walter Brennan, Buddy Ebsen, Lesley Ann Warren, Kurt Russell, Goldie Hawn, Wally Cox, Richard Deacon, Janet Blair; *D:* Michael O'Herlihy. *DIS*

One Arabian Night 🎬🎬🎬 *Sumurun* 1921 When an exotic dancer in a traveling carnival troupe is kidnapped into a harem, a dwarf acts on his unrequited love and avenges her death by murdering the sheik who killed her. Secured a place in American filmmaking for director Lubitsch. 85m/B VHS, Beta. *GE* Pola Negri, Ernst Lubitsch, Paul Wegener; *D:* Ernst Lubitsch. *VYY, GPV, GLV*

One Armed Executioner 🎬🎬 1980 (R) An Interpol agent seeks revenge on his wife's murderers. 90m/C VHS, Beta. Franco Guerrero, Jody Kay; *D:* Bobby A. Auarez. *NO*

One Away 🎬 1980 (PG) Gypsy escapes from a South African prison and the police are in hot pursuit. 83m/C VHS, Beta. Elke Sommer, Bradford Dillman, Dean Stockwell. *NO*

One Body Too Many 🎬🎬 1944 A mystery spoof about a wacky insurance salesman who's mistaken for a detective. The usual comedy of errors ensues. A contrived mish-mash—but it does have Lugosi going for it. 75m/B VHS, Beta. Jack Haley, Jean Parker, Bela Lugosi, Lyle Talbot; *D:* Frank McDonald. *NOS, SNC, HHT*

One Brief Summer WOOF! 1970 (R) Love triangles and intrigues abound on a spectacular country manor. An aging woman is mortified by her father's interest in a young seductress, who finds herself attracted to the old man, but not only him. 86m/C VHS. Clifford Evans, Felicity Gibson, Jennifer Hilary, Jan Holden, Peter Egan; *D:* John MacKenzie. *NO*

One Cooks, the Other Doesn't 🎬🎬 1983 A most unlikely story of a man's ex-wife and his son moving back into his house, where he's now living with his new wife. Made for television. 96m/C VHS, Beta. Suzanne Pleshette, Joseph Bologna, Rosanna Arquette, Oliver Clark; *D:* Richard Michaels. *ART*

One Crazy Night 🎬🎬½ 1993 (PG-13) In 1964, five Australian teenagers try to get into the Melbourne hotel where the Beatles are staying on tour. They wind up trapped in the basement, swapping secrets, and finding out how much they have in common. *CW:* Language and teen sensuality. 92m/C VHS. *AU* Noah Taylor, Beth Champion, Malcolm Kennard, Danni Minogue, Malcolm Braly; *D:* Michael Pattinson. *THV*

100

One Crazy Summer ♪♪½ **1986 (PG)** A group of wacky teens spends a fun-filled summer on Nantucket Island in New England. Follow-up to "Better Off Dead" is offbeat and fairly charming, led by Cusack's perplexed cartoonist and with comic moments delivered by Goldthwait. **94m/C VHS, Beta, LV, Closed Caption.** John Cusack, Demi Moore, William Hickey, Curtis Armstrong, Bob(cat) Goldthwait, Mark Metcalf, Joel Murray, Tom Villard, Joe Flaherty; **D:** Steve Holland; **W:** Steve Holland; **M:** Cory Lerios. *WAR*

One Dark Night ♪½ *Entity Force; Mausoleum* **1982 (R)** Two high school girls plan an initiation rite for one of their friends who is determined to shed her "goody-goody" image. West is the caped crusader of TV series "Batman" fame. **94m/C VHS, Beta.** Meg Tilly, Adam West, David Mason Daniels, Robin Evans, Elizabeth Daily; **D:** Tom McLoughlin. *NO*

One Day in the Life of Ivan Denisovich ♪♪♪ **1971** The film version of Nobel Prize-winner Alexander Solzhenitsyn's novel about a prisoner's experiences in a Soviet labor camp. A testament to human endurance. Photography by Sven Nykvist. **105m/C VHS, LV.** *NO GB* Tom Courtenay, Alfred Burke, Espen Skjonberg, James Maxwell, Eric Thompson; **D:** Caspar Wrede; **W:** Ronald Harwood; **C:** Sven Nykvist. *NO*

One Deadly Owner ♪ **1974** A made-for-television film about a possessed Rolls-Royce torturing its new owner. Quite a vehicle for the usually respectable set of wheels. **80m/C VHS, Beta.** Donna Mills, Jeremy Brett, Robert Morris, Laurence Payne. *ART*

One Deadly Summer ♪♪♪ *L'Ete Meurtrier* **1983 (R)** Revenge drama about a young girl who returns to her mother's home village to ruin three men who had assaulted her mother years before. Very well acted. From the novel by Sebastien Japrisot. In French with English subtitles. **134m/C VHS, Beta, Closed Caption.** *FR* Isabelle Adjani, Alain Souchon, Suzanne Flon; **D:** Jean Becker; **M:** Georges Delerue. Cesar Awards '84: Best Actress (Adjani), Best Supporting Actress (Flon), Best Writing. *USH*

One Down, Two to Go! woof! **1982 (R)** When the mob is discovered to be rigging a championship karate bout, two dynamic expert fighters join in a climactic battle against the hoods. Example of really bad "blaxploitation" that wastes talent, film, and the audience's time. **84m/C VHS, Beta.** Jim Brown, Fred Williamson, Jim Kelly, Richard Roundtree; **D:** Fred Williamson. *RHI, HHE*

187 ♪♪½ **1997 (R)** Jackson's a Brooklyn high school teacher who is brutally attacked by one of his students. His physical scars are healed, but his emotional state is marred as he takes some pretty unorthodox teaching methods to a troubled L.A. school. Very dark, psychological drama with a powerful performance by Jackson. Tough film whose title refers to the California penal code number for murder. First film from director Reynolds after his "Waterworld" fiasco. **CW:** Violence, strong language, drug use and brief nudity. **119m/C VHS, LV, Closed Caption.** Samuel L. Jackson, John Heard, Kelly Rowan, Clifton Gonzalez Gonzalez, Tony Plana; **D:** Kevin Reynolds; **W:** Scott Yagemann; **C:** Ericson Core. *WAR*

One-Eyed Jacks ♪♪♪½ **1961** An often engaging, but lengthy, psychological western about an outlaw who seeks to settle the score with a former partner who became a sheriff. Great acting by all, particularly Brando, who triumphed both as star and director. Stanley Kubrick was the original director, but Brando took over mid-way through the filming. The photography is wonderful and reflects the effort that went into it. **141m/C VHS, Beta, LV.** Marlon Brando, Karl Malden, Katy Jurado, Elisha Cook Jr., Slim Pickens, Ben Johnson, Pina Pellicer, Timothy Carey; **D:** Marlon Brando; **W:** Calder Willingham; **C:** Charles B(ryant) Lang. Nominations: Academy Awards '61: Best Color Cinematography. *PAR*

One-Eyed Soldiers ♪ **1967** Young woman, criminal, and dwarf follow trail to mysterious key to unlock $15 million treasure. Much cheesy intrigue. **83m/C VHS.** *GB YU* Dale Robertson, Luciana Paluzzi; **D:** Jean Christopher. *NO*

One-Eyed Swordsman ♪ **1963** A handicapped samurai battles shogun warriors. With English subtitles. **95m/C VHS, Beta.** *JP* Tetsuro Tamba, Haruko Wanibuchi; **D:** Seiichiro Uchikawa. *VDA*

One False Move ♪♪♪ **1991 (R)** Black psycho Pluto, his white-trash partner Ray, and Ray's biracial lover Fantasia are three low-level drug dealers on the streets of Los Angeles who get involved in murder. Fleeing the city for Fantasia's small hometown in Arkansas, they come up against the local sheriff and two L.A. cops sent to bring them back. Not a typical crime thriller, first-time feature director Franklin is more interested in a psychological character study of racism and smalltown mores than in your average shoot 'em up action picture. Good performances, especially by Williams as the deceptive bad girl. **CW:** Strong language and strong violence and drug content. **105m/C VHS, LV, Closed Caption.** Bill Paxton, Cynda Williams, Michael Beach, Jim Metzler, Earl Billings, Billy Bob Thornton, Natalie Canderday, Robert Ginnaven, Robert Anthony Bell, Kevin Hunter; **D:** Carl Franklin; **W:** Billy Bob Thornton, Tom Epperson; **C:** James L. Carter. Independent Spirit Awards '93: Best Director (Franklin); MTV Movie Awards '93: Best New Filmmaker Award (Franklin). *COL, FCT*

One Fine Day ♪♪½ **1996 (PG)** Marshmallows. That's what this movie is like—light, fluffy, not much substance, but enjoyable when you're in the mood. Nod to the classic screwball comedies of the '40s and '50s throws harried single mom/architect Pfeiffer and political columnist/weekend dad Clooney together when their kids, who attend the same school, miss a class field trip. Naturally, they take an instant dislike to each other, but are forced to cooperate to solve the daycare situation. An accidental switching of cell phones provides the chance for repeated encounters, and growing mutual interest. Predictable, but pleasantly so. No matter how hard she tries, Pfeiffer always looks good, and Clooney has that cocked head, devilish grin thing working overtime. Screenplay by Neil Simon's daughter Ellen supplies all the elements for a fine date movie. **108m/C VHS, Closed Caption.** Michelle Pfeiffer, George Clooney, Alex D. Linz, Mae Whitman, Charles Durning, Jon Robin Baitz, Ellen Greene, Joe Grifasi, Pete Hamill, Anna Maria Horsford, Sheila Kelley, Barry Kivel, Robert Klein, George Martin, Michael Massee, Amanda Peet, Bitty Schram, Holland Taylor, Rachel York; **D:** Michael Hoffman; **W:** Terrel Seltzer, Ellen Simon; **C:** Oliver Stapleton; **M:** James Newton Howard. Nominations: Academy Awards '96: Best Song ("For the First Time"); Golden Globe Awards '97: Best Song ("For the First Time"). *FXV*

One Flew Over the Cuckoo's Nest ♪♪♪♪ **1975 (R)** Touching, hilarious, dramatic, and completely effective adaptation of Ken Kesey's novel. Nicholson is a two-bit crook, who, facing a jail sentence, feigns insanity to be sentenced to a cushy mental hospital. The hospital is anything but cushy, with a tyrannical head nurse out to squash any vestige of the patients' independence. Nicholson proves to be a crazed messiah and catalyst for these mentally troubled patients and a worthy adversary for the head nurse. Classic performs superbly on numerous levels. **129m/C VHS, Beta, LV.** Jack Nicholson, Brad Dourif, Louise Fletcher, Will Sampson, William Redfield, Danny DeVito, Christopher Lloyd, Scatman Crothers, Vincent Schiavelli, Michael Berryman, Peter Brocco, Louisa Moritz; **D:** Milos Forman; **W:** Ken Kesey, Bo Goldman; **C:** Haskell Wexler, Bill Butler, William A. Fraker; **M:** Jack Nitzsche. Academy Awards '75: Best Actor (Nicholson), Best Actress (Fletcher), Best Adapted Screenplay, Best Director (Forman), Best Picture; British Academy Awards '76: Best Actor (Nicholson), Best Actress (Fletcher), Best Director (Forman), Best Film, Best Supporting Actor (Dourif); Directors Guild of America Awards '75: Best Director (Forman); Golden Globe Awards '76: Best Actor—Drama (Nich-

olson) Best Actress—Drama (Fletcher), Best Director (Forman), Best Film—Drama, Best Screenplay; National Board of Review Awards '75: Best Actor (Nicholson), National Film Registry '93;; New York Film Critics Awards '75: Best Actor (Nicholson); National Society of Film Critics Awards '75: Best Actor (Nicholson); Writers Guild of America '75: Best Adapted Screenplay; Nominations: Academy Awards '75: Best Cinematography, Best Film Editing, Best Supporting Actor (Dourif), Best Original Score. *REP, BTV, FCT*

One Frightened Night ♪♪½ **1935** An eccentric millionaire informs his family members that he is leaving each of them one million dollars...as long as his long-lost granddaughter doesn't reappear. Guess who comes to dinner. **69m/B VHS, Beta.** Mary Carlisle, Wallace Ford, Hedda Hopper, Charley Grapewin; **D:** Christy Cabanne. *NOS, BAR, VYY*

One from the Heart ♪♪ **1982 (R)** The film more notable for sinking Coppola's Zoetrope Studios than for its cinematic context. Garr and Forrest are a jaded couple who seek romantic excitement with other people. An extravagant (thus Coppola's finance problems) fantasy Las Vegas set, pretty to look at but does little to enhance the weak plot. Score by Waits, a much-needed plus. **100m/C VHS, Beta, LV.** Teri Garr, Frederic Forrest, Nastassia Kinski, Raul Julia, Lainie Kazan, Rebecca DeMornay, Harry Dean Stanton; **D:** Francis Ford Coppola; **W:** Armyan Bernstein, Francis Ford Coppola; **M:** Tom Waits, Robert Alcivar. Nominations: Academy Awards '82: Original Song Score and/or Adaptation. *COL*

One Good Cop ♪♪½ **1991 (R)** A noble, inconsistent attempt to do a police thriller with a human face, as a young officer and his wife adopt the three little daughters of his slain partner from the force. But it reverts to a routine action wrapup, with 'Batman' Keaton even donning a masked-avenger getup to get revenge. **CW:** Language and violence and drug content. **105m/C VHS, Beta, LV, Closed Caption.** Michael Keaton, Rene Russo, Anthony LaPaglia, Kevin Conway, Rachel Ticotin, Grace Johnston, Blair Swanson, Rhea Silver-Smith, Tony Plana, Benjamin Bratt, Charlaine Woodard; **D:** Heywood Gould; **W:** Heywood Gould; **C:** Ralf Bode; **M:** William Ross. *HPH*

One Good Turn ♪♪ **1995 (R)** Matt Forrest (Von Dohlen) and his wife Laura (Amis) seemingly have it all only to have their fortunes take a radical turn for the worse. Matt "accidentally" runs into Simon Jury (Remar), the man who saved his life 12 years before. But the seemingly friendly Jury is actually intent on destroying everything they have. **CW:** Some strong sexuality and violence. **90m/C VHS, Closed Caption.** Lenny Von Dohlen, James Remar, Suzy Amis, John Savage; **D:** Tony Randel; **W:** Jim Piddock; **C:** Jacques Haitkin; **M:** Joel Goldsmith. *BMG*

100 Men and a Girl ♪♪♪ **1937** Charming musical features Durbin as the daughter of an unemployed musician, who decides she will try to persuade Leopold Stokowski to help her launch an orchestra that will employ her father and his musician friends. Beautiful mix of classical and pop music. Based on a story by Hans Kraly. ♪Hungarian Rhapsody No. 2; Symphony No. 5; Alleluja; It's Raining Sunbeams; A Heart That's Free. **85m/B VHS.** Deanna Durbin, Leopold Stokowski, Adolphe Menjou, Alice Brady, Eugene Pallette, Mischa Auer, Billy Gilbert, Alma Kruger, Christian Rub, Jed Prouty, Jack Mulhall; **D:** Henry Koster; **C:** Joseph Valentine. Academy Awards '37: Best Score; Nominations: Academy Awards '37: Best Film Editing, Best Picture, Best Sound, Best Story. *USH*

100 Rifles ♪♪ **1969 (R)** Native American bank robber and Black American lawman join up with a female Mexican revolutionary to help save the Mexican Indians from annihilation by a despotic military governor. What it lacks in political correctness it makes up for in fits of action. Although quite racy in its day for its interracial sex sizzle of Brown and Rachel, it's tame and overblown by today's standards. **110m/C VHS, Beta.** Jim Brown, Raquel Welch, Burt Reynolds, Fernando Lamas; **D:** Tom Gries; **M:** Jerry Goldsmith. *FOX*

101 Dalmatians 🎬🎬🎬½ 1961 (G) Disney classic is one of the highest-grossing animated films in the history of Hollywood. Dogowners Roger and Anita, and their spotted pets Pongo and Perdita are shocked when their puppies are kidnapped by Cruella de Vil, villainess extraordinaire, to make a simply fabulous spotted coat. The aid of various animals including a dog named Colonel, a horse, a cat, and a goose is enlisted to rescue the doomed pups. Imagine their surprise when they find not only their own puppies, but 84 more as well. You can expect a happy ending and lots of spots—6,469,952 to be exact. Based on the children's book by Dodie Smith. Technically notable for the first time use of the Xerox process to transfer the animator's drawings onto celluloid, which made the film's opening sequence of dots evolving into 101 barking dogs possible. ♫Remember When; Cruella de Vil; Dalmation Plantation; Kanine Krunchies Kommercial. **79m/C VHS, Beta. D:** Clyde Geronimi, Wolfgang Reitherman, Hamilton Luske; **M:** George Bruns; **V:** Rod Taylor, Betty Lou Gerson, Lisa Davis, Ben Wright, Frederick Worlock, J. Pat O'Malley. *DIS, OM*

101 Dalmatians 🎬🎬½ 1996 (G) Yes, it's the live-action Disney version of their own 1961 animated film (based on the book by Dodie Smith) about dog-napping villainess Cruella De Vil (Close) and lots of spotted pups. They're absolutely adorable, of course, Cruella's costumes (and hair) are certainly eye-catching, and the bumbling crooks get their proper comeuppance. Daniels and Richardson have the thankless role of the dogs' human owners, Roger and Anita, and get upstaged at every opportunity. Kids familiar with the cartoon pups may be surprised that the live pups don't talk—and keep in mind that Close, while terrific, may be too scary for the little ones. The Hound is always happy to see another dog movie but still feels some classics should be left alone. **103m/C VHS, Closed Caption.** Glenn Close, Jeff Daniels, Joely Richardson, Joan Plowright, Hugh Laurie, Mark Williams; **D:** Stephen Herek; **W:** John Hughes; **C:** Adrian Biddle; **M:** Michael Kamen. Nominations: Golden Globe Awards '97: Best Actress—Musical/Comedy (Close). *TOU*

125 Rooms of Comfort 🎬🎬 1983 A mental patient has bizarre fantasies that create havoc among those who stand in his way. **82m/C VHS, Beta.** Tim Henry, Jackie Burroughs, Bob Warner, Bob Silverman, Les Barker; **D:** Patrick Loubert; **W:** Patrick Loubert, Bill Freut. *TWE*

One in a Million 🎬🎬🎬 1936 Debut film of Norwegian skating star Henie centers around a Swiss girl whose father is training her for the Olympics. Features good comedy by the Ritz Brothers and Sparks, as well as the beautiful skating of Henie. ♫One in a Million; We're Back in Circulation Again; Who's Afraid of Love; Lovely Lady in White; The Moonlight Waltz. **95m/B VHS.** Sonja Henie, Adolphe Menjou, Jean Hersholt, The Ritz Brothers, Arline Judge, Don Ameche, Ned Sparks, Montagu Love, Leah Ray; **D:** Sidney Lanfield; **W:** Leonard Praskins, Mark Kelly. *FXV*

One in a Million: The Ron LeFlore Story 🎬🎬½ 1978 The true story of Detroit Tigers' star Ron LeFlore, who rose from the Detroit ghetto to the major leagues. Adaptation of LeFlore's autobiography, "Breakout." A well-acted and compelling drama with Burton in a standout performance. **95m/C VHS, Beta.** LeVar Burton, Madge Sinclair, Billy Martin, James Luisi; **D:** William A. Graham; **C:** Jordan Cronenweth. *NO*

One Last Run 🎬½ 1989 It's drama on the slopes as a variety of individuals confront their pasts/fears/personal demons via extreme skiing. Features the performances of champion skiers Franz Weber and Scot Schmidt. **82m/C VHS, Beta.** Russell Todd, Ashley Laurence, Craig Branham, Jimmy Aleck, Tracy Scoggins, Nels Van Patten, Chuck Connors; **D:** Peter Winograd, Glenn Gebhard; **W:** Peter Winograd, Glenn Gebhard.

One Little Indian 🎬🎬 1973 An AWOL cavalry man and his Indian ward team up with a widow and her daughter in an attempt to cross the New Mexican desert. A tepid presentation from the usually high quality Disney studio. **90m/C VHS, Beta.** James Garner, Vera Miles, Jodie Foster, Clay O'Brien, Andrew Prine, Bernard McEveety; **D:** Bernard McEveety; **M:** Jerry Goldsmith. *DIS*

One Magic Christmas 🎬🎬½ 1985 (G) Disney feel-good film about a disillusioned working woman whose faith in Christmas is restored when her guardian angel descends to Earth and performs various miracles. Somewhat cliched and tiresome, but partially redeemed by Stanton and Steenburgen's presence. **88m/C VHS, Beta, LV, Closed Caption.** Mary Steenburgen, Harry Dean Stanton, Gary Basaraba, Michelle Meyrink, Arthur Hill, Elisabeth Harnois, Robbie Magwood; **D:** Phillip Borsos; **W:** Thomas Meehan; **M:** Michael Conway Baker. *DIS*

One Man Army 🎬½ 1993 (R) Kickboxer goes to visit gramps in small town, only to discover the old guy has been murdered and corruption and cover-ups abound. So he decides to kick some butt and set things right. **95m/C VHS.** Jerry Trimble; **D:** Cirio H. Santiago. *NHO*

One Man Force 🎬🎬 1989 (R) L.A. narcotics cop Jake Swan goes on a vigilante spree. Huge in body and vengeful in spirit, he makes his partner's murderers pay! **92m/C VHS, Beta, LV.** John Matuszak, Ronny Cox, Charles Napier, Sharon Farrell, Sam Jones, Chance Boyer, Richard Lynch, Stacey Q; **D:** Dale Trevillion; **W:** Dale Trevillion; **M:** Charles Fox.

One Man Jury 🎬 1978 (R) LAPD lieutenant, wearied by an ineffective justice system, becomes a one-man vigilante avenger. Pale Dirty Harry rip-off with over acting and an overdose of violence. **95m/C VHS, Beta.** Jack Palance, Chris Mitchum, Joe Spinell, Pamela Shoop; **D:** Charles Martin. *VCI*

One Man Out 🎬🎬 1989 (R) An ex-CIA agent diverts his psychological problems into his new job: assassin for a South American despot. His jaded view of life changes when he meets and falls in love with an American journalist. Trouble in paradise when he is ordered to kill her. One man out was not enough, they should have done away with the entire crew of this stinker. **90m/C VHS, Beta, LV.** Stephen McHattie, Deborah Van Valkenburgh, Aharon Ipale, Ismael Carlo, Michael Champion, Dennis A. Pratt; **D:** Michael Kennedy. *COL*

One Man's Justice 🎬🎬½ 1995 (R) Army drill sergeant John North (Bosworth) heads for the streets of Venice, California to get the drug-dealing, gun-running scum who killed his wife and daughter. And a streetwise 10-year-old may be his best chance for finding them. **100m/C VHS, LV, Closed Caption.** Brian Bosworth, Bruce Payne, Jeff Kober, DeJuan Guy, Hammer; **D:** Kurt Wimmer; **W:** Steven Selling; **M:** Anthony Marinelli. *ART*

One Man's War 🎬🎬 1990 (PG-13) A human-rights crusader in repressive Paraguay won't be silenced, even after government thugs torture and murder his son. He fights obsessively to bring the killers to justice. The true story of the Joel Filartiga family is heartfelt but ultimately a dramatic letdown; an epilogue proves that full story hasn't been told. **91m/C VHS, Closed Caption.** Anthony Hopkins, Norma Aleandro, Fernanda Torres, Ruben Blades; **D:** Sergio Toledo. *HBO*

One Man's Way 🎬🎬½ 1963 Murray is appropriately devout as charasmatic religious leader Norman Vincent Peale. With the support of his wife (Hyland), he survives the adulations and accusations of blasphemy for his rather unorthodox theological ideas and his book, "The Power of Positive Thinking." Based on the book "Norman Vincent Peale: Minister to Millions" by Arthur Gordon. **105m/B VHS, Beta.** Don Murray, Diana Hyland, William Windom, Virginia Christine, Carol Ohmart, Veronica Cartwright, Liam Sullivan, June Dayton, Ian Wolfe; **D:** Denis Sanders; **W:** Eleanore Griffin, John W. Bloch. *MGM, FCT, BTV*

One Million B.C. 🎬🎬½ *The Cave Dwellers; Cave Man; Man and His Mate* 1940 The strange saga of the struggle of primitive cavemen and their battle against dinosaurs and other monsters. Curiously told in flashbacks, this film provided stock footage for countless dinosaur movies that followed. Portions of film rumored to be directed by cinematic pioneer D. W. Griffith. **80m/B VHS, Beta.** Victor Mature, Carole Landis, Lon Chaney Jr.; **D:** Hal Roach, Hal Roach Jr. Nominations: Academy Awards '40: Best Original Score. *RXM*

One Million Years B.C. 🎬🎬½ 1966 (R) It's Welch in a fur bikini and special FX expert Ray Harryhausen doing dinosaurs so who cares about a plot (which involves Welch and her boyfriend, who's from a rival clan). Remake of the 1940 film "One Million B.C." **100m/C VHS, Closed Caption.** *GB* Raquel Welch, John Richardson, Percy Herbert, Robert Brown, Martine Beswick; **D:** Don Chaffey. *FXV*

One Minute Before Death 🎬 1988 A woman is buried in a catatonic state, and returns from the grave to exact retribution. Supposedly based loosely on Poe. **87m/C VHS, Beta.** Giselle MacKenzie. *NO*

One Minute to Zero 🎬🎬 1952 Korean War action film divides its time between an army romance and war action. The lukwarm melodrama features Mitchum as a colonel in charge of evacuating American civilians but who ends up bombing refugees. **105m/B VHS, Beta.** Robert Mitchum, Ann Blyth, William Talman, Charles McGraw, Margaret Sheridan, Richard Egan, Eduard Franz, Robert Osterloh, Robert Gist; **D:** Tay Garnett. *TTC*

One More Chance 🎬½ 1990 While he was in jail, an ex-con's family moves away without leaving a forwarding address. When he's released he strikes up a friendship with a woman from the neighborhood who knows where they've gone. **102m/C VHS, Beta.** Kirstie Alley, John Lamotta, Logan Clarke, Michael Pataki, Hector Maisonette; **D:** Sam Firstenberg. *WAR, OM*

One More Saturday Night 🎬 1986 (R) Franken and Davis, "Saturday Night Live" alumni, wrote this film about a small town going wild on the weekend. Dry, taxing, and unfunny. Averages about one laugh per half hour—at one-and-a-half hours, that's way too long. **96m/C VHS, Beta, LV, Closed Caption.** Al Franken, Tom Davis, Nan Woods, Dave Reynolds; **D:** Dennis Klein; **W:** Al Franken, Tom Davis. *NO*

One Night in the Tropics 🎬🎬½ 1940 The film debut of radio stars Abbott & Costello who play secondary roles to a love triangle (set to music). Jones is an insurance salesman who falls in love with Kelly, the fiance of Cummings. Based on the novel "Love Insurance" by Earl Derr Biggers. ♫Back in My Shell; Remind Me; You and Your Kiss; Your Dream is the Same as My Dream. **83m/B VHS, Beta.** Allan Jones, Robert Cummings, Nancy Kelly, Bud Abbott, Lou Costello, Mary Boland, Peggy Moran, William Frawley, Leo Carrillo; **D:** Edward Sutherland; **W:** Kathryn Scola, Gertrude Purcell, Charles Grayson, Francis Martin. *USH, FCT*

One Night of Love 🎬🎬🎬½ 1934 Moore's best quasi-operetta, about a young American diva rebelling in response to her demanding Italian teacher. "Pygmallion"-like story has her falling in love with her maestro. Despite being nearly 60 years old, this film is still enchanting and fresh. ♫One Night of Love; Ciri-Biri-Bin; Sempre Libera; Sextet; Indian Love Call; 'Tis the Last Rose of Summer; Habanera; Un bel di; None But the Lonely Heart. **95m/B VHS, Beta, LV.** Grace Moore, Tullio Carminati, Lyle Talbot, Jane Darwell, Nydia Westman, Mona Barrie, Jessie Ralph, Luis Alberni; **D:** Victor Schertzinger. Academy Awards '34: Best Sound, Best Score; Nominations: Academy Awards '34: Best Actress (Moore), Best Director (Schertzinger), Best Film Editing, Best Picture. *COL*

One Night Only 1984 A gorgeous law student decides to make big money by hiring herself and her friends out as hookers to the school football team. 87m/C VHS, Beta. Lenore Zann, Jeff Braunstein, Grant Alianak; D: Timothy Bond. FOX

One Night Stand 1977 Woman's chance encounter with a man in a singles bar leads to an evening of unexpected terror. Adapted from a play for Canadian television. Billed as a horror flick, it is really more of a drama. 90m/C VHS, Beta. CA Chapelle Jaffe, Brent Carver. TWE

One Night Stand 🎬🎬🎬 1984 Four young people attempt to amuse themselves at the empty Sydney Opera House on the New Year's Eve, that night WWIII begins. An odd commentary on nuclear war that sees the bomb as the ultimate bad joke. Features an appearance by alternative rock group Midnight Oil. 94m/C VHS, Beta. Tyler Coppin, Cassandra Delaney, Jay Hackett, Saskia Post; D: John Duigan.

One Night Stand 🎬🎬½ 1995 (R) Lonely Michelle (Sheedy) visits a nightclub and allows herself to be picked up by your basic handsome stranger, Jack (Martinez) in this case. She wakes up alone and learns from building owner Josslyn (Forrest) that the apartment is up for lease. Obsessed with finding her mystery man, Michelle discovers Jack's wife was murdered—possibly by him or maybe by Josslyn, who turns out to be the dead woman's father. Debut feature for director Shire covers familiar territory, with Sheedy giving a strong performance.*CW:* Nudity, language, violence, sexual situations. 92m/C VHS. Ally Sheedy, A. Martinez, Frederic Forrest, Don Novello, Diane Salinger, Millie Slavin; D: Talia Shire; W: Marty Casella; C: Arthur Albert; M: David Shire. NHO

One Night Stand 🎬🎬🎬 1997 (R) Max (Snipes) is a commercial director in New York on business. While visiting his friend Charlie (Downey), a choreographer dying of AIDS, he meets willowy beauty Karen (Kinski). This chance meeting leads to, you guessed it, a one night stand. When Max returns home to L.A., he realizes how empty and stale his life is. One year later, he and wife Mimi (Wen) return to visit the quickly fading Charlie. They meet Charlie's brother Vernon (McLachlan) and his wife...Karen. Good performances (especially by Downey) and characterization make this more than a morality play about the ramifications of a sexual fling. Although paid for his original material, Joe Eszterhas didn't take any writing credit after Figgis totally rewrote the script. 103m/C VHS, LV, Closed Caption, DVD. Wesley Snipes, Nastassia Kinski, Ming-Na Wen, Robert Downey Jr., Kyle MacLachlan, Glenn Plummer, Amanda Donohoe, Thomas Haden Church, Julian Sands, John Ratzenberger, Annabelle Gurwitch, Donovan Leitch, Ione Skye, Xander Berkeley, Zoe Nathenson, Vincent Ward, Susan Barnes; *Cameos:* Mike Figgis; D: Mike Figgis; W: Mike Figgis; C: Declan Quinn; M: Mike Figgis. WAR

1-900 🎬🎬 1994 Based on the play "06" by Doesburg, which refers to the Dutch exchange for phone-sex numbers. Sarah (Schluter) and Thomas (van Kempen) are both lonely professionals who "meet" when Thomas answers Sarah's personal ad. Their weekly phone chats lead to descriptions of sexual fantasies but relationship issues begin to intrude as time passes. Dutch with subtitles. 80m/C VHS. NL Ariane Schluter, Ad van Kempen; D: Theo van Gogh; W: Ariane Schluter, Ad van Kempen, Johan Doesburg, Marcel Otten; C: Tom Erisman; M: Ruud Bos. FXL

One of My Wives Is Missing 🎬🎬½ 1976 An ex-New York cop tries to solve the mysterious disappearance of a newlywed socialite. Things become strange when she reappears but is discovered as an imposter. Above average acting in a film adapted from the play, "The Trap for a Lonely Man." 97m/C VHS, Beta. Jack Klugman, Elizabeth Ashley, James Franciscus; D: Glenn Jordan. ORI

One of Our Aircraft Is Missing 🎬🎬½ 1941 The crew of an R.A.F. bomber downed in the Netherlands, struggle to escape Nazi capture. A thoughtful study of wars and the men who fight them, with an entertaining melodramatic plot. Look for the British version, which runs 106 minutes. Some of the American prints only run 82 minutes. 103m/B VHS. GB Godfrey Tearle, Eric Portman, Hugh Williams, Pamela Brown, Googie Withers, Peter Ustinov; D: Emeric Pressburger, Michael Powell. Nominations: Academy Awards '42: Best Original Screenplay. NOS, MRV, REP

One of Our Dinosaurs Is Missing 🎬🎬 1975 (G) An English nanny and her cohorts help British Intelligence retrieve a microfilm—concealing dinosaur fossil from the bad guys that have stolen it. Disney film was shot on location in England. 101m/C VHS, Beta. Peter Ustinov, Helen Hayes, Derek Nimmo, Clive Revill, Robert Stevenson, Joan Sims; D: Robert Stevenson. DIS

One on One 🎬🎬½ 1977 (PG) A Rocky-esque story about a high school basketball star from the country who accepts an athletic scholarship to a big city university. He encounters a demanding coach and intense competition. Light weight drama that is economically entertaining. 100m/C VHS, Beta. Robby Benson, Annette O'Toole, G.D. Spradlin, Gail Strickland, Melanie Griffith; D: Lamont Johnson; W: Robby Benson; M: Charles Fox. WAR

One Plus One 🎬 *Exploring the Kinsey Report* 1961 A dramatization, believe it or not, of the Kinsey sex survey of the 1950s. Participants in a sex lecture talk about and demonstrate various "risque" practices, such as premarital sex and extramarital affairs. Despite this film, the sexual revolution went on as planned. 114m/B VHS, Beta. CA Leo G. Carroll, Hilda Brawner, William Traylor, Kate Reid, Ernest Graves; D: Arch Oboler; W: Arch Oboler. SNC

One-Punch O'Day 🎬 1926 Boxing boy tries to buy back hometown's oil livelihood by winning prizefight. Much patient waiting by his honey. 60m/B VHS, Beta. Billy Sullivan, Jack Herrick, Charlotte Merriam; D: Harry Joe Brown. GPV, FCT, GVV

One Rainy Afternoon 🎬🎬 1936 A bit-player kisses the wrong girl in a Paris theatre causing a massive uproar that brands him as a notorious romantic "monster." Patterned after a German film, the story lacks depth and zest. 80m/B VHS, Beta. Francis Lederer, Ida Lupino, Hugh Herbert, Roland Young, Donald Meek; D: Rowland V. Lee. NOS, MRV, VYY

One Russian Summer woof! 1973 (R) During the Russian Revolution, a cripple seeks revenge on the corrupt land baron who murdered his parents. An unfortunate attempt to dramatize a novel by M. Lermontov. 112m/C VHS, Beta. Oliver Reed, Claudia Cardinale, John McEnery, Carole Andre, Ray Lovelock; D: Antonio Calenda. VCI

One Shoe Makes It Murder 🎬🎬 1982 A shady casino owner hires ex-cop Mitchum to investigate the disappearance of his unfaithful wife. Adapted from Eric Bercovici's novel, the story does little to enhance Mitchum's TV debut. 100m/C VHS, Beta. Robert Mitchum, Angie Dickinson, Mel Ferrer, Howard Hesseman, Jose Perez; D: William Hale; M: Bruce Broughton. ART

One Sings, the Other Doesn't 🎬🎬½ *L'Une Chante, L'Autre Pas* 1977 Seeking contentment, a conservative widow and a liberal extrovert help each other cope in a man's world. Endearing characters, but a superficial treatment of dated feminist issues. In French with English subtitles. 105m/C VHS, Beta. FR BE Valerie Mairesse, Therese Liotard, Robert Dadies, Ali Affi, Jean-Pierre Pellegrin, Francois Wertheimer; D: Agnes Varda; W: Agnes Varda; C: Charlie Van Damme; M: Francois Wertheimer. COL

One Step Beyond 1959 This creepy anthology series featured stories of the occult and supernatural which were supposedly based on true incidents. Two episodes per tape. Includes "Message from Clara" starring Barbara Baxley

and Robert Ellenstein and "The Sorcerer" with Christopher Lee and Martin Benson. 60m/B VHS. D: John Newland. MOV, HEG

One Step to Hell 🎬½ *Caccia Ai Violenti; King of Africa* 1968 Good cop rescues gold-miner's widow from three escaped convicts. Beautiful African scenery helps save an otherwise mediocre film. 90m/C VHS, Beta. Ty Hardin, Rossano Brazzi, Pier Angeli, George Sanders, Tab Hunter, Sandy Howard. NO

One Summer Love 🎬½ *Dragonfly* 1976 Man checks out from loony bin, searches for family ties and befriends beautiful woman who works in a moviehouse. 95m/C VHS. Beau Bridges, Susan Sarandon, Mildred Dunnock, Ann Wedgeworth, Michael B. Miller, Linda Miller, James Noble, Frederick Coffin; D: Gilbert Cates; W: N. Richard Nash. HBO

One That Got Away 🎬🎬🎬 1957 A loyal German Luftwaffe pilot captured by the British becomes obsessed with escape. Fast paced and exciting. Based on a true story. 111m/B VHS, Beta. Hardy Kruger, Colin Gordon, Alec Gordon; D: Roy Ward Baker. NO

One Third of a Nation 🎬🎬½ 1939 Depression era film contrasts the conditions of slum life with those in high society. A young entrepreneur inherits a city block in ruins, only to fall in love with a young woman who lives there and help her crippled brother. Timely social criticism. 79m/B VHS. Sylvia Sidney, Leif Erickson, Myron McCormick, Sidney Lumet; D: Dudley Murphy. NOS, PAR, MLB

1001 Arabian Nights 🎬🎬½ 1959 In this Arabian nightmare, the nearsighted Mr. Magoo is known as "Azziz" Magoo, lamp dealer and uncle of Aladdin. 76m/C VHS, Beta. D: Jack Kinney; M: George Duning; V: Jim Backus, Kathryn Grant, Hans Conried, Herschel Bernardi. COL

One Too Many 🎬 *The Important Story of Alcoholism; Killer With a Label* 1951 Exploitation film depicting the evils of alcoholism. Campy, but slick. ?m/C VHS. Ruth Warrick, Richard Travis, Victor Kilian, Onslow Stevens, Lyle Talbot. SNC

One Touch of Venus 🎬🎬½ 1948 Love fills a department store when a window dresser kisses a statue of the goddess Venus—and she comes to life. Appealing adaptation of the Broadway musical. 🎵Speak Low; The Trouble with Women; That's Him; Don't Look Now But My Heart Is Showing; My Week. 82m/B VHS. Ava Gardner, Robert Walker, Eve Arden, Dick Haymes, Olga San Juan, Tom Conway; D: William A. Seiter; M: Kurt Weill, Ogden Nash. REP, MLB

One Trick Pony 🎬🎬½ 1980 (R) Once-popular rock singer/songwriter struggles to keep his head above water in a turbulent marriage and in the changing currents of popular taste. Simon wrote the autobiographical screenplay and score, but let's hope he is more sincere in real life. A good story. 100m/C VHS, Beta. Paul Simon, Blair Brown, Rip Torn, Joan Hackett, Mare Winningham, Lou Reed, Harry Shearer, Allen (Goorwitz) Garfield, Daniel Stern; D: Robert M. Young. WAR

One, Two, Three 🎬🎬🎬½ 1961 Cagney, an American Coca-Cola exec in Germany, zealously pursues any opportunity to run Coke's European operations. He does the job too well and loses his job to a Communist hippie turned slick capitalist. Fast-paced laughs, wonderful cinematography, and a fine score. 110m/B VHS, Beta, LV, Letterbox. James Cagney, Horst Buchholz, Arlene Francis, Pamela Tiffin; D: Billy Wilder; W: Billy Wilder, I.A.L. Diamond; C: Daniel F. Fapp; M: Andre Previn. Nominations: Academy Awards '61: Best Black and White Cinematography. MGM

One Way Out 🎬🎬 1995 Frank (Gwaltney) gets out of jail, teams up with Bobby (Monahan) and his stripper girlfriend Eve (Golden), and the trio go to visit Frank's brother, Snooky (Turano). When Frank learns that Snooky's lowlife boss (Ironside) has been ripping him off, they plan to even the score. Naturally, the heist goes wrong and they wind up with a hostage (Gillies) on the lam. 106m/C VHS. Jack Gwaltney, Jeff Monahan, Annie Golden, Robert Turano, Michael Ironside, Isabel Gillies; **D:** Kevin Lynn. *AVI*

One Wild Moment 🐾🐾½ 1978 (R) Comic

complications arise when a divorced man is seduced by his best friend's daughter while vacationing. Warm and charming. Later re-made as "Blame It on Rio." In French with English subtitles. **88m/C VHS, Beta.** *FR* Jean-Pierre Marielle, Victor Lanoux, Agnes Soral, Christine Dejoux, Martine Sarcey; **D:** Claude Berri; **W:** Claude Berri. *COL*

One Wish Too Many 🐾🐾½ 1955 A

young boy finds a marble that grants wishes. He has the time of his life with his teachers and the school bullies, but runs into trouble when he creates a giant steam roller which overruns London. Winner of Best Children's Film, 1956 Venice Film Festival, but it is hard to say why. **55m/B VHS, Beta.** *GB* Anthony Richmond, Rosalind Gourgey, John Pike; **D:** John Durst. *SNC*

One Woman or Two 🐾🐾½ *Une Femme*

ou Deux 1985 (PG-13) Paleontologist Depardieu is duped by beautiful ad-exec who plans to use his findings to push perfume. Remake of "Bringing Up Baby," this screwball comedy has a few screws loose. Dubbed. **100m/C VHS, Beta.** *FR* Gerard Depardieu, Sigourney Weaver, Dr. Ruth Westheimer, Michel Aumont, Zabou; **D:** Daniel Vigne; **W:** Elisabeth Rappeneau, Daniel Vigne. *ART, VES, TPV*

Onibaba 🐾🐾🐾 *The Demon; The Devil Woman*

1964 A brutal parable about a mother and her daughter-in-law in war-ravaged medieval Japan who subsist by murdering stray soldiers and selling their armor. One soldier beds the daughter, setting the mother-in-law on a vengeful tirade. Review of the film varied widely, hailed by some as a masterpiece and by others as below average; in Japanese with subtitles. **103m/B VHS, Beta.** *JP* Nobuko Otowa, Yitsuko Yoshimura, Kei Sato; **D:** Kaneto Shindo. *HMV, CVC, TPV*

The Onion Field 🐾🐾🐾½ 1979 (R) True

story about the mental breakdown of an ex-cop who witnessed his partner's murder. Haunted by the slow process of justice and his own feelings of insecurity, he is unable to get his life together. Based on the novel by Joseph Wambaugh, who also wrote the screenplay. Compelling script and excellent acting. **126m/C VHS, Beta, LV.** John Savage, James Woods, Ronny Cox, Franklyn Seales, Ted Danson; **D:** Harold Becker. *NLC*

Only Angels Have Wings 🐾🐾🐾🐾

1939 Melodramatic adventure about a broken-down Peruvian air mail service. Large cast adds to the love tension between Grant, a pilot, and Arthur, a showgirl at the saloon. Nominated for special effects, a category recognized by the academy that year for the first time. William Rankin and Eleanor Griffin are uncredited writers. **121m/B VHS, Beta.** Cary Grant, Thomas Mitchell, Richard Barthelmess, Jean Arthur, Noah Beery Jr., Rita Hayworth, Sig Rumann, John Carroll, Allyn Joslyn; **D:** Howard Hawks; **W:** Jules Furthman; **M:** Dimitri Tiomkin. Nominations: Academy Awards '39: Best Black and White Cinematography, Best Special Effects. *COL*

Only Once in a Lifetime 🐾 1983 A

love story about an Hispanic immigrant painter looking for success in America. **90m/C VHS, Beta.** Miguel Robelo, Estrellita Lopez, Sheree North. *VHE, MOV*

Only One Night 🐾🐾 *En Enda Natt* 1942

Upon finding out that he's the illegitimate son of an aristocrat, a happy-go-lucky carousel operator in a circus joins high society and is promptly matched with a beautiful but repressed woman. In Swedish with English subtitles. **87m/B VHS, Beta, LV.** *SW* Ingrid Bergman, Edvin Adolphson, Aino Taube, Olof Sandborg, Erik Berglund, Marianne Lofgren, Magnus Kester; **D:** Gustaf Molander. *WAC, LUM*

Only the Brave 🐾🐾 1994 Gay coming-of-

age story about two teenaged, working-class girls living on the seedy fringes of Melbourne. Alex (Manadalis) has wild best friend Vicki (Kaskanis), and their equally tough girlfriends seem to spend most of their time hanging out, smoking dope, and

getting into trouble. But Alex slowly recognizes her feelings for Vicki are also sexual, and their friendship drastically changes. **62m/C VHS.** *AU* Elena Mandalis, Dora Kaskanis, Moudo Davey, Bob Bright; **D:** Ana Kokkinos; **W:** Ana Kokkinos, Mira Robertson. *FRF*

Only the Lonely 🐾🐾½ 1991 (PG) Middle-

aged cop, Candy, falls in love with a shy undertaker's assistant, Sheedy, and is torn between love and dear old Mom, O'Hara, in her first role in years. Candy is an unlikely leading man and even the jokes are forced. But the restaurant scene makes the whole thing well worth seeing. **104m/C VHS, Beta, LV, Letterbox.** John Candy, Ally Sheedy, Maureen O'Hara, Anthony Quinn, Kevin Dunn, James Belushi, Milo O'Shea, Bert Remsen, Macaulay Culkin, Joe V. Greco; **D:** Chris Columbus; **W:** Chris Columbus; **M:** Maurice Jarre. *WAR, OM*

Only the Strong 🐾½ 1993 (PG-13) Louis

(Dacascos) is a special forces officer who has mastered capoeira, a Brazilian form of kung fu. In Miami, he works with his old teacher (Lewis) to instill discipline in the 12 toughest punks in school by teaching them his martial arts skills. A neighborhood drug lord, related to two of the students, decides to cause trouble for Louis. Dacascos displays some charm along with his physical abilities but the story's ridiculous and the movie hastily put together. **CW:** Gang violence. **96m/C VHS, LV, Closed Caption.** Mark Dacascos, Stacy Travis, Todd Susman, Geoffrey Lewis, Paco Christian Prieto; **D:** Sheldon Lettich; **W:** Sheldon Lettich, Luis Esteban; **M:** Harvey W. Mason. *FOX*

Only the Valiant 🐾🐾 1950 Action-

packed story of a cavalry officer who struggles to win his troops respect while warding off angry Apaches. Fast-paced Western fun requires little thought. **105m/B VHS, LV.** Gregory Peck, Ward Bond, Gig Young, Lon Chaney Jr., Barbara Payton, Neville Brand; **D:** Gordon Douglas; **C:** Lionel Lindon. *REP*

Only Two Can Play 🐾🐾🐾 1962 Sellers

is a hilarious Casanova librarian who puts the moves on a society lady to get a promotion. Funny, of course, and based on Kingsley Amis' novel "That Uncertain Feeling." **106m/C VHS, Beta.** *GB* Peter Sellers, Virginia Maskell, Mai Zetterling, Richard Attenborough; **D:** Sidney Gilliat; **M:** Richard Rodney Bennett. *COL*

The Only Way 🐾🐾½ 1970 (G) A semi-

documentary account of the plight of the Jews in Denmark during the Nazi occupation. Despite German insistence, the Danes succeeded in saving most of their Jewish population from the concentration camps. **86m/C VHS, Beta.** Jane Seymour, Martin Potter, Benjamin Christiansen; **M:** Carl Davis. *VCI*

The Only Way Home 🐾🐾 1972 (PG)

Two bikers end up in big trouble when one of them kills a wealthy man, and they kidnap his wife. Filmed entirely in Oklahoma. **86m/C VHS, Beta.** Bo Hopkins, Beth Brickell, Steve Sandor, G.D. Spradlin; **D:** G.D. Spradlin. *NO*

Only When I Laugh 🐾🐾🐾 *It Hurts Only*

When I Laugh 1981 (R) Neil Simon reworked his Broadway flop "The Gingerbread Lady" to produce this poignant comedy about the relationship between an aging alcoholic actress and her teenage daughters. **120m/C VHS, Beta, LV.** Marsha Mason, Kristy McNichol, James Coco, Joan Hackett, David Dukes, Kevin Bacon, John Bennett Perry; **D:** Glenn Jordan; **W:** Neil Simon; **M:** David Shire. Golden Globe Awards '82: Best Supporting Actress (Hackett); Nominations: Academy Awards '81: Best Actress (Mason), Best Supporting Actor (Coco), Best Supporting Actress (Hackett). *COL*

Only with Married Men 🐾 1974

Carne's hassle-free dating routine is disrupted when a sly bachelor pretends that he's married to get a date. A middle-aged persons answer to a teenage sex comedy. Pretty bad. **74m/C VHS, Beta.** David Birney, Judy Carne, Gavin MacLeod, John Astin; **D:** Jerry Paris. *ORI*

Only You 🐾½ 1992 (PG-13) A shy guy has

always searched for true romance. But his cup runneth over when he meets, and must choose between, two beautiful women—your basic beach babe and a sensible beauty. What's a guy to do? **85m/C VHS, Closed Caption.** Andrew McCarthy, Kelly Preston, Helen Hunt; **M:** Wendy Blackstone. *ART*

Only You 🐾🐾½ *Him; Just in Time* 1994 (PG)

According to her ouija board, young Faith's (Tomei) soul mate is named Damon Bradley. But as the years pass, Faith is about to settle for a podiatrist—until an old school friend of her fiance's calls from Venice, Italy, with best wishes. Guess what his name is. So Faith and best friend Kate (Hunt) hop on a plane in search of Mr. Right. Then Faith meets charming shoe salesman Peter Wright (Downey) and wonders if ouija got things wrong. Slight romantic comedy with Jewison creating satisfactory chemistry with charming Downey and the somewhat miscast Tomei (and the Venetian scenery is gorgeous). **108m/C VHS, LV, Closed Caption, DVD.** Marisa Tomei, Robert Downey Jr., Bonnie Hunt, Fisher Stevens, Billy Zane, Joaquim de Almeida; **D:** Norman Jewison; **W:** Diane Drake. *COL*

Open All Hours 🐾 1983 A British televi-

sion comedy about a small corner shop and its viciously greedy, opportunistic owner. **85m/C VHS, Beta.** *GB* Ronnie Barker, Lynda Baron, David Jason, Stephenie Cole. *FOX*

Open City 🐾🐾🐾🐾 *Roma, Citta Aperta; Rome,*

Open City 1945 A leader in the Italian underground resists Nazi control of the city. A stunning film, making Rossellini's realistic style famous. In Italian with English subtitles. **103m/B VHS, Beta.** *IT* Anna Magnani, Aldo Fabrizi, Marcel Pagliero, Maria Michi, Vito Annicchiarico, Nando Bruno, Harry Feist; **D:** Roberto Rossellini; **W:** Federico Fellini, Sergio Amidei. New York Film Critics Awards '46: Best Foreign Film; Nominations: Academy Awards '46: Best Screenplay. *VYY, NOS, DVT*

Open Doors 🐾🐾🐾½ *Porte Aperte* 1989 (R)

Bitter review of Fascist rule and justice. The Fascist regime promises security, safety, and tranquility. So, on the morning that a white collar criminal murders his former boss, murders the man who got his job, and then rapes and murders his wife, tensions rise and the societal structures are tested. The people rally for his death. A judge and a juror struggle to uphold justice rather than serve popular passions. Winner of four Donatello Awards, Italian Golden Globes for Best Film, Best Actor, and Best Screenplay, and many international film awards. In Italian with English subtitles. **109m/C VHS.** *IT* Gian Marie Volonte, Ennio Fantastichini, Lidia Alfonsi; **D:** Gianni Amelio; **W:** Gianni Amelio. Nominations: Academy Awards '90: Best Foreign Language Film. *ORI, FCT*

Open Fire 🐾🐾 1994 (R) Alex McNeil (Win-

cott) is an ex-FBI agent, haunted by the death of his partner. But when a group of terrorists threaten to release a cloud of nerve gas over L.A. and hold McNeil's father hostage, he comes back full force. **93m/C VHS, LV, Closed Caption.** Jeff Wincott, Patrick Kilpatrick, Lee DeBroux, Mimi Craven, Arthur Taxier. *REP*

Open House 🐾 1986 Radio psychologist

and beautiful real estate agent search for the killer of real estate agents and their clients. A mystery-thriller for the very patient. **95m/C VHS, Beta.** Joseph Bottoms, Adrienne Barbeau, Mary Stavin, Rudy Ramos; **D:** Jag Mundhra.

Open Season 🐾🐾 1995 (R) Stuart Sain

(Wuhl) is an ambitious executive at Fielding, a TV ratings company (think Nielsen) whose boxes turn out to be defective. The ratings error causes public television programming to be number one, forcing the networks to counter-program culturally in order to regain their market share. Meanwhile, the public TV executives get overconfident and everything's just up for grabs. Flawed satire. **CW:** Language and some sexuality. **97m/C VHS, Closed Caption.** Robert Wuhl, Rod Taylor, Gailard Sartain, Maggie Han, Joe Piscopo, Helen Shaver, Dina Merrill, Saul Rubinek, Steven C. White, Timothy Arrington, Barry Flatman,

Tom Selleck, Alan Thicke, Jimmie Walker; **D:** Robert Wuhl; **W:** Robert Wuhl; **C:** Stephen Lighthill; **M:** Marvin Hamlisch. *REP*

Open Secret 🎬🎬 **1948** Jewish residents are plagued by a gang of anti-semitic thugs. Violence and destruction escalate until a fed up police lieutenant, tenaciously played by Ireland, and a victimized shop owner (Tyne) join forces to just say no more. When the gang learns the shopkeeper has caught their dastardly deeds on camera, the battle begins in earnest. Fast-paced and intriguing suspense. **70m/B VHS, Beta.** John Ireland, Jane Randolph, Roman Bohnen, Sheldon Leonard, George Tyne, Morgan Farley, Ellen Lowe, Anne O'Neal, Arthur O'Connell; **D:** John Reinhardt. *SNC*

Opening Night 🎬🎬½ **1977 (PG-13)** Very long study about an actress (Rowlands) and the play she's about to open in on Broadway. Backstage turmoil increases her own insecurities and the bad luck persists when an adoring fan dies in an accident on opening night. Performances carry this neurotic epic along, including Cassavetes as Rowland's co-star and Blondell as the playwright. **144m/C VHS, Beta, Closed Caption.** Gena Rowlands, John Cassavetes, Joan Blondell, Ben Gazzara, Paul Stewart, Zohra Lampert, Laura Johnson; **D:** John Cassavetes; **W:** John Cassavetes; **C:** Frederick Elmes. *TOU, BTV*

Opera do Malandro **1987** A lavish Brazilian take off of "The Threepenny Opera." Married hustler falls for a beautiful entrepreneur longing to get rich off of American goods. Based on Chico Buarque's musical play. In Portuguese, with subtitles. **106m/C VHS, Beta, LV, Closed Caption.** BR Edson Celulari, Claudia Ohana, Elba Ramalho, Ney Latorraca; **D:** Ruy Guerra. *NO*

Operation Amsterdam 🎬🎬 **1960** Four agents have 14 hours to snare $10 million in diamonds from under the noses of local Nazis. Based on a true story. Full of 1940s wartime action and suspense. **103m/B VHS, Beta.** Peter Finch, Eva Bartok, Tony Britton, Alexander Knox; **D:** Michael McCarthy.

Operation C.I.A. 🎬🎬 *Last Message From Saigon* **1965** A plot to assassinate the U.S. ambassador in Saigon inspires brave CIA agent Reynolds to wipe out the bad guys. Action-packed and somewhat exciting. **90m/C VHS, Beta, Closed Caption.** Burt Reynolds, John Hayt, Kieu Chinh, Danielle Aubry; **D:** Christian Nyby. *FOX, DVT, HEG*

Operation Condor 🎬🎬 *Armor of God 2: Operation Condor* **1991 (PG-13)** Secret agent Jackie (Chan) is sent by the United Nations to retrieve 240 tons of gold buried by the Nazis in a Moroccan desert during WWII. Naturally, he's not the only one after the treasure. Lots of typically exuberant stunts and laughable dialogue (dubbed into English from Cantonese).**CW:** Martial arts action and some shootings, and for sensuality. **92m/C VHS, LV, Closed Caption.** Jackie Chan, Carol Cheng, Eva Cabo De Garcia, Ikeda Shoko; **D:** Jackie Chan; **W:** Edward Tang, Jackie Chan; **C:** Wong Ngok Tai; **M:** Stephen Endelman. *TOU*

Operation Cross Eagles 🎬🎬 *Unakrsna Vatra* **1969** Routine WWII military thriller with Conte and Calhoun on a mission to rescue an American general in exchange for their German prisoner. Their mission is complicated by a traitor in the group. Conte's only directorship. **90m/C VHS.** YU Richard Conte, Rory Calhoun, Aili King, Phil Brown; **D:** Richard Conte. *NO*

Operation Crossbow 🎬🎬🎬 *The Great Spy Mission; Code Name: Operation Crossbow* **1965** Action-packed espionage tale in which a trio of agents are assigned to destroy a Nazi munitions installation. Exciting ending and sensational pyrotechnics. **116m/C VHS, Closed Caption.** Sophia Loren, George Peppard, Trevor Howard, John Mills, Richard Johnson, Tom Courtenay, Jeremy Kemp, Anthony Quayle, Helmut Dantine; **D:** Michael Anderson Sr. *MGM*

Operation Dames 🎬½ **1959** A squadron of soldiers must go behind Korean enemy lines to locate a missing U.S.O. troupe and bring them to safety. Low budget and not very funny for a supposed comedy. **73m/B VHS.** Eve Meyer, Chuck Henderson, Don Devlin, Ed Craig, Cindy Girard; **D:** Louis Clyde Stouman. *COL*

Operation: Delta Force 🎬🎬 **1997 (R)** Nash (Lara) and his South African terrorist band have stolen two vials of the Ebola virus in order to provide some cleansing of the population. So the Delta Force, lead by Lang (Fahey), are flown into Mozambique to stop 'em. Macho guys and lots of firepower.**CW:** Pervasive combat violence and some language. **93m/C VHS, LV, Closed Caption.** Jeff Fahey, Ernie Hudson, Frank Zagarino, Joe Lara, Todd Jensen, Hal Holbrook; **D:** Sam Firstenberg; **W:** David Sparling; **C:** Yossi Wein; **M:** Serge Colbert. *ART*

Operation Dumbo Drop 🎬🎬½ *Dumbo Drop* **1995 (PG)** It's 1968 and tough Green Beret captain (Glover), rescued by Vietnamese villagers, promises to replace their prized elephant, which was killed during his mission. He and a group of commandos use land, sea, and air to transport the reluctant beast, learning way more about elephant hygiene and eating habits than they ever wanted to know in the process. Wincer, who also directed "Free Willy," seems to be going for the title of "greatest large mammal director of all time." Anything with good-guy U.S. troops, a paratrooper elephant, and a family-friendly plot should be a Bob Dole favorite. **107m/C VHS, LV, Closed Caption.** Danny Glover, Ray Liotta, Doug E. Doug, Denis Leary, Corin "Corky" Nemec, Thein Le Dihn; **D:** Simon Wincer; **W:** Jim Kouf, Gene Quintano; **C:** Russell Boyd; **M:** David Newman. *DIS*

Operation Golden Phoenix 🎬 **1994 (R)** A security specialist (Mehri) is betrayed in his assignment is to protect one half of a valuable medallion. Seems the medal reveals the location in Lebanon of a ancient mountain of gold—desired by a ruthless warlord (Hong). Martial arts fights are well done in this routine actioner.**CW:** Graphic shootings, martial arts violence; some language. **95m/C VHS, LV, Closed Caption.** Jalal Merhi, James Hong, Al Waxman, Loren Avedon; **D:** Jalal Merhi. *USH*

Operation Haylift 🎬🎬 **1950** The true story of the U.S. Air Force's efforts to rescue starving cattle and sheep herds during Nevada's blizzards of 1949. The Air Force provided realism for the film with planes, equipment, and servicemen. **73m/B VHS, Beta, LV.** Bill Williams, Tom Brown, Ann Rutherford, Jane Nigh; **D:** William (Lester Williams) Berke. *NO*

Operation Intercept 🎬½ **1995 (R)** Francesca (Andreichenko) suspects that the government is behind her father's murder after he develops technology that causes enemy planes to crash. So she threatens to destroy civilian aircraft until the killer is brought to justice. **94m/C VHS.** Natasha Andreichenko, Bruce Payne, John Stockwell, Lance Henriksen, Dennis Christopher, Michael Champion, Curt Lowens, Corbin Bernsen; **D:** Paul Levine; **W:** Paul Levine; **C:** John Newby. *THV*

Operation Julie 🎬½ **1985** A detective searches out a huge drug ring that manufactures LSD. **100m/C VHS, Beta.** Colin Blakely, Lesley Nightingale, Clare Powney; **D:** Bob Mahoney. *ART*

Operation 'Nam 🎬🎬 **1985** A group of bored Vietnam vets return to 'Nam to rescue their leader from a POW camp. Nothing special, but features John Wayne's son. **85m/C VHS.** Oliver Tobias, Christopher Connelly, Manfred Lehman, John Steiner, Ethan Wayne, Donald Pleasence; **D:** Larry Ludman. *IMP*

Operation Orient 🎬½ **19??** A statue laden with drugs is stolen when an international drug smuggler tries to bring it to the U.S. **94m/C VHS, Beta.** Gianni Gori, Gordon Mitchell; **D:** Elia Milonakos.

Operation Petticoat 🎬🎬🎬½ **1959** Submarine captain Grant teams with wheeler-dealer Curtis to make his sub seaworthy. They're joined by a group of Navy women, and the gags begin. Great teamwork from Grant and Curtis keeps things rolling. Jokes may be considered sexist these days. Later remake and TV series couldn't hold a candle to the original. **120m/C VHS, LV, Closed Caption.** Cary Grant, Tony Curtis, Joan O'Brien, Dina Merrill, Gene Evans, Arthur O'Connell, Virginia Gregg; **D:** Blake Edwards. Nominations: Academy Awards '59: Best Story & Screenplay. *REP*

Operation Thunderbolt 🎬🎬½ *Entebbe: Operation Thunderbolt* **1977** Israeli-produced depiction of Israel's July 14, 1976 commando raid on Entebbe, Uganda to rescue the passengers of a hijacked plane. Better than the American versions "Raid on Entebbe" and "Victory at Entebbe" in its performances as well as the information provided, much of it unavailable to the American filmmakers. **120m/C VHS, Beta.** Yehoram Gaon, Assaf Dayan, Ori Levy, Klaus Kinski; **D:** Menahem Golan. Nominations: Academy Awards '77: Best Foreign Language Film. *MGM*

Operation War Zone 🎬 **1989** A platoon of soldiers uncovers a plot by corrupt officers to continue the Vietnam war and sell weapons. **86m/C VHS, Beta.** Joe Spinell.

The Oppermann Family 🎬🎬½ **1982** On two tapes, the long epic made for German television about a family trying to survive in Berlin during the rise of Hitler. In German with subtitles. **238m/C VHS, Beta.** GE **D:** Egon Monk. *FCT*

The Opponent 🎬🎬 **1989 (R)** A young boxer saves a young woman's life, not realizing that she has mob connections, thus embroiling him in a world of crime. **102m/C VHS, LV.** IT Daniel Greene, Ernest Borgnine, Julian Gemma, Mary Stavin, Kelly Shaye Smith; **D:** Sergio Martino. *THV*

Opportunity Knocks 🎬🎬½ **1990 (PG-13)** Carvey's first feature film has him impersonating a friend of a rich suburbanite's family while hiding from a vengeful gangster. They buy it, and give him a job and the daughter. Not hilarious, but not a dud either. **105m/C VHS, Beta, LV, Closed Caption.** Dana Carvey, Robert Loggia, Todd Graff, Milo O'Shea, Julia Campbell, James Tolkan, Doris Belack, Sally Gracie, Del Close; **D:** Donald Petrie; **W:** Mitchel Katlin, Nat Bernstein; **M:** Miles Goodman. *USH*

Opposing Force 🎬🎬½ *Hellcamp* **1987 (R)** The commander of an Air Force camp simulates prisoner-of-war conditions for realistic training, but he goes too far, creating all too real torture situations. He preys on the only female in the experiment, raping her as part of the training. A decent thriller. **97m/C VHS, Beta.** Tom Skerritt, Lisa Eichhorn, Anthony Zerbe, Richard Roundtree, Robert Wightman, John Considine, George Kee Chueng, Paul Joynt, Jay Louden, Ken Wright, Dan Hamilton; **D:** Eric Karson; **W:** Gil Cowan; **M:** Mark Donohue. *HBO*

The Opposite of Sex 🎬🎬½ **1998 (R)** Teenaged terror Dedee (Ricci) wreaks havoc with the life of gay half-brother Bill (Donovan). She seduces his boyfriend Matt (Sergei), gets pregnant, steals his savings, and nearly costs him his high school teacher's job. Then she takes off for L.A., with Bill, his best friend Lucia (Kudrow), and sheriff Carl (Lovett) in pursuit. Quirky black comedy isn't shy, especially when Ricci's vamping across the screen, and features fine work by Kudrow (in a welcome departure from the dumb blonde roles) and Ricci (who can definitely remove the words "child actress" from her resume). Dedee's acerbic narration is another highlight.**CW:** Strong language and sex related dialogue and sexuality. **105m/C VHS.** Christina Ricci, Martin Donovan, Lisa Kudrow, Ivan Sergei, Lyle Lovett, Johnny Galecki, William Lee Scott; **D:** Don Roos; **W:** Don Roos; **C:** Hubert Taczanowski; **M:** Mason Daring. *NYR*

The Opposite Sex 🎬🎬 **1956** Bevy of women battle mediocre script in adaptation of 1939's "The Women." Laserdisc includes original trailer and letterboxed screen. ♫The Opposite Sex; Dere's Yellow Gold on de Trees (De Banana); A Perfect Love; Rock and Roll Tumbleweed; Now! Baby, Now; Jungle Red; Young Man with a Horn. **115m/C VHS, LV, Letterbox.** June Allyson, Joan Collins, Dolores Gray, Ann Sheridan, Ann Miller, Leslie

Nielsen, Agnes Moorehead, Joan Blondell; **D:** David Miller; **W:** Fay Kanin, Michael Kanin. *MGM, FCT*

The Opposite Sex and How to Live With Them
🎬 1993 (R) Yuppies (Gross and Cox) from different backgrounds (he's Jewish, she's a WASP) meet, fall in love, fight, break up, and reunite, inspiring yawning disinterest. All this while their two best buddies (Pollak and Brown) offer what are meant to be "candid insights" delivered directly to the camera. Flat and formulaic romantic comedy wants to sparkle, but script lacks both purpose and point, and worse, takes way too much time not getting there. Winner of the annual Grammar Police award for the worst example of a semantically incorrect title in recent years. **CW:** Language and sexual dialogue. **86m/C VHS.** Arye Gross, Courteney Cox, Kevin Pollak, Julie Brown, Mitchell Ryan, Philip Bruns, Mitzi McCall, B.J. Ward; **D:** Matthew Meshekoff; **W:** Noah Stern; **M:** Ira Newborn. *HBO*

Options
🎬🎬 1988 (PG) Nerdy Hollywood agent Salinger treks to Africa to "option" a princess's life story—hence the title. He gets mixed up with her kidnapping and with her. Misplaced cameos by Roberts and Anton drag down the overall comedy content, which isn't to high to begin with. **105m/C VHS, LV.** Matt Salinger, Joanna Pacula, John Kani, James Keach; **Cameos:** Susan Anton, Eric Roberts; **D:** Camilo Vila; **W:** Edward Decter. *ART, VES*

The Oracle
🎬 1985 A woman takes a new apartment only to find that the previous occupant's spirit is still a resident. The spirit tries to force her to take revenge on his murderers. Not bad for a low-budget thriller, but bad editing is a distraction. **94m/C VHS, Beta.** Caroline Capers Powers, Roger Neil; **D:** Roberta Findlay. *ART*

Oranges Are Not the Only Fruit
🎬🎬½ 1989 Lesbian coming of age story about young Jess (Coleman), who must escape her evangelical religious upbringing and mother (McEwan) in order to be true to herself. When the teenaged Jess gets a schoolgirl crush on her friend Melanie, the congregation finds out and condemns the girls until Jess finds the strength to break away. Based on the novel by Winsterson, who also wrote the screenplay. Made for TV. **165m/C VHS.** *GB* Charlotte Coleman, Geraldine McEwan, Cathryn Bradshaw, Kenneth Cranham, Freda Dowie, Richard Henders, Elizabeth Spriggs, Sophie Thursfield; **D:** Beeban Kidron; **W:** Jeanette Winterson; **M:** Rachel Portman. *FOX*

Orca
woof! *Orca—Killer Whale; The Killer Whale* 1977 (PG) Ridiculous premise has a killer whale chasing bounty hunter Harris to avenge the murder of its pregnant mate. Great for gore lovers, especially when the whale chomps Derek's leg off. **92m/C VHS, Beta, LV.** Richard Harris, Charlotte Rampling, Bo Derek, Keenan Wynn, Will Sampson, Robert Carradine; **D:** Michael Anderson Sr.; **W:** Sergio Donati, Luciano Vincenzoni; **C:** Ted Moore; **M:** Ennio Morricone. *PAR*

Orchestra Rehearsal
🎬🎬 *Prova d'Orchestra* 1978 Italian orchestra musicians gather in a 13th-century chapel to film a television documentary, protest the increasing authoritarianism of their German conductor, but are eventually persuaded to play amidst the chaos. Rota's last score. Italian with subtitles. **72m/C VHS.** *IT* Balduin Baas, Clara Colosimo, Elisabeth Labi, Ronaldo Bonacchi, Ferdinando Villella, Giovanni Javarone, David Mauhsell, Francesco Aluigi; **D:** Federico Fellini; **W:** Federico Fellini, Brunello Rondi; **C:** Giuseppe Rotunno; **M:** Nino Rota. *FXL, FCT*

Orchestra Wives
🎬🎬🎬 1942 A drama bursting with wonderful Glenn Miller music. A woman marries a musician and goes on the road with the band and the other wives. Trouble springs up with the sultry singer who desperately wants the woman's new husband. The commotion spreads throughout the group. 🎵People Like You and Me; At Last; Serenade in Blue; I've Got a Gal in Kalamazoo. **98m/B VHS, Beta, LV, Closed Caption.** George Montgomery, Glenn Miller, Lynn Bari, Carole Landis, Jackie Gleason, Cesar Romero, Ann Rutherford,

Virginia Gilmore, Mary Beth Hughes, Harry (Henry) Morgan; **D:** Archie Mayo. Nominations: Academy Awards '42: Best Song ("I've Got a Gal in Kalamazoo"). *FCT*

Ordeal by Innocence
🎬½ 1984 (PG-13) Sutherland is an amateur sleuth in 1950s England convinced he has proof that a convicted murderer is innocent, but no one wishes to reopen the case. Big-name cast is essentially wasted. Based on an Agatha Christie story. **91m/C VHS, Beta, LV.** Donald Sutherland, Christopher Plummer, Faye Dunaway, Sarah Miles, Ian McShane, Diana Quick, Annette Crosbie, Michael Elphick; **D:** Desmond Davis; **C:** Billy Williams; **M:** Pino Donaggio. *MGM*

Ordeal in the Arctic
🎬🎬½ 1993 (PG) Military transport plane, piloted by Capt. John Couch (Chamberlain), crashes into the remote glaciers of the Arctic. The survivors face a blizzard and freezing to death unless a rescue team can get to them quickly. Made for cable. **93m/C VHS.** Richard Chamberlain, Melanie Mayron, Catherine Mary Stewart; **D:** Mark Sobel. *THV*

The Ordeal of Dr. Mudd
🎬🎬🎬 1980 His name was Mudd—a fitting moniker after he unwittingly aided President Lincoln's assassin. Dr. Mudd set John Wilkes Boothe's leg, broken during the assassination, and was jailed for conspiracy. He became a hero in prison for his aid during yellow fever epidemics and was eventually released. A strong and intricate performance by Weaver keeps this made-for-television drama interesting. Mudd's descendants are still trying to completely clear his name of any wrongdoing in the Lincoln assassination. **143m/C VHS, Beta.** Dennis Weaver, Susan Sullivan, Richard Dysart, Michael McGuire, Nigel Davenport, Arthur Hill; **D:** Paul Wendkos. *ART*

Order of the Black Eagle
🎬½ 1987 (R) A Bond-ish spy and his sidekick, Typhoon the Baboon, battle neo-Nazis planning to bring Hitler back to life in this silly tongue-in-cheek thriller. **93m/C VHS, Beta.** *GB* Ian Hunter, Charles K. Bibby, William T. Hicks, Jill Donnellan; **D:** Worth Keeter. *CEL*

Order of the Eagle
🎬½ 1989 An innocent scouting trip turns into a non-stop nightmare when an Eagle Scout uncovers some dangerous information. **88m/C VHS, Beta.** Frank Stallone.

Order to Kill
🎬🎬½ 1973 A gambling boss puts out a contract on a hit man. **110m/C VHS, Beta.** Jose Ferrer, Helmut Berger, Sydne Rome, Kevin McCarthy; **D:** Jose Maesso. *NO*

Ordet
🎬🎬🎬½ *The Word* 1955 A man who believes he is Jesus Christ is ridiculed until he begins performing miracles, which result in the rebuilding of a broken family. A statement on the nature of religious faith vs. fanaticism by the profoundly religious Dreyer, and based on the play by Kaj Munk. In Danish with English subtitles. **126m/B VHS, Beta.** *DK* Henrik Malberg; **D:** Carl Theodor Dreyer. Golden Globe Awards '56: Best Foreign Film; Venice Film Festival '55: Best Film. *NOS, WFV, HEG*

Ordinary Heroes
🎬🎬½ 1985 The story is familiar but the leads make it worthwhile. Anderson is strong as a blinded Vietnam vet readjusting to life at home. Bertinelli's portrayal of his former girlfriend is eloquent. Nice work on an overdone story. **105m/C VHS.** Richard Dean Anderson, Doris Roberts, Valerie Bertinelli; **D:** Peter H. Cooper. *HBO*

Ordinary Magic
🎬🎬½ 1993 Teenaged Jeffrey was raised in India, picking up more than a little eastern wisdom along the way. After the death of his parents Jeffrey comes to the U.S. to live with his aunt where he sticks out not only as the new kid but as a decided oddball. But he manages to make some new friends and teach a few lessons about individuality along the way. Adapted from the novel by Malcolm Bosse. **96m/C VHS.** David Fox, Glenne Headly, Heath Lamberts, Ryan Reynolds; **Cameos:** Paul Anka; **D:** Giles Walker; **W:** Jefferson Lewis. *TRI*

Ordinary People
🎬🎬🎬½ 1980 (R) Powerful, well-acted story of a family's struggle to deal with one son's accidental death and the other's subsequent guilt-ridden suicide attempt. Features

strong performances by all, but Moore is especially believable as the cold and rigid mother. McGovern's film debut as well as Redford's directorial debut. Based on the novel by Judith Guest. **124m/C VHS, Beta, LV.** Mary Tyler Moore, Donald Sutherland, Timothy Hutton, Judd Hirsch, M. Emmet Walsh, Elizabeth McGovern, Adam Baldwin, Dinah Manoff, James B. Sikking; **D:** Robert Redford; **W:** Alvin Sargent; **C:** John Bailey; **M:** Marvin Hamlisch. Academy Awards '80: Best Adapted Screenplay, Best Director (Redford), Best Picture, Best Supporting Actor (Hutton); Directors Guild of America Awards '80: Best Director (Redford); Golden Globe Awards '81: Best Actress—Drama (Moore), Best Director (Redford), Best Film—Drama, Best Supporting Actor (Hutton); Los Angeles Film Critics Association Awards '80: Best Supporting Actor (Hutton); National Board of Review Awards '80: Best Director (Redford); New York Film Critics Awards '80: Best Film; Writers Guild of America '80: Best Adapted Screenplay; Nominations: Academy Awards '80: Best Actress (Moore), Best Supporting Actor (Hirsch). *PAR, BTV*

Oregon Trail
1939 A western serial in 15 chapters, each 13 minutes long. **195m/B VHS, Beta.** Johnny Mack Brown, Fuzzy Knight; **D:** Ford Beebe. *VCN, DVT, MLB*

The Organization
🎬🎬🎬 1971 (PG) Poitier's third and final portrayal of Detective Virgil Tibbs, first seen in "In the Heat of the Night." This time around he battles a drug smuggling ring with a vigilante group. Good action scenes and a realistic ending. **108m/C VHS, Beta, Closed Caption.** Sidney Poitier, Barbara McNair, Sheree North, Raul Julia; **D:** Don Medford; **C:** Joseph Biroc. *MGM, FOX*

Organized Crime & Triad Bureau
🎬🎬 *Chungon Satluk Linggei* 1993 Determined Lee and his cop team seal off crowded Hong Kong island Cheung Chai to trap mob boss Tung and his tootsie. And the bystanders better just get out of his way. Lots of action; Chinese with subtitles. **91m/C VHS, LV.** *HK* Danny Lee, Anthony Wong, Cecilia Yip; **D:** Kirk Wong. *TAI*

The Organizer
🎬🎬 *I Compagni; Comrades* 1964 In 19th-century Turin, impoverished aristocratic professor Mastroianni unites a group of textile workers striking against unsafe working conditions. Italian with subtitles. **127m/B VHS.** *IT* Marcello Mastroianni, Annie Girardot, Renato Salvatori, Bernard Blier, Francois Perier, Folco Lulli; **D:** Mario Monicelli; **W:** Mario Monicelli; **C:** Giuseppe Rotunno. *HTV*

Orgy of the Dead
woof! 1965 Classic anti-canon film scripted by Ed Wood, Jr., from his own novel. Two innocent travelers are forced to watch an even dozen nude spirits dance in a cardboard graveyard. Hilariously bad. **90m/C VHS, Beta.** Criswell, Fawn Silver, William Bates, Pat Barringer; **D:** A.C. Stephen; **W:** Edward D. Wood Jr. *RHI*

Orgy of the Vampires
🎬 *Vampire's Night Orgy* 1973 (R) Tourists wander into village during cocktail hour. **86m/C VHS.** *SP* Jack Taylor, Charo Soriano, Dianik Zurakowska, John Richard; **D:** Leon Klimovsky. *SNC*

Oriane
🎬🎬 1985 A troubled Venezuelan woman must leave France for her native soil when her aunt dies. Once there, in the place where she spent youthful summers, she begins to recall her incestuous past. Spanish with subtitles. **88m/C VHS.** Deniela Sliverio, Doris Wells, Philippe Rouleau, David Crotto; **D:** Fina Torres. *FCT*

The Original Fabulous Adventures of Baron Munchausen
🎬🎬½ *The Fabulous Baron Munchausen* 1961 An adventure fantasy that takes the hero all over, from the belly of a whale, eventually landing him on the surface of the moon. **84m/C VHS, LV.** *CZ* Milos Kopecky, Jana Brejchova, Rudolph Jelinek, Jan Werich; **D:** Karel Zeman. *NO*

The Original Flash Gordon Collection
1991 Four vintage Flash Gordon serials from the 1930s were recently re-edited into feature length films and released as this collection. Great stuff, including "Spaceship to the Unknown," "Deadly Ray From Mars," "Peril From Planet Mongo," and "Purple Death From Outer Space." **366m/B VHS.** Buster Crabbe. *QHV, FCT*

Original Gangstas 🐾🐾 1996 (R) In Hollywood, everything old eventually becomes new again. John Bookman (Williamson) returns to his old neighborhood in Gary, Indiana, after his father is brutally shot by a gang leader. Things have changed from Bookman's days of gang banging, with the streets swarming with young machine gun-toting lowlifes. Bent on revenge, cigar-chewing Bookman, aided by childhood friends Jake (Brown), Slick (Roundtree), and Bubba (O'Neal), decide to take back their streets with a little help from Foxy Brown herself (Grier), as a greiving mother. The nostalgia quotient is high watching these '70s blaxploitation stars together in one movie, older, more gray and a little wider, but still able to kick butt. Serious topic (gang violence) is lost in a conventional vigilante vehicle, which sacrifices a message for an all-too-familiar and bloody showdown. **CW:** Non-stop violence and pervasive strong language. 98m/C VHS, LV, Closed Caption. Jim Brown, Fred Williamson, Pam Grier, Ron O'Neal, Richard Roundtree, Paul Winfield; **D:** Larry Cohen; **W:** Aubrey Rattan; **C:** Carlos Gonzalez; **M:** Vladimir Horunzhy. ORI

Original Intent 🐾🐾 1991 (PG) A successful lawyer, facing a mid-life crisis, jeopardizes both his family and career when he decides to defend a homeless shelter from eviction proceedings. What might have been a powerful drama about one man's crusade to help the homeless instead merely melodramtic. Actor/activist Sheen appears briefly as a homeless man. 97m/C VHS, Beta, Closed Caption. Jay Richardson, Candy Clark, Kris Kristofferson, Vince Edwards, Cindy Pickett, Robert DoQui, Joseph Campanella; **Cameos:** Martin Sheen; **D:** Robert Marcarelli; **W:** Robert Marcarelli. PAR

Orlando 🐾🐾🐾 1992 (PG-13) Potter's sumptuous film adaptation of Virginia Woolf's 1928 novel, which covers 400 years in the life of an English nobleman, who not only defies death but evolves from a man to a woman in the intervening years. Orlando (Swinton) is first seen as a young man in the court of Queen Elizabeth I (Crisp) but after a deep sleep it's suddenly 40 years later. Things like this just keep happening and by 1750 he is now a she (and remains so), finding and losing love, and eventually gaining fulfillment in the 20th century. Elaborate productions never overwhelm Swinton's serene, self-assured performance. **CW:** Some sensuality. 93m/C VHS, LV, Letterbox, Closed Caption. GB Tilda Swinton, Charlotte Valandrey, Billy Zane, Lothaire Bluteau, John Wood, Quentin Crisp, Heathcote Williams, Dudley Sutton, Thom Hoffman, Peter Eyre, Jimmy Somerville; **D:** Sally Potter; **W:** Sally Potter; **C:** Alexei Rodionov; **M:** Bob Last. Nominations: Academy Awards '93: Best Art Direction/Set Decoration, Best Costume Design; Independent Spirit Awards '94: Best Foreign Film. COL

The Orphan 🐾½ 1979 A young orphaned boy seeks revenge against his cruel aunt who is harassing him with sadistic discipline. 80m/C VHS, Beta. Mark Evans, Joanna Miles, Peggy Feury; **D:** John Ballard. RHI

An Orphan Boy of Vienna 🐾½ 1937 A homeless street urchin with a beautiful singing voice is accepted into the wonderful world of the Choir, but is later unjustly accused of stealing. Performances by the Vienna Boys' Choir redeem the melodramatic plot. In German with English subtitles. 87m/B VHS, Beta. GE **D:** Max Neufeld. VYY, IHF, GLV

Orphan Train 🐾🐾🐾 1979 A woman realizes her New York soup kitchen can't do enough to help the neighborhood orphans, so she takes a group of children out West in hopes of finding families to adopt them. Their journey is chronicled by a newspaper photographer and a social worker. Based on the actual "orphan trains" of the mid- to late 1800s. From the novel by Dorothea G. Petrie. Made for television. 150m/C VHS. Jill Eikenberry, Kevin Dobson, Glenn Close, Linda Manz; **D:** William A. Graham. KAR, HHE

Orphans 🐾🐾🐾 1977 A sensitive edge-of-your/out portrait of a young boy's discovery of love, friendship, and literature. In Russian with English subtitles. 97m/C VHS, Beta. RU Nikolai Gubenko, Y. Boudraitis, A. Tcherstvov, A. Kaliaguine, E. Bourkov, J. Bolotova, R. Bikov, E. Evstigneev; **D:** Nikolai Gubenko; **C:** Alexander Kniajinsky. FCT

Orphans 🐾🐾🐾 1987 (R) A gangster on the run is kidnapped by a tough New York orphan but soon takes control by befriending his abductor's maladjusted brother. Eventually both brother realizes his need for the older man, who has become a father figure to them. This very quirky film is salvaged by good performances. Based on the play by Lyle Kessler. 116m/C VHS, Beta, LV, Closed Caption. Albert Finney, Matthew Modine, Kevin Anderson; **D:** Alan J. Pakula; **W:** Lyle Kessler; **M:** Michael Small. ORI, WAR

Orphans of the North 🐾 1940 The story of Bedrock Brown's search for gold and his lost partner. Filmed on location in Alaska with nonprofessional actors. Impressive footage of America's "last frontier," including the flora and fauna. 56m/C VHS, Beta, 8mm. **D:** Norman Dawn; **W:** Susan Denis. VYY

Orphans of the Storm 🐾🐾🐾½ 1921 Two sisters are separated and raised in opposite worlds—one by thieves, the other by aristocrats. Gish's poignant search for her sister is hampered by the turbulent maelstrom preceding the French Revolution. Silent. Based on the French play "The Two Orphans." 190m/B VHS, LV. Lillian Gish, Dorothy Gish, Monte Blue, Joseph Schildkraut; **D:** D.W. Griffith. KIV, MRV, MCB

Orpheus 🐾🐾½ Orphee 1949 Cocteau's fascinating, innovative retelling of the Orpheus legend in a modern, though slightly askew, Parisian setting. Classic visual effects and poetic imagery. In French with English subtitles. 95m/B VHS, Beta, 8mm. Jean Marais, Francois Perier, Maria Casares; **D:** Jean Cocteau. SNC, NOS, VYY

Orpheus Descending 🐾🐾½ 1991 Lust and hatred in small Southern town. Confusing, poorly paced, but interesting for Anderson as Elvis-style drifter and Redgrave as woman addicted to love. Made-for-cable version of the 1989 Broadway revival of Tennessee Williams play. 117m/C VHS, Closed Caption. Vanessa Redgrave, Kevin Anderson, Anne Twomey, Miriam Margolyes, Brad Sullivan, Sloane Shelton, Patti Allison; **D:** Peter Hall; **W:** Peter Hall, Tennessee Williams. TTC, FCT

Osa 🐾½ 1985 Yet another post-nuke flick with the usual devastated landscape, leather-clad survivors, and hokey dialog. It's sometimes funny, despite everyone's effort to make it dramatic. The supposed plot centers on one woman's efforts to break up a man's monopoly on clean water. 94m/C VHS. Kelly Lynch, Daniel Grimm, Phillip Vincent, Etienne Chicot, John Forristal, Pete Walker, David Hausman, Bill Moseley; **D:** Oleg Egorov; **M:** Mason Daring. NO

Osaka Elegy 🐾🐾½ Woman of Osaka 1936 A study of Japanese cultural rules when society condemns a woman for behavior that is acceptable for a man. In Japanese with English subtitles. 71m/B VHS. JP Isuzu Yamada; **D:** Kenji Mizoguchi. NO

The Oscar 🐾½ 1966 (R) Unless you enjoy razzing bad acting, this is not for you. Meant as a comeuppance for Hollywood, by Hollywood, this story of a star climbing the ladder of success and squashing fingers on every rung is too schlocky to succeed. The climax, when the scumbag star thinks he's won an Oscar and stands up, only to find it's for someone else, was based on Frank Capra's embarrassing experience with the same situation. 119m/C VHS, Beta. Stephen Boyd, Elke Sommer, Jill St. John, Tony Bennett, Milton Berle, Eleanor Parker, Joseph Cotten, Edie Adams, Ernest Borgnine, Ed Begley Sr., Walter Brennan, Broderick Crawford, James Dunn, Peter Lawford, Merle Oberon, Bob Hope, Frank Sinatra; **D:** Russel Rouse; **C:** Joseph Ruttenberg. Nominations: Academy Awards '66: Best Art Direction/Set Decoration (Color), Best Costume Design (Color).

Oscar 🐾🐾 1991 (PG) The inimitable casting of Stallone in a 1930s style crime farce (an attempt to change his image) is hard to believe. Stallone has little to do as he plays the straight man in this often ridiculous story of a crime boss who swears he'll go straight. Cameos aplenty, with Curry's the most notable. Based on a French play by Claude Magnier. 109m/C VHS, LV, Closed Caption. Sylvester Stallone, Ornella Muti, Peter Riegert, Vincent Spano, Marisa Tomei, Kirk Douglas, Art LaFleur, Ken Howard, Chazz Palminteri, Tim Curry, Don Ameche, Richard Romanus; **D:** John Landis; **W:** Michael Barrie, Jim Mulholland; **C:** Mac Ahlberg; **M:** Elmer Bernstein. COL, IME, TOU

Oscar and Lucinda 🐾🐾½ 1997 (R) A priest and a glassworks heiress are united by a shared passion for gambling; together they attempt to transport a glass church through 1860s Australian wilderness. Fiennes' performance as the vulnerable and flailing Oscar is particularly good. Narrated by Geoffrey Rush. Based on the Booker Prize-winning novel by Peter Carey. **CW:** A scene of sexuality, and brief violence. 131m/C VHS. Ralph Fiennes, Cate Blanchett, Ciaran Hinds, Tom Wilkinson, Richard Roxburgh, Clive Russell, Bille Brown, Josephine Byrnes, Barnaby Kay, Barry Otto, Linda Bassett; **D:** Gillian Armstrong; **W:** Laura Jones; **C:** Geoffrey Simpson; **M:** Thomas Newman. Nominations: Academy Awards '97: Best Costume Design. FXV

Oscar's Greatest Moments: 1971-1991 1992 Collection of highlights from the Oscar ceremonies, featuring footage from the past 21 years. Proceeds from video sales benefit the Center for Motion Picture Study. 110m/C VHS, LV, 8mm, Closed Caption. **D:** Jeff Margolis. COL, BTV

O.S.S. 🐾🐾🐾 1946 John Martin (Ladd) has been recruited by Commander Brady (Knowles) as a would-be spy for the new Office of Strategic Services. Martin's teamed with Ellen Rogers (Fitzgerald) and they parachute into France with orders to obtain information on German troop movements and destroy an important railroad tunnel. A turncoat Gestapo agent sells them information but German colonel Meister (Hoyt) is after them and it's a race to see if their mission can be completed before they're caught. The O.S.S. allowed Paramount studio a look at their WWII files for story purposes and numerous ex-agents served as technical advisors. 108m/B VHS, Closed Caption. Alan Ladd, Geraldine Fitzgerald, Patric Knowles, John Hoyt, Richard Benedict, Gloria Saunders, Bobby Driscoll, Don Beddoe; **D:** Irving Pichel; **W:** Richard Maibaum; **C:** Lionel Linden; **M:** Daniele Amfitheatrof. USH

Ossessione 🐾🐾🐾½ 1942 An adaptation of "The Postman Always Rings Twice," transferred to Fascist Italy, where a drifter and an innkeeper's wife murder her husband. Visconti's first feature, which initiated Italian neo-realism, was not released in the U.S. until 1975 due to a copyright dispute. In Italian with English subtitles. 135m/B VHS, Beta. IT Massimo Girotti, Clara Calamai, Juan deLanda, Elio Marcuzzo; **D:** Luchino Visconti. FCT, TPV

The Osterman Weekend 🐾🐾 1983 (R) Peckinpah was said to have disliked the story and the script in this, his last film, which could account for the convoluted and confusing end result. Adding to the problem is the traditional difficulty of adapting Ludlum's complex psychological thrillers for the screen. The result: cast members seem to not quite "get it" as they portray a group of friends, one of whom has been convinced by the CIA that the others are all Soviet spies. 102m/C VHS, Beta, LV. Burt Lancaster, Rutger Hauer, Craig T. Nelson, Dennis Hopper, John Hurt, Chris Sarandon, Meg Foster, Helen Shaver; **D:** Sam Peckinpah; **M:** Lalo Schifrin. NO

Otaku no Video Fan's Video 1991 Fictionalized animated history of the famed Japanese animation studio Gainax, including strange interviews with rabid fans who want to "Otakunize" the human race. Contains both episodes: "Otaku no Video" (1982) and "More Otaku no Video" (1985). In Japanese with English subtitles. 100m/C VHS. JP ANI

Otello 🎬🎬🎬½ **1986 (PG)** An uncommon film treat for opera fans, with a stellar performance by Domingo as the troubled Moor who murders his wife in a fit of jealous rage and later finds she was never unfaithful. Be prepared, however, for changes from the Shakespeare and Verdi stories, necessitated by the film adaptation. Highly acclaimed and awarded; in Italian with English subtitles. **123m/C VHS, Beta, LV.** *IT* Placido Domingo, Katia Ricciarelli, Justino Diaz; **D:** Franco Zeffirelli. Nominations: Academy Awards '86: Best Costume Design. *HMV, MVD*

Othello 🎬🎬½ **1922** A silent version of Shakespeare's tragedy, featuring Jannings as the tragic Moor. Titles are in English; with musical score. **81m/B VHS, Beta.** *GE* Emil Jannings, Lya de Putti, Werner Krauss; **D:** Dimitri Buchowetzki. *VYY, NOS, DVT*

Othello 🎬🎬🎬 **1952** Welles' striking adaptation of the Shakespeare tragedy casts him as the self-deluding Moor, with MacLiammoir as the despicable Iago and Cloutier as innocent victim, Desdemona. Welles filmed his epic over a four-year period due to budget difficulties, which also resulted in his filming in a number of different countries and settings. The film underwent a $1 million restoration, supervised by Welles' daughter, prior to its limited theatrical re-release in 1992. **90m/B VHS, LV.** Orson Welles, Michael MacLiammoir, Suzanne Cloutier, Robert Coote, Hilton Edwards, Michael Lawrence, Nicholas Bruce, Fay Compton, Doris Dowling, Jean Davis, Joseph Cotten, Joan Fontaine; **D:** Orson Welles. Cannes Film Festival '52: Best Film.

Othello 🎬🎬🎬½ **1965** Olivier (in blackface) gives another towering performance as Shakespeare's tragic Moor, led to disaster by his own jealousy. He's ably supported by Finlay's insinuating performance as Iago, Smith as a sweetly vulnerable Desdemona, and Jacobi as unwitting rival Cassio. The production, however, doesn't stray far from its stage-bound roots. **150m/C VHS.** Laurence Olivier, Frank Finlay, Maggie Smith, Derek Jacobi, Joyce Redman, Anthony Nicholls, Sheila Reid, Roy Holder; **D:** Stuart Burge; **W:** Margaret Unsworth; **C:** Geoffrey Unsworth; **M:** Richard Hampton. Nominations: Academy Awards '65: Best Actor (Olivier), Best Supporting Actor (Finlay), Best Supporting Actress (Smith, Redman). *WMI*

Othello 🎬🎬🎬 **1995 (R)** Fishburne stars as Shakespeare's tragic Moor, with Branagh as silken agitator Iago, and Jacob as the tragic Desdemona. First time director Oliver Parker (brother Nathaniel is also in the film) drastically cut the play, rearranging scenes (and even adding material)—purists will no doubt scream, but performances carry the production. Through the clever use of asides directed at the camera, Branagh's Iago makes the viewer feel like an accomplice in the plot. French-speaking Jacob, however, seems to have a hard time pronouncing the Shakespearean dialogue. Fishburne's imposing performance as Othello is the first by an actor of African descent in a major motion picture. **CW:** Contains violence, sexuality, and nudity. **125m/C VHS, LV, Closed Caption.** Laurence "Larry" Fishburne, Irene Jacob, Kenneth Branagh, Nathaniel Parker, Michael Maloney, Anna Patrick, Nicholas Farrell, Indra Ove, Michael Sheen, Andre Oumansky, Philip Locke, John Savident, Gabriele Ferzetti, Pierre Vaneck; **D:** Oliver Parker; **W:** Oliver Parker; **C:** David Johnson; **M:** Charlie Mole. Nominations: Screen Actors Guild Award '95: Best Supporting Actor (Branagh). *COL*

The Other 🎬🎬🎬 **1972 (PG)** Eerie, effective thriller adapted by Tryon from his supernatural novel. Twin brothers represent good and evil in a 1930s Connecticut farm town beset with gruesome murders and accidents. A good scare. **100m/C VHS, Beta.** Martin Udvarnoky, Chris Udvarnoky, Uta Hagen, Diana Muldaur, Norma Connolly, Victor French, John Ritter, Loretta Leversee, Lou Frizzell, Portia Nelson, Jenny Sullivan; **D:** Robert Mulligan; **W:** Tom Tryon; **C:** Robert L. Surtees; **M:** Jerry Goldsmith. *FOX*

Other Hell 🎬 **1985 (R)** Schlocky Italian-made chiller has the devil inhabiting a convent where he does his damnest to upset the nuns. Gross, but not scary—lots of cliche dark-hallway

scenes and fright music. **88m/C VHS, Beta.** *IT* Carlo De Meyo, Francesca Carmeno; **D:** Stefan Oblowsky. *ART, VES*

Other People's Money 🎬🎬½ **1991 (R)** DeVito is "Larry the Liquidator," a corporate raider with a heart of stone and a penchant for doughnuts. When he sets his sights on a post-smokestack era, family-owned cable company, he gets a taste of love for the first time in his life. He and Miller, the daughter of the company president and also its legal advisor, court one another while sparring over the fate of the company. Unbelievably clipped ending mars otherwise enterprising comedy about the triumph of greed in corporate America. Based on the off-Broadway play by Jerry Sterner. **CW:** Language and sex-related dialogue. **101m/C VHS, LV, 8mm, Letterbox, Closed Caption.** Danny DeVito, Penelope Ann Miller, Dean Jones, Gregory Peck, Piper Laurie, Tom Aldredge, R.D. Call; **D:** Norman Jewison; **W:** Alvin Sargent; **C:** Haskell Wexler; **M:** David Newman. *WAR, CCB*

The Other Side of Midnight woof! **1977 (R)** The dreary, depressingly shallow life story of a poor French girl, dumped by an American GI, who sleeps her way to acting stardom and a profitable marriage, then seeks revenge for the jilt. Based on Sidney Sheldon's novel, it's not even titillating—just a real downer. **160m/C VHS, Beta, LV, Letterbox.** Susan Sarandon, Marie-France Pisier, John Beck, Raf Vallone, Clu Gulager, Sorrell Booke; **D:** Charles Jarrott; **W:** Daniel Taradash; **C:** Fred W. Koenekamp. Nominations: Academy Awards '77: Best Costume Design. *FOX*

The Other Side of Sunday 🎬🎬 **1996** A small town in 1959 Norway is the setting for this coming of age comedy. Maria (Thiesen) is the eldest daughter of conservative priest Johannes (Sundquist). Fun doesn't seem to be part of their religion but puberty is hitting Maria hard and she longs to join in with the livelier crowd of her school friend Brigit (Salvesen), who listens to rock 'n' roll, wears makeup, and makes out with boys. Maria does find a compassionate listener in Mrs. Tunheim (Riise), who urges the teenager to learn how to think for herself. Based on the novel "Sunday" by Reidun Nortvedt. Norwegian with subtitles. **103m/C VHS.** *NO* Marie Theisen, Bjorn Sundquist, Hildegunn Riise, Sylvia Salvesen; **D:** Berit Nesheim; **W:** Berit Nesheim, Lasse Glomm; **C:** Arne Borsheim; **M:** Geir Bohren, Bent Aserud. Nominations: Academy Awards '96: Best Foreign Language Film. *NYR*

The Other Side of the Law 🎬🎬 **1995 (R)** Man makes a wilderness hideout with his son after killing his wife's murderer. But when the boy grows up, dad decides to send him back into civilization for education, leading to nothing but trouble. **CW:** Adventure violence. **96m/C VHS.** Juergen Prochnow; **D:** Gilles Carle. *THV*

The Other Side of the Mountain 🎬🎬 *A Window to the Sky* **1975 (PG)** Tear-jerking true story of Olympic hopeful skier Jill Kinmont, paralyzed in a fall. Bridges helps her pull her life together. A sequel followed two years later. Based on the book "A Long Way Up" by E.G. Valens. **102m/C VHS, Beta.** Marilyn Hassett, Beau Bridges, Dabney Coleman, John David Garfield, Griffin Dunne; **D:** Larry Peerce; **W:** David Seltzer; **M:** Charles Fox. Nominations: Academy Awards '75: Best Song ("Richard's Window"). *USH*

The Other Side of the Mountain, Part 2 🎬🎬 **1978 (PG)** Quadriplegic Jill Kinmont, paralyzed in a skiing accident that killed her hopes for the Olympics, overcomes depression and the death of the man who helped her to recover. In this chapter, she falls in love again and finds happiness. More tears are jerked. **99m/C VHS, Beta.** Marilyn Hassett, Timothy Bottoms; **D:** Larry Peerce. *USH*

Other Voices, Other Rooms 🎬🎬½ **1995** Adaptation of Truman Capote's 1948 novel (his first) is the semi-autobiographical story of a young boy's search for his father set against the

backdrop of a decaying Bayou mansion. Southern saga, narrated by Capote sound-alike Kingdom, starts when 12-year-old Joel's mother dies and he is sent by his aunts to live with his father. Instead of being greeted by his father, Joel (Speck) instead meets an odd collection of guests, including Amy (Thomson), a fragile and pretty Southern belle and her cousin Randolph (Bluteau), a sensitive, effete, and charming alcoholic. Pic deals with the secrets of the father's illness and what lies behind the unhappiness of the two cousins, who try to keep the child from fleeing the wacky "family." Lacks the danger and suspense of Capote's novel, but sets proper mood and shows off actors talents. Best known as a documentary director/producer, this is Rocksavage's feature debut. **98m/C VHS.** Lothaire Bluteau, Anna Thomson, David Speck, April Turner, Aubrey Dollar, Bob Kingdom; **D:** David Rocksavage; **W:** David Rocksavage, Sara Flanigan; **C:** Paul Ryan; **M:** Chris Hajian. *NYR*

The Other Woman 🎬½ **1992 (R)** Investigative reporter Jessica is working on a murder case when she finds incriminating sex photos showing her husband with another woman. She becomes obsessed with finding the woman in the pictures but it would be dangerous for Jessica to forget there's still a murderer on the loose. **CW:** Language and strong sexuality. **90m/C VHS, Closed Caption.** Adrian Zmed, Lee Ann Beaman, Daniel Moriarty, Jenna Persaud, Sam Jones; **D:** Jag Mundhra. *IMP*

Oubliette **1914** A peripheral version of Francois Villon, in what is a recently discovered and restored film, the earliest extant Chaney film. **35m/B VHS, Beta.** Lon Chaney Sr. *GVV, LSV*

Our Daily Bread 🎬🎬🎬 *Miracle of Life* **1934** Vidor's sequel to the 1928 "The Crowd." A young couple inherit a farm during the Depression and succeed in managing the land. A near-classic, with several sequences highly influenced by directors Alexander Dovshenko and Sergei Eisenstein. Director Vidor also co-scripted this film, risking bankruptcy to finance it. **80m/B VHS, Beta, LV.** Karen Morley, Tom George Duryea Keene, John Qualen, Barbara Pepper, Addison Richards; **D:** King Vidor; **W:** King Vidor. *NOS, BAR, VYY*

Our Dancing Daughters 🎬🎬½ **1928** Flapper (Crawford on the brink of stardom) falls hard for millionaire who's forced into arranged marriage, but obliging little missus kicks bucket so Crawford can step in. **98m/B VHS, Beta.** Joan Crawford, Johnny Mack Brown, Nils Asther, Dorothy Sebastian, Anita Page; **D:** Harry Beaumont; **C:** George Barnes. Nominations: Academy Awards '29: Best Cinematography, Best Writing. *MGM, FCT*

Our Family Business 🎬🎬 **1981** Made for television and meant as a series pilot, this generally plodding "Godfather"-type story is saved by good performances by Wanamaker and Milland. **74m/C VHS.** Sam Wanamaker, Vera Miles, Ray Milland, Ted Danson, Chip Mayer; **D:** Robert Collins. *ART*

Our Gang **1926** Two silent "Our Gang" comedies, including "Thundering Fleas" and "Shivering Spooks." **57m/B VHS, Beta, 8mm.** Joe Cobb, Farina Hoskins, Mary Kornman, Mickey Daniels, Scooter Lowry. *VYY*

Our Gang Comedies **194?** The five shorts on this cassette show the gang at their comedic best. They include "The Big Premiere," "Bubbling Troubles," "Clown Princes," "Don't Lie" and "Farm Hands." **53m/B VHS, Beta, LV.** Robert (Bobby) Blake, Billie "Buckwheat" Thomas, George "Spanky" McFarland, Darla Hood, Carl "Alfalfa" Switzer, Tommy "Butch" Bond, Eugene "Porky" Lee, Shirley "Muggsy" Coates, Joe "Corky" Geil, Billy "Froggy" Lauglin. *MGM, VTR*

Our Gang Comedy Festival **1988** A 20-year span of comedy from the Little Rascals, including rare silent features. **45m/B VHS.** Joe Cobb, Farina Hoskins, Mary Kornman, Mickey Daniels, Scooter Lowry. *GKK*

Our Gang Comedy Festival 2 1989 More riotous good times with The Little Rascals, including silent footage. 45m/B VHS. Joe Cobb, Farina Hoskins, Mary Kornman, Mickey Daniels, Scooter Lowry. *GKK*

Our Hospitality ✂✂✂✂ 1923 One of Keaton's finest silent films, with all the elements in place. William McKay (Keaton) travels to the American South on a quaint train (a near-exact replica of the Stephenson Rocket), to claim an inheritance as the last survivor of his family. En route, a young woman traveler informs him that her family has had a long, deadly feud with his, and that they intend to kill him. McKay resolves to get the inheritance, depending on the Southern rule of hospitality to guests to save his life until he can make his escape. Watch for the river scene where, during filming, Keaton's own life was really in danger. By the way, Keaton married his leading lady in real life. 74m/B VHS, LV. Buster Keaton, Natalie Talmadge, Joe Keaton, Buster Keaton Jr., Kitty Bradbury, Joe Roberts; *D:* Buster Keaton, John Blystone. *HBO*

Our Little Girl ✂✂ 1935 (PG) A precocious little tyke tries to reunite her estranged parents by running away to their favorite vacation spot. Sure to please Shirley Temple fans, despite a lackluster script. 65m/B VHS, Beta, Closed Caption. Shirley Temple, Joel McCrea, Rosemary Ames, Lyle Talbot, Erin O'Brien Moore; *D:* John S. Robertson. *FOX*

Our Man Flint ✂✂ 1966 James Bond clone Derek Flint uses gadgets and his ingenuity to save the world from an evil organization, GALAXY, that seeks world domination through control of the weather. The plot moves quickly around many bikini-clad women, but still strains for effect. Spawned one sequel: "In Like Flint." 107m/C VHS, Beta, LV, Letterbox. James Coburn, Lee J. Cobb, Gila Golan, Edward Mulhare, Benson Fong, Shelby Grant, Sigrid Valdis, Gianna Serra, James Brolin, Helen Funai, Michael St. Clair; *D:* Daniel Mann; *C:* Daniel F. Fapp; *M:* Jerry Goldsmith. *FOX*

Our Miss Brooks ✂✂½ 1956 Quietly pleasing version of the television series. Miss Brooks pursues the "mother's boy" biology professor. The father of the child she begins tutoring appears taken with her. The professor takes notice. 85m/B VHS. Eve Arden, Gale Gordon, Nick Adams, Richard Crenna, Don Porter; *D:* Al Lewis. *WAR*

Our Modern Maidens ✂✂½ 1929 Scandalous jazz-age drama in which Crawford and Fairbanks both fall in love with other people before their wedding is to take place. This sequel to "Our Dancing Daughters" features beautiful gowns and lush, opulent Art Deco interiors. Based on a story by Josephine Lovett. 75m/B VHS, Closed Caption. Joan Crawford, Rod La Rocque, Douglas Fairbanks Jr., Anita Page, Josephine Dunn; *D:* Jack Conway; *W:* Josephine Lovett. *MGM*

Our Mother's Murder ✂✂½ 1997 (PG-13) Title says it all in this made for cable drama based on the true story of publishing heiress Anne Scripps Douglas (Hart) who, in 1989, marries volatile young carpenter, Scott (Wilder), and begins an abusive four-year marriage that will end with her beating death in 1993. Scripps Douglas' two daughters by her first marriage, Alexandra and Annie (portrayed on screen by Clarke and Combs), cooperated with the production. *CW:* Scenes of domestic violence, substance abuse and brief sensuality. 92m/C VHS, Closed Caption. Roxanne Hart, Holly Marie Combs, Sarah Chalke, James Wilder, Johnathan Scarfe; *D:* Bill W.L. Norton; *W:* Richard DeLong Adams. *USH*

Our Relations ✂✂✂½ 1936 Confusion reigns when Stan and Ollie meet the twin brothers they never knew they had, a pair of happy-go-lucky sailors. Laurel directs the pair through madcap encounters with their twins' wives and the local underworld. One of the pair's best efforts, though not well-remembered. Based on a story by W.W. Jacobs. 94m/B VHS, Beta. Stan Laurel, Oliver

Hardy, Alan Hale, Sidney Toler, James Finlayson, Daphne Pollard; *D:* Harry Lachman. *OOD, MLB*

Our Sons ✂✂½ 1991 Two middle-aged moms strike up an unlikely friendship over their gay sons in this TV weeper. Arkansas waitress Luanna (Ann Margret) hasn't talked to son Donald (Ivanek) in years—now he's dying of AIDS. Successful career woman Audrey (Andrews in her TV-movie debut) has seemingly accepted son James' (Grant) life with Donald and it's James who urges his mother to make contact with Luanna and persuade her to see Donald one last time. 100m/C VHS. Julie Andrews, Ann-Margret, Hugh Grant, Zeljko Ivanek, Tony Roberts; *D:* John Erman; *W:* John Erman, William Hanley.

Our Time ✂✂½ *Death of Her Innocence* 1974 An exclusive girls finishing school in the '50s is the setting for the friendship of Abby (Martin) and Muffy (Slade) and their first stirrings of romance. But when Muffy gets pregnant, tragedy awaits. Sappy. 91m/C VHS. Pamela Sue Martin, Betsey Slade, Parker Stevenson, George O'Hanlon Jr., Roderick Cook, Edith Atwater, Meg Wyllie, Debralee Scott, Nora Heflin, Kathryn Holcomb, Robert Walden; *D:* Peter Hyams; *W:* Jane C. Stanton. *WAR*

Our Town ✂✂✂ 1940 Small-town New England life in Grover's Corners in the early 1900s is celebrated in this well-performed and directed adaptation of the Pulitzer Prize-winning play by Thornton Wilder. Film debut of Scott. 90m/B VHS, Beta. Martha Scott, William Holden, Thomas Mitchell, Fay Bainter, Guy Kibbee, Beulah Bondi, Frank Craven; *D:* Sam Wood; *M:* Aaron Copland. Nominations: Academy Awards '40: Best Actress (Scott), Best Interior Decoration, Best Picture, Best Sound, Best Score. *CNG, MRV, NOS*

Our Town ✂✂✂ 1977 Television version of Thornton Wilder's classic play about everyday life in Grovers Corners, a small New England town at the turn of the century. It hews more closely to the style of the stage version than the earlier film version. 120m/C VHS, Beta, LV. Ned Beatty, Sada Thompson, Ronny Cox, Glynnis O'Connor, Robby Benson, Hal Holbrook, John Houseman; *D:* Franklin J. Schaffner. *MAS*

Our Town ✂✂½ 1989 Filmed TV version of the Tony Award-winning Lincoln Center production of the Thornton Wilder play focusing on small-town life in Grover's Corners, New Hampshire. Gray is the omniscient Stage Manager, with Stolz and Miller as the young couple brought together by the everyday cycle of happiness and hardship. 104m/C VHS. Eric Stoltz, Penelope Ann Miller, Spalding Gray; *D:* Gregory Mosher. *MAS*

Our Very Own ✂✂ 1950 At eighteen, and about to graduate from high school, Gail (Blyth) discovers she was adopted. So she decides to find her birth mother and then comes to realize what her foster parents really mean to her. Pretty sappy all the way 'round. 93m/B VHS. Ann Blyth, Jane Wyatt, Donald Cook, Farley Granger, Ann Dvorak, Joan Evans, Natalie Wood, Martin Milner, Phyllis Kirk; *D:* David Miller; *W:* F. Hugh Herbert; *C:* Lee Garmes; *M:* Victor Young. *HBO*

Our Vines Have Tender Grapes ✂✂✂½ 1945 A change of pace role for the volatile Robinson who plays a kind Norwegian farmer, living in Wisconsin with his daughter, the spunky O'Brien. The film is made-up of small-town moments as O'Brien learns a few of life's lessons, eased by the thoughtful compassion of Robinson. Based on the novel "For Our Vines Have Tender Grapes" by George Victor Martin. 105m/B VHS. Edward G. Robinson, Margaret O'Brien, James Craig, Agnes Moorehead, Jackie "Butch" Jenkins, Morris Carnovsky, Frances Gifford, Sara Haden, Louis Jean Heydt; *D:* Roy Rowland; *W:* Dalton Trumbo; *C:* Robert L. Surtees. *MGM, MOV, BTV*

Out ✂✂½ 1988 A drifter's travels throughout the U.S. from the '60s to the '80s. Successfully manages to satirize just about every conceivable situation but keeps from posturing by not taking itself too seriously. Adapted from an experimental novel by Ronald Sukenick. 88m/C VHS. Peter Coyote, Danny Glover, O-Lan Shepard, Jim Haynie, Scott Beach,

Semu Haute; *D:* Eli Hollander; *W:* Eli Hollander; *M:* David Cope. *NO*

Out Cold ✂✂½ 1989 (R) Black comedy follows the misadventures of a butcher who believes he has accidentally frozen his business partner; the iced man's girlfriend, who really killed him; and the detective who tries to solve the crime. Too many poor frozen body jokes may leave the viewer cold. 91m/C VHS, Beta, LV. John Lithgow, Teri Garr, Randy Quaid, Bruce McGill; *D:* Malcolm Mowbray; *M:* Michel Colombier. *HBO*

Out for Blood ✂✂ 1993 (R) Attorney John Decker is living a happy life until his family is murdered by drug dealers. He turns vigilante, dubbed "Karateman" by the press, and finds himself hunted by the cops and the criminals. ?m/C VHS, Closed Caption. Don "The Dragon" Wilson, Shari Shattuck, Michael Delano, Kenneth McLeod, Todd Curtis, Timothy Baker, Howard Jackson, Bob Schott, Eric Lee; *D:* Richard W. Munchkin; *W:* David S. Green. *PMH*

Out for Justice ✂✂½ 1991 (R) A psycho Brooklyn hood goes on a murder spree, and homeboy turned lone-wolf cop Seagal races other police and the mob to get at him. Bloodthirsty and profane, it does try to depict N.Y.C.'s Italian-American community—but 90 percent of them are dead by the end so what's the point? Better yet, why does it open with a quote from Arthur Miller? Better still, what's Daffy Duck doing on this tape peddling Warner Bros. T-shirts to kid viewers?! *CW:* Strong language, strong violence and drug use, and sensuality. 91m/C VHS, Beta, LV, 8mm, Letterbox. Steven Seagal, William Forsythe, Jerry Orbach, Julianna Margulies, Gina Gershon, John Leguizamo, Julie Strain. *WAR*

Out of Africa ✂✂✂ 1985 (PG) An epic film of the years spent by Danish authoress Isak Dinesen (her true name is Karen Blixen) on a Kenya coffee plantation. She moved to Africa to marry, and later fell in love with Denys Finch-Hatten, a British adventurer. Based on several books, including biographies of the two lovers. Some critics loved the scenery and music; others despised the acting and the script. A definite "no" for those who love action. 161m/C VHS, Beta, LV, Closed Caption. Meryl Streep, Robert Redford, Klaus Maria Brandauer, Michael Kitchen, Malick Bowens, Michael Gough, Suzanna Hamilton, Rachel Kempson, Graham Crowden, Shane Rimmer, Donal McCann, Iman, Joseph Thiaka, Stephen Kinyanjui; *D:* Sydney Pollack; *W:* Kurt Luedtke; *C:* David Watkin; *M:* John Barry. Academy Awards '85: Best Adapted Screenplay, Best Art Direction/Set Decoration, Best Cinematography, Best Director (Pollack), Best Picture, Best Sound, Best Original Score; British Academy Awards '86: Best Adapted Screenplay; Golden Globe Awards '86: Best Film—Drama, Best Supporting Actor (Brandauer), Best Score; Los Angeles Film Critics Association Awards '85: Best Actress (Streep), Best Cinematography; National Board of Review Awards '85: Best Supporting Actor (Brandauer); New York Film Critics Awards '85: Best Cinematography, Best Supporting Actor (Brandauer); Nominations: Academy Awards '85: Best Actress (Streep), Best Costume Design, Best Film Editing, Best Supporting Actor (Brandauer). *USH, BTV*

Out of Annie's Past ✂✂½ 1994 (R) Successful career woman Annie Carver (Stewart) has managed to hide a dreadful secret from family and co-workers for some 10 years. But now the past is back to haunt her—seems Annie was once the prime suspect in a murder. Made for cable. *CW:* Some violence. 91m/C VHS. Catherine Mary Stewart, Dennis Farina, Scott Valentine, Carsten Norgaard, Michel Flynn; *D:* Stuart Cooper; *W:* Pablo F. Fenjves. *USH*

Out of Bounds ✂✂½ 1986 (R) An Iowa farmboy picks up the wrong bag at the Los Angeles airport, and is plunged into a world of crime, drugs, and murder. Plenty of action, but the fast pace can't hide huge holes in the script or the silliness of Hall playing a tough kid on the run from the law. 93m/C VHS, Beta, LV, Closed Caption. Anthony Michael Hall, Jenny Wright, Jeff Kober; *D:* Richard Tuggle; *C:* Bruce Surtees; *M:* Stewart Copeland. *COL*

Out of Control 🎬 1985 (R) A plane full of rich teenagers crash on a secluded island and must battle a gang of vicious smugglers to survive. A teen sex theme keeps working its way in, leaving the viewer as confused as the actors and actresses appear to be. 78m/C VHS, Beta, LV. Betsy Russell, Martin Hewitt, Claudia Udy, Andrew J. Lederer; **D:** Allan Holzman; **W:** Vicangelo Bullock; **C:** John A. Alonzo. *VTR*

Out of Order 🎬½ 1984 A German-made film about people stuck in an office building's malevolent, free-thinking elevator. Dubbed. 87m/C VHS, Beta. *GE* Renee Soutendijk, Goetz George, Wolfgang Kieling, Hannes Jaenicke; **D:** Carl Schenkel. *ART, VES*

Out of Season 🎬🎬 *Winter Rates* 1975 (R) Mother and teenage daughter compete for the attentions of the mother's mysterious ex-lover. We never know who wins the man in this enigmatic drama set in an English village, and hints of incest make the story even murkier. Had only a short run in the U.S. 90m/C VHS, Beta. *GB* Cliff Robertson, Vanessa Redgrave, Susan George; **D:** Alan Bridges. *VCI*

Out of Sight 1998 (R) Follows charming bank robber Jack Foley (Clooney) as he escapes from prison and takes a female federal marshal (Lopez) as a (temporary) hostage. The two fall in love but she's still determined to bring him to justice, even as he plans his next heist. Adapted from the novel by Elmore Leonard. Not yet reviewed.**CW:** Language and some strong violence. ?m/C VHS. George Clooney, Jennifer Lopez, Ving Rhames, Dennis Farina, Don Cheadle, Albert Brooks, Steve Zahn, Catherine Keener, Luis Guzman, Nancy Allen, Isaiah Washington; **D:** Steven Soderbergh; **W:** Scott Frank; **C:** Elliot Davis; **M:** Cliff Martinez. *NYR*

Out of Sight, Out of Her Mind 🎬🎬 1989 (R) After witnessing her daughter burned alive, Alice is released from a mental institution. She tries to start a new life, but her daughter won't let her—she keeps appearing, crying out for help. 94m/C VHS, Beta, LV. Susan Blakely, Eddie Albert, Wings Hauser. *PAR*

Out of Sync 🎬½ 1995 (R) Deejay Jason St. Julian gets in trouble with his bookies and L.A. detectives, one of whom forces him into an undercover job with a drug-dealing club owner. Then Jason falls for the dealer's girlfriend. Hip-hop soundtrack may provide the only interest.**CW:** Strong sexuality, language and violence. 105m/C VHS, LV, Closed Caption. L.L. Cool J., Victoria Dillard, Howard Hesseman, Ramy Zada, Don Yesso, Yaphet Kotto; **D:** Debbie Allen; **W:** Robert E. Dorn; **M:** Steve Tyrell. *ART*

Out of the Blue 🎬🎬½ 1947 There's trouble in paradise for a married man when a shady lady passes out in his apartment. Thinking she is dead, he tries to get rid of the body. The antics with his neighbor and wife provide plenty of laughs. 86m/B VHS, Beta, LV. George Brent, Virginia Mayo, Carole Landis, Turhan Bey, Ann Dvorak; **D:** Leigh Jason.

Out of the Blue 🎬🎬🎬 1980 (R) A harsh, violent portrait of a shattered family. When an imprisoned father's return fails to reunite this Woodstock-generation family, the troubled teenage daughter takes matters into her own hands. "Easy Rider" star Hopper seems to have reconsidered the effects of the 1960s. 94m/C VHS, Beta. Dennis Hopper, Linda Manz, Raymond Burr; **D:** Dennis Hopper.

Out of the Body 🎬 1988 (R) A man is possessed by a spirit that likes to kill young, beautiful women. This makes him (and the viewer) uncomfortable. 91m/C VHS, LV. Mark Hembrow, Tessa Humphries; **D:** Brian Trenchard-Smith. *NO*

Out of the Dark 🎬½ 1988 (R) The female employees of a telephone-sex service are stalked by a killer wearing a clown mask in this tongue-in-cheek thriller. A few laughs amid the slaughter. Look for Divine. 98m/C VHS, Beta, LV, Closed Caption. Cameron Dye, Divine, Karen Black, Bud Cort, Lynn Danielson, Geoffrey Lewis, Paul Bartel, Tracey Walter, Silvania Gallardo, Starr Andreeff, Lainie Kazan, Tab Hunter;

D: Michael Schroeder; **W:** James DeFelice; **M:** Paul Antonelli. *COL*

Out of the Darkness 🎬🎬🎬 1985 (R) A television movie about the personal life of the New York detective who hunted and arrested sexual killer Son of Sam. Sheen shines in a tight suspenser. 96m/C VHS, Beta, LV. Martin Sheen, Hector Elizondo, Matt Clark, Jennifer Salt, Eddie Egan, Robert Trebor; **D:** Jud Taylor; **W:** T.S. Cook. *VTR, THV*

Out of the Past 🎬🎬🎬½ *Build My Gallows High* 1947 A private detective gets caught in a complex web of love, murder, and money in this film noir classic. The plot is torturous but clear thanks to fine directing. Mitchum became an overnight star after this film, which was overlooked but now considered one of the best in its genre. Based on Geoffrey Homes' novel "Build My Gallows High." Remade in 1984 as "Against All Odds." 97m/B VHS, Beta, LV. Robert Mitchum, Kirk Douglas, Jane Greer, Rhonda Fleming, Steve Brodie, Dickie Moore; **D:** Jacques Tourneur; **W:** Geoffrey Homes. National Film Registry '91. *TTC*

Out of the Rain 🎬🎬½ 1990 (R) A small town becomes a hotbed of deceit and lies due to the influence of drugs. A man and and a woman engage in a passionate struggle to free themselves from the town's grip. 91m/C VHS, Beta, LV. Bridget Fonda, Michael O'Keefe, John E. O'Keefe, John Seitz, Georgine Hall, Al Shannon; **D:** Gary Winick; **W:** Shem Bitterman. *CCB, ART*

Out of the Shadows 🎬🎬½ 199? Scotland Yard Chief Inspector Michael Hayden (Dance) investigates a series of international art thefts that lead him to believe the goods are being smuggled out of the country through diplomatic channels. 95m/C VHS. *GB* Charles Dance, Alexandra Paul, Wanda Ventham. *VCO*

The Out-of-Towners 🎬🎬🎬 1970 (G) A pair of Ohio rubes travels to New York City and along the way everything that could go wrong does. Lemmon's performance is excellent and Simon's script is, as usual, both wholesome and funny. 98m/C VHS, Beta, LV. Jack Lemmon, Sandy Dennis, Anne Meara, Sandy Baron, Billy Dee Williams; **D:** Arthur Hiller; **W:** Neil Simon. Writers Guild of America '70: Best Original Screenplay. *PAR*

Out on a Limb 🎬🎬 1987 MacLaine plays herself in this made-for-television miniseries based on her best-selling book by the same name. In the midst of love affairs with an unnamed British politician and a mysterious teacher, she learns about her past, present, and future through meditation and her beliefs in reincarnation. Features footage of psychics performing spiritual channeling. Beautiful scenery filmed on location in California, Hong Kong, London, Hawaii, Sweden, and Peru, but the acting is just average, and the movie is slow in some parts. A 234-minute special collector's edition is also available. 160m/C VHS, Beta, Closed Caption. Shirley MacLaine, Charles Dance, John Heard, Anne Jackson, Jerry Orbach; **D:** Robert Butler. *WSH*

Out on a Limb 🎬 1992 (PG) Lame comedy follows the misadventures of financial whiz Bill Campbell (Broderick). His young sister is convinced their stepfather is a criminal and persuades her brother to return home. On his way, Bill is robbed and abandoned by a woman hitchhiker, then found by two moronic brothers. It also turns out his stepfather has a twin brother who wants revenge for past crimes. Frantic chase scenes and lots of noise do not a comedy make. Broderick and Jones also appeared together in "Ferris Bueller's Day Off." 82m/C VHS, Beta, LV, Closed Caption. Matthew Broderick, Jeffrey Jones, Heidi Kling, John C. Reilly, Marian Mercer, Larry Hankin, David Margulies; **D:** Francis Veber. *MGM*

Out on Bail 🎬½ 1989 (R) A law-abiding citizen witnesses a murder, only to discover the crooked town council is behind the slaying. 102m/C VHS, Beta. Robert Ginty, Kathy Shower, Tom Badal,

Sydney Lassick; **D:** Gordon Hessler; **W:** Tom Badal, Jason Booth. *TWE*

Out There 🎬🎬½ 1995 (PG-13) Cable sci-fi comedy finds photographer Delbert Mosley (Campbell) buying a Brownie camera at a garage sale and discovering the 25-year-old film shows pictures of a UFO encounter. Mosley then tries to verify the photos with a supermarket tabloid, the military, and UFO fanatics all on his trail. Fast-paced amusement with appealing performances.**CW:** Nude images and crude language. 98m/C VHS, Beta, Closed Caption. Bill Campbell, Wendy Schaal, Julie Brown, David Rasche, Paul Dooley, Bill Cobbs, Bob(cat) Goldthwait, Rod Steiger, June Lockhart, Jill St. John, Carel Struycken, Billy Bob Thornton, P.J. Soles; **D:** Sam Irvin; **W:** Thomas Strelich, Alison Nigh; **C:** Gary Tieche; **M:** Deborah Holland, Frankie Blue. *PAR*

Out to Sea 🎬🎬½ 1997 (PG-13) Charlie (Matthau) persuades brother-in-law Herb (Lemmon) to become a dance instructor aboard a cruise ship so they can meet women and con them out of money. Charlie sets his sights on feisty socialite Liz (Cannon), while Herb romances Vivian (DeHaven), who's tagging along on her daughter's honeymoon. Both of these "salty old dogs" have to avoid the wrath of militaristic cruise director Gil (Spiner). The duo still has great comic timing, as they continue to defy the odds that this is the one that's gonna flop. Great supporting cast, which includes O'Connor in a couple of nifty dance scenes, seems to be having a great time.**CW:** Language and sex-related humor. 109m/C VHS, Closed Caption. Walter Matthau, Jack Lemmon, Dyan Cannon, Gloria De Haven, Brent Spiner, Elaine Stritch, Hal Linden, Donald O'Connor, Rue McClanahan, Estelle Harris; **D:** Martha Coolidge; **W:** Robert Nelson Jacobs, Danny Jacobson; **C:** Lajos Koltai; **M:** David Newman. *FOX*

Outbreak 🎬🎬🎬 1994 (R) Smuggled African monkey spits on someone who kisses someone else who sneezes on a bunch of people, thus initiating the spread of a highly infectious mystery disease in a northern California 'burb. Hoffman leads a team of scientists in a search for the antiserum, but it's a secret government plot to exterminate the victims that literally sends Hoffman and crew into action movie cliche overdrive (add "helicopter" to the list of chase scene vehicles). Not that that's so bad—if the beat-the-clock tempo doesn't grab you, paranoia certainly will. But Hoffman's hardly a threat to Arnold or Sylvester as the next action hero, and the talented Russo remains suspiciously ravishing even with festering pustules. Based on two books: Richard Preston's "The Hot Zone" and Laurie Garrett's "The Coming Plague."**CW:** Language; ugly sick people. 128m/C VHS, LV, Closed Caption, DVD. Dustin Hoffman, Rene Russo, Morgan Freeman, Donald Sutherland, Cuba Gooding Jr., Kevin Spacey, J.T. Walsh; **D:** Wolfgang Petersen; **W:** Robert Roy Pool, Laurence Dworet; **C:** Michael Ballhaus; **M:** James Newton Howard. New York Film Critics Awards '95: Best Supporting Actor (Spacey). *WAR*

The Outcast 🎬🎬 1954 A young tough heads west to seize the family ranch wrongfully held by a conniving uncle. Of course he finds love as well, and enjoys gun and fistfights in this exciting though unspectacular western. 90m/C VHS. John Derek, Jim Davis, Joan Davis; **D:** William Witney. *REP*

The Outcast 🎬½ 1984 Story of three brothers who live by the ax, love from the heart, hate with passion, and die violently. Trouble is they have to recite from a script written in crayon. 86m/C VHS, Beta. Ben Dekker, Sandra Prinsloo. *REP*

The Outcasts 🎬🎬🎬 1986 A Taiwanese film about young gay boys in an urban jungle who are given shelter and protection by an aging photographer. In Chinese with English subtitles. 102m/C VHS, Beta. *TW* **D:** Yu Kan-Ping. *FCT*

Outcasts of the City 🎬🎬 1958 The sort of negligible film filler that TV killed off. An American officer in post-WWII Germany romances a German girl, then gets blamed for the death of her Boche beau. 61m/B VHS. Osa Massen, Robert Hutton,

Maria Palmer, Nestor Paiva, John Hamilton, George Neise, Norbert Schiller, George Sanders; **D:** Boris L. Petroff. *NOS*

Outcasts of the Trail *&½* 1949 When Tom White (Gallaudet) is jailed for robbing the stage, his children are shunned by the town even after Tom decides to return the stolen cash after his release. So, it's up to stagecoach driver Pat Garrett (Hale) to clear up the family's trouble. **61m/B VHS, Closed Caption.** Monte Hale, John Gallaudet, Roy Barcroft, Jeff Donnell, T.V. Tommy Ivo, Paul Hurst; **D:** Philip Ford; **W:** Olive Cooper, Stanley Wilson; **C:** Bud Thackery. *REP*

The Outer Limits: Galaxy Being
1963 "There is nothing wrong with your TV set..." in this sci-fi series which ran from 1963-65. In the show's pilot episode, an obsessed scientist transmits a pure-energy being from Andromeda into our universe, and chaos ensues. Additional episodes are available. **53m/B VHS, Beta.** Cliff Robertson, Jacqueline Scott, Lee Philips, William O. Douglas Jr.; **D:** Leslie Stevens. *MGM, MOV*

The Outer Limits: Sandkings *&&&*
Sandkings 1995 Made-for-cable revival of the '60s sci-fi series is creepier than ever with this tale of loony scientist Simon Kress (Bridges). He discovers tiny alien eggs while doing an analysis of Martian soil samples and decides to take his research home with him when the government cuts off funding. Big mistake—the critters he successfully hatches in his barn are mean and hungry. Features both dad Lloyd and Beau's 10-year-old son, Dylan, in roles. **93m/C VHS, Closed Caption.** Beau Bridges, Lloyd Bridges, Helen Shaver, Dylan Bridges, Kim Coates; **D:** Stuart Gillard; **W:** Melinda M. Snodgrass. *MGM*

The Outfit *&&½* 1993 (R) It's the 1930s and a mob war is brewing between Lucky Luciano, Legs Diamond and Dutch Schultz. A maverick FBI agent gets in good with Diamond and works to end their reign of crime—only he winds up being the spark to light a war between the rival bosses.**CW:** Language, gangster violence, and sexuality. **92m/C VHS, LV, Closed Caption.** John Christian, Billy Drago, Lance Henriksen, Martin Kove, Josh Moby, Rick Washburne; **D:** J. Christian Ingvordsen; **W:** J. Christian Ingvordsen, Steven Kaman, Whitney Ransick. *USH, SGE*

The Outing *&&* The Lamp 1987 (R) A group of high school kids sneaks into a museum at night to party, and get hunted down by a 3,000-year-old genie-in-a-lamp. The genie idea is original enough to make things interesting. Mediocre special effects and run-of-the-mill acting. **87m/C VHS, Beta.** Deborah Winters, James Huston, Andra St. Ivanyi, Scott Bankston, Mark Mitchell, Andre Chimene, Damon Merrill, Barry Coffing; **D:** Tom Daley; **W:** Warren Chaney; **C:** Herbert Raditschnig. *ART*

Outland *&&* 1981 (R) On a volcanic moon of Jupiter, miners begin suffering from spells of insanity. A single federal marshal begins an investigation that threatens the colony's survival. No more or less than a western in space, and the science is rather poor. Might make an interesting double feature with "High Noon," though. **109m/C VHS, Beta, LV, Letterbox, Closed Caption.** Sean Connery, Peter Boyle, Frances Sternhagen, James B. Sikking; **D:** Peter Hyams; **W:** Peter Hyams; **M:** Jerry Goldsmith. Nominations: Academy Awards '81: Best Sound. *WAR*

The Outlaw *&&* 1943 Hughes's variation on the saga of Billy the Kid, which spends more time on Billy's relationship with girlfriend Rio than the climactic showdown with Pat Garrett. The famous Russell vehicle isn't as steamy as it must have seemed to viewers of the day, but the brouhaha around it served to keep it on the shelf for six years. Also available colorized. **123m/B VHS, Beta, LV.** Jane Russell, Jack Buetel, Walter Huston, Thomas Mitchell; **D:** Howard Hughes. *CNG, MRV, NOS*

The Outlaw and His Wife *&&½* 1917 An early silent film about a farmer, accused of a petty crime, who flees with his wife into the mountains to escape the police. This powerful drama was a breakthrough film for the early Swedish

movie industry. **73m/B VHS, Beta, LV.** *SW* Victor Sjostrom, Edith Erastoff; **D:** Victor Ojoutrom. *KIV, FCT*

The Outlaw Bikers—Gang Wars *&*
1970 The original road warriors take it to the streets as rival biker gangs square off. **90m/C VHS, Beta.** Clancy Syrko, Des Roberts, King John III, Linda Jackson; **D:** Lawrence Merrick.

Outlaw Blues *&&* 1977 (PG) An ex-convict becomes a national folk hero when he sets out to reclaim his stolen hit song about prison life. St. James is charming in her first major movie role. A grab bag of action, drama, and tongue-in-cheek humor. **101m/C VHS, Beta.** Peter Fonda, Susan St. James, Johnny Crawford, Michael Lerner, James Callahan; **D:** Richard T. Heffron; **M:** Charles Bernstein. *WAR*

Outlaw Country *&&½* 1949 LaRue has a dual role as the marshal who is after a band of counterfeiters and an outlaw who's part of the gang. **72m/B VHS.** Lash LaRue, Al "Fuzzy" St. John, House Peters Jr., Ted Adams, Dan White, Steve Dunhill; **D:** Ray Taylor. *GPV*

The Outlaw Deputy *&½* 1935 The law-abiding McCoy as an outlaw! It's really a mistake and Lane helps him clear his name. Based on the story "King of Cactusville" by Johnston McCulley. **55m/B VHS.** Tim McCoy, Nora Lane, Bud Osborne, Si Jenks, George Offerman Jr.; **D:** Otto Brower. *GPV*

Outlaw Express *&½* 1938 After the annexing of California, a U.S. marshall is sent to stop a gang of outlaws who have been raiding Spanish landowners. **57m/B VHS, Beta.** Bob Baker, Cecilia Callejo, Leroy Mason, Don Barclay, Carleton Young; **D:** George Waggner. *DVT*

Outlaw Force *&* 1987 (R) A Vietnam veteran country singer tracks down the vicious rednecks that kidnapped his daughter and raped and killed his wife. Heavener did all the work in this low-budget, low-quality take-off on "Death Wish." **95m/C VHS, Beta.** David Heavener, Frank Stallone, Paul Smith, Robert Bjorklund, Devin Dunsworth; **D:** David Heavener. *TWE*

Outlaw Fury *&½* 1950 Another Shamrock Ellison epic, this time dealing with a coward proving himself by killing the bad guys. **55m/B VHS, Beta, LV.** James Ellison, Russell Hayden. *NO*

Outlaw Gang *&½* 1949 A marshal investigates a rash of rancher killings, leading to a conflict between Indians and local land and water companies. **59m/B VHS, Beta, LV.** Donald (Don "Red") Barry, Robert Lowery, Betty Adams. *NO*

The Outlaw Josey Wales *&&&½*
1976 (PG) Eastwood plays a farmer with a motive for revenge—his family was killed and for years he was betrayed and hunted. His desire to play the lone killer is, however, tempered by his need for family and friends. He kills plenty, but in the end finds happiness. Considered one of the last great Westerns, with many superb performances. Eastwood took over directorial chores during filming from Kaufman, who co-scripted. Adapted from "Gone to Texas" by Forest Carter. **135m/C VHS, Beta, LV.** Clint Eastwood, Chief Dan George, Sondra Locke, Matt Clark, John Vernon, Bill McKinney, Sam Bottoms; **D:** Clint Eastwood; **W:** Philip Kaufman; **C:** Bruce Surtees. National Film Registry '96;. Nominations: Academy Awards '76: Best Original Score. *WAR, TLF*

Outlaw Justice *&* 1932 Worn oater plot has our hero infiltrating a gang of outlaws to bring them to justice and save the heroine. **56m/C VHS, Beta.** Jack Hoxie, Dorothy Gulliver, Donald Keith, Kermit Maynard, Charles "Blackie" King, Tom London; **D:** Armand Schaefer. *GPV*

Outlaw of Gor *&½* 1987 (PG) Once again, the mild professor is transported to Gor, where he has new, improved, bloody adventures. Lots of sword-play, but no magic. Sequel to "Gor." From the novel by John Norman. **89m/C VHS, Beta, Closed Caption.** Rebecca Ferratti, Urbano Barberini, Jack Palance, Donna Denton; **D:** John Cardos; **W:** R.J. Marx. *WAR*

Outlaw of the Plains *&* 1946 Another of Crabbe's cowboy pictures in which he played hero Billy Carson, now bailing his trouble-prone sidekick out of a land swindle. Very plain indeed. **56m/B VHS.** Buster Crabbe, Al "Fuzzy" St. John, Patti McCarty, Charles "Blackie" King, Karl Hackett, John Cason, Bud Osborne, Budd Buster, Charles "Slim" Whitaker; **D:** Sam Newfield. *NOS*

Outlaw Riders *&* 1972 (PG) Three outlaw bikers take it on the lam after committing a series of disastrous bank robberies. **84m/C VHS, Beta.** Sonny West, Darlene Duralia, Bambi Allen, Bill Bonner; **D:** Tony Houston. *NO*

Outlaw Roundup *&* 1944 The Texas Rangers battle an outlaw gang. Guess who wins. **51m/B VHS, Beta.** Tex O'Brien, James Newill, Guy Wilkerson, Helen Chapman, Jack Ingram, I. Stanford Jolley; **D:** Harry Fraser. *NOS, MRV, VDM*

Outlaw Rule *&½* 1936 Standard action-packed western adventure pitting outlaws against the law of the West. **61m/B VHS, Beta.** Reb Russell, Betty Mack, Yakima Canutt, Jack Rockwell, John McGuire, Alan Bridge; **D:** S. Roy Luby. *NOS, VCN, HEG*

The Outlaw Tamer *&* 1933 Even though Chandler is on the run he still helps capture some horse thieves. **56m/B VHS, Beta.** Lane Chandler, J.P. McGowan, Janet Morgan, George "Gabby" Hayes; **D:** J.P. McGowan. *GPV, VCN*

Outlaw Trail *&½* 1944 The Trail Blazers put an end to a counterfeiter's evil ways. **53m/B VHS, Beta.** Hoot Gibson, Bob Steele, Chief Thundercloud, Jennifer Holt, Cy Kendall; **D:** Robert Emmett Tansey. *NOS, DVT*

Outlaw Women *&* 1952 A western town is run by a woman who won't let male outlaws in—until one wins her heart. **76m/C VHS, Beta.** Marie Windsor, Jackie Coogan, Carla Balenda; **D:** Sam Newfield. *NO*

The Outlaws Is Coming! *&&½* 1965 Three magazine staffers (Larry, Moe, and Curly Joe) and their editor (West) encounter Wyatt Earp, Wild Bill Hickock, Jesse James, and Annie Oakley when they journey out West to save the buffalo. Last, and one of the best, of the Three Stooges feature films. **90m/B VHS.** Moe Howard, Larry Fine, Joe DeRita, Adam West, Nancy Kovack, Emil Sitka, Henry Gibson; **D:** Norman Maurer. *COL*

Outlaws of Sonora *&½* 1938 A man transports money to a neighboring town while his outlaw double tries to steal it from him. **58m/B VHS.** Bob Livingston, Ray Corrigan, Max Terhune, Jack Mulhall, Otis Harlan; **D:** George Sherman. *NOS, DVT*

Outlaws of the Desert *&½* 1941 Having run out of bad guys in the Old West, Hoppy and his pals head to Arabia to buy some horses. Once there, they get involved in a kidnapping. Russell Hayden is replaced as Hoppy's sidekick by Brad King. Duncan ("The Cisco Kid") Renaldo plays the sheik. **66m/B VHS.** William Boyd, Brad King, Andy Clyde, Forrest Stanley, Jean Phillips, Duncan Renaldo, George Lewis; **D:** Howard Bretherton. *NOS*

Outlaws of the Range *&½* 1936 Action western featuring outlaws who terrorize the countryside. **60m/B VHS, Beta.** Bill Cody, Catherine Cotter, William McCall, Gordon Griffith; **D:** Al(bert) Herman. *VCN*

Outlaw's Paradise *&&* 1939 Cowboy hero McCoy plays not only a lawman out to catch mail thieves, but also the chief outlaw he's hunting! That's one way to keep the budget low. **62m/B VHS.** Tim McCoy, Benny Corbett, Joan Barclay, Ted Adams, Forrest Taylor, Bob Terry; **D:** Sam Newfield. *NOS, LOO, RXM*

Outpost in Morocco *&½* 1949 A desert soldier is sent to quiet the restless natives and falls for the rebel leader's daughter. The good guys win, but the love interest is sacrificed. Glory before love boys, and damn the story. **92m/B VHS.** George Raft, Marie Windsor, Akim Tamiroff, John Litel, Eduard Franz; **D:** Robert Florey. *NOS, MRV, MGM*

Outrage! ♂♂½ 1986 An upstanding citizen guns down his daughter's killer and turns himself in to police. His ambitious lawyer fights an open-and-shut homicide case with both fair and foul means. Not a shootout like the cassette box suggests, but an okay courtroom drama attacking excesses of the legal system. From a novel by Henry Denker, made for TV by producer Irwin Allen. 96m/C VHS. Robert Preston, Beau Bridges, Anthony Newley, Mel Ferrer, Burgess Meredith, Linda Purl, William Allen Young; **D:** Walter Grauman. THV

Outrage ♂♂ Dispara 1993 (R) Journalist Marco Vallez's (Banderas) latest assignment is a story about a traveling circus. Bored with the usual acts, he's intrigued by equestrian/sharpshooter Anna (Neri) and asks her for an interview, which leads to passion. While Marco is on assignment in Barcelona, Anna is attacked and raped in her trailer. Rather than calling the police, Anna decides to take her own revenge. Spanish with subtitles or dubbed. **CW:** Violence, including a brutal rape scene; sexuality and language. 108m/C VHS. SP Antonio Banderas, Francesca Neri; **D:** Carlos Saura; **W:** Carlos Saura; **C:** Javier Aguirresarobe. APX

Outrageous! ♂♂♂ 1977 (R) An offbeat, low-budget comedy about the strange relationship between a gay female impersonator and his pregnant schizophrenic friend. The pair end up in New York, where they feel right at home. Russell's impersonations of female film stars earned him the best actor prize at the Berlin Film Festival. 100m/C VHS, Beta. CA Craig Russell, Hollis McLaren, Richard Easley, Allan Moyle, Helen Shaver; **D:** Richard Benner. COL

Outrageous Fortune ♂♂ 1987 (R) Two would-be actresses—one prim and innocent and one wildly trampy—chase after the same two-timing boyfriend and get involved in a dangerous CIA plot surrounding a deadly bacteria. Tired plot. Mediocre acting and formula jokes, but somehow still funny. Disney's first foray into comedy for grown-ups. 112m/C VHS, Beta, LV, Closed Caption. Shelley Long, Bette Midler, George Carlin, Peter Coyote; **D:** Arthur Hiller; **W:** Leslie Dixon; **M:** Alan Silvestri. TOU

Outside Chance ♂ 1978 A soapy, sanitized remake of Mimieux's film, "Jackson County Jail," wherein an innocent woman is persecuted in a small Southern jail. Made for television. 92m/C VHS, Beta. Yvette Mimieux, Royce D. Applegate; **D:** Michael Miller. NLC

Outside Chance of Maximillian Glick ♂♂ 1988 (G) A sentimental Canadian comedy about a boy's dreams and his tradition-bound Jewish family. 94m/C VHS, Beta. CA Noam Zylberman, Fairuza Balk, Saul Rubinek; **D:** Allan Goldstein; **C:** Ian Elkin. Toronto-City Award '88: Best Canadian Feature Film.

The Outside Man ♂♂ Un Homme Est Mort 1973 (PG) A French hit man is called to Los Angeles to knock off a crime boss, which he does. But then an American hit man is hired to do in the Frenchman. The climatic showdown is set around the crime boss' body, which happens to be embalmed in a sitting position. Decidely offbeat. 104m/C VHS. FR Jean-Louis Trintignant, Roy Scheider, Ann-Margret, Angie Dickinson, Georgia Engel, Carlo De Meyo, Umberto Orsini, Ted de Corsia, Felice Orlandi, John Hillerman; **D:** Jacques Deray. MGM

Outside the Law ♂♂ 1921 Lon Chaney plays dual roles of the underworld hood in "Black Mike Sylva," and a Chinese servant in "Ah Wing." Silent. 77m/B VHS. Lon Chaney Sr., Priscilla Dean, Ralph Lewis, Wheeler Oakman; **D:** Tod Browning. KIV, CCB, VYY

Outside the Law ♂½ 1995 (R) Maverick cop Brad Kingsbury (Bradley) crosses the line when he falls for luscious Tanya Borgman (Thomson), who's the prime suspect in a murder investigation. Also available unrated. 94m/C VHS, LV, Closed Caption. David Bradley, Anna Thomson, Ashley Laurence; **D:** Boaz Davidson; **W:** Dennis Dimster Denk; **C:** Avi Karpik; **M:** Blake Leyh. TTC, NLC, IME

The Outsiders ♂♂½ 1983 (PG) Based on the popular S.E. Hinton book, the story of a teen gang from the wrong side of the tracks and their conflicts with society and each other. Melodramatic and over-done, but teenagers still love the story. Good soundtrack and cast ripples with up and coming stars. Followed by a television series. Coppola adapted another Hinton novel the same year, "Rumble Fish." 91m/C VHS, Beta, LV, Letterbox. C. Thomas Howell, Matt Dillon, Ralph Macchio, Patrick Swayze, Diane Lane, Tom Cruise, Emilio Estevez, Rob Lowe, Tom Waits, Leif Garrett; **D:** Francis Ford Coppola; **W:** Kathleen Rowell; **C:** Stephen Burum; **M:** Carmine Coppola. WAR

Outtakes ♂½ 1985 (R) A piecemeal compilation of comedy skits, concentrating on sex and genre parody. 85m/C VHS, Beta. Forrest Tucker, Bobbi Wexler, Joleen Lutz; **D:** Jack M. Sell. NO

The Oval Portrait ♂½ 1988 An adaptation of the Edgar Allan Poe suspense tale about a Civil War-era maiden, her illicit love for a Confederate soldier and her eventual death. 89m/C VHS, Beta. Giselle MacKenzie, Barry Coe; **D:** Regelio A. Gonzalez Jr. NO

Over Indulgence ♂♂ 1987 (R) A young woman witnesses a murder in an affluent society in British East Africa. 95m/C VHS, Beta. Denholm Elliott, Holly Aird, Michael Byrne, Kathryn Pogson; **D:** Ross Devenish. MCG

Over the Brooklyn Bridge ♂♂ My Darling Shiksa 1983 (R) A young Jewish man (Gould) must give up his Catholic girlfriend (Hemingway) in order to get his uncle (Caesar) to lend him the money he needs to buy a restaurant in Manhattan. Nowhere near as funny as it should be, and potentially offensive to boot. 100m/C VHS, Beta. Elliott Gould, Sid Caesar, Shelley Winters, Margaux Hemingway, Carol Kane, Burt Young; **D:** Menahem Golan; **M:** Pino Donaggio. MGM

Over the Edge ♂♂♂½ 1979 (PG) The music of Cheap Trick, The Cars, and The Ramones highlights this realistic tale of alienated suburban youth on the rampage. Dillon makes his screen debut in this updated, well-done "Rebel Without a Cause." Shelved for several years, the movie was finally released after Dillon made it big. Sleeper with excellent direction and dialogue. 91m/C VHS, Beta. Michael Kramer, Matt Dillon, Pamela Ludwig, Vincent Spano; **D:** Jonathan Kaplan. WAR

Over the Hill ♂♂½ 1993 (PG) Dukakis stars as Alma, an eccentric widow who decides to leave her well-meaning son's restrictive home in Maine to visit her estranged daughter Elizabeth in Sydney, Australia. Embarrassed by her peculiarities Elizabeth arranges a holiday away but Mom has her own plans. She wants to "loop the loop," and make a complete circuit around the Australian continent. Soon Alma is on the road, meeting fellow eccentrics and experiencing a variety of adventures. 102m/C VHS, LV, Closed Caption. Olympia Dukakis, Sigrid Thornton, Derek Fowlds, Pippa Grandison; **D:** George Miller; **W:** Robert Caswell; **C:** David Connell. NLC, COL, IME

Over the Summer ♂♂½ 1985 Strong drama about a troubled teen who escapes the city for a summer with her grandparents. No cliches here—the grandfather lusts after the granddaughter and eventually kills himself, and problems remain at the end. Intelligent and entertaining, though marred by needless nude scenes. 97m/C VHS, Beta. Laura Hunt, Johnson West, Catherine Williams, David Romero; **D:** Teresa Sparks. ART, VES

Over the Top ♂½ 1986 (PG) The film that started a nationwide arm-wrestling craze. A slow-witted trucker decides the only way he can retain custody of his estranged son, as well as win the boy's respect, is by winning a big arm-wrestling competition. Stallone is an expert at grinding these movies out by now, and the kid (General Hospital's Mikey) is all right, but the end result is boredom, as it should be with an arm-wrestling epic. 94m/C VHS, Beta, LV, Closed Caption. Sylvester Stallone, Susan Blakely, Robert Loggia, David Mendenhall; **D:** Menahem Golan; **W:** Sylvester Stallone, Gary Conway, Stirling Silliphant. Golden Raspberry Awards '87: Worst Supporting Actor (Mendenhall), Worst New Star (Mendenhall). WAR

Over the Wire ♂½ 1995 Telephone lineman Bruce (Christensen) accidentally overhears a conversation where a woman hires a hitman to kill her sister. He finds out that the sisters live together and tries to figure out just who the target is before it's too late (of course, he has to seduce both of them to accomplish this). 90m/C VHS. David Christensen, Shauna O'Brien, Landon Hall, Tim Abell, John Lazar; **D:** Nicholas Medina. TRI

Overboard ♂♂ 1987 (PG) A wealthy, spoiled woman falls off of her yacht and into the arms of a low-class carpenter who picks her up and convinces her she is in fact his wife, and mother to his four brats. Just when she learns to like her life, the tables are turned again. Even though it's all been done before, you can't help but laugh at the screwy gags. 112m/C VHS, Beta, LV, Letterbox, Closed Caption. Goldie Hawn, Kurt Russell, Katherine Helmond, Roddy McDowall, Edward Herrmann; **D:** Garry Marshall; **W:** Leslie Dixon; **C:** John A. Alonzo; **M:** Alan Silvestri. MGM, HMV, FOX

The Overcoat ♂♂♂½ 1959 An adaptation of Nikolai Gogol's classic story about the dehumanizing life endured in 20th-century bureaucracy. All a menial civil servant wants is a new overcoat. When he finally gets one, this treasured article not only keeps him warm but makes him feel self-satisfied as well. In Russian with English subtitles. 93m/B VHS, Beta. RU Rolan Bykov; **D:** Alexei Batalov. HTV

Overdrawn at the Memory Bank ♂♂ 1983 In a futuristic tyranny, a romantic rebel becomes somehow fused with the spirit of Humphrey Bogart in the milieu of "Casablanca," and lives out a cliched version of the film character's adventures. 84m/C VHS, Beta. Raul Julia, Linda Griffiths; **D:** Douglas Williams. VTR

Overexposed ♂♂ 1990 (R) All the wackos love the sultry soap star Oxenburg; one is a killer. Eighty minutes and a bunch of bodies later the killer is unmasked. Plenty of suspense and some original gore. Based on the true stories of fans who stalk celebrities. 83m/C VHS. Catherine Oxenberg, David Naughton, Jennifer Edwards, Karen Black; **D:** Larry Brand; **W:** Larry Brand. MGM

Overkill ♂ 1986 (R) A detective and the vengeance-minded brother of a dead Japanese-American fight back against the controlling Yakuza in Little Tokyo. 81m/C VHS. Steve Rally, John Nishio, Laura Burkett, Roy Summerset; **D:** Ulli Lommel. NO

Overkill ♂♂ 1996 (R) Burnt-out cop Norris heads for vacation in the South American jungle and winds up being the prey for demented hunter Nouri. **CW:** Action violence and for some language. 92m/C VHS. Aaron Norris, Michael Nouri; **D:** Dean Ferrandini. THV

Overland Mail 1941 Fifteen episodes of the vintage serial filled with western action. 225m/B VHS, Beta. Lon Chaney Jr., Helen Parrish. NOS, VCN, MLB

Overland Stage Raiders ♂♂♂ 1938 The "Three Mesquiteers" ride again, this time to guard a Greyhound bus! The trio must protect a shipment of gold from hijackers. This is the last film for Brooks, who had starred in the German masterpiece "Pandora's Box" in 1929. 55m/B VHS. John Wayne, Ray Corrigan, Max Terhune, Louise Brooks, John Archer, Frank LaRue, Yakima Canutt; **D:** George Sherman. REP, NOS

Overlanders ♂♂♂ 1946 The Japanese may invade, but rather than kill 1,000 head of cattle, these Aussies drive the huge herd across the continent, facing danger along the way. Beautifully photographed, featuring the "Australian Gary Cooper" and a stampede scene to challenge "Dances with Wolves." 91m/B VHS, Beta. AU Chips Rafferty, Daphne Campbell, Jean Blue, John Nugent Hayward; **D:** Harry Watt. NOS, DVT, HEG

Overnight Delivery 🐾🐾 1996 (PG-13) Convinced his girlfriend (Taylor) has been cheating on him Wyatt (Rudd) sends her a nasty breakup letter via overnight mail. But when he realizes he's been wrong, Wyatt enlists the aid of friendly stripper Ivy (Witherspoon) to help him retrieve the letter. **CW:** Some crude sexual material. 87m/C VHS. Reese Witherspoon, Paul Rudd, Christine Taylor; **D:** Jason Bloom. WAR

Overnight Sensation 🐾🐾 1983 A modern adaptation of the W. Somerset Maugham story about a traditional marriage being tested by the wife's sudden literary success. 30m/C VHS, Beta. Louise Fletcher, Robert Loggia, Shari Belafonte. PYR

Overseas: Three Women with Man Trouble 🐾🐾🐾 1990 Three beautiful sisters in French colonial Algeria surround themselves in a life of luxury to avoid the incredible social changes going on around them. Each sister has a different perspective on her life, and the perspectives are graphically revealed. Lush photography set in the Mediterranean. In French with English subtitles. 96m/C VHS. **FR** Nicole Garcia, Marianne Basler, Philippe Galland, Pierre Doris, Brigitte Rouan; **D:** Brigitte Rouan; **W:** Brigitte Rouan. Cannes Film Festival '90: Best Film. FXL, BTV, BFV

Overthrow 🐾🐾½ 1982 (R) American sportswriter finds himself caught up in violence and intrigue in Buenos Aires. 90m/C VHS, Beta. John Phillip Law, Lewis Van Bergen, Roger Wilson; **D:** Larry Ludman. IMP, HHE, VTR

Overture 1975 An episode of "The Persuaders." Brett and Danny are tricked into helping a retired judge. This adventure leads them to the Mediterranean and a gorgeous gal. 52m/C VHS. GB Roger Moore, Tony Curtis. NO

Overture to Glory 🐾🐾½ Der Vilner Shtot Khazn 1940 A Jewish cantor longs for the world of opera. He leaves his wife and son to fulfill his passion, but eventually he loses his voice and humbly returns home on Yom Kippur, the Jewish Day of Atonement. He learns that his son has passed away. Grief-stricken, he goes to the synagogue. There, the cantor regains his voice as he performs Kol Nidre in a passionate and melodious rendering. In Yiddish with English subtitles. 85m/B VHS, Beta. Helen Beverly, Florence Weiss. ERG, TPV

The Owl and the Pussycat 🐾🐾🐾 1970 (PG) Nerdy author gets the neighborhood hooker evicted from her apartment. She returns the favor, and the pair hit the street—and the sack—in Buck Henry's hilarious adaptation of the Broadway play. Streisand's first non-singing role. 96m/C VHS, Beta, LV. Barbra Streisand, George Segal, Robert Klein, Allen (Goorwitz) Garfield; **D:** Herbert Ross; **W:** Buck Henry; **C:** Harry Stradling, Andrew Laszlo. GKK

The Ox 🐾🐾½ 1991 Slow-moving, simple tale, set in rural Sweden in the 1860s during a famine. Desperate to feed his family a tenant farmer kills his employer's ox. Consumed by guilt, the man is quickly found out and sentenced to life imprisonment. Pardoned after six years, the farmer returns to his family, to find out his wife has survived by doing things she finds difficult to forgive. Based on a true story. Directorial debut of Nykvist, the longtime cinematographer for Ingmar Bergman, well displays his familiarity with composition and lighting to heighten mood. In Swedish with English subtitles. 93m/C VHS. SW Stellan Skarsgard, Ewa Froling, Lennart Hjulstrom, Max von Sydow, Liv Ullmann, Bjorn Granath, Erland Josephson; **D:** Sven Nykvist; **W:** Lasse Summanen, Sven Nykvist. Nominations: Academy Awards '91: Best Foreign Language Film. ICA, FCT

The Ox-Bow Incident 🐾🐾🐾🐾 Strange Incident 1943 A popular rancher is murdered, and a mob of angry townspeople can't wait for the sheriff to find the killers. They hang the young men, despite the protests of Fonda, a cowboy with a conscience. Excellent study of mob mentality with strong individual characterizations. A brilliant western based on a true story by Walter Van Til-

burg Clark. Also see "Twelve Angry Men"—less tragic but just as moving. 75m/B VHS, Beta, LV, Closed Caption. Henry Fonda, Harry (Henry) Morgan, Dana Andrews, Anthony Quinn, Frank Conroy, Harry Davenport, Jane Darwell, William Eythe, Mary Beth Hughes; **D:** William A. Wellman; **W:** Lamar Trotti; **C:** Arthur C. Miller; **M:** Cyril Mockridge. National Board of Review Awards '43: Best Director (Wellman); Nominations: Academy Awards '43: Best Picture. FOX

Oxford Blues 🐾🐾 1984 (PG-13) An American finagles his way into England's Oxford University and onto the rowing team in pursuit of the girl of his dreams. Beautiful scenery, but the plot is wafer-thin. Remake of "Yank at Oxford." 98m/C VHS, Beta, LV, Closed Caption. Rob Lowe, Ally Sheedy, Amanda Pays, Julian Sands, Michael Gough, Gail Strickland, Cary Elwes; **D:** Robert Boris; **W:** Robert Boris; **M:** John Du Prez. FOX

Pace That Kills 🐾 1928 An anti-drug cautionary drama from the Roaring '20s, one of many now marketed on cassette as campy fun. Beware, though, a little bit of this stuff goes a long way. A young man goes to the big city to find his missing sister and winds up hooked on heroin. 87m/B VHS, Beta, 8mm. Owen Gorin, Virginia Roye, Florence Turner. GVV

Pacific Heights 🐾🐾🐾 1990 (R) Young San Francisco couple takes on mammoth mortgage assuming tenants will write their ticket to the American dream, but psychopathic tenant Keaton moves in downstairs and redecorates. He won't pay the rent and he won't leave. Creepy psychothriller has lapses but builds to effective climax. It's a treat to watch mother/daughter actresses Hedren and Griffith work together. Watch for D'Angelo as Keaton's lover. **CW:** Adult situations; language, brief nudity, and violence. 103m/C VHS, LV, Closed Caption. Melanie Griffith, Matthew Modine, Michael Keaton, Mako, Nobu McCarthy, Laurie Metcalf, Carl Lumbly, Dorian Harewood, Luca Bercovici, Tippi Hedren, Sheila McCarthy, Dan Hedaya, Beverly D'Angelo, Nicholas Pryor, Miriam Margolyes; **D:** John Schlesinger; **W:** Daniel Pyne; **M:** Hans Zimmer. FOX

Pacific Inferno 🐾🐾 1985 During WWII, American POWs endeavor to break out of a Japanese prison camp in the Philippines. Their goal is to prevent their captors from retrieving millions of dollars worth of sunken U.S. gold. Made for cable television. 90m/C VHS, Beta. Jim Brown, Richard Jaeckel, Tim Brown; **D:** Rolf Bayer. NO

The Pack 🐾🐾½ The Long, Dark Night 1977 (R) A group of dogs become wild when left on a resort island. A marine biologist leads the humans who fight to keep the dogs from using vacationers as chew toys. Fine production values keep it from going to the dogs. Made with the approval of the American Humane Society who helped with the treatment of stage hands. 99m/C VHS, Beta. Joe Don Baker, Hope Alexander-Willis, R.G. Armstrong, Richard B. Shull; **D:** Robert Clouse; **W:** Robert Clouse. WAR

The P.A.C.K. 🐾🐾 1996 The P.A.C.K. are alien warriors who mistakenly land on earth, which doesn't prevent them from killing all but one of a team of government agents sent to investigate. Now lone agent Rachel (Bergman) reluctantly teams up with a second alien who's been sent to destroy the P.A.C.K. 90m/C VHS. Sandahl Bergman, Ted Prior, Red West. SWI

Pack Up Your Troubles 🐾🐾½ We're in the Army Now 1932 Laurel and Hardy make good on a promise to help find the grandfather of a girl whose father was killed in WWI. All they know is the grandfather's last name though—Smith. Wholesome R and R. 68m/B VHS, Beta. Stan Laurel, Oliver Hardy, James Finlayson, Jacquie Lyn; **D:** George Marshall. FCT, MLB, VTR

The Package 🐾🐾½ 1989 (R) An espionage thriller about an army sergeant who loses the prisoner he escorts into the U.S. When he tries to track him down, he uncovers a military plot to start WWIII. Hackman is believable in his role as the sergeant. 108m/C VHS, Beta, LV, Closed Caption. Gene Hackman, Tommy Lee Jones, Joanna Cas-

sidy, Dennis Franz, Pam Grier, John Heard, Ron Silver, Thalmus Rasulala, Ike Pappas, Kevin Crowley; **D:** Andrew Davis; **W:** John Bishop; **M:** James Newton Howard. ORI

Packin' It In 🐾🐾 1983 A Los Angeles family is in for a rude awakening when they leave the city for a quieter life in the Oregon woods. There they encounter a band of survivalists with semicomedic results. 97m/C VHS, Beta. Richard Benjamin, Paula Prentiss, Molly Ringwald, Tony Roberts, Andrea Marcovicci; **D:** Jud Taylor. NO

Paco 🐾½ 1975 (G) A young, South American boy heads for the city, where he meets his uncle. He discovers his uncle is the leader of a gang of youthful thieves. Predictable and sluggish. 89m/C VHS, Beta. Jose Ferrer, Panchito Gomez, Allen (Goorwitz) Garfield, Pernell Roberts, Andre Marquis; **D:** Robert Vincent O'Neil.

Paddy 🐾🐾 Goodbye to the Hill 1970 (PG) A young Irish lad realizes his sexual potential by seducing every woman he can find. Freudians will have a field day. 97m/C VHS, Beta. IR Des Cave, Milo O'Shea, Darbnia Molloy, Peggy Cass; **D:** Daniel Haller. NO

Padre Nuestro 🐾🐾½ 1985 Religious satire about a dying priest who wishes to reunite his family, who include an atheist brother, a mistress from his youth, and his illegitimate daughter who's a notorious prostitute. In Spanish with English subtitles. 91m/C VHS. SP Fernando Rey, Francesco Rabal, Victoria Abril; **D:** Francisco Regueiro. CVC, FCT

Padre Padrone 🐾🐾🐾½ Father Master; My Father, My Master 1977 The much acclaimed adaptation of the Gavino Ledda autobiography about his youth in agrarian Sardinia with a brutal, tyrannical father. Eventually he overcomes his handicaps, breaks the destructive emotional ties to his father and successfully attends college. Highly regarded although low budget; in an Italian dialect (Sardinian) with English subtitles. 113m/C VHS, Beta. IT Omero Antonutti, Saverio Marconi, Marcella Michelangeli, Fabrizio Forte; **D:** Paolo Taviani, Vittorio Taviani; **W:** Paolo Taviani, Vittorio Taviani; **C:** Mario Masini; **M:** Egisto Macchi. Cannes Film Festival '77: Best Film. FXL

Pagan Island 🐾 1960 A man is stranded on a desert island with 30 beautiful girls who tie him up and abandon him. Maki, to be sacrificed by the rest, saves Dew and they fall in love. They go off in search of a reputed treasure, which they find, but at a deadly cost. 67m/B VHS. Eddie Dew, Nani Maka; **D:** Barry Mahon; **W:** Clelle Mahon. SMW, TPV

Pagan Love Song 🐾 1950 A dull musical which finds Keel in Tahiti taking over his uncle's coconut plantation and falling in love with Williams. Surprise! Williams performs one of her famous water ballets, which is the only saving grace in this lifeless movie. ♫The House of Singing Bamboo; Singing in the Sun; Etiquette; Why is Love So Crazy; Tahiti; The Sea of the Moon; Pagan Love Song; Coconut Milk. 76m/C VHS. Esther Williams, Howard Keel, Minna Gombell, Rita Moreno; **D:** Robert Alton. MGM

The Pagemaster 🐾½ 1994 (G) Timid Richard (Macaulay) is basically scared of his own shadow but, during a storm, he's forced to take refuge in a mysterious library with an even odder librarian, Mr. Dewey (Lloyd). Richard's intrigued by the library's mural, which turns out to be the doorway to an animated universe where the wizardly Pagemaster (voiced by Lloyd) and other literary characters help Richard discover his strengths and overcome his fears. Mildly amusing but kids may not know who the characters refer to unless they're readers (a good intro, perhaps?) 76m/C VHS, LV. Macaulay Culkin, Christopher Lloyd, Ed Begley Jr., Mel Harris; **D:** Joe Johnston, Maurice Hunt; **W:** David Casci, David Kirschner, Ernie Contreras; **M:** James Horner; **V:** Christopher Lloyd, Whoopi Goldberg, Patrick Stewart, Frank Welker, Leonard Nimoy. Nominations: Golden Raspberry Awards '94: Worst Actor (Culkin). FOX

Paid to Kill 🐾🐾 Five Days 1954 A failing businessman hires a thug to kill him in order to leave his family insurance money, but when the business picks up, he can't contact the thug to cancel the contract. The actors' lack of talent is matched only by the characters' lack of motivation. **71m/B VHS, Beta, LV.** *GB* Dane Clark, Paul Carpenter, Thea Gregory; *D:* Montgomery Tully. *RXM*

Pain in the A— 𝄞𝄞𝄞 **1977 (PG)** A hit man helps a suicidal shirt salesman solve his marital problems in this black comedy that was later Americanized as "Buddy, Buddy." Not for all tastes, but has acquired a reputation for its dark wit. In French with English subtitles. **90m/C VHS, Beta.** *FR IT* Lino Ventura, Jacques Brel, Caroline Cellier; *D:* Edouard Molinaro; *W:* Francis Veber, Edouard Molinaro. *FRF, COL*

Paint It Black 𝄞𝄞½ **1989 (R)** A violent/ steamy mystery and action flick from the director of "River's Edge," in which a young man from the silver-spoon set develops a fascination for an artist. **101m/C VHS, Beta, LV.** Sally Kirkland, Rick Rossovich, Martin Landau, Doug Savant, Peter Frechette, Jason Bernard, Julie Carmen, Monique Van De Ven; *D:* Tim Hunter. *ART, VES*

The Paint Job 𝄞𝄞 **1993 (R)** Wesley, the lonely house painter, falls in love with his neighbor, Margaret. Unfortunately, Margaret is married—to Wesley's boss Willy. Margaret is drawn to Wesley and bored with Willy. But one of the men turns out to be a serial killer. What's a gal in love to do? **90m/C VHS.** Will Patton, Bebe Neuwirth, Robert Pastorelli; *D:* Micheal Taav; *W:* Micheal Taav; *M:* John Wesley Harding. *COL*

Paint Your Wagon 𝄞𝄞½ **1969 (PG)** Big-budget western musical-comedy about a gold mining boom town, and two prospectors sharing the same Mormon wife complete with a classic Lerner and Lowe score. Marvin chews up the sagebrush and Eastwood attempts to sing, although Seberg was mercifully dubbed. Overlong, with patches of interest, pretty songs, and plenty of panoramic scenery. Adapted from the L & L play. 𝄞I Talk To the Trees; I Still See Elisa; I'm On My Way; Hand Me Down That Can O' Beans; Whoop-Ti-Ay; They Call the Wind Maria; There's a Coach Comin' In; Wandrin' Star; Best Things. **164m/C VHS, Beta, LV.** Lee Marvin, Clint Eastwood, Jean Seberg, Harve Presnell; *D:* Joshua Logan; *W:* Paddy Chayefsky; *M:* Frederick Loewe, Andre Previn, Alan Jay Lerner. Nominations: Academy Awards '69: Scoring of a Musical. *PAR*

Painted Desert 𝄞𝄞 **1931** Gable's first film role of any consequence came in this early sound western. Gable plays a villain opposite "good guy" William Boyd. **80m/B VHS, Beta.** William Boyd, Helen Twelvetrees, George O'Brien, Clark Gable, William Farnum; *D:* Howard Higgin. *NOS, MRV, HHT*

Painted Hero 𝄞𝄞½ **1995 (R)** Rodeo clown Virgil Kidder (Yoakum) has to watch out for more than rampaging bulls when he returns to Waco, where he's accused of murder and reunites with the mother of his now-dead son.*CW:* Language, some sexuality and violence. **105m/C VHS, Closed Caption.** Dwight Yoakam, Bo Hopkins, Cindy Pickett, Michelle Joyner; *D:* Terry Benedict; *W:* Terry Benedict; *C:* David Bridges; *M:* Rick Marotta. *CAF*

The Painted Hills 𝄞𝄞½ **1951 (G)** Lassie outsmarts crooked miners and rescues her friends. Surprise, Surprise! Overly sentimental, but action packed and beautifully shot. Lassie's last outing with MGM. **70m/C VHS, Beta.** Paul Kelly, Bruce Cowling, Gary Gray, Art Smith, Ann Doran, Lassie; *D:* Harold F. Kress. *MGM, BPG, FCT*

The Painted Stallion 1937 This 12-chapter serial features a mysterious figure on a painted stallion who attempts to maintain peace between Mexicans and Indians. **212m/B VHS, LV.** Ray Corrigan, Hoot Gibson, Duncan Renaldo, Leroy Mason, Yakima Canutt; *D:* William Witney, Ray Taylor. *NOS, VDM, REP*

The Painted Veil 𝄞𝄞½ **1934** Adaptation of a W. Somerset Maugham story. Garbo, once again the disillusioned wife turning to the affections of another man, is magnificent, almost eclipsing the weak script. Lost money at the box office, but for Garbo fans, an absolute must. **83m/B VHS, Beta.** Greta Garbo, Herbert Marshall, George Brent, Warner Oland, Jean Hersholt; *D:* Richard Boleslawski; *C:* William H. Daniels. *MGM, FCT*

Pair of Aces 𝄞𝄞½ **1990** Kristofferson is a Texas Ranger who's on the trail of a serial killer. His only other problem is being saddled with Nelson, a philosophical safecracker who's awaiting trial and in the reluctant cop's custody. Low-key western with good buddy pairing of Nelson and Kristofferson. Made for television. **94m/C VHS, Closed Caption.** Willie Nelson, Kris Kristofferson, Rip Torn, Helen Shaver, Jane Cameron, Sonny Carl Davis, Lash LaRue, Emily Warfield, Michael Marich; *D:* Aaron Lipstadt. *WAR*

Paisan 𝄞𝄞𝄞 **1946** Six episodic tales of life in Italy, several featuring Allied soldiers and nurses during WWII. One of the stories tells of a man who tries to develop a relationship without being able to speak Italian. Another focuses on a young street robber who is confronted by one of his victims. Strong stories that covers a wide range of emotions. In Italian with English subtitles. **115m/B VHS.** *IT* Maria Michi, Carmela Sazio, Gar Moore, William Tubbs, Harriet White, Robert Van Loon, Dale Edmonds, Carla Pisacane, Dots Johnson; *D:* Roberto Rossellini; *W:* Federico Fellini, Roberto Rossellini. National Board of Review Awards '48: Best Director (Fellini); New York Film Critics Awards '48: Best Foreign Film; Nominations: Academy Awards '49: Best Story & Screenplay. *HTV, HHT, CAB*

The Pajama Game 𝄞𝄞𝄞½ **1957** A spritely musical about the striking workers of a pajama factory and their plucky negotiator, who falls in love with the boss. Based on the hit Broadway musical, which was based on Richard Bissell's book "Seven and a Half Cents" and adapted for the screen by Bisell and Abbott. Bob Fosse choreographed the dance numbers. 𝄞I'm Not at All in Love; Small Talk; There Once Was a Man; Steam Heat; Hernando's Highway; Hey There; Once-a-Year Day; Seven and a Half Cents; I'll Never Be Jealous Again. **101m/C VHS, Beta, LV, Closed Caption.** Doris Day, John Raitt, Eddie Foy Jr., Reta Shaw, Carol Haney; *D:* Stanley Donen, George Abbott; *C:* Harry Stradling. *WAR*

Pajama Party 𝄞𝄞 **1964** Followup to "Bikini Beach" takes the party inside in this fourth entry in the popular "Beach Party" series. Plot is up to beach party realism. Funicello is Avalon-less (although he does have a cameo) so she falls for Martian Kirk instead. He's scouting for an alien invasion, but after he falls into Annette's lap decides to save the planet instead. Typical fluff with the usual beach movie faces present; look for a young Garr as a dancer. Followed by the classic "Beach Blanket Bingo." 𝄞It's That Kind of Day; There Has to Be a Reason; Where Did I Go Wrong?; Pajama Party; Beach Ball; Among the Young; Stuffed Animal. **82m/C VHS, LV.** Tommy Kirk, Annette Funicello, Elsa Lanchester, Harvey Lembeck, Jesse White, Jody McCrea, Donna Loren, Susan Hart, Bobbi Shaw, Cheryl Sweeten, Luree Holmes, Candy Johnson, Dorothy Lamour, Toni Basil, Teri Garr, Ben Lessy; *Cameos:* Buster Keaton, Frankie Avalon, Don Rickles; *D:* Don Weis; *W:* Louis M. Heyward; *C:* Floyd Crosby; *M:* Les Baxter. *NO*

Pajama Tops 𝄞𝄞½ **1983** A stage production of the classic French bedroom farce, taped live at the Music Hall Theatre in Toronto, Canada. Includes all the trials of marriage including adultery and deceit. **105m/C VHS.** Robert Klein, Susan George, Pia Zadora. *NO*

Pal Joey 𝄞𝄞𝄞 **1957** Musical comedy about an opportunistic singer who courts a wealthy socialite in hopes that she will finance his nightclub. His play results in comedic complications. Stellar choreography, fine direction, and beautiful costumes complement performances headed by Hayworth and Sinatra. Oscar overlooked his pal Joey when awards were handed out. Songs include some of Rodgers and Hart's best. Based on John O'Hara's book and play. 𝄞Zip; Bewitched, Bothered and Bewildered; I Could Write a Book; That Terrific Rainbow; Whad Do I Care for a Dame?; Happy Hunting Horn; Plant You Now, Dig You Later; Do It the Hard Way; Take Him. **109m/C VHS, Beta, LV.** Frank Sinatra, Rita Hayworth, Kim Novak; *D:* George Sidney; *M:* Richard Rodgers, Lorenz Hart. Golden Globe Awards '58: Best Actor—Musical/Comedy (Sinatra); Nominations: Academy Awards '57: Best Art Direction/ Set Decoration, Best Costume Design, Best Film Editing, Best Sound. *COL*

Palais Royale 𝄞½ **1988** Craven plays an ad exec who gets involved in the world of gangsters in the late 50s. **100m/C VHS.** *CA* Matt Craven, Kim Cattrall, Dean Stockwell; *D:* Martin Lavut; *M:* Jonathan Goldsmith. *REP*

Pale Blood 𝄞𝄞½ **1991 (R)** A serial killer in Los Angeles is leaving his victims drained of blood. Could it be that a vampire is stalking the modern American metropolis, or is this merely the workings of a bloodthirsty psychopath? **93m/C VHS, LV.** George Chakiris, Wings Hauser, Pamela Ludwig, Diana Frank, Darcy Demoss, Earl Garnes; *D:* V.V. Dachin Hsu; *W:* V.V. Dachin Hsu, Takashi Matsuoka. *COL, OM*

Pale Rider 𝄞𝄞𝄞 **1985 (R)** A mysterious nameless stranger rides into a small California gold rush town to find himself in the middle of a feud between a mining syndicate and a group of independent prospectors. Christ-like Eastwood evokes comparisons to "Shane." A classical western theme treated well complemented by excellent photography and a rock-solid cast. **116m/C VHS, Beta, LV, 8mm, Closed Caption.** Clint Eastwood, Michael Moriarty, Carrie Snodgress, Sydney Penny, Richard Dysart, Richard Kiel, Christopher Penn, John Russell, Charles Hallahan, Douglas McGrath, Fran Ryan; *D:* Clint Eastwood; *W:* Michael Butler, Dennis Shryack; *C:* Bruce Surtees; *M:* Lennie Niehaus. *WAR, TLF*

The Paleface 𝄞𝄞𝄞 **1948** A cowardly dentist becomes a gunslinging hero when Calamity Jane starts aiming for him. A rip-roarin' good time as the conventions of the Old West are turned upside down. Includes the Oscar-winning song "Buttons and Bows." The 1952 sequel is "Son of Paleface." Remade in 1968 as "The Shakiest Gun in the West." 𝄞Buttons and Bows; Get a Man!; Meetcha 'Round the Corner. **91m/C VHS, Beta, LV.** Jane Russell, Bob Hope, Robert Armstrong, Iris Adrian, Robert Watson; *D:* Norman Z. McLeod; *C:* Ray Rennahan. Academy Awards '48: Best Song ("Buttons and Bows"). *USH*

The Palermo Connection 𝄞𝄞 **1991 (R)** Not the action-thriller the cassette box claims, but a cynical study of a crusading N.Y.C. mayoral candidate who honeymoons in Mafia-haunted Sicily and learns that the war on crime has already been lost. Remote adaptation of "To Forget Palermo" by Edmonde Charles-Roux. **100m/C VHS, LV, Closed Caption.** James Belushi, Mimi Rogers, Joss Ackland, Philippe Noiret, Vittorio Gassman, Caroline Rosi; *D:* Francesco Rosi; *W:* Gore Vidal. *ART*

The Pallbearer 𝄞𝄞½ **1995 (PG-13)** You probably liked this one better when it was called "The Graduate," as this one shares some key plot points with, but lacks the edge and cultural impact of the 1967 classic. Basset-faced Schwimmer plays Tom, who is asked to be a pallbearer for an old high school classmate whom he can't quite remember. He is then seduced by the mother (Hershey) of the deceased, while trying to kindle a romance with the fabulous Julie DeMarco (Paltrow), an old classmate who can't quite remember him. The spurned older woman then begins to exact her revenge, while Tom tries to figure out how to court Julie while living at home with his mom. Good performances make it watchable.*CW:* Some sexuality and language. **98m/C VHS, LV, Closed Caption.** David Schwimmer, Gwyneth Paltrow, Barbara Hershey, Michael Rapaport, Carol Kane, Toni Collette, Michael Vartan; *D:* Matt Reeves; *W:* Matt Reeves, Jason Katims; *C:* Robert Elswit; *M:* Stewart Copeland. *TOU*

Palm Beach 𝄞𝄞 **1979** The lives of two petty thieves, a runaway, and a private detective intertwine at Palm Beach Down Under. Best appreciated by fans of things Aussie. **90m/C VHS, Beta.**

AU Bryan Brown, Nat Young, Ken Brown, Amanda Berry; *D:* Albie Thomas.

The Palm Beach Story 🎬🎬🎬 1942
Colbert and McCrea play a married couple who have everything—except money. The wife decides to divorce her current husband, marry a rich man, and finance her former husband's ambitions. She decides the best place to husband-hunt is Palm Beach. A Sturges classic screwball comedy. 88m/B VHS, Beta, LV. Claudette Colbert, Joel McCrea, Mary Astor, Rudy Vallee, William Demarest, Franklin Pangborn; *D:* Preston Sturges; *C:* Victor Milner. *USH*

Palm Springs Weekend 🎬🎬½ 1963 A
busload of love-hungry kids head south and get involved in routine hijinks. Actually shot in Palm Springs with above average performances by a handful of stars. 100m/C VHS, Beta, LV. Troy Donahue, Ty Hardin, Connie Stevens, Stefanie Powers, Robert Conrad, Jack Weston, Andrew Duggan; *D:* Norman Taurog. *WAR*

Palmetto 🎬½ 1998 (R) Another contempo-
noir that misses the mark has bitter ex-con Harry (Harrelson) partnered with seductress Rhea (Shue) in a phony kidnapping of her step-daughter Odette (Sevigny). Newly released from the joint after a rotten frame-up job, Harry is lured back to the steamy backwater that sent him up the river in the first place by ex Nina (Gershon), where he, once again, winds up in trouble as all three women go to work on him. Originality and character development go AWOL, as the normally adept Harrelson flounders for an identity alongside Shue's broad characterization of a vamp who teeters on high heels and the brink of satire, and Gershon in an unaccustomed good girl role. Tropical, southern Florida backdrop makes this feel like Tennessee Williams as written by Joe Eszterhas. Adaptation of Rene Raymond's (a.k.a. James Hadley Chase) novel, "Just Another Sucker." *CW:* Sexuality, language and some violence. 114m/C VHS. Angela Featherstone, Woody Harrelson, Elisabeth Shue, Michael Rapaport, Gina Gershon, Chloe Sevigny, Rolf Hoppe, Tom Wright; *D:* Volker Schlondorff; *W:* E. Max Frye; *C:* Thomas Kloss; *M:* Klaus Dolinger. *WAR*

Palmy Days 🎬🎬½ 1931 Shy Eddie (Can-
tor) is involved in a phony medium, a scam involving a bakery, theft, romance, singing, and a disguise as a woman (the other bakery workers are the Goldwyn Girls, including Betty Grable). Silly fun, with choreography by Busby Berkeley. ♫Bend Down, Sister; Goose Pimples; Dunk Dunk Dunk; My Honey Said Yes, Yes; There's Nothing Too Good for My Baby. 77m/B VHS. Eddie Cantor, Charlotte Greenwood, Charles Middleton, George Raft, Harry Woods, Spencer Charters, Barbara Weeks, Paul Page; *D:* Edward Sutherland; *W:* Morrie Ryskind, Keene Thompson, Eddie Cantor; *C:* Gregg Toland. *HBO*

Palombella Rossa 🎬🎬 1989 Political
comedy about the fate of Italian communism. When communist politician Michele loses his memory in a car crash, he finds himself trying to reconstruct his life during a game of water polo as well as trying to answer political questions and keep track of the people from his life who randomly appear and disappear. In Italian with English subtitles. 87m/C VHS. *IT D:* Nanni Moretti. *FXL, ORI, FCT*

Palooka 🎬🎬½ Joe Palooka: The Great Schnozzle
1934 (G) Based on the comic strip, this film portrays a fast-talking boxing manager and his goofy, lovable protege. The young scrapper fights James Cagney's little brother. Durante sings his classic tune, "Inka-Dinka-Doo," and packs a punch in the lead. A two-fisted comedy with a witty dialogue and fine direction. Not a part of the Palooka series of the 1940s. 86m/B VHS, Beta. Jimmy Durante, Stuart Erwin, Lupe Velez, Robert Armstrong, Thelma Todd, William Cagney; *D:* Ben Stoloff. *NOS, RXM, VYY*

Palookaville 🎬🎬🎬 1995 (R) Nostalgic com-
edy of three under-employed friends who take up crime, temporarily, just until they can secure legit work. Using a little-known 1950s crime movie as

their tutor, the trio of criminal cretins encounter a variety of setbacks on their way to financial security. Planning an elaborate scheme to rob an armored car, they decide to use toy guns, so Jerry (Trese) rounds up a most intimidating assortment of the neon orange plastic variety. Later, while chiseling through a wall to a jewelry store, they find themselves in the bakery next door, with Jerry delighted to score some pastries instead. The other two aren't much brighter—Russ (Gallo) is the leader of the three and a small-time ladies man while Sid (Forsythe) is a devout dog lover whose dreams of a taxi service for the aged are shattered when customers are driven away by his kennel on wheels. Adapted from short stories written in the 1940s by the Italian Italo Calvino, modern adaptation manages to retain a '40s feel and charm. *CW:* Language. 92m/C VHS, Closed Caption. William Forsythe, Vincent Gallo, Adam Trese, Lisa Gay Hamilton, Frances McDormand, David Boulton, James David Hilton; *D:* Alan Taylor; *W:* David Epstein; *C:* John Thomas; *M:* Rachel Portman. *EVE*

Pals 🎬🎬 1987 Old friends stumble across $3
million in cash and learn the predictable lesson that money can't buy happiness. A terribly trite TV-movie with an exceptional cast. 90m/C VHS. Don Ameche, George C. Scott, Sylvia Sidney, Susan Rinell, James Greene; *D:* Lou Antonio. *THV*

Pals of the Range 🎬 1935 A framed
ranch owner breaks out of jail in order to catch the real cattle thieves. Ho hum in the Old West. 55m/B VHS, Beta. Rex Lease. *NOS*

Pals of the Saddle 🎬🎬½ 1938 The in-
trepid trio go after enemy agents who are trying to smuggle chemicals for poisonous gas into Mexico. This is the first of the series in which the Duke played the part of Stony Brooke. Somewhat convoluted plot, but nevertheless enjoyable. 55m/B VHS. John Wayne, Ray Corrigan, Max Terhune, Doreen McKay, Josef Forte, Ted Adams, Curly Dresden; *D:* George Sherman. *NOS*

The Pamela Principle 🎬🎬 1991 (R) A
bored, middle-aged man thinks his prayers are answered when he meets a sexy 20-year-old model and begins a sordid affair with her. Soon, however, he finds himself in a tense situation when he must choose between his family or his fantasy. Also available in an unrated version. *CW:* Language and strong sexuality. ?m/C VHS, LV, Closed Caption. J.K. Dumont, Veronica Cash, Shelby Lane, Troy Donahue, Frank Pesce; *D:* Toby Phillips. *IMP*

Panama Hattie 🎬🎬 1942 Screen adapta-
tion of Cole Porter's delightful Broadway musical. Unfortunately, something (like a plot) was lost in transition. Southern runs a saloon for our boys down in Panama. Among the musical numbers and vaudevillian acts some spies show up. Several screenwriters and directors, including Vincente Minnelli, worked uncredited on this picture, to no avail. Horne's second screen appearance. ♫It Was Just One of Those Things; Fresh as a Daisy; I've Still Got My Health; Let's Be Buddies; Make It Another Old Fashioned; Hattie from Panama; Good Neighbors; I'll Do Anything for You; The Son of a Gun Who Pick on Uncle Sam. 79m/B VHS. Ann Sothern, Dan Dailey, Red Skelton, Virginia O'Brien, Rags Ragland, Alan Mowbray, Ben Blue, Carl Esmond, Lena Horne; *D:* Norman Z. McLeod; *M:* George Bassman, Cole Porter. *MGM, CCB*

Panama Lady 🎬½ 1939 Ball stars as the
sexy, sultry "Panama Lady" in this old-fashioned romance. She gets involved in some shady business south of the border. A lackluster remake of "Panama Flo." 65m/B VHS, Beta. Lucille Ball, Evelyn Brent. *NO*

Panama Menace 🎬 South of Panama 1941
An agent heads to Panama to thwart spies who are after a special paint that makes things invisible. Poor effort all around, in spite of Beaumont's presence. 68m/B VHS, Beta. Roger Pryor, Virginia Vale, Lionel Royce, Lucien Prival, Duncan Renaldo, Lester Dorr, Hugh Beaumont; *D:* Jean Yarbrough. *SNC, VYY*

Panama Patrol 🎬🎬½ 1939 Just as they
are about to be married, two Army officers are called to duty in Panama. It seems that the Chinese have infiltrated the area with spies and something's got to be done. Too much attention to minor parts of the plot slows the story occasionally, but performances and photography compensate for some of the sluggishness. 67m/B VHS, Beta. Leon Ames, Charlotte Wynters, Weldon Heyburn, Adrienne Ames, Abner Biberman, Hugh McArthur, Donald (Don "Red") Barry; *D:* Charles Lamont. *SNC*

Panamint's Bad Man 🎬 1938 Ballaw is
a poor man's Gary Cooper fighting for justice against stagecoach robbers. Almost as much flavor as tumbleweed. 59m/B VHS, Beta. Smith Ballew, Evelyn Daw, Noah Beery Sr.; *D:* Ray Taylor. *NOS, VDM, DVT*

Pancho Barnes 🎬🎬½ 1988 (PG) Routine
biography of one of the first female pilots of the 1920s. Barnes is a bored debutante who finds her challenge in life when she learns to fly, becoming a barnstormer and movie stunt pilot. Her ambitions naturally get in the way of her romantic life. Good flying scenes. Made for television. 150m/C VHS. Valerie Bertinelli, Ted Wass, Sam Robards, James Stephens, Cynthia Harris, Geoffrey Lewis; *D:* Richard T. Heffron; *W:* John Michael Hayes. *ORI*

Pancho Villa 🎬🎬½ 1972 (PG) Savalas has
the lead in this fictional account of the famous Mexican. He leads his men on a raid on an American fort after being hoodwinked in an arms deal. Connors tries to hold the fort against him. The finale, in which two trains crash head on, is the most exciting event in the whole darn movie. 92m/C VHS. *SP* Telly Savalas, Clint Walker, Anne Francis, Chuck Connors, Angel Del Pozo, Luis Davila; *D:* Eugenio Martin; *W:* Julian Zimet. *NO*

Pancho Villa Returns 🎬🎬 1950 It's
1913, and noble Mexican General Pancho Villa leads his merry men against the assassins of President Madera. This Mexican production (filmed in English) paints a partisan portrait of title character as a good-hearted revolutionary folk hero, not the roving bandit later notorious north of the border. 95m/B VHS. *MX* Leo Carrillo, Esther Fernandez, Jeanette Comber, Rodolfo Acosta; *D:* Miguel Contreras Torres; *W:* Miguel Contreras Torres. *NOS, LOO*

Pandemonium 🎬🎬½ Thursday the 12th 1982
(PG) A spoof of teen slasher films involving murder at Bambi's Cheerleading School. Seems that nationwide, cheerleaders have been brutally eliminated from their squads, leaving Bambi's as the last resort for the terminally perky. Smothers is interesting and more intelligent than his TV persona (although not by much) as the Mountie hero, assisted by Paul Reubens in a pre-Pee-Wee role. Kane steals the show as Candy, a pleasant lass with hyperkinetic powers. 82m/C VHS, Beta. *CA* Tom Smothers, Carol Kane, Miles Chapin, Paul (Pee Wee Herman) Reubens, Judge Reinhold, Tab Hunter, Marc McClure, Donald O'Connor, Eve Arden, Eileen Brennan, Edie McClurg; *D:* Alfred Sole. *MGM*

Pandora and the Flying
Dutchman 🎬🎬½ 1951 Feverish romantic
fantasy has playgirl/nightclub singer Pandora Reynolds (Gardner) living in '30s Spain and being romanced by every man in sight. Naturally, she cares for none of them until she meets enigmatic Dutch captain Hendrick van der Zee (Mason) who is, in fact, the legendary Flying Dutchman—condemned to wander the seas forever unless a woman is willing to give up her life for him. Gardner is, as usual, exotically lovely. 123m/C VHS. Ava Gardner, James Mason, Nigel Patrick, Sheila Sim, Harold Warrender, Mario Cabre; *D:* Albert Lewin; *W:* Albert Lewin; *C:* Jack Cardiff; *M:* Alan Rawsthorne. *KIV*

Pandora's Box 🎬🎬🎬🎬 Die Buechse Der
Pandora 1928 This silent classic marked the end of the German Expressionist era and established Brooks as a major screen presence. She plays the tempestuous Lulu, who destroys everyone she comes in contact with, eventually sinking to

prostitution and a fateful meeting with Jack the Ripper. Silent with orchestral score. **110m/B VHS, Beta.** *GE* Louise Brooks, Fritz Kortner, Francis Lederer, Carl Goetz, Alice Roberts, Gustav Diesl; **D:** G.W. Pabst; **W:** G.W. Pabst. *GPV, MRV, VDM*

Panic 🎬½ **1983** A scientist terrorizes a small town when he becomes hideously deformed by one of his bacteria experiments. He should have known better. **90m/C VHS, Beta.** David Warbeck, Janet Agren. *MPI*

Panic Button 🎬½ **1962** Mel Brooks took the plot from this film and made "The Producers," which was much better. Italian gangsters produce a television show and stack the deck so that it will fail. Unbeknownst to them, the star has figured out what they are doing and works to make it a success. Shot in Italy, mainly in Venice and Rome. **90m/B VHS.** *IT* Maurice Chevalier, Eleanor Parker, Jayne Mansfield, Mike Connors, Akim Tamiroff; **D:** George Sherman. *NO*

Panic in Echo Park 🎬🎬 **1977** A doctor races against time to find the cause of an epidemic that is threatening the health of a city. Good performances compensate for a predictable plot. Made for television. **78m/C VHS.** Dorian Harewood, Robin Gammell, Catlin Adams, Ramon Bieri, Movita; **D:** John Llewellyn Moxey. *NO*

Panic in Needle Park 🎬🎬🎬 **1975 (R)** Drugs become an obsession for a young girl who goes to New York for an abortion. Her new boyfriend is imprisoned for robbery in order to support both their habits. She resorts to prostitution to continue her drug habit, and trouble occurs when her boyfriend realizes she was instrumental in his being sent to jail. Strikes a vein in presenting an uncompromising look at drug use. May be too much of a depressant for some. Pacino's first starring role. **90m/C VHS, LV.** Al Pacino, Kitty Winn, Alan Vint, Richard Bright, Kiel Martin, Warren Finnerty, Raul Julia, Paul Sorvino; **D:** Jerry Schatzberg; **W:** Joan Didion, John Gregory Dunne; **C:** Adam Holender. Cannes Film Festival '71: Best Actress (Winn). *FOX*

Panic in the Streets 🎬🎬🎬 **1950** The Black Death threatens New Orleans in this intense tale. When a body is found on the waterfront, a doctor (Widmark) is called upon for a diagnosis. The carrier proves to be deadly in more ways than one. Fine performances, taut direction (this was one of Kazan's favorite movies). Filmed on location in New Orleans. **96m/B VHS, LV, Closed Caption.** Richard Widmark, Jack Palance, Barbara Bel Geddes, Paul Douglas, Zero Mostel; **D:** Elia Kazan; **W:** Edward Anhalt. Academy Awards '50: Best Story. *FOX, FCT*

Panic in the Year Zero! 🎬🎬½ *End of the World* **1962** Milland and family leave Los Angeles for a fishing trip just as the city is hit by a nuclear bomb. Continuing out into the wilderness for safety, the family now must try to survive as their world crumbles around them. Generally considered the best of Milland's five directorial efforts. **92m/B VHS.** Ray Milland, Jean Hagen, Frankie Avalon, Mary Mitchell, Joan Freeman, Richard Garland, Rex Holman; **D:** Ray Milland; **M:** Les Baxter. *FRG*

Panic on the 5:22 🎬🎬 **1974** Wealthy commuters are kidnapped and held hostage by terrorist hoodlums in a suburban train club car. Standard made for television vehicle. **78m/C VHS, Beta.** Lynda Day George, Laurence Luckinbill, Ina Balin, Bernie Casey; **D:** Harvey Hart. *WOV*

Panic Station 🎬🎬 *The Plains of Heaven* **1982** Two guys get lonely at remote satellite relay station. **90m/C VHS.** *AU* Richard Moir, Reg Evans, Gerard Kennedy; **D:** Ian Pringle.

Panique 🎬🎬🎬 *Panic* **1947** A study of mob psychology in slums of post-WWII Paris. Two lovers frame a stranger for murder. Dark and tautly paced thriller taken from the novel by Georges Simenon. In French with English subtitles. **87m/B VHS, Beta.** *FR* Michel Simon, Viviane Romance; **D:** Julien Duvivier. *NOS, HHT, CAB*

Pantaloons 🎬🎬 **1957** A man who fancies himself to be irresistible chases women for sport. A quaint and lively period film. **93m/C VHS.** *FR* Fernandel, Carmen Sevilla, Fernando Rey; **D:** John Berry. *VYY*

Panther 🎬🎬 **1995 (R)** The Van Peebles family teaches Oliver Stone History 101 with a fictionalized account of the Black Panthers' emergence as a voice for African Americans and as a fixture on the FBI's most wanted list in the late '60s. Judge (Hardison), a Vietnam vet forced by the FBI to become an informant, chronicles the activities of leaders Bobby Seale (Vance) and Huey P. Newton (Chong) and serves as witness to the Panthers' rise and subsequent fall into corruption and disintegration. Scatter-shot editing is meant to signify the chaos of the times, but instead adds to the action-flick feel and further detracts from the professed intent of being a message movie.**CW:** Strong violence and language. **124m/C VHS.** Kadeem Hardison, Marcus Chong, Courtney B. Vance, Bokeem Woodbine, Joe Don Baker, Anthony Griffith, Nefertiti, James Russo, Richard Dysart, M. Emmet Walsh, Mario Van Peebles; **D:** Mario Van Peebles; **W:** Melvin Van Peebles; **C:** Edward Pei; **M:** Stanley Clarke. *PGV*

Panther Squad 🎬 **1984** Litter of sex kittens led by Danning get into major scraps to save world. **77m/C VHS.** Sybil Danning. *NO*

The Panther's Claw 🎬🎬 **1942** Murder befalls an opera troupe, but a sleuth with the memorable name of Thatcher Colt is on the case. A quick-moving mystery quickie that delivers on its own modest terms. **72m/B VHS.** Sidney Blackmer, Byron Foulger, Rick Vallin, Herbert Rawlinson; **D:** William Beaudine. *NOS, LOO*

Papa's Delicate Condition 🎬🎬🎬 **1963** Based on the autobiographical writings of silent screen star Corinne Griffith. Gleason is Papa whose "delicate condition" is a result of his drinking. His antics provide a constant headache to his family. A paean to turn-of-the-century family life. No I.D.s required as the performances are enjoyable for the whole family. Features the Academy Award-winning song "Call Me Irresponsible." ♫Call Me Irresponsible; Bill Bailey, Won't You Please Come Home?. **98m/C VHS, Beta, Closed Caption.** Jackie Gleason, Glynis Johns, Charlie Ruggles, Laurel Goodwin, Elisha Cook Jr., Murray Hamilton; **D:** George Marshall; **W:** Jack Rose; **C:** Loyal Griggs. Academy Awards '63: Best Song ("Call Me Irresponsible"). *BAR*

The Paper 🎬🎬🎬 **1994 (R)** Another crowd pleaser from director Howard follows a red letter day in the life of an editor at the tabloid New York Sun (modeled on the trashy Post). Fresh, fast-moving script by the Koepp brothers (who appear as reporters) offers a fairly accurate portrayal of the business of journalism (including the "brisk" language), with a few Hollywood exceptions. Pace suffers from cutaways to life outside, while script and direction sometimes coast past targets. Propelled by a fine cast, with cola-swigging editor Keaton the focus as he juggles his personal and professional lives. As a managing editor married to her work and ready to run over anyone in her way, Close is both funny and scary. Duvall contributes salt as the old newsroom warhorse. Tons of cameos, though those outside of the business may not notice them.**CW:** Strong language. **112m/C VHS, LV, Letterbox, Closed Caption, DVD.** Michael Keaton, Robert Duvall, Marisa Tomei, Glenn Close, Randy Quaid, Jason Robards Jr., Jason Alexander, Spalding Gray, Catherine O'Hara, Lynne Thigpen; **D:** Ron Howard; **W:** David Koepp, Steven Koepp; **M:** Randy Newman. Nominations: Academy Awards '94: Best Song ("Make Up Your Mind"). *USH*

The Paper Brigade 🎬🎬½ **1996 (PG)** Fifteen-year-old Gunther (Howard) gets a paper route to pay for the concert tickets he bought to impress a girl. Now he has to contend with his crazy neighbor (Englund) and a gang of bullies, as well as other obstacles. **89m/C VHS, Closed Caption.** Kyle Howard, Robert Englund, Travis Wester; **D:** Blair Treu. *WAR*

The Paper Chase 🎬🎬🎬 **1973 (PG)** Students at Harvard Law School suffer and struggle through their first year. A realistic, sometimes acidly humorous look at Ivy League ambitions, with Houseman stealing the show as the tough professor. Wonderful adaptation of the John Jay Osborn novel which later became the basis for the acclaimed television series. **111m/C VHS, Beta, LV.** Timothy Bottoms, Lindsay Wagner, John Houseman, Graham Beckel, Edward Herrmann, James Naughton, Craig Richard Nelson, Bob Lydiard; **D:** James Bridges; **W:** James Bridges; **C:** Gordon Willis; **M:** John Williams. Academy Awards '73: Best Supporting Actor (Houseman); Golden Globe Awards '74: Best Supporting Actor (Houseman); National Board of Review Awards '73: Best Supporting Actor (Houseman); Nominations: Academy Awards '73: Best Adapted Screenplay, Best Sound.*FOX, BTV*

Paper Lion 🎬🎬½ **1968** A comedy "documentary" about bestselling writer George Plimpton's tryout game as quarterback with the Detroit Lions. Film debut of Alan Alda. Helped Karras make the transition from the gridiron to the silver screen. Moves into field goal range but doesn't quite score. **107m/C VHS, Beta.** Alan Alda, Lauren Hutton, Alex Karras, Ann Turkel, John Gordy, Roger Brown, "Sugar Ray" Robinson, Roy Scheider, David Doyle; **D:** Alex March. *NO*

Paper Man 🎬🎬 **1971** A group of college students create a fictitious person in a computer for a credit card scam. The scheme snowballs, resulting in murder and hints of possible artificial intelligence. But it's just standard network TV fare, with a creepy performance by Stockwell as a computer whiz. **90m/C VHS.** Dean Stockwell, Stefanie Powers, James Stacy, Elliot Street, Tina Chen, James Olson, Ross Elliott; **D:** Walter Grauman. *XVC, VTR*

Paper Marriage 🎬🎬½ **1988** In Canada, a less than successful Chinese boxer agrees to marry a Hong Kong girl for a promise of payment in order that she may become a citizen. The money never comes, but the nearly betrothed pair discover that they love each other, after all. In Cantonese with English subtitles. **102m/C VHS.** *CH* Sammo Hung, Maggie Cheung; **D:** Alfred Cheung. *FCT, MOV*

Paper Marriage 🎬🎬½ **1993** Yet another variation on the marriage in order to gain citizenship but yes we're going to fall in love film. A young Polish woman has fallen for an upper-crust English doctor she's met in Warsaw. When Alicja arrives in England, she's promptly dumped by the cad. She's ambitious and wants to stay in England so Alicja arranges a marriage of convenience with small-time crook Aiden, who finds his new bride is more than he bargained for. **88m/C VHS.** *GB PL* Gary Kemp, Joanna Trepechinska, Rita Tushingham, Richard Hawley, David Horovitch, William Ilkley, Mark McKellen, Ann Mitchell, Sadie Frost; **D:** Krzysztof Lang; **W:** Marek Kreutz, Krzysztof Lang.

Paper Mask 🎬🎬½ **1991 (R)** When a promising young doctor is killed in an auto accident, an unscrupulous, psychotic porter assumes his identity. He uses said identity to, among other things, initiate an affair with a sultry co-worker. How long will this madman play his unholy game, and at what cost?**CW:** Language and some sensuality. **105m/C VHS.** *GB* Paul McGann, Amanda Donohoe, Frederick Treves, Barbara Leigh-Hunt, Jimmy Yuill, Tom Wilkinson; **D:** Christopher Morahan; **W:** John Collee; **M:** Richard Harvey.

Paper Moon 🎬🎬🎬½ **1973 (PG)** Award-winning story set in depression-era Kansas with Ryan O'Neal as a Bible-wielding con who meets up with a nine-year-old orphan. During their travels together, he discovers that the orphan (his daughter, Tatum) is better at "his" game than he is. Irresistible chemistry between the O'Neals, leading to Tatum's Oscar win (she is the youngest actor ever to take home a statue). Cinematically picturesque and cynical enough to keep overt sentimentalism at bay. Based on Joe David Brown's novel, "Addie Pray." The director's version contains a prologue by director Bogdanovich. **102m/B VHS, Beta, LV.** Ryan O'Neal, Tatum O'Neal,

Madeline Kahn, John Hillerman, Randy Quaid; **D:** Peter Bogdanovich; **W:** Alvin Sargent. Academy Awards '73: Best Supporting Actress (O'Neal); Writers Guild of America '73: Best Adapted Screenplay; Nominations: Academy Awards '73: Best Adapted Screenplay, Best Sound, Best Supporting Actress (Kahn). *PAR, BTV*

Paper Tiger 🎬🎬 **1974** Niven plays an imaginative English tutor who fabricates fantastic yarns fictionalizing his past in order to impress his student, the son of the Japanese ambassador to a Southeast Asian country. Poorly executed karate, misdirection, and a simplistic storyline work against it. **104m/C VHS, Beta.** *GB* David Niven, Toshiro Mifune, Eiko Ando, Hardy Kruger; **D:** Ken Annakin; **W:** Jack Davies. *NO*

A Paper Wedding 🎬🎬🎬 *Les Noces de Papier* **1989** A middle-aged literature professor with a dead-end career and equally dead-end romance with a married man is persuaded by her lawyer sister to marry a Chilean political refugee to avoid his deportation. Of course, they must fool an immigration official and their fake marriage does turn into romance, but this is no light-hearted "Green Card." Bujold shines. In French and Spanish with English subtitles. **90m/C VHS, LV, Closed Caption.** *CA* Genevieve Bujold, Manuel Aranguiz, Dorothee Berryman; **D:** Michel Brault. *CTL, LUM*

Paperback Hero 🎬🎬 **1973** A hot-shot hockey player turns to crime when his team loses its financial backing. Choopy storyline could use a Zamboni, while Dullea should be penalized for occasionally losing his rustic accent. Still the supporting actors skate through their roles and, for periods, it works. A slapshot that ultimately clangs off the goal post. **94m/C VHS.** *CA* Keir Dullea, Elizabeth Ashley, John Beck, Dayle Haddon; **D:** Peter Pearson. *NO*

Paperback Romance 🎬🎬½ *Lucky Break* **1996 (R)** Sophie (Carides) is a writer of erotica who doesn't act on her own impulses because she's embarrassed by her polio-crippled leg. But when she breaks her leg, the cast allows her to pass the injury off as a skiing accident and Sophie decides to go after the man of her dreams, a charmingly shady jewelry dealer named Eddie (LaPaglia)—who just happens to be engaged. **CW:** Sexuality and related dialogue. **99m/C VHS, Closed Caption.** *AU* Gia Carides, Anthony LaPaglia, Rebecca Gibney; **D:** Ben Lewin; **W:** Ben Lewin; **C:** Vincent Monton; **M:** Paul Grabowsky. *ORI*

The Paperboy 🎬🎬 **1994 (R)** Melissa Thorpe (Paul) returns to her small hometown to settle her mother's estate, only to become the obsession of Johnny (Marut), the 12-year-old paperboy she mistakenly befriends. Seems he becomes psychotically jealous when Melissa takes up with an old flame (Katt) and dead bodies become as common as old newspapers. **93m/C VHS, LV, Closed Caption.** *CA* Alexandra Paul, Marc Marut, William Katt, Brigid Tierney; **D:** Douglas Jackson; **W:** David Peckinpah; **M:** Milan Kymlicka. *REP*

Paperhouse 🎬🎬🎬 **1989** An odd fantasy about a young girl plagued by recurring dreams that begin to influence real life. Very obtuse, British-minded film with "Twilight Zone" feel that manages to capture genuine dream-ness. Not for all audiences, but intriguing nonetheless. Based on the novel "Marianne Dreams" by Catherine Storr. **92m/C VHS, Beta, LV.** *GB* Glenne Headly, Ben Cross, Charlotte Burke, Elliott Spiers, Gemma Jones, Sarah Newbold; **D:** Bernard Rose; **W:** Matthew Jacobs; **M:** Hans Zimmer, Stanley Myers. *ART, VES*

Papillon 🎬🎬🎬 **1973 (PG)** McQueen is a criminal sent to Devil's Island in the 1930s determined to escape from the Lemote prison. Hoffman is the swindler he befriends. A series of escapes and recaptures follow. Boxoffice winner based on the autobiographical writings of French thief Henri Charriere. Excellent portrayal of prison life and fine performances from the prisoners. Certain segments would have been better left on the cutting room floor. The film's title refers to the lead's butterfly tattoo. **150m/C VHS, Beta, LV.** Steve McQueen, Dustin Hoffman, Victor Jory, George Coulouris, Anthony Zerbe; **D:** Franklin J. Schaffner; **C:** Fred W. Koonekamp; **M:** Jerry Goldsmith. Nominations: Academy Awards '73: Best Original Dramatic/Comedy Score. *FOX, WAR*

Parade 🎬🎬🎬 **1974** A series of vignettes in a circus, "Parade" is actually a play within a play, meshing the action with events offstage. The laserdisc edition includes Rene Clement's 1936 "Soigne Ton Gauche," Tati's inspiration. **85m/C VHS, LV.** *FR* Jacques Tati; **D:** Jacques Tati; **W:** Jacques Tati. *HMV, CRC, FCT*

The Paradine Case 🎬🎬½ **1947** A passable Hitchcock romancer about a young lawyer who falls in love with the woman he's defending for murder, not knowing whether she is innocent or guilty. Script could be tighter and more cohesive. Seventy thousand dollars of the three million budget were spent recreating the original Bailey courtroom. Based on the novel by Robert Hichens. **125m/B VHS, Beta, LV, Closed Caption.** Gregory Peck, Alida Valli, Ann Todd, Louis Jourdan, Charles Laughton, Charles Coburn, Ethel Barrymore, Leo G. Carroll; **D:** Alfred Hitchcock; **C:** Lee Garmes. Nominations: Academy Awards '47: Best Supporting Actress (Barrymore). *FOX*

Paradise 🎬🎬 **1982 (R)** Young American boy and beautiful English girl on a 19th-century jaunt through the Middle East are the sole survivors when their caravan is massacred. Left to their own devices, they discover a magnificent oasis and the joys of frolicking naked and experience (surprise) their sexual awakening. Do a doubletake: it's the "Blue Lagoon" all over, with a bit more nudity and a lot more sand. **96m/C VHS, Beta, LV.** Phoebe Cates, Willie Aames, Richard Curnock, Tuvio Tavi; **D:** Stuart Gillard. *COL*

Paradise 🎬🎬🎬 **1991 (PG-13)** Young boy is sent to the country to live with his pregnant mother's married friends (real life husband and wife Johnson and Griffith). From the outset it is clear that the couple are experiencing marital troubles, making the boy's assimilation all the more difficult. Help arrives in the form of a sprightly ten-year-old girl, with whom he forms a charming relationship. Largely predictable, this remake of the French film "Le Grand Chemin" works thanks to the surprisingly good work of its ensemble cast, and the gorgeous scenery of South Carolina, where the movie was filmed. **112m/C VHS, Beta, Closed Caption.** Melanie Griffith, Don Johnson, Elijah Wood, Thora Birch, Sheila McCarthy, Eve Gordon, Louise Latham, Greg Travis, Sarah Trigger; **D:** Mary Agnes Donoghue; **W:** Mary Agnes Donoghue; **M:** David Newman. *TOU*

Paradise Alley 🎬🎬 **1978 (PG)** Rocky tires of boxing, decides to join the WWF. Three brothers brave the world of professional wrestling in an effort to strike it rich and move out of the seedy Hell's Kitchen neighborhood of New York, circa 1946. Stallone wrote, stars in, and makes his directorial debut in addition to singing the title song. He makes a few good moves as director, but is ultimately pinned to the canvas. **109m/C VHS, Beta, LV.** Sylvester Stallone, Anne Archer, Armand Assante, Lee Canalito, Kevin Conway; **D:** Sylvester Stallone; **W:** Sylvester Stallone; **M:** Bill Conti. *USH*

Paradise Canyon 🎬½ **1935** Early Wayne "B" thriller, in which he plays an undercover government agent sent to track down a group of counterfeiters. **59m/B VHS.** John Wayne, Yakima Canutt, Marion Burns. *COL, NOS, REP*

Paradise, Hawaiian Style 🎬½ **1966 (G)** Out-of-work pilot returns to Hawaii, where he and a buddy start a charter service with two helicopters. Plenty of gals are wooed by "the Pelvis." Filmed four years after Elvis's first Pacific piece, "Blue Hawaii." Presley, showing the first signs of slow-down, displays no surprises here. 🎵Paradise, Hawaiian Style; Scratch My Back (Then I'll Scratch Yours); Stop Where You Are; This Is My Heaven; House of Sand; Queenie Wahine's Papaya; Datin'; Drums of the Islands; A Dog's Life. **91m/C VHS, Beta.** Elvis Presley, Suzanna Leigh, James Shigeta, Donna Butterworth, Irene Tsu, Julie Parrish, Philip Ahn, Mary Treen, Marianna Hill, John Doucette, Grady Sutton; **D:** Michael Moore. *FOX, MVD*

Paradise in Harlem 🎬½ **1940** All-black musical in which a cabaret performer witnesses a gangland murder, sees his sick wife die, and is pressured into leaving town by the mob. Have a nice day. **83m/B VHS, Beta.** Frank Wilson, Mamie Smith, Edna Mae Harris, Juanita Hall; **D:** Joseph Seiden. *VYY, FCT, VCN*

Paradise Island 🎬 **1930** Down-scale musical romance about an ingenue on her way to join her fiance in the South Seas, only to find that he has gambled away his money. The opportunistic saloon owner tries to put the moves on her. Will the two lovers be reunited? 🎵I've Got a Girl in Every Port; Drinking Song; Lazy Breezes; Just Another Dream. **68m/B VHS.** Kenneth Harlan, Marceline Day, Thomas Santschi, Paul Hurst, Victor Potel, Gladden James, Will Stanton; **D:** Bert Glennon. *GPV, NOS*

Paradise Motel 🎬½ **1984 (R)** Teen exploitation film centered around a local motel predominantly used for one-night rendezvous. High school heroes and jocks battle for the affections of a beautiful classmate. **87m/C VHS, Beta, Closed Caption.** Gary Hershberger, Jonna Leigh Stack, Robert Krantz; **D:** Cary Medoway; **C:** James L. Carter. *FOX*

Paradise Park 🎬🎬½ **199?** A whimsical comedy about the inhabitants of a West Virginia trailer park who dream of better lives while coping with their depressing surroundings. An English teacher (Groce) wishes he was a writer, an elderly woman (Basquette) dreams of winning a TV quiz show, and a mechanic wants to be a race car driver. Director Boyd sprinkles in appearances of non-Hollywood notables Porter Waggoner, Johnny Paycheck, Webb Wilder, and wrestler Dusty Rhodes. Includes some black and white fantasy sequences. **100m/C VHS.** Lena Basquette, Larry Groce, Jennifer Gurney; **Cameos:** Johnny Paycheck, Webb Wilder, Dusty Rhodes, Porter Waggoner; **D:** Daniel Boyd. *MTH*

Paradise Road 🎬🎬 **1997 (R)** Fleeing Singapore during WWII, a group of British, American, and Australian women straggle to the shore of Sumatra after their ship is bombed, where they're taken prisoner by the Japanese. Headed by Close, the prisoners form a vocal ensemble that crosses their collective national differences and attempts to lift the spirits of the brutalized women. Familiar ground is trod in this prisoner-of-war saga, but the music is genuinely moving, and excellent performances from the cast help sustain interest. The symphonic choral pieces were taken from actual sheet music used by a similar group of real-life WWII prisoners. **CW:** Prisoner of war brutality and violence. **115m/C VHS, Closed Caption.** Glenn Close, Frances McDormand, Julianna Margulies, Pauline Collins, Jennifer Ehle, Elizabeth Spriggs, Tessa Humphries, Sab Shimono; **D:** Bruce Beresford; **W:** Bruce Beresford; **C:** Peter James. *FOX*

Paradisio 🎬½ **1961 (R)** Dying inventor wills Oxford professor an authentic pair of X-ray specs. Spies come gunning for the professor, chasing him through Europe. Doc keeps forgetting he's being chased while using the special specs to see (sometimes in 3-D) through the clothing of young women. Meager plot does not get in way of 3-D nudie exploitation. **82m/C VHS, Beta.** Arthur Howard, Eva Waegner. *VDM*

The Parallax View 🎬🎬🎬½ **1974 (R)** A reporter tries to disprove a report which states that a presidential candidate's assassination was not a conspiracy. As he digs deeper and deeper, he uncovers more than he bargained for and becomes a pawn in the conspirators' further plans. Beatty is excellent and the conspiracy is never less than believable. A lesser-known, compelling political thriller that deserves to be more widely seen. **102m/C VHS, Beta.** Warren Beatty, Hume Cronyn, William Daniels, Paula Prentiss, Kenneth Mars, Bill McKinney, Anthony Zerbe, Walter McGinn; **D:** Alan J. Pakula; **C:**

Gordon Willis. National Society of Film Critics Awards '74: Best Cinematography. *PAR*

Parallel Corpse 🐾 **1983** A mortuary attendant finds a murder victim hidden in a coffin and blackmails the remorseless killer. **89m/C VHS, Beta.** Buster Larsen, Jorgen Kiil, Agneta Ekmanner, Masja Dessau.

Parallel Lives 🐾🐾½ **1994 (R)** Sorority sisters and frat brothers (and their various spouses and lovers), from the classes of both 1948 and 1973, gather for an on-campus weekend reunion and discover old and new jealousies, rivalries, and lots of lust (requited and not). There's also an unexpected death and a police investigation as well. Director Yellen had her cast improvise much of their dialogue—the same method she used in "Chantilly Lace." Made for cable TV.***CW:*** Strong language; scene of sexuality. **105m/C VHS, Beta, Closed Caption.** James Belushi, James Brolin, LeVar Burton, Lindsay Crouse, Jill Eikenberry, Ben Gazzara, Jack Klugman, David Lansbury, Liza Minnelli, Dudley Moore, Gena Rowlands, Ally Sheedy, Helen Slater, Mira Sorvino, Paul Sorvino, Robert Wagner, Patricia Wettig, JoBeth Williams, Treat Williams; *D:* Linda Yellen; *W:* Gisella Bernice; *M:* Patrick Seymour. *PAR*

Paralyzed 🐾🐾 **197?** An unconscious journalist, mistaken for dead in a hospital emergency room, flashes back to the investigation that embroiled him in his predicament. **90m/C VHS, Beta.** Ingrid Thulin, Jean Sorel, Mario Adorf; *D:* Aldo Lado; *W:* Aldo Lado. *MPI*

Paramedics 🐾½ **1988 (PG-13)** A motley crew of cavorting paramedics battle their evil captain. Another parody of people in uniform. A comedy with little pulse. **91m/C VHS, Beta.** George Newbern, Christopher McDonald, John P. Ryan, Ray Walston, Lawrence-Hilton Jacobs; *D:* Stuart Margolin. *ART, VES*

Paranoia 🐾 *Orgasmo; A Beautiful Place to Kill; A Quiet Place to Kill* **1969** Beautiful jet-set widow is trapped in her own Italian villa by a young couple who drug her to get her to perform in various sex orgies, which are probably the most interesting part of this muddled affair. **94m/C VHS, Beta.** *IT* Carroll Baker, Lou Castel, Colette Descombes; *D:* Umberto Lenzi. *REP*

Paranoiac 🐾🐾½ **1962** Greed and terror set in a country mansion. Simon (Reed) wants the family inheritance all to himself even if it means driving sister Eleanor (Scott) insane. This may not be so hard—she's claiming to see their dead brother Tony. Surprise! Tony (Davion) shows up (really throwing Simon for a loop). Reed's evil is tinged with humor although the numerous plot twists can get confusing. First directorial effort for cinematographer Francis. **80m/B VHS, Closed Caption.** *GB* Oliver Reed, Janette Scott, Alex Davion, Liliane Brousse, Sheila Burell, Maurice Denham; *D:* Freddie Francis; *W:* Jimmy Sangster; *C:* Arthur Grant; *M:* Elisabeth Lutyens. *USH*

Parasite woof! **1982 (R)** A small town is beset by giant parasites. An "Alien" ripoff originally filmed in 3-D, during that technique's brief return in the early '80s. Bad films like this killed it both the first and second times. An unpardonable mess that comes off as a stinky sixth-grade film project. **90m/C VHS, Beta, LV, Closed Caption.** Bob Glaudini, Demi Moore, Luca Bercovici, Cherie Currie, Gale Robbins, James Davidson, Al Fann, Cheryl "Rainbeaux" Smith, Vivian Blaine; *D:* Charles Band; *W:* Alan J. Adler, Frank Levering, Michael Shoob; *C:* Mac Ahlberg; *M:* Richard Band. *PAR*

Pardners 🐾🐾½ **1956** Spoiled New York millionaire (Lewis) becomes the sheriff of small western town, with Martin as a ranch foreman. The two team up to rid the town of bad guys and romance two local cuties. Western spoof (with music) is a remake of 1936's "Rhythm on the Range." ♫Buckskin Beauty; Pardners; The Wind! The Wind!; Me 'N You 'N the Moon. **90m/C VHS, Closed Caption.** Jerry Lewis, Dean Martin, Lori Nelson, Jackie Loughery, Jeff Morrow, John Baragrey, Agnes Moorehead, Lon Chaney Jr., Milton Frome, Lee Van Cleef, Jack Elam,

Bob Steele, Emory Parnell; *D:* Norman Taurog; *W:* Sidney Sheldon, Jerry Davis. *PAR*

Pardon Mon Affaire 🐾🐾🐾 *Un Elephant a Trompe Enormement* **1976 (PG)** When a middle-aged civil servant gets a look at a model in a parking garage, he decides it's time to cheat on his wife. Enjoyable French farce. Re-made as in the United States "The Woman in Red" and followed by "Pardon Mon Affair, Too!" Subtitled. **107m/C VHS, Beta, LV.** *FR* Jean Rochefort, Claude Brasseur, Guy Bedos, Victor Lanoux, Daniele Delorme, Martine Sarcey, Anny Duperey; *D:* Yves Robert; *M:* Vladimir Cosma. Cesar Awards '77: Best Supporting Actor (Brasseur).

Pardon Mon Affaire, Too! 🐾🐾½ *We Will All Meet in Paradise* **1977** Pale sequel to the first popular French comedy, "Pardon Mon Affair." This time the four fantasy-minded buddies withstand the trials of marriage and middle-class life. With English subtitles or dubbed. **105m/C VHS, Beta.** *FR* Jean Rochefort, Claude Brasseur, Guy Bedos; *D:* Yves Robert; *M:* Vladimir Cosma.

Pardon My Gun 🐾½ **1930** Cowpoke falls for the boss' daughter but has a rival in a wealthy rancher, who isn't above sabotage to get the girl. **64m/B VHS.** Tom George Duryea Keene, Harry Woods, Sally Starr, Lee Moran, Mona Ray; *D:* Robert De Lacy; *W:* Hugh Cummings. *GPV*

Pardon My Sarong 🐾🐾½ **1942** Bud and Lou star as Chicago bus drivers who end up shipwrecked on a South Pacific island when they get involved with notorious jewel thieves. The island natives think Lou is a god! Standard Abbott & Costello fare. **83m/B VHS.** Bud Abbott, Lou Costello, Virginia Bruce, Robert Paige, Lionel Atwill, Leif Erickson, William Demarest, Samuel S. Hinds; *D:* Erle C. Kenton; *C:* Milton Krasner. *USH*

Pardon My Trunk 🐾🐾 *Hello Elephant; Bvongiorno, Elefante* **1952** Struggling against poverty on his teacher's salary, a man and his family receive a gift from a Hindu prince—an elephant. De Sica carries this silly premise beyond mere slapstick. Dubbed. **85m/B VHS, Beta.** *IT* Sabu, Vittorio De Sica; *D:* Gianni Franciolini. *VYY*

Pardon Us 🐾🐾½ *Jail Birds* **1931** Laurel and Hardy are thrown into prison for bootlegging. Plot meanders along aimlessly, but the duo have some inspired moments. The first Laurel and Hardy feature. **78m/B VHS, Beta.** Stan Laurel, Oliver Hardy, June Marlowe, James Finlayson; *D:* James Parrott. *CCB, MLB*

The Parent Trap 🐾🐾½ **1961** Mills plays a dual role in this heartwarming comedy as twin sisters who conspire to bring their divorced parents together again. Well-known Disney fluff. Followed by several made-for-television sequels featuring the now grown-up twins. **127m/C VHS, Beta, LV, Closed Caption.** Hayley Mills, Maureen O'Hara, Brian Keith, Charlie Ruggles, Una Merkel, Leo G. Carroll; *D:* David Swift. Nominations: Academy Awards '61: Best Film Editing, Best Sound. *DIS*

The Parent Trap **1998** Updated remake of Disney's 1961 family film about long-separated identical twins, Hallie and Annie, who meet accidentally at camp and decide to reunite their divorced parents. Quaid is Napa vineyard-owning dad while mom is London fashion designer Richardson, with newcomer Lohan the identity-swapping twins. Not yet reviewed. **?m/C VHS.** Dennis Quaid, Natasha Richardson, Lindsay Lohan, Polly Holliday, Joanna Barnes, Elaine Hendrix, Ronnie Stevens, Lisa Ann Walter; *D:* Nancy Meyers; *W:* Nancy Meyers, Charles Shyer; *C:* Dean Cundey. *NYR*

Parenthood 🐾🐾🐾 **1989 (PG-13)** Four grown siblings and their parents struggle with various levels of parenthood. From the college drop-out, to the nervous single mother, to the yuppie couple raising an overachiever, every possibility is explored, including the perspective from the older generation, portrayed by Robards. Genuinely funny with dramatic moments that work most of the time, with an affecting performance from Martin and Wiest. Director Howard has four kids and was

inspired to make this film when on a European jaunt with them. **124m/C VHS, Beta, LV, Closed Caption, DVD.** Steve Martin, Mary Steenburgen, Dianne Wiest, Martha Plimpton, Keanu Reeves, Tom Hulce, Jason Robards Jr., Rick Moranis, Harley Jane Kozak, Joaquin Rafael (Leaf) Phoenix, Paul Linke, Dennis Dugan; *D:* Ron Howard; *W:* Lowell Ganz, Babaloo Mandel, Ron Howard; *M:* Randy Newman. Nominations: Academy Awards '89: Best Song ("I Love to See You Smile"), Best Supporting Actress (Wiest). *USH*

Parents 🐾🐾🐾 **1989 (R)** Dark satire of middle class suburban life in the '50s, centering on a young boy who discovers that his parents aren't getting their meat from the local butcher. Gives new meaning to leftovers and boasts a very disturbing barbecue scene. Balaban's debut is a strikingly visual and creative gorefest with definite cult potential. The eerie score is by Badalamenti, who also composed the music for "Blue Velvet," "Wild at Heart," and the television series "Twin Peaks." **81m/C VHS, Beta, LV.** Randy Quaid, Mary Beth Hurt, Bryan Madorsky, Sandy Dennis, Kathryn Grody, Deborah Rush, Graham Jarvis, Juno Mills-Cockell; *D:* Bob Balaban; *W:* Christopher Hawthorne; *C:* Robin Vidgeon; *M:* Angelo Badalamenti, Jonathan Elias. *ART, HHE*

Paris Belongs to Us 🐾🐾½ *Paris Nous Appartient; Paris is Ours* **1960** An early entry in the French "new wave" of naturalistic cinema, this psychological mystery drama has a woman investigating a suicide linked to a possible worldwide conspiracy. Interesting, if somewhat dated by Cold War elements. **120m/B VHS.** *FR* Jean-Claude Brialy, Betty Schneider, Gianni Esposito, Francoise Prevost; *D:* Jacques Rivette; *W:* Jacques Rivette, Jean Gruault. *VDM*

Paris Blues 🐾🐾½ **1961** Two jazz musicians, one white, one black, strive for success in Paris and become involved with American tourists who want to take them back to the States. Score by Duke Ellington and an appearance by Armstrong make it a must-see for jazz fans. **100m/B VHS, Beta, Closed Caption.** Paul Newman, Sidney Poitier, Joanne Woodward, Diahann Carroll, Louis Armstrong, Barbara Lange; *D:* Martin Ritt; *W:* Jack Sher, Walter Bernstein; *M:* Duke Ellington. Nominations: Academy Awards '61: Scoring of a Musical. *MGM, FCT*

Paris Express 🐾🐾½ *The Man Who Watched Trains Go By* **1953** When a man steals money from his employer, he boards the Paris Express to escape from the police. A bit convoluted, but well acted. Based on the George Simenon novel. **82m/C VHS, Beta.** Claude Rains, Herbert Lom, Felix Aylmer, Marius Goring, Anouk Aimee, Marta Toren; *D:* Harold French. *SNC, NOS, MRV*

Paris, France 🐾🐾 **1994 (NC-17)** Lucy (Hope) is a frustrated writer, living in Toronto, who decides the pursuit of sexual passion will unleash her blocked creative urges. Her main partner is poet Sloan (Outerbridge), the young man Lucy is trying to fashion in the image of a deceased Parisian lover, and also the man whose poetry her husband (and publisher) Michael (Ertmanis) is promoting. Lots of self-delusion and literary pretensions as well as erotic grappling. Adapted from the novel by Tom Walmsley.***CW:*** Explicit sexual content. **111m/C VHS.** *CA* Leslie Hope, Peter Outerbridge, Victor Ertmanis, Raoul Trujillo, Dan Lett; *D:* Gerard Ciccoritti; *W:* Tom Walmsley; *M:* John McCarthy. *APX*

Paris Holiday 🐾🐾½ **1957** An actor heading for Paris to buy a noted author's latest screenplay finds mystery and romance. Entertaining chase scenes as the characters try to find the elusive script. **100m/C VHS, Beta.** Bob Hope, Fernandel, Anita Ekberg, Martha Hyer, Preston Sturges; *D:* Gerd Oswald. *UNI*

Paris Is Burning 🐾🐾🐾 **1991 (R)** Livingston's documentary portrayal of New York City's transvestite balls where men dress up, dance, and compete in various categories. Filmed between 1985 and 1989, this is a compelling look at a subculture of primarily black and Hispanic men and the one place they can truly be themselves. Madonna noted this look and attitude (much watered down) in her song "Vogue." **CW:** Language and sexuality. **71m/C VHS.** Dorian Corey, Pepper Labeijn, Venus Xtravaganza, Octavia St. Laurant, Willi Ninja, Anji Xtravaganza, Freddie Pendavis, Junior Labeija; **D:** Jennie Livingston. National Society of Film Critics Awards '91: Best Feature Documentary; Sundance Film Festival '91: Grand Jury Prize. *FCT*

Paris, Texas 🎬🎬🎬½ **1983 (PG)** After four years a drifter returns to find his son is being raised by his brother because the boy's mother has also disappeared. He tries to reconnect with the boy. Introspective script acclaimed by many film critics, but others found it to be too slow. **145m/C VHS, Beta, LV, Closed Caption.** *FR GE* Harry Dean Stanton, Nastassia Kinski, Dean Stockwell, Hunter Carson, Aurore Clement; **D:** Wim Wenders; **W:** Sam Shepard, L.M. Kit Carson. British Academy Awards '84: Best Director (Wenders); Cannes Film Festival '84: Best Film. *FOX*

Paris Trout 🎬🎬½ **1991 (R)** Believing himself above the law, southern Trout (Hopper) shoots the mother and sister of a young black man who reneged on his IOU. Lawyer Harris is forced to defend a man he knows deserves to be punished, and wife Hershey suffers long. Adapted by Pete Dexter from his National Book Award-winning novel. Made for cable.**CW:** Brief language, violence, and sexuality. **98m/C VHS, Beta, LV, Closed Caption.** Dennis Hopper, Barbara Hershey, Ed Harris, Tina Lifford, Darnita Henry, Eric Ware, Ray McKinnon; **D:** Stephen Gyllenhaal; **W:** Pete Dexter; **C:** Robert Elswit. *FCT, VTR*

Paris When It Sizzles 🎬🎬 **1964** A screenwriter and his secretary fall in love while working on a film in Paris, confusing themselves with the script's characters. Star-studded cast deserves better than this lame script. Shot on location in Paris. Holden's drinking—he ran into a brick wall while under the influence—and some unresolved romantic tension between him and Hepburn, affected shooting. Dietrich, Sinatra, Astaire, Ferrer, and Curtis show up for a party on the set. **110m/C VHS, Beta.** William Holden, Audrey Hepburn, Gregoire Aslan, Raymond Bussieres, Tony Curtis, Fred Astaire, Frank Sinatra, Noel Coward, Marlene Dietrich, Mel Ferrer; **D:** Richard Quine; **W:** George Axelrod. *PAR*

Park Avenue Logger 🎬½ **1937** Silly story has blue-blood Ingraham believing son O'Brien is a panty-waist, so he sends him to a lumber camp to prove his manhood. But junior is actually a wrestling champ (known as The Masked Marvel) and manages just fine, even winning the gal. **65m/B VHS.** George O'Brien, Beatrice Roberts, Lloyd Ingraham, Ward Bond, Willard Robertson, Bert Hanlon; **D:** David Howard. *GPV*

The Park Is Mine 🎬🎬 **1985** A deranged and desperate Vietnam vet takes hostages in Central Park. Semi-infamous film, notable for being the first movie made for HBO on cable and for being filmed in Toronto, before the inexpensive practice of filming in Canada became widespread. **102m/C VHS, Beta, Closed Caption.** Tommy Lee Jones, Yaphet Kotto, Helen Shaver; **D:** Steven Hilliard Stern; **M:** Tangerine Dream. *FOX*

Parker 🎬🎬 **1984** An executive is kidnapped, then released, but does not know why. Unable to live with the mystery, he tracks his kidnappers down into a world of blackmail, drugs, and intrigue. **100m/C VHS, Beta.** Bryan Brown, Kurt Raab. *ORI*

Parlor, Bedroom and Bath 🎬🎬
Romeo in Pyjamas **1931** A family tries to keep a young woman from seeing that her love interest is flirting with other prospects. Doesn't live up to the standard Keaton set in his silent films. Keaton spoke French and German for foreign versions. **75m/B VHS.** Buster Keaton, Charlotte Greenwood, Cliff Edwards, Reginald Denny; **D:** Edward Sedgwick. *NOS, VYY, VDM*

Parole, Inc. 🎬🎬 **1949** FBI takes on the underground in this early crime film. Criminals on parole have not served their sentences, and the mob is responsible. A meagerly financed yawner.

71m/B VHS. Michael O'Shea, Evelyn Ankers, Turhan Bey, Lyle Talbot; **D:** Alfred Zeisler. *NOS, SNC*

Paroled to Die 🎬½ **1937** A man frames a young rancher for a bank robbery and a murder he committed in this wild west saga. Predictable and bland. **66m/B VHS, Beta.** Bob Steele, Kathleen Elliott. *NOS, DVT*

Parrish 🎬½ **1961** Parrish McLean (Donohue) is a very ambitious young man, determined to make it in the rich world of the tobacco growers of the Connecticut River Valley. But his ruthless tobacco king stepfather (Malden) would like to thwart his plans. As befits Donohue's teen idol status, he also gets to romance three beautiful girls. Very silly and much too long. Based on the novel by Mildred Savage. **138m/C VHS.** Troy Donahue, Claudette Colbert, Karl Malden, Dean Jagger, Diane McBain, Connie Stevens, Sharon Hugueny, Dub Taylor, Hampton Fancher, Bibi Osterwald, Madeline Sherwood, Sylvia Miles, Carroll O'Connor, Vincent Gardenia; **D:** Delmer Daves; **W:** Delmer Daves; **C:** Harry Stradling; **M:** Max Steiner. *WAR*

Parting Glances 🎬🎬🎬 **1986 (R)** Low-budget but acclaimed film shows the relationship between two gay men and how they deal with a close friend's discovery of his exposure to the AIDS virus. Touching and realistic portrayals make this a must see. In 1990 Sherwood died of AIDS without completing any other films. **90m/C VHS, Beta, Closed Caption.** John Bolger, Richard Ganoung, Steve Buscemi, Adam Nathan, Patrick Tull; **D:** Bill Sherwood; **W:** Bill Sherwood. *FOX, FRF*

Partner 🎬🎬🎬 **1968** An extremely shy young man invents a strong alter ego to cope with the world but this second personality comes to dominate—with tragic results. In Italian with English subtitles. **110m/C VHS.** *IT* Pierre Clementi, Stefania Sandrelli, Tina Aumont; **D:** Bernardo Bertolucci; **M:** Ennio Morricone. *TPV*

Partners 🎬🎬 **1982 (R)** A straight, macho cop must pose as the lover of a gay cop to investigate the murder of a gay man in Los Angeles' homosexual community. Sets out to parody "Cruising"; unfortunately, the only source of humor the makers could find was in ridiculous homosexual stereotypes that are somewhat offensive and often unfunny. **93m/C VHS, Beta.** Ryan O'Neal, John Hurt, Kenneth McMillan, Robyn Douglass, Jay Robinson, Rick Jason; **D:** James Burrows; **W:** Francis Veber; **M:** Georges Delerue. *PAR*

Partners of the Trail 🎬½ **1944** U.S. marshals Brown and Hatton try to find out who's murdering ranchers which leads them to gunplay with Ingraham's band of outlaws. **57m/B VHS.** Johnny Mack Brown, Raymond Hatton, Lloyd Ingraham, Christine McIntyre, Robert Frazer; **D:** Lambert Hillyer. *GPV*

The Party 🎬🎬🎬 **1968** Disaster-prone Indian actor wreaks considerable havoc at a posh Hollywood gathering. Laughs come quickly in this quirky Sellers vehicle. **99m/C VHS, Closed Caption.** Peter Sellers, Claudine Longet, Marge Champion, Sharron Kimberly, Denny Miller, Gavin MacLeod, Carol Wayne; **D:** Blake Edwards; **W:** Blake Edwards; **M:** Henry Mancini. *MGM, TVC*

Party Animal 🎬 **1983 (R)** A college stud teaches a shy farm boy a thing or two about the carnal aspects of campus life. **78m/C VHS, Beta.** Timothy Carhart, Matthew Causey, Robin Harlan; **D:** David Beaird; **W:** David Beaird; **C:** Bryan England. *ART*

Party Camp 🎬 **1987 (R)** A rowdy summer camp counselor endeavors to turn a tame backwoods camp into a non-stop party. Late entry in the "Meatballs"-spawned genre fails to do anything of even minor interest. **96m/C VHS, Beta.** Andrew Ross, Billy Jacoby, April Wayne, Kirk Cribb; **D:** Gary Graver. *ART*

Party Favors woof! **1989 (R)** Erotic dancing, strip tease acts, and general hilarity are featured in this party tape. **83m/C VHS, Beta.** Jeannie Winters, Marjorie Miller, Gail Thackray; **D:** Ed Hansen. *ART, VES*

Party Girl 🎬🎬🎬½ **1958** A crime drama involving an attorney representing a 1920s crime boss and his henchmen when they run afoul of the law. The lawyer falls in love with a nightclub dancer who successfully encourages him to leave the mob, but not before he is wounded in a gang war attack, arrested, and forced to testify against the mob as a material witness. The mob then takes his girlfriend hostage to prevent his testifying, leading to an exciting climax. Must-see viewing for Charisse's steamy dance numbers. **99m/C VHS, Beta, LV, Letterbox.** Robert Taylor, Cyd Charisse, Lee J. Cobb, John Ireland, Kent Smith, Claire Kelly, Corey Allen; **D:** Nicholas Ray. *MGM*

Party Girl 🎬🎬½ **1994 (R)** In the "girls just wanna have fun" category comes this spritely saga of 20-something Manhattan club gal Mary (Posey), who needs some steady income after the cops bust her for throwing an illegal rent party. So, since Mary's godmother is a librarian, she gets a job as a library clerk and discovers the wonders of the Dewey Decimal system (no, I'm not joking but presumably director Mayer is). Parker's Mary is a properly flaunting poseur but a little nightlife tends to a go a long way.**CW:** Language and drug content. **99m/C VHS, LV, Closed Caption.** Parker Posey, Omar Townsend, Anthony De Sando, Guillermo Diaz, Sasha von Scherler, Liev Schreiber; **D:** Daisy von Scherler Mayer; **W:** Harry Birckmayer, Daisy von Scherler Mayer; **C:** Michael Slovis; **M:** Anton Sanko. *COL*

Party Girls 🎬½ **1929** Escort service girls run afoul of the law in this hokey melodrama. **67m/B VHS, Beta.** Douglas Fairbanks Jr., Jeanette Loff, Judith Barrie, Marie Prevost, John St. Polis, Lucien Prival; **D:** Victor Halperin. *NOS, LOO, SNC*

Party Girls for Sale 🎬🎬 *Violated* **1954** Mystery thriller in which a young girl's body is found on the beach in Rio de Janeiro. **?m/C VHS.** Raymond Burr, Scott Brady, Johanna Matz. *SNC*

Party Incorporated 🎬🎬 *Party Girls* **1989 (R)** Marilyn Chambers (of "Behind the Green Door" fame) stars as a young widow with a huge tax load who gives parties to pay it off. Also known as "Party Girls." **80m/C VHS, LV.** Marilyn Chambers, Kurt Woodruff, Christine Veronica, Kimberly Taylor; **D:** Chuck Vincent. *VTR, IME*

Party Line 🎬 **1988 (R)** A veteran police captain and a district attorney team up to track down a pair of killers who find their victims through party lines. **90m/C VHS, Beta.** Richard Hatch, Shawn Weatherly, Richard Roundtree, Leif Garrett, Greta Blackburn; **D:** William Webb; **W:** Richard Brandes. *NO*

Party! Party! **1983** A bunch of kids go nuts and have a party when their parents leave. **100m/C VHS.** *GB* **M:** Sting, David Bowie, Joe Jackson, Elvis Costello.

Party Plane 🎬 **1990** Softcore fun-fest about a plane full of oversexed stewardesses. **81m/C VHS, Beta, LV.** Kent Stoddard, Karen Annarino, John Goff, Jill Johnson; **D:** Ed Hansen. *VES*

Pas Tres Catholique 🎬🎬 *Something Fishy* **1993** Pleasant comedy finds 40ish, chain-smoking, unconventional P.I. Maxine (Anemone) investigating her ex-husband for an insurance scram, drawing closer to her estranged son, and trying to decide romantically between long-time friend Florence and handsome economist Jacques. French with subtitles. **100m/B VHS.** *FR* Anemone, Christine Boisson, Michel Didym, Gregoire Colin, Denis Podalydes, Roland Bertin, Bernard Verley, Michel Roux; *Cameos:* Micheline Presle; **D:** Tonie Marshall; **W:** Tonie Marshall; **C:** Dominique Chapuis. Nominations: Cesar Awards '95: Best Actress (Anemone). *NYR*

Pascali's Island 🎬🎬🎬½ **1988 (PG-13)** A Turkish spy becomes involved with an adventurer's plot to steal rare artifacts, then finds himself ensnared in political and personal intrigue. Superior tragedy features excellent performances from Kingsley, Dance, and Mirren. **106m/C VHS, Beta, LV.** *GB* Ben Kingsley, Helen Mirren, Charles Dance, Sheila Allen, Vernon Dobtcheff; **D:** James Dearden; **W:** James Dearden; **C:** Roger Deakins; **M:** Loek Dikker. *ART*

Pass the Ammo 🎬🎬½ **1988 (R)** Entertaining comedy about a young couple who attempt to steal back $50,000 of inheritance money that a televangelist swindled from the family. One of the more creative satires on this religious TV phenomenon. **93m/C VHS, Beta, LV.** Bill Paxton, Tim Curry, Linda Kozlowski, Annie Potts, Anthony Geary, Dennis Burkley, Glenn Withrow, Richard Paul; *D:* David Beaird; *W:* Neil Cohen, Joel Cohen; *M:* Carter Burwell. *ART*

A Passage to India 🎬🎬🎬 **1984 (PG)** An ambitious adaptation of E.M. Forster's complex novel about relations between Brits and Indians in the 1920s. Drama centers on a young British woman's accusations that an Indian doctor raped her while serving as a guide in some rather ominous caves. Film occasionally flags, but is usually compelling. Features particularly strong performances from Bannerjee, Fox, and Davis. **163m/C VHS, Beta, LV, Closed Caption.** GB Peggy Ashcroft, Alec Guinness, James Fox, Judy Davis, Victor Banerjee, Nigel Havers; *D:* David Lean; *M:* Maurice Jarre. Academy Awards '84: Best Supporting Actress (Ashcroft), Best Original Score; British Academy Awards '85: Best Actress (Ashcroft); Golden Globe Awards '85: Best Foreign Film, Best Supporting Actress (Ashcroft), Best Score; Los Angeles Film Critics Association Awards '84: Best Supporting Actress (Ashcroft); National Board of Review Awards '84: Best Actor (Banerjee), Best Actress (Ashcroft), Best Director (Lean); New York Film Critics Awards '84: Best Actress (Ashcroft), Best Director (Lean), Best Film; Nominations: Academy Awards '84: Best Actress (Davis), Best Adapted Screenplay, Best Art Direction/Set Decoration, Best Cinematography, Best Costume Design, Best Director (Lean), Best Film Editing, Best Picture, Best Sound. *COL, BTV, HMV*

Passage to Marseilles 🎬🎬🎬 **1944** Hollywood propaganda in which convicts escape from Devil's Island and help French freedom fighters combat Nazis. Routine but entertaining. What else could it be with Bogart, Raines, Greenstreet, and Lorre, who later made a pretty good film set in Casablanca? **110m/B VHS, Beta.** Humphrey Bogart, Claude Rains, Sydney Greenstreet, Peter Lorre, Helmut Dantine, George Tobias, John Loder, Eduardo Ciannelli, Michele Morgan; *D:* Michael Curtiz; *C:* James Wong Howe; *M:* Max Steiner. *FOX*

Passed Away 🎬½ **1992 (PG-13)** Family patriarch Jack Scanlan dies and his entire family gets together for the funeral and a big Irish wake. The family, of course, is made up of a weird group of characters, good steadfast son Hoskins, dimwitted but good-looking son Petersen, rebellious daughter Reed, and a left-wing nun who works in Central America and is accompanied by an illegal alien (McDormand). Throw in a mysterious female mourner and a pregnant granddaughter who goes into labor at the graveside and you come up with a movie that manages to use every comic death cliche ever imagined. Talented cast is wasted in a movie that should have passed away. **96m/C VHS, Beta, Closed Caption.** Bob Hoskins, Jack Warden, William L. Petersen, Helen Lloyd Breed, Maureen Stapleton, Pamela Reed, Tim Curry, Peter Riegert, Blair Brown, Patrick Breen, Nancy Travis, Teri Polo, Frances McDormand; *D:* Charlie Peters; *W:* Charlie Peters; *C:* Arthur Albert; *M:* Richard Gibbs. *HPH*

Passenger 🎬🎬🎬 *Pasazerka* **1961** While on a cruise ship Lisa (Slaska), a former camp guard at Auschwitz, realizes that fellow passenger Martha (Ciepielewska) was once one of her prisoners. Their meeting triggers a series of flashbacks to the Holocaust and to domination, suffering, and resistance. Director Munk was killed in a car crash during filming, which was completed by his colleague Witold Lesiewicz. Based on the novel by Zofia Posmysz-Piasecka; Polish with subtitles. **63m/B VHS.** PL Aleksandra Slaska, Anna Ciepielewska, Marek Walezewski, Jan Kreczewski, Irena Malkiewicz; *D:* Andrzej Munk; *W:* Andrzej Munk, Zofia Posmysz-Piasecka; *C:* Krzysztof Winiewicz; *M:* Tadeusz Baird. *HTV*

The Passenger 🎬🎬🎬½ *Profession: Reporter* **1975 (PG)** A dissatisfied television reporter changes identities with a dead man while on assignment in Africa, then learns that he is posing as a gunrunner. Mysterious, elliptical production from Italian master Antonioni, who co-wrote. Nicholson is fine in the low-key role, and Schneider is surprisingly winning as the woman drawn to him. The object of much debate, hailed by some as quintessential cinema and by others as slow and unrewarding. **119m/C VHS, Beta.** *IT* Jack Nicholson, Maria Schneider, Ian Hendry, Jenny Runacre, Steven Berkoff; *D:* Michelangelo Antonioni; *W:* Mark Peploe, Michelangelo Antonioni; *M:* Claude Bolling. *WAR*

Passenger 57 🎬 **1992 (R)** Classic movie-of-the-week fare. Anti-terrorist specialist John Cutter (Snipes) leaves his profession because of his wife's murder, and coincidentally boards the same plane as Charles Rane (Payne), an apprehended evil terrorist headed to trial in L.A. Somehow, Rane's thugs have also sneaked aboard with plans to hijack the plane, and it's up to Cutter to use his skills and save the day. Athletic Snipes is convincing in his role but can't make up for the plot's lack of premise. *CW:* Language and terrorist violence. **84m/C VHS, LV, Letterbox, Closed Caption.** Wesley Snipes, Bruce Payne, Tom Sizemore, Alex Datcher, Bruce Greenwood, Robert Hooks, Elizabeth Hurley, Michael Horse; *D:* Kevin Hooks; *W:* David Loughery, Dan Gordon; *M:* Stanley Clarke. *WAR*

The Passing 🎬🎬½ **1988** Two men find themselves trapped in the darker vicissitudes of life. The two lead almost parallel lives until an extraordinary event unites them. **96m/C VHS.** James Plaster, Welton Benjamin Johnson, Lynn Dunn, Albert B. Smith; *D:* John Huckert. *NO*

The Passing of Evil 🎬🎬½ *The Grasshopper; Passions* **1970 (R)** Bisset is a starstruck Canadian undone by the bright lights and big cities of America. By age 22, she's a burnt-out prostitute in Las Vegas. Cheerless but compelling. **96m/C VHS.** Jacqueline Bisset, Jim Brown, Joseph Cotten, Corbett Monica, Ramon Bieri, Christopher Stone, Roger Garrett, Stanley Adams, Dick Richards, Tim O'Kelly, Ed Flanders; *D:* Jerry Paris; *C:* Sam Leavitt; *M:* Billy Goldenberg. *WAR*

The Passing of the Third Floor Back 🎬🎬 **1936** Boarding house tenants improve their lives after being inspired by a mysterious stranger. They revert, though, when he leaves. Now you know. Based on a Victorian morality play. **80m/B VHS, Beta.** GB Conrad Veidt, Rene Ray, Frank Cellier, Anna Lee, John Turnbull, Cathleen Nesbitt; *D:* Berthold Viertel. *SNC*

Passion 🎬🎬½ **1919** Paris, and the decadent Louis XV falls for the lovely Jeanne, making her his mistress, much to the scandal of the nation. Respectable silent version of "Madame DuBarry" is a relatively realistic costume drama, but it doesn't rate with the best German films of this period. **135m/B VHS, Beta.** GE Pola Negri, Emil Jannings, Harry Liedtke; *D:* Ernst Lubitsch. *VYY, GLV, GVV*

Passion 🎬🎬 **1954** When a rancher's young family falls victim to rampaging desperadoes, he enlists an outlaw's aid to avenge the murders of his loved ones. **84m/C VHS, Beta.** Raymond Burr, Cornel Wilde, Yvonne De Carlo, Lon Chaney Jr., John Qualen; *D:* Allan Dwan. *NO*

Passion 🎬½ **1992** Linda decides she married the wrong brother. So she plots to kill her husband and marry her in-law instead. **90m/C VHS.** Kristine Rose, Robert Labrosse, Kristine Frischhertz, Jack Ciolini; *D:* Joe D'Amato. *TSR*

Passion Fish 🎬🎬🎬 **1992 (R)** McDonnell plays May-Alice, a soap opera actress who is paralyzed after a taxi accident in New York. Confined to a wheelchair, the bitter woman moves back to her Louisiana home and alienates a number of live-in nurses until Chantelle (Woodard), who has her own problems, comes along. Blunt writing and directing by Sayles overcome the story's inherent sentimentality as do the spirited performances of the leads, including Curtis-Hall as the rogue romancing Chantelle and Strathairn as the Cajun bad boy McDonnell once loved. The laserdisc is available in letterbox format. **136m/C VHS, LV, Letterbox, Closed Caption.** Mary McDonnell, Alfre Woodard, David Strathairn, Vondie Curtis-Hall, Nora Dunn, Sheila Kelley, Angela Bassett, Mary Portser, Maggie Renzi, Leo Burmester, Shauntisa Willis, John Henry, Michael Laskin; *D:* John Sayles; *W:* John Sayles; *M:* Mason Daring. Independent Spirit Awards '93: Best Supporting Actress (Woodard); Nominations: Academy Awards '92: Best Actress (McDonnell), Best Original Screenplay. *COL, MOV, BTV*

Passion Flower 🎬🎬 **1986 (PG-13)** A tropical romantic melodrama made for network TV and set in Singapore, where an ambitious banker falls in love with the daughter of island's wealthiest smuggler. The mixture of high finance, low-dealing and lust only proves moderately passionate. **95m/C VHS.** Bruce Boxleitner, Barbara Hershey, Nicol Williamson; *D:* Joseph Sargent; *M:* Miles Goodman. *THV*

Passion for Life 🎬🎬½ *L'Ecole Buissonniere; I Have a New Master* **1948** A new teacher uses revolutionary methods to engage students, but draws ire from staid parents in rural France. Worthwhile drama. In French with English subtitles. **89m/B VHS, Beta.** Bernard Blier, Julliette Faber, Edouard Delmont; *D:* Jean-Paul LeChanois. *FCT*

Passion for Power **1985** Two men involved in a drug-smuggling syndicate attempt to take over the business. Complications arise when they both fall for a beautiful, deceitful woman who turns them against one another. **94m/C VHS.** SP Hector Suarez, Sasha Montenegro, Manuel Capetillo, Alejandra Peniche. *NO*

Passion in Paradise 🎬🎬½ **1989** Fact-based mystery set in the Bahamas in 1943. Stewart is a spoiled rich girl who marries a handsome gigolo (Assante), much to daddy big bucks' (Steiger) displeasure. Then daddy is murdered and the son-in-law becomes the key suspect. Trashy, but Assante's fine. Made for television. **100m/C VHS, LV.** Armand Assante, Catherine Mary Stewart, Rod Steiger, Mariette Hartley, Wayne Rogers; *D:* Harvey Hart. *APX*

The Passion of Anna 🎬🎬🎬 **1970 (R)** A complicated psychological drama about four people on an isolated island. Von Sydow is an ex-con living a hermit's existence when he becomes involved with a crippled widow (Ullmann) and her two friends—all of whom have secrets in their pasts. Brutal and disturbing. Wonderful cinematography by Sven Nykvist. Filmed on the island of Faro. In Swedish with English subtitles. **101m/C VHS.** SW Max von Sydow, Liv Ullmann, Bibi Andersson, Erland Josephson, Erik Hell; *D:* Ingmar Bergman; *W:* Ingmar Bergman; *C:* Sven Nykvist. National Society of Film Critics Awards '70: Best Director (Bergman). *MGM, BTV*

The Passion of Darkly Noon 🎬½ **1995** Strange religious/sexual allegory. Running through the woods, Darkly Noon (Fraser) stumbles across the rural home of Callie (Judd) and Clay (Mortensen). Callie sees that the young man is ill and allows him to stay, discovering his parents have recently died and he's escaped from the ultra-religious community where he was raised. The sexy Callie is an uncomfortable attraction for the naive lad and when he meets a crazy old woman, Roxy (Zabriskie), in the woods, he's inclined to listen to her ravings against Callie, leading Darkly to believe he's been sent to punish the transgressors. **106m/C VHS.** GB GE BE Brendan Fraser, Ashley Judd, Viggo Mortensen, Grace Zabriskie, Loren Dean; *D:* Philip Ridley; *W:* Philip Ridley; *C:* John de Borman; *M:* Nick Bicat. *TTC*

The Passion of Joan of Arc 🎬🎬🎬🎬 **1928** Masterful silent film relates the events of St. Joan's trial and subsequent martyrdom. Moving, eloquent work features legendary performace by Falconetti. Also rates among master Dreyer's finest efforts. A classic. Silent with music. **114m/B VHS, Beta.** FR Maria Falconetti, Eugena Sylvaw, Maurice Schultz, Antonin Artaud; *D:* Carl Theodor Dreyer. *VYY, MRV, NOS*

Passion of Love ✔✔✔ *Passione d'Amore* 1982 Military captain becomes the obsession of his commander's mysterious cousin when he reports to an outpost far from home. Daring and fascinating. An unrelentingly passionate historical romance guaranteed to heat up the VCR. Available dubbed or with subtitles. 117m/C VHS, Beta. *IT FR* Laura Antonelli, Bernard Giraudeau, Valeria D'Obici, Jean-Louis Trintignant; **D:** Ettore Scola; **W:** Ettore Scola. *VES, CIG, KIV*

A Passion to Kill ✔✔½ *Rules of Obsession* 1994 (R) Formulaic thriller finds psychologist David (Bakula) getting sexually involved with his best friend Jerry's (Getz) wife, who has a lurid past. Seems Diana (Field) stuck a kitchen knife into her abusive first husband and now Jerry's prospects don't look too good.**CW:** Strong sexuality; some violence and language. 93m/C VHS. Scott Bakula, Chelsea Field, Sheila Kelly, John Getz, Rex Smith, France Nuyen, Michael Warren; **D:** Rick King; **W:** William F. Delligan. *APX*

Passionate Thief ✔✔½ *Risate de Gioia; Joyous Laughter* 1960 Two pickpockets and a bumbling actress plan to rip off the guests at a posh New Year's Eve party with slightly comic results. Not much to recommend in this slow moving flick. 100m/C VHS, Beta. *IT* Anna Magnani, Ben Gazzara, Fred Clark, Toto, Edy Vessel; **D:** Mario Monicelli. *NLC*

The Passover Plot ✔✔ 1975 (PG) A controversial look at the crucifixion of Christ which depicts him as a Zealot leader who, aided by his followers, faked his death and then "rose" to win new converts. 105m/C VHS, Beta. Harry Andrews, Hugh Griffith, Zalman King, Donald Pleasence, Scott Wilson; **D:** Michael Campus; **M:** Alex North. Nominations: Academy Awards '76: Best Costume Design.

Passport to Pimlico ✔✔½ 1949 Farce about a London neighborhood's residents who discover an ancient charter proclaiming their right to form their own country within city limits. Passable comedy. 81m/B VHS, Beta. *GB* Stanley Holloway, Margaret Rutherford, Hermione Baddeley, Naunton Wayne, Basil Radford; **D:** Henry Cornelius. Nominations: Academy Awards '49: Best Story & Screenplay. *NOS, DVT, AIM*

Past Midnight ✔✔ 1992 (R) Richardson plays a social worker who believes recently paroled killer Hauer was wrongly convicted. She attempts to prove his innocence while also falling in love—a dangerous combination. Richardson's beautiful and Hauer's making a successful career out of playing handsome psychos.**CW:** Language, violence, and sensuality. 100m/C VHS, LV, Letterbox, Closed Caption. Natasha Richardson, Rutger Hauer, Clancy Brown, Guy Boyd; **D:** Jan Eliasberg; **W:** Frank Norwood; **M:** Steve Bartek. *COL*

Past Perfect ✔✔½ 1998 (R) Gun battles, car chases, and fights move this actioner right along. Cop Dylan Cooper's (Roberts) job is made harder because his city is overrun with juvenile crime. But even he's shocked when the young criminals start turning up dead. Then Cooper discovers a group of futuristic bounty hunters have been sent back in time to eliminate these violent delinquents before they become adult killers. 92m/C VHS, LV, Closed Caption. Eric Roberts, Nick Mancuso, Saul Rubinek; **D:** Jonathan Heap; **W:** John Penney; **C:** John Houtman; **M:** Christophe Beck. *ART*

Past Tense ✔✔½ 1994 (R) Complicated thriller about a cop with a gorgeous but mysterious neighbor, a murder to solve, and problems separating reality from his nightmares. Made for cable television. 91m/C VHS, LV, Closed Caption. Scott Glenn, Lara Flynn Boyle, Anthony LaPaglia, David Ogden Stiers, Sheree J. Wilson, Marita Geraghty, Stephen Graziano; **D:** Graeme Clifford. *REP*

Past the Bleachers ✔✔½ 1995 (PG) Sentimental TV movie finds Anderson starring as Bill Parish—a man still lost by the death of his 11-year-old son. Reluctantly, he agrees to coach the Little League team his son had played on, with the help of an opinionated senior citizen (scene-stealer Hughes), and is drawn to the boy who turns out

to be the team's star player. The appropriately named Lucky Diamond (Fitula) is both mute and of a mysterious family background, and bonding proves therapeutic for both Bill and the youngster. Based on a novel by Christopher A. Bohjalian. 120m/C VHS, LV, Closed Caption. Richard Dean Anderson, Barnard Hughes, Grayson Fricke, Glynnis O'Connor, Ken Jenkins; **D:** Michael Switzer; **W:** Don Rhymer; **M:** Stewart Levin. *HMK*

Pastime ✔✔✔ *One Cup of Coffee* 1991 (PG) A bittersweet baseball elegy set in the minor leagues in 1957. A boyish 41-year-old pitcher can't face his impending retirement and pals around with the team pariah, a 17-year-old black rookie. Splendidly written and acted, it's a melancholy treat whether you're a fan of the game or not, and safe for family attendance. The only drawback is a grungy, low-budget look. 94m/C VHS, LV. William Russ, Scott Plank, Glenn Plummer, Noble Willingham, Jeffrey Tambor, Deirdre O'Connell, Ricky Paull Goldin; *Cameos:* Ernie Banks, Harmon Killebrew, Duke Snider, Bob Feller, Bill Mazeroski, Don Newcombe; **D:** Robin B. Armstrong; **W:** Robin B. Armstrong. Sundance Film Festival '91: Audience Award. *COL*

Pat and Mike ✔✔✔ 1952 War of the sexes rages in this comedy about a leathery sports promoter who futilely attempts to train a woman for athletic competition. Tracy and Hepburn have fine chemistry, but supporting players contribute too. Watch for the first on-screen appearance of Bronson (then Charles Buchinski) as a crook. 95m/B VHS, Beta, LV, Closed Caption. Spencer Tracy, Katharine Hepburn, Aldo Ray, Jim Backus, William Ching, Sammy White, Phyllis Povah, Charles Bronson, Chuck Connors, Mae Clarke, Carl "Alfalfa" Switzer; **D:** George Cukor; **W:** Ruth Gordon, Garson Kanin; **C:** William H. Daniels. Nominations: Academy Awards '52: Best Story & Screenplay. *MGM*

Pat Garrett & Billy the Kid ✔✔✔ 1973 Coburn is Garrett, one-time partner of Billy the Kid (Kristofferson), turned sheriff. He tracks down and eventually kills the outlaw. The uncut director's version which was released on video is a vast improvement over the theatrically and television versions. Dylan's soundtrack includes the now famous "Knockin' on Heaven's Door." 106m/C VHS, Beta, LV, Letterbox. Kris Kristofferson, James Coburn, Bob Dylan, Richard Jaeckel, Katy Jurado, Chill Wills, Charles Martin Smith, Slim Pickens, Harry Dean Stanton; **D:** Sam Peckinpah; **W:** Rudy Wurlitzer; **M:** George Duning. *MGM*

A Patch of Blue ✔✔½ 1965 A kind-hearted blind girl falls in love with a black man without acknowledging racial differences. Good performances from Hartman and Poitier are film's strongest assets. 108m/C VHS, Beta. Sidney Poitier, Elizabeth Hartman, Shelley Winters, Wallace Ford, Ivan Dixon, John Qualen, Elisabeth Fraser, Kelly Flynn; **D:** Guy Green; **C:** Robert Burks; **M:** Jerry Goldsmith. Academy Awards '65: Best Supporting Actress (Winters); Nominations: Academy Awards '65: Best Actress (Hartman), Best Art Direction/Set Decoration (B & W), Best Black and White Cinematography, Best Original Score. *MGM, BTV*

Patchwork Girl of Oz ✔✔ 1914 A very early silent film production by Baum that brought his own Oz books to the screen. 80m/B VHS, Beta. **D:** L. Frank Baum. *NOS, DVT, VYY*

Paternity ✔✔ 1981 (PG) Routine comedy about middle-aged manager of Madison Square Gardens (Reynolds) who sets out to find a woman to bear his child, no strings attached. The predictability of the happy ending makes this a yawner. 94m/C VHS, Beta, LV. Burt Reynolds, Beverly D'Angelo, Lauren Hutton, Norman Fell, Paul Dooley, Elizabeth Ashley; **D:** David Steinberg; **W:** Charlie Peters; **M:** David Shire. Golden Raspberry Awards '81: Worst Song ("Baby Talk"). *PAR*

Path to Paradise ✔✔ 1997 (R) Cable drama based on the true story of the 1993 World Trade Center bombing, which focuses on both the terrorists and the FBI investigators. FBI agent John Anticev (Gallagher) is investigating a rabbi's murder, which leads to Islamic extremists. An

informant warns Anticev that the group are planning terrorist activities in Manhattan but the conspirators are closer to their target than the FBI imagine.**CW:** Some violence and language. 95m/C VHS. Peter Gallagher, Art Malik, Ned Eisenberg, Marcia Gay Harden, Paul Guilfoyle, Andreas Katsulas, Shiek Mahmud-Bey, Mike Starr; **D:** Larry Williams, Leslie Libman; **W:** Ned Curren; **C:** Jean De Segonzac. *HBO*

Pather Panchali ✔✔✔✔ *The Song of the Road; The Saga of the Road; The Lament of the Path* 1954 Somber, moving story of a young Bengali boy growing up in impoverished India. Stunning debut from India's master filmmaker Ray, who continued the story in "Aparajito" and "World of Apu." A truly great work. In Bengali with English subtitles. 112m/B VHS, Beta. *IN* Kanu Banerjee, Karuna Banerjee, Uma Das Gupta, Subir Banerji, Runki Banerji, Chunibala Devi; **D:** Satyajit Ray; **W:** Satyajit Ray; **M:** Ravi Shankar. *NOS, FCT, MRV*

Pathfinder ✔✔✔½ 1987 A young boy in Lapland of 1,000 years ago comes of age prematurely after he falls in with cutthroat nomads who already slaughtered his family and now want to wipe out the rest of the village. Gripping adventure in the ice and snow features stunning scenery. In Lappish with English subtitles and based on an old Lapp fable. 88m/C VHS. *NO* Mikkel Gaup, Nils Utsi, Svein Scharffenberg, Helgi Skulason, Sara Marit Gaup, Sverre Porsanger; **D:** Nils Gaup; **W:** Nils Gaup. Nominations: Academy Awards '87: Best Foreign Language Film. *FXL, FCT*

The Pathfinder ✔✔½ 1994 (PG-13) TV adaptation of the 1840 James Fenimore Cooper novel that finds legendary woodsman Natty Bumppo, his adoptive Indian father Chingachgook, and lovely Mabel Dunham trying to aid a beseiged British fort during the French and Indian wars. If this sounds familiar, it's because Cooper's "Leatherstocking Tales" were also the basis for "The Last of the Mohicans."**CW:** Some frontier violence. 104m/C VHS. Kevin Dillon, Graham Greene, Jaimz Woolvett, Laurie Holden, Russell Means, Stacy Keach; **D:** Donald Shebib; **W:** James Mitchell Miller, Thomas W. Lynch; **M:** Reg Powell. *HMK*

Paths of Glory ✔✔✔✔ 1957 Classic anti-war drama set in WWI France. A vain, ambitious officer imposes unlikely battle strategy on his hapless troops, and when it fails, he demands that three soldiers be selected for execution as cowards. Menjou is excellent as the bloodless French officer, with Douglas properly heroic as the French officer who knows about the whole disgraceful enterprise. Fabulous, wrenching fare from filmmaking great Kubrick, who co-wrote. Based on a true story from Humphrey Cobb's novel of the same name. 86m/B VHS, Beta, LV, Closed Caption. Kirk Douglas, Adolphe Menjou, George Macready, Ralph Meeker, Richard Anderson, Wayne Morris, Timothy Carey, Susanne Christian, Bert Freed; **D:** Stanley Kubrick; **W:** Calder Willingham, Stanley Kubrick. National Film Registry '92. *MGM, FOX*

Paths to Paradise ✔✔✔ 1925 Compson and Griffith share criminal past, reunite at gala event to snatch priceless necklace and head south of the border. World- class chase scene. 78m/B VHS, Beta. Raymond Griffith, Betty Compson, Thomas Santschi, Bert Woodruff, Fred Kelsey; **D:** Clarence Badger. *GPV*

Patrick ✔½ 1978 (PG) Coma patient suddenly develops strange powers and has a weird effect on the people he comes in contact with. 115m/C VHS, Beta. *AU* Robert Helpmann, Susan Penhaligon, Rod Mullinar; **D:** Richard Franklin; **M:** Brian May. *NO*

The Patriot ✔½ 1986 (R) An action film about an ex-Navy commando who battles a band of nuclear-arms smuggling terrorists. Edited via George Lucas' electronic editor, Edit Droid. 88m/C VHS, Beta, LV. Jeff Conaway, Michael J. Pollard, Leslie Nielsen, Greg Henry, Simone Griffeth; **D:** Frank Harris; **W:** Andy Ruben, Katt Shea Ruben; **M:** Jay Michael Ferguson. *ART, VES*

Patriot Games ✂✂✂ 1992 (R) Jack Ryan, retired CIA analyst, takes his wife and daughter to England on a holiday and ends up saving a member of the Royal Family from assassination by IRA extremists. Ryan, who has killed one of the terrorists, then becomes the target of revenge by the dead man's brother. Good action sequences but otherwise predictable adaptation of the novel by Tom Clancy. Companion to "The Hunt for Red October," with Ford taking over the role of Ryan from Alec Baldwin. Since this movie did well, we can probably expect two more from Ford, who's becoming the king of trilogies. Followed by "Clear and Present Danger." *CW:* Language, violence, and sexuality. **117m/C VHS, Beta, CD-I, Closed Caption.** Harrison Ford, Anne Archer, Patrick Bergin, Thora Birch, Sean Bean, Richard Harris, James Earl Jones, James Fox, Samuel L. Jackson, Polly Walker; *D:* Phillip Noyce; *W:* W. Peter Iliff, Donald Stewart; *M:* James Horner. *PAR*

The Patriots ✂✂✂ 1933 A German prisoner works as a shoemaker in a small village during WWI. A lyrical drama in German and Russian with English titles. **82m/B VHS, Beta.** *RU D:* Boris Barnet. *FCT, IHF*

The Patsy ✂✂ 1964 Shady producers attempt to transform a lowly bellboy into a comedy superstar. Not one of Lewis's better efforts; Lorre's last film. **101m/C VHS, Beta.** Jerry Lewis, Ina Balin, Everett Sloane, Phil Harris, Keenan Wynn, Peter Lorre, John Carradine, Hans Conried, Richard Deacon, Scatman Crothers, Del Moore, Neil Hamilton, Buddy Lester, Nancy Kulp, Norman Alden, Jack Albertson; *D:* Jerry Lewis; *W:* Jerry Lewis. *IME*

Pattern for Plunder ✂✂½ *The Bay of Saint Michel* 1962 Ex-commando leader rounds up his former comrades to head back to Normandy in search of buried Nazi plunder. **73m/B VHS.** *GB* Keenan Wynn, Mai Zetterling, Ronald Howard, Edward Underdown; *D:* John Ainsworth; *W:* Christopher Davis. *SNC*

Patterns ✂✂✂ *Patterns of Power* 1956 Realistic depiction of big business. Heflin starts work at a huge New York office that is under the ruthless supervision of Sloane. Serling's astute screenplay (adapted from his TV play) is adept at portraying ruthless, power-struggling executives and the sundry workings of a large corporation. Film has aged slightly, but it still has some edge to it. Originally intended for television. **83m/B VHS.** Van Heflin, Everett Sloane, Ed Begley Sr., Beatrice Straight, Elizabeth Wilson; *D:* Fielder Cook; *W:* Rod Serling; *C:* Boris Kaufman. *NOS, MGM, MRV*

Pattes Blanches ✂✂½ *White Paws* 1949 A reclusive aristocrat always wears white spats, causing ridicule in the small fishing village where he lives. Trouble comes when a local saloonkeeper becomes resentful of the rich man's advances on his girlfriend. Moody, sensual French melodrama exploring class, money and sex. Adaptation of a play by Jean Anouilh. In French with English subtitles. **92m/B VHS.** *FR* Suzy Delair, Fernand Ledoux, Paul Bernard, Michel Bouquet; *D:* Jean Gremillon. *INT, FCT*

Patti Rocks ✂✂✂ 1988 (R) Offbeat, realistic independent effort concerns a foul chauvinist who enlists a friend to accompany him on a visit to a pregnant girlfriend who turns out to be less than the bimbo she's portrayed as en route. Mulkey shines as the sexist. Same characters featured earlier in "Loose Ends." **86m/C VHS, Beta, LV.** Chris Mulkey, John Jenkins, Karen Landry, David L. Turk, Stephen Yoakam; *D:* David Burton Morris; *W:* Chris Mulkey, John Jenkins, Karen Landry, David Burton Morris; *M:* Doug Maynard. *NO*

Patton ✂✂✂½ *Patton—Lust for Glory; Patton: A Salute to a Rebel* 1970 (PG) Lengthy but stellar bio of the vain, temperamental American general who masterminded significant combat triumphs during WWII. "Old Blood and Guts," who considered himself an 18th-century commander living in the wrong era, produced victory after victory in North Africa and Europe, but not without a decided im-

pact upon his troops. Scott is truly magnificent in the title role, and Malden shines in the supporting role of General Omar Bradley. Not a subtle film, but neither is its subject. Interesting match-up with the 1986 made-for-TV movie "The Last Days of Patton," also starring Scott. **171m/C VHS, Beta, LV, Letterbox.** George C. Scott, Karl Malden, Stephen Young, Michael Strong, Frank Latimore, James Edwards, Lawrence Dobkin, Michael Bates, Tim Considine; *D:* Franklin J. Schaffner; *W:* Francis Ford Coppola, Edmund H. North; *C:* Fred W. Koenekamp; *M:* Jerry Goldsmith. Academy Awards '70: Best Actor (Scott), Best Art Direction/Set Decoration, Best Director (Schaffner), Best Film Editing, Best Picture, Best Sound, Best Story & Screenplay; Directors Guild of America Awards '70: Best Director (Schaffner); Golden Globe Awards '71: Best Actor—Drama (Scott); National Board of Review Awards '70: Best Actor (Scott); New York Film Critics Awards '70: Best Actor (Scott); National Society of Film Critics Awards '70: Best Actor (Scott); Writers Guild of America '70: Best Original Screenplay; Nominations: Academy Awards '70: Best Cinematography, Best Original Score. *TLF, BTV, HMV*

Patty Hearst ✂✂½ 1988 (R) Less than fascinating, expressionistic portrait of Hearst from her kidnapping through her brainwashing and eventual criminal participation with the SLA. An enigmatic film that seems to only make Hearst's transformation into a Marxist terrorist all the more mysterious. Based on Hearst's book, "Every Secret Thing." **108m/C VHS, Beta, LV.** Natasha Richardson, William Forsythe, Ving Rhames, Frances Fisher, Jodi Long, Dana Delany; *D:* Paul Schrader; *W:* Nicholas Kazan; *C:* Bojan Bazelli.

Paul and Michelle ✂ 1974 (R) The equally dull sequel to "Friends" finds the two lovers a little older but no wiser. Paul has graduated from his British school and returns to France to seek out Michelle and their child. They try to rekindle their romance but the stresses of everyday life cause them problems. **102m/C VHS, Closed Caption.** *GB FR* Sean Bury, Anicee Alvina, Keir Dullea, Ronald Lewis, Catherine Allegret, Georges Beller; *D:* Lewis Gilbert; *M:* Michel Colombier. *PAR*

Paul Bartel's The Secret Cinema ✂✂½ *The Secret Cinema* 1969 A woman cannot determine whether her life is real or a film by a maniacal director. Offbeat, creative, and a little disturbing. Followed by Bartel's short "Naughty Nurse." **37m/B VHS, Beta.** *D:* Paul Bartel. *RHI*

Paul Robeson ✂✂ 197? Major events in the life of the popular actor are recounted in this one-man performance. Originally staged by Charles Nelson Reilly. **118m/C VHS, Beta.** James Earl Jones; *D:* Lloyd Richards. *KAR*

Paulie ✂✂½ 1998 (PG) Dreamworks follows up "Mouse Hunt" with this tale of a conversant parrot (voiced by Mohr) whose mouth keeps getting him in trouble. Trapped in a dingy basement, Paulie tells a lonely Russian janitor (Shalhoub) the story of his cross-country quest to return to his original owner, the little girl (Eisenberg) who raised him from a fledgling. After the girl's parents send him away, Paulie goes through a procession of owners: a smart-aleck pawn shop owner (Hackett); a kindly old woman (Rowlands) who drives him to L.A in her RV; a petty criminal (Mohr again); a taco stand owner (Marin) who manages a parrot dancing act; and a scientist (Davison) looking to cash in on the bird's talent. Not a whole lot of action for a kiddie movie, and some of the jokes may go over their heads, but fine performances all around and a charming story keep pic aloft. **91m/C VHS.** Jay Mohr, Gena Rowlands, Tony Shalhoub, Richard "Cheech" Marin, Hallie Kate Eisenberg, Bruce Davison, Trini Alvarado, Buddy Hackett, Matt Craven, Bill Cobbs, Laura Harrington, Tia Texada; *D:* John Roberts; *W:* Laurie Craig; *C:* Tony Pierce-Roberts; *M:* John Debney; *V:* Jay Mohr. *NYR*

Pauline at the Beach ✂✂✂½ *Pauline a la Plage* 1983 (R) A young woman accompanies her more experienced cousin to the French coast for a summer of sexual hijinks. Contemplative, not

coarse, though the leads look great in—and out—of their swimsuits. Breezy, typically talky fare from small-film master Rohmer. In French with English subtitles. **95m/C VHS, Beta, LV.** *FR* Amanda Langlet, Arielle Dombasle, Pascal Greggory, Rosette; *D:* Eric Rohmer; *W:* Eric Rohmer; *C:* Nestor Almendros. *XVC*

The Pawnbroker ✂✂✂½ 1965 A Jewish pawnbroker in Harlem is haunted by his grueling experiences in a Nazi camp during the Holocaust. Powerful and well done. Probably Steiger's best performance. Adapted from a novel by Edward Lewis Wallant. **120m/B VHS, LV, Closed Caption.** Rod Steiger, Brock Peters, Geraldine Fitzgerald, Jaime Sanchez, Thelma Oliver; *D:* Sidney Lumet; *C:* Boris Kaufman; *M:* Quincy Jones. Berlin International Film Festival '65: Best Actor (Steiger); British Academy Awards '66: Best Actor (Steiger); Nominations: Academy Awards '65: Best Actor (Steiger). *REP*

Pawnshop 1916 Charlie is employed as a pawnbroker's assistant. Silent with music track. **20m/B VHS, Beta.** Charlie Chaplin. *CAB, GVV*

Pay Off ✂ 1989 A lunatic psychiatrist seeks murderous revenge on his ex-patient/girlfriend and her family. **87m/C VHS, Beta.** Michael Fitzpatrick, Veronika Mattson, Margareta Krook; *D:* George Tirl. *TWE*

Pay or Die 1983 (R) A crime boss' men turn on him and kidnap his daughter. **92m/C VHS, Beta.** Dick Adair, Johnny Wilson; *D:* Bobby Suarez. *ART*

Payback ✂ 1989 A brawny young man uses firepower to avenge those who have wronged him. **90m/C VHS, Beta.** Jean Carol. *NO*

Payback ✂✂½ 1990 (R) A convict sets out to avenge his brother's death, and creates all sorts of mayhem in the process. Produced by Bob "Newlywed Game" Eubanks and scored by Daryl "Captain and Tenille" Dragon. *CW:* Language and violence. **94m/C VHS, Closed Caption.** Corey Michael Eubanks, Michael Ironside, Teresa Blake, Bert Remsen, Vincent Van Patten, Don Swayze; *D:* Russell Solberg; *M:* Daryl Dragon. *REP*

Payback ✂✂½ 1994 (R) An old, dying con (Armstrong) tells fellow inmate Oscar Bonsetter (Howell) the whereabouts of a fortune if he'll promise to kill cruel jail guard Gully (Bell) who made the geezer's life a misery. Years later, the now ex-con finds the ex-guard running a diner near the spot where the money is buried and decides to carry out his plan for revenge. If Oscar doesn't get too distracted by Gully's hot-to-trot wife, Rose (Severance), first. Also available in an unrated version. *CW:* Violence; nudity; language; explicit sex. **92m/C VHS, LV, Closed Caption.** C. Thomas Howell, Joan Severance, Marshall Bell, R.G. Armstrong; *D:* Anthony Hickox; *W:* Sam Bernard; *C:* David Bridges. *THV*

Payday ✂✂½ 1972 Torn stars as a declining country music star on tour in this portrayal of the seamy side of show business, from groupies to grimy motels. Well-written script and fine performances make this an engaging, if rather draining, drama not easily found on the big screen. **98m/C VHS, Beta.** Rip Torn, Ahna Capri, Michael C. Gwynne, Jeff Morris; *D:* Daryl Duke. *NO*

The Payoff ✂½ 1943 The old-fashioned newspaper-reporter-as-crime-fighter routine. When the city's special prosecutor is murdered a daring newshawk investigates and tracks the bad guys. But will he spell their names right? **74m/B VHS.** Lee Tracy, Tom Brown, Tina Thayer, Evelyn Brent, Jack LaRue, Ian Keith, John Maxwell; *D:* Arthur Dreifuss. *NOS, LOO*

Payoff ✂✂ 1991 (R) An ex-cop discovers the identity of gangsters who killed his parents. He traces them to a Lake Tahoe resort and plots revenge. Familiar crime story with a good cast. *CW:* Language, violence, and sensuality. **111m/C VHS, Beta, LV, Closed Caption.** Keith Carradine, Kim Greist, Harry Dean Stanton, John Saxon, Jeff Corey; *D:* Stuart Cooper; *W:* Douglas S. Cook; *M:* Charles Bernstein. *FXL*

P.C.U. 🎬🎬 1994 (PG-13) Satire on campus political correctness follows frochman Tom Law rence's (Young) adventures as he navigates the treacherous waters of Port Chester University (PCU). He falls in with the gang from the Pit, the militantly non-PC dorm, who encourage bizarre and offensive behavior. Essentially a modern up-date of "National Lampoon's Animal House," but without the brilliance; add half a bone for tackling the thorny sensitivity issue in a humorous way that parodies, but shouldn't offend. Actor Bochner's directorial debut. **CW:** Language, drug-content, and some sensuality. 81m/C VHS, LV, **Closed Caption.** Jeremy Piven, Chris Young, David Spade, Sarah Trigger, Jessica Walter, Jon Favreau, Megan Ward, Jake Busey, Alex Desert; **Cameos:** George Clinton; **D:** Hart Bochner; **W:** Adam Leff, Zak Penn; **M:** Steve Vai. FXV

Peacekillers 🎬½ 1971 A mean bunch of bikers visit a commune to kidnap a young woman. The gang has a big surprise in store for them when the girl escapes. 86m/C VHS, Beta. Michael Ontkean, Clint Ritchie, Paul Krokop; **D:** Douglas Schwartz. VTR

Peacemaker 🎬 1990 (R) Two aliens masquerading as human cops stalk each other through a major city. 90m/C VHS, Beta, LV. Robert Forster, Lance Edwards, Hilary Shepard, Bert Remsen, Robert Davi; **D:** Kevin S. Tenney; **W:** Kevin S. Tenney.

The Peacemaker 🎬🎬½ 1997 (R) First-time feature director Leder teams up with fellow "ER" vet Clooney on the first theatrical release for Dreamworks SKG (the brainchild of Steven Spielberg, Jeffrey Katzenberg, and David Geffen). Clooney's Army Intel officer Lt. Col. Thomas Devoe works with White House nuke expert Dr. Julia Kelly (Kidman) when a renegade Russian colonel diverts some nuclear warheads, scheduled for dismantling, into the hands of a Bosnian diplomat (lures) with a grudge against the West. Plenty of well-constructed action set pieces and a reasonably plausible plot overcome a lack of snappy dialogue. Extra credit for making the terrorist human instead of the usual evil caricature, and for letting the two leads work together without having to sleep together. **CW:** Strong violence and some language. 123m/C VHS, **Closed Caption.** George Clooney, Nicole Kidman, Armin Mueller-Stahl, Marcel Iures, Alexander Baluyev, Randall Batinkoff, Jim Haynie, Michael Boatman, Gary Werntz, Holt McCallany, Joan Copeland, Carlos Gomez, Rene Medvesek, Alexander Strobele; **D:** Mimi Leder; **W:** Michael Schiffer; **C:** Dietrich Lohmann; **M:** Hans Zimmer. USH

The Peacock Fan 🎬½ 1929 The Peacock Fan is protected by a deadly curse, with certain death to anyone who possesses it. 50m/B VHS, Beta. Lucian Preval. SNC, VYY

The Peanut Butter Solution 🎬🎬½ 1985 (PG) An imaginative 11-year-old boy investigates a strange old house which is haunted by friendly ghosts who are in possession of a magic potion. 96m/C VHS, Beta. Matthew Mackay, Siluck Saysanasy, Alison Podbrey, Michael Maillot, Griffith Brewer, Michael Hogan, Helen Hughes; **D:** Michael Rubbo; **W:** Michael Rubbo; **M:** Lewis Furey. VTR, HHE

The Pearl 🎬🎬🎬 1948 Based on a John Steinbeck story, a Mexican fisherman, living in poverty, finds a magnificent pearl and he thinks it will improve the lives of his family. He is bewildered by what this pearl really brings—liars and thieves. Simple, yet larger-than-life film, beautifully photographed; a timeless picture capturing human nature. 77m/B VHS. MX Pedro Armendariz Sr., Maria Elena Marques, Fernando Wagner, Charles Rooner; **D:** Emilio Fernandez. FCT, MAS

The Pearl of Death 🎬🎬½ 1944 Holmes and Watson investigate the theft of a precious pearl. 69m/B VHS, Beta, **Closed Caption.** Basil Rathbone, Nigel Bruce, Dennis Hoey, Miles Mander, Rondo Hatton, Evelyn Ankers; **D:** Roy William Neill. FOX

Pearl of the South Pacific 🎬🎬 South Sea Woman 1955 A trio of adventurers destroy a quiet and peaceful island when they ransack it for pearl treasures. 85m/C VHS, Beta. Dennis (Stanley

Morner) Morgan, Virginia Mayo, David Farrar; **D:** Allan Dwan; **W:** Edwin Blum. NO

The Pebble and the Penguin 🎬🎬½ 1994 (G) Animated musical about a shy, romantic penguin named Hubie (Short), who must present his lady love Marina (Golden) with a beautiful pebble to win her hand forever before the villainous Drake (Curry) can claim her. Hubie is helped along the way by a cantankerous new friend (Belushi) he meets when stranded on a boat to Tahiti. Together the two race back to Antarctica fighting enemies and the elements along the way. Based on a true mating custom of the Adeli penguins, the story is satisfying for younger viewers, but does not have the animation magic of other recents films to keep adults interested. Beware of the sugary Manilow tunes. 74m/C VHS, LV, **Closed Caption. W:** Rachel Koretsky, Steve Whitestone; **M:** Barry Manilow, Bruce Sussman, Mark Watters; **V:** Martin Short, Annie Golden, Tim Curry, James Belushi. MGM

Peck's Bad Boy 🎬🎬 1921 Impudent, precocious brat causes his parents considerable grief. Someone should lock this kid in a room with W.C. Fields or the Alien. Silent film based on the stories by George Wilbur Peck. 51m/B VHS, Beta, LV. Jackie Coogan, Thomas Meighan, Raymond Hatton, Wheeler Oakman, Lillian Leighton; **D:** Sam Wood. NOS, MRV, CCB

Peck's Bad Boy 🎬🎬½ 1934 A wedge is driven between a young boy and his adoptive father when the man's sister and her son move in. The aunt wants her son to be number one, causing much discord. Cooper is excellent in his role as the adopted son. 70m/B VHS. Thomas Meighan, Jackie Cooper, Dorothy Peterson, Jackie Searl, O.P. Heggie, Harvey Clark, Lloyd Ingraham; **D:** Eddie Cline. NOS, MLB

Peck's Bad Boy with the Circus 🎬🎬 1938 The circus will never be the same after the mischievous youngster and his buddies get done with it. Gilbert and Kennedy provide the high points. 67m/B VHS, Beta. Tommy Kelly, Ann Gillis, George "Spanky" McFarland, Edgar Kennedy, Billy Gilbert; **D:** Eddie Cline. NOS, VYY, DVT

Pecos Bill 1986 Meet the man who used the Grand Canyon for a swimmin' hole, dug the Rio Grande and used the Texas panhandle for a fryin' pan. From Shelly Duvall's "Tall Tales and Legends" series. Originally made for cable television. 50m/C VHS, **Closed Caption.** Steve Guttenberg, Martin Mull, Claude Akins, Rebecca DeMornay. FOX, COL

Pecos Kid 🎬 1935 A child has his parents killed, and grows up embittered, vengeful and thirsty for blood. 56m/B VHS, Beta, LV. Fred Kohler Jr. NOS

Pedale Douce 🎬🎬½ What a Drag 1996 Irreverant comedy features a romantic triangle involving content gay businessman Adrien (Timsit), whose confidante is the liberal Eva (Ardant), owner of a trendy Paris eatery with an all-gay staff and predominatly gay clientele. Adrien persuades Eva to pose as his wife in order to close a deal with conservative, married banker Alexandre (Berry). Alexandre becomes enchanted with Eva and begins to pursue her, causing a comedy of errors and unexpected jealousy for Adrien, who tries to derail their affair. French with subtitles. 102m/C VHS. FR Patrick Timsit, Fanny Ardant, Richard Berry, Michele Laroque, Jacques Gamblin; **D:** Gabriel Aghion; **W:** Patrick Timsit, Gabriel Aghion, Pierre Palmade; **C:** Fabio Conversi; **M:** Herve Masini, Philippe Chopin. Cesar Awards '97: Best Actress (Ardant); Nominations: Cesar Awards '97: Best Actor (Timsit), Best Film. NYR

Peddlin' in Society 🎬🎬 Da Bancarella a Bancarotta 1947 A fruit vendor makes it big on the black market and lives the good life, until poor investments force her back to her old means. Strong perfomances by Magnani and De Sica. In Italian with English subititles. 85m/B VHS. IT Anna Magnani, Vittorio De Sica, Virgilio Riento, Laura Gore; **D:** Gennaro Righelli. DVT, HEG

The Pedestrian 🎬🎬🎬½ Der Fussgaenger 1973 (PG) A prominent German industrialist is exposed as a Nazi officer who supervised the wholesale devastation of a Greek village during WWII. Impressive debut for director Schell, who also appears in a supporting role. 97m/C VHS, Beta. GE SI Maximilian Schell, Peggy Ashcroft, Lil Dagover, Francoise Rosay, Elisabeth Bergner; **D:** Maximilian Schell; **M:** Manos Hadjidakis. Golden Globe Awards '74: Best Foreign Film; Nominations: Academy Awards '73: Best Foreign Language Film. GLV, SWC

The Pee Wee Herman Show 1982 The original HBO special which introduced Pee Wee to the world. Hilarious stuff, with help from Captain Carl (Hartman), Miss Yvonne, and other assorted pals. Warning: Not to be confused with Pee Wee's children's show. 60m/C VHS. Paul (Pee Wee Herman) Reubens, Phil Hartman, John Paragon. NO

Pee Wee's Big Adventure 🎬🎬🎬½ 1985 (PG) Zany, endearing comedy about an adult nerd's many adventures while attempting to recover his stolen bicycle. Chock full of classic sequences, including a barroom encounter between Pee Wee and several ornery bikers, and a tour through the Alamo. A colorful, exhilerating experience. 92m/C VHS, Beta, LV, **Closed Caption.** Paul (Pee Wee Herman) Reubens, Elizabeth Daily, Mark Holton, Diane Salinger, Judd Omen, Cassandra Peterson, James Brolin, Morgan Fairchild, Tony Bill, Jan Hooks; **D:** Tim Burton; **W:** Paul (Pee Wee Herman) Reubens, Phil Hartman, Michael Varhol; **M:** Danny Elfman. WAR

Pee Wee's Playhouse Festival of Fun 1988 Five fun-filled episodes of the playhouse! 123m/C VHS, Beta, **Closed Caption.** Paul (Pee Wee Herman) Reubens.

Peephole 🎬 1993 Prison psychiatrist is asked by the DA to keep Rick, who committed a sex crime against a little girl, in jail any way he can. So he visits Rick's prostitute girlfriend Sheena for info but instead winds up one of her clients. Meanwhile, Rick has been released and a little girl has been found dead, but nothing's that clear cut. Based on director/writer Bitterman's play. 90m/C VHS. Patrick Husted, Rick Dean, William Dennis Hunt, Kristen Trucksess, Peter Crook; **D:** Shem Bitterman; **W:** Shem Bitterman. LEO

Peeping Tom 🎬🎬🎬½ 1960 Controversial, unsettling thriller in which a psychopath lures women before his film camera, then records their deaths at his hand. Unnerving subject matter is rendered impressively by British master Powell. A classic of its kind, but definitely not for everyone. This is the original uncut version of the film, released in the U.S. in 1979 with the assistance of Martin Scorsese. 88m/C VHS, Beta, LV. Karl-Heinz Boehm, Moira Shearer, Anna Massey, Maxine Audley, Esmond Knight, Shirley Anne Field, Brenda Bruce, Pamela Green, Jack Watson, Nigel Davenport, Susan Travers, Veronica Hurst, Martin Miller, Miles Malleson; **Cameos:** Michael Powell; **D:** Michael Powell; **W:** Leo Marks; **C:** Otto Heller. HMV

Peg O' My Heart 🎬🎬 1922 Taylor portrays the motherless Irish charmer sent to live with her mother's English relatives during the Irish rebellion. Of course, she must overcome their upper-class English snobbery to become a part of the family. 85m/B VHS. Laurette Taylor, Mahlon Hamilton, Russell Simpson, Ethel Grey; **D:** King Vidor; **C:** George Barnes. NO

Peggy Sue Got Married 🎬🎬½ 1986 (PG-13) Uneven but entertaining comedy about an unhappily married woman seemingly unable to relive her life when she falls unconscious at a high school reunion and awakens to find herself back in school. Turner shines, but the film flags often, and Cage isn't around enough to elevate entire work. O'Connor scores, though, as a sensitive biker. Look for musician Marshall Crenshaw as part of the reunion band. 103m/C VHS, Beta, LV, **Closed Caption.** Kathleen Turner, Nicolas Cage, Catherine Hicks, Maureen O'Sullivan, John Carradine, Helen Hunt, Lisa Jane Persky, Barbara Harris, Joan Allen, Kevin J. O'Connor, Barry Miller, Don Murray, Leon Ames, Sofia Coppola, Sachi Parker, Jim Carrey; **D:** Francis Ford Coppola; **W:** Jerry Leichtling, Arlene Sarner; **C:** Jordan Cronenweth; **M:** John Barry. National Board of Review Awards '86: Best Actress (Turner); Nominations: Academy Awards '86: Best Actress (Turner), Best Cinematography, Best Costume Design. *FOX*

The Peking Blond 🎬½ *The Blonde From Peking; Le Blonde de Pekin* 1968 French-fried spyfilm boasts lousy acting unencumbered by plot. Amnesiac may or may not hold secrets coveted by Americans, Russians and Chinese. **80m/C VHS.** *FR* Mireille Darc, Claudio Brook, Edward G. Robinson, Pascale Roberts; **D:** Nicolas Gessner; **W:** Nicolas Gessner, Marc Behm. *MRV*

The Pelican Brief 🎬🎬½ 1993 (PG-13) Tulane law student Darby Shaw (Roberts) writes a speculative brief on the murders of two Supreme Court justices that results in more murder and sends her running for her life. Fairly faithful to the Grisham bestseller, but the multitude of characters is confusing. Pakula adds style and starpower, but much will depend on your tolerance for paranoid political thrillers and ability to accept Roberts as the smart cookie who hits on the right answer and then manages to keep herself alive while bodies are dropping all around her. Washington is sharp as reporter Gray Grantham, the guy Roberts looks like she falls hard for (but the book's romance is nowhere to be seen).**CW:** Momentary language and some violence. **141m/C VHS, LV, 8mm, Letterbox, Closed Caption, DVD.** Julia Roberts, Denzel Washington, John Heard, Tony Goldwyn, Stanley Tucci, James B. Sikking, William Atherton, Robert Culp, John Lithgow, Sam Shepard; **Cameos:** Hume Cronyn; **D:** Alan J. Pakula; **W:** Alan J. Pakula; **C:** Stephen Goldblatt; **M:** James Horner. Nominations: MTV Movie Awards '94: Best Female Performance (Roberts), Most Desirable Male (Washington). *WAR*

Pelle the Conqueror 🎬🎬🎬🎬 1988 Overpowering tale of a Swedish boy and his widower father who serve landowners in late 19th-century Denmark. Compassionate saga of human spirit contains numerous memorable sequences. Hvenegaard is wonderful as young Pelle, but von Sydow delivers what is probably his finest performance as a sympathetic weakling. American distributors foolishly trimmed the film by some 20 minutes (140 minute version). From the novel by Martin Anderson Nexo. In Swedish with English subtitles. **160m/C VHS, Beta, LV.** *SW DK* Max von Sydow, Pelle Hvenegaard, Erik Paaske, Bjorn Granath, Axel Strobye, Astrid Villaume, Troels Asmussen, John Wittig, Anne Lise Hirsch Bjerrum, Kristina Tornqvist, Morten Jorgensen; **D:** Bille August; **W:** Bille August. Academy Awards '88: Best Foreign Language Film; Cannes Film Festival '88: Best Film; Golden Globe Awards '89: Best Foreign Film; Nominations: Academy Awards '88: Best Actor (von Sydow). *HBO*

The Penalty 🎬🎬½ 1920 Legless madman Blizzard (Chaney) is after revenge on his family, doctor, and society. Chaney's properly creepy. **60m/B VHS.** Lon Chaney Sr., Claire Adams, Kenneth Harlan, Charles Clary; **D:** Wallace Worsley. *FCT*

Penalty Phase 🎬🎬 1986 An up-for-election judge must decide a murder case in which his future, as well as the defendant's, is in question. Made for television. **94m/C VHS, Beta, Closed Caption.** Peter Strauss, Melissa Gilbert, Jonelle Allen; **D:** Tony Richardson; **M:** Ralph Burns. *VTR*

Pendulum 🎬🎬 1969 (PG) A police captain struggles to prove himself innocent of his wife's—and his wife's lover's—murders. Wow. **106m/C VHS, Beta, LV.** George Peppard, Jean Seberg, Richard Kiley, Madeline Sherwood, Charles McGraw, Marj Dusay; **D:** George Schaefer; **C:** Lionel Lindon. *COL*

The Penitent 🎬🎬 1988 (PG-13) A remote village's annual reenactment of the crucifixion of Christ serves as the backdrop for Assante's affair with his friend's (Julia) wife. Quirky little tale that focuses a shade too much on the romantic problems of the trio rather than the intriguing religious practices going on around them. **94m/C VHS, Beta.**

Raul Julia, Armand Assante, Rona Freed, Julie Carmen; **D:** Cliff Osmond; **M:** Alex North. *ART*

Penitentiary 🎬🎬½ 1979 (R) A realistic story of a black fighter who survives his prison incarceration by winning bouts against the other prisoners. Well-made and executed, followed by two progressively worse sequels. **99m/C VHS, Beta.** Leon Isaac Kennedy, Jamaa Fanaka; **D:** Jamaa Fanaka; **W:** Jamaa Fanaka. *UNI, FCT*

Penitentiary 2 🎬 1982 (R) A welterweight fighter is after the man who murdered his girlfriend, who, luckily, is incarcerated in the same prison as Our Hero. Sometimes things just work out right. **108m/C VHS, Beta.** Leon Isaac Kennedy, Mr. T, Leif Erickson, Ernie Hudson, Glynn Turman; **D:** Jamaa Fanaka; **W:** Jamaa Fanaka. *MGM, HHE*

Penitentiary 3 🎬½ 1987 (R) Once again, Kennedy as the inmate boxer extraordinaire punches his way out of various prison battles. Another punch-drunk sequel. **91m/C VHS, Beta, Closed Caption.** Leon Isaac Kennedy, Anthony Geary, Steve Antin, Ric Mancini, Kessler Raymond, Jim Bailey; **D:** Jamaa Fanaka; **W:** Jamaa Fanaka. *WAR*

Penn and Teller Get Killed 🎬🎬 1990 (R) The comedy team with a cult following are pursued by an assassin through dozens of pratfalls in this dark comedy. **91m/C VHS, Beta, LV, Closed Caption.** Penn Jillette, Teller, Caitlin Clarke, Leonardo Cimino, David Patrick Kelly; **D:** Arthur Penn. *WAR*

Pennies From Heaven 🎬🎬🎬½ 1981 (R) Underrated, one-of-a-kind musical about a horny sheet-music salesman in Chicago and his escapades during the Depression. Extraordinary musical sequences have stars lip-synching to great effect. Martin is only somewhat acceptable as the hapless salesman, but Peters and Harper deliver powerful performances as the women whose lives he ruins. Walken brings down the house in a stunning song-and-dance sequence. Adapted by Dennis Potter from his British television series. ♫The Clouds Will Soon Roll By; Did You Ever See A Dream Walking?; Yes, Yes; Pennies From Heaven; Love Is Good for Anything That Ails You; I Want to Be Bad; Let's Misbehave; Life Is Just a Bowl of Cherries; Let's Face the Music and Dance. **107m/C VHS, Beta, LV.** Steve Martin, Bernadette Peters, Christopher Walken, Jessica Harper, Vernel Bagneris; **D:** Herbert Ross; **W:** Dennis Potter; **C:** Gordon Willis; **M:** Ralph Burns, Marvin Hamlisch. Golden Globe Awards '82: Best Actress—Musical/Comedy (Peters); National Society of Film Critics Awards '81: Best Cinematography; Nominations: Academy Awards '81: Best Adapted Screenplay, Best Costume Design, Best Sound. *MGM, FCT*

Penny Serenade 🎬🎬🎬 1941 Newlyweds adopt a child, but tragedy awaits. Simplistic story nonetheless proves to be a moving experience. They don't make 'em like this anymore, and no one plays Grant better than Grant. Shine is adequate. Also available colorized. **120m/B VHS, LV.** Cary Grant, Irene Dunne, Beulah Bondi, Edgar Buchanan; **D:** George Stevens. Nominations: Academy Awards '41: Best Actor (Grant).*CNG, NOS, VYY*

Pentathlon 🎬🎬½ 1994 (R) East German Olympic athlete Eric Brogar (Lundgren) defects to the U.S. a year before the crash of the Berlin Wall, causing embarrassed German authorities to seek revenge on him and his family.**CW:** Violence; language. **101m/C VHS, LV, Closed Caption.** Dolph Lundgren, David Soul, Roger E. Mosley, Renee Coleman; **D:** Bruce Malmuth. *ART*

Penthouse 🎬🎬🎬 *Crooks in Clover* 1933 Baxter is a corporation lawyer who, for a change of pace, defends a gangland boss (Pendleton). His success loses him his high-society clientele but wins him Pendleton's respect and protection. But Baxter then gets involved in a further series of gang-related crimes, which nearly cost him his life. Also aiding Baxter is Loy, playing a smart-cookie gun moll, who would take her wisecracks to "The Thin Man" the following year. Good combo of melodrama, suspense, and humor. **90m/B LV.** Warner Baxter, Myrna Loy, Nat Pendleton, C. Henry

Gordon, Mae Clarke, Charles Butterworth, Phillips Holmes; **D:** Woodbridge S. Van Dyke. *MGM*

The Penthouse 🎬🎬 1992 Givens stars as a wealthy young woman stalked by an old boyfriend who just happens to have escaped from a mental institution. When he traps her in her home, she has two choices—love him or die. Based on the novel by Elleston Trevor. **93m/C VHS, Closed Caption.** Robin Givens, David Hewlett, Cedric Smith, Donnelly Rhodes, Robert Guillaume; **D:** David Greene. *TTC*

The People 🎬🎬½ 1971 A young teacher takes a job in a small town and finds out that her students have telepathic powers and other strange qualities. Adapted from a novel by Zenna Henderson. Good atmosphere, especially for a TV movie. **74m/C VHS, Beta.** Kim Darby, Dan O'Herlihy, Diane Varsi, William Shatner; **D:** John Korty; **M:** Carmine Coppola.

People Are Funny 🎬🎬 1946 Battling radio producers vie to land the big sponsor with an original radio idea. Comedy ensues when one of them comes up with a great idea—stolen from a·local station. **94m/B VHS, Beta.** Jack Haley, Rudy Vallee, Ozzie Nelson, Art Linkletter, Helen Walker; **D:** Sam White. *NO*

The People Next Door 🎬🎬 1970 Seventies attempt at exposing the drug problems of suburban youth. Typical middle-class parents Wallach and Harris are horrified to discover that daughter Winters is strung out on LSD. They fight to expose the neighborhood pusher while struggling to understand their now-alien daughter. Based on J.P. Miller's television play. **93m/C VHS.** Deborah Winters, Eli Wallach, Julie Harris, Stephen McHattie, Hal Holbrook, Cloris Leachman, Nehemiah Persoff; **D:** David Greene. *NO*

The People That Time Forgot 🎬🎬½ 1977 (PG) Sequel to "The Land That Time Forgot," based on the Edgar Rice Burroughs novel. A rescue team returns to a world of prehistoric monsters to rescue a man left there after the first film. **90m/C VHS, Beta.** *GB* Doug McClure, Patrick Wayne, Sarah Douglas, Dana Gillespie, Thorley Walters, Shane Rimmer; **D:** Kevin Connor.

The People Under the Stairs 🎬🎬½ 1991 (R) Adams is part of a scheme to rob a house in the slums owned by a mysterious couple (Robie and McGill, both of "Twin Peaks" fame). After his friends are killed off in a gruesome fashion, he discovers that the couple aren't the house's only strange inhabitants—homicidal creatures also lurk within.**CW:** Terror/violence. **102m/C VHS, Beta, LV, Closed Caption.** Everett McGill, Wendy Robie, Brandon Adams, Ving Rhames, A.J. Langer, Sean Whalen, Kelly Jo Minter; **D:** Wes Craven; **W:** Wes Craven; **C:** Sandi Sissel; **M:** Don Peake. *USH*

The People vs. Jean Harris 🎬🎬🎬 1981 Follows the trial of Jean Harris. Shortly before this film was released, she had been convicted of murder in the death of Dr. Herman Tarnower, the author of "The Scarsdale Diet." Harris was headmistress in a private school all the while. Made for television. Burstyn was nominated for an Emmy Award for best actress. **147m/C VHS, Beta.** Ellen Burstyn, Martin Balsam, Richard Dysart, Peter Coyote, Priscilla Morrill, Sarah Marshall, Millie Slavin; **D:** George Schaefer; **M:** Brad Fiedel. *NO*

The People vs. Larry Flynt 🎬🎬🎬 1996 (R) Controversy surrounded director Forman's look at unrepentant pornographer and Hustler Magazine publisher, Larry Flynt (Harrelson). While feminists decried what they saw as a whitewash of Flynt's career, Forman insisted his movie was about Flynt's legal battles concerning the First Amendment and freedom of speech. If you can set aside your prejudices, you'll find a master storyteller at work and some great performances from Harrelson as Flynt, Love as his drug-addicted and ultimately tragic wife Althea, and Norton as Flynt's sometimes impatient attorney, Alan Isaacman, who does get his big moment before the U.S. Supreme Court (his speeches are taken from actual court transcripts).**CW:** Strong sexual material, nudity, language and drug use. **130m/C VHS, LV, Closed Caption, DVD.** Woody Harrelson, Courtney Love, Edward Norton, James Cromwell, Crispin Glover, Brett Harrelson, James Carville, Vincent Schiavelli, Richard Paul, Donna Hanover, Norm MacDonald, Miles Chapin, Jan Triska; *Cameos:* Larry Flynt; *D:* Milos Forman; *W:* Larry Karaszewski, Scott Alexander; *C:* Philippe Rousselot; *M:* Thomas Newman. Golden Globe Awards '97: Best Director (Forman), Best Screenplay; Los Angeles Film Critics Association Awards '96: Best Supporting Actor (Norton); National Board of Review Awards '96: Best Supporting Actor (Norton); New York Film Critics Awards '96: Best Supporting Actress (Love); Nominations: Academy Awards '96: Best Actor (Harrelson), Best Director (Forman); Golden Globe Awards '97: Best Actor—Drama (Harrelson), Best Actress—Drama (Love), Best Film—Drama; MTV Movie Awards '97: Breakthrough Performance (Love); Screen Actors Guild Award '96: Best Actor (Harrelson). COL

People Who Own the Dark woof!

1975 (R) A group of wealthy men and a coterie of call girls are having an orgy in the basement of an old home when a nuclear war breaks out. Everyone outside is blinded by the blast but some survivors manage to make their way to the house where they try to attack the inhabitants. Don't bother. **87m/C VHS.** Paul Naschy, Tony Kendall, Maria Perschy, Terry Kemper, Tom Weyland, Anita Brock, Paul Mackey; *D:* Armando de Ossorio; *W:* Armando de Ossorio. SUN, MRV

People Will Talk 🎬🎬🎬½ 1951 Grant

plays Dr. Noah Praetorius, a doctor and educator who believes that the mind is a better healer than medicine. Archenemy Cronyn is the fellow instructor with a vengeance. Sickened by Grant's goodwill and the undying attention he receives, Cronyn reports Grant's unconventional medical practices to the higher-ups in hopes of ruining his reputation as doctor/educator. Witty and satirical, this well-crafted comedy-drama is chock-full of interesting characters and finely tuned dialogue. Adapted from the play "Dr. Praetorius" by Curt Goetz. **110m/B VHS.** Cary Grant, Jeanne Crain, Finlay Currie, Hume Cronyn, Walter Slezak, Sidney Blackmer, Basil Ruysdael, Katherine Locke, Margaret Hamilton, Carleton Young, Billy House, Stuart Holmes; *D:* Joseph L. Mankiewicz; *W:* Joseph L. Mankiewicz; *C:* Milton Krasner. FXV

People's Choice 🎬🎬 1946 A small town

boy suffers laryngitis, becomes a radio personality via his new huskiness, and claims he's a notorious criminal. **68m/B VHS, Beta, LV.** Drew Kennedy, Louise Arthur, George Meeker, Rex Lease, Fred Kelsey. NO

Pepe Le Moko 🎬🎬🎬 1937 An influential

French film about a notorious gangster holed up in the Casbah, emerging at his own peril out of love for a beautiful woman. Stirring film established Gabin as a matinee idol. Cinematography is particularly fine too. Based upon the D'Ashelbe novel. The basis for both "Algiers," the popular Boyer-Lamarr melodrama, and the musical "The Casbah." In French with English subtitles. **87m/B VHS, Beta, 8mm.** *FR* Jean Gabin, Mireille Balin, Gabriel Gabrio, Lucas Gridoux; *D:* Julien Duvivier. VYY, NOS, HHT

Pepi, Luci, Bom and Other Girls on the Heap 🎬½ *Pepi, Luci, Bom y Otras Chicas del Monton* **1980** Almodovar's low-budget directorial debut will be of interest primarily to the director's aficionados. Pepi (Maura's debut role) is a Madrid heiress who gets in trouble when her neighbor, a policeman, notices her marijuana plants. She offers sexual favors in return for silence but is raped instead. Pepi later decides on revenge by seducing Luci, the policeman's wife, aided by her girlfriend, Bom. There's lots of partying, drugs, promiscuity, and violence, none of it very involving. In Spanish with English subtitles. **80m/C VHS.** *SP* Carmen Maura, Eva Siva, Olivido Gara, Felix Rotaeta; *D:* Pedro Almodovar; *W:* Pedro Almodovar. FCT, CCN

Pepper and His Wacky Taxi 🎬½

1972 (R) Father of four buys a 59 Cadillac and starts a cab company. Time-capsule fun. **79m/C VHS, Beta.** John Astin, Frank Sinatra Jr., Jackie Gayle, Alan Sherman; *D:* Alex Grasshof. UNI

Peppermint Soda 🎬🎬🎬 1977 Kurys' af-

fecting directorial debut is a semi-autobiographical tale of two teenaged sisters set in 1963 Paris. Seen through the eyes of the 13-year-old Anne, who lives with 15-year-old sister Frederique and their divorced mother, this is the year of first loves, strict teachers, dreaded family vacations, and a general awareness of growing up. Sweet look at adolescence and all its embarassing tribulations. In French with English subtitles. **97m/C VHS.** *FR* Eleonore Klarwein, Odile Michel, Anouk Ferjac, Tsilla Chelton, Coralie Clement, Marie-Veronique Maurin, Puterflam; *D:* Diane Kurys; *W:* Diane Kurys; *C:* Philippe Rousselot. NYF, BTV, FCT

Percy & Thunder 🎬🎬½ 1993 Percy

Banks (Jones) is an old-school boxing trainer who believes in hard work and he sees a likely prospect in Wayne "Thunder" Carter (Vance), a middleweight with a chance to be a champ. That is, if big time boxing promotion doesn't get in the way. **90m/C VHS, Closed Caption.** James Earl Jones, Billy Dee Williams, Courtney B. Vance, Robert Wuhl, Gloria Foster, Zakes Mokae, Gloria Reuben; *D:* Ivan Dixon; *W:* Art Washington; *M:* Tom Scott. TTC

The Perez Family 🎬🎬½ 1994 (R) Juan

Paul Perez (Molina) has spent 20 years in Cuban jails, dreaming of being reunited with wife Carmela (Huston) and daughter Teresa (Alvarado) who successfully escaped to Miami. Part of the 1980 Mariel exodus, Juan meets exuberant Dottie (Tomei), who learns families get sponsored first at the refugee camps. She convinces Juan to pose as her husband, while Carmela, who's being wooed by cop Pirelli (Palminteri), mistakenly believes Juan has literally missed the boat. Tomei's spunky (but with a garish accent), Huston's regal, Palminteri courtly, and Molina morose. The film's inconsistently whimsical, wistful, and clunky. From the novel by Christine Bell. **CW:** Some sexuality, discreet nudity, and language. **135m/C VHS, Closed Caption.** Marisa Tomei, Alfred Molina, Anjelica Huston, Chazz Palminteri, Trini Alvarado, Celia Cruz; *D:* Mira Nair; *W:* Robin Swicord; *C:* Stuart Dryburgh; *M:* Alan Silvestri. HMK

Perfect 🎬½ 1985 (R) A "Rolling Stone" re-

porter goes after the shallowness of the Los Angeles health club scene, and falls in love with the aerobics instructor he is going to write about. "Rolling Stone" publisher Wenner plays himself. As bad as it sounds. **120m/C VHS, Beta, LV, Closed Caption.** John Travolta, Jamie Lee Curtis, Carly Simon, Marilu Henner, Laraine Newman, Jann Wenner, Anne DeSalvo; *D:* James Bridges; *W:* James Bridges, Aaron Latham; *C:* Gordon Willis; *M:* Ralph Burns. COL

Perfect Alibi 🎬🎬½ 1994 Woman's suspi-

cions of her husband's affair leads to murder. **90m/C VHS.** Teri Garr, Hector Elizondo, Kathleen Quinlan, Anne Ramsey, Rigg Kennedy; *D:* Kevin Meyer. AVE

The Perfect Bride 🎬½ 1991 (R) A pretty

young nurse prepares to marry her fiance, but his sister thinks she is hiding a secret. Could the bride-to-be have murder on her mind? Made for cable. **95m/C VHS, Beta, LV, Closed Caption.** Sammi Davis, Kelly Preston, Linden Ashby, Marilyn Rockafellow, Ashley Tillman; *D:* Terrence O'Hara; *M:* Richard Bronskill. VTR

Perfect Crime 🎬🎬 1978 A Scotland Yard

inspector must find out who has been killing off executives of a powerful world trust. **90m/C VHS, Beta.** Joseph Cotten, Anthony Steel, Janet Agren. NO

Perfect Crime 🎬🎬 1997 (PG-13) Navy in-

vestigator Joanne Jensen (Kapture) is assigned to look into the disappearance of a black Marine captain (Guy) and all fingers point to her white, alcoholic, ex-Marine estranged husband (Searcy). Though Jensen doesn't have a body, murder weapon, or confession, she stills decides to take

the case to trial. Made for cable drama based on a 1989 true story. **CW:** A scene of violence, and for thematic elements involving spousal abuse. **92m/C VHS.** Mitzi Kapture, Nick Searcy, Jasmine Guy, Andrew Masset. PAR

The Perfect Daughter 🎬🎬½ 1996

(PG-13) A near-fatal hit-and-run accident reintroduces Alexandra Michelson (Gold) to her family—mother, Jill (Armstrong), father, Tom (Joy), and younger brother, Josh (Shulman). They'd cut the ties to the troubled drug abuser and runaway but the accident has erased Alexandra's memory of her recent life. Unfortunately for them all, Alex's sordid and dangerous past will leave neither her nor her family alone. Made for cable. **CW:** Drug content and some violence. **90m/C VHS, Closed Caption.** Tracey Gold, Bess Armstrong, Mark Joy, Michael Shulman, Harold Pruett, Jay Edward Anthony, Brian Gamble; *D:* Harry S. Longstreet. USH

Perfect Family 🎬🎬 1992 (R) Standard

woman-and-kids-in-peril-from-psycho tale. Maggie is a recent widow with two young daughters who's looking for a nanny and a handyman. She hires brother and sister combo Janice and Alan, who, of course, are too good to be true. One is a sociopath who has murdered a family once before. Guess along with Maggie who the nut might be. **CW:** Violence and terror. **92m/C VHS, Beta, Closed Caption.** Jennifer O'Neill, Bruce Boxleitner, Joanna Cassidy, Juliana Hansen, Shiri Appleby; *D:* E.W. Swackhamer; *W:* Christian Stoianovich, Phoebe Dorin; *M:* Nicholas Pike. PAR

The Perfect Furlough 🎬🎬½ *Strictly for*

Pleasure **1959** Paul Hodges (Curtis) is an Army corporal who wins three weeks in Paris with a movie star (Cristal) as a publicity gimmick. It's the idea of a female Army psychologist (Leigh), who thinks the guys need a morale booster. Pretty bizarre, but it works. **93m/C VHS, Closed Caption.** Tony Curtis, Janet Leigh, Keenan Wynn, Linda Cristal, Elaine Stritch, Marcel Dalio, King Donovan; *D:* Blake Edwards; *W:* Stanley Shapiro. USH, MLB, BAR

The Perfect Gift 🎬🎬 1995 (R) Suzanne

decides to fulfill her boyfriend's menage-a-trois fantasy and discovers that the partner they involve just may be the woman of her dreams. **CW:** Strong sexuality; sex-related dialogue. **90m/C VHS.** John McCafferty, Kim Dawson, Monique Parent. SWI

Perfect Harmony 🎬🎬½ 1991 Racial con-

flict at an exclusive Southern boys school in 1950s South Carolina is overcome through friendship and the love of music in this sentimental tale. Made for cable television. **93m/C VHS, Beta, Closed Caption.** Peter Scolari, Darren McGavin, Catherine Mary Stewart, Moses Gunn, Cleavon Little, Justin Whalin, David Faustino, Richie Havens, Eugene Boyd; *D:* Will MacKenzie. DIS

Perfect Killer 🎬½ *Satanic Mechanic* **1977 (R)**

Van Cleef stars as a world weary Mafia hit-man who is double-crossed by his girl, set up by his best friend, and hunted by another hired assassin. **85m/C VHS, Beta.** Lee Van Cleef, Tita Barker, John Ireland, Robert Widmark; *D:* Marlon Sirko.

Perfect Lies 🎬½ 1997 Trying to pull her life

back together, private eye Toby Merck (Friese) winds up being blackmailed by her former lover, an FBI agent, who wants her to infiltrate a drug kingpin's operation. **94m/C VHS.** Brettanya Friese. LEO

A Perfect Little Murder 🎬🎬½ *A Quiet*

Little Neighborhood, A Perfect Little Murder **1990** Marsha is expecting an uneventful life of barbecues and Little League when her family settles into the suburbs. But then she overhears a murder plot and someone finds out she knows. Made for television. **94m/C VHS, Closed Caption.** Teri Garr, Robert Urich, Susan Ruttan, Jeffrey Tambor, Tom Poston, Florence Stanley, Gail Edwards, Alex Rocco; *D:* Anson Williams; *W:* Mark Stein. TTC

The Perfect Marriage 🐾🐾 **1946** Tired comedy about a perfect couple who decide they can't stand each other anymore after ten years of marriage. Good cast makes the most of weak script. Based on the play by Samuel Raphaelson. **88m/B VHS, Closed Caption.** Loretta Young, David Niven, Eddie Albert, Charlie Ruggles, ZaSu Pitts, Jerome Cowan, Rita Johnson; **D:** Lewis Allen; **W:** Leonard Spigelgass. *USH*

Perfect Match 🐾🐾 **1988 (PG)** A timid young woman and an unambitious young man meet each other through the personal ads and then lie to each other about who they are and what they do for a living. **93m/C VHS, Beta.** Marc McClure, Jennifer Edwards, Diane Stilwell, Rob Paulsen, Karen Witter; **D:** Mark Deimel. *MCG*

A Perfect Murder 🐾🐾 **1998 (R)** Steven Taylor (Douglas), a rich commodities trader about to lose his fortune, is married to young, rich, Emily (Paltrow), who's having a torrid affair with hippie artist David (Mortensen). The love triangle gets shaken when Steven devises a solution to both his wife's infidelities and his financial woes by paying David to kill Emily. Things go a little astray, and the psychological cat and mouse game begins. Glossy production is only eye candy while the unsympathetic characters (led by a weak protagonist in Paltrow) march to the beat of many plot points that all come together in a rushed and dull climax. Douglas, the aged yet sturdy centerpiece of the film, shines as the pompous rich dude devoid of morals, and overpowers his youthful supporting players. Inspired by Hitchcock's 1954 film, "Dial M for Murder." **CW:** Violence, sexuality and language. **105m/C VHS.** Michael Douglas, Gwyneth Paltrow, Viggo Mortensen, David Suchet, Sarita Choudhury, Constance Towers, Novella Nelson; **D:** Andrew Davis; **W:** Patrick Smith Kelly; **C:** Darius Wolski; **M:** James Newton Howard. *NYR*

A Perfect Spy 🐾🐾½ *John Le Carre's A Perfect Spy* **1988** In this BBC miniseries, John Le Carre takes a break from the world of George Smiley to take a look at spying from a personal view. Magnus Pym (Evan) would seem to be the perfect English gentleman; having gone to the right schools he proceeds to join the covert world of espionage. But Magnus hides the secret that his estranged father is a con man par excellence and it leads him to his own betrayals. Adapted from the novel, which Le Carre is said to have drawn from his own past. On three cassettes. **360m/C VHS.** *GB* Peter Egan, Ray McAnally, Frances Tomelty, Benedict Taylor, Tim Healy; **W:** Arthur Hopcraft. *FOX, SIG, VCO*

Perfect Strangers 🐾🐾 *Blind Alley* **1984 (R)** Thriller develops around a murder and the child who witnesses it. The killer attempts to kidnap the young boy, but problems arise when he falls in love with the lad's mother. **90m/C VHS, Beta.** Anne Carlisle, Brad Rijn, John Woehrle, Matthew Stockley, Ann Magnuson, Stephen Lack; **D:** Larry Cohen; **W:** Larry Cohen. *NLC*

Perfect Target 🐾½ **1998 (R)** An ex-CIA agent is forced to work as a mercenary, protecting the president of Santa Brava. Naturally, this assignment doesn't go well and he becomes the fall guy for the politico's murder. Only he doesn't intend to stay that way. **97m/C VHS.** Daniel Bernhardt, Robert Englund, Brian Thompson, Dara Tomanovich; **D:** Sheldon Lettich. *AVA*

Perfect Timing woof! **1984** Soft-core film about a fledgling photographer who can't turn his orgy-like photo sessions into anything profitable. **87m/C VHS, Beta.** Stephen Markle, Michelle Scarabelli; **D:** Rene Bonniere. *ART*

Perfect Victims 🐾 **1987 (R)** Beautiful models are being hunted by a killer, and a police officer wants to catch the psychopath before he strikes again. **100m/C VHS, Beta, LV.** Deborah Shelton, Clarence Williams III, Lyman Ward; **D:** Shuki Levy.

The Perfect Weapon 🐾🐾 **1991 (R)** Kenpo karate master Speakman severs family ties and wears funny belt in order to avenge underworld murder of his teacher. **CW:** Some language and martial arts violence. **85m/C VHS, Beta, LV, Closed Caption.** Jeff Sanders, Jeff Speakman; **D:** Mark DiSalle; **W:** David Wilson; **C:** Russell Carpenter; **M:** Gary Chang. *PAR*

Perfect Witness 🐾🐾½ **1989** A restaurant owner witnesses a mob slaying and resists testifying against the culprit to save his family and himself. Made for cable television. Filmed in New York City. **104m/C VHS, Beta, LV.** Brian Dennehy, Aidan Quinn, Stockard Channing, Laura Harrington, Joe Grifasi; **D:** Robert Mandel; **M:** Brad Fiedel. *HBO*

A Perfect World 🐾🐾½ **1993 (PG-13)** Butch Haynes (Costner) is an escaped con who takes eight-year-old fatherless Phillip (Lowther) as a hostage in 1963 Texas and is pursued by Texas Ranger Red Garnett (Eastwood). Butch is a bad guy and the film never tries to make him heroic but it also allows him to grow attached to Phillip and acknowledge him as a surrogate son. Costner gives a quiet and strong performance and the remarkable Lowther never goes wrong in his role as the needy little boy. Eastwood's role is strictly secondary as the well tested lawman who understands justice without seeking vengeance. Somewhat draggy—especially the protracted final scene. **CW:** Language, some violence, and sexual content. **138m/C VHS, LV, Letterbox, Closed Caption.** Kevin Costner, T.J. Lowther, Clint Eastwood, Laura Dern, Keith Szarabajka, Leo Burmester, Paul Hewitt, Bradley Whitford, Ray McKinnon, Wayne Dehart, Jennifer Griffin, Linda Hart; **D:** Clint Eastwood; **W:** John Lee Hancock; **C:** Jack N. Green; **M:** Lennie Niehaus. *WAR*

Perfectly Normal 🐾🐾 **1991 (R)** Two friends end up in hilarious situations when one opens an eccentric restaurant with a mysterious, newly found fortune. **CW:** Language and sensual scene. **106m/C VHS, Beta, LV.** Michael Riley, Robbie Coltrane, Kenneth Welsh, Eugene Lipinski; **D:** Yves Simoneau; **W:** Eugene Lipinski, Paul Quarrington.

Performance 🐾🐾🐾½ **1970 (R)** Grim and unsettling psychological account of a criminal who hides out in a bizarre house occupied by a peculiar rock star and his two female companions. Entire cast scores high marks, with Pallenberg especially compelling as a somewhat mysterious and attractive housemate to mincing Jagger. A cult favorite, with music by Nitzsche under the direction of Randy Newman. **104m/C VHS, Beta, LV.** *GB* James Fox, Mick Jagger, Anita Pallenberg; **D:** Donald Cammell, Nicolas Roeg; **W:** Donald Cammell; **M:** Jack Nitzsche. *WAR*

Perfume 🐾½ **1991** Five beautiful, black childhood friends join together to conquer the cosmetics industry with their new perfume, Sassy. But can they resist all the temptations success brings and keep both their company and their friendship? **98m/C VHS.** Cheryl Francis Harrington, Kathleen Bradley Overton, Shy Jefferson, Lynn Marlin, Eugina Wright, Ted Lange; **D:** Roland S. Jefferson. *XVC*

Perfumed Nightmare 🐾🐾🐾 **1989** Unique, appealing fable about a Filipino youth who discovers the drawbacks of social and cultural progress when he moves to Paris. Director Tahimik also plays the lead role. Imaginative, yet remarkably economical, this film was produced for $10,000 and received the International Critics Award at the Berlin Film Festival. In Tagalog with English dialogue and subtitles. **93m/C VHS.** *PH* Kidlat Tahimik, Dolores Santamaria, Georgette Baudry, Katrin Muller, Harmut Lerch; **D:** Kidlat Tahimik. *UWA*

Peril 🐾🐾½ *Peril en la Demeure* **1985 (R)** From the novel "Sur La Terre Comme Au Ciel" by Rene Belletto. Deals with a music teacher's infiltration into a wealthy family and the sexually motivated, back-stabbing murder plots that ensue. DeVille does poorly with avant-garde technique. In French with English subtitles. **100m/C VHS, Beta.** *FR* Michel Piccoli, Christophe MaLavoy, Richard Bohringer, Ni-

cole Garcia, Anais Jeanneret; **D:** Michel DeVille; **W:** Michel DeVille. Cesar Awards '86: Best Director (DeVille). *NO*

The Perils of Gwendoline 🐾🐾½ *Gwendoline; The Perils of Gwendoline in the Land of the Yik-Yak* **1984 (R)** A young woman leaves a convent to search for her long-lost father, in this adaptation of a much funnier French comic strip of the same name. What ends up on the screen is merely a very silly rip-off of the successful "Raiders of the Lost Ark," and of primary interest for its numerous scenes of amply endowed Kitaen in the buff. **88m/C VHS, Beta, LV.** *FR* Tawny Kitaen, Brent Huff, Zabou, Bernadette LaFont, Jean Rougerie; **D:** Just Jaeckin; **M:** Pierre Bachelet. *ART, VES*

The Perils of Pauline 🐾🐾½ **1934** All 12 episodes of this classic melodrama/adventure serial in one package, featuring dastardly villains, cliff-hanging predicaments, and worldwide chases. **238m/B VHS, Beta.** Evelyn Knapp, Robert Allen, James Durkin, Sonny Ray, Pat O'Malley; **D:** Ray Taylor. *NOS, VYY, MLB*

The Perils of Pauline 🐾🐾 **1947** A musical biography of Pearl White, the reigning belle of silent movie serials. Look for lots of silent film stars. **96m/C VHS, Beta.** Betty Hutton, John Lund, Constance Collier, William Demarest, Billy DeWolfe; **D:** George Marshall; **C:** Ray Rennahan; **M:** Frank Loesser. Nominations: Academy Awards '47: Best Song ("I Wish I Didn't Love You So"). *NOS, HHT, BAR*

Perils of the Darkest Jungle 🐾🐾½ *The Tiger Woman; Jungle Gold* **1944** Tiger Woman battles money-mad oil profiteers to protect her tribe. This 12-episode serial comes on two tapes. **180m/B VHS, Beta.** Linda Stirling, Allan "Rocky" Lane, Duncan Renaldo, George Lewis; **D:** Spencer Gordon Bennet. *REP, MLB*

Period of Adjustment 🐾🐾🐾 **1962** Heartwarming comedy about young newlyweds adjusting to the pressures of domestic life and trying to help the troubled marriage of an older couple. Based on the play by Tennessee Williams. **112m/B VHS.** Anthony (Tony) Franciosa, Jane Fonda, Jim Hutton, Lois Nettleton, John McGiver, Jack Albertson; **D:** George Roy Hill; **W:** Isobel Lennart. Nominations: Academy Awards '62: Best Art Direction/Set Decoration (B & W). *MGM*

Permanent Record 🐾🐾½ **1988 (PG-13)** Hyper-sincere drama about a popular high schooler's suicide and the emotional reactions of those he left behind. Great performance from Reeves. **92m/C VHS, Beta, LV, Closed Caption.** Alan Boyce, Keanu Reeves, Michelle Meyrink, Jennifer Rubin, Pamela Gidley, Michael Elgart, Richard Bradford, Barry Corbin, Kathy Baker, Dakin Matthews; **D:** Marisa Silver; **W:** Jarre Fees, Alice Liddle, Larry Ketron; **C:** Frederick Elmes; **M:** Joe Strummer. *PAR*

Permanent Vacation 🐾🐾½ **1984** A young man disenchanted with New York City decides to escape to Europe to forget about his problems. **80m/C VHS, Beta.** John Lurie, Chris Parker; **D:** Jim Jarmusch; **W:** Jim Jarmusch; **M:** John Lurie. *NO*

Permission To Kill 🐾🐾½ **1975 (PG)** Grim spy drama features Bogard as an agent determined to prevent the return of a third-world radical to a totalitarian state. **96m/C VHS, Beta.** *GB* Dirk Bogarde, Ava Gardner, Timothy Dalton, Frederic Forrest; **D:** Cyril Frankel; **C:** Frederick A. (Freddie) Young; **M:** Richard Rodney Bennett.

Perry Mason Returns 🐾🐾🐾 **1985** Perry Mason returns to solve another baffling mystery. This time he must help his longtime assistant, Della Street, when she is accused of killing her new employer. **95m/C VHS, Beta.** Raymond Burr, Barbara Hale, William Katt, Patrick O'Neal, Richard Anderson, Cassie Yates, Al Freeman Jr.; **D:** Ron Satlof. *MCG*

Perry Mason: The Case of the Lost Love 🐾🐾½ **1987** Super-lawyer Mason defends the husband of a former lover he hadn't seen in 30 years. The solution to the mystery may catch viewer off guard. **98m/C VHS.** Raymond Burr, Barbara Hale, William Katt, Jean Simmons, Gene Barry,

Robert Walden, Stephen Elliott, Robert Mandan, David Ogden Stiers; **D:** Ron Satlof. *VTR*

Persona 🐾🐾🐾🐾 1966 A famous actress turns mute and is treated by a talkative nurse at a secluded cottage. As their relationship turns increasingly tense, the women's personalities begin to merge. Memorable, unnerving—and atypically avant garde—fare from cinema giant Bergman. First of several collaborations between the director and leading lady Ullman. In Swedish with English subtitles. **100m/C VHS, Beta, 8mm.** *SW* Bibi Andersson, Liv Ullmann, Gunnar Bjornstrand, Margareta Krook; **D:** Ingmar Bergman; **W:** Ingmar Bergman; **C:** Sven Nykvist. National Society of Film Critics Awards '67: Best Actress (Andersson), Best Director (Bergman), Best Film. *MGM, VYY, VDM*

Personal Best 🐾🐾🐾 1982 (R) Lesbian lovers compete while training for the 1990 Olympics. Provocative fare often goes where few films have gone before, but overly stylized direction occasionally overwhelms characterizations. It gleefully exploits locker-room nudity, with Hemingway in her pre-implant days. Still, an ambitious, often accomplished production. Towne's directorial debut. **126m/C VHS, Beta.** Mariel Hemingway, Scott Glenn, Patrice Donnelly; **D:** Robert Towne; **W:** Robert Towne; **C:** Michael Chapman; **M:** Jack Nitzsche. *WAR*

Personal Exemptions 🐾½ 1988 (PG) In this stock comedy a frenzied IRS auditor learns that her daughter is smuggling aliens into the country, her son is brokering with some businessmen she's targeted for tax fraud, and her husband is having an affair with a high-school girl. **100m/C VHS, Beta.** Nanette Fabray, John Cotton; **D:** Peter Rowe.

Personal Property 🐾🐾½ *The Man in Possession* 1937 Taylor tries every trick in the book to win Harlow over in this MGM romantic fluff. Not that big on laughs, but plenty of good shots of Harlow and a beefcake scene of Taylor in a bathtub, who was the darling of the MGM lot and worked with every leading lady. This was the only film Harlow and Taylor made together. Remake of the 1931 film "The Man in Possession." **84m/B VHS, Closed Caption.** Robert Taylor, Jean Harlow, Reginald Owen, Una O'Connor, E.E. Clive, Henrietta Crosman, Cora Witherspoon; **D:** Woodbridge S. Van Dyke; **W:** Hugh Mills. *MGM*

Personal Services 🐾🐾½ 1987 (R) A bawdy satire loosely based on the life and times of Britain's modern-day madam, Cynthia Payne, and her rise to fame in the world of prostitution. Payne's earlier years were featured in the film "Wish You Were Here." **104m/C VHS, Beta, LV.** *GB* Julie Walters, Alec McCowen, Shirley Stelfox, Tim Woodward, David Atkins, Danny Schiller, Victoria Hardcastle; **D:** Terry Jones; **W:** David Leland; **C:** Roger Deakins; **M:** John Du Prez. *ART, VES*

The Personals 🐾🐾½ 1983 (PG) A recently divorced young man takes out a personal ad in a newspaper to find the woman of his dreams. But it isn't quite that simple in this independent comedy shot entirely in Minneapolis. **90m/C VHS, Beta.** Bill Schoppert, Karen Landry, Paul Eiding, Michael Laskin, Vickie Dakil; **D:** Peter Markle.

Personals 🐾🐾 1990 Chilling drama that casts O'Neill as an unnoticed librarian, until she begins to meet (and kill) the men who answer her ads. Zimbalist is a widow who is determined to learn the truth. Made for television. **93m/C VHS, Beta, LV, Closed Caption.** Stephanie Zimbalist, Jennifer O'Neill, Robin Thomas, Clark Johnson, Gina Gallego, Rosemary Dunsmore, Colm Feore; **D:** Steven Hilliard Stern. *PAR*

The Persuaders 1971 The first two episodes of Moore and Curtis as international playboy crime fighters. **52m/C VHS, Beta.** *GB* Roger Moore, Tony Curtis, Alex Scott, Joan Collins, Robert Hutton; **D:** Basil Dearden. *NO*

Persuasion 🐾🐾🐾½ 1995 (PG) Charming British costume romance, based on Jane Austen's final novel, deals with the constricted life of practical, plain, put-upon Anne Elliot (Root). Thanks to well-meaning interference, Anne refused the marriage proposal of the manly Frederick Wentworth (Hinds) and instead stuck by her snobbish and demanding family. Eight years later, Anne is given a second chance at love when the now-wealthy Wentworth happens back into her life—but she still has her obnoxious relations to contend with. It's wonderful to see Anne blossom from mouse to lioness although the swirl of supporting players (and settings) provide some confusion. **104m/C VHS, LV, Closed Caption.** *GB* Amanda Root, Ciaran Hinds, Susan Fleetwood, Corin Redgrave, Fiona Shaw, John Woodvine, Phoebe Nicholls, Sam West, Sophie Thompson, Judy Cornwell, Felicity Dean, Simon Russell Beale, Victoria Hamilton, Emma Roberts; **D:** Roger Mitchell; **W:** Nick Dear, Jeremy Sams; **C:** John Daly. *COL*

Persuasion 🐾🐾½ 19?? Practical Anne Elliott is always at the beck-and-call of her snobbish and helpless family. She even turned down a marriage proposal for their sake. Now Captain Wentworth has come back into Anne's life and she has a second chance. But will she be strong enough to take it? Made for BBC TV. **225m/C VHS.** *GB* Ann Firbank, Basil Dignam, Valerie Gearon, Marian Spence, Charlotte Mitchell. *VCO*

The Perverse Countess 🐾 *La Comtesse Perverse* 1973 Romay is a bored tourist who spends a free weekend on a fling with Woods, who procures human flesh for the cannibalistic Count and Countess Zaroff (Vernon and Arno). Romay accompanies her lover to the haunted castle on a delivery, not realizing she is the package. When the Countess sees what a succulent bon-bon Romay is, she faces difficult choices. Subtitled in English. **86m/C VHS.** *FR* Lina Romay, Robert Woods, Howard Vernon, Alice Arno, Caroline Riviere; **D:** Jess (Jesus) Franco. *VSM*

The Pest 🐾 1996 (PG-13) Movie certainly lives up to its title. A hyperkinetic Leguizamo stars as Pestario (Pest) Vargas, a small-time Miami con man, who owes 50 large to the mob. Eccentric German businessman Gustav Shank (Jones) offers the money to Pest—the catch being that Pest will become the human prey for Gustav's private island hunting party. You'll be rooting for the hunter. **CW:** Crude sexual, scatological and ethnic humor. **85m/C VHS, Closed Caption.** John Leguizamo, Jeffrey Jones, Edoardo Ballerini, Freddy Rodriguez, Joe Morton, Charles Hallahan, Tammy Townsend, Aries Spears; **D:** Paul Miller; **W:** David Bar Katz; **C:** Roy Wagner; **M:** Kevin Kiner. *COL*

Pet Sematary 🐾🐾 1989 (R) A quirky adaptation of Stephen King's bestseller about a certain patch of woods in the Maine wilderness that rejuvenates the dead, and how a newly located college MD eventually uses it to restore his dead son. Mildly creepy. **103m/C VHS, Beta, LV, 8mm, Closed Caption.** Dale Midkiff, Fred Gwynne, Denise Crosby, Blaze Berdahl, Brad Greenquist, Miko Hughes, Stephen King; **D:** Mary Lambert; **W:** Stephen King; **C:** Peter Stein; **M:** Elliot Goldenthal. *PAR*

Pet Sematary 2 🐾½ 1992 (R) Lame sequel to original Stephen King flick. After seeing his mother electrocuted, a teen and his veterinarian father move to the Maine town where the legendary Pet Sematary is located. Horror begins when the boy's friend's dog is shot by his stepfather, and the boys bury the dog in the "sematary." King wasn't involved with this film, so the story isn't very coherent, but shock value and special effects are great. Not recommended for those with a weak stomach. **CW:** Language, strong horror violence, and sexuality. **102m/C VHS, Beta, LV, Closed Caption.** Anthony Edwards, Edward Furlong, Clancy Brown, Jared Rushton, Darlanne Fluegel, Lisa Waltz, Jason McGuire, Sarah Trigger; **D:** Mary Lambert; **W:** Richard Outten; **C:** Russell Carpenter. *PAR*

Pet Shop 🐾🐾½ 1994 (PG) Pair of evil, galaxy-travelling aliens take over the local pet store in a remote desert town and plan to abduct all the kids by bewitching them with a spaceship full of intergalactic creatures. Only Dena (aided by the good alien furballs) can stop the bad guys from making space pets of the earthlings. **88m/C VHS,**

Beta, Leigh Ann Orsi, Spencer Vrooman, David Wagner, Joanne Baron, Jane Morris, Terry Kiser, Jeff Michalski, Shashawnee Hall, Sabrina Wiener, Cody Burger; **D:** Hope Perello; **W:** Mark Goldstein, Greg Suddeth, Brent Friedman; **M:** Reg Powell. *PAR*

Pete Kelly's Blues 🐾🐾 1955 A jazz musician in a Kansas City speakeasy is forced to stand up against a brutal racketeer. The melodramatic plot is brightened by a nonstop flow of jazz tunes sung by Lee and Fitzgerald and played by an all-star lineup that includes Dick Cathcart, Matty Matlock, Eddie Miller and George Van Eps. ♫Sugar; Sombody Loves Me; Bye Bye Blackbird; What Can I Say After I Say I'm Sorry?; He Needs Me; Sing a Rainbow; Pete Kelly's Blues. **96m/C VHS, Beta, LV, Letterbox.** Jack Webb, Janet Leigh, Edmond O'Brien, Lee Marvin, Martin Milner, Peggy Lee, Ella Fitzgerald, Jayne Mansfield; **D:** Jack Webb. Nominations: Academy Awards '55: Best Supporting Actress (Lee). *WAR*

Pete 'n' Tillie 🐾🐾 1972 (PG) Amiable comedy turns to less appealing melodrama as couple meets, marries, and endures tragedy. Film contributes little to director Ritt's hit-and-miss reputation, but Matthau and Burnett shine in leads. Adapted by Julius J. Epstein from a Peter de Vries' story. **100m/C VHS, Beta.** Walter Matthau, Carol Burnett, Geraldine Page, Barry Nelson, Rene Auberjonois, Lee Montgomery, Henry Jones, Kent Smith; **D:** Martin Ritt; **W:** Julius J. Epstein; **C:** John A. Alonzo; **M:** John Williams. British Academy Awards '73: Best Actor (Matthau); Nominations: Academy Awards '72: Best Adapted Screenplay, Best Supporting Actress (Page). *USH*

Pete Townshend: White City 1985 The Who guitarist portrays a musician who helps bring a close friend and his estranged wife back together. This semi-autobiographical film includes music from Townsend. **60m/C VHS, Beta, LV.** Pete Townshend, Andrew Wilde, Frances Barber; **D:** Richard Lowenstein. *MVD, VES*

Peter and Paul 🐾🐾½ 1981 TV miniseries follows the lives of the two apostles, Peter (Foxworth) and Paul (Hopkins), from the Crucifixion through the next three decades as they travel spreading the word of Christ, until both are executed in Rome. Tries valiantly, but falls a bit short. **194m/C VHS.** Anthony Hopkins, Robert Foxworth, Eddie Albert, Raymond Burr, Jose Ferrer, Jon Finch, David Gwillim, Herbert Lom, Jean Peters; **D:** Robert Day; **W:** Christopher Knopf. *USH, GFV*

Peter Gunn 🐾🐾 1989 Detective Peter Gunn returns, only to himself being hunted by both the mob and the Feds. A TV movie reprise of the vintage series that has none of the original cast members. **97m/C VHS.** Peter Strauss, Barbara Williams, Jennifer Edwards, Charles Cioffi, Pearl Bailey, Peter Jurasik, David Rappaport; **D:** Blake Edwards; **M:** Henry Mancini. *VTR*

Peter Lundy and the Medicine Hat Stallion 🐾🐾½ *The Medicine Hat Stallion; Pony Express* 1977 A teenaged Pony Express rider must outrun the Indians and battle the elements in order to carry mail from the Nebraska Territory to the West Coast in this made-for-television film. Good family entertainment. **85m/C VHS, Beta.** Leif Garrett, Mitchell Ryan, Bibi Besch, John Quade, Milo O'Shea; **D:** Michael O'Herlihy. *ART, VES*

Peter Pan 🐾🐾🐾 1953 (G) Disney classic about a boy who never wants to grow up. Based on J.M. Barrie's book and play. Still stands head and shoulders above any recent competition in providing fun family entertainment. Terrific animation and lovely hummable music. **76m/C VHS, Beta, LV, Closed Caption. D:** Hamilton Luske; **V:** Bobby Driscoll, Kathryn Beaumont, Hans Conried, Heather Angel, Candy Candido. *DIS, HMV*

Peter Pan 🐾🐾🐾½ 1960 A TV classic, this videotape of a performance of the 1954 Broadway musical adapted from the J.M. Barrie classic features Mary Martin in one of her most famous incarnations, as the adolescent Peter Pan. Songs include "I'm Flying," "Neverland," and "I Won't Grow Up." **100m/C VHS, Beta, LV, Closed Caption.**

Mary Martin, Cyril Ritchard, Sondra Lee, Heather Halliday, Luke Halpin; **D:** Vincent J. Donehue. *GKK, COL, MLT*

Peter the First: Part 1 1937 The first half of Petrov's Soviet epic about the early years of Tsar Peter I's reign. Lavish, in Russian with English subtitles. 95m/B VHS, Beta. *RU* **D:** Vladimir Petrov. *FCT*

Peter the First: Part 2 🎬🎬 *The Conquests of Peter the Great* 1938 The second half of Petrov's epic, covering the triumphs and final years of the famous Tsar. In Russian with English subtitles. 104m/B VHS, Beta. *RU* **D:** Vladimir Petrov. *FCT*

Peter the Great 🎬🎬🎬 1986 Dry but eye-pleasing TV mini-series follows the life of Russia's colorful, very tall ruler from childhood on. Much of the interesting cast is wasted in tiny roles. 371m/C VHS. Maximilian Schell, Laurence Olivier, Omar Sharif, Vanessa Redgrave, Ursula Andress. *VTR*

Peter's Friends 🎬🎬½ 1992 (R) Peter has recently inherited a grand manor house located outside London and invites some chums to celebrate a New Year's Eve weekend, ten years after they've been at university together. So begins another nostalgic trip down memory lane ala "The Big Chill," but unlike other clones, this one can stand on its own, with a lightweight and sly script by talented comedienne Rudner (in her film debut) and her husband Bergman. If the script sometimes falls a little flat, the fine cast will make up for it. Thompson's mother, actress Law, plays the housekeeper. **CW:** Language and some sexuality. 102m/C VHS, LV, Closed Caption. *GB* Kenneth Branagh, Rita Rudner, Emma Thompson, Stephen Fry, Hugh Laurie, Imelda Staunton, Alphonsia Emmanuel, Tony Slattery, Alex Lowe, Alex Scott, Phyllida Law, Richard Briers; **D:** Kenneth Branagh; **W:** Rita Rudner, Martin Bergman; **M:** Jacques Offenbach. *HBO, BTV*

Pete's Dragon 🎬🎬½ 1977 (G) Elliot, an enormous, bumbling dragon with a penchant for clumsy heroics, becomes friends with poor orphan Pete. Combines brilliant animation with the talents of live actors for an interesting effect. 128m/C VHS, Beta, LV, Closed Caption. Helen Reddy, Shelley Winters, Mickey Rooney, Jim Dale, Red Buttons, Sean Marshall, Jim Backus, Jeff Conaway; **D:** Don Chaffey; **W:** Malcolm Marmorstein; **V:** Charlie Callas. Nominations: Academy Awards '77: Best Song ("Candle on the Water"), Original Song Score and/or Adaptation. *DIS, FCT*

Petit Con 🎬🎬½ 1984 (R) A live-action version of the popular French comic strip wherein a young rebel drops out of society to live with aging hippies. With English subtitles. 90m/C VHS, Beta. *FR* Guy Marchand, Michel Choupon, Caroline Cellier, Bernard Brieux, Souad Amidou; **D:** Gerard Lauzier. *ORI*

Petrified Forest 🎬🎬🎬 1936 Patrons and employees are held captive by a runaway gangster's band in a desert diner. Often gripping, with memorable performances from Davis, Howard, and Bogart. Based on the play by Robert Sherwood with Howard and Bogart recreating their stage roles. 83m/B VHS, Beta. Bette Davis, Leslie Howard, Humphrey Bogart, Dick Foran, Charley Grapewin, Porter Hall; **D:** Archie Mayo. *FOX, MGM*

Petulia 🎬🎬🎬🎬 1968 (R) Overlooked, offbeat drama about a flighty woman who spites her husband by dallying with a sensitive, recently divorced surgeon. Classic '60s document and cult favorite offers great performance from the appealing Christie, with Scott fine as the vulnerable surgeon. On-screen performances by the Grateful Dead and Big Brother. Among idiosyncratic director Lester's best. From the novel "Me and the Arch Kook Petulia" by John Haase. 105m/C VHS, Beta. George C. Scott, Richard Chamberlain, Julie Christie, Shirley Knight, Arthur Hill, Joseph Cotten, Pippa Scott, Richard Dysart, Kathleen Widdoes, Austin Pendleton, Rene Auberjonois; **D:** Richard Lester; **W:** Lawrence B. Marcus; **C:** Nicolas Roeg; **M:** John Barry. *WAR*

Peyton Place 🎬🎬🎬 1957 Passion, scandal, and deception in a small New England town set the standard for passion, scandal, and deception in soap operadom. Shot on location in Camden, Maine. Performances and themes now seem dated, but produced a blockbuster in its time. Adapted from Grace Metalious' popular novel and followed by "Return to Peyton Place." 157m/C VHS, LV, Letterbox, Closed Caption. Lana Turner, Hope Lange, Lee Philips, Lloyd Nolan, Diane Varsi, Lorne Greene, Russ Tamblyn, Arthur Kennedy, Terry Moore, Barry Coe, David Nelson, Betty Field, Mildred Dunnock, Leon Ames, Alan Reed Jr.; **D:** Mark Robson; **W:** John Michael Hayes; **C:** William Mellor. Nominations: Academy Awards '57: Best Actress (Turner), Best Adapted Screenplay, Best Cinematography, Best Director (Robson), Best Picture, Best Supporting Actor (Kennedy, Tamblyn), Best Supporting Actress (Lange, Varsi). *FOX, FCT*

Phaedra 🎬🎬 1961 Loose and updated adaptation of Euripides' "Hippolytus." Mercouri, the second wife of a rich Greek shipping magnate, is dispatched to London to convince her husband's adult son (Perkins) to come home to Greece. Mercouri and Perkins immediately begin a steamy affair but their return home brings problems for all. Dubbed. 116m/B VHS. *GR FR* Melina Mercouri, Anthony Perkins, Raf Vallone, Elizabeth Ercy; *Cameos:* Jules Dassin; **D:** Jules Dassin; **W:** Jules Dassin, Margarita Liberaki; **M:** Mikis Theodorakis. Nominations: Academy Awards '62: Best Costume Design (B & W). *FCT*

Phantasm 🎬🎬½ 1979 (R) A small-budgeted, hallucinatory horror fantasy about two parentless brothers who discover weird goings-on at the local funeral parlor, including the infamous airborne, brain-chewing chrome ball. Creepy, unpredictable nightmare fashioned on a shoestring by young independent producer Coscarelli. Scenes were cut out of the original film to avoid an "X" rating. Followed by "Phantasm II." 90m/C VHS, Beta, LV. Michael Baldwin, Bill Thornbury, Reggie Bannister, Kathy Lester, Terrie Kalbus, Ken Jones, Susan Harper, Lynn Eastman, David Arntzen, Angus Scrimm, Bill Cone; **D:** Don A. Coscarelli; **W:** Don A. Coscarelli; **C:** Don A. Coscarelli. *COL*

Phantasm II 🎬🎬 1988 (R) Teen psychic keeps flashing on villainous Tall Man. A rehash sequel to the original, cultishly idiosyncratic fantasy, wherein more victims are fed into the inter-dimensional abyss and Mike discovers that the horror is not all in his head. Occasional inspired gore; bloodier than its predecessor. More yuck for the buck. 97m/C VHS, Beta, LV, Closed Caption. James LeGros, Reggie Bannister, Angus Scrimm, Paula Irvine, Samantha Phillips, Ken Tigar; **D:** Don A. Coscarelli; **W:** Don A. Coscarelli; **C:** Daryn Okada. *USH*

Phantasm III: Lord of the Dead 🎬½ 1994 (R) Murderous mortician The Tall Man and his killer silver spheres return once again in this continuing gore fest. Mike, whose brother Jody was one of The Tall Man's victims, teams up with the cynical Reggie and martial arts expert Rocky to try to defeat the creep. That's if they can get past his zombie cohorts and flesh-eating ghouls. 91m/C VHS, LV, Closed Caption. Reggie Bannister, A. Michael Baldwin, Bill Thornbury, Gloria Henry, Kevin Connor, Angus Scrimm; **D:** Don A. Coscarelli; **W:** Don A. Coscarelli. *USH*

The Phantom 🎬🎬 1931 Rare cheapie of a hooded killer terrorizing a group of people in a haunted house. 62m/C VHS. Guinn "Big Boy" Williams, Wilfrid Lucas, Sheldon Lewis, William Gould; **D:** Alan James. *SNC, GPV*

The Phantom 🎬🎬½ 1996 (PG) Based on the Lee Falk comic created in 1936. Deep in the Bengalla jungle, a mysterious costumed figure honors a 400-year-old legacy by fighting piracy, greed, and evil. With the help of a beautiful newspaper heiress (Swanson), the latest guardian (Zane) must keep an American industrialist (Williams) and a secret brotherhood of pirates from finding three sacred skulls that contain the power to dominate the world. Old-fashioned swashbuckling story is helped along by Zane's enthusiastic portrayal of the stalwart hero. Action set pieces, while done more dynamically elsewhere, are fun and exciting. Older kids (read: teenagers) may find the proceedings a bit hokey, but everyone seems to be having a good time. 100m/C VHS, LV, Closed Caption. Billy Zane, Kristy Swanson, Treat Williams, Catherine Zeta-Jones, James Remar, Jon Tenney, Patrick McGoohan, Samantha Eggar, Cary-Hiroyuki Tagawa, Robert Coleby, David Proval; **D:** Simon Wincer; **W:** Jeffrey Boam; **C:** David Burr; **M:** David Newman. *PAR*

The Phantom Broadcast 🎬🎬½ *Phantom of the Air* 1933 A popular radio crooner is murdered. The main suspect is his hunchbacked accompanist and manager, who had all along secretly pre-recorded his own velvet voice for the crooner to lip-sync along with. A tightly plotted minor thriller that holds up surprisingly well. 63m/B VHS, Beta, 8mm. Ralph Forbes, Gail Patrick, Vivienne Osborne, Guinn "Big Boy" Williams, George "Gabby" Hayes; **D:** Phil Rosen. *VYY, NOS, FCT*

Phantom Brother 🎬½ 1988 A semi-spoof about a teenager left orphaned by a car crash that wiped out his entire family, and who is subsequently haunted by his dead brother. Even thinner than it sounds. 92m/C VHS, Beta. Jon Hammer, Patrick Molloy, John Gigante, Mary Beth Pelshaw; **D:** William Szarka. *NO*

The Phantom Bullet 🎬½ 1926 Hoot wants to holler at his father's murderers. 60m/B VHS, Beta. Hoot Gibson. *GPV*

The Phantom Chariot 🎬🎬½ 1920 A fantasy depicting the Swedish myth about how Death's coach must be driven by the last man to die each year. Silent. 89m/B VHS, Beta. *SW* **D:** Victor Sjostrom. *SNC, FCT, GVV*

The Phantom Creeps 1939 Evil Dr. Zorka, armed with a meteorite chunk which can bring an army to a standstill, provides the impetus for this enjoyable serial in 12 episodes. 235m/B VHS, Beta. Bela Lugosi, Dorothy Arnold, Robert Kent, Regis Toomey; **D:** Ford Beebe, Saul Goodkind. *NOS, SNC, VCN*

The Phantom Empire *Radio Ranch* 1935 Autry faces the futuristic "Thunder Riders" from the subterranean city of Murania, located 20,000 feet beneath his ranch. A complete serial in 12 episodes. If you only see one science-fiction western in your life, this is the one. Also available in an edited theatrical version at 80 minutes. 245m/B VHS, Beta. Gene Autry, Frankie Darro, Betsy King Ross, Smiley Burnette; **D:** B. Reeves Eason, Otto Brower. *NOS, SNC, VYY*

Phantom Empire 🎬🎬 1987 (R) A woman who rules over a lost city takes a bunch of scientists prisoner and forces them to be slaves. 85m/C VHS, Beta. Ross Hagen, Jeffrey Combs, Dawn Wildsmith, Robert Quarry, Susan Stokey, Michelle (McClellan) Bauer, Russ Tamblyn, Sybil Danning; **D:** Fred Olen Ray; **W:** Fred Olen Ray, T.T. Lankford.

Phantom Express 🎬🎬 1932 Experienced old engineer is dismissed from his job because no one believes his explanation that a mysterious train caused the wreck of his own train. He aims to find justice. 65m/B VHS, Beta. J. Farrell MacDonald, Sally Blane, William Collier Jr., Hobart Bosworth; **D:** Emory Johnson. *NO*

Phantom Fiend 🎬½ 1935 A gentle musician becomes a suspect when a series of Jack-the-Ripper type murders terrorize London. Is he the nice guy known by his girlfriend and the people in his lodging house, or is the musician really JTR? Based on the novel "The Lodger" by Marie Belloc-Lowndes. 70m/B VHS. *GB* Ivor Novello, Elizabeth Allan, A.W. Baskcomb, Jack Hawkins, Barbara Everest, Peter Gawthorne, P. Kynaston Reeves; **D:** Maurice Elvey. *FCT, RXM*

The Phantom Flyer 🎬½ 1928 Stunt pilot helps out a cattle-owning frontier family bedeviled by rustlers. Silent. 58m/B VHS, Beta, 8mm. Al Wilson. *VYY, GPV, RXM*

Phantom from Space 🎬½ 1953 An invisible alien lands on Earth, begins killing people, and is pursued by a pair of scientists. 72m/B VHS. Ted Cooper, Rudolph Anders, Noreen Nash, James Seay, Harry Landers; **D:** W. Lee Wilder; **C:** William Clothier. *EEL, SNC, NOS*

The Phantom from 10,000 Leagues 🌑 1959 Slimy sea monster attacks swimmers and fishermen; investigating oceanographer pretends not to notice monster is hand puppet. Early AIP release, when still named American Releasing Company. **80m/B VHS.** Kent Taylor, Cathy Downs, Michael Whalen, Helene Stanton, Phillip Pine; **D:** Dan Milner. *VYY, SNC, MLB*

Phantom Gold 🌑½ 1938 The wicked Whitaker claims to have struck it rich but it's really a scam to lure unsuspecting miners to the claim and then rob and murder them. Luden's suspicious and proves Whitaker's a bad guy. **56m/B VHS.** Jack Luden, Charles "Slim" Whitaker, Beth Marion, Hal Taliaferro, Art Davis; **D:** Joseph Levering. *GPV*

The Phantom in the House 🌑🌑 1929 A woman commits a murder and has her inventor husband take the rap. While he's in prison, she gets rich off of his work. Things get hairy when he is released 15 years later and is introduced to his daughter as a friend of the family. Melodramatic film was originally made with and without sound. **64m/B VHS, Beta.** Ricardo Cortez, Nancy Welford, Henry B. Walthall, Grace Valentine; **D:** Phil Rosen. *SNC*

Phantom Killer 🌑🌑 1942 A district attorney tries to hang a murder rap on a most improbable suspect. When the man is aquitted, the DA quits his job to find the truth, which takes a disturbing twist. The plot is a thinly veiled rehash of "The Sphinx" (1933). **61m/B VHS.** Dick Purcell, Joan Woodbury, John Hamilton, Warren Hymer, Kenneth Harlan, J. Farrell MacDonald, Mantan Moreland; **D:** William Beaudine. *NOS*

Phantom Lady 🌑🌑🌑 1944 After an argument with his wife Scott Henderson (Curtis) walks into a bar and chats up a mystery woman (Helm). When he returns home, the police are there and his wife has been strangled with his necktie. Since he doesn't know his bar mate's name and no one professes to remember her, Scott is quickly convicted of the crime. Only his loyal secretary Carol (Raines) believes him and she sets out to solve the crime. Based on the novel by Cornell Woolrich. **87m/B VHS.** Ella Raines, Alan Curtis, Franchot Tone, Thomas Gomez, Elisha Cook Jr., Fay Helm, Aurora Miranda, Andrew Tombes, Regis Toomey, Joseph Crehan, Virginia Brissac, Gordon Oliver; **W:** Bernard C. Schoenfeld; **C:** Woody Bredell. *USH*

The Phantom Light 🌑🌑½ 1935 A lighthouse keeper is murdered under strange circumstances and a mysterious light keeps appearing at the scene. Detective Hale joins up with a navy man and another lighthouse keeper to solve the crime. A low-budget mystery with good atmosphere and some humor. **75m/B VHS.** GB Binnie Hale, Gordon Harker, Ian Hunter, Donald Calthrop; **D:** Michael Powell. *HCV*

Phantom of Chinatown 🌑 1940 Mr. Wong is called in to solve another murder in the final entry in the series. The first to have an Asian actor portray the lead, as Luke replaced Boris Karloff. **61m/B VHS.** Keye Luke, Lotus Long, Grant Withers, Paul McVey, Charles Miller; **D:** Phil Rosen. *NOS, SNC, HEG*

Phantom of Death 🌑½ 1987 (R) A brilliant pianist, stricken by a fatal disease that causes rapid aging, goes on a murderous rampage. **95m/C VHS, Beta.** IT Michael York, Donald Pleasence, Edwige Fenech; **D:** Ruggero Deodato; **M:** Pino Donaggio. *THV*

The Phantom of 42nd Street 🌑🌑 1945 An actor and a cop team up to find the killer of a wealthy uncle. **58m/B VHS.** Dave O'Brien, Kay Aldridge, Alan Mowbray, Frank Jenks; **D:** Al(bert) Herman. *SNC, NOS, MRV*

Phantom of Liberty 🌑🌑🌑½ *Le Fantome de la Liberte; The Specter of Freedom* 1974 Master surrealist Bunuel's episodic film wanders from character to character and from event to event. Animals wander through a man's bedroom, soldiers conduct military exercises in an inhabited area, a missing girl stands before her parents even as they futilely attempt to determine her whereabouts, and an assassin is found guilty, then applauded and led to freedom. They don't get much more surreal than this. If you think you may like it, you'll probably love it. Bunuel, by the way, is among the firing squad vicitms in the film's opening enactment of Goya's May 3, 1808. In French with English subtitles. **104m/C VHS, Beta, LV.** FR Adriana Asti, Jean-Claude Brialy, Michel Piccoli, Adolfo Celi, Monica Vitti, Milena Vukotic, Michel Lonsdale, Claude Pieplu, Julien Bertheau, Paul Frankeur, Paul Leperson, Bernard Verley; **D:** Luis Bunuel; **W:** Luis Bunuel, Jean-Claude Carrière; **C:** Edmond Richard. *XVC*

The Phantom of Soho 🌑🌑 *Das Phantom von Soho* 1964 A Scotland Yard detective investigates the murders of several prominent businessmen and is assisted by a beautiful mystery writer. **92m/B VHS, Beta.** GE Dieter Borsche, Barbara Rutting, Hans Sohnker, Peter Vogel, Helga Sommerfeld, Werner Peters; **D:** Franz Gottlieb. *SNC*

Phantom of the Air 1933 Twelve chapters of high-flying adventure with Tom Tyler! **230m/B VHS.** Tom Tyler, Gloria Shea, William Desmond, Leroy Mason, Walter Brennan; **D:** Ray Taylor. *GPV, MLB*

Phantom of the Mall: Eric's Revenge 🌑 1989 A murderous spirit haunts the local mall. Gore flows like water. **91m/C VHS, Beta, LV.** Morgan Fairchild, Kari Whitman, Jonathan Goldsmith, Derek Rydell; **D:** Richard S. Friedman.

The Phantom of the Opera 🌑🌑🌑 1925 Deranged, disfigured music lover haunts the sewers of a Parisian opera house and kills to further the career of an unsuspecting young soprano. First of many film versions still packs a wallop, with fine playing from Chaney, Sr. Silent with two-color Technicolor "Bal Masque" sequence. Versions with different running times are also available, including 79 and 88 minutes. **101m/B VHS, LV.** Lon Chaney Sr., Norman Kerry, Mary Philbin, Gibson Gowland, Arthur Edmund Carewe, Snitz Edwards; **D:** Rupert Julian; **W:** Elliot J. Clawson, Raymond L. Schrock; **C:** Virgil Miller. *KIV, NOS, FUS*

The Phantom of the Opera 🌑🌑🌑 1943 Second Hollywood version—the first with talking—of Gastron Leroux novel about a madman who promotes fear and mayhem at a Paris opera house. Raines is good in lead; Eddy warbles away. **92m/C VHS, Beta, LV.** Nelson Eddy, Susanna Foster, Claude Rains, Edgar Barrier, Leo Carrillo, Hume Cronyn, J. Edward Bromberg; **D:** Arthur Lubin; **W:** Samuel Hoffenstein, Eric Taylor; **C:** Hal Mohr, William Howard Greene. Academy Awards '43: Best Color Cinematography, Best Interior Decoration; Nominations: Academy Awards '43: Best Sound, Scoring of a Musical. *USH*

The Phantom of the Opera 🌑🌑½ 1962 Hammer version of the Gaston Leroux novel transfers the action from Paris to London but keeps the basic story of a young singer (Sears) and her masked benefactor (Lom), who lives in the sewers beneath the opera house. There's also the wimpy fiance (De Souza) to come between them. Good gothic melodrama. Sears' singing was dubbed by opera performer Pat Clark; producer Hinds used the pseudonym John Elder for his screenplay. **85m/C VHS, Closed Caption.** Herbert Lom, Heather Sears, Edward De Souza, Thorley Walters, Michael Gough, Martin Miller, Ian Wilson; **D:** Terence Fisher; **W:** Anthony John Elder Hinds; **C:** Arthur Grant; **M:** Edwin Astley. *USH*

The Phantom of the Opera 🌑½ 1989 (R) A gory, "Elm Street"-ish version of the Gaston Leroux classic, attempting to cash in on the success of the Broadway musical. **93m/C VHS, Beta, LV, Closed Caption.** Robert Englund, Jill Schoelen, Alex Hyde-White, Bill Nighy, Terence Harvey, Stephanie Lawrence; **D:** Dwight Little; **W:** Duke Sandefur; **C:** Elemer Ragaly. *COL*

The Phantom of the Opera 🌑🌑½ 1990 Yet another version of the tragic tale of a disfigured mask-wearing opera lover, who lurks in the depths of the Paris Opera House, and his desire for lovely young singer, Christine. Dance plays the Phantom as doomed romantic, with Lancaster his protective father. Kopit adapted from his 1983 play. Made for TV drama, originally shown in two parts. **200m/C VHS.** GB Charles Dance, Burt Lancaster, Teri Polo, Ian Richardson, Andrea Ferreol, Adam Storke, Jean-Pierre Cassel; **D:** Tony Richardson; **W:** Arthur Kopit; **M:** John Addison. *AVE*

Phantom of the Paradise 🌑🌑 1974 (PG) A rock 'n' roll parody of "Phantom of the Opera." Splashy, only occasionally horrific spoof in which cruel music executive Williams, much to his everlasting regret, swindles a songwriter. Violence ensues. Not for most, or even many, tastes. Graham steals the film as rocker Beef. A failure at the boxoffice, and now a cult item (small enthusiastic cult with few outside interests) for its oddball humor and outrageous rock star parodies. Williams also wrote the turgid score. 🎵Goodbye, Eddie, Goodbye; Faust; Upholstery; Special to Me; Old Souls; Somebody Super Like You; Life At Last; The Hell of It; The Phantom's Theme (Beauty and the Beast). **92m/C VHS, Beta, LV.** Paul Williams, William Finley, Jessica Harper, Gerrit Graham; **D:** Brian DePalma; **W:** Brian DePalma; **M:** Paul Williams. Nominations: Academy Awards '74: Original Song Score and/or Adaptation. *FOX*

The Phantom of the Range 🌑½ 1938 Marion is trying to sell her grandfather's ranch only his "ghost" is scaring everyone away. She and cowpoke Tyler find out a group of evil treasure hunters are searching the property for hidden gold. **59m/B VHS.** Tom Tyler, Beth Marion, Charles "Blackie" King, Forrest Taylor, John Elliott, Soledad Jiminez, Sammy Cohen; **D:** Robert F. "Bob" Hill. *GPV*

Phantom of the Ritz 🌑🌑 1988 (R) Bizarre accidents begin to take place when Ed Blake and his girlfriend start renovating the old Ritz Theatre. It seems the theatre is inhabited by a rather angry ghost and somebody's got to deal with it before the Ritz can rock and roll. Features the fabulous sounds of the '50s. **89m/C VHS, Beta, Closed Caption.** Peter Bergman, Deborah Van Valkenburgh; **D:** Allen Plone.

Phantom of the West 🌑🌑 1931 Ten-episode serial about a rancher who becomes "The Phantom of the West" in order to smoke out his father's killer. **166m/B VHS, Beta.** William Desmond, Thomas Santschi, Tom Tyler; **D:** David Ross Lederman. *VYY, NOS, VCN*

Phantom Patrol 🌑½ 1936 A mystery writer is kidnapped and someone impersonates him. Mountie Maynard must come to the rescue. **60m/B VHS, Beta.** Kermit Maynard, Joan Barclay, Paul Fix, Julian Rivero, Eddie Phillips, Roger Williams; **D:** Charles Hutchinson. *DVT, NOS*

The Phantom Planet 🌑½ 1961 An astronaut crash-lands on an asteroid and discovers a race of tiny people living there. Having breathed the atmosphere, he shrinks to their dimunitive size and aids them in their war against brutal invaders. Infamously peculiar. **82m/B VHS, Beta.** Dean Fredericks, Coleen Gray, Tony Dexter, Dolores Faith, Francis X. Bushman, Richard Kiel; **D:** William Marshall. *NOS, SNC*

Phantom Rancher 🌑½ 1939 Roaring melodrama finds Maynard donning a mask to find the real Phantom, who is causing havoc. **61m/B VHS, Beta.** Ken Maynard. *VCI, VCN*

Phantom Ranger 🌑½ 1938 A federal agent masquerades as a crook to catch a band of counterfeiters. **54m/B VHS.** Tim McCoy, Suzanne Kaaren, Karl Hackett, John St. Polis, John Merton, Harry Strang; **D:** Sam Newfield. *NOS, DVT*

The Phantom Rider 1937 Mystery fills the old West in this serial composed of 15 chapters. **152m/B VHS, Beta.** Buck Jones, Marla Shelton. *REP, MLB, VCN*

The Phantom Rider 🌑½ 1946 The masked do-gooder rides the plains protecting the local Indians from some surly settlers. A 12-episode serial. **167m/C VHS.** Robert Kent, Peggy Stewart, Leroy Mason, Chief Thundercloud. *MOV*

Phantom Thunderbolt �½ **1933** A man who has falsely spread the rumor that he's a gunfighter is hired to chase away some good-for-nothings. **62m/B VHS, Beta.** Ken Maynard, Frances Lee, Frank Rice, William Gould, Robert F. (Bob) Kortman; *D:* Alan James. *NOS, DVT, MTX*

Phantom Tollbooth ✶✶✶ **1969 (G)** A young boy drives his car into an animated world, where the numbers are at war with the letters and he has been chosen to save Rhyme and Reason, to bring stability back to the Land of Wisdom. Completely unique and typically Jonesian in its intellectual level and interests. Bright children will be interested, but this is really for adults who will understand the allegory. Based on Norman Justers' metaphorical novel. **89m/C VHS, Beta.** *D:* Chuck Jones; *V:* Mel Blanc, Hans Conried. *MGM*

Phantom 2040 Movie: The Ghost Who Walks ✶✶½ **1995** Teenager Kit Walker discovers his destiny when a mysterious stranger tells him about his late father and how Kit must carry on his father's legacy as a superhero called the Phantom. A purple suit renders Kit invisible and he finds himself battling his dad's old nemesis, Rebecca Madison, who's out to destroy the Earth's resources. Based on the television and comic book series. **97m/C VHS.** *V:* Scott Valentine, Margot Kidder, Ron Perlman, Carrie Snodgress, Mark Hamill. *FHE, ART*

Phantoms ✶ **1997 (R)** Dr. Jennifer Pailey (Going) and her sister Lisa (McGowan) arrive in a Colorado resort town and discover that the entire population has been wiped out by a mysterious force. They team up with local sheriff Hammond (Affleck) and his odd deputy (Schrieber) to battle the evil force thingie, which also seems to have an adverse affect on acting ability. Peter O'Toole appears as an expert on ancient plagues, and to show the rest of the cast what a real actor looks like. Schrieber plays the part of the squirmy deputy very well, but the rest of the characters are cheap plywood. Will they stop the amorphous monster who is taking over the corpses of its victims? Will they remember their lines if someone drops the cue card? Based on the novel by Dean Koontz, who also adapted it for the screen and produced.*CW:* Sci-fi violence/gore and language. **95m/C** Peter O'Toole, Joanna Going, Rose McGowan, Ben Affleck, Liev Schreiber, Nicky Katt, Clifton Powell; *D:* Joe Chappelle; *W:* Dean Koontz; *C:* Richard Clabaugh; *M:* David Williams. *NYR*

Phar Lap ✶✶½ *Phar Lap: Heart of a Nation* **1984 (PG)** Saga of a legendary Australian racehorse who rose from obscurity to win nearly 40 races in just three years before mysteriously dying in 1932. American version runs 10 minutes shorter than the Aussie one. **107m/C VHS, Beta, Closed Caption.** *AU* Ron Leibman, Tom Burlinson, Judy Morris, Celia de Burgh; *D:* Simon Wincer; *W:* David Williamson; *C:* Russell Boyd. *FOX*

Pharaoh ✶✶ **1966** An expensive Polish epic about the power plays of royalty in ancient Egypt. Dubbed. **125m/B VHS, Beta.** *PL* Jerzy Zelnick; *D:* Jerzy Kawalerowicz. *FCT*

Pharmacist ✶✶½ **1932** A day in the life of a hapless druggist undone by disgruntled customers and robbers. Typical Fields effort. **19m/B VHS, Beta.** Elise Cavanna, Babe Kane, W.C. Fields, Grady Sutton. *CCB*

Pharoah's Army ✶✶½ **1995 (PG-13)** Five Union soldiers are foraging for food at a small Kentucky farm when one young soldier (Fox) is badly injured and his captain, John Abston (Cooper), is forced to stay put while he treats the wounds. The farm is home to Sarah Anders (Clarkson) and her young son (Lucas), while her husband is off fighting for the Confederates. Sarah isn't happy about the arrangement but the decent Alston, a farmer himself in peacetime, begins slowly to win her over. Their friendship, however, doesn't sit well with either his men nor Sarah's son. Fine performances in a restrained dra-

ma.*CW:* Brief violence and sexual references. **90m/C VHS.** Chris Cooper, Patricia Clarkson, Kris Kristofferson, Richard Tyson, Huckleberry Fox, Will Lucas; *D:* Robby Henson; *W:* Robby Henson; *C:* Doron Schlair. *ORI*

Phase 4 ✶✶ **1974 (PG)** A tale of killer ants retaliating against the humans attempting to exterminate them. **84m/C VHS, Beta, LV.** Nigel Davenport, Michael Murphy, Lynne Frederick; *D:* Saul Bass. *PAR*

Phat Beach ✶✶½ **1996 (R)** Generic but basically harmless buddies-at-the-beach comedy with a hip-hop beat. Fast-talking, slickster Durrell (Hooks) manipulates sensitive, overweight pal Benny (Hopkins, who's real life nickname is "Huggy") into emptying his savings, "borrowing" his dad's Mercedes convertible, and taking off for some Southern California fun. Scores of scantily clad beach bunnies aren't the only ones threadbare—so's the whole premise of this flick—but that's not the point of this lighthearted romp. The likable Hopkins/Hooks comedy team is a hit with precise, lowbrow humor. Coolio, prominent in the ads, is barely window dressing with minimal screen time. Kickin' soundtrack includes E-40, Biz Markie, and SugaT featuring The Click.*CW:* Sexuality, nudity and strong language. **99m/C VHS.** Jermaine Hopkins, Brian Hooks, Jennifer Lucienne, Claudia Kaleem, Gregg D. Vance, Tommy (Tiny) Lister, Erick Fleeks, Alma Collins, Candice Merideth, Sabrina De Pina; *Cameos:* Coolio; *D:* Doug Ellin; *W:* Doug Ellin, Brian E. O'Neal, Ben Morris; *C:* Jurgen Baum; *M:* Paul Stewart. *ART*

Phedre ✶✶½ **1968** Jean Racine's adaptation of the Greek legend involving Phedre, Theseus, and Hippolyte. Bell is the only one worth watching in this weak and stagy picture. In French with English subtitles. **93m/C VHS, Beta.** Marie Bell; *D:* Pierre Jourdan. *VYY*

Phenomenal and the Treasure of Tutankamen ✶✶ **1977 (R)** Fiendish criminal genius steals priceless golden mask of King Tut. Superhero Phenomenal is less than dry spaghetti sci-fi. **90m/C VHS.** *IT* Mauro Parenti, Lucretia Love. *NO*

Phenomenon ✶✶½ **1996 (PG)** Average small town schmoe George Malley (Travolta) is turned into a genius when he's struck by a bright light on his 37th birthday. This development brings him to the attention of the scientific community and, of course, the military. The locals scorn him, thus fulfilling the Hollywood stereotype of rural folks fearing anything they don't understand. Good-natured weeper plays the Gump card (but turns too paranoid) and wins as Travolta gets to be the nice guy, while attractive Sedgwick is fine as romantic interest Lace. **123m/C VHS, LV, Closed Caption.** John Travolta, Robert Duvall, Kyra Sedgwick, Forest Whitaker, Richard Kiley, Brent Spiner; *D:* Jon Turteltaub; *W:* Phedon Papamichael; *M:* Thomas Newman. Nominations: MTV Movie Awards '97: Best Male Performance (Travolta), Best Song ("Change the World"), Best Kiss (John Travolta/Kyra Sedgwick). *TOU*

Phffft! ✶✶½ **1954** Holliday and Lemmon are a bored couple who decide to divorce, date others, and take mambo lessons. By no stretch of plausibility, they constantly run into each other and compete in the same mambo contest. **91m/B VHS.** Judy Holliday, Jack Lemmon, Jack Carson, Kim Novak, Luella Gear, Merry Anders; *D:* Mark Robson; *W:* George Axelrod; *C:* Charles B(ryant) Lang. *GKK*

Philadelphia ✶✶✶½ **1993 (PG-13)** AIDS goes Hollywood as hot-shot corporate attorney Andrew Beckett (Hanks), fired because he has the disease, hires brilliant but homophobic personal injury attorney Washington as his counsel when he sues for discrimination. Boxoffice winner was criticized by some gay activists as too mainstream, which is the point. It doesn't probe deeply into the gay lifestyle, focusing instead on justice and compassion. Boasts a good script, make-up that transforms Hanks, sure direction, great soundtrack, and a strong supporting cast, but all would mean little without Hanks' superb performance, his best to date. ♫Streets of Philadelphia. **125m/C VHS, LV, 8mm, Closed Caption.** Tom Hanks,

Denzel Washington, Antonio Banderas, Jason Robards Jr., Joanne Woodward, Mary Steenburgen, Ron Vawter, Robert Ridgely, Obba Babatunde, Robert Castle, Daniel Chapman, Roger Corman, John Bedford Lloyd, Roberta Maxwell, Warren Miller, Anna Deavere Smith, Kathryn Witt, Andre B. Blake, Ann Dowd, Bradley Whitford, Chandra Wilson, Charles Glenn, Peter Jacobs, Paul Lazar, Dan Olmstead, Joey Perillo, Lauren Roselli, Bill Rowe, Lisa Talerico, Daniel von Bargen, Tracey Walter; *Cameos:* Karen Finley, David Drake, Quentin Crisp; *D:* Jonathan Demme; *W:* Ron Nyswaner; *C:* Tak Fujimoto; *M:* Howard Shore. Academy Awards '93: Best Actor (Hanks), Best Song ("Streets of Philadelphia"); Berlin International Film Festival '94: Best Actor (Hanks); Golden Globe Awards '94: Best Actor—Drama (Hanks), Best Song ("Streets of Philadelphia"); MTV Movie Awards '94: Best Male Performance (Hanks); Blockbuster Entertainment Awards '95: Drama Actor, Video (Hanks); Nominations: Academy Awards '93: Best Makeup, Best Original Screenplay, Best Song ("Philadelphia"); Golden Globe Awards '94: Best Screenplay; MTV Movie Awards '94: Best Film, Best On-Screen Duo (Tom Hanks/Denzel Washington), Best Song ("Streets of Philadelphia"); Writers Guild of America '93: Best Original Screenplay. *COL*

The Philadelphia Experiment ✶✶½ **1984 (PG)** A WWII sailor falls through a hole in time and lands in the mid-1980s, whereupon he woos a gorgeous woman. Sufficient chemistry between Pare and Allen, but PG rating is an indication of the film's less-than-graphic love scenes. **101m/C VHS, Beta, LV.** Michael Pare, Nancy Allen, Eric Christmas, Bobby DiCicco; *D:* Stewart Raffill; *W:* Don Jakoby. *VTR*

Philadelphia Experiment 2 ✶✶½ **1993 (PG-13)** Melodramatic sci-fi what-ifer has Germany winning WWII by dropping a bomb on Washington. So southern California is now one big labor camp with an evil mad scientist (Graham) and a beleaguered hero (Johnson) who must time-travel back to 1943 to prevent the Germans from dropping that bomb. **98m/C VHS, LV, Closed Caption.** Brad Johnson, Gerrit Graham, Marjean Holden, James Greene, Geoffrey Blake, John Christian Grass, Cyril O'Reilly; *D:* Stephen Cornwell; *W:* Kevin Rock, Nick Paine; *M:* Gerald Gouriet. *THV*

The Philadelphia Story ✶✶✶✶ **1940** A woman's plans to marry again go awry when her dashing ex-husband arrives on the scene. Matters are further complicated when a loopy reporter—assigned to spy on the nuptials—falls in love with the blushing bride. Classic comedy, with trio of Hepburn, Grant, and Stewart all serving aces. Based on the hit Broadway play by Philip Barry, and remade as the musical "High Society" in 1956 (stick to the original). Also available colorized. **112m/B VHS, Beta, LV.** Katharine Hepburn, Cary Grant, James Stewart, Ruth Hussey, Roland Young, John Howard, John Halliday, Virginia Weidler, Henry Daniell, Hillary Brooke, Mary Nash; *D:* George Cukor; *W:* Donald Ogden Stewart; *C:* Joseph Ruttenberg; *M:* Franz Waxman. Academy Awards '40: Best Actor (Stewart), Best Screenplay, National Film Registry '95;; New York Film Critics Awards '40: Best Actress (Hepburn); Nominations: Academy Awards '40: Best Actress (Hepburn), Best Director (Cukor), Best Picture, Best Supporting Actress (Hussey). *MGM, BTV, HMV*

Philby, Burgess and MacLean: Spy Scandal of the Century ✶✶½ **1984** The true story of the three infamous British officials who defected to the Soviet Union in 1951, after stealing some vital British secrets for the KGB. **83m/C VHS, Beta.** *GB* Derek Jacobi, Anthony Bate, Michael Culver; *D:* Gordon Flemyng. *BFA*

Phobia WOOF! **1980 (R)** Patients at a hospital are mysteriously being murdered. Stupid and unpleasant story that lasts too long and probably should never have started. **91m/C VHS, Beta, Closed Caption.** *CA* Paul Michael Glaser, Susan Hogan; *D:* John Huston; *W:* Peter Bellwood, Lew Lehman, Gary Sherman, Ronald Shusett, Jimmy Sangster. *PAR*

Phoenix ✶½ **1978** Aging queen summons her marksman to find the Phoenix, a mythical bird that she believes will bring her eternal life. With English subtitles. **137m/C VHS, Beta.** *JP* Tatsuya Nakadai, Tomisaburo Wakayama, Raoru Yumi, Reiko Ohara. *VDA*

Phoenix 🐾🐾 1995 The Titus 4 deep-space outpost has problems when the creators of a killing machine are targeted for death by their creation, which has begun to think for itself. **94m/C VHS.** Stephen Nichols, Billy Drago, William Sanderson, Brad Dourif; **D:** Troy Cook; **W:** Troy Cook, Jimmy Lifton. *MNC*

The Phoenix and the Magic Carpet 🐾🐾½ 1995 (PG) Visiting England to settle her father's estate, Mrs. Wilson and her three children discover an egg from which a phoenix emerges. This mythical firebird proceeds to take the children on a magic adventure. Adapted from the book by Edith Nesbit. **80m/C VHS, Closed Caption.** Dee Wallace Stone, Timothy Hegeman, Nick Klein, Laura Kamrath, Peter Ustinov; **D:** Zoran Perisic; **W:** Florence Fox; **M:** Alan Parker. *PAR*

Phoenix Team 🐾 1980 Two agents discover their mutual attraction can be deadly in the spy business. **90m/C VHS, Beta.** Don Francks, Elizabeth Shepherd. *TWE*

Phoenix the Ninja 🐾 198? A young girl grows up to be a ninja warrior and battles everyone who would stoop to impede her. **92m/C VHS, Beta.** Sho Kosugi. *TWE*

Phoenix the Warrior 🐾 1988 Sometime in the future, female savages battle each other for control of the now ravaged earth. A newcomer seeks the tribe most worthy of receiving the last man on the planet, thereby continuing the human race. **90m/C VHS.** Persis Khambatta, James H. Emery, Peggy Sands, Kathleen Kinmont; **D:** Robert Hayes. *NO*

The Phone Call 🐾🐾 1989 (R) 900-number morality tale about high-powered executive who calls phone sex line and is connected with escaped homicidal maniac who takes a toll on him and his family. **CW:** Menacing violence. **95m/C VHS.** Michael Sarrazin, Linda Smith, Ron Lea, Lisa Jakub; **D:** Allan Goldstein. *NO*

Phone Call from a Stranger 🐾🐾½ 1952 After a plane crash, a survivor visits the families of three of the victims whom he met during the flight. **96m/B VHS, Beta, Closed Caption.** Bette Davis, Gary Merrill, Michael Rennie, Shelley Winters, Hugh Beaumont, Keenan Wynn, Eve Arden, Craig Stevens; **D:** Jean Negulesco; **W:** Nunnally Johnson; **C:** Milton Krasner. *FOX*

Photographer 🐾 1975 (PG) A photographer turns into a murderer, showing the negative side of his personality. **94m/C VHS, Beta.** Michael Callan; **D:** William B. Hillman. *NLC*

Physical Evidence 🐾🐾 1989 (R) A lawyer finds herself falling for an ex-cop turned murder suspect while she tries to defend him for a crime he doesn't remember committing. **99m/C VHS, Beta, LV, Closed Caption.** Burt Reynolds, Theresa Russell, Ned Beatty, Kay Lenz, Ted McGinley; **D:** Michael Crichton; **W:** Bill Phillips; **C:** John A. Alonzo; **M:** Henry Mancini. *ART, VES, HHE*

Pi 🐾🐾 1998 Definitely a first—a religious/mathematical thriller about a man obsessed with decoding the real name of God. Max (Gullette) is a genius mathematician who believes everything can be understood in terms of numbers, so he works on his homebuilt supercomputer to unravel the stock market. Max begins to suffer hallucinations and blackouts just as his work draws the interest of both a high-powered Wall Street firm and a Hasidic cabalistic sect. **85m/B VHS.** Sean Gullette, Mark Margolis, Ben Shenkman, Pamela Hart; **D:** Darren Aronofsky; **W:** Darren Aronofsky; **C:** Matthew Libatique; **M:** Clint Mansell. Sundance Film Festival '98: Best Director (Aronofsky). *NYR*

P.I. Private Investigations 🐾 1987 (R) Corrupt, drug-dealing cops stalk another cop who can finger them. **91m/C VHS, Beta.** Martin Balsam. *FOX*

Piaf 1981 (PG) Musical drama chronicles the life of Edith Piaf, France's legendary singer of the Roaring '20s. Her rise from the streets, bout with temporary blindness, and many self-destructive

attempts at experiencing life are retold in music. 111m/B VHS, Beta. Jane Lapotaire. *FOX*

The Piano 🐾🐾🐾½ 1993 (R) In the 1850s, Ada (Hunter), a mute Scottish widow with a young daughter, agrees to an arranged marriage with Stewart (Neill), a colonial landowner in New Zealand. The way she expresses her feelings is by playing her cherished piano, left behind on the beach by her new husband. Another settler, George (Keitel), buys it, arranges for lessons with Ada, and soon the duo begin a grand passion leading to a cruelly calculated revenge. Fiercely poetic and well acted (with Keitel in a notably romantic role), though the film may be too dark and intense for some. Fine original score with Hunter doing her own piano playing. **CW:** Extremely graphic sexuality. **120m/C VHS, LV, Closed Caption, DVD.** AU Holly Hunter, Harvey Keitel, Sam Neill, Anna Paquin, Kerry Walker, Genevieve Lemon; **D:** Jane Campion; **W:** Jane Campion; **C:** Stuart Dryburgh; **M:** Michael Nyman. Academy Awards '93: Best Actress (Hunter), Best Original Screenplay, Best Supporting Actress (Paquin); Australian Film Institute '93: Best Actor (Keitel), Best Actress (Hunter), Best Cinematography, Best Costume Design, Best Director (Campion), Best Film, Best Film Editing, Best Screenplay, Best Sound, Best Score; British Academy Awards '93: Best Actress (Hunter), Cannes Film Festival '93: Best Actress (Hunter), Best Film; Golden Globe Awards '94: Best Actress—Drama (Hunter); Independent Spirit Awards '94: Best Foreign Film; Los Angeles Film Critics Association Awards '93: Best Actress (Hunter), Best Cinematography, Best Director (Campion), Best Screenplay, Best Supporting Actress (Paquin); National Board of Review Awards '93: Best Actress (Hunter); New York Film Critics Awards '93: Best Actress (Hunter), Best Director (Campion), Best Screenplay; National Society of Film Critics Awards '93: Best Actress (Hunter), Best Screenplay; Writers Guild of America '93: Best Original Screenplay; Nominations: Academy Awards '93: Best Cinematography, Best Costume Design, Best Director (Campion), Best Film Editing, Best Picture; British Academy Awards '94: Best Director (Campion), Best Film, Best Original Screenplay, Best Score; Directors Guild of America Awards '93: Best Director (Campion); Golden Globe Awards '94: Best Director (Campion), Best Film—Drama, Best Screenplay, Best Supporting Actress (Paquin), Best Score. *ART*

A Piano for Mrs. Cimino 🐾🐾🐾 1982 Declared senile and incompetent, a widowed woman fights for control of her own life. Good script helps this made for TV soaper. **100m/C VHS, Beta.** Bette Davis, Keenan Wynn, Alexa Kenin, Penny Fuller, Christopher Guest, George Hearn; **D:** George Schaefer; **M:** James Horner. *GEM*

The Piano Lesson 🐾🐾🐾 1994 (PG) The prized heirloom of the Charles family is an 80-year-old, ornately carved upright piano, jealously guarded by widowed Berniece (Woodard), and housed in the Pittsburgh home of Uncle Doaker (Gordon). When Berniece's brother Willie Boy (Dutton) visits from Mississippi, it's to persuade her to sell the piano in order to buy some land that their grandfather had worked on as a slave. But the past, carved into the piano's panels, has a strong hold—one that Berniece refuses to give up. Set in 1936. Adaptation by Wilson of his 1990 Pulitzer Prize-winning play. **99m/C VHS, LV, Closed Caption.** Alfre Woodard, Charles S. Dutton, Courtney B. Vance, Carl Gordon, Tommy Hollis, Zelda Harris, Lou Myers, Rosalyn Coleman, Tommy La Fitte; **D:** Lloyd Richards; **W:** August Wilson; **M:** Stephen James Taylor, Dwight Andrews. *REP*

Picasso Trigger 🐾🐾 1989 (R) An American spy tries to catch an elusive murderer. The sequel to "Hard Ticket to Hawaii" and "Malibu Express." **99m/C VHS.** Steve Bond, Dona Speir, John Aprea, Hope Marie Carlton, Guich Koock, Roberta Vasquez, Bruce Penhall; **D:** Andy Sidaris. *WAR*

Pick a Star 🐾🐾 *Movie Struck* 1937 Lawrence is a small-town girl who wins a contest and is off to Hollywood. Only no one pays any attention to her except for publicity man Haley, who arranges her screen test. Naturally, she knocks the studio bosses for a loop and becomes a star. Laurel & Hardy are featured in a couple of comedy segments showing the newcomer some backstage

silliness and movie business on the set of a Western they're filming with Finlayson, better known as a director, cast as the duo's director). **70m/B VHS.** Rosina Lawrence, Jack Haley, Patsy Kelly, Mischa Auer, Stan Laurel, Oliver Hardy, Charles Halton, Tom Dugan, Russell Hicks, James Finlayson; **D:** Edward Sedgwick. *MGM, NOS, CAB*

The Pick-Up Artist 🐾🐾½ 1987 (PG-13) The adventures of a compulsive Don Juan who finds he genuinely loves the daughter of an alcoholic who's in debt to the mob. Standard story with no surprises. **81m/C VHS, Beta, LV, Closed Caption.** Robert Downey Jr., Molly Ringwald, Dennis Hopper, Harvey Keitel, Danny Aiello, Vanessa L(ynne) Williams, Robert Towne, Mildred Dunnock, Lorraine Bracco, Joe Spinell, Victoria Jackson, Polly Draper, Brian Hamill; **D:** James Toback; **W:** James Toback; **C:** Gordon Willis; **M:** Georges Delerue. *FOX*

Pick-Up Summer 🐾 *Pinball Summer; Pinball Pick-Up* 1979 (R) Two suburban boys cruise their town after school lets out, chasing a pair of voluptuous sisters. **99m/C VHS, Beta.** CA Michael Zelniker, Carl Marotte; **D:** George Mihalka.

The Pickle 🐾 1993 (R) Self-indulgent comedy about a midlife crisis. Aiello stars as a middle-aged manic-depressive director certain that his new film is going to be an abysmal flop (as have all his recent pictures). He seeks comfort and reassurance from various ex-wives, children, lovers, and others, though he abuses them all. This dispirited tale also shows clips of the director's dreadful film about children who launch a giant pickle into space. It couldn't possibly be worse that what Mazursky actually put up on the screen. **CW:** Some language and sexual scene. **103m/C VHS, LV, Letterbox, Closed Caption.** Danny Aiello, Dyan Cannon, Clothilde Courau, Shelley Winters, Barry Miller, Jerry Stiller, Christopher Penn, Rebecca Miller; **Cameos:** Ally Sheedy, Little Richard, Spalding Gray, Griffin Dunne, Isabella Rossellini, Dudley Moore; **D:** Paul Mazursky; **W:** Paul Mazursky; **M:** Michel Legrand. *COL*

Pickpocket 🐾🐾🐾½ 1959 Slow moving, documentary-like account of a petty thief's existence is a moral tragedy inspired by "Crime and Punishment." Ending is particularly moving. Classic filmmaking from Bresson, France's master of austerity. In French with English subtitles. **75m/B VHS.** FR Martin LaSalle, Marika Green, Pierre Leymarie; **D:** Robert Bresson. *NYF, FCT, TPV*

Pickup on South Street 🐾🐾🐾 1953 Petty thief Widmark lifts woman's wallet only to find it contains top secret Communist micro-film for which pinko agents will stop at nothing to get back. Intriguing look at the politics of the day. The creme of "B" movies. **80m/B VHS, Beta.** Richard Widmark, Jean Peters, Thelma Ritter, Murvyn Vye, Richard Kiley, Milburn Stone; **D:** Samuel Fuller; **W:** Samuel Fuller. Nominations: Academy Awards '53: Best Supporting Actress (Ritter). *FOX, FCT*

The Pickwick Papers 🐾🐾½ 1954 Comedy based on the Dickens classic wherein Mrs. Bardell sues the Pickwick Club for breach of promise. **109m/B VHS, Beta.** GB James Hayter, James Donald, Nigel Patrick, Hermione Gingold, Hermione Baddeley, Kathleen Harrison; **D:** Noel Langley. Nominations: Academy Awards '55: Best Costume Design (B & W). *VCI*

Picnic 🐾🐾🐾½ 1955 A wanderer arrives in a small town and immediately wins the love of his friend's girl. The other women in town seem interested too. Strong, romantic work, with Holden excelling in the lead. Novak provides a couple pointers too. Lavish Hollywood adaptation of the William Inge play, including the popular tune "Moonglow/Theme from Picnic." **113m/C VHS, Beta, LV, Letterbox.** William Holden, Kim Novak, Rosalind Russell, Susan Strasberg, Arthur O'Connell, Cliff Robertson, Betty Field, Verna Felton, Reta Shaw, Nick Adams, Phyllis Newman, Raymond Bailey; **D:** Joshua Logan; **W:** Daniel Taradash; **C:** James Wong Howe; **M:** George Duning. Academy Awards '55: Best Art Direction/Set Decoration (Color), Best Film Editing; Golden Globe Awards '56: Best Director (Logan); Nominations: Academy Awards '55: Best Director (Logan), Best Picture, Best Supporting Actor (O'Connell), Best Original Dramatic/Comedy Score. *COL*

Picnic at Hanging Rock 🐾🐾🐾 1975
(PG) School outing in 1900 into a mountainous region ends tragically when three girls disappear. Eerie film is strong on atmosphere, as befits mood master Weir. Lambert is extremely photogenic—and suitable subdued—as one of the girls to disappear. Otherwise beautifully photographed on location. From the novel by Joan Lindsey. **110m/C VHS, Beta.** *AU* Margaret Nelson, Rachel Roberts, Dominic Guard, Helen Morse, Jacki Weaver, Vivean Gray, Anne Lambert; **D:** Peter Weir; **C:** Russell Boyd; **M:** Bruce Smeaton. *FCT*

Picnic on the Grass 🐾🐾 *Le Dejeuner sur l'Herbe; Lunch on the Grass* 1959 A strange, whimsical fantasy heavily evocative of the director's Impressionist roots; a science-minded candidate for the president of Europe throws a picnic as public example of his earthiness, and falls in love with a peasant girl. In French with English subtitles. **92m/C VHS, Beta.** *FR* Paul Meurisse, Catherine Rouvel, Fernand Sardou, Jacqueline Morane, Jean-Pierre Granval; **D:** Jean Renoir. *FCT, INT, TPV*

Picture Bride 🐾🐾½ 1994 (PG-13) Familiar immigrant saga finds 17-year-old Japanese Riyo (Kudoh) setting off for Hawaii in 1918 as a "picture bride" to a husband she's never met but with whom she's exchanged photos (hence the title). Riyo's shocked to discover her intended, sugarcane worker Matsuji (Takayama), has deceived her with an out-of-date picture and is at least 25 years older than she. She refuses to consummate the marriage and goes to work in the fields, intending to earn money for her passage home but of course things don't work out quite as Riyo intends. Japanese with subtitles. **CW:** Partial nudity and sexual situations. **95m/C VHS, LV, Closed Caption.** *JP* Yoko Sugi, Youki Kudoh, Akira Takayama, Tamlyn Tomita, Cary-Hiroyuki Tagawa; **Cameos:** Toshiro Mifune; **D:** Kayo Hatta; **W:** Kayo Hatta, Mari Hatta, Diane Mark; **C:** Claudio Rocha; **M:** Cliff Eidelman. Sundance Film Festival '95: Audience Award; Nominations: Independent Spirit Awards '96: Best First Feature. *TOU*

Picture Mommy Dead 🐾🐾 1966 Well acted melodrama involving a scheming shrew who struggles to drive her mentally disturbed stepdaughter insane for the sake of cold, hard cash. **85m/C VHS, Beta.** Don Ameche, Zsa Zsa Gabor, Martha Hyer, Susan Gordon; **D:** Bert I. Gordon; **C:** Ellsworth Fredericks. *NLC*

Picture of Dorian Gray 🐾🐾🐾 1945
Hatfield plays the rake who stays young while his portrait ages in this adaptation of Oscar Wilde's classic novel. Lansbury steals this one. **110m/B VHS, Beta, LV.** Hurd Hatfield, George Sanders, Donna Reed, Angela Lansbury, Peter Lawford, Lowell Gilmore, Miles Mander; **D:** Albert Lewin; **W:** Albert Lewin; **C:** Harry Stradling. Academy Awards '45: Best Black and White Cinematography; Golden Globe Awards '46: Best Supporting Actress (Lansbury); Nominations: Academy Awards '45: Best Interior Decoration, Best Supporting Actress (Lansbury). *MGM, FHE, TVC*

Picture of Dorian Gray 🐾🐾🐾 1974
Another version of Wilde's renowned novel about a man who retains his youthful visage while his portrait shows the physical ravages of aging. Davenport is particularly appealing in the lead. Made for television. **130m/C VHS, Beta.** Shane Briant, Nigel Davenport, Charles Aidman, Fionnula Flanagan, Linda Kelsey, Vanessa Howard; **D:** Glenn Jordan. *ART, MPI*

Picture Perfect 🐾🐾½ 1996 (PG-13) While trying to impress her new boss, ad exec Kate (Aniston) claims Nick (Mohr), the man standing with her in a photo, is her fiance. Unfortunately, the boss now wants to meet the guy (a stranger who was at the same party) and she must find him and get him to play along. The story's cliched, but Aniston's appealing screen presence perks things up a bit. **CW:** Sensuality and related dialogue. **100m/C VHS, Closed Caption.** Jennifer Aniston, Jay Mohr, Kevin Bacon, Illeana Douglas, Olympia Dukakis, Kevin Dunn, Faith Prince, Anne Twomey; **D:** Glenn Gordon Caron;

W: Glenn Gordon Caron; **C:** Paul Sarossy; **M:** Carter Burwell, Carter Burwell. *FOX*

Picture Windows 🐾🐾 1995 (R) Three short cable movies inspired by works of art. "Lightning," based on Frederic Remington sketches and a Zane Grey short story, finds western codger Keith striking gold with the help of his trusty mule. A David Hockney painting suggested "Armed Response," which features a confrontation between a wealthy lawyer (Loggia) and a burglar (Zahn). And an anonymous 16th-century canvas "Two Nudes Bathing" is given an imaginative history. **CW:** Some sexuality/nudity. **95m/C VHS.** Brian Keith, Robert Loggia, Steve Zahn, Charley Boorman; **D:** Joe Dante, Bob Rafelson, John Boorman. *HMK*

Pictures 🐾🐾½ 198? The silent-film era in England is spoofed in this look at ambitious waitress Ruby Sears, who's determined to be a film star, and writer Bill Trench, who winds up a novice screenwriter. Bill's first movie script is based on Ruby's life and she desperately wants to star in the production, if only she can convince the producer and the drunken male lead that she has the talent. Made for British television; seven episodes on four cassettes. **208m/C VHS.** *GB* Wendy Morgan, Peter McEnery, Harry Towb, Anton Rodgers, Annette Badland, Malcom Jamieson, Marc Smith; **W:** Roy Clarke. *TVC, SIG, VCO*

Pie In the Sky 🐾🐾½ 1995 (R) Charles Dunlap (Charles) is a traffic geek, fascinated by the flow of cars on the nearby freeway, whose hero is local traffic reporter Alan Davenport (Goodman), with whom he eventually gets a job in L.A. Charles' other interest is dancer/waitress Amy (Heche)—their first attempt at romance goes awry but persistence pays off. Optimistic and corny. **CW:** Sexuality. **94m/C VHS, LV, Closed Caption.** Josh Charles, Anne Heche, John Goodman, Christine Lahti, Peter Riegert, Christine Ebersole, Wil Wheaton, Bob Balaban, Dey Young; **D:** Bryan Gordon; **W:** Bryan Gordon; **C:** Bernd Heinl; **M:** Michael Covertino. *NLC*

Piece of Cake 🐾🐾½ 1990 Adaptation of the Derek Robinson novel follows the flyboys of the RAF Hornet Squadron during the early years of WWII. They have trouble taking the war seriously but tangles with the Luftwaffe and increasing casualties put a strain on everyone. Great aerial photography and the British planes are vintage Spitfires but not repros. Made for British TV miniseries on six cassettes. **312m/C VHS.** *GB* Tom Burlinson, Tim Woodward, Boyd Gaines, Nathaniel Parker, Neil Dudgeon, David Horovitch, Richard Hope, Jeremy Wortham, Michael Elwyn, Corinne Dacla, Helena Michell. *SIG, VCO*

A Piece of Pleasure 🐾🐾🐾 1970 Marriage declines due to a domineering husband in this familiar domestic study from French master Chabrol. Good, but not among the director's best efforts. In French with English subtitles. **100m/C VHS, Beta.** **D:** Claude Chabrol. *FCT*

Piece of the Action 🐾🐾½ 1977 (PG) An ex-cop beats two con men at their own game when he convinces them to work for a Chicago community center. **135m/C VHS, Beta.** Sidney Poitier, Bill Cosby, James Earl Jones, Denise Nicholas, Hope Clarke, Tracy Reed, Titos Vandis, Ja'net DuBois; **D:** Sidney Poitier; **M:** Curtis Mayfield. *WAR*

Pieces woof! 1983 (R) Chain-saw wielding madman roams a college campus in search of human parts for a ghastly jigsaw puzzle. Gory and loathsome. **90m/C VHS, Beta.** *IT SP* Christopher George, Lynda Day George, Paul Smith; **D:** J. Piquer Simon. *VES*

The Pied Piper of Hamelin 🐾🐾 1957
The evergreen classic of the magical piper who rids a village of rats and then disappears with the village children into a mountain when the townspeople fail to keep a promise. **90m/C VHS, Beta.** Van Johnson, Claude Rains, Jim Backus, Kay Starr, Lori Nelson; **D:** Bretaigne Windust. *KAR, NOS, FOX*

The Pied Piper of Hamelin 1984 From Shelley Duvall's "Faerie Tale Theatre" comes the story of how a man with a magic flute charmed the rats out of Hamelin. **60m/C VHS, Beta, Closed Caption.** Eric Idle; **D:** Nicholas Meyer. *FOX, FCT*

Pier 23 🐾🐾 1951 A private eye is hired to bring a lawless ex-convict to a priest's custody, but gets an imposter instead. A web of intrigue follows. **57m/B VHS, Beta, LV.** Hugh Beaumont, Ann Savage, David Bruce, Raymond Greenleaf, Joi Lansing. *NO*

Pierrot le Fou 🐾🐾🐾½ 1965 A woman fleeing a gangster joins a man leaving his wife in this stunning, occasionally confusing classic from iconoclast Godard. A hallmark in 1960s improvisational filmmaking, with rugged Belmondo and always-photogenic Karina effortlessly excelling in leads. In French with English subtitles. **110m/C VHS, LV, Letterbox.** *FR IT* Samuel Fuller, Jean-Pierre Leaud, Jean-Paul Belmondo, Anna Karina, Dirk Sanders; **D:** Jean-Luc Godard; **M:** Antoine Duhamel. *FXL, FCT, IME*

Pigalle 🐾🐾 1995 Dridi's feature debut focuses on the red light district of Paris and the company of various lowlifes, including pickpocket Fifi (Renaud), who's involved with both stripper Vera (Brile) and transvestite hooker Divine (Li). There's also an increasingly violent turf war between a couple of drug dealers that takes in everyone around. Violent and sordid melodrama. French with subtitles. **93m/C VHS.** *FR* Francis Renaud, Vera Briole, Bianca Li, Raymond Gil, Younesse Boudache, Philippe Ambrosini, Jean-Claude Grenier; **D:** Karim Dridi; **W:** Karim Dridi; **C:** John Mathieson. *FCT*

Pigs 🐾½ *Daddy's Deadly Darling; The Killers* 1973 Young woman who has escaped from a mental hospital teams up with an evil old man to go on a murdering spree. They complement each other beautifully. She kills them and he disposes of the bodies by making pig slop out of them. **90m/C VHS, Beta.** Toni Lawrence, Marc Lawrence, Jesse Vint, Katharine Ross; **D:** Marc Lawrence; **W:** Marc Lawrence; **M:** Charles Bernstein. *MRV*

A Pig's Tale 🐾½ *Summer Camp* 1994 (PG) Rich kids rule at Kamp Kipperman but one 13-year-old forms the Pig Pen club and the club members decide to turn the tables on their overbearing rivals. **94m/C VHS.** Joe Flaherty, Graham Sack; **D:** Paul Tassie. *PGV*

Pigskin Parade 🐾🐾½ 1936 Fifteen-year-old Garland's first feature is a lighthearted musical combining college and football. Winston Winters (Haley) coaches the Texas State U team, which has been mistakenly invited to play Yale, and goes to great lengths to give his team a chance by recruiting a farmboy (Erwin) who's a natural phenom. (Garland's the boy's singing sister.) ♫Balboa; The Texas Tornado; It's Love I'm After; You're Simply Terrific; You Do the Darndest Things, Baby; T.S.U. Alma Mater; Hold That Bulldog; Down with Everything; We'd Rather Be In College. **95m/B VHS.** Jack Haley, Patsy Kelly, Stuart Erwin, Judy Garland, Johnny Downs, Betty Grable, Arline Judge, Tony Martin, Fred Kohler Jr., Elisha Cook Jr.; **D:** David Butler; **W:** Harry Tugend, Jack Yellen; **C:** Arthur C. Miller. Nominations: Academy Awards '36: Best Supporting Actor (Erwin). *FOX*

Pilgrim, Farewell 🐾🐾½ 1982 Dramatic story about a dying woman who needs to tie up loose ends before her death and goes looking for her estranged teenage daughter. Made for television for PBS' "American Playhouse." **110m/C VHS, Beta.** Elizabeth Huddle, Christopher Lloyd, Laurie Pranage, Lesley Paxton, Shelley Wyant, Robert Brown; **D:** Michael Roemer. *HMV*

The Pillow Book 🐾🐾 1995 (NC-17)
Greenaway's usual chilliness gives way to some true erotic heat that still keeps to arcane subjects, violence and dazzling visuals. Japanese model Nagiko (Wu) longs for the childhood rituals enacted by her calligrapher father (Ogata) as he literally painted birthday greetings on her face with brush and ink. As an adult, Nagiko searches out calligrapher/lovers willing to use her body as their

paper but she's still unsatisfied until she meets bisexual Englishman Jerome (McGregor) and he insists Nagiko write on him. When Nagiko learns Jerome's male lover is the publisher (Oida) who was once involved with her father, her jealousy triggers tragic consequences. Title refers to the 10th century diary "The Pillow Book of Sei Shonagon." Some subtitled Japanese dialogue. **126m/C VHS. NL FR GB** Vivian Wu, Ewan McGregor, Yoshi Oida, Ken Ogata, Hideko Yoshida, Judy Ongg, Ken Mitsuishi, Yutaka Honda, Ronald Guttman; **D:** Peter Greenaway; **W:** Peter Greenaway; **C:** Sacha Vierny. *COL*

Pillow Talk 🐾🐾🐾½ **1959** Sex comedy in which a man woos a woman who loathes him. By the way, they share the same telephone party line. Narrative provides minimal indication of the film's strengths, which are many. Classic '50s comedy with masters Day and Hudson exhibiting considerable rapport, even when fighting. Lighthearted, constantly funny. **102m/C VHS, Beta, LV, Letterbox.** Rock Hudson, Doris Day, Tony Randall, Thelma Ritter, Nick Adams, Lee Patrick; **D:** Michael Gordon. Academy Awards '59: Best Story & Screenplay; Nominations: Academy Awards '59: Best Actress (Day), Best Art Direction/Set Decoration (Color), Best Supporting Actress (Ritter), Best Original Dramatic/Comedy Score. *USH, CCB*

Pilot 🐾½ **1984** Young girl discovers the debilitating effects of dishonesty when she becomes a break-dancing champion. **27m/C VHS, Beta.** Kelly Jo Minter, Adolph "Oz" Alvarez, Katie Rich. *PAU*

Pimpernel Smith 🐾🐾½ *Mister V* **1942** Seemingly scatterbrained archaeology professor is actually a dashing agent rescuing refugees from evil Nazis in WWII France. Howard is well cast, but the film is somewhat predictable, and it's too long. Wonderful scene, though, in which a Nazi officer champions Shakespeare as Aryan. **121m/B VHS, Beta.** *GB* Leslie Howard, Mary Morris, Francis L. Sullivan, David Tomlinson; **D:** Leslie Howard. *VYY*

Pin... 🐾🐾½ **1988 (R)** A boy's imaginary friend assists in the slaying of various enemies. Horror effort could be worse. **103m/C VHS, Beta, LV.** Cyndy Preston, David Hewlett, Terry O'Quinn, Bronwen Mantel, Helene Udy, Patricia Collins, Steven Bednarski, Katie Shingler, Jacob Tierney, Michelle Anderson; **D:** Sandor Stern; **W:** Sandor Stern; **C:** Guy Defaux. *VTR, IME*

Pin Down Girls 🐾 *Racket Girls* **1951** Great schlock about girl wrestlers. **?m/C VHS.** Clara Mortensen, Rita Martinez. *SNC*

Pin-Up Girl 🐾🐾 **1944** Grable plays a secretary who becomes an overnight sensation during WWII. Loosely based on her famous pinup poster that was so popular at the time, the movie didn't even come close to being as successful. The songs aren't particularly memorable, although Charlie Spivak and his Orchestra perform. ♫Once Too Often; Yankee Doodle Dandy; I'll Be Marching to a Love Song; You're My Little Pin Up Girl; Story of the Very Merry Widow; Time Alone Will Tell; Don't Carry Tales Out of School; Red Robins, Bob Whites and Blue Birds. **83m/C VHS, LV, Closed Caption.** Betty Grable, Martha Raye, Jon Harvey, Joe E. Brown, Eugene Pallette, Mantan Moreland; **D:** H. Bruce Humberstone; **C:** Ernest Palmer. *FOX*

Ping Pong 🐾🐾½ **1987 (PG)** A Chinese patriarch drops dead in London's Chinatown, leaving a young law student to disentangle his will, and get mixed up with his cross-cultured family. **100m/C VHS, Beta, LV.** David Yip, Lucy Sheen, Robert Lee, Lam Fung, Victor Kan, Ric Young; **D:** Po Chich Leong. *NO*

Pink Cadillac 🐾🐾½ **1989 (PG-13)** A grizzled, middle-aged bondsman is on the road, tracking down bail-jumping crooks. He helps the wife and baby of his latest target escape from her husband's more evil associates. Eastwood's performance is good and fun to watch, in this otherwise lightweight film. **121m/C VHS, Beta, LV, 8mm, Closed Caption.** Clint Eastwood, Bernadette Peters, Timothy Carhart, Michael Des Barres, William Hickey, John Dennis Johnston, Geoffrey Lewis, Jim Carrey, Bill Robinson, Angela Louise Robinson; **D:** Buddy Van Horn; **W:** John Eskow; **M:** Stephen Dorff. *WAR*

The Pink Chiquitas 🐾 **1986 (PG-13)** Scifi spoof about a detective battling a mob of meteorite-traveling Amazons. **86m/C VHS, Beta.** Frank Stallone, Eartha Kitt, Bruce Pirrie, McKinlay Robinson, Elizabeth Edwards, Claudia Judy; **D:** Anthony Currie.

Pink Flamingos 🐾🐾 **1972 (NC-17)** Divine, the dainty 300-pound transvestite, faces the biggest challenge of his/her career when he/she competes for the title of World's Filthiest Person. Tasteless, crude, and hysterical film; this one earned Waters his title as "Prince of Puke." If there are any doubts about this honor—or Divine's rep—watch through to the end to catch Divine chewing real dog excrement, all the time wearing a you-know-what grin. The 25th anniversary special edition on laserdisc includes commentary by John Waters, deleted footage, and scenes from the recent documentary "Divine Trash: The Making of 'Pink Flamingos'"; the disc also has a remastered soundtrack and widescreen presentation. **95m/C VHS, Beta, LV, Letterbox.** Divine, David Lochary, Mary Vivian Pearce, Danny Mills, Mink Stole, Edith Massey, Cookie Mueller, Channing Wilroy, Paul Swift, Susan Walsh, Linda Olgierson, Elizabeth Coffey, Steve Yeager; **D:** John Waters; **W:** John Waters; **C:** John Waters. *CRC*

Pink Floyd: The Wall 🐾🐾½ **1982 (R)** Film version of Pink Floyd's 1979 LP, "The Wall." A surreal, impressionistic tour-de-force about a boy who grows up numb from society's pressures. The concept is bombastic and overwrought, but Geldof manages to remain somewhat likeable as the cynical rock star and the Gerald Scarfe animation perfectly complements the film. Laserdisc edition includes the original theatrical trailer and the letterboxed format of the film. **95m/C VHS, Beta, LV, Letterbox.** *GB* Bob Geldof, Christine Hargreaves, Bob Hoskins; **D:** Alan Parker; **C:** Peter Biziou; **M:** Michael Kamen. *MVD, MGM*

The Pink Jungle 🐾🐾½ **1968** Ben Morris (Garner) is a fashion photographer on assignment with model Alison (Renzi) in South America where they become entangled with eccentric Sammy Ryderbeit (Kennedy) who's searching for a lost diamond mine. Caught up in the adventure, the duo accompany Sammy and find the mine, only to discover Raul Ortega (Ansara) and his band of revolutionaries have gotten there first. Based on the novel "Snake Water" by Alan Williams. **104m/C VHS, Closed Caption.** James Garner, Eva Renzi, George Kennedy, Michael Ansara, Nigel Green, George Rose; **D:** Delbert Mann; **W:** Charles Williams; **C:** Russell Metty; **M:** Ernie Freeman. *USH*

Pink Motel woof! *Motel* **1982 (R)** Several people spend a night meant to be romantic at a pink stucco motel that caters to couples. Comic stiff with Diller and Pickens as the owners of said pink motel. **90m/C VHS, Beta.** Phyllis Diller, Slim Pickens, Terri Berland, Squire Fridell; **D:** Mike MacFarland. *NO*

Pink Nights 🐾 **1987 (PG)** A high school nebbish is suddenly pursued by three beautiful girls, and his life gets turned upside-down. **87m/C VHS, Beta, LV.** Shaun Allen, Kevin Anderson, Larry King, Johnathan Jamcovic Michaels; **D:** Philip Koch. *VTR*

The Pink Panther 🐾🐾🐾 **1964** Bumbling, disaster-prone inspector invades a Swiss ski resort and becomes obsessed with capturing a jewel thief hoping to lift the legendary "Pink Panther" diamond. Said thief is also the inspector's wife's lover, though the inspector doesn't know it. Slick slapstick succeeds on strength of Sellers' classic portrayal of Clouseau, who accidentally destroys everything in his path while speaking in a funny French accent. Followed by "A Shot in the Dark," "Inspector Clouseau" (without Sellers), "The Return of the Pink Panther," "The Pink Panther Strikes Again," "Revenge of the Pink Panther," "Trail of the Pink Panther," and "Curse of the Pink Panther." Memorable theme supplied by Mancini. **113m/C VHS, Beta, LV, Letterbox.** *GB* Peter Sellers, David Niven, Robert Wagner, Claudia Cardinale, Capucine, Brenda de Banzie; **D:** Blake Edwards; **W:** Blake Edwards; **M:** Henry Mancini. Nominations: Academy Awards '64: Best Original Score. *MGM, FOX, TVC*

The Pink Panther Strikes Again 🐾🐾🐾 **1976 (PG)** Fifth in the series has the incompetent inspector tracking his former boss, who has gone insane and has become preoccupied with destroying the entire world. A must for Sellers buffs and anyone who appreciates slapstick. **103m/C VHS, Beta, LV.** *GB* Peter Sellers, Herbert Lom, Lesley-Anne Down, Colin Blakely, Leonard Rossiter, Burt Kwouk; **D:** Blake Edwards; **W:** Edwards Waldman, Frank Waldman; **M:** Henry Mancini. Writers Guild of America '76: Best Adapted Screenplay; Nominations: Academy Awards '76: Best Song ("Come to Me"). *FOX, TVC*

Pink String and Sealing Wax 🐾🐾 **1945** A brutish pub owner in Victorian England is poisoned by his abused wife. She tries to involve the son of a chemist with the idea of blackmailing the father. Fine period flavor. **89m/B VHS, Beta.** *GB* Mervyn Johns, Mary Merrall, Gordon Jackson, Googie Withers, Sally Ann Howes, Catherine Lacey, Garry Marsh, Frederick Piper, Don Stannard, Valentine Dyall; **D:** Robert Hamer; **W:** Robert Hamer. *SNC*

Pinky 🐾🐾🐾 **1949** Early Hollywood treatment of the tragic choice made by some black Americans to pass as white in order to attain a better life for themselves and their families. The story is still relevant today. Waters and Barrymore also star, but the lead black character is portrayed by a white actress. Based on the novel "Quality" by Cyd Ricketts Sumner. **102m/B VHS.** Jeanne Crain, Ethel Barrymore, Ethel Waters, Nina Mae McKinney, William Lundigan; **D:** Elia Kazan; **W:** Philip Dunne, Dudley Nichols; **M:** Alfred Newman. Nominations: Academy Awards '49: Best Actress (Crain), Best Supporting Actress (Barrymore, Waters). *FXL*

Pinocchio 🐾🐾🐾🐾 **1940 (G)** Second Disney animated film featuring Pinocchio, a little wooden puppet, made with love by the old woodcarver Geppetto, and brought to life by a good fairy. Except Pinocchio isn't content to be just a puppet—he wants to become a real boy. Lured off by a sly fox, Pinocchio undergoes a number of adventures as he tries to return safely home. Has some scary scenes, including Geppetto, Pinocchio, and their friend Jiminy Cricket getting swallowed by a whale, and Pleasure Island, where naughty boys are turned into donkeys. An example of animation at its best and a Disney classic that has held up over time. ♫When You Wish Upon a Star; Give a Little Whistle; Turn on the Old Music Box; Hi-Diddle-Dee-Dee (An Actor's Life For Me); I've Got No Strings. **87m/C VHS, Beta, LV, Closed Caption.** **D:** Ben Sharpsteen; **V:** Dick Jones, Cliff Edwards, Evelyn Venable, Walter Catlett, Frankie Darro, Charles Judels, Don Brodie, Christian Rub. Academy Awards '40: Best Song ("When You Wish Upon a Star"), Best Original Score, National Film Registry '94. *DIS*

Pinocchio **1983** Pee Wee Herman is the puppet who wants to be a real little boy in this "Faerie Tale Theatre" adaptation of this children's classic. **60m/C VHS, Beta, Closed Caption.** Paul (Pee Wee Herman) Reubens, James Coburn, Carl Reiner, Lainie Kazan; **D:** Peter Medak. *FOX, FCT*

Pinocchio's Revenge 🐾 **1996 (R)** Man murders his child and buries the body with a wooden Pinocchio puppet. Somehow before his execution, his lawyer, Jennifer Garrick (Allen), and her cute daughter Zoe (Smith) wind up with the grisly toy and Jennifer allows her daughter to keep it. Naturally, this is not a good thing. **96m/C VHS.** Rosalind Allen, Brittany Alyse Smith, Todd Allen, Lewis Van Bergen, Aaron Lustig, Ron Canada; **D:** Kevin S. Tenney; **W:** Kevin S. Tenney; **M:** Dennis Michael Tenney. *THV*

Pinocchio's Storybook Adventures 🐾½ **1979** Pinocchio takes over for an ailing puppet master and puts on a show for a group of children. **80m/C VHS, Beta.** **D:** Ron Merk. *VTR*

Pinto Canyon ♪½ **1940** An honest sheriff does away with a band of cattle rustlers. 55m/B VHS. Bob Steele, Louise Stanley, Kenne Duncan, Ted Adams, Steve Clark, Budd Buster; **D:** Raymond K. Johnson. *NOS, DVT*

Pinto Rustlers ♪½ **1936** A cowboy left orphaned by a gang of rustlers seeks revenge. 52m/C VHS, Beta. Tom Tyler, Catherine Cotter. *NOS, DVT*

Pioneer Marshal ♪ **1949** Lawman Hale disguises himself as a criminal to track down an embezzler. 60m/B VHS, Beta. Monte Hale, Paul Hurst. *DVT*

Pioneer Woman ♪♪ *Pioneers* **1973** A family encounters hostility when they set up a frontier homestead in Nebraska in 1867. Told from the feminine perspective, the tale is strewn with hurdles, both personal and natural. 74m/C VHS, Beta. Joanna Pettet, William Shatner, David Janssen; **D:** Buzz Kulik. *WOV*

The Pioneers ♪½ **1941** Ritter sets out to protect a wagon train. 59m/B VHS, Beta. Tex Ritter. *VCN*

Pipe Dreams ♪♪ **1976 (PG)** A couple tries to repair their broken marriage against the backdrop of the Alaskan pipeline's construction. 89m/C VHS, Beta. Gladys Knight, Barry Hankerson, Bruce French, Sally Kirkland, Sherry Bain; **D:** Stephen Verona. *COL*

Pippi Goes on Board ♪♪½ **1975 (G)** The fourth and last film in the Swedish series finds Pippi's father arriving one day to take her sailing to Taka-Kuka, his island kingdom. She can't bear to leave her friends and jumps off the ship to return home. The series is poorly dubbed and technically flawed, which the kids probably won't notice. Based on the books by Astrid Lindgren. Preceded by "Pippi Longstocking," "Pippi in the South Seas," and "Pippi on the Run." 83m/C VHS, Beta. **SW** Inger Nilsson; **D:** Olle Hellbron. *GEM, MOV, TPV*

Pippi in the South Seas ♪♪½ *Pippi Langstrump Pa de Sju Haven* **1974 (G)** Pippi, a fun-loving, independent, red haired little girl, and her two friends decide to rescue her father, who is being held captive by a band of pirates on a South Sea island. Naturally, clever Pippi saves the day. Poorly dubbed and edited. Based on the children's book by Astrid Lindgren. Follows "Pippi Longstocking" and precedes "Pippi on the Run" and "Pippi Goes on Board." 99m/C VHS, Beta. **SW** Inger Nilsson; **D:** Olle Hellbron. *GEM, MOV, TPV*

Pippi Longstocking ♪♪½ **1973 (G)** This little red-headed, pigtailed terror is left alone by her sailor father as he heads out to sea. Not that Pippi minds, since it gives her the chance to create havoc in her town through the antics of her pets, a monkey and a horse. Pippi's antics may amuse the kiddies but adults will find her obnoxious. Poorly dubbed and technically somewhat shaky. Based on the children's book by Astrid Lindgren. Followed by "Pippi in the South Seas," "Pippi on the Run," and "Pippi Goes on Board." 99m/C VHS, Beta. **SW** Inger Nilsson; **D:** Olle Hellbron. *GEM, MOV, TPV*

Pippi on the Run ♪♪½ **1974 (G)** The third film in the series finds Pippi on the trail of two friends who have run away from home. The three have many adventures before deciding home is best. Preceded by "Pippi Longstocking" and "Pippi in the South Seas," followed by "Pippi Goes on Board." Films lacks technical and dubbing skills. Based on the children's book by Astrid Lindgren. 99m/C VHS, Beta. **SW** *GEM, MOV, TPV*

Pippin ♪♪♪ **1981** Video version of the stage musical about the adolescent son of Charlemagne finding true love. Adequate record of Bob Fosse's Broadway smash. Features Vereen recreating his original Tony Award-winning role. 120m/C VHS, Beta, LV. Ben Vereen, William Katt, Martha Raye, Chita Rivera. *VCI, FHE, FCT*

Piranha ♪♪½ **1995 (R)** Genetically enhanced piranha terrorize the resort community of Lost River. Scientists Paul (Katt) and Maggie (Paul) have accidentally released the vicious fishies but everyone ignores their warnings until some swimmers become din-din. Remake of Roger Corman's 1978 cult item and based on John Sayles' original screenplay. **CW:** Violence/gore and some nudity. 81m/C VHS. Alexandra Paul, William Katt, Soleil Moon Frye, Monte Markham, Darlene Carr, James Karen, Kevin McCarthy, William Kilpatrick; **D:** Scott Levy. *NHO*

Piranha ♪♪½ **1978 (R)** A rural Texas resort area is plagued by attacks from ferocious man-eating fish which a scientist created to be used as a secret weapon in the Vietnam War. Spoofy horror film features the now-obligatory Dante film in-jokes in the background. 90m/C VHS, Beta. Bradford Dillman, Heather Menzies, Kevin McCarthy, Keenan Wynn, Barbara Steele, Dick Miller, Paul Bartel, John Sayles; **D:** Joe Dante; **W:** John Sayles; **C:** Jamie Anderson; **M:** Pino Donaggio. *WAR, OM*

Piranha 2: The Spawning ♪½ *Piranha 2: Flying Killers* **1982 (R)** Diving instructor and a biochemist seek to destroy piranha mutations that are murdering tourists at a club. Early Cameron exercise in gore tech that's a step down from original "Piranha." 88m/C VHS, Beta, LV. Tricia O'Neil, Steve Marachuk, Lance Henriksen, Ricky Paul; **D:** James Cameron; **W:** H.A. Milton; **C:** Roberto D'Ettorre Piazzoli. *NLC*

The Pirate ♪♪♪ **1948** A traveling actor poses as a legendary pilot to woo a lonely woman on a remote Caribbean island. Minnelli always scores with this type of fare, and both Garland and Kelly make the most of the Cole Porter score. ♫Be a Clown; Nina; Mack the Black; You Can Do No Wrong; Sweet Ices, Papayas, Berry Man; Sea Wall; Serafin; The Ring; Judy Awakens. 102m/C VHS, Beta, LV. Judy Garland, Gene Kelly, Walter Slezak, Gladys Cooper, George Zucco, Reginald Owen, Nicholas Brothers; **D:** Vincente Minnelli; **C:** Harry Stradling. Nominations: Academy Awards '48: Scoring of a Musical.*MGM*

Pirate Movie ♪♪½ **1982 (PG)** Gilbert and Sullivan's "The Pirates of Penzance" is combined with new pop songs in this tale of fantasy and romance. Feeble attempt to update a musical that was fine the way it was. 98m/C VHS, Beta. Kristy McNichol, Christopher Atkins, Ted Hamilton, Bill Kerr, Garry McDonald; **D:** Ken Annakin; **M:** Tony Britten. Golden Raspberry Awards '82: Worst Director (Annakin), Worst Song ("Pumpin' and Blowin'").*FOX*

Pirate Ship ♪½ *The Mutineers* **1949** Slow-moving story has sailor Hall discovering new captain Reeves is involved with a gang of gun-runners and counterfeiters. 60m/C VHS. Jon Hall, George Reeves, Adele Jergens, Noel Cravat, Tom Kennedy, Lyle Talbot; **D:** Jean Yarbrough. *GPV*

Pirate Warrior ♪♪ **1964** Grade-B pirate flick about slavery and the evil Tortuga. 86m/C VHS, Beta. Ricardo Montalban, Vincent Price, Liana Orfei; **D:** Mary Costa. *NO*

Pirates ♪½ **1986 (PG-13)** Blustery, confused effort at a big-budgeted retro-adventure, about a highly regarded pirate and his gains and losses on the high seas. Broad comedy, no story to speak of. 124m/C VHS, Beta. Walter Matthau, Cris Campion, Damien Thomas, Richard Pearson, Charlotte Lewis, Olu Jacobs, David Patrick Kelly, Roy Kinnear, Bill Fraser, Jose Santamaria; **D:** Roman Polanski; **W:** Gerard Brach, Roman Polanski. Cesar Awards '87: Best Art Direction/Set Decoration, Best Costume Design; Nominations: Academy Awards '86: Best Costume Design. *ART*

The Pirates of Penzance ♪♪ **1983 (G)** Gilbert and Sullivan's comic operetta is the story of a band of fun-loving pirates, their reluctant young apprentice, the "very model of a modern major general," and his lovely daughters. An adaptation of Joseph Papp's award-winning Broadway play. 112m/C VHS, Beta, LV. Kevin Kline, Angela Lansbury, Linda Ronstadt, Rex Smith, George Rose; **D:** Wilford Leach. *USH, FOX*

Pirates of the Coast ♪½ **1961** A Spanish naval commander teams up with a group of pirates to even the score with an evil governor during the 1500s. 102m/C VHS, Beta. Lex Barker, Estella Blain, Livio Lorenzon, Liana Orfei; **D:** Domenico Paolella. *UNI*

Pirates of the High Seas ♪½ **1950** Crabbe helps a friend save his shipping line from sabotage. A serial in 15 chapters. ?m/C VHS. Buster Crabbe, Lois Hall, Tommy Farrell, Gene Roth, Tristram Coffin; **D:** Spencer Gordon Bennet, Thomas Carr. *MLB*

Pirates of the Seven Seas ♪½ **1962** In the further tales of "Sandokan the Great," the pirate hero helps save the heroine's father from an evil English Imperialist. 90m/C VHS, Beta. Steve Reeves, Jacqueline Sassard, Andrea Bosic; **D:** Umberto Lenzi. *NO*

Pistol: The Birth of a Legend ♪♪½ **1990 (G)** Biography of "Pistol" Pete Maravich, the basketball star who defied age limitations in the 1960s to play on his varsity team. 104m/C VHS, Beta, Closed Caption. Adam Guier, Nick Benedict, Boots Garland, Millie Perkins; **D:** Frank C. Schroeder; **W:** Darrel A. Campbell. *COL*

Pistoleros Asesinos ♪♪ **1987** Plenty of action, plus a little romance, when a man falls in love with a crooked landowner's daughter and must battle her father's henchmen for her hand. 83m/C VHS, Beta. **SP** Maria de Lourdes, Federico Villa, Victor Alcocer, Arturo Benavides, Polo Ortin, Rosa Gloria. *MAD*

The Pit ♪½ **1981 (R)** Autistic boy gets his chance for revenge. The townspeople who humiliate him are in for a surprise after he stumbles across a huge hole in the forest, at the bottom of which are strange and deadly creatures. 96m/C VHS, Beta. Sammy Snyders, Sonja Smits, Jeannie Elias, Laura Hollingsworth; **D:** Lew Lehman. *VTR*

The Pit and the Pendulum ♪♪♪ **1961** A woman and her lover plan to drive her brother mad, and he responds by locking them in his torture chamber, which was built by his loony dad, whom he now thinks he is. Standard Corman production only remotely derived from the classic Poe tale, with the cast chewing on a loopy script. A landmark in Gothic horror. 80m/C VHS, Beta. Vincent Price, John Kerr, Barbara Steele, Luana Anders, Antony Carbone; **D:** Roger Corman; **W:** Richard Matheson; **C:** Floyd Crosby; **M:** Les Baxter. *WAR, OM*

The Pit & the Pendulum ♪♪½ **1991 (R)** Retelling of the classic Poe short story, mixed with his "A Cask of Amantillado" and set during the Spanish Inquisition. Great special effects and professional scary guy, Lance Henriksen.**CW:** Language, nudity, and torture scenes. 97m/C VHS, LV, Closed Caption. Lance Henriksen, Rona De Ricci, Jonathan Fuller, Jeffrey Combs, Tom Towles, Stephen Lee, Frances Bay, Oliver Reed; **D:** Stuart Gordon; **W:** Dennis Paoli; **M:** Richard Band. *FLL*

Pitfall ♪♪♪ **1948** Gritty tale in which an insurance salesman, bored with his routine suburban life and family, follows his less noble instincts—and finds himself up to his ears in stolen goods, adultery and murder. 85m/B VHS, LV. Dick Powell, Jane Wyatt, Lizabeth Scott, Raymond Burr, John Litel, Byron Barr, Ann Doran, Jimmy Hunt, Selmer Jackson, Margaret Wells, Dick Wassel; **D:** Andre de Toth; **W:** Karl Kamb; **C:** Harry Wild; **M:** Louis Forbes. *REP, FCT*

Pittsburgh ♪♪ **1942** Slow-moving drama about a love triangle combined with class differences. Dietrich loves Wayne, but he's more interested in the coal and steel business, so rival Scott steps in. Although limited by standard plot, picture works because of excellent performances by leads. Based on a screen story by George Owen and Tom Reed. 98m/B VHS, Closed Caption. Marlene Dietrich, Randolph Scott, John Wayne, Frank Craven, Louise Allbritton, Shemp Howard, Thomas Gomez, Ludwig Stossel; **D:** Lewis Seiler; **W:** Kenneth Gamet, Tom Reed, John Twist. *USH, FCT*

Pixote 🐾🐾🐾🐾 1981 Wrenching, documentary-like account of an orphan-boy's life on the streets in a Brazil metropolis. Graphic and depressing, it's not for all tastes but nonetheless masterfully done. In Portuguese with English subtitles. 127m/C VHS, Beta. *BR* Fernando Ramos Da Silva, Marilia Pera, Jorge Juliao, Gilberto Moura, Jose Nilson dos Santos, Edilson Lino; *D:* Hector Babenco; *W:* Hector Babenco; *M:* John Neschling. Los Angeles Film Critics Association Awards '81: Best Foreign Film; New York Film Critics Awards '81: Best Foreign Film; National Society of Film Critics Awards '81: Best Actress (Pera). *FCT, COL*

Pizza Man 🐾½ 1991 (PG-13) Pizza deliveryman Elmo Bunn is minding his own business, delivering an extra large with anchovies and sausage, when he finds himself mixed up in a political scandal. Lawton directed under alias "J.D. Athens." *CW:* Violence. 90m/C VHS. Bill Maher, Annabelle Gurwitch; *D:* J.F. Lawton; *W:* J.F. Lawton. *MNC*

P.K. and the Kid 🐾🐾 1985 A runaway kid meets up with a factory worker on his way to an arm wrestling competition and they become friends. 90m/C VHS, Beta, LV. Molly Ringwald, Paul Le-Mat, Alex Rocco, John Madden, Esther Rolle; *D:* Lou Lombardo; *W:* Neal Barbera; *M:* James Horner. *ORI, WAR*

A Place Called Glory 🐾🐾 *Die Holle von Manitoba* 1966 Barker comes to the aid of the local townsfolk in Glory city who have their hands full with a gang of bloodthirsty outlaws. 92m/C VHS. Lex Barker, Pierre Brice, Marianne Koch. *SNC*

A Place Called Today 🐾 *City in Fear* 1972 Sordid tale of big city politics where violence and fear in the streets is at the heart of the campaign. 105m/C VHS, Beta. Cheri Caffaro, J. Herbert Kerr Jr., Lana Wood, Richard Smedley, Tim Brown; *D:* Don Schain. *NO*

A Place for Annie 🐾🐾½ 1994 (PG) Lots of tears in this drama of devoted pediatrics nurse Susan Lansing (Spacek) who decides to become the foster mother of abandoned baby girl Annie, who's been diagnosed as HIV-positive. Then Annie's destitute birth mom (Parker), a former junkie dying of AIDS, resurfaces and decides she wants her daughter back. Sputters into melodrama but good performances by strong women, including Plowright as the nanny and Merkerson as a concerned hospital social worker. Based on a true story. Made for television. 98m/C VHS, Closed Caption. Sissy Spacek, Mary-Louise Parker, Joan Plowright, S. Epatha Merkerson, Jack Noseworthy; *D:* John Gray; *W:* Cathleen Young, Lee Guthrie. *REP*

Place in Hell 🐾½ 1965 The Japanese armed forces camouflage a Pacific island beach which they are holding and invite the American forces to invade it during WWII. 106m/C VHS, Beta. Guy Madison, Helene Chanel, Monty Greenwood. *UNI*

A Place in the Sun 🐾🐾🐾 1951 Melodramatic adaptation of "An American Tragedy," Theodore Dreiser's realist classic about an ambitious laborer whose aspirations to the high life with a gorgeous debutante are threatened by his lower-class lover's pregnancy. Clift is magnificent in the lead, and Taylor and Winters also shine in support. Burr, however, grossly overdoes his role of the vehement prosecutor. Still, not a bad effort from somewhat undisciplined director Stevens. 120m/B VHS, Beta, LV. Montgomery Clift, Elizabeth Taylor, Shelley Winters, Raymond Burr, Anne Revere; *D:* George Stevens; *C:* William Mellor; *M:* Franz Waxman. Academy Awards '51: Best Black and White Cinematography, Best Costume Design (B & W), Best Director (Stevens), Best Film Editing, Best Screenplay, Best Original Dramatic/Comedy Score; Directors Guild of America Awards '51: Best Director (Stevens); Golden Globe Awards '52: Best Film—Drama, National Film Registry '91; Nominations: Academy Awards '51: Best Actor (Clift), Best Actress (Winters), Best Picture. *PAR, BTV*

A Place in the World 🐾🐾🐾 1992 Returning from exile to their native Argentina during a military dictatorship, Mario and Ana (Luppi and Roth) work to help the less advantaged in their society, determined to make a difference. Story is seen as a flashback from point-of-view of the cou- ples' son Ernesto (Batyi). Well-crafted, finely acted piece exploring political, social, and interpersonal themes. 1993 Oscar bid retracted due to controversy over country of film's origin. 120m/C VHS. *AR* Jose Sacristan, Federico Luppi, Cecilia Roth, Leonor Benedetto, Gaston Batyi, Lorena Del Rio; *D:* Adolfo Aristarain; *W:* Alberto Lecchi, Adolfo Aristarain; *C:* Ricardo De Angelis; *M:* Emilio Kauderer. *NYF, FCT*

Place of Weeping 🐾🐾½ 1986 (PG) Early entry in the anti-apartheid sweepstakes (made in South Africa, no less). A South African woman opposes her nation's racist policies. A reporter supports her. 88m/C VHS, Beta. *SA* James Whylie, Geini Mhlophe; *D:* Darrell Roodt. *VTR, FCT*

Places in the Heart 🐾🐾🐾 1984 (PG) A young widow determines to make the best of a bad situation on a small farm in Depression-era Texas, fighting poverty, racism, and sexism while enduring back-breaking labor. Support group includes a blind veteran and a black drifter. Hokey but nonetheless moving film is improved significantly by strong performances by virtually everyone in the cast. In his debut, Malkovich shines through this stellar group. Effective dust-bowl photography by Nestor Almendros. 113m/C VHS, Beta, LV, Closed Caption. Sally Field, John Malkovich, Danny Glover, Ed Harris, Lindsay Crouse, Amy Madigan, Terry O'Quinn; *D:* Robert Benton; *W:* Robert Benton; *C:* Nestor Almendros; *M:* Howard Shore. Academy Awards '84: Best Actress (Field), Best Original Screenplay; Golden Globe Awards '85: Best Actress—Drama (Field); National Board of Review Awards '84: Best Supporting Actor (Malkovich); New York Film Critics Awards '84: Best Screenplay; National Society of Film Critics Awards '84: Best Supporting Actor (Malkovich); Nominations: Academy Awards '84: Best Costume Design, Best Director (Benton), Best Picture, Best Supporting Actor (Malkovich), Best Supporting Actress (Crouse). *FOX, BTV, HMV*

The Plague 🐾½ 1992 (R) An outbreak of bubonic plague has turned the South American city of Oran into a prison, with no one permitted to leave until the disease has run its course. Hurt is the doctor trying to balance his duties with his own fears. Necessarily bleak adaptation of the Albert Camus novel is also slow-moving and long-winded—an equally deadly combination for the viewer. *CW:* Some language, nudity, and grim images. 105m/C VHS, Closed Caption. *FR SP* William Hurt, Robert Duvall, Raul Julia, Sandrine Bonnaire, Jean-Marc Barr; *D:* Luis Puenzo. *ART, FCT, BTV*

The Plague Dogs 🐾🐾½ 1982 Two dogs carrying a plague escape from a research center and are tracked down in this unlikely animated film. A bit ponderous. And yes, that is Hurt's voice. From the novel by Richard Adams, author of "Watership Down." 99m/C VHS, Beta, Closed Caption. *D:* Martin Rosen; *W:* Martin Rosen; *M:* Patrick Gleeson; *V:* John Hurt, Christopher Benjamin, Judy Geeson, Barbara Leigh-Hunt, Patrick Stewart. *NLC*

Plague of the Zombies 🐾🐾½ 1966 The local doctor in a Cornish village gets suspicious when its inhabitants begin suddenly dying off and the local squire refuses to allow any autopsies. That's because he's learned voodoo rites while staying in Haiti and is turning the dead locals into zombies. 90m/C VHS. *GB* Andre Morell, John Carson, Diane Clare, Alex Davion, Jacqueline Pearce, Brook Williams, Michael Ripper, Marcus Hammond, Roy Royston; *D:* John Gilling; *W:* Peter Bryan, John Elder; *C:* Arthur Grant; *M:* James Bernard. *VTR*

Plain Clothes 🐾🐾½ 1988 (PG) An undercover cop masquerades as a high school student to solve the murder of a teacher. He endures all the trials that made him hate high school the first time around. 98m/C VHS, Beta, Closed Caption. Arliss Howard, George Wendt, Suzy Amis, Diane Ladd, Seymour Cassel, Larry Pine, Jackie Gayle, Abe Vigoda, Robert Stack; *D:* Martha Coolidge; *M:* Scott Wilk. *PAR*

The Plainsman 🐾🐾½ 1937 Western legends Wild Bill Hickock, Buffalo Bill, and Calamity Jane team up for adventure in this big, empty venture. Just about what you'd expect from splashy director DeMille. 113m/B VHS, Beta, LV. Gary Cooper, Jean Arthur, Charles Bickford, Anthony Quinn, George "Gabby" Hayes, Porter Hall, James Mason; *D:* Cecil B. DeMille; *C:* Victor Milner. *USH, MLB*

Plan B 🐾🐾½ 1997 Comedy, set between Halloween and New Year's Eve, about a group of 30-ish friends who realize their lives aren't going the way they'd planned. Waiter Stuart (Cryer) despairs of being a serious writer and has instead penned a lurid serial killer novel; aspiring actor Ricky (Matheison) freaks about growing older; Gina (Mornell) is successful in business but unlucky in love; while Gina's older sister Clare (Darr) is happily married to Jack (Guest) but fretting over not being a mother yet. It's pretty familiar but not a complete waste of time, thanks to the appealing cast. 102m/C VHS. Jon Cryer, Mark Matheison, Sara Mornell, Lisa Darr, Lance Guest; *D:* Gary Leva; *W:* Gary Leva; *C:* Yoram Astrakhan; *M:* Andrew Rose. *MNC*

Plan 9 from Outer Space woof! *Grave Robbers from Outer Space* 1956 Two or three aliens in silk pajamas conspire to resurrect several slow-moving zombies from a cardboard graveyard in order to conquer the Earth. Spaceships that look suspiciously like paper plates blaze across the sky. Pitiful, inadvertently hilarious fright worth a look if you're desperate to kill time since it's in the running for the "dumbest movie ever made" award. Lugosi's actual screen time is under two minutes, since he had the good sense to die before the film was complete. Enjoy the taller and younger replacement (the chiropractor of Wood's wife) they found for Lugosi, who remains hooded to protect his identity. 78m/B VHS, LV. Bela Lugosi, Tor Johnson, Lyle Talbot, Vampira, Gregory Walcott, Tom George Duryea Keene, Dudley Manlove, Mona McKinnon, Duke Moore, Joanna Lee, Bunny Breckinridge, Criswell, Carl Anthony, Paul Marco, Norma McCarty, David DeMering, Conrad Brooks, Edward D. Wood Jr.; *D:* Edward D. Wood Jr.; *W:* Edward D. Wood Jr.; *C:* William C. Thompson. *RHI, EEL, SNC*

Plan 10 from Outer Space 🐾½ 1995 The play on the infamous Ed Wood title is the only connection between the two fringe features as director Harris takes aim at his hometown of Salt Lake City, Utah. Heroine Lucinda (Russell) discovers a mysterious bronze plaque buried near the Great Salt Lake and uncovers a UFO conspiracy loosely conforming to Mormon mythology. There's a basic mass hysteria/alien invasion scene, cheesy special effects, dumb sexual humor, and not much else. 82m/C VHS. Stefene Russell, Pat Collins, Curtis James, Karen Black; *D:* Trent Harris; *W:* Trent Harris; *C:* Bryan Duggan; *M:* Fred Myrow. *LEO*

Planes, Trains & Automobiles 🐾🐾½ 1987 (R) One-joke Hughes comedy saved by Martin and Candy. A straight-laced businessman (played straight by Martin) on the way home for Thanksgiving meets up with a oafish, bad-luck-ridden boor who turns his efforts to get home upside down. Martin and Candy both turn in fine performances, and effectively straddle a thin line between true pathos and hilarious buffoonery. Bacon and McClurg, both Hughes alumni, have small but funny roles. 93m/C VHS, Beta, LV, 8mm, Closed Caption. Steve Martin, John Candy, Edie McClurg, Kevin Bacon, Michael McKean, William Windom, Laila Robins, Martin Ferrero, Charles Tyner, Dylan Baker, Ben Stein, Lyman Ward; *D:* John Hughes; *W:* John Hughes; *C:* Don Peterman; *M:* Ira Newborn. *PAR*

Planet Burg 🐾🐾½ 1962 A classic Soviet sci-fi flick about a space exploration team landing on Venus. Their job becomes a rescue mission when one of the crew is stranded. Although there are some silly moments, some good plot twists and acting make up for them. In Russian with English subtitles. 90m/C VHS, Beta. *RU* Vladimir Temelianov, Gennadi Vernov, Kyunna Ignatova; *D:* Pavel Klushantsev. *SNC*

Planet Busters 🐾 1985 Japanimation feature. Haphazardly developed swift-paced science fiction adventure about a magic sword, a royal heir apparent, a couple of bounty hunters, and evil robots. 80m/C VHS. *JP STP, TPV*

Planet Earth 🦴🦴½ 1974 In the year 2133, a man who has been in suspended animation for 154 years is revived to lead the troops against a violent group of women (and mutants, too!). 78m/C **VHS.** John Saxon, Janet Margolin, Ted Cassidy, Diana Muldaur, Johana DeWinter, Christopher Gary; *D:* Marc Daniels. UNI

Planet of Blood 🦴🦴 *Queen of Blood* 1966 Space opera about an alien vampire discovered on Mars by a rescue team. If you've ever seen the Soviet film "Niebo Zowiet," don't be surprised if some scenes look familiar; the script was written around segments cut from that film. 81m/C **VHS.** John Saxon, Basil Rathbone, Judi Meredith, Dennis Hopper, Florence Marly; *D:* Curtis Harrington. SNC, NOS, MRV

Planet of Dinosaurs 🦴½ 1980 (PG) Survivors from a ruined spaceship combat huge savage dinosaurs on a swampy uncharted planet. 85m/C **VHS, Beta.** James Whitworth; *D:* James K. Shea. VTR

Planet of the Apes 🦴🦴🦴 1968 (G) Astronauts crash land on a planet where apes are masters and humans are merely brute animals. Superior science fiction with sociological implications marred only by unnecessary humor. Heston delivers one of his more plausible performances. Superb ape makeup creates realistic pseudo-simians of McDowall, Hunter, Evans, Whitmore, and Daly. Adapted from Pierre Boulle's novel "Monkey Planet." Followed by four sequels and two television series. 112m/C **VHS, Beta, LV, Letterbox, Closed Caption.** Charlton Heston, Roddy McDowall, Kim Hunter, Maurice Evans, Linda Harrison, James Whitmore, James Daly; *D:* Franklin J. Schaffner; *W:* Rod Serling, Michael G. Wilson; *C:* Leon Shamroy; *M:* Jerry Goldsmith. Nominations: Academy Awards '68: Best Costume Design, Best Original Score. FOX, FUS

Planet of the Vampires 🦴🦴½ *Terror in Space; Terreur dans l'Espace; Space Mutants; The Demon Planet* 1965 Astronauts search for missing comrades on a planet dominated by mind-bending forces. Acceptable atmospheric filmmaking from genre master Bava, but it's not among his more compelling ventures. 86m/C **VHS, Beta.** IT Barry Sullivan, Norman Bengell, Angel Aranda, Evi Marandi; *D:* Mario Bava. ORI

Planet on the Prowl 🦴 *War Between the Planets* 1965 A fiery planet causes earthly disasters, so a troop of wily astronauts try to destroy it with the latest technology. They fail, leading one sacrificial soul to do it himself. 80m/C **VHS, Beta.** IT Giacomo "Jack" Rossi-Stuart, Amber Collins, Peter Martell, John Bartha, Halina Zalewska, James Weaver; *D:* Anthony (Antonio Margheriti) Dawson. NO

Planets Against Us 🦴½ *I Pianeti Contro di Noi; The Man with the Yellow Eyes; Hands of a Killer; The Monster with Green Eyes* 1961 Science fiction tale of escaped alien humanoid robots who take refuge on Earth, but whose touch is fatal. Good special effects. 85m/B **VHS.** IT FR Michel Lemoine, Maria Pia Luzi, Jany Clair; *D:* Romano Ferrara. SNC

Platinum Blonde 🦴🦴🦴 1931 Screwball comedy in which a newspaper journalist (Williams) marries a wealthy girl (Harlow) but finds that he doesn't like the restrictions and confinement of high society. Yearning for a creative outlet, he decides to write a play and hires a reporter (Young) to collaborate with him. The results are funny and surprising when Young shows up at the mansion flanked by a group of hard-drinking, fun-loving reporters. 86m/B **VHS, Closed Caption.** Loretta Young, Robert Williams, Jean Harlow, Louise Closser Hale; *D:* Frank Capra; *W:* Jo Swerling, Dorothy Howell. COL

Platinum High School 🦴½ *Trouble at 16; Rich, Young, and Deadly* 1960 Divorced father Rooney is appalled when his son is "accidentally" killed while off at an exclusive military academy. His suspicions are aroused by the prevaricating school commander and he discovers some horrible truths about his son's death and life at the school. 91m/B **VHS.** Mickey Rooney, Terry Moore, Dan Duryea, Conway Twitty, Warren Berlinger, Yvette Mimieux,

Jimmy Boyd, Richard Jaeckel, Harold Lloyd Jr., Elisha Cook Jr., Jimmy Murphy; *D:* Charles Haas; *W:* Robert Smith; *M:* Van Alexander. REP

Platoon 🦴🦴🦴½ 1986 (R) A grunt's view of the Vietnam War is provided in all its horrific, inexplicable detail. Sheen is wooden in the lead, but both Dafoe and Berenger are resplendent as, respectively, good and bad soldiers. Strong, visceral filmmaking from fearless director Stone, who based the film on his own GI experiences. Highly acclaimed; considered by many to be the most realistic portrayal of the war on film. 113m/C **VHS, Beta, LV, Closed Caption.** Charlie Sheen, Willem Dafoe, Tom Berenger, Francesco Quinn, Forest Whitaker, John C. McGinley, Kevin Dillon, Richard Edson, Reggie Johnson, Keith David, Johnny Depp; *D:* Oliver Stone; *W:* Oliver Stone; *C:* Robert Richardson; *M:* Georges Delerue. Academy Awards '86: Best Director (Stone), Best Film Editing, Best Picture, Best Sound; British Academy Awards '87: Best Director (Stone); Directors Guild of America Awards '86: Best Director (Stone); Golden Globe Awards '87: Best Director (Stone), Best Film—Drama, Best Supporting Actor (Berenger); Independent Spirit Awards '87: Best Cinematography, Best Director (Stone), Best Film, Best Screenplay; Nominations: Academy Awards '86: Best Cinematography, Best Original Screenplay, Best Supporting Actor (Berenger, Dafoe). ART, BTV

Platoon Leader 🦴🦴 1987 (R) A battle-drenched portrait of a West Point lieutenant in Vietnam. When he first arrives, he must win the trust of his men, who have been on their tours for a much longer time. As time goes on, he slowly becomes hardened to the realities of the brutal life in the field. Made on the heels of the widely acclaimed "Platoon," but it doesn't have the same power. Norris is martial arts king Chuck Norris' brother. 97m/C **VHS, Beta, LV.** Michael Dudikoff, Brian Libby, Robert F. Lyons, Rick Fitts, Jesse Dabson, William Smith, Michael De Lorenzo; *D:* Aaron Norris; *W:* R.J. Marx; *M:* George S. Clinton. VTR

Platoon the Warriors 🦴 1988 The underworld rages with violence when two kingpins, Rex and Bill, become bitter and declare war over a botched drug deal. 90m/C **VHS, Beta.** David Coley, Dick Crown, James Miller, Don Richard, Alex Sylvian; *D:* Philip Ko. NO

Platypus Cove 🦴 1986 An adopted boy tracks down the culprits responsible for the sabotage of his family's boat, a crime for which he was suspected. Australian. 72m/C **VHS, Beta.** Paul Smith; *D:* Peter Maxwell.

Play Dead 🦴 *Satan's Dog* 1981 Poor Yvonne De Carlo plays a psychotic woman who trains a dog to rip people to shreds. 89m/C **VHS.** Yvonne De Carlo, Stephanie Dunham, David Cullinane, Glenn Kezer, Ron Jackson, Carolyn Greenwood; *D:* Peter Wittman.

Play It Again, Charlie Brown 1971 The Peanuts gang goes bananas when Lucy enlists Schroeder to play rock music at a PTA meeting. 25m/C **VHS, Beta.** Charles M. Schulz. VTR

Play It Again, Sam 🦴🦴🦴½ 1972 (PG) Allen is—no surprise—a nerd, and this time he's in love with his best friend's wife. Modest storyline provides a framework of endless gags, with Allen borrowing heavily from "Casablanca." Bogey even appears periodically to counsel Allen on the ways of wooing women. Superior comedy isn't hurt by Ross directing instead of Allen, who adapted the script from his own play. 85m/C **VHS, Beta, LV, 8mm.** Woody Allen, Diane Keaton, Tony Roberts, Susan Anspach, Jerry Lacy, Jennifer Salt, Joy Bang, Viva, Herbert Ross; *D:* Herbert Ross; *W:* Woody Allen; *C:* Owen Roizman; *M:* Billy Goldenberg. PAR

Play Misty for Me 🦴🦴🦴 1971 (R) A radio deejay obliges a psychotic woman's song request and suddenly finds himself the target of her obsessive behavior, which rapidly turns from seductive to murderous. Auspicious directorial debut for Eastwood, borrowing from the Siegel playbook (look for the director's cameo as a barkeep). Based on a story by Heims. 102m/C **VHS, Beta, LV.** Jessica Walter, Donna Mills, John Larch, Irene Hervey, Jack Ging, Clint Eastwood; *Cameos:* Donald Siegel; *D:* Clint

Eastwood; *W:* Jo Heims, Dean Riesner; *C:* Bruce Surtees; *M:* Dee Barton. USH, TLF

Play Murder for Me 🦴🦴 1991 (R) Saxophonist performing in a seedy Buenos Aires nightclub has his world turned upside down when a former lover suddenly re-enters his life. She still has her eye on him, but she's now the woman of a notorious mobster. Soon the musician finds himself drawn into the usual deadly world of crime, deceit, and unharnessed passion. *CW:* Language, violence, and strong sexuality. 80m/C **VHS.** Jack Wagner, Tracy Scoggins; *D:* Hector Olivera. NHO

Play Nice 🦴½ 1992 (R) A detective hunts down a murderous psychopath but is shocked when he discovers his suspect is a woman—and someone he knows. Also available in an unrated version. *CW:* Language, violence, and strong sexuality. 90m/C **VHS.** Ed O'Ross. THV

Play Time 🦴 1994 Jeannie, Lindsay, and their husbands are on vacation in Palm Springs where they get up to some naughty sexual games that test the limits of friendship. Available in an unedited version at 95 minutes. 90m/C **VHS.** Monique Parent, Craig Stepp. TRI

Playback 🦴🦴½ 1995 (R) Young couple think they've finally captured the gold ring when hubby David (Grant) gets a chance at a million dollar merger deal. But David's set-up by sexy co-worker Karen (Whirry) and his slimy boss Gil (Hamilton) tries to seduce his wife Sara (Kitaen). *CW:* Strong sexuality and language. 91m/C **VHS, Beta, Closed Caption.** Charles Grant, Shannon Whirry, George Hamilton, Tawny Kitaen, Harry Dean Stanton; *D:* Oley Sassone; *W:* Oley Sassone, David DuBos; *C:* Russ Brandt. PAR

Playboy of the Western World 🦴🦴½ 1962 An innkeeper's daughter is infatuated with a young man who says he murdered her father. Adapted from the classic play by John Millington Synge. 96m/C **VHS, Beta.** IR Siobhan McKenna, Gary Raymond; *D:* Brian Desmond Hurst. NO

The Playboys 🦴🦴🦴 1992 (PG-13) In 1957 in a tiny Irish village, unmarried Tara Maguire causes a scandal by having a baby. Her beauty attracts lots of men—there's a former beau who kills himself, the obsessive, middle-aged Sergeant Hegarty, and the newest arrival, Tom Castle, an actor with a rag-tag theatrical troupe called the Playboys. Slow-moving and simple story with particularly good performances by Wright as the strong-willed Tara and Finney as Hegarty, clinging to a last chance at love and family. The Playboys' hysterically hammy version of "Gone With the Wind" is a gem. Directorial debut of Mackinnon. Filmed in the village of Redhills, Ireland, the hometown of co-writer Connaughton. 114m/C **VHS.** Albert Finney, Aidan Quinn, Robin Wright Penn, Milo O'Shea, Alan Devlin, Niamh Cusack, Ian McElhinney, Niall Buggy, Adrian Dunbar; *D:* Gilles Mackinnon; *W:* Shane Connaughton, Kerry Crabbe; *C:* Jack Conroy; *M:* Jean-Claude Petit. HBO, FCT

The Player 🦴🦴🦴½ 1992 (R) Clever, entertaining, and biting satire of the movie industry and the greed that controls it. Robbins is dead-on as Griffin Mill, a young studio exec who becomes the chief suspect in a murder investigation. He personifies Hollywood's ethics (or lack thereof) in a performance both cold and vulnerable, as he looks for the right buttons to push and the proper back to stab. Strong leading performances are supplemented by 65 star cameos. Some viewers may be put off by the inside-Hollywood jokes, but Altman fans will love it. The laserdisc version includes commentary by Altman, interviews with 20 screenwriters, and celebrity cameos that didn't make the final cut. *CW:* Language and sensuality. 123m/C **VHS, LV, Letterbox, Closed Caption, DVD.** Tim Robbins, Greta Scacchi, Fred Ward, Whoopi Goldberg, Peter Gallagher, Brion James, Cynthia Stevenson, Vincent D'Onofrio, Dean Stockwell, Richard E. Grant, Dina Merrill, Sydney Pollack, Lyle Lovett, Randall Batinkoff, Gina Gershon; *Cameos:* Michael Tolkin, Louise Fletcher, Dennis

Franz, Malcolm McDowell, Ray Walston, Rene Auberjonois, David Alan Grier, Jayne Meadows, Michael Bowen, Steve James, Brian Tochi, Burt Reynolds, Cher, Nick Nolte, Jack Lemmon, Lily Tomlin, Marlee Matlin, Julia Roberts, Bruce Willis, Anjelica Huston, Elliott Gould, Sally Kellerman, Steve Allen, Richard Anderson, Harry Belafonte, Shari Belafonte, Karen Black, Gary Busey, Robert Carradine, James Coburn, Cathy Lee Crosby, John Cusack, Brad Davis, Peter Falk, Teri Garr, Leeza Gibbons, Scott Glenn, Jeff Goldblum, Joel Grey, Buck Henry, Kathy Ireland, Sally Kirkland, Andie MacDowell, Martin Mull, Mimi Rogers, Jill St. John, Susan Sarandon, Rod Steiger, Joan Tewkesbury, Robert Wagner; **D:** Robert Altman; **W:** Michael Tolkin; **C:** Jean Lepine; **M:** Thomas Newman. British Academy Awards '92: Best Adapted Screenplay; Cannes Film Festival '92: Best Actor (Robbins), Best Director (Altman); Golden Globe Awards '93: Best Actor—Musical/Comedy (Robbins), Best Film—Musical/Comedy (Altman); Independent Spirit Awards '93: Best Film; New York Film Critics Awards '92: Best Cinematography, Best Director (Altman), Best Film; Writers Guild of America '92: Best Adapted Screenplay; Nominations: Academy Awards '92: Best Adapted Screenplay, Best Director (Altman), Best Film Editing. *NLC, CRC, MOV*

Players 🐾 **1979 (PG)** Young tennis hustler touring Mexico hooks up with beautiful and mysterious older woman. They seem to be from different worlds yet their love grows. She inspires him enough to enter Wimbledon. Several tennis pros appear, including Guillermo Vilas, John McEnroe, and Ilie Nastase. Almost as boring as watching a real tennis game. **120m/C VHS, Beta.** Ali MacGraw, Dean Paul Martin, Maximilian Schell, Pancho Gonzales; **D:** Anthony Harvey; **W:** Arnold Schulman; **M:** Jerry Goldsmith. *PAR*

The Players Club 🐾🐾🐾 **1998 (R)** Rapper-turned-auteur Ice Cube directs this look at the seamy and steamy world of strip clubs from his own screenplay. Diana (LisaRaye) is a single mom and college student by day, and a dancer at a strip club owned by the bombastic Dollar Bill (Mac) by night. When her naive cousin Ebony (Calhoun) is lured into turning tricks by fellow stripper Ronnie (Wilson), trouble starts. Blue (Foxx) is the deejay who falls for Diana, and is persuaded to act honorably by Diana's disapproving (and target shooting) father (Williams). Ice Cube appears as a customer who inadvertently lights the fuse for the movie's climax. While not in Woody Allen territory yet, Mr. Cube brings both humor and reality to the seedy world of strip joints.**CW:** Strong language, sexual content and violence. **107m/C VHS.** LisaRaye, Bernie Mac, Monica Calhoun, A.J. Johnson, Jamie Foxx, Ice Cube, Dick Anthony Williams, Tommy (Tiny) Lister, John Amos, Faizon Love, Alex Thomas, Chrystale Wilson, Adele Givens, Larry McCoy; **D:** Ice Cube; **W:** Ice Cube; **C:** Malik Hassan Sayeed. *NYR*

Playgirl Killer 🐾 *Decoy for Terror* **1966** After impulsively murdering a restless model, an artist continues to kill indiscriminately, keeping his spoils on ice. Sedaka croons between kills and luxuriates poolside—seemingly oblivious to the plot of the movie—while a female decoy is sent to bait the killer for the police. For adult viewers. **86m/C VHS, Beta.** **CA** William Kerwin, Jean Christopher, Andree Champagne, Neil Sedaka; **D:** Erick Santamaria.

Playing Away 🐾 **1987** A team of Caribbean cricket players meet a team of stuffy Brits on the field in a clash of the cultures. **100m/C VHS, Beta, LV.** **GB** Norman Beaton, Robert Urquhart; **D:** Horace Love. *NLC*

Playing Dangerous 🐾½ **1995 (PG-13)** Eleven-year-old computer whiz must outsmart computer thieves with the aid of a water gun and a remote-controlled car.**CW:** Terror/violence; some sexual situations; brief strong language. **86m/C VHS.** David Keith Miller; **D:** Lawrence Lanoff. *THV*

Playing Dead 🐾🐾½ **1915** Drew and his wife portray a married couple in this silent farce. The insecure husband decides to fake his death so his wife can be with the man he thinks she loves. **58m/B VHS.** Sidney Drew, Lucille Drew, Alice Lake, Donald Hall, Harry English, Isadore Marcil; **D:** Sidney Drew. *GPV*

Playing for Keeps 🐾 **1986 (PG-13)** Three high school grads turn a dilapidated hotel into a rock 'n' roll resort. Music by Pete Townshend, Peter Frampton, Phil Collins, and others. **103m/C VHS, Beta, LV, Closed Caption.** Daniel Jordano, Matthew Penn, Leon Grant, Harold Gould, Jimmy Baio; **D:** Bob Weinstein. *USH*

Playing for Time 🐾🐾🐾 **1980** Compelling, award-winning television drama based on actual experiences of a Holocaust prisoner who survives by leading an inmate orchestra. Strong playing from Redgrave and Mayron. Pro-Palestinian Redgrave's political beliefs made her a controversial candidate for the role of Jewish Fania Fenelon, but her stunning performance is on the mark. **148m/C VHS, Beta.** Vanessa Redgrave, Jane Alexander, Maud Adams, Viveca Lindfors, Melanie Mayron; **D:** Daniel Mann; **M:** Brad Fiedel. *NO*

Playing God 🐾🐾½ **1996 (R)** Eugene (Duchovny), a disgraced junkie doctor who has lost his license, saves the life of a hood in a bar while trying to score more drugs. This brings him to the attention of Raymond (Hutton), the head of a counterfeiting and smuggling ring, who hires Eugene as his own personal emergency room. While patching up crooks so they don't get arrested at the hospital, Eugene develops more than a doctor-patient relationship with Raymond's pillow-lipped girlfriend Claire (Jolie). Things begin to get a little slicey and dicey for Eugene, until he saves the life of an undercover cop. While sufficiently bloody and nasty, flick tries too hard to be offbeat and hip.**CW:** Strong graphic violence, gore, pervasive language and some drug use. **94m/C VHS, LV, Closed Caption.** David Duchovny, Timothy Hutton, Angelina Jolie, Michael Massee, Peter Stormare, Andrew Tiernan, John Hawkes, Gary Dourdan; **D:** Andy Wilson; **W:** Mark Haskell Smith; **C:** Anthony B. Richmond; **M:** Richard Hartley. *TOU*

Playing with Fire 🐾 **197?** A young girl gets caught up in drugs, casual sex, and murder. **87m/C VHS, Beta.** Karen Tungay, Danny Keogh, Sam Marais; **D:** Alan Nathanson. *NO*

Playmaker 🐾½ **1994 (R)** Jaime (Rubin) is a struggling actress whose coach Talbert (Firth) guarantees success as long as she follows his bizarre training methods, which include seduction, abuse, and betrayal. Good chemistry between the leads but a mishmash of a script.**CW:** Language; nudity; sex. **91m/C VHS.** Jennifer Rubin, Colin Firth, John Getz, Jeffery Perry; **D:** Yuri Zeltser; **W:** Yuri Zeltser; **C:** Ross Berryman; **M:** Mark Snow. *ORI*

Playmates 🐾 **1941** Barrymore is practically wasted in his last film as a down-on-his-luck actor who agrees to turn bandleader Kyser into a Shakespearean actor. Bizarre comedy is funny at times, but leaves the audience wondering what Barrymore thought he was doing. ♫Humpty Dumpty Heart; How Long Did I Dream?; Que Chica?; Romeo Smith and Juliet Jones; Thank Your Lucky Stars and Stripes. **96m/B VHS, Beta.** Kay Kyser, John Barrymore, Ginny Simms, Lupe Velez, May Robson, Patsy Kelly, Peter Lind Hayes, George Cleveland; **D:** David Butler. *TTC*

Playmates 🐾🐾½ **1972** Two divorced buddies fall in love with each other's ex-wives in this made for television flick. Typical Alda vehicle isn't bad. **78m/C VHS, Beta.** Doug McClure, Alan Alda, Connie Stevens, Barbara Feldon, Eileen Brennan, Tiger Williams, Severn Darden; **D:** Theodore J. Flicker. *THV*

Playroom 🐾🐾 **1990 (R)** Archaeologist McDonald is completing his father's search for the tomb of a medieval boy-prince. But someone, or something, has been waiting for him for a long, long time. When he finally reaches the long-sought-after tomb, he discovers that it is a torture chamber where his worst nightmares become realities. The demonic prince who was buried in the tomb has picked Chris as his playmate, and the rest of the staff as his personal toys. **87m/C VHS, LV, Closed Caption.** Lisa Aliff, Aron Eisenberg, Christo-

pher McDonald, James Purcell, Jamie Rose, Vincent Schiavelli; **D:** Manny Coto; **C:** James L. Carter. *REP*

Playtime 🐾🐾🐾 **1967** Occasionally enterprising comedy in which the bemused Frenchman Hulot tries in vain to maintain an appointment in an urban landscape of glass and steel. The theme of cold, unfeeling civilization is hardly unique, but the film is nonetheless enjoyable. The third in the Hulot trilogy, preceded by "Mr. Hulot's Holiday" and "Mon Oncle." In French with English subtitles. **108m/C VHS, Beta.** **FR** Jacques Tati, Barbara Dennek, Jacqueline Lecomte, Jack Gautier; **D:** Jacques Tati. *HMV, NLC*

Plaza Suite 🐾🐾🐾 **1971 (PG)** Three alternating skits from Neil Simon's play about different couples staying at the New York hotel. Matthau shines in all three vignettes. Some of Simon's funnier stuff, with the first sketch being the best: Matthau and Stapleton are a couple celebrating their 24th anniversary. She's sentimental, while he's yearning for his mistress. Number two has producer Matthau putting the make on old flame Harris, while the finale has father Matthau coaxing his anxious daughter out of the bathroom on her wedding day. **114m/C VHS, Beta, LV.** Walter Matthau, Maureen Stapleton, Barbara Harris, Lee Grant, Louise Sorel; **D:** Arthur Hiller; **W:** Neil Simon; **M:** Maurice Jarre. *PAR*

Please Don't Eat My Mother woof! *Hungry Pets; Glump* **1972** A softcore remake of "Little Shop of Horrors" in which a lonely voyeur plays host to a human-eating plant. **95m/C VHS.** Buck Kartalian, Renee Bond; **D:** Carl Monson. *MOV, VDM, TPV*

Please Don't Eat the Daisies 🐾🐾½ **1960** City couple and kids leave the Big Apple for the country and are traumatized by flora and fauna. Goofy '60s fluff taken from Jean Kerr's book and the basis for the eventual TV series. **111m/C VHS, Beta, LV, Letterbox.** Doris Day, David Niven, Janis Paige, Spring Byington, Richard Haydn, Patsy Kelly, Jack Weston, Margaret Lindsay; **D:** Charles Walters. *MGM, FCT*

Pleasure 🐾🐾 **1931** A saga of love, treachery, and melodrama in English society where self-indulgence held priority and good manners were the rule. **53m/B VHS, Beta, LV.** Conway Tearle, Roscoe Karns, Carmel Myers, Lena Basquette. *NOS*

A Pleasure Doing Business 🐾 **1979 (R)** Three high school buddies, now in their 40s, are reunited at a stag party, where they decide to go into business as managers in "the oldest profession." **86m/C VHS, Beta.** Conrad Bain, John Byner, Alan Oppenheimer, Misty Rowe, Phyllis Diller, Tom Smothers; **D:** Steve Vagnino. *VHE*

Pleasure Palace 🐾🐾 **1980** A gambling lady's-man (Sharif) meets his match when he helps a woman casino owner (Lange). Made for television. **96m/C VHS, Beta.** Omar Sharif, Victoria Principal, J.D. Cannon, Gerald S. O'Loughlin, Jose Ferrer, Hope Lange, Alan King; **D:** Walter Grauman. *ART*

Pledge Night 🐾🐾 **1990 (R)** Tale of horror and revenge. Killed years before in a fraternity hazing, Sid returns for the brothers who did him in. Gory and violent. **90m/C VHS, LV.** Will Kempe, Shannon McMahon, Todd Eastland; **D:** Paul Ziller. *IMP*

Plenty 🐾🐾½ **1985 (R)** Difficult but worthwhile film with Streep in top form as a former member of the French Resistance, who upon returning to England finds life at home increasingly tedious and banal and begins to fear her finest hours may be behind her. Gielgud is flawless as the aging career diplomat. Adapted by David Hare from his play, an allegory to British decline. **119m/C VHS, Beta, LV.** Meryl Streep, Tracey Ullman, Sting, John Gielgud, Charles Dance, Ian McKellen, Sam Neill, Burt Kwouk; **D:** Fred Schepisi; **W:** David Hare; **C:** Ian Baker; **M:** Bruce Smeaton. Los Angeles Film Critics Association Awards '85: Best Supporting Actor (Gielgud); National Society of Film Critics Awards '85: Best Supporting Actor (Gielgud). *REP*

The Plot Against Harry 🐾🐾🐾 **1969** Jewish racketeer Harry Plotnik checks out of prison, and finds the outside world ain't what it used to be. Attempting to lead an honest life only makes matters worse. Completely overlooked when first released in 1969 (and quickly shelved) because it was considered to have no commercial potential, Roemer's crime comedy found an enthusiastic audience when it was rediscovered 20 years later. 81m/B VHS. Martin Priest, Ben Lang, Maxine Woods, Henry Nemo; **D:** Michael Roemer; **W:** Michael Roemer. *NYF, FCT*

The Ploughman's Lunch 🎬🎬🎬 1983 A BBC news reporter claws and lies his way to the top. He then discovers that he is the victim of a far more devious plan. Engrossing and well made, although some of the political views are simplistic. 107m/C VHS, Beta. Jonathan Pryce, Charlie Dore, Tim Curry, Rosemary Harris, Frank Finlay, Bill Paterson; **D:** Richard Eyre.

Plughead Rewired: Circuitry Man 2 🎬🎬 *Circuitry Man 2* 1994 (R) Earth's atmosphere has been destroyed and survivors are forced underground, where they're terrorized by the humanoid Plughead, who likes to literally plug into the minds of his victims. Plughead wants to rule what's left of life on Earth and all that stands in his way is the android Circuitry Man and FBI agent Kyle. Special effects are strictly bargain basement level. 97m/C VHS. Vernon Wells, Deborah Shelton, Jim Metzler, Dennis Christopher, Nicholas Worth, Traci Lords; **D:** Steven Lovy, Robert Lovy; **W:** Steven Lovy, Robert Lovy. *COL*

Plumber 🎬🎬½ 1979 A plumber who makes a house call extends his stay to psychologically torture the woman of the house. Originally made for Australian television. 76m/C VHS, Beta. *AU* Judy Morris, Ivar Kants, Robert Coleby; **D:** Peter Weir; **W:** Peter Weir.

Plunder Road 🎬🎬½ 1957 A pair of crooks cook up a plan to rob a train bound for the San Francisco Mint that's carrying a fortune in gold bullion. Top notch B-film noir. 76m/B VHS. Gene Raymond, Jeanne Cooper, Wayne Morris, Elisha Cook Jr.; **D:** Hubert Cornfield. *REP*

Plunge Into Darkness 🎬½ 1977 Quiet weekend in the mountains turns into a nightmare for an ex-Olympic runner and his family. 77m/C VHS, Beta. Bruce Barry, Olivia Hamnett, Ashley Greenville, Wallace Eaton, Tom Richards; **D:** Peter Maxwell. *NO*

Plutonium Baby 🎬 1987 A mutated kid, whose mother was killed by the same radiation exposure that infected him, tracks down the guilty party in New York in this comic-book style film. 85m/C VHS, Beta. Patrick Molloy, Danny Guerra; **D:** Ray Hirschman. *TWE*

Plutonium Incident 🎬🎬 1982 A female technician at a nuclear power plant suspects the facility to be less safe than it appears, and faces a diabolical plan of harassment when she attempts to bring attention to the hazards. 90m/C VHS, Beta. Janet Margolin, Powers Boothe, Bo Hopkins, Joseph Campanella; **D:** Richard Michaels. *TLF*

Pocahontas 🎬🎬🎬 1995 (G) It's 1607 and spirited Powhatan maiden Pocahontas and British settler Captain John Smith strike an unlikely but doomed romance in Disney's 33rd animated feature, its first based on the life of a historical figure. Lovely Poca, a virtual post-adolescent Native American superbabe, introduces the roguish captain (spoken and sung by Gibson) to the wonders of unspoiled nature and serves as peacemaker in the clash of European and Native American cultures. Disney puts its spin on history but maintains cultural sensitivity: several characters are voiced by Native American performers, including Chief Powhatan, spoken by American Indian activist Means, who led the 1973 siege at Wounded Knee, and Bedard as Pocahontas. Just don't tell the kids the real Pocahontas married someone else, moved to England, and died of smallpox at 21. Stunningly animated, but its mediocre soundtrack and decidedly somber tone leave it lacking in typical Disney majesty and charm. Premiered at New York's Central Park, for the usual theatre crowd of 100,000 or so. 90m/C VHS, Closed Caption. **D:** Mike Gabriel, Eric Goldberg; **W:** Carl Binder, Susannah

Grant, Philip LaZebnik; **M:** Alan Menken, Stephen Schwartz; **V:** Irene Bedard, Judy Kuhn, Mel Gibson, Joe Baker, Christian Bale, Billy Connolly, James Apaumut Fall, Linda Hunt, John Kassir, Danny Mann, Bill Cobbs, David Ogden Stiers, Michelle St. John, Gordon Tootoosis, Frank Welker. Academy Awards '95: Best Song ("Colors of the Wind"), Best Original Score; Golden Globe Awards '96: Best Song ("Colors of the Wind"); Nominations: Golden Globe Awards '96: Best Score. *DIS*

Pocahontas: The Legend 🎬🎬½ 1995 Live-action version of the increasingly familiar story of the Native American girl who aids Virginia settler, John Smith. 101m/C VHS. *CA* Sandrine Holt, Miles O'Keeffe, Tony Goldwyn, Gordon Tootoosis; **D:** Daniele Suissa; **W:** Daniele Suissa. *GKK*

The Pocatello Kid 🎬½ 1931 Maynard stretches in a dual role as the wrongly convicted Kid and the Kid's no-good sheriff brother. 60m/B VHS, Beta. Ken Maynard, Marceline Day, Charles "Blackie" King, Lafe McKee; **D:** Phil Rosen. *NOS, VCN, VDM*

Pocket Money 🎬🎬 1972 (PG) Down-on-their-luck cowpokes foolishly do business with crooked rancher in attempt to make comeback in faltering acting careers. Star-powered, moderately entertaining modern western-comedy based on the novel "Jim Kane" by J.K.S. Brown. 100m/C VHS, Beta. Paul Newman, Lee Marvin, Strother Martin, Christine Belford, Wayne Rogers, Hector Elizondo, Gregory Sierra; **D:** Stuart Rosenberg; **W:** Terrence Malick; **M:** Alex North. *WAR, FCT*

Pocketful of Miracles 🎬🎬🎬 1961 Capra's final film, a remake of his 1933 "Lady for a Day," is just as corny and sentimental but doesn't work quite as well. Davis is delightful as Apple Annie, a down-on-her-luck street vendor who will go to any extreme to hide her poverty from the well-married daughter she adores. Ford is terrific as the man who transforms Annie into a lady in time for her daughter's visit. Touching. Maybe too touching. Also marks Ann-Margret's film debut. 136m/C VHS, Beta, LV, Letterbox, Closed Caption. Bette Davis, Glenn Ford, Peter Falk, Hope Lange, Arthur O'Connell, Ann-Margret, Thomas Mitchell, Jack Elam, Edward Everett Horton, David Brian, Mickey Shaughnessy; **D:** Frank Capra. Golden Globe Awards '62: Best Actor—Musical/Comedy (Ford); Nominations: Academy Awards '61: Best Costume Design (Color), Best Song ("Pocketful of Miracles"), Best Supporting Actor (Falk). *MGM, FOX, CCB*

A Pocketful of Rye 🎬🎬 *Agatha Christie's Miss Marple: A Pocketful of Rye* 1987 Based on Agatha Christie's novel featuring the sleuthing Miss Marple. She faces another murderous puzzle, this one based on an old nursery rhyme. Made for British television. 101m/C VHS, Beta, Closed Caption. *GB* Joan Hickson; **D:** Guy Slater. *FOX, HMV, VCO*

Poco 🎬 1977 The story of Poco, a shaggy little dog who travels across the country to search for the young girl who owns him. 88m/C VHS, Beta. Chill Wills, Michelle Ashburn, John Steadman. *ART, VES*

Poetic Justice 🎬🎬½ 1993 (R) Justice (Jackson in movie debut, for better or worse) gives up college plans to follow a career in cosmetology after her boyfriend's brutal murder. She copes with her loss by dedicating herself to poetry writing (provided by no less than poet Maya Angelou) and meets postal worker Shakur. Singleton's second directorial effort is about the girlz n the hood and boasts a lighter script (well, it is about a hairdresser) focusing less on the Boyz-style morality and more on the trials and tribulations of Justice. Production stopped on the South Central L.A. set during the '92 riots, but the aftermath provided poignant pictures for later scenes. **CW:** Strong language, violence, and sex. 109m/C VHS, LV, 8mm, Closed Caption. Janet Jackson, Tupac Shakur, Tyra Ferrell, Regina King, Joe Torry, Norma Donaldson; **D:** John Singleton; **W:** John Singleton; **C:** Peter Collister; **M:** Stanley Clarke. MTV Movie Awards '94: Best Female Performance (Jackson), Most Desirable Female (Jackson); Golden Raspberry Awards '93: Worst New Star (Jackson); Nominations: Academy Awards '93: Best Song ("Again"); Golden Globe Awards '94: Best Song ("Again"). *COL, BTV*

Pogo for President: "I Go Pogo" 🎬🎬½ 1984 (PG) Animated adventure with Walt Kelly's Pogo Possum becoming an unlikely presidential candidate when Howland Owl proclaims him the winner of a election. 120m/C VHS, Beta. **V:** Jonathan Winters, Vincent Price, Ruth Buzzi, Stan Freberg, Jimmy Breslin, Arnold Stang. *DIS*

Poil de Carotte 🎬🎬🎬 *The Red Head* 1931 A semi-famous French melodrama about a young boy harassed by his overbearing mother to the point of disaster, redeemed finally by the love of his father. In French with English subtitles. 90m/B VHS, Beta. *FR* Harry Baur, Robert Lynen, Catherine Fontenoy; **D:** Julien Duvivier. *NOS, FCT, MRV*

The Point 1971 Charming and sincere made-for-television animated feature about the rejection and isolation of a round-headed child in a world of pointy-headed people. Excellent score. 74m/C VHS, Beta, LV. **D:** Fred Wolf; **M:** Harry Nilsson; **V:** Paul Frees. *FHE, VES, MLT*

Point Blank 🎬🎬½ 1967 Adapted from Stark's "The Hunter." The film's techniques are sometimes compared to those of Resnais and Godard. Double-crossed and believed dead, gangster Marvin returns to claim his share of the loot from the Organization. Hard-nosed examination of the depersonalization of a mechanized urban world. 92m/C VHS, Beta, Letterbox, Closed Caption. Lee Marvin, Angie Dickinson, Keenan Wynn, Carroll O'Connor, Lloyd Bochner, Michael Strong, James B. Sikking; **D:** John Boorman. *MGM*

Point Break 🎬🎬½ 1991 (R) If you can suspend your disbelief—and you'd need a crane—then this crime adventure is just dandy. Reeves is a young undercover FBI kid sent to infiltrate a gang of bank-robbing surfer dudes. Swayze is the leader of the beach subculture, a thrillseeker who plays cat-and-mouse with the feds in a series of excellent action scenes. Silly brain candy. **CW:** Language, brief nudity, and violence. 117m/C VHS, LV, Letterbox, Closed Caption. Patrick Swayze, Keanu Reeves, Gary Busey, Lori Petty, John C. McGinley, Chris Pederson, Bojesse Christopher, Julian Reyes, Daniel Beer, Sydney Walsh, Vincent Klyn, James LeGros, John Philbin; **D:** Kathryn Bigelow; **W:** W. Peter Iliff; **M:** Mark Isham. MTV Movie Awards '92: Most Desirable Male (Reeves). *FOX*

Point of Impact 🎬🎬 1993 (R) A Miami customs officer is killed in an explosion and his partner is blamed. He knows a Cuban crime boss was actually behind it and goes undercover to bring the criminal organization down. But there's also the temptation of the criminal's sexy ladyfriend. Also available in an unrated version. **CW:** Language, strong violence, and strong sexuality. 96m/C VHS, LV, Closed Caption. Michael Pare, Barbara Carrera, Michael Ironside. *THV*

Point of No Return 🎬🎬½ 1993 (R) Fonda is Maggie, a drugged-out loser condemned to death for her part in a murder spree, but if she agrees to work as a government assassin, she'll be given a reprieve. Fonda displays a certain perkiness as the assassin and is better in her early surly scenes; Keitel is creepy as another assassin. Flashy, exacting, but ultimately innocuous remake of the 1990 French thriller "La Femme Nikita." **CW:** Language, strong violence, and sexuality. 108m/C VHS, Beta, LV, Letterbox, Closed Caption. Bridget Fonda, Gabriel Byrne, Dermot Mulroney, Miguel Ferrer, Anne Bancroft, Olivia D'Abo, Harvey Keitel, Richard Romanus, Lorraine Toussaint, Geoffrey Lewis, Calvin Levels; **D:** John Badham; **W:** Robert Getchell, Alexandra Seros; **C:** Michael Watkins; **M:** Hans Zimmer. *WAR*

Point of Terror 🎬 1971 (R) A handsome rock singer seduces a record company executive's wife in order to further his career. 88m/C VHS, Beta. Peter Carpenter, Dyanne Thorne, Lory Hansen, Leslie Simms; **D:** Alex Nicol. *NO*

The Pointsman 🎬🎬½ *De Wisselwachter* 1986 (R) A quirky, small film based on the novel by Jean Paul Franssens. A beautiful Scandinavian woman accidentally gets off a train in Northern Scotland, where the only shelter is a small railway outpost, and the only company is a mysterious pointsman who lives by the comings and goings of the trains. The couple's increasing isolation as winter falls and their lack of a common language persists is portrayed with both humor and poignancy. **95m/C VHS, Beta, LV. NL** Jim Van Der Woude, Stephane Excoffier, John Kraaykamp, Josse De Pauw, Ton Van Dort; **D:** Jos Stelling. **ART, VES**

Poison 🎞🎞🎞 **1991 (R)** A controversial, compelling drama weaving the story of a seven year-old boy's murder of his father with two other tales of obsessive, fringe behavior. From the director of the underground hit "Superstar: The Karen Carpenter Story," which was shot using only a cast of "Barbie" dolls. **CW:** Strong language, sexual violence, and sensuality. **85m/C VHS.** Edith Meeks, Larry Maxwell, Susan Norman, Scott Renderer, James Lyons, Millie White, Buck Smith, Anne Giotta, Al Quagliata, Michelle Sullivan, John R. Lombardi, Tony Pemberton, Andrew Harpending; **D:** Todd Haynes; **W:** Todd Haynes; **C:** Maryse Alberti; **M:** James Bennett. Sundance Film Festival '91: Grand Jury Prize. **FXL**

Poison Ivy 🎞🎞 **1985** A routine, made for television comedy about a chaotic and lusty summer camp. **97m/C VHS, Beta.** Michael J. Fox, Nancy McKeon, Robert Klein, Caren Kaye; **D:** Larry Elikann; **M:** Miles Goodman. **NO**

Poison Ivy 🎞🎞 **1992 (R)** Barrymore is right on target as a junior femme fatale in this trashy tale of a wayward teenager and her takeover of her best friend's family. Ivy has no discernable family life and quickly attaches herself to the lonely, neglected Cooper (Gilbert) who ends up watching as she systematically seduces both her mother (emotionally) and her father (physically). But when Ivy's homewrecking turns lethal, Cooper must fight her "friend" to save herself. Glossy, over-done pulp. An unrated version is also available. **CW:** Language and sensuality. **91m/C VHS.** Drew Barrymore, Sara Gilbert, Tom Skerritt, Cheryl Ladd; **D:** Katt Shea Ruben; **W:** Katt Shea Ruben, Andy Ruben; **C:** Phedon Papamichael. **COL, NLC, PMS**

Poison Ivy 2: Lily 🎞½ **1995 (R)** Art student Lily (Milano) finds the provocative Ivy's diary and becomes intrigued enough to decide to take a walk on the wild side herself, which gets her into all sorts of trouble. Also available unrated. **CW:** Strong sexuality, and for language. **110m/C VHS, LV, Closed Caption.** Alyssa Milano, Xander Berkeley, Johnathon Schaech, Belinda Bauer; **D:** Anne Goursaud; **W:** Chloe King; **M:** Joseph Williams. **NLC**

Poison Ivy 3: The New Seduction 🎞½ **1997 (R)** Now Ivy has a long-lost sister, appropriately named Violet (Pressly), who heads to their childhood home to get revenge on those she believes betrayed them. Naturally, it's all sex and men being led around by their...zippers. Also available unrated. **CW:** Strong sexuality, and for some language and drug content. **93m/C VHS, LV, Closed Caption.** Jaime Pressly, Megan Edwards, Michael Des Barres, Greg Vaughan; **D:** Kurt Voss. **NLC**

Poker Alice 🎞🎞 **1987** A lively Western starring Elizabeth Taylor as a sometime gambler who wins a brothel in a poker game. **100m/C VHS, Beta, Closed Caption.** Elizabeth Taylor, George Hamilton, Tom Skerritt, Richard Mulligan, David Wayne, Susan Tyrrell, Pat Corley; **D:** Arthur Seidelman; **W:** James Lee Barrett. **VTR**

The Polar Bear King 🎞🎞½ **1994 (PG)** When a handsome prince refuses to marry the evil witch of Summerland, the wicked woman uses her power to turn him into a polar bear. The polar bear prince embarks on a journey to Winterland where he meets and falls in love with a beautiful princess. Together they return to Summerland and try to break the witch's spell. Filmed on location in Norway and Sweden. **87m/C VHS, LV.** Maria Bonnevie, Jack Fjeldstad, Tobias Hoesl, Anna-Lotta Larsson; **D:** Ola Solum.

Poldark 🎞🎞🎞 **1975** Tempestuous love, political intrigue, and family struggles all set in 18th-century Cornwall, then the copper-producing center of England. Heroic Ross Poldark has just returned from fighting upstart Americans in the Revolutionary War only to discover that his father has died and the family mines are about to be sold to the scheming Warleggan family. Ross struggles to pay off family debts, reclaim his heritage, resolve his feelings for an old love, and fight his attraction to the beguiling, but completely unsuitable, Demelza. Adapted from the novels by Winston Graham. Made for British television; 12 episodes on six cassettes. **720m/C VHS. GB** Robin Ellis, Angharad Rees, Jill Townsend, Judy Geeson, Ralph Bates, Richard Morant, Clive Francis, Paul Curran, Tilly Tremayne, Mary Wimbush; **D:** Paul Annett, Christopher Barry, Kenneth Ives; **W:** Paul Wheeler, Jack Russell, Peter Draper, Jack Pulman. **TVC, SIG**

Poldark 2 🎞🎞🎞 **1975** The further adventures of Ross Poldark, wife Demelza, and assorted family, friends, and enemies, all set in 18th-century Cornwall. Demelza's two meddlesome younger brothers come to live at Nampara, enemy George Warleggan and Ross' old love Elizabeth move too close for comfort, and the uncertainties of the copper mining economy all bring their share of trouble. Adapted from the novels by Winston Graham. Made for British TV; six cassettes. **720m/C VHS. GB** Robin Ellis, Angharad Rees, Jill Townsend, Judy Geeson, Ralph Bates, Kevin McNally, Brian Stirner, Michael Cadman, Jane Wymark, David Delve, Christopher Biggins, Trudie Styler; **D:** Philip Dudley, Roger Jenkins; **W:** Alexander Baron, John Wiles, Martin Worth. **TVC**

Police 🎞🎞½ **1985** French police drama with the intense Depardieu as a cop hunting an Algerian drug boss. Matters grow complicated when he falls for the elusive crook's girlfriend. Sometimes gripping, but uneven; the actors were encouraged to improvise. Inspired by the novel "Bodies Are Dust" by P.J. Wolfson. In French with English subtitles. **113m/C VHS. FR** Gerard Depardieu, Sophie Marceau, Sandrine Bonnaire, Richard Anconina, Pascale Rocard; **D:** Maurice Pialat; **W:** Catherine Breillat. Venice Film Festival '85: Best Actor (Depardieu). **NYF, FCT**

Police Academy 🎞½ **1984 (R)** In an attempt to recruit more cops, a big-city police department does away with all its job standards. The producers probably didn't know that they were introducing bad comedy's answer to the "Friday the 13th" series, but it's hard to avoid heaping the sins of its successors on this film. Besides, it's just plain dumb. **96m/C VHS, Beta, LV, 8mm, Closed Caption.** Steve Guttenberg, Kim Cattrall, Bubba Smith, George Gaynes, Michael Winslow, Leslie Easterbrook, Georgina Spelvin, Debralee Scott; **D:** Hugh Wilson; **W:** Hugh Wilson, Pat Proft, Neal Israel; **M:** Robert Folk. **WAR**

Police Academy 2: Their First Assignment 🎞 **1985 (PG-13)** More predictable idiocy from the cop shop. This time they're determined to rid the precinct of some troublesome punks. No real story to speak of, just more high jinks in this mindless sequel. **87m/C VHS, Beta, LV, Closed Caption.** Steve Guttenberg, Bubba Smith, Michael Winslow, Art Metrano, Colleen Camp, Howard Hesseman, David Graf, George Gaynes; **D:** Jerry Paris; **W:** Barry W. Blaustein. **WAR**

Police Academy 3: Back in Training 🎞 **1986 (PG)** In yet another sequel, the bumbling cops find their alma mater is threatened by a budget crunch and they must compete with a rival academy to see which school survives. The "return to school" plot allowed the filmmakers to add new characters to replace those who had some scruples about picking up yet another "Police Lobotomy" check. Followed by three more sequels. **84m/C VHS, Beta, LV, Closed Caption.** Steve Guttenberg, Bubba Smith, David Graf, Michael Winslow, Marion Ramsey, Art Metrano, Bob(cat) Goldthwait, Leslie Easterbrook, George Gaynes, Shawn Weatherly; **D:** Jerry Paris; **W:** Gene Quintano; **M:** Robert Folk. **WAR**

Police Academy 4: Citizens on Patrol 🎞 **1987 (PG)** The comic cop cutups from the first three films aid a citizen's patrol group in their unnamed, but still wacky, hometown. Moronic high jinks ensue. Fourth in the series of five (or is it six?) that began with "Police Academy." **88m/C VHS, Beta, LV, Closed Caption.** Steve Guttenberg, Bubba Smith, Michael Winslow, David Graf, Tim Kazurinsky, George Gaynes, Colleen Camp, Bob(cat) Goldthwait, Sharon Stone; **D:** Jim Drake; **W:** Gene Quintano; **M:** Robert Folk. **WAR**

Police Academy 5: Assignment Miami Beach woof! **1988 (PG)** The fourth sequel, wherein the misfits-with-badges go to Miami and bumble about in the usual manner. It's about time these cops were retired from the force. **89m/C VHS, Beta, LV, Closed Caption.** Bubba Smith, David Graf, Michael Winslow, Leslie Easterbrook, Rene Auberjonois, Marion Ramsey, Janet Jones, George Gaynes, Matt McCoy; **D:** Alan Myerson; **W:** Stephen J. Curwick; **M:** Robert Folk. **WAR**

Police Academy 6: City Under Siege 🎞 **1989 (PG)** In what is hoped to be the last in a series of bad comedies, the distinguished graduates pursue three goofballs responsible for a crime wave. **85m/C VHS, LV, Closed Caption.** Bubba Smith, David Graf, Michael Winslow, Leslie Easterbrook, Marion Ramsey, Matt McCoy, Bruce Mahler, G.W. Bailey, George Gaynes; **D:** Peter Bonerz; **W:** Stephen J. Curwick; **M:** Robert Folk. **WAR**

Police Academy: Mission to Moscow 🎞 **1994 (PG)** The seventh in the series is another inept comedy, which finds the chaotic crew tackling a Russian mobster on his Moscow turf—all because of a popular computer game with some sinister software. Like you'll care about the plot anyway. **83m/C VHS.** George Gaynes, Michael Winslow, David Graf, Leslie Easterbrook, G.W. Bailey, Charlie Schlatter, Ron Perlman, Christopher Lee; **D:** Alan Metter; **W:** Michele S. Chodos, Randolph Davis; **M:** Robert Folk. **WAR**

Police Court 🎞🎞 **1937** The son of a faded, alcoholic screen star tries to bring the old fellow back to prominence. **62m/B VHS, Beta, LV.** Nat Barry, Henry B. Walthall, Leon Janney. **NO**

Police Squad! Help Wanted! **1982** Three episodes from the brilliant, short-lived television spoof, with the patented pun-a-second style of humor typical of the makers of "Airplane!" and "The Naked Gun," which was based on this show. Episodes included: "A Substantial Gift," "Ring of Fear," and "Rendezvous at Big Gulch." See also "More! Police Squad." **75m/C VHS, LV.** Leslie Nielsen, Alan North, Ed Williams, William Duell; **D:** Jerry Zucker, David Zucker, Jim Abrahams; **W:** Jerry Zucker, David Zucker, Jim Abrahams. **PAR**

Police Story 🎞🎞½ Jackie Chan's Police Force; Police Force; Jackie Chan's Police Story **1985 (PG-13)** Chopsocker Chan's assigned to protect a witness in a drug case. Faced by unsavory thugs, he flies through the air with the greatest of ease. Very cool stunts. **92m/C VHS. HK** Jackie Chan, Bridget Lin, Maggie Cheung, Cho Yuen, Bill Tung, Kenneth Tong; **D:** Jackie Chan. **NLC, TAI**

Policewoman Centerfold 🎞 **1983** Exploitative rendering based on the true story of a cop who posed for a pornographic magazine. Anderson is appealing in the lead. **100m/C VHS, Beta.** Melody Anderson, Ed Marinaro, Donna Pescow, Bert Remsen, David Spielberg; **D:** Reza Badiyi. **NO**

Policewomen 🎞½ **1973 (R)** Female undercover agent must stop a ring of gold smugglers. **99m/C VHS, Beta.** Sondra Currie, Tony Young, Phil Hoover, Elizabeth Stuart, Jeanne Bell; **D:** Lee Frost. **NO**

A Polish Vampire in Burbank 🎞🎞 **1980** A shy vampire in Burbank tries again and again to find blood and love. Wacky. **84m/C VHS, Beta.** Mark Pirro, Lori Sutton, Eddie Deezen; **D:** Mark Pirro. **NO**

Pollyanna 🎬🎬½ 1920 A young orphan girl is adopted by her cold, embittered aunt and does her best to bring joy and gladness to all the new people she meets. Silent with music score. **60m/B VHS, Beta, LV.** Mary Pickford; **C:** Charles Rosher. **CCB**

Pollyanna 🎬🎬🎬½ 1960 Based on the Eleanor Porter story about an enchanting young girl whose contagious enthusiasm and zest for life touches the hearts of all she meets. Mills is perfect in the title role and was awarded a special Oscar for outstanding juvenile performance. A distinguished supporting cast is the icing on the cake in this delightful Disney confection. Original version was filmed in 1920 with Mary Pickford. **134m/C VHS, Beta, LV, Closed Caption.** Hayley Mills, Jane Wyman, Richard Egan, Karl Malden, Nancy Olson, Adolphe Menjou, Donald Crisp, Agnes Moorehead, Kevin Corcoran; **D:** David Swift. **DIS, BTV**

Poltergeist 🎬🎬🎬🎬 1982 (PG) This production has Stephen Spielberg written all over it. A young family's home becomes a house of horrors when they are terrorized by menacing spirits who abduct their five-year-old daughter...through the TV screen! Roller-coaster thrills and chills, dazzling special effects, and perfectly timed humor highlight this stupendously scary ghost story. **114m/C VHS, Beta, LV, Letterbox, DVD.** JoBeth Williams, Craig T. Nelson, Beatrice Straight, Heather O'Rourke, Zelda Rubinstein, Dominique Dunne, Oliver Robbins, Richard Lawson, James Karen, Michael McManus; **D:** Tobe Hooper; **W:** Steven Spielberg, Michael Grais, Mark Victor; **C:** Matthew F. Leonetti; **M:** Jerry Goldsmith. Nominations: Academy Awards '82: Best Original Score. **MGM**

Poltergeist 2: The Other Side 🎬🎬½ 1986 (PG-13) Adequate sequel to the Spielburg-produced venture into the supernatural, where demons follow the Freeling family in their efforts to recapture the clairvoyant young daughter Carol Anne. The film includes sojourns into Indian lore and a four-foot high agave worm designed by H.R. Giger. The movie was followed by "Poltergeist 3" in 1988. **92m/C VHS, Beta, LV, Letterbox, Closed Caption.** Craig T. Nelson, JoBeth Williams, Heather O'Rourke, Will Sampson, Julian Beck, Geraldine Fitzgerald, Oliver Robbins, Zelda Rubinstein; **D:** Brian Gibson; **W:** Mark Victor, Michael Grais; **C:** Andrew Laszlo; **M:** Jerry Goldsmith.

Poltergeist 3 🎬½ 1988 (PG-13) Wrestling with the supernatural has finally unnerved Carol Ann and she's sent to stay with her aunt and uncle in Chicago where she attends a school for gifted children with emotional disorders. Guess who follows her? Uninspired acting, threadbare premise, and one ghastly encounter too many. Oddly, O'Rourke died suddenly four months before the film's release. **97m/C VHS, Beta, LV, Closed Caption.** Tom Skerritt, Nancy Allen, Heather O'Rourke, Lara Flynn Boyle, Zelda Rubinstein; **D:** Gary Sherman; **W:** Gary Sherman, Brian Taggert; **C:** Alex Nepomniaschy. **MGM**

Poltergeist: The Legacy 🎬🎬½ 1996 Premiere episode of the cable TV series about a secret international society, the Legacy, which is devoted to the paranormal and to protecting mankind from supernatural evil. Derek Rayne (De Lint), the head of the San Francisco Legacy house, must find the last of five sepulchers containing the evil spirits of five fallen angels. This takes him and his cohorts to Ireland where Rachel Corrigan (Shaver) and her young psychic daughter Kat (Purvis) come into unwitting possession of the fifth box and untold danger. **86m/C VHS, Closed Caption.** Derek De Lint, Helen Shaver, Alexandra Purvis, Martin Cummins, Robbi Chong, Patrick Fitzgerald, Jordan Bayne, William Sadler, Daniel Pilon, Chad Krowchuk; **D:** Stuart Gillard; **W:** Brad Wright; **C:** Manfred Guthe. **MGM**

Polyester 🎬🎬½ 1981 (R) Amusing satire on middle-class life, described by producer, director and writer Waters as "'Father Knows Best' gone berserk." Forlorn housewife Divine pines for the man of her dreams while the rest of her life is falling apart at the seams. Filmed in "Odorama," a hilarious gimmick in which theatre goers were provided with scratch-n-sniff cards, containing specific scents corresponding to key scenes. Video watchers will have to use their imagination in experiencing a wide range of smells. The first of Waters' more mainstream films. Features songs by Murray and Harry. **86m/C VHS, Beta, LV.** Divine, Tab Hunter, Edith Massey, Mink Stole, Stiv Bators, David Samson, Mary Garlington, Kenneth King, Joni-Ruth White; **D:** John Waters; **W:** John Waters; **M:** Bill Murray, Deborah Harry, Michael Kamen. **NLC**

Pom Pom Girls 🎬½ 1976 (R) High school seniors, intent on having one last fling before graduating, get involved in crazy antics, clumsy romances, and football rivalries. **90m/C VHS, Beta.** Robert Carradine, Jennifer Ashley, Michael Mullins, Cheryl "Rainbeaux" Smith, Dianne Lee Hart, Lisa Reeves, Bill Adler; **D:** Joseph Ruben. **NO**

The Pompatus of Love 🎬🎬½ 1995 (R) Remember Steve Miller's song "The Joker"?—well, that's where the title comes from—and we still don't know what it means. But the film's about four New York guys and the mystery of women. They may be (reasonably) bright and literate but they still don't have a clue about love or how to grow-up. Naturally, the women they know—or meet—are all too smart for them. **CW:** Nudity, sexuality and language. **99m/C VHS.** Jon Cryer, Tim Guinee, Adrian Pasdar, Adam Oliensis, Kristen Wilson, Dana Wheeler-Nicholson, Paige Turco, Mia Sara, Kristin Scott Thomas, Arabella Field, Jennifer Tilly, Roscoe Lee Browne; **D:** Richard Schenkman; **W:** Jon Cryer, Adam Oliensis, Richard Schenkman; **C:** Russell Fine; **M:** John Hill. **BMG**

Ponette 🎬🎬 1995 Four-year-old Ponette (Thivisol) is hard-pressed to understand what's happening to her family after her mother is killed in a car accident. Her father can't seem to explain it properly, so Ponette comes to her own acceptance with the help of some school friends. Film drew some controversy when the very young Thivisol was awarded the best actress award at the Venice Film Festival—since Thivisol was thought by some critics to be too young to "act," director Doillon was accused of manipulating the youngster in order to get a performance. French with subtitles. **107m/C VHS.** **FR** Victoire Thivisol, Marie Trintignant, Claire Nebout, Xavier Beauvois; **D:** Jacques Doillon; **W:** Jacques Doillon. New York Film Critics Awards '97: Best Foreign Film; Venice Film Festival '96: Best Actress (Thivisol). **NYR**

Pontiac Moon 🎬½ 1994 (PG-13) Danson plays a high school teacher who takes his son on a road trip to Spires of the Moon National Park hoping to arrive simultaneously with the astronauts' first lunar landing. His wife (Steenburgen) decides to follow them, although she's phobic about leaving the house and hasn't set foot outside in seven years. Sincere yet tedious film about father-son bonding has a few heartfelt moments, but not enough to sustain interest for entire viewing period. Best (and only) reason for watching: Monument Valley scenery. **108m/C VHS, Beta, Closed Caption.** Ted Danson, Mary Steenburgen, Ryan Todd, Eric Schweig, Cathy Moriarty, Max Gail, Lisa Jane Persky; **D:** Peter Medak; **W:** Finn Taylor, Jeffrey Brown; **M:** Randy Edelman. **PAR**

The Pony Express 🎬🎬½ 1925 Melodramatic western about an evil senator (Hart) who's out to establish his own empire. His scheme is thwarted by pony express rider Cortez. Based on the novel by Henry James Forman and Walter Woods. **67m/B VHS, Beta.** Ricardo Cortez, Al Hart, Betty Compson, Ernest Torrence, Wallace Beery, George Bancroft, Frank Lackteen; **D:** James Cruze; **W:** Walter Woods. **GPV**

Pony Express 🎬🎬🎬 1953 Buffalo Bill Cody and Wild Bill Hickok join forces to extend the Pony Express mail route west to California through rain and sleet, snow and hail. Far from a factual account but good for extending the myth of the Old West. **101m/C VHS, Beta.** Charlton Heston, Rhonda Fleming, Jan Sterling, Forrest Tucker; **D:** Jerry Hopper; **C:** Ray Rennahan. **PAR, BAR, HHE**

Pony Express Rider 🎬🎬🎬 1976 (G) Young man with a mission joins up with the Pony Express hoping to bag the male responsible for killing his pa. The well-produced script boasts a bevy of veteran western character actors, all lending, solid, rugged performances. **100m/C VHS.** Stewart Peterson, Henry Wilcoxon, Buck Taylor, Maureen McCormick, Joan Caulfield, Ken Curtis, Slim Pickens, Dub Taylor, Jack Elam; **D:** Robert Totten. **TPI**

Pony Post 🎬½ 1940 Standard horse opera has Brown running a pony express station where he battles Indians and typical villains. **59m/B VHS.** Johnny Mack Brown, Fuzzy Knight, Nell O'Day, Dorothy Short, Kermit Maynard, Lane Chandler; **D:** Ray Taylor; **W:** Sherman Lowe. **GPV**

Pool Hustlers 🎬½ 1983 A romantic comedy about an amateur billiards whiz who finds love and successfully defeats the national champ. In Italian with English subtitles. **101m/C VHS, Beta.** **IT** Francesco Nuti, Guiliana de Sio, Marcello Loti; **D:** Maurizio Ponzi. **XVC**

Pool Sharks 🎬🎬½ 1915 W.C. Fields' first film features the comedian's antics while playing a pool game to win the love of a woman. Silent. **10m/B VHS, Beta.** W.C. Fields. **HMV, GVV**

Poor Girl, a Ghost Story 🎬🎬 1974 A young girl takes a job as a governess at an English mansion and is besieged by all manner of strange goings-on. **52m/C VHS, Beta.** **AU** Lynn Miller, Angela Thorne; **D:** Michael Apted.

A Poor Little Rich Girl 🎬🎬🎬 1917 Mary Pickford received raves in this film, in which she portrayed Gwendolyn, with everything money could buy, except the attention of her family. Gwendolyn has a bizarre dream in which she sees a number of horrors and is tempted by death. Elaborate sets and special effects, as well as Pickford's delicate performance, make this one special. Organ score. **64m/B VHS, Beta, Closed Caption.** Mary Pickford, Madeline Traverse, Charles Wellesley, Gladys Fairbanks; **D:** Maurice Tourneur. National Film Registry '91. **CCB, VYY**

The Poor Little Rich Girl 🎬🎬½ 1936 A motherless rich girl wanders away from home and is "adopted" by a pair of struggling vaudevillians. With their help, they rise to the big time. Also available with "Heidi" on laserdisc. ♫ Oh My Goodness; Buy a Bar of Barry's; Wash Your Neck With a Cake of Peck's; Military Man; When I'm with You; But Definitely; You've Gotta Eat Your Spinach, Baby. **79m/B VHS, Beta, Closed Caption.** Shirley Temple, Jack Haley, Alice Faye, Gloria Stuart, Michael Whalen, Sara Haden, Jane Darwell; **D:** Irving Cummings. **FOX**

Poor Little Rich Girl: The Barbara Hutton Story 🎬🎬½ 1987 Bio-drama of the one-time richest woman in America, Woolworth heiress Hutton (Fawcett), and her extravagant lifestyle. She married seven times (including actor Cary Grant) until falling into self-destructive alcohol and drug addictions. Lavishly presented but superficial. Based on the book by C. David Heymann. Originally a two-part television movie. **98m/C VHS.** Farrah Fawcett, Bruce Davison, Kevin McCarthy, Burl Ives, James Read, Stephane Audran, Anne Francis, David Ackroyd, Tony Peck, Zoe Wanamaker, Amadeus August; **D:** Charles Jarrott; **W:** Dennis Turner; **M:** Richard Rodney Bennett. **ART**

Poor Pretty Eddie 🎬½ *Black Vengeance; Heartbreak Motel; Redneck County* 1973 (R) A young black singer gets waylaid and taken in by a twisted white Southern clan. An incredibly sleazy movie which boasts Shelly Winters performing a strip act. **90m/C Beta.** Leslie Uggams, Shelley Winters, Michael Christian, Ted Cassidy, Slim Pickens, Dub Taylor; **D:** Richard Robinson. **MRV**

Poor White Trash 🎬½ *Bayou* 1957 An architect arrives in bayou country with plans to design a new building. He meets with resistance from the locals but falls for the sensual daughter of one of his staunchest detractors. **83m/B VHS,**

Beta. Peter Graves, Lita Milan, Douglas Fowley, Timothy Carey, Jonathan Haze; **D:** Harold Daniels. *NO*

Poor White Trash 2 🎬 *Scum of the Earth* 1975 (R) A young couple, vacationing in Louisiana's bayou country, are introduced to an unusual brand of southern hospitality by the eponymous group of locals. **90m/C VHS, Beta.** Gene Ross, Ann Stafford, Norma Moore, Camilla Carr; **D:** S.F. Brownrigg. *TPV*

Pop Always Pays 🎬🎬 1940 A father gets in a jam when he has to make good on a bet with his daughter's boyfriend. **67m/B VHS.** Walter Catlett, Dennis O'Keefe, Leon Errol, Adele Pearce; **D:** Leslie Goodwins. *MLB*

Pop Goes the Cork 1922 Three films by the man Chaplin referred to as his "professor," Max Linder: "Be My Wife," "Seven Years Bad Luck," and "The Three Must-Get-Theres." Linder was the foremost film comedian in early 20th-century France, and made these three films during a stay in America. **87m/B VHS.** Max Linder. *CCB*

Popcorn 🎬🎬 1989 (R) A killer stalks a movie audience who is unaware that his crimes are paralleling those in the very film they are watching.**CW:** Some language and strong violence. **93m/C VHS, LV, 8mm.** Jill Schoelen, Tom Villard, Dee Wallace Stone, Derek Rydell, Elliott Hurst, Kelly Jo Minter, Malcolm Danare, Ray Walston, Tony Roberts, Karen Witter; **D:** Mark Herrier, Alan Ormsby; **W:** Alan Ormsby. *COL*

Pope John Paul II 🎬🎬 1984 A made-for-television biography of the Pontiff, from childhood to world eminence. **150m/C VHS, Beta.** Albert Finney, Michael Crompton, Nigel Hawthorne, John McEnery, Brian Cox; **D:** Herbert Wise. *IGP*

The Pope Must Diet 🎬½ *The Pope Must Die* 1991 (R) Coltrane stars as a misfit who accidentally becomes Pope Dave I. Living up to the benevolence suggested by his title, Pope Dave proposes to use Vatican money to create a children's fund. But there are those in the organization who have different, less noble plans for the cash, and soon Dave finds himself the target of a mob hit. Frantic comedy caused a stir with its original title "The Pope Must Die," with many newspapers refusing to run ads for the film. This, coupled with lukewarm critical reviews, led to a very brief stint at the boxoffice. **CW:** Language and sensuality. **87m/C VHS, Beta, LV, Closed Caption.** *GB* Robbie Coltrane, Alex Rocco, Beverly D'Angelo, Herbert Lom, Paul Bartel, Salvatore Cascio, Balthazar Getty; **D:** Peter Richardson; **M:** Anne Dudley. *VTR*

The Pope of Greenwich Village 🎬🎬½ 1984 (R) Two Italian-American cousins (Rourke and Roberts) struggle to escape the trap of poverty in New York's Greenwich Village. When a small crime goes wrong in a big way, the two must learn about deception and loyalty. Mostly character study; Page is exceptional. Inferior re-run of the "Mean Streets" idea does have its moments. **122m/C VHS, Beta, LV.** Eric Roberts, Mickey Rourke, Daryl Hannah, Geraldine Page, Tony Musante, M. Emmet Walsh, Kenneth McMillan, Burt Young; **D:** Stuart Rosenberg; **W:** Vincent Patrick; **C:** John Bailey; **M:** Dave Grusin. Nominations: Academy Awards '84: Best Supporting Actress (Page). *CCB, MGM*

Popeye 🎬🎬 1980 (PG) The cartoon sailor brought to life is on a search to find his long-lost father. Along the way, he meets Olive Oyl and adopts little Sweet Pea. Williams accomplishes the near-impossible feat of physically resembling the title character, and the whole movie does accomplish the maker's stated goal of "looking like a comic strip," but it isn't anywhere near as funny as it should be. **114m/C VHS, Beta, LV.** Robin Williams, Shelley Duvall, Ray Walston, Paul Dooley, Bill Irwin, Paul Smith, Linda Hunt, Richard Libertini; **D:** Robert Altman; **W:** Jules Feiffer; **M:** Harry Nilsson. *PAR*

Popi 🎬🎬🎬 1969 (G) Arkin is the heart and soul of this poignant charmer in his role as a Puerto Rican immigrant hell-bent on securing a better life outside the ghetto for his two sons. His zany efforts culminate in one outrageous scheme

---

to set them adrift off the Florida coast in hopes they will be rescued and raised by a wealthy family. Far fetched, but ultimately heartwarming. **115m/C VHS, Beta.** Alan Arkin, Rita Moreno, Miguel Alejandro, Ruben Figueroa; **D:** Arthur Hiller. *NO*

The Poppy Is Also a Flower 🎬½ *Poppies Are Also Flowers; Opium Connection* 1966 (PG) A star-laden, antidrug drama produced by the United Nations. Filmed on location in Iran, Monaco, and Italy. Based on a drug trade thriller by Ian Fleming that explains how poppies, converted into heroin, are brought into the United States. Made for television. **100m/C VHS, Beta.** E.G. Marshall, Trevor Howard, Gilbert Roland, Eli Wallach, Marcello Mastroianni, Angie Dickinson, Rita Hayworth, Yul Brynner, Trini Lopez, Bessie Love; **D:** Terence Young. *NO*

Porcile 🎬🎬 *Pigsty* 1969 Pasolini intertwines the story of a soldier cannibal living in a medieval age with the son of an ex-Nazi industrialist in present day Germany. Both the soldier and the young German (who prefers pigs to his fiance) become sacrificial victims of their differing societies. A grotesque fable on Pasolini's hatred of middle class mores and the 20th century. In Italian with English subtitles. **90m/C VHS, LV.** *IT* Pierre Clementi, Franco Citti, Jean-Pierre Leaud, Anna Wiazemsky, Ugo Tognazzi, Marco Ferreri; **D:** Pier Paolo Pasolini; **W:** Pier Paolo Pasolini; **C:** Tonino Delli Colli. *WBF*

Pork Chop Hill 🎬🎬🎬 1959 A powerful, hard-hitting account of the last hours of the Korean War. Peck is totally believable as the man ordered to hold his ground against the hopeless onslaught of Chinese Communist hordes. A chilling, stark look in the face of a no-win situation. Top notch cast and masterful directing. **97m/B VHS, Beta, LV, Closed Caption.** Gregory Peck, Harry Guardino, Rip Torn, George Peppard, James Edwards, Bob Steele, Woody Strode, Robert (Bobby) Blake, Martin Landau, Norman Fell, Bert Remsen; **D:** Lewis Milestone; **C:** Sam Leavitt. *MGM*

Porky's 🎬🎬½ 1982 (R) Investigation of teen horniness set in South Florida during the fab '50s. Irreverent comedy follows the misadventures of six youths imprisoned in Angel Beach High School who share a common interest: girls. Their main barrier to sexual success: the no-touch babes they lust after and the incredibly stupid adults who run the world. Fairly dumb and tasteless with occasional big laughs that earned mega bucks at the drive-in and created perceived popular outcry for more porky: "Porky's II: The Next Day" (1983) and "Porky's Revenge" (1985). **94m/C VHS, Beta, LV.** *CA* Dan Monahan, Wyatt Knight, Scott Colomby, Tony Ganios, Mark Herrier, Cyril O'Reilly, Roger Wilson, Alex Karras, Bob (Benjamin) Clark, Kim Cattrall, Kaki Hunter; **D:** Bob (Benjamin) Clark; **W:** Bob (Benjamin) Clark. *FOX*

Porky's 2: The Next Day 🎬🎬 1983 (R) More tame tomfoolery about teenage sex drives, Shakespeare, fat high school teachers, the Ku Klux Klan, and streaking in the Florida high school where it all began. Outright caricature shares the stage with juvenile humor, some of which may induce laughter. **100m/C VHS, Beta, LV.** *CA* Bill Wiley, Dan Monahan, Wyatt Knight, Cyril O'Reilly, Roger Wilson, Tony Ganios, Mark Herrier, Scott Colomby; **D:** Bob (Benjamin) Clark; **W:** Alan Ormsby, Bob (Benjamin) Clark. *FOX*

Porky's Revenge 🎬 1985 (R) The Angel Beach High School students are out to get revenge against Porky who orders the school basketball coach to throw the championship game. The second of the "Porky's" sequels. **95m/C VHS, Beta, LV, Closed Caption.** *CA* Dan Monahan, Wyatt Knight, Tony Ganios, Nancy Parsons, Chuck "Porky" Mitchell, Kaki Hunter, Kimberly Evenson, Scott Colomby; **D:** James Komack. *FOX*

The Pornographers 🎬🎬🎬 1966 Bizzare, black comedy focuses on a part-time porno filmmaker lusting after the daughter of the widow he lives with and trying to cope with his family, the world, and himself. A perversely fascinating exploration of contemporary Japanese society and

---

the many facets of sexual emotion. In Japanese with English subtitles. **128m/B VHS.** *JP* Shoichi Ozawa, Massaomi Konda, Sumiko Sakamoto, Haruo Tanaka, Keiko Sagowa; **D:** Shohei Imamura. *CVC, TPV*

Porridge 🎬🎬 *Doing Time* 1991 A British comedy inspired by the popular BBC situation comedy of the title, about a habitual criminal and convict who makes the most of his time in prison. **105m/C VHS.** *GB* Ronnie Barker, Fulton Mackay, Peter Vaughan, Julian Holloway, Geoffrey Bayldon; **D:** Dick Clement. *VCO*

Port of Call 🎬🎬🎬 1948 Early Bergman drama about a seaman on the docks who falls for a troubled woman whose wild, unhappy past has earned her an unsavory reputation. The hopeful, upbeat tone seems incongruous with the grim harbor/slum setting. It's minor Bergman but the seeds of his trademark themes can be seen taking shape, making it a must-see for avid fans. In Swedish with English subtitles. **100m/B VHS, Beta.** *SW* Ivine-Christine Jonsson, Bengt Eklund, Erik Hell, Berta Hall, Mimi Nelson; **D:** Ingmar Bergman. *NLC*

The Port of Missing Girls 🎬 1938 A young woman implicated in a murder stows away on a freighter. There she becomes caught up in a waterfront world of pirates, smugglers and other assorted undesirables. **56m/B VHS, Beta, 8mm.** Harry Carey Sr., Judith Allen, Milburn Stone, Betty Compson; **D:** Karl Brown. *VYY*

Port of New York 🎬🎬 1949 A narcotics gang is smuggling large quantities of drugs into New York. A government agent poses as a gang member in order to infiltrate the mob and get the goods on them. Brynner's film debut. **82m/B VHS, Beta.** Scott Brady, Yul Brynner, K.T. Stevens; **D:** Laslo Benedek. *NOS, VYY, DVT*

Portfolio 1988 (R) Real-life models star in this gritty drama about rising to the top of the fashion heap. Music by Eurythmics, Fun Boy Three and others. **83m/C VHS, LV.** Paulina Porizkova, Julie Wolfe, Carol Alt, Kelly Emberg. *NO*

Portnoy's Complaint 🎬½ 1972 (R) Limp screen adaptation of Philip Roth's novel follows the frustrating experiences of a sexually obsessed young man as he relates them to his psychiatrist. **101m/C VHS, Beta.** Richard Benjamin, Karen Black, Lee Grant, Jeannie Berlin, Jill Clayburgh; **D:** Ernest Lehman; **W:** Ernest Lehman. *WAR*

The Portrait 🎬🎬🎬 1993 Longtime real-life friends Bacall and Peck on-screen together for the first time in 37 years prove they are still shining stars as they play aging parents to Peck's real-life daughter, Cecilia Peck. The younger Peck is an artist preparing for a exhibition and asks her parents to sit for a portrait. This is the pole around which their relationships and reconciliations swing in this emotional made-for-cable-tv drama based loosely on Tina Howe's 1983 off-Broadway play, "Painting Churches." **89m/C VHS, LV, Closed Caption.** Lauren Bacall, Gregory Peck, Cecilia Peck, Paul McCrane, Joyce O'Connor, Donna Mitchell, Mitchell Laurance, William Prince, Augusta Dabney; **D:** Arthur Penn; **W:** Lynn Roth, Jack Darcus; **M:** Michael Conway Baker. *TTC, BTV*

Portrait in Black 🎬🎬½ 1960 Invalid shipping magnate Matthew Cabot (Nolan) is contempuous of second wife Sheila (Turner), who can't leave the marriage because of young son Peter (Kohler). She finds comfort in the arms of her husband's doctor, David Rivera (Quinn), and the duo decide the only way to find happiness is to kill off Cabot, which they do. Then Sheila begins to get anonymous letters accusing her of murder. Turner's glamor can't hide the gaping holes in the contrived plot. Adapted from the Goff/Roberts play. **113m/C VHS, Closed Caption.** Lana Turner, Lloyd Nolan, Anthony Quinn, Richard Basehart, Sandra Dee, John Saxon, Ray Walston, Anna May Wong, Virginia Grey, Dennis Kohler; **D:** Michael Gordon; **W:** Ivan Goff, Ben Roberts; **C:** Russell Metty; **M:** Frank Skinner. *USH*

Portrait in Terror ⭐½ 1966 A master thief and a deranged artist plan a heist of a Titian painting in an oddball suspense piece. Not a great success, but atmospheric and weird. **81m/B VHS.** Patrick Magee, William Campbell, Anna Pavane; **D:** Jack Hill. *SMW*

Portrait of a Hitman ⭐ *Jim Buck* 1977 Aspiring painter leads a double life as a professional hitman. Ragged feature feels more abandoned than finished, as if most of the movie had been shot and then the money ran out. All leads turn in paycheck performances, no more. **85m/C VHS, Beta.** Jack Palance, Rod Steiger, Richard Roundtree, Bo Svenson, Ann Turkel; **D:** Allan A. Buckhantz. *NO*

Portrait of a Lady ⭐⭐½ 1967 A spirited young American woman is taken to England and insists on complete freedom to choose her own future and make her own choices. Based on the 1881 novel by Henry James. On two cassettes. **240m/C VHS.** *GB* Richard Chamberlain, Suzanne Neve, Edward Fox. *VCO, TVC*

Portrait of a Lady ⭐⭐⭐ 1996 (PG-13) Adapted from the century-old Henry James novel, "Portrait" paints the story of independent and newly wealthy American, Isabel Archer (Kidman). Abroad in Europe, she falls under the influence of the bitter, opportunistic Madame Merle (Hershey, in a strong portrayal), who manages to steer the innocent Isabel into a disastrous marriage with Gilbert Osmond (Malkovich). From there, film deals with Isabel's efforts to flee the domineering Osmond and find herself again. Kidman plays her role with never-before-seen efficiency. Malkovich is suitably evil but plays his villain card a bit too early. Director Campion's modern voice carries the film through, but is sometimes out of place, as in the opening segment. Filmed in England and Italy. **CW:** Sensuality and some brief nudity. **142m/C VHS, LV, Letterbox, Closed Caption, DVD.** *GB* Nicole Kidman, John Malkovich, Barbara Hershey, Martin Donovan, Christian Bale, Shelley Winters, Shelley Duvall, Mary-Louise Parker, Richard E. Grant, John Gielgud, Viggo Mortensen; **D:** Jane Campion; **W:** Laura Jones; **C:** Stuart Dryburgh; **M:** Wojciech Kilar. Los Angeles Film Critics Association Awards '96: Best Supporting Actress (Hershey); National Society of Film Critics Awards '96: Best Supporting Actor (Donovan), Best Supporting Actress (Hershey); Nominations: Academy Awards '96: Best Costume Design, Best Supporting Actress (Hershey); Golden Globe Awards '97: Best Supporting Actress (Hershey). *PGV*

Portrait of a Rebel: Margaret Sanger ⭐⭐½ 1982 TV docudrama about the struggle of Margaret Sanger to repeal the Comstock Act of 1912, which prohibited the distribution of birth control information. **96m/C VHS, Beta.** Bonnie Franklin, David Dukes, Milo O'Shea; **D:** Virgil W. Vogel. *TLF*

Portrait of a Showgirl ⭐⭐ 1982 Inexperienced showgirl learns the ropes of Las Vegas life from a veteran of the Vegas stages. Made for television. **100m/C VHS, Beta.** Lesley Ann Warren, Rita Moreno, Tony Curtis, Dianne Kay, Howard Morris; **D:** Steven Hilliard Stern.

Portrait of a Stripper ⭐ 1979 A widowed mother works part-time as a stripper to support her son. Trouble arises when her father-in-law attempts to prove that she is an unfit mother. **100m/C VHS, Beta.** Lesley Ann Warren, Edward Herrmann, Vic Tayback, Sheree North; **D:** John Alonzo. *VES*

Portrait of a White Marriage ⭐⭐½ 1988 An extended made-for-cable comedy special revamping certain old "Mary Hartman, Mary Hartman" and "Fernwood 2-Night" conventions; a moronic talk show host moves his cheap show to his hometown of Hawkins Falls in order to boost the ratings. **81m/C VHS, Beta.** Martin Mull, Mary Kay Place, Fred Willard, Michael McKean, Harry Shearer, Jack Riley, Conchata Ferrell; **D:** Harry Shearer. *USH*

Portrait of Grandpa Doc ⭐⭐½ 1977 As a young artist prepares for his first one-man show, he struggles to complete a painting which he especially wants to have ready for the show—

a portrait of his grandfather, who died seven years earlier. Well, okay. **28m/C VHS, Beta.** Melvyn Douglas, Bruce Davison, Barbara Rush, Anne Seymour, Keith Blanchard. *BFA, ECU*

Portrait of Jennie ⭐⭐⭐½ *Jennie; Tidal Wave* 1948 In this haunting, romantic fable, a struggling artist is inspired by and smitten with a strange and beautiful girl who he also suspects may be the spirit of a dead woman. A fine cast works wonders with what could have been a forgettable story. The last reel was tinted green in the original release with the last scene shot in technicolor. Oscar-winning special effects. **86m/B VHS, Beta, LV, Closed Caption.** Joseph Cotten, Jennifer Jones, Cecil Kellaway, Ethel Barrymore, David Wayne, Lillian Gish, Henry Hull, Florence Bates, Felix Bressart, Anne Francis; **D:** William Dieterle; **C:** Joseph August. Academy Awards '48: Best Special Effects; Venice Film Festival '49: Best Actor (Cotten); Nominations: Academy Awards '48: Best Black and White Cinematography. *FOX*

Portrait of Teresa ⭐⭐⭐ 1979 Havana housewife has to balance motherhood, textile job, and cultural group activities without the cooperation of her husband. Vega skillfully portrays the lingering archaic attitudes and insulting assumptions that still confront post-revolution women. A fine eye for the revealing moments and movements of everyday life. In Spanish with English subtitles. **115m/C VHS.** Daisy Granados, Aldolfo Llaurado, Alina Sanchez, Alberto Molina; **D:** Pastor Vega. *NYF, FCT*

Portraits of a Killer ⭐⭐ *Portraits of Innocence* 1995 Attorney Elaine Taylor (Grey) is getting all hot and bothered by her client—photographer George Kendell (Mandylor), who's suspected in the murders of five hookers. But the detective (Ironside) on the case thinks she's just asking for trouble. **93m/C VHS, LV, Closed Caption.** Jennifer Grey, Costas Mandylor, Michael Ironside, Patricia Charbonneau, Kenneth Welsh, M. Emmet Walsh; **D:** Bill Corcoran. *ART*

Posed for Murder ⭐⭐ 1989 (R) A young centerfold is stalked by a psycho who wants her all for himself. **90m/C VHS, Beta.** Charlotte J. Helmkamp, Carl Fury, Rick Gianisi, Michael Merrins; **D:** Brian Thomas Jones.

The Poseidon Adventure ⭐⭐½ 1972 (PG) The cruise ship Poseidon is on its last voyage from New York to Athens on New Year's Eve when it is capsized by a tidal wave. The ten survivors struggle to escape the water-logged tomb. Oscar-winning special effects, such as Shelley Winters floating in a boiler room. Created an entirely new genre of film making—the big cast disaster flick. ♫The Morning After. **117m/C VHS, Beta, LV, Letterbox.** Gene Hackman, Ernest Borgnine, Shelley Winters, Red Buttons, Jack Albertson, Carol Lynley, Roddy McDowall; **D:** Ronald Neame; **W:** Wendell Mayes, Stirling Silliphant; **M:** John Williams. Academy Awards '72: Best Song ("The Morning After"), Best Visual Effects; Golden Globe Awards '73: Best Supporting Actress (Winters); Nominations: Academy Awards '72: Best Art Direction/Set Decoration, Best Cinematography, Best Costume Design, Best Film Editing, Best Sound, Best Supporting Actress (Winters), Best Original Dramatic/Comedy Score. *FOX*

Positive I.D. ⭐⭐ 1987 (R) A troubled housewife learns that the man who raped her years before is getting released on parole. She devises a second persona for herself with which to entrap him and get her revenge. **96m/C VHS, Beta.** Stephanie Rascoe, John Davies, Steve Fromholz; **D:** Andy Anderson; **W:** Andy Anderson. *USH*

The Positively True Adventures of the Alleged Texas Cheerleader-Murdering Mom ⭐⭐⭐½ 1993 (R) Satirical melodrama about Texas housewife Wanda Holloway (Hunter), accused of hiring a hitman to murder the mother of her daughter's chief cheerleading rival. She figures the girl will be so distraught that her own daughter can easily replace her. Ruthless and hilarious, this fact-based made-for-cable movie goes way over the top in satirizing suburban life-style excess and media overkill. Hunter, complete with whiney Texas twang, is

perfect in her role as self-absorbed Wanda and Bridges is great as her loopy ex-brother-in-law and partner in planned homicide. A riot compared to the usual dramatic movies served up by the networks. **CW:** Language. **99m/C VHS.** Holly Hunter, Beau Bridges, Swoosie Kurtz, Greg Henry, Matt Frewer, Frankie Ingrassia, Elizabeth Ruscio, Megan Berwick; **D:** Michael Ritchie; **W:** Jane Anderson; **M:** Lucy Simon. *HBO, FCT, BTV*

Posse ⭐⭐⭐ 1975 (PG) There's a hidden agenda, fueled by political ambition, in a lawman's (Douglas) dauntless pursuit of an escaped bandit (Dern). An interesting contrast between the evil of corrupt politics and the honesty of traditional lawlessness. Well performed, well photographed, and almost insightful. **94m/C VHS, Beta, LV, Closed Caption.** Kirk Douglas, Bruce Dern, James Stacy, Bo Hopkins, Luke Askew, David Canary, Alfonso Arau, Kate Woodville, Mark Roberts; **D:** Kirk Douglas; **W:** William Roberts; **M:** Maurice Jarre. *PAR*

Posse ⭐⭐⭐ 1993 (R) Big, brawny western shot with MTV in mind that tells the tale in part of how more than 8,000 black cowboys helped tame the American frontier. Or, as the advertising put it, "The untold story of the wild West." Or, spaghetti western meets blaxploitation meets the magnificent seven meets the L.A. riots, with characters actually saying, "No justice, no peace" and "Can't we all get along." However categorized, the intent is to show a side of Americana seldom seen, a goal realized. Strode, perhaps the greatest black Western star, appears at both the beginning and ending, while several other veteran black performers, including Russell, appear in cameos. Hunky Van Peebles is the leader of the usual misfits in the "Dirty Dozen" tradition, infantry deserters holding a load of gold. Between them and freedom is a gang of goons led by Zane. Lots of flash and dash, but lacking soul. **CW:** Language, strong violence, and strong sexuality. **113m/C VHS, LV, Closed Caption.** Mario Van Peebles, Stephen Baldwin, Charles Lane, Tommy (Tiny) Lister, Big Daddy Kane, Billy Zane, Blair Underwood, Tone Loc, Salli Richardson, Reginald Hudlin, Richard Edson, Reginald Vel Johnson, Warrington Hudlin; **Cameos:** Melvin Van Peebles, Pam Grier, Isaac Hayes, Robert Hooks, Richard Jordan, Paul Bartel, Nipsey Russell, Woody Strode, Aaron Neville, Stephen J. Cannell; **D:** Mario Van Peebles; **W:** Sy Richardson, Dario Scardapane; **C:** Peter Menzies Jr.; **M:** Michel Colombier. *PGV, FCT*

Possessed ⭐⭐½ 1931 A poor factory girl becomes a wealthy Park Avenue sophisticate when she falls in love with a rich lawyer who wants to be governor. Not to be confused with Crawford's 1947 movie of the same name, but worth a look. Gable and Crawford make a great couple! **77m/B VHS, Beta.** Joan Crawford, Clark Gable, Wallace Ford, Richard "Skeets" Gallagher, John Miljan; **D:** Clarence Brown. *MGM*

The Possessed ⭐⭐⭐ 1947 Crawford is at her melodramatic best as a crazed gal who can't find happiness with either hunk Heflin or bland Massey. First film for Brooks. From the story "One Man's Secret" by Rita Weiman. **109m/B VHS, LV.** Joan Crawford, Van Heflin, Raymond Massey, Geraldine Brooks, Stanley Ridges, John Ridgely, Nana Bryant, Moroni Olsen; **D:** Curtis Bernhardt; **C:** Joseph Valentine. Nominations: Academy Awards '47: Best Actress (Crawford). *MGM*

The Possessed ⭐½ 1977 (PG-13) Farentino is a priest who loses his faith, but regains it after an apparently fatal auto accident. Hackett is the headmistress of a private girls' school which is in need of an exorcist, since one of her student's appears to be possessed, and Farentino seems just the man for the job. Fairly tame, since originally made for TV. **75m/C VHS, Beta.** James Farentino, Joan Hackett, Diana Scarwid, Claudette Nevins, Eugene Roche, Ann Dusenberry, Dinah Manoff, P.J. Soles; **D:** Jerry Thorpe. *UNI*

Possessed by the Night ✱✱ 1993 (R) Kinky sex games ensue between a married writer and a sexy other woman thanks to a mysterious fetish object. Unrated version also available. **84m/C VHS, LV, Closed Caption.** Ted Prior, Shannon Tweed, Sandahl Bergman, Chad McQueen, Henry Silva; **D:** Fred Olen Ray. *COL*

Possession ✱ 1981 (R) Returned from a long mission, a secret agent notices that his wife is acting very strangely. She's about to give birth to a manifestation of the evil within her! Gory, hysterical, over-intellectual and often unintelligible. Originally shown in a longer version in Europe. **97m/C VHS, Beta.** *FR GE* Isabelle Adjani, Sam Neill, Heinz Bennent, Margit Carstensen, Shaun Lawtor; **D:** Andrzej Zulawski. Cesar Awards '82: Best Actress (Adjani). *ART, VES*

The Possession of Joel Delaney ✱✱½ 1972 (R) Blend of occult horror and commentary on social mores works for the most part, but some viewers may be put off by the low production values and spottiness of the script. MacLaine is a wealthy divorcee who must deal with the mysterious transformations affecting her brother. Skeptical at first, she begins to suspect he is the victim of Caribbean voodoo. **105m/C VHS, Closed Caption.** Shirley MacLaine, Perry King, Michael Hordern, David Elliott, Robert Burr; **D:** Waris Hussein. *PAR*

Possession: Until Death Do You Part ✱ 1990 When one man's attraction for a beautiful young woman becomes an obsession, a bizarre series of inexplicable events unravels a terrifying account of passion and revenge. **93m/C VHS.** Monica Marko, John R. Johnston, Sharlene Martin, Cat Williamson; **D:** Michael Mazo, Lloyd A. Simanol. *NO*

Postal Inspector ✱✱ 1936 An extraordinary tale of a postal inspector's life. Crime, romance, and natural disaster all overtake this civil servant. Catch the song "Let's Have Bluebirds On All Our Wallpaper." **58m/B VHS.** Carlos Cortez, Patricia Ellis, Michael Loring, Bela Lugosi, David Oliver, Wallis Clark; **D:** Otto Brower. *SNC, LSV*

Postcards from America ✱✱ 1995 (R) Traces the non-artistic aspects of the life of writer/artist David Wojnarowicz, who died of AIDS. Neophyte McLean concentrates on troubled childhood with an abusive father and teen years spent as a street hustler years. Choppy narrative uses little of Wojnarowicz's dialogue, save the voice-over narration by the lead character. Based on two semi-autobiographical novels by the artist. **93m/C VHS.** James Lyons, Michael Tighe, Olmo Tighe, Michael Imperioli, Michael Ringer, Maggie Low; **D:** Steve McLean; **W:** Steve McLean; **C:** Ellen Kuras; **M:** Stephen Endelman. *NYR*

Postcards from the Edge ✱✱✱½ 1990 (R) Fisher adapted her best-selling novel, tamed and tempered, for the big screen with a tour-de-force of talent. Streep very fine as a delightfully harried actress struggling with her career, her drug dependence, and her competitive, overwhelming show-biz mother. Autobiographical script is bitingly clever and filled with refreshingly witty dialogue. Lots of cameos by Hollywood's hippest. **101m/C VHS, Beta, LV, 8mm, Closed Caption.** Meryl Streep, Shirley MacLaine, Dennis Quaid, Gene Hackman, Richard Dreyfuss, Rob Reiner, Mary Wickes, Conrad Bain, Annette Bening, Michael Ontkean, Dana Ivey; **Cameos:** Robin Bartlett, Anthony Heald, Oliver Platt, CCH Pounder; **D:** Mike Nichols; **W:** Carrie Fisher; **C:** Michael Ballhaus. Nominations: Academy Awards '90: Best Actress (Streep), Best Song ("I'm Checkin' Out"). *COL, FCT*

The Postman ✱✱✱½ *Il Postino* 1994 (PG) Bittersweet, charming film about Mario (Troisi), a shy villager who wangles the personal postman of poet Pablo Neruda (Noiret), who is exiled from his beloved Chile in 1952, granted asylum by the Italian government, and who finds himself living in the tiny Italian community of Isla Negra. The tongue-tied Mario has fallen in love with barmaid Beatrice (Cucinotta) and asks the poet's help in wooing the dark-eyed beauty, striking up an un-

likely friendship with the worldly Neruda. Based on the novel "Burning Patience" by Antonio Skarmeta. Italian with subtitles. Troisi, a beloved comic actor in his native Italy, was gravely ill, needing a heart transplant, during the making of the film (all-too apparent from his gaunt appearance) and died the day after filming was completed. **115m/C VHS.** *IT* Massimo Troisi, Philippe Noiret, Maria Grazia Cucinotta, Linda Moretti, Renato Scarpa, Anna Buonaiuto, Mariana Rigillo; **D:** Michael Radford; **W:** Massimo Troisi, Michael Radford, Furio Scarpelli, Anna Pavignano, Giacomo Scarpelli; **C:** Franco Di Giacomo; **M:** Luis Bacalov. Academy Awards '95: Best Original Dramatic/Comedy Score; British Academy Awards '95: Best Director (Radford), Best Foreign Film, Best Score; Broadcast Film Critics Association Awards '95: Best Foreign Film; Nominations: Academy Awards '95: Best Actor (Troisi), Best Adapted Screenplay, Best Director (Radford), Best Picture; British Academy Awards '95: Best Actor (Troisi), Best Adapted Screenplay; Cesar Awards '97: Best Foreign Film; Directors Guild of America Awards '95: Best Director (Radford); Screen Actors Guild Award '95: Best Actor (Troisi). *TOU*

The Postman ✱ 1997 (R) It's postapocalypse time (the year's 2013), with a nameless drifter (Costner) assuming the role of a postal carrier in order to bring hope to a devasted town terrorized by marauding hooligans, led by General Bethlehem (Patton). If you fancy deadpan dialogue and can swallow the image of a mail carrier as the symbol for patriotism, then this one's for you. Overall, Costner offers nothing new to the genre of the stranger offering hope, and soon flick becomes a cornball exercise and extravagent waste of time for all involved. Costner's first directing effort since "Dances with Wolves." It's time someone told Kevin to get out of the epic business and stick to the "everyday Joe" roles. **CW:** Mature themes, language, violence, sexual situations, nudity. **170m/C VHS, LV, Letterbox, Closed Caption, DVD.** Kevin Costner, Larenz Tate, Will Patton, Olivia Williams, James Russo, Tom Petty, Daniel von Bargen, Scott Bairstow, Giovanni Ribisi, Roberta Maxwell, Joe Santos, Peggy Lipton, Ron McLarty, Rex Linn, Todd Allen; **D:** Kevin Costner; **W:** Brian Helgeland, Eric Roth; **C:** Stephen Windon; **M:** James Newton Howard. Golden Raspberry Awards '97: Worst Picture, Worst Actor (Costner), Worst Director (Costner), Worst Screenplay, Worst Song (Entire Song Score). *WAR*

The Postman Always Rings Twice ✱✱✱½ 1946 Even without the brutal sexuality of the James M. Cain novel, Garfield and Turner sizzle as the lust-laden lovers in this lurid tale of fatal attraction. Garfield provides the show as the streetwise drifter who blows into town and lights a fire in Turner. As their affair steams up the two conspire to do away with her husband and circumstances begin to spin out of control. Tense and compelling. A classic. **113m/B VHS, Beta, LV, Closed Caption.** Lana Turner, John Garfield, Cecil Kellaway, Hume Cronyn, Leon Ames, Audrey Totter, Alan Reed; **D:** Tay Garnett; **M:** George Bassman. *MGM*

The Postman Always Rings Twice ✱✱ 1981 (R) It must be true because he's ringing again in Mamet's version of James M. Cain's depression-era novel. This time Nicholson plays the drifter and Lange the amoral wife with an aged husband. Truer to the original story than the 1946 movie in its use of brutal sex scenes, it nevertheless lacks the power of the original. Nicholson works well in this time era and Lange adds depth and realism to the character of Cora. But in the end it remains dreary and easily forgettable. **123m/C VHS, Beta, LV.** Jack Nicholson, Jessica Lange, John Colicos, Anjelica Huston, Michael Lerner, John P. Ryan, Christopher Lloyd; **D:** Bob Rafelson; **W:** David Mamet; **C:** Sven Nykvist. *FOX, WAR*

Postmark for Danger ✱✱½ *Portrait of Alison* 1956 Detectives do their best to smash a diamond smuggling ring that operates between Britain and the U.S. Along the way a number of people are killed. **84m/B VHS, Beta.** *GB* Terry Moore, Robert Beatty, William Sylvester, Josephine Griffin, Geoffrey Keen, Henry Oscar; **D:** Guy Green. *SNC*

Postmark for Danger/Quicksand ✱✱ 1956 A "film noire" double feature. In "Postmark for Danger," a young actress returns from the dead to find a criminal, while in "Quicksand," a mechanic becomes indebted to the mob when he borrows extra money for a date. **155m/B VHS, Beta.** *GB* Terry Moore, Robert Beatty, Mickey Rooney, Jeanne Cagney, Peter Lorre; **D:** Guy Green. *SNC*

Pot O' Gold ✱✱ *The Golden Hour* 1941 Stewart plays a wealthy young man who signs on with a struggling band. He convinces his uncle, who has a radio program, to let the band perform during a radio giveaway show he has concocted. Slight comedy, Stewart notwithstanding. **87m/B VHS, Beta.** Paulette Goddard, James Stewart, Charles Winninger, Horace Heidt, Art Carney; **D:** George Marshall. *NOS, CCB, VYY*

Pot, Parents, and Police ✱ 1971 A 13-year-old boy goes crazy when his dog dies and soon gets in with a hippie crowd, drops acid, and gets in trouble with the cops. **m/C VHS.** Phillip Pine, Robert Mantell, Madelyn Keen; **D:** Phillip Pine; **W:** Phillip Pine. *SMW, MOV, TPV*

Pound Puppies and the Legend of Big Paw 1988 The Pound Puppies, known for breaking dogs out of pounds and delivering them to safe and secure homes, are featured in their first full-length musical (and merchandising effort). Fifties music. **76m/C VHS. D:** Pierre de Celles; **W:** Jim Carlson; **V:** Nancy Cartwright, George Rose, B.J. Ward, Ruth Buzzi, Brennan Howard. *FHE*

Pouvoir Intime ✱✱½ 1987 (PG-13) What happens when robbers of an armored car lock the guard in the vehicle, and he decides to fight back? This film offers one possible scenario. Available in dubbed or subtitled versions. **86m/C VHS.** *FR* Marie Tifo, Pierre Curzi, Yvan Ponton, Jaques Lussier; **D:** Yves Simoneau. *TPV*

P.O.W. Deathcamp ✱✱ 1989 A combat unit is captured and tortured by the Vietcong in this typical Vietnam story. **92m/C VHS.** Charles Black, Bill Balbridge, Rey Malonzo; **D:** Jett C. Espirtu. *ATL*

The P.O.W. Escape ✱½ *Behind Enemy Lines* 1986 (R) The adventures of a surly American commander captured as a POW during the final days of the Vietnam War. **90m/C VHS, Beta, LV.** David Carradine, Mako, Charles R. Floyd, Steve James; **D:** Gideon Amir; **W:** Malcolm Barbour, James Bruner, Jeremy Lipp, John Langley. *VTR*

Powaqqatsi: Life in Transformation ✱✱✱½ 1988 (G) Director Reggio's follow-up to "Koyaanisqatsi" doesn't pack the wallop of its predecessor. Still, the cinematography is magnificent and the music of Philip Glass is exquisitely hypnotic as we are taken on a spellbinding video collage of various third world countries and see the price they've paid in the name of progress. Part 2 of a planned trilogy. **95m/C VHS, Beta. D:** Godfrey Reggio; **M:** Philip Glass.

Powder ✱✱ 1995 (PG-13) An electromagnetic albino with an I.Q. off the charts is discovered living in his grandparents' cellar and brought to live in a school for troubled teens. Despite harrassment from the crude locals, Powder (Flanery) manages to exude compassion and electricity all over the place with the help of sensitive school director Steenbergen and wacky science teacher Goldblum. Hyper-sentimentality, convoluted and contradictory writing, absurd messianic overtones, and a cop-out climax barely scratch the surface of film's problems. Revelations of Salva's criminal conviction for child molestation cast some scenes in a disturbing light and caused major headaches for Disney's publicity department. **CW:** Contains intense, sometimes frightening elements of theme and strong language. **111m/C VHS.** Sean Patrick Flanery, Mary Steenburgen, Lance Henriksen, Jeff Goldblum, Brandon Smith, Bradford Tatum, Susan Tyrrell, Missy Crider, Ray Wise, Esteban Louis Powell; **D:** Victor Salva; **W:** Victor Salva; **C:** Jerzy Zielinski; **M:**

Jerry Goldsmith. Nominations: MTV Movie Awards '96: Breakthrough Performance (Flanery). *TOU*

Powder Burn 🎬½ **1996** Detective Jack Becker seeks to protect a Beverly Hills client's young daughter when he uncovers unsavory goings-on at her home. And then discovers he's being set up to be the patsy for a murder. **92m/C VHS.** Jay Irwin, Elizabeth Barry. *LEO*

Powder Keg 🎬🎬 **1970** Railroad company hires a rowdy team of investigators to retrieve a hijacked train. Action never quits. The idea for the television pilot "The Bearcats" came from this movie. **93m/C VHS, Beta.** Rod Taylor, Dennis Cole, Michael Ansara, Fernando Lamas, Tisha Sterling; **D:** Douglas Heyes. *SIM, WOV*

Powdersmoke Range 🎬🎬½ **1935** Crooked frontier politician plots to steal valuable ranch property. The new owners, however, have other ideas. First in "The Three Mesquiteer" series. **71m/B VHS, Beta.** Harry Carey Sr., Hoot Gibson, Tom Tyler, Guinn "Big Boy" Williams, Bob Steele, Sam Hardy, Patricia "Boots" Mallory, Franklyn Farnum, William Desmond, William Farnum, Buzz Barton, Wally Wales, Art Mix, Buffalo Bill Jr., Buddy Roosevelt; **D:** Wallace Fox. *RXM*

Power 🎬🎬½ **1928** Two dam-building construction workers vie with each other for the local girls. Silent. **60m/B VHS, Beta.** William Boyd, Alan Hale, Carole Lombard, Joan Bennett; **D:** Howard Higgin. *FCT, GPV, GVV*

Power 🎬🎬½ *Jew Suss* **1934** A Jewish ghetto inhabitant in 18th-century Wurtemburg works his way out of the gutter and into some authority by pleasing the whims of an evil duke. Based on the novel by Leon Fuechtwangler. **105m/B VHS.** *GB* Conrad Veidt, Benita Hume, Frank Vosper, Cedric Hardwicke, Gerald du Maurier, Pamela Ostrer, Joan Maude, Paul Graetz, Mary Clare, Percy Parsons, Dennis Hoey, Gibb McLaughlin, Francis L. Sullivan; **D:** Lothar Mendes. *DVT*

The Power 🎬½ **1980 (R)** An ancient clay idol that was created by the Aztecs and possesses incredible destructive power is unleashed on modern man. **87m/C VHS.** Warren Lincoln, Susan Stokey, Lisa Erickson, Jeffrey Obrow; **D:** Stephen Carpenter; **W:** Stephen Carpenter, John Penney. *ART, VES*

Power 🎬🎬½ **1986 (R)** A study of corporate manipulations. Gere plays a ruthless media consultant working for politicians. Fine cast can't find the energy needed to make this great, but it's still interesting. Lumet did better with same material in "Network." **111m/C VHS, Beta, LV, Closed Caption.** Richard Gere, Julie Christie, E.G. Marshall, Gene Hackman, Beatrice Straight, Kate Capshaw, Denzel Washington, Fritz Weaver, Michael Learned, E. Katherine Kerr, Polly Rowles, Matt Salinger, J.T. Walsh; **D:** Sidney Lumet; **W:** David Himmelstein; **C:** Andrzej Bartkowiak; **M:** Cy Coleman. *ORI, WAR*

Power 98 🎬 **1996 (R)** L.A. shock-jock Karlin Pickett (Roberts) takes inexperienced Jon Price (Gedrick) as his protege, much to the dismay of girlfriend Sharon (Garth). Since Pickett will do anything to get higher ratings, she's right to worry, especially after a caller confesses to murder during Pickett's show. Roberts refrains from scenery-chewing but co-stars Gedrick and Garth give new meaning to bland. **CW:** Strong sexuality, language and some violence. **89m/C VHS.** Eric Roberts, Jason Gedrick, Jennie Garth, Larry Drake, Stephen Tobolowsky; **D:** Jaime Hellman; **W:** Jaime Hellman; **C:** Kent Wakeford; **M:** Jeff Beal. *WAR*

Power of Attorney 🎬🎬 **1994 (R)** Ambitious up-from-the-streets lawyer Paul Diehl (Koteas) decides to defend Mafia don Joseph Scassi (Aiello) against federal charges of murder and extortion, convincing himself that the mobster is telling the truth. But Scassi decides to make certain his lawyer will do his best by threatening Diehl's drug-dealing brother Frankie (Wilson). **CW:** Sexuality, language. **97m/C VHS.** Danny Aiello, Elias Koteas, Nina Siemaszko, Rae Dawn Chong, Roger Wilson; **D:** Howard Himelstein; **W:** George Erschbamer, Jeff Barmash; **M:** Hal Beckett. *TTC*

The Power of One 🎬🎬 **1992 (PG-13)** Good cast is generally wasted in liberal white look at apartheid. Set in South Africa during the 1940s, P.K. is a white orphan of British descent who is sent to a boarding school run by Afrikaaners (South Africans of German descent). Humiliated and bullied, particularly when England and Germany go to war, P.K. is befriended by a German pianist and a black boxing coach who teach him to box and stand up for his rights. Preachy and filled with stereotypes. Based on the novel by Bryce Courtenay. **126m/C VHS, LV, Closed Caption.** Stephen Dorff, Armin Mueller-Stahl, Morgan Freeman, John Gielgud, Fay Masterson, Marius Weyers, Tracy Brooks Swope, John Osborne, Daniel Craig, Dominic Walker, Alois Mayo, Ian Roberts, Maria Marais; **D:** John G. Avildsen; **W:** Robert Mark Kamen. *WAR*

The Power of the Ninjitsu 🎬 **1988** A young man inherits the leadership of a martial arts crime gang, the Scorpions, but the elder members muscle him out of his place. He returns for revenge and has the old ones running scared. Power to the Ninjitsu! **90m/C VHS, Beta.** Britton Lee, Adam Frank, Peter Ujaer; **D:** Joseph Lai. *IME*

Power, Passion & Murder 🎬½ **1983** A young, glamorous movie star has an affair with a married man which begins the end of her career in 1930s Hollywood. **104m/C VHS, Beta, LV.** Michelle Pfeiffer, Darren McGavin, Stella Stevens; **D:** Paul Bogart, Leon Ichaso. *THV, IME, HHE*

Power Play 🎬½ *Operation Overthrow* **1981** Young army colonel from a small European country joins forces with rebels to overthrow the government. After the coup, the group discovers that in their midst is a traitor. So who is it? Suspense never builds adequately. **95m/C VHS, Beta.** *CA GB* Peter O'Toole, David Hemmings, Donald Pleasence, Barry Morse; **D:** Martyn Burke; **W:** Martyn Burke.

The Power Within 🎬½ **1979** An electrified stuntman finds he can send electrical shocks from his hands and becomes the victim of a kidnapping plot. **90m/C VHS, Beta.** Eric (Hans Gudegast) Braeden, David Hedison, Susan Howard, Art Hindle; **D:** John Llewellyn Moxey.

The Power Within 🎬🎬½ **1995 (PG-13)** Evil Raymond Vonn has stolen an ancient ring of power but to acquire its complete strength he needs to find a second, matching ring. This is in the possession of teenaged Stan Dryer (Roberts), who must discover the ring's power if he expects to defeat Vonn. **CW:** Martial arts violence. **97m/C VHS, Closed Caption.** Ted Jan Roberts, Karen Valentine, Keith Coogan, John O'Hurley, Gary Morgan, Sean Fitzgerald; **D:** Art Camacho; **W:** Susan Bowen, Jacobsen Hart; **M:** Jim Halfpenny. *PMH*

Powwow Highway 🎬🎬🎬½ **1989 (R)** Remarkably fine performances in this unusual, thought-provoking, poorly titled foray into the plight of Native Americans. Farmer shines as the unassuming, amiable Cheyenne traveling to New Mexico in a beat-up Chevy with his Indian activist buddy, passionately portrayed by Martinez. On the journey they are constantly confronted with the tragedy of life on a reservation. A sobering look at government injustice and the lingering spirit of a people lost inside their homeland. **105m/C VHS, Beta.** Gary Farmer, A. Martinez, Amanda Wyss, Rene Handren-Seals, Graham Greene; **D:** Joanelle Romero, Jonathan Wacks; **W:** Janet Heaney, Jean Stawarz; **C:** Toyomichi Kurita; **M:** Barry Goldberg. Sundance Film Festival '89: Filmmakers Trophy. *FCT*

The Practice of Love 🎬🎬 **1984** A woman journalist's investigation of a murder casts suspicion on her two male lovers. The film raises the question of whether love is even possible in a world dominated by men's struggles for power. In German with English subtitles. **90m/C VHS.** *GE* **D:** Valie Export. *FCT, MOV*

Prairie Badmen 🎬½ **1946** Outlaws are after a treasure map in the possession of the owner of a medicine show. It's up to our hero to stop them. One of the "Billy Carson" western series. **55m/B VHS, Beta.** Buster Crabbe. *VCN*

The Prairie King 🎬½ **1927** Will grants three people the same gold mine but stipulates only one may own it. Silent quandary. **58m/B VHS, Beta.** Hoot Gibson, Barbara Worth, Charles Sellon, Albert Priscoe. *GPV*

Prairie Moon 🎬½ **1938** Autry becomes the guardian of three tough kids from Chicago after they inherit a ranch. The kids help Autry round up a gang of rustlers. **58m/B VHS, Beta.** Gene Autry, Smiley Burnette. *CCB, VCN, DVT*

Prairie Pals 🎬½ **1942** Deputies go undercover to rescue a kidnapped scientist. **60m/B VHS, Beta.** William Boyd, Lee Powell, Art Davis, Charles "Blackie" King, John Merton, Kermit Maynard, Al "Fuzzy" St. John; **D:** Sam Newfield. *GPV, VCN*

The Prairie Pirate 🎬🎬½ **1925** Carey is the western hero tracking down the dirty dogs who murdered his sister. Fast-paced. **59m/B VHS.** Harry Carey Sr., Lloyd Whitlock, Jean Dumas, Trilby Clark; **D:** Edmund Mortimer. *GPV*

Prancer 🎬🎬 **1989 (G)** An eight-year-old girl whose mother has recently died thinks an injured reindeer she has found belongs to Santa. She lovingly nurses him back to health. Harmless family entertainment. **102m/C VHS, Beta, LV, 8mm, Closed Caption.** Sam Elliott, Rebecca Harrell, Cloris Leachman, Rutanya Alda, John Joseph Duda, Abe Vigoda, Michael Constantine, Ariana Richards, Mark Rolston; **D:** John Hancock; **M:** Maurice Jarre. *COL, ORI, FCT*

Pray for Death 🎬🎬 **1985 (R)** When a mild-mannered Japanese family is victimized by a crime syndicate in L.A., a master ninja comes to the rescue. Higher quality production than most ninja adventures. **93m/C VHS, Beta.** James Booth, Robert Ito, Sho Kosugi, Shane Kosugi, Kane Kosugi, Donna Kei Benz; **D:** Gordon Hessler; **W:** James Booth. *NO*

Pray for the Wildcats 🎬½ **1974** Three advertising executives' promotional trip from (or to?) Hell. Anything to please a client. **96m/C VHS, Beta.** Andy Griffith, William Shatner, Angie Dickinson, Janet Margolin, Marjoe Gortner, Lorraine Gary; **D:** Robert Lewis. *REP*

Pray TV 🎬🎬 *KGOD* **1980 (PG)** A sly con man turns a failing television station into a profitable one when the station starts to broadcast around-the-clock religious programming. Made for television. **92m/C VHS, Beta, LV.** Dabney Coleman, Archie Hahn, Joyce Jameson, Nancy Morgan, Roger E. Mosley, Marcia Wallace; **D:** Rick Friedberg; **W:** Nick Castle. *VES*

Pray TV 🎬 **1982** A television movie expose of broadcast religion in which a young preacher chooses between orthodox religion and lots of money. Not as cutting an indictment as it could have been. **100m/C VHS, Beta.** John Ritter, Ned Beatty, Madolyn Smith, Richard Kiley, Louise Latham, Jonathan Prince, Michael Currie, Lois Areno; **D:** Robert Markowitz.

A Prayer for Katarina Horovitzova 🎬🎬½ **1969** Stunning tale of a Polish singer who struggles to find the meaning and beauty of life while working to trade Nazi prisoners in U.S. jails for Jews hoping to emigrate. Based on the Arnost Lustig novel. Confiscated by the Czech Communist government and kept from the screen for 21 years. In Czechoslovakian with English subtitles. **60m/C VHS.** *CZ* Jiri Adamira, Lenka Fiserova, Cestmir Randa. *FCT*

Prayer for the Dying 🎬🎬½ **1987 (R)** An IRA hitman longs to quit, but he has to complete one last assignment. The hit is witnessed by a priest who becomes an unwitting associate when the hitman hides out at the church. Fine performances from Bates and Rourke, though Hodges and Rourke were not satisfied with finished film. **104m/C VHS, Beta, LV, Closed Caption.** Mickey Rourke, Alan Bates, Bob Hoskins, Sammi Davis,

Liam Neeson, Alison Doody, Christopher Fulford; **D:** Mike Hodges; **W:** Edmund Ward, Martin Lynch; **M:** Bill Conti. NO

A Prayer in the Dark ✶✶½ 1997 (PG-13) Pious Quaker wife and mother, Emily Hayworth (Carter), is taken hostage in her own home by a former Quaker friend, Jimmy (Ferguson). He's escaped from prison with two armed cons, demanding that Emily steal four million dollars from the bank where she works. Since they're also holding her family, she agrees. But when Emily's out of the house, she and others in the Quaker community try to find a peaceful solution to the volatile situation. Cable movie. **CW:** Violence. 91m/C VHS. Lynda Carter, Colin Ferguson, Teri Polo. PAR

Prayer of the Rollerboys ✶✶½ 1991 (R) Violent, futuristic, funky action as Haim infiltrates a criminal gang of syncopated roller-blading neo-nazi youth with plans for nationwide domination. Though routinely plotted and predictable, it's got great skating stunts and a wry vision of tomorrow's shattered USA—broke, drug-soaked, homeless, foreign-owned; even sharper when you realize this is a Japanese-American co-production. **CW:** Language, violence and drug content, and sensuality. 94m/C VHS, LV. Corey Haim, Patricia Arquette, Christopher Collet, Julius W. Harris, J.C. Quinn, Jake Dengel, Devin Clark, Mark Pellegrino, Morgan Weisser; **D:** Rick King; **W:** Peter Iliff; **C:** Phedon Papamichael; **M:** Stacy Widelitz.

Praying Mantis ✶✶ 1983 (PG-13) The professor's scheming nurse murdered his family and plans to marry him for his money. She enlists the aid of the professor's assistant in her evil plot. **CW:** Some violence and terror and scene of sensuality. 119m/C VHS, Beta. Jonathan Pryce, Cherie Lunghi, Ann Cropper, Carmen Du Sautoy, Pinkas Braun; **D:** Jack Gold; **M:** Carl Davis. NO

Praying Mantis ✶✶½ 1993 (PG-13) Seymour stars as a femme fatale who likes to get married and then, in a rage against her own abusive childhood, kill her new husbands off. So far her total is five dead hubbies with number six (Bostwick) in her sights. Only this time, her almost-sister-in-law (Fisher) is very suspicious of the bride-to-be. Made for cable television. 90m/C VHS, Beta, Closed Caption. Jane Seymour, Barry Bostwick, Frances Fisher, Chad Allen; **D:** James Keach; **W:** Duane Poole, William F. Delligan; **M:** John Debney. PAR

Pre-Madonnas: Rebels Without a Clue ✶✶½ Social Suicide 1995 (PG-13) Kim Sterling (Sturges) decides to rig the Beverly Hills Las Madonnas debutante ball to teach the snobs a lesson. 98m/C VHS, LV, Closed Caption. Shannon Sturges, Bobbie Bresee, Peter Anthony Elliott, Kenn Cooper; **D:** Lawrence Foldes. AVE

Preacherman ✶½ 1983 (R) Phony preacher travels through the South, fleecing gullible congregations (and providing for their sexual desires) wherever he goes. 90m/C VHS. Amos Huxley, Marian Brown, Adam Hesse, Ilene Kristen, W. Henry Smith; **D:** Albert T. Viola; **W:** Albert T. Viola, Harvey Flaxman; **M:** W. Henry Smith, Roland Pope. TTV

The Preacher's Wife ✶✶ 1996 (PG) Remake of 1947's "The Bishop's Wife" finds troubled Newark minister Henry Biggs (Vance) praying for heavenly intervention. His prayers are answered with angel Dudley (Washington)—who isn't so holy that he can't appreciate the minister's choir-leading wife Julia (Houston). While trying to save his cash-strapped church from a greedy developer (Hines), Rev. Biggs is so mired in material problems that he is unable to believe that Dudley is actually an angel. Washington is the dictionary definition of debonair as the angel with a touch of the devil in his eye. All problems are, of course, wrapped up neatly with a bow on top in the end. The real stars of this Christmas tale, however, are Houston's vocal cords. Fans of her singing will love this movie, while others may want to rent the original. 124m/C VHS, LV, Closed Caption. Denzel Washington, Whitney Houston, Courtney B. Vance, Gregory

Hines, Jenifer Lewis, Loretta Devine, Lionel Richie, Paul Bates, Justin Pierre Edmund, Darvel Davis Jr., William James Siggers Jr.; **D:** Penny Marshall; **W:** Nat Mauldin, Allan Scott; **C:** Miroslav Ondricek; **M:** Hans Zimmer. Nominations: Academy Awards '96: Best Original Score. TOU

Precious Find ✶✶ 1996 (R) In 2049 there's a new gold rush—this time into outer space. The moon's enclosed city is a staging area for mining operations throughout the solar system and draws the attention of three prospectors: Ben, who can "smell" gold, Crille (Hauer), who has a high-tech treasure map, and Sam (James), who owns a space hauler. They're all anxious to cash in when a newly discovered asteroid turns out to be a literal gold mine as is claim jumper Camilla (Chen). 90m/C VHS, Closed Caption. Rutger Hauer, Brion James, Harold Pruett, Joan Chen; **D:** Philippe Mora; **W:** Brian Rix, Jane Ubell, John Remark; **C:** Walter Bal; **M:** Roy Hay. REP

Predator ✶✶½ 1987 (R) Schwarzenegger leads a team of CIA-hired mercenaries into the Central American jungles to rescue hostages. They encounter an alien force that begins to attack them one by one. Soon it's just Arnold and the Beast in this attention-grabbing, but sometimes silly, suspense film. 107m/C VHS, Beta, LV, Letterbox, Closed Caption. Arnold Schwarzenegger, Jesse Ventura, Sonny Landham, Bill Duke, Elpidia Carrillo, Carl Weathers, R.G. Armstrong, Richard Chaves, Shane Black, Kevin Peter Hall; **D:** Jim McTiernan; **W:** Jim Thomas, John Thomas; **C:** Donald McAlpine; **M:** Alan Silvestri. NO

Predator 2 ✶✶ 1990 (R) Tough cop takes time away from battling drug dealers to deal with malicious extraterrestrial who exterminated Arnold's band of commandos in "Predator." Missbilled as sequel, its only resemblance to the original is that the predator has inexplicably returned (this time to the thick of L.A.). Gory action aplenty, little logic. Fine cast dominated by minority performers can't save this one. **CW:** Strong language, strong violence and drug content, and sensuality. 105m/C VHS, Beta, LV, Letterbox, Closed Caption. Danny Glover, Gary Busey, Ruben Blades, Maria Conchita Alonso, Bill Paxton, Robert Davi, Adam Baldwin, Kent McCord, Morton Downey Jr., Calvin Lockhart, Teri Weigel; **D:** Stephen Hopkins; **W:** John Thomas, Jim Thomas. FXV, CCB

Prefontaine ✶✶½ 1996 (PG-13) Sports bio has appeal, thanks to lead actor Leto, in covering the brief career of early '70s runner Steve Prefontaine. Cocky and outspoken, the charismatic University of Oregon star soon owns every American record for distances between 2,000 and 10,000 meters. He's expected to gold at the 1972 Munich Olympics but falters, thanks in part to the tragedy surrounding the games. Returning home, the flamboyant Pre becomes a sports activist for athletes' rights before dying in a car crash in 1975 at the age of 24. Relatively straight narrative and little psychological insight make for few lasting impressions. **CW:** Brief strong language. 107m/C VHS, LV, Closed Caption. Jared Leto, R. Lee Ermey, Ed O'Neill, Amy Locane, Lindsay Crouse, Laurel Holloman, Breckin Meyer, Kurtwood Smith, Brian McGovern, Peter Anthony Jacobs; **D:** Steve James; **W:** Steve James, Eugene Corr; **C:** Peter Gilbert; **M:** Mason Daring. TOU

Prehistoric Bimbos in Armageddon City woof! 1993 Trianna and her tribe of Prehistoric Bimbos must prevent post-nuclear domination in Old Chicago City, the last remaining civilization after WWIII, by defeating the evil ruler Nemesis and his cyborgs. "Enough bimbos to fill two post-nuclear action comedies." So bad its gotta be good. 70m/C VHS, Beta. Robert Vollrath, Tonia Monahan, Deric Bernier. TEM

Prehistoric Women woof! Slave Girls 1950 A tribe of prehistoric women look for husbands the old-fashioned way—they drag them back to their caves from the jungle. So bad it's almost good. 74m/C VHS, Beta. Laurette Luez, Allan Nixon, Mara Lynn, Joan Shawlee, Judy Landon; **D:** Greg Tallas. FHE, NOS, RHI

Prehysteria ✶✶½ 1993 (PG) Fantasy/adventure about a widower, his 11-year-old son and teenage daughter, and what happens when some mysterious eggs from South America accidentally wind up at their farm. Imagine their surprise when the eggs hatch and out pop a brood of pygmy dinosaurs. The dinosaurs are cute (as is the family), the villain is dumb, and the violence minimal. 84m/C VHS, Beta, LV, Closed Caption. Brett Cullen, Austin O'Brien, Samantha Mills, Colleen Morris, Tony Longo, Stuart Fratkin, Stephen Lee; **D:** Albert Band, Charles Band; **W:** Greg Suddeth, Mark Goldstein. PAR

Prehysteria 2 ✶✶½ 1994 (PG) While their adoptive family is on vacation the pygmy dinosaurs get loose and aid a lonely rich boy whose governess is plotting to send him to military boarding school. 81m/C VHS, Beta, Closed Caption. Kevin R. Connors, Jennifer Harte, Dean Scofield, Bettye Ackerman, Larry Hankin, Greg Lewis, Alan Palo, Michael Hagiwara, Owen Bush; **D:** Albert Band; **W:** Brent Friedman, Michael Paul Davis; **M:** Richard Band. PAR

Prehysteria 3 ✶✶½ 1995 (PG) The mini-dinos take up miniature golf. Seems Thomas MacGregor's (Willard) putt-putt business is about to sink when his daughter Ella (Anderson) finds the pygmy dinosaurs and a promotional bonanza is born. But Thomas' evil brother Hal (Weitz) hatches a plot to take over the now-successful enterprise. 85m/C VHS, Closed Caption. Fred Willard, Bruce Weitz, Whitney Anderson, Pam Matteson; **D:** Julian Breen; **W:** Michael Paul Davis, Neil Ruttenberg. PAR

Prelude to a Kiss ✶✶ 1992 (PG-13) Disappointing screen adaptation of Craig Lucas' hit play features Baldwin and Ryan as young lovers in this romantic fantasy. Ryan is Rita, a free-spirited bartender and Baldwin is Peter, a conservative writer, who decide to marry after a whirlwind courtship. At their wedding reception, Rita obligingly kisses one of their guests, an old man (Walker). Then, on their honeymoon, Peter begins to notice a number of changes to Rita's character and comes to realize this is truly not the girl he married. The delicate fantasy which worked on stage struggles to survive the "opening up" of the screen adaptation though Baldwin (who reprises his stage role) and Ryan are appealing. 106m/C VHS, LV, Closed Caption. Alec Baldwin, Meg Ryan, Sydney Walker, Ned Beatty, Patty Duke, Kathy Bates, Stanley Tucci; **D:** Norman Rene; **M:** Howard Shore. FXV

Prelude to War 1942 A compact look at the events of 1931-39; includes a series of contrasts between free societies and totalitarian governments. From the "Why We Fight" series. 53m/B VHS, Beta. **D:** Frank Capra. Academy Awards '42: Best Feature Documentary. REP, MPI, HHT

Premature Burial ✶✶ 1962 A cataleptic Englishman's worst fears come true when he is buried alive. He escapes and seeks revenge on his doctor and his greedy wife. Based upon the story by Edgar Allan Poe. 81m/C VHS, Beta, LV. Ray Milland, Richard Ney, Hazel Court, Heather Angel, Alan Napier, John Dierkes, Dick Miller; **D:** Roger Corman; **W:** Charles Beaumont, Ray Russell; **C:** Floyd Crosby. ART, MLB

Premonition ✶½ 1971 (PG) Three drug-riddled '60s college students experience similar premonitions of death, and subsequently either die or become tormented. 83m/C VHS, Beta. Carl Crow, Tim Ray, Winfrey Hester Hill, Victor Izay; **D:** Alan Rudolph; **W:** Alan Rudolph; **C:** John Bailey. NO

The Premonition ✶✶✶ 1975 (PG) Parapsychologist searching for a missing child is drawn into a frightening maze of dream therapy and communication with the dead. Well-done paranorm tale filmed in Mississippi. 94m/C VHS, Beta. Richard Lynch, Sharon Farrell, Jeff Corey, Ellen Barber, Edward Bell, Danielle Brisebois; **D:** Robert Allen Schnitzer; **W:** Anthony Mahon.

Prep School ✶ 1981 (PG-13) A very proper New England prep school is turned topsy-turvy by two rambunctious co-eds. They're determined to break every one of the school's cardinal rules.

97m/C VHS, Beta. Leslie Hope, Andrew Sabiston; **D:** Paul Almond.

The Preppie Murder 🎬🎬½ **1989** Made for TV crime drama based on the killing of Jennifer Levin in New York City's Central Park in 1987, with Baldwin cast as prep school grad Robert Chambers. Amid sensational headlines, the story told of drugs, sexual games, and idle and disaffected youth. **100m/C VHS, Closed Caption.** William Baldwin, Lara Flynn Boyle, Danny Aiello, Joanna Kerns, Dorothy Fielding, James Handy, William Devane; **D:** John Herzfeld. *TTC*

Preppies 🎬½ **1982 (R)** Yet another teen sex comedy, but this time Ivy Leaguer Drake must pass his exams to receive his $50 million inheritance. Lots of skirt chasing as his conniving cousin leads him astray. **83m/C VHS, Beta.** Dennis Drake, Peter Brady Reardon, Steven Holt, Nitchie Barrett, Cindy Manion, Katt Shea Ruben, Lynda Wiesmeier; **D:** Chuck Vincent. *ART, VES*

Prescott Kid 🎬🎬 **1936** Legendary western star McCoy plays a law-abiding cowboy mistaken for the new Marshall in the outlaw town of San Lorenzo, which has been targeted by a gang of cattle rustling killers. **58m/B VHS.** Tim McCoy, Sheila Mannors, Alden Chase, Hooper Atchley, Walter Brennan; **D:** David Selman; **W:** Ford Beebe. *COL*

Presenting Lily Mars 🎬🎬 **1943** A small-town girl comes to New York to make it on Broadway. Based on the Booth Tarkington novel. 🎵When I Look at You; Three O'Clock in the Morning; Kulebiaka; Is It Love? (Or The Gypsy in Me); Broadway Rhythm; Sweethearts of America; Where There's Music; Every Little Movement Has a Meaning All Its Own; Tom, Tom the Piper's Son. **105m/B VHS, Beta.** Judy Garland, Van Heflin, Fay Bainter, Richard Carlson, Tommy Dorsey; **D:** Norman Taurog; **C:** Joseph Ruttenberg. *MGM*

The President's Analyst 🎬🎬🎬½ **1967** A superbly written, brilliantly executed satire from the mind of Theodore J. Flicker, who wrote as well as directed. Coburn steals the show as a psychiatrist who has the dubious honor of being appointed "secret shrink" to the President of the U.S. Pressures of the job steadily increase his paranoia until he suspects he is being pursued by agents and counter agents alike. Is he losing his sanity or...? Vastly entertaining. **104m/C VHS.** James Coburn, Godfrey Cambridge, Severn Darden, Joan Delaney, Pat Harrington, Will Geer, William Daniels; **D:** Theodore J. Flicker; **W:** Theodore J. Flicker; **M:** Lalo Schifrin. *PAR*

President's Mistress 🎬½ **1978** A security agent searches for his sister's murderer, while trying to obscure the fact that she was having an affair with the President. **97m/C VHS, Beta.** Beau Bridges, Susan Blanchard, Larry Hagman, Joel Fabiani, Karen Grassle; **D:** John Llewellyn Moxey. *NO*

The President's Mystery 🎬½ *One For All* **1936** A lawyer decides to turn his back on society by giving up his practice and his marriage. Eventually he meets and falls in love with another woman. The most interesting aspect of the film is that it is based on a story by Franklin D. Roosevelt, which was published in "Liberty" magazine. The story was supposedly better than its screen adaptation. **80m/B VHS, Beta.** Henry Wilcoxon, Betty Furness, Sidney Blackmer, Evelyn Brent; **D:** Phil Rosen. *SNC*

The President's Plane Is Missing 🎬🎬 **1971** When Air Force One disappears, the less than trustworthy Vice President takes control. Could there be a dire plot in the making? Based on a novel by Rod Serling's brother Robert J. Serling. **100m/C VHS.** Buddy Ebsen, Peter Graves, Arthur Kennedy, Rip Torn, Louise Sorel, Raymond Massey, James Wainwright, Mercedes McCambridge, Dabney Coleman, Joseph Campanella; **D:** Daryl Duke. *REP*

President's Target 🎬🎬 **1993** An anti-drug mission in South America is ambushed and CIA operative Peter Caine is the only survivor. Now he's out to see who planned the double-cross and how best to get his revenge. **82m/C VHS, Closed Caption.** John Coleman, Martin Kove, Bo Hopkins, Brigitte Audrey; **D:** Yvan Chiffre.

The Presidio 🎬🎬 **1988 (R)** An easy going police detective must investigate a murder on a military base where he and the base commander have sparred before. The commander becomes downright nasty when his daughter shows an interest in the detective. Good action scenes in San Francisco almost covers up script weaknesses, but not quite. **97m/C VHS, Beta, LV, 8mm, Closed Caption.** Sean Connery, Mark Harmon, Meg Ryan, Jack Warden, Mark Blum, Jenette Goldstein; **D:** Peter Hyams; **W:** Larry Ferguson; **M:** Bruce Broughton. *PAR*

Pressure Point 🎬🎬🎬 **1962** Poitier stars as a prison psychiatrist treating an inmate who is a racist and a member of the Nazi party. Darin gives an excellent performance as the Nazi patient in this intelligent drama based on a true case. **87m/B VHS, Closed Caption.** Sidney Poitier, Bobby Darin, Peter Falk, Carl Benton Reid, Barry Gordon, Howard Caine, Mary Munday; **D:** Hubert Cornfield; **M:** Ernest Gold. *MGM*

Presumed Guilty 🎬 **1991** An innocent man is released from prison only to find he is once again a wanted man! So he gets his gal, who happens to be the sheriff's daughter, is beaten up and in the end winds up living happily ever after. **91m/C VHS, LV.** Jack Vogel, Holly Floria, Sean Holton, Wayne Zanelotti, Bradley Rockwell, Sharon Young, Al Schuerman; **D:** Lawrence L. Simeone; **W:** Lawrence L. Simeone.

Presumed Innocent 🎬🎬🎬 **1990 (R)** Assistant district attorney is the prime suspect when a former lover turns up brutally murdered. Coverups surround him, the political climate changes, and friends and enemies switch sides. Slow-paced courtroom drama with excellent performances from Ford, Julia, and Bedelia. Skillfully adapted from the best-seller by Chicago attorney Scott Turow. **CW:** Adult situations; language; nudity, and sexual situations. **127m/C VHS, Beta, LV, 8mm, Letterbox, Closed Caption.** Harrison Ford, Brian Dennehy, Bonnie Bedelia, Greta Scacchi, Raul Julia, Paul Winfield, John Spencer, Joe Grifasi, Anna Maria Horsford, Sab Shimono, Christine Estabrook, Michael Tolan, Tom Mardirosian; **D:** Alan J. Pakula; **W:** Frank Pierson, Alan J. Pakula; **C:** Gordon Willis; **M:** John Williams. *WAR, FCT*

Pretty Baby 🎬🎬🎬 **1978 (R)** Shield's launching pad and Malle's first American film is a masterpiece of cinematography and style, nearly upstaged by the plodding storyline. Carradine manages to be effective but never succeeds at looking comfortable as the New Orleans photographer besotted with, and subsequently married to, an 11-year-old prostitute (Shields). Low key, disturbingly intriguing story, beautifully photographed by Sven Nykvist. **109m/C VHS, Beta, LV.** Brooke Shields, Keith Carradine, Susan Sarandon, Barbara Steele, Diana Scarwid, Antonio Fargas; **D:** Louis Malle; **C:** Sven Nykvist. Nominations: Academy Awards '78: Original Song Score and/or Adaptation. *PAR*

Pretty in Pink 🎬🎬½ **1986 (PG-13)** More teen angst from the pen of Hughes. Poor girl falls for a rich guy. Their families fret, their friends are distressed, and fate conspires against them. If you can suspend your disbelief that a teenager with her own car and answering machine is financially inferior, then you may very well be able to accept the entire premise. Slickly done and adequately, if not enthusiastically, acted. In 1987, Hughes essentially remade this film and put himself in the director's chair with "Some Kind of Wonderful," the same story with the rich/pauper characters reversed by gender. **96m/C VHS, Beta, LV, 8mm, Closed Caption.** Molly Ringwald, Andrew McCarthy, Jon Cryer, Harry Dean Stanton, James Spader, Annie Potts, Andrew Dice Clay, Margaret Colin, Alexa Ke-

nin, Gina Gershon, Dweezil Zappa; **D:** Howard Deutch; **W:** John Hughes; **C:** Tak Fujimoto; **M:** Michael Gore. *PAR*

Pretty Poison 🎬🎬🎬½ **1968** You won't need an antidote for this one. Original, absorbing screenplay, top-notch acting, and on target direction combine to raise this low-budget, black comedy above the crowd. Perkins at his eerie best as a burned-out arsonist who cooks up a crazy scheme and enlists the aid of a hot-to-trot high schooler, only to discover too late she has some burning desires of her own. Weld is riveting as the turbulent teen. **89m/C VHS.** Anthony Perkins, Tuesday Weld, Beverly Garland, John Randolph, Dick O'Neill; **D:** Noel Black. New York Film Critics Awards '68: Best Screenplay. *ING, MLB*

Pretty Smart woof! **1987 (R)** Two diametrically opposed sisters at a European finishing school team up against a drug-dealing, voyeuristic teacher. Pretty lame. **84m/C VHS, Beta.** Tricia Leigh Fisher, Patricia Arquette, Dennis Cole, Lisa Lorient; **D:** Dimitri Logothetis; **M:** Eddie Arkin. *VTR*

Pretty Village, Pretty Flame 🎬🎬🎬 *Lepa Sela, Lepo Gore* **1996** Powerful story of the Bosnian conflict that is loosely based on a true incident. Story flashes from the days of Yugoslavian unity under Marshal Tito to 1992 when members of a Serbian patrol are trapped (along with an American journalist) by Muslim militiamen in a tunnel connecting Zagreb and Belgrade with no hope for escape. Serbo-Croatian with subtitles. **125m/C VHS.** Dragan Bjelogric, Nikola Kojo, Bata Zivojinovic, Dragan Maksimovic, Zoran Cvijanovic, Nikola Pejakovic, Lisa Moncure; **D:** Srdjan Dragojevic; **W:** Srdjan Dragojevic, Vanja Bulic, Nikola Pejakovic; **C:** Dusan Joksimovic; **M:** Lazar Ristovski. *FXL*

Pretty Woman 🎬🎬🎬 **1990 (R)** An old story takes a fresh approach as a successful but stuffy business man hires a fun-loving, energetic young hooker to be his companion for a week. The film caused some controversy over its upbeat portrayal of prostitution, but its popularity at the boxoffice catapulted Roberts to stardom. **CW:** Adult situations; language. **117m/C VHS, Beta, LV, Closed Caption.** Richard Gere, Julia Roberts, Ralph Bellamy, Jason Alexander, Laura San Giacomo, Hector Elizondo, Alex Hyde-White, Elinor Donahue, Larry Miller, Jane Morris; **D:** Garry Marshall; **W:** J.F. Lawton; **M:** James Newton Howard. Golden Globe Awards '91: Best Actress—Musical/Comedy (Roberts); Nominations: Academy Awards '90: Best Actress (Roberts). *TOU*

Prettykill woof! **1987 (R)** A confusing storyline with numerous subplots involves detective with a paramour/prostitute (Hubley) attempting to stalk a mad killer while contending with her split personality. **95m/C VHS, Beta, LV.** David Birney, Susannah York, Season Hubley, Yaphet Kotto, Suzanne Snyder, Germane Honde; **D:** George Kaczender; **W:** Sandra K. Bailey; **C:** Joao Fernandes. *WAR*

The Prey 🎬 **1980 (R)** Poorly done horror show about a predator who is looking for a mate in the Colorado Rockies and kills five campers in the process. **80m/C VHS, Beta.** Debbie Thurseon, Steve Bond, Lori Lethin, Jackie Coogan; **D:** Edwin Scott Brown; **W:** Edwin Scott Brown, Summer Brown. *NO*

Prey for the Hunter 🎬 **1992 (R)** Four businessmen on a big-game hunt decide they're bored with their usual prey. They persuade a photojournalist to join them in a game with paint pellet guns except they decide to use real bullets and the journalist becomes their new target. An old and tired plot with nothing new to distinguish it. **CW:** Language. **90m/C VHS.** Todd Jensen, Andre Jacobs, Michelle Bestbier, Evan J. Klisser, David Butler, Allan Granville; **D:** John H. Parr. *COL*

Prey of the Chameleon 🎬 **1991 (R)** A female serial killer escapes from her asylum, ready to rip more men to shreds. However a tough lady cop has other ideas and goes all out to put an end to the madwoman's doings. Can she stop this fiend before the man she loves becomes the next victim? **CW:** Violence and strong sensuality. **91m/C VHS, Beta, Closed Caption.** Daphne Zuniga,

James Wilder, Alexandra Paul, Don Harvey; **D:** Fleming Fuller.

A Price above Rubies 🐶🐶½ 1997 (R)

Evils of patriarchal society are exposed in this tale of an Orthodox Jewish wife who seeks fulfillment outside the lonely and oppressive world in which she lives. Zellweger shines as Sonia, who defies her frigid Hasidic husband Mendel (Fitzgerald) to take a job as a jeweler, then falls in love with a Puerto Rican artist (Payne). Eccleston is Mendel's brother who has a strange relationship with Sonia, and Margulies is nice mother figure who tries to help Sonia fit in with their way of life. Interesting, though not earth-shatteringly deep, characterization beyond film's female lead is scanty, with one-dimensional male models on display here. Second feature from writer/director Yakin.**CW:** Sexuality and brief language. **117m/C VHS.** Renee Zellweger, Christopher Eccleston, Glenn Fitzgerald, Allen Payne, Julianna Margulies, Kim Hunter, John Randolph, Kathleen Chalfant, Edie Falco, Tim Jerome, Phyllis Newman; **D:** Boaz Yakin; **W:** Boaz Yakin; **C:** Adam Holender; **M:** Lesley Barber. *NYR*

Priceless Beauty 🐶🐶½ 1990 (R)

Musician Lambert was only looking when he spotted the bottle which changed his life. Beautiful genie (Lane) lives inside, and is waiting just for him! Fun premise, good score, nice chemistry between the actors. **94m/C VHS, LV, Closed Caption.** Christopher Lambert, Diane Lane, Francesco Quinn, J.C. Quinn, Claudia Ohana, Monica Scattini, Joaquin D'Almeida; **D:** Charles Finch. *REP*

Prick Up Your Ears 🐶🐶🐶 1987 (R)

Film biography of popular subversive playwright Joe Orton depicts his rise to fame and his eventual murder at the hands of his homosexual lover in 1967. Acclaimed for its realistic and sometimes humorous portrayal of the relationship between two men in a society that regarded homosexuality as a crime, the film unfortunately pays scant attention to Orton's theatrical success. The occasional sluggishness of the script detracts a bit from the three leads' outstanding performances. **110m/C VHS, Beta, LV.** Gary Oldman, Alfred Molina, Vanessa Redgrave, Julie Walters, Lindsay Duncan, Wallace Shawn, James Grant, Frances Barber, Janet Dale, David Atkins; **D:** Stephen Frears; **W:** Alan Bennett; **M:** Stanley Myers. New York Film Critics Awards '87: Best Supporting Actress (Redgrave).*NO*

Pride and Prejudice 🐶🐶🐶½ 1940

Classic adaptation of Austen's classic novel of manners as a young marriageable woman spurns the suitor her parents choose for her. Excellent cast vividly recreates 19th century England, aided by the inspired set design that won the film an Oscar. **114m/B VHS, Beta, LV.** Greer Garson, Laurence Olivier, Edmund Gwenn, Edna May Oliver, Mary Boland, Maureen O'Sullivan, Ann Rutherford, Frieda Inescort; **D:** Robert Z. Leonard; **C:** Karl Freund. Academy Awards '40: Best Interior Decoration. *MGM*

Pride and Prejudice 🐶🐶½ 1985 BBC

mini-series adaptation of Jane Austen's novel about 19th century British mores and the attempts of five sisters to get married. **226m/C VHS, Beta, LV, Closed Caption.** GB Elizabeth Garvie, David Rintoul; **D:** Cyril Coke. *FOX, SIG, TVC*

Pride and Prejudice 🐶🐶🐶 1995 Lavish

TV adaptation of the Jane Austen novel finds bright Elizabeth Bennet (Ehle) unwillingly smitten by the wealthy, mysterious, and arrogant Mr. Darcy (Firth). Her family, filled with unmarried daughters, is rather silly and, of course, Elizabeth should be looking to get married (or at least not hinder her sisters' chances). Filmed on location in Derbyshire. On six cassettes. **300m/C VHS.** GB Jennifer Ehle, Colin Firth, Susannah Harker, Alison Steadman, Julia Sawalha, Benjamin Whitrow, Crispin Bonham Carter, Anna Chancellor, David Bamber, David Bark-Jones, Polly Maberly, Lucy Briers, Barbara Leigh-Hunt, Adrian Lukis; **D:** Simon Langton; **W:** Andrew Davies; **C:** John Kenway; **M:** Carl Davis. *AEH, PBS, VIF*

The Pride and the Passion 🐶🐶

1957 A small group of resistance fighters battling for Spanish independence in 1810 must smuggle a 6-ton cannon across the rugged terrain of Spain. Miscasting, especially of Sinatra as a Spanish peasant, hurts this film. **132m/C VHS, Beta.** Cary Grant, Frank Sinatra, Sophia Loren; **D:** Stanley Kramer; **W:** Edward Anhalt. *MGM*

Pride of Jesse Hallum 🐶½ 1981 A

made-for-television film about an illiterate man, played by country singer Cash, who learns, after much trial and tribulation, to read. **105m/C VHS, Beta, Closed Caption.** Johnny Cash, Brenda Vaccaro, Eli Wallach; **D:** Gary Nelson. *FOX*

Pride of St. Louis 🐶🐶 1952 A romanti-

cized and humorous portrait of famed baseball player-turned-commentator Dizzy Dean. **93m/B VHS, Beta.** Dan Dailey, Joanne Dru, Richard Crenna, Richard Haydn, Hugh Sanders; **D:** Harmon Jones; **W:** Herman J. Mankiewicz. Nominations: Academy Awards '52: Best Story. *FOX*

Pride of the Bowery 🐶 Here We Go Again

1941 The Dead End Kids versus a boxing hopeful in training camp. **60m/B VHS, Beta.** Leo Gorcey, David Gorcey, Huntz Hall, Gabriel Dell, Billy Halop, Bobby Jordan; **D:** Joseph H. Lewis. *NOS, CAB, DVT*

Pride of the Clan 🐶🐶½ 1918 Silent dra-

ma with Pickford and Moore as Scottish sweethearts battling a bit of adversity. When Pickford's father is lost at sea, she moves onto his fishing boat. She meets Moore, a fishing boy, and falls in love. But, he inherits a fortune and his parents forbid him to see Pickford. He goes off to live the good life but comes back to dramatically rescue Pickford. **80m/B VHS, Beta.** Mary Pickford, Matt Moore; **D:** Maurice Tourneur *GPV*

The Pride of the Yankees 🐶🐶🐶½

1942 Excellent portrait of baseball great Lou Gehrig. Beginning as he joined the Yankees in 1923, the film follows this great American through to his moving farewell speech as his career was tragically cut short by the disease that bears his name. Cooper is inspiring in the title role. **128m/B VHS, Beta, LV, Closed Caption.** Gary Cooper, Teresa Wright, Babe Ruth, Walter Brennan, Dan Duryea; **D:** Sam Wood. Academy Awards '42: Best Film Editing; Nominations: Academy Awards '42: Best Actor (Cooper), Best Actress (Wright), Best Black and White Cinematography, Best Interior Decoration, Best Picture, Best Screenplay, Best Sound, Best Story, Best Original Dramatic/Comedy Score. *FOX*

Priest 🐶🐶 1994 (R) Father Greg (an intense

performance by Roache) is a young, idealistic priest who gets a rude awakening when he's assigned to a tough inner-city Liverpool parish. His superior, Father Matthew (Wilkinson), is a middle-aged rabble rouser who's openly having an affair with their black housekeeper Maria (Tyson). But Father Greg has a secret of his own—despite struggles with his sexuality he gets involved with Graham (Carlyle), a man he meets in the local gay bar. Greg's inner turmoil is heightened when a young parishoner confesses that her father is sexually abusing her but, because of the seal of the confessional, the priest cannot report the problem. Director Bird walks a fine line between criticism and condemnation of Catholic doctrine. British TV feature provoked a storm of controversy in the U.S.; originally released at 105 minutes.**CW:** Mature themes involving sexuality. **98m/C VHS.** Linus Roache, Tom Wilkinson, Cathy Tyson, Robert Carlyle, James Ellis, John Bennett, Rio Fanning, Jimmy Coleman, Lesley Sharp, Robert Pugh, Christine Tremarco; **D:** Antonia Bird; **W:** Jimmy McGovern; **C:** Fred Tammes; **M:** Andy Roberts. Nominations: Australian Film Institute '95: Best Foreign Film. *TOU*

Priest of Love 🐶🐶½ 1981 (R) Arty ac-

count of the final years of the life of then-controversial author D.H. Lawrence, during which time he published "Lady Chatterly's Lover." A slow-moving but interesting portrayal of this complex man and his wife as they grapple with his imminent death from tuberculosis. **125m/C VHS, Beta.** GB Ian McKellen, Janet Suzman, John Gielgud, Helen Mirren,

Jorge Rivero; **D:** Christopher Miles; **W:** Alan Plater; **O:** Ted Moore. *HBO*

Primal Fear 🐶🐶 1996 (R) Chicago defense

attorney Martin Vail (Gere) is torn between the fight for justice and the lure of fame. He seems to have found the spotlight when a gentle altar boy (newcomer Norton is a standout) is accused of savagely murdering an archbishop. This leads to some courtroom fireworks due, in part, to the fact that the prosecutor (Linney) is Vail's former lover. Gere turns in a satisfying performance but, except when he's with his client, can't keep the script afloat. Lame plot revelations and an obvious "shocker" ending don't help matters. Feature directorial debut of Hoblit, Emmy winner for TV's "Hill Street Blues," "L.A. Law," and "NYPD Blue." Adapted from the book by William Diehl.**CW:** Profanity, violence, sexual situations and nudity. **130m/C VHS, Beta, Closed Caption.** Richard Gere, Laura Linney, Edward Norton, John Mahoney, Alfre Woodard, Frances McDormand, Terry O'Quinn, Andre Braugher, Steven Bauer, Joe Spano, Tony Plana, Stanley Anderson, Maura Tierney, Jon Seda; **D:** Gregory Hoblit; **W:** Steve Shagan, Ann Biderman; **C:** Michael Chapman; **M:** James Newton Howard. Golden Globe Awards '97: Best Supporting Actor (Norton); Los Angeles Film Critics Association Awards '96: Best Supporting Actor (Norton); National Board of Review Awards '96: Best Supporting Actor (Norton); Nominations: Academy Awards '96: Best Supporting Actor (Norton); British Academy Awards '96: Best Supporting Actor (Norton); MTV Movie Awards '97: Best Villain (Norton). *PAR*

Primal Impulse 🐶½ 1974 An astronaut,

stranded on the moon because of a sinister experimental double-cross, unleashes a mental scream which possesses a young woman's mind back on earth. **90m/C VHS, Beta.** Klaus Kinski *NO*

Primal Rage 🐶 1990 (R) A student is bitten

by an experimental monkey, and begins to manifest his primal urges physically. Special effects by Carlo Rimbaldi.**CW:** Strong language and strong violence. **92m/C VHS, Beta.** Bo Svenson, Patrick Lowe, Mitch Watson, Cheryl Arutt, Sarah Buxton; **D:** Vittoria Rambaldi. *WAR*

Primal Scream 🐶½ Hellfire 1987 (R) The

Year is 1993. Earth's fuel sources are rapidly decaying and the top secret project to mine a revolutionary new energy source is underway—independently managed by a corrupt corporation. **95m/C VHS.** Kenneth John McGregor, Sharon Mason, Julie Miller, Jon Maurice, Mickey Shaughnessy; **D:** William Murray. *NO*

Primal Secrets 🐶🐶½ Trick of the Eye 1994

Artist Tilly, who specializes in illusionary trompe l'oeil paintings, is commissioned to paint a mural for reclusive socialite/widow Burstyn but there's a lot of mystery surrounding the job, especially when Burstyn begins to take an overly avid interest in Tilly's life. Based on the novel by Jane Stanton Hitchcock. Made for TV. **93m/C VHS.** Meg Tilly, Ellen Burstyn, Barnard Hughes; **D:** Ed Kaplan. *HMK*

Primary Colors 🐶🐶½ 1998 (R) Joe

Klein's anonymously published political satire is adapted for the big screen, starting off humorously and shifting into somber. Southern good ole boy, Gov. Jack Stanton (Travolta), and his savvy wife (Thompson) are after the presidential nomination and surrounded by crazy associates, including skeptical first-time campaign manager Henry Burton (Lester). More about Henry's political baptism by fire than anything else, as he tries to accommodate his conscience to the continuous scandals and double-dealing. It really doesn't matter whether Travolta's channeling Clinton or if Thompson acts like Hilary, since the film has bigger problems. The change in tone is jarring, characters and situations disappear without warning. And given that the press act like salivating wolverines at the merest hint of scandal, the situation surrounding opponent Fred Picker (Hagman) seems far-fetched at best. Still the goings-on will hold your attention until they're over—and you realize it's all smoke-and-mirrors.**CW:** Strong language and sexual references. **134m/C VHS.** John

Travolta, Emma Thompson, Adrian Lester, Kathy Bates, Billy Bob Thornton, Larry Hagman, Maura Tierney, Stacy Edwards, Diane Ladd, Gia Carides, Paul Guilfoyle, Tommy Hollis, Robert Klein, J.C. Quinn, Rob Reiner, Caroline Aaron, Allison Janney, Mykelti Williamson, Tony Shalhoub, John Vargas, Ben Jones, Bonnie Bartlett; *D:* Mike Nichols; *W:* Elaine May; *C:* Michael Ballhaus; *M:* Ry Cooder. *NYR*

Primary Motive 🐾 1992 **(R)** Taut political thriller with Nelson as Andy Blumenthal, a press secretary who finds that an opposing candidate's campaign is covered by a web of lies. Blumenthal exposes the lies, but the candidate denies them and pulls further ahead in the polls. When the candidate's wife gives Blumenthal an extremely damaging piece of information, will the polls finally turn against him? *CW:* Language. 93m/C VHS, Beta, LV. Judd Nelson, Richard Jordan, Sally Kirkland, Justine Bateman, John Savage; *D:* Daniel Adams; *W:* William Snowden III, Daniel Adams; *M:* John Cale. *FXV, VTR*

Primary Target 🐾 1989 **(R)** A mercenary reunites his 'Nam guerilla unit to rescue a diplomat's wife kidnapped by a Laotian jungle lord. 85m/C VHS, Beta. John Calvin, Miki Kim, Joey Aresco, Chip Lucio, John Ericson, Colleen Casey; *D:* Clark Henderson. *MGM*

Prime Cut 🐾🐾½ 1972 **(R)** Veritable orgy of drug trafficking, prostitution, extortion, loan sharking, fisticuffs and gangsters getting ground into mincemeat. Sleazy but well-made crime melodrama has its followers, but is best known as Spacek's film debut. 86m/C VHS, Beta, **Closed Caption.** Lee Marvin, Gene Hackman, Sissy Spacek, Angel Tompkins, Gregory Walcott; *D:* Michael Ritchie; *W:* Robert Dillon; *M:* Lalo Schifrin. *FOX*

Prime Evil 🐾🐾 1988 **(R)** A brave and determined nun infiltrates a sect of devil worshiping monks in an attempt to end their demonic sacrifices. The question is, will this sister slide beneath Satan's cleaver? 87m/C VHS, LV. William Beckwith, Christine Moore; *D:* Roberta Findlay. *VTR*

The Prime of Miss Jean Brodie 🐾🐾🐾 1969 **(PG)** Oscar-winning performance by Smith as a forward-thinking teacher in a Scottish Girls' school during the 1920s. She captivates her impressionable young students with her fascist ideals and free-thinking attitudes in this adaptation of the play taken from Muriel Spark's novel. 116m/C VHS, **Closed Caption.** *GB* Maggie Smith, Pamela Franklin, Robert Stephens, Celia Johnson, Gordon Jackson, Jane Carr; *D:* Ronald Neame; *W:* Jay Presson Allen; *C:* Ted Moore. Academy Awards '69: Best Actress (Smith); British Academy Awards '69: Best Actress (Smith), Best Supporting Actress (Johnson); Golden Globe Awards '70: Best Song ("Jean"); National Board of Review Awards '69: Best Supporting Actress (Franklin); Nominations: Academy Awards '69: Best Song ("Jean"). *FXV, BTV*

Prime Risk 🐾½ 1984 **(PG-13)** A young engineer who discovers an electronic method to break into automated teller machines finds that it leads to more trouble when she discovers that foreign agents are hot on her trail. 98m/C VHS, Beta. Toni Hudson, Lee Montgomery, Sam Bottoms; *D:* W. Farkas; *C:* Mac Ahlberg. *ART*

Prime Suspect 🐾🐾 1982 An honest citizen becomes the prime suspect after the coverage of a murder by an over-ambitious television reporter. 100m/C VHS, Beta. Mike Farrell, Teri Garr, Veronica Cartwright, Lane Smith, Barry Corbin, James Sloyan, Charles Aidman; *D:* Noel Black. *NO*

Prime Suspect 🐾🐾 1988 A young man escapes from a mental institution to clear his name after being wrongfully accused of murdering his girlfriend. 89m/C VHS. Susan Strasberg, Frank Stallone, Billy Drago, Doug McClure; *D:* Mark Rutland. *NO*

Prime Suspect 🐾🐾🐾 1992 Mirren stars as Detective Chief Inspector Jane Tennison in this British television police procedural. When a male inspector dies of a heart attack while investigating a rape-murder, Tennison, the only woman of senior police status, wants the case. But she runs into multiple obstructions, not the least being the smug male police system. Then the case really takes a turn when it appears Tennison is

searching for a serial killer. But Jane is no quitter and she has both the brains and the guts to back up her orders. Adapted from the book by Lynda La Plante, who also wrote the teleplay. 240m/C VHS. *GB* Helen Mirren, Tom Bell, Zoe Wanamaker, John Bowe, Tom Wilkinson, Ralph Fiennes; *D:* Christopher Menaul; *W:* Lynda La Plante. *SIG, FXL*

Prime Suspect 2 🐾🐾🐾 1993 DCI Jane Tennison (Mirren) returns in another British made for TV police drama. Jane has been off at a police seminar where she has a brief liaison with a black police detective, Robert Oswalde (Salmon). She is recalled to investigate the decomposed body of a young woman found in one of London's Afro-Caribbean neighborhoods and must deal with their resentment of the police. When detective Oswalde is reassigned to Jane's department, she begins having trouble separating her public and private feelings, while trying to obtain a confession from her most likely suspect. Based on a story by Lynda La Plante. 240m/C VHS. *GB* Helen Mirren, Colin Salmon, Tom Watson, Ian Fitzgibbon, Philip Wright, Jack Ellis, Craig Fairbrass; *D:* John Strickland; *W:* Allan Cubitt. *SIG, FXL*

Prime Suspect 3 🐾🐾🐾 1993 The BBC returns Jane Tennison to the beat (as does her portrayer Mirren) in another intriguing police drama. Tennison has transferred from homicide to the vice squad but still can't escape murder investigations—or male chauvinists. Oh yes, Tennison has a new team of macho colleagues to contend with and she's still getting heat from her bosses about her job. Still, this is one copper who lets nothing stand in her way. Made for British TV; on three cassettes. 205m/C VHS. *GB* Helen Mirren, Tom Bell, Peter Capaldi, David Thewlis, Ciaran Hinds, Terrence Hardiman, Mark Strong, Karen Tomlin, Struan Rodger, Liza Sadovy, Andrew Woodall, Kelly Hunter; *D:* David Drury; *W:* Lynda La Plante; *M:* Stephen Warbeck. *TVC, PBS*

Prime Suspect 5: Errors of Judgment 🐾🐾🐾 1996 Detective Superintendent Jane Tennison (Mirren) has been transferred to Manchester where her first project is to deal with the death of a drug dealer and the problems caused by an arrogant young gang leader, known as "The Street" (Mackintosh). But Jane's making more than her share of professional errors and, as usual, her personal life's a mess of her own making—this time by starting an affair with her married boss, Martin Ballinger (McArdle). 240m/C VHS. *GB* Helen Mirren, John McArdle, Steven Mackintosh, David O'Hara, Julia Lane, Joseph Jones, Ray Emmet Brown, Marsha Thomson; *D:* Philip Davis; *W:* Guy Andrews; *C:* Barry McCann; *M:* Stephen Warbeck. *PBS, VIF*

Prime Suspect: Inner Circles 🐾🐾½ 1995 Jane Tennison (Mirren) finds herself caught up in suburban fraud and murder and once again on the outs with her bosses. Two drugged-up youths are accused of murdering a country club manager. The powers that be are satisfied but Tennison isn't—and rightly so because the murder is merely the tip of a very large and nasty iceberg. TV movie. 102m/C VHS. *GB* Helen Mirren, Jill Baker, Anthony Bate, John Benfield, Richard Hawley, James Laurenson, Kelly Reilly, Sophie Stanton, Nick Patrick, Tom Russell; *D:* Sarah Pia Anderson; *W:* Eric Deacon; *C:* David Odd; *M:* Stephen Warbeck. *VTR*

Prime Suspect: The Lost Child 🐾🐾🐾 1994 Jane Tennison (Mirren), promoted to Detective Chief Inspector, is caught up in a drama that strikes a little too close to her well-schooled emotions. A young mother's (Edney) 14-month-old daughter has been abducted—has the child been kidnapped for ransom or is this the work of a pedophile? Suspicion falls on released sex offender Chris (Glenister) but things aren't that simple—even as tensions rise among Tennison's own detectives. Made for TV. 102m/C VHS. *GB* Helen Mirren, Beatie Edney, Robert Glenister, Lesley Sharp, Jack Ellis, Stuart Wilson, John Benfield, Richard Hawley; *D:* John Madden; *W:* Paul Billing; *M:* Stephen Warbeck. *VTR*

Prime Suspect: The Scent of Darkness 🐾🐾🐾 1995 Could this be curtains for the career of the irascible Jane Tennison? Not bloody likely but she's got more than her fair share of trouble when a new wave of murders are in the same modus operandi as multiple killer George Marlow—whom Tennison put away four years before (in "Prime Suspect"). Now Marlow's conviction is called into question, as are Jane's methods, so she's placed on suspension. But that isn't going to stop her from getting to the truth. 102m/C VHS. *GB* Helen Mirren, Tim Woodward, Stuart Wilson, Richard Hawley, John Benfield, Christopher Fulford, Joyce Redman, Stephen Boxer; *D:* Paul Marcus. *VTR*

Prime Target 🐾🐾 1991 **(R)** Small-town cop John Bloodstone (Heavener) is recruited by the FBI to transfer a mafia boss (Curtis) from a safehouse to the courthouse. He has to keep the former mobster alive long enough to testify against the "family." Their cross-country adventure is heightened by a murderous confrontation with evil forces that want them both dead. *CW:* Violence and sensuality. 87m/C VHS, **Closed Caption.** David Heavener, Tony Curtis, Isaac Hayes, Jenilee Harrison, Robert Reed, Andrew (Andy) Robinson, Don Stroud; *D:* David Heavener; *W:* David Heavener; *M:* Chris Boardman.

The Prime Time woof! 1960 Horrid film about a teen girl who leaves home and gets involved with a teen gang and a slimy detective. She's also kidnapped by a weird beatnik artist who forces her to pose nude. Black's film debut. Also known as "Hellkitten." 76m/B VHS. JoAnn LeCompte, Frank Roche, James Brooks, Ray Gronwold, Maria Pavelle, Robert Major, Karen Black; *D:* Herschell Gordon Lewis. *SNC*

Prime Time 🐾½ 1980 **(R)** Forgotten satirical comedy about what would happen if the censors took a day off from American television. 73m/C VHS, Beta. Warren Oates, David Spielberg. *NO*

Prime Time Murder 🐾½ 1992 **(R)** Freelance TV journalist hooks up with eccentric ex-cop to trail a psycho stalking street people. *CW:* Graphic stabbings. 95m/C VHS. Tim Thomerson, Sally Kirkland, Anthony Finetti, Laura Reed; *D:* Gary Skeen Hall.

The Primitive Lover 🐾🐾 1916 Early silent comedy about young wife who decides she deserves more than her marriage is giving her. 67m/B VHS, Beta. Constance Talmadge, Kenneth Harlan, Harrison Ford; *D:* Sidney Franklin. *GPV*

Primrose Path 🐾🐾½ 1940 Melodramatic soaper with comedic touches about a wrong-side-of-the-tracks girl falling for and then losing an ambitious young go-getter running a hamburger stand. 93m/B VHS, Beta. Ginger Rogers, Joel McCrea, Marjorie Rambeau, Henry Travers, Miles Mander, Queenie Vassar, Joan Carroll, Vivienne Osborne; *D:* Gregory La Cava. Nominations: Academy Awards '40: Best Supporting Actress (Rambeau). *TTC*

Prince and the Great Race 🐾🐾 1983 Three Australian children search the outback to find their kidnapped horse who is scheduled to run in the big New Year's Day Race. 91m/C VHS, Beta. *AU* John Ewart, John Howard, Nicole Kidman. *ART*

The Prince and the Pauper 🐾🐾🐾 1937 Satisfying adaptation of the classic Mark Twain story of a young street urchin who trades places with the young king of England. Wonderful musical score by noted composer Korngold who provided the music for many of Flynn's adventure films. Also available in a computer-colorized version. 118m/B VHS, Beta, LV. Errol Flynn, Claude Rains, Alan Hale, Billy Mauch, Montagu Love, Henry Stephenson, Barton MacLane; *D:* William Keighley; *M:* Erich Wolfgang Korngold. *FOX, MLB, CCB*

The Prince and the Pauper 🐾🐾 1962 A prince and a poor young boy swap their clothes and identities, thus causing a lot of confusion for their families. Based on the story by Mark Twain. 93m/C VHS, Beta. Guy Williams, Laurence Naismith, Donald Houston, Jane Asher, Walter Hudd. *DIS*

The Prince and the Pauper ✓✓½
Crossed Swords **1978 (PG)** Remake of the 1937 Errol Flynn film employing lavish sets and a tongue-in-cheek attitude among the all-star cast, who occasionally wander adrift when the director stops for tea. When an English prince and a pauper discover that they have identical appearances, they decide to trade places with each other. From Mark Twain's classic. **113m/C VHS, Beta. GB** Oliver Reed, Raquel Welch, Mark Lester, Ernest Borgnine, George C. Scott, Rex Harrison, Charlton Heston, Sybil Danning; *D:* Richard Fleischer; *C:* Jack Cardiff; *M:* Maurice Jarre.

The Prince and the Showgirl ✓✓½
1957 An American showgirl in 1910 London is wooed by the Prince of Carpathia. Part of the "A Night at the Movies" series, this tape simulates a 1957 movie evening, with a Sylvester the Cat cartoon, "Greedy for Tweety," a newsreel and coming attractions for "Spirit of St. Louis." **127m/C VHS, Beta, LV.** Laurence Olivier, Marilyn Monroe, Sybil Thorndike, Jeremy Spenser, Richard Wattis; *D:* Laurence Olivier; *W:* Terence Rattigan; *C:* Jack Cardiff. *WAR*

Prince Brat and the Whipping Boy ✓✓✓
The Whipping Boy **1995 (G)** Orphaned Jemmy (Munro) is living on the streets of the 18th-century German town of Brattenburg with his younger sister Annyrose (Salt). Neglected, spoiled Prince Horace (Knight) has been causing mischief in the castle but instead of being punished himself, the king's men catch Jemmy and use him as a punishment stand-in. Jemmy escapes the castle to get back to his sister and the Prince decides to go along for the adventure. Filmed on location in North Rhine-Westphalia and Burgundy, Germany. Adventurous TV movie with spunky leads; adapted from Sid Fleischman's novella. **96m/C VHS, LV, Closed Caption.** Truan Munro, Nic Knight, Karen Salt, George C. Scott, Kevin Conway, Vincent Schiavelli, Andrew Bicknell, Jean Anderson, Mathilda May; *D:* Syd Macartney; *W:* Max Brindle; *M:* Lee Holdridge. *COL*

Prince Jack ✓✓
1983 Profiles the turbulent political career of President John F. Kennedy. **100m/C VHS, Beta.** Lloyd Nolan, Dana Andrews, Robert Guillaume, Cameron Mitchell; *D:* Bert Lovitt; *M:* Elmer Bernstein. *ART*

Prince of Bel Air ✓½
1987 (R) A pool-cleaning playboy who makes a habit of one night stands meets a woman and starts falling in love with her. Originally a made-for-television movie. **95m/C VHS, Beta, LV.** Mark Harmon, Kirstie Alley, Robert Vaughn, Patrick Laborteaux, Deborah Harmon; *D:* Charles Braverman; *M:* Robert Folk.

The Prince of Central Park ✓✓✓
1977 Two young orphans are forced by circumstance to live in a tree in New York's Central Park until they are befriended by a lonely old woman. An above-average made for television adaptation of the novel by Evan H. Rhodes, the story was later used for a Broadway play. **76m/C VHS, Beta.** Ruth Gordon, T.J. Hargrave, Lisa Richards, Brooke Shields, Marc Vahanian, Dan Hedaya; *D:* Harvey Hart. *ART*

Prince of Darkness ✓½
1987 (R) University students release Satan, in the form of a mysterious chemical, unwittingly on the world. Written by Martin Quatermass (a pseudonym of Carpenter). Strong personnel does not save this dreary and slow-moving cliche plot. **102m/C VHS, Beta, LV.** Donald Pleasence, Lisa Blount, Victor Wong, Jameson Parker, Dennis Dun, Susan Blanchard, Anne Howard, Ken Wright, Dirk Blocker; *Cameos:* Alice Cooper; *D:* John Carpenter; *W:* John Carpenter; *C:* Gary B. Kibbe; *M:* John Carpenter. *USH*

Prince of Pennsylvania ✓½
1988 (R) A mild comedy about a spaced-out youth who kidnaps his own father in hopes of nabbing a family inheritance. **113m/C VHS, Beta, LV.** Keanu Reeves, Fred Ward, Amy Madigan, Bonnie Bedelia, Jeff Hayenga; *D:* Ron Nyswaner; *W:* Ron Nyswaner; *M:* Thomas Newman. *COL*

Prince of the City ✓✓✓
1981 (R) Docudrama of a police officer who becomes an informant in an effort to end corruption within his narcotics unit, but finds he must pay a heavy price. Based on the true story told in Robert Daly's book, the powerful script carries the tension through what would otherwise be an overly long film. Excellent performances make this a riveting character study. **167m/C VHS, Beta, LV.** Treat Williams, Jerry Orbach, Richard Foronjy, Don Billett, Kenny Marino, Lindsay Crouse, Lance Henriksen; *D:* Sidney Lumet; *W:* Jay Presson Allen, Sidney Lumet; *C:* Andrzej Bartkowiak. New York Film Critics Awards '81: Best Director (Lumet); Nominations: Academy Awards '81: Best Adapted Screenplay. *WAR*

The Prince of Thieves ✓✓
1948 Robin Hood helps Lady Marian extricate herself from a forced marriage in this adventure made with younger audiences in mind. **72m/C VHS.** Jon Hall, Patricia Morison, Adele Jergens, Alan Mowbray, Michael Duane; *D:* Howard Bretherton. *COL*

The Prince of Tides ✓✓✓½
1991 (R) Conroy's sprawling southern-fried saga is neatly pared down to essentials in this tale of the dysfunctional Wingo family, whose dark tragedies are gradually revealed as twins Tom and Savannah come to grips with personal demons under the ministering aid of psychiatrist Streisand. Bravura performance by Nolte in what may be his best role to date; Streisand is restrained in both her performance and direction although a subplot dealing with her bad marriage and rebellious son is a predictable distraction. The South Carolina low country, and even New York City, never looked better. Conroy adapted the screenplay from his novel of the same name with Johnston's help. *CW:* Strong language and sex-related violence scene. **132m/C VHS, Beta, LV, 8mm, Closed Caption.** Nick Nolte, Barbra Streisand, Blythe Danner, Kate Nelligan, Jeroen Krabbe, Melinda Dillon, George Carlin, Jason Gould, Brad Sullivan; *D:* Barbra Streisand; *W:* Pat Conroy, Becky Johnston; *M:* James Newton Howard. Golden Globe Awards '92: Best Actor—Drama (Nolte); Los Angeles Film Critics Association Awards '91: Best Actor (Nolte); Nominations: Academy Awards '91: Best Actor (Nolte), Best Adapted Screenplay, Best Art Direction/Set Decoration, Best Cinematography, Best Picture, Best Supporting Actress (Nelligan), Best Original Score. *COL*

Prince Valiant ✓✓½
1954 (PG-13) When his royal dad is exiled by an evil tyrant, brave young Wagner brushes aside bangs and journeys to Camelot to seek the help of King Arthur. Based on Harold Foster's classic comic strip. *CW:* Medieval action violence. **100m/C VHS, Beta.** James Mason, Janet Leigh, Robert Wagner, Debra Paget, Sterling Hayden, Victor McLaglen, Donald Crisp, Brian Aherne, Barry Jones, Mary Philips; *D:* Henry Hathaway; *W:* Dudley Nichols. *FCT*

Prince Valiant ✓✓½
1997 (PG-13) We're back at Camelot with a lot of colorful pageantry and old-fashioned action. Young orphaned Valiant (Moyer) is the squire to Sir Gawain (Hickox), one of King Arthur's (Fox) knights. He is given the task of escorting Princess Ilene (Heigl) to her home in Wales and naturally the young twosome fall in love. Meanwhile, the sword Excalibur has been stolen by Viking leader Thagnar (Kretschmann) and somehow become embedded in his castle's stone floor. Then Ilene gets kidnapped and it's up to Valiant to rescue both Ilene and Excalibur. Based on the comic strip created by Harold R. Foster. **91m/C VHS, Closed Caption. GB** Stephen Moyer, Katherine Heigl, Thomas Kretschmann, Edward Fox, Benjamin Pullen, Anthony Hickox, Udo Kier, Warwick Davis, Zach Galligan, Gavan O'Herlihy, Joanna Lumley, Ron Perlman, Walter Gotell; *D:* Anthony Hickox; *W:* Michael Frost Beckner, Anthony Hickox; *C:* Roger Lanser; *M:* David Bergeaud. *FXV*

Princes in Exile ✓✓½
1990 (PG-13) Young people struggle with their life-threatening illnesses at a special summer camp. They find that love and friendship hold the key to dreams about the future. Excellent cast of newcomers.

Based on a novel of the same name by Mark Schreiber. **103m/C VHS, Beta, LV, Closed Caption. CA** Zachary Ansley, Nicholas Shields, Stacy Mistysyn, Alexander Chapman, Chuck Shamata; *D:* Giles Walker. *FCT*

Princess Academy ✓
1987 (R) A self-respecting young debutante battles the ways of her elitist finishing school. **91m/C VHS, Beta. FR** Eva Gabor, Lu Leonard, Richard Paul, Lar Park Lincoln, Carole Davis; *D:* Bruce Block; *M:* Paul Antonelli, Roger Bellon. *ART*

The Princess & the Call Girl ✓✓
1984 A call girl asks her look-alike roommate to take her place in Monaco for a lavishly erotic weekend. **90m/C VHS, Beta.** Carol Levy, Shannah Hall, Victor Bevine; *D:* Radley Metzger. *MON*

The Princess and the Goblin ✓✓½
1994 (G) Little kiddies may enjoy this animated adventure but it's a bland story with mediocre animation. Groups of ugly, underground-dwelling goblins like nothing better than to scare humans, especially castle-dwelling Princess Irene. Brave working-class Curdie helps to save the day. Based on a book by George MacDonald. **82m/C VHS. GB HU V:** Sally Ann Marsh, Peter Murray, Claire Bloom.

The Princess and the Pea ✓✓✓
1983 From "Faerie Tale Theatre" comes the story of a princess who tries to prove that she's a blueblood by feeling the bump of a tiny pea under the thickness of 20 mattresses. **60m/C VHS, Beta, LV, Closed Caption.** Liza Minnelli, Tom Conti, Tim Kazurinsky, Pat McCormick, Beatrice Straight; *D:* Tony Bill. *FOX, FCT*

The Princess and the Pirate ✓✓✓
1944 Hope at his craziest as a vaudvillian who falls for a beautiful princess while on the run from buccaneers on the Spanish Main. Look for Crosby in a closing cameo performance. Available in digitally remastered stereo with original movie trailer. **94m/C VHS, Beta, LV.** Bob Hope, Walter Slezak, Walter Brennan, Virginia Mayo, Victor McLaglen; *Cameos:* Bing Crosby; *D:* David Butler; *C:* Victor Milner. Nominations: Academy Awards '44: Best Interior Decoration, Best Original Dramatic/Comedy Score. *HBO*

The Princess and the Swineherd ✓½
1960 A German adaptation of the Brothers Grimm fairy tale about a young suitor who tries to please a materialistic princess. **82m/B VHS, Beta. GE VYY**

The Princess Bride ✓✓✓½
1987 (PG) A modern update of the basic fairy tale crammed with all the cliches, this adventurously irreverent love story centers around a beautiful maiden and her young swain as they battle the evils of the mythical kingdom of Florin to be reunited with one another. Great dueling scenes and offbeat satire of the genre make this fun for adults as well as children. Based on William Goldman's cult novel. **98m/C VHS, Beta, LV, 8mm, Letterbox, Closed Caption.** Cary Elwes, Mandy Patinkin, Robin Wright Penn, Wallace Shawn, Peter Falk, Andre the Giant, Chris Sarandon, Christopher Guest, Billy Crystal, Carol Kane, Fred Savage, Peter Cook, Mel Smith; *D:* Rob Reiner; *W:* William Goldman; *M:* Mark Knopfler. Nominations: Academy Awards '87: Best Song ("Storybook Love"). *COL, HMV*

Princess Caraboo ✓✓½
1994 (PG) Fluffy quasi-fairy tale (but based on a true story) finds an exotic beauty (Cates) appearing in an English village in 1817. She speaks a language no one understands and is taken under the wing of the local gentry, the Worralls, who believe she is an Asian princess washed ashore during a shipwreck. Meanwhile, the local journalist (Rea) is suspicious but protective, an Oxford linguist (Lithgow) is determined to prove her a fraud, and she must put up with the Worrall family's pompous Greek butler (Cate's husband Kline at his showy best). **97m/C VHS, LV, Closed Caption.** Phoebe Cates, Stephen Rea, John Lithgow, Kevin Kline, Jim Broadbent, Wendy Hughes, Peter Eyre, Jacqueline Pearce, John Lynch, John Sessions, Arkie Whiteley, John Wells; *D:* Michael Austin; *W:* John Wells, Michael Austin; *M:* Richard Hartley. *COL*

Princess Cinderella 🐾🐾 193? A live-action dramatization of the famous fantasy. Dubbed in English. **75m/B VHS, Beta.** *SP* Silvana Jachino, Roberto Villa. *JEF*

The Princess Comes Across 🐾🐾🐾 1936 Deft comedy-mystery finds Brooklyn actress Lombard deciding to take an ocean voyage and pass herself off as a Swedish princess in the hopes of furthering her career. Bandleader Mac-Murray is smitten but an old beau recognizes the ruse and demands hush money. Then he turns up dead and the duo fall under the suspicious eye of a German passenger (Rumann) who happens to be a detective. From the novel by Louis Lucien Rogger. **77m/B VHS, Closed Caption.** Carole Lombard, Fred MacMurray, Alison Skipworth, Sig Rumann, Douglass Dumbrille, William Frawley, Porter Hall, George Barbier, Lumsden Hare, Mischa Auer, Tetsu Komai; *D:* William K. Howard; *W:* Walter DeLeon, Francis Martin, Frank Butler, Don Hartman; *C:* Ted Tetzlaff. *USH*

Princess Daisy 🐾 1983 Made for television movie about a beautiful model who claws her way to the top of her profession while trying to find true love and avoid the clutches of her rotten halfbrother. Adapted from Judith Krantz's glitzy bestselling novel. **200m/C VHS, Beta.** Merete Van Kamp, Lindsay Wagner, Claudia Cardinale, Stacy Keach, Ringo Starr, Barbara Bach; *D:* Waris Hussein. *VTR, FOX, MOV*

Princess Tam Tam 🐾🐾🐾 1935 Pleasing French adaptation of Shaw's "Pygmalion," as a beautiful native African woman is "westernized" by a handsome writer and then introduced to high society as an exotic princess. A musical notable for its spectacular choreography and on-location Tunisian scenery. Story by Pepito Abatino, who was then Baker's husband. In French with English subtitles. **77m/B VHS, Beta, LV.** *FR* Josephine Baker, Albert Prejean, Germaine Aussey, Viviane Romance; *D:* Edmond T. Greville. *MVD, TPV, KIV*

The Princess Who Never Laughed 1984 A stern king holds a laugh-off contest to make his morose daughter happy in this adaptation of the Brothers Grimm story from the "Faerie Tale Theatre" series. **60m/C VHS, Beta, Closed Caption.** Ellen Barkin, Howard Hesseman, Howie Mandel, Mary Woronov. *FOX, FCT*

Princess Yang Kwei Fei 🐾🐾🐾 *Yokihi; The Empress Yang Kwei Fei* 1955 Set in 8th-century China and based on the life of the last T'ang emperor and the beautiful servant girl he loves and makes his bride. She falls victim to court jealousies and he to his greedy family, though even death cannot end their love. Beautifully filmed and acted romantic tragedy. In Japanese with English subtitles. **91m/C VHS.** *JP* Machiko Kyo, Masayuki Mori, Sakae Ozawa, So Yamamura; *D:* Kenji Mizoguchi. *NYF*

The Principal 🐾🐾½ 1987 (R) A tough, down-on-his-luck high school teacher is hired as the principal of a relentlessly violent, uncontrollable high school. Naturally he whips it into shape. **109m/C VHS, Beta, LV.** James Belushi, Louis Gossett Jr., Rae Dawn Chong, Michael Wright, Esai Morales, J.J. Cohen, Troy Winbush; *D:* Christopher Cain; *W:* Frank Deese; *C:* Arthur Albert; *M:* Jay Gruska. *COL*

Prison 🐾½ 1988 (R) The zombified body of an unjustly executed inmate haunts Creedmore Prison, stalking the guard that killed him. His search is aided by the terrified inmates. **102m/C VHS, Beta, LV, Closed Caption.** Lane Smith, Chelsea Field, Viggo Mortensen, Lincoln Kilpatrick, Tom Everett, Tommy (Tiny) Lister; *D:* Renny Harlin; *W:* C. Courtney Joyner; *C:* Mac Ahlberg; *M:* Richard Band.

Prison Break 🐾🐾 1938 A convict plans a daring prison escape in order to clear his name for a murder he did not commit. **72m/B VHS, Beta.** Barton MacLane, Glenda Farrell, Ward Bond. *SNC, NOS, MRV*

Prison for Children 🐾🐾½ 1993 Sixteen-year-old Chris is orphaned and put into a boys home where a supervisor sees his potential and helps him achieve it. **96m/C VHS.** Raphael Sbarge, Kenny Ransom, Jonathan Chapin, Josh Brolin,

James Callahan, Betty Thomas, John Ritter; *D:* Larry Peerce. *USH*

Prison Planet 🐾½ 1992 (R) In the year 2200 Earth is under the dictatorship of an evil king, with only a band of intrepid rebels to oppose him. Blaine, one of the rebels, gets himself arrested and sent to prison in search of the true ruler, the king's brother. But the prison is protected by a brutal warlord and his equally sadistic warriors, whom Blaine must battle if he ever hopes to find truth and justice. **90m/C VHS.** James Phillips, Jack Willcox, Michael Foley, Deborah Thompson-Carlin; *D:* Armand Gazarian; *W:* Armand Gazarian. *COL*

Prison Shadows 🐾 1936 Contrived programmer about a fighter (Nugent) who attempts to make a comeback after having served three years of a five-year sentence for killing an opponent in the boxing ring. He makes his comeback, but deals yet another mortal blow. Turns out that a gambling ring is behind the bizarre murders of the fighters and Nugent is their next victim. **67m/B VHS.** Eddie Nugent, Lucille Lund, Joan Barclay, Forrest Taylor, Syd Saylor, Monte Blue; *D:* Robert F. "Bob" Hill; *W:* Al Martin. *SNC*

Prison Stories: Women on the Inside 🐾🐾🐾 1991 Three short dramatic stories depict the life of women inside prison walls. "New Chicks," directed by Spheeris, tells the story of two lifelong friends and partners in crime. "Esperanza," directed by Deitch, tells the story of a woman on the inside trying to prevent her family from following the same destructive path. Silver's "Parole Board" features Davidovich as a murderess up for parole but reluctant to leave the security of the prison. Blunt and gritty portrayal of prison gangs, the lifestyle of female inmates, and their fears of returning to life on the outside. Originally produced for cable TV. **94m/C VHS, Beta, Closed Caption.** Rae Dawn Chong, Annabella Sciorra, Lolita Davidovich, Talisa Soto, Rachel Ticotin, Grace Zabriskie, Silvania Gallardo, Francesca Roberts; *D:* Donna Deitch, Penelope Spheeris, Joan Micklin Silver; *W:* Dick Beebe.

Prison Train 🐾🐾½ *People's Enemy* 1938 Travelogue of a convicted murderer's cross-country journey to begin his prison sentence at Alcatraz. **84m/B VHS.** Fred Keating, Linda (Dorothy Comingore) Winters, Clarence Muse, Faith Bacon, Alexander Leftwich, Nestor Paiva, Franklyn Farnum; *D:* Gordon Wiles. *VYY, MOV*

The Prisoner 🐾🐾🐾 1955 Gritty drama about a Cardinal imprisoned in a Soviet bloc country as his captors attempt to break his determination not to be used as a propaganda tool. Interactions between the prisoner and his interogator are riveting. Based on the real-life experiences of Cardinal Mindszenty, a Hungarian activist during and after WWII. **91m/B VHS.** *GB* Alec Guinness, Jack Hawkins, Raymond Huntley, Wilfred Lawson; *D:* Peter Glenville. *COL*

The Prisoner: Arrival 1968 Introductory episode of the cult television series. McGoohan stars as a former British spy abducted and held captive in a mysterious village where everyone is assigned a number. As Number 6 he tries to figure out what's going on and how he can get out. Additional episodes available. **52m/C VHS, Beta, LV.** *GB* Patrick McGoohan, Virginia Maskell, Guy Doleman, Paul Eddington, George Baker, Angelo Muscat, Barbara Yu Ling, Stephanie Randall; *D:* Don Chaffey. *MPI, MOV, TVC*

Prisoner Cell Block H 1980 Popular Australian television soap opera set in Wentworth Detention Center, a women's prison. Primary characters include Franky, a violent lesbian biker in for armed robbery; Karen, who murdered her husband and is the object of Franky's affection; and naive Lynn, accused of kidnapping and attempted murder. Two episodes per cassette. **95m/C VHS.** *AU* Carol Burns, Kerry Armstrong, Patsy King, Gerard Maguire, Barry Quin, Mary Ward, Monica Maughan, Fiona Spence, Val Lehman, Pieta Tommano. *MPI, MOV*

Prisoner in the Middle 🐾🐾 1974 (PG) Janssen is the only man who can stop a nuclear warhead from falling into the hands of rival Middle East factions. Originally released as "Warhead." **87m/C VHS, Beta, LV, 8mm.** David Janssen, Karin Dor, Christopher Stone, Turia Tan, David Semadar, Art Metrano; *D:* John O'Conner. *MTX*

Prisoner of Honor 🐾🐾🐾 1991 (PG) A made-for-cable-TV retelling of notorious Dreyfus Affair, in which a Jewish officer in the 19th-century French military was accused of treason based on little evidence and lots of bigotry. George Piquart (Dreyfuss), the anti-semitic counterintelligence head, grows to realize Dreyfuss' innocence and fights zealously for the truth. Russell's flamboyant direction takes the heroic tale into the realm of the surreal; this may not be a thoroughly accurate account, but it's one of the more eye-filling. **90m/C VHS.** Richard Dreyfuss, Oliver Reed, Peter Firth, Jeremy Kemp, Brian Blessed, Peter Vaughan, Kenneth Colley, Lindsay Anderson; *D:* Ken Russell. *HBO*

Prisoner of Rio 🐾🐾 1989 The made-for-cable-TV satire about scruple-less television evangelists and their nefarious schemes at acquiring their audience's money. **90m/C VHS, Beta, LV.** Steven Berkoff, Paul Freeman; *D:* Lech Majewski; *M:* Hans Zimmer. *MOV*

Prisoner of Second Avenue 🐾🐾½ 1974 (PG) A New Yorker in his late 40s faces the future, without a job or any confidence in his ability, with the help of his understanding wife. Based on the Broadway play by Neil Simon. **98m/C VHS, Beta, LV, Letterbox.** Jack Lemmon, Anne Bancroft, Gene Saks, Elizabeth Wilson, Sylvester Stallone, F. Murray Abraham; *D:* Melvin Frank; *W:* Neil Simon; *M:* Marvin Hamlisch. *WAR*

Prisoner of the Mountains 🐾🐾🐾 *Kavkazsky Plennik; Prisoner of the Caucasus* 1996 (R) A modern-day, freely adapted version of Leo Tolstoy's novella "Prisoner of the Caucasus." Two Russian soldiers find themselves taken hostage in a remote Muslim village when their captor, Abdul-Mourant (Sikharulidze), wishes to exchange them for his own captive son. Seasoned veteran Sacha (Menshikov) and young recruit Vanya (Bodrov Jr.) slowly form a bond, not only with each other but gradually with their captors. But there's a tragic inevitability to the entire untenable situation. Russian with subtitles. *CW:* Some violence and language. **98m/C VHS, LV, Letterbox.** *RU* Sergei Bodrov Jr., Oleg Menshikov, Djemal Sikharulidze, Susanna Mekhralieva, Alexander Burejev; *D:* Sergei Bodrov; *W:* Sergei Bodrov, Arif Aliev, Boris Giller; *C:* Pavel Lebeshev; *M:* Leonid Desyatnikov. Nominations: Academy Awards '96: Best Foreign Language Film; Golden Globe Awards '97: Best Foreign Film. *ORI, MET*

Prisoner of Zenda 🐾🐾🐾½ 1937 An excellent cast and splendid photography make this the definitive film adaptation of Anthony Hope's swashbuckling novel. A British commoner is forced to pose as his cousin, the kidnapped king of a small European country, to save the throne. Complications of the romantic sort ensue when he falls in love with the queen. Excellent acting, robust sword play, and beautifully designed costumes make this an enjoyable spectacle. **101m/B VHS, Beta, LV.** Ronald Colman, Douglas Fairbanks Jr., Madeleine Carroll, David Niven, Raymond Massey, Mary Astor, Sir C. Aubrey Smith, Montagu Love, Byron Foulger, Alexander D'Arcy, Charles Halton; *D:* John Cromwell; *W:* Donald Ogden Stewart, John Balderston, Wells Root; *C:* James Wong Howe. National Film Registry '91;; Nominations: Academy Awards '37: Best Interior Decoration, Best Score. *MGM*

Prisoner of Zenda 🐾🐾½ 1952 Less-inspired remake of the 1937 version of Anthony Hope's novel, of a man resembling the monarch of a small country who is forced to pose as King during the coronation ceremony, becomes enamored with the queen, and finds himself embroiled in a murder plot. Worth watching for the luxurious costumes and lavish sets. Cast as a Cardinal here, Stone starred in the 1922 version. **101m/C**

VHS, Beta, LV. Stewart Granger, Deborah Kerr, Louis Calhern, James Mason, Jane Greer, Lewis Stone; D: Richard Thorpe; C: Joseph Ruttenberg. MGM

Prisoner of Zenda 🎬🎬 1979 (PG) Flat

comedic interpretation of Anthony Hope's swash-buckling tale of two identical men who switch places, only to find things complicated by a murder. Sellers stars in the double role of Prince Rudolph of Ruritania and Syd, the cockney cab driver who doubles for Rudolph when the Prince is imprisoned by his jealous brother Michael. 108m/C VHS, Beta. Peter Sellers, Jeremy Kemp, Lynne Frederick, Lionel Jeffries, Elke Sommer; D: Richard Quine; W: Dick Clement, Ian LaFrenais; M: Henry Mancini. USH

Prisoners of Inertia 🎬🎬½ 1989 (R) Two

newlyweds travel to New York city and find themselves caught up in a whirlwind adventure in this well-acted but lazily scripted comedy drama. 92m/C VHS. Amanda Plummer, Christopher Rich, John C. McGinley; D: Jay Noyles Seles. BTV

Prisoners of the Lost Universe 🎬½

1984 Talk-show hostess and her buddy are transported to a hostile universe by a renegade scientist. The two terrified humans search desperately for the dimensional door that is their only hope of escape. Made for television. 94m/C VHS, Beta. Richard Hatch, Kay Lenz, John Saxon; D: Terry Marcel. NO

Prisoners of the Sun 🎬🎬🎬 Blood Oath

1991 (R) Right after WWII an Australian captain fights to convict Japanese officers for atrocities against Allied POWs, but he's stonewalled by both the U.S. military and still-defiant enemy prisoners. This fiery drama from Down Under packs a punch as it questions whether wartime justice even exists; similar in that way to Brown's earlier "Breaker Morant." Takei (Sulu of the original "Star Trek") makes an imposing Japanese admiral. CW: Momentary strong violence. 109m/C VHS, Beta. AU Bryan Brown, George Takei, Terry O'Quinn, John Back, Toshi Shioya, Deborah Kara Unger; D: Stephen Wallace. PAR

Private Affairs 🎬 1989 (R) The mistress of

a well-known surgeon becomes jealous when the doctor decides to have a fling with a gorgeous young swim instructor. Italian-made cheapie. 83m/C VHS, Beta. IT Giuliana de Sio, Kate Capshaw, David Naughton, Luca Barbareschi, Michele Placido; D: Francesco Massaro.

The Private Affairs of Bel

Ami 🎬🎬🎬 1947 "This is the story of a scoun-

drel," proclaims the opening. Sanders is ideally cast as a suave cad who rises in 1880s Parisian society, largely through the strategic seduction of prominent women. Moralistically minded Old Hollywood toned down the talky adaptation of the Guy de Maupassant novel, but it's still drama of a high order. 112m/B VHS. George Sanders, Angela Lansbury, Ann Dvorak, Frances Dee, John Carradine, Susan Douglas, Hugo Haas, Marie Wilson, Albert Basserman, Warren William, Katherine Emery, Richard Fraser; D: Albert Lewin; W: Albert Lewin. REP, FCT

Private Benjamin 🎬🎬½ 1980 (R) Light-

hearted fare about a pampered New York Jewish princess who impulsively enlists in the U.S. Army after her husband dies on their wedding night. Hawn, who also produced, creates a character loveable even at her worst moments and brings a surprising amount of depth to this otherwise frivolous look at high society attitudes. The basis for the television series. 110m/C VHS, Beta, LV. Goldie Hawn, Eileen Brennan, Albert Brooks, Robert Webber, Armand Assante, Barbara Barrie, Mary Kay Place, Sally Kirkland, Craig T. Nelson, Harry Dean Stanton, Sam Wanamaker; D: Howard Zieff; W: Nancy Meyers, Charles Shyer, Harvey Miller; M: Bill Conti. Writers Guild of America '80: Best Original Screenplay; Nominations: Academy Awards '80: Best Actress (Hawn), Best Original Screenplay, Best Supporting Actress (Brennan). WAR

Private Buckaroo 🎬🎬 1942 War time en-

tertainment in which Harry James and his orchestra get drafted. They decide to put on a show for the soldiers and get help from the Andrews Sisters. ♫ Don't Sit Under the Apple Tree with Any-

one Else But Me; Three Little Sisters; Private Buckaroo; Johnny Get Your Gun Again; We've Got a Job to Do; You Made Me Love You; Six Jerks in a Jeep; That's the Moon My Son; I Love the South. 70m/B VHS, Beta. The Andrews Sisters, Harry James, Joe E. Lewis, Dick Foran, Shemp Howard, Mary Wickes, Donald O'Connor; D: Eddie Cline. NOS, HEG, CAB

Private Contentment 🎬🎬 1983 This is a

drama about a young soldier's experiences before he goes off to war in 1945. 90m/C VHS, Beta. Trini Alvarado, Peter Gallagher, John McMartin, Kathryn Walker; D: Vivian Matalon. HMV

Private Duty Nurses 🎬½ Young L.A.

Nurses 1 1971 (R) Three nurses take on racism, war wounds, and a menage-a-trois (between one nurse, a doctor, and a drug addict). Second in Roger Corman's "nurse" quintet takes itself too seriously to be entertaining, but the gals make good use of those exciting new inventions, waterbeds. Preceded by "The Student Nurses" and followed by "Night Call Nurses," "The Young Nurses," and "Candy Stripe Nurses." 80m/C VHS, Beta. Kathy Cannon, Joyce Williams, Pegi Boucher, Joseph Kaufmann, Dennis Redfield, Herbert Jefferson Jr., Paul Hampton, Paul Gleason; D: George Armitage; W: George Armitage. NLC

The Private Eyes 🎬½ 1980 (PG) Light

and uneven comedic romp with Knotts and Conway as bungling sleuths engaged to investigate two deaths. They're led on a merry chase through secret passages to a meeting with a ghostly adversary. 91m/C VHS, Beta, LV. Don Knotts, Tim Conway, Trisha Noble, Bernard Fox; D: Lang Elliott; W: Tim Conway, John Myhers. VES

The Private Files of J. Edgar

Hoover 🎬🎬½ 1977 (PG) Scandal-mongering

"biography" of J. Edgar Hoover's private, sex-filled life. 112m/C VHS. Broderick Crawford, Dan Dailey, Jose Ferrer, Rip Torn, Michael Parks, Raymond St. Jacques, Ronee Blakley; D: Larry Cohen; W: Larry Cohen. HBO

A Private Function 🎬🎬½ 1984 (PG) A

ribald gag-fest dealing with Palin as a Yorkshire-man who steals and fattens a wily contraband pig against the backdrop of post-WWII rationing. The satire ranges from biting to downright nasty, but Palin is always likeable in the center of it all. 96m/C VHS, Beta. GB Michael Palin, Maggie Smith, Denholm Elliott, Bill Paterson, Liz Smith; D: Malcolm Mowbray; W: Alan Bennett; C: Tony Pierce-Roberts; M: John Du Prez. British Academy Awards '84: Best Actress (Smith), Best Supporting Actor (Elliott), Best Supporting Actress (Smith). PAR, TVC, FCT

Private Hell 36 🎬🎬 1954 Two detectives

become guilt-ridden after keeping part of some stolen money recovered after a robbery. Co-produced by Lupino. 81m/B VHS, LV. Ida Lupino, Howard Duff, Steve Cochran; D: Donald Siegel; W: Ida Lupino. REP

The Private History of a Campaign

That Failed 🎬½ 1987 Adaptation of the

Mark Twain story about a cowardly troop of Confederate soldiers. 89m/C VHS, Beta. Pat Hingle, Edward Herrmann. USH

Private Investigations 🎬½ 1987 (R) A

made-for-video thriller about a nosey reporter who gets himself and his adult son in trouble while investigating drug-pushing cops. 91m/C VHS, Beta, Closed Caption. Ray Sharkey, Clayton Rohner, Talia Balsam, Anthony Zerbe, Paul LeMat; D: Nigel Dick; W: John Dahl, David Warfield. MGM, FOX

Private Lessons 🎬🎬 1981 (R) Teenage

boy is left alone for the summer in the care of an alluring maid and a scheming chauffeur. 83m/C VHS, Beta, LV. Eric Brown, Sylvia Kristel, Howard Hesseman; D: Alan Myerson; C: Jan De Bont. USH

Private Lessons 19?? A boy can't concen-

trate on his piano lessons when he gets a beautiful new teacher. You won't be able to concentrate on anything but comedy. 90m/C VHS, Beta. Carroll Baker. JEF

Private Lessons, Another

Story 🎬½ 1994 (R) A New York photographer

(Morgan) is sick of her philandering husband and decides to experience some sexual excitement of her own by heading off to Miami. All that tropical heat inspires passion with her Cuban chauffeur (Garaza). CW: Strong sexuality. 86m/C VHS, Closed Caption. Mariana Morgan, Ray Garaza, Theresa Morris; D: Dominique Othenin-Girard; W: William Mernit. PAR

Private Life 🎬🎬½ Chastnaya Zhizn 1982 Sud-

denly with time on his hands, a Soviet official scrutinizes his relationships. After a number of revelations, he is forced to make new choices based on what he has learned. Oscar nominee in 1983. In Russian with English subtitles. 103m/C VHS. RU Mikhail Ulyanov, Ita Sanvina, Irina Gubanova; D: Edgar Ryazanov; W: Andrew Davies. Nominations: Academy Awards '82: Best Foreign Language Film. KIV, FCT

Private Life of Don Juan 🎬🎬 Don

Juan 1934 Appropriately slow-moving British costume drama set in 17th-century Spain finds an aging Don Juan struggling to maintain his usual antics in the pursuit of beautiful women. Furthermore, his reputation is being upstaged by a young imposter. Notable only as the last film appearance by Douglas Fairbanks Sr., and based on the play by Henri Bataille. 87m/B VHS, Beta. GB Douglas Fairbanks Sr., Merle Oberon, Binnie Barnes, Melville Cooper, Joan Gardner, Benita Hume, Athene Seyler; D: Alexander Korda; C: Georges Perinal. CNG, NOS, GPV

The Private Life of Henry

VIII 🎬🎬🎬🎬 1933 Lavish historical spectacle

lustily portraying the life and lovers of notorious British Monarch, King Henry VIII. A tour de force for Laughton as the robust 16th-century king, with outstanding performances by the entire cast. 97m/B VHS, Beta, LV. GB Charles Laughton, Binnie Barnes, Elsa Lanchester, Robert Donat, Merle Oberon, Miles Mander, Wendy Barrie, John Loder, Lady Tree, Franklin Dyall, Claud Allister, William Austin, Gibb McLaughlin, Sam Livesey, Lawrence Hanray, Everley Gregg, Judy Kelly, John Turnbull, Frederick Culley, Hay Petrie, Wally Patch; D: Alexander Korda; W: Arthur Wimperis, Lajos Biro; C: Georges Perinal. Academy Awards '33: Best Actor (Laughton); Nominations: Academy Awards '33: Best Picture. HBO, NOS, VHE

The Private Life of Sherlock

Holmes 🎬🎬🎬½ 1970 (PG-13) A unique per-

spective on the life of the famous detective reveals a complex character. Beautifully photographed, with fine performances by the supporting cast, the film boasts a haunting musical score but received suprisingly little recognition despite Wilder's high caliber direction. CW: Brief, drug-related plot material. 125m/C VHS, LV. GB Robert Stephens, Colin Blakely, Genevieve Page, Irene Handl, Stanley Holloway, Christopher Lee, Clive Revill, Catherine Lacey, Tamara Toumanova, Mollie Maureen, Michael Balfour; D: Billy Wilder; W: Billy Wilder, I.A.L. Diamond; M: Miklos Rozsa. FOX

Private Lives 🎬🎬🎬½ 1931 Stylish adap-

tation of Noel Coward play starring Shearer and Montgomery as a couple with a tempestuous relationship. Although once married, they have since divorced and married other mates. While honeymooning at the same french hotel (Quelle coincidence!), they have trouble showing affection to their new spouses and realize they still feel passionately about one another. Excellent acting combined with Coward's witty dialogue makes this film a treat. 92m/B VHS, LV, Closed Caption. Norma Shearer, Robert Montgomery, Reginald Denny, Una Merkel, Jean Hersholt; D: Sidney Franklin. MGM

The Private Lives of Elizabeth &

Essex 🎬🎬 1939 Cast reads like a Who's

Who in Hollywood in this lavishly costumed dramatization of the love affair between Queen Elizabeth I and the Second Earl of Essex. Forced to choose between her Kingdom and her lover, Davis' monarch is the epitome of a regal women. Fobray made her first film appearance as an adult in the adaptation of Maxwell Anderson's "Elizabeth the Queen." 106m/C VHS, Beta. Bette Davis, Errol

Flynn, Vincent Price, Nanette Fabray, Olivia de Havilland, Alan Hale, Donald Crisp, Leo G. Carroll; **D:** Michael Curtiz. Nominations: Academy Awards '39: Best Color Cinematography, Best Sound, Best Special Effects, Best Score. *FOX*

Private Manoeuvres woof! 1983 A comely Swiss military adviser gives her all to uplift the morale of the men at Camp Samantha. 79m/C VHS, Beta. Zachi Noy, Joseph Shiloah, Dvora Bekon. *MGM*

A Private Matter 🎬🎬🎬 1992 (PG-13) Based on the true story of Sherri Finkbine (hostess of TV's "Romper Room") and the controversy surrounding her decision to terminate her pregnancy in 1962. Pregnant with her fifth child, she discovered her sleeping medication contained thalidomide, known to cause severe birth defects. Although technically illegal, her doctor agreed to quietly perform an abortion. Sherri warned a local newspaper reporter about the drug's dangers and her identity was mistakenly revealed. A storm of adverse publicity forced her to Sweden for the abortion. Great performances highlight this complex and traumatic issue. Made for cable television. 89m/C VHS, LV, Closed Caption. Sissy Spacek, Aidan Quinn, Estelle Parsons, Sheila McCarthy, Leon Russom, William H. Macy; **D:** Joan Micklin Silver; **W:** William Nicholson. *HBO*

Private Obsession 🎬½ 1994 (R) Model Emanuelle Griffith (Whirry) is missing—kidnapped by obsessed admirer Richard (Christian) who wants the beauty for himself alone. Emanuelle may be blonde but she's not dumb and she decides to turn the tables on her captor. **CW:** Strong sexuality and language. 93m/C VHS. Shannon Whirry, Michael Christian, Bo Svenson, Rip Taylor; **D:** Lee Frost. *TRI*

Private Parts 🎬🎬 1972 (R) A bizarre first attempt at feature length for Bartel. Black comedy featuring a runaway, a voyeuristic photographer and a hotel full of strange people who participate in murder and a variety of freakish sexual acts. 87m/C VHS. Ayn Ruymen, Lucille Benson, John Ventantonio, Laurie Main, Stanley Livingston, Charles Woolf; **D:** Paul Bartel. *FRG, MGM*

Private Parts 🎬🎬½ *Howard Stern's Private Parts* 1996 (R) Stern makes his movie debut as...himself! Self-effacing yet self-aggrandizing bio traces Stern's rise from gawky kid to gawky college student to awkward small-market DJ to New York madman to inauguration as self-proclaimed King of All Media. Funny, and at times, touching flick features good performances by the rookie actors in Stern's inner circle, as well as by the pros. Giamatti is exceptional as the young WNBC exec assigned to tame Howard. Script manages to show Stern's outrageousness and still make him likeable. While this is clearly a whitewash job, and under other circumstances Stern himself might make fun of its sentimentality, pic should please everyone but the most rabid Stern-hater. **CW:** Strong language, nudity, and crude sexual humor. 109m/C VHS, Beta, Closed Caption. Howard Stern, Robin Quivers, Mary McCormack, Paul Giamatti, Fred Norris, Gary Dell'Abate, Bobby Borriello, Michael Maccarone, Matthew Friedman, Jackie Martling, Carol Alt, Richard Portnow, Kelly Bishop, Henry Goodman, Jonathan Hadary, Paul Hecht, Allison Janney, Michael Murphy, James Murtaugh, Reni Santoni, Lee Wilkof, Theresa Lynn, Amber Smith; **D:** Betty Thomas; **W:** Len Blum, Michael Kalesniko; **C:** Walt Lloyd; **M:** Van Dyke Parks. Nominations: Golden Raspberry Awards '97: Worst New Star (Stern). *PAR*

Private Passions 🎬 1985 A sultry woman gives her teenaged cousin a lesson in love during his European vacation. 86m/C VHS, Beta. Sybil Danning.

Private Resort 🎬🎬 1984 (R) Curious house detective and a bumbling thief interrupt the highjinks of two girl-crazy teens on a quest for fun at an expensive Miami hotel. Occasionally funny plodder. 82m/C VHS, Beta, LV. Johnny Depp, Rob Morrow, Karyn O'Bryan, Emily Longstreth, Tony Azito, Hector Elizondo, Dody Goodman, Leslie Easterbrook, Andrew Dice Clay; **D:** George Bowers. *COL*

Private Road: No Trespassing 1987 (R) A stock car racer and a top engineer compete over a military project, cars and a rich heiress. 90m/C VHS, Beta. George Kennedy, Greg Evigan, Mitzi Kapture; **D:** Raphael Nussbaum. *TWE*

Private School 🎬½ 1983 (R) Two high school girls from the exclusive Cherryvale Academy for Women compete for the affections of a young man from nearby Freemount Academy for Men, while Cherryvale's headmistress is trying to raise funds to build a new wing. Banal teen sexploitation comedy with better-than-average cast. 89m/C VHS, Beta, LV. Phoebe Cates, Betsy Russell, Kathleen Wilhoite, Sylvia Kristel, Ray Walston, Matthew Modine, Michael Zorek, Fran Ryan, Jonathan Prince, Kari Lizer, Richard Stahl; **D:** Noel Black; **C:** Walter Lassally. *USH*

The Private Secretary 🎬½ 1935 Horton is a mild-mannered clergyman who finds out his identity has been usurped by a young man with a great many angry creditors. Horton has some amusing comic bits but the film, based on a popular Victorian farce "Der Bibliotheker" by Van Moser, did not translate well to the screen. 70m/B VHS. GB Edward Everett Horton, Barry Mackay, Oscar Asche, Judy Gunn, Michael Shepley, Alastair Sim; **D:** Henry Edwards. *HCV*

Private War 🎬½ 1990 (R) Training for an elite force turns deadly when the commanding officer makes the rules. Now it's a private war between two brutal fighting machines. Adapted from a Jan Guillou story. 95m/C VHS. Martin Hewitt, Joe Dallesandro, Kimberly Beck; **D:** Frank De Palma; **W:** Frank De Palma, Terry Borst. *REP*

The Private War of Major Benson 🎬🎬½ 1955 Tough Army officer Major Bernard Benson (Heston) has his work cut out for him when he's ordered to take over an ROTC program at a military academy. First he finds out the school's run by nuns and then he treats his young cadets as he would adult troops, which naturally makes him very unpopular. But he manages to unbend enough to try for a romance with the school's doctor (Adams). And of course the kids teach him how to become a human being. Remade in 1995 as "Major Payne." 104m/C VHS, Closed Caption. Charlton Heston, Julie Adams, Milburn Stone, Nana Bryant, William Demarest, Tim Considine, Sal Mineo; **D:** Jerry Hopper; **W:** William Roberts, Richard Alan Simmons; **C:** Harold Lipstein. Nominations: Academy Awards '55: Best Story. *USH*

Private Wars 🎬🎬 1993 (R) A law-abiding community falls victim to gangland violence until the inhabitants hire a down-and-out private eye (Railsback) to show them how to fight back. He finds out that a greedy land developer (Whitman) has bribed the Chief of Police (Champion) to let his goons do anything to get the people out so he can redevelop the land. 94m/C VHS, LV, Closed Caption. Steve Railsback, Michael Champion, Stuart Whitman, Holly Floria, Dan Tullis Jr., Michael Delano, James Lew, Brian Patrick Clark; **D:** John Weidner; **W:** Ken Lamplugh, John Weidner. *PMH, IME*

Privates on Parade 🎬🎬½ 1984 (R) Film centering around the comic antics of an Army song-and-dance unit entertaining the troops in the Malayan jungle during the late '40s. Occasionally inspired horseplay based on Peter Nichols play. 107m/C VHS, Beta. GB John Cleese, Denis Quilley, Simon Jones, Joe Melia, Nicola Pagett, Julian Sands; **D:** Michael Blakemore. *PAR, TVC*

Prix de Beaute 🎬½ *Miss Europe* 1930 A woman's boyfriend does not know that she has won a beauty contest. Brooks' last starring role and the only film she did in France. In French with English subtitles. 93m/B VHS, Beta. FR Louise Brooks, Jean Bradin, George Charlia, Gaston Jacquet; **D:** Augusto Genina. *INT*

The Prize 🎬🎬🎬 1963 Gripping spy story laced with laughs based on a novel by Irving Wallace (adapted by Lehman). In Stockholm, writer accepts the Nobel prize for dubious reasons and then finds himself in the midst of political intrigue.

Newman and Sommer turn in great performances in this action drama. 136m/C VHS. Paul Newman, Edward G. Robinson, Elke Sommer, Leo G. Carroll, Diane Baker, Micheline Presle, Gerard Oury, Sergio Fantoni; **D:** Mark Robson; **W:** Ernest Lehman; **C:** William H. Daniels; **M:** Jerry Goldsmith. *MGM, REP, MLB*

Prize Fighter 🎬🎬 1979 (PG) Comedy team of Knotts and Conway take on Depression-era boxing. Fight manager Knotts and his pugilistic protege Conway unknowingly get involved with a powerful gangster, who convinces them to fight in a fixed championship match. Most enjoyable if intelligence is suspended at onset. 99m/C VHS, Beta. Tim Conway, Don Knotts; **D:** Michael Preece; **W:** Tim Conway.

Prize of Peril 🎬🎬 1984 A French television game show rewards it winners with wealth and its losers with execution. Not always the best policy to learn what's behind Door #1. 95m/C VHS, Beta. FR Michel Piccoli, Marie-France Pisier; **D:** Yves Boisset. *ART*

The Prize Pulitzer 🎬🎬 *Roxanne: The Prize Pulitzer* 1989 Watered-down, made-for-television account of the scandalous divorce between publishing heir Herbert "Pete" Pulitzer and his young wife Roxanne. Based on the book "The Prize Pulitzer" by Roxanne Pulitzer. 95m/C VHS. Perry King, Chynna Phillips, Courteney Cox, Betsy Russell, Sondra Blake, Caitlin Brown; **D:** Richard A. Colla. *CAF*

The Prizefighter and the Lady 🎬🎬🎬 *Every Woman's Man* 1933 In his first film role boxer Baer (who won the heavyweight boxing crown in 1934) is a natural as a fighter who falls for a beautiful nightclub singer (Loy). Baer and Loy get, but don't stay, together but she does turn out to be his lucky charm in the big fight finale. Fellow professional boxer Carnera, Baer's opponent in the climatic fight scene, refused to lose as the script indicated and the film ending was eventually rewritten. The likeable Baer later earned his living as an actor. 102m/B LV. Max Baer Sr., Myrna Loy, Otto Kruger, Primo Carnera, Walter Huston, Vince Barnett, Muriel Evans; **D:** Woodbridge S. Van Dyke. Nominations: Academy Awards '33: Best Story. *MGM*

Prizzi's Honor 🎬🎬 1985 (R) Highly stylized, sometimes leaden black comedy about an aging and none-to-bright hit man from a New York mob family who breaks with family loyalties when he falls for an upwardly mobile tax consultant who's also a hired killer. Skirting caricature in every frame, Nicholson is excellent in his portrayal of the thick-skulled mobster, as are Angelica Huston as the hot-to-trot Mafia daughter and Hickey as the Don. Adapted by Richard Condon and Janet Roach from Condon's novel. 130m/C VHS, Beta, LV, Closed Caption. Jack Nicholson, Kathleen Turner, Robert Loggia, John Randolph, Anjelica Huston, Lawrence Tierney, William Hickey, Lee Richardson, Michael Lombard, Joseph Ruskin, CCH Pounder; **D:** John Huston; **W:** Richard Condon, Janet Roach; **C:** Andrzej Bartkowiak; **M:** Alex North. Academy Awards '85: Best Supporting Actress (Huston); British Academy Awards '85: Best Adapted Screenplay; Golden Globe Awards '86: Best Actor—Musical/Comedy (Nicholson), Best Actress—Musical/Comedy (Turner), Best Director (Huston), Best Film—Musical/Comedy; Los Angeles Film Critics Association Awards '85: Best Supporting Actress (Huston); New York Film Critics Awards '85: Best Actor (Nicholson), Best Director (Huston), Best Supporting Actress (Huston); National Society of Film Critics Awards '85: Best Actor (Nicholson), Best Director (Huston), Best Supporting Actress (Huston); Writers Guild of America '85: Best Adapted Screenplay; Nominations: Academy Awards '85: Best Actor (Nicholson), Best Adapted Screenplay, Best Costume Design, Best Director (Huston), Best Film Editing, Best Picture, Best Supporting Actor (Hickey). *PAR, VES, BTV*

Probable Cause 🎬🎬 1995 (R) A knife-wielding serial killer specializes in murdering cops and the clues seem to point to a troubled veteran cop (Ironside), newly paired with a beautiful detective (Vernon). Some unexpected twists and a surprise ending. **CW:** Violence; a rape scene; language; some nudity. 90m/C VHS, Closed Caption. Michael Ironside, Kate Vernon, Kirk Baltz, Craig T. Nelson, M.

Emmet Walsh; *D:* Paul Ziller; *W:* Hal Salwen; *C:* Danny Nowak. *ART*

Probation 🐾🐾 *Second Chances* 1932 A dashing young man in trouble with the law receives an unusual sentence; he must become a chauffeur for a spoiled society girl. Grable's first film role is a small one. **60m/B VHS, Beta.** Sally Blane, J. Farrell MacDonald, Eddie Phillips, Clara Kimball Young, Betty Grable; *D:* Richard Thorpe. *NOS, SNC*

Probe 🐾🐾½ 1972 A detective uses computer-age technology to apprehend criminals. Pilot for the television series "Search." **95m/C VHS.** Hugh O'Brian, Elke Sommer, John Gielgud, Burgess Meredith, Angel Tompkins, Lilia Skala, Kent Smith, Alfred Ryder, Jaclyn Smith; *D:* Russ Mayberry; *W:* Leslie Stevens. *UNI*

Problem Child 🐾½ 1990 (PG) Ritter decides to adopt Oliver out of the goodness of his heart, but it seems young Oliver's already got a father figure named Beelzebub. Potential for laughs is unmet. **81m/C VHS, LV, Closed Caption.** John Ritter, Michael Oliver, Jack Warden, Amy Yasbeck, Gilbert Gottfried, Michael Richards, Peter Jurasik; *D:* Dennis Dugan; *W:* Scott Alexander, Larry Karaszewski; *C:* Peter Collister; *M:* Miles Goodman. *USH*

Problem Child 2 🐾 1991 (PG-13) Ritter and his nasty adopted son are back, but this time there's an equally malevolent little girl. They team up to prevent Ritter's upcoming marriage to a socialite. Low slapstick junk. **91m/C VHS, Beta, LV, Closed Caption.** John Ritter, Michael Oliver, Laraine Newman, Amy Yasbeck, Jack Warden, Ivyann Schwan, Gilbert Gottfried, James Tolkan, Charlene Tilton, Alan Blumenfeld, Paul Sutera; *D:* Brian Levant; *W:* Scott Alexander, Larry Karaszewski. *USH*

The Prodigal 🐾🐾½ 1955 Luke's New Testament Bible story of the son seduced by greed slickly transfered to the silver screen by MGM. A colorful cast is the main attraction. **113m/C LV.** Lana Turner, Edmund Purdom, Louis Calhern, Audrey Dalton, Neville Brand, Walter Hampden, Taina Elg, Francis L. Sullivan, Joseph Wiseman, Sandy Descher, John Dehner, Cecil Kellaway, Henry Daniell, Paul Cavanagh, Tracey Roberts, Jay Novello, Dorothy Adams, Richard Devon; *D:* Richard Thorpe; *C:* Joseph Ruttenberg. *MGM*

The Prodigal 🐾🐾 1983 (PG) A born-again family drama in which a sundered family is brought together by the return of a once-estranged son. **109m/C VHS, Beta, LV.** John Hammond, Hope Lange, John Cullum, Morgan Brittany, Ian Bannen, Arliss Howard, Joey Travolta, Billy Graham; *M:* Bruce Broughton. *ART*

Prodigal Boxer: The Kick of Death 🐾 1973 (R) A son must avenge his father's death by facing two kung fu masters. **90m/C VHS, Beta, LV.** Meng Fei, Pa Hung, Suma Wah Lung. *GEM, MRV*

The Prodigal Planet 🐾 1988 Small group of believers continue their struggle against the world government UNTIE by disrupting their communication network. Sequel to "Thief in the Night," "A Distant Thunder," and "Image of the Beast." **67m/C VHS, Beta.** William Wellman Jr., Linda Beatie, Cathy Wellman, Thom Rachford; *D:* Donald W. Thompson. *RDF, HHE*

The Prodigal Son 🐾🐾½ 1982 Small-town martial arts champ Biao learns all his fights were fixed by his wealthy father. Determined to prove himself fairly, Biao learns the true wisdom and skills of kung fu from traveling entertainer Ying. Typically over-the-top fight scenes. Chinese with subtitles or dubbed. **100m/C VHS, LV, Letterbox.** HK Yuen Biao, Lam Ching Ying, Sammo Hung; *D:* Sammo Hung. *TAI*

The Producers 🐾🐾🐾½ 1968 Considered one of Brooks' best films, this hilarious farce follows an attempted swindle by a con artist and his accountant who attempt to stage a Broadway flop only to have it backfire. Achieving cult status, the film is known for musical interlude "Springtime for Hitler." The phony play was later actually produced by Alan Johnson. **90m/C VHS, Beta, LV, 8mm, Letterbox.** Zero Mostel, Gene Wilder, Dick Shawn, Kenneth Mars, Estelle Winwood; *D:* Mel Brooks; *W:* Mel Brooks.

Academy Awards '68: Best Story & Screenplay, National Film Registry '96;; Writers Guild of America '96;; Nominations: Academy Awards '68: Best Original Screenplay; Nominations: Academy Awards '68: Best Supporting Actor (Wilder). *COL, CRC*

The Professional 🐾🐾 *Leon* 1994 (R) Leon (Reno) is an eccentric French hit man, working New York's mean streets, when his 12-year-old neighbor Mathilda (Portman) comes knocking. Seems her family has been murdered by minions of crooked drug enforcement agent Stansfield (Oldman) and she'd like Leon to teach her how to be a "cleaner" so she can get revenge. And Leon obliges. The lovely young Portman (in her film debut) is a little too Lolita-ish for comfort as she manipulates the stolid Reno, with Oldman suitably extravagant in the role of sadistic psycho. *CW:* Great deal of graphic violence; language. **109m/C VHS, LV, DVD.** FR Jean Reno, Natalie Portman, Gary Oldman, Danny Aiello, Michael Badalucco, Ellen Greene; *D:* Luc Besson; *W:* Luc Besson; *C:* Thierry Arbogast; *M:* Eric Serra. Nominations: Cesar Awards '94: Best Actor (Reno), Best Director (Besson), Best Film. *COL*

The Professional: Golgo 13 1983 Animated mystery & suspense film. Leonard Dawson vows revenge for his son's death and must battle Duke Togo, a professional hitman better known as "Golgo 13." Dubbed. **94m/C VHS.** *JP*

Professional Killers 1 🐾 1973 Trio of hired assassins wanders about the countryside killing people during Japan's Feudal Era. **87m/C VHS, Beta.** Jiro Tamiya, Koji Takahashi. *NO*

The Professionals 🐾🐾🐾½ 1966 (PG) Action and adventure count for more than a storyline in this exciting western about four mercenaries hired by a wealthy cattle baron to rescue his young wife from Mexican kidnappers. Breathtaking photography recreates turn-of-the-century Mexico in this adaptation of the Frank O'Rourke novel. **117m/C VHS, Beta, LV, Letterbox.** Burt Lancaster, Lee Marvin, Claudia Cardinale, Jack Palance, Robert Ryan, Woody Strode, Ralph Bellamy; *D:* Richard Brooks; *W:* Richard Brooks; *C:* Conrad Hall; *M:* Maurice Jarre. Nominations: Academy Awards '66: Best Adapted Screenplay, Best Color Cinematography, Best Director (Brooks). *COL*

Professionals 🐾 1976 When the daily rigors of cocaine smuggling begin to dampen their spirits, the "Professionals" plan an exciting plutonium heist. From the British Action Show. **104m/C VHS, Beta, LV.** Gordon Jackson, Martin Shaw, Lewis Collins. *TWE*

The Professor 🐾🐾 1958 Rare sci-fi thriller featuring a werewolf, an eccentric scientist and a communist plot. Also includes several 'werewolf' oriented movie trailers. **30m/C VHS.** Doug Hobart, John Copeland, Irene Barr. *SNC*

Profile 🐾🐾½ 1954 A newsman gets an editorial job for a magazine called "Profile," and promptly falls in love with the boss's daughter. Complications arise when the boss's wife puts the moves on him. As if that isn't trouble enough, he finds himself accused of embezzlement. Average entertainment with some notable performances and an interesting chase scene. **65m/B VHS, Beta.** John Bentley, Kathleen Byron, Thea Gregory, Stuart Lindsell; *D:* Francis Searle. *SNC*

Profile for Murder 🐾🐾 1996 (R) Psychiatrist-cop-babe gets involved with a businessman who is also a suspected serial killer. Made for cable, with lots of nudity and sex. *CW:* Violence, language and strong sexuality. **95m/C VHS.** Joan Severance, Lance Henriksen, Jeff Wincott; *D:* David Winning; *W:* Steve Fisher; *C:* Bruce Worrall; *M:* Barron Abramovitch. *ART*

The Program 🐾🐾½ 1993 (R) Sensitive tearjerker about college football players getting caught up in the drive for a championship. As the season takes its toll on both mind and body, players prepare for the Big Game. Caan is the team's gruff coach, who's willing to look the other way as long as his boys are winning. Film sparked controversy when the Disney studio pulled and recut it after release because one scene, where Shef-

fer's character lies down in traffic, sparked copy cat actions and several deaths. The scene was not restored for the video version. *CW:* Language. **110m/C VHS, Beta, LV, Closed Caption.** James Caan, Craig Sheffer, Kristy Swanson, Halle Berry, Omar Epps, Duane Davis, Abraham Benrubi, Jon Maynard Pennell, Andrew Bryniarski, Joey Lauren Adams; *D:* David S. Ward; *W:* David S. Ward, Aaron Latham; *M:* Michel Colombier. *TOU*

Programmed to Kill 🐾🐾 *Retaliator* 1986 (R) A beautiful terrorist is captured by the CIA and transformed into a buxom bionic assassin. **91m/C VHS, Beta, Closed Caption.** Robert Ginty, Sandahl Bergman, James Booth, Louise Caire Clark; *D:* Allan Holzman.

Project A-ko 1986 Set in the near future, this Japanese animated feature, which is intended for adults, concerns teenagers with strange powers, an alien spaceship, and lots of action. Seventeen year-old A-ko possesses superhuman strength and a ditzy sidekick, C-ko. B-ko, the spoiled and rich daughter of a business tycoon, decides to fight A-ko for C-ko's companionship. Meanwhile, an alien spaceship is headed toward Earth with unknown intentions. Somehow, everything ties together—watch and see how. In Japanese with English subtitles. **86m/C VHS, LV.** JP CPM, FUS, TPV

Project A: Part 2 1987 Dragon Ma, the only honest cop in Hong Kong on the high seas at the turn of the century is back with a new set of adventures. In Cantonese with English subtitles. **101m/C VHS.** CH Jackie Chan, Maggie Cheung, Carina Lau, David Lam; *D:* Jackie Chan; *W:* Edward Tang, Jackie Chan. *FCT*

Project: Alien 🐾🐾 1989 (R) Science fiction fans in search of a good extraterrestrial flick should avoid this teaser, for it has nothing to do with aliens. As the film begins, Earth is allegedly being attacked by beings from space, and a vast array of scientists, militia and journalists track the aliens. What's actually happening revolves around the testing of deadly biological weapons. Shot in Yugoslavia. **92m/C VHS, LV.** Michael Nouri, Darlanne Fluegel, Maxwell Caulfield, Charles Durning; *D:* Frank Shields; *W:* Anthony Able. *THV*

Project: Eliminator 🐾½ 1991 (R) A group of terrorists kidnap a designer of "smart" weapons, and it's up to a hard-hitting special forces unit to get him back. Filmed in New Mexico. *CW:* Language, violence, and sensual scene. **89m/C VHS.** David Carradine, Frank Zagarino, Drew Snyder, Hilary English, Vivian Schilling; *D:* H. Kaye Dyal; *W:* H. Kaye Dyal; *M:* Morris Asgar.

Project: Genesis 🐾🐾½ 1993 Pascal and a beautiful Alien Woman are shipwrecked on a desolate planet in the 23rd century. As they watch the worlds around them clash in war, they know it is up to them to create a new beginning at the end of the Universe. **79m/C VHS, LV.** David Ferry, Olga Prokhorova; *D:* Philip Jackson; *W:* Philip Jackson; *M:* Andy McNeill.

Project: Kill! 🐾 1977 Head of a murder-for-hire squad suddenly disappears and his former assistant is hired to track him down dead or alive. **94m/C VHS.** Leslie Nielsen, Gary Lockwood, Nancy Kwan. *QVD*

Project Metalbeast: DNA Overload 🐾🐾½ 1994 (R) A CIA agent, cryogenically frozen for 10 years, becomes the guinea pig when a group of scientists decide to unthaw him for a DNA experiment involving living metallic skin. Too bad he turns into a metal beast by the light of the full moon. Sci-fi take on the werewolf saga. *CW:* Monster violence and gore. **92m/C VHS.** Kim Delaney, Barry Bostwick; *D:* Alessandro DeGaetano; *W:* Timothy E. Sabo; *M:* Conrad Pope.

Project Moon Base 🐾½ 1953 Espionage runs rampant on a spaceship headed by a female officer. Eventually the ship is stranded on the moon. Actually filmed for a television series "Ring Around the Moon." A cold-war sexist relic. **64m/B VHS.** Donna Martell, Hayden Rourke; *D:* Richard Talmadge. *EEL*

Project: Nightmare ♪½ **1985** Seems not all dreams are wish fulfillment, when these nightmares start coming true. 75m/C VHS. Elly Koslo, Lance Dickson; **D:** Donald M. Jones. *MOV*

Project: Shadowchaser ♪½ **1992 (R)** Action-packed would-be thriller about a billion dollar android who escapes from a top secret government laboratory. Programmed with superhuman strength and no human emotions the android and five terrorists take over a hospital (located in a skyscraper no less). Their hostages include the President's daughter and the terrorists demand a $50 million ransom. With a four-hour deadline the FBI calls in the hospital architect to advise them—only they've got the wrong man—and the android's creator, who wants his creation back—no matter what the cost. A low budget Terminator clone. **CW:** Action violence. 97m/C VHS, Closed Caption. Martin Kove, Meg Foster, Frank Zagarino, Paul Koslo, Joss Ackland; **D:** John Eyres.

Project Shadowchaser 3000 ♪½ **1995 (R)** Deep space satellite station collides with a mining vessel carrying a killer android. The seven surviving crew are then hunted by the android as the ship's nuclear core is also threatening to explode. **CW:** Language, sci-fi violence and gore. 99m/C VHS, LV, Closed Caption. Frank Zagarino, Sam Bottoms, Christopher Atkins, Musetta Vander, Christopher Neame; **D:** John Eyres; **W:** Nick Davis; **M:** Steve Edwards. *TTC, NLC*

Project Vampire ♪½ **1993** Vampire concocts a serum that will change humans into vampires within three days. His first guinea pig fights to stop the evil from succeeding. 90m/C VHS. Brian Knudson, Mary-Louise Gemmill, Christopher Cho, Myron Natwick; **D:** Peter Flynn.

Project X ♪♪½ **1987 (PG)** A bemused Air Force pilot is assigned to a special project involving chimpanzees. He must decide where his duty lies when he realizes the semi-intelligent chimps are slated to die. 107m/C VHS, Beta, LV, Closed Caption. Matthew Broderick, Helen Hunt, William Sadler, Johnny Ray McGhee, Jonathan Stark, Robin Gammell, Stephen Lang, Jean Smart, Dick Miller; **D:** Jonathan Kaplan; **W:** Stanley Weiser, Lawrence Lasker; **C:** Dean Cundey; **M:** James Horner. *FOX*

The Projectionist ♪♪♪ **1971 (PG)** A must-see for movie buffs, Dangerfield made his screen debut in this story about a projectionist in a seedy movie house whose real-life existence begins to blur into the films he continuously watches. Made on a limited budget, this creative effort by Hurwitz was the first film to utilize the technique of superimposition. 84m/C VHS, Beta. Rodney Dangerfield, Chuck McCann, Ina Balin; **D:** Harry Hurwitz; **W:** Harry Hurwitz. *ART, VES*

Prom Night ♪♪ **1980 (R)** A masked killer stalks four high school girls during their senior prom as revenge for a murder which occurred six years prior. Sequelled by "Hello Mary Lou: Prom Night 2," "Prom Night 3: The Last Kiss," and "Prom Night 4: Deliver Us from Evil." 91m/C VHS, Beta, LV. CA Jamie Lee Curtis, Leslie Nielsen, Casey Stevens, Eddie Benton, Antoinette Bower, Michael Tough, Pita Oliver, David Mucci, Joy Thompson, Mary Beth Rubens; **D:** Paul Lynch; **W:** William Gray; **C:** Robert New. *NLC*

Prom Night 3: The Last Kiss ♪ **1989** The second sequel, in which the reappearing high school ghoul beguiles a lucky teenager. 97m/C VHS, Beta, LV. Tim Conlon, Cyndy Preston, Courtney Taylor, David Stratton, Dylan Neal, Jeremy Ratchford; **D:** Ron Oliver, Peter Simpson; **W:** Ron Oliver; **C:** Rhett Morita. *ART*

Prom Night 4: Deliver Us from Evil ♪ **1991 (R)** Yet another gory entry in the Prom series (one would hope it will be the last). Another group of naive teens decide that they can have more fun at a private party than at the prom. They host the party in a summer home that was once a monastery, but the festive affair soon turns into a night of terror when an uninvited guest crashes the party. For true fans of slasher flicks. **CW:** Language, violence, and sensuality. 95m/C VHS, Closed Caption. CA Nikki DeBoer, Alden Kane, Joy Tanner, Alle Ghadban, James Carver; **D:** Clay Borris; **W:** Richard Beattie. *ART*

The Promise ♪♪½ *Face of a Stranger* **1979 (PG)** Weepie outdated story about star-crossed lovers Michael (Collins) and Nancy (Quinlan). A car accident leaves Michael comatose and Nancy badly disfigured. Michael's mother (Straight), who loathes Nancy, sees her chance to finally break them up. She offers to pay for Nancy's plastic surgery if she'll leave Michael forever, then Mom tells her son his girlfriend's dead. A year later Nancy, with her new face and new identity, and Michael meet. From the novel by Danielle Steele. 97m/C VHS. Stephen Collins, Kathleen Quinlan, Beatrice Straight, Laurence Luckinbill, William Prince, Michael O'Hare; **D:** Gilbert Cates; **W:** Garry Michael White; **M:** David Shire. Nominations: Academy Awards '79: Best Song ("Theme from The Promise: I'll Never Say Goodbye"). *USH*

The Promise ♪♪½ *Das Versprechen* **1994 (R)** Young lovers Konrad (Zoller and Zirner) and Sophie (Harfouch and Becker) find themselves separated by the Berlin Wall after a botched escape attempt in 1961. The estranged lovers meet only four times during the next three decades as they adjust to the systems under which they're forced to live. Somewhat contrived and cliched, this bittersweet romance uses Konrad and Sophie as symbols of the social and political turmoil and triumphs of the divided Germany. Received some criticism from East Germans who found the film's severe portrayal of Communist rule too harsh. Gets points for being the first post-fall film to explore the Wall's legacy. **CW:** Contains sexual situations and strong language. 115m/C VHS, LV, Closed Caption. GE Corinna Harfouch, Meret Becker, August Zirner, Anian Zollner, Jean-Yves Gautier, Eva Mattes, Suzanne Uge, Hans Kremer, Pierre Besson, Tina Engel, Otto Sander, Hark Bohm; **D:** Margarethe von Trotta; **W:** Peter Schneider, Margarethe von Trotta; **C:** Franz Rath; **M:** Jurgen Knieper. *NLC*

Promise Her Anything ♪♪ **1966** A widow (Caron) with a baby decides to make her boss (Cummings), a child psychologist who hates kids, her new husband. So she stashes the kid with her upstairs neighbor (Beatty), a would-be filmmaker who earns his living making blue movies. But the filmmaker has romantic designs on the widow and decides the baby may be his way to make a good impression. Beatty isn't very believable in this type of light-romantic comedy and the farcical situations are forced. 98m/C VHS. GB Warren Beatty, Leslie Caron, Robert Cummings, Hermione Gingold, Lionel Stander, Keenan Wynn, Cathleen Nesbitt; **D:** Arthur Hiller; **W:** William Peter Blatty. *PAR*

Promise to Murder ♪½ **1956** An early murder-drama episode from the "Climax" television series. 60m/B VHS, Beta. Peter Lorre, Louis Hayward, Ann Harding. *NOS, DVT*

Promised a Miracle ♪♪½ **1988 (PG)** Based on the true story of a religious couple who sought help for their diabetic son through prayer rather than conventional medical means. Following the boy's death in 1974 the couple were charged with manslaughter. From the non-fiction account "We Let Our Son Die" by Larry Parker. Made for television. 94m/C VHS, LV, Closed Caption. Rosanna Arquette, Judge Reinhold, Tom Bower, Gary Bayer, Maria O'Brien, Giovanni Ribisi; **D:** Stephen Gyllenhaal; **W:** David Hill; **C:** Thomas Burstyn. *REP*

Promised Land ♪♪♪ *Young Hearts* **1988 (R)** Two high school friends from the rural northwestern U.S. come together several years after graduation under tragic circumstances. Writer Hoffman's semi-autobiographical, disillusioned look at the American Dream was re-discovered by movie goers due to its excellent dramatic performances, notable also as the first film produced by Robert Redford's Sundance Institute. 110m/C VHS, Beta, LV. Kiefer Sutherland, Meg Ryan, Tracy Pollan, Jason Gedrick, Googy Gress, Deborah Richter, Sandra Seacat, Jay Underwood, Oscar Rowland; **D:** Michael Hoffman; **W:** Michael Hoffman; **M:** James Newton Howard. *ART, VES*

Promises in the Dark ♪♪½ **1979 (PG)** Drama focusing on the complex relationship between a woman doctor and her 17-year-old female patient who is terminally ill with cancer. Hellman's directorial debut. 118m/C VHS, Beta. Marsha Mason, Ned Beatty, Kathleen Beller, Susan Clark, Paul Clemens, Donald Moffat, Michael Brandon; **D:** Jerome Hellman. *WAR*

Promises! Promises! ♪½ *Promise Her Anything* **1963** Having difficulty getting pregnant, a woman goes on a cruise with her husband. While on board, they meet another couple, all get drunk, and change partners. Of course, both women find themselves pregnant, leaving the paternity in doubt. Famous primarily as the movie Mansfield told "Playboy" magazine she appeared "completely nude" in. 90m/B VHS, Beta. Jayne Mansfield, Marie McDonald, Tommy Noonan, Fritz Feld, Claude Stroud. *NO*

The Promoter ♪♪♪ *The Card* **1952** Horatio Alger comedy stars Guinness as an impoverished student who gives himself a surreptitious leg up in life by altering his high school entrance exam scores. Outstanding performances enliven this subtle British comedy of morals. 87m/B VHS, Beta. GB Alec Guinness, Glynis Johns, Petula Clark, Valerie Hobson, Michael Hordern; **D:** Ronald Neame. Nominations: Academy Awards '52: Best Sound. *HMV*

Pronto ♪♪½ **1997 (R)** Semi-retired bookie Harry Arno (Falk) is forced to head out of Miami when his mobster boss realizes Harry's been skimming. So he takes off for the Italian Riviera with ex-stripper girlfriend Joyce (Headly), while being trailed by doofus U.S. Marshal Raylan Givens (LeGros), who's trying to keep Harry alive so the feds can get his testimony against his gangster cohorts. Falk's gruff, Headly's smart, LeGros is a laugh, and the cable movie's vivid since it's taken from Elmore Leonard's 1993 novel. **CW:** Violence, sexuality and language. 100m/C VHS, Closed Caption. Peter Falk, Glenne Headly, James LeGros, Sergio Castellitto, Bradford Tatum; **D:** Jim McBride. *PAR*

Proof ♪♪♪ **1991 (R)** Directorial debut of Moorhouse tells a tale of manipulation, friendship, and obsessive love between a blind photographer, Martin, his housekeeper, and the young man he befriends. Martin, mistrustful of the world around him, takes photographs as "proof" of the reality of his life. A chance meeting with Andy provides Martin with his "eyes" and the opportunity to expand his world and emotions—something his housekeeper, Celia, would be only too happy to help him with. Unhealthy triangle leads all three to a re-evaluation of their lives. Propelled by terrific performances and enough humor to balance its emotional content. **CW:** Some language and sensuality. 90m/C VHS, LV, Closed Caption. AU Hugo Weaving, Genevieve Picot, Russell Crowe, Heather Mitchell, Jeffrey Walker, Frank Gallacher; **D:** Jocelyn Moorhouse; **W:** Jocelyn Moorhouse. Australian Film Institute '91: Best Actor (Weaving), Best Director (Moorhouse), Best Film, Best Film Editing, Best Screenplay, Best Supporting Actor (Crowe). *NLC, COL*

Proof of the Man ♪ **1984** A Japanese co-production about a murder in Tokyo that takes on international importance. 100m/C VHS, Beta. JP George Kennedy, Broderick Crawford, Toshiro Mifune. *VCD*

Prophecy ♪½ **1979 (PG)** A doctor and his wife travel to Maine to research the effects of pollution caused by the lumber industry. They encounter several terrifying freaks of nature and a series of bizarre human deaths. Laughable horror film. 102m/C VHS, Beta. Talia Shire, Robert Foxworth, Armand Assante, Victoria Racimo, Richard Dysart, George Clutesi; **D:** John Frankenheimer; **W:** David Seltzer; **C:** Harry Stradling Jr. *NO*

The Prophecy 🎬🎬½ 1995 (R) Modern variation of "Paradise Lost" carries a heavy load including possession, Native American mythology, and Walken as the archangel Gabriel. Not surprisingly, it stumbles under the weight. Gabriel is at odds with good angel Simon (Stolz) over the souls of humans, a battle that has its final showdown in a small Arizona community and crosses the paths of a homicide detective Thomas Dagget (Koteas) and school teacher Katherine (Madsen). Successfully mixes humor and horror, but biblical jargon can lose horror fans just looking for a cheap thrill. Directorial debut of screenwriter Widen.**CW:** Violence and gore; some language. 97m/C VHS, LV, **Closed Caption.** Christopher Walken, Eric Stoltz, Elias Koteas, Virginia Madsen, Amanda Plummer, Viggo Mortensen; **D:** Gregory Widen; **W:** Gregory Widen; **C:** Bruce Douglas Johnson, Richard Clabaugh; **M:** David Williams. MAX

The Prophecy 2: Ashtown 🎬🎬½ 1997 (R) It's post-apocalyptic L.A. and power-hungry fallen angel Gabriel (Walken) returns from hell to stop the creation of a half-human/half-angelic child who's prophesized as the new savior of mankind. Angel Daniel (Wong) is intended as the dad while nurse Valerie (Beals) is the woman chosen as the mother. The good guys get some help from angel Michael (Roberts). Lots of action and good special effects, though viewers who haven't seen the first film may be confused.**CW:** Strong violence and gore, and a strong sex scene. 83m/C VHS, LV, **Closed Caption.** Christopher Walken, Russell Wong, Eric Roberts, Jennifer Beals, Bruce Abbott, Brittany Murphy, Steve Hytner, Glenn Danzig; **D:** Greg Spence; **W:** Greg Spence, Matt Greenberg; **M:** David Williams. TOU

A Propos de Nice 🎬🎬🎬 1929 First film by French director Vigo, the silent film parodies French travelogues in a manner that indicates the director's later brilliance. 25m/B VHS, Beta. FR **D:** Jean Vigo. FST, MRV

The Proposition 🎬🎬½ 1996 (R) Unless widow Catherine Morgan (Russell) can find the money to pay her late husband's gambling debts, she and her two daughters will be evicted from their Welsh farm. She refuses to take the easy way and marry local sheriff Huw (Lynch), instead making a bargain with her rakish, drunken bastard brother Rhys (Bergin) to drive her cattle to Gloucester market. Huw takes exception to this plan and tries every dirty trick he can to thwart them and naturally, Catherine and Rhys become more than antagonistic allies along the rough journey.**CW:** Strong sex scene, partial nudity, violence. 99m/C VHS. Theresa Russell, Patrick Bergin, Richard Lynch, Richard Harrington, Jennifer Vaughan, Ifan Huw Dafydd, Nick McGaughey, Owen Garmon; **D:** Strathford Hamilton; **W:** Paul Matthews; **C:** David Lewis; **M:** Ben Heneghan, Ian Lawson. APX

The Proposition 🎬🎬 Tempting Fate; Shakespeare's Sister 1997 (R) Convoluted and clunky story centering on wealthy-but-sterile Boston industrialist Hurt and his feminist writer wife Stowe, who decide to hire a surrogate (Harris) to get Stowe pregnant. But faltering priest Branagh, whom the couple consult, has some concerns. After the surrogate is murdered, the melodrama starts to fly and the movie plays out like a daytime soap opera, complete with dirty little secrets and earth-shaking revelations dropped with the sublety usually reserved for an anvil on Wile E. Coyote. Hurt and Stowe give their characters a little fire, but everybody else seems to be wandering around on their own little acting planet.**CW:** Some sexual content. 110m/C VHS. Kenneth Branagh, William Hurt, Madeleine Stowe, Blythe Danner, Neil Patrick Harris, Robert Loggia, Josef Sommer, David Byrd; **D:** Leslie Linka Glatter; **W:** Rick Ramage; **C:** Peter Sova; **M:** Stephen Endelman. NYR

The Proprietor 🎬🎬 1996 (R) Thinly disguised as a returning-to-your-roots and facing-your-ghosts drama, film is actually a celluloid shrine to its Gallic star, the legendary Moreau,

who plays a legendary Gallic novelist, Adrienne Mark. Mark, after residing in New York for 30 years, reclaims her Jewish identity and returns to Paris to buy the home in which she grew up with her mother, who was killed in World War II. Famous for writing the novel, "Call Me French" which became a highly acclaimed French film and a current American remake, Mark's primary struggle to come to grips with her mother's death is overshadowed by a bevy of subplots that compete with one another. Young as a sassy and somewhat stereotypical Hollywood producer; Carter as Milly the loyal housekeeper; Waterston, an antique dealer; and Billy, NYC video artist and adoring Mark fan, all add to the confusion. Moreau tries her best to give life to the saintly lead figure, but the coma-inducing sugar level of her character's goodness is overwhelming. Director Merchant's sophomore effort, though well-acted, is a good idea, poorly told.**CW:** Brief sexuality. 105m/C VHS, **Closed Caption.** Jeanne Moreau, Sean Young, Sam Waterston, Nell Carter, Austin Pendleton, Pierre Vaneck, Christopher Cazenove, Jean-Pierre Aumont, Josh Hamilton, Marc Tissot; **D:** Ismail Merchant; **W:** Jean-Marie Besset, George Trow; **C:** Larry Pizer; **M:** Richard Robbins. WAR

Prospero's Books 🎬🎬🎬 1991 (R) Greenaway's free-ranging adaptation of Shakespeare's "The Tempest" has all his usual hallmarks of the bizarre. Gielgud is the aged Prospero, exiled to a magical island with his innocent daughter Miranda, and 24 beloved books containing the magician's recipe for life, each of which becomes a separate chapter in the film. Greenaway mixes film and high-definition video to create, with cinematographer Sacha Vierny, dazzling visuals that threaten to overwhelm but don't quite, thanks to both Greenaway's skill and the astonishing performance of the then 87-year-old Gielgud.**CW:** Pervasive nudity. 129m/C VHS, Beta, LV. John Gielgud, Michel Blanc, Erland Josephson, Isabelle Pasco, Tom Bell, Kenneth Cranham, Michael Clark, Mark Rylance; **D:** Peter Greenaway; **W:** Peter Greenaway; **C:** Sacha Vierny; **M:** Michael Nyman. FXV, FCT, VTR

Protector 🎬 1985 (R) A semi-martial arts cops 'n' robbers epic about the cracking of a Hong Kong-New York heroin route. 94m/C VHS, Beta, LV, **Closed Caption.** Jackie Chan, Danny Aiello; **D:** James Glickenhaus. WAR

Proteus 🎬 1995 (R) Survivors of a boat wreck wash up on an off-shore oil rig that's actually a secret lab financed by loony millionaire Bradley, who's seeking immortality. His DNA experiments have led to the creation of a disgusting parasite that travels from body to body. Naturally, the boat survivors also seek to survive this latest health threat.**CW:** Violence, gore and language. 97m/C VHS, **Closed Caption.** GB Doug Bradley, Craig Fairbrass, Toni Barry; **D:** Bob Keen. THV

Protocol 🎬🎬 1984 (PG) A series of comic accidents lead a Washington cocktail waitress into the U.S. State Department's employ as a protocol official. Once there she is used as a pawn to make an arms deal with a Middle Eastern country. Typical Hawn comedy with an enjoyable ending. 100m/C VHS, Beta, LV, **Closed Caption.** Goldie Hawn, Chris Sarandon, Andre Gregory, Cliff DeYoung, Ed Begley Jr., Gail Strickland, Richard Romanus, Keith Szarabajka, James Staley, Kenneth Mars, Kenneth McMillan, Archie Hahn, Amanda Bearse; **D:** Herbert Ross; **W:** Charles Shyer, Buck Henry, Nancy Meyers, Harvey Miller; **M:** Basil Poledouris. WAR

Prototype 🎬🎬🎬 1983 Made-for-television revision of the Frankenstein legend has award-winning scientist Plummer as the creator of the first android. Fearful of the use the military branch of government has in mind for his creation, he attempts to steal back his discovery, in this suspenseful adventure. 100m/C VHS, LV. Christopher Plummer, David Morse, Frances Sternhagen, James Sutorius; **D:** David Greene; **M:** Billy Goldenberg. ART

Prototype X29A 🎬½ 1992 (R) The year is 2067 in a desolate, lawless Los Angeles. A research scientist is conducting experiments on a crippled ex-soldier named Hawkins when they suddenly go awry, turning him into a half-man, half-machine robot. Known as Prototype, the creature goes on a hunting and killing spree. Lame "Terminator" & "Robocop" takeoff.**CW:** Language, strong violence, and strong sexuality. 98m/C VHS, LV, **Closed Caption.** Brenda Swanson, Robert Tossberg, Lane Lenhart; **D:** Phillip J. Roth; **W:** Phillip J. Roth. THV

The Proud and the Damned 🎬 Proud, Damned, and Dead 1972 (PG) Five Civil-War-veteran mercenaries wander into a Latin American war and get manipulated by both sides. 95m/C VHS, Beta. Chuck Connors, Aron Kincaid, Cesar Romero; **D:** Ferde Grofe Jr. NOS, VCI, MRV

Proud Men 🎬🎬 1987 A cattle rancher and his expatriate son are separated by bitterness toward each other. Good acting from Heston and Strauss, and good action sequences, but ordinary script. 95m/C VHS, **Closed Caption.** Charlton Heston, Peter Strauss, Nan Martin, Alan Autry, Belinda Balaski, Red West; **D:** William A. Graham. TTC

The Proud Ones 🎬🎬½ Les Orgueilleux 1953 An aristocratic French woman and her husband are traveling through Mexico when he suddenly dies of a mysterious illness. Left penniless in a decaying seaside town, she falls for the local doctor who is mourning the death of his wife. Adaptation of the Satre novel "L'Amour Redempteur." In French with English subtitles. 105m/B VHS. FR Gerard Philipe, Michele Morgan, Victor Manuel Mendoza; **D:** Yves Allegret. Nominations: Academy Awards '56: Best Story.FCT, INT

Proud Rebel 🎬🎬🎬 1958 A character study of a stubborn widower who searches for a doctor to aid him in dealing with the problems of his mute son, and of the woman who helps to tame the boy. Ladd's real-life son makes his acting debut. 99m/C VHS, Beta. Alan Ladd, Olivia de Havilland, Dean Jagger, Harry Dean Stanton; **D:** Michael Curtiz.

Providence 🎬🎬🎬 1977 (R) An interesting score highlights this British fantasy drama of a dying writer envisioning his final novel as a fusion of the people from his past with the circumstances he encounters on a daily basis. The first English-language effort by French director Resnais. 104m/C VHS, Beta. GB John Gielgud, Dirk Bogarde, Ellen Burstyn, David Warner, Elaine Stritch; **D:** Alain Resnais; **M:** Miklos Rozsa. Cesar Awards '78: Best Art Direction/Set Decoration, Best Director (Resnais), Best Film, Best Sound, Best Writing, Best Score; New York Film Critics Awards '77: Best Actor (Gielgud).COL

Provincial Actors 🎬🎬 1979 Ambitious Christopher is the leading actor of a rural theatre troupe, who dreams of moving to the city and becoming a star. But his wife Anna is fed up with his dreams and leaves and Christopher must make a choice between his career and his marriage. Polish with subtitles. 104m/C VHS. PL Tadeysz Huk, Halina Labonarska, Ewa Dalkowska, Jerzy Stuhr; **D:** Agnieszka Holland. NYF

Provocateur 🎬 1996 (R) Story revolves around the 1994 power struggle in North Korea. Spy March, with close ties to dictator Kim Il Sung, takes a job as a nanny in order to get access to sensitive info from her boss, a U.S. colonel. But her loyalties are torn when she befriends her young charge and then falls in love with the colonel's son (Brancato). When her true identity is revealed, there's trouble for all.**CW:** Violence, a strong sex scene and language. 104m/C VHS, **Closed Caption.** Jane March, Nick Mancuso, Lillo Brancato, Cary-Hiroyuki Tagawa; **D:** Jim Donovan. ART

Provoked 🎬🎬½ 1989 What would you do if your husband were being held hostage by a gang of ruthless, but stupid, escaped cons? Well, Maranne actually wants her husband back (maybe 'cause they're newlyweds) and no by-the-book police chief (Jones) is gonna stop her. This bride gets her hands on some automatic weaponry and look out! Shot in eight days with a $130,000 budget. **90m/C VHS, Beta.** Cindy Maranne, McKeiver Jones III, Harold W. Jones, Sharon Blair, Bob Fall, Joe Sprosty, Phyllis Durant, Tara Untiedt; **D:** Rick Pamplin; **W:** Tara Untiedt, Steve Pake. *VTR, HHE*

Prowler 🐾🐾½ **1951** Heflin is a cop who responds to a prowler scare and finds the beautiful married Keyes worried about an intruder. He learns she will inherit a lot of money if anything happens to her husband so he seduces her and then "accidentally" kills her husband, supposedly mistaking him for a prowler. Keyes then marries Heflin but when she learns the truth her own life is in danger. Tidy thriller with Heflin doing a good job as the unpredictable villain. **92m/B VHS, Beta.** Van Heflin, Evelyn Keyes, Katherine Warren, John Maxwell; **D:** Joseph Losey; **C:** Arthur C. Miller. *NO*

The Prowler 🐾 *Rosemary's Killer* **1981 (R)** A soldier returns from duty during WWII, only to find his girl in bed with another guy. He kills them, and for unclear reasons, returns to the same town 35 years later to kill more people. An effects-fest for Tom Savini. **87m/C VHS.** Vicky Dawson, Christopher Goutman, Cindy Weintraub, Farley Granger, John Seitz, Lawrence Tierney; **D:** Joseph Zito; **W:** Neal Barbera; **M:** Richard Einhorn. *VHE*

Prudential Family Playhouse 1950 Presentation of Sinclair Lewis' "Dodsworth." Tells the story of a wealthy American couple who travel from their small town to Europe. **53m/B VHS, Beta.** Ruth Chatterton, Walter Abel, Cliff Hall, Eva Marie Saint. *VYY*

PSI Factor 🐾🐾½ **1980** A civilian researcher working at the NASA space track station observes and records signals coming from planet Serius B. **91m/C VHS.** Peter Mark Richman, Gretchen Corbett, Tommy Martin; **D:** Bryan Trizers; **W:** Quentin Masters. *NO*

Psych-Out 🐾🐾½ **1968** A deaf girl searches Haight-Ashbury for her runaway brother. She meets hippies and flower children during the Summer of Love. Psychedelic score with Strawberry Alarm Clock and The Seeds. Somewhere in the picture, Nicholson whangs on lead guitar. **95m/C VHS, Beta, LV.** Jack Nicholson, Bruce Dern, Susan Strasberg, Dean Stockwell, Henry Jaglom; **D:** Richard Rush; **W:** Richard Rush. *HBO*

The Psychic woof! **1968** An ad executive gains psychic powers after he falls off a ladder and tries to conquer the world. A later effort by gore-king Lewis, notable only for sex scenes inserted by Lewis to make the movie salable. **90m/C VHS, Beta.** Dick Genola, Robin Guest, Bobbi Spencer; **D:** Herschell Gordon Lewis. *NO*

The Psychic 🐾 **1978 (R)** A psychic envisions her own death and attempts to alter the prediction. **90m/C VHS, Beta.** Jennifer O'Neill, Marc Porel, Evelyn Stewart, Gabriele Ferzetti, Gianni "John" Garko; **D:** Lucio Fulci. *NO*

Psychic 🐾½ **1991 (R)** A college student with psychic powers believes he knows who the next victim of a demented serial killer will be. The problem is: no one will believe him. And the victim is the woman he loves. **CW:** Violence and sensuality. **92m/C VHS, Closed Caption.** Michael Nouri, Catherine Mary Stewart, Zach Galligan. *THV*

Psychic Killer 🐾½ **1975 (PG)** A wrongfully committed asylum inmate acquires psychic powers and decides to use them in a deadly revenge. Good cast in cheapie horror flick. **89m/C VHS, Beta.** Jim Hutton, Paul Burke, Julie Adams, Neville Brand, Aldo Ray, Rod Cameron, Della Reese; **D:** Ray Danton. *NO*

Psycho 🐾🐾🐾🐾 **1960** Hitchcock counted on his directorial stature and broke all the rules in this story of violent murder, transvestism, and insanity. Based on Robert Bloch's novelization of an actual murder, Leigh plays a fleeing thief who stops at the secluded Bates Motel where she meets her death in Hitchcock's classic "shower scene." Shot on a limited budget in little more than a month, "Psycho" changed the Hollywood

horror film forever. Followed by "Psycho 2" (1983), "Psycho 3" (1986), "Psycho 4: The Beginning" (1990), and a made-for-television movie. **109m/B VHS, Beta, LV, DVD.** Anthony Perkins, Janet Leigh, Vera Miles, John Gavin, John McIntire, Martin Balsam, Simon Oakland, Ted Knight, John Anderson, Frank Albertson, Patricia Hitchcock; **D:** Alfred Hitchcock; **W:** Joseph Stefano; **C:** John L. Russell; **M:** Bernard Herrmann. Golden Globe Awards '61: Best Supporting Actress (Leigh), National Film Registry '92;; Nominations: Academy Awards '60: Best Art Direction/Set Decoration (B & W), Best Black and White Cinematography, Best Director (Hitchcock), Best Supporting Actress (Leigh). *USH, TLF*

Psycho 2 🐾🐾 **1983 (R)** This sequel to the Hitchcock classic finds Norman Bates returning home after 22 years in an asylum to find himself haunted by "mother" and caught up in a series of murders. In a surprisingly good horror film, Perkins and Miles reprise their roles from the original "Psycho." Perkins went on to direct yet another sequel, "Psycho 3." **113m/C VHS, Beta, LV.** Claudia Bryar, Anthony Perkins, Vera Miles, Meg Tilly, Robert Loggia, Dennis Franz; **D:** Richard Franklin; **W:** Tom Holland; **C:** Dean Cundey; **M:** Jerry Goldsmith. *USH*

Psycho 3 🐾🐾 **1986 (R)** The second sequel to Hitchcock's "Psycho" finds Norman Bates drawn into his past by "mother" and the appearance of a woman who reminds him of this original victim. Perkins made his directorial debut in this film that stretches the plausibility of the storyline to its limits, but the element of parody throughout makes this an entertaining film for "Psycho" fans. **93m/C VHS, Beta, LV, Closed Caption.** Anthony Perkins, Diana Scarwid, Jeff Fahey, Roberta Maxwell, Robert Alan Browne, Hugh Gillin, Lee Garlington; **D:** Anthony Perkins; **W:** Charles Edward Pogue; **C:** Bruce Surtees; **M:** Carter Burwell. *USH*

Psycho 4: The Beginning 🐾🐾 **1990 (R)** Prequels "Psycho" when, at the behest of a radio talk show host, Norman Bates recounts his childhood and reveals the circumstances that aided in the development of his peculiar neuroses. Stefano wrote the original screenplay and the original score is used, but this doesn't even come close to the original. **CW:** Violence and sensuality. **96m/C VHS, LV.** Anthony Perkins, Henry Thomas, Olivia Hussey, CCH Pounder, Warren Frost, Donna Mitchell; **D:** Mick Garris; **W:** Joseph Stefano; **C:** Rodney Charters; **M:** Bernard Herrmann, Graeme Revell. *USH*

Psycho Cop 🐾½ **1988** Six college undergrads on a weekend retreat are menaced and picked off one at a time by a crazed local cop. **89m/C VHS, Beta.** Bobby Ray Shafer; **D:** Wallace Potts. *NO*

Psycho Cop 2 🐾½ **1994 (R)** Four buddies plan a raunchy bachelor party, commandeering the company conference room for an after-hours orgy. Only Psycho Cop is on their case. Gore. **80m/C VHS.** Bobby Ray Shafer, Barbara Lee Alexander, Julie Strain; **D:** Rif Adam Rifkin Coogan. *COL*

Psycho from Texas 🐾 *The Butcher* **1983 (R)** Quiet Southern town is disrupted by the kidnapping of a wealthy oil man, followed by a string of meaningless murders. **85m/C VHS, Beta.** King John III, Candy Dee, Janel King. *NO*

Psycho Girls 🐾 **1986 (R)** Very low budget horror flick redeemed by spurts of weird black humor. Crazed woman is released from institution to seek out sister who should have been put away in the first place. She crashes anniversary celebration and, well, let's just say she's not the life of the party. Never released theatrically. **87m/C VHS, Beta.** *CA* John Haslett Cuff, Darlene Mignacco, Agi Gallus, Rose Graham, Silvio Oliviero, Michael Hoole, Pier Giorgia DiCicco, Fernne Kane; **D:** Gerard Ciccoritti; **W:** Gerard Ciccoritti, Michael Boekner. *MGM*

Psychomania 🐾½ *Violent Midnight* **1963** Semi-limpid mystery thriller about a former war hero and painter who is suspected of being the demented killer stalking girls on campus. To prove his innocence, he tracks the killer himself. **95m/C VHS, Beta.** Lee Philips, Shepperd Strudwick, Jean

Hale, Dick Van Patten, Sylvia Miles, James Farentino; **D:** Richard Hilliard. *SNC, HHT*

Psychomania 🐾🐾 *The Death Wheelers* **1973 (R)** A drama of the supernatural, the occult, and the violence which lies just beyond the conventions of society for a group of dead motorcyclists, the Living Dead, who all came back to life after committing suicide with the help of the devil. **89m/C VHS, Beta.** *GB* George Sanders, Beryl Reid, Nicky Henson, Mary Laroche, Patrick Holt; **D:** Don Sharp. *MRV*

Psychopath 🐾½ **1968** A film about a modern-day, slightly unhinged, Robin Hood and his escapades, stealing from other thieves and giving to the victimized. **90m/C VHS, Beta.** *GB* Klaus Kinski, George Martin, Ingrid Schoeller; **D:** Guido Zurli. *NO*

Psychopath 🐾 *An Eye for an Eye* **1973 (PG)** A nutso children's television personality begins to murder abusive parents. Fairly gory, and definitely not for family viewing. **85m/C VHS, Beta.** Tom Basham, Gene Carlson, Gretchen Kanne; **D:** Larry G. Brown; **M:** John Williams.

Psychos in Love woof! **1987** A psychotic murderer who hates grapes of any kind finds the woman of his dreams—she's a psychotic murderer who hates grapes! Together they find bliss—until the plumber discovers their secret! **90m/C VHS, Beta.** Carmine Capobianco, Debi Thibeault, Frank Stewart; **D:** Gorman Bechard. *NO*

The Psychotronic Man 🐾🐾½ **1991** An innocent man suddenly finds he possesses amazing and dangerous powers, enabling him to control outside events with a thought. **88m/C VHS.** Peter Spelson, Christopher Carbis, Curt Colbert, Robin Newton, Paul Marvel; **D:** Jack M. Sell. *UNI*

PT 109 🐾🐾 **1963** The WWII exploits of Lieutenant (j.g.) John F. Kennedy in the South Pacific. Part of the "A Night at the Movies" series, this tape simulates a 1963 movie evening, with a Foghorn Leghorn cartoon ("Banty Raids"), a newsreel on the JFK assassination, and coming attractions for "Critic's Choice" and "Four for Texas." **159m/C VHS, Beta, LV, Letterbox.** Cliff Robertson, Ty Hardin, Ty Hardin, Robert (Bobby) Blake, Robert Culp, James Gregory; **D:** Leslie Martinson. *WAR*

Pterodactyl Woman from Beverly Hills 🐾 **1997 (R)** California housewife Pixie Chandler (D'Angelo) is the victim of an eccentric witch doctor (James) when her paleontologist husband Dick (Wilson) disturbs an ancient burial site and the doc curses Pixie by turning her into a dinosaur. This is the first so-called family release from those madcap Troma people who brought you the Toxic Avenger. **CW:** Language and some sexual content. **97m/C VHS.** Beverly D'Angelo, Brion James, Brad Wilson, Moon Zappa, Aron Eisenberg; **D:** Philippe Mora; **W:** Philippe Mora; **C:** Walter Bal; **M:** Roy Hay. *TTV*

Puberty Blues 🐾🐾½ **1981 (R)** Two Australian girls become part of the local surfing scene in order to be accepted by the "in crowd" at their high school. **86m/C VHS, Beta.** *AU* Neil Schofield, Jad Capelja; **D:** Bruce Beresford. *USH*

Public Access 🐾🐾 **1993 (R)** Newcomer Whitley Pritcher (Marquette) manages to cause trouble in the small town of Brewster when he begins broadcasting a call-in program over a public-access cable station that encourages complaining about the town's problems. Skeletons start falling out of closets, leading to unexpected tragedy. Feature-film directorial debut of Singer. **90m/C VHS.** Ron Marquette, Dina Brooks, Burt Williams, Charles Kavanaugh, Larry Maxwell, Brandon Boyce; **D:** Bryan Singer; **W:** Bryan Singer, Christopher McQuarrie, Michael Feit Dougan; **C:** Bruce Douglas Johnson; **M:** John Ottman. Sundance Film Festival '93: Grand Jury Prize. *TRI*

A Public Affair 🐾½ **1962** Exposes the evils and abuses of collection agencies without even a shred of humor. Certainly gets its point across, but will bore any audience to tears or spontaneous naps. **71m/B VHS, Beta.** Myron McCormick, Edward Binns, Harry Carey Jr. *VYY*

Public Cowboy No. 1 *♪♪½* 1937 Cattle thieves use a radio, airplanes, and refrigerator trucks in their updated rustling schemes. **54m/B VHS, Beta.** Gene Autry, William Farnum. *NOS, VCN, DVT*

Public Enemies *♪♪* 1996 (R) It's nefarious Ma Barker (Russell) and her boys on a '30s crime spree that gets even bigger when they hook up with criminal Alvin Karpis (Stallone). But when Ma's lover Arthur (Roberts) dreams up a kidnapping plot, it's a fast road to ruin.*CW:* Language, violence, nudity, sexual situations. **95m/C VHS.** Theresa Russell, Eric Roberts, Frank Stallone, Alyssa Milano, Joseph Lindsey, Richard Eden, James Marsden, Dan Cortese; *D:* Mark L. Lester; *W:* C. Courtney Joyner; *M:* Christopher Franke. *THV*

Public Enemy *♪♪♪½ Enemies of the Public* 1931 Cagney's acting career was launched by this story of two Irish boys growing up in a Chicago shantytown to become hoodlums during the prohibition era. Cagney and Woods hook up with molls Clarke and Blondell on their rise to the top. Considered the most realistic "gangster" film, Wellman's movie is also the most grimly brutal due to its release prior to Hollywood censorship. The scene where Cagney smashes a grapefruit in Clarke's face was credited with starting a trend in abusing film heroines. **85m/B VHS, Beta, LV.** James Cagney, Edward Woods, Leslie Fenton, Joan Blondell, Mae Clarke, Jean Harlow; *D:* William A. Wellman. Nominations: Academy Awards '31: Best Story. *MGM, FOX*

The Public Eye *♪♪♪½* 1992 (R) Underappreciated film noir homage casts Pesci as a crime photographer with an unsuspected romantic streak. It's 1942 in NYC and cynical freelancer Leon "Bernzy" Bernstein's always looking for the perfect shot. Hershey's the recent widow whose nightclub-owner husband had mob ties and decides Pesci would be a likely patsy for helping her out. Hershey seems decorative and the romantic angle never quite develops, but Pesci delivers a rich, low-key performance as the visionary, hardboiled artist. Climatic mob shootout is cinematic bullet ballet. Based loosely on the career of '40s photog Weegee, who defined New York and its times in his work.*CW:* Violence. **98m/C VHS, LV, Letterbox.** Joe Pesci, Barbara Hershey, Stanley Tucci, Richard Foronjy, Richard Riehle, Jared Harris, Jerry Adler, Dominic Chianese, Gerry Becker; *D:* Howard Franklin; *W:* Howard Franklin; *M:* John Barry. *USH*

Pucker Up and Bark Like a Dog *♪* 1989 (R) A young artist and his inspirationally lovely actress girl-friend find themselves in strange and crazy situations. Good cast gives this potential. **94m/C VHS, Closed Caption.** Lisa Zane, Jonathan Gries, Paul Bartel, Robert Culp; *D:* Paul S. Parco. *BTV*

Pudd'nhead Wilson *♪½* 1987 An adaptation of a Mark Twain story about a small-town lawyer who discovers the illicit exchange of a white infant for a light-skinned negro infant by a slave woman. Made for television as an "American Playhouse" presentation on PBS. **87m/C VHS, Beta.** Ken Howard; *D:* Alan Bridges. *USH*

Pueblo Affair *♪♪♪* 1973 A dramatization of the capture of the American spy ship "Pueblo" by the North Koreans, during which time the crew was tortured, imprisoned, and all intelligence documents were confiscated. **99m/C VHS, Beta.** Hal Holbrook, Andrew Duggan, Richard Mulligan, George Grizzard, Gary Merrill, Mary Fickett; *D:* Anthony Page. *NO*

Pulp *♪♪½* 1972 (PG) Caine, playing a mystery writer, becomes a target for murder when he ghostwrites the memoirs of a movie gangster from the 1930s, played deftly by Rooney. **95m/C VHS, Beta.** *GB* Michael Caine, Mickey Rooney, Lionel Stander, Lizabeth Scott, Nadia Cassini, Dennis Price, Al Lettieri; *D:* Mike Hodges; *W:* Mike Hodges. *NO*

Pulp Fiction *♪♪♪♪* 1994 (R) Tarantino moves into the cinematic mainstream with his trademark violence and '70s pop culture mindset intact in this stylish crime trilogy. A day in the life of a criminal community unexpectedly shifts from outrageous, esoteric dialogue to violent mayhem with solid scripting that takes familiar stories to unexplored territory. Offbeat cast offers superb performances, led by Travolta, in his best role to date as a hit man whose adventures with partner Jackson tie the seemingly unrelated stories together. Clever, almost gleeful look at everday life on the fringes of mainstream society. Inspired by "Black Mask" magazine. A special collector's edition includes never-before-seen footage and commentary by Tarantino.*CW:* Ultra-violence, ugly drug overdose (and treatment thereof), language, homosexual rape. **154m/C VHS, LV, Closed Caption.** John Travolta, Samuel L. Jackson, Uma Thurman, Harvey Keitel, Tim Roth, Amanda Plummer, Maria De Medeiros, Ving Rhames, Eric Stoltz, Rosanna Arquette, Christopher Walken, Bruce Willis, Frank Whaley, Steve Buscemi, Peter Greene, David Arquette, Julia Sweeney, Quentin Tarantino; *D:* Quentin Tarantino; *W:* Quentin Tarantino, Roger Roberts Avary; *C:* Andrzej Sekula. Academy Awards '94: Best Original Screenplay; British Academy Awards '94: Best Original Screenplay, Best Supporting Actor (Jackson); Cannes Film Festival '94: Best Film; Golden Globe Awards '95: Best Screenplay; Independent Spirit Awards '95: Best Actor (Jackson), Best Director (Tarantino), Best Film, Best Screenplay; Los Angeles Film Critics Association Awards '94: Best Actor (Travolta), Best Director (Tarantino), Best Film, Best Screenplay; MTV Movie Awards '95: Best Film, Best Dance Sequence (John Travolta/Uma Thurman); National Board of Review Awards '94: Best Director (Tarantino), Best Film; New York Film Critics Awards '94: Best Director (Tarantino), Best Screenplay; National Society of Film Critics Awards '94: Best Director (Tarantino), Best Film, Best Screenplay; Nominations: Academy Awards '94: Best Actor (Travolta), Best Director (Tarantino), Best Film Editing, Best Picture, Best Supporting Actor (Jackson), Best Supporting Actress (Thurman); Australian Film Institute '95: Best Foreign Film; Directors Guild of America Awards '94: Best Director (Tarantino); Golden Globe Awards '95: Best Actor—Drama (Travolta), Best Director (Tarantino), Best Film—Drama, Best Supporting Actor (Jackson), Best Supporting Actress (Thurman); Independent Spirit Awards '95: Best Supporting Actor (Stoltz); MTV Movie Awards '95: Best Male Performance (Travolta), Best Female Performance (Thurman), Best On-Screen Duo (John Travolta/Samuel L. Jackson), Best Song ("Girl, You'll Be A Woman Soon"); Screen Actors Guild Award '94: Best Actor (Travolta). *MAX*

Pulse *♪♪* 1988 (PG-13) Electricity goes awry in this science-fiction thriller about appliances and other household devices that become supercharged and destroy property and their owners. **90m/C VHS, Beta, LV, Closed Caption.** Cliff DeYoung, Roxanne Hart, Joey Lawrence, Charles Tyner, Dennis Redfield, Robert Romanus, Myron Healey; *D:* Paul Golding; *C:* Peter Collister; *M:* Jay Michael Ferguson. *COL*

Pulsebeat woof! 1985 Flick about warring health club owners. As boring as it sounds unless you're in the mood for lots of on-screen aerobics. If so, rent Jane Fonda instead. Dubbed. **90m/C VHS, Beta.** *SP* Daniel Greene, Lee Taylor Allen, Bob Small, Alice Moore, Helga Line, Alex Intriago, Peter Lupus; *D:* Marice Tobias. *ART*

The Puma Man woof! 1980 Puma Man is a super hero who must stop the evil Dr. Kobras from using an ancient mask in his attempt to become ruler of the world. Unreleased theatrically in the U.S., this low budget sci-fi/horror mix is so bad one wonders why an actor like Pleasence would sign on. Special effects these days are so extraordinary that the ones employed here are laughable. **80m/C VHS, Beta.** *IT* Donald Pleasence, Walter George Alton, Sydne Rome, Miguel Angel Fuentes; *D:* Alberto De Martino.

Pump Up the Volume *♪♪½* 1990 (R) High school newcomer leads double life as Hard Harry, sarcastic host of an illegal radio broadcast and Jack Nicholson soundalike. Anonymously popular with his peers, he invites the wrath of the school principal due to his less than flattering comments about the school administration. Slater seems to enjoy himself as defiant deejay while youthful cast effectively supports. **105m/C VHS, LV, 8mm, Closed Caption.** Christian Slater, Scott Paulin, Ellen Greene, Samantha Mathis, Cheryl Pollak, Annie Ross, Andy Romano, Mimi Kennedy; *D:* Allan Moyle; *W:* Allan Moyle. *COL, FCT, MVD*

Pumping Iron 1976 (PG) A widely acclaimed documentary look at the sport of bodybuilding, following the behind-the-scenes action surrounding the competition for the Mr. Olympia title. The grueling training ritual and the constant striving for perfection are all explored. **90m/C VHS, Beta, LV.** Arnold Schwarzenegger, Mike Katz, Franco Columbu, Lou Ferrigno; *D:* George Butler. *COL, SCH, RHI*

Pumping Iron 2: The Women 1985 This sequel to "Pumping Iron" takes an in-depth look at the world of female body building. The documentary also follows the ladies to a competition held at Caesar's Palace in Las Vegas. **107m/C VHS, Beta, LV, Closed Caption.** Lori Bowen, Bev Francis, Rachel McLish, Carla Dunlap, Lydia Cheng; *D:* George Butler. *VES*

The Pumpkin Eater *♪♪♪* 1964 British housewife Jo (Bancroft) has seemingly found contentment with her third husband, famous and wealthy writer Jake (Finch), and her eight children. But as Jo struggles to face middle age she discovers Jake is chronically unfaithful and goes into an emotional tailspin. Last film for Hardwicke. Slow-paced film with fine performances; based on the novel by Penelope Mortimer. **110m/C VHS, Closed Caption.** *GB* Anne Bancroft, Peter Finch, James Mason, Richard Johnson, Cedric Hardwicke, Maggie Smith, Alan Webb, Eric Porter; *D:* Jack Clayton; *W:* Harold Pinter; *C:* Oswald Morris; *M:* Georges Delerue. British Academy Awards '64: Best Screenplay; Nominations: Academy Awards '64: Best Actress (Bancroft). *COL*

Pumpkinhead *♪♪½ Vengeance: The Demon* 1988 (R) A farmer evokes a demon from the earth to avenge his son's death. When it continues on its murdering rampage, the farmer finds he no longer has any control over the vicious killer. **89m/C VHS, Beta, LV, Closed Caption.** Lance Henriksen, John DiAquino, Kerry Remsen, Matthew Hurley, Jeff East, Kimberly Ross, Cynthia Bain, Joel Hoffman, Florence Schauffler, Buck Flower, Tom Woodruff Jr.; *D:* Stan Winston; *W:* Gary Gerani, Mark Patrick Carducci; *C:* Bojan Bazelli; *M:* Richard Stone. *MGM*

Pumpkinhead 2: Blood Wings *♪½* 1994 (R) Five typically stupid teenagers resurrect a demon and the creature goes on a bloodthirsty rampage. His leaves his signature, a calling card in the shape of wings, at each murder scene. **88m/C VHS, LV, Closed Caption.** Ami Dolenz, Andrew (Andy) Robinson, Kane Hodder, R.A. Mihailoff, Linnea Quigley, Steve Kanaly, Caren Kaye, Gloria Hendry, Soleil Moon Frye, Mark McCracken, Roger Clinton; *D:* Jeff Burr; *W:* Ivan Chachornia, Constantin Chachornia. *ART*

Punch the Clock *♪♪* 1990 (R) Attractive female thief finds her bail bondsman very exciting; he's ready to help her any way he can. **88m/C VHS.** Michael Rogan, Chris Moore, James Lorinz; *D:* Eric L. Schlagman. *NO*

Punchline *♪♪* 1988 (R) A look at the lives of stand-up comics, following the career ups-and-downs of an embittered professional funny-man and a frustrated housewife hitting the stage for the first time. Some very funny and touching moments and some not-so-funny and touching as the movie descends into melodrama without a cause. **100m/C VHS, Beta, LV, Closed Caption.** Tom Hanks, Sally Field, John Goodman, Mark Rydell, Kim Greist, Barry Sobel, Paul Mazursky, Pam Matteson, George Michael McGrath, Taylor Negron, Damon Wayans; *D:* David Seltzer; *W:* David Seltzer; *C:* Reynaldo Villalobos. Los Angeles Film Critics Association Awards '88: Best Actor (Hanks). *COL*

The Punisher *♪* 1990 (R) Lundgren portrays Frank Castle, the Marvel Comics anti-hero known as the Punisher. When his family is killed by the mob Castle set his eyes on revenge. Filmed in Australia. **92m/C VHS, Beta, LV, Closed Caption.** Dolph Lundgren, Louis Gossett Jr., Jeroen Krabbe, Kim Miyori; *D:* Mark Goldblatt; *C:* Ian Baker. *ART*

Punk Rock Movie 1978 The musical explosion known as punk rock is documented here in its early days (circa 1977) at the Roxy in England. Includes a look at leading punk rock artists such as the Sex Pistols, the Clash, Slits, and others, and at the entire counterculture that was punk. 80m/C VHS, Beta. *MVD, SUN*

Punk Vacation 🐾 1990 A gang of motorcycle mamas terrorize a small town. The usual biker stuff. 90m/C VHS, Beta, LV. Stephen Falchi, Roxanne Rogers, Don Martin, Sandra Bogan; *D:* Stanley Lewis. *NO*

Puppet Master 🐾🐾½ 1989 (R) Four psychics are sent to investigate a puppet maker who they think may have discovered the secret of life. Before they know it, they are stalked by evil puppets. Great special effects, not-so-great script. 90m/C VHS, Beta, LV, Closed Caption. Paul LeMat, Jimmie F. Skaggs, Irene Miracle, Robyn Frates, Barbara Crampton, William Hickey, Matt Roe, Kathryn O'Reilly; *D:* David Schmoeller; *W:* Joseph G. Collodi; *C:* Sergio Salvati; *M:* Richard Band. *FLL*

Puppet Master 2 🐾🐾 1990 (R) Puppets on a rampage turn hotel into den of special effects. Less effective string pulling than in original. Long live Pinocchio. 90m/C VHS, Beta, LV, Closed Caption. Elizabeth MacLellan, Collin Bernsen, Greg Webb, Charlie Spradling, Nita Talbot, Steve Welles, Jeff Weston; *D:* David Allen; *W:* David Pabian; *M:* Richard Band. *PAR*

Puppet Master 3: Toulon's Revenge 🐾🐾 1990 (R) Prequel about the origin of the whole gory Puppet Master shebang, set in Nazi Germany. The weapon-hungry Third Reich tries to wrest secrets of artificial life from sorceror Andre Toulon, who sics his deadly puppets on them. Toulon's a good guy here, one of many contradictions in the series. Fine cast, but strictly for the followers.*CW:* Violence and sensuality. 86m/C VHS, LV, Closed Caption. Guy Rolfe, Ian Abercrombie, Sarah Douglas, Richard Lynch, Walter Gotell; *D:* David DeCoteau; *M:* Richard Band. *PAR*

Puppet Master 4 🐾🐾 1993 (R) It's the puppets versus the totems, equally loathsome midget creatures who derive their power from the same eternal force as the puppets. No one wants to share and there's lots of gore while they battle for supremacy.*CW:* Language and horror violence. 80m/C VHS, Beta, Closed Caption. Gordon Currie, Chandra West, Jason Adams, Teresa Hill, Guy Rolfe; *D:* Jeff Burr; *W:* Todd Henschell, Steven E. Carr, Jo Duffy, Dough Aarniokoski, Keith Payson; *M:* Richard Band. *PAR*

Puppet Master 5: The Final Chapter 🐾½ 1994 Greedy Dr. Jennings has come to Bodega Bay Inn to capture the puppets and discover the secret formula for their animation so he can sell it to the highest bidder. But he's not the only threat, it seems the demonic Eyad, a being from another dimension, also wants the secret and has sent his own evil puppet to kill the puppet master and steal their magic. 81m/C VHS, Beta, LV, Closed Caption. Gordon Currie, Chandra West, Ian Ogilvy, Teresa Hill, Nicholas Guest, Willard Pugh, Diane McBain, Kaz Garas, Guy Rolfe; *D:* Jeff Burr; *M:* Richard Band. *PAR*

The Puppet Masters 🐾🐾 *Robert A. Heinlein's The Puppet Masters* 1994 (R) Government official (Sutherland) discovers aliens are taking over the bodies of humans and if he doesn't find a way to stop the parasites they'll soon rule the Earth. Yes, it does sound like "Invasion of the Body Snatchers" but the film is based on Robert A. Heinlein's 1951 novel, written five years before. The parasites are sufficiently yucky but, unfortunately, this adaptation is mediocre and generally wastes a talented cast. 109m/C VHS, LV, Closed Caption. Donald Sutherland, Eric Thal, Julie Warner, Keith David, Will Patton, Richard Belzer, Yaphet Kotto; *D:* Stuart Orme; *W:* Terry Rossio, David S. Goyer, Ted Elliott; *M:* Colin Towns. *HPH*

Puppet on a Chain 🐾🐾 1972 (PG) American narcotics officer busts an Amsterdam drug ring and the leader's identity surprises him. Slow-moving thriller based on the Alistair MacLean novel. 97m/C VHS, Beta. *GB* Sven-Bertil Taube, Barbara Parkins, Alexander Knox, Patrick Allen, Geoffrey Reeve; *D:* Geoffrey Reeve; *C:* Jack Hildyard.

The Puppetoon Movie 1987 (G) A compilation of George Pal's famous Puppetoon cartoons from the 1940s, marking his stature as an animation pioneer and innovator. Hosted by Gumby, Pokey, Speedy Alka Seltzer and Arnie the Dinosaur in newly directed scenes. 80m/C VHS, Beta, LV. *D:* Arnold Leibovit; *M:* Buddy Baker. *FHE*

The Purchase Price 🐾🐾 1932 After a less than amorous beginning, farmer Brent and mail order bride Stanwyck fall into love and financial despair in this drama bordering on comedy. Good neighbor Landau is willing to help the poor agriculturalist out in exchange for Stanwyck. Tragedy strikes again when Stanwyck's bootlegger ex-boyfriend shows up and further disasters continue to test the couple's commitment. Based on the story "The Mud Lark" by Arthur Stringer. 70m/B VHS. Barbara Stanwyck, George Brent, Lyle Talbot, Hardie Albright, David Landau; *D:* William A. Wellman; *W:* Robert Lord. *MGM*

Pure Country 🐾🐾½ 1992 (PG) An easygoing movie about a familiar subject is held together by the charm of Strait (in his movie debut) and the rest of the cast. Strait plays a country music superstar, tired of the career glitz, who decides to get out and go back to his home in Texas. He falls in love with the spunky Glasser and decides to run his career his own way. Warren is effective as his tough manager and old-time cowboy Calhoun is finely weathered as Glasser's gruff dad. 113m/C VHS, Beta, LV, Letterbox, Closed Caption. George Strait, Isabel Glasser, Lesley Ann Warren, Rory Calhoun, Kyle Chandler, John Doe, Molly McClure; *W:* Rex McGee; *C:* Rick Bota; *M:* Stephen Dorff. *WAR, MVD*

Pure Danger 🐾🐾½ 1996 (R) Short order cook Johnny (Howell) and his waitress girlfriend Becky (Linn) stumble upon a bag of diamonds and think all their troubles are over. Wrong—they're just beginning, since some very nasty men want the jewels and don't care who they kill to get them. Howell keeps his directorial debut fast-paced and surprisingly entertaining.*CW:* Action violence, language and some nudity. 99m/C VHS, Closed Caption. C. Thomas Howell, Teri Ann Linn, Leon, Michael Russo; *D:* C. Thomas Howell; *W:* William Applegate Jr., John Barmettler; *C:* Ken Blakey; *M:* K. Alexander Wilkinson. *PMH*

A Pure Formality 🐾🐾 *Una Pura Formalita; Une Pure Formalite* 1994 (PG-13) Murky psycho-drama finds a disheveled man (Depardieu) winding up at an isolated police station in a nameless country (in the middle of a rainstorm, no less). The Inspector (Polanski) suspects him of a local murder, especially after he claims to be a famous writer named Onoff, yet, can remember nothing. The Inspector wants a confession and spends the night trying to exact one from his guileful suspect. French with subtitles. Film is rated at a much younger level than will possibly understand or enjoy it.*CW:* Brief shocking violence; momentary language. 111m/C VHS, LV. *FR IT* Gerard Depardieu, Roman Polanski, Sergio Rubini; *D:* Giuseppe Tornatore; *W:* Giuseppe Tornatore, Pascal Quignard; *C:* Basco Giurato; *M:* Ennio Morricone. *COL*

The Pure Hell of St. Trinian's 🐾🐾½ 1961 In this sequel to "Blue Murder at St. Trinian's," a sheik who desires to fill out his harem tries recruiting at a rowdy girls' school. Although it isn't as funny as the first, due to the lack of Alistair Sim, it is still humorous. Followed by "The Great St. Trinian's Train Robbery." Based on the cartoon by Ronald Searle. 94m/B VHS. *GB* Cecil Parker, Joyce Grenfell, George Cole, Thorley Walters; *D:* Frank Launder; *M:* Malcolm Arnold. *FCT*

Pure Luck 🐾½ 1991 (PG) A who-asked-for-it remake of a 1981 Franco-Italian film called "La Chevre." The premise is the same: an accident-prone heiress disappears in Mexico, and her father tries to locate her using an equally clumsy accountant. The nebbish and an attendant tough private eye stumble and bumble south of the border until the plot arbitrarily ends. Pure awful. 96m/

C VHS, Beta, LV, Closed Caption. Martin Short, Danny Glover, Sheila Kelley, Scott Wilson, Sam Wanamaker, Harry Shearer; *D:* Nadia Tass; *W:* Herschel Weingrod, Timothy Harris. *USH*

Purgatory 🐾 1989 While travelling abroad, two innocent women find themselves unjustly jailed. During their confinement they are tortured and raped. 90m/C VHS, Beta, LV. Tanya Roberts, Julie Pop; *D:* Ami Artzi; *W:* Paul Aratow. *NO*

Purlie Victorious 🐾🐾 1963 Presentation of the award-winning Broadway hit, which takes a look at racial integration. 93m/C VHS, Beta. Ossie Davis, Ruby Dee, Godfrey Cambridge, Alan Alda; *D:* Nicholas Webster. *NO*

The Purple Heart 🐾🐾½ 1944 An American Air Force crew is shot down over Tokyo and taken into brutal POW camps. Intense wartime melodramatics. 99m/B VHS, Beta. Dana Andrews, Richard Conte, Farley Granger, Donald (Don "Red") Barry, Sam Levene, Kevin O'Shea, Tala Birell, Nestor Paiva, Benson Fong, Marshall Thompson, Richard Loo; *D:* Lewis Milestone; *C:* Arthur C. Miller. *FOX*

Purple Hearts 🐾½ 1984 (R) Wahl stars as a Navy doctor who falls in love with nurse Ladd against the backdrop of the Vietnam war. Overlong and redundant. 115m/C VHS, Beta. Cheryl Ladd, Ken Wahl, Stephen Lee, Annie McEnroe, Paul McCrane, Cyril O'Reilly; *D:* Sidney J. Furie; *W:* Sidney J. Furie, Ron Nyswaner; *M:* Robert Folk. *WAR*

The Purple Monster Strikes 🐾🐾 1945 A martian plots to conquer Earth to save his dying planet. Serial in 15 episodes. 188m/B VHS. Dennis Moore, Linda Stirling, Roy Barcroft; *D:* Spencer Gordon Bennet. *REP, VCN, MLB*

Purple Noon 🐾🐾🐾 *Plein Soleil; Lust for Evil* 1960 (PG-13) Don't let the ratings fool you, this isn't teen fodder. The gorgeous Delon stars as opportunistic Tom Ripley, who's hired by the father of his rich, arrogant playboy friend Philippe (Ronet) to persuade him to return home to San Francisco. Instead, Ripley covets the man's yacht, beautiful girlfriend Marge (Laforet), and money, so when Philippe pushes Tom too far he disposes of him and tries to divert police suspicions. Film noir set in the hedonistic Mediterranean sun. Based on the novel "The Talented Mr. Ripley" by Patricia Highsmith. French with subtitles. 118m/C VHS, LV. *FR* Alain Delon, Maurice Ronet, Marie Laforet, Erno Crisa, Billy Kearns; *D:* Rene Clement; *W:* Rene Clement, Paul Gegauff; *C:* Henri Decae; *M:* Nino Rota. *TOU*

Purple People Eater 🐾 1988 (PG) The alien of the title descends to earth to mix with young girls and rock 'n' roll. Based on the song of the same name whose performer, Sheb Wooley, appears in the film. Harmless, stupid fun for the whole family. 91m/C VHS, Beta, LV. Ned Beatty, Shelley Winters, Neil Patrick Harris, Kareem Abdul-Jabbar, Little Richard, Chubby Checker, Peggy Lipton; *D:* Linda Shayne. *VTR*

Purple Rain 🐾🐾½ 1984 (R) A quasi-autobiographical video showcase for the pop-star Prince. Film tells the tale of his struggle for love, attention, acceptance, and popular artistic recognition in Minneapolis. Not a bad film, for such a monumentally egotistical movie. 113m/C VHS, Beta, LV, Closed Caption, DVD. Prince, Apollonia, Morris Day, Olga Karlatos, Clarence Williams III; *D:* Albert Magnoli; *W:* William Blinn; *C:* Donald E. Thorin; *M:* Michel Colombier. Academy Awards '84: Original Song Score and/or Adaptation. *MVD, WAR*

The Purple Rose of Cairo 🐾🐾🐾 1985 (PG) A diner waitress, disillusioned by the Depression and a lackluster life, escapes into a film playing at the local movie house where a blond film hero, tiring of the monotony of his role, makes a break from the celluloid to join her in the real world. The ensuing love story allows director-writer Allen to show his knowledge of old movies and provide his fans with a change of pace. Farrow's film sister is also her real-life sister Stephanie, who went on to appear in Allen's "Zelig." 82m/C VHS, Beta, LV, Closed Caption. Mia Farrow, Jeff Daniels, Danny Aiello, Dianne Wiest, Van Johnson, Zoe Caldwell, John Wood, Michael Tucker, Edward Herrmann, Milo O'Shea, Glenne Headly, Karen Akers, Deborah Rush; *D:* Woody Allen; *W:* Woody Allen & Gordon Willis; *M:* Dick Hyman. British Academy Awards '85: Best Film, Best Original Screenplay; Cesar Awards '86: Best Foreign Film; Golden Globe Awards '86: Best Screenplay; New York Film Critics Awards '85: Best Screenplay; Nominations: Academy Awards '85: Best Original Screenplay. *ART, VES, HMV*

The Purple Taxi 🦴🦴½ **1977 (R)** Romantic drama revolving around several wealthy foreigners who have taken refuge in beautiful southern Ireland. From Michel Deon's bestselling novel. **93m/C VHS, Beta.** *FR* Fred Astaire, Charlotte Rampling, Peter Ustinov, Philippe Noiret, Edward Albert; *D:* Yves Boisset. *COL*

Purple Vigilantes 🦴½ *The Purple Riders* **1938** The Three Mesquiteers uncover a gang of vigilantes. Part of the series. **54m/B VHS, Beta.** Bob Livingston, Ray Corrigan, Max Terhune. *VCN, DVT*

Pursued 🦴🦴🦴 **1947** Excellent performances by Mitchum and Wright mark this suspenseful Western drama of a Spanish-American war veteran in search of his father's killer. **105m/B VHS, Closed Caption.** Teresa Wright, Robert Mitchum, Judith Anderson, Dean Jagger, Alan Hale, Harry Carey Jr., John Rodney; *D:* Raoul Walsh; *C:* James Wong Howe; *M:* Max Steiner. *REP, HEG*

Pursuit 🦴🦴🦴 **1972** A terrorist threatens to release a toxic nerve gas throughout a city hosting a political convention. Tension mounts as federal agents must beat the extremists' countdown to zero. Based on the novel by Crichton. **73m/C VHS, Beta.** Ben Gazzara, E.G. Marshall, Martin Sheen, Joseph Wiseman, William Windom; *D:* Michael Crichton; *M:* Jerry Goldsmith. *REP*

Pursuit 🦴🦴🦴 **1990 (R)** A mercenary comes out of retirement to join a renegade team recovering stolen gold. But they turn on him, stealing the treasure and taking a hostage. Now he must track them down, or there's no movie. *CW:* Language, violence, and sensuality. **94m/C VHS, Closed Caption.** James Ryan, Andre Jacobs; *D:* John H. Parr. *HBO*

The Pursuit of D.B. Cooper 🦴🦴 **1981 (PG)** Based on an actual hijacking that occurred on Thanksgiving Eve in 1971 in which J.R. Meade (alias D.B. Cooper) parachuted out of an airliner with $200,000 of stolen money. Although his fate and whereabouts have remained a mystery, this story speculates about what may have happened. **100m/C VHS, Beta, LV.** Robert Duvall, Treat Williams, Kathryn Harrold, Ed Flanders; *D:* Roger Spottiswoode; *C:* Harry Stradling Jr.; *M:* James Horner. *ART, VES*

The Pursuit of Happiness 🦴🦴½ **1970 (PG)** An idealistic man is convicted of manslaughter after accidentally running down a woman. Once in prison, he's faced with the decision to try to escape. **85m/C VHS, Beta.** Michael Sarrazin, Arthur Hill, E.G. Marshall, Barbara Hershey, Robert Klein; *D:* Robert Mulligan. *NO*

Pursuit of the Graf Spee 🦴🦴½ *The Battle of the River Plate* **1957** Three small British ships destroy the mighty Graf Spee, a WWII German battleship. **106m/C VHS, Beta.** *GB* Anthony Quayle, Peter Finch, Ian Hunter; *D:* Michael Powell. *NO*

Pursuit to Algiers 🦴🦴½ **1945** The modernized Holmes and Watson guard over the King of fictional Rovenia during a sea voyage, during which assassins close in. **65m/B VHS, Beta, Closed Caption.** Basil Rathbone, Nigel Bruce, Martin Kosleck, Marjorie Riordan, Rosalind Ivan, John Abbott; *D:* Roy William Neill. *FOX*

Pushed to the Limit 🦴½ **1992 (R)** Harry Lee, the most feared gangster in Chinatown, is about to meet his match in martial-arts queen Lesseos. She's out for revenge when she learns that Lee is responsible for her brother's murder but first she must get by Lee's lethal bodyguard, the equally skilled Inga. *CW:* Martial arts violence/drug content. **88m/C VHS, LV.** Mimi Lesseos. *IMP*

Pushing Hands 🦴🦴½ **1992** Aging tai chi master Mr. Chu (Lung) leaves Beijing to live with his son Alex (Wang) and daughter-in-law Martha (Snyder) in suburban New York. High-strung Martha doesn't understand her tranquilly stubborn father-in-law, nor does Chu find disposable American society much to his liking. Naturally, and slowly, some accomodations are made. The title is a tai chi reference to keeping your opponent off-balance while maintaining your own equilibrium. Director Lee's debut feature is also the first in his trilogy of family films—followed by the more accomplished "The Wedding Banquet" and "Eat Drink Man Woman." English and Mandarin Chinese with subtitles. **100m/C VHS, LV.** Sihung Lung, Deb Snyder, Bo Z. Wang, Lai Wang; *D:* Ang Lee; *W:* Ang Lee; *C:* Jong Lin; *M:* Xiao-Song Qu. *TRI*

Puss 'n Boots **1984** From "Faerie Tale Theatre" comes the story of a cat who makes his poor master a rich land-owning nobleman. **60m/C VHS, Beta, Closed Caption.** Ben Vereen, Gregory Hines; *D:* Robert Iscove. *FOX, FCT*

Putney Swope 🦴🦴🦴 **1969 (R)** Comedy about a token black ad man mistakenly elected Chairman of the board of a Madison Avenue ad agency who turns the company upside-down. A series of riotous spoofs on commercials is the highpoint in this funny, though somewhat dated look at big business. **84m/B VHS, Beta.** Arnold Johnson, Laura Greene, Stanley Gottlieb, Mel Brooks; *D:* Robert Downey. *COL*

Puzzle 🦴🦴½ **1978** Franciscus searches for the urn that contains the remains of Buddha but instead finds danger and intrigue. Made for television. **90m/C VHS.** *AU* James Franciscus, Wendy Hughes, Robert Helpmann, Peter Gwynne, Gerald Kennedy, Kerry McGuire; *D:* Gordon Hessler.

Pygmalion 🦴🦴🦴½ **1938** Oscar-winning film adaptation of Shaw's play about a cockney flower-girl who is transformed into a "lady" under the guidance of a stuffy phonetics professor. Shaw himself aided in writing the script in this superbly acted comedy that would be adapted into the musical, "My Fair Lady," first on Broadway in 1956 and for the screen in 1964. **96m/B VHS, Beta, LV.** *GB* Leslie Howard, Wendy Hiller, Wilfred Lawson, Marie Lohr, Scott Sunderland, David Tree, Everley Gregg, Leueen McGrath, Jean Cadell, Eileen Beldon, Frank Atkinson, O.B. Clarence, Esme Percy, Violet Vanbrugh, Iris Hoey, Viola Tree, Irene Browne, Kate Cutler, Cathleen Nesbitt, Cecil Trouncer, Stephen Murray, Wally Patch, H.F. Maltby; *D:* Anthony Asquith, Leslie Howard; *W:* W.P. Lipscomb, Anatole de Grunwald, Cecil Lewis, Ian Dalrymple, George Bernard Shaw; *C:* Harry Stradling. Academy Awards '38: Best Screenplay; Venice Film Festival '38: Best Actor (Howard); Nominations: Academy Awards '38: Best Actor (Howard), Best Actress (Hiller), Best Picture. *MON, NOS, COL*

Pyrates 🦴 **1991 (R)** Real life husband-wife team of Bacon and Sedgwick try to provide fireworks as hot, but there's none in the forgettable one. For the price of this one you can buy a newspaper and chewing gum instead. Use both at the same time and you'll be ahead of everyone involved in this senseless hoot. *CW:* Language and sensuality. **98m/C VHS.** Kevin Bacon, Kyra Sedgwick, Bruce Martyn Payne, Kristin Datillo; *D:* Noah Stern. *VES, ART*

A Pyromaniac's Love Story 🦴🦴 **1995 (PG)** Offbeat tale of romance has a neigborhood bakery burning down and every major character confessing to the crime. Earnest working stiffs, snotty rich kids, and kindly old shop owners all have really confusing reasons for wanting to take the heat, most of which have to do with unrequited love. At times charming, but ultimately too whimsical for its own good. The quirky characters and goofy plot twists sabotage any attempt to ignite much interest. **99m/C VHS, LV, Closed Caption.** John Leguizamo, Sadie Frost, William Baldwin, Erika Eleniak, Michael Lerner, Joan Plowright, Armin Mueller-Stahl, Richard Crenna; *D:* Joshua Brand; *W:* Morgan Ward; *C:* John Schwartzman; *M:* Rachel Portman. *TOU*

Python Wolf 🦴🦴 *C.A.T. Squad: Python Wolf* **1988 (R)** It's non-stop action in South Africa as a counter-terrorist group sets out to thwart a drug smuggler's plans to export plutonium. As usual, intense pacing from director Friedkin. Made for television. Sequel to "C.A.T. Squad" (1986). **100m/C VHS, LV.** Joe Cortese, Jack Youngblood, Steve James, Deborah Van Valkenburgh, Miguel Ferrer, Alan Scarfe; *D:* William Friedkin; *M:* Ennio Morricone. *THV*

The Pyx 🦴🦴🦴 *The Hooker Cult Murders* **1973 (R)** Canadian suspense thriller about the murder of a prostitute with satanic overtones. Poice sergeant investigates the crime and enters a world of devil worship and decadence. Based on the novel by John Buell. **111m/C VHS.** *CA* Karen Black, Christopher Plummer, Donald Pilon; *D:* Harvey Hart.

Q & A 🦴🦴 **1990 (R)** Semi-taut thriller with Nolte playing a totally corrupt, hair-trigger cop trying to make his murder of a drug dealer look like self-defense. Assigned to the case is an ex-cop turned assistant DA (Hutton) who's supposed to sweep the case under the rug. Then he finds out another dealer (Assante) is a witness and he happens to be romancing Hutton's former girlfriend (film debut of director Lumet's daughter). Lots of violence and raw language. **132m/C VHS, Beta, LV, Closed Caption.** Nick Nolte, Timothy Hutton, Armand Assante, Patrick O'Neal, Lee Richardson, Luis Guzman, Charles S. Dutton, Jenny Lumet, Paul Calderone, Fyvush Finkel; *D:* Sidney Lumet; *W:* Sidney Lumet; *C:* Andrzej Bartkowiak; *M:* Ruben Blades. *HBO, WAR*

Q Ships 🦴🦴½ **1928** Silent German drama about a submarine commander who has inner conflicts with his country's war effort. Uses actual WWI footage. **78m/B VHS, Beta.** *GE* J.P. Kennedy, Roy Travers, Johnny Butt, Philip Hewland; *D:* Geoffrey Barkas, Michael Barringer. *GPV, DVT, GLV*

Q (The Winged Serpent) 🦴🦴🦴 *Q: The Winged Serpent* **1982 (R)** A cult of admirers surrounds this goony monster flick about dragonlike Aztec god Quetzlcoatl, summoned to modern Manhattan by gory human sacrifices, and hungry for rooftop sunbathers and construction teams. Direction and special effects are pretty ragged, but witty script helps the cast shine, especially Moriarty as a lowlife crook who's found the beast's hidden nest. **92m/C VHS, Beta.** Michael Moriarty, Candy Clark, David Carradine, Richard Roundtree; *D:* Larry Cohen; *W:* Larry Cohen. *USH*

QB VII 🦴🦴🦴½ **1974** A knighted physician brings a suit for libel against a novelist for implicating him in war crimes. Hopkins as the purportedly wronged doctor and Gazzara as the writer are both superb. Ending is stunning. Adapted from the novel by Leon Uris. Over five hours long; made for TV. Available only as a three-cassette set. **313m/C VHS, Beta, LV.** Anthony Hopkins, Ben Gazzara, Lee Remick, Leslie Caron, Juliet Mills, John Gielgud, Anthony Quayle; *D:* Tom Gries; *M:* Jerry Goldsmith. *COL, SWC*

Quackser Fortune Has a Cousin in the Bronx 🦴🦴🦴 *Fun Loving* **1970 (R)** An Irish fertilizer salesman meets an exchange student from the U.S., who finds herself attracted to this unlearned, but not unknowing, man. An original love story with drama and appeal. **88m/C VHS, Beta, LV.** *IR* Gene Wilder, Margot Kidder; *D:* Waris Hussein. *VCI*

Quadrophenia 🦴🦴🦴 **1979 (R)** Pete Townshend's excellent rock opera about an alienated youth looking for life's meaning in Britain's rock scene circa 1963. Music by The Who is powerful and apt. Fine performance by Sting in his acting debut. **115m/C VHS, Beta, LV.** *GB* Phil Daniels, Mark Wingett, Philip Davis, Leslie Ash, Sting; *D:* Franc Roddam; *C:* Brian Tufano. *MVD, COL, RHI*

Quake 🦴½ **1992 (R)** Railsback stars as a stalker who takes advantage of the 1990 San Francisco earthquake to finally obtain the woman of his dreams. A surveillance expert, he's after a beautiful lawyer (Anderson) and when the earthquake leaves her trapped he rushes to rescue her—only to hold her captive himself. *CW:* Language, violence, and sexuality. **83m/C VHS.** Steve Railsback, Erika Anderson, Eb Lottimer, Dick Miller; **D:** Louis Morneau; **W:** Mark Evan Schwartz. *COL*

Quality Street 🐾🐾 **1937** English lovers Tone and Hepburn are separated when he leaves to fight in the Napoleonic Wars. When Tone returns years later, he's forgotten his erstwhile heartthrob. He also fails to recognize that the 16-year old coquette who's caught his eye is his old beloved in disguise. Cast works hard to overcome the absurd premise, based on the play by Sir James Barrie. **84m/B VHS, LV.** Katharine Hepburn, Franchot Tone, Fay Bainter, Eric Blore, Cora Witherspoon, Estelle Winwood, Florence Lake, Bonita Granville; **D:** George Stevens; **W:** J.M. Barrie. Nominations: Academy Awards '37: Best Score.*NOS, FCT, TTC*

Quarantine 🐾🐾½ **1989 (R)** Quarantine camps for carriers of a fatal virus are the serious measures taken by the nation. The solution is clear to a rebel and an inventor; all must be liberated or exterminated. **92m/C VHS.** Beatrice Boepple, Garwin Sanford, Jerry Wasserman, Charles Wilkinson; **D:** Charles Wilkinson; **W:** Charles Wilkinson. *REP*

The Quarrel 🐾🐾½ **1993** Chaim Kovler is a New York poet visiting Montreal in 1948. In a park he notices a group of Orthodox Jews and discovers one is his childhood friend Hersh. Fifteen years earlier their friendship broke over Chaim's decision to give up the religious life for his writing. Having lost their families to the Holocaust in Poland, both men have immigrated to new lives in North America. They immediately pick up their quarrel over religious faith and its value, particularly in light of the Holocaust. The two characters serve too much as careful ideologues to be compelling and the story turns cloyingly sentimental. Based on a short story by Yiddish writer Chaim Grade. **88m/C VHS.** CA Saul Rubinek, R.H. Thomson; **D:** Eli Cohen; **W:** David Brandes; **M:** William Goldstein. *BMG*

Quarterback Princess 🐾🐾 **1985** Workaday made-for-TV telling of the real-life girl who goes out for football and becomes homecoming queen. Heartwarming, if you like that kinda stuff, but not exciting, except for the early appearances of such '90s stars as Helen Hunt (as said quarterback), Daphne Zuniga as her sister, and Tim Robbins as a teammate. **96m/C VHS, Beta, Closed Caption.** Helen Hunt, Don Murray, John Stockwell, Barbara Babcock, Daphne Zuniga, Kathleen Wilhoite, Tim Robbins; **D:** Noel Black. *FOX*

Quartet 🐾🐾🐾 **1981 (R)** A young French woman is taken in by an English couple after her husband goes to prison. The husband seduces her, and she becomes trapped emotionally and socially. Superbly acted, claustrophobic drama based on a Jean Rhys novel. **101m/C VHS, Beta.** GB FR Isabelle Adjani, Alan Bates, Maggie Smith, Anthony Higgins; **D:** James Ivory; **W:** Ruth Prawer Jhabvala. Cannes Film Festival '81: Best Actress (Adjani). *WAR*

Quartier Mozart 🐾🐾 **1992** Sexual farce presenting the assimilation of African American pop-culture into African traditions. A local sorceress uses witchcraft to give Queen of the 'Hood a first-hand look at sexual politics. The young girl enters the body of a boy struggling to find his place in the male hierarchy established by neighborhood Casanovas. In French with English subtitles. **80m/C VHS. D:** Jean-Pierre Bekolo. *KIV*

Quatermass 2 🐾🐾🐾 *Enemy from Space* **1957** In the well made sequel to "Quatermass Experiment," (also known as "The Creeping Unknown") Professor Quatermass battles blobs and brainwashed zombies to rescue government officials whose bodies have been invaded by aliens. "Five Million Years to Earth" concluded the trilogy. **84m/B VHS, Beta, LV.** GB Brian Donlevy, John Longden, Sidney James, Bryan Forbes, William Franklyn, Vera Day, John Van Eyssen, Michael Ripper, Michael Balfour; **D:** Val Guest; **M:** James Bernard. *FCT, CTH, SNC*

Quatermass and the Pit 🐾🐾½ **1958** From the original BBC production. Professor Quatermass is up to his ears in trouble as a Martian spacecraft is found by subway workers. Not long after a monster stalks the streets of London. Remade cinematically in 1968 as "Five Million Years to Earth." **180m/B VHS.** GB Andre Morell, Cec Linder. *VTR, MRV, SNC*

Quatermass Conclusion 🐾🐾 **1979** An elderly British scientist comes out of retirement to stop an immobilizing death ray from outer space from destroying Earth. Edited version of a television miniseries continues earlier adventures of Quatermass on film and television. **105m/C VHS, Beta.** GB John Mills, Simon MacCorkindale, Barbara Kellerman, Margaret Tyzack; **D:** Piers Haggard. *NO*

The Quatermass Experiment 🐾🐾🐾 *The Creeping Unknown* **1956** Excellent British production about an astronaut who returns to Earth carrying an alien infestation that causes him to turn into a horrible monster. Competent acting and tense direction. Followed by "Enemy From Space." **78m/B VHS.** GB Brian Donlevy, Margia Dean, Jack Warner, Richard Wordsworth; **D:** Val Guest; **M:** James Bernard. *MGM, SNC, NOS*

Quatorze Juliet 🐾🐾½ **1932** A taxi driver and a flower girl meet on Bastille Day and fall in love. When he becomes involved with gangsters, she steers him back to virtue in this minor French relic from director Clair. **85m/B VHS.** FR Anabella Rigaud, Jorge Rigaud; **D:** Rene Clair. *VDM, FCT*

Que Viva Mexico 🐾🐾🐾 **1932** Eisenstein's grand unfinished folly on the history of Mexico, reconstructed and released in 1979 by his protege, Grigori Alexandrov. Divided into four sections: "Sandunga" covers the Tehuantepec jungles and its inhabitants; "Manguei" is about a peasant and his bride; "Fiesta" devotes itself to bullfighting and romance; and "Soldadera" depicts the 1910 Mexican revolution through frescoes. Along with "Greed" and "Napoleon," it remains as one of cinema's greatest irrecoverable casualties. Russian narration with English subtitles. **85m/B VHS, Beta.** RU D: Sergei Eisenstein, Grigori Alexandrov. *KIV*

Queen Bee 🐾🐾½ **1955** Crawford is at her manipulative best as Southern belle Eva Phillips, married to wealthy Georgia mill owner Avery (Sullivan). The ruthless Eva is despised by her bitter, tippling husband who finds a chance at romance when cousin Jennifer (Marlow) comes to visit. Naturally, Eva can't stand any competition, though she doesn't care about Avery, and tries to break up the duo even as she seeks to renew her own affair with a former lover (Ireland). Based on the novel by Edna Lee. **94m/B VHS, Closed Caption.** Joan Crawford, Barry Sullivan, John Ireland, Lucy Marlow, Betsy Palmer, Fay Wray; **D:** Ranald MacDougall; **W:** Ranald MacDougall; **C:** Charles B(ryant) Lang; **M:** George Duning. Nominations: Academy Awards '55: Best Black and White Cinematography, Best Costume Design (B & W).*COL*

Queen Boxer 🐾 **1973 (R)** A female kickboxer beats up those who reprehensibly enslaved her family. **92m/C VHS, Beta.** Judy Lee, Peter Yang Kwan. *ART*

Queen Christina 🐾🐾🐾½ **1933** A stylish, resonant star vehicle for Garbo, portraying the 17th-century Swedish queen from ascension to the throne to her romance with a Spanish ambassador. Alternately hilarious and moving, it holds some of Garbo's greatest and most memorable moments. Gilbert's second to last film and his only successful outing after the coming of sound. **101m/B VHS, Beta, LV.** Greta Garbo, John Gilbert, Lewis Stone, Sir C. Aubrey Smith, Ian Keith, Reginald Owen, Elizabeth Young; **D:** Rouben Mamoulian; **C:** William H. Daniels. *MGM*

Queen for a Day 🐾🐾½ *Horsie* **1951** Three differing vignettes, based on a rather notorious radio and TV game show of the time, in which "deserving" (or sufficiently pathetic) working-class women were rewarded for their sel-

flessness. Part one concerns a perfect suburban family whose son contracts polio. Part two has a teen spooking his immigrant parents by working as a carnival high diver to earn college cash. The finale is a Dorothy Parker farce about a homely but kindhearted nurse caring for the child of an unappreciative couple. So popular was this segment that the film was retitled after the main character. Overall, not bad considering the source. **107m/B VHS.** Phyllis Avery, Darren McGavin, Tristram Coffin, Adam Williams, Tracey Roberts, Jack Bailey, Jim Morgan, Fort Pearson; **D:** Arthur Lubin. *NOS*

Queen Kelly 🐾🐾🐾 **1929** The popularly known, slapdash version of von Stroheim's famous final film, in which an orphan goes from royal marriage to white slavery to astounding wealth. Never really finished, the film is the edited first half of the intended project, prepared for European release after von Stroheim had been fired. Even so, a campy, extravagant and lusty melodrama. Silent. **113m/B VHS, Beta, LV, 8mm.** Gloria Swanson, Walter Byron, Seena Owen, Tully Marshall, Madame Sul Te Wan; **D:** Erich von Stroheim. *NOS, KIV, VYY*

Queen Margot 🐾🐾🐾½ *La Reine Margot* **1994 (R)** Blood-soaked period of French history is duly rendered on screen in big-budget costume epic. Beautiful Catholic, Marguerite de Valois (Adjani), is the pawn of her devious mother, the widowed queen Catherine de Medici (Lisi), who skillfully manipulates unstable son Charles IX (Anglade), the nominal ruler of 1570s France, while she plots to marry Margot off to Protestant Henri de Navarre (Auteuil). Margot is contemptuous of her new husband, preferring to find her amatory amusements in the Paris streets, where she takes a handsome lover (Perez). But both Margot and Henri are united against the Queen when Catherine's minions order the murder of the rival Huguenots—a notably violent affair known as the St. Bartholomew's Day Massacre. The history's confusing, the violence graphic, the acting flamboyant, and the visuals top-notch. Based on the novel by Alexandre Dumas. French with subtitles; originally released at 161 minutes.*CW:* Nudity; strong sexuality; graphic scenes of massacre. **135m/C VHS, LV.** FR Isabelle Adjani, Daniel Auteuil, Virna Lisi, Jean-Hugues Anglade, Vincent Perez, Pascal Greggory, Miguel Bose, Dominique Blanc, Claudio Amendola, Asia Argento, Julien Rassam, Jean-Claude Brialy; **D:** Patrice Chereau; **W:** Patrice Chereau, Daniele Thompson; **M:** Goran Bregovic. Cannes Film Festival '94: Special Jury Prize, Best Actress (Lisi); Cesar Awards '95: Best Actress (Adjani), Best Cinematography, Best Costume Design, Best Supporting Actor (Anglade), Best Supporting Actress (Lisi); Nominations: Academy Awards '94: Best Costume Design; British Academy Awards '95: Best Foreign Film; Cesar Awards '95: Best Director (Chereau), Best Film, Best Supporting Actress (Blanc); Golden Globe Awards '95: Best Foreign Film. *MAX*

Queen of Diamonds 🐾🐾 **198?** A woman pulls off the biggest diamond heist of all time. **90m/C VHS, Beta.** Claudia Cardinale, Stanley Baker, Henri Charriere. *NO*

Queen of Diamonds 🐾🐾 **1991** The "Queen of Diamonds" is an alienated blackjack dealer in Vegas who, in between dealing cards, casually searches for her missing husband and looks after an old man in a motel. **77m/C VHS.** Tinka Menkes; **D:** Nina Menkes; **W:** Nina Menkes. *FCT*

Queen of Hearts 🐾🐾🐾½ **1989 (PG)** Excellent, original romantic comedy is a directorial triumph for Amiel in his first feature. An Italian couple defy both their families and marry for love. Four children later, we find them running a diner in England. Humorous, dramatic, sad—everything a move can and should be. Fine performances. **112m/C VHS, Beta, LV.** GB Anita Zagaria, Joseph Long, Eileen Way, Vittorio Duse, Vittorio Amandola, Ian Hawkes; **D:** Jon Amiel; **M:** Michael Convertino. *NO*

The Queen of Mean 🐾½ *Leona Helmsley: The Queen of Mean* **1990** Tabloid TV-movie based on Ransdell Pierson's scandal-sheet bio of the hotel magnate and convicted tax cheat. See Leona connive. See Leona bitch. See Leona get hers.

What's the point? If you ask that you're too bright to watch. **94m/C VHS, Closed Caption.** Suzanne Pleshette, Lloyd Bridges, Bruce Weitz, Joe Regalbuto; *D:* Richard Michaels; *D:* Thomas Baer.

Queen of Outer Space woof! 1958 Notorious male-chauvinist sci-fi cheapie starts out slow, but then the laughs keep coming as the cast plays the hyperdumb material straight. Space cadets crash on Venus, find it ruled by women—and the dolls have wicked plans in store for mankind. Don't be surprised if you've seen the sets before since they were borrowed from "Forbidden Planet," "World Without End," and "Flight to Mars." **80m/C VHS, Beta.** Zsa Zsa Gabor, Eric Fleming, Laurie Mitchell, Paul Birch, Barbara Darrow, Dave Willcock, Lisa Davis, Patrick Waltz, Marilyn Buferd, Marjorie Durant, Lynn Cartwright, Gerry Gaylor; *D:* Edward L. Bernds. *FOX*

The Queen of Spades 🎬🎬🎬 1949 Mystical drama about a Russian soldier who ruins his life searching for winning methods of card playing. Well-made version of the Pushkin story. **95m/B VHS, LV.** *GB* Anton Walbrook, Edith Evans, Ronald Howard, Mary Jerrold, Yvonne Mitchell, Anthony Dawson; *D:* Thorold Dickinson. *NO*

Queen of the Amazons 🎬½ 1947 A girl searches for her fiance and finds him reluctantly held captive by a tribe of women who rule the jungle. **60m/B VHS, Beta, LV.** Robert Lowery, Patricia Morison, J. Edward Bromberg, John Miljan. *SNC, NOS*

Queen of the Jungle 🎬 1935 Re-edited adventure serial featuring a white woman cast off in a hot-air balloon and landing in Africa, where she is hailed as a Queen. High camp, starring ex-Our Ganger Korman. **85m/B VHS, Beta, 8mm.** Mary Kornman, Reed Howes; *D:* Robert F. "Bob" Hill. *VYY, NOS, MLB*

Queen of the Road 🎬🎬 1984 A feisty Aussie schoolteacher starts a new life as a tractor-trailer driver. **96m/C VHS, Beta.** *AU* Joanne Samuel, Amanda Muggleton; *D:* Bruce Best. *ART, VES*

Queen of the Stardust Ballroom 🎬🎬🎬 1975 Well-made television drama about a lonely widow who goes to a local dance hall, where she meets a man and begins an unconventional late love. **98m/C Beta.** Maureen Stapleton, Charles Durning, Michael Strong, Charlotte Rae, Sam O'Steen; *D:* Michael Brandon; *M:* Billy Goldenberg.

Queenie 🎬🎬½ 1987 Television miniseries loosely based on the life of actress Merle Oberon, exploring her road to stardom. Based on the best-selling novel by Michael Korda, Oberon's nephew by marriage. Many long, dry passages fit for leaving the room for snacks. **233m/C VHS.** Mia Sara, Kirk Douglas, Martin Balsam, Claire Bloom, Chaim Topol, Joel Grey, Sarah Miles, Joss Ackland; *D:* Larry Peerce; *M:* Georges Delerue. *VTR*

Queens Logic 🎬🎬½ 1991 (R) Ensemble comedy in the tradition of "The Big Chill" featuring the trials and tribulations of the "old-neighborhood" gang, who gather again on hometurf and reminisce. Most of the film centers around Olin and girlfriend Webb and whether or not he will chicken out of their wedding. Not bad comedy, with Mantegna delivering most of the good lines. **116m/C VHS, LV, Closed Caption.** John Malkovich, Kevin Bacon, Jamie Lee Curtis, Linda Fiorentino, Joe Mantegna, Ken Olin, Tom Waits, Chloe Webb, Ed Marinaro, Kelly Bishop, Tony Spiridakis; *D:* Steve Rash; *W:* Tony Spiridakis; *M:* Joe Jackson. *ART*

Querelle 🎬🎬½ 1983 (R) Querelle, a handsome sailor, finds himself involved in a bewildering environment of murder, drug smuggling, and homosexuality in the port of Brest. Highly stylized and erotic sets, along with a dark look, give the film an interesting feel. Nice performances by Davis, Nero, and Moreau. Fassbinder's controversial last film, based on the story by Jean Genet. Strange, difficult narrative (such as it is), alternately boring and engrossing. **106m/C VHS, Beta.** *GE* Brad Davis, Jeanne Moreau, Franco Nero, Laurent Malet; *D:* Rainer Werner Fassbinder; *M:* Peer Raben. *COL, GLV*

The Quest 🎬🎬 1986 (PG) Australian film never released theatrically in the United States. A young boy (Thomas, of "E.T." fame) raised in the outback investigates a local Aboriginal superstition about a monster living in an ancient cemetery. Not bad, just dull. **94m/C VHS, Beta, Closed Caption.** *AU* Henry Thomas, Tony Barry, John Ewart, Rachel Friend, Tamsin West, Dennis Miller, Katya Manning; *D:* Brian Trenchard-Smith. *NLC*

The Quest 🎬🎬 1996 (PG-13) In his directorial debut, Van Damme plays pickpocket Christopher Dubois, who finds his adventures just beginning when he hops a freighter heading for the Far East in order to escape police trouble. He learns about a prestigious martial arts competition, where the prize could set him up for life, if he can manage to get into the invitation-only event. After many films set in the future, Van Damme chose to set this one in the '20s, with fairly good results. He piles on the beautiful location shots until the inevitable martial arts melee toward the end. Pacing is sketchy but Van Damme does display directorial talent.*CW:* Adventure violence and martial arts fights. **95m/C VHS, LV, Letterbox, Closed Caption, DVD.** Jean-Claude Van Damme, Roger Moore, Aki Aleong, James Remar, Jack McGee, Janet Gunn, Abdel Qissi, Louis Mandylor; *D:* Jean-Claude Van Damme; *W:* Stuart Klein, Paul Mones; *C:* David Gribble; *M:* Randy Edelman. *USH*

Quest for Camelot 🎬🎬½ 1998 (G) Camelot's future lies in the hands of heroine Kayley who sees an opportunity to win a spot at King Arthur's roundtable when Excalibur is stolen by evil knight Ruber (Oldman). On her quest to recover the sword, she meets a range of characters including blind hermit Garrett and two-headed dragon Devon and Cornwall (Idle and Rickles). With an all-star cast, this first full-length animated feature from Warner Bros. wants to be a contender for the Disney animation crown, but can't quite overcome its familar story, one-dimensional villain, and forgettable songs. Kayley and Garrett are strong, non-stereotypical characters that children and adults will welcome, and there are some bona fide chuckles from the mismatched Idle and Rickles that add to the film's likeable, innocent appeal. Based on the children's novel "The King's Damosel" by Vera Chapman. **85m/C VHS.** *D:* Frederick Du Chan; *W:* Kirk De Micco, William Schifrin, Jacqueline Feather, David Seidler; *M:* Patrick Doyle; *V:* Jessalyn Gilsig, Cary Elwes, Gary Oldman, Eric Idle, Don Rickles, Jane Seymour, Pierce Brosnan, Gabriel Byrne, Bronson Pinchot, Jaleel White, John Gielgud. *NYR*

Quest for Fire 🎬🎬🎬 1982 (R) An interesting story sans the usual dialogue thing. A group of men during the Ice Age must wander the land searching for fire after they lose theirs fending off an attack. During their quest, they encounter and battle various animals and tribesmen in order to survive. The special language they speak was developed by Anthony Burgess, while the primitive movements were Desmond "The Naked Ape" Morris. Perlman went on to become the Beast in TV's "Beauty and the Beast"; Chong is the daughter of Tommy Chong of the comic duo Cheech and Chong. **75m/C VHS, Beta, LV, Letterbox.** *FR* Everett McGill, Ron Perlman, Nameer El-Kadi, Rae Dawn Chong; *D:* Jean-Jacques Annaud; *W:* Gerard Brach. Academy Awards '82: Best Makeup; Genie Awards '83: Best Actress (Chong). *FOX*

Quest for Love 🎬🎬½ 1971 Quirky sci-fi story of a man who passes through a time warp and finds himself able to maintain two parallel lives. Based on John Wyndham's short story. **90m/C VHS, Beta.** *GB* Joan Collins, Tom Bell, Denholm Elliott, Laurence Naismith; *D:* Ralph Thomas. *NO*

Quest for the Mighty Sword 🎬 1990 (PG-13) A warrior battles dragons, demons and evil wizards. **94m/C VHS, Beta, LV.** Eric Allen Kramer, Margaret Lenzey, Donald O'Brien, Dina Marrone, Chris Murphy; *D:* David Hills. *COL*

Quest of the Delta Knights 🎬🎬1½ 1993 (PG) Swashbuckling fantasy about a kingdom suffering under an evil ruler and his equally sinister queen. They are opposed by the heroic Delta Knights whose only chance to defeat the fiendish powers of darkness is by unearthing a legendary storehouse containing technology from the age of Atlantis and all the powers of the Ancients. **97m/C VHS.** David Warner, Olivia Hussey, Corbin Allred, Brigid Conley Walsh, David Kriegel; *D:* James Dodson; *W:* Redge Mahaffey.

A Question of Attribution 🎬🎬½ 1991 Sir Anthony Blunt (Fox) is an internationally respected art expert who also serves as an art adviser to Queen Elizabeth II. His life unravels when an on-going British Intelligence investigation reveals him to be the fourth man in the Burgess-Maclean-Philby scandal involving Englishmen who spied for, and eventually defected to, the USSR. The investigation of Blunt's covert past is paralleled with his own art investigation of a painting attributed to Titian. Three men are depicted in the art work—with a fourth male figure discovered to have been painted over. Alan Bennett adapted his play for the television drama. **90m/C VHS.** *GB* James Fox, David Calder, Geoffrey Palmer, Prunella Scales, Mark Payton, Jason Flemyng, Edward De Souza, Ann Beach; *D:* John Schlesinger; *W:* Alan Bennett. *FOX*

Question of Faith 🎬🎬½ 1993 A happily married woman is diagnosed with a rare form of cancer. Much to her family's dismay, she turns to some unconventional medical therapies in order to heal herself. Based on a true story. Basically noble, Archer and Neill lift this tearjerker out of most of its maudlin aspects. **90m/C VHS, Closed Caption.** Anne Archer, Sam Neill, Frances Lee McCain, James Tolkan, James Hong, CCH Pounder, Louis Giambalvo, Norman Parker, Michael Constantine; *D:* Stephen Gyllenhaal; *W:* Bruce Hart. *WOV*

A Question of Guilt 🎬🎬 1978 When her child turns up dead, a free-wheeling divorcee is the prime suspect. Made-for-television soaper. **100m/C VHS.** Tuesday Weld, Ron Leibman, Peter Masterson, Alex Rocco, Viveca Lindfors, Lana Wood; *D:* Robert Butler. *ART*

Question of Honor 🎬🎬½ 1980 Under governmental pressures, an honest narcotics cop decides to inform on his department's corruption. Co-written and produced by ex-cop Sonny Grosso, on whom "The French Connection" was based. Made for television and based on the book, "Point Blank," by Grosso and Philip Rosenberg. **134m/C VHS, Beta.** Ben Gazzara, Paul Sorvino, Robert Vaughn, Tony Roberts, Danny Aiello, Anthony Zerbe; *D:* Jud Taylor; *W:* Budd Schulberg. *NO*

A Question of Love 🎬🎬🎬 1978 Fine performances in this well-done television movie about two lesbians—one of whom is fighting her ex-husband for custody of their child. **100m/C VHS.** Gena Rowlands, Jane Alexander, Ned Beatty, Clu Gulager, Bonnie Bedelia, James Sutorius, Jocelyn Brando; *D:* Jerry Thorpe; *M:* Billy Goldenberg. *NO*

Question of Silence 🎬🎬🎬 *De Stilte Rond Christine M* 1983 (R) Three women, strangers to each other, stand trial for a murdering a man. Intricately analyzed courtroom drama with much to say about male domination. In Dutch with English subtitles or dubbed. **92m/C VHS, Beta.** *NL* Cox Habrema, Nelly Frijda, Henriette Tol, Edda Barends; *D:* Marleen Gorris. *FRF*

Qui Etes Vous, Mr. Sorge? 🎬🎬 1961 The story of German journalist Richard Sorge, who was hanged by the Japanese in 1944 for being a Soviet spy. Uninteresting docudrama which focuses on the opinions of various witnesses as to the accuracy of the espionage charge. In French with English subtitles. **130m/B VHS, Beta.** *FR* Thomas Holtzman, Keiko Kishi; *D:* Andre Girard. *BAR*

Quick 🎬🎬½ **1993 (R)** Polo stars as Quick, a professional assassin whose latest job is Herschel (Donovan), a mob accountant turned federal witness. When Quick is double-crossed, she takes off with Herschel as her insurance and a couple of bad guys (Fahey and Davi) on her trail. Not too much sex and lots of violence to go along with the fast pacing. **99m/C VHS.** Teri Polo, Martin Donovan, Jeff Fahey, Robert Davi, Tia Carrere; **D:** Rick King; **W:** Frederick Bailey; **M:** Robert Sprayberry.

The Quick and the Dead 🎬🎬 **1987** Based on a Louis L'Amour story, this made-for-cable western features a lone gunslinger who protects a defenseless settler's family from the lawless West, only to become a source of sexual tension for the wife. **91m/C VHS, Beta.** Sam Elliott, Tom Conti, Kate Capshaw, Kenny Morrison, Matt Clark; **D:** Robert Day; **M:** Stephen Dorff. **ORI, WAR**

The Quick and the Dead 🎬🎬 **1994 (R)** Stone is a tough gal gunslinger (ala a female Clint Eastwood) out to avenge the murder of her father. Ellen arrives in the frontier town of Redemption where arch-villain Herod (Hackman) rules by means of violence and intimidation. Director Raimi packs in so many cliches that you're amazed that it's not a parody of the spaghetti westerns it tries to emulate. Maybe if Stone and Raimi didn't take this film so seriously, it would have been a better movie. One redeeming quality of the film is its wildly staged gunfights. **CW:** Extreme gunplay violence. **105m/C VHS, LV, 8mm, Closed Caption.** Sharon Stone, Gene Hackman, Leonardo DiCaprio, Russell Crowe, Kevin Conway, Lance Henriksen, Roberts Blossom, Pat Hingle, Keith David, Michael Stone; **Cameos:** Gary Sinise; **D:** Sam Raimi; **W:** Simon Moore; **C:** Dante Spinotti. **COL**

Quick Change 🎬🎬½ **1990 (R)** Murray, Davis, and Quaid form bumbling trio of New York bank robbers who can't seem to exit the Big Apple with loot. Based on Jay Cronley's book, it's Murray's directing debut (with help from screenwriter Franklin). Engaging minor caper comedy displaying plenty of NYC dirty boulevards. **89m/C VHS, Beta, LV, 8mm, Closed Caption.** Bill Murray, Geena Davis, Randy Quaid, Jason Robards Jr., Bob Elliott, Victor Argo, Kathryn Grody, Philip Bosco, Phil Hartman, Kurtwood Smith, Jamey Sheridan; **D:** Bill Murray, Howard Franklin; **W:** Howard Franklin; **C:** Michael Chapman; **M:** Randy Edelman, Howard Shore. **WAR**

Quick, Let's Get Married woof! **Seven Different Ways; The Confession 1971** Quick, let's not watch this movie. Even the people who made it must have hated it: they waited seven years to release it. Rogers runs a whorehouse; Eden is a gullible, pregnant prostitute; Gould in his big-screen debut(!) is a deaf-mute. A must-not-see. **96m/C VHS, Beta, LV.** Ginger Rogers, Ray Milland, Barbara Eden, Carl Schell, Michael Ansara, Walter Abel, Scott Meyer, Cecil Kellaway, Elliott Gould; **D:** William Dieterle. **NO**

Quicker Than the Eye 🎬🎬 **1988** When a magician gets mixed up in an assassination plot, he must use his wit, cunning, and magic to get out of it. **94m/C VHS, Beta.** Ben Gazzara, Mary Crosby, Catherine Jarrett, Ivan Desny, Eb Lottimer, Sophie Carle, Wolfram Berger, Dinah Hinz, Jean Yanne; **D:** Nicolas Gessner.

Quicksand 🎬🎬½ **1950** Mechanic Rooney borrows $20 from his boss's cash register, intending to return it. One thing leads to another, the plot thickens, and it's downhill (for Rooney) from there. Good, tense suspense drama. **79m/B VHS.** Mickey Rooney, Peter Lorre, Jeanne Cagney; **D:** Irving Pichel. **EEL, NOS, MRV**

Quicksand: No Escape 🎬🎬 **1991 (PG-13)** Scott Reinhardt (Matheson) is a successful architect whose partner decides to secure a building contract by bribing a city official. When his partner is murdered Reinhardt is approached by a former cop (Sutherland) asking a lot of money for some incriminating evidence. Reinhardt is then drawn ever deeper into the illicit dealings, endangering his life. **93m/C VHS, Beta, LV, Closed Caption.** Tim Matheson, Donald Sutherland, Jay Acovone,

Timothy Carhart, John Finn, Marc Alaimo, Felicity Huffman, Al Pugliese; **D:** Michael Pressman; **W:** Peter Baloff, Dave Wollert. **USH**

Quicksilver 🎬½ **1986 (PG)** A young stockbroker loses all, then quits his job to become a city bicycle messenger. Pointless, self-indulgent yuppie fantasy. **106m/C VHS, Beta, LV, Closed Caption.** Kevin Bacon, Jami Gertz, Paul Rodriguez, Rudy Ramos, Andrew Smith, Gerald S. O'Loughlin, Laurence "Larry" Fishburne, Louie Anderson; **D:** Tom Donnelly; **W:** Tom Donnelly; **M:** Tony Banks. **COL**

Quiet Cool 🎬 **1986 (R)** When his former girlfriend's family is killed, a New York cop travels to a sleepy California town run by a pot-growing tycoon. He subsequently kills the bad guys in a Rambo-like fit of vengeance. Dopey exercise in sleepy-eyed bloodshed. **80m/C VHS, Beta, LV.** James Remar, Daphne Ashbrook, Adam Coleman Howard, Jared Martin, Fran Ryan; **D:** Clay Borris; **W:** Clay Borris; **M:** Jay Michael Ferguson. **COL**

Quiet Day In Belfast 🎬🎬🎬 **1974** Tragedy occurs when northern Irish patriots and British soldiers clash in an Irish betting parlor. Kidder plays a dual role: an Irish woman in love with a British soldier and the woman's twin sister. Convincingly adapted from a Canadian stage play. **92m/C VHS, Beta.** **CA** Barry Foster, Margot Kidder; **D:** Milad Bessada.

A Quiet Duel 🎬🎬 **A Silent Duel; Shizuka Naru Ketto 1949** Kyoji (Mifune), a young, idealistic doctor working as an army surgeon, contracts syphilis from the blood of a patient during an operation. Because the disease was virtually incurable at the time, the tormented Kyoji abandons his fiance and decides to dedicate himself to his work. Based on a play by Kazuo Kikuta. Japanese with subtitles. **95m/B VHS.** **JP** Toshiro Mifune, Takashi Shimura, Kenjiro Uemura; **D:** Akira Kurosawa; **W:** Senkichi Taniguhi, Akira Kurosawa; **M:** Akira Ifukube. **FCT**

The Quiet Earth 🎬🎬🎬 **1985 (R)** Serious science fiction film about a scientist who awakens to find himself seemingly the only human left on earth as the result of a misfired time/space government experiment. He later finds two other people, a girl and a Maori tribesman, and must try to repair the damage in order to save what's left of mankind. **91m/C VHS, Beta, LV, Closed Caption.** **NZ** Bruno Lawrence, Alison Routledge, Peter Smith; **D:** Geoff Murphy; **W:** Bruno Lawrence, Sam Pillsbury, Bill Baer; **M:** John Charles. **FOX**

Quiet Fire 🎬½ **1991 (R)** A health-club owner tries to get the goods on the arms-dealing congressman who killed his best friend. Hilton-Jacobs looks properly pumped up since his sweathog days on TV's "Welcome Back Kotter." **100m/C VHS.** Lawrence-Hilton Jacobs, Robert Z'Dar, Nadia Marie, Karen Black, Lance Lindsay; **D:** Lawrence-Hilton Jacobs. **PMH**

The Quiet Man 🎬🎬🎬🎬 **1952** The classic incarnation of Hollywood Irishness, and one of Ford's best, and funniest films. Wayne is Sean Thornton, a weary American ex-boxer who returns to the Irish hamlet of his childhood and tries to take a spirited lass as his wife, despite the strenuous objections of her brawling brother (McLaglen). Thornton's aided by the leprechaun-like Fitzgerald and the local parish priest, Bond. A high-spirited and memorable film filled with Irish stew, wonderful banter, and shots of the lush countryside. Listen for the Scottish bagpipes at the start of the horse race, a slight geographic inaccuracy. **129m/C VHS, LV, Closed Caption.** John Wayne, Maureen O'Hara, Barry Fitzgerald, Victor McLaglen, Arthur Shields, Jack MacGowran, Ward Bond, Mildred Natwick, Ken Curtis, Mae Marsh, Sean McClory, Francis Ford; **D:** John Ford; **W:** Frank Nugent; **C:** Archie Stout; **M:** Victor Young. Academy Awards '52: Best Color Cinematography, Best Director (Ford); Directors Guild of America Awards '52: Best Director (Ford); Venice Film Festival '52: Best Director (Ford); Nominations: Academy Awards '52: Best Art Direction/Set Decoration (Color), Best Picture, Best Screenplay, Best Sound, Best Supporting Actor (McLaglen). **REP, TLF, CCB**

The Quiet Room 🎬🎬 **1996 (PG)** A nameless seven-year-old girl (Chloe Ferguson) refuses to speak when she learns her constantly quarreling parents are separating. Film is shown from only the child's perspective and her fantasies of a different life as she goes about her daily routine. Although the girl remains silent, she answers her parents in her thoughts (the voiceover lets the viewer into the girl's world) and she has flashbacks to her younger self (played by Ferguson's sister Phoebe) and when her parents loved each other. **91m/C VHS, LV, Closed Caption.** **AU** Chloe Ferguson, Celine O'Leary, Paul Blackwell, Phoebe Ferguson; **D:** Rolf de Heer; **W:** Rolf de Heer; **C:** Tony Clark; **M:** Graham Tardiff. **NLC**

Quiet Thunder 🎬 **1987 (PG-13)** A hard-drinking bush pilot in Africa and a beautiful senator's wife are thrown together on the run after both witness an assassination. Mindless, thoroughly derivative "adventure." **94m/C VHS, Beta, LV.** Wayne Crawford, June Chadwick, Victor Steinbach; **D:** David Rice. **ART**

Quigley Down Under 🎬🎬½ **1990 (PG-13)** A Western sharpshooter moves to Australia in search of employment. To his horror, he discovers that he has been hired to kill aborigines. Predictable action is somewhat redeemed by the terrific chemistry between Selleck and San Giacomo and the usual enjoyable theatrics from Rickman as the landowner heavy. **121m/C VHS, Beta, LV, 8mm, Letterbox, Closed Caption.** **AU** Tom Selleck, Laura San Giacomo, Alan Rickman, Chris Haywood, Ron Haddrick, Tony Bonner, Roger Ward, Ben Mendelsohn, Jerome Ehlers, Conor McDermottroe; **D:** Simon Wincer; **W:** John Hill; **C:** David Eggby; **M:** Basil Poledouris. **MGM**

The Quiller Memorandum 🎬🎬🎬 **1966** An American secret agent travels to Berlin to uncover a deadly neo-Nazi gang. Refreshingly different from other spy tales of its era. Good screenplay adapted from Adam Hall's novel, "The Berlin Memorandum." **103m/C VHS, Beta, Closed Caption.** George Segal, Senta Berger, Alec Guinness, Max von Sydow, George Sanders; **D:** Michael Anderson Sr.; **W:** Harold Pinter; **M:** John Barry. **FOX**

Quilombo 🎬🎬½ **1984** The title refers to a legendary settlement of runaway slaves in 17th-century Brazil; an epic chronicles its fortunes as leadership passes from a wise ruler to a more militant one who goes to war against the government. Stunning scenery, tribal images, and folk songs, but the numerous characters seldom come to life as personalities. One of Brazil's most expensive films, in Portuguese with English subtitles. **114m/C VHS.** **BR** Vera Fischer, Antonio Pompeo, Zeze Motta, Toni Tornado; **D:** Carlos Diegues; **W:** Carlos Diegues. **NYF, FCT**

Quintet 🎬🎬 **1979** Atypical Altman sci-fi effort. The stakes in "Quintet," a form of backgammon, are high—you bet your life. Set during the planet's final ice age. Newman and wife Fossey wander into a dying city and are invited to play the game, with Fossey losing quickly. Bizarre and pretentious, with heavy symbolic going. **118m/C VHS, Beta.** Paul Newman, Bibi Andersson, Fernando Rey, Vittorio Gassman, David Langton, Nina Van Pallandt, Brigitte Fossey; **D:** Robert Altman; **W:** Lionel Chetwynd, Patricia Resnick, Robert Altman, Frank Barhydt. **FOX**

Quiz Show 🎬🎬🎬🎬 **1994 (PG-13)** Redford's intelligent, entertaining, and morally complex film about the TV game show scandals of the late '50s is his most accomplished work to date. At the center of the film is Charles Van Doren (Fiennes), an intellectual, golden boy who dethrones Herbert Stempel (Turturro), the reigning champion of the rigged "Twenty-One." The program's sponsor felt Stempel, a nerdy Jewish grad's everyman qualities were wearing thin and wanted a more polished image, which they found in handsome, sophisticated Van Doren. Federal investigator Goodwin (Morrow) suspects Van Doren's reign is a sham and sets out to expose him as a fraud. Acting is of the highest caliber with Fiennes, Turturro, and Morrow all giving beautiful performances. Notable among supporting cast is Scofield as Van Doren's Pulitzer prize-winning father. With strong script and gorgeous lensing, this modern Faust story is a brilliant reflection on corporate greed, class rivalry, and the powers of television. Based on the book "Remembering America: A Voice From the Sixties" by Richard N. Goodwin. **CW:** Some strong language. **133m/C VHS, LV, Closed Caption.** John Turturro, Rob Morrow, Ralph Fiennes, Paul Scofield, David Paymer, Hank Azaria, Christopher McDonald, Johann Carlo, Elizabeth Wilson, Mira Sorvino, Griffin Dunne, Martin Scorsese, Barry Levinson; *D:* Robert Redford; *W:* Paul Attanasio; *C:* Michael Ballhaus; *M:* Mark Isham. British Academy Awards '94: Best Adapted Screenplay; New York Film Critics Awards '94: Best Film; Nominations: Academy Awards '94: Best Adapted Screenplay, Best Director (Redford), Best Picture, Best Supporting Actor (Scofield); Directors Guild of America Awards '94: Best Director (Redford); Golden Globe Awards '95: Best Director (Redford), Best Film—Drama, Best Screenplay, Best Supporting Actor (Turturro); Writers Guild of America '94: Best Adapted Screenplay. *HPH*

Quo Vadis 🐾🐾½ 1912 One of the first truly huge Italian silent epics. The initial adaptation of the Henryk Sienkiewicz novel about Nero and ancient Rome. Probably the cinema's first great financial success. **45m/B VHS, Beta.** *D:* Enrico Guazzoni. *FCT*

Quo Vadis 🐾🐾🐾 1951 Larger-than-life production about Nero and the Christian persecution. Done on a giant scale: features exciting fighting scenes, romance, and fabulous costumes. Definitive version of the classic novel by Henryk Siekiewicz. Remade for Italian television in 1985. **171m/C VHS, Beta, Closed Caption.** Robert Taylor, Deborah Kerr, Peter Ustinov, Patricia Laffan, Finlay Currie, Abraham Sofaer, Marina Berti, Buddy Baer, Felix Aylmer, Nora Swinburne; *Cameos:* Sophia Loren, Elizabeth Taylor; *D:* Mervyn LeRoy; *C:* Robert L. Surtees; *M:* Miklos Rozsa. Golden Globe Awards '52: Best Supporting Actor (Ustinov); Nominations: Academy Awards '51: Best Art Direction/Set Decoration (Color), Best Color Cinematography, Best Costume Design (Color), Best Film Editing, Best Picture, Best Supporting Actor (Ustinov), Best Original Dramatic/Comedy Score. *MGM, IGP*

Quo Vadis 🐾🐾½ 1985 (R) Third screen version of Henryk Sienkiewicz's book. See the other two first. This one is slow and perfunctory. Brandauer is memorable as Nero; Quinn (in the lead) is the son of Anthony. **122m/C VHS, Beta, LV.** *IT* Klaus Maria Brandauer, Frederic Forrest, Christina Raines, Marie Therese Relin, Francesco Quinn, Barbara DeRossi, Phillippe LeRoy, Max von Sydow, Gabriele Ferzetti, Massimo Girotti, Leopoldo Trieste; *D:* Franco Rossi.

Rabbit Test 🐾½ 1978 (PG) In Rivers' first directorial effort, a clumsy virginal guy becomes the world's first pregnant man. So irreverent it's almost never in good taste, and so poorly written it's almost never funny. **86m/C VHS, Beta, LV.** Billy Crystal, Roddy McDowall, Imogene Coca, Paul Lynde, Alex Rocco, George Gobel; *D:* Joan Rivers. *COL*

Rabid 🐾🐾½ *Rage* 1977 (R) A young girl undergoes a radical plastic surgery technique and develops a strange and unexplained lesion in her armpit. She also finds she has an unusual craving for human blood. **90m/C VHS, Beta.** *CA* Marilyn Chambers, Frank Moore, Joe Silver, Howard Ryshpan, Patricia Gage, Susan Roman; *D:* David Cronenberg; *W:* David Cronenberg; *C:* Rene Verzier. *WAR*

Rabid Grannies woof! 1989 (R) Wicked satire about two aging sisters who receive a surprise birthday gift from their devilworshipping nephew. The gift turns their party into a gorefest as they rip into various family members—literally. Any humor will be lost on any but the most diehard Troma fans. Dubbed. **89m/C VHS, Beta, LV.** *BE* Catherine Aymerie, Caroline Brackman, Danielle Daven, Raymond Lescot, Anne Marie Fox, Richard Cotica, Patricia Davie; *D:* Emmanuel Kervyn; *W:* Emmanuel Kervyn. *VTR*

Race for Glory 🐾½ 1989 (R) A young motorcyclist builds a super-bike he hopes will help him win a world championship race. Will he win? Can you stand the suspense? Let's just say

there's a happy ending. **102m/C VHS, Beta.** Alex McArthur, Peter Berg, Pamela Ludwig; *D:* Rocky Lang; *M:* Jay Michael Ferguson. *HBO*

Race for Life 🐾½ *Mask of Dust* 1955 A race car driver attempts to make a comeback despite objections from his wife. He races around Europe (great scenery); she leaves him; he tries to win her back and salvage his career. Standard, ungripping story. Car scenes are great. **69m/B VHS, Beta, LV.** *GB* Richard Conte, Mari Aldon, George Coulouris; *D:* Terence Fisher. *NO*

Race for Your Life, Charlie Brown 🐾🐾½ 1977 (G) Another in the popular series of "Peanuts" character films. This one features Charlie Brown, Snoopy, and all the gang spending an exciting summer in the American wilderness. **76m/C VHS, Beta, LV.** *D:* Bill Melendez, Phil Roman; *W:* Charles M. Schulz; *M:* Ed Bogas; *V:* Gail Davis, Melanie Kohn, Duncan Watson, Gregory Felton, Stuart Brotman, Liam Martin, Ed Bogas. *PAR*

Race the Sun 🐾🐾 1996 (PG) There's nothin' new under this sun. Tired story of a group of young losers who band together to beat the odds and compete in an unusual contest is trotted out once again for populist amusement. This time it's a Hawaiian high school solar car team traveling to Australia to go for the prize against the big shots and snobs. Based on true events, it features some nice scenery from Berry and the main locations, but not much else. Uninspired but basically harmless, this one's fine for the kids. **100m/C VHS, LV, Closed Caption.** Halle Berry, James Belushi, Casey Affleck, Eliza Dushku, Kevin Tighe, Anthony Michael Ruivivar, J. Moki Cho, Dion Basco, Sara Tanaka, Nadja Pionilla, Steve Zahn, Bill Hunter; *D:* Charles Kanganis; *W:* Barry Morrow; *C:* David Burr; *M:* Graeme Revell. *COL*

Race to Freedom: The Story of the Underground Railroad 🐾🐾½ 1994 Story of four fugitive slaves, in 1850, who struggle to get from North Carolina to the safety of Canada through a network of safe-houses and people willing to risk smuggling them to asylum. Made for cable TV. **90m/C VHS.** Courtney B. Vance, Janet Bailey, Glynn Turman, Michael Riley, Dawnn Lewis, Ron White; *Cameos:* Tim Reid; *D:* Don McBrearty; *W:* Nancy Trite Botkin, Diana Braithwaite. *XVC*

Race with the Devil 🐾½ 1975 (PG) Vacationers are terrorized by devil worshippers after they witness a sacrificial killing. Heavy on car chases; light on plot and redeeming qualities. Don't waste your time. **88m/C VHS, Beta, Closed Caption.** Peter Fonda, Warren Oates, Loretta Swit, Lara Parker, R.G. Armstrong; *D:* Jack Starrett; *W:* Wes Bishop, Lee Frost; *C:* Robert C. Jessup. *FOX, FCT*

The Racers 🐾🐾½ *Such Men are Dangerous* 1955 Douglas brings power to the role of a man determined to advance to the winners' circle. Exciting European location photography, but not much plot. **112m/C VHS, Closed Caption.** Gilbert Roland, Kirk Douglas, Lee J. Cobb, Cesar Romero, Bella Darvi; *D:* Henry Hathaway; *W:* Alex North. *FOX, FCT*

Rachel and the Stranger 🐾🐾🐾 1948 A God-fearing farmer declares his love for his wife when a handsome stranger (Mitchum) nearly woos her away. Well-cast, well-paced, charming Western comedy-drama. **93m/B VHS, Beta, LV.** Loretta Young, Robert Mitchum, William Holden, Gary Gray; *D:* Norman Foster. *TTC*

The Rachel Papers 🐾🐾🐾 1989 (R) Based on the Martin Amis novel, this is the funny/sad tale of an Oxford youth who plots via his computer the seduction of a beautiful American girl. For anyone who has ever loved someone just out of their reach. **92m/C VHS, Beta, Closed Caption.** Dexter Fletcher, Ione Skye, James Spader, Jonathan Pryce, Bill Paterson, Michael Gambon, Lesley Sharp; *D:* Damian Harris; *W:* Damian Harris; *M:* Chaz Jankel. *FOX*

Rachel, Rachel 🐾🐾🐾½ 1968 (R) Rachel teaches by day, wearing simple, practical dresses and her hair up. By night she caters to her domineering mother by preparing refreshments for her parties. This sexually repressed, spinster school-

teacher, however, gets one last chance at romance in her small Connecticut town. Woodward mixes just the right amounts of loneliness and sweetness in the leading role. A surprising award-winner that was an independent production of Newman. Based on Margaret Laurence's "A Jest of God." **102m/C VHS, Beta.** Joanne Woodward, James Olson, Estelle Parsons, Geraldine Fitzgerald, Donald Moffat; *D:* Paul Newman; *W:* Stewart Stern. Golden Globe Awards '69: Best Actress—Drama (Woodward), Best Director (Newman); New York Film Critics Awards '68: Best Actress (Woodward), Best Director (Newman); Nominations: Academy Awards '68: Best Actress (Woodward), Best Adapted Screenplay, Best Picture, Best Supporting Actress (Parsons). *WAR*

Rachel River 🐾🐾½ 1987 (PG-13) A divorced radio personality struggles to make something of her life in her small Minnesota town. **88m/C VHS, LV.** Pamela Reed, Craig T. Nelson, Viveca Lindfors, James Olson, Zeljko Ivanek, Jo Henderson, Alan North, Jon DeVries; *D:* Sandy Smolan; *W:* Judith Guest; *M:* Arvo Part.

Rachel's Man 🐾 1975 A big-screen version of the Biblical love story of Jacob and Rachel. **115m/C VHS, Beta.** Mickey Rooney, Rita Tushingham, Leonard Whiting; *D:* Moshe Mizrahi. *ART*

Racing Luck 🐾 *Red Hot Tires* 1935 While working at a race track, a man is framed and forced to work for another stable. **56m/B VHS, Beta.** William Boyd, Barbara Worth, George Ernest, Esther Muir, Dick Curtis; *D:* Sam Newfield. *GPV*

Racing with the Moon 🐾🐾🐾 1984 (PG) Sweet, nostalgic film about two buddies awaiting induction into the Marines in 1942. They have their last chance at summer romance. Benjamin makes the most of skillful young actors and conventional story. Great period detail. Keep your eyes peeled for glimpses of many rising young stars including Hannah and Carvey. **108m/C VHS, Beta, LV, Closed Caption.** Sean Penn, Elizabeth McGovern, Nicolas Cage, John Karlen, Rutanya Alda, Max Casey Adams Showalter, Crispin Glover, Suzanne Adkinson, Page Hannah, Michael Madsen, Dana Carvey, Carol Kane, Michael Talbott; *D:* Richard Benjamin; *W:* Steven Kloves; *C:* John Bailey; *M:* Dave Grusin. *PAR*

The Racket 🐾🐾🐾 1951 Police captain Mitchum tries to break up mob racket of gangster Ryan. Internecine strife on both sides adds complexity. Mitchum and especially Ryan are super; fine, tense melodrama. **88m/B VHS, Beta, LV.** Robert Ryan, Robert Mitchum, Lizabeth Scott, Ray Collins, William Conrad, Don Porter; *D:* John Cromwell. *TTC*

The Racketeer 🐾🐾½ 1929 A racketeer falls in love with a pretty girl and attempts to win her over. As part of his plan, the gangster arranges to help the girl's boyfriend begin his musical career in exchange for the girl's promise to marry him. **68m/C VHS, Beta.** Carole Lombard, Robert Armstrong, Hedda Hopper; *D:* Howard Higgin. *SNC, NOS, CAB*

Racketeers of the Range 🐾½ 1939 Cattleman fights a crooked attorney who wants to sell his client's stock to a large meat packing company. **62m/B VHS, Beta.** George O'Brien, Marjorie Reynolds, Chill Wills, Ray Whitley; *D:* David Ross Lederman.

Racquet 🐾 1979 Tennis pro Convy searches for true love and a tennis court to call his own in Beverly Hills. Lame, sophomoric, and unfunny. **87m/C VHS, Beta.** Bert Convy, Edie Adams, Lynda Day George, Phil Silvers, Bobby Riggs, Bjorn Borg, Tanya Roberts; *D:* David Winters. *NO*

Rad 🐾½ 1986 (PG) Teenage drama revolving around BMX racing and such dilemmas as: can the good guys beat the bad guys, who's got the fastest bike, must you cheat to win, and should our hero miss his SAT tests to compete in "the big race.." Directed by stunt-expert Needham. **94m/C VHS, Beta, LV, Closed Caption.** Bill Allen, Bart Conner, Talia Shire, Jack Weston, Lori Loughlin; *D:* Hal Needham; *W:* Sam Bernard. *NLC*

Radar Men from the Moon *Retik, the Moon Menace* 1952 Commando Cody, with his jet-pack, fights to defend the earth from invaders from the moon. Twelve-episode serial on two tapes. Silly sci-fi. **152m/B VHS, LV.** George Wallace, Aline Towne, Roy Barcroft, William "Billy" Bakewell, Clayton Moore; **D:** Fred Brannon. *NOS, REP, SNC*

Radar Patrol vs. Spy King 1949 Special agent Alyn and his buxom Vargas girl Jean Dean battle the deadly Baroda and his ring of saboteurs, hell-bent on destroying America. 12 episodes of the serial edited onto two cassettes. **167m/B VHS.** Kirk Alyn, Jeanne Dean. *REP, MLB*

Radar Secret Service *♂♂½* 1950 Two servicemen witness the hijacking of a truck loaded with nuclear material. **59m/B VHS, Beta, LV.** John Howard, Adele Jergens, Tom Neal, Ralph Byrd. *NO*

Radio Days *♂♂♂* 1987 (PG) A lovely, unpretentious remembrance of the pre-television radio culture. Allen tells his story in a series of vignettes centering around his youth in Brooklyn, his eccentric extended family, and the legends of radio they all followed. The ubiquitous Farrow is a young singer hoping to make it big. **96m/C VHS, Beta, LV.** Mia Farrow, Dianne Wiest, Julie Kavner, Michael Tucker, Wallace Shawn, Josh Mostel, Tony Roberts, Jeff Daniels, Kenneth Mars, Seth Green, William Magerman, Diane Keaton, Renee Lippin, Danny Aiello, Gina DeAngelis, Kitty Carlisle Hart, Mercedes Ruehl, Tito Puente; **D:** Woody Allen; **W:** Woody Allen; **C:** Carlo DiPalma. Nominations: Academy Awards '87: Best Art Direction/Set Decoration, Best Original Screenplay. *HBO*

Radio Flyer *♂♂½* 1992 (PG-13) It's 1969 and Mike and Bobby have just moved to northern California with their divorced mom. Everything would be idyllic if only their mother hadn't decided to marry a drunken child abuser who beats Bobby whenever the mood strikes him. Mike decides to help Bobby escape by turning their Radio Flyer wagon into a magic rocketship that will carry Bobby to safety, but ultimately proves tragic. Appealing version of childhood dreams sans the child abuse angle (toned down though it was), which is abruptly and unsatisfactorily handled. **114m/C VHS, LV, Closed Caption.** Elijah Wood, Joseph Mazzello, Lorraine Bracco, Adam Baldwin, John Heard, Ben Johnson; **D:** Richard Donner. *COL*

Radio Inside *♂♂½* 1994 Aimless Matthew (McNamara) comes to live with older brother Michael (Walsh) after their dad's death. Matthew needs someone to listen to him but, unfortunately, his picks his brother's neglected girlfriend Natalie (Shue). Aimless story, as well. Made for cable TV. **91m/C VHS, LV, Closed Caption.** William McNamara, Dylan Walsh, Elisabeth Shue, Gil Goldstein; **D:** Jeffrey Bell; **W:** Jeffrey Bell. *MGM*

Radio Patrol 1937 Plenty of action and thrills abound in this 12-chapter serial. Pinky Adams, radio cop, is assisted by his trusty canine partner, Irish (Silverwolf). A cop's best friend is his dog. **235m/B VHS, Beta.** Mickey Rentschler, Adrian Morris, Monte Montague, Jack Mulhall, Grant Withers, Catherine Hughes; **D:** Ford Beebe, Cliff Smith. *NOS, VDM, MLB*

Radioactive Dreams *♂♂* 1986 (R) Surreal, practically senseless fantasy wherein two men, trapped in a bomb shelter for 15 years with nothing to read but mystery novels, emerge as detectives into a post-holocaust world looking for adventure. **94m/C VHS, Beta, LV.** John Stockwell, Michael Dudikoff, Lisa Blount, George Kennedy, Don Murray, Michelle Little; **D:** Albert Pyun; **W:** Albert Pyun. *ART, VES*

Radioland Murders *♂♂½* 1994 (PG) Looks overwhelm weak plot in this mystery-comedy about 1939 Chicago radio station WBN. Lots of stock types (befuddled director, preening announcer, lusty vamp) with Masterson as Penny, the secretary holding everything together except for her marriage to head writer Roger (Benben). Then bodies start piling up during the live broadcast and everyone runs around frantically trying to solve the crimes and keep the broadcast going. Tiring and cliched. **112m/C VHS, LV, Closed Caption.**

Brian Benben, Mary Stuart Masterson, Ned Beatty, George Burns, Brion James, Michael Lerner, Michael McKean, Jeffrey Tambor, Scott Michael Campbell, Anita Morris, Stephen Tobolowsky, Christopher Lloyd, Larry Miller, Corbin Bernsen; **Cameos:** Robert Klein, Harvey Korman, Peter MacNicol, Joey Lawrence, Bob(cat) Goldthwait; **D:** Mel Smith; **W:** Willard Huyck, Gloria Katz, Jeff Reno, Ron Osborn; **C:** David Tattersall; **M:** Joel McNeely. *USH*

Rafferty & the Gold Dust Twins *♂½* *Rafferty and the Highway Hustlers* 1975 (R) Two women kidnap a motor vehicle inspector at gunpoint in Los Angeles and order him to drive to New Orleans. En route, they become pals. Wandering, pointless female buddy flick. **91m/C VHS, Beta, Closed Caption.** Alan Arkin, Sally Kellerman, MacKenzie Phillips, Charles Martin Smith, Harry Dean Stanton; **D:** Dick Richards; **M:** Artie Butler. *WAR*

The Raffle *♂♂½* 1994 (R) Frank and David travel the globe to find the world's most beautiful woman, who'll be the prize date of the lucky guy with the winning raffle ticket. **CW:** Some strong language; nudity. **100m/C VHS, LV.** Nicholas Lea, Bobby Dawson, Jennifer Clement, Teri-Lynn Rutherford, Jay Underwood, Mark Hamill; **D:** Gavin Wilding; **W:** John Fairley; **M:** Robert O. Ragland. *APX*

Raffles *♂♂♂* 1930 Debonair and dashing gentleman thief A.J. Raffles (Coleman) is a famed cricket player by day and a cat burglar by night, who's always been successful at eluding Scotland Yard. Then he falls for beautiful socialite Lady Gwen Manders (Francis) and gets invited to a weekend house party where Lady Kitty Melrose (Skipworth) just happens to own a very valuable necklace and one of the other guests is suspicious Scotland Yard inspector McKenzie (Torrance). Naturally Raffles goes after the jewels. Based on the novel "The Amateur Cracksman" by Ernest William Hornung. Director D'Arrast was fired by producer Goldwyn and Fitzmaurice finished the film. **72m/B VHS.** Ronald Colman, Kay Francis, Alison Skipworth, David Torrence, Bramwell Fletcher, Frances Dade; **D:** Harry D'Abbadie D'Arrast, George Fitzmaurice; **W:** Sidney Howard; **C:** George Barnes, Gregg Toland. *HBO*

The Rag Nymph *♂♂½* *Catherine Cookson's The Rag Nymph* 1996 Aggie Winkowski finds 10-year-old Millie Forrester abandoned on the streets. Knowing how dangerous the child's life could become, Aggie decides to take Millie in. TV movie based on the novel by Catherine Cookson. **150m/C VHS.** *GB* Honeysuckle Weeks, Val McLane, Alec Newman, Perdita Weeks, Crispin Bonham Carter. *VCO*

Rage *♂♂* 1972 (PG) Scott's directorial debut. A military helicopter sprays peace-loving rancher Scott and his son with nerve gas. The son's death is covered up; the rancher embarks on a vengeful rampage. Scott's sudden transformation to avenging killer is implausible and overwrought. **100m/C VHS, Beta.** George C. Scott, Richard Basehart, Martin Sheen, Barnard Hughes, Kenneth Tobey, Ed Lauter, Nicholas Beauvy, Dabbs Greer; **D:** George C. Scott; **C:** Fred W. Koenekamp. *WAR*

Rage *♂* 1980 Well-acted, well-written, nerve-wracking drama about a convicted rapist who finds help through difficult therapy. Focuses on how the sex-offender discovers the "whys" behind his assaults. Made for television. **100m/C VHS, Beta.** David Soul, James Whitmore, Yaphet Kotto, Caroline McWilliams, Vic Tayback, Sharon Farrell, Craig T. Nelson, Garry Walberg; **D:** William A. Graham; **C:** Allen Daviau. *WAR*

Rage *♂½* 1995 (R) When Alex Gainer (Daniels) is kidnapped he becomes the target of a high-tech lab experiment. Injected with chemicals that induce blind and killing rages, Alex escapes and unwillingly goes on a murderous rampage. Now he must find the antidote and clear his name before it happens again. **CW:** Non-stop action/violence, language. **94m/C VHS, Closed Caption.** Gary Daniels, Ken Tigar, Jillian McWhirter, Fiona Hutchinson, Peter Jason, Mark Metcalf; **D:** Joseph Merhi; **W:** Jacobsen Hart, Joseph John Barmettler Jr.; **C:** Ken Blakey; **M:** Louis Febre. *PMH*

The Rage *♂♂* 1996 (R) Nick Travis (Lamas) is a burned-out FBI agent with a brand new partner Kelly McCord (Cloke), who has no field experience, and a tough assignment. He's after a gang of anti-government killers led by psycho Dacy (Busey). Good action sequences substitute for the lack of plot sense. **CW:** Strong violence, including some grisly images of mutilated victims, and for strong language. **95m/C VHS, Closed Caption.** Lorenzo Lamas, Gary Busey, Kristen Cloke, Roy Scheider; **D:** Sidney J. Furie. *TOU*

Rage and Honor *♂♂* 1992 (R) Rothrock stars as Kris Fairfield, a high-school teacher who spends her spare time tutoring students in the martial-arts. Her present students are a group of cops, including Aussie visitor Preston Michaels. When Michaels witnesses a drug deal, he gets set-up by the dealers for a murder he didn't commit and only Kris can help him prove his innocence. **CW:** Language and violence. **93m/C VHS, LV, Letterbox, Closed Caption.** Cynthia Rothrock, Richard Norton, Brian Thompson, Terri Treas, Catherine Bach, Alex Datcher; **D:** Terence H. Winkless; **W:** Terence H. Winkless. *COL, PMS*

Rage and Honor 2: Hostile Takeover *♂♂½* 1993 (R) Rothrock returns as black-belt CIA operative Kris Fairfield, whose latest assignment takes her to Jakarta where a banker is involved in a large-scale drug money laundering operation. She teams up with Preston Michaels (Norton), a renegade Australian cop, and winds up following a trail that leads to a fortune in diamonds and lots of trouble. **98m/C VHS.** Cynthia Rothrock, Richard Norton, Patrick Muldoon, Frans Tumbuan, Ron Vreeken, Alex Tumundo; **D:** Guy Norris; **W:** Louis Sun, Steven Reich. *COL*

Rage at Dawn *♂♂½* *Seven Bad Men* 1955 An outlaw gang is tracked by a special agent who must "bend" the rules a little in order to get the bad guys. Not surprisingly, he gets his girl as well. A solid standard of the genre, with some clever plot twists. **87m/C VHS.** Randolph Scott, Forrest Tucker, Mala Powers, J. Carrol Naish, Edgar Buchanan; **D:** Tim Whelan. *NOS, MRV, HEG*

A Rage in Harlem *♂♂♂* 1991 (R) The crime novels of Chester A. Himes were translated into the best movies of the early '70s blaxploitation era. Now, a Himes story gets the big budget Hollywood treatment with juice and aplomb. A voluptuous lady crook enters Harlem circa 1950 with a trunkful of stolen gold sought by competing crooks, and the chase is on, with one virtuous soul (Whitaker) who only wants the girl. Great cast and characters, much humor, but unsparing in its violence. **CW:** Language, violence, and sensuality. **108m/C VHS, LV, Closed Caption.** Forest Whitaker, Gregory Hines, Robin Givens, Zakes Mokae, Danny Glover, Tyler Collins, Ron Taylor, T.K. Carter, Willard Pugh, Samm-Art Williams, Jay Hawkins, Badja Djola, John Toles-Bey, Stack Pierce, George Wallace; **D:** Bill Duke; **W:** John Toles-Bey, Bobby Crawford; **M:** Elmer Bernstein. *HBO, FCT*

Rage of Angels *♂♂* 1983 Lengthy television miniseries adaptation of the Sidney Sheldon novel about an ambitious female attorney, her furs, and her men. Followed by "Rage of Angels: The Story Continues" (1986). **192m/C VHS, Beta.** Jaclyn Smith, Ken Howard, Armand Assante, Ronald Hunter, Kevin Conway, George Coe, Deborah May; **D:** Buzz Kulik; **M:** Billy Goldenberg. *COL*

Rage of Angels: The Story Continues *♂♂* 1986 In this sequel to the Sidney Sheldon trash-with-flash television miniseries, Smith reprises her role as the beautiful lady lawyer who always gets involved with the wrong men. This time she tries to hide the fact of her illegitimate son from his father, who's about to become Vice President of the United States. **200m/C VHS.** Jaclyn Smith, Ken Howard, Michael Nouri, Susan Sullivan, Brad Dourif, Angela Lansbury, Mason Adams; **D:** Paul Wendkos; **C:** Jack Priestley; **M:** Billy Goldenberg. *VTR*

Rage of Honor 🎬 1987 **(R)** A high-kicking undercover cop seeks vengeance on bad guys for his partner's murder. Standard of its type; why bother? 92m/C VHS, Beta. Sho Kosugi, Lewis Van Bergen, Robin Evans, Gerry Gibson; **D:** Gordon Hessler; **W:** Wallace C. Bennett. *VTR*

The Rage of Paris 🎬🎬🎬 1938 Scheming ex-actress and head waiter hope to gain by helping a beautiful French girl (Darrieux) snag a rich hubby. She comes to her senses, realizing that love, true love, matters more than wealth. Well-acted, quaint comedy. 78m/B VHS, Beta. Danielle Darrieux, Douglas Fairbanks Jr., Mischa Auer, Helen Broderick; **D:** Henry Koster; **C:** Joseph Valentine. *NOS, DVT, CAB*

Rage of Wind 🎬 1982 Master boxer seeks revenge on a Japanese commandant who kidnaps his wife during WWII. 97m/C VHS, Beta. Chen Hsing, Yasuka Kurata, Irene Ryder. *WVE*

Rage to Kill 🎬½ 1988 **(R)** Jingoistic retelling of the 1982 Grenada invasion, complete with helpless American med students. Good-guy race car driver whips them into shape to fight the Soviet-supplied general (he's the bad guy). Guess who wins. 94m/C VHS, Beta. Oliver Reed, James Ryan, Henry Cele, Cameron Mitchell; **D:** David Winters.

Raggedy Ann and Andy: A Musical Adventure 🎬 1977 **(G)** The fun-filled exploits of America's favorite fictional dolls, transformed into an enchanting animated musical. Includes 16 songs by Joe Raposo. 87m/C VHS, Beta, Closed Caption. **D:** Richard Williams; **V:** Didi Conn, Joe Silver. *FOX*

Raggedy Man 🎬🎬🎬 1981 **(PG)** Spacek in her signature role as a lonely small-town woman. Here she's raising two sons alone in a small Texas town during WWII. Spacek's strong acting carries a well-scripted story, unfortunately marred by an overwrought ending. 94m/C VHS, Beta, LV. Sissy Spacek, Eric Roberts, Sam Shepard, Tracey Walter, William Sanderson, Henry Thomas; **D:** Jack Fisk; **W:** William D. Wittliff; **C:** Ralf Bode; **M:** Jerry Goldsmith. *USH*

The Raggedy Rawney 🎬🎬½ 1990 **(R)** A young Army deserter dresses in women's clothing and hides out as a mad woman with a band of gypsies. Good first directing effort by English actor Bob Hoskins. Unpretentious and engaging. 102m/C VHS. Bob Hoskins, Dexter Fletcher, Zoe Nathenson, David Hill, Ian Dury, Zoe Wanamaker, J.G. Devlin, Perry Fenwick; **D:** Bob Hoskins; **W:** Bob Hoskins, Nicole De Wilde; **M:** Michael Kamen.

Ragin' Cajun 🎬 1990 Retired kickboxer is forced into a death match to save his girlfriend. 91m/C VHS. David Heavener, Charlene Tilton, Sam Bottoms, Samantha Eggar; **D:** William B. Hillman. *HHE*

Raging Angels 🎬 1995 **(R)** L.A. couple Chris (Flanery) and Lila (Mazur) are struggling rock 'n' rollers when Lila gets a job as a backup singer to star Colin (Pare), who's part of a cult called the Coalition for World Unity. Turns out they're a recruiting org for Satan and are looking for new souls. Our young duo are aided by flamboyant evangelist Sister Kate (Ladd) but it all comes down to a sky battle over downtown L.A. between a good angel and a satanic creature. Lots of unintentional laughs. The director wisely opted for the industry's Smithee pseudonym. **CW:** Language and some violence. 97m/C VHS, Closed Caption. Sean Patrick Flanery, Monet Mazur, Michael Pare, Diane Ladd, Shelley Winters, Arielle Dombasle; **D:** Alan Smithee; **W:** Kevin Rock, David Markov, Chris Bittler; **C:** Bryan England; **M:** Terry Plumeri. *THV*

Raging Bull 🎬🎬🎬🎬 1980 **(R)** Scorsese's depressing but magnificent vision of the dying American Dream and suicidal macho codes in the form of the rise and fall of middleweight boxing champ Jake LaMotta, a brutish, dull-witted animal who can express himself only in the ring and through violence. A photographically expressive, brilliant drama, with easily the most intense and brutal boxing scenes ever filmed. De Niro provides a vintage performance, going from the young LaMotta to the aging has-been, and is ably accompanied by Moriarty as his girl and Pesci as his loyal, much beat-upon bro. 128m/B VHS, Beta, LV, 8mm, Letterbox, DVD. Robert De Niro, Cathy Moriarty, Joe Pesci, Frank Vincent, Nicholas Colasanto, Theresa Saldana; **D:** Martin Scorsese; **W:** Paul Schrader, Mardik Martin; **C:** Michael Chapman. Academy Awards '80: Best Actor (De Niro), Best Film Editing; Golden Globe Awards '81: Best Actor—Drama (De Niro); Los Angeles Film Critics Association Awards '80: Best Actor (De Niro), Best Film; National Board of Review Awards '80: Best Actor (De Niro), Best Supporting Actor (Pesci), National Film Registry '90;; New York Film Critics Awards '80: Best Film (De Niro), Best Actor (De Niro), Best Supporting Actor (Pesci, Pesci); National Society of Film Critics Awards '80: Best Cinematography, Best Director (Scorsese), Best Supporting Actor (Pesci); Nominations: Academy Awards '80: Best Cinematography, Best Director (Scorsese), Best Picture, Best Sound, Best Supporting Actor (Pesci), Best Supporting Actress (Moriarty). *MGM, FOX, BTV*

Rags to Riches 🎬 1987 A wealthy Beverly Hills entrepreneur decides to improve his public image by adopting six orphan girls. TV pilot. 96m/C VHS, Beta. Joseph Bologna, Tisha Campbell. *VTR*

Ragtime 🎬🎬🎬 1981 **(PG)** The lives and passions of a middle class family weave into the scandals and events of 1906 America. A small, unthinking act represents all the racist attacks on one man, who refuses to back down this time. Wonderful period detail. From the E.L. Doctorow novel, but not nearly as complex. Features Cagney's last film performance. 156m/C VHS, Beta, LV. Howard E. Rollins Jr., Kenneth McMillan, Brad Dourif, Mary Steenburgen, James Olson, Elizabeth McGovern, Pat O'Brien, James Cagney, Debbie Allen, Jeff Daniels, Moses Gunn, Donald O'Connor, Mandy Patinkin, Norman Mailer; **D:** Milos Forman; **W:** Michael Weller; **M:** Randy Newman. Nominations: Academy Awards '81: Best Adapted Screenplay, Best Art Direction/Set Decoration, Best Cinematography, Best Costume Design, Best Song ("One More Hour"), Best Supporting Actor (Rollins), Best Supporting Actress (McGovern), Best Original Score. *PAR, FCT*

Raid on Entebbe 🎬🎬🎬 1977 **(R)** Dramatization of the Israeli rescue of passengers held hostage by terrorists at Uganda's Entebbe Airport in 1976. A gripping actioner all the more compelling because true. Finch received an Emmy nomination in this, his last film. Made for television. 113m/C VHS, Beta. Charles Bronson, Peter Finch, Horst Buchholz, John Saxon, Martin Balsam, Jack Warden, Yaphet Kotto, Sylvia Sidney; **D:** Irvin Kershner; **C:** Bill Butler; **M:** David Shire. *NO*

Raid on Rommel 🎬½ 1971 **(PG)** A British soldier (Burton) poses as a Nazi and tries to infiltrate Rommel's team with his rag-tag brigade of misfits. Predictable drivel. Contains action footage from the 1967 film "Tobruk." 98m/C VHS, Beta. Richard Burton, John Colicos, Clinton Greyn, Wolfgang Preiss; **D:** Henry Hathaway. *USH*

Raiders in Action 🎬 1971 Tale following the activities of a band of allied commandos in the closing days of the war. 89m/C VHS, Beta. Paul Smith. *TWE*

Raiders of Atlantis 🎬 *The Atlantis Interceptors* 1983 Battles break out when the lost continent surfaces in the Caribbean. The warriors in these apocalyptic frays deploy atomic arsenals. 100m/C VHS, Beta. Christopher Connelly; **D:** Roger Franklin.

Raiders of Ghost City 🎬½ 1944 Serial in 13 chapters involves a Union Secret Service Agent when a ring of gold robbers who are posing as Confederate soldiers during the end of the Civil War. ?m/C VHS. Dennis Moore, Lionel Atwill, Regis Toomey, Wanda McKay. *MOV*

Raiders of Red Gap 🎬½ 1943 A cattle company tries running homesteaders off their land to get control of it. The Lone Rider saves the day. 56m/B VHS, Beta. Al "Fuzzy" St. John, Bob Livingston. *DVT, VYY, VCN*

Raiders of Sunset Pass 🎬🎬 1943 Wartime western quickie makes an interesting novelty today. With most cowboys off fighting the Axis, the ladies form the Women's Army of the Plains to watch out for 4-F rustlers. 57m/B VHS. Eddie Dew, Smiley Burnette, Jennifer Holt, Roy Barcroft, Mozelle Cravens, Beverly Aadland, Nancy Worth, Kenne Duncan, Jack Rockwell, Budd Buster, Jack Ingram; **D:** John English. *NOS, HEG*

Raiders of the Border 🎬 1944 A white-hatted cowboy must prevent the takeover of a trading post. 55m/B VHS, Beta. Johnny Mack Brown, Raymond Hatton, Ellen Hall. *VDM*

Raiders of the Lost Ark 🎬🎬🎬🎬 1981 **(PG)** Classic '30s-style adventure reminiscent of early serials spawned two sequels and numerous rip-offs. Made Ford a household name as dashing hero and intrepid archeologist Indiana Jones. He battles mean Nazis, decodes hieroglyphics, fights his fear of snakes, and even has time for a little romance in his quest for the biblical Ark of the Covenant. Allen is perfectly cast as his feisty ex-flame, more than a little irritated with the smooth talker who dumped her years earlier. Asks viewers to suspend belief as every chase and stunt tops the last. Unrelated opening sequence does a great job of introducing the character. Followed by "Indiana Jones and the Temple of Doom." 115m/C VHS, Beta, LV, 8mm, Closed Caption. Harrison Ford, Karen Allen, Wolf Kahler, Paul Freeman, John Rhys-Davies, Denholm Elliott, Ronald Lacey, Anthony Higgins, Alfred Molina; **D:** Steven Spielberg; **W:** George Lucas, Philip Kaufman; **M:** John Williams. Academy Awards '81: Best Art Direction/Set Decoration, Best Film Editing, Best Sound, Best Visual Effects; Nominations: Academy Awards '81: Best Cinematography, Best Director (Spielberg), Best Picture, Best Original Score. *PAR*

Raiders of the Sun 🎬 1992 **(R)** After the Earth has been ruined in a biological disaster, a futuristic warrior arrives to help restore world peace and order. Cheap "Mad Max" ripoff. **CW:** Language, war violence, and sensuality. 80m/C VHS, Closed Caption. Richard Norton, Rick Dean, William Steis, Blake Boyd, Brigitta Stenberg; **D:** Cirio H. Santiago. *NHO*

Railroaded 🎬🎬 1947 The police seek a demented criminal who kills his victims with perfumed-soaked bullets. Tense, excellent noir Anothony Mann crime drama. 72m/B VHS, Beta, LV. John Ireland, Sheila Ryan, Hugh Beaumont, Ed Kelly; **D:** Anthony Mann. *KIV, NOS, DVT*

Railrodder 🎬🎬🎬 1965 Buster Keaton as the railroader in this slapstick short fumbles his way across Canada. As in the days of the silents, he speaks not a word. 25m/C VHS, Beta. Buster Keaton. *NFB*

The Railway Children 🎬🎬🎬½ 1970 At the turn of the century in England, the father of three children is framed and sent to prison during Christmas. The trio and their mother must survive on a poverty stricken farm near the railroad tracks. They eventually meet a new friend who helps them prove their father's innocence. Wonderfully directed by Jeffries. From the classic Edith Nesbitt children's novel. 104m/C VHS, Beta. GB Jenny Agutter, William Mervyn, Bernard Cribbins, Dinah Sheridan, Iain Cuthbertson, Sally Thomsett, Peter Bromilow, Ann Lancaster, Gary Warren, Gordon Whiting, David Lodge; **D:** Lionel Jeffries. *NO*

The Railway Station Man 🎬🎬🎬 1992 Set in present-day Ireland. Christie plays a widowed artist struggling to put her life back together after her husband's death in a terrorist bombing. She meets a mysterious American (Sutherland) who's working on restoring the local railway station and finds herself falling in love. When she stumbles upon an IRA bombing plot she also finds out some unpleasant truths about her new lover. Wonderful performances, tragic story. Shot on location in County Donegal, Northern Ireland. Based on the novel by Jennifer Johnston. Made for cable television. 93m/C VHS, Beta, LV, Closed Caption. Julie Christie, Donald Sutherland, John Lynch, Mark Tandy, Frank McCusker, Niall Cusack; **D:** Michael Whyte; **W:** Shelagh Delaney. *TTC*

Rain 🎬🎬½ **1932** W. Somerset Maugham's tale of a puritanical minister's attempt to reclaim a "lost woman" on the island of Pago Pago. Crawford and Huston work up some static. Remake of the 1928 silent film "Sadie Thompson." Remade again in 1953 as "Miss Sadie Thompson." **92m/B VHS, Beta.** Joan Crawford, Walter Huston, William Gargan, Guy Kibbee, Beulah Bondi, Walter Catlett; **D:** Lewis Milestone. *MON, NOS, CNG*

The Rain Killer 🎬 **1990 (R)** Big city cop and fed don goloshes to track serial killer who slays rich ladies during heavy precipitation. Soggy story. **94m/C VHS, LV.** Ray Sharkey, David Beecroft, Maria Ford, Woody Brown, Tania Coleridge; **D:** Ken Stein; **W:** Ray Cunneff. *COL*

Rain Man 🎬🎬🎬½ **1988 (R)** When his father dies, ambitious and self-centered Charlie Babbit finds he has an older autistic brother who's been institutionalized for years. Needing him to claim an inheritance, he liberates him from the institution and takes to the road, where both brothers undergo subtle changes. The Vegas montage is wonderful. Critically acclaimed drama and a labor of love for the entire cast. Cruise's best performance to date as he goes from cad to recognizing something wonderfully human in his brother and himself. Hoffman is exceptional. **128m/C VHS, Beta, LV, 8mm, Closed Caption, DVD.** Dustin Hoffman, Tom Cruise, Valeria Golino, Jerry Molen, Jack Murdock, Michael D. Roberts, Ralph Seymour, Lucinda Jenney, Bonnie Hunt, Kim Robillard, Beth Grant; **D:** Barry Levinson; **W:** Ronald Bass, Barry Morrow; **C:** John Seale; **M:** Hans Zimmer. Academy Awards '88: Best Actor (Hoffman), Best Director (Levinson), Best Original Screenplay, Best Picture; Berlin International Film Festival '88: Golden Berlin Bear; Directors Guild of America Awards '88: Best Director (Levinson); Golden Globe Awards '89: Best Actor—Drama (Hoffman), Best Film—Drama; Nominations: Academy Awards '88: Best Art Direction/Set Decoration, Best Cinematography, Best Film Editing, Best Original Score. *MGM, BTV, HMV*

The Rain People 🎬🎬🎬 **1969 (R)** Pregnant housewife Knight takes to the road in desperation and boredom; along the way she meets retarded ex-football player Caan. Well directed by Coppola from his original script. Pensive drama. **102m/C VHS, Beta.** Shirley Knight, James Caan, Robert Duvall; **D:** Francis Ford Coppola; **W:** Francis Ford Coppola; **C:** Bill Butler. *WAR*

Rain Without Thunder 🎬🎬½ **1993 (PG-13)** Imagine the year 2042, a time when abortion is illegal and a fertilized egg has full Constitutional rights. Now imagine sitting through an 87 minute fake documentary that follows the story of a mother and daughter team who have been jailed for trying to go to Sweden so that the daughter can get an abortion. A one-sided, militant pro-choice effort that is neither entertaining nor informational.**CW:** Theme. **87m/C VHS.** Betty Buckley, Jeff Daniels, Ali Thomas, Frederic Forrest, Carolyn McCormick, Linda Hunt, Robert Earl Jones, Graham Greene, Iona Morris, Austin Pendleton; **D:** Gary Bennett; **W:** Gary Bennett; **M:** Randall Lynch, Allen Lynch. *ORI*

Rainbow 🎬🎬 **1978** Broadway's "Annie" is badly miscast as Judy Garland from her early years in vaudeville to her starring years at M.G.M. Based on the book by Christopher Finch. Made for television; directed by sometime Garland flame Jackie Cooper. **100m/C VHS, Beta, LV.** Andrea McArdle, Jack Carter, Don Murray; **D:** Jackie Cooper; **M:** Charles Fox. *NO*

The Rainbow 🎬🎬🎬 **1989 (R)** Mature, literate rendering of the classic D.H. Lawrence novel about a young woman's sexual awakening. Beautiful cinematography. Companion/prequel to director Russell's earlier Lawrence adaptation, "Women in Love" (1969). **104m/C VHS, LV.** *GB* Sammi Davis, Amanda Donohoe, Paul McGann, Christopher Gable, David Hemmings, Glenda Jackson, Kenneth Colley; **D:** Ken Russell; **W:** Vivian Russell, Ken Russell; **C:** Billy Williams; **M:** Carl Davis. *VES, IME*

Rainbow Bridge 🎬 **1971 (R)** The adventures of a group of hippies searching for their consciousness in Hawaii. Features concert footage from Jimi Hendrix's final performance. **74m/C VHS, Beta. D:** Chuck Wein. *RHI, FCT*

Rainbow Drive 🎬🎬½ **1990 (R)** Made for cable tv cop thriller promises great things but fails to deliver. Weller is a good cop trapped in the political intrigues of Hollywood. He discovers five dead bodies; when the official count is four, he detects funny business. From the novel by Roderick Thorp.**CW:** Language, violence, and sensuality. **93m/C VHS.** Peter Weller, Sela Ward, Bruce Weitz, David Caruso, James Laurenson, Chris Mulkey, Kathryn Harrold; **D:** Bobby Roth; **W:** Roderick Thorp, Bill Phillips, Bennett Cohen; **M:** Tangerine Dream. *BTV, THV*

The Rainbow Gang 🎬 **1973** A trio of unlikely prospectors heads into a legendary mine in search of riches and fame. **90m/C VHS, Beta.** Donald Pleasence, Don Calfa, Kate Reid.

Rainbow Over Broadway **1933** A former Broadway star mother is set against having her son and daughter try their luck on Broadway. **52m/C VHS.** Joan Marsh, Frank Albertson, Lucien Littlefield, Grace Hayes, Dell Henderson, Harry Myers, Gladys Blake, Glen Boles, Nat Carr; **D:** Richard Thorpe. *GPV*

Rainbow Ranch 🎬½ **1933** A Navy boxer returns home to his ranch to find murder and corruption. Needless to say, he rides off to seek revenge. **54m/B VHS.** Rex Bell, Cecilia Parker, Robert F. (Bob) Kortman, Henry Hall, Gordon DeMain; **D:** Harry Fraser. *NOS, DVT, HEG*

Rainbow Warrior 🎬🎬½ **1994 (PG)** True story of the bombing of the Greenpeace vessel and the two men who set out to solve the crime. **90m/C VHS.** Sam Neill, Jon Voight, Kerry Fox, Bruno Lawrence; **D:** Michael Tuchner.

Rainbow's End 🎬🎬 **1935** Gibson must defend Gale, the female rancher, from an evil adversary who is trying to run Gale and her invalid father off of their land. Things get complicated when Gibson discovers that Richmond works for his father! **54m/B VHS.** Hoot Gibson, June Gale, Oscar Apfel, Ada Ince, Charles Hill, Warner Richmond; **D:** Norman Spencer. *NOS, DVT*

Raining Stones 🎬🎬 **1993** A hard-up plumber becomes obsessed with buying an expensive first communion dress for his daughter and gets involved in numerous misadventures trying to get the money. Another of Loach's comedydramas about the British working class and their struggle to survive with dignity. **90m/C VHS.** *GB* Bruce Jones, Julie Brown, Ricky Tomlinson, Tom Hickey, Gemma Phoenix, Jonathan James; **D:** Ken Loach; **W:** Jim Allen; **C:** Barry Ackroyd; **M:** Stewart Copeland. Cannes Film Festival '93: Special Jury Prize; Nominations: British Academy Awards '93: Best Film. *ORI*

The Rainmaker 🎬🎬🎬 **1956** Reminiscent of "Elmer Gantry" in his masterful performance, Lancaster makes it all believable as a con man who comes to a small midwestern town and works miracles not only on the weather but on spinster Hepburn, although both were a little long in the tooth for their roles. Written by Nash from his own play. **121m/C VHS, LV, Closed Caption.** Burt Lancaster, Katharine Hepburn, Wendell Corey, Lloyd Bridges, Earl Holliman, Cameron Prudhomme, Wallace Ford; **D:** Joseph Anthony; **W:** N. Richard Nash; **C:** Charles B(ryant) Lang; **M:** Alex North. Golden Globe Awards '57: Best Supporting Actor (Holliman); Nominations: Academy Awards '56: Best Actress (Hepburn), Best Original Dramatic/Comedy Score. *PAR, CCB*

The Rains Came 🎬🎬½ **1939** Living within a loveless marriage in the mythical Indian city of Ranchipur, English socialite Loy pursues extramarital love interests, including the compassionate doctor Power, potential heir to the maharajah's throne. When an earthquake hits and brings major destruction to the city, Loy aids the doctor in helping the injured. Hankies should be kept handy. Adapted from the Louis Bromfield novel. **104m/B VHS.** Myrna Loy, Tyrone Power, George Brent,

Brenda Joyce, Nigel Bruce, Maria Ouspenskaya, Joseph Schildkraut, Laura Hope Crews, Marilyn Nash, Jane Darwell, Marjorie Rambeau, Henry Travers, H.B. Warner, William Royle, Montague Shaw, Harry Hayden, Abner Biberman, George Regas; **D:** Clarence Brown; **W:** Philip Dunne, Julien Josephson; **C:** Arthur C. Miller; **M:** Alfred Newman. Academy Awards '40: Best Special Effects (Sersen); Nominations: Academy Awards '39: Best Black and White Cinematography, Best Film Editing, Best Sound, Best Original Score. *FXV*

Raintree County 🎬🎬½ **1957** A lavish, somewhat overdone epic about two lovers caught up in the national turmoil of the Civil War. An Indiana teacher (Clift) marries a southern belle (Taylor) just after the outbreak of war. The new wife battles mental illness. Producers had hoped this would be another "Gone With the Wind." Adapted from the novel by Ross Lockridge, Jr. Film was delayed in mid-production by Clift's near-fatal and disfiguring car crash. **175m/C VHS, Beta, LV, Letterbox.** Elizabeth Taylor, Montgomery Clift, Eva Marie Saint, Lee Marvin, Nigel Patrick, Rod Taylor, Agnes Moorehead, Walter Abel; **D:** Edward Dmytryk; **C:** Robert L. Surtees. Nominations: Academy Awards '57: Best Actress (Taylor), Best Art Direction/Set Decoration, Best Costume Design, Best Score.*MGM*

Rainy Day 🎬🎬 **1979** A successful actress' return home for her father's funeral brings back unpleasant childhood memories that force her to face the truth about herself. **35m/C VHS, Beta.** Mariette Hartley. *BFA*

Raise the Red Lantern 🎬🎬🎬½ **1991 (PG)** Set in 1920s China, Zhang explores its claustrophobic world of privilege and humiliation. Songlian, an educated 19-year-old beauty, is forced into marriage as the fourth wife of a wealthy and powerful old man. She discovers that the wives have their own separate quarters and servants, and spend most of their time battling to attract their husband's attention. Over the course of a year, Songlian's fury and resentment grow until self-defeating rebellion is all she has. Gong Li is exquisite as the young woman struggling for dignity in a portrayal which is both haunting and tragic. **125m/C VHS, LV, Closed Caption.** *CH* Gong Li, Ma Jingwu, He Caifei, Cao Cuifeng, Jin Shuyuan, Kong Lin, Ding Weimin; **D:** Zhang Yimou. British Academy Awards '92: Best Foreign Film; Los Angeles Film Critics Association Awards '92: Best Cinematography; New York Film Critics Awards '92: Best Foreign Film; National Society of Film Critics Awards '92: Best Cinematography, Best Foreign Film; Nominations: Academy Awards '91: Best Foreign Language Film. *ORI, BTV*

Raise the Titanic woof! **1980 (PG)** A disaster about a disaster. Horrible script cannot be redeemed by purported thrill of the ship's emergence from the deep after 70 years. It's a shame, because the free world's security hangs in the balance. Based on Clive Cussler's best seller. **112m/C VHS, Beta, LV.** Jason Robards Jr., Richard Jordan, Anne Archer, Alec Guinness, J.D. Cannon; **D:** Jerry Jameson; **M:** John Barry. *FOX*

A Raisin in the Sun 🎬🎬🎬🎬 **1961** Outstanding story of a black family trying to make a better life for themselves in an all-white neighborhood in Chicago. The characters are played realistically and make for a moving story. Each person struggles with doing what he must while still maintaining his dignity and sense of self. Based on the Broadway play by Hansberry, who also wrote the screenplay. **128m/B VHS, Beta, LV.** Diana Sands, John Fiedler, Ivan Dixon, Louis Gossett Jr., Sidney Poitier, Claudia McNeil, Ruby Dee; **D:** Daniel Petrie; **W:** Lorraine Hansberry. National Board of Review Awards '61: Best Supporting Actress (Dee). *COL, HMV*

A Raisin in the Sun 🎬🎬🎬 **1989** An "American Playhouse," made for television presentation of the Lorraine Hansberry play about a black family threatened with dissolution by the outside forces of racism and greed when they move into an all-white neighborhood in the 1950s. **171m/C VHS, Beta, Closed Caption.** Danny Glover, Esther Rolle, Starletta DuPois; **D:** Bill Duke. *MON*

Raising Arizona 🎬🎬🎬½ 1987 (PG-13)
Hi's an ex-con and the world's worst hold-up man. Ed's a policewoman. They meet, fall in love, marry, and kidnap a baby (one of a family of quints). Why not? Ed's infertile and the family they took the baby from has "more than enough," so who will notice? But unfinished furniture tycoon Nathan Arizona wants his baby back, even if he has to hire an axe-murderer on a motorcycle to do it. A brilliant, original comedy narrated in notorious loopy deadpan style by Cage. Innovative camerawork by Barry Sonnenfeld. Wild, surreal and hilarious. **94m/C VHS, Beta, LV, Closed Caption.** Nicolas Cage, Holly Hunter, John Goodman, William Forsythe, Randall "Tex" Cobb, Trey Wilson, M. Emmet Walsh, Frances McDormand; **D:** Joel Coen; **W:** Ethan Coen, Joel Coen; **M:** Carter Burwell. *FOX*

Raising Cain 🎬🎬 1992 (R) Thriller evoking poor man's Hitchcock about a child psychiatrist who just happens to be nuts features Lithgow in five roles. Seems his supposedly dead Norwegian father has come to the United States and needs his son's help to steal babies for a child development experiment, so the son's alter ego, Cain, shows up to commit the nasty deed. Unfortunately Lithgow also catches his wife with another man, and that's when the bodies start piling up. **CW:** Language, terror violence, and sexuality. **95m/C VHS, Beta, LV, Letterbox, Closed Caption.** John Lithgow, Lolita Davidovich, Steven Bauer, Frances Sternhagen, Cindy Girard, Tom Bower, Mel Harris, Gabrielle Carteris, Barton Heyman; **D:** Brian DePalma; **W:** Brian DePalma; **C:** Stephen Burum; **M:** Pino Donaggio. *USH*

Raising Heroes 🎬🎬 1997 Josh (Sistillio) and Paul (White) are about to finalize their adoption of a child when Josh witnesses a mob hit. Now he's a target, trying to stay alive while being next on the mob's hit list and protect his family as well. **85m/C VHS.** Troy Sistillio, Henry White; **D:** Douglas Langway; **W:** Douglas Langway. *WBF*

Rambling Rose 🎬🎬🎬 1991 (R) Dern is Rose, a free-spirited, sexually liberated before her time young woman taken in by a Southern family in 1935. Rose immediately has an impact on the male members of the clan, father Duvall and son Haas, thanks to her insuppressible sexuality. This causes consternation with the strait-laced patriarch, who attempts to control his desire for the girl. Eventually Rose decides she must try to stick to one man, but this only causes further problems. Dern gives her best performance yet in this excellent period piece, and solid support is offered from the rest of the cast, in particular Duvall and Dern's real-life mother Ladd. **115m/C VHS, LV.** Laura Dern, Diane Ladd, Robert Duvall, Lukas Haas, John Heard, Kevin Conway, Robert John Burke, Lisa Jakub, Evan Lockwood; **D:** Martha Coolidge; **W:** Calder Willingham; **M:** Elmer Bernstein. Independent Spirit Awards '92: Best Director (Coolidge), Best Film, Best Supporting Actress (Ladd); Nominations: Academy Awards '91: Best Actress (Dern), Best Supporting Actress (Ladd). *ART*

Rambo: First Blood, Part 2 🎬🎬
1985 (R) If anyone can save Our Boys still held prisoner in Asia it's John Rambo. Along the way he's tortured, flexes biceps, grunts, and then disposes of the bad guys by the dozen in one of filmdom's bigger dead body parades. Mindless action best enjoyed by testosterone-driven fans of the genre. Sequel to "First Blood" (1982), followed by "Rambo 3" (1988). **93m/C VHS, Beta, LV, Closed Caption.** Sylvester Stallone, Richard Crenna, Charles Napier, Steven Berkoff, Julia Nickson-Soul, Martin Kove; **D:** George P. Cosmatos; **W:** Sylvester Stallone, James Cameron; **C:** Jack Cardiff; **M:** Jerry Goldsmith. Golden Raspberry Awards '85: Worst Picture, Worst Actor (Stallone), Worst Screenplay, Worst Song ("Peace In Our Life"). *ART*

Rambo 3 🎬½ 1988 (R) John Rambo, the famous Vietnam vet turned Buddhist monk, this time invades Afghanistan to rescue his mentor. Meets up with orphan and fights his way around the country. Typically exploitative, kill now, ask questions later Rambo attack, lacking the sheer volume of no-brainer action of the first two Rambos. At the time, the most expensive film ever made, costing $58 million. Filmed in Israel. **102m/C VHS, Beta, LV.** Sylvester Stallone, Richard Crenna, Marc De Jonge, Kurtwood Smith, Spiros Focas; **D:** Peter McDonald; **W:** Sylvester Stallone; **M:** Jerry Goldsmith. Golden Raspberry Awards '88: Worst Actor (Stallone). *ART*

Rampage 🎬🎬 1987 (R) Seemingly all-American guy Charles Reece (McArthur) goes on a murder spree, killing and then mutiliating his victims. Fraser (Biehn) is a liberal district attorney who questions his own views as he argues during the trial that Reece was sane when he committed the murders and deserves the death penalty. Director Friedkin makes no bones about his concerns that the criminal insanity defense often spares the perpetrator while denying justice to the victims. Adapted from the book by William P. Wood and loosely based on killer Richard Chase. Filmed in 1987, the movie wasn't released until 1992 due to the production company's financial difficulties. **CW:** Strong violence. **92m/C VHS, Beta, LV, Closed Caption.** Michael Biehn, Alex McArthur, Nicholas Campbell, Deborah Van Valkenburgh, John Harkins, Art LaFleur; **D:** William Friedkin; **W:** William Friedkin; **M:** Ennio Morricone. *PAR, BTV*

Ramparts of Clay 🎬🎬🎬 1971 (PG) A young woman in Tunisia walks the line between her village's traditional way of life and the modern world just after her country's independence from France. Brilliantly shot on location; exquisitely poignant. In Arabic with English subtitles. **87m/C VHS, Beta.** *FR* Jean-Louis Bertucelli. *COL*

Ramrod 🎬🎬 1947 Lake is a tough ranch owner at odds with her father, who is being manipulated by a big-time cattleman in trying to put them out of business. She fights back, and McCrea is caught in the middle as the only good guy. Nothing special. **94m/B VHS.** Veronica Lake, Joel McCrea, Arleen Whelan, Don DeFore, Preston Foster, Charlie Ruggles, Donald Crisp, Lloyd Bridges; **D:** Andre de Toth. *REP*

The Ramrodder 🎬 *Ramrodders* 1969 An adult western spoof. **92m/C VHS, Beta.** *VDM, TPV*

Ran 🎬🎬🎬🎬 1985 (R) The culmination of Kurosawa's career stands as his masterpiece. Loosely adapting Shakespeare's "King Lear," with plot elements from "Macbeth," he's fashioned an epic, heartbreaking statement about honor, ambition, and the futility of war. Aging medieval warlord Hidetora gives control of his empire to his oldest son, creating conflict with two other sons. Soon he's an outcast, as ambition and greed seize the two sons. Stunning battle scenes illuminate the full-blown tragedy of Kurosawa's vision. Superb acting with a scene-stealing Harada as the revenge-minded Lady Kaede; period costumes took three years to create. Japanese with English subtitles. **160m/C VHS, Beta, LV, Letterbox, Closed Caption.** *JP FR* Tatsuya Nakadai, Akira Terao, Jinpachi Nesu, Daisuke Ryu, Meiko Harada, Hisashi Igawa, Peter; **D:** Akira Kurosawa; **W:** Akira Kurosawa, Hideo Oguni, Masato Ide; **M:** Toru Takemitsu. Academy Awards '85: Best Costume Design; British Academy Awards '86: Best Foreign Film; Los Angeles Film Critics Association Awards '85: Best Foreign Film; National Board of Review Awards '85: Best Director (Kurosawa); New York Film Critics Awards '85: Best Foreign Film; National Society of Film Critics Awards '85: Best Cinematography, Best Film; Nominations: Academy Awards '85: Best Art Direction/Set Decoration, Best Cinematography, Best Director (Kurosawa). *FXL, HMV*

Rana: The Legend of Shadow Lake 🎬 1975 Gold at the bottom of a lake is guarded by a frog-monster, but treasure hunters try to retrieve it anyway. **96m/C VHS, Beta.** Alan Ross, Karen McDiarmid, Jerry Gregoris.

The Ranch 🎬🎬 1988 (PG-13) An executive who loses everything inherits a dilapidated ranch and renovates it into a health spa. **97m/C VHS, Beta.** Andrew Stevens, Gary Fjellgaard, Lou Ann Schmidt, Elizabeth Keefe; **D:** Stella Stevens.

Rancho Deluxe 🎬🎬🎬 1975 Off-beat western spoof starring Bridges and Waterston as two carefree cowpokes. Cult favorite featuring music by Buffett, who also appears in the film. **93m/C VHS, Closed Caption.** Jeff Bridges, Sam Waterston, Elizabeth Ashley, Charlene Dallas, Clifton James, Slim Pickens, Harry Dean Stanton, Richard Bright, Jimmy Buffett; **D:** Frank Perry; **W:** Thomas McGuane; **M:** Jimmy Buffett. *MGM*

Rancho Notorious 🎬🎬🎬 1952 Kennedy, on the trail of his girlfriend's murderer, falls for dance hall girl Dietrich. Fine acting. A "period" sample of '50s westerns, but different. A must for Dietrich fans. **89m/C VHS, Beta, LV.** Marlene Dietrich, Arthur Kennedy, Mel Ferrer, William Frawley, Jack Elam, George Reeves; **D:** Fritz Lang; **W:** Daniel Taradash; **C:** Hal Mohr. *NO*

Random Harvest 🎬🎬🎬 1942 A masterful, tearjerking film based on the James Hilton novel. A shell-shocked WWI amnesiac meets and is made happy by a beautiful music hall dancer. He regains his memory and forgets about the dancer and their child. This is Garson's finest hour, and a shamelessly potent sobfest. **126m/B VHS, Beta.** Greer Garson, Ronald Colman, Reginald Owen, Philip Dorn, Susan Peters, Henry Travers, Margaret Wycherly, Bramwell Fletcher; **D:** Mervyn LeRoy; **C:** Joseph Ruttenberg. Nominations: Academy Awards '42: Best Actor (Colman), Best Director (LeRoy), Best Interior Decoration, Best Picture, Best Screenplay, Best Supporting Actress (Peters), Best Original Dramatic/Comedy Score. *MGM*

Randy Rides Alone 🎬🎬 1934 Very young Wayne is good in this slappable but pleasant B effort. Wayne single-handedly cleans up the territory and rids the land of a passel o'bad guys. **53m/B VHS, Beta.** John Wayne, Alberta Vaughn, George "Gabby" Hayes; **D:** Harry Fraser. *COL, NOS, VCN*

Range Busters 🎬 1940 Range Busters are called in to find the identity of the phantom killer. **55m/B VHS, Beta.** Ray Corrigan, Max Terhune. *NOS, VCN, DVT*

Range Feud 🎬½ 1931 Wayne is a ranch owner's son falsely accused of murder. Just as he's about to hang, Jones, as the heroic sheriff, saves the day and reveals the real killer's identity. **58m/B VHS.** Buck Jones, John Wayne, Susan Fleming, William Walling, Wallace MacDonald, Harry Woods, Ed LeSaint; **D:** David Ross Lederman. *COL*

The Range Feud/Two Fisted Law 🎬🎬 1931 Two early, short Wayne oaters which reveal the Duke developing the drawl, gait and pleasingly profane style that would carry him to fame. In "Feud" he is a young rancher accused of murdering a cattle rustler. "Law" finds him playing a character named Duke who loses his land and girl to a neighboring land grabber. **112m/C VHS.** Buck Jones, Tim McCoy, John Wayne, Susan Fleming, Alice Faye, Walter Brennan; **D:** David Ross Lederman. *COL*

Range Law 🎬 1931 Another entry in the infamous Maynard series of horseplay, cliche, and repetitive plot elements. **60m/B VHS, Beta.** Ken Maynard, Charles "Blackie" King, Lafe McKee. *GPV, VCI, DVT*

Range Law 🎬½ 1944 Ranchers are being terrorized for their silver mine and its up to Brown and Hatton to catch the villains. **59m/B VHS.** Johnny Mack Brown, Raymond Hatton, Lloyd Ingraham, Sarah Padden, Ellen Hall, Steve Clark, Jack Ingram, Bud Osborne; **D:** Lambert Hillyer. *GPV*

Range Renegades 🎬½ 1948 Sheriff Wakely and his pals have their hands full when his deputy gets involved with the leader of a gang of outlaw women. Predictable B oater reflects the then developing trend of using wicked female characters in westerns. Paved the way for films like "Johnny Guitar" and "Rancho Notorious." **54m/B VHS.** Jimmy Wakely, Dub Taylor, Dennis Moore, Jennifer Holt, John James, Steve Clark, Frank LaRue; **D:** Lambert Hillyer; **W:** Ronald Davidson, William Lively. *MOV*

Range Rider 1952 Eight episodes of the series are on four tapes, including "Greed Rides the Range," "Silver Blade" and "Fatal Bullet." 60m/B VHS, Beta. Jock Mahoney. *DVT*

Range Riders 1935 A gunman poses as a wimp and cleans out an outlaw gang. 46m/B VHS, Beta. Buddy Roosevelt. *NO*

Rangeland Empire ♂♂ 1950 Shamrock and Lucky are at it again, implicated as being members of an outlaw gang until that gang attacks them. 59m/B VHS, Beta, LV. James Ellison, Russell Hayden, Stanley Price, John Cason. *NO*

Rangeland Racket ♂♂½ 1941 The Lone Rider (Houston) has been wrongly accused of a crime. 60m/B VHS, Beta. George Houston, Hillary Brooke, Al "Fuzzy" St. John. *VYY*

Ranger and the Lady ♂♂½ 1940 Texas Ranger Rogers romances the woman who is the leader of a wagon train. 54m/B VHS, Beta. Roy Rogers, George "Gabby" Hayes; *D:* Joseph Kane. *NOS, DVT*

Ranger's Roundup ♂♂ 1938 The Rangers prove their courage by rounding up an outlaw gang. 57m/B VHS, Beta. Fred Scott, Al "Fuzzy" St. John. *NOS, DVT*

The Rangers Step In ♂♂½ 1937 Allen leaves the Texas Rangers when a feud between his family and that of the girl he loves heats up again. Turns out rustlers are stirring things up in order to get some of the disputed land. 56m/B VHS, Robert Allen, Eleanor Stewart, John Merton, Hal Taliaferro, Jack Ingram, Jack Rockwell, Lafe McKee, Robert F. (Bob) Kortman; *D:* Spencer Gordon Bennet. *GPV*

Rangers Take Over ♂♂½ 1943 Gunlords are driven out by the Texas Rangers. 62m/B VHS, Beta. Dave O'Brien, James Newill. *NOS, VYY, DVT*

Ransom ♂♂♂ 1996 (R) Tight and crafty thriller proves millionaire airline magnate Tom Mullen (Gibson) is a force to be reckoned with when son Sean (Nolte, son of actor Nick) is kidnapped. A vigilante Donald Trump (only gorgeous and brave), Mullen treats this like a high-stakes business deal and decides to get his kid back by announcing on TV that the $2 million ransom demand will instead become a bounty on the kidnappers. Wife Kate (Russo), predictably flips out but Mullen, after a few encounters with the heinous abductors, has sized them up and is convinced he's done the right thing. Lindo is a by-the-book fed with bad dialogue and Sinise is a bad cop playing for the other team. Gibson's emergency appendectomy delayed filming but he was soon leaping over cars for director Howard's well-staged action scenes. Based on the 1956 flick starring Glenn Ford. *CW:* Graphic bloody violence and strong language. 121m/C VHS, LV, Closed Caption. Mel Gibson, Rene Russo, Gary Sinise, Delroy Lindo, Brawley Nolte, Lili Taylor, Liev Schreiber, Evan Handler, Dan Hedaya, Paul Guilfoyle, Jose Zuniga, Donnie Wahlberg, Michael Gaston, Nancy Ticotin; *Cameos:* Richard Price; *D:* Ron Howard; *W:* Richard Price, Alexander Ignon; *C:* Piotr Sobocinski; *M:* James Horner. Nominations: Golden Globe Awards '97: Best Actor—Drama (Gibson). *TOU*

Ransom Money ♂♂½ 1988 A kidnapping scheme involving millions of dollars, in and around the Grand Canyon, backfires. 87m/C VHS, Beta. Broderick Crawford, Rachel Romen, Gordon Jump, Randy Whipple; *D:* DeWitt Lee. *NO*

Ranson's Folly ♂♂½ 1926 Barthelmess makes a wager that he can impersonate a famous outlaw well enough to rob a stage with only a pair of scissors. When the army paymaster is killed, guess who gets caught with his swash unbuckled? 80m/B VHS, Beta. Richard Barthelmess, Dorothy Mackaill, Anders Randolf, Pat Hartigan, Brooks Benedict; *D:* Sidney Olcott. *GPV*

Rapa Nui ♂♂½ 1993 (R) The title refers to the Polynesian name for Easter Island, with the film set in the 17th century (before Dutch explorers discovered the island). It depicts the annual rituals of the mysterious people who built the Island's moai—the famous giant stone statues.

Lee plays the heroic Noroinia, with Morales as his rival Make, and Holt as Ramana, the object of their desires. Faux primitive but with some great on-location filming. *CW:* Tribal violence and sexuality. 107m/C VHS, LV, Closed Caption. Jason Scott Lee, Esai Morales, Sandrine Holt; *D:* Kevin Reynolds; *W:* Kevin Reynolds, Tim Rose Price; *M:* Stewart Copeland. *WAR*

Rape ♂ 198? Two guys investigate a third pal's mysterious death. They discover that his supernatural-power-imbued girlfriend is at the root of the matter. 90m/C VHS, Beta. Rick Joss, Gil Vidal. *NO*

Rape and Marriage: The Rideout Case ♂♂½ 1980 The true story of an Oregon wife who accused her husband of rape. Thoughtfully explores the legal and moral questions raised by the case. Interpreted well enough, though not superbly, by a decent cast. although Rourke is a little too intense. Made for television. 96m/C VHS, Beta. Mickey Rourke, Linda Hamilton, Rip Torn, Eugene Roche, Conchata Ferrell, Gail Strickland, Bonnie Bartlett, Alley Mills; *D:* Peter Levin. *ART*

Rape of Love ♂♂♂½ 1979 The story begins with one of the most chilling rape scenes on film and then attempts to analyze the emotional impact of rape on its victim. Well-acted and directed. In French with English subtitles. 117m/C VHS, Beta. *FR* Nathalie Nell, Alain Foures; *D:* Yannick Bellon. *COL*

The Rape of the Sabines woof! *El Rapto de las Sabinas; The Mating of the Sabine Women; Shame of the Sabine Women* 1961 The story of Romulus, king of Rome, and how he led the Romans to capture the women of Sabina. The battles rage, the women plot, and Romulus fights and lusts. Dubbed in English. 101m/C VHS, Beta. *IT FR* Roger Moore, Mylene Demongeot, Jean Marais; *D:* Richard Pottier. *UNI*

Rapid Fire ♂♂ 1989 Cheap, made-for-video quickie about a good guy U.S. agent who battles terrorists. Easy to skip. 90m/C VHS, Beta. Joe Spinell, Michael Wayne, Ron Waldron; *D:* David A. Prior.

Rapid Fire ♂♂♂½ 1992 (R) Lee (son of martial arts cult idol Bruce Lee) is a Chinese-American art student who also happens to be a martial arts expert. He's tapped by the police to help stem the violence between the Asian and Italian gangs fighting for control over Chicago's drug trade. Typical martial arts movie is made better by uniquely choreographed action sequences and Lee's attractive presence. *CW:* Language, violence, and sexuality. 96m/C VHS, LV, Closed Caption. Brandon Lee, Powers Boothe, Nick Mancuso, Raymond J. Barry, Kate Hodge, Tzi Ma, Tony Longo, Michael Paul Chan, Dustin Nguyen, John Vickery; *D:* Dwight Little; *W:* Alan B. McElroy, Cindy Cirile, Paul Attanasio; *M:* Christopher Young. *FXV*

Rappin' ♂♂ 1985 (PG) Ex-con Van Peebles gets into it with the landlord and a street gang leader. Forgettable action/music drivel. ♫Rappin'; Two of a Kind; Call Me; Born to Love; Killer; Itching for a Scratch; Snack Attack; Dodge; Golly Gee. 92m/C VHS, Beta. Mario Van Peebles, Tasia Valenza, Harry Goz, Charles Flohe; *D:* Joel Silberg. *MGM*

The Rapture ♂♂ 1991 (R) A beautiful telephone operator engages in indiscriminate sexual adventures to relieve the boredom of her job and life. She becomes curious by, and eventually converted to, evangelical Christianity, which leads her to a contented marriage and the birth of a daughter. When her husband is tragically killed she becomes convinced that she and her child will be taken by God into heaven if she only waits for the proper sign. *CW:* Some language, violence, and strong sensuality. 100m/C VHS, LV. Mimi Rogers, David Duchovny, Patrick Bauchau, Will Patton; *D:* Michael Tolkin; *W:* Michael Tolkin; *C:* Bojan Bazelli. *COL*

Rapunzel 1982 A beautiful young woman locked in a tall tower is saved by the handsome prince who climbs her golden tresses. Part of Shelly Duvall's "Faerie Tale Theatre" series. 60m/C VHS, Beta, LV, Closed Caption. Shelley Duvall, Gena Rowlands, Jeff Bridges. *KUI, FOX, FCT*

The Rare Breed ♂♂½ 1966 Plodding but pleasant Western. A no-strings ranch hand (Stewart) agrees to escort a Hereford Bull to Texas, where the widow of an English breeder plans to crossbreed the bull with longhorn cattle. The widow (O'Hara) insists that she and her daughter accompany Stewart on the trip, which features every kind of western calamity imaginable. When all others believe the attempt to crossbreed has failed, Stewart sets out to prove them wrong. 97m/C VHS, Beta, Closed Caption. James Stewart, Maureen O'Hara, Brian Keith, Juliet Mills, Jack Elam, Ben Johnson; *D:* Andrew V. McLaglen; *C:* William Clothier; *M:* John Williams. *USH*

A Rare Breed ♂♂½ 1981 (PG) Real-life story of a kidnapped horse in Italy and a young girl's quest to retrieve it. Directed by David Nelson of television's "Ozzie and Harriet" fame, this movie is cute and old-fashioned. 94m/C VHS, Beta. George Kennedy, Forrest Tucker, Tracy Vaccaro, Tom Hallick, Don DeFore; *D:* David Nelson. *VTR, ART*

Rascal Dazzle 1981 Montage-like tribute to that best-loved group of children, the Our Gang kids. Includes scenes with Spanky, Alfalfa, Darla, and the rest of the gang. 100m/B VHS, Beta, LV.

The Rascals ♂♂♂½ 1981 (R) An irrepressible youth at a rural Catholic boys' school comes of age. 93m/C VHS, Beta. *FR* Thomas Chabrol; *D:* Bernard Revon.

Rashomon ♂♂♂♂ *In the Woods* 1951 In 12th century Japan, two travelers attempt to discover the truth about an ambush/rape/murder. They get four completely different versions of the incident from the three people involved in the crime and the single witness. An insightful masterpiece that established Kurosawa and Japanese cinema as major artistic forces. Fine performances, particularly Mifune as the bandit. Visually beautiful and rhythmic. Remade as a western, "The Outrage," in 1964. In Japanese with English subtitles. 83m/B VHS, Beta, LV. *JP* Machiko Kyo, Toshiro Mifune, Masayuki Mori, Takashi Shimura; *D:* Akira Kurosawa; *W:* Akira Kurosawa. Academy Awards '51: Best Foreign Language Film; National Board of Review Awards '51: Best Director (Kurosawa); Venice Film Festival '51: Best Film; Nominations: Academy Awards '52: Best Art Direction/Set Decoration (B & W). *CRC, NLC*

Rasputin ♂♂♂ *Agoniya* 1985 The long-censored and banned film of the story of the mad monk and his domination of the royal family before the Russian Revolution. Petrenko is superb. First released in the United States in 1988. In Russian with English subtitles. 104m/C VHS, Beta. *RU* Alexei Petrenko, Anatoly Romashin, Velta Linne, Alice Freindlikh; *D:* Elem Klimov; *W:* Semyon Lunghin, Ilya Nusinov; *M:* Alfred Shnitke. *NO*

Rasputin and the Empress ♂♂♂ *Rasputin: The Mad Monk* 1933 Lavish historical epic teamed the three Barrymore sibs for the first and only time, as they vied for scene-stealing honors. Ethel is Empress Alexandra of Russia, tied to the weak-willed Nicholas II (Morgan) and under the spell of Rasputin, played by Lionel. John is a nobleman who seeks to warn the Russian rulers of their perilous perch on the throne, made only worse by Rasputin's spreading power and corruption. Ethel's first talkie and Wynyard's first film role. Uncredited director Charles Brabin was replaced by Boleslawski due to his incompatability with the imperious Ethel. 123m/B VHS. Ethel Barrymore, John Barrymore, Lionel Barrymore, Ralph Morgan, Diana Wynyard, Tad Alexander, C. Henry Gordon, Edward Arnold, Gustav von Seyffertitz, Anne Shirley, Jean Parker, Henry Kolker; *D:* Richard Boleslawski; *W:* Charles MacArthur; *C:* William H. Daniels. Nominations: Academy Awards '33: Best Story. *MGM, MOV*

Rasputin: Dark Servant of Destiny ♂♂♂ 1996 (R) Charismatic Russian peasant/mystic Grigori Rasputin (a mesmerizing Rickman), having received a vision of the Virgin Mary, comes to St. Petersburg in order to relieve the suffering of young hemophiliac, Prince Alexei

(Findlay). Tsarina Alexandra (Scacchi) approves of anyone who can help her stricken son while Tsar Nicholas II (McKellen) tentatively agrees to accept the self-proclaimed holy man into the Russian court. Fine performances and beautiful photography make this one of the better made-for-cable efforts. Filmed in St. Petersburg. **120m/C VHS.** Alan Rickman, Ian McKellen, Greta Scacchi, Freddie Findlay, David Warner, John Wood, James Frain, Diana Quick, Ian Hogg, Peter Jeffrey, Ian McDiarmid, Julian Curry; **D:** Uli Edel; **W:** Peter Bruce; **C:** Elemer Ragaly; **M:** Brad Fiedel. *HBO*

Rasputin the Mad Monk 🐾🐾 1966
Hammer's version of Russian history of course emphasizes the evil powers of the mad Russian monk (Lee) who gains entry into the court of the czar. Poor script but Lee's good. **90m/B VHS, Letterbox.** *GB* Christopher Lee, Barbara Shelley, Richard Pasco, Francis Matthews, Suzan Farmer, Nicholas Pennell, Renee Asherson, Derek Francis; **D:** Don Sharp; **W:** John Elder; **C:** Michael Reed; **M:** Don Banks. *VTR*

Rat Pfink a Boo-Boo woof! 1966
Parody on "Batman" in which a bumbling superhero and his sidekick race around saving people. Notoriously inept. Title story is legendary—it was misspelled accidentally and Steckler didn't have the cash to fix it. **72m/B VHS, Beta.** Vin Saxon, Carolyn Brandt, Titus Moede, Mike Kannon; **D:** Ray Dennis Steckler. *NO*

The Rat Race 🐾🐾🐾 1960
A dancer and a musician venture to Manhattan to make it big, and end up sharing an apartment. Their relationship starts pleasantly and becomes romantic. Enjoyable farce. Well photographed and scripted, with the supporting characters stealing the show. **105m/C VHS.** Tony Curtis, Debbie Reynolds, Jack Oakie, Kay Medford, Don Rickles, Joe Bushkin; **D:** Robert Mulligan; **C:** Robert Burks; **M:** Elmer Bernstein. *PAR*

Ratboy 🐾🐾½ 1986 (PG-13)
An unscrupulous woman attempts to transform a boy with a rat's face into a celebrity, with tragic results. First directorial effort by Locke that gradually loses steam. **105m/C VHS, Beta, Closed Caption.** Sondra Locke, Sharon Baird, Robert Townsend; **D:** Sondra Locke; **W:** Rob Thompson; **C:** Bruce Surtees; **M:** Lennie Niehaus. *WAR*

Rate It X 1986 (R)
Sexism in a variety of national institutions, from pornography to consumerism, is revealed through the average man on the street via microphone interviews. **95m/C VHS, Beta.** **D:** Lucy Winer, Paula de Koenigsberg. *ART*

Ratings Game 🐾🐾 *The Mogul* 1984
A bitter, out-of-work actor and a woman who works at the ratings service manage to mess up the television industry. Early directorial effort by DeVito is uneven but funny. Made for cable television. **102m/C VHS, Beta, LV, Closed Caption.** Danny DeVito, Rhea Perlman, Gerrit Graham, Kevin McCarthy, Jayne Meadows, Steve Allen, Ronny Graham, George Wendt; **D:** Danny DeVito; **W:** Michael Barrie, Jim Mulholland. *PAR*

Rats 🐾🐾 1983
In 2225, the beleaguered survivors of a nuclear holocaust struggle with a mutant rodent problem. **100m/C VHS, Beta.** Richard Raymond, Richard Cross; **D:** Vincent Dawn. *NO*

The Rats Are Coming! The Werewolves Are Here! woof! 1972 (R)
Low-budget schlock revolves around a family of werewolves and the daughter who decides to put an end to the curse. Imaginative title promises much more than movie delivers. The killer rats were thrown in as an afterthought to increase the run time. **92m/C VHS, Beta.** Hope Stansbury, Jackie Skarvellis, Noel Collins, Joan Ogden, Douglas Phair, Bernard Kaler; **D:** Andy Milligan; **W:** Andy Milligan. *NO*

A Rat's Tale 🐾🐾 1998 (G)
"Romeo & Juliet" for rats. A regular Joe, Manhattanite Monty Mad-Rat meets Isabella Noble-Rat, the daughter of the rat President, and soon Monty is a goner for this out-of-reach rodent whose family disapproves of the common sewer creature. Adding to the intrigue, a land developer (Ostendorf) appears with a scheme to obliterate the rat population and build a parking garage. The rats band together to raise money to buy their land and prevent ratricide. Admirably lo-tech, kid pic nonetheless suffers from the cute but expressionless and very much wired marionettes playing the rats—they're no muppets—and the broadly characterized roles of the human actors (Hutton, Stiller and D'Angelo). Marionettes complements of Germany's Augsburger Puppet Theatre. Based on the book by Tor Seidler. **90m/C VHS.** **GE** Lauren Hutton, Jerry Stiller, Beverly D'Angelo, Josef Ostendorf; **D:** Michael F. Huse; **W:** Werner Morganrath, Peter Scheerbaum; **C:** Piotr Lenar; **V:** Dee Bradley Baker, Lynsey Bartilson, Donald Arthur, Ray Guth, Scott MacDonald. *WAR*

Rattle of a Simple Man 🐾🐾½ 1964
A naive, chaste, middle-aged bachelor (Corbett) who lives in London must spend the night with a waitress (Cilento) to win a bet. She knows of the bet and kindly obliges. Enjoyable sex comedy. **91m/B VHS, Beta.** **GB** Harry H. Corbett, Diane Cilento, Michael Medwin, Thora Hird; **D:** Muriel Box. *NO*

Rattled 🐾🐾½ 1996 (PG-13)
Indiana Jones won't be the only snake-hater after seeing what hundreds of rattlesnakes can do. When their den is disturbed by construction on a new water project, hundreds of rattlers slither down the mountainside ready to attack anyone in their path. Based on the book "Rattlers" by Joseph Gilmore. **CW:** Terrifying snake attacks. **90m/C VHS, Closed Caption.** William Katt, Shanna Reed, Michael Galeota, Monica Creel, Clint Howard, Ian Abercrombie, Ed Lauter, Bibi Besch, Zack Eginton; **D:** Tony Randel; **W:** Jim Wheat, Ken Wheat. *USH*

Rattler Kid 🐾 197?
Cavalry sergeant wrongly accused of murdering his commanding officer escapes from prison and finds the real killer. **86m/C VHS, Beta.** Richard Wyler, Brad Harris. *UNI*

Rattlers 🐾 1976 (PG)
Made for television movie featuring poisonous rattlesnakes who attack at random. **82m/C VHS, Beta.** Sam Chew, Elizabeth Chauvet, Dan Priest; **D:** John McCauley. *NO*

Ravager 🐾½ 1997 (R)
When a space transport ship crashlands in the desert, former lovers Cooper Wayne (Payne) and Avedon Hammond (Butler), along with their crew, search for help. They discover an underground storage facility and some leaking hazardous material labeled "Ravenger" that infects one of their technicians. When they return the infected crewman to the ship, they also bring back a contagion that threatens the survival of everyone aboard. **CW:** Sci-fi violence and gore. **92m/C VHS, Beta, Closed Caption.** Bruce Payne, Yancy Butler, Juliet Landau, Salvator Xuereb; **D:** James D. Deck; **W:** James D. Deck. *PAR*

Rave Review 🐾🐾 1995
Desperate L.A. theatrical director wants to scare a powerful critic into giving his latest production a glowing review so that his small theatre company can remain in business. Too bad he scares the critic to death. **91m/C VHS.** Jeff Seymour, Ed Begley Jr., Leo Rossi, Joe Spano, Bruce Kirby, James Handy; **D:** Jeff Seymour; **W:** Jeff Seymour.

The Raven 🐾🐾 1915
An early, eccentric pseudo-biography of author Edgar Allan Poe. The film opens with a look at Poe's ancestors and follows the author to maturity when he turns to alcohol for solace. His drunken stupor produces hallucinations that lead to his tale of "The Raven." Silent with added music track. **80m/B VHS.** Henry B. Walthall, Wanda Howard; **D:** Charles Brabin. *GPV, HEG, GVV*

The Raven 🐾🐾🐾 1935
A lunatic surgeon (Lugosi), who has a dungeon full of torture gadgets inspired by Edgar Allan Poe's stories, is begged by a man to save his daughter's life. The surgeon does, and then falls in love with the girl. But when he rejects her love (she's already engaged), he plans revenge in his chamber of horrors. Karloff plays the criminal who winds up ruining the mad doctor's plans. Lugosi is at his prime in this role, and any inconsistencies in the somewhat shaky script can be overlooked because of his chilling performance. **62m/B VHS, LV.** Boris Karloff, Bela Lugosi, Irene Ware, Lester Matthews, Samuel S. Hinds, D. Lew (Louis Friedlander) Landers; **W:** David Boehm, Jim Tully; **C:** Charles Stumar. *USH*

The Raven 🐾🐾🐾 1963
This could-have-been monumental teaming of horror greats Karloff, Lorre, and Price is more of a satire than a true horror film. One of the more enjoyable of the Corman/Poe adaptations, the movie takes only the title of the poem. As for the storyline: Price and Karloff play two rival sorcerers who battle for supremacy, with Lorre as the unfortunate associate turned into the bird of the title. **86m/C VHS, Beta, LV.** Vincent Price, Boris Karloff, Peter Lorre, Jack Nicholson, Hazel Court, Olive Sturgess; **D:** Roger Corman; **W:** Richard Matheson; **C:** Floyd Crosby; **M:** Les Baxter. *MLB*

Raven 🐾½ 1997 (R)
Covert mercenary team codenamed Raven is after a Soviet satellite decoder. They're double-crossed by renegade CIA agents and their leader Reynolds decides to get his own brand of justice. **CW:** Violence, language, sexual situations, nudity. **93m/C VHS, LV, Closed Caption.** Burt Reynolds, Krista Allen, Richard Gant, David Ackroyd, Matt Battaglia; **D:** Russell Solberg; **W:** Jacobsen Hart; **C:** John Dirlam. *NLC*

Ravenhawk 🐾🐾 1995 (R)
Native American Ravenhawk (McLish) is falsely accused of murdering her parents and sent to a maximum security asylum. Twelve years later she returns to her home and learns that corporate slimeball Philip Thorne (Atherton) framed her. Now, he's built a nuclear waste plant on Shoshone land over the objections of the tribe and Ravenhawk is determined to even the score. **CW:** Violence; language; brief nudity. **88m/C VHS, LV.** Rachel McLish, John Enos, William Atherton, Ed Lauter, Mitch Pileggi; **D:** Albert Pyun; **W:** Kevin Elders; **C:** George Mooradian; **M:** Johnny Harris. *COL*

Ravishing Idiot 🐾🐾 *Agent 38-24-36; Adorable Idiot; The Warm-Blooded Spy; Bewitching Scatterbrain* 1964
An unemployed bank clerk becomes mixed up with Soviet spies. **99m/B VHS, Beta.** **FR** Brigitte Bardot, Anthony Perkins; **D:** Edouard Molinaro. *NO*

Raw Courage 🐾 *Courage* 1984
Three long-distance runners relax in New Mexico, but are kidnapped by vigilantes. Loosely based on a James Dickey novel. **90m/C VHS, Beta, LV.** Ronny Cox, Lois Chiles, Art Hindle, Tim Maier, M. Emmet Walsh; **D:** Robert L. Rosen. *VTR*

Raw Deal 🐾🐾🐾 1948
Sadistic Rick Coyle (Burr) framed one-time associate Joe Sullivan (O'Keefe), who wound up in prison. Joe's moll Pat (Trevor) helps him to escape and they take prison social worker Ann (Hunt), who's befriended Joe, as a hostage. They go after Coyle and Joe begins to fall for the demure dame, who finds the underworld life exciting and even saves Joe from one of Coyle's henchmen. No good guys here but it is fine film noir. **79m/B VHS.** Dennis O'Keefe, Claire Trevor, Raymond Burr, Marsha Hunt, John Ireland, Curt Conway, Whit Bissell; **D:** Anthony Mann; **W:** John C. Higgins, Leopold Atlas; **C:** John Alton; **M:** Paul Sawtell. *KIV*

Raw Deal 🐾½ 1986 (R)
Don't ever give Schwarzenegger a raw deal! FBI agent Schwarzie infiltrates the mob and shoots lots of people. **106m/C VHS, Beta, LV, Closed Caption.** Arnold Schwarzenegger, Kathryn Harrold, Darren McGavin, Sam Wanamaker, Paul Shenar, Steven Hill; **D:** John Irvin; **W:** Gary De Vore, Patrick Edgeworth. *TLF*

Raw Force 🐾 *Shogun Island* 1981 (R)
Three karate buffs visit an island inhabited by a sect of cannibalistic monks who have the power to raise the dead (it could happen). They fix the villains by kicking them all in the head. **90m/C VHS, Beta.** **PH** Cameron Mitchell, Geoffrey Binney, John Dresden, John Locke, Ralph Lombardi; **D:** Edward Murphy.

Raw Justice 🐾🐾 1993 (R)
When the daughter of a powerful Southern mayor is murdered, tough ex-cop Mace (Keith) is hired to get the killer. Mace enlists the reluctant help of call girl Sarah (Anderson) to help him trap Mitch (Hayes), his prime suspect. Only things don't work out as Mace planned and the wary three-

some must work together to save themselves from certain death. **92m/C VHS, LV, Closed Caption.** David Keith, Pamela Anderson, Robert Hayes, Leo Rossi, Charles Napier, Stacy Keach; **D:** David A. Prior; **W:** David A. Prior. *REP*

Raw Nerve 🎦 **1991 (R)** A cast with possibilities can't overcome this poorly reasoned suspenser. A young man has visions of the local serial killer, but when he reports them to police he becomes the suspect. There are a few twists beyond that, none too thrilling. **CW:** Language and violence and drug content. **91m/C VHS, Beta, LV.** Glenn Ford, Traci Lords, Sandahl Bergman, Randall "Tex" Cobb, Ted Prior, Jan-Michael Vincent; **W:** David A. Prior. *REP*

Raw Target 🎦½ **1995 (R)** Ex-kickboxer Johnny Rider (Cook) finds himself a police decoy in a drug bust and then learns that the drug gang's leader Sparks (Hill) was also involved in his brother's death. **CW:** Bloody shootings and martial arts violence, a sex scene, and language. **92m/C VHS.** Dale "Apollo" Cook, Ron Hall, Nick Hill, Mychelle Charters; **D:** Tim Spring; **W:** Larry Maddox; **C:** Bruce Dorfman; **M:** Jun Lupito. *THV*

Rawhead Rex 🎦½ **1987 (R)** An ancient demon is released from his underground prison in Ireland by a plowing farmer, and begins to decapitate and maim at will. Adapted by Clive Barker from his own short story. But, Barker later disowned the film, so make your own judgment. **89m/C VHS, Beta, LV.** David Dukes, Kelly Piper; **D:** George Pavlou; **W:** Clive Barker; **M:** Colin Towns. *ART, VES*

Rawhide 🎦🎦 **1938** Rancher's Protection Association forces landowners to knuckle under resulting in friction. Lou Gehrig plays a rancher in a western released the year before he died. Bandleader Ballew could be more gripping in the lead. **60m/B VHS, Beta.** Lou Gehrig, Smith Ballew, Evalyn Knapp; **D:** Ray Taylor. *NOS, CCB, DVT*

Rawhide 🎦🎦🎦 *Desperate Siege* **1950** Four escaped convicts hijack a stagecoach way station and hold hostages while waiting for a shipment of gold. A suspenseful B-grade western with a bang-up ending. Well paced and cast with an abundance of good talent. A remake of "Show Them No Mercy" (1938). **86m/B VHS, Beta.** Tyrone Power, Susan Hayward, Hugh Marlowe, Jack Elam, Dean Jagger, George Tobias, Edgar Buchanan, Jeff Corey; **D:** Henry Hathaway; **C:** Milton Krasner. *FOX*

Rawhide Romance 🎦 **1934** Bill finds justice and love in this chap-slappin' opus, which finds him neglecting the thieves operating on the ranch as he romances his girl. Naturally he comes to his senses and goes after the crooks. **47m/B VHS, Beta, LV.** Buffalo Bill Jr., Genee Boutell, Lafe McKee, Si Jenks; **D:** Victor Adamson. *VYY*

The Razor: Sword of Justice 🎦🎦 **1972** Reasonably honest cop Hanzo Itami knows he won't get a promotion under his corrupt boss Inspector Onishi unless he can blackmail him into it. And he finds a way when he discovers condemned prisoner Kanbei is actually living with his mistress Omino, who it turns out is busy with Onishi as well. A little knowledge could get Hanzo killed but he's willing to take the risk. Japanese with subtitles. **90m/C VHS, LV, Letterbox.** **JP** Shintaro Katsu, Asaoka Yukiji, Atsumi Mari, Nishimura Akira; **D:** Kenji Misumi. *ANI, MOV*

Razorback 🎦 **1984 (R)** Young American travels to the Australian outback in search of his missing journalist wife. During his quest, he encounters a giant killer pig that has been terrorizing the area. Firmly establishes that pigs, with little sense of natural timing, make lousy movie villains. **95m/C VHS, Beta.** **AU** Gregory Harrison, Bill Kerr, Arkie Whiteley, Judy Morris, Chris Haywood, David Argue; **D:** Russell Mulcahy; **W:** Everett De Roche; **C:** Dean Semler. *WAR*

The Razor's Edge 🎦🎦🎦 **1946** Adaptation of the W. Somerset Maugham novel. A rich young man spends his time between WWI & WWII searching for essential truth, eventually landing in India. A satisfying cinematic version of

a difficult novel, supported by an excellent cast. Remade in 1984 with Bill Murray in the lead role. **146m/B VHS, Beta, LV, Closed Caption.** Tyrone Power, Gene Tierney, Anne Baxter, Clifton Webb, Herbert Marshall, John Payne, Elsa Lanchester; **D:** Edmund Goulding; **C:** Arthur C. Miller. Academy Awards '46: Best Supporting Actress (Baxter); Golden Globe Awards '47: Best Supporting Actor (Webb), Best Supporting Actress (Baxter); Nominations: Academy Awards '46: Best Interior Decoration, Best Picture, Best Supporting Actor (Webb). *BTV*

The Razor's Edge 🎦🎦½ **1984 (PG-13)** A beautifully filmed but idiosyncratic version of the W. Somerset Maugham novel. WWI-ravaged Larry Darrell combs the world in search of the meaning of life. Murray is a little too old and sardonic to seem really tortured. Russell is great as the loser he rescues. Subtly unique, with real shortcomings. **129m/C VHS, Beta, LV, Closed Caption.** Bill Murray, Catherine Hicks, Theresa Russell, Denholm Elliott, James Keach, Peter Vaughan, Saeed Jaffrey, Brian Doyle-Murray; **D:** John Byrum; **W:** John Byrum; **M:** Jack Nitzsche. *COL*

Re-Animator 🎦🎦🎦 **1984** Based on an H.P. Lovecraft story, this grisly film deals with a medical student who re-animates the dead. It has quickly turned into a black humor cult classic. Also available in an "R" rated version, and followed by "Bride of Re-Animator." **86m/C VHS, Beta, LV.** Jeffrey Combs, Bruce Abbott, Barbara Crampton, David Gale, Robert Sampson, Gerry Black, Carolyn Purdy-Gordon; **D:** Stuart Gordon; **W:** Stuart Gordon, Dennis Paoli, William J. Norris; **C:** Mac Ahlberg; **M:** Richard Band. *ART, VES*

Reach for the Sky 🎦🎦½ **1956** WW II flying ace loses both legs in an accident and learns to fly again. He becomes a hero during the Battle of Britain, then is shot down over France and held prisoner by the Germans. At war's end he returns to England to lead 3,000 planes over London in a victory flight. Inspirationally told true story. **123m/B VHS, Beta.** **GB** Kenneth More, Alexander Knox, Nigel Green; **D:** Lewis Gilbert; **M:** John Addison. British Academy Awards '56: Best Film. *NO*

Reaching for the Moon 🎦🎦½ **1917** A day-dreaming department store employee finds himself in the unlikely position of ruling a kingdom. Vintage Fairbanks fun, based on a story by Anita Loos. Silent. **62m/B VHS, Beta.** Douglas Fairbanks Sr., Eileen Percy, Millard Webb; **D:** John Emerson. *VYY, GPV, GVV*

Reaching for the Moon 🎦🎦½ **1931** Fairbanks is a businessman who falls for liquor and Daniels on a transatlantic cruise. Dull and cruel; not as light-hearted as it intends. One Irving Berlin song sung by Crosby. **62m/B VHS, Beta, 8mm.** Douglas Fairbanks Sr., Bebe Daniels, Bing Crosby, Edward Everett Horton; **D:** Edmund Goulding. *NOS, VYY, CAB*

Reactor 🎦 **1985** A low-budget sci-fi film about kidnapped scientists, alien ships and an activated nuclear reactor. **90m/C VHS, Beta.** Yanti Somer, Melissa Long, James R. Stuart, Robert Barnes, Nick Jordan. *NO*

Ready to Wear 🎦🎦 *Pret-a-Porter* **1994 (R)** Altman travels to Paris to take on the fashion industry with his trademark satire, ensemble cast, and cameo players in tow. The untimely death of a major industry player begins a swirl of random subplots involving a head-spinning array of fashion industry stereotypes. Loren and Mastroianni recreate their "Yesterday, Today and Tomorrow" boudoir striptease scene. Coterie of one-dimensional characters is set adrift with no discernable plot, which might make for interesting people watching, but results in a tedious movie. Altman did it better with "The Player" and "Short Cuts." **CW:** Contains profanity, sexual situations, and nudity. **132m/C VHS, LV, Closed Caption.** Sophia Loren, Marcello Mastroianni, Julia Roberts, Tim Robbins, Kim Basinger, Stephen Rea, Anouk Aimee, Lauren Bacall, Lili Taylor, Sally Kellerman, Tracey Ullman, Linda Hunt, Rupert Everett, Forest Whitaker, Richard E. Grant, Danny Aiello, Teri Garr, Lyle Lovett, Jean Rochefort, Michel Blanc, Anne Canovas, Jean-Pierre Cassel, Francois Cluzet, Rossy de Palma, Kaisa Figura, Sam Robards; **Cameos:** Cher,

Harry Belafonte, Issey Miyake, Sonia Rykiel, Jean-Paul Gaultier, Thierry Mugler; **D:** Robert Altman; **W:** Barbara Shulgasser, Robert Altman; **M:** Michel Legrand. Nominations: Golden Globe Awards '95: Best Film—Musical/Comedy, Best Supporting Actress (Loren). *MAX*

A Real American Hero 🎦½ *Hard Stick* **1978** Made for television story of Tennessee sheriff Buford Pusser, the subject of three "Walking Tall" films. Here, he battles moonshiners, with the usual violence. **94m/C VHS, Beta.** Brian Dennehy, Brian Kerwin, Forrest Tucker; **D:** Lou Antonio. *VTR*

The Real Blonde 🎦🎦½ **1997 (R)** Entertaining, ensemble pic that daringly exposes the business of show features a disillusioned actor, his beleaguered girlfriend, and a successful soap star (Caulfield) searching for a peroxide-free blonde in New York. On-the-outs couple Joe and Mary (Modine and Keener) is main focus but is undercut by the industry mania that surrounds them. Intelligent writing and caustic wit provide a few memorable scenes, such as the "Il Piano" debate in a crowded restaurant over a thinly veiled "acclaimed independent film" and Bob's resolution to his blonde quest. Modine also revs things up in an emotional improv. Thomas stands out from the crowd as a pretentious fashion photog. DiCillo's latest feature tackles the movie biz from the other side of the camera than his 1995 acclaimed satire, "Living in Oblivion." **CW:** Sexuality and language. **105m/C VHS.** Matthew Modine, Catherine Keener, Daryl Hannah, Maxwell Caulfield, Elizabeth Berkley, Marlo Thomas, Buck Henry, Bridgette Wilson, Christopher Lloyd, Kathleen Turner, Denis Leary; **D:** Tom DiCillo; **W:** Tom DiCillo; **C:** Frank Prinzi; **M:** Jim Farmer. *NYR*

Real Bruce Lee **1979 (R)** Contains actual early films of Bruce Lee, once feared lost but recently discovered in the Chinese film archives, (the movies, not Bruce). **108m/C VHS, Beta.** Bruce Lee. *GEM, SUN, VTR*

The Real Buddy Holly Story **1987** Documentary serves as a tribute to the rock 'n' roll legend who met an untimely death in 1959. **90m/C VHS, Beta, LV.** *SMV, IME, MVD*

Real Bullets 🎦 **1990** Stunt team performs the real thing when two members get imprisoned in a bad guy's desert castle. **86m/C VHS, Beta, LV.** John Gazarian, Martin Landau; **D:** Lance Lindsay. *THV*

The Real Charlotte 🎦🎦½ **1991** When young, lovely, and flirtatious Francie Fitzpatrick (Roth) is romantically betrayed by a young English officer, she then sets her mind on the one man (Bergin) whom her plain and middle-aged cousin Charlotte (Crowley) has long loved. Set in Victorian-era Ireland; made for British TV. **240m/C VHS.** **GB** Joanna Roth, Jeananne Crowley, Patrick Bergin. *VTR, WMI*

Real Genius 🎦🎦🎦 **1985 (PG)** Brainy kids in California work with lasers on a class project that is actually intended for use as an offensive military weapon. When they learn of the scheme, they use their brilliant minds to mount an amusingly elaborate strategic defense initiative of their own. Eccentric characters and an intelligent script provide a bevy of laughs for the family. **108m/C VHS, Beta, LV, Closed Caption.** Val Kilmer, Gabe Jarret, Jonathan Gries, Michelle Meyrink, William Atherton, Patti D'Arbanville, Severn Darden; **D:** Martha Coolidge; **W:** Peter Torokvei, Neal Israel, Pat Proft; **M:** Thomas Newman. *COL*

The Real Glory 🎦🎦🎦 **1939** After the U.S. capture of the Philippine islands during the Spanish-American war, an uprising of Moro tribesmen spreads terror. After most of the islands are evacuated only a small group of Army officers is left to lead the Filipino soldiers against the rebels. Cooper plays the heroic doctor, who is not afraid to fight, especially when he comes to the rescue of the beseiged Army fort. Great action sequences and paticularly good performances by Cooper and Niven. **95m/B VHS.** Gary Cooper, Andrea Leeds, David Niven, Reginald Owen, Broderick Crawford; **D:** Henry Hathaway. *MGM, WAR*

Real Life 🎬🎬🎬 **1979 (R)** Writer/comedian Brooks's first feature sags in places, but holds its own as a vehicle for his peculiar talent. Brooks plays a pompous director whose ambition is to make a documentary of a "typical" American family. Good, intelligent comedy. **99m/C VHS, Beta.** Charles Grodin, Frances Lee McCain, Albert Brooks; **D:** Albert Brooks; **W:** Monica Johnson, Harry Shearer, Albert Brooks. *PAR*

The Real McCoy 🎬½ **1993 (PG-13)** Generally awful crime-caper film about female bank robber Karen McCoy (Basinger). Just out of prison, all Karen wants to do is go straight and raise her young son but her plans are thwarted by former associates who kidnap the child to force her into one last heist. Kilmer is the small-time thief, with a crush on Karen, who tries to help her out. Dumb, slow-moving story with a vapid performance by Basinger. **104m/C VHS, LV, Letterbox, Closed Caption.** Kim Basinger, Val Kilmer, Terence Stamp, Zach English, Gailard Sartain; **D:** Russell Mulcahy; **W:** William Davies, William Osborne. *USH*

Real Men 🎬½ **1987 (PG-13)** The junior Belushi brother is a spy forced to recruit ordinary guy Ritter to help him negotiate with aliens to save the world. Bizarre premise shows promise, but spy spoof doesn't fire on all comedic pistons. Nice try. **86m/C VHS, Beta, LV, Closed Caption.** James Belushi, John Ritter, Barbara Barrie; **D:** Dennis Feldman; **C:** John A. Alonzo; **M:** Miles Goodman. *FOX*

The Real Thing 🎬🎬 **1997 (R)** Ex-con Rupert (Russo) is trying the straight and narrow while his kid brother James continues to be a bad guy. But when James is shot, Rupert gets together with some criminal buddies to pull off a New Year's Eve heist to raise the money needed for James' care. This one's kind of dull until the ending shoot-out. **89m/C VHS.** James Russo, Gary Busey, Emily Lloyd, Esai Morales, Jeremy Piven. *THV*

Reality Bites 🎬🎬½ **1994 (PG-13)** Humorous look at four recent college grads living, working, and slacking in Houston. Script by newcomer Childress is at its best when highlighting the trends: 7-Eleven Big Gulps, tacky '70s memorabilia, and games revolving around episodes of old TV shows like "Good Times," to name a few. Definite appeal for those in their early 20s, but anyone over 25 may encounter a "Generation X-er" gap, a noticeable problem since "Reality" claims to speak for the entire 20-something generation. Decent directorial debut for Stiller; good cast, particularly Garofalo, in her film debut. **99m/C VHS, LV, Letterbox, Closed Caption, DVD.** Winona Ryder, Ethan Hawke, Ben Stiller, Janeane Garofalo, Steve Zahn, Swoosie Kurtz, Joe Don Baker, John Mahoney; *Cameos:* David Pirner, Anne Meara, Jeanne Tripplehorn, Karen Duffy, Evan Dando; **D:** Ben Stiller; **W:** Helen Childress; **M:** Karl Wallinger. Nominations: MTV Movie Awards '94: Best Kiss (Ethan Hawke/Winona Ryder). *USH*

Really Weird Tales 🎬🎬½ **1986** Several SCTV alumni highlight this three-story movie, which is science fiction with a satirical edge. **85m/C VHS, Beta.** John Candy, Martin Short, Joe Flaherty, Catherine O'Hara. *VTR*

Reap the Wild Wind 🎬🎬½ **1942** DeMille epic about salvagers off the Georgia coast in the 1840s featuring Wayne as the captain and Massey and a giant squid as the villains. Good cast, lesser story, fine underwater photography. **123m/C VHS, Beta.** Ray Milland, John Wayne, Paulette Goddard, Raymond Massey, Robert Preston, Lynne Overman, Susan Hayward, Charles Bickford, Walter Hampden, Louise Beavers, Martha O'Driscoll, Elisabeth Risdon, Hedda Hopper, Raymond Hatton, Barbara Britton; **D:** Cecil B. DeMille; **C:** Victor Milner. Academy Awards '42: Best Special Effects; Nominations: Academy Awards '42: Best Color Cinematography, Best Interior Decoration. *USH*

Rear Window 🎬🎬🎬🎬 **1954** A newspaper photographer with a broken leg (Stewart) passes the time recuperating by observing his neighbors through the window. When he sees what he believes to be a murder, he decides to solve the crime himself. With help from his beautiful girl-

friend and his nurse, he tries to catch the murderer without getting killed himself. Top drawer Hitchcock blends exquisite suspense with occasional on-target laughs. Based on the story by Cornell Woolrich. **112m/C VHS, Beta, LV.** James Stewart, Grace Kelly, Thelma Ritter, Wendell Corey, Raymond Burr, Judith Evelyn; **D:** Alfred Hitchcock; **W:** John Michael Hayes; **C:** Robert Burks; **M:** Franz Waxman. National Film Registry '97;; Nominations: Academy Awards '54: Best Color Cinematography, Best Director (Hitchcock), Best Screenplay, Best Sound. *USH, TLF, HMV*

A Reason to Believe 🎬🎬 **1995 (R)** Campus date rape drama filmed at writer/director Tirola's alma mater, Miami University. Charlotte (Smith) goes to her boyfriend Wesley's (Quinn) big frat party, even though he's away and asked her not to. She drinks and flirts (a lot) with his best friend Jim (Underwood) and eventually leaves to collapse in a stupor on Wesley's bed. Jim follows and rapes her, though he'll tell his buddies Charlotte was a willing participant, which Wesley angrily believes. Meanwhile, the traumatized Charlotte is taken up by Linda (Emelin), the leader of the student feminist organization who wants the fraternities disbanded. Somewhat preachy and predicatable.**CW:** Strong sexuality, language, substance abuse, a rape. **109m/C VHS.** Allison Smith, Jay Underwood, Daniel Quinn, Georgia Emelin, Obba Babatunde; **D:** Douglas Tirola; **W:** Douglas Tirola; **C:** Sarah Cawley. *THV*

Reason to Die 🎬 **1990 (R)** Bounty hunter uses his own girlfriend as a decoy to trap a psychotic serial killer. **86m/C VHS, LV.** Liam Cundill, Wings Hauser, Anneline Kriel, Arnold Vosloo; **D:** Tim Spring. *THV*

A Reason to Live, a Reason to Die 🎬🎬 *Massacre at Fort Holman; Una Ragione Per Vivere e Una Per Morire* **1973** A bland Italian-French-German-Spanish western in which a group of condemned men attempt to take a Confederate fort. **90m/C VHS, Beta.** James Coburn, Telly Savalas, Bud Spencer, Robert Burton; **D:** Tonino Valerii. *NO*

Rebecca 🎬🎬🎬🎬 **1940** Based on Daphne Du Maurier's best-selling novel about a young unsophisticated girl who marries a moody and prominent country gentleman haunted by the memory of his first wife. Fontaine and Olivier turn in fine performances as the unlikely couple. Suspenseful and surprising. Hitchcock's first American film and only Best Picture Oscar. Laserdisc features: rare screen tests of Vivien Leigh, Anne Baxter, Loretta Young, and Joan Fontaine, footage from Rebecca's winning night at the Academy Awards, original radio broadcasts of film by Orson Welles and David O. Selznick, and commentary of film with interview excerpts with Hitchcock. **130m/B VHS, Beta, LV, Closed Caption.** Joan Fontaine, Laurence Olivier, Judith Anderson, George Sanders, Nigel Bruce, Florence Bates, Gladys Cooper, Reginald Denny, Leo G. Carroll, Sir C. Aubrey Smith, Melville Cooper; **D:** Alfred Hitchcock; **W:** Joan Harrison, Robert Sherwood; **C:** George Barnes; **M:** Franz Waxman. Academy Awards '40: Best Black and White Cinematography, Best Picture; Nominations: Academy Awards '40: Best Actor (Olivier), Best Actress (Fontaine), Best Director (Hitchcock), Best Film Editing, Best Interior Decoration, Best Screenplay, Best Supporting Actress (Anderson), Best Original Score. *FOX, HMV, BTV*

Rebecca 🎬🎬🎬 **1997** Daphne du Maurier's tale of marriage and jealousy makes its second TV incarnation. Worldly widower Maxim de Winter (Dance) takes his nameless, shy young bride (Fox) back to Manderley, the family estate. There she must compete with the ghost of the first Mrs. de Winter—the glamorous Rebecca—family secrets, and obsessive housekeeper, Mrs. Danvers (Rigg). The 1980 TV version (with Jeremy Brett as Maxim) starred Joanna David in the title role, coincidentally newcomer Fox's mother. **240m/C VHS.** GB Emilia Fox, Charles Dance, Diana Rigg, Faye Dunaway, Geraldine James, Jonathan Cake; **D:** Jim O'Brien; **W:** Arthur Hopcraft. *PBS, VIF, TVC*

Rebecca of Sunnybrook Farm 🎬🎬 **1917** The original film version of the tale about an orphan who spreads sunshine and good cheer to all those around her. Silent with organ score. Based on the popular novel by Kate Douglas Wiggin; remade with Shirley Temple in 1938. **77m/B VHS, Beta, LV.** Mary Pickford, Eugene O'Brien, Marjorie Daw, Helen Jerome Eddy; **D:** Marshall Neilan; **M:** Gaylord Carter. *CCB*

Rebecca of Sunnybrook Farm 🎬🎬🎬 **1938** Temple becomes a radio star over her aunt's objections in this bouncy musical that has nothing to do with the famous Kate Douglas Wiggin novel. Temple sings a medley of her hits, and dances the finale with Bill "Bojangles" Robinson. ♫On the Good Ship Lollipop/ When I'm With You/Animal Crackers medley; Crackly Corn Flakes; Alone With You; Happy Ending; Au Revoir; An Old Straw Hat; Come and Get Your Happiness; Parade of the Wooden Soldiers. **80m/B VHS, Beta, LV, Closed Caption.** Shirley Temple, Randolph Scott, Jack Haley, Phyllis Brooks, Gloria Stuart, Slim Summerville, Bill Robinson, Helen Westley, William Demarest; **D:** Allan Dwan; **C:** Arthur C. Miller. *FOX, MLB, MLT*

Rebel 🎬½ **1973 (PG)** Mumbling student radical must decide between his love for a country girl and his loyalty to an underground terrorist organization. Notable (or not) for display of early Stallone. **80m/C VHS, Beta.** Sylvester Stallone, Anthony Page, Rebecca Grimes. *NO*

Rebel 🎬½ **1985 (R)** A U.S. Marine falls in love with a Sydney nightclub singer and goes AWOL during WWII. Stylish but empty and badly cast. **93m/C VHS, Beta, LV, Closed Caption.** AU Matt Dillon, Debbie Byrne, Bryan Brown, Bill Hunter, Ray Barrett; **D:** Michael Jenkins. *ART, VES*

Rebel High 🎬½ **1988 (R)** Hijinks occur at a high school where youngsters study guerilla warfare and teachers wear bullet-proof vests. **92m/C VHS, Beta.** Harvey Berger, Stu Trivax, Larry Gimple, Shawn Goldwater; **D:** Harry Jacobs.

Rebel Love 🎬 **1985** Love grows between a northern widow and a Confederate spy. In better hands it might have been a good story. Here, it's overwrought and embarrassing historical melodrama. **84m/C VHS, Beta.** Terence Knox, Jamie Rose, Fred Ryan; **D:** Milton Bagby Jr.; **W:** Milton Bagby Jr. *ART, VES*

Rebel Rousers 🎬🎬 **1969** A motorcycle gang wreaks havoc in a small town where a dragrace is being held to see who will get the pregnant girlfriend of Dern's high-school buddy as the prize. Young Nicholson in striped pants steals the show. **81m/C VHS, Beta.** Jack Nicholson, Cameron Mitchell, Diane Ladd, Bruce Dern, Harry Dean Stanton; **D:** Martin B. Cohen.

The Rebel Set 🎬🎬½ *Beatsville* **1959** The owner of a beat generation coffeehouse plans an armed robbery with the help of some buddies. Genuinely suspenseful, competently directed. **72m/B VHS, Beta.** Gregg Palmer, Kathleen Crowley, Edward Platt, John Lupton, Ned Glass, Don Sullivan, Vicki Dougan, I. Stanford Jolley; **D:** Gene Fowler Jr.; **C:** Karl Struss. *SNC*

Rebel Storm 🎬 **1990 (R)** A group of freedom fighters team up to rescue America from the totalitarian rulers that are in charge in 2099 A.D. **99m/C VHS, Beta, LV.** Zach Galligan, Wayne Crawford, June Chadwick, Rod McCary, John Rhys-Davies, Elizabeth Kiefer; **D:** Francis Schaeffer.

Rebel Vixens woof! **1985** Even though the war is over, ex-confederate soldiers continue looting and raping, until a brothel-full of prostitutes concoct a plan that has a lot to do with softcore sex. **94m/C VHS, Beta.** Maria Lease, Roda Spain.

Rebel Without a Cause 🎬🎬🎬🎬 **1955** James Dean's most memorable screen appearance. In the second of his three films, he plays a troubled teenager from the right side of the tracks. Dean's portrayal of Jim Stark, a teen alienated from both his parents and peers, is excellent. He befriends outcasts Wood and Mineo in a police station and together they find a commonground. Superb young stars carry this in-the-gut story of adolescence. All three leads met with real-life tragic ends. 111m/C VHS, Beta, LV, Letterbox, Closed Caption. James Dean, Natalie Wood, Sal Mineo, Jim Backus, Nick Adams, Dennis Hopper, Ann Doran, William Hopper, Rochelle Hudson, Corey Allen, Edward Platt; D: Nicholas Ray; W: Stewart Stern; M: Leonard Rosenman. National Film Registry '90;; Nominations: Academy Awards '55: Best Story, Best Supporting Actor (Mineo), Best Supporting Actress (Wood). WAR

The Rebels 🎞🎞 **1979** In the sequel to the television mini series "The Bastard," Philip Kent (Stevens) continues his Revolutionary War battle on the side of American independence. He is assisted by Southerner Judson Fletcher (Johnson) in thwarting an assassination attempt on George Washington. In addition to Bosley's Ben Franklin, "The Rebels" offers Backus as John Hancock. Followed by "The Seekers"; based on the novel by John Jakes. 190m/C VHS, Closed Caption. Andrew Stevens, Don Johnson, Doug McClure, Jim Backus, Richard Basehart, Joan Blondell, Tom Bosley, Rory Calhoun, MacDonald Carey, Kim Cattrall, William Daniels, Anne Francis, Peter Graves, Pamela Hensley, Wilfrid Hyde-White, Nehemiah Persoff, William Smith, Forrest Tucker, Tanya Tucker, Robert Vaughn, Deborah Richter; D: Russ Mayberry. USH

Reborn 🎞🎞 **1978** A faith healer and a talent scout hire actors to be cured of fake ailments. 91m/C VHS, Beta. Dennis Hopper, Michael Moriarty, Francesco Rabal, Antonella Murgia. VES

Rebound: The Legend of Earl "The Goat" Manigault 🎞🎞½ **1996 (R)** Earl "The Goat" Manigault (Cheadle) was a '60s Harlem playground basketball phenom who was taken under the wing of parks director Holcomb Rucker (Whitaker), who tries to steer the young man towards college and a career in the NBA. Unfortunately, the easily influenced Manigault also attracts the attention of local drug dealer Legrand (Beach) and when Manigault's life starts to fall apart, he drops out of college and turns to heroin, eventually winding up in prison. Since this is an inspirational true story, Manigault does turn his life around to found his own basketball tournament in Harlem. Made for cable. CW: Graphic` drug use, strong language, some sexuality and a scene of violence. 111m/C VHS. Don Cheadle, Michael Beach, James Earl Jones, Loretta Devine, Glynn Turman, Clarence Williams III, Forest Whitaker, Eriq La Salle; D: Eriq La Salle; W: Larry Golin, Alan Swyer; C: Alan Kivilo; M: Kevin Eubanks. HBO

Reckless 🎞🎞 **1935** Harlow, in a role originally intended for Joan Crawford, plays a showgirl coveted by a millionaire and secretly loved by her manager. Unfortunately, Harlow couldn't pull off the acting (much less the singing and dancing), although the plot strangely paralleled her own life. Songs include "Reckless," "Ev'rything's Been Done Before," "Trocadero," "Hear What My Heart Is Saying" and "Cyclone." 96m/B VHS, LV. Jean Harlow, William Powell, Franchot Tone, May Robson, Ted Healy, Nat Pendleton, Rosalind Russell; D: Victor Fleming. MGM

Reckless 🎞🎞½ **1984 (R)** A sincere movie about a "good" girl who finds herself obsessed with a rebel from the wrong side of her small town. Differs from 1950s' wrong-side-of-the-track flicks only in updated sex and music. 93m/C VHS, Beta, LV. Aidan Quinn, Daryl Hannah, Kenneth McMillan, Cliff DeYoung, Lois Smith, Adam Baldwin, Dan Hedaya, Jennifer Grey, Pamela Springsteen; D: James Foley; W: Chris Columbus; C: Michael Ballhaus; M: Thomas Newman. MGM

Reckless 🎞🎞 **1995 (PG-13)** Rachel (Farrow) thinks she has a happy marriage and family but her husband (Goldwyn) informs her that he's hired a hit man to kill her. This startling revelation sends her on a 15-year journey in which she meets many other people who are not what they seem. Rene and Lucas go for an ultra-stylized

fable theme, exploring Rachel's (and America's) aversion to dealing with the world as it really is. Quirky characters and situations are at turns amusing and annoying. Adapted by Lucas from his own play. CW: Complex psychological themes and some disturbing images. 91m/C VHS, LV, Closed Caption. Mia Farrow, Scott Glenn, Mary-Louise Parker, Tony Goldwyn, Stephen Dorff, Eileen Brennan, Giancarlo Esposito, Deborah Rush; D: Norman Rene; W: Craig Lucas; C: Frederick Elmes; M: Stephen Endelman. HMK

Reckless 🎞🎞🎞 **1997** British TV production's a combo of farce, romance, and drama that finds young doctor Owen Springer (Green) returning to Manchester to look after his feisty-but-ailing father (Bradley). He has a chance meeting with a beautiful middle-aged woman on the train, and then Anna Fairley (Annis) turns out to be his job interviewer. Reckless Owen falls impulsively in love—before learning Anna is also the wife of his new boss, Dr. Richard Crane (Kitchen). This doesn't deter Owen, and when he learns Crane is having an affair, Owen arranges for Anna to discover her husband's infidelity. Naturally, this leads to Owen and Anna hitting the sheets and things get very complicated. 312m/C VHS. GB Robson Green, Francesca Annis, Michael Kitchen, David Bradley, Julian Rhind-Tutt, Daniela Nardini, Margery Mason, Connor Mullen; D: David Richards, Sarah Harding; W: Paul Abbott. VTR

Reckless Disregard 🎞½ **1984** A doctor whose career is ruined by a news report accusing him of involvement in a drug scam sues the newscaster. Made for television saga based on Dan Rather's "60 Minutes" story and ensuing lawsuit. 92m/C VHS, Beta. Leslie Nielsen, Tess Harper, Ronny Cox, Kate Lynch; D: Harvey Hart. ART, VES

Reckless Kelly 🎞🎞½ **1993 (PG)** Australian bank robber, pop culture hero, and local video store owner Kelly is upset when his gang's island retreat is about to be sold to a Japanese conglomerate, unless he can come up with a higher offer. So he prepares for a last-ditch defense of his home. Slapstick homage to legendary Australian outlaw Ned Kelly. 81m/C VHS, Closed Caption. AU Yahoo Serious, Hugo Weaving, Melora Hardin, Alexei Sayle, Bob Maza, Kathleen Freeman; D: Yahoo Serious; W: Yahoo Serious. WAR

Reckless Moment 🎞🎞🎞 **1949** A mother commits murder to save her daughter from an unsavory older man, and finds herself blackmailed. Gripping, intense thriller. 82m/B VHS, Beta. James Mason, Joan Bennett, Geraldine Brooks; D: Max Ophuls; C: Burnett Guffey. BFA

The Reckless Way 🎞½ **1936** A young woman struggles for her big break into the movies. 72m/B VHS, Beta. Marion Nixon, Kane Richmond, Inez Courtney, Malcolm McGregor, Harry Harvey, Arthur Howard; D: Raymond K. Johnson. GPV

Recoil 🎞🎞 **1997 (R)** L.A. detective Ray Morgan (Daniels) gets in trouble with a crime family and they target his wife and family. So, for Ray it's a kill or be killed situation. CW: Violence, language and a scene of sexuality. 96m/C VHS, Closed Caption. Gary Daniels, Gregory McKinney. PMH

Record of a Tenement Gentleman 🎞🎞 **1947** An abandoned child picks a grumpy, middle-aged widow as a surrogate mother and she and her crazy neighbors come to love the little boy. Surprise ending. Japanese with subtitles. 72m/B VHS. JP Choko Iida, Hohi Aoki, Chishu Ryu, Eitaro Ozawa; D: Yasujiro Ozu. NYF

Recruits 🎞 **1986 (R)** Sophomoric gagfest about an inept Californian police force. Typical '80s-style mindless "comedy": dumb gags ensue from perfunctory premise. 81m/C VHS, Beta, LV. Alan Deveau, Annie McAuley, Lolita Davidovich; D: Rafal Zielinski. ART, VES

The Rector's Wife 🎞🎞 **1994** Anna Bouverie (Duncan) has spent 20 years as a clergyman's wife, scrimping and slaving to raise a family, serve God, and work for the parish on limited

means. Tired of the financial strain she takes a job at a local supermarket causing additional disturbances in her already shaky marriage, disapproval of the parish, and the sudden interest of three different men. Based on the novel by Joanna Trollope; on four cassettes. 208m/C VHS. GB Lindsay Duncan, Jonathan Coy, Simon Fenton, Lucy Dawson, Joyce Redman, Stephen Dillane, Ronald Pickup, Miles Anderson, Prunella Scales, Jonathan Cecil; D: Giles Foster; W: Hugh Whitemore; M: Richard Hartley. SIG, AEH, NEW

Red Alert 🎞🎞½ **1977** Good, suspenseful, topical made for televison thriller about nuclear meltdown. Will Minneapolis be saved? Usually Barbeau's name in the credits is a red alert, but this one is better than most. 95m/C VHS, Beta. William Devane, Ralph Waite, Michael Brandon, Adrienne Barbeau; D: Billy Hale. PAR

The Red and the Black 🎞🎞🎞 *Le Rouge et le Noir* **1957** A big budgeted French adaptation of the classic Stendhal novel. A young man from the country seeks success, first in the Church and later in the employment and seduction of the gentry. In French with English subtitles. 134m/B VHS, Beta. FR Danielle Darrieux, Gerard Philipe; D: Claude Autant-Lara. IVY, MRV, FCT

The Red and the White 🎞🎞🎞 *Csillagosok, Katonak* **1968** Epic war drama about the civil war between the Red Army and the non-communist Whites in Russia in 1918. Told from the perspective of Hungarians who fought alongside the Reds. Little dialogue. In Hungarian with English subtitles. 92m/B VHS, LV, Letterbox. HU D: Miklos Jancso. KIV

The Red Badge of Courage 🎞🎞🎞½ **1951** John Huston's adaptation of the Stephen Crane Civil War novel is inspired, despite cutting room hatchet job by the studio. A classic study of courage and cowardice. Sweeping battle scenes and intense personal drama. 69m/B VHS, Beta. Audie Murphy, Bill Mauldin, Douglas Dick, Royal Dano, Andy Devine; D: John Huston. KUI, MGM, HMV

Red Ball Express 🎞🎞½ **1952** Fast-paced action highlights this WWII story about the transportation corp that must supply the gas, food, and ammunition necessary for General Patton's tank advance on Nazi-held Paris. Tough company leader Lt. Campbell (Chandler) must get the cooperation of both his first sergeant (Nicol), who holds a pre-war grudge, and a black corporal (Poitier), who believes he's the target of racism, in order to accomplish his mission. 84m/B VHS, Closed Caption. Jeff Chandler, Alex Nicol, Sidney Poitier, Charles Drake, Hugh O'Brian, Jack Kelly, Judith Braun, Jacqueline Duval; D: Budd Boetticher; W: John Michael Hayes; C: Maury Gertsman. USH

The Red Balloon 🎞🎞🎞½ **1956** The story of Pascal, a lonely French boy who befriends a wondrous red balloon which follows him everywhere. Lovely, finely done parable of childhood, imagination and friendship. 34m/C VHS, Beta, LV, 8mm. FR Pascal Lamorisse; D: Albert Lamorisse. Academy Awards '56: Best Original Screenplay. HMV, HHT, DVT

Red Balloon/Occurrence at Owl Creek Bridge 🎞🎞🎞½ **1962** Two classic award-winning shorts have been combined on one tape: "The Red Balloon" (color, 1956) and "An Occurrence at Owl Creek Bridge." The former is a children's story about a balloon on the loose; the latter is a perfectly rendered adaptation of the Ambrose Bierce short story of the same title, a taut narration of a Civil War hanging. 60m/C VHS, Beta. FR Pascal Lamorisse, Roger Jacquet; D: Robert Enrico, Albert Lamorisse. VYY, WFV, CAB

Red Barry **1938** A comic strip detective tries to track down criminals who threaten the world. Thirteen episodes on one videotape. ?m/B VHS. Buster Crabbe, Frances Robinson, Edna Sedgwick, Cyril Delevanti, Frank Lackteen; D: Ford Beebe, Alan James. NOS, MLB

Red Beard 🎬🎬🎬 *Akahige* **1965** An uncharacteristic drama by Kurosawa, about a young doctor in Japan awakening to life and love under the tutelage of a compassionate old physician. Highly acclaimed; in Japanese with English subtitles. **185m/B VHS, Beta, LV, Letterbox.** *JP* Toshiro Mifune, Yuzo Kayama, Yoshio Tsuchiya, Reiko Dan; **D:** Akira Kurosawa. *CRC, FCT*

Red Blooded American Girl 🎬 **1990** (R) A scientist develops a virus that turns people into vampires. Those infected hit the streets in search of blood. **89m/C VHS, Beta, LV.** *CA* Christopher Plummer, Andrew Stevens, Heather Thomas, Kim Coates; **D:** David Blyth.

Red Corner 🎬🎬½ **1997** (R) Wrong-man scenario features Gere as an American entertainment lawyer on business in China who is framed for murdering a Chinese model he spent the night with. A colossal bummer, Jack's beautiful, court-appointed attorney (Ling) explains the Chinese legal process: "If you plead not guilty, you will be shot within a week and the cost of the bullet will be charged to your family." Gruesome jail scenes involving excrement and a hell-on-wheels female judge don't help his case much, either. Pic suffers from some of the usual cliches but is aided by an acclaimed performance by Ling and one of the better recent Gere turns. Beijing was recreated on the DreamWorks studio lot in California. *CW:* Some violence and a scene of sexuality. **118m/C VHS.** Richard Gere, Bai Ling, Byron Mann, Bradley Whitford, Peter Donat, Robert Stanton, Tsai Chin, James Hong, Tzi Ma, Richard Venture; **D:** Jon Avnet; **W:** Robert King; **C:** Karl Walter Lindenlaub; **M:** Thomas Newman. *MGM*

Red Dawn 🎬½ **1984** (PG-13) During WWIII, Russian invaders overrun America's heartland and take over the country. Eight small-town teenagers, calling themselves the Wolverines, hide out in the rugged countryside and fight the Russians. Swayze and Grey met again in "Dirty Dancing." **114m/C VHS, Beta, LV, Letterbox.** Patrick Swayze, C. Thomas Howell, Harry Dean Stanton, Powers Boothe, Lea Thompson, Charlie Sheen, Ben Johnson, Jennifer Grey, Ron O'Neal, William Smith; **D:** John Milius; **W:** John Milius, Kevin Reynolds; **M:** Basil Poledouris. *MGM*

Red Desert 🎬 **1950** The Pecos Kid is sent to track down the theft of a shipment of gold. **60m/B VHS, Beta, LV.** Jack Holt, Donald (Don "Red") Barry, Tom Neal, Joseph Crehan, Tom London; **D:** Charles Marquis Warren. *NO*

The Red Desert 🎬🎬🎬 *Il Deserto Rosso* **1964** Antonioni's first color film, depicting an alienated Italian wife who searches for meaning in the industrial lunar landscape of northern Italy, to no avail. Highly acclaimed, and a masterpiece of visual form. In Italian with English subtitles. **120m/C VHS.** *IT* Monica Vitti, Richard Harris, Carlos Chionetti; **D:** Michelangelo Antonioni; **W:** Michelangelo Antonioni, Tonino Guerra; **C:** Carlo DiPalma; **M:** Giovanni Fusco. Venice Film Festival '64: Best Film. *FCT, CVC, TPV*

Red Desert Penitentiary **1983** A spoof of movie-making featuring caricatures of industry-types. **104m/C VHS, Beta.** James Michael Taylor, Cathryn Bissell, Will Rose; **D:** George Sluizer. *NO*

Red Dust 🎬🎬🎬 **1932** The overseer of a rubber plantation in Indochina causes all kinds of trouble when he falls in love with a young engineer's wife. Filled with free-spirited humor and skillfully directed; remarkably original. Remade in 1940 as "Congo Maisie" and in 1954 as "Mogambo." **83m/B VHS, Beta.** Clark Gable, Jean Harlow, Mary Astor, Gene Raymond, Donald Crisp; **D:** Victor Fleming. *MGM*

Red Earth 🎬🎬 **19??** A satire about life under Hungarian socialism. Szanto is a bauxite mixer whose pigs have rooted out high quality bauxite from his backyard. Only the local bauxite prospectors don't want to believe in luck (and pigs) and credit, instead, careful planning. When Szanto's village is turned into a vast open mine, he's blamed. In Hungarian with English subtitles. **105m/C VHS.** *HU* Imre Nemeth, Sandor Kocsis, Kalman Toronyi,

Ferenc Togh, Vilmos Gadori; **D:** Laszlo Vitezy; **W:** Istvan Darday. *FCT*

Red Firecracker, Green Firecracker 🎬🎬½ *Paoda Shuang Deng* **1993** (R) Set in northern China before the 1911 revolution, this gorgeous saga focuses on the fortunes of the Cai family. The family, whose wealth depends on their fireworks business, has no male heirs and is headed by daughter Chun Zhi (Jing). To assume this lofty position, Chun Zhi must dress like a man and is forbidden to marry but that doesn't stop her from falling in love with bold young travelling artist Nie Bao (Gang). The household is thrown into a frenzy by their affair and it's decided that all Chun Zhi's potential suitors must undergo a firecracker ritual in order to win her hand. Mandarin Chinese with subtitles. *CW:* Language. **111m/C VHS.** *HK CH* Ning Jing, Wu Gang, Zhao Xiaorui, Gai Yang; **D:** He Ping; **W:** Da Ying; **C:** Yang Lun. *HMK*

Red Flag: The Ultimate Game 🎬🎬½ **1981** Pilots rival for success in battle simulation training with terrible consequences. Fine performances cover plot weaknesses. Well-written dialogue. Made for television. **100m/C VHS, Beta.** Barry Bostwick, William Devane, Joan Van Ark, Fred McCarren, Debra Feuer, George Coe, Linden Chiles, Arlen Dean Snyder; **D:** Don Taylor. *ART*

The Red Fury 🎬🎬 **197?** Young Indian boy struggles to overcome prejudice and caring for his horse shows him the way. Good family viewing. **105m/C VHS.** William Jordan, Kathy Cannon. *TPV, HHE, BPG*

Red Garters 🎬🎬½ **1954** A musical parody of old-time westerns which doesn't quite come off. Mitchell plays the cowpoke who comes to town to avenge the death of his brother with Clooney as the saloon singer who uses him to make boyfriend Carson jealous. The adequate songs include "Red Garters," "Man and Woman," "A Dime and a Dollar," and "Vaquero." **91m/C VHS, Closed Caption.** Guy Mitchell, Rosemary Clooney, Jack Carson, Gene Barry, Pat Crowley, Joanne Gilbert, Frank Faylen, Reginald Owen, Buddy Ebsen; **D:** George Marshall; **W:** Michael Fessier; **M:** Jay Livingston, Ray Evans. Nominations: Academy Awards '54: Best Art Direction/Set Decoration (Color). *PAR*

The Red Half-Breed 🎬½ **1970** A lonely half-breed Indian, wrongly accused of murder, discovers the real killer while running from the law. **103m/C VHS, Beta.** Daniel Pilon, Genevieve Deloir; **D:** Gilles Carle.

Red Headed Stranger 🎬½ **1987** (R) Willie Nelson vehicle based on his 1975 album. Nelson is a gun-totin' preacher who kills his wife and is led to salvation by a good farm woman. But honestly: Morgan Fairchild as Willie Nelson's wife? Please. **108m/C VHS, Beta, LV, Closed Caption.** Willie Nelson, Katharine Ross, Morgan Fairchild; **D:** William D. Wittliff; **W:** William D. Wittliff. *NLC*

Red Headed Woman 🎬🎬🎬 **1932** Harlow plays an unscrupulous woman who charms her way into the lives of influential men. She causes her boss to divorce his wife and marry her while she sleeps with the chauffeur (Boyer) and others. Audiences loved the scandalous material, but the Hays Office objected to the fact that the immoral woman goes unpunished. Boyer's small but important role salvaged his floundering American film career. Harlow is sultry and funny. **79m/B VHS, Beta.** Jean Harlow, Chester Morris, Lewis Stone, Leila Hyams, Una Merkel, Henry Stephenson, May Robson, Charles Boyer, Harvey Clark; **D:** Jack Conway. *MGM, FCT*

Red Heat 🎬½ **1985** Blair is a tourist in East Germany mistakenly arrested and sent to a rough women's prison. Her fiance tries to free her. Meanwhile, she has to deal with tough-lady fellow jail bird Kristel. Familiar and marginal. **104m/C VHS, Beta, LV.** Linda Blair, Sylvia Kristel, Sue Kiel, William Ostrander; **D:** Robert Collector. *ART, VES*

Red Heat 🎬🎬 **1988** (R) Two cops—one from the Soviet Union, one from Chicago—team up to catch the Eastern Bloc's biggest drug czar. Lots of action, but at times it seems too similar to Hill's earlier hit "48 Hours." Film claims to be the first major U.S. production shot in Red Square, Moscow. **106m/C VHS, Beta, LV, DVD.** Arnold Schwarzenegger, James Belushi, Peter Boyle, Ed O'Ross, Laurence "Larry" Fishburne, Gina Gershon, Richard Bright; **D:** Walter Hill; **W:** Walter Hill; **M:** James Horner. *ART, TLF*

Red Hot 🎬🎬½ **1995** (PG) Alexi (Getty), a young Russian classical musician, is secretly smuggled American rock 'n' roll music (it's 1959) by his uncle. He immediately decides to form a band and plots the first underground Soviet rock concert. Too bad girlfriend Valentina's (Gugino) dad is a disapproving highly ranked Communist Party official and the KGB are giving Alexi the evil eye. **95m/C VHS, LV.** Balthazar Getty, Carla Gugino, Donald Sutherland, Armin Mueller-Stahl; **D:** Paul Haggis; **W:** Paul Haggis, Michael Maurer. *COL*

The Red House 🎬🎬🎬 **1947** Robinson plays a crippled farmer who, after his daughter brings home a suitor, attempts to keep everyone from a mysterious red house located on his property. Madness and murder prevail. Strange film noir about tangled relationships and unsuccessful attempts to bury the horrid past. Based on the novel by George Agnew Chamberlain. **100m/B VHS, Beta.** Edward G. Robinson, Lon McCallister, Judith Anderson, Allene Roberts, Rory Calhoun, Ona Munson, Julie London, Harry Shannon, Arthur Space, Walter Sande, Pat Flaherty; **D:** Delmer Daves; **W:** Delmer Daves; **C:** Bert Glennon; **M:** Miklos Rozsa. *CNG, NOS, SNC*

The Red Inn 🎬🎬 *L'Auberge Rouge* **1951** Yes, it is a comedy. An innkeeper and his wife have a second career involving the robbery and murder of stagecoach travellers staying at their isolated inn. And it's up to a monk (Fernandel) to stop the mayhem. French with subtitles. Yves Montand sings on the soundtrack. **95m/B VHS.** *FR* Fernandel, Francoise Rosay, Julien Carette, Gregoire Aslan, Marie-Claire Olivia, Lud Germain; **D:** Claude Autant-Lara; **W:** Jean Aurenche, Pierre Bost; **C:** Andre Bac; **M:** Rene Cloerec. *FCT*

Red Kimono 🎬🎬 **1925** Exploitative silent melodrama about a young woman ditched by her husband. She becomes a prostitute, but is redeemed by true love. Interesting slice of its period. **95m/B VHS, Beta.** Tyrone Power Sr., Priscilla Boner, Nellie Bly Baker, Mary Carr; **D:** Walter Lang. *NOS, VYY, DVT*

Red King, White Knight 🎬🎬½ **1989** (R) An assassin tries to kill Mikhail Gorbachev during superpower peace talks. Ex-s pook Skerritt returns to duty to thwart him. Better than most "topical" thrill ers. Made for cable television. **106m/C VHS, Beta.** Tom Skerritt, Max von Sydow, Helen Mirren; **D:** Geoff Murphy. *HBO*

Red Kiss 🎬🎬 *Rouge Baiser* **1985** In 1952 Paris, Nadia, a 15-year-old French-Jewish Stalinist of Polish descent falls in love with Stephane, an older, apolitical photographer. She's torn between love and politics; he's worried (rightly) about her being under-age; and to make matters more complicated, her Polish mother has been reunited with her first love and Nadia's family may be split apart. The sensual Valandrey is a real find in her difficult coming-of-age role. In French with English subtitles. **110m/C VHS, LV.** *FR* Charlotte Valandrey, Lambert Wilson, Marthe Keller, Gunter Lamprecht, Laurent Terzieff; **D:** Vera Belmont; **W:** Vera Belmont. Berlin International Film Festival '86: Best Actress (Valandrey). *FXL, FCT*

The Red Light Sting 🎬 **1984** A Justice Department rookie (Bridges) and a call girl (Fawcett) reluctantly team up to con the Mafia in order to convict a San Francisco rackets czar. Goes down easy, but also easily forgotten or skipped. **96m/C VHS, Beta.** Farrah Fawcett, Beau Bridges, Harold Gould, Paul Burke, Sunny Johnson; **D:** Rod Holcomb. *USH*

Red Lights Ahead 1936 Grandpa tries to save the day as he fights against spiritualism and crystal balls to help a friend prove that he is not running a scam. 63m/C VHS. Andy Clyde, Paula Stone, Roger Imhof, Frank "Junior" Coghlan, Ben Alexander, Matty Kemp, Sam Flint, Addison Randall, Lucile Gleason, Dann Doran; *D:* Roland D. Reed. *GPV*

Red Line ⅛½ 1996 (R) Stock-car racer Jim (McQueen) loses his sponsorship, turns to petty crime to settle his debts, and winds up in trouble with the mob when he hooks up with a couple of hoods to steal some diamonds. 102m/C VHS, LV. Chad McQueen, Michael Madsen, Corey Feldman, Jan-Michael Vincent, Roxana Zal, Dom DeLuise, Julie Strain, Robert Z'Dar; *D:* John Sjogren; *W:* John Sjogren, Scott Ziehl, Rolfe Kanefsky. *ORI*

Red Line 7000 ⅛⅛ 1965 High stakes auto racers drive fast cars and date women. Excellent racing footage in otherwise routine four-wheel fest. 110m/C VHS, LV, Closed Caption. James Caan, Laura Devon, Gail Hire, Charlene Holt, John Crawford, Marianna Hill, George Takei; *D:* Howard Hawks; *C:* Milton Krasner. *PAR, FCT*

Red Lion ⅛⅛½ *Akage* 1969 A bumbling horse-tender in feudal Japan impersonates a military officer to impress his family, only to be swept into leading a liberating revolution. In Japanese with English subtitles. 115m/C VHS, Beta. *JP* Toshiro Mifune, Shima Iwashita; *D:* Kihachi Okamoto. *VDA*

The Red Menace woof! 1949 Anti-Communist propaganda, made with unknown actors in documentary style has little to offer today's viewers other than unintentional laughs. Picture the Commies offering naive Americans money and sex to join the party, and you'll have an idea of the intellectual talent that went into this one. 87m/B VHS, LV. Robert Rockwell, Hanne Axman, Shepard Menken, Betty Lou Gerson, Barbara Fuller; *D:* R.G. Springsteen. *REP, FCT*

Red Nightmare ⅛½ 1962 Anti-communist propaganda produced for the Department of Defense by Warner Bros. features the cast of "Dragnet." The story dramatizes the Red Menace, with communists conspiring to take over America, and shows what would happen to life in a small American town if the Commies took over. 30m/B VHS, Beta. Jack Webb, Jack Kelly, Jeanne Cooper, Peter Brown. *VYY, IHF*

Red Nights ⅛ 1987 A country boy goes to Hollywood seeking success and finds instead corruption, decadence, and dishonesty. Excellent soundtrack by Tangerine Dream. 90m/C VHS, Beta. Christopher Parker, Jack Carter, Brian Matthews; *D:* Izhak Hanooka. *TWE*

Red Planet Mars ⅛⅛ 1952 Anti-communist, pro-Christianity story about scientists discovering that the Voice of Radio Free Mars belongs to God. Incoherent film overburdened with messages about politics, religion, and science was ahead of its time. Based on the play "Red Planet" by John L. Balderson and John Hoare. 87m/B VHS. Peter Graves, Andrea King, Marvin Miller, Herbert Berghof, House Peters Jr., Vince Barnett; *D:* Harry Horner; *W:* Anthony Veiller, John Balderston. *MGM, FCT*

The Red Pony ⅛⅛⅛ 1949 A young boy escapes from his family's fighting through his love for a pet pony. Based on the novel by John Steinbeck. Remade for television in 1976. Timeless classic that the whole family can enjoy. 89m/C VHS, LV. Myrna Loy, Robert Mitchum, Peter Miles, Louis Calhern, Shepperd Strudwick, Margaret Hamilton, Beau Bridges; *D:* Lewis Milestone; *C:* Gaetano Antonio "Tony" Gaudio; *M:* Aaron Copland. *REP, KUI*

The Red Pony ⅛⅛⅛ 1976 Excellent TV remake of a classic 1949 adaptation of John Steinbeck. Fonda is superb as a troubled young boy's difficult father. 101m/C VHS, Beta, LV. Henry Fonda, Maureen O'Hara, Clint Howard, Jack Elam, Ben Johnson; *D:* Robert Totten. *BFA*

The Red Raven Kiss-Off ⅛ 1990 (R) A seedy Hollywood detective becomes the key suspect in a movie-making murder. Based on the 1930s' Dan Turner mystery stories. Made for video. 93m/C VHS, Beta. Marc Singer, Tracy Scoggins, Nicholas Worth, Arte Johnson; *D:* Christopher Lewis.

Red Riding Hood ⅛⅛½ 1988 Musical version of story of wolf who has little girl fetish. 81m/C VHS, Beta. Isabella Rossellini, Craig T. Nelson, Rocco Sisto. *MGM*

Red River ⅛⅛⅛⅛ 1948 The classic Hawks epic about a gruelling cattle drive and the battle of wills between father and son. Generally regarded as one of the best westerns ever made, and Wayne's shining moment as a reprehensible, obsessive man. Featuring Clift in his first film. Restored version has eight minutes of previously edited material. Remade for television in 1988 with James Arness and Brian Boxleitner. 133m/B VHS, Beta, LV, Closed Caption. John Wayne, Montgomery Clift, Walter Brennan, Joanne Dru, John Ireland, Noah Beery Jr., Paul Fix, Coleen Gray, Harry Carey Jr., Harry Carey Sr., Chief Yowlachie, Hank Worden; *D:* Howard Hawks; *W:* Borden Chase, Charles Schnee; *M:* Dimitri Tiomkin. National Film Registry '90;; Nominations: Academy Awards '48: Best Film Editing, Best Story. *MGM, TLF, RDG*

Red River Valley ⅛⅛ *Man of the Frontier* 1936 Autry and partner Burnette go undercover to find out who's plaguing a dam construction site with explosions. Not to be confused with a 1941 Roy Rogers pic bearing the same title. 60m/B VHS. Gene Autry, Smiley Burnette, Frances Grant, Boothe Howard, Sam Flint, George Chesebro, Charles "Blackie" King, Eugene Jackson, Frank LaRue, Lloyd Ingraham; *D:* B. Reeves Eason. *NOS, VDM, VCN*

Red Rock Outlaw ⅛ 1947 A sleazy character tries to kill his twin brother and takes his place as an honest rancher. 56m/B VHS, Beta, LV. Lee White. *NO*

Red Rock West ⅛⅛⅛½ 1993 (R) Nothing is what it seems in this stylish and entertaining film noir set in a desolate Wyoming town. Perennial loser and nice guy Michael (Cage) is headed to a job at oil rig, but blows his chance by admitting he has a bad leg. Landing in the tiny burg of Red Rock, he's mistaken for the hit man hired by local barkeep Walsh to kill his pretty wife (Boyle). Then Boyle doubles Walsh's offer—what's a film noir boy to do? And Hopper, the real killer, strides into town. Full of twists, turns, and shades of "El Mariachi," this enjoyable, well-acted thriller is a real gem that escaped directly to cable before being rescued by a San Francisco exhibitor. 98m/C VHS, LV, Closed Caption. Nicolas Cage, Dennis Hopper, Lara Flynn Boyle, J.T. Walsh, Timothy Carhart, Dan Shor, Dwight Yoakam, Bobby Joe McFadden, Craig Reay, Vance Johnson, Robert Apel, Dale Gibson, Ted Parks, Babs Bram, Robert Guajardo, Sarah Sullivan; *D:* John Dahl; *W:* John Dahl, Rick Dahl; *C:* Marc Reshovsky; *M:* William Olvis. Nominations: Independent Spirit Awards '95: Best Director (Dahl), Best Screenplay. *COL*

The Red Rope ⅛½ 1937 A Western hero cuts his honeymoon short to track down some villains. 56m/B VHS. Bob Steele, Lois January, Forrest Taylor, Charles "Blackie" King, Karl Hackett, Bobby Nelson; *D:* S. Roy Luby. *NOS, DVT*

Red Scorpion ⅛ 1989 (R) A Soviet soldier journeys to Africa where he is to assassinate the leader of a rebel group. Will he succeed or switch allegiances? Poor acting and directing abound. 102m/C VHS, LV. Dolph Lundgren, M. Emmet Walsh, Al White, T.P. McKenna, Carmen Argenziano, Brion James, Regopstann; *D:* Joseph Zito; *W:* Arne Olsen, Jack Abramoff, Robert Abramoff; *C:* Joao Fernandes. *VTR*

Red Scorpion 2 ⅛½ 1994 (R) Another "Dirty Dozen" rip-off finds your average ethnically mixed good guys brought together by a government agency to be heroic. In this case the enemy is a neo-fascist businessman who uses skinheads to cause mayhem in minority communities. *CW:* Strong non-stop violence and some sexuality. 90m/C VHS, LV, Closed Caption. Matt McColm, John Savage, Jennifer Rubin, Michael Ironside, Michael Covert, Real

Andrews, George Touliatos; *D:* Michael Kennedy; *W:* Troy Bolotnick, Barry Victor; *M:* George Blondheim. *USH*

Red Shoe Diaries ⅛⅛ 1992 (R) After a woman's suicide her grieving lover discovers her diaries and finds out she led a secret erotic life, revolving around her shoe-salesman lover and a pair of sexy red shoes. Made for cable television; also available in an unrated version. *CW:* Language and strong sexuality. 105m/C VHS, LV, Closed Caption. David Duchovny, Billy Wirth, Brigitte Bako; *D:* Zalman King. *REP*

Red Shoe Diaries 2: Double Dare ⅛⅛ 1992 (R) The erotic sequel to "Red Shoe Diaries" follows the libidinous fancies of three women. Severance begins a sexual affair with a stranger while being torn between love and lust. Johnson gets naked to tease an office worker in the building next door. Crosby is a cop who is rejected by the man she desires—so she arrests and handcuffs him in order to play some kinky games. Also available in an unrated version. *CW:* Language and strong sexuality. 92m/C VHS, LV, Closed Caption. Joan Severance, Laura Johnson, Denise Crosby, Steven Bauer, Arnold Vosloo, David Duchovny; *D:* Zalman King, Tibor Takacs. *REP, PMS*

Red Shoe Diaries 3: Another Woman's Lipstick ⅛⅛ 1993 (R) Another sexual anthology focusing on three stories of desire from the made for cable television series. In "Another Woman's Lipstick" Zoey finds out her husband is having an affair and follows him to his liaison—only to become intrigued with his lover herself. "Just Like That" finds the up-tight Trudie falling for two very opposite men. "Talk to Me Baby" finds Ida and her lover Bud caught up in a very obsessional relationship. Also available in an unrated version. *CW:* Language and erotic content. 90m/C VHS, LV, Closed Caption. Nina Siemaszko, Matthew LeBlanc, Tcheky Karyo, Maryam D'Abo, Richard Tyson, Lydie Denier, Christina Fulton, Kevin Haley, David Duchovny; *D:* Ted Kotcheff, Rafael Eisenman, Zalman King; *W:* Zalman King, Chloe King. *REP*

Red Shoe Diaries 4: Auto Erotica ⅛ 1993 (R) Yet another compilation of erotic tales courtesy of the Zalman King series. The first story finds a maid finding her employer's secret chamber and uncovering a very private fantasy. The second has an architect lured by a mystery woman into a game of seduction and the third finds a couple engaged in competitive obsessions. Also available in an unrated version. 83m/C VHS, Closed Caption. Ally Sheedy, Scott Plank, David Duchovny, Sheryl Lee, Nicholas Chinlund; *D:* Zalman King. *REP*

Red Shoe Diaries 5: Weekend Pass ⅛⅛ 1995 (R) Yet another erotic saga from the cable series that features a model (Barbieri) hustling a pool hustler, a bounty hunter (Stansfield) becoming captivated by her prey, and an army recruit (Pouget) whose furlough involves a sexy drifter. 85m/C VHS, Closed Caption. Paula Barbieri, Claire Stansfield, Ely Pouget, Francesco Quinn, Ron Marquette, Tony Addabbo; *D:* Ted Kotcheff. *REP*

Red Shoe Diaries 6: How I Met My Husband ⅛⅛ 1995 (R) Three more erotic vignettes from the cable series. "How I Met My Husband" finds Alice enrolling in a course on becoming a dominatrix and falling for Giuseppe, who's one of the training objects. Camille has inherited her father's vast fortune in "Naked in the Moonlight" on the condition that she take special care of his '57 Cadillac convertible—and the one mechanic allowed to work on the car. In "Midnight Bells," Claire reminisces about the mystery lover she meets on only one night of the year—New Year's Eve. 85m/C VHS, Closed Caption. Luigi Amodeo, Neith Hunter, Raven Snow, Carsten Norgaard, John Enos, Charlotte Lewis, David Duchovny; *D:* Anne Goursaud, Philippe Angers, Bernard Auroux. *REP*

Red Shoe Diaries 7: Burning Up 🎬🎬 1996 (R) Yet another trilogy of TV eroticism. "Burning Up" finds Lynn becoming obsessed with a handsome fireman. "Kidnap" features the workaholic Sara taken hostage during a bank robbery and finding out that her captor has decided to marry her, Alia is a top model in "Runway," who falls in lust with a cabby. **CW:** Strong sexuality and some language. **90m/C VHS.** Udo Kier, Ron Marquette, Jennifer Ciesar, Amber Smith, Anthony Guidera, Daniel Blasco, Alexandra Tydings, David Duchovny; **D:** Rafael Eisenman. *REP*

Red Shoe Diaries 8: Night of Abandon 🎬🎬 1997 (R) Three more erotic adventures from the cable series. "Night of Abandon" finds Isabelle visiting her grandma in Rio de Janeiro and indulging in Carnival. "Liar's Table" has photjournalist Corey assigned to record L.A.'s sex scene and becoming intriged by a very expensive call gir. Married Kathryn's life changes "In the Blink of an Eye" when she meets a young boxer who's in training with her husband. **CW:** Language and erotic content. **86m/C VHS.** Erika Anderson, Audie England, Daniel Leza, Ann Cockburn, Terrence Sheahan, Laurie Simpson, Julien Maurel, Brian Edwards, David Duchovny; **D:** Rafael Eisenman, Rene Manzor, James Gavin Bedford. *REP*

The Red Shoes 🎬🎬🎬🎬 1948 British classic about a young ballerina torn between love and success. Inspired by the Hans Christian Andersen fairy tale. Noted for its lavish use of Technicolor. **136m/C VHS, Beta, LV, Closed Caption.** *GB* Anton Walbrook, Moira Shearer, Marius Goring, Leonide Massine, Robert Helpmann, Albert Basserman, Ludmila Tcherina, Esmond Knight; **D:** Emeric Pressburger, Michael Powell; **W:** Emeric Pressburger, Michael Powell; **C:** Jack Gardiff. Academy Awards '48: Best Art Direction/Set Decoration (Color), Best Original Dramatic/Comedy Score; Golden Globe Awards '49: Best Score; Nominations: Academy Awards '48: Best Film Editing, Best Picture, Best Story. *PAR, HMV*

Red Signals 🎬🎬 1927 Mystery criminal makes trains collide. **70m/B VHS, Beta.** Wallace MacDonald, Earl Williams, Eva Novak, J.P. McGowan, Frank Rice; **D:** J.P. McGowan. *GPV, FCT*

Red Snow 🎬 1991 High in the Cascade Mountains, Kyle Lewis is the new snowboard instructor for the Hurricane Ridge Ski Resort. The job is fine in the beginning, until Kyle learns of the tragic fate of the last instructor. Before he knows it, Kyle is the next target and is framed for two murders. He secures the help of his fellow snowboard buddies in hopes of solving the mystery and getting the girl, too. High speed ski scenes and dangerous stunts are the film's only redeeming qualities. **86m/C VHS.** Carlo Scandiuzzi, Scott Galloway, Darla Slavens, Mitchell Cox, Tamar Tibbs, Brian Mahoney; **D:** Phillip J. Roth. *VHE*

Red Sonja 🎬½ 1985 (PG-13) Two warriors join forces against an evil queen in this sword and sorcery saga. Big, beautiful bodies everywhere, with Bergman returning from her Conan adventures. Little humor, few special effects, and weak acting make this a poor outing. **89m/C VHS, Beta, LV, Closed Caption.** Arnold Schwarzenegger, Brigitte Nielsen, Sandahl Bergman, Paul Smith; **D:** Richard Fleischer; **M:** Ennio Morricone. Golden Raspberry Awards '85: Worst New Star (Nielsen). *MGM, FOX*

Red Sorghum 🎬🎬🎬½ 1987 A stunning visual achievement, this new wave Chinese film (and Yimou's directorial debut) succeeds on many levels—as an ode to the color red, as dark comedy, and as a sweeping epic with fairy tale overtones. Set in rural China in the 1920s, during the period of the Japanese invasion. The sorghum plot nearby is a symbolic playing field in the movie's most stunning scenes. Here, people make love, murder, betray, and commit acts of bravery, all under the watchful eye of nature. In Mandarin with English subtitles. **91m/C VHS.** *CH* Gong Li, Jiang Wen, Ji Cun Hua; **D:** Zhang Yimou; **C:** Gu Changwei. *NYF*

The Red Squirrel 🎬🎬 *La Ardilla Roja* 1993 Former pop star Jota (Nova) is distraught over breaking up with his girlfriend and contemplating throwing himself off a bridge when he witnesses a motorcycle accident and rushes to help the young woman (Suarez) involved. After learning she's suffering from amnesia, Jota tells both the woman and the hospital that her name is Lisa and he's her lover. Then Jota invents a fictitious life for her, according to his own desires. Spanish with subtitles. **104m/C VHS.** *SP* Nancho Novo, Emma Suarez, Maria Barranco, Carmelo Gomez, Ana Garcia; **D:** Julio Medem; **W:** Julio Medem; **C:** Gonzalo F. Berridi; **M:** Alberto Iglesias. *NYF*

The Red Stallion 🎬½ 1947 Good film for animal lovers, but it loses something when it comes to human relationships. A young boy raises his pony into an award-winning racehorse that saves the farm when it wins the big race. Good outdoor photography. **82m/B VHS.** Robert Paige, Noreen Nash, Ted Donaldson, Jane Darwell; **D:** Lesley Selander. *NOS, MOV, HEG*

Red Sun 🎬🎬 1971 A gunfighter, a samurai, and a French bandit fight each other in various combinations in the 1800s. Ludicrous and boring. **115m/C VHS, Beta.** *FR IT SP* Charles Bronson, Toshiro Mifune, Alain Delon, Ursula Andress; **D:** Terence Young; **W:** William Roberts; **M:** Maurice Jarre. *GEM*

Red Sun Rising 🎬½ 1994 (R) Kyoto cop Thomas Hoshino (Wilson) heads to L.A. in order to extradite a Japanese gangster, Yamata (Oh), and teams up with local detective Karen Ryder (Ferrell). Seems Yamata wants to start a turf war between two L.A. street gangs so he can sell guns to both sides. **CW:** Martial arts and gangster violence; brief language. **95m/C VHS.** Don "The Dragon" Wilson, Terry Farrell, Soon-Teck Oh, Mako, James Lew, Edward Albert, Michael Ironside; **D:** Francis Megahy; **C:** John Newby. *IMP*

Red Surf 🎬🎬 1990 (R) Action abounds in this surfer film. A couple of hard-nosed wave-riders get involved with big money drug gangs and face danger far greater than the tide. **104m/C VHS, Beta, LV.** George Clooney, Doug Savant, Dedee Pfeiffer, Gene Simmons, Rick Najera, Philip McKeon; **D:** H. Gordon Boos.

Red Tent 🎬🎬🎬 *Krasnaya Palatka* 1969 (G) A robust, sweeping man-versus-nature epic based on the true story of the Arctic stranding of Italian explorer Umberto Nobile's expedition in 1928. A Russian-Italian co-production. **121m/C Beta, LV.** Sean Connery, Claudia Cardinale, Peter Finch, Hardy Kruger, Massimo Girotti, Luigi Vannucchi; **D:** Mikhail Kalatozov; **M:** Ennio Morricone. *PAR*

Red, White & Busted 🎬 *Outside In* 1975 Amnesty or prison? That is the scorching, virtually unanswerable question asked by indictment of America. We follow three friends during the Vietnam War and see how they were affected by the events, whether or not they went. **85m/C VHS, Beta, LV.** Darrell Larson, Heather Menzies, Dennia Oliveri, John Bill. *NO*

Red Wind 🎬🎬 1991 (R) Kris Morrow is a psychotherapist whose latest patient, Lila, has a number of disturbing sadomasochistic fantasies. When Kris feels she's getting too close to the situation, she refers Lila to another therapist. But Lila calls and tells Kris she's already acted out one of her fantasies by killing her husband. In order to stop Lila from killing again, Kris goes on a dangerous search for her deadly patient. **CW:** Violent scenes. **93m/C VHS, Closed Caption.** Lisa Hartman Black, Deanna Lund, Philip Casnoff, Christopher McDonald; **D:** Alan Metzger. *USH*

The Redeemer 🎬 1976 Group of adults at their high school reunion play the children's game of hide-and-seek, with deadly results. **80m/C VHS, Beta.** F.G. Finkbinder, Damien Knight, Jeanetta Arnetta; **D:** Constantine S. Gochis.

Redemption: Kickboxer 5 🎬 *Kickboxer 5* 1995 (R) Retired kickboxer Matt Reeves (Dacascos) goes after the scum who murdered a friend. No surprises here. **87m/C VHS.** Mark Dacascos, James Ryan; **D:** Kristine Peterson; **M:** John Massari. *THV*

The Redhead from Wyoming 🎬🎬½ 1953 Spirited sagebrush adventure with fiery-tempered O'Hara as a saloon proprietress with feelings for both a local cattle rustler and the town's sheriff. Based on a story by James. **81m/C VHS, Closed Caption.** Maureen O'Hara, Alex Nicol, William Bishop, Robert Strauss, Alexander Scourby, Jack Kelly, Jeanne Cooper, Dennis Weaver, Stacy Harris; **D:** Lee Sholem; **W:** Polly James, Herb Meadow. *USH*

Redline 🎬🎬 *Deathline* 1997 (R) John Wade (Hauer) is double-crossed and murdered by his partner Merrick (Dacascos), who's involved with a Russian crime syndicate. But Wade is resurrected as a bionically-enhanced creation and hunts for revenge in a seedily futuristic Moscow. **CW:** Strong violence and sexuality, graphic nudity and language. **96m/C VHS.** Rutger Hauer, Mark Dacascos, Yvonne Scio; **D:** Tibor Takacs. *THV*

Redneck 🎬 1973 Implausible, distasteful purported "thriller" about criminals on the run. **92m/C VHS, Beta.** *IT GB* Telly Savalas, Franco Nero, Mark Lester, Ely Galleani, Dulio Del Prete, Maria Michi; **D:** Silvio Narizzano. *NO*

Redneck Zombies 🎬 1988 (R) A bunch of backwoods rednecks become zombies after chug-a-lugging some radioactive beer. Eating local tourists becomes a hard habit to break. Betcha can't have just one! **83m/C VHS, Beta.** Floyd Piranha, Lisa DeHaven, W.E. Benson, William W. Decker, James Housely, Zoofoot, Tyrone Taylor, Perieles Lewnes. *TWE*

Reds 🎬🎬🎬 1981 (PG) The recreation of the life of author John Reed ("Ten Days that Shook the World"), his romance with Louise Bryant, his efforts to start an American Communist party, and his reporting of the Russian Revolution. A sweeping, melancholy epic using dozens of "witnesses" who reminisce about what they saw. See director Sergei Eisenstein's silent masterpiece "Ten Days that Shook the World," based on Reed's book, for the Russian view of some of the events depicted in Beatty's film. **195m/C VHS, Beta, LV, Closed Caption.** Warren Beatty, Diane Keaton, Jack Nicholson, Edward Herrmann, Maureen Stapleton, Gene Hackman, Jerzy Kosinski, George Plimpton, Paul Sorvino, William Daniels, M. Emmet Walsh, Dolph Sweet, Josef Sommer; **D:** Warren Beatty; **W:** Warren Beatty, Warren Beatty; **M:** Dave Grusin, Stephen Sondheim. Academy Awards '81: Best Cinematography, Best Director (Beatty), Best Supporting Actress (Stapleton); British Academy Awards '82: Best Supporting Actor (Nicholson), Best Supporting Actress (Stapleton); Directors Guild of America Awards '81: Best Director (Beatty); Golden Globe Awards '82: Best Director (Beatty); Los Angeles Film Critics Association Awards '81: Best Cinematography, Best Director (Beatty), Best Supporting Actress (Stapleton); National Board of Review Awards '81: Best Director (Beatty), Best Supporting Actor (Nicholson); New York Film Critics Awards '81: Best Film; National Society of Film Critics Awards '81: Best Supporting Actress (Stapleton); Writers Guild of America '81: Best Original Screenplay; Nominations: Academy Awards '81: Best Actor (Beatty), Best Actress (Keaton), Best Art Direction/Set Decoration, Best Costume Design, Best Film Editing, Best Original Screenplay, Best Picture, Best Sound, Best Supporting Actor (Nicholson). *PAR, BTV*

Redwood Curtain 🎬🎬½ 1995 (PG) Geri Riordan (Salonga) is an Amerasian teenager, with a brilliant future as a concert pianist before her, until she becomes obsessed with learning about her past. Her wealthy adoptive father, Laird Riordan (Lithgow), provides understanding but no answers so she turns to her sympathetic Aunt Geneva (Monk), who lives in the redwood forest area of northern California. There Geri encounters homeless Vietnam vet Lyman Fellers (Daniels) and becomes convinced the troubled man is her birth father. Adapted from the play by Lanford Wilson; made for TV. **99m/C VHS, Closed Caption.** Lea Salonga, John Lithgow, Jeff Daniels, Debra Monk, Catherine

Hicks; **D:** John Korty; **W:** Ed Namzug; **M:** Lawrence Shragge. *REP*

Redwood Forest Trail 🐾🐾 **1950** Environmental-themed oater about a camp for under-privileged city boys. The boys of the camp are blamed for the death of a landowner whose daughter then refuses to renew the camp's mortgage. Allen and Switzer set out to prove that the real culprits are sawmill workers out to control the area timber. Smokey the Bear also makes an appearance to lecture about careless forest fires and the need to preserve the woods. **67m/B VHS.** Rex Allen, Jeff Donnell, Carl "Alfalfa" Switzer, Jane Darwell, Marten Lamont, Pierre Watkin; **D:** Philip Ford; **W:** Bradford Ropes. *MOV*

Reed: Insurgent Mexico 🐾🐾 *Reed, Mexico Insurgente* **1973** Dramatization of John Reed's newspaper reporting on the Mexican Revolution. Spanish with subtitles. **104m/B VHS.** *MX* Claudio Obregon, Eduardo Lopez Rojas, Eracio Zepeda; **D:** Paul Leduc. *CVC*

Reefer Madness *Tell Your Children* **1938 (PG)** Considered serious at the time of its release, this low-budget depiction of the horrors of marijuana has become an underground comedy favorite. Overwrought acting and lurid script contribute to the fun. **67m/B VHS.** Dave O'Brien, Dorothy Short, Warren McCollum, Lillian Miles, Thelma White, Carleton Young; **D:** Louis Gasnier. *SNC, NOS, HHT*

Reet, Petite and Gone 🐾🐾 **1947** All-Black musical featuring the music of neglected jive singer Louis Jordan, and his band, The Tympany Five. A girl's mother dies; sneaky lawyer tries to cheat her. Slick and enjoyable. **75m/B VHS, Beta.** Louis Jordan, June Richmond; **D:** William Forest Crouch. *MVD, NOS, VYY*

The Ref 🐾🐾🐾 **1993 (R)** The couple from hell turn the tables on Gus (Leary), a hard-nosed fugitive who takes Caroline (Davis) and her husband Lloyd (Spacey) hostage. Gus then finds himself trapped in the traditional Christmas ordeal of a family suffering from industrial-strength dysfunction. He plots his getaway while masquerading as the couple's marriage counselor, hence the film's title. This sometimes brutal, frequently hysterical satire of male-female relationships, family ties, and compulsory holiday rituals uses consistently sharp dialogue and superb acting to tell an absurd but convincing tale. **CW:** Strong language and crude sexual references. **97m/C VHS, LV, Closed Caption.** Denis Leary, Judy Davis, Kevin Spacey, Glynis Johns, Robert J. Steinmiller Jr., Christine Baranski; **D:** Ted Demme; **W:** Richard LaGravenese, Marie Weiss; **M:** David A. Stewart. *TOU*

The Reflecting Skin 🐾🐾 **1991** In a 1950s prairie town a small boy sees insanity, child-murder, and radiation sickness, leading him to fantasize that the tormented young widow next door is a vampire. The pretentious drama/freak show rationalizes its ghastly events as symbolizing the hero's loss of youthful innocence. But the Hound knows the score; this is "Faces of Death" for the arts crowd, a grotesque menagerie that dares you to watch. The exploding-frog opener is already notorious. Beautiful photography, with vistas inspired by the painting of Andrew Wyeth. **116m/C VHS, LV.** Viggo Mortensen, Lindsay Duncan, Jeremy Cooper; **D:** Philip Ridley; **W:** Philip Ridley; **M:** Nick Bicat. *NO*

A Reflection of Fear 🐾🐾 *Labyrinth* **1972 (PG)** Lame psycho-thriller about a young girl's jealously of her father's girlfriend, with family members dying of supernatural causes. **90m/C VHS, Beta.** Robert Shaw, Sally Kellerman, Sondra Locke, Mary Ure; **D:** William A. Fraker; **W:** Lewis John Carlino. *COL*

Reflections in a Golden Eye 🐾🐾½ **1967** Huston's film adaptation of Carson McCullers novel about repressed homosexuality, madness, and murder at a Southern Army base in 1948. Star-studded cast cannot consistently pull off convoluted lives of warped characters; not for everyone, though it holds some interest. **109m/C**

VHS, Beta. Elizabeth Taylor, Marlon Brando, Brian Keith, Julie Harris; **D:** John Huston; **C:** Oswald Morris. *WAR*

Reflections in the Dark 🐾🐾 *Reflections on a Crime* **1994 (R)** Beautiful Regina (Rogers) is on death row for murdering her overbearing husband James (Terry). On execution-eve, she relates her tale to young guard Colin (Zane), dispatching hubby by a different method each time she varies her story. Takes itself too seriously though Rogers gives a star performance. **CW:** Adult situations, nudity, violence. **83m/C VHS, LV, Closed Caption.** Mimi Rogers, Billy Zane, John Terry, Kurt Fuller, Lee Garlington, Nancy Fish; **D:** Jon Purdy; **W:** Jon Purdy; **C:** Teresa Medina. *NHO*

Reflections of Murder 🐾🐾½ **1974** Evil schoolteacher's wife and mistress decide to kill him off and then are plagued by his phantom. Well done made for television remake of the French film "Diabolique." Suspenseful, with a great ending. **97m/C VHS.** Tuesday Weld, Joan Hackett, Sam Waterston, Lucille Benson, R.G. Armstrong, Michael Lerner, Ed Bernard, Lance Kerwin; **D:** John Badham; **M:** Billy Goldenberg. *REP*

Reform School Girl 🐾 **1957** A young girl ends up behind bars when her boyfriend steals a car to go joy-riding and is involved in a hit-and-run murder. Extremely cheap production and incredulous story. Look for Kellerman in a bit part in her first screen appearance. **71m/B VHS, Closed Caption.** Gloria Castillo, Ross Ford, Edward Byrnes, Ralph Reed, Jack Kruschen, Sally Kellerman; **D:** Edward L. Bernds; **W:** Edward L. Bernds. *NLC*

Reform School Girls 🐾 **1986 (R)** Satiric raucous women's prison film, complete with tough lesbian wardens, brutal lesbian guards, sadistic lesbian inmates, and a single, newly convicted heterosexual heroine. Wendy O. Williams as a teenager? Come on. Overdone, over-campy, exploitative. **94m/C VHS, Beta, LV.** Linda Carol, Wendy O. Williams, Pat Ast, Sybil Danning, Charlotte McGinnis, Sherri Stoner; **D:** Tom De Simone. *VTR*

The Refrigerator 🐾½ **1991** Filmed on a miniscule budget, this comic/horror flick tells the story of the innocent Batemans of Ohio who move into a grubby New York apartment where they discover that their battered Norge refrigerator is actually a doorway to hell. The fridge has a taste for flesh and tends to eat the unwary visitor as well as defrosting blood (very messy). All the previous tenants disappeared without a trace—will the Batemans be next? Cartoon satire is too amateurish to be successful. **86m/C VHS.** David Simonds, Julia McNeal, Angel Caban, Nena Segal, Jaime Rojo, Michelle DeCosta, Phyllis Sanz; **D:** Nicholas A.E. Jacobs; **W:** Nicholas A.E. Jacobs; **C:** Paul Gibson. *NO*

Regarding Henry 🐾🐾🐾 **1991 (PG-13)** A cold-hearted lawyer gets shot in the head during a holdup and survives with memory and personality erased. During recovery the new Henry displays compassion and conscience the old one never had. Though too calculated in its yuppie-bashing ironies, the picture works thanks to splendid acting and low-key, on-target direction. **107m/C VHS, Beta, LV, Letterbox, Closed Caption.** Harrison Ford, Annette Bening, Bill Nunn, Mikki Allen, Elizabeth Wilson, Robin Bartlett, John Leguizamo, Donald Moffat, Nancy Marchand; **D:** Mike Nichols; **W:** Jeffrey Abrams; **C:** Giuseppe Rotunno; **M:** Hans Zimmer. *PAR*

Regeneration 🐾🐾 **1915** Irish hoodlum Owen (Fellowes) is saved from his life of crime by social worker Mamie Rose (Nilsson). Walsh filmed on location in New York's Bowery district and used actual gangsters in roles. Also features the 10-minute 1910 short "The Police Force of New York City," produced by Thomas Edison. **72m/B VHS.** Rockliffe Fellowes, Anna Q. Nilsson; **D:** Raoul Walsh. *KIV*

Regeneration 🐾🐾 **1997 (R)** Focuses on the friendship between WWI soldier/poets Siegfried Sassoon (Wilby) and Wilfred Owen (Bunce), who receive a brief reprieve from the war when they're treated for shell shock at Edinburgh's Craiglock-

hart Hospital in 1917. Another patient is working-class soldier Billy Prior (Miller), made mute from the horrors he's witnessed. But their compassionate doctor, William Rivers (Pryce), is himself becoming increasingly unstable over the ethical concerns his work engenders. If he cures his patients, they go back to the front to fight again. The first book in Pat Barker's war trilogy. **CW:** War-related violent images and some sexuality and language. **110m/C VHS.** *GB CA* Jonathan Pryce, James Wilby, Jonny Lee Miller, Stuart Bunce, Tanya Allen, John Neville, Dougray Scott, David Hayman; **D:** Gilles Mackinnon; **W:** Allan Scott; **C:** Glen MacPherson; **M:** Mychael Danna. Nominations: British Academy Awards '97: Best Film. *NYR*

Reggie Mixes In 🐾🐾🐾 **1916** Wealthy man brawls in bar room and falls for barmaid. Taking a job to be near his beloved, he wipes out local thugs while tending to her welfare. Exhilarating fight scenes in which Fairbanks fists it out with real life boxers. **58m/B VHS, Beta.** Douglas Fairbanks Sr., Bessie Love, Joseph Singleton, William E. Lowery, Wilbur Higby, Frank Bennett; **D:** Christy Cabanne. *GPV, FCT*

Regina 🐾🐾½ **1983** A woman controls all the activities of her husband and son. At age 36, her son is ready to leave home and she refuses to let him. Fine performances in this strange and disturbing film. **86m/C VHS, Beta.** *IT* Anthony Quinn, Ava Gardner, Ray Sharkey, Anna Karina; **D:** Jean-Yves Prate. *THV*

Reg'lar Fellers 🐾🐾 **1941** A gang of kids save the town and soften the heart of their grandmother, too. Production is sloppy. Based on a comic strip by Gene Byrnes. **66m/B VHS.** Billy Lee, Carl "Alfalfa" Switzer, Buddy Boles, Janet Dempsey, Sarah Padden, Roscoe Ates; **D:** Arthur Dreifuss. *NOS, FMT, VYY*

Rehearsal for Murder 🐾🐾½ **1982** Movie star Redgrave is murdered on the night of her Broadway debut. Seems it might have been someone in the cast. Brought to you by the creative team behind "Columbo." Challenging made for television whodunit a twist. Good cast. **96m/C VHS, Beta.** Robert Preston, Lynn Redgrave, Patrick Macnee, Lawrence Pressman, Madolyn Smith, Jeff Goldblum, William Daniels; **D:** David Greene; **M:** Billy Goldenberg. *REP*

Reign of Terror 🐾🐾 *The Black Book* **1949** British-made adventure set during the French Revolution, with everyone after the black book that holds the names of those arch-fiend Robespierre plans to guillotine in his ruthless bid for power. Well-mounted, but historical personages and events are reduced to cartoon form. **89m/B VHS.** Robert Cummings, Arlene Dahl, Richard Hart, Arnold Moss, Richard Basehart; **D:** Anthony Mann; **W:** Philip Yordan; **C:** John Alton. *NOS, MRV, DVT*

Reilly: Ace of Spies 🐾🐾🐾 **1987** Covers the exploits of the real-life superspy and womanizer Sydney Reilly who uncovers Russian secrets in 1901, allowing the Japanese to sink the Russian fleet and invade China. After a lively spying career for the British, Reilly eventually plots against the Bolsheviks and comes close to overthrowing Lenin and installing himself as the new leader of the Russian government. Eleven episodes on four cassettes. **572m/C VHS, Beta, LV.** *GB* Sam Neill, Sebastian Shaw, Jeannane Crowley; **D:** Jim Goddard. *SIG, HBO, FCT*

The Reincarnate 🐾 **1971 (PG)** Cult guarantees lawyer will live forever if he can find a new body. Enter gullible sculptor; lawyer uses skill at persuasion. **89m/C VHS, Beta.** *CA* Jack Creley, Jay Reynolds, Trudy Young, Terry Tweed; **D:** Don Haldane. *NO*

The Reincarnation of Golden Lotus 🐾🐾🐾 *Pan Jin Lian Zhi Qian Shi Jin Sheng* **1989** In this highly erotic story of love and revenge, Wong escapes China for decadent Hong Kong by marrying a wealthy but foolish man. She has numerous sadomasochistic affairs and begins having flashbacks, revealing her to be the reincarnation of Golden Lotus, a courtesan of ancient China. In Mandarin Chinese with English subtitles. 99m/C VHS. *HK* Joi Wong, Eric Tsang, Lam Chen Yen; *D:* Clara Law. *NYF, CVC*

The Reincarnation of Peter Proud 🐾🐾 1975 (R) A college professor has nightmares which lead him to believe the spirit of a murdered man is now possessing him. Kinda scary, but predictable. Screenplay by Ehrlich from his novel. 105m/C VHS, Beta, LV. Michael Sarrazin, Jennifer O'Neill, Margot Kidder, Cornelia Sharpe, Paul Hecht; *D:* J. Lee Thompson; *W:* Max Ehrlich; *C:* Victor Kemper; *M:* Jerry Goldsmith. *ART, VES*

The Reivers 🐾🐾🐾½ 1969 (PG) Young boy and two adult pals journey from small town Mississippi (circa 1905) to the big city of Memphis in a stolen car. Picaresque tale is delightful on-screen, as in William Faulkner's enjoyable last novel. 107m/C VHS, Beta. Steve McQueen, Sharon Farrell, Will Geer, Michael Constantine, Rupert Crosse; *D:* Mark Rydell; *W:* Harriet Frank Jr., Irving Ravetch; *M:* John Williams. Nominations: Academy Awards '69: Best Supporting Actor (Crosse), Best Original Score. *FOX*

The Rejuvenator 🐾🐾½ *Rejuvenatrix* 1988 (R) An oft-told film story: an aging actress discovers a "youth" serum but finds out that the serum affects things other than her aging. Well-done. 90m/C VHS, LV. Marcus Powell, John MacKay, James Hogue, Vivian Lanko, Jessica Dublin; *D:* Brian Thomas Jones; *W:* Simon Nuchtern; *M:* Larry Juris. *NO*

Relative Fear 🐾½ 1995 (R) Little Adam has bad luck with his friends and relatives—they keep getting murdered all around him. His mother begins to suspect something unnatural is going on, and discovers Adam is not her natural child, but the son of a homicidal madwoman. Has Adam inherited some deadly traits? *CW:* Violence involving psychological terror. 94m/C VHS, Closed Caption. Darlanne Fluegel, M. Emmet Walsh, James Brolin, Denise Crosby, Martin Neufeld, Linda Sorensen, Matthew Dupuis; *D:* George Mihalka; *W:* Kurt Wimmer. *REP*

Relentless 🐾🐾 1989 (R) Twisted psycho Nelson, once rejected by the LAPD Academy on psychological grounds, takes his revenge by murdering people and using his police training to cover his tracks. Good acting keeps sporadically powerful but cliched thriller afloat. 92m/C VHS, Beta, LV, Closed Caption. Judd Nelson, Robert Loggia, Meg Foster, Leo Rossi, Pat O'Bryan, Mindy Seeger, Angel Tompkins, Ken Lerner, George Flower; *D:* William Lustig. *COL*

Relentless 2: Dead On 🐾🐾 1991 (R) Rossi, the detective from the first film, tracks yet another murderer whose occult-style mutilations mask an international political conspiracy. So-so slaughter with artsy camerawork. Honestly, how many "Relentless" fans can you name who've been waiting with anticipation? *CW:* Language and violence. 93m/C VHS, LV. Leo Rossi, Ray Sharkey, Meg Foster, Miles O'Keeffe; *D:* Michael Schroeder. *COL*

Relentless 3 🐾🐾 1993 (R) A serial killer (Forsythe) likes to carve up his women victims and send various body parts to taunt the police. Then this sicko decides to really drive the cops crazy by stalking the beautiful girlfriend of the detective (Rossi) investigating the crimes. 84m/C VHS, Closed Caption. William Forsythe, Leo Rossi, Tom Bower, Robert Costanzo, Signy Coleman; *D:* James Lemmo; *W:* James Lemmo. *NLC*

Relentless 4 🐾½ 1994 (R) A psychiatrist with a secret (Janssen) is the only clue Detective Sam Dietz (Rossi) has to a serial killer. Seems all the victims knew the shrink but what does she know? 91m/C VHS, LV, Closed Caption. Leo Rossi, Famke Janssen, Ken Lerner, Colleen Coffey; *D:* Oley Sassone; *W:* Mark Sevi, Terry Plumeri. *NLC*

The Relic 🐾🐾 1996 (R) Quiz time! Which is more implausible: a huge reptilian creature from South American mythology who is crazy for decapitations running amok in a Chicago museum, or Miller as an evolutionary biologist? That's right! Both are equally implausible. But we're forced to accept both after a ship from Brazil arrives with crates for the museum and a completely headless crew (extra credit if you said it's implausible for people with no heads to pilot a ship). Superstitious police detective Vincent D'Agosto (Sizemore) decides to close down the museum's exhibit of...Superstition. That does not sit well with museum director Ann Cuthbert (Hunt), who decides she needs grant money (and the movie needs victims). The monster proceeds to suck brains until the sassy scientist decides she's had enough and takes off her high heels, which everyone knows means the end is near for the creature. Sound interesting? Only if you like Lifestyles of the Rich and Headless. *CW:* Monster violence and gore and language. 110m/C VHS, Beta, Closed Caption. Penelope Ann Miller, Tom Sizemore, Linda Hunt, James Whitmore, Clayton Rohner, Thomas Ryan, Lewis Van Bergen, Chi Muoi Lo, Robert Lesser; *D:* Peter Hyams; *W:* Amy Holden Jones, John Raffo, Rick Jaffa, Amanda Silver; *C:* Peter Hyams; *M:* John Debney. *PAR*

The Reluctant Agent 🐾🐾 1995 Waitress Linda (Jackee) is persuaded to take the place of injured twin sister Charlene, an FBI agent hot on the trail of shady-but-attractive businessman C. Gabriel Dash (Lawson). So, she goes undercover with the questionable assistance of agent John Fraser (Hedaya) to bring their criminal to justice. 94m/C VHS. Jackee, Richard Lawson, Dan Hedaya, Bill Fagerbakke, Harold Sylvester, Cynthia Stevenson, Sharon Barr, Eda Reiss Merin; *D:* Paul Lynch; *W:* Jeff Cohn, Kristi Kane; *M:* Tim Truman.

The Reluctant Astronaut 🐾½ 1967 Roy Fleming (Knotts) is a carnival worker who operates the spaceship ride. Dad's upset the kid has no ambition and sends an application for Roy to NASA. Everyone's surprised when Roy gets accepted and he heads off to Florida but it turns out the job is janitorial. Still Roy does make friends with astronaut Red (Nielsen), who persuades NASA that Roy would be the perfect civilian to send up in an experimental capsule. Too bad Roy's terrified to fly in anything. 103m/C VHS, Closed Caption. Don Knotts, Leslie Nielsen, Joan Freeman, Arthur O'Connell, Jesse White, Jeanette Nolan, Joan Shawlee; *D:* Edward Montagne; *W:* James Fritzell, Everett Greenbaum; *C:* Rexford Wimpy; *M:* Vic Mizzy. *USH*

The Reluctant Debutante 🐾🐾🐾 1958 Harrison and Kendall are the urbane parents of Dee who are trying to find a suitable British husband for their girl. It seems their choices just won't do however, and Dee falls for American bad boy musician Saxon. A very lightweight yet extremely enjoyable romantic comedy thanks to Harrison and in particular his real-life wife Kendall, who unfortunately died the following year. 96m/C VHS, Beta, LV, Letterbox. Rex Harrison, Kay Kendall, John Saxon, Sandra Dee, Angela Lansbury, Diane Clare; *D:* Vincente Minnelli; *C:* Joseph Ruttenberg. *MGM*

The Reluctant Dragon 1941 Classic Disney short about a fun-loving dragon, based on the Kenneth Grahame story; accompanied also by the Disney short "Morris, the Midget Moose." Not to be confused with the full-length 1941 Disney feature film. 28m/C VHS, Beta. *D:* Alfred Werker. *DIS, KUI*

The Remains of the Day 🐾🐾🐾 1993 (PG) If repression is your cup of tea then this is the film for you. Others may want to shake British butler par excellence Stevens (Hopkins) and tell him to express an emotion. In the 1930s, Stevens is the rigidly traditional butler to Lord Darlington (Fox). When Miss Kenton (Thompson) the almost vivacious new housekeeper expresses a quietly personal interest in Stevens his loyalty to an unworthy master prevents him from a chance at happiness. A quiet movie, told in flashback. Hopkins' impressive performance gets by strictly on nuance with Thompson at least allowed a small amount of natural charm. Based on the novel by Kazuo Ishiguro. 135m/C VHS, LV, 8mm, Letterbox, Closed Caption. *GB* Anthony Hopkins, Emma Thompson, James Fox, Christopher Reeve, Peter Vaughan, Hugh Grant, Michael Lonsdale, Tim Pigott-Smith; *D:* James Ivory; *W:* Ruth Prawer Jhabvala; *C:* Tony Pierce-Roberts; *M:* Richard Robbins. British Academy Awards '93; Best Actor (Hopkins); Los Angeles Film Critics Association Awards '93: Best Actor (Hopkins); National Board of Review Awards '93: Best Actor (Hopkins); Nominations: Academy Awards '93: Best Actor (Hopkins), Best Actress (Thompson), Best Adapted Screenplay, Best Art Direction/Set Decoration, Best Costume Design, Best Director (Ivory), Best Picture, Best Original Score; British Academy Awards '94: Best Actress (Thompson), Best Adapted Screenplay, Best Director (Ivory), Best Film; Directors Guild of America Awards '93: Best Director (Ivory); Golden Globe Awards '94: Best Actor—Drama (Hopkins), Best Actress—Drama (Thompson), Best Director (Ivory), Best Film—Drama, Best Screenplay; Writers Guild of America '93: Best Adapted Screenplay. *COL*

Rembrandt 🐾🐾🐾 1936 Necessarily very visual biography of the great Dutch painter, Rembrandt. Superb acting by Laughton. 86m/B VHS, Beta, LV. *GB* Charles Laughton, Elsa Lanchester, Gertrude Lawrence, Walter Hudd; *D:* Alexander Korda; *C:* Georges Perinal.

Rembrandt—1669 🐾🐾 1977 A recreation of the controversial artist's last year, with his egotism clashing with his artistic impulses. In Dutch with English subtitles. 114m/C VHS. *NL* Frans Stelling, Tom de Koff, Aye Fil; *D:* Jos Stelling. *CVC*

Remedy for Riches 🐾🐾 1940 The fourth "Dr. Christian" comedy, has the small-town doctor trying to uncover a real estate fraud before it bankrupts his community. Mildly funny. 66m/B VHS, Beta, 8mm. Jean Hersholt, Dorothy Lovett, Edgar Kennedy, Jed Prouty, Walter Catlett; *D:* Erle C. Kenton. *NOS, VYY*

Remember Me 🐾 1985 Just as a woman is starting to gain control of her life, her husband returns home from the mental hospital. 95m/C VHS, Beta. Robert Grubb, Wendy Hughes, Richard Moir; *D:* Lex Marinos. *NO*

Remember the Night 🐾🐾🐾 1940 Another Sturges-scripted winner in which assistant D.A. MacMurray falls for sophisticated shoplifter Stanwyck, who has stolen a diamond bracelet amidst the Christmas holiday bustle. On a promise that she will return for the trial MacMurray postpones the trial and offers her a ride home for the holidays. Stanwyck is turned away by her mother and MacMurray brings her home for a real family Christmas, where love blooms. A sentimental, funny romance that boisters holiday cheer any time of year. 94m/B VHS, Closed Caption. Barbara Stanwyck, Fred MacMurray, Beulah Bondi, Elizabeth Patterson, Willard Robertson, Sterling Holloway; *D:* Mitchell Leisen; *W:* Preston Sturges; *C:* Ted Tetzlaff; *M:* Friedrich Hollander. *USH*

Remington Steele, Vol. 1: License to Steele 1982 Pilot episode to the light-hearted detective TV series starring Zimbalist as Laura Holt, a female PI who sets up her agency under the name of her fictitious male boss. Then a mystery man appears claiming to be the real Remington Steele (Brosnan) and the two decide to join forces. Also in the first episode are Read as Laura's suspicious assistant, Murphy Michaels, and DeMay as Bernice Fox, the agency secretary. 60m/C VHS. Stephanie Zimbalist, Pierce Brosnan, James Read, Janet DeMay. *MOV, MTM*

Remo Williams: The Adventure Begins 🐾🐾 1985 (PG-13) Adaptation of "The Destroyer" adventure novel series with a Bond-like hero who can walk on water and dodge bullets after being instructed by a Korean martial arts master. Funny and diverting, and Grey is excellent (if a bit over the top) as the wizened oriental. The title's assumption is that the adventure will continue. 121m/C VHS, Beta, LV. Fred Ward, Joel Grey, Wilford Brimley, Kate Mulgrew; *D:* Guy Hamilton. Nominations: Academy Awards '85: Best Makeup. *NO*

Remolina de Pasiones 🐾🐾 1987 A young woman is driven to suicide after succumbing to her mother's persistent lover. 89m/C VHS, Beta. *SP* Amparo Rivelles, Carlos Pinar, Susana Dosamantes. *MAD*

Remote ✒✒½ **1993 (PG)** Thirteen-year-old Randy is a whiz designing high-tech remote-control gadgets. When one of his toys wipes out a friend's science project, Randy's parents try to put a halt to his tinkering but the kid has other plans. Innocuous rip-off of "Honey, I Shrunk the Kids" with some "Home Alone" thrown in as well. **80m/C VHS, Beta, Closed Caption.** Chris Carrara, Jessica Bowman, John Diehl, Derya Ruggles, Tony Longo, Stuart Fratkin; **D:** Ted Nicolaou; **W:** Mike Farrow; **M:** Richard Band. *PAR*

Remote Control ✒½ **1988 (R)** A circulating videotape of a 1950s sci-fi flick is turning people into murderous zombies, thanks to some entrepreneurial aliens. Silly, but performed by young actors with gusto. **88m/C VHS, Beta, LV.** Kevin Dillon, Deborah Goodrich, Christopher Wynne, Jennifer Tilly; **D:** Jeff Lieberman; **M:** Peter Bernstein. *ART, HHE*

Remote Control ✒✒½ **1994** Quiet Axel lives with his mom, whose life revolves around the TV set, and his sister Maeja, who spends most of her time partying in a seedy club called Sodoma. Sodoma is run by three amateur gangsters who are anxious to get rid of a rival, Moli. Meanwhile, Axel falls in love with Moli's sister Unnur (who also happens to be Maeja's best friend). Then the gangsters kidnap Unnur and Axel sets out to rescue her. Icelandic with English subtitles. **85m/C VHS.** **IC** Bjorn Fridbjornsson, Margret H. Gustavsdottir, Helgi Bjornsson, Soley Eliasdottir; **D:** Oskar Jonasson; **W:** Oskar Jonasson. *COL*

Renaissance Man ✒✒½ **1994 (PG-13)** Skeptical new teacher inspires a classroom of underachievers and finds his true calling. Based loosely on the experiences of screenwriter Burnstein at a base in Michigan. Civilian Bill Rago (DeVito) is an unemployed ad exec assigned to teach Shakespeare to a group of borderline Army recruits led by Hardison. Add half a bone for the recruits and their Hamlet rap, a breath of fresh air in an otherwise stale plot. Some funny moments, reminiscent of "Stripes," but not quite as wacky. On the other hand, Marshall does endearing well. Look for rapper Marky Mark with his shirt on (hard to recognize). Shot with the cooperation of the Army.**CW:** Language. **128m/C VHS, LV, Closed Caption.** Danny DeVito, Gregory Hines, James Remar, Stacey Dash, Ed Begley Jr., Mark Wahlberg, Lillo Brancato, Kadeem Hardison, Richard T. Jones, Khalil Kain, Peter Simmons, Jenifer Lewis; **Cameos:** Cliff Robertson; **D:** Penny Marshall; **W:** Jim Burnstein, Ned Mauldin; **M:** Hans Zimmer. *TOU*

Rendez-Moi Ma Peau ✒✒½ **1981** A modern-day witch transposes two people's personalities with comic results. In French with subtitles. **82m/C VHS, Beta.** **FR D:** Patrick Schulmann. *FCT*

Rendez-vous ✒✒✒ **1985 (R)** A racy, dark film about the sensitive balance between sex and exploitation, the real world and the stage world. Some may be disturbed by chillingly explicit scenes. Impressive tour de force of imagination, direction, and cinematography. In French with English subtitles. **82m/C VHS, LV.** **FR** Juliette Binoche, Lambert Wilson, Wadeck Stanczak, Jean-Louis Trintignant; **D:** Andre Techine; **W:** Olivier Assayas; **C:** Philippe Angers. Cannes Film Festival '85: Best Director (Techine). *CVC, TPV*

Rendezvous in Paris ✒✒ *Les Rendezvous de Paris* **1995** Includes three stories by Rohmer about the complications and disappointments of love. "Le Rendez-vous de 7 heures" finds Esther (Bellar) upset when boyfriend Horace (Basler) is spotted with another girl at a cafe. She decides to make him jealous by showing up at the same cafe with another man. A woman (Rauscher) decides to leave her boring fiance in "Les Bancs de Paris" and tries to decide on a possible new romance with a provincial professor (Renko). In "Mere et Enfant 1907," a painter (Kraft) goes to an art gallery where he spots a woman (Loyen) admiring Picasso's painting "Mother and Child" and he decides to pursue her. French with subtitles. **100m/C VHS.** **FR** Clara Bellar, Antoine Basler, Mathias Megard, Judith Chancel, Aurore Rauscher, Serge Renko, Michael Kraft, Benedicte Loyen, Veronika Johansson; **D:** Eric Rohmer; **W:** Eric Rohmer; **C:** Diane Baratier; **M:** Sebastien Erms. *NYF*

Renegade Girl ✒ **1946** A special agent is sent west to capture the female head of a band of outlaws. **65m/B VHS, Beta, LV.** Alan Curtis, Ann Savage, Edward Brophy, Ray Corrigan, Jack Holt; **D:** William (Lester Williams) Berke. *NOS, RXM, VYY*

Renegade Monk ✒½ **1982 (R)** Invincible warrior-monk dispenses his own brand of justice with his fists of aluminum foil. **90m/C VHS, Beta.** Liu Chang Liang, Huang Hsing Shaw, Ko Shou Liang, Lang Shih Chia, Hsu Chung Hsing. *GEM*

Renegade Ninja ✒ **1983** A man whose father was murdered kicks everyone within reach in his quest for revenge. **109m/C VHS, Beta.** Kensaku Marita; **D:** Sadao Nakajima.

Renegade Ranger/Scarlet River ✒½ **1938** A western double feature: A Texas Ranger and his singing sidekick attempt to help out a woman accused of murder in the "The Renegade Ranger," and a cowboy tries to free his sweetheart from a band of cattle rustlers in "Scarlet River." **113m/B VHS, Beta.** Rita Hayworth, Tim Holt, George O'Brien, Ray Whitley, Tom George Duryea Keene, Lon Chaney Jr., Myrna Loy, Bruce Cabot, Betty Furness; **D:** David Howard. *TTC*

Renegade Trail ✒✒ **1939** Hopalong Cassidy helps a marshall and a pretty widow round up ex-cons and rustlers. The King's Men, radio singers of the era, perform a fistful of songs. **61m/B VHS.** William Boyd, George "Gabby" Hayes, Russell Hayden, Charlotte Wynters, Russell Hopton, Sonny Bupp, Jack Rockwell, Roy Barcroft, Eddie Dean; **D:** Lesley Selander. *NOS*

Renegades ✒✒ **1989 (R)** A young cop from Philadelphia and a Lakota Indian begrudgingly unite to track down a gang of ruthless crooks. Good action, and lots of it; not much story. **105m/C VHS, Beta, LV, Closed Caption.** Kiefer Sutherland, Lou Diamond Phillips, Rob Knepper, Jami Gertz, Bill Smitrovich; **D:** Jack Sholder; **C:** Phil Meheux; **M:** Michael Kamen. *USH*

Renfrew of the Royal Mounted ✒ **1937** A Canadian Mountie goes after counterfeiters and sings a few songs in this mild adaptation of a popular kids' radio serial. Newill was a popular tenor of the day, but the Hound thinks Renfrew's dog 'Lightning' should have been the star. **57m/B VHS, Beta.** Carol Hughes, James Newill, Kenneth Harlan; **D:** Al(bert) Herman. *DVT, GPV, HEG*

Renfrew on the Great White Trail ✒½ *On the Great White Trail; Renfrew of the Royal Mounted on the Great White Trail* **1938** A frustrated fur trader takes off after a pack of thieves. **58m/B VHS.** James Newill, Terry Walker, Robert Frazer, Richard Alexander; **D:** Al(bert) Herman. *NOS, DVT*

Reno and the Doc ✒✒½ **1984** Enjoyable comedy about two endearingly cranky middle-aged men battling mid-life crises join together and test their mettle in the world of professional skiing. **88m/C VHS, Beta.** **CA** Ken Walsh, Henry Ramer, Linda Griffiths; **D:** Charles Dennis.

Renoir Shorts ✒✒ **1927** Two early silent Renoir fantasies: "The Little Matchgirl," a lyrical adaptation of the Hans Christian Anderson fairy tale, and "Charleston," in which a space-traveling African and Parisian girl dance comically. **50m/B VHS, Beta.** Catherine Hessling; **D:** Jean Renoir. *NOS, FCT*

Rent-A-Cop ✒✒ **1988 (R)** A cop (Reynolds) is bounced from the force after he survives a drug-bust massacre under suspicious circumstances. He becomes a security guard and continues to track down the still-at-large killer with help from call girl Minnelli. **95m/C VHS, Beta, LV, Closed Caption.** Burt Reynolds, Liza Minnelli, James Remar, Richard Masur, Bernie Casey, John Stanton, John P. Ryan, Dionne Warwick, Robby Benson; **D:** Jerry London; **W:** Michael Blodgett; **M:** Jerry Goldsmith. Golden Raspberry Awards '88: Worst Actress (Minnelli). *HBO*

Rent-A-Kid ✒✒½ **1995 (G)** Businessman Harry Haber (Nielsen) is asked by his son to keep an eye out on the Mid-Valley Orphanage for a week. Then Harry meets a young couple who are unsure about having a family so, since Harry's business is renting all sorts of things, he decides to rent the couple three orphans so they can get a taste of parenting. **89m/C VHS, LV, Closed Caption.** Leslie Nielsen, Christopher Lloyd, Matt McCoy, Sherry Miller, Amos Crawley, Cody Jones, Tabitha Lupien, Tony Rosato; **D:** Fred Gerber; **W:** Paul Bernbaum; **C:** Rene Ohashi; **M:** Ron Ramin. *REP*

Rentadick ✒✒ **1972** A precursor to the Monty Python masterpieces, written by future members Chapman and Cleese. Private eye spoof isn't as funny as later Python efforts; but it is an indication of what was yet to come and fans should enjoy it. **94m/C VHS.** **GB** James Booth, Julie Ege, Ronald Fraser, Donald Sinden, Michael Bentine, Richard Briers, Spike Milligan; **D:** Jim Clark; **W:** Graham Chapman, John Cleese; **M:** Carl Davis. *NO*

Rented Lips ✒ **1988 (R)** Two documentary filmmakers sell out, taking over the production of a porno film at the request of a public television producer who promises to help their careers. Mull and Shawn are well supported by an impressive cast, but everyone's effort is wasted in unfunny attempt at comedy. **82m/C VHS, Beta, LV.** Martin Mull, Dick Shawn, Jennifer Tilly, Kenneth Mars, Edy Williams, Robert Downey Jr., June Lockhart, Shelley Berman, Mel Welles, Pat McCormick, Eileen Brennan; **D:** Robert Downey. *NO*

Repentance ✒✒✒ *Pokayaniye; Confession* **1987 (PG)** A popular, surreal satire of Soviet and Communist societies. A woman is arrested for repeatedly digging up a dead local despot, and put on trial. Wickedly funny and controversial; released under the auspices of glasnost. In Russian with English subtitles. **151m/C VHS, Beta, LV.** **RU** Avtandil Makharadze, Zeinab Botsvadze, Ia Ninidze, Edisher Giorgobiani, Ketevan Abuladze, Kakhi Kavsadze; **D:** Tengiz Abuladze. Cannes Film Festival '87: Grand Jury Prize.

The Replacement Killers ✒✒½ **1998 (R)** Hong Kong action star Chow Yun-Fat makes his American debut in this somewhat disappointing first feature from director Antoine Fuqua. Chow stars as John Lee, an assassin working for crime boss Mr. Wei (Tsang). When Lee decides not to carry out a hit on a cop's (Rooker) son, he becomes the target of the men sent to replace him. Needing a passport to get back to China, Lee goes to forger Meg Coburn (Sorvino). Before she can finish the papers, Wei's men begin the first of many high body count gun battles. Fuqua, who was heavily influenced by John Woo (one of the film's exec producers), does a passable job of conveying the style of Chow and Woo's Hong Kong work, but doesn't leave much room for the substance. Chow's sublety and charisma are crammed into a mechanical action plot, and only his talent saves the whole thing from imploding.**CW:** Strong violence and for language. **86m/C VHS, LV, Closed Caption, DVD.** Chow Yun-Fat, Mira Sorvino, Michael Rooker, Kenneth Tsang, Juergen Prochnow, Danny Trejo, Til Schweiger, Clifton Gonzalez Gonzalez, Carlos Gomez, Frank Medrano; **D:** Antoine Fuqua; **W:** Ken Sanzel; **C:** Peter Collister; **M:** Harry Gregson-Williams. *COL*

Replikator: Cloned to Kill ✒½ **1994 (R)** In the 21st century, a ruthless criminal gets hold of replication techology that can duplicate anything, including people. So it's up to a cop and two cyberpunks to stop the destruction.**CW:** Rated R for nudity and futuristic violence. **96m/C VHS, Closed Caption.** Michael St. Gerard, Brigitte Bako, Ned Beatty; **D:** G. Philip Jackson; **W:** Tony Johnston, Michelle Bellerose, John Dawson.

Repo Jake ✒½ **1990** Jake Baxter learns the myth of the carefree life of a repossession man in this action thriller. His illusion is destroyed by angry clients, pornography, a deadly underworld racetrack, and a sinister crime boss. **90m/C VHS.** Dan Haggerty, Robert Axelrod. *PMH*

Repo Man ✶✶✶½ **1983 (R)** An inventive, perversely witty portrait of sick modern urbanity, following the adventures of a punk rocker taking a job as a car repossessor in a barren city. The landscape is filled with pointless violence, no-frills packaging, media hypnosis and aliens. Executive producer: none other than ex-Monkee Michael Nesmith. **93m/C VHS, Beta, LV.** Emilio Estevez, Harry Dean Stanton, Sy Richardson, Tracey Walter, Olivia Barash, Fox Harris, Jennifer Balgobin, Vonetta McGee, Angelique Pettyjohn; **D:** Alex Cox; **W:** Alex Cox. USH

The Report on the Party and the Guests ✶✶✶✶ **1966** A controversial, widely banned political allegory, considered a masterpiece from the Czech new wave. A picnic/lawn party deteriorates into brutality, fascist intolerance and persecution. Many Czech film makers, some banned at the time, appear. Based on a story by Ester Krumbachova, who also co-wrote the screenplay. In Czech with English subtitles. **71m/B VHS, Beta.** CZ Jiri Nemec, Evald Schorm, Ivan Vyskocil, Jan Klusak, Zdena Skvorecka, Pavel Bosek; **D:** Jan Nemec; **W:** Jan Nemec. FCT

Report to the Commissioner ✶✶✶ Operation Undercover **1974 (R)** A rough, energetic crime-in-the-streets cop thriller. A young detective accidentally kills an attractive woman who turns out to have been an undercover cop, then is dragged into the bureaucratic cover-up. **112m/C VHS, Beta.** Michael Moriarty, Yaphet Kotto, Susan Blakely, Hector Elizondo, Richard Gere, Tony King, Michael McGuire, Stephen Elliott; **D:** Milton Katselas; **W:** Abby Mann; **M:** Elmer Bernstein. MGM

Repossessed ✶✶ **1990 (PG-13)** A corny, occasionally funny takeoff on the human-possessed-by-the-devil films with Blair, as usual, as the afflicted victim. Nielsen, in another typecast role, plays the goofy man of the cloth who must save the day. Numerous actors appear in brief comedy sequences which lampoon current celebrities and constitute the film's highlights. For fans of "Airplane" and "The Naked Gun"; not necessarily for others. **89m/C VHS, LV, Closed Caption.** Linda Blair, Ned Beatty, Leslie Nielsen, Anthony Starke, Jesse Ventura; **D:** Bob Logan; **W:** Bob Logan; **M:** Charles Fox. Golden Raspberry Awards '90: Worst Song ("He's Comin' Back (The Devil!)"). ART

The Reptile ✶✶ **1966** The inhabitants of yet another Cornish village are turning up dead—mysteriously from snakebite. When Harry (Barrett) investigates his brother's death, he finds out Anna (Pearce) is the victim of a curse, which causes her to turn into a snake. Rather sympathetic characters for the horror genre. **90m/C VHS.** GB Jacqueline Pearce, Ray Barrett, Noel Willman, Jennifer Daniel, Michael Ripper, John Laurie, Marne Maitland, Charles Lloyd Pack, George Woodbridge, David Baron; **D:** John Gilling; **W:** John Elder; **C:** Arthur Grant; **M:** Don Banks. VTR

Repulsion ✶✶✶½ **1965** Character study of a young French girl who is repulsed and attracted by sex. Left alone when her sister goes on vacation, her facade of stability begins to crack, with violent and bizarre results. Polanski's first film in English and his first publicly accepted full-length feature. Suspenseful, disturbing and potent. **105m/B VHS, LV.** GB Catherine Deneuve, Yvonne Furneaux, Ian Hendry, John Fraser, Patrick Wymark, James Villiers, Renee Houston, Helen Fraser, Mike Pratt, Valerie Taylor; **D:** Roman Polanski; **W:** Roman Polanski, Gerard Brach, David Stone; **C:** Gilbert Taylor. COL

Requiem for a Heavyweight ✶✶✶ **1956** The original television version of the story about an American Indian heavyweight boxer played by Palance who risks blindness in order to help his manager pay off bookies. Highly acclaimed teleplay written for "Playhouse 90." **90m/B VHS, Beta.** Jack Palance, Keenan Wynn, Ed Wynn, Kim Hunter, Ned Glass; **D:** Ralph Nelson; **W:** Rod Serling. FUS, BTV, RHI

Requiem for a Heavyweight ✶✶✶ **1962** After 17 years Mountain Rivera (Quinn) is a washed-up heavyweight risking his life if he continues boxing. He tries to find another job but his manager, Maish Rennick (Gleason), owes the mob big, and persuades the fighter to help him pay off his debts by joining the wrestling circuit, so Mountain humiliates himself to help out his old friend. The 1956 TV version is still more compelling but the film's performances are all first-rate. **100m/B VHS.** Anthony Quinn, Jackie Gleason, Mickey Rooney, Julie Harris, Stanley Adams, Muhammad Ali; **D:** Ralph Nelson; **W:** Rod Serling; **C:** Arthur Ornitz; **M:** Laurence Rosenthal. COL

Requiem for Dominic ✶✶✶½ Requiem fur Dominic **1991 (R)** A Communist-bloc country in the midst of revolution accuses a man of terrorist activities. Can his friend, exiled for years, help him discover the truth? Interesting and timely premise matched with outstanding ensemble acting make for a superior thriller. Amnesty International receives partial proceeds from all sales of this video. In German with English subtitles. **CW:** Graphic views of a massacred corpse. **88m/C VHS, LV.** GE Felix Mitterer, Viktoria Schubert, August Schmolzer, Angelica Schutz; **D:** Robert Dornhelm.

The Rescue ✶½ **1988 (PG)** An elite team of U.S. Navy Seals is captured after destroying a disabled submarine. When the U.S. government writes off the men, their children decide to mount a rescue. Puerile, empty-headed trash for teens. **97m/C VHS, Beta, LV, Closed Caption.** Marc Price, Charles Haid, Kevin Dillon, Christina Harnos, Edward Albert; **D:** Ferdinand Fairfax; **W:** Jim Thomas, John Thomas; **C:** Russell Boyd; **M:** Bruce Broughton. TOU, HHE

Rescue Force ✶✶ **1990** A crack team of anti-terrorists, led by Lt. Col. Steel, takes on the kidnappers of an American ambassador. Action filled excitement. **85m/C VHS.** Richard Harrison. NO

Rescue Me ✶✶½ **1993 (PG-13)** Geek photographer Fraser carries a torch for high school honey Ginny and just happens to be on the scene (with camera) when she's kidnapped. So he persuades a scruffy Vietnam vet to help him rescue his damsel in distress. Likeable adventure with lots of chases. **CW:** Mild language and violence. **99m/C VHS, LV.** Michael Dudikoff, Stephen Dorff, Peter DeLuise, Ami Dolenz, William Lucking, Dee Wallace Stone; **D:** Arthur Seidelman; **W:** Michael Snyder; **M:** Al Kasha, Joel Hirschhorn; David Waters. WAR

The Rescuers ✶✶✶ **1977 (G)** Bernard and Miss Bianca, two mice who are members of the Rescue Aid Society, attempt to rescue an orphan named Penny from the evil Madame Medusa, who's after the world's biggest diamond. They are aided by comic sidekick, Orville the albatross, and a group of lovable swamp creatures. Very charming in the best Disney tradition. Based on the stories of Margery Sharp. Followed by "The Rescuers Down Under." **76m/C VHS, LV, Closed Caption. D:** Wolfgang Reitherman, John Lounsbery; **M:** Artie Butler; **V:** Bob Newhart, Eva Gabor, Geraldine Page, Jim Jordan, Joe Flynn, Jeanette Nolan, Pat Buttram. Nominations: Academy Awards '77: Best Song ("Someone's Waiting for You"). DIS, OM

The Rescuers Down Under ✶✶½ **1990 (G)** "Crocodile" Dundee goes Disney; the followup to "The Rescuers" places its characters in Australia with only mild results for a Magic Kingdom product. Heroic mice Bernard and Bianca protect a young boy and a rare golden eagle from a poacher. The great bird closely resembles the logo of Republic Pictures. **77m/C VHS, Beta, LV, Closed Caption. D:** Hendel Butoy, Mike Gabriel; **W:** Jim Cox, Karey Kirkpatrick, Joe Ranft, Byron Simpson; **M:** Bruce Broughton; **V:** Bob Newhart, Eva Gabor, John Candy, Tristan Rogers, George C. Scott, Frank Welker, Adam Ryen. DIS, OM

Rescuers: Stories of Courage— Two Women ✶✶✶ **1997 (PG-13)** Fact-based cable drama about Gentiles who sheltered Jews from Nazi persecution during WWII. In "Mamusha" Perkins plays Gertruda, a Catholic nanny in Poland, who poses as the mother of her orphaned Jewish charge. "The Woman on the Bicycle" is Frenchwoman Marie-Rose (Ward), who works for the Resistance and hides a Jewish family in the attic of her home. **CW:** Thematic elements, violence and strong language. **107m/C VHS, Closed Caption.** Elizabeth Perkins, Sela Ward, Fritz Weaver, Anne Jackson, Al Waxman, Gerard Parkes, Michael Landes; **D:** Peter Bogdanovich; **W:** Ernest Kinoy, Terry Norris; **C:** Miroslaw Baszak; **M:** Hummie Mann. PAR

Reservoir Dogs ✶✶✶½ **1992 (R)** Ultra-violent tale of honor among thieves. Six professional criminals known by code names to protect their identities (Misters Pink, White, Orange, Blonde, Blue, and Brown) are assembled by Tierney to pull off a diamond heist. But two of the gang are killed in a police ambush. The survivors regroup in an empty warehouse and try to discover the informer in their midst. In probably the most stomach-churning scene (there is some competition here), a policeman is tortured just for the heck of it to the tune of the Stealers Wheel "Stuck in the Middle with You." Unrelenting; auspicious debut for Tarantino with strong ensemble cast anchored by Keitel as the very professional Mr. White. **CW:** Strong language and strong violence. **100m/C VHS, LV, Letterbox, Closed Caption, DVD.** Harvey Keitel, Tim Roth, Michael Madsen, Steve Buscemi, Christopher Penn, Lawrence Tierney, Kirk Baltz, Quentin Tarantino, Eddie Bunker, Randy Brooks; **D:** Quentin Tarantino; **W:** Quentin Tarantino; **C:** Andrzej Sekula; **V:** Steven Wright. Independent Spirit Awards '93: Best Supporting Actor (Buscemi). ART, BTV

Resistance ✶✶ **1992** Apocalyptic tale of rebels and soldiers. The poor have been driven from abandoned cities into working as farm hands for a large corporation. When the workers rebel, anti-terrorist squads manage to make the situation worse and a full-scale rebellion begins. **112m/C VHS, DVD.** Jack Thompson, Stephen Leeder, Robyn Nevin, Harold Hopkins, Helen Jones, Kris McQuade, Hugh Keays-Byrne; **D:** Paul Elliot. LEO

The Respectful Prostitute ✶✶½ **1952** Sartre's tale of hooker who is cajoled into providing false testimony as a witness in the trial of a member of a prominent family. English language version of French drama. **75m/B VHS.** FR Ivan Desny, Barbara Laage, Walter Bryan; **D:** Marcel Pagliero, Charles Brabant; **W:** Jean-Paul Sartre. XVC, FCT, TPV

Rest in Pieces ✶ **1987 (R)** A young woman inherits a Spanish mansion, and weird things begin to happen. It seems a cult of Satan worshippers is already living on the estate. As one might infer from the title, quite a bit of hacking and slashing ensues. **90m/C VHS, Beta.** Scott Thompson Baker, Lorin Jean, Dorothy Malone; **D:** Joseph Braunstein. ART

Restless ✶ The Beloved **1972** A restless homemaker begins an affair with a childhood friend. Director Cosmatos later oversaw "Rambo." **75m/C VHS, Beta.** GR Raquel Welch, Richard Johnson, Jack Hawkins, Flora Robson; **D:** George P. Cosmatos. THV

The Restless Breed ✶ **1958** Son is restless after dad, a secret service agent, is slain by gunrunners. Routine oater-revenge epic done in by listless script. **86m/C VHS, LV, Closed Caption.** Scott Brady, Anne Bancroft, Jay C. Flippen, Rhys Williams, Jim Davis; **D:** Allan Dwan. IME

Restoration ✶✶✶ **1994 (R)** Set in the 17th century after Charles II is restored to the British throne, the title may instead refer to the restoration of one man's values. After curing one of the king's dogs, physician Downey is elevated to courtier and falls into drunken debauchery. He is soon forced to marry (but not touch) the king's favorite mistress. Unfortunately, he is caught trespassing on his majesty's main squeeze and banished from the court. Cast among the common rabble, he encounters the plague and the Great Fire of London while trying to redeem himself. Strong cast and sumptuous set design help to propel Downey's performance. Adapted from Rose Tremain's 1989 novel. Release was delayed a year because no one could seem to come up with a marketing strategy. **CW:** Sexuality. 118m/C VHS, LV, **Closed Caption.** Robert Downey Jr., Meg Ryan, Sam Neill, Hugh Grant, David Thewlis, Polly Walker, Ian McKellen; **D:** Michael Hoffman; **W:** Rupert Walters; **C:** Oliver Stapleton; **M:** James Newton Howard. Academy Awards '95: Best Art Direction/Set Decoration, Best Costume Design. TOU

The Resurrected ♫♫½ **1991 (R)** One of the best recent H.P. Lovecraft horror adaptations, a fairly faithful try at "The Case of Charles Dexter Ward." Ward learns he has a satanic ancestor who possessed the secret of resurrection and eternal life—but, as the warlock says, it is very messy. Surprisingly tasteful even with occasional gore and truly ghastly monsters; in fact this pic could have used a bit more intensity. **CW:** Language and violence. 108m/C VHS. John Terry, Jane Sibbett, Chris Sarandon, Robert Romanus; **D:** Dan O'Bannon; **M:** Richard Band. ART

Resurrection ♫♫♫ **1980 (PG)** After a near-fatal car accident, a woman finds she has the power to heal others by touch. She denies that God is responsible, much to her Bible Belt community's dismay. Acclaimed and well-acted. 103m/C VHS, Beta. Ellen Burstyn, Sam Shepard, Roberts Blossom, Eva LeGallienne, Clifford David, Richard Farnsworth, Pamela Payton-Wright; **D:** Daniel Petrie; **W:** Lewis John Carlino; **M:** Maurice Jarre. National Board of Review Awards '80: Best Supporting Actress (LeGallienne); Nominations: Academy Awards '80: Best Actress (Burstyn), Best Supporting Actress (LeGallienne). USH

Resurrection of Zachary Wheeler ♫♫½ **1971 (G)** A presidential candidate, who narrowly escaped death in an auto crash, is brought to a mysterious clinic in New Mexico. A reporter sneaks into the clinic and discovers the horrors of cloning. 100m/C VHS, Beta. Angie Dickinson, Bradford Dillman, Leslie Nielsen, Jack Carter, James Daly; **D:** Bob Wynn. NO

Retreat, Hell! ♫♫ **1952** Korean War drama about the retreat from the Changjin Reservoir. Standard gun-ho military orientation with dismal results. 95m/B VHS. Frank Lovejoy, Richard Carlson, Russ Tamblyn, Anita Louise; **D:** Joseph H. Lewis. REP

Retribution ♫½ **1988 (R)** Struggling artist survives suicide attempt only to find himself possessed by the spirit of a criminal who was tortured to death. Seeing the hood's gruesome demise in his dreams, the survivor sets out to bring his murderers face-to-face with their maker. 106m/C VHS, Beta, LV. Dennis Lipscomb, Hoyt Axton, Leslie Wing, Suzanne Snyder; **D:** Guy Magar. NO

Retrievers ♫ **1982** Young man and a former CIA agent team up to expose the unsavory practices of the organization. 90m/C VHS, Beta. Max Thayer, Roselyn Royce. VES

Retroactive ♫♫ **1997 (R)** Scientist Brian (Whaley) has been experimenting with reversing time and finally manages to make his project work. Meanwhile, police psychologist Karen (Travis) has has car trouble and been given a ride by Frank (Belushi) and his wife Rayanne (Whirry). Karen soon realizes Frank is a psycho and escapes, stumbling into Brian's lab. But Brian's just reversed time and Karen winds up back in Frank's car, trying to change the sequence of events. **CW:** Violence and language. 91m/C VHS, **Closed Caption.** James Belushi, Kylie Travis, Shannon Whirry, Frank Whaley, Jesse Borrego, M. Emmet Walsh, Guy Boyd; **D:** Louis Morneau; **W:** Robert Strauss, Phillip Badger; **M:** Tim Truman. ORI

The Return woof! The Alien's Return **1980 (PG)** Vincent and Shepherd meet as adults and discover that they had both, as children, been visited by aliens who had given technology to a cattle-mutilating prospector. A mess with no idea of what sort of film it wants to be. 91m/C VHS, Beta. Cybill Shepherd, Raymond Burr, Jan-Michael Vincent, Martin Landau, Vincent Schiavelli, Zachary Vincent, Farah Bunch, Neville Brand, Susan Kiger; **D:** Greydon Clark. NO

Return ♫♫ **1988 (R)** A woman believes that the man she loves is the reincarnation of her dead grandfather. Interesting concept, but overall, a disappointing mystery. 78m/C VHS, Beta, LV. Frederic Forrest, Anne Francis, Karlene Crockett, John Walcutt, Lisa Richards; **D:** Andrew Silver. NO

Return Engagement ♫♫½ **1978** A lonely middle-aged ancient history professor falls in love with one of her students. 76m/C VHS, Beta. Elizabeth Taylor, Joseph Bottoms, Peter Donat, James Ray; **D:** Joseph Hardy. NO

Return Fire ♫½ **1991 (R)** A former employee of the government finds that he must now fight the system if he wants to save his son. Trivial action fare. 97m/C VHS. Adam West, Ron Marchini.

Return from Witch Mountain ♫½ **1978 (G)** A pair of evil masterminds use a boy's supernatural powers to place Los Angeles in nuclear jeopardy. Sequel to Disney's ever-popular "Escape to Witch Mountain." 93m/C VHS, Beta. Christopher Lee, Bette Davis, Ike Eisenmann, Kim Richards, Jack Soo; **D:** John Hough; **W:** Malcolm Marmorstein. DIS

The Return of a Man Called Horse ♫♫ **1976 (PG)** Sequel to "A Man Called Horse" tells the story of an English aristocrat who was captured and raised by Sioux Indians, and then returned to his native homeland. Contains more of the torture scenes for which this series is famous, but not much of Harris. 125m/C VHS, Beta. Richard Harris, Gale Sondergaard, Geoffrey Lewis; **D:** Irvin Kershner; **W:** Jack DeWitt; **C:** Owen Roizman. FOX

The Return of Boston Blackie ♫½ **1927** The oft-filmed crook/detective tries to retrieve an heiress's stolen jewels. Silent. 77m/B VHS, Beta. Raymond Glenn, Corliss Palmer, Strongheart, Rosemary Cooper, Coit Albertson; **D:** Harry Hoyt. VYY, GPV, FCT

Return of Captain Invincible ♫♫½ Legend in Leotards **1983 (PG)** Arkin is a derelict super-hero persuaded to fight crime again in this unique spoof. One liners fly faster than a speeding bullet. Lee gives one of his best performances as the mad scientist. Musical numbers by Rocky Horror's O'Brien and Hartley sporadically interrupt. Made on a shoe-string budget, offbeat film is entertaining but uneven. 90m/C VHS, Beta, LV. AU Alan Arkin, Christopher Lee, Kate Fitzpatrick, Bill Hunter, Graham Kennedy, Michael Pate, Hayes Gordon, Max Phipps, Noel Ferrier; **D:** Philippe Mora; **W:** Steven E. de Souza. NO

The Return of Casey Jones ♫♫ Train 2419 **1934** Early adventure film featuring lots of great railroad action. 64m/B VHS. Charles Starrett, Ruth Hall, George "Gabby" Hayes, Robert Elliott, Margaret Seddon, Jackie Searl; **D:** John P. McCarthy. GPV

Return of Chandu ♫ **1934** This serial in 12 chapters features Bela Lugosi as Chandu, who exercises his magical powers to conquer a religious sect of cat worshippers inhabiting the island of Lemuria. In the process, he fights to save the Princess Nadji from being sacrificed by them. 156m/B VHS, Beta. Bela Lugosi, Maria Alba, Clara Kimball Young; **D:** Ray Taylor. DVT, NOS, SNC

The Return of Count Yorga ♫♫ **1971 (R)** The vampire Count returns, taking up residence in a decrepit mansion nearby an orphanage. There he spies the toothsome Cynthia and Yorga decides to make her a vampiric bride. But the Count reckons without Cynthia's noble boyfriend who wants to keep his honey on this side of the grave. Preceded by "Count Yorga, Vampire." **CW:** Some horror violence. 97m/C VHS. Robert Quarry, Mariette Hartley, Roger Perry, Yvonne Wilder, Rudy DeLuca, George Macready, Walter Brooke, Tom Toner, Karen Huston, Paul Hansen, Craig T. Nelson; **D:** Bob Kelljan; **W:** Bob Kelljan, Yvonne Wilder; **C:** Bill Butler. ORI

The Return of Dr. Mabuse ♫♫½ Im Stahlnetz Des Dr. Mabuse; Phantom Fiend **1961** The evil doctor is back, this time sending his entranced slaves to attack a nuclear power plant. Frobe, the inspector, and Barker, the FBI man, team up to thwart him. Fun for fans of serial detective stories. 88m/B VHS, Beta. GE FR IT Gert Frobe, Lex Barker, Daliah Lavi, Wolfgang Preiss, Fausto Tozzi, Rudolph Forster; **D:** Harald Reinl. SNC

Return of Dracula ♫♫ The Curse of Dracula; The Fantastic Disappearing Man **1958** Low-budget film about the Count killing a Czech artist and assuming his identity as he makes his way to the States. Once there, he moves in with the dead man's family and begins acting rather strangely. Retitled "The Curse of Dracula" for TV. 77m/C VHS. Francis Lederer, Norma Eberhardt, Ray Stricklyn, Jimmie Baird, John Wengraf, Virginia Vincent, Greta Granstedt; **D:** Paul Landres; **W:** Pat Fielder; **C:** Jack MacKenzie. MGM, FCT

Return of Draw Egan ♫½ **1916** Vintage silent western wherein Hart is an outlaw-turned-greenhorn sheriff of a lawless town. Music score. 64m/B VHS, Beta, 8mm. William S. Hart, Louise Glaum; **D:** William S. Hart. VYY, GPV, GVV

The Return of Eliot Ness ♫♫½ **1991** Ness comes out of retirement in 1947 Chicago to track down a friend's killer. And with Al Capone dead, Chicago mob bosses are fighting for their piece of illegal turf. Stack reprises his "The Untouchables" TV role from the early '60s in this made for TV movie. 94m/C VHS. Robert Stack, Charles Durning, Philip Bosco, Jack Coleman, Lisa Hartman Black, Anthony De Sando; **D:** James A. Contner. APX

Return of Frank Cannon ♫♫ **1980** Portly private eye Frank Cannon comes out of retirement to investigate the alleged suicide of an old friend. Made for television. 96m/C VHS, Beta. William Conrad, Diana Muldaur, Joanna Pettet, Allison Argo, Arthur Hill, Ed Nelson; **D:** Corey Allen; **M:** Bruce Broughton. WOV

Return of Frank James ♫♫♫ **1940** One of Lang's lesser Hollywood works, this is nonetheless an entertaining sequel to 1939's "Jesse James." Brother Frank tries to go straight, but eventually has to hunt down the culprits who murdered his infamous outlaw sibling. Tierney's first film. 92m/C VHS, Beta, LV, **Closed Caption.** Henry Fonda, Gene Tierney, Jackie Cooper, Henry Hull, John Carradine, Donald Meek, J. Edward Bromberg; **D:** Fritz Lang. FOX

The Return of Grey Wolf ♫♫ **1922** A wild dog must fight for survival in Northern Quebec and is befriended by a fur trapper. An intelligent hound, he repays the trapper's generosity by helping him put the moves on some fur thieves. Silent. 62m/B VHS, Beta, 8mm. Helen Lynch, Henry Pierce. VYY

The Return of Jafar ♫♫ **1994 (G)** Clumsy thief Abis Mal inadvertently releases evil sorcerer Jafar from his lamp prison and now the powerful "genie Jafar" plots his revenge. So it's up to Aladdin and friends to save the Sultan's kingdom once again. Contains five new songs. ♫ Just Forget About Love; Nothing In the World (Quite Like a Friend); I'm Looking Out for Me; You're Only Second Rate; Arabian Nights. 66m/C VHS, LV, **Closed Caption.** **W:** Kevin Campbell, Mirith J.S. Colao; **V:** Scott Weinger, Linda Larkin, Gilbert Gottfried, Val Bettin, Dan Castellaneta. DIS

Return of Jesse James ♫♫ **1950** Look-alike of dead outlaw Jesse James joins in with some former members of the James Gang, leading townsfolk to believe the notorious bank robber never died. It's up to brother Frank James, now an upstanding citizen, to set the record straight. A little slow moving at times, but still worth viewing. 77m/B VHS, Beta. John Ireland, Ann Dvorak, Reed Hadley, Henry Hull, Hugh O'Brian, Tommy Noonan, Peter Marshall; **D:** Arthur Hilton. NO

The Return of Josey Wales ♫ **1986 (R)** No match for the original featuring Clint Eastwood, the title character is played woodenly by Parks. This installment finds Wales pitted against a bumbling lawman. Sequel to 1976's "The Outlaw Josey Wales." 90m/C VHS. Michael Parks, Rafael

Campos, Bob Magruder, Paco Vela, Everett Sifuentes, Charlie McCoy; **D:** Michael Parks. HHE

The Return of Martin Guerre 🏕🏕🏕½ Le Retour de Martin Guerre 1983
In this medieval tale, a dissolute village husband disappears soon after his marriage. Years later, someone who appears to be Martin Guerre returns, allegedly from war, and appears much kinder and more educated. Starring in a love story of second chances, Depardieu does not disappoint, nor does the rest of the cast. In French with English subtitles. Based on an actual court case. Remade in 1993 as "Sommersby." 111m/C VHS, **Letterbox.** FR Gerard Depardieu, Roger Planchon, Maurice Jacquemont, Barnard Pierre Donnadieu, Nathalie Baye; **D:** Daniel Vigne; **W:** Daniel Vigne, Jean-Claude Carriere. Cesar Awards '83: Best Writing, Best Score; National Society of Film Critics Awards '83: Best Actor (Depardieu); Nominations: Academy Awards '83: Best Costume Design. FXL, HMV

The Return of Our Gang 🏕½ 1925
Contains three vintage silent Pathe "Our Gang" shorts: "The School Play (Stage Fright)," "Summer Daze (The Cobbler)," and "Dog Days." 57m/B VHS, Beta, 8mm. Joe Cobb, Ernie Morrison, Mickey Daniels, Farina Hoskins, Mary Kornman, Jackie Condon, Jack Davis, Jannie Hoskins, Andy Samuels, Eugene Jackson. VYY

The Return of Peter Grimm 🏕🏕½
1935 Man returns from death to try to tidy up the mess he left behind. Enjoyable if trite fantasy based on a play by David Belasco. 82m/B VHS. Lionel Barrymore, Helen Mack, Edward Ellis, Donald Meek, George Breakston, James Bush; **D:** George Nicholls Jr. TTC, FCT

The Return of Spinal Tap 🏕🏕½
1992 Cult-fave mock rock group Spinal Tap is back with a feature-length video of performance and backstage footage from its recent reunion concert tour promoting their album "Break Like the Wind." Sequel to "This Is Spinal Tap" features lots of heavy metal songs including the title track, "Majesty of Rock," "Bitch School," "Diva Fever," "Clam Caravan," and "Stinkin' Up the Great Outdoors." Not as great as the original satire, but will appeal to Spinal Tap fans. 110m/C VHS, **LV.** Christopher Guest, Michael McKean, Harry Shearer, Rick Parnell, C.J. Vanston; **Cameos:** Paul Anka, Jeff Beck, Jamie Lee Curtis, Richard Lewis, Martha Quinn, Kenny Rogers, Martin Short, Mel Torme; **W:** Christopher Guest, Michael McKean, Harry Shearer. MPI, MVD

Return of Superfly 🏕 1990 (R) Man with
insect moniker pesters drug dealers and cops in Harlem. Long-awaited sequel to urban epic "Superfly," scored again by Mayfield. 94m/C VHS, **Closed Caption.** Margaret Avery, Nathan Purdee, Sam Jackson; **M:** Ice-T, Curtis Mayfield. THV

The Return of Swamp Thing 🏕½
1989 (PG-13) The DC Comics creature rises again out of the muck to fight mutants and evil scientists. Tongue-in-cheek, and nothing at all like the literate, ecologically oriented comic from which it was derived. 95m/C VHS, Beta, LV, **Closed Caption.** Louis Jourdan, Heather Locklear, Sarah Douglas, Dick Durock; **D:** Jim Wynorski. COL

Return of the Aliens: The Deadly Spawn 🏕 The Deadly Spawn 1983 (R) Aliens infect the earth and violently destroy humans. Extremely violent and gory. Watch out for those officious offspring. 90m/C VHS. Charles George Hildebrandt; **D:** Douglas McKeown. NO

Return of the Ape Man 🏕🏕 1944
Campy fun with Carradine and Lugosi. A mad scientist transplants Carradine's brain into the body of the "missing link." Hams galore. 51m/B VHS. Bela Lugosi, John Carradine, George Zucco, Judith Gibson, Michael Ames, Frank Moran, Mary Currier; **D:** Phil Rosen.

Return of the Bad Men 🏕🏕 1948
Scott is a retired marshall who must fight against a gang of outlaws lead by the Sundance Kid. Sequel to "Badman's Territory." 90m/C VHS, Beta, **Closed Caption.** Randolph Scott, Robert Ryan, Anne Jef-

freys, George "Gabby" Hayes, Jason Robards Sr., Jacqueline White; **D:** Ray Enright. **W:** Charles "Blackie" O'Neal. CCB, TTC

The Return of the Borrowers 🏕🏕🏕
1996 Sweet sequel to 1993's "The Borrowers" finds the six-inch Clock family—father Pod (Holm), mother Homily (Wilton), and teenaged daughter Arrietty (Callard)—having to find a new home. Lots of misadventures ensue as they must avoid nasty humans, a giant bee, a storm, and other dangers on their way to safety. Based on the novels by Mary Norton. 165m/C VHS. GB Ian Holm, Penelope Wilton, Rebecca Callard, Sian Phillips, Tony Haygarth, Judy Parfitt, Ben Chaplin, Paul Cross, Pamela Cundell, Ross McCall, Richard Vernon, Danny Newman; **D:** John Henderson; **W:** Richard Carpenter; **C:** Clive Tucker; **M:** Howard Goodall. TTC

Return of the Chinese Boxer 🏕
1974 Samurai and ninja warriors fight, usually to the death. 93m/C VHS, Beta. Jimmy Wang Yu, Lung Fei, Cheung Ying Chen, Chin Kang. UNI

Return of the Dragon 🏕🏕½ 1973 (R)
In Lee's last picture, a Chinese restaurant in Rome is menaced by gangsters who want to buy the property. On behalf of the owners, Lee duels an American karate champ in the Roman forum. The battle scenes between Lee and Norris are great and make this a must-see for martial arts fans. 91m/C VHS, Beta, LV, **Letterbox, Closed Caption.** CH Bruce Lee, Nora Miao, Chuck Norris; **D:** Bruce Lee. FOX, GEM

Return of the Evil Dead 🏕 Return of the Blind Dead; El Ataque de los Muertos Sin Ojos 1975 The sightless dead priests return to attack still more 1970s' Europeans in this second installment of the "blind dead" trilogy. Preceded by "Tombs of the Blind Dead" and followed by "Horror of the Zombies." Not to be confused with Raimi's "Evil Dead" slasher flicks. 85m/C VHS. SP PT Tony Kendall, Esther Roy, Frank Blake, Fernando Sancho, Lone Fleming, Loreta Tovar, Jose Canalejas; **D:** Armando de Ossorio; **W:** Armando de Ossorio; **C:** Miguel Mila. VTR

Return of the Family Man 🏕 1989 A
mass murderer seems unstoppable as he continues to slash whole families at a time...the family man is redefined in this bloody gore-fest. 90m/C VHS. Ron Smerczak, Liam Cundill, Terence Reis, Michelle Constant; **D:** John Murlowski. NO

Return of the Fly 🏕🏕 1959 The son of
the scientist who discovered how to move matter through space decides to continue his father's work, but does so against his uncle's wishes. He soon duplicates his dad's experiments with similar results. This sequel to "The Fly" doesn't buzz like the original. Followed by "Curse of the Fly." 80m/B VHS, Beta, LV. Vincent Price, Brett Halsey, John Sutton, Dan Seymour, David Frankham, Danielle De Metz, Ed Wolff; **D:** Edward L. Bernds; **W:** Edward L. Bernds, Brydon Baker. FOX, FCT

Return of the Jedi 🏕🏕🏕½ 1983 (PG)
Third film in George Lucas' popular space saga. Against seemingly fearsome odds, Luke Skywalker battles such worthies as Jabba the Hut and heavy-breathing Darth Vader to save his comrades and triumph over the evil Galactic Empire. Han and Leia reaffirm their love and team with C3PO, R2-D2, Chewbacca, Calrissian, and a bunch of furry Ewoks to aid in the annihilation of the Dark Side. The special effects are still spectacular, even the third time around. Sequel to "Star Wars" (1977) and "The Empire Strikes Back" (1980). 132m/C VHS, Beta, LV, **Letterbox, Closed Caption.** Mark Hamill, Carrie Fisher, Harrison Ford, Billy Dee Williams, David Prowse, James Earl Jones, Kenny Baker, Denis Lawson, Anthony Daniels, Peter Mayhew; **D:** Richard Marquand; **W:** George Lucas, Lawrence Kasdan; **M:** John Williams; **V:** Alec Guinness, Frank Oz. Academy Awards '83: Best Visual Effects; Nominations: Academy Awards '83: Best Art Direction/Set Decoration, Best Sound, Best Original Score. FOX, RDG, HMV

Return of the Killer Tomatoes! 🏕
1988 (PG) The man-eating plant-life from 1977's "Attack of the Killer Tomatoes" is back, able to turn into people due to the slightly larger budget. Astin is mad as the scientist. Not as bad as "Attack," representing a small hurdle in the history of filmdom. Followed by "Killer Tomatoes Strike Back." 98m/C VHS, Beta, LV, **Closed Caption.** Anthony Starke, George Clooney, Karen Mistal, Steve Lundquist, John Astin, Charlie Jones, Rock Peace, Frank Davis, C.J. Dillon, Teri Weigel; **D:** John DeBello; **W:** John DeBello. VTR

The Return of the King 1980 The third
and final animated episode of J.R.R Tolkien's Middle Earth Trilogy. This saga features Frodo, relative to Hobbit Bilbo Baggins, and his faithful servant, making middle Earth safe for Orcs, Gollums and other ooky creatures. 120m/C VHS. **D:** Arthur Rankin Jr., Jules Bass; **V:** Orson Bean, Roddy McDowall, John Huston, Theodore Bikel, William Conrad, Glen Yarborough, Paul Frees, Casey Kasem, Sonny Melendrez. XVC, VTR, FAF

Return of the Lash 🏕 1947 Lash LaRue
once again defends settlers' rights from ruthless outlaws. 53m/B VHS, Beta. Lash LaRue, Al "Fuzzy" St. John, Mary Maynard, George Chesebro; **D:** Ray Taylor. COL

Return of the Living Dead 🏕🏕½
1985 (R) Poisonous gas revives a cemetery and a morgue rendering an outrageous spoof on the living-dead sub-genre with fast-moving zombies, punk humor, and exaggerated gore. Its humor does not diminish the fear factor, however. Sequel follows. Directed by "Alien" writer O'Bannon. 90m/C VHS, Beta, LV. Clu Gulager, James Karen, Linnea Quigley, Don Calfa, Jewel Shepard, Beverly Randolph, Miguel Nunez, Brian Peck; **D:** Dan O'Bannon; **W:** Dan O'Bannon; **C:** Jules Brenner. NO

Return of the Living Dead 2 🏕½
1988 (R) An inevitable sequel to the original Dan O'Bannon satire about George Romero-esque brain-eating zombies attacking suburbia with zest and vigor. 89m/C VHS, Beta, LV, **Closed Caption.** Dana Ashbrook, Marsha Dietlein, Philip Bruns, James Karen, Thom Mathews, Suzanne Snyder, Michael Kenworthy, Thor Van Lingen; **D:** Ken Wiederhorn; **W:** Ken Wiederhorn; **C:** Robert Elswit. ORI, WAR

Return of the Living Dead 3 🏕½
1993 (R) When Curt's girlfriend Julie dies in a motorcycle accident you'd think that would be the end of romance. But not when your dad heads a secret project that involves reviving corpses. Only problem is now Julie's a zombie with long metal claws and glass spikes sticking out of various body parts. Hey, if it's true love Curt will get over it. Macabre special effects. Also available unrated. **CW:** Extreme violence. 97m/C VHS, LV, **Closed Caption.** Mindy Clarke, J. Trevor Edmond, Kent McCord, Basil Wallace, Fabio Urena; **D:** Brian Yuzna; **W:** John Penney; **M:** Barry Goldberg. THV

Return of the Man from U.N.C.L.E. 🏕🏕 1983 Those dashing super agents Napoleon Solo and Illya Kuryakin come out of retirement to settle an old score with their nemesis THRUSH. Made for television. 96m/C VHS, Beta. Robert Vaughn, David McCallum, Patrick Macnee, Gayle Hunnicutt, Geoffrey Lewis; **D:** Ray Austin. TWE

The Return of the Musketeers 🏕🏕½ 1989 (PG) Lester's third Musketeers film (after his successful double-act in the '70s) is a good-natured but average costume/comedy/buddy film. Twenty years after D'Artagnan, Athos, Porthos, and Aramis saved the French queen from scandal it's time to do it all over again. Milady DeWinter, who hatched the first plot, is dead but her equally devious daughter Justine is more than able to take mama's scheming place. Just to add a little more excitement Athos' adopted son Raoul meets Justine and passions fly amidst the swordplay. Based on the Alexandre Dumas novel "Twenty Years After." 103m/C VHS, LV, **Closed Caption.** GB FR SP Michael York, Oliver Reed, Frank Finlay, Richard Chamberlain, Kim Cattrall, C. Thomas Howell, Geraldine Chaplin, Roy Kin-

near, Christopher Lee, Philippe Noiret, Jean-Pierre Cassel, Billy Connolly, Eusebio Lazaro; **D:** Richard Lester; **W:** George MacDonald Fraser. *USH, BTV, FCT*

The Return of the Native 🐾🐾½

1994 (PG) Wind-swept moors, a tempestuous heroine, two loves, and requisite tragedy all courtesy of Thomas Hardy's 1878 novel. Beautiful Eustacia Vye (Jones) longs to leave the boredom of Egdon Heath—even though she's involved with the roguish Damon Wildeve (Owen). Then businessman Clym Yeobright (Stevenson) returns from Paris and captures Eustacia's fancy. She marries him in the hope they'll return to the continent but she's bitterly disappointed when Clym wants to remain in Egdon. Meanwhile, Damon has married Clym's gentle cousin Thomasin (Skinner) but he and Eustacia can't seem to stay away from each other, leading to storms for all. **99m/C VHS, Closed Caption.** Catherine Zeta-Jones, Clive Owen, Ray Stevenson, Claire Skinner, Joan Plowright, Steven Mackintosh, Celia Imrie, Paul Rogers; **D:** Jack Gold; **W:** Robert W. Lenski; **M:** Carl Davis. *REP*

Return of the Pink Panther 🐾🐾½

1974 (G) Bumbling Inspector Clouseau is called upon to rescue the Pink Panther diamond stolen from a museum. Sellers manages to produce mayhem with a vacuum cleaner and other devices that, in his hands, become instruments of terror. Clever opening credits. Fourth installment in the Pink Panther series but the first with Sellers since 1964's "A Shot In The Dark." **113m/C VHS, Beta, LV.** Peter Sellers, Christopher Plummer, Catherine Schell, Herbert Lom, Victor Spinetti; **D:** Blake Edwards; **W:** Frank Waldman, Blake Edwards; **C:** Geoffrey Unsworth; **M:** Henry Mancini. *FOX, FHE, FCT*

Return of the Rebels 🐾🐾

1981 Made for television fluff with Eden as a motorcycle matron whose campground is rid of riff-raff by the crow-lined participants in a 25-year reunion of a biker gang. **100m/C VHS.** Barbara Eden, Robert Mandan, Jamie Farr, Patrick Swayze, Don Murray, Christopher Connelly; **D:** Noel Nosseck. *NO*

Return of the Scorpion 🐾

1980 Big trouble abounds as that crazy kung fu guy, the "Scorpion," comes back to town. **90m/C VHS, Beta.** Yang Pan Pan, Lam Men Wei, Philip Ko. *NO*

Return of the Secaucus 7 🐾🐾🐾½

1980 Centers around a weekend reunion of seven friends who were activists during the Vietnam War in the turbulent '60s. Now turning 30, they evaluate their present lives and progress. Writer and director Sayles plays Howie in this excellent example of what a low-budget film can and should be. A less trendy predecessor of "The Big Chill" (1983) which, perhaps, was a few years ahead of its time. **110m/C VHS, Beta.** Mark Arnott, Gordon Clapp, Maggie Cousineau-Arndt, David Strathairn; **D:** John Sayles; **W:** John Sayles; **M:** Mason Daring. Los Angeles Film Critics Association Awards '80: Best Screenplay, National Film Registry '97. *COL*

Return of the Seven 🐾🐾

Return of the Magnificent Seven **1966** The first sequel to "The Magnificent Seven" features the group liberating a compatriot who is held hostage. Yawn. **97m/C VHS, Beta.** Yul Brynner, Warren Oates, Robert Fuller, Claude Akins; **D:** Burt Kennedy; **W:** Larry Cohen; **C:** Paul Vogel; **M:** Elmer Bernstein. Nominations: Academy Awards '66: Best Adapted Score. *MGM*

Return of the Soldier 🐾🐾🐾

1982 A shell-shocked WWI veteran has no memory of his marriage, leaving his wife, his childhood flame, and an unrequited love to vie for his affections. Adapted from the novel by Rebecca West. **101m/C VHS, Beta.** *GB* Glenda Jackson, Julie Christie, Ann-Margret, Alan Bates, Ian Holm, Frank Finlay; **D:** Alan Bridges; **M:** Richard Rodney Bennett. *NO*

Return of the Street Fighter 🐾½

197? Sequel to "The Street Fighter," finds Terry Tsuguri (Chiba) hired by a gang to silence a jailed informer. So, Terry gets arrested, practices his karate and does the guy in, and finds out the gang now wants to silence him. Big mistake! Notice a

pattern yet? Followed by "The Street Fighter's Last Revenge" and "Sister Street Fighter." **88m/C VHS.** Sonny Chiba. *NLC*

Return of the Tall Blond Man With One Black Shoe 🐾🐾½

Le Retour du Grand Blond **1974** Sequel to 1972's "The Tall Blond Man With One Black Shoe." Again a "klutz" is mistaken for a master spy and becomes unknowingly involved in the world of international intrigue. In French with English subtitles. Not quite as good as the original. **84m/C VHS, Beta.** *FR* Pierre Richard, Mireille Darc, Michael Duchaussoy, Jean Rochefort, Jean Carmet; **D:** Yves Robert; **W:** Francis Veber; **M:** Vladimir Cosma. *CVC*

Return of the Tiger 🐾½

1978 The Hover Night Club in Bangkok fronts the operations of an international narcotics group headed by an American. When a rival Chinese gang tries to dominate the drug market, conflict and lots of kicking ensue. **95m/C VHS, Beta.** Bruce Li, Paul Smith, Chaing I, Angela Mao; **D:** Jimmy Shaw.

Return of the Vampire 🐾🐾

1943 A Hungarian vampire and his werewolf servant seek revenge on the family who drove a spike through his heart two decades earlier. **69m/B VHS, Beta, LV.** Bela Lugosi, Nina Foch, Miles Mander, Matt Willis, Frieda Inescort, Roland Varno, Gilbert Emery, Ottola Nesmith; **D:** Lew (Louis Friedlander) Landers; **W:** Griffin Jay; **C:** L.W. O'Connell, John Stumar. *NO*

Return of Wildfire 🐾½

1948 Two sisters are left to run the family horse ranch when their brother is killed. A drifter aids the sisters in bringing the murderer to justice. **83m/B VHS, Beta.** Richard Arlen, Patricia Morison, Mary Beth Hughes. *NO*

Return to Africa 🐾🐾

1989 Rebels threaten the familial paradise of the tightknit Mallory clan. **95m/C VHS, Beta.** Stan Brock, Anne Collings, David Tors, Ivan Tors, Peter Tors, Steven Tors; **D:** Leslie Martinson.

Return to Boggy Creek 🐾🐾

1977 (PG) Townspeople in a small fishing village learn from a photographer that a "killer" beast, whom they thought had disappeared, has returned and is living in Boggy Creek. Some curious children follow the shutterbug into the marsh, despite hurricane warnings, and the swamp monster reacts with unusual compassion. OK for the kiddies. Fictitious story unlike other "Boggy Creek" films, which are billed as semi-documentaries. Sequel to "Legend of Boggy Creek" and features Mary Ann from "Gilligan's Island." **87m/C VHS, Beta.** Dawn Wells, Dana Plato, Louise Belaire, John Hofeus; **D:** Tom Moore. *FOX*

Return to Earth 🐾🐾

1976 Made for television drama deals with the self-doubts faced by Apollo 11 astronaut Buzz Aldrin after his triumphant return to Earth. Based on Aldrin's own novel. **74m/C VHS, Beta.** Cliff Robertson, Shirley Knight, Ralph Bellamy, Stefanie Powers, Charles Cioffi; **D:** Jud Taylor. *TWE*

Return to Eden 🐾🐾

1989 A young woman falls in love with her philosophy tutor, but he can't return her affections. An interesting comparison between the passion of the primitive and the tangle of modern-day romance. **90m/C VHS.** Sam Bottoms, Edward Binns, Renee Coleman; **D:** William Olsen. *NO*

Return to Fantasy Island 🐾½

1977 Boss, boss, it's da plane! The second full-length television treatment of the once popular series wherein three couples get their most cherished fantasy fulfilled by Mr. Roarke. and company. **100m/C VHS, Beta.** Ricardo Montalban, Herve Villechaize, Adrienne Barbeau, Pat Crowley, Joseph Campanella, Karen Valentine, Laraine Day, George Maharis, Horst Buchholz, France Nuyen, Joseph Cotten, Cameron Mitchell, George Chakiris; **D:** George McCowan.

Return to Frogtown WOOF!

1992 (PG-13) Sequel to "Hell Comes to Frogtown" finds Texas Rocket Ranger Ferrigno captured by mutant frogs. As unbelievably bad as it sounds. **90m/C**

VHS. Lou Ferrigno, Charles Napier, Robert Z'Dar, Denice Duff, Don Stroud; **D:** Donald G. Jackson. *TPV, YHV*

Return to Horror High 🐾

1987 (R) A horror movie producer makes a film in an abandoned and haunted high school, where a series of murders occurred years earlier. As in most "return" flicks, history repeats itself. **95m/C VHS, Beta.** Alex Rocco, Vince Edwards, Philip McKeon, Brendan Hughes, Lori Lethin, Scott Jacoby; **D:** Bill Froelich. *VTR*

Return to Lonesome Dove 🐾🐾½

1993 Routine sequel to successful western saga "Lonesome Dove" picks up after the burial of Gus McCrae in Texas by his friend, ex-Texas Ranger Woodrow F. Call (now played by Voight). The original dealt with a cattle drive, this one with horses. Along the way you'll run into the usual sidewinders as well as McCrae's lost love Clara (now Hershey) and Schroder, returning as Call's unacknowledged son Newt. Filmed on loction in Montana. TV production was already underway when author Larry McMurtry gave the producers his then unpublished sequel "Streets of Laredo" which differed from the book and miniseries don't match. **330m/C VHS, LV, Closed Caption.** Jon Voight, William L. Petersen, Rick Schroder, Barbara Hershey, Louis Gossett Jr., Oliver Reed, Reese Witherspoon, Nia Peeples, Dennis Haysbert, Timothy Scott, Barry Tubb, Chris Cooper, CCH Pounder, William Sanderson; **D:** Mike Robe; **W:** John Wilder. *CAF, FUS*

Return to Macon County 🐾🐾

1975 Tale of three young, reckless youths who become involved with drag racing and a sadistic law enforcement officer. Nolte turns in a good performance in his first film, as does Johnson, despite a mediocre script and dialogue. Sequel to 1974's "Macon County Line." **90m/C VHS, Beta.** Nick Nolte, Don Johnson, Robin Mattson; **D:** Richard Compton; **W:** Richard Compton. *ART, VES*

Return to Mayberry 🐾🐾

1985 Andy Taylor returns to Mayberry after 20 years to obtain his old job as sheriff. Sixteen of the original actors reappeared for this nostalgia-fest. Made for television. **95m/C VHS, Beta.** Andy Griffith, Ron Howard, Don Knotts, Jim Nabors, Aneta Corsaut, Jack Dodson, George Lindsey, Betty Lynn; **D:** Bob Sweeney. *MCG*

Return to Oz 🐾🐾½

1985 (PG) Picking up where "The Wizard of Oz" left off, Auntie Em and Uncle Ed place Dorothy in the care of a therapist to cure her "delusions" of Oz. A natural disaster again lands her in the land of the yellow brick road, where the evil Nome King and Princess Mombi are spreading terror and squalor. Based on a later L. Frank Baum book. Enjoyable for the whole family although some scenes may frighten very small children. **109m/C VHS, Beta, LV.** Fairuza Balk, Piper Laurie, Matt Clark, Nicol Williamson, Jean Marsh; **D:** Walter Murch; **C:** David Watkin; **M:** David Shire. *DIS*

Return to Paradise 🐾🐾

1953 Cooper is a soldier of fortune wandering through the Polynesian islands in the late 1920s. On a remote atoll he comes across a crazy missionary intent upon subduing the native population. Cooper falls in love with a native beauty (Haynes in her screen debut) and leads the natives in a revolt against authority. Cliched but with nice scenery from the location shoot in Samoa. Loose adaptation of the short story "Mr. Morgan" by James Michener. **100m/C VHS, Beta.** Gary Cooper, Roberta Haynes, Barry Jones, John Hudson, Moira MacDonald; **D:** Mark Robson; **W:** Charles Kaufman. *MGM, FCT*

Return to Peyton Place 🐾🐾½

1961 A young writer publishes novel exposing town as virtual Peyton Place, and the townsfolk turn against her and her family. Sequel to the scandalously popular '50s original and inspiration for the just-as-popular soap opera. Astor is excellent as the evil matriarch. **122m/C VHS, Closed Caption.** Carol Lynley, Jeff Chandler, Eleanor Parker, Mary Astor, Robert Sterling, Luciana Paluzzi, Tuesday Weld, Brett Halsey, Bob Crane; **D:** Jose Ferrer. *FOX, FCT*

Return to Salem's Lot ✗✗ 1987 (R)
Enjoyable camp sequel to the Stephen King tale, this time involving a cynical scientist and his son returning to the town only to find it completely run by vampires. 101m/C VHS, Beta, **Closed Caption.** Michael Moriarty, Ricky Addison Reed, Samuel Fuller, Andrew Duggan, Evelyn Keyes, Jill Gatsby, June Havoc, Ronee Blakley, James Dixon, David Holbrook; **D:** Larry Cohen; **W:** Larry Cohen, James Dixon; **C:** Daniel Pearl. WAR

Return to Savage Beach ✗½ 1997 (R)
Top secret government agency L.E.T.H.A.L. is sent to retrieve a computer disk containing the location of a hidden treasure. Lots of action, babes, and hard-bodies (you're not expecting acting talent, are you?).**CW:** Nudity, sexuality and some violence. 98m/C VHS. Julie Strain, Julie K. Smith, Shae Marks, Cristian Letelier; **D:** Andy Sidaris. MNC

Return to Snowy River ✗✗✗ 1988
(PG) Continues the love story of the former ranch hand and the rancher's daughter in Australia's Victoria Alps that began in "The Man From Snowy River." Dennehy takes over from Kirk Douglas as the father who aims to keep the lovers apart. The photography of horses and the scenery is spectacular, making the whole film worthwhile. 99m/C VHS, Beta, LV. AU Tom Burlinson, Sigrid Thornton, Brian Dennehy, Nicholas Eadie, Mark Hembrow, Bryan Marshall; **D:** Geoff Burrowes; **W:** Geoff Burrowes. DIS, TVC

Return to the Blue Lagoon ✗ 1991
(PG-13) Neither the acting nor the premise has improved with age. Another photogenic adolescent couple experiences puberty on that island; for continuity, the young man is the son of the lovers in the first "Blue Lagoon." Breathtaking scenery—just turn down the sound. 102m/C VHS, LV, **Closed Caption.** Milla Jovovich, Brian Krause, Lisa Pelikan; **D:** William A. Graham; **C:** Robert Steadman. COL

Return to the Lost World ✗✗½
1993 (PG) Rival scientists Challenger and Summerlee set out for the Lost World and find it threatened by oil prospectors. With a volcano about to explode the scientists set out to save their prehistoric paradise and its dinosaur inhabitants. Based on a story by Sir Arthur Conan Doyle. Sequel to "The Lost World." 99m/C VHS, **Closed Caption.** John Rhys-Davies, David Warner, Darren Peter Mercer, Geza Kovacs; **D:** Timothy Bond. WOV

Return to Two Moon Junction ✗½
1993 (R) New York supermodel Savannah (Clarke) returns to her family's riverfront home in Georgia and promptly sheds her clothing for local sculptor Jake (Schafer). Must be something about the southern heat. This sequel should have the same video success as its predecessor since it keeps to the minimal plot/maximum teasing sex scenes outline.**CW:** Nudity. 96m/C VHS, LV, **Closed Caption.** Mindy Clarke, John Clayton Schafer, Louise Fletcher; **D:** Farhad Mann. THV

Reuben, Reuben ✗✗✗ 1983 (R) Brilliant, but drunken poet Conti turns himself around when he falls in love with earthy college girl McGillis in her film debut. The student's dog Reuben unwittingly alters Conti's progress, however, in the film's startling conclusion. Based on the writings of Peter DeVries. 100m/C VHS, Beta, **Closed Caption.** Tom Conti, Kelly McGillis, Roberts Blossom, E. Katherine Kerr, Cynthia Harris, Joel Fabiani, Kara Wilson, Lois Smith; **D:** Robert Ellis Miller; **W:** Julius J. Epstein; **M:** Billy Goldenberg. National Board of Review Awards '83: Best Actor (Conti); Writers Guild of America '83: Best Adapted Screenplay; Nominations: Academy Awards '83: Best Actor (Conti), Best Adapted Screenplay. FOX

Reunion ✗✗✗ 1988 (PG-13) Robards stars as a Jewish businessman, living in the U.S., who returns to his boyhood home of Stuttgart, Germany some 50 years after his leaving in 1933. He hopes to find out what happened to a boyhood school chum—the son of an aristocractic (and Aryan) German family. Film uses extensive flashbacks to show the the rise of anti-Semitism and how it affects the friendship of both youths. Thoughtfull and well-acted though occasionally

plodding drama based on Fred Uhlman's novel. 120m/C VHS, Beta, LV, Closed Caption. FR GE GB Jason Robards Jr., Christien Anholt, Sam West, Francoise Fabian, Maureen Kerwin, Barbara Jefford, Alexander Trauner; **D:** Jerry Schatzberg; **W:** Harold Pinter; **C:** Bruno de Keyzer. IME, FCT, MOV

Reunion in France ✗✗ Mademoiselle France; Reunion 1942 Parisian dress designer sacrifices her lifestyle to help an American flier flee France after the Nazis invade. Dated patriotic flag-waver. 104m/B VHS, Beta. Joan Crawford, John Wayne, Philip Dorn, Reginald Owen, Albert Basserman, John Carradine, Ann Ayars, J. Edward Bromberg, Henry Daniell, Moroni Olsen, Howard da Silva, Ava Gardner, John Considine; **D:** Jules Dassin. MGM

Revenge ✗½ Terror under the House; After Jenny Died; Inn of the Frightened People 1971 The parents of a girl who was brutally killed take the law into their own hands in this bloody, vengeful thriller. 89m/C VHS, Beta, Letterbox. GB Joan Collins, James Booth, Ray Barrett, Sinead Cusack, Kenneth Griffith; **D:** Sidney Hayers. MRV

Revenge woof! 1986 (R) Sequel to "Blood Cult" about a cult led by horror king Carradine. Seems these dog worshippers want McGowan's land and Senator Carradine will stop at nothing to get it. Woofer filled with gratuitous violence. 104m/C VHS, Beta. Patrick Wayne, John Carradine, Bennie Lee McGowan, Josef Hanet, Stephanie Kropke; **D:** Christopher Lewis. VCI

Revenge ✗✗ 1990 (R) Retired pilot Costner makes the mistake of falling in love with another man's wife. Quinn gives a first-rate performance as the Mexican crime lord who punishes his spouse and her lover, beginning a cycle of vengeance. Sometimes contrived, but artfully photographed with tantalizing love scenes. Based on the Jim Harrison novel. 123m/C VHS, Beta, LV, 8mm. Kevin Costner, Anthony Quinn, Madeleine Stowe, Sally Kirkland, Joe Santos, Miguel Ferrer, James Gammon, Tomas Milian; **D:** Tony Scott; **W:** Jim Harrison; **M:** Jack Nitzsche. COL

Revenge in the House of Usher ✗✗ 1982 House holds grudge. 90m/C VHS. Howard Vernon, Dan Villers; **D:** Jess (Jesus) Franco. MOV

Revenge of a Kabuki Actor ✗✗
1963 When Kabuki actor Kazuo Hasegawa's parents are viciously murdered, he seeks their killer with a vengeance. In Japanese with English subtitles. 114m/C VHS. JP **D:** Kon Ichikawa. FST, FCT

Revenge of Doctor X woof! 198? A man/beast lies waiting for the pretty reporter who seeks her shipwrecked father in the jungles of an uncharted island. 94m/C VHS, Beta. John Ashley, Ronald Remy, Angelique Pettyjohn. NO

The Revenge of Frankenstein ✗✗½ 1958 Frankenstein (Cushing) is rescued from the guillotine by his dwarf servant and decides to relocate to Carlsbruck where he becomes the popular society physician, Dr. Stein. But the misunderstood doc just can't stop his ghoulish experiments and plans to transfer his servant's brain into another sewn together creature. Nicely macabre sequel to "The Curse of Frankenstein"; followed by "The Evil of Frankenstein." 89m/C VHS. GB Peter Cushing, Michael Gwynn, Francis Matthews, Oscar Quitak, Lionel Jeffries, Eunice Gayson, John Welsh; **D:** Terence Fisher; **W:** Jimmy Sangster. COL

Revenge of the Barbarians ✗ 1964
As the barbarians descend on Rome, Olympus must decide whether to save the empire or the beautiful Gallo, the woman he loves. Decisions, decisions. 99m/C Beta. Robert Alda, Anthony Steel.

Revenge of the Barbarians ✗ 1985
A Scandinavian adventure about a young Celt seeking revenge against the Viking hordes that killed his family. 95m/C Beta. **D:** Hrafn Gunnlaugsson. NO

Revenge of the Cheerleaders ✗
1976 (R) The cheerleaders pull out all the stops to save their school from a ruthless land developer. What spirit. 86m/C VHS, Beta. Jerii Woods, Cheryl "Rainbeaux" Smith, Helen Lang, Patrice Rohmer, Susie Elene, Eddra Gale, William Bramley, Carl Ballantine, David Hasselhoff; **D:** Richard Lerner. ART

Revenge of the Creature ✗✗ 1955 In this follow up to "The Creature from the Black Lagoon," the Gill-man is captured in the Amazon and taken to a Florida marine park. There he is put on display for visitors and subjected to heartless experiments. Growing restless in his captive surroundings, the creature breaks free and makes for the ocean. Includes screen debut of Clint Eastwood as a lab technician. Originally shot in 3-D. Based on a story by William Alland. Available on laserdisc as part of a special Encore Edition Double Feature with "The Creature Walks Among Us." 82m/B VHS, LV, **Closed Caption.** John Agar, Lori Nelson, John Bromfield, John Wood, Nestor Paiva, Clint Eastwood, Robert B. Williams, Grandon Rhodes; **D:** Jack Arnold; **W:** Martin Berkeley; **C:** Charles S. Welbourne. USH, FCT

Revenge of the Dead ✗ 1984 (R) European archeological team discovers the existence of a powerful force that allows the dead to return to life. 100m/C VHS, Beta. IT Gabriele Lavia, Anne Canoras; **D:** Pupi Avati. ART

Revenge of the Living Zombies ✗
1988 (R) Teens on a Halloween hayride run headlong into flesh-craving zombies. Available in a slightly edited version. 85m/C VHS, Beta. Bill Hinzman, John Mowod, Leslie Ann Wick, Kevin Kindlan; **D:** Bill Hinzman. NO

Revenge of the Nerds ✗✗½ 1984 (R)
When nerdy college freshmen are victimized by jocks, frat boys and the school's beauties, they start their own fraternity and seek revenge. Carradine and Edwards team well as the geeks in this better than average teenage sex comedy. Guess who gets the girls? Sequel was much worse. 89m/C VHS, Beta, LV, **Closed Caption.** Robert Carradine, Anthony Edwards, Timothy Busfield, Andrew Cassese, Curtis Armstrong, Larry B. Scott, Brian Tochi, Julia Montgomery, Michelle Meyrink, Ted McGinley, John Goodman, Bernie Casey; **D:** Jeff Kanew; **W:** Tim Metcalfe, Jeff Buhai; **M:** Thomas Newman. FOX

Revenge of the Nerds 2: Nerds in Paradise ✗ 1987 (PG-13) The nerd clan from the first film (minus Edwards who only makes a brief appearance) travels to Fort Lauderdale for a fraternity conference. They fend off loads of bullies and jocks with raunchy humor. Boy can Booger belch. Not as good as the first Nerds movie; a few laughs nonetheless. 89m/C VHS, Beta, LV, **Closed Caption.** Robert Carradine, Curtis Armstrong, Timothy Busfield, Andrew Cassese, Ed Lauter, Larry B. Scott, Courtney Thorne-Smith, Anthony Edwards, James Hong; **D:** Joe Roth. FOX

Revenge of the Nerds 3: The Next Generation ✗½ 1992 Adams College has nerd-loathing trustee Downey, Jr. mobilizing those frat boys against the bespectacled geeks, who turn to founding nerd Carradine to save them. Cookie-cutter characters and the gags won't hold your attention. Let's hope this is the last in the series. ?m/C VHS. Robert Carradine, Curtis Armstrong, Ted McGinley, Morton Downey Jr., Julia Montgomery. FOX

Revenge of the Nerds 4: Nerds in Love ✗✗½ 1994 Yes, even nerds deserve a little love. This time the gang get together for Booger's (Armstrong) wedding—complete with nerd bachelor party and wedding shower. Too bad Booger's future father-in-law is so reluctant to have a nerd in the family that he hires a sleazy detective to dig up some dirt. Made for TV. 90m/C VHS, **Closed Caption.** Curtis Armstrong, Robert Carradine, Ted McGinley, Larry B. Scott, Donald Gibb, Joseph Bologna, Julia Montgomery, Corinne Bohrer, Christina Pickles, Jessica Tuck, Robert Picardo; **D:** Steve Zacharias; **W:** Steve Zacharias, Steve Buhai. FXV

Revenge of the Ninja 🎬🎬½ 1983 (R) Ninja Kosugi hopes to escape his past in Los Angeles. A drug trafficker, also ninja-trained, prevents him. The two polish off a slew of mobsters before their own inevitable showdown. Better-than the standard chop-socky fest from Cannon with amusing surreal touches like a battling grandma ninja. Sequel to "Enter the Ninja," followed by "Ninja III." 90m/C VHS, Beta. Sho Kosugi, Arthur Roberts, Keith Vitali, Virgil Frye, Ashley Ferrare, Kane Kosugi, John Lamotta, Grace Oshita, Melvin C. Hampton, Mario Gallo; D: Sam Firstenberg; W: James R. Silke; M: Rob Walsh. MGM

Revenge of the Pink Panther 🎬🎬½ 1978 (PG) Inspector Clouseau survives his own assassination attempt, but allows the world to think he is dead in order to pursue an investigation of the culprits in his own unique, bumbling way. The last "Pink Panther" film before Sellers died, and perhaps the least funny. 99m/C VHS, Beta, LV, Letterbox. Peter Sellers, Herbert Lom, Dyan Cannon, Robert Webber, Burt Kwouk, Robert Loggia; D: Blake Edwards; W: Blake Edwards, Ron Clark, Frank Waldman; M: Henry Mancini. FOX, FCT

Revenge of the Radioactive Reporter 🎬🎬 1991 Nuclear plant honchos don't like journalist who's about to hang their dirty laundry, so they toss him into vat of nuclear waste. He returns as a reporter with a cosmetic peel. 90m/C VHS. David Scammell, Kathryn Boese, Randy Pearlstein, Derrick Strange; D: Craig Pryce. NO

Revenge of the Red Baron 🎬🎬½ 1993 (PG-13) Jim Spencer (Rooney) is the WWI pilot who shot down Germany's fearsome Red Baron. Now aged and infirm he's tormented by what he thinks is his enemy's ghost. A vengeful ghost who takes after Spencer's family. CW: Language and violence. 90m/C VHS, LV. Mickey Rooney, Tobey Maguire, Laraine Newman, Cliff DeYoung; D: Robert Gordon; W: Michael James McDonald; C: Christian Sebaldt. NHO

Revenge of the Stepford Wives 🎬½ 1980 Made for television sequel to the Ira Levin fantasy about suburban husbands who create obedient robot replicas of their wives. In this installment, the wives are not robots, but are simply made docile by drugs. Strange casting pairs Johnson and Kavner as husband and step-ford wife. Begat "The Stepford Children." 95m/C VHS, Beta. Sharon Gless, Julie Kavner, Don Johnson, Audra Lindley, Mason Adams, Arthur Hill; D: Robert Fuest. NLC

Revenge of the Teenage Vixens from Outer Space 🎬🎬 1986 A low-budget film about three sex starved females from another planet who come to earth to find men. When the ones they meet do not live up to their expectations, the frustrated females turn the disappointing dudes are turned into vegetables. 84m/C VHS, Beta. Lisa Schwedop, Howard Scott; D: Jeff Ferrell. NO

Revenge of the Virgins 🎬 1962 A tribe of topless 'Indian' women protect their sacred land from the white men. Exhumed exploitation for bad-film junkies, narrated by Kenne Duncan, an Ed Wood cohort. 53m/B VHS. Jewell Morgan, Charles Veltman, Jodean Russo, Stanton Pritchard; D: Paul Perri. NOS, SMW, VDM

Revenge of the Zombies 🎬½ 1943 In this sequel of sorts to "King of the Zombies," Carradine is creating an army of the undead for use by an evil foreign entity. 61m/B VHS. John Carradine, Robert Lowery, Gale Storm, Veda Ann Borg, Mantan Moreland; D: Steve Sekely. MLB

Revenge of the Zombies 🎬½ 1981 (R) Kung-fu exploitation film featuring man-eating alligators, zombies, mad magicians, and more. ?m/C VHS. Ti Lung, Lily Tu. LOO

The Revenge Rider 🎬🎬 1935 Orphan McCoy goes after the villains who killed his parents. Good performance from McCoy in an otherwise average film. 60m/B VHS. Tim McCoy, Robert Al-

len, Billie Seward, Edward Earle, Jack Clifford, Lafe McKee; D: David Selman. DVT, HEG

The Revenger 🎬 1990 A framed man returns from prison and finds that a mobster has kidnapped his wife and wants $50,000 to give her back. 91m/C VHS, Beta. Oliver Reed, Frank Zagarino; D: Cedric Sundstrom.

Reversal of Fortune 🎬🎬🎬½ 1990 (R) True tale of wealthy socialite Claus von Bulow (Irons) accused of deliberately giving his wife Sunny (Close) a near-lethal overdose of insulin. Comatose Close narrates history of the couple's courtship and married life, a saga of unhappiness and substance abuse, while Silver (as lawyer Dershowitz) et al prepare von Bulow's defense. An unflattering picture of the idle rich that never spells out what really happened. Irons is excellent as the eccentric and creepy defendant and richly deserved his Best Actor Oscar. From the novel by Dershowitz. 112m/C VHS, Beta, LV, 8mm, Closed Caption. Jeremy Irons, Glenn Close, Ron Silver, Annabella Sciorra, Uta Hagen, Fisher Stevens, Julie Hagerty, Jack Gilpin, Christine Baranski; D: Barbet Schroeder; W: Nicholas Kazan. Academy Awards '90: Best Actor (Irons); Golden Globe Awards '91: Best Actor—Drama (Irons); Los Angeles Film Critics Association Awards '90: Best Actor (Irons), Best Screenplay; National Society of Film Critics Awards '90: Best Actor (Irons); Nominations: Academy Awards '90: Best Adapted Screenplay, Best Director (Schroeder). WAR, FCT, BTV

The Revolt of Job 🎬🎬🎬 Job Lazadasa 1984 An elderly Jewish couple adopts an eight-year-old Gentile boy although it is illegal in WWII-torn Hungary and against the beliefs of the orthodox community. Moving story with fine performances. 98m/C VHS, Beta. GE HU Fereno Zenthe, Hedi Tenessy; D: Imre Gyongyossy, Barna Kabay. MGM, SWC

Revolt of the Barbarians 🎬 1964 Ancient Rome is plagued by barbarian invasion and piracy. A consul travels to Gaul to try to put an end to their misdeeds. ?m/C VHS, Beta. IT Roland Carey, Grazia Maria Spina, Mario Feliciani. SNC

Revolt of the Zombies 🎬 1936 A mad scientist learns the secret of bringing the dead to life and musters the zombies into an unique, gruesome military unit during WWI. Strange early zombie flick looks silly by today's standards. 65m/B VHS, Beta. Dorothy Stone, Dean Jagger, Roy D'Arcy, Robert Noland, George Cleveland; D: Victor Halperin; W: Howard Higgin. SNC, MLB, MRV

Revolution 🎬 1985 (R) The American Revolution is the setting for this failed epic centering on an illiterate trapper and his son who find themselves caught up in the fighting. Long and dull, which is unfortunate, because the story had some potential. The cast is barely believable in their individual roles. Where did you get that accent, Al? 125m/C VHS, Beta, LV, Closed Caption. GB Al Pacino, Donald Sutherland, Nastassia Kinski, Annie Lennox, Joan Plowright, Steven Berkoff, Dave King; D: Hugh Hudson; W: Robert Dillon. WAR

Revolution! A Red Comedy 🎬🎬🎬 1991 A group of students are lured away from their revolutionary tendencies by materialistic indulgences. This satirical comedy is in color and black and white. 84m/B VHS. Kimberly Flynn, Christopher Renstrom, Georg Osterman; D: Jeff Kahn; W: Jeff Kahn. NO

Revolver 🎬🎬 1992 (R) FBI agent Nick Sastro is paralyzed by an assassin's bullet when he tries to stop Aldo Testi, an arms and drug smuggler. But Nick decides to come out of retirement when a chance to nail Testi comes his way. 96m/C VHS, Closed Caption. Robert Urich, Dakin Matthews, Steven Williams, Assumpta Serna; D: Gary Nelson. COL

Rhapsody 🎬🎬½ 1954 Taylor plays a wealthy woman torn between a famous young violinist and an equally talented pianist in this long and overdrawn soap opera. Although Taylor gives a superb performance, it's not enough to save this sugarcoated musical romance. Includes lush European scenery and sequences of classical music

dubbed in by Claudio Arrau and Michael Rabin. Based on the adaptation of the Henry Handel Richardson novel "Maurice Guest." 115m/C VHS. Elizabeth Taylor, Vittorio Gassman, John Ericson, Louis Calhern, Michael Chekhov, Barbara Bates, Celia Lovsky; D: Charles Vidor; W: Michael Kanin, Fay Kanin. MGM

Rhapsody in August 🎬🎬½ 1991 (PG) Talky family drama has four children spending the summer with their grandmother Kane in Nagasaki. They become obsessed with the memorials and bomb sites commemorating the dropping of the atomic bomb in 1945 and their grandmother's experiences. Then Kane's Eurasian nephew (Gere) comes for a visit, inciting more family discussions. Adapted from the novel "Nabe-no-Naka" by Kiyoko Murata. Minor Kurosawa; in Japanese with English subtitles. 98m/C VHS, LV. JP Sachiko Murase, Narumi Kayashima, Hisashi Igawa, Richard Gere; D: Akira Kurosawa; W: Akira Kurosawa. ORI

Rhapsody in Blue 🎬🎬🎬 1945 Standard Hollywood biography of the great composer features whitewashed and non-existent characters to deal with the spottier aspects of Gershwin's life. Still, the music is the main attraction and it doesn't disappoint. 🎵Rhapsody in Blue; Concerto in F; The Cuban Overture; Fascinatin' Rhythm; The Man I Love; Yankee Doodle Blues; Somebody Loves Me; Swanee; Mine. 139m/B VHS, LV. Robert Alda, Joan Leslie, Alexis Smith, Charles Coburn, Julie Bishop, Albert Basserman, Morris Carnovsky, Rosemary DeCamp, Herbert Rudley, Charles Halton, Robert Shayne, Johnny Downs, Al Jolson; D: Irving Rapper; W: Howard Koch; M: George Gershwin, Max Steiner, Ira Gershwin. Nominations: Academy Awards '45: Best Sound, Scoring of a Musical. MGM, FCT

Rhinestone 🎬 1984 (PG) A country singer claims she can turn anyone, even a cabbie, into a singing sensation. Stuck with Stallone, Parton prepares her protege to sing at New York City's roughest country-western club, The Rhinestone. Only die-hard Dolly and Rocky fans need bother with this bunk. Some may enjoy watching the thick, New York accented Stallone learn how to properly pronounce dog ("dawg") in country lingo. Yee-haw. 111m/C VHS, Beta, LV, Closed Caption. Sylvester Stallone, Dolly Parton, Ron Leibman, Richard Farnsworth, Tim Thomerson; D: Bob (Benjamin) Clark; W: Sylvester Stallone, Phil Alden Robinson. Golden Raspberry Awards '84: Worst Actor (Stallone), Worst Song ("Drinkenstein"). FOX, SNC

Rhodes 🎬🎬½ Rhodes of Africa 1936 The story of Cecil Rhodes, a man who was instrumental in the Boer War in Africa and established the Rhodes Scholarships with $10 million, is told in this biography. Fine performance by Huston and Homolka. 91m/B VHS. GB Walter Huston, Oscar Homolka, Basil Sydney, Frank Cellier, Peggy Ashcroft, Renne De Vaux, Percy Parsons, Bernard Lee, Ndanisa Kumalo; D: Berthold Viertel. NOS, SNC

Rhodes 🎬🎬½ 1997 British miniseries details the life of 19th-century colonialist, British-born Cecil Rhodes (Shaw), who makes his money in the South African diamond trade and decides to place as much African territory under Britain's flag as possible. Rhodes succeeded in begetting the nation of Rhodesia (now Zimbabwe), became involved in the bloody Boer War, and established the prestigious Rhodes scholarship at Oxford University. On three cassettes. 336m/C VHS. GB Martin Shaw, Frances Barber, Tim Dutton, David Butler, Ken Stott, Raymond Coulthard, Neil Pearson; D: David Drury; W: Antony Thomas; C: Alec Curtis; M: Alan Parker. FOX

Rhythm on the Range 🎬🎬½ 1936 Crosby stars as a singing cowboy who befriends freight car stowaway Farmer while transporting his prize steer back to his ranch in California. He invites her to his domicile and she falls in love with life on the range and with the rancher himself. Filled with lots of musical numbers, including an appearance from the Sons of the Pioneers featuring Roy Rogers. Comedy from Burns and Raye, who makes her feature film debut here, is as entertaining as always. Remade by Dean Martin and Jerry Lewis in 1956 as "Pardners." ♫I'm an Old Cowhand; Empty Saddles; I Can't Escape From You; The House That Jack Built for Jill; If You Can't Sing It You'll Have to Swing It; Round-up Lullaby; Drink It Down; Memories; Hang Up My Saddle. **88m/B VHS, Closed Caption.** Bing Crosby, Frances Farmer, Bob Burns, Martha Raye, Samuel S. Hinds, Warren Hymer, Lucile Watson; **D:** Norman Taurog; **W:** John Moffitt, Sidney Salkow, Walter DeLeon, Francis Martin; **C:** Karl Struss. *USH*

Rhythm on the River ♪♪½ 1940 Famous Broadway songwriter Rathbone has lost his magic touch so he hires melody maker Crosby to ghost for him while also hiring Martin to be the wordsmith. When the two fall in love they decide to strike off on their own but can't get their music heard since everyone assumes they've been copying Rathbone. Lots of backstage jokes with Rathbone terrific as an insecure egomaniac. ♫Rhythm on the River; When the Moon Comes Over Madison Square; Ain't It a Shame About Mame?; What Would Shakespeare Have Said?; Only Forever; That's for Me; I Don't Want to Cry Anymore. **94m/B VHS, Closed Caption.** Bing Crosby, Mary Martin, Basil Rathbone, Oscar Levant, Oscar Shaw, Charley Grapewin, William Frawley, Charles Lane; **D:** Victor Schertzinger; **W:** Dwight Taylor; **M:** Victor Young. Nominations: Academy Awards '40: Best Song ("Only Forever"). *USH*

Rhythm Parade ♪♪ 1943 A woman takes off for Hawaii, leaving her infant in the care of an L.A. nightclub singer. A jealous rival of the singer takes the opportunity to cause problems. The thin plot serves as a vehicle for lots of singing. ♫Tootin' My Own Horn; Petticoat Army; Mimi From Tahiti; You're Drafted; Wait Till the Sun Shines Nellie; Sweet Sue; 'Neath the Yellow Moon In Old Tahiti. **68m/B VHS.** Nils T. Granlund, Gale Storm, Robert Lowery, Margaret Dumont, Chick Chandler, Cliff Nazarro, Jan Wiley, Candy Candido, Yvonne De Carlo; **D:** Howard Bretherton. *NOS, MLB*

Rhythm Thief ♪♪ 1994 No-budget independent film finds alienated New York hustler Simon (Andrews) eking out a living selling tapes of local underground bands he has illegally recorded. He wants to be left alone but circumstances won't allow it. He's got one of the enraged bands after him, he's pestered by local "admirers," and his eccentric former girlfriend Marty (Daniels) suddenly turns up—severely shaking Simon's emotionally barren existence. Quirky character study gets lots of impact from tiny bucks. **88m/B VHS.** Jason Andrews, Eddie Daniels, Kimberly Flynn, Kevin Corrigan, Sean Haggerty, Mark Alfred, Paul Rodriguez, Cynthia Sley; **D:** Matthew Harrison; **W:** Matthew Harrison, Christopher Grimm; **C:** Howard Krupa; **M:** Danny Brenner. Sundance Film Festival '95: Special Jury Prize; Nominations: Independent Spirit Awards '96: Debut Performance (Andrews). *NYR*

Ricco ♪♪ *Summertime Killer* 1974 (PG) A young man swears vengeance against the mobsters who killed his father. He kidnaps the daughter of a mafia kingpin and the battle begins. **90m/C VHS, Beta.** *FR IT SP* Chris Mitchum, Karl Malden, Olivia Hussey, Raf Vallone, Claudine Auger, Gerard Tichy; **D:** Antonio Isasi. *NO*

Rich and Famous ♪♪ 1981 (R) The story of the 25-year friendship of two women, through college, marriage, and success. George Cukor's last film. **117m/C VHS, Beta, LV.** Jacqueline Bisset, Candice Bergen, David Selby, Hart Bochner, Meg Ryan, Steven Hill, Michael Brandon, Matt Lattanzi; **D:** George Cukor; **W:** Gerald Ayres; **M:** Georges Delerue. Writers Guild of America '81: Best Adapted Screenplay. *MGM*

Rich and Strange ♪♪½ *East of Shanghai* 1932 Early Hitchcock movie is not in the same class as his later thrillers. A couple inherits a fortune and journeys around the world. Eventually the pair gets shipwrecked. **92m/B VHS, LV.** *GB* Henry Kendall, Joan Barry, Betty Amann, Percy Marmont, Elsie Randolph; **D:** Alfred Hitchcock; **W:** Alfred Hitchcock, Alma Reville. *REP, SNC, MLB*

Rich Girl ♪♪ 1991 (R) A winsome, wealthy wench hideo her milliono by going to work in a rock 'n' roll bar and falls in love with the local Bruce Springsteen wannabe. Despite the thick coating of music, sex, drugs, and profanity, this consists of cliches that were old before talkies. Too earnestly acted to be campy fun. Poor movie.**CW:** Language, drug content, and sensuality. **96m/C VHS, LV, Closed Caption.** Jill Schoelen, Don Michael Paul, Ron Karabatsos, Sean Kanan, Willie Dixon, Paul Gleason; **D:** Joel Bender. *COL*

Rich Hall's Vanishing America 1986 Funnyman Hall travels across the country looking for the mail-order company that promised to give him a genuine Wilt Chamberlain basketball hoop. **50m/C VHS, Beta.** Rich Hall, M. Emmet Walsh, Peter Isacksen, Harry Anderson, Wilt Chamberlain; **D:** Steve Rash. *PAR*

Rich in Love ♪♪½ 1993 (PG-13) Lighthearted look at the changes in a Southern family after matriarch Helen Odom leaves to pursue her own life, shattering the peaceful existence of those around her. Seen through the eyes of 17-year-old daughter Lucille who assumes the role of "mother" for her sister and father while trying to come to terms with her own confused feelings. Nice performances by newcomer Erbe and Finney can't overcome a mediocre script. Based on the novel by Josephine Humphreys.**CW:** Thematic elements. **105m/C VHS, LV, Letterbox, Closed Caption.** Albert Finney, Jill Clayburgh, Kathryn Erbe, Kyle MacLachlan, Piper Laurie, Ethan Hawke, Suzy Amis, Alfre Woodard; **D:** Bruce Beresford; **W:** Alfred Uhry; **M:** Georges Delerue. *MGM, BTV, FCT*

Rich Kids ♪♪½ 1979 (PG) A young girl trying to cope with the divorce of her parents is aided by a boyfriend whose parents have already split. **97m/C VHS, Beta.** John Lithgow, Kathryn Walker, Trini Alvarado, Paul Dooley, David Selby, Jill Eikenberry, Olympia Dukakis; **D:** Robert M. Young; **C:** Ralf Bode. *MGM*

Rich Man, Poor Man ♪♪♪ 1976 Classic television miniseries covers 20, sometimes bitter, years in the lives of the two Jordache brothers. It's 1945 in quiet Port Phillip, New York with embittered German baker Axel (Asner), his unfulfilled wife Mary (McGuire), and sons Tom (Nolte) and Rudy (Strauss). Tom is wild and irresponsible, Rudy is ambitious and college-bound, and Julie Prescott (Blakely), Rudy's girl, overshadows both their lives. Based on the novel by Irwin Shaw. The first series contained 12 episodes. A second series, of 21 episodes, primarily followed the tribulations of the next generation, although Strauss returned as Rudy. **720m/C VHS.** Peter Strauss, Nick Nolte, Susan Blakely, Ed Asner, Dorothy McGuire, Bill Bixby, Robert Reed, Ray Milland, Kim Darby, Talia Shire, Lawrence Pressman, Kay Lenz; **M:** Alex North. *CMB*

The Rich Man's Wife ♪½ 1996 (R) Modern noir strands unhappy wife Josie (Berry) on Martha's Vineyard without her loathsome spouse (McDonald), where she makes the mistake of confiding her marital woes to sympathetic, yet obviously deranged stranger Cole (Greene). She tells Cole sometimes she wishes her husband was dead. Poof! Before you can say "foreshadowing," hubby's murdered and she's the prime suspect. Increasingly nutso Cole stalks our heroine, seemingly innocent, but possibly not as blameless as it appears. Failed mystery/thriller delivers little of either and the attempt at a "Strangers on a Train" premise and a "Usual Suspects" type ending fail miserably.**CW:** Strong violence and language. **95m/C VHS, LV, Closed Caption.** Halle Berry, Christopher McDonald, Clive Owen, Peter Greene, Charles Hallahan, Frankie Faison, Clea Lewis; **D:** Amy Holden Jones; **W:** Amy Holden Jones; **C:** Haskell Wexler; **M:** John Frizzell. *TOU*

Rich, Young and Pretty ♪♪½ 1951 Light-hearted, innocuous musical starring Powell as a Texas gal visiting Paris with her rancher father (Corey). Powell finds romance with Damone (in his screen debut) and a secret—the mother

she has never known (Darrieux) Lamas (in his American screen debut) plays Darrieux's new heartthrob. ♫Dark is the Night; L'Amour Toujours, Tonight For Sure; Wonder Why; I Can See You; Paris; We Never Talk Much; How Do You Like Your Eggs in the Morning?; There's Danger in Your Eyes, Cherie; The Old Piano Roll Blues. **95m/C VHS.** Jane Powell, Danielle Darrieux, Wendell Corey, Vic Damone, Fernando Lamas, Marcel Dalio, Una Merkel, Richard Anderson, Jean Murat, Hans Conried; **D:** Norman Taurog; **W:** Sidney Sheldon, Dorothy Cooper; **M:** Sammy Cahn, Nicholas Brodszky. Nominations: Academy Awards '51: Best Song ("Wonder Why"). *MGM, FCT*

Richard III ♪♪♪½ 1955 This landmark film version of the Shakespearean play features an acclaimed performance by Laurence Olivier, who also directs. The plot follows the life of the mentally and physically twisted Richard of Gloucester and his schemes for the throne of England. **138m/C VHS, Beta, LV, Letterbox.** *GB* Laurence Olivier, Cedric Hardwicke, Ralph Richardson, John Gielgud, Stanley Baker, Michael Gough, Claire Bloom; **D:** Laurence Olivier. British Academy Awards '55: Best Actor (Olivier), Best Director (Olivier), Best Film; Golden Globe Awards '57: Best Foreign Film; Nominations: Academy Awards '56: Best Actor (Olivier). *COL, HMV, FUS*

Richard III ♪♪♪½ 1995 (R) The Brits once again bring the Bard's most notorious monarch to the screen, this time in a new setting. McKellen stars in the title role of the deformed and ruthless English king, now in an imagined 1930s London of swanky Art Deco, Black Shirt thugs and modern media. Purists may resent major dialogue cuts, but famous speeches (such as the "winter of our discontent" opener) arc amusingly staged in this modern take. Gorgeously polished visuals are perfect foil for the slimy, evil goings-on. Based on both Shakespeare's play and Richard Eyre's stage adaptation (in which McKellen also starred).**CW:** Violence and sexuality. **105m/C VHS, LV, Closed Caption.** *GB* Ian McKellen, Annette Bening, Jim Broadbent, Robert Downey Jr., Nigel Hawthorne, Kristin Scott Thomas, Maggie Smith, John Wood; **D:** Richard Loncraine; **W:** Ian McKellen, Richard Loncraine; **C:** Peter Biziou; **M:** Trevor Jones. Nominations: Academy Awards '95: Best Art Direction/Set Decoration, Best Costume Design; British Academy Awards '96: Best Actor (McKellen), Best Adapted Screenplay; Golden Globe Awards '96: Best Actor—Drama (McKellen). *MGM*

Richard Petty Story ♪ 1972 (G) The biography of race car driver Petty, played by himself, and his various achievements on the track. **83m/C VHS, Beta.** Richard Petty, Darren McGavin, Kathie Browne, Lynn Marta, Noah Beery Jr., L.Q. Jones. *GEM*

Richard's Things ♪♪ 1980 (R) A man's wife and his girlfriend find love and comfort in each other after his death. Screenplay by Frederic Raphael, from his novel. Very slow and dreary, with a weak performance from Ullman. **104m/C VHS, Beta.** *GB* Liv Ullmann, Amanda Redman; **D:** Anthony Harvey; **W:** Frederic Raphael; **C:** Frederick A. (Freddie) Young; **M:** Georges Delerue.

Richie Rich ♪♪½ 1994 (PG) Yet another adaptation from the comics. Richie (Culkin), the world's richest boy, takes over the family business when his madcap parents Richard (Herrmann) and Regina (Ebersole) disappear thanks to the devious Laurence Van Dough (Larroquette). But there's kindly valet Cadbury (Hyde) and eccentric live-in inventor Keenbean (McShane) to help Richie save the day. Some silliness but Culkin has clearly outgrown this type of kid role. Biltmore, the 8,000 acre Vanderbilt estate in Asheville, North Carolina, serves as the Rich family home. **94m/C VHS, LV, Closed Caption.** Macaulay Culkin, John Larroquette, Edward Herrmann, Christine Ebersole, Jonathan Hyde, Micheal McShane, Stephi Lineburg; **Cameos:** Reggie Jackson, Claudia Schiffer; **D:** Donald Petrie; **W:** Tom S. Parker, Jim Jennewein; **C:** Don Burgess; **M:** Alan Silvestri. Nominations: Golden Raspberry Awards '94: Worst Actor (Culkin). *WAR*

Ricky 1 🎬½ **1988** Mumbling pugilist spoof. Da Mob wants to make Ricky da fall guy, but uh, he's not as dumb as he looks. **90m/C VHS.** Michael Michaud, Maggie Hughes, James Herbert, Lane Montano; **D:** Bill Naud; **M:** Joel Goldsmith. *TPV, HHE*

Ricochet 🎬🎬🎬 **1991 (R)** Rookie cop Washington causes a sensation when he singlehandedly captures notorious psychopath Lithgow. But this particular criminal is a twisted genius, and from his prison cell he comes up with a plan to destroy the young cop. Teaming up with old friend Ice-T, the rookie tries to outwit his evil arch-nemesis. Genuinely scary, tense and violent thriller. **CW:** Language, strong violence and drug content, and sensuality. **104m/C VHS, LV, 8mm, Closed Caption.** Denzel Washington, John Lithgow, Ice-T, Jesse Ventura, Kevin Pollak, Lindsay Wagner, Mary Ellen Trainor, Josh Evans, Victoria Dillard, John Amos, John Cothran Jr.; **D:** Russell Mulcahy; **W:** Steven E. de Souza; **M:** Alan Silvestri. *HBO, CCB*

Riddance 🎬🎬🎬 **1973** The second of Meszaros' trilogy, about a Hungarian couple, an upper-class male student, and a factory-working young woman, and their difficulties in meshing their lives together. In Hungarian with English subtitles. **84m/C VHS, Beta.** *HU D:* Marta Meszaros. *KIV*

The Riddle of the Sands 🎬🎬½ **1979** Two English yachtsmen in 1903 inadvertently stumble upon a German plot to invade England by sea. British film based on the Erskine Childers spy novel. **99m/C VHS, Beta.** *GB* Michael York, Jenny Agutter, Simon MacCorkindale, Alan Badel; **D:** Tony Maylam; **M:** Howard Blake. *MOV, BMV*

Ride 🎬🎬 **1998 (R)** This sometimes-amusing but mostly-rude road comedy seems to be merely an excuse for getting MTV veejays and rap stars together without actually showing any videos. Freddy B (Campbell) is a superstar looking for street cred, so his director Bleau (Brown) sends Leta (DeSousa) to Harlem to bring a group of young street talents to Miami for a video shoot. There are too many story lines in the busload of passengers to develop fully, so they are skimmed over and defused with a mixture of generic road movie brawls and narrow escapes combined with sexual and scatalogical humor. Yoba does a good job as Poppa, who's trying to watch over reckless little brother Geronimo (Starr) while keeping the rest of the crew in line. **CW:** Pervasive strong language including sex related dialogue. **83m/C VHS.** Malik Yoba, Melissa De Sousa, Fredro Starr, John Witherspoon, Cedric the Entertainer, Sticky Fingaz, Kellie Williams, Idalis de Leon, Julia Garrison, Guy Torrey, Reuben Asher, The Lady of Rage, Dartanyan Edmonds, Downtown Julie Brown; **Cameos:** Snoop Doggy Dogg; **D:** Millicent Shelton; **W:** Millicent Shelton; **C:** Frank Byers; **M:** Dunn Pearson Jr. *NYR*

Ride a Wild Pony 🎬🎬🎬 **1975 (G)** A poor Australian farmer's son is allowed to pick a horse of his own from a neighboring rancher's herd. After he trains and grows to love the pony, the rancher's daughter, a handicapped rich girl, decides to claim it for herself. Enjoyable Disney story is based on the tale "Sporting Proposition," by James Aldridge. **86m/C VHS, Beta.** *AU* John Meillon, Michael Craig, Robert Bettles, Eva Griffith, Graham Rouse; **D:** Don Chaffey; **C:** Jack Cardiff; **M:** John Addison. *DIS*

Ride 'Em Cowboy 🎬🎬½ **1942** Two peanut and hotdog vendors travel west to try their hand as cowpokes. Usual Abbott and Costello fare with a twist—there are lots of great musical numbers. ♫A Tisket, A Tasket; I'll Remember April; Wake Up Jacob; Beside the Rio Tonto; Rock 'n' Reelin'; Give Me My Saddle; Cow Boogie. **86m/B VHS.** Bud Abbott, Lou Costello, Anne Gwynne, Samuel S. Hinds, Dick Foran, Richard Lane, Johnny Mack Brown, Ella Fitzgerald, Douglass Dumbrille; **D:** Arthur Lubin. *USH*

Ride 'Em Cowgirl 🎬🎬 **1941** Singing cowgirl, Page, enters a horse race to expose the crook who cheated her father. **51m/B VHS.** Dorothy Page, Vince Barnett, Milton Frome; **D:** Samuel Diege. *VCN*

Ride Him, Cowboy 🎬🎬🎬 **1932** Entertaining oater has Wayne saving horse Duke from being sentenced to death. This was the first of six series films Wayne made for Warner's, all of which costarred his white wonder horse, Duke. Remake of the 1926 Ken Maynard silent "The Unknown Cavalier." Based on the story by Kenneth Perkins. **55m/B VHS, Closed Caption.** John Wayne, Ruth Hall, Henry B. Walthall, Harry Gribbon, Otis Harlan, Charles Sellon; **D:** Fred Allen; **W:** Scott Mason. *MGM, GPV*

Ride in a Pink Car 🎬 **1974 (R)** When a Vietnam vet returns home, he discovers that his welcoming committee is really a lynch mob. **83m/C VHS, Beta.** Glenn Corbett, Morgan Woodward, Ivy Jones; **D:** Robert Emery.

Ride in the Whirlwind 🎬🎬 **1967** Three cowboys are mistaken for members of a gang by a posse. Screenplay for the offbeat western by Nicholson. **83m/C Beta, LV.** Jack Nicholson, Cameron Mitchell, Millie Perkins, Katherine Squire, Harry Dean Stanton; **D:** Monte Hellman; **W:** Jack Nicholson. *HHT, DVT, WFV*

Ride Lonesome 🎬🎬½ **1959** The heroic Scott is a bounty hunter looking for a killer (Best). It's not just the money, Scott hopes Best will lead him to the man who murdered Scott's wife. Along the trail he meets a pretty widow and two outlaws who hope if they capture Best, they'll get a pardon. A well-done example of a "B" western with good performances; Coburn's film debut. **73m/C VHS.** Randolph Scott, James Best, Karen Steele, Pernell Roberts, Lee Van Cleef, James Coburn; **D:** Budd Boetticher; **W:** Burt Kennedy. *MOV*

Ride, Ranger, Ride 🎬½ **1936** Texas Ranger Autry is out to stop a group of Comanches from raiding a wagon train. **56m/B VHS, Beta.** Gene Autry, Smiley Burnette, Kay Hughes, Max Terhune, Monte Blue, Chief Thundercloud; **D:** Joseph Kane. *NOS, VYY, DVT*

Ride the High Country 🎬🎬🎬🎬 *Guns in the Afternoon* **1962** The cult classic western about two old friends who have had careers on both sides of the law. One, Joel McCrea, is entrusted with a shipment of gold, and the other, Randolph Scott, rides along with him to steal the precious cargo. Although barely promoted by MGM, the film became a critics' favorite. Grimacing and long in the tooth, McCrea and Scott enact a fitting tribute and farewell to the myth of the grand ol' West. The laserdisc edition carries the film in widescreen format along with the original movie trailer. **93m/C VHS, Beta, LV, Letterbox.** Randolph Scott, Joel McCrea, Mariette Hartley, Edgar Buchanan, R.G. Armstrong, Ronald Starr, John Anderson, James Drury, L.Q. Jones, Warren Oates; **D:** Sam Peckinpah; **C:** Lucien Ballard; **M:** George Bassman. National Film Registry '92. *MGM*

Ride the Man Down 🎬½ **1953** Story of a murderous land war between neighboring landowners tells the same old story: Greed knows no boundaries. **90m/C VHS.** Brian Donlevy, Chill Wills, Jack LaRue, Rod Cameron, Ella Raines, Barbara Britton; **D:** Joseph Kane. *REP*

Ride the Wild Surf 🎬🎬½ **1964** It's fun in the sun when surfers Fabian, Hunter, and Brown head to Hawaii in search of the ultimate waves. Throw in a little romance and a cool title song by Jan and Dean and you've got your better than average beach movie. The surfing footage is excellent. Cowabunga! **101m/C VHS, Closed Caption.** Fabian, Tab Hunter, Barbara Eden, Peter Brown, Susan Hart, Shelley Fabares, Jim Mitchum; **D:** Don Taylor. *COL*

Ride the Wind 🎬🎬 **1966** "Bonanza" gang goes to the aid of the Pony Express. **120m/C VHS, Beta.** Michael Landon, Lorne Greene, Dan Blocker. *REP*

Ride to Glory 🎬🎬 *The Deserter; La Spina Dorsale del Diavolo* **1971** In 1886, a cavalry officer deserts his troops to seek revenge on the Apaches that brutally killed his family. Hearing this, a general offers to pardon him if he will lead a dangerous group of men on a mission against the Apaches. Fast-paced and very bloody. **90m/C VHS.**

Bekim Fehmiu, Richard Crenna, Chuck Connors, Ricardo Montalban, Ian Bannen, Slim Pickens, Woody Strode, Patrick Wayne, John Huston; **D:** Burt Kennedy. *SIM, PAR, HHE*

Rider from Tucson 🎬🎬 **1950** Two rodeo riders head out to Colorado for a friend's wedding. They find out the bride has been kidnapped by a bunch of claim jumpers after control of a gold mine. **60m/B VHS, Beta.** Tim Holt, Richard Martin, Elaine Riley, Douglas Fowley, Veda Ann Borg; **D:** Lesley Selander. *NO*

Rider of the Law 🎬 **1935** A government agent poses as a greenhorn easterner to nab a gang of outlaws. **56m/B VHS, Beta.** Bob Steele. *NO*

Rider on the Rain 🎬🎬🎬 *Lepassager de la Pluie* **1970** A young housewife is viciously raped by an escaped sex maniac. She kills him and disposes of his body, not knowing that he is being relentlessly pursued by mysterious American Bronson. Suspenseful, French-made thriller featuring one of Bronson's best performances. **115m/C VHS, Beta.** *FR* Marlene Jobert, Charles Bronson, Jill Ireland; **D:** Rene Clement. Golden Globe Awards '71: Best Foreign Film. *FCT*

Riders of Death Valley 🎬🎬½ **1941** Splendid western action serial in 15 episodes. Foran, Jones, and Carillo head a passel o'men watching for thieves and claim jumpers in a mining area. **320m/B VHS, Beta.** Dick Foran, Buck Jones, Leo Carrillo, Lon Chaney Jr.; **D:** Ford Beebe, Ray Taylor. *NOS, VCN, DVT*

Riders of Destiny 🎬🎬½ **1933** Wayne plays a government agent sent to find out who is stealing water from the local farmers. Very early Wayne has the Duke looking awfully young as an agent securing water rights for ranchers. **59m/B VHS.** John Wayne, George "Gabby" Hayes, Cecilia Parker, Forrest Taylor, Al "Fuzzy" St. John; **D:** Robert North Bradbury. *COL, NOS, REP*

Riders of Pasco Basin 🎬½ **1940** Outlaws are tricking ranchers out of their money by falsely promising to build a dam. So Brown and his cohorts come to set things right. **56m/B VHS.** Johnny Mack Brown, Fuzzy Knight, Bob Baker, Frances Robinson, Arthur Loft, Frank LaRue, Lafe McKee, Kermit Maynard; **D:** Ray Taylor; **W:** Ford Beebe. *GPV*

Riders of the Desert 🎬🎬½ **1932** Steele tracks down the loot from a stagecoach robbery. **57m/B VHS, Beta.** Bob Steele. *VYY, VCN*

Riders of the Purple Sage 🎬🎬½ **1925** When Texas Ranger Jim Lassiter's (Mix) sister and niece are kidnapped by the evil Walters (Oland), he devotes his life to finding them. While working on a ranch (and falling in love with the beautiful ranch owner), he learns Walters has changed his name and is passing himself off as a judge. Promptly shooting the skunk dead, Lassiter and his sweetie must run from a posse. Based on the Zane Grey novel. **63m/B VHS.** Tom Mix, Warner Oland, Mabel Ballin, Beatrice Burnham, Arthur Morrison, Fred Kohler Sr.; **D:** Lynn F. Reynolds; **W:** Edfrid Bingham. *GPV*

Riders of the Purple Sage 🎬🎬½ **1996** Legendary gunman (are there any other kind?) Lassiter (Harris) helps save Bern (Thomas) from a beating in a town run by a conservative religious sect, led by Deacon Tull (Weisser). Seems Bern's befriended ranch owner (and nonmember) Jane (Madigan) and the Deacon is not only after Bern but her considerable land and cattle holdings. Lassiter rides to the rescue. Properly brooding TV adaptation of the 1912 Zane Grey novel (the Grey novel specifies that the sect are Mormons but this caused considerable fuss). Filmed in Utah. **90m/C VHS.** Ed Harris, Amy Madigan, Henry Thomas, Norbert Weisser, Robin Tunney, G.D. Spradlin; **D:** Charles Haid; **W:** Gill Dennis; **C:** William Wages; **M:** Arthur Kempel. *TTC*

Riders of the Range 🎬🎬 **1924** Sheep invade the cattle range and a range war flares up between those who would herd and the ranchers. Silent flick of interest because of the stars. **62m/B VHS, Beta.** Edmund Cobb, Dolly Dale; **D:** Otis Thayer. *GPV*

Riders of the Range 🎬 **1949** Cowboy rides into town just in time to save a girl's brother from gamblers. **60m/B VHS, Beta.** Tim Holt, Richard Martin. *NO*

Riders of the Range/Storm Over Wyoming 🎬½ **1950** A double feature package of Tim Holt Westerns. **120m/B VHS, Beta.** Tim Holt, Richard Martin, Jacqueline Wells. *TTC*

Riders of the Rockies 🎬🎬½ **1937** An honest cowboy turns rustler in order to trap a border gang. One of Ritter's very best cowboy outings; good fun, and a very long fistfight with King. **60m/B VHS, Beta.** Tex Ritter, Yakima Canutt, Louise Stanley, Charles "Blackie" King, Snub Pollard; **D:** Robert North Bradbury. *NOS, VCI, VCN*

Riders of the Storm 🎬½ *The American Way* **1988 (R)** A motley crew of Vietnam vets runs a covert television broadcasting station from an in-flight B-29, jamming America's legitimate airwaves. Interesting premise with boring result. **92m/C VHS, Beta, LV.** Dennis Hopper, Michael J. Pollard, Eugene Lipinski, James Aubrey, Nigel Pegram; **D:** Maurice Phillips; **W:** Scott Roberts. *NLC*

Riders of the Timberline 🎬🎬 **1941** Unusual for a Hopalong Cassidy programmer in that it puts him in timber country. Yes, he's a lumberjack and he's okay, as he fights against land-grabbing crooks all day. **59m/B VHS.** William Boyd, Brad King, Andy Clyde, J. Farrell MacDonald, Elaine Stewart, Anna Q. Nilsson, Hal Taliaferro, Tom Tyler, Victor Jory; **D:** Lesley Selander. *NOS*

Riders of the West 🎬 **1942** An honest cowpoke fights off a band of rustlers. **58m/B VHS.** Buck Jones, Tim McCoy, Raymond Hatton, Sarah Padden, Harry Woods; **D:** Howard Bretherton. *NOS, DVT*

Riders of the Whistling Pines 🎬🎬 **1949** Our ever-so-bland hero solves a murder perpetrated by a passel of lumber thieves and saves the day for yet another damsel in distress. **70m/B VHS, Beta.** Gene Autry, Patricia White, Jimmy Lloyd; **D:** John English. *NOS, DVT*

Riders of the Whistling Skull 🎬🎬½ *The Golden Trail* **1937** The Three Mesquiteers are guiding an expedition to an ancient Indian city. A gang of rustlers looting the city are holding an archeology professor hostage, and the Mesquiteers must rescue him. Swell cast; nifty, creepy plot; solid-as-usual leads. **58m/B VHS, Beta.** Bob Livingston, Ray Corrigan, Max Terhune, Yakima Canutt, Roland Winters; **D:** Mack V. Wright. *SNC, NOS, VCN*

Riders to the Sea 🎬½ **1988** A mother envisions the death of her last son in the same manner her other sons died—by drowning. Based on the play by Irish dramatist John Millington Synge. **90m/C VHS, Beta.** Geraldine Page, Amanda Plummer, Sachi Parker, Barry McGovern; **D:** Ronan O'Leary. *NO*

Ridicule 🎬🎬🎬½ **1996 (R)** Fish-out-of-water drama has minor country aristocrat Pondeludon (Berling) enter the depraved world of the 18th century court at Versailles. There, he hopes, the king will aid him in his quest to drain the disease-ridden swamps at his estate. The naive provincial finds he must master the weapons of choice for success within the court—wit, deadly ridicule, and impeccable lineage. After initial missteps due to lack of finesse, he quickly adapts, and finds some influential allies: the beautiful Madame de Blayac (Ardant) and sympathetic Marquis de Bellegarde (Rochefort). When the Marquis' spirited and attractive daughter, Mathilde (Godreche), shows up, the smitten Pondeludon must stop her loveless marriage of convenience. Perfectly cast, director Leconte's highly lauded period piece has all the emotional and technical elements of an engaging film. In French with subtitles. **CW:** Graphic nudity, some sexuality and brief violence. **102m/C VHS, LV, Closed Caption. FR** Charles Berling, Jean Rochefort, Fanny Ardant, Bernard Giraudeau, Judith Godreche, Bernard Dheran, Carlo Brandt, Jacques Mathou; **D:** Patrice Leconte; **W:** Remi Waterhouse, Michel Fessler, Eric Vicaut; **C:** Thierry Arbogast; **M:** Antoine Duhamel. British

Academy Awards '96: Best Foreign Film; Cesar Awards '97: Best Director (Leconte), Best Film; Broadcast Film Critics Association Awards '96: Best Foreign Film; Nominations: Academy Awards '96: Best Foreign Film; Cesar Awards '97: Best Actor (Berling); Golden Globe Awards '97: Best Foreign Film. *TOU*

Ridin' Down the Canyon 🎬🎬½ **1942** Standard but entertaining entry in Rogers' popular series. It's Rogers to the rescue when a gang of outlaws are rustling cattle and selling to the government for wartime profits. Roy, along with the Sons of the Pioneers, also manages to croon a few tunes. Based on a story by Robert Williams and Norman Houston. **54m/B VHS.** Roy Rogers, George "Gabby" Hayes, Linda Hayes, Addison Richards, Adrian Booth, James Seay; **D:** Joseph Kane; **W:** Albert De Mond. *MOV*

Ridin' on a Rainbow 🎬½ **1941** Has-been performer on a steamboat decides to rob a bank in the hopes of starting a new life for himself and his daughter. The money he robs had just been deposited by some cattlemen, one of whom joins the steamboat's crew, wins the daughter's heart, and gets to the father. Slow and dull, with too much singing, and too little plot and scenery. **79m/B VHS, Beta.** Gene Autry, Smiley Burnette, Mary Lee; **D:** Lew (Louis Friedlander) Landers. Nominations: Academy Awards '41: Best Song ("Be Honest With Me"). *REP, CCB, VCN*

Ridin' the California Trail 🎬½ **1947** The Cisco Kid is wanted dead or alive in several states. **40m/B VHS, Beta.** Gilbert Roland. *DVT*

Ridin' the Lone Trail woof! **1937** Steele attempts to stop some criminals who've been harassing a stagecoach line. Republic was better than this weak western would lead us to believe. Steele, who went on to better things, is a bright spot in a film that sounds and looks bad. Keep your ears open for the sound of airplanes—apparently Newfield forgot they hadn't been invented in the time of the wild west. From a story by E.B. Mann. **56m/B VHS.** Bob Steele, Claire Rochelle, Charles "Blackie" King, Ernie Adams, Lew Meehan, Julian Rivero; **D:** Sam Newfield; **W:** Charles Francis Royal. *NOS, DVT*

Ridin' the Trail 🎬 **1940** Scott stars as a cowboy out to rid the countryside of bad guys in this western. **60m/B VHS, Beta.** Fred Scott, Iris Lancaster, Harry Harvey, Jack Ingram, John Ward; **D:** Raymond K. Johnson. *NOS, DVT*

Ridin' Thru 🎬🎬 **1935** Another Tom Tyler western, in which the hero does battle with unscrupulous villains. **60m/B VHS, Beta.** Tom Tyler, Ruth Hiatt, Lafe McKee, Philo McCullough, Lew Meehan, Bud Osborne; **D:** Harry S. Webb. *NOS, DVT, HEG*

The Riding Avenger 🎬½ **1936** To gain the love of a beautiful lady, a cowboy vows never to fight again, but is forced to break his promise when the town is terrorized. Aw, shucks. **56m/B VHS, Beta.** Hoot Gibson, Ruth Mix, Buzz Barton; **D:** Harry Fraser. *VCN*

Riding High 🎬🎬½ **1950** Capra remade his 1934 film "Broadway Bill" as this light-hearted musical. Horse trainer Crosby falls for the wealthy Gray who demands he choose between her and his horse. Bing chooses the horse who proves his loyalty by winning the big race and making Crosby a rich man. 🎵Someplace on Anywhere Road; Sunshine Cake; We've Got a Sure Thing; The Horse Told Me; The Whiffenpoof Song; De Camptown Races. **112m/B VHS, Beta, Closed Caption.** Bing Crosby, Coleen Gray, Charles Bickford, William Demarest, Frances Gifford, Raymond Walburn, James Gleason, Ward Bond, Percy Kilbride, Harry Davenport, Margaret Hamilton, Douglass Dumbrille, Gene Lockhart, Charles Lane, Frankie Darro, Paul Harvey, Marjorie Lord, Dub Taylor, Max Baer Sr., Oliver Hardy; **D:** Frank Capra; **W:** Robert Riskin, Melville Shavelson, Jack Rose; **C:** George Barnes. *TTC*

Riding High 🎬 **1978** It's a battle for supremacy between the kings of the motorcycle stunt world. Made for television movie's soundtrack includes songs from The Police, Dire Straits, Jerry Lee Lewis, and more. **92m/C VHS, Beta.** Murray

Salem, Marella Oppenheim, Eddie Kidd, Irene Handl; **D:** Ross Cramer. *ART*

Riding On 🎬🎬 **1937** Hayseed falls for the daughter of his father's arch rival. While his father battles it out over cattle, he pines for his enemy's daughter. Lots of action which is typical fare in mediocre western production. **59m/B VHS.** Tom Tyler, Germaine Greer, Rex Lease, John Elliott, Earl Dwire; **D:** Harry S. Webb. *NOS, DVT*

Riding on Air 🎬🎬 **1937** Small-town newspaper editor Brown discovers that his bumbling methods get him the right results. Smugglers and crazy inventions in a ho-hum Brown entry. **58m/B VHS, Beta.** Joe E. Brown; **D:** Edward Sedgwick. *NOS, BAR, FCT*

Riding Speed 🎬 **1935** Our hero breaks up a gang of smugglers along the Mexican border. **50m/B VHS, Beta, LV.** Buffalo Bill Jr. *NO*

Riding the Sunset Trail 🎬🎬🎬 **1941** Top-notch tale of Keene trying to stop a con from cashing in on his dead half-brother's fortune. Solid production values and an enthusiastic performance by Keene make this one of his best films after a string of flops. **56m/B VHS.** Tom George Duryea Keene, Betty Miles, Frank Yaconelli, Sugar Dawn, Slim Andrews, Kenne Duncan; **D:** Robert Emmett Tansey; **W:** Robert Emmett, Frances Kavanaugh. *MOV*

The Riding Tornado 🎬🎬½ **1932** Bronc rider McCoy takes a job on Grey's ranch, promptly falling for her. Ranch foreman Oakman, who's really the leader of a gang of rustlers, kidnaps Grey and McCoy goes after them. **63m/B VHS.** Tim McCoy, Shirley Grey, Wheeler Oakman, Wallace MacDonald, Russell Simpson, Montagu Love, Lafe McKee, Bud Osborne; **D:** David Ross Lederman. *GPV*

Riding with Death **1976** A man who can become invisible, thanks to a military experiment, uses his power to uncover a dastardly plot by a mad scientist. So-so TV pilot. **97m/C VHS, Beta.** Ben Murphy, Andrew Prine, Katherine Crawford, Richard Dysart; **D:** Alan J. Levi. *USH*

Riel 🎬🎬 **1979** The story of Louis Riel, a half-French, half-Indian visionary who challenged the Canadian army in his fight for equality and self-rule. **150m/C VHS, Beta.** Raymond Cloutier, Arthur Hill, William Shatner, Christopher Plummer, Leslie Nielsen; **D:** George Bloomfield.

Riff Raff 🎬🎬 *Riffraff* **1935** Melodramatic story about the relationship of two waterfront workers in the tuna fishing business. Confusing script saddled with too many characters, but there is some good sharp dialogue between the leads. Also features the scenic California waterfront. **80m/B VHS, Closed Caption.** Jean Harlow, Spencer Tracy, Joseph Calleia, Una Merkel, Mickey Rooney, Victor Kilian, J. Farrell MacDonald, Roger Imhof; **D:** J. Walter Ruben. *MGM*

Riff-Raff 🎬🎬½ **1947** Various dramatic and comic complications arise when a dying man gives Panama City con man O'Brien a map to oil deposits. Interesting and quick-moving melodrama. **80m/B VHS, Beta.** Pat O'Brien, Walter Slezak, Anne Jeffreys, Jason Robards Sr., Percy Kilbride, Jerome Cowan; **D:** Ted Tetzlaff. *TTC*

Riff Raff 🎬🎬🎬 **1992** Unsparing black comedy about the British working-class by director Loach. Ex-con Stevie comes to London from Scotland to look for work and escape his thieving past. He finds a nonunion job on a construction site, takes up squatter's rights in an abandoned apartment, and finds a girlfriend in equally struggling singer Susie, who turns out to be a junkie. Loach's characters deal with their unenviable lot in life through rough humor and honest sentiment. Regional accents are so thick that the film is subtitled. **96m/C VHS, LV. GB** Robert Carlyle, Emer McCourt, Jimmy Coleman, George Moss, Ricky Tomlinson, David Finch, Bill Jesse; **D:** Ken Loach; **W:** Bill Jesse; **M:** Stewart Copeland. *NLC, COL, IME*

Rififi 🎬🎬🎬½ *Du Rififi Chez les Hommes* **1954** Perhaps the greatest of all "heist" movies. Four jewel thieves pull off a daring caper, only to fall prey to mutual distrust. The long scene of the actual theft, completely in silence, will have your heart in your throat. In French with English subtitles. **115m/B VHS, Beta.** *FR* Jean Servais, Carl Mohner, Robert Manuel, Jules Dassin; *D:* Jules Dassin; *W:* Jules Dassin. Cannes Film Festival '55: Best Director (Dassin). *VYY, NOS, HHT*

Rift ⚔½ 1996 Bland romantic triangle set among Manhattan 20-somethings. Shy Tom (Sage) pines for Lisa (Bransford), the wife of his best friend, Bill (Cavanaugh). In fact, Tom begins having overwhelming nightmares, involving murder, about the situation. Not that you'll care since Tom is a mope, Lisa's a whiner, and Bill's a nasty-tempered bore. **87m/C VHS.** William Sage, Timothy Cavanaugh, Jennifer Bransford, Alan Davidson; *D:* Edward S. Barkin; *W:* Edward S. Barkin; *C:* Lee Daniel. *LEO*

The Right Connections ⚔⚔½ 1997 (PG) Kik N Bak Flash (Hammer) is a retired music star who gets a chance at a comeback when he helps a group of kids who've entered a hip hop contest to get the money to help their financially-strapped mom. **97m/C VHS, Closed Caption.** Hammer, Melissa Joan Hart, Meshach Taylor. *PAR*

The Right Hand Man ⚔½ 1987 (R) A brother and sister must deal with their crusty patriarch's demise in the Victorian-era Australian outback. Disappointing and overwrought. **101m/C VHS, Beta.** *AU* Rupert Everett, Hugo Weaving, Arthur Dignam; *D:* Di Drew. *VTR*

Right of Way ⚔⚔½ 1984 Stewart plays an elderly man who makes a suicide pact with his wife (Davis) when he learns of her terminal illness. Davis and Stewart's first film together is disappointing and stodgy, with an abrupt ending that looks like bad editing by a frightened studio. Made for TV. **102m/C VHS, Beta.** James Stewart, Bette Davis, Priscilla Morrill, Melinda Dillon; *D:* George Schaefer; *M:* Brad Fiedel. *NO*

The Right Stuff ⚔⚔⚔ 1983 (PG) A rambunctious adaptation of Tom Wolfe's nonfiction book about the beginnings of the U.S. space program, from Chuck Yeager's breaking of the sound barrier to the last of the Mercury missions. Featuring an all-star cast and an ambitious script. Rowdy, imaginative, and thrilling, though broadly painted and oddly uninvolving. Former astronaut John Glenn was running for president when this was out. **193m/C VHS, Beta, LV, Letterbox, Closed Caption, DVD.** Ed Harris, Dennis Quaid, Sam Shepard, Scott Glenn, Fred Ward, Charles Frank, William Russ, Kathy Baker, Barbara Hershey, Levon Helm, David Clennon, Kim Stanley, Mary Jo Deschanel, Veronica Cartwright, Pamela Reed, Jeff Goldblum, Harry Shearer, Donald Moffat, Scott Paulin, Lance Henriksen, Scott Wilson, John P. Ryan, Royal Dano; *D:* Philip Kaufman; *W:* Philip Kaufman; *C:* Caleb Deschanel; *M:* Bill Conti. Academy Awards '83: Best Film Editing, Best Sound, Best Original Score; Nominations: Academy Awards '83: Best Art Direction/Set Decoration, Best Cinematography, Best Picture, Best Supporting Actor (Shepard). *WAR*

The Right to Remain Silent ⚔⚔ 1995 (R) Rookie cop Christine Paley (Thompson) learns all about human foibles in her job processing incoming suspects. Based on a play by Brent Briscoe and Mark Fauser. *CW:* Language and brief violence. **96m/C VHS, Closed Caption.** Lea Thompson, Amanda Plummer, Christopher Lloyd, Laura San Giacomo, Judge Reinhold, Carl Reiner, L.L. Cool J., Patrick Dempsey, Fisher Stevens, Robert Loggia; *D:* Hubert de la Bouillerie. *REP*

Rikisha-Man ⚔⚔⚔½ *Rickshaw Man; Muhomatsu no Issho* 1958 A tragic melodrama about a rickshaw puller who helps raise a young boy after his father has died, and loves the boy's mother from afar. Inagaki's remake of his original 1943 version. In Japanese with English subtitles. **105m/B VHS, Beta.** *JP* Toshiro Mifune; *D:* Hiroshi Inagaki. *FCT*

Rikky and Pete ⚔⚔½ 1988 (R) An engaging Australian comedy about a bizarre, precociously eccentric brother and sister. He's a Rube Goldberg-style mentor; she's a scientist-cum-country singer. They move together to the outback and meet a score of weird characters. A worthy follow-up to director Tass's "Malcolm." **103m/C VHS, Beta, LV, Closed Caption.** *AU* Nina Landis, Stephen Kearney, Tetchie Agbayani, Bruce Spence, Bruno Lawrence, Bill Hunter, Dorothy Allison, Don Reid, Lewis Fitz-gerald; *D:* Nadia Tass; *W:* David Parker; *M:* Phil Judd. *MGM, FOX*

Rikyu ⚔⚔⚔ 1990 Set in 16th century Japan, Rikyu is a Buddhist priest who elevated the tea ceremony to an art form. To him it is a spiritual experience, to his master, Lord Hideyoshi Toilyotomi, the ruler of Japan, mastery of the ceremony is a matter of prestige. Conflict arises between Rikyu's ideal of profound simplicity, symbolized by the ceremony, and Toilyotomi's planned conquest of China, which Rikyu opposes. In Japanese with English subtitles. **116m/C VHS, LV.** *JP* Rentaro Mikuni, Tsutomu Yamazaki; *D:* Hiroshi Teshigahara. *CTL, LUM*

Rim of the Canyon ⚔½ 1949 Autry has a dual role as a lawman tracking villains who were jailed by his father years before. **70m/B VHS, Beta.** Gene Autry, Nan Leslie, Thurston Hall, Clem Bevans, Walter Sande, Jock Mahoney, Alan Hale Jr., Denver Pyle; *D:* John English. *NOS, DVT, TIM*

Rimfire ⚔⚔½ 1949 An undercover agent tracks down some stolen U.S. Army gold, aided by the ghost of a wrongly hanged gambler. Fun B western. **65m/B VHS, Beta, LV.** Mary Beth Hughes, Henry Hull, Fuzzy Knight, James Millican, Victor Kilian, Margia Dean, Jason Robards Sr., Reed Hadley; *D:* B. Reeves Eason. *NO*

Rin Tin Tin, Hero of the West ⚔⚔ 1955 In one of his last adventures, the famous German Shepherd proves his courage and hypercanine intelligence. Colorized. **75m/C VHS, Beta.** James Brown, Lee Aaker. *MON*

The Ring ⚔⚔½ 1927 Very early Hitchcock about boxer who marries carnival girl, loses carnival girl, and wins carnival girl back again. Standard romantic punch and roses yarn interesting as measure of young director's developing authority. **82m/B VHS.** *GB* Carl Brisson, Lillian Hall-Davis, Ian Hunter, Gordon Harker; *D:* Alfred Hitchcock; *W:* Alfred Hitchcock. *VEC, MLB*

The Ring ⚔⚔½ 1952 Poignant early fight movie that gives a lesson in prejudice against Chicanos. The main character feels that the only way to get respect from the world is to fight for it. Well-directed and perceptive. **79m/B VHS.** Gerald Mohr, Rita Moreno, Kiri Te Kanawa, Robert Arthur, Art Aragon, Jack Elam; *D:* Kurt Neumann. *MOV, DVT, HEG*

Ring of Bright Water ⚔⚔⚔ 1969 (G) Well done story of a pet otter from Gavin Maxwell's autobiography. The film stars the couple that made the delightful "Born Free." Beautiful Scottish Highlands photography adds to this captivating and endearing tale of a civil servant who purchases an otter from a pet store and moves to the country. **107m/C VHS, Beta.** *GB* Bill Travers, Virginia McKenna, Peter Jeffrey, Archie Duncan; *D:* Jack Couffer. *FCT, SIG, TVC*

Ring of Death ⚔½ 1972 A tough cop investigating a routine case becomes a hunted man after someone kills the man he is following. **93m/C VHS, Beta.** Franco Nero, Florinda Bolkan, Adolfo Celi. *CNG, MRV, GEM*

Ring of Fire ⚔½ 1991 (R) Wilson is one of very few modern American kung-fu heroes of Asian descent, and he works messages against prejudice into this interracial Romeo-and-Juliet chopsocky tale. What foot through yonder window breaks? **100m/C VHS, LV, Closed Caption.** Don "The Dragon" Wilson, Maria Ford, Vince Murdocco, Dale Jacoby, Michael Delano, Eric Lee; *D:* Richard W. Munchkin. *IMP, HMV*

Ring of Fire 2: Blood and Steel ⚔½ 1992 (R) Wilson returns as Dr. Johnny Wu in this martial-arts actioner which finds the good doctor the witness to a robbery. When one of the robbers is killed, the gang's leader kidnaps Johnny's fiance and holds her for ransom. He decides to bypass the police and use his own expertise to rescue her. *CW:* Language and martial arts violence. **94m/C VHS, Closed Caption.** Don "The Dragon" Wilson, Maria Ford, Sy Richardson, Michael Delano, Dale Jacoby, Vince Murdocco, Evan Lorie, Gary Robbins, Charlie Ganis, Ron Yuan; *D:* Richard W. Munchkin. *PMH*

Ring of Fire 3: Lion Strike ⚔½ 1994 (R) Johnny Wu is supposed to be on vacation with his son and a beautiful forest ranger when they find themselves in the way of a violent group known as the Global Mafia. Seems Johnny has a computer disk that the gangsters want. *CW:* Violence; language. **90m/C VHS, LV, Closed Caption.** Don "The Dragon" Wilson, Bobbie Phillips, Robert Costanzo; *D:* Rick Jacobson. *PMH*

Ring of Steel ⚔⚔ 1994 (R) Alex, a one-time Olympic hopeful in fencing, is enticed into combat by the mysterious owner of a decadent nightclub where gladiator-type matches are staged for the thrill of the bored and jaded super-rich. Unaware of the high stakes, Alex wins a duel and is showered with money and the attention of a beautiful, yet dangerous woman. When Alex discovers the club's dark secret, he no longer wants to fight, but blackmail draws him in even deeper. **94m/C VHS, LV, Closed Caption.** Joe Don Baker, Carol Alt, Robert Chapin, Gary Kasper, Darlene Vogel; *D:* David Frost; *W:* Robert Chapin; *M:* Jeff Beal. *USH*

Ring of Terror ⚔ 1962 College boy who wants to join a fraternity must survive the initiation rights, which include stealing a ring from a corpse. Unfortunately, this seemingly invincible guy has a deadly terror of the dead. Cheaply made flop allegedly based on a composite of actual hazing incidents. **72m/B VHS.** George Mather, Esther Furst, Austin Green, Joseph Conway; *D:* Clark Paylow. *NOS, SNC*

Ring of the Musketeers ⚔⚔½ 1993 (PG-13) Contemporary spoof of the Musketeers saga finds three descendants of the swashbuckling heroes carrying on the family tradition of protecting the weak and innocent. They even get stuck with a Musketeer-wannabe when they come to the rescue of a young boy who is kidnapped to prevent his dad from testifying against mobsters. *CW:* Action violence. **86m/C VHS, Closed Caption.** David Hasselhoff, Alison Doody, Thomas Gottschalk, Richard "Cheech" Marin, Corbin Bernsen, John Rhys-Davies; *D:* John Paragon; *W:* Joel Surnow. *COL*

Ringside ⚔½ 1949 A concert pianist turns boxer to avenge his brother who was blinded in a fight. **64m/B VHS, Beta, LV.** Donald (Don "Red") Barry, Sheila Ryan, Tom Brown. *SNC*

The Rink ⚔⚔⚔ 1916 Chaplin plays a waiter who spends his lunch hour on roller skates. Silent with musical soundtrack added. **20m/B VHS, Beta.** Charlie Chaplin; *D:* Charlie Chaplin. *CAB, GVV*

Rink/Immigrant 191? Two Chaplin shorts: "The Rink" (1916), in which Charlie defends his girlfriend's honor at a local roller skating rink; "The Immigrant" (1917), features Charlie as a newcomer to America. **56m/B VHS, Beta.** Charlie Chaplin, Mack Swain, Edna Purviance. *VYY*

Rio Bravo ⚔⚔⚔½ 1959 The sheriff of a Texas border town (Wayne) takes a brutal murderer into custody and faces a blockade of hired gunmen determined to keep his prisoner from being brought to justice. Long, but continually entertaining. Generally regarded as an American film classic, with an all-star cast, didn't impress the critics at the time. Sequel: "El Dorado." Semi-remake was called "Assault on Precinct 13." **140m/C VHS, Beta.** John Wayne, Dean Martin, Angie Dickinson, Ricky Nelson, Walter Brennan, Ward Bond, Claude Akins, Bob Steele, John Russell; *D:* Howard Hawks. *WAR, TLF*

Rio Conchos ⚔⚔⚔ 1964 Nifty nonstop action in this western set in Texas after the Civil War. Three Army buddies search for 2,000 stolen rifles. Boone is understated, O'Brien is good, and Brown memorable in his debut. **107m/C VHS, Beta.** Richard Boone, Stuart Whitman, Edmond O'Brien, Anthony (Tony) Franciosa, Jim Brown; *D:* Gordon Douglas; *M:* Jerry Goldsmith. *FOX*

Rio Diablo 🐾🐾½ 1993 Country Western singers abound in—what else—a made-for-TV Western movie. A bounty hunter (Rogers) and newlywed groom (Tritt) set off after a gang of thieving kidnappers who have snatched the young bride (Harring). Judd shows up as the owner of a desert hostelry, who happens to cross paths with the hunters. Watch out—this could be more fun than a Partridge Family reunion. 120m/C VHS. Kenny Rogers, Travis Tritt, Naomi Judd, Stacy Keach, Brion James, Bruce Greenwood, Laura Harring; **M:** Larry Brown. CAF, MVD

Rio Grande 🐾🐾🐾 1950 The last entry in Ford's cavalry trilogy following "Fort Apache" and "She Wore a Yellow Ribbon." A U.S. cavalry unit on the Mexican border conducts an unsuccessful campaign against marauding Indians. The commander (Wayne) faces an unhappy wife and is estranged from his son, a new recruit. Featuring an excellent Victor Young score and several songs by the Sons of the Pioneers. 105m/B VHS, LV, Closed Caption. John Wayne, Maureen O'Hara, Ben Johnson, Claude Jarman Jr., Harry Carey Jr., Victor McLaglen, Chill Wills, J. Carrol Naish; **D:** John Ford. REP, TLF, RXM

Rio Grande Raiders 🐾 1946 A Stagecoach driver discovers that his kid brother is working for a crooked rival stage company. 54m/B VHS, Beta. Sunset Carson, Linda Stirling, Bob Steele. DVT, RXM

Rio Lobo 🐾🐾½ 1970 (G) Hawks's final film takes place after the Civil War, when Union Colonel Wayne goes to Rio Lobo to take revenge on two traitors. Disappointing. The Duke has to carry weak supporting performances on his brawny shoulders—and nearly does. 114m/C VHS, Beta, LV, Closed Caption. John Wayne, Jorge Rivero, Jennifer O'Neill, Jack Elam, Chris Mitchum, David Huddleston, George Plimpton; **D:** Howard Hawks; **C:** William Clothier; **M:** Jerry Goldsmith. FOX

Rio Rattler 🐾½ 1935 Tyler takes the place of a murdered lawman in order to find his killer. 60m/B VHS, Beta. Tom Tyler, Marion Shilling, Eddie Gribbon, William Gould, Tom London; **D:** Franklin Shamray. VCN, GPV

Rio Rita 🐾🐾½ 1942 Abbott & Costello are working on a ranch and somehow become involved with Nazi spies. Provides a few original comic bits for the duo but is otherwise mediocre. An updated remake of the 1929 Wheeler & Woolsey comedy. 91m/B VHS. Bud Abbott, Lou Costello, Kathryn Grayson, John Carroll, Patricia Dane, Tom Conway, Peter Whitney; **D:** Sylvan Simon. MGM

Riot 🐾🐾½ 1969 (R) Men in cages throw tantrums until warden returns from vacation. Filmed in Arizona State Prison with real convicts as extras. Strong performances by fullback Brown and durable Hackman. Based on story by ex-con Frank Elli. Too oft-played theme song sung by Bill Medley of the Righteous Brothers. 97m/C VHS. Gene Hackman, Jim Brown, Mike Kellin, Ben Carruthers, Frank Eyman; **D:** Buzz Kulik; **W:** James Poe. PAR

Riot 🐾 1996 (R) Dumb actioner set on Christmas Eve, 1999, amidst some L.A. riots. British Special Air Service officer Shane Alcott (Daniels) must rescue his kidnapped ex-girlfriend Anna-Lisa (Rowland), who just happens to be the British ambassador's daughter. She's being held by ghetto gangster Leon (Sanders), whose gang turn out to be pawns for IRA leader O'Flaherty (Kilpatrick), who has a score to settle. Predictable fights, lots of explosions. 95m/C VHS, Closed Caption. Gary Daniels, Ray "Sugar Ray" Leonard, Patrick Kilpatrick, Paige Rowland, Dex Elliot Sanders, Charles Napier; **D:** Joseph Merhi; **W:** John Barmettler, William Applegate Jr.; **C:** Ken Blakey; **M:** Jim Halfpenny. PMH

Riot in Cell Block 11 🐾🐾🐾 1954 A convict leads four thousand prisoners in an uprising to improve prison conditions. Based on producer/ex-con Walter Wanger's own experience. Powerful and still timely. Filmed at Folsom Prison. 80m/B VHS, Beta. Neville Brand, Leo Gordon, Emile Meyer, Frank Faylen; **D:** Donald Siegel. REP

Riot in the Streets 🐾🐾 *Riot* 1996 (R) Four intertwined stories revolving around the 1992 Los Angeles riots, on the day the Rodney King verdict was announced. Concerned are an African-American family, a white police officer, a Latino family, and Asian-American shopowners. Documentary footage of the actual riots is also included. **CW:** Violence and pervasive strong language. 95m/C VHS. Mario Van Peebles, Melvin Van Peebles, Cicely Tyson, Luke Perry, Peter Dobson, Dante Basco, Mako, Kieu Chinh, Alexis Cruz, Douglas Spain, Yelba Osorio, John Ortiz; **D:** C. David Johnson, Richard Dilello, Galen Yuen, Alex Munoz; **W:** C. David Johnson, Richard Dilello, Galen Yuen, Joe Vasquez; **C:** Paul Elliott. EVE

Riot Squad 🐾🐾 1941 An intern poses as a doctor in order to find out who was responsible for putting a mob hit on a police captain. 55m/B VHS, Beta. Richard Cromwell, Rita Quigley, John Miljan, Mary Ruth, Herbert Rawlinson, Mary Gordon, Arthur Space; **D:** Edward Finney. SNC, RXM

Rip-Off 🐾 1977 Two Greek wanderers enter the American way of life via sex, drugs, syndicated crime, and terrorism. 78m/C VHS, Beta. Michael Benet, Michelle Simone, James Masters, Johnny Dark; **D:** Manolis Tsafos. UNI

The Rip Off 🐾 1978 (R) A colorful gang of hoodlums goes for the biggest heist of their lives—six million bucks in diamonds! 99m/C VHS, Beta. Lee Van Cleef, Karen Black, Robert Alda, Edward Albert; **D:** Anthony (Antonio Margheriti) Dawson. WOV

Rip Roarin' Buckaroo 🐾 1936 A fighter sets out to avenge himself when he is framed in a dishonest fight. 51m/B VHS, Beta. Tom Tyler, B.J. Quinn Jr., Beth Marion, Charles "Blackie" King; **D:** Robert F. "Bob" Hill. NOS, DVT, RXM

Rip van Winkle 1985 Sleepy Coppola adaptation of the Washington Irving story about a man who falls asleep for 20 years after a group of ghosts get him drunk. From the "Faerie Tale Theatre" series. 60m/C VHS, Beta, Closed Caption. Harry Dean Stanton, Talia Shire; **D:** Francis Ford Coppola. KUI, FOX, FCT

Ripe 🐾🐾 1997 (R) Fourteen-year-old fraternal twins Violet (Keena) and Rosie (Eagan) decide to make it on their own after their abusive parents are killed in a car crash. They wind up on a derelict southern army base where they're befriended by caretaker Pete (Currie) and M.P. Ken (Brice), who may not have the most innocent of intentions. **CW:** Sexuality involving young teens, language and some violence. 93m/C VHS. Monica Keena, Daisy Eagan, Gordon Currie, Ron Brice, Karen Gorney; **D:** Mo Ogrodnik; **W:** Mo Ogrodnik; **C:** Wolfgang Held; **M:** Anton Sanko. THV

The Ripper woof! 1986 The spirit of Jack the Ripper possesses a university professor's body. Ultra-violent. Shot on videotape for the video market. 90m/C VHS, Beta. Wade Tower, Tom Schreir, Mona Van Pernis, Andrea Adams; **D:** Christopher Lewis. NO

The Ripper 🐾🐾 1997 (R) Yet another version of the Jack the Ripper saga, this time made for cable. In 1888 London, ambitious Scotland Yard inspector Jim Hansen (Bergin) is investigating the murders of several East End prostitutes. Clues direct him to a member of the nobility, in fact, Queen Victoria's grandson, Prince Edward (West), but pursuing his inquiries could lead to the end of Hansen's career. **CW:** Violence and sexuality. 120m/C VHS. Patrick Bergin, Gabrielle Anwar, Michael York, Sam West, Essie Davis, Olivia Hamnett; **D:** Janet Meyers; **W:** Robert Rodat; **C:** Martin McGrath; **M:** Mason Daring. USH

Ripper Man 🐾½ 1996 (R) Ex-cop is accused of murder when he finds a body at a nightclub and then becomes the killer's next target. 93m/C VHS. Mike Norris. TTC

Ripping Yarns 1975 Three episodes of the popular British comedy series written by Monty Python's Terry Jones and Michael Palin: "Tomkinson's Schooldays," "Escape from Stalag Luft 112B," and "Golden Gordon." The subsequent episodes are released as "More Ripping Yarns" and "Even More Ripping Yarns." 90m/C VHS, Beta, Closed Caption. GB Michael Palin, Gwen Watford, Ian Ogilvy, Roy Kinnear, Bill Fraser; **D:** Terry Hughes, Jimmy Franklin, Alan Bell; **W:** Michael Palin, Terry Jones. FOX, VCO

Riptide 🐾🐾🐾 1934 Shearer is a carefree American married to stuffy English lord Marshall. He goes off to America on a business trip, she's bored and goes to a costume party (everyone dresses as insects!) where she meets old flame Montgomery. He gets drunk, follows her home in an effort to rekindle their passion, and winds up in the hospital after a drunken fall. The returning Marshall is appalled by the scandalous press and instigates divorce proceedings. Eventually, they come to their senses and decide they do love each other. Quality production with an entertaining cast. 90m/B VHS. Norma Shearer, Herbert Marshall, Robert Montgomery, Richard "Skeets" Gallagher, Ralph Forbes, Lilyan Tashman; **D:** Edmund Goulding; **W:** Edmund Goulding. MGM

The Rise and Fall of Legs Diamond 🐾🐾½ 1960 Not quite historically accurate but fast-paced and entertaining gangster bio of legendary booze trafficker Legs Diamond. Danton's debut. 101m/B VHS, LV. Ray Danton, Karen Steele, Jesse White, Simon Oakland, Robert Lowery, Elaine Stewart; **D:** Budd Boetticher. Nominations: Academy Awards '60: Best Costume Design (B & W). WAR, FCT

The Rise & Rise of Daniel Rocket 🐾🐾 1986 A exceptional young boy believes he can fly without the aid of a flying machine. From the "American Playhouse" series. 90m/C VHS, Beta. Tom Hulce, Timothy Daly, Valerie Mahaffey; **D:** Emile Ardolino. PBS

The Rise of Louis XIV 🐾🐾🐾 *La Prise de Pouvoir Par Louis XIV* 1966 A masterful docudrama detailing the life and court intrigues of Louis XIV of France. Successfully captures the attitudes and mores of the royalty at the time. One of a series of historical films directed by Rossellini. Made for French television. In French with English subtitles. 100m/C VHS. FR Jean-Marie Patte, Raymond Jourdan, Dominique Vincent, Silvagni, Pierre Barrat; **D:** Roberto Rossellini. HTV, FCT

Rising Son 🐾🐾🐾 1990 A family man who loves his job faces trauma when his factory closes at the same time his son informs him he's quitting medical school. Solid family drama and parable of economic hard times of the early '80s, sustained by top-drawer performances by Dennehy, Damon, and Laurie. Well directed by Coles. Made for cable. 92m/C VHS, Beta, Closed Caption. Brian Dennehy, Matt Damon, Piper Laurie, Graham Beckel, Ving Rhames, Jane Adams, Richard Jenkins, Emily Longstreth; **D:** John David Coles; **W:** Bill Phillips. TTC

Rising Sun 🐾🐾🐾 1993 (R) When a prostitute is found murdered in the boardroom of a powerful Japanese-owned corporation, seasoned cop (and Japanese expert) Connery and new partner Snipes are sent to investigate. Complicated yarn about business, prejudice, cops, and the differences between east and west. Filmed with stylized camera techniques, quick action, and good rapport between the two leads. Based on the book by Crichton, which offered ominous theories about international politics and business. These aspects had the film labeled as Japan-bashing, one of the reasons the script was rewritten to focus more on the murder mystery. **CW:** Language, some violence, and strong sexuality. 129m/C VHS, LV, Letterbox, Closed Caption. Sean Connery, Wesley Snipes, Tia Carrere, Harvey Keitel, Kevin Anderson, Stan Egi, Mako, Cary-Hiroyuki Tagawa, Ray Wise, Tatjana Patitz; **D:** Philip Kaufman; **W:** Michael Backes, Michael Crichton, Philip Kaufman; **C:** Michael Chapman; **M:** Toru Takemitsu. FOX, BTV, FCT

Risk 🐾🐾🐾 1994 Maya (Sillas) is a struggling, emotionally distant, New York artist when she meets overly friendly Joe (Ilku) on a bus. He follows her home and manages to entice Maya into letting him spend the night but Joe has some psychological problems, including criminal behavior, which manifests itself when he steals a car. Maya, nevertheless, agrees to drive with him to his older sister's home in rural Connecticut and finds bad blood and more mental anguish that she knows how to deal with. Terrifically honest performance by Sillas and an equally touching one by Ilku are highlights of this adult attempt at romance. **85m/C VHS.** Karen Sillas, David Ilku, Molly Price, Jack Gwaltney; **D:** Deirdre Fishel; **W:** Deirdre Fishel; **C:** Peter Pearce; **M:** John Paul Jones. *LEO*

Risky Business 🎬🎬 **1928** Fortune-seeking mother disapproves of daughter's doctor fiance, and educates girl in marital woes. Video includes early Pollard short "Sold at Auction." **104m/B VHS, Beta, LV.** Vera Reynolds, ZaSu Pitts, Ethey Clayton; **D:** Alan Hale. *GPV, FCT, WAR*

Risky Business 🎬🎬🎬 **1983 (R)** With his parents out of town and awaiting word from the college boards, a teenager becomes involved in unexpected ways with a quick-thinking prostitute, her pimp, and assorted others. Cruise is likeable, especially when dancing in his underwear. Funny, well-paced, stylish prototypical '80s teen flick reintroduced Ray-Bans as the sunglasses for the wannabe hip. What a party! **99m/C VHS, Beta, LV, 8mm, Letterbox.** Tom Cruise, Rebecca DeMornay, Curtis Armstrong, Bronson Pinchot, Joe Pantoliano, Kevin Anderson, Richard Masur, Raphael Sbarge, Nicholas Pryor, Janet Carroll; **D:** Paul Brickman; **W:** Paul Brickman; **C:** Reynaldo Villalobos; **M:** Tangerine Dream. *WAR*

Rita Hayworth: The Love Goddess 🎬½ **1983** Made for television drama details the tragic life of the beautiful film star. Carter, lovely though she is, plays Rita weakly and without depth. **100m/C VHS, Beta.** Lynda Carter, Michael Lerner, Alejandro Rey, John Considine; **D:** James Goldstone. *ART*

Rita, Sue & Bob Too 🎬🎬🎬 **1987 (R)** A middle-aged Englishman gets involved in a menage a trois with two promiscuous teenagers, until the whole town gets wind of it. A raunchy, amoral British comedy. **94m/C VHS, Beta, LV.** *GB* Michelle Holmes, George Costigan, Siobhan Finneran, Lesley Sharp, Willie Ross, Patti Nicholls, Kulvinder Ghir; **D:** Alan Clarke; **W:** Andrea Dunbar; **M:** Michael Kamen. *ORI, WAR*

The Rite 🎬🎬 *The Ritual; Riten* **1969** Members of a famous theatrical troupe are called before a judge to answer charges that a production is obscene. The judge's interrogation exposes their private and painful neuroses until the performers decide to turn on their accuser. Pessimistic even by Bergman standards and the first film the director made specifically for TV. Swedish with subtitles. **75m/B VHS.** *SW* Ingrid Thulin, Gunnar Bjornstrand, Erik Hell, Anders Ek; **D:** Ingmar Bergman; **W:** Ingmar Bergman; **C:** Sven Nykvist. *HMV*

Rituals 🎬½ *The Creeper* **1979** Group of five calm, rational men suddenly turn desperate after a chain of nightmarish events on a camping trip. Yet another low-budget "Deliverance" rip off. **100m/C VHS, Beta.** *CA* Hal Holbrook, Lawrence Dane; **D:** Peter Carter. *VTR*

The Ritz 🎬🎬🎬 **1976 (R)** Weston tries to get away from his gangster brother-in-law by hiding out in a gay bathhouse in New York. Moreno plays a talentless singer Googie Gomez, who performs in the bathhouse while waiting for her big break. Moreno is great reprising her Tony-winning stage role, and Lester's direction is spiffy. Written by Terence McNally from his play. **91m/C VHS, Beta, LV, Closed Caption.** Rita Moreno, Jack Weston, Jerry Stiller, Kaye Ballard, Treat Williams, F. Murray Abraham; **D:** Richard Lester. *WAR*

Rivals 🎬½ *Deadly Rivals* **1972 (R)** Shallow, unconvincing drama about a stepfather challenged by his stepson, who wants to kill this new contender for his mother's love. Nice handling of cast credits, but other details—like acting, directing and photography—leave much to be desired. **103m/C VHS, Beta.** Robert Klein, Joan Hackett, Scott Jacoby; **D:** Krishna Shah. *TPI*

Rivals of the Silver Fox 🎬½ **1980** Young kickers prove no match for their hoary, hard-chopping elder. **90m/C VHS, Beta.** Casanova Wong, Barry Lam, Chen Shao Ping, Lee Fat Yuen. *NO*

The River 🎬🎬🎬🎬 **1951** A massively lauded late film by Renoir about three British girls growing up in Bengal, India, all developing crushes on a one-legged American vet. Lyrical and heartwarming, with hailed cinematography by Claude Renoir. Rumer Godden wrote the novel, and co-scripted the screenplay with director Renoir. Satyajit Ray, one of India's greatest filmmakers, assisted Renoir. **99m/C VHS, Beta, LV.** *FR* Patricia Walters, Adrienne Corri, Nora Swinburne, Radha, Arthur Shields, Thomas E. Breen, Esmond Knight; **D:** Jean Renoir; **W:** Jean Renoir; **C:** Claude Renoir. *HMV, CRC*

The River 🎬🎬 **1984 (PG)** Farmers battle a river whose flood threatens their farm. Spacek, as always, is strong and believable as the wife and mother, but Gibson falters. Beautiful photography. The third in an onslaught of films in the early '80s that dramatized the plight of the small American farmer. "The River" isn't as strong as "Country" and "Places in the Heart" which managed to convey important messages less cloyingly. **124m/C VHS, Beta, LV, Closed Caption.** Mel Gibson, Sissy Spacek, Scott Glenn, Billy Green Bush; **D:** Mark Rydell; **W:** Julian Barry, Robert Dillon; **C:** Vilmos Zsigmond; **M:** John Williams. Nominations: Academy Awards '84: Best Actress (Spacek), Best Cinematography, Best Sound, Best Original Score. *USH*

River Beat 🎬🎬 **1954** A woman aboard an American freighter is unwittingly used as diamond smuggler, and is arrested when the ship docks in London. An inspector does his best to clear the hapless woman. **70m/B VHS, Beta.** Phyllis Kirk, John Bentley, Robert Ayres, Lenny White, Glyn Houston, Charles Lloyd Pack; **D:** Guy Green. *SNC*

The River Niger 🎬🎬½ **1976 (R)** Jones is riveting, and Tyson is good in an otherwise muddling adaptation of the Tony-award winning play about black ghetto life. Realistic emotions and believable characters. **105m/C VHS.** James Earl Jones, Cicely Tyson, Glynn Turman, Louis Gossett Jr., Roger E. Mosley, Jonelle Allen; **D:** Krishna Shah. *NO*

River of Death 🎬½ **1990 (R)** Absurd adventure, based on an Alistair McLean novel, about a white man entering the Amazon jungle world of a forgotten tribe in search of wealth, tripping over Neo-Nazi scientists and war criminals. Too complex to be harmlessly enjoyable; too mindless for the complexity to be worth unraveling. **103m/C VHS, Beta, LV, Closed Caption.** Michael Dudikoff, Robert Vaughn, Donald Pleasence, Herbert Lom, L.Q. Jones, Cynthia Erland, Sarah Maur-Thorp; **D:** Steve Carver. *MGM, WAR*

River of Diamonds 🎬 **1990** A daring adventurer, with the standard beautiful woman at his side, battles evil curses and Nazis buried alive to find a fortune in diamonds. Yeah, sure. Another miserable "Indiana Jones" rip off. **88m/C VHS, Closed Caption.** Dack Rambo, Angela O'Neill, Ferdinand "Ferdy" Mayne, Graham Clark, David Sherwood, Tony Caprari, Dominique Tyawa; **D:** Robert J. Smawley. *TTC*

River of Evil 🎬½ **1964** Action/adventure in which a young girl travels through the Amazon jungle searching for clues to her father's death. **?m/C VHS.** Barbara Rutting, Harald Leipnitz. *SNC*

River of Grass 🎬½ **1994** No-budget noirish crime/romance set in the swampy, low-rent Florida area between Miami and the Everglades. Uncaring and frankly dumb housewife/mom Cozy (Bowman) hooks up with the boozing Lee Ray (Fessenden) and the dim duo take an illegal dip in a private pool. Cozy manages to fire off Lee's gun and thinks she hit a man who suddenly appeared. Not bothering to find out if this is true, they decide to hold up in a motel until they can figure out what to do. You won't really care but director Reichardt does have a way with visuals so things aren't a total loss. **80m/C VHS.** Lisa Bowman, Larry Fessenden, Dick Russell; **D:** Kelly Reichardt; **W:** Jesse Hartman, Kelly

Reichardt; **C:** Jim Denault. Nominations: Independent Spirit Awards '96: Best First Feature, Debut Performance (Bowman). *FCT*

River of No Return 🎬🎬½ **1954** During the gold rush, an itinerant farmer and his young son help a heart-of-gold saloon singer search for her estranged husband. Rather crummy script is helped by the mere presence of Mitchum and Monroe. Marilyn sings the title song, "Down in the Meadow," and "I'm Going to File My Claim." **91m/C VHS, Beta, LV.** Robert Mitchum, Marilyn Monroe, Tommy Rettig, Rory Calhoun, Murvyn Vye, Douglas Spencer; **D:** Otto Preminger; **C:** Joseph LaShelle. *FOX*

River of Unrest 🎬🎬½ *Ourselves Alone* **1937** Remarkable visual expressiveness and emotional power mark this depiction of terrorism and open warfare during the Irish Rebellion. Based on a play, hence slow; but good acting pulls it up half a bone. **69m/B VHS, Beta.** John Lodge, John Loder, Antoinette Cellier. *VYY*

The River Pirates 🎬🎬½ **1994 (PG)** Mississippi boy discovers a lot about life over the summer of his 12th birthday in 1942. He finds the secret hiding place of a band of river thieves, endures a tornado, has some adventures with his friends, and finds out that his crush on the prettiest girl in town is reciprocated. Based on a novel by Willie Morris. **108m/C VHS, LV.** Ryan Francis, Richard Farnsworth, Gennie James, Doug Emerson, Anne Ramsey, Maureen O'Sullivan; **D:** Tom G. Robertson. *THV*

The River Rat 🎬🎬½ **1984 (PG)** Ex-con Jones is reunited with his daughter after spending 13 years in prison. There's something in there about stashed loot that should have been jettisonned in favor of more getting-to-know-you father-daughter drama, which is good. **93m/C VHS, Beta, LV, Closed Caption.** Tommy Lee Jones, Brian Dennehy, Martha Plimpton, Shawn Smith, Melissa Davis; **D:** Tom Rickman. *PAR*

A River Runs Through It 🎬🎬🎬½ **1992 (PG)** Contemplative exploration of family ties and coming of age with impact falling just short of the novel's is another well-crafted American tale directed by Redford. Set in Montana during the early part of the century, a Presbyterian minister teaches his two sons, one troubled and one on his way to success, about life and religion via fly-fishing. Based on the novel by Norman Maclean. The laserdisc version includes commentary by Redford. **123m/C VHS, LV, 8mm, Letterbox, Closed Caption.** Craig Sheffer, Brad Pitt, Tom Skerritt, Brenda Blethyn, Emily Lloyd, Edie McClurg, Stephen Shellan, Susan Taylor; **D:** Robert Redford; **W:** Richard Friedenberg; **C:** Philippe Rousselot; **M:** Mark Isham. Academy Awards '92: Best Cinematography; Nominations: Academy Awards '92: Best Adapted Screenplay, Best Original Score. *COL, CRC, BTV*

River Street 🎬🎬 **1995** Ambitious real estate agent Ben Egan (Young) is engaged to marry Sharon (MacIntosh), his shady boss Vincent Pierce's (Hunter) daughter. But when he blows a big deal and winds up striking a cop, Ben's sentenced to community service at a dilapidated center for street kids. He takes an interest in good-hearted center director Wendy (Davis) but can't change his ways so easily. The center stands on valuable river front property and if Ben can get the land, he'll get back both his job and Sharon. The relationships don't convince and Ben's change of heart seems forced. **88m/C VHS.** *AU* Aden Young, Bill Hunter, Essie Davis, Tammy MacIntosh, Sullivan Stapleton, Lois Ramsey; **D:** Tony Mahood; **W:** Philip Ryall; **C:** Martin McGrath; **M:** David Bridie, John Phillips. Nominations: Australian Film Institute '96: Best Actor (Young). *NYR*

The River Wild 🎬🎬½ **1994 (PG-13)** Dissatisfied wife Gail (Streep) plans a family whitewater rafting vacation with 10-year-old son Roarke (Mazzello) and workaholic husband Tom (Strathairn). A former guide (and white-water expert) Gail comes to the aid of river novices Wade (boyishly menacing Bacon) and Terry (Reilly), who quickly turn out to be violent criminals needing Gail's help with their escape. Slow start leads to nonstop thrills with Streep an adept action heroine, though undercut by the flic's need to do something with Strathairn's thankless role. Beautiful Montana and Oregon settings. **CW:** Some violence, threatening moments. **111m/C VHS, LV, Closed Caption, DVD.** Meryl Streep, David Strathairn, Joseph Mazzello, Kevin Bacon, John C. Reilly, Benjamin Bratt; **D:** Curtis Hanson; **W:** Raynold Gideon; **C:** Robert Elswit; **M:** Jerry Goldsmith. Nominations: Golden Globe Awards '95: Best Actress—Drama (Streep), Best Supporting Actor (Bacon); Screen Actors Guild Award '94: Best Actress (Streep). *USH*

Riverbend ♫♫ 1989 (R) A renegade black Army major escapes a rigged court martial only to be persecuted by racist whites in a small Southern town. Made for television. **106m/C VHS, Beta.** Steve James, Tony Frank, Julius Tennon, Margaret Avery; **D:** Sam Firstenberg. *PAR*

River's Edge ♫♫♫ 1987 (R) Drug-addled high school student strangles his girlfriend and casually displays the corpse to his apathetic group of friends, who leave the murder unreported for days. Harrowing and gripping; based on a true story. Aging biker Hopper is splendid. **99m/C VHS, Beta, LV, 8mm, Closed Caption.** Keanu Reeves, Crispin Glover, Daniel Roebuck, Joshua Miller, Dennis Hopper, Ione Skye, Roxana Zal, Tom Bower, Constance Forslund, Leo Rossi, Jim Metzler; **D:** Tim Hunter; **W:** Neal Jimenez; **C:** Frederick Elmes; **M:** Jurgen Knieper. Independent Spirit Awards '88: Best Film, Best Screenplay; Sundance Film Festival '87: Special Jury Prize. *NLC*

Road Agent ♫½ *Texas Road Agent* 1926 Hoxie is the Kansas Kid, a fugitive hired by a crooked lawyer to pose as the long-lost heir to a ranching fortune. Only the Kid develops a soft spot for his "family" and may not be able to go through with the evil plot. **70m/B VHS, Beta.** Al Hoxie; **D:** J.P. McGowan. *NOS, DVT, MLB*

Road Games ♫♫ 1981 (PG) Trucker Keach is drawn into a web of intrigue surrounding a series of highway "Jack the Ripper"-style murders. Curtis is a hitchhiker. Nothing special. Director Franklin later helmed "Psycho II." **100m/C VHS, Beta.** *AU* Stacy Keach, Jamie Lee Curtis; **D:** Richard Franklin; **M:** Brian May. *COL, NLC*

The Road Home ♫♫½ 1995 (PG) Depression-era heart-tugger features two orphaned brothers who ride the rails from New York to Nebraska in search of a new home at Father Flanagan's Boys Town. **90m/C VHS, Closed Caption.** Keegan Macintosh, Will Estes, Kris Kristofferson, Charles Martin Smith, Danny Aiello, Dee Wallace Stone, Mickey Rooney; **D:** Dean Hamilton. *REP*

Road House ♫♫½ 1948 Nightclub singer Lupino inspires noir feelings between jealous road house owner Widmark and his partner Wilde. Widmark sets up Wilde to take the fall for a faked robbery, convinces the law to release him into his custody, then dares him to escape. **95m/B VHS, Beta.** Richard Widmark, Ida Lupino, Cornel Wilde, Celeste Holm, O.Z. Whitehead; **D:** Jean Negulesco. *FOX, FCT*

Road House ♫½ 1989 (R) Bouncer Swayze is hired to do the impossible: clean up the toughest bar in Kansas City. When he lays down his rules he makes a lot of enemies, including ex-bar employees and local organized crime. Ample violence; an example of formula filmmaking at its most brain-numbing, with a rock soundtrack. **115m/C VHS, Beta, LV, 8mm, Letterbox.** Patrick Swayze, Sam Elliott, Kelly Lynch, Ben Gazzara, Kevin Tighe, Marshall Teague, Julie Michaels, Jeff Healey; **D:** Rowdy Herrington; **C:** Dean Cundey; **M:** Michael Kamen. *MGM*

Road Kill USA ♫♫½ 1993 Two sleazy drifters on a cross-country murder spree pick up a hitchhiking college student and expect him to join in the fun. When he refuses, he has two choices: kill or be killed. **98m/C VHS.** Andrew Porter, Sean Bridges, Deanna Perry; **D:** Tony Elwood.

The Road Killers ♫♫ 1995 (R) Sickening psycho Cliff (well-played by Sheffer) is head of a brutal quartet that terrorizes a family driving along a remote desert highway. Cliff kidnaps the family

daughter and her mild-mannered dad (Lambert) must rescue her. **CW:** violence; language. **89m/C VHS, LV, Closed Caption.** Christopher Lambert, Craig Sheffer, Adrienne Shelly; **D:** Deran Sarafian; **W:** Tedi Sarafian. *WEA, ART*

Road Racers ♫♫ 1959 The roar of the engine, fast cars, and family ties combine in this movie about the thrill of speed. **73m/B VHS.** Joel Lawrence, Marian Collier, Skip Ward; **D:** Arthur Swerdloff; **W:** Stanley Kallis, Ed Lasko. *COL*

Road Show ♫♫½ 1941 Menjou stars as a young man wrongfully committed to an insane asylum. He escapes and joins a bankrupt carnival owned by Landis. Some really zany stuff keeps this from being just standard fare. Co-written by silent film comic Langdon. **87m/B VHS.** Adolphe Menjou, Carole Landis, John Hubbard, Charles Butterworth, Patsy Kelly, George E. Stone, Polly Ann Young, Edward Norris, Marjorie Woodworth, Florence Bates; **D:** Hal Roach; **W:** Harry Langdon. *NOS*

The Road to Bali ♫♫♫ 1953 Sixth Bob-n-Bing road show, the only one in color, is a keeper. The boys are competing for the love of—that's right—Lamour. She must be some gal, cuz they chase her all the way to Bali, where they meet cannibals and other perils, including the actual Humphrey Bogart. Jones's debut, in a bit role. ♫Moonflowers; Chicago Style; Hoots Mon; To See You; The Merry-Go-Runaround; Chorale for Brass, Piano, and Bongo (instrumental). **90m/C VHS, Beta.** Bob Hope, Bing Crosby, Dorothy Lamour, Murvyn Vye, Ralph Moody, Jane Russell, Jerry Lewis, Dean Martin, Carolyn Jones; **D:** Hal Walker. *UNI, DVT, MLB*

The Road to Galveston ♫♫♫ 1996 (PG-13) Texas widow Jordan Roosevelt (Tyson) needs to pay her mortgage so she turns her home into a residence for three Alzheimer patients. When her financial problems only worsen, Jordan decides to fulfill her lifetime goal and takes everyone on a trip to Galveston to see the ocean. Sentimental, fact-based TV movie cuts the saccharine through compelling performances. **CW:** Thematic elements. **93m/C VHS, Beta, Closed Caption.** Cicely Tyson, Piper Laurie, Tess Harper, Salle Ellis, Starletta DuPois, James McDaniel, Penny Johnson, Clarence Williams III, Stephen Root; **D:** Michael Toshiyuki Uno; **W:** Tony Lee; **M:** Stanley Clarke. *PAR*

The Road to Hong Kong ♫♫½ 1962 Last of the Crosby/Hope team-ups shows some wear, but still manages charm and humor. Lamour appears only briefly in this twisted comedy of hustlers caught in international espionage and cosmic goings-on. ♫Teamwork; Let's Not Be Sensible; It's The Only Way to Travel; We're On the Road to Hong Kong; Warmer Than a Whisper. **91m/B VHS, LV.** Bob Hope, Bing Crosby, Joan Collins, Dorothy Lamour, Peter Sellers; **D:** Norman Panama; **W:** Norman Panama; **C:** Jack Hildyard. *MGM, BTV, FCT*

The Road to Lebanon ♫♫ 1960 An original musical comedy featuring many stars, spoofing the famous Hope-Crosby "Road" films. **50m/B VHS, Beta.** Danny Thomas, Bing Crosby, Bob Hope, Hugh Downs, Claudine Auger, Sheldon Leonard. *NOS, VYY, DVT*

The Road to Life ♫♫ *Putyovka V Zhizn* 1931 In the turmoil caused by Russia's Revolutionary and Civil wars, thousands of orphans roam the countryside resorting to petty crime to survive. One group is sent to a collective as part of an experimental program where they can be reformed and learn a trade but their criminal pasts seem inescapable. Russian with subtitles. **100m/B VHS.** *RU* Nikolai Batalov, Maria Gonfa, Tsifan Kyria; **D:** Nicolai Ekk; **W:** Nicolai Ekk; **M:** Yakov Stollyar. *FCT*

The Road to Morocco ♫♫♫ 1942 The third in the road movie series finds Hope and Crosby in Morocco, stranded and broke. To get some money, Crosby sells Hope into slavery to be the princess's (Lamour) personal plaything. Feeling guilty, Crosby returns to the palace to rescue Hope, only to find that he and the princess are getting married because the royal astrologer

said it was in the stars. Crosby then tries to woo Lamour and, when the astrologer discovers the stars were mistaken, these two decide to marry. Quinn, however, also wants her and hilarious scenes ensue when the boys rescue Lamour from him. One of the funniest in the series. Watch for the camel at the end. ♫Constantly; Moonlight Becomes You; Ain't Got a Dime to My Name; Road to Morocco. **83m/C VHS, LV.** Bing Crosby, Bob Hope, Dorothy Lamour, Anthony Quinn, Dona Drake, Vladimir Sokoloff, Yvonne De Carlo; **D:** David Butler; **C:** William Mellor. National Film Registry '96;; Nominations: Academy Awards '42: Best Original Screenplay, Best Sound. *USH*

Road to Nashville ♫♫ 1967 (G) An agent travels to Nashville to enlist talent for a new musical. Why do so many of these semi-musicals insist on having a plot? Good music. **110m/C VHS, Beta.** Marty Robbins, Johnny Cash, Doodles Weaver, Connie Smith, Marty Robbins, Richard Arlen; **D:** Robert Patrick. *NO*

Road to Nhill ♫♫ 1997 Very Aussie comedy filled with eccentric characters. An isolated, rural community is thrown into a tizzy when four female members of the local bowling team are in an accident that traps them in their overturned car. Volunteer emergency services rush into action but head off in the wrong direction and the women finally manage to free themselves, with various local yokels inept aid at the scene. Ensemble cast is fine. **95m/C VHS.** *AU* Lynette Curran, Patricia Kennedy, Lois Ramsey, Monica Maugham, Paul Chubb, Bill Hunter, Kerry Walker, Matthew Dyktynski, Terry Norris, Bill Young, Tony Barry, Alwyn Kurts; **D:** Sue Brooks; **W:** Alison Tilson; **C:** Nicolette Freeman; **M:** Elizabeth Drake. Nominations: Australian Film Institute '97: Best Original Screenplay, Best Score. *NYR*

The Road to Rio ♫♫♫½ 1947 The wisecracking duo travel to Rio de Janeiro to prevent Spanish beauty Lamour (there she is again) from going through with an arranged marriage. Top-notch entry; fifth in the "Road" series. ♫But Beautiful; You Don't Have To Know the Language; For What?; Experience; Apalachicola, Florida; Cavaquinho; Brazil. **100m/B VHS, Beta.** Bing Crosby, Bob Hope, Dorothy Lamour, Gale Sondergaard, Frank Faylen, The Andrews Sisters; **D:** Norman Z. McLeod; **W:** Jack Rose; **C:** Ernest Laszlo. Nominations: Academy Awards '47: Best Original Dramatic/Comedy Score. *COL*

The Road to Ruin ♫♫ 1928 The evils of smoking and drinking plummet a girl into a life of prostitution in this melodramatic, moralistic tale. An unintentional laugh-riot right up there with "Reefer Madness." Silent. **45m/B VHS, Beta.** Helen Foster, Grant Withers, Virginia Roye; **D:** Norton S. Parker; **W:** Erik Anjou. *SNC, NOS, VYY*

Road to Ruin ♫♫ 1991 (R) A rich playboy pretends to lose all his money to see if his girlfriend loves him for himself or for his wealth. But when his business partner embezzles his fortune, he must regain both his money and his girlfriend's trust. **CW:** Sexuality. **94m/C VHS.** Peter Weller, Carey Lowell, Michael Duchaussoy; **D:** Charlotte Brandstrom. *ART*

Road to Salina ♫♫♫ 1968 (R) A drifter is mistaken for (and might actually be) a desert-restaurant owner's long-lost son. He plays along, eventually seducing the family's daughter, who might be his sister. **97m/C VHS, Beta.** *FR* Robert Walker Jr., Rita Hayworth, Mimsy Farmer, Ed Begley Sr.; **D:** Georges Lautner. *NLC*

The Road to Singapore ♫♫½ 1940 This is the movie that started it all. Crosby and Hope decide to swear off women and escape to Singapore to enjoy the free life. There they meet Lamour, a showgirl who is abused by Quinn. The boys rescue Lamour, but soon find they are both falling for her. She's in love with one of them, but won't reveal her feelings. Who will get the girl? Not as funny as some of the other road movies, but it's great for a first try. ♫Captain Custard; The Moon and the Willow Tree; Sweet Potato Piper; Too Romantic; Kaigoon. **84m/C VHS, LV.** Bing Crosby, Bob Hope, Dorothy Lamour, Charles Coburn, Judith Barrett, Anthony Quinn, Jerry Colonna, Johnny Arthur,

Pierre Watkin; **D:** Victor Schertzinger; **C:** William Mellor. *USH*

The Road to Utopia 🎬🎬🎬 1946
Fourth of the "Road" films, wherein the boys wind up in Alaska posing as two famous escaped killers in order to locate a secret gold mine. One of the series' funniest and most spontaneous entries, abetted by Benchley's dry, upper-crust comments. 🎵Put It There, Pal; Welcome to My Dreams; Would You?; Personality; Sunday, Monday, or Always?; Goodtime Charlie; It's Anybody's Spring. **90m/B VHS, Beta, LV.** Bing Crosby, Bob Hope, Dorothy Lamour, Jack LaRue, Robert Benchley, Douglass Dumbrille, Hillary Brooke; **D:** Hal Walker; **W:** Norman Panama; **C:** Lionel Linden. Nominations: Academy Awards '46: Best Original Screenplay. *USH*

The Road to Wellville 🎬🎬 1994 (R)
Corn flake magnate John Harvey Kellogg takes good health to an intestine-invading extreme in this spa satire featuring Hopkins as the buck-toothed Kellogg. Broderick and Fonda portray a wealthy couple who visit the turn-of-the-century sanitarium in search of Kellogg's cure, but receive only sexual frustration and anal humiliations. Bowel jokes and an essentially plotless scenario overshadow a gifted, but helpless cast. Adapted from T. Coraghessan Boyle's not-so-easily-adaptable novel.**CW:** Contains nudity, sexual situations, and incessant bathroom humor. **120m/C VHS, LV, Closed Caption.** Anthony Hopkins, Bridget Fonda, Matthew Broderick, John Cusack, Dana Carvey, Michael Lerner, Colm Meaney, John Neville, Lara Flynn Boyle, Traci Lind, Roy Brocksmith, Norbert Weisser; **D:** Alan Parker; **W:** Alan Parker; **C:** Peter Biziou; **M:** Rachel Portman. *COL*

The Road to Yesterday 🎬🎬½ 1925
Two couples together on a crashing train are somehow thrown into the 18th century in roles parallel to their own lives. DeMille's first independent film; intriguing action/melodrama. Silent with musical soundtrack. **136m/B VHS, Beta.** Joseph Schildkraut, William Boyd, Jetta Goudal, Vera Reynolds, Iron Eyes Cody; **D:** Cecil B. DeMille. *GPV, VYY*

Road to Yesterday/The Yankee Clipper 🎬🎬½ 1927
Four train passengers are transported back to previous lives in "The Road to Yesterday." "The Yankee Clipper" races the British Lord of the Isles from China to New England to capture the tea trade. Both of these pictures are abridged versions. Silent. **56m/B VHS, Beta.** William Boyd, Elinor Fair, Joseph Schildkraut, Jetta Goudal, Vera Reynolds; **D:** Cecil B. DeMille. *CCB*

The Road to Zanzibar 🎬🎬🎬 1941
After selling a fake diamond mine to a criminal, Crosby and Hope flee to Zanzibar, where they meet up with Lamour and Merkel. The guys put up the money for a safari, supposedly to look for Lamour's brother, but they soon discover that they too have been tricked. Deciding to head back to Zanzibar, Crosby and Hope find themselves surrounded by hungry cannibals. Will they survive, or will they be someone's dinner? Not as funny as the other road movies, but amusing nonetheless. 🎵It's Always You; You're Dangerous; On the Road to Zanzibar; You Lucky People You; Birds of a Feather; African Etude. **92m/C VHS, LV.** Bing Crosby, Bob Hope, Dorothy Lamour, Una Merkel, Eric Blore, Iris Adrian, Lionel Royce; **D:** Victor Schertzinger. *USH*

The Road Warrior 🎬🎬🎬½ 1982 (R)
The first sequel to "Mad Max" takes place after nuclear war has destroyed Australia. Max helps a colony of oil-drilling survivors defend themselves from the roving murderous outback gangs and escape to the coast. The climactic chase scene is among the most exciting ever filmed; this film virtually created the "action-adventure" picture of the 1980s. **95m/C VHS, Beta, LV, Letterbox, DVD.** Mel Gibson, Bruce Spence, Emil Minty, Vernon Wells; **D:** George Miller; **W:** George Miller; **C:** Dean Semler; **M:** Brian May. Los Angeles Film Critics Association Awards '82: Best Foreign Film. *WAR*

Roadhouse Girl 🎬 *Marilyn* 1953
A sexy woman kindles a romance with one of her husband's employees and the result is murder. Reminiscent of "The Postman Always Rings Twice," but with poor production values and performances. **70m/B VHS, Beta.** *GB* Maxwell Reed, Sandra Dorne, Leslie Dwyer, Vida Hope, Ferdinand "Ferdy" Mayne; **D:** Wolf Rilla; **W:** Wolf Rilla. *SNC*

Roadhouse 66 🎬½ 1984 (R)
Utterly unoriginal broke-down-in-a-hick-town nonsense. Snooty Reinhold and scruffy Dafoe go through the motions, and of course find a pair of female companions. Soundtrack features Los Lobos, the Pretenders, and Dave Edmunds. **90m/C VHS, Beta.** Willem Dafoe, Judge Reinhold, Karen Lee, Kate Vernon, Stephen Elliott; **D:** John Mark Robinson; **C:** Thomas Ackerman. *FOX*

Roadie 🎬½ 1980 (PG)
Supposedly a look at the back-stage world of rock 'n' roll, but the performance and direction leave a lot to be desired. Meatloaf is a roadie who desperately wants to meet Alice Cooper, and spends the movie trying to do so. Features Art Carney, and musical names like Blondie, Roy Orbison, Hank Williams, Jr., and Don Cornelius (of "Soul Train" fame). **105m/C VHS.** Meat Loaf, Kaki Hunter, Art Carney, Gailard Sartain, Alice Cooper, Roy Orbison, Hank Williams Jr., Ramblin' Jack Elliot; **D:** Alan Rudolph; **W:** Alan Rudolph, Michael Ventura. *MVD, MGM*

Roadkill 🎬 1989
Cheap thriller about Ramona (Buhagiar), a concert promoter who tries to find a lost band, "The Children of Paradise," in the Canadian north woods. Along the way, she meets a would-be serial killer and other assorted weirdos. **85m/B VHS.** *CA* Valerie Buhagiar, Don McKellar, Bruce McDonald; **D:** Bruce McDonald; **W:** Don McKellar. Toronto-City Award '89: Best Canadian Feature Film. *NO*

Roadracers 🎬🎬½ 1994 (R)
Homage/satire of 1950s teen-rebel drive-in movies. Rebellious, wrong-side-of-the-tracks Dude Delaney (Arquette) plays rock 'n' roll guitar, has a sexy Hispanic girlfriend, Donna (Hayek), and wants to leave his small Texas hometown in his rearview mirror. But first Dude gets into trouble with gang leader Teddy (Wiles), whose dad just happens to be the self-righteous local sheriff, Sarge (Sadler). Originally shown as part of Showtime's "Rebel Highway" series.**CW:** Language and some violence. **93m/C VHS, LV, Closed Caption.** David Arquette, Salma Hayek, William Sadler, Jason Wiles, John Hawkes, Karen Landry, Lance LeGault, Helen Shaver, O'Neal Compton, Johnny Reno; **D:** Robert Rodriguez; **W:** Robert Rodriguez, Tommy Nix; **C:** Roberto Schaefer; **M:** Paul Boll, Johnny Reno. *TOU*

Roads to the South 🎬🎬½ *Les Routes du Sud* 1978
One-time Spanish revolutionary turned screenwriter returns to his homeland to fight fascism, but finds himself attracted to his son's beautiful girlfriend. Much soul searching. In French with English subtitles. **100m/C VHS, LV.** *FR* Yves Montand, Miou-Miou, Laurent Malet; **D:** Joseph Losey; **W:** Jorge Semprun; **M:** Michel Legrand. *CVC, FCT, IME*

Roadside Prophets 🎬🎬½ 1992 (R)
Counter-culture road trip, striving to be the '90s version of "Easy Rider," follows factory worker/biker Joe (Doe) on his mission to transport the ashes of a fellow biker to Nevada. He is accompanied by the pesky younger Sam (Horovitz), and together they meet up with lots of eccentrics and stay at lots of cheap motels. Interesting cast meanders through sentimental and slow-moving buddy flick from debut director Wool, who wrote "Sid and Nancy." Cusack completes the cameo hat trick, with appearances here and in 1992's "The Player" and "Shadows and Fog." **CW:** Language and drug use scene. **96m/C VHS, LV, Closed Caption.** John Doe, Adam Horovitz, David Carradine, Timothy Leary, Arlo Guthrie, Barton Heyman, Jennifer Balgobin; *Cameos:* John Cusack; **D:** Abbe Wool; **W:** Abbe Wool. *NLC*

The Roamin' Cowboy 🎬🎬 1937
In a town where the local ranchers are being threatened, a drifter comes to their rescue and wins both a girl and a job. **56m/B VHS.** Fred Scott, Al "Fuzzy" St. John, Lois January, Forrest Taylor, Roger Williams; **D:** Robert F. "Bob" Hill. *NOS, DVT*

Roamin' Wild 🎬🎬½ 1936
Exciting, action-packed early western with marshal Tyler saving a lady's stagecoach line from unsavory varmints. **60m/B VHS, Beta.** Tom Tyler, Carol Wyndham, Al Ferguson, George Chesebro, Max Davidson, Fred Parker; **D:** Bernard B. Ray. *NOS, DVT*

Roanoak 🎬🎬½ 1986
A dramatization in three parts of the mysterious fate of the early English settlement of Roanoke in North Carolina, which disappeared without a trace. Long, but intriguing. Made for PBS: "American Playhouse." **180m/C Beta.** Will Sampson, Victoria Racimo, Porky White, Adrian Sparks, Patrick Kilpatrick; **D:** Jan Egleson. *PBS*

Roarin' Lead 🎬½ 1937
Three Mesquiteers fight with a gang of rustlers while helping the orphans' and cattlemen's associations. **54m/B VHS, Beta.** Bob Livingston, Ray Corrigan, Max Terhune. *VCN*

Roaring City 🎬½ 1951
A hard-boiled detective searches for the person behind the murders of gangsters and prize fighters. **58m/B VHS, Beta, LV.** Hugh Beaumont, Edward Brophy, Richard Travis; **D:** William (Lester Williams) Berke. *NO*

Roaring Guns 🎬🎬 1936
An unflappable McCoy rides in to thwart a despicable landowner trying to drive all the small ranchers out of business. Low-budget fun. **66m/B VHS, Beta.** Tim McCoy, Rex Lease, Wheeler Oakman; **D:** Sam Newfield. *NOS, VCN, DVT*

Roaring Ranch 🎬½ 1930
Gibson is trying to protect his ranch from the evil Oakman while attempting to care for a baby as well. **65m/B VHS.** Hoot Gibson, Wheeler Oakman, Sally Eilers, Bobby Nelson, Frank Clark; **D:** B. Reeves Eason; **W:** B. Reeves Eason. *GPV*

The Roaring Road 🎬🎬½ 1919
Romantic comedy about a car salesman named Toodles, who drives for his company in a big race. Vintage racing footage; silent with original organ music. **57m/B VHS, 8mm.** Wallace Reid, Ann Little, Theodore Roberts; **D:** James Cruze. *VYY, GPV, GVV*

Roaring Roads 🎬 1935
An heir to a fortune acquires a lust for race car driving, and his family thinks, a reckless death wish. **60m/B VHS, Beta, LV.** Gertrude Messinger, David Sharpe. *NO*

Roaring Six Guns 🎬½ 1937
Maynard protects his property against his crooked partner and his fiancee's father. **60m/B VHS, Beta.** Kermit Maynard, Mary Hayes, John Merton, Edward Cassidy. *NOS, DVT, VCN*

Roaring Speedboats 🎬 *Mile a Minute Love* 1937
Bakewell is a speedboat racer up against crooks who want to con him out of his money by tinkering with his invention. **62m/B VHS, Beta, 8mm.** William "Billy" Bakewell, Arletta Duncan, Duncan Renaldo, Vivien Oakland, Wilfrid Lucas; **D:** Elmer Clifton. *VYY*

The Roaring Twenties 🎬🎬🎬 1939
Three WWI buddies find their lives intersecting unexpectedly in Prohibition-era New York. Cagney becomes a bootlegger and vies with Bogart for status as crime boss. Lynn is the attorney working to prosecute them. Greatest of all gangster flicks. Cheesy script delivered with zest by top pros. **106m/B VHS, Beta, LV, Closed Caption.** James Cagney, Humphrey Bogart, Jeffrey Lynn, Priscilla Lane, Gladys George, Frank McHugh; **D:** Raoul Walsh. *MGM, FOX*

Rob Roy 🎬🎬🎬 1995 (R)
Kilt-raising though overlong tale of legendary Scot Robert Roy MacGregor mixes love and honor with bloodlust and revenge. Neeson's rugged clan leader fends off a band of dastardly nobles led by Cunningham (Roth), a foppish twit with an evil bent. Misty highland scenery and intense romantic interplay between Neeson and Lange as the spirited Mary MacGregor lend a passionate twist to an other-

wise earthy, robust adventure of lore capped by one of the best sword fights in years. Both Neeson and Lange provide a gutsy substance to their characters: Neeson's Celtic hero is sexy and steadfast (and generally sports an Irish accent), while Lange inhabits a soulful and tenacious Mary. Roth's delightfully hammy performance as MacGregor's loathsome, bewigged nemesis delivers zip amid the high-minded speeches, plot lulls, and separated body parts. Visually stunning, with on-location shooting in the Scottish Highlands. More ambience is provided by Buswell's evocative score. **CW:** Sexuality and violence, including a rape scene and a lot of bloody swordplay. **144m/C VHS, LV, Closed Caption.** Liam Neeson, Jessica Lange, Tim Roth, John Hurt, Eric Stoltz, Andrew Keir, Brian Cox, Brian McCardie, Gilbert Martin, Vicki Masson, David Hayman; **D:** Michael Caton-Jones; **W:** Alan Sharp; **C:** Karl Walter Lindenlaub. British Academy Awards '95: Best Supporting Actor (Roth); Nominations: Academy Awards '95: Best Supporting Actor (Roth); Golden Globe Awards '96: Best Supporting Actor (Roth). *MGM*

Rob Roy—The Highland Rogue 🐾½ *Rob Roy* 1953 In the early 18th century, Scottish Highlander Rob Roy must battle against the King of England's secretary, who would undermine the MacGregor clan to enact his evil deeds. Dull Disney drama. **84m/C VHS, Beta.** Richard Todd, Glynis Johns, James Robertson Justice, Michael Gough; **D:** Harold French. *DIS*

Robbers of the Sacred Mountain 🐾🐾 *Falcon's Gold* 1983 TV rip-off of "Raiders of the Lost Ark," loosely based on Arthur Conan Doyle's story "Challenger's Gold." Adventurers seek meteorites in the Mexican jungle. Billed as the first made for cable movie. **95m/C VHS, Beta.** John Marley, Simon MacCorkindale, Louise Vallance, George Touliatos; **D:** Bob Schulz.

Robbery 🐾🐾½ 1967 Unoriginal but competent rendition of the hackneyed British Royal Mail robbery. Thieves plan and execute a heist of a late-night mail train carrying $10 million. **113m/C VHS, Beta.** **GB** Stanley Baker, James Booth, Joanna Pettet, Frank Finlay, Barry Foster; **D:** Peter Yates. *NLC*

Robbery 🐾 1985 A six-man platoon of Vietnam war veterans endeavors to assault and rob a mob of shiftless looters. **91m/C VHS, Beta.** Jim Sheerin, Tony Rickards, Tim Hughes; **D:** Michael Thornhill. *ART*

Robbery Under Arms 🐾🐾½ 1957 From Australia in the 1800s, similar to the American wild west, comes a tale of love and robbery. Finch is the leader of a band of outlaws. Rather dull story redeemed by excellent photography of beautiful landscape. **83m/C VHS.** **GB** Peter Finch, Ronald Lewis, Laurence Naismith, Maureen Swanson, David McCallum, Jill Ireland; **D:** Jack Lee. *IMP*

Robby 🐾🐾 1968 A young white boy and a young black boy shipwrecked on an island form a strong friendship that sees them through a series of adventures. **60m/C VHS, Beta.** Warren Raum, Ryp Siani, John Garces; **D:** Ralph Blumke. *FCT*

The Robe 🐾🐾½ 1953 This moving, religious portrait follows the career and religious awakening of drunken and dissolute Roman tribune Marcellus (Burton), after he wins the robe of the just-crucified Christ in a dice game. Mature plays Burton's slave surprisingly well, and reprised the role in the sequel, "Demetrius and the Gladiators"; Burton is wooden. "The Robe" was the first movie to be filmed in CinemaScope. Based on the novel by Lloyd C. Douglas. **133m/C VHS, Beta, LV, Letterbox.** Richard Burton, Jean Simmons, Victor Mature, Michael Rennie, Richard Boone, Dean Jagger, Jeff Morrow, Jay Robinson, Dawn Addams, Ernest Thesiger; **D:** Henry Koster; **W:** Albert Maltz, Philip Dunne; **C:** Leon Shamroy. Academy Awards '53: Best Art Direction/Set Decoration (Color), Best Costume Design (Color); Golden Globe Awards '54: Best Film—Drama; National Board of Review Awards '53: Best Actress (Simmons); Nominations: Academy Awards '53: Best Actor (Burton), Best Color Cinematography, Best Picture. *FOX, IGP*

Robert et Robert 🐾🐾🐾 1978 Two 'ineligible' bachelors resort to using a computerized matrimonial agency to find the girls of their dreams. They become friends while they wait for their dates. Sensitive tale of loneliness and friendship. Warm and witty with fine performances throughout. French with English subtitles. **105m/C VHS, Beta.** **FR** Charles Denner, Jacques Villeret, Jean-Claude Brialy, Macha Meril, Germaine Montero, Regine; **D:** Claude Lelouch; **W:** Claude Lelouch; **C:** Jacques Lefrancois. Cesar Awards '79: Best Supporting Actor (Villeret). *COL*

Robert Kennedy and His Times 🐾🐾½ 1990 Another look at the Kennedy clan, this time from the Bobby angle. Good acting. Based on the book by Arthur Schlesinger. **309m/C VHS.** Brad Davis, Veronica Cartwright, Cliff DeYoung, Ned Beatty, Beatrice Straight, Jack Warden; **D:** Marvin J. Chomsky. *COL, PBS*

Roberta 🐾🐾🐾 1935 A football player inherits his aunt's Parisian dress shop and finds himself at odds with an incognito Russian princess. Dumb plot aside, this is one of the best Astaire-Rogers efforts. A later remake was titled "Lovely to Look At." ♫Let's Begin; Yesterdays; Smoke Gets in Your Eyes; I'll Be Hard to Handle; I Won't Dance; Lovely to Look At; Back Home Again in Indiana; The Touch of Your Hand; You're Devasting. **85m/B VHS, Beta.** Fred Astaire, Ginger Rogers, Irene Dunne, Lucille Ball, Randolph Scott; **D:** William A. Seiter; **M:** Max Steiner. Nominations: Academy Awards '35: Best Song ("Lovely to Look At"). *MGM*

Robin and Marian 🐾🐾 1976 (PG) After a separation of 20 years, Robin Hood is reunited with Maid Marian, who is now a nun. Their dormant feelings for each other are reawakened as Robin spirits her to Sherwood Forest. In case you wanted to see Robin Hood robbed of all magic, spontaneity, and fun. Connery is dull, dull, dull, working with an uninspired script. **106m/C VHS, Beta, LV.** **GB** Sean Connery, Audrey Hepburn, Robert Shaw, Richard Harris, Denholm Elliott, Ian Holm, Nicol Williamson, Ronnie Barker; **D:** Richard Lester; **C:** David Watkin; **M:** John Barry. *COL, FOX*

Robin and the 7 Hoods 🐾🐾½ 1964 Runyon-esque Rat Pack version of 1920s Chicago, with Frank and the boys as do-good gangsters in their last go-round. Fun if not unforgettable. ♫Bang! Bang!; Style; Mister Booze; Don't be a Do-Badder; My Kind of Town. **124m/C VHS, Beta, LV, Letterbox.** Frank Sinatra, Bing Crosby, Dean Martin, Sammy Davis Jr., Peter Falk, Barbara Rush, Allen Jenkins; **D:** Gordon Douglas. Nominations: Academy Awards '64: Best Adapted Score, Best Song ("My Kind of Town"). *WAR*

Robin Hood 🐾🐾🐾 1922 Extravagant production casts Fairbanks as eponymous gymnastic swashbuckler who departs for Crusades as Earl of Huntington and returns as the hooded one to save King Richard's throne from the sinister Sheriff of Nottingham. Best ever silent swashbuckling. **110m/B VHS, Beta.** Douglas Fairbanks Sr., Wallace Beery, Sam DeGrasse, Enid Bennett, Paul Dickey, William E. Lowery, Roy Coulson, Bill Bennett, Merrill McCormick, Wilson Benge, Willard Louis, Alan Hale, Maine Geary, Lloyd Talman; **D:** Allan Dwan. *NOS, GPV, FCT*

Robin Hood 🐾🐾🐾 1973 This time the Sherwood Forest crew are portrayed by appropriate cartoon animals, hence, Robin is a fox, Little John a bear, etc. Good family fare, but not as memorable as other Disney features. **83m/C VHS, Beta, LV, Closed Caption. D:** Wolfgang Reitherman; **M:** George Bruns; **V:** Roger Miller, Brian Bedford, Monica Evans, Phil Harris, Andy Devine, Carol Shelley, Peter Ustinov, Terry-Thomas, Pat Buttram, George Lindsey, Ken Curtis. Nominations: Academy Awards '73: Best Song ("Love"). *DIS, FCT, RDG*

Robin Hood 🐾🐾🐾 1991 Dark version of the medieval tale. Bergin's Prince of Thieves is well developed and Thurman is a graceful Marion. Three studios announced plans to remake "Robin Hood" in 1990 and two were completed, including this one which was scaled down for cable television. **116m/C VHS, Beta, LV.** Patrick Bergin, Uma Thur-

man, Juergen Prochnow, Edward Fox, Jeroen Krabbe, Jeff Nuttal, David Morrisey, Owen Teale; **D:** John Irvin; **M:** Geoffrey Burgon. *FCT*

Robin Hood: Men in Tights 🐾🐾½ *Men in Tights* 1993 (PG-13) Brooksian rendition of the classic legend inspires guffaws, but doesn't hit the bullseye on all it promises. Hood afficionados will appreciate the painstaking effort taken to spoof the 1938 Errol Flynn classic while leaving plenty of room to poke fun at the more recent Costner non-classic "Robin Hood: Prince of Thieves." Elwes, last seen swinging swords in "The Princess Bride," is well cast as the Flynn look-alike. Expect the usual off-color humor that's so prevalent in all Brooks outings. **CW:** Off-color humor. **105m/C VHS, Closed Caption.** Cary Elwes, Richard Lewis, Roger Rees, Amy Yasbeck, Dave Chappelle, Isaac Hayes, Tracey Ullman, Mark Blankfield, Megan Cavanagh, Eric Allen Kramer, Tony Griffin, Dick Van Patten, Mel Brooks; **D:** Mel Brooks; **W:** Mel Brooks, J. David Shapiro, Evan Chandler; **M:** Hummie Mann. *FOX*

Robin Hood of Texas 🐾🐾½ 1947 Autry finds his calm life disturbed when he is falsely accused of robbing a bank. Pretty good plot for once, in Autry's last Republic western, and plenty of action. **71m/B VHS, Beta.** Gene Autry, Lynn (Mary Hart) Roberts, Sterling Holloway, Adele Mara; **D:** Lesley Selander. *NO*

Robin Hood of the Pecos 🐾🐾½ 1941 Ex-Confederate soldier takes on northern post-war politicians and carpetbaggers. Decent Rogers/Hayes outing. **56m/B VHS, Beta.** Roy Rogers, George "Gabby" Hayes, Marjorie Reynolds, Jay Novello, Roscoe Ates; **D:** Joseph Kane. *NOS, DVT, VYY*

Robin Hood: Prince of Thieves 🐾🐾½ 1991 (PG-13) Costner is the politically correct Rebel with a Cause, but a thinker, not a doer—and therein lies the problem. His quiet thoughtfulness doesn't add up to leadership and Rickman easily overpowers him as the wicked, crazed Sheriff of Nottingham. Freeman is excellent as a civilized Moor who finds England, and its people, inhospitable, dangerous, and not a little stupid. Mastrantonio, a last minute choice, excels as the lovely Lady Marian. Great action sequences, a gritty and morbid picture of the Middle Ages, and some fun scenes with the Merry Men. Revisionist in its ideas about the times and people, critics generally disapproved of the changes in the story and Costner's performance, though their comments about his lack of an English accent seem nitpicky in light of some basic plot problems. Still has lots of fun for lovers of action, romance and fairy tales. **144m/C VHS, LV, Letterbox, Closed Caption.** Kevin Costner, Morgan Freeman, Mary Elizabeth Mastrantonio, Christian Slater, Alan Rickman, Geraldine McEwan, Micheal McShane, Brian Blessed, Michael Wincott, Nick Brimble, Harold Innocent, Jack Wild; **Cameos:** Sean Connery; **D:** Kevin Reynolds; **W:** Pen Densham, John Watson; **M:** Michael Kamen. British Academy Awards '91: Best Supporting Actor (Rickman); MTV Movie Awards '92: Best Song ("(Everything I Do) I Do for You"); Golden Raspberry Awards '91: Worst Actor (Costner); Nominations: Academy Awards '91: Best Song ("(Everything I Do) I Do It for You"). *WAR, RDG*

Robin Hood: The Movie 1955 A colorized and re-mixed version of several episodes of the British television series adds up to a fine version of the classic tale. Excellent cast, clever editing and stunning colorization. **90m/C VHS.** **GB** Richard Greene, Bernadette O'Farrell, Alan Wheatley; **D:** Ralph Smart, Daniel Birt, Terence Fisher. *GKK*

Robin Hood...The Legend: Herne's Son 🐾🐾½ 1985 When Robin Hood is killed by the Sheriff of Nottingham, he begs Robert of Huntington (Connery) to continue his work. Connery refuses, the band dissolves, Maid Marion is kidnapped, and they reunite to save her. Good entry in the BBC series. **101m/C VHS, Beta, Closed Caption.** **GB** Jason Connery, Oliver Cotton, Michael Craig, Nickolas Grace, George Baker; **D:** Robert M. Young. *FOX, FCT, TVC*

Robin Hood...The Legend: Robin Hood and the Sorcerer 🎬🎬½ 1983

Robin Hood is chosen by the mystical Herne the Hunter to thwart the evil Sheriff of Nottingham and protect the English peasantry. He must defeat the supernatural powers of a sorcerer and gather together his men in this introduction to the made for British television series. **115m/C VHS, Closed Caption.** *GB* Michael Praed, Anthony Valentine, Nickolas Grace, Clive Mantle, Peter Williams; *D:* Ian Sharp. FOX, FCT, TVC

Robin Hood...The Legend: The Swords of Wayland 🎬🎬½ 1983

A wicked sorceress provides a supernatural threat to Robin and his merry men. Second entry in the BBC series. Convoluted, breathless plot makes for swashbuckling fun and much derring-do. **115m/C VHS, Beta, Closed Caption.** *GB* Michael Praed, Rula Lenska, Nickolas Grace; *D:* Robert M. Young. FOX, FCT

Robin Hood...The Legend: The Time of the Wolf 🎬🎬½ 1985

Robin Hood finds out that an old enemy is about to release his evil doings on the world and only he can stop him, while Maid Marian comes to a momentous decision. **105m/C VHS, Beta, Closed Caption.** *GB* Jason Connery, Nickolas Grace, Richard O'Brien; *D:* Syd Roberson. FOX, FCT, TVC

Robin of Locksley 🎬🎬½ 1995 (PG)

A modern-day, teenaged Robin Hood (Sawa) battles the bullies at his private boys school (thanks to his archery prowess), meets a girl named Marian, and takes on sinister FBI agent Nottingham. **97m/C VHS.** Devon Sawa, Sarah Chalke, Joshua Jackson; *D:* Michael Kennedy. HMK

Robinson Crusoe 🎬🎬 1936

A real oddity: a British silent film originally made in 1927, re-edited ten years later. Music and sound effects were added, along with a narration by children's radio personality Carney. Follows the plot of the famous adventure story by Daniel Defoe. **34m/B VHS, Beta.** VYY

Robinson Crusoe & the Tiger 🎬½ 1972 (G)

A tiger tells the famous story of how Robinson Crusoe became stranded on a desert island. **109m/C VHS, Beta, Closed Caption.** Hugo Stiglitz, Ahui; *D:* Rene Cardona Jr.

Robinson Crusoe of Clipper Island 🎬🎬 1936

Fourteen-episode serial featuring the investigative expertise of Mala, a Polynesian in the employ of the U.S. Intelligence Service. Each episode runs 16 minutes. Shortened version titled "Robinson Crusoe of Mystery Island." **256m/B VHS, LV.** Mala, Rex, Buck, Kate Greenfield, John Ward, Tracy Lane, Robert F. (Bob) Kortman, Herbert Rawlinson; *D:* Mack V. Wright. SNC, NOS, REP

Robinson Crusoe of Mystery Island 🎬🎬 1936

A Polynesian employed by the U.S. Intelligence Service investigates saboteurs on a mysterious island. Would-be cliffhanger is a yawner; where are the chills and thrills? Edited from the serial "Robinson Crusoe of Clipper Island." **100m/B VHS, Beta.** Mala, Rex, Buck, Herbert Rawlinson, Ray Taylor; *D:* Mack V. Wright. VCN

Robinson Crusoe on Mars 🎬 1964

Sci-fi interpretation of Defoe classic. West is one of two daring scientists who take a monkey with them on a mission to outer space. When a meteor strikes their ship, it hurtles out of control towards the red planet and only Mantee and Mona survive the wreckage. They meet Lundin, an escaped slave and teach him English until evil slave traders spoil the fun. **109m/C LV.** Adam West, Vic Lundin, Paul Mantee; *D:* Byron Haskin; *W:* Ib Melchior, John C. Higgins; *C:* Winton C. Hoch; *M:* Nathan Van Cleave. IME

Robo-Chic Cyber-Chic 1989

A woman who is part cop, part machine, becomes a defender of justice. **90m/C VHS, Beta.** Kathy Shower, Jack Carter, Burt Ward, Lyle Waggoner; *D:* Ed Hansen, Jeffrey Mandel.

RoboCop 🎬🎬🎬 1987 (R)

A nearly dead Detroit cop is used as the brain for a crime-fighting robot in this bleak vision of the future. Humor, satire, action, and violence keep this moving in spite of its underlying sadness. Slick animation techniques from Phil Tippet. Verhoeven's first American film. **103m/C VHS, Beta, LV, Letterbox, Closed Caption.** Peter Weller, Nancy Allen, Ronny Cox, Kurtwood Smith, Ray Wise, Miguel Ferrer, Dan O'Herlihy, Robert DoQui, Felton Perry, Paul McCrane, Del Zamora; *D:* Paul Verhoeven; *W:* Michael Miner, Edward Neumeier; *C:* Jan De Bont; *M:* Basil Poledouris. Nominations: Academy Awards '87: Best Film Editing, Best Sound. ORI

RoboCop 2 🎬🎬 1990 (R)

Grimer, more violent sequel to the initial fascinating look at the future, where police departments are run by corporations hungry for profit at any cost. A new and highly addictive drug has made Detroit more dangerous than ever. Robocop is replaced by a stronger cyborg with the brain of a brutal criminal. When the cyborg goes berserk, Robocop battles it and the drug lords for control of the city. Dark humor and graphic savagery, with little of the tenderness and emotion of the original. **117m/C VHS, Beta, LV, Closed Caption.** Peter Weller, Nancy Allen, Belinda Bauer, Dan O'Herlihy, Tom Noonan, Gabriel Damon, Galyn Gorg, Felton Perry, Patricia Charbonneau; *D:* Irvin Kershner; *W:* Walon Green. ORI

RoboCop 3 🎬½ 1991 (PG-13)

Robocop's new Japanese owners plan to build a huge, new, ultra-modern city (in place of the decrepit 21st-century Detroit) but first must evict thousands of people in this third installment of the "Robocop" films (which sat on the studio shelf before finally being released in 1993). There's an android Ninja warrior to do battle with Robo who's gone over to the rebel underground but the plot and action sequences are rehashed from better films. Watch the original. **104m/C VHS, LV, Closed Caption.** Robert John Burke, Nancy Allen, John Castle, CCH Pounder, Bruce Locke, Rip Torn, Remi Ryan, Felton Perry; *D:* Fred Dekker; *W:* Fred Dekker, Frank Miller; *M:* Basil Poledouris. ORI

RoboCop the Series: The Future of Law Enforcement 1994

Premiere episode of the TV series, based on the movie about the unstoppable 21st-century Detroit robocop with the human touch. A murderous corporate creep and a mad doctor team up for nefarious corporate shenanigans. Helping out our hero is a murdered secretary who is merged into the city's central computer as Neuro-Brain. **?m/C VHS, LV.** Richard Eden, Andrea Roth, Cliff DeYoung, John Rubinstein. ORI

Roboman 🎬🎬½ Who? 1975 (PG)

American scientist gets in car crash in Soviet Union. When he returns to the States as a cyborg, his friends seem to notice a change. **91m/C VHS.** *GB* Elliott Gould, Trevor Howard, Joe Bova, Ed Grover, James Noble, John Lehne; *D:* Jack Gold. ACE, MTX

Robot Holocaust 🎬🎬 1987

Somewhere in the doomed future, after the Earth is laid waste by robots with superior intelligence, a human survivor dares to challenge them. If you're doomed to watch this, you just might survive; it's so-so, unsurprisingly sci-fi. **79m/C VHS, Beta.** Norris Culf, Nadine Hart, Joel von Ornsteiner, Jennifer Delora, Andrew Howarth, Angelika Jager, Rick Gianisi; *D:* Tim Kincaid; *W:* Tim Kincaid. NO

Robot in the Family 🎬🎬 1994

Slapstick comedy about Alex and his wacky but endearing robot who embark on a race against time through the streets of New York to track down a priceless antique that could save Alex's family from financial ruin. **92m/C VHS.** Joe Pantoliano, John Rhys-Davies, Danny Gerard, Amy Wright, Tom Signorelli, Peter Maloney, John Wylie, David Shuman, Matthew Locricchio; *D:* Mark Richardson, Jack Shaoul; *W:* Jack Shaoul; *M:* Papo Gely, Ted Mason; *V:* Don Peoples. APX

Robot Jox 🎬½ 1990 (PG)

Two futuristic warriors battle to the finish in giant mechanical robots. Preteen fare. **84m/C VHS, LV, Closed Caption.** Gary Graham, Anne-Marie Johnson, Paul Koslo, Robert Sampson, Danny Kamekona, Hilary Mason, Michael All-

dredge; *D:* Stuart Gordon; *W:* Joe Haldeman; *C:* Mac Ahlberg. COL

Robot Monster 🎬🎬½ Monsters From the Moon 1953

Ludicrous cheapie is widely considered one of the worst films of all time, as a single alien dressed in a moth-eaten gorilla suit and diving helmet conspires to take over the Earth from his station in a small, bubble-filled California cave. Available in original 3-D format. **84m/B VHS, LV.** George Nader, Claudia Barrett, Gregory Moffett, Selena Royle; *D:* Phil Tucker; *M:* Elmer Bernstein. EEL, RHI, FCT

Robot Pilot 🎬 Emergency Landing 1941

Tuck-er stars as a WWII test pilot trying to promote a friend's invention. Along the way, he's involved in a subplot with enemy agents who steal a bomber. He also finds time to become romantically entangled with the boss' spoiled daughter. **68m/B VHS, Beta, 8mm.** Forrest Tucker, Carol Hughes, Evelyn Brent, Emmett Vogan, William Halligan; *D:* William Beaudine. VYY, SNC

The Robot vs. the Aztec Mummy woof! El Robot Humano; La Momia Azteca Contra el Robot Humano 1959

Grade-Z Mexican horror film pits a jealous mummy who guards a tomb against tomb robbers and the robot they invent. Special effects are laughable today—the robot's ears are lightbulbs—but true mummy movie fans might want to watch this one. Everyone else will probably be better off skipping it. **65m/B VHS, Beta.** *MX* Ramon Gay, Rosita Arenas, Crox Alvarado, Luis Aceves Cantaneda, Emma Rolden; *D:* Rafael Portillo; *W:* Alfredo Salazar. SNC, AOV, MRV

Robot Wars 🎬🎬 1993 (PG)

When what seems to be the last mega-robot on earth falls into enemy hands, a renegade pilot unearths another with the help of an engineer and archeologist to fight for the future of mankind. **106m/C VHS, Beta, LV, Closed Caption.** Don Michael Paul, Barbara Crampton, James Staley, Lisa Rinna, Danny Kamekona, Yuji Okumoto, J. Downing, Peter Haskell; *D:* Albert Band. PAR

Rocco and His Brothers 🎬🎬🎬½ Rocco et Ses Freres; Rocco E I Suoi Fratelli 1960

A modern classic from top director Visconti, about four brothers who move with their mother from the Italian countryside to Milan. Very long, sometimes ponderous, but engrossing, complex drama. Available shortened to 90 minutes, but the unedited version is much more rewarding. In Italian with English subtitles. **175m/B VHS, LV, Letterbox.** *IT* Alain Delon, Renato Salvatori, Annie Girardot, Katina Paxinou, Claudia Cardinale, Roger Hanin; *D:* Luchino Visconti; *M:* Nino Rota. VDM, CVC, TPV

The Rock 🎬🎬🎬 1996 (R)

Cage follows up his Oscar win with a big-budget action turn, with great results. In an attempt to get benefits for the families of soldiers killed in various covert operations, a decorated general (Harris) and his commando squad occupy Alcatraz island, taking hostages and threatening to unleash a deadly gas bomb on San Francisco. Biochemical weapons expert Stanley Goodspeed (Cage) is called in to disarm the rockets, aided by John Patrick Mason (Connery), only man to successfully escape from the island prison. Like most Simpson/Bruckheimer productions, credibility is stretched to the limit, but the action scenes and crisp pacing don't leave much time for pondering details, anyway. Connery, cool as ever, hasn't lost a step. Cage effectively plays up his character's inexperience at being the hero. Co-producer Don Simpson died of drug overdose during production. *CW:* Strong violence, language and a sex scene. **136m/C VHS, LV, Letterbox, Closed Caption.** Nicolas Cage, Sean Connery, Ed Harris, Michael Biehn, William Forsythe, David Morse, John Spencer, John C. McGinley, Tony Todd, Bokeem Woodbine, Danny Nucci, Vanessa Marcil, Claire Forlani, Gregory Sporleder; *D:* Michael Bay; *W:* Jonathan Hensleigh; *C:* John Schwartzman; *M:* Nick Glennie-Smith. MTV Movie Awards '97: Best On-Screen Duo (Sean Connery/Nicolas Cage); Nominations: Academy Awards '96: Best Sound; MTV Movie Awards '97: Best Film, Best Action Sequence. TOU

Rock-a-Doodle 🎬🎬½ 1992 (G) Little Edmond is knocked out during a storm and has an Elvis-influenced vision. He sees Chanticleer, the sun-raising rooster, tricked into neglecting his duties by an evil barnyard owl. Humiliated and scorned, the earnest young fowl leaves the farm and winds up in a Las Vegas-like city as an Elvis-impersonating singer (complete with pompadour) where he meets with success and all its trappings. Mildly amusing, but bland by today's standards of animation, with music which is certainly nothing to crow about. 77m/C VHS, LV. **D:** Don Bluth; **W:** David A. Weiss; **M:** Robert Folk; **V:** Glen Campbell, Christopher Plummer, Phil Harris, Sandy Duncan, Ellen Greene, Charles Nelson Reilly, Eddie Deezen, Toby Scott Granger, Sorrell Booke. HBO, MVD

Rock All Night 🎬🎬 1957 Typically trashy Corman quickie (filmed in five days on one set) about some wild '50s teens and, in this case, a couple of murderers. Seems Cloud Nine, the local teen hangout, is invaded by a couple of murderers who hold the kids hostage. It's up to the hipster bartender, known as Shorty because he's five-foot-one, to save the day. Unrelated concert footage of the Platters and the Blockbusters opens the film. 62m/B VHS. Dick Miller, Abby Dalton, Russell Johnson, Jonathan Haze, Robin Morse; **D:** Roger Corman. COL, MOV, MVD

Rock & Roll Cowboys 🎬 1992 Set in the near-future. Mickey LaGrange is a roadie who has dreams of playing his own songs and becoming a rock and roll star himself. When he meets the mysterious Damien Shard he just may get the opportunity and a lot more besides. Shard is the inventor of an instrument that taps directly into the brain to transform thought into music. When Mickey uses the instrument he becomes an instant success—until he notices some horrifying side effects. 83m/C VHS. Peter Phelps, David Franklin, John Doyle; **D:** Robert Stewart. MOV

Rock & Rule 🎬🎬 1983 Animated sword & sorcery epic with a rock soundtrack. Voices are provided by Deborah Harry, Cheap Trick, Lou Reed, and Iggy Pop. 85m/C VHS, Beta, LV. **D:** Clive A. Smith; **M:** Deborah Harry, Lou Reed, Iggy Pop; **V:** Paul LeMat, Susan Roman, Don Francks, Dan Hennessey, Chris Wiggins, Catherine Gallant, Catherine O'Hara. MGM

Rock & the Money-Hungry Party Girls 🎬 1989 A struggling musician battles against Gabor-sister-worshipping bimbos in an effort to find unpublished songs by a '50s music legend. 90m/C VHS, Beta. Paul Sercu, Adam Small, Judi Durand, Mary Baldwin, Debra Lamb; **D:** Kurt MacCarley. NO

Rock, Baby, Rock It 🎬 1957 Weak and silly rock-and-roll crime drama about teens trying to fight the Mafia in Dallas in 1957. Features performances by many regional bands including Kay Wheeler, the Cell Block Seven, Johnny Carroll, Preacher Smith and the Deacons, and the Five Stars. If you grew up in Dallas in the '50s, the musical groups may bring back some fond memories; otherwise, this obscure film probably isn't worth your time. 84m/B VHS, Beta. Kay Wheeler, John Carroll; **D:** Murray Douglas Sporup. RHI

Rock House 🎬🎬 1992 (R) When an L.A. narcotics officer's wife is murdered by drug runners he goes on an obsessive revenge mission to destroy the city's cocaine operations. 98m/C VHS. Joseph Jennings, Michael Robbin, Alan Shearer; **D:** Jack Vacek; **W:** Jack Vacek.

Rock Hudson's Home Movies 1992 Farr re-creates the character of the late actor over numerous film clips used to suggest homoerotic themes in Hudson's movies. Low-budget and high camp. 93m/C VHS. Eric Farr; **D:** Mark Rappaport; **W:** Mark Rappaport. WBF, PPI

Rock 'n' Roll High School 🎬🎬🎬 1979 (PG) The music of the Ramones highlights this non-stop high-energy cult classic about a high school trying to thwart the principal at every turn. If it had been made in 1957, it would have been the ultimate rock 'n' roll teen movie. As it is, its 1970s' milieu works against it, but the performances are perfect for the material and the Ramones are great. Songs include "Teenage Lobotomy," "Blitzkrieg Bop," "I Wanna Be Sedated," and the title track, among others. Followed less successfully by "Rock 'n' Roll High School Forever." 94m/C VHS, Beta, Closed Caption, DVD. The Ramones, P.J. Soles, Vincent Van Patten, Clint Howard, Dey Young, Mary Woronov, Alix Elias, Dick Miller, Paul Bartel; **D:** Allan Arkush; **C:** Dean Cundey. NHO, LUM

Rock 'n' Roll High School Forever 🎬 1991 (PG-13) Jesse Davis and his band just want to rock 'n' roll, but the new principal doesn't share their enthusiasm. Way late, way lame sequel to "Rock 'n' Roll High School" doesn't come close to the originality that made it a cult classic. Soundtrack includes music from The Divinyls, Dee Dee Ramone, Mojo Nixon, Will and the Bushmen, The Pursuit of Happiness, and more. 94m/C VHS, Beta, LV, Closed Caption. Corey Feldman, Mary Woronov, Mojo Nixon, Evan Richards, Michael Ceveris, Patrick Malone, Larry Linville, Sarah Buxton; **D:** Deborah Brock; **W:** Deborah Brock. ART, IME

Rock 'n' Roll Nightmare 🎬½ The Edge of Hell 1985 (R) A rock band is pursued by demons from another dimension. The usual lame garbage. 89m/C VHS, Beta. CA Jon Mikl Thor, Paula Francescatto, Rusty Hamilton; **D:** John Fasano.

Rock, Pretty Baby 🎬 1956 Early rock-'n'-roll movie about a teenage band and high school riots. 89m/B VHS, Beta. Sal Mineo, John Saxon, Rod McKuen, Luana Patten, Fay Wray, Edward Platt, Alan Reed Jr.; **D:** Richard Bartlett; **M:** Henry Mancini. BAR

Rock River Renegades 🎬 1942 The Range Busters capture a band of renegades and restore peace to the territory once more. 59m/B VHS, Beta. Ray Corrigan, John "Dusty" King. NOS, DVT

Rock, Rock, Rock 🎬🎬½ 1956 A young girl tries to earn enough money for a prom gown after her father closes her charge account. Screen debut of Tuesday Weld. Ultra-low-budget, but a classic after a fashion. Includes classic musical numbers performed by Chuck Berry and other rock 'n' roll pioneers. 78m/B VHS, Beta. Alan Freed, Chuck Berry, Fats Domino, Tuesday Weld; **D:** Will Price. MVD, MRV, SNC

Rockabye 🎬🎬½ 1986 Single mother Bertinelli is visiting New York with her two-year-old son when she's attacked and her child stolen. In her search for the boy, she discovers a black market in baby selling. ?m/C VHS. Valerie Bertinelli, Rachel Ticotin, Jason Alexander, Ray Baker, Dick Latessa, James Rebhorn, Lynne Thigpen; **D:** Richard Michaels. BFV

Rocket Attack U.S.A. woof! 1958 Antiquated and ridiculous tale of nuclear warfare about the time of Sputnik, with Russia's first strike blowing up New York City and environs. Mercifully short, with time for a little romance. Everything about this movie is so bad it's good for a laugh. 70m/B VHS, Beta. Monica Davis, John McKay, Dan Kern, Edward Czerniuk, Art Metrano; **D:** Barry Mahon. NO

Rocket Gibraltar 🎬🎬🎬 1988 (PG) On the occasion of a crusty patriarch's birthday, a large family unites on his remote estate to carry out his special birthday wish. Fine performance by Lancaster. Supported by a solid cast, overcomes a slim story, Culkin, later of "Home Alone," is loveable as the precocious five-year-old. Picturesque Long Island scenery. 92m/C VHS, Beta, Closed Caption. Burt Lancaster, Bill Pullman, John Glover, Suzy Amis, Macaulay Culkin, Patricia Clarkson, Frances Conroy, Sinead Cusack, Bill Martin, Kevin Spacey; **D:** Daniel Petrie; **W:** Amos Poe; **M:** Andrew Powell. COL

Rocket to the Moon 🎬🎬 1986 An adaptation of the Clifford Odets story about the mundane life of a 30-year-old Manhattan dentist and how he comes to terms with his life. From the PBS "American Playhouse" series. 118m/C VHS, Beta. Judy Davis, John Malkovich, Eli Wallach; **D:** John Jacobs. PBS

The Rocketeer 🎬🎬🎬 1991 (PG) Light headed fun. A stunt flyer in the 1930s finds a prototype jet backpack sought by Nazi spies. Donning a mask, he becomes a flying superhero. Breezy family entertainment with stupendous effects; even better if you know movie trivia, as it brims with Hollywood references, like a great villain (Dalton) clearly based on Errol Flynn. 109m/C VHS, Beta, LV, Letterbox, Closed Caption. Bill Campbell, Jennifer Connelly, Alan Arkin, Timothy Dalton, Paul Sorvino, Melora Hardin, Tiny Ron, Terry O'Quinn, Ed Lauter, James Handy; **D:** Joe Johnston; **W:** Danny Bilson, Paul DeMeo; **M:** James Horner. DIS, CCB, IME

RocketMan 🎬½ Rocket Man 1997 (PG) Houston, we have a gastrointestinal problem. Well, dumb astronaut Fred Z. Randall (Williams) does, anyway. The bumbling computer geek is picked to go on the first manned mission to Mars, much to the dismay of crew commander "Wild Bill" Overbeck (Sadler) and specialist Julie Ford (Lundy). Beau Bridges plays Bud Nesbitt, the veteran astronaut back at NASA headquarters who is Randall's only supporter. While too much of the humor revolves around flatulence, Williams shows some talent while raiding the Disney archive for impressions. Remember, in space no one can hear you...pull my finger. 93m/C VHS, LV, Closed Caption. Harland Williams, Jessica Lundy, Beau Bridges, William Sadler, Jeffrey DeMunn, James Pickens Jr., Peter Onorati; **D:** Stuart Gillard; **W:** Craig Mazin, Greg Erb; **C:** Steven Poster; **M:** Michael Tavera. TOU

Rocketship 🎬🎬 1936 Flash Gordon battles sea monsters, ray guns, and robots in this sci-fi adventure, which is an edited version of a Flash serial. ?m/B VHS. Buster Crabbe, Jean Rogers, Charles Middleton. LOO, HEG

Rocketship X-M 🎬🎬½ Expedition Moon 1950 A lunar mission goes awry and the crew lands on Mars, where they discover ancient ruins. Well acted and nicely photographed. Contains footage, a tinted sequence and previews of coming attractions from classis science fiction files. 77m/B VHS, LV. Lloyd Bridges, Osa Massen, John Emery, Hugh O'Brian, Noah Beery Jr.; **D:** Kurt Neumann. EEL, RXM

The Rockford Files: Backlash of the Hunter 1974 The two-part episode which launched the TV series about ex-con turned PI Jim Rockford, who lives (and works) in a beach trailer and only takes clients who have real trouble and real money. His first is a seemingly simple investigation into a man's death. His daughter wants to know if dad was murdered or really did commit suicide. 90m/C VHS. James Garner, Lindsay Wagner, William Smith, Nita Talbot, Joe Santos; **D:** Richard T. Heffron; **W:** Stephen J. Cannell. USH

Rockin' Road Trip 🎬 1985 (PG-13) A guy meets a girl in a Boston bar, and finds himself on a drunken, slapstick road trip down the Eastern seaboard with a rock band. 101m/C VHS, Beta. Garth McLean, Katherine Harrison, Margaret Currie, Steve Boles. FOX

The Rocking Horse Winner 🎬🎬½ 1949 Poignant tale of a young boy who discovers he can predict racehorse winners by riding his rocking horse. His spendthrift mother's greed leads to tragedy. Based on the short story by D.H. Lawrence. 91m/B VHS. GB John Howard Davies, Valerie Hobson, Hugh Sinclair; **D:** Anthony Pelissier. HMV

Rocktober Blood 🎬½ 1985 (R) A convicted and executed rock star comes back from the grave and starts killing people all over again. Yet another gorefest. 88m/C VHS, Beta. Donna Scoggins, Tray Loren, Nigel Benjamin, Beverly Sebastian; **D:** Ferd Sebastian. ART, VES

Rockula 🎬½ 1990 (PG-13) Teen rock comedy about a young-yet-300-year-old vampire looking to lose his virginity. Recommended only for hardcore Diddley fans. 90m/C VHS, Beta, LV, Closed Caption. Dean Cameron, Bo Diddley, Tawny Fere, Susan Tyrrell, Thomas Dolby, Toni Basil; **D:** Luca Bercovici; **W:** Luca Bercovici. MGM, WAR

Rockwell: A Legend of the Wild West ♂♂½ 1993 Black heroics in the wild west. U.S. Marshall Porter Rockwell and his posse of sharp shooters are after a vicious gang murdering supposed claim jumpers who just happen to be Rockwell's friends. **?m/C VHS, LV, Closed Caption.** Randy Gleave, Karl Malone, Michael Rudd, George Sullivan. *IMP*

Rocky ♂♂♂½ 1976 (PG) Boxoffice smash about a young man from the slums of Philadelphia who dreams of becoming a boxing champion. Stallone plays Rocky, the underdog hoping to win fame and self-respect. Rags-to-riches story seems to parallel Stallone's life; he had been previously virtually unknown before this movie. Intense portrayal of the American Dream; loses strength in the subsequent (and numerous) sequels. **125m/C VHS, Beta, LV, 8mm, DVD.** Sylvester Stallone, Talia Shire, Burgess Meredith, Burt Young, Carl Weathers; **D:** John G. Avildsen; **W:** Sylvester Stallone; **M:** Bill Conti. Academy Awards '76: Best Director (Avildsen), Best Film Editing, Best Picture; Directors Guild of America Awards '76: Best Director (Avildsen); Golden Globe Awards '77: Best Film—Drama; Los Angeles Film Critics Association Awards '76: Best Film; National Board of Review Awards '76: Best Supporting Actress (Shire); New York Film Critics Awards '76: Best Supporting Actress (Shire); Nominations: Academy Awards '76: Best Actor (Stallone), Best Actress (Shire), Best Original Screenplay, Best Song ("Gonna Fly Now"), Best Sound, Best Supporting Actor (Meredith, Young). *MGM, FOX, BTV*

Rocky 2 ♂♂ 1979 (PG) Time-marking sequel to the boxoffice smash finds Rocky frustrated by the commercialism that followed his match to Apollo, but considering a return bout. Meanwhile, his wife fights for her life. The overall effect is to prepare you for the next sequel. **119m/C VHS, Beta, LV.** Sylvester Stallone, Talia Shire, Burt Young, Burgess Meredith, Carl Weathers; **D:** Sylvester Stallone; **W:** Sylvester Stallone; **C:** Bill Butler; **M:** Bill Conti. *MGM, FOX*

Rocky 3 ♂♂½ 1982 (PG) Rocky is beaten by big, mean Clubber Lang (played to a tee by Mr. T). He realizes success has made him soft, and has to dig deep to find the motivation to stay on top. Amazingly, Stallone regains his underdog persona here, looking puny next to Mr. T, who is the best thing about the second-best "Rocky" flick. **103m/C VHS, Beta, LV.** Sylvester Stallone, Talia Shire, Burgess Meredith, Carl Weathers, Mr. T, Leif Erickson, Burt Young; **D:** Sylvester Stallone; **W:** Sylvester Stallone; **C:** Bill Butler; **M:** Bill Conti. Nominations: Academy Awards '82: Best Song ("Eye of the Tiger"). *MGM, FOX*

Rocky 4 ♂♂½ 1985 (PG) Rocky travels to Russia to fight the Soviet champ who killed his friend during a bout. Will Rocky knock the Russkie out? Will Rocky get hammered on the head a great many times and sag around the ring? Will Rocky ever learn? Lundgren isn't nearly as much fun as some of Rocky's former opponents and Stallone overdoes the hyper-patriotism and relies too heavily on uplifting footage from earlier "Rocky" movies. **91m/C VHS, Beta, LV, Closed Caption.** Sylvester Stallone, Talia Shire, Dolph Lundgren, Brigitte Nielsen, Michael Pataki, Burt Young, Carl Weathers; **D:** Sylvester Stallone; **W:** Sylvester Stallone; **C:** Bill Butler. Golden Raspberry Awards '85: Worst Actor (Stallone), Worst Supporting Actress (Nielsen), Worst Director (Stallone), Worst Screenplay, Worst New Star (Nielsen). *MGM, FOX*

Rocky 5 ♂♂ 1990 (PG) Brain damaged and broke, Rocky finds himself back where he started on the streets of Philadelphia. Boxing still very much in his blood, Rocky takes in a protege, training him in the style that made him a champ (take a lickin' and keep on tickin'). However an unscrupulous promoter has designs on the young fighter and seeks to wrest the lad from under the former champ's wing. This eventually leads to a showdown between Rocky and the young boxer in a brutal streetfight. Supposedly the last "Rocky" film, it's clear the formula has run dry. **105m/C VHS, Beta, LV, 8mm, Closed Caption.** Sylvester Stallone, Talia Shire, Burt Young, Sage Stallone, Tom Morrison, Burgess Meredith; **D:** John G. Avildsen; **W:** Sylvester Stallone; **C:** Steven Poster; **M:** Bill Conti. *MGM*

The Rocky Horror Picture Show ♂♂♂ 1975 (R) When a young couple take refuge in a haunted castle, they find themselves the unwilling pawns in a warped scientist's experiment. Cult camp classic has been a midnight movie favorite for years and has developed an entire subculture built around audience participation. The tape includes a seven-minute short detailing the story behind the movie's popularity. May not be as much fun watching it on the little screen unless you bring the rice and squirt guns. ♪The Time Warp; Science Fiction Double Feature; Wedding Song; Sweet Transvestite; The Sword of Damocles; Charles Atlas Song; Whatever Happened to Saturday Night; Touch-a Touch-a Touch-a Touch Me; Eddie's Teddy. **105m/C VHS, LV, Closed Caption.** Tim Curry, Susan Sarandon, Barry Bostwick, Little Nell, Richard O'Brien, Patricia Quinn, Jonathan Adams, Peter Hinwood, Meat Loaf; **D:** Jim Sharman; **W:** Jim Sharman, Richard O'Brien; **C:** Peter Suschitzky; **M:** Richard O'Brien. *FOX, FCT*

Rocky Jones, Space Ranger 1954 This syndicated space series followed the adventures of Rocky Jones, commander of the spaceship Orbit Jet, who worked for the United Worlds. The first three half-hour television episodes chronicle the story of how Rocky met his beautiful assistant Vena. Entitled "Beyond the Curtain of Space." Additional episodes available. **78m/B VHS, Beta.** Richard Crane, Sally Mansfield, Scotty Beckett. *MVC, MOV*

Rocky Jones, Space Ranger: Renegade Satellite ♂½ 1954 Nostalgia freaks may embrace this revived edition of the infamous early live-TV space cadet show. Rocky squares off against enemies of the United Solar System like Dr. Reno and Rudy DeMarco. Really cheap. **69m/B VHS.** Richard Crane, Sally Mansfield, Maurice Cass. *VDM*

Rocky Mountain Rangers ♂♂ 1940 The Three Mesquiteers do what they do best: save a town from bad guys. **58m/B VHS.** Bob Livingston, Raymond Hatton, Duncan Renaldo, Leroy Mason, Dennis Moore, John St. Polis; **D:** George Sherman. *NOS*

Rodan ♂♂ *Radon; Radon the Flying Monster* 1956 A gigantic prehistoric bird is disturbed from his slumber by H-bomb tests. He awakens to wreak havoc on civilization. Big bugs also run amok. From the director of "Godzilla" and a host of other nuclear monster movies. **74m/C VHS, Beta, LV.** JP Kenji Sahara, Yumi Shirakawa; **D:** Inoshiro Honda. *PAR, MLB, VES*

Rodeo Girl ♂♂½ 1980 Ross is a restless housewife who joins the rodeo in this television drama based on the life of cowgirl Sue Pirtle. Particularly strong supporting cast of Hopkins, Clark, and Brimley. **100m/C VHS, Beta.** Katharine Ross, Bo Hopkins, Candy Clark, Jacqueline Brookes, Wilford Brimley, Parley Baer; **D:** Jackie Cooper. *ART*

Rodrigo D.: No Future ♂♂ 1991 Gritty, realistic portrayal of the youth-killing culture of Medellin, Columbia. Minimal plot involves a young drummer and his drug-running friends. The actors used are actual untrained street kids, several of whom died after the film's completion. In Spanish with English subtitles. **92m/C VHS.** Ramiro Meneses, Carlos Mario Resrepo; **D:** Victor Gaviria. *KIV*

Roe vs. Wade ♂♂♂ 1989 Hunter is excellent as the single woman from Texas who successfully challenged the nation's prohibitive abortion laws in a landmark Supreme Court case. Television drama based on the actual 1973 case of Norma McCorvey. **92m/C VHS, Beta, LV, Closed Caption.** Holly Hunter, Amy Madigan, Terry O'Quinn, Stephen Tobolowsky, Dion Anderson, Kathy Bates, James Gammon, Chris Mulkey; **D:** Gregory Hoblit. *PAR*

Roger & Me ♂♂♂½ 1989 (R) Hilarious, controversial and atypical semi-documentary details Moore's protracted efforts to meet General Motors president Roger Smith and confront him with the poverty and despair afflicting Flint, Michigan, after GM closed its plants there. Includes some emotionally grabbing scenes: a Flint family is evicted just before Christmas; a woman makes a living by selling rabbits for food or pets; and a then soon-to-be Miss America addresses the socioeconomic impact of GM's decision. One of the highest-grossing non-fiction films ever released, and Moore's first. **91m/C VHS, Beta, LV, Closed Caption.** Michael Moore, Bob Eubanks, Pat Boone, Anita Bryant; **D:** Michael Moore; **W:** Michael Moore. *WAR*

RoGoPaG ♂♂ 1962 Four episodic films by four European masters (the title refers to their last names), satirizing the human condition. Rosselini's "Virginity" finds an airline stewardess (Schiaffino) fending off an amorous passenger (Balabin). Godard's "The New World" features a post-nuclear Paris and its effect on romance. "La Ricotta" is Pasolini's controversial take on religion with Welles as the director of a religious epic. Gregoretti's "The Range Grown Chicken" finds Tognazzi the frazzled head of a family beset by consumerism. A mixed bag with Pasolini and Godard offering the most disturbing essays. **122m/B VHS.** IT Orson Welles, Ugo Tognazzi, Rosanna Schiaffino, Alexandra Stewart, Jean-Mark Bory, Renato Salvatori, Lisa Gastoni, Bruce Balabin; **D:** Roberto Rossellini, Jean-Luc Godard, Pier Paolo Pasolini, Ugo Gregoretti; **W:** Roberto Rossellini, Jean-Luc Godard, Pier Paolo Pasolini, Ugo Gregoretti; **M:** Carlo Ristichelli. *KIV*

Rogue ♂ 1976 (R) The Rogue is a ruthless man who can make beautiful women do anything that he desires; so, of course, he does. **87m/C VHS, Beta.** Milan Galvonic, Barbara Bouchet, Margaret Lee; **D:** Gregory Simpson. *NO*

Rogue Lion ♂½ 1975 A quasi-incompetent game warden more than meets his match when a voraciously carnivorous lion begins stalking an African community. **89m/C VHS, Beta.** VCI

Rogue Male ♂♂½ 1976 TV movie finds '30s British aristocrat O'Toole plotting to assassinate Hitler. When his plan fails, he's on the run from both the Gestapo and the British police. Based on the novel by Geoffrey Household. **100m/C VHS.** GB Peter O'Toole, Alastair Sim, John Standing, Cyd Hayman; **D:** Clive Donner; **W:** Frederic Raphael. *FCT*

Rogue of the Range ♂ 1936 A lawman pretends that he is a bandit in order to track down an outlaw gang. **60m/B VHS, Beta.** Johnny Mack Brown. *NOS, DVT, RXM*

Rogue of the Rio Grande ♂♂½ 1930 Musical western in which the renowned bandit El Malo arrives in the peace-loving town of Sierra Blanca. One of Loy's earlier films. ♪Argentine Moon; Carmita; Song of the Bandoleros. **60m/B VHS, Beta.** Myrna Loy, Jose Bohr, Raymond Hatton, Carmelita Geraghty. *VCN*

Rogue's Gallery ♂♂ 1944 A reporter and photographer covering the story of an inventor and his latest device are caught up in intrigue when he is found murdered. **60m/B VHS, Beta.** Frank Jenks, Robin Raymond, H.B. Warner, Ray Walker, Davison Clark, Robert E. Homans, Frank McGlynn, Pat Gleason, Edward Keane; **D:** Al(bert) Herman. *SNC, RXM*

Rogue's Tavern ♂♂ 1936 In this grade B curio, a blood-thirsty killer stalks the occupants of a country inn, bodies are found with their throats crushed, and a psycho psychic is on the loose. Surprise ending. **70m/B VHS, Beta.** Wallace Ford, Joan Woodbury, Clara Kimball Young, Barbara Pepper, Jack Mulhall, John Elliott; **D:** Robert F. "Bob" Hill. *NOS, DVT, HEG*

Rogue's Yarn ♂♂ 1956 An investigator probes the death of a woman, ostensibly the result of a boating accident. Gradually he uncovers a plot involving the woman's husband and his mistress in this semi-entertaining British mystery. **80m/B VHS, Beta.** GB Nicole Maurey, Derek Bond, Elwyn Brook-Jones, Hugh Latimer; **D:** Vernon Sewell. *SNC*

Roland the Mighty 🎬½ 1958 Muscular, Herculeanesque hero takes on all comers in this sword and sandal epic set in the Asian steppes. ?m/C VHS, Beta. *IT* Rick Battaglia. *SNC*

Roll Along Cowboy 🎬½ 1937 A vintage sagebrush saga about a cowboy caught by love. Based on Zane Grey's "The Dude Ranger." 55m/B VHS, Beta. Smith Ballew, Cecilia Parker; *D:* Gus Meins. *NOS, CCB, VDM*

Roll of Thunder, Hear My Cry 🎬🎬½ 1978 A black family struggles to survive in Depression-era Mississippi in this inspiring, if somewhat predictable, television production. Look for the always impressive Freeman in a supporting role. Set in the South of 1933 and based on the novels of Mildred Taylor. 110m/C VHS, Beta. Claudia McNeil, Janet MacLachlan, Morgan Freeman; *D:* Jack Smight. *ART, BFA*

Roll on Texas Moon 🎬 1946 A cowpoke is hired to prevent a feud between the sheep men and the cattle ranchers. 68m/B VHS. Roy Rogers, George "Gabby" Hayes, Dale Evans, Dennis Hoey; *D:* William Witney. *NOS, DVT, MTX*

Roll, Wagons, Roll 🎬½ 1939 Tex Ritter leads a wagon train to Oregon. 52m/B VHS, Beta. Tex Ritter; *D:* Al(bert) Herman. *NOS, VCN*

Roller Blade 🎬 1985 In a post-holocaust world a gang of Amazon-style nuns, who worship a "have a nice day" happy face, battle the forces of evil with martial arts and mysticism. Has to be seen to be believed. Extremely low-budget outing. 88m/C VHS, Beta. Suzanne Solari, Jeff Hutchinson, Shaun Mitchelle; *D:* Donald G. Jackson.

Roller Blade Warriors: Taken By Force 🎬🎬 1990 Roller babes battle evil mutant while balancing on big boots with small wheels. 90m/C VHS. Kathleen Kinmont, Rory Calhoun, Abby Dalton, Elizabeth Kaitan. *NO*

Roller Boogie woof! 1979 (PG) A truly awful film made at the time of the mercifully brief roller-disco craze. Blair runs away from home and winds up helping some friends thwart a businessman looking to close the local roller rink. Everything about this one reeks amateur. 103m/C VHS. Linda Blair, Jim Bray, Beverly Garland, Roger Perry, James Van Patten, Kimberly Beck, Mark Goddard, Stoney Jackson, Sean McClory; *D:* Mark L. Lester; *W:* Barry Schneider; *C:* Dean Cundey. *MGM*

Rollerball 🎬🎬½ 1975 (R) Caan is utterly convincing in this futuristic tale in which a brutal sport assumes alarming importance to a sterile society. Flashy, violent, sometimes exhilirating. 123m/C VHS, Beta, LV, Letterbox. James Caan, John Houseman, Maud Adams, Moses Gunn, John Beck; *D:* Norman Jewison; *M:* Andre Previn. *USH*

Rollercoaster 🎬🎬 1977 (PG) A deranged extortionist threatens to sabotage an amusement park ride. Plucky Segal must stop him. Video renters will be spared the nauseating effects of film's original "Sensurround." 119m/C VHS, Beta, LV, Letterbox. George Segal, Richard Widmark, Timothy Bottoms, Henry Fonda, Susan Strasberg, Harry Guardino; *D:* James Goldstone; *W:* William Link; *M:* Lalo Schifrin. *USH*

Rollin' Plains 🎬 1938 A Texas Ranger tries to settle a feud between cattlemen and sheepmen over water rights. 60m/B VHS, Beta. Tex Ritter; *D:* Al(bert) Herman. *NOS, VCN, VCI*

Rolling Home 🎬🎬 1948 Tame tale about aging cowpoke, his grandson, and a really swell horse. Saddle up and snooze. 71m/B VHS, Beta, LV. Jean Parker, Russell Hayden, Pamela Blake, Buss Henry, Raymond Hatton. *VYY*

Rolling Thunder 🎬🎬½ 1977 (R) Vietnam vet turns vigilante when he arrives home from POW camp and sees his family slaughtered. Graphically violent, potentially cathartic. Typical of screenwriter Paul Schrader. 99m/C VHS, Beta, LV. William Devane, Tommy Lee Jones, Linda Haynes; *D:* John Flynn; *W:* Paul Schrader, Heywood Gould; *C:* Jordan Cronenweth. *ART, VES*

Rolling Vengeance 🎬½ 1987 (R) Enterprising fellow constructs powerful truck to better facilitate the extermination of gang members who earlier slaughtered his family. Keep on truckin'. 90m/C VHS, Beta, LV. Don Michael Paul, Ned Beatty, Lawrence Dane, Lisa Howard; *D:* Steven Hilliard Stern. *NLC*

Rollover 🎬½ 1981 (R) Turgid big-budget drama about Arab undermining of American economy. Kristofferson is lifeless, Fonda is humorless. Supporting players Sommer and Cronyn fare better. 117m/C VHS, Beta. Jane Fonda, Kris Kristofferson, Hume Cronyn, Bob Gunton, Josef Sommer, Martha Plimpton; *D:* Alan J. Pakula. *WAR*

Roman Holiday 🎬🎬🎬½ 1953 Hepburn's first starring role is a charmer as a princess bored with her official visit to Rome who slips away and plays at being an "average Jane." A reporter discovers her little charade and decides to cash in with an exclusive story. Before they know it, love calls. Blacklisted screenwriter Trumbo was "fronted" by Ian McLellan Hunter, who accepted screen credit and the Best Story Oscar in Trumbo's stead. The Academy voted to posthumously award Trumbo his own Oscar in 1993. 118m/B VHS, Beta, LV, 8mm. Audrey Hepburn, Gregory Peck, Eddie Albert, Tullio Carminati; *D:* William Wyler; *W:* Dalton Trumbo. Academy Awards '53: Best Actress (Hepburn), Best Costume Design (B & W), Best Story; British Academy Awards '53: Best Actress (Hepburn); Golden Globe Awards '54: Best Actress—Drama (Hepburn); New York Film Critics Awards '53: Best Actress (Hepburn); Nominations: Academy Awards '53: Best Art Direction/Set Decoration (B & W), Best Black and White Cinematography, Best Director (Wyler), Best Film Editing, Best Picture, Best Screenplay, Best Supporting Actor (Albert). *PAR, BTV, HMV*

Roman Scandals 🎬🎬½ 1933 A penniless young man daydreams himself back to ancient Rome with uproarious results. Lucille Ball appears as one of the Goldwyn Girls. Dance sequences were choreographed by Busby Berkeley. ♫ No More Love; Build A Little Home; Keep Young and Beautiful; Rome Wasn't Built in a Day; Put a Tax on Love. 91m/B VHS. Eddie Cantor, Ruth Etting, Gloria Stuart, Edward Arnold, Lucille Ball, Busby Berkeley; *D:* Frank Tuttle; *C:* Gregg Toland. *HBO*

Roman Spring of Mrs. Stone 🎬🎬🎬 *The Widow and the Gigolo* 1961 An aging actress determines to revive her career in Rome but finds romance with a gigolo instead in this adaptation of Tennessee Williams's novella. Leigh and Beatty are compelling, but Lenya nearly steals the show as Leigh's distinctly unappealing confidant. 104m/C VHS, Beta. Warren Beatty, Vivien Leigh, Lotte Lenya, Bessie Love, Jill St. John; *D:* Jose Quintero; *W:* Gavin Lambert. Nominations: Academy Awards '61: Best Supporting Actress (Lenya). *WAR, FHE*

Romance 🎬🎬 1930 In only her second talkie, Garbo stars as an Italian opera star who seduces a young priest. Poor story and weak acting from everyone with the exception of Garbo. Even she can't save this one. Adapted from the play "Signora Cacllini." 77m/B VHS. Greta Garbo, Lewis Stone, Gavin Gordon, Elliott Nugent, Florence Lake, Clara Blandick; *D:* Clarence Brown; *C:* William H. Daniels. Nominations: Academy Awards '30: Best Actress (Garbo), Best Director (Brown). *MGM*

Romance in Manhattan 🎬🎬 1934 Recent immigrant to New York struggles to build new life, in spite of unemployment, language barriers, and loneliness. He meets Broadway chorine Rogers and song and dance ensues. America, ain't it a great place? 78m/B VHS. Ginger Rogers, Francis Lederer, J. Farrell MacDonald; *D:* Stephen Roberts; *M:* Max Steiner. *TTC, FCT*

Romance of a Horsethief 🎬🎬½ 1971 (PG) Brynner leads this entertaining but slow-paced "Fiddler on the Roof" comedic romp without the music. In 1904 Poland, a Cossack captain takes horses for the Russo-Japanese war. The residents of the town rise up, goaded on by Birkin. 100m/C VHS. *YU* Yul Brynner, Eli Wallach, Jane Birkin, Oliver Tobias, Lainie Kazan, David Opatoshu; *D:* Abraham Polonsky. *ACE, MOV*

Romance on the High Seas 🎬🎬🎬 1948 A woman is scheduled to take a cruise vacation but skips the boat when she believes her husband is cheating on her. Her husband believes she is taking the cruise to cheat on him and hires a private detective to follow her. Pleasant comedy features the film debut of Doris Day. ♫ It's Magic; It's Your or No One; The Tourist Trade; Put 'Em in a Box, Tie 'Em with a Ribbon, and Throw 'Em in the Deep Blue Sea; Two Lovers Met in the Night; Run, Run, Run; I'm in Love; Cuban Rhapsody. 99m/C VHS, LV. Jack Carson, Janis Paige, Don DeFore, Doris Day, Oscar Levant, S.Z. Sakall, Eric Blore, Franklin Pangborn, Leslie Brooks, Michael "Billy" Bakewell; *D:* Michael Curtiz; *W:* Julius J. Epstein. Nominations: Academy Awards '48: Best Song ("It's Magic"), Scoring of a Musical. *FOX, FCT*

Romance on the Orient Express 🎬½ 1989 Sparks fly when former lovers meet again on the Orient Express. Don't expect any flesh, though, as film was made for television. 96m/C VHS, Beta. Cheryl Ladd, Stuart Wilson, John Gielgud; *D:* Lawrence Gordon Clark. *TTC*

Romance on the Range 🎬½ 1942 Rogers sets out to trap a gang of fur thieves and finds romance. 60m/B VHS. Roy Rogers, George "Gabby" Hayes, Sally Payne. *NOS, VCN, REP*

Romance with a Double Bass 🎬🎬🎬 1974 When a musician and a princess take a skinny dip in the royal lake and get their clothes stolen, comic complications arise. Reminiscent of Cleese's sojourn as a Monty Python member, with surreal, frequently raunchy humor. 40m/C VHS, Beta, LV. *GB* John Cleese, Connie Booth, Graham Crowden, Desmond Jones, Freddie Jones, Andrew Sachs; *D:* Robert M. Young. *FCT, SIG*

Romancing the Stone 🎬🎬🎬 1984 (PG) Uptight romance novelist lives out her fantasies after she receives a mysterious map from her murdered brother-in-law and her sister is kidnapped in South America—the ransom being the map. Out to rescue her sister, she's helped and hindered by an American soldier of fortune (Douglas) whose main concern is himself and the hidden treasure described in the map. Great chemistry between the stars and loads of clever dialogue in this appealing adventure comedy. First outing with Turner, Douglas, and DeVito. Followed by "The Jewel of the Nile." 106m/C VHS, Beta, LV, Letterbox, Closed Caption. Michael Douglas, Kathleen Turner, Danny DeVito, Zack Norman, Alfonso Arau, Ron Silver; *D:* Robert Zemeckis; *M:* Alan Silvestri. Golden Globe Awards '85: Best Actress—Musical/Comedy (Turner), Best Film—Musical/Comedy; Los Angeles Film Critics Association Awards '84: Best Actress (Turner); Nominations: Academy Awards '84: Best Film Editing. *FOX, HMV*

Romantic Comedy 🎬🎬 1983 (PG) Writing duo never seem to synchronize their desires for each other in this dull comedy. Engaging stars don't inspire each other much, and supporting cast can't make up the difference. Adapted from the Bernard Slade play. 102m/C VHS, Beta, Closed Caption. Dudley Moore, Mary Steenburgen, Frances Sternhagen, Ron Leibman; *D:* Arthur Hiller; *M:* Marvin Hamlisch. *MGM, FOX*

Romantic Englishwoman 🎬🎬🎬 1975 (R) Literate comedy-drama about the intertwined lives of several sophisticated and restrained Brits. Caine is a successful novelist with writer's block whose wife falls for another man while on a trip alone. He then invites his wife's lover to stay with them in order to generate ideas for his writing until his jealousy begins to surface. 117m/C VHS, Beta. *GB* Glenda Jackson, Michael Caine, Helmut Berger, Kate Nelligan; *D:* Joseph Losey; *W:* Tom Stoppard, Thomas Wiseman. *WAR, OM*

Rome Adventure 🎬🎬 *Lovers Must Learn* 1962 Spinster librarian Pleshette takes Roman vacation hoping to meet handsome prince. Donahue takes shine to her while girlfriend Dickinson is away, as does suave Roman Brazzi. Soapy, ill-paced romance. **119m/C VHS, LV, Closed Caption.** Troy Donahue, Angie Dickinson, Suzanne Pleshette, Rossano Brazzi, Constance Ford, Al Hirt, Chad Everett; *D:* Delmer Daves; *W:* Delmer Daves; *M:* Max Steiner. *PAR, FCT, WAR*

Rome '78 🎬🎬½ 1978 Acclaimed underground film centered around Caligula and the Queen of Sheba in ancient Rome. **60m/C VHS.** Eric Mitchell; *D:* James Nares. *MWF*

Romeo and Juliet 🎬🎬🎬½ 1936 One of MGM producer Irving Thalberg's pet projects (and starring Thalberg's wife, Norma Shearer), this Shakespeare classic was given the spare-no-expense MGM treatment. Physically too old to portray teenage lovers, both Howard and Shearer let their acting ability supply all necessary illusions. Also notable is Barrymore's over-the-top portrayal of Mercutio. **126m/B VHS, LV.** Leslie Howard, Norma Shearer, John Barrymore, Basil Rathbone, Edna May Oliver; *D:* George Cukor; *C:* William H. Daniels. Nominations: Academy Awards '36: Best Actress (Shearer), Best Interior Decoration, Best Picture, Best Supporting Actor (Rathbone). *MGM, CCB*

Romeo and Juliet 🎬🎬 1954 Unfulfilling adaptation of Shakespeare's timeless drama of young love cast against family antagonisms. Peculiar supporting cast features both Cabot and ubiquitous master Gielgud. **138m/C VHS, Beta.** *IT* Laurence Harvey, Susan Shantall, Aldo Zollo, Sebastian Cabot, Flora Robson, Mervyn Johns, Bill Travers, John Gielgud; *D:* Renato Castellani; *C:* Robert Krasker. National Board of Review Awards '54: Best Director (Castellani). *BFA*

Romeo and Juliet 🎬🎬🎬½ 1968 (PG) Young couple share love despite prohibitive conflict between their families in this adaptation of Shakespeare's classic play. Director Zeffirelli succeeds in casting relative novices Whiting and Hussey in the leads, but is somewhat less proficient in lending air of free-wheeling '60s appeal to entire enterprise. Kudos, however, to cinematographer Pasquale De Santis and composer Nina Rota. Also available in a 45-minute edited version. **138m/C VHS, Beta, LV.** *GB IT* Olivia Hussey, Leonard Whiting, Michael York, Milo O'Shea; *D:* Franco Zeffirelli; *C:* Pasquale De Santis; *M:* Nino Rota. Academy Awards '68: Best Cinematography, Best Costume Design; Golden Globe Awards '69: Best Foreign Film; National Board of Review Awards '68: Best Director (Zeffirelli); Nominations: Academy Awards '68: Best Director (Zeffirelli), Best Picture. *PAR, HMV, PBC*

Romeo Is Bleeding 🎬🎬½ 1993 (R) Jack (Oldman) is a police detective accepting mobster payoffs from boss Falcone (Scheider) for fingering federally protected witnesses. But the next target proves Jack's undoing—hitwoman Mona (Olin), who's more than a match for any man. Oldman's character is played for a patsy by everyone while Olin's is a kinky psycho-villainess with an enjoyment of violence, red lipstick, and a constant, maniacal laugh. Sciorra is generally wasted as Jack's unhappy wife while Lewis is annoying as his young and vacuous mistress. Part homage, part satire of film noir is overly stylized with intrusive narration but some effective shocks.*CW:* Strong language, strong violence, and strong sexuality. **111m/C VHS, LV, Closed Caption.** Gary Oldman, Lena Olin, Annabella Sciorra, Juliette Lewis, Roy Scheider, Michael Wincott, David Proval, Paul Butler, Will Patton, Larry Joshua, James Cromwell, Ron Perlman; *D:* Peter Medak; *W:* Hilary Henkin; *C:* Darius Wolski; *M:* Mark Isham. Nominations: MTV Movie Awards '94: Best Action Sequence. *PGV*

Romero 🎬🎬½ 1989 Julia is riveting as the Salvadoran archbishop who championed his destitute congregation despite considerable political opposition. A stirring biography financed by the United States Roman Catholic Church. **102m/C VHS, Beta, LV, Closed Caption.** Raul Julia, Richard Jordan, Ana Alicia, Eddie Velez, Alejandro Bracho, Tony Plana, Lucy Reina, Harold Gould, Al Ruscio, Robert Viharo; *D:* John Duigan; *W:* John Sacret Young; *C:* Geoff Burton; *M:* Gabriel Yared. *THV*

Romola 🎬🎬½ 1925 Silent adventure. After Powell and his father are attacked by pirates, Powell escapes. But instead of rescuing his father, he opts for a life of corruption. Dad eventually escapes and returns to exact vengeance. A rather expensive film in its day, troubled by modern-day sights in what was supposed to be old Florence. Gish's drowning scene had to be re-shot because she wouldn't sink. Colman arranged for his then-wife Raye to have a bit part, but they were divorced soon after the film was finished. **120m/B VHS, Beta.** Lillian Gish, Dorothy Gish, William Powell, Ronald Colman, Charles Lane, Herbert Grimwood, Bonaventure Ibanez, Frank Puglia, Thelma Raye; *D:* Henry King. *NO*

Romper Stomper 🎬🎬 1992 (R) Violent confrontations between Australian skinheads and the Vietnamese community mixed in with a disturbed love story. Suburban rich girl Gabe (McKenzie) is drawn to the charasmatic Hando (Crowe), the certifiably loony leader of a group of Melbourne's skinheads. Any romance takes a backseat to the carnage brought by the skinheads' attacks on the local Asian community, who fight back with equal force. Disquieting look at a brutal world which can't be ignored. Film caused a furor upon its Australian release with debates about whether the extreme violence was intended to titilate or explicate the plot. An unrated version at 89 minutes is also available. **85m/C VHS.** *AU* Russell Crowe, Jacqueline McKenzie, Daniel Pollock; *D:* Geoffrey Wright; *W:* Geoffrey Wright. Australian Film Institute '92: Best Actor (Crowe), Best Sound, Best Score. *FCT*

Romy and Michele's High School Reunion 🎬½ 1997 (R) Two vacuous ditz queens, Romy (Sorvino) and Michele (Kudrow), best friends and roommates since high school, decide they must impress at their 10-year Tucson high school reunion by passing themselves off as wealthy and successful. Since they're barely bright enough to walk and chew gum at the same time, this proves to be a challenge, especially when the arrival of cynical Heather (Garofalo), who knows the truth, threatens their deception. Music's good, and there are a (very) few funny moments, but you'll concentrate most on trying to ignore those annoying accents. You don't laugh with these would-be babes, you laugh at them. And even then, not all that much. Based on Schiff's play "The Ladies' Room."*CW:* Language. **91m/C VHS, LV, Closed Caption.** Mira Sorvino, Lisa Kudrow, Janeane Garofalo, Alan Cumming, Julia Campbell, Elaine Hendrix, Jacob Vargas; *D:* David Mirkin; *W:* Robin Schiff; *C:* Reynaldo Villalobos; *M:* Steve Bartek. Nominations: MTV Movie Awards '98: Best Dance Sequence (Lisa Kudrow/Mira Sorvino/Alan Cumming). *TOU*

Ronnie and Julie 🎬🎬½ 1997 (PG) Yet another contemporary variation of "Romeo & Juliet" with high-school sweethearts Ronnie and Julie's relationship threatened by their respective parents political rivalry in a mayoral campaign. At least this one has a happy ending. **99m/C VHS.** Teri Garr, Joshua Jackson, Margot Finlay, Alexandra Purvis, Tom Butler, Garwin Sanford; *D:* Philip Spink. *HMK*

The Roof 🎬🎬 1956 Uninteresting outing about a young couple who married against their families' wishes and find that setting up a home of their own is more difficult than they thought. In Italian with English subtitles. **98m/B VHS, Beta.** *IT* Gabriella Pallotti, Giorgio Listuzzi; *D:* Vittorio De Sica. *NOS, HHT*

Rooftops 🎬½ 1989 (R) Peculiar but predictable, centering on love between Hispanic girl and white youth who has mastered martial arts dancing. Director Wise is a long way from his earlier "West Side Story." See this one and be the only person you know who has. **108m/C VHS, Beta, LV.** Jason Gedrick, Troy Beyer, Eddie Velez, Tisha Campbell; *D:* Robert Wise; *W:* Allan Goldstein, Terrence (Terry) Brennan; *M:* Michael Kamen. *ART*

The Rookie 🎬🎬 1990 (R) Routine cop drama has worldly veteran and wide-eyed newcomer team to crack stolen-car ring managed by Germans. Eastwood and Sheen are reliable, but Hispanics Julia and Braga, though miscast, nonetheless steal this one as the German villains. **121m/C VHS, Beta, LV, 8mm, Letterbox, Closed Caption.** Clint Eastwood, Charlie Sheen, Raul Julia, Sonia Braga, Lara Flynn Boyle, Pepe Serna, Marco Rodriguez, Tom Skerritt, Roberta Vasquez; *D:* Clint Eastwood. *WAR*

Rookie of the Year 🎬🎬½ 1993 (PG) Kid's fluff fantasy come true. Twelve-year-old baseball fanatic Henry has dreams of making it to the big league. He falls, breaks his arm, and when it heals strangely is blessed with a pitching arm so spectacular he finds himself not only playing for the Chicago Cubs, but leading them to the World Series. Enjoyable family outing for first-time director Stern (who also plays a seasoned and very incredulous ballplayer). Keep your eyes peeled for appearances by real-live sluggers Pedro Guerrero, Barry Bonds, and others. **103m/C VHS, LV, Closed Caption.** Thomas Ian Nicholas, Daniel Stern, Gary Busey, Dan Hedaya; *D:* Daniel Stern; *W:* Sam Harper; *C:* Jack N. Green; *M:* Bill Conti. Blockbuster Entertainment Awards '95: Family Movie, Video.*FOX*

The Room 🎬🎬 1987 Altman takes on Pinter in this brooding mini-play about two young strangers who try to rent the room already occupied by a disconnected woman and her semi-catatonic husband. Made for television. **48m/C VHS, Beta.** Julian Sands, Linda Hunt, Annie Lennox, David Hemblen, Donald Pleasence; *D:* Robert Altman; *W:* Harold Pinter.

Room at the Top 🎬🎬🎬½ 1959 Ambitious factory man forsakes true love and marries boss's daughter instead in this grim drama set in industrial northern England. Cast excels, with Harvey and Sears as the worker and his wife. Signoret is also quite compelling as the abandoned woman. Adapted from John Braine's novel and followed by "Life at the Top" and "Man at the Top." **118m/B VHS.** *GB* Laurence Harvey, Simone Signoret, Heather Sears, Hermione Baddeley, Avril Ungar, Donald Wolfit, Wendy Craig, Allan Cuthbertson, Ian Hendry, Donald Houston, Raymond Huntley, Miriam Karlin, Wilfred Lawson, Richard Pasco, Mary Peach, Prunella Scales, Beatrice Varley, John Westbrook; *D:* Jack Clayton; *W:* Neil Paterson; *C:* Freddie Francis; *M:* Mario Nascimbene. Academy Awards '59: Best Actress (Signoret), Best Adapted Screenplay; British Academy Awards '58: Best Actress (Signoret), Best Film; Cannes Film Festival '59: Best Actress (Signoret); Nominations: Academy Awards '59: Best Actor (Harvey), Best Director (Clayton), Best Picture, Best Supporting Actress (Baddeley). *NO*

Room 43 🎬½ *Passport to Shame* 1958 Campy fable about a British cab driver who falls in love with a French girl, and stumbles onto a white-slavery ring when she falls victim to it. Features a young Caine and future novelist Collins in bit parts. **93m/B VHS, Beta.** Diana Dors, Herbert Lom, Eddie Constantine, Michael Caine, Jackie Collins; *D:* Alvin Rakoff. *VDM, TPV*

Room Service 🎬🎬½ 1938 The Marx Brothers provide less than the usual mayhem here with Groucho as a penniless theatrical producer determined to remain in his hotel room until he can secure funds for his next play. Ball doesn't help matters much either. Not bad, but certainly not up to the zany Marx clan's usual stuff. **78m/B VHS, Beta, LV.** Groucho Marx, Harpo Marx, Chico Marx, Lucille Ball, Ann Miller, Frank Albertson, Donald MacBride, Charles Halton; *D:* William A. Seiter. *CCB, TTC*

Room to Let 🎬🎬 1949 An elderly woman and her daughter take in boarders in Victorian England. They rent a room to a man who claims to be a doctor, but the two women eventually become prisoners of fear, believing the man is actually Jack the Ripper. Will there be a vacancy soon? Somewhat disturbing and suspenseful. **68m/B VHS, Beta.** *GB* Jimmy Hanley, Valentine Dyall, Christine Silver, Merle Tottenham, Charles Hawtrey, Connie Smith, Laurence Naismith; *D:* Godfrey Grayson. *NOS, SNC*

A Room with a View *🎬🎬🎬🎬* 1986
Engaging adaptation of E.M. Forster's novel of requited love. Carter stars as the feisty British idealist who rejects dashing Sands for supercilious Day Lewis, then repents and finds (presumably) eternal passion. A multi-Oscar nominee, with great music (courtesy of Puccini), great scenery (courtesy of Florence), and great performances (courtesy of practically everybody, but supporters Smith, Dench, Callow, and Elliott must be particularly distinguished). Truly romantic, and there's much humor too. **117m/C VHS, Beta, LV, Closed Caption.** *GB* Helena Bonham Carter, Julian Sands, Denholm Elliott, Maggie Smith, Judi Dench, Simon Callow, Daniel Day-Lewis, Rupert Graves, Rosemary Leach; *D:* James Ivory; *W:* Ruth Prawer Jhabvala; *C:* Tony Pierce-Roberts. Academy Awards '86: Best Adapted Screenplay, Best Art Direction/Set Decoration, Best Costume Design; British Academy Awards '86: Best Actress (Smith), Best Film, Best Supporting Actress (Dench); Golden Globe Awards '87: Best Supporting Actress (Smith); Independent Spirit Awards '87: Best Foreign Film; National Board of Review Awards '86: Best Supporting Actor (Day-Lewis); New York Film Critics Awards '86: Best Cinematography, Best Supporting Actor (Day-Lewis); Writers Guild of America '86: Best Adapted Screenplay; Nominations: Academy Awards '86: Best Cinematography, Best Director (Ivory), Best Picture, Best Supporting Actor (Elliott). *FOX, HMV*

Roommate 1984 A valedictorian church-goer and a rebellious iconoclast room together at Northwestern University in 1952, with the expected humorous results. Public television presentation based on a John Updike story. **96m/C VHS, Beta.** Lance Guest, Barry Miller, Elaine Wilkes, Melissa Ford, David Bachman; *D:* Neil Cox. *ART, VES*

Roommates *🎬🎬½* 1995 (PG) Rocky Holeczek (Falk) is a cantankerous coot who, at age 75, decides to care for orphaned seven-year-old grandson Michael. Over the 30 years they are together, they fight over Rocky's old school ways and a grown-up Michael's (Sweeney) attempt to have a family of his own. But despite their bickering, Michael soon realizes that his 107-years-old grandfather's words are truly pearls of wisdom when faced with tragedy. Film hits the right sentimental buttons without going overboard with the tissues and Falk's performance, underneath the layers of film make-up, is charmingly irascible. Based on co-writer Apple's own grandfather. **108m/C VHS, LV, Closed Caption.** Peter Falk, D.B. Sweeney, Julianne Moore, Ellen Burstyn; *D:* Peter Yates; *W:* Max Apple, Stephen Metcalfe; *C:* Mike Southon; *M:* Elmer Bernstein. Nominations: Academy Awards '95: Best Makeup. *TOU*

Rooster Cogburn *🎬🎬½* 1975 (PG) A Bible-thumping schoolmarm joins up with a hard-drinking, hard-fighting marshal in order to capture a gang of outlaws who killed her father. Tired sequel to "True Grit" but the chemistry between Wayne and Hepburn is right on target. **107m/C VHS, Beta, LV, DVD.** John Wayne, Katharine Hepburn, Richard Jordan, Anthony Zerbe, John McIntire, Strother Martin, Paul Koslo; *D:* Stuart Millar; *C:* Harry Stradling Jr. *USH, TLF*

Rooster: Spurs of Death! woof! 1983 (PG) An expose on cock fighting, in which a young idealist tries to stop the thriving sport in a small southern town. Dog of a movie that (not surprisingly) went straight to video. **90m/C VHS, Beta.** Vincent Van Patten, Ty Hardin, Kristine DeBell, Ruta Lee. *NO*

Roosters *🎬🎬½* 1995 (R) Gallo Morales (Olmos) is returning home, after serving seven years in prison for manslaughter, anxiously awaited by wife Juana (Braga), 20-year-old rebellious son Hector (Nucci), neglected adolescent daughter Angela (Lassez), and sexy sister Chata (Alonso). Gallo is a noted breeder of fighting cocks, which for him represent machismo and power but, to his resentment, it's Hector who owns a potential prize-winning bird, precipitating some explosive family conflicts. Adapted by Sanchez-Scott from her 1987 play. *CW:* Some disturb-

ing images of violence and sexuality. **93m/C VHS, Closed Caption.** Edward James Olmos, Sonia Braga, Maria Conchita Alonso, Danny Nucci, Sarah Lassez; *D:* Robert M. Young; *W:* Milcha Sanchez-Scott; *C:* Reynaldo Villalobos; *M:* David Kilay. *CAF*

Rootin' Tootin' Rhythm *🎬* *Rhythm on the Ranch* 1938 All's not quiet on the range, but Autry comes along to sing things back to normal. Goofy, clumsy, ubiquitous sidekick Burnette is a symbol for this whole effort. **55m/B VHS, Beta.** Gene Autry, Smiley Burnette, Monte Blue; *D:* Mack V. Wright. *NOS, VYY, DVT*

Roots *🎬🎬🎬🎬* 1977 The complete version of Alex Haley's made for television saga following a black man's search for his heritage, revealing an epic panorama of America's past. Available on six tapes, complete at 570 minutes. **90m/C VHS, Beta.** Ed Asner, Lloyd Bridges, LeVar Burton, Chuck Connors, Lynda Day George, Lorne Greene, Burl Ives, O.J. Simpson, Cicely Tyson, Ben Vereen, Sandy Duncan; *D:* David Greene; *M:* Quincy Jones. *WAR, MOV, PBS*

Roots of Evil *🎬½* 1991 (R) This erotic thriller follows a cop on the trail of a murderer who specializes in killing Hollywood's most beautiful prostitutes. Also available in unrated and Spanish-language versions. *CW:* Language, strong violence, and strong sexuality. *?m/C VHS.* Alex Cord, Delia Sheppard, Charles Dierkop, Jillian Kesner; *D:* Gary Graver.

Roots: The Gift *🎬🎬* 1988 It's Christmas, 1770, and Kunte Kinte (Burton) and Fiddler (Gossett) try to escape slavery via the Underground Railroad. In their attempt, they wind up giving the gift of freedom to several of their fellow slaves. A made for television movie based on the Alex Haley characters. **94m/C VHS.** Louis Gossett Jr., LeVar Burton, Michael Learned, Avery Brooks, Kate Mulgrew, Shaun Cassidy, John McMartin; *D:* Kevin Hooks; *C:* John A. Alonzo. *WAR, FCT*

Roots: The Next Generation *🎬🎬🎬* 1979 Sequel to the landmark television miniseries continuing the story of author Alex Haley's ancestors from the Reconstruction era of the 1880s to 1967, culminating with Haley's visit to West Africa where he is told the story of Kunta Kinte. On seven tapes. **685m/C VHS.** Georg Stanford Brown, Lynne Moody, Henry Fonda, Richard Thomas, Marc Singer, Olivia de Havilland, Paul Koslo, Beah Richards, Stan Shaw, Harry (Henry) Morgan, Irene Cara, Dorian Harewood, Ruby Dee, Paul Winfield, James Earl Jones, Debbie Allen; *Cameos:* Al Freeman Jr., Marlon Brando. *MOV*

Rope *🎬🎬🎬½* 1948 (PG) In New York City, two gay college students murder a friend for kicks and store the body in a living room trunk. They further insult the dead by using the trunk as the buffet table and inviting his parents to the dinner party in his honor. Very dark humor is the theme in Hitchcock's first color film, which he innovatively shot in uncut ten-minute takes, with the illusion of a continuous scene maintained with tricky camera work. Based on the Patrick Hamilton play and on the Leopold-Laeb murder case. **81m/C VHS, Beta, LV.** James Stewart, John Dall, Farley Granger, Cedric Hardwicke, Constance Collier; *D:* Alfred Hitchcock; *W:* Arthur Laurents. *USH*

Rorret *🎬🎬🎬* 1987 "Rorret" is "terror" spelled backwards—a good indication of the psychological and physical terror Mr. Rorret, the owner of the Peeping Tom Cinema, inflicts upon his female patrons. The Cinema is devoted to the horror film and Rorret himself dresses like Peter Lorre in "M"; lives behind the movie screen, watching the films in mirror image; and enjoys the frightened reactions of his female patrons. He enjoys their reactions so much that he later stalks the women for real. Highlighted by recreated sequences from such psycho-terror classics as "Psycho," "Dial M for Murder," "Strangers on a Train," and "Peeping Tom." In Italian with English subtitles. **105m/C VHS.** *IT* Lou Castel, Anna Galiena, Massimo Venturiello; *D:* Fulvio Wetzl; *W:* Fulvio Wetzl. *NYF*

Rosa Luxemburg *🎬🎬* 1986 Based on the life of the Jewish political radical, murdered in 1919. Involving herself with the German Social Democratic Party, Luxemburg undergoes numerous imprisonments and maintains a tempestuous personal life. Based primarily on Luxemburg's letters and speeches; charismatic performance by Sukowa. In German with English subtitles. **122m/C VHS.** *GE* Barbara Sukowa, Daniel Olbrychski, Otto Sander, Adelheid Arndt; *D:* Margarethe von Trotta; *W:* Margarethe von Trotta. Cannes Film Festival '86: Best Actress (Sukowa). *NYF, FCT*

Rosalie *🎬🎬½* 1938 A gridiron great from West Point falls for a mysterious beauty from Vassar. He soon learns that her father reigns over a tiny Balkan nation. Expensive, massive, imperfect musical; exotic romantic pairing fails to conceal plot's blah-ness. Oh well, at least Porter's music is good. *🎵* I've a Strange New Rhythm in My Heart; Why Should I Care?; Spring Love Is in the Air; Rosalie; It's All Over But the Shouting; Who Knows?; In the Still of the Night; To Love or Not to Love; Close (instrumental). **118m/B VHS, Beta.** Nelson Eddy, Eleanor Powell, Frank Morgan, Ray Bolger, Ilona Massey, Reginald Owen, Edna May Oliver, Jerry Colonna; *D:* Woodbridge S. Van Dyke; *M:* Cole Porter. *MGM*

Rosalie Goes Shopping *🎬🎬🎬* 1989 (PG-13) Satire about American consumerism hiding behind slapstick comedy, and it works, most of the time. Misplaced Bavarian (Sagebrecht) moves to Arkansas and begins spending wildly and acquiring "things." Twisty plot carried confidently by confident wackiness from Sagebrecht and supporters. **94m/C VHS, LV.** *GE* Marianne Saegebrecht, Brad Davis, Judge Reinhold, Willie Harlander, Alex Winter, Erika Blumberger, Patricia Zehntmayr; *D:* Percy Adlon; *W:* Eleonore Adlon, Percy Adlon; *M:* Bob Telson. *THV*

The Rosary Murders *🎬🎬* 1987 (R) Based on the William X. Kienzle mystery about a serial killer preying on nuns and priests. Father Koesler (Sutherland) must betray the confessional to stop him. Interesting, though sometimes muddled and too rarely tense. Filmed on location in Detroit. **105m/C VHS, Beta, LV, Closed Caption.** Donald Sutherland, Charles Durning, Belinda Bauer, Josef Sommer, James Murtaugh, John Danelle, Addison Powell, Kathleen Tolan; *D:* Fred Walton; *W:* Fred Walton, Elmore Leonard. *VTR*

The Rose *🎬🎬🎬* 1979 (R) Modeled after the life of Janis Joplin, Midler plays a young, talented and self-destructive blues/rock singer. Professional triumphs don't stop her lonely restlessness and confused love affairs. The best exhibition of the rock and roll world outside of documentaries. Electrifying film debut for Midler features an incredible collection of songs. *🎵* Fire Down Below; I've Written A Letter to Daddy; Let Me Call You Sweetheart; The Rose; Stay With Me; Camellia; Sold My Soul To Rock 'n' Roll; Keep On Rockin'; When A Man Loves a Woman. **134m/C VHS, Beta, LV, Closed Caption.** Bette Midler, Alan Bates, Frederic Forrest, Harry Dean Stanton, David Keith; *D:* Mark Rydell; *C:* Vilmos Zsigmond. Golden Globe Awards '80: Best Actress—Musical/Comedy (Midler), Best Song ("The Rose"); National Society of Film Critics Awards '79: Best Supporting Actor (Forrest); Nominations: Academy Awards '79: Best Actress (Midler), Best Film Editing, Best Sound, Best Supporting Actor (Forrest). *FOX*

The Rose and the Jackal *🎬🎬* 1990 Fun, intriguing fictionalization about the founder of the Pinkerton detective agency. During the Civil War, bearded, Scottish Reeve tries to persuade a wealthy Southern lady to help save the Union. Made for cable television. **94m/C VHS, Beta, Closed Caption.** Christopher Reeve, Madolyn Smith, Granville Van Dusen, Carrie Snodgress, Kevin McCarthy; *D:* Jack Gold. *TTC*

The Rose Garden *🎬🎬½* 1989 (PG-13) In modern Germany, a Holocaust survivor is put on trial for assaulting an elderly man. The victim, it turns out, was a Nazi guilty of heinous war crimes. Ullmann and Schell lend substance, though treatment of a powerful theme is inadequate. **112m/C VHS, Beta, LV.** Liv Ullmann, Maximilian Schell, Peter Fonda, Jan Niklas, Kurt Hubner; *D:* Fons Rademakers; *W:* Paul Hengge; *M:* Egisto Macchi.

Rose Marie 🎸🎸🎸 *Indian Love Call* 1936

An opera star falls in love with the mountie who captured her escaped convict brother. Hollywood legend has it that when a British singer was presented with the first line in "Indian Love Song," which is "When I'm calling you-oo-oo-oo-oo-oo-oo," the confused performer sang, "When I'm calling you, double oh, double oh, double oh..." Maybe true, maybe not, but funny anyway. Classic MacDonald-Eddy operetta. Remade in 1954. 🎵Indian Love Call; Pardon Me, Madame; The Mounties; Rose Marie; Totem Tom Tom; Just for You; Tex Yeux; St. Louis Blues; Dinah. **112m/B VHS, Beta, LV.** Jeanette MacDonald, Nelson Eddy, James Stewart, Allan Jones, David Niven, Reginald Owen; *D:* Woodbridge S. Van Dyke; *C:* William H. Daniels; *M:* Rudolf Friml. *MGM*

Rose Marie 🎸🎸🎸 1954 (G)

Blyth is a lonely Canadian woman wooed by a mean spirited fur trapper and a gallant mountie. Unremarkable remake of the Eddy/MacDonald musical is saved by specatular technicolor and CinemaScope photography. Choreography by Busby Berkeley. 🎵Rose Marie; Indian Love Call; Totem Tom Tom; The Mounties; I Have the Love; The Right Place For A Girl; Free to be Free; The Mountie Who Never Got His Man. **115m/C VHS, LV, Letterbox.** Ann Blyth, Howard Keel, Fernando Lamas, Bert Lahr, Marjorie Main, Joan Taylor, Chief Yowlachie, Abel Fernandez, Al Ferguson, Dabbs Greer, Lumsden Hare; *D:* Mervyn LeRoy; *C:* Paul Vogel. *MGM, MLB*

Rose of Rio Grande 🎸 1938

A western musical about a Mexican gang that avenges the deaths of members of the upper strata. **60m/B VHS, Beta.** John Carroll, Movita, Antonio Moreno, Lena Basquette, Duncan Renaldo; *D:* William Nigh. *GPV*

Rose of Washington Square 🎸🎸½ 1939

Singer Faye gets involved with the no-account Power, much to the dismay of her friend Jolson. They marry, and she becomes a singing sensation in the Ziegfeld Follies while he becomes an embarassment, eventually winding up on the wrong side of the law. Jolson stole the movie, singing some of his best numbers. This thinly disguised portrait of Fanny Brice caused the performer to sue for defamation of character; she eventually settled out of court. 🎵California, Here I Come; My Mammy; Pretty Baby; Toot Toot Tootsie Goodbye; Rock-A-Bye Your Baby with a Dixie Melody; My Man; I'm Just Wild About Harry; I Never Knew Heaven Could Speak; Rose of Washington Square. **86m/B VHS.** Alice Faye, Tyrone Power, Al Jolson, William Frawley, Joyce Compton, Hobart Cavanaugh, Moroni Olsen; *D:* Gregory Ratoff; *W:* Nunnally Johnson; *C:* Karl Freund. *FXV*

The Rose Tattoo 🎸🎸🎸½ 1955

Magnani, in her U.S. screen debut, is just right as a Southern widow who cherishes her husband's memory, but falls for virile trucker Lancaster. Williams wrote this play and screenplay specifically for Magnani, who was never as successful again. Interesting character studies, although Lancaster doesn't seem right as an Italian longshoreman. **117m/B VHS, Beta, LV, Closed Caption.** Anna Magnani, Burt Lancaster, Marisa Pavan, Ben Cooper, Virginia Grey, Jo Van Fleet; *D:* Daniel Mann; *W:* Tennessee Williams, Hal Kanter; *C:* James Wong Howe; *M:* Alex North. Academy Awards '55: Best Actress (Magnani), Best Art Direction/Set Decoration (B & W), Best Black and White Cinematography; British Academy Awards '56: Best Actress (Magnani); Golden Globe Awards '56: Best Actress—Drama (Magnani), Best Supporting Actress (Pavan); New York Film Critics Awards '55: Best Actress (Magnani); Nominations: Academy Awards '55: Best Costume Design (B & W), Best Film Editing, Best Picture, Best Supporting Actress (Pavan), Best Original Dramatic/Comedy Score. *PAR, FCT, BTV*

Roseanne: An Unauthorized Biography 🎸 1994

Boring TV movie about the boorish (ex-)duo of Tom Arnold and Roseanne Barr Pentland Arnold. Recounts her trou-

bled upbringing in Salt Lake City, her stormy marriage, and her long slog toward fame as a "domestic goddess" stand-up comedienne and TV series star. Miscasting of both leads hurts any chance this poor substitute had. **90m/C VHS.** Denny Dillon, David Graf, John Walcutt, John Karlen, Judith Scarpone, Danielle Harris. *PGV*

Rosebud 🎸 1975 (PG)

Embarassingly dull film finds a group of PLO terrorists kidnapping five young women who were vacationing aboard O'Toole's yacht. He's supposedly a journalist but actually works for the CIA. Action ping-pongs between the plight of the victims and what's being done to rescue them but it's so boring you won't care. "Rosebud" is the name of the yacht. Based on a novel by Joan Hemingway and Paul Bonnecarrere. **126m/C VHS.** Peter O'Toole, Richard Attenborough, Kim Cattrall, Brigitte Ariel, Isabelle Huppert, Lalla Ward, Deborah Berger, Cliff Gorman, Claude Dauphin, Peter Lawford, Raf Vallone, Adrienne Corri; *D:* Otto Preminger; *W:* Eric Lee Preminger, Marjorie Kellogg. *MGM*

Rosebud Beach Hotel 🎸 *The Big Lobby; The No-Tell Hotel* 1985 (R)

Wimpy loser tries his hand at managing a run-down hotel in order to please his demanding girlfriend. Camp is okay, but this soft-porn excuse is horrible in every other way. **82m/C VHS, Beta, LV.** Colleen Camp, Peter Scolari, Christopher Lee, Fran Drescher, Eddie Deezen, Chuck McCann, Hank Garrett, Hamilton Camp, Cherie Currie; *D:* Harry Hurwitz; *C:* Joao Fernandes. *ART, VES*

Roseland 🎸🎸🎸 1977 (PG)

Three interlocking stories, set at New York's famous old Roseland Ballroom, about lonely people who live to dance. Not fully successful, but strong characters, especially in the second and third stories, make it worth watching, although it lacks energy. **103m/C VHS, Beta, LV.** Christopher Walken, Geraldine Chaplin, Joan Copeland, Teresa Wright, Lou Jacobi; *D:* James Ivory; *W:* Ruth Prawer Jhabvala. *VES, CVC*

Rosemary's Baby 🎸🎸🎸🎸 1968 (R)

A young woman, innocent and religious, and her husband, ambitious and agnostic, move into a new apartment. Soon the woman is pregnant, but she begins to realize that she has fallen into a coven of witches and warlocks, and that they claim the child as the antichrist. Gripping and powerful, subtle yet utterly horrifying, with luminous performances by all. Polanski's first American film; from Levin's best-seller. **134m/C VHS, Beta, LV.** Mia Farrow, John Cassavetes, Ruth Gordon, Sidney Blackmer, Maurice Evans, Patsy Kelly, Elisha Cook Jr., Charles Grodin, William Castle, Ralph Bellamy; *D:* Roman Polanski; *W:* Roman Polanski; *C:* William A. Fraker; *M:* Krzysztof Komeda. Academy Awards '68: Best Supporting Actress (Gordon); Golden Globe Awards '69: Best Supporting Actress (Gordon); Nominations: Academy Awards '68: Best Adapted Screenplay. *PAR, MLB, BTV*

Rosencrantz & Guildenstern Are Dead 🎸🎸🎸 1990 (PG)

Playwright Stoppard adapted his own absurdist 1967 play to film—which at first look makes as much sense as a "Swan Lake" ballet on radio. Patience is rewarded for those who stick with it. Two tragicomic minor characters in "Hamlet" squabble rhetorically and misperceive Shakespeare's plot tightening fatally around them. Uprooted from the stage environment, it's arcane but hilarious if you're paying attention. Roth and Oldman are superb as the doomed duo. **118m/C VHS, Beta, LV, Closed Caption.** Gary Oldman, Tim Roth, Richard Dreyfuss, Iain Glen; *D:* Tom Stoppard; *W:* Tom Stoppard; *C:* Peter Biziou. Venice Film Festival '91: Best Picture. *TOU, FCT*

Roses Bloom Twice 🎸½ 1977

When a middle-aged widow decides to make up for some of the wild living that she missed during her marriage, she shocks her children. **87m/C VHS, Beta.** Glynis McNicoll, Michael Craig, Diane Craig, John Allen, Jennifer West; *D:* David Stevens. *NO*

Rosewood 🎸🎸🎸 1996 (R)

Based on the true story of the well-off African American community of Rosewood, Florida, which was destroyed by a white mob in 1923. Rhames is Mr. Mann, a war vet and Voight a white shopkeeper who, to-

gether, try to save innocent people from the tragic massacre that begins when a woman falsely accuses a black man of rape. Accurately shows the tensions present between blacks and whites of the time. Voight's character is not overly romanticized as the great white hope. The real hero is the reticent Rhames, a fictitious blend of real-life characters and Hollywood machismo. Both performances are strong and film succeeds as a detailed visual reminder of country's tragic history. Real-life survivors of the bloodshed finally won reparation from the Florida legislature in 1993. Singleton's location shoots in the Florida swamps caused problems for the crew, one of whom was sent to the hospital after a snake bite. *CW:* Violence and some sexuality. **142m/C VHS, LV, Closed Caption.** Ving Rhames, Jon Voight, Don Cheadle, Michael Rooker, Bruce McGill, Loren Dean, Esther Rolle, Elise Neal, Catherine Kellner, Akosua Busia, Paul Benjamin, Mark Boone Jr., Muse Watson, Badja Djola, Kathryn Meisle, Jaimz Woolvett; *D:* John Singleton; *W:* Gregory Poirier; *C:* Johnny E. Jensen; *M:* John Williams. *WAR*

Rosie: The Rosemary Clooney Story 🎸🎸½ 1982

Above average biography of Clooney's up-and-down career. Locke lip-synches Clooney's voice in songs. Orlando doesn't help matters portraying Jose Ferrer. Made for television. **100m/C VHS, Beta.** Sondra Locke, Tony Orlando, Penelope Milford, Katherine Helmond, Kevin McCarthy, John Karlen, Cheryl Anderson, Robert Ridgely, Joey Travolta; *D:* Jackie Cooper; *Performed by:* Rosemary Clooney. *ART*

Roswell: The U.F.O. Cover-Up 🎸🎸½ 1994 (PG-13)

Fact-based drama finds intelligence officer Major Jesse Marcel (McLachlan) investigating the wreckage of a craft near his Roswell, New Mexico air base in the summer of 1947. Marcel believes the craft is extraterrestrial—as are the strange bodies recovered from the wreckage. An Air Force press release announces a UFO but is quickly retracted and Marcel's suspicions ridiculed. A 30-year reunion still finds him obsessed and seeking to clear his name but this time Marcel's investigations may finally lead to the truth. Made for TV; based on the book "UFO Crash at Roswell" by Kevin D. Randle and Donald R. Schmitt. *CW:* Brief strong language. **91m/C VHS, LV, Closed Caption.** Kyle MacLachlan, Dwight Yoakam, Kim Greist, Martin Sheen, Xander Berkeley, J.D. Daniels, Doug Wert, John M. Jackson, Peter MacNicol, Bob Gunton, Charles Martin Smith; *D:* Jeremy Paul Kagan; *W:* Jeremy Paul Kagan, Arthur Kopit, Paul Davids; *C:* Steven Poster; *M:* Elliot Goldenthal. *REP*

R.O.T.O.R. 🎸 1988

R.O.T.O.R. (Robotic Officer of Tactical Operations Research) is a law enforcement robot that is supposed to stop criminals. But watch out! It might go beserk and wreck your town. **90m/C VHS, LV.** Richard Gesswein, Margaret Trigg, Jayne Smith; *D:* Cullen Blaine. *IMP*

Rough Cut 🎸🎸 1980 (PG)

American diamond thief Reynolds lives in London, pursued by an aging Scotland Yard detective who wants to end his career in a blaze of glory. A beautiful lady is the decoy. Good chemistry; lousy script. **112m/C VHS, Beta, LV.** Burt Reynolds, Lesley-Anne Down, David Niven, Timothy West, Joss Ackland, Patrick Magee; *D:* Donald Siegel; *W:* Larry Gelbart; *C:* Frederick A. (Freddie) Young. *PAR*

Rough Justice 🎸½ 1987

Spaghetti western about a lone gunfighter tracking down three killers. Kinski is a sexually aroused bad guy in this miserable excuse. What could he have been thinking? **95m/C VHS, Beta.** *IT* Klaus Kinski, Steven Tedd; *D:* Mario Costa. *TWE*

Rough Magic 🎸🎸 *Miss Shumway; Jette un Sort* 1995 (PG-13)

Fantasy-noir-romance-comedy-on-the-road-movie-nostalgia-fest can't decide what it wants to be when it grows up. Fonda is a magician's assistant, with latent powers of her own, who flees to Mexico after witnessing a murder. Her fiance (Moffett) turns out to be the culprit and he hires drifter Crowe to track her down. Along the way, they meet a quack doctor (Broadbent) trying to find a magic Mayan potion, a garage owner who becomes a sausage, and a one man. Sure, it's confusing, but the performances are good, and you could always play "Name That Genre" afterwards. Adapted from the novel "Miss Shumway Waves a Wand" by James Hadley Chase.**CW:** Sex-related content and some violence. **104m/C VHS.** *GB FR* Bridget Fonda, Russell Crowe, Jim Broadbent, D.W. Moffett, Paul Rodriguez, Euva Anderson; **D:** Clare Peploe; **W:** Clare Peploe, Robert Mundy, William Brookfield; **C:** John Campbell; **M:** Richard Hartley. *COL*

Rough Night in Jericho ♂♂½ 1967
Martin plays unredeemable scum in this cliched western. He's an ex-lawman trying to take over the town of Jericho and all that's left to own is the stagecoach line run by Simmons and McIntire. Coming to Simmons aid is Peppard, a former deputy marshall turned gambler. Predicatably violent. **104m/C VHS, Closed Caption.** Dean Martin, Jean Simmons, George Peppard, John McIntire, Slim Pickens, Don Galloway; **D:** Arnold Laven; **W:** Sydney Boehm, Marvin H. Albert. *USH, FCT*

Rough Riders ♂♂½ 1997 Cable TV miniseries covering the adventures of the Volunteer Cavalry, led by a pre-presidential Teddy Roosevelt (Berneger), and their travails during the Spanish-American War in 1898. Fighting in Cuba, the Calvary were a mixture of western outlaws and cowboys and eastern bluebloods—all of whom would have to learn to fight together. Filmed on locations in Texas. **240m/C VHS.** Tom Berenger, Sam Elliott, Gary Busey, Brad Johnson, Christopher Noth, Brian Keith, George Hamilton, R. Lee Ermey, Nicholas Chinlund, Dale Dye, Holt McCallany, Illeana Douglas, Geoffrey Lewis, William Katt, Adam Storke, Dakin Matthews, Francesco Quinn, Titus Welliver, Mark Moses; **D:** John Milius; **W:** John Millus, Hugh Wilson; **C:** Tony Richmond; **M:** Peter Bernstein. *WAR*

Rough Riders of Cheyenne ♂½ 1945 Sunset Carson ends the feud between the Carsons and the Sterlings. **54m/B VHS, Beta.** Sunset Carson, Peggy Stewart.

Rough Riders' Roundup ♂♂ 1939 Roy and the boys rid a mining town of its crooked manager. Less yodeling than later Roger's outings; also better all around. **54m/B VHS, Beta.** Roy Rogers, Raymond Hatton, Lynn (Mary Hart) Roberts, Dorothy Sebastian, Duncan Renaldo, George Montgomery; **D:** Joseph Kane. *NOS, VDM, DVT*

Rough Ridin' Rhythm ♂½ 1937 Wallace is kidnapped to care for the orphaned child of a bandit's sister with Maynard being accused of having murdered the woman. But he's innocent and fights the gang to clear his name. Based on the story "Getting a Start in Life" by James Oliver Curwood. **58m/B VHS.** Kermit Maynard, Beryl Wallace, Ralph Peters, Betty Mack, Curly Dresden; **D:** J.P. McGowan. *GPV*

Rough Riding Rangers ♂½ *The Secret Stranger* 1935 Threatening letters plague a western ranch family. **57m/B VHS, Beta.** Rex Lease, Janet Chandler. *VCN*

Roughnecks ♂½ 1980 A team of Texas oil drillers attempt to dig the deepest oil well in history and chase women on the side. Too long, and not particularly action-packed or gripping. Made for television. **240m/C VHS, Beta.** Sam Melville, Cathy Lee Crosby, Vera Miles, Harry (Henry) Morgan, Steve Forrest, Stephen McHattie, Wilford Brimley; **D:** Bernard McVeety.

Round Midnight ♂♂♂ 1986 (R) An aging, alcoholic black American jazz saxophonist comes to Paris in the late 1950s seeking an escape from his self-destructive existence. A devoted young French fan spurs him to one last burst of creative brilliance. A moody, heartfelt homage to such expatriate bebop musicians as Bud Powell and Lester Young. In English and French with English subtitles. Available in a Spanish-subtitled version. **132m/C VHS, Beta, LV, Closed Caption.** *FR* Dexter Gordon, Lonette McKee, Francois Cluzet, Martin Scorsese, Herbie Hancock, Sandra Reaves-Phillips; **D:**

Bertrand Tavernier; **W:** Bertrand Tavernier, David Rayfiel; *C:* Bruno de Keyzer; *M:* Herbie Hancock. Academy Awards '86: Best Original Score; Nominations: Academy Awards '86: Best Actor (Gordon). *MVD, WAR, FCT*

Round Numbers ♂♂½ 1991 (R) Judith Schweitzer believes her husband "Big Al the Muffler King" is having an affair with the gorgeous Muffler Mate of the Month, Mitzi (Playboy Playmate Hope Marie Carlton). Determined to get revenge, Judith books herself into the same health spa that Mitzi attends and the result is pure comedy.**CW:** Language. **98m/C VHS, Closed Caption.** Kate Mulgrew, Samantha Eggar, Marty Ingels, Hope Marie Carlton, Shani Wallis, Natalie Barish, Debra Christofferson; **D:** Nancy Zala; **W:** Nancy Zala.

Round Trip to Heaven ♂♂ 1992 (R) Party guy Larry (Feldman) and his innocent cousin (Galligan) take off in a borrowed Rolls Royce to go meet Larry's dream centerfold in a super model contest. Unfortunately, the Rolls' trunk is loaded with stolen money and Stoneface (Sharkey), the felon who stashed the cash, wants the money back. With Stoneface in pursuit these guys are in for the ride of their lives. For the teen set only. Also available with Spanish subtitles.**CW:** Langauge, nudity, violence, and some sexuality. **97m/C VHS, LV, Closed Caption.** Corey Feldman, Zach Galligan, Julie McCullough, Rowanne Brewer, Ray Sharkey; **D:** Alan Roberts.

The Round Up ♂♂½ *Szegenylegenyek Nehezeletuck; The Hopeless Ones; The Poor Outlaws* 1966 Brutal tale spins a realistic political web of fear. Set in 1868 in a prison camp, suspected Hungarian subversives, largely peasants and herdsmen, are thrown into jail and tortured. A direct and shocking exploration of life under dehumanizing, totalitarian rule. In Hungarian with English subtitles. **90m/B VHS.** *HU* Janos Gorbe, Tibor Molnar, Andras Kozak; **D:** Miklos Jancso; **W:** Gyula Hernadi. *FST, HTV*

Round-Up Time in Texas ♂♂ 1937 Autry delivers a herd of horses to his diamond-prospector brother in South Africa and has to deal with bandits after the jewels. Typical early Autry entry, with singin' on the side. **54m/B VHS, Beta.** Gene Autry, Smiley Burnette; **D:** Joseph Kane. *NOS, VCN, VYY*

The Rounders ♂♂½ 1965 Two aging, no-account cowboys (Ford and Fonda) dream of giving up their bronco-busting ways to open a bar in Tahiti where they can watch the world go by. But they have a habit of blowing all their money on women, whiskey, and bad bets. An ornery unbreakable horse may be the key to changing their luck. Mild-mannered comedy with beautiful Arizona scenery. **85m/C VHS, Closed Caption.** Glenn Ford, Henry Fonda, Sue Ane Langdon, Hope Holiday, Chill Wills, Edgar Buchanan, Kathleen Freeman, Joan Freeman, Denver Pyle; **D:** Burt Kennedy; **W:** Burt Kennedy; **C:** Paul Vogel. *MGM*

Rounding Up the Law ♂♂½ 1922 Good guy dupes bad guy while organ plays. **62m/B VHS, Beta, 8mm.** Russell Gordon, Chet Ryan, Patricia Palmer, William McCall, Guinn "Big Boy" Williams; **D:** Charles Seeling. *VYY, GPV*

Roustabout ♂♂½ 1964 (PG) A roving, reckless drifter joins a carnival and romances the owner's daughter. Elvis rides on good support from Stanwyck et al. Welch has a bit part in her film debut; look for Terri Garr as a dancer. ♫Roustabout; Poison Ivy League; One Track Heart; Little Egypt; Wheels on My Heels; It's a Wonderful World; It's Carnival Time; Hard Knocks; There's a Brand New Day on the Horizon. **101m/C VHS, Beta.** Elvis Presley, Barbara Stanwyck, Joan Freeman, Leif Erickson, Sue Ane Langdon, Pat Buttram, Joan Staley, Dabbs Greer, Steve Brodie, Jack Albertson, Marianna Hill, Beverly Adams, Billy Barty, Richard Kiel, Raquel Welch; **D:** John Rich. *FOX, MVD*

The Rousters ♂♂½ 1990 (PG) Descendants of Wyatt Earp run a carnival in a small Western town. Comic misadventures arise when a modern varmint named Clayton comes looking

for action. Cannell (of "The A-Team" and "Riptide" fame) co-wrote and produced—with his usual extraordinary mix of the absurd and the dangerous. Unusual vehicle for Rogers, but she keeps her style and humor. Made for TV. **72m/C VHS, LV.** Jim Varney, Mimi Rogers, Chad Everett, Maxine Stuart, Hoyt Axton; **D:** E.W. Swackhamer; **W:** E.W. Swackhamer, Stephen J. Cannell. *THV*

Rover Dangerfield ♂♂ 1991 (G) Lovable Las Vegas hound Rover Dangerfield searches for respect but finds none. The results are hilarious. Quality animation from a project developed by Rodney Dangerfield and Harold Ramis. **78m/C VHS, LV, 8mm. D:** Jim George; **W:** Harold Ramis; **M:** David Newman; **V:** Rodney Dangerfield. *WAR*

Roxanne ♂♂♂ 1987 (PG) A modern comic retelling of "Cyrano de Bergerac." The romantic triangle between a big nosed, small town fire chief, a shy fireman and the lovely astronomer they both love. Martin gives his most sensitive and believable performance. Don't miss the bar scene where he gets back at a heckler. A wonderful adaptation for the modern age. **107m/C VHS, Beta, LV, 8mm, Closed Caption.** Steve Martin, Daryl Hannah, Rick Rossovich, Shelley Duvall, Michael J. Pollard, Fred Willard, John Kapelos, Max Alexander, Damon Wayans, Matt Lattanzi, Kevin Nealon; **D:** Fred Schepisi; **W:** Steve Martin; **C:** Ian Baker; **M:** Bruce Smeaton. Los Angeles Film Critics Association Awards '87: Best Actor (Martin); National Society of Film Critics Awards '87: Best Actor (Martin); Writers Guild of America '87: Best Adapted Screenplay. *COL*

Roxie Hart ♂♂½ 1942 Sassy '20s Chicago dance hall girl Roxie (Rogers) decides to take the fall when hubby (Chandler) murders a man. (She sees it as a publicity boost to her career). Slick lawyer Billy Flynn (Menjou) knows he can get the tootsie off if she justs flashes the jury her considerable sex appeal. Montgomery's a smitten reporter who catches Roxie's eye. Based on the play "Chicago" by Maurine Watkins and previously filmed in 1927. Bob Fosse later adapted the play for a Broadway musical. **75m/B VHS.** Ginger Rogers, Adolphe Menjou, George Montgomery, Lynne Overman, Nigel Bruce, Phil Silvers, Sara Allgood, William Frawley, Spring Byington, George Chandler; **D:** William A. Wellman; **W:** Nunnally Johnson; **C:** Leon Shamroy; **M:** Alfred Newman. *FXV*

The Royal Bed ♂♂½ *The Queen's Husband* 1931 King Eric's queen really wears the pants in the family, and when she leaves on a trip, he's left helpless and hapless. A revolution erupts, and his daughter announces she plans to marry a commoner. What's a king to do? **74m/B VHS, Beta.** Lowell Sherman, Nance O'Neil, Mary Astor, Anthony Bushell, Gilbert Emery, Robert Warwick, J. Carrol Naish; **D:** Lowell Sherman. *VYY*

Royal Deceit ♂½ *Prince of Jutland* 1994 (R) Young Amled (Bale) is heir to the 6th century kingdom of Jutland. But when his father is murdered by Amled's jealous uncle Fenge (Byrne), the youth feigns insanity to save himself and then begins to plot his revenge. Very familiar story doesn't arouse more than mild interest despite the cast.**CW:** Some violence and scenes of nudity. **85m/C VHS, LV, Closed Caption.** Gabriel Byrne, Helen Mirren, Christian Bale, Brian Cox, Kate Beckinsale; **D:** Gabriel Axel. *TOU*

Royal Flash ♂♂♂ 1975 (PG) Satirical adventure picture, witty and fast paced, with a few real life period characters thrown in for good measure. Cowardly swashbuckler Flashman, wanting to enter high society, is used to advance a political cause when he is forced to impersonate a Prussian nobleman and marry a duchess. Script by Fraser and based on his series of novels featuring the Flashman character. **98m/C VHS.** *GB* Malcolm McDowell, Alan Bates, Florinda Bolkan, Oliver Reed, Britt Ekland, Lionel Jeffries, Tom Bell, Alastair Sim, Michael Hordern, Joss Ackland, Christopher Cazenove, Bob Hoskins; **D:** Richard Lester; **W:** George MacDonald Fraser; **C:** Geoffrey Unsworth. *NO*

A Royal Scandal ⵛⵛ½ **1996** And you thought Chuck and Di made a hash of their marriage. The British should be used to marital scandal as this saga on the disasters befalling Princess Caroline of Brunswick (Lynch) and Prince George (Grant), aptly demonstrates. The extravagant George is forced to marry through political and financial pressure but loathes the unrefined Caroline practically on sight. As soon as a royal heir is on the way, they cease to live together and George goes back to his mistresses. But although Caroline will agree to a settlement, she refuses a divorce and when George becomes King George IV, Caroline fully intends to be Queen. **60m/C VHS.** *GB* Richard E. Grant, Susan Lynch, Frances Barber, Michael Kitchen, Denis Lawson, Oliver Ford Davies, Irene Richards; *D:* Sheree Folkson; *W:* Stanley Price; *C:* John Daly; *M:* John Altman. *FOX*

Royal Warriors ⵛⵛ *In the Line of Duty; Police Assassins; Ultra Force; Huang Jia Zhan Shi* **1986** Watch Michelle kick major butt! Policewoman Yeoh teams up with a retired Japanese cop and an airport security officer to prevent a terrorist highjacking. When the terrorist's associates decide to get even, the three must continue to fight together to save themselves. Chinese with subtitles or dubbed. **85m/C VHS, LV, DVD.** *HK* Michelle Yeoh, Henry Sanada, Michael Wong; *D:* David Chung. *TAI*

Royal Wedding ⵛⵛⵛ *Wedding Bells* **1951** Astaire and Powell play a brother-and-sister dance team who go to London during the royal wedding of Princess Elizabeth, and find their own romances. Notable for the inspired songs and Astaire's incredible dancing on the ceiling and walls; Lerner's first screenplay. The idea came from Adele Astaire's recent marriage to a British Lord. ♫Too Late Now; Sunday Jumps; How Can You Believe Me When I Said I Love You When You Know I've Been A Liar All My Life?; You're All the World to Me; The Happiest Day of My Life; Open Your Eyes; Ev'ry Night at Seven; I Left My Hat in Haiti; What A Lovely Day For A Wedding. **93m/C VHS, Beta, LV.** Fred Astaire, Jane Powell, Peter Lawford, Keenan Wynn, Sarah Churchill; *D:* Stanley Donen; *W:* Alan Jay Lerner. Nominations: Academy Awards '51: Best Song ("Too Late Now"). *MGM, NOS, CAB*

Royce ⵛⵛ **1993 (R)** After a successful mission, Royce's CIA team is disbanded. But some former agents aren't happy with early retirement and decide to go into business for themselves.***CW:*** Language, topless dance scene, and violence. **98m/C VHS, Closed Caption.** James Belushi, Chelsea Field, Miguel Ferrer, Peter Boyle; *D:* Rod Holcomb; *W:* Paul Bernbaum. *PAR*

R.P.M.* **(*Revolutions Per Minute)** ⵛ½ **1970 (R)** Another chance to relive the '60s. Student activists force the university hierarchy to appoint their favorite radical professor president. Hip prof-turned-prez Quinn is between a rock and a hard place, and allows police to crack down. Could have been intriguing, but loses steam; in any case, the script and direction both stink. **90m/C VHS, Beta.** Anthony Quinn, Paul Winfield, Gary Lockwood, Ann-Margret, Rigg Kennedy; *D:* Stanley Kramer; *W:* Erich Segal; *M:* Perry Botkin. *COL*

R.S.V.P. ⵛ½ **1984 (R)** Hollywood party honoring a writer turns tragic when a body is found in the guest of honor's pool. Most interesting part is watching the porn stars who make up most of the cast fail at acting while dressed. **87m/C VHS, Beta, LV.** Harry Reems, Lynda Wiesmeier; *D:* Lem Amero. *ART, VES*

Rubberface ⵛ **1981 (PG)** Tony Maroni (Carrey) is a real bad but very determined comedian. And he may just catch a break when he teams up with joke writer Janet (Glassbourg). Made for Canadian TV. **48m/C VHS, Closed Caption.** *CA* Jim Carrey, Adah Glassbourg; *D:* Glen Salzman, Rebecca Yates. *THV*

Rubdown ⵛⵛ **1993** An ex-baseball player, turned Beverly Hills masseur, finds himself the victim of a frame-up when one of his clients is murdered. **88m/C VHS, Beta, Closed Caption.** Jack Coleman, Michelle Phillips, Kent Williams, Alan Thicke, Catherine Oxenberg, William Devane; *D:* Stuart Cooper; *W:* Clyde Allen Hayes; *M:* Gerald Gouriet. *PAR*

Rubin & Ed ⵛⵛ **1992 (PG-13)** Ed is a real estate groupie who bribes the eccentric Rubin to attend a get-rich-quick seminar. Rubin decides to cash in on the favor by taking Ed on the road in search of the perfect gravesite for Rubin's long-dead feline. If that sounds wacky, just wait—the fun really begins when the duo is stranded in Death Valley and begins to suffer from sunstroke and hallucinations. Those who dream of weirdos bonding in the desert may be enthused but other viewers may thirst for something more. **82m/C VHS, LV.** Crispin Glover, Howard Hesseman, Karen Black, Michael Greene, Brittney Lewis; *D:* Trent Harris; *W:* Trent Harris; *C:* Bryan Duggan. *COL, FCT*

Ruby ⵛⵛ **1977 (R)** A young woman, christened in blood and raised in sin, has a love affair with the supernatural and murders up a storm at a drive-in. Confused, uneven horror a step up from most similar flicks. **85m/C VHS, Beta.** Roger Davis, Janet Baldwin, Piper Laurie, Stuart Whitman; *D:* Curtis Harrington; *W:* Barry Schneider. *NO*

Ruby ⵛⵛ½ **1992 (R)** Another in the increasing number of Kennedy assassination and conspiracy dramas—this one told from the viewpoint of Jack Ruby, Lee Harvey Oswald's killer. Confusing plot, somewhat redeemed by the performances of Aiello and Fenn. Combines actual footage of Ruby shooting Oswald with black-and-white filmed scenes. Based on the play "Love Field" by Stephen Davis.***CW:*** Language. **111m/C VHS, LV, Closed Caption.** Danny Aiello, Sherilyn Fenn, Arliss Howard, Tobin Bell, David Duchovny, Richard Sarafian, Joe Cortese, Marc Lawrence; *D:* John MacKenzie; *W:* Stephen Davis; *C:* Phil Meheux; *M:* John Scott. *COL*

Ruby Gentry ⵛⵛ½ **1952** White-trash girl Jones, cast aside by man-she-loves Heston, marries wealthy Malden to spite him, then seeks revenge. Classic Southern theme of comeuppance, good direction and acting lift it a notch. **82m/B VHS, Beta.** Charlton Heston, Jennifer Jones, Karl Malden; *D:* King Vidor. *FOX*

Ruby in Paradise ⵛⵛⵛ **1993 (R)** Leaving her dead-end life in Tennessee, Gissing (Judd) moves to Panama City, Florida and lands a job selling souvenirs for no-nonsense Mildred Chambers (Lyman). Although pursued by two very different men, Ruby concentrates more on self-exploration, recording her thoughts in a journal. A seemingly effortless portrayal of Ruby Lee by Judd (daughter of Naomi and sister of Wynonna Judd) makes for a pleasurable character study of a young woman on her own.***CW:*** Some language and some sexuality. **115m/C VHS, LV, Closed Caption.** Ashley Judd, Todd Field, Bentley Mitchum, Allison Dean, Dorothy Lyman, Betsy Dowds; *D:* Victor Nunez; *W:* Victor Nunez; *C:* Alex Vlacos; *M:* Charles Engstrom. Independent Spirit Awards '94: Best Actress (Judd); Sundance Film Festival '93: Grand Jury Prize; Nominations: Independent Spirit Awards '94: Best Cinematography, Best Director (Nunez), Best Film, Best Screenplay, Best Supporting Actor (Field). *REP*

Ruby Jean and Joe ⵛⵛ **1996 (PG-13)** Aging rodeo star Joe Wade (Selleck) doesn't want to leave the circuit even though it's obvious that his body can't take the punishment anymore. Joe gets more depressed until he picks up hitchhiker Ruby Jean (Johnson), a sarcastic teenager in search of a future. The unlikely duo form a friendship that may offer salvation to them both. Made for cable.***CW:*** Brief nudity, sensuality and language. **100m/C VHS, LV, Closed Caption.** Tom Selleck, JoBeth Williams, Rebekah Johnson, Ben Johnson; *D:* Geoffrey Sax; *W:* James Lee Barrett; *C:* James L. Carter; *M:* Stephen Graziano. *REP*

Ruby's Dream ⵛⵛ **1992** A bowling alley and nightclub owner dreams of making it big in Las Vegas. After his dreams crash to the ground, however, he realizes what is truly important in life. **100m/C VHS.** Joe Pesci. *QVD*

Ruckus ⵛⵛ *The Loner* **1981 (PG)** A Vietnam vet uses his training to defend himself when he runs into trouble in a small Alabama town. Less obnoxious than "First Blood," (which came later), but basically the same movie. **91m/C VHS, Beta.** Dirk Benedict, Linda Blair, Ben Johnson, Richard Farnsworth, Matt Clark; *D:* Max Kleven; *C:* Don Burgess. *NO*

Ruddigore ⵛⵛ **197?** The Lords of Ruddigore have been bound for centuries by a terribly inconvenient curse; they must commit a crime every day or die a horribly painful death. When the Lord of Ruddigore passes his mantle on to the new heir, the young heir loses both his good reputation and his very proper fiancee. A new version of Gilbert and Sullivan's opera. **112m/C VHS, Beta.** Vincent Price, Keith Michell, Sandra Dugdale. *FOX*

Rude ⵛⵛ **1996 (R)** Rude's (Lewis) a Jamaican-Canadian pirate-radio DJ in Toronto, who narrates three stories about urban life: window dresser Maxine (Crawford) struggles to recover from an abortion after her lover leaves her; frightened boxer Jordan (Chevolleau) tries to deal with his own homosexuality after participating with friends in a gay bashing; and ex-con Luke (Wint) returns to his wife (now a police officer) and young son. He tries to resist returning to his drug dealing past and cope with a jealous younger brother (Johnson). Debut for director Virgo.***CW:*** Strong graphic language, drug use, sexuality, and some violence. **90m/C VHS, LV.** *CA* Sharon M. Lewis, Richard Chevolleau, Rachael Crawford, Maurice Dean Wint, Stephen Ellen, Clark Johnson, Melanie Nicholls-King, Stephen Shellan; *D:* Clement Virgo; *W:* Clement Virgo; *C:* Barry Stone; *M:* Aaron David. *APX*

Rude Awakening ⵛⵛ½ **1981** A real estate agent is tortured by bizarre nightmares which lead to an unusual series of events. Part of the "Thriller Video" series. **60m/C VHS, Beta.** Denholm Elliott, James Laurenson, Pat Heywood; *D:* Peter Sasdy. *ART*

Rude Awakening ⵛⵛ **1989 (R)** Hippies Cheech and Roberts (where's Chong?) settled in a South American commune 20 years ago. Now they're back, and don't know what to make of old pals Carradine and Hagerty who have become—that's right—yuppies. Rip Van Winkle-ian farce draws a few yuks, but could have been much funnier. Points for trying. **100m/C VHS, Beta, LV.** Eric Roberts, Richard "Cheech" Marin, Julie Hagerty, Robert Carradine, Buck Henry, Louise Lasser, Cindy Williams, Andrea Martin, Cliff DeYoung; *D:* Aaron Russo, David Greenwalt; *W:* Richard LaGravenese; *M:* Jonathan Elias. *HBO*

Rudolph & Frosty's Christmas in July **1982** More animated adventures of Rudolph and friends. This time they are transported to a glittering, sunny seashore for a magical summer weekend that almost turns into tragedy. **97m/C VHS, Beta.** *V:* Red Buttons, Ethel Merman, Mickey Rooney, Jackie Vernon, Shelley Winters. *ART, TLF*

Rudolph the Red-Nosed Reindeer **1964** The durable Christmas story of the nasally enhanced reindeer who saved the holiday; colorful stop-motion animation and character voices bring it to life, with a memorable guest visit from an abominable snowman. Made for television. **53m/C VHS, Beta, LV, 8mm, Closed Caption.** *D:* Larry Roemer. *FHE, LME*

Rudy ⵛⵛ½ **1993 (PG)** Likeable, true story about a little guy who triumphs over big odds. Daniel "Rudy" Ruettiger (Astin) dreams of playing football for Notre Dame, no matter how farfetched the dream. He's a mediocre student, physically unsuitable for big time college ball, but sheer determination helps him attain his dream. Astin delivers an engaging performance and is backed up by a good supporting cast. Sentimental story stretches the truth with typical shameless Hollywood manipulation, but is still entertaining. From the director and writer of another David boots Goliath sports film, "Hoosiers." 112m/C VHS, LV, 8mm, Closed Caption. Sean Astin, Ned Beatty, Charles S. Dutton, Lili Taylor, Robert Prosky, Jason Miller, Ron Dean, Chelcie Ross, Jon Favreau, Greta Lind, Scott Benjaminson, Christopher Reed; **D:** David Anspaugh; **W:** Angelo Pizzo; **M:** Jerry Goldsmith. COL

Rudyard Kipling's The Jungle Book 🗡🗡½ The Jungle Book 1994 (PG)
Respectable live-action version from Disney of the Rudyard Kipling tale of Mowgli (Lee), the boy who's raised by a wolf pack after getting lost in an Indian jungle. This time around Mowgli gets to grow up—enough to have a romantic interest in the lovely Kitty (Headey), the daughter of British officer, Major Brydon (Neill). His rival is the supercilious Captain Boone (Elwes), who learns Mowgli knows the location of a hidden jungle treasure. Now Mowgli must count on his friends, Grey Brother the wolf, Baloo the bear, and Bagheera the black panther, to defeat the greedy Boone and win Kitty. Filmed in India. 111m/C VHS, LV, Closed Caption. Jason Scott Lee, Cary Elwes, Sam Neill, Lena Headey, John Cleese; **D:** Stephen Sommers; **W:** Stephen Sommers. DIS

Rudyard Kipling's the Second Jungle Book: Mowgli and Baloo 🗡🗡 Jungle Book 2; Mowgli and Baloo: Jungle Book 2; The Second Jungle Book: Mowgli and Baloo 1997 (PG)
Actually a prequel to "Rudyard Kipling's The Jungle Book," the story centers on the ten-year-old Mowgli (Williams) and his efforts to stay among his animal friends in the jungle. After he is spotted by a scout for P.T. Barnum's circus (Campbell), he must elude the hastily organized group that's out to capture and exploit him. He must also dodge the Bandars, a group of funky monkeys who want to make Mowgli their unwilling leader. The special effects are nowhere near as good as its predecessor, with matte shots that make some of the animals look like they were added with magic markers. The story is a classic, however, and the performances (especially Williams') are good. 88m/C VHS, Closed Caption. Jamie Williams, Bill Campbell, Roddy McDowall, Cornelia Hayes O'Herlihy, David Paul Francis, Gulsham Grover, Dyrk Ashton, B.J. Hogg, Al Robbins, Hal Fowler; **D:** Duncan McLachlan; **W:** Bayard Johnson, Matthew Horton; **C:** Adolfo Bartoli; **M:** John Scott. COL

The Rue Morgue Massacres 🗡½
1973 (R) A modern reprise of the Poe story with touches of Frankensteinia thrown in; plenty of gore. 90m/C VHS, Beta. SP Paul Naschy, Rossana Yanni, Maria Perschy, Vic Winner, Mary Ellen Arpon; **D:** Javier Aguirre. NO

Ruggles of Red Gap 🗡🗡🗡🗡 1935
Classic comedy about an uptight British butler who is "won" by a barbarous American rancher in a poker game. Laughton as the nonplussed manservant is hilarious; supporting cast excellent. Third and far superior filming of Harry Leon Wilson story. One of the all-time great comedies, the film was remade musically with Bob Hope and Lucille Ball as "Fancy Pants" (1950). 90m/B VHS, Beta. Charles Laughton, Mary Boland, Charlie Ruggles, ZaSu Pitts, Roland Young, Leila Hyams, James Burke, Maude Eburne; **D:** Leo McCarey; **W:** Walter DeLeon; **M:** Ralph Rainger. New York Film Critics Awards '35: Best Actor (Laughton); Nominations: Academy Awards '35: Best Picture. USH

Rule #3 🗡🗡 1993 "Never believe everything you see." That's the rule con artist Travis West lives by. This time he's got two scams planned—a Las Vegas real estate swindle and a cash ripoff of a former nemesis. Double- and triple-crosses abound. Based on the true story of West, who swindled more than $9 million in 15 years. 93m/C VHS. Mitchell Cox, Marcia Swayze; **D:** Mitchell Cox. AVI

Rulers of the City 🗡 1971 Young gangster avenges his father's death. 91m/C VHS, Beta. Jack Palance, Edmund Purdom, Al Cliver, Harry Baer. VDC

The Rules of the Game 🗡🗡🗡🗡 Le Regle du Jeu 1939 Renoir's masterpiece, in which a group of French aristocrats, gathering for a weekend of decadence and self-indulgence just before WWII, becomes a metaphor for human folly under siege. The film was banned by the French government, pulled from distribution by the Nazis, and not restored to its original form until 1959, when it premiered at the Venice Film Festival. A great, subtle, ominous film landmark. In French with English subtitles. The laserdisc version includes a commentary by director Peter Bogdanovich. Heavily copied and poorly remade in 1989 as "Scenes from the Class Struggle in Beverly Hills." 110m/B VHS, Beta, LV, 8mm. Marcel Dalio, Nora Gregor, Jean Renoir, Mila Parely, Julien Carette, Gaston Modot, Roland Toutain, Paulette Dubost, Odette Talazac; **D:** Jean Renoir; **W:** Jean Renoir. NOS, HHT, VYY

The Ruling Class 🗡🗡🗡½ 1972 (PG)
The classic cult satire features O'Toole as the unbalanced 14th Earl of Gurney, who believes that he is either Jesus Christ or Jack the Ripper. Tongue-in-cheek look, complete with dance and music, at eccentric upper-class Brits and their institutions. Uneven, chaotic, surreal and noteworthy. 154m/C VHS, Beta, LV. GB Peter O'Toole, Alastair Sim, Arthur Lowe, Harry Andrews, Coral Browne, Nigel Green; **D:** Peter Medak. National Board of Review Awards '72: Best Actor (O'Toole); Nominations: Academy Awards '72: Best Actor (O'Toole). WBF

Rumble Fish 🗡🗡🗡 1983 (R) A young street punk worships his gang-leading older brother, the only role model he's known. Crafted by Coppola into an important story of growing up on the wrong side of town, from the novel by S.E. Hinton. Ambitious and experimental, with an atmospheric music score; in black and white. 94m/B VHS, Beta, LV. Matt Dillon, Mickey Rourke, Dennis Hopper, Diane Lane, Vincent Spano, Nicolas Cage, Diana Scarwid, Christopher Penn, Tom Waits; **D:** Francis Ford Coppola; **W:** Francis Ford Coppola; **C:** Stephen Burum; **M:** Stewart Copeland. USH

Rumble in the Bronx 🗡🗡½ 1996 (R)
Singapore action star Chan plays a Hong Kong cop who comes to the South Bronx to attend his uncle's wedding and winds up caught in a crime war between the mob and a vicious motorcycle gang. Living special effect Chan choreographed and performed all of his own stunts, and they are remarkable (pay special attention to the hovercraft scene). Over-the-top cheesy dubbing and streets that are obviously not New York (filmed in Vancouver) add to the cartoonish fun. After several attempts to break into the American market, this is Chan's first release in the United States.**CW:** Some language and violent sequences. 91m/C VHS, LV, Letterbox, Closed Caption, DVD. HK Jackie Chan, Anita Mui, Francoise Yip, Bill Tung, Morgan Lam, Marc Akerstream; **D:** Stanley Tong; **W:** Edward Tang, Fibe Ma; **C:** Jingle Ma; **M:** J. Peter Robinson. NLC

Rumble in the Streets 🗡½ 1996 (R)
Street-smart young Rowe discovers that a psycho cop has decided to clean up the streets of Dallas by hunting down and killing kids like her and she must use her own toughness to survive. 74m/C VHS. Kimberly Rowe, David Courtemarche, Patrick DeFazio; **D:** Bret McCormick. NHO

The Rumor Mill 🗡🗡½ Malice in Wonderland 1986 The careers and titanic rivalry of influential Hollywood gossip writer Hedda Hopper and Louella Parsons, played with verve by Taylor and Alexander. Fictionalized script based on the book "Hedda and Louella" by George Eels. Made for TV. 94m/C VHS, Beta, LV. Elizabeth Taylor, Jane Alexander, Richard Dysart, Joyce Van Patten; **D:** Gus Trikonis; **W:** Jaqueline Feather, David Seidler; **M:** Charles Bernstein. THV

A Rumor of War 🗡🗡🗡½ 1980 The first big Vietnam drama for TV is a triumph, portraying the real-life experience of author Philip Caputo (based on his bestseller), from naive youth to seasoned soldier to bitter murder suspect at court

martial. Succeeds where Stone's later much-ballyhooed "Born on the Fourth of July" fails. Adapted by John Sacret Young. 195m/C VHS, Beta. Brad Davis, Keith Carradine, Michael O'Keefe, Stacy Keach, Steve Forrest, Richard Bradford, Brian Dennehy, John Friedrich, Perry Lang, Chris Mitchum, Dan Shor, Jeff Daniels; **D:** Richard T. Heffron.

Rumpelstiltskin 1982 From "Faerie Tale Theatre" comes the story of a woman who can spin straw into gold (Duvall) and the strange man who saves her life (Villechaize). Enjoyable for the whole family. 60m/C VHS, Beta, LV, Closed Caption. Bud Cort, Ned Beatty, Shelley Duvall, Herve Villechaize, Paul Dooley. FOX, FCT

Rumpelstiltskin 🗡🗡 1986 (G) Musical retelling of the classic Brother Grimm fairy tale. Irving plays a young girl who says she can spin straw into gold. Barty is a dwarf who helps her. The catch: she must give up her first born to pay him. Lackluster direction and uninspired acting make this version a yawner. Irving's real-life mother (Pointer) and brother have roles too. 84m/C VHS, Beta, LV, Closed Caption. Amy Irving, Billy Barty, Robert Symonds, Priscilla Pointer, Clive Revill, John Moulder-Brown; **D:** David Irving.

Rumpelstiltskin woof! 1996 (R) First director Jones inflicts "Leprechaun" upon us and now there's another warped dwarf on the loose. Single L.A. mom Shelly (Johnston-Ulrich) finds a wishing stone in a thrift shop and unwittingly summons up the little demon, who immediately tries to steal her young son. 91m/C VHS, Closed Caption. Kim Johnston-Ulrich, Tommy Blaze, Max Grodenchik, Allyce Beasley; **D:** Mark Jones; **W:** Mark Jones; **C:** Doug Milsome; **M:** Charles Bernstein. REP

Rumpole of the Bailey 198? John Mortimer's famed British barrister comes to life in McKern's portrait in two episodes taken from the television series. In "Rumpole and the Genuine Article," Rumpole is called on to defend an embittered artist in a forgery case. "Rumpole and the Old Boy Network" has the barrister drawn into blackmail and deception when a brothel is discovered in a respectable London neighborhood. Additional episodes available. 104m/C VHS. GB Leo McKern. MOV, SIG, TVC

Rumpole of the Bailey: Rumpole's Return 🗡🗡🗡 1990 A feature-length film based on the popular British television series. A middle aged barrister refuses to settle for less than justice. Based on the character created by John Mortimer. 106m/C VHS. GB Leo McKern. FCT

Run 🗡½ 1991 (R) A high energy action cartoon, with little plot but lots of stunts. Dempsey is a super-smart law student hired to drive a car to Atlantic City. A stop on the way starts trouble. Instant romance with a local girl balances mayhem from crime boss. Expect no more than physical feats and you'll be happy with this lightweight fare. 91m/C VHS, Beta, LV, Closed Caption. Patrick Dempsey, Kelly Preston, Ken Pogue, Alan C. Peterson, Sean McCann; **D:** Geoff Burrowes; **W:** Michael Blodgett; **C:** Bruce Surtees. HPH

Run, Angel, Run! 🗡🗡½ 1969 (R) Ex-biker Angel is on the run from his former gang after he helps expose them in a magazine article. He settles on a sheep ranch with his girl and then the gang shows up with revenge in mind. Prime drive-in fare with title song sung by none other than Ms. Tammy Wynette. 90m/C VHS, Beta. William Smith, Margaret Markov, Valerie Starrett; **D:** Jack Starrett. NO

Run for the Dream: The Gail Devers Story 🗡🗡½ 1996 (PG-13) Inspirational made-for-cable biopic on U.S. track star Devers (Woodard) who won a gold medal in the 100m sprint in the 1992 Olympics. But 17 months before, Devers suffers complications from a debilitating thyroid condition, Graves' Disease, which could not only cost her her career but her life. 99m/C VHS, Closed Caption. Alfre Woodard, Louis Gossett Jr., Robert Guillaume. HMK

Run for the Roses ⚗½ *Thoroughbred* 1978 **(PG)** "National Velvet" clone about a young Puerto Rican boy and a champion race horse in Kentucky. Cheery family fare. **93m/C VHS, Beta.** Lisa Eilbacher, Vera Miles, Stuart Whitman, Sam Groom; *D:* Henry Levin. *ART*

Run If You Can ⚗ 1987 **(R)** A woman sees a brutal murderer killing his victims on her television. Will she be next? **92m/C Beta.** Martin Landau, Yvette Nipar, Jerry Van Dyke; *D:* Virginia Lively Stone.

Run of the Arrow ⚗⚗ *Hot Lead* 1956 Rather than surrender to the North at the end of the Civil War, an ex-Confederate soldier (Steiger) joins the Sioux nation, engaged in war against the white man. Steiger's Irish brogue is weird and distracting, and the intriguing premise fails to satisfy, but the cast is competent and interesting. **85m/C VHS, Beta, LV.** Rod Steiger, Brian Keith, Charles Bronson, Ralph Meeker, Tim McCoy; *D:* Samuel Fuller; *W:* Samuel Fuller. *NO*

The Run of the Country ⚗⚗⚗ 1995 **(R)** Amid the scenic splendor of a small town south of the North Irish border in County Cavan, Danny (Keeslar) comes of age, sometimes the hard way. His relationship with his bullying dad (Finney), the local Garda officer, begins to crumble after the tragic death of his mum. So he runs away to live with the town malcontent Prunty (Brophy) and falls in love with the beautiful Annagh (Smurfit), who lives north of the border. Life gets even more complicated when Annagh learns she's pregnant. Director Yates, reunited with Finney for the first time since they won Oscars for "The Dresser," sometimes digs too deep into a big crock of standard Irish stew, occasionally delivering Celtic melodrama instead of poignant slice of life. The usual themes of family dysfunction, religious rebellion and moral dilemma are augmented by the occasional appearance of the IRA. As the frustrated, violent father, Finney shines. In their debut, Keeslar and Smurfit are fine, but Brophy's Prunty is the one you'll remember. Adapted by Connaughton (who used similar geography for "The Playboys") from his novel. *CW:* Strong sex scene and some language. **109m/C VHS, LV, Closed Caption.** Albert Finney, Matt Keeslar, Victoria Smurfit, Anthony Brophy, David Kelly; *D:* Peter Yates; *W:* Shane Connaughton; *C:* Mike Southon; *M:* Cynthia Millar. *COL*

Run, Rebecca, Run ⚗⚗½ 1981 Interesting family adventure yarn for the family about a South American refugee who tries to stop a young girl from leaving from an Australian island where they are both stranded. She eventually befriends him, and attempts to get permission for him to enter the country. **90m/C VHS, Beta.** *AU* Simone Buchanan, Henri Szeps; *D:* Peter Maxwell. *NO*

Run Silent, Run Deep ⚗⚗⚗ 1958 Submarine commander Gable battles his officers, especially the bitter Lancaster who vied for the same command, while stalking the Japanese destroyer that sunk his former command. Top-notch WWII sub action, scripted from Commander Edward L. Beach's novel. **93m/B VHS, Beta.** Burt Lancaster, Clark Gable, Jack Warden, Don Rickles, Brad Dexter; *D:* Robert Wise; *W:* John Gay. *MGM*

Run, Stranger, Run ⚗⚗ *Happy Mother's Day, Love, George* 1973 **(PG)** The inhabitants of a seaside house in Nova Scotia are paralyzed with fear when a number of brutal murders occur. A couple of sicko slasher scenes, but hard to swallow. **110m/C VHS.** Ron Howard, Patricia Neal, Cloris Leachman, Bobby Darin; *D:* Darren McGavin; *C:* Walter Lassally. *COL*

Runaway ⚗½ 1984 **(PG-13)** A cop and his sidekick track down a group of killer robots wreaking havoc. Self-serious, sorry sci-fi. Features Simmons of the rock group KISS. **100m/C VHS, Beta, LV, Closed Caption.** Tom Selleck, Cynthia Rhodes, Gene Simmons, Stan Shaw, Kirstie Alley; *D:* Michael Crichton; *W:* Michael Crichton; *C:* John A. Alonzo; *M:* Jerry Goldsmith. *COL*

Runaway 1989 A boy blames himself for his friend's accidental death and runs away to live in the subway tunnels of New York City. After four months of life underground, a disabled veteran and a waitress lend the boy a hand. Adapted from the novel "Slake's Limbo" by Felice Holman. Made for PBS and aired as part of the "Wonderworks" series. **58m/C VHS, Closed Caption.** Charles S. Dutton, Jasmine Guy, Gavin Allen; *D:* Gilbert Moses. *HMV, COL, FCT*

The Runaway Barge ⚗⚗ 1975 Tiresomely ordinary TV yarn about three adventurers earning their living on a riverboat. The usual cliches are present, including a gang of bad guys. **78m/C VHS.** Bo Hopkins, Tim Matheson, Jim Davis, Nick Nolte, Devon Ericson, Christina Hart, James Best; *D:* Boris Sagal. *ART*

The Runaway Bus ⚗⚗ 1954 Filled with the requisite motley crew of passengers, including a gold-carrying thief and the ever-befuddled Margaret Rutherford, a bus gets lost between airports and ends up in a deserted village. Would-be wacky comedy. **78m/B VHS, Beta.** *GB* Frankie Howerd, Margaret Rutherford, Petula Clark, George Coulouris; *D:* Val Guest. *VYY, FCT*

Runaway Father ⚗⚗½ 1991 Pat Bennett's husband fakes his own death in an attempt to abandon his family. When Bennett discovers he's alive she works to set a legal precedent—17 years worth of back child support. Based on a true story. Made for television. **94m/C VHS, Closed Caption.** Donna Mills, Jack Scalia, Chris Mulkey, Jenny Lewis; *D:* John Nicolella. *WOV*

Runaway Nightmare ⚗ 1984 Two western worm ranchers are kidnapped by a female gang whose members torture and initiate them, then talk about their plan to steal from organized criminals. Just another typical worm rancher flick. **104m/C VHS.** Michael Cartel, Al Valletta; *D:* Michael Cartel. *NO*

Runaway Train ⚗⚗⚗ 1985 **(R)** A tough jailbird and his sidekick break out of the hoosegow and find themselves trapped aboard a brakeless freight train heading for certain derailment in northwestern Canada. Harrowing existential action drama based on a screenplay by Akira Kurosawa. Voigt is superb. **112m/C VHS, Beta, LV, Letterbox, Closed Caption.** Jon Voight, Eric Roberts, Rebecca DeMornay, John P. Ryan, T.K. Carter, Kenneth McMillan; *D:* Andrei Konchalovsky; *W:* Andrei Konchalovsky, Djordje Milicevic, Edward Bunker; *M:* Trevor Jones. Golden Globe Awards '86: Best Actor—Drama (Voight); Nominations: Academy Awards '85: Best Actor (Voight), Best Film Editing, Best Supporting Actor (Roberts). *MGM*

The Runaways ⚗⚗ 1975 A boy runs away from an unhappy foster home situation and becomes friends with a leopard that has escaped from an animal park. Sentimental but well-done family fun. **76m/C VHS, Beta.** Dorothy McGuire, John Randolph, Neva Patterson, Josh Albee; *D:* Harry Harris. *NO*

Runaways ⚗ 1984 A corrupt politician's wife falls in love with the man who saved her when she attempted suicide. The two try to escape her husband's wrathful vengeance. **95m/C VHS, Beta.** Steve Oliver, Jennifer Ashley, Jim Russell. *NO*

The Runestone ⚗⚗ 1991 **(R)** After the eponymous viking relic is unearthed, an archaeologist's meddling frees a long-imprisoned wolfbeast that terrorizes New York. An adequate horror flick that taps the seldom-explored vein of Norse mythology. Based on a novel by Mark E. Rogers. **105m/C VHS, LV, Closed Caption.** Peter Riegert, Joan Severance, William Hickey, Tim Ryan, Chris Young, Alexander Godunov; *D:* Willard Carroll; *W:* Willard Carroll; *M:* David Newman. *ART*

The Runner Stumbles ⚗½ 1979 **(R)** Dated melodrama about a priest who goes on trial for murdering the nun with whom he fell in love in a mining town in the 1920s. Based on a true incident, from the play by Milan Stiff. Van Dyke in an unwanted serious role is miserably grim and wooden. **109m/C VHS, Beta, Closed Caption.** Dick Van Dyke, Kathleen Quinlan, Maureen Stapleton, Ray Bolger, Beau Bridges, Tammy Grimes; *D:* Stanley Kramer; *M:* Ernest Gold. *FOX*

The Runnin' Kind ⚗⚗½ 1989 **(R)** A yuppie expecting to inherit his father's Ohio law firm goes on a wild spree with an all-girl rock band. Sexy drummer Howard shows him the sights of certain parts of L.A. Original, fun comedy. Independent. **89m/C VHS, Beta.** David Packer, Pleasant Gehman, Brie Howard, Susan Strasberg; *D:* Max Tash. *FOX*

Running Against Time ⚗⚗½ 1990 **(PG)** A teacher tries to change history (and erase his brother's Vietnam War death) by time-warping back to 1963 and preventing JFK's murder. The made for cable TV movie takes an offhanded gee-whiz approach to a tantalizing premise, as temporal paradoxes multiply in "Back to the Future" style. No assassination-conspiracy theories, by the way, but Lyndon Johnson fans may not like his portrayal here. Based on the novel "A Time to Remember" by Stanley Shapiro. **93m/C VHS.** Robert Hays, Catherine Hicks, Sam Wanamaker, James DiStefano, Brian Smiar; *D:* Bruce Seth Green; *W:* Robert Glass. *USH*

Running Away ⚗⚗ 1989 **(PG-13)** Bittersweet story of WWII romance, with a twist of adventure. Strong cast creates good chemistry, but somehow the story is not engaging. Loren and Penny are mother and daughter, leaving Rome for the hills and encountering dangers. **101m/C VHS, LV, Closed Caption.** Sophia Loren, Sydney Penny, Robert Loggia, Andrea Occhipinti; *D:* Dino Risi. *PAR, FCT*

Running Blind ⚗⚗ 197? Espionage/adventure thriller has a double agent and a beautiful woman on the run in Iceland. **120m/C VHS.** *GB* Stuart Wilson, Heidi Steindorsottir. *FCT, VCO*

Running Brave ⚗⚗ 1983 **(PG)** The true story of Billy Mills, a South Dakota Sioux Indian who won the Gold Medal in the 10,000 meter run at the 1964 Tokyo Olympics. Not bad, but hokey in the way of many of these plodding true-story flicks. **90m/C VHS, Beta, LV.** Robby Benson, Claudia Cron, Pat Hingle, Denis Lacroix; *D:* D.S. Everett; *W:* Henry Bean. *DIS, TPV*

Running Cool ⚗⚗ 1993 **(R)** Two easy-going bikers join up with an old friend to protect his wetlands property from a lowlife developer and his stooges. Chicks (there's a romance with a local biker babe), motorcycles, fighting, and saving the environment—what more could you want? **106m/C VHS, Beta, Closed Caption.** Andrew Divoff, Tracy Sebastian, Dedee Pfeiffer, James Gammon, Paul Gleason, Arlen Dean Snyder, Bubba Baker; *D:* Beverly Sebastian, Ferd Sebastian; *W:* Beverly Sebastian, Ferd Sebastian. *PAR*

Running Delilah ⚗⚗½ 1993 Delilah (Cattrall) is a secret agent who is apparently killed by a vicious arms dealer. Only her fellow agent (Zane) resurrects her and Delilah is transformed into a cybernetic super agent. And her assignment is to go after a terrorist who's building a nuclear weapon with plutonium supplied by Delilah's killer. **85m/C VHS, Closed Caption.** Kim Cattrall, Billy Zane, Diana Rigg.

Running Free ⚗½ 1994 **(PG)** Sullen Garrett joins his naturalist mother in the Alaskan wilderness and establishes a friendship with a wolverine cub (who's smarter than the kid). **90m/C VHS, LV, Closed Caption.** Jesse Montgomery Sythe, Jayme Lee Misfeldt, Michael Pena; *D:* Steve Kroschel. *THV*

Running Hot ⚗⚗½ *Highway to Hell; Lucky 13* 1983 **(R)** Seventeen-year-old convicted murderer Stoltz gets love letter in prison from older woman Carrico. When he escapes, they flee the law together. Quick-paced and entertaining. **88m/C VHS, Beta.** Monica Carrico, Eric Stoltz, Stuart Margolin, Virgil Frye, Richard Bradford, Sorrels Pickard, Juliette Cummins; *D:* Mark Griffiths; *W:* Mark Griffiths. *ART, VES*

The Running Man ⚗⚗½ 1987 **(R)** Special-effects-laden adaptation of the Stephen King novel about a futuristic television game show. Convicts are given a chance for pardon—all they have to do is survive an on going battle with specially trained assassins in the bombed-out sections of Los Angeles. Sci-fi with an attitude 101m/C VHS, Beta, LV. Arnold Schwarzenegger, Richard Dawson, Maria Conchita Alonso, Yaphet Kotto, Mick Fleetwood, Dweezil Zappa, Jesse Ventura, Jim Brown; *D:* Paul Michael Glaser; *W:* Steven E. de Souza; *C:* Thomas Del Ruth; *M:* Harold Faltermeyer. ART

Running Mates ✍✍✍ 1986 (PG-13) Occasionally intriguing drama of two teens who fall in love, but are kept apart by their fathers' local political rivalry. Could have been better, but cardboard characters abound. 90m/C VHS, Beta. Greg Webb, Barbara Howard, J. Don Ferguson, Clara Dunn; *D:* Thomas L. Neff. VTR

Running Mates ✍✍✍ 1992 (PG-13) Cynically amusing political satire about a bachelor politician and his too intelligent lady love. Harris is Hugh, a U.S. senator looking forward to the presidential primaries when he meets widowed children's novelist Aggie (Keaton). He hates politics and he's Mr. Slick, although decent enough behind the political expediency. Aggie, however, has a potentially damaging secret in her past which causes the scandal-scenting pack of press hounds to bay in salivating anticipation. Will Hugh stick by Aggie and will Aggie overcome her natural political distaste for everything to end happily? A well-played romp. Made for cable television.*CW:* Language and sensuality. 116m/C VHS, LV, Closed Caption. Ed Harris, Diane Keaton, Ed Begley Jr., Ben Masters, Robert Harper, Brandon Maggart, Russ Tamblyn; *D:* Michael Lindsay-Hogg; *W:* A.L. Appling. HBO

Running on Empty ✍✍✍ 1988 (PG-13) Two 1960s radicals are still on the run in 1988 for a politically motivated Vietnam War-era crime. Though they have managed to stay one step ahead of the law, their son wants a "normal" life, even if it means never seeing his family again. Well-performed, quiet, plausible drama. 116m/C VHS, Beta, LV, 8mm, Closed Caption. Christine Lahti, River Phoenix, Judd Hirsch, Martha Plimpton, Jonas Arby, Ed Crowley, L.M. Kit Carson, Steven Hill, Augusta Dabney, David Margulies, Sidney Lumet; *D:* Sidney Lumet; *W:* Naomi Foner; *M:* Tony Mottola. Golden Globe Awards '89: Best Screenplay; Los Angeles Film Critics Association Awards '88: Best Actress (Lahti); National Board of Review Awards '88: Best Supporting Actor (Phoenix); Nominations: Academy Awards '88: Best Original Screenplay, Best Supporting Actor (Phoenix). WAR

Running Out of Luck ✍½ 1986 (R) A light, song-packed story about a rock star very much like Jagger who is abandoned in South America and believed dead, until he returns to his world. Features songs from Jagger's solo album "She's the Boss." 88m/C VHS, Beta, LV. Mick Jagger, Dennis Hopper, Jerry Hall, Rae Dawn Chong; *D:* Julien Temple. MVD, FOX

Running Scared ✍✍ 1979 (PG) Two young men, returning from military service as stowaways aboard an Army cargo plane, are caught by an intelligence agent and thought to be spies, because Reinhold has unknowingly photographed a secret U.S. base with his stolen Army-issue camera. Not-bad spy thriller with a twist—the "spies" are hapless nobodies, now on the lam. 92m/C VHS, Beta, LV. Ken Wahl, Judge Reinhold, John Saxon, Annie McEnroe, Bradford Dillman, Pat Hingle; *D:* Paul Glickler. NO

Running Scared ✍✍½ 1986 (R) Hip, unorthodox Chicago cops Hines and Crystal have to handle an important drug arrest before taking an extended vacation in Key West. Not as relentless as "48 Hrs.," but more enjoyable in some ways. Ever wonder what it's like to ride in a car at high speed on the tracks? Find out here. 107m/C VHS, Beta, LV, Letterbox, Closed Caption. Gregory Hines, Billy Crystal, Dan Hedaya, Jimmy Smits, Darlanne Fluegel, Joe Pantoliano, Steven Bauer; *D:* Peter Hyams; *W:* Gary De Vore. MGM

Running Wild ✍✍ 1927 Early silent comedy starring mustachioed Fields as an eternal coward who suddenly turns into a lion by hypnosis. Odd, often unfunny Fields entry sometimes hits

the mark. He's awfully mean, though. 68m/B VHS, Beta W.C. Fields, Mary Brian, Claud Buchanan, D. Gregory La Cava; *M:* Gaylord Carter. PAR

Running Wild ✍✍½ 1973 (G) A free-lance photographer becomes involved in a dispute to save a corral of wild mustang horses. The usual great Colorado scenery enhances a good, family-view story. 102m/C VHS, Beta. Lloyd Bridges, Dina Merrill, Pat Hingle, Gilbert Roland, Morgan Woodward; *D:* Robert McCahon; *W:* Robert McCahon.

Running Wild ✍ 1994 (R) Beautiful woman abandons her much older fiance to go on a wild road trip with his son that includes sex and crime.*CW:* Strong sexuality and language. 91m/C VHS, LV. Jennifer Barker, Daniel Dupont, Daniel Spector, Eliot Keener; *D:* Philippe Blot. APX

Rush ✍ 1984 A post-nuclear world war movie in which a rebel named Rush battles the rulers of a slave colony. 83m/C VHS. IT Conrad Nichols, Gordon Mitchell, Laura Trotter, Rita Furlan; *D:* Tonino Ricci. NO

Rush ✍✍✍ 1991 (R) Texas drug culture, circa 1975, is portrayed in this bleak cop drama. Rookie narcotics officer Kristen Cates (Leigh) goes undercover with the experienced Raynor (Patric) to catch a big-time dealer, menacingly played by Allman, and their bosses don't much care how they do it. Cates falls in love with Raynor and is drawn ever deeper into the drug-addicted world they are supposed to destroy. Fine performances and a great blues score by Clapton. The directorial debut of Zanuck. Based on ex-narcotics cop Kim Wozencraft's autobiographical novel.*CW:* Language, violence and graphic drug use, and sensuality. 120m/C VHS. Jason Patric, Jennifer Jason Leigh, Gregg Allman, Max Perlich, Sam Elliott, Tony Frank, William Sadler; *D:* Lili Fini Zanuck; *W:* Pete Dexter; *M:* Eric Clapton. MGM

Rush Hour 1998 Action-comedy features Tucker as an L.A. cop who must keep Hong Kong interloper Chan away from an FBI investigation concerning the Chinese consul's daughter. Not yet reviewed. ?m/C VHS. Jackie Chan, Chris Tucker, Tzi Ma, Julia Hsu, Philip Baker Hall, Rex Linn, Elizabeth Pena, Mark Rolston, Tom Wilkinson; *D:* Brett Ratner; *W:* Jim Kouf, Ross LaManna, Jeff Nathanson; *C:* Adam Greenberg. NYR

Rush It ✍½ 1977 Scriptwriters ponder possible plots over capucino: "I've got it! 'Bike Messengers in Love'!" "Nah. The title's too obvious. Why don't we call it 'Rush It'?" Much hard work and many months later, the result is forgettable. 78m/C VHS, Beta. Tom Berenger, Jill Eikenberry. UNI

Rush Week ✍ 1988 (R) Dead coeds populate campus during frat week. Greg Allman has bit part and the Dickies perform two songs. 93m/C VHS, LV. Dean Hamilton, Gregg Allman, Kathleen Kinmont, Roy Thinnes, Pamela Ludwig; *D:* Bob Bravler. COL

The Russia House ✍✍½ 1990 (R) Russian scientist Brandauer attempts to publish book debunking Soviet Union's claims of military superiority by passing it through ex-lover Pfeiffer to British editor Connery, apparently unaware of impending glasnost. Star-studded spy thriller aspires to heights it never quite reaches. Adapted from John Le Carre's novel, Stoppard's screenplay is very fine, actually making some aspects of the novel work better.*CW:* Langauge. 122m/C VHS, LV, 8mm, Letterbox, Closed Caption. Sean Connery, Michelle Pfeiffer, Roy Scheider, James Fox, John Mahoney, Klaus Maria Brandauer, Ken Russell, J.T. Walsh, Michael Kitchen, David Threlfall, Ian McNeice, Christopher Lawford; *D:* Fred Schepisi; *W:* Tom Stoppard; *C:* Ian Baker; *M:* Jerry Goldsmith. MGM, FCT

Russian Roulette ✍✍ 1975 The Russian premier is visiting Vancouver in 1970, and the Mounties must prevent a dissident KGB terrorist from assassinating him. Un-thrilling spy yarn fails to deliver on intriguing premise. 100m/C VHS, Beta. George Segal, Christina Raines, Bo Brundin, Denholm Elliott, Louise Fletcher; *D:* Lou Lombardo. FOX

Russian Roulette ✍✍½ 1993 Routine story about an American woman on vacation in Russia who finds herself in the middle of a plot to locate a hidden Czarist artifact and smuggle it out of the country. Everyone on her tour group is suspect, an American businessman becomes involved, and a killer starts eliminating the number of players. Great location scenery. 89m/C VHS. Susan Blakely, Barry Bostwick, E.G. Marshall, Jeff Altman; *D:* Greydon Clark. MNC

The Russian Terminator ✍ 1990 (R) An FBI agent is up against a one-man "death squad." 90m/C VHS. Helena Michaelson, Frederick Offrein, Harley Melin, Tina Tjung; *D:* Mats Helge; *W:* Mats Helge. XVC, DMP

The Russians Are Coming, the Russians Are Coming ✍✍✍ 1966 Based on the comic novel "The Off-Islanders" by Nathaniel Benchley, this is the story of a Russian sub which accidentally runs aground off the New England coast. The residents falsely believe that the nine-man crew is the beginning of a Soviet invasion, though the men are only looking for help. A memorable set of silly events follows the landing, engineered by a gung-ho police chief and a town filled with overactive imaginations. 126m/C VHS, Beta, Closed Caption. Alan Arkin, Carl Reiner, Theodore Bikel, Eva Marie Saint, Brian Keith, Paul Ford, Jonathan Winters, Ben Blue, Tessie O'Shea, Doro Merande, John Phillip Law; *D:* Norman Jewison; *C:* Joseph Biroc. Golden Globe Awards '67: Best Actor—Musical/Comedy (Arkin), Best Film—Musical/Comedy; Nominations: Academy Awards '66: Best Actor (Arkin), Best Adapted Screenplay, Best Film Editing, Best Picture. FOX, MLB

Russkies ✍½ 1987 (PG) A jolly comedy about three adorable American kids who capture, and eventually grow to like, a stranded Russian sailor. Friendly and peace-loving, but dull. 98m/C VHS, Beta, LV, Closed Caption. Joaquin Rafael (Leaf) Phoenix, Whip Hubley, Peter Billingsley, Stefan DeSalle, Susan Walters; *D:* Rick Rosenthal; *M:* James Newton Howard. ORI, WAR

Rustler's Hideout ✍ *Rustler's Roundup* 1944 One of numerous westerns starring Crabbe as cowboy do-gooder Billy Carson, here plodding through standard histrionics against rustlers, a cardsharp, and a business fraud. 60m/C VHS, Beta. Buster Crabbe, Al "Fuzzy" St. John, Charles "Blackie" King, John Merton, Lane Chandler, Hal Price, Edward Cassidy, Bud Osborne; *D:* Sam Newfield. GPV

Rustlers of Red Dog ✍✍½ 1935 A 12-chapter western serial about Indian wars and cattle rustlers. 235m/B VHS. Johnny Mack Brown, Raymond Hatton, Joyce Compton, Walter Miller, Harry Woods, William Desmond, Wally Wales, Chief Thundercloud, Art Mix, Bill Patton, Bud Osborne, Lafe McKee; *D:* Lew (Louis Friedlander) Landers. GPV

Rustler's Paradise ✍ 1935 Carey seeks revenge on the man who stole his wife and daughter. 59m/B VHS, Beta, LV. Harry Carey Sr., Gertrude Messinger, Edmund Cobb; *D:* Harry Fraser. NOS

Rustler's Rhapsody ✍✍ 1985 (PG) A singing cowboy rides into a small western town and encounters all kinds of desperados in this earnest would-be satire of '40s B-movie westerns. 89m/C VHS, Beta, LV, Closed Caption. Tom Berenger, Patrick Wayne, G.W. Bailey, Andy Griffith, Marilu Henner; *D:* Hugh Wilson; *W:* Hugh Wilson; *C:* Jose Luis Alcaine; *M:* Stephen Dorff. PAR

Rustler's Roundup ✍½ 1933 Mix rides to the rescue of Sinclair, whose daddy has been murdered by villains out to steal the ranch. 58m/B VHS. Tom Mix, Diane Sinclair, Noah Beery Jr., Douglass Dumbrille, Roy Stewart, Nelson McDowell, William Desmond, Frank Lackteen, Pee Wee Holmes, Bud Osborne; *D:* Henry MacRae. GPV

Rustler's Valley ✍✍ 1937 Hopalong Cassidy is a ranch foreman who tries to save his employer from the clutches of a crooked lawyer. Pretty fair ordinary range-ridin' saga. 59m/B VHS, Beta. William Boyd, George "Gabby" Hayes, Lee J. Cobb; *D:* Nate Watt. VYY

Rusty's Birthday 🎬🎬½ **1949** Danny searches for the lost Rusty who's been taken in by a family of transient workers. When Danny discovers his pal, he finds the young son of the family doesn't want to give Rusty up. **61m/B VHS.** Ted Donaldson, John Litel, Ann Doran, Jimmy Hunt, Ray Teal; **D:** Seymour Friedman; **W:** Brenda Weisberg. COL

The Rutanga Tapes 🎬½ **1990 (R)** Soviet bloc country has representatives in Africa producing deadly chemicals used for war and a dissident has taped evidence of native deaths. Reporter babe Simpson wants an exclusive, Petersen wants the dissident, Libyan agents want the tapes, you'll want to fast forward to the end.**CW:** Violence. **88m/C VHS.** Henry Cele, Arnold Vosloo, Wilson Dunster, David Dukes, Susan Anspach; **D:** David Lister.

The Rutherford County Line 🎬 **1987** A tough small-town sheriff searches for the killer of his deputies. **98m/C VHS, Beta.** Earl Owensby; **D:** Thom McIntyre. USH

The Ruthless Four 🎬🎬 Every Man For Himself; Each One For Himself; Sam Cooper's Gold; Each Man For Himself **1970** Quartet of unlikely mining partners match wills and wits and battle the elements. Not-so-hot spaghetti western, with good lead from Heflin. **97m/C VHS, Beta.** IT Van Heflin, Klaus Kinski, Gilbert Roland, George Hilton; **D:** Giorgio Capitani. MON

Ruthless People 🎬🎬🎬 **1986 (R)** DeVito and his mistress spend a romantic evening plotting his obnoxious wife's untimely demise. Before he can put his plan into action, he's delighted to discover she's been kidnapped by some very desperate people—who don't stand a chance with Bette. High farcical entertainment is a variation on the story "The Ransom of Red Chief," by O. Henry. **93m/C VHS, Beta, LV.** Bette Midler, Danny DeVito, Judge Reinhold, Helen Slater, Anita Morris, Bill Pullman; **D:** David Zucker, Jim Abrahams, Jerry Zucker; **W:** Dale Launer; **C:** Jan De Bont; **M:** Michel Colombier. TOU

Ruyblas 🎬🎬 **1948** Revenge and romance beset the court of Charles II in this tale of mistaken identity (with Marais in a dual role). Based on the novel by Victor Hugo. **90m/B VHS.** FR Jean Marais, Danielle Darrieux; **D:** Pierre Billon; **W:** Jean Cocteau. FCT

Ryan's Daughter 🎬🎬½ **1970 (PG)** Irish woman (Miles) marries a man she does not love and then falls for a shell-shocked British major who arrives during the 1916 Irish uprising to keep the peace. Not surprisingly, she is accused of betraying the local IRA gunrunners to her British lover. Tasteful melodrama with lots of pretty scenery that goes on a bit too long. **194m/C VHS, Beta, LV, Letterbox.** GB Sarah Miles, Robert Mitchum, John Mills, Trevor Howard, Christopher Jones, Leo McKern; **D:** David Lean; **W:** Robert Bolt; **C:** Frederick A. (Freddie) Young; **M:** Maurice Jarre. Academy Awards '70: Best Cinematography, Best Supporting Actor (Mills); Golden Globe Awards '71: Best Supporting Actor (Mills); Nominations: Academy Awards '70: Best Supporting Actor (Mills); Best Sound. MGM, BTV

Ryder P.I. **1988 (PG-13)** P.I Ryder and his sidekick fight crime and solve weird cases in the big city. **92m/C VHS, Beta.** Bob Nelson. MOV, VTR

Sabaka 🎬🎬 The Hindu **1955** Adventure set in India about a scary religious cult. Karloff and the cast of stalwart "B" movie performers have fun with this one, and you should, too. **81m/C VHS.** Boris Karloff, Reginald Denny, Victor Jory, Lisa Howard, Jeanne Bates, Jay Novello, June Foray; **D:** Frank Ferrin. SNC

Sabotage 🎬🎬🎬 Woman Alone **1936** Early Hitchcock thriller based on Conrad's "The Secret Agent." A woman who works at a movie theatre (Sidney) suspects her quiet husband (Homolka) might be the terrorist planting bombs around London. Numerous sly touches of the Master's signature humor. **81m/B VHS, Beta, LV, 8mm.** Oscar Homolka, Sylvia Sidney, John Loder, Desmond Tester, Joyce Barbour, Matthew Boulton, S. J. Warmington, William Dewhurst, Austin Trevor, Torin Thatcher, Aubrey Mather, Peter Bull, Charles Hawtrey, Martita Hunt, Hal Walters, Frederick Piper; **D:** Alfred Hitchcock; **W:** Charles Bennett, Ian Hay,

Alma Reville, E.V.H. Emmett, Helen Simpson. SNC, NOS, HHT

Saboteur 🎬🎬🎬 **1942** A man wrongly accused of sabotaging an American munitions plant during WWII sets out to find the traitor who framed him. Hitchcock uses his locations, including Boulder Dam, Radio City Music Hall, and the Statue of Liberty, to greatly intensify the action. Stunning resolution. **108m/B VHS, Beta, LV.** Priscilla Lane, Robert Cummings, Otto Kruger, Alan Baxter, Norman Lloyd, Charles Halton; **D:** Alfred Hitchcock; **W:** Alfred Hitchcock, Peter Viertel; **C:** Joseph Valentine. USH

Sabre Jet 🎬🎬 **1953** Run-of-the-mill wartime drama of hubbies flying combat missions in Korea and long-suffering spouses on the home front. **90m/C VHS, Beta.** Robert Stack, Amanda Blake, Louis King; **D:** Louis King. NO

Sabrina 🎬🎬🎬 Sabrina Fair **1954** Two wealthy brothers, one an aging businessman (Bogart) and the other a dissolute playboy (Holden), vie for the attention of their chauffeur's daughter (Hepburn), who has just returned from a French cooking school. Typically acerbic, in the Wilder manner, with Bogart and Holden cast interestingly against type (but it's Hepburn's picture anyway). Based on the play "Sabrina Fair" by Samuel Taylor. **113m/B VHS, Beta, LV.** Audrey Hepburn, Humphrey Bogart, William Holden, Walter Hampden, Francis X. Bushman, John Williams, Martha Hyer, Marcel Dalio; **D:** Billy Wilder; **W:** Billy Wilder, Ernest Lehman; **C:** Charles B(ryant) Lang. Academy Awards '54: Best Costume Design (B & W); Directors Guild of America Awards '54: Best Director (Wilder); Golden Globe Awards '55: Best Screenplay; National Board of Review Awards '54: Best Supporting Actor (Williams); Nominations: Academy Awards '54: Best Actress (Hepburn), Best Art Direction/Set Decoration (B & W), Best Black and White Cinematography, Best Director (Wilder), Best Screenplay. PAR

Sabrina 🎬🎬½ **1995 (PG)** Updated version of Billy Wilder's 1954 fairytale that starred a luminous Audrey Hepburn. This time around the pretty Ormond is the chauffeur's daughter who gets closely involved with the wealthy Larrabees. And this time the emphasis is more on workaholic business mogul Linus (Ford), who plays a dangerous game when he decides to transfer Sabrina's affections from his feckless engaged brother David (Kinnear) to himself in order to protect a business merger. Ford's a little too stodgy (you'll wonder why Sabrina bothers except she's probably just too nice to say no) but Kinnear's suitably charming (in his film debut) and Marchand properly matriarchal. **127m/C VHS, Beta, Closed Caption.** Harrison Ford, Julia Ormond, Greg Kinnear, Nancy Marchand, John Wood, Richard Crenna, Angie Dickinson, Lauren Holly, Fanny Ardant, Dana Ivey, Patrick Bruel, Miriam Colon, Elizabeth Franz; **D:** Sydney Pollack; **W:** David Rayfiel, Barbara Benedek; **C:** Giuseppe Rotunno; **M:** John Williams. Nominations: Academy Awards '95: Best Song ("Moonlight"), Best Original Score; Golden Globe Awards '96: Best Actor—Musical/Comedy (Ford), Best Film—Musical/Comedy, Best Song ("Moonlight"). PAR

Sabrina the Teenage Witch 🎬🎬½ **1996 (PG)** Based on the Archie Comics, this lighthearted cable movie finds 16-year-old Sabrina (Hart) being told by her two eccentric aunts, Hilda (Miller) and Zelda (Fernetz), that she is a witch, descended from a long line of good witches and warlocks. Sabrina's having enough trouble fitting in at Riverdale High without this kind of news but she does find that her magical powers have their advantages. The pilot for the TV series. **90m/C VHS, Closed Caption.** Melissa Joan Hart, Charlene Fernetz, Sherry Miller, Michelle Beaudoin, Ryan Reynolds, Tobias Mehler, Lalainia Lindbjerg; **D:** Tibor Takacs; **W:** Barney Cohen, Kathryn Wallack, Nicholas Factor. HMK

Sacco & Vanzetti 🎬🎬 Sacco e Vanzetti **1971 (PG)** Two Italian immigrants and acknowledged anarchists are caught amidst communist witch-hunts and judicial negligence when they are tried and executed for murder in 1920s America. Based on the true-life case, considered by some a flagrant miscarriage of justice and political mar-

tyrdom, by others, honest American judicial-system proceedings. Well-made and acted. Joan Baez sings the title song "The Ballad of Sacco and Vanzetti." **120m/C VHS, Beta.** Gian Marie Volonte, Riccardo Cucciolla, Milo O'Shea, Cyril Cusack, Geoffrey Keen; **D:** Guiliano Montaldo; **M:** Ennio Morricone. Cannes Film Festival '71: Best Actor (Cucciolla). NO

The Sacketts 🎬🎬½ **1979** Follows the adventures of three Tennessee brothers who migrate to the West after the Civil War. Based on two Louis L'Amour novels. Made for television. **198m/C VHS.** Jeffery Osterhage, Tom Selleck, Sam Elliott, Glenn Ford, Ben Johnson, Mercedes McCambridge, Ruth Roman, Jack Elam, Gilbert Roland; **D:** Robert Totten. WAR, HHE

Sacred Ground 🎬🎬 **1983 (PG)** A trapper and his pregnant Apache wife unknowingly build shelter on the Paiute Indians' sacred burial ground. When the wife dies in childbirth, the pioneer is forced to kidnap a Paiute woman who has just buried her own deceased infant. Average western drama. **100m/C VHS, Closed Caption.** Tim McIntire, Jack Elam, L.Q. Jones, Mindi Miller; **D:** Charles B. Pierce; **W:** Charles B. Pierce. FOX

Sacred Mountain/White Flame 🎬🎬🎬 **1931** Two short films starring Riefenstahl, featuring mostly fluid dance sequences and Teutonic mountain boy/girl plots. Silent. **60m/B VHS, Beta.** GE Leni Riefenstahl. FCT, GLV, MRV

The Sacrifice 🎬🎬🎬 **1986 (PG)** Tarkovsky's enigmatic final film, released after his death. Deals with a retired intellectual's spiritually symbolic efforts at self-sacrifice in order to save his family on the eve of a nuclear holocaust. Stunning cinematography by Nykvist. Acclaimed, but sometimes slow going; not everyone will appreciate Tarkovsky's visionary spiritualism. In Swedish and Russian with English subtitles. **145m/C VHS, LV, Letterbox.** FR SW Erland Josephson, Susan Fleetwood, Valerie Mairesse, Allan Edwall, Gudrun Gisladottir, Sven Wollter, Filippa Franzen; **D:** Andrei Tarkovsky; **C:** Sven Nykvist. British Academy Awards '87: Best Foreign Film. KIV, TPV

Sacrilege 🎬½ **1986** A nun and a nobleman engage in a hot love affair that fosters scandal, murder and, revenge. Cynical use of religious theme masks otherwise ordinary sex/romance flick. Controversial Italian-made erotic drama. **104m/C VHS, Beta.** IT Myriem Roussel, Alessandro Gassman; **D:** Luciano Odorisio.

The Sad Sack 🎬🎬 **1957** A bumbling hero with a photographic memory winds up in Morocco as a member of the French Foreign Legion. Although a success at the box office, Lewis's second movie (without partner Dean Martin) seems jerky and out of sorts today. Based on the comic strip character by George Baker, but not effectively. **98m/B VHS.** Jerry Lewis, Phyllis Kirk, David Wayne, Peter Lorre, Gene Evans, Mary Treen; **D:** George Marshall; **C:** Loyal Griggs; **M:** Burt Bacharach, Hal David. COL

Sadat 🎬🎬½ **1983 (PG)** Gossett, Jr., well plays his title role of Egyptian leader and Nobel Peace Prize winner Anwar el Sadat. But the controversial life and peace efforts of the president (assassinated in 1981) are given a quick overview in this average drama. Made for television. **195m/C VHS.** Louis Gossett Jr., John Rhys-Davies, Jeremy Kemp, Nehemiah Persoff, Madolyn Smith, Anne Heywood, Jeffrey Tambor, Barry Morse; **D:** Richard Michaels; **M:** Charles Bernstein. COL

Saddle Buster 🎬🎬 **1932** A rodeo cowboy loses his nerve after being thrown by a tough horse, but gets it back again by the end of the hour. Actual rodeo footage is incorporated into this low-budget bronco saga. **59m/B VHS.** Tom Tyler, Rosita(?), Helen Foster, Charles Quigley, Marie Quillen, Robert Frazer, Charles "Slim" Whitaker; **D:** Fred Allen. NOS, HEG

Saddle Mountain Round-Up ✍ 1941 The Range Busters are on the trail again as they smoke out a murderer. 61m/B VHS, Beta. Ray Corrigan, John "Dusty" King, Max Terhune. *NOS, DVT, RXM*

Sadie McKee ✍✍✍ 1934 A melodrama with Crawford as a maid searching for love in the big city. She falls for a self-destructive ne'er-do-well, marries an alcoholic millionaire, and eventually finds true love with the wealthy Tone (who would become Crawford's third husband). Professional acting and directing elevate the story. 90m/B VHS. Joan Crawford, Franchot Tone, Gene Raymond, Edward Arnold; *D:* Clarence Brown. *BTV*

Sadie Thompson ✍✍✍ 1928 Swanson plays a harlot with a heart of gold, bawdy and good-natured, in the South Seas. A zealot missionary (Barrymore) arrives and falls in love with her. The last eight minutes of footage have been recreated by using stills and the original title cards, to replace the last reel which had decomposed. Remade as "Rain," "Dirty Gertie From Harlem," and "Miss Sadie Thompson." Based on W. Somerset Maugham's "Rain." 97m/B VHS, LV. Gloria Swanson, Lionel Barrymore, Raoul Walsh, Blanche Frederici, Charles Lane, James Marcus; *D:* Raoul Walsh. Nominations: Academy Awards '28: Best Actress (Swanson), Best Cinematography. *KIV, MOV*

The Sadist ✍✍½ *The Profile of Terror* 1963 Three teachers on their way to Dodger Stadium find themselves stranded at a roadside garage and terrorized by a snivelling lunatic. Tense and plausible. 95m/B Beta. Arch Hall Jr., Helen Hovey, Richard Alden, Marilyn Manning; *D:* James Landis; *W:* James Landis; *C:* Vilmos Zsigmond. *SNC, RHI*

Safari 3000 ✍½ 1982 (PG) "Playboy" writer is assigned to do a story on a three-day, 3,000 kilometer car race in Africa. Doesn't take itself so seriously, and neither should we. Dumb, dull, and disjointed. 91m/C VHS, Beta. Stockard Channing, David Carradine, Christopher Lee; *D:* Harry Hurwitz; *M:* Ernest Gold. *MGM*

Safe ✍✍✍ 1995 (R) Surburban California housewife Carol (Moore) literally becomes allergic to her environment and winds up seeking relief in a holistic center in Albuquerque, where director Haynes takes a shot at the New Age and finds a link to the AIDS crisis. Serious, stylistically detached look at a near future riddled with environmental toxins is led by Moore's performance as the sunny suburbanite undone by the unseen. *CW:* Sex scene; brief language. 119m/C VHS, LV, Closed Caption. Julianne Moore, Peter Friedman, Xander Berkeley, Susan Norman, James LeGros, Mary Carver, Kate McGregor Stewart, Jessica Harper, Brandon Cruz; *D:* Todd Haynes; *W:* Todd Haynes; *C:* Alex Nepomniaschy; *M:* Ed Tomney. Nominations: Independent Spirit Awards '96: Best Actress (Moore), Best Director (Haynes), Best Film, Best Screenplay. *COL*

Safe Passage ✍✍ 1994 (PG-13) Grueling family drama with Sarandon and Shepherd portraying an unhappily married couple who are the parents of seven sons, one of whom is missing and presumed dead in the Sinai Desert war. One by one the grown boys arrive home to await any further news. They rehash memories, watch old videos, open old wounds, and generally affirm life. None of the performances, with the exception of Sarandon, are truly believable. She is the only one that brings any depth to her character as the tough matriarch that holds the family together. Feels like a TV movie, albeit one with classier names. Based on the novel by Ellyn Bache. *CW:* Profanity; scene of marijuana use. 98m/C VHS, LV, Closed Caption. Susan Sarandon, Sam Shepard, Robert Sean Leonard, Sean Astin, Marcia Gay Harden, Nick Stahl, Jason London, Philip Bosco, Matt Keeslar; *D:* Robert Ackerman; *W:* Deena Goldstone; *C:* Ralf Bode; *M:* Mark Isham. *TTC, NLC*

Safety Last ✍✍✍ 1923 Lloyd silent comedy about an average guy who goes to the big city to become a success, and his misadventures. Hilarious and still awe-inspiring building climbing scene set new standards for movies in sight gags

and comedy-thrill stunts, which became Lloyd's trademark. 78m/B VHS. Harold Lloyd, Mildred Davis, Bill Strothers, Noah Young; *D:* Fred Newmeyer, Sam Taylor. National Film Registry '94. *NO*

Saga of Death Valley ✍✍½ 1939 Rogers battles a band of outlaws and discovers that their leader is his own brother. Exciting and likeable early Rogers western. 56m/B VHS, Beta. Roy Rogers, George "Gabby" Hayes, Donald (Don "Red") Barry, Doris Day; *D:* Joseph Kane. *NOS, VDM, VCN*

The Saga of the Draculas ✍ *Dracula Saga; Dracula: The Bloodline Continues...; The Saga of Dracula* 1972 (R) An aging vampire wishes to continue his bloodline and seeks to convert his niece's baby to his bloodsucking ways. 90m/C VHS. *SP* Narciso Ibanez Menta, Tina Sainz, Tony Isbert, Maria Koski, Cristina Suriani, Helga Line; *D:* Leon Klimovsky. *SNC*

Saga of the Vagabond ✍ *Sengoku Gunto-Den* 1959 Arranged by master director Akira Kurosawa. A band of ruthless outlaws careen across a civil war-torn countryside. With English subtitles. 115m/C VHS, Beta. *JP* Toshiro Mifune, Michiyo Aratama; *D:* Toshio Sugie. *VDA*

Sagebrush Law ✍½ 1943 Western yarn has Holt playing a young man trying to clear the name of his bank president father. Barclay serves as the love interest and "Ukulele Ike" Edwards provides needed comic and music relief. 56m/B VHS. Tim Holt, Cliff Edwards, Joan Barclay, Edward Cassidy, Karl Hackett, Roy Barcroft, Ernie Adams; *D:* Sam Nelson; *W:* Bennett Cohen. *MOV*

Sagebrush Trail ✍✍✍ 1933 Wayne's second-ever western; complete with all sorts of tumbleweed and white-hat cliches. Our hero is wrongly accused of killin' a man, and busts out of the hoosegow to clear his name. Interesting plot twists makes for fun, compelling viewing. 53m/B VHS, LV. John Wayne, Yakima Canutt, Wally Wales; *D:* Armand Schaefer. *COL, REP, NOS*

Sahara ✍✍✍ 1943 A British-American unit must fight the Germans for their survival in the Libyan desert during WWII. Plenty of action and suspense combined with good performances makes this one a step above the usual war movie. 97m/B VHS, Beta. Humphrey Bogart, Dan Duryea, Bruce (Herman Brix) Bennett, Lloyd Bridges, Rex Ingram, J. Carrol Naish, Richard Nugent; *D:* Zoltan Korda; *M:* Miklos Rozsa. Nominations: Academy Awards '43: Best Black and White Cinematography, Best Sound, Best Supporting Actor (Naish). *COL*

Sahara woof! 1983 (PG) Disappointing "Perils of Pauline" type adventure. Shields disguises herself as a man (sure) to complete a race across the desert in honor of her late father, and a sheik captures her. 111m/C VHS, Beta, LV. Brooke Shields, Lambert Wilson, Horst Buchholz, John Rhys-Davies, Ronald Lacey, John Mills, Steve Forrest, Perry Lang, Cliff Potts; *D:* Andrew V. McLaglen; *W:* James R. Silke; *M:* Ennio Morricone. *MGM*

Saigon Commandos ✍ 1988 (R) Commandos, on the eve of the fall of Saigon in the 1970s, attempt to prevent heroin dealers from toppling the already-shaky government. So-so war/action flick. 84m/C VHS, Beta, LV. Richard Young, P.J. Soles, John Allen Nelson, Jimi B Jr.; *D:* Clark Henderson.

Saigon: Year of the Cat ✍ 1987 A made for British television drama about an American ambassador, a CIA operative, and a British bank clerk who try to leave Saigon in 1974 before the Vietcong enter the city. 106m/C VHS, Beta. *GB* Frederic Forrest, E.G. Marshall, Judi Dench; *D:* Stephen Frears; *W:* David Hare; *M:* George Fenton. *HBO*

Sailing Along ✍✍ 1938 British musical about a young starlet who sacrifices her career for true love. 80m/B VHS. *GB* Jessie Matthews, Barry Mackay, Jack Whiting, Roland Young, Noel Madison, Athene Seyler, Patrick Barr; *D:* Sonnie Hale. *FCT*

Sailor-Made Man/Grandma's Boy 192? Silent comedy shorts. In "A Sailor-Made Man" (1921) Lloyd joins the Navy. As shy "Grandma's Boy" (1922), he is given courage

and good advice to win the hand of a girl and defeat a bully. 83m/B VHS, Beta. Harold Lloyd. *TLF*

The Sailor Who Fell from Grace with the Sea ✍✍ 1976 (R) Perverse tale of a disillusioned sailor who rejects the sea for the love of a lonely young widow and her troubled son. Graphic sexual scenes. Based on the novel by Yukio Mishima, the film suffers from the transition of Japanese culture to an English setting. 105m/C VHS, Beta, LV. *GB* Sarah Miles, Kris Kristofferson, Jonathan Kahn, Margo Cunningham; *D:* Lewis John Carlino; *W:* Lewis John Carlino. *VTR, FOX*

The Saint 1967 Dashing and sophisticated Simon Templar (Moore), AKA "The Saint," is a gentlemanly hero/crook who takes on the causes of those who have been taken advantage of—and whose methods are often less than legal. Based on a popular series of mystery novels by Leslie Charteris, which debuted in the 1930s. Each volume from the British series contains two 50-minute episodes. 100m/C VHS. *GB* Roger Moore, Ivor Dean. *PGV*

The Saint ✍✍ 1968 Moore is Simon Templar, Leslie Charteris' mysterious British detective/hero in this adventure tale that takes him to Naples. Revival of and improvement on earlier movie series, and based on the very popular British television show. 98m/C VHS. *GB* Roger Moore, Ian Hendry. *FOX*

The Saint ✍✍½ 1997 (PG-13) The plot makes about as much sense as that of "Mission: Impossible," the villains are average ego-driven bad guys, and Shue's naive scientist/babe is totally unbelievable (she's like a deer caught in a car's headlights). The only reason the movie works at all is due to the debonair, if angst-ridden, charms of Kilmer as super-thief and master of disguise Simon Templar. He's hired by Russian strongman Ivan Tretiak (Serbedzija) to steal the formula for cold fusion from scientist Emma Russell (Shue) so that Tretiak can save a freezing Moscow by delivering cheap energy and thus make Russia a formidable power once again (with himself as leader, natch). Only problem is Templar, who names all his alter egos after saints, falls for Emma and tries to get them out of harm's way by double-crossing Tretiak. At least the Moscow and Oxford settings are scenic. Templar's exploits are featured in a series of novels by Leslie Charteris, and previously appeared in earlier movies and on TV. *CW:* Action violence, brief strong language, some sensuality and drug content. 118m/C VHS, Beta, Closed Caption. Val Kilmer, Elisabeth Shue, Rade Serbedzija, Valery Nikolaev, Henry Goodman, Alun Armstrong, Michael Byrne, Eugene Lazarev, Charlotte Cornwell, Irina Apexímova, Emily Mortimer; *D:* Phillip Noyce; *W:* Jonathan Hensleigh, Wesley Strick; *C:* Phil Meheux; *M:* Graeme Revell. Nominations: Golden Raspberry Awards '97: Worst Actor (Kilmer). *PAR*

St. Benny the Dip ✍✍½ *Escape If You Can* 1951 Three con-men evade police by posing as clergymen, and end up going straight after a series of adventures in a skid row mission. Funny in parts but extremely predictable. Still, good for a few laughs. 80m/B VHS. Dick Haymes, Nina Foch, Roland Young, Lionel Stander, Freddie Bartholomew; *D:* Edgar G. Ulmer. *NOS, FCT, HEG*

St. Elmo's Fire ✍✍½ 1985 (R) Seven Georgetown graduates confront adult problems during their first post-graduate year. Reminiscent of "The Big Chill," but a weak story wastes lots of talent and time. 110m/C VHS, Beta, LV, Closed Caption. Rob Lowe, Demi Moore, Andrew McCarthy, Judd Nelson, Ally Sheedy, Emilio Estevez, Mare Winningham, Martin Balsam, Jenny Wright, Joyce Van Patten, Andie MacDowell, Anna Maria Horsford; *D:* Joel Schumacher; *W:* Joel Schumacher; *C:* Stephen Burum; *M:* David Foster. Golden Raspberry Awards '85: Worst Supporting Actor (Lowe). *COL*

Saint-Ex: The Story of the Storyteller 🐾🐾 1995 (PG)
Ambitious bio based on famous French aviator, and author of the children's classic "The Little Prince," Antoine de Saint-Exupery (Ganz). Flashbacks show his childhood obsession with flying that eventually lead to Saint-Exuprey's perilous North African mail flights that is his passion for flying during WWII. Beyond his passion for flying is his marriage to Consuelo (Richardson), who comes to resent his frequent absences, and the later, more-supportive love of Genevieve (McTeer). Striking visuals but that's about all. **90m/ C VHS.** *GB* Bruno Ganz, Miranda Richardson, Janet McTeer, Ken Scott, Katrin Cartlidge, Eleanor Bron, Brid Brennan, Karl Johnson; *D:* Anand Tucker; *W:* Frank Cottrell Boyce; *C:* David Johnson; *M:* Barrington Pheloung. *BWE*

St. Helen's, Killer Volcano 🐾🐾½
1982 A young man and an old man develop a deep friendship amid the devastation, fear, greed, and panic surrounding the eruption of the Mt. St. Helen's volcano. Based on the true story of Harry Truman (!), who refused to leave his home. Pretty good. **95m/C VHS.** Art Carney, David Huffman, Cassie Yates, Bill McKinney, Ron O'Neal, Albert Salmi, Cesare Danova; *D:* Ernie Pintoff. *VES*

The Saint in London 🐾🐾 1939 The
Saint investigates a gang trying to pass counterfeit banknotes. The third in "The Saint" series. **72m/B VHS, Beta.** George Sanders, Sally Gray; *D:* John Paddy Carstairs.

The Saint in New York 🐾🐾 1938 The
Saint, Simon Templar, turns Robin Hood to help the Civic Committee clean up a gang of desperados. First of "The Saint" series. **71m/B VHS, Beta.** Louis Hayward, Kay Sutton, Jack Carson, Charles Halton; *D:* Ben Holmes.

St. Ives 🐾🐾 1976 (PG) Former police reporter Bronson agrees to recover some stolen ledgers and finds himself dealing with betrayal and murder. Bisset is sultry and the tale is slickly told, but dumb. Co-stars Travanti, later of TV's "Hill Street Blues." **94m/C VHS, Beta.** Charles Bronson, Jacqueline Bisset, John Houseman, Harry Guardino, Maximilian Schell, Harris Yulin, Elisha Cook Jr., Daniel J. Travanti; *D:* J. Lee Thompson; *W:* Barry Beckerman; *M:* Lalo Schifrin. *WAR*

Saint Jack 🐾🐾🐾 1979 (R) The story of a
small-time pimp with big dreams working the pleasure palaces of late-night Singapore. Engrossing and pleasant. Based on Paul Theroux's novel. **112m/C VHS, Beta.** Ben Gazzara, Denholm Elliott, Joss Ackland, George Lazenby; *D:* Peter Bogdanovich; *W:* Peter Bogdanovich. *ART, VES*

Saint Joan 🐾🐾 1957 Film of the George
Bernard Shaw play, adapted by Graham Greene, about the French Maid of Orleans at her trial. Otto Preminger went on a nationwide talent hunt for his leading actress and chose the inexperienced Seberg (her screen debut). A good thing for her career, but not for this ill-begotten, overambitious opus. Seberg doesn't fit. Also available colorized. **131m/B VHS, Beta.** Jean Seberg, Anton Walbrook, Richard Widmark, John Gielgud, Harry Andrews, Felix Aylmer, Richard Todd; *D:* Otto Preminger; *C:* Georges Perinal. *WAR*

St. Michael Had a Rooster 🐾🐾 1972 *San Michele Aveva un Gallo* In 19th-century Italy, idealist anarchist Giulio Manieri (Brogi) hopes to inspire the local peasantry through armed raids. Imprisoned for his trouble, Manieri learns upon his release after 10 years that his political struggles have been forgotten and he has to make a difficult adjustment to life on the outside. Based on the Leo Tolstoy story "The Divine and the Human." Italian with subtitles. **87m/C VHS.** *IT* Giulio Brogi, Danielle Dublino, Renato Scarpa; *D:* Paolo Taviani, Vittorio Taviani; *W:* Paolo Taviani, Vittorio Taviani; *C:* Mario Masini. *FXL, FCT*

The Saint of Fort Washington 🐾🐾½ 1993 (R) Sweetly naive
and schizophrenic Matthew (Dillon) is homeless and through government screw-ups is sent to the Fort Washington Armory, which houses more than 700 homeless men. Harassed by others,

Matthew is befriended by Jerry, a kindly Vietnam vet, who tries to care for him. Subject is taken seriously but slips into mawkishness; good performances by the leads. *CW:* Langauge. **104m/C VHS, Beta, LV, Letterbox, Closed Caption.** Danny Glover, Matt Dillon, Rick Aviles, Nina Siemaszko, Ving Rhames, Joe Seneca; *D:* Tim Hunter; *W:* Lyle Kessler; *C:* Frederick Elmes; *M:* James Newton Howard. *WAR*

The Saint Strikes Back 🐾🐾 1939
Sanders debuts as the mysterious Simon Templar in this competent series. On a trip to San Francisco, the Saint aims to clear the name of a murdered man. The second in the series. **67m/B VHS.** George Sanders, Wendy Barrie, Jonathan Hale, Jerome Cowan, Neil Hamilton, Barry Fitzgerald, Edward Gargan, Robert Strange; *D:* John Farrow. *MOV*

The Saint Strikes Back: Criminal Court 🐾🐾 1946 A suspense double feature:
The Saint helps a daughter clear the name of her murdered father, a San Francisco police commissioner in "The Saint Strikes Back," and a young lawyer becomes involved in murder in "Criminal Court." **127m/B VHS.** George Sanders, Wendy Barrie, Barry Fitzgerald, Tom Conway, Steve Brodie; *D:* John Farrow. *TTC*

The Saint Takes Over 🐾🐾 1940 More
adventures with the British mystery man; this time involving racetrack gambling. An original story that wasn't based on a Leslie Charteris novel as were the others. **69m/B VHS.** George Sanders, Jonathan Hale, Wendy Barrie, Paul Guilfoyle, Morgan Conway, Cy Kendall; *D:* Jack Hively. *MOV*

The St. Tammany Miracle 🐾🐾½
1994 Predictable, good-natured sports film about young coach Lootie Pfannder (Luner) who takes a job at a prep school and turns the losing girls basketball team into winners. Her broadcaster boyfriend Carl (Grosselaar) thinks she's crazy but aided by her assistant (Frye), Lootie is determined to prove everyone wrong. **90m/C VHS.** Jamie Luner, Mark Paul Gosselaar, Soleil Moon Frye, Jeffrey Meek, Julie McCullough; *Cameos:* Steve Allen; *D:* Joy Houck Jr.; *W:* Jim McCullough Jr.; *M:* Jay Weigel. *VCI*

The St. Valentine's Day Massacre 🐾🐾½ 1967 Corman's big studio
debut recreates the events leading to one of the most violent gangland shootouts in modern history: the bloodbath between Chicago's Capone and Moran gangs on February 14, 1929. Uninspired and unremittingly violent. Watch for Jack Nicholson's bit part. **100m/C VHS, Beta.** Jason Robards Jr., Ralph Meeker, Jean Hale, Joseph Campanella, Bruce Dern, Clint Ritchie, Richard Bakalayan, George Segal; *D:* Roger Corman; *C:* Milton Krasner. *FOX, FCT*

Saints and Sinners 🐾½ 1995 (R) Street-
smart "Pooch" Puccia (Chapa) returns to his 'hood as an undercover cop to set up childhood buddy, drug dealer Big Boy Baynes (Plank), and winds up getting involved with seductive bad girl Eve (Rubin), who's also bedding Baynes. Then Pooch discovers his police contact is in the pay of the mob. Lots of macho posturing (attractive actors). *CW:* Strong violence, sexuality and language. **99m/C VHS, LV, Closed Caption.** Damian Chapa, Scott Plank, Jennifer Rubin, Damon Whitaker, Panchito Gomez, William Atherton; *D:* Paul Mones; *W:* Paul Mones; *C:* Michael Bonvillain. *ART*

The Saint's Double Trouble 🐾🐾
1940 Leslie Charteris' suave detective becomes embroiled in another mystery, this one involving jewel thieves. Sanders plays a dual role as the hero and the crook. The fourth in the series. **68m/B VHS.** George Sanders, Helene Whitney, Jonathan Hale, Bela Lugosi, Donald MacBride, John Hamilton; *D:* Jack Hively.

The Saint's Vacation/The Narrow Margin 🐾🐾 1952 A mystery double feature. In "The Saint's Vacation," Simon Templar prevents a valuable secret from getting into the wrong hands, and in "The Narrow Margin," strange things happen to a detective when he takes a train ride with a witness to Chicago. Sinclair took over the

sleuth's role from George Sanders in this series. **148m/B VHS, Beta.** Hugh Sinclair, Sally Gray, Charles McGraw, Marie Windsor, Jacqueline White. *TTC*

Sakharov 🐾🐾🐾 1984 The true story of the
Russian physicist who designed the H-bomb and then rose to lead the Soviet dissident movement and win the Nobel Peace Prize. Robards is excellent. Made for cable; topical and powerful. **120m/C VHS, Beta.** Glenda Jackson, Jason Robards Jr., Michael Bryant; *D:* Jack Gold; *M:* Carl Davis.

Sakura Killers 🐾 1986 Killer Ninjas steal a
valuable gene-splicing formula and are hunted down by an American colonel. **87m/C VHS, Beta.** Chuck Connors, Mike Kelly, Brian Wong, Thomas Lung; *D:* Richard Ward. *FOX*

Salaam Bombay! 🐾🐾🐾 1988 A gritty film
about a child street beggar in the slums of Bombay trying to raise enough money to return to his mother's house in the country. The boy experiences every variety of gutter life imaginable, from humiliation to love. Moving and searing. Filmed on location, with actual homeless children; Nair's first feature. In Hindi with subtitles. **114m/C VHS, Beta, LV.** *IN GB* Shafiq Syed, Hansa Vithal, Chanda Sharma, Nana Patekar, Aneeta Kanwar, Sarfuddin Quarassi, Raju Barnad, Raghubir Yadav; *D:* Mira Nair; *W:* Sooni Taraporevala; *C:* Sandi Sissel; *M:* L. Subramaniam. Nominations: Academy Awards '88: Best Foreign Language Film. *NO*

The Salamander 🐾½ 1982 (R) A French
detective tries to find the assassin of the leaders of a neo-fascist underground movement in Italy and follows clues that lead back to WWII. Disappointing, overwrought adaptation of a Morris West novel. **101m/C VHS, Beta.** *GB* Franco Nero, Anthony Quinn, Martin Balsam, Sybil Danning, Christopher Lee, Cleavon Little, Paul Smith, Claudia Cardinale, Eli Wallach; *D:* Peter Zinner; *M:* Jerry Goldsmith. *NLC*

Salammbo 🐾🐾½ 1914 An early silent epic
in the grand Italian tradition. Loosely based on Flaubert's novel about ancient Carthage. **49m/B VHS, Beta.** *IT* Ernesto Pagani; *D:* Giovanni Pastrone. *FCT*

Salem's Lot 🐾🐾½ 1979 (PG) *Blood Thirst*
Based on Stephen King's novel about a sleepy New England village which is infiltrated by evil. A mysterious antiques dealer takes up residence in a forbidding hilltop house—and it becomes apparent that a vampire is on the loose. Generally creepy; Mason is good, but Soul only takes up space in the lead as a novelist returning home. Also available in the original television miniseries version at 190 minutes on two cassettes. **112m/C VHS, Beta, LV.** David Soul, James Mason, Lance Kerwin, Bonnie Bedelia, Lew Ayres, Ed Flanders, Elisha Cook Jr., Reggie Nalder, Fred Willard, Kenneth McMillan, Marie Windsor; *D:* Tobe Hooper; *W:* Paul Monash; *C:* Jules Brenner. *WAR*

Sallah 🐾🐾🐾 1963 A North African Jew takes
his family to Israel in 1949 in hopes of making his fortune. He finds himself in a transit camp and runs up against the local bureaucracy in a quest for permanent housing as well as the European work ethic. Amusing and enjoyable satire. In Hebrew with English subtitles. **105m/B VHS, Beta.** *IS* Chaim Topol, Geula Noni, Gila Almagor, Arik Einstein, Shraga Friedman, Esther Greenberg; *D:* Ephraim Kishon; *C:* Floyd Crosby. Golden Globe Awards '65: Best Foreign Film; Nominations: Academy Awards '64: Best Foreign Language Film. *MOV, ERG, NCJ*

Sally of the Sawdust 🐾🐾½ 1925
Fields' first silent feature; he is carnival barker Professor Eustace McGargle who's the guardian of orphaned Sally (Dempster). Then Sally's wealthy grandfather (Alderson), a stern judge, becomes determined to claim her from showbiz lowlifes. Fields gets to demonstrate his talent for juggling, conning customers, and car chasing. Interesting movie caught director Griffith on the decline and Fields on the verge of stardom. Remade as a talkie in 1936 entitled "Poppy." Includes musical score. **113m/B VHS, Beta.** W.C. Fields, Carol Dempster, Erville Alderson; *D:* D.W. Griffith. *KIV, VYY, CCB*

Salmonberries ♂½ 1991 (R) East German Roswitha (Zech) is devastated when her lover is killed trying to scale the Berlin Wall. She manages to escape and finds herself stuck in a remote Eskimo community in Alaska where she becomes involved with Kotzebue (lang in her film debut), who poses as a man to work on the Alaskan pipeline. The title has something to do with preserved berries—don't bother, it makes about as much sense as the entire movie. English and German with English subtitles. **94m/C VHS.** *GE CA* Rosel Zech, k.d. lang, Chuck Connors; *D:* Percy Adlon; *W:* Percy Adlon, Felix Adlon. *FCT*

Salo, or the 120 Days of Sodom ♂♂ 1975 Extremely graphic film follows 16 children (eight boys and eight girls) who are kidnapped by a group of men in Fascist Italy. On reaching a secluded villa in the woods, the children are told to follow strict rules and then subjected to incredible acts of sadomasochism, rape, violence, and mutilation. This last film of Pasolini's was taken from a novel by the Marquis de Sade. Viewers are strongly recommended to use their utmost discretion when watching this controversial film. In Italian with English subtitles. **117m/C VHS, LV.** *IT* Giorgio Cataldi, Umberto P. Quinavalle, Paolo Bonacelli; *D:* Pier Paolo Pasolini; *C:* Tonino Delli Colli; *M:* Ennio Morricone. *FCT, HHE, WBF*

Salome ♂♂½ 1922 Garish silent rendition of Oscar Wilde's scandalous tale. **54m/B VHS, Beta.** Alla Nazimova, Rose Dione, Mitchell Lewis, Earl Schenck; *D:* Charles Bryant. *GPV, FCT, VYY*

Salome ♂♂ 1953 An over-costumed version of Oscar Wilde's Biblical story about King Herod's lascivious stepdaughter who danced her way to stardom and tried to save the life of John the Baptist. Talented cast can't overcome hokey script. **103m/C VHS, Beta.** Rita Hayworth, Stewart Granger, Charles Laughton, Judith Anderson, Cedric Hardwicke, Basil Sydney, Maurice Schwartz; *D:* William Dieterle; *C:* Charles B(ryant) Lang; *M:* George Duning. *COL, CCB*

Salome ♂½ 1985 (R) An updated and graphic version of the Oscar Wilde historical fantasy about the temptress Salome who helped topple Herod's Biblical kingdom with her dance of the Seven Veils. Not really a remake of the 1953 film since this is set during the 1940s. **100m/C VHS, Beta.** Jo Ciampa, Tomas Milian, Pamela Salem; *D:* Claude D'Anna; *C:* Pasquale De Santis. *MGM*

Salome/Queen Elizabeth 1923 Two famous silent shorts: "Salome" (1923), an atmospheric adaptation of Oscar Wilde's tale, with sets designed after Aubrey Beardsley; and "Queen Elizabeth" (1912), Bernhardt's famous, and famously stilted, singular film appearance. **91m/B VHS, Beta, 8mm.** Alla Nazimova, Sarah Bernhardt, Lou Tellegen, Mitchell Lewis, Nigel de Brulier; *D:* Charles Bryant, Henri Desfontaines, Louis Mercanton. *VYY*

Salome, Where She Danced ♂ 1945 Set during the Franco-Prussian war. A European dancer helps an American reporter in a spy scheme. She eventually relocates to America and becomes the toast of San Francisco. Somehow, De Carlo managed to spring from this ridiculous camp outing to stardom. **90m/C VHS, Beta.** Yvonne De Carlo, Rod Cameron, David Bruce, Walter Slezak; *D:* Charles Lamont; *C:* William Howard Greene, Hal Mohr. *NOS, BAR, DVT*

Salome's Last Dance ♂♂ 1988 (R) A theatrical, set-surreal adaptation of the Wilde story. Typically flamboyant Russell. **113m/C VHS, Beta, LV.** Glenda Jackson, Stratford Johns, Nickolas Grace, Douglas Hodge, Imogen Millais Scott; *D:* Ken Russell; *W:* Ken Russell. *ART, IME, VES*

Salsa ♂♂ 1988 (PG) An auto repairman would rather dance in this "Dirty Dancing" clone. Rosa was formerly a member of the pop group Menudo. **97m/C VHS, Beta, LV.** Robby Rosa, Rodney Harvey, Magali Alvarado, Miranda Garrison, Moon Orona; *D:* Boaz Davidson; *W:* Boaz Davidson, Tomas Benitez. *MGM*

Salt of the Earth ♂♂♂½ 1954 Finally available in this country after being suppressed for 30 years, this controversial film was made by a group of blacklisted filmmakers during the McCarthy era. It was deemed anti-American, communist propaganda. The story deals with the anti-Hispanic racial strife that occurs in a New Mexico zinc mine when union workers organize a strike. **94m/B VHS, Beta, LV, CD-I.** Rosaura Revueltas, Will Geer, David Wolfe; *D:* Herbert Biberman. National Film Registry '92. *IHF, NOS, MPI*

Salty ♂♂ 1973 A lovable but mischievous sea lion manages to complicate two brothers' lives when they volunteer to help a friend renovate a Florida marina, which is threatened by a mortgage foreclosure. Straightforward and inoffensive tale. **93m/C VHS, Beta.** Clint Howard, Mark Slade, Nina Foch; *D:* Ricou Browning. *NO*

Salut l'Artiste ♂♂♂ 1974 Two bad actors try to make it in the industry. Delightfully funny with an excellent cast, especially Mastroianni. Snide and irreverant, yet loving and comic look at the world of acting. In French with English subtitles. **96m/C VHS.** *FR* Marcello Mastroianni, Jean Rochefort, Francoise Fabian, Carla Gravina; *D:* Yves Robert; *M:* Vladimir Cosma. *FCT, CVC*

Salute John Citizen ♂♂♂ 1942 The life of an average English family during the early days of WWII is depicted, focusing on the deprivation and horror of the Nazi blitzkrieg. **74m/B VHS, Beta.** Peggy Cummins, Stanley Holloway, Dinah Sheridan, Jimmy Hanley. *VYY*

Salute to the "King of the Cowboys," Roy Rogers 197? Glimpses of Roy from song clips, home movies, trailers, out-takes, and other sources. **60m/B VHS, Beta.** Roy Rogers. *DVT*

Salvador ♂♂♂½ 1986 (R) Photo journalist Richard Boyle's unflinching and sordid adventures in war-torn El Salvador. Boyle (Woods) must face the realities of social injustice. Belushi and Woods are hard to like, but excellent. Early critical success for director Stone. **123m/C VHS, Beta, LV, Closed Caption.** James Woods, James Belushi, John Savage, Michael Murphy, Elpidia Carrillo, Cynthia Gibb, Tony Plana, Colby Chester, Will MacMillan, Jose Carlos Ruiz, Jorge Luke, Juan Fernandez, Valerie Wildman; *D:* Oliver Stone; *W:* Oliver Stone, Richard Boyle; *C:* Robert Richardson; *M:* Georges Delerue. Independent Spirit Awards '87: Best Actor (Woods); Nominations: Academy Awards '86: Best Actor (Woods), Best Original Screenplay. *ART, IME, VES*

Salvation! ♂♂½ 1987 (R) *Salvation! Have You Said Your Prayers Today?* A mean-tempered, timely satire about a money-hungry television evangelist beset by a family of fervent, equally money-hungry followers, who proceed to cheat, seduce and blackmail him. Occasionally quite funny, but sloppy and predictable. Underground director Beth B's first above-ground feature. **80m/C Beta.** Stephen McHattie, Exene Cervenka, Dominique Davalos, Viggo Mortensen, Rockets Redglare, Billy Bastiani; *D:* Beth B; *W:* Beth B. *NO*

The Salzburg Connection ♂½ 1972 (PG) A list of Nazi collaborators is discovered in Austria. A vacationing American lawyer is caught up in the battle for its possession. Filmed on location, it's still a poor, cheesy adaptation of the Helen MacInnes novel. **94m/C VHS, Beta.** Barry Newman, Anna Karina, Klaus Maria Brandauer, Karen Jensen; *D:* Lee H. Katzin. *FOX*

Samantha ♂♂½ 1992 (PG) Twenty-one year-old Samantha discovers she was left on her parents' doorstep in a basket and decides to find out where she came from. Good cast and high charm quotient help this film along. **101m/C VHS, Beta, Closed Caption.** Martha Plimpton, Dermot Mulroney, Hector Elizondo, Mary Kay Place, Ione Skye; *D:* Steven La Rocque; *W:* John Golden, Steven La Rocque.

Samar ♂♂½ 1962 (PG) A liberal penal colony commandant rebels against his superiors by leading his prisoners through the Philippine jungles to freedom. Original action drama with an interesting premise. **89m/C VHS, Beta.** George Montgomery, Gilbert Roland, Joan O'Brien, Ziva Rodann; *D:* George Montgomery. *NOS*

Samaritan: The Mitch Snyder Story ♂♂♂ 1986 Effective television drama based upon the true story of Vietnam vet Mitch Snyder (Sheen) who battles various government agencies and ultimately fasts to call national attention to his crusade against homelessness. Tyson appears as bag lady; Snyder eventually committed suicide. **90m/C VHS, Beta, Closed Caption.** Martin Sheen, Roxanne Hart, Joe Seneca, Stan Shaw, Cicely Tyson; *D:* Richard T. Heffron.

Same Old Song ♂♂♂ *On Connait la Chanson* 1997 Amusing melodrama that replaces some dialogue with lip-synched popular song lyrics ala Dennis Potter's "Pennies from Heaven" and "The Singing Detective." (Pic is dedicated to Potter.) Camille (Jaoui) is helping her sister Odile (Azema) and brother-in-law Claude (Arditti) look for a new Paris apartment, while beginning an affair with real estate broker Marc (Wilson) and ignoring the overtures of love-sick Simon (Dussollier). Meanwhile, Nicolas (Bacri), Odile's now-married ex-flame is also apartment hunting and Odile's vulnerable since Claude doesn't love her anymore. Everybody lies to everybody else (and themselves) and misinterprets all the situations. **122m/C VHS.** *FR* Agnes Jaoui, Jean-Pierre Bacri, Andre Dussollier, Sabine Azema, Lambert Wilson, Pierre Arditti, Jane Birkin, Jean-Paul Roussillon; *D:* Alain Resnais; *W:* Agnes Jaoui, Jean-Pierre Bacri; *M:* Bruno Fontaine. Cesar Awards '98: Best Actor (Dussollier), Best Film, Best Film Editing, Best Screenplay, Best Sound, Best Supporting Actor (Bacri), Best Supporting Actress (Jaoui). *NYR*

Same Time, Next Year ♂♂♂ 1978 A chance meeting between an accountant and a housewife results in a sometimes tragic, always sentimental 25-year affair in which they meet only one weekend each year. Well-cast leads carry warm, touching story based on the Broadway play by Bernard Slade. **119m/C VHS, Beta, LV.** Ellen Burstyn, Alan Alda; *D:* Robert Mulligan; *C:* Robert L. Surtees; *M:* Marvin Hamlisch. Golden Globe Awards '79: Best Actress—Musical/Comedy (Burstyn); Nominations: Academy Awards '78: Best Actress (Burstyn), Best Adapted Screenplay, Best Cinematography, Best Song ("The Last Time I Felt Like This"). *USH*

Sammy & Rosie Get Laid ♂♂♂ 1987 An unusual social satire about a sexually liberated couple living in London whose lives are thrown into turmoil by the arrival of the man's father—a controversial politician in India. Provides a confusing look at sexual and class collisions. From the makers of "My Beautiful Laundrette." **97m/C VHS, Beta, LV.** *GB* Shashi Kapoor, Frances Barber, Claire Bloom, Ayub Khan Din, Roland Gift, Wendy Gazelle, Meera Syal; *D:* Stephen Frears; *W:* Hanif Kureishi; *M:* Stanley Myers. *ORI, WAR*

Sammy, the Way-Out Seal ♂♂ 1962 Two young boys bring a mischievous seal to live in their beach house and try to keep it a secret from their parents. Disney in its early '60s phase. **89m/C VHS, Beta.** Michael McGreevey, Billy Mumy, Patricia Barry, Robert Culp; *D:* Norman Tokar. *DIS*

Sam's Son ♂♂ 1984 (PG) Sentimental, autobiographical tale about how a young man's athletic prowess opens the door for an acting career in Hollywood. Good performance by Wallach as the boy's father. Self-indulgent, though entertaining. **107m/C VHS, Beta.** Eli Wallach, Anne Jackson, Timothy Patrick Murphy, Hallie Todd, James Karen, Allan Hayes, Joanna Lee, Michael Landon; *D:* Michael Landon; *W:* Michael Landon. *WOV*

Samson ♂ 1961 Samson attempts to keep wits and hair about him. **90m/C VHS.** *IT* Brad Harris, Brigitte Corey, Alan Steel, Serge Gainsbourg, Mara Berni; *D:* Gianfranco Parolini. *SNC, MRV*

Samson Against the Sheik 1962 Samson survives long enough to battle a sheik in the Middle Ages. **?m/C VHS, Beta.** *IT* Ed Fury. *SNC*

Samson and Delilah 🐾🐾🐾 1950 The biblical story of the vindictive Delilah, who after being rejected by the mighty Samson, robbed him of his strength by shearing his curls. Delivered in signature DeMille style. Wonderfully fun and engrossing. Mature is excellent. **128m/C VHS, Beta, LV.** Victor Mature, Hedy Lamarr, Angela Lansbury, George Sanders, Henry Wilcoxon, Olive Deering, Fay Holden; *D:* Cecil B. DeMille; *C:* George Barnes. Academy Awards '50: Best Art Direction/Set Decoration (Color), Best Costume Design (Color); Nominations: Academy Awards '50: Best Color Cinematography, Best Original Dramatic/Comedy Score. *PAR*

Samson and Delilah 🐾🐾 1984 A made for television version of the Biblical romance, semi-based on DeMille's 1950 version. Original Samson (Mature) plays Samson's father. Too long but inoffensive; see the DeMille version instead. **95m/C VHS, Beta.** Antony Hamilton, Belinda Bauer, Max von Sydow, Jose Ferrer, Victor Mature, Maria Schell; *D:* Lee Philips; *M:* Maurice Jarre.

Samson and Delilah 🐾🐾 1996 Another in TNT's biblical retellings, this time with Israelite shepherd Samson (Thal), who also the strongest man alive, falling for beautiful-but-treacherous Philistine Delilah (Hurley). Seems Samson is causing havoc with General Tariq's (Hopper) Philistine army and Delilah is to discover the secret of his strength. **180m/C VHS, Closed Caption.** Eric Thal, Elizabeth Hurley, Dennis Hopper, Michael Gambon, Diana Rigg, Ben Becker, Paul Freeman, Daniel Massey, Pinkas Braun, Debora Caprioglio, Alessandro Gassman, Mark McGann, Jonathan Rhys Myers; *D:* Nicolas Roeg; *W:* Allan Scott; *C:* Raffaele Mertes; *M:* Marco Frisina. *TTC, VIF*

Samson and His Mighty Challenge 🐾½ 1964 In this rarely seen muscle epic, Hercules, Maciste, Samson and Ursus all take part in a battle royale. **?m/C VHS, Beta.** *IT* Alan Steel. *SNC*

Samson and the 7 Miracles of the World 🐾🐾 *Maciste Alla Corte Del Gran Khan; Maciste at the Court of the Great Khan; Goliath and the Golden City* 1962 This time the hero known as Maciste (renamed Samson for Americans) is in the 13th century battling brutal Tartar warlords. The very Earth itself shakes when our hero goes into battle! **80m/C VHS, Beta.** *FR IT* Gordon Scott, Yoko Tani, Gabriele Antonini, Leonardo Severini, Valeri Inkizhinov, Helene Chanel; *D:* Riccardo (Robert Hampton) Freda; *M:* Les Baxter. *SNC*

Samson in the Wax Museum 🐾½ *Santo en el Museo de Cera; Santo in the Wax Museum* 1963 Masked Mexican wrestling hero Santo (here called Samson) does battle with a scientist who has discovered a way to make wax monsters come to life. **92m/B VHS.** *MX* Santo, Claudio Brook, Ruben Rojo, Norma Mora, Roxana Bellini; *D:* Alfonso Corona Blake. *SNC, HHT*

Samson vs. the Vampire Women 🐾½ 1961 Santo (here called Samson) the masked hero and athlete, battles the forces of darkness as a horde of female vampires attempt to make an unsuspecting girl their next queen. Not bad if you're into the Mexican wrestling genre. **89m/B VHS, Beta.** *MX* Santo, Lorena Velasquez, Jaime Fernandez, Maria Duval; *D:* Alfonso Corona Blake. *SNC, HHT*

Samurai 🐾 1945 Truly bad spy-exploitation film about a Japanese orphan who was raised in America, turns traitor, and helps plot the invasion of California. **?m/C VHS.** Paul Fung, Luke Chan, David Chow. *SNC, TPV*

Samurai 1: Musashi Miyamoto 🐾🐾🐾½ 1955 The first installment in the film version of Musashi Miyamoto's life, as he leaves his 17th century village as a warrior in a local civil war only to return beaten and disillusioned. Justly award-winning. In Japanese with English subtitles. **92m/C VHS, Beta, LV.** *JP*

Toshiro Mifune; *D:* Hiroshi Inagaki. Academy Awards '55: Best Foreign Language Film. *NLC, HMV*

Samurai 2: Duel at Ichijoji Temple 🐾🐾🐾½ 1955 Inagaki's second film depicting the life of Musashi Miyamoto, the 17th century warrior, who wandered the disheveled landscape of feudal Japan looking for glory and love. In Japanese with English subtitles. **102m/C VHS, Beta, LV.** *JP* Toshiro Mifune; *D:* Hiroshi Inagaki. *NLC, HMV*

Samurai 3: Duel at Ganryu Island 🐾🐾🐾½ 1956 The final film of Inagaki's trilogy, in which Musashi Miyamoto confronts his lifelong enemy in a climactic battle. Depicts Miyamoto's spiritual awakening and realization that love and hatred exist in all of us. In Japanese with English subtitles. **102m/C VHS, Beta, LV.** *JP* Toshiro Mifune, Koji Tsurata; *D:* Hiroshi Inagaki. *NLC, HMV*

Samurai Cowboy 🐾🐾 1993 Sato (Go) is a successful Japanese businessman who worships the American western ideal so he decides to give up the rat race by moving to Running Moose, Montana, and buying a cattle ranch. Talk about culture shock! Inoffensive fish-out-of-water comedy. Go is a popular singer in his native Japan. **101m/C VHS, Beta.** Hiromi Go, Catherine Mary Stewart, Robert Conrad, Conchata Ferrell, Matt McCoy; *D:* Michael Keusch; *W:* Michael Keusch; *M:* Osamu Kitajima. *MNC*

Samurai Rebellion 🐾🐾🐾 *Rebellion* 1967 Isaburo (Mifune) is a reknowned swordsman in 18th-century Japan who is the model of loyalty until his overlord demands the return of a former mistress, who is now Isaburo's daughter-in-law. This insult to his family forces Isaburo to take a deadly stand, which turns out to be against his best friend (Nakadai) who's trying to uphold the feudal code. Lots of swordplay. Last in Kobayashi's trilogy following "Harakiri" (1962) and "Kwaidan" (1964). Japanese with subtitles. **121m/B VHS.** *JP* Toshiro Mifune, Tatsuya Nakadai; *D:* Masaki Kobayashi; *W:* Shinobu Hashimoto. *HMV*

Samurai Reincarnation 1981 After the Shogunate government kills 18,000 Christian rioters in the revolt of 1638, and publicly beheads the leader Shiro Amakusa, Shiro reincarnates during a monstrous thunderstorm. Consumed with hatred, he discards the teachings of Jesus Christ and seeks revenge. In Japanese with English subtitles. **122m/C VHS.** *JP D:* Kinji Fukasaku. *FCT*

San Antonio 🐾🐾 1945 A bad girl working in a dance hall turns over a new leaf on meeting the good guy. Trite plot, but good production. **105m/C VHS, Beta, Closed Caption.** Errol Flynn, Alexis Smith, S.Z. Sakall, Victor Francen, Florence Bates, John Litel, Paul Kelly; *D:* David Butler; *M:* Max Steiner. Nominations: Academy Awards '45: Best Interior Decoration, Best Song ("Some Sunday Morning"). *MGM, FCT, MLB*

San Demetrio, London 🐾🐾½ 1947 Set in 1940, the crew of a crippled tanker endures harrowing situations to reach port. A decent antiwar movie in its time, it's now showing its age. Based on a true story, the plot sags with unbelievable scenes and holes on the plot side. **76m/B VHS.** Walter Fitzgerald, Mervyn Johns, Ralph Michael, Robert Beatty, Charles Victor, Frederick Piper; *D:* Charles Frend. *NOS*

San Fernando Valley 🐾🐾 *San Fernando* 1944 Another lawman-in-evil-town epic. Rogers received his first on-screen kiss in 1944's biggest western. Fairly typical, pleasant cowboy tale. **54m/B VHS, Beta.** Roy Rogers, Dale Evans. *NOS, DVT*

San Francisco 🐾🐾🐾½ 1936 The San Francisco Earthquake of 1906 serves as the background for a romance between an opera singer and a Barbary Coast saloon owner. Somewhat overdone but gripping tale of passion and adventure in the West. Wonderful special effects. Finale consists of historic earthquake footage. Also available colorized. ♫San Francisco; A Heart That's Free; Would You?; Air des Bijoux; Sempre Libera. **116m/B VHS, Beta, LV.** Jeanette Mac-

Donald, Clark Gable, Spencer Tracy, Jack Holt, Jessie Ralph, Al Shean; *D:* Woodbridge S. Van Dyke; *W:* Anita Loos. Academy Awards '36: Best Sound; Nominations: Academy Awards '36: Best Actor (Tracy), Best Director (Van Dyke), Best Picture, Best Story. *MGM*

Sanctuary of Fear 🐾½ *Girl in the Park* 1979 A priest in New York City helps an actress subjected to a series of terrorizing incidents. Uninspired would-be TV pilot based on Chesterton's "Father Brown" series. **98m/C VHS, Beta.** George Hearn, Barnard Hughes, Kay Lenz, Michael McGuire, Robert Schenkkan, David Rasche, Fred Gwynne, Elizabeth Wilson; *D:* John Llewellyn Moxey. *FOX*

Sand and Blood 🐾🐾½ *Blood and Sand; De Sable et de Sang* 1987 A young matador who wishes to escape poverty and a young, cultivated doctor, who despises bullfighting, meet and eventually become friends. A woman enters the picture and completes the love triangle. Widely praised by critics. Interesting and moving. In French with English subtitles. **101m/C VHS, Beta.** *FR* Sami Frey, Andre Dussollier, Clementine Celarie, Patrick Catalifo, Maria Casares, Catherine Rouvel; *D:* Jeanne Labrune; *W:* Jeanne Labrune. *NYF, FCT*

The Sand Pebbles 🐾🐾🐾½ 1966 An American expatriate engineer, transferred to a gunboat on the Yangtze River in 1926, falls in love with a missionary teacher. As he becomes aware of the political climate of American imperialism, he finds himself at odds with his command structure; the treatment of this issue can be seen as commentary on the situation in Vietnam at the time of the film's release. Considered one of McQueen's best performances, blending action and romance. **193m/C VHS, Beta, LV.** Steve McQueen, Richard Crenna, Richard Attenborough, Candice Bergen, Marayat Andriane, Gavin MacLeod, Larry Gates, Mako, Simon Oakland; *D:* Robert Wise; *W:* Robert Anderson; *M:* Jerry Goldsmith. Golden Globe Awards '67: Best Supporting Actor (Attenborough); Nominations: Academy Awards '66: Best Actor (McQueen), Best Art Direction/Set Decoration (Color), Best Color Cinematography, Best Film Editing, Best Picture, Best Sound, Best Supporting Actor (Mako), Best Original Score. *FOX, FCT*

Sandakan No. 8 🐾🐾🐾 *Brothel 8; Sandakan House 8* 1974 A Japanese woman working as a journalist befriends an old woman who was sold into prostitution in Borneo in the early 1900s. Justly acclaimed feminist story dramatizes the role of women in Japanese society. Japanese with English subtitles. **121m/C VHS, Beta.** *JP* Kinuyo Tanaka, Yoko Takakashi, Komake Kurihara, Eitaro Ozawa; *D:* Kei Kumai. Berlin International Film Festival '75: Best Actress; Nominations: Academy Awards '75: Best Foreign Language Film. *FCT*

Sanders of the River 🐾🐾🐾 *Bosambo* 1935 A British officer in colonial Africa must work with the local chief to quell a rebellion. Tale of imperialism. Dated but still interesting and of value. Robeson is very good; superb location cinematography. **80m/B VHS, Beta.** *GB* Paul Robeson, Leslie Banks, Robert Cochran; *D:* Zoltan Korda; *C:* Georges Perinal. *NOS, VYY, CAB*

Sandflow 🐾🐾½ 1937 Well-made Western with Jones playing a man whose father has cheated many ranchers. Jones is out to avenge all of his father's misdeeds and build a new life for himself in this above-average oater. **58m/B VHS.** Buck Jones, Lita Chevret, Robert F. (Bob) Kortman, Arthur Aylesworth, Robert Terry, Enrique DeRosas; *D:* Lesley Selander. *GPV*

The Sandlot 🐾🐾🐾 1993 (PG) Young Scotty (Guiry) moves to a new neighborhood in California in 1962 and tries to make friends despite not knowing anything about playing baseball. His scrappy teammates include the friendly Benny (Vitar), a chubby loud-mouthed catcher named Ham (Renna), and Squints (Leopardi), a would-be Lothario before his time. Action revolves around Scotty's attempt to get baseball autographed by Babe Ruth out of the clutches of giant killer junkyard dog owned by Jones before dad Leary discovers it's missing. Small wonder is nostalgic without being sentimental, and tells its tale with grace and humor, supported by a period sound track. 101m/C VHS, LV, Letterbox, Closed Caption. Tom Guiry, Mike Vitar, Patrick Renna, Chauncey Leopardi, Marty York, Brandon Adams, Karen Allen, James Earl Jones, Maury Wills, Art LaFleur, Marlee Shelton; *Cameos:* Denis Leary, Brooke Adams; **D:** David Mickey Evans; **W:** Robert Gunter, David Mickey Evans; **M:** David Newman; **V:** Arliss Howard. FOX

The Sandpiper 🎬🎬 1965 Free-spirited artist Taylor falls in love with Burton, the married headmaster of her son's boarding school. Muddled melodrama offers little besides starpower. Filmed at Big Sur, California. ♫The Shadow of Your Smile. 117m/C VHS, Beta. Elizabeth Taylor, Richard Burton, Charles Bronson, Eva Marie Saint, Robert Webber, Morgan Mason; **D:** Vincente Minnelli; **C:** Milton Krasner. Academy Awards '65: Best Song ("The Shadow of Your Smile"). MGM

Sandra of a Thousand Delights 🎬🎬 *Sandra; Of a Thousand Delights; Vaghe Stelle Dell'Orsa* 1965 Haunting drama with strong women (and weak men). Sandra returns to Italy from her American home in order to attend a ceremony honoring her father—a Jewish scientist who died in a Nazi concentration camp. Back with her family, Sandra tries to deal with her past, including her mother's possible betrayal of her father and her brother's incestuous longings. Italian with subtitles. 100m/B VHS. *IT* Claudia Cardinale, Jean Sorel, Marie Bell, Michael Craig, Renzo Ricci; **D:** Luchino Visconti; **W:** Luchino Visconti, Suso Cecchi D'Amico; **M:** Cesar Franck. FCT

Sands of Iwo Jima 🎬🎬🎬½ 1949 Wayne earned his first Oscar nomination as a tough Marine sergeant, in one of his best roles. He trains a squad of rebellious recruits in New Zealand in 1943. Later they are responsible for the capture of Iwo Jima from the Japanese—one of the most difficult campaigns of the Pacific Theater. Includes striking real war footage. 109m/B VHS, LV, Closed Caption. John Wayne, Forrest Tucker, John Agar, Richard Jaeckel; **D:** Allan Dwan. Nominations: Academy Awards '49: Best Actor (Wayne), Best Film Editing, Best Sound, Best Story. REP, TLF, RDG

Sands of Sacrifice 🎬🎬½ *Tangled Trails* 1921 Hart, a Northwest Mountie, seeks an unscrupulous promoter who's selling worthless mining stock. 56m/B VHS. Neal Hart, Violet Palmer, Gladys Hampton, Jules Cowles, Jean Bary, Ed Roseman; **D:** Charles Bartlett. GPV

Sanjuro 🎬🎬🎬 *Tsubaki Sanjuro* 1962 In this offbeat, satiric sequel to "Yojimbo," a talented but lazy samurai comes to the aid of a group of naive young warriors. The conventional ideas of good and evil are quickly tossed aside; much less earnest than other Kurosawa Samurai outings. In Japanese with English subtitles. 96m/B VHS, Beta, LV. *JP* Toshiro Mifune, Tatsuya Nakadai; **D:** Akira Kurosawa. NOS, HHT, HEG

Sans Soleil 🎬🎬🎬 *Sunless* 1982 A female narrator reads and comments on the letters she receives from a friend, a freelance cameraman traveling through Japan, West Africa, and Iceland. The cameraman meditates on the cultural dislocation he feels and the meaning of his work and of life itself. Both narrator and cameraman remain unseen with the visuals being the cameraman's work in progress. 100m/C VHS. *FR* **D:** Chris Marker; **W:** Chris Marker. NYF, BTV

Sanshiro Sugata 🎬🎬🎬 1943 Kurosawa's first film. A young man learns discipline in martial arts from a patient master. Climactic fight scene is early signature Kurosawa. In Japanese with English subtitles. 82m/B VHS. *JP* Denjiro Okochi, Yukiko Todoroki, Ranko Hanai, Ryonosuke Tsukigata, Sugisaku Aoyama, Kokuten Kodo, Susumo Fusuita, Takashi Shimura; **D:** Akira Kurosawa. HMV, FCT, COL

Sansho the Bailiff 🎬🎬🎬🎬 *The Bailiff; Sansho Dayu* 1954 A world masterpiece by Mizoguchi about feudal society in 11th century Japan. A woman and her children are sold into prostitution

and slavery. As an adult, the son seeks to right the ills of his society. Powerful and tragic, and often more highly esteemed than "Ugetsu." In Japanese with English subtitles. 132m/B VHS, Beta, LV. *JP* Kinuyo Tanaka, Yoshiaki Hanayagi, Kyoko Kagawa, Eitaro Shindo, Ichiro Sugai; **D:** Kenji Mizoguchi; **W:** Yoshikata Yoda; **M:** Fumio Hayasaka. HMV

Santa Claus woof! 1959 Santa Claus teams up with Merlin the Magician to fend off an evil spirit who would ruin everyone's Christmas. Mexican camp classic. 94m/C VHS, Beta. *MX* Jose Elias Moreno, Cesareo Quezadas; **D:** Rene Cardona Sr. SNC, MLB

Santa Claus Conquers the Martians 🎬 *Santa Claus Defeats the Aliens* 1964 A Martian spaceship comes to Earth and kidnaps Santa Claus and two children. Martian kids, it seems, are jealous that Earth tykes have Christmas. Features then-child star Pia Zadora. 80m/C VHS, Beta. John Call, Pia Zadora, Leonard Hicks, Vincent Beck, Victor Stiles, Donna Conforti; **D:** Nicholas Webster. COL, SNC, MRV

Santa Claus Is Coming to Town 1970 Kris Kringle takes you along on his quest to give toys to the citizens of Sombertown. An animated classic. 53m/C VHS, Beta, LV, Closed Caption. **D:** Arthur Rankin Jr., Jules Bass; **V:** Mickey Rooney, Keenan Wynn, Paul Frees. FHE, LME

Santa Claus: The Movie 🎬🎬 1985 (PG) A big-budgeted spectacle about an elf who falls prey to an evil toy maker and almost ruins Christmas and Santa Claus. Boring, 'tis-the-season fantasy-drama meant to warm our cockles. 112m/C VHS, Beta, LV, Closed Caption. Dudley Moore, John Lithgow, David Huddleston, Judy Cornwell, Burgess Meredith; **D:** Jeannot Szwarc; **W:** David Newman; **M:** Henry Mancini.

The Santa Clause 🎬🎬½ 1994 (PG) If you like Allen, you'll enjoy this lightweight holiday comedy about divorced workaholic dad Scott Calvin and eight-year-old son Charlie (Lloyd). Seems Santa injures himself falling off the Calvin roof and dad winds up putting on Santa's suit. But as it turns out when you put on Santa's suit, you become Santa, including a noticeable weight gain, a fluffy beard, and all those reindeer and elves to deal with (but where's Mrs. Claus?). 97m/C VHS, Closed Caption. Tim Allen, Eric Lloyd, Judge Reinhold, Wendy Crewson, David Krumholtz, Mary Gross; **D:** John Pasquin; **W:** Leo Benvenuti, Steve Rudnick; **M:** Michael Convertino. Blockbuster Entertainment Awards '95: Male Newcomer, Theatrical (Allen); Nominations: MTV Movie Awards '95: Breakthrough Performance (Allen), Best Comedic Performance (Allen). TOU

Santa Fe 🎬🎬 1951 Action-packed western with Scott playing a Confederate soldier who heads West to take a job with the Santa Fe Railroad. However, his brothers, with their wounded rebel pride, have different ideas for forgetting the defeat. Refusing to take money from Northern businesses, they become outlaws. Based on a story by Louis Stevens and the novel by James Marshall. 89m/C VHS. Randolph Scott, Janis Carter, Jerome Courtland, Peter Thompson, John Archer, Warner Anderson, Roy Roberts, Billy House; **D:** Irving Pichel; **W:** Kenneth Gamet. COL

Santa Fe 🎬🎬½ 1997 Muddled romantic drama with an appealing cast. It's taken cop Paul Thomas (Cole) eight months to recover from bullet wounds suffered in a shoot-out with a local cult. In the meantime, wife Leah's (Kelley) distanced herself from the marriage but still urges Paul into group counseling with charismatic Eleanor (Davidovich). Despite Paul's mistrust of her guru-like status, he's naturally drawn to Eleanor (and she to him). There's some tedious subplot stuff but the leads do fine. 97m/C VHS. Gary Cole, Lolita Davidovich, Sheila Kelley, Tina Majorino, Jere Burns, Pamela Reed, Phyllis Frelich, Mark Medoff, Tony Plana, Jeffrey Jones; **D:** Andrew Shea; **W:** Andrew Shea, Mark Medoff; **C:** Paul Elliott; **M:** Mark Governor. NYR

Santa Fe Bound 🎬🎬 1937 Tyler must work to clear his name when he is falsely accused of having murdered a man. 58m/B VHS. Tom Tyler, Jeanne Martel, Richard Cramer, Charles "Slim" Whitaker, Edward Cassidy, Lafe McKee, Dorothy Woods, Charles "Blackie" King; **D:** Harry S. Webb. DVT, HEG, GPV

Santa Fe Marshal 🎬🎬 1940 The 27th Hopalong Cassidy movie, if anyone's counting. In the title job the Hopster goes undercover with a medicine show to smash a criminal gang. A little different than usual, right up to the surprise identity of the crooked mastermind. 66m/B VHS. William Boyd, Russell Hayden, Marjorie Rambeau, Bernadene Hayes, Earle Hodgins, Kenneth Harlan, Eddie Dean; **D:** Lesley Selander. NOS

Santa Fe Stampede 🎬🎬½ 1938 The Three Mesquiteers join an old prospector in his claim but when he is killed, one of them (Wayne) is framed. The photography makes up for the weak story line and direction. 58m/B VHS. John Wayne, Ray Corrigan, Max Terhune, William Farnum, June Martel, Leroy Mason, Yakima Canutt, Curly Dresden; **D:** George Sherman. NOS

Santa Fe Trail 🎬🎬½ 1940 Historically inaccurate but entertaining tale about the pre-Civil War fight for "bloody Kansas." The action-adventure depicts future Civil War Generals J.E.B. Stuart (Flynn) and George Armstrong Custer (Reagan!) as they begin their military career (although Custer was really just a youth at this time). Good action scenes. Also available colorized. 110m/B VHS, Beta. Errol Flynn, Olivia de Havilland, Ronald Reagan, Van Heflin, Raymond Massey, Alan Hale; **D:** Michael Curtiz; **M:** Max Steiner. MGM, NOS, HHT

Santa Fe Uprising 🎬🎬½ 1946 Red Ryder has to save Little Beaver from kidnappers. Good first entry for Lane in the "Red Ryder" series. 54m/B VHS, Beta. Allan "Rocky" Lane, Robert (Bobby) Blake.

Santa Sangre 🎬🎬🎬 1990 (R) A circus in Mexico City, a temple devoted to a saint without arms, and a son who faithfully dotes upon his armless mother are just a few of the bizarre things in this wildly fantastic film. Fenix acts as his mother's arms, plays the piano for her, and carries out any wish she desires—including murder. Visually intoxicating but strange outing may prove too graphic for some viewers. Not as rigorous as other Jodorowsky outings. Also available in an NC-17 version. *CW:* Bizarre graphic violence/drug use and bizarre graphic sensuality. 123m/C VHS, LV, Closed Caption. *IT MX* Axel Jodorowsky, Sabrina Dennison, Guy Stockwell, Blanca Guerra, Thelma Tixou, Adan Jodorowsky, Faviola Tapia, Jesus Juarez; **D:** Alejandro Jodorowsky; **W:** Robert Leoni, Claudio Argento, Alejandro Jodorowsky; **C:** Danielle Nannuzzi; **M:** Simon Boswell. REP, FCT

Santa with Muscles 🎬½ 1996 (PG) Cartoonish holiday-themed comedy finds the Hulkster as Scrooge-like millionaire Blake Thorne. Through a series of stupid circumstances, Thorne winds up in a Santa suit in a shopping mall hiding from the cops. But a blow to the head makes him believe he's the Jolly-Old-Elf himself and he comes to the aid of a local orphanage, whose tykes are about to be evicted. Silly's the kindest thing to say. 97m/C VHS. Hulk Hogan, Don Stark, Ed Begley Jr., Clint Howard, Robin Curtis, Garrett Morris, Adam Wylie; **D:** John Murlowski; **W:** Jonathan Bond, Fred Mata, Dorrie Krum Raymond; **C:** Michael Gfelner; **M:** James Covell. CAF

Santee 🎬🎬 1973 (PG) A father-son relationship develops between a bounty hunter and the son of a man he killed. Good, but not great, Western. 93m/C VHS, Beta. Glenn Ford, Dana Wynter, Jay Silverheels, John Larch, Michael Burns; **D:** Gary Nelson. HHE

The Saphead 🎬🎬½ 1921 Keaton's first outing as the rich playboy has him playing the none-to-bright son of a Wall Street mogul. Some great moments provide a glimpse of cinematic greatness to come from the budding comedic genius. Based on the play "The New Henrietta" by Winchell Smith and Victor Mapes. Silent. **70m/B VHS.** William H. Crane, Buster Keaton, Carol Holloway, Edward Connelly, Irving Cummings; *D:* Herbert Blache. *NO*

Sapphire ✶✶✶ **1959** Two Scotland Yard detectives seek the killer of a beautiful black woman who was passing for white. Good mystery and topical social comment; remains interesting and engrossing. Superbly acted all around. **92m/C VHS, Beta.** *GB* Nigel Patrick, Yvonne Mitchell, Michael Craig, Paul Massie, Bernard Miles; *D:* Basil Dearden. British Academy Awards '59: Best Film. *NO*

Saps at Sea ✶✶½ **1940** A doctor advises Ollie to take a rest away from his job at a horn factory. He and Stan rent a boat, which they plan to keep tied to the dock, until an escaped criminal happens by and uses the boys (and their boat) for his getaway. Cramer is a good bad guy; Stan and Ollie cause too much trouble, as always. **57m/B VHS, Beta, LV.** Stan Laurel, Oliver Hardy, James Finlayson, Ben Turpin, Richard Cramer; *D:* Gordon Douglas. *CCB, VTR, FCT*

Sara Dane ✶✶ **1981** A strong young woman in the 18th century rises in the world through marriage and business acumen. Interesting but imperfect and slow. **150m/C VHS, Beta.** *AU* Harold Hopkins, Brenton Whittle, Barry Quin, Sean Scully; *D:* Rod Hardy, Gary Conway.

Sarafina! ✶✶✶ **1992 (PG-13)** Part coming-of-age saga, part political drama, part musical, and all emotionally powerful. Sarafina is a young girl in a township school in Soweto, South Africa in the mid-'70s, gradually coming into a political awakening amid the Soweto riots. Khumalo recreates her stage role as the glowing and defiant Sarafina with both Goldberg and Makeba good in their roles as Sarafina's outspoken and inspirational teacher and her long-suffering mother, respectively. Adapted from Ngema's stage musical. *CW:* Apartheid-driven violence. **98m/C VHS, Beta, LV, Closed Caption.** Leleti Khumalo, Whoopi Goldberg, Miriam Makeba, John Kani, Mbongeni Ngema; *D:* Darrell Roodt; *W:* Mbongeni Ngema, William Nicholson; *M:* Stanley Myers. *TOU*

The Saragossa Manuscript ✶✶½
Rekopis Znaleziony W Saragossie **1965** Ambitious fantasy based on the 1813 novel "Sanatorium under the Hourglass" by Bruno Schultz. A romantic Belgian army officer, travelling to Spain, meets two beautiful princesses who send him on a fantastic journey to prove himself worthy of their affections. Polish with subtitles. **174m/B VHS.** *PL* Zbigniew Cybulski, Iga Cembrzynska, Joanna Jedryka, Slawomir Linder; *D:* Wojciech Has; *W:* Tadeusz Kwiatkowski; *M:* Krzysztof Penderecki. *FCT*

Sarah, Plain and Tall ✶✶✶ **1991 (G)**
New England school teacher (Close) travels to Kansas circa 1910 to care for the family of a widowed farmer who has advertised for a wife. Superior entertainment for the whole family. Adapted for television from Patricia MacLachlan's novel of the same name by MacLachlan and Carol Sobieski. Nominated for nine Emmy Awards. A "Hallmark Hall of Fame" presentation. **98m/C VHS, LV, Closed Caption.** Glenn Close, Christopher Walken, Lexi Randall, Margaret Sophie Stein, Jon DeVries, Christopher Bell; *D:* Glenn Jordan. *REP*

Sarah's Child ✶✶½ **1996** Sarah LaMere is devastated to learn that she can never have children. While husband Michael tries to accept, Sarah's upbringing has led her to believe that's her only purpose in life and she becomes increasingly unbalanced. Seemingly out of nowhere children's clothes and toys appear in their home and soon a strange young girl named Melissa appears, whom Sarah treats as her own child. When their landlady dies horribly after questioning Melissa, Michael is afraid the line between reality and fantasy has been breached but just how can he fight? **90m/C VHS.** Mary Parker Williams, Michael Berger, Ruth Hale, Bryce Chamberlain; *D:* Ron Beckstrom; *W:* Muffy Mead Thomas; *C:* Gregg Stouffer; *M:* Jim Ball, Glenn Workman.

Saratoga ✶✶½ **1937** Gable plays a bookie and Harlow the daughter of an impoverished horse breeder in this romantic comedy centered around the race tracks. This was the final film appearance for Harlow, who died before the film's completion. Mary Dees was chosen as her stand-in and had to finish many of the scenes. "Saratoga" was released just a month after Harlow's death and became one of the biggest moneymakers of the year. **94m/B VHS.** Jean Harlow, Clark Gable, Lionel Barrymore, Walter Pidgeon, Frank Morgan, Una Merkel, Cliff Edwards, George Zucco, Hattie McDaniel, Jonathan Hale; *D:* Jack Conway; *W:* Anita Loos, Robert Hopkins. *MGM*

Saratoga Trunk ✶✶½ **1945** Lavish, if slow-moving, version of Edna Ferber's romance novel reteams Cooper and Bergman (who starred in "For Whom the Bell Tolls"). It's 1875 New Orleans and bitter Clio, the half-Creole illegitimate daughter of a local, is determined to marry rich. But first, she gets involved with Texas gambler Clint Maroon (Cooper). He's in a business deal with wealthy Van Steed (Warburton), about the Saratoga railroad line, and Clio decides to go after him. Of course, she really wants Clint and they go through lots of bother before ending up together. Filmed in 1943 but release was delayed because of WWII. **135m/B VHS, Closed Caption.** Gary Cooper, Ingrid Bergman, John Warburton, Flora Robson, Florence Bates, Jerry Austin; *D:* Sam Wood; *W:* Casey Robinson; *C:* Ernest Haller; *M:* Max Steiner. Nominations: Academy Awards '46: Best Supporting Actress (Robson). *MGM*

Sardinia Kidnapped ✶✶½ **1975** A beautiful girl is trapped in a clash between two powerful families while on vacation in Sardinia, where the peasants' custom is to kidnap a member of a rival family and then exchange the victim for land. Former documentary maker Mingozzi creates a realistic and uncompromising look at culture and change. In Italian; dubbed. **95m/C VHS, Beta.** *IT* Charlotte Rampling, Franco Nero; *D:* Gianfranco Mingozzi.

Sartana's Here...Trade Your Pistol for a Coffin ✶ **1970** A soldier of fortune searches for a missing shipment of gold in the Old West. **92m/C VHS, Beta.** George Hilton, Charles Southwood, Erika Blanc, Linda Sini. *UNI*

S.A.S. San Salvador ✶ **1984** A CIA agent tries to prevent a psychotic from running amok in El Salvador. **95m/C VHS, Beta.** Miles O'Keeffe, Dagmar Lassander, Catherine Jarrett. *ART, VES*

Sasquatch woof! **1976** Purported "documentary" about the mythical creature Bigfoot. Includes pictures of the "actual" monster. For those real stupid moods. **94m/C VHS, Beta.** George Lauris; *D:* Ed Ragozzini. *NO*

Satan in High Heels ✶½ **1962** Sordid show-biz tale of a carnival dancer (Myles) who dreams of making it big on Broadway. First she finagles her way into a position as a nightclub singer and the mistress of a convenient millionaire. But she loses it all for love when she falls for the millionaire's misbehaving son. Flamboyant performance by Hall as the lesbian nightclub owner. **90m/C VHS.** Meg Myles, Grayson Hall, Del Tenney; *D:* Jerald Intrator; *W:* John T. Chapman. *SMW, TPV*

The Satan Killer ✶½ **1993** A vicious serial killer is targeted by two tough police detectives. What makes it personal is Detective Stephen's fiance is one of the killer's victims and he's not going to let justice stand in the way of his revenge. **90m/C VHS.** Steve Sayre, Billy Franklin, James Westbrook, Belinda Creason, Cindy Healy; *D:* Stephen Calamari.

Satan Met a Lady ✶✶½ **1936** A weak adaptation of Dashiell Hammett's "Maltese Falcon." This version has Davis employing a private detective to track down a mysterious woman. The hunted woman is herself searching for a valuable collectible. **74m/B VHS.** Bette Davis, Warren William, Ali-

son Skipworth, Arthur Treacher, Marie Wilson, Porter Hall, Olin Howlin; *D:* William Dieterle. *MGM, FCT*

The Satanic Rites of Dracula ✶✶
Count Dracula and His Vampire Bride; Dracula Is Dead and Well and Living in London **1973** Count Dracula is the leader of a satanic cult of prominent scientists and politicians who develop a gruesome plague virus capable of destroying the human race. Preceded by "Dracula A.D. 1972" and followed by "The 7 Brothers Meet Dracula." **88m/C VHS.** *GB* Christopher Lee, Peter Cushing, Michael Coles, William Franklyn, Freddie Jones, Joanna Lumley, Richard Vernon, Patrick Barr, Barbara Yo Ling; *D:* Alan Gibson; *W:* Don Houghton; *C:* Brian Probyn. *MLB*

Satanik ✶ **1969 (R)** A hideous old hag is turned into a lovely young woman by a stolen potion, but it doesn't last long and she becomes a monster. **85m/C VHS.** *IT SP* Magda Konopka, Julio Pena, Luigi Montini, Armando Calvo, Umberto Raho; *D:* Piero Vivarelli. *SNC*

Satan's Black Wedding ✶ **1975 (R)**
The ghouls arrive at a Monterey monastery in their Sunday best to celebrate devildom's most diabolical ritual, the "Black Wedding." **61m/C VHS, Beta.** Greg Braddock, Ray Miles, Lisa Milano. *NO*

Satan's Brew ✶✶ *Satansbraten* **1976** Aspiring poet (Raab) murders his mistress and assumes the identity of 19th-century symbolist poet Stefan George, including his idol's homosexual tastes. Fassbinder at his most excessive. German with subtitles. **100m/C VHS.** *GE* Kurt Raab, Margit Carstensen, Volker Spengler, Ingrid Caven, Helen Vita; *D:* Rainer Werner Fassbinder; *W:* Rainer Werner Fassbinder; *C:* Michael Ballhaus; *M:* Peer Raben. *ORI*

Satan's Cheerleaders woof! **1977 (R)** A demonic high school janitor traps a bevy of buxom cheerleaders at his Satanic altar for sacrificial purposes. The gals use all of their endowments to escape the clutches of the evil sheriff and his fat wife. Is it ever campy! **92m/C VHS, Beta.** John Carradine, John Ireland, Yvonne De Carlo, Kerry Sherman, Jacqulin Cole, Hilary Horan, Alisa Powell, Sherry Marks, Jack Kruschen, Sydney Chaplin; *D:* Greydon Clark. *VCI*

Satan's Harvest ✶½ **1965** American detective inherits estate in Johannesburg, only to find the place is being used by drug smugglers. Sidesteps the political climate and shows the beauty of the land. And a good thing: the story is virtually nonexistent. **88m/C VHS, Beta.** George Montgomery, Tippi Hedren; *D:* Ferde Grofe Jr. *NO*

Satan's Princess ✶ **1990** Satanic cult with a female leader runs amuck. Sloppy and forgettable. **90m/C VHS, Beta, Closed Caption.** Robert Forster, Caren Kaye, Lydie Denier, Phillip Glasser, Michael Harris, Ellen Geer, Jack Carter; *D:* Bert I. Gordon; *C:* Stephen Katz. *PAR*

Satan's Sadists ✶ **1969 (R)** Tamblyn and his biker gang terrorize folks in the Southern California desert, including a retired cop, a Vietnam vet and a trio of vacationing coeds. Violent film will probably be best appreciated by Adamson completists. **88m/C VHS.** Russ Tamblyn, Regina Carrol, Gary Kent, Jackie Taylor, Jim Cardos, Kent Taylor, Robert Dix, Scott Brady, Evelyn Frank, Greydon Clark, Bill Bonner, Bobby Clark, Yvonne Stewart, Cheryl Anne, Randee Lynn, Bambi Allen, Breck Warwick; *D:* Al Adamson. *NO*

Satan's School for Girls ✶½ **1973**
When a young woman investigates the circumstances that caused her sister's suicide, it leads her to a satanic girl's academy. Dumb and puerile made for TV "horror." **74m/C VHS, Beta.** Pamela Franklin, Roy Thinnes, Kate Jackson, Lloyd Bochner, Jamie Smith-Jackson, Jo Van Fleet, Cheryl Ladd; *D:* David Lowell Rich. *CNG*

Satan's Touch woof! **1984 (R)** A simpleton worships the Devil and gets burned for his trouble. **86m/C VHS, Beta.** James Lawless, Shirley Venard. *NO*

Satanwar woof! **1979** A fictional look at various forms of Satan worship. **95m/C VHS, Beta.** Bart LaRue, Sally Schermerhorn, Jimmy Drankovitch. *NO*

Satisfaction 🎬 1988 (PG-13) An all-girl, high school rock band play out the summer before college. The Keatons should have sent Bateman to her room for this stunt. 93m/C VHS, Beta, LV, Closed Caption. Justine Bateman, Trini Alvarado, Britta Phillips, Julia Roberts, Scott Coffey, Liam Neeson, Deborah Harry; **D:** Joan Freeman; **W:** Charles Purpura; **M:** Michel Colombier. *FOX*

Saturday Night and Sunday Morning 🎬🎬🎬½ 1960 This "kitchen sink" drama finds the 23-year-old Finney in star form as working-class Arthur Seaton, who's devoted to good times, spending his weekends with boozing, brawling, and willing women. He's having an affair with the older, married Brenda (Roberts) and pursuing the strictly moral Doreen (Field), who refuses to sleep with him without a commitment. Arthur thinks he's falling in love and is (eventually) ready for marriage but not without complications and not before warning Doreen that he's unlikely to completely change his carefree ways. Reisz's first feature film; Sillitoe adapted from his novel. Finney was voted the most promising newcomer at the British Academy's (BAFTA) awards. 98m/B VHS. GB Albert Finney, Rachel Roberts, Shirley Anne Field, Bryan Pringle, Norman Rossington, Hylda Baker, Robert Cowdra, Elsie Wagstaff, Frank Pettitt; **D:** Karel Reisz; **W:** Alan Sillitoe; **C:** Freddie Francis; **M:** John Dankworth. British Academy Awards '60: Best Actress (Roberts), Best Film; National Board of Review Awards '61: Best Actor (Finney). *HMK*

Saturday Night Fever 🎬🎬½ 1977 (R) Brooklyn teenager (Travolta), bored with his daytime job, becomes the nighttime king of the local disco. Based on a story published in "New York Magazine" by Nik Cohn. Acclaimed for its disco dance sequences, memorable soundtrack by the Bee Gees, and carefree yet bleak script; extremely dated, although it made its mark on society in its time. Followed by the sequel "Staying Alive." Also available in a 112-minute "PG" rated version. 🎵Staying Alive; Night Fever; More Than a Woman; How Deep Is Your Love?. 118m/C VHS, Beta, LV. John Travolta, Karen Gorney, Barry Miller, Donna Pescow; **D:** John Badham; **C:** Ralf Bode; **M:** David Shire. National Board of Review Awards '77: Best Actor (Travolta); Nominations: Academy Awards '77: Best Actor (Travolta). *PAR*

Saturday Night Serials 1940 A compilation of excerpts from four serials: "The Phantom Creeps," "The Phantom Empire," "Undersea Kingdom," and "Junior G-Men." 90m/B VHS, Beta. Bela Lugosi, Gene Autry, Ray Corrigan, Lon Chaney Jr. *RHI*

Saturday Night Shockers 1950 Each volume in this series is comprised of two full-length horror flicks, featuring twisted twins, barbarous butchers and sinister snow creatures. Terror abounds. 150m/B VHS, Beta. Daisy Hilton. *RHI*

Saturday Night Sleazies, Vol. 1 1966 Two sleazy films. "College Girl Confidential" (1968) and "Suburban Confidential" (1966) are each directed by the man who helmed "Orgy of the Dead." Also includes sleazy short subjects. 150m/B VHS, Beta. Marsha Jordan, Harvey Shane; **D:** A.C. Stephen; **W:** A.C. Stephen. *RHI*

Saturday Night Special 🎬½ 1992 (R) Country singer/songwriter Travis (played by Nashville stalwart Burnette) gets a job fronting the house band of Tennessee tavern owner T.J. (Dean). Travis also takes up with ambitious Darlene (Ford), who happens to be T.J.'s wife. But it's Darlene who has the brains in this unpleasant trio, she decides to get rid of hubby and sets Travis up to take the fall. It's all been done before (and better).**CW:** Language, some violence, and strong sexuality. 75m/C VHS. Billy Burnette, Maria Ford, Rick Dean; **D:** Dan Golden; **W:** Jonathan Banks; **M:** Billy Burnette, Nicholas Rivera. *NHO*

Saturday the 14th 🎬½ 1981 (PG) A parody of the popular axe-wielding-maniac genre, about a family inheriting a haunted mansion. Poorly made; not funny or scary. Followed by

even worse sequel: "Saturday the 14th Strikes Back." 91m/C VHS, Beta. Richard Benjamin, Paula Prentiss, Severn Darden; **D:** Howard R. Cohen; **W:** Howard R. Cohen, Jeff Begun.

Saturday the 14th Strikes Back 🎬 1988 Continuing the name, but not the storyline, cast, or characters of the original, this one concerns the invasion of a birthday party by a vampire (Stonebrook) and her monstrous friends. The monsters decide that the birthday boy (Presson) should be their new leader. Pretty lame, even by the original's standards. 91m/C VHS, Beta. Ray Walston, Avery Schreiber, Patty McCormack, Julianne McNamara, Jason Presson, Pamela Stonebrook; **D:** Howard R. Cohen; **W:** Howard R. Cohen. *MGM*

Saturn 3 🎬½ 1980 (R) Two research scientists create a futuristic Garden of Eden in an isolated sector of our solar system, but love story turns to horror story when a killer robot arrives. Sporadically promising, but ultimately lame; dumb ending. For Farrah fans only. 88m/C VHS, Beta, LV. GB Farrah Fawcett, Kirk Douglas, Harvey Keitel, Ed Bishop; **D:** Stanley Donen; **W:** Martin Amis; **C:** Billy Williams; **M:** Elmer Bernstein. *FOX*

Saul and David *Saul e David* 1968 Beautifully filmed story of David's life with King Saul, the battle with Goliath, and the tragic end of Saul. From the "Bible" series. 120m/C VHS, Beta. Norman Wooland, Gianni "John" Garko. *VCI, MOV, KEP*

Savage! woof! *Black Valor* 1973 (R) A savage foreign mess with ex-baseball star Iglehart killing people with grenades and guns, abetted by an army full of murderous models. 81m/C VHS, Beta. MX James Iglehart, Lada Edmund, Carol Speed, Rossana Ortiz, Sally Jordan, Aura Aurea, Vic Diaz; **D:** Cirio H. Santiago. *NLC*

Savage 🎬🎬 1996 (R) Mad scientist discovers the gateway to a future world, which unleashes a powerful guardian known known as the Savage (Gruner). The Savage must prevent the doorway between the worlds from exploding and causing an apocalypse, even as he hunts his nemesis.**CW:** Continuous strong violence, a graphic sex scene and language. 103m/C VHS, Closed Caption. Olivier Gruner, Kario Salem, Jennifer Grant, Sam McMurray, Kristin Minter; **D:** Avi Nesher; **W:** Patrick Highsmith, Peter Sagal; **C:** Peter Fornborger; **M:** Roger Neill. *REP*

Savage Abduction 🎬 1973 (R) Two girls visiting Los Angeles are kidnapped by a bizarre man. 84m/C VHS, Beta. Tom Drake, Stephen Oliver, Sean Kenney; **D:** John Lawrence.

Savage Attraction 🎬½ *Hostage: The Christine Maresch Story; Hostage* 1983 (R) True story of a 16-year-old girl forced to marry an ex-Nazi, and her hellish life thereafter. Frustrating because it could have been much better. 93m/C VHS, Beta. AU GE Kerry Mack, Ralph Schicha; **D:** Frank Shields. *VTR*

Savage Beach 🎬 1989 (R) A pair of well-endowed female federal agents battle assorted buccaneers on a remote Pacific isle over a rediscovered cache of gold from WWII. Exploitative, pornographic, and degrading to watch. Sequel to "Picasso Trigger." 90m/C VHS, Beta, LV. Dona Speir, Hope Marie Carlton, Bruce Penhall, Rodrigo Obregon, John Aprea, Teri Weigel, Lisa London; **D:** Andy Sidaris. *COL*

The Savage Bees 🎬🎬 1976 A South American ship harbored at New Orleans during Mardi Gras unleashes killer bees into the celebratory crowds. Not bad, relatively exciting, TV thriller. 90m/C VHS, Beta. Ben Johnson, Michael Parks, Paul Hecht, Horst Buchholz, Gretchen Corbett; **D:** Bruce Geller. *ART*

Savage Capitalism 🎬🎬 *Capitalismo Salvaje* 1993 Melodramatic romance between a reporter and a mining company exec crumbles when the exec's presumed dead wife returns. Meanwhile, the reporter uncovers the truth behind the company's plans to mine in the interior of Brazil, which could cause ecological ruin. Portuguese with subtitles. 86m/C VHS. BR Fernanda Torres, Jose

Mayer, Marisa Orth, Marcelo Tass; **D:** Andre Klotzel; **W:** Andre Klotzel, Djalma Batista. *FCT*

Savage Dawn 🎬½ 1984 (R) In yet another desert town, yet another pair of combat-hardened vets are confronted by yet another vicious motorcycle gang. Haven't we seen this one before? 102m/C VHS, Beta. George Kennedy, Karen Black, Richard Lynch, Lance Henriksen, William Forsythe; **D:** Simon Nuchtern. *VTR*

Savage Drums 🎬½ 1951 Sabu returns to his South Seas island to help end tribal warfare there. Dated and dumb, but fun-to-watch melodrama/action. 70m/B VHS, Beta, LV. Sabu, Lita Baron; **D:** William (Lester Williams) Berke. *NO*

Savage Fury *Call of the Savage* 1933 Feature-length version of the popular movie serial. 80m/B VHS, Beta. Noah Beery Jr., Dorothy Short. *NOS, DVT, HEG*

The Savage Girl 🎬 1932 A hunter journeys through the darkest jungle in search of prey. Instead, he stumbles across a beautiful white jungle girl, falls in love with her and attempts to take her back with him. 64m/B VHS. Rochelle Hudson, Walter Byron, Harry Myers, Ted Adams, Adolph Milar, Floyd Schackleford; **D:** Harry Fraser. *SNC, NOS, DVT*

Savage Hearts 🎬½ 1995 Terminally ill mob hitwoman Beatrice Baxter (D'Abo) has six months left to live and she wants her last days to be spent in style. So she steals $2 million from her mob employer Roger Focely (Harris)—who's determined to get the money back. 90m/C VHS. Maryam D'Abo, Richard Harris, Myriam Cyr, Jerry Hall; **D:** Mark Ezra. *TRI*

Savage Hunger 🎬 1984 Ten plane crash survivors struggle to survive in the Baja desert. 90m/C VHS, Beta. Chris Makepeace, Scott Hylands, Anne Lockhart; **D:** Sparky Green. *VES*

Savage Instinct 🎬🎬 1991 A woman stumbles across a drug ring and becomes a target when they fear she could expose them. Only Mongo and his crew are even more surprised when she decides to fight back. 95m/C VHS. Debra Sweaney, Brian Oldfield. *MOV*

Savage Intruder 🎬 1968 (R) A wandering opportunist worms his way into the heart and home of a rich ex-movie star. She soon discovers that he's a sexual deviant who mutilates and murders for fun. Twisted doings with Hopkins in her final role. 90m/C VHS. John David Garfield, Miriam Hopkins, Gale Sondergaard, Florence Lake, Joe Besser, Minta Durfee; **D:** Donald Wolfe. *UNI*

Savage Is Loose woof! 1974 (R) Drivel about a scientist, his wife, and their son stranded on a deserted island for 20 years. Not surprisingly, as junior matures he realizes there isn't a woman for him—or is there? Completely lacking in redeeming qualities. Absurd pseudo-Freudian claptrap produced by Scott. 114m/C VHS, Beta. George C. Scott, Trish Van Devere, John David Carson, Lee Montgomery; **D:** George C. Scott. *MLB*

Savage Island 🎬½ 1985 (R) Women's prison in the tropics sets the scene for the usual exploitative goings-on. Blair is actually in the film only for a few minutes. Chopped-up, even worse version of "Escape From Hell." 74m/C VHS. SP IT Nicholas Beardsley, Linda Blair, Anthony Steffen, Ajita Wilson, Christina Lai, Leon Askin; **D:** Edward Muller; **W:** Nicholas Beardsley. Golden Raspberry Awards '85: Worst Actress (Blair). *NO*

Savage Journey 🎬½ 1983 (PG) A wagon train of pioneers has difficulty on its westward journey. Simple story with no real appeal. 99m/C VHS, Beta. Richard Moll, Maurice Grandmaison, Faith Clift; **D:** Tom McGowan.

Savage Justice 🎬 1988 A young woman seeks revenge against leftist rebels (boo, hiss) in a Southeast Asian country who killed her parents and raped her. She hooks up with an ex-Green Beret, and they fight and love their way through the jungle. The usual nudity and violence; derivative and dumb. 90m/C Beta. Julia Montgomery, Steven Memel. *VTR*

Savage Land ⅜½ **1994 (PG)** Family western finds a young brother and sister travelling by stage to meet up with their father. The stage is robbed by some bumbling bad guys, who then pursue the kids and two other passengers across the frontier. The kids, of course, are smarter than most of the adults, and manage to get the best of the bad hombres. **91m/C VHS, LV.** Graham Greene, Corbin Bernsen, Vivian Schilling, Mercedes McNab, Corey Carrier, Brion James, Bo Svenson, Charlotte Ross.

Savage Messiah ⅜⅜⅜ **1972 (R)** Bio of young French sculptor Henri Gaudier and his intense, though platonic, affair with a refined Polish woman 20 years his senior. Stylized drama is spared most of director Russell's noted excesses but he manages to believably show their magnetic attraction. Gaudier was killed in WWI at the age of 24. Based on the biography by H.S. Ede. **96m/C VHS. GB** Scott Antony, Dorothy Tutin, Helen Mirren, Lindsay Kemp, Peter Vaughan, Michael Gough; **D:** Ken Russell; **W:** Christopher Logue. *MGM*

Savage Run *Run, Simon, Run* **1970** Reynolds is Papago Indian framed and imprisoned for his brother's murder. Sprung from the pen, he heads back to the reservation to find the real killers and to avenge his brother's death. Convincing made for televisiondrama. Stevens' last role before her suicide. **73m/C VHS.** Burt Reynolds, Inger Stevens, James Best, Rodolfo Acosta, Don Dubbins, Joyce Jameson, Barney Phillips, Eddie Little Sky; **D:** George McCowan. *SIM*

Savage Sam ⅜⅜ **1963** Intended as a sequel to "Old Yeller." Sam, the offspring of the heroic dog named Old Yeller, tracks down some children kidnapped by Indians. Fun, but not fully successful. **103m/C VHS, Beta.** Tommy Kirk, Kevin Corcoran, Brian Keith, Dewey Martin, Jeff York, Marta Kristen; **D:** Norman Tokar; **C:** Edward Colman. *DIS*

The Savage Seven ⅜⅜ **1968** An underground classic where everyone loses. A motorcycle gang rides into an Indian town which is at the mercy of corrupt businessmen. The gang's leader becomes involved in the Indians' problems but the businessmen and the cops cause trouble for all concerned. Less than memorable. Produced by Dick Clark. **96m/C VHS.** Larry Bishop, Joanna Frank, Adam Roarke, Robert Walker Jr.; **D:** Richard Rush. *NO*

Savage Streets ⅜½ **1983 (R)** Blair seeks commando-style revenge on the street gang that raped her deaf sister. Extended rape scene betrays the exploitative intentions, though other bits are entertaining, in a trashy kind of way. **93m/C VHS, Beta, LV.** Linda Blair, John Vernon, Sal Landi, Robert Dryer, Debra Blee, Linnea Quigley; **D:** Danny Steinmann; **M:** John D'Andrea. Golden Raspberry Awards '85: Worst Actress (Blair). *ART, VES*

Savage Weekend woof! *The Killer Behind the Mask; The Upstate Murders* **1980 (R)** A killer behind a ghoulish mask stalks human prey in the boonies, of course. Astoundingly, there is one interesting role—William Sanderson's lonely. Otherwise, throw this one no bones. **88m/C VHS, Beta.** Christopher Allport, James Doerr, Marilyn Hamlin, Caitlin Kathleen Heaney O'Heaney, David Gale, William Sanderson; **D:** David Paulsen, John Mason Kirby; **W:** David Paulsen. *PRG*

Savage Wilderness ⅜⅜½ *The Last Frontier* **1955** When a trio of fur trappers lose a year's worth of skins to a band of marauding Indians, they decide to take scouting jobs at a cavalry outpost. But they find the new commander (Preston) hasn't gotten his nickname as the "Butcher of Shiloh" without reason. Adapted from the novel "The Gilded Rooster" by Richard Emery Roberts. **98m/C VHS.** Victor Mature, Robert Preston, Guy Madison, James Whitmore, Anne Bancroft, Russell Collins, Peter Whitney, Pat Hogan, Manuel Donde, Guy Williams; **D:** Anthony Mann; **W:** Philip Yordan, Russell S. Hughes; **M:** Leigh Harline. *COL*

The Savage Woman ⅜⅜ **1991** Marianna escapes from a desperate situation and is found unconscious in the woods by Elysee. He nurses her back to health, learns her terrible secret, and tries to help Marianna decide whether to turn herself into the police or keep running. In French with English subtitles. **100m/C VHS.** *CA* Patricia Tulasne, Matthias Habich; **D:** Lea Pool. *WBF*

Savages ⅜⅜ **1972** A group of savages descend on a palatial mansion, and after living there for some time, become refined ladies and gentlemen. The moral savages and "civilized" men are really the same. **106m/C VHS.** Lewis J. Stadlen, Anne Francine, Thayer David, Salome Jens, Susan Blakely, Kathleen Widdoes, Sam Waterston; **D:** James Ivory; **C:** Walter Lassally. *CVC, FCT*

Savages ⅜⅜½ **1975** Griffith as a demented nut-case stalking another man in the desert? That's right, Opie. "The Most Dangerous Game" remade-sort of-for TV. **74m/C VHS, Beta.** Andy Griffith, Sam Bottoms, Noah Beery Jr.; **D:** Lee H. Katzin.

Savages from Hell ⅜ *Big Enough and Old Enough* **1968 (R)** Greasy biker dude beats up a young black guy because he was flirting with the biker's woman. The biker also tries to rape a migrant farmworker's daughter because he lusts after her. Trashy exploitation film. **79m/C VHS.** Bobbie Byers, Cyril Poitier, Diwaldo Myers, Viola Lloyd, William P. Kelley; **D:** Joseph Prieto; **W:** Joseph Prieto. *SNC, TPV*

Savannah Smiles ⅜⅜½ **1982 (PG)** Poor little rich girl Anderson runs away from home, into the clutches of two ham-handed crooks. She melts their hearts, and they change their ways. Decent, sentimental family drama. **104m/C VHS, Beta, LV.** Bridgette Anderson, Mark Miller, Donovan Scott, Peter Graves, Chris Robinson, Michael Parks; **D:** Pierre De Moro. *NLC*

Save Me ⅜⅜ **1993 (R)** Jim Stevens' (Hamlin) wife has left him and his boss is involved in some dirty deals that could cost Jim his job. So things couldn't get worse, could they? Well, of course they could—and do. Because Jim meets Ellie (Anthony), a sexual adventuress just destined to bring trouble to a lonely guy. Also available in an unrated version. **89m/C VHS, LV, Closed Caption.** Harry Hamlin, Lysette Anthony, Michael Ironside, Olivia Hussey, Bill Nunn, Steve Railsback; **D:** Alan Roberts; **W:** Neil Ronco; **M:** Rick Marvin. *COL*

Save the Lady ⅜⅜ **1982** Plucky kids fight city hall to save an old ferry, the Lady Hope, from the scrap heap. Nothing offensive here—just a pleasant family flick. **76m/C VHS, Beta.** Matthew Excell, Robert Clarkson, Miranda Cartledge, Kim Clifford; **D:** Leon Thau. *NO*

Save the Tiger ⅜⅜⅜ **1973 (R)** A basically honest middle-aged man sees no way out of his failing business except arson. The insurance settlement will let him pay off his creditors, and save face. David, as the arsonist, and Gilford, as Lemmon's business partner, are superb. Lemmon is also excellent throughout his performance. **100m/C VHS, Beta, LV.** Jack Lemmon, Jack Gilford, Laurie Heineman, Patricia Smith, Norman Burton, Thayer David; **D:** John G. Avildsen; **M:** Marvin Hamlisch. Academy Awards '73: Best Actor (Lemmon); Writers Guild of America '73: Best Original Screenplay; Nominations: Academy Awards '73: Best Story & Screenplay, Best Supporting Actor (Gilford). *PAR, BTV*

Saved by the Light ⅜⅜½ **1997** On September 17, 1975, ruthless Dannion Brinkley's (Roberts) life was changed forever—he died. Struck by a bolt of lightning, Brinkley was declared dead, only to wake up 28 minutes later in the morgue. A changed man, which some of Brinkley's acquaintances find hard to believe, he becomes a public speaker, telling about his trip to heaven and his belief in love and salvation. TV movie based on Brinkley's book about his near-death experience. **95m/C VHS.** Eric Roberts, Lynette Walden, K. Callan; **D:** Lewis Teague. *BWE*

Saving Grace ⅜⅜ **1986 (PG)** A tale of the fictional youngest Pope of modern times, Pope Leo XIV (Conti). Beset by duty, he decides to shed his robes and get in touch with the world's peasantry. Improbable, but that's okay; the mortal sin is that it's improbable and slow and boring. **112m/C VHS, Beta, LV, 8mm, Closed Caption.** Tom Conti, Fernando Rey, Giancarlo Giannini, Erland Josephson, Donald Hewlett, Edward James Olmos; **D:** Robert M. Young; **W:** David S. Ward; **M:** William Goldstein. *NLC*

Saving Private Ryan **1998 (R)** Big-budget WWII Spielberg epic finds eight soldiers, lead by army captain Hanks, forced to go behind enemy lines in order to rescue downed paratrooper James Ryan (Damon). He's the sole surviving brother of four soldier siblings and the government wants some good PR—the men pulling the duty are less than enthusiastic, however. Film opens with a 25-minute graphic depiction of Omaha Beach on D-Day and the actors went through a week of boot camp in England in order to get the proper attitude. Not yet reviewed. **CW:** Intense prolonged realistically graphic sequences of war violence, and for language. **?m/C VHS.** Tom Hanks, Matt Damon, Edward Burns, Tom Sizemore, Jeremy Davies, Giovanni Ribisi, Adam Goldberg, Barry Pepper, Vin Diesel, Ted Danson, Dale Dye; **D:** Steven Spielberg; **W:** Robert Rodat, Frank Darabont. *NYR*

Sawbones ⅜ **1995 (R)** Medical school reject Willy Knapp (Harvey) takes out his frustrations by murdering people and then performing gruesome surgeries on the bodies. Cop But Miller (Baldwin) investigates. Made for cable. **CW:** Sadistic violence and gore; some language. **78m/C VHS.** Don Harvey, Adam Baldwin, Barbara Carrera, Nina Siemaszko, Nicholas Sadler, Don Stroud, Christopher Baffa; **D:** Catherine Cyran. *NHO*

Sawdust & Tinsel ⅜⅜⅜ *The Naked Night; Sunset of a Clown; Gycklarnas Afton* **1953** Early Bergman film detailing the grisly, humiliating experiences of a traveling circus rolling across the barren Swedish countryside. Lonely parable of human relationships. In Swedish with English subtitles. **87m/B VHS, Beta, LV.** *SW* Harriet Andersson, Ake Gronberg; **D:** Ingmar Bergman; **W:** Ingmar Bergman. *HMV, NLC, FCT*

Sawmill/The Dome Doctor ⅜⅜½ **1922** Two silent comedies starring the inimitable klutz of the golden era, Larry Semon, whose name has been nearly forgotten today. **71m/B VHS, Beta.** Larry Semon, Dorothy Dwan. *VYY*

Say Anything ⅜⅜⅜ **1989 (PG-13)** A semimature, successful teen romance about an offbeat loner interested in the martial arts (Cusack, in a winning performance) who goes after the beautiful class brain of his high school. Things are complicated when her father is suspected of embezzling by the IRS. Joan Cusack, John's real-life sister, also plays his sister in the film. Works well on the romantic level without getting too sticky. **100m/C VHS, Beta, LV, Closed Caption.** John Cusack, Ione Skye, John Mahoney, Joan Cusack, Lili Taylor, Richard Portnow, Pamela Segall, Jason Gould, Loren Dean, Bebe Neuwirth, Aimee Brooks, Eric Stoltz, Chynna Phillips, Joanna Frank; **D:** Cameron Crowe; **W:** Cameron Crowe; **M:** Anne Dudley, Richard Gibbs, Nancy Wilson. *FOX*

Say Goodbye, Maggie Cole ⅜⅜½ **1972** A widow goes to work as a doctor in a Chicago street clinic and becomes emotionally involved with a dying child. Hayward's final role in moving made-for-TV drama. **78m/C VHS, Beta.** Susan Hayward, Darren McGavin, Michael Constantine, Nichelle Nichols, Dane Clark; **D:** Jud Taylor. *THV*

Say Hello to Yesterday ⅜½ **1971 (PG)** A May-December romance that takes place entirely in one day. An unhappy housewife meets an exciting young traveler while both are in London. Cast and director try hard but fail to get the point across to the audience. **91m/C VHS, Beta. GB** Jean Simmons, Leonard Whiting, Evelyn Laye; **D:** Alvin Rakoff.

Say Yes! 🎬½ 1986 (PG-13) A nutty millionaire (Winters) bets €660 million that his inept nephew cannot get married within 24 hours. Three times the length of usual wacky sitcom, alas. 87m/C VHS, Beta, LV. Jonathan Winters, Art Hindle, Logan Ramsey, Lissa Layng; **D:** Larry Yust. NO

Sayonara 🎬🎬🎬 1957 An Army major is assigned to a Japanese airbase during the Korean conflict at the behest of his future father-in-law. Dissatisfied with his impending marriage, he finds himself drawn to a Japanese dancer and becomes involved in the affairs of his buddy who, against official policy, marries a Japanese woman. Tragedy surrounds the themes of bigotry and interracial marriage. Based on the novel by James Michener. 147m/C VHS, Beta. Marlon Brando, James Garner, Ricardo Montalban, Patricia Owens, Red Buttons, Miyoshi Umeki, Martha Scott; **D:** Joshua Logan; **C:** Ellsworth Fredericks. Academy Awards '57: Best Art Direction/Set Decoration, Best Sound, Best Supporting Actor (Buttons), Best Supporting Actress (Umeki); Golden Globe Awards '58: Best Supporting Actor (Buttons); Nominations: Academy Awards '57: Best Actor (Brando), Best Adapted Screenplay, Best Cinematography, Best Director (Logan), Best Film Editing, Best Picture. FOX, BTV

The Scalawag Bunch 🎬 1975 Yet another retelling of Robin Hood and his Merry Men and their adventures in Sherwood Forest. 100m/C VHS, Beta. IT Mark Damon, Luis Davila, Silvia Dionisio; **D:** George Ferron. MON, HHE

Scalp Merchant 🎬 1977 Private investigator Cliff Rowan hunts for a missing payroll. Someone would rather see him dead than successful. 108m/C VHS, Beta. Cameron Mitchell, John Waters, Elizabeth Alexander, Margaret Nelson; **D:** Howard Rubie. NO

Scalpel 🎬 False Face 1976 (R) After his daughter's death, a plastic surgeon creates her image on another woman to get an inheritance. Violent and graphic, with a surprise ending. Not too bad; interesting premise. 95m/C VHS, Beta. Robert Lansing, Judith Chapman, Arlen Dean Snyder, Sandy Martin, David Scarroll; **D:** John Grissmer; **W:** John Grissmer. NLC

The Scalphunters 🎬🎬½ 1968 Semi-successful, semi-funny western about an itinerant trapper (Lancaster) who is forced by Indians to trade his pelts for an educated black slave (Davis); many chases and brawls ensue. Good performances. 102m/C VHS, Beta. Burt Lancaster, Ossie Davis, Telly Savalas, Shelley Winters, Nick Cravat, Dabney Coleman, Paul Picerni; **D:** Sydney Pollack; **W:** William W. Norton Sr.; **M:** Elmer Bernstein. MGM

Scalps 🎬🎬 1983 (R) Hunted Indian princess and man whose family was killed by Indians form uneasy alliance in old West. 90m/C VHS, Beta. Karen Wood, Albert Farley, Benny Cardosa, Charlie Bravo, Vassili Garis; **D:** Werner Knox. IMP, HHE

Scam 🎬🎬½ 1993 (R) Maggie and her partner Barry are con artists making their living scamming high rollers in Miami Beach. Then Maggie tries to pull a con on the wrong man. Jack Shanks is an ex-FBI agent with a score to settle and he blackmails Maggie into helping her. 102m/C VHS. Christopher Walken, Lorraine Bracco, Miguel Ferrer; **D:** John Flynn. FOX

Scandal 🎬🎬 Shuban 1950 Handsome artist (Mifune) and beautiful concert singer (Yamaguchi) become the victims of a libelous article in a gossip magazine. The artist decides to sue but, being softhearted, chooses a questionable lawyer because the man's young daughter is dying. Then the unethical lawyer accepts a bribe to prejudice the case. Japanese with subtitles. 105m/B VHS. JP Toshiro Mifune, Takashi Shimura, Yoshiko Yamaguchi; **D:** Akira Kurosawa; **W:** Ryuzo Kikushima, Akira Kurosawa; **M:** Fumio Hayasaka. FCT

Scandal 🎬🎬🎬 1989 (R) A dramatization of Britain's Profumo government sex scandal of the 1960s. Hurt plays a society doctor who enjoys introducing pretty girls to his wealthy friends. One of the girls, Christine Keeler, takes as lovers both a Russian government official and a British Cabinet Minister. The resulting scandal eventually overturned an entire political party, and led to disgrace, prison, and death for some of those concerned. Also available in an unedited 115-minute version which contains more controversial language and nudity. Top-notch performances make either version well worth watching. 105m/C VHS, Beta, LV. GB John Hurt, Joanne Whalley, Ian McKellen, Bridget Fonda, Jeroen Krabbe, Britt Ekland, Roland Gift, Daniel Massey, Leslie Phillips; **D:** Michael Caton-Jones; **W:** Michael Thomas; **M:** Carl Davis. HBO

Scandal in a Small Town 🎬🎬 1988 A cocktail waitress in a small town has to defend herself and her daughter from the town's critical eye and hateful actions. Self-righteous made for TV drama rehashes several earlier plots. 90m/C VHS, LV. Raquel Welch, Christa Denton, Peter Van Norden, Ronny Cox; **D:** Anthony Page. THV

Scandal Man 🎬🎬½ 1967 A French photographer gets in over his head when he snaps the daughter of an American KKK leader embracing a black man in a nightclub. In French with English subtitles. 86m/C VHS, Beta. Maurice Ronet; **D:** Richard Balducci. FCT

Scandalous 🎬½ 1984 (PG) A bumbling American television reporter becomes involved with a gang of British con artists. Starts well but peters out. Look for the scene where Gielgud attends a Bow Wow Wow concert. 93m/C VHS, Beta, LV. Robert Hays, Pamela Stephenson, John Gielgud, Jim Dale, M. Emmet Walsh; **D:** Rob Cohen; **W:** Rob Cohen, Larry Cohen, John Byrum; **C:** Jack Cardiff; **M:** Dave Grusin. ART, VES

Scandalous 🎬 1988 A duke and his uncle work together to find a secretary who disappeared after witnessing a murder. 90m/C VHS, Beta. Albert Fortell, Lauren Hutton, Ursula Carven, Capucine; **D:** Robert W. Young. VTR

Scandalous John 🎬🎬 1971 (G) Comedy western about a last cattle drive devised by an aging cowboy (Keith) in order to save his ranch. Keith's shrewd acting as the ornery cattle man who won't sell to developers carries this one. 113m/C VHS, Beta. Brian Keith, Alfonso Arau, Michele Carey, Rick Lenz, John Ritter, Harry (Henry) Morgan; **D:** Robert Butler. DIS

Scanner Cop 🎬½ 1994 (R) When deranged scientist Sigmund Glock escapes from prison, he's determined to take revenge on Peter Harrigan, the cop who put him behind bars. With the aid of an evil assistant and a mind-altering drug, Glock kidnaps and programs innocent citizens into cop-killing maniacs. Harrigan's only weapon is a rookie cop with the Scanner power to read minds—and then destroy them. 94m/C VHS, LV, Closed Caption. Daniel Quinn, Darlanne Fluegel, Richard Lynch, Mark Rolston, Hilary Shepard, Gary Hudson, Cyndi Pass, Luca Bercovici, Brion James; **D:** Pierce David; **W:** John Bryant, George Saunders. REP

Scanner Cop 2: Volkin's Revenge 🎬🎬 1994 (R) Scanner cop Sam Staziak (Quinn) has become curious about his family, asking Carrie Goodart (Haje) to find out what she can. But Carrie's attacked by evil scanner Carl Volkin (Kilpatrick), whom Sam once sent to prison, and left in a coma. Then Sam discovers Volkin is draining the life force of other scanners in order to make himself invincible when he and Sam have their final showdown. **CW:** Language; sci-fi violence and gore. 95m/C VHS. Daniel Quinn, Patrick Kilpatrick, Khrystyne Haje, Robert Forster, Stephen Mendel; **D:** Steve Barnett; **W:** Mark Sevi; **C:** Thomas Jewett. REP

Scanners 🎬🎬½ 1981 (R) "Scanners" are telepaths who can will people to explode. One scanner in particular harbors Hitlerian aspirations for his band of psychic gangsters. Gruesome but effective special effects. 102m/C VHS, Beta, LV. CA Stephen Lack, Jennifer O'Neill, Patrick McGoohan, Lawrence Dane, Michael Ironside, Robert A. Silverman; **D:** David Cronenberg; **W:** David Cronenberg; **C:** Mark Irwin; **M:** Howard Shore. COL

Scanners 2: The New Order 🎬🎬 1/2 1991 (R) This not-bad sequel to the 1981 cult classic finds a power-mad police official out to build a psychic militia of captured Scanners. More story than last time, plus more and better special effects. **CW:** Strong violence and sci-fi action. 104m/C VHS, Beta, LV, Closed Caption. CA David Hewlett, Deborah Raffin, Yvan Ponton, Isabelle Mejias, Valentin Trujillo, Tom Butler, Vlasta Vrana, Dorothee Berryman, Raoul Trujillo; **D:** Christian Duguay; **W:** B.J. Nelson; **M:** Marty Simon. IME, VTR

Scanners 3: The Takeover 🎬½ 1992 (R) The third sequel in which Scanner siblings battle for control of the world. Lacks the creativity and storyline of the first two films. **CW:** Horror violence and sensuality. 101m/C VHS, LV, Closed Caption. Steve Parrish, Liliana Komorowska, Valerie Valois; **D:** Christian Duguay. REP

Scanners: The Showdown 🎬½ 1994 (R) Carl Volkin (Kilpatrick), the "scanner" killer, has escaped jail and is stalking the streets of L.A. His ultimate target is Sam Staziak (Quinn), the scanner cop who sent him away. Since Volkin's powers grow with every kill, Staziak better get to Volkin in a hurry. 95m/C VHS, Closed Caption. Patrick Kilpatrick, Daniel Quinn, Khrystyne Haje, Stephen Mendel, Brenda Swanson, Jewel Shepard, Robert Forster; **D:** Steve Barnett; **W:** Mark Sevi. REP

The Scar 🎬🎬½ Hollow Triumph 1948 A cunning criminal robs the mob, then hides by "stealing" the identity of a lookalike psychologist. But he's overlooked one thing...or two. Farfetched film noir showcases a rare villainous role for Henreid (who also produced). Based on a novel by Murray Forbes. 83m/B VHS. Paul Henreid, Joan Bennett, Eduard Franz, Leslie Brooks, John Qualen, Mabel Paige, Herbert Rudley; **D:** Steve Sekely. REP, FCT, NOS

Scar of Shame 🎬🎬 1927 Explores the ill-fated romance between a successful black concert pianist and the lower-class woman he marries. Gives a look at the color caste system and divisions within the black community of the era. 90m/B VHS. Harry Henderson, Lucia Lynn Moses, Ann Kennedy, Norman Johnstone; **D:** Frank Peregini. FCT, BTV

Scaramouche 🎬🎬🎬½ 1952 Thrilling swashbuckler about a nobleman (Granger, very well cast) searching for his family during the French Revolution. To avenge the death of a friend, he joins a theatre troupe where he learns swordplay and becomes the character "Scaramouche." Features a rousing six-and-a-half-minute sword battle. 111m/C VHS, LV. Stewart Granger, Eleanor Parker, Janet Leigh, Mel Ferrer, Henry Wilcoxon, Nina Foch, Richard Anderson, Robert Coote, Lewis Stone, Elisabeth Risdon, Howard Freeman; **D:** George Sidney; **C:** Charles Rosher. FCT

Scarecrow 🎬🎬½ 1973 (R) Two homeless drifters (Hackman and Pacino) walk across America, heading toward a car wash business they never reach. An oft-neglected example of the early 70s extra-realistic subgenre initiated by "Midnight Cowboy." Engrossing until the end, when it falls flat. Filmed on location in Detroit. 112m/C VHS, Beta. Gene Hackman, Al Pacino, Ann Wedgeworth, Eileen Brennan, Richard Lynch; **D:** Jerry Schatzberg; **C:** Vilmos Zsigmond. Cannes Film Festival '73: Best Film. WAR

Scared Stiff 🎬🎬🎬 1953 Fleeing a murder charge, Martin and Lewis find gangsters and ghosts on a Caribbean island. Funny and scary, a good remake of "The Ghost Breakers," with cameos by Hope and Crosby. ♫San Domingo; Song of the Enchilada Man; Mama Yo Quiero; You Hit the Spot; I Don't Care If the Sun Don't Shine; I'm Your Pal; When Somebody Thinks You're Wonderful. 108m/B VHS. Dean Martin, Jerry Lewis, Lizabeth Scott, Carmen Miranda, Dorothy Malone; **Cameos:** Bob Hope, Bing Crosby; **D:** George Marshall. PAR, MLB, REP

Scared Stiff 🎬 1987 (R) Three people move into a mansion once owned by a sadistic slave trader. Once there, they become unwilling victims of a voodoo curse. Bad special effects and script, not redeemed by decent but unoriginal story. 85m/

C VHS, LV. Andrew Stevens, Mary Page Keller; *D:* Richard S. Friedman; *W:* Richard S. Friedman, Mark Frost, Daniel F. Bacaner. REP

Scared to Death 🎬½ 1946
Begins with a woman dying of fright when shown the death mask of the man she framed. Dead woman then proceeds to narrate remainder of the story, which focuses on events leading up to her unfortunate, untimely, and fairly uninteresting demise. Memorable as Lugosi's only color film. DVD version is paired with 1941's "The Devil Bat." 60m/C VHS, Beta, DVD. Bela Lugosi, George Zucco, Douglas Fowley, Nat Pendleton, Joyce Compton; *D:* Christy Cabanne. NOS, SNC, EEL

Scared to Death 🎬 1980 (R)
A scientific experiment goes awry as a mutation begins killing off the residents of Los Angeles. 93m/C VHS, Beta. John Stinson, Diana Davidson, David Moses, Kermit Eller; *D:* William Malone; *M:* Tom Chase.

Scared to Death/Dick Tracy's Dilemma 🎬🎬 1947
On one tape, two '40s programs: Lugosi's only color film, about a psychotic magician who tortures a young girl, and a standard black-and-white Tracy entry. 125m/C VHS, Beta. Bela Lugosi, George Zucco, Ralph Byrd, Kay Christopher, Ian Keith. AOV

Scarface 🎬🎬🎬 Scarface: The Shame of a Nation 1931
The violent rise and fall of a 1930s Chicago crime boss (based on the life of notorious gangster Al Capone). Release was held back by censors due to the amount of violence and its suggestion of incest between the title character and his sister. Producer Howard Hughes recut and filmed an alternate ending, without director Hawks' approval, to pacify the censors, and both versions of the film were released at the same time. Almost too violent and intense at the time. Remains brilliant and impressive. Remade in 1983. 93m/B VHS, Beta, LV. Paul Muni, Ann Dvorak, Karen Morley, Osgood Perkins, George Raft, Boris Karloff; *D:* Howard Hawks; *C:* Lee Garmes. National Film Registry '94. USH

Scarface 🎬🎬🎬 1983 (R)
Al Pacino is a Cuban refugee who becomes powerful in the drug trade until the life gets the better of him. A remake of the 1932 classic gangster film of the same name, although the first film has more plot. Extremely violent, often unpleasant, but not easily forgotten. 170m/C VHS, Beta, LV, Letterbox, DVD. Al Pacino, Steven Bauer, Michelle Pfeiffer, Robert Loggia, F. Murray Abraham, Mary Elizabeth Mastrantonio, Harris Yulin, Paul Shenar, Oliver Stone; *D:* Brian DePalma; *W:* Oliver Stone; *C:* John A. Alonzo. USH

Scarface Mob 🎬🎬 Tueur de Ch Icago 1962
This is the original television pilot film for the popular series "The Untouchables," about Eliot Ness's band of good guys battling Chicago's crime lord, Al Capone. Still strong stuff. Narrated by Walter Winchell. 120m/B VHS, Beta. Robert Stack, Neville Brand, Barbara Nichols; *D:* Phil Karlson; *W:* Paul Monash. PAR

The Scarlet & the Black 🎬🎬½ 1983
A priest clandestinely works within the shield of the Vatican's diplomatic immunity to shelter allied soldiers from the Nazis in occupied Rome. His efforts put him at odds with the Pope and target him for Gestapo assassination. Swashbuckling adventure at its second-best. Made for television. Based on the nonfiction book "The Scarlet Pimpernel of the Vatican" by J.P. Gallagher. 145m/C VHS, Beta, Closed Caption. Gregory Peck, Christopher Plummer, John Gielgud, Raf Vallone; *D:* Jerry London; *M:* Ennio Morricone. FOX, FCT, IGP

The Scarlet Car 🎬🎬 1917
Chaney is a bank cashier who discovers his boss has been embezzling funds. A fight causes Chaney to believe he has killed his employer and he hides out in a remote cabin where guilt preys on his mind. 50m/B VHS, Beta. Lon Chaney Sr., Franklyn Farnum, Edith Johnson, Sam DeGrasse; *D:* Joseph DeGrasse. SNC, GPV, FCT

Scarlet Claw 🎬🎬🎬 Sherlock Holmes and the Scarlet Claw 1944
Holmes and Watson solve the bloody murder of an old lady in the creepy Canadian village of Le Mort Rouge. The best and most authentic of the Sherlock Holmes films. 74m/B VHS, Beta, Closed Caption. Basil Rathbone, Nigel Bruce, Miles Mander, Gerald Hamer, Kay Harding; *D:* Roy William Neill. FOX

The Scarlet Clue 🎬🎬 1945
A better script and faster pacing improved this Monogram entry in the Chan series. Charlie investigates a series of mysterious deaths which lead to a plot to steal secret government radar plans. 65m/B VHS. Sidney Toler, Benson Fong, Mantan Moreland, Robert E. Homans, Helen Devereaux; *D:* Phil Rosen. MGM

Scarlet Dawn 🎬🎬½ 1932
Lavish sets and costumes abound in this romantic drama starring Fairbanks as a Russian aristocrat and Carroll as his maid servant. Together they flee Russia during the Revolution, marry, and settle into the life of the common working class. Restless under his new status, Fairbanks pursues Tashman and tries his hand at swindling. A slow but interesting love story. Adapted from the novel "Revolt" by Mary McCall. 58m/B VHS. Douglas Fairbanks Jr., Nancy Carroll, Lilyan Tashman, Sheila Terry, Guy Kibbee, Richard Alexander, Frank Reicher; *D:* William Dieterle; *W:* Douglas Fairbanks Jr., Niven Busch, Erwin Gelsey. MGM

Scarlet Empress 🎬🎬🎬½ 1934
One of Von Sternberg's greatest films tells the story of Catherine the Great and her rise to power. Dietrich stars as the beautiful royal wife who outwits her maniacal husband to become empress of Russia. Incredibly rich decor is a visual feast for the eye, as perfectionist von Sternberg fussed over every detail. Dietrich is excellent as Catherine, and von Sternberg's mastery of lighting and camerawork makes for a highly extravagant film. Based on the diary of Catherine the Great. 110m/B VHS, Closed Caption. Marlene Dietrich, John Lodge, Sam Jaffe, Louise Dresser, Maria Sieber, Sir C. Aubrey Smith, Ruthelma Stevens, Olive Tell; *D:* Josef von Sternberg; *W:* Manuel Komroff. USH, FCT

The Scarlet Letter 🎬🎬 1934
Unlikely comic relief provides only measure of redemption for this poorly rendered version of Hawthorne's classic novel about sin and Hester Prynne. 69m/B VHS, Beta. Colleen Moore, Hardie Albright, Henry B. Walthall, Alan Hale, Cora Sue Collins, Betty Blythe; *D:* Robert G. Vignola. NOS, BAR, VYY

The Scarlet Letter 🎬🎬🎬 1973
A studied, thoughtful, international production of the Nathaniel Hawthorne classic about a woman's adultery which incites puritanical violence and hysteria in colonial America. Fine modernization by Wenders. In German with English subtitles. 90m/C VHS, Beta. SP GE Senta Berger, Lou Castel, Yella Rottlaender, William Layton, Yelena Samarina, Hans-Christian Blech; *D:* Wim Wenders. FCT, GLV

The Scarlet Letter 🎬🎬🎬 1979
Faithful yet passionate TV adaptation of Hawthorne's classic novel of 17th-century New England. Hester Prynne (Foster) is condemned by her Puritan fellows for having a child out of wedlock and is forced to wear a scarlet letter A for adultery. Secretly sharing Hester's torment is the Rev. Arthur Dimmesdale (Heard), the baby's father, and Hester's vengeful back-from-the-dead husband, Roger Chillingsworth (Conway). 240m/C VHS, Closed Caption. Meg Foster, John Heard, Kevin Conway, Josef Sommer; *D:* Rick Hauser; *W:* Allan Knee, Alvin Sapinsley; *M:* John Morris. WGB, PBS

The Scarlet Letter woof! 1995 (R)
Ewwwwww—ego-driven stinker of '95 ("Showgirls" not-withstanding). Feisty Hester Prynne (Moore) is condemned to wear the scarlet letter "A" of adultery by her 17-century Puritan neighbors because she bore a child out of wedlock. Oldman is the lusty Reverend Arthur Dimmesdale (her partner in illicit passion) while Duvall chews scenery as Hester's wronged hubby. This "freely adapted" version of the 1850 American classic should have set author Nathaniel Hawthorne spinning in his grave as his moral saga of sin and redemption meets 20th-century moviemaking by having the passion made explicit and a happy ending tacked on.CW: Violence and sexuality. 135m/C VHS, LV, Closed Caption. Demi Moore, Gary Oldman, Robert Duvall, Robert Prosky, Edward Hardwicke, Joan Plowright, Roy Dotrice, Dana Ivey, Sheldon Peters Wolfchild, Diane Salinger, Lisa Jolliff-Andoh, Amy Wright, Tim Woodward; *D:* Roland Joffe; *W:* Douglas Day Stewart; *C:* Alex Thomson; *M:* John Barry. Golden Raspberry Awards '95: Worst Remake/Sequel. HPH

The Scarlet Pimpernel 🎬🎬🎬½ 1934
"The Scarlet Pimpernel," supposed dandy of the English court, assumes a dual identity to outwit the French Republicans and aid innocent aristocrats during the French Revolution. Classic rendering of Baroness Orczy's novel, full of exploits, 18th century costumes, intrigue, damsels, etc. Produced by Alexander Korda, who fired the initial director, Rowland Brown. Remade for television in 1982. Available in colorized version. 95m/B VHS, Beta. GB Leslie Howard, Joan Gardner, Merle Oberon, Raymond Massey, Anthony Bushell, Nigel Bruce, Bramwell Fletcher, Walter Rilla, O.B. Clarence, Ernest Milton, Edmund Breon, Melville Cooper, Gibb McLaughlin, Morland Graham, Allan Jeayes; *D:* Harold Young; *W:* Robert Sherwood, Arthur Wimperis, Lajos Biro. CNG, NOS, HHT

The Scarlet Pimpernel 🎬🎬🎬 1982
Remake of the classic about a British dandy who saved French aristocrats from the Reign of Terror guillotines during the French Revolution. Made for British television version is almost as good as the original 1935 film, with beautiful costumes and sets and good performances from Seymour and Andrews. 142m/C VHS, Beta, LV. GB Anthony Andrews, Jane Seymour, Ian McKellen, James Villiers, Eleanor David; *D:* Clive Donner; *M:* Nick Bicat. ART, VES, FUS

Scarlet Spear woof! 1954
Filmed in Nairobi National Park in Kenya. A great white hunter convinces a young African chief that the ancient practices of his people are uncivilized. Pathetically stated and culturally offensive by today's standards. 78m/C VHS, Beta. John Bentley, Martha Hyer, Morasi; *D:* George Breakston.

Scarlet Street 🎬🎬🎬 1945
A mild-mannered, middle-aged cashier becomes an embezzler when he gets involved with a predatory, manipulating woman. Lang remake of Jean Renoir's "La Chienne" (1931). Set apart from later attempts on the same theme by excellent direction by Lang and acting. Also available Colorized. 95m/B VHS, Beta. Edward G. Robinson, Joan Bennett, Dan Duryea, Samuel S. Hinds; *D:* Fritz Lang; *C:* Milton Krasner. CNG, NOS, HHT

Scarlett 🎬🎬½ 1994 (PG-13)
Well, fiddle-dee-dee. While purists may object to any tampering of "Gone With the Wind," this epic TV miniseries, from the Alexandra Ripley novel, manages to be good if overlong fun for those willing to sit back and relax. Scarlett tries to get back Tara and Rhett (they divorce but still battle continuously); explores her Irish family ties and even moves to Ireland; then gets involved with the wrong man and is accused of murder so Rhett can save her and everything can turn out okay (there's lots more). The big budget is up on-screen with lavish costumes and sets and a big cast—although why two Brits got the leads in this Southern melodrama is anyone's guess (Whalley-Kilmer and Dalton try hard).CW: Violence including sexual abuse, sensuality and a childbirth. 360m/C VHS, Closed Caption. Joanne Whalley, Timothy Dalton, Ann-Margret, Barbara Barrie, Sean Bean, Brian Bedford, Stephen Collins, John Gielgud, Annabeth Gish, George Grizzard, Julie Harris, Tina Kellegher, Melissa Leo, Colm Meaney, Esther Rolle, Jean Smart, Elizabeth Wilson, Paul Winfield, Betsy Blair, Peter Eyre, Pippa Guard, Ronald Pickup, Gary Raymond, Dorothy Tutin; *D:* John Erman; *W:* William Hanley; *M:* John Morris. CAF

Scarred 🎬½ *Street Love; Red on Red* **1984 (R)** Unwed teenage mother becomes prostitute to support baby. Predictable plot and acting pull this one down. 85m/C VHS, Beta. Jennifer Mayo, Jackie Berryman, David Dean; *D:* Rosemarie Turko; *W:* Rosemarie Turko. *ART, VES*

The Scars of Dracula 🎬🎬½ **1970 (R)** A young couple tangles with Dracula in their search for the man's missing brother. Gory, creepy, violent, sexy tale from the dark side. Don't see it late at night. Preceded by "Taste the Blood of Dracula" and followed by "Dracula A.D. 1972." Available on laserdisc with "The Horror of Frankenstein." 96m/C VHS, Beta, LV. *GB* Christopher Lee, Jenny Hanley, Dennis Waterman, Wendy Hamilton, Patrick Troughton, Michael Gwynn, Anouska Hempel, Michael Ripper, Christopher Matthews, Delta Lindsay; *D:* Roy Ward Baker; *W:* Anthony John Elder Hinds; *M:* James Bernard. *REP, MLB*

Scavenger Hunt 🎬 **1979 (PG)** Action begins when a deceased millionaire's will states that his 15 would-be heirs must compete in a scavenger hunt, and whoever collects all the items first wins the entire fortune. Big cast wanders about aimlessly. 117m/C VHS, Beta. Richard Benjamin, James Coco, Ruth Buzzi, Cloris Leachman, Cleavon Little, Roddy McDowall, Scatman Crothers, Tony Randall, Robert Morley, Richard Mulligan, Dirk Benedict, Willie Aames, Vincent Price; *D:* Michael A. Schultz; *M:* Billy Goldenberg. *FOX*

Scavengers 🎬 **1987 (PG-13)** A man and a woman become involved in a spy plot and wind up in all sorts of danger. Pathetic excuse for a "thriller." 94m/C VHS, Beta, LV. Kenneth Gilman, Brenda Bakke, Ken Gampu, Norman Anstey, Crispin De Nys; *D:* Duncan McLachlan.

Scenario du Film Passion 🎬🎬🎬 **1982** A classically self-analyzing video piece by Godard, in which he recreates on tape the scenario for his film "Passion," resulting in a reflexive, experimental essay on the process of image-making and conceptualizing films, especially Godard's. In French with English subtitles. 54m/C VHS, Beta. *D:* Jean-Luc Godard, Anne-Marie Mieville, Barnard Menoud.

Scene of the Crime 🎬🎬½ **1985** Three short mysteries, which the audience is asked to solve: "The Newlywed Murder," "Medium Is the Murder" and "Vote for Murder." Made for television. 74m/C VHS, Beta. Markie Post, Alan Thicke, Ben Piazza; *D:* Walter Grauman. *USH*

Scene of the Crime 🎬🎬🎬 **1987** Beautiful widow, trapped in small French town, is sexually awakened by escaped convict hiding out near her home. Acclaimed, but sometimes distracting camera technique and slow pace undermine the film. In French with English subtitles. 90m/C VHS. *FR* Catherine Deneuve, Danielle Darrieux, Wadeck Stanczak, Victor Lanoux, Nicolas Giraudi, Jean Bousquet, Claire Nebout; *D:* Andre Techine; *W:* Olivier Assayas. *KIV, FCT*

Scenes from a Mall 🎬 **1991 (R)** Conspicuous consumers spend 16th wedding anniversary waltzing in mall while marriage unravels with few laughs. Surprisingly superficial comedy given the depth of talent of Allen and Midler. 87m/C VHS, Beta, LV, Closed Caption. Woody Allen, Bette Midler, Bill Irwin, Daren Firestone, Rebecca Nickels; *Cameos:* Fabio Lanzoni; *D:* Paul Mazursky; *W:* Paul Mazursky; *C:* Fred Murphy. *TOU, IME*

Scenes from a Marriage 🎬🎬🎬🎬 **1973 (PG)** Originally produced in six one-hour episodes for Swedish television, this bold and sensitive film excruciatingly portrays the painful, unpleasant, disintegration of a marriage. Ullmann is superb. Realistic and disturbing. Dubbed. 168m/C VHS, Beta. *SW* Liv Ullmann, Erland Josephson, Bibi Andersson, Jan Malmsjo, Anita Wall; *D:* Ingmar Bergman; *W:* Ingmar Bergman; *C:* Sven Nykvist. Golden Globe Awards '75: Best Foreign Film; New York Film Critics Awards '74: Best Actress (Ullmann), Best Screenplay; National Society of Film Critics Awards '74: Best Actress (Ullmann), Best Film, Best Screenplay, Best Supporting Actress (Andersson). *HMV*

Scenes from a Murder 🎬½ **1972** A killer (Savalas) stalks a beautiful actress (Heywood). Dull excuse for a suspense flick. 91m/C VHS, Beta. *IT* Telly Savalas, Anne Heywood, Giorgio Piazza; *D:* Alberto De Martino. *NO*

Scenes from the Class Struggle in Beverly Hills 🎬🎬½ **1989 (R)** Social satire about the wealthy, their servants, and their hangers-on in two Hollywood households. Two chauffeurs spend their spare time lusting after their lovely employers, and bet to see who can accomplish reality first. All kinds of erotic capers result. Usually funny and irreverent; occasionally misfires or takes itself too seriously. Reunites the trio from cult classic "Eating Raoul": Bartel, Woronov, and Beltran. Remake of Renoir's "The Rules of the Game." 103m/C VHS, Beta, LV. Jacqueline Bisset, Ray Sharkey, Mary Woronov, Robert Beltran, Ed Begley Jr., Wallace Shawn, Paul Bartel, Paul Mazursky, Arnetia Walker, Rebecca Schaeffer, Edith Diaz; *Cameos:* Little Richard; *D:* Paul Bartel; *W:* Bruce Wagner; *C:* Steven Fierberg; *M:* Stanley Myers. *NO*

Scenes from the Goldmine 🎬½ **1987 (R)** A young woman joins a rock band and falls in love with its lead singer. Realistic but bland; music not memorable (performed mostly by the actors themselves). 99m/C VHS, Beta, LV. Catherine Mary Stewart, Cameron Dye, Joe Pantoliano, John Ford Coley, Steve Railsback, Timothy B. Schmit, Jewel Shepard, Alex Rocco, Lee Ving, Lesley-Anne Down; *D:* Marc Rocco. *NLC*

The Scent of a Woman 🎬🎬½ *Sweet Smell of Woman; Profumo di Donna* **1975** An acclaimed dark comedy that may be an acquired taste for some. A blinded military officer and his valet take a sensual tour of Italy, the sightless man seducing beautiful women on the way. But at the end of the journey awaits a shock, and the real point of the tale, based on a novel by Giovanni Arpino. In Italian with English subtitles. Remade in 1992 as "Scent of a Woman." 103m/C VHS. *IT* Vittorio Gassman; *D:* Dino Risi. Nominations: Academy Awards '75: Best Adapted Screenplay, Best Foreign Language Film. *NYF*

Scent of a Woman 🎬🎬🎬 **1992 (R)** Pacino is a powerhouse (verging on caricature) in a story that, with anyone else in the lead, would be your run-of-the-mill, overly sentimental coming of age/redemption flick. Blind, bitter, and semi-alcoholic Pacino is a retired army colonel under the care of his married niece. He's home alone over Thanksgiving, under the watchful eye of local prep school student Charlie (O'Donnell). Pacino's abrasive (though wonderfully intuitive and romantic) colonel makes an impact on viewers that lingers like a woman's scent long after the last tango. O'Donnell is competently understated in key supporting role, while the tango lesson between Pacino and Anwar dances to the tune of "classic." Boxoffice winner is a remake of 1975 Italian film "Profumo di Donna." The laserdisc version is available in letterbox format. *CW:* Language. 157m/C VHS, LV, Letterbox, Closed Caption, DVD. Al Pacino, Chris O'Donnell, James Rebhorn, Gabrielle Anwar, Philip S. Hoffman, Richard Venture, Bradley Whitford, Rochelle Oliver, Margaret Eginton, Tom Riis Farrell, Frances Conroy; *D:* Martin Brest; *W:* Bo Goldman; *C:* Donald E. Thorin; *M:* Thomas Newman. Academy Awards '92: Best Actor (Pacino); Golden Globe Awards '93: Best Actor—Drama (Pacino), Best Film—Drama, Best Screenplay; Nominations: Academy Awards '92: Best Adapted Screenplay, Best Director (Brest), Best Picture; British Academy Awards '93: Best Adapted Screenplay. *USH, MOV, BTV*

The Scent of Green Papaya 🎬🎬🎬 **1993** Tranquil film, set in 1951 Vietnam, follows 10-year-old peasant girl Mui as she spends the next 10 years as a servant in a troubled family, gracefully accommodating herself to the small changes in her life. At 20, she finds a fairy-tale romance with her next employer, a young pianist. Presents a romanticized view of the stoicism of Vietnamese women but is visually beautiful. Directorial debut of Hung is based on his childhood memories of Vietnam, which he re-created on a

soundstage outside Paris. In Vietnamese with English subtitles. 104m/C VHS, LV. *VT* Tran Nu Yen-Khe, Lu Man San, Truong Thi Loc, Vuong Hoa Hoi; *D:* Tran Anh Hung; *W:* Tran Anh Hung, Patricia Petit. Nominations: Academy Awards '93: Best Foreign Language Film. *COL*

Schemes 🎬🎬 **1995 (R)** Grieving widower Paul Stewart (McCaffrey) becomes interested in Laura Pierce (Hope), a lovely young woman who said she knew his late wife. Then, Paul's business partner Evelyn (Draper) discovers Laura's not on the up and up and is really interested in Paul's substantial insurance payoff. Leslie's part of a con job set up by volatile Victor (Glover), but since Evelyn's also in love with Paul, things aren't at all what they seem. *CW:* Language, some sexuality. 95m/C VHS. John Glover, Polly Draper, Leslie Hope, James McCaffrey, John de Lancie, Allison Mackie; *D:* Derek Westervelt; *W:* Derek Westervelt; *C:* Claudio Obregon; *M:* Mark Chait. *PEG*

Scherzo **1939** One of McLaren's earliest films, an abstract meditation lost in 1939 and subsequently found and reconstructed in 1984. 2m/C VHS, Beta. *D:* Norman McLaren. *NFB*

Schindler's List 🎬🎬🎬🎬 **1993 (R)** Spielberg's staggering evocation of the Holocaust finds its voice in Oscar Schindler (Neeson), womanizing German businessman and aspiring war profiteer, who cajoled, bribed, and bullied the Nazis into allowing him to employ Jews in his Polish factories during WWII. By doing so he saved over 1,000 lives. The atrocities are depicted matter of factly as a by-product of sheer Nazi evil. Shot in black and white and powered by splendid performances. Neeson uses his powerful physique as a protective buffer; Kingsley is watchful as his industrious Jewish accountant; and Fiennes personifies evil as Nazi Amon Goeth. Based on the novel by Thomas Keanally, which itself was based on survivor's memories. Filmed on location in Cracow, Poland; due to the sensitive nature of the story, sets of the Auschwitz concentration camp were reconstructed directly outside the camp after protests about filming on the actual site. A tour de force and labor of love for Spielberg, who finally garnered the attention and respect as a filmmaker he deserves. *CW:* Language, actuality violence, and some sexuality. 195m/B VHS, LV, Letterbox, Closed Caption. Liam Neeson, Ben Kingsley, Ralph Fiennes, Embeth Davidtz, Caroline Goodall, Jonathan Sagalle, Mark Ivanir; *D:* Steven Spielberg; *W:* Steven Zaillian; *C:* Janusz Kaminski; *M:* John Williams. Academy Awards '93: Best Adapted Screenplay, Best Art Direction/Set Decoration, Best Cinematography, Best Director (Spielberg), Best Film Editing, Best Picture, Best Original Score; British Academy Awards '93: Best Adapted Screenplay, Best Director (Spielberg), Best Film, Best Supporting Actor (Fiennes); Directors Guild of America Awards '93: Best Director (Spielberg); Golden Globe Awards '94: Best Director (Spielberg), Best Film—Drama, Best Screenplay; Los Angeles Film Critics Association Awards '93: Best Cinematography, Best Film; National Board of Review Awards '93: Best Film; New York Film Critics Awards '93: Best Cinematography, Best Film, Best Supporting Actor (Fiennes); National Society of Film Critics Awards '93: Best Cinematography, Best Director (Spielberg), Best Film, Best Supporting Actor (Fiennes); Writers Guild of America '93: Best Adapted Screenplay; Nominations: Academy Awards '93: Best Actor (Neeson), Best Costume Design, Best Makeup, Best Sound, Best Supporting Actor (Fiennes); British Academy Awards '94: Best Actor (Neeson), Best Adapted Screenplay, Best Supporting Actor (Kingsley), Best Score; Golden Globe Awards '94: Best Actor—Drama (Neeson), Best Supporting Actor (Fiennes), Best Score; MTV Movie Awards '94: Best Film, Breakthrough Performance (Fiennes). *USH*

Schizo 🎬 *Amok; Blood of the Undead* **1977 (R)** Devious intentions abound as a middle-aged man is overcome by weird scenes and revelations, caused by the impending wedding of the figure skater he adores. Confusing tale of insanity, obsession, and skating. 109m/C VHS, Beta. *GB* Lynne Frederick, John Leyton, Stephanie Beacham, John Fraser, Jack Watson, John McEnery; *D:* Pete Walker; *W:* John M. Watson Sr.; *C:* Peter Jessop.

Schizoid *♂* *Murder by Mail* 1980 (R) Advice-to-the-lovelorn columnist Hill receives a series of threatening letters causing her to wonder whether psychiatrist Kinski is bumping off his own patients. Boring blood dripper that's difficult to follow. **91m/C VHS, Beta.** Klaus Kinski, Marianna Hill, Craig Wasson; **D:** David Paulsen. *USH*

Schizopolis *♂♂* 1997 Experimental, empty satire on modern spirituality and communication combines a number of weird and wacky devices that are not particularly entertaining. In an interesting premise, Soderbergh takes the lead in a dual role as Fletcher Munson, a manically neurotic employee of a self-help guru and his own look-alike, a ho-hum dentist having an affair with Fletcher's wife. Soderburgh's real-life ex, actress Brantley, plays his wife, who also has a double that shows up at the dentist. Things grow more bizarre for no apparent reason, as secondary cast members speak in other languages or just complete nonsense while strange sound effects confuse, in a film which also lists no credits (the title is shown in film on a character's t-shirt). Soderburgh, who wrote, directed and lensed this surrealist homage, shot on a super-low $250,000 budget as a way of expressing ideas not allowed in bigger budget, conventional films. To most, this just looks like expensive therapy. **96m/C VHS.** Steven Soderbergh, Betsy Brantley, David Jensen; **D:** Steven Soderbergh; **W:** Steven Soderbergh; **C:** Steven Soderbergh. *FXL*

Schlock *♂♂* *The Banana Monster* 1973 (PG) Accurately titled horror parody is first directorial effort for Landis, who does double duty as a missing link who kills people and falls in love with blind girl. Look for cameo appearance by Forrest J. Ackerman; ape-makeup by Rick Baker. **78m/C VHS.** John Landis, Saul Kahan, Joseph Piantadosi, Eliza Garrett; **Cameos:** Forrest J. Ackerman; **D:** John Landis; **W:** John Landis. *NO*

Schnelles Geld *♂*½ 1984 A mild-mannered guy gets involved with a prostitute, and is plunged into a world of crime and drugs. In German with English subtitles. **90m/C VHS, Beta.** *GE VCD, GLV*

School Daze *♂♂♂* 1988 (R) Director/writer/star Lee's second outing is a rambunctious comedy (with a message, of course) set at an African-American college in the South. Skimpy plot revolves around the college's homecoming weekend and conflict among frats and sororities and African-Americans who would lose their racial identity and others who assert it. Entertaining and thought provoking. A glimpse at Lee's "promise," fulfilled in "Do the Right Thing." **114m/C VHS, Beta, LV, Closed Caption.** Spike Lee, Laurence "Larry" Fishburne, Giancarlo Esposito, Tisha Campbell, Ossie Davis, Joe Seneca, Art Evans, Ellen Holly, Branford Marsalis, Bill Nunn, Kadeem Hardison, Darryl M. Bell, Joie Lee, Tyra Ferrell, Jasmine Guy, Gregg Burge, Kasi Lemmons, Samuel L. Jackson, Phyllis Hyman; **D:** Spike Lee; **W:** Spike Lee; **M:** Bill Lee. *COL, FCT*

School for Scandal *♂♂* 1965 British television adaptation of Richard Sheridan's comedic play of the morals and manners of 18th century England. **100m/B VHS, Beta.** *GB* Joan Plowright, Felix Aylmer. *VYY*

School Spirit *♂* 1985 (R) A hormonally motivated college student is killed during a date. He comes back as a ghost to haunt the campus, disrupt the stuffy president's affair, and fall in love. Forgettable, lame, low-grade teen sex flick. **90m/C VHS, Beta.** Tom Nolan, Elizabeth Foxx, Larry Linville; **D:** Allan Holleb; **W:** Geoffrey Baere; **M:** Tom Bruner.

School Ties *♂♂♂* 1992 (PG-13) Encino man Fraser does a dramatic turn as a talented 1950s quarterback who gets a scholarship to the elite St. Matthew prep school. To conform with the closed-mindedness of the McCarthy era, both his father and coach suggest that he hide his Jewish religion. Fraser's compliance results in his big-man-on-campus status, until his rival in football

and his love interest both find out that he is Jewish, creating an ugly rift in the school. What easily could have been just another teen hunk flick looks at much more than just Fraser's pretty face in successful, unflinching treatment of anti-Semitism. **110m/C VHS, Beta, LV, Letterbox, Closed Caption.** Brendan Fraser, Matt Damon, Chris O'Donnell, Randall Batinkoff, Andrew Lowery, Cole Hauser, Ben Affleck, Anthony Rapp, Amy Locane, Peter Donat, Zeljko Ivanek, Kevin Tighe, Michael Higgins, Ed Lauter; **D:** Robert Mandel; **W:** Dick Wolf, Darryl Ponicsan; **M:** Maurice Jarre. *PAR*

Schtonk *♂♂* 1992 Hermann Willie is a down-and-out journalist who thinks he's come upon the find of the century when he's given what are supposedly Hitler's diaries. Based on the 1983 scandal when the German publication "Der Stern" paid $5 million and printed what turned out to be not-very-clever forgeries. Director Dietl mocks the greedy gullibility of the journal, the ingenuity of the forger, as well as the nostalgia of the ex- and neo-Nazis of the modern Germany. The title is a meaningless expletive uttered by Charlie Chaplin in "The Great Dictator." German with subtitles. **115m/C VHS.** *GE* Goetz George, Uwe Ochsenknecht, Rolf Hoppe; **D:** Helmut Dietl; **W:** Helmut Dietl. Berlin International Film Festival '92: Best Actor (George), Best Director (Dietl), Best Film; Nominations: Academy Awards '92: Best Foreign Language Film. *NYR*

Sci-Fighters *♂♂*½ 1996 (R) Renegade cop Cameron Grayson (Piper) is tracking rapist Adrian Dunn (Drago) in 2009 Boston and discovers that Dunn has been exposed to a deadly, mutating virus. It's actually changing the bad guy into an alien methane-breathing lifeform that, of course, wants to inhabit the earth. Appropriately gross alien makeup and some decent special effects. **CW:** Violence/gore and some strong sexuality. **94m/C VHS, LV.** Roddy Piper, Billy Drago, Jayne Heitmeyer; **D:** Peter Svatek. *TRI, ORI*

Science Crazed *♂*½ 1990 A scientist creates a monster who could conceivably destroy the world. **90m/C VHS, Beta.** *CA* Cameron Klein; **D:** Ron Switzer. *NO*

Scissors *♂*½ 1991 (R) Yes, this Hitchcock imitation needs trimming. An unstable young woman contends with a rapist, devious lookalikes, birds, and a prison-like apartment, not all of which are relevant to the plot. An unsharp stab at suspense from novelist/filmmaker DeFelitta. **105m/C VHS, Beta, Closed Caption.** Sharon Stone, Steve Railsback, Michelle Phillips, Ronny Cox; **D:** Frank de Felitta; **W:** Frank de Felitta. *PAR*

Scorchers *♂♂* 1992 (R) Back in the bayou, Splendid (Lloyd), a newlywed who won't sleep with her husband, and her cousin Talbot (Tilly), a preacher's daughter whose husband prefers the town whore Thais (Dunaway), find their lives intertwined because of their marital and sexual problems. A real "scorcher." **CW:** Language and sexuality. **81m/C VHS, Beta, LV.** Faye Dunaway, Denholm Elliott, James Earl Jones, Emily Lloyd, Jennifer Tilly, Leland Crooke, James Wilder, Anthony Geary; **D:** David Beaird; **W:** David Beaird. *FXV, VTR*

Scorchy *♂* 1976 (R) Low-budget female cop action flick about a narcotics agent (Stevens) on the trail of a drug kingpin. Blood and guts, guns, and violence. Poor casting. **100m/C VHS, Beta.** Connie Stevens, William Smith, Cesare Danova, Marlene Schmidt; **D:** Howard (Hikmet) Avedis; **W:** Howard (Hikmet) Avedis. *ART*

Score *♂♂* 1972 Swinging marrieds Jack and Elvira turn their attention to a newlywed couple in order to indulge their sexual desires. Campy, culty erotica. **89m/C VHS.** Calvin Culver, Claire Wilbur, Lynn Lowry, Gerald Grant, Carl Parker; **D:** Radley Metzger. *FRF*

Scorned *♂♂* 1993 (R) Seductive Patricia Langley loves her husband Truman so much that she'll do anything to help him get that promotion, including seducing another man. Too bad Alex Weston gets the promotion instead. Really too bad, since Patricia decides Alex has ruined her life and she's going to get revenge by ruining his.

Also available in an unrated version. **100m/C VHS, LV.** Shannon Tweed, Andrew Stevens, Michael D. Arenz, Kim Morgan Greene, Stephen Young, Daniel McVicar; **D:** Andrew Stevens; **W:** Barry Avrich.

Scorned 2 *♂♂*½ 1996 (R) Amanda (McClure) seems happily married to psych prof Mark—even if she is having those bad dreams. But when her hubby is tempted by a pretty coed and Amanda finds out—well this is one woman that should never be scorned. **CW:** Strong sexuality, and for violence and gore. **105m/C VHS.** Tane McClure, Wendy Schumacher, Myles O'Brien, John McCook, Andrew Stevens, Seth Jaffe; **D:** Rodney McDonald; **W:** Sean McGinley; **C:** Gary Graver; **M:** Patrick Seymour. *APX*

Scorpio *♂♂*½ 1973 (PG) Okay cat-and-mouse espionage tale about a wily, veteran CIA agent (Lancaster) who may have turned traitor. He's set-up to be killed by a CIA boss but the assassin, code-name Scorpio (Delon), has some trouble fulfilling his assignment. Cross- and double-cross abound. **114m/C VHS.** Burt Lancaster, Alain Delon, Paul Scofield, John Colicos, Gayle Hunnicutt, J.D. Cannon, Joanne Linville, Melvin Stewart, James B. Sikking, Vladek Sheybal, William Smithers, Celeste Yarnall; **D:** Michael Winner. *MGM*

The Scorpio Factor *♂♂* 1990 Murder and mayhem follow microchip heist. **87m/C VHS.** Attila Bertalan, David Nerman, Wendy Dawn Wilson. *NO*

Scorpion *♂* 1986 (R) A karate-master and anti-terrorist expert defuses a skyjacking and infiltrates international assassination conspiracies. Ex-real life karate champ Tulleners is a ho-hum hero, and the story is warmed over. **98m/C VHS, Beta, LV.** Tonny Tulleners, Allen Williams, Don Murray; **D:** William Reed. *COL, HHE*

Scorpion Spring *♂♂* 1996 (R) Drug runner Astor (Morales) is on the lam through the desert with a beautiful hostage (Aviles) when two unsuspecting travelers (Molina and McGaw) offer the stranded duo a ride. But drug lord El Rojo (McConaughey) wants Astor dead and doesn't care who gets in his way and there's also a border patrol officer (Blades) on their trail as well. **CW:** Violence, language and some nudity. **89m/C VHS, LV, Closed Caption.** Esai Morales, Alfred Molina, Patrick McGaw, Matthew McConaughey, Angel Aviles, Ruben Blades, Miguel Sandoval, Richard Edson, John Doe; **D:** Brian Cox; **W:** Brian Cox; **C:** Nancy Schreiber; **M:** Lalo Schifrin. *NLC*

Scorpion with Two Tails *♂* 1982 In an underworld of terror, people die grotesque deaths that a woman dreams of. **99m/C VHS.** John Saxon, Van Johnson. *NO*

The Scorpion Woman *♂♂* 1989 A female Viennese judge becomes entwined in an unusual case which partially parallels her own life. Her new young lover turns out to be bisexual. Not gripping. In German with English subtitles. **101m/C VHS, Beta.** *GE* Angelica Domrose, Fritz Hammel; **D:** Susanne Zanke. *NO*

The Scorpion's Tail *♂* 1971 Graphic murder scenes rev up this early thriller by Martino filmed with plot twists and visual games. Dubbed in English. **90m/C VHS.** *IT SP* Evelyn Stewart, Anita Strindberg, George Hilton, Luigi Pistilli, Janine Reynaud; **D:** Sergio Martino; **W:** Sauro Scavolini, Ernesto Gastaldi; **M:** Bruno Nicolai. *VSM*

Scotland Yard Inspector *♂♂* *Lady in the Fog* 1952 An American newspaperman (Romero) in London looks for a killer. Nothing special. **73m/B VHS, Beta, LV.** *GB* Cesar Romero, Bernadette O'Farrell; **D:** Sam Newfield. *MLB*

Scott of the Antarctic *♂♂*½ 1948 Drama of doomed British expedition of 1911 struggling to be the first group to reach the South Pole. Much of the stunning location filming was shot in the Swiss Alps. Story is authentic, but oddly uninvolving, as though seen from afar. **111m/C VHS, Beta.** *GB* John Mills, Christopher Lee, Kenneth More, Derek Bond; **D:** Charles Frend; **C:** Geoffrey Unsworth. *REP, DVT, NOS*

Scott Turow's The Burden of Proof 🎬🎬½ *The Burden of Proof* 1992 Attorney Alejandro "Sandy" Stern (Elizondo) struggles to discover the reasons behind his wife's baffling suicide and deal with the problems caused by the federal investigation of his brother-in-law's commodities business. The character of Stern was also featured in the film "Presumed Innocent" (played by Raul Julia). TV movie; on two cassettes. **184m/C VHS.** Hector Elizondo, Brian Dennehy, Mel Harris, Stefanie Powers, Victoria Principal, Adrienne Barbeau, Anne Bobby, Gail Strickland, Concetta Tomei, Jeffrey Tambor; **D:** Mike Robe; **C:** Kees Van Oostrum. *TVC*

Scoumoune 🎬🎬½ 1974 The local "fixer" and heavy gets into trouble and no one comes to help. A movie that searches for honesty. Dubbed in English. **87m/C VHS, Beta.** *FR* Jean-Paul Belmondo, Claudia Cardinale. *NO*

The Scout 🎬🎬 1994 (PG-13) Brooks is an about-to-be-canned scout for the New York Yankees who discovers a weird, though genuine, phenom pitcher (Fraser) on a trip to Mexico. He convinces the Yankees to take the phenom on, though he's not sure whether Fraser isn't a few innings shy of a complete game. But with a 100 mph fast ball and a bat that would have made Babe Ruth envious, who cares? Film straddles sports comedy and melodrama territories, satisfying in neither. Fraser plays variation on Encino Man. Brooks rewrote part of the script, adding much needed biting humor, but not enough. Bombastic real-life team owner Steinbrenner plays himself. **101m/C VHS, Closed Caption.** Albert Brooks, Brendan Fraser, Dianne Wiest, Lane Smith, Michael Rapaport, Steve Garvey, Bob Costas, Roy Firestone, Anne Twomey, Tony Bennett; **D:** Michael Ritchie; **W:** Albert Brooks, Andrew Bergman, Monica Johnson; **M:** Bill Conti. *FXV*

Scout's Honor 🎬🎬 1980 An orphan (Coleman) is determined to become the best Cub Scout ever when he joins a troop led by an executive who dislikes children. Harmless, enjoyable family tale includes several former child stars as Scout parents. Made for television. **96m/C VHS, Beta.** Gary Coleman, Katherine Helmond, Wilfrid Hyde-White, Pat O'Brien, Joanna Moore, Meeno Peluce, Jay North, Harry (Henry) Morgan, Angela Cartwright; **D:** Henry Levin. *NO*

Scrambled Feet 🎬🎬½ 1983 An uninhibited satire of the world of show business. **100m/C VHS, Beta.** Madeline Kahn. *TTC*

Scream 🎬 1983 (R) Vacationers on a raft trip down the Rio Grande are terrorized by a mysterious murderer. Hopelessly dull. **86m/C VHS, Beta.** Pepper Martin, Hank Worden, Alvy Moore, Woody Strode, John Ethan Wayne; **D:** Byron Quisenberry. *ART, VES*

Scream 🎬🎬🎬 *Scary Movie* 1996 (R) Director Craven playfully tweaks the cliches of teen slasher pics (which he helped create with "Nightmare on Elm Street") with this tongue-in-cheek thriller. Yep, where there's a mad slasher on the loose, there must be a group of teenagers "just out for a good time." The difference is both the killer and the victims have been raised on '80s splatter movies and, therefore, know all the rules. Sexual activity and/or substance abuse? Start picking out coffins. The stalker uses his cellular phone to terrorize his victims. He also uses it to ask his prey trivia questions or offer critiques of low-grade horror movies. Campbell plays the virginal heroine in the tight sweater, with Ulrich playing opposite as the sexually frustrated boyfriend. More fun than a bucket full of Karo syrup with red dye #3.**CW:** Strong graphic horror violence and gore, and for language. **111m/C VHS, LV, Closed Caption.** Drew Barrymore, Neve Campbell, Courteney Cox, David Arquette, Skeet Ulrich, Rose McGowan, Henry Winkler, Liev Schreiber, W. Earl Brown, Jamie Kennedy, Lawrence Hecht; *Cameos:* Wes Craven, Linda Blair; **D:** Wes Craven; **W:** Kevin Williamson; **C:** Mark Irwin; **M:** Marco Beltrami. MTV Movie Awards '97: Best Film; Nominations: MTV Movie Awards '97: Best Female Performance (Campbell). *TOU*

Scream 2 🎬🎬🎬 *Scream Again* 1997 (R) Sidney (Campbell) trades psychotherapy for college, only to be harassed by a lunatic willing to duplicate her nightmares from the original. All the cast that survived the first pic are back (and some new faces, with O'Connell as Sidney's new boyfriend) including TV-tabloider Gale Weathers (Cox), who has turned a best-seller about the murders into a movie called "Stab"; lovable, huggable sheriff Dewey (Arquette); and horror film fanatic Randy (Kennedy). Director Craven and writer Williamson add more of the satirical spark that propelled its predecessor into boxoffice success. By following the rules of sequels, they increase the suspense (everyone is a suspect) and gore to tantalizing fun, making this entry to the popular franchise a hard one to top.**CW:** Language and strong bloody violence. **120m/C VHS, LV, Closed Caption, DVD.** Courteney Cox, Neve Campbell, Jerry O'Connell, David Arquette, Jada Pinkett Smith, Jamie Kennedy, Liev Schreiber, Sarah Michelle Gellar, Laurie Metcalf, Elise Neal, Lewis Arquette, Duane Martin, Omar Epps, David Warner; *Cameos:* Tori Spelling; **D:** Wes Craven; **W:** Kevin Williamson; **C:** Peter Deming; **M:** Marco Beltrami. MTV Movie Awards '98: Best Female Performance (Campbell). *TOU*

Scream and Scream Again 🎬🎬½ *Screamer* 1970 (PG) Price is a sinister doctor who tries to create a super race of people devoid of emotions. Cushing is the mastermind behind the plot. Lee is the agent investigating a series of murders. Three great horror stars, a psychedelic disco, great '60s fashions; it's all here. **95m/C VHS, Beta.** *GB* Vincent Price, Christopher Lee, Peter Cushing, Judy Huxtable, Alfred Marks, Anthony Newlands, Uta Levka, Judi Bloom, Yutte Stensgaard; **D:** Gordon Hessler; **W:** Christopher Wicking; **C:** John Coquillon. *ART, ORI*

Scream, Baby, Scream 🎬 *Nightmare House* 1969 An unsuccessful artist switches from sculpting clay to carving young models' faces into hideous deformed creatures. **86m/C VHS, Beta.** Ross Harris, Eugenie Wingate, Chris Martell, Suzanne Stuart, Larry Swanson, Brad Grinter; **D:** Joseph Adler. *NO*

Scream Blacula Scream 🎬🎬 1973 (R) Blacula returns from his dusty undoing in the original movie to once again suck the blood out of greater Los Angeles. A voodoo priestess (Grier) is the only person with the power to stop him. A weak follow up to the great "Blacula," but worth a look for Marshall and Grier. **96m/C VHS.** William Marshall, Don Mitchell, Pam Grier, Michael Conrad, Richard Lawson, Lynne Moody, Janee Michelle, Barbara Rhoades, Bernie Hamilton; **D:** Bob Kelljan. *ORI, FCT*

Scream Bloody Murder woof! 1972 (R) A young boy grinds his father to death with a tractor but mangles his own hand trying to jump off. After receiving a steel claw and being released from a mental institution he continues his murderous ways in and around his home town. Inspiring. **90m/C VHS, Beta.** Fred Holbert, Leigh Mitchell, Robert Knox, Suzette Hamilton; **D:** Robert Emery. *VCI*

Scream Dream 🎬 1989 (R) A beautiful rock star uses her supernatural powers to control her fans, turning them into revenge-seeking monsters when she wants to. Heavy on the blood and skin; heavily exploitative. **80m/C VHS.** Melissa Moore, Carole Carr, Nikki Riggins, Jesse Ray; **D:** Donald Farmer; **W:** Donald Farmer. *NO*

Scream for Help 🎬 1986 (R) A young girl discovers that her cheating stepfather is plotting to murder her mother, but no one will believe her. Is she paranoid? So bad it's funny; otherwise, it's just bad, and far from suspenseful. **95m/C VHS, Beta, LV.** Rachael Kelly, David Brooks, Marie Masters; **D:** Michael Winner; **W:** Tom Holland. *ORI, WAR*

Scream of Fear 🎬🎬🎬 *Taste of Fear* 1961 A wheelchair-bound young woman goes to visit her father and new stepmother only to find her father is away on business. But she believes she sees her father's corpse. Is someone trying to drive her mad? Abounds in plot twists and mistaken identities. A truly spooky film, suspenseful, and well-made. **81m/B VHS, Beta.** *GB* Susan Strasberg, Ronald Lewis, Ann Todd, Christopher Lee; **D:** Seth Holt; **W:** Jimmy Sangster. *COL, MLB*

Scream of the Demon Lover woof! 1971 (R) A young biochemist has a busy day as she works for a reclusive Baron. She fantasizes about him, tries to track down a murderer, and eventually discovers a mutant in the cellar. About as bad as they come, but short! **75m/C VHS, Beta.** Jennifer Hartley, Jeffrey Chase; **D:** J.L. Merino. *NLC*

Screamer 🎬 1974 A woman wants revenge after she is viciously attacked and raped. Now every man she sees is her attacker as she becomes more and more unbalanced. **71m/C VHS, Beta.** Pamela Franklin, Donal McCann. *NO*

Screamers 🎬 *L'Isola Degli Uomini Pesce; Island of the Fishmen; Something Waits in the Dark* 1980 (R) A mad scientist on a desert island gleefully turns escaped convicts into grotesque monstrosities. Gory and gratuitous. **83m/C VHS, Beta.** Richard Johnson, Joseph Cotten, Barbara Bach; **D:** Dan T. Miller, Sergio Martino.

Screamers 🎬🎬 1996 (R) In the year 2078, Colonel Joe Hendriksson (Weller) and a small band of survivors fight a civil war on the radiation contaminated planet Sirius 6B. They run up against the screamers—mechanical creatures with razor-sharp claws, originally designed to protect humans. The screamers are bent on destroying all life in the universe while somehow mutating and breeding on their own. Unfortunately, director Duguay doesn't give any indication how this is taking place. Some fine stunt work and special effects redeem standard action adventure. Based on the novella "Second Variety" by Philip K. Dick ("Blade Runner").**CW:** Profanity, violence and gore. **107m/C VHS, LV, 8mm, Closed Caption.** Peter Weller, Jennifer Rubin, Andrew Lauer, Charles Powell, Ron White, Michael Caloz; **D:** Christian Duguay; **W:** Dan O'Bannon, Miguel Tejada-Flores; **C:** Rodney Gibbons; **M:** Normand Corbeil. Nominations: Genie Awards '96: Best Art Direction/Set Decoration, Best Supporting Actor (White), Best Score. *COL*

The Screaming Dead 🎬 *Dracula vs. Frankenstein* 1972 Monsters rise from the tomb to do battle with planet Earth and each other. Not to be confused with the Al Adamson epic "Dracula vs. Frankenstein." **84m/C VHS.** *SP* Dennis Price, Howard Vernon, Alberto Dalbes, Mary Francis, Genevieve Deloir, Josianne Gibert, Fernando Bilbao; **D:** Jess (Jesus) Franco. *NO*

The Screaming Skull 🎬½ 1958 Man redecorates house with skulls in attempt to drive already anxious wife insane. **68m/B VHS.** William Hudson, Peggy Webber, Toni Johnson, Russ Conway, Alex Nicol; **D:** Alex Nicol; **M:** Ernest Gold. *NOS, SNC*

Screams of a Winter Night 🎬 1979 (PG) Ghostly tale of an evil monster from the lake and the terror he causes. **92m/C VHS, Beta.** Matt Borel, Gil Glasco. *NO*

Screamtime 🎬 1983 (R) Two fiendish friends filch a trilogy of horror tapes for home viewing. After the show, real scary things happen. **89m/C VHS, Beta.** Jean Anderson, Robin Bailey, Dora Bryan, David Van Day; **D:** Al Beresford. *ART*

Screen Test woof! 1985 (R) Oversexed silly teenagers arrange fake screen tests in order to meet girls. **84m/C VHS, Beta, LV.** Michael Allan Bloom, Robert Bundy, Paul Lueken, David Simpatico; **D:** Sam Auster; **W:** Sam Auster. *COL*

Screwball Academy 🎬½ 1986 (R) A beautiful female director makes a soft-core film on a secluded island, and gets trouble from thugs, evangelists, horny crew members and others. Former "SCTV" director John Blanchard understandably used a pseudonym to direct this lame effort. **90m/C VHS, Beta.** Colleen Camp, Kenneth Welsh, Christine Cattall; **D:** Reuben Rose. *TWE*

Screwballs 🎬 1983 (R) Freewheeling group of high school boys stirs up trouble for their snooty and virginal homecoming queen. Another inept teen sex comedy with no subtlety whatsoever. Sequel: "Loose Screws." **80m/C VHS, Beta.** Peter

Keleghan, Lynda Speciale; **D:** Rafal Zielinksi; **W:** Jim Wynorski. *WAR*

Scrooge ♫♫♫ **1935** On Christmas Eve a miser changes his ways after receiving visits from the ghosts of Christmas past, present, and future. Co-scripter Hicks gives an interesting performance as Ebeneezer Scrooge. Based on the classic novel "A Christmas Carol" by Charles Dickens. **61m/B VHS, Beta.** *GB* Seymour Hicks, Maurice Evans, Robert Cochran, Donald Calthrop, Mary Glynne, Oscar Asche; **D:** Henry Edwards; **W:** Seymour Hicks. *VYY, CCB, DVT*

Scrooge ♫♫½ **1970 (G)** Well done musical version of Charles Dickens' classic "A Christmas Carol," about a miserly old man who is faced with ghosts on Christmas Eve. Finney is memorable in the title role. ♫The Beautiful Day; Happiness; Thank You Very Much; A Christmas Carol; Christmas Children; I Hate People; Farver Chris'mas; See the Phantoms; December the 25th. **86m/C VHS, Beta, LV, Closed Caption.** Albert Finney, Alec Guinness, Edith Evans, Kenneth More; **D:** Ronald Neame; **W:** Leslie Bricusse; **C:** Oswald Morris; **M:** Leslie Bricusse. Golden Globe Awards '71: Best Actor—Musical/Comedy (Finney); Nominations: Academy Awards '70: Best Art Direction/Set Decoration, Best Costume Design, Best Song ("Thank You Very Much"), Original Song Score and/or Adaptation. *FOX, FUS*

Scrooged ♫♫ **1988 (PG-13)** Somewhat disjointed big-budgeted version of the hallowed classic. A callous television executive staging "A Christmas Carol" is himself visited by the three ghosts and sees the light. Kane is terrific as one of the ghosts. Film is heavy-handed, Murray too sardonic to be believable. **101m/C VHS, Beta, LV, 8mm, Closed Caption.** Bill Murray, Carol Kane, John Forsythe, David Johansen, Bob(cat) Goldthwait, Karen Allen, Michael J. Pollard, Brian Doyle-Murray, Alfre Woodard, John Glover, Robert Mitchum, Buddy Hackett, Robert Goulet, Jamie Farr, Mary Lou Retton, Lee Majors; **D:** Richard Donner; **W:** Mitch Glazer, Michael O'Donoghue; **C:** Michael Chapman; **M:** Danny Elfman. *PAR*

Scrubbers ♫ **1982 (R)** Young girl is sent to reform school where she's forced to survive in a cruel and brutal environment. Low-budget "reform school" movie with no point, but lots of lesbianism. **93m/C VHS, Beta.** *GB* Amanda York, Chrissie Cotterill, Elizabeth Edmonds, Kate Ingram, Debbie Bishop, Dana Gillespie; **D:** Mai Zetterling. *NO*

Scruffy 1980 An orphan and his dog survive with the help of two crooks who are reformed through their love for the little boy. Animated. **72m/C VHS, Beta. V:** Alan Young, June Foray, Hans Conried, Nancy McKeon. *WOV, GKK*

Scruples ♫♫½ **1980** Set in the glamorous, jet-setting world of Beverly Hills, this top-rated miniseries follows the career of Billy Ikehorn (Wagner) as she weds a wealthy industrialist and opens a clothing boutique named "Scruples." She caters to high society's haute couture, and encounters unscrupulous individuals who threaten to dethrone her from her position of power and privilege. Based on the best-selling novel by Judith Krantz. **279m/C VHS, Beta, Closed Caption.** Lindsay Wagner, Barry Bostwick, Kim Cattrall, Gavin MacLeod, Connie Stevens, Efrem Zimbalist Jr., Gene Tierney; **M:** Charles Bernstein. *WAR*

The Sculptress ♫♫ **1997** Troubled writer Rosalind Leigh (Goodall) prepares to interview convicted killer Olive Martin (Quirke), who five years before was found with the dead bodies of her mother and sister. Nicknamed "The Sculptress" for the gruesome nature of the murders, the equally troubled Olive is also a convincing liar. Although Olive says she's guilty, Roz is certain she's hiding something and becomes determined to discover the truth. Very creepy. Made for British TV; based on the novel by Minette Walters. **180m/C VHS.** *GB* Caroline Goodall, Pauline Quirke, Christopher Fulford, Dermot Crowley, David Horovitch, Jay Villiers, Lynda Rooke; **D:** Stuart Orme; **W:** Reg Gadney; **C:** Gavin Finney; **M:** Colin Towns. *VTR*

Scum ♫♫♫ **1979** Adapted from Roy Minton's acclaimed play, this British production looks at the struggle among three young men in a British Borstal (a prison for young convicts.) Portrays the physical, sexual, and psychological violence committed. Horrifying and powerful. **96m/C VHS, Beta.** *GB* Phil Daniels, Mick Ford, Ray Winstone; **D:** Alan Clarke.

Sea Chase ♫♫½ **1955** An odd post-war sea adventure, wherein a renegade German freighter captain is pursued by British and German navies as he leaves Australia at the outbreak of WWII. A Prussian Wayne rivaled only by his infamous Genghis Khan in "The Conqueror" for strange character selection. Turner is on board as Wayne's girlfriend. **117m/C VHS, Beta, LV, Letterbox.** John Wayne, Lana Turner, Tab Hunter, James Arness, Lyle Bettger, David Farrar, Richard Davalos, Claude Akins, John Qualen; **D:** John Farrow; **C:** William Clothier. *WAR*

Sea Devils ♫ **1931** Sentenced to prison for a crime he didn't commit, a man escapes and joins a boatload of treasure hunters, but mutiny is afoot. Don't get soaked by this cheapie. **77m/B VHS.** Walter Long, Edmund Burns, Henry Otto, James Donnelly; **D:** Joseph Levering. *SNC, NOS*

Sea Devils ♫♫ **1937** The tale of a sea captain and his lovely daughter who have differing opinions on whom she should marry. While her father would like her to marry a tame gentlemen under his command, she has her heart set on another beau. Sound predictable? It is, but fun. **88m/B VHS.** Victor McLaglen, Preston Foster, Ida Lupino, Donald Woods, Gordon Jones; **D:** Ben Stoloff.

Sea Devils ♫♫ **1953** A smuggler and a beautiful spy come together during the Napoleonic Wars in this sea romance filled with intrigue and adventure. **86m/C VHS, Beta.** *GB* Rock Hudson, Yvonne De Carlo, Maxwell Reed; **D:** Raoul Walsh.

Sea Gypsies ♫♫ **1978 (G)** A sailing crew of five is shipwrecked off the Aleutian Islands. They must escape before winter or learn to survive. Passable family drama. **101m/C VHS, Beta.** Robert F. Logan, Mikki Jamison-Olsen, Heather Rattray, Cjon Damitri; **D:** Stewart Raffill; **W:** Stewart Raffill. *WAR*

The Sea Hawk ♫♫♫½ **1940** An English privateer learns the Spanish are going to invade England with their Armada. After numerous adventures, he is able to aid his queen and help save his country, finding romance along the way. One of Flynn's swashbuckling best. Available colorized. **128m/B VHS, Beta, LV.** Errol Flynn, Claude Rains, Donald Crisp, Alan Hale, Flora Robson, Brenda Marshall, Henry Daniell, Gilbert Roland, James Stephenson, Una O'Connor; **D:** Michael Curtiz; **W:** Howard Koch. Nominations: Academy Awards '40: Best Interior Decoration, Best Sound, Best Score. *MGM, TTC, FOX*

Sea Hound 1947 A 15-part series set in the late 1940s that charts the voyage of a group of pirates searching for buried treasure. Everything goes well until Crabbe emerges to wreck their hopes. **?m/B VHS.** Buster Crabbe, Jimmy Lloyd, Pamela Blake; Ralph Hodges, Bob Barron; **D:** Walter B. Eason, Mack V. Wright. *MLB, GPV*

Sea Lion ♫♫ **1921** A vicious sea captain, embittered by a past romance, becomes sadistic and intolerable, until the truth emerges. Lots of action, but plodding, rehashed plot. Silent. **50m/B VHS, Beta.** Hobart Bosworth. *VYY*

Sea of Dreams ♫ **1990** Don't expect much in the way of a script from this soft-core production. **80m/C VHS, Beta.** Jon Rodgers, Chad Scott, Jacky Peel, Renee O'Neil. *HHE*

Sea of Love ♫♫♫½ **1989 (R)** A tough, tightly wound thriller about an alcoholic cop with a mid-life crisis. While following the track of a serial killer, he begins a torrid relationship with one of his suspects. Pacino doesn't stand a chance when Barkin heats up the screen. **113m/C VHS, Beta, LV, Letterbox, Closed Caption, DVD.** Al Pacino, Ellen Barkin, John Goodman, Michael Rooker, William Hickey, Richard Jenkins; **D:** Harold Becker; **W:** Richard Price; **M:** Trevor Jones. *USH*

Sea of Sand ♫♫½ *Desert Patrol* **1958** Typical actioner set in WWII finds a British desert patrol's latest mission is to blow up Rommel's fuel supply before the battle of El Alamein. Lots of heroics against the Nazis and stiff upper lips. **97m/B VHS.** *GB* Richard Attenborough, John Gregson, Michael Craig, Vincent Ball, Ray McAnally; **D:** Guy Green; **W:** Robert Westerby; **C:** Wilkie Cooper; **M:** Clifton Parker. *FCT*

Sea Prince and the Fire Child ♫♫ **1982** Japanese animated film follows two young lovers who set off on an adventure to escape the disapproval of their parents. **70m/C VHS, Beta.** *JP COL*

Sea Racketeers ♫½ **1937** Soggy old tribute to the Coast Guard inadvertently makes them look like a bunch of bumblers, as they belatedly uncover a fur-smuggling racket working under their noses from a floating nightclub. **64m/B VHS, Beta.** Weldon Heyburn, Jeanne Madden, Warren Hymer, Dorothy McNulty, J. Carrol Naish, Joyce Compton, Charles Trowbridge, Syd Saylor, Lane Chandler, Benny Burt; **D:** Hamilton MacFadden. *SNC*

The Sea Serpent ♫½ **1985** A young sea captain and a crusty scientist unite to search out a giant sea monster awakened by atomic tests. Not one of Milland's better films. **92m/C VHS, Beta.** *SP* Timothy Bottoms, Ray Milland, Jared Martin; **D:** Gregory Greens. *ART*

The Sea Shall Not Have Them ♫♫½ **1955** A British bomber crashes into the North Sea during WWII. Film tells of the survivors' rescue by the Air-Sea Rescue Unit. Decent drama/adventure. **92m/B VHS.** Michael Redgrave, Dirk Bogarde; **D:** Lewis Gilbert; **M:** Malcolm Arnold. *REP*

The Sea Wolf ♫♫♫½ **1941** Jack London's adventure novel about brutal, canny Captain Wolf Larsen (Robinson), his rebellious crew, and some unexpected passengers. Knox and Lupino are shipwreck survivors, picked up by Robinson and forced into working aboard his ship, the aptly named "Ghost." Crewman Garfield falls for Lupino and tries to rally his shipmates into resisting the meglomaniacal Robinson. Fine performances by all, especially Robinson as the personification of malevolent ego. Screen debut of Knox. Director Curtiz filmed entirely in studio tanks, sets, and pervasive fog machines. Previously filmed three times; later remade as "Barricade" and "Wolf Larsen." **90m/C VHS.** Edward G. Robinson, Alexander Knox, John Garfield, Ida Lupino, Gene Lockhart, Barry Fitzgerald, Stanley Ridges, Francis McDonald, David Bruce, Howard da Silva, Frank Lackteen, Ralf Harolde; **D:** Michael Curtiz; **W:** Robert Rossen. *MGM, MOV, BTV*

The Sea Wolf ♫♫ **1993** Yet another adaptation of Jack London's classic battle of wills tale. Captain Wolf Larsen (Bronson) commands a surly ship of seal hunters through sheer ruthlessness and ego. He rescues snobbish theatre critic Van Weyden (Reeve) and pretty scam artist Flaxen (Stewart) from a capsized ferry. The self-educated captain wants to test out his theories about survival of the fittest by making the rich Van Weyden his cabin boy (Flaxen gets leered at). Lots of teeth-gnashing and bellowing in this turgid TV remake, although Revill has fun as the sniveling Cookie. See the Edward G. Robinson version instead. **120m/C VHS.** Charles Bronson, Christopher Reeve, Catherine Mary Stewart, Clive Revill; **D:** Michael Anderson Sr.; **W:** Andrew J. Fenady; **M:** Charles Bernstein. *TTC*

Sea Wolves ♫♫½ **1981 (PG)** True WWII story about a commando-style operation undertaken by a group of middle-aged, retired British cavalrymen in India in 1943. Decent acting, though Peck's British accent fades in and out, with Moore as Bond. **120m/C VHS, Beta, Closed Caption.** *GB* Gregory Peck, Roger Moore, David Niven, Trevor Howard, Patrick Macnee; **D:** Andrew V. McLaglen; **W:** Reginald Rose. *FOX, WAR*

The Seagull 🎬🎬🎬 1971 A pensive, sensitive adaptation of the famed Chekhov play about the depressed denizens of an isolated country estate. In Russian with English subtitles. **99m/B VHS, Beta.** Alla Demidova, Lyudmila Savelyeva, Yuri Yakovlev; **D:** Yuri Karasik. FCT, MRV, AUD

Seance on a Wet Afternoon 🎬🎬🎬½ 1964 Dark, thoughtful film about a crazed pseudo-psychic who coerces her husband into a kidnapping so she can gain recognition by divining the child's whereabouts. Directed splendidly by Forbes, and superb acting from Stanley and Attenborough, who co-produced with Forbes. **111m/B VHS, Beta.** *GB* Kim Stanley, Richard Attenborough, Margaret Lacey, Maria Kazan, Mark Eden, Patrick Magee; **D:** Bryan Forbes; **M:** John Barry. British Academy Awards '64: Best Actor (Attenborough); National Board of Review Awards '64: Best Actress (Stanley); New York Film Critics Awards '64: Best Actress (Stanley); Nominations: Academy Awards '64: Best Actress (Stanley). HMV, BTV

The Search 🎬🎬🎬½ 1948 Clift, an American solider stationed in post-WWII Berlin, befriends a homeless nine-year-old amnesiac boy (Jandl) and tries to find his family. Meanwhile, his mother has been searching the Displaced Persons camps for her son. Although Clift wants to adopt the boy, he steps aside, and mother and son are finally reunited. "The Search" was shot on location in the American Occupied Zone of Germany. Jandl won a special juvenile Oscar in his first (and only) film role. This was also Clift's first screen appearance, although this movie was actually filmed after his debut in "Red River," it was released first. **105m/B VHS.** Montgomery Clift, Aline MacMahon, Ivan Jandl, Jarmila Novotna, Wendell Corey; **D:** Fred Zinnemann; **W:** Paul Jarrico. Academy Awards '48: Best Story, Golden Globe Awards '49: Best Screenplay; Nominations: Academy Awards '48: Best Actor (Clift), Best Director (Zinnemann), Best Screenplay. MGM

Search and Destroy 🎬 *Striking Back* 1981 (PG) Deadly vendetta is begun by a Vietnamese official during the war. It is continued in the U.S. as he hunts down the American soldiers he feels betrayed him. Sub-par, forgettable war/action flick. **93m/C VHS, Beta, LV.** Perry King, Don Stroud, Park Jong Soo, George Kennedy, Tisa Farrow; **D:** William Fruet. VES

Search and Destroy 🎬 1988 (R) Sci-fi action flick about the capture of a secret biological warfare research station. Lotsa action, that's for sure—where's the plot? **87m/C VHS, Beta.** Stuart Garrison Day, Dan Kuchuck, Peggy Jacobsen; **D:** J. Christian Ingvordsen. MCG

Search and Destroy 🎬🎬 1994 (R) Complex story finds bankrupt businessman Martin Mirkheim (Dunne) trying to overcome his financial woes by making a film based on a book by self-help guru, Dr. Luther Waxling (Hopper). Of course, since Martin's broke, he first has to find someone willing to invest in his venture, and the shady duo (Walken and Turturro) do does just leave him with more problems. Tediously stagy adaptation of Howard Korders' play. Directorial debut by artist Salle at least looks great and provides some quirky moments.**CW:** Strong language; some violence, nudity, and drug content. **91m/C VHS, LV, Closed Caption.** Griffin Dunne, Dennis Hopper, Rosanna Arquette, Christopher Walken, John Turturro, Illeana Douglas, Ethan Hawke; **Cameos:** Martin Scorsese; **D:** David Salle; **W:** Michael Almereyda; **C:** Michael Spiller, Bobby Bukowski; **M:** Elmer Bernstein. HMK

The Search for Bridey Murphy 🎬🎬 1956 Long before channelers, Ramtha and New-Age profiteers, there was a Colorado housewife who under hypnosis described a previous life as an Irish girl. Her famous claim was never proven—but that didn't stop this well-acted but dull dramatization. Neither sensationalist, nor likely to persuade skeptics. Based on the book by Morey Bernstein, hypnotist in the case. **84m/B VHS, Closed Caption.** Teresa Wright, Louis Hayward, Nancy Gates,

Kenneth Tobey, Richard Anderson; **D:** Noel Langley; **W:** Noel Langley; PAR, FCT

The Search for One-Eyed Jimmy 🎬🎬 1996 (R) Good-natured slice-of-life comedy about lowlife friends in the Brooklyn neighborhood of Red Hook. Film school grad Les (McCallany) returns to his old stomping grounds to make a documentary and decides missing local character Jimmy (Rockwell) will be his topic. Only no one except Jimmy's parents seem really concerned and Les' friends are such dimwits that they couldn't find a hole in the ground anyway.**CW:** Language, adult situations. **86m/C VHS, Closed Caption.** Holt McCallany, Nicholas Turturro, Steve Buscemi, Michael Badalucco, Ray "Boom Boom" Mancini, Anne Meara, John Turturro, Samuel L. Jackson, Sam Rockwell; **D:** Sam Henry Kass; **W:** Sam Henry Kass; **C:** Charles Levey; **M:** William Bloom. CAF

Search for Signs of Intelligent Life in the Universe 🎬🎬🎬 1991 (PG-13) Tomlin's brilliant one-woman show has been expanded into a wonderful film. As Tomlin's cast of 12 female and male characters meet and interact, they show every viewer his/her own humanity. **120m/C VHS.** Lily Tomlin; **D:** John Bailey; **W:** Jane Wagner; **M:** Jerry Goodman. WLF, BTV

Search for the Gods 🎬🎬 1975 A dig in the Southwest turns interesting when one of the archeologists comes across an exquisite ancient medallion that could answer questions about alien visitors. Pilot for a television series that didn't make it. **100m/C VHS.** Kurt Russell, Stephen McHattie, Ralph Bellamy, Victoria Racimo, Raymond St. Jacques; **D:** Jud Taylor. UNI, HHE

The Searchers 🎬🎬🎬🎬 1956 The classic Ford western, starring John Wayne as a hard-hearted frontiersman who spends years doggedly pursuing his niece, who was kidnapped by Indians. A simple western structure supports Ford's most moving, mysterious, complex film. Many feel this is the best western of all time. **119m/C VHS, Beta, LV, Letterbox.** John Wayne, Jeffrey Hunter, Vera Miles, Natalie Wood, Ward Bond, John Qualen, Harry Carey Jr., Olive Carey, Antonio Moreno, Henry Kleinbach Brandon, Hank Worden, Lana Wood, Dorothy Jordan, Patrick Wayne; **D:** John Ford; **W:** Frank Nugent; **C:** Winton C. Hoch; **M:** Max Steiner. National Film Registry '89. WAR, TLF

Searching for Bobby Fischer 🎬🎬🎬½ 1993 (PG) Seven-year-old Josh Waitzkin (Pomeranc, in his debut) shows an amazing gift for chess, stunning his parents, who must then try to strike the delicate balance of developing his abilities while also allowing him a "normal" childhood. Excellent cast features Mantegna and Allen as his parents, Kingsley as demanding chess teacher Pandolfini, and Fishburne as an adept speed-chess hustler. Pomeranc is great, and his knowledge of chess (he's a ranked player) brings authenticity to his role. Title comes from Pandolfini's belief that Josh may equal the abilities of chess whiz Bobby Fischer. Underrated little gem based on a true story and adapted from the book by Waitzkin's father. **111m/C VHS, Beta, LV, Closed Caption.** Joe Mantegna, Max Pomeranc, Joan Allen, Ben Kingsley, Laurence "Larry" Fishburne, Robert Stephens, David Paymer, William H. Macy; **D:** Steven Zaillian; **W:** Steven Zaillian; **C:** Conrad Hall; **M:** James Horner. MTV Movie Awards '94: Best New Filmmaker Award (Zaillian); Nominations: Academy Awards '93: Best Cinematography. PAR

Seaside Swingers 🎬½ *Every Day's a Holiday* 1965 A group of teenagers at a seaside resort work to win a talent competition on television. But where is the talent? Dumb teen romance comedy with accidental plot. ♪All I Want Is You; A Girls Needs a Boy; Second Time Around; Indubitably Me; Love Me, Please; Now, Ain't That Somethin'—Caw Blimey; Romeo Jones; What's Cookin. **94m/C VHS, Beta.** *GB* Michael Sarne, Grazina Frame, John Leyton; **D:** James Hill. NLC

Season for Assassins 🎬½ 1971 Police commissioner Castroni is the only man who can stop a wave of violence enveloping Rome. **102m/C VHS, Beta.** Joe Dallesandro, Martin Balsam. ART

Season of Change 🎬½ 1994 Tepid coming of age saga set in rural Montana, circa 1946. Thirteen-year-old Sally Mae (Tom) notices the tensions between her Bible-bound mother (Anderson) and war vet dad (Madsen), who's worried about finding a job to support his family. Sally Mae tries to understand all these adult notions even as she herself becomes attracted to teen mechanic Bobby (Randall). Cliched script and awkward performances don't help. **93m/C VHS.** Nicholle Tom, Michael Madsen, Jo Anderson, Hoyt Axton, Ethan Randall; **D:** Robin Murray; **W:** Shirley Hillard. MNC

Season of Fear 🎬½ 1989 (R) A young man visits his estranged father's home. Abandoned as a child, he's embroiled in a murder scheme engineered by his father's beautiful young wife. Intriguing premise, forgettable execution. **89m/C VHS, Beta.** Michael Bowen, Clancy Brown, Clare Wren, Ray Wise, Michael J. Pollard; **D:** Doug Campbell; **W:** Doug Campbell. FOX

Season of the Witch 🎬½ *Hungry Wives; Jack's Wife* 1973 (R) A frustrated housewife becomes intrigued with a neighboring witch and begins to practice witchcraft herself, through murder and seduction. Meant to be suspenseful, thrilling, and topical, it is none of these. Poorly acted at best. Originally 130 minutes! **89m/C Beta.** Jan White, Ray Laine, Bill Thunhurst, Joedda McClain, Virginia Greenwald, Ann Muffly, Neil Fisher, Esther Lapidus, Dan Mallinger, Ken Peters; **D:** George A. Romero; **W:** George A. Romero; **C:** George A. Romero. VTR

Sebastian 🎬🎬½ *Mr. Sebastian* 1968 Mathematics whiz is employed by the British to decipher codes. He falls in love with York, another code breaker, and becomes involved in international intrigue. A bit too fast-paced and busy, but enjoyable spy drama. Sutherland has a small role. **100m/C VHS.** *GB* Dirk Bogarde, Susannah York, Lilli Palmer, John Gielgud, Margaret Johnston, Nigel Davenport, Donald Sutherland; **D:** David Greene; **M:** Jerry Goldsmith. MOV

Sebastiane 🎬🎬🎬 1979 An audacious film version of the legend of St. Sebastian, packed with homoerotic imagery and ravishing visuals. Honest, faithful rendering of the Saint's life and refusal to obey Roman authorities. Jarman's first film, in Latin with English subtitles. **90m/C VHS, Beta.** Leonardo Treviglio, Barney James, Richard James, Neil Kennedy; **D:** Derek Jarman; **M:** Brian Eno. CCN, FCT

The Second Awakening of Christa Klages 🎬🎬 *Das Zweite Erwachen der Christa Klages* 1978 Young divorced mother Christa (Engel) decides to finance her money-troubled day-care center by robbing a bank with her lover Werner (Muller-Westernhagen). Werner's killed and Christa becomes a fugitive, taking refuge with her friend Ingrid (Reize). German with subtitles. **90m/C VHS.** *GE* Tina Engel, Sylvia Reize, Marius Muller-Westernhagen, Peter Schneider; **D:** Margarethe von Trotta; **W:** Margarethe von Trotta, Luisa Francia; **C:** Franz Rath; **M:** Klaus Doldinger. FCT

Second Best 🎬🎬🎬 1994 (PG-13) Quiet, intimate drama about a lonely Welsh postmaster (Hurt) who decides to adopt a son (Miles). James, the 11-year-old boy he considers adopting, comes from a troubled background and is prone to violent outbursts. Graham, the village postmaster, is dealing with emotional demons of his own, and his problems are interwoven with those of the deprived, temperamental James. Although Hurt seems miscast as a shy, middle-aged Welshman, he turns in one of the best performances of his career. Richly acted and flawlessly directed, Menges has created a convincing and effective father-son drama. Based on David Cook's novel.**CW:** Thematic elements. **105m/C VHS, LV, Closed Caption.** *GB* William Hurt, Chris Cleary Miles, Keith Allen,

Prunella Scales, Jane Horrocks, Alan Cumming, John Hurt; **D:** Chris Menges; **W:** David Cook; **M:** Simon Boswell. *WAR*

Second Best Secret Agent in the Whole Wide World 🎬🎬½ *Licensed to Kill*

1965 A klutzy agent attempts to prevent a Swedish anti-gravity formula from falling into Russian hands. Surprisingly good early spoof of the James Bond genre. **93m/C VHS, Beta.** *GB* Tom Adams, Veronica Hurst, Peter Bull, Karel Stepanek, John Arnatt; **D:** Lindsay Shonteff. *NLC*

Second Chance 🎬🎬½ **1953** A former prizefighter (Mitchum) travels to Mexico where he protects a gangster's moll (Darnell) targeted for murder. But Palance is on their trail. Originally released theatrically on a wide screen in 3-D. Good melodrama. **82m/C VHS, Beta, LV.** Robert Mitchum, Linda Darnell, Jack Palance, Reginald Sheffield, Roy Roberts; **D:** Rudolph Mate.

Second Chance 🎬🎬 **1980** When a woman finds her husband is in love with another, her marital happiness is shattered. She leaves her betrayer and struggles to adapt to life as a single mother. Made for British television. **270m/C VHS.** *GB* Susannah York, Ralph Bates; **D:** Gerry Mill, Richard Handford. *NO*

Second Chorus 🎬🎬½ **1940** Rivalry of two trumpet players for a girl and a job with Artie Shaw Orchestra. Music, dance, and romance. Nothing great, but pleasant. 🎵Would You Like to Be the Love of My Life?; Poor Mr. Chisholm; (I Ain't Hep to That Step) But I'll Dig It; Swing Concerto; Sweet Sue; I'm Yours. **83m/B VHS, Beta, LV.** Fred Astaire, Paulette Goddard, Burgess Meredith, Artie Shaw, Charles Butterworth; **D:** H.C. Potter. Nominations: Academy Awards '40: Best Song ("Love of My Life"), Best Score. *NOS, HHT, CAB*

The Second Civil War 🎬🎬½ **1997 (R)** Political satire falls apart at the end but until then manages to provide some dark comedy in this cable movie. In the near future, Idaho Governor Farley (Bridges) closes his state's borders to a planeload of refugee children from a Pakistan-India nuclear war. The President (Hartman), who wants to look tough, gives Farley 72-hours to change his mind and the media, led by executive producer Mel Burgess (Hedaya), puts into a typical frenzy.**CW:** Language and some war violence. **105m/C VHS.** Beau Bridges, Phil Hartman, James Coburn, Dan Hedaya, Elizabeth Pena, Kevin Dunn, Denis Leary, James Earl Jones, Ron Perlman, Joanna Cassidy; **D:** Joe Dante; **W:** Martyn Burke; **C:** Mac Ahlberg; **M:** Hummie Mann. *HBO*

Second Coming of Suzanne 🎬🎬½ **1980** Young actress encounters a hypnotic film director. Her role: to star in a crucifixion—which may be more real than she imagines. Winner of two international film festivals. **90m/C VHS, Beta.** Sondra Locke, Richard Dreyfuss, Gene Barry, Paul Sand, Jared Martin; **D:** Michael Barry; **W:** Michael Barry; **C:** Isidore Mankofsky. *GEM*

Second Fiddle 🎬🎬½ *Irving Berlin's Second Fiddle* **1939** Power is a studio flack who's hired to mount a huge talent search for a girl to star in a new film epic (very clear parallels to the Scarlett O'Hara "Gone With the Wind" hunt). He's sent to smalltown Minnesota where he meets Henie, who lives with her forbidding aunt (Oliver), who doesn't want her niece to go to wicked Hollywood. Nevertheless, Henie gets the part, becomes a success, and falls for her co-star Vallee. But it's all a publicity stunt on his part and Power is the one who really loves the girl. Henie gets to do some skating. 🎵Back to Back; I'm Sorry for Myself; I Poured My Heart Into Song; An Old-Fashioned Tune is Always New; When Winter Comes; Song of the Metronome. **86m/B VHS.** Sonja Henie, Tyrone Power, Rudy Vallee, Edna May Oliver, Mary Healy, Lyle Talbot, Alan Dinehart, Mona Gombell; **D:** Sidney Lanfield; **W:** Harry Tugend; **M:** Irving Berlin. Nominations: Academy Awards '39: Best Song ("I Poured My Heart Into Song"). *FXV*

Second Sight 🎬 **1989 (PG)** A detective (Larroquette) and a goofy psychic (Pinchot) set out to find a kidnapped priest. Flick is sidetracked along the way by such peculiarities as a pixieish nun for romantic, not religious, intrigue. Remember this one? No? That's because you blinked when it was released in theatres. Eminently missable. **84m/C VHS, Beta, LV, Closed Caption.** John Larroquette, Bronson Pinchot, Bess Armstrong, James Tolkan, Christine Estabrook, Cornelia Guest, Stuart Pankin, William Prince, John Schuck; **D:** Joel Zwick; **W:** Patricia Resnick; Tom Schulman. *WAR*

Second Thoughts 🎬 **1983 (PG)** Frustrated woman attorney divorces her stuffy husband and takes up with an aging hippie. She comes to regret her decision when it becomes obvious that her new man has his head firmly stuck in the 60s. Comedy-drama lacking real laughs or drama. **109m/C VHS, Beta.** Lucie Arnaz, Craig Wasson, Ken Howard, Joe Mantegna; **D:** Lawrence Turman; **W:** Steve Brown; **M:** Henry Mancini. *CNG*

Second Time Lucky 🎬 **1984** The devil makes a bet with God that if the world began all over again Adam and Eve would repeat their mistake they made in the Garden of Eden. Bites off a lot, but has no teeth nor laughs. **98m/C VHS, Beta.** *AU NZ* Diane Franklin, Roger Wilson, Robert Morley, Jon Gadsby, Bill Ewens; **D:** Michael Anderson Sr. *ORI*

Second Victory 🎬🎬½ **1987 (PG)** Major Mark Hanlon has been appointed an Occupation Officer in the winter of 1945. He expects this will be his chance to work for peace but when a good friend is brutally murdered all his thoughts turn to revenge. Based on the novel by Morris West. **95m/C VHS, LV, Closed Caption.** Anthony Andrews, Max von Sydow, Renee Soutendijk; **D:** Gerald Thomas.

Second Wind 🎬🎬 **1990 (PG)** Wagner and Naughton are trying to settle into their new life together, but find they must make a variety of difficult choices. **93m/C VHS.** Lindsay Wagner, James Naughton. *NO*

The Second Woman 🎬🎬½ *Here Lies Love; Twelve Miles Out* **1951** An architect, suffering from blackouts and depression, believes himself responsible for the death of his fiancee. Well-done psycho-drama. **91m/B VHS.** Robert Young, Betsy Drake, John Sutton; **D:** James V. Kern. *EEL, NOS, VDM*

Seconds 🎬🎬🎬 **1966 (R)** Aging banker Arthur Hamilton (Randolph) is frantic to escape his dead-end existence and accepts an invitation from a mysterious organization to give him a second chance at life. Through surgery, Arthur's transformed into handsome artist Tony Wilson (Hudson). Uncomfortably living in Malibu, he soons finds out all his new neighbors are also "seconds," who are afraid he'll betray their secrets. Wilson decides he wants out of his new arrangement and back to his former life but it comes at a very high price. Eerie film manages to (mostly) overcome its plot problems, with a fine performance by Hudson. Based on the novel by Donald Ely. **107m/B VHS, Beta, Closed Caption.** Rock Hudson, John Randolph, Salome Jens, Will Geer, Jeff Corey, Richard Anderson, Murray Hamilton, Karl Swenson, Khigh Deigh, Frances Reid, Wesley Addy; **D:** John Frankenheimer; **W:** Lewis John Carlino; **C:** James Wong Howe; **M:** Jerry Goldsmith. Nominations: Academy Awards '66: Best Black and White Cinematography. *PAR*

The Secret 🎬🎬½ **1993** Businessman and political candidate Mike Dunsmore (Douglas) comes to terms with his lifelong battle with dyslexia when his grandson begins to show signs of the same affliction. Set in picturesque New England fishing village. **92m/C VHS, Closed Caption.** Kirk Douglas, Bruce Boxleitner, Brock Peters, Laura Harrington; **D:** Karen Arthur. *CAF*

Secret Admirer 🎬🎬 **1985 (R)** A teenager's unsigned love letter keeps falling into the wrong hands. Intends to be funny, and sometimes is; too often, though, it surrenders to obviousness and predictability. **98m/C VHS, Beta, LV.** C. Thomas Howell, Cliff DeYoung, Kelly Preston, Dee Wallace Stone, Lori

Loughlin, Fred Ward, Casey Siemaszko, Corey Haim, Leigh Taylor-Young; **D:** David Greenwalt. *NO*

The Secret Adversary 🎬🎬 **1983** Set in 1920s London. Ace detectives Tommy and Tuppence Beresford must find a secret treaty before it falls into the wrong hands. Pilot for the "Partners in Crime" series. Based on the characters created by Agatha Christie. **120m/C VHS, Beta.** *GB* Francesca Annis, James Warwick. *TPV*

The Secret Agent 🎬🎬🎬 **1936** Presumed dead, a British intelligence agent (Gielgud) reappears and receives a new assignment. Using his faked death to his advantage, he easily journeys to Switzerland where he is to eliminate an enemy agent. Strange Hitchcockian melange of comedy and intrigue; atypical, but worthy offering from the Master. **83m/B VHS, Beta, LV.** *GB* Madeleine Carroll, Peter Lorre, Robert Young, John Gielgud, Lilli Palmer; **D:** Alfred Hitchcock; **W:** Charles Bennett. *SNC, NOS, HHT*

Secret Agent **1964** Secret agent John Drake embarks upon dangerous and exciting assignments around the world in this mystery-adventure series, which ran during 1965 and 1966. All but two episodes are in black and white. **60m/B VHS, Beta.** Patrick McGoohan, Niall MacGinnis, Dawn Addams, Lelia Goldoni; **D:** Don Chaffey. *MOV*

The Secret Agent 🎬🎬 *Joseph Conrad's The Secret Agent* **1996 (R)** Rain, rain go away. In this waterlogged adaptation of the Conrad novel, Hoskins plays Adolf Verloc, a cowardly agent provocateur who heads a group of anarchists in soggy Victorian England. His real mission, however, is to report the actions of the expatriates to the Russian government. After he is bullied into a terrorist attack on the Greenwich Observatory by his contact at the Russian embassy, the lives of Verloc, his wife Winnie (Arquette) and her mentally disabled brother Stevie (Bale) are blown to pieces (sometimes literally) by the consequences. The only spark in the otherwise dank and gloomy production is Williams (listed as George Spelvin) as the demented explosives expert known only as the Professor. Alfred Hitchcock also used a loose interpretation of Conrad's novel for "Sabotage." **CW:** Some moments of violence. **95m/C VHS, LV, Closed Caption.** *GB* Bob Hoskins, Patricia Arquette, Gerard Depardieu, Robin Williams, Jim Broadbent, Christian Bale, Elizabeth Spriggs, Peter Vaughan, Julian Wadham; **D:** Christopher Hampton; **W:** Christopher Hampton; **C:** Denis Lenoir; **M:** Philip Glass. *FXV*

Secret Agent 00 🎬 *Operation Kid Brother* **1967 (R)** A master criminal plans to blackmail the western world and only special Secret Agent 00 can stop him. Bad spy genre ripoff, interesting only as the screen debut of Sean Connery's brother. **97m/C VHS.** *IT* Neil Connery, Daniela Bianchi, Adolfo Celi; **D:** Alberto De Martino; **M:** Ennio Morricone. *NO*

The Secret Agent Club 🎬½ **1996 (PG)** Secret agent Ray Chase (Hogan) steals a laser gun that evil Eve (Down) is determined to sell to the highest bidder. Ray returns home and, under the pretext of his job as a toy store owner, hides the gun in the store where his son Jeremy (McCurley) assumes it's a new toy. Eve's henchmen manage to capture Ray but not before Jeremy gets the gun and plans a rescue mission with his friends. **90m/C VHS.** Hulk Hogan, Richard Moll, Lesley-Anne Down, Mathew McCurley, Edward Albert, Lyman Ward, James Hong, Barry Bostwick, Jack Nance; **D:** John Murlowski; **W:** Rory Johnston; **C:** S. Douglas Smith. *CAF*

Secret Agent 00-Soul 🎬½ **1989** International spy decides to fulfill his dream of opening a detective agency in his old neighborhood. Release of this direct-to-video mishmash was delayed until '95. **71m/C VHS.** Billy Dee Williams, Amanda Le Flore, Marjean Holden, Tommy (Tiny) Lister; **D:** Julius Le Flore. *XVC*

Secret Agent Super Dragon 🎬 *Super Dragon* **1966** The CIA calls in the agent known as "Super Dragon" when it is discovered that a Venezuelan drug czar plans to spike U.S. gum and

candy with an LSD-like drug. Less than competent production offers some unintended laughter. **95m/C VHS, Beta.** *FR IT GF* Ray Danton, Marisa Mell, Margaret Lee, Jess Hahn, Carlo D'Angelo, Andriana Ambesi; *D:* Calvin Jackson Padget. *SNC*

Secret Beyond the Door 🎬🎬 1948 A
wealthy heiress marries a widower and soon discovers that he murdered his first wife. Understandably, she wonders what plans he might have for her. Capably done chiller, but the plot is hackneyed pseudo-Hitchcock. **99m/B VHS.** Joan Bennett, Michael Redgrave, Barbara O'Neil, Anne Revere; *D:* Fritz Lang; *M:* Miklos Rozsa. *REP*

Secret Ceremony 🎬🎬½ 1969 An aging
prostitute and a young, aimless waif resemble each other's dead mother and dead daughter, respectively, and the relationship goes on, strangely, from there. This original big-screen version is very good Freudian psycho-drama; 101-minute TV version is unfortunately greatly diluted. **109m/C VHS, Beta.** Elizabeth Taylor, Robert Mitchum, Mia Farrow, Pamela Brown, Peggy Ashcroft; *D:* Joseph Losey; *M:* Richard Rodney Bennett. *BAR*

The Secret Code 1942 A 15-chapter serial
with the Black Commando (Kelly) thwarting the Nazis' attempts at sabotage. After each chapter's cliffhanger ending a new form of secret code is explained and decoded. **315m/B VHS.** Paul Kelly, Anne Nagel, Clancy Cooper, Trevor Bardette, Gregory Gay, Ludwig Donath, Ed Parker; *D:* Spencer Gordon Bennet. *GPV*

The Secret Diary of Sigmund
Freud 🎬🎬 1984 Spoofy look at the early years of Sigmund Freud, the father of modern psychoanalysis. Freud (Cort) has an affair with lisping nurse Kane while tending to patient Shawn and answering to mama Baker, who's carrying on with mad doctor Kinski. Talented cast falls asleep on couch. **129m/C VHS, Beta, Closed Caption.** Bud Cort, Carol Kane, Carroll Baker, Klaus Kinski, Marisa Berenson, Dick Shawn, Ferdinand "Ferdy" Mayne; *D:* Danford B. Greene. *FOX*

Secret File of Hollywood 🎬½ *Secret
File: Hollywood* 1962 A down-and-out private eye gets a job taking photos for a sleazy Hollywood scandal sheet and finds himself in the midst of a blackmail plot masterminded by his editor. An often childish potboiler, perhaps inspired by the once-feared Confidential Magazine. **85m/B VHS.** Robert Clarke, Francine York, Syd Mason, Maralou Gray, John Warburton; *D:* Ralph Cushman. *NOS, LOO, TPV*

The Secret Four 🎬🎬 *The Four Just Men*
1940 Three young men seek to avenge the death of their friend at the hands of British traitors, and become involved in a plot to sabotage the Suez canal. Poorly adapted from the novel by Edgar Wallace. **79m/B VHS, Beta.** *GB* Hugh Sinclair, Griffith Jones, Francis L. Sullivan, Frank Lawton, Anna Lee, Alan Napier, Basil Sydney; *D:* Walter Forde. *SNC*

Secret Games 🎬½ 1992 (R) An unhappily
married woman (Brin) is searching for relief from her restrictive marriage. At the "Afternoon Demitasse," an exclusive brothel where women are paid for fulfilling their ultimate fantasies, she meets a man (Hewitt) who pushes her beyond her sexual limits and threatens to totally possess her. **90m/C VHS, Closed Caption.** Martin Hewitt, Michele Brin, Delia Sheppard, Billy Drago; *D:* Alexander Gregory Hippolyte. *IMP*

Secret Games 2: The Escort 🎬½
1993 (R) A performance artist (Hewitt) learns how to seduce women from a beautiful escort (Rochelle). However, he falls for his trainer despite being a star pupil who could have anyone he wanted. Plot conveniently lends itself to lots of steamy love scenes. Also available in an unrated version. **?m/C VHS, Closed Caption.** Martin Hewitt, Amy Rochelle, Sara Suzanne Brown, Marie Leroux; *D:* Alexander Gregory Hippolyte; *W:* Russell Lavalle; *M:* Ashley Irwin. *IMP*

Secret Games 3 🎬½ 1994 (R) A bored
doctor's wife gets her kicks by visiting a club catering to women's fantasies. But then she meets a criminal who wants her all to himself. An unrated version is available at 91 minutes. *CW:* Strong sexuality. **82m/C VHS.** Woody Brown, Brenda Swanson, Rochelle Swanson; *D:* Alexander Gregory Hippolyte.

The Secret Garden 🎬🎬🎬 1949 The
well-loved Frances Hodgson Burnett story has been remade and even revamped as a Broadway musical, but this is considered the definitive version. An orphan girl arrives at her uncle's somber Victorian estate. She starts tending a long-forgotten garden, and with its resurrection joy returns to the household. O'Brien leads an outstanding cast in one of her final juvenile roles. In black and white, with Technicolor for later garden scenes. **92m/B VHS, Beta, LV.** Margaret O'Brien, Herbert Marshall, Dean Stockwell, Gladys Cooper, Elsa Lanchester, Brian Roper; *D:* Fred M. Wilcox. *MGM*

The Secret Garden 🎬🎬½ 1984 Orphaned Mary Lennox is sent to live with her mysterious uncle after her parents die. Mary is willful and spoiled and her uncle's house holds a number of secrets, including a crippled cousin. When Mary discovers a mysteriously abandoned locked garden she makes it her mission to restore the garden to life. Based on the children's classic by Frances Hodgson Burnett. Made for British television. **107m/C VHS.** *GB* Sarah Hollis Andrews, David Patterson; *D:* Katrina Murray. *MOV, SIG, TVC*

The Secret Garden 🎬🎬🎬 1987 (PG)
Lonely orphan Mary Lennox is sent to live with her uncle in England after her parent's deaths. Mary, who has grown up in India, is selfish and unhappy until she discovers two secrets on her uncle's estate. Class production of the children's classic by Frances Hodgson Burnett with wonderful performances; added prologue and afterword showing Mary as an adult are unnecessary, but don't detract either. Made for television as a "Hallmark Hall of Fame" special. **100m/C VHS, LV, Closed Caption.** Gennie James, Barret Oliver, Jadrien Steele, Michael Hordern, Derek Jacobi, Billie Whitelaw, Lucy Gutteridge, Julian Glover, Colin Firth, Alan Grint. *REP*

The Secret Garden 🎬🎬½ 1993 (G) Rekindled interest in Frances Hodgon Burnett's classic tale has prompted a Broadway musical, two TV movies, and this latest big screen version. Mary Lennox is an orphan sent to live in her reclusive uncle's forbidding mansion filled with secrets, including a crippled cousin she didn't know she had. She discovers a secret neglected garden and becomes determined to bring it back to life. Befitting director Holland's reputation this version is beautiful but dark, with children prey to very adult anxieties. **102m/C VHS, Beta, LV, Closed Caption.** Kate Maberly, Maggie Smith, Haydon Prowse, Andrew Knott, John Lynch; *D:* Agnieszka Holland; *W:* Caroline Thompson; *C:* Roger Deakins; *M:* Zbigniew Preisner. Los Angeles Film Critics Association Awards '93: Best Score; Nominations: British Academy Awards '93: Best Supporting Actress (Smith). *WAR, BTV*

Secret Honor 🎬🎬🎬 *Lords of Treason; Secret
Honor: The Last Testament of Richard M. Nixon; Secret Honor: A Political Myth* 1985 Idiosyncratic, single-set, one-man film version adapted by Donald Freed and Arnold Stone from their stage play about Richard Nixon coping with the death of his presidency on the night he's decided to blow his brains out. Made with students at the University of Michigan, and carried by the ranting and raving of Hall as a tragic Shakespearean Nixon with plenty of darkly humorous lines. **90m/C VHS, Beta, LV.** Philip Baker Hall; *D:* Robert Altman; *M:* George Burt. *ART, VES, CRC*

Secret Ingredient 🎬½ 1992 A legendary
cognac recipe is the secret formula of the monks of St. Celare, whose monastery is located in the mountains of Yugoslavia. A wealthy American sends his flighty heiress daughter to pry the secret recipe from the monks but she runs into more

than she bargains for when she falls for a handsome friar and gets caught up with a band of bumbling gypsies and the inept state police. **95m/C VHS.** Rick Rossovich, Catherine Hicks, Gary Kroeger, Jeff Corey, Brad Dexter, Sam Wanamaker; *D:* Slobodan Shijan.

Secret Life of an American
Wife 🎬🎬 1968 A bored housewife (Jackson) tries to seduce a client of her husband's, with less than hilarious results. Too much dialogue, not enough genuine humor. Disappointing inversion of director Axelrod's "The Seven Year Itch." **97m/C VHS, Beta.** Walter Matthau, Anne Jackson, Patrick O'Neal, Edy Williams; *D:* George Axelrod; *W:* George Axelrod. *FOX*

The Secret Life of Walter
Mitty 🎬🎬🎬 1947 An entertaining adaptation of the James Thurber short story about a meek man (Kaye) who lives an unusual secret fantasy life. Henpecked by his fiancee and mother, oppressed at his job, he imagines himself in the midst of various heroic fantasies. While Thurber always professed to hate Kaye's characterization and the movie, it scored at the boxoffice and today stands as a comedic romp for Kaye. Available with digitally remastered stereo and original movie trailer. **110m/C VHS.** Danny Kaye, Virginia Mayo, Boris Karloff, Ann Rutherford, Fay Bainter, Florence Bates; *D:* Norman Z. McLeod; *C:* Lee Garmes. *HBO*

Secret Mission 🎬🎬½ 1942 Four British
intelligence agents are sent into occupied France to assess the strength of Nazi forces. But after discovering the information, their cover is blown and it's a race to get the intelligence into the right hands before the Nazis get to them first. **94m/B VHS.** *GB* James Mason, Hugh Williams, Roland Culver, Michael Wilding, Carla Lehmann, Nancy Price, Percy Walsh, Karel Stepanek, Herbert Lom, Stewart Granger, *D:* Harold French; *W:* Anatole de Grunwald, Basil Bartlett; *C:* Bernard Knowles, Cyril Knowles; *M:* Mischa Spoliansky. *FCT*

Secret Obsession 🎬 1988 (PG) A love triangle among a father, his illegitimate son, and the woman they both love, set in North Africa in 1955. Sounds intriguing, but don't be fooled. Slow, dull, and poorly acted. **82m/C VHS, Beta.** Julie Christie, Ben Gazzara, Patrick Bruel, Jean Carmet; *D:* Henri Vart. *THV*

The Secret of El Zorro 🎬½ 1957 Don
Diego's friend, Don Ricardo, threatens to unmask Zorro's secret identity when he challenges the legendary swordsman to a duel. **75m/B VHS, Beta.** Guy Williams. *DIS*

The Secret of My Success 🎬🎬
1987 (PG-13) Country bumpkin Fox goes to the Big Apple to make his mark. He becomes the corporate mailboy who rises meteorically to the top of his company (by impersonating an executive) in order to win the love of an icy woman executive. He spends his days running frantically between his real job in the mailroom and his fantasy position, with various sexual shenanigans with the boss's wife thrown in to keep the viewer alert. Fox is charismatic while working with a cliche-ridden script that ties up everything very neatly at the end. **110m/C VHS, Beta, LV, Closed Caption.** Michael J. Fox, Helen Slater, Richard Jordan, Margaret Whitton; *D:* Herbert Ross; *W:* Jim Cash, Jack Epps Jr., A.J. Carothers; *C:* Carlo DiPalma; *M:* David Foster. *USH*

The Secret of Navajo Cave 🎬🎬 *Legend of Cougar Canyon* 1976 (G) Fair family adventure. Two young friends explore the mysterious Navajo cave, where one can be assured that a secret awaits. **84m/C VHS.** Holger Kasper, Steven Benally Jr., Johnny Guerro; *D:* James T. Flocker. *XVC*

The Secret of NIMH 🎬🎬🎬 1982 (G)
Animated tale, produced by a staff of Disney-trained artists led by "American Tail's" Bluth; concerns a newly widowed mouse who discovers a secret agency of superintelligent rats (they've escaped from a science lab) who aid her in protecting her family. As is usually the case with Bluth films, the animation is superb while the socially aware plot struggles to keep pace. That aside, it's still an interesting treat for the youngsters. Adapt-

ed from Robert C. O'Brien's "Mrs. Frisby and the Rats of N.I.M.H." **84m/C VHS, Beta, LV, 8mm, Closed Caption.** *D:* Don Bluth; *W:* Don Bluth; *M:* Jerry Goldsmith; *V:* John Carradine, Derek Jacobi, Dom DeLuise, Elizabeth Hartman, Peter Strauss, Aldo Ray, Edie McClurg, Wil Wheaton. *MGM*

The Secret of Roan Inish 🐾🐾🐾½
1994 (PG) Irish myth comes to life in this fantasy about the importance of family and place, seen through the eyes of 10-year-old Fiona Coneelly (newcomer Courtney) who's sent to live with her grandparents in post-WWII County Donegal. Fiona's drawn to her grandfather's stories about the family's ancestral home on the island of Roan Inish and the loss of her baby brother Jamie, who was carried out to sea. Another family tale is about a Selkie—a beautiful seal/woman captured by a Coneelly fisherman who eventually returned to her ocean home. When Fiona visits Roan Inish she becomes convinced that Jamie is alive and being cared for by the island's seals. Director Sayles keeps a firm grip on the cuteness factor while cinematographer Wexler works his usual magic on the sea, sky, and land of Ireland. Based on the 1957 novel "Secret of the Ron Mor Skerry" by Rosalie K. Fry. **102m/C VHS, LV, Closed Caption.** Jeni Courtney, Michael Lally, Eileen Colgan, John Lynch, Richard Sheridan, Susan Lynch, Cillian Byrne; *D:* John Sayles; *W:* John Sayles; *C:* Haskell Wexler; *M:* Mason Daring. Nominations: Independent Spirit Awards '96: Best Director (Sayles), Best Film, Best Screenplay. *COL*

Secret of the Black Trunk 🐾🐾½
1962 Chilling Edgar Wallace story about a series of murders at a famed English hotel. Filmed in Great Britain. **96m/C VHS.** *GE* Joachim Hansen, Senta Berger, Hans Reiser, Leonard Steckel, Peter Carsten; *D:* Werner Klinger. *SNC*

The Secret of the Golden Eagle 🐾🐾
1991 A boy and his new adventurer friend are on a quest to find the strange "Golden Statue" that causes people to grow old before their time. They must take it from criminals who are using it for evil purposes. A good adventure/fantasy for the entire family. **90m/C VHS.** Michael Berryman, Brandon McKay; *D:* Cole McKay. *WLA*

Secret of the Ice Cave 🐾 **1989 (PG-13)**
A motley band of explorers, hijackers and mercenaries go after a secret treasure in the remote mountains. **106m/C VHS, Beta.** Michael Moriarty, Sally Kellerman, David Mendenhall, Virgil Frye, Gerald Anthony, Norbert Weisser; *D:* Radu Gabrea. *MOV*

The Secret of the Loch 🐾½ **1934**
Scottish scientist claims to have seen Loch Ness Monster but everyone thinks his bagpipe's blown a reed. **80m/B VHS.** *GB* Seymour Hicks, Nancy O'Neil, Gibson Gowland, Frederick Peisley; *D:* Milton Rosmer. *NOS, SNC*

The Secret of the Telegian 🐾🐾½
The Telegian **1961** Rare Japanese sci-fi flick about a soldier who uses a teleportation device to kill fellow soldiers who tried to kill him. He could find his victims wherever they hid. **85m/C VHS.** *JP* Koji Tsuruta, Yumi Shirakawa, Akihiko Hirata, Tadao Nakamura; *D:* Jun Fukuda. *SNC*

Secret of Yolanda 🐾 **1982 (R)** Steamy
romance about a young deaf-mute whose guardian and riding instructor both fall for her. **90m/C VHS, Beta.** Aviva Ger, Asher Zarfati, Shraga Harpaz. *MGM*

The Secret Passion of Robert Clayton 🐾🐾 **1992 (R)** When Robert Clayton
Jr. (Valentine) returns to his home town to take the position of D.A., he is forced to go head to head in a lurid murder trial with the defense attorney (Mahoney), who also happens to be his own father. *CW:* Violence and sexuality. **92m/C VHS.** John Mahoney, Scott Valentine, Eve Gordon, Kevin Conroy; *D:* E.W. Swackhamer; *W:* Brian Ross; *C:* Billy Dickson. *PAR*

Secret Passions 🐾½ **1978** A young couple are haunted by a dark, romance-novel-type secret. Made for television. **99m/C VHS, Beta.** John James, Susan Lucci; *D:* Michael Pressman. *NO*

Secret Places 🐾🐾½ **1985 (PG)** On the
brink of WWII, a German girl in an English school finds friendship with a popular classmate. Touching and involving, but somehow unsatisfying. **98m/C VHS, Beta, Closed Caption.** *GB* Maria Therese Relin, Tara MacGowran, Claudine Auger, Jenny Agutter; *D:* Zelda Barron; *W:* Zelda Barron. *FOX*

The Secret Policeman's Other Ball 🐾🐾🐾 **1982 (R)** Engaging live performance by most of the Monty Python troupe and guest rock artists, staged for Amnesty International. Follows 1979's "The Secret Policeman's Ball," and followed by 1987's "The Secret Policeman's Third Ball." **101m/C VHS, Beta, LV.** *GB* John Cleese, Graham Chapman, Michael Palin, Terry Jones, Pete Townshend, Sting, Billy Connolly, Bob Geldof; *D:* Julien Temple; *W:* Michael Palin. *MGM*

Secret Policeman's Private Parts 🐾🐾½ **1981** Various sketches and performances from the various Secret Policeman occasions, featuring classic Python sketches including "I'm a Lumberjack and I'm OK." Also featured are performances by Phil Collins, Pete Townshend, Donovan, and Bob Geldof. Thank you very much. **77m/C VHS, Beta, LV.** *GB* John Cleese, Michael Palin, Terry Jones, Pete Townshend, Julien Temple; *D:* Roger Graef. *USH*

The Secret Rapture 🐾🐾 **1994 (R)** Two
sisters clash in this family drama, adapted by Hare from his 1988 play. The bohemian Isobel (Stevenson) and her estranged sister, the forbidding Marion (Wilton), are brought together by their father's death. While Isobel grieves, Marion seeks to gain advantage in the family business, and both must deal with their young, alcoholic, and volatile stepmother Katherine (Whalley-Kilmer). Emotional intensity with good performances but abrupt shifts in tone. *CW:* Language; nudity; sexual situations. **96m/C VHS, LV.** *GB* Juliet Stevenson, Penelope Wilton, Joanne Whalley, Alan Howard, Neil Pearson, Robert Stephens, Hilton McRae; *D:* Howard Davies; *W:* David Hare; *C:* Ian Wilson; *M:* Richard Hartley. *FXV*

A Secret Space 🐾🐾½ **1988** Story of a
young man, born of secular parents, searching for the meaning of his Jewish roots as he nears his Bar Mitzvah. He is helped along by a group of Jews who are also searching for this meaning. **80m/C VHS, Beta.** Robert Klein, Phyllis Newman, John Matthews, Sam Schacht, Virginia Graham; *D:* Roberta Hodes. *ERG*

The Secret War of Harry Frigg 🐾½
1968 (R) Non-conformist WWII Private Harry Frigg is promoted to general as part of a scheme to help five Allied generals escape from the custody of the Germans. Rare Newman bomb; dismal comedy. **123m/C VHS, Beta.** Paul Newman, Sylva Koscina, John Williams, Tom Bosley, Andrew Duggan; *D:* Jack Smight; *C:* Russell Metty. *USH*

Secret Weapon 🐾🐾 **1990** An Israeli technician flees his country with atomic secrets and a beautiful government agent is sent to induce him to return. Based on the true case of Mordecai Vanunu. Slow-paced and not very suspenseful. Made for cable. **95m/C VHS, Beta, Closed Caption.** Griffin Dunne, Karen Allen, Stuart Wilson, Jeroen Krabbe, Brian Cox, John Rhys-Davies, Ian Mitchell; *D:* Ian Sharp. *TTC*

Secret Weapons 🐾½ *Secrets of the Red Bedroom* **1985** Sexy Russian babes are KGB-trained to get any secret from any man. Strains credibility as well as patience. Made for TV. **100m/C VHS.** Linda Hamilton, Sally Kellerman, Hunt Block, Viveca Lindfors, Christopher Atkins, Geena Davis, James Franciscus; *D:* Don Taylor; *M:* Charles Bernstein. *NO*

The Secretary 🐾½ **1994 (R)** Another bland
variation of "The Temp." Career woman Ellen Bradford (Harris) has a new fast-track job and a highly efficient secretary in Deidre (Kelley). But it turns out Deidre's also lethally efficient in disposing of co-workers through a series of inexplicable accidents and "suicides." So just what's Ellen going to do to show Deidre who's boss? *CW:* Lan-

guage; violence; some sexuality. **94m/C VHS, LV, Closed Caption.** Mel Harris, Sheila Kelley, Barry Bostwick, James Russo; *D:* Andrew Lane; *C:* Steven Bernstein; *M:* Louis Febre. *REP*

Secrets 🐾½ **1971 (R)** A wife, her husband,
and her daughter each have a sexual experience which they must keep secret. Bisset's nude love scene is an eye-opener. Fast forward through the rest of this dull, overwrought drama. **86m/C VHS.** Jacqueline Bisset, Per Oscarsson, Shirley Knight, Robert Powell, Tarka Kings, Martin C. Thurley; *D:* Philip Saville; *M:* Michael Gibbs.

Secrets 🐾 **1977** An unhappy young bride
starts having numerous affairs when her mother dies. Made for television. Hardly worth the effort. **100m/C VHS.** Susan Blakely, Roy Thinnes, Joanne Linville, John Randolph, Anthony Eisley, Andrew Stevens; *D:* Paul Wendkos. *MGM*

Secrets 🐾🐾 **1982** British drama about the
confused life of an innocent schoolgirl who's the victim of a mess of authoritative misunderstandings. One of David Puttnam's "First Love" series. **79m/C VHS, Beta.** *GB* Helen Lindsay, Anna Campbell-Jones, Daisy Cockburn; *D:* Gavin Millar. *MGM*

Secrets 🐾🐾½ **1994 (PG-13)** Teenager Anna
Berter, growing up in turn-of-the-century Iowa, is told by her snobbish mother Etta (Hamel) not to befriend the help, which include the woman who raised Anna alongside her granddaughter Edwina. When Edwina is seduced by a Berter family friend and left pregnant, Etta decides to adopt her baby daughter—whether Edwina wants to let the baby go or not. All this obsessive behavior leads Anna to discover some very unhappy family secrets surrounding her own birth. Made for TV. *CW:* Thematic elements involving sensuality, family issues, and social intolerance. **92m/C VHS.** Veronica Hamel, Julie Harris, Richard Kiley, Thomas Gibson, Shae D'Lyn, Jessica Bowman, Reed Edward Diamond; *D:* Jud Taylor. *HMK*

Secrets and Lies 🐾🐾 **1995 (R)** Too-long
film focusing on family and identity. The adoptive parents of black Yuppie Londoner Hortense (Jean-Baptiste) have just died and she decides it's time to seek out her birth parents. She's warned about the emotional consequences, especially upon discovering her biological mother is white—factory worker Cynthia (Blethyn), who has another daughter, Roxanne (Rushbrook), who doesn't get along with mum. Naturally, when Hortense is introduced to the rest of Cynthia's family, there's lots of dysfunction to explore. Good performances, although Hortense's character is bland, but pacing drags. *CW:* Language. **142m/C VHS.** *GB* Brenda Blethyn, Marianne Jean-Baptiste, Timothy Spall, Claire Rushbrook, Phyllis Logan, Lee Ross, Ron Cook, Leslie Manville, Irene Handl; *Cameos:* Alison Steadman; *D:* Mike Leigh; *W:* Mike Leigh; *C:* Dick Pope; *M:* Andrew Dickson. Australian Film Institute '97: Best Foreign Film; British Academy Awards '96: Best Actress (Blethyn), Best Original Screenplay; Cannes Film Festival '96: Best Actress (Blethyn), Best Film; Golden Globe Awards '97: Best Actress (Blethyn); Los Angeles Film Critics Association Awards '96: Best Actress (Blethyn), Best Director (Leigh), Best Film; Nominations: Academy Awards '96: Best Actress (Blethyn), Best Director (Leigh), Best Original Screenplay, Best Picture, Best Supporting Actress (Jean-Baptiste); British Academy Awards '96: Best Actor (Spall), Best Director (Leigh), Best Film, Best Supporting Actress (Jean-Baptiste); Cesar Awards '97: Best Foreign Film; Directors Guild of America Awards '96: Best Director (Leigh); Golden Globe Awards '97: Best Film—Drama, Best Supporting Actress (Jean-Baptiste); Independent Spirit Awards '97: Best Foreign Film; Screen Actors Guild Award '96: Best Actress (Blethyn); Writers Guild of America Awards '96: Best Original Screenplay. *FXV*

Secrets of a Married Man 🐾 **1984** A
married man's philandering ways are his ruination when he falls hard for a beautiful prostitute. Shatner and Shepherd contain their laughter as they make their way through this hyper-earnest family drama. **96m/C VHS, Beta.** William Shatner, Cybill Shepherd, Michelle Phillips, Glynn Turman; *D:* William A. Graham. *ART*

Secrets of a Soul 🎬🎬½ 1925 A visually impressive presentation of Freudian psychoanalytic theory in which a professor, wanting a child and jealous of his wife's childhood sweetheart, moves toward madness (we did say Freudian) and is cured through dream interpretation. Great dream sequences bring out the arm-chair psychoanalyst. Silent. **94m/B VHS, Beta. GE** Werner Krauss, Ruth Weyher, Jack Trevor; **D:** G.W. Pabst. **FCT**

Secrets of Sweet Sixteen woof! 1974 **(R)** Gag-fest about budding sexuality in high school. **84m/C VHS, Beta.** Suzie Atkins. **NO**

Secrets of Three Hungry Wives 🎬 1978 When a multi-millionaire is killed, the women with whom he was having affairs are suspected. Tacky made for television flick. **97m/C VHS.** Jessica Walter, Gretchen Corbett, Eve Plumb, Heather MacRae, James Franciscus, Craig Stevens; **D:** Gordon Hessler. **NO**

Secrets of Women 🎬🎬🎬 Kvinnors Vantan; Waiting Women 1952 A rare Bergman comedy about three sisters-in-law who tell about their affairs and marriages as they await their husbands at a lakeside resort. His first commercial success, though it waited nine years for release (1961). In Swedish with English subtitles. **114m/B VHS, Beta. SW** Anita Bjork, Karl Arne Homsten, Eva Dahlbeck, Maj-Britt Nilsson, Jarl Kulle; **D:** Ingmar Bergman; **W:** Ingmar Bergman. **HMV, NLC, FCT**

The Secrets of Wu Sin 🎬🎬 1932 A suicidal news writer in Chinatown is given a reason to live by a news editor who gives her a job. She starts investigating a ring smuggling Chinese workers, with the trail leading to, of course, Chinatown. Low-budget crime thriller. **65m/B VHS.** Lois Wilson, Grant Withers, Dorothy Revier, Robert Warwick, Toschia Mori; **D:** Richard Thorpe. **SNC, NOS, DVT**

Seduce Me: Pamela Principle 2 🎬½ Pamela Principle 2 1994 **(R)** Charles is a bored, married, architectural photographer who decides a change of pace is in order. So he starts shooting lingerie fashion spreads and gets seduced by model Pamela, who likes her men married. The only connection to the 1991 film is the married man/affair angle. **CW:** Nudity and sexual situations. **96m/C VHS.** Alina Thompson, Nick Rafter, India Allen; **D:** Edward Holzman. **APX**

Seduced 🎬🎬 1985 When a rich businessman turns up dead, the ambitious politician who was involved with his wife must find the killer. Not memorable or exceptional, but not boring or offensive either. Made for television. **100m/C VHS.** Gregory Harrison, Cybill Shepherd, Jose Ferrer, Adrienne Barbeau, Michael C. Gwynne, Karmin Murcelo, Paul Stewart; **D:** Jerrold Freedman.

Seduced and Abandoned 🎬🎬🎬 Sedotta e Abbandonata 1964 A lothario seduces his fiancee's young sister. When the girl becomes pregnant, he refuses to marry her. Family complications abound. A comic look at the Italian code of honor. In Italian with English subtitles. **118m/B VHS, Letterbox. IT** Saro Urzi, Stefania Sandrelli, Aldo Puglisi, Leopoldo Trieste; **D:** Pietro Germi; **W:** Pietro Germi. Cannes Film Festival '64: Best Actor (Urzi). **HTV, HHT, HEG**

Seduced by Evil 🎬🎬 1994 A journalist (Somers) is investigating a story in a small Southwest town when she encounters a sorcerer (Vargas) who decides he wants her for himself alone. Even if it means destroying everyone she holds dear. Adapted from the novel "Brujo" by Jann Arrington Wolcott. **88m/C VHS, Beta, Closed Caption.** Suzanne Somers, John Vargas, Julie Carmen, James B. Sikking, Mindy Seymour, Nancy Moonves; **D:** Tony Wharmby; **W:** Bill Svanoe. **PAR**

Seduced by Evil 🎬 1994 **(PG-13)** Journalist Somers is plagued by nightmares and discovers they have something to do with the mysterious occultist who wants to possess her. Made for cable. **CW:** Some sensuality; supernatural violence. **88m/C VHS.** Suzanne Somers, James B. Sikking, John Vargas; **D:** Tony Wharmby. **PAR**

The Seducer 🎬🎬 1982 **(R)** Things get dangerous when a playboy's goals turn from love to death. **72m/C VHS.** Christopher Mathews; **D:** Donovan Winters. **NO**

The Seducers 🎬 1970 An acid-dropping mother takes her shy, withdrawn son on a Mediterranean cruise and asks along some of her girlfriends in the hopes of stoking his libido. However, she finds it difficult to control her own impulses. The boy gets a chance when the ship runs aground on a remote island and he meets an innocent native girl. His mother, though, has designs of her own. Dubbed from Italian. **84m/C VHS. GE** Rosalba (Sara Bay) Neri, Edwige Fenech, Maud de Belleroche, Maurizio Bonuglia, Ruggero Miti, Ewa Thulin; **D:** Ottavio Alessi. **SMW, TPV**

Seducers 🎬 Death Game 1977 **(R)** Wealthy, middle-aged man unsuspectingly allows two young lesbians to use his telephone. A night of bizarre mayhem and brutal murder begins. They tease him, tear apart his house, and generally make him miserable. Why? Good question. **90m/C VHS, Beta.** Sondra Locke, Colleen Camp, Seymour Cassel, Beth Brickell; **D:** Peter S. Traynor. **GEM**

The Seduction 🎬 1982 **(R)** Superstar television anchorwoman is harassed by a psychotic male admirer. Usual run of the mill exploitive "B" thriller with no brains behind the camera. **104m/C VHS, Beta.** Morgan Fairchild, Michael Sarrazin, Vince Edwards, Andrew Stevens, Colleen Camp, Kevin Brophy; **D:** David Schmoeller; **W:** David Schmoeller; **C:** Mac Ahlberg; **M:** Lalo Schifrin. **VTR**

The Seduction of Joe Tynan 🎬🎬½ 1979 **(R)** Political drama about a young senator (Alda) torn between his family, his political career, and his mistress (Streep). Alda also wrote the thin screenplay, which reportedly is loosely based on the remarkable life of Ted Kennedy. Relatively shallow treatment of the meaty themes of power, hypocrisy, sex, and corruption in our nation's capital. **107m/C VHS, Beta, LV.** Alan Alda, Meryl Streep, Melvyn Douglas, Barbara Harris, Rip Torn; **D:** Jerry Schatzberg; **W:** Alan Alda; **M:** Bill Conti. Los Angeles Film Critics Association Awards '79: Best Supporting Actor (Douglas), Best Supporting Actress (Streep); National Board of Review Awards '79: Best Supporting Actress (Streep); New York Film Critics Awards '79: Best Supporting Actress (Streep); National Society of Film Critics Awards '79: Best Supporting Actress (Streep). **USH**

Seduction of Mimi 🎬🎬🎬 1972 **(R)** Comic farce of politics and seduction about a Sicilian laborer's escapades with the Communists and the local Mafia. Giannini is wonderful as the stubborn immigrant to the big city who finds himself in trouble. One of the funniest love scenes on film. Basis for the later movie "Which Way is Up?" **92m/C VHS, Beta. IT** Giancarlo Giannini, Mariangela Melato; **D:** Lina Wertmuller; **W:** Lina Wertmuller. **FXL**

Seduction: The Cruel Woman 🎬🎬 1989 A curiously uninvolving look at sexual games and fantasies. Wanda is a dominatrix, who also owns a sado-masochistic gallery where her various friends and current and formers lovers act out their based desires. Stylized, with plenty of graphic sex. Based on the novel "Venus in Furs" by Leopold Sacher-Masoch. In German with English subtitles. **84m/C VHS. GE** Mechthild Grossmann, Carola Regnier, Udo Kier, Sheila McLaughlin; **D:** Elfi Mikesch, Monika Treut; **W:** Elfi Mikesch, Monika Treut. **FRF**

See How She Runs 🎬🎬🎬 1978 Running becomes a central and redefining experience for a 40-year-old divorced schoolteacher (Woodward). Her training culminates with a run in the Boston marathon. Her loved ones, though concerned for her health and sanity, cheer her on. Excellent made for TV drama. Screen daughter Newman is also Woodward's real-life daughter. **92m/C VHS, Beta.** Joanne Woodward, John Considine, Lissy Newman, Barbara Manning; **D:** Richard T. Heffron. **NO**

See No Evil 🎬🎬🎬 Blind Terror 1971 **(PG)** A blind girl gradually discovers the murdered bodies of her uncle's family. Trapped in the family mansion, she finds herself pursued by the killer. Chilling and well crafted. **90m/C VHS, Beta, LV.** Mia Farrow, Dorothy Allison, Robin Bailey; **D:** Richard Fleischer; **W:** Brian Clemens; **M:** Elmer Bernstein. **COL**

See No Evil, Hear No Evil 🎬🎬 1989 **(R)** Another teaming for Pryor and Wilder, in which they portray a blind man and a deaf man both sought as murder suspects. Pryor and Wilder deserve better. **103m/C VHS, Beta, LV, 8mm, Closed Caption.** Gene Wilder, Richard Pryor, Joan Severance, Anthony Zerbe; **D:** Arthur Hiller; **W:** Gene Wilder, Andrew Kurtzman, Eliot Wald, Earl Barret, Arne Sultan; **M:** Stewart Copeland. **COL**

See You in the Morning 🎬½ 1989 **(PG-13)** Ill-conceived romantic comedy-drama about a divorced psychiatrist and a widow, both of whom had unhappy marriages, who meet and marry. They must cope with their respective children, family tragedies, and their own expectations, in order to make this second marriage work. **119m/C VHS, Beta, LV, Closed Caption.** Jeff Bridges, Alice Krige, Farrah Fawcett, Drew Barrymore, Lukas Haas, Macaulay Culkin, David Dukes, Frances Sternhagen, Theodore Bikel, George Hearn, Linda Lavin; **D:** Alan J. Pakula; **W:** Alan J. Pakula. **WAR**

Seedpeople 🎬🎬½ 1992 Mindless horror flick has bloodthirsty plants inhabiting peaceful Comet Valley after their seeds fall from outer space and germinate. These "seedpeople" possess tremendous powers and soon have the rural residents transformed into zombies. Bears an uncanny resemblance to "Invasion of the Bodysnatchers," and is so bad it's almost good. Also available with Spanish subtitles. **87m/C VHS, Beta, Closed Caption.** Sam Hennings, Andrea Roth, Dane Witherspoon, David Dunard, Holly Fields, Bernard Kates, Anne Betancourt, Sonny Carl Davis; **D:** Peter Manoogian; **W:** Jackson Barr; **M:** Bob Mithoff. **PAR**

Seeds of Doubt 🎬🎬½ 1996 **(R)** Formula thriller finds reporter Jennifer Kingsley (Watson) working to free convicted murderer Crawford (Lando) from prison because she thinks he's innocent (and she's fallen for him). Detective Dexter (Coyote) is unsuccessful in convincing her otherwise but Jennifer begins to have her own doubts when a new series of killings begin after Crawford's release. **CW:** Language, violence, sexual situations. **94m/C VHS.** Alberta Watson, Peter Coyote, Joe Lando; **D:** Peter Foldy. **MNC**

Seeds of Evil 🎬🎬 The Gardener 1976 **(R)** Warhol alumnus Dallesandro is a strange gardener who grows flowers that can kill. He can also turn himself into a tree and figures to seduce rich and bored housewife Houghton (niece of Katharine Hepburn) after he finishes tending her garden. Strange, quirky horror flick. **97m/C VHS, Beta.** Katharine Houghton, Joe Dallesandro, Rita Gam; **D:** James H. Kay. **UNI**

The Seekers 🎬🎬 1979 The story of the Kent family continues, as Abraham Kent, his wife and young son are forced to leave the safety of Boston for the rugged, untamed Pacific Northwest. TV movie based on the novel by John Jakes; preceded by "The Bastard" and "The Rebels." **200m/C VHS, Closed Caption.** Randolph Mantooth, Edie Adams, Neville Brand, Delta Burke, John Carradine, George DeLoy, Julie Gregg, Roosevelt Grier, George Hamilton, Alex Hyde-White, Brian Keith, Ross Martin, Gary Merrill, Martin Milner, Vic Morrow, Timothy Patrick Murphy, Hugh O'Brian, Robert Reed, Allen Rich, Barbara Rush, Sarah Rush, Stuart Whitman, Ed Harris, Jeremy Licht, Eric Stoltz; **D:** Sidney Hayers. **USH**

Seems Like Old Times 🎬🎬½ 1980 **(PG)** A sweet lawyer (Hawn) finds herself helping her ex-husband (Chase) when two robbers force him to hold up a bank. Grodin is the new spouse threatened by Chase's appearance and by the heavies he's trying to escape. Better-than-average script, with funny and appealing characters. **102m/C VHS, Beta, LV.** Goldie Hawn, Chevy Chase,

Charles Grodin, Robert Guillaume, Harold Gould, George Grizzard, T.K. Carter; **D:** Jay Sandrich; **W:** Neil Simon; **M:** Marvin Hamlisch. *COL*

Seize the Day 🎬🎬🎬 **1986** A man approaching middle age (Williams) feels that he is a failure. Brilliant performances by all, plus a number of equally fine actors in small roles. Based on the short novel by Saul Bellow. **93m/C VHS, Beta, LV.** Robin Williams, Joseph Wiseman, Jerry Stiller, Glenne Headly, Tony Roberts; **D:** Fielder Cook. *MON*

Seizure 🎬🎬 **1974 (PG)** Three demonic creatures from a writer's dreams come to life and terrorize him and his houseguests at a weekend party. Slick but disjointed; Stone's directorial debut. Interesting cast includes Tattoo from "Fantasy Island." **93m/C VHS, Beta.** *CA* Jonathan Frid, Herve Villechaize, Christina Pickles, Martine Beswick, Joseph Sirola, Troy Donahue, Mary Woronov, Anne Meacham; **D:** Oliver Stone; **W:** Oliver Stone, Edward Andrew Mann; **C:** Roger Racine.

Seizure: The Story of Kathy Morris 🎬🎬 **1982** The real-life anguish and struggle of a young music student who must have brain surgery and comes out of it unable to read or count. Workaday dramatization. **104m/C VHS, Beta.** Leonard Nimoy, Penelope Milford; **D:** Gerald I. Isenberg. *TLF*

Selena 🎬🎬½ **1996 (PG)** Lopez is appealing in the title role of the 23-year-old Tejano superstar singer who was just breaking into international prominence when she was murdered by the president of her fan club in 1995. Flashbacks show dad Abraham's (Olmos) dashed musical aspirations and he serves as a stage father to his children, recognizing his daughter Selena's exceptional voice. Film covers her marriage to guitarist Chris Perez (Seda) and her building success until the final tragedy (which isn't shown). Film concludes with concert footage of the real Selena. **127m/C VHS.** Jennifer Lopez, Edward James Olmos, Jon Seda, Constance Marie, Jacob Vargas, Lupe Ontiveros, Jackie Guerra, Sal Lopez, Rebecca Lee Mezza; **D:** Gregory Nava; **W:** Gregory Nava; **C:** Edward Lachman; **M:** Dave Grusin. Nominations: Academy Awards '98: Best Actress—Musical/Comedy (Lopez); MTV Movie Awards '98: Breakthrough Performance (Lopez). *WAR*

Self-Defense 🎬½ **1988 (R)** When a city's police force goes on strike, the citizens band together into vigilante troops. **85m/C VHS, Beta, LV.** Tom Nardini, Brenda Bazinet.

A Self-Made Hero 🎬🎬🎬 *Un Heros Tres Discret; A Very Discreet Hero* **1995** Albert Delhousse (Kassovitz) is a young Frenchman who manages to avoid military service in WWII. His one great talent is his confidence and his ability as a salesman. So, with some help from a true freedom fighter known as the Captain (Dupontel), he sells himself as a hero of the Resistance in 1945 Paris and manages to do so very effectively for the rest of his life. Kassovitz does an excellent job as the assured imposter. Based on the novel by Jean-Francoise Deniau; French with subtitles. **105m/C VHS, Letterbox.** *FR* Mathieu Kassovitz, Anouk Grinberg, Albert Dupontel, Sandrine Kimberlain, Jean-Louis Trintignant, Nadia Barentin; **D:** Jacques Audiard; **W:** Jacques Audiard, Alain Le Henry; **C:** Jean-Marc Fabre; **M:** Alexandre Desplat. *NYF*

Sell Out 🎬🎬½ **1976 (PG)** A former spy living in Jerusalem is called out of retirement; his protege, who defected to the Soviets, now wants out. **102m/C VHS, Beta.** Richard Widmark, Oliver Reed, Gayle Hunnicutt, Sam Wanamaker; **D:** Peter Collinson.

Semi-Tough 🎬🎬½ **1977 (R)** Likeable, still current social satire involving a couple of pro-football buddies and their mutual interest in their team owner's daughter. Romantic comedy, satire of the sports world, zany highjinks—it's all here, though not enough of any of these. Pleasant and enjoyable. Based on the novel by Dan Jenkins. **107m/C VHS, Beta, LV.** Burt Reynolds, Kris Kristofferson, Jill Clayburgh, Lotte Lenya, Robert Preston, Bert Convy, Richard Masur, Carl Weathers, Brian Dennehy, John Matuszak, Ron Silver; **D:** Michael Ritchie; **W:** Walter Bernstein. *MGM, FOX*

The Senator was Indiscreet 🎬🎬🎬 *Mr. Ashton was Indiscreet* **1947** A farcical comedy concerning a slightly loony senator with presidential aspirations. He thinks he can win the nomination because he keeps a diary that would prove embarrassing to numerous colleagues. The diary then falls into the hands of a journalist. Powell is wonderful as the daffy politician. Playwright Kaufman's only directorial effort. **75m/B VHS.** William Powell, Ella Raines, Hans Conried; **D:** George S. Kaufman; **C:** William Mellor. New York Film Critics Awards '47: Best Actor (Powell). *REP*

Send Me No Flowers 🎬🎬🎬 **1964** Vintage Hudson-Day comedy. Hudson plays a hypochondriac who thinks his death is imminent. He decides to provide for his family's future by finding his wife a rich husband. She thinks he's feeling guilty for having an affair. **100m/C VHS, Beta.** Rock Hudson, Doris Day, Tony Randall, Paul Lynde; **D:** Norman Jewison; **W:** Julius J. Epstein, Philip C. Epstein; **C:** Daniel F. Fapp. *USH, CCB*

The Sender 🎬🎬 **1982 (R)** An amnesiac young man is studied by a psychiatrist. She discovers that her patient is a "sender," who can transmit his nightmares to other patients at a hospital. **92m/C VHS, Beta, LV.** *GB* Kathryn Harrold, Zeljko Ivanek, Shirley Knight, Paul Freeman, Sean Hewitt, Harry Ditson, Marsha Hunt, Al Matthews, Angus MacInnes, Olivier Pierre; **D:** Roger Christian; **W:** Thomas Baum; **M:** Trevor Jones. *PAR*

The Sender 🎬🎬½ **1998 (R)** Naval officer Dallas Grayson (Madsen) and his daughter Lisa are possessed of a mysterious power they may have inherited from Dallas' long-missing father, a Naval pilot shot down in the '60s. Whatever they have, the government wants, and they don't care how they get it. **CW:** Violence. **98m/C VHS, Closed Caption.** Michael Madsen, Dyan Cannon, Robert Vaughn, R. Lee Ermey, Steven Williams, Brian Bloom, Shelli Lether; **D:** Richard Pepin; **W:** Richard Preston Jr., Nathan Long; **C:** Michael Weaver. *PMH*

Senior Trip 🎬 **1981** New York City will never be the same after a bunch of rowdy Midwestern high school seniors tear up the town on their graduation trip. Made for television. **96m/C VHS, Beta.** Scott Baio, Mickey Rooney, Faye Grant, Vincent Spano, Jane Hoffman; **D:** Kenneth Johnson. *WOV*

Senior Week woof! **1988** A batch of girl-hungry teens have a wacky time on their Florida vacation just before graduation. **97m/C VHS, Beta.** Michael St. Gerard, Devon Skye, Leesa Bryte; **D:** Stuart Goldman. *ART, VES*

The Seniors 🎬🎬 **1978 (R)** A group of college students decide to open a phony sex clinic, but the joke is on them when the clinic becomes a success. Better than it sounds. Pretty good acting and much harmless goofiness. **87m/C VHS, Beta.** Dennis Quaid, Priscilla Barnes, Jeffrey Byron, Gary Imhoff; **D:** Rod Amateau. *VES*

Senora Tentacion 🎬🎬 **1949** Musical melodrama about a composer who fights to leave his mother, sister, and girlfriend in order to flee with Hortensia, a famous singer. In Spanish with English subtitles. **82m/B VHS, Beta.** David Silva, Susana Guizar, Ninon Sevilla. *VYY*

Sensation 🎬🎬 **1994 (R)** A college co-ed agrees to participate in a professor's paranormal experiments in order to test her psychic abilities. Unfortunately what she senses is her prof involved in the unsolved sex-murder of a former student. **102m/C VHS, LV, Closed Caption.** Kari Wuhrer, Eric Roberts, Ron Perlman, Ed Begley Jr., Paul LeMat, Claire Stansfield, Kieran Mulroney, Tracey Needham; **D:** Brian Grant; **W:** Doug Wallace; **M:** Arthur Kempel. *COL*

Sensations 🎬🎬 **1987 (R)** A woman and a man who aren't exceptionally fond of one another share a lottery ticket and win. Vincent is best known as a former director of porno flicks, and he manages to work in several sexual overtones. **91m/C VHS, Beta.** Rebecca Lynn, Blake Bahner, Jennifer Delora, Rick Savage, Loretta Palma, Frank Stewart; **D:** Chuck Vincent.

Sensations of 1945 🎬🎬½ *Sensations* **1944** A press agent turns his firm over to one of his clients, a dancer with some wild promotional ideas. Brings together numerous variety and musical acts. W. C. Fields has a cameo in his last film role. Mostly unremarkable, occasionally fun musical. **86m/B VHS, Beta.** Eleanor Powell, Dennis O'Keefe, Sir C. Aubrey Smith, Eugene Pallette, Cab Calloway, Sophie Tucker, Woody Herman, Lyle Talbot, Marie Blake; **Cameos:** W.C. Fields; **D:** Andrew L. Stone. Nominations: Academy Awards '44: Scoring of a Musical. *VDM*

Sense & Sensibility 🎬🎬 **1985** BBC miniseries adaptation of Jane Austen's first novel concerning two sisters striving for happiness in their well-ordered lives. **174m/C VHS, Beta, Closed Caption.** *GB* Irene Richard, Tracey Childs; **D:** Rodney Bennett. *FOX, TVC, HMV*

Sense and Sensibility 🎬🎬🎬½ **1995 (PG)** Thanks to the machinations of greedy relatives, the impecunious Dashwood family is forced to move to a country cottage when father dies. Sensible Elinor (Thompson) looks after the household while overly romantic Marianne (Winslet) pines for passion—ignoring the noble attentions of middle-aged neighbor Brandon (Rickman) for the far more dashing Willoughby (Wise). Elinor has her own hopes for marriage with boyishly ineffectual Edward (Grant) but all three men have secrets that could crush romantic dreams (at least temporarily). Somewhat slow-paced but witty adaptation (by Thompson) of Jane Austen's first novel, well-acted and beautifully photographed (oh, to be in the English countryside). **135m/C VHS, LV, 8mm, Closed Caption, DVD.** *GB* Emma Thompson, Kate Winslet, Hugh Grant, Alan Rickman, Greg Wise, Robert Hardy, Elizabeth Spriggs, Emile Francois, Gemma Jones, James Fleet, Harriet Walter, Imogen Stubbs, Imelda Staunton, Hugh Laurie, Richard Lumsden; **D:** Ang Lee; **W:** Emma Thompson; **C:** Michael Coulter; **M:** Patrick Doyle. Academy Awards '95: Best Adapted Screenplay; British Academy Awards '95: Best Actress (Thompson), Best Film, Best Supporting Actress (Winslet); Golden Globe Awards '96: Best Film—Drama, Best Screenplay; Los Angeles Film Critics Association Awards '95: Best Screenplay; National Board of Review Awards '95: Best Actress (Thompson), Best Director (Lee), Best Film; New York Film Critics Awards '95: Best Director (Lee); Screen Actors Guild Award '95: Best Supporting Actress (Winslet); Writers Guild of America '95: Best Adapted Screenplay; Broadcast Film Critics Association Awards '95: Best Film, Best Screenplay; Nominations: Academy Awards '95: Best Actress (Thompson), Best Cinematography, Best Costume Design, Best Picture, Best Supporting Actress (Winslet), Best Original Dramatic/Comedy Score; British Academy Awards '95: Best Adapted Screenplay, Best Cinematography, Best Director (Lee), Best Supporting Actor (Rickman), Best Supporting Actress (Spriggs); Directors Guild of America Awards '95: Best Director (Lee); Golden Globe Awards '96: Best Actress—Drama (Thompson), Best Director (Lee), Best Supporting Actress (Winslet), Best Score; Screen Actors Guild Award '95: Best Actress (Thompson), Cast. *COL*

A Sense of Freedom 🎬🎬🎬 **1978 (R)** A hopeless racketeering criminal is thrust from institution to institution until the Scottish authorities decide on an innovative style of reform. Based on Jimmy Boyle's autobiographical book. Excellent and disturbing. **81m/C VHS, Beta.** *GB* David Hayman, Alex Norton, Jake D'Arcy, Sean Scanlan, Fulton Mackay; **D:** John MacKenzie. *NO*

Senseless 🎬🎬 **1998 (R)** Darryl (Wayans) is a poverty stricken college student trying to work his way through school while still supporting his family back home. He agrees to be a medical test subject for a procedure intended to heighten the senses. Unfortunately, as one sense is amplified, the others are drowned out, and Darryl becomes a flailing buffoon. Meanwhile he is in a competition against smarmy frat boy Scott (Spade, who looks about ten years late for his last Econ class) that would land him a job on Wall Street. After dealing with sounds that are too loud and smells that are too pungent, his body adjusts itself. The slapstick puns are hit and miss, but the likable Wayans and dislikable Spade prop up the movie fairly well. **CW:** Language and sexual content. 88m/C VHS. Marlon Wayans, David Spade, Matthew Lillard, Rip Torn, Tamara Taylor, Brad Dourif, Ken Lerner, Ernie Lively, Richard McGonagle, Esther Scott, Kenya Moore; **D:** Penelope Spheeris; **W:** Greg Erb, Craig Mazin; **C:** Daryn Okada; **M:** Yello. *NYR*

Senso 🎬🎬🎬 *The Wanton Contessa* 1954 Tragic story of romance and rebellion as Italian patriots battle the Austro-Hungarian empire for independence in 1866. An Italian noblewoman betrays her marriage, and almost her country, to be with a cynical Austrian soldier in this visually stunning piece of cinematography. In Italian with English subtitles or dubbed. 125m/C VHS. *IT* Alida Valli, Massimo Girotti, Heinz Moog, Farley Granger; **D:** Luchino Visconti; **C:** Robert Krasker. *VCD*

The Sensual Man 🎬½ 1974 (R) Hotblooded Italian falls in love and gets married only to find out that his wife cannot consummate their marriage. Exploitative, misogynistic, and unfunny. 90m/C VHS, Beta. Giancarlo Giannini, Rossana Podesta, Lionel Stander; **D:** Marco Vicario. *COL*

Sensual Partners woof! 1987 Young actresses are lured to Tangier by a fake movie producer and sold as sex slaves. Emphasis on softfocus, soft-core flesh. 87m/C VHS, Beta. Gina Jansen, Eric Falk.

The Sensuous Nurse 🎬🎬 1976 (R) Italian comedy about a beautiful nurse hired by the greedy, treacherous relatives of a weak-hearted count in hopes that her voluptuousness will give him a heart attack. It doesn't, and she falls in love. Mindless, but fun and sexy. Dubbed in English. 79m/C VHS, Beta, Closed Caption. *IT* Ursula Andress, Mario Pisu, Dulio Del Prete, Jack Palance; **D:** Nello Rosatti. *FOX*

Sensuous Summer 🎬½ 1993 (R) When Bobby returns home to the town of Elk Lake he finds the family business, run by his brother Nick, is in deep trouble. It seems Alex, an unscrupulous banker, wants to foreclose. But business comes second to pleasure when Bobby is reunited with old flame Jill and Nick takes up again with ex-girlfriend Cindy. **CW:** Language and sexuality. 80m/C VHS. Tom Case, Christina Campbell, Brittany McGrea, Gina Jorand. *CEL*

The Sensuous Teenager woof! *Libido; Forbidden Passions* 1970 (R) Overwhelmingly erotic and uncontrollably seductive, a teenage girl aims to please by releasing all the sensuality within her. 80m/C VHS. Sandra Jullien, Janine Reynaud, Michel Lemoine; **D:** Max Pecas. *SUN*

The Sentinel 🎬🎬 1976 (R) A model, who has moved into a New York City brownstone, encounters an aging priest and some unusual neighbors. When she investigates strange noises she finds out that the apartment building houses the doorway to hell—and that she's intended to be the next doorkeeper. Modest suspense film with a good cast and enough shock and special effects to keep the viewer interested. 92m/C VHS, Beta. Chris Sarandon, Christina Raines, Ava Gardner, Jose Ferrer, Sylvia Miles, John Carradine, Burgess Meredith, Tom Berenger, Beverly D'Angelo, Jeff Goldblum, Arthur Kennedy, Deborah Raffin, Eli Wallach, Christopher Walken; **D:** Michael Winner; **W:** Michael Winner, Jeffrey Konvitz; **C:** Richard Kratina. *USH*

Separate But Equal 🎬🎬🎬½ 1991 (PG) One of TV's greatest history lessons, a powerful dramatization of the 1954 Brown vs. The Board of Education case that wrung a landmark civil rights decision from the Supreme Court. Great care is taken to humanize all the participants, from the humblest schoolchild to NAACP lawyer Thurgood Marshall (Poitier). On two cassettes. 194m/C VHS, LV, Closed Caption. Sidney Poitier, Burt Lancaster, Richard Kiley, Cleavon Little, John McMartin, Graham Beckel, Lynne Thigpen, Albert Hall; **D:** George Stevens Jr.; **W:** George Stevens Jr. *REP, FCT, PTB*

Separate Lives 🎬½ 1994 (R) Psych prof Lauren Porter (Hamilton) is in need of some counseling herself. Seems she has a sexy alter ego calling herself Lena and Lauren fears she may have killed someone in her Lena persona. So she turns to her student Tom (Belushi), who happens to be an ex-cop, for help. Sketchy characters and a tired formula make this one a yawner. **CW:** Scenes of violence and sexuality; strong language. 101m/C VHS. Linda Hamilton, James Belushi, Vera Miles, Elissabeth Moss, Drew Snyder, Mark Lindsay Chapman, Marc Poppel, Elizabeth Arlen; **D:** David Madden; **W:** Steven Pressfield; **M:** William Olvis. *THV*

A Separate Peace 🎬🎬 1973 (PG) Two young men in a New England prep school during WWII come to grips with the war, coming of age, and a tragic accident. Cheap rendition of a not-so-great novel by John Knowles. 104m/C VHS, Beta. John Heyl, Parker Stevenson, William Roerick; **D:** Larry Peerce; **M:** Charles Fox. *PAR, HMV*

Separate Tables 🎬🎬🎬½ 1958 Adaptation of the Terence Rattigan play about a varied cast of characters living out their personal dramas in a British seaside hotel. Guests include a matriarch and her shy daughter, a divorced couple, a spinster, and a presumed war hero. Their secrets and loves are examined in grand style. Fine acting all around. 98m/B VHS, Beta. Burt Lancaster, David Niven, Rita Hayworth, Deborah Kerr, Wendy Hiller, Rod Taylor, Gladys Cooper, Felix Aylmer, Cathleen Nesbitt, Rod Taylor, Audrey Dalton, May Hallatt, Priscilla Morgan, Hilda Plowright; **D:** Delbert Mann; **W:** John Gay; **C:** Charles B(ryant) Lang; **M:** David Raksin. Academy Awards '58: Best Actor (Niven), Best Supporting Actress (Hiller); Golden Globe Awards '59: Best Actor—Drama (Niven); New York Film Critics Awards '58: Best Actor (Niven); Nominations: Academy Awards '58: Best Actress (Kerr), Best Adapted Screenplay, Best Black and White Cinematography, Best Picture, Best Original Dramatic/Comedy Score. *MGM, FOX, FCT*

Separate Tables 🎬🎬½ 1983 (PG) A remake of the 1958 film adapted from Terence Rattigan's play. Separated into two parts, "Table by the Window" and "Table Number Seven." The lives of the lonely inhabitants of a hotel are dramatized through wonderful acting by Christie and Bates. Made for cable television. 50m/C VHS, Beta. Julie Christie, Alan Bates, Claire Bloom, Irene Worth; **D:** John Schlesinger. *MGM*

Separate Vacations 🎬🎬½ 1986 (R) A married man leaves his wife and kids to take a separate vacation, hoping he'll find exciting sex. Wife and kids end up at a ski resort, where romance comes her way. A lightweight, old story. 91m/C VHS, Beta. David Naughton, Jennifer Dale, Mark Keyloun; **D:** Michael Anderson Sr. *ART*

Separate Ways 🎬½ 1982 (R) Unhappily married couple involved in various affairs split up in order to deal with themselves and their marriage. Good cast; bad script wandering down Maudlin Lane. 92m/C VHS, Beta, LV. Karen Black, Tony LoBianco, David Naughton, Sybil Danning; **D:** Howard (Hikmet) Avedis; **C:** Dean Cundey. *VES*

The Separation 🎬🎬 1994 Emotions (and fine performances) rather than action move along this domestic drama. Anne (Huppert) and Pierre (Auteuil) are living together in Paris with their toddler son when Anne suddenly announces that she's involved with another man. Anne doesn't see why this this should cause any rift in their domestic arrangements but Pierre slowly falls to pieces. Adapted from the novel by Dan Franck; French with subtitles. 85m/C VHS. *FR* Isabelle Huppert, Daniel Auteuil, Karin Viard, Jerome Deschamps; **D:** Christian Vincent; **W:** Christian Vincent, Dan Franck; **C:** Denis Lenoir. Nominations: Cesar Awards '94: Best Actor (Auteuil), Best Actress (Huppert). *NYR*

Sepia Cinderella 🎬🎬 1947 A songwriter, who finds himself with a hit, abandons his current life and love to try high society. He finds out it's not what he wants after all. 67m/B VHS, Beta. Sheila Guyse, Rubel Blakely, Freddie Bartholomew, Sid Catlett, Deke Wilson. *NOS, DVT, FCT*

September 🎬🎬½ 1988 (PG-13) Woody does Bergman again with a shuttered, claustrophobic drama about six unhappy people trying to verbalize their feelings in a dark summer house in Vermont. Well-acted throughout and interesting at first, but the whining and angst attacks eventually give way to boredom. Of course, the Woodman went on to "Crimes and Misdemeanors," blending his dark and comedic sides masterfully, so the best way to look at this is as a training film. 82m/C VHS, Beta, LV, Closed Caption. Mia Farrow, Dianne Wiest, Denholm Elliott, Sam Waterston, Elaine Stritch, Jack Warden; **D:** Woody Allen; **W:** Woody Allen; **C:** Carlo DiPalma; **M:** Art Tatum. *ORI*

September Affair 🎬🎬½ 1950 A married engineer and a classical pianist miss their plane from Naples. When the plane crashes, they're presumed dead, and they find themselves free to continue their illicit love affair. They find they cannot hide forever and must make peace with their pasts. Features the hit "September Song," recorded by Walter Huston. 104m/B VHS, LV. Joseph Cotten, Joan Fontaine, Francoise Rosay, Jessica Tandy, Robert Arthur; **D:** William Dieterle; **C:** Charles B(ryant) Lang. Golden Globe Awards '52: Best Score. *PAR*

September Gun 🎬🎬½ 1983 A nun hires an aging gunfighter to escort her and a group of Apache children to a church school two hundred miles away. Preston is excellent as the ornery varmint in this enjoyable, pleasant western comedy. Made for television. 94m/C VHS, Beta. Robert Preston, Patty Duke, Christopher Lloyd, Geoffrey Lewis, Sally Kellerman; **D:** Don Taylor. *WOV*

September 30, 1955 🎬🎬 9/30/55 1977 (PG) A college undergrad (Thomas) in a small Arkansas town is devastated when he learns of the death of his idol, James Dean. (The title refers to the day Dean died.) Jimmy gathers a group of friends together for a vigil which turns into a drinking-binge, resulting in police chases and, finally, tragedy. Film debut of Quaid. 107m/C VHS, Closed Caption. Richard Thomas, Lisa Blount, Deborah Benson, Tom Hulce, Dennis Christopher, Dennis Quaid, Susan Tyrrell; **D:** James Bridges; **W:** James Bridges. *USH*

Sgt. Bilko 🎬🎬½ 1995 (PG) Popular '50s sitcom doesn't march so much as limp to the big screen with Martin leading the troops as the wisecracking title character, crafted so brilliantly by Phil Silvers on the small screen. Martin flims and flams with frenetic energy as he tries to save his base from Washington cutbacks and the film from utter disaster. Enter Major Thorn (Hartman), Bilko's old adversary, who's plotting revenge on the con artist sergeant. Aykroyd's Bilko's naive boss, Col. Hall, but has little to do. Director Lynn finds his usual comic flair on leave this time around—too few laughs, spread too thin. Sentimental stroke has Catherine Silvers, Phil's daughter, playing Lt. Monday. 95m/C VHS, LV, Letterbox, Closed Caption, DVD. Steve Martin, Dan Aykroyd, Phil Hartman, Glenne Headly, Darryl (Chill) Mitchell, Max Casella, Brian Leckner, Pamela Segall, Eric Edwards, Dan Ferro, John Marshall Jones, Brian Ortiz; **D:** Jonathan Lynn; **W:** Andy Breckman; **C:** Peter Sova; **M:** Alan Silvestri. *USH*

Sgt. Kabukiman N.Y.P.D. woof! 1994 When New York cop Harry Griswold (Gianasi) investigates the death of a famous Japanese Kabuki actor, he suddenly finds himself in a kimono, having really bad hair-days, and vested with the powers of "Kabukiman." With the help of his beautiful teacher Lotus (Byun), he learns to channel his commmand of such amazing weapons as suffocating sushi rolls and lethal chopsticks into crime fighting. Stupid and insulting (deliberately so), all at the same time. A PG-13 version runs 95 minutes. 104m/C VHS, DVD. Rick Gianisi, Susan Byun, Brick Bronsky; **D:** Lloyd (Samuel Weil) Kaufman, Michael Herz; **W:** Andrew Osborn, Lloyd (Samuel Weil) Kaufman; **C:** Bob Williams; **M:** Bob Mithoff. *TTV*

Sergeant Matlovich vs. the U.S. Air Force 🎬🎬 1978 A serviceman fights to remain in the Air Force after admitting his homosexuality. Compelling theme (from a true story) and good lead performance from Dourif are not enough to carry a rather flat made for TV script. **100m/C VHS.** Brad Dourif, Marc Singer, Frank Converse, William Daniels, Stephen Elliott, David Spielberg, Rue McClanahan, Mitchell Ryan, David Ogden Stiers; **D:** Paul Leaf. *ART*

Sgt. Pepper's Lonely Hearts Club Band 🐾½ 1978 (PG) "Rip-off" would be putting it kindly. A classic album by one of the greatest rock bands of all time deserves the respect of not having a star-studded extravaganza "filmization" made of it. Gratuitous, weird casting, bad acting give it a surreal feel. And the Bee Gees? Please. A nadir of '70s popular entertainment. ♫Sgt. Pepper's Lonely Hearts Club Band; With a Little Help From My Friends; Fixing a Hole; Getting Better; Here Comes the Sun; I Want You (She's So Heavy); Good Morning, Good Morning; Nowhere Man; Polythene Pam. **113m/C VHS, Beta, LV.** Peter Frampton, The Bee Gees, Steve Martin, George Burns, Donald Pleasence; **D:** Michael A. Schultz. *USH*

Sergeant Rutledge 🐾🐾🐾 1960 The story of a court-martial, told in flashback, about a black cavalry officer on trial for rape and murder. A detailed look at overt and covert racism handled by master director Ford. It is always apparent Strode (as Rutledge) is a heroic, yet human, figure who refuses to be beaten down by circumstances. The courtroom setting is deliberately oppressive but does make the film somewhat static. Based on the novel "Captain Buffalo" by James Warner Bellah. **112m/C VHS.** Woody Strode, Jeffrey Hunter, Constance Towers, Billie Burke, Ward Bond, Carleton Young, Charles Seel, Jan Styne, Mae Marsh; **D:** John Ford; **W:** Willis Goldbeck, James Warner Bellah; **M:** Howard Jackson. *WAR*

Sergeant Ryker 🐾🐾½ 1968 Confident lead acting from Marvin as a U.S. serviceman accused of treason during the Korean War carries this otherwise blah army/courtroom drama. Remake of 1963 TV film "The Case Against Sergeant Ryker." Dillman is good as Marvin's energetic lawyer. **85m/C VHS.** Lee Marvin, Bradford Dillman, Vera Miles, Peter Graves, Lloyd Nolan, Murray Hamilton; **D:** Buzz Kulik; **M:** John Williams. *NO*

Sergeant York 🐾🐾🐾 1941 Timely and enduring war movie based on the true story of Alvin York, the country boy from Tennessee drafted during WWI. At first a pacifist, Sergeant York (Cooper, well cast in an Oscar-winning role) finds justification for fighting and becomes one of the war's greatest heros. Gentle scenes of rural life contrast with horrific battlegrounds. York served as a consultant. **134m/B VHS, Beta.** Gary Cooper, Joan Leslie, Walter Brennan, Dickie Moore, Ward Bond, George Tobias, Noah Beery Jr., June Lockhart, Stanley Ridges, Margaret Wycherly; **D:** Howard Hawks; **W:** Abem Finkel, Harry Chandlee, Howard Koch, John Huston; **M:** Max Steiner. Academy Awards '41: Best Actor (Cooper), Best Film Editing; New York Film Critics Awards '41: Best Actor (Cooper); Nominations: Academy Awards '41: Best Black and White Cinematography, Best Director (Hawks), Best Interior Decoration, Best Original Screenplay, Best Picture, Best Sound, Best Supporting Actor (Brennan), Best Supporting Actress (Wycherly), Best Original Dramatic/Comedy Score. *MGM, FOX, BTV*

Serial 🐾🐾🐾 1980 (R) Fun spoof of hypertrendiness—open marriage, health foods, fad religions, navel-gazing—in Marin County, the really cool place to live across the Golden Gate from San Francisco. Mull in his first lead is the oddly normal guy surrounded by fruits and nuts. Based on Cyra McFadden's novel. **90m/C VHS, Beta, LV.** Martin Mull, Sally Kellerman, Tuesday Weld, Tom Smothers, Bill Macy, Peter Bonerz, Barbara Rhoades, Christopher Lee; **D:** Bill Persky; **W:** Rich Eustis, Michael Elias. *PAR*

Serial Bomber 🐾🐾 1996 (R) A would-be bomber in Seattle targets his ex-girlfriend but his plan is foiled by an FBI agent. So the bomber shifts targets. Based on the novel "Christmas Apocalypse" by Toshiyuki Tajima. **89m/C VHS.** Jason London, Lori Petty, James LeGros, Yuki Amami; **D:** Keoni Waxman. *APX*

Serial Killer 🐾🐾 1995 (R) Selby Younger (Delaney) is able to think like a killer in order to catch them. That's how the beautiful cop captured serial killer William Lucian Morrano (Bell) who has now escaped—Selby's his ultimate target but first he wants revenge. So he uses her friends as bait and leaves the bodies for Selby to discover.*CW:* Violence and terror; language. **94m/C VHS, Closed Caption.** Kim Delaney, Gary Hudson, Tobin Bell, Pam Grier, Marco Rodriguez, Lyman Ward, Cyndi Pass, Andrew Prine; **D:** Pierce David; **W:** Mark Sevi; **C:** Thomas Jewett; **M:** Louis Febre. *REP*

Serial Mom 🐾🐾🐾 1994 (R) June Cleaver-like housewife Turner is nearly perfect, except when someone disrupts her orderly life. Didn't rewind your videotape? Chose the white shoes after Labor Day? Uh oh. Stardom reigns after she's caught and the murderer-as-celebrity phenomenon is exploited to the fullest. Darkly funny Waters satire tends toward the mainstream and isn't as perverse as earlier efforts, but still maintains a shocking edge (vital organs are good for an appearance or two). Turner's chameleonic performance as the perfect mom/crazed killer is right on target, recalling "The War of the Roses." Waterston, Lake, and Lillard are terrific as her generic suburban family.*CW:* Vulgar language, satirical presentation of violence, and sexual episodes. **93m/C VHS, LV, Letterbox, Closed Caption.** Kathleen Turner, Sam Waterston, Ricki Lake, Matthew Lillard, Mink Stole, Traci Lords, Justin Whalin, Susan Lowe, Mary Vivian Pearce; *Cameos:* Suzanne Somers, Joan Rivers, Patty Hearst; **D:** John Waters; **W:** John Waters; **M:** Basil Poledouris. *HBO*

The Serpent and the Rainbow woof! 1987 (R) A good, interesting book (by Harvard ethnobotanist Wade Davis) offering serious speculation on the possible existence and origin of zombies in Haiti was hacked and slashed into a cheap Wes Craven-ized screen semblance of itself. And a shame it is: the result is racist, disrespectful, exploitative, and superficial. **98m/C VHS, Beta, LV.** Bill Pullman, Cathy Tyson, Zakes Mokae, Paul Winfield, Conrad Roberts, Badja Djola, Theresa Merritt, Brent Jennings, Michael Gough; **D:** Wes Craven; **W:** Richard Maxwell, A.R. Simoun; **C:** John Lindley; **M:** Brad Fiedel. *USH*

Serpent Island 🐾½ 1954 Two seamen fight over a Caribbean woman amid voodoo rituals, sea monsters and buried treasure. **63m/C VHS, Beta.** Sonny Tufts.

The Serpent's Egg 🐾½ Das Schlangenei 1978 (R) Big disappointment from the great Bergman in his second film in English. Ullmann is not sultry and Carradine is horrible. Big budget matched by big Bergman ego, making a big, bad parody of himself. The plot concerns a pair of Jewish trapeze artists surviving in Berlin during Hitler's rise by working in a grisly and mysterious medical clinic. **119m/C VHS, Beta.** *GE* David Carradine, Liv Ullmann, Gert Frobe, James Whitmore; **D:** Ingmar Bergman; **W:** Ingmar Bergman; **C:** Sven Nykvist. *ART*

Serpent's Lair 🐾🐾 1995 (R) Tom (Fahey) and Alex (Medway) have just moved into what's supposed to be their dream apartment in L.A. Too bad there's lots of secrets and Tom's soon drawn into the web of sultry beauty Lillith (Lisa B.), who's not just your average femme fatale.*CW:* Sexuality, language and some violence. **90m/C VHS.** Jeff Fahey, Heather Medway, Lisa B, Anthony Palermo, Kathleen Noone, Taylor Nichols, Patrick Bauchau; **D:** Jeff Reiner; **W:** Marc Rosenberg; **C:** Feliks Parnell; **M:** Vinnie Golia. *REP*

Serpico 🐾🐾🐾 1973 (R) Based on Peter Maas's book about the true-life exploits of Frank Serpico, a New York undercover policeman who exposed corruption in the police department. Known as much for his nonconformism as for his honesty, the real Serpico eventually retired from the force and moved to Europe. South Bronx-raised Pacino gives the character reality and strength. Excellent New York location photography. **130m/C VHS, Beta, LV.** Al Pacino, John Randolph, Jack Kehoe, Barbara Eda-Young, Cornelia Sharpe, F. Murray Abraham, Tony Roberts; **D:** Sidney Lumet. Golden Globe Awards '74: Best Actor—Drama (Pacino); National Board of Review Awards '73: Best Actor (Pacino); Writers Guild of America '73: Best Adapted Screenplay; Nominations: Academy Awards '73: Best Actor (Pacino), Best Adapted Screenplay. *PAR*

The Servant 🐾🐾🐾½ 1963 A dark, intriguing examination of British class hypocrisy and the master-servant relationship. A rich, bored playboy is ruined by his socially inferior but crafty and ambitious manservant. Playwright Harold Pinter wrote the adaptation of Robin Maugham's novel in his first collaboration with director Losey. The best kind of British societal navel-gazing. **112m/B VHS, Beta.** *GB* Dirk Bogarde, James Fox, Sarah Miles, Wendy Craig; **D:** Joseph Losey; **W:** Harold Pinter. British Academy Awards '63: Best Actor (Bogarde); New York Film Critics Awards '64: Best Screenplay. *NO*

Servants of Twilight 🐾🐾 1991 (R) Religious zealots target a small boy for assassination because their cult leader says he's the anti-Christ. Adaptation of the Dean R. Koontz novel. Packed with action, its spell on the viewer hinges on a cruel shock ending that undercuts what came before. Made for cable television. **95m/C VHS, Closed Caption.** Bruce Greenwood, Belinda Bauer, Grace Zabriskie, Richard Bradford, Jarrett Lennon, Carel Struycken, Jack Kehoe, Kelli Maroney; **D:** Jeffrey Obrow; **W:** Stephen Carpenter. *THV*

Sesame Street Presents: Follow That Bird Follow That Bird 1985 (G) Television's Big Bird suffers an identity crisis, and leaves Sesame Street to join a family of real birds. He soon misses his home, and returns, in a danger-filled journey. **92m/C VHS, Beta, LV, Closed Caption.** Sandra Bernhard, John Candy, Chevy Chase, Joe Flaherty, Dave Thomas, Waylon Jennings; **D:** Ken Kwapis; **M:** Lennie Niehaus. *WAR*

A Session with the Committee 1969 Collection of skits performed by a Los Angeles comedy troupe. **90m/C VHS.** Peter Bonerz, Barbara Bosson, Garry Goodrow, Carl Gottlieb, Jessica Myerson, Christopher Ross, Melvin Stewart, Melvin Sturdy; **D:** Jack Del. *NO*

Sessions 🐾🐾 1983 Mentally exhausted by her roles as sister, single parent, lover, exercise enthusiast, and high-priced prostitute, Leigh Churchill (Hamel) seeks professional counselling. Hamel's first role after "Hill Street Blues" is only average in this made for TV drama. **96m/C VHS, Beta.** Veronica Hamel, Jeffrey DeMunn, Jill Eikenberry, David Marshall Grant, George Coe, Henderson Forsythe, Deborah Hedwall; **D:** Richard Pearce. *NO*

Set It Off 🐾🐾½ 1996 (R) Lethal "Waiting to Exhale," finds four female friends in Los Angeles pushed over the edge and taking up bank robbery to escape poverty and strike a blow against "the man." The felonious, funky divas of crime include Stony (Pinkett, who seems to be having fun with this role) and Latifah as Cleo, in a powerhouse performance. Butt-kicking action scenes are most entertaining combined with a soundtrack, including Seal, En Vogue, the Fugees and Brandy, to match. Melodramatic sequences, including Stony's romance with Keith (Underwood), drag.*CW:* Strong graphic violence, pervasive language, some sex and drug use. **121m/C VHS.** Jada Pinkett Smith, Queen Latifah, Vivica A. Fox, Kimberly Elise, Blair Underwood, John C. McGinley, Anna Maria Horsford, Ella Joyce, Charles Robinson, Chaz Lamas Shepard, Vincent Baum, Van Baum, Tom Byrd, Samantha MacLachlan; **D:** F. Gary Gray; **W:** Kate Lanier, Takashi Bufford; **C:** Marc Reshovsky; **M:** Christopher Young. Nominations: Independent Spirit Awards '97: Best Supporting Actress (Queen Latifah). *NLC*

The Set-Up 🐾🐾🐾½ 1949 Excellent, original if somewhat overwrought morality tale about integrity set in the world of boxing. Filmed as a continuous narrative covering only 72 minutes in the life of an aging fighter (Ryan). Told to throw a fight, he must battle gangsters when he refuses. Powerful, with fine performances, especially from

Ryan in the lead. Inspired by Joseph Moncure March's narrative poem. **72m/B VHS, Beta, LV.** Robert Ryan, Audrey Totter, George Tobias, Alan Baxter, James Edwards, Wallace Ford; **D:** Robert Wise; **C:** Milton Krasner. *CCB*

The Set Up 🎬🎬½ **1995 (R)** Electronic engineer-turned-cat burglar Charlie Thorpe (Zane) is now apparently reformed after a prison stint and works designing and installing security systems. His latest job is for Chairman Jeremiah Cole (Coburn) at Charter Trust bank where he begins romancing the beautiful Gina (Sara). But she becomes the hostage of Charlie's ex-prison buddy Kliff (Russo), who wants Charlie's help in breaking into the bank. However, there's a doublecross (or maybe even a triplecross) that has Charlie scrambling to save his life. Based on the book "My Laugh Comes Last" by James Hadley Chase. **CW:** Strong sexuality and violent action, and for language. **103m/C VHS, Closed Caption.** Billy Zane, Mia Sara, James Coburn, James Russo; **D:** Strathford Hamilton; **W:** Michael Thoma; **C:** David Lewis; **M:** Conrad Pope. *MGM*

Seven 🎬🎬½ **1979 (R)** Freelance desperado Smith takes $7 million of your tax dollars at work from the feds to get rid of Hawaiian gangsters. Might be tongue in cheek, though sometimes it's hard to tell. Fun action pic unfortunately characterized by bad camera work and over-earnest direction. Features the original of a gag made famous in "Raiders of the Lost Ark." **100m/C VHS, Beta.** William Smith, Barbara Leigh, Guich Koock, Art Metrano, Martin Kove, Richard Le Pore, Susan Kiger; **D:** Andy Sidaris. *ART*

Seven 🎬🎬🎬 *Se7en* **1995 (R)** If this grim thriller can't make you jump, you're dead, and you won't be the only one. Arrogant, ignorant detective David Mills (Pitt) is newly partnered with erudite old-timer William Somerset (Freeman) and they're stuck with the bizarre case of a morbidly obese man who was forced to eat himself to death. The weary Somerset is certain it's just the beginning and he's right—the non-buddy duo are on the trail of a serial killer who uses the seven deadly sins (gluttony, greed, sloth, pride, lust, envy, and wrath) as his modus operandi. Since most of the film is shot in dark, grimy, and unrelentingly rainy circumstances, much of the grotesqueness of the murders is left to the viewer's imagination—which will be in overdrive. **CW:** Grisly afterviews of horrific and bizarre killings, and for strong language. **127m/C VHS, LV, Closed Caption, DVD.** Brad Pitt, Morgan Freeman, Gwyneth Paltrow, Kevin Spacey, R. Lee Ermey, Richard Roundtree, John C. McGinley, Julie Araskog, Reg E. Cathey, Peter Crombie; **D:** David Fincher; **W:** Andrew Kevin Walker; **C:** Darius Khondji; **M:** Howard Shore. MTV Movie Awards '96: Best Film, Most Desirable Male (Pitt), Best Villain (Spacey); National Board of Review Awards '95: Best Supporting Actor (Spacey); New York Film Critics Awards '95: Best Supporting Actor (Spacey); Broadcast Film Critics Association Awards '95: Best Supporting Actor (Spacey); Nominations: Academy Awards '95: Best Film Editing; British Academy Awards '95: Best Original Screenplay; MTV Movie Awards '96: Best On-Screen Duo (Brad Pitt/Morgan Freeman). *NLC*

Seven Alone 🎬🎬½ *House Without Windows* **1975 (G)** Family adventure tale (based on Monroe Morrow's book "On to Oregon," based in turn on a true story) about seven siblings who undertake a treacherous 2000-mile journey from Missouri to Oregon, after their parents die along the way. Inspiring and all that; good family movie. **85m/C VHS, Beta.** Dewey Martin, Aldo Ray, Anne Collins, Dean Smith, Stewart Peterson; **D:** Earl Bellamy. *NO*

Seven Beauties 🎬🎬🎬🎬 *Pasqualino Settebellezze; Pasqualino: Seven Beauties* **1976** Very dark war comedy about a small-time Italian crook in Naples with seven ugly sisters to support. He survives a German prison camp and much else; unforgettably, he seduces the ugly commandant of his camp to save his own life. Good acting and tight direction. **116m/C VHS, Beta, LV.** *IT* Giancarlo Giannini, Fernando Rey, Shirley Stoler, Elena Fiore, Enzo Vi-

tale; **D:** Lina Wertmuller; **W:** Lina Wertmuller; **C:** Tonino Delli Colli. Nominations: Academy Awards '76: Best Actor (Giannini), Best Director (Wertmuller), Best Foreign Language Film, Best Original Screenplay. *COL*

Seven Blows of the Dragon 🎬🎬½ **1973 (R)** The Chinese novel, "All Men Are Brothers," is the basis for this spectacular martial arts epic. **81m/C VHS, Beta.** David Chiang. *WAR*

Seven Brides for Seven Brothers 🎬🎬🎬½ **1954** The eldest of seven fur-trapping brothers in the Oregon Territory brings home a wife. She begins to civilize the other six, who realize the merits of women and begin to look for romances of their own. Thrilling choreography by Michael Kidd—don't miss "The Barn Raising." Charming performances by Powell and Keel, both in lovely voice. Based on Stephen Vincent Benet's story. Thrills, chills, singin', dancin'—a classic Hollywood good time. 🎵 When You're In Love; Spring, Spring, Spring; Sobbin' Women; Bless Your Beautiful Hide; Goin' Co'tin; Wonderful, Wonderful Day; June Bride; Lonesome Polecat Lament. **103m/C VHS, Beta, LV, 8mm, Letterbox.** Howard Keel, Jane Powell, Russ Tamblyn, Julie Newmar, Jeff Richards, Tommy Rall, Virginia Gibson; **D:** Stanley Donen. Academy Awards '54: Scoring of a Musical; Nominations: Academy Awards '54: Best Color Cinematography, Best Film Editing, Best Picture, Best Screenplay. *MGM, HMV*

The 7 Brothers Meet Dracula 🎬½ *Legend of the Seven Golden Vampires* **1973** Seven siblings meet guy with dental anomaly. **110m/C VHS.** *GB* Peter Cushing, David Chiang, Robin Stewart, Julie Ege; **D:** Roy Ward Baker; **M:** James Bernard. *NO*

Seven Chances 🎬🎬🎬½ **1925** Silent classic that Keaton almost didn't make, believing instead that it should go to Harold Lloyd. Lawyer Keaton finds that he can inherit $7 million if he marries by 7:00 p.m. After his girlfriend turns down his botched proposal, chaos breaks loose when he advertises for someone—anyone—to marry him and make him rich. Suddenly he finds what seems to be hundreds of women willing to make the sacrifice, setting up one of the great film pursuits. Memorable boulder sequence was added after preview audience indicated climax was lacking that certain something. **60m/B VHS.** Buster Keaton, T. Roy Barnes, Snitz Edwards, Ruth Dwyer, Frankie Raymond; **D:** Buster Keaton. *NO*

Seven Cities of Gold 🎬🎬 **1955** An expedition of Spanish conquistadors and missionaries descend on 18th-century California, looking for secret Indian caches of gold. Semi-lavish costume epic. **103m/C VHS, Beta.** Anthony Quinn, Michael Rennie, Richard Egan, Rita Moreno, Jeffrey Hunter, Eduardo Noriega, John Doucette; **D:** Robert D. Webb. *FOX*

Seven Days Ashore/Hurry, Charlie, Hurry **1944** A comedy double feature. In "Seven Days Ashore," three merchant marines on leave in San Francisco become romantically involved with three women. In "Hurry, Charlie, Hurry," a henpecked husband finds himself in a lot of trouble. **141m/B VHS, Beta.** Gordon Oliver, Virginia Mayo, Dooley Wilson, Margaret Dumont, Leon Errol, Mildred Coles. *TTC*

Seven Days in May 🎬🎬🎬½ **1964** Topical but still gripping Cold War nuclear-peril thriller. An American general plans a military takeover because he considers the president's pacifism traitorous. Highly suspenseful, with a breathtaking climax. Houseman's film debut in a small role. **117m/B VHS, Beta, LV.** Burt Lancaster, Kirk Douglas, Edmond O'Brien, Fredric March, Ava Gardner, John Houseman; **D:** John Frankenheimer; **W:** Rod Serling; **M:** Jerry Goldsmith. Golden Globe Awards '65: Best Supporting Actor (O'Brien); Nominations: Academy Awards '64: Best Art Direction/Set Decoration (B & W), Best Supporting Actor (O'Brien). *WAR*

Seven Days' Leave 🎬🎬 **1942** Radio star-crammed musical comedy about a soldier who must marry a certain already betrothed gal (Ball) within a week so he can inherit a fortune.

Songs include "Can't Get Out of this Mood," "A Touch of Texas," and "Baby, You Speak My Language." Following the completion of the film, Mature joined the Coast Guard. Lively but not memorable. **87m/B VHS, Beta.** Victor Mature, Lucille Ball, Harold Peary, Mary Cortes, Ginny Simms, Marcy McGuire, Peter Lind Hayes, Walter Reed, Wallace Ford, Arnold Stang, Buddy Clark, Charles Victor; **D:** Tim Whelan. *TTC*

Seven Deadly Sins 🎬🎬🎬 **1953** A collection of tales concerning destructive emotions and the downfalls they cause. Contains shorts from some of Europe's finest directors (five French and two Italian). Stories and their directors are "Avarice and Anger" (de Filippo), "Sloth" (Dreville), "Lust" (Allegret), "Envy" (Rossellini), "Gluttony" (Rim), "Pride" (Autant-Lara) and "The Eighth Sin" (Lacombe). **127m/B VHS.** *FR IT* Eduardo de Filippo, Isa Miranda, Jacqueline Plessis, Louis de Funes, Paolo Stoppa, Frank Villard, Jean Richard, Francoise Rosay, Jean Debucourt, Louis Seigner; **D:** Eduardo de Filippo, Jean Dreville, Yves Allegret, Roberto Rossellini, Carlo Rim, Claude Autant-Lara, Georges Lacombe. *IVY*

Seven Deaths in the Cat's Eye 🎬🎬 **1972** A ravenous beast slaughters people in a small Scottish village. This flick reveals a little-known fact about felines. **90m/C VHS, Beta.** *IT* Anton Diffring, Jane Birkin; **D:** Anthony (Antonio Margheriti) Dawson.

Seven Doors of Death 🎬🎬 · *The Beyond* **1982 (R)** A young woman inherits a possessed hotel. Meanwhile, hellish zombies try to check in. Chilling Italian horror flick. **80m/C VHS, Beta.** *IT* Katherine MacColl, David Warbeck, Farah Keller, Tony St. John; **D:** Louis Fuller. *ART*

Seven Doors to Death 🎬 **1944** Young architect tries to solve a crime to avoid being placed under suspicion. The suspects are six shop owners in this low-budget attempt at a murder mystery. **70m/B VHS, Beta.** Chick Chandler, June Clyde, George Meeker, Gregory Gay, Edgar Dearing; **D:** Elmer Clifton. *VCI, MRV, SNC*

7 Faces of Dr. Lao 🎬🎬🎬 **1963** Dr. Lao is the proprietor of a magical circus that changes the lives of the residents of a small western town. Marvelous special effects and makeup (Randall plays seven characters) highlight this charming family film in the Pal tradition. Charles Finney adapted from his novel. **101m/C VHS, Beta, LV, Closed Caption.** Tony Randall, Barbara Eden, Arthur O'Connell, Lee Patrick, Noah Beery Jr., John Qualen, John Ericson; **D:** George Pal. *MGM*

The Seven Hills of Rome 🎬🎬½ **1958** Quiet story of a television star (Lanza) who follows his girlfriend (Castle) to Rome after a lovers' quarrel, and then falls in love with Allasio. Fantastic music makes up for a weak plot. Based on a story by Giueseppi Amato. 🎵 Arrivederci Roma; Seven Hills of Rome; Never Till Now; Earthbound; Come Dance With Me; Lolita; There's Gonna Be a Party Tonight; Italian Calypso; Questa o Quella. **107m/C VHS.** Mario Lanza, Peggy Castle, Renato Rascel, Marisa Allasio, Clelia Matania, Rosella Como; **D:** Roy Rowland; **W:** Giorgio Prosperi, Art Cohn; **M:** Georgie Stoll. *MGM*

Seven Hours to Judgment 🎬🎬 **1988 (R)** When the punks who murdered his wife go free, a psychotic man (Leibman) decides to take justice into his own hands. He kidnaps the wife of the judge in charge (Bridges, who also directed) and leads him on a wild goose chase. Leibman steals the film as the psycho. Ex-Springsteen spouse Phillips plays the judge's wife. Ambitious but credulity-stretching revenge/crime drama. Screenplay written by de Souza under the pseudonym Elliot Stephens. **90m/C VHS, Beta, LV.** Beau Bridges, Ron Leibman, Julianne Phillips, Al Freeman Jr., Reggie Johnson; **D:** Beau Bridges; **W:** Steven E. de Souza, Walter Halsey Davis; **C:** Hanania Baer; **M:** John Debney. *VTR*

Seven Keys to Baldpate **1917** Early version of the famous stage play by George M. Cohen in which George Washington Magee accepts a challenge that he can finish a novel in 24 hours while staying at the deserted Baldpate Inn. 66m/B VHS. Hugh Ford, Anna Q. Nilsson, George M. Cohan, Hedda Hopper, Corene Uzzell, Joseph Smiley, Armand Cortes, C. Warren Cook; **D:** Mae Gaston. *GPV*

Seven Keys to Baldpate 1929 Early talkie version of the film which was based on the famous stage play of the same name by George M. Cohan which follows an author into a deserted Baldpate Inn on a bet that he can't finish a novel in 24 hours while in the Inn. 70m/B VHS. Richard Dix, Miriam Seegar, Crauford Kent, Margaret Livingston, Lucien Littlefield; **D:** Reginald Barker. *GPV*

The Seven Little Foys *♂♂♂* 1955 Enjoyable musical biography of Eddie Foy (played ebulliantly by Hope) and his famed vaudevillian troupe. Cagney's appearance as George M. Cohan is brief, but long enough for a memorable dance duet with Hope. ♫Mary's a Grand Old Name; I'm a Yankee Doodle Dandy; I'm the Greatest Father of Them All; Nobody; Comedy Ballet; I'm Tired; Chinatown, My Chinatown. 95m/C VHS, Beta. Bob Hope, Milly Vitale, George Tobias, Angela Clark, James Cagney; **D:** Melville Shavelson; **W:** Jack Rose, Melville Shavelson. Nominations: Academy Awards '55: Best Story & Screenplay. *COL*

Seven Magnificent Gladiators *♂* 1984 (PG) Seven gladiators team up to save a peaceful Roman village from total annihilation. Dismal effort at a remake of "The Seven Samurai"—see the original instead, please. Ferrigno was "The Incredible Hulk" on TV. 86m/C VHS, Beta. Lou Ferrigno, Sybil Danning, Brad Harris, Dan Vadis, Carla Ferrigno; **D:** Bruno Mattei. *MGM*

Seven Miles from Alcatraz/Flight from Glory *♂♂* 1943 Dramatic double feature: Two escaped convicts discover a hideout for Nazi spies in "Seven Miles From Alcatraz," and an evil man tries to recruit pilots to fly planes over the Andes Mountains in "Flight From Glory." 127m/B VHS, Beta. James Craig, Bonita Granville, Chester Morris, Van Heflin, Onslow Stevens; **D:** Edward Dmytryk. *TTC*

Seven Minutes in Heaven *♂♂* 1986 (PG) Sensitive love story about a 15-year-old girl who invites her platonic male friend to live in her house, and finds it disturbs her boyfriend, as these things will. Ever so tasteful (unlike most other teen comedies), with gentle comedy—but forgettable. 90m/C VHS, Beta, Closed Caption. Jennifer Connelly, Byron Thames, Maddie Corman, Lauren Holly; **D:** Linda Feferman; **W:** Jane Bernstein; **C:** Steven Fierberg. *WAR*

The Seven-Per-Cent Solution *♂♂♂* 1976 (PG) Dr. Watson persuades Sherlock Holmes to meet with Sigmund Freud to cure his cocaine addiction. Holmes and Freud then find themselves teaming up to solve a supposed kidnapping. Adapted by Nicholas Meyer from his own novel. One of the most charming Holmes films; well-cast, intriguing blend of mystery, drama, and fun. 113m/C VHS, Beta, LV. Alan Arkin, Nicol Williamson, Laurence Olivier, Robert Duvall, Vanessa Redgrave, Joel Grey, Samantha Eggar, Jeremy Kemp, Charles Gray, Regine; **D:** Herbert Ross; **W:** Nicholas Meyer; **C:** Oswald Morris; **M:** John Addison. Nominations: Academy Awards '76: Best Adapted Screenplay, Best Costume Design. *USH*

Seven Samurai *♂♂♂♂* Shichinin No Samurai; The Magnificent Seven 1954 Kurosawa's masterpiece, set in 16th-century Japan. A small farming village, beset by marauding bandits, hires seven professional soldiers to rid itself of the scourge. Wanna watch a samurai movie? This is the one. Sweeping, complex human drama with all the ingredients: action, suspense, comedy. Available in several versions of varying length, all long—and all too short. Splendid acting. In Japanese with English subtitles. 204m/B VHS, Beta, LV, DVD. JP Toshiro Mifune, Takashi Shimura, Yoshio Inaba, Kuninori Kodo, Ko Kimura, Seiji Miyaguchi, Minoru Chiaki; **D:** Akira Kurosawa; **W:** Akira Kurosawa; **M:** Fumio Hayasaka. Venice Film Festival '54: Silver Prize; Nominations: Academy Awards '56: Best Art Direction/Set Decoration (B & W), Best Costume Design (B & W). *HMV, HHT, CAB*

Seven Sinners *♂♂♂* Cafe of the Seven Sinners 1940 A South Seas cabaret singer (Dietrich) attracts sailors like flies, resulting in bar brawls, romance, and intrigue. Manly sailor Wayne falls for her. A good-natured, standard Hollywood adventure. Well cast; performed and directed with gusto. 83m/B VHS, Beta, LV. Marlene Dietrich, John Wayne, Albert Dekker, Broderick Crawford, Mischa Auer, Billy Gilbert, Oscar Homolka; **D:** Tay Garnett. *USH, NOS, BAR*

Seven Thieves *♂♂♂* 1960 Charming performances and nice direction make this tale of the perfect crime especially watchable. Robinson, getting on in years, wants one last big heist. With the help of Collins and Steiger, he gets his chance. From the Max Catto novel "Lions at the Kill." Surprisingly witty and light-hearted for this subject matter, and good still comes out ahead of evil. 102m/C VHS, Closed Caption. Joan Collins, Edward G. Robinson, Eli Wallach, Rod Steiger; **D:** Henry Hathaway; **C:** Sam Leavitt. Nominations: Academy Awards '60: Best Costume Design (B & W). *FOX, FCT*

The Seven-Ups *♂½* 1973 (PG) An elite group of New York City detectives seeks to avenge the killing of a colleague and to bust crooks whose felonies are punishable by jail terms of seven years or more. Unoriginal premise portends ill; plotless cop action flick full of car chases. Scheider tries hard. Directed by the producer of "The French Connection." 109m/C VHS, Beta, LV, Closed Caption. Roy Scheider, Tony LoBianco, Larry Haines, Jerry Leon; **D:** Phil D'Antoni. *FOX*

The Seven Year Itch *♂♂♂* 1955 Classic, sexy Monroe comedy. Stunning blonde model (who else?) moves upstairs just as happily married guy Ewell's wife leaves for a long vacation. Understandably, he gets itchy. Monroe's famous blown skirt scene is here, as well as funny situations and appealing performances. 105m/C VHS, Beta, LV. Marilyn Monroe, Tom Ewell, Evelyn Keyes, Sonny Tufts, Victor Moore, Doro Merande, Robert Strauss, Oscar Homolka, Carolyn Jones; **D:** Billy Wilder; **W:** George Axelrod, Billy Wilder; **C:** Milton Krasner. Golden Globe Awards '56: Best Actor—Musical/Comedy (Ewell). *FOX, FUS, GVV*

Seven Years Bad Luck *♂♂♂* 1920 French comic Linder has the proverbial seven years' bad luck all in one day (!) after he breaks a mirror. Original and quite funny; full of fetching sophisticated sight gags. Silent with music score. 67m/B VHS, Beta. Max Linder. *GPV, VYY*

Seven Years in Tibet *♂♂½* 1997 (PG-13) Big budget epic of a cold-hearted Austrian mountaineer Heinrich Harrer (Pitt) who becomes a WWII POW in a British internment camp in India. When he and fellow climber Peter Aufschnaiter (Thewlis) escape, they travel to Tibet where Harrer bonds with and becomes a tutor to the young Dalai Lama (Wangchuk). Sweeping vistas and snow-capped mountain scenery does little to aid the sluggish and unfocused narrative, which tries to cover too many subplots and doesn't really get going until halfway through. Pitt's screen presence is forceful and his performance capable but hampered by a somewhat labored Austrian accent. Based on Harrer's memoirs, film ran into numerous problems, including the revelation that Harrer had Nazi ties, China's sensitivity to the storyline, and India's refusal to allow filming. Director Annaud wound up substituting the Argentine Andes for the Himalayas.**CW:** Some violent sequences. 131m/C VHS, LV, Closed Caption, DVD. Brad Pitt, David Thewlis, B.D. Wong, Jamyang Jamtsho Wangchuk, Mako, Victor Wong, Ingeborga Dapkounaite; **D:** Jean-Jacques Annaud; **W:** Becky Johnston; **C:** Robert Fraisse; **M:** John Williams. Nominations: Golden Globe Awards '98: Best Original Score. *COL*

1776 *♂♂♂* 1972 (G) A musical comedy about America's first Continental Congress. The delegates battle the English and each other trying to establish a set of laws and the Declaration of Independence. Adapted from the Broadway hit with many members of the original cast. Available in

widescreen format on laserdisc. ♫The Lees of Old Virginia; He Plays the Violin; But, Mr. Adams; Sit Down John; Till Then; Piddle, Twiddle and Resolve; Yours, Yours, Yours; Mama, Look Sharp; The Egg. 141m/C VHS, Beta, LV, Letterbox. William Daniels, Howard da Silva, Ken Howard, Donald Madden, Blythe Danner, Ronald Holgate, Virginia Vestoff, Stephen Nathan, Ralston Hill; **D:** Peter H. Hunt; **C:** Harry Stradling Jr. Nominations: Academy Awards '72: Best Cinematography. *COL, FCT*

The Seventeenth Bride *♂♂* 1984 Set in a Czechoslovakian town; a strong-willed young woman is slowly destroyed by the insanity of war and racism. 92m/C VHS. Lisa Hartman Black, Rosemary Leach; **D:** Israeli Nadav Levitan. *NO*

Seventh Cavalry *♂♂½* 1956 A somewhat different look at Custer's defeat at the Little Big Horn. A soldier who was branded a coward for not taking part in the festivities tries to assuage his guilt by heading up the burial detail. The muddled ending tries to tell us that the Indians were afraid of Custer's horse. 75m/C VHS. Randolph Scott, Barbara Hale, Jay C. Flippen, Jeanette Nolan, Frank Faylen, Leo Gordon, Denver Pyle, Harry Carey Jr., Michael Pate, Donald Curtis, Frank Wilcox, Pat Hogan, Russell Hicks; **D:** Joseph H. Lewis; **C:** Ray Rennahan. *NOS*

The Seventh Coin *♂♂½* 1992 (PG-13) The legendary King Herod minted seven coins bearing his image which have become coin collector Emil Saber's (O'Toole) obsession. (He's a homicidal lunatic who thinks he's the reincarnation of Herod anyway.) Saber has found six of the coins but the seventh has fallen into the unsuspecting hands of Salim (Chowdhry), a pickpocket who has actually snatched it from the equally unsuspecting Ronnie (Powers), an American teenager visiting Jerusalem (good local color). The two become allies when Saber comes after them. They're an appealing couple; O'Toole camps it up shamelessly; and the movie is easygoing escapism.**CW:** One use of strong language, moment of nudity, and some violence. 92m/C VHS, LV. Alexandra Powers, Navin Chowdhry, Peter O'Toole, John Rhys-Davies, Ally Walker; **D:** Dror Soref; **W:** Michael Lewis, Dror Soref; **C:** Avi Karpik.

The 7th Commandment *♂½* 1961 Unlikely melodrama about a man afflicted with amnesia following an auto accident. He becomes a successful evangelist only to be blackmailed by an old girlfriend. Don't you just hate when that happens? 82m/B VHS. Jonathan Kidd, Lynn Statten; **D:** Irvin Berwick. *NOS, LOO*

The Seventh Cross *♂♂♂* 1944 Tracy stars as one of seven men who escape from a German concentration camp. When it is discovered they're gone, the commandant nails seven crosses to seven trees, intending them for the seven escapees. Watch for Tandy ("Driving Miss Daisy") in her first screen appearance. Effective war-time drama. From the novel by Anna Seghers. 110m/B VHS. Spencer Tracy, Signe Hasso, Hume Cronyn, Jessica Tandy, Agnes Moorehead, Herbert Rudley, Felix Bressart, Ray Collins, Alexander Granach, George Macready, Steve Geray, Karen Verne, George Zucco; **D:** Fred Zinnemann; **C:** Karl Freund. Nominations: Academy Awards '44: Best Supporting Actor (Cronyn). *MGM*

The Seventh Floor *♂½* 1993 (R) Kate's computer-controlled apartment becomes her prison when a psycho takes charge of the system. 99m/C VHS. Brooke Shields, Massaya Kato, Craig Pearce, Linda Cropper; **D:** Ian Barry. *APX*

The Seventh Seal *♂♂♂♂* Det Sjunde Inseglet 1956 As the plague sweeps through Europe a weary knight convinces "death" to play one game of chess with him. If the knight wins, he and his wife will be spared. The game leads to a discussion of religion and the existence of God. Considered by some Bergman's masterpiece. Von Sydow is stunning as the knight. In Swedish with English subtitles. Also available on laserdisc with a filmography of Bergman's work and commentary by film historian Peter Cowie. 96m/B VHS, Beta,

LV, 8mm. *SW* Gunnar Bjornstrand, Max von Sydow, Bibi Andersson, Bengt Ekerot, Nils Poppe, Gunnel Lindblom; *D:* Ingmar Bergman; *W:* Ingmar Bergman; *M:* Erik Nordgren. Cannes Film Festival '57: Grand Jury Prize. *VDM, CRC, DVT*

The Seventh Sign 🎬🎬 **1988 (R)** A pregnant woman realizes that the mysterious stranger boarding in her house and the bizarre events that accompany him are connected to Biblical prophesy and her unborn child. Tries hard, but it's difficult to get involved in the supernatural goings-on. 105m/C VHS, Beta, LV, Closed Caption. Demi Moore, Juergen Prochnow, Michael Biehn, John Heard, Peter Friedman, Manny Jacobs, John Taylor, Lee Garlington, Akosua Busia; *D:* Carl Schultz; *W:* W.W. Wicket; *C:* Juan Ruiz-Anchia; *M:* Jack Nitzsche. *COL*

The Seventh Veil 🎬🎬🎬½ **1946** A concert pianist loses the use of her hands in a fire, and with it her desire to live. Through the help of her friends and a hypnotizing doctor, she regains her love for life. Superb, dark psycho-drama. Todd as the pianist and Mason as her guardian are both unforgettable. Wonderful music and staging. 91m/B VHS, Beta. *GB* James Mason, Ann Todd, Herbert Lom, Hugh McDermott, Albert Lieven; *D:* Compton Bennett. Academy Awards '46: Best Original Screenplay. *NO*

The Seventh Victim 🎬🎬🎬 **1943** Another Val Lewton-produced low-budget exercise in shadowy suggestion, dealing with a woman searching for her lost sister, who'd gotten involved with Satanists. The Hays Office's squeamishness regarding subject matter makes the film's action a bit cloudy but it remains truly eerie. 71m/B VHS, Beta, LV. Kim Hunter, Tom Conway, Jean Brooks, Hugh Beaumont, Erford Gage, Isabel Jewell, Evelyn Brent; *D:* Mark Robson; *W:* Charles "Blackie" O'Neal *TTC*

The Seventh Voyage of Sinbad 🎬🎬🎬 **1958 (G)** Sinbad seeks to restore his fiancee from the midget size to which an evil magician (Thatcher) has reduced her. Ray Harryhausen works his animation magic around a well-developed plot and engaging performances by the real actors. Great score and fun, fast-moving plot. 94m/C VHS, Beta, LV. Kerwin Mathews, Kathryn Grant, Torin Thatcher, Richard Eyer; *D:* Nathan (Hertz) Juran; *W:* Kenneth Kolb; *M:* Bernard Herrmann. *COL, MLB, CCB*

Severance 🎬 **1988** An ex-pilot attempts to save his daughter from the world of drugs and violence. 93m/C VHS, Beta. Lou Liotta, Lisa Nicole Wolpe, Linda Christian-Jones; *D:* David Max Steinberg. *NO*

The Severed Arm woof! **1973 (R)** Trapped in a cave, five men are compelled to cut off the arm of a companion in order to ward off starvation. Then as luck would have it, they're rescued. Years later, one by one they meet a bloody demise. Is it the one-armed man? 89m/C VHS, Beta. Deborah Walley, Marvin Kaplan, Paul Carr, John Crawford, David Cannon; *D:* Thomas Alderman. *CNG, MRV, GEM*

Severed Ties 🎬½ **1992 (R)** Brilliant genetic scientist experiments with human limb regeneration in order to re-grow his accidentally severed arm. His strange mixture of lizard and serial-killer genes results in a repulsive repitilian limb with a nasty habit of slithering out of his shoulder. His mother discovers his experiments and tries to sell his discovery to the Nazis but her son escapes into a bizarre subterranean society and vows revenge. So bad it's just bad.*CW:* Language and strong horror violence. 95m/C VHS. Billy Morrissette, Elke Sommer, Oliver Reed, Garrett Morris; *D:* Damon Santostefano. *COL*

Sex 🎬🎬½ **1920** Interesting dated relic. Morality play about a Broadway star who uses her charms to destroy a marriage only to dump her lover for richer prospects. The businessman she lands then shamelessly betrays her. What a title, especially for its time! 87m/B VHS, Beta. Adrienne Renault, Louise Glaum, Irving Cummings, Peggy Pearce, Myrtle Stedman; *D:* Fred Niblo. *CCB, GPV, GVV*

Sex Adventures of the Three Musketeers woof! **198?** Soft-core spoof of the Dumas classic. Dubbed. 79m/C VHS, Beta. Inga Steeger, Achim Hammer, Peter Graf, Jurg Coray.

Sex and Buttered Popcorn **1991 (R)** Stylish and entertaining documentary of the Hollywood sexploitation moguls, and their films, from the 1920s through the 1950s. These films shamelessly catered to audience's prurient interests, but typically delivered saccharin-coated morality messages and stock footage of routine baby births or the horrible effects of sexually transmitted diseases. Hosted by Ned Beatty, and featuring clips from the actual films, plus an interview with the widow of Kroger Babb, the most notorious of the exploiteers. A real hoot. 70m/C VHS. David Friedman; *D:* Sam Harrison. *CPM, FCT*

Sex and the College Girl 🎬 **1964** Folks talk about their relationship problems while vacationing in Puerto Rico. Tame talkfest providing Grodin with his first role. Included as part of Joe Bob Brigg's "Sleaziest Movies in the History of the World" series, probably just for the title. ?m/C VHS. Charles Grodin, Richard Arlen, Luana Anders; *D:* Joseph Adler. *VTR*

Sex and the Other Man 🎬🎬 *Captive* **1995 (R)** Bill's (Eldard) having this little impotence problem, which girlfriend Jessica (Wuhrer) naturally finds frustrating. So much so that she succumbs to the charms of her married boss, Arthur (Tucci). But when Bill catches them together in bed, his reaction is something none of them expected. Based on the play "Captive" by Paul Weitz.*CW:* Strong sexuality and language. 89m/C VHS. Ron Eldard, Kari Wuhrer, Stanley Tucci; *D:* Karl Slovin; *W:* Karl Slovin; *C:* Frank Prinzi; *M:* Anton Sanko. *APX*

Sex and the Single Girl 🎬🎬½ **1964** Curtis is a reporter for a trashy magazine who intends to write an expose on "The International Institute of Advanced Marital and Pre-Marital Studies," an organization run by Wood. Curtis poses as a man having marital trouble, using his neighbor's name and marital problems, in order to get close to Wood. Things get sticky when Wood wants to meet Curtis' wife and three women show up claiming to be her. This confusing but amusing tale twists and turns until it reaches a happy ending. Loosely based on the book by Helen Gurley Brown. 114m/C VHS, LV, Closed Caption. Tony Curtis, Natalie Wood, Henry Fonda, Lauren Bacall, Mel Ferrer, Fran Jeffries, Leslie Parrish, Edward Everett Horton, Larry Storch, Count Basie; *D:* Richard Quine; *C:* Charles B(ryant) Lang; *M:* Neal Hefti. *WAR*

Sex and the Single Parent 🎬½ **1982** St. James and Farrell, both divorced, both with kids, have a relationship. Complications set in— just how does one be a single parent and have a fulfilling sex life in this day and age? Some of these made for TV efforts are so formulaic! 98m/C VHS, Beta. Susan St. James, Mike Farrell, Dori Brenner, Warren Berlinger, Julie Sommars, Barbara Rhoades; *D:* Jackie Cooper. *TLF*

Sex and Zen 🎬🎬 **1993** Softcore Hong Kong sex film based on the 17th century novel "Prayer Mat for the Flesh" by Li Yu. Mei Yang (Ng) gets married to beautiful Yuk Heung (Yip) but intends to commit adultery as often as possible. There's lots of bizarre sexual practices and Yuk ends up in a brothel while Mei finds his decadent lifestyle not quite as entertaining as he imagined. Cantonese with subtitles or dubbed. 99m/C VHS. *HK* Lawrence Ng, Amy Yip, Kent Cheng, Isabella Chow; *D:* Michael Mak; *W:* Lee Ying Kit; *C:* Peter Ngor. *NYF*

Sex Crimes 🎬🎬 **1992** A tough female judge is brutally raped and she keeps the attack a secret. However, she does ask a friendly police detective to teach her how to use a gun. He's suspicious of her reasons and decides to trail her as she sets out for revenge on her attacker. Predictable actioner. 90m/C VHS, Closed Caption. Jeffery

Osterhage, Maria Richwine, Fernando Garzon, Craig Alan, Grace Morley; *D:* David Garcia. *ATV*

Sex, Drugs, and Rock-n-Roll woof! **1984** Several girls frequent a rock club looking for all the action they can get their hands on. 90m/C VHS, Beta. Jeanne Silver, Sharon Kane, Tish Ambrose, Josey Duval. *NO*

Sex, Drugs, Rock & Roll: Eric Bogosian **1991 (R)** Bogosian's 1990 concert performance, taped live at the Wilur Theate in Boston, exhibits the electricity and finely nuanced characters for which he is justly famous. The characters share a depressingly negative side, however, which keeps this film from being strictly belly-laugh territory.*CW:* Language; drug/sex related dialogue. 96m/C VHS. Eric Bogosian; *D:* John McNaughton; *W:* Eric Bogosian. *MPI*

Sex Is Crazy 🎬 **1979** A melange from Italian horror director Franco containing some epic, some horror, some sex, some sitcom, and some documentary. Little green aliens touch down and impregnate earth women in one skit. In another, a gambler's girlfriend demands two thugs ravage her for the sheer sexual thrill. And in a third, a severed hand commands a heroine to martyr herself to the great god Cucufat. Spanish with English subtitles. 81m/C VHS. *SP* Lina Romay, Anthony Mayans, Tony Skios; *D:* Jess (Jesus) Franco. *VSM*

sex, lies and videotape 🎬🎬🎬 **1989 (R)** Acclaimed, popular independent film by first-timer Soderbergh, detailing the complex relations among a childless married couple, the wife's adulterous sister, and a mysterious college friend of the husband's obsessed with videotaping women as they talk about their sex lives. Heavily awarded, including first prize at Cannes. Confidently uses much (too much?) dialogue and slow (too slow?) pace. Available on laserdisc with a deleted scene and interviews with the director; also includes two theatrical trailers and a short film by Soderbergh. 101m/C VHS, Beta, LV, 8mm, Letterbox, Closed Caption. James Spader, Andie MacDowell, Peter Gallagher, Laura San Giacomo, Ron Vawter, Steven Brill; *D:* Steven Soderbergh; *W:* Steven Soderbergh; *C:* Walt Lloyd; *M:* Cliff Martinez. Cannes Film Festival '89: Best Actor (Spader), Best Film; Independent Spirit Awards '90: Best Actress (MacDowell), Best Director (Soderbergh), Best Film, Best Supporting Actress (San Giacomo); Los Angeles Film Critics Association Awards '89: Best Actress (MacDowell); Sundance Film Festival '89: Audience Award; Nominations: Academy Awards '89: Best Original Screenplay. *COL*

Sex, Love and Cold Hard Cash 🎬🎬½ **1993 (PG-13)** Sarah (Williams) is a high-priced hooker whose life savings ($20 million in stocks and bonds) have just been stolen. She hires an ex-con (Denison) to help recover the money and the two partners find themselves on the wrong side of some Mob trouble as well. Enough twists to keep a viewer interested as well as the prerequisite amount of shootings and chase scenes. 86m/C VHS. JoBeth Williams, Anthony John Denison; *D:* Harry S. Longstreet; *W:* Harry S. Longstreet. *USH*

The Sex Machine woof! **1976 (R)** In the year 2037, a scientist finds two of the world's greatest lovers and unites them so he can transform their reciprocating motion into electricity. It worked on paper. 80m/C VHS, Beta. Agostina Belli.

Sex on the Run woof! *Cassanova and Co.; Some Like It Cool* **1978 (R)** Love-starved wife of an oil-rich sheik, stimulated by the idea of having Casanova for her lover, teases her master into delivering him, but Casanova finds peace in the arms of three convent lovelies. Disgusting, amateurish, and offensive. 88m/C VHS, Beta, LV. Tony Curtis, Marisa Berenson, Britt Ekland; *D:* Francosis Legrand. *VES, MON*

Sex Through a Window 🎬 *Extreme Close-Up* **1972 (R)** TV reporter becomes an obsessive voyeur after filing a report on high tech surveillance equipment. Flimsy premise is a yucky, lame excuse to show skin. **81m/C VHS, Beta.** James McMullan, James A. Watson Jr., Kate Woodville, Bara Byrnes, Al Checco, Antony Carbone; **D:** Jeannot Szwarc; **W:** Michael Crichton. *ART, VES*

Sex with a Smile 🎬 1976 (R) Five slapstick episodes by five different directors with lots of sexual satire pointed at religion and politics in Italy. Don't know much about Italy? Then you'll be left out of the joke here. And really, only one episode is funny anyway (the one with Feldman of "Young Frankenstein" fame). **100m/C VHS, Beta.** *IT* Marty Feldman, Edwige Fenech, Alex Marino, Enrico Monterrano, Giovanna Ralli; **D:** Sergio Martino. *GEM*

Sexpot 🎬 1988 (R) A voluptuous woman's rich husbands mysteriously keep dying, but not before they leave their fortunes to her. **95m/C VHS, Beta.** Ruth Collins, Troy Donahue, Joyce Lyons, Gregory Patrick, Frank Stewart, Jack Carter; **D:** Chuck Vincent.

Sextette WOOF! 1978 (PG) Lavish film about an elderly star who is constantly interrupted by former spouses and well-wishers while on a honeymoon with her sixth husband. West unwisely came out of retirement for this last film role, based on her own play. Exquisitely embarrassing to watch. Interesting cast. **91m/C VHS, Beta.** Mae West, Timothy Dalton, Ringo Starr, George Hamilton, Dom DeLuise, Tony Curtis, Alice Cooper, Keith Moon, George Raft, Rona Barrett, Walter Pidgeon; **D:** Ken Hughes; **M:** Artie Butler. *MLB*

Sexton Blake and the Hooded Terror 🎬🎬 1938 Sexton Blake a British private detective a la Holmes, is after "The Snake," a master criminal, and his gang The Hooded Terror. One of a series of melodramatic adventures interesting chiefly for Slaughter's performance as the gangleader. **70m/B VHS, Beta.** *GB* Tod Slaughter, Greta Gynt, George Curzon; **D:** George King. *VYY, SNC, MRV*

Sexual Intent 🎬🎬 1994 (R) Based on the true story of pathological liar John Walsome, known as "the Sweetheart Scammer," who seduced and robbed more than 40 women. This con artist transformed himself into whatever kind of Mr. Right his victim needed—until he picked on the wrong woman. **88m/C VHS.** Gary Hudson, Michele Brin, Sarah Hill; **D:** Kurt MacCarley; **W:** Kurt MacCarley. *COL*

The Sexual Life of the Belgians 🎬🎬½ *La Vie Sexuelle des Belges* 1994 Autobiographical comedy of sexual manners covering 1950 to 1978. Jan Bucquoy (Compere) grows up with a grim mother and immediately takes an interest in sex and beautiful women, which only heightens as he winds up in Brussels during the hedonistic '60s. He has a short, disastrous marriage, lots of affairs, not much sense, and a mocking disregard for Belgian provincialism. French with subtitles. **80m/C VHS.** *BE* Jean-Henri Compere, Isabella Legros, Sophie Schneider, Michele Shor; **D:** Jan Bucquoy; **W:** Jan Bucquoy; **C:** Michel Baudour. *FRF*

Sexual Malice 🎬🎬 1993 (R) Another erotic thriller finds a bored wife involved in an obsessive affair with a mystery man who has murder on his mind. Also available in an unrated version. **96m/C VHS.** Diana Bartori, John Laughlin, Chad McQueen, Edward Albert, Don Swayze, Kathy Shower, Samantha Phillips; **D:** Jag Mundhra; **W:** Carl Austin. *APX*

Sexual Response 🎬🎬 1992 (R) Eve, a radio talk show "sexologist," is ironically unhappy in her marriage but scoffs at her producer's suggestion of an affair. That is until she meets a brash sculptor and they begin a torrid, and increasingly obsessive, romance. Her lover suggests that her husband have an "accident" with his hunting rifle, but Eve refuses and throws him out. The sculptor, however, breaks into the husband's loft to steal the rifle and finds some news clippings about the man's past that could ruin the lives of many. Little more than an excuse for torrid love scenes. Also available in an unrated version.**CW:** Language, violence, and strong sex scenes. **87m/C VHS, LV, Closed Caption.** Shannon

Tweed, Catherine Oxenberg, Vernon Wells, Emile Levisetti; **D:** Yaky Yosha. *COL*

Sexual Roulette 🎬 1996 (R) A distaff and decidedly raunchier "Indecent Proposal." Jed and Sally wind up in money trouble and get in deeper by trying to recoup their loses (and losing bigtime) in a Vegas horse race. Then a rich blonde with some kinky preferences makes Jed an offer he can't afford to refuse. The unrated version is six minutes longer.**CW:** Strong, pervasive sexuality, a scene of violence and some language. **90m/C VHS.** Tane McClure, Tim Abell, Gabriella Hall, Richard Gabai, Myles O'Brien, G. Gordon Brer; **D:** Gary Graver; **W:** Sean McGinley; **C:** Gary Graver. *APX*

S.F.W. 🎬🎬 1994 (R) Get out your cliche-o-meter for another look at Generation X. Suburban teen Cliff Spab (Dorff) unwillingly becomes a media sensation during a terrorist hostage crisis at a convenience store. The phrasemaking teen's apathetic words are adopted by his peers just as he realizes that there is something he actually cares about—fellow hostage Wendy Pfister (Witherspoon), a cheerleader who wouldn't have given him the time of day before. A somewhat heavy-handed commentary on fame in our tabloid-intensive society. Title acronym stands for "So F***Ing What." Many reviewers had a similar reaction. Based on the novel by Andrew Wellman.**CW:** Pervasive strong language; scenes of brutal violence; constant drug and alcohol use; some sexuality. **92m/C VHS, Closed Caption.** Stephen Dorff, Reese Witherspoon, Jake Busey, Joey Lauren Adams, Pamela Gidley, David Barry Gray, Jack Noseworthy, Richard Portnow; **D:** Jefery Levy; **W:** Jefery Levy, James Foley. *PGV*

Shack Out on 101 🎬🎬🎬 1955 A waitress (Moore) in an isolated cafe on a busy highway notices suspicious doings among her customers. What could they be up to? Communist subversion, of course. Of-its-era anti-pinko propaganda, but with a twist: Moore uncovers commie plots, pleases her customers, and fends off unwelcome lecherous advances all in 80 minutes, on a single set! **80m/B VHS.** Lee Marvin, Terry Moore, Keenan Wynn, Frank Lovejoy, Whit Bissell; **D:** Edward Dein. *REP*

Shades of Black 🎬🎬 1993 Young, small-town photographer/athlete Kate becomes the romantic obsession of charismatic, older artist Lilly. But Lilly's manipulations also hide the deeper secret of her mental instability, which soon proves dangerous to Kate. **115m/C VHS. D:** Mary Haverstick. *WBF*

Shades of Fear 🎬🎬 *Great Moments in Aviation* 1993 (R) Adventurous would-be aviatrix Gabriel Angel (Ayola), who's sailing from Grenada to England, is mistakenly assigned a room with Duncan (Pryce) and decides to pose as his wife to avoid a scandal. But a fellow passenger (Hurt) believes Duncan is also the art forger who ran off with his wife and caused her death. Then on their last night at sea there's a final confrontation.**CW:** Sexual situations, nudity, mild violence. **93m/C VHS.** *GB* Jonathan Pryce, Rakie Ayola, John Hurt, Vanessa Redgrave, Dorothy Tutin; **D:** Beeban Kidron. *TOU*

Shadey 🎬🎬½ 1987 (PG-13) The premise for this oddball comedy came to someone in the wee hours: I've got it! Mild-mannered mechanic can film people's thoughts; wants to use his gift only for good, but needs money for a sex-change operation. Assorted bad guys want to use him for evil purposes. Strange, but not bad; Helmond's character is memorable. **90m/C VHS, Beta, Closed Caption.** *GB* Anthony Sher, Billie Whitelaw, Patrick Macnee, Katherine Helmond, Leslie Ash, Larry Lamb, Bernard Hepton; **D:** Philip Saville; **W:** Snoo Wilson; **C:** Roger Deakins; **M:** Colin Towns. *FOX*

The Shadow 🎬🎬½ 1936 Scotland Yard pulls out all the stops to track down a murderous extortionist, enlisting the aid of a novelist in their efforts. Long on talk and short on action. **63m/B VHS, Beta.** *GB* Henry Kendall, Elizabeth Allan, Jeanne Stuart,

Felix Aylmer, Cyril Raymond; **D:** George Cooper. *NOS, SNC*

The Shadow 🎬🎬½ 1994 (PG-13) Who knows what evil lurks in the hearts of men? Why "The Shadow" of course, as is shown in this highly stylized big screen version of the '30s radio show that once starred Orson Welles. Billionaire playboy Lamont Cranston (Baldwin) is a master of illusion and defender of justice thanks to his alter ego. Aided by companion Margo Lane (Miller), da Shadow battles super-criminal Shiwan Khan (Lone), the deadliest descendant of Ghenghis Khan. Numerous and elaborate special effects provide icing on the cake for those in the mood for a journey back to the radio past or a quick superhero fix.**CW:** Fantasy action violence. **112m/C VHS, LV, Closed Caption, DVD.** Alec Baldwin, John Lone, Penelope Ann Miller, Peter Boyle, Ian McKellen, Tim Curry, Jonathan Winters; **D:** Russell Mulcahy; **W:** David Koepp; **C:** Stephen Burum. *USH*

The Shadow Box 🎬🎬🎬 1980 Three terminally ill people at a California hospice confront their destinies. Pulitzer Prize-winning play by Michael Cristofer is actually improved by director Newman and a superb, well-chosen cast. Powerful. **96m/C VHS, Beta.** Joanne Woodward, Christopher Plummer, Robert Urich, Valerie Harper, Sylvia Sidney, Melinda Dillon, Ben Masters, John Considine, James Broderick; **D:** Paul Newman; **M:** Henry Mancini. *KAR*

The Shadow Conspiracy 🎬 1996 (R) Laughable innocent-on-the-run tale of presidential advisor Bobby Bishop (Sheen), who finds himself smack in the middle of an assassination conspiracy against the Prez (Waterston). Accused of murder, Bishop hooks up with ex-gal pal, reporter Amanda Givens (Hamilton) to get to the truth before the police and the bad guys get to them. Hunting the duo is a pro known as "The Agent" (Lang). Lang's lethal Agent comes off as one of the only believable characters here, perhaps because he has absolutely no dialogue to sabotage him. Sutherland fares better than most as Chief of Staff Conrad Jacob. Ludicrous plot twists and unconvincing performances by leads Sheen and Hamilton.**CW:** Violence and language. **103m/C VHS, LV, Closed Caption.** Charlie Sheen, Linda Hamilton, Stephen Lang, Donald Sutherland, Sam Waterston, Ben Gazzara, Nicholas Turturro, Charles Cioffi, Theodore Bikel, Stanley Anderson, Dey Young, Gore Vidal, Paul Gleason, Terry O'Quinn; **D:** George P. Cosmatos; **W:** Rick Gibbs, Wayne Beach; **C:** Buzz Feitshans IV; **M:** Bruce Broughton. *TOU*

Shadow Creature 🎬 1996 (R) Detective investigating a series of grisly murders finds a mad scientist and a mysterious formula that could unlock the secrets of immortality. The downside being the entire mutation of all life on earth into monsters. **?m/C VHS.** Shane Minor. *MTH, LEO*

Shadow Dancer 🎬🎬 1996 (R) Formulaic Corman exploitation finds L.A. stripper Narita (Hall) under investigation for the murder of two fellow dancers.**CW:** Strong sexuality, nudity, language, and some violence. **89m/C VHS.** Gabriella Hall, Robert Donovan, Kate McNeil, Ron Johnson; **D:** Stan Kane. *NHO*

Shadow Dancing 🎬🎬🎬 1988 (PG) The proprietor of the auspicious Beaumont Theater of Dance is haunted by one of his former dancers who died unexpectedly during a performance of "Medusa." Now, over 50 years later, Jessica, the pick for the lead in a new production, begins to take on her predecessor's mannerisms and spirit as she faces her impending doom. Surprisingly believable and suspenseful—and scary! **100m/C VHS, Beta.** Nadine Van Der Velde, James Kee, John Colicos, Shirley Douglas, Christopher Plummer; **D:** John Furey; **M:** Jay Gruska. *NO*

Shadow Force 🎬½ 1992 Homicide detective Rick Kelly is investigating the murders of a district attorney and a police sergeant. With the help of Mary, the usual beautiful female journalist, he uncovers a plot to assassinate key law enforcement officers. **?m/C VHS, LV, Closed Caption.** Dirk Benedict, Lance LeGault, Lise Cutter, Jack Elam, Glenn Corbett, Bob Hastings; **D:** Darrell Davenport. IMP

Shadow Killers 🐾½ **1980** There's no time to fear your own shadow, for there is a far more terrifying darkness stalking the city. **90m/C VHS, Beta.** Chen Ching, Chang Wu Lang, Chen Chiang. NO

The Shadow Man 🐾🐾 *Street of Shadows* **1953** A casino operator in London (Romero) is accused of killing a former girlfriend and works to clear himself. Family conventional action mystery: nothing to write home about. **76m/B VHS, Beta, LV.** GB Cesar Romero, Simone Silva, Kay Kendall, John Penrose, Edward Underdown; **D:** Richard Vernon. NO

Shadow Man 🐾🐾 **1975 (PG)** A mysterious thief, a master of disguise, sets out to steal the Treasure of the Knights Templar and nothing will stand in his way. **89m/C VHS, Beta.** Josephine Chaplin, Gert Frobe, Gayle Hunnicutt.

Shadow of a Doubt 🐾🐾🐾½ **1943** Uncle Charlie has come to visit his relatives in Santa Rosa. Although he is handsome and charming, his young niece slowly comes to realize he is a wanted mass murderer—and he comes to recognize her suspicions. Hitchcock's personal favorite movie; a quietly creepy venture into Middle American menace. Good performances, especially by Cronyn. From the story by Gordon McConnell. **108m/B VHS, Beta, LV.** Teresa Wright, Joseph Cotten, Hume Cronyn, MacDonald Carey, Henry Travers, Wallace Ford; **D:** Alfred Hitchcock; **W:** Thornton Wilder, Sally Benson, Alma Reville; **C:** Joseph Valentine; **M:** Dimitri Tiomkin. National Film Registry '91;; Nominations: Academy Awards '43: Best Story.USH

Shadow of a Scream 🐾🐾 **1997 (R)** Detective Alice Redmond (Massey) goes undercover to investigate a suspected killer (Chokachi) and discovers his rough sexual fantasies appeal to the less staid side of her nature. So much so that she gets a little too up close and personal with this possible murderer.**CW:** Nudity, extreme violence, language. **84m/C VHS.** Athena Massey, David Chokachi, Cyril O'Reilly, Timothy Bottoms; **D:** Howard McCain. NHO

Shadow of Angels 🐾🐾 *Schatten der Engel* **1976** Beautiful prostitute Lily Brest's (Caven) latest client, a wealthy real estate investor (Lowitsch), just wants to talk and Lily's a good listener. So good, that more and more of her clients tell her all their darkest secrets and fears, leaving Lily herself falling into such a deep depression that she wonders if she can go on. Based on Fassbinder's play "The Garbage, the City and Death"; Fassbinder himself appears as a pimp. German with subtitles. **103m/C VHS.** GE Ingrid Caven, Klaus Lowitsch; **Cameos:** Rainer Werner Fassbinder; **D:** Daniel Schmid; **W:** Rainer Werner Fassbinder, Daniel Schmid. WBF

Shadow of Chikara 🐾 *Thunder Mountain; The Curse of Demon Mountain* **1977 (PG)** A Confederate Army Captain and an orphan girl encounter unexpected adventures as they search for a fortune in diamonds hidden in a river in northern Arkansas. **96m/C VHS, Beta, LV.** Joe Don Baker, Sondra Locke, Ted Neeley, Slim Pickens. VTR

Shadow of China 🐾🐾🐾 **1991 (PG-13)** A young man struggles for power and love in Hong Kong, while an English beauty and an Oriental activist hold the keys to his future and a past which could destroy him. Excellent acting, stunning location photography. Exotic and intense. Based on the Japanese best-seller "Snakehead." **100m/C VHS, LV.** John Lone, Sammi Silva, Vivian Wu; **D:** Mitsuo Yanagimachi; **W:** Mitsuo Yanagimachi, Richard Maxwell. COL, NLC

Shadow of Chinatown 🐾½ **1936** Mad scientist creates wave of murder and terror in Chinatown. Edited version of a 15-chapter serial. **70m/B VHS, Beta.** Bela Lugosi, Bruce (Herman Brix) Bennett, Joan Barclay. NOS, SNC, VCN

Shadow of the Eagle 1932 Former wartime flying ace Wayne is accused of being a criminal known as "The Eagle." He's using his flying skills (which include skywriting) to threaten a cor-

poration which has stolen plans for a new invention. But can Wayne really be our villain? 12-chapter serial. **226m/B VHS.** John Wayne, Dorothy Gulliver, Walter Miller; **D:** Ford Beebe. GPV, VYY, VCN

Shadow of the Thin Man 🐾🐾🐾 **1941** In the fourth "Thin Man" film, following "Another Thin Man," Nick and Nora stumble onto a murder at the racetrack. The rapport between Powell and Loy is still going strong, providing us with some wonderful entertainment. Followed by "The Thin Man Goes Home." **97m/B VHS, Beta.** William Powell, Myrna Loy, Barry Nelson, Donna Reed, Sam Levene, Alan Baxter, Dickie Hall, Loring Smith, Joseph Anthony, Henry O'Neill; **D:** Woodbridge S. Van Dyke. MGM

Shadow of the Wolf 🐾🐾 *Agaguk: Shadow of the Wolf* **1992 (PG-13)** Phillips is Agaguk, the son of the village leader, in this epic saga of survival set against the wilderness of the Arctic. Agaguk decides he cannot accept the white man's intrusion, so he sets out on his own. His father believes his departure to be the ultimate betrayal and casts upon him the "curse of the white wolf." Now Agaguk and his companion (Tilly) must face the harsh tundra alone and struggle to stay alive in the Great White North. Based on the novel "Agaguk" by Yves Theriault.**CW:** Violence and sensuality. **108m/C VHS, LV, Letterbox, Closed Caption.** CA Lou Diamond Phillips, Donald Sutherland, Jennifer Tilly, Toshiro Mifune; **D:** Jacques Dorfman; **W:** Rudy Wurlitzer, Evan Jones. Genie Awards '93: Best Art Direction/Set Decoration, Best Costume Design. COL

Shadow on the Sun 🐾½ **1988** The life of Beryl Markham, pioneer female aviator and adventurer of the 1930s. Way too long and boring made for TV answer to "Out of Africa." On two cassettes. **192m/C VHS.** Stefanie Powers, Claire Bloom, Frederic Forrest, James Fox, John Rubinstein, Jack Thompson; **D:** Tony Richardson. VTR

Shadow Play 🐾½ **1986 (R)** A successful female playwright is haunted by visions of a past lover. Her life slowly falls apart, but not before this film does. **98m/C VHS, Beta.** Dee Wallace Stone, Cloris Leachman; **D:** Susan Shadburne; **W:** Susan Shadburne. VTR

The Shadow Riders 🐾🐾 *Louis L'Amour's "The Shadow Riders"* **1982 (PG)** Two brothers who fought on opposite sides during the Civil War return home to find their brother's fiancee kidnapped by a renegade Confederate officer who plans to use her as ransom in a prisoner exchange, and they set out to rescue the woman. Preceded by "The Sacketts" and based on the works of Louis L'Amour. Made for television. **96m/C VHS.** Tom Selleck, Sam Elliott, Ben Johnson, Katharine Ross, Jeffery Osterhage, Gene Evans, R.G. Armstrong, Marshall Teague, Dominique Dunne, Jeanetta Arnetta; **D:** Andrew V. McLaglen. THV

The Shadow Strikes 🐾½ **1937** Adaptation of the radio serial. The sleuth pursues a killer and a gangster. Meanwhile, the police try to pin a robbery on the "Shadow." Who did it? The Shadow knows! **61m/B VHS, Beta.** Rod La Rocque, Lynn Anders. GPV, NOS, CAB

Shadow Warriors 🐾½ **1995 (R)** Greedy security expert Connors (O'Quinn) sells computerized bodyguards that are created from human corpses, aided by doctor Natalie (Graham). Only one of the latest creations has just gone on a killing spree, so they use another "technosapien" (Lurie) to prevent further mayhem.**CW:** Non-stop violence. **80m/C VHS.** Evan Lurie, Terry O'Quinn, Russ Tertyask, Ashley Anne Graham, Timothy Patrick Cavanaugh; **D:** Lamar Card; **C:** M. David Mullen. NHO

A Shadow You Soon Will Be 🐾🐾 *Una Sombra Ya Pronto Seras* **1994** An allegory of the emptiness of contemporary Argentinian society, following the end of military rule, and based on a 1990 novel by Soriano, who co-wrote the screenplay. A man known merely as "The Engineer" (Sola) returns from Europe where he's lived in exile during the military dictatorship. Without family or friends, he wanders through the southern

pampas, briefly communicating with other eccentric travelers, and non-commitally watching the world go by. Spanish with subtitles. **105m/C VHS.** AR Miguel Angel Sola, Eusebio Poncela, Pepe Soriano, Alicia Bruzzo, Luis Brandoni, Diego Torres, Gloria Carra; **D:** Hector Olivera; **W:** Hector Olivera, Osvaldo Soriano; **C:** Felix Monti; **M:** Osvaldo Montes. NYF

Shadowhunter 🐾🐾 **1993 (R)** Glenn stars as a burned-out big city detective who is sent to a Navajo reservation in Arizona to bring a murder suspect back to Los Angeles. When the alleged killer escapes custody Glenn must track him across forbidding desert territory and face his suspect's unusual mystical powers. **98m/C VHS, LV, Closed Caption.** Scott Glenn; **D:** J.S. Cardone; **W:** J.S. Cardone. REP

Shadowlands 🐾🐾🐾 *C.S. Lewis Through the Shadowlands* **1985** A look at the later life of bachelor-scholar C.S. Lewis (also the author of the "Chronicles of Narnia"). A devout proponent of Christianity, the middle-aged Lewis fell in love and married Joy Gresham, a divorced American poet with two young sons. Joy was diagnosed with cancer and her illness provided Lewis with the clearest test of his faith. Wonderful performances by both Ackland and Bloom. **90m/C VHS.** GB Joss Ackland, Claire Bloom, Rupert Baderman; **D:** Norman Stone. FRV, KAR, GFV

Shadowlands 🐾🐾🐾 **1993 (PG)** Touching, tragic story of the late-in-life romance between celebrated author and Christian theologian C.S. Lewis (Hopkins) and brash New York divorcee Joy Gresham (Winger). Attenborough's direction is rather stately and sweeping and Winger is really too young for her role but Hopkins is excellent as (another) repressed man who finds more emotions than he can handle. Critically acclaimed adaptation of Nicholson's play will require lots of kleenex. **130m/C VHS, LV, Closed Caption.** GB Anthony Hopkins, Debra Winger, Edward Hardwicke, Joseph Mazzello, Michael Denison, John Wood, Peter Firth, Peter Howell; **D:** Richard Attenborough; **W:** William Nicholson; **M:** George Fenton. British Academy Awards '93: Best Film; Los Angeles Film Critics Association Awards '93: Best Actor (Hopkins); National Board of Review Awards '93: Best Actor (Hopkins); Nominations: Academy Awards '93: Best Actress (Winger), Best Adapted Screenplay; British Academy Awards '94: Best Actor (Hopkins), Best Actress (Winger), Best Adapted Screenplay, Best Director (Attenborough). HBO

Shadows 🐾🐾 **1922** A Chinese laundryman (Chaney) lives with a group of his countrymen in a New England seacoast village. All is peaceful until the local minister decides to convert the "heathen" Chinese. Ludicrous but worth seeing for Chaney's fun performance. Silent with music score. **70m/B VHS.** Lon Chaney Sr., Harrison Ford; **D:** Tom Forman. KIV, NOS, CCB

Shadows 🐾🐾🐾 **1960** Director Cassavetes' first indie feature finds jazz player Hugh (Hurd) forced to play dives to support his brother Ben (Carruthers) and sister Lelia (Goldoni). Light-skinned enough to pass for white, Lelia takes on the uptown New York art crowd and gets involved with the white Tony (Ray), who leaves when he finds out her true heritage. Meanwhile, Ben drifts along with his friends who abandon him when trouble finds them. Script was improvised by cast. **87m/B VHS.** Hugh Hurd, Lelia Goldoni, Ben Carruthers, Anthony Ray, Rupert Crosse, Tom Allen; **D:** John Cassavetes; **C:** Erich Kollmar; **M:** Charles Mingus, Shifi Hadi. National Film Registry '93. FXL

Shadows and Fog 🐾🐾 **1992 (PG-13)** Offbeat, unpredictable Allen film that is little more than an exercise in expressionistic visual stylings. The action centers around a haunted, alienated clerk (Allen) who is awakened in the middle of the night to join a vigilante group searching the streets for a killer. Although reminiscent of a silent film, Carlo DiPalma's black-and-white cinematography is stunning. Several stars appear briefly throughout this extremely unfocused comedy. **85m/B VHS, LV, Closed Caption.** Woody Allen, Kathy

Bates, John Cusack, Mia Farrow, Jodie Foster, Fred Gwynne, Julie Kavner, Madonna, John Malkovich, Kenneth Mars, Kate Nelligan, Donald Pleasence, Lily Tomlin, Philip Bosco, Robert Joy, Wallace Shawn, Kurtwood Smith, Josef Sommer, David Ogden Stiers, Michael Kirby, Anne Lange; **D:** Woody Allen; **W:** Woody Allen; **C:** Carlo DiPalma. *ORI*

Shadows in the Storm 🎬🎬 1988 (R) A librarian/poet retreats to a secluded forest after losing his job. There he meets an exotically beautiful young woman who becomes his lover. With her love, she brings blackmail, murder, and mystery. **90m/C VHS, LV.** Ned Beatty, Mia Sara, Michael Madsen; **D:** Terrell Tannen. *THV*

Shadows of Death 🎬½ 1945 Crabbe is the hero who must track down a gang of outlaws who kill to grab the land along the path of a new railroad. One of the "Billy Carson" series. **60m/B VHS, Beta.** Buster Crabbe, Al "Fuzzy" St. John. *VCN, VCI*

Shadows of Forgotten Ancestors 🎬🎬🎬 *Tini Zabutykh Predkiv; Shadows of Our Ancestors; Shadows of Our Forgotten Ancestors; Wild Horses of Fire* 1964 Set in rural Russia in the early 20th century. Brings to expressive life the story of a man whose entire life has been overtaken by tragedy. Folk drama about a peasant who falls in with the daughter of his father's killer, then marries another woman. Strange, resonant and powerful with distinctive camera work. In Ukrainian with English subtitles. **99m/C VHS, Beta.** *RU* Ivan Micholaichuk, Larisa Kadochnikova; **D:** Sergei Paradjanov. *CVC, AUD, HMV*

Shadows of the Orient 1937 Two detectives are out to smash a Chinese smuggling ring. **70m/B VHS.** Regis Toomey, Esther Ralston. *SNC, NOS, DVT*

Shadows on the Stairs 🎬🎬 1941 A creepy boarding house is the scene of a number of mystery-drenched murders. A bizarre assortment of suspects make things even crazier. **63m/B VHS, Beta.** Frieda Inescort, Paul Cavanagh, Heather Angel, Bruce Lester, Miles Mander, Lumsden Hare, Turhan Bey; **D:** David Ross Lederman. *SNC*

Shadows Over Shanghai 🎬½ 1938 This adventure relic was set during the Japanese invasion of China prior to WWII and uses much newsreel footage of that infamy. As for the plot, it's a groaner about good guys and bad skulking around the eponymous port in search of a treasure. **66m/B VHS.** James Dunn, Ralph Morgan, Robert Barrat, Paul Sutton, Edward Woods; **D:** Charles Lamont. *NOS, LOO*

Shadows Run Black 🎬½ 1984 A police detective must save a college coed from the clutches of a maniac wielding a meat cleaver. Ordinary slash-'em-up. Bet Costner's embarrassed now about this early role—like Stallone's porno role in "The Italian Stallion." **89m/C VHS, Beta.** William J. Kulzer, Elizabeth Trosper, Kevin Costner; **D:** Howard Heard. *NO*

Shadowzone 🎬🎬 1989 (R) As a result of NASA experiments in dream travel, an interdimensional monster invades our world in search of victims. Begins well, with slightly interesting premise, but degenerates into typical monster flick. Good special effects. **88m/C VHS, Beta, LV, Closed Caption.** Louise Fletcher, David Beecroft, James Hong, Shawn Weatherly, Lu Leonard; **D:** J.S. Cardone; **W:** J.S. Cardone. *PAR*

ShadowZone: The Undead Express 🎬🎬½ 1996 (PG-13) Teenaged Zach (Leopardi) winds up in New York's subway tunnels where he meets the vampire Valentine (Silver) and his fellow bloodsuckers. Based on the book by J.R. Black; made for cable.**CW:** Some horror violence and gore. **98m/C VHS, Closed Caption.** Chauncey Leopardi, Ron Silver, Natanya Ross, Tony T. Johnson, Ron White; **Cameos:** Wes Craven; **D:** Stephen Williams; **W:** Roy Swallows; **C:** Curtis Petersen; **M:** Reg Powell. *EVE*

Shaft 🎬🎬🎬 1971 (R) A black private eye is hired to find a Harlem gangster's kidnapped daughter. Lotsa sex and violence; suspenseful and well directed. Great ending. Academy Award winning theme song by Isaac Hayes, the first music award from the Academy to an African American. Adapted from the novel by Ernest Tidyman. Followed by "Shaft's Big Score" and "Shaft in Africa." ♫Theme From Shaft. **98m/C VHS, Beta.** Richard Roundtree, Moses Gunn, Charles Cioffi; **D:** Gordon Parks; **W:** John D.F. Black. Academy Awards '71: Best Song ("Theme from Shaft"); Golden Globe Awards '72: Best Score; Nominations: Academy Awards '71: Best Original Dramatic/Comedy Score. *MGM*

Shaft in Africa 🎬🎬½ 1973 (R) Violent actioner finds detective Shaft forced into helping an African nation stop some modern-day slave trading. Second sequel, following "Shaft's Big Score." **112m/C VHS.** Richard Roundtree, Frank Finlay, Vonetta McGee, Neda Arneric, Jacques Marin; **D:** John Guillermin; **W:** Stirling Silliphant. *MGM*

Shaft's Big Score 🎬🎬½ 1972 (R) This first sequel to the extremely sucessful "Shaft" has Roundtree's detective trying to mediate between several mobsters while investigating a friend's murder. Lots of action and an exciting Brooklyn chase scene involving cars, helicopters, and boats but still routine when compared to the original. Followed by "Shaft in Africa." **105m/C VHS.** Richard Roundtree, Moses Gunn, Joseph Macolo, Drew Bundi Brown, Wally Taylor, Kathy Imrie, Julius W. Harris, Rosalind Miles, Joe Santos; **D:** Gordon Parks; **W:** Ernest Tidyman; **M:** Gordon Parks. *MGM*

Shag: The Movie 🎬🎬🎬 1989 (PG) The time is 1963, the setting Myrtle Beach, South Carolina, the latest craze shaggin' when four friends hit the beach for one last weekend together. Carson (Cates) is getting ready to marry staid Harley (Power); Melaina (Fonda) wants to be discovered in Hollywood; and Pudge (Gish) and Luanne (Hannah) are off to college. They encounter lots of music, boys, and dancing in this delightful film. Not to be confused with other "teen" movies, this one boasts a good script and an above average cast. **96m/C VHS, Beta, LV.** Phoebe Cates, Annabeth Gish, Bridget Fonda, Page Hannah, Scott Coffey, Robert Rusler, Tyrone Power Jr., Jeff Yagher, Carrie Hamilton, Shirley Anne Field, Leilani Sarelle Ferrer; **D:** Zelda Barron; **W:** Robin Swicord, Lanier Laney, Terry Sweeney. *HBO*

The Shaggy D.A. 🎬🎬 1976 (G) Wilby Daniels is getting a little worried about his canine alter ego as he is about to run for District Attorney. Fun sequel to "The Shaggy Dog." **90m/C VHS, Beta.** Dean Jones, Tim Conway, Suzanne Pleshette, Keenan Wynn; **D:** Robert Stevenson; **M:** Buddy Baker. *DIS, OM*

The Shaggy Dog 🎬🎬½ 1959 (G) When young Wilby Daniels utters some magical words from the inscription of an ancient ring he turns into a shaggy dog, causing havoc for family and neighbors. Disney slapstick is on target at times, though it drags in places. Followed by "The Shaggy D.A." and "Return of the Shaggy Dog." **101m/B VHS, Beta, LV.** Fred MacMurray, Jean Hagen, Tommy Kirk, Annette Funicello, Tim Considine, Kevin Corcoran; **D:** Charles T. Barton; **C:** Edward Colman. *DIS, BTV*

Shaka Zulu 🎬🎬🎬 1983 British miniseries depicting the career of Shaka, king of the Zulus (Cele). Set in the early 19th century during British ascendency in Africa. Good, absorbing cross-cultural action drama would have been better with more inspired directing by Faure. **300m/C VHS, Beta.** *GB* Edward Fox, Robert Powell, Trevor Howard, Christopher Lee, Fiona Fullerton, Henry Cele; **D:** William C. Faure. *FCT*

Shake Hands with Murder 🎬🎬 1944 Three people spend their time bailing criminals out of jail for profit. One is murdered, and the other two become implicated in comedy. **63m/B VHS, Beta.** Iris Adrian, Frank Jenks, Douglas Fowley, Jack Raymond, Claire Rochelle, Herbert Rawlinson, Forrest Taylor; **D:** Al(bert) Herman. *SNC*

Shake Hands with the Devil 🎬🎬🎬 1959 It's the Irish Republican Army against the British Black and Tans as Ireland fights for independence in 1921. Cagney is a teaching surgeon who is secretly a militant, obsessed with the idea of gaining Irish freedom. He urges his students to join with him, which Irish-American Murray does. When Murray learns that Cagney is out to sabotage a peace treaty, he must decide whether to betray Cagney in order to stop further violence. Cagney is excellent as the hard-bitten revolutionary who can't see beyond his own ideals. Filmed on location in Dublin, which further heightens the film's tension. **110m/B VHS.** James Cagney, Don Murray, Dana Wynter, Glynis Johns, Michael Redgrave, Sybil Thorndike, Harry Brogan, Robert Brown; **D:** Michael Anderson Sr.; **W:** Ivan Goff. *MGM, FCT*

Shake, Rattle and Rock 🎬🎬½ 1957 A deejay wants to open a teen music club playing rock 'n' roll, which has all the conservative parents up in arms. A court case follows (which the kids win). Incidental plot to the great music by Fats Domino, Joe Turner, Annita Ray, and Tommy Charles. Songs include "Ain't It a Shame," "Honey Chile," "I'm in Love Again," "Feelin' Happy," and "Sweet Love on My Mind." **76m/C VHS.** Mike Connors, Lisa Gaye, Sterling Holloway, Margaret Dumont, Raymond Hatton, Douglass Dumbrille; **D:** Edward L. Cahn; **W:** Lou Rusoff. *COL, MOV, MVD*

Shakedown 🎬🎬½ 1988 (R) Power-packed action film. An overworked attorney and an undercover cop work together to stop corruption in the N.Y.P.D. Although lacking greatly in logic or plot, the sensational stunts make this an otherwise entertaining action flick. **96m/C VHS, Beta, LV.** Sam Elliott, Peter Weller, Patricia Charbonneau, Antonio Fargas, Blanche Baker, Richard Brooks, Jude Ciccolella, George Loros, Tom Waits, Shirley Stoler, Rockets Redglare, Kathryn Rossetter; **D:** James Glickenhaus; **W:** James Glickenhaus; **M:** Jonathan Elias. *USH*

Shaker Run 🎬½ 1985 A stunt car driver and his mechanic transport a mysterious package. They don't know what to do—they're carrying a deadly virus that every terrorist wants! Car chases galore, and not much else. However, if you like chase scenes... **91m/C VHS, Beta, LV.** *NZ* Leif Garrett, Cliff Robertson, Lisa Harrow; **D:** Bruce Morrison. *NLC*

Shakes the Clown 🎬 1992 (R) Chronicles the rise and fall of Shakes, an alcoholic clown wandering through the all-clown town of Palukaville. Framed for the murder of his boss by his archrival, Binky, Shakes takes it on the lam in order to prove his innocence, aided by his waitress girlfriend Judy, who dreams of becoming a professional bowler. Meant as a satire of substance-abuse recovery programs and the supposed tragedies of a performer's life, the film is sometimes zany, but more often merely unpleasant and unamusing. Williams has an uncredited role as a mime.**CW:** Language and drug use. **83m/C VHS, LV.** Bob(cat) Goldthwait, Julie Brown, Blake Clark, Adam Sandler, Tom Kenny, Sydney Lassick, Paul Dooley, Tim Kazurinsky, Florence Henderson, LaWanda Page; **Cameos:** Robin Williams; **D:** Bob(cat) Goldthwait; **W:** Bob(cat) Goldthwait. *COL*

Shakespeare Wallah 🎬🎬🎬½ 1965 Tender, plausible drama of romance and postcolonial relations in India. A troupe of traveling Shakespeareans quixotically tours India trying to make enough money to return to England. Wonderfully acted and exquisitely and sensitively directed by Ivory. **120m/B VHS, Beta.** Laura Liddell, Geoffrey Kendal, Felicity Kendal, Shashi Kapoor, Madhur Jaffrey; **D:** James Ivory; **W:** Ruth Prawer Jhabvala, James Ivory. *NLC*

The Shakiest Gun in the West 🎬🎬½ 1968 Remake of Bob Hope's "Paleface" has Philadelphia dentist Jesse W. Heywood (Knotts) heading off for a new practice in the wild west of Big Springs. There he unwittingly takes on bad guys and sultry Penny (Rhoades), an undercover government agent who ropes the nervous dentist into marriage for the sake of his job. 101m/C VHS **Closed Caption** Don Knotts, Barbara Rhoades, Jackie Coogan, Donald (Don "Red") Barry, Ruth McDevitt, Dub Taylor, Noriyuki "Pat" Morita; **D:** Alan Rafkin; **W:** James Fritzell, Everett Greenbaum. *USH*

Shaking the Tree 🐾🐾½ 1992 (PG-13)
Group of four high school buddies are still in quest of self-fulfillment ten years after high school as they grapple with problems in the real world of adulthood, seeking distraction in adventure, romance, friendship, and sex. **CW:** Language. 97m/C VHS. Arye Gross, Gale Hansen, Doug Savant, Steven Wilde, Courteney Cox, Christina Haag, Michael Arabian, Nathan Davis; **D:** Duane Clark; **W:** Duane Clark; **M:** David E. Russo.

Shakma 🐾½ 1989
A group of medical researchers involved with experiments on animal and human tendencies toward aggression take a night off to play a quiet game of "Dungeons and Dragons." The horror begins when their main experimental subject comes along and turns things nasty! 101m/C VHS. Roddy McDowall, Christopher Atkins, Amanda Wyss, Ari Meyers; **D:** Hugh Parks. *HHE*

Shalako 🐾🐾 1968
Connery/Bardot pairing promises something special, but fails to deliver. European aristocrats on a hunting trip in New Mexico, circa 1880, are menaced by Apaches. U.S. Army scout tries to save captured countess Bardot. Strange British attempt at a Euro-western. Poorly directed and pointless. Based on a Louis L'Amour story. 113m/C VHS, Beta. Brigitte Bardot, Sean Connery, Stephen Boyd, Honor Blackman, Woody Strode, Alexander Knox; **D:** Edward Dmytryk; **C:** Ted Moore. *FOX*

Shall We Dance 🐾🐾🐾 1937
And shall we ever! Seventh Astaire-Rogers pairing has a famous ballet dancer and a musical-comedy star embark on a promotional romance and marriage, to boost their careers, only to find themselves truly falling in love. Score by the Gershwins includes memorable songs. Thin, lame plot—but that's okay. For fans of good singing and dancing, and especially this immortal pair. ♫Slap That Bass; Beginner's Luck; Let's Call the Whole Thing Off; Walking the Dog; They All Laughed; They Can't Take That Away From Me; Shall We Dance. 116m/B VHS, Beta, LV. Fred Astaire, Ginger Rogers, Edward Everett Horton, Eric Blore; **D:** Mark Sandrich; **M:** George Gershwin, Ira Gershwin. Nominations: Academy Awards '37: Best Song ("They Can't Take That Away From Me"). *TTC, CCB*

Shall We Dance? 🐾🐾🐾 1997
A timid Japanese businessman is lured to ballroom dancing when he glimpses a beautiful, sad-eyed teacher through a window. As much commentary on controlled Japanese society as a spirited discovery of learning to live and dance. Well-drawn, quirky characters and good humor amid the observant social commentary should put this one at the top of the anyone's foreign film dance card. In Japanese with subtitles. 118m/C VHS, LV, **Closed Caption.** JP Koji Yakusho, Tamiyo Kusakari, Naoto Takenaka, Akira Emoto, Eriko Watanabe, Yu Tokui, Hiromasa Taguchi; **D:** Masayuki Suo; **W:** Masayuki Suo; **C:** Naoke Kayano; **M:** Yoshikazu Suo. National Board of Review Awards '97: Best Foreign Film; Broadcast Film Critics Association Awards '97: Best Foreign Film. *TOU*

Shallow Grave 🐾½ 1987 (R)
Four coeds en route to Florida witness a murder in rural Georgia and then are pursued relentlessly by the killer, a local sheriff. Decent premise and talented cast could have offered something better, given a meatier script. 90m/C VHS, Beta. Tony March, Lisa Stahl, Tom Law, Carol Cadby; **D:** Richard Styles. *PAR*

Shallow Grave 🐾🐾½ 1994 (R)
Juliet (Fox), David (Eccleston), and Alex (McGregor), three completely unlikable housemates, face a moral dilemma when their new roomie, Hugo (Allen), turns up dead of a drug overdose, leaving behind a suitcase stuffed with cash. Their decision to chop up the body, bury the bits, and keep the loot leads to a well-deserved descent into paranoia, betrayal, and dementia. Interesting charac-

ter study in which the veneer of civility is totally destroyed at the first hint of temptation. Style wins out over substance as the characters are never humanized before they're demonized. **CW:** Contains scenes of strong, grisly violence; some profanity and nudity. 91m/C VHS. GB Kerry Fox, Christopher Eccleston, Ewan McGregor, Keith Allen, Ken Stott, Colin McCredie, John Hodge; **D:** Danny Boyle; **W:** John Hodge; **C:** Brian Tufano; **M:** Simon Boswell. *PGV*

The Shaman 🐾½ 1987 (R)
Members of a family succumb to the hypnotic spell of the Shaman as he searches for the perfect one to inherit his powers. 88m/C VHS, Beta. Michael Conforti, Elvind Harum, James Farkas, Lynn Weaver; **D:** Michael Yakub. *IMP*

Shame 🐾🐾🐾½ *The Intruder; I Hate Your Guts; The Stranger* 1961
Strangely unsuccessful low-budget Corman effort, starring pre-"Star Trek" Shatner as a freelance bigot who travels around Missouri stirring up opposition to desegregation. Moralistic and topical but still powerful. Adapted from the equally excellent novel by Charles Beaumont. Uses location filming superbly to render a sense of everydayness and authenticity. 84m/B VHS, Beta, LV. William Shatner, Frank Maxwell, Jeanne Cooper, Robert Emhardt, Leo Gordon; **D:** Roger Corman. *NOS, DVT, FCT*

The Shame 🐾🐾🐾½ 1968 (R)
A Bergman masterpiece focusing on the struggle for dignity in the midst of war. Married concert musicians Ullmann and von Sydow flee a bloody civil war for a small island off their country's coast. Inevitably, the carnage reaches them and their lives become a struggle to endure and retain a small measure of civilized behavior as chaos overtakes them. Deeply despairing and brilliantly acted. In Swedish with English subtitles. 103m/C VHS. SW Max von Sydow, Liv Ullmann, Gunnar Bjornstrand, Sigge Furst, Birgitta Valberg, Hans Alfredson, Ingvar Kjellson; **D:** Ingmar Bergman; **W:** Ingmar Bergman; **C:** Sven Nykvist. National Society of Film Critics Awards '68: Best Actress (Ullmann), Best Director (Bergman), Best Film. *MGM, BTV*

Shame 🐾🐾 1987 (R)
Strange Australian revenge drama about a female lawyer/biker who rides into a small town and finds herself avenging the rape of a 16-year-old girl. Is it a genuinely feminist movie about justice and a strong woman taking charge? Or is it exploitative trash using a politically correct theme and "message" as a peg for much—very much—gratuitous violence? Hard to tell. Cultish for sure; made on a B budget. 95m/C VHS, LV. AU Deborra Lee Furness, Tony Barry, Simone Buchanan, Gillian Jones; **D:** Steve Jodrell; **W:** Beverly Blakenship, Michael Brindley. *REP*

Shame 🐾🐾 1992
In a small logging town a group of violent high school thugs get away with rape because the women are too terrified to go to the cops. Then lawyer Diana Cadell (Donohoe) gets stuck in town when her motorcycle breaks down. When she finds out what's been happening, she urges one victim (Balk) to speak out and suddenly they become the targets of both the vicious attackers and a town which would like to hush the entire mess up. Very strong performances by Donohoe and Balk. Made for cable U.S. version of the same-titled 1987 Australian movie. 91m/C VHS. Amanda Donohoe, Fairuza Balk, Dean Stockwell, Dan Gauthier; **D:** Dan Lerner; **W:** Rebecca Soladay.

Shame of the Jungle 1990 (R)
Animated spoof on Tarzan featuring the voices of John Belushi, Bill Murray, and Johnny Weissmuller, Jr. 73m/C VHS. **D:** Boris Szulzinger, Picha; **V:** Johnny Weissmuller Jr., John Belushi, Bill Murray, Brian Doyle-Murray, Christopher Guest, Andrew Duncan. *JEF*

Shame, Shame on the Bixby Boys 🐾½ 1982
Somewhere in the Old West, outside a small town, lives a band of misfits who persist in rustling cattle. The Bixby Boys and their Pa have made a bad habit into a family tradition. 90m/C VHS, Beta. Monte Markham, Sammy Jackson; **D:** Anthony Bowers. *TLF*

Shameless 🐾🐾 *Mad Dogs and Englishmen* 1994 (R)
Wealthy Antonia Dyer (Hurley) is the self-centered, drug addict daughter of aristocrat Sir Harry Dyer (Treves). Her dealer is upper-class Tony Vernon-Smith (Brett), who's involved with Sandy (Delamere), the daughter of corrupt narcotics cop Stringer (Ackland). Stringer discovers the two girls know each other and irrationally blames Antonia for his daughter's heroin habit. Meanwhile, American student Mike (Howell) has been trying to get girlfriend Antonia off the drugs. Hurley's properly snooty and manipulative while Howell seems out-of-place and uncomfortable. **CW:** Strong drug use and for violence, sexuality and language. 99m/C VHS. GB Elizabeth Hurley, C. Thomas Howell, Joss Ackland, Jeremy Brett, Frederick Treves, Claire Bloom, Louise Delamere, Chris Adamson; **D:** Henry Cole; **W:** Tim Sewell; **C:** John Peters; **M:** Barrie Guard. *BMG*

The Shaming 🐾½ *The Sin; Good Luck, Miss Wyckoff* 1971 (R)
Puritanical schoolteacher is raped by a janitor, then develops a voracious sexual appetite. Horrible script, offensive premise can't be saved by good cast. Based on a novel by William Inge. 90m/C VHS, Beta. Anne Heywood, Donald Pleasence, Robert Vaughn, Carolyn Jones; **D:** Marvin J. Chomsky. *NO*

Shampoo 🐾🐾½ 1975 (R)
A satire of morals (and lack thereof) set in Southern California, concerning a successful hairdresser (Beatty) and the many women in his life. A notable scene with Julie Christie is set at a 1968 presidential election-night gathering. Fisher's screen debut, only one year before "Star Wars" made her famous. Has a healthy glow in places and a perky bounce, but too many split ends. 112m/C VHS, Beta, LV, **Letterbox, Closed Caption.** Warren Beatty, Julie Christie, Goldie Hawn, Jack Warden, Lee Grant, Tony Bill, Carrie Fisher, William Castle, Howard Hesseman; **D:** Hal Ashby; **W:** Warren Beatty, Robert Towne; **M:** John Barry. Academy Awards '75: Best Supporting Actress (Grant); National Society of Film Critics Awards '75: Best Screenplay; Writers Guild of America '75: Best Original Screenplay; Nominations: Academy Awards '75: Best Art Direction/Set Decoration, Best Original Screenplay, Best Supporting Actor (Warden). *COL, CRC*

Shamus 🐾🐾 1973 (PG)
Private dick Reynolds investigates a smuggling ring, beds a sultry woman, gets in lotsa fights. Classic Burt vehicle meant as a send-up. Unoriginal but fun. 91m/C VHS, Beta, LV. Burt Reynolds, Dyan Cannon, John P. Ryan; **D:** Buzz Kulik; **W:** Barry Beckerman; **M:** Jerry Goldsmith. *GKK*

Shane 🐾🐾🐾🐾 1953
A retired gunfighter, now a drifter, comes to the aid of a homestead family threatened by a land baron and his hired gun. Ladd is the mystery man who becomes the idol of the family's young son. Classic, flawless western. Pulitzer prize-winning western novelist A.B. Guthrie, Jr. adapted from the novel by Jack Schaefer. Long and stately; worth savoring. 117m/C VHS, Beta, LV. Alan Ladd, Jean Arthur, Van Heflin, Brandon de Wilde, Jack Palance, Ben Johnson, Elisha Cook Jr., Edgar Buchanan, Emile Meyer; **D:** George Stevens; **W:** Jack Sher; **C:** Loyal Griggs; **M:** Victor Young. Academy Awards '53: Best Color Cinematography; National Board of Review Awards '53: Best Director (Stevens); National Film Registry '93; Nominations: Academy Awards '53: Best Director (Stevens), Best Picture, Best Screenplay, Best Supporting Actor (de Wilde, Palance). *PAR, TLF*

The Shanghai Cobra 🐾½ 1945
Below-average mystery has Chan hired by the government to investigate several supposed cobra bite murders. All motives lead to stealing a supply of radium. 64m/B VHS. Sidney Toler, Benson Fong, Mantan Moreland, Walter Fenner, James B. Cardwell, Joan Barclay, James Flavin; **D:** Phil Karlson. *MGM*

Shanghai Express 🐾🐾🐾½ 1932
Dietrich is at her most alluring in this mystical and exotic story that made legends out of both star and director. Dietrich plays Shanghai Lily, a woman of objectionable reputation, who has a reunion of sorts with ex-lover Brook aboard a slow-moving

train through China. Remade as "Peking Express." Based on a story by Harry Hervey. **80m/B VHS.** Marlene Dietrich, Clive Brook, Anna May Wong, Warner Oland, Eugene Pallette, Lawrence Grant, Louise Closser Hale; *D:* Josef von Sternberg; *W:* Jules Furthman; *C:* Lee Garmes. Academy Awards '32: Best Cinematography; Nominations: Academy Awards '32: Best Director (von Sternberg), Best Picture. *USH, FCT*

The Shanghai Gesture ✍✍½ 1942 A wildly baroque, subversive melodrama. An English financier tries to close a gambling den, only to be blackmailed by the female proprietor—who tells him not only is the man's daughter heavily indebted to her, but that she is the wife he abandoned long ago. Based on a notorious Broadway play. Von Sternberg had to make numerous changes to the script in order to get it past the Hays censors; the director's final Hollywood work, and worthy of his oeuvre, but oddly unsatisfying. **97m/B VHS, LV.** Walter Huston, Gene Tierney, Victor Mature, Ona Munson, Albert Basserman, Eric Blore, Maria Ouspenskaya, Phyllis Brooks, Mike Mazurki; *D:* Josef von Sternberg. Nominations: Academy Awards '42: Best Interior Decoration, Best Original Dramatic/Comedy Score. *MFV*

Shanghai Surprise ✍½ 1986 (PG-13) Tie salesman Penn and missionary Madonna (yeah, right) are better than you'd think, and the story (of opium smuggling in China in the '30s) is intrepid and wildly fun, but indifferently directed and unsure of itself. Executive producer George Harrison wrote the songs and has a cameo. **90m/C VHS, Beta, LV.** Sean Penn, Madonna, Paul Freeman, Richard Griffiths; *Cameos:* George Harrison; *D:* Jim Goddard; *W:* Robert Bentley; *M:* George Harrison, Michael Kamen. Golden Raspberry Awards '86: Worst Actress (Madonna). *ART, VES*

Shanghai Triad ✍✍✍½ 1995 (R) Seventh collaboration of director Yimou and star Li takes place in violent crime dynasty of 1930s Shanghai. Here, eight days are seen through the eyes of a young boy (Cuihua) initiated into the Triad to be the lackey of the mob boss's arrogant mistress (Li). The trio and some trusty associates flee to the country after things heat up with a rival mob. Yimou subtly distinguishes the dichotomy between the jaded criminals and the naive youth with the move from the city to the country and his use of color and tone while avoiding cliche. Plot twists are fresh and technical aspects impeccable. Chinese with subtitles. *CW:* Some language and images of violence. **108m/C VHS, LV.** *FR CH* Gong Li, Li Bao-Tian, Li Xuejian, Shun Chun Shusheng, Wang Xiaoxiao Cuihua, Jiang Baoying; *D:* Zhang Yimou; *W:* Bi Feiyu; *C:* Lu Yue; *M:* Zhang Guangtain. Nominations: Academy Awards '95: Best Cinematography; Golden Globe Awards '96: Best Foreign Film. *COL*

Shanty Tramp ✍ 1967 Small-town tramp puts the moves on an evangelist, a motorcycle gang, and a young black man, who risks his life trying to save her from her loose morals. Another cheesy flick made for the drive-in crowd. **72m/B VHS.** Lee Holland, Bill Rogers, Lawrence Tobin; *D:* Joseph Prieto. *SNC, TPV*

Shao Lin Popeye ✍✍ 1994 A poor, but optimistic school boy has a crush on the principal's daughter. The girl's rich and rowdy boyfriend naturally begins to harass the lovesick lad. Much kicking, punching, and yelling ensues. **m/C VHS.** *CH* Ge-Ying Lin, Shao-Wen Haw, Shiao-Long She. *TPV*

Shaolin Ex-Monk ✍ 1982 Renegade Shaolin Monk is pursued by a Kung Fu master and his disciple. **94m/C VHS, Beta.** John Liu, Ko Shou Liang, Huang Hsing Shaw. *WVE*

Shaolin Executioner ✍ 198? Several generations of Shaolin defend the Shaolin Temple against all high-kicking odds. **104m/C Beta.** Chen Kuan-Tai, Lo Lieh; *D:* Lu Chia-Liang. *NO*

Shaolin Kung Fu Mystagogue ✍ 1984 In this action-packed chop-fest, the mysterious "Floating in Blood" weapon enlivens the battle between the Ching Dynasty and Ming rebels. **90m/C VHS, Beta.** *D:* Chang Peng-I. *NO*

Shaolin Temple Strikes Back ✍ 1972 The protective inhabitants of the Shaolin temple defend themselves against invading Manchu Barbarians. **90m/C VHS, Beta.** Chen Chien Chang, Sho Kosugi, Chang Shan, Lung Fei; *D:* Joseph Kuo. *TWE*

Shaolin Traitor ✍½ 1982 (R) Exotic weapons and dazzling martial-arts action are featured in this exciting tale of intrigue and mystery. **99m/C VHS, Beta.** Carter Wong, Shangkuan Ling-Feng, Lung Chun-Eng, Chang Yi, Lung Fei. *GEM*

Shaolin Vengence ✍½ 1982 Framed for murder and deceived into accepting guilt for the crime, a man does penance in a Shaolin temple. When he learns of the deception, he uses his newly learned Shaolin boxing skills to relentlessly pound the creeps who set him up. **?m/C VHS.** Chen Sing. *MGI*

Shark! ✍½ *Man-Eater; Un Arma de Dos Filos* 1968 (PG) American gun smuggler Reynolds, stranded in a tiny seaport in Africa, joins the crew of a marine biologist's boat. He soon discovers the boat's owner and his wife are trying to retrieve gold bullion that lies deep in shark-infested waters. Typical Reynoldsian action-infested dumbness. Like "Twilight Zone: The Movie," earned notoriety because of on-location tragedy: a stunt diver really was killed by a shark. Edited without the consent of Fuller, who disowned it. **92m/C VHS, Beta.** Burt Reynolds, Barry Sullivan, Arthur Kennedy; *D:* Samuel Fuller; *W:* Samuel Fuller. *REP, MRV*

Shark Hunter ✍ 1984 (PG) Shark hunter gets ensnared in the mob's net off the Mexican coast as they race for a cache of sunken millions. The usual garden-variety B-grade adventure. **95m/C VHS, Beta.** Franco Nero, Jorge Luke, Mike Forrest. *MRV*

Shark River ✍½ 1953 A man attempts to get his brother, a Civil War veteran accused of murder, through the Everglades and send him to safety in Cuba. Good photography of the great swamp; disappointing story. **80m/C VHS, Beta.** Steve Cochran, Carole Mathews, Warren Stevens; *D:* John Rawlins; *W:* Lewis Meltzer, Louis Lantz. *NO*

Sharks' Treasure ✍½ 1975 (PG) A band of escaped convicts commandeer a boat filled with gold. Old fashioned sunken-treasure tale unexceptional except as a virtual one man show by writer/actor/director/producer/fitness nut Wilde. **96m/C VHS, Beta.** Cornel Wilde, Yaphet Kotto, John Nellson, Cliff Osmond, David Canary, David Gilliam; *D:* Cornel Wilde. *MGM*

Sharky's Machine ✍✍½ 1981 (R) A tough undercover cop (Reynolds) is hot on the trail of a crooked crime czar. Meanwhile he falls for a high-priced hooker. Well done but overdone action, with much violence. Based on the William Diehl novel. **119m/C VHS, Beta, LV.** Burt Reynolds, Rachel Ward, Vittorio Gassman, Brian Keith, Charles Durning, Bernie Casey, Richard Libertini, Henry Silva, John Fiedler, Earl Holliman; *D:* Burt Reynolds. *WAR*

Sharma & Beyond ✍ 1984 A teenage would-be science fiction writer falls in love with the daughter of a famous sci-fi author. **85m/C VHS, Beta.** Suzanne Burden, Robert Urquhart, Michael Maloney; *D:* Brian Gilbert; *M:* Rachel Portman. *MGM*

Sharon's Secret ✍✍½ 1995 (R) When the mutilated bodies of wealthy Richard Harly and his wife are discovered, investigating detective Thomas McGregor (Henry) looks to place the blame on their traumatized 16-year-old daughter Sharon (Cameron), who'll inherit a fortune. Psychiatrist Laurel O'Connor (Harris) is assigned to help Sharon recover and she's defended by family lawyer Frank Bowdin (McArthur) but it seems everyone has something to hide. Made for cable. *CW:* Some strong violence. **91m/C VHS, Closed Caption.** Candace Cameron, Mel Harris, Greg Henry, Alex McArthur, Paul Regina, Elaine Kagan, James Pickens Jr.; *D:* Michael Scott; *W:* Mark Homer. *USH*

Sharpe's Battle ✍✍½ 1994 Sharpe (Bean) must prepare the Royal Irish company, led by Lord Kiely (Durr) and used to only ceremonial duties, for their first battle. Meanwhile, Kiely's wife (Byrne) goes to Sharpe for help with a personal matter and there's more trouble with the French. Based on the novel by Bernard Cornwell; made for British TV. **100m/C VHS.** *GB* Sean Bean, Daragh O'Malley, Hugh Fraser, Jason Durr, Allie Byrne; *D:* Tom Clegg; *W:* Russell Lewis. *VCO*

Sharpe's Company ✍✍½ 1994 Sharpe (Bean) sets out to rescue Spanish lover Teresa (Serna) and his infant daughter, trapped in the French-held city of Badajoz, which is about to be stormed by British troops. To make matters worse, Sharpe must also deal with the machinations of underhanded madman Sergeant Obadiah Hakeswill (Postlethwaite), an old enemy with a grudge to settle. Based on the novel by Bernard Cornwell; made for British TV. **100m/C VHS.** *GB* Sean Bean, Assumpta Serna, Daragh O'Malley, Pete Postlethwaite, Hugh Fraser, Clive Francis, Louise Germaine; *D:* Tom Clegg; *W:* Charles Wood. *VCO*

Sharpe's Eagle ✍✍½ 1993 Sharpe (Bean) and his chosen band of sharpshooters are once again in the thick of battle against Napoleon's troops but this time they have the misfortune to be led by the imbecilic Sir Henry Simmerson (Cochrane). Thanks to Simmerson's cowardice, the regimental colors are captured and a heroic officer Sharpe admires is killed. Setting out for revenge, Sharpe is determined to capture the French mascot, a carved golden eagle carried into battle, and settle some personal scores. Based on the novel by Bernard Cornwell; made for British TV. **100m/C VHS.** *GB* Sean Bean, Assumpta Serna, Brian Cox, David Troughton, Daragh O'Malley, Michael Cochrane, Katia Caballero; *D:* Tom Clegg; *W:* Eoghan Harris. *VCO*

Sharpe's Enemy ✍✍½ 1994 Sharpe (Bean) is sent to a mountain stronghold, held by a band of deserters, to ransom Isabella (Hurley), the bride of English colonel, Sir Augustus Farthingdale (Child). But the evil Hakeswill (Postlethwaite) is leading the criminals and he refuses to make things easy for our hero—nor will the French troops leave the English soldiers in peace. Based on the novel by Bernard Cornwell; made for British TV. **100m/C VHS.** *GB* Sean Bean, Assumpta Serna, Pete Postlethwaite, Daragh O'Malley, Hugh Fraser, Elizabeth Hurley, Michael Byrne, Jeremy Child, Nicholas Rowe; *D:* Tom Clegg; *W:* Eoghan Harris. *VCO*

Sharpe's Gold ✍✍½ 1994 Circa 1813 and Richard Sharpe (Bean) has now been promoted to Major—still leading his band of renegade sharpshooters. This time they're assigned to trade rifles for deserters held by the partisans and search for hidden Aztec gold, as Wellington (Fraser) prepares to push on into France. Sharpe must also protect Wellington's cousin Bess (Linehan) and her daughter Ellie (Ashbourne) as they search for Bess' missing husband. Based on the novel by Bernard Cornwell; made for British TV. **100m/C VHS.** *GB* Sean Bean, Daragh O'Malley, Hugh Fraser, Rosaleen Linehan, Jayne Ashbourne, Abel Folk, Peter Eyre; *D:* Tom Clegg; *W:* Nigel Kneale. *VCO*

Sharpe's Honour ✍✍½ 1994 Sharpe (Bean) becomes a pawn of French spy Pierre Ducos when he's forced to cross enemy lines, disguised as a Spanish rebel, in order to defend himself against allegations of dishonor. Sharpe's also unable to resist the attractions of the Marquesa Dorada (Krige), who's also part of Ducos' plan. Based on the novel by Bernard Cornwell; made for British TV. **100m/C VHS.** *GB* Sean Bean, Daragh O'Malley, Alice Krige, Hugh Fraser, Michael Byrne, Ron Cook; *D:* Tom Clegg; *W:* Colin MacDonald. *VCO*

Sharpe's Justice ✍✍½ 1997 Having cleared his name, Richard Sharpe (Bean) returns to England and is ordered north where he's to command the local militia. But Sharpe soon has to decide whether to support the local gentry or the working class in a time of social unrest. Based on the novel by Bernard Cornwell. **100m/C VHS.** *GB* Sean Bean, Daragh O'Malley, Abigail Cruttenden, Alexis Denisof, Douglas Henshall, Caroline Langrishe, Philip Glenister; *D:* Tom Clegg. *VCO*

Sharpe's Legend ♂♂½ 1997 Highlights from the British TV series detailing the life, loves, and career of 19th-century British soldier/hero Richard Sharpe (Bean). Narrated by Rifleman Cooper (Mears). **90m/C VHS.** *GB* Sean Bean, Michael Mears; **D:** Paul Wilmshurst. *VCO*

Sharpe's Mission ♂♂½ 1996 Sharpe (Bean) joins with Colonel Brand (Strong) and his men to blow up an ammunition depot as Wellington continues his invasion of France. But Brand arouses Sharpe's suspicions that the supposedly heroic Colonel is actually a French spy. Based on the novel by Bernard Cornwell. **100m/C VHS.** *GB* Sean Bean, Daragh O'Malley, Hugh Fraser, James Laurenson, Mark Strong, Abigail Cruttenden; **D:** Tom Clegg. *VCO*

Sharpe's Regiment ♂♂½ 1996 Wellington prepares for the invasion of France in June, 1813 but the South Essex batallion needs more men. So Sharpe (Bean) and Harper (O'Malley) are sent back to London for recruits and uncover corruption in high places. Based on the novel by Bernard Cornwell. **100m/C VHS.** *GB* Sean Bean, Daragh O'Malley, Nicholas Farrell, Michael Cochrane, Abigail Cruttenden, Caroline Langrishe, James Laurenson; **D:** Tom Clegg. *VCO*

Sharpe's Revenge . ♂♂½ 1997 The Peninsular War is over but Sharpe (Bean) is accused of stealing Napoleon's treasures by old enemy Ducos. Abandoned by his wife when he's convicted of the crime, Sharpe escapes from prison and crosses postwar France in search of the truth. Based on the novel by Bernard Cornwell. **100m/C VHS.** *GB* Sean Bean, Daragh O'Malley, Abigail Cruttenden, Feodor Atkine, Alexis Denisof, Cecile Paoli, Philip Whitchurch; **D:** Tom Clegg. *VCO*

Sharpe's Rifles ♂♂½ 1993 Swashbuckling heroics dominate as the Duke of Wellington's British soldiers battle Napoleon's French forces in the 1809 Penisular War (fought in Spain and Portugal). Common soldier Richard Sharpe (Bean) has just been promoted and given the unenviable task of leading a group of malcontent sharpshooters on a secret mission to aid Britain's Spanish allies. But it's not all hard times for Sharpe since the Spanish commander happens to be a very lovely woman. Adapted from the novel by Bernard Cornwall; made for British TV. **100m/C VHS.** *GB* Sean Bean, Assumpta Serna, Brian Cox, David Troughton, Daragh O'Malley, Julian Fellowes, Timothy Bentinck, Simon Andreu, Michael Mears, John Tams, Jason Salkey, Paul Trussell; **D:** Tom Clegg; **W:** Eoghan Harris. *VCO*

Sharpe's Siege ♂♂½ 1996 In the winter of 1813, Napoleon Bonaparte sends his best spy, Major Ducos (Atkine), to find out where Wellington plans to invade France. The newly married Sharpe (Bean) is forced to leave his ill wife, Jane (Cruttenden), and capture a French fort while preventing Ducos' treachery. Based on the novel by Bernard Cornwell. **100m/C VHS.** *GB* Sean Bean, Daragh O'Malley, Hugh Fraser, Abigail Cruttenden, James Laurenson, Feodor Atkine; **D:** Tom Clegg. *VCO*

Sharpe's Sword ♂♂½ 1994 Sharpe's (Bean) sent to protect Wellington's top spy, El Mirador, and finds himself up against Napoleon's top swordsman Colonel Leroux (Fierry). When Sharpe's wounded, it's up to Lass (Mortimer), a young mute convent girl, to save our hero's life. Based on the novel by Bernard Cornwell; made for British TV. **100m/C VHS.** *GB* Sean Bean, Daragh O'Malley, Patrick Fierry, Emily Mortimer, John Kavanagh; **D:** Tom Clegg; **W:** Eoghan Harris. *VCO*

Sharpe's Waterloo ♂♂½ 1997 Sharpe's (Bean) making a new life with new love Lucille (Paoli) at their French chateau. But when Napoleon returns from exile, Sharpe returns to the army and the Chosen Men to organize a defense before the battle of Waterloo. Based on the novel by Bernard Cornwell. **100m/C VHS.** *GB* Sean Bean, Daragh O'Malley, Hugh Fraser, Cecile Paoli, Alexis Denisof, Paul Bettany; **D:** Tom Clegg. *VCO*

Shattered ♂♂♂ *Scherben* 1921 Key film in Germany's kammerspiel (chamber play) movement, which emphasized naturalism with a minimum number of characters. A railway worker's daughter is seduced by her father's supervisor. When the man abandons her, the girl's father takes revenge. **62m/B VHS.** *GE* Werner Krauss, Edith Posca, Paul Otto; **D:** Lupu Pick; **W:** Carl Mayer. *FCT*

Shattered ♂½ *Something to Hide* 1972 (R) Finch plays Harry, a man blamed for a failed marriage, held hostage in his home by his own paranoia, and driven to bouts of drinking. Slowly his tenuous grip on sanity slips and at any moment his fragile and crumbling life may be shattered. Tired, overwrought domestic drama. **100m/C VHS, Beta.** *GB* Peter Finch, Shelley Winters, Colin Blakely; **D:** Alastair Reid.

Shattered ♂♂ 1991 (R) An architect recovering from a serious automobile accident tries to regain the memory that he has lost. As he begins to put together the pieces of his life, some parts of the puzzle don't quite fit. For example, he recalls his now loving wife's affair as well as his own. He remembers that he hired a private detective to follow his wife and shockingly, he remembers that he once believed his wife had planned to kill him. Are these memories the real thing, or are they all part of some mad, recuperative nightmare? Who knows. **CW:** Language, violence, and sensuality. **98m/C VHS, Beta, LV, 8mm, Letterbox, Closed Caption.** Tom Berenger, Bob Hoskins, Greta Scacchi, Joanne Whalley, Corbin Bernsen, Theodore Bikel; **D:** Wolfgang Petersen; **W:** Wolfgang Petersen. *MGM*

Shattered Dreams ♂♂½ 1994 TV movie about domestic violence finds Wagner as the battered wife of a prominent, high-profile government official. Based on a true story. **94m/C VHS.** Lindsay Wagner, Michael Nouri. *ART*

Shattered Image ♂♂½ 1993 (R) Confusing thriller about the FBI's involvement in the kidnapping of the owner of a model agency, as well as plastic surgery, and a big money scam. Made for cable TV. **CW:** Language, violence, brief nudity, sex. **100m/C VHS, LV, Closed Caption.** Bo Derek, Jack Scalia, John Savage, Dorian Harewood, Ramon Franco, Carol Lawrence, Michael Harris, David McCallum; **D:** Fritz Kiersch. *THV*

Shattered Silence ♂½ *When Michael Calls* 1971 A woman is tormented by phone calls that seem to be coming from her dead son as her life is torn apart by divorce. Leaves unanswered the question: Will there be any suspense? Made for TV. Worthless and dumb. **73m/C VHS.** Elizabeth Ashley, Ben Gazzara, Michael Douglas, Karen Pearson; **D:** Philip Leacock. *CCB*

Shattered Spirits ♂½ 1991 (PG-13) Quiet family man cracks and goes on a rampage through his normally peaceful suburban neighborhood. Been done before and better. **93m/C VHS.** Martin Sheen, Melinda Dillon, Matthew Laborteaux, Roxana Zal, Lukas Haas. *THV*

Shattered Vows ♂♂ 1984 A young nun struggles with her love for a priest and her desire for a child. Bertinelli is convincing as the confused teen in otherwise ordinary TV drama. Adapted from the true story of Dr. Mary Gilligan Wong as told in her book, "Nun: A Memoir." **95m/C VHS, Beta, Closed Caption.** Valerie Bertinelli, David Morse, Caroline McWilliams, Patricia Neal, Millie Perkins, Leslie Ackerman, Lisa Jane Persky; **D:** Jack Bender.

**The Shawshank
Redemption** ♂♂♂½ 1994 (R) Bank veep Andy (Robbins) is convicted of the murder of his wife and her lover and sentenced to the "toughest prison in the Northeast." While there he forms a friendship with lifer Red (Freeman), experiences the brutality of prison life, adapts, offers financial advice to the guards, and helps the warden (Gunton) cook the prison books...all in a short 19 years. In his debut, director Darabont avoids belaboring most prison movie cliches while Robbins' talent for playing ambiguous characters is put to good use, and Freeman brings his usual grace to what could have been a thankless role. Adapted from the novella "Rita Hayworth and the Shawshank Redemption" by Stephen King. **CW:** Profanity; occasional violence. **142m/C VHS, LV, Closed Caption.** Tim Robbins, Morgan Freeman, Bob Gunton, William Sadler, Clancy Brown, Mark Rolston, Gil Bellows, James Whitmore; **D:** Frank Darabont; **W:** Frank Darabont; **C:** Roger Deakins. Nominations: Academy Awards '94: Best Actor (Freeman), Best Adapted Screenplay, Best Cinematography, Best Film Editing, Best Picture, Best Sound, Best Original Score; Directors Guild of America Awards '94: Best Director (Darabont); Golden Globe Awards '95: Best Actor—Drama (Freeman), Best Screenplay; Screen Actors Guild Award '94: Best Actor (Freeman), Best Actor (Robbins); Writers Guild of America '94: Best Adapted Screenplay. *COL*

She ♂♂½ 1921 H. Rider Haggard's famous story about the ageless Queen Ayesha, (Blythe), who renews her life force periodically by walking through a pillar of cold flame. Story and titles by Haggard. Blythe is a stirringly mean queen, and the story remains fresh and fun. Silent film with music score. **69m/B VHS, Beta.** Betty Blythe, Carlyle Blackwell, Mary Odette. *NOS, VYY, DVT*

She ♂♂ 1935 First sound version of H. Rider Haggard's popular 1887 adventure tale, although the film's location was changed from Africa to the frozen Arctic. Explorers Scott and Bruce are searching for a fire that preserves rather than destroys life. They are captured by a mysterious tribe and discover a living goddess—She-Who-Must-Be-Obeyed (Gahagan)—who bathed in the Flame of Life and is now eternal. She falls for Scott, who doesn't return her love, and there's trouble. Fantastic Art Deco sets and special effects. **95m/B VHS.** Helen Gahagan, Randolph Scott, Nigel Bruce, Helen Mack, Gustav von Seyffertitz; **D:** Irving Pichel, Lansing C. Holden; **W:** Dudley Nichols, Ruth Rose; **C:** J. Roy Hunt; **M:** Max Steiner. *KIV*

S*H*E ♂♂ 1979 A flashy made for TV spy thriller. The female agent S*H*E (Securities Hazards Expert) must save the world's oil; good locations, nifty plot and looker Sharpe as the she-Bond add up to a reasonably fun time. Scripted by "Bond"-writer Maibaum. **100m/C VHS, Beta.** Cornelia Sharpe, Robert Lansing, William Taylor, Isabella Rye, Anita Ekberg; **Cameos:** Omar Sharif; **D:** Robert Lewis; **W:** Richard Maibaum; **M:** Michael Kamen.

She ♂ 1983 A beautiful female warrior rules over the men in a post-holocaust world. She is kidnapped by a wealthy merchant who uses her to fight evil mutants. Utter rubbish vaguely based on the Haggard novel. **90m/C VHS, Beta.** Sandahl Bergman, Harrison Muller, Quin Kessler, David Goss; **D:** Avi Nesher. *ART*

She and He ♂♂½ 1963 Hani's look at the oppression of women, marital and spiritual discontent, and class divisions. Naoko is a bored housewife, living in a sterile high-rise apartment with her equally dissatisfied husband, and yearning for something to express her inner feelings. She accidentally meets an old classmate of her husband's who has become a poor ragpicker and tries to aid him. But all her efforts only lead to further tragedies. In Japanese with English subtitles. **110m/C VHS.** *JP* Sachiko Hidari, Eiji Okada, Kikuji Yamashita; **D:** Susumu Hani. *FCT*

The She-Beast ♂½ *Il Lago di Satana; The Revenge of the Blood Beast; La Sorella di Satan; The Sister of Satan* 1965 Burned at the stake in 18th-century Transylvania, a witch returns in the body of a beautiful young English woman on her honeymoon (in Transylvania?!), and once again wreaks death and destruction. Caution, Barbara Steele fans: she appears for all of 15 minutes. Sporadically funny. **74m/C VHS, Beta.** *IT YU* Barbara Steele, Ian Ogilvy, Mel Welles, Lucretia Love; **D:** Michael Reeves. *SNC, MPI*

She Came on the Bus woof! 1969 Young thugs break into a well-kept suburban home and terrorize the housewife through rape and torture. Then they kidnap a bus and pose as the drivers until they can find more victims. Contains scenes of graphic violence which would be considered offensive even by today's standards. **58m/C VHS. D:** Harry Vincent. *SMW, TPV*

She Came to the Valley 🎬 *Texas in Flames* **1977 (PG)** A tough pioneer woman becomes embroiled in political intrigue during the Spanish-American War. Based on Cleo Dawson's book. **90m/C VHS, Beta.** Ronee Blakley, Dean Stockwell, Scott Glenn, Freddy Fender. *CNG*

She Couldn't Say No 🎬🎬 *Beautiful But Dangerous* **1952** A wealthy oil heiress (Simmons) with good intentions plans to give her money away to those friends who had helped her when she was struggling. Things don't go quite as planned; her philanthropy leads to unexpected mayhem in her Arkansas hometown. Passable, but not memorable comedy. Mitchum as a small-town doctor? **88m/B VHS, Beta.** Robert Mitchum, Jean Simmons, Arthur Hunnicutt, Edgar Buchanan, Wallace Ford; **D:** Lloyd Bacon. *CCB*

She Demons woof! **1958** Pleasure craft loaded with babes crashes into a remote island controlled by a mad ex-Nazi scientist who transforms pretty girls into rubber-faced Frankensteins. Incomprehensible, to say the least. **68m/B VHS, Beta.** Irish McCalla, Tod Griffin, Victor Sen Yung; **D:** Richard Cunha. *RHI, SNC, EEL*

She-Devil 🎬🎬½ **1989 (PG-13)** A comic book version of the acidic Fay Weldon novel "The Life and Loves of a She-Devil"; a fat, dowdy suburban wife (Arnold) becomes a vengeful beast when a smarmy romance novelist steals her husband. Uneven comedic reworking of a distinctly unforgiving feminist fiction. Arnold is given too much to handle (her role requires an actual range of emotions); Streep's role is too slight, though she does great things with it. **100m/C VHS, LV, Closed Caption.** Meryl Streep, Roseanne, Ed Begley Jr., Linda Hunt, Elizabeth Peters, Bryan Larkin, A. Martinez, Sylvia Miles; **D:** Susan Seidelman; **W:** Mark Burns, Barry Strugatz; **M:** Howard Shore. *ORI*

She Devils in Chains 🎬🎬 **19?? (R)** A group of traveling female athletes are kidnapped by a groups of sadists who torture and beat them. In the end, however, the girls get their revenge, and it's bloody. **82m/C VHS.** Colleen Camp, Rosanne Katon, Sylvia Anderson, Ken Washington, Leo Martinez; **D:** Cirio H. Santiago. *SIM*

She-Devils on Wheels woof! **1968** Havoc erupts as an outlaw female motorcycle gang, known as "Maneaters on Motorbikes," terrorizes a town—especially the men. Really, really bad biker flick finely honed by Lewis. **83m/C VHS, Beta.** Betty Connell, Christie Wagner, Pat Poston, Nancy Lee Noble, Ruby Tuesday; **D:** Herschell Gordon Lewis. *VTR*

She Done Him Wrong 🎬🎬🎬 **1933** West stars as Lil, an 1890s saloon singer in the screen version of her Broadway hit "Diamond Lily," and imparts on the negligible plot her usual share of double entendres and racy comments. Grant is likeable as the hapless sap she beds. ♫Silver Threads Among the Gold; Masie, My Pretty Daisy; Easy Rider; I Like a Guy What Takes His Time; Frankie and Johnny. **65m/B VHS, Beta, LV.** Mae West, Cary Grant, Owen Moore, Noah Beery Sr., Gilbert Roland, Louise Beavers; **D:** Lowell Sherman; **C:** Charles B(ryant) Lang. National Film Registry '96;; Nominations: Academy Awards '33: Best Picture.*USH, MLB, BTV*

She-Freak 🎬 *Alley of Nightmares* **1967** Remake of Tod Browning's "Freaks." A cynical waitress burns everyone in a circus and gets mauled by the resident freaks. Pales beside its unacknowledged, classic original. **87m/C VHS, Beta.** Claire Brennan, Lynn Courtney, Bill McKinney, Lee Raymond, Madame Lee; **D:** Byron Mabe. *NO*

She Gods of Shark Reef 🎬 *Shark Reef* **1956** Typical no-budget Corman exploitation tale of two brothers shipwrecked on an island inhabited by beautiful pearl-diving women. Filmed in Hawaii. **63m/C VHS.** Bill Cord, Don Durant, Lisa Montell, Carol Lindsay, Jeanne Gerson; **D:** Roger Corman. *SNC, MRV, HEG*

She Goes to War 🎬🎬 **1929** King's first part-sound effort that takes place in the milieu of WWI. Boardman plays a spoiled rich girl who grows up fast when confronted with the horrors of the frontline while working in a canteen. **50m/B VHS, Beta, 8mm.** Eleanor Boardman, Alma Rubens, Al "Fuzzy" St. John; **D:** Henry King. *NOS, GVV, DVT*

She Likes You, Charlie Brown **1986** Romantic travails for Charlie Brown and the gang. Animated. **41m/C VHS, Beta.** *BAR*

She Must Be Seeing Things 🎬🎬 **1987** Filmmaker Jo (Weaver) is making a picture about a 17th-century woman who lived her life as a man. Jo's lover Agatha (Dabney) becomes disturbed when she reads Jo's diary, learns she's been having affairs with men, and begins to fantasize about Jo's unfaithfulness with the men in her film crew. Agatha's insecurities finally lead her to disguising herself as a man in order to spy on Jo—mirroring what's happening in Jo's film. **95m/C VHS.** Sheila Dabney, Lois Weaver, Kyle DiCamp, John Erdman; **D:** Sheila McLaughlin; **W:** Sheila McLaughlin. *TVC, FRF*

She Shall Have Music 🎬½ **1936** A magnate hires a dance band to broadcast from a cruise ship. Features music by Jack Hylton and his band, one of Britain's most popular orchestras of the 1930s. **76m/B VHS, Beta.** GB Jack Hylton, June Clyde, Claude Dampier, Bryan Lawrence, Gwen Farrar. *EEL*

She Waits 🎬🎬 **1971** When a newlywed couple moves into an old house, the bride becomes possessed by the spirit of her husband's first wife. Unoriginal and mediocre horror. Made for television. **74m/C VHS, Beta.** Dorothy McGuire, Patty Duke, David McCallum; **D:** Delbert Mann.

She Wore a Yellow Ribbon 🎬🎬🎬½ **1949** An undermanned cavalry outpost makes a desperate attempt to repel invading Indians. Wayne shines as an officer who shuns retirement in order to help his comrades. Still fun and compelling. The second chapter in director Ford's noted cavalry trilogy, preceded by "Fort Apache" and followed by "Rio Grande." **93m/C VHS, Beta, LV.** John Wayne, Joanne Dru, John Agar, Ben Johnson, Harry Carey Jr., Victor McLaglen, Mildred Natwick, George O'Brien; **D:** John Ford; **C:** Winton C. Hoch. Academy Awards '49: Best Color Cinematography. *TTC, TLF*

Sheba, Baby 🎬🎬 **1975 (PG)** A female dick (Grier) heads to Louisville where someone is trying to threaten her rich father and his loan company. Oddly non-violent for action-flick vet Grier; poorly written and directed. **90m/C VHS, Beta.** Pam Grier, Rudy Challenger, Austin Stoker, D'Urville Martin, Charles Kissinger; **D:** William Girdler. *ORI, FCT*

Sheena woof! **1984 (PG)** Television sportscaster aids a jungle queen in defending her kingdom from being overthrown by an evil prince. Horrid bubble-gum "action" fantasy. **117m/C VHS, Beta, LV, Closed Caption.** Tanya Roberts, Ted Wass, Donovan Scott, Elizabeth Toro; **D:** John Guillermin; **W:** David Newman; **C:** Pasquale De Santis. *GKK*

The Sheep Has Five Legs 🎬🎬½ **1954** Quintuplet brothers return from around the world for a reunion in their small French village. Fernandel plays the father and all five sons; otherwise, comedy is only average-to-good. In French with English subtitles. **96m/B VHS, Beta, 8mm.** FR Fernandel, Edouard Delmont, Louis de Funes, Paulette Dubost; **D:** Henri Verneuil. Nominations: Academy Awards '55: Best Story. *NOS, DVT, VYY*

Sheer Madness 🎬🎬🎬 **1984** Focuses on the intense friendship between a college professor and a troubled artist, both women. Engrossing and subtle exposition of a relationship. Ambiguous ending underscores film's general excellence. Subtitled. **105m/C VHS, Beta.** GE FR Hanna Schygulla, Angela Winkler; **D:** Margarethe von Trotta; **W:** Margarethe von Trotta; **C:** Michael Ballhaus. *MGM*

The Sheik 🎬🎬🎬 **1921** High camp Valentino has English woman fall hopelessly under the romantic spell of Arab sheik who flares his nostrils. Followed by "Son of the Sheik." **80m/B VHS, Beta.** Agnes Ayres, Rudolph Valentino, Adolphe Menjou, Walter Long, Lucien Littlefield, George Waggner, Patsy Ruth Miller; **D:** George Melford. *PAR, GPV*

She'll Be Wearing Pink Pajamas 🎬🎬 **1984** Eight women volunteer for a rugged survival course to test their mettle. The intense shared experience gives them all food for thought. Well acted from a pretty thin story. **90m/C VHS, Beta.** Julie Walters, Anthony Higgins; **D:** John Goldschmidt; **M:** John Du Prez. *ORI*

The Shell Seekers 🎬🎬½ **1989 (PG)** The widowed Penelope Keeling (Lansbury) is recovering from a heart attack and her three grown children want her to take things easy. But the scare has convinced Penelope to revisit her past and the happiness she once knew. So she returns to her childhood home in Cornwall to see what she can discover. Fine cast in a heart-tugger (with some lovely scenery from Cornwall, England and the island of Ibiza). Adapted from the novel by Rosamunde Pilcher. A Hallmark Hall of Fame presentation. **94m/C VHS, Closed Caption.** GB Angela Lansbury, Sam Wanamaker, Anna Carteret, Michael Gough, Christopher Bowen, Patricia Hodge, Denis Quilley, Sophie Ward, Irene Worth; **D:** Waris Hussein; **W:** John Pielmeier. *REP*

Shell Shock 🎬½ **198?** Four GI's fight off the Germans and the longings for home during WWII. **90m/C VHS, Beta.** **D:** John Hayes. *NO*

Shelley Duvall's Bedtime Stories **1992** A series of stories based on popular children's books, narrated by celebrities. Each tape is available individually and contains at least two stories. Nominated for cable's ACE award and an Emmy award. Originally produced for cable television. **25m/C VHS, LV, Closed Caption.** *USH*

Shelter 🎬🎬 **1998 (R)** ATF agent Martin Roberts (Allen) is set up by his commanding officer and has a bounty on his head. He takes refuge with a crime lord (Onorati) and plans how to get even.*CW:* Violence, and for language and sexuality. **92m/C VHS, DVD.** John Allen Nelson, Brenda Bakke, Peter Onorati, Costas Mandylor, Charles Durning, Linden Ashby, Kurtwood Smith; **D:** Scott Paulin. *STE*

The Sheltering Sky 🎬🎬🎬 **1990 (R)** American couple Winger and Malkovich flee the plasticity of their native land for a trip to the Sahara desert where they hope to renew their spirits and rekindle love. Accompanied by socialite acquaintance Scott with whom Winger soon has an affair, their personalities and belief systems deteriorate as they move through the grave poverty of North Africa in breathtaking heat. Based on the existential novel by American expatriate Paul Bowles who narrates and appears briefly in a bar scene. Overlong but visually stunning, with cinematography by Vittorio Storaro. **139m/C VHS, Beta, LV, Letterbox, Closed Caption.** Debra Winger, John Malkovich, Campbell Scott, Jill Bennett, Timothy Spall, Eric Vu-An, Sotigui Koyate, Amina Annabi, Paul Bowles; **D:** Bernardo Bertolucci; **W:** Mark Peploe, Bernardo Bertolucci; **C:** Vittorio Storaro; **M:** Ryuichi Sakamoto, Richard Horowitz. Golden Globe Awards '91: Best Score; New York Film Critics Awards '90: Best Cinematography. *WAR, FCT, CCB*

Shenandoah 🎬🎬🎬 **1965** A Virginia farmer (Stewart, in a top-notch performance) who has raised six sons and a daughter, tries to remain neutral during the Civil War. War takes its toll as the daughter marries a Confederate soldier and his sons become involved in the fighting. Screen debut for Ross. **105m/C VHS, Beta, LV.** James Stewart, Doug McClure, Glenn Corbett, Patrick Wayne, Rosemary Forsyth, Katharine Ross, George Kennedy; **D:** Andrew V. McLaglen; **C:** William Clothier. Nominations: Academy Awards '65: Best Sound. *USH*

Shep Comes Home ⏱ 1949 Shep the wonder canine accompanies an orphan through the Midwest where he nabs a band of bankrobbers. Sequel to "My Dog Shep." **62m/B VHS, LV.** Robert Lowery, Sheldon Leonard. *NO*

The Shepherd of the Hills ⏱⏱⏱ 1941 Young Ozark mountain moonshiner Matt Matthews (Wayne) vows to one day find and kill the unknown father who deserted his family, leading to the early death of Matt's mother. His hatred is so strong that his girlfriend Sammy (Field) refuses to marry him because of it. Then a stranger, Daniel Howitt (Carey Sr.), comes to town and his kind deeds have everyone calling him "The Shepherd." Even Matt warms to the man—until he discovers that Howitt is his father. Based on the novel by Harold Bell Wright. **89m/B VHS.** John Wayne, Harry Carey Sr., Betty Field, Beulah Bondi, James Barton, Marjorie Main, Ward Bond, Fuzzy Knight; *D:* Henry Hathaway; *W:* Grover Jones, Stuart Anthony; *C:* Charles Lang Jr., William Howard Greene; *M:* Gerard Carbonara. *USH*

Sheriff of Tombstone ⏱⏱½ 1941 Trouble begins when a "judge" takes a sharpshooter in a poker game. **60m/B VHS, Beta.** Roy Rogers. *NOS, DVT, RXM*

Sherlock Holmes and the Deadly Necklace ⏱⏱½ *Sherlock Holmes Und Das Halsband des Todes; Valley of Fear* 1962 Once again, Holmes and Watson are up against the evil nemesis Moriarty. This time, Moriarty wants to get his hands on a necklace stolen from Cleopatra's tomb. Not only does Scotland Yard not consider him a suspect, they seek his advice. Enter Holmes and Watson, and the game's afoot. The offbeat casting and direction help make this one of the odder versions of Conan Doyle's work. **84m/B VHS.** *GE* Christopher Lee, Senta Berger, Hans Sohnker, Hans Nielsen, Ivan Desny, Leon Askin, Thorley Walters; *D:* Terence Fisher. *NOS, SNC*

Sherlock Holmes and the Incident at Victoria Falls ⏱⏱½ *Incident at Victoria Falls* 1991 A substandard Holmes excursion brings the Baker Street sleuth out of retirement to transport the world's largest diamond from Africa to London. The resulting mystery involves Teddy Roosevelt, the inventor of radio, and poor plotting. **120m/C VHS.** *GB* Christopher Lee, Patrick Macnee, Jenny Seagrove; *D:* Bill Corcoran. *VES*

Sherlock Holmes and the Secret Weapon ⏱⏱⏱ *Secret Weapon* 1942 Based on "The Dancing Men" by Sir Arthur Conan Doyle. Holmes battles the evil Moriarty in an effort to save the British war effort. Good Holmes mystery with gripping wartime setting. Hoey is fun as bumbling Inspector Lestrade. Available colorized. **68m/B VHS, LV, Closed Caption.** Basil Rathbone, Nigel Bruce, Karen Verne, William Post Jr., Dennis Hoey, Holmes Herbert, Mary Gordon, Henry Victor, Philip Van Zandt, George Eldridge, Leslie Denison, James Craven, Paul Fix, Hugh Herbert, Lionel Atwill; *D:* Roy William Neill. *REP, AOV, MRV*

Sherlock Holmes Faces Death ⏱⏱⏱ 1943 Dead bodies are accumulating in a mansion where the detecting duo are staying. Underground tunnels, life-size dress boards, and unanswered mysteries... Top-notch Holmes. Peter Lawford appears briefly as a sailor. Also available with "Hound of the Baskervilles" on Laser Disc. **68m/B VHS, Beta, LV, Closed Caption.** Basil Rathbone, Nigel Bruce, Hillary Brooke, Milburn Stone, Halliwell Hobbes, Arthur Margetson, Gavin Muir; *D:* Roy William Neill. *FOX*

Sherlock Holmes in Washington ⏱⏱½ 1943 A top-secret agent is murdered; seems it's those blasted Nazis again! Holmes and Watson rush off to Washington, D.C. to solve the crime and to save some vitally important microfilm. Heavily flag-waving Rathbone-Bruce episode. Dr. Watson is dumbfounded by bubble gum. **71m/B VHS, Beta, Closed Caption.** Basil Rathbone, Nigel Bruce, Henry Daniell, George Zucco, Marjorie Lord, John Archer; *D:* Roy William Neill. *FOX*

Sherlock Holmes: The Master Blackmailer ⏱⏱⏱ 1992 Brett returns as the super-sleuth, along with sidekick Dr. Watson, in a tale which has the detective working against the evil scheming of London's most cunning and ruthless blackmailer. When Holmes disguises himself to enter the blackmailer's lair he even finds himself attracting the romantic attentions of a young lady. Based on the story "The Adventure of Charles Augustus Milverton" by Arthur Conan Doyle. Made for television. **120m/C VHS.** *GB* Jeremy Brett, Edward Hardwicke, Robert Hardy. *MPI, SIG*

Sherlock Holmes: The Sign of Four ⏱⏱ 1984 Sherlock Holmes must find the man who murdered Bartholomew Sholto with a poison dart in the neck. **48m/C VHS, Beta.** *V:* Peter O'Toole. *PMS, PAR*

Sherlock Holmes: The Silver Blaze ⏱½ 1941 Sherlock Holmes mystery about the theft of a racehorse known as "The Silver Blaze." Remade in 1977. **70m/B VHS, Beta.** Arthur Wontner, Ian Fleming, Lyn Harding. *NOS, BAR, EEL*

Sherlock Holmes: The Voice of Terror ⏱⏱½ 1942 Holmes and Watson try to decode German radio messages during WWII. First Rathbone-as-Holmes effort for Universal, and first in which we are asked to believe the Victorian sleuth and his hairdo could have lived in this century. Patriotic and all that—and lots of fun. **65m/B VHS, Beta, LV, Closed Caption.** Basil Rathbone, Nigel Bruce, Hillary Brooke, Reginald Denny, Evelyn Ankers, Montagu Love; *D:* John Rawlins. *FOX*

Sherlock Hound: Tales of Mystery 1990 Sherlock, Watson and Moriarty are all dogs in this animated children's adaptation of the popular Arthur Conan Doyle stories. Well worth a howl. **115m/C VHS, Beta.** *JFK*

Sherlock: Undercover Dog ⏱⏱½ 1994 (PG) Billy (Eroen) arrives on Catalina island to spend the summer with his father, an eccentric inventor. He makes a human friend in Emma (Cameron) and a canine companion in Sherlock, a police dog who's able to talk but naturally only to the two kids. Seems Sherlock's policeman master has been kidnapped by bumbling smugglers and its up to the trio to come to the rescue. **80m/C VHS, Closed Caption.** Benjamin Eroen, Brynne Cameron, Anthony Simmons, Margy Moore, Barry Philips; *D:* Richard Harding Gardner; *W:* Richard Harding Gardner; *M:* Lou Forestieri. *COL*

Sherlock's Rivals & Where's My Wife ⏱½ 1927 Double feature includes a detective movie in which two used car dealers become amateur sleuths and a comedy in which a man has a hard time enjoying his weekend at a seashore resort. **53m/B VHS, Beta.** Milburn Morante, Monty Banks. *VYY*

Sherman's March: An Improbable Search for Love 1986 McElwee's "epic" which was originally planned as a historical documentary about General Sherman's catastrophic march through the South, ends up being about the filmmaker himself, and his disastrous quest for love. When his girlfriend dumps him, he puts Sherman's story aside and films his own battle for romance, which includes help from his meddling family. The melodramatic women he meets and the neurotic energy of McElwee make this a very funny, uncensored film. **155m/C VHS.** *D:* Ross McElwee; *W:* Ross McElwee. *FRF*

She's a Good Skate, Charlie Brown 1980 Snoopy becomes Peppermint Patty's ice-skating coach, and he helps her train for the local competition. **30m/C VHS, Beta, Closed Caption.** *D:* Phil Roman. *VTR, HSE*

She's Back ⏱½ 1988 (R) Murderee Fisher pesters hubby Joy from beyond the grave to avenge her death at the hands of a motorcycle gang. Uneven, but occasionally funny. **89m/C VHS, Beta, LV.** Carrie Fisher, Robert Joy; *D:* Tim Kincaid. *VES, ART*

She's Dressed to Kill ⏱⏱ *Someone's Killing the World's Greatest Models* 1979 Beautiful models are turning up dead during a famous designer's comeback attempt at a mountain retreat. Who could be behind these grisly deeds? Suspenseful in a made for TV kind of way, but not memorable. **100m/C VHS.** Eleanor Parker, Jessica Walter, John Rubinstein, Connie Sellecca; *D:* Gus Trikonis. *ART*

She's Gotta Have It ⏱⏱⏱ 1986 (R) Lee wrote, directed, edited, produced and starred in this romantic comedy about an independent-minded black girl in Brooklyn and the three men and one woman who compete for her attention. Full of rough edges, but vigorous, confident, and hip. Filmed entirely in black and white except for one memorable scene. Put Lee on the film-making map. **84m/B VHS, Beta, LV, Closed Caption.** Tracy C. Johns, Spike Lee, Tommy Redmond Hicks, Raye Dowell, John Canada Terrell, Joie Lee, Epatha Merkinson, Bill Lee, Cheryl Burr, Aaron Dugger, Stephanie Covington, Renata Cobbs, Cheryl Singleton, Monty Ross, Lewis Jordan, Erik Dellums, Reginald Hudlin, Eric Payne, Marcus Turner, Gerard Brown, Ernest R. Dickerson; *D:* Spike Lee; *W:* Spike Lee; *C:* Ernest R. Dickerson; *M:* Bill Lee. Independent Spirit Awards '87: Best First Feature. *FOX, FCT*

She's Having a Baby ⏱⏱½ 1988 (PG-13) Newlyweds Bacon and McGovern tread the marital waters with some difficulty, when news of an impending baby further complicates their lives. Told from Bacon's viewpoint as the tortured young writer/husband, who wonders if the yuppie life they lead is trapping him. Hughes' first venture into the adult world isn't as satisfying as his teen angst flicks, although the charming leads help. Major drawbacks are the arguably sexist premise and dull resolution. Great soundtrack; observant viewers will notice the beemer's license plate is the title's acronym: "SHAB." **106m/C VHS, Beta, LV, 8mm, Closed Caption.** Kevin Bacon, Elizabeth McGovern, William Windom, Paul Gleason, Alec Baldwin, Cathryn Damon, Holland Taylor, James Ray, Isabel Lorca, Dennis Dugan, Edie McClurg, John Ashton; *D:* John Hughes; *W:* John Hughes; *M:* Stewart Copeland. *PAR*

She's in the Army Now ⏱ 1981 Farce about military life. Two bubble-headed females undergo basic training. Made for TV "Private Benjamin" ripoff was meant as a series pilot. **97m/C VHS, Beta.** Jamie Lee Curtis, Kathleen Quinlan, Melanie Griffith, Susan Blanchard, Julie Carmen, Janet MacLachlan; *D:* Hy Averback; *M:* Artie Butler. *NLC*

She's Out of Control ⏱½ 1989 Dad Danza goes nuts when teen daughter Dolenz (real-life daughter of Monkee Mickey Dolenz) takes the advice of Dad's girlfriend on how to attract boys. Formulaic plot could almost be an episode of "Who's the Boss?" Danza is appealing, but not enough to keep this one afloat. **95m/C VHS, Beta, LV, 8mm, Closed Caption.** Tony Danza, Catherine Hicks, Wallace Shawn, Dick O'Neill; *D:* Stan Dragoti; *M:* Alan Silvestri. *COL*

She's So Lovely ⏱⏱½ *She's De Lovely; Call It Love* 1997 (R) Troubled young alcoholic Eddie (Penn) disappears for three days on his pregnant wife Maureen (Wright), and returns to discover that she has been brutalized by a neighbor. Retaliation costs him 10 years in a mental institution. Upon his release, Eddie decides to find his now ex-wife and the daughter he's never known. Maureen's moved on—she's happily married to Joey (Travolta), has two daughters by him, and is justifiable worried that Eddie's love (which is as strong as ever) will upset the balance of her new life. Somewhat unevenly directed by Nick Cassavetes from a screenplay written by his late father John, who had already cast Penn and was set to direct when he became ill. Film revels in the style that made the elder Cassavetes famous (or infamous), and is best appreciated as a tribute. Travolta and Penn play well off each other.*CW:* Strong language and some violence. **97m/C VHS, LV, Closed Caption.** Sean Penn, Robin Wright Penn, John Travolta, Harry Dean Stanton, Debi Mazar, James Gandolfini, Gena Rowlands, Kelsey Mulrooney; *D:* Nick Cassavetes;

W: John Cassavetes; **C:** Thierry Arbogast; **M:** Joseph Vitarelli. Cannes Film Festival '97: Best Actor (Penn); Nominations: Screen Actors Guild Award '97: Best Actress (Wright Penn). *TOU*

She's the One 𝗜𝗜½ 1996 (R)
Another Irish family saga from Burns covering lots of the same territory as "The Brothers McMullen." Semi-slacker taxi driver Mickey Fitzpatrick (Burns) impulsively marries passenger Hope (Bahns) and their romance is contrasted with the disintegrating marriage of Mickey's younger brother, buttoned-down stockbroker Francis (McGlone) and his frustrated wife Rene (Aniston). No wonder she's frustrated, Francis is having an affair with slutty Heather (Diaz), who turns out to be Mickey's former flame. Mahoney offers a typically fine performance, along with bad marital advice as the boys' father. Again the blustering men don't have a clue about the usually smarter women. *CW:* Language, including sex-related dialogue. **95m/C VHS, LV, Closed Caption.** Edward Burns, Mike McGlone, Jennifer Aniston, Cameron Diaz, Maxine Bahns, John Mahoney, Leslie Mann, George McCowan, Amanda Peet, Anita Gillette, Frank Vincent; **D:** Edward Burns; **W:** Edward Burns; **C:** Frank Prinzi; **M:** Tom Petty. *FXV*

Shifting Sands 1918
Compelling film tells the tale of a young girl looking to be a successful artist. Her landlord makes constant overtures towards her. She refuses, so he has her thrown in jail for prostitution as an act of revenge. She fears her past may prevent her from obtaining true love. **52m/B VHS, Beta, 8mm.** Gloria Swanson, Joe King, Lillian Langdon. *GPV, YYY, GVV*

Shiloh 𝗜𝗜½ 1997 (PG)
Schmaltzy but redeeming story about small town West Virginia 11-year-old Marty (Heron), who seeks to rescue and care for mistreated hunting dog Shiloh, who belongs to mean hermit Judd (Wilson). Goes beyond the typical "boy and his dog" theme with moral and ethical issues that Marty faces when he takes the dog from its owner. Frannie (who plays Shiloh) is a very cute and expressive beagle. Adapted from the Newberry award-winning novel by Phyllis Reynolds Naylor. **93m/C VHS, Closed Caption.** Blake Heron, Michael Moriarty, Scott Wilson, Rod Steiger, Ann Dowd, Bonnie Bartlett; **D:** Dale Rosenbloom; **W:** Dale Rosenbloom; **C:** Frank Byers; **M:** Joel Goldsmith. *WAR*

Shin Heike Monogatari 𝗜𝗜𝗜𝗜
New Tales of the Taira Clan 1955 Mizoguchi's second to last film, in which a deposed Japanese emperor in 1137 endeavors to win back the throne from the current despot, who cannot handle the feudal lawlessness. Acclaimed; his second film in color. In Japanese with English subtitles. **106m/C VHS, Beta.** *JP* Raizo Ichikawa, Ichijiro Oya, Michiyo Kogure, Eijiro Yanagi, Tatsuya Ishiguro, Yoshiko Kuga; **D:** Kenji Mizoguchi. *FCT*

Shinbone Alley 1970 (G)
Animated musical about Archy, a free-verse poet reincarnated as a cockroach, and Mehitabel, the alley cat with a zest for life. Based on the short stories by Don Marquis. **83m/C VHS, Beta.** **D:** John D. Wilson; **W:** Carol Channing, Eddie Bracken, John Carradine, Alan Reed. *GEM, KAR, HHE*

Shine 𝗜𝗜𝗜½ 1995 (PG-13)
Astonishing true portrayal of musical genius and its cost. Teenaged pianist David Helfgott (Taylor) is a prodigy in his native Australia but is pushed to the limit by his authoritarian father Peter (Mueller-Stahl). Eventually defying his father's strictures, David accepts a scholarship to London's Royal College of Music where he triumphs under the tutelage of professor Cecil Parkes (Gielgud), but then collapses from strain. For 15 years, he is confined to psychiatric hospitals, unable to play the piano, until the now-adult David (Rush) has a chance meeting with the loving Gillian (Redgrave), whose support enables him to resume his career. Helfgott himself plays piano for his screen counterparts. *CW:* Nudity/sensuality and intense thematic elements. **105m/C VHS, LV, Closed Caption, DVD.** *AU* Geoffrey Rush, Noah Taylor, Armin Mueller-Stahl, Lynn

Redgrave, John Gielgud, Googie Withers, Chris Haywood, Sonia Todd, Alex Rafalowicz; **D:** Scott Hicks; **W:** Jan Sardi; **C:** Geoffrey Simpson; **M:** David Hirschfelder. Academy Awards '96: Best Actor (Rush); Australian Film Institute '96: Best Actor (Rush), Best Cinematography, Best Director (Hicks), Best Film, Best Film Editing, Best Original Screenplay, Best Sound, Best Supporting Actor (Mueller-Stahl), Best Score; British Academy Awards '96: Best Actor (Rush); Golden Globe Awards '97: Best Actor—Drama (Rush); Los Angeles Film Critics Association Awards '96: Best Actor (Rush); National Board of Review Awards '96: Best Film; New York Film Critics Awards '96: Best Actor (Rush); Screen Actors Guild Award '96: Best Actor (Rush); Broadcast Film Critics Association Awards '96: Best Actor (Rush); Nominations: Academy Awards '96: Best Director (Hicks), Best Film Editing, Best Original Screenplay, Best Picture, Best Supporting Actor (Mueller-Stahl), Best Original Dramatic/Comedy Score; Australian Film Institute '96: Best Actor (Taylor); British Academy Awards '96: Best Director (Hicks), Best Film, Best Original Screenplay, Best Supporting Actor (Gielgud), Best Supporting Actress (Redgrave); Directors Guild of America Awards '96: Best Director (Hicks); Golden Globe Awards '97: Best Director (Hicks), Best Film—Drama, Best Screenplay, Best Score; Screen Actors Guild Award '96: Best Supporting Actor (Taylor); Cast; Writers Guild of America '96: Best Original Screenplay. *NLC*

Shine on, Harvest Moon 𝗜𝗜 1938
Rogers brings a band of outlaws to justice and clears an old man suspected of being their accomplice. Title bears no relation to storyline. **60m/B VHS, Beta.** Roy Rogers, Lynn (Mary Hart) Roberts, Stanley Andrews; **D:** Joseph Kane. *NOS, VYY, VDM*

The Shining 𝗜𝗜𝗜½ 1980 (R)
Very loose adaptation of the Stephen King horror novel about a writer and his family, snowbound in a huge hotel, who experience various hauntings caused by either the hotel itself or the writer's dementia. Technically stunning, and pretty dang scary, but too long, pretentious and implausible. Nicholson is excellent as the failed writer gone off the deep end. **143m/C VHS, Beta, LV, Closed Caption.** Jack Nicholson, Shelley Duvall, Danny Lloyd, Scatman Crothers, Joe Turkel, Barry Nelson, Philip Stone, Lia Beldam, Billie Gibson, Barry Dennan, David Baxt, Lisa Burns, Alison Coleridge, Kate Phelps, Anne Jackson, Tony Burton; **D:** Stanley Kubrick; **W:** Stanley Kubrick, Diane Johnson; **C:** John Alcott. *WAR*

The Shining Hour 𝗜𝗜½ 1938
A compelling melodrama in which Crawford portrays a New York night club dancer who is pursued by the rather conservative Douglas. His brother tries to persuade him from marrying Crawford, but then he soon finds himself attracted to her. A devastating fire wipes out all problems of family dissension in this intelligent soap opera. **76m/B VHS, Closed Caption.** Joan Crawford, Margaret Sullavan, Melvyn Douglas, Robert Young, Fay Bainter, Allyn Joslyn; **D:** Frank Borzage; **W:** Ogden Nash, Jane Murfin. *MGM*

A Shining Season 𝗜𝗜𝗜 1979
Tearjerker about a potential-packed long-distance runner, John Baker, stricken with cancer. He spends his last year training a girls' track team to a championship. Earnest, well-performed and involving. Based on a true story. Made for TV. **100m/C VHS, Beta.** Timothy Bottoms, Rip Torn, Allyn Ann McLerie, Ed Begley Jr., Benjamin Bottoms, Mason Adams, Constance Forslund, Ellen Geer; **D:** Stuart Margolin; **M:** Richard Bellis. *BTV*

Shining Star 𝗜½
That's the Way of the World 1975 (PG) A recording company is run by the mob. Potentially interesting film is hampered by quality of sound and photography and general lack of purpose or direction. **100m/C VHS.** Harvey Keitel, Ed Nelson, Cynthia Bostick, Bert Parks; **D:** Sig Shore. *ART*

Shining Through 𝗜𝗜 1992 (R)
Baby-voiced Griffith as a spy sent behind enemy lines without training? Douglas as a spy sent behind enemy lines without speaking German? Old-fashioned blend of romance, espionage, and derring-do where noble hero saves spunky heroine from nasty Nazis in WWII Germany works despite thin plot. Series of flash-forwards to an aged Griffith is annoying and tends to stop action cold, but every-

one tries hard and period flavor is authentic. Adapted from best-selling Susan Isaacs novel, but bears little resemblance to book. *CW:* Sensual scene. **133m/C VHS, Closed Caption.** Michael Douglas, Melanie Griffith, Liam Neeson, Joely Richardson, John Gielgud, Francis Guinan, Patrick Winczewski, Sylvia Syms; **D:** David Seltzer; **W:** David Seltzer; **C:** Jan De Bont; **M:** Michael Kamen. Golden Raspberry Awards '92: Worst Picture, Worst Actress (Griffith), Worst Director (Seltzer). *FXV*

Shinobi Ninja 𝗜 1984
Last-surviving member of Koga ninja clan returns to Japan from U.S. to save his homeland from enemy ninja clan. Mediocre pseudo ninja antics. Badly dubbed. **103m/C VHS, Beta.** *JP* Tadashi Yamashita, Eric Lee, Karen Lee Sheperd.

Shiokari Pass 𝗜𝗜 1977
A man has a divine revelation at the pass. In Japanese with English subtitles. **60m/C VHS.** *JP* **D:** Novuru Nakamuru. *REP, VBL*

Ship Ahoy 𝗜𝗜½ 1942
Songs, comedy, a spy spoof, and some patriotism thrown in for good measure. Powell plays a dancer who works with Tommy Dorsey and his orchestra. They're on their way to Puerto Rico, via ocean liner, along with her pulp fiction writer boyfriend (Skelton). Emery, posing as an FBI man, convinces Powell to smuggle a package for him but he's really a spy and the whole thing's a con which turns out to be based on one of Skelton's potboiler plots. An uncredited Frank Sinatra is the singer with the Dorsey band, along with drummer Buddy Rich and trumpeter Ziggy Elman who provide some great musical solos. ♫ Last Call For Love; Poor You; On Moonlight Bay; Tampico; I'll Take Tallulah; Cape Dance; Ship Ahoy. **95m/B VHS.** Eleanor Powell, Red Skelton, Bert Lahr, Virginia O'Brien, John Emery, William Post Jr.; **D:** Edward Buzzell; **W:** Harry Kurnitz, Harry Clork, Irving Brecher. *MGM*

Ship of Fools 𝗜𝗜𝗜 1965
A group of passengers sailing to Germany in the '30s find mutual needs and concerns, struggle with early evidence of Nazi racism, and discover love on their voyage. Twisted story and fine acting maintain interest. Appropriate tunes written by Ernest Gold. Based on the Katherine Ann Porter novel. Leigh's last film role; she died two years later. Kramer grapples with civil rights issues in much of his work. **149m/B VHS, Beta, LV, Closed Caption.** Vivien Leigh, Simone Signoret, Jose Ferrer, Lee Marvin, Oskar Werner, Michael Dunn, Elizabeth Ashley, George Segal, Jose Greco, Charles Korvin, Heinz Ruehmann; **D:** Stanley Kramer; **W:** Abby Mann; **C:** Ernest Laszlo; **M:** Ernest Gold. Academy Awards '65: Best Art Direction/Set Decoration (B & W), Best Black and White Cinematography; National Board of Review Awards '65: Best Actor (Marvin); New York Film Critics Awards '65: Best Actor (Werner); Nominations: Academy Awards '65: Best Actor (Werner), Best Actress (Signoret), Best Adapted Screenplay, Best Costume Design (B & W), Best Picture, Best Supporting Actor (Dunn). *COL, SWC*

Ships in the Night 𝗜𝗜 1928
Logan is the plucky heroine who is searching for her missing brother who has been captured by pirates. She is aided in her search by handsome hero Mower. **86m/B VHS, Beta.** Frank Moran, Jacqueline Logan, Jack Mower, Andy Clyde. *GVV, FCT, GPV*

Shipwreck Island 𝗜𝗜 1961
Eight boys are shipwrecked on a deserted island, then make their way to another island where they must survive against wild animals and the elements for two years. **93m/C VHS.** *HTV, FCT*

Shipwrecked 𝗜𝗜½
Haakon Haakonsen 1990 (PG) Kiddie swashbuckler based on the 1873 popular novel "Haakon Haakonsen." A cabin boy is marooned on an island where he defends the hidden pirate treasure he finds by boobytrapping the island. **93m/C VHS, LV, Letterbox, Closed Caption.** *NO* Gabriel Byrne, Stian Smestad, Louisa Haigh, Trond Munch, Bjorn Sundquist, Eva Von Hanno, Kjell Stormoen; **D:** Nils Gaup; **W:** Nick Thiel, Nils Gaup; **M:** Patrick Doyle. *TOU*

Shirley Temple Festival 1933 A collection of four Shirley Temple short subjects from the 30s: "Dora's Dunkin Doughnuts," "Pardon My Pups," "War Babies" and "Kid N' Africa." 55m/B VHS, Beta. Shirley Temple, Andy Clyde. MRV

Shirley Valentine ♂♂♂ 1989 A lively middle-aged English housewife gets a new lease on life when she travels to Greece without her husband. Collins reprises her London and Broadway stage triumph. The character frequently addresses the audience directly to explain her thoughts and feelings; her energy and spunk carry the day. Good script by Russell from his play. From the people who brought us "Educating Rita." 108m/C VHS, LV, 8mm, Closed Caption. GB Pauline Collins, Tom Conti, Alison Steadman, Julia McKenzie, Joanna Lumley, Bernard Hill, Sylvia Syms; D: Lewis Gilbert; W: George Hadjinassios, Willy Russell; M: Willy Russell. British Academy Awards '89: Best Actress (Collins); Nominations: Academy Awards '89: Best Actress (Collins), Best Song ("The Girl Who Used to Be Me"). PAR, TVC, HMV

The Shock ♂♂½ 1923 Crippled low-life Chaney becomes restored spiritually by a small-town girl and rebels against his Chinese boss. This causes an unfortunate string of melodramatic tragedies, including the San Francisco earthquake of 1906. Silent. Odd, desultory tale with bad special effects is worth seeing for Chaney's good acting. 96m/B VHS, Beta. Lon Chaney Sr., Virginia Valli; D: Lambert Hillyer. SNC, NOS, HEG

Shock! ♂♂ 1946 A psychiatrist is called on to treat a woman on the edge of a nervous breakdown. He then discovers she saw him murder his wife, and tries to keep her from remembering it. Interesting premise handled in trite B style. Price's first starring role. 70m/B VHS, Beta. Vincent Price, Lynn Bari, Frank Latimore, Anabel Shaw; D: Alfred Werker. SNC, NOS, BAR

Shock Corridor ♂♂♂ 1963 A reporter, dreaming of a Pulitzer Prize, fakes mental illness and gets admitted to an asylum, where he hopes to investigate a murder. He is subjected to disturbing experiences, including shock therapy, and does manage to solve the murder. However, he suffers a mental breakdown in the process and is admitted for real. Disturbing and lurid. 101m/B VHS, LV, Letterbox. Peter Breck, Constance Towers, Gene Evans, Hari Rhodes, James Best, Philip Ahn; D: Samuel Fuller; W: Samuel Fuller. National Film Registry '96. HMV, CRC

Shock 'Em Dead ♂♂ 1990 (R) A devil worshipper trades his life to Lucifer for a chance at rock and roll fame and beautiful Miss Lords. Sexy thriller, with a good share of violence and tension. Ironically, ex porn great Lords is one of the few starlets who doesn't disrobe in the film. 94m/C VHS, LV. Traci Lords, Aldo Ray, Troy Donahue, Stephen Quadros, Tim Moffett, Karen Russell, Gina Parks, Laurel Wiley, Tyger Sodipe; D: Mark Freed; W: Andrew Cross, Mark Freed, Dave Tedder; C: Ron Chapman.

Shock! Shock! Shock! ♂ 1987 Another low-budget slasher flick, with a homicidal lunatic wielding a butcher knife. Space alien jewel thieves add an element, for what it's worth. Makes one ponder the cosmic question: What's the diff between a bad slasher flick and a spoof of a bad slasher flick? Whichever this one is, it's really bad! 60m/B VHS, Beta. Brad Issac, Cady McCrossen, Allen Rickman, Brian Fuorry; D: Todd Rutt, Arn McConnell. RHI, MWF

A Shock to the System ♂♂♂ 1990 (R) Business exec. Caine is passed over for a long-deserved promotion in favor of a younger man. When he accidentally pushes a panhandler in front of a subway in a fit of rage, he realizes how easy murder is and thinks it may be the answer to all his problems. Tries to be a satire take on corporate greed, etc., but somehow loses steam. Excellent cast makes the difference; Caine adds class. Based on the novel by Simon Brett. 88m/C VHS, Beta, LV, Closed Caption. Michael Caine, Elizabeth McGovern, Peter Riegert, Swoosie Kurtz,

Will Patton, Jenny Wright, John McMartin, Barbara Baxley; D: Jan Egleson; W: Andrew Klavan; M: Gary Chang. HBO

Shock Treatment ♂½ Traitement de Choc 1981 (PG) Seldom-seen mediocre semi-sequel to the cult classic, "The Rocky Horror Picture Show" (1975). Brad and Janet, now married and portrayed by different leads, find themselves trapped on a TV gameshow full of weirdos. Same writers, same director, and several original cast members do make an appearance. 94m/C VHS, Beta, Closed Caption. Richard O'Brien, Jessica Harper, Cliff DeYoung, Patricia Quinn, Charles Gray, Ruby Wax; D: Jim Sharman. FOX

Shock Waves ♂♂ Death Corps; Almost Human 1977 (PG) Group of mutant-underwater-zombie-Nazi-soldiers terrorizes stranded tourists staying at a deserted motel on a small island. Cushing is the mad scientist intent on recreating the Nazi glory days with the seaweed-attired zombies. Odd B-grade, more or less standard horror flick somehow rises (slightly) above badness. Halpin's name was erroneously listed as Halprin—even on the original movie poster! 90m/C VHS, Beta. Peter Cushing, Brooke Adams, John Carradine, Luke Halpin, Jack Davidson, Fred Buch; D: Ken Wiederhorn; W: Ken Wiederhorn, John Kent Harrison; C: Reuben Trane; M: Richard Einhorn.

Shocker ♂♂½ 1989 (R) Another Craven gore-fest. A condemned serial killer is transformed into a menacing electrical force after being fried in the chair. Practically a remake of Craven's original "Nightmare on Elm Street." Great special effects, a few enjoyable weird and sick moments. What's Dr. Timothy Leary doing here? 111m/C VHS, Beta, LV, Closed Caption. Michael Murphy, Peter Berg, Cami Cooper, Mitch Pileggi, Richard Price, Timothy Leary, Heather Langenkamp, Theodore (Ted) Raimi, Richard Brooks, Sam Scarber; D: Wes Craven; W: Wes Craven; C: Jacques Haitkin; M: William Goldstein. USH

Shocking Asia ♂½ 1975 For the eye-covering delight of Western audiences, Mr. Fox compiles gruesome Asian oddities. 94m/C VHS, Beta. GE D: Emerson Fox. HHE

The Shoes of the Fisherman ♂♂½ 1968 (G) Morris West's interesting, speculative best seller about Russian Pope brought to the big screen at much expense, but with little care or thought. Siberian prison-camp vet Quinn, elected Pope, tries to arrest nuclear war. Director Anderson wasted the prodigious talents of Olivier, Gielgud, et al. Sloppy use of good cast and promising plot. 160m/C VHS, Beta, LV, Letterbox. Anthony Quinn, Leo McKern, Laurence Olivier, John Gielgud, Vittorio De Sica, Oskar Werner, David Janssen; D: Michael Anderson Sr.; M: Alex North. Golden Globe Awards '69: Best Score; National Board of Review Awards '68: Best Supporting Actor (McKern); Nominations: Academy Awards '68: Best Art Direction/Set Decoration, Best Original Score. MGM, FCT

Shoeshine ♂♂♂♂ 1947 Two shoeshine boys struggling to survive in post-war Italy become involved in the black market and are eventually caught and imprisoned. Prison scenes detail the sense of abandonment and tragedy that destroys their friendship. A rich, sad achievement in neo-realistic drama. In Italian with English subtitles. 90m/B VHS, Beta. IT Franco Interlenghi, Rinaldo Smordoni, Anniello Mele, Bruno Ortensi, Pacifico Astrologo; D: Vittorio De Sica; W: Cesare Zavattini, Sergio Amidei, Adolfo Franci, C.G. Viola. Nominations: Academy Awards '47: Best Original Screenplay. FCT

Shogun ♂♂♂½ James Clavell's Shogun 1980 Television miniseries chronicling the saga of a shipwrecked English navigator who becomes the first Shogun, or Samurai warrior chief, from the Western world. Colorfully adapted from the James Clavell bestseller. Also released in a two-hour version, but this full-length version is infinitely better. 550m/C VHS, Beta, LV. Richard Chamberlain, Toshiro Mifune, Yoko Shimada, John Rhys-Davies, Damien Thomas; D: Jerry London; M: Maurice Jarre. PAR

Shogun Assassin ♂♂½ 1980 (R) Story of a proud samurai named Lone Wolf who served his Shogun master well as the Official Decapitator, until the fateful day when the aging Shogun turned against him. Extremely violent, with record-breaking body counts. Edited from two other movies in a Japanese series called "Sword of Vengeance"; a tour de force of the cutting room. The samurai pushes his son's stroller through much of the film-sets it aside to hack and slash. 89m/C VHS, Beta, LV. JP Tomisaburo Wakayama; D: Kenji Misumi, Robert Houston. USH, OM

Shogun's Ninja ♂½ 1983 In 16th-century Japan, an age-old rivalry between two ninja clans sparks a search for a dagger which will lead to one clan's hidden gold. Martial arts performed and directed by Sonny Chiba. In Japanese with usual poor English dubbing. 115m/C VHS, Beta. Henry Sanada, Sue Shiomi, Sonny Chiba; D: Noribumi Suzuki.

Shoot ♂ 1985 (R) Five hunting buddies fall prey to a group of crazed killers after one man is shot by accident. What's the message: Anti-gun? Anti-hunting? Silly, unbelievable, irresponsibly moralistic, and gratuitously violent. 98m/C VHS, Beta. CA Ernest Borgnine, Cliff Robertson, Henry Silva, Helen Shaver; D: Harvey Hart.

Shoot ♂♂ 1992 (R) Photographer Katie Tracy goes undercover to expose an illegal gambling ring fronted by an exotic nightclub. The latest gambling stakes involve the Emperor's pearls, offered in a private auction which could turn deadly, especially when Katie gets involved with the group's handsome ringleader. 90m/C VHS. Dedee Pfeiffer, Miles O'Keeffe, Christopher Atkins; D: Hugh Parks. TRI, TPV

Shoot It Black, Shoot It Blue ♂½ 1974 Rogue cop shoots a black purse snatcher and thinks he has gotten away with it. Unknown to him, a witness has filmed the incident and turns the evidence over to a lawyer. 93m/C VHS, Beta. Michael Moriarty. NO

Shoot Loud, Louder, I Don't Understand! ♂½ Spara Forte, Piu Forte...Non Capisco 1966 A sculptor who has a hard time separating reality from dreams thinks he witnessed a murder. Shenanigans follow. Meant to be a black comedy, but when not dull, it is confusing. Welch looks good, as usual, but doesn't show acting talent here. In Italian with English subtitles. 101m/C VHS, Beta. IT Marcello Mastroianni, Raquel Welch; D: Eduardo de Filippo; M: Nino Rota. NLC

Shoot the Living, Pray for the Dead ♂ 1973 While travelling through Mexico, the leader of a band of killers promises his guide half of a share in stolen gold if he can lead them to it. 90m/C VHS, Beta. Klaus Kinski. CNG

Shoot the Moon ♂♂½ 1982 (R) A successful writer, married and with four children, finds his life unrewarding and leaves his family to take up with a younger woman. The wife must learn to deal with her resentment, the fears of her children, and her own attempt at a new love. Fine acting but a worn-out story. 124m/C VHS, Beta, LV. Diane Keaton, Albert Finney, Karen Allen, Peter Weller, Dana Hill, Viveka Davis, Tracey Gold, Tina Yothers; D: Alan Parker; W: Bo Goldman. MGM

Shoot the Piano Player ♂♂♂♂ Tirez sur le Pianiste; Shoot the Pianist 1962 Former concert pianist (Aznavour, spendidly cast) changes his name and plays piano at a low-class Paris cafe. A convoluted plot ensues; he becomes involved with gangsters, though his girlfriend wants him to try a comeback. Lots of atmosphere, character development, humor, and romance. A Truffaut masterpiece based on a pulp novel by David Goodis. In French with English subtitles. 92m/B VHS, Beta, LV, Letterbox. FR Charles Aznavour, Marie DuBois, Nicole Berger, Michele Mercier, Albert Remy; D: Francois Truffaut; W: Marcel Moussey, Francois Truffaut; M: Georges Delerue. HMV, HHT, WFV

Shoot the Sun Down 𝄞½ 1981 (PG)
Four offbeat characters united in a search for gold turn against each other. "Gilligan's Island"-style assortment of characters (Indian; gunfighter; girl; sea captain) are cast away in a pointless plot from which they never escape. Too bad: talented cast could have done better. 102m/C VHS, Beta. Christopher Walken, Margot Kidder, Geoffrey Lewis, Bo Brundin, Sacheen Little Feather; *D:* David Leeds. *NO*

Shoot to Kill 𝄞𝄞½ 1947 B-grade noir-esque mystery about a crooked D.A. and a gangster who bite the dust. Suspenseful, dark, street-level crime drama uncovered by ambitious journalist Ward. 64m/B VHS, Beta, LV. Russell Wade, Susan Walters, Nestor Paiva, Edmund MacDonald, Vince Barnett; *D:* William (Lester Williams) Berke. *SNC, VYY*

Shoot to Kill 𝄞𝄞𝄞 1988 (R) A city cop (Poitier, better than ever after 10 years off the screen) and a mountain guide (Berenger) reluctantly join forces to capture a killer who is part of a hunting party traversing the Pacific Northwest and which is being led by the guide's unsuspecting girlfriend (Alley). Poitier may be a bit old for the role, but he carries the implausible plot on the strength of his performance. Good action. 110m/C VHS, Closed Caption. Sidney Poitier, Tom Berenger, Kirstie Alley, Clancy Brown, Richard Masur, Andrew (Andy) Robinson, Frederick Coffin, Andrew (Andy) Robinson, Kevin Scannell; *D:* Roger Spottiswoode; *W:* Michael Burton, Harv Zimmel, Dan Petrie Jr.; *C:* Michael Chapman; *M:* John Scott. *TOU*

Shoot to Kill 𝄞𝄞 *Disparen a Matar* 1990 An innocent young man is murdered during a police round-up while his mother watches helplessly. The police try a whitewash—proclaiming the victim a criminal—but she launches a long campaign for justice. Spanish with subtitles. 90m/C VHS. *VZ D:* Carlos Azpurua. *FCT*

Shooters 𝄞 1989 A wacky platoon of misfits is paired off against a group of vicious killers in a "war game" training session. Not completely unfunny or worthless. 84m/C VHS, Beta. Ben Schick, Robin Sims, Aldo Ray.

Shootfighter 2: Kill or Be Killed! 𝄞½ 1996 (R) The Miami underworld is placed on alert when a police chief, seeking to avenge the death of his son, joins with a martial arts master to recruit and train a group of fighters. Then they'll infiltrate the illegal spectator games of to-the-death-combat and see what mayhem they can cause.*CW:* Non-stop violence, a sex scene and some language. 90m/C VHS, LV, Closed Caption. Bolo Yeung, Michael Bernardo, William Zabka; *D:* Paul Ziller; *W:* Peter Shaner, Greg Mellott. *COL*

Shootfighter: Fight to the Death 𝄞½ 1993 (R) Two boys become experts in the martial arts and constant rivals. Now grown-up they take their rivalry to a deadly level in a "shootfight," a game which has no rules and is so brutal it's banned as a sport. Not that this stops them. An unrated version is also available.*CW:* Strong martial arts violence. 94m/C VHS, LV, Closed Caption. Bolo Yeung, Martin Kove, William Zabka, Michael Bernardo, Maryam D'Abo, Edward Albert; *D:* Patrick Allen; *W:* Judd B. Lynn, Larry Feliz Jr., Peter Shaner. *COL*

The Shooting 𝄞𝄞𝄞 1966 A mysterious woman, bent on revenge, persuades a former bounty hunter and his partner to escort her across the desert, with tragic results. Offbeat, small film filled strong by performances of Nicholson and Oates. Filmed concurrently with "Ride in the Whirlwind," with the same cast and director. Bang-up surprise ending. 82m/C VHS, Beta, LV. Warren Oates, Millie Perkins, Jack Nicholson, Will Hutchins; *D:* Monte Hellman. *DVT, HHT, WFV*

Shooting 𝄞 1982 Three boys run away when they think they have killed a man in a hunting accident. 60m/C VHS, Beta. Lynn Redgrave, Lance Kerwin, Barry Primus. *NO*

Shooting Elizabeth 𝄞½ 1992 (PG-13) A fed-up husband decides to shut his loudmouthed wife up—permanently. Only before he can kill her, she disappears. The police don't buy it and want to charge him with murder. Can he find his wife before things really get serious?*CW:* Brief nudity and drug use. 96m/C VHS, LV. Jeff Goldblum, Mimi Rogers; *D:* Baz Taylor. *ART*

Shooting Fish 𝄞𝄞½ 1998 (PG) London con-artists Dylan (Futterman) and Jez (Townsend) hire perky temp Georgie (Beckinsale) to lend an air of authenticity to one of their scams. She charms them both, while figuring out that they're not the legit businessmen they pretend to be. When one of their scams goes awry, landing them in prison, Georgie helps them out. All the while, she's trying to figure out a way to save her retarded brother's home from her greedy fiance. Breezy, fun comedy benefits from great chemistry between the likable leads, but suffers from plot overload near the end. 109m/C VHS. *GB* Dan Futterman, Stuart Townsend, Kate Beckinsale, Dominic Mafham, Claire Cox, Nickolas Grace, Peter Capaldi, Annette Crosbie, Jane Lapotaire; *D:* Stefan Schwartz; *W:* Stefan Schwartz, Richard Holmes; *C:* Henry Braham; *M:* Stanislas Syrewicz. *NYR*

The Shooting Party 𝄞𝄞½ 1977 Told in flashbacks, a story of a crime of passion, an innocent man, and guilty secrets. A magistrate cannot admit his love for a woodsman's daughter so she falls in love in a loveless marriage and a decadent affair. In a fit of passion, the magistrate kills her and then decides to prosecute her innocent husband for the crime. Based on a story by Chekhov. In Russian with English subtitles. 105m/C VHS. *RU* Oleg Yankovsky, Galina Belyayeva; *D:* Emil Loteanu. *CVC, FCT*

The Shooting Party 𝄞𝄞𝄞½ 1985 A group of English aristocrats assemble at a nobleman's house for a bird shoot on the eve of WWI. Splendid cast crowned Mason, in his last role. Fascinating crucible class anxieties, rich with social scheming, personality conflicts, and things left unsaid. Adapted from Isabel Colegate's novel. 97m/C VHS, Beta. *GB* James Mason, Dorothy Tutin, Edward Fox, John Gielgud, Robert Hardy, Cheryl Campbell, Judi Bowker; *D:* Alan Bridges; *W:* Julian Bond. Los Angeles Film Critics Association Awards '85: Best Supporting Actor (Gielgud); National Society of Film Critics Awards '85: Best Supporting Actor (Gielgud).*NO*

Shooting Stars 𝄞 1985 Two actors who play private eyes on television are pushed out of their jobs by a jealous co-star. They take to the streets as "real" crime-fighting dicks. Interesting premise goes nowhere. Made for TV. 96m/C VHS, Beta. Billy Dee Williams, Parker Stevenson, Efrem Zimbalist Jr., Edie Adams; *D:* Richard Lang.

The Shootist 𝄞𝄞𝄞½ 1976 (PG) Wayne, in a supporting last role, plays a legendary gunslinger afflicted with cancer who seeks peace and solace in his final days. Town bad guys Boone and O'Brian aren't about to let him rest and are determined to gun him down to avenge past deeds. One of Wayne's best and most dignified performances about living up to a personal code of honor. Stewart and Bacall head excellent supporting cast. Based on Glendon Swarthout's novel. 100m/C VHS, Beta, LV. John Wayne, Lauren Bacall, Ron Howard, James Stewart, Richard Boone, Hugh O'Brian, Bill McKinney, Harry (Henry) Morgan, John Carradine, Sheree North, Scatman Crothers; *D:* Donald Siegel; *C:* Bruce Surtees; *M:* Elmer Bernstein. Nominations: Academy Awards '76: Best Art Direction/Set Decoration. *PAR, TLF*

Shop Angel 𝄞𝄞 1932 A department store dress designer encounters romance and scandal in this low-budget drama of intrigue and romance. She falls in love with the fiance of her boss's daughter, and schemes to blackmail him (the boss). Competently rendered if unexceptional tale. 66m/B VHS, Beta, 8mm. Marion Shilling, Holmes Herbert, Creighton Hale; *D:* E. Mason Hopper. *VYY*

The Shop Around the Corner 𝄞𝄞𝄞½ 1940 A low-key romantic classic in which Stewart and Sullavan are feuding clerks in a small Budapest shop, who unknowingly fall in love via a lonely hearts club. Charming portrayal of ordinary people in ordinary situations. Adapted from the Nikolaus Laszlo's play "Parfumerie." Later made into a musical called "In the Good Old Summertime" and, on Broadway, "She Loves Me." 99m/B VHS, LV, Closed Caption. Margaret Sullavan, James Stewart, Frank Morgan, Joseph Schildkraut, Sara Haden, Felix Bressart, Charles Halton; *D:* Ernst Lubitsch; *C:* William H. Daniels. *MGM*

The Shop on Main Street 𝄞𝄞𝄞𝄞
The Shop on High Street; Obch Od Na Korze 1965 During WWII, a Slovak takes a job as an "Aryan comptroller" for a Jewish-owned button shop. The owner is an old deaf woman; they slowly build a friendship. Tragedy ensues when all of the town's Jews are to be deported. Sensitive and subtle. Surely among the most gutwrenching portrayals of human tragedy ever on screen. Exquisite plotting and direction. In Czechoslovakian with English subtitles. 111m/B VHS, LV. *CZ* Ida Kaminska, Josef Kroner, Hana Slivkoua, Frantisek Holly, Martin Gregor; *D:* Jan Kadar, Elmar Klos. Academy Awards '65: Best Foreign Language Film; New York Film Critics Awards '66: Best Foreign Film; Nominations: Academy Awards '66: Best Actress (Kaminska). *COL, SWC, HMV*

Shopping 𝄞𝄞½ 1993 (R) A crumbling British industrial city (filmed at London's docklands) is the bleak setting for gangs of aimless youth who steal cars, crash into the windows of various shops, grab whatever comes to hand, and then lead the police on high-speed chases. Adrenaline junkie Billy (Law) is accompanied by thrill-seeking girlfriend Jo (Frost) on one such escapade while fending off rival Tommy (Pertwee), who doesn't like his burgeoning criminal empire disturbed. Tries too hard for that rebel youth feeling.*CW:* Violence/mayhem, pervasive language and some drug content. 86m/C VHS. *GB* Jude Law, Sadie Frost, Sean Pertwee, Fraser James, Sean Bean, Marianne Faithfull, Jonathan Pryce, Danny Newman; *D:* Paul Anderson; *W:* Paul Anderson; *C:* Tony Imi; *M:* Barrington Pheloung. *NHO*

Shopworn Angel 𝄞𝄞𝄞 1938 Weepy melodrama about a sophisticated actress who leads on a naive Texas soldier who's in New York prior to being shipped out for WWI duty. Later, just before she goes on stage, she learns he's been killed at the front. She rallys to sing "Pack Up your Troubles in Your Old Kit Bag and Smile, Smile, Smile." Lots of tears. Adapted from the story "Private Pettigrew's Girl" by Dana Burnet. This remake of the same-titled 1929 film considerably softened the characters. Remade again in 1959 as "That Kind of Woman." 85m/B VHS. Margaret Sullavan, James Stewart, Walter Pidgeon, Nat Pendleton, Alan Curtis, Sam Levene, Hattie McDaniel, Charley Grapewin, Charles D. Brown; *D:* H.C. Potter; *W:* Waldo Salt; *C:* Joseph Ruttenberg. *MGM, MOV*

Shore Leave 𝄞𝄞𝄞 1925 Dressmaker Mackaill isn't getting any younger. Tough-guy sailor Bilge Smith (Barthelmess, in top form) meets her on shore leave; little does he realize her plans for him! She owns a dry-docked ship, you see, and it (and she) will be ready for him when he comes ashore next. Lovely, fun (if rather plodding) romantic comedy. Later made into musicals twice, as "Hit the Deck" and "Follow the Fleet." 74m/B VHS. Richard Barthelmess, Dorothy Mackaill; *D:* John S. Robertson. *GPV, GVV, VYY*

Short Circuit 𝄞𝄞 1986 (PG) A newly developed robot designed for the military is hit by lightning and begins to think it's alive. Sheedy and Guttenberg help it hide from the mean people at the weapons lab who want to take it home. Followed two years later, save Sheedy and Guttenberg, by the lame "Short Circuit 2." 98m/C VHS, Beta, LV, Closed Caption. Steve Guttenberg, Ally Sheedy, Austin Pendleton, Fisher Stevens, Brian McNamara; *D:*

John Badham; **W:** S.S. Wilson, Brent Maddock; **M:** David Shire. *FOX*

Short Circuit 2 ⅕ 1988 (PG) A sequel to the first adorable-robot-outwits-bad-guys tale. The robot, Number Five, makes his way through numerous plot turns without much human assistance or much purpose. Harmless (unless you have to spend time watching it), but pointless and juvenile. Very occasional genuinely funny moments. 95m/C VHS, Beta, LV, Closed Caption. Fisher Stevens, Cynthia Gibb, Michael McKean, Jack Weston, David Hemblen; **D:** Kenneth Johnson; **W:** S.S. Wilson, Brent Maddock; **M:** Charles Fox. *COL*

Short Cuts ⅞⅞⅞½ 1993 (R) Multi-storied, fish-eyed look at American culture with some 22 characters intersecting—profoundly or fleetingly—through each other's lives. Running the emotional gamut from disturbing to humorous, Altman's portrait of the contemporary human condition is nevertheless fascinating. Based on nine stories and a prose poem by Raymond Carver. Available on laserdisc in a movie-only edition or a special edition.**CW:** Graphic sexual language and nudity. 189m/C VHS, LV, Closed Caption. Annie Ross, Lori Singer, Jennifer Jason Leigh, Tim Robbins, Madeleine Stowe, Frances McDormand, Peter Gallagher, Lily Tomlin, Tom Waits, Bruce Davison, Andie MacDowell, Jack Lemmon, Lyle Lovett, Fred Ward, Buck Henry, Huey Lewis, Matthew Modine, Anne Archer, Julianne Moore, Lili Taylor, Christopher Penn, Robert Downey Jr., Jarrett Lennon, Zane Cassidy; **D:** Robert Altman; **W:** Frank Barhydt, Robert Altman; **M:** Mark Isham. Independent Spirit Awards '94: Best Director (Altman), Best Film, Best Screenplay; National Society of Film Critics Awards '93: Best Supporting Actress (Stowe); Venice Film Festival '93: Best Film; Nominations: Academy Awards '93: Best Director (Altman); Golden Globe Awards '94: Best Screenplay; Independent Spirit Awards '94: Best Supporting Actress (Moore). *COL*

Short Eyes ⅞⅞⅞½ *The Slammer* 1979 (R) When a child molester (Davison) enters prison, the inmates act out their own form of revenge against him. Filmed on location at New York City's Men's House of Detention, nicknamed "The Tombs." Script by Manuel Pinero from his excellent play; he also acts in the film. Top-notch performances and respectful direction from Young bring unsparingly realistic prison drama to the screen. Title is prison jargon for child molester. 100m/C VHS, Beta. Bruce Davison, Miguel Pinero, Nathan George, Donald Blakely, Curtis Mayfield, Jose Perez, Shawn Elliott; **D:** Robert M. Young. *ART*

Short Fuse ⅞½ *Good to Go* 1988 (R) A Washington, D.C. reporter uncovers the truth behind the rape and murder of a nurse. Interesting "go-go" music from the Washington D.C. ghetto aids an otherwise uninteresting film. 91m/C VHS, Beta. Art Garfunkel, Robert DoQui, Harris Yulin, Richard Brooks, Reginald Daughtry; **D:** Blaine Novak. *THV*

Short Time ⅞⅞⅞ 1990 (PG-13) Somewhere between "Tango & Cash" and "Airplane" is where you'll find "Short Time." Non-stop action/comedy stars Dabney Coleman and Teri Garr as partners in crime and humor. Coleman is a cop days from retirement; wrongly told he is dying, he tries hard to get killed so his family will be provided for. Coleman is wonderful. Garr, no longer the long-suffering wife of "Oh, God" and "Close Encounters," is appealing here as the indulgent sidekick. 100m/C VHS, LV, Closed Caption. Dabney Coleman, Teri Garr, Matt Frewer, Barry Corbin, Joe Pantoliano, Xander Berkeley, Rob Roy, Kaj-Erik Eriksen; **D:** Gregg Champion; **W:** John Blumenthal, Michael Berry; **M:** Ira Newborn. *IME, ART*

The Shot ⅞⅞½ 1996 Shot in 14 days for $40,000 (and sometimes showing it), this independent release follows out-of-work actors Dern Reel (Bell) and Patrick St. Patrick (Rivkin) as they try to break into the movie business. The foil for the two sensitive artist-types is the shallow but successful director David Egoman. Offended by his brainless action movies, the duo decide to "kidnap" the only print of his latest epic. Although production values are low and the sound is a bit

dicey, indie fans will probably like this depiction of Hollywood's shady side. Gained some publicity when ten reels of Kevin Spacey's "Albino Alligator" were swiped from an airport baggage claim shortly after its release. 84m/C VHS. Dan Bell, Michael Rivkin, Mo Gaffney, Michael DeLuise, Vincent Ward, Jack Kehler, Theodore (Ted) Raimi, Jude Horowitz; **Cameos:** Dana Carvey; **D:** Dan Bell; **W:** Dan Bell; **C:** Alan Caudillo; **M:** Dan Sonis. *PZA*

A Shot in the Dark ⅞½ 1933 A minister suspects murder when a despised miser is thought to have committed suicide. He takes it on himself to investigate in this routine mystery. 53m/B VHS, Beta. GB Dorothy Boyd, O.B. Clarence, Jack Hawkins, Russell Thorndike, Michael Shepley; **D:** George Pearson. *SNC*

A Shot in the Dark ⅞⅞ 1935 When his son is murdered at a New England college, a distraught dad takes it on himself to investigate. Movie cowboy Starrett plays the sleuthing pop in this undistinguished mystery. 69m/B VHS, Beta. Charles Starrett, Robert Warwick, Edward Van Sloan, Marion Shilling, Doris Lloyd, Helen Jerome Eddy, James Bush; **D:** Charles Lamont. *NOS, SNC*

A Shot in the Dark ⅞⅞⅞½ 1964 Second and possibly the best in the classic "Inspector Clouseau-Pink Panther" series of comedies. The bumbling Inspector Clouseau (Sellers, of course) investigates the case of a parlor maid (Sommer) accused of murdering her lover. Clouseau's libido convinces him she's innocent,even though all the clues point to her. Classic gags, wonderful music. After this film, Sellers as Clouseau disappears until 1975's "Return of the Pink Panther" (Alan Arkin played him in "Inspector Clouseau," made in 1968 by different folks). 101m/C VHS, Beta, LV, Letterbox. Peter Sellers, Elke Sommer, Herbert Lom, George Sanders, Bryan Forbes; **D:** Blake Edwards; **W:** William Peter Blatty, Blake Edwards; **M:** Henry Mancini. *FOX, FCT*

Shotgun ⅞⅞½ 1955 A sheriff on the trail of a killer is accompanied by a girl he's saved from Indians. Average western cowritten by western actor Rory Calhoun, who had hoped to star in the film, but was turned down by the studio. 81m/C VHS. Sterling Hayden, Zachary Scott, Yvonne De Carlo; **D:** Lesley Selander; **C:** Ellsworth Fredericks. *PAR*

The Shout ⅞⅞⅞ 1978 (R) From a strange Robert Graves story, an even stranger film. A lunatic befriends a young couple, moves in with them, and gradually takes over their lives. The movie's title refers to the man's ability to kill by shouting, a power he learned from his Australian aboriginal past. 88m/C VHS, Beta. GB Alan Bates, Susannah York, John Hurt, Tim Curry; **D:** Jerzy Skolimowski; **W:** Michael Austin; **M:** Tony Banks. Cannes Film Festival '78: Grand Jury Prize. *COL*

Shout ⅞⅞ 1991 (PG-13) Romance and rebellion set in a sleepy Texas town during the 1950s. Jesse Tucker's (Walters) rebellious ways land him in the Benedict Home for Boys and he seems lost until Jack Cabe (Travolta) enters town. Jack introduces Jesse and the gang to the exciting new sounds of rock 'n' roll. Been done before and better. 93m/C VHS, Beta, LV, Closed Caption. John Travolta, James Walters, Heather Graham, Richard Jordan, Linda Fiorentino, Scott Coffey; **D:** Jeffrey Hornaday; **C:** Robert Brinkmann; **M:** Randy Edelman. *USH*

Shout at the Devil ⅞½ 1976 (PG) English officer Moore and Irish-American adventurer Marvin seek to blow up a German battleship out for repairs in East Africa before the outbreak of WWI. There's also some intrigue about ivory smuggling. From the novel by Wilbur Smith and based on an actual incident, but that doesn't make the comedy adventure any more palatable. Marvin's hamming is ludicrous, Moore is unusually wooden, and the big budget permits any number of fairly pointless action-oriented excursions and explosions. 128m/C VHS, Beta, LV. GB Lee Marvin, Roger Moore, Barbara Parkins, Ian Holm; **D:** Peter Hunt; **M:** Maurice Jarre. *ART, VES*

The Show ⅞⅞ 1995 (R) Choppy and incoherent behind-the-scenes look at the attitude and people who make up the explosive hip-hop and rap scene. Mixes black and white concert footage and interviews with Russell Simmons, LL Cool J and Snoop Doggy Dogg, who discuss their music and fans. Will be a disappointment for those looking for a more in-depth study of the music, as this exercise merely scratches the surface. Includes an abundance of cameos from today's top hip hop artists such as Notorious B.I.G., Naughty by Nature and Wu-Tang Clan.**CW:** Pervasive strong language and some drug content. 90m/B VHS, LV, Closed Caption. Craig Mack, Dr. Dre, Run DMC, Slick Rick, Warren G, Kurtis Blow; **D:** Brian Robbins; **C:** Larry Banks, Steven Consentino, Ericson Core, John L. Demps Jr., Todd A. Dos Reis. *COL*

Show Boat ⅞⅞⅞⅞ 1936 The second of three film versions of the Jerome Kern/Oscar Hammerstein musical (based on the Edna Ferber novel), filmed previously in 1929, about a Mississippi showboat and the life and loves of its denizens. Wonderful romance, unforgettable music. Director Whale also brought the world "Frankenstein." The laser edition includes a historical audio essay by Miles Kreuger, excerpts from the 1929 version, Ziegfeld's 1932 stage revival, "Life Aboard a Real Showboat" (a vintage short), radio broadcasts, and a 300-photo essay tracing the history of showboats. Remade 15 years later. ♫Ol' Man River; Ah Still Suits Me; Bill; Can't Help Lovin' Dat Man; Only Make Believe; I Have the Room Above Her; You Are Love; Gallivantin' Around; Cotton Blossom. 110m/B VHS, Beta, LV. Irene Dunne, Allan Jones, Paul Robeson, Helen Morgan, Hattie McDaniel, Charles Winninger, Donald Cook, Bobs Watson; **D:** James Whale; **W:** Oscar Hammerstein; **M:** Oscar Hammerstein, Jerome Kern. National Film Registry '96. *MGM, CRC, MLB*

Show Boat ⅞⅞½ 1951 Third movie version of the 1927 musical about the life and loves of a Mississippi riverboat theatre troupe. Terrific musical numbers, with fun dance routines from Champion, who went on to great fame as a choreographer. Grayson is somewhat vapid, but lovely to look at and hear. Gardner didn't want to do the part of Julie, although she eventually received fabulous reviews—her singing was dubbed by Annette Warren. The 171-foot "Cotton Blossom" boat was built on the Tarzan lake on the MGM back lot at an astounding cost of $126,468.00. Warfield's film debut—his "Ole Man River"—was recorded in one take. Laserdisc version features the original motion picture trailer, excerpts from "Broadway," "Silent Film," and radio Version of "Show Boat," a documentary featuring life on a real show boat, and a commentary on the performers, the film, and the history of show boats. ♫Make Believe; Can't Help Lovin' Dat Man; I Might Fall Back On You; Ol' Man River; You Are Love; Why Do I Love You?; Bill; Life Upon the Wicked Stage; After the Ball. 115m/C VHS, Beta, LV. Kathryn Grayson, Howard Keel, Ava Gardner, William Warfield, Joe E. Brown, Agnes Moorehead, Gower Champion; **D:** George Sidney; **C:** Charles Rosher; **M:** Jerome Kern, Oscar Hammerstein. Nominations: Academy Awards '51: Best Color Cinematography, Scoring of a Musical. *MGM, TLF, CRC*

Show Business ⅞⅞⅞ 1944 Historically valuable film record of classic vaudeville acts, especially Cantor and Davis. A number of vaudevillians recreate their old acts for director Marin—unforgettable slapstick and songs. All this pegged on a plot that follows Cantor's rise to fame with the Ziegfeld Follies. ♫Alabamy Bound; I Want a Girl (Just Like the Girl Who Married Dear Old Dad); It Had to Be You; Makin' Whoopee; Why Am I Blue; They're Wearing 'Em Higher in Hawaii; The Curse of an Aching Heart; While Strolling in the Park One Day; You May Not Remember. 92m/B VHS, Beta, LV. Eddie Cantor, Joan Davis, George Murphy; **D:** Edwin L. Marin. *CCB, TTC*

A Show of Force ♫♫ 1990 (R) Reporter Irving investigates the coverup of a murder with political ramifications. Brazilian director Barreto cast (surprise!) his girlfriend in the lead; she doesn't exactly carry the day. Phillips is good, but you'll end up feeling cheated if you expect to see much of highly billed Duvall or Garcia. Based on a real incident of 1978, but hardly believable as political realism or even moralism. 93m/C VHS, Beta, LV, Closed Caption. Erik Estrada, Amy Irving, Andy Garcia, Robert Duvall, Lou Diamond Phillips; D: Bruno Barreto; W: Evan Jones; M: Georges Delerue. PAR

The Show-Off ♫½ 1946 Aubrey Piper (Skelton) has big dreams which far out weigh his modest talents. He tells outlandish tales to impress girlfriend Amy (Maxwell) and schemes to make them come true. Dated material which even gifted comedian Skelton can't rescue. Adapted from a play by George Kelly and previously filmed in 1926, 1929, and 1934. 83m/B VHS, Beta. Red Skelton, Marilyn Maxwell, Marjorie Main, Virginia O'Brien, Eddie Anderson, George Cleveland, Leon Ames, Marshall Thompson, Jacqueline White, Lila Leeds, Emory Parnell; D: Harry Beaumont; W: George Wells. MGM, FCT

Show People ♫♫♫ 1928 A pretty girl from the boonies tries to make it big in Tinseltown. But as a slapstick star?! She wanted to be a leading lady! Enjoyable, fun silent comedy shows Davies's true talents. Interesting star cameos, including director Vidor at the end. 82m/B VHS. Marion Davies, William Haines, Dell Henderson, Paul Ralli, William S. Hart, Rod La Rocque; Cameos: King Vidor; D: King Vidor. MGM

Show Them No Mercy ♫♫♫ Tainted Money 1935 A couple and their baby out for a drive unwittingly stumble into a kidnapping that doesn't go as planned. Tense gangster drama reincarnated as the Western "Rawhide." 76m/B VHS. Rochelle Hudson, Cesar Romero, Bruce Cabot, Edward Norris, Edward Brophy, Warren Hymer, Herbert Rawlinson; D: George Marshall. FOX, FCT

The Showdown ♫♫ 1940 The title actually refers to a tricky poker game, the highlight of yet another Hopalong Cassidy versus hoss thieves quickie epic. Kermit Maynard is the brother of cowboy hero Ken Maynard. 65m/B VHS. William Boyd, Russell Hayden, Britt Wood, Morris Ankrum, Jan Clayton, Roy Barcroft, Kermit Maynard; D: Howard Bretherton. NOS

The Showdown ♫♫½ 1950 Elliott plays trail boss Shad Jones who knows one of his fellow cowhands has murdered his brother. Jones is determined to find out who it is and even the score. Brennan is cast against type as a greedy cattle baron. Elliott's last film for Republic. 86m/B VHS. Wild Bill Elliott, Walter Brennan, Marie Windsor, Harry (Henry) Morgan, Rhys Williams, Jim Davis, Leif Erickson, Yakima Canutt; D: Stuart E. McGowan, Dorrell McGowan; W: Stuart E. McGowan, Dorrell McGowan. REP

Showdown ♫♫½ 1973 (PG) Billy Massey (Martin) and Chuck Garvis (Hudson) had been friends since childhood, until they fell out over the attentions of the pretty Kate (Clark), whom Chuck married. Chuck became the honest town sheriff while Billy took to train robbing. Now it's up to Chuck to bring Billy to justice. Director Seaton's final film. 99m/C VHS. Dean Martin, Rock Hudson, Susan Clark, Donald Moffat, John McLiam, Ed Begley Jr.; D: George Seaton; W: Theodore Taylor; C: Ernest Laszlo; M: David Shire. USH, FCT

Showdown ♫½ 1993 (R) A small southern town is taken over by a motorcycle gang whose leader, Kincade, decides to set up his fencing and drug operations there. But the local law enforcement has other ideas, calling in a martial arts expert who wants revenge against Kincade for the death of his partner.CW: Language and martial arts violence. 92m/C VHS. Leo Fong, Werner Hoetzinger, Richard Lynch, Michelle McCormick, Frank Marth, Tom MacDowell, Troy Donahue; D: Leo Fong; W: Leo Fong.

Showdown ♫½ 1993 (R) Ken, the new kid in a particularly nasty high school, gets picked on by the martial-arts expert school bully. After getting beaten up a lot Ken finds out the school janitor can help turn him into a high-kicking fighter. Lots of fast-paced fight scenes which is all the genre demands. An edited PG-13 version is also available.CW: Language and violence. 90m/C VHS, LV, Closed Caption. Ken Scott, Billy Blanks, Patrick Kilpatrick, Kenneth McLeod; D: Robert Radler. IMP

Showdown at Boot Hill ♫♫ 1958 A U.S. Marshal (Bronson) kills a wanted murderer but cannot collect the reward because the townspeople will not identify the victim. 76m/B VHS. Charles Bronson, Robert Hutton, John Carradine; D: Gene Fowler Jr. REP

Showdown at the Equator ♫ 1983 (R) Chinese cops are trained to kill criminals with their feet, and they do. 95m/C VHS, Beta. Lo Lieh, Bruce Liang, Nora Miao, Lee Kan Kwun. GEM

Showdown at Williams Creek ♫♫½ Kootenai Brown 1991 (R) A graphic Canadian Western set in the old Montana territory, where an outcast settler goes on trial for killing an old man. Testimony recounts a shocking history of greed and betrayal. The dark side of the Gold Rush, generally well-acted. Inspired by an actual incident.CW: Language, violence, and sensuality. 97m/C VHS, Closed Caption. CA Tom Burlinson, Donnelly Rhodes, Raymond Burr, Michael Thrush, John Pyper-Ferguson, Alex Bruhanski; D: Allen Kroeker; W: John Gray; M: Michael Conway Baker. REP

Showdown in Little Tokyo ♫♫ 1991 (R) Lundgren stars as a martial arts master/L.A. cop who was raised in Japan, and has all the respect in the world for his "ancestors" and heritage. Brandon Lee (son of Bruce) is Lundgren's partner, and he's a bona fide American-made, pop-culture, mall junkie. Together, they go after a crack-smuggling gang of "yakuza" (Japanese thugs). Lots of high-kicking action and the unique angle on stereotypes make this a fun martial arts film.CW: Language, strong violence and drug use, and sensuality. 78m/C VHS, Beta, LV, 8mm, Closed Caption. Dolph Lundgren, Brandon Lee, Tia Carrere, Cary-Hiroyuki Tagawa; D: Mark L. Lester; W: Caliope Brattlestreet. WAR

The Showgirl Murders ♫♫½ 1995 (R) Stripper Jessica (Ford) goes into management when she turns a failing Las Vegas bar into a money-maker but this femme fatale wants owner Mitch (Preston) to stop sharing the wealth with his boozy wife Carolyn (Case). Meanwhile, blackmailing DEA agent Ridley (McFarland) and hitman Joey (Alber) cause problems.CW: Strong sexuality, including numerous erotic dance sequences, and for violence, language, and brief drug use. 84m/C VHS. Maria Ford, Matt Preston, Jeff Douglas, D.S. Case, Kevin Alber, Bob McFarland; D: Gene Hertel; W: Christopher Wooden. NHO

Showgirls woof! 1995 (NC-17) Long on ridiculous dialogue and bad acting and short on costumes, coming-of-age tale follows one young woman as she nakedly climbs the ladder of success as a Vegas showgirl. Oh, the things she must do to be headliner. Berkley makes the jump from television's "Saved by the Bell" to portray Nomi, the young lap dancer with the gift of pelvic thrust and the will to succeed. Whether cavorting clothed or nude, Berkley is uniformly wooden, a mass of lip gloss and mascara struggling to emote. Gershon, as her sly nemesis, brings some wit and splash to her role as the jaded headliner. Eszterhas script descends below its maker's usual standards, which are not particularly high. Titanic amount of female flesh on display fails to give film even a faint hint of sexuality, proof that there is a hell. Rent it, and be prepared to fast forward (to what, we're not sure, though there is a certain camp element that might have been amusing if not imprisoned here). Also available in "R" and unrated versions.CW: Nudity and erotic sexuality throughout, and for some graphic language and sexual violence. 131m/C VHS, Closed Caption. Elizabeth Berkley, Gina Gershon, Kyle MacLachlan, Glenn Plummer, Alan Rachins, Robert Davi, Gina Ravera; D: Paul Verhoeven; W: Joe Eszterhas; C: Jost Vacano; M: David A. Stewart. Golden Raspberry Awards '95: Worst Picture, Worst Actress (Berkley), Worst Director (Verhoeven), Worst Screenplay, Worst Song ("Walk into the Wind"), Worst New Star (Berkley); Nominations: Golden Raspberry Awards '95: Worst Actor (MacLachlan), Worst Supporting Actor (Davi), Worst Supporting Actress (Gershon). MGM

Shredder Orpheus ♫ 1989 Rock star Orpheus skateboards through hell to stop deadly television transmissions and rescue his wife. 93m/C VHS, Beta. Jesse Bernstein, Robert McGinley, Vera McCaughan, Megan Murphy, Carlo Scandiuzzi; D: Robert McGinley.

Shriek in the Night ♫♫½ 1933 Two rival reporters (Rogers and Talbot, previously paired in "The Thirteenth Guest") turn detective to solve a string of apartment murders. Made on a proverbial shoestring, but not bad. 66m/B VHS, Beta. Ginger Rogers, Lyle Talbot, Harvey Clark; D: Albert Ray. SNC, NOS, BAR

Shriek of the Mutilated woof! 1974 (R) An anthropological expedition on a deserted island turns into a night of horror as a savage beast kills the members of the group one by one. 85m/C VHS, Beta. Alan Brock, Jennifer Stock, Michael Harris; D: Michael Findlay. ART, SNC

Shrieker ♫ 1997 (R) Six college students are squatting in an abandoned hospital that just happens to be the scene of a 50-year-old massacre. So, one gets the bright idea of conjuring up the creature that did the deed after learning that it will only kill five victims—and the sixth will become the creature's master. This one's really lame.CW: Language, violence, gore. 80m/C VHS. Tanya Dempsey, Jamie Gannon, Parry Allen; D: Victoria Sloan; W: Benjamin Carr. AFE

The Shrieking ♫ Hex 1973 (PG) Black magic women hang out with biker types in Nebraska in 1919. 93m/C VHS, Beta, LV. Keith Carradine, Christina Raines, Gary Busey, Robert Walker Jr., Dan Haggerty, John Carradine, Scott Glenn; D: Leo Garen; M: Charles Bernstein. IME

The Shrimp on the Barbie ♫½ 1990 (R) When daddy refuses to bless her marriage to dim bulb boyfriend, Australian Samms hires L.A. low life Marin to pose as new beau. Another pseudonymous Smithee effort.CW: Sensuality. 86m/C VHS, Beta, LV, Closed Caption. Richard "Cheech" Marin, Emma Samms, Vernon Wells, Bruce Spence, Carole Davis; D: Alan Smithee. VTR

Shrunken Heads ♫♫½ 1994 (R) Inspired by their comic book heroes three boys try to take on neighborhood thugs only to be gunned down. But along comes Mr. Sumatra, a retired voodoo specialist, who revives the three (in a somewhat smaller form) so they can fight the good fight once again. Title theme music by director Richard's brother, Danny Elfman. 86m/C VHS, Beta, LV. Aeryk Egan, Meg Foster, Julius W. Harris, Becky Herbst, A.J. Damato, Bo Sharon, Darris Love, Leigh-Allyn Baker, Troy Fromin; D: Richard Elfman; W: Matthew Bright; M: Richard Band. PAR

Shy People ♫♫♫ 1987 (R) An urbanized New York journalist and her spoiled daughter journey to the Louisiana bayou to visit long-lost relatives in order to produce an article for "Cosmopolitan." They find ignorance, madness, and ancestral secrets and are forced to examine their motives, their relationships and issues brought to light in the watery, murky, fantastic land of the bayous. Well-acted melodrama with an outstanding performance by Hershey as the cajun matriarch. 119m/C VHS, Beta, LV, Closed Caption. Jill Clayburgh, Barbara Hershey, Martha Plimpton, Mare Winningham, Merritt Butrick, John Philbin, Don Swayze, Pruitt Taylor Vince; D: Andrei Konchalovsky; W: Gerard Brach, Marjorie David; C: Chris Menges; M: Tangerine Dream. Cannes Film Festival '87: Best Actress (Hershey). WAR

Siberiade �171 1979 Depicts life in a Siberian village from 1909 to 1969 for a wealthy family and a peasant clan and how Soviet society affects them. Rambling narrative with strong characters. In Russian with subtitles. 190m/C VHS. *RU* Vladimir Samoilov, Vitaly Solomin, Nikita Mikhalkov, Ludmila Gurchenko, Nathalia Andretchenko; *D:* Andrei Konchalovsky; *W:* Valentin Yezhov, Andrei Konchalovsky; *M:* Eduard Artemyev. Cannes Film Festival '79: Grand Jury Prize. *KIV*

The Sibling �171 *Psycho Sisters; So Evil, My Sister* 1972 (PG) Two sisters become involved in the accidental murder of a man who was a husband to one woman and lover to the other. Of course, one sister has just been released from the mental rehabilitation clinic. 85m/C VHS, Beta. Susan Strasberg, Faith Domergue, Sydney Chaplin, Steve Mitchell; *D:* Reginald LeBorg. *HHE*

Sibling Rivalry �171 1990 (PG-13) Repressed doctor's wife (redundant) Alley rolls in hay with soon to be stiff stranger upon advice of footloose sister. Stranger expires from heart attack in hay and Alley discovers that the corpse is her long-lost brother-in-law. Slapstick cover-up ensues. 88m/C VHS, Beta, LV, 8mm, Closed Caption. Kirstie Alley, Bill Pullman, Carrie Fisher, Sam Elliott, Jami Gertz, Ed O'Neill, Scott Bakula, Frances Sternhagen, Bill Macy; *D:* Carl Reiner. *COL, NLC*

The Sicilian �171 1987 Adapted from the Mario Puzo novel and based on the life of Salvatore Giuliano. Chronicles the exploits of the men who took on the government, the Catholic Church, and the Mafia in an effort to make Sicily secede from Italy and become its own nation in the 1940s. Pretentious, overdone, and confused. This long, uncut version was unseen in America, but hailed by European critics; the 115-minute, R-rated American release is also available, but isn't as good. See "Salvatore Giuliano" (Francesco Rosi, 1962) instead of either version. 146m/C VHS, Beta, LV. Christopher Lambert, John Turturro, Terence Stamp, Joss Ackland, Barbara Sukowa; *D:* Michael Cimino. *ART, VES*

Sicilian Connection �171 1974 A narcotics agent poses as a nightclub manager to bust a drug-smuggling organization. 100m/C VHS, Beta. *IT* Ben Gazzara, Silvia Monti, Fausto Tozzi. *VCD*

The Sicilian Connection �171 *The Pizza Connection* 1985 (R) Two brothers in the mob serve out vendettas and generally create havoc wherever they go. 117m/C VHS, Beta. Michele Placido, Mark Switzer, Simona Cavallari. *MGM*

Sid & Nancy �171½ 1986 (R) The tragic, brutal, true love story of The Sex Pistols' Sid Vicious and American groupie Nancy Spungen, from the director of "Repo Man." Remarkable lead performances in a very dark story that manages to be funny at times. Depressing but engrossing; no appreciation of punk music or sympathy for the self-destructive way of life is required. Oldman and Webb are superb. Music by Joe Strummer, the Pogues, and Pray for Rain. 111m/C VHS, Beta, LV, Closed Caption. Gary Oldman, Chloe Webb, Debbie Bishop, David Hayman; *D:* Alex Cox; *W:* Alex Cox; *C:* Roger Deakins. National Society of Film Critics Awards '86: Best Actress (Webb). *MVD, NLC*

Side By Side �171 1988 In the same vein as "Cocoon," three senior citizens who aren't ready to retire decide to start their own business and launch a sportswear company designed for seniors. A witty portrayal of graceful aging that is uneven at times. 100m/C VHS, Beta, Closed Caption. Milton Berle, Sid Caesar, Danny Thomas; *D:* Jack Bender. *TRI*

Side Out �171½ 1990 (PG-13) The first major film about volleyball!? What a claim! What a bore. Midwestern college guy spends summer in Southern Cal. working for slumlord uncle; instead enters "the ultimate" beach volleyball touring. Bogus. Don't see it, dude. 100m/C VHS, Beta, Closed Caption. C. Thomas Howell, Peter Horton, Kathy Ireland, Sinjin Smith, Randy Stoklos, Courtney Thorne-

Smith, Harley Jane Kozak, Christopher Rydell; *D:* Peter Israelson. *COL*

Side Show �171 1984 A runaway teen joins the circus, witnesses a murder, and must use his wits to stay out of reach of the killer. Forced "suspense" and "drama" of the bad made for TV ilk. 98m/C VHS, Beta. Lance Kerwin, Red Buttons, Anthony (Tony) Franciosa, Connie Stevens; *D:* William Conrad; *M:* Ralph Burns. *TWE*

Sideburns �171 1991 The Pushkin Club, a group of reactionaries who try to remove the western influence from Russia, attack first a rock band, then innocent civilians as they act as a social cleaning service. Uses humor to try and warn people against the rising fascism in Russia because of the battle between conservative and reformist forces. In Russian with English subtitles. 110m/C VHS. *RU D:* Yuri Mamin. *FCT*

Sidekicks �171 1993 (PG) Cutesy ego vehicle for executive producer Norris. (Brandis) is bullied by the kids at school and doesn't find much support at home from his well-meaning but ineffectual dad. He has a severe case of hero-worship for Norris, who appears as himself in a series of daydream karate sequences, saving the good guy and maiming the bad. Director Norris is actor Norris' brother. Predictable and sappy. 100m/C VHS, LV, 8mm, Closed Caption. Chuck Norris, Jonathan Brandis, Beau Bridges, Mako, Julia Nickson-Soul, Danica McKellar, Richard Moll, Joe Piscopo; *D:* Aaron Norris; *W:* Donald W. Thompson, Lou Illar; *C:* Joao Fernandes; *M:* Alan Silvestri, David Shire. *COL*

Sidewalks of London �171 *St. Martin's Lane* 1938 Laughton's a sidewalk entertainer who takes in homeless waif Leigh and puts her in his act and in his heart. Harrison steals her away and before long she's a star in the music halls. Meanwhile, Laughton has fallen on hard times. Memorable performances. 86m/B VHS, Beta. *GB* Charles Laughton, Vivien Leigh, Rex Harrison, Larry Adler, Tyrone Guthrie, Gus McNaughton, Bart Cormack, Edward Lexy, Maire O'Neil, Basil Gill, Claire Greet, David Burns, Cyril Smith, Ronald Ward, Romilly Lunge, Helen Haye, Jerry Verno; *D:* Tim Whelan; *W:* Clemence Dane; *C:* Jules Kruger; *M:* Arthur Johnson. *KIV, HHT, CAB*

Sidewalks of New York �171½ 1931 A hapless New York millionaire (Keaton) falls for tenement gal Page and tries to win her heart by saving her street urchin brother from joining the local gang of toughs. Keaton was a silent screen classic as a comedian but his talkie career was disappointing as he lost creative control and battled alcohol problems. 74m/B VHS, Beta. Buster Keaton, Anita Page, Cliff Edwards, Frank LaRue, Frank Rowan, Norman Phillips Jr.; *D:* Jules White, Zion Myers. *MGM, FCT*

Sidewinder One �171 1977 (PG) Motocross racing is the setting for a romance between a racer and an heiress. Good racing footage, but where's the plot? If you like cars a whole lot... 97m/C VHS, Beta. Michael Parks, Marjoe Gortner, Susan Howard, Alex Cord, Charlotte Rae; *D:* Earl Bellamy; *W:* Nancy Voyles Crawford. *NLC*

Sidney Sheldon's Bloodline woof!
Bloodline 1979 (R) Wealthy businesswoman Hepburn finds she is marked for death by persons unknown. Exquisitely bad trash from another Sheldon bestseller. 116m/C VHS, Beta. Audrey Hepburn, Ben Gazzara, James Mason, Michelle Phillips, Omar Sharif, Irene Papas, Romy Schneider, Gert Frobe, Maurice Ronet, Beatrice Straight; *D:* Terence Young; *C:* Frederick A. (Freddie) Young; *M:* Ennio Morricone. *PAR*

The Siege of Firebase Gloria �171½ 1989 Story of the Marines who risked their lives defending an outpost against overwhelming odds during the 1968 Tet offensive in Vietnam. Purportedly patriotic war drama made by an Australian director; lead Hauser is a disgusting sadist, and plot is hopelessly hackneyed. 95m/C VHS, Beta, LV. Wings Hauser, R. Lee Ermey; *D:* Brian Trenchard-Smith.

Siegfried �171 *Siegfrieds Tod; Siegfried's Death* 1924 Half of Lang's epic masterpiece "Der Niebelungen," based on German mythology. Title hero bathes in the blood of a dragon he has slain. He marries a princess, but wicked Queen Brumhilde has him killed. Part two, in which Siegfried's widow marries Attila the Hun, is titled "Kriemheld's Revenge." These dark, brooding, archetypal tours de force were patriotic tributes, and were loved by Hitler. Silent with music score. 100m/B VHS, LV. *GE* Paul Richter, Margarete Schoen; *D:* Fritz Lang. *SNC, NOS, GPV*

Siesta �171½ 1987 (R) Barkin is a professional stunt woman who leaves her current lover/manager, played by Sheen, and returns to visit her former lover and trainer, Byrne, on the eve of his marriage to another woman. Her trip, marked by flashbacks and flights of seemingly paranoid fantasy, leads to the discovery of murder, but she cannot remember who, when, why, or where. The film distorts time, reality, and perception in a sometimes fascinating, sometimes frustrating psychological mystery. Attractively filmed by video director Lambert. Barkin and Byrne were married in real life a year after the film's release. 97m/C VHS, Beta, LV, Closed Caption. Ellen Barkin, Gabriel Byrne, Jodie Foster, Julian Sands, Isabella Rossellini, Martin Sheen, Grace Jones, Alexei Sayle; *D:* Mary Lambert; *W:* Patricia Louisianna Knop; *M:* Miles Davis, Marcus Miller. *ORI, WAR*

The Sign of Four �171½ 1983 Sherlock Holmes and the ever-faithful Watson are hired by a young woman who has been anonymously sent an enormous diamond. An inept production which looks good but that's all. 97m/C VHS, Beta, Closed Caption. *GB* Ian Richardson, David Healy, Thorley Walters, Cherie Lunghi; *D:* Desmond Davis. *PAR*

The Sign of the Cross �171½ 1933 Depraved Emperor Nero (Laughton) decides he wants a new city so he burns down Rome—blaming the fire on the Christians he also wants to get rid of (preferably by the lions in the arena). Meanwhile, Marcus (March), the Roman Prefect, has fallen for the virginal Christian Mercia (Landi) and risks his life to save her. Besides Laughton's overwhelmingly hammy performance, Colbert slinks seductively as the emperor's vixenish wife, Poppaea. Again, lots of crowd scenes (DeMille's specialty). Based on the play by Wilson Barrett. 125m/B VHS, Closed Caption. Fredric March, Elissa Landi, Charles Laughton, Claudette Colbert, Ian Keith, Harry Beresford, Arthur Hohl, Nat Pendleton; *D:* Cecil B. DeMille; *W:* Waldemar Young, Sidney Buchman; *M:* Rudolph Kopp. Nominations: Academy Awards '33: Best Cinematography. *USH*

The Sign of Zorro �171 1960 Adventures of the masked swordsman as he champions the cause of the oppressed in early California. Full-length version of the popular late-50s Disney television series. 89m/C VHS, Beta. Guy Williams, Henry Calvin, Gene Sheldon, Romney Brent, Britt Lomond, George Lewis, Lisa Gaye; *D:* Norman Foster, Lewis R. Foster. *DIS*

Signal 7 �171 1983 An improvised, neo-verite document of a night in the lives of two San Francisco taxi drivers. Nilsson's first major release and a notable example of his unique scriptless, tape-to-film narrative technique. 89m/C VHS, Beta. Bill Ackridge, Dan Leegant; *D:* Rob Nilsson; *W:* Rob Nilsson. *WAR*

Signals Through the Flames �171 1983 A film by Sheldon Rochlin and Maxine Harris outlining the tumultuous history of the famous experimental group, The Living Theatre. 97m/C VHS, Beta. Julian Beck, Judith Malina, Maxine Harris; *D:* Sheldon Rochlin. *MFV, TPV*

Signs of Life �171 *Lebenszeichen* 1968 German soldier Stroszek (Brogle), injured during the occupation of Crete, is sent to recuperate on the remote island of Kos. With his Greek wife Nora, Stroszek has nothing to do but guard a deserted fortress and a store of abandoned ammunition.

But soon the suspicious natives and the isolation begin to drive Stroszek to madness and he decides to blow up the ammunition dump (and the island along with it). German with subtitles. **90m/B VHS.** *GE* Peter Brogle, Wolfgang Reichmann, Athina Zacharopoulous, Wolfgang Stumpf; *D:* Werner Herzog; *W:* Werner Herzog; *C:* Thomas Mauch; *M:* Stavros Xarchakos. *NYF*

Signs of Life 🐾🐾½ *One for Sorrow, Two for Joy* 1989 (PG-13)
A boat-building company in Maine closes its doors after centuries in business; the employees and families whose lives have been defined by it for generations learn to cope. Wonderful performances compensate only partly for a week script. An episode on PBS's "American Playhouse." **95m/C VHS, Beta, LV.** Beau Bridges, Arthur Kennedy, Vincent D'Onofrio, Kevin J. O'Connor, Will Patton, Kate Reid, Michael Lewis, Kathy Bates, Mary-Louise Parker, Georgia Engel; *D:* John David Coles; *W:* Mark Malone; *C:* Elliot Davis; *M:* Howard Shore. *ART*

Silas Marner 🐾🐾🐾 1985
Superb made for British television adaptation of the 1861 George Eliot classic about an itinerant weaver subjected to criminal accusation, poverty, and exile. Wonderful detail and splendid acting. Shot on location in the Cotswold district of England. **92m/C VHS, Beta, Closed Caption.** *GB* Ben Kingsley, Jenny Agutter, Patrick Ryecart, Patsy Kensit; *D:* Giles Foster; *M:* Carl Davis. *VCO, FOX, TVC*

The Silence 🐾🐾🐾 *Tystnaden* 1963
A brutal, enigmatic allegory about two sisters, one a nymphomaniac, the other a violently frustrated lesbian, traveling with the former's young son to an unnamed country beset by war. Fascinating and memorable but frustrating and unsatisfying: What is it about? What is it an allegory of? Where is the narrative? The third in Bergman's crisis-of-faith trilogy following "Through a Glass Darkly" and "Winter Light." In Swedish with English subtitles or dubbed. **95m/B VHS, Beta, LV.** *SW* Ingrid Thulin, Gunnel Lindstrom, Birger Malmsten; *D:* Ingmar Bergman; *W:* Ingmar Bergman; *C:* Sven Nykvist. *HMV, NLC*

Silence 🐾🐾 *Crazy Jack and the Boy* 1973 (G)
An autistic boy gets lost in the wilderness and faces an array of difficulties while his foster parents search for him. **82m/C VHS, Beta.** Will Geer, Ellen Geer, Richard Kelton, Ian Geer Flanders, Craig Kelly; *D:* John Korty. *NO*

Silence Like Glass 🐾🐾½ 1990 (R)
Diagnosed with life-threatening illness, two young women struggle to overcome their anger at their fate. They find friendship and together, search for reasons to live. Fine performances, with pacing that keeps the melodrama to a minimum. **102m/C VHS, Beta, LV, Closed Caption.** Jami Gertz, Martha Plimpton, George Peppard, Rip Torn, James Remar; *D:* Carl Schenkel; *M:* Anne Dudley. *VTR*

The Silence of Neto 🐾🐾 *Silencio de Neto* 1994
A sheltered young boy comes of age in Guatemala during the early 1950's, a period marked by political upheaval and Cold War paranoia. His relationship with his socialist-leaning uncle causes family friction as it reflects on a repressive society and calls for reform. Spanish with subtitles. **106m/C VHS.** *D:* Luis Argueta; *W:* Luis Argueta; *C:* Ramon Suarez. *PEG*

Silence of the Hams 🐾½ 1993 (R)
Very feeble parody of "The Silence of the Lambs" and others in the thriller/horror genre. Director/writer Greggio also stars as the murder victim, stabbed in the shower, who narrates the story in flashback. There's an eager FBI recruit, a femme fatale, assorted cameo turns, and DeLuise, chewing more scenery than even Anthony Hopkins could swallow, as nutcase Dr. Animal Cannibal Pizza. *CW:* Language. **85m/C VHS, Closed Caption.** Ezio Greggio, Dom DeLuise, Billy Zane, Joanna Pacula, Charlene Tilton, Martin Balsam; *Cameos:* Stuart Pankin, John Astin, Phyllis Diller, Bubba Smith, Larry Storch, Rip Taylor, Shelley Winters, Mel Brooks, John Landis, John Carpenter, Joe Dante; *D:* Ezio Greggio; *W:* Ezio Greggio; *C:* Jacques Haitkin. *CAF*

Silence of the Heart 🐾🐾🐾 1984
Mother copes with aftermath of suicide of teenage son following her recent divorce. Hartley is captivating in this gripping drama. **100m/C VHS.** Mariette Hartley, Dana Hill, Howard Hesseman, Chad Lowe, Charlie Sheen; *D:* Richard Michaels; *W:* Phil Penningroth; *M:* Georges Delerue. *PMH, HHE, VTR*

The Silence of the Lambs 🐾🐾🐾½ 1991 (R)
Foster is FBI cadet Clarice Starling, a woman with ambition, a cum laude degree in psychology, and a traumatic childhood. When a serial killer begins his ugly rounds, the FBI wants psychological profiles from other serial killers and she's sent to collect a profile from one who's exceptionally clever—psychiatrist Hannibal Lecter, a vicious killer prone to dining on his victims. Brilliant performances from Foster and Hopkins, finely detailed supporting characterizations, and elegant pacing from Demme. Some brutal visual effects. Excellent portrayals of women who refuse to be victims. Based on the Thomas Harris novel. **118m/C VHS, Beta, LV, Letterbox, Closed Caption.** Jodie Foster, Anthony Hopkins, Scott Glenn, Ted Levine, Brooke Smith, Charles Napier, Roger Corman, Anthony Heald, Diane Baker, Chris Isaak; *D:* Jonathan Demme; *W:* Ted Tally; *C:* Tak Fujimoto; *M:* Howard Shore. Academy Awards '91: Best Actor (Hopkins), Best Actress (Foster), Best Adapted Screenplay, Best Director (Demme), Best Picture; British Academy Awards '91: Best Actor (Hopkins), Best Actress (Foster); Directors Guild of America Awards '91: Best Director (Demme); Golden Globe Awards '92: Best Actress—Drama (Foster); National Board of Review Awards '91: Best Director (Demme), Best Film, Best Supporting Actor (Hopkins); New York Film Critics Awards '91: Best Actor (Hopkins), Best Actress (Foster), Best Director (Demme), Best Film; Writers Guild of America '91: Best Adapted Screenplay; Nominations: Academy Awards '91: Best Film Editing, Best Sound. *ORI, FCT, IME*

Silence of the North 🐾🐾½ 1981 (PG)
A widow (Burstyn) with three children struggles to survive under rugged pioneer conditions on the Canadian frontier. The scenery is, not surprisingly, stunning. Based on a true but generic story. **94m/C VHS, Beta.** *CA* Ellen Burstyn, Tom Skerritt; *D:* Allan Winton King; *M:* Michael Conway Baker. *USH*

The Silencer 🐾🐾 1992 (R)
Walden stars as Harley-riding Angel who is out to stop a slavery and prostitution ring that abuses young runaways. Video-arcades hold the clues, and Angel must learn to kill without a conscience. Every time she kills, Angel seeks comfort in the arms of anonymous lovers. However, what she doesn't know is that her demented ex-boyfriend is watching. *CW:* Language, strong violence, and strong sexuality. **85m/C VHS, Closed Caption.** Lynette Walden, Chris Mulkey, Paul Ganus, Morton Downey Jr.; *D:* Amy Goldstein; *W:* Amy Goldstein, Scott Kraft.

The Silencers 🐾🐾½ 1995 (R)
Secret Service agent Chuck Rafferty (Scalia) discovers that his latest enemies, known as the Men In Black, are actually human-appearing aliens seeking to conquer Earth. Now Rafferty's only hope is to team up with inter-galactic peace officer Condor (Christopher) to defeat this evil. *CW:* Action violence. **103m/C VHS.** Jack Scalia, Dennis Christopher, Clarence Williams III, Carlos Lauchu, Lucinda Weist; *D:* Richard Pepin. *PMH*

The Silences of the Palace 🐾🐾🐾 *Les Silences du Palais* 1994
Set in 1950s Tunisia at the end of the ruling monarchy. Twenty-five-year-old Alia (Lacroix) returns to the run-down palace where she was born and grew up as the daughter of a lifelong servant, Khedija (Hedhili), who was also the sexual favorite of her master, Prince Sidi Ali (Fazaa). She remembers the limited, repressed existence they endured and realizes that, ten years after leaving the palace, she has traded one form of subjugation for another and has yet to find her own independence. Arabic with subtitles. **116m/C VHS.** *FR* Ghalia Lacroix, Amel Hedhili, Kamel Fazaa, Hend Sabri, Najia Overghi; *D:* Moufida Tlatli; *W:* Moufida Tlatli, Nouri Bouzid; *C:* Youssef Ben Youssef. *CTL*

Silent Assassins 🐾🐾 1988
Fists and bullets fly when a scientist is kidnapped in order to gain secrets to biological warfare. Chong and Rhee, real-life owners of a martial arts studio, produced and choreographed the film. Blair is here, but doesn't figure much. A notch up from most similar martial arts pics. **92m/C VHS.** Sam Jones, Linda Blair, Jun Chong, Phillip Rhee; *D:* Scott Thomas, Lee Doo-yong. *MCG, VTR*

Silent Code 🐾 1935
A Mountie is framed for the murder of a young miner. **55m/B VHS, Beta.** Tom Tyler. *NO*

The Silent Enemy 🐾🐾½ 1958
The true-life exploits of British frogmen battling Italian foes during WWII. Suspenseful and engrossing; good performances and good rendering of underwater action. Video release snips 20 minutes from the original and adds color. **91m/C VHS, Beta.** *GB* Laurence Harvey, John Clements, Michael Craig, Dawn Addams, Sidney James, Alec McCowen, Nigel Stock; *D:* William Fairchild. *NO*

Silent Fall 🐾½ 1994 (R)
Grisly double murder of his parents is witnessed by autistic nine-year-old, Tim Warden (Faulkner), and his traumatized over-protective teenaged sister Sylvie (Tyler). Retired psychiatrist Jake Rainier (Dreyfuss) is reluctant to get involved, ever since an autistic child in his care died, but when authoritarian rival Dr. Harlinger (Lithgow) is called instead, Jake changes his mind. Second half of film takes a lurid turn as Jake probes Tim's damaged psyche to discover the killer. Trite, clueless whodunit that generally wastes the talent involved; Tyler and Faulkner make their film debuts. *CW:* Strong language; violence. **101m/C VHS, LV, Closed Caption.** Richard Dreyfuss, Ben Faulkner, John Lithgow, Liv Tyler, Linda Hamilton, J.T. Walsh; *D:* Bruce Beresford; *W:* Akiva Goldsman; *M:* Stewart Copeland. *WAR*

Silent Hunter 🐾½ 1994 (R)
Undercover cop Jim Paradine (O'Keeffe) retreats to a remote mountains cabin when his family is killed by a gang of bank robbers. Naturally, the thugs just happen to crash land on Paradine's mountain top with their stolen loot and he goes off to hunt them down. *CW:* Language; sadistic violence; some sexuality. **97m/C VHS, LV, Closed Caption.** Miles O'Keeffe, Fred Williamson, Lynne Adams, Peter Colvey, Jason Cavalier, Sabine Karsenti; *D:* Fred Williamson. *TTC, NLC*

Silent Killers 🐾½ 19??
A scientist is responsible for the deaths of many people because of his research in germ warfare. He's haunted by the ghosts of his victims. Is he losing his mind or is it a sinister plot? **90m/C VHS.** Stephen Soul, Daniel Garfield. *MOV*

Silent Laugh Makers, No. 1 🐾🐾🐾 1915
Four hilarious short movies from the silent era: "Looking for Sally," about an immigrant in search of his best girlfriend; "Lucky Dog," with the young Laurel and Hardy; "His Night Out," about a wild evening with Charlie Chaplin and Ben Turpin; and "Hop-a-Long." Non-stop side-splitting fun. **50m/B VHS, Beta.** Charley Chase, Stan Laurel, Oliver Hardy, Charlie Chaplin, Ben Turpin, Arthur Lake. *VYY*

Silent Laugh Makers, No. 2 🐾🐾🐾 1917
Several short funny films from the silent picture era: "Fluttering Hearts," "Long Live the King," about a king who just can't get along with his nobles, starring Chase and Hardy; and "A Sea Dog Tale." All are unremittingly hilarious. **50m/B VHS, Beta.** Charley Chase, Oliver Hardy, Billy Bevan. *VYY*

Silent Laugh Makers, No. 3 🐾🐾 1919
Four comedy shorts: "Picking Peaches" (1924), directed by Frank Capra, Langdon's first for Mack Sennett; "All Tied Up" (1925), featuring "A Ton of Fun"-four rotund comedians; "Don't Shove" (1919), featuring Harold Lloyd wooing Bebe Daniels; and "Some Baby" (1922), with Snub Pollard. **55m/B VHS, Beta.** Harry Langdon, Harold Lloyd, Bebe Daniels, Snub Pollard. *VYY*

Silent Madness ♂ 1984 (R) A psychiatrist must stop a deranged killer, escaped from an asylum, from slaughtering helpless sellrys aeodu in a sorority house. Meanwhile, hospital execs send orderlies to kill the patient, to conceal their mistake. Ludicrous. 93m/C VHS, Beta. Belinda J. Montgomery, Viveca Lindfors, Sydney Lassick; **D:** Simon Nuchtern.

The Silent Mr. Sherlock Holmes ♂♂ 1912 These two silent shorts are a rare treat for Holmes fans. "The Copper Beeches" was produced with the "personal supervision of Arthur Conan Doyle." In "The Man with the Twisted Lip," Holmes is hired to find out whether a banker was murdered. 68m/B VHS. *GB* Ellie Norwood. VYY

Silent Motive ♂♂½ 1991 Laura is a Hollywood screenwriter who's shocked to discover that a killer is using her recent script as an outline for a series of film-industry murders. She's even more unnerved when a detective makes Laura his number one suspect. 90m/C VHS, Closed Caption. Patricia Wettig, Mike Farrell, Ed Asner, Rick Springfield, David Packer; **D:** Lee Philips; **W:** William Bekkala. WOV

Silent Movie ♂♂ 1976 (PG) A has-been movie director (Brooks) is determined to make a comeback and save his studio from being taken over by a conglomerate. Hilarious at times but uneven. An original idea; not as successful as it could have been. Has music and sound effects, but only one word of spoken dialogue by famous mime Marceau. 88m/C VHS, Beta, LV. Mel Brooks, Marty Feldman, Dom DeLuise, Burt Reynolds, Anne Bancroft, James Caan, Liza Minnelli, Paul Newman, Sid Caesar, Bernadette Peters, Harry Ritz, Marcel Marceau; **D:** Mel Brooks; **W:** Mel Brooks, Ron Clark, Rudy DeLuca, Barry Levinson. FOX

Silent Movies...Just For the Fun of It! 1926 Three short silent films: "The Iron Mule" (1925), "For Sadie's Sake" (1926), and "Hazel from Hollywood" (1918). 56m/B VHS, Beta, 8mm. Jimmie Adams, Dorothy Devore, Al "Fuzzy" St. John. VYY

Silent Night, Bloody Night ♂♂ 1973 (R) An escaped lunatic terrorizes a small New England town, particularly a mansion that was once an insane asylum. Not great, but well done by director Gershuny, with some nail-biting suspense and slick scene changes. 83m/C VHS. Patrick O'Neal, John Carradine, Walter Abel, Mary Woronov, Astrid Heeren, Candy Darling; **D:** Theodore Gershuny. NO

of the Dark Full Moon; Death House 1973 (R) An escaped lunatic terrorizes a small New England town, particularly a mansion that was once an insane asylum. Not great, but well done by director Gershuny, with some nail-biting suspense and slick scene changes. 83m/C VHS. Patrick O'Neal, John Carradine, Walter Abel, Mary Woronov, Astrid Heeren, Candy Darling; **D:** Theodore Gershuny. NO

Silent Night, Deadly Night ♂ 1984 (R) A psycho ax-murders people while dressed as jolly old St. Nick. Violent and disturbing, to say the least. Caused quite a controversy when it was released to theatres. Santa gimmick sold some tickets at the time, but resist the urge to rent it: it's completely devoid of worth, whatever the killer's outfit. As if one were not enough, we've been blessed with four sequels. 92m/C VHS, Beta, LV. Lilyan Chauvin, Gilmer McCormick, Toni Nero; **D:** Charles E. Sellier; **M:** Perry Botkin. ART, IME

Silent Night, Deadly Night 2 ♂ 1987 (R) The psychotic little brother of the psychotic, Santa Claus-dressed killer from the first film exacts revenge, covering the same bloody ground as before. Almost half this sequel consists of scenes lifted whole from the original. 88m/C VHS, Beta, LV. Eric Freeman, James Newman, Elizabeth Cayton, Jean Miller; **D:** Lee Harry; **M:** Michael Armstrong. ART

Silent Night, Deadly Night 3: Better Watch Out! ♂½ 1989 (R) The now grown-up psycho goes up against a young blind woman. Santa is no longer the bad guy, thank goodness. The least bad of the lot, with black humor—though not enough to make it worth seeing. 90m/C VHS, Beta, LV. Richard Beymer, Bill Moseley, Samantha Scully, Eric Da Re, Laura Herring, Robert Culp; **D:** Monte Hellman. ART

Silent Night, Deadly Night 4: Initiation ♂ 1990 (R) A secret L.A. cult of she-demons use the slasher Ricky for their own ends—making for more mayhem and horror. Has

virtually nothing to do with the other "sequels"— which is not to say it's very good. 90m/C VHS, LV. Maud Adams, Allyce Beasley, Clint Howard, Reggie Bannister; **D:** Brian Yuzna. MOV

Silent Night, Deadly Night 5: The Toymaker ♂♂ 1991 (R) A young boy's Christmas is overrun by murderous Santas and viscious stuffed animals. Definitely for fans of the genre only. **CW:** Strong violence and strong sensuality. 90m/C VHS. Mickey Rooney, William Thorne, Jane Higginson. ART

Silent Night, Lonely Night ♂♂ 1969 Two lonely middle-aged people (Bridges and Jones) begin an affair at Christmas to stem the pain of their separately disintegrating marriages. Poignant but not successfully credible. Based on the play by Robert Anderson. Made for television. 98m/C VHS, Beta. Lloyd Bridges, Shirley Jones, Jeff Bridges, Cloris Leachman, Carrie Snodgress, Lynn Carlin; **D:** Daniel Petrie; **M:** Billy Goldenberg. USH

The Silent One ♂♂½ 1986 Featuring underwater photography by Ron and Valerie Taylor, this is the odd story of a mysterious Polynesian boy who has a nautical relationship with a sea turtle. 96m/C VHS, Beta. *NZ* Telo Malese, George Henare; **D:** Yvonne Mackay. NO

The Silent Partner ♂♂♂ 1978 A bank teller (Gould) foils a robbery, but manages to take some money for himself. The unbalanced robber (Plummer) knows it and wants the money. Good script and well directed, with emphasis on suspense and detail. Unexpectedly violent at times. Early, non-comedic role for big guy Candy. 103m/C VHS, Beta, LV. *CA* Elliott Gould, Christopher Plummer, Susannah York, John Candy; **D:** Daryl Duke; **W:** Curtis Hanson; **C:** Billy Williams. FCT, VES

The Silent Passenger ♂♂½ 1935 Amateur sleuth Lord Peter Wimsey makes cinematic debut investigating murder and blackmail on the British railway. Dorothy Sayer's character later inspired BBC mystery series. 75m/B VHS, Beta. *GB* John Loder, Peter Haddon, Mary Newland, Austin Trevor, Donald Wolfit, Leslie Perrins, Aubrey Mather, Ralph Truman; **D:** Reginald Denham. NOS, SNC

Silent Rage ♂ 1982 (R) Sheriff Norris of a small Texas town must destroy killer Libby who has been made indestructible through genetic engineering. Chuck Norris meets Frankenstein, sort of. Nice try, but still thoroughly stupid and boring. 100m/C VHS, Beta, LV, 8mm. Chuck Norris, Ron Silver, Steven Keats, Toni Kalem, Stephen Furst; **D:** Michael Miller; **W:** Joseph Fraley; **M:** Peter Bernstein. COL

Silent Raiders ♂ 1954 A commando unit is sent to France in 1943 to knock out a Nazi communications center. 72m/B VHS, Beta. Richard Bartlett, Earle Lyon, Jeanette Bordeau; **M:** Elmer Bernstein. NO

Silent Rebellion ♂½ 1982 A Greek immigrant (Savalas) and his son return to Greece, where they reunite with mother and brother and re-discover their heritage and each other. Cross-cultural misunderstandings abound; could have been interesting, but the story is just too generic and uninspired. 90m/C VHS, Beta. Telly Savalas, Keith Gordon, Michael Constantine, Yula Gavala. NO

Silent Running ♂♂♂ 1971 (G) Members of a space station orbiting Saturn care for the last vegetation of a nuclear-devastated earth. When orders come to destroy the vegetation, Dern takes matters into his own hands. Speculative sci-fi at its best. Trumbull's directorial debut; he created special effects for "2001" and "Close Encounters." Strange music enhances the alien atmosphere. 90m/C VHS, Beta, LV. Bruce Dern, Cliff Potts, Ron Rifkin; **D:** Douglas Trumbull; **W:** Michael Cimino, Deric Washburn, Steven Bochco; **M:** Prof. Peter Schickele. USH

Silent Scream ♂½ 1980 (R) College kids take up residence with the owners of an eerie mansion complete with obligatory murders. Obvious to the point of being gratuitous—and just plain uninteresting. 87m/C VHS, Beta. Rebecca Balding, Cameron Mitchell, Avery Schreiber, Barbara Steele, Steve Doubet, Brad Reardon, Yvonne De Carlo; **D:** Denny

Harris; **W:** Wallace C. Bennett, Jim Wheat, Ken Wheat; **C:** Michael D. Murphy, David Shore.

Silent Scream ♂ 1984 A former Nazi concentration camp commandant collects unusual animals and humans as a hobby. 60m/C VHS, Beta. *GB* Peter Cushing, Brian Cox, Elaine Donnelly; **D:** Alan Gibson. ART

Silent Tongue ♂♂ 1992 (PG-13) Weird western finds the crazed Talbot Roe (Phoenix) alone in the wilderness, guarding the tree that is the burial place of his half-breed wife Awbonnie (Tousey). Roe's father (Harris) bought his son's bride from her greedy and abusive father McCree (Bates). In an effort to return Talbot to some semblance of normality, Roe offers to buy McCree's other daughter (Arredondo) for his son. But Talbot is haunted by his wife's angry ghost, who wants her spirit set free by ritual burning, and McCree himself fears the vengeance of his one-time Indian wife Silent Tongue (Cardinal). Messy, over-the-top plot with some poignant performances, especially Phoenix's. **CW:** Mildly violent. 101m/C VHS, LV, Closed Caption. River Phoenix, Sheila Tousey, Richard Harris, Alan Bates, Jeri Arredondo, Dermot Mulroney, Tantoo Cardinal; **Cameos:** Bill Irwin, David Shiner; **D:** Sam Shepard; **W:** Sam Shepard; **C:** Jack Conroy; **M:** Patrick O'Hearn. THV

The Silent Touch ♂♂½ 1994 (PG-13) Irascible, aged composer Henry Kesdi (Von Sydow), living in Denmark with his long-suffering wife Helena (Miles), hasn't written a note in 40 years. Music student Stefan (Blutheau) dreams of a composition he believes Henry started but never completed. So Stefan naturally sets out to help Henry finish his symphony by mystically healing his composer's block. Yes, it does sound hokey but the fluff is saved by Von Sydow's buoyantly funny performance. 92m/C VHS. *PL DK GB* Max von Sydow, Lothaire Bluteau, Sarah Miles, Sofie Graboel, Aleksander Bardini, Peter Hesse Overgaard; **D:** Krzysztof Zanussi; **W:** Peter Morgan, Mark Wadlow; **M:** Wojciech Kilar. PEG, FCT

Silent Trigger ♂♂ 1997 (R) Special Forces commando Shooter (Lundgren) becomes a paid assassin for an undercover agency but an ill-fated mission causes him and partner Spotter (Bellman) to question the agency, who then decide the duo are expendable. Fast-paced with some eye-catching action sequences. **CW:** Strong violent content and language, and for some sexuality and drug content. 94m/C VHS, LV, Closed Caption. Dolph Lundgren, Gina Bellman, George Jenesky; **D:** Russell Mulcahy; **W:** Sergio D. Altieri. TOU

Silent Valley ♂ 1935 Adventure of the Old West with American cowboy star Tom Tyler. 60m/B VHS, Beta. Tom Tyler. NOS, VCN, DVT

Silent Victim ♂♂½ 1992 (R) Greene stars as Bonnie Jackson, a Georgia housewife whose marriage has not only gone wrong but turned violent. She takes a drug overdose in a suicide attempt but it results only in a miscarriage. Her furious husband sues her for the murder of their unborn child while an ambitious district attorney petitions the state to charge Bonnie with committing an illegal abortion. Bonnie's torment soon becomes a media circus as she goes on trial. Based on a true story. **CW:** Language, elements of domestic violence, and sexuality. 116m/C VHS, Closed Caption. Michele Greene, Kyle Secor, Ely Pouget, Alex Hyde-White, Dori Brenner, Leann Hunley; **D:** Menahem Golan; **W:** Nelly Adnil, Jonathan Platnick; **M:** William T. Stromberg. COL

Silent Victory: The Kitty O'Neil Story ♂♂♂ 1979 Genuinely stirring real-life-overcoming-adversity story of the deaf woman who became a top stunt woman in Hollywood and holder of the land speed record for women. Channing is very good as O'Neil. Made for television. 96m/C Beta. Stockard Channing, Brian Dennehy, Colleen Dewhurst, Edward Albert, James Farentino; **D:** Lou Antonio. NO

Silent Witness ⅃ 1985 (R) A woman (Bertinelli) witnesses her brother-in-law and his friend rape a young woman. She must decide whether to testify against them or keep the family secret. Exploitative and weakly plotted. Rip-off of the much-discussed Massachusetts barroom rape case. Made for television. **97m/C VHS, Beta.** Valerie Bertinelli, John Savage, Chris Nash, Melissa Leo, Pat Corley, Steven Williams, Jacqueline Brookes, Alex McArthur, Katie McCombs; **D:** Michael Miller.

Silhouette ⅃⅃ 1991 (R) Detained in a small Texas town, a woman witnesses the murder of a local girl—but in silhouette, so the killer's identity takes a feature-length running time to resolve. A fair but contrived made for cable TV thriller that the leading lady co-produced.**CW:** Violence. **89m/C VHS.** Faye Dunaway, David Rasche, John Terry, Carlos Gomez, Ron Campbell, Margaret Blye, Talisa Soto, Ritch Brinkley; **D:** Carl Schenkel; **W:** Victor Buell. *USH*

Silk ⅃ 1986 (R) A beautiful and bloodthirsty detective cuts a swath through local heroin rings. **84m/C VHS, Beta.** Cec Verrell, Bill McLaughlin, Fred Bailey; **D:** Cirio H. Santiago. *MGM*

Silk 2 ⅃ 1989 (R) A foreign-made sequel, in which a beautiful cop stops crime in Honolulu. Ludicrous plot, bad acting, lots of skin and violence—what more could you want? Dreadful. **85m/C VHS, Beta.** Monique Gabrielle, Peter Nelson, Jan Merlin, Maria Clair; **D:** Cirio H. Santiago. *MGM*

Silk Degrees ⅃½ 1994 (R) Actress witnesses a murder and is targeted for elimination by the killer. She's supposed to be protected by a couple of federal agents but it seems there's a traitor around.**CW:** Violence and sexuality. **89m/C VHS, LV, Closed Caption.** Deborah Shelton, Marc Singer, Mark Hamill, Michael Des Barres, Charles Napier, Gilbert Gottfried, Adrienne Barbeau; **D:** Armand Garabidian; **W:** Stuart Gibbs, Douglas J. Sloan, Robert Gottlieb; **M:** Larry Wolff. *IMP*

Silk n' Sabotage ⅃½ 1994 Serious-minded Jamie comes up with a program for a new computer game. When it's stolen by a con artist, Jamie and her frivolous roommates team up to retrieve it. Since the roomies operate a lingerie business there's lots of pulchritude on display. Also available unrated. **70m/C VHS, Beta, LV.** Cherilyn Shea, Stephanie Champlin, Julie Skiru; **D:** Joe Cauley.

The Silk Road ⅃⅃½ 1992 (PG-13) In 11th-century China the ancient trading route leads to Dun Huang, a desert city that is the last Chinese outpost on the road. Zhao, a young scholar, travels in a caravan which is attacked by Chinese mercenaries. His life is spared and when his new home is attacked by a neighboring nation, he hides the city's treasures in nearby caves. Adapted from the novel by Yashushi Inoue, which was based on the Thousand Buddha Caves, where a treasure of Buddhist icons and scrolls were discovered in 1900. Billed as an epic, there's lots of pageantry and some impressive battle scenes but is too stately and overdone to be more than merely interesting. In Japanese with English subtitles. **99m/C VHS, LV.** CH JP Koichi Sato, Toshiyuki Nishida, Anna Nakagawa, Tsunehiko Watase, Daijiro Harada, Takahiro Tamura; **D:** Junya Sato; **M:** Masaru Sato. *THV*

Silk Stockings ⅃⅃⅃ 1957 Splendid musical comedy adaptation of "Ninotchka," with Astaire as a charming American movie man, and Charisse as the cold Soviet official whose commie heart he melts. Music and lyrics by Cole Porter highlight this film adapted from George S. Kaufman's hit Broadway play. Director Mamoulian's last film. ♫Too Bad; Paris Loves Lovers; Fated to Be Mated; The Ritz Roll 'n Rock; Silk Stockings; Red Blues; All of You; Stereophonic Sound; Josephine. **117m/C VHS, LV, Letterbox.** Fred Astaire, Cyd Charisse, Janis Paige, Peter Lorre, George Tobias; **D:** Rouben Mamoulian; **M:** Andre Previn. *MGM, TTC*

Silkwood ⅃⅃⅃ 1983 (R) The story of Karen Silkwood, who died in a 1974 car crash under suspicious circumstances. She was a nuclear plant worker and activist who was investigating shoddy practices at the plant. Streep acts up a storm, disappearing completely into her character. Cher surprises with her fine portrayal of a lesbian co-worker, and Russell is also good. Nichols has a tough time since we already know the ending, but he brings top-notch performances from his excellent cast. **131m/C VHS, Beta, LV.** Meryl Streep, Kurt Russell, Cher, Diana Scarwid, Bruce McGill, Fred Ward, David Strathairn, Ron Silver, Josef Sommer, Craig T. Nelson; **D:** Mike Nichols; **W:** Nora Ephron, Alice Arlen; **M:** Georges Delerue. Golden Globe Awards '84: Best Supporting Actress (Cher); Nominations: Academy Awards '83: Best Actress (Streep), Best Director (Nichols), Best Film Editing, Best Original Screenplay, Best Supporting Actress (Cher). *PAR*

Silver Bandit ⅃ 1947 A bookkeeper is sent to investigate a mine theft. Along the way he sings country and western songs. **54m/B VHS, Beta, LV.** Spade Cooley. *NOS*

Silver Bears ⅃⅃ 1978 (PG) Caine is an unlikely mobster in this comedy. He's sent to Switzerland to buy a bank for laundering purposes and ends up being swindled himself. So-so entry adapted from the novel by Paul Erdman. **114m/C VHS, Beta.** Michael Caine, Cybill Shepherd, Louis Jourdan, Stephane Audran, David Warner, Tom Smothers, Martin Balsam, Jay Leno, Charles Gray, Joss Ackland; **D:** Ivan Passer; **W:** Claude Bolling. *NO*

The Silver Bullet 1934 Follows the adventures of Tom, the sheriff of a small gold mining town. **55m/C VHS.** Tom Tyler, Jayne Regan, Lafe McKee, Charles King, George Chesebro, Charles "Slim" Whitaker, Lew Meehan, Franklyn Farnum, Walt Williams; **D:** Bernard B. Ray. *GPV*

Silver Bullet ⅃⅃ *Stephen King's Silver Bullet* 1985 (R) Adapted from Stephen King's "Cycle of the Werewolf," about a town whose inhabitants are being brutally murdered. It finally dawns on them the culprit is a werewolf. Action moves along at a good clip and the film has its share of suspense. **95m/C VHS, LV, Closed Caption.** Corey Haim, Gary Busey, Megan Follows, Everett McGill, Robin Groves, Leon Russom, Terry O'Quinn, Bill Smitrovich, Kent Broadhurst, Lawrence Tierney; **D:** Daniel Attias; **W:** Stephen King; **C:** Armando Nannuzzi. *PAR*

The Silver Chalice ⅃ 1954 Newman's career somehow survived his movie debut in this bloated, turgid Biblical epic about the momentous events that befall a young Greek sculptor who fashions the cup that will be used at the Last Supper. Newman later took out an ad in Variety to apologize for the film, in which Greene also made his debut. Based on the novel by Thomas Costain. **135m/C VHS, Beta.** Paul Newman, Virginia Mayo, Pier Angeli, Jack Palance, Natalie Wood, Joseph Wiseman, Lorne Greene, E.G. Marshall; **D:** Victor Saville; **M:** Franz Waxman. Nominations: Academy Awards '54: Best Color Cinematography, Best Original Dramatic/Comedy Score. *WAR*

Silver City ⅃⅃ 1984 (PG) A saga depicting the plight of Polish refugees in Australia in 1949. A pair of lovers find each other in a crowded refugee camp. She's married to her friend. Too-complex, slow but earnest effort. **110m/C VHS, Beta.** AU Gosia Dobrowolska, Ivar Kants; **D:** Sophia Turkiewicz. *ORI*

Silver City Bonanza ⅃⅃½ 1951 Lots of action in this outrageous oater that includes a haunted ranch and an undersea battle as plot devices. Singing cowboy Allen and sidekick Ebsen use a seeing-eye dog to track down the killer of a blind man. Since Roy Rogers and Republic parted company the year of this film's release, singing star Allen was groomed to become the new "King of the Cowboys." However, by this time, the singing-cowboy craze was almost old hat. **67m/B VHS, Closed Caption.** Rex Allen, Buddy Ebsen, Mary Ellen Kay, Billy Kimbley, Alix Ebsen, Bill Kennedy, Gregg Barton, Clem Bevans; **D:** George Blair; **W:** Bob Williams. *REP*

Silver City Kid ⅃ 1945 Two mine owners learn about a rich mineral vein under a rancher's land, kill him, and then try to steal the property from his sister. So it's up to ranch foreman Jack Adams (Lane) to expose the plot and bring the guilty to justice. **56m/B VHS, Closed Caption.** Allan "Rocky" Lane. *REP*

Silver Dream Racer ⅃½ 1983 (PG) An English grease monkey wants to win the World Motorcycle Championship title away from an American biker. He's also after someone else's girlfriend. Boring, stilted, unoriginal "Big Race" flick. **103m/C VHS, Beta.** Beau Bridges, David Essex, Christina Raines, Diane Keen, Harry H. Corbett; **D:** David Wickes; **M:** David Essex. *ART, VES*

The Silver Horde ⅃⅃½ 1930 Alaskan salmon fishery owner McCrea battles villainous competitor Gordon for both his livelihood and his ladyfriend—dancehall dame Brent. Arthur's the society gal who briefly catches McCrea's eye. Silent screen star Sweet ended her career with a brief role. Based on a novel by Rex Beach. **80m/B VHS, Beta.** Joel McCrea, Evelyn Brent, Jean Arthur, Gavin Gordon, Louis Wolheim, Raymond Hatton, Blanche Sweet; **D:** George Archainbaud. *FCT*

Silver Lode ⅃⅃½ 1954 A man accused of murder on his wedding day attempts to clear his name while the law launches an intensive manhunt for him. Ordinary story improved by good, energetic cast. **92m/C VHS, Beta.** John Payne, Dan Duryea, Lizabeth Scott, Stuart Whitman; **D:** Allan Dwan. *NO*

Silver Queen ⅃⅃ 1942 A woman finds out her father has gambled away a silver mine and left her with debts. She opens a saloon, only to have her fiance use the money to hunt for more silver. **81m/B VHS, Beta.** Priscilla Lane, George Brent, Bruce Cabot, Eugene Pallette; **D:** Lloyd Bacon. Nominations: Academy Awards '42: Best Interior Decoration, Best Original Dramatic/Comedy Score. *NO*

Silver River ⅃½ 1948 Average western that marked the final collaboration between director Walsh and star Flynn. It never even comes close to their previous works. Flynn plays a no-good, power-hungry cad who will stop at nothing to get what he wants. He happens to want Sheridan, who is married to Bennett, so Flynn schemes to get rid of him. Overall, Flynn acts as though he really isn't interested in the material and had to make a pact with Walsh that he would stay sober until five in the afternoon while filming. Based on an unpublished novel by Stephen Longstreet. **108m/B VHS, Closed Caption.** Errol Flynn, Ann Sheridan, Thomas Mitchell, Bruce (Herman Brix) Bennett, Tom D'Andrea, Barton MacLane, Monte Blue, Jonathan Hale; **D:** Raoul Walsh; **W:** Stephen Longstreet, Harriet Frank Jr.; **M:** Max Steiner. *MGM*

Silver Spurs ⅃½ 1943 Villain tries to get some oil-rich property by murdering the ranch's owner. Ranch foreman Rogers saves the day. **60m/B VHS, Beta.** Roy Rogers, Jerome Cowan, John Carradine, Phyllis Brooks, Smiley Burnette, Joyce Compton; **D:** Joseph Kane. *NOS, VCN, DVT*

Silver Stallion ⅃½ 1941 Thunder the Wonder Horse plays the title character, who fights rattlesnakes, wild dogs and hoss thieves. Too bad he doesn't give acting lessons to the humans in this frail family western with nice scenery and action scenes. **59m/C VHS, Beta.** David Sharpe, Carol Hughes, Leroy Mason, Walter Long; **D:** Edward Finney. *VYY, GPV*

The Silver Stallion: King of the Wild Brumbies ⅃½ *The Silver Brumby* 1993 (G) The adolescent Indi is enthralled as her writer-mother relates each new chapter in the saga of Thara, the amazing silver stallion. And she images each adventure as the horse triumphs over evil men, other horses, and the elements to become leader of the herd. Based on the Australian children's novel "The Silver Brumby" by Elyne Mitchell. **93m/C VHS, Beta, Closed Caption.** AU Caroline Goodall, Ami Daemion, Russell Crowe; **D:** John

Tatoulis; **W:** John Tatoulis, Jon Stephens; **M:** Tassos Ioannides. *PAR*

Silver Star ♂♂ 1955 Man elected sheriff of a western town turns down the job because he is a pacifist. He changes his mind when his defeated opponent hires a trio of killers to come after him. **73m/B VHS, Beta.** Jimmy Wakely, Edgar Buchanan, Marie Windsor. *NO*

Silver Strand ♂♂½ 1995 (R) Hunky Brian Del Piso (Bellows), a naval cadet in the S.E.A.L. training school, makes the big mistake of falling for sexy Michelle (Sheridan), who just happens to be an officer's wife. As if he didn't have enough challenges, should their affair be exposed Brian might just as well kiss his career goodbye. **CW:** Sexuality and strong language. **104m/C VHS, Closed Caption, Beta.** Gil Bellows, Nicolette Sheridan; **D:** George Miller; **W:** Douglas Day Stewart; **C:** David Connell; **M:** Joseph Conlan. *MGM*

The Silver Streak ♂♂ 1934 The sickly son of a diesel train designer needs an iron lung—pronto. A rival's super-fast locomotive is the only hope for the boy. Murders, runaway engines, and a crew that would rather walk enliven this race against time. **72m/B VHS, Beta.** Sally Blane, Charles Starrett, Arthur Lake, Edgar Kennedy, William Farnum; **D:** Thomas Atkins. *CCB*

Silver Streak ♂♂♂ 1976 (PG) Pooped exec Wilder rides a train from L.A. to Chicago, planning to enjoy a leisurely, relaxing trip. Instead he becomes involved with murder, intrigue, and a beautiful woman. Energetic Hitchcock parody features successful first pairing of Wilder and Pryor. **113m/C VHS, Beta, LV.** Gene Wilder, Richard Pryor, Jill Clayburgh, Patrick McGoohan, Ned Beatty, Ray Walston, Richard Kiel, Scatman Crothers; **D:** Arthur Hiller; **W:** Colin Higgins; **M:** Henry Mancini. Nominations: Academy Awards '76: Best Sound. *FOX*

Silverado ♂♂♂ 1985 (PG-13) Affectionate pastiche of western cliches has everything a viewer could ask for—except Indians. Straightforward plot has four virtuous cowboys rise up against a crooked lawman in a blaze of six guns. No subtlety from the first big Western in quite a while, but plenty of fun and laughs. Laserdisc edition features a widescreen film-to-tape transfer monitored by the photography director, set photos, release trailers, and other publicity hoohah as well as a special time-lapse sequence of the set construction, and interviews with the stars and director Kasdan. Letterboxed laserdisc version is available with dolby surround sound. **132m/C VHS, Beta, LV, Letterbox, Closed Caption.** Kevin Kline, Scott Glenn, Kevin Costner, Danny Glover, Brian Dennehy, Linda Hunt, John Cleese, Jeff Goldblum, Rosanna Arquette, Jeff Fahey; **D:** Lawrence Kasdan; **W:** Lawrence Kasdan; **C:** John Bailey; **M:** Bruce Broughton. Nominations: Academy Awards '85: Best Sound, Best Original Score. *COL, CRC*

Simba ♂♂♂ 1955 A young Englishman arrives at his brother's Kenyan farm to find him murdered in a local skirmish between the Mau Maus and white settlers. Well made, thoughtful look at colonialism, racial animosity, and violence. **98m/C VHS, Beta, LV.** *GB* Dirk Bogarde, Donald Sinden, Virginia McKenna, Orlando Martins; **D:** Brian Desmond Hurst; **C:** Geoffrey Unsworth. *NO*

Simon ♂♂½ 1980 (PG) A group of bored demented scientists brainwash a college professor into believing he is an alien from a distant galaxy, whereupon he begins trying to correct the evil in America. Screwball comedy, or semi-serious satire of some kind? Hard to tell. Some terrific set pieces but the movie as a whole doesn't quite hold together. Directorial debut of Brickman, who previously worked as a scriptwriter with Woody Allen ("Sleeper," etc.). **97m/C VHS, Beta.** Alan Arkin, Madeline Kahn, Fred Gwynne, Adolph Green, Wallace Shawn, Austin Pendleton; **D:** Marshall Brickman; **W:** Marshall Brickman, Thomas Baum. *WAR*

Simon Bolivar ♂♂½ 1969 The title character leads the Venezuelan revolution in 1817. **110m/C VHS, Beta.** Maximilian Schell, Rosanna Schiaffino. *UNI*

Simon, King of the Witches ♂♂½ 1971 (R) An L.A. warlock who lives in a sewer drain finds himself the center of attention when his spells actually work. This interesting hippie/witchcraft entry bogs down now and then but Prine's performance is droll and lively. **90m/C VHS, Beta.** Andrew Prine, Brenda Scott, George Paulsin, Norman Burton, Ultra Violet; **D:** Bruce Kessler; **W:** Robert Phippeny; **C:** David L. Butler. *UNI*

Simon of the Desert ♂♂♂½ 1966 Not Bunuel's very best, but worthy of the master satirist. An ascetic stands on a pillar in the desert for several decades—closer to God, farther from temptation. Pinal is a gorgeous devil that tempts Simon. Hilarious, irreverent, sophisticated. What's with the weird ending, though? In Spanish with English subtitles. **46m/B VHS, Beta.** Claudio Brook, Silvia Pinal; **D:** Luis Bunuel; **W:** Luis Bunuel. *HTV, HHT, DVT*

Simple Justice ♂½ 1989 (R) Mindless, justice-in-own-hands anti-liberal hogwash. Overwrought, smug, and violent story of a young couple beaten by robbers who remain at large. **91m/C VHS.** Cesar Romero, John Spencer, Doris Roberts, Candy McClain; **D:** Deborah Del Prete. *JTC*

Simple Men ♂♂♂ 1992 (R) Odd-ball brothers Bill (a petty criminal) and Dennis (a shy college student) decide to track down their missing father in this fractured comedy. Dad, a former big-league baseball player who bombed the Pentagon in the '60s, is a long-time fugitive hiding out somewhere in the wilds of Long Island. Their search leads them to two equally opposite women, the wary Kate, whom Bill immediately falls for, and the sexy Elina, who turns out to know dear old dad quite well. Deliberately deadpan and cliched, Hartley's quirky style can either irritate or illuminate via the weird turnings of his characters' lives. **CW:** Language. **105m/C VHS, LV, Closed Caption.** Robert John Burke, William Sage, Karen Sillas, Elina Lowensohn, Martin Donovan, Mark Bailey, John MacKay; **D:** Hal Hartley; **W:** Hal Hartley; **C:** Michael Spiller; **M:** Hal Hartley. *COL, IME, NLC*

A Simple Story ♂♂♂ *Une Histoire Simple* 1979 A woman faces her 40th birthday with increasing uneasiness, though her life seems perfect from the outside. She evaluates her chances at love, child-bearing, and friendship, after having an abortion and breaking up with her lover. Schneider's performance is brilliant in this gentle, quiet drama. In French with English subtitles. **110m/C VHS, Beta.** *FR* Romy Schneider, Bruno Cremer, Claude Brasseur; **D:** Claude Sautet. Nominations: Academy Awards '79: Best Foreign Language Film; Cesar Awards '79: Best Actress (Schneider). *FRF, COL*

A Simple Twist of Fate ♂♂½ 1994 (PG-13) Comedy drama gives Martin chance to flex serious muscles with this update of George Eliot's "Silas Marner." Adoptive father Michael McMann wants to keep his daughter Mathilda (played by the prerequisite adorable twins) in the face of demands from her biological father (Byrne), who happens to be a local politician. Then revelations brought out at the custody hearing threaten the politician's career. Cuddly dad is hardly Martin's image (in spite of "Parenthood"), though strong cast limits the sugar. **CW:** A drug-related situation. **106m/C VHS, LV, Closed Caption.** Steve Martin, Gabriel Byrne, Catherine O'Hara, Stephen Baldwin, Alana Austin, Alyssa Austin, Laura Linney, Anne Heche, Michael Des Barres, Byron Jennings; **D:** Gilles Mackinnon; **W:** Steve Martin; **M:** Cliff Eidelman. *TOU*

A Simple Wish ♂♂½ 1997 (PG) Equal employment opportunities now even extend to the fairy godmother realm. Anabel (Wilson) knows her dad (Pastorelli) wants to become a Broadway actor. So she wishes for a fairy godmother—and gets stuck with Murray (Short), the first affirmative-action male practitioner, who's really not very good at spellcasting. Both Anabel and Murray have bigger problems—evil fairy godmother Claudia (Turner) is after all the fairy godmother's magic wands so she can rule the world's wishes.

Short's brand of comic energy plays right into the kid audience, and Wilson lights up every scene she's in. **95m/C VHS, LV, Closed Caption, DVD.** Mara Wilson, Martin Short, Kathleen Turner, Robert Pastorelli, Amanda Plummer, Teri Garr, Francis Capra, Jonathan Hadary, Alan Campbell; **D:** Michael Ritchie; **W:** Jeff Rothberg; **C:** Ralf Bode; **M:** Bruce Broughton. *USH*

Sin of Adam & Eve ♂½ 1972 (R) The story of Adam and Eve in the Garden of Eden and their fall from grace. Voice-over narrator is only sound in this strange dialogue-less story of the Adam and Eve, how they got kicked out of the Garden of Eden, and how they lose and then find each other outside. Ancient plot, to say the least. **72m/C VHS, Beta.** Candy Wilson, Jorge Rivero; **D:** Michael Zachary. *VDM*

The Sin of Harold Diddlebock ♂♂½ *Mad Wednesday* 1947 A man gets fired from his job, stumbles around drunk, and wins a fortune gambling. He then buys a circus and uses a lion to frighten investors into backing him. Inventive comedy, but missing the spark and timing of "The Freshman" (1925), of which it is a sequel. The final feature film for Lloyd (who did all his own stunts), made at the urging of director Sturges. **89m/B VHS.** Harold Lloyd, Margaret Hamilton, Frances Ramsden, Edgar Kennedy, Lionel Stander, Rudy Vallee, Franklin Pangborn; **D:** Preston Sturges. *NOS, BAR, AOV*

The Sin of Madelon Claudet ♂♂♂ *The Lullaby* 1931 Hayes plays common thief who works her way into upper crust of Parisian society only to tumble back into the street, all in the name of making a better life for her illegitimate son. Very sudsy stuff, with an outstanding performance by Hayes. **74m/B VHS.** Helen Hayes, Lewis Stone, Neil Hamilton, Robert Young, Cliff Edwards, Jean Hersholt, Marie Prevost, Karen Morley, Charles Winninger, Alan Hale; **D:** Edgar Selwyn. Academy Awards '32: Best Actress (Hayes). *MGM, FCT*

Sin Takes a Holiday ♂♂½ 1930 A woman marries her boss to save him from his girl friend. On a trip to Paris, she finds that she really does love her husband. By today's standards, it doesn't sound like much, but in the '30s, it was pretty sophisticated stuff. **81m/B VHS.** Constance Bennett, Kenneth MacKenna, Basil Rathbone, Rita La Roy, ZaSu Pitts, Fred Walton, Richard Carle, Helen Johnson; **D:** Paul Stein. *NOS, HEG*

Sin You Sinners ♂ 1963 Aging stripper gets ahold of an amulet that allows her to look youthful and manipulate the lives of others. When she loses the amulet, however, bad things happen. Twisted ending. **73m/B VHS.** June Colbourne, Dian Lloyd, Derek Murcott, Beverly Nazarow, Charles Clements; **D:** Anthony Farrar. *SNC*

Sinai Commandos ♂♂½ *Sinai Commandos: The Story of the Six Day War; Ha'Matarah Tiran* 1968 The story of a group of commandos in the Israeli Six-Day War in 1967 who are assigned to destroy important Arab radar installations. Includes actual combat footage. **99m/C VHS.** Robert Fuller; **D:** Raphael Nussbaum. *ATL, FCT*

Sinatra ♂♂½ 1992 Made for television biopic chronicles the stormy life of crooner Frank Sinatra. Begins with his childhood in Hoboken, New Jersey and works its way through his big band tours, bobby soxer days, career skids, and triumphant comeback with his Oscar-winning performance in "From Here to Eternity," as well as his three marriages, "Rat Pack" friends, and mob connections. Executive producer Tina Sinatra, Frank's daughter, doesn't gloss over her father's less savory character points and Casnoff does well with his leading role. Songs are lip-synched to classic Sinatra tunes with a few early recordings redone by actor Tom Burlinson and Frank Sinatra, Jr. **245m/C VHS, Beta, LV, Closed Caption.** Philip Casnoff, Olympia Dukakis, Joe Santos, Gina Gershon, Nina Siemaszko, Marcia Gay Harden, Rod Steiger, Bob Gunton, David Raynr, James F. Kelly, Matthew Posey, Jay Robinson, Robin Gammell, Todd Waring, Joris Stuyck,

Danny Gans, Jeff Corey; **D:** James Sadwith; **W:** William Mastrosimone; **C:** Reynaldo Villalobos. *WAR*

Sinbad 🎬🎬 1971 A sardonic portrait of an aging hedonist as he tries to hold onto the pleasures of drink, sex and gluttony. In Magyar (Hungarian), with English subtitles. 98m/C VHS, Beta. *HU* **D:** Zoltan Huszarik. *KIV, FCT*

Sinbad and the Eye of the Tiger 🎬🎬 1977 (G) The swashbuckling adventures of Sinbad the Sailor as he encounters the creations of Ray Harryhausen's special effects magic. Don't see this one for the plot, which almost doesn't exist. Otherwise, mildly fun. 113m/C VHS, Beta, LV. *GB* Patrick Wayne, Jane Seymour, Taryn Power, Margaret Whiting; **D:** Sam Wanamaker; **W:** Beverley Cross; **C:** Ted Moore. *COL, CCB*

Sinbad of the Seven Seas 🎬½ 1989 Italian muscle epic based on the ancient legends. Ferrigno isn't green, but he's still a hulk, and he still can't act. It's poorly dubbed, which makes little difference; it would be stupid regardless. 90m/C VHS, Beta, LV. *IT* Lou Ferrigno, John Steiner, Leo Gullotta, Teagan Clive; **D:** Enzo G. Castellari. *WAR, OM*

Sinbad, the Sailor 🎬🎬🎬 1947 Fairbanks fits well in this luminent father's swashbuckling shoes, as he searches for the treasure of Alexander the Great. Self-mocking but hamhanded, and confusing if you seek the hidden plot. Still, it's all in fun, and it is fun. 117m/C VHS, Beta, LV. Douglas Fairbanks Jr., Maureen O'Hara, Anthony Quinn, Walter Slezak, George Tobias, Jane Greer, Mike Mazurki, Sheldon Leonard; **D:** Richard Wallace; **C:** George Barnes. *TTC*

Since You Went Away 🎬🎬🎬½ 1944 An American family copes with the tragedy, heartache and shortages of wartime in classic megatribute to the home front. Be warned: very long and bring your hankies. Colbert is superb, as is the photography. John Derek unobtrusively made his film debut, as an extra. 172m/B VHS, Beta, LV, Closed Caption. Claudette Colbert, Jennifer Jones, Shirley Temple, Joseph Cotten, Agnes Moorehead, Monty Woolley, Guy Madison, Lionel Barrymore, Robert Walker, Hattie McDaniel, Keenan Wynn, Craig Stevens, Albert Basserman, Alla Nazimova, Lloyd Corrigan, Terry Moore, Florence Bates, Ruth Roman, Andrew V. McLaglen, Dorothy Dandridge, Rhonda Fleming; **D:** John Cromwell; **W:** David O. Selznick; **M:** Max Steiner. Academy Awards '44: Best Original Dramatic/Comedy Score; Nominations: Academy Awards '44: Best Actress (Colbert), Best Black and White Cinematography, Best Film Editing, Best Interior Decoration, Best Picture, Best Supporting Actor (Woolley), Best Supporting Actress (Jones). *FOX*

Sincerely Charlotte 🎬🎬🎬 *Signe Charlotte* 1986 Huppert directs her sister in this film about a beautiful singer framed for her boyfriend's murder. She enlists an old lover to help her flee across the countryside. Love story/thriller is pleasingly odd and absorbing. In French with English subtitles. 92m/C VHS, Beta, LV, Closed Caption. *FR* Isabelle Huppert, Niels Arestrup, Christine Pascal; **D:** Caroline Huppert; **C:** Bruno de Keyzer. *COL*

Sincerely Yours woof! 1956 Liberace wisely stayed away from acting after inauspiciously debuting in this horrible, maudlin remake of "The Man Who Played God." He plays a pianist who loses his hearing and decides to become a philanthropist to help those less fortunate than himself. Laughably cheesy. Thirty-one musical numbers, including Liberace's inimitable arrangement of "Chopsticks." 116m/C VHS, Beta, LV. Liberace, Joanne Dru, Dorothy Malone, William Demarest; **D:** Gordon Douglas; **W:** Irving Wallace. *WAR*

A Sinful Life 🎬🎬 1989 (R) A strained, offbeat, B-grade comedy about an odd, infantile mother fighting to keep her unusual child from being taken away. Definitely not a must-see; can be irritating and obnoxious, depending on viewer and mood. Morris is at her oddball comedic best as the mother and former show dancer. Adult Tefkin plays her little girl. Based on the play "Just Like the Pom Pom Girls." 112m/C VHS, Beta, LV.

Anita Morris, Rick Overton, Dennis Christopher, Blair Tefkin, Mark Rolston, Cynthia Szigeti; **D:** William Schreiner. *COL*

Sing 🎬½ 1989 (PG-13) The students in the real-life Brooklyn public school "Sing" program endure the trials of adolescence while putting together a musical revue. Hurtles over the edge into cheesiness from the start, with way too much (cheesy) music. From the creator of "Fame" and "Footloose." 111m/C VHS, Beta, LV. Lorraine Bracco, Peter Dobson, Jessica Steen, Louise Lasser, George DiCenzo, Patti LaBelle; **D:** Richard Baskin; **M:** Jay Gruska. *COL*

Sing, Cowboy, Sing 🎬🎬 1937 Decent adventure story about a wagon train heading west that runs into a band of outlaws doing outlaw stuff and must somehow get through. 60m/B VHS, Beta. Tex Ritter. *NOS, DVT*

Sing Sing Nights 🎬½ *Reprieved* 1935 A world-famous journalist is killed with three bullets. Three men have confessed, but only one could have actually done it. A professor sets out to solve the case. 60m/B VHS. Conway Tearle, Mary Doran, Hardie Albright, Patricia "Boots" Mallory, Ferdinand Gottschalk, Berton Churchill, Jameson Thomas; **D:** Lewis D. Collins. *SNC*

Sing Your Worries Away 🎬🎬 1942 Songwriter Ebsen inherits three million dollars and finds the money causes him nothing but trouble. Band of crooks cause the requisite wacky complications. Fun, harmless musical comedy. ♪It Just Happened to Happen; Sally, My Dear Sally; Sing Your Worries Away; Cindy Lou McWilliams; How Do You Fall in Love. 71m/B VHS, Beta. Buddy Ebsen, Bert Lahr, June Havoc, Patsy Kelly, Margaret Dumont; **D:** Edward Sutherland. *CCB*

Singapore 🎬🎬½ 1947 Rather boring romantic drama finds pearl smuggler Matt Gordon (MacMurray) returning to Singapore to resume his illegal trade at the end of WWII. He spots Linda (Gardner), the love of his life, but discovers she's suffering from amnesia and has married another man. Gangsters want Matt's hidden supply of pearls and kidnap Linda to get his cooperation. Remade with equal dullness in 1956 as "Istanbul." 80m/B VHS, Closed Caption. Fred MacMurray, Ava Gardner, Roland Culver, Richard Haydn, Thomas Gomez, Spring Byington, Porter Hall; **D:** John Brahm; **W:** Seton I. Miller, Robert Thoeren; **C:** Maury Gertsman; **M:** Daniele Amfitheatrof. *USH*

Singin' in the Rain 🎬🎬🎬🎬 1952 One of the all-time great movie musicals—an affectionate spoof of the turmoil that afflicted the motion picture industry in the late 1920s during the changeover from silent films to sound. Co-director Kelly and Hagen lead a glorious cast. Music and lyrics by Arthur Freed and Nacio Herb Brown. Served as basis of story by Betty Comden and Adolph Green. Also available on laserdisc with the original trailer, outtakes, behind the scenes footage, and commentary by film historian Ronald Haver. Later a Broadway musical. ♪All I Do is Dream of You; Should I?; Singin' in the Rain; Wedding of the Painted Doll; Broadway Melody; Would You; I've Got a Feelin' You're Foolin'; You Are My Lucky Star; Broadway Rhythm. 103m/C VHS, Beta, LV, Closed Caption, DVD. Gene Kelly, Donald O'Connor, Jean Hagen, Debbie Reynolds, Rita Moreno, King Donovan, Millard Mitchell, Cyd Charisse, Douglas Fowley, Madge Blake, Joi Lansing; **D:** Gene Kelly, Stanley Donen; **W:** Adolph Green, Betty Comden. Golden Globe Awards '53: Best Actor—Musical/Comedy (O'Connor), National Film Registry '89;; Nominations: Academy Awards '52: Best Supporting Actress (Hagen), Scoring of a Musical. *MGM, TLF, CRC*

The Singing Blacksmith 🎬🎬½ 1938 A relic of American Yiddish cinema, adapting popular 1909 play by David Pinski. A married blacksmith is wooed by another woman and falls victim to alcoholism. Overlong, but Oysher and his rich baritone voice still shine. In Yiddish with English subtitles. 95m/B VHS. *PL* Miriam Riselle, Florence Weiss, Moishe Oysher; **D:** Edgar G. Ulmer. *ERG*

Singing Buckaroo 🎬🎬 1937 Dastardly bandits try to pilfer money from pretty blonde damsel and have to battle with yodelin' cowboy. B-level western good guy Scott belts out a few numbers and saves the day. Innocuously pleasant. 58m/B VHS, Beta. Fred Scott, Victoria Vinton, Cliff Nazarro; **D:** Tom Gibson. *NOS, VYY*

Singing Cowboys, Vol. 2 193? Three films starring brave and talented singing cowboys. Rogers saves a young ranch heir from a couple of con artists in "Sunset Serenade." Tex Ritter plays a deputy sheriff trying to catch a gang of claim jumpers in his first singing western, "Song of the Gringo." Autry stars in "Public Cowboy No. 1," which has old fashioned cattle rustlers using airplanes, radios, and trucks to further their thieving ways. 175m/B VHS. Gene Autry, Tex Ritter, Roy Rogers. *BPG*

The Singing Cowgirl 🎬 1939 Band of outlaws murder a ranch owner to get to a gold mine. Heroine Page rides in to save the day but gets shot down by western stereotypes. 60m/B VHS. Dorothy Page, Dave O'Brien, Vince Barnett, Stanley Price; **D:** Samuel Diege; **W:** Arthur Hoerl. *MOV*

The Singing Detective 1986 A musical/mystery/fantasy British miniseries, based on the work by Dennis Potter. Pulp fiction writer Phillip Marlowe (Gambon) is confined to his hospital bed, unable to move due to extreme psoriasis. In his lucid moments he tries to figure out the cause of his condition, but in his elaborate daydreams he's a detective (and big band singer) who's working to solve a series of murders. Six episodes: "Skin," "Heat," "Lovely Days," "Clues," "Pitter Patter," and "Who Done It." 420m/C VHS. *GB* Michael Gambon, Patrick Malahide, Janet Suzman, Joanne Whalley; **D:** Jon Amiel. *FOX, PBS*

The Singing Nun 🎬🎬 1966 The true story of a Belgian nun who takes a liking to a motherless little boy. She writes a song for him, and a kind-hearted priest talks to a record producer to see about getting the song to go somewhere. The song soon becomes an international hit, and the nun ends up on the "Ed Sullivan Show." Sentimental and sugary sweet, but a big boxoffice hit. 98m/C VHS. Debbie Reynolds, Ricardo Montalban, Greer Garson, Agnes Moorehead, Chad Everett, Katharine Ross, Juanita Moore, Ricky Cordell, Michael Pate, Tom Drake; **D:** Henry Koster; **C:** Milton Krasner. Nominations: Academy Awards '66: Best Adapted Score. *MGM*

Singing the Blues in Red 🎬🎬🎬 1987 Dark, pessimistic character study of a protest singer/songwriter who leaves his native East Germany to escape repression and finds his loyalties divided. A moving personal story, as well as insightful, subtle social commentary. In English and German with subtitles. 110m/C VHS, Beta. *GE* Gerulf Pannach, Fabienne Babe, Cristine Rose, Trevor Griffiths; **D:** Ken Loach; **W:** Trevor Griffiths; **C:** Chris Menges. *NO*

Single Bars, Single Women 🎬½ 1984 Utterly formulaic made for TV comedy-drama based on Dolly Parton's song is not entirely without merit. Lonely people gather in a local pick-up joint and share their miseries and hopes. 96m/C VHS, Beta. Shelley Hack, Christine Lahti, Tony Danza, Mare Winningham, Keith Gordon, Paul Michael Glaser; **D:** Harry Winer; **M:** Basil Poledouris. *PAR, VTR*

A Single Girl 🎬🎬½ *La Fille Seule* 1996 Follows, in real time, a young woman as she tells her boyfriend that she's pregnant, (Ledoyen) through her job handling room service at a Paris hotel, then again with her boyfriend after work. French with subtitles. Part sexual hotel fantasy, part observation of an ordinary couple going about daily life. 90m/C VHS. *FR* Virginie Ledoyen, Benoit Magimel, Vera Briole, Dominique Valadie; **D:** Benoit Jacquot; **W:** Benoit Jacquot, Jerome Beaujour; **C:** Caroline Champetier; **M:** Kvarteto Mesta Prahi. *FXL*

Single Room Furnished ♂♂½ 1968 The fall of a buxom blonde from uncorrupted innocence through pregnancies to desperate prostitution. Fails to demonstrate any range of talent in Mansfield, who died before it was completed. Exploitative and pathetic. **93m/C VHS, Beta.** Jayne Mansfield, Dorothy Keller; **D:** Matt Cimber, Matteo Ottaviano. *VCI, HEG*

The Single Standard ♂♂ 1929 San Francisco deb Garbo flings with artsy Asther and finds out the Hayes Code is just around the corner. **93m/B VHS.** Greta Garbo, Nils Asther, Johnny Mack Brown, Dorothy Sebastian, Lane Chandler, Zeffie Tilbury; **D:** John S. Robertson. *MGM, FCT*

Single White Female ♂♂½ 1992 (R) Psycho thriller casts Fonda as chic Manhattan computer consultant Allison Jones, who advertises for a roommate after a falling out with her boyfriend. Leigh is the frumpy, shy, bookstore clerk Hedra who answers the ad and moves into Allie's great Upper West Side apartment. They hit it off, that is until Allie notices Hedra's beginning to look and sound very familiar. Hmm... Derivative, though bonus points for creative murder implements and interesting performances throughout, including Friedman as Allie's gay upstairs neighbor. Based on the novel "SWF Seeks Same" by John Lutz. **CW:** Language, violence, and strong sexuality. **107m/C VHS, Beta, LV, Closed Caption, DVD.** Bridget Fonda, Jennifer Jason Leigh, Steven Weber, Peter Friedman, Stephen Tobolowsky, Frances Bay, Renee Estevez, Kenneth Tobey; **D:** Barbet Schroeder; **W:** Don Roos; **M:** Howard Shore. MTV Movie Awards '93: Best Villain (Leigh). *COL, BTV*

Singles ♂♂♂ 1992 (PG-13) Seattle's music scene is the background for this lighthearted look at single 20-somethings in the '90s. Hits dead on thanks to Crowe's tight script and a talented cast, and speaks straight to its intended audience—the "Generation X" crowd. Real life band Pearl Jam plays alternative band Citizen Dick and sets the tone for a great soundtrack featuring the hot Seattle sounds of Alice in Chains, Soundgarden, and Mudhoney. The video contains six extra minutes of footage after the credits that was thankfully edited out of the final cut. Look for Horton, Stoltz (as a mime), Skerritt, and Burton in cameos. **100m/C VHS, Beta, LV, Letterbox, Closed Caption.** Matt Dillon, Bridget Fonda, Campbell Scott, Kyra Sedgwick, Sheila Kelley, Jim True, Bill Pullman, James LeGros, Ally Walker, Devon Raymond, Camillo Gallardo, Jeremy Piven; **Cameos:** Tom Skerritt, Peter Horton, Eric Stoltz, Tim Burton; **D:** Cameron Crowe; **W:** Cameron Crowe; **M:** Paul Westerberg. *WAR, PMS*

Singleton's Pluck ♂♂♂ *Laughterhouse* 1984 Touching British comedy about a determined farmer who must walk his 500 geese 100 miles to market because of a strike. He becomes a celebrity when the TV stations start covering his odyssey. **89m/C VHS, Beta.** *GB* Ian Holm, Penelope Wilton, Bill Owen, Richard Hope; **D:** Richard Eyre. *VTR*

The Sinister Invasion ♂ *Alien Terror; The Incredible Invasion* 1968 A turn-of-the-century scientist (Karloff) discovers a death ray. Aliens, who would like a closer peek at what makes it work, use a sex-fiend's body to do so. One of Karloff's last four films, made simultaneously in Mexico. The great horror master's final offering. Excruciating. **95m/C VHS, Beta.** *MX* Boris Karloff, Enrique Guzman, Jack Hill; **D:** Juan Ibanez. *SNC*

The Sinister Urge woof! *The Young and the Immortal; Hellborn* 1960 Vice cops Duncan and Moore search for the murderer of three women. Seems the disturbed slayer is unbalanced because he's been looking at pictures of naked ladies. Was this meant to be taken seriously at the time? The last film by camp director Wood, maker of the infamous "Plan 9 from Outer Space." A must see for Wood fans. **82m/B VHS, Beta.** Kenne Duncan, Duke Moore, Jean Fontaine; **D:** Edward D. Wood Jr. *AOV, SNC*

Sink the Bismarck ♂♂♂ 1960 British navy sets out to locate and sink infamous German battleship during WWII. Good special effects with battle sequences in this drama based on real incidents. One of the better of the plethora of WWII movies, with stirring naval battles and stylish documentary-style direction. **97m/B VHS, Beta.** Kenneth More, Dana Wynter, Karel Stepanek, Carl Mohner, Laurence Naismith, Geoffrey Keen, Michael Hordern, Maurice Denham, Esmond Knight; **D:** Lewis Gilbert. *FOX, HMV*

Sinners ♂ 1989 Outrageous portrait of an Italian family in the Big Apple trying to come to terms with the violence that surrounds their neighborhood. **90m/C VHS, Beta.** Joey Travolta, Robert Gallo, Joe Palese, Lou Calvelli, Angie Daglas, Sabrina Ferrand; **D:** Charles Kanganis. *PMH*

Sinner's Blood woof! 1970 (R) Bikers terrorize and torture a small town. **81m/C VHS, Beta.** Stephen Jacques, Crusty Beal, Nancy Sheldon, Parker Herriott, Julie Connors; **D:** Neil Douglas.

Sinners in Paradise ♂♂ 1938 An assortment of trouble-plagued characters alternately hide and face up to their mysterious pasts when their plane crashes on a deserted island. Interesting "crucible" premise runs out of steam, but plucky, resourceful cast and competent direction keep it going. **64m/B VHS, Beta.** Madge Evans, John Boles, Bruce Cabot, Marion Martin, Gene Lockhart, Dwight Frye, Charlotte Wynters, Nana Bryant, Milburn Stone, Donald (Don "Red") Barry, Morgan Conway; **D:** James Whale. *SNC, MLB*

Sins 1985 On her way up the ladder of success in the fashion industry, Helene has stepped on a few toes. Those rivals and her ever-increasing acquisition of power and money make this film an exciting drama. **336m/C VHS, Beta.** Joan Collins, Timothy Dalton, Catherine Mary Stewart, Gene Kelly, James Farentino; **D:** Douglas Hickox. *VTR, HHE*

Sins of Desire ♂♂ 1992 Highly erotic thriller with Roberts going undercover as a nurse in a sex therapy clinic. It seems her sister was a former patient at the clinic and has since died a mysterious death. Linking up with private eye Cassavetes, Roberts sets out to investigate the doctors who treated her sister, searching for clues to her untimely death. **90m/C VHS, Closed Caption.** Tanya Roberts, Jay Richardson, Delia Sheppard, Nick Cassavetes, Jan-Michael Vincent; **D:** Jim Wynorski; **W:** Mark Thomas McGee, Peter Paul Liapis. *COL, THV, PMS*

The Sins of Dorian Gray ♂ 1982 (PG) A modernized adaptation of "The Portrait of Dorian Grey" by Oscar Wilde, with Dorian as a beautiful woman who remains young for 30 years, while a video screen test ages, like the original character's mirror image. Might have been intriguing and stylish; instead, only disappointing and incompetent. Made for television. **95m/C VHS, Beta, Closed Caption.** Belinda Bauer, Joseph Bottoms, Anthony Perkins; **D:** Tony Maylam. *FOX*

Sins of Jezebel ♂ 1954 Biblical epic about Jezebel, who worships an evil god. She marries the king of Israel and brings the kingdom nothing but trouble. **74m/C VHS, Beta, LV.** Paulette Goddard, George Nader, John Hoyt, Eduard Franz; **D:** Reginald LeBorg. *NO*

Sins of Rome ♂♂ 1954 Spartacus risks it all in a bold attempt to free his fellow slaves. Not nearly the equal of Kirk Douglas's "Spartacus," but much better than later Italian adventure epics. **75m/B VHS.** *IT* Ludmila Tcherina, Massimo Girotti, Gianna Maria Canale, Yves Vincent; **D:** Riccardo (Robert Hampton) Freda. *SNC*

Sins of the Mind ♂♂ 1997 (R) Michelle (Crider), the 25-year-old daughter of Eve (Clayburgh) and William (Farrell) Widener, awakens from a coma after a car accident and turns out to have psychological damage. Previously a conservative, hard-working artist, she's now a hedonist, given to erratic impulses and sexual compulsions. Michelle's actions threaten her family but her father is convinced he can still get his little girl back. Made for cable. **CW:** Sexual content. **92m/C VHS.**

Missy Crider, Mike Farrell, Jill Clayburgh, Louise Fletcher, Michael Mantell, Robert Pine, Cyia Batten, Grayson McCouch; **D:** James Frawley. *PAR*

Sins of the Night ♂ 1993 (R) An ex-con insurance investigator is hired to find a sultry exotic dancer. Also available in an unrated version. **82m/C VHS.** Nick Cassavetes, Deborah Shelton.

Sinthia: The Devil's Doll ♂♂ 1970 A little girl is thought to be possessed by a demon after she has horrible dreams about killing her father. **?m/C VHS.** Shula Roan, Diane Webber; **D:** Ray Dennis Steckler. *SNC, TPV*

Sioux City ♂♂½ 1994 (PG-13) Jesse Rainfeather Goldman (Phillips) is a Lakota Sioux adopted away from the reservation of his birth and raised in Beverly Hills by a Jewish family. Jesse's curious when his birth mother suddenly contacts him, but when he arrives at the Sioux City reservation, he discovers she's suddenly died under mysterious circumstances. So Jesse sticks around to find out what's going on and discovers his heritage along the way. Well-meaning but dull. **102m/C VHS, Closed Caption.** Lou Diamond Phillips, Salli Richardson, Melinda Dillon, Ralph Waite, Adam Roarke, Bill Allen, Gary Farmer; **D:** Lou Diamond Phillips; **W:** L. Virginia Browne; **M:** Christopher Lindsey. *CAF*

Sioux City Sue ♂♂ 1946 Talent scouts looking to cast a western musical find Autry, then trick him into being the voice of a singing donkey in an animated production. But, the yodelin' cowboy belts out a number or two, and the poobahs give him the lead. Singin' and fancy ridin' abound in Autry's first post-WWII role. **69m/B VHS, Beta.** Gene Autry, Lynn (Mary Hart) Roberts, Sterling Holloway. *NO*

Sirens ♂♂½ 1994 (R) Staid minister takes Australian artist Norman Lindsay to task for submitting scandalous works to public exhibitions. Noted by one reviewer as "Enchanted April with nipples," comedy of manners is witty but lacks plot and looks remarkably like a centerfold layout. Ample displays of nudity as the models (including supermodel MacPherson in her acting debut) frolic in the buff. Grant is terrific as the seemingly enlightened but easily shocked minister, but Neill's Lindsay is thinly written and too often takes a back seat to the vamping models. Fictionalized account of a true incident from the 1930s; Lindsay's home and some of his artworks were used. Check out writer/director Duigan as a pompous village minister. **CW:** Language, abundant nudity, and sex-related scenes. **96m/C VHS, LV, Closed Caption.** *AU GB* Hugh Grant, Tara Fitzgerald, Sam Neill, Elle Macpherson, Kate Fischer, Portia de Rossi, Pamela Rabe, Ben Mendelsohn, John Polson, Mark Gerber, Julia Stone, Ellie MacCarthy, Vincent Ball; **Cameos:** John Duigan; **D:** John Duigan; **W:** John Duigan; **C:** Geoff Burton; **M:** Rachel Portman. *MAX*

Siringo ♂♂½ 1994 U.S. Deputy Marshal Charlie Siringo (Johnson) is out to capture escaped convict Wade Lewis (Macht). The two antagonists share a nasty history as Siringo, along with a young deputy, heads out to the ranch of former prostitute Kaitlin (Bernard) for a final showdown. **90m/C VHS.** Brad Johnson, Stephen Macht, Chad Lowe, Crystal Bernard; **D:** Kevin G. Cremin. *AVE*

Sirocco ♂♂½ 1951 An American gun-runner (Bogart) stuck in Syria in 1925 matches wits with a French intelligence officer amid civil war and intrigue. About the underbelly of human affairs. **111m/B VHS, Beta, LV.** Humphrey Bogart, Lee J. Cobb, Zero Mostel, Everett Sloane, Gerald Mohr; **D:** Curtis Bernhardt; **C:** Burnett Guffey. *COL*

Sister Act ♂♂½ 1992 (PG) Surprising box-office hit casts Goldberg as a Reno lounge singer and inadvertent witness to a mob murder who hides out in a convent—where she's as comfortable in a habit as a fish is out of water. Much to the dismay of poker-faced Mother Superior Smith, she takes over the rag-tag choir and molds them into a swinging, religious version of a '60s girls group. Stock characters and situations are deflected by some genuinely funny moments and good performances, especially by Najimy and Makkena. Coached by the very clever Shaiman, Whoopie handles her singing bits with gusto, highlight of which is "My God," sung to the tune of "My Guy." **100m/C VHS, Beta, LV, Letterbox, Closed Caption.** Whoopi Goldberg, Maggie Smith, Harvey Keitel, Bill Nunn, Kathy Najimy, Wendy Makkena, Mary Wickes, Robert Miranda, Richard Portnow, Joseph Maher; *D:* Emile Ardolino; *W:* Joseph Howard; *M:* Marc Shaiman. TOU, PMS

Sister Act 2: Back in the Habit 🐾🐾 1993 (PG) Mediocre retread finds Goldberg once again donning her nun's habit and getting a choir rocking. Deloris has established her singing career in Vegas, but she's persuaded by her nun friends to whip the incorrigible music students at a troubled inner-city high school into shape for an all-state choral competition. The musical numbers and singing are catchy and well-done but Goldberg seems to have phoned her work in; given her reported $7,000,000 salary, a little more life is expected. She's still sharp with the one-liners but it's all familiar ground. Geared directly towards young viewers. **107m/C VHS, LV, Closed Caption.** Whoopi Goldberg, Kathy Najimy, James Coburn, Maggie Smith, Wendy Makkena, Barnard Hughes, Mary Wickes, Sheryl Lee Ralph, Michael Jeter, Robert Pastorelli, Thomas Gottschalk, Lauryn Hill, Brad Sullivan; *D:* Bill Duke; *W:* James Orr, Jim Cruickshank, Judi Ann Mason; *M:* Miles Goodman. Blockbuster Entertainment Awards '95: Comedy Actress, Video (Goldberg); Nominations: MTV Movie Awards '94: Best Comedic Performance (Goldberg). TOU

Sister Dora 🐾🐾½ 1977 An idealistic young woman joins a nursing sisterhood in 19th century England but she questions her vocation when she falls in love. Adapted from a popular romance novel. **147m/C VHS. GB** Dorothy Tutin, James Grout, Peter Cellier; *D:* Mark Miller. NO

The Sister-in-Law 🐾🐾 1974 (R) Shady dealings, seduction, and adultery run rampant. Savage (who also wrote and sings the folk score) reluctantly agrees to deliver a package across the Canadian border for his brother. Intriguing. **80m/C VHS, Beta.** John Savage, Anne Saxon, W.G. McMillan, Meredith Baer; *D:* Joseph Rubin.

The Sister-in-Law 🐾🐾½ 1995 (PG-13) Chilling cable suspenser finds the beautiful and evil Sarah Preston (Vernon) assuming the identity of the woman she's just killed—the widow of wealthy George Richards' (McCarthy) estranged son. George is dying and pathetically eager to accept Sarah at face value as is his vulnerable daughter Madlyn (Reed). But Sarah has not chosen the Richards family at random—she has a longtime grudge and plans to take her revenge slowly—so be prepared for a few more bodies to turn up.*CW:* Some violence and sensuality. **95m/C VHS, Beta, Closed Caption.** Kate Vernon, Kevin McCarthy, Shanna Reed, Craig Wasson; *D:* Noel Nosseck; *W:* David Callaway, Megan Marks. PAR

Sister Kenny 🐾🐾🐾 1946 Follows the story of a legendary Australian nurse crusading for the treatment of infantile paralysis. Stirring, well-made screen biography. Based on Elizabeth Kenny's memoir, "And They Shall Walk." **116m/B VHS, Beta, LV.** Rosalind Russell, Dean Jagger, Alexander Knox, Philip Merivale, Beulah Bondi, Charles Halton; *D:* Dudley Nichols; *C:* George Barnes. Golden Globe Awards '47: Best Actress—Drama (Russell); Nominations: Academy Awards '46: Best Actress (Russell). NOS, CCB, TTC

Sister My Sister 🐾🐾 1994 (R) True crime story that served as the inspiration for Jean Genet's play "The Maids." In a French provincial town lives the authoritarian Madame Danzard (Walters), who stifles daughter Isabelle (Thursfield), and subjects her two maids, sisters Christine (Richardson) and Lea (May), to an equally harsh discipline. The tension between the four women reaches a highstrung crescendo, leading to violence. Claustrophobic character study.*CW:* Sexuality and a brutal murder sequence. **89m/C VHS. GB**

Julie Walters, Joely Richardson, Jodhi May, Sophie Thursfield; *D:* Nancy Meckler; *W:* Wendy Kelleman; *C:* Ashley Ropwe; *M:* Stephen Warbeck. APX

Sister, Sister 🐾🐾 1987 (R) A Congressional aide on vacation in Louisiana takes a room in an old mansion. He gradually discovers the secret of the house and its resident sisters. Dark Southern gothicism, full of plot surprises, with a twisted ending. **91m/C VHS, Beta, LV.** Eric Stoltz, Judith Ivey, Jennifer Jason Leigh, Dennis Lipscomb, Anne Pitoniak, Natalija Nogulich; *D:* Bill Condon; *W:* Bill Condon, Joel Cohen, Ginny Cerrella; *M:* Richard Einhorn. VTR

Sister Street Fighter 🐾 1976 Action star Sonny Chiba takes a rest from his "Street Fighter" series in favor of protege Long, who's determined to deliver her own brand of deadly justice in this martial arts fest. **81m/C VHS.** Tina Long; *D:* Kazuhiko Yamaguchi. NLC

The Sisterhood 🐾 1988 (R) A pair of amazons fight for women's rights in a post-nuclear future. Cheap feminist theme laid over warmed-over sci-fi plot. **75m/C VHS, Beta, LV.** Rebecca Holden, Chuck Wagner, Lynn-Holly Johnson, Barbara Hooper; *D:* Cirio H. Santiago.

The Sisters 🐾🐾🐾 1938 Lavish film of three sisters and their marital problems in turn of the century San Francisco. Davis gives a great performance as the oldest sister with the most trouble—notably in the form of unreliable sports reporter Flynn. Look for Susan Hayward in a bit role, as well as Bogart's wife, Mayo Methot. Based on the bestselling novel by Myron Brinig. **98m/B VHS, Closed Caption.** Bette Davis, Errol Flynn, Anita Louise, Jane Bryan, Ian Hunter, Henry Travers, Beulah Bondi, Donald Crisp, Dick Foran, Patric Knowles; *D:* Anatole Litvak; *M:* Max Steiner. MGM

Sisters 🐾🐾🐾 1973 (R) Siamese twins are separated surgically, but one doesn't survive the operation. The remaining sister is scarred physically and mentally with her personality split into bad and good. The bad side commits a murder, witnessed (or was it?) by an investigative reporter. And then things really get crazy. DePalma's first ode to Hitchcock, with great music by Hitchcock's favorite composer, Bernard Herrmann. Scary and suspenseful. **93m/C VHS, Beta.** Margot Kidder, Charles Durning, Barnard Hughes, Jennifer Salt, William Finley, Lisle Wilson, Mary Davenport, Dolph Sweet; *D:* Brian DePalma; *W:* Brian DePalma, Louisa Rose; *C:* Gregory Sandor; *M:* Bernard Herrmann. WAR, OM

Sisters of Death 🐾🐾 1976 (PG) Five members of a sorority gather together for a reunion in a remote California town. Little do they know, a psychopath is stalking them, one by one. Could it have something to do with the terrible secret they each keep? Good, cheap thrills and some Bicentennial features to boot. **87m/C VHS, Beta.** Arthur Franz, Claudia Jennings, Cheri Howell, Sherry Boucher, Paul Carr; *D:* Joseph Mazzuca. VCI

Sisters of Gion 🐾🐾🐾½ 1936 Mizoguchi's most famous and arguably best pre-war film. Two geisha sisters in Tokyo's red-light district reflect the tension in Japanese culture by waging a quiet battle of tradition vs. progressiveness. Highly acclaimed. In Japanese with English subtitles. **69m/B VHS, Beta. JP** Isuzu Yamada, Yoko Umemura; *D:* Kenji Mizoguchi. FCT

Sisters of Satan 🐾🐾½ 1975 (R) The nuns of the infamous convent St. Archangelo choose to survive by trading God for the devil. **91m/C VHS, Beta.** MX Claudio Brook, David Silva, Tina Romero, Susana Kamini; *D:* Juan Lopez Moctezuma. MPI

Sisters of the Gion 🐾🐾 Gion No Shimai 1936 Story follows two geisha sisters, illuminating the plight of women in Japan. Elder sister Umekichi is traditional and dependent on her patrons while her modern younger sister Omocha exploits her customers as much as possible. But no matter the difference in their attitudes, both remain trapped by circumstances. Adapted from the novel "Yama" by Alexander Ivanovich Kuprin. Japanese with subtitles. **66m/B VHS. JP** Isuzu Yamada,

Yoko Umemura, Eitaro Shindo, Benkei Shiganoya; *D:* Kenji Mizoguchi; *W:* Kenji Mizoguchi, Yoshikata Yoda; *C:* Minoru Miki. HMV

Sisters, Or the Balance of Happiness 🐾🐾 Schwestern Oder die Balance des Glucks 1979 Orderly Maria (Lampe) runs the household for her resentful, dependent sister Anna (Gabriel). Opposites in temperment, the dysfunctional duo can neither live with or without each other. When Anna commits suicide, Maria tries to makeover young typist Miriam (Fruh) to take her sister's place. German with subtitles. **97m/C VHS. GE** Jutta Lampe, Gudrun Gabriel, Jessica Fruh; *D:* Margarethe von Trotta; *W:* Margarethe von Trotta; *C:* Franz Rath; *M:* Konstantin Wecker. FCT

Sitting Ducks 🐾🐾🐾 1980 (R) Mild-mannered accountant and lecherous pal rip off and then attempt to outrun the mob—all while swapping songs and confessions. Emil and Norman make it up as they go along; their hilarious repartee is largely improvised. They pick up a gorgeous lady (Townsend) and go about their way. **88m/C VHS, Beta.** Michael Emil, Zack Norman, Patrice Townsend, Richard Romanus, Irene Forrest, Henry Jaglom; *D:* Henry Jaglom; *W:* Henry Jaglom.

Six Days, Seven Nights 🐾🐾½ 1998 (PG-13) Brash magazine editor Robin Monroe (Heche) is on a tropical vacation with fiance Frank (Schwimmer) when a deadline crisis forces her to ask gruff cargo pilot Quinn Harris (Ford) for a lift to Tahiti. The incompatible duo get stranded on a remote island when the plane goes down and naturally need each other to survive. This started out as a routine romantic comedy but the action quotient was upped considerably as filming progressed, thanks to a storyline involving modern-day pirates that's frankly a waste of time. Also a waste are scenes involving fiance Frank with Quinn's bodacious but dumb babe, Angelica (Obradors). Why does the only other woman with a significant part have to be a coochie-coo Charo impersonator? Thankfully, Ford and Heche do have considerable sass between them. Filmed on location in Kauai.*CW:* Language, sensuality and brief violence. **101m/C VHS.** Harrison Ford, Anne Heche, David Schwimmer, Temuera Morrison, Jacqueline Obradors, Allison Janney, Danny Trejo; *D:* Ivan Reitman; *W:* Michael Browning; *C:* Michael Chapman; *M:* Randy Edelman. NYR

Six Degrees of Separation 🐾🐾½ 1993 (R) Some believe that any two people, anywhere in the world, are connected by links to only six other people, hence the six degrees of separation. For the upper crust New Yorker Kittredges, Ouisa (Channing) and Flan (Sutherland), this becomes an issue when they encounter a charming young man (Smith) who claims to be Sidney Poitier's son and a friend of their children. The story unfolds as they realize they've been hustled—and don't understand why. Guare adapted his hit play, but what worked well there is almost too talky here. Channing, reprising her stage role, is very good as the stuffy Ouisa, with Sutherland delivering another interesting performance. Incredibly, the play was based on a true story.*CW:* Language and some sexuality. **112m/C VHS, LV, Closed Caption.** Stockard Channing, Will Smith, Donald Sutherland, Mary Beth Hurt, Bruce Davison, Ian McKellen, Richard Masur, Anthony Michael Hall, Heather Graham, Eric Thal, Anthony Rapp, Osgood Perkins, Kitty Carlisle Hart, Catherine Kellner; *D:* Fred Schepisi; *W:* John Guare; *C:* Ian Baker; *M:* Jerry Goldsmith. Nominations: Academy Awards '93: Best Actress (Channing); Golden Globe Awards '94: Best Actress—Musical/Comedy (Channing). MGM

Six Fois Deux/Sur et Sous la Communication 🐾🐾🐾 1976 A six-part experimental series made for French television, in which Godard and Mieville analyze modern culture and socioeconomics via a free-form essay format, combining interviews, screened text, self-referential devices and news footage. In French with English voice-over. **100m/C VHS, Beta. FR D:** Jean-Luc Godard, Anne-Marie Mieville.

Six Gun Gospel 🎬🎬 1943 Hatton masquerades as a preacher to investigate some shady dealings. Laughs come when the women of the congregation prevail upon him to sing, and he croons a ballad about Jesse James! 59m/B VHS. Johnny Mack Brown, Raymond Hatton, Inna Gest, Eddie Dew, Roy Barcroft, Kenneth MacDonald, Bud Osborne; *D:* Lambert Hillyer. *DVT, HEG*

Six Gun Rhythm 🎬½ 1939 Novelty western plot has football player traveling to Texas to avenge his father's murder. 59m/B VHS, Beta. Tex Fletcher. *NOS, VDM, HEG*

633 Squadron 🎬🎬½ 1964 A skilled R.A.F. pilot attempts to lead his squadron on a mission deep into the fjords of Norway in search of a Nazi fuel plant. Robertson tries hard, as always, but is really not British officer material. Well-made war flick, based on a true story. 102m/C VHS, Beta. Cliff Robertson, George Chakiris, Maria Perschy, Harry Andrews; *D:* Walter Grauman; *W:* James Clavell. *MGM*

Six in Paris 🎬🎬½ *Paris vu Par* 1968 Six short films by acclaimed French New Wave directors, each depicting a different Parisian neighborhood. "Saint-Germain-des-Pres" finds an American girl disillusioned by two French boys. "Gare du Nord" has a woman meeting a handsome stranger who announces he's going to kill himself. A shy dishwasher brings a prostitute to his room in the "Rue Saint-Denis." When a salesman is accosted by a derelict in the "Place de l'Etoile" he hits him with his umbrella and then thinks he's killed the man. "Montparnasse-Levallois" has a woman thinking she's mixed-up her meetings with her two lovers. "La Muette" finds a small boy buying earplugs to shut out the noise of his parents constant arguing. In French with English subtitles. 93m/C VHS. *FR* Barbara Wilkin, Jean-Francois Chappey, Jean-Pierre Andreani, Nadine Ballot, Barbet Schroeder, Gilles Queant, Micheline Dax, Claude Melki, Jean-Michel Rouziere, Marcel Gallon, Joanna Shimkus, Philippe Hiquilly, Serge Davri, Stephane Audran, Gilles Chusseau, Dinah Saril, Claude Chabrol; *D:* Jean Douchet, Jean Rouch, Jean-Daniel Pollet, Eric Rohmer, Jean-Luc Godard, Claude Chabrol; *W:* Jean Douchet, George Keller, Jean Rouch, Jean-Daniel Pollet, Eric Rohmer, Jean-Luc Godard, Claude Chabrol; *C:* Nestor Almendros. *NYF, FCT*

Six of a Kind 🎬🎬🎬 1934 When Flora (Boland) and J. Pinkham Whinney (Ruggles) decide to drive to California for a second honeymoon, they advertise for another couple to share expenses. Unfortunately, it's Burns and Allen and their exceptionally large Great Dane that answer the ad. There's numerous complications, including bank clerk Whinney's being suspected of embezzlement, prompting Sheriff "Honest John" Hoxley (Fields) to go after the supposed criminals. Veteran comedy performers make this one a delight. 63m/B VHS, Closed Caption. Charlie Ruggles, Mary Boland, Gracie Allen, George Burns, W.C. Fields, Alison Skipworth; *D:* Leo McCarey; *W:* Walter DeLeon, Harry Ruskin; *C:* Henry Sharp; *M:* Ralph Rainger. *USH*

Six Pack 🎬½ 1982 (PG) The Gambler goes auto racing. Rogers, in his theatrical debut, stars as Brewster Baker, a former stock car driver. He returns to the racing circuit with the help of six larcenous orphans (the six-pack, get it?) adept at stripping cars. Kinda cute if you're in the mood for sugar-powered race car story. 108m/C VHS, Beta. Kenny Rogers, Diane Lane, Erin Gray, Barry Corbin, Anthony Michael Hall; *D:* Daniel Petrie; *M:* Charles Fox. *FOX*

Six Shootin' Sheriff 🎬🎬 1938 A cowboy framed for bank robbery is released and seeks to rid his town of all evil. And he gets the girl! 59m/B VHS, Beta. Ken Maynard, Marjorie Reynolds, Walter Long; *D:* Harry Fraser. *VYY, VCI, VCN*

Six Weeks 🎬🎬 1982 (PG) A young girl dying of leukemia brings together her work-driven mother and an aspiring married politician. Manipulative hanky-wringer has good acting from both Moores but oddly little substance. 107m/C VHS, Beta, LV. Dudley Moore, Mary Tyler Moore, Katherine Healy; *D:* Tony Bill; *M:* Dudley Moore. *COL*

Six Wives of Henry VIII 🎬🎬🎬 1971 Michell has been called the definitive Henry VIII and this BBC Classic Television Series (shown as part of "Masterpiece Theatre" on PBS) was perhaps the most beloved series on British TV. Henry's wives were: Catherine of Aragon, Anne Boleyn, Jane Seymour, Anne of Cleves, Catherine Howard, and Catherine Parr. Each episode tells of their, sometimes tragic, fates as pawns in Henry's quest for an heir, and his changes from an eager young man to aged, bitter monarch. The 90-minute videos are available individually or as a boxed set. 540m/C VHS. *GB* Keith Michell, Annette Crosbie, Dorothy Tutin, Anne Stallybrass, Elvi Hale, Angela Pleasence, Rosalie Crutchley. *FCT, VCO, TVC*

Sixteen 🎬🎬 *Like a Crow on a June Bug* 1972 (R) A naive country lass is attracted to the glitter and hum of the outside world. Her determination and optimism help her triumph. 84m/C VHS, Beta. Mercedes McCambridge, Parley Baer, Ford Rainey, Beverly Powers, John Lozier, Simone Griffeth, Maidie Norman; *D:* Lawrence Dobkin.

Sixteen Candles 🎬🎬🎬 1984 (PG) Over a decade after hitting the theatres, "Sixteen Candles" is still popular—reaching near cult status among generation X-ers. Hilarious comedy of errors features the pouty Ringwald as an awkard teen who's been dreaming of her 16th birthday. But the rush of her sister's wedding causes everyone to forget, turning her birthday into her worst nightmare. Hughes may not be critically acclaimed, but his movies are so popular they nearly take on a life of their own. Ringwald and Hall are especially charming as the angst-ridden teens, encountering one trauma after another. Great soundtrack includes the title song by The Stray Cats. 93m/C VHS, Beta, LV. Molly Ringwald, Justin Henry, Michael Schoeffling, Haviland Morris, Gedde Watanabe, Anthony Michael Hall, Paul Dooley, Carlin Glynn, Blanche Baker, Edward Andrews, Carole Cook, Max Casey Adams Showalter, Liane Curtis, John Cusack, Joan Cusack, Brian Doyle-Murray, Jami Gertz, Cinnamon Idles, Zelda Rubinstein; *D:* John Hughes; *W:* John Hughes; *M:* Ira Newborn. *USH*

Sixteen Fathoms Deep 🎬🎬 1934 A sponge fisherman risks it all, including his love, when a mean businessman threatens his operation. Good underwater photography, but otherwise undistinguished. 57m/B VHS. Lon Chaney Jr., Sally O'Neil, George Regas, Maurice Black, Russell Simpson; *D:* Armand Schaefer. *VYY, NOS, DVT*

The Sixth Man 🎬½ 1997 (PG-13) College basketball star Antoine Tyler (Hardison) dies but returns as a ghost to help his brother (Wayans) lead their team to the NCAA finals. Basketball seems to be the sport of choice for Hollywood lately, so you'd think they'd be able to get one of these movies right. Once again, they blow the layup. The first half features the requisite flashback and tearjerker death scene, both of which are surprisingly effective. But then the focus turns to "hilarious" on-court hijinks and the all-time sports cliche champion: the second-half rally from an impossible deficit. Hardison and Wayans are the bright spots, displaying fine comic and dramatic chemistry.*CW:* Brief language and some innuendos. 107m/C VHS, LV, Closed Caption. Kadeem Hardison, Marlon Wayans, David Paymer, Michael Michele, Kevin Dunn, Gary Jones, Vladimir Cuk, Chris Spencer, Kirk Baily, Saundra McClain, Lorenzo Orr, Travis Ford, Harold Sylvester; *D:* Randall Miller; *W:* Christopher Reed, Cynthia Carle; *C:* Michael Ozier; *M:* Marcus Miller. *TOU*

'68 🎬 1987 (R) A Hungarian family struggles with the generation gap in 1968 America. 99m/C VHS, Beta, LV. Eric Larson, Terra Vandergaw, Neil Young; *D:* Steven Kovacks. *VTR*

Sizzle 🎬🎬 1981 When her boyfriend is murdered by the mob, nightclub singer Anderson, newly arrived from Hicksville in Roaring '20s Chicago, stops at nothing to get revenge. Bad-guy gangster Forsythe falls for her charms. Fun but unsophisticated. Made for TV. 100m/C VHS, Beta. Loni Anderson, John Forsythe, Leslie Uggams, Roy

Thinnes, Richard Lynch, Michael Goodwin; *D:* Don Medford; *M:* Artie Butler.

Skag 🎬🎬🎬 1979 Disabled following a stroke, a Pittsburgh steel worker confronts a change in family roles and long-ignored family problems during his convalescence. Malden is exceptional and believable as a Joe Lunchbucket in this well-written, well-cast TV movie, pilot for the NBC series. 145m/C VHS, Beta. Karl Malden, Piper Laurie, Craig Wasson, Leslie Ackerman, Peter Gallagher, Kathryn Holcomb, Powers Boothe; *D:* Frank Perry. *NO*

Skateboard 🎬 1977 (PG) A down-and-out Hollywood agent creates a pro skateboarding team and enters them in a race worth $20,000. Quickie premise executed lamely. 97m/C VHS, Beta. Allen (Goorwitz) Garfield, Kathleen Lloyd, Chad McQueen, Leif Garrett, Richard Van Der Wyk, Tony Alva, Antony Carbone; *W:* Dick Wolf. *NO*

The Skateboard Kid 🎬½ 1993 (PG) When an outsider finds a magical talking skateboard, he suddenly becomes the envy of the in-group of skateboarding thrashers. 90m/C VHS. Bess Armstrong, Timothy Busfield; *D:* Larry Swerdlove; *W:* Roger Corman; *V:* Dom DeLuise. *NHO*

The Skateboard Kid 2 🎬🎬 1994 (PG) Mystery creature helps Sammy build his dream skateboard, which turns out to have a mind of its own. 95m/C VHS. Trenton Knight, Dee Wallace Stone, Bruce Davison, Andrew Stevens; *D:* Andrew Stevens. *NHO*

Skeeter 🎬½ 1993 (R) Yes, it's the attack of the killer mosquito! Not just any mosquito of course, but a new gigantic species bred on toxic waste. They're invading the quiet desert town of Mesquite—and they're out for blood! 95m/C VHS, LV. Tracy Griffith, Jim Youngs, Charles Napier, Michael J. Pollard; *D:* Clark Brandon; *W:* Clark Brandon, Lanny Horn; *M:* David Lawrence. *COL*

Skeezer 🎬🎬½ 1982 A dog becomes a key factor in a sympathetic doctor's efforts to communicate with emotionally unstable children. Based on reality, and a good cast makes it believable and moving. Quality family fare. 100m/C VHS. Karen Valentine, Dee Wallace Stone, Tom Atkins, Mariclare Costello, Leighton Greer, Justine Lord; *D:* Peter H. Hunt. *ART*

Skeleton Coast 🎬 *Fair Trade* 1989 (R) Borgnine plays a retired U.S. Marine colonel who organizes a Magnificent Seven-like group of tough mercenaries to go into eastern Africa to save hostages held by Angolan terrorists. Cliches abound, including a token large-breasted woman, Mulford, getting her t-shirt ripped open. No plot and a bad script. 94m/C VHS, LV. Ernest Borgnine, Robert Vaughn, Oliver Reed, Herbert Lom, Daniel Greene, Nancy Mulford, Leon Isaac Kennedy; *D:* John Cardos. *NLC*

Skeletons 🎬🎬 1996 (R) Journalist Peter Crane (Silver) decides to leave New York after suffering a heart attack and moves his family to what he thinks will be the quiet of Saugatuck, Maine. They're settling in when Peter is approached by the mother of a young man, who's standing trial for murder, who claims her son is innocent. When Peter investigates, the townspeople suddenly turn hostile and the man is found hanged in his cell. Turns out this town's skeletons go back 100 years and the secrets are deadly.*CW:* Violence and language. 91m/C VHS. Ron Silver, James Coburn, Christopher Plummer, Dee Wallace Stone, Kyle Howard, Thomas Wilson Brown; *Cameos:* Paul Bartel; *D:* David DeCoteau. *FEI*

Sketch Artist 🎬🎬 1992 (R) Jack Whitfield (Fahey) is a police sketch artist whose latest rendering of a murder suspect looks suspiciously like his wife. Jack decides to keep this information to himself while he does some quiet investigating but he may not have any time. The police have a new murder suspect in mind—Jack! Made for cable television.*CW:* Language and sexuality. 89m/C VHS, Beta, LV, Closed Caption. Jeff Fahey, Sean Young, Drew Barrymore, Frank McRae, Tcheky Karyo, James Tolkan, Charlotte Lewis; *D:* Phedon Papamichael; *W:* Michael Angeli. *FXV, VTR*

Sketch Artist 2: Hands That

See ♂♂½ 1994 Fahey returns as police artist Jack Whitfield, who's asked to draw a sketch of a serial rapist/murderer. Near-victim Emmy (Cox) just happens to be blind but describes to Jack how the rapist looked as she felt his face. Emmy's hubby Glenn (Silverman) is concerned, especially when the creep warns Emmy about her trip to the cops. Solid characters build to good courtroom climax. 95m/C VHS, LV, Closed Caption. Jeff Fahey, Courteney Cox, Jonathan Silverman, Michael Beach, Brion James, James Tolkan, Leilani Sarelle Ferrer, Michael Nicolosi, Scott Burkholder; D: Jack Sholder; W: Michael Angeli; M: Tim Truman. MGM

Sketches of a Strangler ♂½ 1978 A psychotic art student sketches, then murders prostitutes. Interesting lead character but hardly chilling—just horrible to watch. Made for TV. 91m/C VHS, Beta. Allen (Goorwitz) Garfield, Meredith MacRae; D: Paul Leder.

Ski Bum ♂ 1975 (R) A ski bum discovers corruption and violence at a Colorado Rockies resort. Eminently forgettable trash. Scantily based on a novel by Romain Gary. 94m/C VHS, Beta. Charlotte Rampling, Zalman King, Dimitra Arliss, Anna Karina; D: Bruce Clark. NLC

Ski Patrol ♂♂ 1989 (PG) Wacky ski groupies try to stop an evil developer. Good ski action in a surprisingly plotful effort from the crazy crew that brought the world "Police Academy." 85m/C VHS, Beta, LV, Closed Caption. Roger Rose, Yvette Nipar, T.K. Carter, Leslie Jordan, Ray Walston, Martin Mull; D: Richard Correll. COL

Ski School ♂ 1991 (R) Rival ski instructors compete for jobs and babes. Brow lowering.CW: Language and sensuality. 89m/C VHS, LV, Closed Caption. Ava Fabian, Dean Cameron, Tom Breznahan, Stuart Fratkin; D: Damian Lee. HBO

Ski School 2 ♂½ 1994 (R) Former ski instructor Dave finds that both his job and his ex-gal have been acquired by a jerk. So Dave decides to get them both back.CW: Nudity; language. 90m/C VHS. Dean Cameron, Wendy Hamilton, Heather Campbell, Brent Sheppard, Bill Dwyer; D: David Mitchell; W: Jay Naples. MNC

Ski Troop Attack ♂♂ 1960 During WWII, an American ski patrol is sent behind Nazi lines to blow up a German railway bridge. Unexceptional low-budget Corman outing; not among the greatest of war movies. 61m/B VHS, Beta. Michael Forest, Frank Wolff, Sheila Carol. SNC, NOS, DVT

Skier's Dream 1988 This spectacular action-packed film focuses on a young executive in search of the ultimate run. Shot on the most exotic ski locations in the world; covers freestyle skiing, powder skiing, snowboarding, extreme skiing, cliff jumping, paragliding, and wave riding. 75m/C VHS, Closed Caption. John Eaves, Ian Boyd; M: Jimi Hendrix, Tom Cochrane. COL, RAP

Skin ♂½ Howard Beach: Making the Case for Murder 1989 (PG-13) Prosecutor seeks the truth after a black man is chased into highway traffic by a gang of white teenaged thugs from Queens. Based on the true story of the death of a young black man in Howards Beach, Queens. Made for TV. 95m/C VHS. Daniel J. Travanti, Joe Morton, Dan Lauria, William Daniels; C: Ron Fortunato. NHO

Skin Art ♂½ 1993 (R) Very offbeat character study focusing on Will, a tormented tattoo artist who specializes in decorating the backs of the young Asian prostitutes who work in a nearby brothel. Haunted by his memories as a Vietnam POW, Will decides to exorcise some demons on his latest female canvas.CW: Language, violence, and bizarre sexual situations. 90m/C VHS, LV, Closed Caption. Kirk Baltz, Jake Weber, Nora Ariffin; D: W. Blake Herron; W: W. Blake Herron. FXV

Skin Deep ♂½ 1989 (R) A boyish Don Juan tries everything to win back his ex-wife. Ritter whines about his mid-life crisis and seduces women; this substitutes for plot. A few funny slapstick scenes still don't make this worth watching. 102m/

C VHS, Beta, LV. John Ritter, Vincent Gardenia, Julianne Phillips, Alyson Reed, Nina Foch, Chelsea Field, Denise Crosby; D: Blake Edwards; W: Blake Edwards; M: Henry Mancini. CCB, VTR

Skin Game ♂½ 1931 Two British families feud over land rights. Not thrilling; not characteristic of working with Hitchcock. Way too much talking in excruciating, drawn-out scenes. Adapted from the play of the same name. 87m/B VHS, Beta. GB Phyllis Konstam, Edmund Gwenn, Frank Lawton, C.V. France, Jill Esmond, Helen Haye; D: Alfred Hitchcock; W: Alfred Hitchcock. REP, NOS, MLB

Skin Game ♂♂♂ 1971 (PG) A fast talking con-artist (Garner) and his black partner (Gossett) travel throughout the antebellum South setting up scams—Gossett is sold to a new owner by Garner, who helps him escape. Garner and Gossett make a splendid comedy team in this different kind of buddy flick. All is well until Asner turns the tables on them. Finely acted comedy-drama. 102m/C VHS, Beta. James Garner, Louis Gossett Jr., Susan Clark, Ed Asner, Andrew Duggan; D: Paul Bogart; M: David Shire. WAR

Skinheads: The Second Coming of

Hate ♂ 1988 (R) Neo-fascists run rampant. Exploitative effort from schlock-doyen Clark. 93m/C VHS. Chuck Connors, Barbara Bain, Brian Brophy, Jason Culp, Elizabeth Sagal; D: Greydon Clark; W: Greydon Clark. NO

Skinned Alive woof! 1989 A woman and her children travel cross-country to sell leather goods. When a detective discovers where the leather comes from he's hot on their trail. 90m/C VHS, Beta. Mary Jackson, Scott Spiegel; D: Jon Killough; W: Jon Killough. NO

Skinner ♂ 1993 (R) Psychopath Dennis Skinner (Raimi) more than lives up to his grisly name with his penchant for stalking hookers with carving knives and cleavers. Now he's going after his innocent landlady (Lake) and it's up to Heidi (Lords), a victim who managed to get away, to find him before he can kill again. Lords in lingerie (and nasty scars) and some really disgusting skinning scenes.CW: Brutal bizarre violence and gore; some sexuality and language. 89m/C VHS, LV. Theodore (Ted) Raimi, Traci Lords, Ricki Lake; D: Ivan Nagy. APX

Skinner's Dress Suit ♂♂½ 1926 Meek, hen-pecked office clerk tells domineering wife he got a raise so she'll get off his back. She quickly insinuates them into upper crusty social circle, where the fib pays off big. Remake of the 1917 version based on Henry Irving Dodge's novel. 79m/B VHS, Beta. Reginald Denny, Laura La Plante, Arthur Lake, Hedda Hopper; D: William A. Seiter. GPV

Skirts Ahoy! ♂♂ 1952 Williams, Evans, and Blaine are three WAVES who have their eyes set on three handsome men. To get them, of course, they must sing and dance a lot, and Williams must perform one of her famous water ballets. ♫Oh By Jingo; Hold Me Close to You; What Makes a WAVE?; What Good is a Gal Without a Guy?; Skirts Ahoy!; Glad to Have You Aboard; The Navy Waltz; I Get a Funny Feeling; We Will Fight. 109m/C VHS. Esther Williams, Joan Evans, Vivian Blaine, Barry Sullivan, Keefe Brasselle, Billy Eckstine, Debbie Reynolds; D: Sidney Lanfield. MGM

The Skull ♂♂ 1965 Horror abounds when Cushing gets his hands on the skull of the Marquis de Sade that has mysterious, murderous powers. Based on a story by Robert Bloch. 83m/C VHS, Closed Caption. Peter Cushing, Patrick Wymark, Christopher Lee, Nigel Green, Jill Bennett, Michael Gough, George Coulouris, Patrick Magee; D: Freddie Francis. PAR

Skull: A Night of Terror ♂♂ 1988 (R) A cop vows not to use guns after a tragic accident, then single-handed and unarmed, takes on terrorists who kidnap his family. 80m/C VHS, Beta. Nadia Capone, Robert Bideman, Robbie Fox, Paul Sanders; D: Robert Bergman; W: Robert Bergman, Gerard Ciccoritti.

Skull & Crown ♂♂ 1935 Rin Tin Tin, Jr. helps the hero break up a group of smugglers. A favorite of Tin fans everywhere. 58m/B VHS, Beta. Regis Toomey, Jack Mulhall, James Murray. VYY, DVT, HEG

Skullduggery ♂½ 1970 (PG) When a peaceful race of blond ape-people are discovered in New Guinea, a courtroom battle ensues to prevent their slaughter at the hands of developers. Interesting premise sadly flops. 105m/C VHS, Beta. Burt Reynolds, Susan Clark, Roger C. Carmel, Chips Rafferty, Edward Fox, Wilfrid Hyde-White, Rhys Williams; D: Gordon Douglas.

Skullduggery woof! Warlock 1979 (PG) Costume-store minion Haverstock carries a curse that makes him kill and mutilate. The usual unspeakable horror ensues for a group of medieval-game players. 95m/C VHS, Beta. Thom Haverstock, Wendy Crewson, David Calderisi; D: Ota Richter.

The Sky Above, the Mud Below Le Ciel et le Boue 1961 An acclaimed documentary following a band of explorers transversing New Guinea in 1959, and their confrontations with native rituals, heretofore unknown cannibal tribes and physical calamities. In HiFi. 90m/C VHS, Beta. D: Pierre-Dominique Gaisseau. Academy Awards '61: Best Feature Documentary. ORI, WAR, FCT

Sky Bandits ♂½ 1940 Mounties uncover the mystery of a disappearing plane carrying gold from a Yukon mine. Last of the "Renfrew of the Mounties" pictures. 56m/B VHS, Beta, 8mm. James Newill, Dave O'Brien, Louise Stanley. NOS, SNC, VCN

Sky Hei$t ♂♂ 1975 Criminals plan robbery of police helicopter carrying fortune in gold bullion. Made for television. 96m/C VHS. Stefanie Powers, Joseph Campanella, Don Meredith, Larry Wilcox, Frank Gorshin, Shelley Fabares, Ken Swofford, Ray Vitte, Nancy Belle Fuller, Suzanne Somers; D: Lee H. Katzin. UNI

Sky High ♂♂½ 1922 Mix is an immigration agent after a gang smuggling Chinese laborers across the Mexican border. Thrills involve an airplane and mountaintop battles as well as some terrific location footage from the Grand Canyon. 58m/B VHS. Tom Mix, Eva Novak, J. Farrell MacDonald, Sid Jordan; D: Lynn F. Reynolds; W: Lynn F. Reynolds. GPV, GVV

Sky High ♂ 1951 A spy at an Air Force base is trying to get hold of the plans to a secret plane. A GI is recruited to catch him. 60m/B VHS, Beta, LV. Sid Melton, Mara Lynn, Douglas Evans. NO

Sky High ♂ 1984 Three college students become immersed in international intrigue when they pursue them through the C.I.A. and the K.G.B. pursue them through Greece looking for a secret Soviet tape. 103m/C VHS, Beta. Daniel Hirsch, Clayton Norcross, Frank Schultz, Lauren Taylor; D: Nico Mastorakis. ART

Sky Liner ♂ 1949 An FBI agent is trailing a spy who has taken secret documents aboard a west-bound flight. 62m/B VHS, Beta, LV. Richard Travis, Pamela Blake. NO

The Sky Pilot ♂♂½ 1921 Young clergyman sets up a parish on North Pacific coast and finds he must prove himself to the cowboys. He saves young woman from stampede, but her father blames him for her maimed legs and sets the preacher's church on fire, providing girl with excuse to overcome handicap. 63m/B VHS, Beta. John Bowers, Colleen Moore, David Butler, Donald Ian Macdonald; D: King Vidor. GPV, FCT, GVV

Sky Pirates woof! 1987 Space epic deals about pieces of ancient stone left by prehistoric extraterrestrials, now lost in a time warp. Bad stunts, bad script and notably bad acting make it a woofer in any era. 88m/C VHS, Beta, Closed Caption. AU John Hargreaves, Max Phipps, Meredith Phillips; D: Colin Eggleston. FOX

Sky Riders ♂♂½ 1976 (PG) Hang-gliders risk it all to take on a group of political kidnapers. Fine hang-gliding footage and glorious Greek locations make up for garden-variety plot. 93m/C VHS. James Coburn, Susannah York, Robert Culp, Charles

Aznavour, Harry Andrews, John Beck; **D:** Douglas Hickox; **W:** Jack DeWitt, Garry Michael White; **M:** Lalo Schifrin. *FOX*

Skylark 🎞🎞½ 1993 (G) In a sequel to Hallmark Hall of Fame's hugely successful "Sarah, Plain and Tall," the whole Kansas crew shows up for more of their little-farm-on-the-prairie life. After two years in America's squarest state, mail-order bride Sarah (Close) loves Jacob (Walken), but not the scenery and still yearns for the lush greenery of Maine. When drought and fire threaten the farm, Jacob fears for the family's health and safety, and sends them back East for a visit. Close's "tough Yankee" expression grows a bit tiresome in a plot that is a tad predictable, yet the simplistic charm and nostalgia are unresistable and work to propel this quality Hallmark production. 98m/C **VHS, Closed Caption.** Glenn Close, Christopher Walken, Lexi Randall, Christopher Bell, Tresa Hughes, Lois Smith, Lee Richardson, Elizabeth Wilson, Margaret Sophie Stein, Jon DeVries, James Rebhorn, Woody Watson; **D:** Joseph Sargent; **W:** Patricia MacLachlan. *REP, BTV*

Skyline 🎞🎞🎞 *La Linea Del Cielo* 1984 (R) A Spanish photographer comes to New York City to work for a magazine and tries to adjust to his cultural dislocation. Quietly funny, with a startling ending. Partly in Spanish with English subtitles. 84m/C **VHS, Beta, LV.** *SP* Antonio Resines, Beatriz Perez-Porro, Jaime Nos, Roy Hoffman; **D:** Fernando Colombo. *KIV, FCT, TPV*

The Sky's the Limit 🎞🎞½ 1943 Astaire spends his leave in Manhattan and falls in love with fetching journalist Leslie. He's in civvies, so little does she know he's a war hero. Nothing-special semi-musical, with Fred-Ginger spark missing. 🎵One For My Baby; My Shining Hour; I've Got a Lot in Common With You. 89m/B **VHS, Beta.** Fred Astaire, Joan Leslie, Robert Benchley, Robert Ryan, Elizabeth Patterson; **D:** Edward H. Griffith. Nominations: Academy Awards '43: Best Song ("My Shining Hour"), Scoring of a Musical. *TTC, VYY*

Skyscraper 🎞 1995 (R) Gun-wielding helicopter pilot/heroine Carrie Wink (Smith) must battle villainous mercenaries holding hostages in an LA skyscraper. But she stills manages to find time for lots of steamy showers (to best display the only assets the film has).**CW:** Strong action violence, sex scenes and language. 96m/C **VHS, Closed Caption.** Anna Nicole Smith, Richard Steinmetz; **D:** Raymond Martino; **W:** William Applegate Jr.; **C:** Frank Harris; **M:** Jim Halfpenny. *PMH*

Skyscraper Souls 🎞🎞🎞 1932 William stars as David Dwight, a ruthless businessman who manipulates stock prices and double-crosses lovers in order to have complete control of a 100-story office building. He sacrifices everything and everyone in this story of big business. Based on the novel "Skyscraper" by Faith Baldwin. 98m/B **VHS, Closed Caption.** Warren William, Maureen O'Sullivan, Gregory Ratoff, Anita Page, Verree Teasdale, Norman Foster, Jean Hersholt, Wallace Ford; **D:** Edgar Selwyn. *MGM*

Slacker 🎞🎞🎞 1991 (R) Defines a new generation: Overwhelmed by the world and it's demands, "Slackers" react by retreating into lives of minimal expectations. Filmed as a series of improvisational stories about people living on the fringes of the working world and their reactions (or lack thereof) to the life swirling around them. First feature for writer/director Linklater on a budget of $23,000; filmed on location in Austin, Texas with a cast of primarily non-professional actors.**CW:** Language. 97m/C **VHS.** Richard Linklater, Rudy Basquez, Jean Caffeine, Jan Hockey, Stephan Hockey, Mark James, Samuel Dietert; **D:** Richard Linklater; **W:** Richard Linklater; **C:** Lee Daniel. *ORI*

Slam 🎞🎞 1998 (R) Documentarian Levin makes his feature film debut with this part-prison, part-ghetto drama. Street-smart, low-level drug dealer Ray (Williams) is living in gang-ridden D.C. when he's busted for possession and suspicion of murdering his supplier. Jail's just as rough as the streets since two local inside gangs each want Ray's allegiance. Ray wants to keep to himself

and work on his writing—the poetry he composes about what he sees in life. He manages to get bail and then has a lot of hard decisions to make.**CW:** Pervasive language, a sex scene and brief violence. 100m/C **VHS.** Saul Williams, Sonja Sohn, Bonz Malone; **D:** Marc Levin; **W:** Marc Levin, Saul Williams, Sonja Sohn, Richard Stratton; **C:** Mark Benjamin. Sundance Film Festival '98: Grand Jury Prize. *NYR*

Slam Dunk Ernest 🎞½ 1995 (PG-13) Ernest (Varney) becomes a basketball star in a city league exhibition game when the Basketball Angel (Abdul-Jabbar) loans him his magic shoes.**CW:** Mild language. 93m/C **VHS, LV, Closed Caption.** Jim Varney, Kareem Abdul-Jabbar, Jay Brazeau; **D:** John R. Cherry III; **W:** Daniel Butler, John R. Cherry III; **M:** Mark Adler. *TOU*

Slamdance 🎞½ 1987 (R) A struggling cartoonist is framed for the murder of a beautiful young woman while being victimized by the real killer. A complicated murder mystery with a punk beat and visual flash. But the tale is unoriginal—and where's the slamdancing? 99m/C **VHS, Beta, LV, Closed Caption.** Tom Hulce, Virginia Madsen, Mary Elizabeth Mastrantonio, Harry Dean Stanton, Adam Ant, John Doe; **D:** Wayne Wang. *FOX*

Slammer Girls 🎞 1987 (R) In this sex-drenched, unfunny spoof on women's prison films, the inmates of Loch Ness Penitentiary try to break out using their sexual wiles. The actresses are pseudonymous porn stars. 82m/C **VHS, Beta, LV.** Tally Brittany, Jane Hamilton, Jeff Eagle, Devon Jenkin; **D:** Chuck Vincent. *ART*

The Slap *La Gifle* 1976 (PG) French teens learn about love the French way. 103m/C **VHS.** *FR* Isabelle Adjani, Lino Ventura; **D:** Claude Pinoteau; **M:** Georges Delerue.

Slap Shot 🎞🎞🎞 1977 (R) A profane satire of the world of professional hockey. Over-the-hill player-coach Newman gathers an odd-ball mixture of has-beens and young players and reluctantly initiates them, using violence on the ice to make his team win. The strip-tease on ice needs to be seen to be believed. Charming in its own bone-crunching way. 123m/C **VHS, Beta, LV.** Paul Newman, Michael Ontkean, Jennifer Warren, Lindsay Crouse, Jerry Houser, Melinda Dillon, Strother Martin; **D:** George Roy Hill; **M:** Elmer Bernstein. *USH*

Slappy and the Stinkers 🎞🎞½ 1997 (PG) Five young misfits, known as "The Stinkers," are constantly in trouble with their stuffy school principal Morgan Brinway (Wong). On a class trip to the acquarium, the Stinkers meet Slappy the sea lion and decide to liberate him (they think he looks unhappy), stowing Slappy in Mr. Brinway's hot tub. Then the kids find out that evil animal thief Boccoli (McMurray) wants to steal the critter and sell him to a circus. Just as silly as it sounds but Slappy is really cute. 78m/C **VHS, Closed Caption.** B.D. Wong, Bronson Pinchot, Sam McMurray, Joseph Ashton, Travis Tedford, Gary LeRoi Gray, Carl Michael Lindner, Scarlett Pomers, Jennifer Coolidge; **D:** Barnet Kellman; **W:** Michael Scott, Bob Wolterstorff. *COL*

Slapstick 193? An anthology of great moments from Mack Sennett comedy shorts, featuring many great stars in some of their earliest film appearances. 76m/B **VHS, Beta.** Charlie Chaplin, Harold Lloyd, Charley Chase, Buster Keaton, Ben Turpin, Stan Laurel. *REP*

Slapstick of Another Kind 🎞½ 1984 (PG) Lewis and Kahn play dual roles as an alien brother and sister and their adoptive Earth parents, who are being pursued by U.S. agents. Rather miserable rendition of a Kurt Vonnegut novel. 85m/C **VHS, Beta, LV.** Jerry Lewis, Madeline Kahn, Marty Feldman, Jim Backus, Noriyuki "Pat" Morita, Samuel Fuller, Orson Welles; **D:** Steven Paul. *ART, VES*

Slash 🎞½ 1987 Each of four people caught in a political takeover harbors a secret that could harm one of the others. Extremely violent. 90m/C **VHS, Beta.** Romano Kristoff, Michael Monty, Gwen Hung; **D:** John Gale. *NO*

Slashdance woof! 1989 A really pathetic thriller follows a lady cop undercover in a chorus line to find out who's been murdering the dancers. The acting is on the level of pro wrestling. Don't be fooled by the naked babes on the cassette box—there's no nudity. 83m/C **VHS, Beta.** Cindy Maranne, James Carroll Jordan, Queen Kong, Joel von Ornsteiner, Jay Richardson; **D:** James Shyman; **W:** James Shyman. *NO*

Slashed Dreams 🎞🎞 *Sunburst* 1974 (R) Hippie couple travels to California wilderness in search of a friend. A pair of woodsmen assault them and rape the woman, which really messes with their heads. Retitled and packaged as slasher movie. 74m/C **VHS.** Peter Hooten, Katherine Baumann, Ric Carrott, Anne Lockhart, Robert Englund, Rudy Vallee, James Keach, David Pritchard, Peter Brown; **D:** James Polakof; **W:** James Keach, David Pritchard.

The Slasher woof! 1974 A policeman must find the madman who has been killing off unfaithful married women. Miserably gory, pointless slasher (hence the title) interesting only as an early example of its kind. 88m/C **VHS, Beta.** Farley Granger, Sylva Koscina, Susan Scott. *NO*

Slate, Wyn & Me 🎞 1987 (R) Two bank-robbing, kidnapping brothers flee cross-country from the law, and fall in love with the girl they've snatched. Pointless, and pointlessly violent and vulgar. 90m/C **VHS, Beta.** Sigrid Thornton, Simon Burke, Martin Sacks; **D:** Don McLennan; **C:** David Connell. *NLC*

Slaughter 🎞 1972 (R) After his parents are murdered, a former Green Beret goes after their killers. Plenty of brutality. Followed by "Slaughter's Big Ripoff." 92m/C **VHS, Beta, LV.** Jim Brown, Stella Stevens, Rip Torn, Cameron Mitchell, Don Gordon, Marlene Clark; **D:** Jack Starrett. *FOX*

Slaughter High 🎞 1986 (R) A high school nerd is accidentally disfigured by a back-firing prank. Five years later, he returns to exact bloody revenge. Available in an unrated version. 90m/C **VHS, Beta.** Caroline Munro, Simon Scuddamore, Kelly Baker; **D:** George Dugdale. *ART, VES*

Slaughter Hotel 🎞 *Asylum Erotica; La Bestia Uccide a Sangue Freddo* 1971 (R) An asylum already inhabited by extremely bizarre characters is plagued by a series of gruesome murders. Lots of skin and lots of blood; Neri shines as a nymphomaniacal lesbian nurse. 72m/C **VHS, Beta.** Klaus Kinski, Rosalba (Sara Bay) Neri, Margaret Lee, John Ely; **D:** Fernando Di Leo. *MPI, GRG*

Slaughter in San Francisco 🎞 *Chuck Norris vs. the Karate Cop; Yellow Faced Tiger; Karate Cop* 1981 (R) A Chinese-American cop leads a one-man fight against corruption in the department in Daly City, near San Francisco. Norris is the bad guy; made in 1973 but not released until he had an established following (and he still has only some 18 minutes of film footage). Plenty of kicking and karate chops. 92m/C **VHS, Beta.** *CH* Chuck Norris, Don Wong; **D:** William Lowe. *RHI*

Slaughter of the Innocents 🎞🎞 1993 (R) FBI agent Broderick (Glenn) is sent to Salt Lake City to investigate the murders of two children which are found to be connected to a series of bizarre killings that have occurred around Monument Valley. Unbeknownst to his associates, Broderick often uses his 11-year-old whiz-kid son Jesse's (Cameron-Glickenhaus) computer skills to aid his research. Only this time, his inquisitive son gets too close to a serial killer and unless Dad can figure things out on his own, Jesse will be the next victim. 104m/C **VHS, LV, Closed Caption.** Scott Glenn, Jesse Cameron-Glickenhaus, Sheila Tousey, Darlanne Fluegel, Zitto Kazann; **D:** James Glickenhaus; **W:** James Glickenhaus. *USH*

The Slaughter of the Vampires woof! *Curse of the Blood-Ghouls; Curses of the Ghouls* 1962 Newlyweds meet a bloodthirsty vampire in a Viennese chalet. Real, real bad horror flick, poorly dubbed. 81m/C **VHS, Beta.** *IT* Walter Brandi, Dieter Eppler, Graziella Granata; **D:** Robert Mauri; **W:** Robert Mauri. *SNC*

Slaughter Trail �✰✰ 1951 Rancher-turned-stage robber Young shoots two Indians and cavalry colonel Donlevy has to deal with the fallout. Peace returns when Young dies. Ordinary western with balladeer device helping the plot along, or trying to. 78m/C VHS, Beta. Brian Donlevy, Gig Young, Virginia Grey, Andy Devine, Robert Hutton; **D:** Irving Allen. *TTC*

Slaughterday ✰½ 1977 (R) An innocent woman is caught in the middle of an ex-con's elaborate scheme to commit the largest heist of his life. 87m/C VHS, Beta. Rita Tushingham, William Berger, Frederick Jaeger, Michael Hauserman, Gordon Mitchell; **D:** Peter Patzak.

Slaughterhouse woof! 1987 (R) A rotund, pig-loving country boy kills, maims, and eats numerous victims. Features the requisite dumb teens and plenty of blood. 87m/C VHS, Beta. Joe Barton, Sherry Bendorf, Don Barrett; **D:** Rick Roessler. *NLC*

Slaughterhouse Five ✰✰ 1972 (R) A suburban optometrist becomes "unstuck" in time and flits randomly through the experiences of his life, from the Dresden bombing to an extraterrestrial zoo. Noticed at Cannes but not at theatres; ambitious failure to adapt Kurt Vonnegut's odd novel. 104m/C VHS, Beta, LV, DVD. Michael Sacks, Valerie Perrine, Ron Leibman, Eugene Roche, Perry King; **D:** George Roy Hill. Cannes Film Festival '72: Special Jury Prize. *USH, IME*

Slaughterhouse Rock woof! 1988 (R) The ghost of a sexy rock star draws a young man into a confrontation with a sadistic spirit that rules a deserted prison. There's also some cannibalism involved. Music group Devo did the score for this flick. 90m/C VHS, Beta. Nicholas Celozzi, Donna Denton, Toni Basil, Hope Marie Carlton; **D:** Dimitri Logothetis. *NO*

Slaughter's Big Ripoff ✰½ 1973 (R) Slaughter is back battling the Mob with guns, planes and martial arts. This undistinguished sequel features McMahon as a mob boss. 92m/C VHS, Beta. Jim Brown, Brock Peters, Don Stroud, Ed McMahon, Art Metrano, Gloria Hendry; **D:** Gordon Douglas. *FOX*

Slave Girls from Beyond Infinity ✰✰ 1987 (R) In this B-movie spoof, two beautiful intergalactic slave girls escape their penal colony, land on a mysterious planet, and meet a cannibalistic despot. Fun spoof of '50s "B" sci-fi movies. 80m/C VHS, Beta, LV. Elizabeth Cayton, Cindy Beal, Brinke Stevens; **D:** Ken Dixon; **C:** Thomas Callaway. *AFE*

A Slave of Love ✰✰✰ 1978 Poignant love story set in the Crimea as the Bolshevik Revolution rages around a film crew attempting to complete a project. Interesting as ideological cinema but also enjoyable romantic drama. In Russian with English subtitles. 94m/C VHS, Beta. *RU* Elena Solovei, Rodion Nakhapetov, Alexander Kalyagin; **D:** Nikita Mikhalkov; **M:** Eduard Artemyev. *COL, AUD*

Slave of the Cannibal God woof! *Il Montagna di Dio Cannibale; Mountain of Cannibal Gods* 1979 (R) Beautiful Andress is captured by "native" cannibals; Keach must save her. 86m/C VHS, Beta. *IT* Stacy Keach, Ursula Andress, Claudio Cassinelli; **D:** Sergio Martino. *VES*

Slave Trade in the World Today ✰ 1964 Slavery practices in the modern world are shown, including actual scenes of a sheik's harem, slave auctions, and the kidnapping and selling of young women. 87m/C VHS, Beta. **D:** Roberto Malenotti. *VDC, TPV*

Slavers ✰✰ 1977 (R) Detailed depiction of the 19th century African slave trade with a little romance thrown in. 102m/C VHS, Beta. *GE* Trevor Howard, Britt Ekland, Ron Ely, Cameron Mitchell, Ray Milland; **D:** Jurgen Goslar. *VCD*

Slaves in Bondage ✰ 1937 Young country girls are lured into the big city and initiated into a life of ill repute in this exploitation classic. A must for camp fans of the '30s. ?m/C VHS. Lona Andre, Wheeler Oakman. *SNC*

Slaves of New York ✰½ 1989 (R) Greenwich Village artists worry about life and love in the '80s and being artistic enough for New York. Adapted from the stories of Tama Janowitz, who also wrote the screenplay and appears as Abby. Disastrous adaptation of a popular novel. 115m/C VHS, Beta, LV. Bernadette Peters, Chris Sarandon, Mary Beth Hurt, Madeleine Potter, Adam Coleman Howard, Nick Corri, Mercedes Ruehl, Joe Leeway, Charles McCaughan, John Harkins, Anna Katarina, Tama Janowitz; **D:** James Ivory; **W:** Tama Janowitz. *COL*

The Slayer woof! *Nightmare Island* 1982 (R) It's movies like this that give getting back to nature a bad name. That horrible monster is after those nice young people again! This time it's on an island off the coast of Georgia. 95m/C VHS, Beta. **D:** J.S. Cardone; **W:** J.S. Cardone; **M:** Robert Folk. *NO*

The Slayer/The Scalps ✰ 1982 (R) Double feature. "Scalps" is a slasher set in a Native American burial ground. "The Slayer" is about vacationing couples who run into more than they bargained for on their island retreat. 150m/C VHS, Beta. **D:** J.S. Cardone. *NO*

Slayground ✰½ 1984 (R) Man, distraught at the accidental death of his daughter, hires a hitman to exact revenge. Excruciating adaptation of the novel by Richard Stark (Donald E. Westlake). 85m/C VHS, Beta. *GB* Peter Coyote, Mel Smith, Billie Whitelaw, Philip Sayer, Kelli Maroney; **D:** Terry Bedford; **M:** Colin Towns. *REP*

Sleazemania 1985 Compilation of trailers 'n bits reviews some of the sleazier, sicker, and sexier selections of celluloid from the past 50 years. 60m/C VHS, Beta. *RHI*

Sleazemania III: The Good, the Bad & the Sleazy 1986 Another compilation of the cheapest, funniest and scurviest moments, from grade-Z horror films, including "Mondo Psycho" and "Smut Peddler Meets Emmanuel." 90m/B VHS, Beta. *RHI*

The Sleazy Uncle ✰✰ *Lo Zio Indegno* 1989 A successful but bored businessman is energized by an encounter with his vice-ridden uncle, a mooching, womanizing beatnik poet who knows how to enjoy life. An energetic but rather formulaic comedy. In Italian with English subtitles. 104m/C VHS, Beta. *IT* Giancarlo Giannini, Vittorio Gassman, Andrea Ferreol, Stefania Sandrelli; **D:** Franco Brusati. *TRI*

Sledgehammer woof! 1983 A madman is wreaking havoc on a small town, annihilating young women with a sledgehammer. 87m/C VHS, Beta. Ted Prior, Doug Matley, Steven Wright. *NO*

Sleep of Death ✰½ 1979 Young Englishman's pursuit of a blue-blooded woman seems to set off a series of bizarre and mysterious murders. A gothic thriller based on Sheridan Le Fanu's short story. 90m/C VHS, Beta. Brendan Price, Marilu Tolo, Patrick Magee, Curt Jurgens, Per Oscarsson; **D:** Calvin Floyd.

Sleep with Me ✰✰½ 1994 (R) What happens when love comes between friendship? Sarah (Tilly), Joseph (Stoltz), and Frank (Sheffer) are soon to find out. Sarah and Joseph are about to get married when their best friend Frank realizes he's in love with Sarah. So he sets out to seduce her and when Joseph realizes what's going on, he not only questions Frank's friendship but wonders just what signals Sarah's been giving off (although Joseph's hardly blameless). Six writers each wrote one of the social scenes detailing their triangular troubles, including a party where Tarantino does a hilarious riff on the homoerotic subtext in "Top Gun." Kelly's directorial debut. **CW:** Language; nudity; sexuality; drug use. 117m/C VHS, LV. Craig Sheffer, Eric Stoltz, Meg Tilly, Todd Field, Adrienne Shelly, Lewis Arquette, Susan Traylor, Tegan West, Parker Posey, Dean Cameron, Thomas Gibson, June Lockhart, Quentin Tarantino, Joey Lauren Adams; **D:** Rory Kelly; **W:** Rory Kelly, Roger Hedden, Neal Jimenez, Michael Steinberg, Duane Dell'Amico, Joe Keenan; **M:** David Lawrence. *MGM*

Sleepaway Camp ✰ 1983 (R) Crazed killer hacks away at the inhabitants of a peaceful summer camp in this run-of-the-mill slasher. 88m/C VHS, Beta. Mike Kellin, Jonathan Tiersten, Felissa Rose, Christopher Collet.

Sleepaway Camp 2: Unhappy Campers ✰½ 1988 (R) A beautiful camp counselor is actually a blood-thirsty, murdering madwoman. Sequel to the 1983 slasher, "Sleepaway Camp." 82m/C VHS, Beta. Pamela Springsteen, Renee Estevez, Walter Gotell, Brian Patrick Clark; **D:** Michael A. Simpson. *NLC*

Sleepaway Camp 3: Teenage Wasteland woof! 1989 (R) This second sequel is as bad as the first two movies. Another disturbed camper hacks up another bevy of teenagers. Better luck at the Motel Six. 80m/C VHS, Beta, LV. Pamela Springsteen, Tracy Griffith, Michael J. Pollard; **D:** Michael A. Simpson. *NLC*

Sleeper ✰✰✰½ 1973 (PG) Hapless nerd Allen is revived two hundred years after an operation gone bad. Keaton portrays Allen's love interest in a futuristic land of robots and giant vegetables. He learns of the hitherto unknown health benefits of hot fudge sundaes; discovers the truth about the nation's dictator, known as The Leader; and gets involved with revolutionaries seeking to overthrow the government. Hilarious, fast-moving comedy, full of slapstick and satire. Don't miss the "orgasmatron." 88m/C VHS, Beta, LV, Closed Caption. Woody Allen, Diane Keaton, John Beck, Howard Cosell; **D:** Woody Allen; **W:** Woody Allen, Marshall Brickman; **M:** Woody Allen. *MGM, FOX, FUS*

Sleepers ✰✰½ 1996 (R) Tense, gritty drama based on Lorenzo Carcaterra's book about four teenaged friends from Hell's Kitchen who get into trouble and wind up being sent to a reform school, where they're brutalized by guards. John (Eldard) and Tommy (Crudup), who grow up to be hit men, recognize their chief abuser (Bacon) years later and kill him. Their trial is prosecuted by Michael (Pitt), another of the gang, who's now the assistant DA. It's supposed to be a true story (the book is published as non-fiction) but doubt has been cast on Carcaterra's veracity (his character is the fourth member, journalist Lorenzo, played by Patric). De Niro and Hoffman excel in relatively minor, but pivotal, roles. **CW:** Language, graphic violence and two scenes of strong sexual content. 150m/C VHS, LV, Closed Caption, DVD. Brad Pitt, Jason Patric, Ron Eldard, Billy Crudup, Kevin Bacon, Robert De Niro, Dustin Hoffman, Vittorio Gassman, Minnie Driver, Terry Kinney, Brad Renfro, Jonathan Tucker, Joe Perrino, Geoff Wigdor, Bruno Kirby, Aida Turturro, Frank Medrano; **D:** Barry Levinson; **W:** Barry Levinson; **C:** Michael Ballhaus; **M:** John Williams. Nominations: Academy Awards '96: Best Original Dramatic/Comedy Score. *WAR*

Sleeping Beauty ✰✰✰ 1959 (G) Classic Walt Disney version of the famous fairy tale is set to the music of Tchaikovsky's ballet. Lavishly produced. With the voices of Mary Costa, Bill Shirley, and Vera Vague. 75m/C VHS, Beta, LV, Closed Caption. **D:** Clyde Geronimi, Eric Larson, Wolfgang Reitherman, Les Clark; **M:** George Bruns; **V:** Mary Costa, Bill Shirley, Barbara Luddy, Taylor Holmes, Verna Felton, Barbara Jo Allen, Pinto Colvig, Marvin Miller. Nominations: Academy Awards '59: Scoring of a Musical. *DIS*

Sleeping Beauty 1983 Peters is the princess put to sleep by the evil queen. Handsome prince Reeve comes to the rescue in this classy retelling of the Sleeping Beauty legend. Combines live action and animation. From Shelley Duvall's "Faerie Tale Theatre." 60m/C VHS, Beta, LV, Closed Caption. Christopher Reeve, Bernadette Peters, Beverly D'Angelo. *FOX, FCT*

Sleeping Beauty ✰½ 1989 Live action version of the beloved fairy tale, with Welch in the title role. 92m/C VHS. Tahnee Welch, Morgan Fairchild, Nicholas Clay, Sylvia Miles, Kenny Baker. *MGM, CVC*

The Sleeping Car ✱✱ 1990 A vindictive ghost haunts a group of people living in an old railway car. Fairly fun, fairly competent horror. 87m/C VHS, LV. David Naughton, Judie Aronson, Kevin McCarthy, Jeff Conaway, Dani Minnick, John Carl Buechler; **D:** Douglas Curtis. *THV*

Sleeping Car to Trieste ✱✱ 1945 Conspirators in the theft of a diplomat's diary ride the Orient Express, as a wily detective on board tries to piece together murder clues. Based on the story "Rome Express" by Clifford Grey. 95m/B VHS, Beta. Jean Kent, Albert Lieven, David Tomlinson, Finlay Currie; **D:** John Paddy Carstairs. *FCT, BFA*

Sleeping Dogs ✱✱½ 1982 A man in near-future New Zealand finds it hard to remain neutral when he is caught between a repressive government and a violent resistance movement. The first New Zealand film ever to open in the U.S., and a fine debut for director Donaldson. 107m/C VHS, Beta. *NZ* Sam Neill, Ian Mune, Nevan Rowe, Dona Akersten, Warren Oates; **D:** Roger Donaldson. *NO*

The Sleeping Tiger ✱✱½ 1954 A thief breaks into the home of a psychiatrist, who captures him. In exchange for his freedom, the thief agrees to become a guinea pig for the doctor's rehabilitation theories with ultimately tragic results. Director Losey was originally compelled to release the film under a pseudonym, "Victor Hanbury," because he had been blacklisted by Hollywood during the 1950s red scare. First pairing of Losey and Bogarde, who collaborated on several later films, including "Modesty Blaise" (1966) and "Accident" (1967). 89m/B VHS. Alexis Smith, Alexander Knox, Dirk Bogarde, Hugh Griffith; **D:** Joseph Losey; **W:** Harold Buchman, Carl Foreman; **M:** Malcolm Arnold. *NOS, SNC*

Sleeping with Strangers ✱✱½ 1994 (R) Two hoteliers in a small British Columbia town find their rivalry increasing as one hotel gets a boost when a drunken rock star and his Hollywood starlet arrive with their entourage in tow. Of course, the media follows and so does the comedic hysteria.**CW:** Sexuality. 103m/C VHS, Closed Caption. Adrienne Shelly, Neil Duncan, Shawn Thompson, Kymberley Huffman, Scott McNeil; **D:** William T. Bolson; **W:** Joan Carr-Wiggin. *PAR*

Sleeping with the Enemy ✱✱½ 1991 (R) Roberts escapes from abusive husband by faking death, flees to Iowa, falls for drama professor, and gasp, is found by psycho husband. Occasionally chilling but oft predictable thriller based on novel by Nancy Price.**CW:** Wife abuse terror and sex scene. 99m/C VHS, Beta, LV, Closed Caption. Julia Roberts, Kevin Anderson, Patrick Bergin, Elizabeth Lawrence, Kyle Secor, Claudette Nevins; **D:** Joseph Ruben; **W:** Ronald Bass; **M:** Jerry Goldsmith. *IME, FCT*

Sleepless in Seattle ✱✱✱½ 1993 (PG) Witty, sweet romantic comedy explores the differences between men and women when it comes to love and romance. When widower Hanks talks about his wife on a national talk show, recently engaged Ryan responds. Writer/director Ephron's humorous screenplay is brought to life by a perfectly cast ensemble; it also breathed new life into the classic weepie "An Affair to Remember," comparing it to "The Dirty Dozen" in an unforgettable scene. A movie full of fine detail, from Sven Nykvist's camera work to the graphic layout of the opening credits to the great score. Captured millions at the boxoffice, coming in as the fourth highest grossing movie of 1993. 105m/C VHS, LV, 8mm, Letterbox, Closed Caption, DVD. Tom Hanks, Meg Ryan, Bill Pullman, Ross Malinger, Rosie O'Donnell, Gaby Hoffman, Victor Garber, Rita Wilson, Barbara Garrick, Carey Lowell, Rob Reiner, Sarah Trigger; **D:** Nora Ephron; **W:** Jeffrey Arch, Larry Atlas, David S. Ward, Nora Ephron; **C:** Sven Nykvist; **M:** Marc Shaiman. Nominations: Academy Awards '93: Best Original Screenplay, Best Song ("A Wink and a Smile"); British Academy Awards '93: Best Original Screenplay, Best Score; Golden Globe Awards '94: Best Actor—Musical/Comedy (Hanks), Best Actress—Musical/Comedy (Ryan), Best Film—Musical/Comedy; MTV Movie

Awards '94: Best Female Performance (Ryan), Breakthrough Performance (Mulinger), Best On-Screen Duo (Tom Hanks/Meg Ryan), Best Song ("When I Fall in Love"); Writers Guild of America '93: Best Original Screenplay. *COL, BTV, FCT*

Sleepstalker: The Sandman's Last Rites ✱✱ 1994 (R) A serial killer known as the Sandman (Harris) is executed but returns as a shape-shifting horror who can strip the flesh off his victims with whirling sand. He haunts the nightmares of a reporter (Underwood), the only survivor of one of the killer's massacres, who teams up with a photographer (Morris) to learn the creature's origins and defeat him. Good special effects.**CW:** Some terror/violence and language. 101m/C VHS. Jay Underwood, Michael Harris, Kathryn Morris; **D:** Turi Meyer.

Sleepwalk ✱✱ 1988 (R) Odd independent effort about a bored New York desk worker who is given an ancient text of Chinese fairy tales to translate, and finds they're manifesting themselves in dangerous ways in real life. 78m/C VHS, Beta, LV. Suzanne Fletcher, Ann Magnuson; **D:** Sara Driver; **C:** Frank Prinzi, Jim Jarmusch. *NLC, ICA*

Sleepwalkers ✱½ *Stephen King's Sleepwalkers* 1992 (R) When Mary and her son Charles arrive in the small town of Travis, Indiana, ugly things begin to happen. And no wonder, it seems the deadly duo are sleepwalkers—fiendish, cat-like vampire creatures who can only survive by sucking the life force out of unsuspecting virgins. Gory but not without some humor, particularly in Krige's portrayal of the sexy and too-loving mother. Not nearly as good as some of King's other horror classics.**CW:** Language, strong violence, and strong sensuality. 91m/C VHS, LV, Closed Caption. Brian Krause, Madchen Amick, Alice Krige, Jim Haynie, Cindy Pickett, Lyman Ward, Ron Perlman; **Cameos:** Stephen King, Tobe Hooper, Mark Hamill, Glenn Shadix, Joe Dante, Clive Barker, John Landis, Dan Martin; **D:** Mick Garris; **W:** Stephen King; **C:** Rodney Charters. *COL*

Sleepy Eyes of Death: The Chinese Jade ✱✱ 1963 Master swordsman Nemuri Kyoshireo slaughters six would-be ambushers and has the seductive Chisa trying to set him against his master's enemy, Chen Sun, all for the sake of discovering the secret of the Chinese Jade. Adapted from the novel by Shibata Renzaburo. Japanese with subtitles. 82m/C VHS, LV, Letterbox. *JP* Raizo Ichikawa, Tamao Nakamura, Jo Kenzaburo; **D:** Tokuzo Tanaka. *ANI, MOV*

The Slender Thread ✱✱✱ 1965 Based on a true story, Poitier plays a college student who volunteers at a crisis center and must keep would-be suicide Bancroft on the phone until the police can find her. Filmed on location in Seattle. First film for director Pollack. 98m/C VHS, Closed Caption. Sidney Poitier, Anne Bancroft, Telly Savalas, Steven Hill; **D:** Sydney Pollack; **W:** Stirling Silliphant; **C:** Loyal Griggs; **M:** Quincy Jones. Nominations: Academy Awards '65: Best Art Direction/Set Decoration (B & W), Best Costume Design (B & W). *PAR*

Sleuth ✱✱✱½ 1972 (PG) A mystery novelist and his wife's lover face off in ever shifting, elaborate, and diabolical plots against each other, complete with red herrings, traps, and tricks. Playful, cerebral mystery thriller from top director Mankiewicz. Shaffer also scripted "Frenzy" for Hitchcock, from his play. 138m/C VHS, Beta, LV. Laurence Olivier, Michael Caine; **D:** Joseph L. Mankiewicz; **W:** Anthony Shaffer; **C:** Oswald Morris; **M:** John Addison. New York Film Critics Awards '72: Best Actor (Olivier); Nominations: Academy Awards '72: Best Actor (Caine), Best Actor (Olivier), Best Director (Mankiewicz), Best Original Dramatic/Comedy Score. *HMV, VTR*

Sliding Doors ✱✱½ 1997 (R) The sliding doors are those of a London subway train. If Helen (Paltrow) makes it through before they close, her life (and loves) go one way. If she's left on the platform, they go another, and the audience is let in on both options. She'll either dump or stick with cheating boyfriend Gerry (Lynch), who has been sleeping with ultra-bitchy ex-girlfriend Lydia (Trip-

plehorn). And she will either strike up a relationship with a charming stranger (Hannah) on the train and become fabulously successful, or end up slinging hash in a diner while pregnant with her scumbag boyfriend's baby. The concept and story of the dual possibilities is pulled off well, although it is a bit too cute at times. Will you like it? Depends on if it's already been rented when you're at the video store. If it's out, be careful which you pick, because apparently the small stuff really does matter.**CW:** Some sexuality and language. 98m/C VHS. Gwyneth Paltrow, John Lynch, John Hannah, Jeanne Tripplehorn, Virginia McKenna, Zara Turner, Douglas McFerran, Paul Brightwell, Nina Young; **D:** Peter Howitt; **W:** Peter Howitt; **C:** Remi Adefarasin; **M:** David Hirschfelder. *NYR*

Slightly Honorable ✱✱½ 1940 A lawyer gets involved in political scandals and becomes a murder suspect. Snappy comedy-drama with good performances but too many subplots. Based on the novel "Send Another Coffin" by F. G. Presnell. 75m/B VHS, Beta. Pat O'Brien, Broderick Crawford, Edward Arnold, Eve Arden, Evelyn Keyes, Phyllis Brooks; **D:** Tay Garnett. *NOS, VYY, BAR*

A Slightly Pregnant Man ✱✱ 1979 (PG) Comic complications abound as a construction worker becomes the world's first pregnant man. Surprise ending saves this simple and not very exciting film. 92m/C VHS, Beta. Catherine Deneuve, Marcello Mastroianni; **D:** Jacques Demy. *NO*

Slightly Scarlet ✱✱½ 1956 Small-time hood Payne carries out an assignment from boss DeCorsia to smear a law-and-order politico running for mayor. He falls in love with the candidate's secretary, tries to go straight, and ends up running the mob when DeCorsia flees town. A spiffy, low-budget noir crime drama based on the James M. Cain novel "Love's Lovely Counterfeit." 99m/C VHS, Beta. Rhonda Fleming, Arlene Dahl, John Payne, Kent Taylor, Ted de Corsia; **D:** Allan Dwan; **W:** Robert Blees. *NO*

Slime City ✱ 1989 The widow of an alchemist poisons her tenants so they will join her husband in the hereafter. Very low-budget; occasionally funny. 90m/C VHS, Beta. Robert C. Sabin, Mary Huner, T.J. Merrick, Dick Biel; **D:** Gregory Lamberson. *NO*

The Slime People *woof!* 1963 Huge prehistoric monsters are awakened from long hibernation by atomic testing in Los Angeles. They take over the city, creating the fog they need to live. Thank goodness for scientist Burton, who saves the day. Filmed in a butcher shop in Los Angeles. 76m/B VHS, Beta. Robert Hutton, Robert Burton, Susan Hart, William Boyce, Les Tremayne, John Close, Judee Morton; **D:** Robert Hutton; **W:** Vance Skarstedt; **C:** William G. Troiano. *NOS, GEM, RHI*

Sling Blade ✱✱✱½ 1996 (R) Mildly retarded killer Karl Childers (Thornton, making his feature directorial debut) is released from a mental hospital, where he was placed after killing his mother and her lover, after 25 years. Returning to his hometown, he befriends a boy (Black) with problems of his own. His mother is living with a mean, bullying drunkard (Yoakam, in a brilliant performance) who has no use for anyone, least of all mom's openly gay co-worker (Ritter). Thornton's excellent script moves at the slow pace of its hero, providing the superb cast plenty of opportunity to explore the rich characterization and dialogue. Filmed in Thornton's home state of Arkansas. 134m/C VHS, LV, Closed Caption. Billy Bob Thornton, Dwight Yoakam, John Ritter, Lucas Black, Natalie Canerday, James Hampton, Robert Duvall, J.T. Walsh, Rick Dial, Brent Briscoe, Christy Ward, Col. Bruce Hampton, Vic Chesnutt, Mickey Jones, Jim Jarmusch, Ian Moore; **D:** Billy Bob Thornton; **W:** Billy Bob Thornton; **C:** Barry Markowitz; **M:** Daniel Lanois. Academy Awards '96: Best Adapted Screenplay; Independent Spirit Awards '97: Best First Feature; Writers Guild of America '96: Best Adapted Screenplay; Nominations: Academy Awards '96: Best Actor (Thornton); Screen Actors Guild Award '96: Best Actor (Thornton), Cast. *TOU*

The Slingshot 🎿🎿🎿 1993 (R) Quirky coming-of-age tale, set in 1920s Stockholm, finds 12-year-old Roland (Salen) trying to survive childhood dilemmas. His mother (Frydman) is a Russian Jew (who sells condoms illegally) and his father (Skarsgard) is a zealous socialist, so Roland is subjected to unceasing bullying and prejudice. But the resourceful Roland doesn't let society get him down—he uses the contraband condoms in an inventive slingshot design that brings him an unwarranted amount of attention. Based on the novel by Roland Schutt. Swedish with subtitles. 102m/C VHS, LV. SW Jesper Salen, Stellan Skarsgard, Basia Frydman, Niclas Olund, Ernst-Hugo Jaregard, Jacob Leygraf; D: Ake Sandgren; W: Bjorn Isfalt, Ake Sandgren. COL

Slipping into Darkness 🎿½ 1988 (R) Three spoiled, rich college girls are held responsible for a retarded local boy's death. Honest and overwrought. 86m/C VHS, Beta, LV. Belle Mitchell, Laslo Papas, Beverly Ross, T.J. McFadden, Michelle Johnson, John DiAquino; D: Eleanor Gaver; W: Eleanor Gaver. HHE

Slipstream 🎿🎿 1972 "Turgid" and "gloomy" are the words for this romantic drama set in remote Alberta. The minor plot concerns a young woman who teaches a lonely disc jockey a lesson about life and love. This film feels like a long Canadian winter. 93m/C VHS, Beta. CA Julie Askew, Patti Oatman, Eli Rill. TWE

Slipstream 🎿🎿 1989 (PG-13) A sci-fi adventure set on a damaged Earthscape where people seek to escape a giant jetstream. While tracking down a bounty hunter gone bad, a futuristic cop follows his quarry into the dangerous river of wind. Ambitious "Blade Runner" clone with big names (Hamill is good) was never released theatrically in the US. 92m/C VHS, Beta, LV. GB Mark Hamill, Bill Paxton, Bob Peck, Eleanor David, Kitty Aldridge, Robbie Coltrane, Ben Kingsley, F. Murray Abraham; D: Steven Lisberger; W: Tony Kayden; M: Elmer Bernstein. VTR

Slither 🎿🎿🎿 1973 (PG) Caan and Boyle become wrapped up in a scheme to recover $300,000 in cash, stolen seven years previously. Along the way they pick up speed freak Kellerman, who assists them in a variety of loony ways. Frantic chase scenes are the highlight. 97m/C VHS, Beta. James Caan, Peter Boyle, Sally Kellerman, Louise Lasser, Allen (Goorwitz) Garfield, Richard B. Shull, Alex Rocco; D: Howard Zieff; W: W.D. Richter. MGM

Slithis woof! 1978 (PG) Slithis, the nuclear-waste creature, is the menace of Venice, California. Keep your pets (and yourself) indoors! 86m/C VHS, Beta. Alan Blanchard, Judy Motulsky; D: Stephen Traxler; W: Stephen Traxler.

Sliver 🎿½ 1993 (R) Another voyeuristic thriller starring Stone. She's Carly Norris, a lonely book editor who moves into one of Manhattan's toothpick thin buildings (the "sliver" of the title). She meets pulp novelist Jack (Berenger), whose libido is as overheated as his prose, but gets involved in a steamy affair with handsome neighbor Zeke (Baldwin), a computer whiz who also owns the building. Oh, by the way, he's installed video cameras in every unit that reveal many intimate secrets. Lots of sex and murders. Murky and underdeveloped and the ending, which was reshot, still leaves much to be desired. Lots of hype, little to recommend. CW: Language, violence, and strong sexuality. 106m/C VHS, Beta, LV, CD-I, Letterbox, Closed Caption. Sharon Stone, William Baldwin, Tom Berenger, Martin Landau, Polly Walker, Colleen Camp, CCH Pounder, Nina Foch, Keene Curtis; D: Phillip Noyce; W: Joe Eszterhas; C: Vilmos Zsigmond; M: Howard Shore. MTV Movie Awards '94: Most Desirable Male (Baldwin); Nominations: MTV Movie Awards '94: Most Desirable Female (Stone), Best Song ("I Can't Help Falling in Love"). PAR

Sloane woof! 1984 Typical sleazy sex and violence flick. For the record: organized crime baddies kidnap good guy Resnick's girlfriend and he seeks revenge. 95m/C VHS, Beta. Robert Resnick, Debra Blee, Paul Aragon; D: Dan Rosenthal. ART, VES

Slow Burn 🎿🎿 1986 An ex-reporter tries some detective work in the seamy side of Palm Springs, and becomes embroiled in the standard drug, kidnapping, murder routine. Based on the novel "Castles Burning" by Arthur Lyons. Made for cable television. 92m/C VHS, Beta, Closed Caption. Eric Roberts, Beverly D'Angelo, Dan Hedaya, Dennis Lipscomb; D: Matthew Chapman; W: Matthew Chapman; M: Loek Dikker. USH

Slow Burn 🎿 1990 (R) The Mafia and Chinese Triads are having troubles and a tired cop attempts to reach a peaceful solution. 90m/C VHS. William Smith, Anthony James, Ivan Rogers. XVC, DMP

Slow Moves 🎿½ 1984 Slow story of slow people who meet slowly, have sluggish affair, and find tragedy eventually. 93m/C VHS, Beta. Roxanne Rogers; D: Jon Jost. FCT

The Slugger's Wife 🎿½ Neil Simon's The Slugger's Wife 1985 (PG-13) The marriage between an Atlanta Braves outfielder and a rock singer suddenly turns sour when their individual careers force them to make some tough choices. 105m/C VHS, Beta, LV, Closed Caption. Michael O'Keefe, Rebecca DeMornay, Martin Ritt, Randy Quaid, Loudon Wainwright III, Cleavant Derricks, Lynn Whitfield; D: Hal Ashby; W: Neil Simon; C: Caleb Deschanel. COL

Slugs woof! 1987 (R) A health inspector discovers that spilled toxic waste is being helpfully cleaned up by the slug population, saving Uncle Sam countless dollars. But wait! The slugs are mutating into blood-thirsty man-eaters. Is this the answer to military cut-backs? 90m/C VHS, Beta, LV. Michael Garfield, Kim Terry, Philip Machale; D: J. Piquer Simon. VTR

Slumber Party '57 🎿½ 1976 (R) At a slumber party, six girls get together and exchange stories of how they lost their virginity. Lots of great music by the Platters, Big Bopper, Jerry Lee Lewis, the Crewcuts, and Paul and Paula but complete schlock otherwise. 89m/C VHS, Beta, LV. Noelle North, Bridget Hollman, Debra Winger, Mary Ann Appleseth, Cheryl "Rainbeaux" Smith, Janet Wood, R.L. Armstrong, Rafael Campos, Larry Gelman, Will Hutchins, Joyce Jillson, Victor Rogers, Joe E. Ross, Bill Thurman; D: William A. Levey; M: Miles Goodman. MGM, VES

The Slumber Party Massacre 🎿½ 1982 (R) A psychotic killer with a power drill terrorizes a high school girl's slumber party. Contrived and forced, but not always unfunny. 84m/C VHS, Beta. Michele Michaels, Robin Stille, Andre Honore, Michael Villela, Debra Deliso, Gina Mari, Brinke Stevens, Jean Vargas, Rigg Kennedy; D: Amy Holden Jones; W: Rita Mae Brown; C: Stephen Posey.

Slumber Party Massacre 2 woof! 1987 Drowsy babes in lingerie are drilled to death by a perverse madman. Another disappointing sequel. 75m/C VHS, Beta, LV, Closed Caption. Crystal Bernard, Kimberly McArthur, Juliette Cummins, Patrick Lowe; D: Deborah Brock; W: Deborah Brock; C: Thomas Callaway. NLC

Slumber Party Massacre 3 woof! 1990 (R) Parents: Don't let your daughters have any slumber parties! Yes, it's a drill—for the third time. 76m/C VHS, Beta. Keely Christian, Brittain Frye, M.K. Harris, David Greenle, Hope Marie Carlton, Maria Ford; D: Sally Mattison; W: Catherine Cyran. MGM

The Small Back Room 🎿🎿🎿 Hour of Glory 1949 A crippled WWII munitions expert leads a tormented existence and laments government bureaucracy. Powerfully presented adult storyline. 106m/B VHS. David Farrar, Jack Hawkins, Cyril Cusack, Kathleen Byron, Anthony Bushell, Michael Gough, Robert Morley; D: Michael Powell, Emeric Pressburger. VYY, LOO, FCT

Small Change 🎿🎿🎿🎿 1976 (PG) Pudgy, timid Desmouceaux and scruffy, neglected Goldman lead a whole pack of heartwarming tykes. A realistically and tenderly portrayed testament to the great director's belief in childhood as a "state of grace." Criticized for sentimentality, "Small Change" followed Truffaut's gloomy "The Story of Adele H." Steven Spielberg suggested the English translation of "L'Argent de Poche." In French with English subtitles. 104m/C VHS, Beta, LV. FR Geory Desmouceaux, Philippe Goldman, Jean-Francois Stevenin, Chantal Mercier, Claudio Deluca, Frank Deluca, Richard Golfier, Laurent Devlaeminck, Francis Devlaeminck, Sylvie Grezel, Pascale Bruchon, Nicole Felix; D: Francois Truffaut; W: Francois Truffaut, Suzanne Schiffman; C: Pierre William Glenn; M: Maurice Jaubert. MGM, FCT, WAR

A Small Circle of Friends 🎿½ 1980 (R) Three Harvard students struggle through their shifting relationships during their college years in the 1960s. 112m/C VHS, Beta. Brad Davis, Jameson Parker, Karen Allen, Shelley Long; D: Rob Cohen. FOX

Small Faces 🎿🎿🎿 1995 (R) Semi-autobiographical account of three brothers growing up in a working class, gang-ridden section of Glasgow in 1968. Scottish lad Lex MacLean (Robertson) is at the crucial age of 13 and caught between two completely opposite brothers and two warring gangs. Sensitive brother Alan (McFadden) has the stigma of being an artist in a conscientiously macho society, while older brother Bobby (Duffy) has no such problem, being a gang member and all-around punk. When Lex unfortunately injures the eye of gang leader Malky (McKidd) with an air-gun, he unknowingly sets in motion a dangerous chain of events, forcing him to ally with both brothers. Writer/director MacKinnon makes sure even the most tense situations are offset with dark humor, and stages the violent scenes beautifully. Garnering comparisons with other Scottish youth fables like "Trainspotting," film follows somewhat the same storytelling formula, but is much more low-key. Character and plot are given equal attention and film greatly benefits from an outstanding performance by Robertson. CNT Violence and language. CW: Violence and language. 108m/C VHS. GB Iain Robertson, Clare Higgins, Ian McElhinney, Kevin McKidd, Joseph McFadden, J.S. Duffy, Laura Fraser, Garry Sweeney, Mark McConnochie, Steven Singleton, David Walker; D: Gilles Mackinnon; W: Gilles Mackinnon, Billy Mackinnon; C: John de Borman; M: John Keane. EVE

Small Hotel 🎿🎿 1957 After discovering that he is to be replaced as headwaiter by a young woman, Harker plots to save his job through espionage, blackmail and cajolery. Average comedy, adapted from a popular British stage play as a star vehicle for Harker. 59m/B VHS. Gordon Harker, Marie Lohr, John Loder, Irene Handl, Janet Munro, Billie Whitelaw, Francis Matthews, Dora Bryan; D: David MacDonald. NOS

Small Kill 🎿½ 1993 (R) Burghoff leaves his lovable MASH character far behind, testing his acting skills as a psycho who disguises himself as a female fortune teller to rob his victims of their life savings so he can become head druglord of his town (what a goal). Two cops try to stop him/her. 86m/C VHS. Gary Burghoff, Rebecca Ferratti, Donnie Kehr, Jason Miller, Fred Carpenter; D: Robert M. Fresco; W: Fred Carpenter, James McTernan. VCI

A Small Killing 🎿🎿 1981 An undercover cop and a college professor pose as a wino and a bag lady, when trying to put the tabs on a druglord. Made for TV mystery/romance based on "The Rag Bag Clan" by Richard Barth. 100m/C VHS, Beta. Ed Asner, Jean Simmons, Sylvia Sidney, Andrew Prine, J. Pat O'Malley, Anne Ramsey; D: Steven Hilliard Stern. ART

Small Sacrifices 🎿🎿½ 1989 The true story of Diane Downs, an Oregon woman who may have murdered her own three children in 1983. Fine performance from Fawcett, who seems to have made for TV tales of true-life domestic violence as an antidote to her earlier ditzy persona as a Charlie's Angel. Gripping, with a superb script. 159m/C VHS, Beta, LV. Farrah Fawcett, Ryan O'Neal, John Shea, Emily Perkins, Gordon Clapp; D: David Greene; W: Joyce Eliason.

Small Soldiers 1998 Toys gone bad! Prototype commando action figures are meant to interact with their owners. And do they ever—they take on a life of their own and wage war, thanks to being mistakenly implanted with military intelligence chips. Led by Chip Hazard (Jones), these commandos take on the previously quiet town of Winslow Corners, Ohio. Now it's up to teens Alan (Smith) and Christy (Dunst) to battle this miniature menace. Combo of computer animation, Stan Winston's animatronic puppets, and live-action. Not yet reviewed. **?m/C VHS.** Gregory Edward Smith, Kirsten Dunst, Phil Hartman, Ann Magnuson, Jay Mohr, Denis Leary, Kevin Dunn, Wendy Schaal, Dick Miller, David Cross; **D:** Joe Dante; **V:** Tommy Lee Jones. *NYR*

Small Time 🐾🐾 1991 Chronicles the downfall of a young, small-time Harlem thief. Vince knows nothing but the streets and peer pressure, indifference, and police abuse lead him inexorably to a fatal crime. Near documentary style only heightens the tensions. **88m/B VHS.** Richard Barboza, Carolyn Hinebrew, Keith Allen, Scott Ferguson, Jane Wiliams; **D:** Norman Loftis; **W:** Norman Loftis; **M:** Arnold Bieber. *XVC*

Small Town Boy 🐾🐾 1937 The cast does what they can with the brief, hackneyed story of a guy whose personality changes for the worse when he finds a "fortune" (one thousand pre-inflationary dollars). **61m/B VHS.** Stuart Erwin, Joyce Compton, Jed Prouty, Clara Blandick, James "Doc" Blakely; **D:** Glenn Tryon; **W:** Glenn Tryon. *NOS, LOO, VYY*

Small Town Girl 🐾🐾½ *One Horse Town* 1953 Typical romantic musical of the era, as a city slicker picked up for speeding in a hick town is pursued by the sheriff's daughter. Several Busby Berkeley blockbuster musical numbers are shoehorned incongruously into the rural doings. ♪Take Me To Broadway; I've Got To Hear That Beat; My Flaming Heart; Fine, Fine, Fine; The Fellow I'd Follow; Lullaby of the Lord; Small Towns Are Smile Towns; My Gaucho. **93m/C VHS, Beta.** Jane Powell, Farley Granger, Bobby Van, Ann Miller, Billie Burke, Robert Keith, S.Z. Sakall, Fay Wray, Nat King Cole, Chill Wills; **D:** Leslie Kardos; **M:** Andre Previn. Nominations: Academy Awards '53: Best Song ("My Flaming Heart"). *MGM*

A Small Town in Texas 🐾🐾 1976 (PG) An ex-con returns home looking for the sheriff who framed him on a drug charge, and who has stolen his woman. Not-too-violent, predictable revenge flick. **96m/C VHS, Beta.** Timothy Bottoms, Susan George, Bo Hopkins; **D:** Jack Starrett; **W:** William W. Norton Sr.; **M:** Charles Bernstein. *VES, ART*

The Smallest Show on Earth 🐾🐾🐾 *Big Time Operators* 1957 A couple inherit not only an old movie house, but the three people who work there as well. Very funny and charming, with a wonderful cast. Sellers is delightful as the soused projectionist. **80m/B VHS.** GB Bill Travers, Virginia McKenna, Margaret Rutherford, Peter Sellers, Bernard Miles, Leslie Phillips, Stringer Davis, Francis De Wolff, Sidney James, June Cunningham; **D:** Basil Dearden; **W:** William Rose, John Eldridge. *NOS, FCT, VEC*

Smart-Aleck Kill 1985 An episode of the cable television-produced Phillip Marlowe series involving the drug-related murder of a Hollywood actor in the 20s. **53m/C VHS, Beta.** Powers Boothe, Michael J. Shannon, Liza Ross; **D:** Peter Hunt. *FOX*

Smart Alecks 🐾½ 1942 The Bowery Boys get involved with gangsters when Jordan helps capture a crook. The usual wise-cracking from Hall and Gorcey helps keep things moving. **88m/B VHS.** Leo Gorcey, Huntz Hall, Gabriel Dell, Gale Storm, Roger Pryor Jr., Walter Woolf King, Herbert Rawlinson, Joe Kirk, Marie Windsor; **D:** Wallace Fox. *NOS*

Smart Money 🐾🐾½ 1988 A wrongly jailed man enlists the help of his oddball pals to get revenge on the real thief who committed the computer fraud that put him behind bars. They get even while padding their pockets. **88m/C VHS.** Spencer Leigh, Alexandra Pigg, Ken Campbell. *NO*

Smash Palace 🐾🐾½ 1982 A compelling drama of a marriage jeopardized by his obsession with building a race car and her need for love and affection. Melodramatic, but worth watching. Robson as their young daughter is wonderful. **100m/C VHS, Beta, LV.** NZ Bruno Lawrence, Anna Jemison, Greer Robson, Keith Aberdein; **D:** Roger Donaldson; **W:** Bruno Lawrence. *ART, VES*

Smash-Up: The Story of a Woman 🐾🐾🐾 *A Woman Destroyed* 1947 A famous nightclub singer gives up her career for marriage and a family, only to become depressed when her husband's career soars. She turns to alcohol and her life falls apart. When her husband sues for divorce and custody of their child, she fights to recover from alcoholism. Hayward's first major role. **103m/B VHS, Beta.** Susan Hayward, Lee Bowman, Marsha Hunt, Eddie Albert; **D:** Stuart Heisler; **W:** John Howard Lawson. Nominations: Academy Awards '47: Best Actress (Hayward), Best Story. *NOS, DVT, VEC*

Smile 🐾🐾🐾 1975 (PG) Barbed, merciless send-up of small-town America focusing on a group of naive California girls who compete for the "Young American Miss" crown amid rampant commercialism, exploitation and pure middle-class idiocy. Hilarious neglected '70s-style satire. Early role for Griffith. **113m/C VHS, Beta, LV.** Bruce Dern, Barbara Feldon, Michael Kidd, Nicholas Pryor, Geoffrey Lewis, Colleen Camp, Joan Prather, Annette O'Toole, Melanie Griffith, Denise Nickerson; **D:** Michael Ritchie; **W:** Jerry Belson; **C:** Conrad Hall. *MGM*

Smile, Jenny, You're Dead 🐾🐾 1974 Janssen discovers that close friend's son-in-law has been murdered, and falls in love with the daughter, the main suspect. Pilot for Janssen's "Harry-O" detective series. **100m/C VHS.** David Janssen, John Anderson, Howard da Silva, Martin Gabel, Clu Gulager, Zalman King, Jodie Foster, Barbara Leigh; **D:** Jerry Thorpe. *UNI*

A Smile Like Yours 🐾½ 1996 (R) Too-cute yuppie couple Danny and Jennifer (Kinnear and Holly) decide to start a family, only to discover that Danny's "boys" can't swim. Many formulaic and predictable gags about masturbation and the possiblilty of infidelity ensue. Unfortunately, laughs do not. Kinnear comes off as amiable enough, while Holly turns in an aggravatingly over-the-top performance. Thomas and Cusack, as the couple's best friends, fare better than anyone, with the possible exception of scene-stealer Meullerleile as the cranky clinic nurse. Writer/director Samples is the former head of now-defunct Rysher Entertainment (flick's producing company). Coincidence? We think not. **CW:** Sex-related material. **99m/C VHS, Closed Caption.** Greg Kinnear, Lauren Holly, Jill Hennessey, Christopher McDonald, Joan Cusack, Jay Thomas, Donald Moffat, France Nuyen, Marianne Muellerleile; **Cameos:** Shirley MacLaine; **D:** Keith Samples; **W:** Keith Samples, Kevin Meyer; **C:** Richard Bowen; **M:** William Ross. Nominations: Golden Raspberry Awards '97: Worst Actress (Holly). *PAR*

Smiles of a Summer Night 🐾🐾🐾½ *Sommarnattens Leende* 1955 The best known of Bergman's rare comedies; sharp satire about eight Swedish aristocrats who become romantically and comically intertwined over a single weekend. Inspired Sondheim's successful Broadway musical "A Little Night Music," and Woody Allen's "A Midsummer Night's Sex Comedy." In Swedish with English subtitles. **110m/B VHS, Beta, LV.** SW Gunnar Bjornstrand, Harriet Andersson, Ulla Jacobsson, Eva Dahlbeck, Jarl Kulle, Margit Carlquist; **D:** Ingmar Bergman; **W:** Ingmar Bergman. *HMV, DVT, CRC*

Smilin' Through 🐾🐾🐾 1933 First sound version of this melodrama/romance which Franklin had directed as a silent in 1922. Shearer is set to marry Howard when jealous rival March shows up armed at the wedding and accidentally kills the bride. March escapes and Howard spends his years as a recluse until his young niece, the image of his dead fiance (naturally, since she's also played by Shearer) arrives to live with him. She meets a young man who turns out to be March's son (played again by March) and they fall in love. Pure sentiment done with high gloss. Remade in 1941. **97m/B VHS.** Norma Shearer, Fredric March, Leslie Howard, O.P. Heggie, Ralph Forbes, Beryl Mercer, Margaret Seddon; **D:** Sidney Franklin; **C:** Lee Garmes. Nominations: Academy Awards '33: Best Picture. *PCT*

Smilin' Through 🐾🐾½ 1941 Third filming, second with sound, first in color, of a popular melodrama. An embittered man whose wife was murdered on their wedding day raises an orphaned niece, only to have her fall in love with the son of her aunt's murderer. Made MacDonald into a singing star. Songs include title tune and "A Little Love, a Little Kiss." **101m/C VHS, Beta.** Jeanette MacDonald, Brian Aherne, Gene Raymond, Ian Hunter, Frances Robinson; **D:** Frank Borzage. *MGM*

Smiling Madame Beudet/The Seashell and the Clergyman 🐾🐾🐾½ 1928 Two famous shorts by Dulac; the second scripted by Artaud. Both are pioneering examples of surrealistic film. Silent. **62m/B VHS, Beta.** FR Alix Allin; **D:** Germaine Dulac; **W:** Antonin Artaud. *FCT*

Smilla's Sense of Snow 🐾🐾 1996 (R) Thriller starts off well but fails to sustain the suspense of the Peter Hoeg mystery on which it is based. Solitary scientist Smilla Jasperson (Ormond) is a half-Inuit, half-American (Danish in the book) resident of Copenhagen who's an expert on snow and ice. Born and raised in Greenland, Smilla is drawn back to her home when the body of six-year-old Isaiah (Miano), whom she's grudgingly befriended, is discovered at their apartment building. Smilla believes the boy was murdered and when she begins investigating it leads to the Greenland mining company where Isaiah's late father worked and which is run by the suspicious Tork (Harris). Location cinematography is particularly impressive. **CW:** Language, some violence and a sex scene. **121m/C VHS, LV, Closed Caption.** GE DK SW Julia Ormond, Gabriel Byrne, Richard Harris, Vanessa Redgrave, Robert Loggia, Jim Broadbent, Mario Adorf, Bob Peck, Tom Wilkinson, Peter Capaldi, Emma Croft, Clipper Miano; **D:** Bille August; **W:** Ann Biderman; **C:** Jorgen Persson; **M:** Hans Zimmer, Harry Gregson-Williams. *FXV*

Smith! 🐾🐾½ 1969 (G) Naive but well intentioned look at present-day treatment of Native Americans. Rancher Ford becomes embroiled in the trial of murder suspect Ramirez. Based on Paul St. Pierre's novel "Breaking Smith's Quarter Horse." **101m/C VHS, Beta.** Glenn Ford, Frank Ramirez, Keenan Wynn; **D:** Michael O'Herlihy; **M:** Robert F. Brunner. *DIS*

Smithereens 🐾🐾½ 1982 (R) Working-class girl leaves home for New York's music scene. Rugged, hip character study. Director Seidleman's first feature. **90m/C VHS, Beta, LV.** Susan Berman, Brad Rinn, Richard Hell, Christopher Noth; **D:** Susan Seidelman; **W:** Ron Nyswaner, Peter Askin. *FRF, TPV, FCT*

Smoke 🐾🐾½ 1970 A young boy nurses a lost German sheperd back to health with the help of his new stepfather, whom he learns to trust. Then he runs away with the dog when the original owners show up. Made for television Disney fare starring Opie/Richie (and later successful director) Howard. **89m/C VHS, Beta.** Earl Holliman, Ron Howard, Andy Devine; **D:** Vincent McEveety. *DIS*

Smoke 🐾🐾 1993 Three days in the life of Michael, as he travels between fantasy and reality, past and present, searching for love with the perfect older man. **90m/C VHS.** **D:** Mark D'Aruia; **M:** Arnold Bieber. *WBF*

Smoke 🐾🐾 1995 (R) Brooklyn slice of life centers around the local cigar store run by Auggie Wren (Keitel). An ensemble piece, divided into five chapters, which includes such characters as down-to-luck novelist Paul (Hurt), troubled black teenager Rashid (Perrineau Jr.), Auggie's ex-wife Ruby (Channing) and supposed daughter (Judd), and many more (some of whom get lost in the shuffle). Wonderfully acted but the stories tend to disappear in a wisp of smoke. Based on a story by Auster. Wang and Auster also made an impromptu companion film "Blue in the Face." **CW:** Language. **112m/C VHS, LV, Closed**

Caption. Harvey Keitel, William Hurt, Stockard Channing, Forest Whitaker, Harold Perrineau Jr., Ashley Judd, Mary Ward, Victor Argo, Jared Harris, Giancarlo Esposito, Mel Gorham; **D:** Wayne Wang; **W:** Paul Auster; **C:** Adam Holender; **M:** Rachel Portman. Nominations: Independent Spirit Awards '96: Best Supporting Actor (Perrineau); Screen Actors Guild Award '95: Best Supporting Actress (Channing). *TOU*

Smoke in the Wind ⚔️½ 1975 (PG) Subpar western about men accused of complicity with the Union in postbellum Arkansas. Minor role for Brennan was his last; also director Kane's last film. 93m/C VHS, Beta. John Ashley, Walter Brennan, John Russell, Myron Healey; **D:** Joseph Kane.

Smoke Signals ⚔️⚔️ 1998 (PG-13) Serious themes are treated in a deceptively simple and humorous manner, based on stories from Alexie's book "The Lone Ranger and Tonto Fistfight in Heaven." Geeky, orphaned Thomas (Adams) lives on the Coeur d'Alene reservation in Idaho where he's reluctantly looked after by stoic Victor (Beach), whose long-gone father Arnold (Farmer) saved Thomas from the fire that killed his parents. When Victor learns of Arnold's death in Phoenix, Thomas says he'll pay the expenses of the trip if he can accompany Victor. The young men reach an understanding during their travels, while Victor struggles to deal with his complicated feelings about his father and the past.**CW:** Some intense images. 88m/C VHS. Adam Beach, Evan Adams, Irene Bedard, Gary Farmer, Tantoo Cardinal, Michelle St. John, Robert Miano, Molly Cheek, Elaine Miles, Michael Greyeyes, Chief Leonard George, John Trudell; *Cameos:* Tom Skerritt, Cynthia Geary; **D:** Chris Eyre; **W:** Sherman Alexie; **C:** Brian Capener. Sundance Film Festival '98: Audience Award, Filmmakers Trophy. *NYR*

Smokescreen ⚔️⚔️½ 1990 (R) A young ad exec meets the girl of his dreams, and finds himself working for her gangster boyfriend. Competently made and acted, but phoney ending wrecks it. 91m/C VHS, LV, Closed Caption. Kim Cattrall, Dean Stockwell, Matt Craven, Kim Coates, Brian George, Michael Hogan; **D:** Martin Lavut. *COL*

Smokey and the Bandit ⚔️⚔️½ 1977 (PG) If you don't know how to end a movie, you call for a car chase. The first and best of the horrible series about bootlegger Reynolds is one long car chase. Reynolds makes a wager that he can have a truck load of Coors beer—once unavailable east of Texas—delivered to Atlanta from Texas in 28 hours. Gleason is the "smokey" who tries to stop him. Field is the hitchhiker Reynolds picks up along the way. Great stunts; director Needham was a top stunt man. 96m/C VHS, Beta, LV. Burt Reynolds, Sally Field, Jackie Gleason, Jerry Reed, Mike Henry, Paul Williams, Pat McCormick; **D:** Hal Needham; **W:** Charles Shyer. Nominations: Academy Awards '77: Best Film Editing. *USH*

Smokey and the Bandit, Part 2 ⚔️ *Smokey and the Bandit Ride Again* 1980 (PG) Pathetic sequel to "Smokey and the Bandit" proved a box-office winner, grossing $40 million. The Bandit is hired to transport a pregnant elephant from Miami to the Republican convention in Dallas. Sheriff Buford T. Justice and family are in hot pursuit. 101m/C VHS, Beta, LV. Burt Reynolds, Sally Field, Jackie Gleason, Jerry Reed, Mike Henry, Dom DeLuise, Pat McCormick, Paul Williams; **D:** Hal Needham; **W:** Jerry Belson, Michael Kane. *USH*

Smokey and the Bandit, Part 3 ⚔️ 1983 (PG) You thought the second one was bad? Another mega car chase, this time sans Reynolds and director Needham. 88m/C VHS, Beta, LV. Jackie Gleason, Jerry Reed, Paul Williams, Pat McCormick, Mike Henry, Colleen Camp; *Cameos:* Burt Reynolds; **D:** Dick Lowry; **W:** Stuart Birnbaum, David Dashev. *USH*

Smokey & the Hotwire Gang ⚔️½ 1979 A convoy of truckers try to track down a beautiful woman driving a stolen car. 85m/C VHS, Beta. James Keach, Stanley Livingston, Tony Lorea, Alvy Moore, George Barris. *NO*

Smokey & the Judge ⚔️ 1980 (PG) Police officer has his hands full with a trio of lovely ladies. 90m/C VHS. Gene Price, Wayde Preston, Juanita Curiel. *SUN*

Smokey Bites the Dust ⚔️ 1981 (PG) Car-smashing gag-fest about a sheriff's daughter kidnapped by her smitten beau. Near-plotless and literally unoriginal: lifted footage from several other Corman-produced flicks, a technique that can aptly be called garbage picking. 87m/C VHS, Beta. Janet Julian, Jimmy McNichol, Patrick Campbell, Kari Lizer, John Blythe Barrymore Jr.; **D:** Charles B. Griffith; **W:** Max Apple. *NLC*

Smokey Smith ⚔️½ 1936 Ubiquitous Hayes and steely Steele hunt down the slayers of an elderly couple. Ordinary oater directed by Steele's father, Bradbury. 59m/B VHS, Beta. Bob Steele, George "Gabby" Hayes; **D:** Robert North Bradbury. *VCN*

Smoking/No Smoking ⚔️⚔️ 1994 Two linked films director Resnais adapted from writer Alan Ayckbourn's eight-play cycle "Intimate Exchanges" (although the screenwriters have only used six stories). Azema and Arditti plays nine characters in various tableaux on marriage and affairs set at a Yorkshire school. The opening sequence of each episode provides the title tie-in, as faculty wife Celia goes onto the terrace, finds a pack of cigarettes, and decides whether or not to light up. A studio set provides all the frankly fake backdrops. Very slight and very long. French with subtitles. 285m/C VHS. **FR** Sabine Azema, Pierre Arditti; **D:** Alain Resnais; **W:** Jean-Pierre Bacri, Agnes Jaoui. Cesar Awards '94: Best Actor (Arditti), Best Art Direction/Set Decoration, Best Director (Resnais), Best Film, Best Writing.

A Smoky Mountain Christmas ⚔️⚔️ 1986 Dolly gets away from it all in a secluded cabin that has been appropriated by a gang of orphans, and sings a half dozen songs. Innocuous seasonal country fun. Winkler's TV directing debut. 94m/C VHS, Beta, Closed Caption. Dolly Parton, Bo Hopkins, Dan Hedaya, Gennie James, David Ackroyd, Rene Auberjonois, John Ritter, Anita Morris, Lee Majors; **D:** Henry Winkler; **W:** Dolly Parton. *FOX*

Smooth Talk ⚔️⚔️⚔️ 1985 (PG-13) An innocent, flirtatious teenager catches the eye of a shady character, played by Williams. Disturbing and thought-provoking film that caused some controversy when it opened. Dern gives a brilliant performance as the shy, sheltered girl. Based on the Joyce Carol Oates story "Where Are You Going, Where Have You Been?" Made for PBS' "American Playhouse" series. 92m/C VHS, Beta, LV. Laura Dern, Treat Williams, Mary Kay Place, Levon Helm; **D:** Joyce Chopra; **W:** Tom Cole. Sundance Film Festival '86: Grand Jury Prize. *ART, VES*

Smooth Talker WOOF! 1990 (R) A serial killer stalks the women of a 976 party line. Bad acting, bad dialog, not a scare to be found.**CW:** Language and sex-related dialogue, violence, and sensuality. 89m/C VHS, Closed Caption. Joe Guzaldo, Peter Crombie, Stuart Whitman, Burt Ward, Sydney Lassick, Blair Weickgenant; **D:** Tom Milo.

Smouldering Fires ⚔️⚔️½ 1925 A tough businesswoman falls in love with an ambitious young employee, who is 15 years her junior. After they marry, problems arise in the form of the wife's attractive younger sister. Surprisingly subtle melodrama, if that's not an oxymoron. 100m/B VHS, Beta. Pauline Frederick, Laura La Plante, Tully Marshall, Malcolm McGregor, Wanda Hawley, Helen Lynch, George Cooper, Bert Roach; **D:** Clarence Brown. *VYY, GPV*

Smugglers ⚔️ *Lover of the Great Bear* 1975 Opportunistic smugglers take advantage of the Russian Revolution to sack the land and make a bundle. 110m/C VHS, Beta. **IT** Senta Berger, Giuliano Gemma; **D:** Valentino Orsini. *VCD*

Smugglers' Cove ⚔️⚔️⚔️ 1948 Gorcey wrongly believes he has inherited a mansion. He and the Bowery Boys move in, only to stumble across a smuggling ring. Plenty of slapsticks; the boys at their best. 66m/B VHS. Leo Gorcey, Huntz Hall, Gabriel Dell; **D:** William Beaudine. *NO*

Smuggler's Cove ⚔️½ 1983 A young boy doggedly pursues a mysterious trawler captain despite warnings from his parents. 75m/C VHS, Beta. *AU NO*

Snake Eyes 1998 The Secretary of Defense is assassinated during an Atlantic City boxing match and corrupt cop Cage and naval officer pal Sinise take it upon themselves to seal off the arena until the crime is solved. De Palma shot in a Montreal skating arena. Not yet reviewed. ?m/C VHS. Nicolas Cage, Gary Sinise, Carla Gugino, John Heard, Stan Shaw, Kevin Dunn; **D:** Brian DePalma; **W:** David Koepp. *NYR*

The Snake Hunter Strangler ⚔️ 1966 A young girl is rescued after 15 years from an evil cult of snake people. 65m/C VHS, Beta. Guy Madison, Ivan Desny; **D:** Luigi Capuano. *NO*

Snake in the Eagle's Shadow 2 ⚔️ 1983 Three champions of self-defense mount a major offensive and win battle after battle. 89m/C VHS, Beta. Wang Tao, Chen Shing, Lung Fei; **D:** Chang Shinn I. *TWE*

The Snake People ⚔️ *Isle of the Snake People; Cult of the Dead; La Muerte Viviente; Isle of the Living Dead* 1968 A police captain investigates a small island littered with LSD-experimenting scientists, snake-worshippers, and voodoo. One of the infamous quartet of Karloff's final films, all made in Mexico. 90m/C VHS, Beta. **MX** Boris Karloff, Julissa, Carlos East; **D:** Enrique Vergara. *SNC, MPI, HEG*

The Snake Pit ⚔️⚔️⚔️½ 1948 One of the first films to compassionately explore mental illness and its treatment. Following an emotional collapse de Havilland is placed in a mental institution by her husband. The severity of her depression causes her sympathetic doctor to try such treatments as electric shock, hydrotherapy, and drugs, along with the psychoanalysis which gradually allows her to accept her fears and make her recovery. Tour-de-force performance by de Havilland. Based on the novel by Mary Jane Ward. 108m/B VHS. Olivia de Havilland, Mark Stevens, Leo Genn, Celeste Holm, Glenn Langan, Helen Craig, Leif Erickson, Beulah Bondi; **D:** Anatole Litvak; **W:** Frank Partos, Millen Brand; **M:** Alfred Newman. Academy Awards '48: Best Sound; New York Film Critics Awards '48: Best Actress (de Havilland); Nominations: Academy Awards '48: Best Actress (de Havilland), Best Director (Litvak), Best Picture, Best Screenplay, Best Original Dramatic/Comedy Score. *MOV, BTV, FCT*

The Snake Woman ⚔️ 1961 A herpetologist working in a small English village during the 1890s is conducting strange experiments to try to cure his wife's madness. He tries injecting his pregnant wife with snake venom and she gives birth to a cold-blooded daughter, who, when she grows up, has the ability to change herself into a deadly snake. She promptly begins killing the local male populace until Scotland Yard is called in to investigate. The curvy Travers is appropriately snakey but this movie is dull. 68m/C VHS. **GB** John P. McCarthy, Susan Travers, Arnold Marle; **D:** Sidney J. Furie. *CNM*

SnakeEater ⚔️ 1989 (R) Loner cop tracks down swine who killed his parents and kidnapped his sister. "Rambo" rip-off with little plot, but lots of action. Followed by two sequels. 89m/C VHS, Beta. Lorenzo Lamas, Larry Csonka, Ron Palillo; **D:** George Erschbamer. *VTR*

SnakeEater 2: The Drug Buster ⚔️ 1989 (R) A cop goes nuts and kills four drug dealers. As a result he is committed to an institution. Iron bars don't make a prison for this guy though, and he's soon back on the streets fighting crime with his pal "Speedboat." Silly sequel is quite bad; followed by yet another.**CW:** Language and some violence. 93m/C VHS, Beta, Closed Caption. Lorenzo Lamas, Larry B. Scott, Michelle Scarabelli, Harvey Atkin, Jack Blum, Kathleen Kinmont; **D:** George Erschbamer. *PAR*

SnakeEater 3: His Law ✍ 1992 (R) Tough cop Jack Kelly (Lamas), aka SnakeEater, is out to avenge a woman's beating by a gang of thug bikers. Lots of action and violence, not much plot; based on W. Glenn Duncan's novel "Rafferty's Rules."**CW:** Language, strong violence, and sexuality. 109m/C VHS, Beta, Closed Caption. Lorenzo Lamas, Minor Mustain, Tracy Cook, Holly Chester, Scott "Bam Bam" Bigelow; **D:** George Erschbamer; **W:** John Dunning. **PAR**

Snapdragon ✍✍ 1993 (R) Police psychologist is led astray by his libido while investigating a luscious amnesiac. His sensible vice cop girlfriend then discovers the sexpot is actually a psycho serial killer calling herself the Snapdragon but will her boyfriend even care?**CW:** Strong language, strong violence, and strong sexuality. 96m/C VHS, Beta. Steven Bauer, Pamela Anderson, Chelsea Field; **D:** Worth Keeter; **W:** Gene Church.

The Snapper ✍✍✍½ 1993 (R) Originally made for BBC television, Frears creates a small comic gem based on the second inveral of Doyle's Barrytown trilogy. Set in Dublin, 20-year-old Sharon Curley (Kellegher) finds herself unexpectedly pregnant and refuses to name the father. Family and friends are understanding—until they discover the man's identity. Affecting performances, particularly from Meaney as Sharon's dad who takes a much greater interest in the birth of his grandchild than he ever did with his own children. Cheerful semi-sequel to "The Commitments" serves up domestic upheavals graced with humor and a strong sense of family loyalty.**CW:** Language and some sexuality. 95m/C VHS, LV, Closed Caption. IR Tina Kellegher, Colm Meaney, Ruth McCabe, Colm O'Byrne, Pat Laffan, Eanna MacLiam, Ciara Duffy; **D:** Stephen Frears; **W:** Roddy Doyle. Nominations: Golden Globe Awards '94: Best Actor—Musical/Comedy (Meaney). **TOU**

Snapshot ✍ 1977 (R) Typical grade Z sex comedy; a free-lance photographer ogles lots of variously dishabilled young women through his lens. 84m/C VHS, Beta. Jim Henshaw, Susan Petrie. **NO**

Snatched ✍✍ 1972 The wives of three wealthy men are held for ransom, but one man doesn't want to pay, while one of the victims needs insulin. Standard made for television fare. 73m/C VHS. Howard Duff, Leslie Nielsen, Sheree North, Barbara Parkins, Robert Reed, John Saxon, Tisha Sterling; **D:** Sutton Roley; **M:** Randy Edelman. **REP**

Sneakers ✍✍½ 1992 (PG-13) Competent thriller about five computer hackers with questionable pasts and an equally questionable government job. Of course, nothing is as it seems. Rather slow-going considering the talents and suspense involved but includes enough turns to keep a viewer's interest. 125m/C VHS, Beta, LV, Letterbox, Closed Caption, DVD. Robert Redford, Sidney Poitier, River Phoenix, Dan Aykroyd, Ben Kingsley, David Strathairn, Mary McDonnell, Timothy Busfield, George Hearn, Eddie Jones, James Earl Jones, Stephen Tobolowsky; **D:** Phil Alden Robinson; **W:** Lawrence Lasker, Walter F. Parkes, Phil Alden Robinson; **C:** John Lindley; **M:** James Horner, Branford Marsalis. **USH, PMS**

Sniper ✍✍✍ The Deadly Tower 1975 Suspenseful television drama based on true story of Charles Whitman, who shot at University of Texas students from Texas Tower on a summer day in 1966. Disney alumunus Russell breaks type as mass killer, with fine support by Yniguez as a police officer on the scene and Beatty as the passerby who lends a hand. Finely crafted recreation of disturbing, true event. 85m/C VHS. Kurt Russell, Richard Yniguez, John Forsythe, Ned Beatty, Pernell Roberts, Clifton James, Paul Carr, Alan Vint, Pepe Serna; **D:** Jerry Jameson. **XVC**

The Sniper ✍½ 1987 A law-abiding citizen becomes a vigilante killer after witnessing a violent crime. 90m/C VHS, Beta. Claudia Cardinale. **NO**

Sniper ✍½ 1992 (R) Less than compelling shoot-'em-up set in Panama. Lead characters include Sgt. Beckett (Berenger), a seasoned assassin who gets a rush from killing. Also assigned to the case is Richard Miller (Zane), a newcomer who knows his guns but not his jungles. Together they go in search of their target, a politician planning a coup with the help of a druglord. Action is poorly choreographed and plot is cursory at best. The laserdisc version is available letterboxed.**CW:** Language and strong violence. 99m/C VHS, LV, 8mm, Letterbox, Closed Caption. Tom Berenger, Billy Zane, J.T. Walsh, Aden Young, Ken Radley, Reinaldo Arenas, Carlos Alvarez, Roy Edmonds; **D:** Luis Llosa; **W:** Michael Frost Beckner, Crash Leyland; **C:** Bill Butler; **M:** Gary Chang. **COL**

Sno-Line ✍ 1985 (R) A New York gangster moves to Texas and begins to wipe out the competition on his way to building his drug and gambling dynasty. Bo-ring excuse for entertainment. No hope, no redemption, no titillation: just ultra-"realistic" depiction of organized crime, poorly acted. 89m/C VHS, Beta. Vince Edwards, Paul Smith, June Wilkinson; **D:** Douglas F. Oneans. **ART**

Snoopy, Come Home ✍✍✍ 1972 (G) Snoopy leaves Charlie Brown to visit his former owner Lila in the hospital and returns with her to her apartment house. From Charles Schultz's popular comic strip "Peanuts." 80m/C VHS, Beta, LV, Closed Caption. **D:** Bill Melendez; **W:** Charles M. Schulz. **NO**

Snoopy's Getting Married, Charlie Brown 1985 An animated Peanuts adventure wherein Snoopy prepares to get married. 30m/C VHS, Beta. **BAR**

Snow Country ✍✍½ 1957 Romantic drama of an unsuccessful, married artist from Tokyo who travels to a mountain resort to find himself. He requests a Geisha for the evening and, when none are available, the beautiful adopted daughter of the local music teacher is sent to him instead. Based on the novel by Nobel Prize winner Yasunari Kawabata. In Japanese with English subtitles. Remade in 1965. 104m/B VHS, Beta. JP Ryo Ikebe, Keiko Kishi, Akira Kubo, Kaoru Yachigusa, Hisaya Morishige, Mineko Yorozuyo, Etsuko Ichihara, Noriko Sengoku, Kumeko Urabe, Eiko Miyoshi, Akira Tan, Chieko Naniwa, Daisuke Kato, Haruo Tanaka; **D:** Shiro Toyoda. **CVC**

The Snow Creature woof! 1954 Stupid troop of explorers bring back a snow creature from the Himalayas. Critter escapes in L.A. and terrorizes all in its path before blending in with club crowd. Very bad monster epic (the first about a snow monster) that strains credibility frame by frame. Occasionally, depending upon camera angle, light, and viewer mood, monster appears to be something other than guy in bad suit sweating. Directed by Billy Wilder's brother and another argument against genetic consistency. 72m/B VHS, Beta. Paul Langton, Leslie Denison; **D:** W. Lee Wilder. **NOS, SNC**

Snow Kill ✍½ 1990 Five city-dwellers travel into the mountains for a fun survival training weekend, but the fun turns deadly when they accidentally come across a murderous drug gang. Pseudo-'30s suspense adventure fails to thrill or surprise. Made for cable. 90m/C VHS, Beta, Closed Caption. Terence Knox, Patti D'Arbanville, David Dukes; **D:** Thomas J. Wright; **W:** Harv Zimmel. **PAR, TTC**

The Snow Queen 1983 From "Fairie Tale Theatre" comes this adaptation of the Hans Christian Andersen tale. A boy and girl who grow up together are separated by evil when the boy is held captive in the icy palace of the Snow Queen. The girl sets out to rescue him. 60m/C VHS, Beta, Closed Caption. Lauren Hutton, Linda Manz, David Hemmings, Melissa Gilbert, Lee Remick, Lance Kerwin; **D:** Peter Medak. **FOX, FCT**

Snow: The Movie ✍ 1983 Rates creative zero for title, though there is snow, as well as skiing, growing up, romance, and good times among the young people involved. Filmed in Australia. 83m/C VHS, Beta. David Argue, Lance Curtis; **D:** Robert Gibson. **VCD**

Snow Treasure ✍ 1967 (G) With the help of an underground agent, Norwegian children smuggle gold out of the country right under the noses of the Nazis. Based on the novel by Marie McSwigan. 96m/C VHS, Beta. James Franciscus, Paul Anstad; **D:** Irving Jacoby. **ART**

Snow White ✍✍ 1989 The incomparable Rigg stars in this witty retelling of the beautiful girl and her seven little friends. 85m/C VHS. Diana Rigg, Sarah Patterson, Billy Barty; **D:** Michael Berz. **WAR**

Snow White: A Tale of Terror ✍✍½ Snow White in the Black Forest; Grimm Brothers' Snow White 1997 (R) This definitely puts the grim in the Grimm Brothers version of the fairy tale. In medieval Austria, beautiful Claudia (Weaver) marries widowed Frederick who, unfortunately, has an even-more beautiful daughter, Lilli (Keena), who's put out by this rival for her father's affections. The stepmom/stepdaughter battle increases when Claudia's own long-awaited baby is still-born and the wrathful and unbalanced Claudia orders Lilli's death. Only she's rescued by seven outcasts (only one of whom is a dwarf) living in the forest. The witchy Claudia does still like to talk to her mirror, however. Filmed in the Czech Republic.**CW:** Mature themes, violence, language. 101m/C VHS, LV. Sigourney Weaver, Sam Neill, Monica Keena, Gil Bellows, Taryn Davis; **D:** Michael Cohn; **W:** Thomas Szollosi, Deborah Serra; **C:** Mike Southon; **M:** John Ottman. **PGV**

Snow White and the Seven Dwarfs ✍✍✍✍ 1937 (G) Classic adaptation of the Grimm Brothers fairy tale about the fairest of them all. Beautiful animation, memorable characters, and wonderful songs mark this as the definitive "Snow White." Set the stage for other animated features after Walt Disney took an unprecedented gamble by attempting the first animated feature-length film, a project which took over two years to create and $1.5 million to make, and made believers out of those who laughed at the concept. Lifelike animation was based on real stars; Margery Belcher (later Champion) posed for Snow, Louis Hightower was the Prince, and Lucille LaVerne gave the Queen her nasty look. ♫Some Day My Prince Will Come; One Song; With a Smile and a Song; Whistle While You Work; Bluddle-Uddle-Um-Dum; The Dwarfs' Yodel Song; Heigh Ho; I'm Wishing; Isn't This a Silly Song?. 83m/C VHS, LV, Closed Caption. **D:** David Hand; **W:** Ted Sears, Otto Englander, Earl Hurd, Dorothy Blank, Richard Creedon, Dick Richard, Merrill De Maris, Webb Smith; **M:** Frank Churchill, Paul Smith, Larry Morey, Leigh Harline; **V:** Adriana Caselotti, Harry Stockwell, Lucille LaVerne, Moroni Olsen, Billy Gilbert, Pinto Colvig, Otis Harlan, Scotty Matraw, Roy Atwell, Stuart Buchanan, Marion Darlington, Jim Macdonald. National Film Registry '89;; Nominations: Academy Awards '37: Best Score. **DIS, OM**

Snow White and the Seven Dwarfs 1983 From cable television's "Faerie Tale Theatre" comes the story of a princess who befriends seven little men to protect her from the jealous evil queen. 60m/C VHS, Beta, LV, Closed Caption. Elizabeth Ashley, Rex Smith, Vincent Price, Vanessa Redgrave; **D:** Peter Medak. **FOX, FCT, HMV**

Snow White and the Three Stooges ✍ Snow White and the Three Clowns 1961 The Stooges fill in for the Seven Dwarfs when they go off prospecting in King Solomon's mines. Alas, see any Stooge movie but this one. 107m/C VHS, Beta, Closed Caption. Moe Howard, Curly Howard, Larry Fine, Carol Heiss, Patricia Medina; **D:** Walter Lang. **FOX, FCT**

Snowball Express ⅆⅆ 1972 (G) When a New York City accountant inherits a hotel in the Rocky Mountains, he decides to move his family west to attempt to make a go of the defunct ski resort, only to find that the place is falling apart. Run-of-the-mill Disney comedy, based on the novel "Chateau Bon Vivant" by Frankie and John O'Rear. 120m/C VHS, Beta. Dean Jones, Nancy Olson, Harry (Henry) Morgan, Keenan Wynn; **D:** Norman Tokar; **M:** Robert F. Brunner. DIS

Snowballin' ⅆ 1985 A ski instructor gives private lessons to a bunch of snow bunnies. 90m/C VHS, Beta. Seline Lomez, Daniel Pilon. JEF

Snowballing ⅆ 1985 (PG) Part of the polluted wave of teen-sex flicks of the 1980s, this is very mild for the genre but still no prize. Lusty high schoolers at a skiing competition look for action on and off the slopes, end up exposing a resort fraud. 96m/C VHS, Beta. Mary McDonough, Bob Hastings.

Snowbeast ⅆ½ 1977 The residents of a ski resort are being terrorized by a half-human, half-animal beast leaving a path of dead bodies in its wake. "Jaws" hits the slopes. Not scary or even funny. Made for TV. 96m/C VHS, Beta. Bo Svenson, Yvette Mimieux, Sylvia Sidney, Clint Walker, Robert F. Logan; **D:** Herb Wallerstein. WOV

Snowblind ⅆⅆ *Ski Lift to Death* 1978 Two ski gondolas derail, placing the passengers in jeopardy. Among the passengers is a mobster being pursued by an assassin. 98m/C VHS. Deborah Raffin, Charles Frank, Howard Duff, Don Galloway, Gail Strickland, Don Johnson, Veronica Hamel, Clu Gulager, Lisa Reeves, Suzy Chaffee; **D:** John Shepphird; **W:** Rudy Rupak, James Salisko; **C:** Bruno Philip; **M:** Ross Vannelli. COL

Snowboard Academy ⅆ½ 1996 (PG) Chris Barry (Haim), the younger son of a ski resort owner, gets into trouble when his crazy snowboarder pals take over the slopes. Chris' older brother challenges him to start a school that will turn the bumblers into racers in just two weeks. Filmed at Le Chantecler resort in the Laurentian Mountains near Montreal. 89m/C VHS, Closed Caption. Corey Haim, Jim Varney, Brigitte Nielsen, Joe Flaherty, Paul Hopkins; **D:** John Shepphird; **W:** Rudy Rupak, James Salisko; **C:** Bruno Philip; **M:** Ross Vannelli. COL

Snowbound ⅆⅆ½ 1997 Based on a true story, this TV drama follows a couple and their baby fighting for survival when they're trapped in the open by a snowstorm for eight days. 120m/C VHS. Neil Patrick Harris, Kelli Williams, Susan Clark, Michael Gross. BWE

The Snows of Kilimanjaro ⅆⅆⅆ 1952 Called by Hemingway "The Snows of Zanuck," in reference to the great producer, this film is actually an artful pastiche of several Hemingway short stories and novels. The main story, "The Snows of Kilimanjaro," acts as a framing device, in which the life of a successful writer is seen through his fevered flashbacks as he and his rich wife, while on safari, await a doctor to save his gangrenous leg. 117m/C Beta. Gregory Peck, Susan Hayward, Ava Gardner, Hildegarde Neff, Leo G. Carroll, Torin Thatcher, Ava Norring, Helene Stanley, Marcel Dalio, Vincente Gomez, Richard Allen, Leonard Carey; **D:** Henry King; **W:** Casey Robinson; **C:** Leon Shamroy. Nominations: Academy Awards '52: Best Art Direction/Set Decoration (Color), Best Color Cinematography. NOS, GKK, SNC

Snowy River, the MacGregor Saga: The Race 1993 A continuation of the "The Man from Snowy River" set in late 1800s Australia. Matt MacGregor (Clarke) is running a successful cattle ranch with his two grown sons and a teenage daughter. Naturally, there's some family strife as well as a horse race. Edited episodes from the TV series. 87m/C VHS. AU Andrew Clarke. FHE

Snuff-Bottle Connection ⅆ 1982 Russian envoy is spying for the government while delivering a gift to a Ching dynasty emperor. 96m/C VHS, Beta. Hwang Jang Lee, John Liu, Roy Horan. WVE

Snuffy Smith, Yard Bird ⅆ½ *Private Snuffy Smith; Snuffy Smith* 1942 The pint-sized moonshiner finds himself in the Army, clashing with his sergeant. Followed by "Hillbilly Blitzkrieg" later the same year. Duncan is perfect for the part, and Kennedy is right on as his foil. 67m/B VHS. Bud Duncan, Edgar Kennedy, Sarah Padden, Doris Linden, J. Farrell MacDonald, Frank Austin, Jimmie Dodd; **D:** Eddie Cline. NOS, VYY

So Dear to My Heart ⅆⅆⅆ½ 1949 A farm boy and his misfit black sheep wreak havoc at the county fair. Several sequences combine live action with animation. Heartwarming and charming; straightforward and likeable but never sentimental. Wonderful, vintage Disney. ♫Sourwood Mountain; Billy Boy; So Dear To My Heart; County Fair; Stick-To-It-Ivity; Ol' Dan Patch; It's Whatcha Do With Watcha Got; Lavender Blue (Dilly Dilly). 82m/C VHS, Beta, LV. Bobby Driscoll, Burl Ives, Beulah Bondi, Harry Carey Sr., Luana Patten; **D:** Harold Schuster. Nominations: Academy Awards '49: Best Song ("Lavender Blue"). DIS

So Ends Our Night ⅆⅆⅆ 1941 German scorns Nazi ideology, flees Austria, and meets young Jewish couple seeking asylum. Fine adaptation of Erich Maria Remarque's novel "Flotsam," with splendid performances from Sullavan (on loan from Universal) and young Ford. 117m/B VHS. Fredric March, Margaret Sullavan, Frances Dee, Glenn Ford, Anna Sten, Erich von Stroheim; **D:** John Cromwell; **C:** William H. Daniels. Nominations: Academy Awards '41: Best Original Dramatic/Comedy Score. IVY

So Fine ⅆⅆ½ 1981 (R) Absent-minded English professor O'Neal tries to rescue his father's clothing business from going bottom-up. He accidentally invents peek-a-boo bottomed jeans, which become an immediate hit and make him rich. Comedy smorgasbord, setting outing from sometime novelist Bergman, hits and misses. O'Neal is memorable, as is the ubiquitous Warden and his sidekick. 91m/C VHS, Beta. Ryan O'Neal, Jack Warden, Mariangela Melato, Richard Kiel; **D:** Andrew Bergman; **W:** Andrew Bergman; **M:** Ennio Morricone. WAR

So I Married an Axe Murderer ⅆⅆ½ 1993 (PG-13) Combination comedy/romance/thriller. Charlie is a hip bookstore owner with a commitment problem. When he finally falls in love with a butcher, he comes to suspect she's a serial killer and he's in line as her next victim. "Saturday Night Live" star Myers has a dual role: as Charlie and as Scottish dad Stuart, allowing him to be fanatically Scottish as Stuart and somewhat more restrained as the angst-ridden Charlie. One-gag movie counted on Myers' "Wayne's World" popularity, which didn't pan out at the boxoffice. Best appreciated by Myers' fans, this one is better on the small screen. **CW:** Language, nudity, and mock terror. 92m/C VHS, LV, 8mm, Closed Caption. Mike Myers, Nancy Travis, Anthony LaPaglia, Amanda Plummer, Brenda Fricker, Matt Doherty, Charles Grodin; **Cameos:** Phil Hartman, Steven Wright, Alan Arkin; **D:** Thomas Schlamme; **W:** Mike Myers, Robbie Fox; **M:** Bruce Broughton. COL

So Proudly We Hail ⅆⅆⅆ 1943 True story of the lives of three war-front nurses and their heroism under fire during WWII. Colbert is Lt. Davidson in charge of nine Red Cross Army nurses serving in the Pacific. Lake and Goddard play the other leads. With the popularity of its stars and the patriotic spirit of the film, the picture hit boxoffice gold. Critics praised its authenticity, as the film never fell victim to the usual standards of Hollywood glamour. Fans of Lake beware: she has short hair in this film because the government requested that she not appear as a servicewoman with her famous peek-a-boo hair style because female factory workers were getting their long Lake-inspired hair caught in the machinery. 126m/B VHS, Closed Caption. Claudette Colbert, Paulette Goddard, Veronica Lake, George Reeves, Barbara Britton, Walter Abel, Sonny Tufts; **D:** Mark Sandrich; **W:** Allan Scott; **M:** Miklos Rozsa. Nominations: Academy Awards '43: Best Black and White Cinematography, Best Original Screen-

play, Best Special Effects, Best Supporting Actress (Goddard). USH

So This Is Paris ⅆⅆⅆ 1926 Roguish pre-Hayes Code dancing duo seeks spice through alternative lovemates. Classic sophisticated Lubitsch, with outstanding camerawork and a bit of jazz. 68m/B VHS, Beta. Monte Blue, Patsy Ruth Miller, Lilyan Tashman, Andre de Beranger, Myrna Loy; **D:** Ernst Lubitsch. GPV, FCT

So This Is Washington ⅆⅆ½ 1943 The comedy team go to Washington with wacky inventions to help the war effort. Turns out there's too entirely too much nonsense going around, and the boys give 'em a piece of their mind. Fun, featherweight wartime comedy. 70m/B VHS, Beta. Lum & Abner, Alan Mowbray. Nominations: Academy Awards '43: Best Sound. NOS, DVT

Soapdish ⅆⅆⅆ 1991 (PG-13) The backstage lives of a daytime soap opera, "The Sun Also Sets," and its cast. When the soap's ratings fall, a character written out of series via decapitation is brought back to give things a lift. While the writer struggles to make the reincarnation believable, the cast juggles old and new romances, and professional jealousies abound. Some genuinely funny moments as film actors spoof the genre that gave many of them a start. 97m/C VHS, Beta, LV, 8mm, Letterbox, Closed Caption. Sally Field, Kevin Kline, Robert Downey Jr., Cathy Moriarty, Whoopi Goldberg, Elisabeth Shue, Carrie Fisher, Garry Marshall, Teri Hatcher, Paul Johansson, Costas Mandylor, Stephen Nichols, Kathy Najimy, Sheila Kelley; **Cameos:** Leeza Gibbons, John Tesh, Finola Hughes; **D:** Michael Hoffman; **W:** Andrew Bergman, Robert Harling; **M:** Alan Silvestri. PAR

S.O.B. ⅆⅆ½ 1981 (R) Blake Edwards' bitter farce about Hollywood and the film industry wheelers and dealers who inhabit it. When a multi-million dollar picture bombs at the boxoffice, the director turns suicidal, until he envisions re-shooting it with a steamy, X-rated scene starring his wife, a star with a goody-two-shoes image. Edwards used his real-life wife, Julie ("Mary Poppins") Andrews, for the scene in which she bared her breasts. Oft-inspired, but oft-terrible. Zestfully vengeful. William Holden's last film. 121m/C VHS, Beta, LV, Letterbox. William Holden, Robert Preston, Richard Mulligan, Julie Andrews, Robert Webber, Shelley Winters, Robert Vaughn, Larry Hagman, Stuart Margolin, Loretta Swit, Craig Stevens, Larry Storch, Jennifer Edwards, Robert Loggia, Rosanna Arquette, Marisa Berenson; **D:** Blake Edwards; **W:** Blake Edwards; **C:** Harry Stradling Jr.; **M:** Henry Mancini. National Society of Film Critics Awards '81: Best Supporting Actor (Preston). FOX, WAR

Social Error ⅆⅆ 1935 An heiress mistakes her guards for a group of kidnappers. 60m/B VHS, Beta, LV. Gertrude Messinger, David Sharpe. NOS, HEG

The Social Secretary ⅆⅆ½ 1916 Driven from the rat race by lecherous men, Talmadge gets new job as rich woman's secretary, where she down-dresses to avoid further lewd encounters. She falls for her boss's son, but isn't considered marriage material until she proves herself. 56m/B VHS, Beta. Norma Talmadge, Kate Lester, Helen Weir, Gladden James, Herbert Frank; **D:** John Emerson. GPV, FCT

Society ⅆ 1992 (R) A teenager wonders if his visions are real or hallucinations when he believes his family, and everyone else around him, are flesh-eating predators. The puzzle isn't much but wait for the special-effects ladened ending to get your fill of gore. **CW:** Language, bizarre violence, and bizarre sexuality. 99m/C VHS, Closed Caption. Billy Warlock, Devin Devasquez, Evan Richards; **D:** Brian Yuzna. REP

Sodbusters ⅆⅆ½ 1994 (PG-13) Western spoof about homesteaders versus a greedy cattle baron and the railroad in 1875 Colorado. A lascivious farmer's wife and a mysterious gunslinger—as well as a couple of gay cowboys—are included for additional fun. 97m/C VHS, Closed Caption. Kris Kristofferson, John Vernon, Fred Willard, Wendel Meldrum, Max Gail, Steve Landesburg, Don Lake, James Pickens Jr.,

John Hemphill; **D:** Eugene Levy; **W:** John Hemphill, Eugene Levy. *REP*

Sodom and Gomorrah 🎬🎬 *Sodome et Gomorrhe; The Last Days of Sodom and Gomorrah* 1962 The Italian-made, internationally produced epic about Lot, the Hebrews and the destruction of the two sinful biblical cities. Moderately entertaining—but ponderous, to say the least, and very long. **154m/C VHS, Beta, LV, Closed Caption.** *IT* Stewart Granger, Stanley Baker, Pier Angeli, Anouk Aimee, Rossana Podesta; **D:** Robert Aldrich; **M:** Miklos Rozsa. *FOX, IME*

Sofie 🎬🎬½ 1992 Sweet family melodrama about a late 19th Jewish family in Denmark. Sofie (Mynster) is the unmarried 28-year-old daughter of loving, protective parents. She has fallen in love with a gentile artist (Christensen) but gives him up to marry within her faith. Unsuited, Sofie and Jonas (Zeller) lead melancholy lives, which Sofie redeems through her joy in her son. Self-effacing drama is Ullmann's directorial debut. Adapted from the novel "Mendel Philipsen & Son" by Henri Nathansen. In Swedish with English subtitles. **145m/C VHS, Letterbox.** *SW* Karen-Lise Mynster, Ghita Norby, Erland Josephson, Jesper Christensen, Henning Moritzen, Torben Zeller, Stig Hoffmeyer, Kirsten Rolffes, Lotte Herman; **D:** Liv Ullmann; **W:** Liv Ullmann, Peter Poulsen. *FCT, ING*

Soft and Hard 🎬🎬½ 1985 Made for English television, this video by Godard and Mieville intends to address the role of media and television in everyday life via a seemingly informal look at the couple's daily existence and the propensity for image production in it. In French with English subtitles. **48m/C VHS, Beta.** *FR* **D:** Anne-Marie Mieville, Jean-Luc Godard.

Soft Deceit 🎬🎬½ 1994 (R) Master criminal Trent (Bergin) gets caught in the heist of $16 million in mob money. Then Anne (Vernon) shashays into prison offering Trent a deal—half the cash in exchange for breaking him out. She succeeds but maybe a doublecross is next on the agenda.**CW:** Some strong sexuality and language. **95m/C VHS, LV.** Patrick Bergin, Kate Vernon, John Wesley Shipp, Gwynyth Walsh, Nigel Bennett, Damir Andrei; **D:** Jorge Montesi; **W:** Jorge Montesi. *TTC*

The Soft Kill 🎬🎬 1994 (R) LA private eye Jack Ramsey (Bernsen) becomes the prime murder suspect when his girlfriend is strangled. Can he prove his innocence before more bodies pile up and the cops catch him?**CW:** Sexuality; language; violence. **95m/C VHS.** Corbin Bernsen, Brion James, Matt McCoy, Michael Harris, Kim Morgan Greene, Carrie-Anne Moss; **D:** Eli Cohen. *TRI*

The Soft Skin 🎬🎬🎬 *Le Peau Douce; Silken Skin* 1964 A classic portrayal of marital infidelity by the master director. A writer and lecturer has an affair with a stewardess. After the affair ends, his wife confronts him, with tragic results. Cliche plot is forgivable; acted and directed to perfection. Frequent Truffaut star Jean-Pierre Leaud served here as an apprentice director. In French with English subtitles. **120m/B VHS, Beta, LV.** *FR* Jean Desailly, Nelly Benedetti, Francoise Dorleac; **D:** Francois Truffaut; **M:** Georges Delerue. *HMV, FOX*

Soggy Bottom U.S.A. 🎬🎬 1984 (PG) A sheriff has his hands full trying to keep the law enforced in a small Southern town. Quite-good cast keeps the plot from disappearing altogether. **90m/C VHS, Beta.** Don Johnson, Ben Johnson, Dub Taylor, Ann Wedgeworth, Lois Nettleton, Anthony Zerbe; **D:** Theodore J. Flicker. *HHE*

Sois Belle et Tais-Toi 🎬🎬½ 1958 A police detective tracks jewel thieves and falls in love with a young waif. Several interesting and later famous actors have small parts. Light-hearted adventure. Subtitled in English. **110m/B VHS, Beta.** *FR* Henri Vidal, Mylene Demongeot, Jean-Paul Belmondo, Alain Delon; **D:** Marc Allegret. *BAR*

Solar Crisis 🎬🎬½ 1992 (PG-13) Eye-popping special effects highlight this Earth-on-the-edge-of-destruction sci-fier. In 2050 the sun has gone on self-destruct and begins throwing off gi-

ant solar flares which turn the Earth extra-crispy. A space team is sent to divert the flares but the mission may become a victim of sabotage. Director Sarafian actually forgoes credit for the standard Smithee pseudonym. **111m/C VHS, LV, Letterbox, Closed Caption.** Tim Matheson, Charlton Heston, Peter Boyle, Annabel Schofield, Jack Palance, Corin "Corky" Nemec; **D:** Richard Sarafian; **C:** Russell Carpenter; **M:** Maurice Jarre. *THV*

Solar Force 🎬🎬 1994 (R) Cop (Pare), stationed on the moon, is sent to earth to find a stolen chemical that is capable of restoring a destroyed environment. But there are secrets behind the assignment which could cost him his life. **91m/C VHS, LV, Closed Caption.** Michael Pare, Billy Drago, Walker Brandt; **D:** Boaz Davidson; **W:** Terrence Pare; **C:** Avi Karpik; **M:** Don Peake. *HMK*

Solarbabies 🎬 1986 (PG-13) Rollerskating youths in a drought-stricken future vie for a mysterious power that will replenish the Earth's water. Shades of every sci-fi movie you've ever seen, from "Mad Max" to "Ice Pirates." Pathetic. **95m/C VHS, Beta, LV, Closed Caption.** Richard Jordan, Sarah Douglas, Charles Durning, Lukas Haas, Jami Gertz, Jason Patric; **D:** Alan Johnson; **W:** Walon Green; **M:** Maurice Jarre. *MGM*

Solaris 🎬🎬 1972 With this the USSR tried to eclipse "2001: A Space Odyssey" in terms of cerebral science-fiction. Some critics thought they succeeded. You may disagree now that the lumbering effort is available on tape. Adapted from a Stanislaw Lem novel, it depicts a dilapidated space lab orbiting the planet Solaris, whose ocean, a vast fluid "brain," materializes the stir-crazy cosmonauts' obsessions—usually morose ex-girlfriends. Talk, talk, talk, minimal special effects. In Russian with English subtitles. In a two-cassette package, with a letterbox format preserving Tarkovsky's widescreen compositions. **167m/C VHS, LV, Letterbox.** *RU* Donatas Banionis, Natalya Bondarchuk; **D:** Andrei Tarkovsky; **M:** Eduard Artemyev. Cannes Film Festival '72: Grand Jury Prize. *FXL, FCT*

Soldat Duroc...Ca Va Etre Ta Fete! 🎬🎬 *Soldier Duroc* 196? Days after the 1944 liberation of Paris, a French soldier crosses back over the French lines to see his lover, and is caught as a German sympathizer by American troops. **105m/C VHS, Beta.** *FR* Pierre Tornade, Robert Webber, Michel Galabru, Roger Carel. *NO*

The Soldier 🎬 *Codename: The Soldier* 1982 (R) The Russians are holding the world at ransom with a pile of stolen plutonium, and a soldier finds himself in the position to carry out an unauthorized and dangerous plan to preserve the balance of world power. Wildly implausible, gratuitously violent spy trash. **90m/C VHS, Beta, Closed Caption.** Ken Wahl, Klaus Kinski; **D:** James Glickenhaus. *COL*

Soldier Blue 🎬🎬 1970 (R) Two survivors of an Indian attack make their way back to an army outpost. The cavalry then seeks revenge on the Cheyenne tribe accused of the attack. Gratuitously violent Vietnam-era western hits hard on racial themes. Based on the novel "Arrow in the Sun" by Theodore V. Olsen on the Sand Creek Indian massacre. **109m/C VHS, Beta.** Candice Bergen, Peter Strauss, Donald Pleasence, Dana Elcar, Jorge Rivero; **D:** Ralph Nelson; **W:** John Gay; **C:** Robert B. Hauser. *COL*

Soldier Boyz 🎬½ 1995 (R) Ex-Marine Major Howard Tolliver (Dudikoff), who now runs a high-security prison for youthful offenders, is called on to rescue a United Nations worker who's being held hostage by a group of revolutionaries in Vietnam. For help, he takes along six of his toughest prisoners. A variation of "The Dirty Dozen."**CW:** Strong non-stop violence and language. **91m/C VHS.** Michael Dudikoff, Cary-Hiroyuki Tagawa, Tyrin Turner, David Barry Gray, Channon Roe, Cedrick Terrell, Demetrius Navarro, Jacqueline Obradors; **D:** Louis Morneau; **W:** Darryl Quarles. *HBO*

Soldier in Love 🎬🎬 1967 Teleplay from "George Schaefer's Showcase Theatre" is based on the life of John Churchill, first Duke of Marlborough, and his wife Sarah. The ambitious young couple held the favor of Queen Anne for a time, until political intrigue brought about their downfall. **76m/C VHS, Beta.** Jean Simmons, Claire Bloom, Keith Michell; **D:** George Schaefer. *FHS*

Soldier in the Rain 🎬🎬½ 1963 An unusual friendship develops between career sergeant Gleason and wheeler-dealer McQueen. Gleason is in good form, but McQueen is listless, and the story (set in a Southern army camp) is unsatisfying. Weld is the comely teen who makes for an intriguing love triangle. From the novel by William Goldman. **88m/B VHS, Beta, Closed Caption.** Steve McQueen, Jackie Gleason, Tuesday Weld, Tony Bill, Tom Poston, Ed Nelson; **D:** Ralph Nelson; **W:** Blake Edwards; **M:** Henry Mancini. *FOX*

Soldier of Fortune 🎬🎬½ 1955 A woman (Hayward) enlists mercenaries to help find her lost husband in Red China. Late Gable vehicle with the formula beginning to feel the post-war strain and the star looking a trifle long in the tooth. Still, a fun adventure from a top star. Hayward had been among the myriad starlets vying for the Scarlett O'Hara roles nearly two decades earlier. **96m/C VHS, Beta, Closed Caption.** Clark Gable, Susan Hayward, Gene Barry, Alexander D'Arcy, Michael Rennie, Tom Tully, Anna Sten, Russell Collins, Leo Gordon, Jack Kruschen, Robert Quarry; **D:** Edward Dmytryk. *FOX*

Soldier of Orange 🎬🎬🎬 1978 The lives of six Dutch students are forever changed by the WWII invasion of Holland by the Nazis. Based on the true-life exploits of Dutch resistance leader Erik Hazelhoff. Exciting and suspenseful; cerebral; carefully made and well acted. Made Rutger Hauer an international star. **144m/C VHS, Beta, LV.** *NL* Rutger Hauer, Jeroen Krabbe, Edward Fox, Susan Penhaligon; **D:** Paul Verhoeven; **W:** Paul Verhoeven; **C:** Jan De Bont. Los Angeles Film Critics Association Awards '79: Best Foreign Film.

Soldier of the Night 🎬½ 1984 Toy-store worker by day, vigilante killer by night. Israeli thriller set in Tel Aviv lacks vim and is badly dubbed. **89m/C VHS, Beta.** **D:** Dan Wolman. *MGM*

Soldier's Fortune 🎬½ 1991 (R) A traveling gun for hire leaves the combat of Central America for the jungles of Los Angeles, only to find out that his daughter had been taken hostage. That's the last thing these kidnappers will ever do when they are found by this tough guy looking for his child.**CW:** Language and violence. **96m/C VHS, Closed Caption.** Gil Gerard, Charles Napier, Dan Haggerty, P.J. Soles, Barbara Bingham, Janus Blythe; **D:** Arthur N. Mele. *REP*

Soldier's Revenge 🎬🎬 197? A Vietnam vet has a hard time adjusting to life at home. **92m/C VHS, Beta.** John Savage. *TWE*

A Soldier's Story 🎬🎬🎬 1984 (PG) A black army attorney is sent to a Southern base to investigate the murder of an unpopular sergeant. Features WWII, Louisiana, jazz and blues, and racism in and outside the corps. From the Pulitzer-prize winning play by Charles Fuller, with most of the Broadway cast. Fine performances from Washington and Caesar. **101m/C VHS, Beta, LV, Closed Caption.** Howard E. Rollins Jr., Adolph Caesar, Denzel Washington, Patti LaBelle, Robert Townsend, Scott Paulin, Wings Hauser, Art Evans, Larry Riley, David Alan Grier; **D:** Norman Jewison; **C:** Russell Boyd; **M:** Herbie Hancock. Los Angeles Film Critics Association Awards '84: Best Supporting Actor (Caesar); Nominations: Academy Awards '84: Best Adapted Screenplay, Best Picture, Best Supporting Actor (Caesar). *COL, FCT*

A Soldier's Tale 🎬🎬 1991 (R) During WWII, a menage-a-trois develops that can only lead to tragedy, yet the participants find themselves unable to resist. **96m/C VHS, Closed Caption.** Gabriel Byrne, Marianne Basler, Judge Reinhold, Paul Wyett; **D:** Larry Parr; **M:** John Charles. *REP*

Sole Survivor ⚔½ 1984 (R) A group of zombies are searching for a beautiful advertising executive who was the sole survivor of a plane crash. 85m/C VHS, Beta. Anita Skinner, Kurt Johnson, Caren Larkey, Brinke Stevens, Leon Robinson; D: Thom Eberhardt; C: Russell Carpenter. ART

Solid Gold Cadillac ⚔⚔⚔ 1956 Holliday is a winning lead as Laura Patridge, an idealistic, small-time stockholder who discovers that the corporate board of directors is crooked. She makes waves at a stockholders meeting, gets noticed by the press, finds romance with former CEO Edward McKeever (Douglas), and works to oust the scalawags from power. The title comes from Laura's fervent desire to own a—you guessed it—solid gold cadillac. Based on the Broadway play by George S. Kaufman and Howard Teichmann. 99m/B VHS, Closed Caption. Judy Holliday, Paul Douglas, Fred Clark, Neva Patterson, Arthur O'Connell, Ray Collins; D: Richard Quine; W: Abe Burrows; C: Charles B(ryant) Lang; M: Cyril Mockridge. Academy Awards '56: Best Costume Design (B & W); Nominations: Academy Awards '56: Best Art Direction/Set Decoration (B & W). COL

Solitaire for 2 ⚔⚔½ 1994 (R) Sweet-natured romantic comedy about a rogue and a psychic. Handsome Daniel Becker (Frankel) is a behavioral psychologist who specializes in interpreting body language and using his expertise to bed as many beautiful women as happen his way. Uptight paleontologist Katie (Pays) has a problem with men—she can literally read their minds and gets angry at their lewd thoughts. So the path to true commitment is going to get a bit bumpy. CW: Some language and a sex scene. 105m/C VHS, Beta, Closed Caption. GB Mark Frankel, Amanda Pays, Roshan Seth, Maryam D'Abo, Jason Isaacs, Annette Crosbie; D: Gary Sinyor; W: Gary Sinyor; C: Henry Braham; M: David A. Hughes, John Murphy. PAR

The Solitary Man ⚔⚔ 1982 Glum look at a family breakup, from the husband's point of view. Holliman is good, but the exercise at large is regularly blues-inducing, and not especially inspiring or artful. Made for TV. 96m/C VHS, Beta. Earl Holliman, Carrie Snodgress, Lara Parker, Lane Smith, Nicolas Coster, Michelle Pfeiffer; D: John Llewellyn Moxey. TLF

Solo ⚔⚔ 1977 (PG) Young hitchhiker Peers enters the lives of fire patrol pilot Gil and his teenage son. A plotless friendship develops, headed nowhere—like this movie. Great New Zealand scenery might be worth the price of rental. 90m/C VHS, Beta. Vincent Gil, Perry Armstrong, Martyn Sanderson, Lisa Peers; D: Tony Williams. BPG, VES, HHE

Solo ⚔⚔ 1996 (PG-13) Fast-paced actioner stars Van Peebles as Solo, an android assassin with a heart of gold. It seems the muscle-bound, computerized killer is programmed with not only amazing fighting skills but the ability to think and learn. Solo who, being naughty in the sight of one-dimensional government bigwigs, is scheduled for replacement by a fighting machine that won't be so fickle when it comes to pulling the trigger. The chase is on when Solo learns of their plot and takes to the jungles of Central America, where together with the local peasants, the rebellious robot fights to preserve his humanity and his life. Poor man's "Terminator" is sprinkled with the kind of glib one-liners usually reserved for Schwarzenegger, although Van Peebles' performance hikes this rehashed premise up a notch. Adapted from Robert Mason's novel "Weapon." CW: Combat action violence and brief strong language. 106m/C VHS, LV, Closed Caption. Mario Van Peebles, William Sadler, Seidy Lopez, Barry Corbin, Adrien Broady, Abraham Verduzo, Jaime Gomez, Damian Bechir, Joaquin Garrido; D: Norberto Barba; W: David Corley; C: Chris Walling; M: Christopher Franke. COL

Solo Voyage: The Revenge ⚔⚔ 1990 A Russian "Rambo" goes on a murderous rampage, the likes of which humanity has not yet seen. 91m/C VHS. RU Mikhail Nojkine, Alexandre Fatiouchine; D: Mikhail Toumanichulli. NO

Solomon and Sheba ⚔⚔ 1959 King Solomon's brother and the Egyptian Pharaoh send the Queen of Sheba to Israel to seduce King Solomon so they may gain his throne. Tyrone Power had filmed most of the lead role in this silly, overwrought epic when he died of a heart attack. The role was reshot, with Brynner (with a full head of hair) replacing him. Director Vidor's unfortunate last film. Shot on location in Spain. 139m/C VHS, Beta, LV, Letterbox. Yul Brynner, Gina Lollobrigida, Marisa Pavan, George Sanders, Alejandro Rey; D: King Vidor; C: Frederick A. (Freddie) Young; M: Malcolm Arnold. MGM, FOX

The Sombrero Kid ⚔⚔ 1942 The Kid unwittingly gets involved in a murder and is nearly hanged before his friends help him discover the real culprits. Plenty of action in this straight forward, fun western. 54m/B VHS, Beta. Donald (Don "Red") Barry, Lynn Merrick, Rand Brooks; D: George Sherman. VDM

Some Call It Loving ⚔ 1973 (R) Bad, pretentious modern version of Sleeping Beauty, set in L.A. King buys the sleeping girl (Farrow) from a carnival show, but she doesn't live up to his ideal. 103m/C VHS. Zalman King, Carol White, Tisa Farrow, Richard Pryor, Pat Priest; D: James B. Harris. NO

Some Came Running ⚔⚔ 1958 James Jones's follow-up novel to "From Here to Eternity" does not translate nearly as well to the screen. Overlong and with little plot, the action centers around a would-be writer, his floozy girl friend, and the holier-than-thou characters which populate the town in which he grew up and to which he has now returned. Strong performances by all. 136m/C VHS, Beta, LV, Letterbox. Frank Sinatra, Dean Martin, Shirley MacLaine, Martha Hyer, Arthur Kennedy, Nancy Gates; D: Vincente Minnelli; C: William H. Daniels; M: Elmer Bernstein. Nominations: Academy Awards '58: Best Actress (MacLaine), Best Costume Design, Best Song ("To Love and Be Loved"), Best Supporting Actor (Kennedy), Best Supporting Actress (Hyer). MGM

Some Folks Call It a Sling Blade ⚔⚔⚔ 1994 The short film that became 1996's critically acclaimed "Sling Blade." This stark black-and-white short, penned by Billy Bob Thornton and directed by George Hickenlooper ("Hearts of Darkness: A Filmmaker's Apocalypse") premiered at Sundance. The original version only involves a young reporter's interview with Karl Childers, in which he recalls the events that led him to be in the institution. In addition to Thornton as Childers, J.T. Walsh also played the original mysoginistic psycho killer; Molly Ringwald plays the reporter. The tape also includes "The Making of 'Some Folks Call It a Sling Blade'" (color, 13 minutes) which comprises interviews the stars, director, and producer. 29m/B VHS, Letterbox. Billy Bob Thornton, Molly Ringwald, J.T. Walsh, Jefferson Mays, Suzanne Cryer; D: George Hickenlooper; W: Billy Bob Thornton; C: Kent Wakeford; M: Bill Boll. PIC

Some Girls ⚔⚔½ Sisters 1988 (R) A man goes to Quebec to see his college girlfriend who informs him that she is not in love with him anymore. But she has two sisters ready to comfort him! Strange black comedy; Gregory as the girl's father elevates so-so story. 104m/C VHS, Beta. Patrick Dempsey, Andre Gregory, Lila Kedrova, Florinda Bolkan, Jennifer Connelly, Sheila Kelly; D: Michael Hoffman; M: James Newton Howard. MGM

Some Kind of Hero ⚔⚔ 1982 (R) A Vietnam prisoner of war returns home to a changed world. Pryor tries hard, but can't get above this poorly written, unevenly directed film. 97m/C VHS, Beta, LV. Richard Pryor, Margot Kidder, Ray Sharkey, Ronny Cox, Lynne Moody, Olivia Cole; D: Michael Pressman; W: Robert Boris. PAR

Some Kind of Wonderful ⚔⚔ 1987 (PG-13) A high-school tomboy has a crush on a guy who also happens to be her best friend. Her feelings go unrequited as he falls for a rich girl with snobbish friends. In the end, true love wins out. Deutch also directed (and John Hughes also

produced) the teen flick "Pretty in Pink," which had much the same plot, with the rich/outcast characters reversed by gender. OK, but completely predictable. 93m/C VHS, LV, Closed Caption. Eric Stoltz, Lea Thompson, Mary Stuart Masterson, Craig Sheffer, John Ashton, Elias Koteas, Molly Hagan; D: Howard Deutch; W: John Hughes. PAR

Some Like It Hot ⚔⚔⚔⚔ 1959 Two unemployed musicians witness the St. Valentine's Day massacre in Chicago. They disguise themselves as women and join an all-girl band headed for Miami to escape the gangsters' retaliation. Flawless cast includes a fetching Monroe at her best; hilarious script. Curtis does his Cary Grant impression. Classic scenes between Lemmon in drag and Joe E. Brown as a smitten suitor. Brown also has the film's famous closing punchline. Monroe sings "I Wanna Be Loved By You," "Running Wild," and "I'm Through With Love." One of the very funniest movies of all time. 120m/B VHS, Beta, LV, Letterbox, Closed Caption. Marilyn Monroe, Tony Curtis, Jack Lemmon, George Raft, Pat O'Brien, Nehemiah Persoff, Joe E. Brown, Joan Shawlee, Mike Mazurki; D: Billy Wilder; W: Billy Wilder, I.A.L. Diamond; C: Charles Lang Jr.; M: Adolph Deutsch. Academy Awards '59: Best Costume Design (B & W); British Academy Awards '59: Best Actor (Lemmon); Golden Globe Awards '60: Best Actor—Musical/Comedy (Lemmon), Best Actress—Musical/Comedy (Monroe), Best Film—Musical/Comedy, National Film Registry '89;; Nominations: Academy Awards '59: Best Actor (Lemmon), Best Adapted Screenplay, Best Art Direction/Set Decoration (B & W), Best Black and White Cinematography, Best Director (Wilder). MGM, FOX

Some Mother's Son ⚔⚔⚔ Sons and Warriors 1996 (R) Young IRA members Gerard Quigley (Gillen) and Frank Higgins (O'Hara) are sentenced to long prison terms after an attack on the British army. Tough, politically active Annie Higgins (Flanagan) has already lost one son to "The Troubles" and is willing to support Frank in whatever he does. But her son Gerard's involvement takes apolitical schoolteacher Kathleen (Mirren) completely by surprise. When their sons join in a prison hunger strike, the two mothers must face the choice of supporting their sons' possible deaths by starvation or allowing the prison's officials to force-feed them. The leads give tough, terrific performances in a heartwrenching story. CW: Language and some political violence and suffering. 112m/C VHS. IR GB Helen Mirren, Fionnula Flanagan, Aidan Gillen, David O'Hara, John Lynch, Tim Woodward, Ciaran Hinds, Gerard McSorley, Geraldine O'Rawe; D: Terry George; W: Jim Sheridan, Terry George; C: Geoffrey Simpson; M: Bill Whelan. WAR

Somebody Has to Shoot the Picture ⚔⚔⚔ 1990 (R) Photographer Scheider is hired by a convicted man to take a picture of his execution. Hours before the event, Scheider uncovers evidence that leads him to believe the man is innocent. He then embarks in a race against time to save him. Adapted by Doug Magee from his book "Slow Coming Dark." Unpretentious, tough drama. Made for cable. CW: Language and violence. 104m/C VHS, Beta, LV, Closed Caption. Roy Scheider, Bonnie Bedelia, Robert Carradine, Andre Braugher, Arliss Howard; D: Frank Pierson; W: Doug Magee; C: Bojan Bazelli. USH

Somebody to Love ⚔⚔½ 1994 (R) Spunky taxi dancer Mercedes (Perez) wants to be an actress despite the bad luck actor/boyfriend Harry (a subdued Keitel) has. One of her clients is the bumpious Ernesto (De Lorenzo), who quickly becomes infatuated by Mercedes and, to impress her, takes a job with local racketeer Emillio (Quinn). Ernesto even decides to take a contract hit to get the money Mercedes needs to help out Harry, leading to tragedy. Confusing look at the fringes of the L.A. showbiz scene, with lots of missed chances though Perez gets some flashy diva scenes. CW: Pervasive strong language, some violence and sexual content. 103m/C VHS. Rosie Perez, Harvey Keitel, Michael De Lorenzo, Anthony Quinn, Steve Buscemi, Stanley Tucci, Gerardo, Paul Herman; *Cameos:* Angel Aviles, Quentin Tarantino; **D:** Alexandre Rockwell; **W:** Alexandre Rockwell, Sergei Bodrov. *CAF*

Somebody Up There Likes Me 🐾🐾🐾
1956 Story of Rocky Graziano's gritty battle from his poor, street-wise childhood to his prison term and his eventual success as the middleweight boxing champion of the world. Adapted from Graziano's autobiography. Superior performance by Newman (in his third screen role, after the miserable "The Silver Chalice" and forgettable "The Rack"); screen debuts for McQueen and Loggia. **113m/B VHS, Beta, Closed Caption.** Paul Newman, Pier Angeli, Everett Sloane, Eileen Heckart, Sal Mineo, Robert Loggia, Steve McQueen; **D:** Robert Wise; **W:** Ernest Lehman; **C:** Joseph Ruttenberg. Academy Awards '56: Best Art Direction/Set Decoration (B & W), Best Black and White Cinematography; Nominations: Academy Awards '56: Best Film Editing. *MGM*

Someday You'll Find Her, Charlie Brown
1981 Charlie Brown tries to find a beautiful girl he saw on tv. **24m/C VHS.**

Someone at the Door 🐾🐾
1950 Reporter Medwin arranges to be suspected of killing his sister, thus providing him with a good story and advancing his career. His plan almost backfires, when he is almost executed. Remake of a 1936 film of the same name. **65m/B VHS, Beta. GB** Michael Medwin, Garry Marsh, Yvonne Owen, Hugh Latimer; **D:** Francis Searle. *SNC*

Someone Behind the Door 🐾🐾½
Two Minds for Murder; Quelqu' Un Derriere la Porte 1971 (PG) Evil brain surgeon Perkins implants murderous suggestions into psychopathic amnesia victim Bronson's mind, then instructs him to kill his (the surgeon's) wife and her lover. **97m/C VHS, Beta, LV.** Charles Bronson, Anthony Perkins, Jill Ireland, Henri Garcin; **D:** Nicolas Gessner. *UNI, VTR*

Someone Else's America 🐾🐾🐾
1996 (R) Euro-"Grumpy Old Men" explores friendship and the modern immigrant experience in Brooklyn. Bayo (Manojlovic) is a comical, sad-sack Serb who works at the bar of Alonso (Conti), a Spaniard who immigrated with his blind mother (Casares). Story follows Bayo's family as they illegally immigrate to chase the American dream and adapt to life once they arrive. Touchingly funny highlight involves a scheme by the men which enables Alonso's homesick mother to revisit her village in Spain. Filmed in Germany with sets built to resemble Brooklyn, picture has an appealingly unreal quality. Cast and crew together formed its own melting pot, with over 20 nationalities contributing. English and Serbo-Croatian with subtitles.*CW:* Language and brief sexuality. **116m/C VHS. FR GB GE** Tom Conti, Miki Manojlovic, Maria Casares, Zorka Manojlovic, Sergej Trifunovic, Chia-ching Niu, Andjela Stojkovic, Ananda Ellis; **D:** Goran Paskalyevic; **W:** Gordan Mihic; **C:** Yorgos Arvanitis; **M:** Andrew Dickson. *NYF*

Someone I Touched 🐾🐾½
1975 Way-overdone melodrama starring Leachman as a finally pregnant woman who learns her husband and a teenager she slept with have venereal disease. **74m/C VHS, Beta.** Cloris Leachman, James Olson, Glynnis O'Connor, Andrew (Andy) Robinson, Allyn Ann McLerie; **D:** Lou Antonio. *WOV*

Someone to Die For 🐾🐾
1995 (R) Accused murderer (and cop) Bernsen is out to prove his innocence but learns that the real killer may be very close to home.*CW:* Violence, sexuality, and some language. **98m/C VHS.** Corbin Bernsen, Ally Walker, Robert Stewart; **D:** Clay Borris. *AVE*

Someone to Love 🐾🐾
1987 (R) Rootless filmmaker gathers all his single friends together and interviews them about their failed love lives. Welles's last film as an actor. Visually uneven, interesting experiment. **110m/C VHS, Beta, LV, Closed Caption.** Henry Jaglom, Orson Welles, Sally Kellerman, Andrea Marcovicci, Michael Emil, Oja Kodar, Stephen Bishop, Ronee Blakley, Kathryn Harrold, Monte Hellman; **D:** Henry Jaglom; **W:** Henry Jaglom; **C:** Hanania Baer. *PAR*

Someone to Watch Over Me 🐾🐾🐾
1987 (R) After witnessing the murder of a close friend, a beautiful and very wealthy woman must be protected from the killer. The working-class New York detective assigned the duty is more than taken with her, despite the fact that he has both a wife and son at home. A highly watchable, stylish romantic crime thriller. **106m/C VHS, Beta, LV, Closed Caption.** Tom Berenger, Mimi Rogers, Lorraine Bracco, Jerry Orbach, Andreas Katsulas, Tony DiBenedetto, James Moriarty, John Rubinstein; **D:** Ridley Scott; **W:** Howard Franklin; **C:** Steven Poster; **M:** Michael Kamen. *COL*

Something for Everyone 🐾🐾½
The Rook; Black Flowers for the Bride 1970 (R) A corrupt footman uses sex and murder in an attempt to take over the estate of an aristocratic Bavarian family in post-WWII Germany. He nearly succeeds in marrying the countess (Lansbury), but someone has been keeping tabs on him. Funny, ambitious black comedy. From the novel "The Code" by Harry Kressing. **112m/C VHS, Beta.** Angela Lansbury, Michael York, Anthony Corlan, Heidelinde Weis; **D:** Harold Prince; **C:** Walter Lassally. *FOX*

Something in Common 🐾🐾½
1986 A woman discovers her 22-year-old son is having an affair with a woman her own age. Nicely done comedy; Burstyn and Weld both make good use of a solid script. Made for TV. **94m/C VHS, Beta.** Ellen Burstyn, Tuesday Weld, Don Murray, Patrick Cassidy, Eli Wallach; **D:** Glenn Jordan; **W:** Susan Rice; **M:** John Addison. *VTR*

Something in the Wind 🐾🐾½
1947 Mary Collins (Durbin) is a DJ having a sort of romance with Donald Read (Dall), who gets the mistaken idea that she was once his wealthy Uncle Chester's (Winninger) mistress and is still after the family money. O'Connor gets to steal the show as Durbin's ally, Charlie. ♫Something in the Wind; Turntable Song; It's Only Love; You Wanna Keep Your Baby Lookin' Right; Happy Go Lucky and Free. **89m/B VHS, Closed Caption.** Deanna Durbin, Donald O'Connor, John Dall, Charles Winninger, Helena Carter, Margaret Wycherly; **D:** Irving Pichel; **W:** William Bowers, Harry Kurnitz; **C:** Milton Krasner; **M:** Johnny Green. *USH*

Something of Value 🐾🐾🐾
1957 Good ensemble performances in a serious colonial story about the Mau Mau rebellion in Kenya. Hudson and Poitier are torn between their friendship and their opposing loyalties. Drama solidly grounded in fact from the book by Robert Ruark. **113m/B VHS, Beta.** Rock Hudson, Sidney Poitier, Wendy Hiller, Dana Wynter, Juano Hernandez; **D:** Richard Brooks; **W:** Richard Brooks; **M:** Miklos Rozsa. *MGM*

Something Short of Paradise 🐾½
1979 (PG) The owner of a Manhattan movie theatre has an again/off again romance with a magazine writer. Would-be Allenesque romantic comedy is too talky and pretentious. **87m/C VHS, Beta.** David Steinberg, Susan Sarandon, Jean-Pierre Aumont, Marilyn Sokol; **D:** David Helpern; **W:** Fred Barron. *ART, VES*

Something Special 🐾🐾½
Willy Milly; I Was a Teenage Boy 1986 (PG-13) A 14-year-old girl has her wish come true when she is turned into a boy. Charming, original fantasy-comedy is fun for young and old. **93m/C VHS, LV.** Pamela Segall, Patty Duke, Eric Gurry, John Glover, Seth Green; **D:** Paul Schneider; **W:** Walter Carbone. *NO*

Something to Sing About 🐾🐾
Battling Hoofer 1936 Musical melodrama about a New York bandleader's attempt to make it big in Hollywood. Allows Cagney the opportunity to demonstrate his dancing talents; he also sings. Rereleased in 1947. Also available colorized. Frawley was Fred on "I Love Lucy." ♫Any Old Love; Right or Wrong; Loving You; Out of the Blue; Something to Sing About. **84m/B VHS, Beta, LV.** James Cagney, William Frawley, Evelyn Daw, Gene Lockhart; **D:** Victor Schertzinger. Nominations: Academy Awards '37: Best Score. *NOS, VHE, CAB*

Something to Talk About 🐾🐾½
Grass Under Pressure 1995 (R) Romantic comedy/drama finds Grace (Roberts) running her overbearing father Wyly's (Duvall) horsebreeding operation and learning that her husband Eddie (the ever-charming Quaid) is tomcatting around. So Grace tosses him out and makes a temporary move with daughter Caroline (Aull) back home. Tart-tongued sister Emma Rae (Sedgwick) is sympathetic but long-suffering mama Georgia (Rowlands) thinks Grace should make the best of things (the way she's done). Naturally, Eddie wants his family back but the frazzled Grace is just coming to terms with what she wants out of life. Star appeal from both leads lends this familiar plot some spark.*CW:* Brief strong language. **106m/C VHS, LV, Closed Caption.** Julia Roberts, Dennis Quaid, Robert Duvall, Gena Rowlands, Kyra Sedgwick, Brett Cullen, Haley Aull, Muse Watson, Anne Shropshire; **D:** Lasse Hallstrom; **W:** Callie Khouri; **C:** Sven Nykvist; **M:** Hans Zimmer. Nominations: Golden Globe Awards '96: Best Supporting Actress (Sedgwick). *WAR*

Something Weird
woof! 1968 McCabe is disfigured horribly in an electrical accident. A seemingly beautiful witch fixes his face, on condition that he be near her. The accident also gave him ESP—and it gets cheesier from there. **80m/C VHS, Beta.** Tony McCabe, Elizabeth Lee; **D:** Herschell Gordon Lewis. *THV, VDM, TWE*

Something Wicked This Way Comes 🐾🐾
1983 (PG) Two young boys discover the evil secret of a mysterious traveling carnival that visits their town. Bradbury wrote the screenplay for this much-anticipated, expensive adaptation of his own novel. Good special effects, but disappointing. **94m/C VHS, Beta, LV.** Jason Robards Jr., Jonathan Pryce, Diane Ladd, Pam Grier, Richard Davalos, James Stacy, Royal Dano, Vidal Peterson, Shawn Carson; **D:** Jack Clayton; **W:** Ray Bradbury; **C:** Stephen Burum; **M:** James Horner. *DIS*

Something Wild 🐾🐾½
1986 (R) Mild-mannered business exec Daniels is picked up by an impossibly free-living vamp with a Louise Brooks hairdo, and taken for the ride of his uptill-then staid life, eventually leading to explosive violence. A sharp-edged comedy with numerous changes of pace. Too-happy ending wrecks it, but it's great until then. Look for cameos from filmmakers John Waters and John Sayles. **113m/C VHS, Beta, LV, Closed Caption.** Jeff Daniels, Melanie Griffith, Ray Liotta, Margaret Colin, Tracey Walter, Dana Peru, Jack Gilpin, Su Tissue, Kenneth Utt, Sister Carol East; *Cameos:* John Sayles, John Waters; **D:** Jonathan Demme; **W:** E. Max Frye; **C:** Tak Fujimoto; **M:** Laurie Anderson, Rosemary Paul, John Cale. *HBO*

Sometimes a Great Notion 🐾🐾🐾
Never Give an Inch 1971 (PG) Trouble erupts in a small Oregon town when a family of loggers decide to honor a contract when the other loggers go on strike. Newman's second stint in the director's chair; Fonda's first role as an old man. Based on the novel by Ken Kesey. **115m/C VHS, Beta.** Paul Newman, Henry Fonda, Lee Remick, Richard Jaeckel, Michael Sarrazin; **D:** Paul Newman; **W:** John Gay; **M:** Henry Mancini. Nominations: Academy Awards '71: Best Song ("All His Children"), Best Supporting Actor (Jaeckel). *USH*

Sometimes They Come Back 🐾🐾
1991 (R) Another Stephen King tale of terror. Matheson plays a man haunted by the tragedy in his past. A witness to his brother's death, he also witnesses the fiery crash of his brother's killers. Only now the killers have returned from the dead, to take their revenge on him. Made for television.*CW:* Terror violence. **97m/C VHS, LV, Closed Caption.** Tim Matheson, Brooke Adams, Robert Rusler, William Sanderson; **D:** Tom McLoughlin. *THV*

Sometimes They Come Back...Again 🐾½
1996 (R) Psychologist John Porter (Gross) and his teenaged daughter (Swank) return to Porter's hometown after his mother's mysterious death. He should know you can never go home again since they're both soon threatened by a young man (Arquette) involved in

the ritualistic murder of Porter's sister years before. Gruesome special effects are the highlight. **CW:** Strong horror violence and gore, some sexuality and language. **98m/C VHS.** Michael Gross, Hilary Swank, Alexis Arquette, Jennifer Elise Cox; **D:** Adam Grossman; **W:** Adam Grossman; **C:** Christopher Baffa; **M:** Peter Manning Robinson. *THV*

Somewhere I'll Find You 🐾🐾🐾 1942
Clark and Turner heat up the screen as correspondents running all over the war-torn world in their second film together. ("Honky Tonk" was their first.) Notable mainly because Gable's beloved wife, Carole Lombard, was killed in a plane crash only three days into production. Gable forced himself to finish the film and it became one of the studio's biggest hits. Although critics applauded his determination to complete the film, many felt his performance was subdued and strained. Film debut of Wynn. Based on a story by Charles Hoffman. **108m/B VHS.** Clark Gable, Lana Turner, Robert Sterling, Reginald Owen, Lee Patrick, Charles Dingle, Tamara Shayne, Leonid Kinskey, Diana Lewis, Molly Lamont, Patricia Dane, Sara Haden, Keenan Wynn; **D:** Wesley Ruggles; **W:** Walter Reisch, Marguerite Roberts. *MGM*

Somewhere in Sonora 🐾🐾 1933
Early Wayne Western set in Old Mexico. Wayne plays a rodeo performer who joins an outlaw gang to save a friend and a silver mine. Like most of the other films of the series, this was a remake of a Ken Maynard silent. Based on a story and the novel "Somewhere South in Sonora" by Will Levington Comfort. **59m/B VHS, Closed Caption.** John Wayne, Henry B. Walthall, Shirley Palmer, J.P. McGowan, Frank Rice, Billy Franey, Paul Fix, Ralph Lewis; **D:** Mack V. Wright; **W:** Joe Roach. *MGM*

Somewhere in Time 🐾🐾½ 1980 (PG)
Playwright Reeve (in his first post-Clark Kent role) falls in love with a beautiful woman in an old portrait. Through self-hypnosis he goes back in time to 1912 to discover what their relationship might have been. The film made a star of the Grand Hotel, located on Mackinac Island in Michigan, where it was shot. Drippy rip-off of the brilliant novel "Time and Again" by Jack Finney. Reeve is horrible; Seymour is underused. All in all, rather wretched. **103m/C VHS, Beta, LV.** Christopher Reeve, Jane Seymour, Christopher Plummer, Teresa Wright; **D:** Jeannot Szwarc; **W:** Richard Matheson; **M:** John Barry. Nominations: Academy Awards '80: Best Costume Design. *USH*

Somewhere Tomorrow 🐾🐾½ 1985 (PG)
A lonely, fatherless teenage girl is befriended by the ghost of a young man killed in a plane crash. Charming and moving, if not perfect. **91m/C VHS, Beta.** Sarah Jessica Parker, Nancy Addison, Tom Shea; **D:** Robert Wiemer.

Sommersby 🐾🐾🐾½ 1993 (PG-13)
A too-good-to-be-true period romance based on the film "The Return of Martin Guerre." A Civil War veteran (Gere) returns to his wife's (Foster) less-than-open arms. She soon warms up to his kind, sensitive and caring manner, but can't quite believe the change that the war has wrought. Neither can the neighbors, especially the one (Pullman) who had his own eye on Laurel Sommersby. So is he really Jack Sommersby or an all too clever imposter? Lots of hankies needed for the tender-hearted. Strong performance by Foster. Filmed in Virginia (passing for the state of Tennessee.) The laserdisc version is available in letterbox format. **CW:** Sensuality. **114m/C VHS, Beta, LV, 8mm, Letterbox, Closed Caption.** Richard Gere, Jodie Foster, Bill Pullman, James Earl Jones, William Windom, Brett Kelley, Richard Hamilton, Maury Chaykin, Lanny Flaherty, Frankie Faison, Wendell Wellman, Clarice Taylor, R. Lee Ermey; **D:** Jon Amiel; **W:** Nicholas Meyer, Sarah Kernochan; **M:** Danny Elfman. *WAR, FCT*

Son-in-Law 🐾½ 1993 (PG-13)
Surfer-dude comic Shore's a laconic fish out of water as a city-boy rock 'n' roller who falls in love with a country beauty, marries her, and visits the family farm to meet the new in-laws. Once there, he weirds out

family and neighbors before showing everyone how to live, Pauly style. Silly entertainment best appreciated by Shore fans. **CW:** Sexual situations. **95m/C VHS, Beta, LV, Closed Caption.** Pauly Shore, Carla Gugino, Lane Smith, Cindy Pickett, Mason Adams, Patrick Renna, Dennis Burkley, Dan Gauthier, Tiffani-Amber Thiessen; **D:** Steve Rash; **W:** Shawn Schepps, Fax Bahr, Adam Small; **M:** Richard Gibbs. Nominations: MTV Movie Awards '94: Best Comedic Performance (Shore). *HPH*

Son of a Gun 🐾½ 1919
A loveable but ornery cowboy gets banished from the county for disturbing the peace. However, he wins the favor of the townspeople when he stands up to a gang of gambling swindlers. Silent. **68m/B VHS, Beta.** "Broncho" Billy Anderson. *NOS, DVT, RXM*

Son of Ali Baba 🐾🐾 1952
Kashma Baba, son of Ali Baba, enters the military academy to learn to withstand adversity. He has other ideas however, until he must suddenly fill his father's shoes and fight the evil Caliph. He fights bravely with the help of his childhood friend, a beautiful princess, in this swashbuckler. **85m/C VHS, Closed Caption.** Tony Curtis, Piper Laurie, Susan Cabot, Victor Jory, Hugh O'Brian, William Reynolds, Gerald Mohr; **D:** Ross Hunter. *USH, FCT*

Son of Blob 🐾🐾 Beware! The Blob 1972 (PG)
A scientist brings home a piece of frozen blob from the North Pole; his wife accidentally revives the dormant gray mass. It begins a rampage of terror by digesting nearly everyone within its reach. A host of recognizable faces make for fun viewing. Post-Jeannie, pre-Dallas Hagman directed this exercise in zaniness. **87m/C VHS, Beta.** Robert Walker Jr., Godfrey Cambridge, Carol Lynley, Shelley Berman, Larry Hagman, Burgess Meredith, Gerrit Graham, Dick Van Patten; **D:** Larry Hagman. *GEM*

Son of Captain Blood 🐾½ Il Figlio del Capitano Blood 1962 (G)
The son of the famous pirate meets up with his father's enemies on the high seas. The son of the famous actor Errol Flynn—Sean—plays the son of the character the elder Flynn played in "Captain Blood." Let's just say the gimmick didn't work. **90m/C VHS, Beta.** IT SP Sean Flynn, Ann Todd; **D:** Tulio Demicheli. *MLB*

Son of Dracula 🐾🐾🐾 Young Dracula 1943
In this late-coming sequel to the Universal classic, a stranger named Alucard is invited to America by a Southern belle obsessed with eternal life. It is actually Dracula himself, not his son, who wreaks havoc in this spine-tingling chiller. **80m/B VHS, Beta, LV.** Lon Chaney Jr., Evelyn Ankers, Frank Craven, Robert Paige, Louise Allbritton, J. Edward Bromberg, Samuel S. Hinds; **D:** Robert Siodmak; **W:** Eric Taylor; **C:** George Robinson. *USH*

Son of Flubber 🐾🐾½ 1963
Sequel to "The Absent Minded Professor" finds Fred MacMurray still toying with his prodigious invention, Flubber, now in the form of Flubbergas, which causes those who inhale it to float away. Disney's first-ever sequel is high family wackiness. **96m/C VHS, Beta.** Fred MacMurray, Nancy Olson, Tommy Kirk, Leon Ames, Joanna Moore, Keenan Wynn, Charlie Ruggles, Paul Lynde; **D:** Robert Stevenson; **C:** Edward Colman; **M:** George Bruns. *DIS*

Son of Frankenstein 🐾🐾🐾 1939
The second sequel (after "The Bride of Frankenstein") to the 1931 version of the horror classic. The good doctor's skeptical son returns to the family manse and becomes obsessed with his father's work and with reviving the creature. Full of memorable characters and brooding ambience. Karloff's last appearance as the monster. **99m/C VHS, Beta, LV.** Basil Rathbone, Bela Lugosi, Boris Karloff, Lionel Atwill, Josephine Hutchinson, Donnie Dunagan, Emma Dunn, Edgar Norton, Lawrence Grant, Lionel Belmore; **D:** Rowland V. Lee; **W:** Willis Cooper; **C:** George Robinson. *USH*

Son of Fury 🐾🐾🐾 1942
Dashing Ben Blake (Power) is left penniless when his sinister uncle (Sanders) wrongfully takes the family fortune. Ben escapes to sea and then to an island paradise—all the while plotting his revenge. But he still finds time to fall for the beauteous Tierney. Fine 18th-century costumer done in grand style.

Based on the novel "Benjamin Blake" by Edison Marshall. **98m/C VHS.** Tyrone Power, Gene Tierney, George Sanders, Frances Farmer, Roddy McDowall, John Carradine, Elsa Lanchester, Harry Davenport, Kay Johnson, Dudley Digges, Halliwell Hobbes, Marten Lamont, Arthur Hohl, Pedro de Cordoba, Dennis Hoey, Heather Thatcher; **D:** John Cromwell; **W:** Philip Dunne; **M:** Alfred Newman. *FXV*

Son of God's Country 🐾½ 1948
Utterly hackneyed, near-comic attempt at a western. Good-guy U.S. Marshal poses as a crook to get the lowdown on the varmints. **60m/B VHS, Beta.** Monte Hale, Pamela Blake, Adrian Booth. *DVT*

Son of Godzilla 🐾🐾 Gojira no Musuko 1966
Dad and junior protect beauty Maeda from giant spiders on a remote island ruled by a mad scientist. Fun monster flick with decent special effects. **86m/C VHS, Beta.** JP Tadao Takashima, Akira Kubo; **D:** Jun Fukuda. *HHT, DVT*

Son of Ingagi 🐾½ 1940
Lonely ape-man kidnaps woman in search of romance. Early all-black horror film stars Williams of "Amos 'n' Andy." **70m/B VHS.** Zack Williams, Laura Bowman, Alfred Grant, Spencer Williams Jr.; **D:** Richard C. Kahn; **W:** Spencer Williams Jr. *NOS, SNC, MLB*

Son of Kong 🐾🐾½ 1933
King Kong's descendant is discovered on an island amid prehistoric creatures in this often humorous sequel to RKO's immensely popular "King Kong." Hoping to capitalize on the enormous success of its predecessor, director Schoedsack quickly threw this together. As a result, its success at the boxoffice did not match the original's, and didn't deserve to, but it's fun. Nifty special effects from Willis O'Brien, the man who brought them to us the first time. **70m/B VHS, Beta, LV.** Robert Armstrong, Helen Mack; **D:** Ernest B. Schoedsack; **M:** Max Steiner. *NOS, FCT, MLB*

Son of Lassie 🐾🐾½ 1945 (G)
It seems that Lassie's son Laddie just isn't quite as smart as his mother. After the dog sneaks onto his master's plane during WWII, the plane gets shot down, and Lawford parachutes out with Laddie in his arms. The dog goes to get help because Lawford is hurt, but he brings back two Nazis! A sequel to "Lassie Come Home." **102m/C VHS.** Peter Lawford, Donald Crisp, June Lockhart, Nigel Bruce, William Severn, Leon Ames, Donald Curtis, Nils Asther, Robert Lewis; **D:** Sylvan Simon. *MGM*

The Son of Monte Cristo 🐾🐾½ 1941
Illegitimate offspring of the great swashbuckler with Robert Donat proves they made pathetic, pointless sequels even back then. **102m/B VHS, Beta, LV.** Louis Hayward, Joan Bennett, George Sanders, Florence Bates, Montagu Love, Ralph Byrd, Clayton Moore; **D:** Rowland V. Lee. Nominations: Academy Awards '41: Best Interior Decoration. *DVT, BAR, CAB*

Son of Paleface 🐾🐾🐾½ 1952
Hilarious sequel to the original Hope gag-fest, with the Harvard-educated son of the original character (again played by Hope) heading west to claim an inheritance. Hope runs away with every cowboy cliche and even manages to wind up with the girl. Songs include "Buttons and Bows" (reprised from the original), "There's a Cloud in My Valley of Sunshine," and "Four-legged Friend." **95m/C VHS, Beta, LV.** Bob Hope, Jane Russell, Roy Rogers, Douglass Dumbrille, Iron Eyes Cody, Bill Williams, Harry von Zell; **D:** Frank Tashlin. Nominations: Academy Awards '52: Best Song ("Am I in Love"). *COL*

Son of Rusty 🐾🐾½ 1947
Danny and his friends are warned to stay away from the farm of suspicious Jed Barlow. But Rusty keeps running away to see Jed's dog Barb and Danny gets to know Jed. Then Danny must stand by his new friend when word of Jed's past turns folks against him. (Rusty and Barb have puppies too.) **70m/B VHS.** Ted Donaldson. *COL*

Son of Samson 🐾½ Le Geant de la Vallee Das Rois 1962
Man with large pectoral muscles puts an end to the evil Queen of Egypt's reign of terror **89m/C VHS.** FR IT YU Mark Forest, Chelo Alonso, Angelo

Zanolli, Vira Silenti, Frederica Ranchi; **D:** Carlo Campogalliani. *SNC*

Son of Sinbad 🎵🎵 *Nights in a Harem* 1955 Sinbad, captured by the Khalif of Baghdad, must bring him the secret of Greek fire to gain his freedom and free the city from the forces of mighty Tamerlane. About three dozen nubile young women wear very little and gambol with our hero herein; much-anticipated skinfest caused a scandal, nurtured by Howard Hughes for profit. **88m/C VHS, Beta.** Dale Robertson, Sally Forrest, Vincent Price, Lili St. Cyr, Mari Blanchard, Joi Lansing; **D:** Ted Tetzlaff. *NO*

Son of the Morning Star 🎵🎵🎵 1991 (PG-13) Lavish made for TV retelling of Custer's famed-butt kicking. Complex characterizations and unusual points of view, based on the book by Evan S. Connell. **186m/C VHS, LV, Closed Caption.** Gary Cole, Rosanna Arquette, Dean Stockwell, Rodney Grant, Terry O'Quinn, David Strathairn, Stanley Anderson, George American Horse; **D:** Mike Robe. *REP, FCT*

Son of the Pink Panther 🎵½ Blake Edwards' Son of the Pink Panther 1993 (PG) Lame leftover from the formerly popular comedy series. Director Edwards has chosen not to resurrect Inspector Clouseau, instead opting for his son (Benigni), who turns out to be just as much of a bumbling idiot as his father. Commissioner Dreyfus (Lom), the twitching, mouth-foaming former supervisor of the original Clouseau is looking for a kidnapped princess (Farentino) along with Clouseau, Jr., who himself does not know he is the illegitimate son of his partner's dead nemesis. Many of the sketches have been recycled from previous series entrants. Rather than being funny, they seem used and shopworn like a threadbare rug. **115m/C VHS, LV, Closed Caption.** Roberto Benigni, Herbert Lom, Robert Davi, Debrah Farentino, Claudia Cardinale, Burt Kwouk, Shabana Azmi; **D:** Blake Edwards; **W:** Blake Edwards; **M:** Henry Mancini. *MGM*

The Son of the Shark 🎵🎵 Le Fils du Requin 1993 Simon (Da Silva) and Martin Vanderhoes (Vandendaele) have been abandoned by their mother and prefer to live as homeless delinquents rather than with their drunken father. The boys commit petty crimes and vandalism to survive (always escaping from foster homes and institutions) while Martin dreams of running away to his true home in the ocean—proclaiming himself to be "the son of a female shark." Depressing and casually cruel; based on a true story. French with subtitles. **88m/C VHS.** *FR* Ludovic Vandendaele, Erick Da Silva, Sandrine Blancke, Maxime LeRoux; **D:** Agnes Merlet; **W:** Agnes Merlet; **C:** Gerard Simon; **M:** Bruno Coulais. *FXL*

Son of the Sheik 🎵🎵🎵 1926 A desert sheik abducts an unfaithful dancing girl. Valentino's well-done, slightly self-mocking last film. Silent. Sequel to "The Sheik" (1921). **62m/B VHS, Beta, LV.** Rudolph Valentino, Vilma Banky, Agnes Ayres; **D:** George Fitzmaurice; **C:** George Barnes. *NOS, CCB, VCN*

Son of Zorro 1947 Zorro takes the law into his own hands to protect ranchers from bandits. A serial in 13 chapters. **164m/B VHS.** George Turner, Peggy Stewart, Roy Barcroft, Edward Cassidy. *REP, VCN, MLB*

Sonatine 🎵🎵🎵 1996 (R) Middle-age Yakuza mobster Murakama (director Kitano, using his screen name Beat Takeshi) wishes to retire but is instead sent to mediate a low-level gang war. Upon arrival, an attempt is made on his life, so he and his men hole up at a beach house. The young punks of the gang engage in horseplay and antics that indicate their violent natures and signal that all will not remain calm for long. Kitano's performance, writing, and direction are superb, understating the violence while not glamorizing it, and showing the effect it has on the man who carries it out. The relatively tranquil setting of the hideout allows some humor and character development, as well as preventing the cliches that usually pop up in this type of movie. Ever on the prowl for Far East gangster chic, Tarantino's Rolling Thunder brought this one to U.S. shores. **CW:** Bloody

shootings, language and some sexuality. **93m/C VHS.** Takeshi "Beat" Kitano, Aya Kokumai, Tetsu Watanabe, Masanobu Katsumura, Susumu Terashima, Ren Ohsugi, Tonbo Zushi, Eiji Minakata, Kenichi Yajima; **D:** Takeshi "Beat" Kitano; **W:** Takeshi "Beat" Kitano; **C:** Katsumi Yanagishima; **M:** Jo Hasaishi. *NYR*

A Song Is Born 🎵🎵🎵 1948 A group of music professors try to trace the history of music. Kaye is in charge of a U.S. music foundation whose research has led him up to ragtime. He is soon, however, thrust into the sometimes seedy world of jazz joints and night spots, all in the name of research. Enter love interest Mayo, a woman on the run from her gangster boyfriend who hides out at the foundation. Not one of Kaye's funniest or best, but if you enjoy big band music, you'll love this. Includes music by Louis Armstrong and his orchestra, Tommy Dorsey and his orchestra, and Charlie Barnet and his orchestra. This was Kaye's last film for Goldwyn. 🎵A Song is Born; Bach Boogie; Anitra's Dance; I'm Getting Sentimental Over You; Blind Barnabas; Mockin' Bird; Redskin Rhumba; The Goldwyn Stomp; Daddy-O. **113m/B VHS.** Danny Kaye, Virginia Mayo, Benny Goodman, Hugh Herbert, Steve Cochran, J. Edward Bromberg, Felix Bressart; **D:** Howard Hawks; **C:** Gregg Toland. *GVV*

Song o' My Heart 🎵🎵🎵 1929 An early musical starring popular Irish tenor McCormack as a singer forced to abandon his career when he marries a woman he does not love. A tour de force for the lead in his movie debut. 🎵Little Boy Blue; Paddy Me Lad; I Hear You Calling Me; A Fair Story by the Fireside; Just For a Day; Kitty My Love; The Rose of Tralee; A Pair of Blue Eyes; I Feel You Near Me. **91m/B VHS, Beta.** John McCormack, Maureen O'Sullivan, John Garrick, J.M. Kerrigan, Tommy Clifford, Alice Joyce; **D:** Frank Borzage. *VAI, FCT, TVC*

Song of Arizona 🎵🎵 1946 Rogers and the Sons of the Pioneers arrive to aid their pal Hayes against a gang of bank robbers in this modern-day oater. Eight songs perpetually punctuate the perfunctory plot, particularly "Will Ya Be My Darling," "Half-a-Chance Ranch," and the title tune. **54m/B VHS, Beta.** Roy Rogers, Dale Evans, George "Gabby" Hayes, Lyle Talbot, Bob Nolan, The Pioneers; **D:** Frank McDonald. *NOS, VCN, HEG*

The Song of Bernadette 🎵🎵🎵 1943 Depicts the true story of a peasant girl who sees a vision of the Virgin Mary in a grotto at Lourdes in 1858. The girl is directed to dig at the grotto for water that will heal those who believe in its powers, much to the astonishment and concern of the townspeople. Based on Franz Werfel's novel. Directed with tenderness and carefully cast, and appealing to religious and sentimental susceptibilities, it was a boxoffice smash. **156m/B VHS, Beta, LV.** Charles Bickford, Lee J. Cobb, Jennifer Jones, Vincent Price, Anne Revere, Gladys Cooper; **D:** Henry King; Arthur C. Miller; **M:** Alfred Newman. Academy Awards '43: Best Actress (Jones), Best Black and White Cinematography, Best Interior Decoration, Best Original Dramatic/Comedy Score; Golden Globe Awards '44: Best Actress—Drama (Jones), Best Director (King), Best Film—Drama; Nominations: Academy Awards '43: Best Director (King), Best Film Editing, Best Picture, Best Screenplay, Best Sound, Best Supporting Actor (Bickford), Best Supporting Actress (Cooper, Revere). *KEP, IGP, BTV*

Song of Freedom 🎵🎵½ 1936 John Zinga (Robeson) is a British-born black dockworker whose voal gifts are discovered by an opera impresario. After realizing a career as a concert performer, Zinga ventures to Africa to investigate his ancestry and finds he has royal roots, and that his tribe have fallen under the grip of corrupt spiritualists. Robeson turns in a fine performance in what is otherwise an average film. 🎵Sleepy River; Lonely Road; Song of Freedom; The Black Emperor. **80m/B VHS.** *GB* Paul Robeson, Elizabeth Welch, George Mozart; **D:** J. Elder Wills. *KIV, HHT, NOS*

Song of Nevada 🎵🎵½ 1944 Rogers woos the high-society daughter (Evans, of course) of a rancher (Hall). Quintessential Royn-Dale. 🎵It's Love, Love, Love; New Moon Over Nevada; Hi Ho Little Dogies; The Harum Scarum Baron of the Harmonium; What Are We Going to Do?; A Cowboy Has to Yodel in the Morning. **60m/B VHS, Beta.** Roy Rogers, Dale Evans, Thurston Hall; **D:** Joseph Kane. *NOS, HHT, DVT*

Song of Norway 🎵🎵 1970 (G) A dramatization of the early life of the beloved Norwegian Romantic composer Edvard Grieg. Filmed against the beautiful mountains, waterfalls, and forests of Norway and based on the popular '40s stage production. The scenery is the best thing because Grieg's life was dull—even with cinematic liberties taken. 🎵Strange Music; The Song of Norway; The Little House; Be a Boy Again; Three There Were; A Rhyme and a Reason; Wrong to Dream; I Love You; The Solitary Wanderer. **143m/C VHS, Beta.** Toralv Maurstad, Florence Henderson, Edward G. Robinson, Christina Schollin, Frank Porretta, Oscar Homolka, Robert Morley, Harry Secombe; **D:** Andrew L. Stone. *FOX*

Song of Old Wyoming 🎵½ 1945 Three of those songs are presented in the course of an ordinary western about a spunky widow driving badmen out of Wyoming territory. La Rue plays the villainous Cheyenne Kid; this was before he got his own series as the heroic "Lash" La Rue. **65m/C VHS.** Eddie Dean, Sarah Padden, Lash LaRue, Jennifer Holt, Emmett Lynn, John Carpenter, Ian Keith, Bob Barron; **D:** Robert Emmett Tansey. *NOS, HEG*

Song of Texas 🎵½ 1943 When a young woman journeys west to visit her father at "his" ranch, Roy and his pals must keep the father's secret that he is just another hired hand. Whenever possible, everyone breaks into song. **54m/B VHS, Beta.** Roy Rogers, Harry Shannon, Pat Brady, Barton MacLane, Arline Judge; **D:** Joseph Kane. *NOS, VYY, VCN*

Song of the Exile 🎵🎵½ 1990 A Chinese/Japanese student living in London in the early 1970s faces racial discrimination and decides to return to her native Hong Kong. But on the home front, she and her family clash emotionally until daughter and mother come to a gradual understanding of how the past affects the present. In Cantonese and Japanese with English subtitles. **100m/C VHS.** *CH* Maggie Cheung, Shwu-Fen Chang; **D:** Ann Hui. *KIV, FCT*

Song of the Gringo 🎵🎵 The Old Corral 1936 Tex Ritter stars in his first singing western as a sheriff going after a gang of claim jumpers. **57m/B VHS, Beta.** Tex Ritter, Monte Blue, Joan Woodbury, Fuzzy Knight, Richard Adams, Warner Richmond; **D:** John P. McCarthy. *NOS, VCI, VCN*

Song of the Islands 🎵🎵½ 1942 Landing families in Hawaii feud over a beach, while the son of one (Mature) and the daughter of the other (Grable) fall in love. Plenty of songs, and dancing to display Grable's legs. Of course happiness and concord reign at the end. Songs include "O'Brien Has Gone Hawaiian," "Sing Me a Song of the Islands," and "What's Buzzin', Cousin?" **75m/C VHS, Beta, LV, Closed Caption.** Betty Grable, Victor Mature, Jack Oakie, Thomas Mitchell, Billy Gilbert; **D:** Walter Lang. *FOX, MLB*

Song of the Thin Man 🎵🎵½ 1947 The sixth and final "Thin Man" mystery. This time Nick and Nora Charles (Powell and Loy) investigate the murder of a bandleader. Somewhat more sophisticated than its predecessor, due in part to its setting in the jazz music world. Sequel to "The Thin Man Goes Home." **86m/B VHS, Beta.** William Powell, Myrna Loy, Keenan Wynn, Dean Stockwell, Philip Reed, Patricia Morison, Gloria Grahame, Jayne Meadows, Don Taylor, Leon Ames, Ralph Morgan, Warner Anderson; **D:** Edward Buzzell; **C:** Charles Rosher. *MGM*

Song of the Trail ♪½ 1936 Our hero saves an old man hornswoggled at cards. 65m/B **VHS, Beta.** Kermit Maynard, George "Gabby" Hayes, Fuzzy Knight, Wheeler Oakman, Evelyn Brent, Andrea Leeds; **D:** Russell Hopton. NOS, VDM, VCN

Song Spinner ♪♪½ 1995 (G) In a mysterious land, a stranger gives a young girl the power of music, which she hopes to share with the king. But first she must get past the kingdom's noise police. 95m/C **VHS, Closed Caption.** Meredith Henderson, Patti LuPone, John Neville; **D:** Randy Bradshaw. HMK

A Song to Remember ♪♪♪ 1945 With music performed by Jose Iturbi, this film depicts the last years of the great pianist and composer Frederic Chopin, including his affair with famous author George Sand, the most renowned French woman of her day. Typically mangled film biography. ♫Valse in D Flat (Minute Waltz); Mazurka In B Flat, Opus 7, No. 1; Fantasie Impromptu, Opus 66; Etude In A Flat, Opus 25, No. 1 (partial); Polonaise In A Flat, Opus 53 (partial); Scherzo In B Flat Minor; Etude In C Minor, Opus 10, No. 12; Nocturne In C Minor, Opus 48, No. 1; Nocturn In E Flat, Opus 9, No. 2. 112m/C **VHS, Beta, LV.** Cornel Wilde, Paul Muni, Merle Oberon, Nina Foch, George Coulouris; **D:** Charles Vidor; **C:** Gaetano Antonio "Tony" Gaudio; **M:** Miklos Rozsa. Nominations: Academy Awards '45: Best Actor (Wilde), Best Color Cinematography, Best Film Editing, Best Sound, Best Story, Best Original Dramatic/Comedy Score. COL, RDG, TVC

Song Without End ♪♪½ 1960 This musical biography of 19th century Hungarian pianist/composer Franz Liszt is given the Hollywood treatment. The lavish production emphasizes Liszt's scandalous exploits with married women and his life among the royal courts of Europe rather than his musical talents. Features music from several composers including Handel, Beethoven, Bach and Schumann. This film marked the debut of Capucine. Director Vidor died during filming and Cukor stepped in, so there is a noticeable change in style. Although there is much to criticize in the story, the music is beautiful. ♫Mephisto Waltz; Spozalizio; Sonata In B Minor; Un Sospiro; Fantasy on Themes From "Rigoletto"; Consolation in D Flat; Liebestraum; Les Preludes; Piano Concerto No. 1. 130m/C **VHS, LV.** Dirk Bogarde, Capucine, Genevieve Page, Patricia Morison, Ivan Desny, Martita Hunt, Lou Jacobi; **D:** Charles Vidor, George Cukor; **C:** James Wong Howe; **M:** Morris Stoloff, Harry Sukman. Academy Awards '60: Scoring of a Musical; Golden Globe Awards '61: Best Film—Musical/Comedy. COL, TVC

Songs and Bullets ♪½ 1938 Simple zen-like title sums it up. The songs total five in number, the bullets somewhat more as hero cowboys battle rustlers in routine fashion. One of a handful of films (westerns and comedies) produced by funnyman Stan Laurel. 57m/B **VHS.** Fred Scott, Al "Fuzzy" St. John, Alice Ardell, Charles "Blackie" King, Karl Hackett, Frank LaRue, Budd Buster; **D:** Sam Newfield. NOS, HEG

Songwriter ♪♪½ 1984 (R) A high-falutin' look at the lives and music of two popular country singers with, aptly, plenty of country tunes written and performed by the stars. Singer-businessman Nelson needs Kristofferson's help keeping a greedy investor at bay. Never mind the plot; plenty of good music. ♫How Do You Feel About Foolin' Around?; Songwriter; Who'll Buy My Memories; Write Your Own Songs; Nobody Said It Was Going To Be Easy; Good Times; Eye of the Storm; Crossing the Border; Down to Her Socks. 94m/C **VHS, Beta, LV, Closed Caption.** Willie Nelson, Kris Kristofferson, Rip Torn, Melinda Dillon, Lesley Ann Warren; **D:** Alan Rudolph. Nominations: Academy Awards '84: Original Song Score and/or Adaptation. COL

Sonny and Jed ♪ La Banda J.&S. Cronaca Criminale del Far West 1973 (R) An escaped convict and a free-spirited woman travel across Mexico pillaging freely, followed determinedly by shiny-headed lawman Savalas. Lame rip-off of the Bonnie and Clyde legend. 85m/C **VHS, Beta.** IT Tomas Milian, Telly Savalas, Susan George, Rosanna Janni, Laura Betti; **D:** Sergio Corbucci; **M:** Ennio Morricone. NO

Sonny Boy woof! 1987 (R) A transvestite and a psychopath adopt a young boy, training him to do their bidding, which includes murder. 96m/C **VHS, Beta, LV.** IT David Carradine, Paul Smith, Brad Dourif, Conrad Janis, Sydney Lassick, Savina Gersak, Alexandra Powers, Steve Carlisle, Michael Griffin; **D:** Robert Martin Carroll; **W:** Graeme Whifler. TWE

Sonora Stagecoach ♪♪ 1944 Okay sagebrush saga with an interesting lineup; two cowboys, a heroic Indian, and a tough gal pilot escort a murder suspect in the title conveyance and manage to clear him when the real bad guys attack. 61m/B **VHS.** Hoot Gibson, Bob Steele, Chief Thundercloud, Rocky Camron, Betty Miles, Glenn Strange, George Eldridge, Karl Hackett; **D:** Robert Emmett Tansey. NOS, HEG

Sons ♪♪ 1991 A Vietnam veteran's son joins the military, causing strains within the family. ?m/C **VHS. D:** Alexandre Rockwell; **W:** Alexandre Rockwell, Brandon Cole. LRP

Sons of Hercules in the Land of Darkness ♪ 1955 Hercules' sons kill dragons, fight titans, and generally flex up a storm. 74m/B **VHS, Beta.** Dan Vadis. VYY

Sons of Katie Elder ♪♪♪ 1965 After their mother's death, four brothers are reunited. Wayne is a gunman; Anderson is a college graduate; silent Holliman is a killer; and Martin is a gambler. When they learn that her death might have been murder, they come together to devise a way to seek revenge on the killer. The town bullies complicate matters; the sheriff tells them to lay off. Especially strong screen presence by Wayne, in his first role following cancer surgery. One of the Duke's most popular movies of the '60s. 122m/C **VHS, Beta, LV.** John Wayne, Dean Martin, Earl Holliman, Michael Anderson Jr., Martha Hyer, Dennis Hopper, Paul Fix, James Gregory; **D:** Henry Hathaway; **M:** Elmer Bernstein. PAR, TLF

Sons of Steel ♪♪ 1935 Two brothers, owners of a steel mill, lead vastly different lives. They raise their sons in their own images, causing problems. 65m/B **VHS.** Charles Starrett, Polly Ann Young, William "Billy" Bakewell, Walter Walker, Aileen Pringle, Holmes Herbert, Florence Roberts, Adolf Millar, Lloyd Ingraham; **D:** Charles Lamont. NOS

Sons of the Desert ♪♪♪ Sons of the Legion; Convention City; Fraternally Yours 1933 Laurel and Hardy in their best-written film. The boys try to fool their wives by pretending to go to Hawaii to cure Ollie of a bad cold when in fact, they are attending their lodge convention in Chicago. Also includes a 1935 Thelma Todd/Patsy Kelly short, "Top Flat." 73m/B **VHS, Beta.** Stan Laurel, Oliver Hardy, Mae Busch, Charley Chase, Dorothy Christy; **D:** William A. Seiter. MLB, FAF, VTR

Sons of the Pioneers ♪♪ 1942 Small town sheriff Hayes hires cowboy Roy to rid town of outlaws. 61m/B **VHS.** Roy Rogers, George "Gabby" Hayes, Maris Wrixon, Forrest Taylor; **D:** Joseph Kane. REP

Sons of Trinity ♪ 1995 (PG) The two sons, Bambino (Neubert) and Trinity (Kizzier), of legendary cowpokes first meet when Bambino is about to be hung for horse thieving in the town of San Clementino. When Trinity gets his new friend off, they wind up as sheriff and deputy of the same town. Lots of physical comedy. 90m/C **VHS, LV.** Heath Kizzier, Keith Neubert, Ronald Nitschke, Siegfried Rauch; **D:** E.B. Clucher; **C:** Juan Amoros; **M:** Stefano Mainetti. TRI

Sooner or Later ♪½ 1978 13-year-old girl passes herself off as 16 with a local rock idol and must decide whether to go all the way. 100m/C **VHS, Beta.** Rex Smith, Judd Hirsch, Denise Miller, Morey Amsterdam, Lynn Redgrave; **D:** Bruce Hart.

Sophia Loren: Her Own Story ♪♪ 1980 Bio of Sophia Loren, watching her grow from a spindly child in working-class Naples to a world-renowned movie star, beauty queen, and mother. Loren plays herself and her mother in this tedious account. Based on the biography by A.E. Hotchner. Made for TV. 150m/C **VHS, Beta.** Sophia Loren, Armand Assante, Ed Flanders, John Gavin; **W:** Joanna Crawford. NO

Sophie's Choice ♪♪♪½ 1982 (R) A haunting modern tragedy about Sophie Zawistowska, a beautiful Polish Auschwitz survivor settled in Brooklyn after WWII. She has intense relationships with a schizophrenic genius and an aspiring Southern writer. An artful, immaculately performed and resonant drama, with an astonishing, commanding performance by the versatile Streep; a chilling portrayal of the banality of evil. From the best-selling, autobiographical novel by William Styron. 157m/C **VHS, Beta, LV.** Meryl Streep, Kevin Kline, Peter MacNicol, Rita Karin, Stephen D. Newman, Josh Mostel; **D:** Alan J. Pakula; **C:** Nestor Almendros; **M:** Marvin Hamlisch. Academy Awards '82: Best Actress (Streep); Golden Globe Awards '83: Best Actress—Drama (Streep); Los Angeles Film Critics Association Awards '82: Best Actress (Streep); National Board of Review Awards '82: Best Actress (Streep); New York Film Critics Awards '82: Best Actress (Streep), Best Cinematography; National Society of Film Critics Awards '82: Best Actress (Streep); Nominations: Academy Awards '82: Best Adapted Screenplay, Best Cinematography, Best Costume Design, Best Original Score. FOX, SWC

Sophisticated Gents ♪♪ 1981 Nine boyhood friends, members of a black athletic club, reunite after 25 years to honor their old coach and see how each of their lives has been affected by being black men in American society. Based on the novel "The Junior Bachelor Society" by John A. Williams. Originally made for television. 200m/C **VHS.** Paul Winfield, Roosevelt Grier, Bernie Casey, Raymond St. Jacques, Thalmus Rasulala, Dick Anthony Williams, Ron O'Neal, Rosalind Cash, Denise Nicholas, Alfre Woodard, Melvin Van Peebles; **D:** Harry Falk; **W:** Melvin Van Peebles. XVC

Sorcerer ♪♪½ Wages of Fear 1977 (PG) To put out an oil fire, four men on the run in South America agree to try to buy their freedom by driving trucks loaded with nitroglycerin over dangerous terrain—with many natural and man-made obstacles to get in their way. Remake of "The Wages of Fear" is nowhere as good as the classic original, but has exciting moments. Puzzlingly retitled, which may have contributed to the boxoffice failure, and the near demise of Friedkin's directing career. 121m/C **VHS, LV, Closed Caption.** Roy Scheider, Bruno Cremer, Francisco Rabal, Soudad Amidou, Ramon Bieri; **D:** William Friedkin; **W:** Walon Green; **M:** Tangerine Dream. Nominations: Academy Awards '77: Best Sound. USH, FCT

Sorceress woof! 1982 (R) The Harris girls are sisters who use their powers of sorcery and fighting skills to battle demons, dragons, and evil. Yeah, sure. Really, they're just a pair of babes parading for the camera. 83m/C **VHS, Beta.** Leigh Anne Harris, Lynette Harris, Bob Nelson, David Milbern, Bruno Rey, Anna De Sade; **D:** Brian Stuart; **W:** Jim Wynorski. NO

Sorceress ♪♪♪ 1988 A friar in medieval Europe feels insecure in his religious beliefs after encountering a woman who heals through ancient practices. Historically authentic and interestingly moody. Written, produced, and directed by two women: an art history professor and a collaborator of Francois Truffaut's. In French with English subtitles or dubbed. 98m/C **VHS.** Tcheky Karyo, Christine Boisson, Jean Carmet; **D:** Suzanne Schiffman; **W:** Pamela Berger, Suzanne Schiffman. MFV

Sorceress ♪½ 1994 (R) Larry Barnes (Poindexter) is on his way to a partnership at his law firm, especially since his wife Erica (Strain) eliminates his competition—permanently. But Erica goes after the wrong guy when she comes up against Howard Reynolds (Albert). Seems Howard's loving spouse Amelia (Blair) happens to be a witch and she has her own evil spells to cast. **CW:** Sexuality; violence. 93m/C **VHS.** Julie Strain, Larry Poindexter, Linda Blair, Edward Albert; **D:** Jim Wynorski. TRI

Sorority Babes in the Slimeball Bowl-A-Rama 🎬🎬 1987 (R)
An ancient gremlin-type creature is released from a howling alley, and the great-looking sorority babes have to battle it at the mall, with the help of a wacky crew of nerds. Horrible horror spoof shows plenty of skin. 80m/C Beta, LV. Linnea Quigley, Brinke Stevens, Andras Jones, John Wildman; **D:** David DeCoteau; **M:** Guy Moon. *AFE*

Sorority Girl 🎬½ 1957
Camp classic in which beautiful co-ed Cabot is presented as a malicious rich kid involved in everything from petty fights to blackmail. Cheap production from the Corman factory. 60m/B VHS, Closed Caption. Susan Cabot, Dick Miller, Barbara Crane, June Kennedy, Fay Baker, Jeane Wood; **D:** Roger Corman. *NLC*

Sorority House Massacre woof! 1986
(R) A knife-wielding maniac stalks a sorority girl while her more elite sisters are away for the weekend. Yawn—haven't we seen this one before? Unfortunately for us we'll see it again because this one's followed by a sequel. 74m/C VHS, Beta. Angela O'Neill, Wendy Martel, Pamela Ross, Nicole Rio; **D:** Carol Frank. *WAR*

Sorority House Massacre 2: Nighty Nightmare woof! 1992
Another no-brainer with a different cast and director. This time around three lingerie-clad lovelies are subjected to the terrors of a killer their first night in their new sorority house. College just keeps getting tougher all the time. 80m/C VHS. Melissa Moore, Robin Harris, Stacia Zhivago, Dana Bentley; **D:** Jim Wynorski. *NHO*

Sorority House Party 🎬 1992 (R)
A famous rock guitarist is held against his will at the sexiest sorority house on campus. He definitely has mixed feelings about the experience considering the inhabitants saunter around in bikinis and "force" him to party with them. Anders and Attila are transplants from the modeling circuit. 95m/C VHS. Attila, April Lerman, Kim Little, Avalon Anders, Joe Mundi, Rachel Latt, Mark Stulce, Michael Xavier; **D:** David Michael Latt; **W:** John Murdy, Steve Taylor. *APX*

Sorrento Beach 🎬🎬 *Hotel Sorrento* 1995 (R)
A beachside community outside Melbourne, Australia, Sorrento is home to the Moynihans. The three Moynihan sisters—Meg (Goodall), Hillary (Gillmer), and Pippa (Morice)—are reunited after 10 years by their father's sudden death. Lots of tensions, rivalries, and jealousies come to the surface as well as old secrets regarding a family tragedy. Talky film hasn't quite cast off its stage origins (it's adapted from a play by Hannie Rayson) but the performances are noteworthy. **CW:** Language. 112m/C VHS. **AU** Caroline Goodall, Caroline Gillmer, Tara Morice, Joan Plowright, John Hargreaves, Ray Barrett, Ben Thomas; **D:** Richard Franklin; **W:** Richard Franklin, Peter Fitzpatrick; **C:** Geoff Burton; **M:** Nevida Tyson-Chew. Australian Film Institute '95: Best Adapted Screenplay, Best Supporting Actor (Barrett); Nominations: Australian Film Institute '95: Best Actress (Gillmer), Best Actress (Goodall), Best Director (Franklin), Best Film. *THV*

The Sorrow and the Pity 🎬🎬🎬½ 1971
A classic documentary depicting the life of a small French town and its resistance during the Nazi occupation. Lengthy, but totally compelling. A great documentary that brings home the atrocities of war. In French with English narration. 265m/B VHS, Beta. **FR** **D:** Marcel Ophuls. *COL, OM*

Sorrowful Jones 🎬🎬 1949
A "Little Miss Marker" remake, in which bookie Hope inherits a little girl as collateral for an unpaid bet. Good for a few yuks, but the original is much better. 88m/B VHS, Beta. Bob Hope, Lucille Ball, William Demarest, Bruce Cabot, Thomas Gomez, Mary Jane Saunders; **D:** Sidney Lanfield; **W:** Jack Rose, Melville Shavelson; **C:** Daniel F. Fapp. *USH*

Sorrows of Gin 🎬🎬½ 1979
Eight-year-old girl searches for a sense of family amid her parents' lives. Her efforts to deal with alienation and emotional isolation lead her to run away from home. From a short story by John Cheever. 60m/C

VHS, Beta. Edward Herrmann, Sigourney Weaver, Mara Hobel, Eileen Heckart, Rachel Roberts. *HMV*

The Sorrows of Satan 🎬🎬🎬 1926
Dempster and Cortez star as writers in love with each other, but Cortez can't take his poverty and the rejection of publishers. As he is about to end it all, the devil appears to him in disguise and makes an offer he can hardly refuse. He is introduced to London society and winds up marrying a fortune hunter. When he discovers this he goes back to Dempster, who still loves him, and vows to give up everything for her. Menjou then reveals himself to be the devil but Dempster's faith is so strong that the evil is vanquished. 111m/B VHS, Beta. Adolphe Menjou, Carol Dempster, Ricardo Cortez, Lya de Putti; **D:** D.W. Griffith. *GPV*

Sorry, Wrong Number 🎬🎬🎬½ 1948
A wealthy, bedridden wife overhears two men plotting a murder on a crossed telephone line, and begins to suspect that one of the voices is her husband's. A classic tale of paranoia and suspense. Based on a radio drama by Louise Fletcher, who also wrote the screenplay. Remade for television in 1989. 89m/B VHS, Beta, LV. Barbara Stanwyck, Burt Lancaster, Ann Richards, Wendell Corey, Harold Vermilyea, Ed Begley Sr.; **D:** Anatole Litvak. Nominations: Academy Awards '48: Best Actress (Stanwyck). *PAR*

Sorry, Wrong Number 🎬½ 1989
Cable remake of the 1948 Barbara Stanwyck thriller about a bed-ridden woman trying to get help after she realizes she's being stalked by a killer. Offers a new twist (drug dealing), but doesn't even approach the Stanwyck original. From the story by Lucille Fletcher. 90m/C VHS, Beta, LV, Closed Caption. Loni Anderson, Hal Holbrook, Patrick Macnee, Miguel Fernandez, Carl Weintraub; **D:** Tony Wharmby; **W:** Ann Louise Bardach; **M:** Bruce Broughton. *PAR*

S.O.S. Coast Guard 🎬🎬½ 1937
A fiendish scientist creates a disintegrating gas and the U.S. Coast Guard must stop him from turning it over to unfriendly foreigners. Loads of action in this 12-part serial. 224m/B VHS, LV. Ralph Byrd, Bela Lugosi, Maxine Doyle. *NOS, SNC, REP*

S.O.S. Pacific 🎬🎬 1960
A seaplane crashes on a nuclear-test island and the survivors find that they have only five hours before they get nuked. Even though there is plenty of the usual action one would expect from such a film, the story really revolves around the characters. The British and U.S. versions have different endings. 91m/B. **GB** Eddie Constantine, Pier Angeli, Richard Attenborough, John Gregson, Eva Bartok; **D:** Guy Green. *NOS*

S.O.S. Titanic 🎬🎬½ 1979
The story of the Titanic disaster, recounted in flashback, in docudrama style. James Costigan's teleplay of the familiar story focuses on the courage that accompanied the horror and tragedy. Thoroughly professional, absorbing made-for-TV drama. 102m/C VHS, Beta. **GB** David Janssen, Cloris Leachman, Susan St. James, David Warner, Ian Holm, Helen Mirren, Harry Andrews, David Battley, Ed Bishop, Peter Bourke, Shevaun Briars, Nick Brimble, Jacob Brooke, Catherine Byrne, Tony Caunter, Warren Clarke, Nicholas Davies, Deborah Fallender; **D:** Billy Hale; **W:** James Costigan; **C:** Christopher Challis; **M:** Howard Blake. *QHV*

Sotto, Sotto 🎬🎬½ 1985 (R)
A minor Wertmuller comedy about an Italian businessman who is constantly suspicious of his wife's fidelity. As it happens, she's attracted to another woman (de Santis). Massimo Wertmuller is Lina's nephew. Entertaining. In Italian with English subtitles. 104m/C VHS, Beta. **IT** Enrico Montesano, Veronica Lario, Massimo Wertmuller, Luisa de Santis; **D:** Lina Wertmuller; **W:** Lina Wertmuller. *COL*

Soul-Fire 🎬🎬 1925
South Pacific high seas induce Cupid's arrow. Silent. 100m/B VHS, Beta. Richard Barthelmess, Bessie Love, Walter Long, Arthur Metcalfe; **D:** John S. Robertson. *GPV, FCT, GVV*

Soul Food 🎬🎬½ 1997 (R)
In between the mouth watering servings of fried-chicken, collard greens and catfish unfolds the lives of sisters Williams, Fox, and Long. They struggle to hold their family together by keeping up their mother's Sunday dinner tradition after she becomes ill. As mom's health deteriorates, so do the sisters' relationships with their significant others, turning things a bit soapy and predictable. Unfulfilling appetizer for those looking for a stark urban drama, but with an attractive ensemble cast which brings to life truthful characters, it's a hearty feast for those hungry for a heartwarming, contemporary tale. Warmth and humor won over audiences across color lines. Boasts many promising debuts, including director/writer Tillman and young narrator Hammond. Produced by music producer Kenneth (Babyface) Edmonds.**CW:** Some strong sexuality and language. 114m/C VHS, Closed Caption. Vanessa L(ynne) Williams, Vivica A. Fox, Nia Long, Michael Beach, Mekhi Phifer, Irma P. Hall, Jeffrey D. Sams, Gina Ravera, Brandon Hammond, Carl Wright, Mel Jackson, Morgan Michelle Smith, John M. Watson Sr.; **D:** George Tillman Jr.; **W:** George Tillman Jr.; **C:** Paul Elliot; **M:** Wendy Melvoin, Lisa Coleman. Nominations: MTV Movie Awards '98: Best Female Performance (Fox), Best Song ("A Song for Mama"). *FOX*

Soul Hustler woof! 1976 (PG)
A con man becomes rich and famous as a tent-show evangelist. Pathetic drivel. 81m/C VHS, Beta. Fabian, Casey Kasem, Larry Bishop, Nai Bonet; **D:** Burt Topper. *ART*

Soul Man 🎬🎬 1986 (PG-13)
Denied the funds he expected for his Harvard tuition, a young white student (Howell) masquerades as a black in order to get a minority scholarship. As a black student at Harvard, Howell learns about racism and bigotry. Pleasant lightweight comedy with romance thrown in (Chong is the black girl he falls for), and with pretensions to social satire that it never achieves. 101m/C VHS, Beta, LV, Closed Caption. C. Thomas Howell, Rae Dawn Chong, James Earl Jones, Leslie Nielsen, Arye Gross; **D:** Steve Miner; **W:** Carol Black. *VTR*

Soul of the Beast 🎬½ 1923
An elephant repeatedly saves Bellamy from the villainous Beery. Silent with original organ score. 77m/B VHS, Beta, 8mm. Madge Bellamy, Cullen Landis, Noah Beery Sr. *GPV, VYY*

Soul of the Game 🎬🎬🎬 1996
TV movie follows the lives of three talented players in the Negro League during the 1945 season as they await the potential integration of baseball. Brooklyn Dodgers general manager Branch Rickey (Herrmann) has his scouts focusing on three men in particular: flashy, aging pitcher Satchel Paige (Lindo), mentally unstable catcher Josh Gibson (Williamson), and the young, college-educated Jackie Robinson (Underwood). Manages to resist melodrama through terrific performances. 105m/C VHS. Delroy Lindo, Mykelti Williamson, Blair Underwood, Edward Herrmann, R. Lee Ermey, Gina Ravera, Salli Richardson, Obba Babatunde, Brent Jennings; **D:** Kevin Rodney Sullivan; **W:** David Himmelstein; **C:** Sandi Sissel; **M:** Lee Holdridge. *HBO*

Soul Patrol 🎬 1980 (R)
Black newspaper reporter clashes with the all-white police department in a racist city. 90m/C VHS, Beta. Nigel Davenport, Ken Gampu, Peter Dyneley; **D:** Christopher Rowley. *SUN*

Soul Survivor 🎬🎬½ 1995 (PG-13)
Set in Toronto's Jamaican community, this urban drama focuses on 20-something Tyrone (Williams) who's stuck in a custodial job and looking to make some easy money. He goes to work making collections for local gangster Winston (Harris), who tries to reassure his protege that money buys respect. But when Tyrone falls for straight-living social worker Annie (Scott), he begins to see the potholes in the path he's on.**CW:** Sex-related material. 89m/C VHS. **CA** Peter Williams, George Harris, Judith Scott, Clark Johnson, David Smith; **D:** Stephen Williams; **W:** Stephen Williams; **C:** David Franco; **M:** John McCarthy. *MRC*

Soul Vengeance ⵣ *Welcome Home Brother Charles* 1975 Black man is jailed and brutalized for crime he didn't commit and wants revenge when he's released. Many afros and platform shoes. Vintage blaxploitation. **91m/C VHS.** Marlo Monte, Reatha Grey, Stan Kamber, Tiffany Peters, Ven Bigelow, Jake Carter; *D:* Jamaa Fanaka; *W:* Jamaa Fanaka. *XVC*

Souls at Sea ⵣⵣ½ 1937 Good buddy work by Cooper and Raft highlight this complicated seafaring yarn. In the 1840s sailor and abolitionist Nuggin Taylor (Cooper) is secretly sabotaging slave ships, working undercover for the British Navy. With loyal friend Powdah (Raft), Taylor tries to gather evidence against British officer Tarryton (Wilcoxon) even though he's fallen for Tarryton's sister Margaret (Dee). But after a sea disaster, Taylor's accused of murder and brought to trial. Will the truth come out in time to save him? **93m/B VHS, Closed Caption.** Gary Cooper, George Raft, Henry Wilcoxon, Frances Dee, Olympe Bradna, George Zucco, Harry Carey Sr., Robert Cummings, Porter Hall, Joseph Schildkraut; *D:* Henry Hathaway; *W:* Dale Van Every, Grover Jones; *C:* Charles Lang Jr. Nominations: Academy Awards '37: Best Score. *USH*

Soultaker ⵣ½ 1990 (R) The title spirit is after a young couple's souls, and they have just an hour to reunite with their bodies after a car crash. Meanwhile, they're in limbo (literally) between heaven and earth. The ending's OK, if you can make it that far. **CW:** Drug content. **94m/C VHS, LV.** Joe Estevez, Vivian Schilling, Gregg Thomsen, David Shark, Jean Reiner, Chuck Williams, Robert Z'Dar; *D:* Michael Rissi; *W:* Vivian Schilling; *C:* James Rosenthal.

The Sound and the Silence ⵣⵣ½ 1993 Bio of inventor Alexander Graham Bell (Bach). The Scottish Bell's father was a speech specialist and his beloved mother Eliza (Fricker) was severely hearing impaired. Bell himself trained to work with the deaf in Boston and experimented with transmitting speech electronically—a project which only grew when Bell married the deaf Mable Hubbard (Quinn). Bell's lifelong devotion lead to his development of the telephone as well as numerous other inventions (and his founding of "National Geographic" magazine). Bell was hardly a lively character but this made for television drama is lavishly done. In two parts. **93m/C VHS.** John Bach, Elizabeth Quinn, Brenda Fricker, Ian Bannen; *D:* John Kent Harrison; *W:* Tony Foster, William Schmidt, John Kent Harrison; *M:* John Charles. *TTC*

Sound of Horror ⵣ½ *El Sonido de la Muerte; Sound From a Million Years Ago; The Prehistoric Sound* 1964 The Hound usually admires creative efforts to keep budgets down, but this is too much (or too little). A dinosaur egg hatches, and out lashes an invisible predator. Yes, you'll have to use your imagination as archaeologists are slashed to bits by the no-show terror. **85m/B VHS.** *SP* James Philbrook, Arturo Fernandez, Soledad Miranda, Ingrid Pitt; *D:* Jose Antonio Nieves-Conde. *NOS, LOO*

Sound of Love ⵣ 1977 The mutual attraction between a deaf female hustler and a deaf race car driver leads to a deep relationship where they both learn about their own fears and desires. **74m/C VHS, Beta.** Celia de Burgh, John Jarratt.

Sound of Murder 1982 A successful children's book writer wants to exact revenge on his adulterous wife, but is himself murdered before he can "execute" his plan. **114m/C VHS, Beta.** Michael Moriarty, Joanna Miles. *ART*

The Sound of Music ⵣⵣⵣⵣ 1965 The classic film version of the Rodgers and Hammerstein musical based on the true story of the singing von Trapp family of Austria and their escape from the Nazis just before WWII. Beautiful Salzburg, Austria location photography and an excellent cast. Andrews, fresh from her Oscar for "Mary Poppins," is effervescent, in beautiful voice, but occasionally too good to be true. Not Rodgers & Hammerstein's most innovative score, but lovely to hear and see. Plummer's singing was dubbed by Bill Lee. Marni Nixon, behind-the-scenes songstress for "West Side Story" and "My Fair Lady," makes her on-screen debut as one of the nuns. ♫I Have Confidence In Me; Something Good; The Sound of Music; Preludium; Morning Hymn; Alleluia; How Do You Solve A Problem Like Maria?; Sixteen, Going on Seventeen; My Favorite Things. **174m/C VHS, Beta, LV, Letterbox, Closed Caption.** Julie Andrews, Christopher Plummer, Eleanor Parker, Peggy Wood, Charmian Carr, Heather Menzies, Marni Nixon, Richard Haydn, Anna Lee, Norma Varden, Nicholas Hammond, Angela Cartwright, Portia Nelson, Duane Chase, Debbie Turner, Kym Karath; *D:* Robert Wise; *W:* Ernest Lehman; *M:* Richard Rodgers, Oscar Hammerstein. Academy Awards '65: Best Adapted Score, Best Director (Wise), Best Film Editing, Best Picture, Best Sound; Directors Guild of America Awards '65: Best Director (Wise); Golden Globe Awards '66: Best Actress—Musical/Comedy (Andrews), Best Film—Musical/Comedy; Nominations: Academy Awards '65: Best Actress (Andrews), Best Art Direction/Set Decoration (Color), Best Color Cinematography, Best Costume Design (Color), Best Supporting Actress (Wood). *FOX, BTV, RDG*

Sounder ⵣⵣⵣⵣ 1972 (G) The struggles of a family of black sharecroppers in rural Louisiana during the Depression. When the father is sentenced to jail for stealing in order to feed his family, they must pull together even more, and one son finds education to be his way out of poverty. Tyson brings strength and style to her role, with fine help from Winfield. Moving and well made, with little sentimentality and superb acting from a great cast. Adapted from the novel by William Armstrong. **105m/C VHS, Beta, LV, Closed Caption.** Paul Winfield, Cicely Tyson, Kevin Hooks, Taj Mahal, Carmen Mathews, James Best, Janet MacLachlan; *D:* Martin Ritt; *W:* Lonnie Elder III; *C:* John A. Alonzo; *M:* Taj Mahal. National Board of Review Awards '72: Best Actress (Tyson); National Society of Film Critics Awards '72: Best Actress (Tyson); Nominations: Academy Awards '72: Best Actor (Winfield), Best Actress (Tyson), Best Adapted Screenplay, Best Picture. *KUI, PAR, PTB*

Sounds of Silence ⵣⵣ 1991 A young deaf boy fears that a killer arsonist may be at large—but can he prove it? One of a number of obscure oddities featuring former youth idol Donahue. **108m/C VHS, Beta.** Troy Donahue, Peter Nelson. *NO*

Soup for One ⵣⵣ½ 1982 (R) Writer-director Kaufer's first film is a solid entry in the Woody Allen-esque Manhattanite's angst genre. Young Jewish guy Rubinek pines for the woman of his dreams, finds her, is rejected, persists, gets her, wonders if she's what he wants after all. If you like Woody Allen, this is worth seeing. **84m/C VHS, Beta.** Saul Rubinek, Marcia Strassman, Gerrit Graham, Richard Libertini, Andrea Martin; *D:* Jonathan Kaufer. *WAR*

Sour Grapes ⵣⵣ 1998 (R) "Seinfeld" co-creator David's feature directorial debut has cousins Evan and Richie (Weber and Bierko) feuding over an Atlantic City slot machine jackpot. Evan, a successful neurosurgeon lends Richie, an extroverted loser, two quarters for one last pull on the slots. Of course, Richie wins $400,000. Escalating revenge schemes, petty greed, and quirky small talk scream sitcom episode, as do the TV quality production values, and lighting. The dialogue is biting and clever, but on the whole there's not enough here to justify 90 minutes of screen time. Robyn Peterman, the real-life daughter of J. Peterman, plays Richie's girlfriend. If you liked "Seinfeld," this flick's for you. **CW:** Language and sex-related humor. **91m/C VHS.** Steven Weber, Craig Bierko, Karen Sillas, Matt Keeslar, Robyn Peterman, Jennifer Leigh Warren, Richard Gant, James MacDonald, Philip Baker Hall, Ann Guilbert; *D:* Larry David; *W:* Larry David; *C:* Victor Hammer. *NYR*

Sourdough ⵣⵣ 1977 Fur trapper Perry escapes the hustle and bustle of modern life by fleeing to the Alaskan wilderness. Near-plotless travelog depends heavily on scenery—and there's plenty of that, for sure. **94m/C VHS, Beta, LV, Closed Caption.** Gil Perry, Charles Brock, Slim Carlson, Carl Clark; *D:* Martin J. Spinelli. *IMP*

Sous Sol ⵣⵣ *Not Me* 1996 In 1967 Montreal, overly sensitive 11-year-old Rene (Moffatt) spies on his parents while they make love and the next morning learns his father has died. Rene becomes certain that sex leads to death, which puts a crimp in his budding sexuality. As a matter of fact he literally refuses to grow up, remaining in his pre-adolescent state for several years while Mom Reine (Portal) eventually hooks up with a new boyfriend Roch (Godin), who moves in. This causes a few more problems for Rene. French with subtitles. **90m/C VHS.** *CA* Louise Portal, Richard Moffatt, Isabelle Pasco, Christian Godin; *W:* Pierre Gang; *C:* Pierre Mignot; *M:* Anne Bourne, Ken Myrh. Genie Awards '96: Best Original Screenplay; Nominations: Genie Awards '96: Best Actress (Portal). *NYR*

South Beach ⵣⵣ 1992 (R) Two ex-football players turned private eyes are living the good life and partying it up in Miami Beach. However, their leisurely lifestyles are soon disrupted when they accept a mysterious challenge from the beautiful Vanity. **CW:** Strong violence and sexuality. **93m/C VHS.** Fred Williamson, Gary Busey, Vanity, Peter Fonda; *D:* Fred Williamson; *W:* Mark Montgomery; *M:* Joe Renzetti.

South Beach Academy ⵣ 1996 (R) Eye candy focusing on a beach school that specializes in surfing, swimming, and volleyball rather than the usual academics. Maybe that's why the school's about to close—unless the lightly clad student body can come up with a plan to save their alma mater. **91m/C VHS, Closed Caption.** Corey Feldman, Al Lewis, James Hong, Elizabeth Kaitan; *D:* Joe Esposito. *ART*

South Bronx Heroes ⵣ½ *The Runaways; Revenge of the Innocents* 1985 (R) A police officer helps two children when they discover their foster home is the headquarters for a pornography ring. **105m/C VHS, Beta.** Brendan Ward, Mario Van Peebles, Megan Van Peebles, Melissa Esposito, Martin Zurla, Jordan Abeles; *D:* William Szarka. *NO*

South Central ⵣⵣ 1992 (R) A low-budget urban drama set in a gang-infested L.A. neighborhood. Bobby is a young black man, and former gang leader, who has spent ten years in prison for murder. His wife has become a drug addict and his young son Jimmie has begun running with his dad's old gang. Now paroled, Bobby hopes to reestablish the bond with his son—enough to protect him from following in his nowhere-to-go-but-down footsteps. Worthy effort with an emotional ending. Feature debut of director Anderson. Based on the novel "Crips" by Donald Bakeer. **CW:** Language and gang violence and drug content. **99m/C VHS, Beta, LV, Letterbox, Closed Caption.** Glenn Plummer, Carl Lumbly, Christian Coleman, LaRita Shelby, Byron Keith Minns; *D:* Steve Anderson; *W:* Steve Anderson. *WAR, PMS*

South of Hell Mountain ⵣ½ 1970 (R) On the run from a gold mine robbery where they left 20 dead, the McHenry brothers meet a mother-daughter team that slows them down. **87m/C VHS, Beta.** Ann Stewart, Sam Hall, Nicol Britton; *D:* William Sachs, Louis Leahman. *MGM*

South of Monterey ⵣ½ 1947 Western adventure with the Cisco kid. **63m/B VHS, Beta.** Gilbert Roland, Martin Garralaga, Frank Yaconelli, Marjorie Riordan; *D:* William Nigh. *VCN*

South of Pago Pago ⵣⵣ½ 1940 The unsuspecting natives of a tropical isle are exploited by a gang of pirates searching for a seabed of rare pearls. A notch up from most similar adventure outings, with great violent action and excellent cinematography. Leading lady Farmer was thought to be a rising star, but retired at 29 in 1942 because of alcoholism and spent some time in mental institutions. "Frances" (1982), with Jessica Lange, is based on her life. **98m/B VHS, Beta.** Victor McLaglen, Jon Hall, Frances Farmer, Gene Lockhart; *D:* Alfred E. Green. *NO*

South of Reno 🎬🎬½ **1987 (R)** A man living a secluded life in the desert dreams of moving to Reno and learns his wife is cheating on him. Odd, minimal plot. Impressive first feature for Polish diretor Rezyka, who cut his teeth on music videos. **98m/C VHS, LV.** Jeffery Osterhage, Lisa Blount, Joe Phelan, Lewis Van Bergen, Julia Montgomery, Brandis Kemp, Danitza Kingsley, Mary Grace Canfield, Bert Remsen; **D:** Mark Rezyka; **M:** Nigel Holton. **REP**

South of St. Louis 🎬🎬½ **1948** A peaceful cattle rancher turns renegade gunrunner during the Civil War when his stock is destroyed by Union guerrillas. Overplotted but exciting and action-packed western, with Smith dazzling in a plethora of costumes. **88m/C VHS.** Joel McCrea, Zachary Scott, Victor Jory, Douglas Kennedy, Alexis Smith, Alan Hale, Dorothy Malone; **D:** Ray Enright; **C:** Karl Freund; **M:** Max Steiner. **REP**

South of Santa Fe 🎬🎬 **1932** Mexican rebels give the hero a hard time in this standard Western. **60m/B VHS.** Bob Steele, Janis Elliott, Chris-Pin Martin, Jack Clifford, Eddie Dunn, Robert Burns, Hank Bell, Allan Garcia; **D:** Bert Glennon. **NOS**

South of Santa Fe 🎬🎬 **1942** Rogers and friends take on the mob—yes, the mob, armed with machine guns and airplanes—after they are falsely implicated in a crime. In lulls between the rootin' tootin' gunfights, Rogers belts out "We're Headin' for the Home Corral," "Down the Trail," and "Open Range Ahead." **60m/B VHS, Beta.** Roy Rogers, George "Gabby" Hayes, Linda Hayes, Paul Fix, Judy Clark; **D:** Joseph Kane. **NOS, DVT, CAB**

South of the Border 🎬🎬 **1939** Autry and Burnette are government agents sent to Mexico to investigate a possible revolution instigated by foreign agents. Propaganda-heavy singing western appeared just before the U.S. entered WWII; did well at the boxoffice and boosted Autry's career. **70m/B VHS, Beta.** Gene Autry, Smiley Burnette. **CCB, VCN**

South of the Rio Grande 🎬½ **1945** The Cisco Kid rides again as he comes to the aid of a rancher whose horses were stolen. Garden-variety law-and-order western. **60m/B VHS, Beta.** Duncan Renaldo; **D:** Lambert Hillyer. **NO**

South Pacific 🎬🎬🎬½ **1958** A young American Navy nurse and a Frenchman fall in love during WWII. Expensive production included much location shooting in Hawaii. Based on Rodgers and Hammerstein's musical; not as good as the play, but pretty darn good still. The play in turn was based on James Michener's novel "Tales of the South Pacific." ♫My Girl Back Home; Dites-Moi; Bali Ha'i; Happy Talk; A Cockeyed Optimist; Soliloquies; Some Enchanted Evening; Bloody Mary; I'm Gonna Wash That Man Right Out of My Hair. **167m/C VHS, Beta, LV, Letterbox, Closed Caption.** Mitzi Gaynor, Rossano Brazzi, Ray Walston, France Nuyen, John Kerr, Juanita Hall, Tom Laughlin; **D:** Joshua Logan; **C:** Leon Shamroy; **M:** Richard Rodgers, Oscar Hammerstein; **V:** Giorgio Tozzi. Academy Awards '58: Best Sound; Nominations: Academy Awards '58: Best Color Cinematography, Scoring of a Musical. **FOX, RDG, HMV**

South Riding 🎬🎬½ **1937** Estate owner Robert Carne (Richardson) lives with teenaged daughter Midge (Johns) and has money woes from keeping ill wife Madge (Todd) in a mental hospital. A city councilman as well, Carne's drawn into a plan that will supposedly build decent housing for the lower classes but is actually a scam (which he discovers). Adapted from the novel by Winifred Holtby. **85m/B VHS.** **GB** Ralph Richardson, John Clements, Edna Best, Glynis Johns, Ann Todd, Edmund Gwenn, Marie Lohr, Milton Rosmer; **D:** Victor Saville; **W:** Ian Dalrymple; **C:** Harry Stradling; **M:** Richard Addinsell. **KIV**

South Seas Massacre woof! **19??** A cop and a prisoner, shackled together, try to survive modern-day pirates, natives, and each other. They may make it through, but viewers may wish they didn't. **60m/C VHS, Beta.** Troy Donahue; **D:** Pablo Santiago.

Southern Comfort 🎬🎬🎬 **1981 (R)** A group of National Guardsmen are on weekend maneuvers in the swamps of Louisiana. They run afoul of some of the local Cajuns, and are marked for death in this exciting and disturbing thriller. Boothe is excellent in a rare exploration of a little-understood way of life. Lots of blood. If you belong to the National Guard, this could make you queasy. **106m/C VHS, Beta, LV.** Powers Boothe, Keith Carradine, Fred Ward, Franklyn Seales, Brion James, T.K. Carter, Peter Coyote; **D:** Walter Hill; **W:** Walter Hill, David Giler, Michael Kane; **M:** Ry Cooder. **HHE**

A Southern Yankee 🎬🎬½ My Hero **1948** Skelton plays a bumbling bellboy who ends up as a Union spy during the Civil War. Enjoyable comedy, thanks largely to the off-screen input of Buster Keaton. **90m/B VHS, Beta.** Red Skelton, Brian Donlevy, Arlene Dahl, George Coulouris, Lloyd Gough, John Ireland, Minor Watson, Charles Dingle, Art Baker, Reed Hadley, Arthur Space, Addison Richards, Joyce Compton, Paul Harvey, Jeff Corey; **D:** Edward Sedgwick. **MGM**

The Southerner 🎬🎬🎬 **1945** A man used to working for others is given some land by an uncle and decides to pack up his family and try farming for himself. They find hardships as they struggle to support themselves. A superb, naturalistic celebration of a family's fight to survive amid all the elements. From the story "Hold Autumn in Your Hand," by George Sessions Perry. Novelist Faulkner had an uncredited hand in the script. He thought Renoir the best contemporary director, and later said "The Southerner" gave him more pleasure than any of his other Hollywood work (though this is faint praise; Faulkner is said to have hated Hollywood). **91m/B VHS, Beta, 8mm.** Zachary Scott, Betty Field, Beulah Bondi, Norman Lloyd, Bunny Sunshine, Jay Gilpin, Estelle Taylor, Blanche Yurka, Percy Kilbride, J. Carrol Naish; **D:** Jean Renoir; **W:** Hugo Butler, William Faulkner, Jean Renoir. National Board of Review Awards '45: Best Director (Renoir); Venice Film Festival '46: Best Film; Nominations: Academy Awards '45: Best Director (Renoir), Best Sound, Best Original Dramatic/Comedy Score. **NOS, VYY, CAB**

Southward Ho! 🎬🎬 **1939** In the first western to team Rogers with sidekick Gabby Hayes, they portray ranchers investigating bloodshed in their valley. Roy meanwhile yodelin' four tunes. Fun outing. **56m/B VHS, Beta.** Roy Rogers, George "Gabby" Hayes. **NOS, VCN, CAB**

Souvenir 🎬🎬 **1988 (R)** A German soldier returns to France after WWII to find the woman he left behind and the daughter he never saw. Might have been good, but too melodramatic and overwrought, with lukewarm acting. **93m/C VHS, Beta, LV, Closed Caption.** Christopher Plummer, Catherine Hicks, Christopher Cazenove, Michael Lonsdale; **D:** Geoffrey Reeve. **PAR**

Soviet Spy 🎬🎬 **1961** A French docu-drama written by Hans Otto Meissner, Chief of Protocol at the German Embassy in Tokyo during WWII, about the journalist Richard Sorge, a German hanged in 1944 for supplying information to the Soviets. In French with subtitles. **130m/B VHS, Beta.** **FR FCT**

Soylent Green 🎬🎬½ **1973 (PG)** In the 21st Century, hard-boiled police detective Heston investigates a murder and discovers what soylent green—the people's principal food—is made of. Robinson's final film is a disappointing end to a great career. Its view of the future and of human nature is relentlessly dark. Don't watch it with kids. **95m/C VHS, Beta, LV.** Charlton Heston, Leigh Taylor-Young, Chuck Connors, Joseph Cotten, Edward G. Robinson, Brock Peters; **D:** Richard Fleischer. **MGM**

Space Jam 🎬🎬½ **1996 (PG)** Expensive live action-animation combo finds basketball great Jordan forced to play ball against evil intergalactic invaders who are out to capture Bugs Bunny and the rest of the Looney Tunes characters. It's all fairly silly but the kids will enjoy it. **87m/C VHS, DVD.** Michael Jordan, Bill Murray, Wayne Knight, Theresa Randle; **D:** Joe Pytka; **C:** Michael Chapman; **M:** James Newton Howard; **V:** Danny DeVito. Nominations: MTV Movie Awards '96: Best Song ("I Believe I Can Fly"). **WAR**

Space Marines 🎬½ **1996 (R)** Cheesy cable thriller finds intergalactic marines battling 21st century space pirates who've stolen a nuclear cargo and taken hostages. **93m/C VHS, Closed Caption.** Billy Wirth, John Pyper-Ferguson, Meg Foster, Edward Albert, James Shigeta, Cady Huffman; **D:** John Weidner; **C:** Garett Griffin. **REP**

Space Monster woof! First Woman Into Space; Voyage Beyond the Sun **1964** Really bad, low-budget flick with a rubber monster and a climactic crash into a "sea of monsters" which is really a fish tank full of crabs. Ultra cheap production with handed down cast and props. **?m/B VHS.** **SMW**

Space Mutiny 🎬 **1988 (PG)** Spaceship falls under the attack of the mutinous Kalgan. To keep everyone from being sold into slavery, a small band of loyal passengers strike back. Will they be successful in thwarting the attack? Who cares? **93m/C VHS, Beta.** Reb Brown, James Ryan, John Phillip Law, Cameron Mitchell; **D:** David Winters; **W:** Maria Dante.

Space: 1999 **1975** Landau and Bain star as the leaders of Moonbase Alpha, a scientific outpost which is hurled out of orbit by a nuclear explosion. In "Voyager's Return" the crew of Moonbase Alpha discover the original Voyager probe and excitedly prepare to extract its vast knowledge of the universe. To their horror, they discover that it has somehow been transformed into a planet-destroying monster. Bitter aliens are coming to exact their revenge on the machine and the crew is caught in the middle! Additional episodes available. **52m/C VHS, LV.** **GB** Martin Landau, Barbara Bain, Barry Morse, Nick Tate, Jeremy Kemp, Barry Stokes, Alex Scott, Lawrence Trimble; **D:** Bob Kellett. **MOV**

Space: 1999—Alien Attack 🎬🎬🎬 **1979** After an explosion on the moon, Moonbase Alpha loses contact with Earth forever. Pilot episode of the popular British sci-fi series. **109m/C VHS, Beta.** **GB** Martin Landau, Barbara Bain, Barry Morse, Nick Tate, Roy Dotrice, Philip Madoc, Lou Satton, Eric Carte; **D:** Lee H. Katzin. **ART**

Space Ninja: Sword of the Space Ark 🎬½ **1981** A young fighter pilot returns home to his planet under siege and his family dead. He vows to seek revenge and sets out to destroy the evil emperor who is wreaking such havoc. **75m/C VHS, Beta.** **D:** Roger Jenkins. **ART**

Space Patrol **1950** Buzz Corey, Commander-in-Chief of the Space Patrol, tries to maintain interplanetary peace and protect the people of Earth's neighboring planets. These episodes television series include previews of coming attractions from classic science fiction films. Additional episodes are available. **120m/B VHS, Beta.** Edward Kemmer, Lyn Osborn. **MOV**

Space Rage 🎬 Trackers **1986 (R)** A criminal sentenced to life on a prison planet leads a revolt of the inmates. Lame, formula western set in outer space. **78m/C VHS, Beta.** Michael Pare, Richard Farnsworth, John Laughlin, Lee Purcell; **D:** Conrad Palmisano. **ART**

Space Raiders 🎬🎬 Star Child **1983 (PG)** A plucky 10-year-old blasts off into a futuristic world of intergalactic desperados, crafty alien mercenaries, starship battles and cliff-hanging dangers. Recycled special effects (from producer Corman's movie factory) and plot (lifted near-whole from "Star Wars"). **84m/C VHS, Beta.** Vince Edwards, David Mendenhall; **D:** Howard R. Cohen; **W:** Howard R. Cohen. **WAR**

Space Riders woof! **1983 (PG)** Action-adventure about the world's championship motorcycle race, with a rock soundtrack featuring Duran Duran, Simple Minds and Melba Moore. **93m/C VHS, Beta.** Barry Sheene, Gavan O'Herlihy, Toshiya Ito, Stephanie McLean, Sayo Inaba; **D:** Joe Massot. **NO**

Space Soldiers Conquer the Universe 🎞🎞 1940

Edited version of the Flash Gordon serial "Flash Gordon Conquers the Universe." The evil Emperor Ming introduces a horrible plague from outer space called "The Purple Death." Dr. Zarkov, Dale, and Flash Gordon travel from the frozen wastes of Frigia to the palaces of Mongo and must take risk after risk. Twelve chapters at 20 minutes each. **240m/B VHS, Beta.** Buster Crabbe, Charles Middleton, Carol Hughes. *NOS, CAB*

Spaceballs 🎞🎞½ 1987 (PG)

A humorous Brooks parody of recent science fiction pictures, mostly notably "Star Wars," with references to "Alien," the "Star Trek series," and "The Planet of the Apes." Disappointingly tame and tentative, but chuckle-laden enough for Brooks fans. The great man himself appears in two roles, including puny wise man/wise guy Yogurt. **96m/C VHS, Beta, LV, Closed Caption.** Mel Brooks, Rick Moranis, John Candy, Bill Pullman, Daphne Zuniga, Dick Van Patten, John Hurt, George Wyner, Joan Rivers, Lorene Yarnell, Sal Viscuso, Stephen Tobolowsky, Dom DeLuise, Michael Winslow; *D:* Mel Brooks; *W:* Mel Brooks, Ronny Graham, Thomas Meehan; *M:* John Morris. *MGM*

Spaced Invaders 🎞½ 1990 (PG)

Five ultra-cool aliens crash-land in a small midwestern town at Halloween. Local denizens mistake them for trick-or-treaters. Poorly made and a waste of time. **102m/C VHS, Beta, LV, Closed Caption.** Douglas Barr, Royal Dano, Ariana Richards, Kevin Thompson, Jimmy Briscoe, Tony Cox, Debbie Lee Carrington, Tommy Madden; *D:* Patrick Read Johnson; *W:* Scott Lawrence Alexander; *C:* James L. Carter. *TOU*

Spaced Out woof! 1980 (R)

Outer Reach Naughty sci-fi sex comedy that parodies everything from "Star Wars" to "2001," though not very well. The sultry female aliens are visually pleasing, though. Watch this one with the sound turned off. **85m/C VHS, Beta.** Barry Stokes, Glory Annen; *D:* Norman J. Warren. *NO*

Spacehunter: Adventures in the Forbidden Zone 🎞½ 1983 (PG)

Galactic bounty hunter agrees to rescue three damsels held captive by a cyborg. Strauss ain't no Harrison Ford. Filmed in 3-D, but who cares? **90m/C VHS, Beta, LV, Closed Caption.** *CA* Peter Strauss, Molly Ringwald, Michael Ironside, Ernie Hudson, Andrea Marcovicci; *D:* Lamont Johnson; *W:* Len Blum; *M:* Elmer Bernstein. *COL*

Spaceship 🎞½ 1981 (PG)

The Creature Wasn't Nice; Naked Space Misguided attempt to spoof creature-features. Mad scientist tries to protect kindly monster from crazed crew. Not very funny, with the exception of the song-and-dance routine by the monster. **88m/C VHS.** Cindy Williams, Bruce Kimmel, Leslie Nielsen, Gerrit Graham, Patrick Macnee, Ron Kurowski; *D:* Bruce Kimmel. *ART*

Spaceways 🎞½ 1953

Scientist Duff is beset by all sorts of troubles: his experimental rockets explode, his wife has an affair with an ambitious scientist, and when they disappear together, he's accused of killing them and placing their bodies in the exploded rocket. All in all, a pretty bad (and long) day for our hero. Why should we suffer through it with him? **76m/B VHS, Beta, LV.** Howard Duff, Eva Bartok, Ceclie Cheyreau, Andrew Osborn; *D:* Terence Fisher. *MLB*

Spaghetti House 🎞½ 1982

A handful of waiters are held hostage by ruthless killers in this innocuous but worthless Italian comedy. Dubbed. **103m/C VHS, Beta.** *IT* Nino Manfredi, Rita Tushingham; *D:* Giullo Paradisi. *NO*

Spaghetti Western 🎞½ 1969

A farmer and a publisher take on the vile oil baron who is taking over the town. A parody-or is it?—of Eastwoodian B-grade spaghetti westerns. No director credited. **90m/C VHS, Beta.** Franco Nero, Martin Balsam, Sterling Hayden. *VDC*

Spalding Gray: Terrors of Pleasure 1988

The ultra-cool Gray tells the story of one man's dream to own land in his own inimitable way. HBO comedy special. **60m/C VHS, Beta.** Spalding Gray; *D:* Thomas Schlamme. *HBO*

Spangles 🎞 1926

Silent circus drama. **58m/B VHS, Beta.** Marion Nixon, Hobart Bosworth, Pat O'Malley, Gladys Brockwell; *D:* Frank O'Connor. *GPV*

The Spaniard's Curse 🎞🎞½ 1958

When a man is convicted for a murder he did not commit, he puts a curse on the judge and jury responsible. Mysteriously, the marked people begin dying. Is he responsible? Then he dies and the mystery thickens. Intriguing but sloppy murder mystery. **80m/B VHS, Beta.** *GB* Tony Wright, Lee Patterson, Michael Hordern, Ralph Truman, Henry Oscar; *D:* Ralph Kemplen. *SNC*

The Spanish Gardener 🎞🎞🎞 1957

A boy in a prominent family spends more time with the gentle gardner than with the domineering father, so dad arranges for his rival to be framed and sent to prison. An affecting British adaptation of the A.J. Cronin novel, turned into a showcase for Bogarde in the title role. **95m/C VHS.** Dirk Bogarde, Jon Whiteley, Michael Hordern, Cyril Cusack, Maureen Swanson, Lyndon Brook, Josephine Griffin, Bernard Lee; *D:* Philip Leacock. *NOS, VEC*

The Spanish Main 🎞🎞½ 1945

Typical, gusto-laden swashbuckler, RKO's first in Technicolor. Evil Spanish governor Slezak captures Dutch crew led by Henreid. They escape and kidnap his fiancee (O'Hara) off a ship coming from Mexico. Henreid forces her to marry him, but his crew uses the might of the armada and returns O'Hara to Slezak behind Henreid's back. Wow! **100m/C LV.** Paul Henreid, Maureen O'Hara, Walter Slezak, Binnie Barnes, John Emery, Barton MacLane; *D:* Frank Borzage; *C:* George Barnes. Nominations: Academy Awards '45: Best Color Cinematography. *IME*

The Spanish Prisoner 🎞🎞🎞 1997 (PG)

Playwright-filmmaker Mamet goes Hitchcockian in his latest thriller involving an elaborate con game. Naive inventor Joe Ross (Scott) develops a formula for something called "the Process" and soon finds himself a victim of industrial espionage. In a bit of stunt casting that works, Martin plays a sinister, wealthy businessman who befriends Joe and advises him about his coroprate employers. No one is what they appear to be (if they were, it wouldn't be much of a thriller) in this unpredictable and seductive puzzle. Although the staccato dialogue is grating at times, and the emotional payoff is slight, there's enough twists throughout to keep you intrigued. Title comes from an old scam that feeds on the greed and lust of the mark. **112m/C VHS.** Campbell Scott, Steve Martin, Rebecca Pidgeon, Ben Gazzara, Ricky Jay, Felicity Huffman, Ed O'Neill; *D:* David Mamet; *W:* David Mamet; *C:* Gabriel Beristain; *M:* Carter Burwell. *NYR*

Spanking the Monkey 🎞🎞🎞 1994 (R)

"What'd ya do on your summer vacation?" Ray Aibelli (Davies) has an interesting answer in this dark comedy about family dysfunction, sexual politics, incest and masturbation, topics which guarantee it a special place on the video shelf. Returning from his freshman year at M.I.T., Ray learns he must give up a prestigious internship to care for his bedridden mother (Watson) while Dad goes on an extended "business" trip. Much sexual and emotional confusion follows. Mom, it seems, is rather attractive, controlling, and in need of hands-on assistance. Black comedy is understated and sensitive, focusing attention on the story and characters rather than the delicate subject matter, but you'll be aware of the delicate subject matter, nonetheless. Sharp directorial debut by Russell features fine performances by mostly unknown cast, elevating low-budget feel. See it with a relative. *CW:* mature themes, nudity, incest, sexual situations, minor violence **99m/C VHS, LV.** Jeremy Davies, Alberta Watson, Benjamin Hendrickson, Carla Gallo, Matthew Puckett; *D:* David O. Rus-

sell; *W:* David O. Russell. Independent Spirit Awards '95: Best First Feature; Sundance Film Festival '94: Audience Award; Nominations: Independent Spirit Awards '95: Best Supporting Actress (Gallo), Debut Performance (Davies). *NLC, IME*

Spare Parts woof! 1985

Guests at a remote hotel discover that it is run by black marketeers who kill guests and sell the body parts. Of course, they don't bother signing out. **108m/C VHS, Beta.** Judith Speidel, Wolf Roth. *THV*

Sparkle 🎞🎞½ 1976 (PG)

The saga of three singing sisters struggling to rise to the top of the charts in the 1950s. Sound familiar? Well done but cliched fictional version of the Supremes' career. McKee shines. Alcohol, drugs, and mobsters get in the way. Excellent musical score. **98m/C VHS, Beta.** Irene Cara, Lonette McKee, Dwan Smith, Philip Michael Thomas, Mary Alice, Dorian Harewood, Tony King; *D:* Sam O'Steen; *W:* Joel Schumacher; *M:* Curtis Mayfield. *WAR*

Sparrows 🎞🎞🎞 1926

A woman cares for nine orphan children on an impoverished farm, warding off starvation and kidnappers. Silent melodrama features notable performance by Pickford, and a musical score. **81m/B VHS, Beta, LV.** Mary Pickford, Roy Stewart, Gustav von Seyffertitz; *D:* William Beaudine; *C:* Charles Rosher; *M:* William Perry. *NOS, CCB, DVT*

Spartacus 🎞🎞🎞🎞 1960 (PG-13)

The true story of a gladiator who leads other slaves in a rebellion against the power of Rome in 73 B.C. The rebellion is put down and the rebels are crucified. Douglas, whose political leanings are amply on display herein, also served as executive producer, surrounding himself with the best talent available. Magnificent climactic battle scene features 8,000 real, live Spanish soldiers to stunning effect. A version featuring Kubrick's "director's cut" is also available, featuring a restored, controversial homoerotic bath scene with Olivier and Curtis. Anthony Mann is uncredited as co-director. A boxoffice triumph that gave Kubrick much-desired financial independence. **196m/C VHS, Beta, LV, Letterbox, Closed Caption, DVD.** Kirk Douglas, Laurence Olivier, Jean Simmons, Tony Curtis, Charles Laughton, Herbert Lom, Nina Foch, Woody Strode, Peter Ustinov, John Gavin, John Ireland, Charles McGraw, Joanna Barnes; *D:* Stanley Kubrick; *W:* Dalton Trumbo; *C:* Russell Metty; *M:* Alex North. Academy Awards '60: Best Art Direction/Set Decoration (Color), Best Color Cinematography, Best Costume Design (Color), Best Supporting Actor (Ustinov); Golden Globe Awards '61: Best Film—Drama; Nominations: Academy Awards '60: Best Film Editing, Best Original Dramatic/Comedy Score. *USH, BTV*

Spasms woof! 1982 (R)

Death Bite Reed is the unfortunate big game hunter who encounters The Demon Serpent, known as N'Gana Simbu, the deadliest snake in the world. Lame-brained horror fantasy; the producers should have released the nifty Tangerine Dream soundtrack and chucked the movie. Based on the novel "Death Bite" by Michael Maryk and Brent Monahan. **92m/C VHS, Beta.** *CA* Peter Fonda, Oliver Reed, Kerrie Keane, Al Waxman, Miguel Fernandez, Marilyn Lightstone, Laurie Brown, Gerard Parkes; *D:* William Fruet; *W:* Don Enright. *NO*

Spawn 🎞🎞🎞 1997 (PG-13)

Government agent Al Simmons (White) returns to earth, six years after being murdered, in the form of Spawn, a hell-born creature with supernatural powers. He wants to avenge his death and also save his loved ones from the evil Violator (Leguizamo). With green eyes and a friendship with Satan, Spawn's more of a lethal weapon and way more sinister looking than the villain. An unrecognizable Leguizamo and sleazy Sheen team up as adequate adversaries. Extravagant special effects, and a complex, dark story put a unique spin on the over-exposed superhero premise. Adapted from the best-selling comic book. An R-rated director's cut, which includes a "making of" feature and an interview with Todd McFarlane, is also available. *CW:* Thematic elements involving the demonic underworld, violence, intense fantasy action and crude humor. **97m/C VHS, LV, Closed Caption.** Michael Jai White, John Leguizamo, Martin Sheen, Theresa Randle, D.B. Sweeney, Miguel Williamson, Melinda Clarke; **D:** Mark Dippe; **W:** Alan B. McElroy; **C:** Guillermo Navarro; **M:** Graeme Revell. WAR

Spawn of the North ✍✍½ 1938 Alaska's the final frontier in the early 1900s as fisherman Jim Kimmerlee (Fonda) tries to earn an honest buck. But former friend Tyler Dawson (Raft) has joined a group of Russian pirates who plunder the nets of others and the two men are forced into a deadly confrontation. Solid cast, weak script, and a special Oscar for photographic and sound effects (a glacier's involved). Based on the novel by Barrett Willoughby; remade in 1954 as "Alaska Seas." **110m/B VHS, Closed Caption.** Henry Fonda, George Raft, Dorothy Lamour, John Barrymore, Akim Tamiroff, Louise Platt, Fuzzy Knight, Duncan Renaldo; **D:** Henry Hathaway; **W:** Jules Furthman, Talbot Jennings; **C:** Charles Lang Jr.; **M:** Dimitri Tiomkin. USH

The Spawning ✍ 1982 (R) The sequel to "Piranha." At Club Elysium the main course is the vacationers themselves. **88m/C VHS, Beta, LV.** Steve Marachuk; **D:** James Cameron. NO

Speak Easily ✍✍½ 1932 Keaton is bored with his dull life as a college professor. Durante tries to spice things up with a phony inheritance letter, and Keaton decides to spend his supposed money backing a stage show. Keaton is the star, but Durante steals the show. Great supporting cast. **82m/B VHS.** Buster Keaton, Jimmy Durante, Ruth Selwyn, Thelma Todd, Hedda Hopper, Sidney Toler, Lawrence Grant, Henry Armetta, Edward Brophy; **D:** Edward Sedgwick. MGM, GPV, NOS

Speak of the Devil ✍ 1990 A New Orleans evangelist who seduces his followers moves to Los Angeles and strikes a bargain with Satan. Exploitative, unthinking spoof of Swaggart/Bakker scandals of recent years. **99m/C VHS.** Robert Elarton, Jean Miller, Bernice Tamara Goor, Louise Sherill, Walter Kay, Shawn Patrick Greenfield.

Speaking Parts ✍✍✍ 1989 VCR-obsessed laundry worker and another woman battle for the attention of bit-part actor McManus who works in ritzy hotel. A telling picture of the inextricable nature of modern technology. **92m/C VHS, LV, CA** Michael McManus, Arsinee Khanjian, David Hemblen, Gabrielle Rose, Tony Nardi, Patricia Collins, Gerard Parkes; **D:** Atom Egoyan; **W:** Atom Egoyan; **M:** Mychael Danna. FXL, FCT

Special Bulletin ✍✍✍ 1983 A pacifistic terrorist threatens to blow up Charleston, South Carolina with a nuclear warhead. Done quite well in docu-drama style as a TV news bulletin. Interesting examination of the media's treatment of dramatic events. Top-notch made-for-TV fare. **105m/C VHS, Beta.** Ed Flanders, Christopher Allport, Kathryn Walker, Roxanne Hart; **D:** Edward Zwick; **W:** Marshall Herskovitz, Edward Zwick. BAR, ORI, WAR

A Special Day ✍✍✍ Una Giornata Speciale; The Great Day 1977 The day of a huge rally celebrating Hitler's visit to Rome in 1939 serves as the backdrop for an affair between weary housewife Loren and lonely, unhappy homosexual radio announcer Mastroianni. Good performances from two thorough pros make a depressing film well worth watching. In Italian with English subtitles or dubbed. **105m/C VHS, Beta, LV, Letterbox.** ✍ Sophia Loren, Marcello Mastroianni, John Vernon, Francoise Berd; **D:** Ettore Scola; **W:** Ettore Scola, Ruggero Maccari, Maurizio Costanzo; **C:** Pasquale De Santis; **M:** Armando Travaioli. Golden Globe Awards '78: Best Foreign Film; Nominations: Academy Awards '77: Best Actor (Mastroianni), Best Foreign Language Film. COL

Special Delivery ✍✍½ 1976 (PG) Three unemployed Vietnam veterans decide to rob a bank but their getaway plans go awry. Svenson, the only robber who escapes, stashes the cash in a mailbox only to have it discovered by nutty artist, Shepherd, and crooked barkeep Gwynne. **99m/C VHS, Beta.** Bo Svenson, Cybill Shepherd, Vic Tayback, Michael C. Gwynne, Tom Atkins, Sorrell Booke, Dei-

dre Hall, Gerrit Graham, Jeff Goldblum; **D:** Paul Wendkos; **C:** Harry Stradling Jr.; **M:** Lalo Schifrin. ART, VES

Special Effects ✍✍ 1985 (R) A desperate movie director murders a young actress, then makes a movie about her death. Solid, creepy premise sinks in the mire of flawed execution; a good film about Hollywood ego trips and obsession is lurking inside overdone script. **103m/C VHS, Beta.** Zoe Tamerlis, Eric Bogosian, Brad Rijn, Bill Oland, Richard Greene; **D:** Larry Cohen; **W:** Larry Cohen. NLC

Special Forces ✍ Hell in Normandy 1968 Eight specially trained soldiers drop behind enemy lines to rescue prisoners of war in WWII. **90m/C VHS, Beta.** Peter Lee Lawrence, Guy Madison, Erika Blanc, Tony Norton. NO

Special Investigator ✍✍½ 1936 Dix is a criminal attorney who specializes in getting his mob clients freed. Then his FBI brother gets killed by the same criminals he's been defending. So Dix becomes a special agent and sets out to get the mob boss responsible for his brother's murder. Climax is the big shootout at the gang's hideaway. Based on the novel by Earle Stanley Gardner. **60m/B VHS.** Richard Dix, J. Carrol Naish, Margaret Callahan, Erik Rhodes, Owen Davis Jr., Ray Mayer, Joseph Sawyer; **D:** Louis King. GPV

Special Olympics 1978 A father attempts to care for his three sons, one of whom is mentally retarded, following the death of his wife. Made for television. **104m/C VHS, Beta.** Charles Durning, Philip Brown, George Parry, Irene Tedrow, Mare Winningham, Herb Edelman, Debra Winger, Constance McCashin; **D:** Lee Philips. GEM

Special Police ✍✍½ 1985 Police inspector protecting old friend's murder-witnessing sister learns that important politicians are involved with a seedy underground political movement. French thriller also available dubbed. **92m/C VHS.** FR Richard Berry, Carole Bouquet, Fanny Cottencon; **D:** Michael Vianey; **W:** Michael Vianey. FRA, FCT

The Specialist ✍½ 1975 (R) Lawyer West thinks he has seduced stunning Capri, but she has lured him into her clutches—she's been hired to kill him. Campy crud. It's old home week for '60s TV alums: West was Batman; bailiff Moore was Mr. Kimbell on Green Acres. **93m/C VHS, Beta.** Adam West, John Anderson, Ahna Capri, Alvy Moore; **D:** Howard (Hikmet) Avedis. NO

The Specialist ✍½ 1994 (R) Buffed bods do not a movie make—at least not in this mechanical actioner featuring Stone as the revenge-minded May Munro. Seems May's parents were killed by Cuban gangsters, led by father/son thugs Joe (Steiger) and Tomas Leon (Roberts), and she decides ex-CIA bomb specialist Ray Quick (Stallone) is just the man she needs to settle the score. But Quick has his own reasons for accepting—his ex-partner is nutball Ned Trent (Woods), who's now working for the Leons. Things blow up a lot, the two leads show off their toned flesh (but not much acting), and Woods gets to steal the movie with his amusing scenery chewing.**CW:** Violence; sexual scenes; strong language. **110m/C VHS, LV, Letterbox, Closed Caption.** Sylvester Stallone, Sharon Stone, James Woods, Eric Roberts, Rod Steiger; **D:** Luis Llosa; **W:** Alexandra Seros; **M:** John Barry. Golden Raspberry Awards '94: Worst Actress (Stone); Nominations: MTV Movie Awards '95: Most Desirable Female (Stone); Golden Raspberry Awards '94: Worst Picture. WAR

Species ✍✍½ 1995 (R) A "friendly" galactic message containing a recipe on how to combine extraterrestrial DNA with human DNA is sent to scientists on Earth. The scientists, led by Fitch (Kingsley), whip up a batch of genetic material resulting in a sexy half alien, half human procreating/killing machine named Sil (model Henstridge's film debut). Naturally, Sil escapes from the lab, leaving the scientists with the unenviable task of catching her/it. All-star special effects team, including "Alien" designer H. R. Giger, create over-the-top, stomach-churning thrills. Dips liberally into the tricks of many sci-fi classics. For avid

gore-meisters only.**CW:** Sci-fi violence, strong sexuality and some language. **108m/C VHS, LV, Closed Caption, DVD.** Ben Kingsley, Michael Madsen, Alfred Molina, Forest Whitaker, Marg Helgenberger, Natasha Henstridge; **D:** Roger Donaldson; **W:** Dennis Feldman; **C:** Andrzej Bartkowiak; **M:** Christopher Young. MTV Movie Awards '96: Best Kiss (Natasha Henstridge/Anthony Guidera); Nominations: MTV Movie Awards '96: Breakthrough Performance (Henstridge). MGM

Species 2 ✍½ 1998 (R) Genetic scientists, in their quest to see an actual babe who will talk to genetic scientists, create a clone named Eve (Henstridge) from the monster in the original movie. Meanwhile, the U.S. has managed to successfully put an underwear model who can't act on Mars. Astronaut Patrick Ross (Lazard) has been infected with spores of alien DNA. Soon Ross' urge to procreate takes over and nasty alien babies are exploding out of screaming women all over town Government assassin Press Lennox (Madsen) and Dr. Laura Baker (Helgenberger) are once again called in to help track down the new species, with the help of Eve. Can they stop Ross before his brood mature? Can they stop Eve and Ross from making the beast with several scaly slimy multi-appendaged backs? Can they please stop making this movie again?**CW:** Strong sexuality, sci-fi violence/gore and language. **95m/C VHS.** Natasha Henstridge, Justin Lazard, Michael Madsen, Marg Helgenberger, Mykelti Williamson, George Dzundza, James Cromwell, Myriam Cyr, Baxter Harris; **D:** Peter Medak; **W:** Chris Brancato; **C:** Matthew F. Leonetti; **M:** Ed Shearmur. NYR

Specimen ✍✍½ 1995 (R) Twenty-four years ago, aliens impregnated Carol Hillary and she gave birth to a son, Mark. Now, the aliens have returned to claim him, only he doesn't want to go. **85m/C VHS, LV.** Mark Paul Gosselaar, Doug O'Keefe, Michelle Johnson, Andrew Jackson; **D:** John Bradshaw; **W:** Damian Lee, Sheldon Inkol; **C:** Gerald R. Goozie; **M:** Terence Gowan. APX

The Speckled Band ✍✍✍ 1931 Set in 1930, this early talkie is a Sherlock Holmes adventure wherein the great detective must solve the mysterious death of a young woman. Massey makes his screen debut as Holmes, making the sleuth cynical, unhappy and pessimistic. Interesting prototypical Holmes case, faithful to the like-titled Conan Doyle story. **84m/B VHS, Beta, 8mm.** Raymond Massey, Lyn Harding, Athole Stewart, Angela Baddeley, Nancy Price; **D:** Jack Raymond; **C:** Frederick A. (Freddie) Young. SNC, NOS, VYY

Specters ✍ Spettri 1987 Archaeologists excavating the Roman catacombs break open the gates of hell. Hellishly confused plot is unoriginal, to boot; decent production values hardly compensate. **95m/C VHS, Beta.** IT Donald Pleasence, John Pepper, Erna Schurer, Katrine Michelsen; **D:** Marcello Avallone; **W:** Marcello Avallone, Andrea Purgatori, Dardano Sacchetti, Maurizio Tedesco. IMP

Spectre ✍✍ House of the Damned; Roger Corman Presents: House of the Damned 1996 (R) Maura South (Paul) is the heiress to a old mansion in Ireland and when she, husband Will (Evigan), and their young daughter Aubrey (played by Evigan's daughter Briana) move in they discover it's haunted by the vengeful spirit of a young girl. When they discover the girl's body, the family hope a proper burial will set her spirit to rest but the ghost has other ideas. Cable movie filmed in Ireland.**CW:** Scenes of strong terror, violence and sexuality. **82m/C VHS.** Greg Evigan, Alexandra Paul, Briana Evigan, Eamon Draper, Dick Donaghue; **D:** Scott Levy; **W:** Brendan Broderick; **C:** Christopher Baffa; **M:** Christopher Lennertz. NHO

The Spectre of Edgar Allen Poe ✍½ 1973 The horridly fictionalized writer of horror fiction visits the asylum where his love Lenore is being held, and discovers murder and torture. Based very loosely on Poe's own torments. Dorky, rip-off horror. **87m/C VHS, Beta.** Cesar Romero, Robert Walker Jr., Tom Drake; **D:** Mohy Quandour. UNI

Spectre of the Rose ✂✂½ 1946
Strange film set in the world of ballet. An impressario contends with an over-the-hill ballerina and a young male dancer with a deadly affinity for knives. **90m/B VHS, LV.** Judith Anderson, Michael Chekhov, Ivan Kirov, Viola Essen, Lionel Stander; **D:** Ben Hecht; **W:** Ben Hecht. *REP*

Speechless ✂✂½ 1994 (PG-13) Cute romantic comedy about sparring speechwriters who fall in love, and then briefly turn enemies when they discover they're working at professional odds. Davis is the idealistic liberal working for senatorial candidate Wannamaker, while Keaton is a TV sitcom writer doing a one-shot deal for a millionaire businessman, Republican Garvin. Both stars do a likable job; the supporting cast fares better with Reeve as an egotistical TV reporter, as well as Davis's fiance, and Bedelia as Keaton's ex-wife/campaign press secretary. Although the film parallels the real-life romance of rival Bush-Clinton spin doctors Mary Matalin and James Carville, it was written prior to the last presidential race. **CW:** Mild profanity, adult situations. **99m/C VHS, LV, Closed Caption.** Michael Keaton, Geena Davis, Christopher Reeve, Bonnie Bedelia, Ernie Hudson, Charles Martin Smith, Gailard Sartain, Ray Baker, Mitchell Ryan; **D:** Ron Underwood; **W:** Robert King; **M:** Marc Shaiman. Nominations: Golden Globe Awards '95: Best Actress—Musical/Comedy (Davis).*MGM*

Speed ✂✂✂½ 1994 (R) Excellent dude Reeves has grown up (and bulked up) as Los Angeles SWAT cop Jack Traven, up against bomb expert Howard Payne (Hopper, more maniacal than usual), who's after major ransom money. First it's a rigged elevator in a very tall building. Then it's a rigged bus—if it slows, it will blow, bad enough any day, but a nightmare in LA traffic. And that's still not the end. Terrific directorial debut for cinematographer De Bont, who certainly knows how to keep the adrenaline pumping. Fine support work by Daniels, Bullock, and Morton and enough wit in Yost's script to keep you chuckling. Great nonstop actioner from the "Die Hard" school.**CW:** Language and violence. **115m/C VHS, LV, Closed Caption.** Keanu Reeves, Dennis Hopper, Sandra Bullock, Joe Morton, Jeff Daniels, Alan Ruck, Glenn Plummer, Richard Lineback, Beth Grant, Hawthorne James, David Kriegel, Carlos Carrasco, Natsuko Ohama, Daniel Villarreal; **D:** Jan De Bont; **W:** Graham Yost; **C:** Andrzej Bartkowiak; **M:** Mark Mancina. Academy Awards '94: Best Sound; MTV Movie Awards '95: Best Female Performance (Bullock), Most Desirable Female (Bullock), Best On-Screen Duo (Keanu Reeves/Sandra Bullock), Best Villain (Hopper), Best Action Sequence; Blockbuster Entertainment Awards '95: Movie, Video, Action Actress, Video (Bullock), Action Actress, Theatrical (Bullock); Nominations: Academy Awards '94: Best Film Editing; MTV Movie Awards '95: Best Film, Best Male Performance (Reeves), Most Desirable Male (Reeves), Best Kiss (Keanu Reeves/Sandra Bullock). *FXV*

Speed 2: Cruise Control ✂ 1997 (PG-13) Bigger's certainly not better in this lame sequel. Annie's (Bullock) got a new beau, hot-headed cop Alex (Patric), and the twosome decide to go on a Caribbean cruise for a little romance. Annie's luck with transportation holds as the ship is taken over by villainous computer geek-with-a-grudge John Giger (a particularly wild-eyed Dafoe), who sends the liner on a collision course with an oil tanker. Since Alex is off performing heroics, there's not much togetherness and Annie's left to get taken hostage (again). De Bont spent $25 mil on the ship's endless crash into a Caribbean island, which still manages to look fake and only elicits "you've got to be kidding me" disappointment. Bullock's feisty but powerless to save the flick. Patric's bland, and Dafoe is never menacing enough to create any thrills. This sea disaster crashes against the rocks of high expectations and poor execution.**CW:** Frenetic disaster action and violence. **123m/C VHS.** Sandra Bullock, Jason Patric, Willem Dafoe, Temuera Morrison, Brian McCardie, Glenn Plummer, Royale Watkins, Colleen Camp, Lois Chiles, Michael G. Hagerty, Kimmy Ro-

bertson, Christine Firkins; **Cameos:** Tim Conway, Joe Morton; **D:** Jan De Bont, Jeff Nathanson, Randall McCormick; **C:** Jack N. Green; **M:** Mark Mancina. Golden Raspberry Awards '97: Worst Remake/Sequel; Nominations: Golden Raspberry Awards '97: Worst Picture, Worst Actress (Bullock), Worst Supporting Actor (Dafoe), Worst Director (De Bont), Worst Screenplay, Worst Song ("My Dream"). *FOX*

The Speed Lovers ✂ 1968 Stock car driver Lorenzen plays himself as an inspiration to a young man to join the auto racing circuit. More of a pat on the industry's back than a serious drama. Features footage from a number of race tracks around the country although shot principally in Atlanta. ♫Speed Lovers. **102m/C VHS.** Fred Lorenzen, William F. McGaha, Peggy O'Hara, David Marcus, Carol Street, Glenda Brunson; **D:** William F. McGaha; **W:** William F. McGaha, Elaine Wilkerson, Fred Tuch. *SMW, TPV*

Speed Reporter ✂ 1936 Talmadge is the intrepid reporter investigating a phony reform movement that's really a front for a gang of criminals. Mediocre drama with Talmadge's thick German accent a hindrance. **56m/B VHS.** Richard Talmadge, Luana Walters, Richard Cramer; **D:** Bernard B. Ray. *GPV*

The Speed Spook ✂ 1924 Silent ghost races car and steals documents. **85m/B VHS, Beta.** Johnny Hines, Warner Richmond; **D:** Charles Hines. *GPV*

Speed Zone ✂ 1988 (PG) Comic celebrities take over a high speed auto race when a redneck cop locks up the real drivers. Unfunny sequel to "Cannonball Run." **96m/C VHS, Beta, LV.** Melody Anderson, Peter Boyle, Tim Matheson, Donna Dixon, John Candy, Eugene Levy, Joe Flaherty, Matt Frewer, Shari Belafonte, Tom Smothers, Dick Smothers, Brooke Shields, Lee Van Cleef, Jamie Farr, John Schneider, Michael Spinks; **D:** Jim Drake. Golden Raspberry Awards '89: Worst Supporting Actress (Shields). *VTR*

Speeding Up Time ✂ 1971 (R) An angry man wants to ice the dudes who torched his mother's tenement. **90m/C VHS, Beta.** Winston Thrash, Pamela Donegan. *NO*

Speedtrap ✂✂ 1978 (PG) Typical chase scenes and cross-gender sparring characterize this tale of a private detective and a police officer pursuing car thieves. Good cast and fun chemistry between the leads; weak, typical script. **101m/C VHS, Beta.** Joe Don Baker, Tyne Daly, Richard Jaeckel, Robert Loggia, Morgan Woodward, Timothy Carey; **D:** Earl Bellamy.

Speedway ✂✂ 1968 (G) Elvis the stock car driver finds himself being chased by Nancy the IRS agent during an important race. Will Sinatra keep to the business at hand? Or will the King melt her heart? Some cameos by real-life auto racers. Watch for a young Garr. Movie number 27 for Elvis. ♫Speedway; He's Your Uncle, Not Your Dad; There Ain't Nothing Like a Song. **90m/C VHS, Beta.** Elvis Presley, Nancy Sinatra, Bill Bixby, Gale Gordon, William Schallert, Carl Ballantine, Ross Hagen; **Cameos:** Richard Petty, Cale Yarborough, Teri Garr; **D:** Norman Taurog; **C:** Joseph Ruttenberg. *MGM*

Speedy ✂✂✂ 1928 Lloyd comes to the rescue when the last horse car in New York City, operated by his fiance's grandfather, is stolen by a gang. Thoroughly phoney, fun pursuit/action comedy shot on location. Look for a brief appearance by Babe Ruth. **72m/B VHS.** Harold Lloyd, Bert Woodruff, Ann Christy; **D:** Ted Wilde. Nominations: Academy Awards '28: Best Director (Wilde). *FCT*

The Spell ✂✂ 1977 An obese 15-year-old girl has the power to inflict illness and death on the people she hates. Necessarily mean-spirited, if we're being asked to sympathize with the main character. Therein lies the rub. Made for TV. **86m/C VHS, Beta.** Lee Grant, James Olson, Susan Myers, Barbara Bostock, Lelia Goldoni, Helen Hunt; **D:** Lee Philips. *GKK, WOV*

The Spellbinder ✂½ 1988 (R) L.A. lawyer Daly falls in love with a woman he saves from an attacker, then discovers she's a fugitive from a satanic cult that wants her back. Unoriginal, but

slickly made. **96m/C VHS, Beta, Closed Caption.** Timothy Daly, Kelly Preston, Rick Rossovich, Audra Lindley; **D:** Janet Greek; **W:** Tracy Torme; **M:** Basil Poledouris. *FOX*

Spellbound ✂✂ *The Spell of Amy Nugent* 1941 Broken-hearted over dead girlfriend, young college student attempts to contact her through spiritualism, succeeds, and suffers nervous breakdown. **75m/B VHS.** GB Derek Farr, Vera Lindsay, Frederick Leister, Hay Petrie, Felix Aylmer; **D:** John Harlow. *SNC*

Spellbound ✂✂✂½ 1945 Peck plays an amnesia victim accused of murder. Bergman plays the psychiatrist who uncovers his past through Freudian analysis and ends up falling in love with him. One of Hitchcock's finest films of the 1940s, with a riveting dream sequence designed by Salvador Dali. Full of classic Hitchcock plot twists and Freudian imagery. Based on Francis Beeding's novel "The House of Dr. Edwardes." **111m/B VHS, Beta, LV, Closed Caption.** Ingrid Bergman, Gregory Peck, Leo G. Carroll, Michael Chekhov, Wallace Ford, Rhonda Fleming, Regis Toomey; **D:** Alfred Hitchcock; **C:** George Barnes; **M:** Miklos Rozsa. Academy Awards '45: Best Original Dramatic/Comedy Score; New York Film Critics Awards '45: Best Actress (Bergman); Nominations: Academy Awards '45: Best Black and White Cinematography, Best Director (Hitchcock), Best Picture, Best Supporting Actor (Chekhov). *FOX, IME, TLF*

Spellbreaker: Secret of the Leprechauns ✂✂½ 1996 (G) Youngster Mike Dennehy (Smith) is on summer vacation in Fairyhill, Ireland where he meets, what else, a band of leprechauns. He finds out the wee folk are battling sinister sorceress Nula, Queen of the Dead, who wants to seize the leprechauns power and destroy them. But not if Mike can stop her! **85m/C VHS, Beta, Closed Caption.** Gregory Edward Smith, Madeleine Potter, Godfrey James, Tina Martin, Sylvester McCoy, James Ellis; **D:** Ted Nicolaou; **W:** Ted Nicolaou; **C:** Adolfo Bartoli; **M:** Richard Kosinski. *PAR*

Spellcaster ✂ 1991 (R) An evil wizard invites a DJ and a band of rock 'n' roll fanatics to his 1000-year-old Italian castle for an evil and blood-curdling treasure hunt. **83m/C VHS, LV, Closed Caption.** Richard Blade, Gail O'Grady, Harold Pruett, Bunty Bailey, Rafal Zielinksi, Adam Ant; **D:** Rafal Zielinksi. *COL*

Spencer's Mountain ✂✂½ 1963 Fonda plays the larger-then-life patriarch of nine (with O'Hara as his wife), who's inherited the Wyoming mountain land claimed by his father. Fonda's dream is to build a new house large enough to contain his brood but something always gets in his way. This time it's eldest son MacArthur's dream of a college education. Sentimental family fare based on a novel by Earl Hamner, Jr., which also became the basis for the television series "The Waltons." **118m/C VHS.** Henry Fonda, Maureen O'Hara, James MacArthur, Donald Crisp, Wally Cox, Mimsy Farmer, Virginia Gregg, Lillian Bronson, Whit Bissell, Hayden Rorke, Dub Taylor, Victor French, Veronica Cartwright; **D:** Delmer Daves; **W:** Delmer Daves; **M:** Max Steiner. *WAR*

Spenser: Ceremony ✂✂½ 1993 Urich resumes his role as Robert B. Parker's Boston PI, which he played in the TV series "Spenser: For Hire." This time around Spenser is searching for a troubled runaway who's gotten involved in prostitution. But her suburban dad, who has political aspirations, seems reluctant to have her found. Brooks returns as Spenser's menacing associate Hawk. Toronto stands-in for Boston. Made for cable TV; based on Parker's novel "Ceremony." **?m/C VHS.** Robert Urich, Avery Brooks, Barbara Williams, Tanya Allen, David Nichols, Lynne Cormack; **D:** Paul Lynch; **W:** Joan H. Parker, Robert B. Parker. *PAR*

Spenser: Pale Kings & Princes ✂✂½ 1994 Spenser's (Urich) new case involves the murder of a reporter who was investigating a drug-ridden small New England town. But was the journalist killed for what he found out about a Colombian cocaine connection or did his womanizing have deadly consequences? Adapted from Robert B. Parker's novel; made for cable TV. **?m/C VHS.** Robert Urich, Avery Brooks, Barbara Williams. *PAR*

Spetters ✶✶½ 1980 (R) Four Dutch teenagers follow the motorcycle racing circuit and motocross champ Hauer. Misdirected youth film with a spicy performance from Soutendijk. Plenty of violence, sex, and gripping photography. Verhoeven went on to direct "Robocop" and "Total Recall." 108m/C VHS, Beta, LV. *NL* Rutger Hauer, Renee Soutendijk; *D:* Paul Verhoeven; *C:* Jan De Bont.

Sphere ✶✶½ 1997 (PG-13) It must've looked good on paper, but bringing Michael Crichton's decade-old novel to the screen turned out to be a big mistake for all involved. Hoffman, Jackson, and Stone are a team of researchers sent underwater to investigate a mysterious 300-year-old space ship. After realizing the ship has American origins, they stumble across a huge liquid metal sphere that can make their deepest fears come true, in the form of huge squids and sea snakes. Never lives up to the promising premise or high-class looks. Despite three mega-stars and an A-list director, it's a hollow excursion low on thrills and originality, but there's plenty of existential ramblings about the power of the mind. *CW:* Sci-fi action including some startling images. 133m/C VHS. Dustin Hoffman, Sharon Stone, Samuel L. Jackson, Peter Coyote, Queen Latifah, Liev Schreiber; *D:* Barry Levinson; *W:* Paul Attanasio, Stephen Hauser; *C:* Adam Greenberg; *M:* Elliot Goldenthal. *WAR*

The Sphinx ✶✶½ 1933 A murderer causes havoc for his deaf-mute twin (Atwill, good in a dual role) when he frames him for his own crimes. Remade as "The Phantom Killer." 63m/B VHS. Lionel Atwill, Theodore Newton, Sheila Terry, Paul Hurst, Luis Alberni, George "Gabby" Hayes; *D:* Phil Rosen. *SNC, VYY, GPV*

Sphinx woof! 1981 (PG) Woman archaeologist searches for hidden riches in the tomb of an Egyptian king. The scenery is impressive, but otherwise, don't bother. Based on the novel by Robin Cook. 117m/C VHS, Beta. Lesley-Anne Down, Frank Langella, John Gielgud, Maurice Ronet, John Rhys-Davies; *D:* Franklin J. Schaffner; *W:* John Byrum. *WAR*

Spice World: The Movie ✶½ 1997 (PG) Clear some space on the video rack next to "Cool as Ice," the Spice Girls made a movie! Stretching their acting ability, the pop group plays a band of marginally talented singers who are inexplicably thrown to the top of the charts by a bitter twist of pop culture fate. What passes for the plot is stolen from "A Hard Day's Night," by the Beatles, depicting five days before a sellout concert at Albert Hall. The courageous champions of girl power do battle with the hassles of fame, bossy managers, and the media in their quest to get to the show. They find the time to visit a pregnant ex-Spice, change their clothes a kajillion times, and generally poke fun at themselves along the way. Unfortunately (at least for those over 13) they're not poked with anything really sharp. Loads of celebrity cameos (Elton John, Elvis Costello, Bob Hoskins), some of whom run off screen faster than if they were on fire. 93m/C VHS, LV, Closed Caption, DVD. Emma (Baby Spice) Burton, Geri (Ginger Spice) Halliwell, Victoria (Posh Spice) Adams, Melanie (Sporty Spice) Chisholm, Melanie (Scary Spice) Brown, Richard E. Grant, Alan Cumming, George Wendt, Claire Rushbrook, Mark McKinney, Richard O'Brien, Roger Moore, Barry Humphries, Jason Flemyng, Meat Loaf, Bill Paterson, Stephen Fry, Richard Briers, Michael Barrymore, Naoki Mori; *Cameos:* Elvis Costello, Bob Geldof, Bob Hoskins, Elton John; *D:* Bob Spiers; *W:* Kim Fuller; *C:* Clive Tickner; *M:* Paul Newcastle. *COL*

Spices ✶✶✶ 1986 Poor woman Sonbai revolts against the sexist mores of rural colonial India in the 1940s. Features actress Patil in her final role. In Hindi with English subtitles. 98m/C VHS. *IN* Smita Patil; *D:* Ketan Mehta. *MFV, FCT*

The Spider and the Fly ✶✶½ 1994 (PG-13) Mystery writer Dianna Taylor (Harris) and her friends like to play a murder mystery charade known as "The Game." Their latest unsuspecting patsy is crime writer Michael Moore (Shackelford)—who falls for Dianna bigtime. Then their publisher is killed—in the same sort of murder scenario one of them devised. Made for cable television. 87m/C VHS, Beta, Closed Caption. Mel Harris, Ted Shackleford, Kim Coates, Colm Feore, Frankie Faison, Cynthia Belliveau, Kenneth Welsh, Peggy Lipton; *D:* Michael Katleman; *W:* Robert Pucci, Alanna Hamill; *M:* Richard Bellis. *PAR*

Spider Baby ✶ *The Liver Eaters; Spider Baby, or the Maddest Story Ever Told; Cannibal Orgy, or the Maddest Story Ever Told* 1964 A tasteless horror-comedy about a chauffeur who takes care of a psychotic family. Theme song sung by Lon Chaney. 86m/B VHS, Beta. Lon Chaney Jr., Mantan Moreland, Carol Ohmart, Sid Haig, Beverly Washburn, Jill Banner, Quinn Redeker, Mary Mitchell; *D:* Jack Hill. *VTR, MLB, HEG*

Spider Woman ✶✶✶ *Sherlock Holmes and the Spider Woman* 1944 A modernized Holmes and Watson adventure as the duo track down a woman responsible for a series of murders. His adversary uses poisonous spiders to do her work. Zestful, superior Holmes. 62m/B VHS, Beta, Closed Caption. Basil Rathbone, Nigel Bruce, Gale Sondergaard, Dennis Hoey; *D:* Roy William Neill. *FOX*

Spiderman: The Deadly Dust 1978 A live-action episode of Spiderman, from the TV seies, as he attempts to prevent a city-destroying plutonium accident. 93m/C VHS, Beta, Closed Caption. Nicholas Hammond, Robert F. Simon, Chip Fields; *D:* Ron Satlof. *FOX*

Spiders ✶✶✶ 1918 One of the earliest surviving films by director Lang, and predates Indiana Jones by almost 60 years. In these first two chapters ("The Golden Lake" and "The Diamond Ship") of an unfinished 4-part thriller, Carl deVogt battles with the evil Spider cult for a mystically powerful Incan diamond. Restored version has original color-tinted scenes. Silent with organ score. 137m/B VHS, Beta, LV. *GE* Lil Dagover; *D:* Fritz Lang; *M:* Gaylord Carter. *KIV, IME, GLV*

The Spider's Stratagem ✶✶✶ 1970 Thirty years after his father's murder by the facists, a young man returns to a small Italian town to learn why his father was killed. The locals resist his efforts, and he is trapped in a mysterious web where history and lies exert a stranglehold on the truth. Intriguing, high literate thriller; outrageously lovely color photography. Based on a short story by Jorge Luis Borges. In Italian with English subtitles. 97m/C VHS. *IT* Giulio Brogi, Alida Valli; *D:* Bernardo Bertolucci; *W:* Bernardo Bertolucci. *NYF, FCT, AUD*

Spies ✶✶✶½ *Spione* 1928 A sly criminal poses as a famous banker to steal government information and create chaos in the world in this silent Lang masterpiece. Excellent entertainment, tight plotting and pacing, fine performances. Absolutely relentless intrigue and tension. 88m/B VHS, Beta, LV. *GE* Rudolf Klein-Rogge, Lupu Pick, Fritz Rasp, Gerda Maurus, Willy Fritsch; *D:* Fritz Lang. *GPV, NOS, VYY*

Spies, Lies and Naked Thighs ✶½ 1991 A pair of crackpot CIA agents find themselves in a whirlpool of comedic madness when they are assigned to track down a deadly assassin. The problem? The assassin happens to be the ex-wife of one of the guys. Can he go another round with her and this time come out on top? Who cares? 90m/C VHS, LV. Harry Anderson, Ed Begley Jr., Rachel Ticotin, Linda Purl, Wendy Crewson; *D:* James Frawley. *NLC*

Spies Like Us ✶✶½ 1985 (PG) Chase and Aykroyd meet while taking the CIA entry exam. Caught cheating on the test, they seem the perfect pair for a special mission. Pursued by the Soviet government, they nearly start WWIII. Silly, fun homage to the Bing Crosby-Bob Hope "Road" movies that doesn't capture those classics' quota of guffaws, but comes moderately close. Look for several cameos by film directors. 103m/C VHS, Beta, LV, Closed Caption. Chevy Chase, Dan Aykroyd, Steve Forrest, Bruce Davison, William Prince, Bernie Casey, Tom Hatton, Donna Dixon, Frank Oz; *Cameos:* Michael Apted, Constantin Costa-Gavras, Terry Gilliam, Ray Harryhausen, Joel Coen, Martin Brest, Bob Swaim; *D:* John Landis; *W:* Dan Aykroyd, Lowell Ganz, Babaloo Mandel; *M:* Elmer Bernstein. *WAR*

Spike of Bensonhurst ✶✶½ 1988 (R) A Brooklyn street kid dreams of becoming a championship boxer. He tries to gain the mob's help by courting the local Don's daughter. Hip-but-stereotyped Morrissey effort is helped by great cast. 101m/C VHS, Beta, LV. Sasha Mitchell, Ernest Borgnine, Maria Pitillo, Talisa Soto, Sylvia Miles, Anne DeSalvo, Geraldine Smith, Rick Aviles, Antonia Rey; *D:* Paul Morrissey; *W:* Paul Morrissey, Alan Bowne; *C:* Steven Fierberg; *M:* Coati Mundi. *NO*

Spinout ✶✶ *California Holiday* 1966 A pouty traveling singer decides to drive an experimental race car in a rally. Usual Elvis fare with the King being pursued by an assortment of beauties. ♫Adam and Eve; Stop, Look, Listen; All That I Am; Am I Ready; Smorgasbord; Never Say Yes; Beach Shack; I'll Be Back; Spinout. 93m/C VHS, Beta. Elvis Presley, Shelley Fabares, Carl Betz, Diane McBain, Cecil Kellaway, Jack Mullaney, Deborah Walley, Una Merkel, Warren Berlinger, Will Hutchins, Dodie Marshall; *D:* Norman Taurog. *MGM*

The Spiral Staircase ✶✶✶ 1946 A mute servant, working in a creepy Gothic mansion, may be the next victim of a murderer preying on women afflicted with deformities, especially when the next murder occurs in the mansion itself. Great performance by McGuire as the terrified victim. Remade for television in 1975. 83m/B VHS, LV. Dorothy McGuire, George Brent, Ethel Barrymore, Kent Smith, Rhonda Fleming, Gordon Oliver, Elsa Lanchester, Sara Allgood; *D:* Robert Siodmak. Nominations: Academy Awards '46: Best Supporting Actress (Barrymore). *FOX*

Spiral Staircase ✶½ 1975 Mild TV remake of the 1946 classic about a mute servant who is menaced by a psychopathic killer. Why didn't they just show the original? 99m/C VHS, Beta. *GB* Jacqueline Bisset, Christopher Plummer, John Phillip Law, Mildred Dunnock, Sam Wanamaker, Gayle Hunnicutt; *D:* Peter Collinson; *W:* Allan Scott, Chris Bryant. *WAR*

Spirit Lost ✶✶ 1996 (R) John (Leon) and wife Willy (Taylor) move to an old seaside home, where he hopes to find artistic inpiration. Instead, he finds an attractive ghost, Arabella (Williams), who has been hanging around for 200 years after her lover's betrayal. And the jealous Arabella wants to get her new lover's wife out of the way. Yes, ghosts CAN do it. Based on the book by Nancy Thayer. *CW:* Strong sexuality. 90m/C VHS, LV, Closed Caption. Leon, Regina Taylor, Cynda Williams, James Avery, Juanita Jennings; *D:* M. Neema Barnette; *W:* Joyce Renee Lewis; *C:* Yuri Neyman; *M:* Lionel Cole. *ART*

Spirit of St. Louis ✶✶✶ 1957 A lavish Hollywood biography of famous aviator Charles Lindbergh and his historic transatlantic flight from New York to Paris in 1927, based on his autobiography. Intelligent; Stewart shines as the intrepid airman. Inexplicably, it flopped at the boxoffice. 137m/C VHS, Beta. James Stewart, Patricia Smith, Murray Hamilton, Marc Connelly; *D:* Billy Wilder; *W:* Billy Wilder, Wendell Mayes; *M:* Franz Waxman. *WAR, HMV*

Spirit of '76 ✶½ 1991 (PG-13) In the 22nd century, the Earth faces certain disaster as a magnetic storm wipes out all of American culture. Now time travellers must return to 1776 to reacquire the Constitution to fix things up. But when their computer goes on the blink, the do-gooders land, not in 1776, but in 1976 at the beginning of disco fever! 82m/C VHS, LV, Closed Caption. David Cassidy, Olivia D'Abo, Leif Garrett, Geoff Hoyle, Jeff McDonald, Steve McDonald, Liam O'Brien, Barbara Bain, Julie Brown, Thomas Chong, Iron Eyes Cody, Don Novello, Carl Reiner, Rob Reiner, Moon Zappa; *D:* Lucas Reiner; *W:* Lucas Reiner. *NO*

Spirit of the Beehive ✶✶✶ *El Espiritu de la Colmena* 1973 An acclaimed and haunting film about a young Spanish girl enthralled by the 1931 "Frankenstein," embarking on a journey to find the creature in the Spanish countryside. One of the best films about children's inner life; in Spanish with subtitles. 95m/C VHS, Beta, LV. *SP* Fernando

Gomez, Teresa Gimpera, Ana Torrent, Isabel Telleria, Laly Soldevilla; **D:** Victor Erice; **W:** Victor Erice; **C:** Luis Cuadrado; **M:** Luis De Pablo. HMV, CVC, TPV

Spirit of the Eagle 🐾🐾 1990 (PG) Man and young son wander in mountains and make friends with feathered creature. Then boy is kidnapped, creating problems for dad. Somnolent family fare. 93m/C **VHS, LV.** Dan Haggerty, Bill Smith, Don Shanks, Jeri Arredondo, Trever Yarrish; **D:** Boon Collins; **W:** Boon Collins. SGE, IME

Spirit of the West 🐾½ 1932 Rodeo star Gibson and his ranch foreman brother work together to save a fair damsel's land from a gang of rustlers. Routine western of its era. 61m/B **VHS, Beta.** Hoot Gibson, Hooper Atchley; **D:** Otto Brower. NOS, DVT, VCI

The Spirit of West Point 🐾½ 1947 The true story of West Point's two All-American football greats, Doc Blanchard and Glenn Davis (who play themselves), while on leave after graduation from the title school. 77m/B **VHS, Beta, LV.** Felix "Doc" Blanchard, Glenn Davis, Tom Harmon, Alan Hale Jr., Anne Nagel, Robert Shayne; **D:** Ralph Murphy.

The Spirit of Youth 🐾🐾 1937 Joe Louis supports his family with menial jobs until he shows his knack as a fighter. When he's knocked down, his gal appears at ringside to inspire him, and does. 70m/B **VHS, Beta.** Joe Louis, Mantan Moreland. VYY, NOS, VCN

Spirit Rider 🐾🐾🐾 1993 Jesse Threebears is a sullen 16-year-old Ojibway who has been shuttled from foster homes since the age of six. Repatriated to his family's Canadian reservation, he's left in the care of his grandfather, Joe Moon. The entire community works to make Jesse's return successful but there are Jesse's resentments and some family tragedies to be overcome first. Based on the novel "Winners" by Mary-Ellen Lang Collura. 120m/C **VHS.** **CA** Herbie Barnes, Adam Beach, Graham Greene, Tantoo Cardinal, Gordon Tootoosis, Tom Jackson, Michelle St. John. HMV, BTV

Spiritism 🐾🐾 *Espiritismo* 1961 Mother uses one of her three wishes to bring back her dead son. Adapted from the "Monkey's Paw." 85m/B **VHS.** **MX** Nora Veyran, Jose Luis Jimenez, Jorge Mondragon, Rene Cardona Jr.; **D:** Benito Alazraki. SNC

Spirits 🐾½ 1990 (R) A priest tormented by his lust-filled dreams breaks his vows of chastity with a woman who turns out to be a murderer. Bad luck.**CW:** Language and sensuality. 88m/C **VHS, Closed Caption.** Erik Estrada, Carol Lynley, Robert Quarry, Brinke Stevens, Oliver Darrow, Kathrin Lautner; **D:** Fred Olen Ray. THV

Spirits of the Dead 🐾🐾🐾 *Histoires Extraordinaires* 1968 (R) Three Edgar Allan Poe stories adapted for the screen and directed by three of Europe's finest. "Metzengerstein," directed by Roger Vadim stars the Fonda siblings in a tale of incestuous lust. "William Wilson" finds Louis Malle directing Delon and Bardot in the story of a vicious Austrian army officer haunted by a murder victim. Finally, Fellini directs "Never Bet the Devil Your Head" or "Toby Dammit" in which Stamp plays a drunken British film star who has a gruesome date with destiny. Although Fellini's segment is generally considered the best (and was released on its own) all three provide an interesting, atmospheric vision of Poe. 117m/C **VHS.** IT FR Jane Fonda, Peter Fonda, Carla Marlier, Francoise Prevost, James Robertson Justice, Brigitte Bardot, Alain Delon, Katia Christine, Terence Stamp, Salvo Randone; **D:** Roger Vadim, Louis Malle, Federico Fellini; **M:** Nino Rota. WBF, MLB, FRG

Spite Marriage 🐾🐾🐾 1929 When Sebastian's lover dumps her like yesterday's garbage, she marries Keaton out of spite. Much postnuptial levity follows. Keaton's final silent. 82m/B **VHS, Beta, LV.** Buster Keaton, Dorothy Sebastian, Edward Earle, Leila Hyams, William Bechtel, Hank Mann; **D:** Edward Sedgwick. MGM, FCT

Spitfire 🐾🐾🐾 1934 Sentimental comedy-drama starring Hepburn as a hillbilly faith healer from the Ozarks who falls into a love triangle. One in a string of early boxoffice flops for Hepburn. She wanted to play a role other than patrician Eastern Seaboard, and did, but audiences didn't buy it. 90m/B **VHS, Beta, 8mm.** Katharine Hepburn, Robert Young, Ralph Bellamy, Sidney Toler; **D:** John Cromwell; **M:** Max Steiner. NO

Spitfire 🐾🐾🐾 *The First of the Few* 1942 True story of Reginald J. Mitchell, who designed "The Spitfire" fighter plane, which greatly assisted the Allies during WWII. Howard's last film. Heavily propagandist but enjoyable and uncomplicated biography, with a splendid score. 88m/B **VHS, Beta.** **GB** Leslie Howard, David Niven, Rosamund John, Roland Culver, David Horne, J.H. Roberts, Patricia Medina; **D:** Leslie Howard; **C:** Georges Perinal; **M:** William Walton. HMV, NOS, HHT

Spitfire 🐾½ 1994 (R) Feisty gymnast Charlie Case (Phillips) has some super secret info slipped to her by her secret agent father (Henrikson) that is desired by evil Carla Davis (Douglas). With the help of reporter Rex Beacham (Thomerson), Charlie's gonna save the day.**CW:** Language; violence; some nudity. 95m/C **VHS.** Kristie Phillips, Sarah Douglas, Lance Henriksen, Tim Thomerson; **D:** Albert Pyun; **W:** Albert Pyun; **C:** George Mooradian; **M:** Tony Riparetti. THV

The Spitfire Grill 🐾🐾½ *Care of the Spitfire Grill* 1995 (PG-13) Newly released from prison, Perry Talbott (Elliott) moves to smalltown Gilead, Maine, and gets a waitressing job at the Spitfire Grill, run by the cranky Hannah (Burstyn). Perry's upfront about her jail time, which doesn't endear her to the suspicious locals. Particularly censorious is businessman Nahum Goddard (Patton), who sends his downtrodden wife Shelby (Harden) to keep an eye on Perry. There are a number of personal dilemmas that take their toll in this familiar setting—redeemed by strong performances.**CW:** Thematic elements. 117m/C **VHS, LV, Closed Caption.** Alison Elliott, Ellen Burstyn, Marcia Gay Harden, Will Patton, Kieran Mulroney, Gailard Sartain, Louise De Cormier, John M. Jackson; **D:** Lee David Zlotoff; **W:** Lee David Zlotoff; **C:** Rob Draper; **M:** James Horner. Sundance Film Festival '96: Audience Award. COL

Spittin' Image 🐾 1983 After falling from her mean-spirited father's wagon, a young girl befriends a kind mountain man. She learns the ways of the wilderness and tobacco spitting. 92m/C **VHS, Beta.** Sunshine Parker, Trudi Cooper, Sharon Barr, Karen Barr; **D:** Russell Kern.

Splash 🐾🐾½ 1984 (PG) A beautiful mermaid ventures into New York City in search of a man she's rescued twice when he's fallen overboard. Now it's her turn to fall—in love. Charming performances by Hanks and Hannah. Well-paced direction from Howard, with just enough slapstick. Don't miss the lobster scene. 109m/C **VHS, Beta, LV, 8mm.** Tom Hanks, Daryl Hannah, Eugene Levy, John Candy, Dody Goodman, Shecky Greene, Richard B. Shull, Bobby DiCicco, Howard Morris; **D:** Ron Howard; **W:** Babaloo Mandel, Lowell Ganz. National Society of Film Critics Awards '84: Best Screenplay; Nominations: Academy Awards '84: Best Original Screenplay. TOU

Splatter University woof! 1984 A deranged killer escapes from an asylum and begins to slaughter and mutilate comely coeds at a local college. Abysmally motiveless killing and gratuitous sex. Also available in a 78-minute "R" rated version. 79m/C **VHS, Beta.** Francine Forbes, Dick Biel, Cathy Lacommaro, Ric Randing, Dan Eaton; **D:** Richard W. Haines; **M:** Chris Burke. ART, VES

Splendor 🐾🐾½ 1935 Typical romantic weepie finds beautiful-but-poor Phyllis (Hopkins) marrying into the snobby clan of Brighton Lorrimore (McCrea). His family (whose fortunes are sliding) want to break the duo up and push Phyllis towards an affair with wealthy broker Martin (Cavanagh). There's a scandal and the Lorrimore's separate but true love conquers all, as you expect. 77m/B **VHS.** Miriam Hopkins, Joel McCrea, Paul

Cavanagh, Helen Westley, Billie Burke, Katherine Alexander, David Niven, Arthur Treacher; **D:** Elliott Nugent; **W:** Rachel Crothers; **C:** Gregg Toland. HBO

Splendor in the Grass 🐾🐾🐾 1961 A drama set in rural Kansas in 1925, concerning a teenage couple who try to keep their love on a strictly intellectual plane and the sexual and family pressures that tear them apart. After suffering a mental breakdown and being institutionalized, the girl returns years later in order to settle her life. Film debuts of Beatty, Dennis, and Diller. Inge wrote the screenplay specifically with Beatty in mind, after the actor appeared in one of Inge's stage plays. Filmed not in Kansas, but on Staten Island and in upstate New York. 124m/C **VHS, Beta, LV.** Natalie Wood, Warren Beatty, Audrey Christie, Barbara Loden, Zohra Lampert, Phyllis Diller, Sandy Dennis; **D:** Elia Kazan; **W:** William Inge; **C:** Charles Durnham; **M:** David Amram. Academy Awards '61: Best Story & Screenplay; Nominations: Academy Awards '61: Best Actress (Wood).WAR

Split 🐾 1990 Humanoids from another dimension manipulate earth activity. 85m/C **VHS.** John Flynn, Timothy Dwight, Chris Shaw, Joan Bechtel; **D:** Chris Shaw.

Split Decisions 🐾🐾 1988 (R) An Irish family of boxers, dad and his two sons, slug it out emotionally and physically, as they come to terms with career choices and each other. Good scenes in the ring but the drama leans toward melodrama. Decent family drama, but somewhat of a "Rocky" rip-off. 95m/C **VHS, LV, 8mm, Closed Caption.** Gene Hackman, Craig Sheffer, Jeff Fahey, Jennifer Beals, John McLiam, Eddie Velez, Carmine Caridi, James Tolkan; **D:** David Drury; **W:** David Fallon; **M:** Basil Poledouris. WAR

Split Image 🐾🐾🐾 1982 (R) An all-American boy comes under the spell of a cult. His parents then hire a deprogrammer to bring the boy back to reality. Exceptional performances by Dennehy and Woods. This is a worthwhile film that spent far too little time in theatres. 113m/C **VHS, Beta.** Michael O'Keefe, Karen Allen, Peter Fonda, Brian Dennehy, James Woods; **D:** Ted Kotcheff; **W:** Robert Mark Kamen; **M:** Bill Conti.

Split Second 🐾🐾½ 1953 An escaped prisoner holds hostages in a Nevada atomic bomb testing area. McNally's excellent performance as the kidnapper, in addition to strong supporting performances, enhance a solid plot. Powell's directorial debut. 85m/B **VHS, Beta.** Paul Kelly, Richard Egan, Jan Sterling, Alexis Smith, Stephen McNally; **D:** Dick Powell; **W:** William Bowers, Irving Wallace. TTC

Split Second 🐾🐾½ 1992 (R) Hauer is a futuristic cop tracking down a vicious alien serial killer in London in the year 2008. The monster rips out the hearts of his victims and then eats them in what appears to be a satanic ritual in this blood-soaked thriller wanna-be. Hauer gives a listless performance and overall, the action is quite dull. The music soundtrack also manages to annoy with the Moody Blues song "Nights in White Satin" playing at the most inappropriate times. A British/American co-production.**CW:** Language and gore. 91m/C **VHS, Closed Caption.** **GB** Rutger Hauer, Kim Cattrall, Neil Duncan, Michael J. Pollard, Alun Armstrong, Pete Postlethwaite, Ian Dury, Roberta Eaton; **D:** Tony Maylam. HBO

Splitting Heirs 🐾🐾½ 1993 (PG-13) Idle stars as the offspring of titled parents who is accidentally abandoned in a restaurant as an infant and raised by poor Pakistanis. (His mother winds up claiming the wrong abandoned baby.) When he discovers he's actually the 15th Duke of Bournemouth he plots, ineffectually, to kill off the present unknowing imposter, a nitwit American (Moranis). Cleese pops in as a shabby lawyer hired by Idle to help him claim the title with Hershey as Idle's real mother, the addle-brained and sex-starved Duchess. Convoluted plot, bland comedy.**CW:** Sexual dialogue and nudity. 87m/C **VHS, LV, Closed Caption.** Eric Idle, Rick Moranis, Barbara Hershey, John Cleese, Catherine Zeta-Jones, Sadie Frost,

Stratford Johns, Brenda Bruce, William Franklyn, Jeremy Clyde; **D:** Robert M. Young; **W:** Eric Idle; **M:** Michael Kamen. *USH*

Splitz woof! **1984 (PG-13)** An all-girl rock band agrees to help out a sorority house by participating in a series of sporting events. **89m/C VHS, Beta.** Robin Johnson, Patti Lee, Shirley Stoler, Raymond Serra; **D:** Domonic Paris. *ART, VES*

Spoiled Children ♫♫½ *Les Enfants Gates* **1977** A famous film director (Piccoli) tries to work on his new script at home but is too distracted by his family life. So he rents a high-rise apartment for peace and quiet but winds up involved in a tenant/landlord dispute and with a girl half his age. In French with English subtitles. **113m/B VHS.** *FR* Michel Piccoli, Christine Pascal, Michel Aumont, Gerard Jugnot, Arlette Bonnard; **D:** Bertrand Tavernier; **W:** Christine Pascal, Charlotte Dubreuil, Bertrand Tavernier; **M:** Philippe Sarde. *FCT, CVC*

The Spoilers ♫♫½ **1914** Virtually unstaged account of gold hunting in the Alaskan wilderness enhanced by gritty film quality. Was a gold mine when released. **110m/B VHS, Beta.** William Farnum, Kathlyn Williams, Kathlyn Williams, Bessie Eyton, Frank Clark, Wheeler Oakman; **D:** Colin Campbell. *GPV*

The Spoilers ♫♫♫ **1942** Two adventurers in the Yukon are swindled out of their gold mine and set out to even the score. A trademark scene of all versions of the movie (and there are many) is the climactic fistfight, in this case between hero Wayne and bad-guy Scott. One of the better films adapted from the novel by Rex Beach. William Farnum, who starred in both the 1914 and the 1930 versions, has a small part. **88m/B VHS, Beta, LV.** John Wayne, Randolph Scott, Marlene Dietrich, Margaret Lindsay, Harry Carey Sr., Richard Barthelmess, Charles Halton; **D:** Ray Enright; **C:** Milton Krasner. Nominations: Academy Awards '42: Best Interior Decoration. *USH, MLB, FCT*

Spontaneous Combustion ♫♫ **1989 (R)** A grisly horror film detailing the travails of a hapless guy who has the power to inflict the title phenomenon on other people. **97m/C VHS, Beta, LV.** Brad Dourif, Jon Cypher, Melinda Dillon, Cynthia Bain, William Prince, Dey Young, Dick Butkus, John Landis; **D:** Tobe Hooper; **W:** Tobe Hooper, Howard Goldberg; **C:** Levie Isaacks; **M:** Graeme Revell. *VTR*

Spook Busters ♫♫½ **1948** The Bowery Boys take jobs as exterminators, only to find themselves assigned the unenviable task of ridding a haunted house of ghosts. To make matters worse, the resident mad scientist wants to transplant Sach's brain into a gorilla. Essential viewing for anyone who thought "Ghostbusters" was an original story. **68m/B VHS.** Leo Gorcey, Huntz Hall, Douglass Dumbrille, Bobby Jordan, Gabriel Dell, Billy Benedict, David Gorcey, Bernard Gorcey, Tanis Chandler, Maurice Cass, Charles Middleton; **D:** William Beaudine. *WAR, GPV*

The Spook Who Sat By the Door ♫½ **1973 (PG)** A black CIA agent organizes an army of inner-city youths and launches a revolution. Based on the novel by Sam Greenlee. **95m/C VHS, Beta.** Lawrence Cook, Paula Kelly, J.A. Preston; **D:** Ivan Dixon; **M:** Herbie Hancock. *VCD*

Spookies woof! **1985 (R)** An old master sorcerer who lives in a run-down haunted house sacrifices humans to give eternal life to his unconscious bride. He needs only a few more victims when a group of teenagers come along to explore the house. **85m/C VHS, Beta, LV.** Felix Ward, Dan Scott, Maria Pechukas, Brendan Faulkner, Eugine Joseph; **D:** Thomas Doran. *NO*

Spooks Run Wild ♫♫½ **1941** The East Side Kids seek refuge in a spooky mansion owned by the eerie Lugosi. A fun horror-comedy with the Kids' antics playing off Lugosi's scariness quite well. Co-scripter Carl Foreman later co-wrote "High-Noon," "The Bridge on the River Kwai," and "The Guns of Navarone." Not the same movie as "Ghosts on the Loose" which followed in '43 and also featured Lugosi and the Kids. **64m/B VHS, Beta.** Huntz Hall, Leo Gorcey, Bobby Jordan, Sammy Morrison, Dave O'Brien, Dennis Moore, Dola Lugosi, **D:** Phil Rosen; **W:** Carl Foreman. *NOS, SNC, VYY*

The Sporting Club woof! **1972 (R)** A semi-gothic melodrama about a strict all men's club which, during a 100th anniversary party, reverts to savagery and primitive rites. **104m/C VHS, Beta.** Robert Fields, Margaret Blye, Nicolas Coster, Ralph Waite, Jack Warden, Linda Blair; **D:** Larry Peerce. *NLC*

Spotlight Scandals ♫♫ **1943** A barber and a vaudevillian team up and endure the ups and downs of showbiz life in this low-budget musical from prolific B-movie director Beaudine. ♫The Restless Age; Goodnight Now; The Lilac Tree; Tempo of the Trail; Oh Johnny. **79m/B VHS.** Billy Gilbert, Frank Fay, Bonnie Baker; **D:** William Beaudine. *NOS, LOO*

Spraggue ♫♫ **1984** A Boston professor and his eccentric aunt put the moves on a doctor who may have committed murder. Served as a TV pilot for a series that never materialized. **78m/C VHS.** Michael Nouri, Glynis Johns, James Cromwell, Mark Herrier, Patrick O'Neal, Andrea Marcovicci; **D:** Larry Elikann. *ART*

The Spring ♫½ **1989** Two archaeologists search Florida for the fountain of youth after they find new clues to its whereabouts. However, a greedy industrialist and an evil priest are both on their trail, fighting to keep the secret for themselves at any cost. **110m/C VHS, Beta, LV.** Dack Rambo, Gedde Watanabe, Shari Shattuck, Steven Keats; **D:** John D. Patterson. *NO*

Spring Break ♫ **1983 (R)** Four college students go to Fort Lauderdale on their spring vacation and have a wilder time that they bargained for, though viewer is deprived of excitement. **101m/C VHS, Beta, LV.** Perry Lang, David Knell, Steve Bassett, Paul Land, Jayne Modean, Corinne Alphen; **D:** Sean S. Cunningham. *COL*

Spring Fever ♫½ **1981** Heartaches of the junior tennis circuit are brought to the screen in this sports comedy. Previews promised a lot more than this film could ever hope to deliver. Even tennis fans will be disappointed. **93m/C VHS, Beta.** *CA* Susan Anton; **D:** Joseph L. Scanlan. *ART, VES*

Spring Symphony ♫♫½ *Fruhlingssinfonie* **1986 (PG-13)** A moody, fairy-tale biography of composer Robert Schumann, concentrating on his rhapsodic love affair with pianist Clara Weick. Kinski is very good as the rebellious daughter, while the music is even better. Reasonably accurate in terms of history; dubbed. **102m/C VHS, Beta.** *GE* Nastassia Kinski, Rolf Hoppe, Herbert Gronemeyer; **D:** Peter Schamoni. *ART*

Springfield Rifle ♫♫½ **1952** Based on the real-life story of Major Les Kearney, who joined forces with outlaws to catch the thief stealing government weapons. Average. **93m/C VHS.** Gary Cooper, Phyllis Thaxter, David Brian, Lon Chaney Jr., Paul Kelly, Phil Carey, Guinn "Big Boy" Williams; **D:** Andre de Toth; **M:** Max Steiner. *WAR*

Springtime in the Rockies ♫♫ **1937** Autry is a cattle-ranch foreman whose employer decides to try raising sheep. This doesn't set well with the other ranchers, but Autry manages to save the day and sing a little too. **60m/B VHS, Beta, Closed Caption.** Gene Autry, Polly Rowles, Smiley Burnette; **D:** Joseph Kane. *NOS, VCN, DVT*

Springtime in the Rockies ♫♫½ **1942** A Broadway duo just can't get along despite being in love with each other. Top-notch musical, with a touch of romantic tension and comedy. Beautifully filmed in the Canadian Rockies. ♫I Had the Craziest Dream; Run Little Rainrop Run; A Poem Set to Music; Pan American Jubilee; I Like to Be Love by You; Chattanooga Choo Choo; Tic Tac Do Meu Coracao. **91m/C VHS, LV.** Betty Grable, Jon Payne, Carmen Miranda, Cesar Romero, Charlotte Greenwood, Edward Everett Horton, Jackie Gleason; **D:** Irving Cummings; **C:** Ernest Palmer. *FOX, MLB*

Springtime in the Sierras ♫♫½ *Song of the Sierra* **1947** Rogers and Devine band together to fight a gang of poachers who prey on the wildlife of a game preserve. Features a number of songs by Rogers and The Sons of the Pioneers. **54m/B VHS, Beta.** Roy Rogers, Andy Devine, Jane Frazee, Stephanie Bachelor; **D:** William Witney. *NOS, CAB, DVT*

The Sprinter ♫♫½ **1984** A young homosexual, while trying to submerge his confusion in professional track and field, gets to know a homely shot-putter and is seduced by her. In German with English subtitles. **90m/C VHS, Beta.** *VCD, GLV*

Sprung ♫♫ **1996 (R)** The dating scene among four young African Americans is examined in this well-intended, yet unfocused romantic comedy. Couple A are Brandy (Campbell) and Montel (Cundieff) who realize that they have a chance at true love. Couple B are their friends Adina (Parker) and Clyde (Torry) who try to sabotage Brandy and Montel's happiness in order to save them from being "sprung" (in love) with each other. The camaraderie between the couples is funny, some of the time, but the humor often turns from vulgar to juvenile and scenes drag on a bit. Cundieff and Campbell are too bland to carry over the used plot but Torry is a comedic find who makes the film tolerable. **CW:** Some strong sexuality and language. **105m/C VHS.** Tisha Campbell, Paula Jai Parker, Rusty Cundieff, Joe Torry, John Witherspoon, Clarence Williams III; **D:** Rusty Cundieff; **W:** Rusty Cundieff, Darin Scott; **C:** Joao Fernandes; **M:** Stanley Clarke. *THV*

Spurs ♫♫♫ **1930** A rodeo star takes on a whole gang of rustlers and their imposing machine gun. This transitional western was made both with and without sound. **60m/B VHS.** Hoot Gibson, Robert E. Hornans; **D:** B. Reeves Eason. *NOS, DVT, HEG*

Sputnik ♫♫ *A Dog, a Mouse, and a Sputnik* **1961** A Frenchman, amnesiac after a car crash, comes up against Russian scientists, space-bound dogs, and weightlessness. Pleasant and charming family fun though clearly dated. Another fine performance from Auer. Dubbed. **80m/B VHS, Beta.** *FR* Noelia Noel, Mischa Auer, Denise Grey; **D:** Jean Dreville. *NO*

Spy ♫♫ **1989** A former spy who knows too much becomes the target of a renegade agency. Made for television. **88m/C VHS, Beta, LV, Closed Caption.** Ned Beatty, Tim Choate, Bruce Greenwood, Catherine Hicks, Jameson Parker, Michael Tucker; **D:** Philip Frank Messina. *PAR*

Spy Hard ♫ **1996 (PG-13)** Nielsen does yet another genre spoof—this time a combo of "Die Hard" meets James Bond. Agent Dick Steele aka WD40 (Nielsen) is brought out of retirement to thwart the plans of crazed General Rancor (Griffith) for world domination. Not much else plotwise, which ropes Nielsen along in domino fashion through the myriad of unimaginative spoofs on such films as "Speed" and "Pulp Fiction." Minus the charm and pace of parody pioneers Zucker/Abrahams/Zucker, this latest entry should retire the whole genre. Directorial debut of Friedberg. **CW:** Crude humor and sexual innuendo **80m/C VHS, LV, Closed Caption.** Leslie Nielsen, Nicollette Sheridan, Andy Griffith, Charles Durning, Marcia Gay Harden, Barry Bostwick; **D:** Rick Friedberg; **W:** Rick Friedberg, Dick Chudnow, Jason Friedberg, Aaron Seltzer; **C:** John R. Leonetti; **M:** Bill Conti. *TOU*

Spy in Black ♫♫♫ *U-Boat 29* **1939** A German submarine captain returns from duty at sea during WWI and is assigned to infiltrate one of the Orkney Islands and obtain confidential British information. Known in the U.S. as "U-Boat 29," this film is based on a J. Storer Clouston novel. This was the first teaming of director Powell and writer Pressburger, who followed with "Contraband" in 1940. **82m/B VHS, Beta, LV.** *GB* Conrad Veidt, Valerie Hobson, Sebastian Shaw, Marius Goring, June Duprez, Helen Haye, Cyril Raymond, Hay Petrie; **D:** Michael Powell; **M:** Miklos Rozsa. *NOS, VYY, DVT*

Spy of Napoleon 🎬🎬 1936 A French aristocrat agrees to marry the illegitimate daughter of Emperor Napoleon III and finds himself working to uncover traitors to the throne. Based on Baroness Orczy's novel. 77m/B VHS, Beta. *GB* Richard Barthelmess, Dolly Haas, Francis L. Sullivan. *VYY*

Spy Smasher 1942 A war reporter uses his supposed death (and a covenient twin brother) to go underground and fight Nazi counterfeiters trying to wreck the economy. 12-episode serial. "Spy Smasher Returns" is actually a condensedversion not a sequel. 185m/B VHS. Kane Richmond, Marguerite Chapman, Sam Flint, Hans Schumm, Tristram Coffin; *D:* William Witney. *REP*

Spy Smasher Returns 1942 The exciting 12-part serial "Spy Smasher" was cut and edited into feature length and released under this title. The masked marvel and his twin brother battle enemy agents during WWII. This new version is just as exciting as the original cliffhanger. 185m/B VHS. Kane Richmond, Marguerite Chapman, Sam Flint, Hans Schumm, Tristram Coffin; *D:* William Witney. *REP, MLB*

Spy Story 🎬🎬 1986 A Cold War conflict, counter-intelligence, conspiracy, and a nuclear sub chase highlight this tale by Len Deighton. 105m/C VHS, Beta. *MOV*

Spy Trap 🎬🎬½ 1992 Four junior-high school friends concoct bogus military plans using futuristic toys for blueprints. The "secret" plans get sold to the Russians and the kids find themselves chased by the unhappy KGB and the CIA. Family adventure. 96m/C VHS. Elya Baskin, Danielle Du Clos, Jason Kristofer, Cameron Johann, Kimble Joyner; *D:* Arthur Sherman.

The Spy Who Came in from the Cold 🎬🎬🎬½ 1965 The acclaimed adaptation of the John Le Carre novel about an aging British spy who attempts to infiltrate the East German agency. Prototypical Cold War thriller, with emphasis on de-glamorizing espionage. Gritty and superbly realistic with a documentary style which hampered it at the boxoffice. 110m/B VHS, Beta, LV, Closed Caption. Richard Burton, Oskar Werner, Claire Bloom, Sam Wanamaker, Peter Van Eyck, Cyril Cusack, Rupert Davies, Michael Hordern; *D:* Martin Ritt; *C:* Oswald Morris. British Academy Awards '66: Best Film; Golden Globe Awards '66: Best Supporting Actor (Werner); Nominations: Academy Awards '65: Best Actor (Burton), Best Art Direction/Set Decoration (B & W). *PAR*

The Spy Who Loved Me 🎬🎬 1977 (PG) James Bond teams up with female Russian Agent XXX to squash a villain's plan to use captured American and Russian atomic submarines in a plot to destroy the world. The villain's henchman, 7'2" Kiel, is the steel-toothed Jaws. Carly Simon sings the memorable, Marvin Hamlisch theme song, "Nobody Does It Better." 136m/C VHS, Beta, LV, Letterbox. *GB* Roger Moore, Barbara Bach, Curt Jurgens, Richard Kiel, Caroline Munro, Walter Gotell, Geoffrey Keen, Valerie Leon, Bernard Lee, Lois Maxwell, Desmond Llewelyn; *D:* Lewis Gilbert; *M:* Marvin Hamlisch, Paul Buckmaster. Nominations: Academy Awards '77: Best Art Direction/Set Decoration, Best Song ("Nobody Does It Better"), Best Original Score. *MGM, FOX, TLF*

Spy with a Cold Nose 🎬🎬 1966 A sporadically funny spy spoof about a bugged dog passed between British and Soviet intelligence. Hard-working cast keeps it from collapsing. 93m/C VHS, Beta. *GB* Laurence Harvey, Daliah Lavi, Lionel Jeffries; *D:* Daniel Petrie. *NLC*

The Spy Within 🎬🎬 *Flight of the Dove* 1994 (R) Spy Alex (Russell) is working undercover as a call girl and Will (Glenn) is an explosives expert on the run from his past. The two share more than a mutual attraction since a covert organization wants them both dead. Confusing plot but fast-paced action. Railsback's directorial debut. *CW:* Strong sexuality; violence and language. 92m/C VHS. Theresa Russell, Scott Glenn, Lane Smith, Terence Knox, Katherine Helmond, Alex Rocco, Joe Pantoliano, Rudy Ramos; *D:* Steve Railsback; *W:* Lewis Green. *NHO*

Spymaker: The Secret Life of Ian Fleming 🎬🎬½ *Spymaker* 1990 Fictionalized account of the creator of the ultimate spy, James Bond, and his early days in the British Secret Service. Fans of the Bond movies will appreciate the numerous inside jokes. Connery is the son of Sean. Made for British television. 96m/C VHS, Closed Caption. *GB* Jason Connery, Kristin Scott Thomas, Joss Ackland, Patricia Hodge, David Warner, Fiona Fullerton, Richard Johnson; *D:* Ferdinand Fairfax. *TTC*

S*P*Y*S 🎬 1974 (PG) An attempt to cash in on the success of "M*A*S*H," this unfunny spy spoof details the adventures of two bumbling CIA men who botch a Russian defection, and get both sides after them. Usually competent director Kershner had a bad day. 87m/C VHS, Beta. Donald Sutherland, Elliott Gould, Zouzou, Shane Rimmer, Vladek Sheybal, Nigel Hawthorne; *D:* Irvin Kershner; *W:* Malcolm Marmorstein, Lawrence J. Cohen; *M:* Jerry Goldsmith. *FOX*

Squanto: A Warrior's Tale 🎬🎬🎬 1994 (PG) Family adventure fare about 17th-century Massachusetts brave Squanto (Beach), who's captured by English traders and taken to Plymouth, England for display as a "savage." He manages to escape, eventually hiding aboard a trading vessel bound for America, and on returning home even brings about a peace between fearful Pilgrims and a neighboring tribe (which culminates in the first Thanksgiving feast). It may be history lite but it's also a thoughtful, adventurous saga with good performances, and fine location filming in Nova Scotia and Cape Breton, Canada. 101m/C VHS, LV, Closed Caption. Adam Beach, Mandy Patinkin, Michael Gambon, Nathaniel Parker, Eric Schweig, Donal Donnelly, Stuart Pankin, Alex Norton, Irene Bedard; *D:* Xavier Koller; *W:* Darlene Craviotto; *M:* Joel McNeely. *DIS*

Square Dance 🎬🎬½ *Home is Where the Heart Is* 1987 (PG-13) A Texas teenager leaves the farm where she's been raised by her grandfather to live in the city with her promiscuous mother (Alexander, cast against type) where she befriends a retarded young man (yes, it's Lowe, also cast against type). Too slow, but helped by good acting. 118m/C VHS, Beta, LV. Jane Alexander, Jason Robards Jr., Rob Lowe, Winona Ryder, Deborah Richter, Guich Koock, Elbert Lewis; *D:* Daniel Petrie; *W:* Alan Hines; *M:* Bruce Broughton.

Square Dance Jubilee 🎬½ 1951 Television scouts hit Prairie City in search of cowboy stars, and stumble onto cattle rustlers. Twenty-one C&W tunes support a near-invisible plot, suitable for fridge runs. 78m/B VHS, Beta, LV. Mary Beth Hughes, Donald (Don "Red") Barry, Wally Vernon, John Eldridge; *D:* Paul Landres. *NO*

Square Shoulders 🎬½ 1929 Adventures of young military school student with geometric anatomy (Coghlan). 58m/B VHS, Beta. Frank "Junior" Coghlan, Louis Wolheim, Anita Louise, Montague Shaw; *D:* E. Mason Hopper. *GPV, FCT*

The Squeaker 🎬🎬½ *Murder on Diamond Row* 1937 Good Edgar Wallace mystery about a disgraced inspector trying to clear his name. 77m/C VHS. Edmund Lowe, Sebastian Shaw; *M:* Miklos Rozsa. *SNC*

The Squeaker 🎬🎬½ 1965 Complicated but interesting thriller about the underworld goings-on after a big-time diamond heist. German remake of an early (1930) British talkie, also done in 1937, based on the Edgar Wallace novel. 95m/B VHS. *GE* Heinz Drache, Eddi Arent, Klaus Kinski, Barbara Rutting; *D:* Alfred Vohrer. *SNC*

The Squeeze 🎬🎬 1977 (R) Scotland Yard detective Keach, fired for drunkeness, gets a chance to reinstate himself when his ex-wife is caught up in a brutal kidnapping scheme. Slim script gives good cast uphill work. Ordinary thriller. Available with Spanish subtitles. 106m/C VHS, Beta, LV. Stacy Keach, Carol White, David Hemmings, Edward Fox, Stephen Boyd; *D:* Michael Apted. *WAR*

The Squeeze 🎬½ 1980 An aging safecracker is hired for a final job, but learns that his cohorts plan to kill him when the heist is finished. Blah revenge thriller. 93m/C VHS, Beta. *IT* Lee Van Cleef, Karen Black, Edward Albert, Lionel Stander, Robert Alda; *D:* Anthony (Antonio Margheriti) Dawson. *NO*

The Squeeze woof! 1987 (PG-13) Keaton is wasted in this attempt at a comedy about a small-time con artist who discovers a Mafia plan to fix a lottery electromagnetically. 101m/C VHS, Beta, LV, Closed Caption. Michael Keaton, Rae Dawn Chong, John Davidson, Ric Abernathy, Bobby Bass, Joe Pantoliano, Meat Loaf, Paul Herman; *D:* Roger Young; *C:* Arthur Albert; *M:* Miles Goodman. *HBO*

Squeeze 🎬🎬 1997 (R) Self-conscious but not unappealing first effort made on a shoestring budget, with a director who teaches acting at a Boston youth center and who wrote his script based on the lives of his three teeanged lead actors. Tyson (Burton), Hector (Cutanda) and Boa (Duong) lead aimless lives on Boston's meaner streets where trouble finds them despite their efforts to stay (more-or-less) clear. *CW:* Strong violence, pervasive strong language and some drug content. 105m/C VHS, LV, Closed Caption. Tyron Burton, Eddie Cutanda, Phuong Duong, Geoffrey Rhue; *D:* Robert Patton-Spruill; *W:* Robert Patton-Spruill; *C:* Richard Moos; *M:* Bruce Flowers. Nominations: Independent Spirit Awards '98: Debut Performance (Burton), Debut Performance (Cutanda, Duong). *TOU*

Squeeze Play woof! 1979 Group of young women start a softball team and challenge the boyfriends to a game. Standard battle of the sexes takes places, with a wet T-shirt contest thrown in for good measure. Cheap, plotless, offensive trash from Troma. 92m/C VHS, Beta, LV. Al Corley, Jennifer Hetrick, Jim Metzler; *D:* Lloyd (Samuel Weil) Kaufman. *NO*

Squirm 🎬🎬 1976 (R) Storm disrupts a highly charged power cable, electrifying a host of garden-variety worms. The worms then turn themselves into giant monsters that terrorize a small town in Georgia. The opening credits claim it's based on an actual 1975 incident. Yeah, right. Okay entry in the giant worm genre. 92m/C VHS, Beta, LV. Don Scardino, Patricia Pearcy, Jean Sullivan; *D:* Jeff Lieberman; *W:* Jeff Lieberman. *ART, VES*

Squizzy Taylor 🎬🎬 1984 The rise and fall of real-life Australian mob boss Squizzy Taylor in the 1920s. Colorful period gangster drama loses steam about halfway through. 82m/C VHS, Beta. *AU* Jacki Weaver, Alan Cassell, David Atkins; *D:* Kevin J. Dobson; *C:* Dan Burstall. *NO*

S.S. Experiment Camp 2 🎬 1986 Hitler's elite corps of sadists get their kicks torturing and maiming prisoners during the dark days of WWII. 90m/C VHS, Beta. John Braun, Macha Magal. *NO*

SS Girls woof! 1978 After the assassination attempt of July 1944, Hitler does not trust the Wehrmacht and extends the power of the SS over Germany. General Berger entrusts Hans Schillemberg to recruit a specially chosen group of prostitutes who must test the fighting spirit and loyalty of the generals. Seedy exploitation. 82m/C VHS, Beta. Gabriele Carrara, Marina Daunia, Vassilli Karis, Macha Magal, Thomas Rudy, Lucic Bogoljub Benny, Ivano Staccioli.

S.S. Love Camp No. 27 197? A beautiful young girl's life is torn to shreds when she is imprisoned in a Nazi brothel. 90m/C VHS, Beta. *VCD*

Sssssss 🎬🎬½ 1973 (PG-13) Campy, creepy story of snake expert Carl Stoner (Strother Martin) who's developed a serum from cobra venom that just happens to turn human beings into snakes. His latest unwitting guinea pig is reasearch assistant David Blake (Benedict). Cool makeup effects. 99m/C VHS, Closed Caption. Strother Martin, Dirk Benedict, Heather Menzies, Richard B. Shull, Tim O'Connor, Jack Ging; *D:* Bernard L. Kowalski; *W:* Hal Dresner; *C:* Gerald Perry Finnerman; *M:* Patrick Williams. *USH*

Stacey 🐾½ *Stacey and Her Gangbusters* 1973 (R) Ex-Playmate Randall stars as Stacey Hansen, a beautiful, implausibly talented private detective. Hyper-convoluted plot, too much sex and violence detract from a potentially not-wretched whodunit. **87m/C VHS, Beta.** Anne Randall, Marjorie Bennett, Anitra Ford, Alan Landers, James Westmoreland, Christina Raines; *D:* Andy Sidaris. GEM

Stacking 🐾🐾 *Season of Dreams* 1987 (PG) In the 1950s, a Montana family is threatened with losing their farm. Typical, boring '80s farmland tragedy with coming of age tale. **95m/C VHS, Beta, LV.** Christine Lahti, Megan Follows, Frederic Forrest, Peter Coyote, Jason Gedrick; *D:* Martin Rosen; *W:* Victoria Jenkins; *C:* Richard Bowen, Paul Elliott, Richard Bowen; *M:* Patrick Gleeson. NLC

Stacy's Knights 🐾🐾 *Double Down* 1983 (PG) A seemingly shy girl happens to have an uncanny knack for blackjack. With the odds against her and an unlikely group of "knights" to aid her, she sets up an implausible "sting" operation. Blah TV fodder for the big screen. **95m/C VHS, Beta.** Kevin Costner, Andra Millian; *D:* Jim Wilson; *W:* Michael Blake. ART, VES

Stag 🐾🐾 1997 (R) Bachelor party goes out of control and it's every guy for himself. Best man Michael (Van Peebles) surprises groom-to-be Victor (Stockwell) by inviting guys to his bachelor party that he hasn't seen in years—for good reason—such as drug dealer Pete (McCarthy). But when stripper Kelly (McShane) is accidentally killed, Pete's the only one to keep his cool and lay out their options. And this group is a lot more interested in self-preservation than in doing the right thing. *CW:* Strong language, violence, some sex and nudity. **92m/C VHS, Closed Caption.** Mario Van Peebles, Andrew McCarthy, John Stockwell, Kevin Dillon, Taylor Dane, William McNamara, Jerry Stiller, Ben Gazzara, John Henson, Jenny McShane; *D:* Gavin Wilding; *W:* Evan Tylor; *C:* Maryse Alberti; *M:* Paul Zaza. CAF

Stage Door 🐾🐾🐾½ 1937 An energetic ensemble peek at the women of the theatre. A boarding house for potential actresses houses a wide variety of talents and dreams. Patrician Hepburn and wisecracking Rogers make a good team in a talent-packed ensemble. Realistic look at the sub-world of Broadway aspirations includes dialogue taken from idle chat among the actresses between takes. Based on the play by Edna Ferber and George S. Kaufman, who suggested in jest a title change to "Screen Door," since so much had been changed. Watch for young stars-to-be like Ball, Arden, and Miller. **92m/B VHS, Beta.** Katharine Hepburn, Ginger Rogers, Lucille Ball, Eve Arden, Andrea Leeds, Jack Carson, Adolphe Menjou, Gail Patrick; *D:* Gregory La Cava. New York Film Critics Awards '37: Best Director (La Cava); Nominations: Academy Awards '37: Best Director (La Cava), Best Picture, Best Screenplay, Best Supporting Actress (Leeds). TTC, CCB

Stage Door Canteen 🐾🐾½ 1943 The Stage Door Canteens were operated by the American Theatre Wing during WWII for servicemen on leave. They were staffed by some of the biggest stars of the day, 65 of whom are featured here. The slight, hokey plot concerns three soldiers who fall for canteen workers while on furlough in New York City. Many musical numbers, cameos, and walk-ons by a plethora of stars. 🎵We Mustn't Say Goodbye; Bombshell From Brooklyn; The Machine Gun Song; Sleep, Baby, Sleep in Your Jeep; Quick Sands; You're Pretty Terrific Yourself; Don't Worry Island; We Meet in the Funniest Places; A Rookie and His Rhythm. **135m/B VHS, Beta, LV.** Cheryl Walker, William Terry, Marjorie Riordan, Lon McCallister, Sunset Carson, Tallulah Bankhead, Merle Oberon, Katharine Hepburn, Paul Muni, Ethel Waters, Judith Anderson, Ray Bolger; *Cameos:* Helen Hayes, Harpo Marx, Gertrude Lawrence, Ethel Merman, Edgar Bergen, George Raft, Benny Goodman, Peggy Lee, Count Basie, Kay Kyser, Guy Lombardo, Xavier Cugat, Johnny Weissmuller; *D:* Frank Borzage. Nominations: Academy Awards '43: Best Song ("We Mustn't Say Goodbye"), Scoring of a Musical. CNG, NOS, VHE

Stage Fright 🐾🐾🐾 1950 Wyman will stop at nothing to clear her old boyfriend who has been accused of murdering the husband of his mistress, an actress (Dietrich). Disguised as a maid, she falls in love with the investigating detective, and discovers her friend's guilt. Dietrich sings "The Laziest Gal in Town." The Master's last film made in England until "Frenzy" (1971). **110m/B VHS, Beta, LV.** GB Jane Wyman, Marlene Dietrich, Alastair Sim, Sybil Thorndike, Michael Wilding, Kay Walsh; *D:* Alfred Hitchcock. WAR, MLB

Stage Fright 🐾 1983 Bashful actress is transformed into a homicidal killer after a latent psychosis in her becomes active. **82m/C VHS, Beta, LV.** Jenny Neumann, Gary Sweet; *M:* Brian May. NO

Stage Struck 🐾🐾½ 1957 Strasberg reprises the role made famous by Katharine Hepburn as a determined, would-be actress in this mediocre remake of "Morning Glory" (1933). Christopher Plummer's screen debut shows little of his later talent. **95m/B VHS, Beta, LV.** Henry Fonda, Susan Strasberg, Christopher Plummer, Herbert Marshall, Joan Greenwood; *D:* Sidney Lumet; *W:* Alex North. IME

Stage to Mesa City 🐾🐾 1948 Marshal LaRue must find out who is behind the pesky attacks on the stage line to Mesa City. Chesebro, as usual, is a good bad guy. A few chuckles between fist fights and shoot-em-ups. **52m/B VHS, Beta.** Lash LaRue, Al "Fuzzy" St. John, George Chesebro, Jennifer Holt, Russell Arms; *D:* Ray Taylor. COL, GPV

Stagecoach 🐾🐾🐾🐾 1939 Varied group of characters with nothing in common are stuck together inside a coach besieged by bandits and Indians. Considered structurally perfect, with excellent direction by Ford, it's the film that made Wayne a star as the Ringo Kid, an outlaw looking to avenge the murder of his brother and father. The first pairing of Ford and Wayne changed the course of the modern western. Stunning photography by Bert Glennon and Ray Binger captured the mythical air of Monument Valley, a site that Ford was often to revisit. Based on the story "Stage to Lordsburg" by Ernest Haycox. Remade miserably with in 1966 and again—why?—as a TV movie in 1986. **100m/B VHS, Beta, LV.** John Wayne, Claire Trevor, Thomas Mitchell, George Bancroft, John Carradine, Andy Devine, Donald Meek, Louise Platt, Berton Churchill, Tom Tyler, Tim Holt, Chris-Pin Martin, Francis Ford, Jack Pennick; *D:* John Ford. Academy Awards '39: Best Supporting Actor (Mitchell), Best Score, National Film Registry '95;; New York Film Critics Awards '39: Best Director (Ford); Nominations: Academy Awards '39: Best Black and White Cinematography, Best Director (Ford), Best Film Editing, Best Interior Decoration, Best Picture. WAR, VES, TLF

Stagecoach 🐾 1986 A forgettable made-for-television remake of the classic 1939 western about a motley crew of characters in a cross-country coach beset by thieves and Indians. **95m/C VHS, Beta.** Willie Nelson, Waylon Jennings, Johnny Cash, Kris Kristofferson, John Schneider, Elizabeth Ashley, Mary Crosby, Anthony Newley, Anthony (Tony) Franciosa; *D:* Ted Post; *M:* Willie Nelson. THV

Stagecoach to Denver 🐾🐾 1946 Lane as Red Ryder investigates a stagecoach wreck and uncovers a land-grabbing plot led by-who else?—the pillar of the community (Barcroft). Well-directed "Red Ryder" episode. **53m/B VHS, Beta.** Allan "Rocky" Lane, Roy Barcroft, Robert (Bobby) Blake, Peggy Stewart, Martha Wentworth; *D:* R.G. Springsteen. NOS, CAB, VCN

Stagefright 🐾 1987 A maniacal serial killer tries to cover his trail by joining the cast of a play about mass murder. The other actors soon have more to worry about than remembering their lines. Typical low-grade horror. **95m/C VHS, Beta.** David Brandon, Barbara Cupisti, Robert Gligorov; *D:* Michele (Michael) Soavi. IMP

Stairway to Heaven 🐾🐾🐾½ *A Matter of Life and Death* 1946 (PG) Wonderful romantic fantasy features Niven as RAF pilot Peter D. Carter who falls in love with American WAC June (Hunter). Forced to bail out during a mission, Peter is rescued and must undergo a risky operation. What's riskier is an angel (Goring) has made a mistake and realizes that Peter should have died. While on the operating table, Peter's spirit travels to Heaven and pleads his case for life against a harsh prosecutor (Massey) and a group of judges. Terrific work by cinematographer Cardiff. **104m/C VHS.** GB David Niven, Kim Hunter, Marius Goring, Raymond Massey, Roger Livesey, Robert Coote, Kathleen Byron, Richard Attenborough; *D:* Michael Powell, Emeric Pressburger; *W:* Michael Powell, Emeric Pressburger; *C:* Jack Cardiff; *M:* Allan Gray. COL

Stakeout 🐾🐾 1962 An ex-con tries to start life anew, but every time he finds a good job, his past catches up with him. A return to the life of crime looks tempting. Predictable and familiar plot, but performances are sincere. **81m/B VHS.** Bing Russell, Billy Hughes, Bill Hale, Jack Harris; *D:* James Landis; *W:* James Landis. SNC

Stakeout 🐾🐾½ 1987 (R) A sometimes violent comedy-thriller about a pair of detectives who stake out a beautiful woman's apartment, hoping for a clue to the whereabouts of her psycho boyfriend who has broken out of prison. One of them (Dreyfuss) then begins to fall in love with her. Natural charm among Estevez, Dreyfuss, and Stowe that adds to the proceedings, which are palpably implausible and silly. Slapstick sequel "Another Stakeout" followed in 1993. **117m/C VHS, Beta, LV, 8mm, Closed Caption.** Richard Dreyfuss, Emilio Estevez, Madeleine Stowe, Aidan Quinn, Forest Whitaker, Dan Lauria, Earl Billings; *D:* John Badham; *W:* Jim Kouf; *M:* Arthur B. Rubinstein. TOU

Stalag 17 🐾🐾🐾🐾 1953 A group of American G.I.s in a German POW camp during WWII suspects the opportunistic Holden of being the spy in their midst. One of the very best American movies of the 1950s, adapted from the play by Donald Bevan and Edmund Trzcinski. Wilder, so good at comedy, proved himself equally adept at drama, and brought a top-drawer performance out of Holden. Features superb photography from Ernest Laszlo, and a wonderful score. **120m/B VHS, Beta, LV.** William Holden, Don Taylor, Peter Graves, Otto Preminger, Harvey Lembeck, Robert Strauss, Sig Rumann, Richard Erdman, Neville Brand; *D:* Billy Wilder; *W:* Billy Wilder, Edwin Blum; *C:* Ernest Laszlo; *M:* Franz Waxman. Academy Awards '53: Best Actor (Holden); Nominations: Academy Awards '53: Best Director (Wilder), Best Supporting Actor (Strauss). PAR, TLF

Stalag Luft 19?? Senior British officer James Forrester (Fry) is regarded by fellow POWs as a first-class idiot, since he has a record 23 escapes and re-captures. But he's determined to break all 327 prisioners out of their Nazi camp while the nervous German Kommandant keeps one eye on the advancing Allied army and the other on his prisoners. **103m/C VHS.** GB Stephen Fry, Geoffrey Palmer, Nicholas Lyndhurst. VCO

Stalin 🐾🐾½ 1992 The story of the leader of the Soviet Union who ruled with an iron fist from 1924-53. One of the most feared men of the 20th century, he wrenched the largest country in the world singlehandedly from a backward, pastoral farmland to an industrial landscape. He was also responsible for the feared purges of the late 1930s where more than a million people were executed. Also explored is the dictator's relationship with his family, including how marriage to a cunning, sadistic, paranoid tyrant affected his wife. Filmed at actual historical locations in Russia. Made for cable television. **173m/C VHS, LV, Closed Caption.** Robert Duvall, Julia Ormond, Jeroen Krabbe, Joan Plowright, Maximilian Schell, Frank Finlay, Roshan Seth, Daniel Massey, Miriam Margolyes, Jim Carter, Joanna Roth, Andras Balint; *D:* Ivan Passer; *W:* Paul Monash; *C:* Vilmos Zsigmond. MGM, BTV

Stalingrad 🐾🐾 1994 Group of German stormtroopers fall victim to the brutal war of attrition over Stalingrad in 1942 and 1943. Realistic depiction of war is not for the fainthearted. Originally a TV miniseries; German with subtitles. **150m/C VHS.** GE Dominique Horwitz, Thomas Kretschmann, Jochen Nickel; *D:* Joseph Vilsmaier; *W:* Joseph Vilsmaier; *C:* Joseph Vilsmaier; *M:* Norbert J. Schneider. *FXL*

Stalk the Wild Child 🎬½ **1976** Well-intentioned but unconvincing American remake of Truffaut's "The Wild Child," about a child psychologist's efforts to rehabilitate a boy raised by wolves. TV pilot inspired "Lucan," a short-lived series. **78m/C VHS.** David Janssen, Trish Van Devere, Benjamin Bottoms, Joseph Bottoms; *D:* William Hale. *WOV*

Stalked 🎬½ **1994 (R)** Daryl Gleeson (Underwood) saves the life of the widowed Brooke's (D'Abo) young son (Fennell). Naturally, she's grateful—only Daryl takes her gratitude for something more intimate and becomes fixated on her every move.*CW:* Violence; language; some nudity. **95m/C VHS, LV, Closed Caption.** Maryam D'Abo, Jay Underwood, Tod Fennell, Lisa Blount, Alex Karzis, Karen Robinson, Vivian Reis; *D:* Douglas Jackson. *REP*

Stalker 🎬🎬🎬 **1979** A meteorite, crashing to Earth, has caused a wasteland area known as the Zone. The Zone is forbidden to anyone except special guides called Stalkers. Three Stalkers enter the region searching for its center, which contains a room that supposedly reveals fantasies. From the Soviet team that made "Solaris." Filmed with both color and black-and-white sequences. Suspenseful atmosphere due to the director's use of long takes, movement, and color. In Russian with English subtitles. **160m/C VHS.** *RU* Alexander Kaidanovsky, Nikolai Grinko, Anatoli Solonitzin, Alice Freindlikh; *D:* Andrei Tarkovsky; *M:* Eduard Artemyev. *FXL, FCT*

Stalking Danger 🎬½ *C.A.T. Squad* **1986 (PG)** A secret government group must terminate an assassination plot by a terrorist organization. **97m/C VHS, Beta, LV.** Joe Cortese, Steve James, Patricia Charbonneau, Jack Youngblood; *D:* William Friedkin; *M:* Ennio Morricone. *THV*

Stalking Laura 🎬½ *I Can Make You Love Me: The Stalking of Laura Black* **1993** Laura Black (Shields) has just landed her first job at a California engineering firm where she meets co-worker Richard Farley (Thomas). He asks her out—she turns him down—he starts harassing her. Laura reports it to the company, who eventually fire Farley, and obtains a restraining order. He goes on a murderous rampage. Fact-based TV movie with Thomas effective as the dangerous obsessive. **90m/C VHS.** Brooke Shields, Richard Thomas, Viveka Davis, William Allen Young, Richard Yniguez, Scott Bryce.

The Stalking Moon 🎬½ **1969 (G)** Indian scout Peck, ready to retire, meets a woman and her half-breed son who have been captives of the Apaches for 10 years. He agrees to help them escape but learns that the woman's Indian husband is hunting them down. Skeletal plot with little meat on it; great scenery but you wouldn't know it. **109m/C VHS.** Gregory Peck, Eva Marie Saint, Robert Forster, Noland Clay; *D:* Robert Mulligan; *W:* Alvin Sargent. *ACE, WAR*

Stamp Day for Superman 🎬🎬 **1953** Based on the "Superman" television series, this program was made to promote defense savings stamps for kids. A "Superman" cartoon is also included. **25m/B VHS, Beta.** George Reeves, Jack Larson, Robert Shayne. *VDM*

Stamp of a Killer 🎬 **1987 (PG)** A tough cop tries to decipher the pattern of a rampaging serial killer. Made for television. **95m/C VHS.** Jimmy Smits, Judith Light, Audra Lindley, Michael Parks, Rhea Perlman; *D:* Larry Elikann. *VTR*

Stan without Ollie, Vol. 1 **1923** Three silent comedy shorts featuring Laurel on his own, years before teaming with Ollie: "Kill or Cure," "Oranges & Lemons," and "The Noon Whistle." **53m/B VHS, Beta.** Stan Laurel. *VYY*

Stan without Ollie, Vol. 2 **1923** Three silent shorts from Laurel before he met the big guy. **55m/B VHS, Beta.** Stan Laurel. *VYY*

Stan without Ollie, Vol. 3 **1923** Three early Laurel shorts: "White Wings," "Man About Town," and "Smithy." **51m/B VHS, Beta.** Stan Laurel, James Finlayson. *VYY*

Stan without Ollie, Vol. 4 **1925** Three classic pre-Hardy shorts featuring Laurel: "Half a Man," "Yes, Yes, Nanette," and "Save the Ship." **64m/B VHS, Beta, 8mm.** Stan Laurel, Blanche Payson, James Finlayson. *VYY*

Stand Alone 🎬🎬 **1985 (R)** WWII vet Durning battles local dope dealers in his New York neighborhood. Self-serious anti-drug flick miscasts Durning (overweight and looking silly in fight scenes) and Grier. **94m/C VHS, Beta.** Charles Durning, Pam Grier, James Keach; *D:* Alan Beattie; *W:* Roy Carlson. *VTR*

Stand and Deliver 🎬🎬 **1928** War vet joins Greek ranks for the smell of gunpowder in the morning and meets woman of his dreams. Kidnapped by infamous outlaws, he pledges allegiance to them before turning them over to the authorities, and he's free to live happily ever after with heartthrob. **57m/B VHS, Beta.** Rod La Rocque, Lupe Velez, Warner Oland, James Dime, Frank Lanning, Donald Crisp; *D:* Donald Crisp. *GPV*

Stand and Deliver 🎬🎬🎬 **1988 (PG)** A tough teacher inspires students in an East L.A. barrio to take the Advanced Placement Test in calculus. A superb, inspirational true story, with a wonderful performance from Olmos. **105m/C VHS, LV, 8mm, Closed Caption.** Edward James Olmos, Lou Diamond Phillips, Rosana De Soto, Andy Garcia, Will Gotay, Ingrid Oliu, Virginia James, Mark Eliot, Eugene Glazer; *D:* Ramon Menendez; *W:* Ramon Menendez, Tom Musca; *C:* Tom Richmond; *M:* Craig Safan. Independent Spirit Awards '89: Best Actor (Olmos), Best Director (Menendez), Best Film, Best Screenplay, Best Supporting Actor (Phillips), Best Supporting Actress (De Soto); Nominations: Academy Awards '88: Best Actor (Olmos). *WAR, HMV*

Stand By Me 🎬🎬🎬 **1986 (R)** A sentimental, observant adaptation of the Stephen King novella "The Body." Four 12-year-olds trek into the Oregon wilderness to find the body of a missing boy, learning about death and personal courage. Told as a reminiscence by narrator "author" Dreyfuss with solid performances from all four child actors. Too much gratuitous obscenity, but a very good, gratifying film from can't-miss director Reiner. **87m/C VHS, Beta, LV, 8mm, Closed Caption, DVD.** River Phoenix, Wil Wheaton, Jerry O'Connell, Corey Feldman, Kiefer Sutherland, Richard Dreyfuss, Casey Siemaszko, John Cusack; *D:* Rob Reiner; *W:* Raynold Gideon; *M:* Jack Nitzche. Nominations: Academy Awards '86: Best Adapted Screenplay. *COL*

Stand-In 🎬🎬🎬 **1937** When a Hollywood studio is threatened with bankruptcy, the bank sends in timid efficiency expert Howard to save it. Satire of studio executives and big-budget movie making. Bogart is interestingly cast and effective in his first comedy role, playing a drunken producer in love with star Shelton. **91m/B VHS, Beta.** Humphrey Bogart, Joan Blondell, Leslie Howard, Alan Mowbray, Marla Shelton, Jack Carson; *D:* Tay Garnett. *NO*

Stand-In 🎬 **1985** A strange comedy-action film that takes a behind-the-scenes look at sleaze films and organized crime. **87m/C VHS, Beta.** Danny Glover; *D:* Robert Zagone. *NO*

Stand-Ins 🎬🎬½ **1997** Would-be actresses in pre-WWII Hollywood find themselves looking for fame and unwillingly settling for stand-in status. The girls all hang out at Jack's (Mandylor) bar, where Greta Garbo-double, druggie Shirley (Zuniga), battles with cynical Bette Davis stand-in, Monica (Ladd), as they celebrate the birthday of Jean Harlowish Martha Anne (Davis), along with Mae West clone Peggy (Chatton) and Marlene Dietrich stand-in Rhonda (Crider). This desperate gang are bitchy and frustrated and, of course, theatrical. Based on Kelleher's one-act play. **88m/C VHS.** Daphne Zuniga, Jordan Ladd, Sammi Davis, Missy Crider, Charlotte Chatton, Costas Mandylor, Katherine Heigl; *D:* Harvey Keith; *W:* Harvey Keith, Ed Kelleher; *C:* Andrzej Sekula; *M:* Bill Elliott. *NYR*

Stand Off 🎬½ **1989** Two young hoodlums with guns take 18 girls hostage in a dormitory. In Hungarian with English subtitles. **97m/C VHS.** *HU* Ary Beri, Gabor Svidrony, Zbigniew Zapassiewicz, Istvan Szabo; *D:* Gyula Gazdag. *FCT*

Stand Off 🎬🎬½ *April One* **1993 (PG-13)** Dramatization of a 14-hour hostage incident that took place at the Bahamanian High Commission in Ottawa on April Fools Day in 1986. Ex-con David Maltby (Shellen) politely demands that an empty firehall become a shelter for women by taking the High Commissioner for the Bahamas, Jane Briscoe (Sears), as a hostage. Somewhat flawed but psychologically interesting.*CW:* Language, threat of violence. **90m/C VHS.** *CA* Stephen Shellan, Djanet Sears, David Strathairn, Gordon Clapp, Pierre Curzi, Wayne Robson; *D:* Murray Battle; *W:* Murray Battle; *M:* Jonathan Goldsmith. *MNC*

Stand Up and Cheer 🎬🎬½ **1934 (PG)** The new federal Secretary of Entertainment organizes a huge show to raise the country's depressed spirits. Near-invisible plot, fantastic premise are an excuse for lots of imagery, dancing, and comedy, including four-year-old Temple singing "Baby Take a Bow." Also available colorized. ♫I'm Laughing; We're Out of the Red; Broadway's Gone Hillbilly; Baby Take a Bow; This Is Our Last Night Together; She's Way Up Thar; Stand Up and Cheer. **80m/B VHS, Beta, Closed Caption.** Shirley Temple, Warner Baxter, Madge Evans, Nigel Bruce, Stepin Fetchit, Frank Melton, Lila Lee, James Dunn, John Boles, Scotty Beckett; *D:* Hamilton MacFadden; *W:* Will Rogers, Ralph Spence; *C:* Ernest Palmer. *FOX*

Standing Tall 🎬🎬 **1978** A small-time cattle rancher takes on a high-class land baron in this average, made-for-TV western set during the Depression. Playing a "half-breed," Forster carries an otherwise mediocre effort. **100m/C VHS.** Robert Forster, Linda Evans, Will Sampson, L.Q. Jones; *D:* Harvey Hart. *WOV*

Standoff 🎬🎬½ **1997 (R)** A botched FBI raid on a Texas cult stronghold lead the four fed survivors to seek shelter in an abandoned farmhouse. Surrounded by gunfire, they're soon not any safer inside, especially when they capture two of the cult's female recruits.*CW:* Language, violence, brief nudity. **91m/C VHS, LV, Closed Caption.** Robert Sean Leonard, Natasha Henstridge, Dennis Haysbert, Keith Carradine, Tricia Vessey; *D:* Andrew Chapman; *W:* Andrew Chapman. *THV*

Stanley 🎬½ **1972 (PG)** Seminole Vietnam veteran Robinson uses rattlesnakes as his personal weapon of revenge against most of mankind. Thoroughly wretched effort in the gross-pets vein of "Willard" and "Ben." **108m/C VHS, Beta.** Chris Robinson, Alex Rocco, Susan Carroll; *D:* William Grefe. *NO*

Stanley and Iris 🎬🎬½ **1990 (PG-13)** Blue collar recent widow Fonda meets co-worker De Niro, whose illiteracy she helps remedy. Romance follows, inevitably but excruciatingly. Leads' strong presence helps along a very slow, underdeveloped plot. **107m/C VHS, Beta, LV, Letterbox, Closed Caption.** Jane Fonda, Robert De Niro, Swoosie Kurtz, Martha Plimpton, Harley Cross, Jamey Sheridan, Feodor Chaliapin Jr, Zohra Lampert, Loretta Devine, Julie Garfield; *D:* Martin Ritt; *W:* Harriet Frank Jr., Irving Ravetch; *M:* John Williams. *MGM, FCT*

Stanley and Livingstone 🎬🎬🎬 **1939** The classic Hollywood kitsch version of the Victorian legend-based-on-fact. American journalist Tracy sets out into darkest Africa to locate a long lost Brisith explorer. Lavish, dramatically solid fictionalized history. (The real Stanley did not become a missionary—but hey, this is the movies). Tracy is excellent, as usual, and low-key. **101m/B VHS, Beta, Closed Caption.** Spencer Tracy, Cedric Hardwicke, Nancy Kelly, Walter Brennan, Richard Greene, Charles Coburn, Henry Hull, Henry Travers, Miles Mander, Holmes Herbert, Paul Stanton, Brandon Hurst, Joseph Crehan, Russell Hicks; *D:* Henry King; *C:* George Barnes; *M:* Alfred Newman. *FOX*

Star! 🎬🎬 *Those Were the Happy Times* 1968 Campy showbiz extravaganza based on the life of famed musical comedy performer Gertrude Lawrence (Andrews), star of the London and Broadway stage. Film follows Lawrence's adventures from the British music halls to her fateful meeting with Noel Coward (Massey), who would not only become her dearest friend but perform with and write for her as well. A tumultuous private life is also on display. 17 lavishly staged musical numbers helped boost the cost of the film to $14 million—big bucks in '68. Movie was a colossal flop on opening and was recut, deleting 50 minutes, but still didn't recoup its losses. Has gained a cult following. 🎵Down at the Old Bull and Bush; Piccadilly; Star!; Oh, It's a Lovely War; In My Garden of Joy; Forbidden Fruit; Parisian Pierrot; Someday I'll Find You; Has Anybody Seen Our Ship?. 172m/C VHS, LV, Letterbox, Closed Caption. Julie Andrews, Daniel Massey, Richard Crenna, Michael Craig, Robert Reed, Bruce Forsyth, Beryl Reid, John Collin, Alan Oppenheimer, Anthony Eisley, Jenny Agutter, J. Pat O'Malley, Richard Karlan, Lynley Laurence, Harvey Jason, Elizabeth St. Clair; **D:** Robert Wise; **W:** William Fairchild; **C:** Ernest Laszlo; Academy Awards '68: Best Adapted Score, Best Art Direction/Set Decoration, Best Cinematography, Best Costume Design, Best Song ("Star!"), Best Sound, Best Supporting Actor (Massey). *BTV, FCT*

The Star Chamber 🎬🎬 1983 (R) A conscientious judge (Douglas) sees criminals freed on legal technicalities and wonders if he should take justice into his own hands. He finds a secret society that administers justice extra-legally. Implausible yet predictable. 109m/C VHS, Beta, LV. Michael Douglas, Hal Holbrook, Yaphet Kotto, Sharon Gless, James B. Sikking; **D:** Peter Hyams; **W:** Peter Hyams, Roderick Taylor. *FOX*

Star Crash 🎬🎬½ *Stella Star* 1978 (PG) Trio of adventurers (woman, man, and robot) sent by emperor Plummer square off against interstellar evil (Spinell) by using their wits and technological wizardry. Semi-funny and cheesy sci-fi, done with style beyond its limited budget. 92m/C VHS, Beta, LV. *IT* Caroline Munro, Marjoe Gortner, Christopher Plummer, David Hasselhoff, Robert Tessier, Joe Spinell, Nadia Cassini, Judd Hamilton; **D:** Lewis (Luigi Cozzi) Coates; **W:** Lewis (Luigi Cozzi) Coates; **M:** John Barry. *NLC*

Star Crystal 🎬 1985 (R) Aboard a spaceship, an indestructible alien hunts down the human crew. Cheap imitation of "Alien." 93m/C VHS, Beta. C. Jutson Campbell, Faye Bolt, John W. Smith; **D:** Lance Lindsay. *VTR, HHE*

Star 80 🎬🎬½ 1983 (R) Based on the true-life tragedy of Playmate of the Year Dorothy Stratten and her manager-husband Paul Snider as they battle for control of her body, her mind, and her money, with gruesome results. Roberts is overpowering as the vile Snider, but the movie is generally unpleasant. Fosse's last film. 104m/C VHS, Beta, LV. Mariel Hemingway, Eric Roberts, Cliff Robertson, David Clennon, Josh Mostel, Roger Rees, Carroll Baker; **D:** Bob Fosse; **C:** Sven Nykvist; **M:** Ralph Burns. *WAR*

Star Hunter 🎬½ 1995 (R) When a bus filled with football players and cheerleaders takes a wrong turn, it winds up in an intergalactic hunting ground where the humans become the prey. Lots of lame chase and would-be action scenes. 80m/C VHS. Roddy McDowall, Stella Stevens, Ken Stott, Zack Ward, Wendy Schumacher; **D:** Cole McKay. *NHO*

A Star Is Born 🎬🎬🎬 1937 A movie star declining in popularity marries a shy girl and helps her become a star. Her fame eclipses his and tragic consequences follow. Shows Hollywood-behind-the-scenes machinations. Stunning ending is based on the real-life tragedy of silent film star Wallace Reid, who died of a morphine overdose in 1923 at age 31. Remade twice, in 1954 and 1976. 111m/C VHS, Beta, LV. Janet Gaynor, Fredric March, Adolphe Menjou, May Robson, Andy Devine, Lionel Stander, Franklin Pangborn; **D:** William A. Wellman; **W:** William A. Wellman, David O. Selznick, Dorothy Parker; **C:** William Howard Greene; **M:** Max Steiner. Academy Awards '37: Best Story; Nominations: Academy Awards '37:

Best Actor (March), Best Actress (Gaynor), Best Director (Wellman), Best Picture. *GNG, NOS, VYY*

A Star Is Born 🎬🎬🎬½ 1954 (PG) Aging actor helps a young actress to fame. She becomes his wife, but alcoholism and failure are too much for him. She honors his memory. Remake of the 1937 classic was Garland's triumph, a superb and varied performance. Newly restored version reinstates over 20 minutes of long-missing footage, including three Garland musical numbers. 🎵I'll Get By; You Took Advantage of me; Black Bottom; Peanut Vendor; My Melancholy Baby; Swanee; It's A New World; Gotta Have Me Go With You; Somewhere There's Someone. 175m/C VHS, Beta, LV. Judy Garland, James Mason, Jack Carson, Tommy Noonan, Charles Bickford, Emerson Treacy, Charles Halton; **D:** George Cukor; **C:** Sam Leavitt. Golden Globe Awards '55: Best Actor—Musical/Comedy (Mason), Best Actress—Musical/Comedy (Garland); Nominations: Academy Awards '54: Best Actor (Mason), Best Actress (Garland), Best Art Direction/Set Decoration (Color), Best Costume Design (Color), Best Song ("The Man That Got Away"), Scoring of a Musical. *WAR*

A Star Is Born 🎬🎬 1976 (R) Miserable update of the 1937 and 1954 classics permitting Ms. Streisand to showcase her hit song "Evergreen." The tragic story of one rock star (the relentlessly un-hip Streisand) on her way to the top and another (good old boy Kristofferson) whose career is in decline. Kristofferson is miscast, Streisand eventually numbing, but film may interest those looking into big-budget, big-star misfires. 🎵Watch Closely Now; Spanish Lies; Hellacious Acres; With One More Look At You; Woman in the Moon; Queen Bee; Everything; Crippled Cow; I Believe in Love. 140m/C VHS, Beta. Barbra Streisand, Kris Kristofferson, Paul Mazursky, Gary Busey, Sally Kirkland, Oliver Clark, Marta Heflin, Robert Englund; **D:** Frank Pierson; **W:** Frank Pierson, Joan Didion, John Gregory Dunne; **C:** Robert L. Surtees; **M:** Paul Williams. Academy Awards '76: Best Song ("Evergreen"); Golden Globe Awards '77: Best Actor—Musical/Comedy (Kristofferson), Best Actress—Musical/Comedy (Streisand), Best Film—Musical/Comedy, Best Song ("Evergreen"), Best Score; Nominations: Academy Awards '76: Best Cinematography, Best Sound, Original Song Score and/or Adaptation. *WAR*

Star Kid 🎬🎬🎬 *The Warrior of Waverly Street* 1997 (PG) Twelve-year-old Spencer Griffith (Mazzello) is the new wimp in town, with a face that immediately attracts the fists of the biggest bully around, Turbo Bradley (Simmrin). On the run from Turbo, Spencer encounters Cy, an experimental cyber-battlesuit built by cutesy good aliens to save themselves from reptilian bad aliens. After inserting himself into Cy, and solving a few problems common to boy-inside-alien relationships, Spencer takes his first awkward steps, gets some humorous revenge on Turbo, and learns some lessions about confronting one's fears and accepting responsibility. Film delivers enough action and effects to keep everyone happy. 101m/C VHS, LV, DVD. Joseph Mazzello, Alex Daniels, Richard Gilliland, Joey Simmrin, Brian Simpson, Danny Masterson, Corinne Bohrer; **D:** Manny Coto; **W:** Manny Coto; **C:** Ronn Schmidt; **M:** Nicholas Pike. *THV*

Star Knight 🎬 *Starknight* 1985 (PG-13) Weird combo of sci fi and medieval romance. A spaceship lands near a European castle and the local princess falls for one of the visitors—much to her daddy's dismay. Very silly. 92m/C VHS, LV, Closed Caption. **SP** Harvey Keitel, Klaus Kinski, Fernando Rey; **D:** Fernando Colombo. *THV*

The Star Maker 🎬🎬 *The Star Man; L'Uomo delle Stelle* 1995 (R) Con man Joe Morelli (Castellitto) travels through the villages of 1950s Sicily claiming to be a movie talent scout. For a fee, he offers the locals a chance to shoot a screen test, which reveals various bits and pieces of their lives. There's a brief romance and Joe's scam eventually comes to light but the story's more nostalgia than narrative. Italian with subtitles. **CW:** Some strong sexuality, language and a brutal beating. 107m/C VHS, LV, Closed Caption. *IT* Sergio

Castellitto, Tiziana Lodato; **D:** Giuseppe Tornatore; **W:** Giuseppe Tornatore, Fabio Rinaudo, C. Dante Spinotti; **M:** Ennio Morricone. Nominations: Academy Awards '95: Best Foreign Language Film. *TOU*

Star Maps 🎬🎬 1997 (R) Ambitious and ambiguous effort from first-time director Arteta has boyish Carlos (Spain) chase his dreams of movie stardom on the streets of Hollywood. Pimped by his manipulative and brutal father Pepe (Figueroa), Carlos sells "maps of the stars' homes" as a cover for his real job, male prostitute. Dad's hooker mistress (Murphy) mentors him in the family business. Add in a mother (Velez) "recovering" from a nervous breakdown by talking to long-dead Mexican comedy star Cantinflas, and a brother (Chandler) who acts out scenes from Mexican wrestling movies, and it's a wonder he doesn't make his screen debut on Jerry Springer. Despite fine performances and a solid debut effort from Arteta, the tragic elements don't fit well with the attempted comic tone of the rest of the movie. **CW:** Strong sexuality and language, and for violence. 80m/C VHS, LV, Closed Caption. Douglas Spain, Efrain Figueroa, Lysa Flores, Kandeyce Jensen, Martha Velez, Annette Murphy, Vincent Chandler, Al Vincente, Herbert Siguenza, Robin Thomas, Jeff Michalski; **D:** Miguel Arteta; **W:** Miguel Arteta; **C:** Chuy Chavez; **M:** Lysa Flores. Nominations: Independent Spirit Awards '98: Best First Feature, Best Supporting Actor (Figueroa), Debut Performance (Spain, Flores). *FOX*

Star of Midnight 🎬🎬 1935 A lawyer/detective becomes involved in the disappearance of the leading lady in a Broadway show and the murder of a columnist. Powell and Rogers take on characters similar to Nick and Nora Charles, but the pizazz of the "Thin Man" series is missing. 90m/B VHS, Beta, LV. Ginger Rogers, William Powell, Paul Kelly; **D:** Stephen Roberts. *TTC*

The Star Packer 🎬🎬 1934 Wayne puts on a marshal's badge, straightens out a gang of crooks, and still finds time for romance. Implausible and kind of dull early Wayne vehicle. 53m/B VHS, Beta. John Wayne, George "Gabby" Hayes, Earl Dwire, Yakima Canutt; **D:** Robert North Bradbury. *COL, REP, NOS*

Star Portal 🎬🎬 1997 (R) Alien Rena (Massey) comes to Earth seeking blood to help her dying race. Assuming the form of a babe, she falls in love with a hematologist (Bauer), and must battle a law-enforcer from her own planet. **CW:** Violence, sexual situations, nudity. 83m/C VHS. Athena Massey, Steven Bauer, Stephen Davies, Anthony Crivello; **D:** Jon Purdy. *NHO*

Star Quest 🎬 *Beyond the Rising Moon; Space 2074* 1989 A genetically engineered woman fights for freedom from her corporate creators. Mediocre effects and some pointless action; done much better by Ridley Scott in "Blade Runner." 90m/C VHS, Beta, LV. Tracy Davis, Hans Bachman, Michael Mack; **D:** Phillip Cook. *NO*

Star Quest 🎬🎬½ 1994 (R) Eight astronauts, suspended in a cryogenic sleep for nearly 100 years, awaken to find the human race has been destroyed by a nuclear holocaust. 95m/C VHS, LV. Steven Bauer, Emma Samms, Alan Rachins, Brenda Bakke, Ming-Na Wen, Gregory McKinney, Cliff DeYoung; **D:** Rick Jacobson. *NHO*

Star Reporter 🎬½ 1939 A son takes over his father's newspaper when dad is killed by gangsters. The son uses the paper in an attempt to destroy the underworld, but stumbles on some startling personal information that could drastically backfire on him. Generally interesting plot, but has some implausibility and too-broad characterization. 62m/B VHS, Beta. Warren Hull, Marsha Hunt, Morgan Wallace, Clay Clement, Wallis Clark, Virginia Howell, Paul Fix, Joseph Crehan; **D:** Howard Bretherton. *SNC*

Star Slammer 🎬½ 1987 (R) A beautiful woman is unjustly sentenced to a brutal intergalactic prison ship. She leads the convicts to escape amid zany situations. Unevenly funny sci-fi comedy. **85m/C VHS, Beta, LV.** Ross Hagen, John Carradine, Sandy Brooke, Aldo Ray; **D:** Fred Olen Ray. *THV*

Star Spangled Girl ♂½ 1971 (G) One of
Neil Simon's lesser plays, one of his least movies. A pert, patriotic young lady captures the hearts of two left-wing alternative-newspaperguys next door; their political conflicts never rise above bland sitcom level. **94m/C VHS, Closed Caption.** Sandy Duncan, Tony Roberts, Todd Susman, Elizabeth Allen; **D:** Jerry Paris; **W:** Neil Simon; **C:** Sam Leavitt; **M:** Charles Fox. *PAR*

Star Spangled Rhythm ♂♂♂ 1942
Movie studio guard (Moore) has told his son (Bracken), a sailor, that he's actually the head of the studio in this WW2 musical/comedy. When he learns his son and his pals are coming for a visit, he enlists the aid of a friendly studio switchboard operator (Hutton) to pull a fast one. (Luckily, the real studio boss is out of town). Plot doesn't matter anyway since its just an excuse for a lot of studio stars to show up and perform. ♪ A Sweater, a Sarong and a Peek-a-Boo Bang; That Old Black Magic; Hit the Road to Dreamland; Old Glory; On the Swing Shift; Doing It for Defense; Sharp as a Tack; He Loved Me Till the All-Clear Came. **99m/B VHS.** Betty Hutton, Eddie Bracken, Victor Moore, Bing Crosby, Ray Milland, Bob Hope, Veronica Lake, Dorothy Lamour, Susan Hayward, Dick Powell, Mary Martin, Alan Ladd, Paulette Goddard, Cecil B. DeMille, Arthur Treacher, Preston Sturges, Eddie Anderson, William Bendix; **D:** George Marshall. Nominations: Academy Awards '43: Best Song ("That Old Black Magic"), Scoring of a Musical. *USH*

Star Time ♂½ 1992 Henry is a mentally ill
loser who wants to be as happy and famous as his favorite TV stars. Deciding to kill himself, Henry is stopped by the mysterious Sam Bones, who offers him TV stardom—at a steep price. Henry achieves his 15 minutes of fame as a serial killer and his only link to reality is a female social worker. **85m/C VHS.** Michael St. Gerard, John P. Ryan, Maureen Teefy; **D:** Alexander Cassini; **W:** Alexander Cassini; **C:** Fernando Arguelles. *MNC*

Star Trek: The Motion
Picture ♂♂½ 1980 (G) The Enterprise fights a strange alien force that threatens Earth in this first film adaptation of the famous television series. Very slow moving; followed by numerous sequels. Twelve additional minutes of previously unseen footage have been added to this home video version of the theatrical feature. The laserdisc edition offers the film in widescreen format. **143m/C VHS, Beta, LV, Closed Caption.** William Shatner, Leonard Nimoy, DeForest Kelley, James Doohan, Stephen Collins, Persis Khambatta, Nichelle Nichols, Walter Koenig, George Takei; **D:** Robert Wise; **M:** Jerry Goldsmith. Nominations: Academy Awards '79: Best Art Direction/Set Decoration, Best Original Score. *PAR*

Star Trek 2: The Wrath of
Khan ♂♂♂ 1982 (PG) Picking up from the 1967 Star Trek episode "Space Seed," Admiral James T. Kirk and the crew of the Enterprise must battle Khan, an old foe out for revenge. Warm and comradly in the nostalgic mode of its successors. Introduced Kirk's former lover and unknown son to the series plot, as well as Mr. Spock's "death," which led to the next sequel (1984's "The Search for Spock"). Can be seen in widescreen format on laserdisc. **113m/C VHS, Beta, LV, 8mm, Letterbox, Closed Caption.** William Shatner, Leonard Nimoy, Ricardo Montalban, DeForest Kelley, Nichelle Nichols, James Doohan, George Takei, Walter Koenig, Kirstie Alley, Merritt Butrick, Paul Winfield; **D:** Nicholas Meyer; **M:** James Horner. *PAR*

Star Trek 3: The Search for
Spock ♂♂½ 1984 (PG) Captain Kirk hijacks the USS Enterprise and commands the aging crew to go on a mission to the Genesis Planet to discover whether Mr. Spock still lives (supposedly he died in the last movie). Klingons threaten, as usual. Somewhat slow and humorless, but intriguing. Third in the series of six (so far) Star Trek movies. The laserdisc edition carries the film in widescreen format. **105m/C VHS, Beta, LV, 8mm,**

Letterbox, Closed Caption. William Shatner, Leonard Nimoy, DeForest Kelley, James Doohan, George Takei, Walter Koenig, Mark Lenard, Robin Curtis, Merritt Butrick, Christopher Lloyd, Judith Anderson, John Larroquette, James B. Sikking, Nichelle Nichols, Cathie Shirriff, Miguel Ferrer, Grace Lee Whitney; **D:** Leonard Nimoy; **W:** Harve Bennett; **M:** James Horner. *PAR*

Star Trek 4: The Voyage
Home ♂♂♂ 1986 (PG) Kirk and the gang go back in time (to the 1980s, conveniently) to save the Earth of the future from destruction. Filled with hilarious moments and exhilarating action; great special effects enhance the timely conservation theme. Watch for the stunning going-back-in-time sequence. Spock is particularly funny as he tries to fit in and learn the '80s lingo! Can be seen in widescreen format on laserdisc. Also available as part of Paramount's "director's series," in which Nimoy discusses various special effects aspects in the making of the film. The best in the six-part (so far) series. **119m/C VHS, Beta, LV, 8mm, Letterbox, Closed Caption.** William Shatner, DeForest Kelley, Catherine Hicks, James Doohan, Nichelle Nichols, George Takei, Walter Koenig, Mark Lenard, Leonard Nimoy; **D:** Leonard Nimoy; **W:** Nicholas Meyer, Harve Bennett. Nominations: Academy Awards '86: Best Cinematography, Best Sound, Best Original Score. *PAR*

Star Trek 5: The Final Frontier ♂½
1989 (PG) A renegade Vulcan kidnaps the Enterprise and takes it on a journey to the mythic center of the universe. Shatner's big-action directorial debut (he also co-wrote the script) is a poor follow-up to the Nimoy-directed fourth entry in the series. Heavy-handed and pretentiously pseudo-theological. Available in widescreen format on laserdisc. **107m/C VHS, Beta, LV, 8mm, Letterbox, Closed Caption.** William Shatner, Leonard Nimoy, DeForest Kelley, James Doohan, Laurence Luckinbill, Walter Koenig, George Takei, Nichelle Nichols, David Warner; **D:** William Shatner; **W:** William Shatner; **M:** Jerry Goldsmith. Golden Raspberry Awards '89: Worst Picture, Worst Actor (Shatner), Worst Director (Shatner). *PAR*

Star Trek 6: The Undiscovered
Country ♂♂½ 1991 (PG) The final chapter in the long running Star Trek series is finally here. The Federation and the Klingon Empire are preparing a much-needed peace summit but Captain Kirk has his doubts about the true intentions of the Federation's longtime enemies. When a Klingon ship is attacked, Kirk and the crew of the Enterprise, who are accused of the misdeed, must try to find the real perpetrator. Has an exciting, climactic ending. As is typical of the series, the film highlights current events—glasnost—in its plotlines. Meyer also directed Star Trek movie 2 ("The Wrath of Khan") and wrote the screenplay for 4 ("The Voyage Home"). **110m/C VHS, Beta, CD-I, Closed Caption.** William Shatner, Leonard Nimoy, DeForest Kelley, James Doohan, George Takei, Walter Koenig, Nichelle Nichols, Christopher Plummer, Kim Cattrall, Iman, David Warner, Mark Lenard, Grace Lee Whitney, Brock Peters, Kurtwood Smith, Rosana De Soto, John Schuck, Michael Dorn; **D:** Nicholas Meyer; **W:** Nicholas Meyer, Denny Martin Flinn; **M:** Cliff Eidelman. Nominations: Academy Awards '91: Best Makeup. *PAR*

Star Trek Bloopers 1969 The television
cast of "Star Trek" appears in these flubs and goofs that were edited out of the actual episodes. The blooper reels from all three seasons are included on this tape. **25m/C VHS, Beta.** William Shatner, Leonard Nimoy, DeForest Kelley, Nichelle Nichols, James Doohan, George Takei, Walter Koenig, Frank Gorshin. *MOV*

Star Trek Deep Space Nine:
Emissary 1993 The second "Star Trek" spin-off, following "The Next Generation," finds Federation Commander Benjamin Sisko (Brooks) arriving at the space station, which orbits the planet Bajor. Bajor has just undergone a war of independence against the Cardassians, who have left both the planet and the station in a devastated condition. Sisko, naturally, must find a way to deal with a variety of unpleasant situations, crew, and

station residents. The TV pilot is considered episodes one and two of the series; additional episodes are also available. **92m/C VHS, Beta.** Avery Brooks, Colm Meaney, Rene Auberjonois, Nana Visitor, Terry Farrell, Alexander Siddig, Armin Shimerman, Cirroc Lofton. *PAR*

Star Trek: First Contact ♂♂♂ 1996
(PG-13) The eighth big-screen Trek saga is firmly in the hands of the "Next Generation" cast as Picard and the Enterprise cross paths with the Borg and their sinister Queen. It's hard to tell whether the cry "Resistance is Futile" is coming from the Borg, or the Trek franchise itself, as this installment may well bring in new "Trekkers" with its "less techo-babble, more action" approach and the fact that this crew can act. The Borg attempt to change history by travelling back in time (to 2063) to prevent scientist Cromwell from inventing warp drive. While the less-interesting members of the crew stay on Earth to help out with the launch, the battle for the Enterprise rages on up in space. Trademark effects, humor, and idealism are in abundant supply and should please the long-time fan as well as the neophyte. **CW:** Some sci-fi adventure violence. **111m/C VHS, Beta, Closed Caption.** Patrick Stewart, Jonathon Frakes, Brent Spiner, LeVar Burton, Michael Dorn, Marina Sirtis, Gates McFadden, Alfre Woodard, James Cromwell, Alice Krige, Neal McDonough, Robert Picardo, Dwight Schultz; **D:** Jonathon Frakes; **W:** Brannon Braga, Ronald D. Moore; **C:** Matthew F. Leonetti; **M:** Jerry Goldsmith. Nominations: Academy Awards '96: Best Makeup. *PAR*

Star Trek Generations ♂♂♂ 1994 (PG)
The sci-fi phenomena continues with the first film spun off from the recently departed "Star Trek: The Next Generation" TV series and the seventh following the adventures of the Enterprise crew. Captain Kirk is propelled into the future thanks to an explosion and manages to hook up with current starship captain, Picard. Of course, just in time to save the galaxy from the latest space loon, the villainous Dr. Soren (McDowell), renegade Klingons, and your basic mysterious space entity. For comic relief, android Data gets an emotion chip. Terrific special effects (courtesy of Industrial Light and Magic) and yes, the heroic Kirk receives his mandatory grandiose death scene. Other original characters making a brief appearance are Scotty and Chekov. An entertaining romp through time and space. **117m/C VHS, Beta, Closed Caption.** William Shatner, Patrick Stewart, Malcolm McDowell, Whoopi Goldberg, Jonathon Frakes, Brent Spiner, LeVar Burton, Michael Dorn, Gates McFadden, Marina Sirtis, James Doohan, Walter Koenig, Alan Ruck; **D:** David Carson; **W:** Ronald D. Moore, Brannon Braga; **C:** John A. Alonzo; **M:** Dennis McCarthy. *PAR*

Star Trek: The Cage 1965 This cult se-
ries only ran from 1966-69 but it's impact has been lasting. Join Captain Kirk and the crew of the starship Enterprise on its voyages of discovery. Additional episodes available. In this original pilot episode for the series Captain Chris Pike of the Enterprise faces the challenge of his life when he is captured by the telepathic aliens of Talos IV. Never telecast in its original form and later edited to form the flashback sequences of the two-part episode "Menagerie." Some portions are in black and white. Version was long believed to be lost, but was reconstituted from original color footage. **73m/C VHS, Beta, LV.** Jeffrey Hunter, Leonard Nimoy, Susan Oliver, Majel Barrett, Meg Wyllie, John Hoyt, Gene Roddenberry; **D:** Robert Butler. *PAR, MOV*

Star Trek the Next Generation:
Encounter at Farpoint 1987 Roddenberry, the creator of the original "Star Trek" television series, spearheaded this episodic reincarnation for network syndication. Set 80 or so years beyond the original, with an entirely new crew and a modernized vessel, it places less emphasis on violent solutions to conflicts than the original TV series. In this first installment, a powerful life force named "Q" threatens the lives of Captain Picard and his crew as they attempt to figure out what's

going on at Farpoint Station. Look for a cameo by Kelley "Bones" from the original series, as a very old man waxing nostalgic about the old U.S.S. Enterprise. Excellent production values, including fine special effects. Additional episodes available. **96m/C VHS, LV, Closed Caption.** Patrick Stewart, Michael Dorn, Jonathan Frakes, Gates McFadden, Marina Sirtis, Denise Crosby, Brent Spiner, Wil Wheaton, LeVar Burton; *Cameos:* DeForest Kelley; *W:* Gene Roddenberry. *PAR, MOV*

Star Trek the Next Generation, the Final Episode: All Good Things...

1994 Since Q (de Lancie) was there to cause trouble in the first series episode, it seems only fitting that he's up to his usual tricks in the finale. A spatial anomaly has Picard time-traveling between past, present, and future with the very fate of humanity resting on his shoulders—and Q around to tell him that everyone's doomed. **92m/C VHS, Beta, Closed Caption.** Patrick Stewart, LeVar Burton, Brent Spiner, Marina Sirtis, Jonathon Frakes, Gates McFadden, Michael Dorn, John de Lancie, Denise Crosby, Colm Meaney, Andreas Katsulas; *D:* Winrich Kolbe; *W:* Ronald D. Moore, Brannon Braga. *PAR*

Star Trek Voyager: Caretaker 1995

The third TV spinoff from the franchise sci-fi series features the 24th century adventures of Captain Kathryn Janeway (Mulgrew) and the USS Voyager. In the pilot episode, the crew is searching for Maquis rebels in an area of space known as the Badlands when the ship is mysteriously tossed 70,000 lightyears across the galaxy. The Voyager does find the Maquis ship, as well as an alien named Nelix (Phillips) and a planet run by a force called the Caretaker, whose inhabitants all live underground. This episode is currently available only as part of "The Captains Collection," a four-tape set. **92m/C VHS, Closed Caption.** Kate Mulgrew, Robert Beltran, Robert Picardo, Ethan Phillips, Roxann Biggs-Dawson, Robert Duncan McNeill, Tim Russ, Jennifer Lien, Garrett Wang; *D:* Winrich Kolbe. *PAR*

Star Wars 🎬🎬🎬🎬 1977 (PG) First entry

Lucas's "Star Wars" trilogy proved to be one of the biggest boxoffice hits of all time. A young hero, a captured princess, a hot-shot pilot, cute robots, a vile villain, and a heroic and mysterious Jedi knight blend together with marvelous special effects in a fantasy tale about rebel forces engaged in a life or death struggle with the tyrant leaders of the Galactic Empire. Set a new cinematic standard for realistic special effects, making many pre-"Star Wars" effects seem almost laughable in retrospect. Followed by "The Empire Strikes Back" (1980) and "Return of the Jedi" (1983). **121m/C VHS, Beta, LV, Letterbox, Closed Caption.** Mark Hamill, Carrie Fisher, Harrison Ford, Alec Guinness, Peter Cushing, Kenny Baker, James Earl Jones, David Prowse, Anthony Daniels; *D:* George Lucas; *W:* George Lucas; *M:* John Williams. Academy Awards '77: Best Art Direction/Set Decoration, Best Costume Design, Best Film Editing, Best Sound, Best Visual Effects, Best Original Score; Golden Globe Awards '78: Best Score; Los Angeles Film Critics Association Awards '77: Best Film, National Film Registry '89;:; Nominations: Academy Awards '77: Best Director (Lucas), Best Original Screenplay, Best Picture, Best Supporting Actor (Guinness). *FOX, RDG, HMV*

Starbird and Sweet William 🎬🎬

1973 (G) On a solo plane flight, a young Native American crashes in the wilderness. He must fight for survival in the harsh woods with his only friend, a bear cub. Good family fare. **95m/C VHS.** A. Martinez, Louise Fitch, Dan Haggerty, Skip Homeier; *D:* Jack B. Hively. *NO*

Starchaser: The Legend of Orin 🎬🎬½ 1985 (PG) Animated fantasy about a boy who must save the world of the future from malevolent hordes. **107m/C VHS, Beta, LV.** *D:* Steven Hahn; *M:* Andrew Belling. *PAR*

Stardust Memories 🎬🎬½ 1980 (PG) Allen's "8 1/2." A comic filmmaker is plagued with creative blocks, relationships, modern fears and fanatical fans. The last film in Allen's varying self-

analysis, with explicit references to Fellini and Antonioni. **88m/B VHS, Beta, LV.** Woody Allen, Charlotte Rampling, Jessica Harper, Marie-Christine Barrault, Tony Roberts, Helen Hanft, Cynthia Gibb, Amy Wright, Daniel Stern; *D:* Woody Allen; *W:* Woody Allen; *C:* Gordon Willis. *MGM, FOX*

The Starfighters 🎬½ 1963 Air Force Lieutenant Dornan must prove his courage to his disapproving war hero Congressman father. Dornan flies his F-104 through a dangerous storm, thereby earning his father's respect, which leads them to form a bond. **84m/C VHS, Beta.** Robert Dornan, Richard Jordahl, Shirley Olmstead. *NO*

Starflight One 🎬🎬 Starflight: the Plane that Couldn't Land 1983 A space shuttle is called on to save the world's first hypersonic airliner trapped in an orbit above earth. The film features good special effects, but also a predictable "rescue-mission" plot. **155m/C VHS, Beta.** Ray Milland, Lee Majors, Hal Linden, Lauren Hutton, Robert Webber, Terry Kiser; *D:* Jerry Jameson. *ART, VES*

Stargate 🎬🎬 1994 (PG-13) U.S. military probe of a ring-shaped ancient Egyptian artifact (your tax dollars at work) sends he-man colonel Russell and geeky Egyptologist Spader into a parallel universe. There they meet the builders of the pyramids who are enslaved by an evil despot (Davidson) posing as a sun god. Ambitious premise zapped from prepubescent imaginations gets an A for effort, but a silly plot that jumbles biblical epic panoramas and space odyssey special effects with otherworldly mysticism and needless emotional hang-ups trade shlock for style. Spader's shaggy scholar is neurotically fun, Russell's jarhead a bore, and Davidson's vampy villain an unintended hoot. *CW:* Sci-fi action violence. **119m/ C VHS, LV, Closed Caption, DVD.** Kurt Russell, James Spader, Jaye Davidson, Viveca Lindfors, Alexis Cruz, Leon Rippy, John Diehl, Erik Avari, Mili Avital; *D:* Roland Emmerich; *W:* Dean Devlin, Roland Emmerich; *C:* Jeff Okun. *ART*

Starhops 🎬½ 1978 (R) A trio of buxom young women attract business to their drive-in restaurant by wearing skimpy outfits. Surprisingly inoffensive for an "R" rating. **92m/C VHS.** Dorothy Buhrman, Sterling Frazier, Jillian Kesner, Peter Paul Liapis, Paul Ryan, Anthony Mannino, Dick Miller; *D:* Barbara Peeters; *W:* Stephanie Rothman. *NO*

Stark 🎬½ 1985 Wichita detective journeys to Las Vegas in an effort to locate his missing sister. During his search, he finds himself taking on the mob. A television pilot for a series that never happened, and Tidyman's last screenplay. A sequel, "Stark: Mirror Image," was made in 1986. **94m/C VHS, Beta, Closed Caption.** Nicolas Surovy, Dennis Hopper, Marilu Henner, Seth Jaffe; *D:* Rod Holcomb; *W:* Ernest Tidyman. *FOX*

Starlight 🎬½ 1997 Alien envoy searches for a genetic component (found in a half-alien/half-human hybrid) that will allow her people to live in a post-apocalytic Earth's polluted atmosphere. **100m/C VHS.** Rae Dawn Chong, Willie Nelson, Billy Wirth, Jim Byrnes, Deborah Wakeham; *D:* Jonathan Kay. *MNC*

Starlight Hotel 🎬🎬½ 1990 (PG) An unhappy teenage girl sets off to find her father, with the help of a shellshocked veteran wrongly accused of a crime. Set in New Zealand during the Depression. Lovely scenery and good acting highlight nice story of odd friendship. **90m/C VHS, LV.** *NZ* Greer Robson, Peter Phelps, Marshall Napier, Pat Smythe, Alice Fraser; *D:* Sam Pillsbury. *REP*

Starman 🎬🎬🎬 1984 (PG) An alien from an advanced civilization lands in Wisconsin. He hides beneath the guise of a grieving young widow's recently deceased husband. He then makes her drive him across country to rendezvous with his spacecraft so he can return home. Well-acted, interesting twist on the "Stranger in a Strange Land" theme. Bridges is fun as the likeable starman; Allen is lovely and earthy in her worthy follow-up to "Raiders of the Lost Ark." Available in widescreen format on laserdisc. **115m/C VHS, Beta, LV, Letterbox, Closed Caption.** Jeff Bridges, Karen Allen,

Charles Martin Smith, Richard Jaeckel; *D:* John Carpenter; *W:* Bruce A. Evans, Raynold Gideon, *C:* Donald M. Morgan; *M:* Jack Nitzsche. Nominations: Academy Awards '84: Best Actor (Bridges). *COL*

Starring Bugs Bunny! 1948 Bug Bunny teams up with Yosemite Sam and others in some of these great hits. Friz Freleng's "Buccaneer Bunny" and "Hare Force," as well as Chuck Jones' "Hare Tonic." **54m/C VHS.** *D:* Isadore "Friz" Freleng, Chuck Jones, Robert McKimson. *MGM*

Stars and Bars 🎬🎬 1988 (R) O'Connor misfire strands Day-Lewis in the midst of hillbilies. A stuffy English art expert travels from New York to Georgia to price a Renoir, and happens on a bizarre backwoods family marginally run by Stanton. Stereotypical pursuit of humor teeters precariously on the edge of black comedy without actually being funny. Stinky script dooms fine cast to just acting weird in a "Deliverance" sort of way. Based on the novel by William Boyd. **95m/C VHS, Beta, LV, Closed Caption.** Daniel Day-Lewis, Harry Dean Stanton, John Cusack, Joan Cusack, Spalding Gray, Will Patton, Martha Plimpton, Glenne Headly, Laurie Metcalf, Maury Chaykin; *D:* Pat O'Connor; *W:* William Boyd. *COL*

Stars and Stripes Forever 🎬🎬🎬

Marching Along 1952 Sumptious, Hollywoodized bio of composer John Phillip Sousa, based on his memoir "Marching Along," but more concerned with the romantic endeavors of young protege Wagner. Accuracy aside, it's solid entertainment even if you're not mad about march music. ♫Stars and Stripes Forever; El Capitan; Washington Post; King Cotton; The Battle Hymn of the Republic; Dixie; Light Cavalry; Turkey in the Straw; Hail to the Chief. **89m/C VHS, Closed Caption.** Clifton Webb, Debra Paget, Robert Wagner, Ruth Hussey, Finlay Currie; *D:* Henry Koster. *FCT*

The Stars Fell on Henrietta 🎬🎬½

1994 (PG) Down-on-his-luck wildcatter Mr. Cox (Duvall) searches for oil and redemption. He's looking for it on the failing farm of couple Don and Cora Day (Quinn and Fisher) in the middle of the 1930s Texas dustbowl with the reluctant backing of more successful oil man (Dennehy). Quiet character study of an obsessed wheeler-dealer playing with his last poker chip verges on the romantic in its quest for black gold, true to its message about never giving up hope. Directorial debut for Keach is led by typically excellent portrayals by Duvall and Dennehy, but Quinn and Fisher are given little to work with. Marks the first movie Clint Eastwood's Malpaso company has produced in which he didn't star or direct since "Ratboy." **110m/C VHS.** Robert Duvall, Aidan Quinn, Frances Fisher, Brian Dennehy, Lexi Randall, Kaylyn Knowles, Francesca Ruth Eastwood; *D:* James Keach; *W:* Philip Railsback; *C:* Bruce Surtees; *M:* David Benoit. *WAR*

Stars in My Crown 🎬🎬🎬 1950 McCrea provides a moving performance as the pistol-wielding preacher who helps the residents of a 19th-century small town battle a typhoid epidemic and KKK terrorism. Adapted from the novel by Joe David Brown. **89m/B VHS, Closed Caption.** Joel McCrea, Ellen Drew, Dean Stockwell, Alan Hale, Lewis Stone, Amanda Blake, Juano Hernandez, Charles Kemper, Connie Gilchrist, Ed Begley Sr., James Arness, Jack Lambert, Arthur Hunnicutt; *D:* Jacques Tourneur; *W:* Margaret Fitts; *M:* Adolph Deutsch. *MGM*

The Stars Look Down 🎬🎬🎬 1939 A mine owner forces miners to work in unsafe conditions in a Welsh town and disaster strikes. Redgrave is a miner's son running for office, hoping to improve conditions, and to escape the hard life. Forceful, well-directed effort suffered at the boxoffice, in competition with John Ford's similar classic "How Green Was My Valley." From the novel by A.J. Cronin. The original British version was released at 110 minutes. **96m/B VHS, Beta.** *GB* Michael Redgrave, Margaret Lockwood, Emlyn Williams, Cecil Parker; *D:* Carol Reed. *NOS, HHT, CAB*

Starship 🎬 *Lorca and the Outlaws* **1987 (PG)** British sci-fi seems to be an oxymoron. To wit, this lame "Star Wars" ripoff is about human slaves on a planet run by evil robots. **91m/C VHS, Beta.** *GB* John Tarrant, Cassandra Webb, Donough Rees, Deep Roy, Ralph Cotterill; *D:* Roger Christian. *HHE*

Starship Invasions 🎬 **1977 (PG)** Lee leads a group of bad aliens seeking to take over the Earth. He's thwarted by UFO expert Vaughn, who is aided by a group of good aliens. Cheesy special effects have this one looking like a bad sci-fi serial from the '40s. **89m/C VHS.** *CA* Christopher Lee, Robert Vaughn, Daniel Pilon, Helen Shaver, Henry Ramer, Victoria (Vicki) Johnson; *D:* Edward Hunt; *W:* Edward Hunt. *WAR*

Starship Troopers 🎬🎬🎬 **1997 (R)** As Bugs Bunny would say, "Of course you know, this means war!" Giant arachnids prove to be an invincible opponent with zero tolerance for things with less than four legs in Verhoeven's comic-book styled, epic slaughter fest. The futuristic, fascist, co-ed Moblie Infantry, led by renegade Commander Rasczak (Ironside), does battle with the sinister arthropods, usually resulting in much human bloodshed. The high body count includes many young actors, but unlike Verhoeven's "Showgirls," their careers should remain relatively unscathed. The acting is straight out of a Mattel toy factory, but the action and confrontations with the enemy insects are a thrill thanks to computer animated special effects. Cheesy, bloody good fun, if you can ignore the fact that fascists are portrayed as the good guys. Based on the 1959 novel by Robert A. Heinlein. *CW:* Graphic sci-fi violence and gore, and for some language and nudity. **129m/C VHS, LV, Closed Caption, DVD.** Caspar Van Dien, Michael Ironside, Neil Patrick Harris, Clancy Brown, Denise Richards, Dina Meyer, Jake Busey, Patrick Muldoon, Seth Gilliam, Rue McClanahan, Marshall Bell, Eric Bruskotter, Blake Lindsley, Anthony Michael Ruivivar, Dean Norris; *D:* Paul Verhoeven; *W:* Edward Neumeier; *C:* Jost Vacano; *M:* Basil Poledouris. Nominations: Academy Awards '97: Best Visual Effects; MTV Movie Awards '98: Best Action Sequence. *COL*

Starstruck 🎬🎬½ **1982 (PG)** Fun-loving folly about a teen who tries to help his talented cousin make it as a singer. Playfully tweeks Hollywood musicals. Enjoyable and fun. **95m/C VHS.** *AU* Jo Kennedy, Ross O'Donovan, Pat Evison; *D:* Gillian Armstrong; *C:* Russell Boyd. *FXL*

Start the Revolution Without Me 🎬🎬🎬 **1970 (PG)** Hilarious, Moliere-esque farce about two sets of identical twins (Wilder and Sutherland) separated at birth, who meet 30 years later, just before the French Revolution. About as hammy as they come; Wilder is unforgettable. Neglected when released, but now deservedly a cult favorite. **91m/C VHS, Beta.** Gene Wilder, Donald Sutherland, Orson Welles, Hugh Griffith, Jack MacGowran, Billie Whitelaw, Victor Spinetti, Ewa Aulin; *D:* Bud Yorkin; *W:* Lawrence J. Cohen; *M:* John Addison. *WAR*

Starting Over 🎬🎬🎬 **1979 (R)** His life racked by divorce, Phil Potter learns what it's like to be single, self-sufficient, and lonely once again. When a blind date grows into a serious affair, the romance is temporarily halted by his hang-up for his ex-wife. Enjoyable love-triangle comedy loses direction after a while, but Reynolds is subtle and charming, and Bergen good as his ex, a very bad songwriter. Based on a novel by Dan Wakefield. **106m/C VHS, Beta, LV.** Burt Reynolds, Jill Clayburgh, Candice Bergen, Frances Sternhagen, Austin Pendleton, Mary Kay Place, Kevin Bacon, Daniel Stern; *D:* Alan J. Pakula; *W:* James L. Brooks; *C:* Sven Nykvist; *M:* Marvin Hamlisch. Nominations: Academy Awards '79: Best Actress (Clayburgh), Best Supporting Actress (Bergen). *PAR*

Starved 🎬½ **1997** Monica (Beaman) thinks she's found a terrific guy in Scott Dawson (Adams). He gives her flowers, writes her romantic notes, and offers her candle lit dinners. So naturally, Monica falls in love. Too bad, Scott's a sociopath. He takes her prisoner, keeps her in his basement, and uses mind games and starvation to try and break Monica's will. Monica's best friend Jane (Zobel) continues to search for her, even after the police have let the case go. But can she find her in time? Based on a true story. **90m/C VHS.** Lee Ann Beaman, Hal Adams, Toni Zobel. *SPC*

Starvengers **1982** Animated adventures with action and excitement meeting futuristic technology, resulting in the high-powered super-intelligence of the robot Starvenger. **105m/C VHS, Beta.** *JP FUS, FHE, TPV*

State Department File 649 🎬½ **1949** Insipid spy drama set in northern China. Mongolian rebels hold U.S. agent Lundigan captive; he hopes to capture a Chinese warlord. **87m/C VHS, Beta.** Virginia Bruce, William Lundigan; *D:* Sam Newfield. *SNC, NOS, DVT*

State Fair 🎬🎬🎬 *It Happened One Summer* **1945** The second version of the glossy slice of Americana about a family at the Iowa State Fair, featuring plenty of great songs by Rodgers and Hammerstein. Adapted from the 1933 screen version of Phil Stong's novel. Remade again in 1962. ♫ It Might as Well Be Spring; It's a Grand Night for Singing; That's For Me; Isn't It Kinda Fun?; All I Owe Iowa; Our State Fair. **100m/C VHS, Beta.** Charles Winninger, Jeanne Crain, Dana Andrews, Vivian Blaine, Dick Haymes, Fay Bainter, Frank McHugh, Percy Kilbride, Donald Meek, William Marshall, Harry (Henry) Morgan; *D:* Walter Lang; *W:* Oscar Hammerstein; *C:* Leon Shamroy; *M:* Richard Rodgers, Oscar Hammerstein. Academy Awards '45: Best Song ("It Might as Well Be Spring"); Nominations: Academy Awards '45: Scoring of a Musical. *FOX*

State Fair 🎬🎬 **1962** The third film version of the story of a farm family who travel to their yearly state fair and experience life. The original songs are still there, but otherwise this is a letdown. Texas setting required dropping the song "All I Owe Iowa." ♫ Our State Fair; It's a Grand Night for Singing; That's for Me; It Might as Well Be Spring; Isn't It Kinda Fun?; More Than Just a Friend; It's the Little Things in Texas; Willing and Eager; This Isn't Heaven. **118m/C VHS, Beta, Closed Caption.** Pat Boone, Ann-Margret, Bobby Darin, Tom Ewell, Alice Faye, Pamela Tiffin, Wally Cox; *D:* Jose Ferrer; *C:* William Mellor. *FOX*

State of Emergency 🎬🎬½ **1994 (R)** John Novelli (Mantegna) is a cynical, overworked emergency-room doctor for an over-crowded, underequipped big-city hospital. His latest casualty is a head trauma case the hospital is ill-prepared to handle and as the patient's condition worsens both doctor and hospital are put at risk. Made for television. *CW:* Language; graphic depiction of emergency room traumas. **97m/C VHS, LV.** Joe Mantegna, Lynn Whitfield, Paul Dooley; *D:* Leslie Linka Glatter; *W:* Susan Black, Dr. Lance Gentile. *HBO*

State of Grace 🎬🎬🎬 **1990 (R)** Irish hood Penn returns to old NYC neighborhood as undercover cop and becomes involved with an Irish Westies mob in a fight for survival as urban renewal encroaches on their Hell's Kitchen turf. Shrinking client base for shakedown schemes and protection rackets forces them to become contract killers for the Italian mafia. Fine performances, with Penn tense but restrained, gang honcho Harris intense, and Oldman chewing up gritty urban scenery as psycho brother of Harris, but the story is long and meandering. Well-choreographed violence. **134m/C VHS, LV, Closed Caption.** Sean Penn, Ed Harris, Gary Oldman, Robin Wright Penn, John Turturro, Burgess Meredith, John C. Reilly; *D:* Phil Joanou; *W:* Dennis McIntyre; *C:* Jordan Cronenweth; *M:* Ennio Morricone. *ORI*

State of Siege 🎬🎬🎬 *Etat de Siege* **1973** Third pairing of Montand and Costa-Gavras, about the real-life death of USAID employee Daniel Mitrione, suspected to be involved in torture and murder in Uruguay in the '60s. Quietly suspenseful, with snazzy editing; conspiracy-theory premise is similar to Stone's "JFK," and similarly disturbing, whether you believe it or not. Dubbed. **119m/C VHS, Beta, LV.** *FR* Yves Montand, Renato Salvatori, O.E. Hasse, Jacques Perrin; *D:* Constantin Costa-Gavras. *COL*

State of the Union 🎬🎬🎬½ *The World and His Wife* **1948** Liberal multimillionaire Tracy is seeking the Republican presidential nomination. His estranged wife (Hepburn) is asked to return so they can masquerade as a loving couple for the sake of his political career. Hepburn tries to help Tracy, as the backstage political machinations erode his personal convictions. Adapted from a highly successful, topical Broadway play; the writers changed dialogue constantly to reflect the news. Capra and his partners at Liberty Pictures originally hoped to cast Gary Cooper and Claudette Colbert. Hepburn and Menjou were at odds politically (over communist witch hunts in Hollywood) but are fine together onscreen. **124m/B VHS, Beta, LV.** Spencer Tracy, Katharine Hepburn, Angela Lansbury, Van Johnson, Adolphe Menjou, Lewis Stone, Howard Smith; *D:* Frank Capra. *USH*

State of Things 🎬🎬🎬 **1982** Ostensibly a mystery involving a film crew trying to remake a B-movie, "The Most Dangerous Man On Earth," but also an in-depth look at the process of filmmaking, a scathing look at nuclear warfare and an homage to Roger Corman and Hollywood at large. An enigmatic, complex film from Wenders prior to his American years. In German with English subtitles; some dialogue in English. **120m/B VHS, Beta, LV.** *GE* Patrick Bauchau, Allen (Goorwitz) Garfield, Isabelle Weingarten, Viva, Samuel Fuller, Paul Getty III, Roger Corman; *D:* Wim Wenders. Venice Film Festival '82: Best Film. *GLV*

Stateline Motel 🎬½ *Last Chance For a Born Loser* **1975 (R)** Cheap Italian ripoff of "The Postman Always Rings Twice," with a surprise ending but little of great interest. **86m/C VHS, Beta.** *IT* Eli Wallach, Ursula Andress, Fabio Testi, Barbara Bach; *D:* Maurizio Lucidi. *NO*

State's Attorney 🎬🎬½ *Cardigan's Last Case* **1931** A burned-out attorney finds himself falling in love with the least likely person, a prostitute he is defending. Contrived, improbable story succumbs to star-quality lead acting from Barrymore. Remade in 1937 with Lee Tracy as "Criminal Lawyer." **79m/B VHS, Beta.** John Barrymore, Jill Esmond, William "Stage" Boyd, Helen Twelvetrees; *D:* George Archainbaud; *M:* Max Steiner. *TTC*

Static 🎬🎬½ **1987 (PG-13)** A strange, disquieting independent film about an eccentric youth who claims to have built a machine through which one can see heaven. Uneven, with some dull stretches. **89m/C VHS, Beta, LV.** Keith Gordon, Amanda Plummer, Bob Gunton, Jane Hoffman, Barton Heyman, Lily Knight; *D:* Mark Romanek; *W:* Keith Gordon, Mark Romanek. *MCG*

Station 🎬🎬½ **1981** A Japanese detective's love affair is corrupted by his ruthless search for a bloodthirsty cop killer. With English subtitles. **130m/C VHS, Beta.** *JP* Ken Takakura, Chieko Baisho; *D:* Yasuo Furuhata. *NO*

The Station 🎬🎬 **1992** A sophisticated woman, who has just abandoned her fiancee, waits in a tiny station for an early train. The only person around is the young and ordinary stationmaster. Gradually the two are drawn together in a number of charming and comic romantic fantasies. In Italian with English subtitles. **92m/C VHS.** *IT* Margherita Buy, Ennio Fantastichini; *D:* Sergio Rubini; *W:* Sergio Rubini. *FXL*

Station West 🎬🎬🎬 **1948** A disguised Army officer is sent to uncover a mystery of hijackers and murderers. Along the way, he meets up with and falls for a beautiful woman who may be involved in the treachery. Good, solid western with a fine cast and plenty of fun action shot against the requisite beautiful western landscapes. Based on the Luke Short story. Also available colorized. **92m/B VHS, Beta.** Dick Powell, Jane Greer, Agnes Moorehead, Burl Ives, Tom Powers, Raymond Burr; *D:* Sidney Lanfield. *CCB, TTC*

The Stationmaster's Wife 🎬🎬½ 1977 In Germay's Weimar Republic a provincial stationmaster's wife expresses her boredom with her pleasant ineffectual husband by having numerous meaningless affairs. Meant to invoke postwar German dread and the fake bourgeois morality which covered political and social resentments. Originally shown as a 200-minute miniseries for German television. In German with English subtitles. 111m/C VHS. GE Elisabeth Trissenaar, Kurt Raab, Gustal Bayrhammer, Bernard Helfrich, Udo Kier, Volker Spengler; D: Rainer Werner Fassbinder; W: Rainer Werner Fassbinder; C: Michael Ballhaus; M: Peer Raben. NYF, FCT

The Statue 🎬 1971 (R) Famed sculptress unveils a nude rendering of her Nobel Prize-winning husband. Much hilarity in the British vein is meant to ensue, but doesn't. Niven is OK, but this empty, plotless farce should have been much shorter. 84m/C VHS, Beta. GB David Niven, Virna Lisi, Robert Vaughn, Ann Bell, John Cleese; D: Rod Amateau.

Stavisky 🎬🎬🎬 1974 Sumptuously lensed story of Serge Stavisky, a con-artist and bon-vivant whose machinations almost brought down the French government when his corruption was exposed in 1934. Belmondo makes as charismatic an antihero as you could find. Excellent score complements the visuals. In French with English subtitles. 117m/C VHS. Jean-Paul Belmondo, Anny Duperey, Charles Boyer, Francois Perier, Gerard Depardieu; D: Alain Resnais; C: Sacha Vierny; M: Stephen Sondheim. New York Film Critics Awards '74: Best Supporting Actor (Boyer).INT

Stay As You Are 🎬½ 1978 Aging French architect Mastroianni has designs on a teenager who may be his illegitimate daughter from an earlier affair. 95m/C VHS, Beta. FR Marcello Mastroianni, Nastassia Kinski, Francesco Rabal; D: Alberto Lattuada. WAR, OM

Stay Awake 🎬 1987 (R) A demon stalks, haunts and tortures eight young girls sleeping together at a secluded Catholic school. Title might be addressed to the viewer, who will be tempted to snooze. 90m/C VHS, Beta, LV. SA Shirley Jane Harris, Tanya Gordon, Jayne Hutton, Heath Porter; D: John Bernard. NLC

Stay Away, Joe 🎬 1968 (PG) The King is a singing half-breed rodeo star who returns to his reservation where he finds love and trouble. Utterly cliche, embarrassing, and stupid even by Elvis-movie standards. 98m/C VHS, Beta. Elvis Presley, Burgess Meredith, Joan Blondell, Thomas Gomez, L.Q. Jones, Katy Jurado, Henry Jones; D: Peter Tewkesbury. MGM

Stay Hungry 🎬🎬🎬 1976 (R) A wealthy southerner (Bridges) is involved in a real estate deal which depends on the sale of a gym where a number of body builders hang out. He becomes immersed in their world and finds himself in love with the working-class Field. Big Arnold's first speaking role in his own inimitable accent (his first role in "Hercules in New York" was dubbed.) Offbeat and occasionally uneven comedy-drama based on a novel by Charles Gaines is a sleeper. 102m/C VHS, Beta, LV. Jeff Bridges, Sally Field, Arnold Schwarzenegger, Robert Englund, Scatman Crothers; D: Bob Rafelson; W: Bob Rafelson. MGM, FOX

Stay Tuned 🎬 1992 (PG-13) Suburban yuppie couple buys a large-screen TV and satellite dish from Hellvision salesman, are sucked into their dish, and wind up starring in hellish TV shows such as "Wayne's Underworld," "Northern Overexposure," "Sadistic Home Videos," and "My Three Sons of Bitches." If they can survive for 24 hours, they'll be able to return to their normal lives. Clever idea for a film is wasted as this one never really gets off the ground; viewers may not want to stay tuned to the low comedy and frantic yucks. 90m/C VHS, LV, Closed Caption. John Ritter, Pam Dawber, Jeffrey Jones, Eugene Levy, David Tom, Heather McComb; D: Peter Hyams; W: Tom S. Parker; M: Bruce Broughton. WAR

Stay Tuned for Murder 🎬½ 1988 A sexy news reporter gets caught in a web of financial wrongdoings and corruption. The financiers, lawyers, and other sinister types she's investigating decide to give her a story she will never forget—if she ever gets the chance to tell it! 92m/C VHS, Beta. Terry Reeves Wolf, Christopher Ginnaven; D: Gary Jones. IME

Staying Alive 🎬½ 1983 (PG) "Saturday Night Fever" was the ultimate cheesy '70s musical, hence likeable in a dorky way. This pathetic sequel (directed by Stallone from a Rocky-esque script about beating the odds, etc.) is utterly predictable and forgettable. Music mostly by Frank Stallone, the great heir to Rodgers and Hammerstein. ♫The Woman In You; I Love You Too Much; Breakout; Someone Belonging to Someone; Life Goes On; Far From Over; Devils and Seducers; (We Dance) So Close to the Fire; Hope We Never Change. 96m/C VHS, Beta, LV, Closed Caption. John Travolta, Cynthia Rhodes, Finola Hughes, Norma Donaldson; D: Sylvester Stallone; W: Sylvester Stallone; M: Frank Stallone. PAR

Staying On 🎬🎬½ 1980 Based on the Paul Scott novel, this English drama follows the life of a post-colonial British colonel and his wife who chose to remain in India. 87m/C VHS, Beta. GB Trevor Howard, Celia Johnson; D: Irene Shubik. NO

Staying Together 🎬½ 1989 (R) Three midwestern brothers go into a panic when their father decides to sell the restaurant they've worked at all their adult lives. Somehow they manage the transition and learn about life. Sloppy comedy-drama with way too many unresolved subplots. 91m/C VHS, Beta, LV. Dermot Mulroney, Tim Quill, Sean Astin, Stockard Channing, Melinda Dillon, Daphne Zuniga; D: Lee Grant; W: Monte Merrick; M: Miles Goodman. HBO

The Steagle 🎬 1971 (R) The threat of the Cuban missile crisis lets a fantasizing professor loose to enact his wildest dreams. Odd Mitty-esque fantasy comedy might have worked, but ends up confusing and frustrating. 101m/C VHS, Beta. Richard Benjamin, Cloris Leachman; D: Paul Sylbert. NLC

Steal Big, Steal Little 🎬🎬 1995 (PG-13) Twins Robby and Reuben Martinez (Garcia) battle over the California ranch land left to Reuben by their mother. Evil, manipulative Robby, all fancy suits and slicked-back hair, wants to build condos while gentle, less-fashionable Reuben must fight to fulfill his dream of building a home for the migrant workers he employs. Yawn. Writer/director Davis' flashy action movie technique doesn't fit into the dramatic social commentary—it's too fast and forced to work. Garcia's radical character changes are impressive though. Arkin provides comic relief as the good-hearted used-car dealer who tries to save the day, if not the film.CW: Some strong language and a scene involving marijuana use. 130m/C VHS, LV. Andy Garcia, Alan Arkin, Rachel Ticotin, Joe Pantoliano, David Ogden Stiers, Charles Rocket, Holland Taylor; D: Andy Davis; W: Lee Blessing, Jeanne Blake, Terry Kahn, Andy Davis; C: Frank Tidy; M: William Olvis. HBO

Steal the Sky 🎬🎬 1988 Israeli agent Hemingway seduces Iraqi pilot Cross and persuades him to steal a Soviet MIG jet and defect to Israel. Unlikely plot but swell flying scenes. Hemingway is poorly cast, as she often is. Made for cable television. 110m/C VHS, Beta, LV, Closed Caption. Mariel Hemingway, Ben Cross, Etta Ankri; D: John Hancock. HBO

Stealing Beauty 🎬🎬½ 1996 (R) The film's main asset, besides the beautiful Tuscan scenery, is the coltish charm of Tyler, who stars as virginal teenager Lucy Harmon. An innocent abroad, she's spending the summer with family friends after her mother's suicide. Ostensibly artist Ian Grayson (McCann) is doing her portrait but Lucy's more interested in finding romance with neighbor lad Niccolo (Zibetti), who bestowed her first kiss on a previous visit. Lucy's sunny appeal doesn't go unnoticed by the villa's other inhabitants, including dying playwright Alex (Irons), but it seems Lucy's growing up won't be easy on anyone (not even herself).CW: Strong sexuality, nudity, some drug use and language. 118m/C VHS, LV, Closed Caption. IT GB FR Liv Tyler, Jeremy Irons, Donal McCann, Sinead Cusack, Jean Marais, D.W. Moffett, Stefania Sandrelli, Carlo Cecchi, Roberto Zibetti, Joseph Fiennes, Jason Flemyng, Leonardo Treviglio; D: Bernardo Bertolucci; W: Susan Minot, Bernardo Bertolucci; C: Darius Khondji; M: Richard Hartley. FXV

Stealing Heaven 🎬🎬 1988 (R) Based on the lives of Abelard and Heloise. In 12th-century Paris, a theologian and teacher falls in love with a beautiful young woman, and the two must defend their bond from all comers, including her righteous uncle. Steamy; trimmed to 108 minutes after threatened X rating. Attractive and cerebral. Available in a 115 minute-uncut, unrated version. 108m/C VHS, Beta, LV. GB YU Derek De Lint, Kim Thomson, Denholm Elliott, Mark Jax, Bernard Hepton, Kenneth Cranham, Angela Pleasence, Rachel Kempson; D: Clive Donner; W: Chris Bryant; M: Nick Bicat. NO

Stealing Home 🎬🎬½ 1988 (PG-13) A washed-up baseball player learns his former babysitter (who was also his first love and inspiration), has committed suicide. Their bittersweet relationship is told through flashbacks. Foster's superb performance steals the show in this quiet sleeper. 98m/C VHS, LV, Closed Caption. Mark Harmon, Jodie Foster, William McNamara, Blair Brown, Harold Ramis, Jonathan Silverman, John Shea, Helen Hunt, Richard Jenkins, Ted Ross, Thatcher Goodwin, Yvette Croskey; D: Steven Kampmann, Will Aldis; W: Steven Kampmann, Will Aldis; M: David Foster. WAR

Steamboat Bill, Jr. 🎬🎬🎬½ 1928 City-educated student returns to his small home-town and his father's Mississippi river boat, where he's an embarrassment to dad. But bond they do, to ward off the owner of a rival riverboat, whose daughter Keaton falls for. Engaging look at small-town life and the usual wonderful Keaton antics, including braving the big tornado. 75m/B VHS, Beta, LV. Buster Keaton, Ernest Torrence, Marion Byron, Tom Lewis; D: Charles Riesner. NOS, CCB, DVT

Steaming 🎬🎬 1986 (R) Six women get together in a London bathhouse and review their various troubles with men. Unfortunate adaptation of the good play by Nell Dunn. Where are the laughs—and what happened to the dramatic tension? The last film of Dors and director Losey. 102m/C VHS, Beta, Closed Caption. GB Vanessa Redgrave, Sarah Miles, Diana Dors; D: Joseph Losey. VTR

Steel 🎬🎬 Look Down and Die; Men of Steel 1980 (R) Construction workers on a mammoth skyscraper face insurmountable odds and strong opposition. Will they finish their building? Worth watching, if you don't have anything else to do. 100m/C VHS, Beta, LV. Lee Majors, Jennifer O'Neill, Art Carney, George Kennedy, Harris Yulin, Terry Kiser, Richard Lynch, Roger E. Mosley, Albert Salmi, R.G. Armstrong; D: Steve Carver; W: Leigh Chapman; M: Michel Colombier. VES

Steel 🎬½ 1997 (PG-13) Metal specialist John Henry Irons (O'Neal) has designed a top-secret military weapon that falls into the hands of a street gang. Donning a suit of armor he designed, he become super hero Steel and sets out to end the reign of terror of former colleague turned super villian Burke (Nelson). Adaptation of popular DC comic keeps target audience in mind with lots of action and plenty of humor. Shaq proves once again that as an actor he's a pretty good basketball player.CW: Some superhero action violence. 97m/C VHS, LV, Closed Caption. Shaquille O'Neal, Judd Nelson, Annabeth Gish, Richard Roundtree, Irma P. Hall, Charles Napier, Kerrie Keane; D: Kenneth Johnson; W: Kenneth Johnson; C: Mark Irwin; M: Mervyn Warren. Nominations: Golden Raspberry Awards '97: Worst Actor (O'Neal). WAR

Steel and Lace 💿½ **1990 (R)** Davison is the scientist brother of a classical pianist who commits suicide after being raped. He revives her as a cyborg, which promptly sets out to enact its revenge. Depressing, morbid sci-fi. **92m/C VHS, Beta, LV, Closed Caption.** Bruce Davison, Clare Wren, Stacy Haiduk, David Naughton, David Lander; **D:** Ernest Farino; **W:** Joseph Dougherty, Dave Edison; **C:** Thomas Callaway.

Steel Arena 💿 **1972 (PG)** Several real life stunt-car drivers appear in this action-packed film, crammed with spins, jumps, explosions and world-record-breaking, life risking stunts. **99m/C VHS, Beta.** Dusty Russell, Gene Drew, Buddy Love; **D:** Mark L. Lester. *ART, VES*

The Steel Claw 💿💿 **1961** One-handed ex-Marine Montgomery organizes guerilla forces against the Japanese in the Philippines in WWII. Good location shooting and plenty of action. **95m/ C VHS, Beta.** George Montgomery, Charito Luna, Mario Barri; **D:** George Montgomery. *NO*

Steel Cowboy 💿💿 **1978** With his marriage, sanity, and livelihood on the line, an independent trucker agrees to haul a hot herd of stolen steers. Passable made-for-TV macho adventure. **100m/C VHS, Beta.** James Brolin, Rip Torn, Jennifer Warren, Strother Martin, Melanie Griffith, Lou Frizzell; **D:** Harvey Laidman; **M:** Charles Bernstein. *NO*

Steel Dawn 💿½ **1987 (R)** Another "Mad Max" clone: A leather-clad warrior wields his sword over lots of presumably post-apocalyptic desert terrain. Swayze stars with his real-life wife Niemi in unfortunate follow-up to "Dirty Dancing." **90m/C VHS, Beta, LV.** Patrick Swayze, Lisa Niemi, Christopher Neame, Brett Hool, Brion James, Anthony Zerbe; **D:** Lance Hool. *ART, VES*

Steel Fisted Dragon 💿 **1982 (R)** Son seeks revenge on the gang who murdered his mother and burned her house to the ground. **85m/ C VHS, Beta.** Stephen Lee, Johnny Kong Kong, Peter Chan. *NO*

Steel Frontier 💿½ **1994 (R)** Post-apocalypse actioner finds a group of survivors trying to make a new life in a town they call New Hope. But then a group of bandit soldiers take over—until a lone hero comes along to save the day. **CW:** Non-stop action violence; language. **94m/C VHS, LV, Closed Caption.** Joe Lara, Brion James, Bo Svenson, Stacie Foster; **D:** Paul G. Volk, Jacobsen Hart; **W:** Jacobsen Hart. *PMH*

The Steel Helmet 💿💿💿½ **1951** Hurriedly made Korean War drama stands as a top-notch war film. Brooding and dark, GIs don't save the world for democracy or rescue POWs; they simply do their best to survive a horrifying situation. Pointless death, confused loyalties and cynicism abound in writer-director Fuller's scathing comment on the madness of war. **84m/B VHS, Beta, LV.** Gene Evans, Robert Hutton, Steve Brodie, William Chun, James Edwards, Richard Loo, Sid Melton; **D:** Samuel Fuller; **W:** Samuel Fuller. *RXM*

Steel Magnolias 💿💿💿 **1989 (PG)** Julia Roberts plays a young woman stricken with severe diabetes who chooses to live her life to the fullest despite her bad health. Much of the action centers around a Louisiana beauty shop where the women get together to discuss the goings-on of their lives. Screenplay by R. Harling, based on his partially autobiographical play. Sweet, poignant, and often hilarious, yet just as often overwrought. MacLaine is funny as a bitter divorcee; Parton is sexy and fun as the hairdresser. But Field and Roberts go off the deep end and make it all entirely too weepy. **118m/C VHS, Beta, LV, 8mm, Closed Caption.** Sally Field, Dolly Parton, Shirley MacLaine, Daryl Hannah, Olympia Dukakis, Julia Roberts, Tom Skerritt, Sam Shepard, Dylan McDermott, Kevin J. O'Connor, Bill McCutcheon, Ann Wedgeworth, Janine Turner; **D:** Herbert Ross; **W:** Robert Harling; **C:** John A. Alonzo; **M:** Georges Delerue. Golden Globe Awards '90: Best Supporting Actress (Roberts); Nominations: Academy Awards '89: Best Supporting Actress (Roberts). *COL*

Steel Sharks 💿💿 **1997 (R)** It's undersea international terrorim as the superpowers play cat-and-mouse using their nuclear-powered submarines. **94m/C VHS, Closed Caption.** Billy Dee Williams, Gary Busey, Tim Lounibos, Larry Poindexter, Billy Warlock; **D:** Rodney McDonald. *CAF*

Steele Justice 💿 **1987 (R)** A tough 'Nam vet takes on the whole Vietnamese Mafia in Southern California after his friend is murdered. One of those head-scratchers: Should I laugh, or be offended? **96m/C VHS, Beta, LV, Closed Caption.** Martin Kove, Sela Ward, Ronny Cox, Bernie Casey, Joseph Campanella, Sarah Douglas; **D:** Robert Boris; **W:** Robert Boris. *PAR*

Steele's Law 💿💿 **1991 (R)** A loner cop is forced to take the law into his own hands in order to track down an insane international assassin. **CW:** Language, violence, and sensuality. **90m/ C VHS, LV.** Fred Williamson, Bo Svenson, Doran Ingrham, Phyllis Cicero; **D:** Fred Williamson.

Steelyard Blues 💿💿½ *The Final Crash* **1973 (PG)** A motley-crew comedy about a wacky gang that tries to steal an abandoned WW II airplane. Zany pranks abound. Technically flawed direction from Myerson mars a potentially hilarious story. **93m/C VHS, Beta.** Jane Fonda, Donald Sutherland, Peter Boyle, Howard Hesseman, John Savage, Garry Goodrow; **D:** Alan Myerson; **W:** David S. Ward; **M:** David Shire. *WAR*

Stella 💿💿½ **1955** Mercouri's film debut has her as a free-spirited bar singer who gets involved in a tragic romantic triangle with a middle-class writer and a local football hero. Melodramatic but Mercouri's earthy joie de vivre is already apparent. In Greek with English subtitles. **94m/B VHS.** *GR* Melina Mercouri, Yiorgo Fountas, Aiekos Alexandrikis, Sophia Vembo; **D:** Michael Cacoyannis; **M:** Manos Hadjidakis. *FCT*

Stella 💿½ **1989 (PG-13)** Anachronistic remake update of "Stella Dallas" casts Midler as a single mother who sacrifices everything to give her daughter a better life. Barbara Stanwyck did it much better in 1937. Based on Olive Higgins Prouty's novel. **109m/C VHS, Beta, LV, Closed Caption.** Bette Midler, John Goodman, Stephen Collins, Eileen Brennan, Ben Stiller, Trini Alvarado, Marsha Mason; **D:** John Erman; **W:** Robert Getchell; **C:** Billy Williams. *TOU*

Stella Dallas 💿💿💿 **1937** An uneducated woman lets go of the daughter she loves when she realizes her ex-husband can give the girl more advantages. What could be sentimental turns out believable and worthwhile under Vidor's steady hand. Stanwyck never makes a wrong step. From a novel by Olive Higgins Prouty. Remade in 1989 as "Stella," starring Bette Midler. **106m/B VHS, Beta, LV.** Barbara Stanwyck, Anne Shirley, John Boles, Alan Hale, Marjorie Main; **D:** King Vidor. Nominations: Academy Awards '37: Best Actress (Stanwyck), Best Supporting Actress (Shirley).

Stella Maris 💿💿💿 **1918** Pickford plays tattered waif who's a slave to an alcoholic who's married to the man she loves. But he's in love with Pickford playing a sheltered rich invalid. Brimming with the tragic consequences of love. **70m/B VHS, Beta.** Mary Pickford, Conway Tearle, Camille Ankewich, Ida Waterman; **D:** Marshall Neilan. *GPV, FCT*

Step Lively 💿💿½ **1944** A young playwright tries to recover the money he lent to a fast-talking Broadway producer and is forced to take the leading role in his play. Lively musical remake of "Room Service" (1938) was Sinatra's first starring role. Look for Dorothy Malone as a brunette switchboard operator. ♪Some Other Time; As Long As There's Music; Where Does Love Begin?; Come Out, Come Out, Wherever You Are; Why Must There Be an Opening Song?; And Then You Kissed Me; Ask the Madame. **88m/B VHS, Beta, LV.** Frank Sinatra, Gloria De Haven, George Murphy, Walter Slezak, Adolphe Menjou, Anne Jeffreys; **D:** Tim Whelan. Nominations: Academy Awards '44: Best Interior Decoration. *CCB*

The Stepfather 💿💿💿 **1987 (R)** Creepy thriller about a seemingly ordinary stepfather who is actually a homicidal maniac searching for the "perfect family." An independently produced sleeper tightly directed and well written. Followed by two inferior sequels. **89m/C VHS, Beta, LV, Closed Caption.** Terry O'Quinn, Shelley Hack, Jill Schoelen, Stephen Shellan, Charles Lanyer, Stephen E. Miller; **D:** Joseph Ruben; **W:** Donald E. Westlake; **C:** John Lindley; **M:** Patrick Moraz. *COL*

Stepfather 2: Make Room for Daddy 💿½ **1989 (R)** A poor sequel to the suspenseful sleeper, wherein the psychotic family man escapes from an asylum and woos another suburban family, murdering anyone who may suspect his true identity. Followed by yet another sequel. **93m/C VHS, Beta, LV.** Terry O'Quinn, Meg Foster, Caroline Williams, Jonathan Brandis, Henry Brown, Mitchell Laurance; **D:** Jeff Burr; **W:** John P. Auerbach; **C:** Jacek Laskus. *NO*

Stepfather 3: Father's Day 💿 **1992 (R)** The father from Hell is back! Escaping from the loony bin with a surgically altered face, the stepfather settles in a small town and gets a job at a nursery (the plant kind, not the children kind). His favorite gardening tool fast becomes the mulch machine, and soon locals are fertilizing the garden. Well below the original, but it may please fans of this genre. **CW:** Violence and some sensuality. **110m/C VHS, LV, Closed Caption.** Robert Wightman, Priscilla Barnes, Season Hubley; **D:** Guy Magar; **C:** Alan Caso. *THV*

Stephano Quantestorie 💿💿 **1993** Walter Mitty-ish story about daydreaming cop Stephano (Nichetti) who falls for the prime suspect in a robbery he's investigating. He escapes his conflicting feelings by imagining himself living other lives—as a math professor, airline pilot, saxophone player, and thief, but soon all these alter ego are intruding into his work. Italian with subtitles. **90m/C VHS.** *IT* Maurizio Nichetti; **D:** Maurizio Nichetti; **W:** Maurizio Nichetti. *KIV*

Stephen King's Golden Years 💿½ **1991** Stephen King creates a chilling vision of scientific progress gone awry in this shocking techno-thriller. After being accidentally exposed to exotic chemicals in a lab explosion, an aging janitor undergoes an extraordinary transformation and the government will sacrifice anything to learn more about it. Originally a made-for-television miniseries. **232m/C VHS, LV, Closed Caption.** Keith Szarabajka, Frances Sternhagen, Ed Lauter, R.D. Call, Stephen King; **D:** Kenneth Fink, Stephen Tolkin, Allen Coulter, Michael G. Gerrick; **W:** Stephen King, Josef Anderson. *WOV*

Stephen King's It 💿💿½ **1990** A group of small town children, who were terrorized by an evil force in their youth, are traumatized again some 30 years later, when they learn a new series of child murders occurred in their Eastern home town. The adults, who now all have successful and diverse careers, must come to terms with the terrible secret they share, as "IT" has returned to wreak havoc in their New England home town. Based on horror master King's best-selling novel of the same name. **193m/C VHS, Beta, LV.** Tim Reid, Richard Thomas, John Ritter, Annette O'Toole, Richard Masur, Dennis Christopher, Harry Anderson, Olivia Hussey, Tim Curry, Jonathan Brandis, Michael Cole; **D:** Tommy Lee Wallace; **W:** Stephen King; **M:** Richard Bellis. *WAR*

Stephen King's The Langoliers 💿½ *The Langoliers* **1995 (PG-13)** Bloated variation of "Ten Little Indians" finds 10 airline passengers dozing off on their L.A.-to-Boston flight and awakening to find their fellow passengers and the crew have vanished. Of course, one passenger (Morse) is a pilot and he gets them to Bangor, Maine (where the miniseries was filmed), only to discover the airport is deserted and very weird things are going on. Oh yeah, the "langoliers" look like flying cannonballs with piranha teeth and have something to do with neurotic Pinchot's character. Not that you'll care much.**CW:** Violence; some sci-fi terror 180m/C VHS, LV, Closed Caption. David Morse, Bronson Pinchot, Patricia Wettig, Dean Stockwell, Kate Maberly, Christopher Collet, Kimber Riddle, Mark Lindsay Chapman, Frankie Faison, Baxter Harris; **Cameos:** Stephen King, Tom Holland; **D:** Tom Holland; **W:** Tom Holland; **C:** Paul Maibaum; **M:** Vladimir Horunzhy. REP

Stephen King's The Night Flier 🎬🎬

The Night Flier 1996 (R) Portrays bloodsucking beings that prey upon the weakness of mortal men in order to survive. And besides tabloid journalists, there's vampires in it, too! Richard Dees (Ferrer) is a reporter/photographer for a National Enquirer-like paper who is not above staging lurid photos to grab Page One. His editor pits him in a contest with rookie papparazzo Katherine (Entwistle) for a story about a murderer who wears a black cape and tricorn hat, flies into small airports in a sinister black plane and drains his victims' blood. Dees follows the killer's trail in his own plane, stopping to ruthlessly grill survivors and doctor up a few pictures. Genuinely spooky showdown will leave only one monster standing. Who is it? Inquiring minds want to know.**CW:** Horror violence, gore and strong language. 97m/C VHS, Closed Caption. Michael H. Moss, Miguel Ferrer, Julie Entwisle, Dan Monahan, John Bennes, Beverly Skinner, Rob Wilds, Richard Olsen, Elizabeth McCormick; **D:** Mark Pavia; **W:** Mark Pavia, Jack O'Donnell; **C:** David Connell; **M:** Brian Keane. HBO

Stephen King's The Stand 🎬🎬½

The Stand 1994 Ghoulish made for TV adaptation of the King novel about a superflu/plague that decimates the U.S. population. The few survivors are soon divided into two camps—those dreaming of a godly old black woman known as Mother Abigail and others of the satanic Randall Flagg, the Walkin' Dude. Boulder, Colorado (where King was living when he wrote the novel) serves as headquarters for Abigail's brood while Las Vegas (where else) is Flagg territory. It all comes down to a battle of good vs. evil, with the future of mankind at stake. Religious allegory can get tedious but it's a varied cast with some scenes not for those with queasy stomachs. On four cassettes. 360m/C VHS, LV, Closed Caption. Jamey Sheridan, Ruby Dee, Gary Sinise, Molly Ringwald, Rob Lowe, Laura San Giacomo, Rob Lowe, Adam Storke, Matt Frewer, Corin "Corky" Nemec, Ray Walston, Bill Fagerbakke, Ossie Davis, Shawnee Smith, Rick Aviles, John Joe Bob Briggs Bloom, Michael Lookinland; **Cameos:** Ed Harris, Kathy Bates, Kareem Abdul-Jabbar, Stephen King, Sam Raimi; **D:** Mick Garris; **W:** Stephen King; **C:** Edward Pei. REP

Stephen King's The Tommyknockers 🎬🎬½

The Tommyknockers 1993 (R) Another of King's creepy tales, adapted for TV. Bobbi (Helgenberger) and Gard (Smits) live in the small town of Haven, Maine (actually filmed on New Zealand's North Island). She's an aspiring writer; he's a fading poet with a drinking problem and a metal plate in his head (this is important). Walking in the woods, Bobbi stumbles over a long-buried spaceship which begins to take possession of the townspeople—their eyes shine green, their teeth fall out, and they act out their (often violent) fantasies—all but Gard. The whole thing's more silly than scary. The title comes from an old children's rhyme.**CW:** Sci/fi terror/horror. 120m/C VHS, LV, Closed Caption. Jimmy Smits, Marg Helgenberger, Joanna Cassidy, E.G. Marshall, Traci Lords, John Ashton, Allyce Beasley, Cliff DeYoung, Robert Carradine, Leon Woods, Paul McIver; **D:** John Power; **W:** Lawrence D. Cohen. THV, TWV

Stephen King's Thinner 🎬🎬

Thinner 1996 (R) Holland takes all the meat out of this supernatural horror by turning it into a formulaic pursuit-of-justice bore. Porcine lawyer Billy Halleck (Burke) accidentally hits a gypsy with his car and is cursed with a case of perpetual weight loss. Conveniently for Billy, the client he has just gotten an acquittal for is local mobster Richie "The Hammer" Ginelli (Mantegna) who is now determined

to save him. Ponderous plot and lackluster-looking later is redeemed by decent acting. King makes his requisite cameo as Dr. Bangor (get it, Maine?) Originally published in 1984 under King's pseudonym Richard Bachman.**CW:** Horror violence and gore, language and sexuality. 92m/C VHS, LV, Closed Caption. Robert John Burke, Joe Mantegna, Lucinda Jenney, Michael Constantine, Kari Wuhrer, John Horton, Sam Freed, Daniel von Bargen, Elizabeth Franz, Joy Lentz, Jeff Ware; **Cameos:** Stephen King; **D:** Tom Holland; **W:** Michael McDowell, Tom Holland; **C:** Kees Van Oostrum; **M:** Daniel Licht. REP

Stepmonster 🎬½

1992 (PG-13) A boy tries to convince his father that his new stepmother is a monster—literally. Doesn't work any better than "My Stepmother Is an Alien."**CW:** Horror elements. ?m/C VHS, Closed Caption. Alan Thicke, Robin Riker, Corey Feldman, John Astin, Ami Dolenz, George Gaynes. NHO

The Stepmother 🎬½

1971 Yet another Hitchcock ripoff story involving an evil stepmother. Rey is passable, but there's not much else to recommend this dredge. 100m/C VHS. Alejandro Rey, John Anderson, Katherine Justice, John David Garfield, Marlene Schmidt, Claudia Jennings, Larry Linville; **D:** Howard (Hikmet) Avedis. Nominations: Academy Awards '72: Best Song ("Strange Are the Ways of Love").

Steppenwolf 🎬🎬½

1974 (PG) Static, enigmatic film version of the famous Herman Hesse novel about a brooding writer searching for meaning and self-worth. Interesting to watch, but the offbeat novel doesn't translate to the screen; leaves you flat. 105m/C VHS, Beta, LV. SI Max von Sydow, Dominique Sanda, Pierre Clementi, Carla Rominelli, Roy Bosier; **D:** Fred Haines; **W:** Fred Haines; **C:** Tomislav Pinter; **M:** George Gruntz. THV, GLV

Stepping Out 🎬🎬🎬

1991 (PG) Minnelli stars as a would-be Broadway dancer who gives tap dancing lessons in an old church to an assortment of offbeat and interesting characters. When the troupe is asked to perform for a local charity, they make the most of their opportunity. A warm and touching ensemble piece that avoids oversentimentalizing and utilizes its cast to best advantage. 113m/C VHS, Beta, LV, Closed Caption. Liza Minnelli, Shelley Winters, Bill Irwin, Ellen Greene, Julie Walters, Robyn Stevan, Jane Krakowski, Sheila McCarthy, Andrea Martin, Carol Woods, Nora Dunn, Eugene Glazer; **D:** Lewis Gilbert; **W:** Richard Harris; **M:** Peter Matz. PAR

Steps from Hell 🎬

1992 Vald Tempest is an evil immortal in control of a cult of zombie women. He's stolen a sacred map that will lead to a gateway which, when opened, will unleash a supreme evil on the world. Unless the heroic John Clark can find a way to prevent it, of course. 90m/C VHS. Bernardo Rosa, Rocky Tucker, Ron Odell, Philip Cable, Liz Stoeckel, Steve Quimby, Lisa Lund; **D:** James Tucker; **W:** James Tucker. CTC

The Stepsister 🎬🎬

1997 (PG-13) Pediatrician Donna Canfield is lured to her death by one of her young patients. When daughter Darcy (Sofer) comes home to console her dad, Dr. Derek (Rachins), she finds her place usurped by the widowed Joan (Evans) and her sexpot daughter, Melinda (Wilson). Married in unseemly haste, the wealthy Derek dies equally quickly, leaving Darcy suspicious of her new step-family. Cable thriller.**CW:** Violence and some sensuality. 91m/C VHS, Closed Caption. Rena Sofer, Bridgette Wilson, Linda Evans, Alan Rachins. PAR

Stepsisters woof! 1985 Murderous doublecrosses occur among a pilot, his wife, and her sister. 75m/C VHS, Beta. Hal Fletcher, Sharyn Talbert, Bond Gideon. NO

The Sterile Cuckoo 🎬🎬🎬

Pookie 1969 (PG) An aggressive co-ed pursues a shy freshman who seems to embody her romantic ideal. Minnelli's performance is outstanding; Burton as the naive young man is also fine. Pakula's splendid first directing job. 108m/C VHS, Beta, LV. Liza Minnelli, Wendell Burton, Tim McIntire; **D:** Alan J. Pakula; **W:** Alvin Sargent; **C:** Milton Krasner. Nominations: Academy Awards '69:

Best Actress (Minnelli), Best Song ("Come Saturday Morning"). PAR

Steve Martin Live 🎬🎬½

1985 Martin shows veteran comedians his famous Universal Amphitheatre performance and his short "The Absent-Minded Waiter." 58m/C VHS, Beta, LV. Steve Martin, Teri Garr, Buck Henry, David Letterman, Paul Simon. ART, VES

Stevie 🎬🎬

1978 Jackson brings her flawless skill to the role of British poet Stevie Smith. Excellent performance from Washbourne as Stevie's spinster aunt. Wooden, lifeless screen rendition for the Hugh Whitemore stage play is helped greatly by good performances, but is too talky and, frankly, rather dull and self-absorbed. 102m/C VHS. GB Glenda Jackson, Mona Washbourne, Alec McCowen, Trevor Howard; **D:** Robert Enders; **C:** Frederick A. (Freddie) Young. Los Angeles Film Critics Association Awards '78: Best Supporting Actress (Washbourne); Montreal World Film Festival '78: Best Actress (Jackson); New York Film Critics Awards '78: Best Supporting Actress (Washbourne). UAV

Stewardess School woof! 1986 (R) Airline spoof aims at wackiness, but misses the runway. Generic title betrays probable badness which turns out to be all too real. An utter woofer. 84m/C VHS, Beta, LV. Sandahl Bergman, Wendie Jo Sperber, Judy Landers, Julia Montgomery, Corinne Bohrer; **D:** Ken Blancato; **W:** Ken Blancato; **M:** Robert Folk. NO

Stick 🎬½

1985 (R) Ex-con Stick (Reynolds, directing himself) wants to start a new life for himself in Miami. Lots of drug dealers and guns don't help the interest level in this dull underworld tale. Based upon the Elmore Leonard novel. 109m/C VHS, Beta, LV, Closed Caption. Burt Reynolds, Candice Bergen, George Segal, Charles Durning, Dar Robinson; **D:** Burt Reynolds; **W:** Elmore Leonard; **M:** Stephen Dorff. USH

The Stick-Up 🎬

Mud 1977 In 1935, a young American traveling in Great Britain is introduced to some rather illegal fun. Rather sorry attempt at romance/comedy/adventure. 101m/C VHS, Beta. David Soul, Pamela McMyler; **D:** Jeffrey Bloom; **W:** Jeffrey Bloom. HHE

Stickfighter 🎬

1989 (PG) The oppressive reign of an evil Spanish ruler of the Philippines is challenged by the world's best stickfighter. 102m/C VHS. PH Dean Stockwell, Nancy Kwan, Alejandro Rey, Roland Dantes; **D:** Luis Nepomuceno.

Sticky Fingers 🎬

1988 (PG-13) Two female musicians, asked to watch nearly a million bucks in drug money, go on a mega shopping spree. Completely incredible, unlikeable and mean-spirited attempt at zany comedy. 89m/C VHS, beta. Melanie Mayron, Helen Slater, Eileen Brennan, Carol Kane, Christopher Guest, Danitra Vance, Gwen Welles, Stephen McHattie; **D:** Catlin Adams; **W:** Melanie Mayron, Catlin Adams; **M:** Gary Chang.

Stigma 🎬½

1973 "Miami Vice" star Thomas (then 23; later to restore his middle name, Michael) is a young doctor who treats a syphilis epidemic in a small town. He's indistinguishable, but better than anything else here. Ever seen closeups of advanced syphilis? Here's your chance—but it's not pretty. 93m/C Beta. Philip Michael Thomas, Harlan Cary Poe; **D:** David E. Durston. NO

Stiletto 🎬½

1969 (R) Good cast is wasted in this mediocre depiction of the trouble encountered by a contract Mafia assassin when he decides to change careers. Based on the usual pulp cheese by Harold Robbins. 101m/C VHS, Beta. Alex Cord, Britt Ekland, Patrick O'Neal, Joseph Wiseman, Barbara McNair, Roy Scheider, M. Emmet Walsh; **Cameos:** Raul Julia; **D:** Bernard L. Kowalski; **C:** Jack Priestley.

Still Life 🎬🎬

1992 (PG-13) The press has dubbed him "the Art Killer," a serial murderer who makes scupltures out of his victims. He's a sensation—and not ready to stop. This sicko's next "Still Life" may just be a struggling young musician. 83m/C VHS. Jason Gedrick, Jessica Steen, Stephen Shellan; **D:** Graeme Campbell; **M:** Mychael Danna.

Still Not Quite Human 🐾🐾 1992 Teenage android Chip must do battle with unscrupulous industrialists and their robot weapon Spartacus to rescue his inventor father from their deadly clutches. 84m/C VHS, Beta, Closed Caption. Alan Thicke, Christopher Neame, Betsy Palmer, Adam Philipson, Rosa Nevin, Ken Pogue, Jay Underwood; D: Eric Luke; W: Eric Luke. DIS

Still of the Night 🐾🐾 1982 (PG) A Hitchcock-style thriller about a psychiatrist infatuated with a mysterious woman who may or may not be a killer. 91m/C VHS, Beta, LV. Meryl Streep, Roy Scheider, Jessica Tandy, Joe Grifasi, Sara Botsford, Josef Sommer; D: Robert Benton; W: Robert Benton, David Newman; C: Nestor Almendros. MGM

The Stilts 🐾🐾🐾 1984 From modern Spanish cinema's preeminent director, this is a study of sexual dynamics revolving around a doomed love triangle. Aging professor Gomez wants young Del Sol to commit to him, but she won't; she has another, younger lover. Overwrought at times, but well acted. In Spanish with English subtitles. 95m/C VHS, Beta. SP Laura Del Sol, Francesco Rabal, Fernando Gomez; D: Carlos Saura. XVC

The Sting 🐾🐾🐾½ 1973 (PG) Newman and Redford together again in this sparkling story of a pair of con artists in 1930s Chicago. They set out to fleece a big-time racketeer, pitting brain against brawn and pistol. Very inventive, excellent acting, Scott Joplin's wonderful ragtime music adapted by Marvin Hamlisch. The same directorial and acting team from "Butch Cassidy and the Sundance Kid" triumphs again. 129m/C VHS, Beta, LV, Closed Caption, DVD. Paul Newman, Robert Redford, Robert Shaw, Charles Durning, Eileen Brennan, Harold Gould, Ray Walston; D: George Roy Hill; W: David S. Ward; C: Robert L. Surtees; M: Marvin Hamlisch. Academy Awards '73: Best Art Direction/Set Decoration, Best Costume Design, Best Director (Hill), Best Film Editing, Best Picture, Best Story & Screenplay, Original Song Score and/or Adaptation; Directors Guild of America Awards '73: Best Director (Hill); Nominations: Academy Awards '73: Best Actor (Redford), Best Cinematography, Best Sound.USH, BTV

The Sting 2 🐾½ 1983 (PG) Complicated comic plot concludes with the final con game, involving a fixed boxing match where the stakes top a million dollars and the payoff could be murder. Lame sequel to "The Sting" (1973). 102m/C VHS, Beta, LV. Jackie Gleason, Mac Davis, Teri Garr, Karl Malden, Oliver Reed; D: Jeremy Paul Kagan; W: David S. Ward; C: Bill Butler; M: Lalo Schifrin. Nominations: Academy Awards '83: Original Song Score and/or Adaptation. USH

Sting of the Dragon Masters 🐾 1974 (R) Martial arts adventure featuring Bruce Lee's female Kung-Fu counterpart, Angela Mao. 96m/C VHS, Beta. Angela Mao, Thoon Rhee, Carter Huang; D: Huang Feng. VCI

Sting of the West 🐾 1976 (PG) Journeyman con artist swindles his way across the Wild West. 90m/C VHS, Beta. Jack Palance, Timothy Brent, Lionel Stander. MPI

Stingray 🐾½ 1978 (PG) Two guys buy a Corvette, not knowing it's loaded with stolen heroin. Gangsters with an interest in the dope come after them, and the chase is on. Very violent and not all that funny. 105m/C VHS, Beta. Chris Mitchum, Sherry Jackson, Les Lannom; D: Richard Taylor. COL

Stir Crazy 🐾🐾½ 1980 (R) Two down-on-their luck losers find themselves convicted of a robbery they didn't commit and sentenced to 120 years behind bars with a mean assortment of inmates. Wilder and Pryor's second teaming isn't quite as successful as the first go-round, but still provides plenty of laughs. 111m/C VHS, Beta, LV. Richard Pryor, Gene Wilder, Nicolas Coster, Lee Purcell, Craig T. Nelson, JoBeth Williams; D: Sidney Poitier. COL

Stitches 🐾 1985 (R) Adolescent comedy about med students playing practical jokes on the dean using laboratory specimens. So bad the director (actually Rod Holcomb) allegedly did not want his name associated with it. 92m/C VHS, Beta.

Eddie Albert, Parker Stevenson, Geoffrey Lewis, Brian Tochi; D: Alan Smithee; W: Michael Choquette.

The Stolen Children 🐾🐾🐾½ Il Ladro di Bambini 1992 Highly acclaimed Italian neo-realist film that tells the story of a shy carabiniere and two children who have been placed in his care. They are an emotionally battered 11-year-old girl who was forced into prostitution by her mother and her sullen 9-year-old brother. As they journey from Milan to Sicily and gradually get to know each other, all three of the characters undergo a slight transformation. Gracefully executed, this haunting masterpiece explores the overriding themes of guilt and innocence and keeps you thinking about them long after the movie's over. Italian with subtitles. 108m/C VHS. IT Enrico Lo Verso, Valentina Scalici, Giuseppe Ieracitano, Florence Darel, Marina Golovine, Fabio Alessandrini; D: Gianni Amelio; W: Gianni Amelio, Sandro Petraglia, Stefano Rulli; M: Franco Piersanti. Cannes Film Festival '92: Grand Jury Prize. NYR

A Stolen Face 🐾🐾 1952 Creepy, implausible drama of a plastic surgeon, spurned by a beautiful concert pianist, who transforms a female convict to look just like her. The convict runs away, but perhaps there's hope in the future with the pianist. 71m/B VHS, Beta, LV. GB Paul Henreid, Lizabeth Scott, Andre Morell, Susan Stephen; D: Terence Fisher; M: Malcolm Arnold. MLB

Stolen Hours 🐾🐾½ 1963 Inferior remake of Bette Davis' "Dark Victory" casts Hayward as an oil-rich heiress who learns she has a fatal illness. Bring the tissues for this tearjerker. Based on the play "Dark Victory" by George Emerson Brewer, Jr. and Bertram Block. 100m/C VHS, Closed Caption. Susan Hayward, Michael Craig, Diane Baker, Edward Judd, Paul Rogers; D: Daniel Petrie; W: Jessamyn West, Joseph Hayes. MGM, FCT

Stolen Identity 🐾½ 1953 A Viennese cabbie sees his American dream dashed for lack of the proper papers. When an American businessman is murdered in his cab he is quick to seize the moment...and the dead man's identity. In no time at all he finds himself involved with the widow, entangled with the murderer and under suspicion for the killing. Predictable and sluggish, the story inches its way to the foregone conclusion. 81m/B VHS, Beta. Francis Lederer, Donald Buka, Joan Camden, Adrienne Gessner; D: Gunther Fritsch. SNC

Stolen Kisses 🐾🐾🐾½ Baisers Voles 1968 Sequel to "The 400 Blows," the story of Antoine Doinel: his unsuccessful career prospects as a detective in Paris, and his initially awkward but finally successful adventures with women. Made during Truffaut's involvement in a political crisis involving the sack of Cinematique Francais director Henri Langlois. Truffaut dedicated the film to Langlois and the Cinematique, but it is a thoroughly apolitical, small-scale, charming (some say too charming) romantic comedy, Truffaut-style. Followed by "Bed and Board." 90m/C VHS, Beta. FR Jean-Pierre Leaud, Delphine Seyrig; D: Francois Truffaut; M: Antoine Duhamel. National Society of Film Critics Awards '69: Best Director (Truffaut); Nominations: Academy Awards '68: Best Foreign Language Film. COL

A Stolen Life 🐾🐾 1946 Remake of 1939 film of the same title starring Elisabeth Bergner. Oddly, Davis chose this as her first and last producing effort. Implausible tale of an evil twin (Davis) who takes her sister's (Davis) place so she can have the man they both love. Davis pulls it off as both twins; Ford is good as the hapless hubby. 107m/B VHS, Beta. Bette Davis, Glenn Ford, Dane Clark, Walter Brennan, Charlie Ruggles, Bruce (Herman) Bennett, Esther Dale, Peggy Knudsen; D: Curtis Bernhardt; M: Max Steiner. MGM

Stolen Painting 🐾½ 1979 A man's wife is kidnapped by an evil gang while having her portrait painted. Her husband rescues her, and they, in turn, are chased by the kidnappers. 11m/C VHS, Beta. BFA

The Stone Boy 🐾🐾🐾½ 1984 (PG) A boy accidentally kills his older brother on their family's Montana farm. The family is torn apart by sadness and guilt. Sensitive look at variety of reactions during a crisis, with an excellent cast led by Duvall's crystal-clear performance. 93m/C VHS, Beta, Closed Caption. Glenn Close, Robert Duvall, Jason Presson, Frederic Forrest, Wilford Brimley, Linda Hamilton; D: Christopher Cain; W: Gina Berriault; C: Juan Ruiz-Anchia; M: James Horner, John Beal. FOX

Stone Cold WOOF! 1991 (R) Flamboyant footballer Bosworth made his acting debut in this sensitive human document, playing the usual musclebound, one-punk-army terminator cop, out to infiltrate a sadistic band of fascist biker barbarians engaged in drug running and priest shooting. Profane, lewd, gory, self-deifying; a crash course (accent on crashes) in everything despicable about modern action pics.CW: Strong language, strong violence, and sensuality. 91m/C VHS, Beta, LV, 8mm, Closed Caption. Brian Bosworth, Lance Henriksen, William Forsythe, Arabella Holzbog, Sam McMurray; D: Craig R. Baxley. COL

Stone Cold Dead 🐾½ 1980 (R) Rugged cop Crenna battles crime lord Williams (Paul Williams? Yeah, sure) over a prostitution ring. Meanwhile, a sniper starts killing hookers. Unoriginal and thoroughly dull would-be thriller. 100m/C VHS, Beta. Richard Crenna, Paul Williams, Linda Sorensen, Belinda J. Montgomery; D: George Menduluk; W: George Menduluk.

Stone Fox 🐾🐾 1987 Heartwarming family drama in which a young man must win a dogsled race to save the family farm. Based on John Reynolds Gardiner's popular children's book. 96m/ C VHS. Buddy Ebsen, Joey Cramer, Belinda J. Montgomery, Gordon Tootoosis; D: Harvey Hart. WOV

The Stone Killer 🐾🐾½ 1973 (R) Bronson stars as a tough plainclothes cop in this action-packed drama about a Mafia plot to use Vietnam vets in a mass killing. Violent but tense and action-packed revenge adventure set in the underworlds of New York and Los Angeles. 95m/C VHS, Beta, LV. Charles Bronson, Martin Balsam, Norman Fell, Ralph Waite, John Ritter; D: Michael Winner. COL

Stone of Silver Creek 1935 The owner of the Bonanza saloon, T. William Stone (Jones), discovers some of his unsavory patrons are planning to rob him. After a friend is shot trying to help him, Stone decides to even the score. Chapter 3 of "Gordon of Ghost City" finds Mary and Gordon entering a mine owned by Mary's grandfather, which turns out to be rich in gold. A figure sets an explosion and Mary and Gordon get trapped in the mine! 87m/B VHS, Closed Caption. Buck Jones, Noel Francis, Niles Welch, Marion Shilling, Peggy Campbell, Harry Semels, Madge Bellamy, Walter Miller; D: Nick Grinde, Ray Taylor. USH

The Stoned Age 🐾 1994 (R) Buddies look to get wasted and find some chicks. Set in the '70s. 90m/C VHS. Michael Kopelow, China Kantner, Renee Griffen; D: James Melkonian. THV

Stones of Death 🐾 1988 (R) An aboriginal curse is invoked when a subdivision is built too close to an ancient burial site. Teenagers begin having all-too-real nightmares about death. 90m/C VHS, Beta. Tom Jennings, Natalie McCurry, Zoe Carides, Eric Oldfield; D: James Bagle. NO

Stonewall 🐾🐾🐾 1995 (R) Fictional account of the June, 1969 police raid on Greenwich Village gay bar the Stonewall Inn, which is considered to have launched the modern gay rights movement. White-bread, midwestern activist Matty Dean (Weller) arrives in New York and gets thrown in jail for defending streetwise drag queen LaMiranda (Diaz) from harassing cops. They become lovers but Matty is also involved with conservative prepster Ethan (Corbalis), who thinks the flamboyant queens give the gay movement a bad name. Meanwhile, the drag queens at the mob-backed Stonewall are getting fed up with police raids and brutal treatment. Adapted from Martin Duberman's social history "Stonewall." Director Finch died during the final editing stages of the film. *CW:* Violence, sexuality, and language. 93m/C VHS. Frederick Weller, Guillermo Diaz, Brendan Corbalis, Bruce MacVittie, Duane Boutte, Peter Ratray, Luis Guzman; *D:* Nigel Finch; *W:* Rikki Beadle Blair; *C:* Chris Seager; *M:* Michael Kamen. *BMG*

The Stooge 🎬🎬½ 1951 Singer Bill Miller (Martin) asks the antic Ted Rogers (Lewis) to join him in his vaudeville act, where Rogers' clowning has them on the road to success. But then Miller decides he wants to go solo. Sounds more than a little autobiographical. ♫A Girl Named Mary and a Boy Named Bill; Who's Your Little Whozis?; Just One More Chance; With My Eyes Wide Open I'm Dreaming; Louise; I'm Yours. 100m/B VHS, Closed Caption. Dean Martin, Jerry Lewis, Polly Bergen, Marion Marshall, Eddie Mayehoff, Richard Erdman, Frances Bavier; *D:* Norman Taurog; *W:* Martin Rackin, Fred Finklehoffe, Elwood Ullman; *C:* Daniel F. Fapp. *PAR*

Stoogemania 🎬 1985 A nerd becomes so obsessed with the Three Stooges that they begin to take over his life and ruin it. Harmless except as a waste of time. Includes actual Stooge footage including some colorized—but see an old Stooges movie instead. 95m/C VHS, Beta. Josh Mostel, Melanie Chartoff, Sid Caesar; *D:* Chuck Workman; *M:* Hummie Mann. *PAR*

Stooges Shorts Festival 194? This collection of shorts includes "Disorder in the Court" (1936), "Sing a Song of Six Pants" (1947), and "Malice in the Palace" (1949). 55m/B VHS, Beta. *HHT*

The Stooges Story 🎬🎬🎬 1990 "The Stooges Anthology" presents a history of the comedy team, from their vaudevillian beginnings to their television resurgence in the '60s. "Disorder in the Court" finds the trio making a mockery of the United States justice system, and in "Brideless Groom," Shemp must find a bride within 48 hours in order to collect an inheritance. 90m/B VHS. Moe Howard, Larry Fine, Curly Howard, Shemp Howard. *SIM*

Stop! Look! and Laugh! 🎬🎬½ 1960 Paul Winchell and his dummy Jerry Mahoney host a look at some of the Stooges funniest moments. Features the Marquis Chimps' interpretation of Cinderella for some reason. 78m/B VHS. Moe Howard, Curly Howard, Shemp Howard, Larry Fine; *D:* Jules White. *COL*

Stop Making Sense 🎬🎬🎬½ 1984 The Talking Heads perform 18 of their best songs in this concert filmed in Los Angeles. Considered by many to be the best concert movie ever made. The band plays with incredible energy and imagination, and Demme's direction and camera work is appropriately frenzied and original. Features such Talking Heads songs as "Burning Down the House," "Psycho Killer," and "Once in a Lifetime." Band member Tina Weymouth's Tom Tom Club also performs for the audience. 99m/C VHS, Beta, LV. *D:* Jonathan Demme; *C:* Jordan Cronenweth; *Performed by:* David Byrne, Tina Weymouth, Chris Franz, Jerry Harrison. *MVD, COL*

Stop! or My Mom Will Shoot 🎬 1992 (PG-13) Getty is an overbearing mother paying a visit to her cop son (Stallone) in Los Angeles. When mom witnesses a crime she has to stay in town longer than intended, which gives her time to meddle in her son's work and romantic lives. If Stallone wants to change his image this so-called comedy isn't the way to do it—because the joke is only on him. Viewers who rent this may find the joke is on them. 87m/C VHS, Beta, LV, Closed Caption. Sylvester Stallone, Estelle Getty, JoBeth Williams, Roger Rees, Martin Ferrero, Gailard Sartain, Dennis Burkley; *D:* Roger Spottiswoode; *W:* William Osborne, William Davies, Blake Snyder; *M:* Alan Silvestri. Golden Raspberry Awards '92: Worst Actor (Stallone), Worst Supporting Actress (Getty), Worst Screenplay. *USH*

Stop That Cab 🎬½ 1951 Sloppy crooks accidentally leave precious jewels in the back seat of a taxi, and pursue and torture the cabby who found and hid them. Rather mean-spirited, uninteresting comedy. 56m/B VHS, Beta, LV. Sid Melton, Iris Adrian, Tom Neal. *NO*

Stopover Tokyo 🎬🎬 1957 An American intelligence agent uncovers a plot to assassinate the American ambassador while on leave in Japan. Nice location shooting and scenery; limp story and characters. Based on a novel by John P. Marquand. 100m/C VHS, Beta. Robert Wagner, Joan Collins, Edmond O'Brien, Ken Scott; *D:* Richard L. Breen. *FOX*

The Stork Club 🎬🎬 1945 A little song, a little dance, will Betty Hutton find romance? The actors manage to rise above the script in this silly, overdone fable. Hutton stars as the poor but spunky hatcheck girl who unwittingly saves the life of a cynical billionaire. His expressions of gratitude are less than appreciated by her G.I. beau. Done mainly as a vehicle for Hutton's promotion, so Betty's die-hard fans may find it to their liking. ♫Doctor, Lawyer, Indian Chief; Baltimore Oriole; I'm a Square in the Social Circle; If I Had a Dozen Hearts; Love Me; China Boy; In the Shade of the Old Apple Tree. 98m/B VHS. Betty Hutton, Barry Fitzgerald, Don DeFore, Robert Benchley, Bill Goodwin, Iris Adrian, Noel Neill, Andy Russell; *D:* Hal Walker. *NOS*

Storm 🎬½ 1987 (PG-13) Uneven thriller finds college students on a camping trip who must fight for their lives when they are confronted by killer thieves. Somewhat contrived, but interesting ending to this low-budget outing. 99m/C VHS, Closed Caption. CA David Palfy, Stan Kane, Harry Freedman, Lawrence Elion, Tom Schioler; *D:* David Winning; *M:* Amin Bhatia. *WAR*

Storm and Sorrow 🎬🎬 1990 Molly Higgins is known as the "Spiderwoman of the Rockies" for her legendary mountain climbing abilities. Then she joins a team looking to scale the 24,000-foot peaks of Russia's Pamir Mountains. The group meets deadly hazards—both natural and those caused by the ego-driven rivalries of the group's members. A fact-based drama based on the novel by Richard Craig. 96m/C VHS, Closed Caption. Lori Singer, Todd Allen, Steve Anderson, Jay Baker; *W:* Leigh Chapman. *WOV*

Storm in a Teacup 🎬🎬½ 1937 A reporter starts a campaign to save a sheepdog that the town magistrate has ordered killed because the owner, an old woman, is unable to pay the license tax. As the dog's fate hangs in the balance, this often humorous film provides an interesting look at British society of the 1930s. 80m/B VHS. GB Vivien Leigh, Rex Harrison, Cecil Parker, Sara Allgood; *D:* Victor Saville. *HMV, BAR, DVT*

Storm over Asia 🎬🎬🎬 *The Heir to Genghis Khan* 1928 A Mongolian trapper is discovered to be descended from Genghis Khan and is made puppet emperor of a Soviet province. Beautiful and evocative. Silent masterpiece. 70m/B VHS, Beta. RU I. Inkizhinov, Valeri Inkizhinov, A. Christiakov, A. Dedinstev, V. Tzoppi, Paulina Belinskaya; *D:* Vsevolod Pudovkin. *IHF, FST, VYY*

Storm over Wyoming 🎬🎬 1950 The old sheep-and-cattle battle again; Holt and Martin find themselves haplessly embroiled in a Wyoming range war. Action-packed but thin, ordinary western. 60m/B VHS, Beta. Tim Holt, Richard Martin. *NO*

Storm Rider 🎬🎬 1957 A gunman hired to protect a group of ranchers from a powerful rancher falls in love with a local widow. After his job is done, however, he leaves her behind. Typical western fare. 70m/B VHS. Scott Brady, Mala Powers, Bill Williams, Olin Howlin, William "Bill" Fawcett, John Goddard; *D:* Edward L. Bernds; *W:* Edward L. Bernds; *M:* Les Baxter. *NO*

The Storm Within 🎬🎬🎬½ *Les Parents Terribles* 1948 Based on Cocteau's play, many consider this domestic drama of a troubled family's tortured existence to be his finest work. De Bray

plays the domineering mother, Marais plays the son, and Day is the woman he (and his father) love in this complex story of sexuality, parental rivalry and jealousy. With the film set in only two locations, Cocteau creates a claustrophobic intimacy within the walls of de Bray's family apartment and Day's apartment. An inferior remake, "Intimate Relations" was released in Britain in 1953. In French with English subtitles. 98m/B VHS. FR Jean Marais, Yvonne de Bray, Gabrielle Dorziat, Marcel Andre, Josette Day; *D:* Jean Cocteau; *W:* Jean Cocteau. *WBF*

Stormquest woof! 1987 Deep in the jungle, a band of women warriors live without men. When it is discovered that one of the group has a male lover, she is sentenced to death. Her man tries to rescue her, and it turns into a war of the sexes—literally. In Spanish with subtitles. 90m/C VHS. SP Kai Baker, Brent Huff; *D:* Alex Sessa.

Stormswept 🎬½ 1995 Actress Brianna (Hughes) rents a haunted Louisiana mansion housing the spirit of a slave master. When a storm strands Brianna and friends, the spirit causes everyone to get up to all sorts of sexual escapades. 94m/C VHS. Julie Hughes, Melissa Moore, Kathleen Kinmont, Justin Carroll, Lorissa McComas, Ed Wasser, Kim Kopf, Hunt Scarritt; *D:* David Marsh; *W:* David Marsh. *MTH*

Stormy Monday 🎬🎬½ 1988 (R) An American developer conspires to strike it rich in Newcastle, England real estate by resorting to violence and political manipulations. Sting plays the jazz club owner who opposes him. Slow plot, but acted and directed well; interesting photography. 108m/C VHS, Beta, LV, 8mm, Closed Caption. GB Melanie Griffith, Tommy Lee Jones, Sting, Sean Bean, James Cosmo, Mark Long, Brian Lewis; *D:* Mike Figgis; *W:* Mike Figgis; *C:* Roger Deakins; *M:* Mike Figgis. *PAR, OM*

Stormy Nights 🎬½ 1997 (R) Femme fatale Nicole (Spaulding) worms her way into the lives of Jennifer McCormick (Tweed) and her weak-willed hubby (Clark), leading to seduction and betrayal. *CW:* Strong sexuality and violence, and for language. 90m/C VHS. Shannon Tweed, Tracy Spaulding, Brent Baxter Clark; *D:* Alberto Vidaurri; *W:* Michael Meyer; *C:* S. Douglas Smith; *M:* Jay Bolton. *PMH*

Stormy Trails 🎬 1936 Bell battles bellicose bad guys who are after his property. At least all the gunfights should keep a viewer awake! 59m/B VHS, Beta. Rex Bell. *VCN*

Stormy Waters 🎬🎬½ *Remorques* 1941 A romantic French drama about a sea captain falling in love with a woman he rescues from a storm. He goes back to his wife, however, when she becomes critically ill. Director Gremillon insisted on realistic footage of storms at sea; production was delayed because of the difficulties of the German occupation. Dubbed. 75m/B VHS, Beta. FR Jean Gabin, Michele Morgan, Madeleine Renaud; *D:* Jean Gremillon. *VYY*

Stormy Weather 🎬🎬½ 1943 In this cavalcade of black entertainment, the plot takes a back seat to the nearly non-stop array of musical numbers, showcasing this stellar cast at their performing peak. ♫There's No Two Ways About Love; Stormy Weather; Ain't Misbehavin'; Rhythm Cocktail; Rang Tang Tang; Dat, Dot, Dah; That Ain't Right; I Can't Give You Anything But Love, Baby; Digga Digga Doo. 77m/B VHS, Beta, LV, Closed Caption. Lena Horne, Bill Robinson, Fats Waller, Dooley Wilson, Cab Calloway, Nicholas Brothers; *D:* Andrew L. Stone; *C:* Leon Shamroy. *FOX, PTB, FCT*

The Story Lady 🎬🎬½ 1993 (G) A retiree uses her story-telling abilities as a hostess on a public-access children's program. She becomes so popular that two network execs want to exploit her as a spokesperson for a toy company. Only a young girl can help her find a way to resist going commercial. 120m/C VHS. Jessica Tandy, Lisa Jakub, Ed Begley Jr., Charles Durning, Stephanie Zimbalist; *D:* Larry Elikann. *BWE, UNT*

The Story of a Cheat 🎬🎬🎬 1936 The hero of the film discovers at an early age that dishonesty is probably the best policy and he sets out to put his theory into use. Director/writer Guitry also turns in a great performance as the central character. Guitry was a major influence on such different directors as Welles, Resnais and Truffaut. Based on Guitry's novel "Memoires d'Un Tricheur." In French with English subtitles. 83m/B VHS. *FR* Sacha Guitry; *D:* Sacha Guitry; *W:* Sacha Guitry. *INT, FCT*

Story of a Cowboy Angel 🎬 1981 On the Christmas Mountain Ranch, a cowboy angel descends to Earth to bestow various beneficences. 90m/C VHS, Beta. Slim Pickens. *ART, VES*

The Story of a Love Story 🎬🎬½ *Impossible Object* 1973 Bates plays a writer whose imagination gets the better of him when he attempts an extra-marital affair. Was he with her or not? Unusual concept doesn't stand up in the long run. Fine cast is under-utilized. 110m/C VHS. *FR* Alan Bates, Dominique Sanda, Evans Evans, Lea Massari, Michel Auclair, Laurence De Monaghan; *D:* John Frankenheimer; *W:* Alan Bates. *NO*

The Story of a Three Day Pass 🎬🎬½ *La Permission* 1968 A black American GI falls in love with a white French girl he meets in peacetime Paris. Based on Van Peebles book "La Permission." With English subtitles. Made on a low budget and flawed, but poignant and impressive. 87m/B VHS. Harry Baird, Nicole Berger, Pierre Doris; *D:* Melvin Van Peebles; *W:* Melvin Van Peebles. *XVC, FCT, HEG*

Story of Adele H. 🎬🎬🎬 *L'Histoire d'Adele H* 1975 (PG) The story of Adele Hugo, daughter of Victor Hugo, whose love for an English soldier leads to obsession and finally to madness after he rejects her. Sensitive and gentle unfolding of characters and story. Beautiful photography. In French with English subtitles. 97m/C VHS, Beta, LV. *FR* Isabelle Adjani, Bruce Robinson; *D:* Francois Truffaut; *W:* Suzanne Schiffman, Jean Gruault; *C:* Nestor Almendros. National Board of Review Awards '75: Best Actress (Adjani); New York Film Critics Awards '75: Best Actress (Adjani), Best Screenplay; National Society of Film Critics Awards '75: Best Actress (Adjani); Nominations: Academy Awards '75: Best Actress (Adjani). *MGM, FCT*

The Story of Alexander Graham Bell 🎬🎬🎬 1939 Lavish Fox biography on the inventor of the telephone provided Ameche with his most popular role. He's a serious Scot who comes to Boston to teach speech to the deaf and falls in love with the rich, beautiful and hearing impaired Young (whose three sisters, Georgianna, Polly Ann, and Sally are also in the film). Thanks to Young's rich daddy (Coburn), Bell gets the money to work on his invention, aided by enthusiastic assistant Watson (Fonda). No, it's not an entirely accurate retelling but it's well-done. 97m/B VHS. Don Ameche, Loretta Young, Henry Fonda, Charles Coburn, Spring Byington, Gene Lockhart, Sally Blane, Polly Ann Young, Georgianna Young, Bobs Watson, Jonathan Hale, Harry Davenport; *D:* Irving Cummings; *W:* Lamar Trotti; *C:* Leon Shamroy. *FXV*

The Story of Boys & Girls 🎬🎬🎬 *Storia de Ragazzi e di Ragazze* 1991 Two very different families come together for the wedding feast of their children, during which family secrets are revealed and we come to know and care for everyone present. A 20-course meal rivals the food scenes in "Babette's Feast" and is guaranteed to make your mouth water. Fine ensemble of actors, well directed, with a vivid evocation of 1930s Italy. In Italian with English subtitles. 92m/C VHS, LV. *IT* Lucrezia Lante della Rovere, Massimo Bonetti, Davide Bechini, Enrica Maria Modugno, Valeria Bruni Tadeschi, Lina Bernardi, Anna Bonaiuto, Alessandro Haber; *D:* Pupi Avati; *W:* Pupi Avati; *M:* Riz Ortolani. *FXL*

The Story of David 🎬🎬🎬 1976 (PG) Well-done Old Testament Bible drama about the shepherd boy who slew Goliath, overcame the Philistines, and united Israel. Then, as King Da-vid, he winds up involved in an illicit love affair with Bathsheba that threatens to destroy his kingdom. Fine acting and a literate script highlight this made for television production. On two cassettes. 192m/C VHS. Timothy Bottoms, Anthony Quayle, Jane Seymour, Keith Michell, Susan Hampshire; *D:* Alex Segal; *W:* Ernest Kinoy. *COL, VIF*

The Story of Dr. Wassell 🎬🎬½ 1944 Courageous true story of Corydon M. Wassell (Cooper), who won the Navy Cross for humanitarianism in WWII. Stationed in Java when the Japanese overrun the island, Wassell's placed in charge of evacuating the wounded. When he learns that stretcher cases must be left behind, he disobeys orders to rescue some badly wounded soldiers and get them to safety. (Naturally, there has to be some romance, so Cooper's paired with Day as a Red Cross nurse). Based on the book by James Hilton. 137m/C VHS, Closed Caption. Gary Cooper, Laraine Day, Signe Hasso, Dennis O'Keefe, Carol Thurston, Carl Esmond, Stanley Ridges, Paul Kelly, Elliott Reid, Philip Ahn, Barbara Britton; *D:* Cecil B. DeMille; *W:* Charles Bennett, Alan LeMay; *C:* Victor Milner; *M:* Victor Young. *USH*

The Story of Esther Costello 🎬🎬½ *Golden Virgin* 1957 Rich American Margaret Landi (Crawford) is visiting her Irish homeland when she meets Esther (Sears), a young girl rendered deaf, mute, and blind by a childhood trauma. The childless Margaret is persuaded to take Esther in as a surrogate daughter and the waif gradually begins to respond to her care, sparking a media frenzy over the inspirational saga. This brings Carlo (Brazzi), Margaret's estranged and money-grubbing husband, out of the woodwork, with some get-rich-quick schemes. Well-done melodrama adapted from the book by Nicholas Monsarrat. 102m/B VHS. *GB* Joan Crawford, Heather Sears, Rossano Brazzi, Lee Patterson, Ron Randell, Fay Compton, John Loder, Denis O'Dea; *D:* David Miller; *W:* Charles Kaufman; *C:* Robert Krasker; *M:* Georges Auric. *COL*

The Story of Fausta 🎬🎬½ *Romance da Empregada* 1988 (R) An unhappily married cleaning woman in the slums of Rio entices all the money and gifts she can out of an elderly widower. Decidedly grim comedy-drama, well-done but unsparing in its depiction of overwhelming greed. In Portuguese with English subtitles. 90m/C VHS. *BR* Betty Faria, Daniel Filho, Brandao Filho; *D:* Bruno Barreto; *M:* Ruben Blades. *FXL, FCT*

The Story of Jacob & Joseph 🎬🎬🎬 1974 (R) Fine Biblical drama finds brothers Jacob and Esau fighting over their birthright, tearing apart their family for 20 years. When the brothers finally reconcile, it's only to cast an envious eye on youngest brother Joseph, whom they sell into slavery. Taken to Egypt Joseph uses his talents to become the Pharoah's chief advisor but he can never forget his family or what was done to him. All-around good acting, directing, and writing. Made for television. 96m/C VHS. Keith Michell, Tony LoBianco, Julian Glover, Colleen Dewhurst, Herschel Bernardi, Harry Andrews; *D:* Michael Cacoyannis; *W:* Ernest Kinoy. *COL, VIF*

The Story of Louis Pasteur 🎬🎬🎬 1936 Formulaic Hollywood biopic raised a notch or two by Muni's superb portrayal of the famous scientist and his career leading up to his most famous discoveries. Acclaimed in its time; excellent despite low budget. 85m/B VHS, Beta. Paul Muni, Josephine Hutchinson, Anita Louise, Fritz Leiber, Donald Woods, Porter Hall, Akim Tamiroff, Walter Kingsford; *D:* William Dieterle; *C:* Gaetano Antonio "Tony" Gaudio. Academy Awards '36: Best Actor (Muni), Best Story; Nominations: Academy Awards '36: Best Picture. *MGM, BTV*

The Story of O 🎬🎬 1975 A young woman's love for one man moves her to surrender herself to many men, in order to please him. Softcore porn with bondage and S&M beautified by camera work. Based on the classic Freudian-erotic novel by Pauline Reage. 97m/C VHS, Beta, LV. Corinne Clery, Anthony Steel; *D:* Just Jaeckin. *HHE*

The Story of O, Part 2 🎬 1987 A sort-of sequel to the erotic classic, in which the somewhat soiled vixen takes over an American conglomerate by seducing everyone in it. 107m/C Beta, LV. Sandra Wey, Carole James. *ART, VES, HHE*

The Story of Qui Ju 🎬🎬🎬 *Qui Ju Da Guansi* 1991 (PG) A simple story, beautifully directed and acted, about a peasant woman's search for justice. The pregnant Qui Ju's husband is assaulted and injured by the head of their village. Outraged, Qui Ju slowly climbs the Chinese administrative ladder from official to higher official as she insistently seeks redress. Presents a close observance of daily life and customs with a strong female lead. Adapted from the novel "The Wan Family's Lawsuit" by Chen Yuan Bin. In Mandarin Chinese with English subtitles. 100m/C VHS, LV. *CH* Gong Li, Lei Lao Sheng, Liu Pei Qu, Ge Zhi Jun, Ye Jun, Yang Liu Xia, Zhu Qanging, Cui Luowen, Yank Huiquin, Wang Jianfa, Lin Zi; *D:* Zhang Yimou; *W:* Liu Heng; *C:* Chi Xiaonin, Yu Xaioqun; *M:* Zhao Jiping. National Society of Film Critics Awards '93: Best Foreign Film; Venice Film Festival '92: Best Actress (Li), Best Film; Nominations: Independent Spirit Awards '94: Best Foreign Film. *COL*

The Story of Robin Hood & His Merrie Men 🎬🎬🎬 *The Story of Robin Hood* 1952 Well-made swashbuckler based on the English legend was Disney's second live action feature. Almost, but not quite, as memorable as the 1938 Michael Curtiz "Adventures of Robin Hood." Curtiz's version had Errol Flynn, after all. 83m/C VHS, Beta, Closed Caption. Richard Todd, Joan Rice, Peter Finch, Martita Hunt; *D:* Ken Annakin. *DIS*

The Story of Ruth 🎬🎬 1960 Biblical saga of adventures of Ruth as she denounces her pagan gods and flees to Israel. Typically "epic" with overwrought performances. Alternately not too bad to downright boring. 132m/C VHS, Beta, Closed Caption. Elana Eden, Viveca Lindfors, Peggy Wood, Tom Tryon, Stuart Whitman, Jeff Morrow, Thayer David, Eduard Franz; *D:* Henry Koster. *FOX, IGP*

The Story of Seabiscuit 🎬🎬½ *Pride of Kentucky* 1949 The famous racing winner Seabiscuit is featured in a fluffy story of a racetrack romance. Temple is in love with a jockey (McCallister) but wants him to give up racing. Her uncle (Fitzgerald), who is Seabiscuit's trainer, has other things in mind. 93m/C VHS. Shirley Temple, Barry Fitzgerald, Lon McCallister, Rosemary DeCamp; *D:* David Butler. *MGM, BTV*

Story of the Dragon 🎬🎬 1982 How Bruce Lee developed the martial arts technique of Jeet Kune Do. 93m/C VHS, Beta. Bruce Li, Hwang Jang Lee, Carter Wong, Roy Horan. *WVE*

The Story of the Late Chrysanthemum 🎬🎬🎬½ 1939 Classic drama about the son of a Kabuki actor who falls in love with a servant girl against his father's wishes. Their doomed affair is the center of the plot. Acclaimed and sensitive drama, in Japanese with English subtitles. 115m/B VHS, Beta. *JP* Shotaro Hanayagi, Kakuo Mori, Kokichi Takada, Gonjuro Kawarazaki, Yoko Umemura; *D:* Kenji Mizoguchi. *FCT*

The Story of Vernon and Irene Castle 🎬🎬🎬 1939 In this, their last film together for RKO, Astaire and Rogers portray the internationally successful ballroom dancers who achieved popularity in the early 1900s. Irene Castle served as technical advisor for the film and exasperated everyone on the set by insisting that Rogers be a brunette. Still fun, vintage Fred and Ginger. ♫Only When You're In My Arms; Missouri Waltz; Oh, You Beautiful Doll; Nights of Gladness; By the Beautiful Sea; Glow, Little Glow Worm; Destiny Waltz; Row, Row, Row; The Yama Yama Man. 93m/B VHS, Beta, LV. Fred Astaire, Ginger Rogers, Edna May Oliver, Lew Fields, Jack Perrin, Walter Brennan; *D:* H.C. Potter. *TTC*

Story of William S. Hart/Sad Clowns 192? Features William S. Hart as a cowboy in "Hell's Hinges" and "Tumbleweeds" (1925). From "The History of the Motion Picture" series. **50m/B VHS, Beta.** William S. Hart, Buster Keaton, Harry Langdon. *GGR*

The Story of Women 🎗🎗🎗 *Une Affaire de Femmes* 1988 Riveting factual account of a woman (Huppert) who was guillotined for performing abortions in Nazi-occupied France. In French with English subtitles. **110m/C VHS.** *FR* Isabelle Huppert, Francois Cluzet, Marie Trintignant, Nils Tavernier, Louis Ducreux; *D:* Claude Chabrol; *W:* Claude Chabrol, Colo Tavernier O'Hagan; *M:* Matthieu Chabrol. Los Angeles Film Critics Association Awards '89: Best Foreign Film; New York Film Critics Awards '89: Best Foreign Film; Venice Film Festival '88: Best Actress (Huppert). *NYF*

The Story of Xinghua 🎗🎗 1993 Obedient wife Xinghua (Wenli) endures the cruelty of her greedy husband (Guoli) in a northern Chinese village, built within the shadow of the Great Wall. Working in the fields alongside handsome farmer Tulin (Shaojun), Xinghua is drawn to his gentleness and the two become lovers. When her husband hears that gold may be buried beneath one of the wall's watchtowers, he persuades his fellow villagers to help him dig beneath the stones—a decision that leads to tragedy. Mandarin with subtitles. **89m/C VHS.** *CH* Jiang Wehli, Zhang Guoli, Tian Shaoujun; *D:* Yin Li. *EVE*

Storybook 🎗🎗½ 1995 (G) Eight-year-old Brandon finds a magic storybook and enters into a realm of fantasy. He discovers the only way to return home from Storyland is to save the kingdom from the rule of Queen Evilia and along with Woody the Woodsman, Pouch the Boxing Kangaroo, and Hoot the Wise Owl, Brandon just may succeed. **88m/C VHS, Closed Caption.** Sean Fitzgerald, William McNamara, Swoosie Kurtz, Robert Costanzo, James Doohan, Brenda Epperson, Jay Morgan, Richard Moll, Jack Scalia, Milton Berle; *D:* Lorenzo Doumani; *W:* Lorenzo Doumani, Susan Bowen. *REP*

Storyville 🎗½ 1974 (PG) Love and music overcome prostitution and poverty in this turn-of-the-century New Orleans jazz drama, but tragedy prevails. **96m/C VHS, Beta.** Tim Rooney, Jeannie Wilson, Butch Benit, Wayne Mack, Bond Gideon, Oley Sassone; *D:* Jack Weis. *NO*

Storyville 🎗🎗 1992 (R) Southern Gothic tale set in New Orleans about a feckless young lawyer running for a local congressional seat. Neither Cray nor his family are strong candidates for the family values vote. Cray is separated from his wife and willingly indulges in an affair with a beautiful and mysterious young woman. This leads to a blackmail plot when he finds out his lover has been videotaping their antics. There's also a murder investigation and a host of family skeletons rattling around. Robards is fine as the crafty uncle but Spader's low-key attitude works against the story. Directorial debut of Frost.*CW:* Language, violent scene, and sensuality. **112m/C VHS, LV, Closed Caption.** James Spader, Joanne Whalley, Jason Robards Jr., Charlotte Lewis, Michael Warren, Piper Laurie, Michael Parks, Chuck McCann, Woody Strode, Charles Haid; *D:* Mark Frost; *W:* Mark Frost, Lee Reynolds; *M:* Carter Burwell. *COL*

Stowaway 🎗🎗🎗 1936 (G) After her missionary parents are killed in a Chinese revolution, Shirley stows away on a San Francisco-bound liner and plays cupid to a bickering couple who adopt her. 🎜Good Night, My Love; One Never Knows, Does One; You Gotta S-M-I-L-E to Be H-A-P-P-Y; I Wanna Go To the Zoo; That's What I Want For Christmas. **86m/B VHS, Beta, Closed Caption.** Shirley Temple, Robert Young, Alice Faye, Eugene Pallette, Helen Westley, Arthur Treacher, Astrid Allwyn; *D:* William A. Seiter; *C:* Arthur C. Miller. *FOX*

Straight for the Heart 🎗🎗 *A Corps Perdu* 1988 Photojournalist Pierre returns to Montreal after a harrowing assignment in Nicaragua. His homecoming is less than happy when he discovers both his lovers, David and Sarah, have deserted him. Pierre takes to wandering the Montreal streets, taking pictures, hoping they will help him make some sense of his life and help him re-establish a connection with beauty and humanity. In French with English subtitles. **98m/C VHS.** Matthias Habich, Johanne-Marie Tremblay; *D:* Lea Pool. *WBF*

Straight Line 🎗🎗 1988 T.S. Turner is a private investigator who goes after street gangs in order to prevent further violence in this action-packed story. **95m/C VHS.** Mr. T, Sean Roberge, Ron Ryan. *CAF, MOV*

Straight Out of Brooklyn 🎗🎗 1991 (R) A bleak, nearly hopeless look at a struggling black family in a Brooklyn housing project. The son seeks escape through crime, his father in booze. An up-close and raw look at part of society seldom shown in mainstream film, its undeniable power is sapped by ragged production values and a loose narrative prone to melodrama. Rich (seen in a supporting role) was only 19 years old when he completed this, funded partly by PBS-TV's "American Playhouse."*CW:* Language. **91m/C VHS.** George T. Odom, Ann D. Sanders, Lawrence Gilliard, Mark Malone Jr., Reana E. Drummond, Barbara Sanon, Matty Rich; *D:* Matty Rich; *W:* Matty Rich; *C:* John Rosnell; *M:* Harold Wheeler. Independent Spirit Awards '92: Best First Feature; Sundance Film Festival '91: Special Jury Prize. *HBO, FCT, MNR*

Straight Shootin' 🎗🎗½ 1917 Ford's first major effort launched both Carey and Gibson to national fame. Prototypical western; great action, great scenery. Silent. **53m/B VHS, Beta.** Harry Carey Sr., Hoot Gibson, Mollie Malone; *D:* John Ford. *GPV, VCN, DVT*

Straight Talk 🎗🎗½ 1992 (PG) Shirlee (Parton), a down-home gal from Arkansas, heads for Chicago to start life anew. She finds a job as a receptionist at WNDY radio, but is mistaken for the new radio psychologist. Her homespun advice ("Get off the cross. Somebody needs the wood.") becomes hugely popular and soon "Dr." Shirlee is the toast of the town. Parton's advice is the funniest part of this flimsy movie, but she is helped immensely by Dunne and Orbach. Woods, however, is not in his element in a romantic comedy, and holds the movie down. **91m/C VHS, Beta, Closed Caption.** Dolly Parton, James Woods, Griffin Dunne, Michael Madsen, Deirdre O'Connell, John Sayles, Teri Hatcher, Spalding Gray, Jerry Orbach, Philip Bosco, Charles Fleischer, Jay Thomas; *D:* Barnet Kellman; *W:* Craig Bolotin, Patricia Resnick; *M:* Brad Fiedel. *HPH*

Straight Time 🎗🎗🎗 1978 (R) Ex-con Hoffman hits the streets for the first time in six years and finds himself again falling into a life of crime. Well-told, sobering story flopped at the boxoffice and has never received the recognition it deserved. Convincing, realistic portrayal of a criminal. Hoffman was the original director, but gave the reins to Grosbard. Based on the novel "No Beast So Fierce" by Edward Bunker. **114m/C VHS, Beta.** Dustin Hoffman, Harry Dean Stanton, Gary Busey, Theresa Russell, M. Emmet Walsh, Kathy Bates; *D:* Ulu Grosbard; *W:* Jeffrey Boam, Alvin Sargent, Edward Bunker; *C:* Owen Roizman; *M:* David Shire. *WAR*

Straight to Hell 🎗½ 1987 (R) A wildly senseless, anachronistic western spoof about a motley, inept gang of frontier thieves. An overplayed, indiscriminating punk spaghetti oat-opera. **86m/C VHS, Beta, Closed Caption.** Dennis Hopper, Joe Strummer, Elvis Costello, Grace Jones, Jim Jarmusch, Dick Rude, Courtney Love, Sy Richardson; *D:* Alex Cox; *W:* Alex Cox. *FOX, OM*

Straight Up 🎗½ 1990 A musical f/x-ridden attempts to warn MTV-era children about drugs, but visual gimmicks often overwhelm the message. Gossett sings nicely as a cosmic sage of abstinence, who cautions a boy against substance abuse. The smartest segment lambasts cigarette and alcohol ads. **75m/C VHS, Beta.** Chad Allen, Louis Gossett Jr. *RHI*

Strait-Jacket 🎗🎗 1964 After Crawford is released from an insane asylum where she was sent 20 years for axing her husband and his mistress, mysterious axe murders begin to occur in the neighborhood. Coincidence? Aging axist Crawford is the prime suspect, and even she cannot say for sure who's doing it. Daughter Baker is there to help her adjust. Moderately creepy grade B+ slasher is lifted somewhat by Crawford. Written by Robert Bloch ("Psycho"). Never one to miss a gimmick, director Castle arranged for the distribution of cardboard "bloody axes" to all theatre patrons attending the movie. **89m/B VHS, Beta.** Joan Crawford, Leif Erickson, Diane Baker, George Kennedy, Howard St. John, Rochelle Hudson, Edith Atwater, Lee Majors; *D:* William Castle; *W:* Robert Bloch; *C:* Arthur E. Arling; *M:* Van Alexander. *COL*

Stranded 🎗🎗 1987 (PG-13) A group of aliens escaping interplanetary persecution land on Earth and enlist the aid of an Earth family. Solid characters make it more than sci-fi; sort of a parable of intolerance, human (and alien) goodness, etc. **80m/C VHS, Beta, LV, Closed Caption.** Maureen O'Sullivan, Ione Skye, Cameron Dye; *D:* Tex Fuller; *W:* Alan Castle. *COL*

The Strange Affair of Uncle Harry 🎗🎗½ *Uncle Harry* 1945 Small-town gothic with fine acting by Sanders, an aging bachelor who plots murder when his romance is threatened by a jealous sister. A title card asks you not to reveal the 'surprise' ending—a hackneyed twist that appeased the censors but made producer Joan Harrison resign in protest. Based on a play by Robert Job. Tape suffers from poor film-video transfer. **80m/B VHS, LV.** George Sanders, Geraldine Fitzgerald, Ella Raines, Sara Allgood, Moyna MacGill, Samuel S. Hinds, Harry von Zell; *D:* Robert Siodmak. *REP, FCT*

A Strange and Deadly Occurence 🎗½ 1974 Strange things start to happen to a family when they move to a house in a remote area. Made-for-television. **74m/C VHS, Beta.** Robert Stack, Vera Miles, L.Q. Jones, Herb Edelman; *D:* John Llewellyn Moxey. *WOV*

Strange Awakening 🎗 1958 Traveling in France while recuperating from amnesia, Barker is trapped in a plot of fraud and theft. Confused and contrived. **75m/B VHS.** *GB* Lex Barker, Carole Mathews, Nora Swinburne, Richard Molinos, Peter Dyneley; *D:* Montgomery Tully. *SNC*

Strange Bedfellows 🎗🎗½ 1965 Within 24 hours of Carter Hudson (Hudson) arriving to work in London, he's met and married eccentric Italian Toni Vincenti (Lollobrigida). Complete opposites, the marriage is soon over and Carter returns to the States. Seven years later, he's back in London, ready to officially divorce Toni but learns from company PR whiz Dick Bramwell (Young) that his big promotion is contingent on his happy marriage. Carter courts Toni again, and tries to support her liberal causes and friends, but it turns out her latest stunt is aimed at his firm. Supposedly a check of the closing credits shows the film was shot on a Universal back lot and not on location. **104m/C VHS, Closed Caption.** Rock Hudson, Gina Lollobrigida, Gig Young, Edward Judd, Howard St. John, Nancy Kulp, Bernard Fox, Terry-Thomas; *D:* Melvin Frank; *W:* Melvin Frank, Michael Pertwee; *C:* Leo Tover; *M:* Leigh Harline. *USH*

Strange Behavior 🎗🎗 *Dead Kids; Small Town Massacre* 1981 (R) In a small Midwestern town, the police chief follows the clues from a series of murders to the experimental lab of the local college. Seems there's a mad scientist involved... Grisly and creepy, but unduly ballyhooed when it appeared. Shot on location in New Zealand. **105m/C VHS.** Michael Murphy, Louise Fletcher, Dan Shor, Fiona Lewis, Arthur Dignam, Marc McClure, Scott Brady, Dey Young, Charles Lane; *D:* Michael Laughlin; *W:* Michael Laughlin, Bill Condon; *C:* Louis Horvath. *COL, RHI, FCT*

Strange Brew 🎗🎗½ 1983 (PG) The screen debut of the SCTV alumni's characters Doug & Bob MacKenzie, the Great White North duo. They do battle with a powerful, megalomaniacal brew master over—what else?—a case of beer. Dumb, but what did you expect? Watch it, or be a hoser. **91m/C VHS, Beta, LV.** Rick Moranis, Dave Thomas, Max von Sydow, Paul Dooley; *D:* Rick Moranis, Dave Thomas;

W: Rick Moranis, Dave Thomas, Steve DeJarnatt; M: Charles Fox. MGM

Strange Cargo 🐾🐾½ **1940** Convicts escaping from Devil's Island are mystically entranced by a Christ-like fugitive en route to freedom. An odd, pretentious Hollywood fable waiting for a cult following. Gable and Crawford's eighth and final pairing. Adapted by Anita Loos from the book "Not Too Narrow...Not Too Deep" by Richard Sale. **105m/B VHS, Beta.** Clark Gable, Joan Crawford, Ian Hunter, Peter Lorre, Paul Lukas, Albert Dekker, J. Edward Bromberg, Eduardo Ciannelli, Frederick Worlock; D: Frank Borzage. MGM

Strange Case of Dr. Jekyll & Mr. Hyde 🐾🐾 **1968** An adaptation of the classic Robert Louis Stevenson book about a scientist who conducts experiments on himself to separate good from evil. Palance is oddly but appealingly cast; Jarrott's bad direction wrecks it. Made for TV. **128m/C VHS, Beta.** Jack Palance, Leo Genn, Oscar Homolka, Billie Whitelaw, Denholm Elliott; D: Charles Jarrott. ART, MPI

Strange Case of Dr. Jekyll & Mr. Hyde 🐾🐾½ **1989** The Robert Louis Stevenson classic, with Hyde portrayed as an icy, well-dressed sociopath. In Shelley Duvall's "Nightmare Classics" series. More psychological than special effect-y. Made for cable. **60m/C VHS, Beta.** Anthony Andrews, Laura Dern, George Murdock, Nicholas Guest; D: Michael Lindsay-Hogg. WAR, OM

The Strange Case of the End of Civilization as We Know It 🐾🐾½ **1993** Cleese stars as the detective grandson of Sherlock Holmes, who also has a reputation for making a mockery of police investigations. Nevertheless, the police commissioner summons him to capture that diabolical criminal Professor Moriarty. **55m/C VHS.** GB John Cleese, Stratford Johns, Connie Booth, Arthur Lowe. KUL, FCT, SIG

Strange Confession **1945** Contains one of the truly rare Inner Sanctum Mysteries from Universal. **62m/C VHS.** Lon Chaney Jr., Brenda Joyce, J. Carrol Naish, Milburn Stone, Lloyd Bridges; D: John Hoffman; W: M. Coates Webster. GPV

The Strange Countess 🐾🐾 **1961** A girl is almost murdered and no apparent motive can be found until a 20-year-old murder is uncovered in this Edgar Wallace story. **96m/C VHS.** GE Joachim Fuchsberger, Lil Dagover, Marianne Hoppe, Brigitte Grothum; D: Josef von Baky. SNC

Strange Days 🐾🐾🐾 **1995 (R)** It's 1999 in volatile L.A. and vice cop-turned-street-hustler Lenny Nero (Fiennes) is plying his SQUID trade—discs that offer the wearer the chance to experience any vice. The seedily likeable Lenny draws the line at peddling snuff clips until one capturing the murder of his friend, hooker Iris (Bako), shows up. Lenny's in way over his head and turns to self-sufficient security agent Mace (Bassett) to save him. The phenomenal Bassett heats up the screen (and kicks major butt) while the generally cerebral Fiennes shows why someone could care about his desperate lowlife. Bigelow's an action expert and struts on the film's dark visuals while offering some emotional impact with her society-on-the-eve-of-destruction saga.CW: Intense disturbing violence, sexuality, nudity, and profanity. **145m/C VHS, Closed Caption.** Ralph Fiennes, Angela Bassett, Juliette Lewis, Michael Wincott, Brigitte Bako, Vincent D'Onofrio, William Fichtner, Richard Edson, Glenn Plummer, Josef Sommer; D: Kathryn Bigelow; W: James Cameron, Jay Cocks; C: Matthew F. Leonetti; M: Graeme Revell. FXV

The Strange Door 🐾½ **1951** Laughton hams it up as the evil Alan de Maletroit (Laughton), who's imprisoned his brother Edmond (Cavanagh) for the crime of marrying Alan's one love. Now Maletroit wants to destroy his niece Blanche (Forrest) as well. But Edmond's faithful retainer Voltan (Karloff) is determined to stop the evil. Low-budget hokum adapted from the Robert Louis Stevenson story "The Sire de Maletroit's

Door." **81m/B VHS, Closed Caption.** Charles Laughton, Boris Karloff, Paul Cavanagh, Sally Forrest, Richard Stapley, Michael Pate, Alan Napier; D: Joseph Pevney; W: Jerry Sackheim; C: Irving Glassberg. USH

Strange Fruit 🐾🐾 **1979** Based on Lillian Smith's novel, this program tells the story of a black painter in Georgia, 1948, who faces racism. At first avoiding voter registration, he becomes involved and is killed. His death serves as an inspiration to his community. **33m/C VHS, Beta.** BFA

Strange Illusion 🐾🐾½ Out of the Night **1945** Unbalanced teen Lydon believes his mother, about to remarry, was responsible for his father's death. He feigns insanity in a plan to catch her, but is sent to an asylum, where he nearly goes insane for real. Slow and implausible, but creepy enough to hold your interest. **87m/B VHS, Beta.** Jimmy Lydon, Warren William, Sally Eilers, Regis Toomey, Charles Arnt, George Reed; D: Edgar G. Ulmer. SNC

Strange Interlude 🐾🐾🐾 Strange Interval **1932** Shearer is at her best in screen adaptation of talky Eugene O'Neill play in which she portrays a young wife who wants a child, but discovers that insanity runs in her husband's family. Doing the only sensible thing, she decides to have a child by another man (Gable). Interesting because the characters' thoughts are revealed to the audience through voice-overs. **110m/B VHS, Closed Caption.** Norma Shearer, Clark Gable, May Robson, Ralph Morgan, Robert Young, Mary Alden, Maureen O'Sullivan, Henry B. Walthall; D: Robert Z. Leonard; C: Lee Garmes. MGM

Strange Interlude 🐾🐾½ **1990** Slow PBS production of Eugene O'Neill's famous drama covering two decades of the lives and loves of an upper-class family. Excellent performances help to make up for talkiness. On two cassettes. **190m/C VHS.** Glenda Jackson, Jose Ferrer, David Dukes, Ken Howard, Edward Petherbridge; D: Herbert Wise. TVC

Strange Invaders 🐾🐾🐾 **1983 (PG)** Body-snatchers-from-space sci-fi with an attitude—fun spoof of '50s alien flicks. Space folks had taken over a midwestern town in the '50s, assuming the locals' appearance and attire before returning to their ship. Seems one of them married an earthling—but divorced and moved with his half-breed daughter to New York City. So the hicksters from space arrive in Gotham wearing overalls... **94m/C VHS, Beta, LV.** Paul LeMat, Nancy Allen, Diana Scarwid, Michael Lerner, Louise Fletcher, Wallace Shawn, Fiona Lewis, Kenneth Tobey, June Lockhart, Charles Lane, Dey Young, Mark Goddard; D: Michael Laughlin; W: Bill Condon. VES

The Strange Love of Martha Ivers 🐾🐾🐾 **1946** Douglas is good in his screen debut as the wimpy spouse of unscrupulous Stanwyck. Stanwyck shines as the woman who must stay with Douglas because of a crime she committed long ago... Tough, dark melodrama; classic film noir. **117m/B VHS, Beta, LV.** Barbara Stanwyck, Van Heflin, Kirk Douglas, Lizabeth Scott, Judith Anderson; D: Lewis Milestone; C: Victor Milner; M: Miklos Rozsa. Nominations: Academy Awards '46: Best Story. NOS, KIV, DVT

The Strange Love of Molly Louvain 🐾½ Molly Louvain **1932** Unwed mother Dvorak finds herself in hiding after her criminal beau fatally shoots a police officer. She falls in love with the unsuspecting newsman (Tracy) hot on her trail. Good performance from Dvorak but the film in general lacks sparkle. Adapted from the play "Tinsel Girl" by Maurine Watkins. **70m/B VHS.** Ann Dvorak, Lee Tracy, Richard Cromwell, Guy Kibbee, Leslie Fenton, Frank McHugh, Evalyn Knapp, Charles Middleton, Mary Doran, C. Henry Gordon; D: Michael Curtiz; W: Erwin Gelsey, Brown Holmes. MGM

Strange New World 🐾½ **1975** Three astronauts awake from 188 years in the fridge to find cloning has arrived. Made for TV as a pilot for a hoped-for series that might have been even worse. **100m/C VHS.** John Saxon, Kathleen Miller, Keene Curtis, Martine Beswick, James Olson, Catherine Bach, Richard Farnsworth, Ford Rainey; D: Robert Butler. UNI

The Strange One 🐾🐾½ **1957** Appropriate title for this dank drama based on Willingham's novel and play "End as a Man." Jacko De Paris (Gazzara) is the student leader at a Southern military school, who uses his power to intimidate and brutalize fellow cadets, aided by minions Knoble (Hingle) and Gatt (Olson). Finally a group of younger students, led by Marquales (Peppard, in his film debut), go after the tyrant. Also filmed as 1957's "Sorority Girl." **100m/B VHS.** Ben Gazzara, Pat Hingle, James Olson, George Peppard, Peter Mark Richman, Larry Gates, Clifton James, Arthur Storch; D: Jack Garfein; W: Calder Willingham; C: Burnett Guffey; M: Kenyon Hopkins. COL

Strange Shadows in an Empty Room 🐾 Blazing Magnums; Shadows in an Empty Room **1976 (R)** Sleuth Whitman wants answers about the murder of his kid sis. He beats lots of people up, and the viewer leaves the empty living room to look at the inside of the fridge, which is more interesting. **97m/C VHS, Beta.** Stuart Whitman, John Saxon, Martin Landau, Tisa Farrow, Carole Laure, Gayle Hunnicutt; D: Martin Herbert. VES

Strange Tales/Ray Bradbury Theatre 🐾🐾½ **1986 (R)** An anthology of thrillers based on Bradbury stories: "Banshee," "The Screaming Woman," and "The Town Where No One Got Off." **86m/C VHS, Beta.** Jeff Goldblum, Peter O'Toole, Drew Barrymore, Charles Martin Smith. CNG

The Strange Woman 🐾🐾 **1946** Uneventful Hollywood costume drama. Lamarr stalks man after man, but never creates much excitement in spite of Ulmer's fancy camera work and intense pace. **100m/B VHS.** Hedy Lamarr, George Sanders, Louis Hayward, Gene Lockhart, Hillary Brooke, June Storey; D: Edgar G. Ulmer. NOS, FCT

Strange World of Coffin Joe 🐾 O Estranho Mundo de Ze do Caixao **1968** A collection of three shocking horror episodes about a truly disgusting dollmaker who becomes tempted by his human-like creations, a balloon seller's repulsive necrophiliac impulses, and a doctor (the disguised Coffin Joe) with a sadistic gift for excruciating torture. In Portugese with English subtitles. **?m/C VHS.** BR Jose Mojica Marins; D: Jose Mojica Marins. SMW, FCT, TPV

The Strangeness woof! **1985** Miners in search of gold release a "strange" creature from far beneath the earth—eek! Made on a negative budget. **90m/C VHS, Beta.** Dan Lunham, Terri Berland; D: David Michael Hillman. TWE

The Stranger 🐾🐾🐾½ **1946** Notably conventional for Welles, but swell entertainment nonetheless. War crimes tribunal sets Nazi thug Shayne free hoping he'll lead them to his superior, Welles. Robinson trails Shayne through Europe and South America to a small town in Connecticut. Tight suspense made on a tight budget saved Welles's directorial career. **95m/B VHS, Beta.** Edward G. Robinson, Loretta Young, Martha Wentworth, Konstantin Shayne, Richard Long, Orson Welles; D: Orson Welles; C: Russell Metty. Nominations: Academy Awards '46: Best Story. CNG, NOS, VYY

The Stranger 🐾½ **1973** Corbett crashlands on a planet an awful lot like Earth—and must stay on the run. Uneven fugitive thriller in sci-fi drag. Made for TV. **100m/C VHS.** Cameron Mitchell, Glenn Corbett, Sharon Acker, Lew Ayres, George Coulouris, Dean Jagger; D: Lee H. Katzin. NO

The Stranger 🐾🐾🐾 **1987 (R)** Amnesiac car-wreck victim Bedelia begins regaining her memory, and realizes she witnessed several ghostly murders. Is her shrink (Riegert) helping her remember, or keeping something from her? Good, neglected thriller. **93m/C VHS, Beta, 8mm, Closed Caption.** AR Bonnie Bedelia, Peter Riegert, Barry Primus, David Spielberg, Julio de Grazia, Cecilia Roth, Marcus Woinski; D: Adolfo Aristarain; W: Dan Gurskis; M: Craig Safan. COL

The Stranger 🎞🎞½ 1992 Quiet comedy about family loyalties and devalued traditions. The upper-middle-class life of Sudhindra Bose is disturbed by the arrival of his wife Anila's long-lost uncle Manomohan. Although their young son is excited by the visit of this mysterious relative, Anila is bewildered and her husband suspicious—he thinks the man may be an imposter after their money. The independent Manomohan realizes the family's discomfort and slowly turns the tables on all their suspicions. Ray's last film. In Bengali with English subtitles. **100m/C VHS. IN** Deepankar De, Mamata Shankar, Bikram Bhattacharya, Utpal Dutt, Dhritiman Chatterji, Rabi Ghosh, Subrata Chatterji; **D:** Satyajit Ray; **W:** Satyajit Ray. *FRF*

The Stranger 🎞🎞 1995 (R) Mystery woman (Long) rides into small town and rids it of a vicious motorcycle gang. Femme version of the lone hero saga. **CW:** Action violence; strong sex scene; some language. **98m/C VHS, Closed Caption.** Kathy Long, Andrew Divoff, Eric Pierpont, Robin Lynn Heath; **D:** Fritz Kiersch; **W:** Gregory Poirier. *COL*

A Stranger Among Us 🎞🎞 1992 (PG-13) A missing jeweler turns up dead and more than $1 million in diamonds has disappeared. NYPD Detective Emily Eden (Griffith) is called in to solve the case, and she decides she must go undercover in a community of Hasidic Jews to find the perpetrator. She not only finds the criminal, but she also falls in love with one of the group's most devout residents. Griffith is out of her element as a tough cop with her baby voice and cutesy style, but other actors, including Thal (in his movie debut) and Sara, perform splendidly, even though they are held back by a cumbersome script that is similar in many respects to "Witness." **109m/C VHS, Beta, LV, Letterbox, Closed Caption.** Melanie Griffith, Eric Thal, John Pankow, Tracy Pollan, Lee Richardson, Mia Sara, Jamey Sheridan; **D:** Sidney Lumet; **C:** Robert J. Avrech; **M:** Jerry Bock. Golden Raspberry Awards '92: Worst Actress (Griffith). *HPH*

The Stranger and the Gunfighter 🎞🎞 1976 The baddest spaghetti western of all time—or is it a kung fu movie? Alcoholic cowpoke Van Cleef and kung fu master Lieh pair up to find hidden treasure. There is a map, but parts are printed on the assorted fannies of various women. **106m/C VHS, Beta, LV, Closed Caption.** Patty Shepard, Lee Van Cleef, Lo Lieh; **D:** Anthony (Antonio Margheriti) Dawson. *COL*

Stranger by Night 🎞🎞 1994 (R) Detective Bobby Corcoran and his partner are hunting a mutilating serial killer. Since Corcoran suffers from black-outs and fits of rage the evidence begins pointing very close to home. **96m/C VHS.** Steven Bauer, William Katt, Jennifer Rubin, Michael Parks, Michele Greene, J.J. Johnston; **D:** Gregory Brown; **M:** Ashley Irwin. *APX*

The Stranger from Pecos 🎞🎞 1945 Brown fights a cheater who swindles people at poker and then uses the money to buy their mortgages. Meanwhile, his pal Hatton finds a novel way to help a robbery victim buy back his property. **55m/B VHS.** Johnny Mack Brown, Raymond Hatton, Kirby Grant, Christine McIntyre, Steve Clark, Kermit Maynard; **D:** Lambert Hillyer. *DVT, HEG*

The Stranger from Venus woof! *Immediate Disaster; The Venusian* 1954 "The Day the Earth Stood Still" warmed over. Venusian Dantine tells earth lady Neal he's worried about the future of her planet. Real low budget. Includes previews of coming attractions from classic sci-fi. **78m/B VHS.** Patricia Neal, Helmut Dantine, Derek Bond. *EEL, MLB*

Stranger in Paso Bravo 🎞 1973 A distraught drifter returns to a strange Italian town to avenge the murders of his wife and daughter years before. Dubbed. **92m/C VHS, Beta. IT** Anthony Steffen, Giulia Rubini, Eduardo Fajardo, Andriana Ambesi. *UNI*

Stranger in the House 🎞🎞 1997 (R) Jack (Nullabuck) hid a diamond necklace in an old house after his heist went bad. When he gets out of prison and goes to retrieve his loot, he discovers the house is now occupied by Joanna (Greene) and Dan (Dinsmore). Turns out Dan wants to kill Joanna for her money, and Jack's being pursued by an insurance adjuster (Vrana) after the necklace. **CW:** Language, violence. **94m/C VHS, LV, Closed Caption.** Michele Greene, Steve Railsback, Bruce Dinsmore, Vlasta Vrana; **D:** Rodney Gibbons; **W:** Peter Paul Liapis, Steve Pesce; **M:** Marty Simon. *ART*

Stranger in Town 🎞🎞 1957 A young journalist looks into the murder of an American composer in a sleepy English village. He discovers blackmail and intrigue. So-so thriller. Based on the novel "The Uninvited" by Frank Chittenden. **73m/B VHS, Beta. GB** Alex Nicol, Ann Page, Mary Laura Wood, Mona Washbourne, Charles Lloyd Pack; **D:** George Pollock. *SNC*

A Stranger in Town 🎞🎞½ 1995 Single mom Kay Tarses (Smart) has relocated to a small, quiet town with her infant son. But her peace is disturbed by menacing Barnes (Hines), a stranger who seems to know Kay has been lying about her past—and her child. When he seems determined to take her child, Kay has to decide whether to run, accept her fate, or fight. **93m/C VHS.** Jean Smart, Gregory Hines, Jeffrey Nordling, Lucinda Jenney, Richard Riehle; **D:** Peter Levin; **M:** Mark Snow. *PEG*

A Stranger Is Watching 🎞½ 1982 (R) Rapist-murderer Torn holds his victim's 10-year-old daughter hostage, along with a New York television anchorwoman. Complicated and distasteful. Made for TV. **92m/C VHS, Beta.** Rip Torn, Kate Mulgrew, James Naughton; **D:** Sean S. Cunningham. *MGM*

Stranger on the Third Floor 🎞🎞🎞 1940 Reporter McGuire's testimony helped convict cabbie Cook of murder, but he begins to have doubts. Odd, shadowy psycho-thriller considered by some the first film noir. The reporter comes to be suspected of the crime...and his fiancee pounds the pavement to prove him innocent. Average acting, but great camera work gives the whole a deliciously menacing feel. **64m/B VHS, Beta, LV.** Peter Lorre, John McGuire, Elisha Cook Jr., Margaret Tallichet, Charles Halton; **D:** Boris Ingster. *CCB*

Stranger than Paradise 🎞🎞🎞 1984 (R) Regular guy, nerdy sidekick and Hungarian girl cousin traipse around America being bored and having fun and adventure. New York, then—on to Cleveland! The thinking person's mindless flick. Inventive, independent comedy made on quite a low budget was acclaimed at Cannes. **90m/B VHS, Beta, LV, Closed Caption. GE** Richard Edson, Eszter Balint, John Lurie; **D:** Jim Jarmusch; **W:** Jim Jarmusch; **M:** John Lurie. National Society of Film Critics Awards '84: Best Film. *FCT, FOX*

The Stranger Who Looks Like Me 🎞🎞 1974 Adoptees Baxter and Bridges set out to find their real parents. Not-bad TV fare. Blake is Baxter's real-life mom. Look for a young Patrick Duffy. **74m/C VHS, Beta.** Meredith Baxter, Beau Bridges, Whitney Blake; **D:** Larry Peerce. *WOV*

The Stranger Within 🎞½ 1974 Made-for-TV "Rosemary's Baby" rip-off. Eden is in a family way, though hubby Grizzard is impotent. The stranger within begins commanding her to do its bidding, just as if she were a genie. **74m/C VHS, Beta.** Barbara Eden, George Grizzard, Joyce Van Patten, Nehemiah Persoff; **D:** Lee Philips; **M:** Charles Fox. *ART*

The Stranger Wore a Gun 🎞🎞 1953 Hoping to remove a black mark against his name, Jeff Travis (Scott) goes to Arizona and ends up foiling a stagecoach robbery. Features a great action sequence in a burning saloon. Originally shot in 3-D, this is based on the novel "Yankee Gold" by John M. Cunningham. **83m/C VHS.** Randolph Scott, Claire Trevor, Joan Weldon, George Macready, Alfonso Bedoya, Lee Marvin, Ernest Borgnine, Pierre Watkin, Joseph Vitale; **D:** Andre de Toth. *COL*

Strangers 🎞🎞 1990 Australian horror film revolves around a man in a troubled marriage who fools around with another woman, only to realize she is dead set on mating for life. When he hesitates, she vows to murder his wife. Very similar to the smash hit "Fatal Attraction." **83m/C VHS. AU** James Healey, Anne Looby; **D:** Craig Lahiff. *NO*

Strangers 🎞🎞 1991 (R) Features three provocative vignettes that take place far from home. Fiorentino, Chen, and Hutton each star in an erotic story played out in a foreign land. **CW:** Language and sexuality. **85m/C VHS, LV, Closed Caption.** Linda Fiorentino, Joan Chen, Timothy Hutton; **D:** Joan Tewkesbury.

Stranger's Gold 🎞 1971 A mysterious gunslinger eliminates corruption in a western mining town. **90m/C VHS, Beta.** Gianni "John" Garko, Antonio Vilar, Daniela Giordano. *GEM*

Strangers in Good Company 🎞🎞🎞 *The Company of Strangers* 1991 (PG) A loving metaphor to growing older. Director Scott uses non-actors for every role in this quiet little film about a bus-load of elderly women lost in the Canadian wilderness. They wait for rescue without hystrionics, using the opportunity instead to get to know each other and nature. Beautifully made, intelligent, uncommon and worthwhile. **101m/C VHS, Beta, Closed Caption. CA** Alice Diabo, Mary Meigs, Cissy Meddings, Beth Webber, Winifred Holden, Constance Garneau, Catherine Roche, Michelle Sweeney; **D:** Cynthia Scott; **W:** Cynthia Scott, David Wilson, Gloria Demers, Sally Bochner; **M:** Marie Bernard. *TOU*

Strangers in Paradise 🎞½ 1986 A scientist who cryogenically frozen himself to escape the Nazis is thawed out in the present, and his powers are used by a delinquent-obsessed sociopath. **81m/C VHS, Beta. D:** Ulli Lommel; **W:** Ulli Lommel. *ART, VES*

Strangers in the City 🎞🎞 1962 Puerto Ricans newly arrived in New York try to make their way. Serious but slightly overwrought immigrant-family melodrama. **80m/B VHS, Beta.** Robert Gentile, Camilo Delgado, Rosita De Triana; **D:** Rick Carrier. *NLC*

Strangers Kiss 🎞🎞½ 1983 (R) Circa 1955: Hollywood director encourages his two leads to have an off-screen romance to bring reality to his film. Conflict arises when the leading lady's boyfriend, the film's financier, gets wind of the scheme. Intriguing, fun, slightly off-center. Based on Stanley Kubrick's film "Killer Kiss." **93m/C VHS, Beta.** Peter Coyote, Victoria Tennant, Blaine Novak, Dan Shor, Richard Romanus, Linda Kerridge, Carlos Palomino; **D:** Matthew Chapman; **W:** Blaine Novak, Matthew Chapman; **M:** Gato Barbieri. *CNG*

Strangers of the Evening 🎞🎞 1932 In its day this dark comedy/mystery caught flak for its gruesomeness. There's been a mixup at the undertaker's, and the wrong body was buried—possibly alive. Good photography and acting make the humor work, intentionally or not. Based on the novel "The Illustrious Corpse," by Tiffany Thayer. **70m/B VHS.** ZaSu Pitts, Eugene Pallette, Lucien Littlefield, Tully Marshall, Miriam Seegar, Theodore von Eltz; **D:** H. Bruce Humberstone. *SNC, NOS*

Strangers on a Train 🎞🎞🎞🎞 1951 Long before there was "Throw Momma from the Train," there was this Hitchcock super-thriller about two passengers who accidentally meet and plan to "trade" murders. Amoral Walker wants the exchange and the money he'll inherit by his father's death; Granger would love to end his stifling marriage and wed Roman, a senator's daughter, but finds the idea ultimately sickening. What happens is pure Hitchcock. Screenplay co-written by murder-mystery great Chandler. Patricia Hitchcock, the director's only child, plays Roman's sister. The concluding "carousel" scene is a masterpiece. From the novel by Patricia Highsmith. **101m/B VHS, Beta, LV, DVD.** Farley Granger, Robert Walker, Ruth Roman, Leo G. Carroll, Patricia Hitchcock, Marion Lorne; **D:** Alfred Hitchcock; **W:** Raymond Chandler;

C: Robert Burks; *M:* Dimitri Tiomkin. Nominations: Academy Awards '51: Best Black and White Cinematography. *WAR, MLB*

Strangers: The Story of a Mother and Daughter 🐾🐾🐾 1979 Rowlands is the long-estranged daughter of Davis, who won an Emmy for her portrayal of the embittered widow. The great actress truly is at her recent best in this made-for-TV tearjerker, and Rowlands keeps pace. 88m/C VHS, Beta. Bette Davis, Gena Rowlands, Ford Rainey, Donald Moffat; *D:* Milton Katselas. *TLF*

Strangers When We Meet 🐾🐾½ 1960 A married architect and his equally married neighbor begin an affair. Their lives become a series of deceptions. Lavish but uninvolving soaper. Written by Evan Hunter and based on his novel. 117m/B VHS, Beta. Kirk Douglas, Kim Novak, Ernie Kovacs, Walter Matthau, Barbara Rush, Virginia Bruce, Kent Smith; *D:* Richard Quine; *C:* Charles B(ryant) Lang. *COL*

Stranglehold 🐾½ 1994 (R) Cooper (Trimble) is the executive assistant of Congresswoman Fillmore (McWhirter), who becomes the hostage of a nerve gas holding nutcase (Wells). Cooper manages to evade the nutcase's thugs while using his martial arts prowess to rescue his boss. *CW:* Commando and martial arts violence; language; some sexuality. 73m/C VHS. Jerry Trimble, Jillian McWhirter, Vernon Wells; *D:* Cirio H. Santiago. *NHO*

The Strangler 🐾½ 1964 A confused, mother-fixated psychopath strangles young women. Made at the time the Boston Strangler was terrorizing Beantown. The film slayer strangles ten lasses before his love of dolls gives him away. 89m/B VHS, Beta. Victor Buono, David McLean, Diane Sayer, Ellen Corby, Jeanne Bates, James B. Sikking; *D:* Burt Topper. *FOX, FCT*

Strangler of Blackmoor Castle 🐾🐾 1963 Someone is murdering people at an old English castle and Scotland Yard sends an investigator to track down the killer. ?m/C VHS. GE Karin Dor, Ingmar Zeisberg. *SNC*

Strangler of the Swamp 🐾½ 1946 The ghost of an innocent man wrongly hanged for murder returns to terrorize the village where he was lynched. Decidedly B-grade horror features an out-of-focus ghost and Edwards—on the other side of the camera—as one of his would-be victims. 60m/B VHS, Beta. Rosemary La Planche, Blake Edwards, Charles Middleton, Robert Barrat; *D:* Frank Wisbar. *COL*

Strapless 🐾🐾½ 1990 (R) Just-turned-40 American doctor Brown lives and works in London. She has just ended a long-term romance, and takes up with suave foreigner Ganz. Her young sister Fonda, arrives for a visit. Good, interesting if sometimes plodding story of adult relationships. 99m/C VHS, Beta, LV. Blair Brown, Bridget Fonda, Bruno Ganz, Alan Howard, Michael Gough, Hugh Laurie, Suzanne Burden, Camille Coduri, Alexandra Pigg, Billy Roch, Gary O'Brien; *D:* David Hare; *W:* David Hare; *M:* Nick Bicat. *COL*

Strapped 🐾🐾½ 1993 Earnest urban drama about a young man who needs quick cash and turns to selling guns to get it. ("Strapped" in street lingo means both carrying a gun and needing money.) Diquan's (Woodbine) pregnant girlfriend is in jail for selling crack and he doesn't have the bail money. So he and a partner begin selling guns but it turns out Diquan has also cut a deal with the cops and the deal doesn't stay a secret for long. Whitaker's directorial debut. Made for cable television. 102m/C VHS, LV. Bokeem Woodbine, Kia Joy Goodwin, Fred "Fredro" Scruggs, Michael Biehn, Craig Wasson; *D:* Forest Whitaker; *W:* Dena Kleiman. *HBO*

Strategic Air Command 🐾🐾½ 1955 A classic post-WWII chunk of Air Force patriotism. Veteran third baseman Stewart is recalled to flight duty at the hint of a nuclear war. He's already put in his time in the Big One and thinks he's being singled out now, but he answers his Uncle Sam's

call. Allyson plays Stewart's wife for the third time. 114m/C VHS, Beta, LV. James Stewart, June Allyson, Frank Lovejoy, Barry Sullivan; *D:* Anthony Mann; *C:* William H. Daniels. Nominations: Academy Awards '55: Best Story. *PAR*

The Stratton Story 🐾🐾🐾 1949 Stewart and Allyson teamed up for the first of the three pictures they'd make together in this true story of Monty Stratton, the Chicago White Sox pitcher. A baseball phenom, Stratton suffers a devastating hunting accident which leads to the amputation of one leg. Learning to walk with an artificial limb, Stratton also struggles to resume his baseball career. Stewart's fine as always, with Allyson lending noble support as the loving wife. Chisox manager Jimmy Dykes played himself as did pitcher Gene Bearden, lending further authenticity to an excellent production. 106m/B VHS, Beta. James Stewart, June Allyson, Frank Morgan, Agnes Moorehead, Bill Williams, Bruce Cowling; *D:* Sam Wood; *W:* Guy Trosper, Douglas S. Morrow. Academy Awards '49: Best Story. *MGM, FCT, BTV*

Straw Dogs 🐾🐾🐾 1972 (R) An American mathematician, disturbed by the predominance of violence in American society, moves with his wife to an isolated Cornish village. He finds that primitive savagery exists beneath the most peaceful surface. After his wife is raped, Hoffman's character seeks revenge. Hoffman is good, a little too wimpy at times. A violent, frightening film reaction to the violence of the 1960s. 118m/C VHS, Beta, LV. GB Dustin Hoffman, Susan George, Peter Vaughan, T.P. McKenna, David Warner; *D:* Sam Peckinpah; *W:* David Zelag Goodman. Nominations: Academy Awards '71: Best Original Dramatic/Comedy Score. *FOX*

Strawberry and Chocolate 🐾🐾🐾 *Fresa y Chocolate* 1993 (R) Sex, politics, and friendship set in 1979 Havana. University student David (Cruz) is sitting morosely in a cafe eating chocolate ice cream when he's spotted by older, educated, gay, strawberry-eating Diego (Perugorria), who manages to persuade David to visit him at his apartment. Resolutely hetero (and communist), David is appalled not only by Diego's sexuality but by his subversive politics. But gradually David's seduced by Diego's ideas and friendship into questioning the regime's harsh policies (and homophobia). Satiric and sympathetic—not only to the characters but to Cuba itself. Ill with cancer, Gutierrez Alea finished the film with the aid of Tabio. From the short story "The Wolf, the Forest and the New Man" by screenwriter Paz. Spanish with subtitles. *CW:* Language; brief strong sexuality. 110m/C VHS. CU Jorge Perugorria, Vladimir Cruz, Mirta Ibarra, Francisco Gattorno, Jorge Angelino, Marilyn Solaya; *D:* Tomas Gutierrez Alea, Juan Carlos Tabio; *W:* Tomas Gutierrez Alea, Senel Paz; *C:* Mario Garcia Joya; *M:* Jose Maria Vitier. Nominations: Academy Awards '94: Best Foreign Language Film. *TOU*

Strawberry Blonde 🐾🐾🐾 1941 A romantic comedy set in the 1890s, with Cagney as a would-be dentist infatuated with money-grubbing Hayworth (the strawberry blonde of the title), who wonders years later whether he married the right woman (chestnut brunette de Havilland). Attractive period piece remade from 1933's "One Sunday Afternoon," and revived yet again in 1948 by Raoul Walsh. 100m/B VHS, Beta. James Cagney, Olivia de Havilland, Rita Hayworth, Alan Hale, George Tobias, Jack Carson, Una O'Connor, George Reeves; *D:* Raoul Walsh; *W:* Julius J. Epstein, Philip G. Epstein; *C:* James Wong Howe. Nominations: Academy Awards '41: Scoring of a Musical. *MGM*

Strawberry Roan 🐾🐾 1933 Maynard plays a stubborn rodeo cowboy, out to prove he ain't whipped yet. One of Maynard's most popular films. Gene Autry bought the story to help him out in later years; the 1948 Autry "remake" uses only the title. 59m/B VHS. Ken Maynard, Ruth Hall; *D:* Ken Maynard. *NOS, DVT, HEG*

The Strawberry Statement 🐾🐾 1970 (R) Dated message film about a campus radical who persuades a college student to take part in the student strikes on campus during the '60s. Ambitious anti-violence message is lost in too many subplots. Soundtrack features songs by Crosby, Stills, Nash and Young and John Lennon. 109m/C VHS, Beta. Kim Darby, Bruce Davison, Bud Cort, James Coco, Kristina Holland, Bob Balaban, David Dukes, Jeannie Berlin; *D:* Stuart Hagmann; *W:* Israel Horovitz. Cannes Film Festival '70: Special Jury Prize. *MGM*

Stray Dog 🐾🐾🐾 1949 A tense, early genre piece by Kurosawa, about a police detective who has his revolver picked from his pocket on a bus, and realizes soon after it's being used in a series of murders. Technically somewhat flawed, but tense and intense. Mifune's pursuit of the criminal with his gun becomes metaphorically compelling. In Japanese with English subtitles. 122m/B VHS. JP Toshiro Mifune, Takashi Shimura, Isao Kimura; *D:* Akira Kurosawa. *HMV, COL*

Strays 🐾🐾 1991 (R) Here kitty kitty! A young couple move into their dream home, convinced it is the perfect place to raise their daughter. What they don't know is that the area is populated by a pack of wild cats. Before they can get rid of the kitties, one has marked their bedroom as his territory and they find themselves battling a swarm of mean kitties during a bad storm. *CW:* Violence and terror. 83m/C VHS, LV, Closed Caption. Kathleen Quinlan, Timothy Busfield, Claudia Christian; *D:* John McPherson; *W:* Shaun Cassidy. *USH*

Streamers 🐾🐾 1983 (R) Six young soldiers in a claustrophobic army barracks tensely await the orders that will send them to Vietnam. Written by Rabe from his play. Well acted but downbeat and drawn out. 118m/C VHS, Beta, LV. Matthew Modine, Michael Wright, Mitchell Lichtenstein, George Dzundza; *D:* Robert Altman; *W:* David Rabe. *IME, FCT*

The Street 🐾🐾½ 1923 A dark classic of German Kammerspiel film, notable for its expressionist treatment of Paris street life. A middle-aged man decides to abandon his wife and job to see what excitement he can find. He is duped by a prostitute, accused of murder, imprisoned, and nearly commits suicide before being rescued. Silent. 87m/B VHS, Beta. GE *D:* Karl Grune; *W:* Karl Grune. *VYY*

Street Asylum 🐾 1990 (R) Real-life Watergate spook Liddy is pathetically bad as an evil genius who cooks up a scheme to rid the streets of deadbeats and scumbags by implanting cops with a gizmo that makes them kill. Also available in a 94-minute unrated version. 94m/C VHS, Beta, LV. Wings Hauser, Alex Cord, Roberta Vasquez, G. Gordon Liddy, Marie Chambers, Sy Richardson, Jesse Doran, Jesse Aragon, Brion James; *D:* Gregory Brown. *NO*

Street Crimes 🐾🐾 1992 (R) A street-wise cop convinces gang members to put down their weapons and settle their grudges in the boxing ring. But when a gang leader starts shooting down the police and civilians, the cop and his young partner must work together to keep the neighborhood safe. *CW:* Language and violence. ?m/C VHS, LV. Dennis Farina, Max Gail, Mike Worth; *D:* Stephen Smoke; *W:* Stephen Smoke; *M:* John Gonzalez. *PMH*

The Street Fighter 🐾½ 1975 Fast-paced martial arts action finds freelance fighter Terry Tsuguri (Chiba) hired to spring a convicted killer from prison. But after he succeeds, his employers renege on their payment. Big mistake. Dubbed from Japanese. Three sequels: "Return of the Street Fighter," "The Street Fighter's Last Revenge," and "Sister Street Fighter." 91m/C VHS, LV. Sonny Chiba; *D:* Sakae Ozawa. *NLC*

Street Fighter 🐾½ 1994 (PG-13) Yes, it's a movie based on a popular video game (guess no one worried about the colossal flop of "Super Mario Bros"). Van Damme is action-minded Colonel Guile who is assigned to defeat crazed dictator General Bison (Julia in one of his last roles) in order to rescue kidnapped relief workers. Yes, there's lots of cartoon action but the genre's more exciting (and even makes more sense). Shot on location in Australia and Bangkok. **CW:** Non-stop martial arts and action violence. 101m/C **VHS, LV, Letterbox, Closed Caption, DVD.** Jean-Claude Van Damme, Raul Julia, Wes Studi, Ming-Na Wen, Damian Chapa, Simon Callow, Roshan Seth, Kylie Minogue, Byron Mann; **D:** Steven E. de Souza; **W:** Steven E. de Souza; **M:** Graeme Revell. **USH**

The Street Fighter's Last Revenge
🎬 1979 Third in the martial arts series finds Terry Tsuguri (Chiba) hired by a mob boss to do some dirty work and then getting doublecrossed—resulting in the death of Terry's girl. So, Terry hunts the miscreants down one by one. Lots of action, not much acting. Followed by "Sister Street Fighter." 80m/C **VHS.** Sonny Chiba, Sue Shiomi; **D:** Sakae Ozawa. **NLC**

Street Girls
🎬 1975 (R) A father enters the world of urban drugs and prostitution to find his runaway daughter. 77m/C **VHS, Beta.** Carol Case, Christine Souder, Paul Pompian; **D:** Michael Miller. **NLC**

Street Hawk
🎬 1984 A government agent operates an experimental, crime-fighting motorcycle in battling against a high-powered drug smuggling ring. 60m/C **VHS, Beta.** Rex Smith, Jayne Modean, Richard Venture, Christopher Lloyd. **USH**

Street Hero
woof! 1984 A young thug is torn between familial common sense and Mafia connections. 102m/C **VHS, Beta.** Vince Colosimo, Sigrid Thornton, Sandy Gore. **ART, VES**

Street Hitz
🎬½ 1992 Two brothers in the South Bronx find their family loyalties tested. Joey wants to finish college and get away from the violence in the streets while his brother Junior turns to the gangs to survive. 92m/C **VHS.** Angelo Lopez, Melvin Muza, Lyota Ramirez; **D:** Joseph B. Vasquez.

Street Hunter
woof! 1990 (R) Former cop turned freelance fighter quit the force when his integrity was questioned, but he still helps out now and then. Scumbag drug dealers line up a thug to waste him; epic kung fu battle ensues. 120m/C **VHS, LV.** Steve James, Reb Brown, John Leguizamo, Valarie Pettiford, Frank Vincent, Richie Havens; **D:** John A. Gallagher; **C:** Phil Parmet. **COL**

Street Justice
🎬½ 1989 (R) Over-complex tale of a CIA agent on the lam. Returning from years of Russian imprisonment, Ontkean finds his wife remarried, his daughter grown and both battling the corrupt town government. Good performances can't help the confusion of too many characters too flatly developed. 94m/C **VHS, Beta.** Michael Ontkean, Joanna Kerns, Catherine Bach, J.D. Cannon, Jeanette Nolan, Richard Cox, William Windom; **D:** Richard Sarafian. **WAR**

Street Knight
🎬🎬 1993 (R) Gang warfare in L.A. in a routine actioner. Jake is an ex-cop who gets drawn into a battle between two rival gangs when their truce is broken by mysterious murders on both sides. Seems there's an unsuspected third party involved—a para-military band of professional killers that want the gang violence to divert police interest from their own nefarious operations. **CW:** Language, strong violence, and sexuality. 88m/C **VHS, Beta, LV, Closed Caption.** Jeff Speakman, Christopher Neame, Lewis Van Bergen, Bernie Casey, Jennifer Gatti, Richard Coca; **D:** Albert Magnoli. **WAR**

Street Law
🎬 1979 (R) Vivid and violent study of one man's frustrated war on crime. 77m/C **VHS, Beta.** Franco Nero, Barbara Bach, Reno Palmer. **NO**

Street Law
🎬🎬 1995 (R) John Ryan (Wincott) is a down-on-his-luck trial lawyer whose childhood buddy Luis Calderone (Prieto) is willing to lend a helping hand. Too bad Luis is an ex-con who hasn't left his dangerous street ways behind him and now John is caught up in some unsavory action. **CW:** Violence, some strong sexuality, and language. 98m/C **VHS.** Jeff Wincott, Paco Christian Prieto, Christina Cox. **TRI**

Street Music
🎬🎬½ 1981 The elderly people living in an old hotel join forces with a young couple to organize a protest that may save their building. Well-directed urban comedy-drama; good location shooting in San Francisco's Tenderloin. 88m/C **VHS, Beta.** Larry Breeding, Elizabeth Daily, Ned Glass; **D:** Jenny Bowen; **C:** Richard Bowen. Sundance Film Festival '82: Grand Jury Prize. **ART, VES**

Street of Forgotten Women
🎬 1925 Hollywood, in one of its periodic morality binges, came up with this purported expose on prostitution. An innocent girl is seduced and brutalized by a theatrical agent and eventually finds herself walking the pavement for less than moral purposes. Lots of shots of scantily clad showgirls and our heroine in her undies. 55m/B **VHS.** **SNC, VYY**

Street of Shame
🎬🎬🎬½ *Red-Light District; Akasen Chitai* 1956 A portrayal of the abused lives of six Tokyo prostitutes. Typically sensitive to the roles and needs of women and critical of the society that exploits them, Mizoguchi creates a quiet, inclusive coda to his life's work in world cinema. Kyo is splendid as a hardened hooker and has a memorable scene with her father. Kogure is also good. The great director's last finished work was instrumental in the outlawing of prostitution in Japan. In Japanese with English subtitles. 88m/B **VHS.** *JP* Machiko Kyo, Aiko Mimasu, Michiyo Kogure; **D:** Kenji Mizoguchi. **HMV, NLC**

Street People
woof! 1976 (R) Gratuitous car chases and violence do not a movie make, as in this case in point. Utter woofer has Brit Moore cast as a mafiosa. Yeah, right. 92m/C **VHS, Beta.** Roger Moore, Stacy Keach, Ivo Garrani, Ettore Manni; **D:** Maurizio Lucidi. **ART, VES**

Street Scene
🎬🎬🎬 1931 Life in a grimy New York tenement district, circa 1930. Audiences nationwide ate it up when Elmer Rice adapted his own Pulitzer Prize-winning play and top helmsman Vidor gave it direction. 80m/B **VHS, Beta, 8mm.** Sylvia Sidney, William Collier Jr., Estelle Taylor, Beulah Bondi, David Landau; **D:** King Vidor; **C:** George Barnes; **M:** Alfred Newman. **NOS, HHT, CAB**

Street Smart
🎬🎬½ 1987 (R) Reeve was blah as Superman (let's be frank), and he's blah here as a desperate New York freelance writer who fakes a dramatic story about prostitution. When his deception returns to haunt him, he's in trouble with pimps and murderers, as well as the D.A. Freeman and Baker are both superb. Based on screenwriter David Freeman's own experience with "New York" magazine. 97m/C **VHS, Beta, Closed Caption.** Christopher Reeve, Morgan Freeman, Kathy Baker, Mimi Rogers, Andre Gregory, Jay Patterson, Anna Maria Horsford; **D:** Jerry Schatzberg; **W:** David Freeman; **C:** Adam Holender; **M:** Miles Davis. Independent Spirit Awards '88: Best Supporting Actor (Freeman); Los Angeles Film Critics Association Awards '87: Best Supporting Actor (Freeman); New York Film Critics Awards '87: Best Supporting Actor (Freeman); National Society of Film Critics Awards '87: Best Supporting Actor (Freeman), Best Supporting Actress (Baker); Nominations: Academy Awards '87: Best Supporting Actor (Freeman). **IME**

Street Soldiers
🎬½ 1991 (R) Martial artists are out to take back the streets from the punks and scum who now rule them. **CW:** Language and strong violence. 98m/C **VHS, Beta, LV.** Jun Chong, Jeff Rector, David Homb, Jonathan Gorman, Joon Kim, Katherine Armstrong, Joel Weiss; **D:** Lee Harry.

Street Trash
woof! 1987 In Brooklyn, a strange poisonous liquor is being sold cheap to bums, making them melt and explode. A gross, cheap, tongue-in-cheek shocker from the makers of "The Toxic Avenger." 91m/C **VHS, Beta.** R.L. Ryan, Vic Noto, Miriam Zucker, Bill Chepil, Mike Lackey; **D:** Jim Muro. **ART**

Street War
🎬 197? A cop pursues the Mob in the name of revenge as well as duty. 90m/C **VHS, Beta.** James Mason, Cyril Cusack, Raymond Pellegrin. **NO**

Street Warriors
woof! 1987 Ostensibly "serious" look at juvenile crime. Actually miserable, exploitative, offensive junk. 105m/C **VHS, Beta.** Christa Leem, Nadia Windell, Victor Petit, Francisco (Frank) Brana; **D:** Jose Antonio De La Loma. **NO**

Street Warriors, Part 2
woof! 1987 Even worse than its predecessor, and that's saying something. Horrible dubbing from Spanish would be laughable, if the rapes weren't so graphic. 105m/C **VHS, Beta.** Angel Fernandez, Paul Ramirez, Teresa Giminez, Veronica Miriel, Conrad Tortosa; **D:** Jose Antonio De La Loma. **NO**

Street Wars
🎬½ 1991 (R) Violent low-budgeter about 17-year-old Sugarpop, who takes over older brother Frank's Los Angeles drug operation, after Frank is murdered, and finds himself battling a rival gang. 90m/C **VHS, LV.** Alan Joseph, Bryan O'Dell, Clifford Shegog, Jean Pace, Vaughn Cromwell, Cardella Demilo; **D:** Jamaa Fanaka; **W:** Jamaa Fanaka; **C:** John L. Demps Jr.; **M:** Michael Dunlap, Yves Chicha. **TRI**

The Street with No Name
🎬🎬🎬 1948 In follow-up to "Kiss of Death," Widmark confirms rep as one disturbed guy playing psychotic career criminal whose life is grisly trail of murder and brutality. 93m/B **VHS.** Mark Stevens, Richard Widmark, Lloyd Nolan, Barbara Lawrence, Ed Begley Sr., Donald Buka, Joseph Pevney; **D:** William Keighley. **FOX, FCT**

A Streetcar Named Desire
🎬🎬🎬🎬 1951 (PG) Powerful film version of Tennessee Williams' play about a neurotic southern belle with a hidden past who comes to visit her sister and is abused and driven mad by her brutal brother-in-law. Grim New Orleans setting for terrific performances by all, with Malden, Leigh, and Hunter winning Oscars, and Brando making highest impact on audiences. Brando disliked the role, despite the great impact it had on his career. Remade for television in 1984. 122m/B **VHS, Beta, LV, Closed Caption, DVD.** Vivien Leigh, Marlon Brando, Kim Hunter, Karl Malden; **D:** Elia Kazan; **W:** Tennessee Williams; **C:** Harry Stradling; **M:** Alex North. Academy Awards '51: Best Actress (Leigh), Best Art Direction/Set Decoration (B & W), Best Supporting Actor (Malden), Best Supporting Actress (Hunter); British Academy Awards '52: Best Actress (Leigh); Golden Globe Awards '52: Best Supporting Actress (Hunter); New York Film Critics Awards '51: Best Actress (Leigh), Best Director (Kazan), Best Film; Nominations: Academy Awards '51: Best Actor (Brando), Best Black and White Cinematography, Best Costume Design (B & W), Best Director (Kazan), Best Picture, Best Screenplay, Best Sound, Best Original Dramatic/Comedy Score. **FOX, WAR, BTV**

A Streetcar Named Desire
🎬🎬🎬 1984 Excellent made for television adaptation of the Tennessee Williams drama about fading southern belle Blanche du Bois (Ann-Margret in a terrific performance). D'Angelo is her plain sister Stella who lives with brutish husband Stanley (Williams) in the seamy French Quarter of New Orleans. Can't surpass the original but this version does have the advantage of not having to soft-pedal the drama for the '50s censors. 94m/C **VHS.** Ann-Margret, Beverly D'Angelo, Treat Williams, Randy Quaid, Rafael Campos, Erica Yohn; **D:** John Erman; **C:** Bill Butler; **M:** Marvin Hamlisch. **FCT**

A Streetcar Named Desire
🎬🎬½ 1995 Baldwin and Lange recreate their 1992 stage roles of brutal Stanley Kowalski and fragile Southern belle Blanche DuBois from the Broadway revival of Tennessee Williams 1947 Pulitzer Prize-winning play. This TV version is truer to the dialogue and situations of the original production than the censored '51 film. 156m/C **VHS, Closed Caption.** Jessica Lange, Alec Baldwin, Diane Lane, John Goodman, Frederick Coffin; **D:** Glenn Jordan; **C:** Ralf Bode; **M:** David Mansfield. **FXV**

Streetfight
🎬½ *Coonskin* 1975 (R) Semi-animated racist exploitation from the creator of "Fritz the Cat." Features some superb animation. 89m/C **VHS, Beta.** Philip Michael Thomas, Scatman Crothers; **D:** Ralph Bakshi; **W:** Ralph Bakshi.

Streets ✓✓ **1990** (R) Applegate (of Fox TV's "Married...With Children") is believable as an illiterate runaway teen. Good drama set in Venice, California about life on the streets is flawed by near-gratuitous pairing with story of a crazy prostitute-killing cop. **90m/C VHS, Beta.** Christina Applegate, David Mendenhall, Eb Lottimer; *D:* Katt Shea Ruben, Andy Ruben; *W:* Andy Ruben. *MGM*

Streets of Fire ✓✓½ **1984** A soldier of fortune rescues his ex-girlfriend, now a famous rock singer, after she's been kidnapped by a malicious motorcycle gang. Violently energetic in its insistent barrage of imagery. Director Hill's never-never land establishes a retro-futuristic feel and is beautifully photographed, however vacuous the ending may be. **93m/C VHS, Beta, LV, Closed Caption, DVD.** Michael Pare, Diane Lane, Rick Moranis, Amy Madigan, Willem Dafoe, Deborah Van Valkenburgh, Richard Lawson, Rick Rossovich, Bill Paxton, Lee Ving, Stoney Jackson, Robert Townsend, Grand Bush, Mykelti Williamson, Elizabeth Daily, Lynne Thigpen, Marine Jahan, Ed Begley Jr., John Dennis Johnston, Olivia Brown; *D:* Walter Hill; *W:* Walter Hill, Larry Gross; *M:* Ry Cooder. *USH*

Streets of Gold ✓✓½ **1986** (R) Brandauer is good as a Soviet boxer who defected and now washes dishes in Brooklyn. He trains a pair of street youngsters in the hope of beating his old coach in the Olympics. "Rocky"-like in the boxing, and in the rags-to-riches optimism. **94m/C VHS, Beta, LV.** Klaus Maria Brandauer, Adrian Pasdar, Wesley Snipes; *D:* Joe Roth; *W:* Richard Price, Heywood Gould, Tom Cole; *C:* Arthur Albert; *M:* Jack Nitzsche. *ART, VES*

The Streets of L.A. ✓✓½ **1979** A frustrated middle-aged woman teaches some punks from an L.A. barrio a thing or two about pride and motivation when she demands reimbursement for the tires they slashed. Without thoroughly professional Woodward to carry it, there would not be much of a movie. Woodward's character is resourceful, and so is the actress. Made for TV. **94m/C VHS, Beta.** Joanne Woodward, Robert Webber, Michael C. Gwynne; *D:* Jerrold Freedman; *C:* Allen Daviau. *NO*

The Streets of San Francisco ✓✓ **1972** The pilot that spawned the popular TV series. A streetwise old cop and his young college-boy partner (who else but Malden and Douglas as Stone and Keller) investigate the murder of a young woman. Adapted from "Poor, Poor Ophelia" by Carolyn Weston. **120m/C VHS, Beta.** Karl Malden, Robert Wagner, Michael Douglas, Andrew Duggan, Tom Bosley, Kim Darby, Mako; *D:* Walter Grauman. *GKK*

Streets of Sin ✓✓½ *Not Wanted* **1949** Written and produced by movie star Lupino (who also took over directing when credited director Clifton became ill), this morality play tells the story of a naive girl's tribulations when she becomes infatuated with a musician and then becomes pregnant by him. Shunned by the musician, she enters a home for unwed mothers to sort out her life and feelings for a crippled veteran who wants to marry her. **91m/B VHS.** Sally Forrest, Keefe Brasselle, Leonard Penn, Dorothy Adams, Rita Lupino; *D:* Elmer Clifton; *W:* Ida Lupino. *EEL, NOS, KIV*

Streetwalkin' ✓ **1985** (R) Life in the Big Apple isn't always rosy for a brother and sister who must contend with prostitutes, drug dealers, and tough cops. She turns to prostitution to get by. Miserable, exploitative trash. **86m/C VHS, Beta, LV.** Melissa Leo, Dale Midkiff, Leon Robinson, Julie Newmar, Randall Batinkoff, Annie Golden, Antonio Fargas; *D:* Joan Freeman; *W:* Joan Freeman, Robert Alden; *C:* Steven Fierberg. *ART, VES*

Streetwise ✓✓✓½ **1984** Eye-opening and candid documentary inspired by a "Life" magazine article. Frank and honest look at homeless children making a living on the streets. Seattle provides the backdrop to the story as the filmmakers hang around with the kids, earning their trust, and receive the truth from them. Cruel, funny, enraging, but always sobering look into a population of homeless in America. A deservedly acclaimed,

terrifying vision of urban America. **92m/C VHS, Beta, LV.** *D:* Martin Bell; *M:* Tom Waits. *ORI*

Strictly Ballroom ✓✓✓½ **1992** (PG) Offbeat, cheerfully tacky dance/romance amusingly turns every movie cliche slightly askew. Scott (Mercurio) has been in training for the Pan-Pacific ballroom championships since the age of six. While talented, he also refuses to follow convention and scandalizes the stuffy dance establishment with his new steps. When his longtime partner leaves him, Scott takes up with a love-struck beginner (Morice), with some surprises of her own. Ballet dancer Mercurio (in his film debut) is appropriately arrogant yet vulnerable, with Morice as the plain Jane turned steel butterfly. Wonderful supporting cast; great debut for director Luhrmann. **94m/C VHS, LV, Closed Caption.** *AU* Paul Mercurio, Tara Morice, Bill Hunter, Pat Thomsen, Barry Otto, Gia Carides, Peter Whitford, John Hannan, Sonia Kruger-Tayler, Kris McQuade, Pip Mushin, Leonie Page, Antonio Vargas, Armonia Benedito; *D:* Baz Luhrmann; *W:* Craig Pearce, Baz Luhrmann; *M:* David Hirshfelder. Australian Film Institute '92: Best Costume Design, Best Director (Luhrmann), Best Film, Best Film Editing, Best Screenplay, Best Supporting Actor (Otto), Best Supporting Actress (Thomsen); Nominations: Golden Globe Awards '94: Best Film—Musical/Comedy.*MAX, TOU, BTV*

Strictly Business ✓½ **1991** (PG-13) An upwardly mobile black broker has his career aspirations in order until he meets a beautiful club promoter who finds him square and boring. Wanting to impress her he asks the advice of a young man who works in the mail room for the proper way to dress and talk. A low-rent Pygmalion story. **83m/C VHS.** Halle Berry, Tommy Davidson, Joseph C. Phillips; *D:* Kevin Hooks; *M:* Michel Colombier. *WAR, FCT*

Strictly G.I. **1944** A collection of war-time patriotic shorts, including "All Star Bond Rally." The support and perception of WWII is historically intriguing. **45m/B VHS, Beta.** Bing Crosby, Frank Sinatra, Betty Grable, Judy Garland, Harpo Marx, Harry James, Bob Hope, Jerry Colonna. *NOS, DVT, HEG*

Strike ✓✓✓½ **1924** Eisenstein's debut, and a silent classic. Stirring look at a 1912 clash between striking factory workers and Czarist troops. **78m/B VHS, Beta.** *RU D:* Sergei Eisenstein. *NOS, KIV, IHF*

Strike a Pose ✓½ **1993** (R) Erotic thriller finds retired model-turned-fashion photographer Miranda Cross, her boyfriend LAPD detective Nick Carter, and Miranda's model friends stalked by a revenge-minded killer. Also available in an unrated version.*CW:* Violence and sexuality. **?m/C VHS, LV, Closed Caption.** Margie Peterson, Robert Eastwick, Michelle LaMothe; *D:* Dean Hamilton. *PMH*

Strike Back ✓✓ **1980** A convict escapes from prison to find the girl he loves, and is hounded by the police and the mob. **89m/C VHS, Beta.** Dave Balko, Brigette Wollner; *D:* Carl Schenkel. *ART, VES*

Strike Commando woof! **1987** (R) Cheap, exploitative ripoff of the expensive, exploitative mega-action thriller "Rambo." Sleepwalking actors; horrible, overwrought script. **92m/C VHS, Beta.** Reb Brown, Christopher Connelly, Locs Kamme; *D:* Vincent Dawn. *NO*

Strike Force ✓ *Crack* **1975** A New York City cop, a Federal agent and a state trooper work together to battle a large drug ring. Failed made-for-TV pilot. Early Gere appearance; not related to later Robert Stack film with the same title. **74m/C VHS, Beta.** Cliff Gorman, Richard Gere, Donald Blakely; *D:* Barry Shear. *THV*

Strike Force ✓✓ **1981** The jurors on an embezzlement case turn up bloody and headless around town, so a special criminal strike force is brought in to solve the murders. Why do the murders happen only on Tuesdays? Made for TV. **90m/C VHS, Beta.** Robert Stack, Dorian Harewood, Herb Edelman; *D:* Richard Lang.

Strike It Rich ✓½ *Loser Take All* **1990** (PG) A honeymooning couple find themselves resorting to the Monte Carlo gambling tables in order to raise money for the ride home. Lightweight fluff

unfortunately adapted from Graham Greene's short novel "Loser Takes All." Only for hard-core Gielgudites. **86m/C VHS, Beta, LV.** Molly Ringwald, Robert Lindsay, John Gielgud, Max Wall, Simon de la Brosse; *D:* James Scott; *M:* Cliff Eidelman. *HBO*

Strike Me Pink ✓✓ **1936** Shy Eddie Pink (Cantor) decides to change his ways after reading a self-help book and takes on the management of the local amusement park. Then some crooks want to muscle in on the action and Eddie must prove his mettle. Merman as girlfriend Joyce gets to belt out a few songs. ♫The Lady Dances; Shake It Off with Rhythm; You Have Me High, You Have Me Low; Calabash Pipe. **100m/B VHS.** Eddie Cantor, Ethel Merman, Sally Eilers, William Frawley, Parkyakarkus, Brian Donlevy, Jack LaRue; *D:* Norman Taurog; *W:* Frank Butler, Walter DeLeon, Francis Martin; *C:* Gregg Toland, Merritt B. Gerstad; *M:* Harold Arlen. *HBO*

Strike Up the Band ✓✓½ **1940** A high school band turns to hot swing music and enters a national radio contest. Rooney and Garland display their usual charm in this high-energy stroll down memory lane. ♫Over the Waves; The Light Cavalry Overture; Walkin Down Broadway; Five Foot Two, Eyes of Blue; After the Ball; Nobody; Strike Up the Band. **120m/B VHS, Beta, LV.** Judy Garland, Mickey Rooney, Paul Whiteman, William Tracy, June Preisser; *D:* Busby Berkeley. Academy Awards '40: Best Sound; Nominations: Academy Awards '40: Best Song ("Our Love Affair"), Best Score.*MGM*

Striker ✓✓ **1988** (R) Mercenary John "Striker" Slade is sent to Nicaragua to free a captured American journalist, not knowing his superiors have betrayed him to the Contras and the Sandinistas. He battles it out with both groups while seeking revenge on the businessmen who set him up. **90m/C VHS, Beta.** Frank Zagarino, Melanie Rogers, Paul Werner; *D:* Stephen M. Andrews.

Striker's Mountain ✓½ **1987** Story of a sports enthusiast who creates heliskiing and builds it into a business. Great ski scenes, but skip the rest. **99m/C VHS.** Bruce Greenwood, Mimi Kuzyk, Leslie Nielsen, August Schellenberg; *D:* Allen Simmonds. *VTR*

Striking Distance ✓✓½ **1993** (R) Tom Hardy (Willis) is a hard-nosed fifth-generation Pittsburgh homicide cop whose police detective father (Mahoney) is killed, apparently by a serial killer. Hardy insists the perp was really a fellow cop and winds up on the River Rescue squad (at least his partner is the fetching Parker). When the serial killer starts striking at women with some connection to Hardy, he finds scant support from his fellow cops. High action quotient but the killer's identity won't be any surprise.*CW:* Strong language, violence, and one sex scene. **101m/C VHS, LV, 8mm, Closed Caption.** Bruce Willis, Sarah Jessica Parker, Dennis Farina, Tom Sizemore, Brion James, Robert Pastorelli, Timothy Busfield, John Mahoney, Andre Braugher; *D:* Rowdy Herrington; *W:* Marty Kaplan, Rowdy Herrington; *M:* Brad Fiedel. *COL*

Striking Point ✓½ **1994** (R) Police detectives are determined to stop ex-KGB commandoes from smuggling high-tech weapons into the country.*CW:* Some language; sexuality; strong gangster violence. **96m/C VHS.** Chris Mitchum, Tracy Spaulding. *CAF*

Strip Search ✓½ **1997** (R) Police detective Robby (Pare) gets seduced by easy money and sex when he gets involved with sex clubs and underworld gangs.*CW:* Strong violence and sexualtiy, and for language. **90m/C VHS.** Michael Pare, Pam Grier, Caroline Neron, Lucie Laurier, Maury Chaykin, Heidi von Palleske; *D:* Rod Hewitt. *APX*

Stripes ✓✓½ **1981** (R) Feeling like losers and looking to straighten out their lives, two friends enlist in the Army under the mistaken impression that military life is something like a summer camp for grownups. A boxoffice success (despite a poorly written and directed script) due in large part to Murray's charm and his verbal and sometimes physical sparring with Oates, who is good as the gruff-tempered platoon sergeant. Features humorous stints from various "Second City" players, including Candy, whom Murray turns into a "lean, mean fighting machine." 105m/C VHS, Beta, LV, Closed Caption. Bill Murray, Harold Ramis, P.J. Soles, Warren Oates, John Candy, John Larroquette, Judge Reinhold, Sean Young, Dave Thomas, Joe Flaherty; *D:* Ivan Reitman; *W:* Len Blum, Harold Ramis; *C:* Bill Butler; *M:* Elmer Bernstein. COL

Stripped to Kill 🐾🐾 1987 (R) A female cop goes undercover to lure a psycho killing strippers. Not-bad entry from Corman and cohorts. Followed by—you guessed it—"Stripped to Kill II." 88m/C VHS, Beta. Kay Lenz, Greg Evigan, Norman Fell; *D:* Katt Shea Ruben; *W:* Katt Shea Ruben, Andy Ruben. MGM

Stripped to Kill II: Live Girls 🐾 1989 A young woman with extra-sensory powers dreams of murders which she discovers are all too real. A weak sequel, despite the interesting premise. 83m/C VHS, Beta. Maria Ford, Eb Lottimer, Karen Mayo Chandler, Marjean Holden, Birke Tan, Debra Lamb; *D:* Katt Shea Ruben; *W:* Katt Shea Ruben. MGM

The Stripper 🐾🐾½ *Woman of Summer* 1963 A middle-aged stripper in a traveling show returns to the small Kansas town of her youth. Left stranded, she moves in with an old friend whose teenage son promptly falls in love with her. Based on the play "A Loss of Roses" by William Inge. 95m/B VHS, Beta. Joanne Woodward, Richard Beymer, Claire Trevor, Carol Lynley, Robert Webber, Gypsy Rose Lee; *D:* Franklin J. Schaffner; *M:* Jerry Goldsmith. Nominations: Academy Awards '63: Best Costume Design (B & W). FOX

Stripper 🐾🐾½ 1986 (R) A good under-the-covers glimpse of the life and work of several real-life strippers, culminating in the First Annual Stripper's Convention in 1984. 90m/C VHS, Beta. Janette Boyd, Sara Costa, Kimberly Holcomb; *D:* Jerome Gary; *M:* Jack Nitzsche. FOX

Stripshow 🐾 1995 (R) Veteran Vegas stripper shows the ropes to newcomer and then must vie with the upstart for her boyfriend's interest.*CW:* Strong sexuality and some language. ?m/C VHS. Monique Parent, Tane McClure, Steven Tietsort; *D:* Gary Orona; *W:* Gary Orona. MTH

Striptease 🐾🐾½ 1996 (R) Single mom Erin Grant (Moore) loses custody of her daughter Angela (Moore's real-life offspring, Rumer) to her lowlife ex, Darrell (Patrick). In order to raise the money for an appeal, she dances at a Miami strip club, where she runs across politician David Dilbeck (Reynolds), who has a thing for both vaseline and Erin. Unlike "Showgirls," this one's intentionally funny and features some fine script work and performances, which got overlooked amidst all the hype, including Moore's record-setting (for an actress) $12 million paycheck, 4 mil of which reportedly was for agreeing to dance nude. Based on the novel by Carl Hiaasen.*CW:* Nudity, erotic dancing and language. 115m/C VHS, LV, Closed Caption. Demi Moore, Burt Reynolds, Ving Rhames, Armand Assante, Robert Patrick, Rumer Willis; *D:* Andrew Bergman; *W:* Andrew Bergman; *C:* Stephen Goldblatt; *M:* Howard Shore. Golden Raspberry Awards '96: Worst Picture, Worst Actress (Moore), Worst Director (Bergman), Worst Screenplay, Worst Song ("Pussy, Pussy, Pussy (Whose Kitty Cat Are You?)"); Nominations: Golden Raspberry Awards '96: Worst Supporting Actor (Reynolds). COL

Stripteaser 🐾½ 1995 (R) Sicko psycho Dean holds dancers and patrons hostage in an L.A. strip joint where he provides various humiliations for his captives. Ford's the beautiful ecdysiast whose been the object of the fellow's secret obsessions. Also available unrated. 82m/C VHS. Rick Dean, Maria Ford, Lance August; *D:* Dan Golden. NHO

Stroke of Midnight 🐾½ 1990 (PG) Souped-up Cinderella with Lowe as egotistic high fashion designer, Grey as struggling shoe designer and a pumpkin-colored VW Bug. 102m/C VHS, Beta, LV. Rob Lowe, Jennifer Grey, Andrea Ferreol; *D:* Tom Clegg. VTR

Stroker Ace woof! 1983 (PG) Flamboyant stock car driver tries to break an iron clad promotional contract signed with a greedy fried-chicken magnate. Off duty, he ogles blondes as dopey as he is. One of the worst from Reynolds—and that's saying something. 96m/C VHS, Beta. Burt Reynolds, Ned Beatty, Jim Nabors, Parker Stevenson, Loni Anderson, Bubba Smith; *D:* Hal Needham; *W:* Hal Needham, Hugh Wilson. Golden Raspberry Awards '83: Worst Supporting Actor (Nabors). WAR

Stromboli 🐾🐾½ 1950 Bergman is a Czech refugee who marries an Italian fisherman in order to escape from her displaced persons camp. He brings her to his home island of Stromboli where she finds the life bleak and isolated and her marriage a trial. In Italian with English subtitles. The melodrama was even greater off-screen than on; this is the movie which introduced Bergman and Rossellini and began their (then) scandalous affair. 107m/B VHS, Beta. IT Ingrid Bergman, Mario Vitale, Renzo Cesana; *D:* Roberto Rossellini. NO

Strong Man 🐾🐾🐾 1926 A WWI veteran, passing himself off as an unlikely circus strongman, searches an American city for the girl whose letters gave him hope during the war. Perhaps Langdon's best full-length film. 78m/B VHS, Beta, LV. Harry Langdon, Gertrude Astor, Tay Garnett; *D:* Frank Capra. HBO, IME

Strong Medicine 🐾🐾½ 1984 Strange, avant-garde film about a strange, off-written young woman. Cleverly directed experiment that's not for everyone. 84m/C VHS, Beta. Carol Kane, Raul Julia, Wallace Shawn, Kate Manheim, David Warrilow; *D:* Guy Green. NO

Stroszek 🐾🐾🐾 1977 Three German misfits—a singer, a prostitute and an old man—tour the U.S. in search of their dreams. Touching, hilarious comedy-drama with a difference and an attitude. One of Herzog's easiest and also best films. In English and German with English subtitles. 108m/C VHS. GE Eva Mattes, Bruno S, Clemens Scheitz; *D:* Werner Herzog; *M:* Chet Atkins. NYF, FCT

The Structure of Crystals 🐾🐾½ *Struktura Krysztalu* 1969 A member of the scientific elite meets with an old friend who has moved to a remote meteorological station and tries to persuade him to return to the city and resume his work. Zanussi's cerebral first feature was also the first of a series of films to explore the scientific community. In Polish with English subtitles. 76m/B VHS. PL Andrzej Zarnecki, Jan Myslowicz, Barbara Wrzesinska, Wladyslaw Jarema, Daniel Olbrychski; *D:* Krzysztof Zanussi; *W:* Edward Zebrowski, Krzysztof Zanussi. FCT

Struggle 🐾 1931 Unfortunately, Griffith's final directorial effort is a ludicrous melodrama about the evils of alcohol. Because of Prohibition, working man Jimmie Wilson (Skelly) takes to illegal hootch, which turns out to be tainted, causing Jimmie to abuse his wife and daughter and destroy their formerly happy home. 87m/B VHS. Hal Skelly, Zita Johann, Evelyn Baldwin, Charlotte Wynters, Helen Mack, Kate Bruce, Jackson Halliday, Edna Hagan, Claude Cooper, Arthur Lipson, Charles Richman, Dave Manley; *D:* D.W. Griffith; *W:* D.W. Griffith, Anita Loos, John Emerson; *C:* Joseph Ruttenberg; *M:* D.W. Griffith, Philip A. Scheib. KIV

Stryker woof! 1983 (R) The ever-lovin' nuclear holocaust has occurred, and good guys and bad guys battle it out for scarce water. If you liked "Mad Max," go see it again; don't watch this miserable effort. 86m/C VHS, Beta. PH Steve Sandor, Andria Fabio; *D:* Cirio H. Santiago; *W:* Howard R. Cohen. VTR

Stuart Saves His Family 🐾🐾 1994 (PG-13) Fired from his self-help television show on a Chicago public-access station, New-age advice guru Smalley (Franken) returns home to help his pathetically dysfunctional family sort out their problems and an inheritance, a nonplot that gives Smalley a chance to do his 12-step shtick. And that's...O.K. A tolerable installment in the endless parade of mediocre "Saturday Night Live" sketches stretched for the big screen that takes a few surprisingly maudlin turns. Based on Franken's book of Smalley's "daily affirmations," "I'm Good Enough, I'm Smart Enough, and Doggone It, People Like Me!"*CW:* Language; substance abuse. 97m/C VHS, Beta, Closed Caption. Al Franken, Laura San Giacomo, Vincent D'Onofrio, Shirley Knight, Harris Yulin; *D:* Harold Ramis; *W:* Al Franken; *M:* Marc Shaiman. PAR

Stuck on You 🐾 1984 (R) Couple engaged in a palimony suit takes their case to a judge to work out their differences. Wing-clipped angel Gabriel (Corey) comes to earth to help them patch it up. Never mind. 90m/C VHS, Beta. Prof. Irwin Corey, Virginia Penta, Mark Mikulski; *D:* Lloyd (Samuel Weil) Kaufman, Michael Herz.

Stuckey's Last Stand 🐾 1978 (PG) A group of camp counselors prepare to take 22 children on a nature hike they will never forget. Mindless teen fodder. 95m/C VHS, Beta. Whit Reichert, Tom Murray, Rich Casentino. NO

The Stud woof! 1978 (R) Owner of a fashionable "after hours" dance spot hires a young, handsome stud to manage the club and attend to her personal needs. Low-budget look and seemingly scriptless. Faithfully adapted by sister Jackie Collins from her novel. 90m/C VHS, Beta. GB Joan Collins, Oliver Tobias; *D:* Quentin Masters; *W:* Jackie Collins. NO

The Student Affair 🐾 *The Lay of the Land* 1997 (R) Lame would-be comedy based on Shapiro's stage play, which also starred Kellerman. She's college prof M.J. Dankworth, who suspects hubby Harvey (Begley Jr.) is tossing their tired marriage aside to shtupp his well-endowed grad student Muriel (Taylor). So she hires a P.I. (Margolin) to snoop but he's more interested in his client. Then the marrieds seek out (different) psychiatrists for help and M.J. indulges her rage in silly fantasy scenes. Don't waste your time. 94m/C VHS, Closed Caption. CA Sally Kellerman, Ed Begley Jr., Sandra Taylor, Stuart Margolin, Tyne Daly, Rance Howard, Avery Schreiber; *D:* Larry Arrick; *W:* Mel Shapiro; *C:* Frederic Goodich; *M:* Jeff Lass. FXV

Student Affairs woof! 1988 (R) A bunch of highschool misfits vie for roles in a movie about a bunch of high school misfits. 92m/C VHS, Beta. Louie Bonanno, Jim Abele, Alan Fisler, Deborah Blaisdell; *D:* Chuck Vincent. ART, VES

Student Bodies woof! 1981 (R) A "Halloween"-style spoof of high-school horror films, except it's not funny. And what's so funny about bloody murder anyway? When the on-the-set problems and strife arose (which they did), why didn't everyone just cut their losses and go home? 86m/C VHS, Beta, LV. Kristen Riter, Matthew Goldsby, Richard Brando, Joe Flood, Joe Talarowski, Mimi Weddell; *D:* Mickey Rose; *W:* Mickey Rose. PAR

Student Confidential 🐾 1987 (R) A Troma-produced spoof of seedy high school youth movies, new and old, involving four students who are led into the world of adult vices by a mysterious millionaire. Badly made and dull. Douglas and Jackson both have brothers named Michael. 99m/C VHS, Beta. Eric Douglas, Marlon Jackson, Susan Scott, Ronee Blakley, Elizabeth Singer; *D:* Richard Horian.

The Student Nurses 🐾🐾 1970 (R) The adventures, amorous and otherwise, of four last-year nursing students. Followed by four sequels: "Private Duty Nurses," "Night Call Nurses," "The Young Nurses," and "Candy Stripe Nurses." Better than average exploitation fare. First release from Roger Corman's New World studios; it goes down hill from there. 89m/C VHS, Beta. Elaine Giftos, Karen Carlson, Brioni Farrell, Barbara Leigh, Reni Santoni, Richard Rust, Lawrence Casey, Darrell Larson, Paul Camen, Richard Stahl, Scottie MacGregor, Pepe Serna; *D:* Stephanie Rothman. NLC

Student of Prague 🐾🐾🐾 1913 Early silent classic based on the German Faust legend: a student makes a pact with the devil to win a beautiful woman. Poor fellow. With either German or English title cards. Music track. 60m/B VHS, Beta.

GE Lothar Koemer, Grete Berger, Paul Wegener; *D:* Paul Wegener, Stellan Rye. *DVT, GLV, GVV*

The Student Prince *1954* Delightful rendition of Sigmund Romberg's famous operetta in which Purdom stars as the Prince of Heidelberg who falls for barmaid Blyth. Lanza recorded the soundtrack, but could not star in this film because of his weight problem. Previously filmed in 1919 and 1927 without music. ♫Golden Days; Serenade; Deep in My Heart; To the Inn We're Marching; Drink, Drink, Drink; Come Boys, Let's All Be Gay, Boys; Summertime in Heidelberg; Beloved; I Walk With God. **107m/C VHS.** Ann Blyth, Edmund Purdom, John Ericson, Louis Calhern, Edmund Gwenn, S.Z. Sakall, Betta St. John; *D:* Richard Thorpe; *C:* Paul Vogel. *MGM*

The Student Prince in Old Heidelberg 🐾🐾½ *Old Heidelberg 1927* Prince Karl Heinrich silently falls in love with lowly barmaid. **102m/B VHS.** Ramon Novarro, Norma Shearer; *D:* Ernst Lubitsch. *MGM, FCT*

The Student Teachers 🐾½ *1973* Yet another soft-core Corman product. Three student teachers sleep around, on screen. **79m/C VHS, Beta.** Susan Damante Shaw, Brooke Mills, Bob Harris, John Cramer, Chuck Norris; *D:* Jonathan Kaplan.

Studs Lonigan 🐾🐾 *1960* Drifting, too artsy rendering a James T. Farrell's trilogy about an Irish drifter growing up in Chicago in the '20s. Good period detail, but oddly off-kilter and implausible as history. **96m/B VHS, Beta.** Christopher Knight, Frank Gorshin, Jack Nicholson; *D:* Irving Lerner; *W:* Philip Yordan; *M:* Jerry Goldsmith. *MGM*

A Study in Scarlet 🐾🐾 *1933* Owen played Watson the previous year in "Sherlock Holmes"; here he's miscast as Holmes, and the plot differs from the Doyle story of the same title. **77m/B VHS, Beta.** Reginald Owen, Alan Mowbray, Anna May Wong, June Clyde, Alan Dinehart; *D:* Edwin L. Marin; *W:* Reginald Owen. *SNC, NOS, CAB*

A Study in Terror 🐾🐾🐾 *Sherlock Holmes Grosster Fall; Fog 1966* A well-appointed Sherlock Holmes thriller, and the second one in color. Premise has a young, athletic Holmes in pursuit of an educated Jack the Ripper in 1880s London. **94m/C VHS, Beta, LV.** *GE GB* John Neville, Donald Houston, Judi Dench, Anthony Quayle, Robert Morley, Frank Finlay, Cecil Parker; *D:* James Hill. *COL*

The Stuff 🐾½ *1985 (R)* Surreal horror semi-spoof about an ice cream mogul and a hamburger king who discover that the new, fast-selling confection in town zombifies its partakers. Forced, lame satire from producer/director/writer Cohen. **93m/C VHS, Beta, Closed Caption.** Michael Moriarty, Andrea Marcovicci, Garrett Morris, Paul Sorvino, Danny Aiello, Brooke Adams, Patrick O'Neal, Alexander Scourby, Scott Bloom; *D:* Larry Cohen; *W:* Larry Cohen. *VTR*

Stuff Stephanie in the Incinerator 🐾 *1989 (PG-13)* A Troma gagfest about wealthy cretins who torture and kill young women. "Funny" title betrays utter, exploitive mindlessness. **97m/C VHS, Beta, LV.** Catherine Dee, William Dame, M.R. Murphy, Dennis Cunningham; *D:* Don Nardo. *ART*

The Stunt Man 🐾🐾🐾🐾 *1980 (R)* A marvelous and unique exercise in meta-cinematic manipulation. O'Toole, in one of his very best roles, is a power-crazed movie director; Railsback is a fugitive sheltered by him from sherrif Rocco. When a stunt man is killed in an accident, O'Toole prevails on Railsback to replace him, leading Railsback to wonder if O'Toole wants him dead. A labor of love for director-producer Rush, who spent nine years working on it, and waited two years to see it released, by Fox. Based on the novel by Paul Brodeur. **129m/C VHS, Beta, LV.** Peter O'Toole, Steve Railsback, Barbara Hershey, Chuck Bail, Alex Rocco, Allen (Goorwitz) Garfield, Adam Roarke, Sharon Farrell, Philip Bruns; *D:* Richard Rush; *W:* Lawrence B. Marcus, Richard Rush; *M:* Dominic Frontiere. Golden Globe Awards '81: Best Score; Montreal World Film Festival '80: Best Film; National Society of Film Critics Awards '80: Best

Actor (O'Toole); Nominations: Academy Awards '80: Best Actor (O'Toole), Best Adapted Screenplay, Best Director (Rush).*FOX*

Stunt Pilot 🐾🐾 *1939* A young man takes a job at a film studio as a stunt pilot and finds mayhem and romance on and off the ground. One in the "Tailspin Tommy" series. Well-paced and fun to watch. **61m/C VHS.** John Trent, Marjorie Reynolds, Milburn Stone, Jason Robards Sr., Pat O'Malley; *D:* George Waggner. *NOS, MOV*

Stunts 🐾🐾 *Who Is Killing the Stuntman 1977 (PG)* See "The Stunt Man" instead. OK script hides near-invisible plot; stunt man engages in derring-do. **90m/C VHS, Beta.** Robert Forster, Fiona Lewis, Joanna Cassidy, Darrell Fetty, Bruce Glover, James Luisi; *D:* Mark L. Lester; *M:* Michael Kamen. *NO*

Stuntwoman 🐾½ *1981* Welch plays a stuntwoman whose death-defying job interferes with her love life. What ever shall she do? **95m/C VHS.** Raquel Welch, Jean-Paul Belmondo; *D:* Claude Zidi. *NO*

The Stupids 🐾½ *1995 (PG)* In the tradition of "Dumb and Dumber," the aptly named Stupids—dad Stanley (Arnold), mom Joan (Lundy), brother Buster (Hall), and sis Petunia (McKenna)—blunder unwittingly into and out of dangerous adventures involving their garbage. Landing Arnold for the lead seems like the casting coup of the decade but the movie itself is shaky and uninspired. Based on the children's best-selling books. Keep a lookout for Captain Kangaroo (Keeshan) and numerous other cameos. **93m/C VHS, LV, Closed Caption.** Tom Arnold, Jessica Lundy, Bug Hall, Alex McKenna, Mark Metcalf, Matt Keeslar, Frankie Faison, Christopher Lee, Bob Keeshan; *Cameos:* Robert Wise, Norman Jewison, Constantin Costa-Gavras, David Cronenberg, Atom Egoyan, Gillo Pontecorvo; *D:* John Landis; *W:* Brent Forrester; *C:* Manfred Guthe; *M:* Christopher Stone. Golden Raspberry Awards '96: Worst Actor (Arnold); Nominations: Golden Raspberry Awards '96: Worst Picture, Worst Director (Landis), Worst Screenplay. *NLC*

The Subject Was Roses 🐾🐾🐾½ *1968* Outstanding story of family dysfunction and love based on Gilroy's Pulitzer Prize-winning play. Timmy Cleary (Sheen) returns from WWII to find that his parents' marriage has disintegrated into open hostility. Formerly mom Nettie's (Neal) fave, Timmy finally starts to learn about blustery dad John (Albertson) and attempts to moderate between the rancorous duo. But he quickly discovers that each of his parents will use him against the other and Timmy decides the best thing for everyone would be if he strikes out on his own. First film for Neal after her recovery from a series of strokes. **107m/C VHS.** Martin Sheen, Patricia Neal, Jack Albertson; *D:* Ulu Grosbard; *W:* Frank D. Gilroy; *C:* Jack Priestley; *M:* Lee Pockriss. Academy Awards '68: Best Supporting Actor (Albertson); Nominations: Academy Awards '68: Best Actress (Neal). *MOV*

Submarine Seahawk 🐾🐾 *1959* When a group of Japanese warships mysteriously disappear, allied intelligence suspect a big battle is brewing. An inexperienced commander who has been tracking the movement of the Japanese ships is put in charge of the submarine Seahawk, even though the crew lacks faith in his command abilities. His own men may prove a bigger obstacle than any of the Japanese. Lots of action and stock WWII footage. **83m/B VHS.** John Bentley, Brett Halsey, Wayne Heffley, Steve Mitchell, Henry McCann, Frank Gerstle; *D:* Spencer Gordon Bennet. *COL*

Submission 🐾½ *1977 (R)* A pharmacist's sensuality is reawakened when she has a provocative affair with a clerk in her shop. **107m/C VHS, Beta.** *IT* Franco Nero, Lisa Gastoni; *D:* Salvatore Samperi.

Subspecies 🐾½ *1990 (R)* New improved vampire demons descend on earth. The first full-length feature film shot on location in Transylvania. For horror buffs only.*CW:* Nudity and vampire violence. **90m/C VHS, LV, 8mm, Closed Caption.** Laura Tate, Michael Watson, Anders Hove, Michelle McBride, Irina Movila, Angus Scrimm; *D:* Ted Nicolaou. *FLL*

The Substance of Fire 🐾🐾 *1996 (R)* Publisher Isaac Geldhart (Rifkin) is an autocrat in both his business and his personal life, which may be why he's having so much trouble with both. A Holocaust survivor, Geldhart's obsessive about publishing a lavish four-volume history of Nazi medical experiments that will bankrupt the family firm. So his children wind up ousting him from the company and Isaac slowly slips over the edge into madness. Very King Lear, with an astonishing performance by Rifkin who also played the character in Baitz's 1991 Off-Broadway play.*CW:* Language. **100m/C VHS, LV, Closed Caption.** Ron Rifkin, Tony Goldwyn, Timothy Hutton, Sarah Jessica Parker, Ronny Graham, Elizabeth Franz, Gil Bellows; *D:* Daniel Sullivan; *W:* Jon Robin Baitz; *C:* Robert Yeoman; *M:* Joseph Vitarelli. *TOU*

The Substitute 🐾🐾 *1993 (R)* Donohue plays a sexy high-school substitute teacher who turns out to have homicidal tendencies, which she decides to take out on her students. Film debut for rapper/underwear model Mark.*CW:* Terror/violence and some sexuality. **86m/C VHS, Beta, Closed Caption.** Amanda Donohoe, Dalton James, Natasha Gregson Wagner, Eugene Glazer, Mark Wahlberg; *D:* Martin Donovan; *W:* Cynthia Verlaine; *M:* Gerald Gouriet. *PAR*

The Substitute 🐾 *1996 (R)* Berenger plays a Vietnam vet mercenary who poses as a substitute teacher to uncover a drug ring after his girlfriend (Venora) is roughed up by the gang. At one point, he displays his unique teaching style by throwing some unruly students out of the second floor window. Hmm...wonder if that was on the test. Being a concerned teacher, he decides to uncover the kingpin of the unruly drug gang. Being an unruly drug gang, they decide to shoot at him...a lot. Unless you're a fan of heavy weaponry, banal one liners or yelling at the screen in frustration, substitute another movie for this one.*CW:* Strong violence, language and brief nudity. **114m/C VHS, LV, Closed Caption, DVD.** Tom Berenger, Ernie Hudson, Diane Venora, Mark Anthony, Glenn Plummer, Cliff DeYoung, William Forsythe, Raymond Cruz, Sharron Corley, Richard Brooks, Rodney Grant, Luis Guzman; *D:* Robert Mandel; *W:* Roy Frumkes, Rocco Simonelli, Alan Ormsby; *C:* Bruce Surtees; *M:* Gary Chang. *ART*

The Substitute Wife 🐾🐾½ *1994 (PG-13)* Dying Nebraska frontier woman Amy Hightower (Thompson) decides to find her husband Martin (Weller) a new wife to help on the farm and look after their four children. But women are so scarce (and the farm is so isolated) that the only one willing to give it a try is prostitute Pearl (Fawcett), who's fed up with her profession but isn't exactly the motherly time (at least not at first). Amusing relationships develop between the two women and the bewildered husband. Made for TV.*CW:* Some sexual themes and situations. **92m/C VHS.** Farrah Fawcett, Lea Thompson, Peter Weller; *D:* Peter Werner; *W:* Stan Daniels; *C:* Neil Roach; *M:* Mark Snow. *THV*

Subterfuge 🐾🐾 *1968* When a special American security agent goes to England for a "vacation," his presence causes speculation and poses several serious questions for both British Intelligence and the underworld. Nothing special, with the occasional suspenseful moment. **89m/C VHS, Beta.** *GB* Joan Collins, Gene Barry, Richard Todd; *D:* Peter Graham Scott. *REP*

Suburban Commando 🐾🐾 *1991 (PG)* A goofy, muscular alien mistakenly lands on Earth while on vacation. He does his best to remain inconspicuous, resulting in numerous hilarious situations. Eventually he is forced to confront his arch, interstellar nemesis in order to defend the family who befriended him. A harmless, sometimes cute vehicle for wrestler Hogan, which will certainly entertain his younger fans. **88m/C VHS, LV, Closed Caption.** Hulk Hogan, Christopher Lloyd, Shelley Duvall, Larry Miller, William Ball, JoAnn Dearing, Jack Elam, Roy Dotrice, Christopher Neame, Tony Longo; *D:* Burt Kennedy; *W:* Frank Cappello. *COL, NLC*

Suburban Roulette * 1967 "Adults only" footage from splottermanfor Lewis natore in the prurient. Groovy themes like wife swapping and other very daring subjects. Totally '60s. Presented as part of Joe Bob Brigg's "Sleaziest Movies in the History of the World" series. **91m/C VHS. D:** Herschell Gordon Lewis. *VTR*

Suburbia * *The Wild Side* 1983 (R) When a group of punk rockers move into a condemned suburban development, they become the targets of a vigilante group. Low budget, needless violent remake of anyone of many '50s rebellion flicks that tries to have a "message." **99m/C VHS, Beta, LV.** Chris Pederson, Bill Coyne, Jennifer Clay, Timothy Eric O'Brien, Andrew Pece, Don Allen; **D:** Penelope Spheeris. *ART, VES*

subUrbia ** 1996 (R) Ensemble piece featuring three aimless post-high school friends, Jeff (Ribisi), Buff (Zahn), and Tim (Katt) who spend their time hanging out in the parking lot of a convenience store. What's different about this night is that they're joined by Jeff's girlfriend Sooze (Carey) and her friend Bee-Bee (Spybey), and they actually have a purpose for waiting around. The guys are expecting a visit from their old buddy Pony (Bartok), a rock musician just finding success. But when Pony does appear, the fact that he has done something to get out and succeed turns the meeting hostile. Based on the play by Eric Bogosian. **CW:** Strong language including sex and drug references, teen drinking and brief nudity. **121m/C VHS, Closed Caption.** Giovanni Ribisi, Steve Zahn, Nicky Katt, Jayce Bartok, Amie Carey, Dina Spybey, Parker Posey, Ajay Naidu, Samia Shoaib; **D:** Richard Linklater; **W:** Eric Bogosian; **C:** Lee Daniel. Nominations: Independent Spirit Awards '98: Best Supporting Actor (Naidu). *WAR*

Subway *½ 1985 (R) Surreal, MTV-esque vision of French fringe life from the director of "Le Dernier Combat." A spike-haired renegade escapes the law by plunging into the Parisian subway system. Once there, he encounters a bizarre subculture living under the city. Plenty of angry-youth attitude, but where's the point? And frankly, too much bad New Wave music. **103m/C VHS, Beta, LV, Closed Caption.** *FR* Christopher Lambert, Isabelle Adjani, Jean-Hugues Anglade, Jean Reno; **D:** Luc Besson; **W:** Luc Besson. Cesar Awards '86: Best Actor (Lambert), Best Art Direction/Set Decoration, Best Sound; Nominations: Cesar Awards '86: Best Supporting Actor (Anglade). *FOX*

Subway Stories ** 1997 (R) Ten short films based on actual experiences on the New York subway system featuring such topics as harassment, flirtation, sex, food, and money. **CW:** Language. **82m/C VHS.** Bill Irwin, Kris Parker, Denis Leary, Christine Lahti, Steve Zahn, Jerry Stiller, Bonnie Hunt, Lili Taylor, Michael Rapaport, Mercedes Ruehl, Sarita Choudhury, Taral Hicks, Danny Hoch, Mike McGlone, Rosie Perez, Gregory Hines, Anne Heche; **D:** Ted Demme, Abel Ferrara, Jonathan Demme, Julie Dash, Seth Zvi Rosenfeld, Bob Balaban, Alison Maclean, Lucas Platt, Patricia Benoit, Craig McKay; **W:** Danny Hoch, John Guare, Adam Brooks, Julie Dash, Lynn Grossman, Marla Hanson, Seth Zvi Rosenfeld, Joe Viola, Albert Innaurato, Angela Todd; **C:** Ken Kelsch, Adam Kimmel, Tom Hurwitz, Anthony Jannelli. *HBO*

Subway to the Stars **½ *Un Trem Para as Estrelas* 1987 Young saxophonist Fontes searches the back streets of Rio for his missing girlfriend. Realistic and sometimes depressing, if aimless at times. Overall, an intriguing "underworld" flick from Brazil. Portuguese with subtitles. **103m/C VHS.** *BR* Guilherme Fontes, Milton Goncalves, Taumaturgo Ferreira, Ze Trindade, Ana Beatriz Wiltgen; **D:** Carlos Diegues. *FCT*

Success Is the Best Revenge **½ 1984 A Polish film director living in London struggles with his rebellious teenage son. Both struggle with questions of exile and identity. Uneven but worthwhile and based on Skolimowski's own experiences. His better earlier film is "Moonlighting." **95m/C VHS, LV.** *GB* Michael York, Michel Piccoli, Anouk Aimee, John Hurt, Jane Asher,

Joanna Szerbic, Michael Lyndon, George Skolimowski; **D:** Jerzy Skolimowski; **W:** Lesz Sakolski. *JME*

The Sucker ** *Le Corniauds* 1965 Antoine Marechal (Bouvril) is on his way to an Italian vacation when his car is wrecked in an accident. The businessman who smashed his car offers Antoine a Cadillac to drive but this turns him into a smuggler. However, Antoine isn't as dumb as he may appear and he makes the most of his unusual situation. French with subtitles. **90m/C VHS.** *FR* Bourvil, Louis de Funes; **D:** Gerard Oury. *FCT*

Sucker Money *½ *Victims of the Beyond* 1934 Newspaper reporter works to expose phony spiritualist. Good title; little else. Boring. **59m/B VHS, Beta, LV.** Mischa Auer, Phyliss Barrington, Earl McCarthy, Ralph Lewis, Mae Busch; **D:** Dorothy Davenport Reid. *NOS, SNC, VYY*

Sudden Death * 1950 Shamrock and Lucky are back as cowboys posing as hired gunmen in order to foil a wealthy, homesteader-hating land baron. **55m/B VHS, Beta, LV.** James Ellison, Russell Hayden, Stanley Price, Raymond Hatton, Julie Adams. *NO*

Sudden Death * 1977 (R) Two professional insurance merchants put themselves up for hire. **84m/C VHS, Beta.** Robert Conrad, Felton Perry, Don Stroud, Bill Raymond, Ron Vawter, Harry Roskolenko; **D:** Richard Foreman.

Sudden Death * 1985 (R) A beautiful businesswoman decides to kill every rapist she can find after she herself has been attacked. Exploitative in its own fashion; fueled and felled by rage. **95m/C VHS, Beta.** Denise Coward, Frank Runyeon, Jamie Tirelli; **D:** Sig Shore. *ART, VES*

Sudden Death * 1995 (R) Terrorists invade a hockey arena where the Vice President and 17,000 fans, including Fire Marshal Jean-Claude and his kids, are watching the seventh game of the Stanley Cup Finals. The latest in the "Die Hard in a..." genre covers the territory with the now-standard lack of characterization, family member in peril, and ever-increasing body count. Boothe (playing Alan Rickman playing a bad guy) does most of the talking while Van Damme kicks people in the head and plays goalie. Producer Howard Baldwin owns the Pittsburgh Penguins, coincidentally one of the teams on the ice for the second pairing of "Timecop" vets Hyams and Van Damme. **CW:** Substantial amount of strong violence and language. **110m/C VHS, LV, Closed Caption, DVD.** Jean-Claude Van Damme, Powers Boothe, Ross Malinger, Whittni Wright, Raymond J. Barry, Dorian Harewood, Kate McNeil, Audra Lindley; **D:** Peter Hyams; **W:** Gene Quintano; **C:** Peter Hyams; **M:** John Debney. *USH*

Sudden Fear *** 1952 Successful playwright/heiress Myra Hudson (Crawford) has a whirlwind romance, leading to marriage, with oh-so-charming actor Lester Blaine (Palance). But Les is more interested in Myra's money and gets together with former flame Irene (always the bad girl Grahame) to get rid of his new bride and inherit her fortune. But Myra finds out about the plot and puts her writing talent to work in coming up with a new scenario. Good suspenser with fine performances. Adapted from the book by Edna Sherry. **111m/B VHS.** Joan Crawford, Jack Palance, Gloria Grahame, Bruce (Herman Brix) Bennett, Virginia Huston, Mike Connors; **D:** David Miller; **W:** Lenore Coffee, Robert Smith; **C:** Charles B(ryant) Lang; **M:** Elmer Bernstein. Nominations: Academy Awards '52: Best Actress (Crawford), Best Black and White Cinematography, Best Costume Design (B & W), Best Supporting Actor (Palance). *KIV*

Sudden Impact **½ 1983 (R) Eastwood directs himself in this formula thriller, the fourth "Dirty Harry" entry. This time "Dirty Harry" Callahan tracks down a revenge-obsessed murderess and finds he has more in common with her than he expected. Meanwhile, local mobsters come gunning for him. This is the one where he says, "Go ahead. Make my day." Followed by "The Dead Pool." **117m/C VHS, Beta, LV, 8mm, Letterbox, Closed Caption.** Clint Eastwood, Sondra Locke, Pat Hin-

gle, Bradford Dillman; **D:** Clint Eastwood; **W:** Charles B. Plerce, J. Bruce Bonoca, M. Luio Uchitti. *WAR, TLF*

Sudden Terror * *Eyewitness* 1970 (PG) The murder of an African dignitary is witnessed by a young boy who has trouble convincing his parents and the police about the incident. Suspenseful but less than original. Shot on location in Malta. **95m/C VHS, Beta.** *GB* Mark Lester, Lionel Jeffries, Susan George, Tony Bonner; **D:** John Hough. *FOX*

Suddenly ***½ 1954 Crazed gunman Sinatra holds a family hostage in the hick town of Suddenly, California, as part of a plot to kill the president, who's passing through town. Tense thriller is a good display for Sinatra's acting talent. Unfortunately hard to find because Sinatra forced United Artists to take it out of distribution after hearing that Kennedy assassin Lee Harvey Oswald had watched "Suddenly" only days before November 22, 1963. Really, Ol' Blue Eyes should have stuck with making top-notch thrillers like this one, instead of degenerating into the world's greatest lounge singer. **75m/B VHS, Beta.** Frank Sinatra, Sterling Hayden, James Gleason, Nancy Gates, Paul Frees; **D:** Lewis Allen. *SNC, NOS, VEC*

Suddenly, Last Summer ***½ 1959 Brain surgeon is summoned to the mansion of a rich New Orleans matron who wishes him to perform a lobotomy on her niece, supposedly suffering from a mental breakdown. Based on the play by Tennessee Williams. Softened for the censors, though the themes of homosexuality, insanity, and murder, characterizations of evil, and unusual settings presage many movies of the next two decades. Extremely fine performances from Hepburn and Taylor. Clift never completely recovered from his auto accident two years before and does not come across with the strength of purpose really necessary in his character. Still, fine viewing. **114m/B VHS, Beta, LV.** Elizabeth Taylor, Katharine Hepburn, Montgomery Clift, Mercedes McCambridge, Albert Dekker; **D:** Joseph L. Mankiewicz; **W:** Gore Vidal; **C:** Jack Hildyard; **M:** Malcolm Arnold. Golden Globe Awards '60: Best Actress—Drama (Taylor); Nominations: Academy Awards '59: Best Actress (Hepburn), Best Actress (Taylor), Best Art Direction/Set Decoration (B & W). *COL*

Sudie & Simpson *** 1990 Heart-tugging tale of friendship set in rural 1940s Georgia. Twelve-year-old white Sudie's forbidden friendship with the adult black Simpson provides a lot of talk in their small town. Racial barriers finally cause Simpson to be accused of child molestation and the odds of his survival, despite his innocence, don't seem great. Based on Sara Flanigan Carter's autobiographical novel. Made for cable television. **95m/C VHS, Closed Caption.** Sara Gilbert, Louis Gossett Jr., Frances Fisher, John M. Jackson, Paige Danahy, Ken Strong; **D:** Joan Tewkesbury; **W:** Sara Flanigan Carter, Ken Koser. *WOV*

Suds **½ 1920 Pickford is tragic laundress with major crush on a guy who left his shirt at the laundry. **75m/B VHS, Beta, LV.** Mary Pickford, William Austin, Harold Goodwin, Rose Dione, Theodore Roberts; **D:** John Francis Dillon. *GPV*

Suffering Bastards **½ 1990 Buddy and Al have never worked a day in their lives—Mom's nightclub always gave them something to do and a regular paycheck. But when Mom's swindled out of the family business, they decide it's time to take charge. Soon they're caught between bullets, babes, and belly laughs in this action-filled comedy. **95m/C VHS.** Eric Bogosian, John C. McGinley, David Warshofsky.

Sugar Cane Alley *** *Rue Cases Negres* 1983 After the loss of his parents, an 11-year-old orphan boy goes to work with his grandmother on a sugar plantation. She realizes that her young ward's only hope is an education. Set in Martinique in the 1930s among black workers. Poignant and memorable. French with subtitles. **106m/C VHS.** *FR* Garry Cadenat, Darling Legitimus, Douta Seck; **D:** Euzhan Palcy; **W:** Euzhan Palcy; **C:** Dominique Chapuis. *NYF, FCT*

Sugar Cookies woof! 1977 (R) Erotic horror story in which young women are the pawns as a satanic satyr and an impassioned lesbian play out a bizarre game of vengeance, love, and death. 89m/C VHS, Beta. Mary Woronov, Lynn Lowry, Monique Van Vooren; *D:* Michael Herz. *NO*

Sugar Hill ✗✗ 1994 (R) Two brothers (Wright & Snipes) are heroin dealers who have built their own crime empire in the Sugar Hill section of Harlem. Snipes is moved to reconsider his career options when he falls for an aspiring actress (Randle). Jarring editing sequence recaps the seminal event in the brothers' upbringing and serves to explain how the wide-eyed boys became cold-blooded pushers. Good performances by all, but formulaic plot will leave viewers asking themselves if they haven't seen it before and why it was they saw it then. Junkie dad Williams was Linc on "The Mod Squad" on television in the late 1960s and director of "Tales from the Hood." 123m/C VHS, LV, Closed Caption. Wesley Snipes, Michael Wright, Theresa Randle, Clarence Williams III, Abe Vigoda, Ernie Hudson, Larry Joshua, Leslie Uggams, Khandi Alexander, Raymond Serra, Joe Dallesandro, Vondie Curtis-Hall; *D:* Leon Ichaso; *W:* Barry Michael Cooper; *C:* Bojan Bazelli; *M:* Terence Blanchard. *FXV*

Sugarbaby ✗✗✗ *Zuckerbaby* 1985 (R) An acclaimed German film about a fat mortuary attendant living in Munich who transforms herself (but doesn't lose weight) in order to seduce a young, handsome subway conductor. Touching and warm film that introduced Sagebrecht to American audiences. A bit too cutting-edge cinematographically. In German with English subtitles. Remade as "Babycakes." Sagebrecht and director Adlon team up again for "Bagdad Cafe" and "Rosalie Goes Shopping." 103m/C VHS, Beta. *GE* Marianne Saegebrecht, Eisi Gulp, Toni Berger, Will Spendler, Manuela Denz; *D:* Percy Adlon; *W:* Percy Adlon. *ORI, GLV, KIV*

The Sugarland Express ✗✗✗ 1974 (PG) To save her son from adoption, a young woman helps her husband break out of prison. In their flight to freedom, they hijack a police car, holding the policeman hostage. Speilberg's first feature film is a moving portrait of a couple's desperation. Based on a true story, adapted by Hal Barwood and Matthew Robbins. 109m/C VHS, Beta, LV, Letterbox. Goldie Hawn, Ben Johnson, Michael Sacks, William Atherton; *D:* Steven Spielberg; *W:* Steven Spielberg, Matthew Robbins, Hal Barwood; *C:* Vilmos Zsigmond; *M:* John Williams. *USH*

Sugartime ✗✗½ 1995 (R) Based on the true-life romance of '60s Chicago mobster Sam Giacana (Turturro) and song bird Phyllis Maguire (Parker), one of the wholesome Maguire Sisters. Naturally, getting involved with a crime boss did little for her image and Maguire's career hit the skids while Giacana's volatile jealousy brought unwanted attention from both fellow gangsters and the feds. (He was murdered in 1975 but had broken off with Phyllis before that). The real Maguire denounced the inaccuracy of the TV production. Suggested by William F. Roemer, Jr.'s book "Roemer: Man Against the Mob."*CW:* Violence, language, and sexuality. 108m/C VHS. John Turturro, Mary-Louise Parker, Elias Koteas, Maury Chaykin, Louis Del Grande, Christopher Barry, Richard Blackburn; *D:* John N. Smith; *W:* Martyn Burke; *C:* Pierre Letarte. *HBO*

Suicide Battalion/Hell Squad ✗✗ 1958 A war movie double feature. In "Suicide Battalion," American troops must sneak through enemy territory to destroy a captured American command outpost in the Philippines during WWII. Five American soldiers are lost in the North African desert in "Hell Squad." After a series of fights with various enemies, one soldier survives, only to nearly be doublecrossed by a Nazi he meets in the desert. 150m/B VHS. Mike Connors, John Ashley, Russ Bender, Jewell Lain, Bing Russell, Wally Campo, Brandon Carroll, Frederic Galvin; *D:* Edward L. Cahn, Burt Topper; *W:* Burt Topper. *COL*

Suicide Cult woof! 1977 A CIA employee predicts the second coming of Christ, and a battle ensues between the forces of good and evil for possession of the child. 82m/C VHS, Beta. *NO*

Suicide Kings ✗✗ 1997 (R) When the sister of one of four prep school friends is kidnapped, the guys decide to take retired mobster Charlie Barrett (Walken) hostage so he'll help them. The wannabe "Reservoir Pups" lose control almost as soon as the caper begins, and the savvy Barrett takes advantage to turn his captors against each other with news that the girl's abduction may have been an inside job. Maze of a plot, which wanders into "Usual Suspects" is-this-all-real? territory, does nothing to help any of the young actors, who are clearly overmatched by Walken. Not much here for anyone except fans of Walken's patented Gangster Cool.*CW:* Strong violence and language, and for some nudity and drug use. 106m/C VHS. Christopher Walken, Jay Mohr, Henry Thomas, Sean Patrick Flanery, Denis Leary, Jeremy Sisto, Johnny Galecki, Cliff DeYoung, Laura San Giacomo, Nina Siemaszko, Frank Medrano, Brad Garrett, Lisanne Falk; *D:* Peter O'Fallon; *W:* Josh McKinney, Gina Goldman, Wayne Rice; *C:* Christopher Baffa; *M:* Graeme Revell. *NYR*

Suicide Patrol ✗ 197? A small band of saboteurs patrols a German-controlled Mediterranean island during WWII. 90m/C VHS, Beta. Gordon Mitchell, Pierre Richard, Max Dean. *UNI, MOV*

Suicide Ride ✗✗ 1997 Action-movie junkie Barney's (Quill) life is going nowhere, so looking for some real adventure he decides to hire a hitman (Hues) to off him. Only the hitman wants to retire and instead offers Barney his job, which he takes. This causes him lots of trouble. Quirky low-budgeter. 86m/C VHS. Tim Quill, Matthias Hues, Frank Adonis; *D:* Samer Daboul, Trevor Sands. *SPC*

Suite 16 ✗✗ 1994 (R) A penthouse suite in a French Riviera hotel is occupied by rich, manipulative, wheelchair-bound Glover (Postlethwaite). Young gigolo/thief Chris (Kamerling), who believes he's killed his latest trick, is given refuge by Glover in exchange for allowing the aging voyeur to watch Chris (via camera) perform with a succession of prostitutos. Finally, Chris wants to leave but Glover offers him a huge amount of money for one final vicarious—and deadly—thrill. Eurotrash, with corny dialogue, but Postlethwaite's chillingly creepy. Also available in an R-rated version.*CW:* Strong sexuality and language, and for some violence and drug use. 93m/C VHS. *BE GB* Pete Postlethwaite, Antoine Kamerling, Geraldine Pailhas, Tom Jansen; *D:* Dominique Derudddere; *W:* Charles Higson, Lise Mayer; *C:* Jean-Francois Robin; *M:* Walter Hus. *APX*

The Suitors ✗ 1988 When a group of Iranians decide to sacrifice a lamb in their apartment, the New York police send in SWAT team assuming they're terrorists. First time effort by Ebrahimian, in Farsi with English subtitles. 106m/C VHS. *D:* Ghasem Ebrahimian. *FCT*

Sullivan's Travels ✗✗✗✗ 1941 Sturges' masterpiece is a sardonic, whip-quick romp about a Hollywood director tired of making comedies who decides to make a serious, socially responsible film and hits the road masquerading as a hobo in order to know hardship and poverty. Beautifully sustained, inspired satire that mercilessly mocked the ambitions of Depression-era social cinema. Gets a little over-dark near the end before the happy ending; Sturges insisted on 20-year-old Lake as The Girl; her pregnancy forced him to rewrite scenes and design new costumes for her. As ever, she is stunning. 90m/B VHS, Beta, LV. Joel McCrea, Veronica Lake, William Demarest, Robert Warwick, Franklin Pangborn, Porter Hall, Eric Blore, Byron Foulger, Robert Greig, Torben Meyer, Jimmy Conlin, Margaret Hayes, Chester Conklin, Alan Bridge; *D:* Preston Sturges; *W:* Preston Sturges. National Film Registry '90. *USH*

The Sum of Us ✗✗✗ 1994 (R) Sweet and faithful adaptation of David Stevens' stage play about a father and his gay son. Widowed Harry Mitchell (Thompson) shares his house with son Jeff (Crowe), who's never made a secret of his sexual orientation. Affable Harry only wants what's best for his boy, including his over-enthusiastic welcome to Jeff's potential new boyfriend (Polson). Too bad Harry's not so lucky in love—his new woman friend Joyce (Kennedy) has problems with Jeff's sexuality. Well, she just has to adjust. Pervasive feel-good message may leave less well-adjusted viewer addled. Sensitive performances, though the film's antecedents as a play are highlighted by having the main characters talk directly to the camera. Aussie slang provides a challenge.*CW:* Much sex-related dialogue; brief flash of nudity. 99m/C VHS. *AU* Jack Thompson, Russell Crowe, John Polson, Deborah Kennedy, Mitch Mathews, Julie Herbert, Joss Moroney, Rebekah Elmaloglou; *D:* Kevin Dowling, Geoff Burton; *W:* David Stevens; *C:* Geoff Burton; *M:* Dave Faulkner. Australian Film Institute '94: Best Adapted Screenplay; Montreal World Film Festival '94: Best Screenplay; Nominations: Australian Film Institute '94: Best Film, Best Supporting Actor (Polson), Best Supporting Actress (Kennedy). *HMK*

Summer ✗✗✗½ *Le Rayon Vert; The Green Ray* 1986 (R) The fifth and among the best of Rohmer's "Comedies and Proverbs" series. A romantic but glum young French girl finds herself stuck in Paris during the tourist season searching for true romantic love. Takes time and patience to seize the viewer; moving ending makes it all worthwile. In French with English subtitles. 90m/C VHS, Beta, LV. *FR* Marie Riviere, Lisa Heredia, Beatrice Romand, Eric Hamm, Rosette, Isabelle Riviere; *D:* Eric Rohmer; *W:* Eric Rohmer. *FCT, TPV*

Summer Affair ✗½ 1979 Two young lovers run away from their bickering parents and get shipwrecked on a desert island. 90m/C VHS, Beta. *IT* Ornella Muti, Les Rannow; *D:* George S. Casorati. *NO*

Summer and Smoke ✗✗½ 1961 Repressed, unhappy Page falls for handsome doctor Harvey. A tour de force for Page, but that's all; adapted clumsily from the overwrought Tennessee Williams play. 118m/C VHS, Beta, LV, Letterbox, Closed Caption. Laurence Harvey, Geraldine Page, Rita Moreno, Una Merkel, John McIntire, Thomas Gomez, Pamela Tiffin, Lee Patrick, Max Casey Adams Showalter, Earl Holliman, Harry Shannon, Pattee Chapman; *D:* Peter Glenville; *C:* Charles B(ryant) Lang; *M:* Elmer Bernstein. Golden Globe Awards '62: Best Actress—Drama (Page); National Board of Review Awards '61: Best Actress (Page); Nominations: Academy Awards '61: Best Actress (Page), Best Art Direction/Set Decoration (Color), Best Supporting Actress (Merkel), Best Original Dramatic/Comedy Score. *PAR, FCT*

Summer Camp Nightmare ✗½ *The Butterfly Revolution* 1986 (PG-13) See "Lord of the Flies" instead. A young fascist incites children at two summer camps to overthrow and imprison the adults. Barbarism rears its ugly head. Self-serious and anticlimatic. Based on the novel "The Butterfly Revolution" by William Butler. 89m/C VHS, Beta, LV, Closed Caption. Chuck Connors, Charles Stratton, Harold Pruett, Tom Fridley, Adam Carl; *D:* Bert L. Dragin; *C:* Don Burgess. *NLC*

Summer City ✗½ *Coast of Terror* 1977 Fun-and-sun surfing movie complete with romance, hot rods, murder and great shots of the sea features Gibson in his debut. Ever wonder what Australian surf bums do on weekends? The same as their California counterparts—except they talk funny. 83m/C VHS, Beta. *AU* Mel Gibson, Phillip Avalon, John Jarratt, Christopher Fraser. *VCD*

Summer Fantasy ✗ 1984 Mindless TV surf saga about a curvy teen who would rather watch the beach hunks then go to medical school. 96m/C VHS, Beta. Julianne Phillips, Ted Shackleford, Michael Gross, Dorothy Lyman; *D:* Noel Nosseck; *M:* Peter Bernstein. *NO*

Summer Fling 🎬🎬½ 1998 (R) Under-achieving Frankie decides to forget about his grade point average and enjoy himself on summer vacation by cutting loose, making new friends, falling in love, and maybe doing some growing up. 103m/C VHS, **Closed Caption.** Jared Leto, Christina Ricci, Gabriel Byrne, Catherine O'Hara, Colm Meaney, Lorraine Pilkington; **D:** David Keating. TOU

Summer Heat 🎬½ 1987 (R) In rural, mid-Depression North Carolina, a young, lonely wife and mother is seduced by a drifter and together they plot murder. Her husband neglects her, and you should neglect to see this utter yawner. Based on a Louise Shivers novel. 80m/C VHS, Beta, LV. Lori Singer, Anthony Edwards, Bruce Abbott, Kathy Bates; **D:** Michie Gleason; **C:** Elliot Davis. PAR

Summer Holiday 🎬🎬½ 1948 Rooney comes of age with a vengeance during summer vacation in musical rendition of "Ah, Wilderness." Undistinguished musical numbers, inferior to the original, but jazzy Technicolor cinematography. Ended up in the red by over $1.5 million, lotsa money back then. ♫ It's Our Home Town; Afraid to Fall in Love; All Hail, Danville High; The Stanley Steamer; It's Independence Day; I Think You're the Sweetest Kid I've Ever Known; Weary Blues. 92m/C VHS. Mickey Rooney, Gloria De Haven, Walter Huston, Frank Morgan, Jackie "Butch" Jenkins, Marilyn Maxwell, Agnes Moorehead, Selena Royle, Anne Francis; **D:** Rouben Mamoulian. MGM, TTC, FCT

The Summer House 🎬🎬½ 1994 Comedy of manners set in 1959 England about the manipulations of three middle-aged women (Moreau, Plowright, Walters) over the impending marriage of one's dreamy young daughter (Headey) to a dolt (Threlfall). Moreau stirs things up as the spirited and skeptical friend of Walters, the deluded bride's mother whom she must interrupt from her busy nuptial preparations and somehow communicate the obvious. Plowright is perfectly cast as the gimlet-eyed groom's mother, well aware of her son's flaws, who achieves an odd alliance with polar opposite Moreau. Strong performances from all the veterans carry the day. Based on the novel by Alice Thomas Ellis. 85m/C VHS. GB Jeanne Moreau, Joan Plowright, Julie Walters, Lena Headey, David Threlfall, Padraig Casey, Britta Smith, John Wood; **D:** Waris Hussein; **W:** Martin Sherman; **M:** Stanley Myers. HMK

Summer Interlude 🎬🎬🎬½ Illicit Interlude; Summerplay; Sommarlek 1950 A ballerina recalls a romantic summer spent with an innocent boy, who was later tragically killed. Contains many earmarks and visual ideas of later Bergman masterpieces. In Swedish with English subtitles. 95m/B VHS, Beta. SW Maj-Britt Nilsson, Birger Malmsten, Alf Kjellin; **D:** Ingmar Bergman; **W:** Ingmar Bergman. HMV, NLC

Summer Lovers 🎬 1982 (R) Summer vacation finds young couple traveling to the exotic Greek island of Santorini. They meet up with a fun-loving woman and discover three-way sexual tension, but little in the way of plot, dialogue, or acting. From the director of "Grease" and "Blue Lagoon" and best watched late at night while half conscious. 98m/C VHS, Beta, LV. Peter Gallagher, Daryl Hannah, Valerie Quennessen; **D:** Randal Kleiser; **M:** Basil Poledouris. COL

Summer Magic 🎬🎬 1963 An impecunious recent widow is forced to leave Boston and settle her family in a small town in Maine. Typical, forgettable Disney drama; early Mills vehicle. A remake of "Mother Carey's Chickens." 116m/C VHS, Beta. Hayley Mills, Burl Ives, Dorothy McGuire, Deborah Walley, Una Merkel, Eddie Hodges; **D:** James Neilson; **M:** Buddy Baker. DIS

Summer Night 🎬🎬 1987 (R) A female tycoon who is concerned for the environment decides to strike out at the terrorists who are destroying it. This caper turns into one big comedy. In Italian with English subtitles. 94m/C VHS, Beta. IT Mariangela Melato, Michele Placido, Roberto Herlitzka, Massimo Wertmuller; **D:** Lina Wertmuller. ART

Summer Night with Greek Profile, Almond Eyes & Scent of Basil 🎬🎬 1987 (R) A wealthy woman tycoon hires an ex-CIA man to kidnap a high-priced, professional terrorist and hold him for ransom. An ironic battle of the sexes follows. In Italian with English subtitles. 94m/C VHS, Beta. IT Mariangela Melato, Michele Placido, Roberto Herlitzka; **D:** Lina Wertmuller; **W:** Lina Wertmuller. TPV

The Summer of Aviya 🎬🎬 Kayitz Shel Aviya 1988 Ten-year-old Aviya has spent most of her life in orphanages as her partisan Jewish mother fought the Nazis. Now, Aviya faces the prospect of returning to a home and woman she doesn't really know, one who is also balanced on the edge of madness. Based on the memoirs of Almagor. Hebrew with subtitles. Followed by "Under the Domim Tree." 7m/C VHS. IS Kaipo Cohen, Gila Almagor; **D:** Eli Cohen; **W:** Eli Cohen, Gila Almagor. FCT

The Summer of Ben Tyler 🎬🎬½ 1996 (PG) Temple Rayburn (Woods) is an up-and-coming lawyer in a small southern town in 1942 and the protege of influential Spencer Maitland (Cariou). Before his family's black housekeeper dies, Rayburn agrees to take in her mentally handicapped teenaged son, Ben (Mattocks), to the dismay of the white community. Then Maitland insists Rayburn defend his son Junius (Isola) against a drunk driving charge where a woman was killed. TV movie. 134m/C VHS, **Closed Caption.** James Woods, Len Cariou, Elizabeth McGovern, Charles Mattocks, Kevin Isola, Julia McIlvaine, Clifton James; **D:** Arthur Allan Seidelman; **W:** Robert Inman; **C:** Neil Roach; **M:** Van Dyke Parks. HMK

Summer of Fear 🎬🎬 Stranger in Our House 1978 A happy young woman (Blair) must overcome evil forces when her cousin (a teenage witch not akin to Sabrina) comes to live with—and control—her family. Based on a novel by Lois Duncan, who also wrote the source novel for 1997's "I Know What You Did Last Summer." Pretty scary if ordinary, made-for-TV horror from later-famous Craven. 94m/C VHS, Beta. Linda Blair, Lee Purcell, Jeremy Slate, Carol Lawrence, MacDonald Carey, Jeff McCracken, Jeff East, Fran Drescher; **D:** Wes Craven; **M:** Tom D'Andrea. NO

Summer of '42 🎬🎬🎬 1971 (R) Touching if sentimental story about a 15-year-old boy's sexual coming of age during his summer vacation on an island off New England. While his friends are fumbling with girls their own age, he falls in love with a beautiful 22-year-old woman whose husband is off fighting in the war. 102m/C VHS, Beta, LV, **Closed Caption.** Jennifer O'Neill, Gary Grimes, Jerry Houser, Oliver Conant; **D:** Robert Mulligan; **C:** Robert L. Surtees. Academy Awards '71: Best Original Dramatic/Comedy Score; Nominations: Academy Awards '71: Best Cinematography, Best Film Editing, Best Story & Screenplay. WAR

The Summer of Miss Forbes 🎬🎬 El Verano de la Senora Forbes 1988 A governess rules over two young boys with an iron hand by day and cavorts nude and drunk by night. The boys fantasize about her murder, but fate has different plans. In Spanish with English subtitles. 85m/C VHS, LV. SP Hanna Schygulla, Alexis Castanares, Victor Cesar Villalobos, Guadalupe Sandoval, Fernando Balzaretti, Yuriria Munguia; **D:** Jaime Humberto Hermosillo. FXL, FCT

The Summer of My German Soldier 🎬🎬🎬 1978 A young Jewish girl befriends an escaped German prisoner of war in a small town in Georgia during WWII. Occasionally sentimental but more often genuinely moving made for TV drama. Rolle won a deserved Emmy as the housekeeper. Adapted from Bette Green's novel. 98m/C VHS, Beta. Kristy McNichol, Esther Rolle, Bruce Davison; **D:** Michael Tuchner. NO

A Summer Place 🎬🎬 1959 Melodrama about summer liaisons amid the young and middle-aged rich on an island off the coast of Maine. Too slick; romantic drama is little more than skin-deep, and dialogue is excruciating. Donahue's first starring role. Based on the novel by Sloan Wilson. Featuring "Theme from a Summer Place," which was a number-one hit in 1959. 130m/C VHS, Beta, LV. Troy Donahue, Richard Egan, Sandra Dee, Dorothy McGuire, Arthur Kennedy, Constance Ford, Beulah Bondi; **D:** Delmer Daves; **C:** Harry Stradling; **M:** Max Steiner. WAR

Summer Rental 🎬🎬 1985 (PG) That John Candy just can't win, can he? Here, as a hopeless, harried air traffic controller, he tries to have a few days to relax in sunny Florida. Enter mean rich guy Crenna. Candy can add something hefty to the limpest of plots, and does so here. Watch the first hour for yuks, then rewind. 87m/C VHS, Beta, LV, 8mm, **Closed Caption.** John Candy, Rip Torn, Richard Crenna, Karen Austin, Kerri Green, John Larroquette, Pierrino Mascarino; **D:** Carl Reiner; **M:** Alan Silvestri. PAR

Summer School 🎬 1977 (R) A teenaged boy's girlfriend will stop at nothing to prevent him from going out with the pretty new girl in town. 80m/C VHS, Beta. John McLaughlin, Steve Rose, Phoebe Schmidt.

Summer School 🎬🎬½ 1987 (PG-13) A high-school teacher's vacation plans are ruined when he gets stuck teaching remedial English in summer school. It seems all these students are interested in is re-enacting scenes from "The Texas Chainsaw Massacre." Actually, one of the better films of this genre. 98m/C VHS, Beta, LV, **Closed Caption.** Mark Harmon, Kirstie Alley, Nels Van Patten, Courtney Thorne-Smith, Lucy Lee Flippin, Shawnee Smith, Robin Thomas, Dean Cameron; **D:** Carl Reiner; **W:** Jeff Franklin; **M:** Danny Elfman. PAR

Summer School Teachers woof! 1975 (R) Three sultry femmes bounce about Los Angeles high school and make the collective student body happy. Typical Corman doings; sequel to "The Students Teachers." 87m/C VHS, Beta. Candice Rialson, Pat Anderson, Rhonda Leigh Hopkins, Christopher Wales; **D:** Barbara Peeters. NLC

Summer Snow 🎬🎬 Nuiyan, Seisap; Woman, Forty 1994 Broad comedy mixed (not always successfully) with family drama. May (Siao) is forced to take in her father-in-law Sun (Chiao) after his wife dies. The old man immediately causes chaos with his habit of wandering off and bizarre behavior, which is finally diagnosed as being Alzheimer's disease. Working mother May tries to find a practical way to deal with her dilemmas but the strains are beginning to crack the family apart. Cantonese with subtitles. 106m/C VHS. HK Josephine Siao, Roy Chiao, Law Kar-ying, Allen Ting; **D:** Ann Hui; **W:** Chan Man-keung; **C:** Lee Ping-bing; **M:** Yoshihide Otomo. Berlin International Film Festival '94: Best Actress (Siao). NYR

Summer Solstice 🎬🎬½ 1981 Fonda and Loy are splendid as a couple married half a century who revisit the beach where they first met. Fonda especially shines, as a crusty old artist. Yes, it is an awful lot like "On Golden Pond." Made for TV. 75m/C VHS, Beta. Henry Fonda, Myrna Loy, Lindsay Crouse, Stephen Collins; **D:** Ralph Rosenblum. NO

Summer Stock 🎬🎬🎬 If You Feel Like Singing 1950 Garland plays a farm owner whose sister arrives with a summer stock troupe, led by Kelly, to rehearse a show in the family barn. Garland agrees, if the troupe will help her with the farm's harvest. When her sister decamps for New York, guess who steps into the leading lady role open, guess who steps into the breach. Slim plot papered over with many fun song-and-dance numbers. Also features Garland's first MGM short, "Every Sunday," made in 1936 with Deanna Durbin. ♫ Friendly Star; Mem'ry Island; Dig-Dig-Dig For Your Dinner; If You Feel Like Singing, Sing; Howdy Neighbor; Blue Jean Polka; Portland Fancy; You, Wonderful You; Get Happy. 109m/C VHS, Beta, LV. Judy Garland, Gene Kelly, Gloria De Haven, Carleton Carpenter, Eddie Bracken, Phil Silvers, Hans Conried, Marjorie Main, Ray Collins, Deanna Durbin; **D:** Charles Walters. MGM, TTC

A Summer Story 🎬🎬🎬 **1988 (PG-13)** Superbly acted, typically British period drama about beautiful farm girl Stubbs and city lawyer Wilby, who fall in love. But can they overcome difference of social class? From the story "The Apple Tree" by John Galsworthy. **97m/C VHS, Beta, Closed Caption.** *GB* James Wilby, Imogen Stubbs, Susannah York, Sophie Ward, Kenneth Colley, Jerome Flynn; *D:* Piers Haggard; *W:* Penelope Mortimer; *M:* Georges Delerue.

A Summer to Remember 🎬🎬🎬 *Seryozha* **1961** A five-year-old boy spends a summer with his stepfather on a Soviet collective farm. The two become deeply attached. Scenes of collective life will be of more interest to Westerners than the near-sentimental story. Star Bondarchuk later directed the epic, award-winning "War and Peace." **80m/B VHS, Beta.** *RU* Borya Barkhazov, Sergei Bondarchuk, Irana Skobtseva. NO

A Summer to Remember 🎬🎬½ **1984 (PG)** A deaf boy (played by Gerlis, himself deaf since birth) develops a friendship with an orangutan through sign language. Bad guys abduct the friendly ape—but all is right in the end. Nice, innocuous family viewing. Based on a story by Scott Swanton and Robert Lloyd Lewis. **93m/C VHS, Beta, Closed Caption.** Tess Harper, James Farentino, Burt Young, Louise Fletcher, Sean Gerlis, Bridgette Anderson; *D:* Robert Lewis; *M:* Charles Fox. USH

Summer Vacation: 1999 🎬 **1999—** *Nen No Natsu Yasumi* **1988** Four boys are left behind at boarding school during their summer vacation. They experience all the early pangs of adolescence from love to jealousy. Their summer is then disturbed by the arrival of another boy who appears to be the reincarnation of a dead friend. Romantic look at youth caught between innocence and awareness. In Japanese with English subtitles. **90m/C VHS, Beta.** *JP* Eri Miyagima, Miyuki Nakano, Tomoko Otakra, Rie Mizuhara; *D:* Shusuke Kaneko. NYF, FCT

Summer Wishes, Winter Dreams 🎬🎬 **1973 (PG)** Woodward and Balsam are a materially prosperous middle-aged couple with little but tedium in their lives—a tedium accurately replicated, in what feels like real life, in this slow, dull film. The two leads and Sidney—in her first screen role in 17 years—are all excellent, but the story of regret and present unhappiness wears the viewer down. **95m/C VHS, Beta.** Joanne Woodward, Martin Balsam, Sylvia Sidney, Dori Brenner, Ron Richards; *D:* Gilbert Cates; *W:* Stewart Stern. British Academy Awards '74: Best Actress (Woodward); National Board of Review Awards '73: Best Supporting Actress (Sidney); New York Film Critics Awards '73: Best Actress (Woodward); Nominations: Academy Awards '73: Best Actress (Woodward), Best Supporting Actress (Sidney). COL

Summerdog 🎬🎬 **1978 (G)** Harmless family tale about vacationers who rescue a cheerful, lovable mutt named Hobo. And a good thing they found him: He saves them from many perils. Thanks, Hobo! **90m/C VHS, Beta.** James Congdon, Elizabeth Eisenman, Oliver Zabriskie, Tavia Zabriskie; *D:* John Clayton. GEM

Summer's Children 🎬 **1984** Man who suffers from amnesia as a result of a car crash becomes the target of a mysterious killer. Forget about it. **90m/C VHS, Beta.** Tom Haoff, Paully Jardine, Kate Lynch. TWE

Summertime 🎬🎬🎬½ *Summer Madness* **1955** Spinster Hepburn vacations in Venice and falls in love with Brazzi. She is hurt when inadvertently she learns he is married, but her life has been so bleak she is not about to end her one great romance. Moving, funny, richly photographed in a beautiful Old World city. From Arthur Laurents' play "The Time of the Cuckoo." **98m/C VHS, Beta, LV.** Katharine Hepburn, Rossano Brazzi; *D:* David Lean; *C:* Jack Hildyard. New York Film Critics Awards '55: Best Director (Lean); Nominations: Academy Awards '55: Best Actress (Hepburn), Best Director (Lean). CRC, NLC, HMV

Summertree 🎬🎬 **1971 (PG)** Douglas stars as a young musician in the 1960s trying to avoid the draft and the wrath of his parents. Contrived and heavy-handed. Produced by Douglas pere, Kirk. Adapted from the play by Ron Cower. **88m/C VHS, Beta.** Michael Douglas, Jack Warden, Brenda Vaccaro, Barbara Bel Geddes, Kirk Calloway, Bill Vint; *D:* Anthony Newley; *M:* David Shire. WAR, OM

The Sun Comes Up 🎬🎬 **1949** MacDonald, in her last screen appearance, plays a bitter widow whose life is changed by an orphan's love for a collie. Songbird MacDonald manages to sing a number of songs, some of them backed by a chorus of "orphans." Based on short stories by Marjorie Kinnan Rawlings. **93m/C VHS.** Jeanette MacDonald, Lloyd Nolan, Claude Jarman Jr., Lewis Stone, Dwayne Hickman; *D:* Richard Thorpe; *W:* William Ludwig; *M:* Andre Previn. MGM, FCT

Sun Ra & His Intergalactic Solar Arkestra: Space Is the Place 🎬🎬 **1974** Space age flick starring most appropriately Sun Ra, space-age prophet/jazz musician. Sun Ra returns from a space odyssey and embarks on saving black youth from the world's oppressive control by bringing them back into space with him. The shaman's philosophy on film. ♫Watusi; Outer Spaceways Inc.; The Satellites are Spinning. **63m/C VHS.** *D:* John Coney; *W:* Joshua Smith. RHP

The Sun Shines Bright 🎬🎬 **1953** Heavily stereotyped, contrived tale of a Southern judge with a heart of gold who does so many good deeds (defending a black man accused of rape; helping a desperate prostitute) that he jeopardizes his re-election. Set during Reconstruction. An unfortunate remake of Ford's own 1934 "Judge Priest," starring Will Rogers. **92m/B VHS.** Charles Winninger, Arleen Whelan, John Russell, Stepin Fetchit, Milburn Stone, Russell Simpson; *D:* John Ford; *C:* Archie Stout. REP

Sun Valley Serenade 🎬🎬½ **1941** Wartime musical fluff about a band that adopts a Norwegian refugee waif as a publicity stunt. She turns out to be a full-grown man-chaser who stirs up things at a ski resort. Fun, but it ends abruptly—because, they say, Henie fell during the huge skating finale, and Darryl Zanuck wouldn't greenlight a reshoot. One of only two feature appearances by Glenn Miller and his Orchestra (the other was "Orchestra Wives"), on video with a soundtrack restored from original dual-track recordings. ♫Chattanooga Choo Choo; I Know Why and So Do You; It Happened In Sun Valley; The Kiss Polka; In the Mood. **86m/C VHS, Beta, Closed Caption.** Sonja Henie, John Payne, Glenn Miller, Milton Berle, Lynn Bari, Joan Davis, Dorothy Dandridge; *D:* H. Bruce Humberstone. Nominations: Academy Awards '41: Best Black and White Cinematography, Best Song ("Chattanooga Choo Choo"), Scoring of a Musical. FCT, MLB

Sunburn 🎬½ **1979 (PG)** Insurance investigator Grodin hires model Fawcett to pretend to be his wife to get the scoop on a suicide/murder case of a rich guy in Acapulco. Made-for-TV drivel. **110m/C VHS, Beta.** Farrah Fawcett, Charles Grodin, Joan Collins, Art Carney, William Daniels; *D:* Richard Sarafian; *W:* James Booth. PAR

Sunchaser 🎬½ **1996 (R)** Mishmash of medicine and mysticism focuses on yuppie UCLA oncologist Dr. Michael Reynolds (Harrelson) who's kidnapped by 16-year-old patient, Brandon "Blue" Monroe (Seda). Blue is a half-Navajo gangbanger whose cancer is inoperable and he needs the doc to drive him to a reservation in Arizona where he feels a medicine man and the waters of a supposedly magical lake can cure him. Reynolds naturally discovers some humanity on the trip and decides to help his truculent patient. Leads give sincere performances but film is half-baked at best. *CW:* Strong language and some violence. **123m/C VHS, Closed Caption.** Woody Harrelson, Jon Seda, Anne Bancroft, Alexandra Tydings, Matt Mulhern, Talisa Soto, Lawrence Pressman, Michael O'Neill, Harry Carey Jr.; *D:* Michael Cimino; *W:* Charles Leavitt; *C:* Doug Milsome; *M:* Maurice Jarre. WAR

Sundance and the Kid 🎬🎬 **1976 (PG)** Two brothers out to collect an inheritance against all odds. Originally known as "Sundance Cassidy and Butch the Kid." **84m/C VHS, Beta.** John Wade, Karen Blake; *D:* Arthur Pitt. NO

Sunday 🎬🎬 **1996** Basically a two-character study of mistaken identity among lonely, middle-aged people. On a winter's Sunday morning in Queens, depressed Oliver (Suchet) is greeted by failing British actress Madeleine (Harrow), who mistakes him for a director she once met. She invites him to lunch and Oliver, who's actually a homeless former accountant, struggles to maintain the charade. The unstable Madeleine's bitter when she discovers his deception but is also unwillingly to let the connection between them die. **93m/C VHS.** David Suchet, Lisa Harrow, Larry Pine, Jared Harris, Joe Grifasi; *D:* Jonathan Nossiter; *W:* Jonathan Nossiter, James Lasdun; *C:* Michael Barrow, John Foster; *M:* Jonathan Nossiter. Sundance Film Festival '97: Best Screenplay, Grand Jury Prize; Nominations: Independent Spirit Awards '98: Best Actress (Harrow), Best Cinematography. NYR

Sunday, Bloody Sunday 🎬🎬🎬 **1971 (R)** Adult drama centers around the intertwined love affairs of the homosexual Finch, the heterosexual Jackson, and self-centered bisexual artist Head, desired by both. Fully drawn characters brought to life by excellent acting make this difficult story well worth watching—though Head's central character is sadly rather dull. Day-Lewis makes his first (brief) screen appearance as a car vandalizing teenager. Powerful, sincere, and sensitive. **110m/C VHS, LV, Letterbox.** *GB* Glenda Jackson, Peter Finch, Murray Head, Daniel Day-Lewis; *D:* John Schlesinger. British Academy Awards '71: Best Actor (Finch), Best Actress (Jackson), Best Director (Schlesinger), Best Film; Golden Globe Awards '72: Best Foreign Film; New York Film Critics Awards '71: Best Screenplay; National Society of Film Critics Awards '71: Best Actor (Finch), Best Screenplay; Writers Guild of America '71: Best Original Screenplay; Nominations: Academy Awards '71: Best Actor (Finch), Best Actress (Jackson), Best Director (Schlesinger), Best Story & Screenplay. FOX

Sunday Daughters 🎬🎬🎬 **1980** A teenage girl kept in a detention home constantly tries to escape and find some kind of familial love. Strong performances mix with keen direction. In Hungarian with English subtitles. **100m/C VHS, Beta.** *HU* Julianna Nyako; *D:* Janosz Rozsa. FCT

A Sunday in the Country 🎬🎬🎬½ *Un Dimanche a la Campagne* **1984 (G)** A lush, distinctively French affirmation of nature and family life. This character study with a minimal plot takes place during a single summer day in 1910 France. An elderly impressionist painter-patriarch is visited at his country home by his family. Highly acclaimed, though the pace may be too slow for some. Beautiful location photography. In French with English subtitles. **94m/C VHS, Beta.** *FR* Louis Ducreux, Sabine Azema, Michel Aumont; *D:* Bertrand Tavernier; *W:* Bertrand Tavernier, Colo Tavernier O'Hagan; *C:* Bruno de Keyzer. Cannes Film Festival '84: Best Director (Tavernier); Cesar Awards '85: Best Actress (Azema), Best Cinematography, Best Writing; National Board of Review Awards '84: Best Supporting Actress (Azema); New York Film Critics Awards '84: Best Foreign Film. MGM

Sunday in the Park with George 🎬🎬🎬 **1986** Taped theatrical performance of the Tony, Grammy, and Pulitzer Prize-winning musical play, which is based upon impressionist Georges Seurat's painting "A Sunday Afternoon on the Island of Grande Jatte." Features a celebrated music score by Sondheim. **120m/C VHS, Beta, LV.** Mandy Patinkin, Bernadette Peters, Barbara Byrne, Charles Kimbrough; *D:* James Lapine; *M:* Stephen Sondheim. ORI, WAR

Sunday Too Far Away 🎬🎬🎬 **1974** The rivalries between Australian sheep shearers and graziers leads to an ugly strike at a remote outback area in 1955. An uncomplicated story and a joy to watch. **100m/C VHS, Beta.** *AU* Jack

Thompson; **D:** Ken Hannam. Australian Film Institute '74: Best Actor (Thompson), Best Film.

Sundays & Cybele 🐾🐾🐾½ *Les Dimanches de Ville d'Avray; Cybele* 1962 A ragged war veteran and an orphaned girl develop a strong emotional relationship, which is frowned upon by the townspeople. Warm and touching. In French with English subtitles. Also available in a letter-boxed edition. **110m/b VHS, Beta.** *FR* Hardy Kruger, Nicole Courcel; **D:** Serge Bourguignon; **M:** Maurice Jarre. Academy Awards '62: Best Foreign Language Film; Nominations: Academy Awards '63: Best Adapted Score, Best Adapted Screenplay. *NYF, DVT, VYY*

Sunday's Children 🐾🐾🐾½ 1994 Lyrical exploration of childhood continues trilogy that includes "Fanny and Alexander" and "Best Intentions." Wistful childhood memoir takes up the story of Ingmar Bergman's family eight years after the director was born. Many of the same familial issues surface, but story soon narrows its focus to the relationship between little Ingmar, whom everyone calls Pu, and his stern father Henrik. Deeply emotional and intense, film represents the steps toward forgiveness that the elder Bergman is finally able to take regarding the painful relationship he had with his own father. Father-son theme made more poignant with Ingmar's son Daniel making his feature debut as director. **118m/C VHS.** *SW* Thommy Berggren, Lena Endre, Henrik Linnros, Jacob Leygraf, Maria Bolme, Bjorje Ahistedt, Per Myrberg; **D:** Daniel Bergman; **W:** Ingmar Bergman. *FRF*

Sundown 🐾🐾½ 1941 In Africa at the beginning of WWII, a local girl aids the British against a German plot to run guns to the natives and start a rebellion. Engaging performances and efficient direction keep it above the usual cliches. Also available in a colorized version. **91m/B VHS, Beta.** Gene Tierney, Bruce Cabot, George Sanders, Harry Carey Sr., Cedric Hardwicke, Joseph Calleia, Dorothy Dandridge, Reginald Gardiner; **D:** Henry Hathaway; **C:** Charles B(ryant) Lang; **M:** Miklos Rozsa. Nominations: Academy Awards '41: Best Black and White Cinematography, Best Interior Decoration, Best Original Dramatic/Comedy Score. *NOS, VYY, DVT*

Sundown 🐾½ 1991 (R) An ambitious shot at a vampire western fails because it drains almost all vampire lore and winds up resembling a standard oater. Carradine plays a reformed vampire king (guess who) running a desert clinic that weans bloodsuckers away from preying on humans. But undead renegades attack using six-guns and wooden bullets. The climax may outrage horror purists. **104m/C VHS.** David Carradine, Bruce Campbell, Deborah Foreman, Maxwell Caulfield, Morgan Brittany; **D:** Anthony Hickox. *VES*

Sundown Fury 🐾 1942 Young cowboy fights against a group of bandits to hold a telegraph office. **56m/B VHS, Beta.** Donald (Don "Red") Barry. *VCN*

Sundown Kid 🐾½ 1943 A Pinkerton agent goes undercover to break up a counterfeiting operation. Routine western. **55m/B VHS, Beta.** Donald (Don "Red") Barry. *DVT*

Sundown Riders 🐾 1948 Cowhands are victimized by noose-happy outlaws. Filmed in just over a week on a $30,000 budget and originally shot on 16mm to make it accessible to hospitals and schools with basic viewing equipment. The lesson here: it takes time and money to make a good western. **56m/B VHS, Beta, LV.** Russell Wade, Andy Clyde, Jay Kirby; **D:** Lambert Hillyer. *NO*

Sundown Saunders 🐾 1936 A standard oater about a cowboy whose prize for winning a horse race is a ranch. Trouble is, an outlaw wants the homestead as well. **64m/B VHS, Beta.** Bob Steele; **D:** Robert North Bradbury. *NOS, VYY, HEG*

The Sundowners 🐾🐾🐾½ 1960 Slow, beautiful, and often moving epic drama about a family of Irish sheepherders in Australia during the 1920s who must continually uproot themselves and migrate. They struggle to save enough money to buy their own farm and wind up training

a horse they hope will be a money-winner in racing. Well acted by all, with Johns and Ustinov providing some humorous moments. Adapted from the novel by Jon Cleary. Filmed in Australia and London studios. **133m/C VHS, Beta, LV.** Deborah Kerr, Robert Mitchum, Peter Ustinov, Glynis Johns, Dina Merrill, Chips Rafferty, Michael Anderson Jr., Lola Brooks, Wylie Watson; **D:** Fred Zinnemann; **C:** Jack Hildyard; **M:** Dimitri Tiomkin. National Board of Review Awards '60: Best Actor (Mitchum); New York Film Critics Awards '60: Best Actress (Kerr); Nominations: Academy Awards '60: Best Actress (Kerr), Best Adapted Screenplay, Best Director (Zinnemann), Best Picture, Best Supporting Actress (Johns). *WAR, VTR, CCB*

Sunny 🐾🐾 1941 Another glossed-over, love-conquers-all musical with Neagle as a circus star who falls for a wealthy car maker's son. Dad and crew disapprove, putting a damper on the romance. In spite of the weak storyline and flat direction, Kerns' music and Bolger's dancing make it enjoyable. ♫Who?; D'ya Love Me?; Sunny; Two Little Bluebirds. **98m/B VHS.** Anna Neagle, Ray Bolger, John Carroll, Edward Everett Horton, Frieda Inescort, Helen Westley, Benny Rubin, Richard Lane, Martha Tilton; **D:** Herbert Wilcox. Nominations: Academy Awards '41: Scoring of a Musical.*NOS*

Sunny Side Up 🐾🐾½ 1928 As stress of pickle factory work takes toll on woman's friend, she makes heroic effort to help her to the country to recover. **66m/B VHS, Beta.** Vera Reynolds, ZaSu Pitts, Edmund Burns, Sally Rand; **D:** Donald Crisp. *GPV*

Sunny Skies 🐾 1930 Bargain-basement retread has Lease donating a pint of blood. ♫Sunny Days; I Must Have You; Wanna Find a Boy; Must Be Love. **75m/B VHS.** Benny Rubin, Marceline Day, Rex Lease, Marjorie Kane, Wesley Barry; **D:** Norman Taurog. *NOS*

Sunnyside woof! 1979 (R) Travolta plays a street kid trying to bring an end to the local gang warfare so he can move to Manhattan. Features a host of pop tunes in an attempt to ride the coattails of brother John's successful "Saturday Night Fever." Laughably bad. **100m/C VHS.** Joey Travolta, John Lansing, Stacey Pickren, Andrew Rubin, Michael Tucci, Talia Balsam, Joan Darling; **D:** Timothy Galfas. *FOX*

Sunrise 🐾🐾🐾🐾 *Sunrise—A Song of Two Humans* 1927 Magnificent silent story of a simple country boy who, prodded by an alluring city woman, tries to murder his wife. Production values wear their age well. Gaynor won an Oscar for her stunning performance. Remade in Germany as "The Journey to Tilsit." Based on a story by Hermann Suderman. **110m/B VHS, LV.** George O'Brien, Janet Gaynor, Bodil Rosing, Margaret Livingston, J. Farrell MacDonald, Carl Mayer; **D:** F.W. Murnau; **C:** Charles Rosher, Karl Struss. Academy Awards '28: Best Actress (Gaynor), Best Cinematography, National Film Registry '89;; Nominations: Academy Awards '28: Best Interior Decoration. *IME, GPV*

Sunrise at Campobello 🐾🐾🐾 1960 A successful adaptation (with Bellamy and Donehue repeating their roles) of the Tony award-winning play that chronicles Franklin D. Roosevelt's battle to conquer polio and ultimately receive the Democratic presidential nomination in 1924. Garson gives an excellent performance as Eleanor Roosevelt. Screenplay by Schary, who adapted his own play, and also produced. **143m/C VHS, Beta.** Ralph Bellamy, Greer Garson, Hume Cronyn, Jean Hagen, Jack Perrin, Lyle Talbot; **D:** Vincent J. Donehue; **W:** Dore Schary. Golden Globe Awards '61: Best Actress—Drama (Garson); National Board of Review Awards '60: Best Actress (Garson); Nominations: Academy Awards '60: Best Actress (Garson), Best Art Direction/Set Decoration (Color), Best Costume Design (Color), Best Sound. *WAR*

Sunrise Trail 🐾🐾½ 1931 Lots of action with Steele working undercover for the sheriff, trying to stop a rustler. He also finds the time to fall for barmaid Mehaffey. **65m/B VHS, Beta.** Bob Steele, Blanche Mehaffey, Jack Clifford, Eddie Dunn; **D:** John P. McCarthy. *GPV*

The Sun's Burial 🐾🐾🐾 1960 Oshima's stylized and violent drama depicts life in Osaka's worst slum—a teeming underworld populated by teen gangs, prostitutes, and criminals. All want control of the area's most profitable business, an illegal blood-selling operation. In Japanese with English subtitles. **87m/C VHS.** *JP* Kayoko Honoo, Koji Nakahara, Masahiko Tsugawa, Fumio Watanabe; **D:** Nagisa Oshima. *NYF*

Sunset 🐾🐾 1988 (R) Edwards wanders the range in this soft-centered farce about a couple of Western legends out to solve a mystery. On the backlots of Hollywood, silent screen star Tom Mix (Willis) meets aging marshal Wyatt Earp (Garner) and participates in a time-warp western circa 1927. They encounter a series of misadventures while trying to finger a murderer. Garner ambles enjoyably, lifting him a level above the rest of the cast. **101m/C VHS, Beta, LV, Closed Caption.** Bruce Willis, James Garner, Mariel Hemingway, Darren McGavin, Jennifer Edwards, Malcolm McDowell, Kathleen Quinlan, M. Emmet Walsh, Patricia Hodge, Richard Bradford, Joe Dallesandro, Dermot Mulroney; **D:** Blake Edwards; **W:** Blake Edwards, Rod Amateau; **M:** Henry Mancini. Golden Raspberry Awards '88: Worst Director (Edwards); Nominations: Academy Awards '88: Best Costume Design. *COL*

Sunset Boulevard 🐾🐾🐾½ 1950 Famed tale of Norma Desmond (Swanson), aging silent film queen, who refuses to accept that stardom has ended for her and hires a young down-on-his-luck screenwriter (Holden) to help engineer her movie comeback. The screenwriter, who becomes the actress' kept man, assumes he can manipulate her, but finds out otherwise. Reality was almost too close for comfort, as Swanson, von Stroheim (as her major domo), and others very nearly play themselves. A darkly humorous look at the legacy and loss of fame with witty dialog, stellar performances, and some now-classic scenes. Based on the story "A Can of Beans" by Brackett and Wilder. **100m/B VHS, Beta, LV.** Gloria Swanson, William Holden, Erich von Stroheim, Nancy Olson, Buster Keaton, Jack Webb, Cecil B. DeMille, Fred Clark; **D:** Billy Wilder; **W:** Billy Wilder, Charles Brackett, D.M. Marshman Jr. Academy Awards '50: Best Art Direction/Set Decoration (B & W), Best Story & Screenplay, Best Original Dramatic/Comedy Score; Golden Globe Awards '51: Best Actress—Drama (Swanson), Best Director (Wilder), Best Film—Drama, Best Score, National Film Registry '89;; Nominations: Academy Awards '50: Best Actor (Holden), Best Actress (Swanson), Best Black and White Cinematography, Best Director (Wilder), Best Film Editing, Best Picture, Best Supporting Actor (von Stroheim), Best Supporting Actress (Olson). *PAR, HMV*

Sunset Grill 🐾🐾 1992 (R) While investigating his wife's murder, detective Ryder Hart (Weller) discovers a pattern of grisly killings. Sexy singer Loren Duquesne (Singer) leads him south of the border to her boss and his bloody money-making scheme. Unrated version also available.*CW:* Language, violence, and sexuality. **103m/C VHS, Closed Caption.** Peter Weller, Lori Singer, Alexandra Paul, John Rhys-Davies, Michael Anderson Jr., Stacy Keach; **D:** Kevin Connor. *NLC, PMS*

Sunset Heat 🐾🐾 *Midnight Heat* 1992 (R) Former drug dealer (Pare) returns to his home in Los Angeles with a legit job as a photojournalist. He stays with an old friend who turns out to be involved with the obsessed drug czar that Pare used to work for. Trouble comes along when the drug lord is robbed and blames Pare for the crime. Action-packed, with some good plot twists. An unrated version contains two additional minutes of footage.*CW:* Language, strong violence, and strong sensuality. **94m/C VHS, Closed Caption.** Michael Pare, Dennis Hopper, Adam Ant, Daphne Ashbrook, Charlie Schlatter; **D:** John Nicolella. *NLC*

Sunset in El Dorado 🐾½ 1945 Roy and Dale thwart a villainous scheme to defraud farmers of their land. **56m/B VHS, Beta.** Roy Rogers, Dale Evans, George "Gabby" Hayes, Hardie Albright, Roy Barcroft, Tom London, Edmund Cobb; **D:** Frank McDonald. *GPV, VCN*

Sunset Limousine 🎬🎬½ 1983 An out-of-work stand-up comic gets thrown out by his girlfriend, then takes a job as a chauffeur. Standard vehicle with occasional bursts of speed. 92m/C VHS, Beta. John Ritter, Martin Short, Susan Dey, Paul Reiser, Audrie Neehan, Lainie Kazan; D: Terry Hughes. ART

Sunset on the Desert 🎬½ 1942 Rogers gets to wear a white hat and a black hat as both the leader of a gang of outlaws and the hero who brings them to justice. A poor man's Western omelette. 53m/B VHS, Beta. Roy Rogers, George "Gabby" Hayes, Lynne Carver, Frank M. Thomas Sr., Bob Nolan, Beryl Wallace, Glenn Strange, Douglas Fowley, Roy Barcroft, Pat Brady; D: Joseph Kane. VYY

Sunset Park 🎬 1996 (R) Brooklyn phys ed teacher Phyllis Saroka (Perlman) becomes the coach of a high school basketball team that, despite her total lack of knowledge about the game, makes it to the city championships. The cast's excellent performances hold interest, even though the predictable storyline gives away all of its moves before it gets near the hoop. Starr (of the rap group Onyx) is outstanding as the most talented (and most troubled) member of the team. CW: Some language and sexual references. 100m/C VHS, LV, Closed Caption. Rhea Perlman, Carol Kane, Terrence DaShon Howard, Camille Saviola, Fredro Starr, James Harris, Antwon Tanner, Shawn Michael Howard, De'Aundre Bonds; D: Steve Gomer; W: Seth Zvi Rosenfeld, Kathleen McGhee-Anderson; C: Robbie Greenberg; M: Kay Gee, Miles Goodman. COL

Sunset Range 🎬½ 1935 The "World's All-Around Champion Cowboy" of 1912 stars in this chaps-slappin', bit-chompin', dust-raisin' saga of the plains. 59m/B VHS, Beta. Hoot Gibson. NOS, VCN, VCI

Sunset Serenade 🎬🎬 1942 Roy and Gabby outwit murderous duo who plan to eliminate the new heir to a ranch. 60m/B VHS, Beta. Roy Rogers, George "Gabby" Hayes, Helen Parrish; D: Joseph Kane. NOS, HEG, TIM

Sunset Strip 🎬 1985 A photographer investigates a friend's murder, and enters the seamy world of drugs and rock and roll in L.A. 83m/C VHS, Beta. Tom Elpin, Cheri Cameron Newell, John Mayall. ART, VES

Sunset Strip woof! 1991 (R) A young dancer finds a job in a strip club and competes against the other women there to find the man of her dreams. The women take their jobs very seriously—even attending ballet classes to improve their performances. However, the viewer probably won't take this movie very seriously since it is just another excuse to show women in as little clothing as possible. CW: Nudity and sensuality. 95m/C VHS, LV. Jeff Conaway, Michelle Foreman, Shelley Michelle; D: Paul G. Volk; M: John Gonzalez. PMH

Sunset Trail 🎬 1932 Routine Maynard sagebrush saga with the hero protecting a woman rancher from outlaws. 60m/B VHS, Beta. Ken Maynard. NOS, VCI, DVT

The Sunshine Boys 🎬🎬🎬 1975 (PG) Two veteran vaudeville partners, who have shared a love-hate relationship for decades, reunite for a television special. Adapted by Neil Simon from his play. Matthau was a replacement for Jack Benny, who died before the start of filming. Burns, for his first starring role since "Honolulu" in 1939, won an Oscar. 111m/C VHS, Beta, LV. George Burns, Walter Matthau, Richard Benjamin, Lee Meredith, F. Murray Abraham, Carol Arthur, Howard Hesseman; D: Herbert Ross; W: Neil Simon. Academy Awards '75: Best Supporting Actor (Burns); Golden Globe Awards '76: Best Actor—Musical/Comedy (Matthau), Best Film—Musical/Comedy, Best Supporting Actor (Benjamin); Writers Guild of America '75: Best Adapted Screenplay; Nominations: Academy Awards '75: Best Actor (Matthau), Best Adapted Screenplay, Best Art Direction/Set Decoration. MGM, BTV

Sunshine Run 🎬½ Black Rage 1979 (PG) Two escaped slaves and a young widow search for Spanish treasure in the Everglades. 102m/C VHS, Beta. Chris Robinson, Ted Cassidy, David Legge, Phyllis Robinson; D: Chris Robinson. NO

Sunstroke 🎬🎬 1992 (R) Seymour plays a desperate mother searching for her kidnapped child through the Arizona desert. Framed for murder, she cannot contact the police but must track the kidnappers herself, until she meets a drifter with secrets of his own. CW: Violence. 91m/C VHS, Beta, Closed Caption. Jane Seymour, Stephen Meadows, Steve Railsback, Ray Wise, Don Ameche; D: James Keach; W: Duane Poole. PAR

The Super 🎬½ 1991 (R) Pesci stars as a slumlord who faces a prison sentence thanks to his terminal neglect. The option given to him is to live in his own rat hole until he provides reasonable living conditions. This he does, and predictably learns a thing or two about his own greed and the people who suffer as a result of it. Pesci as always gives an animated performance but poor scripting laden with stereotypes and cliches successfully restricts effort. CW: Language. 86m/C VHS. Joe Pesci, Vincent Gardenia, Madolyn Smith, Ruben Blades; D: Rod Daniel; C: Bruce Surtees. FXV, CCB

Super Bitch 🎬½ Mafia Junction 1989 Nasty, cold, and uncaring woman uses men to keep up her expensive habits, then ruthlessly tosses them aside when she is done. She purposely entangles them in her drug trade and thinks nothing of their deaths. Proving once again that you get what you pay for. 90m/C VHS. Stephanie Beacham, Patricia Hayes, Gareth Thomas; D: Massimo Dallamano. ATL

Super Brother 🎬 1990 (R) The feared and respected leader of an oppressed people is imprisoned, much to everyone's regret. 90m/C VHS, Beta. Woody Strode. ELE

Super Force 🎬🎬 1990 When astronaut Zach Stone (Olandt) returns from an assignment on Mars he finds his policeman brother has been murdered. He quits NASA and joins the force to get revenge, battling evil crime boss Tao Satori (Liddy). Stone also moonlights as a vigilante, complete with motorcycle and high-tech armoured suit. It's dumb but there's lots of action. 92m/C VHS, LV. Ken Olandt, G. Gordon Liddy, Larry B. Scott, Lisa Niemi, Marshall Teague; Cameos: Patrick Macnee; D: Richard Compton. USH

Super Fuzz 🎬½ Supersnooper 1981 (PG) Rookie policeman develops super powers after being accidentally exposed to radiation. Somewhat ineptly, he uses his abilities to combat crime. Somewhat ineptly acted, written, and directed as well. 97m/C VHS, Beta. Terence Hill, Joanne Dru, Ernest Borgnine; D: Sergio Corbucci; W: Sergio Corbucci.

Super Mario Bros. 🎬🎬½ 1993 (PG) $42 million adventure fantasy based on the popular Nintendo video game. The brothers are in hot pursuit of the Princess Daisy who's been kidnapped by evil slimebucket Hopper and taken to Dinohattan, a fungi-infested, garbage-strewn, rat-hole version of Manhattan. Hopper will amuse the adults, doing a gleeful reptilian version of Frank Booth from "Blue Velvet." Hoskins and Leguizamo act gamely in broad Nintendo style, enthusiastically partaking in high-tech wizardry and the many gags. Hits bullseye of target audience—elementary and junior high kids—with frenetic pace, gaudy special effects, oversized sets and animatronic monsters. 104m/C VHS, Beta, LV, Letterbox, Closed Caption. Bob Hoskins, John Leguizamo, Samantha Mathis, Fisher Stevens, Richard Edson, Dana Kaminsky, Dennis Hopper, Fiona Shaw, Mojo Nixon, Lance Henriksen; D: Rocky Morton, Annabel Jankel; W: Edward Solomon, Parker Bennett, Terry Runte; M: Alan Silvestri. HPH, BTV, TOU

Super Ninjas 🎬 198? A ninja battles evil hordes of like-trained ninja warriors, and wins over and over again. 104m/C VHS, Beta. Cheng Tien Chi, Lung Tien Hsiang, Chen Pei Hsi. NO

Super Seal 🎬 1977 (G) An injured seal pup disrupts a family's normal existence after the young daughter adopts him. 95m/C VHS, Beta. Foster Brooks, Sterling Holloway, Sarah Brown; D: Michael Dugan. VCI

Super Soul Brother 198? A lazy no-goodnik accidentally ingests a strange potion which turns him into a master thief. 80m/C VHS. Wildman Steve. XVC

Superargo 🎬🎬 Il Re Dei Criminali; Superargo the Giant; The King of Criminals 1967 A wrestler becomes a super-hero with psychic powers and a bulletproof leotard. He fights against a madman who is turning athletes into robots. Successful Italian hero who wouldn't last two minutes in the ring with Batman. 95m/C VHS, Beta. IT SP Guy Madison, Ken Wood, Liz Barrett, Diana Loris; D: Paul Maxwell. SNC, MAD

Superbug Super Agent 🎬½ 1976 Dodo, the wonder car puts the brakes on crime in this silly action-adventure tale. A lemon in a lot full of Herbies. 90m/C VHS, Beta. Robert Mark, Heidi Hansen, George Goodman. JEF

Superchick woof! 1971 (R) Mild-mannered stewardess by day, sexy blonde with karate blackbelt by night. In addition to stopping a skyjacking she regularly makes love to men around the world. A superbomb that never gets off the ground. 94m/C VHS, Beta. Joyce Jillson, Louis Quinn, Thomas Reardon; D: Ed Forsyth.

Supercop 🎬🎬½ Police Story 3: Supercop 1992 (R) Super Hong Kong cop Kevin Chan (Chan) heads to China to assist the authorities in cracking an international drug ring. He's partnered with disciplined-but-beautiful Director Yang (Yeoh), who's also a terrific fighter, and the duo go undercover (as a married couple) to infiltrate the operation, which takes them to a Malaysian resort. Then Chan's girlfriend shows up, blowing their cover. Lots of action-packed fighting and wild chases. The 1996 American release loses about a half-hour of run time from the original. Dubbed from Cantonese. CW: Some violence. 93m/C VHS, LV, Closed Caption. HK Jackie Chan, Michelle Yeoh, Maggie Cheung, Kenneth Tsang, Andrew Kam Yeun Wah; D: Stanley Tong; W: Edward Tang, Fibe Ma, Lee Wai Yee; C: Ardy Lam; M: Joel McNeely. TOU

Superdad 🎬 1973 (G) A middle-aged parent is determined to bridge the generation gap by trying his hand at various teenage activities. Disney family fare that's about as complicated as a television commercial. The adolescents are two-dimensional throwbacks to the fun-loving '50s. 94m/C VHS, Beta. Bob Crane, Kurt Russell, Joe Flynn, Barbara Rush, Kathleen Cody, Dick Van Patten; D: Vincent McEveety; M: Buddy Baker. DIS

Superfly 🎬🎬½ 1972 (R) Controversial upon release, pioneering blaxploitation has Harlem dope dealer finding trouble with gangs and police as he attempts to establish retirement fund from one last deal. Excellent period tunes by Curtis Mayfield. Two lesser sequels. 98m/C VHS, Beta. Ron O'Neal, Carl Lee, Sheila Frazier, Julius W. Harris; D: Gordon Parks Jr.; M: Curtis Mayfield. WAR

Superfly T.N.T. woof! Super Fly T.N.T 1973 (R) This confusing sequel to "Superfly" finds O'Neal returning as Youngblood Priest. The now ex-drug dealer has retired with his girlfriend to Rome where he is approached by an African gun-runner (Browne) for help in a revolution against an oppressive government. Cheap exploitation. 87m/C VHS, Closed Caption. Ron O'Neal, Roscoe Lee Browne, Sheila Frazier, Robert Guillaume, Jacques Sernas, William Berger; D: Ron O'Neal; W: Alex Haley. PAR

Supergirl 🎬½ 1984 (PG) Big-budget bomb in which Slater made her debut and nearly killed her career, with the help of Kryptonite. Unexciting and unsophisticated story of a young woman, cousin to Superman, with super powers, based on the comic book series. She's in pursuit of a magic paperweight, but an evil sorceress wants it too. Dunaway is a terrifically vile villainess with awesome black magic powers. Slater is great to look at, but is much better in almost any other film. 114m/C VHS, Beta, LV, *GB* Faye Dunaway, Helen Slater, Peter O'Toole, Mia Farrow, Brenda Vaccaro, Marc McClure, Simon Ward, Hart Bochner, Maureen Teefy, David Healy, Matt Frewer; *D:* Jeannot Szwarc; *M:* Jerry Goldsmith. *ART*

Supergrass 🐾🐾 1987 (R) A low-brow British farce about a nebbish who poses as a drug smuggler to impress his girlfriend, and is then mistaken for a real one by the authorities. 105m/C VHS, Beta. *GB* Adrian Edmondson, Peter Richardson, Nigel Planer, Jennifer Saunders, Ronald Allen, Dawn French; *D:* Peter Richardson. *NLC*

Superman: The Movie 🐾🐾🐾½ 1978 (PG) The DC Comics legend comes alive in this wonderfully entertaining saga of Superman's life from a baby on the doomed planet Krypton to Earth's own Man of Steel. Hackman and Beatty pair marvelously as super criminal Lex Luthor and his bumbling sidekick. Award-winning special effects and a script that doesn't take itself too seriously make this great fun. Followed by three sequels. 144m/C VHS, Beta, LV, Letterbox. Christopher Reeve, Margot Kidder, Marlon Brando, Gene Hackman, Glenn Ford, Susannah York, Ned Beatty, Valerie Perrine, Jackie Cooper, Marc McClure, Trevor Howard, Sarah Douglas, Terence Stamp, Jack O'Halloran, Phyllis Thaxter; *D:* Richard Donner; *W:* Mario Puzo, Robert Benton, David Newman; *M:* John Williams. Academy Awards '78: Best Visual Effects; Nominations: Academy Awards '78: Best Film Editing, Best Sound, Best Original Score. *WAR*

Superman 2 🐾🐾🐾 1980 (PG) The sequel to "the movie" about the Man of Steel. This time, he has his hands full with three super-powered villains from his home planet of Krypton. The romance between reporter Lois Lane and our superhero is made believable and the storyline has more pace to it than the original. A sequel that often equals the first film—leave it to Superman to pull off the impossible. 127m/C VHS, Beta, LV. Christopher Reeve, Margot Kidder, Gene Hackman, Ned Beatty, Jackie Cooper, Sarah Douglas, Jack O'Halloran, Susannah York, Marc McClure, Terence Stamp, Valerie Perrine, E.G. Marshall; *D:* Richard Lester; *W:* Mario Puzo, David Newman; *M:* John Williams. *WAR*

Superman 3 🐾🐾 1983 (PG) Villainous businessman Vaughn tries to conquer Superman via the expertise of bumbling computer expert Pryor and the judicious use of an artificial form of Kryptonite. Superman explores his darker side after undergoing transformation into sleaze ball. Promising satiric start ultimately defeated by uneven story and direction and boring physical comedy. Notable is the absence of Lois Lane as a main character. Followed by "Superman 4." 123m/C VHS, Beta, LV. Christopher Reeve, Richard Pryor, Annette O'Toole, Jackie Cooper, Margot Kidder, Marc McClure, Annie Ross, Robert Vaughn; *D:* Richard Lester; *W:* David Newman; *M:* John Williams. *WAR*

Superman 4: The Quest for Peace 🐾🐾 1987 (PG) The third sequel, in which the Man of Steel endeavors to rid the world of nuclear weapons, thereby pitting himself against nuclear-entrepreneur Lex Luthor and his superpowered creation, Nuclear Man. Special effects are dime-store quality and it appears that someone may have walked off with parts of the plot. Reeve deserves credit for remaining true to character through four films. 90m/C VHS, Beta, LV, Closed Caption. Christopher Reeve, Gene Hackman, Jon Cryer, Marc McClure, Margot Kidder, Mariel Hemingway, Sam Wanamaker; *D:* Sidney J. Furie; *W:* Mark Rosenthal; *M:* John Williams; *V:* Susannah York. *WAR*

Superman & the Mole Men 🐾🐾½ *Superman and the Strange People* 1951 The cast of the popular 1950s' television show made this rarely seen feature as a "pilot" for the series. Superman faces the danger threatened by the invasion of radioactive mole-men who make their way to the surface world from the bowels of the earth through an oil-well shaft. Simple fun. 58m/C VHS, Beta. George Reeves, Phyllis Coates, Jeff Corey; *D:* Lee Sholem. *WAR*

Superman: The Serial, Vol. 1 1948 Superman was first seen in live action in this 15 part theatrical serial that has been rarely shown since its original release. 248m/B VHS, Beta. Kirk Alyn, Noel Neill, Pierre Watkin, Tommy "Butch" Bond, Thomas Carr; *D:* Spencer Gordon Bennet. *WAR*

Supernatural 🐾🐾½ 1933 Roma (Lombard) falls prey to a phony medium (Dinehart) who promises to call up the spirit of her recently murdered twin brother. At the same moment of the seance a murderess dies in the electric chair and her body is used in Dr. Houston's (Warner) life-after-death experiment. Too bad Roma becomes possessed by the woman's evil spirit. Now the doctor and Roma's fiance (Scott) must undo the curse. A hokey B-grade movie disliked by Lombard. 78m/B VHS, Closed Caption. Carole Lombard, Randolph Scott, H.B. Warner, Alan Dinehart, Vivienne Osborne, Beryl Mercer, William Farnum, Willard Robertson; *D:* Victor Halperin; *W:* Harvey Thew, Brian Marlow; *C:* Arthur Martinelli. *USH*

The Supernaturals 🐾½ 1986 (R) Confederate Civil War-era ghosts, bent on avenging their deaths, haunt a wooded area in which modern Yankee army maneuvers are practiced. Antebellum boredom. 85m/C VHS, Beta, Closed Caption. Maxwell Caulfield, LeVar Burton, Nichelle Nichols; *D:* Armand Mastroianni; *C:* Peter Collister. *NLC*

Supersonic Man woof! 1978 (PG) Incoherent shoestring-budget Superman spoof with a masked hero fighting to save the world from the evil intentions of a mad scientist. 85m/C VHS, Beta. *SP* Michael Coby, Cameron Mitchell, Diana Polakov; *D:* J. Piquer Simon. *VCI*

Superstar: The Life and Times of Andy Warhol 🐾🐾🐾 1990 Even if you didn't grok Andy's 'pop' artwork and self-created celebrity persona, this ironic, kinetic, oft-rollicking documentary paints a vivid picture of the wild era he inspired and exploited. Interviewees range from Warhol cohorts like Dennis Hopper to proud executives at the Campbell Soup plant. One highlight: a Warhol guest shot on "The Love Boat." 87m/C VHS. Tom Wolfe, Sylvia Miles, David Hockney, Taylor Mead, Dennis Hopper; *D:* Chuck Workman. *VES*

Superstition 🐾½ *The Witch* 1982 A reverend and his family move into a vacant house despite warnings about a curse from the townsfolk. Some people never learn. 85m/C VHS, Beta. James Houghton, Albert Salmi, Lynn Carlin; *D:* James Robertson. *ART*

Supervixens 🐾🐾 1975 True to Meyer's low-rent exploitation film canon, this wild tale is filled with characteristic Amazons, sex and violence. A gas station attendant is framed for the grisly murder of his girlfriend and hustles out of town, meeting a succession of well-endowed women during his travels. As if it needed further problems, it's hampered by a tasteless storyline and incoherent writing. 105m/C VHS. Shari Eubank, Charles Napier; *D:* Russ Meyer; *W:* Russ Meyer. *RMF*

Support Your Local Gunfighter 🐾🐾🐾 1971 (G) Garner plays a western con man with his tongue firmly in his cheek. He comes to the small town of Purgatory and is thought to be a notorious gunfighter. He decides to go with the mistaken identity and use it to his profitable advantage. Elam is his bumbling sidekick and Pleshette the love interest. A delightful, deliberately cliche-filled western. A follow-up, not a sequel, to "Support Your Local Sheriff" (1969). 92m/C VHS, Closed Caption. James Garner, Jack Elam, Suzanne Pleshette, Harry (Henry) Morgan, Dub Taylor, John Dehner, Joan Blondell, Ellen Corby, Henry Jones; *D:* Burt Kennedy. *MGM*

Support Your Local Sheriff 🐾🐾🐾½ 1969 (G) Amiable, irreverent western spoof with more than its fair share of laughs. When a stranger stumbles into a gold rush town, he winds up becoming sheriff. Garner is perfect as the deadpan sheriff, particularly in the scene where he convinces Dern to remain in jail, in spite of the lack of bars. Neatly subverts every western cliche it encounters, yet keeps respect for formula western. Followed by "Support Your Local Gunfighter." 92m/C VHS, Beta, LV, Closed Caption. James Garner, Joan Hackett, Walter Brennan, Bruce Dern, Jack Elam, Harry (Henry) Morgan; *D:* Burt Kennedy; *W:* William Bowers; *C:* Harry Stradling Jr. *FOX, MGM*

Suppose They Gave a War and Nobody Came? 🐾🐾½ *War Games* 1970 (G) A small Southern town battles with a local army base in this entertaining but wandering satire. The different acting styles used as the producers wavered on making this a comedy or drama were more at war with one another than the characters involved. 113m/C VHS, LV. Tony Curtis, Brian Keith, Ernest Borgnine, Suzanne Pleshette, Ivan Dixon, Bradford Dillman, Don Ameche; *D:* Hy Averback; *W:* Don McGuire. *FOX*

Surabaya Conspiracy 🐾½ 1975 Mystery and intrigue surround a quest for gold in Africa. 90m/C VHS, Beta. Michael Rennie, Richard Jaeckel, Barbara Bouchet, Mike Preston; *D:* Roy Davis. *NO*

Sure Fire 🐾🐾 1990 Wes (Blair) is a mercurial entrepreneur who thinks he has found the financial ticket to paradise with his vacation home scheme. Much to the chagrin of his wife Ellen (Dezina), he refuses to let anything stand in the way of his sure-fire scheme, even his family. Wes develops a little self-control as he realizes he's beginning to flake out, but it may be too late. Director Jost has put together a surprisingly unpretentious film with a virtually no-name cast, its plot speaking volumes on the American condition while unfolding in the bleak Utah desert. 86m/C VHS. Tom Blair, Kristi Hager, Robert Ernst, Kate Dezina, Phillip R. Brown; *D:* Jon Jost; *W:* Jon Jost. *WAC*

The Sure Thing 🐾🐾🐾 1985 (PG-13) College students who don't like each other end up travelling to California together, and of course, falling in love. Charming performances make up for predictability. Can't-miss director (and ex-Meathead) Reiner's second direct hit at the box-office. 94m/C VHS, Beta, LV, 8mm, Closed Caption. John Cusack, Daphne Zuniga, Anthony Edwards, Boyd Gaines, Lisa Jane Persky, Viveca Lindfors, Nicolette Sheridan, Tim Robbins; *D:* Rob Reiner; *W:* Jonathan Roberts, Steven L. Bloom; *C:* Robert Elswit. *COL*

Surf Nazis Must Die 🐾 1987 A piece of deliberate camp in the Troma mold, about a group of psychotic neo-Nazi surfers taking over the beaches of California in the wake of a devastating earthquake. Tongue-in-cheek, tasteless and cheap, but intentionally so. 83m/C VHS, Beta, Closed Caption, DVD. Barry Brenner, Gail Neely, Michael Sonye, Dawn Wildsmith, Tom Shell, Bobbie Bresee; *D:* Peter George; *W:* John Ayre. *VTR*

Surf Ninjas 🐾🐾½ *Surf Warriors* 1993 (PG) Action comedy for the kiddies finds two young surfer dudes who are actually the long-lost crown princes of the obscure nation of Patu San. The country's incompetent (what a surprise, it's Nielsen) warlord wants the boys to stay lost. Lame jokes and tame martial arts sequences. 87m/C VHS, LV, Closed Caption. Ernie Reyes Jr., Nick Cowen, Leslie Nielsen, Tone Loc, Rob Schneider, John Karlen, Ernie Reyes Sr.; *D:* Neal Israel; *W:* Dan Gordon; *C:* Arthur Albert; *M:* David Kitay. *COL, NLC, IME*

Surf Party 🐾½ 1964 Romance among the sands of Malibu with Vinton as the owner of a surf shop. Risque in 1964; utterly campy today. 🎵 If I Were an Artist; That's What Love Is; Pearly Shells. 68m/C VHS. Bobby Vinton, Jackie De Shannon, Patricia Morrow, Kenny Miller; *D:* Maury Dexter. *MOV*

Surf 2 woof! *Surf 2: The End of the Trilogy* 1984 (R) A most excellent group of surfers get sick from drinking tainted Buzz Cola concocted by demented chemist Deezen in most heinous effort to obliterate surfer population from Southern California. Bogus, dude. No, you didn't miss "Surf 1" (there's not one), the title is the sort of in-joke this exercise in mental meltdown perpetuates as comedy. Ha. 91m/C VHS, Beta. Morgan Paull, Cleavon Little, Lyle Waggoner, Ruth Buzzi, Linda Kerridge, Carol Wayne, Eddie

Deezen, Eric Stoltz, Brandis Kemp, Terry Kiser; **D:** Randall Badat; **W:** Randall Badat; **M:** Peter Bernstein. *MVD*

Surfacing woof! **1984** A girl braves the hostile northern wilderness to search for her missing father. This pseudo-psychological, sex-driven suspense flick makes little sense. **90m/C VHS, Beta.** Joseph Bottoms, Kathleen Beller, R.H. Thomson, Margaret Dragu; **D:** Claude Jutra. *NO*

The Surgeon *Exquisite Tenderness* **1994 (R)** Routine hospital horror finds Dr. Theresa McCann (Glasser) caught up in murder when patients and doctors become poison victims. Aided by toxicologist Benjamin Hendricks (Remar), McCann finds a lollipop left behind and realizes the killer is ex-boyfriend/doctor Julian Matar (Haberle), whose unlawful experiments in tissue regeneration got him suspended. Now he's hiding out in the hospital and killing to get the pituitary glands necessary for his miracle serum. Film's original title "Exquisite Tenderness" is a term for the point when pain becomes so extreme it turns to pleasure—the film merely turns grisly. **CW:** Strong violence and gore, and for sexuality and language. **100m/C VHS.** *GE* Isabel Glasser, James Remar, Sean Haberle, Charles Dance, Peter Boyle, Malcolm McDowell, Charles Bailey-Gates, Gregory West, Mother Love; **D:** Carl Schenkel; **W:** Patrick Cirillo; **C:** Thomas Burstyn; **M:** Christopher Franke. *APX*

Surprise Attack **197?** The Spanish Civil War forms the backdrop for this action opus. **124m/C VHS, Beta.** Simon Andrew, Danny Martin, Patty Shepard; **D:** Joseph Loman. *NO*

Surrender **1987 (PG)** A struggling woman artist and a divorced author fall in love but won't admit it for fear of being hurt again. Jumbled plot, unfortunate casting. Available in a Spanish-subtitled version. **95m/C VHS, Beta, LV, Closed Caption.** Michael Caine, Sally Field, Steve Guttenberg, Peter Boyle, Jackie Cooper, Julie Kavner, Louise Lasser, Iman; **D:** Jerry Belson; **W:** Jerry Belson; **C:** Juan Ruiz-Anchia; **M:** Michel Colombier. *WAR, GVV*

Surrogate **1988** A young couple fights to keep their marriage afloat by turning to a sex surrogate. Strong cast helps carry odd, confusing script, with plenty of (you guessed it) sex, and a mystery to solve. **100m/C VHS, Beta.** *CA* Art Hindle, Shannon Tweed, Carole Laure, Michael Ironside, Marilyn Lightstone; **D:** Don Carmody.

Survival Game **1987** A young combat expert (Chuck Norris's son) gets involved with some ex-hippies in search of a $2 million cache. High-kickin' action. **91m/C VHS, Beta.** Mike Norris, Deborah Goodrich, Seymour Cassel; **D:** Herb Freed.

Survival of a Dragon **197?** A medieval Chinese warrior is transported into the future, where he goes on a kicking rampage. **88m/C VHS, Beta.** Squall Hung, Jaguar Lee. *NO*

Survival of Spaceship Earth **1990** Man, his world and the protection of its ecology are discussed in this beautiful and fascinating film. Winner of numerous international awards due to the strength of its production values and writing. Nominated for ten Emmy awards; winner of two. **63m/C VHS.** Rue McClanahan; **D:** Dirk Summers; **W:** Dirk Summers. *CPM, FCT, CRY*

Survival Quest **1989 (R)** Students in a Rocky Mountain survival course cross paths with a band of bloodthirsty mercenaries-in-training. A battle to the death ensues; you'll wish they'd all put each other out of their misery a lot sooner. **90m/C VHS, Beta, Closed Caption.** Lance Henriksen, Dermot Mulroney, Mark Rolston, Steve Antin, Paul Provenza, Ben Hammer, Traci Lind, Catherine Keener, Reggie Bannister; **D:** Don A. Coscarelli; **W:** Don A. Coscarelli. *FOX*

Survival Run **1980 (R)** Six California teenagers become stranded in the Mexican desert, where they witness Graves and Milland making a shady deal. The chase is on, the story is lame, the gory parts aren't gory—so why bother? **90m/C VHS, Beta.** Peter Graves, Ray Milland, Vincent Van Patten; **D:** Larry Spiegel; **W:** Gerard M. Cahill.

Survival Zone woof! **1984 (R)** Nuclear holocaust survivors battle a violent band of marauding motorcyclists on the barren ranches of the 21st century. Advice to director Rubens and cohorts: Next time, find a plot that's not growing mold. **90m/C VHS, Beta.** Gary Lockwood, Morgan Stevens, Camilla Sparv; **D:** Percival Rubens.

The Survivalist **1987 (R)** An arms-ready survivalist nut defends his family and supplies against a panicked society awaiting nuclear war. Poorly acted, little tension, and ineffective plotting make boredom seem a more critical issue than survival. **96m/C VHS, Beta, LV.** Steve Railsback, Susan Blakely, Marjoe Gortner, David Wayne, Cliff DeYoung; **D:** Sig Shore; **W:** Robert Dillon. *VES*

Surviving Desire **1991** Donovan plays Jude, a neurotic, romantic English professor who falls madly in love with an independently minded student, Sophie. Unfortunately, Sophie is more interested in how the seduction will advance her writing than how it will affect her life. The lovers explore their brief affair by analyzing every emotion and motive in a series of quirky conversations. Intelligent, amusing, and stylized film from director Hartley. The tape also includes two Hartley shorts: "Theory of Achievement" and "Ambition." **86m/C VHS.** Martin Donovan, Mary B. Ward, Matt Malloy, Rebecca Nelson; **D:** Hal Hartley; **C:** Michael Spiller. *FXL*

Surviving Picasso **1996 (R)** Merchant-Ivory team takes time off from bodice-rippers to tear into the personal life of the Cubist legend, Pablo Picasso. Takes an unglamourous look at the mythically famous artist, focusing on the rocky ten-year affair with Francoise Gilot (newcomer McElhone), who met the artist in Nazi-occupied Paris when she was 22 and he was 62. Hopkins is well-cast as the insufferable senior and adds a strong dose of charm to soften his portrayal. Scores high tech credits, especially picture's sumptuous look, compliments of production designer and frequent collaborator Luciana Arrighi. Unfortunately adapted from the decidedly one-sided biography "Picasso: Creator and Destroyer" by controversial author Arianna Huffington. Denied use of the artist's works by his estate, the filmmakers settled for some "work in progress" replicas. **CW:** Scene of nudity and brief sex-related language. **126m/C VHS, LV, Closed Caption.** Anthony Hopkins, Natascha McElhone, Julianne Moore, Joss Ackland, Joan Plowright, Diane Venora, Peter Eyre, Jane Lapotaire, Joseph Maher, Bob Peck; **D:** James Ivory; **W:** Ruth Prawer Jhabvala; **C:** Tony Pierce-Roberts; **M:** Richard Robbins. *WAR*

Surviving the Game **1994 (R)** Poorly made hunt-the-human story. Homeless Ice-T is hired by a group of men to assist them on their annual hunt. But wait, he's the prey. Unbelievable premise pits the streetwise, down and out Ice-T against the savvy and resource rich group—and he beats them at their own game. Few high-impact action sequences. The violence, although there isn't as much as might be expected, is graphic. **94m/C VHS, LV, Closed Caption.** Rutger Hauer, Ice-T, F. Murray Abraham, Gary Busey, Charles S. Dutton, John C. McGinley, William McNamara, Jeff Corey; **D:** Ernest R. Dickerson; **W:** Eric Bernt; **C:** Bojan Bazelli; **M:** Stewart Copeland. *NLC*

Survivor **1980** A jetliner crashes, leaving but one survivor, the pilot, who is then plagued by visions, tragedies, and ghosts of dead passengers. Viewers also suffer. **91m/C VHS, Beta.** *AU* Robert Powell, Jenny Agutter, Joseph Cotten, Angela Punch McGregor; **D:** David Hemmings; **W:** David Ambrose; **M:** Brian May. *ORI, WAR*

Survivor **1987** A lone warrior on a post-nuclear holocaust wasteland battles a megalomaniac ruler. Moll as the evil villian is watchable, but overall the film is a wasteland, too. **92m/C VHS, Beta, LV.** Chip Mayer, Richard Moll, Sue Kiel; **D:** Michael Shackleton. *ART, VES*

Survivors **1983 (R)** Two unemployed men find themselves the target of a hit man, whom they have identified in a robbery attempt. One of the men goes gun-crazy protecting himself. Uneven comedy with Williams and laid-back Matthau. **102m/C VHS, Beta, LV, Closed Caption.** Robin Williams, Walter Matthau, Jerry Reed, John Goodman; **D:** Michael Ritchie; **W:** Michael Leeson; **C:** Billy Williams. *COL*

Susan and God *The Gay Mrs. Trexel* **1940** A selfish socialite returns from Europe and starts practicing a new religion, much to the dismay of her friends and family. Despite her preaching, her own domestic life is falling apart and she realizes that her preoccupation and selfish ways have caused a strain on her marriage and her relationship with her daughter. An excellent script and a fine performance from Crawford make this a highly satisfying film. **115m/B VHS, Closed Caption.** Joan Crawford, Fredric March, Ruth Hussey, John Carroll, Rita Hayworth, Nigel Bruce, Bruce Cabot, Rose Hobart, Rita Quigley, Marjorie Main, Gloria De Haven; **D:** George Cukor; **W:** Anita Loos. *MGM*

Susan Lenox: Her Fall and Rise *The Rise of Helga; Rising to Fame* **1931** Garbo, the daughter of an abusive farmer, falls into the arms of the handsome Gable to escape an arranged marriage. Both stars are miscast, but the well-paced direction keeps the melodrama moving. **84m/B VHS, Beta.** Greta Garbo, Clark Gable, Jean Hersholt, John Miljan, Alan Hale, Hale Hamilton; **D:** Robert Z. Leonard; **C:** William H. Daniels. *MGM, FCT*

Susan Slept Here **1954** While researching a movie on juvenile delinquents, a Hollywood script writer (Powell) is given custody of a spunky 18-year-old delinquent girl (Reynolds) during the Christmas holidays. Cute sex comedy. Based on the play "Susan," by Alex Gottlieb and Steve Fisher. **98m/C VHS, Beta, LV.** Dick Powell, Debbie Reynolds, Anne Francis; **D:** Frank Tashlin. Nominations: Academy Awards '54: Best Song ("Hold My Hand"), Best Sound. *NO*

Susana **1951** Minor though still interesting Bunuel, in which a sexy delinquent young girl is rescued from vagrancy by a Spanish family, and how she subsequently undermines the family's structure through sexual allurement and intimidation. In Spanish with English subtitles. **87m/B VHS, Beta.** *MX* Rosita Quintana, Fernando Soler, Victor Manuel Mendoza, Matilde Palou; **D:** Luis Bunuel. *XVC*

Susanna Pass **1949** Oil deposits underneath a fish hatchery lake attract bad guys. They set off explosions to destroy the fishery, but game warden Rogers investigates. Minor outing for Roy. **67m/C VHS.** Roy Rogers, Dale Evans, Estelita Rodriguez, Martin Garralaga, Robert Emmett Keane, Lucien Littlefield, Douglas Fowley; **D:** William Witney. *REP*

Susannah of the Mounties **1939 (PG)** An adorable young girl is left orphaned after a wagon train massacre and is adopted by a Mountie. An Indian squabble gives Shirley a chance to play little peacemaker and teach Scott how to tap dance, too. Could she be any cuter? Available colorized. **78m/B VHS, Beta, Closed Caption.** Shirley Temple, Randolph Scott, Margaret Lockwood, J. Farrell MacDonald, Moroni Olsen, Victor Jory; **D:** William A. Seiter; **C:** Arthur C. Miller. *NO*

Suspect **1987 (R)** An overworked Washington, DC, public defender (Cher) is assigned to a controversial murder case in which her client is a deaf-mute, skid-row bum. A cynical lobbyist on the jury illegally researches the case himself. They work together to uncover a far-reaching conspiracy. Unrealistic plot, helped along by good performances and tight direction. **101m/C VHS, Beta, LV, 8mm.** Dennis Quaid, Cher, Liam Neeson, E. Katherine Kerr, Joe Mantegna, John Mahoney, Philip Bosco; **D:** Peter Yates; **W:** Eric Roth; **C:** Billy Williams; **M:** Michael Kamen. *COL*

Suspect Device 🎬½ *Roger Corman Presents: Suspect Device* 1995 (R) Nonsensical cable thriller finds government computer researcher Dan (Howell) mistakenly accessing a secret file and becoming an immediate assassination target. Then Dan discovers he isn't even human—he's really a genetically engineered cross between a robot and a nuclear bomb! Part "Terminator," part "Three Days of the Condor," and all silliness. **CW:** Strong violence, a sex scene and language. 90m/C VHS, **Closed Caption.** C. Thomas Howell, Stacy Travis, Jed Allan, John Beck, Marcus Aurelius, Jonathan Fuller; **D:** Rick Jacobson; **W:** Alex Simon; **C:** John Aronson; **M:** Christopher Lennertz. *NHO*

Suspended Alibi 🎬½ *Suspected Alibi* 1956 British crime-drama about an adulterous man unjustly accused when his alibi is murdered. Overlook the convenient coincidence. 64m/B VHS. *GB* Patrick Holt, Honor Blackman, Andrew Keir, Valentine Dyall; **D:** Alfred Shaughnessy. *NOS, SNC*

Suspicion 🎬🎬🎬½ 1941 Alfred Hitchcock's suspense thriller about a woman who gradually realizes she is married to a killer and may be next on his list. An excellent production unravels at the end due to RKO's insistence that Grant retain his "attractive" image. This forced the writers to leave his guilt or innocence undetermined. Available colorized. 99m/B VHS, Beta, LV. Cary Grant, Joan Fontaine, Cedric Hardwicke, Nigel Bruce, May Whitty, Leo G. Carroll, Heather Angel; **D:** Alfred Hitchcock; **C:** Harry Stradling. Academy Awards '41: Best Actress (Fontaine); New York Film Critics Awards '41: Best Actress (Fontaine); Nominations: Academy Awards '41: Best Picture, Best Original Dramatic/Comedy Score. *MLB, BTV, TTC*

Suspicion 🎬🎬 1987 Remake of the chilling Hitchcock tale. Newlywed bride is consumed with fears about her wealthy new husband. The suspense builds as she comes to suspect that she is married to a cold-blooded killer. Curtin in way over her head. 97m/C VHS, Beta. Jane Curtin, Anthony Andrews, Jeremy Northam, Ron Pember, Betsy Blair, Michael Hordern, Vivian Pickles, Jo Anderson; **D:** Andrew Grieve.

Suspicious Agenda 🎬🎬½ 1994 (R) Cop with a past is assigned to a task force that's hunting down a sadistic vigilante. 97m/C VHS. Richard Grieco, Nick Mancuso, Jim Byrnes; **D:** Clay Borris; **W:** Kevin Rock. *AVE*

Suspiria 🎬🎬🎬 1977 (R) An American dancer enters a weird European ballet academy and finds they teach more than movement as bodies begin piling up. Sometimes weak plot is aided by great-but-gory special effects, fine photography, good music, and a chilling opening sequence. Also available in unrated version. 92m/C VHS, Beta, LV, Letterbox, **Closed Caption.** IT Jessica Harper, Joan Bennett, Alida Valli, Udo Kier, Stefania Casini, Flavio Bucci, Barbara Magnolfi, Rudolf Schuendler; **D:** Dario Argento; **W:** Dario Argento, Daria Nicolodi; **C:** Luciano Tovoli. *FXL*

Suture 🎬🎬 1993 Quirky thriller is a homage to late '50s melodramas with its strange tale of mistaken identity. Vincent wants to hide his unsavory past by assuming the identity of his estranged half-brother, Clay, which should be difficult since Vincent is white and Clay is black but the movie's premise is that everyone confuses the two. Vincent tries to kill Clay in an explosion but he survives—with amnesia and with everyone in the hospital assuming he's Vincent. Shifting points of view as he struggles to piece together his memory offer disorientation not just for Clay but the viewer as well. Feature film debut for the directors. 96m/B VHS. Dennis Haysbert, Sab Shimono, Mel Harris, Michael Harris, Dina Merrill, David Graf, Fran Ryan; **D:** Scott McGehee, David Siegel; **W:** Scott McGehee, David Siegel; **C:** Greg Gardiner; **M:** Cary Berger. Sundance Film Festival '94: Best Cinematography; Nominations: Independent Spirit Awards '95: Best Cinematography, Best First Feature. *HMK*

Suzanne 🎬½ 1980 (R) Set in 1950s Quebec, the story of a good woman whose criminal boyfriend leaves her pregnant when he is sent to prison. Ten years later, he returns, threatening her

happy marriage. Confused script can't be saved by valiant cast. 90m/C VHS, Beta. Sondra Locke, Richard Dreyfuss, Gene Barry. *VES*

Suzy 🎬🎬½ 1936 Harlow's fourth film and her only one with Grant is a mixture of romance, action, and comedy set during WWI. Grant plays a French flier who falls in love with Harlow, although she is married to Tone. Excellent air footage and some good funny scenes keep this film moving right along. Even has Grant singing hit song, "Did I Remember?" 99m/B VHS, **Closed Caption.** Jean Harlow, Franchot Tone, Cary Grant, Benita Hume, Lewis Stone, Inez Courtney; **D:** George Fitzmaurice. Nominations: Academy Awards '36: Best Song ("Did I Remember"). *MGM*

Svengali 🎬🎬🎬 1931 A music teacher uses his hypnotic abilities to manipulate one of his singing students and make her a star. Soon the young woman is singing for sell-out crowds, but only if her teacher is present. Barrymore in a hypnotic performance. Adapted from "Trilby" by George Du Maurier. Remade in 1955 and 1983. 76m/B VHS, Beta. John Barrymore, Marian Marsh, Donald Crisp; **D:** Archie Mayo. Nominations: Academy Awards '31: Best Cinematography, Best Interior Decoration. *NOS, GPV, SNC*

Svengali 🎬🎬½ 1955 Limp remake of the 1931 film about Trilby, an artist's model, falling under the mesmerizing spell of the title character, who is determined to make her into a famous singer. Chiefly notable for its visuals which were based on the illustrations from the original novel "Trilby" by George du Maurier. 82m/C VHS. GB Hildegarde Neff, Donald Wolfit, Terence Morgan, Derek Bond, Paul Rogers, David Kossoff; **D:** Noel Langley; **W:** Noel Langley. *NO*

Svengali 🎬🎬½ 1983 Flamboyant but faded music star O'Toole mentors Foster, a young pop singer looking for stardom. Boring, made for television remake of the Barrymore classic. 96m/C VHS. Peter O'Toole, Jodie Foster, Elizabeth Ashley, Larry Joshua, Pamela Blair, Barbara Byrne, Holly Hunter; **D:** Anthony Harvey; **M:** John Barry. *NO*

Swallows and Amazons 🎬🎬½ 1996 The six children comprising the Walker and Blackett families spend the summer together in the English lake district during the 1920s having numerous adventures. Based on the books by Arthur Ransome. 89m/C VHS, **Closed Caption.** *REP*

Swamp Fire 🎬½ 1946 Mississippi riverboat captain Weissmuller, wrestles alligators and battles with Crabbe for the woman he loves in this turgid drama. Look for Janssen in an early screen performance. 69m/B VHS, Beta. Johnny Weissmuller, Virginia Grey, Buster Crabbe, Carol Thurston, Edwin Maxwell, Pedro de Cordoba, Pierre Watkin, David Janssen; **D:** William H. Pine. *NOS, SNC*

Swamp of the Lost Monster 🎬 1965 An incredible Mexican horror/western/musical that features a mouse-like monster that'll scare the cheese out of you. 88m/B VHS, Beta. MX Gaston Santos, Sarah Cabrera, Manuel Donde; **D:** Rafael Baledon. *NOS, SNC*

Swamp Thing 🎬🎬½ 1982 (PG) Overlooked camp drama about scientist accidentally turned into tragic half-vegetable, half-man swamp creature, with government agent Barbeau caught in the middle, occasionally while topless. A vegetarian nightmare or ecology propaganda? You be the judge. Adapted from the comic book by Craven. 91m/C VHS, Beta, LV. Adrienne Barbeau, Louis Jourdan, Ray Wise, Dick Durock; **D:** Wes Craven; **W:** Wes Craven. *COL*

Swamp Women 🎬 *Swamp Diamonds; Cruel Swamp* 1955 Four escaped women convicts, known as the "Nardo Gang," chase after a stash of diamonds in this super cheap, super bad action adventure from cult director Corman. 73m/C VHS. Mike Connors, Marie Windsor, Beverly Garland, Carole Mathews, Susan Cummings; **D:** Roger Corman. *SNC*

The Swan 🎬🎬½ 1925 Princess' arranged marriage with a prince is complicated by a poor man also in love with her. Classic romantic comedy of the silent era. Remade in 1956. Based on a play by Ferenc Molnar. 50m/B VHS, Beta. Adolphe Menjou, Ricardo Cortez, Frances Howard; **D:** Dimitri Buchowetzki. *NOS, DVT*

The Swan 🎬🎬🎬 1956 A twist on the Cinderella story with Kelly (in her last film before her marriage) as the charming beauty waiting for her prince. Both Guinness, as the crown prince, and Jourdan, as her poor tutor, want her hand (and the rest of her). Attractive cast, but story gets slow from time to time. Remake of a 1925 silent film. The laserdisc version also includes "Wedding in Monaco," the news short showing Kelly's wedding to Prince Rainier. 112m/C VHS, LV. Grace Kelly, Louis Jourdan, Alec Guinness, Jessie Royce Landis, Brian Aherne, Estelle Winwood; **D:** Charles Vidor; **C:** Joseph Ruttenberg, Robert L. Surtees. *MGM*

The Swan Princess 🎬🎬½ 1994 (G) Formulaic prince-and-princess love story based loosely on "Swan Lake" takes a modern twist: Princess Odette, offended by the emphasis her intended, Prince Derek, places on her beauty, flees the kingdom. She's kidnapped by the evil Rothbart, an enchanter who turns her into a swan able to take human form only when touched by moonlight. A snappy trio of animal characters eventually helps Odette reunite with her newly P.C. love, with lots of zesty musical numbers and various Disney-inspired plot points along the way. Adults may yawn, but kiddies will be charmed just the same. 90m/C VHS, **Closed Caption. D:** Richard Rich; **W:** Richard Rich, Brian Nissen; **M:** Lex de Azevedo; **V:** Jack Palance, Michelle Nicastro, Howard McGillin, Liz Callaway, John Cleese, Steven Wright, Steve Vinovich, Dakin Matthews, Sandy Duncan, Mark Harelik, James Arrington, Davis Gaines, Joel McKinnon Miller. Nominations: Golden Globe Awards '95: Best Song ("Far Longer than Forever"). *TTC*

The Swan Princess 2: Escape from Castle Mountain 🎬🎬½ 1997 (G) Heroine Odette changes back into a swan to help husband Derek defeat evil magician Clavius. Some humor, some action, some nice tunes, and decent animation should keep the kids happy. ♬That's What You Do for a Friend; The Magic of Love; You Gotta Love It. 75m/C VHS. **D:** Richard Rich; **W:** Brian Nissen; **M:** Lex de Azevedo; **V:** Michelle Nicastro, Douglas Sills, Jake Williamson, Christy Landers. *WAR*

Swann 🎬½ 1996 Too many loose ends and weak direction from Benson Gyles (in her feature film debut) waste the efforts of a talented cast. Chicago-based writer Sarah Maloney (Richardson) is doing a biography of Mary Swann, wife/murder victim of a backwater Ontario farmer, who secretly wrote poetry (and gets compared to Emily Dickinson). Sarah heads to Nadeau to meet with Mary's friend Rose (Fricker) and discovers she may have altered some of the published poetry but there's not much there to really care about. Based on a novel by Carol Shields. 98m/C VHS. GB CA Miranda Richardson, Brenda Fricker, Michael Ontkean, Sean McCann, John Neville, Sean Hewitt, Kyra Harper, David Cubitt, Geny Walter; **D:** Anna Benson Gyles; **W:** David Young; **C:** Gerald Packer; **M:** Richard Rodney Bennett. Nominations: Genie Awards '96: Best Actress (Fricker), Best Art Direction/Set Decoration, Best Costume Design, Best Supporting Actor (McCann), Best Score. *NYR*

Swann in Love 🎬🎬½ *Un Amour De Swann* 1984 (R) A handsome, wealthy French aristocrat makes a fool of himself over a beautiful courtesan who cares nothing for him. Elegant production lacks spark. Based upon a section of Marcel Proust's "Remembrance of Things Past." In French with English subtitles or an English language version. 110m/C VHS, Beta. FR GE Jeremy Irons, Ornella Muti, Alain Delon, Fanny Ardant, Marie-Christine Barrault; **D:** Volker Schlondorff; **W:** Peter Brook, Jean-Claude Carriere; **C:** Sven Nykvist. Cesar Awards '85: Best Art Direction/Set Decoration, Best Costume Design. *XVC*

The Swap 🎬½ 1971 (R) Ex-con searches for his brother's killer. Muddled story uses clips from early De Niro film "Sam's Song." 120m/C VHS. Robert De Niro, Jered Mickey, Jennifer Warren, Terrayne Crawford, Martin Kelley; **D:** Jordan Leondopoulos. MGM

Swap Meet 🎬 1979 (R) Wacky teen sex comedy about shenanigans at a small town swap meet. Strictly bargain basement. 86m/C VHS. Ruth Cox, Deborah Richter, Danny Goldman, Cheryl Rixon, Jonathan Gries; **D:** Brice Mack. NO

The Swarm 🎬 1978 (PG) Low-brow insect contest as scientist Caine fends off a swarm of killer bees when they attack metro Houston. The bees are really just black spots painted on the film. And the movie is terrible. "B" movie on bees, but it's still better than "The Bees." 116m/C VHS, **Beta.** Michael Caine, Katharine Ross, Richard Widmark, Lee Grant, Richard Chamberlain, Olivia de Havilland, Henry Fonda, Fred MacMurray, Patty Duke, Ben Johnson, Jose Ferrer, Slim Pickens, Bradford Dillman, Cameron Mitchell; **D:** Irwin Allen; **W:** Stirling Silliphant; **C:** Fred W. Koenekamp; **M:** Jerry Goldsmith, John Williams. Nominations: Academy Awards '78: Best Costume Design. WAR

Swashbuckler 🎬 Scarlet Buccaneer 1976 (PG) Jaunty pirate returns from sea to find his friends held captive by dastardly dictator for their political views. He rescues them, and helps them overthrow the erstwhile despot. 101m/C VHS, LV, **Letterbox.** Robert Shaw, James Earl Jones, Peter Boyle, Genevieve Bujold, Beau Bridges, Geoffrey Holder; **D:** James Goldstone; **W:** Jeffrey Bloom; **M:** John Addison. USH

Swashbuckler 🎬½ The Scarlet Buccaneer 1984 Eighteenth-century pirate fracas that can't compete with Errol Flynn. 100m/C VHS. FR Jean-Paul Belmondo, Marlene Jobert, Laura Antonelli, Michel Auclair, Julien Guiomar; **D:** Jean-Paul Rappeneau. USH

Sweater Girls woof! 1978 (R) Sex comedy about two girls starting their own club called the "Sweater Girls." Terrible teen exploitaiton film. 90m/C VHS, **Beta.** Charlene Tilton, Harry Moses, Meegan King, Noelle North, Kate Sarchet, Carol Seflinger, Tamara Barkley, Julie Parsons; **D:** Donald M. Jones. NO

Swedenhielms 🎬🎬½ 1935 A poor Swedish scientist struggles to support his family while hoping to win a Nobel prize, while his two sons get involved in a moneylending scandal. Bergman is the rich fiance of one son, to whom poverty is a puzzlement. Fine performances by Ekman and the 20-year-old Bergman (in her third film). In Swedish with English subtitles. 92m/B VHS, LV, **Beta.** SW Gosta Ekman, Karin Swanstrom, Bjorn Berglund, Hakan Westergren, Tutta Rolf, Ingrid Bergman, Sigurd Wallen; **D:** Gustaf Molander. WAC, LUM

Sweeney Todd: The Demon Barber of Fleet Street 1984 A filmed performance of Sondheim's Tony-winning Broadway musical. Creepy thriller about a demon barber, his razor, and his wife's meatpies. 139m/C VHS, Beta, LV. GB Angela Lansbury, George Hearn; **D:** Harold Prince; **M:** Stephen Sondheim. MVD, STS, TTC

The Sweeper 🎬🎬½ 1995 (R) LA cop Mark Goddard (Howell) has a problem—his suspects have a bad habit of dying in his custody. Then he's recruited by a secret police organization whose aim is to dispense their own brand of deadly justice and Mark discovers a key to his troubled past and the murder of his cop father (Fahey).**CW:** Violence, some sexuality and language. 101m/C VHS. C. Thomas Howell, Ed Lauter, Cynda Williams, Jeff Fahey; **D:** Joseph Merhi; **W:** William Applegate Jr.; **C:** Ken Blakey; **M:** K. Alexander Wilkinson. PMH

Sweet Adeline 🎬🎬 1926 Smalltime hayseed makes it big in the music business while brother steals his girl back home. Not easily put off, young songster perseveres. 60m/B VHS, Beta. Charles Ray, Gertrude Olmsted, Jack Clifford, Ida Lewis; **D:** Jerome Storm. GPV, FCT

Sweet Adeline 🎬🎬½ 1935 Dunne attracts all the men in her father's Hoboken beer garden but Woods plays the songwriter with whom she finds real love. Wonderful score. 🎵Play Us a Pol-

ka; Dot; Here Am I; We Were So Young; Why Was I Born?; Mollie O'Donahue; Lonely Feet; 'Twas Not So Long Ago; Don't Ever Leave Me. 87m/B VHS. Irene Dunne, Donald Woods, Hugh Herbert, Ned Sparks, Joseph Cawthorn, Louis Calhern; **D:** Mervyn LeRoy; **M:** Jerome Kern, Oscar Hammerstein. MGM

Sweet Beat 🎬 The Amorous Sex 1962 A young woman gets a chance to become a singer when she reaches the finals of a British beauty contest. Pedestrian story enlivened by music from popular British bands of the time. 66m/B VHS, Beta. Julie Amber, Sheldon Lawrence, Irv Bauer, Billy Myles. NOS, INC, TPV

Sweet Bird of Youth 🎬🎬🎬 1962 An acclaimed adaptation of the Tennessee Williams play about Chance Wayne, a handsome drifter who travels with an aging movie queen to his small Florida hometown, hoping she'll get him started in a movie career. However, coming home turns into a big mistake, as the town boss wants revenge on Chance for seducing his daughter, Heavenly. Williams' original stage ending was cleaned up, providing a conventional "happy" movie ending for the censors. Remade for television in 1989 with Elizabeth Taylor and Mark Harmon in the lead roles. 120m/C VHS, Beta, LV, Letterbox. Paul Newman, Geraldine Page, Ed Begley Sr., Mildred Dunnock, Rip Torn, Shirley Knight, Madeline Sherwood; **D:** Richard Brooks; **W:** Richard Brooks; **C:** Milton Krasner. Academy Awards '62: Best Supporting Actor (Begley); Golden Globe Awards '63: Best Actress—Drama (Page); Nominations: Academy Awards '62: Best Actress (Page), Best Supporting Actress (Knight).MGM, BTV, TRI

Sweet Bird of Youth 🎬🎬 1989 (R) Made for television remake of the Tennessee Williams' play, which was filmed for the big screen in 1962, with Harmon and Taylor having the unenviable task of following in the roles played by Paul Newman and Geraldine Page. She is an egotistical, has-been movie star and is her ambitious gigolo who wants a movie career of his own. Unfortunately, the trouble that drove him from his Florida hometown is still there when he reappears, actress in tow. Things don't bode well. The television production uses Williams' original ending, which was cleaned up for a "happier" version in the '62 film.**CW:** Sexuality. 95m/C VHS. Elizabeth Taylor, Mark Harmon, Rip Torn, Valerie Perrine, Ruta Lee, Seymour Cassel, Kevin Geer, Michael Wilding Jr.; **D:** Nicolas Roeg; **W:** Gavin Lambert; **M:** Ralph Burns. TRI

Sweet Charity 🎬🎬🎬 1969 An ever-optimistic dime-a-dance girl has a hard time finding a classy guy to marry. MacLaine is appealing in this big-budget version of the popular Broadway musical by Neil Simon (derived from Fellini's "Notti di Cabiria"). Fosse's debut as film director. Watch for Cort as a flower child. 🎵My Personal Property; It's a Nice Face; Hey, Big Spender; Rich Man's Frug; If My Friends Could See Me Now; There's Gotta Be Something Better Than This; Rhythm of Life; Sweet Charity; I'm a Brass Band. 148m/C VHS, Beta, LV. Shirley MacLaine, Chita Rivera, John McMartin, Paula Kelly, Sammy Davis Jr., Ricardo Montalban, Bud Cort; **D:** Bob Fosse; **C:** Robert L. Surtees; **M:** Cy Coleman; Nominations: Academy Awards '69: Best Art Direction/Set Decoration, Best Costume Design, Scoring of a Musical. USH

Sweet Country 🎬½ 1987 (R) During the overthrow of the Allende government in Chile, the lives of a Chilean family and an American couple intertwine. Heavy-going propaganda is a cross between tragedy and unintentional comedy. Made by the director of "Zorba the Greek." 147m/C VHS, Beta, LV. Jane Alexander, John Cullum, Carole Laure, Franco Nero, Joanna Pettet, Randy Quaid, Irene Papas, Jean-Pierre Aumont, Pierre Vaneck, Katia Dandoulaki; **D:** Michael Cacoyannis. NO

Sweet Country Road 🎬½ 1981 A rock singer journeys to Nashville to try to cross over into country music. 95m/C VHS, Beta. Buddy Knox, Kary Lynn, Gordy Trapp, Johnny Paycheck, Jeanne Pruett.

Sweet Creek County War 🎬 1982 Retired sheriff must leave his quiet ranch to battle a greedy businessman. 90m/C VHS, Beta. Richard Egan, Albert Salmi, Nita Talbot, Slim Pickens. NO

Sweet Dreams 🎬🎬 1985 (PG-13) Biography of country singer Patsy Cline, focusing mostly on her turbulent marriage. Her quick rise to stardom ended in an early death. Fine performances throughout. Cline's original recordings are used. 🎵Walking After Midnight; Crazy; Sweet Dreams; San Antonio Rose; Blue Moon of Kentucky; Lovesick Blues; Seven Lonely Days; Foolin' Around; Your Cheatin' Heart. 115m/C VHS, Beta, LV. Jessica Lange, Ed Harris, Ann Wedgeworth, David Clennon; **D:** Karel Reisz; **W:** Robert Getchell; **C:** Robbie Greenberg. Nominations: Academy Awards '85: Best Actress (Lange). NO

Sweet Ecstasy 🎬½ Douce Violence; Sweet Violence 1962 Wealthy shenanigans on the French Riviera. Pezy is the upright young man who can't sleep with anyone unless he's in love, much to Sommer's dismay. 75m/B VHS. FR Elke Sommer, Pierre Brice, Christian Pezy, Claire Maurier; **D:** Max Pecas. NO

Sweet Evil 🎬½ 1995 (R) Naomi and Mike seek the help of a surrogate after a number of failed fertility treatments. Jenny seems to be perfect but after she moves into their home, they learn Jenny's got a nasty secret. 92m/C VHS. Bridgette Wilson, Peter Boyle, Scott Cohen, Eiko Matsuda; **D:** Rene Eram. NO

Sweet 15 1990 A young Hispanic girl learns that there is more to growing up than parties when she learns her father is an illegal alien. Originally aired on PBS as part of the "Wonderworks" family movie series. 120m/C VHS. Karla Montana, Panchito Gomez, Tony Plana, Jenny Gago, Susan Ruttan; **D:** Victoria Hochberg. HMV, FCT

Sweet Georgia 🎬 1972 Soft-core star Jordan is a lusty wife whose husband is an alcoholic, so she has a roll in the hay with almost every other cast member. Lots of action, too, including a pitchfork fight. Ride 'em cowboy. 80m/C VHS. Marsha Jordan. VDM

Sweet Hearts Dance 🎬🎬 1988 (R) Parallel love stories follow two long-time friends, one just falling in love, the other struggling to keep his marriage together. Charming performances from all, but a slow pace undermines the film. 95m/C VHS, Beta, LV, Closed Caption. Don Johnson, Jeff Daniels, Susan Sarandon, Elizabeth Perkins, Justin Henry, Holly Marie Combs; **D:** Robert Greenwald; **W:** Ernest Thompson; **M:** Richard Gibbs. COL

The Sweet Hereafter 🎬🎬🎬½ 1996 (R) A schoolbus crash kills 14 children in the small town of Sam Dent, British Columbia. Big city lawyer Mitchell Stephens (Holm) arrives to persuade the townspeople to begin a class-action suit targeting city authorities and the bus manufacturer, while struggling to deal with his drug-addicted daughter Zoe (Banks). Paralyzed teenaged survivor Nicole Burnell (Polley) tries to cope with the aftermath of the tragedy as does widower Billy Ansell (Greenwood), whose two children died in the crash. But the case soon begins to tear the reeling town apart as everyone struggles with loss and fate. Egoyan's intimate, lyrical adaptation of the novel by Russell Banks, is filled with wonderful performances, particularly by Polley.**CW:** Sexuality and some language. 110m/C VHS, LV, Closed Caption, DVD. CA Ian Holm, Sarah Polley, Bruce Greenwood, Tom McCamus, Arsinee Khanjian, Alberta Watson, Gabrielle Rose, Maury Chaykin, David Hemblen, Earl Pastko, Peter Donaldson, Caerthan Banks; **D:** Atom Egoyan; **W:** Atom Egoyan; **C:** Paul Sarossy; **M:** Mychael Danna. Cannes Film Festival '97: Grand Jury Prize; Genie Awards '97: Best Actor (Holm), Best Cinematography, Best Director (Egoyan), Best Film, Best Film Editing, Best Sound, Best Original Score; Independent Spirit Awards '98: Best Foreign Film; Toronto-City Award '97: Best Canadian Feature Film; Nominations: Academy Awards '97: Best Adapted Screenplay, Best Director (Egoyan); Genie Awards '97: Best Actor (Greenwood), Best Actress (Polley, Rose), Best Screenplay. NLC

Sweet Hostage √√½ 1975 Escaped mental patient kidnaps uneducated farm girl and holds her captive in a remote cabin. Blair and Sheen turn in good performances. Adaptation of Nathaniel Benchley's "Welcome to Xanadu." Made-for-television. **93m/C VHS.** Linda Blair, Martin Sheen, Jeanne Cooper, Lee DeBroux, Dehl Berti, Bert Remsen; **D:** Lee Philips. *IMP*

Sweet Justice √½ 1992 (R) This time its the women who get to be commandos, have all the adventures, and get revenge on various scum. The nominal plotline has Sunny Justice (Carter) and her group of gal-warriors avenging the sadistic murder of a friend. Martial arts, weapons, and action galore. **CW:** Violence and sexuality. **92m/C VHS.** Finn Carter, Kathleen Kinmont, Marc Singer, Frank Gorshin; **Cameos:** Mickey Rooney; **D:** Allen Plone; **W:** Allen Plone, Jim Tabilio. *TRI*

Sweet Killing √√ 1993 (R) A banker murders his shrewish wife to be with another woman. He thinks he has the perfect alibi, but then his fictitious excuse comes to life when a mysterious stranger begins stalking him. Based on the novel "Qualthrough" by Agnes Hall. **CW:** Language and sexuality. **87m/C VHS, Beta, Closed Caption.** Anthony Higgins, F. Murray Abraham, Leslie Hope, Michael Ironside, Andrea Ferreol; **D:** Eddy Matalon; **W:** Eddy Matalon. *PAR*

Sweet Liberty √√ 1986 (PG) Alda's hometown is overwhelmed by Hollywood chaos during the filming of a movie version of his novel about the American Revolution. Pleasant but predictable. **107m/C VHS, Beta, LV, Closed Caption.** Alan Alda, Michael Caine, Michelle Pfeiffer, Bob Hoskins, Lillian Gish; **D:** Alan Alda; **M:** Bruce Broughton. *USH*

Sweet Lies √½ 1988 (R) An insurance investigator tracking a scam artist in Paris is preyed upon by a group of single women betting one another that any man can be seduced. Slow comedy. **86m/C VHS, Beta, Closed Caption.** Treat Williams, Joanna Pacula, Julianne Phillips, Laura Manszky, Norbert Weisser, Marilyn Dodd-Frank; **D:** Nathalie Delon; **M:** Trevor Jones. *FOX*

Sweet Light in a Dark Room √√√ *Romeo, Julia a Tma; Romeo, Juliet and Darkness* 1960 A student in Prague during the Nazi Occupation hides a Jewish girl. He falls in love with her but becomes the suspect in the murder of a Nazi officer. Directed by the great Czech filmmaker Weiss who was himself forced to leave his country during Nazi occupation. In Czech with English subtitles. **93m/B VHS.** *CZ* Ivan Mistrik, Dana Smutna; **D:** Jiri Weiss. *FCT, DVT, HEG*

Sweet Lorraine √√√ 1987 (PG-13) A bittersweet, nostalgic comedy about the staff and clientele of a deteriorating Catskills hotel on the eve of its closing. **91m/C VHS, Beta.** Maureen Stapleton, Lee Richardson, Trini Alvarado, Freddie Roman, John Bedford Lloyd, Giancarlo Esposito, Edie Falco, Todd Graff, Evan Handler; **D:** Steve Gomer; **W:** Michael Zettler, Shelly Altman; **M:** Richard Robbins. *PAR*

Sweet Love, Bitter √√½ *It Won't Rub Off, Baby; Black Love, White Love* 1967 The downfall of a black jazz saxophonist in the 1950s. The character is loosely based on the life of legendary musician Charlie "Bird" Parker. Alto sax man Charles McPherson dubs Gregory's solos. Adapted from the novel "Night Song" by John A. Williams. **92m/C VHS.** Dick Gregory, Don Murray, Diane Varsi, Robert Hooks; **D:** Herbert Danska; **W:** Lewis Jacobs, Herbert Danska; **M:** Mal Waldron. *RHP, MVD, FCT*

Sweet Movie √√ 1975 A provocative cult classic concerning a South African tycoon who purchases a virgin bride and then exploits her sexually. In English and French with subtitles. **120m/C VHS, Beta.** *YU* Carole Laure, Pierre Clementi, Sami Frey; **D:** Dusan Makavejev; **W:** Dusan Makavejev; **M:** Manos Hadjidakis. *FCT, MOV*

Sweet Murder woof! 1993 (R) "Single White Female" rip-off features Udy allowing Davidtz to share her apartment—with nasty consequences. **CW:** Language, stabbing scenes, and

sexuality. **101m/C VHS.** Helene Udy, Embeth Davidtz, Russell Todd; **D:** Percival Rubens. *THV*

Sweet Nothing √√√ 1996 (R) Wall Street up-and-comer Angel (Imperioli) is given some crack by a buddy (Calderon) to celebrate the birth of his child. This starts a downward spiral into addiction and dealing. At first, his wife Monika (Sorvino) goes along, but as Angel deteriorates, she learns not to trust him. Excellent performances by Imperioli and Sorvino avoid over-the-top theatrics. Script provides a realistic look at how addiction affects real people, and steers clear of obvious cliches. Based on diaries found in a Bronx apartment building. Film's producers tracked down the author and paid for his rehab. **CW:** Mature themes, drug use, violence, language. **89m/C VHS, Closed Caption.** Michael Imperioli, Mira Sorvino, Paul Calderone, Billie Neal; **W:** Lee Drysdale. *WAR*

Sweet Perfection √√ 1990 (R) Jackson plans a big promotion for her beauty contest. Who will be voted the "Perfect Woman?" Tired premise, but it has its moments. **90m/C VHS.** Stoney Jackson, Anthony Norman McKay, Catero Colbert, Liza Crusat, Reggie Theus, Tatiana Tumbtzen. *XVC, HHE*

Sweet Poison √√ 1991 (R) Bobby Stiles is a ruthless criminal who has just broken out of prison. He wants to get home and settle the score with his brother, who actually committed the crime Bobby was imprisoned for. Henry and Charlene Odell are traveling cross-country when Bobby crosses their path and forces them to drive him home. Bobby's not too busy eluding the police to notice that his captives' marriage is a little shaky—and that Charlene is attractive and sexy. As Bobby and Charlene get closer husband Henry just becomes another problem. **CW:** Strong violence and strong sexuality. **101m/C VHS, Closed Caption.** Steven Bauer, Patricia Healy, Edward Herrmann; **D:** Brian Grant. *USH*

Sweet Revenge √√ 1987 (R) TV journalist kidnapped by a white slavery ring in the Asian jungles. After escaping, she returns for vegeance. Meek drama. **79m/C VHS, Beta.** Ted Shackleford, Nancy Allen, Martin Landau; **D:** Mark Sobel.

Sweet Revenge √√ 1990 When a judge tells a divorced couple that the woman must pay the man alimony, she hires an actress to marry her ex. The tables are turned in this way-out marriage flick, reminiscent of the screwball comedies of the 1940s. **89m/C VHS, Beta, Closed Caption.** Rosanna Arquette, Carrie Fisher, John Sessions; **D:** Charlotte Brandstrom; **W:** Janet Brownell; **M:** Hubert Bougis. *TTC*

Sweet Rosie O'Grady √√½ 1943 Musical-comedy star Grable has returned to New York after success in England, where she caught the eye of nobleman Gardiner. Ex-boyfriend Young is a tabloid reporter who's expected to get the scoop on her past. Seems she used to perform in Bowery saloons although that's not what Grable's been telling everyone. Slight story, charming performers, and lots of songs. Remade in 1948 as "That Wonderful Urge." ♫My Heart Tells Me; My Sam; Oh Where is the Groom?; The Wishing Waltz; Going to the Country Fair; Get Your Police Gazette; Battle Cry; Sweet Rosie O'Grady; Two Little Girls in Blue. **74m/C VHS.** Betty Grable, Robert Young, Adolphe Menjou, Reginald Gardiner, Virginia Grey, Phil Regan, Sig Rumann, Alan Dinehart; **D:** Irving Cummings; **C:** Ernest Palmer. *RXM*

Sweet 16 √√ 1981 (R) Serial killings in Texas town begin to set off muffled alarms in big head of sheriff Hopkins. Sixteen-year-old Melissa has recently moved into town. She's beautiful, mysterious, and promiscuous, and she has a big problem—all her boyfriends end up dead. No real puzzle. **90m/C VHS, Beta.** Susan Strasberg, Bo Hopkins, Don Stroud, Dana Kimmell, Patrick Macnee, Larry Storch; **D:** Jim Sotos. *VES*

Sweet Smell of Success √√√½ 1957 Evil New York City gossip columnist J.J. Hunsecker (Lancaster) and sleazy press agent (Curtis) cook up smear campaign to ruin career of jazz musician in love with J.J.'s sister. Engrossing performances, great dialogue. **96m/C VHS, LV.** Burt Lancaster, Tony Curtis, Martin Milner, Barbara Nichols, Sam Levene; **D:** Alexander MacKendrick; **W:** Ernest Lehman, Clifford Odets; **C:** James Wong Howe; **M:** Elmer Bernstein. National Film Registry '93. *MGM*

Sweet Spirits woof! 198? Soft-sell European fluff about a modern mannequin having a raucous affair with an artist. **87m/C VHS, Beta.** Erika Blanc, Farley Granger.

Sweet Sugar √½ *Chaingang Girls; Captive Women 3: Sweet Sugar* 1972 (R) Slave girls try to escape from a Costa Rican sugar cane plantation and its cruel owner. Needless to say, vulgar exploitation runs hither and yon in this film. **90m/C VHS.** Phyllis E. Davis, Ella Edwards, Pamela Collins, Cliff Osmond, Timothy Brown; **D:** Michel Levesque. *NO*

Sweet Sweetback's Baadasssss Song √√√ 1971 A black pimp kills two policemen who beat up a black militant. He uses his street-wise survival skills to elude his pursuers and escape to Mexico. A thriller, but racist, sexist, and violent. **97m/C VHS, Beta.** Melvin Van Peebles, Simon Chuckster, John Amos; **D:** Melvin Van Peebles; **W:** Melvin Van Peebles. *XVC*

Sweet Talker √√½ 1991 (PG) Following his release from prison, a charming con man shows up in a small coastal village, thinking the townsfolk will be ripe for the picking. What he doesn't know is they can do some sweet talking of their own, and he soon finds himself caring for a pretty widow and her son. Enjoyable light comedy works thanks to likable leads. **91m/C VHS, LV, Closed Caption.** *AU* Bryan Brown, Karen Allen, Chris Haywood, Bill Kerr, Bruce Spence, Bruce Myles, Paul Chubb, Peter Hehir, Justin Rosniak; **D:** Michael Jenkins; **W:** Tony Morphett; **M:** Richard Thompson, Peter Filleul. *ART*

Sweet Trash woof! 1989 (R) A vice cop, having an affair with a 17-year-old prostitute, is blackmailed by an underworld figure. Lives up to its name. **80m/C VHS.** Sebastian Gregory, Sharon Matt, Luke Perry, Bonnie Clark, Gene Blackey; **D:** John Hayes. *NO*

Sweet William √√√ 1979 (R) A philandering and seemingly irresistible young man finds that one sensitive woman hasn't the patience or time for his escapades. Adult comedy concerned with sex without displaying any on the screen. **88m/C VHS, Beta.** *GB* Sam Waterston, Jenny Agutter, Anna Massey, Arthur Lowe; **D:** Claude Whatham; **W:** Beryl Bainbridge.

Sweet Young Thing 19?? Young students at a French girls' school receive all sorts of attention from the male staff. **83m/C VHS, Beta.** Jean Tolzac, Bernard Musson.

Sweetheart of the Navy √½ 1937 Sailors help a cafe singer out of a jam, with one of them almost giving up his career for her. Standard fare, but Parker is well worth listening to. **63m/B VHS.** Eric Linden, Cecilia Parker, Roger Imhof, Bernadene Hayes, Jason Robards Sr., Don Barclay; **D:** Duncan Mansfield. *NOS*

Sweethearts √√√ 1938 MacDonald and Eddy star as married stage actors trying to get some time off from their hectic schedule in this show-within-a-show. Trouble ensues when their conniving producer begs, pleads and tricks them into staying. Lots of well-staged musical numbers. ♫Wooden Shoes; Every Lover Must Meet His Fate; Sweethearts; Pretty as a Picture; Summer Serenade; On Parade. **114m/C VHS, LV.** Jeanette MacDonald, Nelson Eddy, Frank Morgan, Florence Rice, Ray Bolger, Mischa Auer; **D:** Woodbridge S. Van Dyke. Nominations: Academy Awards '38: Best Sound, Best Score. *MGM*

Sweetie 🐾🐾🐾 1989 (R) Bizarre, expressive Australian tragicomedy about a pair of sisters—one a withdrawn, paranoid Plain Jane, the other a dangerously extroverted, overweight sociopath who re-enters her family's life and turns it upside down. Campion's first feature. 97m/C VHS, Beta, LV. *AU* Genevieve Lemon, Karen Colston, Tom Lycos, Jon Darling, Dorothy Barry, Michael Lake, Andre Pataczek; *D:* Jane Campion; *W:* Gerard Lee, Jane Campion; *M:* Martin Armiger. Nominations: Academy Awards '91: Best Foreign Language Film. *ART*

Swept Away... 🐾🐾🐾 *Swept Away...By an Unusual Destiny in the Blue Sea of August* 1975 (R) A rich and beautiful Milanese woman is shipwrecked on a desolate island with a swarthy Sicilian deck hand, who also happens to be a dedicated communist. Isolated, the two switch roles, with the wealthy woman dominated by the crude proletarian. Sexy and provocative. Italian with subtitles. 116m/C VHS, Letterbox. *IT* Giancarlo Giannini, Mariangela Melato; *D:* Lina Wertmuller; *W:* Lina Wertmuller; *C:* Julio Battiferri; *M:* Piero Piccioni. *FXL*

Swept from the Sea 🐾🐾½ *Amy Foster* 1997 (PG-13) Shipwrecked foreigner (Perez) and ostracized servant girl (Weisz) are star-crossed lovers in 19th century Cornwall. Told in flashback by Dr. Kennedy (McKellen) to Kathy Bates' invalid Miss Swaffer, he recalls how the native Ukrainian Yanko, who could speak no English, was thought to be an idiot by all in town, except the kind and gentle Amy, who found him washed up on the shore. Kennedy and Yanko bond through a game of chess, and the kindly doctor teaches him English. Armed with the native words of love, Yanko goes a'courtin' Miss Amy. Definitely for die-hard romantics, the films throws in all the melodrama it can muster and then some, but performances are worthy (especially McKellen's). Based on a short story by Joseph Conrad. *CW:* Elements of theme and some sensuality. 115m/C VHS, Closed Caption, DVD. *GB* Vincent Perez, Rachel Weisz, Kathy Bates, Ian McKellen, Joss Ackland, Tom Bell, Zoe Wanamaker, Tony Haygarth, Fiona Victory; *D:* Beeban Kidron; *W:* Tim Willocks; *C:* Dick Pope; *M:* John Barry. *NYR*

Swift Justice 🐾🐾 1988 Mayor of a small town thinks he's gotten away with murder after leaving a young girl for dead in a junk yard. However, the mayor and his violent pals are soon hunted by an ex-Green Beret with a penchant for justice. 90m/C VHS, Beta. Jon Greene, James Daughton, Jenny Neumann, Kim Day, Buster Crabbe; *D:* James Polakof.

Swifty 🐾½ 1936 A cowpoke is accused of murder but escapes to track down the real culprit and win the hand of the girl he loves. 60m/B VHS, Beta. Hoot Gibson. *VCN*

Swim Team 🐾 1979 New coach for a terminally inept school swimming team whips them into shape. Doesn't hold much water. 81m/C VHS, Beta. Stephen Furst, James Daughton, Jenny Neumann, Kim Day, Buster Crabbe; *D:* James Polakof.

The Swimmer 🐾🐾🐾½ 1968 (PG) A lonely suburbanite swims an existential swath through the pools of his neighborhood landscape in an effort at self-discovery. A surreal, strangely compelling work based on a story by John Cheever. 94m/C VHS, Beta, LV. Burt Lancaster, Janice Rule, Janet Landgard, Marge Champion, Kim Hunter, Rose Gregorio, John David Garfield; *D:* Frank Perry; *M:* Marvin Hamlisch. *GKK*

Swimming Pool 🐾🐾½ 1970 (PG) Two men and two women spend a weekend in a villa on the French Riviera, manipulating each other, playing sexual games, and changing partners. Their escapades end in murder. Romantic melodrama is sensuous if slow-moving. French film dubbed in English. 85m/C VHS, Beta. *FR* Romy Schneider, Alain Delon, Maurice Ronet, Jane Birkin; *D:* Jacques Deray. *NLC*

Swimming to Cambodia 🐾🐾🐾 1987 Gray tells the story of his bit part in "The Killing Fields," filmed in Cambodia, and makes ironic observations about modern life. It works. 87m/C VHS, Beta, LV, Closed Caption. Spalding Gray; *D:* Jonathan Demme; *C:* John Bailey; *M:* Laurie Anderson. *ORI, WAR*

Swimming with Sharks 🐾🐾🐾 *The Buddy Factor* 1994 (R) Budding screenwriter Guy (Whaley) goes to work for notoriously insulting movie producer Buddy (Spacey). Soon, Guy grows tired of his boss's demeaning treatment and cruel means of communication and devises a scheme which would even the score. Hollywood satire has more bite than "The Player," and a devious cilmax, but it's mostly an opportunity for Spacey to hang his hams, which he does with glee. Debut for director Huang, who based his script on his experience as a production assistant. See it with your boss. *CW:* Some scenes of psychological/physical torture; pervasive strong language. 93m/C VHS, LV, Closed Caption. Kevin Spacey, Frank Whaley, Michelle Forbes, Benicio Del Toro; *D:* George Huang; *W:* George Huang; *C:* Steven Firestone. New York Film Critics Awards '95: Best Supporting Actor (Spacey); Nominations: Independent Spirit Awards '96: Best Actor (Spacey). *THV*

Swimsuit: The Movie 🐾½ 1989 A young ad executive decides to revitalize a swimsuit company's failing business by sponsoring a contest for the perfect swimsuit model. Made-for-television fluff. 100m/C VHS. William Katt, Catherine Oxenberg, Cyd Charisse, Nia Peeples, Tom Villard, Cheryl Pollak, Billy Warlock, Jack Wagner; *D:* Chris Thomson; *W:* Robert Schiff; *M:* John D'Andrea.

The Swindle 🐾🐾 *Il Bidone* 1955 Three Italian conmen pull capers in Rome trying to make a better life for themselves. Dark overtones permeate one of Fellini's lesser efforts. Good can't bring up the level of this film. In Italian with English subtitles. 92m/C VHS, LV. *IT* Broderick Crawford, Giulietta Masina, Richard Basehart, Franco Fabrizi; *D:* Federico Fellini; *W:* Federico Fellini, Tullio Pinelli, Ennio Flaiano; *M:* Nino Rota. *IME, CVC, TPV*

Swindle 🐾 1992 Two life-long friends set up scam after scam in their quest for sex and money. Their latest con involves a phony marriage broker business, which provides the opportunity to meet a lot of lovely ladies. Only it turns out the hustlers may be the ones getting hustled. 85m/C VHS. Robby West, Britt Houston, Elaina Dunn, Samantha Fong, Bobby Tess, Donna Thomas; *D:* Jason Holt. *CEL*

Swing High, Swing Low 🐾🐾½ 1937 A trumpet player fights the bottle and the dice to become a hit in the jazz world and marry the woman he loves. Solid drama. From the stage play "Burlesque." Made first as "The Dance of Life," then as "When My Baby Smiles At Me." 95m/B VHS, Beta. Carole Lombard, Fred MacMurray, Charles Butterworth, Dorothy Lamour; *D:* Mitchell Leisen. *NOS, HHT, DVT*

Swing It, Professor 🐾🐾½ *Swing it Buddy* 1937 A stodgy music professor refuses to recognize jazz as a valid musical form and subsequently loses his job. During his unemployment, he wanders into a nightclub and discovers jazz isn't so bad after all. Nice camera work. 🎵I'm Sorta Kinda Glad I Met You; An Old-Fashioned Melody; Richer Than A Millionaire. 62m/B VHS. Pinky Tomlin, Paula Stone, Mary Kornman, Milburn Stone, Pat Gleason; *D:* Marshall Neilan. *NOS, DVT, HEG*

Swing It, Sailor! 🐾🐾 1937 Two footloose sailors go after the same woman while on shore leave. Decent screwball comedy. 61m/B VHS, Beta. Wallace Ford, Ray Mayer, Isabel Jewell, Mary Treen; *D:* Raymond Cannon. *VYY, NOS*

Swing Kids 🐾🐾 1993 (PG-13) In 1939 in Germany, big band or "swing" music is the instrument used by a group of young people to rebel against the conformity demanded by Hitler. Highlights the politics of the era, but concentrates mainly on three teenagers and the strains that Nazi power put on their friendship. Although the premise is based in historic fact, there is still something disturbingly silly about the entire production. Dance sequences are lively and well-choreographed. Branagh (in an uncredited role) plays a smooth-talking Gestapo chief. Filmed on location in Prague, Czechoslovakia (as a substitute for Hamburg, Germany). 114m/C VHS, Beta, LV, Closed Caption. Robert Sean Leonard, Christian Bale, Frank Whaley, Barbara Hershey, Tushka Bergen, David Tom, Kenneth Branagh; *D:* Thomas Carter; *W:* Jonathan Marc Feldman; *M:* James Horner. *HPH*

Swing Parade of 1946 🐾½ 1946 One of the multitude of 1940s musicals. Young songwriter falls in love with club owner. Highlights include an appearance by the Three Stooges. 🎵Stormy Weather; Just a Little Fond Affection; Don't Worry About the Mule; A Tender Word Will Mend It All; On the Sunny Side of the Street; Oh, Brother; After All This Time; Caledonia. 74m/B VHS. Gale Storm, Phil Regan, Moe Howard, Edward Brophy, Connee Boswell; *D:* Phil Karlson. *NO*

Swing Shift 🐾🐾½ 1984 (PG) When Hawn takes a job at an aircraft plant after her husband goes off to war, she learns more than riveting. Lahti steals the film as her friend and co-worker. A detailed reminiscence of the American home front during WWII that never seems to gel. Produced by Hawn. 100m/C VHS, Beta, LV. Goldie Hawn, Kurt Russell, Ed Harris, Christine Lahti, Holly Hunter, Chris Lemmon, Belinda Carlisle, Fred Ward, Roger Corman, Lisa Pelikan; *D:* Jonathan Demme; *W:* Ron Nyswaner, Bo Goldman; *C:* Tak Fujimoto. New York Film Critics Awards '84: Best Supporting Actress (Lahti); Nominations: Academy Awards '84: Best Supporting Actress (Lahti). *WAR*

Swing Time 🐾🐾🐾 1936 Astaire, a dancer who can't resist gambling, is engaged to marry another woman, until he meets Ginger. One of the team's best efforts. Laserdisc version includes: production photos and stills, commentary on Fred Astaire and musical films, and excerpts from "Hooray for Love" featuring Bill "Bojangles" Robinson and Fats Waller. 🎵The Way You Look Tonight; Waltz in Swing Time; Never Gonna Dance; Pick Yourself Up; A Fine Romance; Bojangles of Harlem. 103m/B VHS, Beta, LV. Fred Astaire, Ginger Rogers, Helen Broderick, Betty Furness, Eric Blore, Victor Moore; *D:* George Stevens; *M:* Jerome Kern, Dorothy Fields. Academy Awards '36: Best Song ("The Way You Look Tonight"). *TTC, CRC*

Swingers 🐾🐾🐾 1996 (R) Hip, hilarious, and highly entertaining low-budget comedy features five young showbiz wannabes on the prowl for career breaks and beautiful "babies" in the Hollywood retro club scene. Mike (screenwriter Favreau) is a struggling actor/comedian from New York who's having trouble getting over his ex. His slick, handsome friend Trent (Vaughn, in a star-making turn) and the rest of his neo-Rat Pack buddies try to get him back in the game with nightly parties and lounge-hopping. Witty script and clever camera work make this one "money, baby, money!" *CW:* Language throughout. 96m/C VHS, LV, Closed Caption. Jon Favreau, Vince Vaughn, Ron Livingston, Patrick Van Horn, Alex Desert, Brooke Langton, Heather Graham, Deena Martin, Katherine Kendall, Blake Lindsley; *D:* Doug Liman; *W:* Jon Favreau; *C:* Doug Liman; *M:* Justin Reinhardt. MTV Movie Awards '97: Best New Filmmaker Award (Liman). *TOU*

A Swingin' Summer 🐾½ 1965 A bunch of groovy guys and gals go-go to the beach for a vacation of fun and sun and end up starting a rock 'n' roll concert series. Everybody gets part of the action...even the bespectacled Welch, who gets a chance to sing. Performances from the Righteous Brothers and rock semi-legends Donnie Brooks, Gary Lewis and the Playboys, and the Rip Chords. 🎵Red Hot Roadster; Justine; Penny the Poo; Out to Lunch; Nitro; Ready to Groove. 81m/C VHS. James Stacy, William Wellman Jr., Quinn O'Hara, James West, Mary Mitchell, Allan Jones, Raquel Welch; *D:* Robert Sparr; *W:* Leigh Chapman. *NO*

The Swinging Cheerleaders 1974 (PG) A group of amorous cheerleaders turn on the entire campus in this typical sexploiter. 90m/C VHS, Beta. Cheryl "Rainbeaux" Smith, Colleen Camp, Jo Johnston; *D:* Jack Hill. MON

Swinging Wives 1979 (R) Ribald humor for the discriminating viewer. 84m/C VHS, Beta. Gale Mayberrie, Ron James. NO

Swiss Conspiracy ⅗⅗ 1977 (PG) Against the opulent background of the world's richest financial capital and playground of the wealthy, one man battles to stop a daring and sophisticated blackmailer preying on the secret bank account set. Fast-paced, if sometimes confusing. 92m/C VHS, Beta. *GE* David Janssen, Senta Berger; *D:* Jack Arnold. NO

The Swiss Family Robinson ⅗⅗⅗ 1960 A family, seeking to escape Napoleon's war in Europe, sets sail for New Guinea, but shipwrecks on a deserted tropical island. There they build an idyllic life, only to be confronted by a band of pirates. Lots of adventure for family viewing. Filmed on location on the island of Tobago. Based on the novel by Johann Wyss. 126m/C VHS, Beta, LV, Letterbox. John Mills, Dorothy McGuire, James MacArthur, Tommy Kirk, Janet Munro, Sessue Hayakawa; *D:* Ken Annakin. DIS, IGP

Swiss Miss ⅗⅗½ 1938 Stan and Ollie are mousetrap salesmen on the job in Switzerland. Highlights include Stan's tuba serenade and the gorilla-on-the-bridge episode. Also included on this tape is a 1935 Thelma Todd/Patsy Kelly short, "Hot Money." 97m/B VHS, Beta. Stan Laurel, Oliver Hardy, Della Lind, Walter Woolf King, Eric Blore, Thelma Todd, Patsy Kelly; *D:* John Blystone. CCB, FCT, MLB

The Switch ⅗⅗ 1989 (R) An escaped convict takes the place of a talented conman and chaos ensues. ?m/C VHS. Anthony Quinn, Adriano Celentano, Capucine, Corinne Clery. NO

Switch ⅗⅗⅗ 1991 (R) A chauvinist louse, slain by the girlfriends he misused, is sent back to Earth as an alluring female to learn the other side's point of view. The plot may lack urgency, but this is a sparkling adult comedy that scores as it pursues the gimmicky concept to a logical, outrageous and touching conclusion. Barkin's act as swaggering male stuck in a woman's body is a masterwork of physical humor. *CW:* Language. 104m/C VHS, LV, Closed Caption. Ellen Barkin, Jimmy Smits, JoBeth Williams, Lorraine Bracco, Perry King, Bruce Martyn Payne, Tony Roberts; *D:* Blake Edwards; *W:* Blake Edwards; *M:* Henry Mancini. HBO, WAR

Switchback ⅗⅗ *Going West in America* 1997 (R) FBI agent Frank Lacrosse (Quaid) pursues the serial killer who kidnapped his son. Against the backdrop of a Texas sheriff's election and a Colorado snowstorm, the killer, who may or may not be a former rail worker (Glover) or the hitchhiking ex-doctor (Leto) he picked up leads Lacrosse on a convoluted cat-and-mouse game with no apparent logic or motive. First-time director Stuart, who wrote "Die Hard" and "The Fugitive," wrote this one in film school, and it shows. Connect-the-dots set pieces and plot twists only provide Quaid more time to perfect his Harrison Ford impression and Glover more scenery and dialogue to chew. Ermey is impressive as the put-upon small town sherriff. Stunt work is well-done and the Colorado countryside looks great. 120m/C VHS, Beta, Closed Caption. Dennis Quaid, Danny Glover, Jared Leto, R. Lee Ermey, William Fichtner, Ted Levine, Leo Burmester, Merele Kennedy, Julio Mechoso; *D:* Jeb Stuart; *W:* Jeb Stuart; *C:* Oliver Wood; *M:* Basil Poledouris. PAR

Switchblade Sisters woof! *The Jezebels; Playgirl Gang* 1975 Crime gang of female ex-cons wreaks pseudo-feminist havoc. Bruce is Lenny Bruce's daughter. 90m/C VHS. Robbie Lee, Joanne Nail, Monica Gayle, Kitty Bruce, Asher Brauner, Chase Newhart, Marlene Clark, Janice Karman, Don Stark, Kate Murtagh, Bill Adler; *D:* Jack Hill; *W:* F.X. Maier; *C:* Stephen M. Katz; *M:* Les Baxter, Medusa, Chuck Day, Richard Person. TOU, HHE

Switched at Birth ⅗⅗½ 1991 (PG) A fact-based made for television drama about two girls, switched in a hospital nursery at birth. Only when one girl dies, a decade later, do her parents discover that she could not have been their biological child. Their search for their daughter leads to an emotional conflict between the girl, the man that raised her, and the biological parents who seek to claim her. Beware of the sappy Hollywood ending, five years later the story of Kimberly Mays is still going through the U.S. judicial system. 200m/C VHS. Bonnie Bedelia, Brian Kerwin, Ed Asner, Caroline McWilliams, John M. Jackson, Lois Smith, Eve Gordon, Judith Hoag, Ariana Richards; *D:* Waris Hussein. COL, PMS

Switching Channels ⅗⅗½ 1988 (PG) A modernized remake of "His Girl Friday," and therefore the fourth version of "The Front Page." Beautiful television anchorwoman (Turner) wants to marry handsome tycoon (Reeve), but her scheming ex-husband (Reynolds) gets in the way. Weak performances from everyone but Beatty and lackluster direction render this oft-told story less funny than usual. 108m/C VHS, Beta, LV, Closed Caption. Burt Reynolds, Kathleen Turner, Christopher Reeve, Ned Beatty, Henry Gibson, George Newbern, Al Waxman, Ken James, Joe Silver, Charles Kimbrough, Tony Rosato; *D:* Ted Kotcheff; *W:* Jonathan Reynolds; *M:* Michel Legrand. COL

Swoon ⅗⅗⅗ 1991 Kalin's directorial debut is a stylish rendering of the sensational 1924 kidnapping and murder of Bobby Franks by Richard Loeb and Nathan Leopold Jr. and their subsequent trial and imprisonment. Core elements of the case remain but Kalin imposes contemporary styles and morals on the past, particularly his protest against the homophobic attitudes influencing the trial while acknowledging the jaded and dispassionate behavior of the two young men. Previous cinematic versions of the murder case include "Rope" and "Compulsion" but Kalin graphically portrays the characters homosexuality, which was only hinted at in the earlier films. 95m/B VHS, LV, Closed Caption. Daniel Schlachet, Craig Chester, Ron Vawter, Michael Kirby, Michael Stumm, Valda Z. Drabla, Natalie Stanford; *D:* Tom Kalin; *W:* Tom Kalin; *C:* Ellen Kuras; *M:* James Bennett. Sundance Film Festival '92: Best Cinematography. NLC, IME

The Sword and the Cross ⅗½ 1958 A grade-B adventure about the life of Mary Magdelene. 93m/B VHS, Beta. Yvonne De Carlo, George Mistral; *D:* Carlo L. Bragaglia. NO

Sword & the Dragon ⅗⅗ *Ilya Mouromets* 1956 A young warrior must battle any number of giant mythical creatures. 81m/C VHS, Beta. *RU* Boris Andreyer, Andrei Abrikosov; *D:* Alexander Ptushko. VCI, SNC

The Sword & the Rose ⅗⅗½ *When Knighthood Was in Flower* 1953 Mary Tudor, sister of King Henry VIII, shuns the advances of a nobleman for the love of a commoner. Johns is an obstinate princess; Justice, a fine king. Based on the book "When Knighthood Was in Flower." 91m/C VHS, Beta, LV. Richard Todd, Glynis Johns, Michael Gough, Jane Barrett, James Robertson Justice; *D:* Ken Annakin; *C:* Geoffrey Unsworth. DIS, HHE, BTV

Sword & the Sorcerer ⅗½ 1982 (R) Young prince strives to regain control of his kingdom, now ruled by an evil knight and a powerful magician. Mediocre script and acting is enhanced by decent special effects. 100m/C VHS, Beta, LV. Lee Horsley, Kathleen Beller, George Maharis, Simon MacCorkindale, Richard Lynch, Richard Moll, Robert Tessier, Nina Van Pallandt, Anna Bjorn, Jeff Corey; *D:* Albert Pyun; *W:* Albert Pyun. USH

The Sword in the Stone ⅗⅗⅗ 1963 (G) The Disney version of the first volume of T.H. White's "The Once and Future King" wherein King Arthur, as a boy, is instructed in the ways of the world by Merlin and Archimedes the owl. Although not in the Disney masterpiece fold, boasts the usual superior animation and a gripping mythological tale. 79m/C VHS, Beta, LV, Closed Caption. *D:* Wolfgang Reitherman; *M:* George Bruns; *V:* Ricky Sorenson, Sebastian Cabot, Karl Swenson, Junius Matthews, Alan Napier, Norman Alden, Martha Wentworth, Barbara Jo Allen. Nominations: Academy Awards '63: Best Adapted Score. DIS, KUI, HMV

Sword of Doom ⅗⅗⅗ *Daibosatsu Toge* 1967 A rousing samurai epic detailing the training of an impulsive, bloodlusting warrior by an elder expert. In Japanese with English subtitles. 120m/B VHS, Beta. *JP* Tatsuya Nakadai, Toshiro Mifune; *D:* Kihachi Okamoto. NLC

The Sword of El Cid ⅗½ *La Spada del Cid* 1962 Not much dash and very little daring-do in this poorly plotted, overly dramatic saga of good vs. evil, Spanish style. Rightful heir to the crown threatens, challenges and enevitably crosses swords with the pretender to his throne. Costume mavens may find something to hold their interest. 86m/C VHS, Beta. *SP IT* Roland Carey, Sandro Moretti, Chantal Deberg, Iliana Grimaldi, Jose Luis Pellicena, Daniela Bianchi; *D:* Miguel Iglesias. SNC

Sword of Fury II ⅗½ 1973 The sequel. Two samurai fight to the death to determine who will become the premier swordsman of all Japan. With English subtitles. 77m/C VHS, Beta. *JP* Hideki Takahashi, Jiro Tamiya. NO

Sword of Gideon ⅗⅗½ 1986 An action packed and suspenseful made for television film about an elite commando group who set out to avenge the Munich Olympic killings of 1972. Adapted from "Vengeance" by George Jonas. 148m/C VHS, Closed Caption. Steven Bauer, Michael York, Rod Steiger, Colleen Dewhurst, Robert Joy, Laurent Malet, Lino Ventura, Leslie Hope; *D:* Michael Anderson Sr.; *W:* Chris Bryant; *M:* Georges Delerue. NO

Sword of Honor ⅗½ 1994 (R) Undercover cop and martial arts expert Johnny Lee (Leigh) investigates his partner's mysterious death amidst the tawdry glamor of Vegas. *CW:* Bloody shootings; martial arts violence; sexuality and language. ?m/C VHS, LV, Closed Caption. Steven Leigh, Sophia Crawford, Angelo Tiffe, Jerry Tiffe, Jeff Pruitt, Debbie Scofield; *D:* Robert Tiffe; *W:* Robert Tiffe, Clay Ayers; *M:* David Rubinstein. PMH

Sword of Lancelot ⅗⅗½ *Lancelot and Guinevere* 1963 A costume version of the Arthur-Lancelot-Guinevere triangle, with plenty of swordplay and a sincere respect for the old legend. 115m/C VHS, Beta. *GB* Cornel Wilde, Jean Wallace, Brian Aherne, George Baker; *D:* Cornel Wilde. USH

Sword of Monte Cristo ⅗½ 1951 Masked female avenger, seeking the liberty of the French people, discovers a valuable sword that holds the key to a vast fortune. But the sword is also desired by an evil government minister. 80m/C VHS, Beta. George Montgomery, Rita (Paula) Corday; *D:* Maurice Geraghty. VHE

Sword of Sherwood Forest ⅗⅗½ 1960 The Earl of Newark plots the murder of the Archbishop of Canterbury in yet another rendition of the Robin Hood legend. Cushing is truly evil as the villain. 80m/C VHS. *GB* Richard Greene, Peter Cushing, Niall MacGinnis, Richard Pasco, Jack Gwillim, Sarah Branch, Nigel Green, Oliver Reed; *D:* Terence Fisher. COL, MLB

Sword of the Valiant ⅗⅗ 1983 (PG) The Green Knight arrives in Camelot to challenge Gawain. Remake of "Gawain And The Green Knight." Connery adds zest to a minor epic. 102m/C VHS, Beta. *GB* Sean Connery, Miles O'Keeffe, Cyrielle Claire, Leigh Lawson, Trevor Howard, Peter Cushing, Wilfrid Brambell, Lila Kedrova, John Rhys-Davies; *D:* Stephen Weeks; *W:* Philip M. Breen; *C:* Frederick A. (Freddie) Young. MGM

Sword of Venus ⅗ *Island of Monte Cristo* 1953 Uninspired production finds the son of the Count of Monte Cristo the victim in a scheme to deprive him of his wealth. 73m/B VHS. Robert Clarke,

Catherine McLeod, Dan O'Herlihy, William Schallert; **D:** Harold Daniels. *FCT*

Swords of Death 𝒵𝒵 **1971** Final film by Uchida, released posthumously, deals with the adventurous period exploits of the irrepressible Miyamoto Musashi. With English subtitles. **76m/C VHS, Beta.** *JP* Kinnosuke Nakamura, Rentaro Mikuni; **D:** Tomu Uchida. *VDA*

The Swordsman 𝒵𝒵½ **1992 (R)** The quest to return the stolen sword of the legendary Alexander the Great to a museum is muscular detective Lamas' assignment. Turns out the detective and his evil millionaire antagonist have been chasing each other through time in their endless quest for revenge and power. **CW:** Language and violence. **98m/C VHS, LV.** Lorenzo Lamas, Claire Stansfield, Michael Champion; **D:** Michael Kennedy; **W:** Michael Kennedy. *REP*

Sworn Enemies 𝒵𝒵½ **1996 (R)** Clifton Santier (Greene) goes on a killing spree in a small town where the local sheriff turns out to be his ex-partner, Pershing Quinn (Pare). The two enemies decide that only death will settle their old (and new) scores. **101m/C VHS, LV.** Peter Greene, Michael Pare, Macha Grenon; **D:** Shimon Dotan; **W:** Rod Hewitt; **C:** Sylvain Brault; **M:** Walter Christian Rothe, Richard Anthony Boast. *APX*

Sybil 𝒵𝒵𝒵 **1976** Fact-based story of a woman who developed 16 distinct personalities, and the supportive psychiatrist who helped her put the pieces of her ego together. Excellent made-for-television production with Field's Emmy-winning performance. **122m/C VHS, Beta.** Sally Field, Joanne Woodward, Brad Davis, Martine Bartlett, Jane Hoffman; **D:** Daniel Petrie. *FOX*

Sylvester 𝒵𝒵 **1985 (PG)** A 16-year-old girl and a cranky stockyard boss team up to train a battered horse named Sylvester for the National Equestrian trials. Nice riding sequences and good performances can't overcome familiar plot, but the kids will enjoy this one. **104m/C VHS, Beta, LV, Closed Caption.** Melissa Gilbert, Richard Farnsworth, Michael Schoeffling, Constance Towers; **D:** Tim Hunter. *COL*

Sylvia 𝒵𝒵½ **1986 (PG)** Biography of author/educator Sylvia Ashton-Warner, and her efforts to teach Maori children in New Zealand to read via unorthodox methods. David is a marvel. Based on Ashton-Warner's books "Teacher" and "I Passed This Way." **99m/C VHS, Beta, Closed Caption.** *NZ* Eleanor David, Tom Wilkinson, Nigel Terry, Mary Regan; **D:** Michael Firth. *FOX*

Sylvia and the Phantom 𝒵𝒵𝒵 *Sylvia and the Ghost* **1945** A charming French comedy about a lonely young girl who is befriended by the ghost of a man killed decades earlier in a duel over the girl's grandmother. Based on the play by Alfred Adam. In French with English subtitles. **88m/B VHS, Beta.** *FR* Odette Joyeux, Jacques Tati, Francois Perier; **D:** Claude Autant-Lara. *HMV, NLC*

Sylvia Scarlett 𝒵𝒵½ **1935** An odd British comedy about a woman who masquerades as a boy while on the run with her father, who causes all kinds of instinctive confusion in the men she meets. **94m/B VHS, Beta, LV.** Katharine Hepburn, Cary Grant, Brian Aherne, Edmund Gwenn, Natalie Paley, Dennie Moore, Lennox Pawle, Daisy Belmore, Nola Luxford; **D:** George Cukor; **C:** Russell Metty. *FCT, TTC*

Sympathy for the Devil 𝒵𝒵 *One Plus One* **1970** Rolling Stones provide music for confused, revolutionary documentary. Episodic jumble is odd, sometimes fascinating. **110m/C VHS, Beta.** *FR* Mick Jagger, Rolling Stones; **D:** Jean-Luc Godard. *FOX, OM*

Symphony in the Mountains 𝒵𝒵½ **1935** An early German sound romance, where an Austrian singing teacher falls in love with the sister of one of his student's. Featuring choral work by the Vienna Boys' Choir. In German with English subtitles. **75m/B VHS, Beta.** *GE FCT, IHF, GLV*

Synapse 𝒵𝒵 **1995 (R)** Black-marketeer Andre (Makepeace) is doublecrossed by a partner and arrested by Life Corp., which runs this futuristic civilization. As an experimental punishment, his mind is implanted into the body of Celeste (Duffy), who manages to escape and join up with a band of revolutionaries determined to destroy the evil corporation. Fast-paced story and good special effects. **CW:** Strong violence, and for sexuality and language. **89m/C VHS.** Karen Duffy, Saul Rubinek, Matt McCoy, Chris Makepeace; **D:** Allan Goldstein. *AVE*

Syngenor 𝒵½ **1990 (R)** Syngenor stands for Synthesized Genetic Organism, to differentiate it from all other organisms. Created by science, it escapes, and a crack team of scientists and gung-ho military types are mobilized to track it down. **98m/C VHS.** Starr Andreeff, Michael Laurence, David Gale, Charles Lucia, Riva Spier, Jeff Doucette, Bill Gratton, Lewis Arquette, Jon Korkes, Melanie Shatner; **D:** George Elanjian Jr.; **M:** Tom Chase, Steve Rucker.

T-Bird Gang 𝒵½ **1959** A high school student goes undercover to infiltrate a teen gang. When his cover is blown, things get hairy. Laughable sleazebag production. **75m/B VHS.** Ed Nelson, John Brinkley, Pat George, Beach Dickerson, Tony Miller; **D:** Richard Harbinger; **M:** Shelley Manne. *SNC*

T Bone N Weasel 𝒵𝒵 **1992 (PG-13)** Hines and Lloyd play not-so-ex-cons who steal a car and try to lead a life of ease. Crime doesn't pay. Made for cable television. **94m/C VHS, LV.** Gregory Hines, Christopher Lloyd. *TTC*

T-Force 𝒵𝒵½ **1994 (R)** T-Force is a successful cybernetic law enforcement team set up in the year 2007. But when innocent people get caught in the T-Force crossfire, a team shutdown is ordered, causing the members to turn renegade and fight for their survival instead. The plot rarely gets in the way of the hard-hitting action. **CW:** Non-stop sci-fi violence; some sexuality. **101m/C VHS, LV, Closed Caption.** Jack Scalia, Erin Gray, Evan Lurie, Daron McBee; **D:** Richard Pepin. *PMH*

T-Men 𝒵𝒵𝒵 **1947** Treasury Department agents Dennis O'Brien (O'Keefe) and Tony Genaro (Ryder) infiltrate a mob counterfeiting gang. Filmed in semi-documentary style, exciting tale serves also as an effective commentary on the similarities between the agents and those they pursue. Mann and cinematographer Alton do especially fine work here. **96m/B VHS, LV.** Alfred Ryder, Dennis O'Keefe, June Lockhart, Mary Meade, Wallace Ford, Charles McGraw; **D:** Anthony Mann; **C:** John Alton. Nominations: Academy Awards '47: Best Sound. *KIV*

Table for Five 𝒵𝒵½ **1983 (PG)** A divorced father takes his children on a Mediterranean cruise and while sailing, he learns that his ex-wife has died. The father and his ex-wife's husband struggle over who should raise the children. Sentimental and well-acted. **120m/C VHS, Beta, LV.** Jon Voight, Millie Perkins, Richard Crenna, Robbie Kiger, Roxana Zal, Son Hoang Bui, Marie-Christine Barrault, Kevin Costner; **D:** Robert Liebmann; **W:** David Seltzer; **M:** Miles Goodman. *FOX*

Table Settings 𝒵𝒵 **1984** A taped performance of James Lapines' comedy about the lives of three generations of a Jewish family. **90m/C VHS, Beta.** Robert Klein, Stockard Channing, Dinah Manoff, Eileen Heckart. *NO*

Tabloid! 𝒵½ **1988** Unorthodox woman prints and sells racy trash for enquiring minds. **99m/C VHS.** Scott Davis, Glen Cobum; **D:** Bret McCormick, Matt Shaffen. *HHE*

Tabu: A Story of the South Seas 𝒵𝒵𝒵½ **1931** Fascinating docudrama about a young pearl diver's ill-fated romance. The gods have declared the young woman he desires "taboo" to all men. Filmed on location in Tahiti. Authored and produced by Murnau and Flaherty. Flaherty left in mid-production due to artistic differences with Murnau, who was later killed in an auto accident one week before the premiere of film. **81m/B VHS, Beta. D:** Robert Flaherty, F.W. Murnau;

C: Floyd Crosby. Academy Awards '31: Best Cinematography, National Film Registry '94. *MIL, GVV, LUM*

Taffin 𝒵½ **1988 (R)** An Irish bill collector battles a group of corrupt businessmen who want to replace the local soccer field with a hazardous chemical plant. Pretty dull fare, overall, with Brosnan much less charismatic than usual. **96m/C VHS, Beta, LV.** *GB* Pierce Brosnan, Ray McAnally, Alison Doody, Patrick Bergin; **D:** Francis Megahy; **W:** David Ambrose. *MGM*

Tag: The Assassination Game 𝒵½ **1982 (PG)** An exciting new game has been discovered by a group of university students. Players act as spies and assassins, "killing" each other to make points. But a school newspaper sportswriter finds the game has become more real than make-believe. Timely topic in the early '80s when Dungeons and Dragons and other "war" games were popular on college campuses across the nation. **92m/C VHS, Beta.** Robert Carradine, Linda Hamilton, Michael Winslow, Kristine DeBell, Perry Lang; **D:** Nick Castle; **W:** Nick Castle.

Tagget 𝒵 **1990 (PG-13)** A former CIA operative who has erased his nightmarish stint in Vietnam gradually begins to recall his past. When pieces of the puzzle begin to come together, he remembers a few things that the government would prefer he forget. Soon, CIA men are on his trail and their mission is to see that he forgets his past—permanently. Made for cable television. **89m/C VHS, Closed Caption.** Daniel J. Travanti, William Sadler, Roxanne Hart, Stephen Tobolowsky, Peter Michael Goetz, Sarah Douglas, Noel Harrison; **D:** Richard T. Heffron. *USH*

Tai Chi 2 𝒵½ **19??** Young Tai Chi master (Wu) battles corrupt officials and English merchants who are flooding the country with opium. And then he turns around and battles a bunch of high-kicking rivals for the love of a beautiful revolutionary (Chung). Chinese with subtitles or dubbed. **95m/C VHS.** *HK* Jacky Wu, Christy Chung, Sibelle Hu; **D:** Yuen Woo Ping. *TAI*

Tai-Pan 𝒵½ **1986 (R)** A 19th century Scottish trader and his beautiful Chinese mistress are the main characters in this confusing attempt to dramatize the story of Hong Kong's development into a thriving trading port. Too many subplots and characters are introduced in a short time to do justice to James Clavell's novel of the same name, the basis for the movie. The first American production completely filmed in China. **130m/C VHS, Beta, LV, Closed Caption.** Bryan Brown, Joan Chen, John Stanton, Kyra Sedgwick, Tim Guinee, Russell Wong, Bert Remsen; **D:** Daryl Duke; **W:** John Briley; **C:** Jack Cardiff; **M:** Maurice Jarre. *VES*

Tails You Live, Heads You're Dead 𝒵𝒵 **1995 (R)** Cable thriller features Bernsen as psycho Neil Jones, who kills at random—and tells a stranger, Jeff Quint (McGinley), whom he met at a bar that the man is his next victim. After several unsuccessful attempts on his life, Quint turns to private detective McKinley (Matheson) for help. Based on the short story "Liar's Dice" by Bill Pronzini. **CW:** Some violence. **91m/C VHS, Beta, Closed Caption.** Corbin Bernsen, Ted McGinley, Tim Matheson, Maria Del Mar; **D:** Tim Matheson; **W:** Miguel Tejada-Flores; **C:** Francois Protat; **M:** David Michael Frank. *PAR*

Tailspin: Behind the Korean Airline Tragedy 𝒵 **1989** Made-for-TV docudrama on the 1983 downing of Korean Aire flight 007 in Soviet airspace. Purports to show the U.S. government's reaction to what became a major international incident. **82m/C VHS, Beta, LV.** Michael Moriarty, Michael Murphy, Chris Sarandon, Harris Yulin, Gavan O'Herlihy, Ed O'Ross; **D:** David Darlow; **M:** David Ferguson. *PAR*

Tailspin Tommy 1934 Features 12 chapters of the great action serial. **?m/B VHS.** Maurice Murphy, Noah Beery Jr., Walter Miller, Patricia Farr, Grant Withers, John Davidson, William Desmond, Charles A. Browne; **D:** Lew (Louis Friedlander) Landers. *GPV*

Tainted *√½* 1988 Small-town woman tries to endure after being raped. Both her husband and the attacker are killed, and she is forced to conceal their deaths. Poorly scripted. 90m/C VHS, Beta. Shari Shattuck, Park Overall, Gene Tootle, Magilla Schaus, Blaque Fowler; *D:* Orestes Matacena.

Tainted Blood *√√* 1993 (R) Welch stars as an investigative reporter whose latest story has her attempting to find the teenage twin of a psychotic killer. *CW:* Violence. 86m/C VHS, Beta, Closed Caption. Raquel Welch, Alley Mills, Kerri Green, Natasha Gregson Wagner, Joan Van Ark; *D:* Matthew Patrick; *W:* Kathleen Rowell, Ginny Cerrella; *C:* Billy Dickson. PAR

Tainted Image *√√* 1991 Artist woman starts to lose sanity with help of boyfriend, psycho neighbor and rash of bizarre deaths. She turns to canvas for solace and decides she needs secret ingredient that can't be found in art supply store to complete masterpiece. 95m/C VHS. Tom Saunders, Sandra Frances, Annetta Arpin, Ken La Mothe, Heidi Emerich, Steve Kornacki. HHT, DMP

The Take *√√* 1990 (R) Recovering alcoholic cop faces wrath of drug lord and marriage on the rocks. 91m/C VHS. Ray Sharkey, R. Lee Ermey, Lisa Hartman Black, Larry Manetti, Joe Lala; *D:* Leon Ichaso; *W:* Edward Anhalt, Handel Glassberg; *M:* David Beal. USH

Take a Hard Ride *√½* 1975 (R) Dull spaghetti western about a cowboy transporting money to Mexico, evading bandits and bounty hunters. 103m/C VHS, Beta. Jim Brown, Lee Van Cleef, Fred Williamson, Jim Kelly, Barry Sullivan; *D:* Anthony (Antonio Margheriti) Dawson; *M:* Jerry Goldsmith. FOX

Take Down *√√* 1979 (PG) Hermann is charming as a high school English teacher turned reluctant wrestling coach. 96m/C VHS, Beta. Lorenzo Lamas, Kathleen Lloyd, Maureen McCormick, Edward Herrmann; *D:* Keith Merrill. UNI

Take It Big *√½* 1944 Uninspired B-musical starring the Tin Man from the "Wizard of Oz." Haley is an impoverished actor who inherits a ranch and saves it by—surprise—putting on a show. ♫Sunday, Monday, and Always; Love and Learn; Life Can Be Beautiful; Take It Big; I'm a Big Success with You. 75m/B VHS, Beta. Jack Haley, Harriet Hilliard Nelson, Mary Beth Hughes, Arline Judge, Nils T. Granlund, Fuzzy Knight, Ozzie Nelson; *D:* Frank McDonald. NOS, VYY, DVT

Take Me Back to Oklahoma *√* 1940 Musical western with comedy. 64m/B VHS, Beta. Tex Ritter, Terry Walker, Karl Hackett, George Eldridge; *D:* Al(bert) Herman. NOS, VCN, VYY

Take Me Out to the Ball Game *√√½* Everybody's Cheering 1949 Williams manages a baseball team, locks horns with players Sinatra and Kelly, and wins them over with song. Naturally, there's a water ballet scene. Contrived and forced, but enjoyable. ♫Take Me Out to the Ball Game; The Hat My Father Wore on St. Patrick's Day; O'Brien to Ryan to Goldberg; The Right Girl for me; It's Fate, Baby, It's Fate; Yes, Indeedy; Strictly U.S.A. 93m/C VHS, Beta, LV. Frank Sinatra, Gene Kelly, Esther Williams, Jules Munshin, Betty Garrett, Edward Arnold, Tom Dugan, Richard Lane; *D:* Busby Berkeley. MGM

Take the Money and Run *√√√* 1969 (PG) Allen's directing debut; he also co-wrote and starred. "Documentary" follows a timid, would-be bank robber who can't get his career off the ground and keeps landing in jail. Little plot, but who cares? Nonstop one-liners and slapstick. 85m/C VHS, Beta, LV. Woody Allen, Janet Margolin, Marcel Hillaire, Louise Lasser; *D:* Woody Allen; *W:* Woody Allen; *M:* Marvin Hamlisch. FOX

Take This Job & Shove It *√√* 1981 (PG) The Johnny Paycheck song inspired this story of a hot-shot efficiency expert who returns to his hometown to streamline the local brewery. Encounters with old pals inspire self-questioning. Alternately inspired and hackneyed. Cameos by Paycheck and other country stars. 100m/C VHS, Beta, Closed Caption. Robert Hays, Art Carney, Barbara Hershey, David Keith, Martin Mull, Eddie Albert, Penelope

Milford; *Cameos:* Johnny Paycheck, David Allen Coe, Charlie Rich, Lacy J. Dalton; *D:* Gus Trikonis; *W:* Barry Schneider. COL

Take Two *√* 1987 (R) A woman has an affair with her husband's twin brother. Interesting metaphysically: Are you my husband or my lover? But is an adultery/murder drama with Frank Stallone worth 101 minutes of your time? 101m/C VHS, Beta, LV. Grant Goodeve, Robin Mattson, Frank Stallone, Warren Berlinger, Darwyn Swalve, Nita Talbot; *D:* Peter Rowe.

Take Your Best Shot *√½* 1982 Standard TV fare about an out-of-work actor struggling with his low self-esteem and his failing marriage. Made-for-television comedy. 96m/C VHS, Beta. Robert Urich, Meredith Baxter, Jeffrey Tambor, Jack Bannon, Claudette Nevins; *D:* David Greene. ART

Taken Away *√√½* 1989 Struggling young divorcee Stephanie Monroe waits tables during the day and studies to be a computer tech at night in order to provide her eight-year-old daughter Abby with a better life. Unable to afford child care, Stephanie leaves Abby alone in the afternoon until she can get home from work. But when the welfare system finds out Stephanie is accused of child neglect and must fight a bureaucratic nightmare in order to get her child back. Made for television. 94m/C VHS, LV. Valerie Bertinelli, Kevin Dunn, Joshua Maurer, Anna Maria Horsford, Juliet Sorcey, Nada Despotovich, Matthew Faison, James Arone; *D:* John D. Patterson; *W:* Robert Freedman, Selma Thomson. USH

The Takeover *√½* 1994 (R) East coast crime boss Danny Stein (Drago) decides to take over the L.A. operations of rival Tony Valachi (Mancuso). Lots of mayhem ensues. *CW:* Gangster violence, sexuality, and language. 91m/C VHS, LV, Closed Caption. Billy Drago, Nick Mancuso, John Savage, Eric Da Re, Cali Timmins, David Amos, Gene Mitchell; *D:* Troy Cook; *W:* Gene Mitchell; *M:* Jimmy Lifton. ART

Takin' It All Off woof! 1987 In this sequel to "Takin' It Off," Kitten does it again with unbelievable bumps and grinds. 90m/C VHS. Francesca "Kitten" Natividad; *D:* Ed Hansen. ART, VES

Taking Care of Business *√½* Filofax 1990 (R) Too familiar tale of switched identity has crazed Cubs fan Belushi find Grodin's Filofax, allowing him to pose as businessman. Old jokes and a story full of holes. 108m/C VHS, Beta, LV, Closed Caption. James Belushi, Charles Grodin, Anne DeSalvo, Loryn Locklin, Veronica Hamel, Hector Elizondo, Mako, Gates McFadden, Stephen Elliott; *D:* Arthur Hiller; *W:* Jeffrey Abrams. HPH

The Taking of Beverly Hills *√½* 1991 (R) Deranged billionaire Bat Masterson designs a bogus toxic spill that leaves the wealth of Beverly Hills his for the taking. Football hero Boomer Hayes teams up with renegade cop Ed Kelvin to try and stop Masterson and save the city of Beverly Hills. *CW:* Language and some violence. 96m/C VHS, LV, Letterbox, Closed Caption. Ken Wahl, Matt Frewer, Robert Davi, Harley Jane Kozak, Lee James, Branscombe Richmond, Lyman Ward, Michael Bowen, William Prince, Ken Swofford, George Wyner; *D:* Sidney J. Furie; *W:* Sidney J. Furie, David Burke. COL, NLC

The Taking of Flight 847: The Uli Derickson Story *√√√* The Flight 1988 Wagner plays the stewardess who acted as a go-between for the passengers during a 1985 terrorist hijacking, saving all but one life. True-story drama is suspenseful and entertaining, nominated for several Emmys. Made-for-television drama. 100m/C VHS, LV. Laurie Walters, Sandy McPeak, Ray Wise, Leslie Easterbrook, Lindsay Wagner, Eli Danker, Joseph Naser; *D:* Paul Wendkos; *W:* Norman Merrill. IME

The Taking of Pelham One Two Three *√√√* 1974 (R) A hijack team, lead by the ruthless Shaw, seizes a New York City subway car and holds the 17 passengers for one million dollars ransom. Fine pacing keeps things on the edge. New cinematic techniques used by cameraman Owen Roizman defines shadowy areas like never before. 105m/C VHS, Beta. Robert

Shaw, Walter Matthau, Martin Balsam, Hector Elizondo, James Broderick, Earl Hindman, Dick O'Neill, Jerry Stiller, Tony Roberts, Doris Roberts, Kenneth McMillan, Julius W. Harris, Sal Viscuso; *D:* Joseph Sargent; *C:* Owen Roizman; *M:* David Shire. MGM, FOX

Taking the Heat *√√½* 1993 (R) When mobster Arkin kills a sporting-goods dealer with a golf club the murder is witnessed by yuppie Goldwyn. Whitfield is the ambitious cop who wants Goldwyn to testify against the gangster—if she can keep him alive long enough to get him to court. One long chase scene. Made for cable television. 91m/C VHS. Lynn Whitfield, Tony Goldwyn, Alan Arkin, George Segal, Peter Boyle; *D:* Tom Mankiewicz; *W:* Dan Gordon. FOX

Tale of a Vampire *√√½* 1992 (R) In present day London, ageless vampire Alex (Sands) still mourns his long-lost vampiric love, Virginia, when he meets Anne (Hamilton) (who resembles Virginia). Alex doesn't know he's being stalked by Virginia's husband, Edgar (Cranham), also a vampire. Edgar decides to use Anne (with whom Alex has fallen in love) as bait, in a revenge plot. A tiny budget and slow pacing mar the film's fine visual style and good work by the two male leads. Film debut for director Sato. *CW:* Vampire violence and gore. 93m/C VHS. GB Julian Sands, Kenneth Cranham, Suzanna Hamilton; *D:* Shimako Sato; *W:* Jane Corbett, Shimako Sato; *M:* Julian Joseph. THV

The Tale of Ruby Rose *√√√* 1987 (PG) Living in the mountains of Tasmania, Ruby Rose, her husband Henry, and their adopted son Gem, struggle to survive the '30s depression by hunting and trapping. Having spent all her life in the mountains, Ruby Rose has a very superstitious view of life and a terror of nightfall. But after an argument with her husband, Ruby Rose sets out on a cross-country journey to find her grandmother and discover the secrets of her past. 101m/C VHS. AU Melita Jurisic, Chris Haywood; *D:* Roger Sholes; *W:* Roger Sholes; *M:* Paul Schutze. NO

A Tale of Springtime *√√½* 1992 (PG) Comedy-romance is the first film in Rohmer's planned new series, the "Tales of the Four Seasons," not to be confused with his "Six Moral Tales" or his "Comedies and Proverbs." Centers around Jeanne, a high school philosophy teacher; Natacha, a young student; and Igor, Natacha's father. As characteristic of Rohmer films, texture and character largely overshadow linear plots and social messages. However, the efficiency and directness of his camerawork make it a pleasure to watch. 107m/C VHS, Closed Caption. FR Anne Teyssedre, Hugues Quester, Florence Darel, Eloise Bennett, Sophie Robin; *D:* Eric Rohmer; *W:* Eric Rohmer. ORI

The Tale of the Frog Prince *√√√½* 1983 Superb edition of Shelley Duvall's "Faerie Tale Theatre" finds Williams the victim of an angry fairy godmother's spell. Garr to the rescue as the self-centered princess who saves him with a kiss. Directed and written by Idle of Monty Python fame. 60m/C VHS, Beta, LV, Closed Caption. Robin Williams, Teri Garr; *D:* Eric Idle; *W:* Eric Idle. FOX

A Tale of Two Cities *√√√√* 1936 Lavish production of the Dickens' classic set during the French Revolution, about two men who bear a remarkable resemblance to each other, both in love with the same girl. Carefree lawyer Sydney Carton (Colman) roused to responsibility, makes the ultimate sacrifice. A memorable Madame DeFarge from stage star Yurka in her film debut, with assistance from other Dickens' film stars Rathbone, Oliver, and Walthall. 128m/B VHS, Beta. Ronald Colman, Elizabeth Allan, Edna May Oliver, Reginald Owen, Isabel Jewell, Walter Catlett, H.B. Warner, Donald Woods, Basil Rathbone, Blanche Yurka, Henry B. Walthall; *D:* Jack Conway; *W:* W.P. Lipscomb, S.N. Behrman; *M:* Herbert Stothart. Nominations: Academy Awards '36: Best Film Editing, Best Picture. MGM, KUI, IGP

A Tale of Two Cities 🎬🎬🎬 1958 A well-done British version of the Dickens' classic about a lawyer who sacrifices himself to save another man from the guillotine during the French Reign of Terror. The sixth remake of the tale. 117m/B VHS, Beta. **GB** Dirk Bogarde, Dorothy Tutin, Christopher Lee, Donald Pleasence, Ian-Bannen, Cecil Parker; **D:** Ralph Thomas. BFA, FHS

A Tale of Two Cities 🎬🎬½ 1980 Impressive looking but bloodless adaptation of the Dickens novel set in the French Revolution. Sardon takes on the dual role of sacrificing English lawyer Carton and French nobleman Darnay, with Krige as the lovely woman caught between the two. Made for television. 156m/C VHS. Chris Sarandon, Alice Krige, Peter Cushing, Kenneth More, Barry Morse, Flora Robson, Billie Whitelaw; **D:** Jim Goddard; **W:** John Gay. ART, FUS

A Tale of Two Cities 🎬🎬🎬 1991 Masterpiece Theatre production of the classic Dickens tale. The French revolution was a time of revenge and brutality, but also provided the proving ground for a love greater than life. Terrific cast and perfectly detailed production. On two cassettes. 240m/C VHS, **Closed Caption.** James Wilby, Serena Gordon, John Mills, Jean-Pierre Aumont, Anna Massey. PBS, VIF, TVC

Tale of Two Cities/In the Switch Tower 🎬½ 1915 A package of two medium-length silent films, the latter featuring a rare acting appearance by director Borzage. 70m/B VHS, Beta, 8mm. Walter Edwards, Maurice Costello, Florence Turner, Frank Borzage, Norma Talmadge, Leo Delaney. VYY

Tale of Two Sisters 🎬🎬½ 1989 Sheen narrates sensual drama about two beautiful, ambitious sisters. 90m/C VHS. Valerie Breiman, Claudia Christian, Sydney Lassick, Jeff Conaway. NO

A Tale of Winter 🎬🎬½ Conte D'Hiver 1992 Portrays the romantic trials of a young French woman who cannot choose between her two smitten lovers and her one true love, the long disappeared father of her child. Felicie (Very) hopelessly loves Charles (Van Den Driessche), whom she met five years before, but mistakenly gave the wrong address. Rohmer's trademark conversation-filled scenes find her brooding over her predicament, running from one lover and back again, until a revelation during a viewing of Shakespeare's "The Winter's Tale." A charming cast carries the story to a surprise twist of an ending. Second in the series "Tales of the Four Seasons." In French with English subtitles. 114m/C VHS. **FR** Charlotte Very, Frederic Van Dren Driessche, Michel Voletti, Herve Furic, Ava Loraschi, Jean-Luc Revol, Haydee Caillot, Jean-Claude Biette, Rosette, Marie Riviere; **D:** Eric Rohmer; **W:** Eric Rohmer; **C:** Luc Pages; **M:** Sebastien Erms. NYF

Talent for the Game 🎬🎬½ 1991 (PG) A slight but handsomely produced baseball pleasantry about a talent scout who recruits a phenomenal young pitcher, then sees the kid exploited by the team owner. More like an anecdote than a story, with an ending that aims a little too hard to please. Good for sports fans and family audiences. 91m/C VHS, Beta, LV, **Closed Caption.** Edward James Olmos, Lorraine Bracco, Jeff Corbett, Jamey Sheridan, Terry Kinney; **D:** Robert M. Young; **W:** David Himmelstein, Tom Donnelly, Larry Ferguson; **M:** David Newman. PAR

Tales from a Parallel Universe: Eating Pattern 🎬🎬 Eating Pattern 1997 (R) The Lexx space cruiser is part machine and part organic matter, so it needs nourishment, as does its crew. But Zev and Stanley make a big mistake stopping for food at the planet Klaagya. Seems the inhabitants are controlled by parasitic worms that feed on their brains and they're always interested in a fresh meal. Now it's up to Kai to come to the rescue. Third episode in the series. 93m/C VHS, **Closed Caption.** Brian Downey, Eva Habermann, Michael McManus, Rutger Hauer. PAR

Tales from a Parallel Universe: Giga Shadow 🎬🎬 Giga Shadow 1997 (R) The Lexx crew must make a dangerous attempt to replenish Kai's supply of proto-blood, which brings them perilously near their arch-enemy, His Shadow. **CW:** Violence/gore and sexual symbolism. 93m/C VHS, **Closed Caption.** Brian Downey, Eva Habermann, Michael McManus, Malcolm McDowell; **D:** Robert Sigl. PAR

Tales from a Parallel Universe: I Worship His Shadow 🎬🎬 I Worship His Shadow 1997 (R) Space rebels try to unseat a tyrannical ruler known as His Shadow in this cable movie that's the first of a four-part series. A prophecy states that the ruler will be defeated by a dying race and aiding that prediction are rebel leader Thodin (Bostwick), cowardly Stanley Tweedle (Downey), warrior Kai (McManus) and Zev (Habermann), His Shadow's unwilling love slave. Followed by the "Super Nova" episode. **CW:** Sci-fi violence and gore. 95m/C VHS, **Closed Caption.** Brian Downey, Eva Habermann, Michael McManus, Barry Bostwick, Ellen Dubin; **D:** Paul Donovan; **W:** Paul Donovan; **C:** Les Krizsan; **M:** Marty Simon. PAR

Tales from a Parallel Universe: Super Nova 🎬🎬 Super Nova 1997 (R) A continuation of the "I Worship His Shadow" episode, which finds the rebels in possession of the mile-long spacecraft known as The Lexx, which also happens to be the most destructive weapon in the universe. But they don't want to destroy the craft, instead they use the Lexx to visit the lost planet of Brunnis in hopes of restoring their lost leader to life. Only the rebels get captured by the Poet Man (Curry), and their deaths could lead to the total annihilation of the universe. **CW:** Sex-related material and brief violence. 93m/C VHS, **Closed Caption.** Brian Downey, Eva Habermann, Michael McManus, Ellen Dubin, Tim Curry; **D:** Ron Oliver; **W:** Paul Donovan; **C:** Les Krizsan. PAR

Tales from Avonlea, Vol. 1: The Journey Begins Road to Avonlea; Avonlea 1990 From the producer of the popular "Anne of Green Gables" movie and its sequel comes this weekly TV series, a collaboration of the Disney channel and CBC Television. In "The Journey Begins," Sara meets her stuffy Aunt Hetty and her cousins Felix and Felicity. Unhappy with her life, she decides whether to stay or run away. "The Proof of the Pudding" finds the grownups away and Felicity in charge of her siblings and Sara for the weekend. The same attention to detail, particularly in scenic views of lovely Prince Edward Island and the costumes, is shown in the series. Based on the writings of Lucy Maud Montgomery. 106m/C VHS, Beta, **Closed Caption. CA** Sarah Polley, Jackie Burroughs, Gema Zamprogna. DIS, BTV

Tales from the Crypt 🎬🎬🎬 1972 (PG) A collection of five scary stories from the classic EC comics that bear the movie's title. Richardson tells the future to each of five people gathered in a cave, each tale involving misfortune and, of course, gore. 92m/C VHS, Beta. **GB** Ralph Richardson, Joan Collins, Peter Cushing, Richard Greene, Ian Hendry; **D:** Freddie Francis.

Tales from the Crypt 1989 Three contemporary tales of the macabre, "The Man Who Was Death," "'Twas the Night Before," and "Dig That Cat...He's Real Gone," linked together by a special-effects host. Ry Cooder provides the musical score for the second episode. Based on stories published by William M. Gaines in EC Comics; made-for-cable-television. 81m/C VHS, Beta, LV. William Sadler, Mary Ellen Trainor, Larry Drake, Joe Pantoliano, Robert Wuhl, Gintas Vintas; **D:** Richard Donner, Walter Hill, Robert Zemeckis; **M:** Ry Cooder, Alan Silvestri. HBO

Tales from the Crypt Presents Bordello of Blood 🎬🎬 Bordello of Blood 1996 (R) Detective Rafe Guttman (Miller) is on the case of a Bible thumper's (Eliniak) missing brother (Feldman). The trail leads to a unique establishment, a brothel presided over by vampire queen Lilith (Everhart), whose clients all wind up dead (but probably with smiles on their faces), and the strange Reverend Current (Sarandon, who made a fine vampire himself in "Fright Night"). Crypt Keeper's second big screen outing showcases Miller's slant on the leading man gig and serves up campy fun with the blood. **CW:** Horror violence and gore, sexuality, nudity, and strong language. 87m/C VHS, LV, **Closed Caption.** Dennis Miller, Angie Everhart, Chris Sarandon, Corey Feldman, Erika Eleniak; **D:** Gilbert Adler; **W:** Gilbert Adler, A.L. Katz; **C:** Tom Priestley; **M:** Chris Boardman. USH

Tales from the Crypt Presents Demon Knight 🎬🎬 Demon Knight; Demon Keeper 1994 (R) Gruesomely garish big-screen version of the TV series that was inspired by the lurid 1950s E.C. comics. Horrormeister Crypt Keeper offers his usual pun-filled introduction to a tale set in a seedy boarding-house. Brayker (Sadler) is the guardian of an ancient key that keeps the forces of darkness from overwhelming mankind, a key desired by the charismatic Collector (Zane), who unleashes a disgusting mix of demons against the house's inhabitants. Curious hybrid of spoof/splatter pic that doesn't quite work in either genre. **CW:** Violence; gore; nudity; strong language. 93m/C VHS, LV, **Closed Caption.** Billy Zane, William Sadler, Jada Pinkett Smith, Brenda Bakke, CCH Pounder, Dick Miller, Thomas Haden Church, John Schuck, Gary Farmer, Charles Fleischer; **D:** Ernest R. Dickerson; **W:** Ethan Reiff, Cyrus Voris, Mark Bishop; **C:** Rick Bota; **M:** Ed Shearmur; **V:** John Kassir. USH

Tales from the Crypt, Vol. 3 1990 Three more tales of terror from the made-for-cable-television series. "Dead Right" has Moore as a golddigger who takes a fortuneteller's advice and marries a penniless slob. "Cutting Cards" has Tighe and Hendricksen involved in a very high stakes game. "The Switch" features Hickey as a wealthy old man bartering for a new body to woo the beautiful Preston. 80m/C VHS, Beta, **Closed Caption.** Demi Moore, William Hickey, Kelly Preston, Jeffrey Tambor, Rick Rossovich, Lance Henriksen, Kevin Tighe; **D:** Arnold Schwarzenegger, Walter Hill, Howard Deutch. WAR, MOV

Tales from the Darkside 1985 Each episode of this series features several short Twilight Zone-esque stories of fantasy and suspense. Additional tapes available. 70m/C VHS, Beta, LV. ART, MOV

Tales from the Darkside: The Movie 1990 (R) Three short stories in the tradition of the ghoulish TV show are brought to the big screen, with mixed results. The plot centers around a boy who is being held captive by a cannibal. In order to prolong his life, he tells her horror stories. The tales were written by Sir Arthur Conan Doyle, Stephen King, and Michael McDowell. 93m/C VHS, Beta, LV, **Closed Caption.** Deborah Harry, Christian Slater, David Johansen, William Hickey, James Remar, Rae Dawn Chong, Julianne Moore, Robert Klein, Steve Buscemi, Matthew Lawrence; **D:** John Harrison; **W:** George A. Romero, Michael McDowell. PAR

Tales from the Gimli Hospital 🎬🎬 1988 A smallpox outbreak at the turn of the century finds Einar and Gunnar sharing a hospital room. They begin telling each other increasingly bizarre personal secrets and develop a serious rivalry. Sharp dialogue with some equally grotesque imagery. Director Maddin's first feature film. 72m/B VHS, **Closed Caption.** Kyle McCulloch, Michael Gottli; **D:** Guy Maddin. KIV, FCT

Tales from the Hood 🎬🎬 1995 (R) Horror anthology with that urban twist. Three young thugs search for lost drugs inside a funeral parlor run by creepy Mr. Simms (Williams III) and instead walk into a world of four chilling and funny stories of fright dealing with racism and black on black crime. Tales aren't very original and are often too preachy for true enjoyment, but its nice to see someone attempt to breath life into an old and familiar genre. Williams III, with his pop-eyed stares and Don King coif, is fitting as the eerie storyteller. *CW:* Graphic brutal violence and strong language. **97m/C VHS.** Clarence Williams III, Corbin Bernsen, David Alan Grier, Wings Hauser, Rosalind Cash, Rusty Cundieff, Joe Torry, Anthony Griffith; *D:* Rusty Cundieff; *W:* Rusty Cundieff, Darin Scott; *C:* Anthony B. Richmond; *M:* Christopher Young. HBO

Tales from the Snow Zone 1991
"Tales from the Snow Zone" is the latest feature length ski film from RAP producers Jon Long and James Angrove. Filmed entirely in the 1991 ski season, this film captures the essence of the sport and lifestyle. "Tales" covers true extreme skiing, radical free skiing, moguls, downhill ski racing, telemarking, snowboarding, and monoskiing. Filmed in Europe and North America, "Tales" features skiers from the United States, Canada, France, Sweden, and Australia. **70m/C VHS.** RAP

Tales of Beatrix Potter 🎬🎬🎬½
Peter Rabbit and Tales of Beatrix Potter 1971 **(G)** The Royal Ballet Company of England performs in this adaptation of the adventures of Beatrix Potter's colorful and memorable creatures. Beautifully done. **90m/C VHS.** GB *D:* Reginald Mills. REP, HMV

Tales of Erotica 🎬🎬
Die Erotische Geschichten 1993 **(R)** Four stories made for German TV. "The Dutch Master" finds New Yorker Teresa (Sorvino) becoming obsessed with a Vermeer-style painting at a museum. She begins to dress like the lively characters and eventually disappears into the picture itself. "The Insatiable Mrs. Kirsch" finds a vacationing writer (Shepherd) becoming fascinated by a fellow guest (Baynes), who seems to be hiding something. In "Vroom Vroom Vroom" luckless Leroy (Barboza) asks a voodoo doctor for help with the girls and winds up with a motorcycle that transforms itself into a beautiful woman when ridden. "Wet" has bathroom-fixture salesman Bruce (Howard) enticed by persistent customer Davida (Williams), who insists they both try out the showroom hot tub before she'll consider buying. *CW:* Scenes of sexuality and nudity, and for some language. **104m/C VHS.** GE Mira Sorvino, Aida Turturro, Simon Shepherd, Hetty Baynes, Ken Russell, Richard Barboza, Arliss Howard, Cynda Williams; *D:* Ken Russell, Susan Seidelman, Melvin Van Peebles, Bob Rafelson; *W:* Susan Seidelman, Melvin Van Peebles, Bob Rafelson, Jonathan Brett; *C:* Maryse Alberti, Hong Manley, Igor Sunara; *M:* Melvin Van Peebles, Wendy Blackstone, David McHugh. THV

The Tales of Hoffmann 🎬🎬½
1951 A ballet-opera consisting of three stories by Jacques Offenbach covering romance, magic and mystery arising out of a poet's misadventures in love. Lavishly designed and highly stylized. **138m/C VHS, LV.** Robert Rounseville, Robert Helpmann, Moira Shearer; *D:* Michael Powell, Emeric Pressburger. Nominations: Academy Awards '51: Best Art Direction/Set Decoration (Color), Best Costume Design (Color). HMV

Tales of Manhattan 🎬🎬🎬
1942 Star-studded anthology about a tailor who curses a tailcoat that then travels, with varying degrees of good and bad fortune, from owner to owner. There's a love triangle, a love match, a concert appearance, a down-on-his-luck lawyer, a swanky party, a crook, and a windfall for some sharecroppers. Fields' party episode (he wears the coat to give a lecture and winds up wreaking havoc) was cut out of the original theatrical release. **118m/C VHS, Closed Caption.** Charles Boyer, Rita Hayworth, Thomas Mitchell, Ginger Rogers, Henry Fonda, Cesar Romero, Elsa Lanchester, Charles Laughton, Edward G. Robinson, George Sanders, James Gleason, J. Carrol Naish, Paul Robeson, Ethel Waters, Eddie Anderson, W.C. Fields, Margaret Dumont; *D:* Julien Duvivier; *W:* Ben Hecht, Donald Ogden Stewart, Samuel Hoffenstein, Ferenc Molnar, Alan Campbell; *C:* Joseph Walker; *M:* Sol Kaplan. FXV

Tales of Ordinary Madness 🎬
1983 Gazzara as a poet who drinks and sleeps with assorted women. Based on the stories of Charles Bukowski. Pretentious and dull. **107m/C VHS, Beta.** Ben Gazzara, Ornella Muti, Susan Tyrrell, Tanya Lopert,

Roy Brocksmith, Katya Berger; *D:* Marco Ferreri; *C:* Tonino Delli Colli. ART, VES

Tales of Robin Hood 🎬½
1952 A low-budget depiction of the Robin Hood legend. **59m/B VHS, Beta, LV.** Robert Clarke, Mary Hatcher; *D:* James Tinling. NO

Tales of Terror 🎬🎬
Poe's Tales of Terror 1962 Three tales of terror based on stories by Edgar Allan Poe: "Morella," "The Black Cat," and the "The Case of M. Valdemar." Price stars in all three segments and is excellent as the bitter and resentful husband in "Morella." **90m/C VHS, Beta.** Vincent Price, Peter Lorre, Basil Rathbone, Debra Paget, Joyce Jameson; *D:* Roger Corman; *W:* Richard Matheson; *C:* Floyd Crosby; *M:* Les Baxter. MLB, ORI

Tales of the Klondike: In a Far Country 🎬🎬
1987 An adaptation of Jack London's story exploring the fears, dangers, and joys experienced by prospectors in the harsh wilderness of northwest Canadian gold country. **60m/C VHS, Beta.** Robert Carradine, Scott Hylands; *D:* Janine Manatis.

Tales of the Klondike: Race for Number One 🎬🎬
1987 Two men compete in a highly contested dog-sled race—the goal of which is to be the first to reach a tract of gold-laden land. Adapted from a story by Jack London. **60m/C VHS, Beta.** David Ferry, John Ireland; *D:* David Cobham.

Tales of the Klondike: The Scorn of Women 🎬🎬
1987 An available man is enthusiastically courted by every single woman in Dawson City, Alaska. From a story by Jack London. **60m/C VHS, Beta.** Tom Butler, Eva Gabor; *D:* Claude Fournier.

Tales of the Klondike: The Unexpected 🎬🎬
1987 Five gold prospectors grow rich, but lose all that is most valuable through overwhelming greed. Adapted from a story by Jack London. **60m/C VHS, Beta.** John Candy, Cherie Lunghi; *D:* Peter Pearson.

Tales of the Unexpected 🎬🎬½
1991 Four tales designed to startle the senses and provoke the imagination. Episodes include "People Don't Do Such Things," about a marriage gone awry, "Youth from Vienna," about a weird fountain of youth, "Skeleton in the Cupboard," which tells of a man desperately trying to hide some strange secret and finally, "Bird of Prey," in which a pet parrot leaves its owners an enormous egg before dying. **101m/C VHS, Beta, LV.** Arthur Hill, Samantha Eggar, Don Johnson, Dick Smothers, Sharon Gless, James Carroll Jordan, Charles Dance, Zoe Wanamaker, Sondra Locke, Frank Converse; *D:* Gordon Hessler, Norman Lloyd, Paul Annett, Ray Danton. IME

Tales That Witness Madness 🎬🎬½
1973 **(R)** An asylum is the setting for four tales of horror, as a doctor tells a visitor how four patients ended up in his clinic. Stories are "Mr. Tiger," "Penny Farthing," "Mel" and "Luau." At the time this was Novak's first film appearance in four years. **90m/C VHS, Closed Caption.** GB Jack Hawkins, Donald Pleasence, Suzy Kendall, Joan Collins, Kim Novak, Mary Tamm, Georgia Brown, Donald Houston, David Wood, Peter McEnery; *D:* Freddie Francis. PAR

Talion 🎬🎬
An Eye for an Eye 1966 **(PG)** A western revenge movie that features two disabled men, a rancher and a bounty hunter, who team up to find the gang that slaughtered the rancher's family. **92m/C VHS, Beta.** Robert Lansing, Slim Pickens, Patrick Wayne; *D:* Michael Moore. COL, NLC

Talk 🎬🎬
1994 Sharp conversation between two 30-something women as they wander around the streets of Sydney. Stephanie (Milliken) and Julia (Longley) are collaborators on graphic novels—Stephanie's single and adventurous while Julia is seemingly settled in the country with her lover and child. As they talk, the women learn that both their lives have conflicts. Fantasy sequences, which slow the story down, find the women stepping into their own comic-book adventures. **86m/C VHS.** AU Victoria Longley, Angie Millik-

en, Richard Roxburgh, Jacqueline McKenzie, John Jarratt; *D:* Susan Lambert; *W:* Jan Cornall; *C:* Ron Hagen, *M:* John Clifford White. NYR

Talk of the Town 🎬🎬🎬
1942 A brilliantly cast, strange mixture of screwball comedy and lynch-mob melodramatics. An accused arsonist, a Supreme Court judge and the girl they both love try to clear the former's name and evade the cops. **118m/B VHS, Beta, LV.** Ronald Colman, Cary Grant, Jean Arthur, Edgar Buchanan, Glenda Farrell, Rex Ingram, Emma Dunn; *D:* George Stevens. Nominations: Academy Awards '42: Best Black and White Cinematography, Best Film Editing, Best Interior Decoration, Best Picture, Best Screenplay, Best Story, Best Original Dramatic/Comedy Score. COL

Talk Radio 🎬🎬🎬
1988 **(R)** Riveting Stone adaptation of Bogosian's one-man play. An acidic talk radio host confronts America's evil side and his own past over the airwaves. The main character is loosely based on the life of Alan Berg, a Denver talk show host who was murdered by white supremacists. **110m/C VHS, Beta, LV.** Eric Bogosian, Alec Baldwin, Ellen Greene, John Pankow, John C. McGinley, Michael Wincott, Leslie Hope; *D:* Oliver Stone; *W:* Eric Bogosian, Oliver Stone; *C:* Robert Richardson; *M:* Stewart Copeland. USH

Talk to Me 🎬½
1982 A successful New York accountant checks into the Hollins Communication Institute to cure his stuttering. While there, he meets and falls in love with a squirrel-hunting stuttering woman from Arkansas. **90m/C VHS, Beta, Closed Caption.** Austin Pendleton, Michael Murphy, Louise Fletcher, Brian Backer, Clifton James. FOX

Talkin' Dirty After Dark 🎬🎬
1991 **(R)** Sexy comedy starring Lawrence as a suave comedian who will do anything to get a late-night spot at Dukie's comedy club. *CW:* Strong language and sexual dialogue and sex scenes. **89m/C VHS, Closed Caption.** Martin Lawrence, Jedda Jones, Phyllis Stickney, Darryl Sivad; *D:* Topper Carew; *W:* Topper Carew. NLC, FCT

Talking About Sex 🎬🎬½
1994 Publishing party for a shrink's self-help manual sparks many conversations about sex and romance among a group of fashionable Los Angelenos. The breezy party chatter is broken up by B&W pseudo-documentary interludes of women exchanging confidences. **83m/C VHS.** Kim Wayans, Marcy Walker, Daniel Beer, Randy Powell, Kerry Ruff, Joe Richards, Daria Lynn; *D:* Aaron Speiser; *W:* Aaron Speiser, Carl Nelson; *M:* Tim Landers. LEO

Talking Walls 🎬½
Motel Vacancy 1985 A college sociology student uses high-tech surveillance equipment to spy on the clients of a seedy motel, in order to complete his thesis on human sexuality. **85m/C VHS, Beta.** Stephen Shellan, Marie Laurin, Barry Primus, Sally Kirkland; *D:* Stephen Verona. VTR

The Tall Blond Man with One Black Shoe 🎬🎬🎬
Le Grand Blond avec une Chaussure Noire 1972 **(PG)** A violinist is completely unaware that rival spies mistakenly think he is also a spy, and that he is the center of a plot to booby-trap an overly ambitious agent at the French Secret Service. A sequel followed called "Return of the Tall Blond Man with One Black Shoe" which was followed by a disappointing American remake, "The Man with One Red Shoe." In French with English subtitles or dubbed. **90m/C VHS, Beta, 8mm.** FR Pierre Richard, Bernard Blier, Jean Rochefort, Mireille Darc, Jean Carmet; *D:* Yves Robert; *W:* Francis Veber; *M:* Vladimir Cosma. CVC, VYY, FCT

Tall, Dark and Deadly 🎬🎬½
1995 **(R)** TV cable movie finds Roy (Scalia) romancing Maggie (Delaney), a young woman he's met in a bar. The viewer's already clued in that Roy's a bad 'un (seein' as how he's killed one woman) and when he chains Maggie to a sink, she picks up on the idea that he's a wacko. Basic damsel-in-distress with a cast that manages to keep straight faces in the most preposterous of circumstances. *CW:* Violence, terror, and sexuality. **89m/C VHS, Closed Caption.** Jack Scalia, Kim Delaney, Todd Allen, Gina Mastrogiacomo, Ely Pouget; *D:* Kenneth Fink;

W: MaryAnne Kasica, Michael Scheff; M: Joseph Vitarelli. PAR

The Tall Guy 🎬🎬🎬 1989 (R)
Goldblum is a too-tall actor who tries the scene in London and lands the lead in a musical version of 'The Elephant Man,' becoming an overnight success. Not consistently funny, but good British comedy, including an interesting sex scene. 92m/C VHS, LV. Jeff Goldblum, Emma Thompson, Rowan Atkinson, Geraldine James, Kim Thomson, Anna Massey; D: Mel Smith; W: Richard Curtis; M: Peter Brewis. COL, FCT

Tall in the Saddle 🎬🎬½ 1944
A misogynist foreman (Wayne) finds himself accused of murder. Meanwhile, he falls in love with his female boss' niece. An inoffensive and memorable western. 79m/B VHS, Beta, LV. John Wayne, Ella Raines, George "Gabby" Hayes, Ward Bond; D: Edwin L. Marin. TTC

Tall Lie 🎬🎬 For Men Only 1953
A student quits a fraternity hazing exercise. He's pursued by a psychotic bunch of his fraternity brothers and is killed in a smash-up. A local doctor goes onto an anti-hazing campaign in the aftermath. 93m/B VHS, Beta, LV. Paul Henreid, Robert Sherman; D: Paul Henreid. NO

The Tall Men 🎬🎬 1955
Standard western features frontier hands on a rough cattle drive confronting Indians, outlaws, and the wilderness while vying with each other for the love of Russell. 122m/C VHS, Beta. Clark Gable, Jane Russell, Robert Ryan, Cameron Mitchell, Mae Marsh; D: Raoul Walsh. FOX

Tall Story 🎬🎬 1960
Perkins is a star basketball player who must pass a crucial test in order to continue to play the game. In addition to the pressure of the exam, he is being pressured by gamblers to throw a game against the Russians. Fonda makes her screen debut as a cheerleader who is so awe-struck by Perkins that she takes the same classes just to be close to him. Based on the play by Howard Lindsay and Russel Crouse, and the novel "The Homecoming Game" by Howard Nemerov. 91m/C VHS, LV. Anthony Perkins, Jane Fonda, Ray Walston, Marc Connelly, Anne Jackson, Tom Laughlin; D: Joshua Logan; W: Julius J. Epstein, Philip C. Epstein; C: Ellsworth Fredericks. WEA

The Tall T 1957
A veteran rancher (Pat) stumbles onto big trouble when by chance he catches a stage coach that is eventually overrun by an evil band of cut-throats. After killing everyone on the coach except Pat and the daughter of a wealthy copper mine owner (Doretta), the renegades decide to leave the scene with the unfortunate two as hostages. Pat and Doretta, although in dire straits, find time to fall in love and devise an intricate plan for their escape. Regarded in certain western-lover circles as a cult classic. 77m/B VHS. Randolph Scott, Richard Boone, Maureen O'Sullivan, Arthur Hunnicutt, Skip Homeier, Henry Silva, Robert Burton, Robert Anderson; D: Budd Boetticher; W: Burt Kennedy. GKK

Tall Tale: The Unbelievable Adventures of Pecos Bill 🎬 1995 (PG)
Having trouble with greedy land ownners out for his pa's land, Daniel Hackett (Stahl) summons the help of three Old West legends: Pecos Bill (Swayze), John Henry (Brown), and Paul Bunyan (Platt) to face off with the evil industrialist J.P. Stiles (Glenn). Disney's variation on the "Wizard of Oz" is riddled with cartoonish characters and sleep-inducing dialogue. It would truly be a tall tale if it were said that this movie was any good. 98m/C VHS, LV, Closed Caption. Patrick Swayze, Oliver Platt, Roger Brown, Nick Stahl, Scott Glenn, Stephen Lang, Jared Harris, Catherine O'Hara; D: Jeremiah S. Chechik; W: Steven L. Bloom, Robert Rodat; C: Janusz Kaminski. DIS

Tall, Tan and Terrific 1946
Things really go crazy when the owner of a nightclub in Harlem is accused of murder. 40m/C VHS, Beta. Mantan Moreland, Monte Hawley, Francine Everett, Dots Johnson; D: Bud Pollard. NOS

Tall Texan 🎬🎬½ 1953
A motley crew seeks gold in an Indian burial ground in the desert. Flawed but interesting and suspenseful. Greed, lust, Indians and desert heat. 82m/B VHS, Beta, LV. Lloyd Bridges, Lee J. Cobb, Marie Windsor, George Steele; D: Elmo Williams; C: Joseph Biroc. RXM

Talons of the Eagle 🎬🎬 1992 (R)
Martial arts adventure centers around three undercover agents who go up against crimelord Mr. Li (Hong). To impress Li, martial arts champion Tyler Wilson (Blanks) and vice detective Michael Reeds (Merhi) enter a deadly martial arts tournament. They later hook up with beautiful agent Cassandra Hubbard (Barnes), who has already investigated Li's drug, gambling, and prostitution rings. Features the most advanced fighting techniques ever filmed. CW: Martial arts violence and sexuality. 96m/C VHS, LV, Closed Caption. Billy Blanks, Jalal Merhi, James Hong, Priscilla Barnes, Matthias Hues; D: Michael Kennedy; W: J. Stephen Maunder. USH, SGE

Tamango 🎬🎬 1959
A confusing drama set on a slave ship travelling from Africa to Cuba in 1830. Jurgens is the ship's captain who takes the black Dandridge as his mistress. Meanwhile, the slaves are plotting a revolt, with Dandridge as a conspirator. The interracial romance does takes a secondary role to the racial conflicts. The title refers to the leader of the slave revolt, played by Cressan. Filmed in both English- and French-language versions. 98m/C VHS. FR Curt Jurgens, Dorothy Dandridge, Jean Servais, Alex Cressan; D: John Berry. IVY

The Tamarind Seed 🎬½ 1974
Andrews and Sharif are star-crossed lovers kept apart by Cold War espionage. Dated, dull and desultory. 123m/C VHS, Beta. Julie Andrews, Omar Sharif, Anthony Quayle, Dan O'Herlihy, Sylvia Syms; D: Blake Edwards; W: Blake Edwards; C: Frederick A. (Freddie) Young; M: John Barry.

The Taming of the Shrew 🎬🎬½ 1929
Historically interesting early talkie featuring sole (if perhaps unfortunate) pairing of Pickford and Fairbanks. Features the legendary credit line "By William Shakespeare, with additional dialogue by Sam Taylor." Re-edited in 1966; 1967 Zeffirelli remake featured Taylor and Burton. 66m/B VHS, Beta, LV. Mary Pickford, Douglas Fairbanks Sr., Edwin Maxwell, Joseph Cawthorn; D: Sam Taylor; C: Karl Struss. NOS, CCB

The Taming of the Shrew 🎬🎬🎬½ 1967
A lavish screen version of the classic Shakespearean comedy. Burton and Taylor are violently physical and perfectly cast as the battling Katherine and Petruchio. At the time the film was made, Burton and Taylor were having their own marital problems, which not only added an inner fire to their performances, but sent the interested moviegoers to the theatres in droves. 122m/C VHS, Beta, LV. IT Elizabeth Taylor, Richard Burton, Michael York, Michael Hordern, Cyril Cusack; D: Franco Zeffirelli; W: Franco Zeffirelli; C: Oswald Morris; M: Nino Rota. Nominations: Academy Awards '67: Best Art Direction/Set Decoration, Best Costume Design. COL, TVC, PBS

The Taming of the Shrew 🎬🎬 1981
The classic Shakespearean comedy about the battle of the sexes where Petruchio attempts to tame his fiery, free-spirited wife, Kate. 152m/C VHS, Beta. D: Peter Dews.

Tammy and the Bachelor 🎬🎬½ 1957
A backwoods Southern girl becomes involved with a romantic pilot and his snobbish family. They don't quite know what to make of her but she wins them over with her down-home philosophy. Features the hit tune, "Tammy." Charming performance by Reynolds. 89m/C VHS, Beta. Debbie Reynolds, Leslie Nielsen, Walter Brennan, Fay Wray, Sidney Blackmer, Mildred Natwick, Louise Beavers; D: Joseph Pevney; W: Oscar Brodney. Nominations: Academy Awards '57: Best Song ("Tammy"). USH

Tammy and the Doctor 🎬🎬 1963
Sandra Dee reprises Debbie Reynolds's backwoods gal ("Tammy and the Bachelor"). Dee becomes a nurse's aide and is wooed by doctor Fonda, in his film debut. 88m/C VHS, Beta. Sandra Dee, Peter Fonda, MacDonald Carey; D: Harry Keller; W: Oscar Brodney. USH

Tammy and the T-Rex 🎬🎬½ 1994 (PG-13)
All Michael (Walker) wanted was a date with the lovely Denise (Richards)—he didn't expect to almost die for her. Nor did he expect a mad scientist to transplant his brain into a mechanical three-ton dinosaur. Part teen angst—part camp horror—all good-natured hooey. CW: Comic monster violence and some sex-related scenes. 82m/C VHS, LV, Closed Caption. Paul Walker, Denise Richards, Terry Kiser, John Franklin; D: Stewart Raffill. IMP

Tampopo 🎬🎬🎬 1986
A hilarious, episodic Japanese comedy. A widowed noodle shop owner is coached by a ten-gallon-hatted stranger in how to make the perfect noodle. Funny, freeform hit that established Itami in the West. In Japanese with English subtitles. 114m/C VHS, LV, Letterbox. JP Ken Watanabe, Tsutomu Yamazaki, Nobuko Miyamoto, Koji Yakusho, Rikiya Yasuoka, Kinzo Sakura, Shoji Otake; D: Juzo Itami. REP

Tangiers 🎬 1983
The disappearance of a British intelligence agent in Gibraltar sets off a chain-reaction of violent incidents. 82m/C VHS. Ronny Cox. WAR

Tangled Destinies 🎬🎬½ 1932
Old dark house thriller involving a deserted mansion, murder, and faux diamonds. Good acting and a decent storyline make it one of the few successful independently made films of its time. 64m/B VHS. Lloyd Whitlock, Glenn Tryon, Vera Reynolds, Doris Hill, Sidney Bracy; D: Frank Strayer; W: Edward T. Lowe. SNC

Tango 🎬🎬½ 1936
An early melodrama follows the ups and down of a chorus girl and the guy who sticks with her through thick and thin and poorly filmed dance routines. Based on a novel by Vida Hurst. 66m/B VHS. Marion Nixon, Chick Chandler, Matty Kemp, Marie Prevost, Warren Hymer, Herman Bing, Franklin Pangborn, George Meeker; D: Phil Rosen. NOS, LOO

Tango and Cash 🎬🎬 1989 (R)
Stallone and Russell are L.A. cops with something in common: they both think they are the best in the city. Forced to work together to beat drug lord Palance, they flex their muscles a lot. Directing completed by Albert Magnoli, after Andrei Konchalovsky left in a huff. 104m/C VHS, Beta, LV, 8mm, Letterbox, Closed Caption. Sylvester Stallone, Kurt Russell, Jack Palance, Brion James, Teri Hatcher, Michael J. Pollard, James Hong, Marc Alaimo, Robert Z'Dar; D: Andrei Konchalovsky; W: Randy Feldman; M: Harold Faltermeyer. WAR

Tango Bar 🎬🎬½ 1988
A romantic triangle between a tango dancer who leaves Argentina during a time of political unrest, his former partner, and his wife, who both stay behind. They are reunited after years of separation. Gives the viewer a detailed vision of the historical and cultural significance of the tango. Charming, interesting and very watchable. In Spanish with English subtitles. 90m/C VHS, Beta. AR Raul Julia, Valeria Lynch, Ruben Juarez; D: Marcos Zurinaga. WAR

The Tango Lesson 🎬🎬½ 1997 (PG)
Semiautobiographical tale of director/star/writer and former dancer Potter ("Orlando" director), as Sally, who finds love and the meaning of life in the tango while living in Paris. While penning a non-commercial script called "Rage" about a paraplegic designer who stalks leggy models, Sally meets a tango instructor (Pablo) without a partner, and soon the two are doing more than just the tango. Sally grooms Pablo to star in her upcoming pic as long as he allows the headstrong director to take the lead while they dance. Occasionally departs from the story to the "Rage" script, played out in color. While light on their toes, performances by the real-life director and real-life tango instructor are as heavy and stilted as some of the dialogue. Using dance as the metaphor for control and power in relationships, Potter falls flat in a pretentious "Lesson." 101m/B VHS.

GB Sally Potter, Pablo Veron, Gustavo Naveira, Fabian Salas, David Toole, Carolina Iotti, Carlos Copello, Peter Eyre, Heathcote Williams; *D:* Sally Potter; *W:* Sally Potter; *C:* Hobby Muller; *M:* Sally Potter, Fred Frith. Nominations: British Academy Awards '97: Best Foreign Film. COL

Tank 🐾🐾½ **1983 (PG)** Retired Army officer Garner's son is thrown into jail on a trumped-up charge by a small town sheriff. Dad comes to the rescue with his restored Sherman tank. Trite and unrealistic portrayal of good versus bad made palatable by Garner's performance. **113m/C VHS, Beta, LV, Closed Caption.** James Garner, Shirley Jones, C. Thomas Howell, Mark Herrier, Sandy Ward, Jenilee Harrison, Dorian Harewood, G.D. Spradlin; *D:* Marvin J. Chomsky; *M:* Lalo Schifrin. USH

Tank Commando 🐾🐾½ **1959** Mediocre WWII actioner, set in Italy, about a demolition squad of battle-hardened Americans trying to locate a secret German crossing point. It turns out to be an underwater bridge and an Italian orphan is the only one, besides the Germans, to know its location. Can the Americans persuade the kid to talk? **79m/B VHS.** Bob Barron, Wally Campo, Maggie Lawrence, Donato Farretta, Leo V. Metranga, Jack Sowards, Anthony Rich, Larry Hudson; *D:* Burt Topper; *W:* Burt Topper. COL

Tank Girl 🐾🐾½ **1994 (R)** Big-budget adaption of the underground British comic book about a brash punker chick (Petty), her mutant friends, and the evil establishment in the post-apocalyptic future. The heavily armed pixie battles the tyrannical Department of Water and Power, run by evil Dr. Kesslee (McDowell), for control of the world's water supply in the year 2033. Straying a bit too far from the source comic, the plot (such as it is) is crammed into a rigid action-movie structure that lacks excitement. Plays like a cheap Gen-X marketing ploy with its bizarre mixture of pop culture references and a hipper-than-thou soundtrack coordinated by Courtney Love. *CW:* Contains violence, profanity, brief nudity, and adult themes. **104m/C VHS, LV, Closed Caption.** Lori Petty, Malcolm McDowell, Ice-T, Naomi Watts, Jeff Kober, Reg E. Cathey, Scott Coffey, Ann Cusack, Don Harvey, Brian Wimmer, Staci Linn Ramsower; *Cameos:* Iggy Pop, Ann Magnuson; *D:* Rachel Talalay; *W:* Tedi Sarafian; *M:* Graeme Revell. MGM

Tanks a Million 🐾🐾 **1941** Despite the title, tanks aren't even mentioned in this. Tracy stars as a wacky genius who gets drafted. His excellent memory keeps getting him into one predicament after another. Though he gets promoted quickly, he shows himself no leader. Lots of time-worn gags, but they still work. **50m/B VHS.** William Tracy, James Gleason, Noah Beery Jr., Joseph Sawyer, Elyse Knox, Douglas Fowley, Frank Faylen, Dick Wessel, Frank Melton, Harold Goodwin, William Gould, Norman Kerry; *D:* Fred Guiol. Nominations: Academy Awards '41: Best Original Dramatic/Comedy Score. NOS

Tanner '88 *Tanner: A Political Fable* **1988** Murphy is excellent as a longshot politician on the trail of the Democratic presidential nomination. Story by Gary Trudeau of Doonesbury fame. A precise political satire made for cable. **120m/C VHS, LV.** Michael Murphy, Pamela Reed, Cynthia Nixon; *D:* Robert Altman. PBS, BTV

Tanya's Island 🐾🐾½ **1981 (R)** Abused girlfriend fantasizes about an ape on deserted island and romance with an ape. Vanity billed as D.D. Winters. **100m/C VHS, Beta.** Vanity, Dick Sargent, Mariette Levesque, Don McCleod; *D:* Alfred Sole. NO

Tap 🐾🐾½ **1989 (PG-13)** The son of a famous tap dancer, a dancer himself, decides to try to get away from his former life of crime by helping an aging hoofer revitalize the art of tap dancing. Fun to watch for the wonderful dancing scenes. Davis' last big screen appearance. Hines is sincere in this old-fashioned story, and dances up a storm. Captures some never-before filmed old hoofers. **106m/C VHS, Beta, LV, Closed Caption.** Gregory Hines, Sammy Davis Jr., Suzanne Douglas, Joe Morton, Terrance McNally, Steve Condos, Jimmy Slyde, Harold Nicholas, Etta James, Savion Glover, Dick Anthony Williams, Sandman

Sims, Bunny Briggs, Pat Rico, Arthur Duncan; *D:* Nick Castle; *W:* Nick Castle; *M:* James Newton Howard. COL, MVD

Tapeheads 🐾🐾½ **1989 (R)** Silly, sophomoric, sexy comedy starring Cusack and Robbins as young wannabe rock-video producers who strike it big. Many big-name cameos; good soundtrack; laughs. **93m/C VHS, Beta, LV.** John Cusack, Tim Robbins, Mary Crosby, Connie Stevens, Susan Tyrrell, Lyle Alzado, Don Cornelius, Katy Boyer, Doug McClure, Clu Gulager, Jessica Walter; *Cameos:* Stiv Bators, Sam Moore, Junior Walker, Martha Quinn, Ted Nugent, Weird Al Yankovic; *D:* Bill Fishman; *C:* Bojan Bazelli. NO

Taps 🐾🐾½ **1981 (PG)** Military academy students led by Hutton are so true to their school they lay siege to it to keep it from being closed. An antiwar morality play about excesses of zeal and patriotism. Predictable but impressive. **126m/C VHS, Beta.** Timothy Hutton, George C. Scott, Ronny Cox, Sean Penn, Tom Cruise; *D:* Harold Becker; *W:* Darryl Ponicsan, Robert Mark Kamen; *M:* Maurice Jarre. FOX

Tar 🐾🐾 **1997** Female cop Prescott and crook Thigpen were high school sweethearts who went their separate ways. But they're reunited when Thigpen hijacks a squad car that just happens to be driven by guess who. There's also a story involving a group of black nationalists who kidnap white businessman and cover them in—you guessed it—tar. Likeable leads, improbable characters. **?m/C VHS.** Kevin Thigpen, Nicole Prescott, Seth Gilliam, Ron Brice, Frank Minucci; *D:* Goetz Grossmann; *W:* Goetz Grossmann; *C:* Lloyd Handwerker; *M:* John Hill. MRC

Tarantula 🐾🐾🐾 **1955** If you're into gigantic killer insect movies this is one of the best with nifty special effects and some good action. Carroll plays a scientist working on a growth formula which he's testing on a spider when it accidentally gets loose. This eight-legged horror grows to 100 feet high and causes havoc in the Arizona desert until the Air Force napalms the sucker. Look for Eastwood in the final sequence as an Air Force pilot. **81m/B VHS, Closed Caption.** Leo G. Carroll, John Agar, Mara Corday, Nestor Paiva, Ross Elliott, Clint Eastwood; *D:* Jack Arnold; *W:* Robert M. Fresco, Martin Berkeley. USH

Tarantulas: The Deadly Cargo 🐾 **1977** Eek! Hairy spiders terrizing our sleepy town and destroying our orange crop! Made-for-TV cheapie not creepy; will make you sleepy. **100m/C VHS.** Claude Akins, Charles Frank, Deborah Winters, Pat Hingle, Sandy McPeak, Bert Remsen, Howard Hesseman, Tom Atkins, Charles Siebert; *D:* Stuart Hagmann. ART

Taras Bulba 🐾🐾½ **1962** Well-photographed costume epic on the 16th century Polish revolution. Brynner as the fabled Cossack; Curtis plays his vengeful son. Good score. Shot on location in Argentina. Based on the novel by Nikolai Gogol. **122m/C VHS, LV, Letterbox.** Tony Curtis, Yul Brynner, Christine Kaufmann, Sam Wanamaker, George Macready, Vladimir Sokoloff, Perry Lopez; *D:* J. Lee Thompson. Nominations: Academy Awards '62: Best Original Score. MGM

Target 🐾🐾 **1985 (R)** Normal dad/hubby Hackman slips into a figurative phone booth and emerges as former CIA when his better half is kidnapped in Paris. Good action scenes, but poorly scripted and too long. **117m/C VHS, Beta, LV, Closed Caption.** Gene Hackman, Matt Dillon, Gayle Hunnicutt, Josef Sommer; *D:* Arthur Penn; *W:* Howard Berk. FOX

Target Eagle 🐾🐾 **1984** Spanish police chief von Sydow hires mercenary Rivero to infiltrate drug ring. Good performances; ho-hum story. **99m/C VHS, Beta.** *SP MX* Max von Sydow, George Peppard, Maud Adams, Chuck Connors, George Rivero, Susana Dosamantes; *D:* J. Anthony Loma. NO

Target: Favorite Son 🐾🐾 **1987 (R)** An attractive, ammunition-laden woman sharpshoots her way to power in this made-for-TV movie. *CW:* Violence and sensuality. **115m/C VHS, Closed Caption.** Linda Kozlowski, Harry Hamlin, Robert Loggia, Ronny Cox, James Whitmore. THV

Target for Killing 🐾🐾 **1966** Mediocre thriller about a secret agent who must protect a young heiress from a Lebanese syndicate that's out to kill her. **93m/C VHS.** Stewart Granger, Curt Jurgens, Molly Peters, Adolfo Celi, Klaus Kinski, Rupert Davies; *D:* Manfred Kohler. SNC

Targets 🐾🐾🐾 **1968 (PG)** Bogdanovich's suspenseful directorial debut. An aging horror film star plans his retirement, convinced that real life is too scary for his films to have an audience. A mad sniper at a drive-in movie seems to prove he's right. Some prints still have anti-gun prologue, which was added after Robert Kennedy's assassination. **90m/C VHS, Beta.** Boris Karloff, James Brown, Tim O'Kelly, Peter Bogdanovich, Mary Jackson, Sandy Baron, Monte Landis, Mike Farrell, Nancy Hsueh, Arthur Peterson, Tanya Morgan; *D:* Peter Bogdanovich; *W:* Peter Bogdanovich; *C:* Laszlo Kovacs. PAR

Tarka the Otter **198?** The story of Tarka the Otter who encounters many dangers as he pursues his favorite eel meals. **91m/C VHS, Beta.** TWE

Tarnished Angels 🐾🐾🐾 **1957** Reporter Burke Devlin (Hudson) is writing a story for the local New Orleans paper about a tormented trio of air circus barnstormers. A former WWI ace, Roger Shumann (Stack) cares more about flying than he does his sizzling wife Laverne (Malone), who's loved-from-afar by loyal mechanic Jiggs (Carson). When Roger's plane cracks up, he uses his wife to obtain use of an experimental aircraft in order to win a race—and brings disaster crashing around them all. Good action, fine cast. Based on William Faulkner's 1930 novel "Pylon." **91m/B VHS, Closed Caption.** Rock Hudson, Robert Stack, Dorothy Malone, Jack Carson, Robert Middleton, Troy Donahue, Alan Reed, Robert J. Wilke, William Schallert; *D:* Douglas Sirk; *W:* George Zuckerman; *C:* Irving Glassberg; *M:* Frank Skinner. USH

Tartuffe 🐾🐾½ **1984** Popular French leading man Depardieu makes directorial debut with Moliere classic about religious hypocrisy and an imposter taking advantage of a wealthy merchant and his family. In French with English subtitles. **140m/C VHS, LV.** *FR* Gerard Depardieu, Francois Perier, Elisabeth Depardieu; *D:* Gerard Depardieu. CVC, FCT, TPV

Tartuffe 🐾🐾½ **1990** Moliere's famous comedy has Tartuffe posing as a holy man who has attracted the incredulous merchant Orgon. Orgon is willing to give Tartuffe anything—money, social position, even his daughter—and Tartuffe is more than happy to accept. **110m/C VHS, Beta.** Anthony Sher, Nigel Hawthorne, Alison Steadman; *D:* Bill Alexander. TTC

Tarzan and His Mate 🐾🐾🐾 **1934** Second entry in the lavishly produced MGM Tarzan series. Weissmuller and O'Sullivan cohabit in unmarried bliss before the Hays Code moved them to a tree house with twin beds. Many angry elephants, nasty white hunters, and hungry lions. Laserdisc includes the original trailer. **93m/B VHS, LV.** Johnny Weissmuller, Maureen O'Sullivan, Neil Hamilton, Paul Cavanagh; *D:* Jack Conway; *C:* Clyde De Vinna. MGM, FCT

Tarzan and the Green Goddess 🐾½ *New Adventures of Tarzan* **1938** Tarzan searches for a statue that could prove dangerous if in the wrong hands. **72m/B VHS, Beta.** Bruce (Herman Brix) Bennett, Ula Holt, Frank Baker; *D:* Edward Kull. HHT, SNC, VYY

Tarzan and the Lost City 🐾🐾½ *Tarzan and Jane; Greystoke 2: Tarzan and Jane* **1998 (PG)** Gorgeous locations in South Africa are a decided plus in this routine hero/adventure story. Lord Greystoke, AKA Tarzan (Van Dien), returns to Africa from England in order to save his home from mercenaries hunting the lost city of Opar. Spunky fiance Jane (March) heads to the jungle after her Ape Man and gets into (and out of) trouble with bad guy Nigel Ravens (Waddington). Not very convincing special effects but Van Dien looks good in his loincloth and has the action moves down cold. **84m/C VHS.** Caspar Van Dien, Jane March, Steven Waddington, Winston Ntshona, Rapulana Seiphemo, Ian Roberts; *D:* Carl Schenkel; *W:* Bayard Johnson, J. Anderson Black; *C:* Paul Gilpin; *M:* Christopher Franke. *NYR*

Tarzan and the Trappers 🐾½ 1958
Bad-guy trappers and would-be treasure-seekers wish they hadn't messed with the ape man. **74m/B VHS, Beta.** Gordon Scott, Eve Brent, Ricky Sorenson, Maurice Marsac; *D:* H. Bruce Humberstone. *SNC, NOS, VYY*

Tarzan Escapes 🐾🐾🐾 1936 Jane is
tricked by evil hunters into abandoning her fairy tale life with Tarzan, so the Ape Man sets out to reunite with his one true love. The third entry in MGM's Weissmuller/O'Sullivan series is still among the better Tarzan movies thanks to the leads, but the Hays Office made sure Jane was wearing a lot more clothes this time around. **95m/B VHS.** Johnny Weissmuller, Maureen O'Sullivan, John Buckler, Benita Hume, William Henry; *D:* Richard Thorpe. *FOX, FCT*

Tarzan Finds a Son 🐾🐾🐾 1939
Weissmuller and O'Sullivan returned to their roles after three years with the addition of the five-year-old Sheffield as Boy. He's an orphan whose awful relatives hope he stays lost so they can collect an inheritance. Jane and Tarzan fight to adopt the tyke and when the new family are captured by a wicked tribe only an elephant stampede can save them! **90m/B VHS.** Johnny Weissmuller, Maureen O'Sullivan, Johnny Sheffield, Ian Hunter, Henry Stephenson, Frieda Inescort, Henry Wilcoxon; *D:* Richard Thorpe. *MGM*

Tarzan of the Apes 🐾🐾 1917 Brawny
Lincoln is the original screen Tarzan. Silent film well done and more faithful to the book than later versions. **63m/B VHS, Beta.** Elmo Lincoln, Enid Markey; *D:* Scott Sidney. *GPV, VYY, WFV*

Tarzan, the Ape Man 🐾🐾🐾 1932 The
definitive Tarzan movie; the first Tarzan talkie; the original of the long series starring Weissmuller. Dubiously faithful to the Edgar Rice Burroughs story, but recent attempts to remake, update or improve it (notably the pretentious 1984 Greystoke) have failed to near the original's entertainment value or even its technical quality. O'Sullivan as Jane and Weissmuller bring style and wit to their classic roles. **99m/B VHS, Beta, LV.** Johnny Weissmuller, Maureen O'Sullivan, Neil Hamilton; *D:* Woodbridge S. Van Dyke; *C:* Clyde De Vinna. *MGM, FCT*

Tarzan, the Ape Man woof! 1981 (R)
Plodding, perverted excuse to see Derek cavort nude in jungle. So bad not even hard-core Tarzan fans should bother. **112m/C VHS, Beta, LV.** Bo Derek, Richard Harris, John Phillip Law, Miles O'Keeffe; *D:* John Derek; *M:* Perry Botkin. Golden Raspberry Awards '81: Worst Actress (Derek). *MGM*

Tarzan the Fearless 🐾½ 1933 Tarzan
(Crabbe) helps a young girl find her missing father. **84m/B VHS, Beta.** Buster Crabbe, Jacqueline Wells, E. Alyn Warren, Edward Woods, Philo McCullough, Matthew Betz; *D:* Robert F. "Bob" Hill. *SNC, NOS, CAB*

Tarzan the Tiger 1929 Series of 15 chap-
ters is loosely based on the Edgar Rice Burroughs novel entitled "Tarzan and the Jewels of Opar." These chapters were filmed as silent pieces, and were later released with a musical score and synchronized sound effects. Here Merrill is the first to sound the cry of the bull ape, Tarzan's trademark. **?m/B VHS.** Frank Merrill, Natalie Kingston, Lilian Worth, Al Ferguson; *D:* Henry MacRae. *NOS, FCT, MOV*

Tarzana, the Wild Girl 🐾 1972 Jungle
cheapie about an expedition that finds a beautiful, scantily clad girl living wildly in the jungle. **87m/C VHS.** Kenneth Clark, Franca Polesello, Frank Ressel, Andrew Ray, James Reed; *W:* Philip Shaw. *SNC*

Tarzan's New York
Adventure 🐾🐾½ 1942 O'Sullivan's final appearance as Jane is a so-so adventure with some humorous moments when Tarzan meets the big city. When Boy is kidnapped by an evil circus

owner, Tarzan, Jane, and Cheta head out to rescue him. Tarzan shows off his jungle prowess by climbing skyscrapers and diving off the Brooklyn Bridge into the Hudson River. Lincoln, the screen's first Tarzan, has a cameo. **70m/B VHS.** Johnny Weissmuller, Maureen O'Sullivan, Johnny Sheffield, Virginia Grey, Charles Bickford, Paul Kelly, Chill Wills, Russell Hicks, Cy Kendall; *Cameos:* Elmo Lincoln; *D:* Richard Thorpe. *MGM*

Tarzan's Revenge 🐾 1938 Morris is a
better Olympic runner than actor; Holm is horrible. Only for serious Tarzan fans. **70m/B VHS, Beta.** Glenn Morris, Eleanor Holm, Hedda Hopper; *D:* David Ross Lederman. *SNC, NOS, VYY*

Tarzan's Secret Treasure 🐾🐾½ 1941
Tarzan saves an expedition from a savage tribe only to be repaid by having the greedy hunters hold Jane and Boy hostage. They want Tarzan's help in finding a secret cache of gold. But Tarzan doesn't take kindly to threats to his family and teaches those evil-doers a lesson! **81m/B VHS.** Johnny Weissmuller, Maureen O'Sullivan, Johnny Sheffield, Reginald Owen, Barry Fitzgerald, Tom Conway, Philip Dorn; *D:* Richard Thorpe. *MGM*

Task Force 🐾🐾½ 1949 History of naval avi-
ation and the development of the aircraft carrier highlighted by actual WWII combat footage (in color). Cooper and his naval buddies try to convince the brass that planes can be landed on the decks of ships. Slowly the Navy goes ahead and when Pearl Harbor is attacked, Cooper is given command of his own aircraft carrier. The use of the carriers proved very effective in Pacific battles and Cooper is finally vindicated. **116m/B VHS, Beta.** Gary Cooper, Jane Wyatt, Wayne Morris, Walter Brennan, Julie London, Bruce (Herman Brix) Bennett, Jack Holt, Stanley Ridges, John Ridgely, Richard Rober, Art Baker, Moroni Olsen; *D:* Delmer Daves; *W:* Delmer Daves. *MGM, FCT*

A Taste for Flesh and Blood 1990 (R)
A monster from outer space comes to earth and is delighted with the easy pickings for his insatiable appetite. A brave boy and girl, and a NASA commander must join forces to take the alien out. This one is billed as a campy salute to '50s B movies. **84m/C VHS.** Rubin Santiago, Lori Karz, Tim Ferrante. *NO*

A Taste for Killing 🐾🐾 1992 (R) Two
boys, both from well-to-do families, decide to take summer jobs on an offshore Texas oil rig. The best friends think a summer of adventure awaits them; however, their lives are made miserable by their blue-collar boss, who is resentful of their high society background. Then they meet Bo Landry, who befriends them and helps them survive. Unfortunately, Bo turns out to be anything but a friend as he reveals himself as a deadly con-artist in this intense psychological thriller. **87m/C VHS, Closed Caption.** Jason Bateman, Henry Thomas, Michael Biehn, Blue Deckert, Helen Cates; *D:* Lou Antonio; *W:* Dan Bronson. *USH*

Taste of Death 🐾 1977 A youth discovers
his courage within when he stands up to the bandits invading his village. **90m/C VHS, Beta.** John Ireland. *NO*

A Taste of Hell 🐾 1973 (PG) Two Ameri-
can soldiers fight a guerilla outfit in the Pacific during WWII. A low-budget film with few redeeming characteristics. **90m/C VHS, Beta.** William Smith, John Garwood. *VTR*

A Taste of Honey 🐾🐾🐾 1961 A plain
working-class girl falls in love with a black sailor. When she becomes pregnant, a homosexual friend helps her out. A moving film with strong, powerful performances. Based on the London and Broadway hit play by Shelagh Delaney. **100m/ B VHS.** GB Rita Tushingham, Robert Stephens, Dora Bryan, Murray Melvin, Paul Danquah; *D:* Tony Richardson; *W:* Tony Richardson, Shelagh Delaney; *C:* Walter Lassally; *M:* John Addison. British Academy Awards '61: Best Film, Best Supporting Actress (Bryan); British Academy Awards '62: Best Screenplay; Cannes Film Festival '62: Best Actor (Melvin), Best Actress (Tushingham).*NO*

The Taste of the Cherry 🐾🐾 Ta'm e
Guilass; Taste of Cherries 1996 Despairing, middle-aged Mr. Badii (Ershadi) is contemplating suicide and looking for someone who will bury his corpse discreetly. (He's already dug his own shallow grave in the countryside.) He drives through the streets and picks up several different men—all of whom remind him that suicide goes against the teachings of Islam. Finally, one old Turkish man relates his own story of attempted suicide and seemingly persuades Badii to rethink his actions. **95m/C VHS.** Homayon Ershadi, Abdolrahma Bagheri; *D:* Abbas Kiarostami; *W:* Abbas Kiarostami; *C:* Homayun Payvar. Cannes Film Festival '97: Best Film. *NYR*

Taste the Blood of Dracula 🐾🐾½
1970 (PG) Lee's Dracula only makes a brief appearance in this Hammer horror film which has three children taking over from the bloodsucker. Three Victorian dandies have killed the wizard who revived Dracula and he seeks their deaths by using their own children as the means of his revenge. Not enough Lee but still creepy. Preceded by "Dracula Has Risen from the Grave" and followed by "Scars of Dracula." **91m/C VHS.** GB Christopher Lee, Ralph Bates, Geoffrey Keen, Gwen Watford, Linda Hayden, John Carson, Peter Sallis, Isla Blair, Martin Jarvis, Roy Kinnear, Anthony Higgins, Anthony Corlan, Michael Ripper; *D:* Peter Sasdy; *W:* Anthony John Elder Hinds; *C:* Arthur Grant; *M:* James Bernard. *WAR*

Tatie Danielle 🐾🐾🐾 1991 Pitch-black
comedy from the director of "Life Is a Long Quiet River" sees a bitter, elderly widow moving in with her young nephew and making his life a hell. In French with yellow English subtitles. **114m/C VHS, LV.** FR Tsilla Chelton, Catherine Jacob, Isabelle Nanty, Neige Dolsky, Eric Prat, Laurence Fevrier; *D:* Etienne Chatiliez; *W:* Etienne Chatiliez. *ART*

The Tattered Web 🐾🐾 1971 A police
sergeant confronts and accidently kills the woman with whom his son-in-law has been cheating. He's then assigned the case. When he tries to frame a wino for the murder, things get more and more messy. Fine performances aid this made-for-television story. **74m/C VHS, Beta.** Lloyd Bridges, Frank Converse, Broderick Crawford, Murray Hamilton, Sallie Shockley; *D:* Paul Wendkos. *ORI*

Tattle Tale 🐾½ 1992 (PG) Vindictive ex-wife
writes book accusing her actor ex of abusing her and he loses out on his career-breaking role. So he decides to disguise himself and seduce her into telling the truth. Even dumber than it sounds. **96m/C VHS, LV.** C. Thomas Howell, Ally Sheedy; *D:* Baz Taylor. *ART*

Tattoo 🐾🐾 1981 (R) A model becomes the
object of obsession for a crazy tattoo artist. He relentlessly pursues her, leaving behind all his other more illustrated clients. Starts out fine, but deteriorates rapidly. Controversial love scene between Dern and Adams. **103m/C VHS, Beta.** Bruce Dern, Maud Adams, Leonard Frey, Rikke Borge, John Getz; *D:* Bob Brooks; *W:* Joyce Bunuel. *FOX*

Tattoo Connection 🐾 1978 (R) A gang of
lethal Oriental diamond thieves is pursued with whip-snapping flamboyance by a taciturn kung-fu investigator. **95m/C VHS, Beta.** Jim Kelly; *D:* Luk Pak Sang. *ORI*

Tattooed Hit Man 🐾 1976 Japanese
gangster violence in a revenge-doesn't-pay action story. **81m/C VHS, Beta.** JP Mayumi Nagisa, Bunta Sugawara, Tsunehiko Watase.

Tax Season 🐾🐾 1990 (PG-13) A small-time
businessman buys a Hollywood tax service sight-unseen, and finds it employing a hooker, a bookie and a variety of other unconventional types. **93m/C VHS, Beta.** Fritz Bronner, James Hong, Jana Grant, Toru Tanaka, Dorie Krum, Kathryn Knotts, Arte Johnson, Rob Stryker; *D:* Tom Law. *PAR*

Taxi Blues 🐾🐾🐾½ 1990 A political allego-
ry with the two protagonists representing the new and old Soviet Union. A hard-working, narrow-minded cabdriver keeps the saxophone of a westernized, Jewish, jazz-loving musician who doesn't

have his fare. The two strike up a wary friendship as each tries to explain his view of life to the other. Good look at the street life of Moscow populated by drunks, punks, and black marketeers. Directorial debut of Lounguine. In Russian with English subtitles. 110m/C VHS. *RU* Piotr Mamonov, Piotr Zaitchenko, Natalia Koliakanova, Vladimir Kachpour; *D:* Pavel Lounguine; *W:* Pavel Lounguine. Cannes Film Festival '90: Best Director (Lounguine). *NYF*

Taxi Dancers 🎬½ 1993 Smalltown Billie arrives in Hollywood with dreams of becoming an actress. Naturally, her dreams turn to despair and she resorts to "dancing" at the Shark Club where she becomes involved with a gambler who owes money to the wrong people. 97m/C VHS, LV. Sonny Landham, Robert Miano, Brittany McCrena, Tina Fite, Mirage Micheaux, Michele Hess, Randall Irwin; *D:* Norman Thaddeus Vane; *W:* Norman Thaddeus Vane; *M:* Larry Blank.

Taxi Driver 🎬🎬🎬 1976 (R) A psychotic New York City taxi driver tries to save a child prostitute and becomes infatuated with an educated political campaigner. He goes on a violent rampage when his dreams don't work out. Repellant, frightening vision of alienation and urban catharsis. On-target performances from Foster and De Niro. The laserdisc version is slightly longer, with commentary by Scorsese and screenwriter Paul Schrader, storyboards, complete screenplay, and Scorsese's production photos. 112m/C VHS, Beta, LV, 8mm, Letterbox, DVD. Robert De Niro, Jodie Foster, Harvey Keitel, Cybill Shepherd, Peter Boyle, Albert Brooks; *D:* Martin Scorsese; *W:* Paul Schrader; *C:* Michael Chapman; *M:* Bernard Herrmann. British Academy Awards '76: Best Supporting Actress (Foster); Cannes Film Festival '76: Best Film; Los Angeles Film Critics Association Awards '76: Best Actor (De Niro), National Film Registry '94;; New York Film Critics Awards '76: Best Actor (De Niro); National Society of Film Critics Awards '76: Best Actor (De Niro), Best Director (Scorsese), Best Supporting Actress (Foster); Nominations: Academy Awards '76: Best Actor (De Niro), Best Picture, Best Supporting Actress (Foster), Best Original Score. *COL, OM*

The Taxi Mystery 🎬 1926 Guy saves Broadway starlet from band of ne'er-do-wells thanks to deserted taxi, then tries to figure out who she is, unaware that her sinister understudy plans to do her in. 50m/B VHS, Beta. Edith Roberts, Robert Agnew, Virginia Pearson, Phillips Smalley; *D:* Fred Windermere. *GPV*

Taxi zum Klo 🎬🎬🎬 1981 An autobiographical semi-documentary about the filmmaker's aimless existence and attempts at homosexual affairs after being fired from his job as a teacher. Explicit. In German with English subtitles. Sordid sexual situations. 98m/C VHS, Beta. *GE* Bernd Broaderup, Frank Ripploh; *D:* Frank Ripploh. *FCT, GLV, CCN*

A Taxing Woman 🎬🎬🎬½ Marusa No Onna 1987 Satiric Japanese comedy about a woman tax collector in pursuit of a crafty millionaire tax cheater. Followed by the equally hilarious "A Taxing Woman's Return." In Japanese with English subtitles. 127m/C VHS, Beta, LV. *JP* Nobuko Miyamoto, Tsutomu Yamazaki; *D:* Juzo Itami; *W:* Juzo Itami. *FXL, LUM, FCT*

A Taxing Woman's Return 🎬🎬🎬 Marusa No Onna II 1988 Funny, sophisticated, action-packed. Miyamoto returns as the dedicated tax investigator to fight industrialists, politicians, and other big swindlers, who have contrived to inflate Tokyo's real estate values. Sequel to "A Taxing Woman." In Japanese with English subtitles. 127m/C VHS, Beta, LV. *JP* Nobuko Miyamoto, Rentaro Mikuni, Masahiko Tsugawa, Tetsuro Tamba, Toru Masuoka, Takeya Nakamura, Hosei Komatsu, Mihoko Shibata; *D:* Juzo Itami; *W:* Juzo Itami. *NYF*

TC 2000 🎬½ 1993 (R) Jason Storm and Zoey Kinsella are cops working for The Controller, who has the unenviable task of protecting the community from roving gangs of vicious punks. When Zoey is killed, The Controller converts her into a super-cybernetic killing machine unleashed on the gangs. Meanwhile Jason is considered a liability and must battle the gangs, The Controller, and cyber Zoey to save himself. Oh, there's also something about saving the Earth's atmosphere from nuclear destruction. Lots of action.*CW:* Some language and continuous violence. 92m/C VHS, LV, Closed Caption. Billy Blanks, Bobbie Philips, Jalal Merhi, Bolo Yeung, Matthias Hues; *D:* T.J. Scott; *W:* T.J. Scott. *USH, SGE*

Tchaikovsky 🎬🎬½ 1971 The glorious music is all that saves this pedestrian biography of the 19th century Russian composer, which ignores his homosexuality and glosses over the dissolution of his marriage. Lead performance by Smoktunovsky does manage to rise above the moribund script. Originally released at 191 minutes. In Russian with English subtitles. 153m/C VHS. *RU* Innokenti Smoktunovsky, Antonina Shuranova, Yevgeny Leonov, Maya Plisetskaya, Vladislav Strzeltchik, Alla Demidova, Kirill Lavrov; *D:* Igor Talankin. Nominations: Academy Awards '71: Best Foreign Language Film, Original Song Score and/or Adaptation. *KIV, FCT*

Tchao Pantin 🎬🎬🎬 1984 An acclaimed French film noir about an ex-cop being drawn into drug smuggling underground via a young Arab. English subtitles. Finely drawn characters skillfully portrayed make this a winner. 100m/C VHS, Beta. *FR* Coluche, Richard Anconina, Agnes Soral; *D:* Claude Berri. Cesar Awards '84: Best Actor (Coluche), Best Cinematography, Best Sound, Best Supporting Actor (Anconina). *FCT*

Tea and Sympathy 🎬🎬🎬 1956 A young prep school student, confused about his sexuality, has an affair with an older woman, his teacher's wife. The three leads recreate their Broadway roles in this tame adaption of the Robert Anderson play which dealt more openly with the story's homosexual elements. 122m/C VHS, LV, Letterbox, Closed Caption. Deborah Kerr, John Kerr, Leif Erickson, Edward Andrews, Darryl Hickman, Norma Crane, Dean Jones; *D:* Vincente Minnelli; *W:* Robert Anderson; *C:* John Alton. *MGM, FCT*

Tea for Three 🎬🎬 1984 (R) Sexual trio develops and seeks therapy after a fledgling doctor has been having sexual relationships with two women, and the females finally meet. 89m/C VHS, Beta. Iris Berben, Mascha Gonska, Heinz Marecek; *D:* Gerhard Janda.

Tea for Two 🎬🎬🎬 1950 This take-off on the Broadway play "No, No, Nanette" features Day as an actress who takes a bet that she can answer "no" to every question for 24 hours (life was less complex back then). If she can, she gets to finance and star in her own Broadway musical. 🎵I Know That You Know; Crazy Rhythm; Charleston; I Only Have Eyes For You; Tea For Two; I Want to be Happy; Oh Me, Oh My; The Call of the Sea; Do Do Do. 98m/C VHS. Doris Day, Gordon MacRae, Gene Nelson, Patrice Wymore, Eve Arden, Billy DeWolfe, S.Z. Sakall, Bill Goodwin, Virginia Gibson, Crauford Kent, Harry Harvey; *D:* David Butler. *WAR, CCB, MVD*

Teach Me 🎬 1997 (R) Erotic romance novelist Sara Kane gets a story idea from observing a troubled couple at a restaurant. Janine's got some sexual fears that are causing problems in her marriage but Sara's willing to intercede and help ease her tensions.*CW:* Strong sexuality. 90m/C VHS. Shannon Leahy, Raasa Leela Shields, Greg Provance; *D:* Gary Delfiner. *APX*

The Teacher 🎬🎬 The Seductress 1974 (R) TV's "Dennis the Menace" (North) has an affair with his high school teacher; the pair is menaced by a deranged killer. Cheap but enjoyable. 97m/C VHS, Beta, LV. Angel Tompkins, Jay North, Anthony James; *D:* Howard (Hikmet) Avedis. *NO*

Teachers 🎬🎬 1984 (R) A lawsuit is brought against a high school for awarding a diploma to an illiterate student. Comedy-drama starts slowly and seems to condemn the school system, never picking up strength or resolving any issues, though Nolte is fairly intense. Shot in Columbus, Ohio. 106m/C VHS, Beta, LV, Closed Caption. Nick Nolte, JoBeth Williams, Lee Grant, Judd Hirsch, Ralph Mac-

chio, Richard Mulligan, Royal Dano, Morgan Freeman, Laura Dern, Crispin Glover, Madeline Otherwood, Zohra Lampert; *D:* Arthur Hiller. *MGM, FOX*

Teacher's Pet 🎬🎬🎬 1958 This charming comedy features a cynical newspaper editor who enrolls in a night college journalism course, believing that it won't teach anything of substance. He later becomes enamored of his instructor. Well written script and superb performance by Young as Gable's rival for Day. 120m/B VHS, Beta. Clark Gable, Doris Day, Mamie Van Doren, Gig Young, Nick Adams; *D:* George Seaton; *W:* Fay Kanin, Michael Kanin. Nominations: Academy Awards '58: Best Story & Screenplay, Best Supporting Actor (Young).*PAR, BAR*

The Teahouse of the August Moon 🎬🎬½ 1956 An adaptation of the John Patrick play. Post-war American troops are assigned to bring civilization to a small village in Okinawa and instead fall for Okinawan culture and romance. Lively cast keeps it generally working, but assessments of Brando's comedic performance vary widely. 123m/C VHS, Beta, LV, Letterbox. Glenn Ford, Marlon Brando, Eddie Albert, Paul Ford, Machiko Kyo, Harry (Henry) Morgan; *D:* Daniel Mann; *C:* John Alton. *MGM*

Teamster Boss: The Jackie Presser Story 🎬🎬🎬 1992 (R) A well-done made-for-cable-television movie powered by a riveting performance by Dennehy. Presser followed Jimmy Hoffa as president of the Teamsters and was equally caught between the mob and the government as he tried to do what he considered best for the union.*CW:* Strong language and some violence. 111m/C VHS, LV, Closed Caption. Brian Dennehy, Jeff Daniels, Maria Conchita Alonso, Eli Wallach, Robert Prosky, Donald Moffat, Tony LoBianco, Kate Reid, Henderson Forsythe, Al Waxman; *D:* Alastair Reid. *HBO, PMS*

Tearaway 🎬½ 1987 (R) Australian story of a street punk with an alcoholic father. Story has potential, but ends up going nowhere. 100m/C VHS, Beta. *NZ AU* Matthew Hunter, Mark Pilisi, Peter Bland, Kim Willoughby, Rebecca Saunders; *D:* Bruce Morrison. *ORI, WAR*

Tears in the Rain 🎬🎬 1988 Casey Cantrell (Stone) travels to London to deliver a deathbed letter from her mother to Lord Richard Bredon. While in England, she is pursued by two men, an heir to the Bredon fortune, and his wealthy friend. After she finds a love which is forbidden, she makes a bizarre discovery that changes her life forever. Made for British television. 100m/C VHS. *GB* Sharon Stone, Christopher Cazenove, Leigh Lawson, Paul Daneman; *D:* Don Sharp. *VCO*

Tecumseh: The Last Warrior 🎬🎬½ 1995 Oh-so-noble TV biography of the Shawnee leader (1768-1813) and his refusal to give up the battle against white settlement of the Indiana Territory. North Carolina substitutes for Ohio and Indiana. Based on the book "Panther in the Sky" by James Alexander Thom. 90m/C VHS. Jesse Borrego, David Clennon, Tantoo Cardinal, David Morse, Holt McCallany, August Schellenberg, Jimmie F. Skaggs, Jeri Arredondo; *D:* Larry Elikann; *W:* Paul F. Edwards; *M:* David Shire. *TTC*

Ted & Venus 🎬🎬½ 1993 (R) Cort plays Ted, an oddball cult poet in love with Linda, a beach beauty who finds him repulsive. The more she rejects him, the more obsessed about her Ted gets, especially when his equally oddball friends offer him romantic advice.*CW:* Strong language and sexual dialogue, some drug content, and sensuality. 100m/C VHS. Bud Cort, Kim Adams, Rhea Perlman, James Brolin, Carol Kane; *Cameos:* Gena Rowlands, Martin Mull, Woody Harrelson, Andrea Martin, Timothy Leary, Cassandra Peterson; *D:* Bud Cort; *W:* Bud Cort, Paul Ciotti. *COL*

Teddy at the Throttle 🎬🎬 1916 Teddy, the Great Dane, must rescue Gloria Swanson from a villain who has tied up her boyfriend. Silent. 20m/B VHS, Beta. Bobby Vernon, Gloria Swanson, Wallace Beery; *D:* Clarence Badger. *CCB*

Teddy at the Throttle/Speeding Along 🎬🎬 1917 A silent comedy about stealing fortunes from innocent heroines and another about racing cars in a farm area. 54m/B VHS, Beta. Gloria Swanson, Wallace Beery, Bobby Vernon. *VYY*

Teen Alien 🎬 *The Varrow Mission* 1988 (PG) On Halloween, a young boy and his friends run into a hostile alien. It could happen. 88m/C VHS, Beta. Vern Adix; *D:* Peter Senelka.

Teen Vamp 🎬 1988 Dorky high schooler is bitten by a prostitute; becomes a cool vampire. Mindless "comedy." 87m/C VHS, Beta. Clu Gulager, Karen Carlson, Angela Brown; *D:* Samuel Bradford. *VTR*

Teen Witch 🎬🎬 1989 (PG-13) A demure high schooler uses black magic to woo the most popular guy in school. 94m/C VHS, Beta. Robin Lively, Zelda Rubinstein, Dan Gauthier, Joshua Miller, Dick Sargent; *D:* Dorian Walker; *W:* Robin Menken. *VTR*

Teen Wolf 🎬🎬½ 1985 (PG) A nice, average teenage basketball player begins to show werewolf tendencies which suddenly make him popular at school when he leads the team to victory. The underlying message is be yourself, regardless of how much hair you have on your body. Lighthearted comedy carried by the Fox charm; followed by subpar "Teen Wolf Too." 92m/C VHS, Beta, LV, 8mm, Closed Caption. Michael J. Fox, James Hampton, Scott Paulin, Susan Ursitti; *D:* Rod Daniel; *M:* Miles Goodman. *PAR*

Teen Wolf Too 🎬🎬 1987 (PG) The sequel to "Teen Wolf" in which the Teen Wolf's cousin goes to college on a boxing scholarship. More evidence that the sequel is rarely as good as the original. 95m/C VHS, Beta, Closed Caption. Jason Bateman, Kim Darby, John Astin, Paul Sand; *D:* Christopher Leitch; *W:* Timothy King. *PAR*

Teenage 🎬 1944 Low budget juvenile schlock film that tries to figure out what's wrong with modern youth. Pure camp. ?m/C VHS. Herbert Heyes, Wheeler Oakman. *SNC*

Teenage Bad Girl 🎬🎬½ *Bad Girl; My Teenage Daughter* 1959 A woman who edits a magazine for teenagers can't control her own daughter. The kid does time in the pen after staying out all night and generally running around with the wrong crowd. Syms first lead performance is memorable in an otherwise routine teensploitation flick. 100m/B VHS, Beta. Anna Neagle, Sylvia Syms, Norman Wooland, Wilfrid Hyde-White, Kenneth Haigh, Julia Lockwood; *D:* Herbert Wilcox. *SNC, DVT*

Teenage Bonnie & Klepto Clyde 🎬½ 1993 (R) Like their '30s namesakes, Clyde Barrow and Bonnie Parker are just two high-spirited kids who let their need for excitement get in the way of their better judgment (ha!). Bonnie and Clyde meet in a fast-food joint, become shoplifting buddies, fall in love, graduate to armed robbery, try to run for the border, and die. 90m/C VHS. Maureen Flannigan, Scott Wolf; *Cameos:* Don Novello. *THV*

Teenage Caveman 🎬🎬 *Out of the Darkness; Prehistoric World* 1958 A teenage boy living in a post-apocalypse yet prehistoric world journeys across the river, even though he was warned against it, and finds an old man who owns a book about past civilizations in the 20th Century. Schlocky, and one of the better bad films around. The dinosaur shots were picked up from the film "One Million B.C." 66m/B VHS. Robert Vaughn, Darrah Marshall, Leslie Bradley, Frank De Kova; *D:* Roger Corman. *COL*

Teenage Crime Wave 🎬 1955 Route 66 provides thrills for a couple of teen punks, but things get out of hand when they blow a sheriff's head off. They scoop up a couple of babes and hightail it with the police close behind, ultimately confronting their destiny at a mountain top observatory. 77m/B VHS, Beta. Tommy Cook, Mollie McCart, Sue England, Frank Griffin, James Bell, Kay Riehl; *D:* Fred F. Sears. *SNC, AOV*

Teenage Devil Dolls 🎬 1953 A cheap exploitation teenage flick wherein an innocent girl is turned on to reefer and goofballs, and eventually ends up on the street. 70m/C VHS, Beta. Barbara Marks, Bramlef L. Price Jr.; *D:* B. Lawrence Price. *RHI*

Teenage Doll 🎬🎬 1957 Good old Corman teen exploitation pic features a good girl who's tired of being good and gets mixed up with some street punks. She even manages to set off a gang war by accidentally killing a beat girl from a rival group. 71m/B VHS. Fay Spain, John Brinkley, June Kennedy, Collette Jackson, Barbara Wilson, Ed Nelson, Richard Devon, Ziva Rodann; *D:* Roger Corman; *W:* Charles B. Griffith; *C:* Floyd Crosby. *EEL*

Teenage Exorcist 🎬½ 1993 Tired horror spoof finds the prim Diane (Stevens) renting a creepy house from an equally creepy real estate agent (Berryman). After she moves in, Diane begins having horrible nightmares and calls her family for help. When they arrive Diane has turned into a chainsaw-wielding seductress. The family is so distressed that they misdial the phone and wind up with a pizza delivery geek (Deezen) instead of the exorcist they need. 90m/C VHS, LV. Brinke Stevens, Eddie Deezen, Michael Berryman, Robert Quarry, Jay Richardson, Tom Shell, Elena Sahagun; *D:* Grant Austin Waldman; *W:* Brinke Stevens.

Teenage Frankenstein 🎬½ 1958 A descendent of Dr. Frankenstein makes his own scramble-faced monster out of a teenage boy. Lurid '50s drive-in fare (companion to "I Was a Teenage Werewolf") is campy fun in small doses only. 72m/B VHS. Whit Bissell, Phyllis Coates, Robert Burton, Gary Conway, George Lynn, John Cliff; *D:* Herbert L. Strock. *COL*

Teenage Gang Debs 🎬 1966 These chicks throw a sleazy coming out party the likes of which defy description. Simply the most important social function of 1966. 77m/B VHS. Diana Conti, Linda Gale, Eileen Scott, Sandra Kane, Robin Nolan, Linda Cambi, Sue McManus, Geri Tyler, Joey Naudic, John Batis, Tom Yourk, Thomas Andrisano, George Winship, Doug Mitchell, Tom Eldred, Frank Spinella, Alec Primrose, Gene Marrin, Lyn Kennedy, Janet Banzet; *D:* Sande N. Johnson; *W:* Hy Cahl. *SMW, TPV*

Teenage Mother woof! 1967 A Swedish sex education teacher comes to town and poisons the minds of the local high school kids. Naturally one becomes pregnant and has to try to trick the father into marrying her. More awful stuff from the director of "Girl On a Chain Gang." 78m/C VHS, Beta. Arlene Sue Farber, Frederick Riccio, Julie Ange, Howard Le May, George Peters; *D:* Jerry Gross. *SNC, TPV*

Teenage Mutant Ninja Turtles: The Movie 🎬🎬½ 1990 (PG) Four sewer-dwelling turtles that have turned into warrior ninja mutants due to radiation exposure take it upon themselves to rid the city of crime and pizza. Aided by a television reporter and their ninja master, Splinter the Rat, the turtles encounter several obstacles, including the evil warlord Shredder. A most excellent live-action version of the popular comic book characters which will hold the kids' interest. Much head-kicking and rib-crunching action as Leonardo, Donatello, Raphael, and Michelangelo fight for the rights of pre-adolescents everywhere. Combines real actors with Jim Henson creatures. 95m/C VHS, Beta, LV, 8mm, Closed Caption. Judith Hoag, Elias Koteas; *D:* Steven Barron; *W:* Todd W. Langen; *C:* John Fenner; *M:* John Du Prez; *V:* Robbie Rist, Corey Feldman, Brian Tochi, Kevin Clash, David McCharen. *FHE, ART*

Teenage Mutant Ninja Turtles 2: The Secret of the Ooze 🎬🎬 1991 (PG) Amphibious pizza-devouring mutants search for the toxic waste that turned them into marketable martial artist ecologically correct kid idols. Same formula as the first go-round with some new characters tossed in. Animatronic characters from the laboratory of Jim Henson, first screen appearance by rapper Vanilla Ice. Marked end of pre-teen turtle craze. 88m/C VHS, Beta, Closed Caption. Francois

Chau, David Warner, Paige Turco, Ernie Reyes Jr., Vanilla Ice; *D:* Michael Pressman. *COL, NLC*

Teenage Mutant Ninja Turtles 3 🎬🎬 1993 (PG) Check it out dudes; the Teenage Mutant Ninja Turtles hit 17th century Japan to rescue loyal friend, reporter April O'Neil. Plenty of smoothly executed, blood-free martial arts moves keep the pace rolling, while the turtles battle an evil lord and English pirates. Seeing the TMNT's use a little more of their reptilian grey matter, and snarf a little less pizza should contribute to a relatively high adult tolerance level (considering the genre), and loads of good clean fun for the kiddies. 96m/C VHS, LV, Letterbox. Elias Koteas, Paige Turco, Stuart Wilson, Sab Shimono, Vivian Wu; *D:* Stuart Gillard; *W:* Stuart Gillard; *M:* John Du Prez; *V:* Randi Mayem Singer, Matt Hill, Jim Raposa, David Fraser. *NLC, COL, IME*

Teenage Strangler woof! 1964 A homicidal teen terrorizes his school. Cheap film features drag races, rumbles, dances, babes, rock 'n' roll and more. One for the "bad enough to be fun" category. 61m/C VHS, Beta. Bill A. Bloom, Jo Canterbury, John Ensign; *D:* Bill Posner. *SNC, SMW*

Teenage Wolfpack 🎬½ 1957 Boring film about German juvenile delinquents, robbery, violence, and murder. 90m/C VHS. GE Horst Buchholz, Karin Baal, Christian Doermer; *D:* Georg Tressler. *SNC*

Teenage Zombies woof! 1958 Mad scientist on remote island kidnaps teenagers and uses her secret chemical formula to turn them into zombies as part of her plan to enslave the world. Not as good as it sounds. 71m/B VHS, Beta. Don Sullivan, Katherine Victor, Chuck Niles; *D:* Jerry Warren; *W:* Jacques LeCotier. *NOS, SNC, VYY*

Teenager 🎬 1974 (R) Three desperate, reckless individuals, all caught up in making a low budget movie, interact and eventually self-destruct. 91m/C VHS, Beta. Andrea Cagan, Reid Smith, Susan Bernard; *D:* Gerald Seth Sindell.

Teenagers from Outer Space woof! *The Gargon Terror* 1959 Low-budget sci-fi effort finds extraterrestrial youngsters visiting earth to conquer it and find food for their "monstrous pets" (they're really lobster shadows.) So cheaply made and melodramatic that it just may be good for a laugh. 86m/B VHS. Tom Graeff, Dawn Anderson, Harvey B. Dunn, Bryant Grant, Thomas Lockyear; *D:* Tom Graeff. *EEL, SNC*

TekWar 🎬🎬½ 1994 It's 2044 and society is plagued by "Tek," an illegal, addictive drug-like computer disk that creates powerful but destructive virtual-reality fantasies. Jake Cardigan (Evigan) is an cop framed on drug and murder charges, fresh out of prison, who's trying to both clear his name and find out what happened to his now ex-wife and son. Shatner, who wrote the Tek novels, guests as Walter Bascom, the head of a detective agency who promises to help Cardigan if Jake helps find a missing scientist. Made for TV. 92m/C VHS. Greg Evigan, Eugene C. Clark, Torri Higginson, William Shatner; *D:* William Shatner. *USH*

Telefon 🎬🎬 1977 (PG) Suspenseful, slick spy tale. Soviet agents battle a lunatic comrade who tries to use hypnotized Americans to commit sabotage. Daly, later of TV's "Cagney and Lacey," is memorable. 102m/C VHS, Beta. Charles Bronson, Lee Remick, Donald Pleasence, Tyne Daly, Patrick Magee, Sheree North; *D:* Donald Siegel; *W:* Stirling Silliphant, Peter Hyams; *M:* Lalo Schifrin. *MGM*

Telegraph Trail 🎬½ 1933 Weak Wayne entry about an Army scout who helps some workers complete the first transcontinental wire line. Of course, Wayne ends up getting tough with some Indians. Cheaply made, with most of the action footage lifted from the 1926 silent, "The Red Raiders." 60m/B VHS, Closed Caption. John Wayne, Marceline Day, Frank McHugh, Otis Harlan, Yakima Canutt, Lafe McKee; *D:* Tenny Wright; *W:* Kurt Kempler. *MGM*

The Telephone woof! 1987 (R) A neurotic out-of-work actress begins a comedic chain of events via a few prank phone calls. Goldberg has managed to salvage some bad material with the strength of her comedic performances, but not so here. In fact, she sued to prevent this version from ever seeing the light of day. Too bad she didn't have a better lawyer. Tom's directorial debut. **96m/C VHS, Beta, LV, Closed Caption.** Whoopi Goldberg, Elliott Gould, John Heard, Amy Wright; **D:** Rip Torn; **W:** Terry Southern. *VTR*

Tell It to the Judge *♪♪½* 1949 Russell plays the exuberant ex-wife of lawyer Cummings. They repeatedly try reconciling but ditzy blonde McDonald always manages to catch Cummings' eye. Fed up Russell takes off for a holiday in the mountains where she meets Young. When her ex-hubby follows her, she decides to try and make him jealous using Young as the bait. **87m/B VHS.** Rosalind Russell, Robert Cummings, Gig Young, Marie McDonald, Harry Davenport, Louise Beavers; **D:** Norman Foster. *FCT*

Tell Me a Riddle *♪♪½* 1980 (PG) A dying woman attempts to reconcile with her family in this poignant drama about an elderly couple rediscovering their mutual love after 47 years of marriage. Fine acting; Grant's directorial debut. **94m/C VHS, Beta.** Melvyn Douglas, Lila Kedrova, Brooke Adams, Peter Coyote; **D:** Lee Grant; **W:** Joyce Eliason.

Tell Me That You Love Me *♪½* 1984 (R) A tear-jerking portrait of a disintegrating modern marriage. **88m/C VHS, Beta.** Nick Mancuso, Barbara Williams, Belinda J. Montgomery; **D:** Tzipi Trope. *ART, VES*

Tell Me Where It Hurts *♪♪* 1974 A middle-aged housewife changes her life when she forms a women's consciousness-raising group with her friends. The script won an Emmy. Stapleton's performance is redeeming in this otherwise slow movie. **78m/C VHS, Beta.** Maureen Stapleton, Paul Sorvino; **D:** Paul Bogart; **M:** David Shire. *BFA*

The Tell-Tale Heart *♪♪½ The Hidden Room of 1,000 Horrors* 1962 Daydreaming author fantasizes about falling for major babe and killing his best friend for her. Adapted Poe tale. **78m/B VHS.** **GB** Laurence Payne, Adrienne Corri, Dermot Walsh, Selma Vaz Dias, John Scott, John Martin, Annette Carell, David Lander; **D:** Ernest Morris; **W:** Brian Clemens. *NOS, SNC, LOO*

Tell Them Willie Boy Is Here *♪♪♪* 1969 (PG) Western drama set in 1909 California about a Paiute Indian named Willie Boy and his white bride. They become the objects of a manhunt (led by the reluctant local sheriff, Redford) after Willie kills his wife's father in self-defense. This was once-blacklisted Polonsky's first film in 21 years. **98m/C VHS, Beta, LV, Letterbox.** Robert Redford, Katharine Ross, Robert (Bobby) Blake, Susan Clark, Barry Sullivan, John Vernon, Charles McGraw; **D:** Abraham Polonsky; **W:** Abraham Polonsky; **C:** Conrad Hall; **M:** Dave Grusin. *USH*

Telling Lies in America *♪♪* 1996 (PG-13) Semiautobiographical Esterhaus-penned coming-of-ager allies a star-struck and naive Hungarian immigrant teen with dirty deejay on the take in early 60s Cleveland. Karchy Jones (Renfro) worships the slick polyester prince of the airwaves Billy Magic (Bacon), and through a contest at school, wins a chance to become his eager-beaver lackey. The twisted rock-n-roll mentor shows Karchy his own, highly cynical version of attaining the American Dream which, naturally, leads to trouble. Universally acclaimed performance by Bacon, who takes a one-dimensional persona and runs with it. Flockhart plays the "it" girl of Karchy's dreams. Smoothly told story suffers from a few of the usual cliches, but makes up for in heart. **CW:** Sex-related situations. **101m/C VHS.** Kevin Bacon, Brad Renfro, Maximilian Schell, Calista Flockhart, Paul Dooley, Jonathan Rhys Myers, Luke Wilson; **D:** Guy Ferland; **W:** Joe Eszterhas; **C:** Reynaldo Villalobos; **M:** Nicholas Pike. *BMG*

The Temp woof! 1993 (R) Unbelievably bad attempt at office horror. Beautiful, mysterious Kris temps for Hutton, a junior exec at the Mrs. Appleby baked goods company. She's almost too good

to be true with unbelievable organizational skills and her dead serious ambition to climb the corporate ladder. Psycho drama has psycho, but lacks drama, direction, plot development, intelligent dialogue, and anything resembling motive. While Hutton is tolerable, we nominate ex-Twin Peaker Boyle for the bad acting hall of shame as the conniving psycho. **CW:** Language and violent scenes. **99m/C VHS, Beta, LV, Letterbox, Closed Caption.** Timothy Hutton, Lara Flynn Boyle, Faye Dunaway, Dwight Schultz, Oliver Platt, Steven Weber, Scott Coffey, Colleen Flynn, Dakin Matthews, Maura Tierney; **D:** Tom Holland; **W:** Kevin Falls. Golden Raspberry Awards '93: Worst Supporting Actress (Dunaway). *PAR*

The Tempest *♪♪♪* 1928 A Russian peasant soldier rises through the ranks to become an officer, only to be undone by his love for the daughter of his commanding officer. Silent with musical score. **105m/B VHS, Beta.** John Barrymore, Louis Wolheim; **D:** Sam Taylor; **C:** Charles Rosher. Academy Awards '28: Best Interior Decoration; Nominations: Academy Awards '28: Best Cinematography. *NOS, CCB, VYY*

The Tempest *♪♪½* 1963 Shakespeare's classic tale of the fantasy world of spirits, sorcerers, maidens, monsters, and scheming noblemen is brought to life in George Schaefer's ethereal production. **76m/C VHS, Beta.** Maurice Evans, Richard Burton, Roddy McDowall, Lee Remick, Tom Poston; **D:** George Schaefer. *TVC, FHS*

The Tempest *♪♪♪* 1982 (PG) A New York architect, fed up with city living, chucks it all and brings his daughter to live with him on a barren Greek island. Based on Shakespeare's play of the same name. Well-written, thoughtfully acted, and beautifully filmed. **140m/C VHS, Beta, LV.** John Cassavetes, Gena Rowlands, Susan Sarandon, Vittorio Gassman, Molly Ringwald, Paul Stewart, Sam Robards, Raul Julia; **D:** Paul Mazursky; **W:** Paul Mazursky, Leon Capetanos. *COL*

The Tempest/The Eagle *♪♪♪* 1927 A Russian soldier during the Revolution is betrayed and humiliated by the woman he loves in "The Tempest." In "The Eagle," an outcast guardsman becomes the Russian version of Robin Hood. **56m/B VHS, Beta.** John Barrymore, Camilla Horn, Rudolph Valentino, Louise Dresser; **D:** Sam Taylor, Clarence Brown. *CCB*

Temptation *♪♪* 1994 (R) Ex-con Eddie (Fahey) gets hired to work on a luxury yacht, which helps him keep track of his double-crossing former partner. Too bad for Eddie that the guy's wife is such a distraction. **91m/C VHS, Beta, LV, Closed Caption.** Jeff Fahey, Alison Doody, Philip Casnoff, David Keith, Patricia Durham, W. Paul Bodie; **D:** Strathford Hamilton. *ART*

Temptation of a Monk *♪♪* 1994 Costume drama about China's 7th-century Tang Dynasty finds General Shi (Hsin-kuo) duped into an assassination plot against the crown prince. After a massacre, the General flees and finds sanctuary with a group of Buddhist monks at a remote temple. There's also the General's sometime lover and a mystery woman (both played by Chen). Sometimes slow-moving and confusing but with exotic visuals. Based on a novel by Lilian Lee; Mandarin with subtitles. **118m/C VHS.** **CH** Wu Hsin-kuo, Joan Chen, Zhang Fengyi, Michael Lee; **D:** Clara Law; **C:** Andrew Lesnie. *FXL*

The Tempter *♪ L'Anticristo; The Antichrist* 1974 (R) Mirrors the gruesomeness of "The Exorcist," with story following an invalid's adventures with witchcraft, bestiality, and Satanism. **96m/C VHS, Beta.** **IT** Mel Ferrer, Carla Gravina, Arthur Kennedy, Alida Valli, Anita Strindberg, George Coulouris; **D:** Alberto De Martino; **M:** Ennio Morricone.

The Temptress *♪♪½* 1949 A doctor attempting to find a cure for polio is coerced by an irresistible woman into murder and blackmail. Well-told story, if somewhat grim. **85m/B VHS, Beta.** **GB** Joan Maude, Arnold Bell, Don Stannard, Shirley Quentin, John Stuart, Ferdinand "Ferdy" Mayne; **D:** Oswald Mitchell. *SNC*

Temptress *♪♪* 1995 (R) Photographer Karin Swann (Delaney) returns from a spiritual retreat in India obsessed with the deadly goddess Kali. Karin's new overtly sexual personality startles lover Matthew (Sarandon) while her work has also undergone some changes. When a friend is murdered, Matthew begins to wonder if Kali's evil powers have overtaken Karin. **93m/C VHS, Beta, Closed Caption.** Kim Delaney, Chris Sarandon, Corbin Bernsen, Dee Wallace Stone, Jessica Walter, Ben Cross; **D:** Lawrence Lanoff; **W:** Melissa Mitchell; **M:** Michael Stearns. *PAR*

Temptress Moon *♪♪ Feng Yue* 1996 (R) 1920s Shanghai is displayed in all its decadence with opium-addicted Ruyi (Li) forced to officially head the Pang family after the death of her father. Power actually lies with distant male cousin Duanwen (Lin), who manages the household and is drawn to his cold relative. Ruyi's childhood playmate and fellow addict, Zhongliang (Cheung), is now a professional gigolo and blackmailer, working for a gangster (Tian) who wants him to seduce Ruyi and steal the Pang fortune. What happens is an obsessive affair between two beautiful manipulators. Chilly high-style soap opera. Mandarin with subtitles. **CW:** Some intense images of sexuality and opium use. **113m/C VHS, LV, Closed Caption.** **HK** Gong Li, Leslie Cheung, Kevin Lin, Xie Tian, Zhou Jie, He Saifei; **D:** Chen Kaige; **W:** Shu Kei; **C:** Christopher Doyle; **M:** Zhao Jiping. *TOU*

10 *♪♪½* 1979 (R) A successful songwriter who has everything finds his life is incomplete without the woman of his dreams, the 10 on his girl-watching scale. His pursuit brings surprising results. Also popularizes Ravel's "Bolero." **121m/C VHS, Beta, LV, DVD.** Dudley Moore, Julie Andrews, Bo Derek, Dee Wallace Stone, Brian Dennehy, Robert Webber; **D:** Blake Edwards; **W:** Blake Edwards; **M:** Henry Mancini. Nominations: Academy Awards '79: Best Song ("Song from 10 (It's Easy to Say)"), Best Original Score. *WAR, FCT*

Ten Brothers of Shao-lin *♪* 198? Martial arts adventure from the days of warlords and warriors, when men were fierce and strong and struggles to the death occurred several times a day. **90m/C VHS, Beta.** Chia Ling, Wang Tao, Chang Yi. *NO*

The Ten Commandments *♪♪½* 1923 The silent epic that established DeMille as a popular directorial force and which he remade 35 years later as an even bigger epic with sound. Follows Moses' adventures in Egypt, plus a modern story of brotherly love and corruption. Features a new musical score by Gaylord Carter. Remade in 1956. **146m/B VHS, Beta.** Theodore Roberts, Richard Dix, Rod La Rocque, Edythe Chapman, Nita Naldi; **D:** Cecil B. DeMille; **C:** Archie Stout; **M:** Gaylord Carter. *PAR*

The Ten Commandments *♪♪♪* 1956 (G) DeMille's remake of his 1923 silent classic (and his last film) is a lavish Biblical epic that tells the life story of Moses, who turned his back on a privileged life to lead his people to freedom outside of Egypt. Exceptional cast, with Fraser Heston (son of Charlton) as the baby Moses. Parting of Red Sea rivals any modern special effects. Available in widescreen on laserdisc. A 35th Anniversary Collector's Edition is available uncut at 245 minutes, in widescreen format and Dolby Surround stereo, and 1,000 copies of an Autographed Limited Edition that includes an engraved bronze plaque and an imprinted card written and personally signed by Charlton Heston are also available. **219m/C VHS, Beta, LV, Letterbox.** Charlton Heston, Yul Brynner, Anne Baxter, Yvonne De Carlo, Nina Foch, John Derek, H.B. Warner, Henry Wilcoxon, Judith Anderson, John Carradine, Douglass Dumbrille, Cedric Hardwicke, Martha Scott, Vincent Price, Debra Paget; **D:** Cecil B. DeMille; **C:** Loyal Griggs; **M:** Elmer Bernstein. Academy Awards '56: Best Special Effects; Nominations: Academy Awards '56: Best Art Direction/Set Decoration (Color), Best Color Cinematography, Best Costume Design (Color), Best Film Editing, Best Picture, Best Sound. *PAR, FUS, IGP*

Ten Days That Shook the World 🐾🐾🐾½ *October* 1927 Silent masterpiece based on American author John Reed's book of the same name. Eisenstein, commissioned by the Soviet government, spared no expense to chronicle the Bolshevik Revolution of 1917 (in a flattering Communist light, of course). He was later forced to cut his portrayal of Leon Trotsky, who was then an enemy of the state. Includes rare footage of the Czar's Winter Palace in Leningrad. Haunting score, combined with some of Eisenstein's most striking work. See Warren Beatty's "Reds" for a fictional look at Reed and the Russian Revolution. 104m/B VHS, Beta, LV. *RU* Nikandrov, N. Popov, Boris Livanov; *D:* Grigori Alexandrov, Sergei Eisenstein; *M:* Dimitri Shostakovich. VYY, IHF, WFV

Ten Days Wonder 🐾🐾½ *La Decade Prodigieuse* 1972 (PG) Mystery/drama focuses on the patriarch of a wealthy family (Welles), his young wife, and his adopted son (Perkins), who is having an affair with his stepmother. It also turns out that Perkins is certifiable and is trying to break all of the Ten Commandments, which he succeeds in doing before killing himself (gruesomely). Based on the mystery novel by Ellery Queen. 101m/C VHS. *FR* Orson Welles, Anthony Perkins, Marlene Jobert, Michel Piccoli, Guido Alberti; *D:* Claude Chabrol. MOV, CVC, TPV

Ten Little Indians 🐾🐾½ *And Then There Were None* 1975 (PG) Ten people are gathered in an isolated inn under mysterious circumstances. One by one they are murdered, each according to a verse from a children's nursery rhyme. British adaptation of the novel and stage play by Agatha Christie. 98m/C VHS, Beta, LV. *GB* Herbert Lom, Richard Attenborough, Oliver Reed, Elke Sommer, Charles Aznavour, Stephane Audran, Gert Frobe, Adolfo Celi, Orson Welles; *D:* Peter Collinson. NLC

Ten Little Indians 🐾🐾 *Agatha Christie's Ten Little Indians* 1989 (PG) A group of prize-winning vacationers find themselves embarking on an African adventure. They all wind up at the same camp, and realize that they are being murdered one by one. Based on the work of Agatha Christie. 100m/C VHS, Beta, LV. Donald Pleasence, Brenda Vaccaro, Frank Stallone, Herbert Lom, Sarah Maur-Thorp; *D:* Alan Birkinshaw.

The Ten Million Dollar Getaway 🐾🐾 1991 (PG-13) True story of the 1978 Lufthansa robbery at Kennedy Airport in which the criminals were forced to leave 10 of their 20-million-dollar heist behind when a pick-up van didn't show. Standard made-for-cable fare produced to cash in on the same scenario played out in "Goodfellas." 93m/C VHS, Beta, Closed Caption. John Mahoney, Karen Young, Tony LoBianco, Gerry Bamman, Joseph Carberry, Terrence Mann, Kenneth John McGregor, Christopher Murney; *D:* James A. Contner; *W:* Christopher Canaan. PAR

Ten Nights in a Bar Room 🐾🐾 1913 The evils of alcohol are dramatized when they ruin a man's life. One of many propaganda films about alcohol and the problems that it caused that were made during the prohibition era. Silent, with a musical score. Remade in 1931. 68m/B VHS, Beta. Robert Lawrence, Marie Trado. VCN

Ten Nights in a Bar-Room 🐾🐾 1931 A turn-of-the-century mill owner succumbs to alcoholism and ruins his life and family. Later, he sees the error of his ways and gives up drinking. This was one of many films made during this era that chronicled the evils of alcohol and fanned the flames of the prohibition debate. Remake of the 1913 silent film. 60m/B VHS, Beta. William Farnum, Thomas Santschi, John Darrow, Robert Frazer; *D:* William O'Connor. VYY, GPV

Ten North Frederick 🐾🐾½ 1958 A shrewish wife (Fitzgerald) forces her gentle lawyer husband (Cooper) into cut-throat politics. He consoles himself in the arms of a much younger woman. Good performances, hokey script, based on the John O'Hara novel. 102m/B VHS. Gary Cooper, Diane Varsi, Suzy Parker, Geraldine Fitzgerald, Tom Tully, Stuart Whitman; *D:* Philip Dunne; *W:* Philip Dunne. FXL

10 Rillington Place 🐾🐾🐾 1971 (PG) A grimy, upsetting British film about the famed serial killer John Christie and the man wrongly hanged for his crimes, the incident that led to the end of capital punishment in England. Impeccably acted. One of Hurt's earliest films. 111m/C VHS, Beta, LV. *GB* Richard Attenborough, John Hurt, Judy Geeson, Gabrielle Daye, Andre Morell; *D:* Richard Fleischer. MOV

Ten Speed 🐾🐾 1976 Two advertising executives compete in a bicycle race from San Francisco to Malibu. 89m/C VHS, Beta. William Woodbridge, Patricia Hume, David Clover. ART

Ten to Midnight 🐾🐾 1983 (R) Vigilante Bronson is on the prowl again, this time as a police officer after a kinky serial murderer. The psychotic killer stalks his daughter and Dad's gonna stop him at any cost. 101m/C VHS, Beta, LV. Charles Bronson, Wilford Brimley, Lisa Eilbacher, Andrew Stevens; *D:* J. Lee Thompson; *W:* William Roberts. MGM

10 Violent Women woof! 1979 (R) Ten women who take part in a million dollar jewelry heist are tossed into a women's prison where brutal lesbian guards subject them to degradation and brutality. 97m/C VHS, Beta. Sherri Vernon, Dixie Lauren, Sally Gamble; *D:* Ted V. Mikels. NO

Ten Wanted Men 🐾 1954 A successful cattle baron is confronted by a pistol-wielding landowner determined to ruin him. Standard fare, with better than average performances from Scott and Boone. 80m/C VHS, Beta, LV. Randolph Scott, Jocelyn Brando, Richard Boone, Skip Homeier, Leo Gordon, Jack Perrin, Donna Martell; *D:* H. Bruce Humberstone; *W:* Harriet Frank Jr., Irving Ravetch. COL

Ten Who Dared 🐾🐾 1960 Ten Civil War heroes brave the Colorado River in an effort to chart its course. Although it's based on an actual historic event, the film is poorly paced and lacks suspense. 92m/C VHS, Beta. Brian Keith, John Beal, James Drury; *D:* William Beaudine. DIS

The Tenant 🐾🐾🐾½ *Le Locataire* 1976 (R) Disturbing story of a hapless office worker who moves into a spooky Paris apartment house. Once lodged inside its walls, he becomes obsessed with the previous occupant, who committed suicide, and the belief that his neighbors are trying to kill him. Based on a novel by Roland Topor. 126m/C VHS, Beta. *FR* Roman Polanski, Isabelle Adjani, Melvyn Douglas, Jo Van Fleet, Bernard Fresson, Shelley Winters; *D:* Roman Polanski; *W:* Gerard Brach, Roman Polanski; *C:* Sven Nykvist. NO

The Tenant of Wildfell Hall 🐾🐾½ 1996 Anne Bronte gets her turn in the spotlight with this TV adaptation of her 1848 novel. When the mysterious Helen Graham (Fitzgerald) and her young son become the new tenants of decaying Wildfell Hall, they naturally elicit lots of gossip in their rural community. Then young farmer Gilbert Markham (Stephens) becomes romantically interested in Helen and she's eventually forced to reveal her secret—she's run away from her alcoholic and abusive husband Arthur Huntingdon (Graves), who has now kidnapped their son to force Helen to return. 180m/C VHS, Closed Caption. *GB CA* Tara Fitzgerald, Toby Stephens, Rupert Graves; *D:* Mike Barker; *M:* Richard G. Mitchell. WMI, FOX

The Tender Age 🐾🐾 *The Little Sister* 1984 Troubled 18-year-old girl gets out of a detention home and is put on probation. She captivates her idealistic probation officer, whose interest may extend beyond professional concern. Fine idea, but under-played. 103m/C VHS, Beta. John Savage, Tracy Pollan, Roxanne Hart, Richard Jenkins; *D:* Jan Egleson; *W:* Jan Egleson. ART

Tender Comrade 🐾🐾 1943 Flag-waving violin-accompanied tearjerker about five women who live together to make ends meet while their men do manly things during WWII. Intended to puff your heart up with patriotic gusto. Ironically,

thanks to the girls' communal living arrangement, director Dmytryk was later accused of un-American activities. 101m/B VHS. Ginger Rogers, Robert Ryan, Ruth Hussey, Patricia Collinge, Mady Christians, Kim Hunter, Jane Darwell, Mary Forbes, Richard Martin; *D:* Edward Dmytryk. TTC, FCT

Tender Is the Night 🐾🐾½ 1955 A television-special adaptation of the F. Scott Fitzgerald classic, set in the roaring '20s, in which a psychiatrist marries one of his patients and then heads down the road to ruin, driven by his marriage and the times in which he lives. An entry from the "Front Row Center" series. 60m/B VHS, Beta. Mercedes McCambridge, James Daly. NOS, DVT

Tender Loving Care 🐾 1973 Three nurses dispense hefty doses of T.L.C. in their hospital, and the patients aren't the only ones on the receiving end. 72m/C VHS, Beta. Donna Desmond, Leah Simon, Anita King; *D:* Don Edmunds.

Tender Mercies 🐾🐾🐾 1983 (PG) A down-and-out country western singer finds his life redeemed by the love of a good woman. Aided by Horton Foote's script, Duvall, Harper and Barkin keep this from being simplistic and sentimental. Duvall wrote as well as performed the songs in his Oscar-winning performance. Wonderful, life-affirming flick. 88m/C VHS, Beta, LV. Robert Duvall, Tess Harper, Betty Buckley, Ellen Barkin, Wilford Brimley; *D:* Bruce Beresford; *W:* Horton Foote; *C:* Russell Boyd; *M:* George Dreyfus. Academy Awards '83: Best Actor (Duvall), Best Original Screenplay; Golden Globe Awards '83: Best Actor—Drama (Duvall); Los Angeles Film Critics Association Awards '83: Best Actor (Duvall); New York Film Critics Awards '83: Best Actor (Duvall); Writers Guild of America '83: Best Original Screenplay; Nominations: Academy Awards '83: Best Director (Beresford), Best Picture, Best Song ("Over You"). REP, BTV, HMV

The Tender Trap 🐾🐾½ 1955 Charlie Reader (Sinatra) is a bachelor not content with the many women in his life. He meets the innocent Julie Gillis (Reynolds) and falls head over heels for her. He then torments himself over a marriage proposal, unwilling to let go of his freedom. 111m/C VHS, LV, Letterbox. Frank Sinatra, Debbie Reynolds, Celeste Holm, David Wayne, Carolyn Jones, Lola Albright, Tom Helmore, Howard St. John, Willard Sage, James Drury, Benny Rubin, Frank Sully, David White; *D:* Charles Walters; *W:* Julius J. Epstein; *C:* Paul Vogel. Nominations: Academy Awards '55: Best Song ("(Love Is) The Tender Trap"). MGM, MOV

The Tender Warrior 🐾🐾 1971 (G) A beautifully photographed animal adventure with Haggerty as the woodsman. 85m/C VHS, Beta. Dan Haggerty, Charles Lee, Liston Elkins; *D:* Stewart Raffill. VCD

The Tender Years 🐾🐾 1947 Sentimental drama of a minister trying to outlaw dog fighting, spurred on by his son's fondness for a particular dog. 81m/B VHS, Beta. Joe E. Brown, Richard Lyon, Noreen Nash, Charles Drake, Josephine Hutchinson; *D:* Harold Schuster. FXL

Tennessee Stallion 🐾 1978 A low-class horse-trainer breaks into the world of aristocratic thoroughbred racing. 87m/C VHS, Beta. Audrey Landers, Judy Landers, James Van Patten. ART, VES

Tennessee's Partner 🐾🐾 1955 Enjoyable, unexceptional buddy Western. Reagan intervenes in an argument and becomes Payne's pal. Adapted from a story by Bret Harte. 87m/C VHS, Beta. Ronald Reagan, Rhonda Fleming, John Payne; *D:* Allan Dwan. NO

Tension at Table Rock 🐾🐾 1956 Accused of cowardice, a lone gunman must prove he killed in self-defense. Well-cast serious Western. 93m/C VHS, Beta. Richard Egan, Dorothy Malone, Cameron Mitchell; *D:* Charles Marquis Warren. NO

Tentacles woof! 1977 (PG) Cheesy Italian version of "Jaws" lacking only the suspense and cogent storytelling. Huston slums as the investigator charged with finding the octopus gone mad, while Fonda collects check and makes a quick exit. Hopkins is in charge of the killer whales that

save the day. You'll cheer when Winters is devoured by sea pest. From the director of an "Exorcist" rip-off, "Beyond the Door" (that's not a recommendation). 00m/O V113, Beta. *I!* John Huston, Shelley Winters, Bo Hopkins, Henry Fonda, Cesare Danova; *D:* Oliver Hellman; *W:* Steven W. Carabatsos. *ART, VES*

Tentacles of the North ♂♂½ **1926** Two ships are trapped in the ice of the Arctic with the only survivor of one ship being a fearful young girl. Tinted print. 54m/B VHS. Gaston Glass, Alice Calhoun, Al Ferguson, Joseph Girard; *D:* Louis Chaudet. *GPV*

The Tenth Man ♂♂½ **1988** Hopkins stars as a wealthy French lawyer, captured by the Nazis and sentenced to death. He discovers a fellow prisoner who is willing to take his place in exchange for Hopkins' wealth going to support the man's family. After his release, Hopkins returns to his old home, now occupied by the dead man's family, but doesn't reveal his true identity. When an imposter appears, claiming to be Hopkins, another twist is added. Slow-going but the usual excellent performances by Hopkins and Jacobi. Based on a novella by Graham Greene. Made for television. 99m/C VHS, Beta, LV, Closed Caption. Anthony Hopkins, Kristin Scott Thomas, Derek Jacobi, Cyril Cusack, Brenda Bruce, Paul Rogers; *D:* Jack Gold. *MGM*

Tenth Month ♂♂ **1979** Carol Burnett plays a divorced, middle-aged woman who becomes pregnant by a married man. She refuses help, choosing instead to live alone and keep an ever hopeful vigil for the birth of her child. Sappy but touching made-for-TV drama. 123m/C VHS, Beta. Carol Burnett, Keith Michell, Dina Merrill; *D:* Joan Tewkesbury. *TLF*

10th Victim ♂♂♂ *La Decima Vittima; La Dixieme Victime* **1965** Sci-fi cult film set in the 21st century has Mastroianni and Andress pursuing one another in a futuristic society where legalized murder is used as the means of population control. Intriguing movie where Andress kills with a double-barreled bra, the characters hang out at the Club Masoch, and comic books are considered literature. Based on "The Seventh Victim" by Robert Sheckley. 92m/C VHS, Beta. *IT* Ursula Andress, Marcello Mastroianni, Elsa Martinelli, Salvo Randone, Massimo Serato; *D:* Elio Petri; *W:* Tonino Guerra. *NLC*

Teorema ♂♂ **1968** Scathing condemnation of bourgeois complacency. Stamp, either a devil or a god, mysteriously appears and enters into the life of a well-to-do Milanese family and raises each member's spirituality by sleeping with them. Ultimately, the experience leads to tragedy. In Italian with English subtitles. 98m/C VHS. *IT* Terence Stamp, Silvana Mangano, Massimo Girotti, Anna Wiazemsky, Laura Betti, Andres Jose Cruz; *D:* Pier Paolo Pasolini; *M:* Ennio Morricone. *TPV, CVC*

Tequila Sunrise ♂♂♂½ **1988 (R)** Towne's twisting film about two lifelong friends and a beautiful woman. Gibson is a (supposedly) retired drug dealer afraid of losing custody of his son to his nagging ex-wife. Russell is the cop and old friend who's trying to get the lowdown on a drug shipment coming in from Mexico. Pfeiffer runs the poshest restaurant on the coast and is actively pursued by both men. Questions cloud the plot and confuse the viewer; loaded with double-crosses, intrigue and surprises around every corner, still the photogenic leads are pleasant to watch. Steamy love scene between Pfeiffer and Gibson. 116m/C VHS, Beta, LV, 8mm, Closed Caption. Mel Gibson, Kurt Russell, Michelle Pfeiffer, Raul Julia, Arliss Howard, Arye Gross, J.T. Walsh, Ann Magnuson; *D:* Robert Towne; *W:* Robert Towne; *C:* Conrad Hall; *M:* Dave Grusin. Nominations: Academy Awards '88: Best Cinematography. *WAR*

Teresa Venerdi ♂♂♂ **1941** An unusual Italian comedy about a man and his financial difficulties. His mistress, his fiance and a young girl make his troubles more confusing. Unusually sweet and humorous DeSica. 90m/B VHS, Beta. *IT D:* Vittorio De Sica. *CIG*

Teresa's Tattoo ♂ **1994** A bimbo (Shelly) with a Chinese dragon tattoo somehow obtains a pair of earrings containing details of the U.S. space program. She's kidnapped by inept thugs and dies in a freak accident. Now the kidnappers need a look-alike for their extortion scheme so they kidnap another girl (Shelly again) and drug and tattoo her. Naturally, when she wakes up she manages to escape. Thin farce striving too hard to be madcap and whimsical. 88m/C VHS. Adrienne Shelly, C. Thomas Howell, Nancy McKeon, Lou Diamond Phillips, Casey Siemaszko, Jonathan Silverman; *Cameos:* Majel Barrett, Anthony Clark, Nanette Fabray, Tippi Hedren, k.d. lang, Joe Pantoliano, Mary Kay Place, Mare Winningham, Kiefer Sutherland; *D:* Julie Cypher; *W:* Georgie Huntington; *M:* Melissa Etheridge. *THV*

Tereza ♂♂♂ **1961** In politically chaotic Czechoslovakia, a female police detective tries to solve an intricate murder mystery. In Czech with English subtitles. 91m/B VHS, Beta. *CZ* Jirina Svorcova; *D:* Pavel Blumenfeld. *FCT, IHF*

Terminal Bliss ♂½ **1991 (R)** Teen heartthrob Perry stars as a spoiled rich druggie in this "Less Than Zero" knock-off. Perry and childhood pal Owen grow up sharing everything—lacrosse, girlfriends, and drugs. However, their friendship is really put to the test when a beautiful new girl (Chandler) moves to town just before graduation. Release was delayed, but obviously wants to capitalize on Perry's popularity. *CW:* Language, violence and drug use, and sexuality. 94m/C VHS, LV, Closed Caption. Luke Perry, Timothy Owen, Estee Chandler, Sonia Curtis, Micah Grant, Alexis Arquette; *D:* Jordan Alan; *W:* Jordan Alan; *C:* Greg Smith; *M:* Frank Becker. *WAR*

Terminal Choice ♂½ **1985 (R)** Staff at a hospital conduct a betting pool on patients' life expectancies. Someone decides he should win more often and uses a computer to help hedge his bets. Wasted cast on this unsuspenseful and bloody film. 98m/C VHS, Beta. Joe Spano, Diane Venora, David McCallum, Ellen Barkin; *D:* Sheldon Larry; *W:* Neal Bell. *VES*

Terminal Entry ♂½ **1987 (R)** Teen computer geeks accidentally find a terrorist online network, and inadvertently begin transmitting instructions to destroy U.S. targets. The premise is intriguing but poorly done. 95m/C VHS, Beta. Edward Albert, Yaphet Kotto, Kabir Bedi; *D:* John Kincade; *C:* James L. Carter. *CEL*

Terminal Exposure ♂♂ **1989 (R)** Predictable but likeable comedy-mystery. A pair of Venice, CA, beach denizens capture a murder on film and try to solve it. 105m/C VHS, Beta, LV. Steve Donmyer, John Vernon, Ted Lange, Joe Phelan, Hope Marie Carlton, Mark Hennessy, Scott King; *D:* Nico Mastorakis. *ART, VES*

Terminal Force ♂ **1988 (R)** Stupid, poorly executed story of kidnapping and the mob. So bad it never saw the inside of a theatre; went straight to video. 83m/C VHS, LV. Troy Donahue, Richard Harrison, Dawn Wildsmith; *D:* Fred Olen Ray. *VTR*

Terminal Impact ♂♂ **1995 (R)** Bounty hunters Saint (Zagarino) and Max (Genesse) agree to a high-paying assignment at Delta Tech Labs without asking any questions. They discover that the lab's chairman Sheen (Roberts) is messing around with DNA and has been implanting insect DNA into unwilling human subjects, which turns them into killer cyborgs as well. 94m/C VHS, LV, Closed Caption. Bryan Genesse, Frank Zagarino, Jennifer Miller, Ian Roberts; *D:* Yossi Wein; *W:* Jeff Albert, Dennis Dimster Denk; *C:* Rod Stewart. *NLC*

Terminal Island ♂½ **1973 (R)** Tough southern California penal colony is crowded with inmates from death row. When prison becomes coed, violence breaks out. Exploitative and unappealing. 88m/C VHS, Beta. Phyllis E. Davis, Tom Selleck, Don Marshall, Ena Hartman, Marta Kristen; *D:* Stephanie Rothman. *NO*

The Terminal Man ♂♂½ **1974 (R)** A slick, visually compelling adaptation of the Michael Crichton novel. A scientist plagued by violent mental disorders has a computer-controlled regulator implanted in his brain. The computer malfunctions and he starts a murdering spree. Futuristic vision of man-machine symbiosis gone awry. Well acted, but still falls short of the novel. 107m/C VHS, Beta. George Segal, Joan Hackett, Jill Clayburgh, Richard Dysart, James B. Sikking, Norman Burton; *D:* Mike Hodges; *W:* Mike Hodges. *WAR*

Terminal Velocity ♂♂ **1994 (PG-13)** Skydiving instructor Ditch Brodie (Sheen) thinks he sees student Chris Morrow (Kinski) plummet to her death, only it turns out she's not dead and certainly not a beginner. Upon further investigation, he finds the usual web of international intrigue descending upon him, and that the KGB definitely wants him to mind his own business. Still, he pushes on. Another no-brainer actioner with few surprises satisfies the guilty pleasures of action addicts only. *CW:* Scenes of strong action/violence; brief strong language. 132m/C VHS, LV, Closed Caption. Charlie Sheen, Nastassia Kinski, James Gandolfini, Christopher McDonald, Melvin Van Peebles; *D:* Deran Sarafian; *W:* David N. Twohy; *M:* Joel McNeely. *HPH*

Terminal Virus ♂♂ **1996 (R)** A deadly sexually transmitted disease has made reproduction impossible, so humanity is on the verge of extinction. It's up to an outlaw and a scientist to convince a suspicious population that a new serum is the cure everyone's been waiting for. *CW:* Violence, some sexuality and language. 74m/C VHS. James Brolin, Richard Lynch, Bryan Genesse. *NHO*

The Terminator ♂♂♂ **1984 (R)** Futuristic cyborg is sent to present-day Earth. His job: kill the woman who will conceive the child destined to become the great liberator and arch-enemy of the Earth's future rulers. The cyborg is also pursued by another futuristic visitor, who falls in love with the intended victim. Cameron's pacing is just right in this exhilarating, explosive thriller which displays Arnie as one cold-blooded villain who utters a now famous line: "I'll be back." Followed by "Terminator 2: Judgment Day." 108m/C VHS, Beta, LV, Letterbox. Arnold Schwarzenegger, Michael Biehn, Linda Hamilton, Paul Winfield, Lance Henriksen, Bill Paxton, Rick Rossovich, Dick Miller, Earl Boen; *D:* James Cameron; *W:* James Cameron; *M:* Brad Fiedel. *NO*

Terminator 2: Judgment Day ♂♂♂½ **1991 (R)** He said he'd be back and he is, programmed to protect the boy who will be mankind's post-nuke resistance leader. But the T-1000, a shape-changing, ultimate killing machine, is also on the boy's trail. Twice the mayhem, five times the special effects, ten times the budget of the first, but without Arnold it'd be half the movie. The word hasn't been invented to describe the special effects, particularly THE scariest nuclear holocaust scene yet. Worldwide megahit, but the $100 million budget nearly ruined the studio; Arnold accepted his $12 million in the form of a jet. Laserdisc features include pan and scan, widescreen and a "Making of T-2" short. *CW:* Language and strong sci-fi action and violence. 139m/C VHS, LV, 8mm, Closed Caption, DVD. Arnold Schwarzenegger, Linda Hamilton, Edward Furlong, Robert Patrick, Earl Boen, Joe Morton; *D:* James Cameron; *W:* James Cameron; *M:* Brad Fiedel. Academy Awards '91: Best Makeup, Best Sound, Best Sound Effects Editing, Best Visual Effects; MTV Movie Awards '92: Best Film, Best Male Performance (Schwarzenegger), Best Female Performance (Hamilton), Breakthrough Performance (Furlong), Most Desirable Female (Hamilton), Best Action Sequence; Nominations: Academy Awards '91: Best Cinematography, Best Film Editing. *ART*

Termini Station ♂♂½ **1989** Dewhurst gives an excellent performance as the alcoholic matriarch of a small-town Canadian family. She drinks all day and dreams of traveling to Italy, while her children work and believe there is something more to life than their mundane existence. When they finally do leave, they discover an intriguing new world. Dewhurst and Follows also appear together in "Anne of Green Gables" and "Anne of Avonlea." **105m/C VHS, Closed Caption.** *CA* Colleen Dewhurst, Megan Follows, Gordon Clapp, Hannah Lee, Leon Pownall, Debra McGrath, Elliott Smith, Norma Dell'Agnese; *D:* Allen King; *M:* Mychael Danna. *FXL, FCT*

Terms of Endearment 🐾🐾🐾 **1983 (PG)** A weeper following the changing relationship between a young woman and her mother, over a 30-year period. Beginning as a comedy, turning serious as the years go by, this was Brooks' debut as screenwriter and director. Superb supporting cast headed by Nicholson's slyly charming neighbor/ astronaut, with stunning performances by Winger and MacLaine as the two women who often know and love each other too well. Adapted from Larry McMurtry's novel. **132m/C VHS, Beta, LV, Closed Caption.** Shirley MacLaine, Jack Nicholson, Debra Winger, John Lithgow, Jeff Daniels, Danny DeVito; *D:* James L. Brooks; *W:* James L. Brooks; *C:* Andrzej Bartkowiak; *M:* Michael Gore. Academy Awards '83: Best Actress (MacLaine), Best Adapted Screenplay, Best Director (Brooks), Best Picture, Best Supporting Actor (Nicholson); Directors Guild of America Awards '83: Best Director (Brooks); Golden Globe Awards '84: Best Actress—Drama (MacLaine), Best Film—Drama, Best Screenplay, Best Supporting Actor (Nicholson); Los Angeles Film Critics Association Awards '83: Best Actress (MacLaine), Best Director (Brooks), Best Film, Best Screenplay, Best Supporting Actor (Nicholson); National Board of Review Awards '83: Best Actress (MacLaine), Best Director (Brooks), Best Supporting Actor (Nicholson); New York Film Critics Awards '83: Best Actress (MacLaine), Best Film, Best Supporting Actor (Nicholson); National Society of Film Critics Awards '83: Best Actress (Winger), Best Supporting Actor (Nicholson); Writers Guild of America '83: Best Adapted Screenplay; Nominations: Academy Awards '83: Best Actress (Winger), Best Art Direction/Set Decoration, Best Film Editing, Best Sound, Best Supporting Actor (Lithgow), Best Original Score. *PAR, BTV, HMV*

Terraces 🐾🐾½ **1977** TV series pilot about high-rise tenants whose balconies are their only common ground. Good performances. **90m/C VHS, Beta.** Lloyd Bochner, Eliza Garrett, Julie Newmar, Tim Thomerson; *D:* Lila Garrett. *WOV*

Terranova 🐾🐾 **1991** Six characters in search of themselves, with the profound changes in their lives coming through an unlikely friendship. Rosetta is the poor matriarch of an Italian immigrant family while wealthy Noemi is an aristocratic landowner. But they share similiar frustrations and the desire to change their lives. Set in a rural Venezuelan town in the 1950s; Spanish with subtitles. **96m/C VHS.** *IT* Marisa Laurito, Mimi Lazo, Antonio Banderas, Patrick Bauchau, Massimo Bonetti, Nathalia Martinez; *D:* Calogero Salvo. *CCN*

Terrified 🐾🐾½ **1994 (R)** Erotic thriller about a nympho being stalked by a mystery assailant. Genuinely creepy. *CW:* Some strong violence and sexuality, and for language. **90m/C VHS.** Heather Graham, Lisa Zane, Rustam Branaman, Tom Breznahan; *Cameos:* Max Perlich, Balthazar Getty, Richard Lynch, Don Calfa; *D:* James Merendino; *W:* James Merendino, Megan Heath. *APX*

The Terror 🐾🐾 **1938** A hostelry is the scene of a number of brutal murders. Remake of a 1928 film and based on a play by Edgar Wallace. Good story, but weak version of it. **63m/B VHS, Beta.** *GB* Wilfred Lawson, Bernard Lee, Arthur Wontner, Linden Travers, Henry Oscar, Alastair Sim; *D:* Richard Bird. *SNC*

The Terror 🐾🐾 *Lady of the Shadows* **1963** A lieutenant in Napoleon's army chases a lovely maiden and finds himself trapped in a creepy castle by a mad baron. Movie legend has it Corman directed the movie in three days as the sets (from his previous movie "The Raven") were being torn down around them. **81m/C VHS, Beta.** Boris Karloff, Jack Nicholson, Sandra Knight, Dick Miller, Dorothy Neumann, Jonathan Haze; *D:* Roger Corman, Jack Hill, Francis Ford Coppola, Monte Hellman, Dennis Jacob, Jack Nicholson; *W:* Leo Gordon, Jack Hill; *C:* John M. Nickolaus Jr. *NOS, SNC, HHT*

The Terror woof! **1979 (R)** After 100 years, a man reveals in a film that his family killed a witch. Friends who see the film are attacked by supernatural forces. Originally double-billed with "Dracula's Dog." **86m/C VHS, Beta.** John Nolan, Carolyn Courage, James Aubrey, Glynis Barber, Sarah Keller, Tricia Walsh; *D:* Norman J. Warren. *VCI, VCD, HHE*

Terror at London Bridge 🐾🐾 *Bridge Across Time; Arizona Ripper* **1985** London Bridge is transported brick by brick to Arizona. It carries its history with it, including the havoc-wreaking spirit of Jack the Ripper. Campy made-for-TV effort. **96m/C VHS, Beta.** David Hasselhoff, Stephanie Kramer, Adrienne Barbeau, Randolph Mantooth; *D:* E.W. Swackhamer; *C:* Gil Hubbs.

Terror at Red Wolf Inn 🐾🐾 *Club Dead; Terror House; The Folks at Red Wolf Inn* **1972 (R)** Young woman wins a vacation; finds she's been invited for dinner, so to speak. Not campy enough to overcome stupidity. **90m/C VHS, Beta.** Linda Gillin, Arthur Space, John Neilson, Mary Jackson, Janet Wood, Margaret Avery; *D:* Bud Townsend; *W:* Allen Actor.

Terror at Tenkiller 🐾 **1986** Two girls vacationing in the mountains are seemingly surrounded by a rash of mysterious murders. Made for video. **87m/C VHS, Beta.** Mike Wiles, Stacey Logan. *VCI*

Terror at the Opera 🐾½ *Opera* **1988 (R)** A bizarre staging of Verdi's "Macbeth" is plagued by depraved gore murders. But the show must go on, as one character chirps in badly dubbed English. Italian horrormeister Argento's ever-fluid camera achieves spectacular shots, but the lurid, ludicrous script make this one for connoisseurs only. The operatic scenes employ the voice of Maria Callas. Available in an edited "R" rated version. *CW:* Terror and violence and sensual scene. **107m/C VHS.** Christina Marsillach, Ian Charleson, Urbano Barberini, William McNamara, Antonella Vitale, Barbara Cupisti, Coralina Cataldi Tassoni, Daria Nicolodi; *D:* Dario Argento; *W:* Dario Argento, Franco Ferrini; *C:* Ronnie Taylor. *FCT*

Terror Beach 🐾 **198?** A doctor and his bride move to a coastal village, only to find it enmeshed in witchcraft and devil worship. **90m/C VHS, Beta.** Victor Petit, Julie James, Mary Costi, Sandra Mozar. *NO*

Terror Beneath the Sea 🐾🐾½ *Kaitei Daisenso; Water Cyborgs* **1966** A mad scientist wants to rule the world with his cyborgs. American and Japanese scientists unite to fight him. Fine special effects, especially the transformation from human to monster. **85m/C VHS, Beta.** *JP* Sonny Chiba, Peggy Neal, Franz Gruber, Gunther Braun, Andrew Hughes, Mike Daneen; *D:* Hajime Sato. *DVT*

Terror by Night 🐾🐾½ **1946** Holmes and Watson attempt to solve the murder of the owner of a gigantic, beautiful jewel. Their investigation must be completed before their train arrives at its destination, where the murderer can escape. **60m/ B VHS, LV, Closed Caption.** Basil Rathbone, Nigel Bruce; *D:* Roy William Neill. *CNG, REP, FOX*

Terror by Night/Meeting at Midnight 🐾🐾 **1946** In "Terror by Night" (1946), Sherlock Holmes and Dr. Watson board a train to protect a fabulous diamond. In "Meeting at Midnight" (1944), Charlie Chan becomes involved in magic and murder. **122m/B VHS, Beta.** Basil Rathbone, Nigel Bruce, Sidney Toler; *D:* Roy William Neill.

Terror Creatures from the Grave 🐾 **1966** Husband summons medieval plague victims to rise from the grave to drop in on his unfaithful wife. Should've been better. **85m/C VHS.** *IT* Barbara Steele, Riccardo Garrone, Walter Brandi; *D:* Ralph Zucker. *SNC*

Terror Eyes 🐾½ **1987 (PG-13)** Spoof-thriller revolves around an "agent from Hell," sent to Earth to recruit writers for a horror film. **90m/C VHS, Beta.** Daniel Roebuck, Vivian Schilling, Dan Bell, Lance August.

Terror in a Texas Town 🐾🐾½ **1958** George Hansen (Hayden) is a Swedish seaman who returns home to discover his farmer father has been gunned down by the greedy Johnny Crale (Young), who's after the land so he can drill for oil. So Hansen's out for revenge. There's a final showdown that not only includes six-shooters but a harpoon. **120m/B VHS.** Sterling Hayden, Nedrick Young, Sebastian Cabot, Victor Millan; *D:* Joseph H. Lewis; *W:* Ben L. Perry; *C:* Ray Rennahan; *M:* Gerald Fried. *MGM*

Terror in Beverly Hills woof! **1990** When the President's daughter is kidnapped, it's up to an ex-marine to save her. The trouble is, the head terrorist hates the marine's guts as he blames him for the deaths of his wife and children. So incredibly bad it's campy and fun. **88m/C VHS, Beta, LV.** Frank Stallone, Cameron Mitchell, William Smith; *D:* John Myhers; *W:* John Myhers.

Terror in Paradise 🐾½ **1990 (R)** Jason and Vickie think they're going to have a romantic holiday on a beautiful island paradise. But they've picked the wrong spot to vacation. It seems the island harbors a terrorist group and when they see more than they should the lovers become the next targets. **?m/C VHS.** Joanna Pettet, Gary Lockwood, David Anthony Smith, Leslie Ryan; *D:* Peer J. Oppenheimer. *NHO*

Terror in the Haunted House 🐾🐾½ *My World Dies Screaming* **1958** Newlyweds move into an old house. The bride remembers it from her nightmares. First release featured the first use of Psychorama, a technique in which scary words or advertising messages were flashed on the screen for a fraction of a second—just long enough to cause subliminal response. The technique was banned later in the year. **90m/C VHS, Beta.** Gerald Mohr, Cathy O'Donnell, William Ching, John Qualen, Barry Bernard; *D:* Harold Daniels; *W:* Robert C. Dennis; *C:* Frederick E. West. *RHI, MLB, CCB*

Terror in the Jungle 🐾 **1968 (PG)** Plane crashes in Peruvian wilds and young boy survivor meets Jivaro Indians who think he's a god. Much struggling to survive and battling with horrible script. **95m/C VHS.** Jimmy Angle, Robert Burns, Fawn Silver; *D:* Tom De Simone; *M:* Les Baxter.

Terror in the Swamp 🐾 **1985 (PG)** When not hanging out in the local murky waters, a swamp creature terrorizes the residents of a small town. **89m/C VHS, Beta, LV.** Billy Holliday; *D:* Joe Catalanotto. *VTR*

Terror in the Wax Museum woof! **1973 (PG)** The owner of a wax museum is killed while mulling over the sale of the museum. The new owner has little better luck as the bodies continue to pile up. Production uses every out-of-work horror film actor of the time. The most suspenseful part of this low-budget flick is waiting to see how long the "wax dummies" can hold their breath. **94m/C VHS, Beta.** Ray Milland, Broderick Crawford, Elsa Lanchester, Louis Hayward, Maurice Evans, John Carradine; *D:* Georg Fenady; *W:* Jameson Brewer; *M:* George Duning. *ART*

Terror in Toyland 🐾½ *Christmas Evil; You Better Watch Out* **1985** Once again a knife-wielding lunatic dresses as Santa Claus to strike terror and death into the hearts of children. **90m/C VHS, Beta.** Brandon Maggart, Jeffrey DeMunn, Dianne Hull, Scott McKay, Peter Friedman, Joe Jamrog; *D:* Lewis Jackson; *W:* Lewis Jackson.

Terror Is a Man 🐾🐾 *Blood Creature* **1959** A mad scientist attempts to turn a panther into a man on a secluded island. Early Filipino horror attempt inspired by H.G. Wells' "The Island of Doctor Moreau." **89m/B VHS.** *PH* Francis Lederer, Greta Thyssen, Richard Derr, Oscar Keesee; *D:* Gerardo (Gerry) De Leon. *SNC*

Terror of Mechagodzilla 🐾½ *Monsters from the Unknown Planet; The Escape of Megagodzilla; Mekagojira No Gyakushu* **1978 (G)** It's monster vs. machine in the heavyweight battle of the universe as a huge mechanical Godzilla built by aliens is pitted against the real thing. The last Godzilla movie made until "Godzilla 1985." **79m/C VHS, Beta.** JP Katsuhiko Sasakai, Tomoko Ai. *PAR*

Terror of Rome Against the Son of Hercules 🎥 **1964** Muscle-bound gladiators battle it out in this low-budget Italian action flick. Dubbed. **100m/C VHS, Beta.** *FR IT* Mark Forest, Marilu Tolo; **D:** Mario Ciano. *SNC, NLC*

Terror of the Bloodhunters 🎥 **1962** A French author is sentenced to Devil's Island for a crime he didn't commit. The warden's daughter takes a liking to him and arranges for him and a friend to escape, but numerous perils await them in the jungle. **60m/B VHS, Beta.** Robert Clarke, Steve Conte, Dorothy Haney; **D:** Jerry Warren; **W:** Jerry Warren. *SNC*

Terror of the Steppes 🎥 **1964** Yet another sword and sandal extravaganza in which a musclebound hero conquers all. **?m/C VHS, Beta.** *IT* Kirk Morris. *SNC*

Terror of Tiny Town 🎥🎥 **1938** Main characteristic of this musical/western is its entire midget cast, all members of Jed Buell's Midgets. Otherwise the plot is fairly average and features a bad guy and the good guy who finally teaches him a lesson. Newfield plays up the cast's short stature—they walk under saloon doors and ride Shetland ponies. **65m/B VHS, Beta.** Bill Curtis, Yvonne Moray; **D:** Sam Newfield. *SNC, NOS, DVT*

Terror on Alcatraz 🎥 **1986** The only prisoner to successfully escape from Alcatraz Island returns to retrieve the safety deposit box key he needs to get his stolen loot. And anyone who gets in his way is in for trouble. **96m/C VHS.** Veronica Porsche Ali, Sandy Brooke, Aldo Ray, Scott Ryder; **D:** Philip Marcus. *TWE, HHE*

Terror on the 40th Floor 🎥 **1974** Seven people make an attempt to escape from the 40th floor of an inflamed skyscraper. Poorly done re-hash of "Towering Inferno." Uninspired. **98m/C VHS, Beta.** John Forsythe, Anjanete Comer, Don Meredith, Joseph Campanella; **D:** Jerry Jameson.

Terror on Tour woof! **1983** The Clowns, a rock group on their way up, center their stage performance around sadistic, mutilating theatrics. When real murders begin, they become prime suspects. Exploitive, bloody, disgusting. **90m/C VHS, Beta.** Dave Galluzzo, Richard Styles, Rick Pemberton; **D:** Don Edmunds.

Terror Out of the Sky 🎥½ **1978** A scientist must disguise himself as one of the insects to divert the attention of a horde of killing bees from a busload of elementary children. Sub-par sequel to "The Savage Bees." **95m/C VHS, Beta.** Efrem Zimbalist Jr., Dan Haggerty; **D:** Lee H. Katzin; **M:** William Goldstein. *ART*

Terror Ship 🎥🎥 **1954** Three people find an abandoned yacht which they believe was used for smuggling. While searching it, they find that it was used to transport stolen uranium. Before the police can arrive, the thieves show up. Not a very good handling of what was actually an interesting idea. Released as "Dangerous Voyage" in Great Britain. **72m/B VHS.** *GB* William Lundigan, Naomi Chance, Vincent Ball, Jean Lodge, Richard Stewart; **D:** Vernon Sewell. *NOS*

Terror Squad 🎥🎥 **1987** An unsuspecting high school population is put under siege by Libyan terrorists. The students get a hands-on lesson in revolution and guerrilla war tactics. **95m/C VHS.** Kerry Brennan, Bill Calvert, Chuck Connors, Greer Brodie; **D:** Peter Maris. *MCG, VTR*

Terror Stalks the Class Reunion 🎥🎥½ **1993 (PG-13)** Kay (Nelligan) is a teacher who disappears at a class reunion. Police dismiss the case as a runaway wild streak, except for Virginia (Beals), a young detective (Beals) who doesn't accept that theory. And she's right—Kay is held hostage in a remote cabin by an obsessed former student (Davies). Kay needs all her wits to fend off her deranged and possibly deadly suitor

while Virginia races to find her. Based on the novel by Mary Higgins Clark. **CW:** Some violence and terror. **95m/C VHS, Closed Caption.** Kate Nelligan, Jennifer Beals, Geraint Wyn Davies. *REP*

Terror Street 🎥 **1954** An Air Force pilot's wife is murdered. He has 36 hours to clear his name and find the killer. **84m/B VHS, Beta, LV.** Dan Duryea, Elsy Albiin, Ann Gudrun, Eric Pohlmann. *NO*

Terror Trail 🎥½ **1933** As usual, Mix uses guns and fists to bring bad guys to justice, and gets the girl in the bargain. **62m/B VHS.** Tom Mix, Naomi Judge, Arthur Rankin, Raymond Hatton, Francis McDonald, Robert F. (Bob) Kortman, John St. Polis, Lafe McKee, Buffalo Bill Jr.; **D:** Armand Schaefer. *GPV, HEG, DVT*

Terror Train 🎥🎥 *Train of Terror* **1980 (R)** A masquerade party is held on a chartered train. But someone has more than mask-wearing in mind as a series of dead bodies begin to appear. Copperfield provides magic, Curtis provides screams in this semi-scary slasher movie. **97m/C VHS, Beta, LV.** Jamie Lee Curtis, Ben Johnson, Hart Bochner, David Copperfield, Vanity, Howard Busgang, Michael Shanks, Amanda Tapping, Troy Kennedy Martin, Anthony Sherwood, Timothy Webber; **D:** Roger Spottiswoode; **W:** Alec Curtis; **C:** John Alcott. *FOX*

The Terror Within 🎥 **1988 (R)** Reptilian mutants hit the streets searching for human women to breed with. Have the Teenage Mutant Ninja Turtles grown up? **90m/C VHS, Beta.** George Kennedy, Andrew Stevens, Starr Andreeff, Terri Treas; **D:** Thierry Notz; **W:** Thomas McKelvey Cleaver; **M:** Rick Conrad. *MGM*

The Terror Within 2 🎥½ **1991 (R)** In a world destroyed by biological warfare, a warrior and the woman he rescued traverse the badlands occupied by hideous mutants. What they don't know is that the real terror comes from within. How can they possibly survive? Not without decent dialogue, that's for sure. **CW:** Language, strong violence and gore, and sensuality. **90m/C VHS.** Andrew Stevens, Stella Stevens, Chick Vennera, R. Lee Ermey; **D:** Andrew Stevens. *VES, ART*

Terrorgram 🎥 **1990 (R)** Not a very special delivery. An offscreen James Earl Jones introduces three lesser tales of terror. Best seg: a sleazy filmmaker gets trapped in the world of his own exploitation scripts. The other two are bloody but negligible revenge-from-the-grave yarns. All start off with the receipt of a sinister package, hence a postal motif. **CW:** Language, horror violence and drug content, and sensuality. **88m/C VHS.** Michael Hartson, J.T. Wallace. *NO*

The Terrorists 🎥½ **1974 (PG)** Just as later he was a Scottish Lithuanian sub-commander in "The Hunt for Red October" (1990), here Connery is a Scottish Norwegian security chief. Good cinematography and premise are wasted; generic title betrays sloppy execution. **89m/C VHS, Beta, Closed Caption.** Sean Connery, Ian McShane, John Quentin; **D:** Caspar Wrede; **M:** Jerry Goldsmith. *FOX*

Terrorists 🎥 **1983** An Army investigator discovers a plot to assassinate the President. It's up to him to move quickly enough to stop it. Brutal action. **61m/C VHS, Beta.** Marland Proctor, Irmgard Millard. *NO*

The Terrornauts woof! **1967** When man begins space exploration, Earth is attacked by aliens. The defenders are taken to an out-dated fortress where they learn that their forebears were similarly attacked. Juvenile, lackluster, contrived, and really dumb. **77m/C VHS, Beta.** *GB* Simon Oates, Zena Marshall, Charles Hawtrey, Stanley Meadows; **D:** Montgomery Tully. *NLC*

Terrorvision woof! **1986 (R)** OUR TV GAVE BIRTH TO SPACE ALIENS! It's amazing what modern technology can do: Suburban family buys a fancy satellite dish; bad black comedy and gory special effects result. **84m/C VHS, Beta.** Gerrit Graham, Mary Woronov, Diane Franklin, Bert Remsen, Alejandro Rey; **D:** Ted Nicolaou; **W:** Ted Nicolaou; **M:** Richard Band. *ART*

The Terry Fox Story 🎥🎥🎥 **1983** In the spring of 1980, a young man who had lost his right leg to cancer dipped his artificial limb into the Atlantic Ocean and set off on a fund-raising "Marathon of Hope" across Canada, drawing national attention. Inspiring made-for-TV true story is well-scripted and avoids corniness. Good acting from real-life amputee Fryer and, as usual, from Duvall. **96m/C VHS, Beta.** Eric Fryer, Robert Duvall, Chris Makepeace, Michael Zelniker, Rosalind Chao; **D:** Ralph L. Thomas; **M:** Bill Conti. Genie Awards '84: Best Actor (Fryer), Best Film, Best Supporting Actor (Zelniker). *VES*

Tess 🎥🎥🎥 **1980 (PG)** Sumptuous adaptation of the Thomas Hardy novel "Tess of the D'Ubervilles." Kinski is wonderful as an innocent farm girl who is seduced by the young aristocrat she works for and then brings marriage to a man of her own class only brings more grief. Polanski's direction is faithful and artful. Nearly three hours long, but worth every minute. **170m/C VHS, Beta, LV.** *GB FR* Nastassia Kinski, Peter Firth, Leigh Lawson, John Collin; **D:** Roman Polanski; **W:** Roman Polanski, Gerard Brach; **C:** Ghislan Cloquet, Geoffrey Unsworth. Academy Awards '80: Best Art Direction/Set Decoration, Best Cinematography, Best Costume Design; Cesar Awards '80: Best Cinematography, Best Director (Polanski), Best Film; Golden Globe Awards '81: Best Foreign Film; Los Angeles Film Critics Association Awards '80: Best Cinematography, Best Director (Polanski); New York Film Critics Awards '80: Best Cinematography; Nominations: Academy Awards '80: Best Director (Polanski), Best Picture, Best Original Score. *COL*

Test of Donald Norton 🎥🎥½ **1926** Good early Western. A young man raised by Indians finds work with the Hudson's Bay Company and does well, but is haunted by suspicions that he is a half-breed. **68m/B VHS, Beta, 8mm.** George Walsh, Tyrone Power Sr., Eugenia Gilhert, Robert Graves, Virginia True Boardman; **D:** B. Reeves Eason. *GPV, VYY*

A Test of Love 🎥🎥 *Annie's Coming Out* **1984 (PG)** Incorrectly diagnosed as retarded, a young woman with cerebral palsy struggles to adjust to life outside an institution. Predictable but touching and well-acted. **93m/C VHS, Beta.** *AU* Angela Punch McGregor, Drew Forsythe, Tina Arhondis; **D:** Gil Brealey; **W:** Chris Borthwick. Australian Film Institute '84: Best Film. *USH*

Test Pilot 🎥🎥🎥½ **1938** Gable and Spencer star as daring test pilot and devoted mechanic respectively. When Gable has to land his experimental craft in a Kansas cornfield, he meets and falls in love with farm girl Loy. The two marry and raise a family, all the while she worries over his dangerous profession. When the Air Force asks him to test their new B-17 bomber, she refuses to watch, thinking the test will end in tragedy. Superb aviation drama featuring excellent cast. **118m/B VHS, Beta.** Clark Gable, Myrna Loy, Spencer Tracy, Lionel Barrymore, Samuel S. Hinds; **D:** Victor Fleming. Nominations: Academy Awards '38: Best Film Editing, Best Picture, Best Story. *MGM, TLF, CCB*

Test Tube Babies woof! **1948** A married couple's morals begin to deteriorate as they mourn the fact they can't have a child. The day is saved, however, when they learn about the new artificial insemination process. Amusing, campy propaganda in the vein of "Reefer Madness." Rereleased in 1967 as "The Pill" with extra scenes featuring Monica Davis and John Maitland. **83m/B VHS, Beta.** Dorothy Dube, Timothy Farrell, William Thompson; **D:** W. Merle Connell. *GVV, SNC, DVT*

Test Tube Teens from the Year 2000 🎥 *Virgin Hunters* **1993 (R)** When sex is banned in the year 2000, horny teenagers are left with no choice but to travel through time for some action. **CW:** Strong sexuality. **74m/C VHS, Beta, LV, Closed Caption.** Morgan Fairchild, Ian Abercrombie, Brian Bremer, Christopher Wolf, Michelle Matheson, Sara Suzanne Brown, Don Dowe; **D:** Ellen Cabot; **W:** Kenneth J. Hall; **M:** Reg Powell. *PAR*

Testament 🎥🎥🎥 **1983 (PG)** Well-made and thought-provoking story of the residents of a small California town struggling to survive after a nuclear bombing. Focuses on one family who tries to accept the reality of post-holocaust life. We see the devastation but it never sinks into sensationalism. An exceptional performance from Alexander. **90m/C VHS, Beta, LV, Closed Caption.** Jane Alexander, William Devane, Ross Harris, Roxana Zal, Kevin Costner, Rebecca DeMornay; **D:** Lynne Littman; **W:** John Sacret Young; **M:** James Horner. Nominations: Academy Awards '83: Best Actress (Alexander). **PAR**

The Testament of Dr. Cordelier 🎬🎬🎬 1959
A strange, experimental fantasy about a Jekyll and Hyde-type lunatic stalking the streets and alleys of Paris. Originally conceived as a television play, Renoir attempted to create a new mise-en-scene, using multiple cameras covering the sequences as they were performed whole. In French with English subtitles. **95m/C VHS, Beta.** *FR* Jean-Louis Barrault; **D:** Jean Renoir. **FCT**

Testament of Dr. Mabuse 🎬🎬½
The Crimes of Dr. Mabuse; The Last Will of Dr. Mabuse 1962 The director of an asylum is controlled by the evil genius, Dr. Mabuse, who hypnotizes him in this well-done remake of Lang's 1933 classic. **?m/C VHS.** Gert Frobe, Wolfgang Preiss, Senta Berger. **SNC, LSV**

The Testament of Orpheus 🎬🎬🎬½
1959 Superb, personal surrealism; writer-director Cocteau's last film. Hallucinogenic, autobiographical dream-journey through time. Difficult to follow, but rewarding final installment in a trilogy including "The Blood of the Poet" and "Orpheus." In French with English subtitles. **80m/B VHS, Beta.** *FR* Jean Cocteau, Edouard Dermithe, Maria Casares, Francois Perier, Yul Brynner, Jean-Pierre Leaud, Daniel Gelin, Jean Marais, Pablo Picasso, Charles Aznavour; **D:** Jean Cocteau. **HMV, FCT, HEG**

Tetsuo 2: Body Hammer 🎬🎬 1997
Taniguchi (Yaguchi) strikes back at the cyborgs who kidnapped and killed his young son by transforming himself into a killer robotic machine man. Japanese with subtitles. **83m/C VHS.** *JP* Tomoroh Taguchi; **D:** Shinya Tsukamoto; **W:** Shinya Tsukamoto; **C:** Shinya Tsukamoto. **CPM**

Tetsuo: The Iron Man 🎬🎬 1992
A weird live-action science-fiction cartoon about a white-collar Japanese worker who finds himself being gradually transformed into a walking metal collection of cables, drills, wires, and gears. The newly formed metal creature then faces off with an equally bizarre metals fetishist (played by the director). In Japanese with English subtitles. **67m/B VHS.** *JP* Tomoroh Taguchi, Kei Fujiwara, Shinya Tsukamoto; **D:** Shinya Tsukamoto; **W:** Shinya Tsukamoto. **FXL**

Tevye 🎬🎬½
Teyve der Milkhiker 1939 Sholom Aleichem's story of Jewish family life, intermarriage, and turmoil in Poland. When Khave, the daughter of Tevye the dairyman, seeks to marry a Ukrainian peasant, Tevye must come to terms with his love for his daughter and his faith and loyalty to tradition. Also the basis for the musical "Fiddler on the Roof." In Yiddish with English subtitles. **96m/B VHS, Beta.** Maurice Schwartz, Miriam Riselle; **D:** Maurice Schwartz. National Film Registry '91. **ERG, NCJ, TPV**

Tex 🎬🎬½ 1982 (PG)
Fatherless brothers in Oklahoma come of age. Dillon is excellent. Based on the novel by S.E. Hinton. **103m/C VHS, Beta, LV.** Matt Dillon, Jim Metzler, Meg Tilly, Bill McKinney, Frances Lee McCain, Ben Johnson, Emilio Estevez; **D:** Tim Hunter; **M:** Pino Donaggio. **DIS, OM**

Tex Rides with the Boy Scouts 🎬½ 1937
Scouts aid Ritter in capturing gold bandits with a little bit of singing thrown in for good measure. **60m/B VHS, Beta.** Tex Ritter. **NOS, DVT**

The Texans 🎬🎬½ 1938
Ex-Confederate soldier Kirk Jordan (Scott) struggles to make a new life for himself as a trail boss, aiming to get 10,000 head of cattle to the railroad in Abilene. But there's temptation in the form of Ivy Preston (Bennett) and a scheme to reignite the war. Remake of 1924 silent "North of '36." **93m/B VHS,**

Closed Caption. Randolph Scott, Joan Bennett, Walter Brennan, May Robson, Robert Cummings, Raymond Hatton, Robert Barrat, Harvey Stephens, Chris-Pin Martin, Francis Ford; **D:** James Hogan; **W:** Bertram Millhauser, Paul Sloane, William Haines. **USH**

Texas 🎬🎬🎬 1941
Two friends wander through the West after the Civil War getting into scrapes with the law and eventually drifting apart. Ford takes a job on a cattle ranch run by Trevor and discovers Holden has joined a gang of rustlers aiming to steal her herd. The two men vie for Trevor's affections. Although friends, a professional rivalry also existed between the two leading actors and they competed against each other, doing their own stunts during filming. Well-acted, funny, and enthusiastic Western. **94m/B VHS, Beta.** William Holden, Glenn Ford, Claire Trevor, Edgar Buchanan, George Bancroft; **D:** George Marshall. **COL**

Texas 🎬🎬½
James A. Michener's Texas 1994 Stephen Austin (Duffy) sets up a colony in 1821 Texas, with Mexican law requiring the settlers to become Mexican citizens. Eventually, calls for statehood begin and Austin's initial resistance is overturned by rebellion and prodding from Sam Houston (Keach) and Jim Bowie (Keith). Lots of action amidst the history, including the battle for the Alamo, but it's a routine extravaganza. Made for TV miniseries adapted from Michener's novel. Filmed on location in Del Rio, Texas. **180m/C VHS, LV, Closed Caption.** Patrick Duffy, Stacy Keach, David Keith, Maria Conchita Alonso, Anthony Michael Hall, Rick Schroder, Benjamin Bratt, Chelsea Field, John Schneider, Grant Show, Randy Travis, Woody Watson; **D:** Richard Lang; **W:** Sean Meredith; **M:** Lee Holdridge. **REP**

Texas Across the River 🎬🎬½ 1966
Sam Hollis (Martin) is a wise-cracking gun runner who, along with Indian sidekick Kronk (Bishop), is recruiting men to help him ship guns through hostile Comanche territory. Don Andrea, a Spanish nobleman (played by Frenchman Delon) wrongly accused of murder, joins up and much comic misadventure ensues. **101m/C VHS, LV, Letterbox.** Dean Martin, Alain Delon, Joey Bishop, Rosemary Forsyth, Tina Aumont, Peter Graves, Michael Ansara, Linden Chiles, Andrew Prine, Richard Farnsworth; **D:** Michael Gordon; **W:** Ben Starr, Wells Root, Harold Greene; **C:** Russell Metty. **USH, BTV, FCT**

Texas Bad Man 🎬½ 1932
Sheriff Mix goes undercover to get in with Kohler's gang of outlaws and bring them to justice. **60m/B VHS.** Tom Mix, Fred Kohler Sr., Lucille Powers, Ed LeSaint, Richard Alexander; **D:** Edward Laemmle. **GPV**

Texas Buddies 🎬½ 1932
Steele plays a former military pilot who uses his trusty monoplane to round up outlaws. Interesting twist on standard oater, but suffers from poor execution. **57m/B VHS.** Bob Steele, Nancy Drexel, George "Gabby" Hayes, Francis McDonald, Harry Semels; **D:** Robert North Bradbury; **W:** Robert North Bradbury. **MOV, GPV**

Texas Carnival 🎬🎬 1951
Williams and Skelton star as carnival performers who operate the dunk tank. When Skelton is mistaken for an oil tycoon, he lives high on the hog until the mistake is discovered. Believe it or not, this musical has only one water ballet sequence. Songs include "It's Dynamite," "Whoa! Emma," and "Young Folks Should Get Married." **77m/C VHS.** Esther Williams, Red Skelton, Howard Keel, Ann Miller, Paula Raymond, Keenan Wynn, Tom Tully; **D:** Charles Walters. **MGM**

The Texas Chainsaw Massacre 🎬🎬½ 1974 (R)
The movie that put the "power" in power tools. An idyllic summer afternoon drive becomes a nightmare for a group of young people pursued by a chainsaw-wielding maniac. Made with tongue firmly in cheek, this is nevertheless a mesmerizing saga of gore, flesh, mayhem, and violence. **86m/C VHS, LV, Closed Caption.** Marilyn Burns, Allen Danzinger, Paul A. Partain, William Vail, Teri McMinn, Edwin Neal, Jim Siedow, Gunnar Hansen, John Dugan, Jerry Lorenz; **D:** Tobe Hooper; **W:** Tobe Hooper, Ken Henkel; **C:** Daniel Pearl; **M:** Wayne Bell. **MPI**

Texas Chainsaw Massacre 2 woof! 1986 (R)
A tasteless, magnified sequel to the notorious blood-bucket extravaganza, about a certain family in southern Texas who kill and eat passing travelers. Followed by "Leatherface: The Texas Chainsaw Massacre 3." **90m/C VHS, Beta, LV, Closed Caption.** Dennis Hopper, Caroline Williams, Bill Johnson, Jim Siedow, Bill Moseley, Lou Perry; **D:** Tobe Hooper; **W:** L.M. Kit Carson; **C:** Richard Kooris; **M:** Tobe Hooper. **VTR**

The Texas Chainsaw Massacre 4: The Next Generation 🎬🎬
Return of the Texas Chainsaw Massacre 1995 (R) Heroine Jenny (Zellweger) and her three friends take a wrong turn down a dark country road and wind up in the nightmare clutches of homicidal tow-truck driver Vilmer (McConaughey), his accomplice Darla (Perenski), and the infamous Leatherface (Jacks). No restraint here—as the borderline sadism and tension builds to, unfortunately, something of a letdown. Feature debut for Henkel, who co-wrote Tobe Hooper's 1977 horror classic. Film finally got a release in 1997 after both McConaughey and Zellweger became stars in more mainstream films. **CW:** Demented mayhem and torture; strong language. **94m/C VHS, Closed Caption.** Renee Zellweger, Matthew McConaughey, Tony Perenski, Robert Jacks, Lisa Newmyer; **D:** Kim Henkel; **W:** Kim Henkel; **C:** Levie Isaacks. **COL**

Texas Cyclone 🎬🎬 1932
A stranger rides into a town that turns out to be incredibly friendly. Later he realizes the entire town thinks he is a prominent citizen who disappeared years ago. **58m/B VHS.** Tim McCoy, Wheeler Oakman, Shirley Grey, Walter Brennan, John Wayne, Wallace MacDonald, Vernon Dent, Mary Gordon; **D:** David Ross Lederman. **COL, DVT, NOS**

Texas Detour 🎬 1977
On a trip across country, a trio of young Californians have their van stolen. They decide to take the law into their own hands when the redneck sheriff gives them no help. Dull, undistinguished "action" flick. **90m/C VHS, Beta.** Cameron Mitchell, Priscilla Barnes, Patrick Wayne, Mitch Vogel, Lindsay Bloom, R.G. Armstrong; **D:** Howard (Hikmet) Avedis.

Texas Gunfighter 🎬🎬 1932
Your basic western from the Maynard series, with everything a western could have. **60m/B VHS, Beta.** Ken Maynard. **NOS, VCI, DVT**

Texas Guns 🎬🎬
Once Upon a Texas Train 1990 (PG) A gritty western about an old-time gunman (Nelson) and his quest for one last robbery, killing those who stand in his way and some just for fun. Also watch for Cassidy's comeback. **96m/C VHS, LV.** Willie Nelson, Richard Widmark, Shaun Cassidy, Angie Dickinson, Kevin McCarthy, Royal Dano, Chuck Connors, Ken Curtis, Dub Taylor. **THV**

Texas Jack 🎬½ 1935
The head of a medicine show tries to trace the disappearance of his sister. **55m/B VHS.** Jack Perrin, Jayne Regan, Nelson McDowell, Budd Buster, Lew Meehan; **D:** Bernard B. Ray. **GPV**

Texas John Slaughter: Geronimo's Revenge 🎬🎬 1960
An Indian-loving rancher frets and fights when Geronimo attacks innocent settlers. Compiled fom Walt Disney television episodes. **77m/C VHS, Beta.** Tom Tryon, Darryl Hickman, Betty Lynn; **D:** Harry Keller. **DIS**

Texas John Slaughter: Stampede at Bitter Creek 🎬🎬 1962
Good guy Texas John Slaughter meets a variety of threatening obstacles when he tries to move his cattle herd into New Mexico. Originally from the "Walt Disney Presents" television series. **90m/C VHS, Beta.** Tom Tryon; **D:** Harry Keller. **DIS**

Texas Justice 🎬½ 1942
The "Lone Rider" cavorts around in the desert, dispensing justice in the guise of a monk. **60m/B VHS, Beta.** George Houston, Al "Fuzzy" St. John, Dennis Moore, Wanda McKay, Claire Rochelle; **D:** Sam Newfield. **NOS, DVT**

Texas Kid ☆½ 1943 A typical western. Hero helps a vengeance-minded kid catch the robber-gang who robbed and killed his father. Yee-Haw. 53m/B VHS, Beta. Johnny Mack Brown, Kermit Maynard, Raymond Hatton, Shirley Patterson, Edmund Cobb, Charles "Blackie" King; **D:** Lambert Hillyer. *VDM, GPV*

Texas Lady ☆☆ 1956 When a woman wins $50,000 gambling, she buys a Texas newspaper on the stipulation that she can edit it in this standard fare western. Good vehicle for Colbert to look beautiful, but the plot and script are average and uninspired. 86m/C VHS. Claudette Colbert, Barry Sullivan, Gregory Walcott; **D:** Tim Whelan. *REP*

Texas Layover woof! 1975 Impossible-to-describe western/exploitation entry from trashmeister Adamson involving multiple stewardesses and the remnants of the Ritz Brothers. 88m/C VHS. Yvonne De Carlo, Bob Livingston, Donald (Don "Red") Barry, Connie Hoffman, Regina Carrol, Jimmy Ritz, Harry Ritz; **D:** Al Adamson. *NO*

Texas Legionnaires ☆☆ *Man from Music Mountain* 1943 Roy comes back to his home town and gets caught between feuding cattle and sheep herders. 71m/B VHS. Roy Rogers, Ruth Terry, Paul Kelly, Ann Gillis, George Cleveland, Pat Brady; **D:** Joseph Kane. *NOS, DVT*

Texas Lightning ☆½ 1981 (R) Innocuous B-grade touching movie about a father and son and their family woes. 93m/C VHS, Beta. Cameron Mitchell, Channing Mitchell, Maureen McCormick, Peter Jason.

Texas Masquerade ☆☆ 1944 Standard good cowboys versus land-grabbers action filler. William Boyd plays Hopalong Cassidy. Andy Clyde plays California Carson. Jimmy Rogers plays...Jimmy Rogers. 59m/B VHS. William Boyd, Andy Clyde, Jimmy Rogers, Mady Correll, Don Costello, Russell Simpson, Nelson Leigh, Francis McDonald, J. Farrell MacDonald; **D:** George Archainbaud. *NOS, RXM*

Texas Payback ☆☆ 1995 (R) Convicted killer Cody Giles (Hudson) busts out of prison in order to get revenge on the now-retired-and-working-in-Vegas Texas Ranger Louis Gentry (Jones) who put him away. **CW:** Violence and nudity. 96m/C VHS, Closed Caption. Sam Jones, Gary Hudson, Kathleen Kinmont, Bo Hopkins; **D:** Richard W. Munchkin; **W:** Brian Page; **C:** Mark Morris; **M:** Jim Halfpenny. *CAF*

Texas Pioneers ☆½ *The Blood Brother* 1932 A frontier scout is sent to an outpost town besieged by crooks. 54m/B VHS, Beta. Bill Cody. *VDM*

The Texas Rangers ☆☆½ 1936 Banditos Jim Hawkins (MacMurray) and Wahoo Jones (Oakie) roam the Texas frontier until the Rangers come in, establishing order. So, they switch over to the good guys but are then told to bring in their old partner-in-crime Sam McGee (Nolan). Lots of confronting villains and battling varmints. Based on the book by Walter Prescott Webb. Followed by "The Texas Rangers Ride Again" and remade as "The Streets of Laredo" (1949). 99m/B VHS, Closed Caption. Fred MacMurray, Jack Oakie, Lloyd Nolan, Jean Parker, Edward Ellis, Fred Kohler Sr., George "Gabby" Hayes; **D:** King Vidor; **W:** Louis Stevens. Nominations: Academy Awards '36: Best Sound. *USH*

The Texas Rangers ☆☆ 1951 A prisoner is given the opportunity to capture the notorious Sam Bass gang in exchange for freedom. Good B Western; lotsa shootin'. 68m/C VHS, Beta. George Montgomery, Gale Storm, Jerome Courtland, Noah Beery Jr.; **D:** Phil Karlson. *GKK*

The Texas Rangers Ride Again ☆☆½ 1940 When cattle keep disappearing from the Dangerfield ranch, owner Robson secretly calls in the Texas Rangers to find out what's going on. Howard and Crawford work undercover to root out the criminals while Howard also finds the time to make goo-goo eyes at Robson's granddaughter Drew. 68m/B VHS, Closed Caption. John Howard, Broderick Crawford, May Robson, Ellen Drew, Anthony Quinn, Akim Tamiroff, Charley Grapewin, Harvey Stephens; **D:** James Hogan; **W:** William R. Lipman, Horace McCoy. *USH*

Texas Terror ☆☆ 1935 Young Wayne resigns his badge when he mistakenly believes he has shot and killed his friend. He later rescues his friend's sister, learns the truth, and (naturally) finds true love. 50m/B VHS. John Wayne, George "Gabby" Hayes, Lucille Browne. *COL, CNG, NOS*

Texas to Bataan ☆½ 1942 The Range Busters ship horses to the Philippines and encounter enemy spies. Part of the "Range Busters" series. 56m/B VHS, Beta. John "Dusty" King, David Sharpe, Max Terhune; **D:** Robert Emmett Tansey. *VYY*

Texas Trouble 193? Standard matinee fare with cowboy Bob Steele. 0m/B VHS, Beta. Bob Steele. *VCN*

Texas Wildcats ☆☆½ 1939 A cowboy helps make sure that sinister adversaries are brought to justice on the American Frontier. 60m/B VHS, Beta. Tim McCoy. *NOS, DVT, MOV*

Texasville ☆☆½ 1990 (R) Sequel to "The Last Picture Show" finds the characters still struggling after 30 years, with financial woes from the energy crisis, mental illness inspired by the Korean War, and various personal tragedies. Lacks the melancholy sensitivity of its predecessor, but has some of the wit and wisdom that comes with age. Based again on a Larry McMurtry novel. Not well received during its theatrical release. 120m/C VHS, LV, Closed Caption. Timothy Bottoms, Jeff Bridges, Annie Potts, Cloris Leachman, Eileen Brennan, Randy Quaid, Cybill Shepherd, William McNamara; **D:** Peter Bogdanovich; **W:** Peter Bogdanovich. *COL, THV*

The Texican ☆½ 1966 Former sheriff Jess Carlin (Murphy) is living in Mexico but must return to the Texas town of Rim Rock when his newspaperman brother is murdered. Town boss Luke Starr (Crawford) is behind the crime but the townspeople are too scared to help Carlin out—except for saloon gal Kit (Lorys). 86m/C VHS. Audie Murphy, Broderick Crawford, Diana Lorys, Aldo Sambrel, Antonio Casas; **D:** Lesley Selander; **W:** John C. Champion; **C:** Francis Marin. *COL*

Thank God He Met Lizzie ☆☆½ 1997 Predictable wedding comedy has thirty-something Guy (Roxburgh) searching for the perfect woman. Finally he meets Lizzie (Blanchett) and the twosome are soon involved in lavish wedding preparations before they really have a chance to get to know each other. In fact, Guy begins dreaming of former love, Jenny (O'Connor), in the middle of the ceremony! 88m/C VHS. AU Richard Roxburgh, Cate Blanchett, Frances O'Connor, Linden Wilkinson, Michael Ross, John Gaden, Genevieve Mooy, Rhett Walton, Deborah Kennedy; **D:** Cherie Nowlan; **W:** Alexandra Long; **C:** Kathryn Milliss; **M:** Martin Armiger. Australian Film Institute '97: Best Supporting Actress (Blanchett); Nominations: Australian Film Institute '97: Best Actress (O'Connor), Best Art Direction/Set Decoration, Best Costume Design, Best Film Editing. *NYR*

Thank God It's Friday ☆½ 1978 (PG) Episodic and desultory disco-dancing vehicle which won the Best Song Oscar for Donna Summer's rendition. Life is irony. Co-produced by Motown. ♫Last Dance; After Dark; Find My Way; It's Serious; Let's Make A Deal; Romeo and Juliet; You're the Reason I Feel Like Dancing; From Here to Eternity; Dance All Night. 100m/C VHS, Beta. Valerie Landsburg, Teri Nunn, Chick Vennera, Jeff Goldblum, Debra Winger; **D:** Robert Klane; **W:** Armyan Bernstein. Academy Awards '78: Best Song ("Last Dance"). *COL*

Thank You & Good Night 1991 Director Oxenberg gathers members of her own family around a purple armchair of grandma's to talk about life, love, and family memories, including grandma's illness and recent death. 81m/C VHS. **D:** Jan Oxenberg; **W:** Jan Oxenberg; **C:** Claudia Rashke. *ORI, BTV, FXL*

Thank Your Lucky Stars ☆☆☆ 1943 A lavish, slap-dash wartime musical that emptied out the Warner's lot for an array of uncharacteristic celebrity turns. Features Shore in her movie debut. ♫They're Either Too Young or Too Old;

Blues in the Night; Hotcha Cornia; Ridin' For A Fall; We're Staying Home Tonight; Goin' North; Love Isn't Born, It's Made; No You, No Me; Ice Cold Katie. 127m/B VHS, Beta, LV. Eddie Cantor, Dinah Shore, Joan Leslie, Errol Flynn, Bette Davis, Edward Everett Horton, Humphrey Bogart, John Garfield, Alan Hale, Ann Sheridan, Ida Lupino, Jack Carson, Dennis (Stanley Morner) Morgan, Olivia de Havilland; **D:** David Butler; **W:** Norman Panama. Nominations: Academy Awards '43: Best Song ("They're Either Too Young or Too Old"). *MGM*

Tharus Son of Attila ☆ 1987 A couple of sword-wielding barbarians battle each other and an evil emperor. 89m/C VHS, Beta. Jerome Courtland, Rik von Nutter, Lisa Gastoni; **D:** Robert Montero. *TWE*

That Brennan Girl ☆½ 1946 A maudlin soap opera about how a girl's upbringing by an inconsiderate mother makes her a devious little wench. Fortunately her second husband had a better mom, and redemption is at hand. 95m/B VHS. James Dunn, Mona Freeman, William Marshall, June Duprez, Frank Jenks, Charles Arnt; **D:** Alfred Santell. *NOS*

That Certain Age ☆☆½ 1938 Alice (Durbin) is charmed by her newspaper-owning father's houseguest, older and sophisticated journalist Vincent Bullitt (Douglas). She gets a big crush and dumps boyfriend Ken (Cooper), causing much consternation to all. ♫That Certain Age; You're as Pretty as a Picture; Be a Good Scout; Has Anybody Ever Told You Before?; My Own. 101m/B VHS, Closed Caption. Deanna Durbin, Melvyn Douglas, Jackie Cooper, John Halliday, Irene Rich, Nancy Carroll, Jackie Searl, Charles Coleman; **D:** Edward Ludwig; **W:** Bruce Manning; **C:** Joseph Valentine. Nominations: Academy Awards '36: Best Song ("My Own"); Academy Awards '38: Best Sound. *USH*

That Certain Thing ☆☆½ 1928 Very early silent Capra comedy about a bachelor with a silver spoon in his mouth who loses his inheritance when he marries for love. It's got that certain Capra screwball feeling. 65m/B VHS, Beta. Viola Dana, Ralph Graves, Burr McIntosh, Aggie Herring, Syd Crossley; **D:** Frank Capra. *GPV*

That Certain Woman ☆☆½ 1937 Sentimental drama with Davis portraying a gangster's widow who wants to make a new life for herself. Fonda plays the rich playboy with whom she falls in love. Because of Davis' star power, she demanded that Fonda play opposite her. It seems Davis had a real life crush on him when they were both players in a stock company several years earlier. Remake of Goulding's "The Trespasser" which starred Gloria Swanson. 91m/B VHS, Closed Caption. Bette Davis, Henry Fonda, Ian Hunter, Anita Louise, Donald Crisp, Katherine Alexander, Minor Watson; **D:** Edmund Goulding; **W:** Edmund Goulding; **M:** Max Steiner. *MGM*

That Championship Season ☆☆ 1982 (R) Long-dormant animosities surface at the reunion of a championship basketball team. Unfortunate remake of Miller's Pulitzer-prize winning play, with none of the fire which made it a Broadway hit. 110m/C VHS, Beta. Martin Sheen, Bruce Dern, Stacy Keach, Robert Mitchum, Paul Sorvino, Jason Miller; **D:** Jason Miller; **C:** John Bailey; **M:** Bill Conti. *MGM*

That Cold Day in the Park ☆☆½ 1969 (R) Early Altman. An unhappy woman takes in a homeless young man from the park near her home. The woman (Dennis) is obsessive and odd; so is the film. Dennis is excellent. Reminiscent of "The Collector." 91m/C VHS, Beta. Sandy Dennis, Michael Burns, Susanne Benton, Michael Murphy, John David Garfield; **D:** Robert Altman. *REP, FCT*

That Darn Cat ☆☆½ 1965 (G) Vintage Disney comedy about a Siamese cat that helps FBI Agent Jones thwart kidnappers. Could be shorter, but suspenseful and funny with characteristic Disney slapstick. Based on the book "Undercover Cat" by The Gordons. 115m/C VHS, Beta. Hayley Mills, Dean Jones, Dorothy Provine, Neville Brand, Elsa Lanchester, Frank Gorshin, Roddy McDowall; **D:** Robert Stevenson; **C:** Edward Colman; **M:** Robert F. Brunner. *DIS*

That Darn Cat ♪♪½ 1996 (PG) Innocuous Disney remake of the 1965 Disney comedy falls into the "why bother" category. Bored 16-year-old Patti (Ricci) finds some unexpected excitement when her alley-wandering cat D.C. (for Darned Cat) returns home from a prowl with a wristwatch around his neck. Turns out it's a clue in a bungled kidnapping and Patti manages to convince rookie FBI agent Zeke (Doug) to investigate. Jones, who played the FBI agent in the original, is the wealthy husband of would-be kidnap victim Cannon. Ricci's appealing as the sarcastic teen and Elvis the cat has a certain scrappy charm as well. Based on the novel "Undercover Cat" by Mildred and Gordon Gordon. **89m/C VHS, LV, Closed Caption.** Christina Ricci, Doug E. Doug, Dean Jones, George Dzundza, Peter Boyle, Michael McKean, Bess Armstrong, Dyan Cannon, John Ratzenberger, Estelle Parsons, Rebecca Schull, Tom Wilson, Brian Haley, Mark Christopher Lawrence; **D:** Bob Spiers; **W:** Scott Alexander, Larry Karaszewski; **C:** Jerzy Zielinski; **M:** Richard Gibbs. DIS

That Darn Sorceress ♪ 1988 A child witch has grown up, and so has her power. To keep her disciples, she must perform increasingly horrible feats. **89m/C VHS, Beta.** Pauline Adams, Betty Page; **D:** Whitney Bain. NO

That Eye, the Sky ♪♪ 1994 Alice (Harrow) and Sam (Fairall) Flack live on a small farm with their two children and senile grandmother. Sam's in a serious car crash and is eventually returned home still in a deep coma. Alice, who's having trouble coping, is grateful when wandering evangelist Harry Warburton (Coyote) shows up on her doorstep offering his help. But is this mystery man offering a miracle or more heartache? Based on the book by Tim Winton. **105m/C VHS.** AU Lisa Harrow, Peter Coyote, Mark Fairall, Jamie Croft, Amanda Douge, Alethea McGrath; **D:** John Ruane; **W:** John Ruane, Jim Barton; **C:** Ellery Ryan; **M:** David Bridie. Australian Film Institute '95: Best Supporting Actress (Douge); Nominations: Australian Film Institute '95: Best Actress (Harrow), Best Director (Ruane), Best Film. NYR

That Forsyte Woman ♪♪ The Forsyte Saga 1950 Based on the novel "A Man of Property" by John Galsworthy, a married Victorian woman falls for an architect engaged to be wed. Remade later, and better for BBC-television as "The Forsythe Saga." **112m/C VHS.** Errol Flynn, Greer Garson, Walter Pidgeon, Robert Young, Janet Leigh, Harry Davenport, Stanley Logan, Lumsden Hare, Aubrey Mather, Matt Moore; **D:** Compton Bennett; **C:** Joseph Ruttenberg. Nominations: Academy Awards '50: Best Costume Design (Color). MGM, CCB

That Gang of Mine ♪♪ 1940 "East Side Kids" episode about gang member Mugg's ambition to be a jockey. Good racing scenes. **62m/ B VHS, Beta.** Bobby Jordan, Leo Gorcey, Clarence Muse, Dave O'Brien; **D:** Joseph H. Lewis. NOS, DVT, HEG

That Girl from Paris ♪♪½ 1936 An opera singer from Paris stows away on an ocean liner to be near the swing bandleader she has fallen in love with. An entertaining film with many songs; remade as "Four Jacks and a Jill." ♪Una Voce Poco Fa; The Blue Danube; Love and Learn; The Call to Arms; Seal It With A Kiss; My Nephew From Nice; Moon Face; Tarantella. **105m/ B VHS, Beta.** Lily Pons, Gene Raymond, Jack Oakie, Herman Bing, Lucille Ball, Mischa Auer, Frank Jenks; **D:** Leigh Jason. Nominations: Academy Awards '36: Best Sound. TTC

That Hamilton Woman ♪♪♪ Lady Hamilton 1941 Screen biography of the tragic 18th-century love affair between British naval hero Lord Nelson and Lady Hamilton. Korda exaggerated the film's historical distortions in order to pass the censor's production code about adultery. Winston Churchill's favorite film which paralleled Britain's heroic struggles in WWII. **125m/B VHS, Beta, LV.** Laurence Olivier, Vivien Leigh, Gladys Cooper, Alan Mowbray, Sara Allgood, Henry Wilcoxon; **D:** Alexander Korda; **M:** Miklos Rozsa. Academy Awards '41: Best Sound;

Nominations: Academy Awards '41: Best Black and White Cinematography, Best Interior Decoration. HBO

That Long Night in '43 ♪♪½ 1960 A gripping story of fascist terror during WWII. **110m/ B VHS, Beta. D:** Florestano Vancini. CIG

That Lucky Touch ♪♪ 1975 York is a reporter covering NATO games; Moore is Bond warmed over as an arms dealer. Sexual and professional tension becomes unlikely romance. Slight and dull. Cobb's last film. **92m/C VHS, Beta.** Roger Moore, Susannah York, Shelley Winters, Lee J. Cobb, Jean-Pierre Cassel, Raf Vallone, Sydne Rome; **D:** Christopher Miles; **W:** John Briley. TWE

That Man from Rio ♪♪½ L'Homme de Rio; L'Uomo di Rio 1964 Engaging adventure spoof with Belmondo as a pilot whose girlfriend (Dorleac) has just been kidnapped. Her father led an expedition to South America in search of an Amazon treasure and the kidnappers think she knows how to find it. So of course Belmondo does some international adventuring in order to rescue her. In French with English subtitles. **114m/C VHS.** FR IT Jean-Paul Belmondo, Francoise Dorleac, Jean Servais, Simone Renant; **D:** Philippe de Broca; **W:** Philippe de Broca, Jean-Paul Rappeneau; **M:** Georges Delerue. New York Film Critics Awards '64: Best Foreign Film; Nominations: Academy Awards '64: Best Story & Screenplay. MGM

That Midnight Kiss ♪♪½ 1949 Glossy production of a musical romance featuring Lanza in his film debut. Thin plot has Lanza starring as a singing truck driver who is discovered by opera diva Grayson. ♪They Didn't Believe Me; I Know, I Know, I Know; Three O'Clock in the Morning; Santa Lucia; Down Among the Sheltering Palms; Revolutionary Etude; Cara Nome; Celeste Aida; Una Furtiva Lacrima. **96m/C VHS.** Kathryn Grayson, Jose Iturbi, Ethel Barrymore, Mario Lanza, Keenan Wynn, J. Carrol Naish, Jules Munshin; **D:** Norman Taurog; **C:** Robert L. Surtees. MGM

That Naughty Girl ♪♪ 1958 The bored daughter of a nightclub owner decides to experience all life has to offer. **77m/C VHS, Beta.** FR Brigitte Bardot, Jean Bretonniere, Francoise Fabian; **D:** Michel Boisrond. JEF

That Night ♪♪½ 1993 (PG-13) A view of romance through the eyes of a young girl, circa 1961. Ten-year-old Alice (Dushku) is the confidant of rebellious 17-year-old neighbor Cheryl (Lewis), who enlists the young girl's aid as a go-between with her wrong-side-of-the-tracks boyfriend Rick (Howell). 21 soundtrack oldies are featured. Directorial debut for screenwriter Bolotin. Based on a novel by Alice McDermott. **89m/C VHS, Beta, LV, Closed Caption.** C. Thomas Howell, Juliette Lewis, Eliza Dushku, Helen Shaver, John Dossett; **D:** Craig Bolotin; **W:** Craig Bolotin. WAR

That Obscure Object of Desire ♪♪♪½ Cet Obscur Objet Du Desir 1977 (R) Bunuel's last film, a comic nightmare of sexual frustration. A rich Spaniard obtains a beautiful girlfriend who, while changing physical identities, refuses to sleep with him. Based on a novel by Pierre Louys, which has been used as the premise for several other films, including "The Devil is a Woman," "La Femme et le Pantin," and "The Female." Available with subtitles or dubbed. **100m/ C VHS, Beta, LV, Letterbox.** SP Fernando Rey, Carole Bouquet, Angela Molina; **D:** Luis Bunuel; **W:** Luis Bunuel, Jean-Claude Carriere. Los Angeles Film Critics Association Awards '77: Best Foreign Film; National Board of Review Awards '77: Best Director (Bunuel); National Society of Film Critics Awards '77: Best Director (Bunuel); Nominations: Academy Awards '77: Best Adapted Screenplay, Best Foreign Language Film. COL

That Old Feeling ♪♪ 1996 (PG-13) Bitter ex-spouses Lilly (Midler) and Dan (Farina) are reunited at the wedding of their daughter and things turn ugly. They cause a scene and are sent out of the reception to cool down. Instead, their old passion flares up and they're found reeling in that old feeling in the back seat of a Porshe. After leaving to see where their whirlwind of romance takes them, they are trailed by their daughter

(Marshall), her weenie husband (Denton), and their respective current spousal units Rowena (O'Grady) and Alan (Rasche). Fluffy romantic comedy carried mostly by the performances of Midler and Farina. **CW:** Language and sex-related material. **105m/C VHS, LV, Closed Caption, DVD.** Bette Midler, Dennis Farina, Danny Nucci, Paula Marshall, Gail O'Grady, David Rasche, Jayne Eastwood; **D:** Carl Reiner; **W:** Leslie Dixon; **C:** Steve Mason; **M:** Patrick Williams. USH

That Sinking Feeling ♪♪♪ 1979 (PG) A group of bored Scot teenagers decide to steal 90 sinks from a plumber's warehouse. Well received early film from Forsyth is genuinely funny as the boys try to get rid of the sinks and turn a profit. **82m/C VHS, Beta, LV.** GB Robert Buchanan, John Hughes, Billy Greenlees, Alan Love; **D:** Bill Forsyth; **W:** Bill Forsyth; **C:** Michael Coulter.

That Summer of White Roses ♪♪½ 1990 (R) Compelling action drama about a lifeguard working at a resort in Nazi-occupied Yugoslavia and his love for a woman resistance fighter and her child. **98m/C VHS, Beta, LV, Closed Caption.** Tom Conti, Susan George, Rod Steiger; **D:** Rajko Grlic. IME, VTR

That Thing You Do! ♪♪♪ 1996 (PG) The Wonders, a small-town foursome, hit the big time in 1964 after a substitute drummer (like that could ever happen) adds some kick to the band's new song and sets the local kids a-fruggin'. Developed by freshman director/screenwriter Hanks (who also plays the band's Svengali-like record exec) as a diversion from Oscar hype, it's nostalgic and uncomplicated to a fault, but engaging nonetheless. Hanks clone Scott puts the beat into the charmingly wholesome quartet, while the underused Tyler is disarming as the put-upon girlfriend. Look quick or you'll miss bosom buddy Scolari as a TV host. Can't-get-it-out-of-your-head title track (played 11 times in the film) was selected from over 300 submissions after Hanks put out the call to music publishers. **110m/C VHS, LV, Closed Caption.** Tom Everett Scott, Johnathon Schaech, Liv Tyler, Steve Zahn, Ethan Embry, Tom Hanks, Charlize Theron, Obba Babatunde, Peter Scolari, Alex Rocco, Bill Cobbs, Rita Wilson, Chris Isaak, Kevin Pollak; **D:** Tom Hanks; **W:** Tom Hanks; **C:** Tak Fujimoto; **M:** Howard Shore. Nominations: Academy Awards '96: Best Song ("That Thing You Do!"); Golden Globe Awards '97: Best Song ("That Thing You Do!"). FXV

That Touch of Mink ♪♪½ 1962 In New York City, an unemployed secretary finds herself involved with a business tycoon. On a trip to Bermuda, both parties get an education as they play their game of "cat and mouse." Enjoyable romantic comedy. **99m/C VHS, LV, Letterbox.** Cary Grant, Doris Day, Gig Young, Audrey Meadows, John Astin, Dick Sargent; **D:** Delbert Mann; **C:** Russell Metty. Golden Globe Awards '63: Best Film—Musical/Comedy; Nominations: Academy Awards '62: Best Art Direction/Set Decoration (Color), Best Sound, Best Story & Screenplay. REP, MLB

That Uncertain Feeling ♪♪½ 1941 Light comedy about a couple's marital problems increasing when she develops the hiccups and a friendship with a flaky piano player. A remake of the earlier Lubitsch silent film, "Kiss Me Again." Available colorized. **86m/B VHS, Beta.** Merle Oberon, Melvyn Douglas, Burgess Meredith, Alan Mowbray, Eve Arden, Sig Rumann, Harry Davenport; **D:** Ernst Lubitsch; **C:** George Barnes. Nominations: Academy Awards '41: Best Original Dramatic/Comedy Score. NOS, VYY, DVT

That Was Then...This Is Now ♪♪ 1985 (R) Lame adaptation of S.E. Hinton teen novel about a surly kid who is attached to his adoptive brother and becomes jealous when the brother gets a girlfriend. **102m/C VHS, Beta, LV, Closed Caption.** Emilio Estevez, Craig Sheffer, Kim Delaney, Jill Schoelen, Barbara Babcock, Frank Howard, Larry B. Scott, Morgan Freeman; **D:** Christopher Cain; **W:** Emilio Estevez. PAR

That'll Be the Day ⚥⚥½ 1973 (PG) The early rock 'n' roll of the 1950s is the only outlet for a frustrated young working-class Brit. Prequel to "Stardust." Good, meticulous realism, engrossing story. 91m/C VHS, Beta, LV. Ringo Starr, Keith Moon, David Essex, Rosemary Leach, James Booth, Billy Fury, Rosalind Ayres, Robert Lindsay, Brenda Bruce, Verna Harvey, James Ottoway, Deborah Watling, Beth Morris, Daphne Oxenford, Kim Braden, Ron Hackett, Johnny Shannon, Susan Holderness, The Debonairs; **D:** Claude Whatham; **W:** Ray Connolly; **C:** Peter Suschitzsky. REP, TVC, CNG

That's Adequate ⚥⚥ 1990 (R) Mock documentary about a fictional film studio. Lampoons just about every movie made in the last 60 years. Premise might have been adequate for a sketch, but hardly for a feature-length film. Zaniness gets old quickly. 82m/C VHS. Tony Randall, Robert Downey, Rocky Aoki, Bruce Willis, Robert Townsend, James Coco, Jerry Stiller, Peter Riegert, Susan Dey, Richard Lewis, Robert Vaughn, Renee Taylor, Stuart Pankin, Brother Theodore, Anne Bloom, Chuck McCann, Anne Meara; **D:** Harry Hurwitz; **W:** Harry Hurwitz.

That's Dancing! 1985 (G) This anthology features some of film's finest moments in dance from classical ballet to break-dancing. 104m/C VHS, Beta, LV. Fred Astaire, Ginger Rogers, Ruby Keeler, Cyd Charisse, Gene Kelly, Shirley MacLaine, Liza Minnelli, Sammy Davis Jr., Mikhail Baryshnikov, Ray Bolger, Jennifer Beals, Dean Martin; **D:** Jack Haley Jr.; **M:** Henry Mancini. MGM

That's Entertainment 1974 (G) A compilation of scenes from the classic MGM musicals beginning with "The Broadway Melody" (1929) and ending with "Gigi" (1958). Great fun, especially for movie buffs. 132m/C VHS, Beta, LV, Letterbox. Judy Garland, Fred Astaire, Frank Sinatra, Gene Kelly, Esther Williams, Bing Crosby; **D:** Jack Haley Jr.; **M:** Henry Mancini. MGM

That's Entertainment, Part 2 1976 (G) A cavalcade of great musical and comedy sequences from MGM movies of the past. Also stars Jeanette MacDonald, Nelson Eddy, the Marx Brothers, Laurel and Hardy, Jack Buchanan, Ann Miller, Mickey Rooney, Louis Armstrong, Oscar Levant, Cyd Charisse, Elizabeth Taylor, Maurice Chavalier, Bing Crosby, Jimmy Durante, Clark Gable, and the Barrymores. Not as unified as its predecessor, but priceless nonetheless. 129m/C VHS, Beta, LV. Fred Astaire, Gene Kelly. MGM

That's Entertainment, Part 3 1993 (G) Third volume contains 62 MGM musical numbers from over 100 films, hosted by nine of the original stars, and is based on outtakes and unfinished numbers from studio archives. One new technique used here is a split-screen showing both the actual film with a behind-the-scenes shot that includes cameramen, set designers, and dancers scurrying around. Although it has its moments, TE3 doesn't generate the same reverence for Hollywood's Golden Age that its predecessors managed to do. That 18-year gap between sequels may say something about what the studio execs thought of their film vault's remainders. 113m/C VHS, Beta, LV, Closed Caption. **D:** Bud Friedgen, Michael J. Sheridan; **W:** Bud Friedgen, Michael J. Sheridan; **M:** Marc Shaiman. MGM

That's Life! ⚥⚥ 1986 (PG-13) A lackluster semi-home movie starring Edwards' family and friends. A single weekend in the lives of a writer who's turning 60, his singer wife who has been diagnosed with cancer, and their family. 102m/C VHS, Beta, LV, Closed Caption. Jack Lemmon, Julie Andrews, Sally Kellerman, Chris Lemmon, Emma Walton, Rob Knepper, Robert Loggia, Jennifer Edwards; **D:** Blake Edwards; **W:** Blake Edwards; **M:** Henry Mancini. Nominations: Academy Awards '86: Best Song ("Life in a Looking Glass"). CCB, ART, VES

That's My Baby! ⚥ 1988 (PG-13) A man wants his girlfriend to have their baby, but the only thing she wants is a career. War between the sexes poorly done. 97m/C VHS, Beta. Sonja Smits, Timothy Webber; **D:** Edie Yolles, John Bradshaw. TWE

That's Singing: The Best of Broadway 1984 A tribute to the American musical theatre featuring performances of memorable songs from 20 Broadway shows. 111m/C VHS, Beta, LV. ORI, WAR

Theatre of Blood ⚥⚥⚥ *Much Ado about Murder* 1973 (R) Critics are unkind to Shakespearian ham Price, and he eliminates them by various Bard-inspired methods with the assistance of his lovely daughter. Top drawer comedy noir. 104m/C VHS, LV. GB Vincent Price, Diana Rigg, Ian Hendry, Robert Morley, Dennis Price, Diana Dors, Milo O'Shea, Harry Andrews, Coral Browne, Robert Coote, Jack Hawkins, Michael Hordern, Arthur Lowe; **D:** Douglas Hickox; **W:** Anthony Greville-Bell; **C:** Wolfgang Suschitzky. MGM

Theatre of Death ⚥⚥½ *Blood Fiend; Female Fiend* 1967 Horror master Lee is back, this time as a theatre director in Paris. Meanwhile, police are baffled by a series of mysterious murders, each bearing a trace of vampirism. Well-plotted suspense. A racy voodoo dance sequence, often cut, is available on some video versions. 90m/C VHS, Beta. Christopher Lee, Lelia Goldoni, Julian Glover, Evelyn Laye, Jenny Till, Ivor Dean; **D:** Samuel Gallu. REP, SNC

Thelma & Louise ⚥⚥⚥ 1991 (R) Hailed as the first "feminist-buddy" movie, Sarandon and Davis bust out as best friends who head directly into one of the better movies of the year. Davis is the ditzy Thelma, a housewife rebelling against her dominating, unfaithful, abusive husband (who, rather than being disturbing, provides some of the best comic relief in the film). Sarandon is Louise, a hardened and world-weary waitress in the midst of an unsatisfactory relationship. They hit the road for a respite from their mundane lives, only to find violence and a part of themselves they never knew existed. Outstanding performances from Davis and especially Sarandon, with Pitt notable as the stud who gets Davis' motor revved. Director Scott has a fine eye for set details. **CW:** Strong language, some violence, and sensuality. 130m/C VHS, Beta, LV, 8mm, Letterbox, Closed Caption. Susan Sarandon, Geena Davis, Harvey Keitel, Christopher McDonald, Michael Madsen, Brad Pitt, Timothy Carhart, Stephen Tobolowsky, Lucinda Jenney; **D:** Ridley Scott; **W:** Callie Khouri; **M:** Hans Zimmer. Academy Awards '91: Best Original Screenplay; National Board of Review Awards '91: Best Actress (Sarandon), Best Actress (Davis); National Society of Film Critics Awards '91: Best Supporting Actor (Keitel); Writers Guild of America '91: Best Original Screenplay; Nominations: Academy Awards '91: Best Actress (Davis), Best Actress (Sarandon), Best Cinematography, Best Director (Scott), Best Film Editing. MGM, OM

Them! ⚥⚥⚥ 1954 A group of mutated giant ants wreak havoc on a southwestern town. The first of the big-bug movies, and far surpassing the rest, this is a classic fun flick. See how many names you can spot among the supporting cast. 93m/B VHS, Beta, LV. James Whitmore, Edmund Gwenn, Fess Parker, James Arness, Onslow Stevens, Jack Perrin, Joan Weldon, Sean McClory, Sandy Descher, Dub Taylor, William Schallert, Leonard Nimoy; **D:** Gordon Douglas; **W:** Ted Sherdeman; **C:** Sid Hickox. WAR

The Theme ⚥⚥⚥ *Tema* 1979 Esenin is a mediocre middle-aged playwright who knows his success comes from kow-towing to the party line. Trying to find inspiration he visits his native village where he meets the young Sasa, an artist who has refused to compromise. Although Esenin falls for her, Sasa has only contempt for his lack of principles and stays with her poet/lover, who is reduced to digging graves and has decided to emigrate to Israel. The film went unreleased for eight years because of its themes of artistic freedom and emigration. In Russian with English subtitles. 100m/C VHS. RU Mikhail Ulyanov, Inna Churikova, Stanislav Lyubshin, Evgeny Vesnik, Sergei Nikonenko, Natalya Selezneva; **D:** Gleb Panfilov. Berlin International Film Festival '79: Golden Berlin Bear. KIV, FCT

Theodora Goes Wild ⚥⚥⚥ 1936 Tiny, priggish Lynnfield Connecticut is abashed to discover that a scandalous best seller about small-town life has been written pseudonymously by their very own Theodora Lynn (Dunne). When Theodora gets a chance to meet sophisticated New Yorker Michael Grant (Douglas), who did the illustrations for her book, she falls for him. But both must throw aside their own (and everyone else's) expectations and limitations for them to be happy. Dunne's first comedic lead role. 94m/B VHS. Irene Dunne, Melvyn Douglas, Thomas Mitchell, Thurston Hall, Rosalind Keith, Spring Byington, Elisabeth Risdon, Margaret McWade; **D:** Richard Boleslawski; **W:** Sidney Buchman; **C:** Joseph Walker; **M:** Morris Stoloff. Nominations: Academy Awards '36: Best Actress (Dunne), Best Film Editing. COL

Theodore Rex ⚥⚥½ 1995 (PG) Futuristic comedy finds cynical, seasoned cop Katie Coltrane (Goldberg) furious at being teamed with Teddy, who just happens to be an eight-foot-tall, three-ton, returned-from-extinction Tyrannosaurus Rex (who has a taste for cookies). And Teddy's not exactly the brightest dinosaur on the block, which makes Katie's job all the harder when they stumble across a major crime caper. 92m/C VHS, LV, Closed Caption. Whoopi Goldberg, Armin Mueller-Stahl, Richard Roundtree, Juliet Landau; **D:** Jonathan Betuel; **W:** Jonathan Betuel; **C:** David Tattersall; **M:** Robert Folk. Nominations: Golden Raspberry Awards '96: Worst Actress (Goldberg). NLC

There Goes Barder ⚥⚥ 1964 Constantine plays a con-man who's hired by a crooked ship owner to be a security agent. ?m/C VHS. FR Eddie Constantine, May Britt. SNC, VYY

There Goes Kelly ⚥½ 1945 Moran and Miller are page boys at a radio station who try to get the station receptionist a singing job. When the vocalist on a popular show is murdered, the duo not only get their protege a break but get themselves a mystery to solve as well. 62m/B VHS. Jackie Moran, Sidney Miller, Wanda McKay, Ralph Sanford, Jan Wiley, Anthony Warde; **D:** Phil Karlson. GPV

There Goes My Baby ⚥⚥½ 1992 (R) Eight California high school grads confront their futures on two nights in '65 (as the Watts riots ignite). There are Vietnam protests, flower children, would-be rock stars, friendships, and romantic complications. Yes, it sounds a lot like "American Graffiti" but the cast are winning and there's a good deal of affection without sinking to mawkishness. 99m/C VHS, LV, Closed Caption. Dermot Mulroney, Rick Schroder, Kelli Williams, Jill Schoelen, Noah Wyle, Kristin Minter, Lucy Deakins, Kenny Ransom, Seymour Cassel, Paul Gleason, Frederick Coffin, Andrew (Andy) Robinson, Shon Greenblatt, J.E. Freeman; **D:** Floyd Mutrux; **W:** Floyd Mutrux. ORI

There Goes the Neighborhood ⚥⚥½ 1992 (PG-13) A dying convict tells prison psychiatrist Daniels where he has buried 8.5 million dollars—under the home of neighbor O'Hara. Daniels and O'Hara try to discreetly dig up the fortune but when the neighborhood finds out everyone wants a chance at the cash. 88m/C VHS, Beta, Closed Caption. Jeff Daniels, Catherine O'Hara, Dabney Coleman, Hector Elizondo, Judith Ivey, Rhea Perlman, Harris Yulin, Jonathan Banks, Chazz Palminteri, Mary Gross; **D:** Bill Phillips; **M:** David Bell. PAR

There was a Crooked Man ⚥⚥⚥½ 1970 (R) An Arizona town gets some new ideas about law and order when an incorruptible and innovative warden takes over the town's prison. The warden finds he's got his hands full with one inmate determined to escape. Offbeat western black comedy supported by an excellent and entertaining production, with fine acting all around. 123m/C VHS, LV. Kirk Douglas, Henry Fonda, Warren Oates, Hume Cronyn, Burgess Meredith, John Randolph, Arthur O'Connell, Alan Hale Jr., Lee Grant; **D:** Joseph L. Mankiewicz; **W:** Robert Benton, David Newman; **C:** Harry Stradling Jr. WAR

Theremin: An Electronic Odyssey

🎵🎵🎵 1995 (PG) Profiles the life of Russian scientist Leon Theremin (who died in 1993), founder of electronic music, and his revolutionary musical invention, the Theremin. Martin located the 95-year-old Theremin in Moscow in 1991, interviewed him on camera, then brought him back to the U.S. to film reunions with friends and colleages he hadn't seen in 50 years. Martin's focus is on the impact of the Theremin on Hollywood movie scores heard in '50s sci-fi and thriller classics ("The Day the Earth Stood Still") and in popular music (The Beach Boys' "Good Vibrations" is commented on by Brian Wilson). Theremin's life proves as curious as his instrument, with his controversial interracial marriage to a ballet star, abduction by Russian agents, and imprisonment in a Soviet mental hospital. "Theremin" provides a fascinating and heartfelt tribute to the man's work and life. **84m/C VHS, LV, Closed Caption.** *D:* Steven M. Martin; *W:* Steven M. Martin; *C:* Robert Stone, Edward Lachman, Chris Lombardi; *M:* Hal Willner. *ORI*

There's a Girl in My Soup

🎵🎵 1970 (R) Sellers is a gourmet who moonlights as a self-styled Casanova. Early post "Laugh-In" Hawn is the young girl who takes refuge at his London love nest when her boyfriend dumps her. Lust ensues. Has its funny parts, but not a highlight of anyone's career. Based on the hit play. **95m/C VHS, Beta.** *GB* Peter Sellers, Goldie Hawn, Diana Dors; *D:* Roy Boulting. *GKK*

There's No Business Like Show Business

🎵🎵🎵 1954 A top husband and wife vaudevillian act make it a family affair. Filmed in CinemaScope, allowing for full and lavish musical numbers. Good performances and Berlin's music make this an enjoyable film. 🎵When the Midnight Choo-Choo Leaves for Alabam; Let's Have Another Cup of Coffee; Play a Simple Melody; After You Get What You Want You Don't Want It; You'd Be Surprised; A Sailor's Not a Sailor; A Pretty Girl is Like a Melody; If You Believe Me; A Man Chases a Girl Until She Catches Him. **117m/C VHS, Beta, LV, Letterbox, Closed Caption.** Ethel Merman, Donald O'Connor, Marilyn Monroe, Dan Dailey, Johnny Ray, Mitzi Gaynor, Frank McHugh, Hugh O'Brian; *D:* Walter Lang. Nominations: Academy Awards '54: Best Costume Design (Color), Best Story, Scoring of a Musical. *FOX, FCT*

There's No Time for Love, Charlie Brown

1987 An animated adventure with the Peanuts gang as they travel to a museum on a class trip. **30m/C VHS, Beta.** *BAR*

There's Nothing Out There

🎵🎵 1990 A group of seven teenagers spends Spring Break at a secluded mountain cabin. It sounds wonderful, but one of the boys (who claims to have seen every horror movie on video) knows the signs of a horror movie just waiting to happen. **91m/C VHS, Beta, LV.** Craig Peck, Wendy Bednarz, Mark Collver, Bonnie Bowers, John Carhart III, Claudia Flores, Jeff Dachis; *D:* Rolfe Kanefsky; *W:* Rolfe Kanefsky.

There's Something About Mary

1998 (R) Stiller had a disastrous prom date with Diaz but, years later, still decides he wants detective Dillon to find out what happened to her. But when Dillon falls in love with Diaz, he lies to Stiller, who finds out about the ruse and goes after the girl. Not yet reviewed.*CW:* Strong comic sexual content and language. **?m/C VHS.** Ben Stiller, Matt Dillon, Cameron Diaz, Chris Elliott; *D:* Bobby Farrelly, Peter Farrelly; *W:* Edward Decter, John J. Strauss. *NYR*

Therese

🎵🎵🎵 1986 Stylish biography of a young French nun and her devotion to Christ bordering on romantic love. Explores convent life. Real-life Therese died of TB and was made a saint. A directorial tour de force for Cavalier. In French with English subtitles. **90m/C VHS, Beta.** *FR* Catherine Mouchet, Aurore Prieto, Sylvie Habault, Ghislaine Mona; *D:* Alain Cavalier; *W:* Alain Cavalier. Cannes Film Festival '86: Special Jury Prize; Cesar Awards '87: Best

Cinematography, Best Director (Cavalier), Best Film, Best Writing. *TPV*

Therese & Isabelle

🎵🎵½ 1967 Story of growing love and physical attraction between two French schoolgirls. On holiday together, they confront their mutual desires. Richly photographed soft porn based on the novel by Violet Leduc. Not vulgar, but certainly for adults. French with subtitles. **118m/B VHS.** Essy Persson, Anna Gael, Barbara Laage, Anne Vernon; *D:* Radley Metzger. *FRF*

These Girls Won't Talk

192? Three female stars of early silent pictures are featured separately in: "Her Bridal Nightmare," "Campus Carmen," and "As Luck Would Have It." **50m/B VHS, Beta.** Colleen Moore, Carole Lombard, Betty Compson. *VYY*

These Three

🎵🎵🎵½ 1936 A teenaged girl ruins the lives of two teachers by telling a malicious lie. Excellent cast. Script by Lillian Hellman, based on her play "The Children's Hour." Remade by the same director as "The Children's Hour" in 1961. **92m/B VHS, Beta, LV.** Miriam Hopkins, Merle Oberon, Joel McCrea, Bonita Granville, Marcia Mae Jones, Walter Brennan, Margaret Hamilton; *D:* William Wyler; *C:* Gregg Toland. Nominations: Academy Awards '36: Best Supporting Actress (Granville). *COL*

They

🎵 *Invasion from Inner Earth; Hell Fire* 1977 Beings from beneath the earth's crust take their first trip to the surface. **88m/C VHS, Beta.** Paul Dentzer, Debbie Pick, Nick Holt; *D:* Ito Rebane. *NO*

They All Kissed the Bride

🎵🎵½ 1942 Tough cookie Margaret Drew (Crawford) must take over the family's trucking business when dad dies and support her ditzy mother (Burke) and younger sister Vivian (Parrish). Crusading newspaperman Michael Holmes (Douglas) blasts Margaret's business practices in print but when they finally meet, the sparks fly. Crawford manages the physical comedy well and Douglas is suitably charming. **87m/B VHS.** Joan Crawford, Melvyn Douglas, Billie Burke, Helen Parrish, Roland Young, Allen Jenkins, Emory Parnell; *D:* Alexander Hall; *W:* Andrew Solt, P.J. Wolfson; *C:* Joseph Walker; *M:* Werner R. Heymann. *COL*

They All Laughed

🎵🎵 1981 (PG) Three detectives become romantically involved with the women they were hired to investigate. Essentially light-hearted fluff with little or no script. Further undermined by the real-life murder of Stratten before the film's release. **115m/C VHS, Beta, LV.** Ben Gazzara, John Ritter, Audrey Hepburn, Colleen Camp, Patti Hansen, Dorothy Stratten, Elizabeth Pena; *D:* Peter Bogdanovich; *W:* Peter Bogdanovich. *VES*

They Bite

woof! 1995 (R) A pornographic filmmaker's latest epic about lustful gill-men is filming at the same Florida beach where a zoologist is investigating reports of man-like fish monsters killing swimmers. Just a coincidence? Ultra- (and deliberately) cheesy; an unrated version is also available.*CW:* Nudity, language, mild violence. **96m/C VHS.** Donna Frotscher, Nick Baldasare, Charlie Barnett, Ron Jeremy; *D:* Bret Piper; *W:* Bret Piper. *MTH*

They Call It Sin

🎵🎵 *The Way of Life* 1932 Often told story of a young country girl heading to the Big Apple in search of her big break and "Mr. Right." Young is a chorus line girl romantically involved with her married producer (Calhern) while faithful admirer Brent waits nearby. Predictable plot adapted from the novel by Alberta Stedman Eagan. **68m/B VHS.** Loretta Young, George Brent, David Manners, Louis Calhern, Una Merkel, Joseph Cawthorn, Helen Vinson; *D:* Thornton Freeland; *W:* Lillie Hayward, Howard J. Green. *MGM*

They Call Me Bruce?

🎵🎵 *A Fist Full of Chopsticks* 1982 (PG) A bumbling Bruce Lee lookalike meets a karate-chopping Mafia moll in this farce. Silly premise creates lots of laughs. Followed by a sequel, "They Still Call Me Bruce." **88m/C VHS, Beta.** Johnny Yune, Margaux Hemingway; *D:* Elliot Hong; *W:* Tim Clawson. *VES*

They Call Me Mr. Tibbs!

🎵🎵 1970 (R) Lieutenant Virgil Tibbs (Poitier) investigates the murder of a prostitute. The prime suspect is his friend, the Reverend Logan Sharpe (Landau). He is torn between his duty as a policeman, his concern for the reverend, and the turmoil in his domestic life. Less tense, less compelling sequel to "In the Heat of the Night."*CW:* Violent scene with nudity. **108m/C VHS, Beta.** Sidney Poitier, Barbara McNair, Martin Landau, Juano Hernandez, Anthony Zerbe, Ed Asner, Norma Crane, Jeff Corey; *D:* Gordon Douglas; *W:* Alan R. Trustman; *M:* Quincy Jones. *MGM, FOX*

They Call Me Trinity

🎵🎵½ *Lo Chiamavano Trinita* 1972 (G) Lazy drifter-gunslinger and his outlaw brother join forces with Mormon farmers to rout bullying outlaws. Spoofs every western cliche with relentless comedy, parodying "The Magnificent Seven" and gibing the spaghetti western. Followed by "Trinity is Still My Name." Dubbed. **110m/C VHS, Beta.** *IT* Terence Hill, Bud Spencer, Farley Granger, Steffen Zacharias; *D:* E.B. Clucher. *CCB, HHE*

They Came from Beyond Space

🎵 1967 Aliens invade the earth and possess the brains of humans. They only want a few slaves to help them repair their ship which crashed on the moon. The only person able to stop them is a scientist with a steel plate in his head. Silly and forgettable. **86m/C VHS, Beta.** *GB* Robert Hutton, Michael Gough; *D:* Freddie Francis.

They Came from Within

🎵🎵½ *Shivers; The Parasite Murders* 1975 (R) The occupants of a high-rise building go on a sex and violence spree when stricken with an aphrodisiac parasite. Queasy, sleazy, and weird. First major film by Cronenberg. **87m/C VHS, Beta.** *CA* Paul Hampton, Joe Silver, Lynn Lowry, Barbara Steele, Susan Petrie, Allan Magicovsky; *D:* David Cronenberg; *W:* David Cronenberg; *C:* Robert Saad. *ART, VES*

They Came to Cordura

🎵🎵½ 1959 Mexico, 1916: a woman and six American soldiers—five heroes and one who has been branded a coward—begin a journey to the military headquarters in Cordura. Slow journey brings out personalities. Look for "Bewitched" hubby Dick York. Based on Glendon Swarthout's best-seller. **123m/C VHS, Beta, LV.** Gary Cooper, Rita Hayworth, Van Heflin, Tab Hunter, Dick York, Richard Conte; *D:* Robert Rossen. *COL*

They Died with Their Boots On

🎵🎵🎵 1941 The Battle of Little Big Horn is recreated Hollywood style. Takes liberties with historical fact, but still an exciting portrayal of General Custer's last stand. The movie also marks the last time de Havilland worked with Flynn. Also available colorized. **141m/B VHS, Beta.** Errol Flynn, Sydney Greenstreet, Anthony Quinn, Hattie McDaniel, Arthur Kennedy, Gene Lockhart, Regis Toomey, Olivia de Havilland, Charley Grapewin; *D:* Raoul Walsh; *M:* Max Steiner. *MGM, MLB, FOX*

They Drive by Night

🎵🎵🎵½ *The Road to Frisco* 1940 Two truck-driving brothers break away from a large company and begin independent operations. After an accident to Bogart, Raft is forced to go back to the company where Lupino, the boss's wife, becomes obsessed with him and kills her husband to gain the company and win Raft. When he rejects her, she accuses him of the murder. Well-plotted film with great dialogue. Excellent cast gives it their all. **97m/B VHS, Beta.** Humphrey Bogart, Ann Sheridan, George Raft, Ida Lupino, Alan Hale, Gale Page, Roscoe Karns, Charles Halton; *D:* Raoul Walsh. *FOX, FCT*

They Got Me Covered

🎵🎵 1943 Two WWII-era journalists get involved in a comic web of murder, kidnapping and romance. Hope is very funny and carries the rest of the cast. Look for Doris Day in a bit part and listen for Bing Crosby singing whenever Hope opens his cigarette case. **95m/B VHS.** Bob Hope, Dorothy Lamour, Otto Preminger, Eduardo Ciannelli, Donald Meek, Walter Catlett; *D:* David Butler. *HBO*

They Knew What They Wanted 🎬🎬🎬 1940 A lonely San Francisco waitress begins a correspondence romance with a grape grower and agrees to marry him after he sends her a photo which shows him as being young and handsome. She arrives to discover Laughton had sent her a picture of another man. An accident, an affair, and a pregnancy provide further complications before a satisfactory ending is suggested. Flawed adaptation of Sidney Howard's play still has strong performances from Lombard and Laughton. 96m/B VHS, Beta. Charles Laughton, Carole Lombard, Harry Carey Sr., Karl Malden, William Gargan; D: Garson Kanin; C: Harry Stradling. Nominations: Academy Awards '40: Best Supporting Actor (Gargan). NO

They Live 🎬🎬½ 1988 (R) A semi-serious science-fiction spoof about a drifter who discovers an alien conspiracy. They're taking over the country under the guise of Reaganism, capitalism and yuppiedom. Screenplay written by Carpenter under a pseudonym. Starts out fun, deteriorates into cliches and bad special effects makeup. 88m/C VHS, Beta, LV. Roddy Piper, Keith David, Meg Foster, George Flower, Peter Jason, Raymond St. Jacques, John Lawrence, Sy Richardson, Jason Robards III, Larry Franco; D: John Carpenter; W: Frank Armitage, John Carpenter; M: Alan Howarth, John Carpenter. USH

They Live by Night 🎬🎬🎬½ The Twisted Road; Your Red Wagon 1949 A young fugitive sinks deeper into a life of crime thanks to his association with two hardened criminals. Classic film noir was Ray's first attempt at directing. Based on Edward Anderson's novel "Thieves Like Us," under which title it was remade in 1974. Compelling and suspenseful. 95m/B VHS, Beta, LV. Cathy O'Donnell, Farley Granger, Howard da Silva, Jay C. Flippen, Helen Craig; D: Nicholas Ray. HHT

They Made Me a Criminal 🎬🎬½ I Became a Criminal; They Made Me a Fugitive 1939 A champion prizefighter, believing he murdered a man in a drunken brawl, runs away. He finds refuge in the West with the Dead End Kids. Remake of "The Life of Jimmy Dolan." Berkeley was best-known for directing and choreographing musicals and surprisingly did very well with this movie. 92m/B VHS, Beta, LV. John Garfield, Ann Sheridan, Claude Rains, Leo Gorcey; D: Busby Berkeley; C: James Wong Howe; M: Max Steiner. NOS, VHE, KAR

They Meet Again 🎬🎬 1941 The final segment of the Dr. Christian series. The country doctor sets out to prove the innocence of a man who has been wrongly accused of stealing money. Slow moving and not particularly exciting. 68m/B VHS, Beta, 8mm. Jean Hersholt, Dorothy Lovett; D: Erle C. Kenton. NOS, VYY, VYY

They Met in Bombay 🎬🎬½ 1941 Two jewel thieves team up in this romantic action-comedy, complete with exotic locations and two big boxoffice stars. A Japanese invasion makes Russell reconsider her life of crime and gives Gable a chance to play hero. Look for Alan Ladd in a bit part in his pre-"This Gun for Hire" days. Based on a story by John Kafka. 86m/B VHS. Clark Gable, Rosalind Russell, Peter Lorre, Jessie Ralph, Reginald Owen, Eduardo Ciannelli, Alan Ladd; D: Clarence Brown; W: Anita Loos, Edwin Justus Mayer, Leon Gordon. MGM

They Might Be Giants 🎬🎬🎬 1971 (G) Woodward is a woman shrink named Watson who treats retired judge Scott for delusions that he is Sherlock Holmes. Scott's brother wants him committed so the family loot will come to him. Very funny in places; Woodward and Scott highlight a solid cast. 98m/C VHS, Beta. George C. Scott, Joanne Woodward, Jack Gilford, Eugene Roche, Kitty Winn, F. Murray Abraham, M. Emmet Walsh; D: Anthony Harvey; M: John Barry. USH

They Never Come Back 🎬½ 1932 A boxer is thrown in jail and then stages a comeback. 62m/B VHS, Beta, LV. Regis Toomey, Dorothy Sebastian. SNC

They Only Kill Their Masters 🎬🎬½ 1972 (PG) Garner plays a California police chief investigating the death of a wild beach town resident, supposedly killed by her doberman pinscher. He discovers the woman was actually drowned and there are any number of secrets to uncover. Mild whodunit. 98m/C VHS. James Garner, Katharine Ross, June Allyson, Hal Holbrook, Harry Guardino, Christopher Connelly, Tom Ewell, Peter Lawford, Edmond O'Brien, Arthur O'Connell, Ann Rutherford, Art Metrano; D: James Goldstone; M: Perry Botkin. MGM

They Paid with Bullets: Chicago 1929 🎬½ 197? The story of one man's rise to power, and eventual downfall as a Mafia consigliatore. 88m/C VHS, Beta. Peter Lee Lawrence, Ingrid Schoeller. CNG

They Saved Hitler's Brain woof!
Madmen of Mandoras; The Return of Mr. H 1964 Fanatical survivors of the Nazi holocaust gave eternal life to the brain of their leader in the last hours of the war. Now it's on a Caribbean island giving orders again. One of the truly great "bad" movies. Shot in pieces in the U.S., the Philippines, and elsewhere, with chunks of other films stuck in to hold the "story" together. 91m/B VHS, Beta, 8mm. Walter Stocker, Audrey Caire; D: David Bradley. VYY

They Shall Have Music 🎬🎬 Melody of Youth; Ragged Angels 1939 A poverty-stricken child hears a concert by violinist Heifetz and decides to become a musician. He joins Brennan's nearly bankrupt music school and persuades Heifetz to play at a benefit concert. Hokey but enjoyable Goldwyn effort to bring classical music to the big screen. 🎵 Rondo Capriccioso; Hora Staccato; Estrellita; Melody; Concerto in E Minor for Violin and Orchestra; Waltz in D Flat, Opus 64, No. 1; Cara Nome; Casta Diva. 101m/B VHS, Beta. Walter Brennan, Joel McCrea, Gene Reynolds, Jascha Heifetz, Marjorie Main, Porter Hall, Andrea Leeds, Terence Kilburn; D: Archie Mayo. Nominations: Academy Awards '39: Best Score. HBO

They Shoot Horses, Don't They? 🎬🎬🎬½ 1969 (R) Powerful period piece depicting the desperation of the Depression Era. Contestants enter a dance marathon in the hopes of winning a cash prize, not realizing that they will be driven to exhaustion. Fascinating and tragic. 121m/C VHS, LV. Jane Fonda, Michael Sarrazin, Susannah York, Gig Young, Red Buttons, Bonnie Bedelia, Bruce Dern, Allyn Ann McLerie, Chaing I, Al Lewis, Michael Conrad; D: Sydney Pollack. Academy Awards '69: Best Supporting Actor (Young); British Academy Awards '70: Best Supporting Actress (York); Golden Globe Awards '70: Best Supporting Actor (Young); New York Film Critics Awards '69: Best Actress (Fonda); Nominations: Academy Awards '69: Best Actress (Fonda), Best Adapted Screenplay, Best Art Direction/Set Decoration, Best Costume Design, Best Director (Pollack), Best Film Editing, Best Supporting Actress (York), Scoring of a Musical. FOX, MLB

They Still Call Me Bruce 🎬 1986 (PG) A Korean searches for the American who saved his life when he was young and instead becomes big brother to an orphan. Supposedly a sequel to "They Call Me Bruce," but has little in common with it. Poorly done and not particularly entertaining. 91m/C VHS, Beta. Johnny Yune, Robert Guillaume, Pat Paulsen; D: Johnny Yune. VTR

They Watch 🎬🎬½ They 1993 (PG-13) Workaholic Bergin neglects his family and suffers the consequences when his young daughter dies in an auto accident. In fact, he's so distressed that he relies on blind psychic Redgrave to get in touch with his little girl's spirit. Based on the story "They" by Rudyard Kipling. Made for television. 100m/C VHS. Patrick Bergin, Vanessa Redgrave, Valerie Mahaffey; D: John Korty; W: Edithe Swensen; M: Gerald Gouriet. COL

They Went That-a-Way & That-a-Way woof! 1978 (PG) Two bumbling deputies pose as convicts in this madcap prison caper. Terrible re-hash of Laurel-and-Hardy has nothing going for it. 96m/C VHS, Beta. Tim Conway, Richard Kiel, Chuck McCann; D: Edward Montagne; W: Tim Conway.

They Were Expendable 🎬🎬🎬½ 1945 Two American captains pit their PT boats against the Japanese fleet. Based on the true story of a PT boat squadron based in the Philippines during the early days of WWII. One of the best (and most underrated) WWII films. Also available in a colorized version. 135m/B VHS, Beta. Robert Montgomery, John Wayne, Donna Reed, Jack Holt, Ward Bond, Cameron Mitchell, Leon Ames, Marshall Thompson; D: John Ford. Nominations: Academy Awards '45: Best Sound. MGM

They Were So Young 🎬🎬½ 1955 European models become the pawns of wealthy Brazilian magnates when they are sent to South America. They are threatened with death if they do not cooperate. The scenes were shot in Italy and Berlin. Well acted and believable, although rather grim story. 78m/B VHS, Beta, LV. GE Scott Brady, Johanna Matz, Raymond Burr; D: Kurt Neumann. NO

They Were Ten 🎬🎬½ 1961 Ten Soviet Jews make Palestine their home in the 1800s despite Arab and Turkish persecution and pressures among themselves. In Hebrew with English subtitles. 105m/B VHS, Beta. IS Ninette, Oded Teomi, Leo Filer, Yosef Safra; D: Baruch Dienar. ERG, FCT

They Won't Believe Me 🎬🎬🎬 1947 A man plots to kill his wife, but before he does, she commits suicide. He ends up on trial for her "murder." Interesting acting by Young and Hayward against type. Surprising, ironic ending. 95m/B VHS, Beta, LV. Robert Young, Susan Hayward, Rita Johnson, Jane Greer; D: Irving Pichel. TTC

They Won't Forget 🎬🎬🎬½ 1937 When a young girl is murdered in a southern town, personal interests take precedence over justice. Turner is excellent in her first billed role, as are the other actors. Superb script, and expert direction by LeRoy pulls it all together. Based on Ward Greene's "Death in the Deep South." 95m/B VHS. Claude Rains, Otto Kruger, Lana Turner, Allyn Joslyn, Elisha Cook Jr., Edward Norris; D: Mervyn LeRoy; W: Robert Rossen, Aben Kandel. WAR, OM

They're Playing with Fire woof! 1984 (R) An English teacher seduces a student and gets him involved in a murder plot to gain an inheritance. Turns out someone else is beating them to the punch. Sleazy semi-pornographic slasher. 96m/C VHS, Beta. Sybil Danning, Eric Brown, Andrew Prine, Paul Clemens, K.T. Stevens, Alvy Moore; D: Howard (Hikmet) Avedis; W: Howard (Hikmet) Avedis. VTR

Thicker Than Water 🎬🎬 1993 Eerie psychological thriller exploring the relationship between identical twins. Sam Crawford (Pryce) is a successful doctor, happily married to Jo (Russell), whose sister Debbie (Russell again) is completely different in temperament. The two share a strong psychic bond, however, and when Jo dies in a suspicious hit-and-run accident Debbie feels compelled to make Sam her own. Based on the novel by Dylan Jones. 150m/C VHS. GB Theresa Russell, Jonathan Pryce, Robert Pugh; D: Marc Evans; W: Trevor Preston. TVC

The Thief 🎬🎬 1952 An American commits treason and is overcome by guilt. Novel because there is not one word of dialogue, though the gimmick can't sustain the ordinary story. A product of the Communist scare of the 1950s, it tends to be pretentious and melodramatic. 84m/B VHS, LV. Ray Milland, Rita Gam, Martin Gabel, Harry Bronson, John McKutcheon; D: Russel Rouse; C: Sam Leavitt. Nominations: Academy Awards '52: Best Original Dramatic/Comedy Score. EEL, VCI

Thief 1971 A successful businessman (Crenna) attempts to put his criminal past behind him. He's trapped when looking for a quick way to get some money to pay off a gambling debt. Made for television drama that's well-written and directed with tepid acting. 74m/C VHS, Beta. Richard Crenna, Angie Dickinson, Cameron Mitchell, Hurd Hatfield, Robert Webber; D: William A. Graham. ORI

Thief 🎞️🎞️🎞️ *Violent Streets* **1981 (R)** A big-time professional thief likes working solo, but decides to sign up with the mob in order to make one more big score and retire. He finds out it's not that easy. Taut and atmospheric thriller is director Mann's feature film debut. **126m/C VHS, Beta, LV.** James Caan, Tuesday Weld, Willie Nelson, James Belushi, Elizabeth Pena, Robert Prosky; **D:** Michael Mann; **W:** Michael Mann; **C:** Donald E. Thorin. *MGM, FOX*

The Thief and the Cobbler 🎞️🎞️🎞️½ **1996 (G)** Musically animated fairy tale about Tack, a humble cobbler (Broderick) who aids the clever and beautiful Princess Yum Yum (Beals) when their town's golden treasures are stolen. Legendary villain Price lends his voice to the evil Zig Zag. Three time Oscar winning director Williams (of "Who Framed Roger Rabbit?" fame), and a team of animators led by Harris (part of the team that created Bugs Bunny) created sophisticated optical illusions that the team dubbed "two and a half dimensional." Incorporating intricate lighting, shadows and smooth motion, the project took almost three decades to complete. Soundtrack performed by the London Symphony Orchestra. **72m/C VHS, Closed Caption. D:** Richard Williams; **W:** Richard Williams; **C:** John Leatherbarrow; **M:** Robert Folk; **V:** Vincent Price, Matthew Broderick, Jennifer Beals, Eric Bogosian, Toni Collette, Jonathan Winters, Clive Revill, Kenneth Williams, Clinton Sundberg, Thick Wilson. *TOU*

The Thief of Bagdad 🎞️🎞️🎞️½ **1940** A wily young thief enlists the aid of a powerful genie to outwit the Grand Vizier of Baghdad. An Arabian Nights spectacular with lush photography, fine special effects, and striking score. Outstanding performance by Ingram as the genie. **106m/C VHS, Beta, LV.** Sabu, Conrad Veidt, June Duprez, Rex Ingram; **D:** Tim Whelan, Michael Powell, Ludwig Berger; **C:** Georges Perinal; **M:** Miklos Rozsa. Academy Awards '40: Best Color Cinematography; Nominations: Academy Awards '40: Best Original Score. *MLB, FUS*

The Thief of Baghdad 🎞️🎞️🎞️ **1924** The classic silent crowd-pleaser, about a roguish thief who uses a genie's magic to outwit Baghdad's evil Caliph. With famous special effects in a newly struck print, and a new score by Davis based on Rimsky-Korsakov's "Scheherazade." Remade many times. **153m/B VHS, Beta, LV.** Douglas Fairbanks Sr., Snitz Edwards, Charles Belcher, Anna May Wong, Etta Lee, Brandon Hurst, Sojin, Julanne Johnston; **D:** Raoul Walsh; **M:** Carl Davis. National Film Registry '96. *SNC, NOS, CCB*

Thief of Baghdad 🎞️🎞️ *Il Ladro Di Bagdad; Le Voleur De Bagdad* **1961** An Arabian Nights fantasy about a thief in love with a Sultan's daughter who has been poisoned. He seeks out the magical blue rose which is the antidote. Not as lavish as the previous two productions with this title, nor as much fun. **89m/C VHS, Beta.** *IT* Georgia Moll, Steve Reeves; **D:** Arthur Lubin.

The Thief of Baghdad 🎞️🎞️½ **1978 (G)** A fantasy-adventure about a genie, a prince, beautiful maidens, a happy-go-lucky thief, and magic. Easy to take, but not an extraordinary version of this oft-told tale. Made for television. **101m/C VHS, Beta.** Peter Ustinov, Roddy McDowall, Terence Stamp, Frank Finlay, Ian Holm; **D:** Clive Donner. *GEM*

Thief of Hearts 🎞️🎞️ **1984 (R)** A thief steals a woman's diary when he's ransacking her house. He then pursues the woman, using his secret knowledge. Slick, but too creepy. Re-edited with soft porn scenes in some video versions. Stewart's first film. **101m/C VHS, Beta, LV, Closed Caption.** Steven Bauer, Barbara Williams, John Getz, Christine Ebersole, George Wendt; **D:** Douglas Day Stewart; **M:** Harold Faltermeyer. *PAR*

The Thief Who Came to Dinner 🎞️🎞️ **1973 (PG)** A computer analyst and a wealthy socialite team up to become jewel thieves and turn the tables on Houston's high society set. Comedy plot gets complex, though O'Neal and Bisset are likeable. Early Clayburgh

role as O'Neal's ex. Based on a novel by Terence Lore Smith. **103m/C VHS, Beta.** Ryan O'Neal, Jacqueline Bisset, Warren Oates, Jill Clayburgh, Ned Beatty, Gregory Sierra, Michael Murphy, Austin Pendleton, John Hillerman, Charles Cioffi; **D:** Bud Yorkin; **W:** Walter Hill; **M:** Henry Mancini. *WAR*

Thieves Like Us 🎞️🎞️🎞️½ **1974 (R)** Story of doomed lovers during the Depression is thoughtfully told by Altman. Older criminals Remsen and Schuck escape from jail with young killer Carradine. They only know one way to make a living—robbing banks—and it isn't long before they're once more working at their trade. They get a lot of press but they have a distinct problem. They're not really very good at what they do. Cops on their trail, the gang tries, unsuccessfully, to survive. Fletcher's film debut as Remsen's sister-in-law. Good period atmosphere and strong characters. Based on the novel by Edward Anderson and previously filmed as "They Live by Night." **123m/C VHS.** Keith Carradine, Shelley Duvall, Bert Remsen, John Schuck, Louise Fletcher, Anne Latham, Tom Skerritt; **D:** Robert Altman; **W:** Joan Tewkesbury, Calder Willingham, Robert Altman. *MGM*

Thieves of Fortune woof! **1989 (R)** Former Miss Universe stars as a contestant in a high stakes fortune hunt that spans half the globe. She meets with more than her share of action-packed encounters among the ruffians who compete for the $28 million purse. Implausible; horrible script; cliched. **100m/C VHS, Beta, LV.** Michael Nouri, Lee Van Cleef, Shawn Weatherly.

The Thin Blue Line 🎞️🎞️🎞️½ **1988** The acclaimed docudrama about the 1977 shooting of a cop in Dallas County, and the incorrect conviction of Randall Adams for the crime. A riveting, spellbinding experience. Due to the film's impact and continued lobbying by Morris, Adams is now free. **101m/C VHS, Beta, LV, Closed Caption. D:** Errol Morris; **M:** Philip Glass. *HBO, CCB*

Thin Ice 🎞️🎞️🎞️ **1937** Successful musical romance featuring European prince Power falling for commoner Henie. A fine score, solid script, and Henie's excellent ice skating routines make this her best film. Based on the play "Der Komet" by Attila Obok. 🎵I'm Olga from the Volga; My Swiss Hillbilly; My Secret Love Affair; Over Night. **78m/B VHS.** Sonja Henie, Tyrone Power, Arthur Treacher, Raymond Walburn, Joan Davis, Alan Hale, Sig Rumann, Melville Cooper, Maurice Cass, George Givot, Torben Meyer; **D:** Sidney Lanfield; **W:** Boris Ingster, Milton Sperling. *FXV*

A Thin Line Between Love and Hate 🎞️ **1996 (R)** Writer/director/star Lawrence shows that there's no line between a crude, foul-mouthed ego trip and an unfunny, unsuspenseful film. Darnell Wright is a smooth talker constantly on the lookout for women to conquer and discard. Eventually, he meets the wrong lady (Whitfield), a classic movie psycho who turns his life upside down. Drawing heavily from "Fatal Attraction," this halfhearted effort offers bad pacing, a weak script, and totally unsympathetic characters, which could almost be overlooked if it was at all funny. Whitfield holds the flick's only redeeming value as the femme fatale. **CW:** Violence, profanity and nudity. **106m/C VHS, LV, Closed Caption.** Martin Lawrence, Lynn Whitfield, Regina King, Bobby Brown, Della Reese, Roger E. Mosley, Malinda Williams, Darryl (Chill) Mitchell, Simbi Khali; **D:** Martin Lawrence; **W:** Martin Lawrence, Bentley Kyle Evans, Kenny Buford, Kim Bass; **C:** Francis Kenny; **M:** Roger Troutman. *TTC*

The Thin Man 🎞️🎞️🎞️½ **1934** Married sleuths Nick and Nora Charles investigate the mysterious disappearance of a wealthy inventor. Charming and sophisticated, this was the model for all husband-and-wife detective teams that followed. Don't miss Asta, their wire-hair terrier. Based on the novel by Dashiell Hammett. Its enormous popularity triggered five sequels, starting with "After the Thin Man." **90m/B VHS, Beta, LV.** William Powell, Myrna Loy, Maureen O'Sullivan, Cesar Romero, Porter Hall, Nat Pendleton, Minna Gombell, Nata-

lie Moorhead, Edward Ellis; **D:** Woodbridge S. Van Dyke; **C:** James Wong Howe. National Film Registry '97;; Nominations: Academy Awards '34: Best Actor (Powell), Best Adapted Screenplay, Best Director (Van Dyke), Best Picture. *MGM, HMV*

The Thin Man Goes Home 🎞️🎞️½ **1944** Married sleuths Nick and Nora Charles solve a mystery with Nick's disapproving parents looking on in the fifth film from the "Thin Man" series. Despite a three-year gap and slightly less chemistry between Powell and Loy, audiences welcomed the skinny guy. Sequel to "Shadow of the Thin Man"; followed by "Song of the Thin Man." **100m/B VHS, Beta.** William Powell, Myrna Loy, Lucile Watson, Gloria De Haven, Anne Revere, Harry Davenport, Helen Vinson, Lloyd Corrigan, Donald Meek, Edward Brophy, Charles Halton; **D:** Richard Thorpe. *MGM*

The Thing 🎞️🎞️🎞️½ *The Thing from Another World* **1951** One of the best of the Cold War allegories and a potent lesson to those who won't eat their vegetables. Sci fi classic about an alien craft and creature (Arness in monster drag), discovered by an Arctic research team. The critter is accidentally thawed and then wreaks havoc, sucking the blood from sled dog and scientist alike. It's a giant seed-dispersing vegetable run amuck, unaffected by missing body parts, bullets, or cold. In other words, Big Trouble. Excellent direction, assisted substantially by producer Hawks, and supported by strong performances. Available colorized; remade in 1982. Loosely based on "Who Goes There?" by John Campbell. **87m/B VHS, Beta, LV, Letterbox.** James Arness, Kenneth Tobey, Margaret Sheridan, Dewey Martin, Robert Cornthwaite; **D:** Christian Nyby, Howard Hawks; **W:** Charles Lederer, Ben Hecht; **C:** Russell Harlan; **M:** Dimitri Tiomkin. *NO*

The Thing 🎞️🎞️½ **1982 (R)** A team of scientists at a remote Antarctic outpost discover a buried spaceship with an unwelcome alien survivor still alive. Bombastic special effects overwhelm the suspense and the solid cast. Less a remake of the 1951 science fiction classic than a more faithful version of John Campbell's short story "Who Goes There?," since the seeds/spores take on human shapes. **109m/C VHS, Beta, LV.** Kurt Russell, Wilford Brimley, T.K. Carter, Richard Masur, Keith David, Richard Dysart, David Clennon, Donald Moffat, Thomas G. Waites, Charles Hallahan; **D:** John Carpenter; **W:** Bill Lancaster; **C:** Dean Cundey; **M:** Ennio Morricone. *USH*

The Thing Called Love 🎞️🎞️½ **1993 (PG-13)** Take last year's surprise hit "Singles" and replace grunge rock and Seattle with Country/Western and Nashville for this unsentimental tale of four 20-something singles trying to make their mark in the world of country music. The idea for the plot comes from the real-life Bluebird Cafe—the place where all aspiring singers and songwriters want to perform. Phoenix, Mathis, Mulroney, and Bullock did their own singing; look for Oslin as the Cafe owner. Phoenix's last completed film role. **CW:** Some language. **116m/C VHS, Beta, LV, Closed Caption.** River Phoenix, Samantha Mathis, Sandra Bullock, Dermot Mulroney, K.T. Oslin, Anthony Clark, Webb Wilder; **Cameos:** Trisha Yearwood; **D:** Peter Bogdanovich; **W:** Allan Moyle, Carol Heikkinen. *PAR*

Things 🎞️ **198?** A man creates a monster during his freakish experiments with artificial insemination. The monster returns to his house seeking revenge, and the man's visiting brother and a friend disappear, probably a clever move given their lackluster circumstances. **90m/C VHS, Beta.** Barry Gillis, Amber Lynn, Doug Bunston, Bruce Roach; **D:** Andrew Jordan. *NO*

Things 🎞️🎞️½ **1993** Two horror tales told by a jilted wife who's holding her husband's mistress hostage. "The Box" finds evil Mayor Black (Delama) incensed about a newly opened brothel in his hick Nevada town. So he decides to teach the hookers a lesson with the help of a bizarre, boxed creature that's with him at all times. "Thing in a Jar" finds an abusive husband and his mistress plotting to kill his mousy wife. Only the murder victim comes back to haunt the deadly duo—at least parts of her do. Nicely grotesque special effects courtesy of Mike Tristano. **90m/C VHS.** Neil Delama, Trey Howard, Debra Stevens, Courtney Lercara, Kinder Hunt; *Cameos:* Jeff Burr; *D:* Dennis Devine, Jay Woelfel; *W:* Steve Jarvis, Steve Jarvis, Mike Bowler. *VSE*

Things 2 🎬🎬½ 1997 Sequel to 1993's "Things." When a pizza delivery girl gets stranded at the creepy home of a strange horror novelist he entertains her with two tales of terror. Oh yes, if the girl can solve the mysteries within the stories, she gets to live. If not, well... The first has a cheating wife plotting to rid herself of hubby by using the ferocious small creature (with big teeth) she's trained to kill on her command. But the creature has other ideas. The second story finds a fashion photographer suspecting that a serial killer stalking her neighborhood may not be human. **85m/C VHS.** Angela Eads, David Hussey, Rich Ward, Margie Rey; *D:* Steve Jarvis, Dennis Devine, Mike Bowler; *W:* Steve Jarvis, Dennis Devine, Mike Bowler; *C:* Craig Incardone; *M:* Adam Karpel. *CIN*

Things Change 🎬🎬🎬 1988 (PG) An old Italian shoeshine guy agrees, for a fee, to be a fall guy for the Mafia. A lower-echelon mob hood, assigned to watch over him, decides to give the old guy a weekend of fun in Vegas before going to jail. Director Mamet co-wrote the screenplay with Silverstein, best-known for his children's books ("Where the Sidewalk Ends," "The Giving Tree"). Combines charm and menace with terrific performances, especially from Ameche and Mantegna. **114m/C VHS, Beta, LV, Closed Caption.** Joe Mantegna, Don Ameche, Robert Prosky, J.J. Johnston, Ricky Jay, Mike Nussbaum, Jack Wallace, Dan Conway, J.T. Walsh; *D:* David Mamet; *W:* Shel Silverstein, David Mamet; *M:* Alaric Jans. Venice Film Festival '80: Best Actor (Ameche); Venice Film Festival '88: Best Actor (Mantegna). *COL*

Things Happen at Night 🎬 1948 Scientist and insurance investigator determine that friendly ghost has possessed a family's youngest daughter. Not much happens. **79m/B VHS, Beta.** *GB* Gordon Harker, Alfred Drayton, Robertson Hare, Olga Lindo, Wylie Watson; *D:* Francis Searle. *NOS, SNC*

Things in Their Season 🎬🎬½ 1974 Made for TV melodrama about the imminent death of the mother of a Wisconsin farm family who makes those around her realize the value of happiness. Neal is excellent, rest of cast better than average in a well-told and sincere film. **79m/C VHS, Beta.** Patricia Neal, Ed Flanders, Marc Singer, Meg Foster; *D:* James Goldstone. *BFA*

The Things of Life 🎬🎬🎬 *Les Choses De La Vie* 1970 A car crash makes a man re-evaluate his life, goals, and loves. In the end he must choose the course of his future and decide between his wife and mistress. In French with English subtitles. **90m/C VHS, Beta, LV, Letterbox.** *FR* Romy Schneider, Michel Piccoli, Lea Massari; *D:* Claude Sautet. *CVC*

Things to Come 🎬🎬🎬½ 1936 Using technology, scientists aim to rebuild the world after a lengthy war, followed by a plague and other unfortunate events. Massey and Scott each play two roles, in different generations. Startling picture of the world to come, with fine sets and good acting. Based on an H.G. Wells story, "The Shape of Things to Come." **92m/B VHS, Beta.** *GB* Raymond Massey, Margaretta Scott, Ralph Richardson, Cedric Hardwicke, Derrick DeMarney; *D:* William Cameron Menzies; *C:* Georges Perinal. *NOS, SNC, VYY*

Things to Do In Denver When You're Dead 🎬🎬🎬 1995 (R) Jimmy the Saint (Garcia) is an ex-mobster gone straight who is called upon by his former boss, the Man With the Plan (Walken), to do one last easy-money job. Jimmy agrees and rounds up his old gang, a colorfully off-color group which includes Pieces (Lloyd), a porn movie projectionist and Critical Bill (Williams), a hair-trigger psycho who works in a funeral parlor. The job goes awry and the group becomes a target of hitman Mr. Shhh (Buscemi). Hipster dialogue, crime-gone-wrong formula, and

the presence of Buscemi instantly scream Tarantino rip-off, but the performances make it a worthwhile genre entry *CW.* Strong graphic violence and language, and for brief images of a sex film. **115m/C VHS, LV, Closed Caption.** Andy Garcia, Christopher Lloyd, William Forsythe, Bill Nunn, Treat Williams, Jack Warden, Steve Buscemi, Fairuza Balk, Gabrielle Anwar, Christopher Walken, Glenn Plummer, Don Cheadle, Bill Cobbs; *D:* Gary Fleder; *W:* Scott Rosenberg; *C:* Elliot Davis; *M:* Michael Convertino. *TOU*

Think Big 🎬🎬½ 1990 (PG-13) Former professional wrestlers, the Pauls are truck drivers in this silly, enjoyable comedy. They pick up a brilliant teenager running from bad guys. Mayhem ensues. **86m/C VHS, Beta, LV.** Peter Paul, David Paul, Martin Mull, Ari Meyers, Richard Kiel, David Carradine, Richard Moll, Peter Lupus; *W:* Jim Wynorski, R.J. Robertson. *ART, VTR*

Think Dirty 🎬🎬 *Every Home Should Have One* 1970 (R) Lascivious comedy about advertising executive Feldman's attempt to develop a series of sexy commercials to sell cereal. At the same time his wife forms a "clean up television" group. Not very interesting or funny. **93m/C VHS, Beta.** *GB* Marty Feldman, Judy Cornwell, Shelley Berman; *D:* Jim Clark. *COL*

Thinkin' Big 🎬 1987 (R) Guys and gals cavort on the Texas coast, except for one lonely fat guy who tries to increase his sexual prowess. The usual teen sex frenzy. **96m/C VHS, Beta.** Bruce Anderson, Kenny Sargent, Randy Jandt, Nancy Buechler, Darla Ralston; *D:* S.F. Brownrigg. *VTR*

Third Degree Burn 🎬🎬 1989 A made-for-cable-television mystery about a small-time detective hired by a businessman to follow a woman, only to become a suspect when the woman's real husband is killed. **97m/C VHS, Beta, LV, Closed Caption.** Treat Williams, Virginia Madsen, Richard Masur; *D:* Roger Spottiswoode. *PAR*

The Third Key 🎬🎬½ *The Long Arm* 1957 A solid British crime drama follows a dogged detective as he probes serial safe-crackings, with a climax set at London's Festival Hall. Based on the book by Robert Barr, who co-scripted. **96m/B VHS.** Jack Hawkins, Dorothy Allison, Geoffrey Keen, Richard Leech, Ian Bannen; *D:* Charles Frend. *NOS*

The Third Man 🎬🎬🎬🎬 1949 An American writer of pulp westerns (Cotten) arrives in post-war Vienna to take a job with an old friend, but discovers he has been murdered. Or has he? Based on Graham Greene's mystery, this classic film noir thriller plays on national loyalties during the Cold War. Welles is top-notch as the manipulative Harry Lime, blackmarket drugdealer extraordinare. The underground sewer sequence is not to be missed. With a haunting (sometimes irritating) theme by Anton Karas on unaccompanied zither. Special edition features trailer. **104m/B VHS, Beta, LV, 8mm.** Joseph Cotten, Orson Welles, Alida Valli, Trevor Howard, Bernard Lee, Wilfrid Hyde-White, Ernst Deutsch, Erich Ponto, Siegfried Breuer, Hedwig Bleibtreu, Paul Hoerbiger, Frederick Sehreicker, Herbert Halbik, Jenny Werner, Nelly Arno, Alexis Chesnakov, Leo Bieber, Paul Hardtmuth; *D:* Carol Reed; *W:* Graham Greene; *C:* Robert Krasker; *M:* Anton Karas. Academy Awards '50: Best Black and White Cinematography; British Academy Awards '49: Best Film; Cannes Film Festival '49: Best Film; Directors Guild of America Awards '49: Best Director (Reed); Nominations: Academy Awards '50: Best Director (Reed), Best Film Editing. *SNC, REP, HHT*

Third Man on the Mountain 🎬🎬½ *Banner in the Sky* 1959 (G) A family epic about mountain climbing, shot in Switzerland and based on James Ramsey Ullman's "Banner in the Sky." A young man is determined to climb the "Citadel" as his ancestors have. He finds there's more to climbing than he imagined. Look for Helen Hayes (MacArthur's mother) in a cameo. Standard Disney adventure drama. **106m/C VHS, Beta.** James MacArthur, Michael Rennie, Janet Munro, James Donald, Herbert Lom, Laurence Naismith; *Cameos:* Helen Hayes; *D:* Ken Annakin. *DIS*

The Third Sex 🎬 1959 One of the first films to deal with homosexuality in which parents try to "straighten out" their gay son. **?m/C VHS.** Paul Dahlke, Paula Wesley. *SNC*

Third Solution 🎬🎬 *Russicum* 1989 (R) An Italian-made film about the discovery of a secret pact made between the Kremlin and the Vatican that may start WWIII. Well-cast, but poorly conceived spook drama, with music by Vangelis. **93m/C VHS, Beta, LV, Letterbox.** *IT* Treat Williams, F. Murray Abraham, Danny Aiello, Nigel Court, Rita Rusic, Rossano Brazzi; *D:* Pasquale Squitieri; *M:* Vangelis. *COL*

Third Walker 🎬🎬🎬 1979 A desperate woman sacrifices her marriage to immerse herself in efforts to reunite her twin sons, who were inadvertently separated at birth. An original and intriguing directorial debut by McLuhan. **85m/C VHS, Beta.** William Shatner, Colleen Dewhurst; *D:* Marshall McLuhan. *NO*

Thirst 🎬🎬 1987 (R) A girl is abducted by a secret society that wants her to become their new leader. There is just one catch: she has to learn to like the taste of human blood. Chilling but weakly plotted. **96m/C VHS, Beta.** David Hemmings, Henry Silva, Chantal Contouri; *D:* Rod Hardy.

The Thirsty Dead woof! *The Blood Cult of Shangri-La; Blood Hunt* 1974 (PG) Maybe they could learn to like Gatorade. An eternally young jungle king is looking for a wife. She can be young forever too, if she's not above vampirism and sacrificing virgins. In spite of the jungle vampire slant, this Filipino-made movie is a woofer. **90m/C VHS, Beta.** *PH* John Considine, Jennifer Billingsley, Judith McConnell, Fredricka Meyers, Tani Phelps Guthrie; *D:* Terry Becker. *NO*

13 Ghosts 🎬🎬½ 1960 A dozen ghosts need another member to round out their ranks. They have four likely candidates to choose from when a family moves into the house inhabited by the ghoulish group. Originally viewed with "Illusion-O," a technology much like 3-D, which allowed the viewing of the ghosts only through a special pair of glasses. **88m/C VHS, Beta.** Charles Herbert, Jo Morrow, Martin Milner, Rosemary DeCamp, Donald Woods, Margaret Hamilton; *D:* William Castle. *GKK*

13 Rue Madeleine 🎬🎬 1946 Cagney plays a WWII spy who infiltrates Gestapo headquarters in Paris in order to find the location of a German missile site. Actual OSS footage is used in this fast-paced early postwar espionage propaganda piece. Rex Harrison rejected the part taken by Cagney. **95m/B VHS, Beta.** James Cagney, Annabella, Richard Conte, Frank Latimore, Walter Abel, Sam Jaffe, Melville Cooper, E.G. Marshall, Karl Malden, Red Buttons; *D:* Henry Hathaway. *FOX, FCT*

Thirteenth Day of Christmas 1985 A made-for-British-television yarn about a psychotic boy left alone by his parents on Christmas night. **60m/C VHS, Beta.** *GB* Patrick Allen, Elizabeth Spiggs.

The 13th Floor 🎬½ 1988 (R) A young girl fuses with the spirit of a young boy her father ruthlessly killed years before, and together they wreak havoc. **86m/C VHS, Beta.** Lisa Hensley, Tim McKenzie, Miranda Otto; *D:* Chris Roach. *PAR*

13th Guest 🎬🎬 *Lady Beware* 1932 Two people try to solve a murder that occurred at a dinner party. An incredibly creaky early talkie melodrama that created some of the cliches of the genre. **70m/ B VHS, Beta.** Ginger Rogers, Lyle Talbot, J. Farrell MacDonald, Paul Hurst; *D:* Albert Ray. *SNC, NOS, VYY*

The Thirteenth Man 🎬🎬½ 1937 When a journalist investigating the murder of a district attorney is also killed, the paper's gossip columnist takes the case. Entertaining, fast-paced mystery. **70m/B VHS, Beta.** Weldon Heyburn, Inez Courtney, Selmer Jackson, Milburn Stone, Matty Fain; *D:* William Nigh. *NOS, SNC, MLB*

The 13th Mission 🎬½ 1991 A low-budget overseas combat adventure, no better than the first 12. **95m/C VHS, Beta.** Robert Marius, Jeff Griffith, Michael Monty, David Morrison, Paul Home, John Falch, Albert Bronski, Chantal Manz; *D:* Antonio Perez. *VTR*

Thirteenth Reunion 🎬 1981 A newspaperwoman uncovers a bizarre secret society when she does a routine story on a health spa. 60m/C VHS, Beta. Julia Foster, Dinah Sheridan, Richard Pearson; **D:** Peter Sasdy. ART

The Thirty-Nine Steps 🎬🎬½ 1979 Hitchcock remake is a visually interesting, but mostly uninvolving, mystery. Powell is the man suspected of stealing plans to begin WWI. Above average, but not by much. 98m/C VHS, Beta. GB Robert Powell, David Warner, Eric Porter, Karen Dotrice, John Mills, Andrew Keir; **D:** Don Sharp. VYY, CNG

The 30-Foot Bride of Candy Rock 🎬 1959 A junk dealer invents a robot, catapults into space and causes his girlfriend to grow to 30 feet in height. Lightweight, whimsical fantasy was Costello's only solo starring film, and his last before his untimely death. 73m/B VHS, Beta. Lou Costello, Dorothy Provine, Gale Gordon; **D:** Sidney Miller. GKK

30 Is a Dangerous Age, Cynthia 🎬🎬½ 1968 Dudley Moore stars as a nightclub pianist who spends a lot of his time daydreaming about being rich, famous, and married to a beautiful woman. Moore determines to attain all these dreams before his 30th birthday, which is only six weeks away. 85m/C VHS, Beta. GB Dudley Moore, Suzy Kendall, Eddie Foy Jr.; **D:** Joseph McGrath; **W:** Dudley Moore; **M:** Dudley Moore. NO

Thirty Seconds Over Tokyo 🎬🎬🎬 1944 Dated but still interesting classic wartime flagwaver details the conception and execution of the first bombing raids on Tokyo by Lt. Col. James Doolittle and his men. Look for Blake Edwards as well as Steve Brodie in his first screen appearance. Based on a true story. 138m/B VHS, Beta. Spencer Tracy, Van Johnson, Robert Walker, Robert Mitchum, Phyllis Thaxter, Scott McKay, Stephen McNally, Louis Jean Heydt, Leon Ames, Paul Langton; **D:** Mervyn LeRoy; **W:** Dalton Trumbo; **C:** Robert L. Surtees. Academy Awards '44: Best Special Effects; Nominations: Academy Awards '44: Best Black and White Cinematography. MGM, FCT, TLF

32 Short Films about Glenn Gould 🎬🎬🎬 1993 Perceptive docudrama about the iconoclastic Canadian classical pianist who secluded himself in the studio, forsaking live performances for much of his career. A combination of dramatic recreation, archival material, and interviews depict the biographical details of the driven artist who died at the age of 50. Feore is memorable in the title role, especially since he's never actually shown playing the piano. Title and film structure refer to Bach's "Goldberg" Variations, a recording which made Gould's reputation. 94m/C VHS, LV. CA Colm Feore, Gale Garnett, David Hughes, Katya Ladan, Gerry Quigley, Carlo Rota, Peter Millard, Yehudi Menuhin, Bruno Monsaingeon; **D:** Francois Girard; **W:** Don McKellar, Francois Girard; **C:** Alan Dostie. Genie Awards '93: Best Cinematography, Best Director (Girard), Best Film, Best Film Editing; Nominations: Independent Spirit Awards '95: Best Foreign Film. COL

36 Fillete 🎬🎬🎬 1988 Lili, an intellectually precocious 14-year-old French girl who's literally bursting out of her children's dress size 36 fillete, discovers her sexuality. So while on vacation with her family she becomes determined to see if she can seduce a middle-aged playboy. In French with English subtitles. 88m/C VHS. FR Delphine Zentout, Etienne Chicot, Oliver Parniere, Jean-Pierre Leaud; **D:** Catherine Breillat. FXL

Thirty-Six Hours of Hell 🎬½ 1977 A troop of Marines battle Japanese forces in the South Pacific during WWII. Dubbed. 95m/C VHS, Beta. Richard Harrison, Pamela Tudor; **D:** Roberto Marrtero. UNI

'38: Vienna Before the Fall 🎬🎬½ 1988 Wartime Vienna explodes with love and politics. Academy Award Nominee for best foreign language film. In German with English subtitles. 97m/C VHS, LV. GE Tobias Engel, Sunnyi Melles; **D:** Wolfgang Gluck. LUM

The 39 Steps 🎬🎬🎬 1935 The classic Hitchcock mistaken-man-caught-in-intrigue thriller, featuring some of his most often copied set-pieces and the surest visual flair of his pre-war British period. The laserdisc version includes a 20-minute documentary tracing the director's British period. Remade twice, in 1959 and 1979. 81m/B VHS, Beta, LV, 8mm. GB Robert Donat, Madeleine Carroll, Godfrey Tearle, Lucie Mannheim, Peggy Ashcroft, John Laurie, Wylie Watson, Helen Haye, Frank Cellier, Gus McNaughton, Jerry Verno, Peggy Simpson, Hilda Trevelyan, John Turnbull, Elizabeth Inglis, Wilfrid Brambell; **D:** Alfred Hitchcock; **W:** Charles Bennett, Alma Reville, Ian Hay; **M:** Louis Levy. CNG, NOS, VHE

This Boy's Life 🎬🎬🎬 1993 (R) Carolyn and her teenage son are in search of a new life, far from her abusive ex-boyfriend. In the town of Concrete, just outside Seattle, she meets ex-military man Dwight (De Niro), a slick but none too suave mechanic who might be the answer to her dreams, but then again, he might not. Nicely crafted performances from all, but keep your eye on DiCaprio (great in his first major role) as the confused and abused teen divided between dreams of prep school and the allure of the going-nowhere crowd. Based on the memoirs of Tobias Wolff; director Caton-Jones sensitively illustrates the skewed understanding of masculinity in the 1950s. Vintage soundtrack takes you back.**CW:** Strong language and strong sexuality. 115m/C VHS, Beta, LV, Letterbox, Closed Caption. Robert De Niro, Ellen Barkin, Leonardo DiCaprio, Jonah Blechman, Eliza Dushku, Chris Cooper, Carla Gugino, Zachary Ansley, Tracey Ellis, Kathy Kinney, Gerrit Graham; **D:** Michael Caton-Jones; **W:** Robert Getchell; **C:** David Watkin; **M:** Carter Burwell. WAR, FCT, BTV

This Could Be the Night 🎬🎬½ 1957 Rocco and Tony are two small-fry gangsters who run a nightclub. Anne is a prim schoolteacher who takes a part-time job as their secretary. She falls for the handsome Tony much to the dismay of Rocco who knows his partner's less-than-sterling character. Sweet but minor comedy. Franciosa's first film. ♫This Could Be The Night; Hustlin' News Gal; I Got It Bad; I'm Gonna Live Till I Die; Taking a Chance on Love; Trumpet Boogie; Mamba Combo; Blue Moon; Dream Dancing. 105m/B VHS, LV, Letterbox. Jean Simmons, Paul Douglas, Anthony (Tony) Franciosa, Joan Blondell, Julie Wilson, Neile Adams, J. Carrol Naish, Rafael Campos, ZaSu Pitts, Tom Helmore; **D:** Robert Wise. MGM, MOV

This England 🎬½ 1942 Patriotic morale booster is a rather dull jog through Britain's fight for freedom as an American journalist, visiting England, learns a village's history from a country squire, including surviving the Norman conquest, Spanish Armada, Napoleonic Wars, WWI, and the 1940 air attacks. 84m/B VHS. GB Emlyn Williams, John Clements, Constance Cummings; **D:** David MacDonald. FCT

This Gun for Hire 🎬🎬🎬½ 1942 In his first major film role, Ladd plays a hired gun seeking retribution from a client who betrays him. Preston is the cop pursuing him and hostage Lake. Ladd's performance as the cold-blooded killer with a soft spot for cats is stunning; his train-yard scene is an emotional powerhouse. Based on Graham Greene's novel "A Gun for Sale." Remade as "Short Cut to Hell." The first of several films using the Ladd-Lake team, but the only one in which Ladd played a villain. 81m/B VHS, Beta, LV. Alan Ladd, Veronica Lake, Robert Preston, Laird Cregar; **D:** Frank Tuttle; **W:** Albert Maltz, W.R. Burnett. USH, FCT

This Gun for Hire 🎬🎬 1990 (R) A professional assassin finds that he has been duped into killing a powerful political figure, whom he was told was a New Orleans mobster. Now on the run, he takes a nightclub performer hostage, unaware that she is the fiance of the FBI agent who is after him. All odds are against him, but the special relationship he forms with the woman may just be his ticket out. Adapted from novel by Graham Greene.**CW:** Violence and sensuality. 89m/C VHS.

Robert Wagner, Nancy Everhard, Frederic Lehne, John Harkins; **D:** Lou Antonio. USH

This Happy Breed 🎬🎬🎬½ 1947 A celebrated film version of Noel Coward's classic play depicts the changing fortunes of a large family in England between the world wars. Happiness, hardships, triumph and tragedy mix a series of memorable episodes, including some of the most cherished moments in popular British cinema, though its appeal is universal. 114m/C VHS. GB Robert Newton, Celia Johnson, John Mills, Kay Walsh, Stanley Holloway, Amy Veness, Alison Leggatt, Eileen Erskine, John Blythe, Guy Verney, Betty Fleetwood, Merle Tottenham; **D:** David Lean; **W:** David Lean, Noel Coward, Ronald Neame; **C:** Ronald Neame; **M:** Noel Coward, Muir Mathieson. HMV, FCT

This Happy Feeling 🎬🎬½ 1958 Reynolds is a young woman who is romantically attracted to both Jurgens, a sophisticated retired actor, and Saxon, a younger suitor who is Jurgens' neighbor. Good acting all around. Charming telling of old tale. 83m/C VHS, Beta. Curt Jurgens, Debbie Reynolds, John Saxon, Alexis Smith, Mary Astor, Estelle Winwood; **D:** Blake Edwards; **W:** Blake Edwards. BAR, FCT

This Is a Hijack 🎬 1975 (PG) Gambler hijacks the plane carrying his wealthy boss to help pay his debts. What it lacks in suspense, it lacks in performance and direction as well. 90m/C VHS, Beta. Adam Roarke, Neville Brand, Jay Robinson, Lynn Borden, Dub Taylor. NO

This Is Elvis 🎬🎬 1981 (PG) The life of Elvis, combining documentary footage with dramatizations of events in his life. Includes more than three dozen songs. Generally seen as an attempt to cash in on the myth, but was well-received by his fans. 144m/C VHS, Beta. Elvis Presley; **D:** Malcolm Leo, Andrew Solt; **W:** Malcolm Leo, Andrew Solt; **C:** Gil Hubbs. MVD, WAR

This Is My Life 🎬🎬 1992 (PG-13) The story of a working mother torn between her skyrocketing career as a stand-up comic and her two daughters. Kavner plays the divorced mom who is determined to chuck her cosmetic sales job for comic success. Her career starts to really take off; she hires an agent and makes appearances on talk shows. As offers pour in, she eventually realizes that her girls are suffering as a result of her success. Good performances highlight an otherwise average drama. 105m/C VHS, Closed Caption. Julie Kavner, Samantha Mathis, Carrie Fisher, Dan Aykroyd, Gaby Hoffman; **D:** Nora Ephron; **W:** Nora Ephron, Delia Ephron. FXV

This Is Not a Test 🎬🎬 1962 When news comes of an impending nuclear attack, a state trooper at a roadblock offers sanctuary to passing travellers. The effectiveness of the film's social commentary is hindered by its small budget. 72m/B VHS, Beta. Seamon Glass, Mary Morlass, Thayer Roberts, Aubrey Martin; **D:** Frederic Gadette. SNC

This Is Spinal Tap 🎬🎬🎬½ Spinal Tap 1984 (R) Pseudo-rockumentary about heavy-metal band Spinal Tap, profiling their career from "England's loudest band" to an entry in the "where are they now file." Hilarious satire, featuring music performed by Guest, McKean, Shearer, and others. Included are Spinal Tap's music video "Hell Hole," and an ad for their greatest hits album, "Heavy Metal Memories." Features great cameos, particularly David Letterman's Paul Schaefer as a record promoter and Billy Crystal as a surly mime. First feature for Reiner (Meathead on "All in the Family"). Followed by "The Return of Spinal Tap." 82m/C VHS, Beta, LV, 8mm. Michael McKean, Christopher Guest, Harry Shearer, Tony Hendra, Bruno Kirby, Rob Reiner, June Chadwick, Howard Hesseman, Dana Carvey, Ed Begley Jr., Patrick Macnee, Fran Drescher; **Cameos:** Billy Crystal, Paul Shaffer, Anjelica Huston; **D:** Rob Reiner; **W:** Christopher Guest. MVD, NLC

This Is the Army 🎵🎵½ **1943** A robust tribute to the American soldier of WWII based on the hit play by Irving Berlin. Murphy, who later was a senator from California, played Reagan's father. 🎵Your Country and My Country; My Sweetie; Poor Little Me, I'm on K.P.; We're On Our Way to France; What Does He Look Like?; This is the Army, Mr. Jones; I'm Gettin' Tired So I Can Sleep; Mandy; Ladies of the Chorus. **105m/C VHS, Beta.** George Murphy, Joan Leslie, Ronald Reagan, Alan Hale, Kate Smith, George Tobias, Irving Berlin, Joe Louis; **D:** Michael Curtiz; **M:** Max Steiner. Academy Awards '43: Scoring of a Musical; Nominations: Academy Awards '43: Best Interior Decoration, Best Sound. **NOS, DVT, CAB**

This Island Earth 🎵🎵½ **1955** The planet Metaluna is in desperate need of uranium to power its defense against enemy invaders. A nuclear scientist and a nuclear fission expert from Earth are kidnapped to help out. The first serious movie about interplanetary escapades. Bud Westmore created pulsating cranium special effects makeup. **86m/C VHS, Beta, LV.** Jeff Morrow, Faith Domergue, Rex Reason, Russell Johnson; **D:** Joseph M. Newman; **M:** Herman Stein. **USH, MLB**

This Land Is Mine 🎵🎵🎵 **1943** A timid French schoolteacher gathers enough courage to defy the Nazis when they attempt to occupy his town. Laughton's characterization is effective as the meek fellow who discovers the hero within himself in this patriotic wartime flick. **103m/B VHS, Beta, LV.** Charles Laughton, Maureen O'Hara, George Sanders, Walter Slezak, George Coulouris, Una O'Connor; **D:** Jean Renoir. Academy Awards '43: Best Sound. **TTC**

This Lightning Always Strikes Twice 1985 An elegant murder mystery made for British television. **60m/C VHS, Beta.** **GB** Claire Bloom, Trevor Howard, Charles Dance.

This Man Must Die 🎵🎵🎵½ *Que La Bete Meure; Uccidero Un Uomo* **1970 (PG)** A man searches relentlessly for the driver who killed his young son in a hit-and-run. When found, the driver engages him in a complex cat-and-mouse chase. Another stunning crime and punishment tale from Chabrol. **112m/C VHS, Beta.** **FR** Michael Duchaussoy, Caroline Cellier, Jean Yanne; **D:** Claude Chabrol. **FOX**

This Property Is Condemned 🎵🎵 **1966** It's a hot time down south once again in this adaptation of the Tennessee Williams play. Wood is the overly flirtatious southern charmer who takes a shine to the latest tenant of her loathsome mama's boardinghouse. And since it's Redford, who can blame her. Things steam up when he returns her interest but there's trouble a'brewin'. Both leads are lovely but the film itself is overly southern-fried. Williams was reportedly unhappy with the script and wanted his name removed from the film. **109m/C VHS, Beta, LV, Closed Caption.** Robert Redford, Natalie Wood, Charles Bronson, Kate Reid, Mary Badham, Jon Provost, Robert (Bobby) Blake, John Harding; **D:** Sydney Pollack; **W:** Francis Ford Coppola, Edith Sommer, Fred Coe. **PAR**

This Special Friendship 🎵🎵½ *Les Amities Particulieres* **1967** Powerful, if overdone French drama about an emotionally sensitive young man at a Catholic boarding school. His sexual relationship with another boy leads to tragedy. Based on the novel by Roger Peyrefitte. **99m/B VHS, Beta.** **FR** Francis Lacombrade, Didier Haudepin, Lucien Nat, Louis Seigner, Michel Bouquet, Francois Leccia; **D:** Jean Delannoy. **FCT**

This Sporting Life 🎵🎵🎵 **1963** A gritty, depressing portrait of a former coal miner who breaks into the violent world of professional rugby, and whose inability to handle social differences causes problems. He begins an affair with the widow from whom he rents a room but finds they are capable of only a physical attachment. One of the best of the British early '60s working-class angry young man melodramas. **134m/B VHS, Beta.** **GB** Richard Harris, Rachel Roberts, Alan Badel, William Hartnell, Colin Blakely, Vanda Godsell, Arthur Lowe; **D:** Lindsay Anderson; **W:** David Storey. British Academy Awards '63: Best Actress (Roberts); Cannes Film Festival

'63: Best Actor (Harris); Nominations: Academy Awards '63: Best Actor (Harris), Best Actress (Roberts). **RAD**

This Stuff'll Kill Ya! woof! **1971 (PG)** A backwoods preacher who believes in free love and moonshining runs into trouble with the locals when a series of gruesome religious murders are committed. Southern drive-in material from one of the genre's masters. Holt's last film. **100m/C VHS.** Jeffrey Allen, Tim Holt, Gloria King, Ray Sager, Eric Bradly, Terence McCarthy; **D:** Herschell Gordon Lewis; **W:** Herschell Gordon Lewis. **TWE, FRG, TPV**

This Sweet Sickness 🎵🎵½ *Dites-Lui Que Je L'Aime* **1977** Destructive passion and sexual delusion is explored in this adaptation of the Patricia Highsmith novel. David seems to be a hardworking loner who is loved by the sweet Juliette. Rejected by him, Juliette then discovers that David has built a remote mountain chalet for the woman he does love, Lise, who's married and unaware of David's obsessional devotions. Extravagant emotions lead to tragedy. In French with English subtitles. **107m/C VHS.** **FR** Gerard Depardieu, Miou-Miou, Dominique Laffin, Claude Pieplu, Christian Clavier, Jacques Denis, Josiane Balasko, Veronique Silver, Jacqueline Jeanne, Michel Such; **D:** Claude Miller; **W:** Claude Miller, Luc Beraud. **WAC, FCT**

This Time I'll Make You Rich 🎵 **1975 (PG)** Two American hoodlums work out a drug-ring heist in the Far East. **97m/C VHS, Beta.** Tony Sabato, Robin McDavid; **D:** Frank Kramer. **NLC**

This World, Then the Fireworks 🎵🎵½ **1997 (R)** Long on style but short on substance, overwrought neo-noir tells the tragic tale of traumatized twins living a totally debauched life. After seeing their father murdered in a romantic triangle, which left their mother (McClanahan) with physical and emotional scars, brother Marty (Zane) and sister Carol (Gershon) cling to each other as they grow up and engage in an implied incestuous relationship. The duo winds up grifters, murdering and pillaging their way through a small coastal town in the 1950s. Lee plays a messed-up cop who, tragically, becomes an easy mark for Marty. Based on a 1955 short story by Jim Thompson, director Oblowitz's debut gets too caught up in the excesses of pulp and focuses on slick visuals and dramatic score over a coherent story. Well-cast performances are universally solid and engaging.**CW:** Extreme violence, nudity, sexual situations, language. **100m/C VHS, Closed Caption.** Billy Zane, Gina Gershon, Sheryl Lee, Rue McClanahan, Seymour Cassel, Will Patton, Richard Edson, William Hootkins; **D:** Michael Oblowitz; **W:** Larry Gross; **C:** Tom Priestley; **M:** Pete Rugolo. **ORI**

The Thomas Crown Affair 🎵🎵🎵 *Thomas Crown and Company; The Crown Caper* **1968 (R)** A multi-millionaire (McQueen) decides to plot and execute the perfect theft, a daring daylight robbery of a bank. Dunaway is the gorgeous and efficient insurance investigator determined to nab him. One of the best visual scenes is the chess match between the two as they begin to fall in love. Strong production with Oscar-winning theme "The Windmills of Your Mind." 🎵The Windmills of Your Mind. **102m/C VHS, Beta.** Steve McQueen, Faye Dunaway, Jack Weston, Yaphet Kotto; **D:** Norman Jewison; **W:** Alan R. Trustman; **C:** Haskell Wexler. Academy Awards '68: Best Song ("The Windmills of Your Mind"); Golden Globe Awards '69: Best Song ("The Windmills of Your Mind"); Nominations: Academy Awards '68: Best Original Score. **MGM, FCT, FOX**

Thomas Graal's Best Film 🎵🎵🎵 **1917** The famous comical adventures of a film scriptwriter wooing his secretary, followed by "Thomas Graal's First Child." Silent. **70m/B VHS, Beta.** **SW** Victor Sjostrom, Karin Molander; **D:** Mauritz Stiller. **FCT, GPV**

Thomas Graal's First Child 🎵🎵🎵 **1918** The sequel to "Thomas Graal's Best Film." The comical screenwriter and actress couple attempt to raise a baby. Silent. **70m/B VHS, Beta.** Victor Sjostrom, Karin Molander; **D:** Mauritz Stiller. **FCT**

Thompson's Last Run 🎵¼ **1990** Boyhood friends grow up on either side of the law. They come face-to-face, though, when one is assigned to transport the other to prison. Made for television. **95m/C VHS, Beta, LV.** Robert Mitchum, Wilford Brimley, Kathleen York, Susan Tyrrell; **D:** Jerrold Freedman; **M:** Miles Goodman. **NO**

Thor and the Amazon Women 🎵 **1960** The mighty Thor leads his enslaved men on an attack against the evil Queen Nera and her female-dominated Amazon society. **85m/C VHS.** Joe Robinson, Susy Anderson.

The Thorn 🎵½ **1973 (R)** The Virgin Mary and Joseph try to raise Jesus Christ in the modern world. **90m/C VHS, Beta.** Bette Midler, John Bassberger. **NO**

The Thorn Birds 🎵🎵🎵 **1983** Pioneers find danger and romance in the Australian outback as they struggle to begin a dynasty. Charismatic priest sometimes hurts, sometimes helps them. One of Stanwyck's last performances; Ward's American television debut. Originally a ten-hour television epic based on Colleen McCullough novel. Emmy nominations for Actor Chamberlain, Supporting Actor(s) Brown and Plummer, Supporting Actress Laurie, direction, photography, music, costume design, and editing. On four cassettes. **486m/C VHS, Beta, Closed Caption.** Rachel Ward, Richard Chamberlain, Jean Simmons, Ken Howard, Mare Winningham, Richard Kiley, Piper Laurie, Bryan Brown, Christopher Plummer, Barbara Stanwyck; **D:** Daryl Duke; **C:** Bill Butler; **M:** Henry Mancini. **WAR, MOV, TVC**

Thoroughbreds Don't Cry 🎵🎵½ **1937** Rooney plays a jockey who throws a race so his no-good father can win enough money to pay for his supposed medical problems. The owner of the horse then drops dead from a heart attack. Rooney feels guilty, so he asks his father to loan the owner's grandson $1,000 to run in another race. His father says no, so Rooney steals the money from him, and when the father finds out he tells the track officials that Rooney threw the race. Garland is Rooney's best friend and moral support, and she sings a few songs too! A fairly good horse racing story. **80m/B VHS.** Judy Garland, Mickey Rooney, Sophie Tucker, Sir C. Aubrey Smith, Ronald Sinclair, Forrester Harvey; **D:** Alfred E. Green. **MGM, MVD**

Thoroughly Modern Millie 🎵🎵½ **1967 (G)** Andrews is a young woman who comes to New York in the early 1920s where she meets another newcomer, the innocent Moore. Andrews decides to upgrade her image to that of a "modern" woman, a flapper, and sets out to realize her ambition, to become a stenographer and marry the boss. Meanwhile, Moore has become an object of interest to Lillie, who just happens to run a white-slavery ring. Lots of frantic moments and big production numbers in this campy film. Channing and Lillie are exceptional fun. 🎵Thoroughly Modern Millie; The Tapioca; Jimmy; The Jewish Wedding Song; Baby Face; Do It Again; Poor Butterfly; Rose of Washington Square; I Can't Believe That You're In Love With Me. **138m/C VHS, Beta, LV.** Julie Andrews, Carol Channing, Mary Tyler Moore, John Gavin, Beatrice Lillie, James Fox, Noriyuki "Pat" Morita; **D:** George Roy Hill; **W:** Richard Morris; **M:** Elmer Bernstein. Academy Awards '67: Best Original Score; Golden Globe Awards '68: Best Supporting Actress (Channing); Nominations: Academy Awards '67: Best Art Direction/Set Decoration, Best Costume Design, Best Song ("Thoroughly Modern Millie"), Best Sound, Best Supporting Actress (Channing), Best Original Score. **USH**

Those Calloways 🎵🎵½ **1965 (PG)** A small town family attempts to establish a sanctuary for the flocks of wild geese who fly over the woods of Swiftwater, Maine. Fine Disney family fare, with good cast. Based on Paul Annixter's novel "Swiftwater." **131m/C VHS, Beta.** Brian Keith, Vera Miles, Brandon de Wilde, Walter Brennan, Ed Wynn, John Qualen, Linda Evans; **D:** Norman Tokar; **C:** Edward Colman; **M:** Max Steiner. **DIS**

Those Daring Young Men in Their Jaunty Jalopies ⅆⅆ *Monte Carlo or Bust; Quei Temerari Sulle Loro Pazze, Scatenate, Scalcinate Carriole* 1969 (G) Daring young men in noisy slow cars trek 1500 miles across country in the 1920s and call it a race. 125m/C VHS, LV, Closed Caption. GB Tony Curtis, Susan Hampshire, Terry-Thomas, Eric Sykes, Gert Frobe, Peter Cook, Dudley Moore, Jack Hawkins; D: Ken Annakin; W: Ken Annakin, Jack Davies. PAR, FCT

Those Endearing Young Charms ⅆⅆ 1945 Romance develops between a young Air Corps mechanic and a salesgirl. Complications arise when another man enters the scene. Light romantic comedy. Based on the play by Edward Chodorov. 82m/B VHS, Beta. Robert Young, Laraine Day, Anne Jeffreys, Lawrence Tierney; D: Lewis Allen. CCB

Those Fantastic Flying Fools ⅆⅆ½ *Blast-Off; Jules Verne's Rocket to the Moon* 1967 A mad race to be the first on the moon brings hilarious results. Loosely based on a Jules Verne story. 95m/C VHS. GB Burl Ives, Troy Donahue, Gert Frobe, Terry-Thomas, Hermione Gingold, Daliah Lavi, Lionel Jeffries; D: Don Sharp. NO

Those Glory, Glory Days ⅆ½ 1983 An English woman, secure in her position as an outstanding sports journalist, reminisces about the days when she and her friends idolized the boys on the soccer team. Nothing extraordinary, but nicely made. 92m/C VHS, Beta. GB Zoe Nathenson, Liz Campion, Cathy Murphy; D: Philip Saville; M: Trevor Jones. MGM

Those Lips, Those Eyes ⅆⅆ½ 1980 (R) A pre-med student takes a job as a prop boy in a summer stock company and winds up falling in love with the company's lead dancer. Sub-plot about aging actor is more interesting, better played by Langella. O'Connor is appropriately lovely. Nicely made, charming sleeper of a film. 106m/C VHS, Beta. Frank Langella, Tom Hulce, Glynnis O'Connor, Jerry Stiller, Kevin McCarthy; D: Michael Pressman. MGM

Those Magnificent Men in Their Flying Machines ⅆⅆⅆ 1965 In 1910, a wealthy British newspaper publisher is persuaded to sponsor an air race from London to Paris. Contestants come from all over the world and shenanigans, hijinks, double-crosses, and romance are found along the route. Skelton has fun in prologue, while Terry-Thomas is great as the villain. Fun from start to finish. 138m/C VHS, Beta, LV, Letterbox. GB Stuart Whitman, Sarah Miles, Robert Morley, Alberto Sordi, James Fox, Gert Frobe, Jean-Pierre Cassel, Flora Robson, Sam Wanamaker, Terry-Thomas, Irina Demick, Benny Hill, Gordon Jackson, Millicent Martin, Red Skelton; D: Ken Annakin; W: Ken Annakin, Jack Davies. Nominations: Academy Awards '65: Best Story & Screenplay. FOX

Thou Shalt Not Kill...Except ⅆ 1987 A Vietnam vet seeks revenge on the violent cult who kidnapped his girlfriend. 84m/C VHS, Beta. Brian Schulz, Robert Rickman, John Manfredi, Tim Quill, Cheryl Hansen, Sam Raimi, Cheryl Hansen, Perry Mallette, Theodore (Ted) Raimi, Glenn Barr; D: Josh Becker; W: Josh Becker, Glenn Barr; M: Joseph LoDuca.

Thoughts Are Free ⅆⅆⅆ½ 1984 (PG) A young soldier, wounded in WWII, escapes from the train that is transporting him and his comrades to a Soviet labor camp and rejoins his family. Under the repressive communist regime, he plots his family's escape to the West but his plans are thwarted when the Berlin Wall is erected, leaving him in the West and his wife and daughter in the East. As the years go by, they can get together only by outwitting the bureaucrats. The film's title is taken from an old German folk song "Die Gedanken sind frei." 93m/C VHS, Beta. Herbert Ludwig, Kathrin Kratzer; D: Josef Sommer. NO

A Thousand Acres ⅆⅆ 1997 (R) Based on Jane Smiley's Pulitzer Prize-winning novel, it's "King Lear" set on an Iowa farm. Sisters (Pfeiffer, Lange, and Leigh) discover that their father has decided to divide the family's thousand-acre farm amongst the three of them. Then stranger Firth comes to town and divides Pfeiffer and Lange even further by showing an interest in both of them. Melodramatic and contrived, with every hot-button women's issue imaginable thrown into the mix. Director Moorhouse purportedly considered removing her name from the picture. CW: Some strong sexual language and situations. 105m/C VHS, LV, Closed Caption. Jessica Lange, Michelle Pfeiffer, Jennifer Jason Leigh, Colin Firth, Jason Robards Jr., Keith Carradine, Pat Hingle, Kevin Anderson, John Carroll Lynch, Anne Pitoniak, Vyto Ruginis, Michelle Williams, Elissabeth Moss; D: Jocelyn Moorhouse; W: Laura Jones; C: Tak Fujimoto; M: Richard Hartley. Nominations: Golden Globe Awards '98: Best Actress (Lange). TOU

A Thousand and One Nights ⅆⅆ 1945 Handsome Aladdin (Wilde) falls in love with beautiful Princess Armina (Jergens) but fate steps in and Aladdin and sidekick Abdullah (Silvers) are off in search of a magic lamp. This time around the genie is a beautiful woman (Keyes), who falls for Aladdin herself and tries to thwart his would-be romance. Clever fun. 92m/C VHS. Cornel Wilde, Evelyn Keyes, Adele Jergens, Phil Silvers, Rex Ingram, Dennis Hoey, Philip Van Zandt, Gus Schilling; D: Alfred E. Green; W: Jack Henley, Richard English; C: Ray Rennahan; M: Marlin Skiles. COL

A Thousand Clowns ⅆⅆⅆ 1965 A nonconformist has resigned from his job as chief writer for an obnoxious kiddie show in order to enjoy life. But his independence comes under fire when he becomes guardian for his young nephew and social workers take a dim view of his lifestyle. Balsam won an Oscar for his role as Robard's agent brother. Adapted from Herb Gardner's Broadway comedy. 118m/B VHS, Beta. Jason Robards Jr., Barry Gordon, William Daniels, Barbara Harris, Gene Saks, Martin Balsam; D: Fred Coe; W: Herb Gardner. Academy Awards '65: Best Supporting Actor (Balsam); Nominations: Academy Awards '65: Best Adapted Score, Best Adapted Screenplay, Best Picture. MGM, FOX, BTV

The Thousand Eyes of Dr. Mabuse ⅆⅆ½ *The Secret of Dr. Mabuse; The Diabolical Dr. Mabuse; The Shadow Versus the Thousand Eyes of Dr. Mabuse* 1960 Lang's last film is a return to his pre-war German character, the evil Dr. Mabuse. A series of strange murders occur in a Berlin hotel and police believe the killer thinks he's a reincarnation of the doctor. Disorienting chiller. 103m/B VHS. GE Dawn Addams, Peter Van Eyck, Gert Frobe, Wolfgang Preiss; D: Fritz Lang. FCT, GPV

A Thousand Heroes ⅆⅆ½ 1994 (PG) Based on the true story of United Airlines Flight 232 which took off on a flight from Denver to Chicago and then suffered engine explosions over Iowa. The jumbo jet crashed in a fiery explosion but some 200 people survived. 95m/C VHS, LV. Richard Thomas, Charlton Heston, James Coburn. NHO

Thousand Pieces of Gold ⅆⅆⅆ 1991 (PG-13) A young Chinese woman is sold by her father to a marriage broker, but instead of a respectable marriage she is shipped to America and expected to work as a prostitute in an Idaho mining town. Instead she works taking in laundry as she tries to make her way in a man's world, finding a sweet romance of opposites along the way. Based on a true story. Excellent performances by Chao and Cooper. 105m/C VHS, LV, Closed Caption. Rosalind Chao, Dennis Dun, Michael Paul Chan, Chris Cooper, Jimmie F. Skaggs, William Oldham, David Hayward, Beth Broderick; D: Nancy Kelly; W: Anne Makepeace; C: Bobby Bukowski; M: Gary Remal Malkin.

Thousands Cheer ⅆⅆ½ 1943 A flag-waving wartime musical about a tap-dancing Army private who falls in love with the colonel's daughter, culminating with an all-star (MGM) USO show. Songs include "Honeysuckle Rose," sung by Horne, and "The Joint Is Really Jumping Down at Carnegie Hall," sung by Garland. 126m/C VHS, Beta, LV. Gene Kelly, Kathryn Grayson, Judy Garland, Mickey Rooney, Mary Astor, John Boles, Lucille Ball, Eleanor Powell, Virginia O'Brien, Margaret O'Brien, Red Skelton, Lionel Barrymore, June Allyson, Frank Morgan, Kay Kyser, Bob Crosby, Lena Horne, Donna Reed; D: George Sidney; W: Paul Jarrico. Nominations: Academy Awards '43: Best Color Cinematography, Best Interior Decoration, Scoring of a Musical. MGM

Thrashin' ⅆ 1986 (PG-13) A new-to-L.A. teen must prove himself to a tough gang on skateboards by skateboarding a certain treacherous race. For skateboarding fans only. 93m/C VHS, Beta. Josh Brolin, Pamela Gidley, Robert Rusler, Chuck McCann; D: David Winters; W: Paul Brown; M: Barry Goldberg. NO

Threads ⅆⅆⅆ 1985 The famed dramatic recreation of the effects of nuclear war on a British city and two of its families. A disturbing, uncompromising, and somewhat plausible drama. Made for British television. 110m/C VHS, Beta. GB Karen Meagher, Rita May, David Brierly, Reece Dinsdale, Harry Beety; D: Mick Jackson. NO

Threat ⅆⅆ½ 1949 A killer escapes from jail and returns to settle the score with those who convicted him. Tense, fast-moving thriller. 66m/B VHS, Beta. Michael O'Shea, Virginia Grey, Charles McGraw; D: Felix Feist. NO

Three Ages ⅆⅆⅆ 1923 A parody of D.W. Griffith's 1916 film "Intolerance." Keaton's first feature film casts him in prehistoric days, ancient Rome, and in modern times. Silent with musical score. 59m/B VHS, Beta. Wallace Beery, Oliver Hardy, Buster Keaton; D: Buster Keaton, Eddie Cline. NOS, VDM, DVT

Three Amigos ⅆⅆ 1986 (PG) Three out-of-work silent screen stars are asked to defend a Mexican town from bandits; they think it's a public appearance stint. Spoof of Three Stooges and Mexican bandito movies that at times falls short, given the enormous amount of comedic talent involved. Generally enjoyable with some very funny scenes. Co-written by former "Saturday Night Live" producer Michaels. Short's first major film appearance. 105m/C VHS, Beta, LV, Closed Caption. Chevy Chase, Steve Martin, Martin Short, Joe Mantegna, Patrice Martinez, Jon Lovitz, Alfonso Arau, Randy Newman; D: John Landis; W: Steve Martin, Randy Newman, Lorne Michaels; M: Elmer Bernstein. HBO

The Three Avengers ⅆⅆ½ 1980 (R) Hung Tack (Lee) is the master of a kung fu school in a town plagued by two evil businessmen, who force Hung to take on the local gangs. During a fight, he's spotted by a talent scout and starts a career in the movies but is around to rescue a friend who's gotten into trouble. Hey, the fighting's the important part anyway. 93m/C VHS. Bruce Lee. FCT

Three Broadway Girls ⅆⅆⅆ *The Greeks Had a Word for Them* 1932 Three gold-diggers go husband-hunting. Well-paced, very funny telling of this old story. Remade many times, including "How to Marry a Millionaire," "Three Blind Mice," "Moon Over Miami," and "Three Little Girls in Blue." 78m/B VHS, Beta. Joan Blondell, Ina Claire, Madge Evans, David Manners, Lowell Sherman; D: Lowell Sherman. NOS, CAB, BAR

Three Brothers ⅆⅆⅆ 1980 (PG) An acclaimed Italian film by veteran Rosi about three brothers summoned to their small Italian village by a telegram saying their mother is dead. Sensitive and compassionate. In Italian with English subtitles. Adapted from Platonov's story "The Third Son." 113m/C VHS, Beta. IT Philippe Noiret, Charles Vanel, Michele Placido, Vittorio Mezzogiorno, Andrea Ferreol; D: Francesco Rosi; W: Francesco Rosi; C: Pasquale De Santis. Nominations: Academy Awards '81: Best Foreign Language Film.

Three Bullets for a Long Gun ⅆ½ 1973 (PG) Two prairie renegades battle bandits as they search for an inherited gold mine. 89m/C VHS, Beta. Keith Van Der Wat, Beau Brummel, Patrick Munhardt; D: Peter Henkel; W: Keith Van der Wat. COL, NLC, SIM

Three by Hitchcock ✂✂ 1928 Condensed versions of three of Hitchcock's early films (1927-28). Consists of "The Ring," "Champagne," and "The Manxman," his last silent film. 90m/B VHS, Beta. **D:** Alfred Hitchcock. *GVV*

The Three Caballeros ✂✂½ 1945 Donald Duck stars in this journey through Latin America. Full of music, variety, and live-action/animation segments. Stories include "Pablo the Penguin," "Little Gauchito," and adventures with Joe Carioca, who was first introduced in Disney's "Saludos Amigos." Today this film stands as one of the very best pieces of animation ever created. Great family fare. "Saludos Amgios" is available on the laserdisc version. ♫The Three Caballeros; Baia. 71m/C VHS, Beta, LV. **D:** Norman Ferguson; **V:** Sterling Holloway, Aurora Miranda. Nominations: Academy Awards '45: Best Sound, Scoring of a Musical. *DIS*

Three Came Home ✂✂✂ 1950 Colbert is an American married to a British administrator in the Far East during WWII. Conquering Japanese throw the whole family into a brutal POW concentration camp, and their confinement is recounted in harrowing and unsparing detail. Superior drama, also laudable for a fairly even-handed portrayal of the enemy captors. Based on an autobiographical book by Agnes Newton-Keith. 106m/B VHS. Claudette Colbert, Patric Knowles, Sessue Hayakawa; **D:** Jean Negulesco. *NOS, HEG*

Three Cases of Murder ✂✂✂ 1955 Three fast-paced tales of mayhem. "In the Picture" features a deranged taxidermist, a creepy house, and a hapless museum guide. From a story by Roderick Wilkinson. Two friends are in love with the same girl in "You Killed Elizabeth" and when she turns up dead it's clear one of them is guilty. From a story by Brett Halliday. The best features Welles as "Lord Mountdrago," who destroys the career of a fellow Parliament Member and is haunted by fears of retaliation. Based on a story by W. Somerset Maugham. 99m/B VHS. Alan Badel, John Gregson, Orson Welles, Elizabeth Sellars, Hugh Pryse, Jack Lambert; **D:** Wendy Toye, David Eady, George More O'Ferrell; **W:** Donald Wilson, Sidney Carroll, Ian Dalrymple; **C:** Georges Perinal; **M:** Doreen Carwithen. *HMV*

Three Charlies and One Phoney! 1918 Three of Charlie Chaplin's best comedy shorts, plus one featuring his best-known imitator—Billy West. Included are "Recreation" ("Fun is Fun") ("Spring Fever"), "His Musical Career" ("The Piano Movers") ("Musical Tramps"), "The Bond" (featuring Charlie in a Liberty Bond appeal) and "His Day Out" with Billy West imitating Chaplin. All but "His Day Out" were written and directed by Chaplin. 69m/B VHS, Beta, 8mm. Charlie Chaplin, Mack Swain, Charley Chase, Edna Purviance, Sydney Chaplin, Albert Austin; **D:** Charlie Chaplin; **W:** Charlie Chaplin. *VYY*

Three Coins in the Fountain ✂✂½ 1954 Three women throw money into fountain and get romantically involved with Italian men. Outstanding CinemaScope photography captures beauty of Italian setting. Sammy Cahn theme song sung by Frank Sinatra. ♫Three Coins in the Fountain. 102m/C VHS, Beta. Clifton Webb, Dorothy McGuire, Jean Peters, Louis Jourdan, Maggie McNamara, Rossano Brazzi; **D:** Jean Negulesco; **C:** Milton Krasner. Academy Awards '54: Best Color Cinematography, Best Song ("Three Coins in the Fountain"); Nominations: Academy Awards '54: Best Picture. *FOX*

Three Comrades ✂✂✂ 1938 Taylor, Tone, and Young are three friends, reunited in bleak, post-WWI Germany, who meet and befriend Sullavan, a tubercular beauty. Reluctant to marry because of her health, she's finally persuaded to wed Taylor, amidst the country's increasing unrest. Tragedy strikes Sullavan and the politicized Young and the two remaining comrades face an uncertain future. Bleak but forceful and passionate drama. Sullavan's performance is superb. Based on the novel by Erich Maria Rem-

arque. Fitzgerald's script was heavily re-written because both Sullavan and producer Mankiewicz found his approach too literary with unspeakable dialogue. 99m/B VHS. Robert Taylor, Margaret Sullavan, Robert Young, Franchot Tone, Lionel Atwill, Guy Kibbee, Henry Hull, George Zucco, Monty Woolley, Charley Grapewin, Spencer Charters, Sarah Padden; **D:** Frank Borzage; **W:** F. Scott Fitzgerald, Edward Paramore; **C:** Joseph Ruttenberg; **M:** Franz Waxman. New York Film Critics Awards '38: Best Actress (Sullavan); Nominations: Academy Awards '38: Best Actress (Sullavan). *MGM, MOV, BTV*

Three Daring Daughters ✂✂½ 1948 When her husband leaves her and she almost misses her daughter's graduation due to a fainting spell, MacDonald takes hiatus on a cruise ship where she meets and marries pianist Iturbi. Unknowing, the three daughters at home conspire to get Dad back in the family. Enraged when Mom returns with newfound hubby, the threesome do all in their power to make the newlyweds as miserable as possible. Happily ended musical-comedy is chock full of memorable tunes. Based on the play "The Bees and the Flowers" by Kohner and Albert Manning. ♫Route 66; The Dickey Bird Song; Alma Mater; Fleurette; Passepied; Where There's Love; Ritual Fire Dance; You Made Me Love You; Happy Birthday. 115m/C VHS, **Closed Caption.** Jeanette MacDonald, Jose Iturbi, Jane Powell, Edward Arnold, Harry Davenport, Moyna MacGill, Elinor Donahue, Ann Todd; **D:** Fred M. Wilcox; **W:** Sonya Levien, John Meehan, Albert Mannheimer, Frederick Kohner. *MGM*

Three Days in Beirut ✂ 1983 (PG) A soldier of fortune and a beautiful interpreter join forces against a backdrop of Middle Eastern politics, espionage, and violence. 94m/C VHS, Beta. Diana Sands, Calvin Lockhart; **D:** Michael A. Schultz.

Three Days of the Condor ✂✂✂ 1975 (R) CIA researcher Redford finds himself on the run from unknown killers when he is left the only survivor of the mass murder of his office staff. Good performance by Dunaway as the photographer who shelters him. Excellent suspense tale. Based on "Six Days of the Condor" by James Grady. 118m/C VHS, Beta, LV, Letterbox, **Closed Caption.** Robert Redford, Faye Dunaway, Cliff Robertson, Max von Sydow, John Houseman; **D:** Sydney Pollack; **W:** David Rayfiel; **C:** Owen Roizman; **M:** Dave Grusin. Nominations: Academy Awards '75: Best Film Editing. *PAR*

Three Days to a Kill ✂✂ 1991 (R) Calvin Sims is a mercenary hired to rescue a kidnapped ambassador—by any means necessary. **CW:** Language, violence, and some sexuality. 90m/C VHS, LV, **Closed Caption.** Fred Williamson, Bo Svenson, Henry Silva, Chuck Connors, Van Johnson, Sonny Landam; **D:** Fred Williamson. *HBO*

Three Desperate Men ✂✂ 1950 Three brothers accused of murder become outlaws. Not innovative, but satisfactory tale of the Old West. 71m/B VHS, Beta. Preston Foster, Virginia Grey, Jim Davis; **D:** Sam Newfield. *NO*

The Three Faces of Eve ✂✂✂½ 1957 An emotionally disturbed woman seeks the help of a psychiatrist, who discovers she has three distinct personalities. Powerful performances highlight this fascinating study based on a true story. 91m/B VHS, LV. Joanne Woodward, David Wayne, Lee J. Cobb, Nancy Kulp, Vince Edwards; **D:** Nunnally Johnson. Academy Awards '57: Best Actress (Woodward); Golden Globe Awards '58: Best Actress—Drama (Woodward). *FXL, BTV*

Three Faces West ✂✂ *The Refugee* 1940 A dust bowl community is helped by a Viennese doctor who left Europe to avoid Nazi capture. He's aided by the Duke in this odd combination of Western frontier saga and anti-Nazi propaganda. Works only part of the time. 79m/B VHS. John Wayne, Charles Coburn, Sigrid Gurie, Sonny Bupp, Russell Simpson; **D:** Bernard Vorhaus. *REP*

3:15—The Moment of Truth ✂✂ 1986 (R) A vicious high school gang is confronted by an angry ex-member in this so-so teen delinquent film. 86m/C VHS, Beta. Adam Baldwin, Deborah

Foreman, Rene Auberjonois, Danny De La Paz; **D:** Larry Gross, R. Sam Bernard; **M:** Gary Chang.

357 Magnum ✂ 1977 Jonathan Hightower, the CIA's special investigator in the Far East, speaks softly and carries a very big gun. 71m/C VHS, Beta. Marland T. Stewart, James Whitworth, Kathryn Hayes. *NO*

Three for Bedroom C ✂✂ 1952 A movie star and a scientist make romance on a train bound for Los Angeles. Swanson's follow-up to "Sunset Boulevard." 74m/C VHS, Beta. Gloria Swanson, Fred Clark, Steve Brodie, Hans Conried, Margaret Dumont; **D:** Milton Bren. *ART*

Three for the Road ✂✂ 1987 (PG) A young aspiring political aide and his roommate must escort a Senator's ill-mannered and spoiled daughter to a reform institution. On the road, they run into more than a few obstacles. Good performances elevate a bland script. Sheen made this movie before his riveting performance as a young GI in "Platoon." 98m/C Beta, LV. Charlie Sheen, Kerri Green, Alan Ruck, Sally Kellerman; **D:** Bill W.L. Norton; **W:** Tim Metcalfe; **M:** Barry Goldberg. *NO*

Three Fugitives ✂✂ 1989 (PG-13) An ex-con holdup man determined to go straight is taken hostage by a bungling first-time bank robber, who is only attempting the holdup in order to support his withdrawn young daughter. Ex-con Nolte winds up on the lam with the would-be robber and his daughter. The comedy is fun, the sentimental moments too sweet and slow. Remake of French "Les Fugitifs." 96m/C VHS, Beta, LV, **Closed Caption.** Nick Nolte, Martin Short, James Earl Jones, Kenneth McMillan, Sarah Rowland Doroff, Alan Ruck; **D:** Francis Veber; **W:** Francis Veber; **C:** Haskell Wexler. *TOU*

Three Godfathers ✂✂✂ 1948 A sweet and sentimental western have three half-hearted outlaws on the run, taking with them an infant they find in the desert. Dedicated to western star and Ford alumni Harry Carey, Sr. (whose son is one of the outlaws in the film), who died of cancer the year before. Ford had first filmed the tale with Carey Sr. as "Marked Men" in 1919. 82m/C VHS, Beta. John Wayne, Pedro Armendariz Sr., Harry Carey Jr., Ward Bond, Mae Marsh, Jane Darwell, Ben Johnson, Mildred Natwick, Guy Kibbee; **D:** John Ford; **C:** Winton C. Hoch. *MGM*

Three Guys Named Mike ✂✂ 1951 Wyman plays an overly enthusiastic airline stewardess who finds herself the object of affection from three guys named Mike, including an airline pilot, an advertising man, and a scientist. A cute comedy. 89m/B VHS. Jane Wyman, Van Johnson, Barry Sullivan, Howard Keel, Phyllis Kirk, Jeff Donnell; **D:** Charles Walters; **W:** Sidney Sheldon. *VDM*

The 317th Platoon ✂✂✂ 1965 An emotionally gripping war drama of the French-Vietnamese War in which the 317th Platoon of the French Army, consisting of four French commanders and 41 Laotians, is ordered to retreat to camp Dien Bien Phu. The men begin their march and slowly succomb to the elements and ambushes. Days later, when what is left of the platoon finally reaches Dien Bien Phu, the camp is in enemy hands and the remnants of the 317th Platoon are killed in cold blood. Director Shoendoerffer portrays this struggle, conflict, and the quiet haunting tension of war with great skill. In French with English subtitles. 100m/B VHS, LV. *FR* Jacques Perrin, Bruno Cremer, Pierre Fabre, Manuel Zarzo; **D:** Pierre Schoendoerffer; **W:** Pierre Schoendoerffer. *INT, IME, FCT*

Three Husbands ✂✂½ 1950 A deceased playboy leaves letters for the title characters incriminating their wives in extramarital affairs. The men's reactions are pure farce—even though this same concept was played straight with a sex change in the earlier "A Letter to Three Wives." 79m/B VHS. Eve Arden, Ruth Warrick, Vanessa Brown, Howard da Silva, Shepperd Strudwick, Jane Darwell; **D:** Irving Reis. *NOS, VDM*

Three in the Attic ♪½ 1968 (R) A college student juggles three girlfriends at the same time. When the girls find out they are being two-timed, they lock their boyfriend in an attic and exhaust him with forced sexual escapades. Then they talk. Limited trashy and foolish appeal. **92m/C VHS, Beta.** Christopher Jones, Yvette Mimieux, John Beck; **D:** Richard Wilson. *NO*

Three in the Cellar ♪♪ *Up in the Cellar* 1970 (R) A disgruntled college student seeks revenge on the school president by seducing his wife, daughter and mistress. Good screenplay helps carry it off. **92m/C VHS, Beta.** Wes Stern, Joan Collins, Larry Hagman, Judy Pace; **D:** Theodore J. Flicker. *HBO*

Three in the Saddle ♪½ 1945 Ritter and the Texas Rangers fight for law and order. **61m/B VHS, Beta.** Tex Ritter, Dave O'Brien, Charles "Blackie" King; **D:** Harry Fraser. *NOS, VCN*

Three Kinds of Heat ♪ 1987 (R) Three Interpol agents track down a warring Asian crime lord. Alternately tongue-in-cheek and silly. Never released in theatres—it found it's home on video. Stevens created "The Outer Limits" for television. **88m/C VHS, Beta, Closed Caption.** Robert Ginty, Victoria Barrett, Shakti; **D:** Leslie Stevens. *WAR*

Three Legionnaires ♪½ *Three Crazy Legionnaires* 1937 Three soldiers cavort in a post-WWI Siberian tank town. **67m/B VHS, Beta, LV.** Robert Armstrong, Lyle Talbot, Fifi d'Orsay, Anne Nagel, Donald Meek. *VYY*

The Three Little Pigs 1984 From "Faerie Tale Theatre" comes the story of three little pigs, the houses they lived in and the wolf that tried to do them in. **60m/C VHS, Beta, Closed Caption.** Billy Crystal, Jeff Goldblum, Valerie Perrine; **D:** Howard Storm. *KUI, FOX, FCT*

Three Little Words ♪♪½ 1950 A musical biography of songwriting team Harry Ruby and Bert Kalmar, filled with Kalmar-Ruby numbers. Helen Kane (famous for her boop-boop-de-boops) dubbed "I Wanna Be Loved By You" for Reynolds. A musical in the best MGM tradition. ♪ I Wanna Be Loved By You; Who's Sorry Now?; Three Little Words; I Love You So Much; She's Mine, All Mine; So-Long, Oo-Long; Hooray for Captain Spaulding; Up In the Clouds; All Alone Monday. **102m/C VHS, Beta.** Fred Astaire, Red Skelton, Vera-Ellen, Arlene Dahl, Keenan Wynn, Gloria De Haven, Debbie Reynolds, Gale Robbins; **D:** Richard Thorpe; **M:** Andre Previn. Golden Globe Awards '51: Best Actor—Musical/Comedy (Astaire); Nominations: Academy Awards '50: Scoring of a Musical. *MGM*

Three Lives and Only One Death ♪♪½ *Trois Vies et une Seule Mort* 1996 Surrealist film features Mastroianni in four roles. Salesman Mateo Strano walks out on his wife Maria (Paredes) and doesn't see her for 20 years. When he finally returns, Mateo wants her back, although Maria's got a new husband, Andre (Atkine). Then there's Georges Vickers, negative anthropology professor-turned street tramp who takes up with hooker Tania (Galiena), who also has another identity. Then he's a butler who's trying to murder a young couple and steal their child and finally, Mastroianni's a rich industrialist who seems to be suffering from multiple personalities. And yes, somehow all the stories do tie together. French with subtitles. **124m/C VHS.** *FR* Marcello Mastroianni, Anna Galiena, Marisa Paredes, Melvil Poupaud, Chiara Mastroianni, Arielle Dombasle, Feodor Atkine, Jean-Yves Gautier, Pierre Bellemare, Lou Castel, Jacques Pielier; **D:** Raul Ruiz; **W:** Raul Ruiz, Pascal Bonitzer; **C:** Laurent Machuel; **M:** Jorge Arriagada. *NYF*

The Three Lives of Karen ♪♪½ 1997 (PG-13) Cable thriller finds Karen Winthrop (O'Grady) engaged to state trooper Matt (Guinee) and seemingly happy until Paul Riggs (Boutsikaris) shows up. He has proof that Karen is actually his wife Emily who disappeared four years before, abandoning him and their daughter Jessica (Bugajski). So the confused Karen returns with Paul to try and remember what happened to her. She

learns that she's actually disappeared twice before and the flashbacks Karen has of her past are terrifying. **CW:** Violent episodes and a sexual situation. **89m/C VHS, Closed Caption.** Gail O'Grady, Dennis Boutsikaris, Tim Guinee, Monica Bugajski; **D:** David Burton Morris; **W:** David Chisholm. *USH*

The Three Lives of Thomasina ♪♪♪ 1963 (PG) In turn-of-the-century Scotland, a veterinarian orders his daughter's beloved cat destroyed when the pet is diagnosed with tetanus. After the cat's death (with scenes of kitty heaven), a beautiful and mysterious healer from the woods is able to bring the animal back to life and restore the animal to the little girl. Lovely Disney fairy tale with good performances by all. **95m/C VHS, Beta, Closed Caption.** Patrick McGoohan, Susan Hampshire, Karen Dotrice, Matthew Garber; **D:** Don Chaffey. *DIS, TVC*

Three Men and a Baby ♪♪♪ 1987 (PG) The arrival of a young baby forever changes the lives of three sworn bachelors living in New York. Well-paced, charming and fun, with good acting from all. A remake of the French movie "Three Men and a Cradle." **102m/C VHS, Beta, LV, 8mm, Closed Caption.** Tom Selleck, Steve Guttenberg, Ted Danson, Margaret Colin, Nancy Travis, Philip Bosco, Celeste Holm, Derek De Lint, Cynthia Harris, Lisa Blair, Michelle Blair; **D:** Leonard Nimoy; **W:** James Orr, Jim Cruickshank; **M:** Marvin Hamlisch. *TOU*

Three Men and a Cradle ♪♪♪½ 1985 *Trois Hommes et un Couffin* (PG-13) Remade in the U.S. in 1987 as "Three Men and a Baby," this French film is about three bachelors living together who suddenly find themselves the guardians of a baby girl. After the initial shock of learning how to take care of a child, they fall in love with her and won't let her go. Fans of the American version may find themselves liking the original even more. In French with English subtitles. **100m/C VHS, LV.** *FR* Roland Giraud, Michel Boujenah, Andre Dussollier; **D:** Coline Serreau; **W:** Coline Serreau. Cesar Awards '86: Best Film, Best Supporting Actor (Boujenah), Best Writing; Nominations: Academy Awards '85: Best Foreign Language Film. *ART, MGM*

Three Men and a Little Lady ♪♪½ 1990 (PG) In this sequel to "Three Men and a Baby," the mother of the once abandoned infant decides that her child needs a father. Although she wants Selleck, he doesn't get the message and so she chooses a snooty British director. The rest of the movie features various semi-comic attempts to rectify the situation. **100m/C VHS, Beta, LV, Closed Caption.** Tom Selleck, Steve Guttenberg, Ted Danson, Nancy Travis, Robin Weisman, Christopher Cazenove, Fiona Shaw, Sheila Hancock, John Boswall, Jonathan Lynn, Sydney Walsh; **D:** Emile Ardolino; **W:** Charlie Peters, Sara Parriott, Josann McGibbon; **M:** James Newton Howard. *TOU*

Three Men on a Horse ♪♪♪ 1936 Comedy classic about mild-mannered McHugh's ability to predict horse races and the bettors that try to take advantage of him. Blondell is great as the Brooklynese girlfriend of one of the bettors. Lots of laughs, but don't watch for the horse-racing scenes, because there aren't many. **88m/B VHS, Closed Caption.** Frank McHugh, Joan Blondell, Carol Hughes, Allen Jenkins, Guy Kibbee, Sam Levene; **D:** Mervyn LeRoy. *MGM*

The Three Musketeers ♪♪ *D'Artagnan* 1916 One of the many movie adaptation of Alexandre Dumas' adventure, but this one comes from the hand of famed movie pioneer Ince. D'Artagnan joins the title characters in saving France's Queen Anne from a nefarious plot. Silent with the original organ score. **74m/B VHS, Beta, 8mm.** Orin Johnson, Dorothy Dalton, Louise Glaum, Walt Whitman; **D:** Charles Swickard. *VYY, GPV, DVT*

The Three Musketeers ♪♪♪½ 1921 D'Artagnan swashbuckles silently amid stylish sets, scores of extras and exquisite costumes. Relatively faithful adaptation of Alexandre Dumas novel, slightly altered in favor of D'Artagnan's lover. Classic Fairbanks, who also produced. **120m/B**

VHS, Beta, LV. Douglas Fairbanks Sr., Leon Barry, George Siegmann, Eugene Pallette, Boyd Irwin, Thomas Holding, Sidney Franklin, Charles Stevens, Nigel de Brulier, Willis Robards; **D:** Fred Niblo. *GPV, FCT, KIV*

The Three Musketeers 1933 Modern adaptation of the classic tale by Alexander Dumas depicts the three friends as members of the Foreign Legion. Weakest of Wayne serials, in 12 parts. **215m/B VHS, Beta.** John Wayne, Raymond Hatton, Lon Chaney Jr. *NOS, VCN, VDM*

The Three Musketeers ♪♪ 1935 Three swordsmen, loyal to each other, must battle the corrupt Cardinal Richelieu. Generally regarded as the least exciting adaptation of Alexander Dumas' classic tale. The first talking version. **95m/B VHS, Beta, LV.** Walter Abel, Paul Lukas, Moroni Olsen, Ian Keith, Margot Grahame, Heather Angel, Onslow Stevens, Miles Mander; **D:** Rowland V. Lee; **M:** Max Steiner. *IME, TTC*

The Three Musketeers ♪♪½ *The Singing Musketeer* 1939 Musical-comedy version of the famed Alexandre Dumas swashbuckling saga. Ameche is a singing D'Artagnan and the three Ritz brothers are the inept and cowardly Musketeers (who turn out to be phonies, after all). Silly fun. ♪ My Lady; Song of the Musketeers; Voila; Chicken Soup. **73m/B VHS.** Don Ameche, The Ritz Brothers, Binnie Barnes, Lionel Atwill, Miles Mander, Gloria Stuart, Pauline Moore, Joseph Schildkraut, John Carradine, Douglass Dumbrille; **D:** Allan Dwan; **W:** M.M. Musselman, William A. Drake, Sam Hellman. *FXV*

The Three Musketeers ♪♪½ 1948 The three musketeers who are "all for one and one for all" join forces with D'Artagnan to battle the evil Cardinal Richelieu in this rambunctious adaptation of the classic tale by Alexander Dumas. Good performances by the cast, who combined drama and comedy well. Turner's first color film. **126m/C VHS, Beta, LV.** Lana Turner, Gene Kelly, June Allyson, Gig Young, Angela Lansbury, Van Heflin, Keenan Wynn, Robert Coote, Reginald Owen, Frank Morgan, Vincent Price, Patricia Medina; **D:** George Sidney. Nominations: Academy Awards '48: Best Color Cinematography. *MGM, CCB*

The Three Musketeers ♪♪♪½ 1974 (PG) Extravagant and funny version of the Dumas classic. Three swashbucklers and their country cohort, who wishes to join the Musketeers, set out to save the honor of the French Queen. To do so they must oppose the evil cardinal who has his eyes on the power behind the throne. A strong cast leads this winning combination of slapstick and high adventure. Followed by "The Four Musketeers" and "The Return of the Musketeers." **105m/C VHS, Beta.** Richard Chamberlain, Oliver Reed, Michael York, Raquel Welch, Frank Finlay, Christopher Lee, Faye Dunaway, Charlton Heston, Geraldine Chaplin, Simon Ward, Jean-Pierre Cassel; **D:** Richard Lester; **C:** David Watkin. Golden Globe Awards '75: Best Actress—Musical/Comedy (Welch). *FXL*

The Three Musketeers ♪♪½ 1993 (PG) Yet another version of the classic swashbuckler with Porthos, Athos, Aramis, and the innocent D'Artanan banding together against the evil Cardinal Richelieu and the tempting Milady DeWinter to save France. Cute stars, a little swordplay, a few jokes, and cartoon bad guys. Okay for the younger crowd. **105m/C VHS, LV, Closed Caption.** Kiefer Sutherland, Charlie Sheen, Chris O'Donnell, Oliver Platt, Rebecca DeMornay, Tim Curry, Gabriel Anwar, Julie Delpy, Michael Wincott; **D:** Stephen Herek; **W:** David Loughery; **M:** Michael Kamen. Nominations: MTV Movie Awards '94: Best Song ("All for Love"). *DIS*

3 Ninjas ♪♪½ 1992 (PG) Lively kid's action-er about three brothers who are trained as ninjas by their grandpa. When a group of bad guys tries to kidnap the boys, they're in for trouble. Sort of a cross between "The Karate Kid" and "Home Alone" that is suitable for family viewing. Followed by "3 Ninjas Kick Back." **84m/C VHS, Beta, LV, Closed Caption.** Victor Wong, Michael Treanor, Max Elliott Slade, Chad Power, Rand Kingsley, Alan McRae, Margarita

Franco, Toru Tanaka, Patrick Laborteaux; **D:** Jon Turteltaub; **W:** Edward Emanuel; **M:** Rick Marvin. *TOU, PMS*

Three Ninjas: High Noon at Mega Mountain 🎬🎬½ *Three Ninjas: Showdown at Mega Mountain* **1997 (PG)** Fourth installment of the kid-fantasy franchise finds brothers Rocky (Botuchis), Colt (O'Laskey), and Tum-Tum (Roeske) in the middle of a takeover at an amusement park. The ninja trained brothers, along with a computer-whiz neighbor (Earlywine) and retiring action hero Dave Dragon (Hogan) must save the day when Medusa (Anderson) and her henchmen ransom the park and its guests. Typically, the adults are incompetent when they're not busy being nasty. Pre-pubescent kids are the only ones likely to find this entertaining—if they're not too discriminating. The "action" is somewhere between cartoon and pro wrestling. Varney stands out as Medusa's lead henchman. **93m/C VHS, Closed Caption.** Hulk Hogan, Loni Anderson, Jim Varney, Victor Wong, Mathew Botuchis, Michael J. O'Laskey II, J.P. Roeske II, Chelsey Earlywine, Alan McRae, Margarita Franco, Kirk Baily; **D:** Sean McNamara; **W:** Sean McNamara, Jeff Phillips; **C:** Blake T. Evans; **M:** John Coda. *COL*

3 Ninjas Kick Back 🎬🎬½ **1994 (PG)** Sequel to the popular "3 Ninjas." Three brothers help their grandfather protect a ceremonial knife won in a ninja tournament in Japan 50 years earlier. Gramps' ancient adversary in that tournament, now an evil tycoon, wants the sword back and he's willing to enlist the aid of his three American grandchildren, members of garage band Teenage Vomit, to get it. The showdown eventually heads to Japan, where "Kick Back," unlike predecessors, dispenses with the Japan-bashing. High-spirited action fare that kids will enjoy. **95m/C VHS, LV, Closed Caption.** Victor Wong, Max Elliott Slade, Sean Fox, Evan Bonifant, Sab Shimono, Dustin Nguyen, Jason Schombing, Caroline Junko King, Angelo Tiffe; **D:** Charles Kanganis; **W:** Mark Saltzman; **M:** Rick Marvin. *COL*

3 Ninjas Knuckle Up 🎬🎬½ **1992 (PG-13)** Brothers Rocky (Treanor), Tum Tum (Power), and Colt (Slade) spend their summer vacation with ever-wise Grandpa Mori (Wong) and get to practice their martial arts skills on a variety of villains. Seems a waste management company has been illegally dumping toxins onto the nearby Indian reservation where the boys' friend Jo (Lightning) lives and have even kidnapped her dad (Shanks) to keep him silent. So it's our pint-sized heroes to the rescue. Filmed in '92 but released after "3 Ninjas Kick Back," which explains why Treanor and Power are missing from the second film. **CW:** Non-stop ninja action. **94m/C VHS, LV.** Victor Wong, Michael Treanor, Chad Power, Max Elliott Slade, Crystle Lightning, Patrick Kilpatrick, Don Shanks, Charles Napier, Nick Ramus, Vincent Schiavelli; **D:** Simon S. Sheen; **W:** Alex S. Kim; **C:** Eugene Shlugleit; **M:** Gary Stevan Scott. *COL*

Three Nuts in Search of a Bolt 🎬½ **1964 (R)** Three neurotics send a surrogate to a comely psychiatrist for help, but the shrink thinks the surrogate's a three-way multiple personality. Raunchy monkey-shines ensue. Includes Van Doren's infamous beer bath scene. **78m/C VHS, Beta.** Mamie Van Doren, Tommy Noonan, Paul Gilbert, Alvy Moore; **D:** Tommy Noonan. *NO*

301, 302 🎬 **1994** Confusing horror story told in flashbacks focuses on two women in neighboring high-rise apartments. A young policeman is investigating the disappearance of the woman from apartment 302 (Hwang). He questions the tenant across the hall in 301 (Pang), an obsessive cook who tries to share her culinary results with Hwang, who happens to be an anorexic writer. Both have dark secrets in their pasts, which they share, leading to a grotesque resolution of their friendship. **99m/C VHS.** Eun-Jin Bang, Sin-Hye Hwang, Chu-Ryun Kim; **D:** Chul-Soo Park; **W:** Suh-Goon Lee. *EVE*

Three O'Clock High 🎬🎬½ **1987 (PG)** A nerdy high school journalist is assigned a profile of the new kid in school, who turns out to be the biggest bully, too. He approaches his task with great unease. Silly teenage farce is given souped-up direction by Spielberg protege Joanou. Features decent work by the young cast. **97m/C VHS, Beta, LV.** Casey Siemaszko, Anne Ryan, Stacey Glick, Jonathan Wise, Richard Tyson, Jeffrey Tambor, Philip Baker Hall, John P. Ryan; **D:** Phil Joanou; **W:** Richard Christian Matheson, Thomas Szollosi; **M:** Tangerine Dream. *USH*

Three of Hearts 🎬½ **1993 (R)** Slick look at love in contemporary downtown New York. The triangle consists of Connie (Lynch), just dumped by bisexual girlfriend Ellen (Fenn), who is in turn seduced by hired escort Joe (Baldwin), who will break her heart, causing her to turn back to the sympathetic Connie. But guess what happens. Highly superficial plot is transparent although you don't want to know what happens since the film was shot with two endings. The U.S. release pairs Joe and Ellen for a typically American happy ending; the European release doesn't. **CW:** Strong language and strong sexuality. **102m/C VHS, LV.** Kelly Lynch, William Baldwin, Sherilyn Fenn, Joe Pantoliano, Gail Strickland, Cec Verrell, Claire Callaway, Tony Amendola; **D:** Yurek Bogayevicz; **W:** Philip C. Epstein, Adam Greenman; **M:** Richard Gibbs. *COL, IME, FCT*

Three on a Match 🎬🎬🎬 **1932** An actress, a stenographer and a society woman get together for a tenth year reunion. They become embroiled in a world of crime when Blondell's gangster boyfriend takes a liking to Dvorak. She leaves her husband and takes up with the crook. The results are tragic. Bogart's first gangster role. **64m/B VHS, Beta.** Joan Blondell, Warren William, Ann Dvorak, Bette Davis, Lyle Talbot, Humphrey Bogart, Patricia Ellis, Grant Mitchell; **D:** Mervyn LeRoy. *MGM, FCT*

Three on a Meathook woof! **1972** When a young man and his father living on an isolated farm receive female visitors, bloodshed is quick to follow. Essentially a remake of "Psycho," and very loosely based on the crimes of Ed Gein. Filmed in Louisville, Kentucky. **85m/C VHS, Beta.** Charles Kissinger, James Pickett, Sherry Steiner, Carolyn Thompson; **D:** William Girdler; **W:** William Girdler. *NO*

The Three Penny Opera 🎬🎬🎬 *Die Dreigroschenoper* **1962** Mack the Knife presides over an exciting world of thieves, murderers, beggars, prostitutes and corrupt officials in a seedy section of London. Based on the opera by Kurt Weill and Bertold Brecht, which was based on "The Beggar's Opera" by John Gay. Remake of "The Threepenny Opera" (1931). **124m/C VHS, Beta, LV.** Curt Jurgens, Hildegarde Neff, Gert Frobe, June Ritchie, Lino Ventura, Sammy Davis Jr. *MVD, FCT*

Three Secrets 🎬🎬½ **1950** A plane crashes and the only survivor is a five-year-old boy. Three women, each with a secret, seek to claim him as the child each gave up for adoption five years before. Tearjerker with good cast. **98m/B VHS.** Eleanor Parker, Patricia Neal, Ruth Roman, Frank Lovejoy, Leif Erickson; **D:** Robert Wise. *REP*

The Three Sisters 🎬🎬½ **1965** A stage production from the Actor's Studio of Chekhov's play about unhappy siblings in turn-of-the-century Russia. The three sisters believe all their problems are caused by living in the provinces and would be solved if they could return to their childhood home in Moscow. **167m/B VHS.** Shelley Winters, Sandy Dennis, Geraldine Page, Kevin McCarthy, Kim Stanley, Luther Adler, Robert Loggia, James Olson, Gerald Hiken; **D:** Paul Bogart. *HTV, FCT*

Three Smart Girls 🎬🎬🎬½ **1936** Fast-moving musical features three high-spirited sisters who attempt to bring their divorced parents back together. Their plan is thwarted when they learn of their father's plan to marry a gold digger. 15-year-old singing sensation Durbin made her debut in this film. Based on a story by Commandi-

ni. Followed by "Three Smart Girls Grow Up" (My Heart Is Singing, Someone to Care for Me. **84m/B VHS.** Deanna Durbin, Binnie Barnes, Alice Brady, Ray Milland, Charles Winninger, Mischa Auer, Nan Grey, Barbara Read; **D:** Henry Koster; **W:** Adele Comandini, Austin Parker; **C:** Joseph Valentine. Nominations: Academy Awards '36: Best Picture, Best Sound, Best Story. *USH*

Three Smart Girls Grow Up 🎬🎬🎬 **1939** Durbin once again plays matchmaker, this time for her two older sisters and their fellas. A delightful mix of comedy and song, this lighthearted sequel turned out to be one of the top-grossing films of the year. Durbin sings "Because," which became one of her biggest hits. **88m/B VHS.** Deanna Durbin, Charles Winninger, Nan Grey, Helen Parrish, Robert Cummings, William Lundigan, Ernest Cossart; **D:** Henry Koster; **W:** Felix Jackson, Bruce Manning. *USH*

Three Sovereigns for Sarah 🎬🎬½ **1985** Witch-hunters tortured and toasted Sarah's two sisters for practicing witchcraft in the past. Now, accused of witchery herself, she struggles to prove the family's innocence. Excellent, made-for-PBS. Fine performances from all, especially Redgrave. **152m/C VHS, Beta.** Vanessa Redgrave, Phyllis Thaxter, Patrick McGoohan; **D:** Philip Leacock. *PBS*

Three Stooges Comedy Capers: Vol. 1 **194?** Compilation includes: "Disorder in the Court" (1936), "Malice in the Palace" (1949), "Sing a Song of Six Pants" (1947), and "The Brideless Groom" (1947). **80m/B VHS, Beta.** Moe Howard, Larry Fine, Curly Howard, Shemp Howard. *NOS*

Three Stooges Comedy Classics **1949** The antics of the Stooges are featured in this collection of five original shorts, along with an early Ted Healy comedy that features all four Stooges: "Hollywood on Parade," "Disorder in the Court," "Malice in the Palace," "Brideless Groom," and "Sing a Song of Six Pants." **79m/B VHS.** Moe Howard, Larry Fine, Curly Howard, Shemp Howard, Ted Healy. *REP*

Three Stooges: Cookoo Cavaliers and Other Nyuks **1940** The boys star in "Cookoo Cavaliers," "Busy Buddies," and "Booby Dupes." **55m/B VHS.** Moe Howard, Curly Howard, Larry Fine. *COL*

Three Stooges Festival **1949** Three original shorts by the comedy trio, including: "Disorder in the Court" (1936-Curly), "Sing a Song of Six Pants" (1949-Shemp) and "Malice in the Palace" (1949-Shemp). **60m/B VHS, Beta.** Moe Howard, Larry Fine, Shemp Howard, Curly Howard. *AOV, VYY*

Three Stooges: From Nurse to Worse and Other Nyuks **1945** The irrepressible Stooges star in "From Nurse to Worse," "Crash Goes the Hash," and "G.I. Wanna Go Home." **55m/B VHS.** Moe Howard, Larry Fine, Curly Howard. *COL*

The Three Stooges: Half-Wit's Holiday and Other Nyuks **1935** Includes, "Half-Wit's Holiday," "Horse Collars," and "How High Is Up?" **55m/B VHS.** Moe Howard, Larry Fine. *COL*

The Three Stooges: Idiots Deluxe and Other Nyuks **1940** Curly, Larry and Moe star in, "Idiots Deluxe," "I Can Hardly Wait," and "Idle Roomers." **55m/B VHS.** Moe Howard, Curly Howard, Larry Fine. *COL*

Three Stooges in Orbit 🎬🎬½ **1962** Three television performers (you know who) looking for a schtick and a place to live, encounter a crazy scientist with a rocket-like invention. In a shocking plot twist, the boys accidently launch the rocket and must battle Martians to save the world and their TV career. **87m/B VHS.** Moe Howard, Larry Fine, Joe DeRita, Emil Sitka, Carol Christensen, Edson Stroll; **D:** Edward L. Bernds. *COL*

The Three Stooges Meet Hercules 🎬🎬½ **1961** The Three Stooges are transported back to ancient Ithaca by a time machine with a young scientist and his girlfriend. When the girl is captured, they enlist the help of

Hercules to rescue her. **80m/B VHS, Beta.** Moe Howard, Larry Fine, Joe DeRita, Vicki Trickett, Quinn Redeker; **D:** Edward L. Bernds. GKK, COL

The Three Stooges: Nutty but Nice and Other Nyuks 1936 The boys star in "Nutty but Nice," "The Sitter-Downers," and "Slippery Silks." **55m/B VHS.** Moe Howard, Curly Howard, Larry Fine. COL

The Three Stooges: They Stooge to Conga and Other Nyuks 1940 WWII madness from the Stooges in "They Stooge to Conga," "You Natzy Spy!" and "I'll Never Heil Again." **55m/B VHS.** Moe Howard, Curly Howard, Larry Fine. COL

Three Stops to Murder ♘ 1953 An FBI agent investigates the murder of a beautiful model in this early, unspectacular Hammer production. **76m/B VHS, Beta.** GB Tom Conway, Mila Parely, Naomi Chance, Eric Pohlmann, Andrew Osborn, Richard Wattis, Eileen Way, Delphi Lawrence; **D:** Terence Fisher. SNC, MLB

Three Strange Loves ♘♘♘ Thirst 1949 Men and women struggle with loneliness, old age, and sterility. Sometimes disjointed, but for the most part, well-made. Finely acted. In Swedish with English subtitles. **88m/B VHS, Beta.** SW Eva Henning, Brigit Tengroth, Birger Malmsten; **D:** Ingmar Bergman. NOS, HHT, NLC

3:10 to Yuma ♘♘♘½ 1957 In order to collect $200 he desperately needs, a poor farmer has to hold a dangerous killer at bay while waiting to turn the outlaw over to the authorities arriving on the 3:10 train to Yuma. Stuck in a hotel room with the outlaw's gang gathering outside, the question arises as to who is the prisoner. Farmer Heflin is continually worked on by the outlaw Ford, in a movie with more than its share of great dialogue. Suspenseful, well-made action western adapted from an Elmore Leonard story. **92m/B VHS, Beta, LV.** Glenn Ford, Van Heflin, Felicia Farr, Richard Jaeckel; **D:** Delmer Daves; **M:** George Duning. GKK

Three Texas Steers ♘½ Danger Rides the Range 1939 A circus owner inherits some land that the government wants for a water project and her manager tries to get it for himself. Enter the terrific trio to set things right. Last of the series for Terhune. The scenes of the circus fire were taken from "Circus Girl" (1937). **59m/B VHS.** John Wayne, Ray Corrigan, Max Terhune, Carole Landis, Ralph Graves, Roscoe Ates; **D:** George Sherman. NOS

Three the Hard Way ♘♘½ 1974 (R) An insane white supremacist has a plan to eliminate blacks by contaminating water supplies. A big blaxploitation money maker and the first to team Brown, Williamson, and Kelly, who would go on to make several more pictures together. **93m/C VHS.** Jim Brown, Fred Williamson, Jim Kelly, Sheila Frazier, Jay Robinson, Alex Rocco; **D:** Gordon Parks. XVC

Three Violent People ♘♘ 1957 Family feud set in post-Civil War Old West features Heston and Baxter impulsively marrying and returning to run the family ranch. Heston's brother (Tryon) wants to sell the ranch in order to get his share of the inheritance and then Heston finds out Baxter was once a prostitute. In this case family squabbles don't make for an exciting film. **100m/C VHS, Closed Caption.** Charlton Heston, Anne Baxter, Gilbert Roland, Tom Tryon, Forrest Tucker, Elaine Stritch, Bruce (Herman Brix) Bennett, Barton MacLane; **D:** Rudolph Mate; **W:** James Edward Grant; **C:** Loyal Griggs; **M:** Walter Scharf. PAR

Three Warriors ♘½ 1977 Young Native American boy is forced to leave the city and return to the reservation, where his contempt for the traditions of his ancestors slowly turns to appreciation and love. **100m/C VHS, Beta.** Charles White Eagle, Lois Red Elk, McKee "Kiko" Red Wing, Christopher Lloyd, Randy Quaid. NO

Three Way Weekend ♘ 1981 (R) Two young girls set off on a back-packing trip through the mountains of Southern California to enjoy camping and romance. **78m/C VHS, Beta.** Dan Diego,

---

Jody Lee Olhava, Richard Blye, Blake Parrish; **D:** Emmett Alston.

The Three Weird Sisters ♘♘ 1948 The three weird sisters from "Macbeth" strive to maintain their life of luxury by plotting to kill their half-brother for the inheritance. Not a bad effort for Birt's first time out as director; script co-written by his wife, Louise and poet Thomas. **82m/B VHS.** GB Nancy Price, Mary Clare; **D:** Daniel Birt; **W:** Dylan Thomas, Louise Birt. VDM, SNC, THV

Three Wishes ♘♘ 1995 (PG) Mysterious—and perhaps mystical—stranger Jack (Swayze) moves into the lives of a 1950s suburban widow (Mastrantonio) and her kids (Mazzello and Mumy) after she hits him with her car. Jack proceeds to use Zen philosophy, stories of a genie disguised as a dog, and nude sunbathing to help the kids' Little League team, make a boy fly, and scandalize the neighborhood. Adults will recognize the beatnik, Kerouac-influenced philosophy of nonconformity. They'll also recognize the sellout of that ideal with the sickeningly sappy ending. Mumy is the son of former "Lost in Space" child star Billy Mumy. **115m/C VHS, LV, Closed Caption.** Patrick Swayze, Mary Elizabeth Mastrantonio, Joseph Mazzello, David Marshall Grant, Michael O'Keefe, John Diehl, Jay O. Sanders, Diane Venora, Seth Mumy; **D:** Martha Coolidge; **W:** Elizabeth Anderson; **C:** Johnny E. Jensen; **M:** Cynthia Millar. HBO

Three Word Brand ♘♘ 1921 Hart plays three roles in this film, a homesteader who is killed by Indians and his twin sons, who are separated after their father's death and reunited many years later. Silent with musical score. **75m/B VHS, Beta.** William S. Hart, Jane Novak, S.J. Bingham; **D:** Lambert Hillyer. GPV, VYY

The Three Worlds of Gulliver ♘♘½ The Worlds of Gulliver 1959 A colorful family version of the Jonathan Swift classic about an Englishman who discovers a fantasy land of small and giant people. Visual effects by Ray Harryhausen. **100m/C VHS, Beta, LV.** Kerwin Mathews, Jo Morrow, Basil Sydney, Mary Ellis; **D:** Jack Sher; **W:** Arthur Ross, Jack Sher; **M:** Bernard Herrmann. COL, MLB, CCB

The Threepenny Opera ♘♘ Die Dreigroschenoper; L'Opera De Quat'Sous; Beggars' Opera 1931 A musical about the exploits of gangster Mack the Knife. Adapted from Bertolt Brecht's play and John Gay's "The Beggar's Opera." In German with English subtitles. **107m/B VHS.** Rudolph Forster, Lotte Lenya, Carola Neher, Reinhold Schunzel, Fritz Rasp, Valeska Gert; **D:** G.W. Pabst. VDM, AUD, HEG

Three's Trouble ♘♘ 1985 A middle-class family erupts when a young male babysitter enters to care for its three mischievous sons. **93m/C VHS, Beta.** AU John Waters, Jacki Weaver, Steven Vidler; **D:** Chris Thomson.

Threesome woof! 1994 (R) Another Generation X movie that tries hard to be hip, but fails miserably. Due to a college administrative error, Alex (Boyle) winds up sharing a suite with two male roommates, Eddy (Charles) and Stuart (Baldwin). Despite having completely different personalities, they soon become best friends and form one cozy little group, with cozy being the key word. Sexual tension abounds—Alex wants Eddy who wants Stuart who wants Alex. Filled with pathetic dialogue (most of it relating to bodily functions and body parts) and shallow, obnoxious characters, this menage a trois film is a flop. **93m/C VHS, LV, 8mm, Letterbox, Closed Caption.** Lara Flynn Boyle, Stephen Baldwin, Josh Charles, Alexis Arquette, Mark Arnold, Martha Gehman, Michelle Matheson; **D:** Andrew Fleming; **W:** Andrew Fleming; **M:** Thomas Newman. COL

Threshold ♘♘½ 1983 (PG) An internationally acclaimed research biologist is frustrated by his inability to save a dying 20-year-old woman born with a defective heart. She becomes the recipient of the first artificial heart. Solid performances. **97m/C VHS, Beta.** CA Donald Sutherland, Jeff Goldblum, John Marley, Mare Winningham; **D:** Richard Pearce. Genie Awards '83: Best Actor (Sutherland). FOX

The Thrill Killers woof! The Monsters Are Loose; The Maniacs Are Loose 1965 Young murderous thugs rampage through Los Angeles suburbs, killing indiscriminately. Pretentious and exploitative. Sometimes shown with Hallucinogenic Hypo-Vision—a prologue announcing the special effect would be shown before the film, and on cue, hooded ushers would run through the theatre with cardboard axes. Weird. **82m/C VHS, Beta.** Cash Flagg, Liz Renay, Brick Bardo, Carolyn Brandt, Atlas King; **D:** Ray Dennis Steckler. NO

Thrill of a Romance ♘♘ 1945 Johnson, an Army hero, meets Williams, a swimming instructor of all things, at a resort in the Sierra Nevadas. The only problem is that she's married. Typical swim-romance vehicle. ♫Please Don't Say No, Say Maybe; I Should Care; Lonely Night; Vive L'Amour; Schubert's Serenade; The Thrill of a Romance. **105m/C VHS.** Esther Williams, Van Johnson, Frances Gifford, Henry Travers, Spring Byington, Lauritz Melchior; **D:** Richard Thorpe. MGM

The Thrill of It All! ♘♘½ 1963 An average housewife becomes a star of television commercials, to the dismay of her chauvinist husband, a gynecologist. Fast and funny, with numerous acidic jokes about television sponsors and programs. **108m/C VHS, Beta.** James Garner, Doris Day, Arlene Francis, Edward Andrews, Carl Reiner, Elliott Reid, Reginald Owen, ZaSu Pitts; **D:** Norman Jewison; **W:** Carl Reiner; **C:** Russell Metty. USH

Thrilled to Death ♘½ 1988 (R) An utterly naive husband and wife get caught in the middle of a lethal game when they befriend a scheming couple. **90m/C VHS.** Blake Bahner, Rebecca Lynn, Richard Maris, Christine Moore; **D:** Chuck Vincent. REP

Thrillkill ♘ 1984 A young girl is enmeshed in a multi-million-dollar burglary scheme after her computer-whiz/embezzler sister disappears. **88m/C VHS, Beta.** Robin Ward, Gina Massey, Anthony Kramroither; **D:** Anthony D'Andrea.

Throne of Blood ♘♘♘♘ Kumonosujo, Kumonosu-djo; Cobweb Castle; The Castle of the Spider's Web 1957 Kurosawa's masterful adaptation of "Macbeth" transports the story to medieval Japan and the world of the samurai. Mifune and Chiaki are warriors who have put down a rebellion and are to be rewarded by their overlord. On their way to his castle they meet a mysterious old woman who prophesizes that Mifune will soon rule—but his reign will be short. She is dismissed as crazy but her prophesies come to pass. So steeped in Japanese style that it bears little resemblance to the Shakespearean original, this film is an incredibly detailed vision in its own right. In Japanese with English subtitles. **105m/B VHS, Beta, LV.** JP Toshiro Mifune, Isuzu Yamada, Takashi Shimura, Minoru Chiaki, Akira Kubo; **D:** Akira Kurosawa; **W:** Hideo Oguni, Shinobu Hashimoto, Riyuzo Kikushima, Akira Kurosawa; **M:** Masaru Sato. HMV, CRC, IHF

Throne of Fire woof! 1982 A mighty hero battles the forces of evil to gain control of the powerful Throne of Fire. Dubbed. **91m/C VHS, Beta.** IT Peter McCoy, Sabrina Siani; **D:** Franco Prosperi. MGM

Through a Glass Darkly ♘♘♘ 1961 Oppressive interactions within a family sharing a holiday on a secluded island: a woman recovering from schizophrenia, her husband, younger brother, and her psychologist father. One of Bergman's most mysterious, upsetting and powerful films. In Swedish with English subtitles. Part of Bergman's Silence-of-God trilogy followed by "Winter Light" and "The Silence." **91m/B VHS, Beta.** SW Harriet Andersson, Max von Sydow, Gunnar Bjornstrand, Lars Passgard; **D:** Ingmar Bergman; **W:** Ingmar Bergman; **C:** Sven Nykvist. Academy Awards '61: Best Foreign Language Film; Nominations: Academy Awards '62: Best Story & Screenplay. NOS, NLC

Through Naked Eyes ♘♘½ 1987 Made-for-television thriller about two people who spy on each other. They witness a murder and realize that someone else is watching them. What a coincidence. **91m/C VHS, Beta.** David Soul, Pam Dawber; **D:** John Llewellyn Moxey.

Through the Breakers ✍½ 1928
Heartbroken woman suffers silently on South Pacific isle. **55m/B VHS, Beta.** Margaret Livingston, Holmes Herbert, Clyde Cook, Natalie Joyce. *GPV, FCT*

Through the Eyes of a Killer ✍✍½
1992 (R) Laurie Fisher (Helgenberger) has dumped cheating boyfriend Jerry (Pantoliano) and has declared her independence by finding a spacious but crummy New York apartment in desperate need of renovation. Enter handsome handyman Ray Bellano (Anderson), who's happy to work on the apartment—and Laurie as well. But where Laurie sees a fling, Ray sees true love, and since brooding Ray's got the prerequisite mystery past, you know Laurie's in for the shock of her life. Long-time nice guy Anderson does a credible turn as an obsessive psycho. Based on the short story "The Master Builder" by Christopher Fowler; made for TV. **CW:** Terror/violence and some sexuality. **94m/C VHS, Beta, Closed Caption.** Richard Dean Anderson, Marg Helgenberger, Joe Pantoliano, David Marshall Grant, Melinda Culea, Tippi Hedren; **D:** Peter Markle; **W:** John Pielmeier; **M:** George S. Clinton. *PAR*

Through the Olive Trees ✍✍✍ *Under the Olive Trees; Zire Darakhtan Zeyton* 1994 (G) Film-within-a-film is the last of a trilogy concerned with Persian village life, following "Where Is My Friend's House?" and "And Life Goes On." Director, filming in an earthquake-ravaged village, discovers that the young bricklayer playing the bridegroom in his film is actually in love with the local girl who's playing the bride. However, she's turned down his real-life marriage proposal, feeling that the uneducated man is beneath her. Farsi with subtitles. It may be rated G but considering the subject matter and the fact that the film is subtitled, don't consider this one for the kiddies. **104m/C VHS.** Zarifeh Shivah, Hossein Rezai, Mohamad Ali Keshavarz, Taherek Ladania; **D:** Abbas Kiarostami; **W:** Abbas Kiarostami; **C:** Hossein Jafarian, Farhad Saba. Nominations: Independent Spirit Awards '96: Best Foreign Film. *NYR*

Throw Momma from the Train ✍✍✍ 1987 (PG-13) DeVito plays a man, henpecked by his horrific mother, who tries to persuade his writing professor (Crystal) to exchange murders. DeVito will kill Crystal's ex-wife and Crystal will kill DeVito's mother. Only mama isn't going to be that easy to get rid of. Fast-paced and entertaining black comedy. Ramsey steals the film. Inspired by Hitchcock's "Strangers on a Train." **88m/C VHS, Beta, LV, Closed Caption.** Danny DeVito, Billy Crystal, Anne Ramsey, Kate Mulgrew, Kim Greist, Branford Marsalis, Rob Reiner, Bruce Kirby; **D:** Danny DeVito; **W:** Stu Silver; **M:** David Newman. Nominations: Academy Awards '87: Best Supporting Actress (Ramsey). *ORI*

The Throwback ✍½ 1935 When Jones was a lad the townspeople accused his father of cattle rustling. When he returns as an adult he sets out to clear his father's name. **61m/B VHS.** Buck Jones, Muriel Evans, Eddie Phillips, George "Gabby" Hayes, Bryant Washburn, Paul Fix, Frank LaRue; **D:** Ray Taylor. *GPV*

Thumb Tripping ✍✍ 1972 (R) A dated '60s/hippie film. Two flower children hitchhike and encounter all kinds of other strange people in their travels on the far-out roads. **94m/C VHS, Beta.** Meg Foster, Michael Burns, Bruce Dern, Marianna Hill, Michael Conrad, Joyce Van Patten; **D:** Quentin Masters. *NLC*

Thumbelina 1982 From "Faerie Tale Theatre" comes the story of a tiny girl who gets kidnapped by a toad and a mole, but meets the man of her dreams in the nick of time. Adapted from the classic tale by Hans Christian Andersen. Made for television. **60m/C VHS, Beta, LV, Closed Caption.** Carrie Fisher, William Katt, Burgess Meredith; **D:** Michael Lindsay-Hogg. *KUI, FOX, FCT*

Thumbelina ✍✍½ *Hans Christian Andersen's Thumbelina* 1994 (G) Ornery little girl named Mia gets magically sucked into the pages of the "Thumbelina" storybook she's reading and finds all sorts of adventures. Loose adaptation of Hans Christian Andersen fairy tale from Bluth is lackluster, with acceptable songs. Not up to the level of recent Disney animated features, but pleasant enough for the kids. **86m/C VHS, Beta, LV, Letterbox, Closed Caption. D:** Don Bluth, Gary Goldman; **W:** Don Bluth; **M:** William Ross, Barry Manilow, Barry Manilow, Jack Feldman, Bruce Sussman; **V:** Jodi Benson, Gary Imhoff, Charo, Gilbert Gottfried, Carol Channing, John Hurt, Will Ryan, June Foray, Kenneth Mars. Golden Raspberry Awards '94: Worst Song ("Marry the Mole"). *WAR*

Thunder Alley ✍½ 1985 In middle America, two friends and their rock group struggle for success. One of the friends dies after an accidental overdose and the other's grief propels him to stardom. ♪Can't Look Back; Just Another Pretty Boy; Sometimes in the Night; Heart to Heart; Can You Feel My Heart Beat; Do You Feel Alright?; Danger, Danger; Summertime; Gimme Back My Heart. **102m/C VHS, Beta.** Roger Wilson, Leif Garrett, Jill Schoelen; **D:** J.S. Cardone; **W:** J.S. Cardone. *MGM*

Thunder and Lightning ✍✍ 1977 (PG) A mismatched young couple chase a truckload of poisoned moonshine. Action-packed chases ensue. Nice chemistry between Carradine and Jackson. **94m/C VHS, Beta, Closed Caption.** David Carradine, Kate Jackson, Roger C. Carmel, Sterling Holloway, Eddie Barth; **D:** Corey Allen. *FOX*

Thunder & Mud 1989 Female mud wrestlers battle over their favorite rock band. Hahn's attempt to cash in on her notoriety after the Bakker scandal. **90m/C VHS, Beta, LV.** Jessica Hahn; **D:** Penelope Spheeris. *COL*

Thunder Bay ✍✍✍ 1953 Stewart and Duryea are a pair of Louisiana wildcat oil drillers who believe there is oil at the bottom of the Gulf of Mexico off the coast of the town of Port Felicity. They decide to construct an oil platform which the shrimp fisherman of the town believe will interfere with their livelihoods. Tensions rise between the two groups and violence seems likely. Action packed, with timely storyline as modern oil drillers fight to drill in waters that have historically been off-limits. **82m/C VHS, Beta.** James Stewart, Joanne Dru, Dan Duryea, Gilbert Roland, Marcia Henderson; **D:** Anthony Mann; **W:** John Michael Hayes; **C:** William H. Daniels. *USH*

Thunder County ✍½ 1974 Federal agents and drug runners are after a group of four convicts who have just escaped from prison. **78m/C VHS, Beta.** Mickey Rooney, Ted Cassidy, Chris Robinson.

Thunder in God's Country ✍ 1951 A dishonest gambler eyes a peaceful western town as the next Vegas-like gambling capital. Before this occurs he is exposed as a cheat. **67m/B VHS, Beta.** Rex Allen, Mary Ellen Kay. *DVT*

Thunder in Paradise ✍✍½ 1993 (PG-13) R.J. Hurricane Spencer (Hogan) is a soldier of fortune who heads into Cuba to help a woman and child escape political imprisonment, using his high-tech, weapon-filled speedboat. He has to fight off a small army and manages to find a buried treasure as well. Simple-minded TV pilot. **CW:** Language, some action, and sensuality. **104m/C VHS, LV.** Hulk Hogan, Robin Weisman, Chris Lemmon, Carol Alt, Patrick Macnee, Sam Jones, Charlotte Rae; **D:** Douglas Schwartz. *THV*

Thunder in Paradise 2 ✍½ 1994 (PG) Damsel sends up a distress signal and it's the Hulkster and his pal to the rescue. Unfortunately, their commando raid fails and now they need an escape plan. From the syndicated TV series. **90m/C VHS, Closed Caption.** Hulk Hogan, Chris Lemmon, Carol Alt, Patrick Macnee; **D:** Douglas Schwartz. *THV*

Thunder in Paradise 3 ✍½ 1994 (PG-13) Hogan is on a top secret mission to capture a drug lord who's holding his daughter hostage. **88m/C VHS.** Hulk Hogan. *THV*

Thunder in the City ✍✍✍ 1937 Robinson is an intense American promoter in the sales game who is sent to London by his employers to learn a more subdued way of doing business. Instead, he meets a pair of down-on-their-luck aristocrats whose only asset is an apparently worthless Rhodesian mine. Robinson, however, comes up with a way to promote the mine and get enough capital together to make it profitable. Good satire with Robinson well cast. Robinson wasn't taken with the script in its original form and persuaded his friend, playwright Robert Sherwood, to re-write it. **85m/B VHS, Beta.** *GB* Edward G. Robinson, Nigel Bruce, Ralph Richardson, Constance Collier; **D:** Marion Gering; **M:** Miklos Rozsa. *NOS, DVT, BAR*

Thunder in the Desert ✍ 1938 A cowhand joins an outlaw gang in order to catch his uncle's killer. **56m/C VHS, Beta.** Bob Steele, Louise Stanley, Don Barclay, Charles "Blackie" King, Lew Meehan, Budd Buster; **D:** Sam Newfield. *NOS, DVT, GPV*

Thunder in the Pines ✍ 1949 Two lumberjack buddies send for the same French girl to marry, unbeknownst to each other. When she arrives, the dismayed men agree to a contest to see who will marry her. Meanwhile the French girl falls for the local saloon owner and his jilted girlfriend vows to get even. She does, with the help of the lumberjacks. **61m/B VHS, Beta, LV.** Denise Darcel, George Reeves, Ralph Byrd, Lyle Talbot, Michael Whalen, Roscoe Ates, Vince Barnett; **D:** Robert Edwards. *NO*

Thunder Mountain ✍½ 1935 Zane Grey's novel about two prospectors who are bushwhacked on their way to file a claim comes to life on the screen. **56m/B VHS, Beta.** George O'Brien. *DVT, HHE, MLB*

Thunder Over Texas ✍ 1934 The cowboy hero gets embroiled in a railroad scandal that involves a kidnapping. Directed by Edgar G. Ulmer, who used the alias John Warner because he was moonlighting. His first western; previously he was best known for "The Black Cat." **52m/B VHS, Beta.** Marion Shilling, Helen Westcott, Victor Potel, Tiny Skelton; **D:** Edgar G. Ulmer. *VDM*

Thunder Pass ✍✍ 1937 Gold and greed are the motives for murder as two young brothers become separated when their wagon train is attacked and their family is slaughtered. One brother searches for the other and finds him several years later. Based on the novel "Arizona Ames" by Zane Grey. Also released as "Thunder Trail." **58m/B VHS.** Charles Bickford, Marsha Hunt, Gilbert Roland, Monte Blue; **D:** Charles T. Barton. *NOS, VDM, DVT*

Thunder Pass ✍✍ 1954 Routine story about a wagon train threatened by hostile Indians and the Army officer who leads them to safety. Based on a story by George Van Marter. **76m/B VHS.** Dane Clark, Dorothy Patrick, Andy Devine, Raymond Burr, John Carradine, Mary Ellen Kay; **D:** Frank McDonald; **W:** Tom Hubbard, Fred Eggers. *MOV*

Thunder River Feud ✍✍ 1942 The Rangebusters help two ranchers avoid a range war. Part of "The Rangebusters" series. **58m/B VHS, Beta.** Ray Corrigan, John "Dusty" King, Max Terhune. *NOS, VCN, DVT*

Thunder Road ✍✍✍ 1958 (PG) Mitchum comes home to Tennessee from Korea and takes over the family moonshine business, fighting both mobsters and federal agents. An exciting chase between Mitchum and the feds ends the movie with the appropriate bang. Robert Mitchum not only produced, wrote and starred in this best of the moonshine-running films, but also wrote the theme song "Whippoorwill" (which later became a radio hit). Mitchum's son, James, made his film debut, and later starred in a similar movie "Moonrunners." A cult favorite, still shown in many drive-ins around the country. **92m/B VHS, Beta.** Robert Mitchum, Jacques Aubuchon, Gene Barry, Keely Smith, Trevor Bardette, Sandra Knight, Jim Mitchum, Betsy Holt, Frances Koon; **D:** Arthur Ripley; **W:** Robert Mitchum. *MGM*

Thunder Run 🎦 1986 (PG-13) When a load of uranium needs to be transferred across Nevada, a retired trucker takes on the job. The trip is made more difficult since terrorists are trying to hijack the shipment to use for a bomb. 84m/C VHS, Beta. Forrest Tucker, John Ireland, John Shepherd, Jill Whitlow, Wally Ward, Cheryl Lynn; D: Gary Hudson; W: Charles Davis.

Thunder Trail 1937 Set of twins, separated by a wagon trail massacre, meet up years later on opposite sides of the law. 58m/C VHS. Gilbert Roland, Charles Bickford, Marsha Hunt, J. Carrol Naish, James Craig, Monte Blue; D: Charles T. Barton. GPV

Thunder Warrior 🎦 Thunder 1985 (R) A young Indian turns into a one-man army determined to punish the local authorities who are abusing his fellow tribe members. 84m/C VHS, Beta. Raymond Harmstorf, Bo Svenson, Mark Gregory; D: Larry Ludman. TWE

Thunder Warrior 2 🎦 1985 (PG-13) A tough Native American is provoked to violence by small-town prejudice. 114m/C VHS, Beta. IT Mark Gregory, Karen Reel, Bo Svenson; D: Larry Ludman. TWE

Thunder Warrior 3 🎦 1988 The Indian Thunder has vowed to live in peace, but forswears the oath when his wife is kidnapped and family is terrorized. Revenge is the top priority as he torments the bad guys. 90m/C VHS. Mark Gregory, John Phillip Law, Ingrid Lawrence, Werner Pochat, Horts Schon; D: Larry Ludman. IMP

Thunderball 🎦🎦½ 1965 (PG) The fourth installment in Ian Fleming's James Bond series finds 007 on a mission to thwart SPECTRE, which has threatened to blow up Miami by atomic bomb if 100 million pounds in ransom is not paid. One of the more tedious Bond entries but a big boxoffice success. Tom Jones sang the title song. Remade as "Never Say Never Again" in 1983 with Connery reprising his role as Bond after a 12-year absence. 125m/C VHS, Beta, LV, Letterbox. GB Sean Connery, Claudine Auger, Adolfo Celi, Luciana Paluzzi, Rik von Nutter, Martine Beswick, Molly Peters, Guy Doleman, Bernard Lee, Lois Maxwell, Desmond Llewelyn; D: Terence Young; W: John Hopkins, Richard Maibaum; C: Ted Moore; M: John Barry. Academy Awards '65: Best Visual Effects. MGM, TLF

Thunderbolt & Lightfoot 🎦🎦🎦 1974 (R) Eastwood is an ex-thief on the run from his former partners (Kennedy and Lewis) who believe he's made off with the loot from their last job, the robbery of a government vault. He joins up with drifter Bridges, who helps him to escape. Later, Eastwood manages to convince Kennedy he doesn't know where the money is. Bridges then persuades the men that they should plan the same heist and rob the same government vault all over again, which they do. But their getaway doesn't go exactly as planned. All-around fine acting; notable is Bridges' scene dressed in drag. First film for director Cimino. 115m/C VHS, Beta, LV, Letterbox. Clint Eastwood, Jeff Bridges, George Kennedy, Geoffrey Lewis, Gary Busey; D: Michael Cimino; W: Michael Cimino; M: Dee Barton. Nominations: Academy Awards '74: Best Supporting Actor (Bridges). MGM

Thunderground 🎦 1989 (R) A beautiful con artist teams with a fighter and together they travel to New Orleans to arrange a bout with the king of bare-knuckled fighting. 92m/C VHS, LV. Paul Coufos, Margaret Langrick, Jesse Ventura, M. Emmet Walsh; D: David Mitchell. IME

Thunderheart 🎦🎦🎦 1992 (R) Young FBI agent Kilmer is sent to an Oglala Sioux reservation to investigate a murder. He is himself part Sioux, but resents being chosen for the assignment because of it. Aided by a veteran partner (Shepard), Ray learns, professionally and personally, from a shrewd tribal police officer (well played by Greene). Set in the late '70s, the film is loosely based on actual events plaguing the violence-torn Native American community at that time. Great cinematography by Roger Deakins. Filmed on the Pine Ridge Reservation in South Dakota. Director Apted deals with the actual incidents this film is based on in his documentary about Leonard Peltier, "Incident at Oglala."CW: Language and some areas of violence. 118m/C VHS, LV. Val Kilmer, Sam Shepard, Graham Greene, Fred Ward, Fred Dalton Thompson, Sheila Tousey, Chief Ted Thin Elk, John Trudell, Dennis Banks, David Crosby; D: Michael Apted; W: John Fusco; C: Roger Deakins; M: James Horner. COL, FCT, BTV

Thundering Forest 🎦🎦 1941 Australian actioneer pitting loggers against saboteurs. ?m/C VHS. AU Frank Leighton. LOO

Thundering Gunslingers 🎦 1940 A group of gunmen terrorizing townspeople finally meet their match in this Western. 61m/B VHS, Beta. Buster Crabbe. NOS, DVT

Thundering Ninja 🎦½ 198? Three secret agents fight off an army of ninjas. Plenty of heel-to-head antics. 89m/C VHS, Beta. Bernard Geurts, Joe Redner, Klaus Mutter, Ken Kerr, Jimmy Wang Yu; D: Joseph Kong. TWE

Thundering Trail 🎦 Thunder on the Trail 1951 Two cowboys encounter plenty of trouble before they take the President's newly appointed territorial governor to his office. 55m/B VHS, Beta. Lash LaRue, Al "Fuzzy" St. John, Sally Anglim, Archie Twitchell, Ray Bennett. NOS, DVT

Thundersquad 🎦 1985 Mercenaries help a South American rebel leader rescue his kidnapped son. 90m/C VHS, Beta. Sal Borgese, Julia Fursich, Antonio Sabato Jr. NO

Thursday's Child 🎦🎦 1943 A child's success in films causes trouble for her family. Melodramatic and sappy, but Howes, as the kid, is excellent. One of Granger's early supporting roles. 95m/B VHS, Beta. GB Stewart Granger, Sally Ann Howes, Wilfred Lawson, Kathleen O'Regan, Eileen Bennett, Marianne Davis, Gerhard Kempinski, Felix Aylmer, Margaret Yarde, Vera Bogetti, Percy Walsh, Ronald Shiner; D: Rodney Ackland; W: Rodney Ackland. NOS, DVT, HEG

Thursday's Game 🎦🎦🎦 1974 (PG) Two crisis-besieged businessmen meet every Thursday, using poker as a ruse to work on their business and marital problems. Wonderful cast; intelligently written. Made for television. 99m/C VHS, Beta, LV. Gene Wilder, Ellen Burstyn, Bob Newhart, Cloris Leachman, Nancy Walker, Valerie Harper, Rob Reiner; D: James L. Brooks; W: James L. Brooks. THV

THX 1138 🎦🎦🎦 1971 (PG) In the dehumanized world of the future, people live in underground cities run by computer, are force-fed drugs to keep them passive, and no longer have names—just letter/number combinations (Duvall is THX 1138). Emotion is also outlawed and when the computer-matched couple THX 1138 and LUH 3417 discover love, they must battle the computer system to escape. George Lucas' first film, which was inspired by a student film he did at USC. The laserdisc format carries the film in widescreen. 88m/C VHS, Beta, LV, Letterbox. Robert Duvall, Donald Pleasence, Maggie McOmie; D: George Lucas; W: George Lucas; M: Lalo Schifrin. WAR, FUS

Tiara Tahiti 🎦🎦 1962 Intrigue, double-cross, romance, and violence ensue when two old army acquaintances clash in Tahiti. Very fine performances from the two leading men. 100m/C VHS, Beta. James Mason, John Mills, Claude Dauphin, Rosenda Monteros, Herbert Lom; D: Ted Kotcheff.

The Ticket 🎦🎦 1997 (PG-13) Keith Reicker (Marshall) works as a pilot for a financially ailing charter company. His marriage to CeCe (Doherty) is rocky but when Keith wins a lottery worth $23 million, he's certain his life has finally turned around. He persuades CeCe and their 13-year-old son to fly with him and collect the money but the plane is sabotaged. Now they must not only survive the wilderness but whoever is out to steal the ticket and make certain the Reickers don't get out alive. Cable thriller. 88m/C VHS, Closed Caption. James Marshall, Shannen Doherty, Heidi Swedberg. PAR

Ticket of Leave Man 🎦🎦 1937 London's most dangerous killer fronts a charitable organization designed to help reform criminals. It actually steers them into a crime syndicate that cheats philanthropists out of their fortunes. 71m/B VHS, Beta. GB Tod Slaughter, John Warwick, Marjorie Taylor. VYY, SNC

Ticket to Heaven 🎦🎦🎦 1981 (PG) A young man, trying to deal with the painful breakup of a love affair, falls under the spell of a quasi-religious order. His friends and family, worried about the cult's influence, have him kidnapped in order for him to be de-programmed. Mancuso is excellent, as are his supporting players Rubinek and Thomson. 109m/C VHS, Beta. CA Nick Mancuso, Meg Foster, Kim Cattrall, Saul Rubinek, R.H. Thomson, Jennifer Dale, Guy Boyd; D: Ralph L. Thomas; W: Anne Cameron. Genie Awards '82: Best Actor (Mancuso), Best Film, Best Supporting Actor (Rubinek). MGM

Ticket to Tomahawk 🎦🎦½ 1950 A gunslinger is hired by a stagecoach company to sabotage a railroad. Look for Marilyn Monroe as a chorus girl in a musical number. 90m/C VHS. Anne Baxter, Rory Calhoun, Walter Brennan, Charles Kemper, Connie Gilchrist, Arthur Hunnicutt, Victor Sen Yung; D: Richard Sale. FXL

Tickle Me 🎦½ 1965 An unemployed rodeo star finds work at an all-girl health spa and dude ranch. He falls in love with a young lady who has a treasure map and keeps her safe from the evil men who want her fortune. For die-hard Elvis fans only. ♫ (It's a) Long, Lonely Highway; Night Rider; It Feels So Right; Dirty, Dirty Feeling; (Such an) Easy Question; Put the Blame on Me; I'm Yours; I Feel That I've Known You Forever; Slowly but Surely. 90m/C VHS, Beta. Elvis Presley, Julie Adams, Jack Mullaney; D: Norman Taurog. FOX, MVD

Ticks 🎦½ Infested 1993 (R) Mammoth mutant killer insects terrorize a Northern California campground! The predatory woodticks are the victims of steroids dumped in the water supply and a group of unwary teen campers fall prey to their deadly venom! And if that's not bad enough, a forest fire breaks out, trapping the teens! 85m/C VHS, LV, Closed Caption. Ami Dolenz, Rosalind Allen, Alfonso Ribeiro, Peter Scolari; D: Tony Randel. REP

Tidal Wave 🎦½ Nippon Chinbotsu; The Submersion of Japan; Japan Sinks 1975 (PG) Scientists discover that Japan is slowly sinking and order the island to be evacuated. Originally a popular Japanese production, the American version is a poorly dubbed, re-edited mess. 82m/C VHS. JP Lorne Greene, Keiju Kobayashi, Rhonda Leigh Hopkins, Hiroshi Fujioka, Shiro Moriana; D: Andrew Meyer.

The Tide of Life 🎦🎦 Catherine Cookson's The Tide of Life 1996 TV adaptation of Catherine Cookson's novel finds young Emily Kennedy entering service as a maid to the McGilby family and weathering various tragedies, romantic and otherwise. 156m/C VHS. GB Gillian Kearney, Ray Stevenson, John Bowler, James Purefoy, Diana Hardcastle. WMI, PBS

Tides of War 🎦 1990 In the twilight of the second world war, a German officer begins to question his role in a proposed missile attack on Washington in light of the S.S. brutality he witnesses. 90m/C VHS. Yvette Heyden, Rodrigo Obregon, David Soul, Bo Svenson; D: Neil Rossati. NO

Tidy Endings 🎦½ 1988 A man who died from AIDS leaves behind his male lover and his ex-wife. The two form a friendship as they both try to cope with the man's death. Based on the play by Fierstein. 54m/C VHS, Beta. Harvey Fierstein, Stockard Channing; D: Gavin Millar; W: Harvey Fierstein.

Tie Me Up! Tie Me Down! 🎦🎦½ Atame 1990 (NC-17) A young psychiatric patient kidnaps a former porno actress he has always had a crush on, and holds her captive, certain that he can convince her to love him. Black comedy features a fine cast and is well directed. At least one fairly explicit sex scene and the bondage theme caused the film to be X-rated, although it was originally released unrated by the distributor. In

Spanish with English subtitles. *CW:* Adult situations; substance abuse, nudity, violence, and sexual situations. 105m/C VHS, LV, Letterbox *SR* Victoria Abril, Antonio Banderas, Loles Leon, Francesco Rabal, Julieta Serrano, Maria Barranco, Rossy de Palma; *D:* Pedro Almodovar; *W:* Pedro Almodovar; *C:* Jose Luis Alcaine; *M:* Ennio Morricone. COL

The Tie that Binds 🐾 1995 (R) Insipid thriller is a cheap imitation of its cousin, "The Hand that Rocks the Cradle" (made by the same producers), but what the former movie did to the nanny business, this flick does to a whole genre. Leanne and John Netherwood (Hannah and Carradine) are psycho parents out to reclaim their daughter from the lame-brain yuppie couple (Spano and Kelly) who adopted her. Out of all the children there, they choose the one who likes to sleep with a butcher knife under her pillow. Duh! Every "family in danger from psychotic" cliche is employed in a vain attempt to build suspense for the silly conclusion. Dismal directorial debut of screenwriter Strick. *CW:* Strong terror/violence; language; scene of sexuality. 98m/C VHS, LV, Closed Caption. Daryl Hannah, Keith Carradine, Moira Kelly, Vincent Spano, Julia Devin, Ray Reinhardt, Cynda Williams; *D:* Wesley Strick; *W:* Michael Auerbach; *C:* Bobby Bukowski; *M:* Graeme Revell. MAX

Tiefland 🐾🐾½ 1944 Melodrama based on the libretto for D'Albert's opera about a gypsy dancer and her loves. Unreleased until 1954, this film is the last of Riefenstahl's career; she subsequently turned to still photography. In German with English subtitles. 98m/B VHS, Beta. *GE* Leni Riefenstahl, Franz Eichberger, Bernard Minetti, Maria Koppenhofer, Luise Rainer; *D:* Leni Riefenstahl. NOS, FCT, GLV

Tiffany Jones 🐾 1975 (R) Tiffany Jones is a secret agent who has information that presidents and revolutionaries are willing to kill for. 90m/C VHS, Beta. Anouska Hempel, Ray Brooks, Eric Pohlmann, Martin Benson, Susan Sneers; *D:* Pete Walker. MON

Tiger and the Pussycat 🐾🐾½ *Il Tigre* 1967 (R) A successful Italian businessman's infatuation with an attractive American art student leads him to marital and financial woes. 110m/C VHS, Beta. Ann-Margret, Vittorio Gassman, Eleanor Parker; *D:* Dino Risi. HHE

Tiger Bay 🐾🐾🐾 1959 A young Polish sailor, on leave in Cardiff, murders his unfaithful girlfriend. Lonely ten-year-old Gillie sees the crime and takes the murder weapon, thinking it will make her more popular with her peers. Confronted by a police detective, she convincingly lies but eventually the sailor finds Gillie and kidnaps her, hoping to keep her quiet until he can get aboard his ship. A delicate relationship evolves between the child and the killer as she tries to help him escape and the police close in. Marks Hayley Mills' first major role and one of her finest performances. 107m/B VHS, Beta. *GB* John Mills, Horst Buchholz, Hayley Mills, Yvonne Mitchell, Megs Jenkins, Anthony Dawson, Kenneth Griffith, Michael Anderson Jr.; *D:* J. Lee Thompson; *W:* John Hawkesworth; *C:* John Hawkesworth; *M:* Laurie Johnson. PAR

Tiger Claws 🐾½ 1991 (R) The pretty, petite Rothrock has been called the female Bruce Lee. Perhaps, but at least he got a good script every once in a while. This time Rothrock's a kung-fu cop investigating the strange ritual-murders of martial-arts champions. *CW:* Language and violence. 93m/C VHS, Beta, LV, Closed Caption. Cynthia Rothrock, Bolo Yeung, Jalal Merhi; *D:* Kelly Markin. USH

Tiger Fangs 🐾½ 1943 When Nazis threaten the Far East rubber production with man-eating tigers, real-life big game hunter Frank Buck comes to the rescue. 57m/B VHS. Frank Buck, June Duprez, Duncan Renaldo; *D:* Sam Newfield. SNC, NOS, DVT

Tiger Heart 🐾🐾½ 1996 (PG-13) Teenaged karate champ Eric Chase (Roberts) is looking forward to a lazy summer with girlfriend Stephanie (Lyons) before heading off to college. But when

his neighborhood comes under attack from an unscrupulous developer and Stephanie runs afoul of his goons, Eric decides to take action. *CW:* Martial arts violence and menace. 90m/C VHS, Closed Caption. Ted Jan Roberts, Jennifer Lyons, Robert LaSardo, Carol Potter, Timothy Williams; *D:* Georges Chamchoum; *W:* William Applegate Jr.; *M:* John Gonzalez. PMH

Tiger Joe 🐾 1985 There's trouble in Southeast Asia, and the U.S military confuses things even more. 96m/C VHS. Alan Collins, David Warbeck; *D:* Anthony (Antonio Margheriti) Dawson. ART

Tiger of the Seven Seas 🐾🐾 1962 A female pirate takes over her father's command and embarks on adventures on the high seas. Generous portions of action, intrigue, and romance. Sequel to "Queen of the Pirates." 90m/C VHS. *IT FR* Gianna Maria Canale, Anthony Steel, Grazia Maria Spina, Ernesto Calindri; *D:* Luigi Capuano. NO

Tiger Town 🐾🐾½ 1983 (G) A baseball player, ending an illustrious career with the Detroit Tigers, sees his chance of winning a pennant slipping away. A young fan, however, proves helpful in chasing that elusive championship. Made for the Disney cable station. 76m/C VHS, Beta. Roy Scheider, Justin Henry, Ron McLarty, Bethany Carpenter, Noah Moazezi; *D:* Alan Shapiro; *C:* Robert Elswit. DIS

A Tiger Walks 🐾🐾½ 1964 A savage tiger escapes from a circus and local children start a nationwide campaign to save its life. Notable for its unflattering portrayal of America's heartland and small town dynamics. Radical departure from most Disney films of the period. 88m/C VHS, Beta. Sabu, Pamela Franklin, Brian Keith, Vera Miles, Kevin Corcoran, Peter Brown, Una Merkel, Frank McHugh, Edward Andrews; *D:* Norman Tokar; *M:* Buddy Baker. DIS

Tiger Warsaw 🐾½ *The Tiger* 1987 (R) A young man returns to the town where he once lived, before he shot his father. He hopes to sort out his life and repair family problems. Muddled and sappy. 92m/C VHS, Beta, LV. Patrick Swayze, Barbara Williams, Piper Laurie, Bobby DiCicco, Kaye Ballard, Lee Richardson, Mary McDonnell; *D:* Amin Q. Chaudhri. COL

Tigers in Lipstick 🐾½ *Wild Beds* 1980 (R) Seven short vignettes featuring the beautiful actresses as aggressive women and the men that they influence. 88m/C VHS, Beta. *IT* Laura Antonelli, Monica Vitti, Ursula Andress, Sylvia Kristel; *D:* Luigi Zampa. MON

A Tiger's Tale 🐾½ 1987 (R) A middle-aged divorced nurse begins an affair with her daughter's ex-boyfriend. 97m/C VHS, Beta, LV, Closed Caption. Ann-Margret, C. Thomas Howell, Charles Durning, Kelly Preston, Ann Wedgeworth, Tim Thomerson, Steven Kampmann, Traci Lind, Angel Tompkins; *D:* Peter Douglas; *C:* Tony Pierce-Roberts. NO

Tigershark 🐾 1987 (R) A martial arts expert goes to Southeast Asia to rescue his girlfriend, who has been kidnapped by communist forces and held captive for arms and ammunition. Strictly for fans of the martial arts. 97m/C VHS, Beta. Mike Stone, John Quade, Pamela Bryant; *D:* Emmett Alston; *W:* Ivan Rogers. NO

Tight Spot 🐾🐾🐾 1955 Been-around-the-block model Sherry Conley (Rogers) is serving time for a crime she didn't commit when she's offered a deal by U.S. attorney Lloyd Hallett (Robinson) if she'll testify against mob boss Benjamin Costain (Greene). But since no other potential witness lived to the trial date, Sherry's against cooperating. However, Hallett puts her up in a hotel with bodyguard Vince Striker (Keith) in hopes she'll change her mind. But Costain has a lot of clout and is determined to get to Sherry. Rogers gives an excellent performance in a dramatic role with fine support from the rest of the cast. 97m/B VHS. Ginger Rogers, Edward G. Robinson, Brian Keith, Lorne Greene, Katherine Anderson; *D:* Phil Karlson; *W:* William Bowers; *C:* Burnett Guffey; *M:* George Duning. COL

Tightrope 🐾🐾🐾 1984 (R) Police inspector Wes Block pursues a killer of prostitutes in New Orleans' French Quarter. The film is notable both as a thriller and as a fascinating vehicle for Eastwood, who experiments with a disturbing portrait of a cop with some peculiarities all his own. 115m/C VHS, Beta, LV, Closed Caption. Clint Eastwood, Genevieve Bujold, Dan Hedaya, Jennifer Beck, Alison Eastwood, Randi Brooks, Regina Richardson, Jamie Rose; *D:* Richard Tuggle; *C:* Bruce Surtees; *M:* Lennie Niehaus. WAR, TLF

The Tigress 🐾½ 1993 (R) In 1920s Berlin two con artists set out to scam a rich American using sex as a lure. Things don't go as planned. Also available in an unrated version. *CW:* Language and sexuality. 89m/C VHS, LV, Closed Caption. Valentina Vargas, James Remar, George Peppard. THV

Til There Was You 🐾½ 1996 (PG-13) You know what most great romance movies have in common? The couples actually meet each other before the end of the movie. Not here. That's one of the reasons this one isn't even good. Ghostwriter Gwen (Tripplehorn) and architect Nick (McDermott), although seemingly destined for one another, have more near-misses than a drunken, near-sighted airline pilot. They're shown in the same room, in adjoining rooms, leaving a room as soon as the other enters, etc., etc. Meanwhile, minor characters appear, speak some ham-fisted dialogue and then disappear. This happens for 20 years. Then they meet and the movie is (thankfully) over. Parker, however, does an excellent job as a rehab-addicted former child star who has ties to both characters. Feature directorial debut for Winant. *CW:* Sensuality, language and drug references. 113m/C VHS, Closed Caption. Dylan McDermott, Sarah Jessica Parker, Jeanne Tripplehorn, Jennifer Aniston, Ken Olin, Craig Bierko, Nina Foch, Alice Drummond, Christine Ebersole, Michael Tucker, Patrick Malahide; *D:* Scott Winant; *W:* Winnie Holzman; *C:* Bobby Bukowski; *M:* Miles Goodman, Terence Blanchard. PAR

Tilai 🐾🐾 *The Law* 1990 When Saga returns to his African village after a long absence, it's to discover that his young fiancee, Nogma, has been forced into marriage with his own father. According to his tribe's code of honor Saga can do nothing but love won't be denied and they begin an affair, which is deemed incestuous by the village. So Saga and Nogma flee, hoping to live out of the reach of tribal law. 81m/C VHS. *D:* Idrissa Ouedraogo. Cannes Film Festival '90: Grand Jury Prize. NYF

Till Death Do Us Part 🐾½ 1972 (PG) Three married couples spend a weekend at a counseling retreat, unaware that the proprietor is a murderous maniac. 77m/C VHS, Beta. James Keach, Claude Jutra, Matt Craven; *D:* Timothy Brand. VES

Till Death Do Us Part 🐾🐾 1992 (R) An ex-cop turns into an evil killer who seduces unsuspecting women and murders them for their insurance money. Contains footage not seen in the TV movie. Based on a true story and the book by Vincent Bugliosi. *CW:* Violence and sexual scene. 93m/C VHS, Beta. Treat Williams, Arliss Howard, Rebecca Jenkins; *D:* Yves Simoneau. TRI

Till Marriage Do Us Part 🐾🐾½ *Dio Mio, Come Sono Caduta in Basso; How Long Can You Fall?* 1974 (R) An innocent couple discovers on their wedding night that they are really brother and sister. Since they can't in good conscience get a divorce or consummate their marriage, they must seek sexual gratification elsewhere. Antonelli is deliciously tantalizing in this silly satire. In Italian with English subtitles. 97m/C VHS, Beta, LV. *IT* Laura Antonelli, Alberto Lionello, Jean Rochefort, Michele Placido, Karin Schubert; *D:* Luigi Comencini. VES

Till Murder Do Us Part 🐾🐾½ *A Woman an Scorned: The Betty Broderick Story* 1992 (PG-13) Based on the true story of Betty Broderick, an obsessively devoted wife and mother whose husband leaves her for another woman. Even after a bitter divorce, Betty refuses to let go. Until she commits murder. Made for television. **95m/C VHS.** Meredith Baxter, Stephen Collins, Michelle Johnson, Kelli Williams, Stephen Root; *D:* Dick Lowry. *NHO*

Till the Clouds Roll By 🎭🎭½ 1946
An all-star, high-gloss musical biography of songwriter Jerome Kern, that, in typical Hollywood fashion, bears little resemblance to the composer's life. Filled with wonderful songs from his Broadway hit. ♫Showboat Medley; Till the Clouds Roll By; Howja Like to Spoon with Me?; The Last Time I Saw Paris; They Didn't Believe Me; I Won't Dance; Why Was I Born?; Who?; Sunny. **137m/C VHS, Beta, LV.** Robert Walker, Van Heflin, Judy Garland, Frank Sinatra, Lucille Bremer, Kathryn Grayson, June Allyson, Dinah Shore, Lena Horne, Virginia O'Brien, Tony Martin; *D:* Richard Whorf; *C:* Harry Stradling. *CNG, NOS, MGM*

Till the Clouds Roll By/A Star Is Born 🎭🎭🎭 1946
Ostensibly concerns the life and career of songwriter Jerome Kern. Highlighted by stellar performances from a number of musical stars of the day. Maudlin and unconcerned with factual accuracy, the film nonetheless is an exuberant celebration of Kern's talent. **249m/C VHS, Beta.** Judy Garland, Frank Sinatra, Robert Walker, Fredric March, Janet Gaynor, Andy Devine, Lionel Stander, Franklin Pangborn, Van Heflin, Lucille Bremer, Kathryn Grayson, Lena Horne, Tony Martin, Angela Lansbury, Dinah Shore, Virginia O'Brien, Cyd Charisse, Adolphe Menjou; *D:* William A. Wellman, Richard Whorf. *DVT*

Till the End of the Night 🎭½ 1994 (R)
D'arcy (Enos) is an ex-con who will do anything to get back his ex-wife Diana Davenport (Lang) and it doesn't matter that she has a new husband, John (Valentine) and two kids. D'arcy manages to kidnap Diana and it's up to John to save his wife. **90m/C VHS.** John Enos, Katherine Kelly Lang, Scott Valentine, David Keith; *D:* Larry Brand; *W:* Larry Brand. *COL*

Till the End of Time 🎭🎭½ 1946
Three GIs have trouble adjusting to civilian life in their home town after WWII. Fine performances and excellent pacing. Popular title song. Adapted from "They Dream of Home" by Niven Busch. **105m/C VHS, Beta, LV.** Robert Mitchum, Guy Madison, Bill Williams, Dorothy McGuire, William Gargan, Tom Tully; *D:* Edward Dmytryk. *TTC*

Till There was You 🎭 1991 (PG-13)
A struggling musician travels to a faraway tropical isle to solve the mystery of his brother's death. **94m/C VHS, Closed Caption.** Mark Harmon, Deborah Kara Unger, Jeroen Krabbe, Shane Briant; *D:* John Seale; *M:* Graeme Revell. *USH*

Tillie Wakes Up 🎭🎭½ 1917
Third in the Tillie series, following "Tillie's Punctured Romance" and "Tillie's Tomato Surprise." Tillie (Dressler) decides she needs a little fun in her life so she asks her hen-pecked neighbor Mr. Pipkin (Hines) to spend the day with her on Coney Island. **48m/B VHS.** Marie Dressler, Johnny Hines, Frank Beamish, Ruby de Remer; *D:* Harry Davenport; *W:* Frances Marion. *GPV*

Tillie's Punctured Romance 🎭🎭 1914
The silent comedy which established Chaplin and Dressler as comedians. Chaplin, out of his Tramp character, is the city slicker trying to put one over on farm girl Dressler, who pursues revenge. First feature length comedy film. Followed by "Tillie's Tomato Surprise" and "Tillie Wakes Up," which starred Dressler but not Chaplin. **73m/B VHS, Beta, LV.** Charlie Chaplin, Marie Dressler, Mabel Normand, Mack Swain, Chester Conklin; *D:* Mack Sennett. *NOS, CCB, HHT*

Tilt 🎭 1978 (PG)
Flimsy storyline concerns a young runaway's adventures with an aspiring rock star. Shields' pinball expertise eventually leads her to a match against pinball champ Durning. **111m/C VHS.** Charles Durning, Ken Marshall, Brooke Shields, Geoffrey Lewis; *D:* Rudy Durand; *W:* Rudy Durand, Donald Cammell. *NO*

Tim 🎭🎭½ 1979
Follows the relationship between a handsome, mentally retarded young man and an attractive older businesswoman. Sappy storyline is redeemed by Gibson's fine debut per-

formance. Based on Colleen McCullough's first novel. **94m/C VHS, Beta.** AU Mel Gibson, Piper Laurie, Peter Gwynne, Alwyn Kurts, Pat Evison; *D:* Michael Pate. Australian Film Institute '79: Best Actor (Gibson). *WAR, OM*

Tim Tyler's Luck 1937
Lost but not forgotten serial in its 12-chapter entirety. The fearless Tim Tyler uses whatever he can to do battle with the sinister Spider Web gang. **235m/B VHS.** Frankie Thomas Jr., Frances Robinson, Al Shean, Norman Willis, Earl Douglas, Jack Mulhall, Frank Mayo, Pat O'Brien; *D:* Ford Beebe, Wyndham Gittens. *NOS, GPV, FCT*

Timber Queen 🎭🎭 1944
A WWII flier comes home and aids his best friend's widow, who must make a quota of timber or lose her sawmill to gangsters. Old-fashioned. **66m/B VHS.** Richard Arlen, Mary Beth Hughes, June Havoc, Sheldon Leonard, George E. Stone, Dick Purcell; *D:* Frank McDonald. *NOS, LOO*

Time After Time 🎭🎭🎭 1979 (PG)
In Victorian London, circa 1893, H.G. Wells is experimenting with his time machine. He discovers the machine has been used by an associate, who turns out to be Jack the Ripper, to travel to San Francisco in 1979. Wells follows to stop any further murders and the ensuing battle of wits is both entertaining and imaginative. McDowell is charming as Wells and Steenburgen is equally fine as Well's modern American love interest. **112m/C VHS, Beta, LV.** Malcolm McDowell, David Warner, Mary Steenburgen, Patti D'Arbanville, Charles Cioffi; *D:* Nicholas Meyer; *W:* Nicholas Meyer; *M:* Miklos Rozsa. *WAR*

Time Bandits 🎭🎭½ 1981 (PG)
A group of dwarves help a young boy to travel through time and space with the likes of Robin Hood, Napoleon, Agamemnon, and other time-warp playmates. Epic fantasy from Monty Python alumni. **110m/C VHS, Beta, LV, Closed Caption.** GB John Cleese, Sean Connery, Shelley Duvall, Katherine Helmond, Ian Holm, Michael Palin, Ralph Richardson, Kenny Baker, Peter Vaughan, David Warner; *D:* Terry Gilliam; *W:* Michael Palin, Terry Gilliam; *C:* Peter Biziou. *PAR*

Time Chasers 🎭🎭 1995
Nick Miller (Burch) invents a device that permits his airplane to travel through time. But, after selling his invention, he soon discovers that it has turned the future into a desolate wasteland. Now Nick must try to regain control and put things back to normal. **90m/C VHS.** Matthew Burch, Bonnie Pritchard, Peter Harrington; *D:* David Giancola. *SDE*

Time Fighters 🎭½ 1985
A time machine has the ability to travel at the speed of light from prehistoric times to the distant future. This is a great help to the Time fighters. **60m/C VHS, Beta.**

Time Flies When You're Alive 1989
A made-for-cable-television presentation of actor Linke's performance monologue detailing the traumas and experiences he and his family underwent as his wife Francesca slowly died of cancer. **79m/C VHS, Beta.** Paul Linke; *D:* Roger Spottiswoode. *HBO*

A Time for Miracles 🎭½ 1980
Dramatic biography of the first native-born American saint, Elizabeth Bayley Seton, who was canonized in 1975. Made for television. **97m/C VHS, Beta.** Kate Mulgrew, Lorne Greene, Rossano Brazzi, John Forsythe, Jean-Pierre Aumont, Milo O'Shea; *D:* Michael O'Herlihy. *NLC*

Time for Revenge 🎭🎭½ 1982
A demolitions worker attempts to blackmail his corrupt employer by claiming a workplace explosion made him speechless. He finds himself in a contest of silence and wits. In Spanish with English subtitles. **112m/C VHS, Beta.** AR Federico Luppi, Haydee Padilla, Julio de Grazia, Ulises Dumont; *D:* Adolfo Aristarain. Montreal World Film Festival '82: Best Film. *XVC, AUD*

The Time Guardian 🎭½ 1987 (PG)
Time-travelers of the future arrive in the Australian desert in 1988, intent on warning the local populace of the impending arrival of killer cyborgs from the 40th century. Muddled and confusing. **89m/C VHS, Beta, LV, 8mm.** Tom Burlinson, Carrie Fisher,

Dean Stockwell, Nikki Coghill; *D:* Brian Hannant; *W:* Brian Hannant, John Baxter; *C:* Geoff Burton. *COL, NLC*

Time Indefinite 🎭🎭 1993
Cinema verite effort once again follows filmmaker McElwee who returns to his Southern roots to confront personal tragedy by recording every moment on film. It is an emotional journey in which he discovers that his camera may not be enough to protect him from his own feelings. Moving, with occasional lapses into self-absorption. Companion film to McElwee's "Sherman's March." **117m/C VHS.** *D:* Ross McElwee; *W:* Ross McElwee. *FRF*

Time Is Running Out 🎭🎭 1952
A man races against the clock in this taut thriller. **?m/C VHS.** Dave Clark, Mike Smith, Lenny Davidson. *SNC*

Time Lock 🎭🎭 1957
An expert safecracker races against time to save a child who is trapped inside a bank's pre-set time-locked vault. Canada is the setting, although the film was actually made in England. Based on a play by Arthur Hailey. **73m/B VHS, Beta.** GB Sean Connery, Robert Beatty, Lee Patterson, Betty McDowall, Vincent Winter; *D:* Gerald Thomas. *NO*

The Time Machine 🎭🎭🎭 1960
English scientist living near the end of the 19th century invents time travel machine and uses it to travel into various periods of the future. Rollicking version of H.G. Wells' classic cautionary tale boasts Oscar-winning special effects. Remade in 1978. **103m/C VHS, Beta, LV, Letterbox.** Rod Taylor, Yvette Mimieux, Whit Bissell, Sebastian Cabot, Alan Young; *D:* George Pal; *C:* Paul Vogel. Academy Awards '60: Best Special Effects. *MGM, MLB*

Time Machine 🎭½ 1978 (G)
Yet another adaptation of H.G. Wells' classic novel about a scientist who invents a machine that enables him to travel through time. Inferior remake of the 1960 version. **99m/C VHS, Beta.** John Beck, Priscilla Barnes, Andrew Duggan; *D:* Henning Schellerup. *NO*

A Time of Destiny 🎭🎭 1988 (PG-13)
During WWII, an American soldier vows to kill his brother-in-law, who he believes caused his father's death. Meanwhile, the two men have become good friends in the army, never realizing their connection. A strange, overblown family saga from the director of "El Norte." Beautiful photography, terrific editing. **118m/C VHS, Beta, LV, 8mm.** William Hurt, Timothy Hutton, Melissa Leo, Stockard Channing, Megan Follows, Francesco Rabal; *D:* Gregory Nava; *W:* Gregory Nava, Anna Thomas; *M:* Ennio Morricone. *COL*

Time of Indifference 🎭🎭 *Gli Indifferenti;*
Les Deux Rivales 1964 Based on the novel by Alberto Moravia. Tale of the disintegration of values in 1920s Italy is unable to take full advantage of its fine cast or potentially thought-provoking themes. **84m/B VHS.** IT Rod Steiger, Shelley Winters, Claudia Cardinale, Paulette Goddard, Tomas Milian; *D:* Francesco Maselli. *GKK*

Time of the Apes 🎭 1987
A Japanese-made horror film about a woman and two kids thrust into an underground world ruled by intelligent gorillas. **98m/C VHS, Beta.** JP *CEL*

Time of the Gypsies 🎭🎭🎭 *Dom Za Vesanje* 1990 (R)
Acclaimed Yugoslavian saga about a homely, unlucky Gypsy boy who sets out to steal his way to a dowry large enough to marry the girl of his dreams. Beautifully filmed, magical, and very long. In the Gypsy language, Romany, it's the first feature film made in the Gypsy tongue. **136m/C VHS, Beta, LV.** YU Davor Dujmovic, Sinolicka Trpkova, Ljubica Adzovic, Hunsija Hasimovic, Bora Todorovic; *D:* Emir Kusturica. Cannes Film Festival '89: Best Director (Kusturica). *COL*

The Time of Their Lives 🎭🎭½ *The Ghost Steps Out* 1946
A pair of Revolutionary War-era ghosts haunt a modern country estate. One of the best A & C comedies. **82m/B VHS, Beta.** Bud Abbott, Lou Costello, Marjorie Reynolds, Binnie Barnes, Gale Sondergaard, John Shelton; *D:* Charles T. Barton. *USH*

The Time of Your Life 🎬🎬🎬½ 1948
The only Cagney film that ever lost money. A simple but engaging story of people trying to live their dreams. Cagney is delightful as a barroom philosopher who controls the world around him from his seat in the tavern. Although it was not very popular with audiences at the time, the critics hailed it as an artistic achievement. Based on William Saroyan's play. 109m/B VHS. James Cagney, William Bendix, Jeanne Cagney, Broderick Crawford, Ward Bond, James Barton, Paul Draper, Natalie Schafer; **D:** H.C. Potter. NOS, VEC, HEG

Time Out for Love 🎬🎬½ Les Grandes
Personnes; The Five Day Lover 1961 An American girl travels to Paris in search of romance, but discovers more than she bargained for. In French with English subtitles. 91m/B VHS. IT FR Jean Seberg, Micheline Presle, Maurice Ronet, Francoise Prevost, Annibale Ninchi, Fernando Bruno; **D:** Jean Valere; **M:** Georges Delerue. DVT, HEG

Time Runner 🎬🎬 1992 (R) It's 2022 and the Earth is being used as target practice by alien invaders. Space captain Hamill manages to find a hole in time and slip back to 1992 where he can battle the first of the alien infiltrators and maybe change Earth's destiny. The time-travel theme (including Hamill watching his own birth) is fun and the special effects are well done. **CW:** Language and violence. 90m/C VHS, LV, Closed Caption. Mark Hamill, Brion James, Rae Dawn Chong; **D:** Michael Mazo. NLC, COL

Time Stands Still 🎬🎬🎬 1982 Two brothers experience troubled youth in Budapest. Artful, somberly executed, with American pop soundtrack. Subtitled in English. 99m/C VHS, Beta. HU Istvan Znamenak, Henrik Pauer, Aniko Ivan, Sander Soth, Peter Galfy; **D:** Peter Gothar. New York Film Critics Awards '82: Best Foreign Film. COL

Time to Die 🎬½ Seven Graves for Rogan 1983 (R) WWII victim of heinous war crimes, obsessed with revenge, stalks his prey for a final confrontation, while eluding U.S. intelligence. Disappointing despite good cast working with Mario Puzo story. 89m/C VHS, Beta. Edward Albert, Rex Harrison, Rod Taylor, Raf Vallone; **D:** Matt Cimber; **M:** Ennio Morricone.

A Time to Die 🎬½ 1991 (R) Lords plays a police photographer who, well, photographs the police. But her camera catches one in the act of murder. Routine crime thriller. **CW:** Violence and drug content and sensuality. 93m/C VHS, LV. Traci Lords, Jeff Conaway, Richard Roundtree, Bradford Bancroft, Nitchie Barrett; **D:** Charles Kanganis; **W:** Charles Kanganis; **M:** Ennio Morricone. PMH

Time to Kill Tempo di Uccidere 1989 (R) A young soldier in Africa wanders away from his camp and meets a woman whom he rapes and kills. But when he returns to his outfit he finds he can't escape his tormenting conscience. **CW:** Occasional strong language and one scene of brute sexuality. 110m/C VHS, LV, Closed Caption. Nicolas Cage, Giancarlo Giannini, Robert Liensol; **D:** Guiliano Montaldo; **W:** Furio Scarpelli; **M:** Ennio Morricone. REP

A Time to Kill 🎬🎬🎬½ 1996 (R) Powerful story of revenge, racism, and the question of justice in the "new south." John Grisham had a lot of clout when he finally sold his first and favorite novel to the movies, including veto power over the leading man—director Schumacher was for Woody Harrelson, Grisham was opposed but both finally agreed on newcomer McConaughey. He's outstanding as idealistic smalltown Mississippi lawyer Jake Brigance, called to defend anguished father Carl Lee Hailey (Jackson), who's accused of killing the rednecks who raped his young daughter. Jake's assisted by former mentor Lucien Wilbanks (Sutherland) and ambitious northern law student Ellen Roark (Bullock) against ruthless prosecutor Rufus Buckley (Spacey). Is it emotionally manipulative? You betcha. But Grisham's done well on screen and Schumacher (who also did "The Client") knows how to get the most from his cast and script. **CW:** Violence and some

graphic language. 150m/C VHS, LV, Closed Caption, DVD. Matthew McConaughey, Samuel L. Jackson, Sandra Bullock, Kevin Spacey, Donald Sutherland, Brenda Fricker, Oliver Platt, Charles S. Dutton, Kiefer Sutherland, Chris Cooper, Ashley Judd, Patrick McGoohan, Rae'ven Kelly, John Diehl, Tonea Stewart, M. Emmet Walsh, Anthony Heald, Kurtwood Smith; **D:** Joel Schumacher; **W:** Akiva Goldsman; **C:** Peter Menzies Jr.; **M:** Elliot Goldenthal. MTV Movie Awards '97: Breakthrough Performance (McConaughey); Nominations: Golden Globe Awards '97: Best Supporting Actor (Jackson); MTV Movie Awards '97: Best Female Performance (Bullock), Best Villain (Sutherland). MGM

A Time to Live 🎬½ 1985 Made-for-television adaptation of Mary Lou Weisman's "Intensive Care" about a family's adjustment to a young boy's fight with Muscular Dystrophy. Minnelli's first appearance in a television movie. 97m/C VHS. Liza Minnelli, Jeffrey DeMunn, Swoosie Kurtz, Corey Haim, Scott Schwartz; **D:** Rick Wallace; **M:** Georges Delerue. NO

A Time to Live and a Time to Die 🎬🎬 Tong Nien Wang Shi 1985 Family from southern mainland China emigrate to Taiwan in the '40s to escape from hardship and are unable to return after the communist takeover. They find themselves cut off from their cultural heritage, and though the years pass, everyone still thinks of the mainland as home. Taiwanese with subtitles. 137m/C VHS. CH **D:** Hou Hsaio-hsien. FCT

A Time to Love & a Time to Die 🎬🎬½ 1958 Lush adaptation of Erich Maria Remarque novel about WWII German soldier who falls in love with a young girl during furlough. The two are married, only to be separated when he is forced to return to the Russian front. Sympathetic treatment of Germans opposed to Hitler's policies. Hutton's first film, credited to his real name, Dana J. Hutton. 133m/C VHS, Beta. John Gavin, Lilo (Liselotte) Pulver, Jock Mahoney, Keenan Wynn, Klaus Kinski, Jim Hutton; **D:** Douglas Sirk; **M:** Miklos Rozsa. Nominations: Academy Awards '58: Best Sound. BAR

A Time to Remember 🎬½ 1990 Sticky with sentiment, this family film tells of a boy with a gift for singing, encouraged by a priest, discouraged by his father. At one point the kid loses his voice—he probably choked on the pathos. 90m/C VHS. Donald O'Connor, Morgana King. IGP

Time Tracers 🎬½ 1997 A group of scientists, detectives, and a reporter time travel back to the Civil War and the Jurassic period to correct a glitch that could alter earth's future. El tacky production reminiscent of Saturday matinee filler that uses stock footage for its monsters. 93m/C VHS. Jeffrey Combs, Rocky Patterson, T.J. Myers, Tyler Mason; **D:** Bret McCormick. MTH

Time Trackers 🎬🎬 1988 (PG) A Roger Corman cheapie about a race through time, from present-day New York to medieval England, to recover a time machine before it alters the course of history. 87m/C VHS, Beta. Kathleen Beller, Ned Beatty, Will Shriner; **D:** Howard R. Cohen. MGM

The Time Travelers 🎬🎬 Time Trap 1964 Scientists discover and pass through a porthole leading to earth's post-armageddon future where they encounter unfriendly mutants. Frightened, they make a serious effort to return to the past. Remade as "Journey to the Center of Time." 82m/C VHS, Beta. Preston Foster, Phil Carey, Merry Anders, John Hoyt, Joan Woodbury, Dolores Wells, Dennis Patrick; **D:** Ib Melchior. NO

Time Troopers 🎬 Morgen Grauen; Morning Terror 1989 (R) In another post-nuke society, special police must execute anyone who has misused their allotted "energy clips" for illicit behavior. Dime-store budget sci-fi. 90m/C VHS, Beta. AT Albert Fortell, Hannelore Elsner; **D:** L.E. Neiman.

Time Walker 🎬 1982 (PG) An archaeologist unearths King Tut's coffin in California. An alien living inside is unleashed and terrorizes the public. 86m/C VHS, Beta. Ben Murphy, Nina Axelrod, Kevin Brophy, James Karen, Austin Stoker; **D:** Tom Kennedy; **W:** Tom Friedman, Karen Levitt; **M:** Richard Band. NLC

Time Without Pity 🎬🎬½ 1957 Anti-capital punishment plea finds desperate alcoholic David Graham (Redgrave) discovering that his son Alec (McCowen) is about to be executed for murder. But David doesn't believe in the boy's guilt and has 24 hours to find the real killer. The audience knows Alec is innocent from the get-go, making for a certain suspense. Based on the play "Someone Waiting" by Emlyn Williams. 88m/B VHS. GB Michael Redgrave, Alec McCowen, Ann Todd, Leo McKern, Peter Cushing, Renee Houston, Paul Daneman, Lois Maxwell, Richard Wordsworth, George Devine, Joan Plowright; **D:** Joseph Losey; **W:** Ben Barzman; **C:** Freddie Francis; **M:** Tristram Cary. HMV, TVC

Timebomb 🎬🎬½ 1991 (R) When someone attempts to kill Biehn, he turns to a beautiful psychiatrist for help. She triggers flashbacks that send her hunted patient on a dangerous, perhaps deadly, journey into his past. **CW:** Occasional strong language, graphic violence, and strong sensuality. 96m/C VHS, Beta, LV, Closed Caption. Michael Biehn, Patsy Kensit, Tracy Scoggins, Robert Culp, Richard Jordan, Raymond St. Jacques, Jim Maniaci, Billy Blanks, Ray "Boom Boom" Mancini, Steven J. Oliver; **D:** Avi Nesher; **W:** Avi Nesher; **M:** Patrick Leonard. MGM

Timecop 🎬🎬½ 1994 (R) "Terminator" rip-off is fodder for Van Damme followers with lots of action and special effects (you weren't expecting acting too). 2004 policeman Max Walker (Van Damme) must travel back in time to prevent corrupt politician Aaron McComb (Silver) from altering history for personal gain. It's also Walker's chance to alter his personal history since his wife Melissa (Sara) was killed in an explosion he can now prevent. Futuristic thriller based on a Dark Horse comic. 98m/C VHS, LV, Closed Caption, DVD. Jean-Claude Van Damme, Ron Silver, Mia Sara, Bruce McGill, Scott Lawrence, Kenneth Welsh, Gabrielle Rose, Duncan Fraser, Ian Tracey, Gloria Reuben, Scott Bellis, Jason Schombing, Kevin McNulty, Sean O'Byrne, Malcolm Stewart, Alfonso Quijada, Gien Roald, Theodore Thomas; **D:** Peter Hyams; **W:** Mark Verheiden, Gary De Vore. USH

Timemaster 🎬🎬½ 1995 (PG-13) The orphaned 12-year-old Jesse (Cameron-Glickenhaus) dreams his parents are alive in another time, so he asks inventor Isaiah (Morita) for help. The duo discover Jesse's parents are being held hostage by a galactic dictator (Dorn), who's using them in sinister virtual-reality games and Jesse must time-travel to rescue them. **CW:** Some strong action-adventure violence. 100m/C VHS, LV, Closed Caption. Jesse Cameron-Glickenhaus, Noriyuki "Pat" Morita, Joanna Pacula, Michael Dorn, Duncan Regehr, Michelle Williams; **D:** James Glickenhaus; **W:** James Glickenhaus. USH

Timepiece 🎬🎬 1965 This tape features one of Jim Henson's earlier films about an overworked, young executive. 10m/C VHS, Beta. Jim Henson. FLL

Timerider 🎬½ The Adventure of Lyle Swan 1983 (PG) Motorcyclist riding through the California desert is accidentally thrown back in time to 1877, the result of a scientific experiment that went awry. There he finds no gas stations and lots of cowboys. Co-written and co-produced by Michael Nesmith, best known for his days with the rock group "The Monkees." 93m/C VHS, Beta, LV. Fred Ward, Belinda Bauer, Peter Coyote, Richard Masur, Ed Lauter, L.Q. Jones, Tracey Walter; **D:** William Dear; **W:** William Dear. NO

Times of Harvey Milk 1983 A powerful and moving documentary about the life and career of San Francisco supervisor and gay activist Harvey Milk. The film documents the assassination of Milk and Mayor George Moscone by Milk's fellow supervisor, Dan White. Highly acclaimed by both critics and audiences, the film gives an honest and direct look at the murder and people's reactions. News footage of the murders and White's trial is included. 90m/C VHS, Beta, LV. **D:** Robert Epstein. Academy Awards '83: Best Feature Documentary. TPV

Times Square 1980 (R) A 13-year-old girl learns about life on her own when she teams up with a defiant, anti-social child of the streets. Unappealing and unrealistic, the film features a New Wave music score. 111m/C VHS, Beta. Tim Curry, Trini Alvarado, Robin Johnson, Peter Coffield, Elizabeth Pena, Anna Maria Horsford; *D:* Allan Moyle; *W:* Jacob Brackman. NO

Times to Come 🎞🎞🎞 *Lo Que Vendra* 1981 Taut thriller reminiscent of bleak futuristic movies like "Clockwork Orange." Three people try to survive in a desolate, aggressive, and unstable future. In Spanish with English subtitles. 98m/C VHS. *AR* Hugo Soto, Juan Leyrado, Charly Garcia; *D:* Gustavo Mosquera. CCN, FCT, TPV

Timestalkers 🎞🎞½ 1987 A college professor's infatuation with a young woman is complicated by their pursuit of a criminal from the 26th century into the past. Mildly entertaining adventure. Tucker's last film. Made for television. 100m/C VHS. William Devane, Lauren Hutton, Klaus Kinski, John Ratzenberger, Forrest Tucker, Gail Youngs; *D:* Michael A. Schultz.

Tin Cup 🎞🎞🎞 1996 (R) You've got your romantic triangle, you've got your sports, you've got Costner reteamed with Shelton—"Bull Durham" on a golf course? Can lightening strike twice? Ron "Tin Cup" McAvoy (Costner) is a West Texas golf hustler who has the ability but not the steadiness to be on the pro tour. When McAvoy decides on a last-ditch effort to qualify for the U.S. Open, he turns to psychologist Dr. Molly Griswold (Russo) to get his game together. And the fact that Molly is the girlfriend of McAvoy's longtime rival—and successful PGA player—Don Simms (Johnson), well Tin Cup isn't adverse to playing for the lady's affections either. The U.S. Open scenes were filmed at Houston's Kingwood Country Club and the actors do hit their own shots. *CW:* Language and brief nudity. 133m/C VHS, LV, **Closed Caption.** Kevin Costner, Don Johnson, Rene Russo, Richard "Cheech" Marin, Linda Hart, Dennis Burkley, Rex Linn, Lou Myers, Richard Lineback, Mickey Jones; *D:* Ron Shelton; *W:* Ron Shelton, John Norville; *C:* Russell Boyd; *M:* William Ross. Nominations: Golden Globe Awards '97: Best Actor—Musical/Comedy (Costner). MGM

The Tin Drum 🎞🎞🎞🎞 *Die Blechtrommel* 1979 (R) German child in the 1920s wills himself to stop growing in response to the increasing Nazi presence in Germany. He communicates his anger and fear by pounding on a tin drum. Memorable scenes, excellent cast. In German with English subtitles. Adapted from the novel by Gunter Grass. 141m/C VHS, Beta. GE David Bennent, Mario Adorf, Angela Winkler, Daniel Olbrychski, Katharina Thalbach, Heinz Bennent, Andrea Ferreol, Charles Aznavour; *D:* Rainer Werner Fassbinder, Volker Schlondorff; *W:* Jean-Claude Carriere, Volker Schlondorff; *M:* Maurice Jarre. Academy Awards '79: Best Foreign Language Film; Cannes Film Festival '79: Best Film; Los Angeles Film Critics Association Awards '80: Best Foreign Film. KIV, GLV, AUD

Tin Man 🎞🎞½ 1983 Garage mechanic born totally deaf designs and builds a computer that can both hear and speak for him. His world is complicated, however, when a young speech therapist introduces him to new and wonderful sounds and unscrupulous and exploitative computer salesmen. Interesting premise and nice performances. 95m/C VHS, Beta. Timothy Bottoms, Deana Jurgens, Troy Donahue; *D:* John G. Thomas.

Tin Men 🎞🎞½ 1987 (R) Set in Baltimore in the 1960s, this bitter comedy begins with two aluminum-siding salesmen colliding in a minor car accident. They play increasingly savage pranks on each other until one seduces the wife of the other, ruining his marriage. Like "Diner," the movie is full of Levinson's idiosyncratic local Baltimore color. 112m/C VHS, Beta, LV, **Closed Caption.** Richard Dreyfuss, Danny DeVito, Barbara Hershey, John Mahoney, Jackie Gayle, Stan Brock, Seymour Cassel, Bruno Kirby, J.T. Walsh, Michael Tucker; *D:* Barry Levinson; *W:* Barry Levinson; *C:* Peter Sova; *M:* David Steele. TOU

Tin Pan Alley 🎞🎞½ 1940 Tin Pan Alley songwriters Oakie and Payne meet singing sisters Faye and Grable, who agree to plug their material. At first their music business thrives but when the women head off to sing in a hit London show, the business goes downhill. Since WWI has been declared, the boys enlist and wind up in England, where they get a second chance to see their gals. The first teaming of Faye and Payne, who would star together in three more films. Remade as "I'll Get By." 🎵The Sheik of Araby; You Say the Sweetest Things, Baby; America I Love You; Goodbye Broadway, Hello France; K-K-K-Katy; Moonlight Bay; Honeysuckle Rose; Moonlight and Roses. 92m/B VHS. Alice Faye, John Payne, Betty Grable, Jack Oakie, Allen Jenkins, Esther Ralston, John Loder, Elisha Cook Jr., Fred Keating, Billy Gilbert; *D:* Walter Lang; *W:* Robert Ellis, Helen Logan; *C:* Leon Shamroy; *M:* Alfred Newman. Academy Awards '40: Best Score. FXV

The Tin Soldier 🎞🎞½ 1995 (PG) Updated version of the Hans Christian Andersen story finds 12-year-old Billy (Knight) moving with his widowed mom (Sheedy) to a tough L.A. neighborhood. He's intimidated by the school bully to join a gang and smitten by a pretty girl who doesn't like his new friends. What's a guy to do? Why meet a mysterious toy shop owner (DeLuise), who gives Billy a tin soldier that magically transforms into a very real medieval knight named Yarik (Voight). Good intentions—no subtlety. Voight's directorial debut; made for cable TV. 99m/C VHS, **Closed Caption.** Trenton Knight, Ally Sheedy, Dom DeLuise, Jon Voight; *D:* Jon Voight. REP

The Tin Star 🎞🎞🎞 1957 Perkins is the young sheriff who persuades veteran bounty hunter Fonda to help him rid the town of outlaws. Excellent Mann western balances humor and suspense. 93m/B VHS, Beta. Henry Fonda, Anthony Perkins, Betsy Palmer, Neville Brand, Lee Van Cleef, John McIntire, Michel Ray; *D:* Anthony Mann; *C:* Loyal Griggs; *M:* Elmer Bernstein. Nominations: Academy Awards '57: Best Story & Screenplay. PAR, BAR

The Tingler 🎞🎞🎞 1959 Coroner Price discovers that a creepy creature is capable of growing on the human spine and increasing in size through fear. The only way to get rid of it is through constant screaming. Price takes what is probably the screen's first LSD trip and a partial color sequence fights nice red blood pouring from a faucet. One of Castle's cheesy best that originally wowed movie audiences in "Percepto" format, which consisted of installing electric buzzers under the seats for that true tingling sensation. 82m/B VHS. Vincent Price, Darryl Hickman, Judith Evelyn, Philip Coolidge, Patricia Cutts, Pamela Lincoln; *D:* William Castle; *W:* Robb White; *C:* Wilfred M. Kline. COL

Tintorera...Tiger Shark woof! *Tintorera; Tintorera...Bloody Waters* 1978 (R) Three shark hunters attempt to discover why buxom swimmers are disappearing. Phony takeoff of "Jaws." 91m/C VHS, Beta. GB MX Susan George, Fiona Lewis, Jennifer Ashley; *D:* Rene Cardona Jr.

Tiny Toon Adventures: How I Spent My Vacation 🎞🎞🎞 1991 How the tiny toons of Acme Acres spend their summer vacation in this animated adventure that spoofs several popular films and amusements. Plucky Duck and Hampton Pig journey to "Happy World Land" (a takeoff on Walt Disney World), Babs and Buster Bunny's water adventure parodies "Deliverance," there's a spoof of "The Little Mermaid," and the Road Runner even makes a cameo appearance. Parents will be equally entertained by the level of humor and the fast-paced action. Based on the Steven Spielberg TV cartoon series, this is the first made-for-home-video animated feature ever released in the United States. 80m/C VHS, Beta, LV, 8mm, **Closed Caption.** WAR

The Tioga Kid 🎞½ 1948 Dean takes on two roles here, that of a Texas Ranger and an outlaw who goes by the name of "The Tioga Kid." Andy Parker and the Plainsmen provide the cowboy tunes. 54m/B VHS. Eddie Dean, Roscoe Ates, Jennifer Holt, Dennis Moore, William "Bill" Fawcett; *D:* Ray Taylor; *W:* Ed Earl Repp. MOV

The Tip-Off 🎞🎞½ 1931 Lovable boxer (Armstrong) and vivacious girlfriend (Rogers) save less-than-bright friend from getting involved with mean mobster's girlfriend. Major chemistry between Rogers and Armstrong. 75m/B VHS. Eddie Quillan, Robert Armstrong, Ginger Rogers, Joan Peers, Ernie Adams; *D:* Albert Rogell. TTC, FCT

'Tis a Pity She's a Whore 🎞🎞½ *Addio, Fratello, Crudele* 1973 (R) A brother and sister engage in an incestuous affair. She becomes pregnant and is married off. Her husband, however, becomes infuriated when he learns of his wife's pregnancy. Photography is by Vittorio Storaro in this highly stylized drama set in Renaissance Italy. 102m/C VHS, Beta. IT Charlotte Rampling, Oliver Tobias, Fabio Testi, Antonio Falsi, Rick Battaglia, Angela Luce, Rino Imperio; *D:* Giuseppe Patroni Griffi; *M:* Ennio Morricone.

Titanic 🎞🎞🎞 1953 Hollywoodized version of the 1912 sinking of the famous luxury liner sets the scene for the personal drama of a mother (Stanwyck) who wants to flee her husband (Webb) for a new life in America. Story gets a little too melodramatic, but it's not a bad retelling of the sea tragedy. Film is quite effective in conveying the panic and the calm of the actual sinking. A 20-foot-long model of the ship was built for the re-creation of that fateful moment when the "Titanic" hit the inevitable iceberg. 98m/B VHS. Clifton Webb, Barbara Stanwyck, Robert Wagner, Richard Basehart, Audrey Dalton, Thelma Ritter, Brian Aherne; *D:* Jean Negulesco; *W:* Charles Brackett, Walter Reisch, Richard L. Breen. Academy Awards '53: Best Story & Screenplay; Nominations: Academy Awards '53: Best Art Direction/Set Decoration (B & W), Best Screenplay, Best Story. FXV

Titanic 🎞½ 1996 (PG-13) Dull and draggy TV version of the 1912 tragedy between the luxury liner and an iceberg that resulted in the deaths of more than 1000 passengers. There are the usual romantic subplots, villains, and heroes, and Scott is properly noble as the veteran captain making his last voyage before retirement. Otherwise you've seen this many times before. *CW:* Scene of sexual assault and other violent elements. 165m/C VHS. George C. Scott, Peter Gallagher, Catherine Zeta-Jones, Eva Marie Saint, Tim Curry, Roger Rees, Harley Jane Kozak, Marilu Henner, Felicity Waterman, Scott Hylands, Kevin McNulty, Malcolm Stewart; *D:* Robert Lieberman; *W:* Ross LaManna, Joyce Eliason; *C:* David Hennings; *M:* Lennie Niehaus. EVE

Titanic 🎞🎞🎞 1997 (PG-13) Skipper Cameron's mega-budget three-hour tour has had its own brushes with disaster with a mammoth budget (it's the most expensive movie ever made at $285 million) and a theatrical release that seemed unattainable. But instead of reaping hordes of criticism for what many thought was a joke, Cameron has accumulated praise and a boatload of Oscar hardware for his labor of love. A love story that happens to have the sinking of the historic ship as a backdrop, real characters and fictional characters are blended for a detailed re-enactment of the luxury liner's first and last voyage. The two lovebirds, Jack Dawson (DiCaprio) and debutante Rose Bukater (Winslet) are from different ends of the economic and social ladder. DiCaprio and Winslet are dynamic as the star-crossed lovers and make the running time less a chore to sit through. The special effects are impressive with a life-size version of the ship built just for this film. Cameron's prowess as a storyteller keeps the outcome of the ship suspenseful and tense even though the ending is no secret. Film has gone on to break boxoffice records set by "Star Wars" and "ET." *CW:* Disaster related peril and violence, nudity, sensuality and brief language. 197m/C VHS,

Closed Caption. Kate Winslet, Leonardo DiCaprio, Billy Zane, Kathy Bates, Frances Fisher, Gloria Stuart, Jonathan Hyde, Danny Nucci, David Warner, Bill Paxton, Bernard Hill Victor Garber, Suzy Amis, Bernard Fox; **D:** James Cameron; **W:** James Cameron; **C:** Russell Carpenter; **M:** James Horner. Academy Awards '97: Best Art Direction/Set Decoration, Best Cinematography, Best Costume Design, Best Director (Cameron), Best Film Editing, Best Picture, Best Song ("My Heart Will Go On"), Best Sound, Best Sound Effects Editing, Best Visual Effects, Best Original Score; Directors Guild of America Awards '97: Best Director (Cameron); Golden Globe Awards '98: Best Director (Cameron), Best Film—Drama, Best Song ("My Heart Will Go On"), Best Original Score; MTV Movie Awards '98: Best Film, Best Male Performance (DiCaprio); Screen Actors Guild Award '97: Best Supporting Actress (Stuart); Broadcast Film Critics Association Awards '97: Best Director (Cameron); Nominations: Academy Awards '97: Best Actress (Winslet), Best Makeup, Best Supporting Actress (Stuart); British Academy Awards '97: Best Cinematography, Best Costume Design, Best Director (Cameron), Best Film, Best Film Editing, Best Sound, Best Score; Golden Globe Awards '98: Best Actor (DiCaprio), Best Actress (Winslet), Best Screenplay, Best Supporting Actress (Stuart); MTV Movie Awards '98: Best Female Performance (Winslet), Best On-Screen Duo (Kate Winslet/Leonardo DiCaprio), Best Villain (Zane), Best Song ("My Heart Will Go On"), Best Kiss (Kate Winslet/Leonardo DiCaprio), Best Action Sequence; Screen Actors Guild Award '97: Best Actress (Winslet), Cast; Writers Guild of America '97: Best Original Screenplay. *PAR*

Title Shot 🎬 1981 (R) A crafty manager convinces a millionaire to bet heavily on the guaranteed loss of his heavyweight contender in an upcoming fight. He doesn't realize the boxer is too stupid to throw the fight. 88m/C VHS, Beta. Tony Curtis, Richard Gabourie, Susan Hogan, Robert Delbert; **D:** Les Rose. *ART*

Tito and Me 🎬🎬🎬 1992 Ten-year-old Zoran lives in 1954 Belgrade and is fascinated by Yugoslavian leader Marshall Tito. Crowded into a flat with his extended family, Zoran learns about volatility firsthand. Then there's romance—he has a crush on a classmate who breaks up with him when she is chosen as one of Tito's Young Pioneers, which means a two-week trip to the country. Political indoctrination means nothing but love—ahh. Debut role for the young Vojnov, who carries the weight of the movie with perfect aplomb. In Serbo-Croation with English subtitles. 104m/C VHS. *YU* Dimitrie Vojnov, Lazar Ristovski, Anica Dobra, Predrag Manojlovic, Olivera Markovic; **D:** Goran Markovic; **W:** Goran Markovic. *FXL, FCT*

TNT Jackson woof! 1975 (R) A kung fu mama searches for her brother while everyone in Hong Kong tries to kick her out of town. 73m/C VHS, Beta. Jeanne Bell; **D:** Cirio H. Santiago. *NLC*

To All a Goodnight woof! 1980 (R) Five young girls and their boyfriends are planning an exciting Christmas holiday until a mad Santa Claus puts a damper on things. Total gorefest, with few, if any, redeeming virtues. 90m/C VHS, Beta. Jennifer Runyon, Forrest Swanson, Linda Gentile, William Lover; **D:** David Hess.

To All My Friends on Shore 🎬🎬🎬 1971 A made-for-television story about a father dealing with his young son's sickle cell anemia. Fine performances, realistic script make this an excellent outing. 74m/C VHS, Beta. Bill Cosby, Gloria Foster, Dennis Hines; **D:** Gilbert Cates. *NO*

To Be or Not to Be 🎬🎬🎬½ 1942 Sophisticated black comedy set in wartime Poland. Lombard and Benny are Maria and Josef Tura, the Barrymores of the Polish stage, who use the talents of their acting troupe against the invading Nazis. The opening sequence is regarded as a cinema classic. One of Benny's finest film performances, the movie marks Lombard's final screen appearance. Classic Lubitsch. Remade in 1983. 102m/B VHS, Beta. Carole Lombard, Jack Benny, Robert Stack, Sig Rumann, Lionel Atwill, Felix Bressart, Helmut Dantine, Tom Dugan, Charles Halton; **D:** Ernst Lubitsch. National Film Registry '96;; Nominations: Academy Awards '42: Best Original Dramatic/Comedy Score. *VES, WAR*

To Be or Not to Be 🎬🎬½ 1983 (PG) In this remake of the 1942 film, Bancroft and Brooks are actors in Poland during WWII. They accidently become involved with the Polish Resistance and work to thwart the Nazis. Lots of laughs, although at times there's a little too much slapstick. 108m/C VHS, Beta, LV, Closed Caption. Mel Brooks, Anne Bancroft, Charles Durning, Jose Ferrer, Tim Matheson, Christopher Lloyd; **D:** Alan Johnson; **W:** Ronny Graham. Nominations: Academy Awards '83: Best Supporting Actor (Durning). *FOX*

To Be the Best 🎬½ 1993 (R) Eric, a member of the U.S. Kickboxing Team, lets his love for the beautiful Cheryl and his hot temper get the best of him. When a ruthless gambler threatens to kill Cheryl if Eric doesn't throw his big match, he joins with his family, fellow teammates, and most feared opponent, to set things right. 99m/C VHS, Closed Caption. Mike Worth, Martin Kove, Phillip Troy, Brittney Powell, Alex Cord, Steven Leigh; **D:** Joseph Merhi; **W:** Michael January. *PMH*

To Catch a Killer 🎬🎬🎬 1992 A chilling performance by Dennehy highlights this true-crime tale of a detective's relentless pursuit of serial killer John Wayne Gacy, who preyed on young men and hid the bodies in his home. Made for television. 95m/C VHS, LV. Brian Dennehy, Michael Riley, Margot Kidder, Meg Foster; **D:** Eric Till. *WOV*

To Catch a King 🎬🎬 1984 Garr is a singer working in Wagner's nightclub in 1940s' Lisbon. The pair becomes involved in trying to foil the Nazi plot to kidnap the vacationing Duke and Duchess of Windsor. Average made-for-cable fare. 120m/C VHS, Beta. Robert Wagner, Teri Garr, Horst Janson, Barbara Parkins, John Standing; **D:** Clive Donner; **M:** Nick Bicat.

To Catch a Thief 🎬🎬🎬 1955 On the French Riviera, a reformed jewel thief falls for a wealthy American woman, who suspects he's up to his old tricks when a rash of jewel thefts occur. Oscar-winning photography by Robert Burks, a notable fireworks scene, and snappy dialogue. A change of pace for Hitchcock, this charming comedy-thriller proved to be as popular as his other efforts. Kelly met future husband Prince Rainier during shooting in Monaco. Based on the novel by David Dodge. 103m/C VHS, Beta, LV. Cary Grant, Grace Kelly, Jessie Royce Landis, John Williams, Charles Vanel, Brigitte Auber; **D:** Alfred Hitchcock; **W:** John Michael Hayes; **C:** Robert Burks. Academy Awards '55: Best Color Cinematography; Nominations: Academy Awards '55: Best Art Direction/Set Decoration (Color), Best Costume Design (Color). *PAR, MLB, HMV*

To Catch a Yeti 🎬½ 1995 (PG) Big game hunter Meat Loaf is all set for a trip to the Himalayas when the Yeti winds up being spotted in the canyons of Manhattan (and it turns out to be very tiny). 88m/C VHS. Meat Loaf; **D:** Bob Keen. *PGV*

To Cross the Rubicon 🎬🎬½ 1991 Romantic comedy finds Kendall (Royce) getting dumped by David (Souther), her boyfriend of eight years, who then reconciles with former flame, Claire (Devon). Meanwhile, Kendall involves herself with James (Burke), a young musician, and becomes new best friends with—you guessed it—Claire. But will David and Kendall's previous relationship cause friction? 120m/C VHS. Patricia Royce, J.D. Souther, Lorraine Devon, Billy Burke; **D:** Barry Caillier; **W:** Patricia Royce, Lorraine Devon. *MTH*

To Dance with the White Dog 🎬🎬🎬 1993 (PG) Robert Samuel Peek (Cronyn) is a pecan-tree grower from rural Georgia who has been married to Cora (Tandy) for 57 years. Then she dies and their fussing daughters (Baranski and Wright) wonder how their father will survive. But Sam's increasing loneliness is checked when he befriends a stray white dog that it seems no one else can see. Based on the novel by Terry Kay. Made for television. 98m/C VHS, Closed Caption. Hume Cronyn, Jessica Tandy, Christine Baranski, Amy Wright, Esther Rolle, Harley Cross, Frank Whaley, Terry Beaver, Dan Albright, David Dwyer; **D:** Glenn Jordan; **W:** Susan Cooper; **C:** Neil Roach. *REP*

To Die For 🎬½ Dracula: The Love Story 1989 (R) A vampire stalks, woos, and snacks on a young real estate woman. 99m/C VHS, Beta, LV. Brendan Hughes, Scott Jacoby, Duane Jones, Steve Bond, Sydney Walsh, Amanda Wyss, Ava Fabian; **D:** Deran Sarafian; **W:** Leslie King; **C:** Jacques Haitkin; **M:** Cliff Eidelman.

To Die For 🎬🎬🎬 1995 (R) Beauteous, manipulative Suzanne Stone (Kidman) wants to be somebody—preferably a big TV personality—and nothing will stop her. She recruits a scruffy threesome to help her ice sweet-but-dim hubby, Larry (Dillon), even if it does means seducing aimless teenager Jimmy (Phoenix). Black comedy, loosely based on the Pamela Smart murder case and adapted from the novel by Joyce Maynard, takes on the media-obsessed culture with a wicked grin. Van Sant retains his fresh and hip storytelling in his first film for a major studio. Backed by Henry's zesty script, all the actors shine—with standout performances from Kidman as the monstrous Suzanne and Phoenix (River's younger brother) as the lost/horny Jimmy. Shot entirely in Canada.*CW:* Strong sexual content; language. 103m/C VHS, LV, 8mm, Closed Caption. Nicole Kidman, Matt Dillon, Joaquin Rafael (Leaf) Phoenix, Casey Affleck, Alison Folland, Illeana Douglas, Dan Hedaya, Wayne Knight, Kurtwood Smith, Holland Taylor, Maria Tucci, Susan Traylor; **Cameos:** George Segal, Buck Henry; **D:** Gus Van Sant; **W:** Buck Henry, Johnny Burne; **C:** Eric Alan Edwards; **M:** Danny Elfman. Golden Globe Awards '96: Best Actress—Musical/Comedy (Kidman); Broadcast Film Critics Association Awards '95: Best Actress (Kidman); Nominations: British Academy Awards '95: Best Actress (Kidman); MTV Movie Awards '96: Most Desirable Female (Kidman). *COL*

To Die For 2: Son of Darkness 🎬½ Son of Darkness: To Die For 2 1991 (R) This far outclasses part one in terms of acting and production values, but the plot still isn't back from the grave. Strange, because all the vampires are; despite their fiery deaths last time they flock around the adoptive mother of a baby secretly sired by a bloodsucker. 95m/C VHS, Closed Caption. Rosalind Allen, Steve Bond, Scott Jacoby, Michael Praed, Jay Underwood, Amanda Wyss, Remy O'Neill, Vince Edwards; **D:** David F. Price. *THV*

To Die Standing 🎬½ 1991 (R) Two mavericks team up to do what the D.E.A. and cops simply cannot... capture a dangerous international drug lord. High action. 87m/C VHS, LV. Cliff DeYoung, Robert Beltran, Jamie Rose, Gerald Anthony, Orlando Sacha, Michael Ford; **D:** Louis Morneau; **W:** Ross Bell, Daryl Haney. *COL*

To Each His Own 🎬🎬🎬 1946 Top-notch melodrama finds middle-aged business-woman Josephine Norris (de Havilland) recalling her past as she carries on through London's blitz. As a young woman, Josephine fell in love with a dashing WWI pilot (Lund), became pregnant, and had her lover killed in action. To avoid scandal, she gives the baby up for adoption, although she stays in touch with his adoptive mother (Anderson) and befriends the boy. When Gregory (Lund again) grows up, he too becomes a pilot and visits Josephine—who's still longing to tell him the truth. Lund's film debut. 100m/B VHS. Olivia de Havilland, John Lund, Mary Anderson, Roland Culver, Virginia Welles, Bill Goodwin, Phillip Terry; **D:** Mitchell Leisen; **W:** Charles Brackett, Jacques Thery; **C:** Daniel F. Fapp; **M:** Victor Young. Academy Awards '46: Best Actress (de Havilland); Nominations: Academy Awards '46: Best Original Screenplay. *USH*

To Forget Venice 🎬🎬½ 1979 Portrays the sensitive relationships among four homosexuals, and their shared fears of growing older. Dubbed in English. 90m/C VHS, Beta. *IT* Erland Josephson, Mariangela Melato, David Pontremoli, Elenora Giorgi; **D:** Franco Brusati. Nominations: Academy Awards '79: Best Foreign Language Film. *COL*

To Gillian on Her 37th Birthday 🎬🎬 1996 (PG-13) Overly sentimental weeper explores the effects of a mother's death on the ones she's left behind. Gillian's been dead for two years but widower David Lewis (Gallagher) hasn't been able to let her spirit go and daughter Rachel (Danes) is having trouble growing up with a father who spends more time on the beach with his dead wife's ghost than with her. Enter nosy sister-in-law Esther (Baker) and annoying husband (Altman) who try to set him up on the anniversary of Gillian's death and you've got a mental family breakdown coming. Pfeiffer appears as Gillian in this script by husband Kelley, based on the play by Michael Brady. **CW:** Scene involving strong language, and for some sensuality and teen drinking. **92m/C VHS, LV, Closed Caption.** Peter Gallagher, Claire Danes, Kathy Baker, Wendy Crewson, Bruce Altman; *Cameos:* Michelle Pfeiffer; **D:** Michael Pressman; **W:** David E. Kelley; **C:** Tim Suhrstedt; **M:** James Horner. *COL*

To Grandmother's House We Go ♫♫½ **1994** The Olsen twins want to give mom a restful Christmas vacation so they decide to visit Grandma (on their own) and wind up in the hands of a pair of bumbling kidnappers. Made for TV movie. **89m/C VHS, Closed Caption.** Ashley Olsen, Mary-Kate Olsen, Cynthia Geary, Rhea Perlman, J. Eddie Peck, Stuart Margolin; *Cameos:* Bob Saget, Lori Loughlin; **D:** Jeff Franklin; **W:** Jeff Franklin. *WAR*

To Have & Have Not ♫♫♫½ **1944** Martinique charter boat operator gets mixed up with beautiful woman and French resistance fighters during WWII. Top-notch production in every respect. Classic dialogue and fiery romantic bouts between Bogart and Bacall. Bacall's first film. Based on a story by Ernest Hemingway. Remade in 1950 as "The Breaking Point" and in 1958 as "The Gun Runners." **100m/B VHS, Beta, LV.** Humphrey Bogart, Lauren Bacall, Walter Brennan, Hoagy Carmichael, Marcel Dalio, Dolores Moran, Sheldon Leonard, Dan Seymour; **D:** Howard Hawks. *MGM*

To Heal a Nation ♫♫½ **1988** The story of veteran Jan Scruggs, who spearheaded the movement to build the Vietnam Veterans memorial. The then little-known Ross Perot provided major financial support for Scruggs' dream. Made for television. **100m/C VHS.** Eric Roberts, Conrad Bachmann, Glynnis O'Connor, Marshall Colt, Scott Paulin, Lee Purcell, Laurence Luckinbill, Linden Chiles, Brock Peters; **D:** Michael Pressman; **W:** Lionel Chetwynd. *TTC*

To Hell and Back ♫♫½ **1955** Adaptation of Audie Murphy's autobiography. Murphy plays himself, from his upbringing to WWII, where he was the most-decorated American soldier. Features realistic battle sequences punctuated with grand heroics. **106m/C VHS, Beta.** Audie Murphy, Marshall Thompson, Jack Kelly; **D:** Jesse Hibbs. *USH, TLF*

To Joy ♫♫♫ **1950** The rocky marriage of a violinist and his wife illuminate the problems of the young in Swedish society. Early Bergman. In Swedish with English subtitles or dubbed. **90m/B VHS, Beta, LV.** *SW* **D:** Ingmar Bergman. *NO*

To Kill a Clown ♫♫ **1972** (R) Painter and his wife working to save their marriage are trapped on an isolated island and terrorized by a crazed Vietnam veteran. This helps pull them together. Some holes in the plot, but generally effective. **82m/C VHS, Beta.** Alan Alda, Blythe Danner, Heath Lamberts; **D:** George Bloomfield.

To Kill a Mockingbird ♫♫♫♫ **1962** Faithful adaptation of powerful Harper Lee novel, both an evocative portrayal of childhood innocence and a denunciation of bigotry. Peck's performance as southern lawyer defending a black man accused of raping a white woman is flawless. Duvall debuted as the dim-witted Boo Radley. Lee based her characterization of "Dill" on Truman Capote, a childhood friend. **129m/B VHS, Beta, LV, DVD.** Gregory Peck, Brock Peters, Phillip Alford, Mary Badham, Robert Duvall, Rosemary Murphy, William Windom, Alice Ghostley, John Megna, Frank Overton, Paul Fix, Collin Wilcox; **D:** Robert Mulligan; **W:** Horton Foote; **M:** Elmer Bernstein. Academy Awards '62: Best Actor (Peck), Best Adapted Screenplay, Best Art Direction/Set Decoration (B & W); Golden Globe Awards '63: Best Actor—Drama (Peck), Best Score, National Film Registry '95;; Nominations: Academy Awards '62: Best Black and White Cinematography,

Best Director (Mulligan), Best Picture, Best Supporting Actress (Badham), Best Original Score. *KUI, USH, BTV*

To Kill a Priest ♫♫ **1989** (R) Based on the true story of Father Jerzy Popieluszko, a young priest in 1984 Poland who defies his church and speaks out publicly on Solidarity. He is killed by the government as a result. Harris is good as the menacing police official. **110m/C VHS, Beta, LV, Closed Caption.** Christopher Lambert, Ed Harris, David Suchet, Tim Roth, Joanne Whalley, Pete Postlethwaite, Cherie Lunghi, Joss Ackland; **D:** Agnieszka Holland; **W:** Agnieszka Holland; **C:** Adam Holender; **M:** Georges Delerue. *COL*

To Kill a Stranger ♫♫ **1984** A beautiful pop singer is stranded in a storm, and then victimized by a mad rapist/murderer. **100m/C VHS, Beta.** Donald Pleasence, Dean Stockwell, Angelica Maria, Aldo Ray, Sergio Aragones. *NO*

To Live ♫♫♫♫ *Huozhe* **1994** Superb drama follows the lives of one family—weak but adaptable Fugui (You), his strong-willed wife Jiazhen (Li), and their young daughter and son—from prerevolutionary China in the 1940s through the '60s Cultural Revolution. Fugui loses the family fortune in the gambling houses, actually a blessing when the Communists come to power, and the family must struggle to survive financial and increasingly difficult political changes, where fate can change on a whim. Subtle saga about ordinary human lives reacting to terrifying conditions boasts extraordinary performances and evocative imagery. Adapted from the novel "Lifetimes" by Yu Hua. Chinese with subtitles. **130m/C VHS, LV.** *CH* Ge You, Gong Li, Niu Ben, Guo Tao, Jiang Wu; **D:** Zhang Yimou; **W:** Lu Wei, Yu Hua; **M:** Zhao Jiping. British Academy Awards '94: Best Foreign Film; Cannes Film Festival '94: Best Actor (You), Grand Jury Prize; Nominations: Golden Globe Awards '95: Best Foreign Film. *HMK, IME*

To Live and Die in Hong Kong ♫½ **1989** Two sailors arrive in Hong Kong for a little R & R, until they are mistaken for spies by both the Hong Kong police and the Chinese mob. Action-packed tale. **98m/C VHS.** Rowena Cortes, Lawrence Jan, Mike Kelly, Laurens C. Postma; **D:** Lau Shing Hon. *ELV*

To Live & Die in L.A. ♫♫ **1985** (R) Fast-paced, morally ambivalent tale of cops and counterfeiters in L.A. After his partner is killed shortly before his retirement, a secret service agent sets out to track down his ruthless killer. Lots of violence; some nudity. Notable both for a riveting car chase and its dearth of sympathetic characters. **114m/C VHS, Beta, LV, Closed Caption.** William L. Petersen, Willem Dafoe, John Pankow, Dean Stockwell, Debra Feuer, John Turturro, Darlanne Fluegel, Robert Downey; **D:** William Friedkin; **W:** William Friedkin. *ART, VES*

To Love Again ♫½ **1980** A middle-aged love story about a reclusive college professor and the campus handyman. **96m/C VHS, Beta.** Lynn Redgrave, Brian Dennehy, Conchata Ferrell; **D:** Joseph Hardy. *NLC*

To Paris with Love ♫♫½ **1955** A British man and his son fall in love with a shop girl and his boss while on vacation in Paris. Charming and humorous, with a witty performance from Guinness. **75m/C VHS, Beta.** Alec Guinness, Odile Versois, Vernon Gray; **D:** Robert Hamer; **M:** Edwin Astley. *NO*

To Play or To Die ♫♫ **1991** The introverted Kees attends an all-boy school where powerful bullies and sadomasochistic games are the rule. Kees is fascinated by the handsome Charel, the bullies leader. He invites Charel to his home, intending to turn the tables on his tormentor, but nothing goes as planned. Intense and controversial look at gay teens. Directorial debut of Krom. In Dutch with English subtitles. **150m/C VHS.** *NL* Geert Hunaerts, Tjebbo Gerritsma; **D:** Frank Krom; **W:** Anne Van De Putte, Frank Krom. *WBF*

To Play the King ♫♫♫ **1993** Sequel to "The House of Cards" finds Francis Urquhart (Richardson), having murdered his way to the Prime Ministery, now bored with his political situation. But things may be changing—the Queen has been succeeded by her liberal son (Kitchen) and Francis, goaded by his equally vicious wife (Fletcher), plots treachery to bring down the monarchy. Followed by "The Final Cut"; adapted from the novel by Michael Dobbs. **212m/C VHS, Closed Caption.** *GB* Ian Richardson, Michael Kitchen, Diane Fletcher, Kitty Aldridge, Bernice Stegers, Colin Jeavons, Rowena King, Erika Hoffman, Nicholas Farrell; **D:** Paul Seed; **W:** Andrew Davies. *FOX, TVC*

To Please a Lady ♫♫½ *Red Hot Wheels* **1950** Romantic comedy-drama about race car driver Gable and reporter Stanwyck. Although leads do their best with the script, they're unable to generate any sparks. However, race track scenes are excellent. Filmed at the Indianapolis Speedway, the spectacular racing footage makes up for overall average film. **91m/B VHS.** Clark Gable, Barbara Stanwyck, Adolphe Menjou, Will Geer, Roland Winters; **D:** Clarence Brown; **W:** Barre Lyndon, Marge Decker. *MGM*

To Protect and Serve ♫♫ **1992** (R) When crooked cops start getting killed, two young cops are assigned to investigate. Suspicion points to a rookie (Howell), who just may have decided to clean things up his own way. **CW:** Language, violence and drug use, and sexuality. **93m/C VHS.** C. Thomas Howell, Leslie Deane, Richard Romanus, Joe Cortese; **D:** Eric Weston. *ART*

To Race the Wind ♫♫ **1980** Blind man wants to be treated like a normal person as he struggles through Harvard Law School. Based upon Harold Krents' autobiography "Butterflies Are Free." Made for television. **97m/C VHS, Beta.** Steve Guttenberg, Lisa Eilbacher, Randy Quaid, Barbara Barrie; **D:** Walter Grauman. *UNI*

To See Paris and Die ♫♫ **1993** Elena Orekhova (Vasilyeva) is a Russian stage mother who will do absolutely anything to ensure pianist son Yuri gets chosen for a prestigious competition in Paris—even though she knows secrets from her past could place a blight on his career. Russian with subtitles. **110m/C VHS.** *RU* Tatyana Vasilyeva, Dimitry Malikov; **D:** Alexander Proshkin. *NYF, FCT*

To See Such Fun **1981** Hilarious excerpts from 80 years of the greatest British movie comedies. **90m/C VHS, Beta.** *GB* Peter Sellers, Marty Feldman, Benny Hill, Eric Idle, Alec Guinness, Margaret Rutherford, Dirk Bogarde, Spike Milligan. *NO*

To Sir, with Love ♫♫½ **1967** Teacher in London's tough East End tosses books in the wastebasket and proceeds to teach his class about life. Skillful and warm performance by Poitier as idealistic teacher; supporting cast also performs nicely. Based on the novel by E.R. Braithwaite. LuLu's title song was a big hit in 1967-68. **105m/C VHS, Beta.** *GB* Sidney Poitier, Lulu, Judy Geeson, Christian Roberts, Suzy Kendall, Faith Brook; **D:** James Clavell; **W:** James Clavell. *COL*

To Sleep with a Vampire ♫♫ **1992** (R) A Los Angeles bloodsucker is tired of his violent existence and craves the one thing he can't have—daylight. As he stalks his latest victim, a stripper, he decides to take her home and have her tell him about living in daytime. When she realizes what's going on, the intended victim decides to fight for her life. Action and eroticism raises this one above the norm. Remake of "Dance of the Damned." **CW:** Language, violence, and sexuality. **90m/C VHS.** Scott Valentine, Charlie Spradling, Richard Zobel, Ingrid Vold, Stephanie Hardy; **D:** Adam Friedman; **W:** Patricia Harrington. *NHO*

To Sleep with Anger ♫♫♫½ **1990** (PG) At first a comic, introspective look at a black middle-class family going about their business in the heart of Los Angeles. Sly charmer Glover shows up and enthralls the entire family with his slightly sinister storytelling and a gnawing doom gradually permeates the household. Insightful look into the conflicting values of Black America. Glover's best performance. **105m/C VHS, Beta, Closed Caption.** Danny Glover, Mary Alice, Paul Butler, Richard Brooks, Carl Lumbly, Vonetta McGee, Sheryl Lee Ralph; *D:* Charles Burnett; *W:* Charles Burnett; *C:* Walt Lloyd. Independent Spirit Awards '91: Best Actor (Glover), Best Director (Burnett), Best Screenplay, Best Supporting Actress (Ralph); National Society of Film Critics Awards '90: Best Screenplay; Sundance Film Festival '90: Special Jury Prize. *COL, FCT, IME*

To the Death 🎬½ 1993 **(R)** A kickboxer wants to retire from the boxing tournaments but the corrupt promoters refuse to let him go unless he manages to kill his rivals in the ring. **90m/C VHS, LV, Closed Caption.** John Barrett, Michael Quissi; *D:* Darrell Roodt.

To the Devil, a Daughter 🎬🎬 *Child of Satan* 1976 **(R)** A nun is put under a spell by a priest who has been possessed by Satan. She is to bear his child. A writer on the occult intervenes. Based on the novel by Dennis Wheatley. One of Kinski's early films. **93m/C VHS, Beta.** Richard Widmark, Christopher Lee, Nastassia Kinski, Honor Blackman, Denholm Elliott, Michael Goodliffe; *D:* Peter Sykes; *W:* Christopher Wicking; *C:* David Watkin. *REP, MLB*

To the Last Man 🎬 1933 An early Scott sagebrush epic, about two feuding families. Temple is seen in a small role. Based on Zane Grey's novel of the same name. **70m/B VHS, Beta.** Randolph Scott, Esther Ralston, Jack LaRue, Noah Beery Sr., Buster Crabbe, Gail Patrick, Barton MacLane, Fuzzy Knight, John Carradine, Jay Ward, Shirley Temple; *D:* Henry Hathaway. *NOS, DVT, MLB*

To the Lighthouse 🎬🎬 1983 The Ramsay family's annual proper British holiday at their Cornwall home turns into a summer of disillusionment in this adaptation of the Virginia Woolf novel. Made for British TV. **115m/C VHS, Beta.** Rosemary Harris, Michael Gough, Suzanne Bertish, Lynsey Baxter, T.P. McKenna, Kenneth Branagh; *D:* Colin Gregg. *MON*

To the Limit 🎬 1995 **(R)** Actioner finds the pulchritudinous Colette (Smith) revealing to mobster Frank (Travolta) that she's a CIA agent (and if you believe that I have a bridge in Brooklyn to sell you) and that they are the targets of a rogue agent (Richmond). No, Smith can't act but since she takes lots of showers and is supported by some professionals who can, this gets by on trash value alone. *CW:* Strong sexuality, violence and language. **96m/C VHS.** Anna Nicole Smith, Joey Travolta, Michael Nouri, Branscombe Richmond, John Aprea, Kathy Shower, Rebecca Ferratti, David Proval; *D:* Raymond Martino; *W:* Joey Travolta, Raymond Martino; *M:* Jim Halfpenny. *PMH*

To the Shores of Hell 🎬🎬 1965 Leaving his sweetheart behind, Major Greg Donahue attacks Da Nang and plots to rescue his brother from the Viet Cong. **82m/C VHS, Beta.** Marshall Thompson, Kiva Lawrence, Richard Jordahl. *NO*

To the Shores of Tripoli 🎬🎬 1942 Wartime propaganda in the guise of drama, in which a smarmy playboy is transformed into a Marine in boot camp. **82m/C VHS, Beta.** John Payne, Maureen O'Hara, Randolph Scott, Nancy Kelly, Harry (Henry) Morgan, Maxie "Slapsie" Rosenbloom, William Tracy, Minor Watson, Alan Hale Jr., Hugh Beaumont, Hillary Brooke; *D:* H. Bruce Humberstone. Nominations: Academy Awards '42: Best Color Cinematography. *FOX, MLB*

To Wong Foo, Thanks for Everything, Julie Newmar 🎬🎬½ 1995 **(PG-13)** Hot on the high heels of "The Adventures of Priscilla, Queen of the Desert," comes the sanitized for your protection Yankee version. And its all about hanging on to your dreams and how we're all the same inside, with politically correct gay drag queens doing the sermonizing. Yes, this is the feel-good drag road movie for the 90s. Den mother Vida (Swayze), tough beauty queen Noxeema (Snipes), and hot-blooded Chi Chi (Leguizamo doing his best Rosie Perez) head to Hollywood in a 1967 Cadillac convertible that inconveniently breaks down in a tiny Nebraska town. The "girls" work their magic, and presum-

ably the people of this uncultured, anachronistic backwater will never be the same. One-dimensional characters, flat direction, and inconsistent script undercut exceptional efforts by Swayze and Leguizamo. *CW:* Subject matter involving men living in drag; brief scene of spousal abuse; some language. **108m/C VHS, LV, Closed Caption.** Wesley Snipes, Patrick Swayze, John Leguizamo, Stockard Channing, Blythe Danner, Melinda Dillon, Arliss Howard, Jason London, Christopher Penn; *Cameos:* Julie Newmar, Robin Williams; *D:* Beeban Kidron; *W:* Douglas Carter Beane; *M:* Rachel Portman. Nominations: Golden Globe Awards '96: Best Actor—Musical/Comedy (Swayze), Best Supporting Actor (Leguizamo). *USH*

The Toast of New Orleans 🎬🎬½ 1950 A poor fisherman rises to stardom as an opera singer. Likable, though fluffy production features a plethora of musical numbers. 🎵Be My Love; Tina Lina; I'll Never Love You; The Toast of New Orleans; Song of the Bayou; Boom Biddy Boom Boom. **97m/C VHS, Beta.** Kathryn Grayson, Mario Lanza, David Niven, Rita Moreno, J. Carrol Naish; *D:* Norman Taurog. Nominations: Academy Awards '50: Best Song ("Be My Love"). *MGM*

Toast of New York 🎬🎬🎬 1937 Arnold plays Jim Fisk, a New England peddler who rises to become one of the first Wall Street giants of industry. Atypical Grant performance. **109m/B VHS, Beta, LV.** Edward Arnold, Cary Grant, Frances Farmer, Jack Oakie, Donald Meek, Billy Gilbert; *D:* Rowland V. Lee. *TTC*

Tobor the Great 🎬½ 1954 Sentimental and poorly executed, this film tells the tale of a boy, his grandfather, and Tobor the robot. Villainous communists attempt to make evil use of Tobor, only to be thwarted in the end. **77m/B VHS, LV.** Charles Drake, Billy Chapin, Karin Booth, Taylor Holmes, Joan Gerber, Steve Geray; *D:* Lee Sholem. *REP*

Tobruk 🎬 1966 American GI's endeavor to knock out the guns of Tobruk, to clear the way for a bombing attack on German fuel supply depots of North Africa in this WWII actioner. **110m/C VHS, Beta.** Rock Hudson, George Peppard, Guy Stockwell, Nigel Green; *D:* Arthur Hiller. *USH*

Toby McTeague 🎬🎬 1987 **(PG)** A story about an Alaskan family that breeds Siberian Huskies. When his father is injured, the youngest son tries to replace him in the regional dog-sled race. **94m/C VHS, Beta, LV.** Winston Rekert, Wannick Bisson, Timothy Webber; *D:* Jean-Claude Lord; *W:* Djordje Milicevic, Jamie Brown. *COL, NLC*

Toby Tyler 🎬🎬🎬 1959 **(G)** A boy runs off to join the circus, and teams up with a chimpanzee. A timeless and enjoyable Disney film that still appeals to youngsters. Good family-fare. **93m/C VHS, Beta.** Kevin Corcoran, Henry Calvin, Gene Sheldon, Bob Sweeney; *D:* Charles T. Barton. *DIS*

Today I Hang 🎬 1942 A man is framed for murder and sentenced to hang. His buddies on the outside do their best to prove his innocence. Meanwhile, in prison, the accused encounters any number of interesting characters. **67m/B VHS, Beta.** Walter Woolf King, Mona Barrie, William Farnum, Harry Woods, James Craven; *D:* Oliver Drake. *SNC*

Today We Kill, Tomorrow We Die 🎬 1971 **(PG)** A rancher is unjustly sent to prison; when his sentence is over he hires a gang to relentlessly track down the culprit who framed him. **95m/C VHS, Beta.** Montgomery Ford, Bud Spencer, William Berger, Tatsuya Nakadai, Wayde Preston; *D:* Tonino Cervi.

Today We Live 🎬🎬½ 1933 Triangle love story set in WWI. Crawford is a hedonistic Brit having a fling with her naval brother's (Tone) friend (Young). When American flyer Cooper appears she sets her sights on him but soon he's off to combat in France where he's reported killed. Crawford returns to Young but, naturally, reports of Cooper's death have been greatly exaggerated and the two eventually reunite. Faulkner co-scripted from his story "Turn About" which had no fe-

male character and concerned the rivalry between naval officers and fly boys. **113m/B VHS, Beta.** Gary Cooper, Joan Crawford, Franchot Tone, Robert Young, Roscoe Karns, Louise Closser Hale; *D:* Howard Hawks; *W:* Dwight Taylor, William Faulkner, Edith Fitzgerald. *MGM, FCT*

The Todd Killings 🎬½ *A Dangerous Friend; Skipper* 1971 **(R)** A psychotic young man commits a series of murders involving young women. Sleazy, forgettable picture wastes a talented cast. **93m/C VHS.** Robert F. Lyons, Richard Thomas, Barbara Bel Geddes, Ed Asner, Sherry Miles, Gloria Grahame, Belinda J. Montgomery; *D:* Barry Shear; *W:* Joel Oliansky. *WAR*

Todd McFarlane's Spawn *Spawn* 1997 McFarlane's comic book creation makes his cable TV animated debut. Hellspawn was once human CIA assassin Al Simmons, murdered in the line of duty, who sold his soul to see his wife one last time. When he comes back from the grave with superhuman powers it's again as a killer with attitude, who leaves a high body count. A PG-13 version clocks in at 90 minutes. **147m/C VHS.** *D:* Eric Radomski; *W:* Alan B. McElroy, Gary Hardwick; *V:* Keith David, Richard Dysart, Ronny Cox. *HBO*

Toga Party 🎬 1979 **(R)** Fraternity house throws a wild toga party in this raunchy low-rent depiction of college life. **82m/C VHS, Beta.** Bobby H. Charles, Mary Mitchell. *NO*

Together? 🎬½ 1979 **(R)** Divorced woman and a male chauvinist test the limits of their sexual liberation as well as viewer patience. **91m/C VHS, Beta.** *IT* Maximilian Schell, Jacqueline Bisset, Terence Stamp, Monica Guerritore; *D:* Armenia Balducci; *M:* Burt Bacharach.

Togetherness 🎬½ 1970 Two wealthy, good-for-nothing playboys chase after the same blonde, a Communist, in Greece. **101m/C VHS, Beta, LV.** George Hamilton, Peter Lawford, Olinka Berova, John Banner, Jesse White; *D:* Arthur Marks. *NO*

The Toilers and the Wayfarers 🎬🎬 1997 New Ulm, Minnesota is an ultraconservative German-American community where the teen-aged Dieter (Klemp) is the object of affection for best friend Phillip (Woodhouse). Although Dieter thinks he might be gay, he rejects Phillip, who soon takes off for Minneapolis. This leaves Dieter open to the attentions of slightly older, free-spirited Udo (Schirg). Dieter's father strongly disapproves and the young man leaves to join Phillip in the big bad city, with Udo in tow. But since none of the boys have any money, they're soon working the streets to survive. English and German with subtitles. **85m/C VHS.** Matt Klemp, Ralf Schirg, Andrew Woodhouse; *D:* Keith Froelich; *W:* Keith Froelich; *C:* Jim Tittle; *M:* Chan Poling. *AWA*

Tokyo Decadence 🎬½ 1991 **(NC-17)** Ai is a high-paid prostitute working in Tokyo for an agency that specializes in sado-masochism. Film follows her various sexual escapades in humiliating detail as well as her drug-addled search for a client Ai thinks she's in love with. Since Ai remains a cipher, the film also remains unfocused except for its creepy and explicit sex scenes. Adaptation of director Murakami's novel "Topaz." In Japanese with English subtitles or dubbed. *CW:* Sexually explicit. **92m/C VHS, LV.** *JP* Miho Nikaido, Tenmei Kano, Yayoi Kusama, Sayoko Amano; *D:* Ryu Murakami; *W:* Ryu Murakami; *M:* Ryuichi Sakamoto. *TRI, FCT*

Tokyo Drifter 🎬🎬 *Tokyo Nagaremono* 1966 Surreal yakuza film follows an honorable gangster hunted by both his own bosses and a rival mob, who chase him across Japan. Lots of camera trickery. Japanese with subtitles. **83m/C VHS, Letterbox.** *JP* Eiji Go, Chieko Matsubara, Tetsuya Watari; *D:* Seijun Suzuki. *HMV*

Tokyo-Ga 🎬🎬🎬½ 1985 Impelled by his love for the films of Yasujiro Ozu, Wenders traveled to Tokyo and fashioned a caring document of both the city and of Ozu's career, using images that recall and comment on Ozu's visual motifs.

92m/C VHS, Beta. **D:** Wim Wenders; **W:** Wim Wenders. TPV

Tokyo Joe ♂♂½ 1949 A war hero/nightclub owner returns to Tokyo and becomes ensnared in blackmail and smuggling while searching for his missing wife and child. Slow-moving tale has never been considered one of Bogart's better movies. 88m/B VHS, Beta, LV. Humphrey Bogart, Florence Marly, Alexander Knox, Sessue Hayakawa, Jerome Courtland, Lore Lee Michel; **D:** Stuart Heisler. COL

Tokyo Olympiad 1966 A monumental sports documentary about the 1964 Olympic Games in its entirety. Never before available for home viewing. Letterboxed with digital sound. In Japanese with English subtitles. 170m/C VHS, Beta, LV, Letterbox. JP **D:** Kon Ichikawa. TPV, WFV, CRC

Tokyo Pop ♂♂½ 1988 (R) A punk rocker travels to Japan to find stardom and experiences a series of misadventures. Enjoyable in its own lightweight way. Hamilton is the daughter of Carol Burnett. 99m/C VHS, LV, Closed Caption. Carrie Hamilton, Yutaka Tadokoro, Chieko Shiragama, So Yamamura, Masumi Harukawa; **D:** Fran Rubel Kazui; **W:** Lynn Grossman, Fran Rubel Kazui; **M:** Alan Brewer. WAR

Tokyo Story 1953 Poignant story of elderly couple's journey to Tokyo where they receive little time and less respect from their grown children. Masterful cinematography, and sensitive treatment of universally appealing story. In Japanese with English subtitles. 134m/B VHS. JP Chishu Ryu, So Yamamura, Haruko Sugimura, Setsuko Hara; **D:** Yasujiro Ozu; **W:** Yasujiro Ozu. NYF, FCT

Tol'able David ♂♂ 1921 A simple tale of mountain folk, done in the tradition of Mark Twain stories. A family of hillbillies is embroiled in a feud with a clan of outlaws. When the community's mail is stolen by the troublesome ruffians, the family's youngest member, who harbors dreams of becoming a mail driver, comes to the rescue. Silent film. 79m/B VHS, Beta. Richard Barthelmess, Gladys Hulette, Ernest Torrence; **D:** Henry King. NOS, VYY, CCB

Toll Gate ♂♂½ 1920 Quick on the draw outlaw Hart risks capture to rescue drowning child, and consequently gets involved with the boy's mother. Silent classic. 55m/B VHS, Beta. William S. Hart, Anna Q. Nilsson, Jack Richardson, Joseph Singleton; **D:** Lambert Hillyer. GPV, VCN

Toll of the Desert ♂ 1935 A lawman learns that his father is a ruthless, back-stabbing renegade. Now he must try and catch him. 58m/B VHS, Beta, LV. Roger Williams, Ted Adams, Edward Cassidy, Tom London, John Elliott, Earl Dwire, Betty Mack, Fred Kohler Jr.; **D:** William (Lester Williams) Berke. NOS, DVT

Tollbooth ♂♂ 1994 (R) Romantic dreamer Jack (Von Dohlen) mans a tollbooth on a stretch of Florida Keys highway while his equally longing honey Doris (Balk) works at a nearby gas station and has a thing going on the side with bait salesman Dash (Patton). The return of Doris' longgone daddy Leon (Cassel) causes some family problems while Jack's new associate Vic (Wilder) has a scam that's drawing interest from the state police. Thin plot but lots of charm from the two leads helps hold interest in Breziner's first film. **CW:** Scene of strong sexuality and for language and some gore. 108m/C VHS, LV, Closed Caption. Fairuza Balk, Lenny Von Dohlen, Will Patton, Seymour Cassel, James Wilder, Louise Fletcher, William Katt; **D:** Salome Breziner; **W:** Salome Breziner; **C:** Henry Vargas; **M:** Adam Gorgoni. NLC

Tom and Huck ♂♂♂ 1995 (PG) Tom Sawyer and pal Huck Finn are the only witnesses to a murder. Tom's friend Muff is framed for the crime and the boys are being tracked by the real killer, Injun Joe. They must decide to come forward, expose the true fiend, and risk their own hides or run away and let an innocent man hang. True to the Twain story, Thomas plays a mischievious Tom to Renfro's troublemaking Huck. Film was shot in Mooresville, Alabama, popula-

tion 69, just down the road a piece from the Hannibal, Missouri of Twain fame. 91m/C VHS, Closed Caption. Jonathan Taylor Thomas, Brad Renfro, Eric Schweig, Charles Rocket, Amy Wright, Micheal McShane, Marian Seldes, Rachel Leigh Cook, Lanny Flaherty, Courtland Mead, Peter M. MacKenzie, Heath Lamberts; **D:** Pete Hewitt; **W:** Stephen Sommers, David Loughery; **C:** Bobby Bukowski; **M:** Stephen Endelman. TOU

Tom and Jerry: The Movie ♂♂ 1993 (G) Everybody's favorite animated cat/mouse duo (who began life in a 1940 MGM short "Puss Gets the Boot") hit the big screen, this time talking (unlike their animated shorts). Rather than cartoon mayhem our two protagonists are goodytwo-shoes (with songs yet!) but still retain their charm. Kids will like it, but true "Tom and Jerry" fans should probably stick to the original cartoons. 84m/C VHS, Closed Caption. **D:** Phil Roman; **W:** Dennis Marks; **M:** Henry Mancini, Leslie Bricusse; **V:** Richard Kind, Dana Hill, Charlotte Rae, Henry Gibson, Rip Taylor, Howard Morris, Edmund Gilbert, David Lander. FHE

Tom & Viv ♂♂♂ 1994 (PG-13) American T.S. Eliot (Dafoe) is an Oxford student in 1914 when he meets the moody, monied Vivien Haigh-Wood (Richardson). After a whirlwind courtship, they marry—disastrously. Eliot begins to establish himself as a poet, while Vivien serves as muse/ typist and unsuccessfully battles her misdiagnosed illnesses with too much drinking and drugs, as well as embarrassing public scenes. As Eliot gains success, he increasingly distances himself from the unhappy Viv, until finally committing her to an asylum. Dafoe is fine as the chilly, withdrawn poet but Richardson steals the film as his flamboyant, lost wife. Based on the play by Michael Hastings, who co-wrote the screenplay. **CW:** Mature thematic elements. 115m/C VHS, LV, Closed Caption. GB Willem Dafoe, Miranda Richardson, Rosemary Harris, Tim Dutton, Nickolas Grace, Philip Locke, Clare Holman, Joanna McCallum; **D:** Brian Gilbert; **W:** Michael Hastings, Adrian Hodges; **M:** Debbie Wiseman. National Board of Review Awards '94: Best Actress (Richardson), Best Supporting Actress (Harris); Nominations: Academy Awards '94: Best Actress (Richardson), Best Supporting Actress (Harris); British Academy Awards '93: Best Actress (Richardson), Best Film; Golden Globe Awards '95: Best Actress—Drama (Richardson). TOU

Tom Brown's School Days ♂♂½ Adventures at Rugby 1940 Depicts life among the boys in an English school during the Victorian era. Based on the classic novel by Thomas Hughes. Remade in 1951. 86m/B VHS, Beta. GB Cedric Hardwicke, Jimmy Lydon, Freddie Bartholomew; **D:** Robert Stevenson. NOS, HHT, CAB

Tom Brown's School Days ♂♂♂ 1951 Tom enrolls at Rugby and is beset by bullies in classic tale of English school life. British remake of the 1940 version. Based on the novel by Thomas Hughes. 93m/B VHS, Beta. GB Robert Newton, John Howard Davies, James Hayter; **D:** Gordon Parry. VCI

Tom, Dick, and Harry ♂♂½ 1941 Dreamy girl is engaged to three men and unable to decide which to marry. It all depends on a kiss. Remade as "The Girl Most Likely." 86m/B VHS, Beta, LV. Ginger Rogers, George Murphy, Burgess Meredith, Alan Marshal, Phil Silvers; **D:** Garson Kanin; **W:** Paul Jarrico. Nominations: Academy Awards '41: Best Story. CCB, TTC, FCT

Tom Horn ♂♂ 1980 (R) The final days of one of the Old West's legends. Gunman Tom Horn, hired by Wyoming ranchers to stop cattle rustlers, goes about his job with a zeal that soon proves embarrassing to his employers. Beautifully photographed and authentic in its attention to details of the period, the film nonetheless takes liberties with the facts of Horn's life and is lacking in other aspects of production. 98m/C VHS, Beta. Steve McQueen, Linda Evans, Richard Farnsworth, Billy Green Bush, Slim Pickens; **D:** William Wiard; **W:** Thomas McGuane; **C:** John A. Alonzo; **M:** Ernest Gold. WAR

Tom Jones ♂♂♂♂ 1963 Bawdy comedy based on Henry Fielding's novel about a rustic playboy's wild life in 18th century England. Hilarious and clever with a grand performance by Finney. One of the sexiest eating scenes ever. Redgrave's debut. Theatrically released at 129 minutes, the film was recut by the director, who decided it needed tightening before its 1992 re-release on video. 121m/C VHS, Beta, LV. GB Albert Finney, Susannah York, Hugh Griffith, Edith Evans, Joan Greenwood, Diane Cilento, George Devine, David Tomlinson, Joyce Redman, Lynn Redgrave, Julian Glover, Peter Bull, David Warner; **D:** Tony Richardson; **W:** John Osborne; **C:** Walter Lassally; **M:** John Addison. Academy Awards '63: Best Adapted Screenplay, Best Director (Richardson), Best Picture, Best Original Score; British Academy Awards '63: Best Film, Best Screenplay; Directors Guild of America Awards '63: Best Director (Richardson); Golden Globe Awards '64: Best Film—Musical/Comedy, Best Foreign Film; National Board of Review Awards '63: Best Director (Richardson); New York Film Critics Awards '63: Best Actor (Finney), Best Director (Richardson), Best Film; Nominations: Academy Awards '63: Best Actor (Finney), Best Art Direction/Set Decoration (Color), Best Supporting Actor (Griffith), Best Supporting Actress (Cilento, Evans, Redman). HBO, FOX, BTV

Tom Jones ♂♂♂ 1998 Cable miniseries based on the Henry Fielding novel goes further than the hit 1963 movie by including Fielding (Sessions) as the narrator of Tom's bawdy adventures. Tom (Beesley) is an 18th-century orphan with a heart of gold, an affinity for trouble, and an eye for the ladies. His true love is Sophie (Morton), the daughter of the boisterous Squire Western (Blessed). But of course, the path of true love never runs smooth. Lavish adaptation and lots of fun. 300m/C VHS, Closed Caption. GB Max Beesley, Samantha Morton, Brian Blessed, John Sessions, Benjamin Whitrow, Frances De La Tour; **D:** Metin Huseyin; **W:** Simon Burke. AEH

Tom Mix Compilation 1916 This compilation of six "Great American Cowboy" films from Tom Mix's early period includes: "Jimmy Hayes and Muriel," "The Stagecoach Driver and the Girl," "Sagebrush Tom," "An Arizona Wooing," "Roping a Bride" and "Local Color." 60m/B VHS, Beta. Tom Mix. GVV

Tom Mix Compilation 2 1916 Five films from Tom Mix's early period include "Never Again," "An Angelic Attitude," "A Western Masquerade," "A $5,000 Elopement," and "Local Color." 60m/B VHS, Beta. Tom Mix. GVV

Tom Sawyer ♂♂♂ 1930 Winning adaptation of Mark Twain's oft told tale of boyhood in Hannibal, Missouri. Cast reprised their roles the following year in "Huckleberry Finn." 86m/B VHS, Beta. Jackie Coogan, Mitzie Green, Lucien Littlefield, Tully Marshall; **D:** John Cromwell; **C:** Charles B(ryant) Lang. MGM

Tom Sawyer ♂♂½ 1973 (G) Musical version of the Mark Twain tale of the boisterous Tom, his friend Becky Thatcher, and various adventures, including the fence whitewashing. Amusing kid fare shot on location in Missouri. ♫River Song; Gratification; Tom Sawyer; Freebootin'; Aunt Polly's Soliloquy; If n I Was God; A Man's Gotta Be What He's Born To Be; How Come?; Hannibal, Mo. 104m/C VHS, LV, Letterbox. Johnny Whitaker, Jodie Foster, Celeste Holm, Warren Oates, Jeff East; **D:** Don Taylor; **M:** John Williams. Nominations: Academy Awards '73: Best Art Direction/Set Decoration, Best Costume Design, Original Song Score and/or Adaptation. MGM

Tom Thumb ♂♂♂ 1958 Diminutive boy saves village treasury from bad guys. Adapted from classic Grimm fairy tale. Special effects combine live actors, animation, and puppets. 92m/C VHS, Beta, LV. GB Russ Tamblyn, Peter Sellers, Terry-Thomas; **D:** George Pal; **C:** Georges Perinal. Academy Awards '58: Best Special Effects. MGM

Tomahawk ♂♂♂½ 1951 Indian sympathizer Jim Bridger (Heflin) is a local scout who anticipates trouble when the government decides to build a wagon route straight through Sioux hunting grounds in order to reach Montana's gold mines. The touchy situation is made worse by cavalry officer Dancy (Nigel) who thinks the only good Indian is a dead one. **82m/C VHS, Closed Caption.** Van Heflin, Preston Foster, Yvonne De Carlo, Alex Nicol, Jack Oakie, Tom Tully, Rock Hudson, Ann Doran; **D:** George Sherman; **W:** Maurice Geraghty, Silvia Richards; **C:** Charles P. Boyle; **M:** Hans J. Salter. *USH*

Tomb ✂✂ 1986 Fortune seekers disturb the slumber of a magical, sadistic princess much to their everlasting regret. Adapted from a Bram Stoker novel. **106m/C VHS, Beta.** Cameron Mitchell, John Carradine, Sybil Danning, Richard Hench, Michelle (McClellan) Bauer, Susan Stokey, David Pearson, Francesca "Kitten" Natividad; **D:** Fred Olen Ray; **C:** Paul Elliott. *TWE*

Tomb of Ligeia ✂✂✂ *Tomb of the Cat* 1964 The ghost of a man's first wife expresses her displeasure when groom and new little missus return to manor. One of the better Corman adaptations of Poe. Also available with "The Conqueror Worm" on Laser Disc. **82m/C VHS, Beta, LV.** *GB* Vincent Price, Elizabeth Shepherd, John Westbrook, Oliver Johnston, Richard Johnson; **D:** Roger Corman; **W:** Robert Towne. *MLB*

Tomb of the Undead ✂½ 1972 The sadistic guards of a prison camp are rudely awakened by the prisoners they tortured to death when they return as flesh-eating zombies looking to settle the score. **60m/C VHS, Beta.** *GB* Duncan McLeod, Lee Frost, John Dennis; **D:** John Hayes. *NOS, INC*

Tomb of Torture woof! *Metempsycose* 1965 Murdered countess is reincarnated in the body of a newspaperman's mistress. Together they investigate monster reports in a murder-ridden castle. The butler may have something to do with it. Filmed in Sepiatone and dubbed. **88m/B VHS, Beta.** Annie Albert, Thony Maky, Mark Marian; **D:** William Grace.

The Tomboy ✂½ 1924 A young woman behaves boyishly in Colonial America. **64m/B VHS, Beta.** Dorothy Devore, Lotta Williams, Herbert Rawlinson, Harry Gribbon, Lee Moran; **D:** David Kirkland. *GPV, FCT*

Tomboy ✂ 1940 Shy country boy and a not-so-shy city girl meet, fall in love, and overcome obstacles that stand in their path. **70m/B VHS, Beta.** Jackie Moran, Marcia Mae Jones. *VYY*

Tomboy woof! 1985 (R) A pretty auto mechanic is determined to win not only the race but the love and respect of a superstar auto racer. **91m/C VHS, Beta.** Betsy Russell, Eric Douglas, Jerry Dinome, Kristi Somers, Richard Erdman, Toby Iland; **D:** Herb Freed. *ART, VES*

Tomboy & the Champ ✂✂ 1958 Despite many obstacles, a music-loving calf becomes a prize winner with the help of its loving owner. Kids will love it, but adults will find this one a little sugary. **82m/C VHS, Beta.** Candy Moore, Ben Johnson, Jesse White; **D:** Francis D. Lyon. *VCI*

Tombs of the Blind Dead ✂✂½ *The Blind Dead; La Noche dell Terror Ciego; La Noche de la Muerta Ciega; Crypt of the Blind Dead; Night of the Blind Dead* 1972 (PG) Blinded by crows for using human sacrifice in the 13th century, zombies rise from the grave to wreak havoc upon 20th-century Spaniards. Atmospheric chiller was extremely popular in Europe and spawned three sequels. The sequels, also on video, were "Return of the Evil Dead" and "Horror of the Zombies." **102m/C VHS, Beta.** *SP PT* Caesar Burner, Lone Fleming, Helen Harp, Joseph Thelman, Rufino Ingles, Maria Silva; **D:** Armando de Ossorio; **W:** Armando de Ossorio; **C:** Pablo Ripoll. *VTR*

Tombstone ✂✂✂ 1993 (R) Saga of Wyatt Earp and his band of law-abiding large moustaches beat the Kasdan/Costner vehicle to the big screen by several months. Legendary lawman Wyatt (Russell) moves to Tombstone, AZ aiming to start a new life with his brothers, but alas, that's not to be. The infamous gunfight at the OK Corral is here, and so is best buddy Doc Holliday, gunslinger and philosopher, a role designed for sce-

nery chewing (Kilmer excels). Romance is supplied by actress Delany, though Delany lacks the necessary romantic spark. Russell spends a lot of time looking troubled by the violence while adding to the body count. Too self-conscious, suffers from '90s western revisionism, but blessed with a high energy level thanks to despicable villains Lang, Biehn, and Boothe. **CW:** Strong western violence. **130m/C VHS, LV, Closed Caption.** Kurt Russell, Val Kilmer, Michael Biehn, Sam Elliott, Dana Delany, Bill Paxton, Powers Boothe, Stephen Lang, Jason Priestley, Dana Wheeler-Nicholson, Billy Zane, Thomas Haden-Church, Joanna Pacula, Michael Rooker, Harry Carey Jr., Billy Bob Thornton, Charlton Heston, Robert John Burke, John Corbett, Buck Taylor, Terry O'Quinn, Pedro Armendariz Jr., Chris Mitchum, Jon Tenney; **D:** George P. Cosmatos; **W:** Kevin Jarre; **M:** Bruce Broughton. Nominations: MTV Movie Awards '94: Best Male Performance (Kilmer), Most Desirable Male (Kilmer). *HPH*

Tombstone Canyon ✂½ 1935 Death rides the range until Maynard and his horse Tarzan put a halt to it. **60m/B VHS, Beta.** Ken Maynard, Sheldon Lewis, Cecilia Parker. *SNC, NOS, RXM*

Tombstone Terror ✂ 1934 A cowboy is beleaguered by a case of mistaken identity. **55m/B VHS, Beta.** Bob Steele. *NO*

Tomcat: Dangerous Desires ✂✂ 1993 (R) Tom (Grieco) suffers from a rare degenerative condition and agrees to become a guinea pig in a secret, genetic imprinting experiment that has him injected with feline RNA. Tom's health is restored but the side effects give him the predatory instincts of a cat and the need to kill to stay alive. **96m/C VHS, LV, Closed Caption.** Richard Grieco, Maryam D'Abo, Natalie Radford. *REP*

Tommy ✂✂ 1975 (PG) Peter Townsend's rock opera as visualized in the usual hyper-Russell style about the deaf, dumb, and blind boy who becomes a celebrity due to his amazing skill at the pinball machines. A parade of rock musicians perform throughout the affair, with varying degrees of success. Despite some good moments, the film ultimately falls prey to ill-conceived production concepts and miscasting. ♫Underture; Captain Walker Didn't Come Home; It's A Boy; '51 is Going to Be A Good Year; What About the Boy?; The Amazing Journey; Christmas; See Me, Feel Me; Eyesight to the Blind. **108m/C VHS, Beta, LV.** Ann-Margret, Elton John, Oliver Reed, Tina Turner, Roger Daltrey, Eric Clapton, Keith Moon, Pete Townshend, Jack Nicholson, Robert Powell, Paul Nicholas, Barry Winch, Victoria Russell, Ben Aris, Mary Holland, Jennifer Baker, Susan Baker, Arthur Brown, John Entwhistle; **D:** Ken Russell; **W:** Ken Russell, Keith Moon, John Entwhistle; **C:** Dick Bush; **M:** Pete Townshend. Golden Globe Awards '76: Best Actress—Musical/Comedy (Ann-Margret); Nominations: Academy Awards '75: Best Actress (Ann-Margret), Original Song Score and/or Adaptation. *COL, MVD, WME*

Tommy Boy ✂✂ 1995 (PG-13) Not-too-bright rich kid Tommy (Farley) teams up with snide, officious accountant Richard (Spade) to save the family auto parts business after dad (Dennehy) buys the farm. Tommy and Richard must deal with a conniving stepmom and stepbrother (Derek and Lowe), a ruthless rival (Aykroyd), and a road trip from hell to drum up some new business. Not as bad as it sounds, but inconsistent direction and too-familiar characters offset the amusing chemistry between Farley and Spade. **CW:** Sex-related humor; some drug content and nudity. **98m/C VHS, Beta, Closed Caption.** Chris Farley, David Spade, Brian Dennehy, Bo Derek, Dan Aykroyd, Julie Warner, Rob Lowe; **D:** Peter Segal; **W:** Bonnie Turner, Terry Turner; **M:** David Newman. MTV Movie Awards '96: Best On-Screen Duo (Chris Farley/David Spade); Nominations: MTV Movie Awards '96: Best Comedic Performance (Farley). *PAR*

Tomorrow ✂✂✂ 1972 (PG) Powerful tale of the love of two lonely people. Outstanding performance by Duvall as lumber mill worker who falls for a pregnant woman. Based on the neglected Faulkner story. **102m/B VHS, Beta.** Robert Duvall, Olga

Bellin, Sudie Bond; **D:** Joseph Anthony; **W:** Horton Foote. *MON*

Tomorrow at Seven ✂✂½ 1933 A mystery writer is determined to discover the identity of the Ace of Spades, a killer who always warns his intended victim, then leaves an ace of spades on the corpse as his calling card. **62m/B VHS, Beta.** Chester Morris, Vivienne Osborne, Frank McHugh, Allen Jenkins, Henry Stephenson; **D:** Ray Enright. *SNC, NOS, VYY*

Tomorrow Is Forever ✂✂½ 1946 Welles and Colbert marry shortly before he goes off to fight in WWI. Badly wounded and disfigured, he decides to stay in Europe while Colbert, believing Welles dead, eventually marries Brent. Fast forward to WWII when Brent, a chemical manufacturer, hires a new scientist to work for him in the war effort (guess who). This slow-moving melodrama wastes a good cast. Six-year-old Wood debuts as Colbert's daughter. **105m/B VHS.** Claudette Colbert, Orson Welles, George Brent, Lucile Watson, Richard Long, Natalie Wood; **D:** Irving Pichel; **C:** Joseph Valentine; **M:** Max Steiner. *MGM*

Tomorrow Never Comes ✂½ 1977 When he discovers his girlfriend has been unfaithful, a guy goes berserk and eventually finds himself in a stand-off with the police. Violent. **109m/C VHS, Beta.** Oliver Reed, Susan George, Raymond Burr, John Ireland, Stephen McHattie, Donald Pleasence; **D:** Peter Collinson. *UNI, HHE*

Tomorrow Never Dies ✂✂ 1997 (PG-13) 18th installment of the James Bond series is all style and little else packaged in a tedious action adventure. Our villain is a media mogul (Pryce) who plans to start World War III in order to increase his newspaper revenues. (Rupert Murdoch, start your lawyers!) In between the blatant product placements (from Heineken to Visa), our secret agent Bond (Bronsan, who seems bored with the role in his second appearance) sets out to foil the nutty plans. Bond gets help from Hong Kong action queen Yeoh as a Chinese agent, and a bevy of toys from the antiquated Q, including a BMW controlled by remote. Direction and flow is on autopilot after the opening scene and despite Yeoh's energetic high-kicks and the sleek techno toys, it can't revitalize what has become a third-class imitator of its predecessors. **CW:** Intense sequences of action violence, sexuality and innuendo. **119m/C VHS, Closed Caption.** Pierce Brosnan, Jonathan Pryce, Michelle Yeoh, Teri Hatcher, Judi Dench, Colin Salmon, Samantha Bond, Desmond Llewelyn, Joe Don Baker, Ricky Jay, Vincent Schiavelli, Geoffrey Palmer; **D:** Roger Spottiswoode; **W:** Bruce Feirstein; **C:** Robert Elswit; **M:** David Arnold. Nominations: Golden Globe Awards '98: Best Song ("Tomorrow Never Dies"); MTV Movie Awards '98: Best Action Sequence, Best Fight (Michelle Yeoh/bad guys). *WAR*

Tomorrow's Child ✂✂ 1982 Made-for-television drama about in vitro fertilization (test-tube babies) and surrogate motherhood. **100m/C VHS, Beta, Closed Caption.** Stephanie Zimbalist, William Atherton, Bruce Davison, Ed Flanders, Salome Jens, James Shigeta, Susan Oliver, Arthur Hill; **D:** Joseph Sargent. *FOX*

Tomorrow's Children ✂ 1934 An alarmist melodrama warning against the threat of government-induced female sterilization asks the question: if a woman's family is weird, should her tubes be tied? **55m/B VHS, Beta.** Sterling Holloway, Diana Sinclair, Sarah Padden, Don Douglas; **D:** Crane Wilbur. *SNC, NOS, VYY*

The Tong Man ✂✂½ 1919 Robbins owes the tong money and Hayakawa, as the tong's executioner, is sent to kill him when he won't pay up. Only it turns out Hayakawa is in love with Eddy, Robbins daughter, and refuses. Then the tong decide to kill him for disobeying their orders. **58m/B VHS.** Sessue Hayakawa, Helen Jerome Eddy, Marc Robbins, Toyo Fujita; **D:** William Worthington. *GPV*

Tongs: An American Nightmare *ℐ* 1988 (R) Chinese-American street gangs in Chinatown battle over turf and drug shipments. 80m/C VHS, Beta. Ian Anthony Leung, Christopher O'Conner, Simon Yam; **D:** Philip Chan.

Toni *ℐℐℐ½* 1934 An Italian worker falls for his landlady and they make plans to marry. A grim turn of events, however, brings tragic consequences. Based on the lives of several townsfolk in the village of Les Martiques, the film was shot in the town and members of the local populace were used as characters. In French with English subtitles. 90m/B VHS, Beta. **FR** Charles Blavette, Jenny Helia, Edouard Delmont, Celia Montalvan; **D:** Jean Renoir. DVT

Tonight and Every Night *ℐℐ½* 1945 Cabaret singer and RAF pilot fall in love during WWII. Her music hall post puts her in the midst of Nazi bombing, and her dedication to her song and dance career puts a strain on the romance. Imaginative production numbers outweigh pedestrian storyline. ♫Cry and You Cry Alone; What Does an English Girl Think of a Yank; Anywhere; The Boy I Left Behind; You Excite Me; Tonight and Every Night. 92m/C VHS, Beta. Rita Hayworth, Lee Bowman, Janet Blair, Marc Platt, Leslie Brooks; **D:** Victor Saville. Nominations: Academy Awards '45: Best Song ("Anywhere"), Scoring of a Musical. COL

Tonight for Sure *ℐ½* 1961 Coppola made this nudie, his first film, as a student at UCLA. Two men, one who spies on women and the other who imagines nude women everywhere, plan an escapade. 66m/B VHS, Beta. **D:** Francis Ford Coppola; **W:** Francis Ford Coppola; **M:** Carmine Coppola. VYY, TPV

Tonio Kroger *ℐℐ* 1965 A young writer travels through Europe in search of intellectual and sensual relationships and a home that will suit him. He must balance freedom and responsibility. Works best if one is familiar with the Thomas Mann novel on which film is based. In German with English subtitles. 92m/B VHS, Beta. **GE** Jean-Claude Brialy, Nadja Tiller, Gert Frobe; **D:** Rolf Thiele. VYY, GLX

Tonka *ℐℐ½* A Horse Named Comanche 1958 A children's story about a wild horse tamed by a young Indian, only to have it recruited for the Battle of Little Bighorn. Mineo is fine as the Indian brave determined to be reunited with his steed. The film also makes a laudable effort to portray the Indians as a dignified race. The movie, however, stumbles at its conclusion and is contrived throughout. 97m/C VHS, Beta. Sal Mineo, Phil Carey, Jerome Courtland; **D:** Lewis R. Foster. DIS

Tonto Basin Outlaws *ℐℐ* 1941 The Range Busters team up with Teddy Roosevelt's Rough Riders in order to stop a gang of cattle rustlers. Standard oater material. Based on the story by Earle Snell. 60m/B VHS, Beta. Ray Corrigan, John "Dusty" King, Max Terhune, Jan Wiley, Tristram Coffin, Edmund Cobb; **D:** S. Roy Luby; **W:** John Vlahos. MOV

The Tonto Kid *ℐ* 1935 Action-packed western featuring Rex Bell. 56m/B VHS, Beta. Rex Bell, Ruth Mix, Buzz Barton, Joseph Girard, Jack Rockwell, Murdock McQuarrie; **D:** Harry Fraser. NOS, DVT, VDM

Tony Draws a Horse *ℐℐ½* 1951 An eight-year-old draws an anatomically correct horse on the door of his father's office, leading to a rift between the parents as they argue how to handle the heartbreak of precociousness. Somewhat uneven but engaging comedy, based on a play by Lesley Storm. 90m/B VHS. Cecil Parker, Anne Crawford, Derek Bond, Barbara Murray, Mervyn Johns, Barbara Everest, David Hurst; **D:** John Paddy Carstairs. NOS

Tony Rome *ℐℐ½* 1967 The Marvin H. Albert private eye agency investigates a millionaire's daughter's disappearance and her involvement in organized crime. Entertaining and complex plot, although the cast is a numbingly large one. 110m/C VHS, Beta. Frank Sinatra, Jill St. John, Simon Oakland, Gena Rowlands, Richard Conte, Lloyd Bochner, Jeffrey Lynn, Sue Lyon; **D:** Gordon Douglas. FOX

Too Beautiful for You *ℐℐ* Trop Belle Pour Toi 1988 (R) A successful car salesman, married for years to an extraordinarily beautiful woman, finds himself head over heels for his frumpy secretary. Depardieu plays the regular guy who finds he's never believed in the love and fidelity of a woman he thinks is too beautiful for him. In French with English subtitles. 91m/C VHS. **FR** Gerard Depardieu, Josiane Balasko, Carole Bouquet, Roland Blanche; **D:** Bertrand Blier; **W:** Bertrand Blier. Cannes Film Festival '89: Grand Jury Prize; Cesar Awards '90: Best Actress (Bouquet), Best Director (Blier), Best Film, Best Writing. ORI, FXL, FCT

Too Far to Go *ℐℐℐ* 1979 Terrific TV adaptation of a series of John Updike stories focusing on the rocky longtime marriage of not-so-proper New Englanders Danner and Moriarty. 98m/C VHS. Blythe Danner, Michael Moriarty, Glenn Close, Ken Kercheval; **W:** William Hanley. MON

Too Fast, Too Young *ℐ* 1996 (R) L.A. police captain Floyd Anderson (Ironside) finds himself shouldering the blame when violent offender Dalton (Tiller) escapes from prison and goes on a cop-killing spree. **CW:** Graphic violence, profanity, nudity, sexual situations. 90m/C VHS. Michael Ironside, Patrick Tiller, James Wellington, Kaisa Figura, Marshall Bell; **D:** Tim Everitt; **W:** Tim Everitt. MNC

Too Hot to Handle *ℐℐℐ* 1938 Two rival photographers searching for a beautiful lady-pilot's missing brother wind up in Brazil, where they encounter a dangerous tribe of voodoo types. Amusing, if exaggerated, picture of the lengths to which reporters will go for a story. Classic Gable. 105m/B VHS, Closed Caption. Clark Gable, Myrna Loy, Walter Pidgeon, Walter Connolly, Leo Carrillo, Virginia Weidler; **D:** Jack Conway. MGM, FCT

Too Hot to Handle *ℐ* 1976 Voluptuous lady contract killer fights against the mob with all the weapons at her disposal. Filmed on location in Manila. 88m/C VHS, Beta. Cheri Caffaro, Aharon Ipale, Vic Diaz, Corinne Calvet; **D:** Don Schain. WAR

Too Late for Tears *ℐℐ* Killer Bait 1949 An honest husband and his not so honest wife stumble on a load of mob-stolen cash and become entangled in a web of deceit and murder as the wife resorts to increasingly desperate measures to keep her newfound fortune. Atmospheric and entertaining film noir albeit sometimes confusing. 99m/B VHS, Beta. Lizabeth Scott, Don DeFore, Dan Duryea, Arthur Kennedy, Kristine Miller, Barry Kelley, Denver Pyle, Jimmy Ames, Billy Halop, Jimmie Dodd; **D:** Byron Haskin; **W:** Roy Huggins; **C:** William Mellor; **M:** Dale Butts. SNC, VDM, NOS

Too Late the Hero *ℐℐℐ* Suicide Run 1970 (PG) Unlikely band of allied soldiers battle Japanese force entrenched in the Pacific during WWII. Rousing adventure, fine cast. 133m/C VHS, Beta. Michael Caine, Cliff Robertson, Henry Fonda, Ian Bannen, Harry Andrews, Denholm Elliott; **D:** Robert Aldrich; **C:** Joseph Biroc. FOX

Too Many Crooks *ℐℐ* 1959 A British spoof of crime syndicate films. Crooks try to extort, but bungle the job. Terry-Thomas is fun, as always. 85m/B VHS, Beta. **GB** Terry-Thomas, Brenda de Banzie, George Cole; **D:** Mario Zampi. NO

Too Many Girls *ℐℐ½* 1940 Beautiful heiress goes to a small New Mexico college to escape from a cadre of gold-digging suitors. Passable adaptation of the successful Rodgers and Hart Broadway show, with many original cast members and the original stage director. Lucy and Desi met while making this film, and married shortly after. ♫Spic and Spanish; Heroes in the Fall; Pottawatomie; 'Cause We All Got Cake; Love Never Went to College; Look Out; I Didn't Know What Time It Was; The Conga; You're Nearer. 85m/B VHS, Beta, LV. Lucille Ball, Richard Carlson, Eddie Bracken, Ann Miller, Desi Arnaz Sr., Hal LeRoy, Libby Bennett, Frances Langford, Van Johnson; **D:** George Abbott; **M:** George Bassman, Richard Rodgers, Lorenz Hart. TTC

Too Much Sun *ℐ½* 1990 (R) A dying man can prevent his fortune from falling into the hands of a corrupt priest simply by having one of his two children produce an heir. The problem is, they're both gay! 97m/C VHS, LV. Robert Downey Jr., Ralph Macchio, Eric Idle, Andrea Martin, Laura Ernst, Jim Haynie; **D:** Robert Downey. COL

Too Pretty to Be Honest *ℐℐ* Trop Jolie pour Etre Honette 1972 Four women sharing an apartment witness a robbery and begin to suspect that their neighbor is the culprit. So they decide to steal the money from him. In French with subtitles. 95m/C VHS, Beta. **FR** Jane Birkin, Bernadette LaFont, Serge Gainsbourg; **D:** Richard Balducci; **M:** Serge Gainsbourg. FCT

Too Scared to Scream *ℐ½* 1985 (R) Policeman and an undercover agent team up to solve a bizarre series of murders at a Manhattan apartment house. 104m/C VHS, Beta. Mike Connors, Anne Archer, Leon Isaac Kennedy, John Heard, Ian McShane, Maureen O'Sullivan, Murray Hamilton; **D:** Tony LoBianco; **W:** Neal Barbera. ART, VES

Too Shy to Try *ℐℐ* 1982 (PG) A incredibly shy man meets his dream girl, and enrolls in a psychology course to overcome his ineptitude. A ribald, slapstick French comedy. 89m/C VHS, Beta. **FR** Pierre Richard, Aldo Maccione; **D:** Pierre Richard.

Too Wise Wives *ℐℐ* 1921 A story of would-be marital infidelity and misunderstandings. Silent. 90m/C VHS, Beta. Louis Calhern, Claire Windsor; **D:** Lois Weber. GVV

Too Young to Die *ℐℐ* 1990 (R) Teenager Amanda (Lewis) hooks up with the wrong guy in sleazy Billy (Pitt), who hooks her on drugs and turns her into a prostitute. She meets nice guy Mike (O'Keefe), who briefly takes her away from the life but when their relationship falls apart, Amanda goes back to Billy. Billy eggs her on to get revenge for being dumped and Amanda winds up on trial for murder. Fact-based TV movie. **CW:** Intense plot material involving a minor. 92m/C VHS, Closed Caption. Juliette Lewis, Brad Pitt, Michael Tucker, Michael O'Keefe, Emily Longstreth, Alan Fudge; **D:** Robert Markowitz; **W:** David Hill; **C:** Eric Van Haren Noman; **M:** Charles Bernstein. REP

The Toolbox Murders *ℐ* 1978 (R) Unknown psychotic murderer brutally claims victims one at a time, leaving police mystified and townsfolk terrified. Sick and exploitative, with predictably poor production values. 93m/C VHS, Beta. Cameron Mitchell, Pamelyn Ferdin, Wesley Eure, Nicholas Beauvy, Aneta Corsaut, Tim Donnelly, Evelyn Guerrero; **D:** Dennis Donnelly. VCI, VTR

Toothless *ℐℐ½* 1997 Katherine Lewis (Alley) is a work-obsessed dentist who is struck by a car and wakes up in Limbo Land (yes, she's dead). The supervisor, Ms. Rogers (Redgrave), informs Katherine that because she had no emotional connections in life her entry into heaven will have to wait—and she's going to do her time as the Tooth Fairy. Katherine is not supposed to intervene with her charges but this sarcastic lady, who doesn't much care for her princess-like Tooth Fairy attire, does get involved with 12-year-old Bobby (Mallinger) and his widowed dad (Midkiff). 85m/C VHS, Closed Caption. Kirstie Alley, Ross Malinger, Dale Midkiff, Lynn Redgrave, Darryl (Chill) Mitchell, Melanie Mayron, Kimberly Scott, Helen Slater; **W:** Mark S. Kaufman. TOU

Tootsie *ℐℐℐℐ* 1982 (PG) A stubborn, unemployed actor disguises himself as a woman to secure a part on a soap opera. As his popularity on television mounts, his love life becomes increasingly soap operatic. Hoffman is delightful, as is the rest of the stellar cast. Debut of Davis; Murray's performance unbilled. Laserdisc version features audio commentary by director Sidney Pollack, behind the scenes footage and photographs, and complete coverage of Tootsie's production. 110m/C VHS, Beta, LV, Letterbox, Closed Caption. Dustin Hoffman, Jessica Lange, Teri Garr, Dabney Coleman, Bill Murray, Charles Durning, Geena Davis, George

Gaynes, Estelle Getty, Christine Ebersole, Sydney Pollack; *D:* Sydney Pollack; *W:* Larry Gelbart, Murray Schisgal, Don McGuire; *C:* Owen Roizman; Mr Dave Grusin. Academy Awards '82: Best Supporting Actress (Lange); British Academy Awards '83: Best Actor (Hoffman); Golden Globe Awards '83: Best Actor—Musical/Comedy (Hoffman), Best Film—Musical/Comedy, Best Supporting Actress (Lange); Los Angeles Film Critics Association Awards '82: Best Screenplay; New York Film Critics Awards '82: Best Director (Pollack), Best Screenplay, Best Supporting Actress (Lange); National Society of Film Critics Awards '82: Best Actor (Hoffman), Best Film, Best Screenplay, Best Supporting Actress (Lange); Writers Guild of America '82: Best Original Screenplay; Nominations: Academy Awards '82: Best Actor (Hoffman), Best Cinematography, Best Director (Pollack), Best Film Editing, Best Original Screenplay, Best Picture, Best Song ("It Might Be You"), Best Sound, Best Supporting Actress (Garr). *COL, CRC, BTV*

Top Dog ♂½ **1995 (PG-13)** Another cop-and-dog-team-up-to-get-the-bad-guys flick. This one, however, is meant to appeal to the kids who liked "Sidekicks." That raises a problem with the unfortunately topical right-wing-hate group-bombing plot. Jake Wilder (Norris), a beer-swillin' karate-choppin' loner cop, teams up with canine Reno, whose ex-partner was killed by the neo-Nazi terrorists. Weak script and erratic storyline can't find a comfortable balance between the too-cute pooch scenes and the (admittedly toned-down) violence. Reno steals every scene he's in, and provides the flick's few redeeming moments.*CW:* Shootings and martial arts violence; strong language. **93m/C VHS, LV, Closed Caption.** Chuck Norris, Clyde Kusatsu, Michele Lamar Richards, Carmine Caridi, Peter Savard Moore, Erik von Detten, Herta Ware, Kai Wulff, Francesco Quinn, Timothy Bottoms; *D:* Aaron Norris; *W:* Ron Swanson; *C:* Joao Fernandes. *ART*

Top Gun ♂♂½ **1986 (PG)** Young Navy pilots compete against one another on the ground and in the air at the elite Fighter Weapons School. Cruise isn't bad as a maverick who comes of age in Ray Bans, but Edwards shines as his buddy. Awesome aerial photography and high-cal beefcake divert from the contrived plot and stock characters. The Navy subsequently noticed an increased interest in fighter pilots. Features Berlin's Oscar-winning song "Take My Breath Away." ♫Take My Breath Away; Danger Zone; Destination Unknown; Heaven in Your Eyes; Hot Summer Nights; Mighty Wings; Playing with the Boys; Through the Fire; Top Gun Anthem. **109m/C VHS, Beta, LV, 8mm, Closed Caption.** Tom Cruise, Kelly McGillis, Val Kilmer, Tom Skerritt, Anthony Edwards, Meg Ryan, Rick Rossovich, Michael Ironside, Barry Tubb, Whip Hubley, John Stockwell, Tim Robbins, Adrian Pasdar; *D:* Tony Scott; *W:* Jim Cash, Jack Epps Jr.; *M:* Harold Faltermeyer. Academy Awards '86: Best Song ("Take My Breath Away"); Golden Globe Awards '87: Best Song ("Take My Breath Away"); Nominations: Academy Awards '86: Best Film Editing, Best Sound. *PAR*

Top Hat ♂♂♂♂ **1935** Ginger isn't impressed by Fred's amorous attentions since she's mistaken him for a friend's other half. Many believe it to be the duo's best film together. Choreography by Astaire and score by Berlin makes this one a classic Hollywood musical. Look for a young Lucille Ball as a clerk in a flower shop. ♫Cheek to Cheek; Top Hat, White Tie and Tails; Isn't This A Lovely Day; The Piccolino; No Strings. **97m/B VHS, Beta, LV, 8mm.** Fred Astaire, Ginger Rogers, Erik Rhodes, Helen Broderick, Edward Everett Horton, Eric Blore, Lucille Ball; *D:* Mark Sandrich; *W:* Dwight Taylor, Allan Scott; *M:* Irving Berlin, Max Steiner. National Film Registry '90;; Nominations: Academy Awards '35: Best Interior Decoration, Best Picture, Best Song ("Cheek to Cheek"). *TTC, HMV*

Top of the Heap ♂ **1972 (R)** A cop is denied a promotion and gets angry. Deciding to chuck the laws of due process, he goes on a criminal-killing rampage. **91m/C VHS, Beta.** Christopher St. John, Paula Kelly, Patrick McVey; *D:* Christopher St. John. *NO*

Top Secret! ♂♂♂ **1984 (PG)** Unlikely musical farce parodies spy movies and Elvis Presley films. Young American rock star Nick Rivers goes to Europe on goodwill tour and becomes involved with Nazis, the French Resistance, an American refugee, and more. Sophisticated it isn't. From the creators of "Airplane!" **90m/C VHS, Beta, LV, Closed Caption.** Val Kilmer, Lucy Gutteridge, Christopher Villiers, Omar Sharif, Peter Cushing, Jeremy Kemp, Michael Gough; *D:* Jim Abrahams, Jerry Zucker, David Zucker; *W:* Jim Abrahams, Jerry Zucker, David Zucker, Martyn Burke; *M:* Maurice Jarre. *PAR*

Topaz ♂♂♂ **1969 (PG)** American CIA agent and French intelligence agent combine forces to find information about Russian espionage in Cuba. Cerebral and intriguing, but not classic Hitchcock. Based on the novel by Leon Uris. Laserdisc includes two alternate endings. **126m/C VHS, Beta, LV.** John Forsythe, Frederick Stafford, Philippe Noiret, Karin Dor, Michel Piccoli; *D:* Alfred Hitchcock; *C:* Jack Hildyard; *M:* Maurice Jarre. National Board of Review Awards '69: Best Director (Hitchcock), Best Supporting Actor (Noiret). *USH*

Topaze ♂♂♂ **1933** American adaptation of the Marcel Pagnol play, about an innocent, doltish schoolmaster who becomes the unknowing front for a baron's illegal business scam. Remade in two French versions, in 1933, and in 1951 by Pagnol. **127m/B VHS, Beta, LV, Closed Caption.** John Barrymore, Myrna Loy, Jobyna Howland, Jackie Searl; *D:* Harry D'Abbadie D'Arrast. *FOX*

Topaze ♂♂♂ **1933** A shy, depressed teacher is fired from his job at a private school and takes a new job, unaware that his boss is using him in a business scam. From the French play by Marcel Pagnol. An American version was also filmed in 1933; Pagnol produced his own version in '51. In French with English subtitles. **92m/B VHS, Beta, Closed Caption.** FR Louis Jouvet, Edwige Feuillere, Marcel Vallee; *D:* Louis Gasnier; *W:* Marcel Pagnol; *M:* Max Steiner. *INT, FOX, HEG*

Topaze ♂♂♂½ **1951** After losing his job, a pathetic school teacher gets involved with the mob and winds up a powerful businessman. Remake of two earlier versions, one French and one American. Based on the play by director Pagnol. In French with English subtitles. **95m/B VHS, Closed Caption.** FR Fernandel, Helen Perdriere, Pierre Larquey; *D:* Marcel Pagnol. *DVT*

The Topeka Terror ♂♂ **1945** Lane stars as a federal agent who joins forces with a frontier lawyer to stop greedy land-grabber Barcroft from ripping off a group of homesteaders. Based on a story by Patricia Harper. **55m/B VHS.** Allan "Rocky" Lane, Linda Stirling, Roy Barcroft, Earle Hodgins, Bud Geary; *D:* Howard Bretherton; *W:* Patricia Harper, Norman S. Hall. *MOV*

Topkapi ♂♂♂ **1964** An international bevy of thieves can't resist the treasures of the famed Topkapi Palace Museum, an impregnable fortress filled with wealth and splendor. Comic thriller based on Erie Ambler's "The Light of Day." **122m/C VHS, Beta.** Melina Mercouri, Maximilian Schell, Peter Ustinov, Robert Morley, Akim Tamiroff; *D:* Jules Dassin; *M:* Manos Hadjidakis. Academy Awards '64: Best Supporting Actor (Ustinov). *FOX*

Topper ♂♂♂½ **1937** George and Marion Kerby return as ghosts after a fatal car accident, determined to assist their pal Cosmo Topper. Immensely popular at the boxoffice; followed by "Topper Takes a Trip" and "Topper Returns." The series uses trick photography and special effects to complement the comedic scripts. Inspired a television series and remade in 1979 as television movie. Also available colorized. **97m/B VHS, Beta.** Cary Grant, Roland Young, Constance Bennett, Billie Burke, Eugene Pallette, Hoagy Carmichael; *D:* Norman Z. McLeod. Nominations: Academy Awards '37: Best Sound, Best Supporting Actor (Young). *CCB, VTR*

Topper Returns ♂♂♂ **1941** Cosmo Topper helps ghost find the man who mistakenly murdered her and warns her friend, the intended victim. Humorous conclusion to the trilogy preceded

by "Topper" and "Topper Takes a Trip." Followed by a television series. Also available colorized. **87m/B VHS, Beta, LV.** Roland Young, Joan Blondell, Dennis O'Keefe, Carole Landis, Eddie Anderson, H.B. Warner, Billie Burke; *D:* Roy Del Ruth. Nominations: Academy Awards '41: Best Sound. *SNC, NOS, CAB*

Topper Takes a Trip ♂♂♂ **1939** Cosmo Topper and his wife have falling out and ghosts Kerby help them get back together. The special effects sequences are especially funny. Followed by "Topper Returns." Also available colorized. **85m/B VHS, Beta.** Constance Bennett, Roland Young, Billie Burke, Franklin Pangborn, Alan Mowbray; *D:* Norman Z. McLeod. Nominations: Academy Awards '39: Best Special Effects. *VTR*

Topsy Turvy ♂½ **1984 (R)** A comedy about reckless romance and not much else. **90m/C VHS, Beta.** Lisbet Dahl, Ebbe Rode; *D:* Edward Fleming. *ART, VES*

Tor ♂½ **1964** Medieval barbarian endeavors to free an enslaved village from a band of murderous hoodlums. **94m/C VHS, Beta.** Joe Robinson, Bella Cortez, Harry Baird; *D:* Antonio Leonuiola. *TWE*

Tora! Tora! Tora! ♂♂♂ **1970 (G)** The story of events leading up to December 7, 1941, is retold by three directors from both Japanese and American viewpoints in this tense, large-scale production. Well-documented and realistic treatment of the Japanese attack on Pearl Harbor that brought the U.S. into WWII; notable for its good photography but lacks a storyline equal to its epic intentions. **144m/C VHS, Beta, LV.** Martin Balsam, Soh Yomamura, Joseph Cotten, E.G. Marshall, Tatsuya Mihashi, Wesley Addy, Jason Robards Jr., James Whitmore, Leon Ames, George Macready; *D:* Richard Fleischer, Toshio Masuda, Kinji Fukasaku; *M:* Jerry Goldsmith. Academy Awards '70: Best Visual Effects; Nominations: Academy Awards '70: Best Art Direction/Set Decoration, Best Cinematography, Best Film Editing, Best Sound. *FOX, TLF, HMV*

The Torch ♂♂½ **1950** Mexican revolutionary restores law and order when he captures a small town but then finds himself in turmoil as he falls for an aristocratic young woman. **90m/C VHS.** MX Gilbert Roland, Paulette Goddard, Pedro Armendariz Sr., Walter Reed; *D:* Emilio Fernandez. *FCT*

Torch Song ♂♂ **1953** In this muddled melodrama, a tough, demanding Broadway actress meets her match when she is offered true love by a blind pianist. Contains a couple of notoriously inept musical numbers. Made to show off Crawford's figure at age 50. Crawford's singing in the movie is dubbed. **90m/C VHS, LV.** Joan Crawford, Michael Wilding, Marjorie Rambeau, Gig Young, Harry (Henry) Morgan, Dorothy Patrick, Benny Rubin, Nancy Gates; *D:* Charles Walters. Nominations: Academy Awards '53: Best Supporting Actress (Rambeau).*MGM*

Torch Song Trilogy ♂♂½ **1988 (R)** Adapted from Fierstein's hit Broadway play about a gay man who "just wants to be loved." Still effective, but the rewritten material loses something in the translation to the screen. Bancroft heads a strong cast with a finely shaded performance as Fierstein's mother. **126m/C VHS, Beta, LV, Closed Caption.** Anne Bancroft, Matthew Broderick, Harvey Fierstein, Brian Kerwin, Karen Young, Charles Pierce; *D:* Paul Bogart; *W:* Harvey Fierstein; *C:* Mikael Salomon; *M:* Peter Matz. *COL*

Torchlight ♂ **1985 (R)** A young couple's life begins to crumble when a wealthy art dealer teaches them how to free base cocaine. Heavy-handed treatment of a subject that's been tackled with more skill elsewhere. **90m/C VHS, Beta, LV.** Pamela Sue Martin, Steve Railsback, Ian McShane, Al Corley, Rita Taggart; *D:* Thomas J. Wright.

Torero ♂ *Bullfighter* **1956** A young man becomes a bullfighter to overcome his fear of bulls. **89m/B VHS, Beta.** MX Luis Procuna, Manolete, Dolores Del Rio, Carlos Arruza; *D:* Carlos Velo; *W:* Carlos Velo, Hugo Butler. *MAD*

Torment ♂♂♂ *Hets; Frenzy* **1944** Tragic triangle has young woman in love with fellow student and murdered by sadistic teacher. Atmospheric tale hailed by many as Sjoberg's finest film. Ingmar Bergman's first filmed script. In Swedish with English subtitles. **90m/B VHS, Beta. SW D:** Alf Sjoberg; **W:** Ingmar Bergman. *HMV, NLC*

Torment 🎬 **1985 (R)** A mild-mannered fellow is secretly a mass murderer specializing in young lovers. He struggles to hide his secret as his daughter approaches dating age and a relentless detective gets closer to the truth. A low-budget slasher. **85m/C VHS, Beta.** Taylor Gilbert, William Witt, Eve Brenner; **D:** Samson Aslanian, John Hopkins; **W:** Samson Aslanian, John Hopkins. *VTR*

Tormented 🎬½ **1960** Man pushes his mistress out of a lighthouse, killing her. Her ethereal body parts return to haunt him. **75m/B VHS.** Richard Carlson, Susan Gordon, Juli Reding; **D:** Bert I. Gordon. *SNC*

The Tormentors woof! **198? (R)** Vaguely neo-Nazi gangs rape and murder a man's family, and he kills them all in revenge. **78m/C VHS, Beta.** James Craig, Anthony Eisley, Chris Nole; **D:** Boris Eagle. *NO*

Torn Apart 🎬🎬 **1989 (R)** Traditional Middle East hatreds undermine the love affair between two young people. Excellent performances from the principals highlight this drama. Adapted from the Chayin Zeldis novel "A Forbidden Love." **95m/C VHS, Beta.** Adrian Pasdar, Cecilia Peck, Machram Huri, Arnon Zadok, Barry Primus; **D:** Jack Fisher; **M:** Peter Arnow. *WAR, BTV*

Torn Between Two Lovers 🎬🎬 **1979** A beautiful married woman has an affair with an architect while on a trip. Remick is enjoyable to watch, but it's a fairly predictable yarn. Made for television. **100m/C VHS.** Lee Remick, Joseph Bologna, George Peppard, Giorgio Tozzi; **D:** Delbert Mann. *ART*

Torn Curtain 🎬🎬½ **1966** American scientist poses as a defector to East Germany in order to uncover details of the Soviet missile program. He and his fiancee, who follows him behind the Iron Curtain, attempt to escape to freedom. Derivative and uninvolving. **125m/C VHS, Beta, LV.** Paul Newman, Julie Andrews, Lila Kedrova, David Opatoshu; **D:** Alfred Hitchcock; **W:** Brian Moore; **M:** John Addison. *USH*

Tornado 🎬 **1983** An army sergeant revolts against his superiors and the enemy when his captain leaves him stranded in Vietnam. **90m/C VHS, Beta.** Timothy Brent, Tony Marsina, Alan Collins; **D:** Anthony (Antonio Margheriti) Dawson. *ART*

Tornado! 🎬½ **1996 (PG)** TV movie with cheesy special effects chronicles a week with tornado chaser Campbell, meteorologist Hudson, and government accountant Sturges who wants to stop funding for Hudson's new storm-warning device. Lame attempt to capture some of the "Twister" audience fails miserably. **90m/C VHS, LV.** Bruce Campbell, Ernie Hudson, Shannon Sturges, L.Q. Jones, Bo Eason; **D:** Noel Nosseck; **W:** John Logan; **C:** Paul Maibaum; **M:** Garry Schyman. *HMK*

Torpedo Alley 🎬🎬 **1953** A guilt-ridden WWII Navy pilot feels responsible for the deaths of his crew. After the war, he joins a submarine crew and gradually learns to deal with his guilt. Average drama with plenty of submarine footage. **84m/B VHS.** Dorothy Malone, Mark Stevens, Charles Winninger, Bill Williams; **D:** Lew (Louis Friedlander) Landers. *REP*

Torpedo Attack 🎬 **1972** Greek sailors, in an outdated submarine, bravely but hopelessly attack Mussolini's Italy during WWII. **88m/C VHS, Beta.** GR John Ferris, Sidney Kazan; **D:** George Law. *ART*

Torpedo Run 🎬🎬 **1958** Standard submarine melodramatics, about a U.S. sub that must torpedo a Japanese aircraft carrier which holds some of the crew's family members. Sometimes slow, generally worthwhile. **98m/C VHS, Beta.** Glenn Ford, Ernest Borgnine, Dean Jones, Diane Brewster, L.Q. Jones; **D:** Joseph Pevney. *MGM*

Torrents of Spring 🎬🎬 **1990 (PG-13)** Based on an Ivan Turgenev story, this lavishly filmed and costumed drama concerns a young Russian aristocrat circa 1840 who is torn between

two women. Predictably, one is a good-hearted innocent, the other a scheming seductress. **102m/C VHS, Beta, LV.** Timothy Hutton, Nastassia Kinski, Valeria Golino, William Forsythe, Urbano Barberini, Francesca De Sapio, Jacques Herlin; **D:** Jerzy Skolimowski. *NO*

Torso woof! *I Corpi Presentano Tracce Di Violenza Carnale* **1973 (R)** Crazed psychosexual killer stalks beautiful women and dismembers them. Fairly bloodless and uninteresting, in spite of lovely Kendall. Italian title translates: The Bodies Showed Signs of Carnal Violence—quite an understatement for people missing arms and legs. **91m/C VHS, Beta.** IT Suzy Kendall, Tina Aumont, John Richardson; **D:** Sergio Martino; **W:** Ernesto Gastaldi, Sergio Martino.

Tortilla Flat 🎬🎬🎬 **1942** Based on the John Steinbeck novel of the same name, two buddies, Tracy and Garfield, struggle to make their way on the wrong side of the tracks in California. Garfield gets a break by inheriting a couple of houses, Tracy schemes to rip-off a rich, but eccentric, dog owner. In the meantime, both fall for the same girl, Lamarr, in perhaps the finest role of her career. Great performances from all, especially Morgan. **105m/B VHS.** Spencer Tracy, Hedy Lamarr, John Garfield, Frank Morgan, Akim Tamiroff, Sheldon Leonard, John Qualen, Donald Meek, Connie Gilchrist; **D:** Victor Fleming; **C:** Karl Freund. Nominations: Academy Awards '42: Best Supporting Actor (Morgan). *MGM, CCB*

Torture Chamber of Baron Blood 🎬🎬½ *Baron Blood; Gli Orrori del Castello di Norimberga; The Blood Baron; Chamber of Tortures; The Thirst of Baron Blood* **1972 (PG)** Baron with gorgeous thirst for the red stuff is reanimated and lots of innocent bystanders meet a grisly fate in this spaghetti gorefest. Familiar story has that certain Bava feel. **90m/C VHS, Beta.** IT Joseph Cotten, Elke Sommer, Massimo Girotti, Rada Rassimov, Antonio Cantafora; **D:** Mario Bava; **W:** Vincent Fotre, William Bairn; **M:** Les Baxter. *VTR*

The Torture Chamber of Dr. Sadism 🎬🎬½ *Blood Demon; Castle of the Walking Dead; Die Schlangengrube und das Pendel* **1969** Decapitated and drawn and quartered for sacrificing 12 virgins, the evil Count Regula is pieced together 40 years later to continue his wicked ways. Great fun, terrific art direction. Very loosely based on Poe's "The Pit and the Pendulum." Beware of the heavily edited video version. **120m/C VHS, Beta.** GE Christopher Lee, Karin Dor, Lex Barker, Carl Lange, Vladimir Medar, Christiane Rucker, Dieter Eppler; **D:** Harald Reinl. *NO*

Torture Dungeon 🎬 **1970 (R)** Director Milligan tortures audience with more mindless medieval pain infliction from Staten Island. **80m/C VHS, Beta.** Jeremy Brooks, Susan Cassidy; **D:** Andy Milligan. *NO*

Torture Garden 🎬🎬 **1967** A sinister man presides over an unusual sideshow where people can see what is in store if they allow the evil side of their personalities to take over. Written by Bloch ("Psycho") and based on four of his short stories. **93m/C VHS, Beta, LV.** GB Jack Palance, Burgess Meredith, Peter Cushing, Beverly Adams; **D:** Freddie Francis; **W:** Robert Bloch; **M:** Don Banks, James Bernard. *MCA*

The Torture of Silence 🎬🎬½ *Mater Dolorosa* **1917** A simple little drama about a doctor's neglected wife seeking out the doctor's best friend for love, remade by Gance again in 1932; both originally titled "Mater Dolorosa." Silent. **55m/B VHS, Beta. D:** Abel Gance. *FCT*

Torture Ship 🎬½ **1939** Director Halperin, who earlier made the minor horror classic "White Zombie," was all at sea in this becalmed thriller about a mad doctor who uses convicts for glandular experiment on his shipboard laboratory. Based on the short story "A Thousand Deaths" by Jack London. **57m/B VHS, Beta.** Lyle Talbot, Irving Pichel, Jacqueline Wells, Sheila Bromley; **D:** Victor Halperin. *NOS, LOO*

Torture Train 🎬½ **1983 (R)** Mayhem, murder, and knife-wielding psychosis occurs on board a train. **78m/C VHS, Beta.** Patty Edwards, Kay Beal. *JEF*

Total Eclipse 🎬 **1995 (R)** Unfortunate look at the mutually destructive relationship between 19th-century French poets Arthur Rimbaud (DiCaprio) and Paul Verlaine (Thewlis). Rimbaud was a 16-year-old Parisian sensation for his iconoclastic work but what's presented is an obnoxious showoff, while the older, married Verlaine is a drunken lout who abuses his teenaged wife Mathilde (Bohringer). There's lots of dissolute, violent behavior and absolutely no insight into their work (which is the only reason to care). Ugly film wastes a lot of talent. **CW:** Strong sexuality and nudity, language, and some startling violence. **111m/C VHS, Closed Caption.** Leonardo DiCaprio, David Thewlis, Romane Bohringer, Dominique Blanc; **D:** Agnieszka Holland; **W:** Christopher Hampton; **C:** Yorgos Arvanitis. *NLC*

Total Exposure 🎬 **1991 (R)** Total idiocy involving unclad babes and hormonally imbalanced men in blackmail and murder. 1990 Playboy Playmate Deborah Driggs proves there is life of sorts after playmatedom. **CW:** Some language, violence, and sensuality. **96m/C VHS, LV, Closed Caption.** Michael Nouri, Season Hubley, Christian Bocher, Robert Prentiss, Deborah Driggs, Jeff Conaway; **D:** John Quinn. *REP*

Total Recall 🎬🎬🎬 **1990 (R)** Mind-bending sci-fi movie set in the 21st century. Construction worker Quaid (Schwarzenegger) dreams every night about the colonization of Mars, so he decides to visit a travel service that specializes in implanting vacation memories into its clients' brains and buy a memory trip to the planet. Only during the implant, Quaid discovers his memories have been artificially altered and he must find out just what's real and what's not. Intriguing plot and spectacular special effects. Laced with graphic violence. Based on Phillip K. Dick's "We Can Remember It for You Wholesale." **CW:** Adult situations; language, nudity, gore effects, and sexual situations. **113m/C VHS, Beta, LV, 8mm, Closed Caption, DVD.** Arnold Schwarzenegger, Rachel Ticotin, Sharon Stone, Michael Ironside, Ronny Cox, Roy Brocksmith, Marshall Bell, Mel Johnson Jr.; **D:** Paul Verhoeven; **W:** Gary Goldman, Dan O'Bannon; **C:** Jan De Bont; **M:** Jerry Goldsmith. Academy Awards '90: Best Visual Effects; Nominations: Academy Awards '90: Best Sound. *IME, FUS, ART*

Totally F*ed Up** 🎬🎬 **1994** The first of director Araki's teen trilogy, followed by "The Doom Generation" and "Nowhere," concerns itself with the teen angst experienced by a loose group of friends—four gays and a lesbian couple. In short chapters, they meet, talk, and wander through a soulless L.A. as one of their group, film school student Steven (Luna), makes a video documentary about their situation (footage of which is intercut throughout the film). **80m/C VHS.** James Duval, Gilbert Luna, Lance May, Roko Belic, Susan Behshid, Jenee Gill, Alan Boyce; **D:** Gregg Araki; **W:** Gregg Araki; **C:** Gregg Araki. *FCT, SHV*

Toto le Heros 🎬🎬🎬 *Toto the Hero* **1991 (PG-13)** Bitter old man, who as a child fantasized that he was a secret agent named Toto, harbors deep resentment over not living the life he's convinced he should have had. He maintains a childhood fantasy that he and his rich neighbor were switched at birth in the confusion of a fire at the hospital. Series of flashbacks and fast forwards show glimpses of his life, not necessarily as it was, but how he perceived it. Sounds complex, but it's actually very clear and fluid. Mix of comedy and tragedy, with lots of ironic twists, and precise visuals. In French with English subtitles. **90m/C VHS, Beta, LV, Closed Caption.** FR Michel Bouquet, Jo De Backer, Thomas Godet, Mireille Perrier, Sandrine Blancke, Didier Ferney, Hugo Harold Harrisson, Gisela Uhlen, Peter Bohlke; **D:** Jaco Van Dormael; **W:** Jaco Van Dormael. Cesar Awards '91: Best Foreign Film. *PAR, BTV*

The Touch 🎬½ *Be Roringen* **1971 (R)** Straightforward story of a woman who is satisfied with her husband until the arrival of a stranger. The stranger soon has her yearning for a life she has never known. Bergman's first English film lacks the sophistication of his earlier work. 112m/C VHS, Beta SW Bibi Andersson, Elliott Gould, Max von Sydow; D: Ingmar Bergman; W: Ingmar Bergman; C: Sven Nykvist. FOX

Touch 🎬🎬½ 1996 (R) Sleazebags, fundamentalists, and a maybe saint would seem to make for a surefire success in this easygoing adaptation of the offbeat Elmore Leonard novel. And while individual scenes and performances shine, the film doesn't completely hang together. Young Juvenal (Ulrich) is a former monk, now working at an L.A. alcohol rehab center, who possesses the stigmata and seems to have an authentic gift for healing. Naturally, this brings the crazies and the scammers out of the woodwork, including former preacher Bill Hill (Walken), whose partner (Fonda) falls for the lad, and paramilitary religious fanatic August Murray (Arnold). CW: Some sexuality, language and a scene of violence. 96m/C VHS, Closed Caption. Skeet Ulrich, Bridget Fonda, Christopher Walken, Tom Arnold, Gina Gershon, Lolita Davidovich, Paul Mazursky, Janeane Garofalo, John Doe, Conchata Ferrell, Mason Adams, Breckin Meyer, Anthony Zerbe; D: Paul Schrader; W: Paul Schrader; C: Edward Lachman; M: David Grohl. Nominations: Independent Spirit Awards '98: Best Director (Schrader), Best Screenplay. MGM

Touch & Go 🎬🎬 1980 (PG) Three beautiful women commit grand larceny in order to raise funds for underprivileged children. 92m/C VHS, Beta. AU Wendy Hughes; D: Peter Maxwell; W: Alan Ormsby. NO

Touch and Go 🎬½ 1986 (R) Sentimental drama about a self-interested hockey pro who learns about love and giving through a young delinquent and his attractive mother. 101m/C VHS, Beta, LV, Closed Caption. Michael Keaton, Maria Conchita Alonso, Ajay Naidu, Maria Tucci, Max Wright, John C. Reilly; D: Robert Mandel; W: Harry Colomby. NO

Touch Me Not 🎬 The Hunted 1974 (PG) A neurotic secretary is used by an industrial spy to gain information on her boss. Weak thriller. 84m/C VHS. GB Lee Remick, Michael Hinz, Ivan Desny, Ingrid Garbo; D: Douglas Fifthian. NO

A Touch of Class 🎬🎬🎬 1973 (PG) Married American insurance adjustor working in London plans quick and uncommitted affair but finds his heart doesn't obey the rules. Jackson and Segal create sparkling record of a growing relationship. 105m/C VHS, Beta. George Segal, Glenda Jackson, Paul Sorvino, Hildegarde Neil, K. Callan, Mary Barclay, Cec Linder; D: Melvin Frank; W: Jack Rose. Academy Awards '73: Best Actress (Jackson); Golden Globe Awards '74: Best Actor—Musical/Comedy (Segal), Best Actress—Musical/Comedy (Jackson); Writers Guild of America '73: Best Original Screenplay; Nominations: Academy Awards '73: Best Picture, Best Song ("All That Love Went to Waste"), Best Story & Screenplay, Best Original Dramatic/Comedy Score.

Touch of Evil 🎬🎬🎬🎬 1958 (PG-13) Stark, perverse story of murder, kidnapping and police corruption in Mexican border town. Welles portrays a police chief who invents evidence to convict the guilty. Filled with innovative photography reminiscent of "Citizen Kane," as filmed by Russell Metty. CW: Some violence and drug content. 108m/B VHS, Beta, LV. Charlton Heston, Orson Welles, Janet Leigh, Joseph Calleia, Akim Tamiroff, Marlene Dietrich, Valentin de Vargas, Dennis Weaver, Zsa Zsa Gabor, Mort Mills, Victor Milian, Joanna Moore, Joi Lansing; Cameos: Ray Collins, Mercedes McCambridge, Joseph Cotten; D: Orson Welles; W: Orson Welles; C: Russell Metty; M: Henry Mancini. National Film Registry '93. USH

The Touch of Satan 🎬 The Touch of Melissa; Night of the Demon; Curse of Melissa 1970 (PG) Lost on the road, a young man meets a lovely young woman and is persuaded to stay at her nearby farmhouse. Things there are not as they seem, including the young woman—who turns out to be a very old witch. 90m/C VHS, Beta. Michael Berry, Emby Mallay, Lee Amber, Yvonne Wilson, Jeanne Gerson; D: Don Henderson. NO

Touched 🎬🎬 1982 (R) Two young people struggle with the outside world after their escape from a mental institution. Although melodramatic and poorly scripted, the film is saved by fine performances by Hays and Beller. 89m/C VHS, Beta. Robert Hays, Kathleen Beller, Ned Beatty, Gilbert Lewis; D: John Flynn.

Touched by Love 🎬🎬½ To Elvis, With Love 1980 (PG) The true story of a handicapped child who begins to communicate when her teacher suggests she write to Elvis Presley. Sincere and well performed. 95m/C VHS, Beta. Deborah Raffin, Diane Lane, Christina Raines, Clu Gulager, John Amos; D: Gus Trikonis; W: Hesper Anderson; M: John Barry. COL

Tough and Deadly 🎬½ 1994 (R) CIA agent teams up with bounty hunter to stop a drug ring. CW: Non-stop acts of violence; strong language; drug use. 92m/C VHS. Billy Blanks, Roddy Piper. USH

Tough Assignment 🎬 1949 A reporter in the West discovers and infiltrates a gang of organized rustlers who are forcing butchers to buy inferior meat. 64m/B VHS, Beta, LV. Donald (Don "Red") Barry, Marjorie Steele, Steve Brodie. NO

Tough Enough 🎬🎬 1983 (PG) A country-western singer and songwriter decides to finance his fledgling singing career by entering amateur boxing matches. Insipid and predictable, with fine cast wasted. 107m/C VHS, Beta. Dennis Quaid, Charlene Watkins, Warren Oates, Pam Grier, Stan Shaw, Bruce McGill, Wilford Brimley, Bob Watson; D: Richard Fleischer. FOX

Tough Guy 🎬 1953 Based on the play by Bruce Walker, a London hood carouses, mugs, breaks hearts and personifies his generation's anxiety. 73m/B VHS, Beta. GB James Kenney, Hermione Gingold, Joan Collins; D: Lewis Gilbert. UNI

Tough Guy 🎬 197? Two undercover policemen battle local gangsters in a bid to smash their crime ring. 90m/C VHS, Beta. Chen Ying, Charlie Chiang; D: Chieng Hung. NO

Tough Guys 🎬🎬½ 1986 (PG) Two aging ex-cons, who staged America's last train robbery in 1961, try to come to terms with modern life after many years in prison. Amazed and hurt by the treatment of the elderly in the 1980s, frustrated with their inability to find something worthwhile to do, they begin to plan one last heist. Tailor-made for Lancaster and Douglas, who are wonderful. Script becomes cliched at end. 103m/C VHS, Beta, LV. Burt Lancaster, Kirk Douglas, Charles Durning, Eli Wallach, Jake Steinfeld, Dana Carvey, Alexis Smith, Darlanne Fluegel, Billy Barty, Monty Ash; D: Jeff Kanew; W: James Orr, Jim Cruickshank; M: James Newton Howard. TOU

Tough Guys Don't Dance 🎬🎬½ 1987 (R) Mailer directed this self-satiric mystery thriller from his own novel. A writer may have committed murder—but he can't remember. So he searches for the truth among various friends, enemies, lovers, and cohorts. 110m/C VHS, Beta, LV, Closed Caption. Ryan O'Neal, Isabella Rossellini, Wings Hauser, Debra Sandlund, John Bedford Lloyd, Lawrence Tierney, Clarence Williams III, Penn Jillette, Frances Fisher; D: Norman Mailer; W: Norman Mailer; C: John Bailey; M: Angelo Badalamenti. Golden Raspberry Awards '87: Worst Director (Mailer). CDV, VTR

Tough Kid 🎬 1939 A bad kid with gang connections attempts to shield his boxer brother from corruption at the hands of the same gang. Poor production all around. 61m/B VHS, Beta. Frankie Darro, Dick Purcell, Judith Allen, Lillian Elliot; D: Howard Bretherton. SNC

Tough to Handle 🎬½ 1937 ...And no picnic to watch, either. A reporter cracks a criminal racket that rips off lottery sweepstakes winners. A laughably inept production. 58m/B VHS. Frankie Darro, Kane Richmond, Phyllis Fraser, Harry Worth; D: S. Roy Luby. NOS, LOO

Tougher than Leather 🎬 1988 (R) The rap triumvirate battles criminals, vigilante-style, in their home neighborhood. Poorly executed and exploitative fare. 92m/C VHS, Beta. Run DMC, The

Beastie Boys, Slick Rick, Richard Edson, Jenny Lumet; D: Rick Rubin. COL

Toughlove 🎬🎬 1985 The parents of a juvenile delinquent organize a tough parental philosophy and a support group for other parents having a difficult time with their teens. Made for television. 100m/C VHS, Beta. Lee Remick, Bruce Dern, Piper Laurie, Louise Latham, Dana Elcar, Jason Patric, Eric Schiff, Dedee Pfeiffer; D: Glenn Jordan.

Touki Bouki 🎬🎬 Journey of the Hyena 1973 Feeling alienated from their African society, Mory and Anta see freedom in the flashy consumerism of European culture and embark on a quest to meet happiness in Paris. A Bonnie & Clyde-like story symbolizing Africa's advancement toward a technological civilization. In Wolof with English subtitles. 85m/C VHS. D: Djibril Diop Mambety. KIV

Tour of Duty 🎬🎬½ 1987 Follows the trials that the members of an American platoon face daily during the Vietnam war. The pilot movie for a television series. 93m/C VHS, Beta, LV. Terence Knox, Stephen Caffrey, Joshua Maurer, Ramon Franco; D: Bill W.L. Norton. HHE

Tourist Trap 🎬 1979 (PG) While traveling through the desert, a couple's car has a flat. A woman's voice lures the man into an abandoned gas station, where he discovers that the voice belongs to a mannequin. Or is it? Not very interesting or suspenseful. 90m/C VHS, Beta, LV, Closed Caption. Tanya Roberts, Chuck Connors, Robin Sherwood, Jocelyn Jones, Jon Van Ness, Dawn Jeffory, Keith McDermott; D: David Schmoeller; W: David Schmoeller; M: Pino Donaggio. PAR

Tournament 🎬🎬½ Le Tournoi dans la Cite 1929 Renoir's second-to-last silent film, in which Protestants and Catholics joust with their differences in era of Catherine de Medici. 90m/B VHS, Beta. FR Aldo Nadi; D: Jean Renoir. FCT

Tous les Matins du Monde 🎬🎬🎬 All the Mornings of the World 1992 Haunting tale of two 17th century French baroque composers and their relationship with each other and their music. Gerard Depardieu plays Marin Marais who eventually becomes a court composer at Versailles. As a young man, he studies under Sainte Colombe, a private and soulful musician, about whom little is known even today. Depardieu's son Guillaume (in his film debut) plays the young Marais, who startles the quiet Sainte Colombe home and has an affair with one of his daughters (Brochet). Filmmaker Corneau lends a quiet austere tone which parallels the life and music of Sainte Colombe. In French with English subtitles. 114m/C VHS, LV. FR Gerard Depardieu, Guillaume Depardieu, Jean-Pierre Marielle, Anne Brochet, Caroline Sihol, Carole Richert, Violaine Lacroix, Nadege Teron, Miriam Boyer, Michel Bouquet; D: Alain Corneau; W: Pascal Quignard, Alain Corneau; C: Yves Angelo; M: Jordi Savall. Cesar Awards '92: Best Cinematography, Best Director (Corneau), Best Film, Best Supporting Actress (Brochet), Best Score. TOU

Toute Une Nuit 🎬🎬🎬 All Night Long 1982 Assorted people stumble melodramatically in and out of one another's lives on steamy summer night in Brussels. Fine combination of avant-garde technique and narrative. In French with English subtitles. 90m/C VHS. BE FR Aurore Clement, Tcheky Karyo, Veronique Silver, Angelo Abazoglou, Natalia Ackerman; D: Chantal Akerman; W: Andra Akers. WAC, FCT

Toward the Terra 🎬🎬 1980 In the distant future mankind is forced to evacuate Earth and settles on the planet Atarakusha. Society ruthlessly suppresses anything which could destabilize it in an effort to prevent the mistakes which destroyed the Earth. The most destablizing presence is the MU, a new race with incredible mental powers, who are ruthlessly hunted and eliminated. But the leader of the MU reaches out to a human with his own inexplicable powers to aid in establishing a new world. In Japanese with subtitles. 112m/C VHS. JP CPM

Tower of Evil woof! *Horror on Snape Island; Beyond the Fog* 1972 **(R)** Anthropologists and treasure hunters unite in search of Phoenician hoard on Snape Island. Suddenly, inanimate bodies materialize. Seems the island's single inhabitant liked it quiet. Cult favorite despite uneven performances. So bad it's not bad. **86m/C VHS, Beta.** *GB* Bryant Halliday, Jill Haworth, Jack Watson, Mark Edwards, George Coulouris; *D:* James O'Connolly. *NO*

The Tower of London 𝒜𝒜½ 1939 Tells the story of Richard III (Rathbone), the English monarch who brutally executed the people who tried to get in his way to the throne. This melodrama was considered extremely graphic for its time, and some of the torture scenes had to be cut before it was released. **93m/B VHS.** Basil Rathbone, Boris Karloff, Barbara O'Neil, Ian Hunter, Vincent Price, Nan Grey, John Sutton, Leo G. Carroll, Miles Mander; *D:* Rowland V. Lee; *W:* Robert N. Lee; *C:* George Robinson. *USH*

Tower of London 𝒜𝒜 1962 A deranged lord (Price) murdering his way to the throne of England is eventually crowned Richard III. Sophisticated and well-made Poe-like thriller. More interesting as historic melodrama than as horror film. A remake of the 1939 version starring Basil Rathbone, in which Price played a supporting role. **79m/B VHS, Beta.** Vincent Price, Michael Pate, Joan Freeman, Robert Brown, Sandra Knight, Justice Watson; *D:* Roger Corman; *W:* Leo Gordon, F. Amos Powell, James B. Gordon; *C:* Arch R. Dalzell. *MGM, FCT*

Tower of Screaming Virgins 𝒜 1968 The Queen of France maintains a tower in which she has her lovers killed—after she makes love to them. An extremely loose adaptation of a Dumas novel; with English subtitles. **89m/C VHS, Beta, 8mm.** *GE* Terry Torday, Jean Piat. *VYY, VDM, SNC*

Tower of Terror 𝒜½ 1942 **(NC-17)** Woman escapes from a German concentration camp and takes refuge in a lighthouse. The proprietor sees an uncanny resemblance to his late wife, whom he killed, and soon plots to do away with her. Story hampered by poor acting. **62m/B VHS, Beta.** *GB* Wilfred Lawson, Movita, Michael Rennie, Morland Graham, John Longden, George Woodbridge; *D:* Lawrence Huntington. *NOS, SNC*

The Towering Inferno 𝒜𝒜 1974 **(PG)** Raging blaze engulfs the world's tallest skyscraper on the night of its glamorous dedication ceremonies. Allen had invented the disaster du jour genre two years earlier with "The Poseidon Adventure." Features a new but equally noteworthy cast. ♫We May Never Love Like This Again. **165m/C VHS, Beta, LV, Letterbox, Closed Caption.** Steve McQueen, Paul Newman, William Holden, Faye Dunaway, Fred Astaire, Jennifer Jones, Richard Chamberlain, Susan Blakely, O.J. Simpson, Robert Vaughn, Robert Wagner; *D:* John Guillermin, Irwin Allen; *W:* Stirling Silliphant; *C:* Joseph Biroc, Fred W. Koenekamp; *M:* John Williams. Academy Awards '74: Best Cinematography, Best Film Editing, Best Song ("We May Never Love Like This Again"); British Academy Awards '75: Best Supporting Actor (Astaire); Golden Globe Awards '75: Best Supporting Actor (Astaire); Nominations: Academy Awards '74: Best Art Direction/Set Decoration, Best Picture, Best Sound, Best Supporting Actor (Astaire), Best Original Dramatic/Comedy Score. *FOX*

A Town Called Hell 𝒜 *A Town Called Bastard* 1972 **(R)** Two men hold an entire town hostage while looking for "Aguila," the Mexican revolutionary. Greed, evil, and violence take over. Shot in Spain. Whatever you call it, just stay out of it. **95m/C VHS, Beta.** *GB SP* Robert Shaw, Stella Stevens, Martin Landau, Telly Savalas, Fernando Rey; *D:* Robert Parrish. *GEM*

A Town Like Alice 𝒜𝒜½ 1985 An Australian miniseries based on a novel by Nevil Shute. The story follows women prisoners of war during WWII. Jean Paget is a British prisoner in the camps of Malaya when she meets and falls in love with a fellow prisoner, the rugged Australian, Joe. Separated by their captors, they reunite years later and try to see if their love has survived. Remake of a 1951 film of the same name

that is also known as "Rape of Malaya." **301m/C VHS, Beta.** *AU* Bryan Brown, Helen Morse, Gordon Jackson; *D:* David Stevens. *SIG, IME, VTR*

Town that Dreaded Sundown 𝒜𝒜½ 1976 **(R)** A mad killer is on the loose in a small Arkansas town. Based on a true story, this famous 1946 murder spree remains an unsolved mystery. **90m/C VHS, Beta.** Ben Johnson, Andrew Prine, Dawn Wells, Jimmy Clem, Charles B. Pierce; *D:* Charles B. Pierce; *W:* Earl E. Smith; *C:* Jim Roberson. *WAR, OM*

The Toxic Avenger 𝒜½ 1986 **(R)** Tongue-in-cheek, cult fave has 98-pound weakling fall into barrel of toxic waste to emerge as a lumbering, bloodthirsty hulk of sludge and mire. He falls for a blind babe and sets out to do good (and get revenge). Billed as "The first Super-Hero from New Jersey." Two sequels followed: "The Toxic Avenger, Part 2" and "The Toxic Avenger, Part 3: The Last Temptation of Toxie." **90m/C VHS, Beta, LV, DVD.** Mitchell Cohen, Andree Maranda, Jennifer Baptist, Robert Prichard, Cindy Manion; *D:* Michael Herz, Lloyd (Samuel Weil) Kaufman; *W:* Joe Ritter. *TRO, TTV*

The Toxic Avenger, Part 2 𝒜½ 1989 **(R)** Sequel to "Toxic Avenger." Hulky slimer targets Japanese corporations that built toxic chemical dump in Tromaville. Followed by "The Toxic Avenger, Part 3: The Last Temptation of Toxie." **90m/C VHS, Beta, LV, Closed Caption, DVD.** Ron Fazio, Phoebe Legere, Rick Collins, John Altamura; *D:* Michael Herz, Lloyd (Samuel Weil) Kaufman; *W:* Lloyd (Samuel Weil) Kaufman, Gay Partington Terry. *TRO, TTV*

The Toxic Avenger, Part 3: The Last Temptation of Toxie 𝒜½ 1989 **(R)** Unemployed superhero is tempted to sell out to greedy capitalists when his cutie Claire needs an eye operation. Also available in an unrated version. **102m/C VHS.** Ron Fazio, Phoebe Legere, John Altamura, Rick Collins, Lisa Gaye, Jessica Dublin; *D:* Michael Herz, Lloyd (Samuel Weil) Kaufman; *W:* Lloyd (Samuel Weil) Kaufman, Gay Partington Terry. *TRO, TTV*

The Toy 𝒜½ 1982 **(PG)** Penniless reporter finds himself the new "toy" of the spoiled son of a multimillionaire oil man. Unfortunate casting of Pryor as the toy owned by Gleason, with heavy-handed lecturing about earning friends. Slow and terrible remake of the Pierre Richard comedy "Le Jouet." **99m/C VHS, Beta, LV, 8mm.** Richard Pryor, Jackie Gleason, Ned Beatty, Wilfrid Hyde-White; *D:* Richard Donner. *COL*

Toy Soldiers 𝒜½ 1984 **(R)** A group of college students are held for ransom in a war-torn Central American country. When they escape, they join forces with a seasoned mercenary who leads them as a vigilante force. **85m/C VHS, Beta, LV.** Cleavon Little, Jason Miller, Tim Robbins, Tracy Scoggins; *D:* David Fisher. *VTR*

Toy Soldiers 𝒜𝒜 1991 **(R)** This unlikely action tale stops short of being laughable but still has a fair share of silliness. South American narco-terrorists seize an exclusive boys' school. The mischievous students turn their talent for practical jokes to resistance-fighting. Orbach has an uncredited cameo. Based on a novel by William P. Kennedy. *CW:* Language and violence. **104m/C VHS, Beta, LV, 8mm, Closed Caption.** Sean Astin, Wil Wheaton, Keith Coogan, Andrew Divoff, Denholm Elliott, Louis Gossett Jr.; *Cameos:* Jerry Orbach; *D:* Dan Petrie Jr.; *W:* Dan Petrie Jr.; *C:* Thomas Burstyn; *M:* Robert Folk. *COL*

Toy Story 𝒜𝒜𝒜𝒜 1995 **(G)** First feature length, wholly computer animated film confirms what we suspected all along—toys do have lives of their own when we're not around. Pull-string cowboy Woody (Hanks), as favorite toy, presides over his fellow playthings in Andy's room. Enter new toy on the block, Buzz Lightyear (Allen), a space ranger action figure who thinks he's real. Jealous Woody and his delusional, high-tech companion soon find themselves in the outside world, where they must join forces to survive. Funny, intelligent script and voice characterizations that rival many live-action movies in depth and emotion. All this, and Don Rickles berating an

actual hockey puck. **84m/C VHS, LV, Closed Caption.** *D:* John Lasseter; *W:* Joss Whedon, Joel Cohen, Alec Sokolow; *M:* Randy Newman; *V:* Tom Hanks, Tim Allen, Annie Potts, John Ratzenberger, Wallace Shawn, Jim Varney, Don Rickles, John Morris, R. Lee Ermey, Laurie Metcalf, Erik von Detten. Nominations: Academy Awards '95: Best Original Screenplay, Best Song ("You've Got a Friend"), Best Original Score; Golden Globe Awards '96: Best Film—Musical/Comedy, Best Song ("You Got a Friend in Me"); MTV Movie Awards '96: Best On-Screen Duo (Tom Hanks/Tim Allen). *TOU*

Toys 𝒜½ 1992 **(PG-13)** Disappointingly earnest comedy about Leslie (Williams), the whimsical son of a toy manufacturer who must fight to keep the playful spirit of the factory alive after it passes into the hands of his deranged uncle (Gambon). This uncle is a general who attempts to transform the factory into an armaments plant. Leslie receives assistance in this battle from his sister Alsatia (Cusack) and his cousin Patrick (L.L. Cool J). Flat characters; generally falls short by trying too hard to send a message to viewers about the folly of war. Does have extremely vivid and intriguing visuals and special effects. **121m/C VHS.** Robin Williams, Joan Cusack, Michael Gambon, L.L. Cool J., Robin Wright Penn; *Cameos:* Donald O'Connor; *D:* Barry Levinson; *W:* Valerie Curtin, Barry Levinson. Nominations: Academy Awards '92: Best Art Direction/Set Decoration, Best Costume Design. *FXV*

Toys in the Attic 𝒜𝒜½ 1963 A man returns to his home in New Orleans with his child bride, where they will live with his two impoverished, spinster sisters. Toned-down version of the Lillian Hellman play. **88m/B VHS, Closed Caption.** Dean Martin, Geraldine Page, Yvette Mimieux, Wendy Hiller, Gene Tierney, Nan Martin, Larry Gates, Frank Silvera; *D:* George Roy Hill; *W:* James Poe; *C:* Joseph Biroc. Nominations: Academy Awards '63: Best Costume Design (B & W). *MGM*

Traces of Red 𝒜𝒜 1992 **(R)** Set in affluent Palm Beach, and filled with dead bodies, colorful suspects, and red herrings. The complex plot, often so serious it's funny, leads viewers through a convoluted series of events. Cop Jack Dobson (Belushi) is found dead in the opening scene; in homage to "Sunset Boulevard," his corpse acts as the narrator, a vehicle which unfortunately doesn't work as well here. He promises to recount the events leading up to his death which circle around a series of murders, and the people in his life who are possible suspects. Although Belushi's performance is average, Goldwyn, as Dobson's partner, shows off the talent he displayed in "Ghost." *CW:* Language, violence, and sexuality. **105m/C VHS, LV, Closed Caption.** James Belushi, Lorraine Bracco, Tony Goldwyn, William Russ, Michelle Joyner, Joe Lisi, Jim Piddock; *D:* Andy Wolk; *M:* Graeme Revell. *HBO*

Track of the Moonbeast 𝒜𝒜 1976 An American Indian uses mythology to capture the Moonbeast, a lizard-like creature that is roaming the deserts of New Mexico. **90m/C VHS, Beta.** Chase Cordell, Donna Leigh Drake; *D:* Richard Ashe.

Track of the Vampire 𝒜½ *Blood Bath* 1966 Half an hour of leftover footage from a Yugoslavian vampire movie stuck into the story of a California painter who kills his models. Gripping and atmospheric, but disjointed. **80m/B VHS.** *YU* William Campbell, Jonathan Haze, Sid Haig, Marissa Mathes, Lori Saunders, Sandra Knight; *D:* Stephanie Rothman, Jack Hill. *SNC*

Track 29 𝒜½ 1988 **(R)** A confusing black comedy about a lonely woman, her husband who has a model train fetish, and a stranger who claims to be her son. Filmed in North Carolina. **90m/C VHS.** Theresa Russell, Gary Oldman, Christopher Lloyd, Colleen Camp, Sandra Bernhard, Seymour Cassel, Leon Rippy, Vance Colvig; *D:* Nicolas Roeg; *W:* Dennis Potter. *MGM*

The Tracker 𝒜𝒜½ *Dead or Alive* 1988 HBO western about a retired gunman/tracker who must again take up arms. His college-educated son joins him as he searches for a murdering religious fanatic. Fairly decent for the genre. Made for cable television. **102m/C VHS, Beta, Closed Caption.** Kris Kristofferson, Scott Wilson, Mark Moses, David Huddleston, John Quade, Don Swayze, Brynn Thayer; **D:** John Guillermin. *HBO, WAR*

The Trackers 🎬½ **1971** A frontier man searches for the people who kidnapped his daughter and killed his son. He is joined by a cocky black tracker. Borgnine brings strength to his character as the rancher seeking revenge. Made for television. **73m/C VHS, Beta.** Sammy Davis Jr., Ernest Borgnine, Julie Adams, Connie Kreski, Jim Davis; **D:** Earl Bellamy. *FOX*

Tracks 🎬½ **1976 (R)** Vietnam veteran accompanies the body of a buddy on a long train ride home. He starts suffering flashbacks from the war and begins to think some of the passengers are out to get him. **90m/C VHS, Beta, Closed Caption.** Dennis Hopper, Dean Stockwell, Taryn Power, Zack Norman, Michael Emil, Barbara Flood; **D:** Henry Jaglom; **W:** Henry Jaglom; **C:** Paul Glickman. *PAR*

Tracks of a Killer 🎬🎬 **1995 (R)** David (Brolin) and Clair (LeBrock) Hawker are vacationing at their isolated winter retreat with corporate climber Patrick (Larsen) and his wife Bella (Taylor). When Bella is killed on David's snowmobile in an accident-that's-no-accident, it turns out Patrick is after David's company in the worst possible way.**CW:** Sadistic violence, a sex scene and language. **100m/C VHS, LV, Closed Caption.** Kelly Le Brock, James Brolin, Wolf Larson, Courtney Taylor, George Touliatos; **D:** Harvey Frost; **W:** Michael Cooney; **C:** Bruce Worrall; **M:** Barron Abramovitch. *ART*

Trade Off 🎬🎬 **1995 (R)** Beautiful, unhappily married Jackie (Russell) seduces equally miserable married businessman Thomas (Baldwin) and jokes about getting rid of their respective spouses. Then Thomas' wife is killed in a car crash and Thomas learns Jackie caused the "accident." He should have watched "Strangers on a Train" to see where trading murders can get you.**CW:** Sexuality; language; some violence. **92m/C VHS, LV, Closed Caption.** Theresa Russell, Adam Baldwin, Megan Gallagher, Barry Primus, Pat Skipper; **D:** Andrew Lane. *REP*

Trade Secrets 🎬🎬 **199?** Special investigator Jerry Morrison is assigned to probe the mysterious death of an heiress to a wine fortune. His investigation leads to the secrets and private fantasies of the woman's family and friends. **91m/C VHS.** Sam Waterston, Marisa Berenson, Lauren Hutton, Arielle Dombasle; **D:** Claude Feraldo; **W:** Claude Feraldo. *TRI*

Trader Horn 🎬🎬½ **1931** Early talkie was the first Hollywood picture to be filmed in Africa. Carey and Renaldo are traders who tangle with a native tribe while searching for the long-lost daughter of a missionary, who turns out to be a tribal goddess. Based on a novel by Alfred Aloysius Horn and Ethelreda Lewis. Boring remake in 1973. **105m/B VHS.** Harry Carey Sr., Duncan Renaldo, Edwina Booth, Sir C. Aubrey Smith, Mutia Omoolu, Olive Golden Carey; **D:** Woodbridge S. Van Dyke; **W:** Cyril Hume, Richard Schayer, Dale Van Every, John Thomas Neville; **C:** Clyde De Vinna. Nominations: Academy Awards '31: Best Picture. *MGM*

Trader Tom of the China Seas **1954** A young island trader and a shipwrecked beauty get involved in espionage while helping the UN to safeguard the Asian corridor. A 12-part serial on two cassettes. **167m/B VHS.** Harry Lauter, Aline Towne, Lyle Talbot, Fred Graham. *REP*

Trading Favors 🎬🎬 **1997 (R)** Seductress Alex (Arquette) talks eager high-school student Lincoln (Gummersall) into giving her a ride, not knowing she's trying to escape from her violent boyfriend (Greene). But that's only the beginning of the trouble.**CW:** Language, violence, sexual situations, nudity. **103m/C VHS.** Rosanna Arquette, Devon Gummersall, George Dzundza, Peter Greene; **D:** Sondra Locke. *THV*

Trading Hearts 🎬🎬 **1987 (PG)** Over-the-hill baseball player falls for an unsuccessful singer and single mom at a Florida training camp set in the 1950s. **88m/C VHS, Beta, LV.** Beverly D'Angelo, Raul Julia, Jenny Lewis, Parris Buckner, Robert Gwaltney; **D:** Neil Leifer; **W:** Frank Deford. *ART*

Trading Mom 🎬🎬½ **1994 (PG)** Harried single parent Spacek is erased from the lives of her three kids, who decide they want a parent who's more fun. So, thanks to some magic, they head off to the Mommy Mart to try out a trio of bizarre choices. This gives Spacek a chance at three more roles before the kids come to their senses. Based on "The Mommy Market" by Nancy Brelis; directorial debut for daughter Tia. **82m/C VHS, LV, Closed Caption.** Sissy Spacek, Anna Chlumsky, Aaron Michael Metchik, Asher Metchik, Maureen Stapleton; **D:** Tia Brelis; **W:** Tia Brelis; **M:** David Kitay. *THV*

Trading Places 🎬🎬½ **1983 (R)** Two elderly businessmen wager that environment is more important than heredity in creating a successful life, using a rich nephew and an unemployed street hustler as guinea pigs. Curtis is winning as a hooker-with-a-heart-of-gold who helps the hapless Aykroyd. Oft-told tale succeeds thanks to strong cast. Murphy's second screen appearance. **118m/C VHS, Beta, LV, 8mm, Letterbox, Closed Caption.** Eddie Murphy, Dan Aykroyd, Jamie Lee Curtis, Ralph Bellamy, Don Ameche, Denholm Elliott, Paul Gleason, James Belushi; **D:** John Landis; **W:** Herschel Weingrod, Timothy Harris; **M:** Elmer Bernstein. British Academy Awards '83: Best Supporting Actor (Elliott), Best Supporting Actress (Curtis); Nominations: Academy Awards '83: Original Song Score and/or Adaptation. *PAR*

Traenen in Florenz 🎬 *Tears in Florence* **1984** A woman involved in a car accident winds up falling in love with the man who injured her, only to discover later that they are actually brother and sister, long separated. In German with English subtitles. **90m/C VHS, Beta.** *GE* **D:** Marianne Schafer. *VCD, GLV*

Traffic 🎬🎬½ **1971** Eccentric auto designer Monsieur Hulot tries to transport his latest contraption from Paris to Amsterdam for an international auto show. As usual, everything goes wrong. Tati's last feature film and his fifth to feature Hulot. French with subtitles. **89m/C VHS.** *FR* Jacques Tati, Maria Kimberly, Marcel Fraval; **D:** Jacques Tati. *HMV*

Traffic in Souls 🎬🎬🎬 **1913** A silent melodrama dealing with white slavery. Immigrants and gullible country girls are lured into brothels where they are trapped with no hope of escape until, in a hail of bullets, the police raid the dens of vice and rescue them. **74m/B VHS, Beta.** Matt Moore, Jane Gail, William Welsh; **D:** George Tucker. *GPV, KIV*

Traffic Jam 🎬🎬½ *Jutai* **1991** A light comedy about a Japanese family's attempt to travel on a holiday weekend. Tokyo couple and their two young children decide to visit the husband's family who happen to live on a distant island. Naturally, traffic's horrendous, they have very little time, and things continuously go wrong. Japanese with subtitles. **108m/C VHS.** *JP* Kenichi Hagiwara, Hitomi Kuroki, Ayako Takarada, Shingo Yazawa, Eiji Okada; **D:** Mitsuo Kurotsuchi. *WBF*

Traffik 🎬🎬🎬 **1990** A tense, unnerving look at the international world of heroin smuggling. The British drama follows the lives of three men involved in the drug trade: a farmer in the poppy fields of Pakistan, a drug smuggler in Hamburg, and a Tory cabinet minister who heads his government's anti-drug cabinet and then comes to realize his own daughter is an addict. On three cassettes. Made for British television. **360m/C VHS.** *GB* Lindsay Duncan, Bill Paterson, Jamal Shah, Talat Hussain, Fritz Muller-Scherz, Julia Ormond; **D:** Alastair Reid. *SIG, TVC, PBS*

The Tragedy of a Ridiculous Man 🎬 *La Tragedia di un Uomo Ridicolo* **1981 (PG)** The missing son of an Italian cheese manufacturer may or may not have been kidnapped by terror-

ists. Lesser Bertolucci effort may or may not have a point. In Italian with English subtitles. **116m/C VHS.** *IT* Ugo Tognazzi, Anouk Aimee, Victor Cavallo, Ricardo Tognazzi, Laura Morante; **D:** Bernardo Bertolucci; **W:** Bernardo Bertolucci; **C:** Carlo DiPalma; **M:** Ennio Morricone. Cannes Film Festival '81: Best Actor (Tognazzi). *WAR, FCT*

Tragedy of Flight 103: The Inside Story 🎬🎬🎬 **1991 (PG)** Dramatization of the events surrounding the destruction of Pan Am flight 103 over Lockerbie, Scotland, due to a terrorist-planted bomb. **89m/C VHS.** Ned Beatty, Peter Boyle, Vincent Gardenia, Timothy West, Michael Wincott, Harry Ditson, Aharon Ipale, John Shrapnel; **D:** Leslie Woodhead. *MGM*

Trahir 🎬🎬🎬 *Betrayal* **1993** In 1948 Romania journalist George Vlaicu (Leysen) writes a controversial article on the death of democracy in his country and is imprisoned for 11 years. In 1959 he's offered a deal, go free as long as he talks weekly to a police inspector (Repan). He begins a new career as a poet and marries his former typist, Laura (Perrier), but after a tragedy learns that his meetings with the inspector aren't as innocuous as they've seemed. Excellent performances and a cold look at how a police state is able to control its artists and writers. Filmed primarily in Romania. Director Mihaileanu's first feature film. French with subtitles. **104m/C VHS.** *FR SI SP RO* Johan Leysen, Mireille Perrier, Alexandru Repan, Razvan Vasilescu, Maia Morgenstern, Radu Beligan; **D:** Radu Mihaileanu; **W:** Laurent Moussard, Radu Mihaileanu; **M:** Temistocle Popa. Montreal World Film Festival '93: Best Actor (Leysen), Best Film. *NYR*

Trail Beyond 🎬½ **1934** A cowboy and his sidekick go on the trek to the northwest to find a girl and a gold mine. **57m/B VHS.** John Wayne, Noah Beery Sr., Verna Hillie; **D:** Robert North Bradbury. *COL, REP, NOS*

Trail Drive 🎬 **1935** Adventures of a cowboy during a big cattle drive. **63m/B VHS, Beta.** Ken Maynard. *NOS, VCN, CAB*

Trail of Robin Hood 🎬🎬½ **1950** Rogers sees to it that poor families get Christmas trees, in spite of the fact that a big business wants to raise the prices. Features a number of western stars, including Holt playing himself. **67m/C VHS.** Roy Rogers, Penny Edwards, Gordon Jones, Jack Holt, Emory Parnell, Rex Allen, Allan "Rocky" Lane, Clifton Young, Monte Hale, Kermit Maynard, Tom George Duryea Keene, Ray Corrigan, William Farnum; **D:** William Witney. *REP*

Trail of Terror 🎬 **1935** G-Man poses as an escaped convict to get the goods on a gang. **60m/B VHS, Beta, LV.** Bob Steele, Beth Marion, Forrest Taylor, Charles "Blackie" King, Lloyd Ingraham, Charles French; **D:** Robert North Bradbury. *GPV*

Trail of the Hawk 🎬 **1937** Saga of frontier justice and love on the plains. **50m/B VHS, Beta.** Yancey Lane, Betty Jordan, Dick Jones; **D:** Edward Dmytryk. *NOS, DVT, RXM*

The Trail of the Lonesome Pine 🎬🎬🎬 **1936** The first outdoor film to be shot in three-color Technicolor. Two backwoods Kentucky clans, the Tolliver and the Falins, have been feuding so long no one remembers what started the fuss. But young engineer Jack Hale (MacMurray) gets stuck in the middle when he comes to build a railroad through the Blue Ridge Mountains. Hale saves the life of Dave Tolliver (Fonda) but Dave's not happy when the city slicker starts mooning over Dave's sister, June (Sidney). And the Falins aren't happy about the railroad, which leads to even more fighting. Based on the novel by John Fox, Jr. and previously filmed in 1916 and 1923. **102m/C VHS.** Henry Fonda, Fred MacMurray, Sylvia Sidney, Robert Barrat, Fred Stone, Nigel Bruce, Beulah Bondi, George "Spanky" McFarland, Fuzzy Knight; **D:** Henry Hathaway; **W:** Grover Jones, Horace McCoy, Harvey Thew; **C:** William Howard Greene, Robert C. Bruce. Nominations: Academy Awards '36: Best Song ("A Melody from the Sky"). *USH*

Trail of the Mounties ✍ 1947 A Mountie gallops smack into a murdering slew of fur thieves. 41m/B VHS, Beta, LV. Donald (Don "Red") Barry, Robert Lowery, Tom Neal, Russell Hayden. NO

Trail of the Pink Panther ✍✍ 1982 (PG) The sixth in Sellers' "Pink Panther" series. Inspector Clouseau disappears while he is searching for the diamond known as the Pink Panther. Notable because it was released after Sellers' death, using clips from previous movies to fill in gaps. Followed by "Curse of the Pink Panther." 97m/C VHS, Beta, LV, Closed Caption. Peter Sellers, David Niven, Herbert Lom, Capucine, Burt Kwouk, Robert Wagner, Robert Loggia; D: Blake Edwards; W: Blake Edwards, Frank Waldman; M: Henry Mancini. MGM

Trail of the Silver Spurs ✍½ 1941 A lone man remaining in a ghost town discovers gold and becomes rich. Part of the "Range Busters" series. 57m/B VHS. Ray Corrigan, John "Dusty" King, Max Terhune, I. Stanford Jolley, Dorothy Short; D: S. Roy Luby. NOS, DVT

Trail Riders ✍½ 1942 The Range Busters set a trap to capture a gang of outlaws who killed the son of the town marshal during a bank robbery. Part of the "Range Busters" series. 55m/B VHS, Beta. John "Dusty" King, David Sharpe, Max Terhune, Evelyn Finley, Forrest Taylor, Charles "Blackie" King. NOS, VYY, DVT

Trail Street ✍½ 1947 Scott is Bat Masterson, the western hero. He aids the struggle of Kansans as they conquer the land and local ranchers. 84m/B VHS, Beta. Randolph Scott, Robert Ryan, Anne Jeffreys, George "Gabby" Hayes, Madge Meredith, Jason Robards Sr.; D: Ray Enright. CCB

Trailin' ✍✍½ 1921 Mix stars as a cowboy in search of his parentage. Based on the Max Brand story. 58m/B VHS. Tom Mix, Eva Novak, James Gordon; D: Lynn F. Reynolds. GPV

Trailing Double Trouble ✍½ 1940 A corrupt attorney murders a rancher to pursue a business scheme. Three ranch hands kidnap the rancher's orphaned baby to keep her safe from the attorney. The second entry in the "Range Busters" series. 56m/B VHS, Beta. Ray Corrigan, John "Dusty" King, Max Terhune. NOS, VDM, VYY

Trailing Trouble ✍½ 1930 Gibson is a cowpoke who gets robbed of the money he received for a cattle sale. When he rescues a Chinese girl from danger she helps him recover the money. He also has to battle a rival for his girlfriend's affections. He should have battled for a better script. 58m/B VHS. Hoot Gibson, Margaret Quimby, Peter Morrison, Olive Young, William McCall; D: Arthur Rosson. GPV, VYY, DVT

The Train ✍✍✍✍ Le Train; Il Treno 1965 During the German occupation of Paris in 1944, a German colonel (Scofield) is ordered to ransack the city of its art treasures and put them on a train bound for Germany. Word gets to the French Resistance who then persuade the train inspector (Lancaster) to sabotage the train. A battle of wills ensues between Scofield and Lancaster as each becomes increasingly obsessed in outwitting the other—though the cost to all turns out to be as irreplaceable as the art itself. Filmed on location in France. Frankenheimer used real locomotives, rather than models, throughout the film, even in the spectacular crash sequences. 133m/C VHS, LV, Letterbox. Burt Lancaster, Paul Scofield, Jeanne Moreau, Michel Simon, Suzanne Flon, Wolfgang Preiss, Albert Remy; D: John Frankenheimer; W: Frank Davis, Walter Bernstein; M: Maurice Jarre. Nominations: Academy Awards '65: Best Story & Screenplay. MGM

The Train Killer ✍ 1983 A mad Hungarian is bent on destroying the Orient Express. 90m/C VHS, Beta. Michael Sarrazin; D: Sandor Simo. VES

Train of Events ✍✍½ 1949 An interesting look at lives affected by a train wreck just outside London, taking the form of four short episodes. Three are frankly somber, depressing tales of the ill-fated train driver, a murderer and an escaped prisoner-of-war. The fourth segment is a refreshingly lighthearted piece about romantic jealousies in a traveling dance orchestra. A precursor to the later swarm of crass disaster movies, except here emphasis is on character over special effects. 89m/B VHS. Jack Warner, Gladys Henson, Susan Shaw, Patric Doonan, Miles Malleson, Leslie Phillips, Joan Dowling, Laurence Payne, Valerie Hobson, John Clements, Peter Finch, Mary Morris, Laurence Naismith, Michael Hordern; D: Sidney Cole, Basil Dearden, Charles Crichton. NOS, FCT

Train Robbers ✍✍ 1973 (PG) A widow employs the services of three cowboys to help her recover some stolen gold in order to clear her late husband's name. At least that's what she says. 92m/C VHS, Beta, LV, Letterbox. John Wayne, Ann-Margret, Rod Taylor, Ben Johnson, Christopher George, Ricardo Montalban, Bobby Vinton, Jerry Gatlin; D: Burt Kennedy; W: Burt Kennedy; C: William Clothier. WAR

Train Station Pickups ✍ 197? Trashy film about young girls who hook at a local train depot, until something goes wrong. 96m/C VHS. Marco Knoger, Katja Carrol, Ingeborg Steinbach, Benjamin Carwath; D: Walter Boos.

Train to Hollywood ✍✍✍ 1986 Marilyn Monroe-obsessed young Polish girl daydreams incessantly as she works on dining car. Funny and surreal. Polish dialogue with English subtitles. 96m/C VHS. PL D: Radoslaw Piwowarski. FCT

Train to Tombstone ✍ 1950 A train running from Albuquerque to Tombstone carries a motley mob of the usual characters. 60m/B VHS, Beta, LV. Donald (Don "Red") Barry, Judith Allen, Robert Lowery, Tom Neal; D: Charles F. Reisner. NO

Trained to Kill ✍½ 1988 Two brothers seek revenge on the mean streets of L.A. 94m/C VHS, LV. Frank Zagarino, Glen Eaton, Lisa Aliff, Marshall Teague, Robert Z'Dar, Henry Silva, Arlene Golonka, Ron O'Neal, Harold Diamond, Chuck Connors; D: H. Kaye Dyal; W: H. Kaye Dyal, Arthur Webb.

Trained to Kill, U.S.A. ✍½ 1983 (R) Vietnam veteran relives his war experiences when a gang of terrorists threaten his hometown. 88m/C VHS, Beta. Stephen Sander, Heidi Vaughn, Rockne Tarkington. NO

Trainspotting ✍✍✍ 1995 (R) From the same team who offered the violently comedic "Shallow Grave," comes an equally destructive look at a group of Edinburgh junkies and losers. Heroin-user Mark Renton (McGregor) once again decides to get off junk but to do so he has to get away from his friends: knife-wielding psycho Begbie (Carlyle), Sick Boy (Miller), Spud (Bremner), and Tommy (McKidd). He heads for a semi-respectable life in London but Begbie and Spud wind up involving him in a serious money drug deal that spells trouble. Strong fantasy visuals depict drug highs and lows with heavy Scottish accents (and humor) may prove difficult. Based on the 1993 cult novel by Irvine Welsh. Film drew much controversy for supposedly being pro-heroin but the junkie's life is hardly portrayed as being attractive in any way. CW: Graphic heroin use and resulting depravity, strong language, sex, nudity, and some violence. 94m/C VHS, LV, Closed Caption. GB Ewan McGregor, Ewen Bremmer, Jonny Lee Miller, Robert Carlyle, Kevin McKidd, Kelly Macdonald, Shirley Henderson, Pauline Lynch; D: Danny Boyle; W: John Hodge; C: Brian Tufano. British Academy Awards '95: Best Adapted Screenplay; Nominations: Academy Awards '96: Best Adapted Screenplay; Australian Film Institute '96: Best Foreign Film; British Academy Awards '95: Best Film; Independent Spirit Awards '97: Best Foreign Film; MTV Movie Awards '97: Breakthrough Performance (McGregor); Writers Guild of America '96: Best Adapted Screenplay. TOU

The Traitor ✍½ 1936 Undercover man joins a gang of bandits. 57m/B VHS, Beta. Tim McCoy; D: Sam Newfield. NOS, VCI, VCN

Tramp & a Woman ✍✍ 1915 Two shorts made for the Essanay Company in 1915 which offer the Little Tramp wooing Purviance in typical Chaplin fashion. Silent with musical score. 45m/B VHS, Beta. Charlie Chaplin, Edna Purviance. VYY

Tramp at the Door ✍✍½ 1987 Delightful drama about a wandering, magical man who enters the lives of an embittered family. He helps them sort the skeletons in their closets, and works wonders on their relationships. 81m/C VHS, Beta. Ed McNamara, August Schellenberg, Monique Mercure, Eric Peterson; D: Allen Kroeker. NO

Tramplers ✍ 1966 A rebel father and son split over the hanging of a Yankee during the Civil War. Italian made spaghetti western without much plot and lots of gratuitous gunplay. 103m/C VHS, Beta. IT Joseph Cotten, Gordon Scott; D: Albert Band, Mario Sequi. COL, HHE

Trancers ✍✍ Future Cop 1984 (PG-13) A time-traveling cult from the future goes back in time to 1985 to meddle with fate. Only Jack Deth, defender of justice, can save mankind. Low-budget "Blade Runner." Followed by two sequels. 76m/C VHS, Beta, LV, Closed Caption. Tim Thomerson, Michael Stefoni, Helen Hunt, Art LaFleur, Telma Hopkins; D: Charles Band; W: Danny Bilson. ART, VES

Trancers 2: The Return of Jack Deth ✍ 1990 (R) Retro cop is back from the future again, but seems to have lost his wit and nerve in between sequels. Ward is miscast and the pacing undermines whatever suspense that might have been. CW: Violence. 85m/C VHS, Beta, LV, Closed Caption. Tim Thomerson, Helen Hunt, Megan Ward, Biff Manard, Martine Beswick, Jeffrey Combs, Barbara Crampton, Richard Lynch; D: Charles Band. PAR

Trancers 3: Deth Lives ✍½ 1992 (R) In the third film of the "Trancers" series, time-traveling cop Jack Deth fights the deadliest form of government-sponsored Trancer yet—it has a brain. CW: Language, strong violence, and sexuality. 83m/C VHS, Beta, LV, Closed Caption. Tim Thomerson, Melanie Smith, Andrew (Andy) Robinson, Tony Pierce, Dawn Ann Billings, Helen Hunt, Megan Ward, Stephen Macht, Telma Hopkins; D: C. Courtney Joyner; W: C. Courtney Joyner; M: Richard Band. PAR

Trancers 4: Jack of Swords ✍✍½ 1993 (R) Time-traveling cop Jack Deth finds himself in a mystical new dimension where the blook-sucking Trancers have enslaved the local population as feeders. If Jack expects to conquer he'll first need to survive an ancient wizard's prophecy of death. Filmed on location in Romania. 74m/C VHS, Beta, Closed Caption. Tim Thomerson, Stacie Randall, Ty Miller, Terri Ivens, Mark Arnold, Clare Hartley, Alan Oppenheimer, Stephen Macht, David Nutter; W: Peter David; M: Gary Fry. PAR

Trancers 5: Sudden Deth ✍✍½ 1994 (R) Irreverant time-travelling cop Jack Deth (Thomerson) returns to help the Tunnel Rats occupy the castle of Caliban. But the evil Lord Caliban is resurrected and his only desire is to destroy Jack. This is supposedly the final chapter of Deth's saga. CW: Language. 73m/C VHS, Beta, Closed Caption. Tim Thomerson, Stacie Randall, Ty Miller, Terri Ivens, Mark Arnold, Clare Hartley, Alan Oppenheimer, Jeff Moldovan, Lochlyn Munro, Stephen Macht; D: David Nutter; W: Peter David; M: Gary Fry. PAR

Transatlantic Merry-Go-Round ✍✍ 1934 An early semi-musical mystery about an eclectic assortment of passengers aboard a luxury liner. ♫It Was Sweet of You; Rock and Roll; Moon Over Monte Carlo; Oh Leo, It's Love; If I Had a Million Dollars. 90m/B VHS, Beta. Jack Benny, Gene Raymond, Nancy Carroll, Boswell Sisters, Ralph Morgan, Sidney Blackmer; D: Ben Stoloff. NO

Transatlantic Tunnel ✍✍½ The Tunnel 1935 An undersea tunnel from England to America is attempted, despite financial trickery and undersea disasters. Made with futuristic sets which were advanced for their time. 94m/B VHS, Beta. GB Richard Dix, Leslie Banks, Madge Evans, Helen Vinson, Sir C. Aubrey Smith, George Arliss, Walter Huston; D: Maurice Elvey. VYY, SNC, HHT

Transformations ✍½ 1988 (R) An interplanetary pilot battles a deadly virus that threatens life throughout the universe. Obscure space jetsam. CW: Language, violence, and sensuality.

84m/C VHS, LV. Rex Smith, Patrick Macnee, Lisa Langlois, Christopher Neame; **D:** Jay Kamen; **W:** Mitch Brian. *VTR*

Transformers: The Movie 🎵 1986 (G)
A full-length animated film featuring the universe-defending robots fighting the powers of evil. These robots began life as real toys, so there's some marketing going on. **85m/C VHS, Beta. D:** Nelson Shin; **V:** Orson Welles, Eric Idle, Judd Nelson, Leonard Nimoy, Robert Stack. *FHE*

Transmutations 🎵 *Underworld* 1985 (R) Mad scientist Elliott develops a mind-altering drug which is tested by a group of young people. They find out too late that the drug causes horrible facial disfigurement, as well as leaving them hopelessly addicted, and they hide out underground, plotting their revenge. Cowper, a young hooker in the group, turns out to be immune to the side effects and works with her ex-mobster boss to get help. Confusing. Barker co-scripted from one of his stories but later disowned the film. **103m/C VHS, Beta, LV. GB** Denholm Elliott, Steven Berkoff, Miranda Richardson, Nicola Cowper, Larry Lamb, Art Malik, Ingrid Pitt, Irina Brook, Paul Brown; **D:** George Pavlou; **W:** Clive Barker, James Caplin; **C:** Syd Macartney. *ART*

Transport from Paradise 🎵🎵½ *Transport Z Raje* 1965 Follows the story of Jewish life in the Terezin ghetto before the inhabitants are imprisoned and shipped off to Auschwitz as part of Hitler's final solution. Based on a novel by Arnold Lustig. In Czech with English subtitles. **93m/B VHS, Beta. CZ D:** Zbynek Brynych. *FCT*

Transylvania 6-5000 🎵 1985 (PG) Agreeably stupid horror spoof about two klutzy reporters who stumble into modern-day Transylvania and encounter an array of comedic creatures. Shot in Yugoslavia. **93m/C VHS, Beta, LV, Closed Caption.** Jeff Goldblum, Joseph Bologna, Ed Begley Jr., Carol Kane, John Byner, Geena Davis, Jeffrey Jones, Norman Fell; **D:** Rudy DeLuca; **W:** Rudy DeLuca. *VTR*

Transylvania Twist 🎵½ 1989 (PG-13) Moronic comedy about vampires, teenage vampire hunters and half-naked babes. **90m/C VHS, Beta.** Robert Vaughn, Teri Copley, Steve Altman, Ace Mask, Angus Scrimm, Jay Robinson, Brinke Stevens; **D:** Jim Wynorski; **W:** R.J. Robertson. *MGM*

The Trap 🎵🎵 1922 Chaney kidnaps the son of a man he's sent to prison on false charges. Rather than give up the kid when the man is released, he plans a trap. **?m/C VHS.** Lon Chaney Sr., Alan Hale, Irene Rich. *SNC, GVV*

The Trap 🎵🎵½ *The Baited Trap* 1959 In trying to escape justice, a ruthless crime syndicate boss holds a small desert town in a grip of fear. **84m/C VHS, Beta.** Richard Widmark, Tina Louise, Lee J. Cobb, Earl Holliman, Lorne Greene, Carl Benton Reid; **D:** Norman Panama; **W:** Norman Panama. *BAR*

Trap 🎵🎵 *L'Aventure Sauvage* 1966 A trapper buys a mute girl as his wife. Together they try to make a life for themselves in the Canadian wilderness. Fine telling of interesting western tale. Unusual and realistic. **106m/C VHS, Beta. GB CA** Rita Tushingham, Oliver Reed, Rex Sevenoaks; **D:** Sidney Hayers; **C:** Robert Krasker. *NO*

Trap on Cougar Mountain 🎵 1972 (G) A young boy begins a crusade to save his animal friends from the traps and bullets of hunters. **97m/C VHS, Beta, LV.** Erik Larsen, Keith Larsen, Karen Steele; **D:** Keith Larsen. *VTR*

Trap Them & Kill Them 🎵 1984 American group traveling through the Amazon jungle encounter a terrifying aborigine tribe. Point of trip undergoes considerable reexamination. **90m/C VHS, Beta.** Gabriele Tinti, Susan Scott, Donald O'Brien. *TWE*

Trapeze 🎵🎵🎵 1956 Lancaster is a former trapeze artist, now lame from a triple somersault accident. Curtis, the son of an old friend, wants Lancaster to teach him the routine. Lollobrigida, an aerial acrobat, is interested in both men. Exquisite European locations, fine camera work. The actors perform their own stunts. **105m/C VHS, Beta, LV, Letterbox.** Burt Lancaster, Tony Curtis, Gina Lol-

lobrigida, Katy Jurado, Thomas Gomez; **D:** Carol Reed; **C:** Robert Krasker; **M:** Malcolm Arnold. *MGM, FOX*

Trapped 🎵🎵½ 1949 Semi-documentary crime drama shows in semi-documentary style how the feds hunt down a gang of counterfeiters by springing one of their comrades from prison. Well-paced, suspenseful and believable. **78m/B VHS.** Lloyd Bridges, Barbara Payton, John Hoyt, James Todd; **D:** Richard Fleischer. *NOS, DVT, HEG*

Trapped 🎵½ 1989 (R) A woman working late in her high-rise office is stalked by a killer and must rely on her ingenuity to outwit him. Made-for-cable-television thriller. **93m/C VHS, Beta.** Kathleen Quinlan, Bruce Abbott, Katy Boyer, Ben Loggins; **D:** Fred Walton; **W:** Fred Walton. *USH*

Trapped Alive 🎵½ 1993 Robin and Monica are abducted by three escaped convicts who want their car as a getaway vehicle. Trying to avoid a police roadblock the car crashes through the cover of a long-abandoned mine. When the group try to find their way out of the maze of tunnels they realize they're not down there alone. **92m/C VHS.** Alex Kubik, Elizabeth Kent, Michael Nash, Randolph Powell, Mark Witsken, Sullivan Hester, Laura Kallison, Cameron Mitchell; **D:** Leszek Burzynski; **W:** Leszek Burzynski.

Trapped by the Mormons 🎵🎵 *The Mormon Peril* 1922 Mormons seduce innocent young girls to add to their harems. An interesting piece of paranoid propaganda. Silent with original organ music. **97m/B VHS, Beta, 8mm.** Evelyn Brent, Lewis Willoughby. *GPV, VYY, NOS*

Trapped In Paradise 🎵½ 1994 (PG-13) Three bungling brothers make off with a bundle of cash from the Paradise—the town, not the afterlife—bank on Christmas Eve. The locals, naive refugees from a Rockwell painting, don't recognize the buffoons as criminals, and reward their crime with hospitality that would make Frank Capra proud. Chase scenes and subplots abound as the boys spend what seems an eternity trying to make their getaway. Routine, humdrum comedy is hampered by an obvious plot. Watchable only because of Carvey, Lovitz, and Cage. **CW:** Contains mild profanity. **111m/C VHS, LV, Closed Caption.** Nicolas Cage, Jon Lovitz, Dana Carvey, John Ashton, Madchen Amick, Donald Moffat, Richard Jenkins, Florence Stanley, Angela Paton, Vic Manni, Frank Pesce, Sean McCann, Paul Lazar, Richard B. Shull; **D:** George Gallo; **W:** George Gallo; **M:** Robert Folk. *FXV*

Trapped in Silence 🎵🎵 1986 Young Sutherland, abused since childhood, stops speaking to protect himself mentally and physically. Psychologist Mason is determined to break down the walls to help him confront his pain. Interesting cameo by Silver as a gay counselor forced out of his job when his sexual preference is discovered. Mildly melodramatic made-for-TV message drama. **94m/C VHS.** Marsha Mason, Kiefer Sutherland, John Mahoney, Amy Wright; **Cameos:** Ron Silver; **D:** Michael Tuchner. *TTC*

Trapped in Space 🎵🎵½ 1994 (PG-13) On a mission to Venus a space shuttle is damaged by a meteor strike, leaving only enough oxygen for one person. So, what's everyone else suppose to do? Based on a short story by Arthur C. Clarke. **91m/C VHS, Beta, Closed Caption.** Jack Wagner, Jack Coleman, Craig Wasson, Sigrid Thornton, Kay Lenz; **D:** Arthur Seidelman; **W:** John Vincent Curtis, Melinda M. Snodgrass; **M:** Jay Gruska. *PAR*

Trapper County War 🎵🎵 1989 (R) A city boy and a Vietnam vet band together to rescue a young woman held captive by a backwoods clan. **98m/C VHS, LV.** Robert Estes, Bo Hopkins, Ernie Hudson, Betsy Russell, Don Swayze; **D:** Worth Keeter. *REP*

Traps 🎵🎵½ 1993 (R) Australian journalist Michael Duffield (Reynolds) and his English photographer wife Louise (Reeves) arrive for an assignment in 1950 French Indochina. Michael is to write about life on a French-owned rubber plantation, managed by Daniel (Frey), who lives with his rather peculiar daughter Viola (McKenzie). The

plantation is troubled by the increasingly militant Viet-Minh rebels and it becomes clear that the four characters all have their own emotional difficulties to deal with, as well. Loosely adapted from the novel "Dreamhouse" by Kate Grenville. Feature film directing debut for Chan. **CW:** Strong sexuality, nudity, and some violence. **95m/C VHS. AU** Saskia Reeves, Robert Reynolds, Sami Frei, Jacqueline McKenzie; **D:** Pauline Chan; **W:** Pauline Chan, Robert Carter; **C:** Kevin Hayward; **M:** Douglas Stephen Rae. *NYR*

Trash 🎵🎵 1970 Andy Warhol's profile of a depraved couple (Warhol-veteran Dallesandro and female impersonator Woodlawn) living in a lower east side basement and scouting the streets for food and drugs. Not for those easily offended by nymphomaniacs, junkies, lice, and the like; a must for fans of underground film and the cinema verite style. **110m/C VHS, Beta.** Joe Dallesandro, Holly Woodlawn, Jane Forth, Micael Sklar, Geri Miller, Bruce Pecheur; **D:** Paul Morrissey. *PAR*

Trauma 🎵½ 1962 A girl suffers amnesia after the trauma of witnessing her aunt's murder. She returns to the mansion years later to piece together what happened. A sometimes tedious psychological thriller. **93m/C VHS, Beta.** John Conte, Lynn Bari, Lorrie Richards, David Garner, Warren Kemmerling, William Bissell, Bond Blackman, William Justine; **D:** Robert M. Young. *VES*

Traveling Man 🎵🎵 1989 A made-for-cable-television drama about a veteran traveling salesman who's assigned an eager young apprentice when his sales go down. Lithgow gives a great performance as the burnt-out traveling salesman. **105m/C VHS, Beta.** John Lithgow, Jonathan Silverman, Margaret Colin, John Glover; **D:** Irvin Kershner; **M:** Miles Goodman. *HBO*

Traveller 🎵🎵🎵 1996 (R) Deriving its name from the real-life group of wily Irish-American con men who prowl the Southeast, this view into the lives and clannish ways of its members may have you checking that brand-spankin' new driveway sealant. Their basic philosophy is: if you're not one of us, we're allowed to take all of your money. Bokky (Paxton) is the jack-of-all-tricks who takes the younger Pat (Wahlberg) under his wing after the boy is shunned by the rest of the group. Pat's father married outside the clan, and that's not allowed. Bokky falls into the same trap, however, when a beautiful bartender (Margulies), who he has just fleeced, steals his heart. Rather violent ending dims the good feeling that builds and may leave you feeling...well, cheated. Directorial debut of long-time Clint Eastwood cinematographer Jack Green, who also shot "Twister" with Paxton. **CW:** Strong language and violence. **100m/C VHS, Closed Caption.** Bill Paxton, Mark Wahlberg, Julianna Margulies, James Gammon, Luke Askew, Michael Shaner, Nikki Deloach, Danielle Wiener; **D:** Jack N. Green; **W:** Jim McGlynn; **C:** Jack N. Green; **M:** Andy Paley. *EVE*

Travelling North 🎵🎵 1987 (PG-13) A belligerent retiree falls in love with a divorcee and they move together to a rustic retreat. They have an idyllic existence until the man discovers he has a serious heart condition. Adaptation of David Williamson's play has fine performances. **97m/C VHS, Beta.** **AU** Leo McKern, Julia Blake; **D:** Carl Schultz; **W:** David Williamson. Australian Film Institute '87: Best Actor (McKern); Montreal World Film Festival '87: Best Actor (McKern). *NO*

Travels with My Aunt 🎵🎵½ 1972 (PG) A banker leading a mundane life is taken on a wild, whirlwind tour of Europe by an eccentric woman claiming to be his aunt. Based on Graham Greene's best-selling novel. **109m/C LV, Letterbox.** Maggie Smith, Alec McCowen, Louis Gossett Jr., Robert Stephens, Cindy Williams; **D:** George Cukor; **W:** Jay Presson Allen. Academy Awards '72: Best Costume Design; Nominations: Academy Awards '72: Best Actress (Smith), Best Art Direction/Set Decoration, Best Cinematography. *MGM*

Traxx ⚔ 1987 (R) Satire about an ex-cop soldier of fortune. Not surprisingly, Stevens doesn't do much with this lame script. 84m/C VHS, Beta. Shadoe Stevens, Priscilla Barnes, William E. Pugh, John Hancock, Robert Davi, Rick Overton; **D:** Jerome Gary; **W:** Gary De Vore; **M:** Jay Gruska. HBO

Treacherous Crossing ⚔⚔ 1992 (PG) When her husband disappears on their honeymoon cruise heiress Wagner tries to get the ship's crew to help her. They think she's crazy, but aided by new friend Dickinson, Wagner intends to find out just what's going on. Based on the radio play "Cabin B-13" by John Dickson Carr. 88m/C VHS, Beta, Closed Caption. Lindsay Wagner, Angie Dickinson, Grant Show, Joseph Bottoms, Karen Medak, Charles Napier, Jeffrey DeMunn; **D:** Tony Wharmby; **W:** Elisa Bell. PAR, PMS

Treasure Island ⚔⚔⚔½ 1934 Fleming's adaptation of Robert Louis Stevenson's 18th-century English pirate tale of Long John Silver is a classic. Beery is great as the pirate; Cooper has trouble playing the boy. Also available colorized. Multitudinous remakes. 102m/B VHS, Beta, LV. Wallace Beery, Jackie Cooper, Lionel Barrymore, Lewis Stone, Otto Kruger, Douglass Dumbrille, Chic Sale, Nigel Bruce; **D:** Victor Fleming; **C:** Clyde De Vinna. MGM, TLF, HMV

Treasure Island ⚔⚔½ 1950 (PG) Spine-tingling Robert Louis Stevenson tale of pirates and buried treasure, in which young cabin boy Jim Hawkins matches wits with Long John Silver. Some editions excise extra violence. Stevenson's ending is revised. Full Disney treatment, excellent casting. 96m/C VHS, Beta, LV, Closed Caption. Bobby Driscoll, Robert Newton, Basil Sydney, Walter Fitzgerald, Denis O'Dea, Ralph Truman, Finlay Currie; **D:** Byron Haskin; **C:** Frederick A. (Freddie) Young. DIS, IGP

Treasure Island ⚔⚔ La Isla Del Tesoro 1972 (G) Unexceptional British reheat of familiar pirate tale. Welles' interpretation of Long John Silver may be truer to Stevenson, but it's one heckuva blustering binge. 94m/C VHS. GB Orson Welles, Kim Burfield, Walter Slezak, Lionel Stander; **D:** John Hough; **W:** Orson Welles. BTV

Treasure Island ⚔⚔½ 1989 Excellent made for cable version of the classic Robert Louis Stevenson pirate tale with Heston as Long John Silver. Written, produced and directed by Fraser Heston, son of Charlton. 131m/C VHS, Beta, Closed Caption. Charlton Heston, Christian Bale, Julian Glover, Richard Johnson, Oliver Reed, Christopher Lee, Clive Wood, Nicholas Amer, Michael Halsey; **D:** Fraser Heston; **W:** Fraser Heston. TTC

Treasure of Arne ⚔⚔½ 1919 A 16th century Scottish mercenary kills and loots the estate of rich, well-to-do property owner Sir Arne. Famous early Swedish silent that established Stiller as a director. 78m/B VHS, Beta. SW **D:** Mauritz Stiller. FCT

The Treasure of Bengal ⚔½ 1953 Sabu attempts to stop his chief from trading the village's precious gem (the largest ruby in the world) for firearms. 72m/C VHS. Sabu. NO

Treasure of Fear ⚔½ Scared Stiff 1945 A bungling newspaper reporter gets involved with four jade chessmen once owned by Kubla Khan. A few laughs in this contrived haunted house story. 66m/B VHS, Beta. Jack Haley, Barton MacLane, Ann Savage, Veda Ann Borg; **D:** Frank McDonald. SNC, NOS, FCT

The Treasure of Jamaica Reef ⚔½ 1974 (PG) Adventurers battle sharks and other nasty fish as they seek a sunken Spanish galleon and its cache of golden treasure. 96m/C VHS, Beta. Cheryl Ladd, Stephen Boyd, Roosevelt Grier, David Ladd, Darby Hinton; **D:** Virginia Lively Stone. NO

The Treasure of Matecumbe ⚔⚔ 1976 (G) A motley crew of adventurers led by a young boy search for buried treasure as they are pursued by Indians and other foes. Filmed in the Florida Key Islands. 107m/C VHS, Beta. Billy Attmore,

---

Robert Foxworth, Joan Hackett, Peter Ustinov, Vic Morrow; **D:** Vincent McEveety; **M:** Buddy Baker. DIS

Treasure of Monte Cristo ⚔⚔ 1950 A woman marries a seaman said to be an ancestor of the Count for his inheritance. Instead, she finds love and mystery. 78m/B VHS, Beta, LV. GB Adele Jergens, Steve Brodie, Glenn Langan; **D:** William (Lester Williams) Berke. NO

Treasure of Pancho Villa ⚔½ 1955 An American adventurer plots a gold heist to help Villa's revolution. He encounters every obstacle in the West while on his way to help the Mexican rebel. 96m/C VHS, Beta. Rory Calhoun, Shelley Winters, Gilbert Roland; **D:** George Sherman. NO

The Treasure of the Amazon ⚔½ El Tesoro del Amazones 1984 Three fortune hunters embark on a perilous search for wealth in the South American jungles. Silly and unnecessarily violent. 105m/C VHS, Beta. MX Stuart Whitman, Donald Pleasence, Ann Sydney, Bradford Dillman, John Ireland; **D:** Rene Cardona Jr. ART, VES

Treasure of the Four Crowns ⚔ 1982 (PG) Aging history professor hires a team of tough commandos to recover four legendary crowns containing the source of mystical powers. The crowns are being held under heavy guard by a crazed cult leader. 97m/C VHS, Beta. SP Tony Anthony, Anna Obregon, Gene Quintano; **D:** Ferdinand Baldi; **W:** Lloyd Battista, James Bryce; **M:** Ennio Morricone. MGM

Treasure of the Golden Condor ⚔⚔½ 1953 A swashbuckler heads to the jungles of 18th-century Guatemala in search of ancient treasure. Contains interesting footage of Mayan ruins, but otherwise ordinary. A remake of "Son of Fury." 93m/C VHS. Cornel Wilde, Connie Smith, Fay Wray, Anne Bancroft, Leo G. Carroll, Robert (Bobby) Blake; **D:** Delmer Daves. FXL

Treasure of the Lost Desert ⚔½ 1983 A Green Beret crushes a terrorist operation in the Middle East. 93m/C VHS, Beta. Bruce Miller, Susan West, Larry Finch; **D:** Tony Zarindast. ART

Treasure of the Moon Goddess woof! 1988 (R) A dizzy nightclub singer is mistaken by Central American pirates and natives for the earthly manifestation of their Moon Goddess. 90m/C VHS, Beta. Don Calfa, Joann Ayres, Asher Brauner; **D:** Joseph Louis Agraz. THV

Treasure of the Sierra Madre ⚔⚔⚔⚔ 1948 Three prospectors in search of gold in Mexico find suspicion, treachery and greed. Bogart is superbly believable as the paranoid, and ultimately homicidal, Fred C. Dobbs. Huston directed his father and wrote the screenplay, based on a B. Traven story. 126m/B VHS, Beta, LV. Humphrey Bogart, Walter Huston, Tim Holt, Bruce (Herman Brix) Bennett, Barton MacLane, Robert (Bobby) Blake, Alfonso Bedoya; **D:** John Huston; **W:** John Huston; **M:** Max Steiner. Academy Awards '48: Best Director (Huston), Best Screenplay, Best Supporting Actor (Huston); Golden Globe Awards '49: Best Director (Huston), Best Film—Drama, Best Supporting Actor (Huston); National Board of Review Awards '48: Best Director (Huston), Best Film; National Film Registry '90;; New York Film Critics Awards '48: Best Director (Huston), Best Film; Nominations: Academy Awards '48: Best Picture. MGM, FOX, TLF

Treasure of the Yankee Zephyr ⚔⚔ Race for the Yankee Zephyr 1983 (PG) Trio joins in the quest for a plane that has been missing for 40 years...with a cargo of $50 million. They have competition in the form of Peppard and cronies. Decent cast muddles through the predictable plotting. 108m/C VHS, Beta. AU NZ Ken Wahl, George Peppard, Donald Pleasence, Lesley Ann Warren, Bruno Lawrence, Grant Tilly; **D:** David Hemmings; **M:** Brian May. ART, VES

The Treasure Seekers ⚔ 1979 Four rival divers set off on a perilous Caribbean expedition in search of the legendary treasure of Morgan the Pirate. 88m/C VHS, Beta. Rod Taylor, Stuart Whitman, Elke Sommer, Keenan Wynn, Jeremy Kemp. MGM

A Tree Grows in Brooklyn ⚔⚔⚔½ 1945 (PG) Sensitive young Irish lass growing up in turn-of-the-century Brooklyn tries to rise above her tenement existence. Based on the novel by Betty Smith. Kazan's directorial debut. 128m/B VHS, Beta, LV, Closed Caption. Peggy Ann Garner, James Dunn, Dorothy McGuire, Joan Blondell, Lloyd Nolan, Ted Donaldson, James Gleason, John Alexander, Charles Halton; **D:** Elia Kazan; **C:** Leon Shamroy; **M:** Alfred Newman. Academy Awards '45: Best Supporting Actor (Dunn); Nominations: Academy Awards '45: Best Screenplay. BTV, HMV

The Tree of Wooden Clogs ⚔⚔⚔½ L'Albero Degli Zoccoli 1978 Epic view of the lives of four peasant families living on an estate in turn of the century Northern Italy. The title comes from the shoes the peasants wear. When a young boy breaks a shoe, his father risks punishment by cutting down one of his landlord's trees to make a new pair of clogs. Slow moving and beautiful, from former industrial filmmaker Olmi. In Italian with English subtitles. 185m/C VHS, Beta, LV. IT Luigi Ornaghi, Francesca Moriggi, Omar Brignoli, Antonio Ferrari; **D:** Ermanno Olmi; **W:** Ermanno Olmi. Cannes Film Festival '78: Best Film; New York Film Critics Awards '79: Best Foreign Film. FXL

Tree's Lounge ⚔⚔½ 1996 (R) First time director/writer Buscemi takes a look at the downward spiraling life of Tommy Basilio (Buscemi), a working-class misfit who loses his job and then spends most of his time hanging out at the dreary local bar. He finally winds up driving an ice cream truck, only leading to more trouble when his teenaged helper, Debbie (Sevigny), develops a crush on him—a situation her hot-headed father Jerry (Baldwin) takes exception to. And the irresponsible Tommy is finally forced to realize that his ill-concerned actions have consequences. **CW:** Plentiful strong language and some drug content. 94m/C VHS. Steve Buscemi, Chloe Sevigny, Daniel Baldwin, Elizabeth Bracco, Anthony LaPaglia, Debi Mazar, Carol Kane, Seymour Cassel, Mark Boone Jr., Mimi Rogers, Kevin Corrigan, Samuel L. Jackson; **D:** Steve Buscemi; **W:** Steve Buscemi; **C:** Lisa Rinzler; **M:** Evan Lurie. Nominations: Independent Spirit Awards '97: Best First Feature. ART

Tremors ⚔⚔½ 1989 (PG-13) A tiny desert town is attacked by giant man-eating worm-creatures. Bacon and Ward are the handymen trying to save the town. Amusing, with good special effects. 96m/C VHS, Beta, LV, Closed Caption, DVD. Kevin Bacon, Fred Ward, Finn Carter, Michael Gross, Reba McEntire, Bibi Besch, Bobby Jacoby, Charlotte Stewart, Victor Wong, Tony Genaros, Ariana Richards; **D:** Ron Underwood; **W:** S.S. Wilson, Brent Maddock; **C:** Alexander Grusynski; **M:** Ernest Troost. USH

Tremors 2: Aftershocks ⚔⚔½ 1996 (PG-13) They're baaaaack! The Graboids have resurfaced to eat their way through Mexican oil fields and it's up to tough guys Earl Bassett (Ward) and Burt Gummer (Gross) to get rid of the toothy worms once and for all. Same mix of tongue-in-cheek humor and special effects as the first film. **CW:** Sci-fi creature violence and gore. 100m/C VHS, LV, Closed Caption. Fred Ward, Michael Gross, Helen Shaver, Christopher Gartin, Marcelo Tubert; **D:** S.S. Wilson; **W:** S.S. Wilson, Brent Maddock. USH

Trenchcoat ⚔½ 1983 Aspiring mystery writer travels to Malta to research her new novel and is drawn into a real-life conspiracy. Silly and contrived spoof of the detective genre. 95m/C VHS, Beta. Margot Kidder, Robert Hays; **D:** Michael Tuchner; **W:** Jeffrey Price, Peter S. Seaman; **M:** Charles Fox. DIS, OM

Trespass ⚔⚔ Looters 1992 (R) Violent crime tale set in East St. Louis, Illinois. Two redneck firemen learn about stolen gold artifacts supposedly hidden in an abandoned building and go on a treasure hunt. When they witness a murder they also get involved in a battle between two crime lords—who want these interlopers dead. What follows is a deadly game of cat-and-mouse. Lots of action but it's all fairly routine. Original release date of summer 1992 was delayed until the winter because of unfortunate similarities to the L.A. riots. *CW:* Language and violence. **104m/C VHS, Beta, LV, Letterbox.** Ice Cube, Ice-T, William Sadler, Bill Paxton, Art Evans; *D:* Walter Hill; *W:* Robert Zemeckis, Bob Gale; *C:* Lloyd Ahern; *M:* Ry Cooder. *USH*

Trespasser 🐾🐾 1985 A painter has an affair with a young woman. He comes to regret destroying his family and their life together. Based on a D.H. Lawrence novel. **90m/C VHS, Beta.** Alan Bates, Dinah Stabb, Pauline Morgan, Margaret Whiting. *NO*

Trespasses 🐾 1986 (R) A rape victim and a cattleman get involved and become the target of her husband's revenge. Murder and lust in a small Texas town in this tedious film. **90m/C VHS, Beta.** Lou Diamond Phillips, Robert Kuhn, Ben Johnson, Adam Roarke, Mary Pillot, Van Brooks; *D:* Lauren Bivens. *MTX, VTR*

The Trial 🐾🐾🐾 *Le Proces; Der Prozess; Il Processo* 1963 Expressionistic Welles adaptation of classic Kafka novella about an innocent man accused, tried, and convicted of an unknown crime in an unnmaed exaggeratedly bureaucratic country. Another Welles project that met with constant disaster in production, with many lapses in continuity. **118m/B VHS.** *FR* Anthony Perkins, Jeanne Moreau, Orson Welles, Romy Schneider, Akim Tamiroff, Elsa Martinelli; *D:* Orson Welles. *CVC, HHT, WFV*

The Trial 🐾🐾 1993 Spare adaptation of Franz Kafka's novel finds Prague bank clerk Joseph K (MacLachlan) arrested on unknown charges. His increasing guilt and paranoia fit well into a world where the most illogical things happen in the most matter of fact way. Good visuals. **120m/C VHS, LV.** Kyle MacLachlan, Anthony Hopkins, Jason Robards Jr., Polly Walker, Juliet Stevenson, Alfred Molina; *D:* David Jones; *W:* Harold Pinter. *ORI*

Trial & Error 🐾🐾½ *The Dock Brief* 1962 Comedic satire, based on the play by John Mortimer, finds hapless lawyer Morgenhall (Sellers) thinking he's finally got his big chance when he defends murderer Fowle (Attenborough). Fowle wants to plead guilty but Morgenhall dreams of being a court star and insists on pleading his client innocent. It's a disaster just waiting to happen. **78m/B VHS.** *GB* Peter Sellers, Richard Attenborough, Beryl Reid, David Lodge, Frank Pettingell, Eric Woodburn; *D:* James Hill; *W:* Pierre Rouve; *C:* Edward Scaife; *M:* Ron Grainer. *FXL*

Trial and Error 🐾🐾½ 1992 Peter Hudson (Matheson) is an overly zealous prosecutor who successfully convicts a small time criminal of murder, sending him to death row. This launches Hudson's political career and five years later he's about to be nominated for Lieutenant Governor, just as the felon's execution draws near. Suddenly, new evidence points to the man's innocence, but if Hudson investigates it could ruin his political future. But he's got a bigger problem—the real killer decides to make Hudson's wife his next victim. **91m/C VHS, Beta, Closed Caption.** Tim Matheson, Helen Shaver, Sean McCann, Eugene C. Clark; *D:* Mark Sobel. *USH*

Trial and Error 🐾🐾½ 1996 (PG-13) Courtroom comedy may remind you of another law oriented movie. No, not "Kramer vs. Kramer." It's "My Cousin Vinny," also directed by Lynn. Both feature fake lawyers defending hopeless clients in small towns. In this case, lawyer Charles Tuttle (Daniels) is too messed up from his bachelor party to make it to court for a case in which the defendent Benny (Torn), a relative of Chuck's bigwig future father-in-law, is accused of selling mailorder "commemorative copper Lincoln engravings" which are actually pennies. His best bud Richard (Richards), an actor, decides to stand in for him, and the legal slip-and-pratfalls ensue. Richards as the physical comedian and Daniels as the white bread straight man have great comic chemistry, but the plot won't surprise you much. *CW:* Some sexual content. **98m/C VHS, LV, Closed Caption.** Michael Richards, Jeff Daniels, Rip Torn, Charlize Theron, Jessica Steen, Austin Pendleton, Alexan-

dra Wentworth, Lawrence Pressman, Dale Dye, Max Casella, Jennifer Coolidge; *D:* Jonathan Lynn; *W:* Sarah Bernstein, Gregory Bernstein; *D:* Gabriel Bernstein; *M:* Phil Marshall. *NLC*

Trial by Jury 🐾🐾½ 1994 (R) Strong cast, lame script. Idealistic single mother Valerie Alston (Whalley-Kilmer) winds up on the jury trying notorious mobster Rusty Pirone (Assante). Rusty's henchman, Tommy Vesey (Hurt), lets Valerie know that her son is in mortal danger if she doesn't find his boss innocent. Of course DA Daniel Graham (Byrne) is equally adamant about a conviction and is willing to use Valerie any way he has to. *CW:* Language and violence. **107m/C VHS, LV, Closed Caption.** Joanne Whalley, William Hurt, Gabriel Byrne, Armand Assante, Kathleen Quinlan, Stuart Whitman, Margaret Whitton, Ed Lauter, Joe Santos, Richard Portnow; *D:* Heywood Gould; *W:* Heywood Gould; *C:* Frederick Elmes; *M:* Terence Blanchard. *WAR*

The Trial of Billy Jack WOOF! 1974 (PG) Billy Jack takes on the feds and beats the hell out of a lot of people to prove that the world can live in peace. Awful, pretentious film. **175m/C VHS.** Tom Laughlin, Delores Taylor, Victor Izay, Teresa Laughlin, William Wellman Jr.; *D:* Frank Laughlin; *M:* Elmer Bernstein. *NO*

The Trial of Lee Harvey Oswald 🐾🐾 1977 What would've happened if Jack Ruby had not shot Oswald. Oswald's trial and its likely results are painstakingly created. In two volumes. Made for television. **192m/C VHS, Beta.** Ben Gazzara, Lorne Greene, John Pleshette, Lawrence Pressman; *D:* Gordon Davidson. *WOV*

Trial of the Catonsville Nine 🐾🐾½ 1972 (PG) Riveting political drama that focuses on the trial of nine anti-war activists, including Father Daniel Berrigan, during the Vietnam War days of the late 1960s. Imperfect, but involving. **85m/C VHS, Beta.** Ed Flanders, Douglas Watson, William Schallert, Peter Strauss, Richard Jordan; *D:* Gordon Davidson. *COL*

The Trial of the Incredible Hulk 🐾🐾 1989 The Hulk returns to battle organized crime and is aided by his blind superhero/lawyer friend Daredevil. Followed by "The Death of the Incredible Hulk." Made for television. **96m/C VHS.** Bill Bixby, Lou Ferrigno, Rex Smith, John Rhys-Davies, Marta DuBois, Nancy Everhard, Nicholas Hormann; *D:* Bill Bixby. *VTR*

The Trials of Oscar Wilde 🐾🐾🐾 *The Man with the Green Carnation; The Green Carnation* 1960 Finch is the highlight as playwright/wit Wilde, who ill-advisedly sues the Marquis of Queensbury (Jeffries) for libel when the peer accuses him of being a sodomite. Wilde is, in fact, having an affair with the Marquis' son, Lord Alfred Douglas (Fraser), which eventually leads to Wilde's imprisonment and the destruction of his life. Based on the play "The Stringed Lute" by John Furnell and the book "The Trials of Oscar Wilde" by Montgomery Hyde. **123m/C VHS.** *GB* Peter Finch, John Fraser, Lionel Jeffries, Nigel Patrick, James Mason, Yvonne Mitchell, Maxine Audley, James Booth, Paul Rogers, Ian Fleming, Laurence Naismith; *D:* Ken Hughes; *W:* Ken Hughes; *C:* Ted Moore; *M:* Ron Goodwin. *FCT*

The Triangle Factory Fire Scandal 🐾🐾 1979 Based on the true-life Triangle factory fire at the turn of the century. The fire killed 145 garment workers and drastically changed industrial fire and safety codes. Made for television. **100m/C VHS.** Tom Bosley, David Dukes, Tovah Feldshuh, Janet Margolin, Stephanie Zimbalist, Lauren Front, Stacey Nelkin, Ted Wass, Charlotte Rae, Milton Selzer, Valerie Landsburg; *D:* Mel Stuart. *ART*

Tribes 🐾🐾½ *The Soldier Who Declared Peace* 1970 A made-for-television movie about a hippie drafted into the Marines. Despite the furious efforts of his drill sergeant, he refuses to conform to military life. Soon his boot-camp mates are trying his methods of defiance and survival. Well-made mix of comedy and social commentary. **90m/C VHS, Beta.** Jan-Michael Vincent, Darren McGavin, Earl Holliman; *D:* Joseph Sargent. *MGM, FOX*

Tribute 🐾🐾 1980 (PG) A dying man is determined to achieve a reconciliation with his estranged son. Adapted by Bernard Slade from his play. **125m/C VHS, Beta, LV.** *CA* Jack Lemmon, Robby Benson, Lee Remick, Kim Cattrall; *D:* Bob (Benjamin) Clark. Nominations: Academy Awards '80: Best Actor (Lemmon). *VES, FCT*

Tribute to a Bad Man 🐾🐾🐾 1956 Hard-nosed rancher Cagney will stop at nothing to retain his worldly possessions in this 1870s Colorado territory western. His ruthless behavior drives girlfriend Papas into the arms of hired hand Dubbins. Spencer Tracy and Grace Kelly were originally cast for the roles of Jeremy Rodock and Jocasta Constantine, but Kelly backed out and Tracy was fired due to differences with director Wise. Based on the short story by Jack Schaefer. **95m/C VHS, Closed Caption.** James Cagney, Don Dubbins, Stephen McNally, Irene Papas, Vic Morrow, Royal Dano, Lee Van Cleef, James Griffith, Onslow Stevens, James Bell, Jeanette Nolan, Bud Osborne, Tom London, Dennis Moore, Buddy Roosevelt, Carl Pitti; *D:* Robert Wise; *W:* Michael Blankfort; *M:* Miklos Rozsa. *MGM*

A Tribute to the Boys 1992 An all-star salute to the comedy of Laurel & Hardy featuring clips from more than 30 of their comedies, including scenes from their silent film days. Guests include Johnny Carson, Steve Allen, Walter Matthau, Rich Little, Henny Youngman, Robert Klein, Bronson Pinchot, and The Smothers Brothers. **85m/C VHS.** *CAF*

Tricheurs 🐾🐾 *Cheaters* 1984 Scam artists hit largest casino in the world and look forward to golden years of retirement. From the director of "Reversal of Fortune." In French with English subtitles. **95m/C VHS, Beta.** *FR* Jacques Dutronc, Bulle Ogier, Kurt Raab, Virgilio Teixeira, Steve Baes; *D:* Barbet Schroeder. *WAR, BTV, FCT*

Trick or Treat 🐾½ 1986 (R) A high school student is helped to exact violent revenge against his bullying contemporaries. His helper is the spirit of a violent heavy metal rock star who he raises from the dead. Sometimes clever, not terribly scary. **97m/C VHS, Beta, Closed Caption.** Tony Fields, Marc Price, Ozzy Osbourne, Gene Simmons, Elaine Joyce, Glenn Morgan, Lisa Orgolini, Doug Savant; *D:* Charles Martin Smith; *W:* Joel Soisson, Michael S. Murphy, Rhet Topham; *C:* Robert Elswit. *ORI, WAR*

Trick or Treats WOOF! 1982 (R) Young boy's pranks on his terrified babysitter backfire on Halloween night. His deranged father, escaped from an asylum, shows up to help him "scare" her. Giroux doesn't look very frightened in this extremely tedious film from Welles' best cameraman. **90m/C VHS, Beta.** Carrie Snodgress, David Carradine, Jackie Giroux, Steve Railsback, Chris Graver, Peter Jason, Jillian Kesner, Paul Bartel; *D:* Gary Graver. *ART*

Tricks 🐾🐾 1997 (R) Once a Las Vegas showgirl, Jackie (Rogers) is now a gift shop clerk in Reno, making some extra dough by turning tricks at night. After being beaten by a john, Jackie loses her job and has trouble finding work. Her roommate (Daly) introduces her to old-time gangster (Walston), who offers to help her get even with the guy who beat her but it's not that easy. *CW:* Sexuality, nudity, a brutal beating and some language. **96m/C VHS, Closed Caption.** Mimi Rogers, Tyne Daly, Ray Walston; *D:* Kenneth Fink. *PAR*

Tricks of the Trade 🐾🐾 1988 (R) Goody-two-shoe housewife and hooker accomplice search for husband's murderer. Racy made-for-television fodder. **100m/C VHS, LV.** Cindy Williams, Markie Post, Chris Mulkey, James Whitmore Jr., Scott Paulin, John Ritter, Apollonia; *D:* Jack Bender.

Trident Force 🐾 1988 International counter-terrorism team is ordered to destroy the Palestinian Revolutionary Legion by any means possible. **90m/C VHS, Beta.** Anthony Alonzo, Mark Gil, Nanna Anderson, Steve Rogers, Eddie M. Gaerlan; *D:* Richard Smith. *NO*

The Trigger Effect 🎬½ 1996 (R) Nightmare in yuppiedom when a suspicious electromagnetic pulse knocks out all electrical power, telephone, and broadcast signals for hundreds of miles around a tranquil southern California community, which becomes increasingly unsettled. Matt (MacLachlan), wife Annie (Shue), and friend Joe (Mulroney) hang out together during the mystery power outage with lots of mounting tension both within and without. Film, however dread-producing, doesn't really make that much sense. *CW:* Language and some violence. 103m/C VHS, LV, **Closed Caption.** Kyle MacLachlan, Elisabeth Shue, Dermot Mulroney, Michael Rooker, Richard T. Jones, Bill Smitrovich, William Lucking, Molly Morgan, Richard Schiff; *D:* David Koepp; *W:* David Koepp; *C:* Newton Thomas Sigel; *M:* James Newton Howard. *USH*

Trigger Happy 🎬½ *Mad Dog Time* 1996 (R) Director Bishop (son of Rat-Packer Joey, who's in the film) tells a tale of crime lord Vic (Dreyfuss) and various gangsters in what should be a knowingly cool story but isn't. Vic's about to get out of the loony bin and has informed his enforcer, Ben London (Byrne), to get rid of his rivals and disloyal fellow mobsters in time for his return. Meanwhile, his chief of staff, Mickey (Goldblum), has been romancing both Vic's gal Grace (Lane) and her jealous older sister, Rita (Barkin). This situation does not make Vic happy. The movie won't make you happy either. *CW:* Violence, language, and sexuality. 93m/C VHS, **Closed Caption.** Richard Dreyfuss, Gabriel Byrne, Jeff Goldblum, Diane Lane, Ellen Barkin, Gregory Hines, Kyle MacLachlan, Larry Bishop, Burt Reynolds, Henry Silva; *Cameos:* Joey Bishop, Angie Everhart, Michael J. Pollard, Richard Pryor, Rob Reiner, Billy Idol; *D:* Larry Bishop; *W:* Larry Bishop; *C:* Frank Byers; *M:* Earl Rose. *MGM*

Trigger, Jr. 🎬🎬½ 1950 Rogers and his Western Show find themselves in the middle of a dispute between intimidated ranchers and an evil local range patrol office. When Trigger is injured by a killer stallion, Roy turns to two unlikely allies—a 10-year-old boy who's scared of horses and frisky Trigger, Jr. 67m/B VHS, **Closed Caption.** Roy Rogers, Dale Evans, Grant Withers, Pat Brady, Gordon Jones, Peter Miles, George Cleveland; *D:* William Witney; *W:* Gerald Geraghty. *REP*

Trigger Men 🎬½ *Billy the Kid's Fighting Pals* 1941 Steele, Young, and St. John find a dying U.S. marshal who has been ambushed by the villainous Peil. Seems Peil and his gang have taken over a small border town in order to set up a smuggling operation with Mexico. So the trio avenge the marshal by putting a stop to the nefarious doings. Newfield directed under the pseudonym Sherman Scott. 59m/B VHS. Bob Steele, Al "Fuzzy" St. John, Carleton Young, Edward Peil Sr., Phyllis Adair, Charles "Blackie" King, Curly Dresden, Hal Price, George Chesebro, Forrest Taylor, Budd Buster; *D:* Sam Newfield. *GPV, DVT*

Trigger Pals 🎬½ 1939 Jarrett stars in this basic oater about bringing a gang of rustlers to justice. Besides the usual gunplay, he also attempts to sing a few songs. 58m/B VHS. Art Jarrett, Lee Powell, Al "Fuzzy" St. John, Dorothy Fay, Charles "Blackie" King, Frank LaRue; *D:* Sam Newfield. *GPV, VCN, DVT*

Trigger Tricks 🎬½ 1930 Gibson's brother becomes the victim of a vicious cattleman and Hoot is out for revenge. 60m/B VHS. Hoot Gibson, Sally Eilers, Neal Hart, Monte Montague, Peter Morrison, Robert E. Homans, Jack Richardson; *D:* B. Reeves Eason. *GPV, DVT*

The Trigger Trio 🎬½ 1937 Rancher with diseased cattle kills a ranch inspector. The Three Mesquiteers are called in to crack the case. 54m/B VHS, Beta. Ray Corrigan, Max Terhune, Ralph Byrd, Robert Warwick, Cornelius Keefe, Wally Wales; *D:* William Witney. *VCN, DVT, GPV*

Trilby 🎬🎬🎬 1917 Original screen production of Du Maurier's classic tale of Svengali. 59m/B VHS, Beta. Clara Kimball Young, Wilton Lackaye, Chester Barnett; *D:* Maurice Tourneur. *GPV, FCT*

Trilogy of Terror 🎬🎬½ 1975 Black shows her versatility as she plays a tempting seductress, a mousy schoolteacher and the terrified victim of an African Zuni fetish doll in three horror shorts. Made for television. 78m/C VHS, Beta. Karen Black, Robert Burton, John Karlen, Gregory Harrison, George Gaynes, James Storm, Kathryn Reynolds, Tracy Curtis; *D:* Dan Curtis; *W:* Richard Matheson. *NO*

Trilogy of Terror 2 🎬🎬 1996 (R) Curtis follows up his 1975 TV movie with an okay sequel headed by Anthony. "Graveyard Rats" features flesh-eating, cemetery-dwelling rodents and a greedy wife who bumped off her wealthy husband, a mother strikes a fiendish bargain to bring her drowned son back to life in "Bobby," and the deadly African Zuni fetish doll returns in "He Who Kills." *CW:* Violence and terror. 90m/C VHS, Beta, **Closed Caption.** Lysette Anthony, Richard Fitzpatrick, Geraint Wyn Davies, Matt Clark, Geoffrey Lewis, Blake Heron; *D:* Dan Curtis; *W:* Dan Curtis, William F. Nolan, Richard Matheson; *M:* Robert Cobert. *PAR*

Trinity Is Still My Name 🎬🎬½ *Continuavamo A Chiamarlo Trinita* 1975 (G) Sequel to "They Call Me Trinity." Insouciant bumbling brothers Trinity and Bambino, oblivious to danger and hopeless odds, endure mishaps and adventures as they try to right wrongs. A funny parody of Western cliches that never becomes stale. 117m/C VHS, Beta, LV. *IT* Bud Spencer, Terence Hill, Harry Carey Jr.; *D:* E.B. Clucher. *CCB, HHE*

Trio 🎬🎬🎬 1950 Sequel to "Quartet," featuring the W. Somerset Maugham stories "The Verger," "Mr. Knowall," and "Sanatorium Acclaimed." 88m/B VHS, Beta. Jean Simmons, Michael Rennie, Bill Travers, James Hayter, Kathleen Harrison, Felix Aylmer, Nigel Patrick, Finlay Currie, John Laurie; *D:* Ken Annakin, Harold French; *C:* Geoffrey Unsworth, Reg Wyer. Nominations: Academy Awards '50: Best Sound. *NO*

The Trip 🎬🎬 1967 A psychedelic journey to the world of inner consciousness, via drugs. A television director, unsure where his life is going, decides to try a "trip" to expand his understanding. Hopper is the drug salesman, Dern, the tour guide for Fonda's trip through sex, witches, torture chambers and more. Great period music. 85m/C VHS, Beta. Peter Fonda, Dennis Hopper, Susan Strasberg, Dick Miller, Peter Bogdanovich, Bruce Dern; *D:* Roger Corman; *W:* Jack Nicholson; *M:* Barry Goldberg. *ART, VES*

The Trip to Bountiful 🎬🎬🎬 1985 (PG) An elderly widow, unhappy living in her son's fancy modern home, makes a pilgrimage back to her childhood home in Bountiful, Texas. Based on the Horton Foote play. Fine acting with Oscar-winning performance from Page. 102m/C VHS, Beta, LV, 8mm, **Closed Caption.** Geraldine Page, Rebecca DeMornay, John Heard, Carlin Glynn, Richard Bradford; *D:* Peter Masterson; *W:* Horton Foote; *C:* Fred Murphy. Academy Awards '85: Best Actress (Page); Independent Spirit Awards '86: Best Actress (Page), Best Screenplay; Nominations: Academy Awards '85: Best Adapted Screenplay. *COL, BTV, NLC*

Triple Cross 🎬🎬🎬 1967 Plummer is a British safecracker imprisoned on the channel islands at the outbreak of WWII. When the Germans move in, he offers to work for them if they set him free. The Germans buy his story and send him to England, but once there he offers his services to the British as a double agent. Based on the exploits of Eddie Chapman, adapted from his book, "The Eddie Chapman Story." 91m/C VHS, Beta. *FR GB* Christopher Plummer, Romy Schneider, Trevor Howard, Gert Frobe, Yul Brynner, Claudine Auger, Georges Lycan, Jess Hahn, Howard Vernon; *D:* Terence Young. *ACE, MOV, HHE*

Triple Echo 🎬🎬½ *Soldier in Skirts* 1977 (R) A young woman falls for an army deserter who is hiding from the military police by dressing as a woman. Mistrust and deception get the best of some of the involved parties. 90m/C VHS, Beta. *GB* Glenda Jackson, Oliver Reed, Brian Deacon; *D:* Michael Apted; *W:* Robin Chapman. *NO*

Triple Impact 🎬 1992 Hall, Cook, and Riley are three martial-arts experts who join forces against illegal gambling syndicates who are staging full-contact bloodmatches. Their alliance leads them to Asia where the prize is death—or a fortune in gold. 97m/C VHS, LV. Dale "Apollo" Cook, Ron Hall, Bridgett "Baby Doll" Riley, Robert Marius, Steve Rogers, Nick Nicholson, Ned Hourani, Mike "Cobra" Cole; *D:* David Hunt; *W:* Steve Rogers.

Triple Trouble/Easy Street 1918 Two of Chaplin's classic two-reel silent comedy shorts are shown on video. 60m/B VHS, Beta, 8mm. Charlie Chaplin, Edna Purviance, Eric Campbell. *VYY*

TripleCross 🎬½ 1985 Three former cops strike it rich and although they love the money, they miss the game, so they get involved in a murder case. These wealthy detectives encounter high-level gangsters, a baseball scandal, and a hit man in their race to solve the perfect crime. 97m/C VHS, Beta, Closed Caption. Ted Wass, Markie Post, Gary Swanson; *D:* David Greene.

Triplecross 🎬🎬½ 1995 (R) Jewel thief Jimmy Ray (Bergin) is after a fortune in diamonds and obsessive FBI agent Oscar (Williams) is looking to bring him down. Oscar decides to use Jimmy Ray's ex-cell mate Teddy (Pare) but Teddy gets involved with J.R.'s girlfriend Julia (Laurence) instead of tending to business. Wooden crime caper made for cable TV. *CW:* Strong violence, language, and a scene of sexuality. 95m/C VHS. Patrick Bergin, Billy Dee Williams, Michael Pare, Ashley Laurence; *D:* Jeno Hodl. *HMK*

Tripods: The White Mountains 🎬½ 1984 Sci-fi thriller about the takeover of earth by alien tripods. The conquerors start controlling human minds, but not until after they are 16 years old. Two boys seek to end the terror. 150m/C VHS, Beta, LV. John Shackley, Jim Baker, Ceri Seel; *D:* Graham Theakston. *IME*

Tripwire 🎬½ 1989 (R) A vengeance-crazed government agent tracks down the terrorist who murdered his wife. 120m/C VHS, Beta, LV. Terence Knox, David Warner, Charlotte Lewis, Isabella Hoffman, Yaphet Kotto, Thomas Chong, Meg Foster; *D:* James Lemmo. *COL*

Tristana 🎬🎬🎬 1970 (PG) Allegorical tale of a beautiful girl (Deneuve) who moves in with a hypocritical benefactor following the death of her mother. She is quickly exploited and seduced by the one who would protect her, but runs away with an artist in pursuit of love. Searing in its commentary on Catholicism, death, lust, and the woebegone place of humanity in the world, the movie is also widely seen as a depiction of fascist Spain's attempt to find its place in the 20th century. Based on the novel by Benito Perez Galdos. In Spanish with English subtitles. 98m/C VHS. *SP IT FR* Catherine Deneuve, Fernando Rey, Franco Nero, Lola Gaos, Antonio Casas, Jesus Fernandez, Vincent Solder; *D:* Luis Bunuel; *W:* Luis Bunuel. Nominations: Academy Awards '70: Best Foreign Language Film. *HTV*

The Triumph of Sherlock Holmes 🎬🎬½ 1935 Wontner and Fleming teamed for an early series of Holmesian romps. In one of their best outings, Sherlock Holmes comes out of retirement as a series of bizarre murders of Pennsylvania coal miners lure him back into action. From "The Valley of Fear" by Sir Arthur Conan Doyle. 84m/B VHS, Beta. *GB* Arthur Wontner, Ian Fleming; *D:* Leslie Hiscott. *SNC, NOS, CAB*

Triumph of the Son of Hercules 1963 All other victories pale when compared to this, the Son of Hercules' greatest! ?m/C VHS, Beta. *IT* Kirk Morris, Cathia Caro. *SNC*

Triumph of the Spirit 🎬🎬🎬 1989 (R) Gritty account of boxer Salamo Arouch's experiences in Auschwitz. The boxer became champion in matches between prisoners conducted for the amusement of Nazi officers. Filmed on location in Auschwitz. 115m/C VHS, Beta, LV. Willem Dafoe, Robert Loggia, Edward James Olmos, Wendy Gazelle, Kelly Wolf, Costas Mandylor, Kario Salem; *D:* Robert M. Young; *W:*

Andrzej Krakowski, Laurence Heath, Arthur Coburn, Millard Lampell, Robert M. Young, Shimon Arama; **M:** Cliff Eidelman. COL

Triumph of the Will Triumph des Willens 1934

Director Riefenstahl's formidable, stunning film, documenting Hitler and the Sixth Nazi Party Congress in 1934 in Nuernberg, Germany. The greatest and most artful propaganda piece ever produced. German dialogue. Includes English translation of the speeches. 115m/B VHS, Beta. GE **D:** Leni Riefenstahl. NOS, VYY, BAR

Triumphs of a Man Called Horse ✓✓ 1983 (R)

An Indian must save his people from prospectors in order to keep his title as Peace, Chief of the Yellow Hand Sioux. Inadequate sequel to two previous films: "A Man Called Horse" and "The Return of a Man Called Horse." 91m/C VHS, Beta. MX Richard Harris; **D:** John Hough; **W:** Carlos Aured, Jack DeWitt, Kenneth G. Blackwell. NO

Trois Couleurs: Blanc ✓✓✓ White;

Three Colors: White 1994 (R) Bittersweet comedic rags-to-riches tale spiced with revenge and lasting love. "White" focuses on equality and begins when a bewildered Polish hairdresser is divorced by his disdainful French wife, who takes him for everything he has. Returning to his family in Poland, Karol doggedly works his way into wealth. Then he decides to fake his death and leave his fortune to the ex he still loves—or does he? In Polish and French with English subtitles. Part 2 of Kieslowski's trilogy, following "Trois Couleurs: Bleu" and followed by "Trois Couleurs: Rouge." **CW:** Language and sexuality. 92m/C VHS. FR SI PL Zbigniew Zamachowski, Julie Delpy, Janusz Gajos, Jerzy Stuhr, Aleksander Bardini, Grzegorz Warchol, Cezary Harasimowicz, Jerzy Nowak, Jerzy Trela, Cezary Pazura, Michel Lisowski, Philippe Morier-Genoud; **Cameos:** Juliette Binoche, Florence Pernel; **D:** Krzysztof Kieslowski; **W:** Krzysztof Kieslowski, Krzysztof Piesiewicz; **C:** Edward Klosinski; **M:** Zbigniew Preisner. Berlin International Film Festival '94: Best Director (Kieslowski). MAX

Trois Couleurs: Bleu ✓✓✓ Three Col-

ors: Blue; Blue 1993 (R) First installment of director Kieslowski's trilogy inspired by the French tricolor flag. "Blue" stands for liberty—here freedom is based on tragedy as Julie (Binoche) reshapes her life after surviving an accident which killed her famous composer husband and their young daughter. Excellent performance by Binoche, which relies on the internalized grief and brief emotion which flits across her face rather than overwhelming displays for expression. In French with English subtitles. 98m/C VHS, LV, Letterbox. FR Juliette Binoche, Benoit Regent, Florence Pernel, Charlotte Very, Helene Vincent, Phillippe Volter, Claude Duneton, Hugues Quester, Florence Vignon, Isabelle Sadoyan, Yann Tregouet, Jacek Ostaszewski; **Cameos:** Emmanuelle Riva; **D:** Krzysztof Kieslowski; **W:** Krzysztof Kieslowski, Krzysztof Piesiewicz, Slawomir Idziak, Agnieszka Holland, Edward Zebrowski; **C:** Slawomir Idziak. Cesar Awards '94: Best Actress (Binoche), Best Film Editing, Best Sound; Los Angeles Film Critics Association Awards '93: Best Score; Venice Film Festival '93: Best Actress (Binoche), Best Film; Nominations: Golden Globe Awards '94: Best Actress—Drama (Binoche), Best Foreign Film, Best Score. TOU

Trois Couleurs: Rouge ✓✓✓½ Three

Colors: Red; Red 1994 (R) "Red" is for fraternity in the French tricolor flag and, in director Kieslowski's last film in his trilogy, emotional connections are made between unlikely couples. There's law student Auguste and his girlfriend Karin, young fashion model Valentine, and a nameless retired judge, brought together by circumstance and destined to change each other's lives. Subtle details make for careful viewing but it's a rewarding watch and a visual treat (keep an eye on cinematographer Sobocinski's use of the color red). Binoche and Delpy, who starred in the earlier films, also make an appearance, as Kieslowski uses the finale to tie up loose ends. In French with English subtitles. **CW:** Brief but strong sex scene. 99m/C VHS, LV. FR PL SI Irene Jacob, Jean-Louis Trintignant, Frederique Feder, Jean-Pierre Lorit, Samuel Lebihan, Mar-

ion Stalens, Teco Celio, Bernard Escalon, Jean Schlegel, Elzbieta Jasinska; **Cameos:** Juliette Binoche, Julie Delpy, Benoit Regent, Zbigniew Zamachowski; **D:** Krzysztof Kieslowski; **W:** Krzysztof Kieslowski, Krzysztof Piesiewicz; **C:** Piotr Sobocinski; **M:** Zbigniew Preisner. Cesar Awards '94: Best Score; Independent Spirit Awards '95: Best Foreign Film; Los Angeles Film Critics Association Awards '94: Best Foreign Film; New York Film Critics Awards '94: Best Foreign Film; National Society of Film Critics Awards '94: Best Cinematography, Best Director (Kieslowski), Best Original Screenplay; Cesar Awards '94: Best Actor (Trintignant), Best Actress (Jacob), Best Director (Kieslowski), Best Film; Golden Globe Awards '95: Best Foreign Film. MAX

Trojan Eddie ✓✓✓ 1996

Stephen Rea puts his perpetual hangdog mug to good use as the hapless Trojan Eddie, so named for the make of the van in which he transports and sells stolen goods. He is married to the shrewish town tramp, who helps little in raising their two girls and makes fun of his dream of opening his own business. His boss is John Power (Harris), leader of a group of clannish con men. He is teamed with Power's nephew Dermot (Townsend), who's secretly romancing his uncle's much younger wife-to-be. The young lovers take off with the cache of wedding loot on the night of the nuptials, and Power involves Eddie in an all-out search for the couple. After they're caught and pardoned by Power, however, the spiral of betrayal and violence spins faster than ever, with Eddie always eyeing the chance to escape. Excellent rapport between Rea and Harris as their fortunes shift and reverse. 103m/C VHS. Stephen Rea, Richard Harris, Brendan Gleeson, Sean McGinley, Angeline Ball, Brid Brennan, Stuart Townsend, Aislin McGuckin; **D:** Gilles Mackinnon; **W:** Billy Roche; **C:** John de Borman; **M:** John Keane. NYR

Trojan War ✓✓½ 1997 (PG-13)

Yes, the title does refer to the condom brand. High schooler Friedle has finally convinced dream girl Shelton to get romantic—if he has the proper protection, of course. But as his search is continually thwarted, this gives his best gal pal Hewitt (who would like to be something more) the chance to show who really loves him. Harmless, although sexually overt, teen fluff.**CW:** Sexual themes, language. 90m/C VHS, Closed Caption. Jennifer Love Hewitt, Will Friedle, Marlee Shelton; **D:** George Huang. WAR

Trojan Women ✓✓ 1971 (G)

Euripides' tragedy on the fate of the women of Troy after the Greeks storm the famous city. The play does not translate well to the screen, in spite of tour-de-force acting. 105m/C VHS, Beta. Katharine Hepburn, Vanessa Redgrave, Irene Papas, Genevieve Bujold, Brian Blessed, Patrick Magee; **D:** Michael Cacoyannis. National Board of Review Awards '71: Best Actress (Papas). FHS

Troll ✓½ 1986 (PG-13)

A malevolent troll haunts an apartment building and possesses a young girl in hopes of turning all humans into trolls. Sometimes imaginative, sometimes embarrassing. Followed by a sequel. 86m/C VHS, Beta, LV. Noah Hathaway, Gary Sandy, Anne Lockhart, Sonny Bono, Shelley Hack, June Lockhart, Michael Moriarty, Jennifer Beck, Phil Fondacaro, Brad Hall, Julia Louis-Dreyfus; **D:** John Carl Buechler; **W:** Ed Naha; **C:** Romano Albani; **M:** Richard Band. ART, VES

Troll 2 ✓½ 1992 (PG-13)

A young boy can only rely on his faith in himself when no one believes his warnings about an evil coming to destroy his family. Entering into a nightmare world, Joshua must battle witches' spells and the evil trolls who carry out their bidding. 95m/C VHS, Closed Caption. Michael Stephenson, Connie McFarland; **D:** Drago Floyd; **W:** Clyde Anderson. COL

A Troll in Central Park ✓✓½ 1994 (G)

Animated fantasy about Stanley the troll, who is cast out of his kingdom (because he's a good guy) and winds up in New York's Central Park. There, Stanley brings happiness to a little girl and her skeptical brother, all the while battling the evil troll queen. Strictly average family fare. 76m/C VHS, LV, Closed Caption. **D:** Don Bluth, Gary Goldman; **W:** Stu Krieger; **M:** Robert Folk; **V:** Dom DeLuise, Cloris Leachman, Jonathan Pryce, Hayley Mills, Charles Nelson

Reilly, Phillip Glasser, Robert Morley, Sy Goraleb, Tawney Sunshine Glover, Jordan Metzner. WAR

Troma's War woof! 1988 (R)

The survivors of an air crash find themselves amid a tropical terrorist-run civil war. Also available in a 105-minute, unrated version. Devotees of trash films shouldn't miss this one. 90m/C VHS. Ara Romanoff, Michael Ryder, Carolyn Beauchamp, Sean Bowen; **D:** Michael Herz, Lloyd (Samuel Weil) Kaufman. TTV

Tromba, the Tiger Man ✓✓½ Tromba

1952 A circus tiger tamer uses a special drug that hypnotizes the critters into obeying his every whim. When he tries the same drug on women, things get out of hand. 62m/B VHS, Beta. GE Rene Deltgen, Angelika Hauff, Gustav Knuth, Hilde Weissner, Grethe Weiser, Gardy Granass, Adrian Hoven; **D:** Helmut Weiss. SNC

Tromeo & Juliet ✓✓ 1995 (R)

There've been many versions of Shakespeare, but the Bard may never recover from being "Tromatized." On the outskirts of New York City, teenaged Tromeo Que (Keenan) falls in lust with babe Juliet Capulet (Jensen), but the family feud is still around to cause major disharmony. There's lots of profanity, perversity, and gore to keep your interest. As the movie's tagline says, "Body Piercing. Kinky Sex. Dismemberment. The things that made Shakespeare great." The unrated version is 105 minutes.**CW:** Strong sexuality, violence/gore, language and some drug content. 95m/C VHS, DVD. Will Keenan, Jane Jensen, Debbie Rochon, Lemmy; **D:** Lloyd (Samuel Weil) Kaufman; **W:** James Gunn; **C:** Brendan Flynt. TTV

Tron ✓✓ 1982 (PG)

A video game designer enters into his computer, where he battles the computer games he created and seeks revenge on other designers who have stolen his creations. Sounds better than it plays. Terrific special effects, with lots of computer-created graphics. 96m/C VHS, Beta, LV. Jeff Bridges, Bruce Boxleitner, David Warner, Cindy Morgan, Barnard Hughes, Dan Shor; **D:** Steven Lisberger. Nominations: Academy Awards '82: Best Costume Design, Best Sound. DIS

Troop Beverly Hills ✓ 1989 (PG)

Spoiled housewife Long isn't really spoiled, just misunderstood. She takes over leadership of her daughter's Wilderness Girls troop and finds the opportunity to redeem herself by offering her own unique survival tips to the uncooperative little brats who make up the troop. Everyone learns meaningful life lessons, Long is finally understood, and everyone lives happily ever after in posh Beverly Hills. Sheer silliness makes this one almost painful to watch, a shame since it boasts a good cast whose talent is totally wasted. 105m/C VHS, Beta, LV, 8mm, Closed Caption. Shelley Long, Craig T. Nelson, Betty Thomas, Mary Gross, Stephanie Beacham, Audra Lindley, Edd Byrnes, Ami Foster, Jenny Lewis, Kellie Martin; **D:** Jeff Kanew; **W:** Pamela Norris, Margaret Grieco Oberman; **M:** Randy Edelman. COL

Tropic of Cancer ✓✓✓ 1970 (NC-17)

Based on Henry Miller's once-banned, now classic novel, this film portrays the sexual escapades of the expatriate author living in 1920s Paris. Torn stars as the carefree, loose-living writer and Burstyn plays his disgusted wife. 87m/C VHS. Rip Torn, James Callahan, Ellen Burstyn, David Bauer, Phil Brown; **D:** Joseph Strick. PAR, FCT

Tropical Heat ✓✓ 1993 (R)

When the Maharajah is killed on safari, his grieving widow (D'Abo) files a five-million-dollar insurance claim before returning to India. She's followed by an investigator (Rossovich) who becomes infatuated with the lovely D'Abo. Through palaces, primitive villages, and ancient jungle temples, they are drawn into a mystery involving blackmail and murder. Based on a story by Jag Mundhra, Michael W. Potts, and Simon Levy.**CW:** Some violence and sexuality. 96m/C VHS. Rick Rossovich, Maryam D'Abo, Lee Ann Beaman, Asha Siewkumar; **D:** Jag Mundhra; **W:** Michael W. Potts; **M:** Del Casher.

Tropical Snow ✂ 1988 (R) A pair of lovers living poorly in Colombia decide to enter the drug trade in exchange for passage to the U.S. offered to them by drug kingpin Carradine. Unfortunately, they get more than they bargained for. Shot on location. 87m/C VHS, Beta, LV, Closed Caption. David Carradine, Madeleine Stowe, Nick Corri, Argemiro Catiblanco; *D:* Ciro Duran. PAR

Trouble Along the Way ✂✂½ 1953 Wayne is a once big-time college football coach who takes a coaching job at a small, financially strapped Catholic college in an effort to retain custody of his young daughter. His underhanded recruiting methods result in his firing—and the probable loss of his daughter. Unusual and sentimental role for Wayne proves he can handle comedy as well as action. 110m/B VHS. John Wayne, Donna Reed, Charles Coburn, Tom Tully, Sherry Jackson, Marie Windsor, Tom Helmore, Dabbs Greer, Leif Erickson, Douglas Spencer; *D:* Michael Curtiz; *W:* Jack Rose, Melville Shavelson; *M:* Max Steiner. WAR

Trouble Bound ✂✂ 1992 (R) Madsen is Harry, a guy just out of prison, on his way to Nevada with trouble dogging him every step. He's got a dead body in the car trunk, drug dealers after him, and when he offers a lift to a pretty cocktail waitress (Arquette) his luck only gets worse. She plans to kill a Mob boss and it's no secret. Chases and violence.*CW:* Language, violence, and sexuality. 90m/C VHS, LV, Closed Caption. Michael Madsen, Patricia Arquette, Florence Stanley, Seymour Cassel, Sal Jenco; *D:* Jeff Reiner; *W:* Darrell Fetty, Francis Delia; *M:* Vinnie Golia. FOX

Trouble Busters ✂ 1933 Troubled locals worry about who to call when oil is discovered in their town, bringing evil profiteers with it. The Trouble Busters come into town to set things straight. 51m/B VHS, Beta. Jack Hoxie, Lane Chandler; *D:* Lewis D. Collins. NOS, DVT

Trouble in Mind ✂✂✂ 1986 (R) Stylized romance is set in the near future in a rundown diner. Kristofferson is an ex-cop who gets involved in the lives of a young couple looking for a better life. Look for Divine in one of her/his rare appearances outside of John Waters' works. 111m/C VHS, Beta, LV, 8mm, Closed Caption. Kris Kristofferson, Keith Carradine, Genevieve Bujold, Lori Singer, Divine, Joe Morton, George Kirby, John Considine, Dirk Blocker, Gailard Sartain, Tracy Kristofferson; *D:* Alan Rudolph; *W:* Alan Rudolph; *C:* Toyomichi Kurita; *M:* Mark Isham. Independent Spirit Awards '86: Best Cinematography. COL, NLC

Trouble in Paradise ✂✂ 1988 Welch stars as a widow stranded in a tropical island paradise with an Australian sailor. The two must struggle as they are stalked by a gang of drug smugglers, hence the title. Made for television. 92m/C VHS. Raquel Welch, Jack Thompson, Nicholas Hammond, John Gregg; *D:* Di Drew. CAF

Trouble in Store ✂✂½ 1953 A bumbling department store employee stumbles on a gangster's plot. Fun gags and a good cast. 85m/B VHS. GB Margaret Rutherford, Norman Wisdom, Moira Lister, Megs Jenkins; *D:* John Paddy Carstairs. REP

Trouble in Texas ✂✂ 1937 Outlaws go to a rodeo and try to steal the prize money. Tex wants to find out who killed his brother and in his spare time, sings and tries to stop the crooks. Notable because it is the last film Hayworth made under her original stage name (Rita Cansino). 65m/B VHS, Beta. Tex Ritter, Rita Hayworth, Earl Dwire, Yakima Canutt; *D:* Robert North Bradbury. NOS, DVT, VCI

Trouble in the Glen ✂✂½ 1954 A Scottish-American soldier returns to his ancestral home and becomes involved in a dispute between the town residents and a lord over a closed road. Uneven script undermines comic jabs. 91m/C VHS. GB Orson Welles, Victor McLaglen, Forrest Tucker, Margaret Lockwood; *D:* Herbert Wilcox. REP

The Trouble with Angels ✂✂½ 1966 (PG) Two young girls turn a convent upside down with their endless practical jokes. Russell is everything a Mother Superior should be: understanding, wise, and beautiful. 112m/C VHS, Beta. Hayley Mills, June Harding, Rosalind Russell, Gypsy Rose Lee, Binnie Barnes; *D:* Ida Lupino; *C:* Lionel Lindon; *M:* Jerry Goldsmith. COL

The Trouble with Dick ✂ 1988 (R) An ambitious young science fiction writer's personal troubles begin to appear in his writing. Although the box cover displays a "Festival Winner" announcement, don't be fooled! Story becomes tedious after first five minutes. 86m/C VHS, Beta. Tom Villard, Susan Dey; *D:* Gary Walkow; *M:* Roger Bourland. Sundance Film Festival '87: Grand Jury Prize.

The Trouble with Father *The Stu Erwin Show* 1950 Erwin starred in the classic comedy series about a bumbling father which aired from 1950-55. Two episodes per tape. On this tape: "Yvette," a 1954 episode in which Stu tries to surprise June with a lifelike female mannequin as an aniversary gift and the 1952 episode "What Paper Do you Read" when June enrolls in Stu's evening government classes. 50m/B VHS, Beta. Stuart Erwin, June Collyer Erwin, Sheila James, Ann Todd, Martin Milner, Willie Best. NOS, MOV, DVT

The Trouble with Girls (and How To Get Into It) ✂✂✂ *The Chautauqua* 1969 (G) A 1920s traveling show manager tries to solve a local murder. Not as much singing as his earlier films, but good attention is paid to details. This is definitely one of the better Elvis vehicles. ♫ Almost; Clean Up Your Own Back Yard. 99m/C VHS, Beta. Elvis Presley, Marlyn Mason, Nicole Jaffe, Sheree North, Edward Andrews, John Carradine, Vincent Price, Joyce Van Patten, Dabney Coleman, John Rubinstein, Anthony Teague; *D:* Peter Tewkesbury. MGM

The Trouble with Harry ✂✂✂ 1955 (PG) When a little boy finds a dead body in a Vermont town, it causes all kinds of problems for the community. No one is sure who killed Harry and what to do with the body. MacLaine's film debut and Herrmann's first musical score for Hitchcock. 90m/C VHS, Beta, LV. John Forsythe, Shirley MacLaine, Edmund Gwenn, Jerry Mathers, Mildred Dunnock, Mildred Natwick, Royal Dano; *D:* Alfred Hitchcock; *W:* John Michael Hayes; *C:* Robert Burks; *M:* Bernard Herrmann. USH, HMV

The Trouble with Spies ✂ 1987 (PG-13) A bumbling British spy goes to Ibizia to locate a Russian agent, makes a million mistakes and wins anyway. A loser of a film, wasted a fine cast. Made in 1984; no one bothered to release it for three years. 91m/C VHS, Beta. Donald Sutherland, Malcolm Morley, Lucy Gutteridge, Ruth Gordon, Ned Beatty, Michael Hordern, Robert Morley; *D:* Burt Kennedy; *W:* Burt Kennedy. HBO

Troublemakers ✂½ 1994 (PG) Travis (Hill) is the fastest gun in the west—but his brother Moses (Spencer) is the country's meanest bounty hunter. But their mother loves them, and wants both her boys home for Christmas. So she leaves it up to Travis to lure Moses back to the homestead. 98m/C VHS. Terence Hill, Bud Spencer. TRI

Truck Stop ✂ 19?? This truck stop has all a trucker needs—including the owner, voluptuous Pamela. 80m/C VHS. Nikki Gentile, Elizabeth Turner; *D:* Jean Marie Pallardy.

Truck Stop Women ✂✂ 1974 (R) Female truckers become involved in smuggling and prostitution at a truck stop. The mob wants a cut of the business and will do anything to get their way. Better than it sounds. 88m/C VHS, Beta. Claudia Jennings, Lieux Dressler, John Martino, Dennis Fimple, Dolores Dorn, Gene Drew, Paul Carr, Jennifer Burton; *D:* Mark L. Lester. VES

Truck Turner ✂½ 1974 (R) He's a bounty hunter, he's black and he's up against a threadbare plot. Hayes methodically eliminates everyone involved in his partner's murder while providing groovy soundtrack. Quintessential blaxploi-

tation. 91m/C VHS. Isaac Hayes, Yaphet Kotto, Annazette Chase, Nichelle Nichols, Scatman Crothers, Dick Miller; *D:* Jonathan Kaplan; *W:* Leigh Chapman; *M:* Isaac Hayes. ORI, FCT

Trucker's Woman ✂ 1983 (R) Man takes a job driving an 18-wheel truck in order to find the murderers of his father. 90m/C VHS, Beta. Michael Hawkins, Mary Cannon; *D:* Will Zens. NO

True Believer ✂✂½ 1989 (R) Cynical lawyer, once a '60s radical, now defends rich drug dealers. Spurred on by a young protege, he takes on the hopeless case of imprisoned Asian-American accused of gang-slaying. Tense thriller with good cast. 103m/C VHS, Beta, LV, Closed Caption. James Woods, Robert Downey Jr., Yuji Okumoto, Margaret Colin, Kurtwood Smith, Tom Bower, Miguel Fernandez, Charles Hallahan; *D:* Joseph Ruben; *W:* Wesley Strick; *M:* Brad Fiedel. COL

True Blood ✂✂ 1989 (R) A man returns to his home turf to save his brother from the same ruthless gang who set him up for a cop's murder. 100m/C VHS, Beta, LV. Chad Lowe, Jeff Fahey, Sherilyn Fenn; *D:* Peter Maris. IME

True Colors ✂✂½ 1987 (PG-13) A woman fights for her homeland of France in order to save the country from being taken over by Hitler. 160m/C VHS, Beta. Noni Hazlehurst, John Waters, Patrick Ryecart, Shane Briant, Alan Andrews; *D:* Pino Amenta.

True Colors ✂✂ 1991 (R) Law school buddies take divergent paths in post grad real world. Straight and narrow Spader works for Justice Department while dropout Cusack manipulates friends and acquaintances to further his position as Senator's aid. Typecast, predictable and, moralizing.*CW:* Language and sensuality. 111m/C VHS, Beta, LV, Closed Caption. John Cusack, James Spader, Imogen Stubbs, Mandy Patinkin, Richard Widmark; *D:* Herbert Ross. PAR

True Confessions ✂✂✂ 1981 (R) Tale of corruption pits two brothers, one a priest and the other a detective, against each other. Nice 1940s period look, with excellent performances from De Niro and Duvall. Based on a true case from the Gregory Dunne novel. 110m/C VHS, Beta, LV. Robert De Niro, Robert Duvall, Kenneth McMillan, Charles Durning, Cyril Cusack, Ed Flanders, Burgess Meredith, Louisa Moritz; *D:* Ulu Grosbard; *W:* John Gregory Dunne, Joan Didion; *C:* Owen Roizman; *M:* Georges Delerue. MGM

True Crime ✂✂½ *Dangerous Kiss* 1995 (R) High school student turns detective when a classmate is killed, hooks up with a police cadet, and finds herself on the trail of a serial killer.*CW:* Psychopathic violence; strong sexuality; language. 94m/C VHS. Alicia Silverstone, Kevin Dillon; *D:* Pat Verduci. THV

The True Game of Death 197? A story of the circumstances behind the death of superstar Bruce Lee. 90m/C VHS, Beta. Shou Lung. NO

True Grit ✂✂✂ 1969 (G) Hard-drinking U.S. Marshal Rooster Cogburn (Wayne) is hired by a young girl (Darby) to find her father's killer. Won Wayne his only Oscar. Based on the Charles Portis novel. Prompted sequel, "Rooster Cogburn." 128m/C VHS, Beta, LV. John Wayne, Glen Campbell, Kim Darby, Robert Duvall; *D:* Henry Hathaway; *M:* Elmer Bernstein. Academy Awards '69: Best Actor (Wayne); Golden Globe Awards '70: Best Actor—Drama (Wayne); Nominations: Academy Awards '69: Best Song ("True Grit"). PAR, HHE, TLF

True Heart Susie ✂✂½ 1919 A simple, moving story about a girl who is in love with a man who marries another girl from the city. Silent. 87m/B VHS, Beta. Lillian Gish, Robert "Bobbie" Harron; *D:* D.W. Griffith. NOS, VYY, DVT

True Identity ✂✂ 1991 (R). Henry, a comic superstar in England, stars as an innocent black man marked for death by the Mafia. He hides by disguising himself as white and gets a taste of life on the other side of the color line. The interesting premise was based on a classic Eddie Murphy sketch on "Saturday Night Live," but isn't treated with sufficient imagination or humor here.*CW:* Language. **94m/C VHS, Beta, Closed Caption.** Lenny Henry, Frank Langella, Anne-Marie Johnson, Charles Lane; *D:* Charles Lane; *W:* Andy Breckman. *TOU, FCT*

True Lies 🐾🐾½ **1994 (R)** Brain candy with a bang offers eye popping special effects and a large dose of unbelievability. Sort of like a big screen "Scarecrow and Mrs. King" as supposed computer salesman Ah-nuld keeps his spy work secret from mousy, neglected wife Curtis, who has a few secrets of her own and inadvertently ends up right in the thick of things. Raunchy and extremely sexist, but not without charm; the stupidity is part of the fun. Perfectly cast sidekick Arnold holds his own as a pig, but Heston is wasted as the head honcho. Tons of special effects culminate in a smashing finish. Very loosely adapted from the 1991 French comedy "La Total."*CW:* Some language and a lot of action/violence. **114m/C VHS, LV, Closed Caption.** Arnold Schwarzenegger, Jamie Lee Curtis, Tom Arnold, Bill Paxton, Tia Carrere, Art Malik, Eliza Dushku, Charlton Heston, Grant Heslov; *D:* James Cameron; *W:* James Cameron; *C:* Russell Carpenter. Golden Globe Awards '95: Best Actress—Musical/Comedy (Curtis); Blockbuster Entertainment Awards '96: Action Actress, Video (Curtis); Nominations: Academy Awards '94: Best Visual Effects; MTV Movie Awards '95: Best Female Performance (Curtis), Best Comedic Performance (Arnold), Best Kiss (Arnold Schwarzenegger/Jamie Lee Curtis), Best Action Sequence, Best Dance Sequence (Arnold Schwarzenegger/Tia Carrere). *FXV*

True Love 🐾🐾🐾 **1989 (R)** Low-budget, savagely observed comedy follows the family and community events leading up to a Bronx Italian wedding. Authentic slice-of-life about two young people with very different ideas about what marriage and commitment mean. Acclaimed script and performances. **104m/C VHS, Beta, LV, Closed Caption.** Annabella Sciorra, Ron Eldard, Aida Turturro, Roger Rignack, Michael J. Wolfe, Star Jasper, Kelly Cinnante, Rick Shapiro, Suzanne Costallos, Vinny Pastore; *D:* Nancy Savoca; *W:* Nancy Savoca, Richard Guay; *C:* Lisa Rinzler. Sundance Film Festival '89: Grand Jury Prize.*MGM*

True Romance 🐾🐾½ **1993 (R)** Geeky Clarence (Slater) and wide-eyed whore Alabama (Arquette) meet and fall instantly in love (and marriage). The inept duo skips town after an accidental murder and hit the road to L.A. with the mob in pursuit. Gem performances in small roles include Walken's debonair mafioso who's not adverse to torture; Clarence's dad (Hopper), an ex-cop who runs afoul of Walken; Pitt's space-case druggie; and the ghost of Elvis (Kilmer), whom Clarence talks to in times of stress. Horrific violence mixed with very black humor (courtesy of a script by pre "Reservoir Dogs" Tarantino and "Last Boy Scout" director Scott). An unrated version is also available.*CW:* Strong language, strong violence and drug use, and sexuality. **116m/C VHS, Beta, LV, Closed Caption.** Christian Slater, Patricia Arquette, Gary Oldman, Brad Pitt, Val Kilmer, Dennis Hopper, Christopher Walken, Samuel L. Jackson, Christopher Penn, Bronson Pinchot, Michael Rapaport, Saul Rubinek, Conchata Ferrell, James Gandolfini, Tom Sizemore, Ed Lauter; *D:* Tony Scott; *W:* Quentin Tarantino; *M:* Hans Zimmer. Nominations: MTV Movie Awards '94: Best Kiss (Christian Slater/Patricia Arquette). *WAR, BTV*

True Stories 🐾🐾🐾½ **1986 (PG)** Quirky, amusing look at the eccentric denizens of a fictional, off-center Texas town celebrating its 150th anniversary. Notable are Kurtz as the Laziest Woman in America and Goodman as a blushing suitor. Directorial debut of Byrne. Worth a look. **89m/C VHS, Beta, LV, Closed Caption.** David Byrne, John Goodman, Swoosie Kurtz, Spalding Gray, Annie McEnroe, Pops Staples, Tito Larriva; *D:* David Byrne; *W:* David Byrne, Beth Henley, Stephen Tobolowsky; *M:* David Byrne. *MVD, WAR*

True Vengeance 🐾🐾 **1997 (R)** Navy operative finds himself on the run from a group of bounty hunters. **90m/C VHS.** Daniel Bernhardt, Miles O'Keeffe, Beverly Johnson; *D:* David Worth; *W:* Kurt Johnstad; *C:* David Worth. *FEI*

True West 🐾🐾🐾 **1986** Filmed performance of the acclaimed Sam Shepard play about two mismatched brothers. Made for Television. **110m/C VHS, Beta.** John Malkovich, Gary Sinise; *D:* Allan Goldstein.

True Women 🐾🐾½ **1997 (PG-13)** Sarah McClure (Delany) leaves Georgia with husband Bartlett (Boothe), settles in Texas, and raises her orphaned sister Euphemia (Majorino and Gish), as well as her own family, while Bartlett's off being a Texas Ranger. Euphemia's eventually reunited with her best friend, southern plantation beauty Georgia (Jolie), who's trying to hide the fact that she's part-Cherokee. The ladies suffer through Comanche attacks, the Alamo and the Mexican Army, the Civil War, Reconstruction, and various romantic trials and tribulations, all while being gosh-darn heroic. TV miniseries based on the historical novel by Janice Woods Windle.*CW:* Violence, sensuality and diverse thematic elements. **170m/C VHS, Closed Caption.** Dana Delany, Annabeth Gish, Angelina Jolie, Powers Boothe, Tina Majorino, Rachel Leigh Cook, Jeffrey Nordling, Michael Greyeyes, Tony Todd, Terrence Mann, Michael York, Salli Richardson, Irene Bedard, Charles S. Dutton, Julie Carmen, Matthew Glave, John Schneider; *W:* Christopher Lofton; *C:* Thomas Neuwirth; *M:* Bruce Broughton. *HMK*

Truly, Madly, Deeply 🐾🐾🐾 **1991 (PG)** The recent death of her lover drives a young woman into despair and anger, until he turns up at her apartment one day. Tender and well written tale of love and the supernatural, with believable characters and plot-line. Playwright Minghella's directorial debut. **107m/C VHS.** Juliet Stevenson, Alan Rickman, Bill Paterson, Michael Maloney, Christopher Rozycki, Keith Bartlett, David Ryall, Stella Maris; *D:* Anthony Minghella; *W:* Anthony Minghella; *C:* Remi Adefarasin. Australian Film Institute '92: Best Foreign Film; British Academy Awards '91: Best Original Screenplay.*TOU*

Truman 🐾🐾½ **1995 (PG)** Cable bio follows "Give 'em Hell" Harry (Sinise) from 1917 to 1968. The 33rd U.S. President, derided as a political hack, was determined to prove himself against the odds and by making the tough decisions, including authorizing use of the A-bomb on Japan. Sinise gives the appropriate no-nonsense performance, matched by Scarwid as ever-loyal wife Bess. Based on David McCullough's Pulitzer Prize-winning book. **?m/C VHS.** Gary Sinise, Diana Scarwid, Colm Feore, Richard Dysart, James Gammon, Tony Goldwyn, Pat Hingle, Harris Yulin, Leo Burmester, Zeljko Ivanek, David Lansbury, Marian Seldes, Lois Smith, Richard Venture, Daniel von Bargen; *D:* Frank Pierson; *W:* Tom Rickman; *C:* Paul Elliott; *M:* David Mansfield. *HBO*

The Truman Show 🐾🐾🐾🐾 **1998 (PG)** Flawless execution of an eerie, yet fantastical premise, marked by outstanding performances, make this surreal fable a joy to watch from start to finish. Unbeknowst to insurance salesman resident Truman Burbank, (Carrey) his entire life has been broadcast live for television in a 24-hour soap opera viewed by the world. When evidence of Truman's fabricated life begins to surface, he plans his escape, upsetting the grand scheme of producer, director and charismatic artist Christof (Harris in a stand-out performance). Carrey's sympathetic, low-key portrayal will make people forget the disappointment of "Cable Guy." Weir handles his satirical theme with craftsmen-like precision, never letting his commentary on the power of the tube to become too heavy-handed. Carrey reportedly took a pay cut from his $20 million dollar fee in order to star. **102m/C VHS.** Jim Carrey, Ed Harris, Laura Linney, Noah Emmerich, Natascha McElhone, Holland Taylor, Paul Giamatti, Philip Baker Hall, Brian Delate, Una Damon; *D:* Peter Weir; *W:* Andrew Niccol; *C:* Peter Biziou; *M:* Philip Glass, Burkhard Dallwitz. *NYR*

Trumps 🐾 *Enormous Changes at the Last Minute* **1983 (R)** Three dramas about women and contemporary relationships in New York City. Based on three stories—"Faith's Story," "Virginia's Story," and "Alexandra's Story"—by Grace Paley. **90m/C VHS.** Ellen Barkin, Kevin Bacon, Maria Tucci, Ron

McLarty, Zvee Scooler, David Strathairn, Jeffrey DeMunn, Sudie Bond; *D:* Mirra Bank, Ellen Hovde, Mfc John Bayley, Susan Rice. *HHE*

Trust 🐾🐾 **1991 (R)** An obnoxious girl, tossed out by her family after becoming pregnant, forms a loving bond with a strange, possibly deranged guy from an abusive household. Similar in style and theme to Hartley's "The Unbelievable Truth"—a peculiar sardonic comedy/drama not for every taste. **107m/C VHS, LV, Closed Caption.** Adrienne Shelly, Martin Donovan, Merritt Nelson, Edie Falco, John MacKay, Marko Hunt; *D:* Hal Hartley; *W:* Hal Hartley; *C:* Michael Spiller; *M:* Phil Reed. Sundance Film Festival '91: Best Screenplay. *REP*

Trust Me 🐾🐾 **1989 (R)** A cynical L.A. art dealer decides to promote a young artist's work and then kill him off to increase the value of his paintings. Satirical view of the Los Angeles art crowd. **94m/C VHS, Beta, LV.** Adam Ant, Talia Balsam, David Packer, Barbara Bain, Joyce Van Patten, William DeAcutis; *D:* Bobby Houston. *LEO*

Trusting Beatrice 🐾½ **1992 (PG)** Lame comedy finds feckless landscaper Claude (Jacobs) the bewildered caretaker of Beatrice (Jacob), a Frenchwoman stranded in America without a green card and with a young Cambodian refugee girl. So Claude decides to take Beatrice home to his determinedly eccentric family. Tries for quirky but fails miserably. **86m/C VHS.** Irene Jacob, Mark Evan Jacobs, Leonardo Cimino, Charlotte Moore, Steve Buscemi, Pat McNamara; *D:* Cindy Lou Johnson; *W:* Cindy Lou Johnson. *FRF*

The Truth About Cats and Dogs 🐾🐾🐾 **1996 (PG-13)** Funny, intelligent Abby (Garofalo) hosts a popular radio call-in show for pet lovers. When a handsome Brit photographer (Chaplin) phones in with a Great Dane problem, he becomes intrigued by her voice, and asks for a date. Insecure about her looks, Abby asks her beautiful-but-dim girlfriend Noelle (Thurman) to fill in. Naturally, both women fall for the shy Englishman. Charming, updated version of "Cyrano de Bergerac" theme works because of strong lead performances, especially Garofalo, who steals the show with her dry, self-effacing wit. Entertaining romantic comedy features some nice scenes of Santa Monica, too.*CW:* Sex-related scene and brief strong language. **97m/C VHS, LV, Closed Caption.** Janeane Garofalo, Uma Thurman, Ben Chaplin, Jamie Foxx, Richard Coca, Stanley DeSantis; *D:* Michael Lehmann. Nominations: MTV Movie Awards '97: Best Comedic Performance (Garofalo). *FXV*

Truth About Women 🐾🐾 **1958** An old aristocrat recounts his youthful adventures to his son-in-law. A pale British comedy of manners. **107m/C VHS, Beta.** *GB* Laurence Harvey, Julie Harris, Mai Zetterling, Eva Gabor, Wilfrid Hyde-White, Derek Farr; *D:* Muriel Box. *NOS*

Truth or Consequences, N.M. 🐾 **1997 (R)** Yes, the name of the town is real. No, Bob Barker is not the mayor. Dim parolee Raymond (Gallo) and his even dimmer girlfriend Addy (Dickens) are reunited and just want to settle down, to tell the truth. Instead, they fall immediately back into a life of crime. Along with their accomplices Marcus (Williamson) and Curtis (Sutherland), they plan to rip off a drug dealer for big bucks (no whammies!). The heist, of course, goes bad; they steal an RV and kidnap its owners Gordon (Pollack) and Donna (Phillips). An attempt to unload the drugs on a powerful Mafia boss (Steiger) also goes awry, and that starts a real family feud. As the mob hit man (Sheen), the cops, and the crooks all converge on the eponymous New Mexico town, everyone is in jeopardy. Not logical, not original and not good. Directorial debut for Sutherland, who should really quit playing coked-up psychopathic murderers.*CW:* Substantial amount of strong violence, and for sex, language, and drug use. **106m/C VHS, LV, Closed Caption.** Vincent Gallo, Kim Dickens, Kiefer Sutherland, Mykelti Williamson, Grace Phillips, Kevin Pollak, Martin

Sheen, Rod Steiger; **D:** Kiefer Sutherland; **W:** Brad Mirman; **C:** Ric Waite. COL

Truth or Dare? 🎬 1986 The childhood game of truth or dare turns deadly in this violent thriller. 87m/C **VHS, Beta.** John Brace, Mary Fanaro, Geoffrey Lewis Miller; **D:** Yale Wilson. HHE

Truth or Dare 🎬🎬½ In Bed with Madonna; Madonna Truth or Dare 1991 (R) A quasi-concert-documentary—here is music superstar Madonna tarted up in fact, fiction, and fantasy—exhibitionism to the nth power. Tacky, self-conscious, and ultimately, if you are a Madonna fan, moving. On camera Madonna stings ex-boyfriend Warren Beatty, disses admirer Kevin Costner, quarrels with her father, reminisces, and does sexy things with a bottle. Oh yes, she occasionally sings and dances. Both those who worship and dislike the Material Girl will find much to pick apart here. Available in widescreen format on laserdisc. **CW:** Strong sexual dialogue and strong sexual situations. 118m/C **VHS, LV, Closed Caption, DVD.** Madonna; **D:** Alek Keshishian. ART, FCT

Truth or Die 🎬🎬 Doing Life 1986 (PG-13) This trite, cliched TV movie chronicles the life of convict Jerry Rosenberg, the first prisoner to earn a law degree from his cell. Still, an uncharacteristic role for sitcom guy Danza. Based on Rosenberg's book "Doing Life." 96m/C **VHS, LV, Closed Caption.** Tony Danza, Jon DeVries, Lisa Langlois, Rocco Sisto; **D:** Gene Reynolds. THV

Try and Get Me 🎬🎬 Sound of Fury 1950 A small town is incited into a manhunt for kidnappers who murdered their victim. Suspenseful melodrama analyzes mob rule and the criminal mind. 91m/B **VHS.** Lloyd Bridges, Kathleen Ryan, Richard Carlson, Frank Lovejoy, Katherine Locke; **D:** Cy Endfield. REP

Tryst 🎬½ 1994 (R) Julia plots to kill her husband with the help of a detective, but when her housekeeper's son arrives, Julia decides another pawn is just what her deceitful plan needs. 101m/C **VHS, Closed Caption.** Barbara Carrera, Louise Fletcher, David Warner, Steve Bond, Andy Romano, Johnny LaSpada; **D:** Peter Foldy; **W:** Peter Foldy; **M:** Tom Howard. PAR

The Tsar's Bride 🎬🎬🎬 Tsarskaya Nevesta 1966 A lovely young woman is chosen to be the bride of the horrible Tsar Glebov but when the Tsar's bodyguard falls for her, romantic difficulties ensue. A hybrid of the 1899 Rimsky-Korsakov opera and an 1849 play. 95m/B **VHS.** RU Raisa Nedashkovskaya, Natalya Rudnaya, Otar Koberidze; **D:** Vladimir Gorikker. KUL, MVD, HMV

Tucker: The Man and His Dream 🎬🎬🎬 1988 (PG) Portrait of Preston Tucker, entrepreneur and industrial idealist, who in 1946 tried to build the car of the future and was effectively run out of business by the powers-that-were. Ravishing, ultra-nostalgic lullaby to the American Dream. Watch for Jeff's dad, Lloyd, in a bit role. 111m/C **VHS, Beta, LV, 8mm, Letterbox, Closed Caption.** Jeff Bridges, Martin Landau, Dean Stockwell, Frederic Forrest, Mako, Joan Allen, Christian Slater, Lloyd Bridges, Elias Koteas, Nina Siemaszko, Corin "Corky" Nemec, Marshall Bell, Don Novello, Peter Donat, Dean Goodman, Patti Austin; **D:** Francis Ford Coppola; **W:** Arnold Schulman, David Seidler; **M:** Joe Jackson, Carmine Coppola. Golden Globe Awards '89: Best Supporting Actor (Landau); New York Film Critics Awards '88: Best Supporting Actor (Stockwell); Nominations: Academy Awards '88: Best Art Direction/Set Decoration, Best Costume Design, Best Supporting Actor (Landau). PAR

Tuff Turf 🎬🎬 1985 (R) The new kid in town must adjust to a different social lifestyle and a new set of rules when his family is forced to move to a low-class section of Los Angeles. He makes enemies immediately when he courts the girlfriend of one of the local toughs. Fast-paced with a bright young cast. Music by Jim Carroll, Lene Lovich, and Southside Johnny. 113m/C **VHS, Beta, LV, Closed Caption.** James Spader, Kim Richards, Paul Mones, Matt Clark, Olivia Barash, Robert Downey Jr., Catya Sassoon; **D:** Fritz Kiersch; **M:** Jonathan Elias. VTR

Tulips 🎬½ 1981 (PG) Would-be suicide takes a contract out on himself, and then meets a woman who makes life worth living again. Together they attempt to evade the gangland hit man. Limp comedy. 91m/C **VHS, Beta.** CA Gabe Kaplan, Bernadette Peters, Henry Gibson; **D:** Stan Ferris.

Tulsa 🎬🎬🎬 1949 High-spirited rancher's daughter begins crusade to save her father's oil empire when he's killed. Having become ruthless and determined to succeed at any cost, she eventually sees the error of her ways. Classic Hayward. 96m/C **VHS, Beta.** Susan Hayward, Robert Preston, Chill Wills, Ed Begley Sr., Pedro Armendariz Sr.; **D:** Stuart Heisler; **C:** Winton C. Hoch. NOS, BPG, HHT

Tumbledown Ranch in Arizona 🎬 1941 After a rodeo accident, an unconscious college student dreams of adventure out west. Part of the "Range Busters" series. 60m/B **VHS.** Ray Corrigan, John "Dusty" King, Max Terhune, Sheila Darcy, Marian Kerby; **D:** S. Roy Luby. NOS, DVT

Tumbleweed Trail 🎬½ 1942 Action-packed thundering western. 57m/B **VHS, Beta.** William Boyd, Art Davis, Lee Powell, Jack Rockwell; **D:** Sam Newfield. VCN

Tumbleweeds 🎬🎬🎬 1925 William S. Hart's last western. Portrays the last great land rush in America, the opening of the Cherokee Strip in the Oklahoma Territory to homesteaders. Preceded by a sound prologue, made in 1939, in which Hart speaks for the only time on screen, to introduce the story. Silent, with musical score. 114m/B **VHS, Beta, LV.** William S. Hart, Lucien Littlefield, Barbara Bedford; **D:** King Baggot. GPV, CCB, VYY

Tundra 🎬🎬½ The Mighty Thunder 1936 Quasi adventure-drama/documentary set in the Alaskan tundra. A young man, known only as the "Flying Doctor," tends to the sick in small villages throughout the wilderness. But his own survival is at stake when his small plane crashes. Filmed on location. 72m/B **VHS.** Del Cambre; **D:** Norman Dawn. VYY

The Tune 🎬🎬 1992 30,000 ink and watercolor drawings make up this animated gem which tells the story of Del (Neiden), a failed songwriter who gets a fresh start when he makes a wrong turn on the freeway and winds up in Flooby Nooby. The strange inhabitants of this town teach Del to throw out his rhyming dictionary and write about his experiences. Plympton's first full-length animated feature. Also includes "The Making of The Tune" and the animated short "Draw." 80m/C **VHS. D:** Bill Plympton; **W:** Maureen McElheron, Bill Plympton; **V:** Daniel Neiden, Maureen McElheron, Marty Nelson, Emily Bindiger, Chris Hoffman. TRI

Tune in Tomorrow 🎬🎬 1990 (PG-13) Lovesick young Martin (Reeves) wants to woo divorced older babe aunt-by-marriage Julia (Hershey) and is romantically counseled by wacky soap opera writer Pedro (Falk). Seems even soap operas draw on real life, and Martin's story is immortalized on the airwaves, circa 1951 New Orleans. The story-within-a-story also features Pedro's radio characters coming to hammy life. Sometimes funny, sometimes not (the Albanian jokes are tiresome). Adapted from the novel "Aunt Julia and the Scriptwriter" by Mario Vargas Llosa. 90m/C **VHS, LV, Closed Caption.** Barbara Hershey, Keanu Reeves, Peter Falk, Bill McCutcheon, Patricia Clarkson, Peter Gallagher, Dan Hedaya, Buck Henry, Hope Lange, John Larroquette, Elizabeth McGovern, Robert Sedgwick, Henry Gibson; **D:** Jon Amiel; **W:** William Boyd; **M:** Wynton Marsalis. HBO

Tunes of Glory 🎬🎬🎬½ 1960 Guinness and Mills are wonderful in this well made film about a brutal, sometimes lazy colonel and a disciplined and educated man moving up through the ranks of the British military. York's film debut. From the novel by James Kennaway, who adapted it for the screen. Laserdisc version contains interview with director Neame. 107m/C **VHS, Beta, LV.** GB Alec Guinness, John Mills, Dennis Price, Kay Walsh, Susannah York; **D:** Ronald Neame; **M:** Malcolm Ar-

nold. Nominations: Academy Awards '60: Best Adapted Screenplay. TVC, NLC

Tunes of Glory/Horse's Mouth 1960 Guinness double feature. First, "Tunes of Glory" looks at the relationship between good and bad soldiers vying for the same rank. "Horse's Mouth" takes a much lighter tone. Guinness plays a truly obsessed painter who creates his work on public property. Wildly humorous. 305m/C **VHS, Beta.** Alec Guinness, Kay Walsh, Renee Houston, John Mills, Robert Coote; **D:** James Kennaway, Ronald Neame. CRC

The Tunnel 🎬🎬½ 1989 (R) Obsessive romance film with a trace of suspense. Artist sees the woman of his dreams at a showing of his work. His marriage, and her trepidation, don't keep his obsession from consuming him. 99m/C **VHS, Beta, LV.** Jane Seymour, Peter Weller, Fernando Rey; **D:** Antonio Drove. VES, IME

The Tunnel of Love 🎬🎬½ 1958 Day and Widmark are a married couple who find themselves over their heads in red tape when they try to adopt a baby. A beautiful, disapproving adoption investigator also causes more problems for the couple when she believes Widmark is less than ideal father material. Widmark is not in his element at comedy but Day and Young (as their next-door neighbor) are fine in this lightweight adaptation of the Joseph Fields-Peter DeVries play. 98m/C **VHS, LV, Letterbox.** Doris Day, Richard Widmark, Gig Young, Gia Scala, Elisabeth Fraser, Elizabeth Wilson; **D:** Gene Kelly. MGM, MOV

Tunnel Vision 🎬½ 1995 (R) Detective Kelly Wheatstone (Kensit) and her partner Frank Yanovitch (Reynolds) are after a serial killer whose victims are all beautiful women killed in a ritualistic fashion. But all the clues begin to point to Yanovitch as the one committing the crimes. **CW:** Sexuality, nudity, violence and brief language. 100m/C **VHS.** AU Patsy Kensit, Robert Reynolds, Rebecca Rigg, Shane Briant; **D:** Clive Fleury; **W:** Clive Fleury; **C:** Paul Murphy; **M:** David Hirschfelder. TRI

Tunnelvision 🎬🎬½ 1976 (R) A spoof of television comprised of irreverent sketches. Fun to watch because of the appearances of several now-popular stars. 70m/C **VHS.** Chevy Chase, John Candy, Laraine Newman, Joe Flaherty, Howard Hesseman, Gerrit Graham, Al Franken, Tom Davis, Ron Silver; **D:** Neal Israel. HTV

Turbo: A Power Rangers Movie 🎬 1996 (PG) The Power Rangers must battle the evil Divatox (Turner), who's kidnapped the wizard Lerigot so she can use his power to free her even more evil boyfriend Maligore. It's all around cheesy but if you're a five-year-old you may still enjoy the action. 99m/C **VHS, Closed Caption.** Jason David Frank, Stephen Antonio Cardenas, John Yong Bosch, Catherine Sutherland, Nakia Burrise, Blake Foster, Paul Schrier, Jason Narvy, Amy Jo Johnson, Austin St. John, Hilary Shepard Turner, Jon Simanton; **D:** David Winning, Shuki Levy; **W:** Shuki Levy, Shell Danielson; **C:** Ilan Rosenberg; **M:** Shuki Levy. FOX

Turbulence 🎬½ 1996 (R) When you fly, it's usually the turbulence that makes you throw up. Well, this movie isn't that bad, but you may experience a touch of nausea. Flight attendant Teri (Holly) is pushing the drink cart on a strangely vacant New York to L.A. Christmas Eve run. Among the passengers are convicted felons Ryan (Liotta) and Stubbs (Gleeson), who are either on their way to a more secure prison or fulfilling the "consumption of airline food" portion of their sentence. The prisoners seize a gun from the marshals and accidentally rub out the cockpit crew. With all the passengers locked away, Teri must battle the serial rapist/killer Ryan as well as learn to fly the plane through a horrible storm. Passengers on the left of the screen may look out and see "Passenger 57," while those on the right can see the ancient monument of "Airport 75." **CW:** Terror, strong violence and language. 103m/C **VHS, DVD.** Ray Liotta, Lauren Holly, Hector Elizondo, Brendan Gleeson, Ben Cross, Rachel Ticotin, Jeffrey DeMunn, John Finn, Catherine Hicks; **D:** Robert Butler; **W:** Jonathan Brett;

C: Lloyd Ahern; **M:** Shirley Walker. Nominations: Golden Raspberry Awards '97: Worst Actress (Holly). *HBO*

Turf Boy 🎬🎬 *Mr. Celebrity* 1942 Desperate for cash, a boy and his uncle try to get an old horse into prime condition for racing. A minor equine melodrama, just the right length for an old-time matinee double-feature. **68m/B VHS.** Robert "Buzzy" Henry, James Seay, Doris Day, William Halligan, Gavin Gordon; **D:** William Beaudine. *NOS, LOO*

Turk 182! 🎬½ 1985 (PG-13) The angry brother of a disabled fireman takes on City Hall in order to win back the pension that he deserves. He attacks through his graffiti art. Hutton is too heavy for the over-all comic feel of this mostly silly film. **96m/C VHS, Beta, Closed Caption.** Timothy Hutton, Robert Culp, Robert Urich, Kim Cattrall, Peter Boyle, Darren McGavin, Paul Sorvino; **D:** Bob (Benjamin) Clark. *FOX*

Turkish Delights 🎬🎬½ 1973 Free spirit sculptor falls in love with free spirit gal from bourgeois family and artsy soft porn ensues. That is until a brain tumor puts an end to their fun, and he's left to wallow in flashbacks and more artsy soft porn. Dubbed. Verhoeven later became big boxoffice in the U.S. with "Total Recall." **100m/C VHS.** *NL* Monique Van De Ven, Rutger Hauer, Tonny Huurdeman, Wim Van Den Brink; **D:** Paul Verhoeven; **C:** Jan De Bont. Nominations: Academy Awards '73: Best Foreign Language Film. *NO*

Turn of the Blade 🎬 1997 Predictable thriller photographer Sam Peyton (Christensen) upset that his wife Kelly (Owens) is more interested in her acting career than in having a baby. It may be safer to have the kid, since Kelly's the lust object for a seedy film director and then a dangerous stalker. Meanwhile, Sam has his own problems with his associate Wendy, who wants their relationship to get personal and wants Kelly out of the way. **91m/C VHS.** David Christensen, Crystal Owens, David Keith Miller, Julie Horvath; **D:** Bryan Michael Stoller; **W:** Mark Bark; **C:** Richard A. Jones; **M:** Greg Edmonson. *PEG*

The Turn of the Screw 🎬🎬 1974 Supernatural powers vie with a young governess for control of the souls of the two children in her charge. Redgrave does well in this chilling film adapted from the Henry James story. **100m/C VHS, Beta, LV.** Lynn Redgrave, Jasper Jacobs, Eva Griffith; **D:** Dan Curtis. *ART*

The Turn of the Screw 🎬🎬 1989 (R) The young charges of an English nanny are sought for their souls by a dark, unimaginable evil in the mansion. Another version of the Henry James classic. **60m/C VHS, Beta, LV.** Amy Irving, David Hemmings; **D:** Graeme Clifford.

The Turn of the Screw 🎬🎬 1992 (R) Yet another version of the Henry James classic as a young governess struggles with sexual obsession and the two children in her care who are possessed by evil.**CW:** Images of terror and sexual images. **95m/C VHS, LV, Closed Caption.** Julian Sands, Patsy Kensit, Stephane Audran, Marianne Faithfull; **D:** Rusty Lemorande; **M:** Simon Boswell. *ART*

Turnaround 1987 (R) Unusual action/suspense film set in a small town. Relentless gang rampages the citizens. Finally, a man decides he's had enough, and turns on the heathens with his knowledge of magic. **97m/C VHS, Beta.** Doug McKeon, Tim Maier, Eddie Albert, Gayle Hunnicutt; **D:** Ola Solum. *NO*

Turner and Hooch 🎬🎬 1989 (PG) A dog witnesses a murder, and a fussy cop is partnered with the drooling mutt and a weak script in his search for the culprit. Drool as a joke will only go so far, but Hanks is his usual entertaining self. **99m/C VHS, Beta, LV.** Tom Hanks, Mare Winningham, Craig T. Nelson, Scott Paulin, J.C. Quinn; **D:** Roger Spottiswoode; **W:** Jim Cash, Jack Epps Jr., Michael Blodgett. *TOU*

The Turning 🎬½ *Home Fires Burning* 1992 Twenty-two-year-old Cliff Harnish (Dolan) returns home after a four-year absence to shock his family with his strident Neo-Nazi beliefs. May be of curiosity value to Anderson's "X-Files" fans, since she appears (relatively briefly and partially nude) as the guy's girlfriend in a kitchen sex scene. Based on the play by Ceraso. **92m/C VHS.** Michael Dolan, Raymond J. Barry, Karen Allen, Tess Harper, Gillian Anderson; **D:** L.A. Puopolo; **W:** L.A. Puopolo, Chris Ceraso; **C:** J. Michael McClary. *LEO*

The Turning Point 🎬🎬½ 1977 (PG) A woman who gave up ballet for motherhood must come to terms as her daughter launches a ballet career and falls for the lead male dancer. The mother finds herself threatened by her daughter's affection toward an old friend who sacrificed a family life for the life of a ballerina. Baryshnikov's film debut. Melodramatic ending and problems due to ballet sequences. **119m/C VHS, Beta.** Shirley MacLaine, Anne Bancroft, Tom Skerritt, Leslie Browne, Martha Scott, Marshall Thompson, Mikhail Baryshnikov; **D:** Herbert Ross; **W:** Arthur Laurents; **C:** Robert L. Surtees. Golden Globe Awards '78: Best Director (Ross), Best Film—Drama; Los Angeles Film Critics Association Awards '77: Best Director (Ross); National Board of Review Awards '77: Best Actress (Bancroft), Best Supporting Actor (Skerritt); Writers Guild of America '77: Best Original Screenplay; Nominations: Academy Awards '77: Best Actress (Bancroft), Best Actress (MacLaine), Best Art Direction/Set Decoration, Best Cinematography, Best Director (Ross), Best Film Editing, Best Original Screenplay, Best Picture, Best Sound, Best Supporting Actor (Baryshnikov), Best Supporting Actress (Browne). *FOX*

Turtle Diary 🎬🎬🎬 1986 (PG) Two lonely Londoners collaborate to free giant turtles from the city aquarium with the aid of a zoo-keeper, and the turtles' freedom somehow frees them as well. Jackson and Kingsley are stunning. Adapted by Harold Pinter from the Russell Hoban book. **90m/C VHS, Beta, LV, Closed Caption.** *GB* Ben Kingsley, Glenda Jackson, Michael Gambon, Rosemary Leach, Jeroen Krabbe, Eleanor Bron; **D:** John Irvin; **W:** Harold Pinter; **M:** Geoffrey Burgon. *ART, VES*

Turumba 🎬🎬🎬 1984 A quiet satire about a family of papier-mache animal makers in a Philippine village who get a gargantuan order in time for the Turumba holiday, and desperately try to fill it. In Tagalog with English subtitles. **94m/C VHS, Beta.** *PH* **D:** Kidlat Tahimik. *FFM, FCT*

The Tuskegee Airmen 🎬🎬🎬 1995 (PG-13) Cable drama based on the formation and WWII achievements of the U.S. Army Air Corps' first squadron of black combat fighter pilots, the "Fighting 99th" of the 332nd Fighter Group. They were nicknamed after the segregated military outpost where they trained in Tuskegee, Alabama and distinguished themselves in combat, never losing a single bomber, and receiving more than 800 medals. Cast all do a fine job in what turns out to be essentially a standard action/war movie. Based on a story by former Tuskegee airman, Robert W. Williams.**CW:** Strong language, thematic elements, and brief strong war violence. **107m/C VHS.** Laurence "Larry" Fishburne, Cuba Gooding Jr., Allen Payne, Malcolm Jamal Warner, Courtney B. Vance, Andre Braugher, John Lithgow, Rosemary Murphy, Christopher McDonald; **D:** Robert Markowitz; **W:** Paris Qualles, Ron Hutchinson, Trey Ellis; **C:** Ronald Orieux; **M:** Lee Holdridge. *HBO*

Tusks 🎬½ *Fire in Eden* 1989 (R) A ruthless hunter tries to kill elephants. **99m/C VHS, Beta, LV.** Andrew Stevens, John Rhys-Davies, Lucy Gutteridge, Julian Glover; **D:** Tara Hawkins Moore. *NO*

Tut & Tuttle 🎬½ 1982 Young dabbler in magic is transported to ancient Egypt where he is able to demonstrate courage and wits against the evil Horemheb, who has kidnapped Prince Tut. **97m/C VHS, Beta.** Christopher Barnes, Eric Greene, Hans Conried, Vic Tayback. *NO*

The Tuttles of Tahiti 🎬🎬🎬 1942 The Tuttles lead a life of leisure in the South Seas. Laughton's child becomes enamoured of his rival's offspring, causing problems between the two families. More interesting than it sounds. **91m/C VHS, Beta, LV.** Charles Laughton, Jon Hall, Peggy Drake, Victor Francen, Gene Reynolds, Florence Bates, Mala, Alma Ross, Curt Bois; **D:** Charles Vidor. *HHT*

Tuxedo Warrior 🎬½ 1982 Set in South Africa, this film involves the adventures of a well-dressed mercenary who is caught between the police, diamond thieves, and an old girlfriend's bank robbing. **93m/C VHS, Beta.** John Wyman, Carol Royle, Holly Palance; **D:** Andrew Sinclair. *VTR*

TV's Best Adventures of Superman 1951 This first package of episodes from the original television series, which ran from 1951-1957, contains "Superman on Earth," the black & white series pilot about the Man of Steel's childhood on Krypton and Earth, and "All That Glitters," the series' final episode, wherein Lois Lane and Jimmy Olsen acquire super powers. Also includes the 1941 animated cartoon "Superman," the first-ever screen appearance of the superhero. Additional episodes available. **62m/C VHS, Beta.** George Reeves, Phyllis Coates, Noel Neill, Jack Larson, John Hamilton, Robert Shayne. *WAR, MOV*

Twelfth Night 🎬🎬½ 1996 (PG) Director Nunn's take on Shakespeare's gender-bending, romantic-comedy, which is now set in the 1890s. Shipwrecked on an unfriendly Illyrian shore, Viola (Stubbs), believing twin brother Sebastian (Mackintosh) to be dead, disguises herself in male attire and joins the retinue of the lovesick Duke Orsino (Stephens). He's pining for the Countess Olivia (Bonham Carter) and decides to use Viola-turned-Cesario as a surrogate wooer. Too bad Olivia's becoming more interested in her effeminate pseudo-suitor and that Orsino's having a few sexual quandries of his own. **133m/C VHS, LV, Closed Caption.** *GB* Imogen Stubbs, Helena Bonham Carter, Toby Stephens, Steven Mackintosh, Richard E. Grant, Nigel Hawthorne, Ben Kingsley, Imelda Staunton, Mel Smith, Nicholas Farrell; **D:** Trevor Nunn; **W:** Trevor Nunn; **C:** Clive Tickner; **M:** Shaun Davey. *NLC*

Twelve Angry Men 🎬🎬🎬🎬 1957 Fonda sounds the voice of reason as a jury inclines toward a quick-and-dirty verdict against a boy on trial. Excellent ensemble work. Lumet's feature film debut, based on a television play by Reginald Rose. **95m/B VHS, Beta, LV, Closed Caption.** Henry Fonda, Martin Balsam, Lee J. Cobb, E.G. Marshall, Jack Klugman, Robert Webber, Ed Begley Sr., John Fiedler, Jack Warden, George Voskovec, Edward Binns, Joseph Sweeney; **D:** Sidney Lumet; **W:** Reginald Rose; **C:** Boris Kaufman. Berlin International Film Festival '57: Golden Berlin Bear; British Academy Awards '57: Best Actor (Fonda); Nominations: Academy Awards '57: Best Adapted Screenplay, Best Director (Lumet), Best Picture. *MGM, FOX*

Twelve Angry Men 🎬🎬½ 1997 (PG-13) Cable TV update of the 1954 "Studio One" teleplay/1957 movie (both written by Rose) that brings together an all-male jury (now with four black jurors) to decide the fate of a Latino murder suspect. Lemmon has the Henry Fonda role of the juror with reasonable doubts, determined to provide a fair hearing.**CW:** Language. **117m/C VHS, Closed Caption.** George C. Scott, Jack Lemmon, Hume Cronyn, Tony Danza, Mykelti Williamson, Edward James Olmos, Courtney B. Vance, Ossie Davis, Armin Mueller-Stahl, Dorian Harewood, James Gandolfini, William L. Petersen, Mary McDonnell, Douglas Spain; **D:** William Friedkin; **W:** Reginald Rose. *ORI*

Twelve Chairs 🎬🎬🎬 1970 (PG) Take-off on Russian folktale first filmed in Yugoslavia in 1927. A rich matron admits on her deathbed that she has hidden her jewels in the upholstery of one of 12 chairs that are no longer in her home. A Brooksian treasure hunt ensues. **94m/C VHS, Beta, LV.** Mel Brooks, Dom DeLuise, Frank Langella, Ron Moody, Bridget Brice; **D:** Mel Brooks; **W:** Mel Brooks.

12 Monkeys 🎬🎬🎬 1995 (R) Forty years after a plague wipes out 99 percent of the human population and sends the survivors underground, scientists send prisoner James Cole (Willis) to the 1990s to investigate the connection between the virus and seriously deranged fanatic Jeffrey Goines (Pitt), whose father happens to be a renowned virologist. Director Gilliam's demented vision is a bit tougher and less capricious than usual, and the convoluted plot and accumulated detail require a keen attention span, but as each piece of the puzzle falls into place the story becomes a fascinating sci-fi spectacle. Pitt drops the pretty-boy image with a nutzoid performance that'll make revelers stop swooning in a heartbeat. Inspired by the 1962 French short "La Jetee." *CW:* Contains some nudity and sadistic violence. **131m/C VHS, LV, Closed Caption, DVD.** Bruce Willis, Madeleine Stowe, Brad Pitt, Christopher Plummer, David Morse, Frank Gorshin, Jon Seda; *D:* Terry Gilliam; *W:* David Peoples, Janet Peoples; *M:* Paul Buckmaster. Golden Globe Awards '96: Best Supporting Actor (Pitt); Nominations: Academy Awards '95: Best Costume Design, Best Supporting Actor (Pitt); MTV Movie Awards '96: Best Male Performance (Pitt). *USH*

Twelve O'Clock High 🎬🎬🎬½ 1949 Epic drama about the heroic 8th Air Force, with Peck as bomber-group commander sent to shape up a hard-luck group, forced to drive himself and his men to the breaking point. Compelling dramatization of the strain of military command. Includes impressive footage of actual WWII battles. Best-ever flying fortress movie. **132m/B VHS, Beta, LV.** Gregory Peck, Hugh Marlowe, Gary Merrill, Millard Mitchell, Dean Jagger, Paul Stewart; *D:* Henry King; *C:* Leon Shamroy. Academy Awards '49: Best Sound, Best Supporting Actor (Jagger); Nominations: Academy Awards '49: Best Actor (Peck), Best Picture; New York Film Critics Awards '50: Best Actor (Peck). *FCT, BTV, HMV*

12:01 🎬🎬½ 1993 (PG-13) It's the "Groundhog Day" premise played for thrills. Barry Thompson (Silverman) is an employee at a scientific research firm who finds himself reliving the same 24-hour period over and over again. And what a day it is—he discovers a secret project is causing the mysterious time warp, falls in love with beauteous scientist Lisa (Slater) and watches as she gets murdered. Can Barry figure out how to stop what's going on and change things enough to save her? Adaptation of the short story "12:01" by Richard Lupoff, which was previously made into a short film. Made for television. **92m/C VHS, LV, Closed Caption.** Jonathan Silverman, Helen Slater, Martin Landau, Nicolas Surovy, Jeremy Piven; *D:* Jack Sholder. *NLC, IME*

12 Plus 1 🎬🎬🎬 *The Thirteen Chairs* 1970 (R) A man sells 13 chairs left to him by his aunt, only to find that one of them contained a hidden fortune. He chases across Europe in search of each of them. Some good cameos help move this remake of a Russian folk-tale along, but it remains lightweight. Tate's last movie, before her death at the hands of Manson and his "family." **94m/C VHS, Beta.** *FR IT* Sharon Tate, Orson Welles, Vittorio Gassman, Mylene Demongeot, Terry-Thomas, Tim Brooke; *Cameos:* Vittorio De Sica; *D:* Nicolas Gessner. *NO*

Twentieth Century 🎬🎬🎬🎬 1934 Maniacal Broadway director Barrymore transforms shop girl Lombard into a smashing success adored by public and press. Tired of Barrymore's manic-excessive ways, she heads to the Hollywood hills, pursued by the Profile in fine form. **91m/B Beta.** Carole Lombard, John Barrymore, Walter Connolly, Roscoe Karns, Edgar Kennedy, Ralph Forbes, Charles Lane, Etienne Girardot, Snow Flake; *D:* Howard Hawks; *W:* Charles MacArthur, Ben Hecht. *COL*

Twenty Bucks 🎬🎬🎬 1993 (R) Whimsical film follows a $20 dollar bill from its "birth" at a cash machine to its "death" as it is returned to the bank, tattered and torn, for shredding. The bill is passed from owner to owner, sometimes simply and briefly, sometimes altering fate. The original screenplay is nearly 60 years old: Endre Bohem originally drafted it in 1935, and his son revised and updated it. Clever transitions allow the various stories and characters to blend almost seamlessly. The strongest character is Shue's, a young waitress and aspiring writer. Rosenfeld's directorial debut is worth a look. Filmed in Minneapolis. *CW:* Language and brief violence. **91m/C VHS, Closed Caption.** Linda Hunt, David Rasche, George Morfogen, Brendan Fraser, Gladys Knight, Elisabeth Shue, Steve

Buscemi, Christopher Lloyd, Sam Jenkins, Kamal Holloway, Melora Walters, William H. Macy, Diane Baker, Spalding Gray, Matt Frewer, Concetta Tomei, Nina Siemaszko; *D:* Keva Rosenfeld; *W:* Leslie Bohem, Endre Bohem; *C:* Emmanuel Lubezki; *M:* David Robbins. Independent Spirit Awards '94: Best Supporting Actor (Lloyd). *COL*

Twenty Dollar Star 🎬½ 1991 (R) Steamy thriller about a prominent actress who leads a double life as a cheap hooker, and consequent occupational hazards. The title may as well refer to the budget. *CW:* Sex-related violence and sensuality. **92m/C VHS, Closed Caption.** Rebecca Holden, Bernie White, Eddie Barth, Marilyn Hassett, Dick Sargent; *D:* Paul Leder. *PAR*

20 Million Miles to Earth 🎬🎬½ 1957 A spaceship returning from an expedition to Venus crashes on Earth, releasing a fast-growing reptilian beast that rampages throughout Athens. Another entertaining example of stop-motion animation master Ray Harryhausen's work, offering a classic battle between the monster and an elephant. **82m/B LV.** William Hopper, Joan Taylor, Frank Puglia, John Zaremba; *D:* Nathan (Hertz) Juran. *COL*

20,000 Leagues Under the Sea 🎬🎬🎬 1916 Outstanding silent adaptation of Jules Verne's "20,000 Leagues Under the Sea" and "The Mysterious Island" filmed with a then revolutionary underwater camera. Much octopus fighting. Look for newly mastered edition. **105m/B VHS, Beta.** Matt Moore, Allen Holubar, June Gail, William Welsh, Chris Benton, Dan Hamlon; *D:* Stuart Paton; *W:* Stuart Paton. *KIV, GPV, DVT*

20,000 Leagues Under the Sea 🎬🎬🎬½ 1954 From a futuristic submarine, Captain Nemo wages war on the surface world. A shipwrecked scientist and sailor do their best to thwart Nemo's dastardly schemes. Buoyant Disney version of the Jules Verne fantasy. **127m/C VHS, Beta, LV, Letterbox, Closed Caption.** Kirk Douglas, James Mason, Peter Lorre, Paul Lukas, Robert J. Wilke, Carleton Young; *D:* Richard Fleischer. Academy Awards '54: Best Art Direction/Set Decoration (Color), Best Special Effects; Nominations: Academy Awards '54: Best Film Editing. *DIS*

Twenty-One 🎬🎬½ 1991 (R) Modern morality tale of a young English woman who moves to the U.S. to make a new start, but falls into the same old habits. Kensit is frank and charming, in spite of difficulties with her drug addict boyfriend and the illegal alien she marries. Director Boyd leaves it to the viewer to decide between right and wrong and where Kensit fits. **92m/C VHS, LV.** Patsy Kensit, Jack Shepherd, Patrick Ryecart, Maynard Eziashi, Rufus Sewell, Sophie Thompson, Susan Wooldridge, Julia Goodman; *D:* Don Boyd; *W:* Don Boyd; *M:* Michael Berkeley. *NO*

21 Days 🎬🎬½ *Twenty-One Days Together; The First and the Last* 1937 Dull film somewhat redeemed by its stars. Leigh is a married woman carrying on with Olivier. When her husband confronts them, Olivier accidentally kills him in a fight. They keep quiet but then a mentally deranged man is taken into custody for the crime. Since he will be held 21 days before coming to trial, the lovers decide to spend the time together before Olivier confesses. Based on the play "The First and the Last" by John Galsworthy. **75m/C VHS.** *GB* Vivien Leigh, Laurence Olivier, Leslie Banks, Francis L. Sullivan, Hay Petrie, Esme Percy, Robert Newton; *D:* Basil Dean; *W:* Graham Greene, Basil Dean. *FCT*

21 Hours at Munich 🎬🎬🎬 1976 Made-for-TV treatment of the massacre of Israeli athletes by Arab terrorists at the 1972 Olympics. Well-done. The film was produced using the actual Munich locations. **100m/C VHS.** William Holden, Shirley Knight, Franco Nero, Anthony Quayle, Noel Willman; *D:* William A. Graham. *MOV*

23 1/2 Hours Leave 🎬🎬 1937 Amusing WWI service comedy as a barracks wiseacre bets that by the following morning he'll be breakfasting with a general. It's a song-filled remake of a 1919 film, whose star Douglas MacLean later produced

this. **73m/B VHS.** James Ellison, Terry Walker, Morgan Hill, Arthur Lake, Paul Harvey; *D:* John Blystone. *NOS, LOO*

Twenty-Four Eyes 🎬🎬🎬 *Nijushi No Hitomi* 1954 Miss Oishi (Takamine), a teacher on a remote Japanese island in the 1920s, attempts to transmit peaceful values to her 12 pupils amidst the clamor of a nation gearing up for war. As she watches them grow up, many of them doomed to an early death, she remains a pillar of quiet strength. In Japanese with English subtitles. **158m/B VHS, Beta.** *JP* Hideko Takamine, Chishu Ryu, Toshiko Kobayashi; *D:* Keisuke Kinoshita. *NO*

24 Hours in a Woman's Life 🎬🎬 1961 A girl in love with an irresponsible guy hears a cautionary tale from grandma Bergman, who once had a whirlwind romance with a young gambler and naively thought she could reform him. A static TV adaptation of an oft-filmed Stefan Zweig novel, unusually lavish for its time but on the dull side. **90m/C VHS.** Ingrid Bergman, Rip Torn, John Williams, Lili Darvas, Jerry Orbach; *D:* Silvio Narizzano; *W:* John Mortimer. *FCT*

24 Hours to Midnight 🎬½ 1992 A widow uses her ninja skills to wipe out the crime bosses and henchmen who killed her husband. **91m/C VHS, Closed Caption.** Cynthia Rothrock, Stack Pierce; *D:* Leo Fong.

25 Fireman's Street 🎬🎬🎬 *Almok a hazrol* 1973 An evocative drama about the residents of an old house in Hungary which is about to be torn down, and their evening of remembrances of life before, during and after WWII. In Hungarian with English subtitles. **97m/C VHS, Beta.** *HU* Rita Bekes, Peter Muller, Lucyna Winnicka; *D:* Istvan Szabo; *C:* Sandor Sara. *KIV*

29th Street 🎬🎬½ 1991 (R) Compelling comedy-drama based on the true story of Frank Pesce, a New York actor who won six million dollars in that state's first lottery. Great performance from Aiello, as usual, but the direction falters in the dramatic sequences. Based on the book by Frank Pesce and James Franciscus. **101m/C VHS, Closed Caption.** Danny Aiello, Anthony LaPaglia, Lainie Kazan, Frank Pesce, Donna Magnani, Rick Aiello, Vic Manni, Ron Karabatsos, Robert Forster, Joe Franklin, Pete Antico; *D:* George Gallo; *W:* George Gallo; *C:* Steven Fierberg; *M:* William Olvis. *FXV, CCB*

TwentyFourSeven 🎬🎬 1997 (R) Title is local Midlands English slang for 24 hours a day, seven days a week. And in this case it refers to the boredom suffered by the aimless, unemployed youth who live in the local housing estates in Thatcher's depressed '80s England. Middle-aged ex-boxer Alan Darcy (Hoskins in a sincere and sweet performance) decides to help the lads by reviving the amateur boxing club which saved him in his youth. Although it seems to work for a time, things slide downward as, eventually, does the distraught Darcy himself. Meadows' feature directorial debut. *CW:* Language, violence and some drug content. **96m/B VHS.** *GB* Bob Hoskins, Danny Nussbaum, James Hooton, Darren O. Campbell, Mat Hand, Jimmy Hynd, Justin Brady, Karl Collins, Johann Myers, Anthony Clarke, Bruce Jones, Frank Harper, Pamela Cundell; *D:* Shane Meadows; *W:* Shane Meadows, Paul Fraser; *C:* Ashley Rowe; *M:* Neil MacColl, Boo Hewerdine. Nominations: British Academy Awards '97: Best Film. *NYR*

The 27 Day 🎬🎬 1957 Temperate cold war allegory has aliens deliver five mysterious capsules to five Earthlings from different countries. Each capsule, if opened, is capable of decimating the population of the entire planet, but is rendered ineffective after 27 days or upon the death of the holder. Wild ending. Based on John Mantley novel. **75m/B VHS.** Gene Barry, Valerie French, George Voskovec, Arnold Moss, Stefan Schnabel, Ralph Clanton, Friedrich Ledebur, Mari Tsien. *MOV, MLB*

Twice a Judas 🎬 196? An amnesiac is swindled and has his family killed by a ruthless renegade. He wants to get even, even though he can't remember who anyone is. **90m/C VHS, Beta.** Klaus Kinski. *UNI, MOV*

Twice a Woman 🎬 1979 Man and woman divorce, and then both fall in love with the same provocative young woman. It's complicated. **somC VHS, Beta.** Bibi Andersson, Anthony Perkins, Sandra Dumas.

Twice Dead woof! 1988 A family moves into a ramshackle mansion haunted by a stage actor's angry ghost. The ghost helps them battle some attacking delinquent boys. Uninteresting story, poorly done. Never released in theatres. **94m/C VHS, Beta, LV.** Tom Breznahan, Jill Whitlow, Sam Melville, Brooke Bundy, Todd Bridges, Jonathan Chapin, Christopher Burgard; **D:** Bert L. Dragin; **M:** David Bergeaud. NLC

Twice in a Lifetime 🎬🎬🎬 1985 (R) Middle-aged man takes stock of his life when he's attracted to Ann-Margret. Realizing he's married in name only, he moves in with his new love while his former wife and children struggle with shock, disbelief, and anger. Well-acted, realistic, and unsentimental. **117m/C VHS, Beta, LV, Closed Caption.** Gene Hackman, Ellen Burstyn, Amy Madigan, Ann-Margret, Brian Dennehy, Ally Sheedy; **D:** Bud Yorkin; **W:** Colin Welland. Nominations: Academy Awards '85: Best Supporting Actress (Madigan). ART, VES

Twice-Told Tales 🎬🎬🎬 Nathaniel Hawthorne's "Twice Told Tales" 1963 Horror trilogy based loosely on three Nathaniel Hawthorne tales, "Dr. Heidegger's Experiment," "Rappaccini's Daughter," and "The House of Seven Gables." Price is great in all three of these well-told tales. **120m/C VHS, Beta.** Vincent Price, Sebastian Cabot, Brett Halsey; **D:** Sidney Salkow. MGM, MLB

Twilight 🎬🎬🎬 The Magic Hour 1998 (R) It's a pleasure to see pros at work, even if the story is a familiar one. In the noir world of L.A., ex-cop, ex-drunk, ex-P.I. Harry Ross (Newman) is living above the garage at the estate of movie star marrieds Jack (Hackman) and Catherine (Sarandon) Ames, for whom Harry has done several jobs. The cancer-stricken Jack asks Harry to handle a blackmail payoff, which seems to resurrect the circumstances of femme fatale Catherine's first husband's alleged suicide. Also involved is Harry's colleague Raymond Hope (Garner) and Harry's ex-flame, Verna (Channing), a cop investigating a murder with ties to the entire ugly situation. **CW:** Violence, language, nudity. **94m/C VHS.** Paul Newman, Susan Sarandon, Gene Hackman, James Garner, Stockard Channing, Reese Witherspoon, Giancarlo Esposito, Liev Schreiber, Margo Martindale, John Spencer, M. Emmet Walsh; **D:** Robert Benton; **W:** Robert Benton, Richard Russo; **C:** Piotr Sobocinski; **M:** Elmer Bernstein. NYR

Twilight in the Sierras 🎬🎬½ 1950 Lots of heroics and music in this action-packed western. An ex-outlaw gone straight is kidnapped for his notorious criminal finesse. Rogers must come to rescue. **67m/C VHS.** Roy Rogers, Dale Evans, Estelita Rodriguez, Pat Brady, Russ Vincent, George Meeker; **D:** William Witney. REP

Twilight Man 🎬🎬½ 1996 (R) University professor and novelist Jordan Cooper (Matheson) finds his great life turned upside down when a brief altercation with a stranger turns into a nightmare. Turns out the stranger is very strange indeed—computer hacker Hollis Dietz (Stockwell) has made Cooper his own deadly obsession. Suddenly his medical records say he's schizophrenic and even a killer and Cooper must elude police to clear his name. **CW:** Language and violence. **99m/C VHS, LV, Closed Caption.** Tim Matheson, Dean Stockwell, L. Scott Caldwell, Yvette Nipar, Georgann Johnson; **D:** Craig R. Baxley; **W:** Pablo F. Fenjves, Jim Korris. USH

Twilight of the Cockroaches 🎬½ Gokiburi 1990 Mr. Saito is a slovenly bachelor who winds up leaving the remains of his meals for the anthropomorphic cockroaches that infest his apartment. The cockroaches have had it so good for so long that they don't know about insecticides and fearing humans. That is, until Mr. Saito's fastidious new girlfriend makes her appearance and declares war on the vermin. A lifelessly animated tale too dumb for both children and adults and with decidedly unpleasant subject matter, despite the singing, dancing insects. In Japanese with English subtitles. **105m/C VHS, LV.** JP **D:** Hiroaki Yoshida; **V:** Kaoru Kobayashi, Setsuko Karamsumarau. FCT, STP, LUM

The Twilight of the Golds 🎬🎬½ 1997 (PG-13) The upper-middle class Jewish Gold family seem conventional if fretful: there's doctor dad Walter (Marshall), concerned mom Phyllis (Dunaway), married daughter Suzanne (Beals), and aspiring theatrical producer son David (Fraser), who's gay. It seems everyone's dealt with David's homosexuality until Suzanne's geneticist husband, Rob Stein (Tenney), informs his pregnant wife that tests on their unborn son show genes statistically link to him being gay. (The theory is unproven.) Suzanne considers abortion and David is understandably upset when no one tries to talk her out of it, beginning a family estrangement. Cable movie based on the play by Tolins. **CW:** Thematic elements and brief language. **90m/C VHS, Closed Caption.** Garry Marshall, Faye Dunaway, Jennifer Beals, Brendan Fraser, Jon Tenney, Jack Klugman, Sean O'Bryan, Rosie O'Donnell; **D:** Ross Kagen Marks; **W:** Jonathan Tolins, Seth Bass; **C:** Tom Richmond; **M:** Lee Holdridge. BMG

Twilight on the Rio Grande 🎬 1941 Autry runs into a female knife thrower and some jewel smugglers in this far-fetched western. **54m/B VHS, Beta.** Gene Autry, Sterling Holloway, Adele Mara, Bob Steele; **D:** Frank McDonald. VCN

Twilight on the Trail 🎬🎬 1941 Cattle rustlers disappear and Hopalong Cassidy and his sidekicks become "dude" detectives to solve the crime. **54m/B VHS, Beta.** William Boyd, Brad King, Andy Clyde, Jack Rockwell, Wanda McKay, Howard Bretherton. GVV

Twilight People woof! Beasts 1972 (PG) When a mad scientist's creations turn on him for revenge, he runs for his life. Boring, gory, with bad make-up and even poorer acting. This one should fade away into the night. **84m/C VHS, Beta.** PH John Ashley, Pat Woodell, Jan Merlin, Pam Grier, Eddie Garcia; **D:** Eddie Romero. VCI

The Twilight Zone 1961 Travel through another dimension in Rod Serling's classic science fiction series. Two episodes per tape. On this tape: "The Invaders," written by Richard Matheson, sees a farm house inhabited by a mute woman become the destination of strange, miniature space travellers. In "Nothing in the Dark," written by George Clayton Johnson, an elderly woman is given an interesting lesson regarding her fear of death. **50m/B VHS, Beta, LV.** Agnes Moorehead, Douglas Heyes, Gladys Cooper, Robert Redford, R.G. Armstrong; **D:** Lamont Johnson; **W:** Richard Matheson, George Clayton Johnson. FXV, FOX, MOV

Twilight Zone: The Movie 🎬🎬½ 1983 (PG) Four short horrific tales are anthologized in this film as a tribute to Rod Sterling and his popular television series. Three of the episodes, "Kick the Can," "It's a Good Life" and "Nightmare at 20,000 Feet," are based on original "Twilight Zone" scripts. Morrow was killed in a helicopter crash during filming. **101m/C VHS, Beta, LV.** Dan Aykroyd, Albert Brooks, Vic Morrow, Kathleen Quinlan, John Lithgow, Billy Mumy, Scatman Crothers, Kevin McCarthy, Bill Quinn, Selma Diamond, Abbe Lane, John Larroquette, Jeremy Licht, Patricia Barry, William Schallert, Burgess Meredith, Cherie Currie; **D:** John Landis, Steven Spielberg, George Miller, Joe Dante; **W:** John Landis; **C:** Allen Daviau; **M:** Jerry Goldsmith. WAR

Twilight's Last Gleaming 🎬🎬½ 1977 (R) A maverick general takes a SAC missile base hostage, threatening to start WWIII if the U.S. government doesn't confess to its Vietnam policies and crimes. Gripping film, with good performances. Based on a novel by Walter Wager, "Viper Three." **144m/C VHS, Beta, LV.** Burt Lancaster, Charles Durning, Richard Widmark, Melvyn Douglas, Joseph Cotten, Paul Winfield, Burt Young, Roscoe Lee Browne, Richard Jaeckel, William Marshall, Vera Miles, Leif Erickson, Charles McGraw, William Smith, John Ratzenberger; **D:** Robert Aldrich; **W:** Ronald M. Cohen; **C:** Robert B. Hauser; **M:** Jerry Goldsmith. FOX

Twin Peaks 🎬🎬 1990 Sketchy home video distillation of the eccentric TV series. It preserves much of the setup episode (the murder of teen-queen Laura Palmer and nest of small-town weirdness it reveals), then rushes piecemeal through the rest of the season. There's an altered quasi-solution to the enigma and a bizarre backward sequence not broadcast in the US. In this compressed form it's best for initiates of the TP cult; others won't be converted. **113m/C VHS, LV, Closed Caption.** Kyle MacLachlan, Michael Ontkean, Sherilyn Fenn, Lara Flynn Boyle, Joan Chen, Peggy Lipton, Piper Laurie, Michael Horse, Russ Tamblyn, Richard Beymer, Madchen Amick, Catherine Coulson, Warren Frost, Everett McGill, Jack Nance, Ray Wise, Eric Da Re, Harry Goaz, Sheryl Lee; **D:** David Lynch; **M:** Angelo Badalamenti. WAR, FCT

Twin Peaks 1990 Premiere episode of David Lynch's bizarre TV drama. In this episode, Agent Cooper and Sheriff Truman begin the investigation into the death of prom queen, Laura Palmer. All seven episodes are available in a boxed set. **50m/C VHS.** Michael Ontkean, Kyle MacLachlan, Joan Chen, Piper Laurie, Sherilyn Fenn, Peggy Lipton, Madchen Amick, Lara Flynn Boyle, Michael Horse, Russ Tamblyn, Richard Beymer, Dana Ashbrook, Warren Frost, Everett McGill, Jack Nance, Ray Wise, Eric Da Re, Catherine Coulson, Harry Goaz, Sheryl Lee; **D:** David Lynch; **M:** Angelo Badalamenti. WOV, MOV

Twin Peaks: Fire Walk with Me 🎬🎬 1992 (R) Prequel to the cult TV series is weird and frustrating, chronicling the week before Laura Palmer's death. Suspense is lacking since we know the outcome, but Lynch manages to intrigue with dream-like sequences and interestingly offbeat characters. On the other hand, it's exploitative and violent enough to alienate series fans. Includes extremely brief and baffling cameos by Bowie as an FBI agent and Stanton as the manager of a trailer park. Several of the show's regulars are missing, and others appear and disappear very quickly. On the plus side are the strains of Badalamenti's famous theme music and Isaak as an FBI agent with amazingly acute powers of observation. **CW:** Language, strong violence and drug content, and strong sexuality. **135m/C VHS, LV, Letterbox, Closed Caption.** Kyle MacLachlan, Sheryl Lee, Moira Kelly, Chris Isaak, Ray Wise, Kiefer Sutherland, Peggy Lipton, Dana Ashbrook, James Marshall, David Lynch; **Cameos:** David Bowie, Harry Dean Stanton; **D:** David Lynch; **W:** David Lynch; **M:** Angelo Badalamenti. NLC

Twin Sisters 🎬½ 1991 Woman discovers her missing twin sister was a high-priced prostitute and a detective tries to protect her from the lowlifes sis was involved with. **92m/C VHS, Closed Caption.** Stephanie Kramer, Susan Almgren, Frederic Forrest, James Brolin; **D:** Tom Berry; **M:** Lou Forestieri. THV

Twin Town 🎬🎬½ 1997 Dark comedy about class warfare, escalating revenge, and drug abuse in a small seaside Welsh town features sharp, profane, and very funny dialogue, well-developed and played characters, and uneven direction. Brothers Julian (Evans) and Jeremy (Ifans) like to steal expensive cars and get high on any substance they can find and control. They live with their handyman dad Fatty (Ceredig) and massage parlor receptionist sister (Scorgie) on the wrong side of the tracks. Dad falls off a roof while working for the local contractor/drug kingpin (Thomas) and is not fairly compensated. This starts a cycle of revenge that begins with public urination and gets nasty from there. Sort of a Welsh "Trainspotting," which featured a cameo by "Twin" writer/director Allen. Some scenes may be too much for some viewers (especially animal lovers). **101m/C VHS, LV.** GB Llyr Evans, Rhys Ifans, Huw Ceredig, William Thomas, Dorien Thomas, Dougray

Scott; **D:** Kevin Allen; **W:** Kevin Allen, Paul Durden; **C:** John Mathieson; **M:** Mark Thomas. *PGV*

Twins 🎬🎬½ **1988 (PG)** A genetics experiment gone awry produces twins rather than a single child. One is a genetically engineered superman, the other a short, lecherous petty criminal. Schwarzenegger learns he has a brother, and becomes determined to find him, despite their having been raised separately. The two meet and are immediately involved in a contraband scandal. Amusing pairing of Schwarzenegger and DeVito. **107m/C VHS, Beta, LV, Closed Caption, DVD.** Arnold Schwarzenegger, Danny DeVito, Kelly Preston, Hugh O'Brian, Chloe Webb, Bonnie Bartlett, Marshall Bell, Trey Wilson, Nehemiah Persoff; **D:** Ivan Reitman; **W:** William Davies, William Osborne, Timothy Harris, Herschel Weingrod; **C:** Andrzej Bartkowiak; **M:** Georges Delerue, Randy Edelman. *USH*

Twins of Evil 🎬🎬 *The Gemini Twins; Twins of Dracula; The Virgin Vampires* **1971** Beautiful female twins fall victim to the local vampire, and their God-fearing uncle is out to save/destroy them. Hammer sex and blood-sucking epic starring the Collinsons, who were featured in the October 1970 issue of "Playboy" as the first twin Playmates. **86m/C VHS, Beta.** *GB* Madeleine Collinson, Mary Collinson, Peter Cushing, Kathleen Byron, Dennis Price, Damien Thomas, David Warbeck, Katya Wyeth, Maggie Wright, Luan Peters, Kristen Lindholm, Judy Matheson; **D:** John Hough; **W:** Tudor Gates. *MLB*

Twinsanity 🎬 *Goodbye Gemini* **1970 (R)** Evil twins are charged with the murder of a man who attempted to blackmail them. **91m/C VHS, Beta.** *GB* Judy Geeson, Martin Potter, Alexis Kanner, Michael Redgrave, Freddie Jones, Peter Jeffrey; **D:** Alan Gibson; **W:** Edmund Ward; **M:** Christopher Gunning.

Twinsitters 🎬🎬½ **1995 (PG-13)** Twins Peter and David Falcone (Peter and David Paul) find themselves unexpectedly saving the life of corrupt businessman Frank Hillhurst (Martin). Hillhurst is turning state's evidence on his crooked operations and his disturbed partners have threatened both his life and the lives of his twin 10-year-old nephews. So Hillhurst hires the Falcones to protect his hellacious pint-sized relatives—who manage to get themselves kidnapped. **93m/C VHS, Closed Caption.** Peter Paul, David Paul, Christian Cousins, Joseph Cousins, Jared Martin, George Lazenby, Rena Sofer, Mother Love; **D:** John Paragon; **W:** John Paragon. *COL*

Twirl 🎬🎬 **1981** Satirical look at the cutthroat world of baton twirling. Parents apply relentless pressure on their daughters to win a contest. Decent made-for-TV movie. **100m/C VHS, Beta.** Stella Stevens, Charles Haid, Lisa Whelchel, Erin Moran, Edd Byrnes, Sharon Spelman, Matthew Tobin, Donna McKechnie, Rosalind Chao, Heather Locklear, Deborah Richter, Jamie Rose, Tracy Scoggins; **D:** Gus Trikonis. *ART*

Twist 🎬½ *Folies Bourgeoises* **1976** A tepid French drama chronicling the infidelities of various wealthy aristocrats. It isn't as pretentious as boring, as is the film. In French with English subtitles or dubbed. **105m/C VHS, Beta.** *FR* Bruce Dern, Stephane Audran, Ann-Margret, Sydne Rome, Jean-Pierre Cassel, Curt Jurgens, Maria Schell, Charles Aznavour; **D:** Claude Chabrol; **M:** Manuel De Sica. *ART*

Twist & Shout 🎬🎬🎬 *Hab Og Karlighed* **1984 (R)** Sequel to the popular Danish import "Zappa," in which two teenage lovers discover sex and rock and roll. Transcends the teens discovering sex genre. Danish with English subtitles. Profanity, nudity, and sex. **107m/C VHS, Beta.** *DK* Lars Simonsen, Adam Tonsberg, Ulrikke Juul Bondo, Camilla Soeberg; **D:** Bille August; **W:** Bille August. *NO*

Twisted 🎬🎬 **1986 (R)** This curio from Slater's early career came out on tape to take advantage of his rising stardom. He's properly creepy as a brilliant but evil teen using electronics, psychology, and swordplay to terrorize victims. The suspense isn't too bad when direction doesn't go overboard, which unfortunately is half the time. Based on the play "Children! Children!" by Jack Horrigan. **87m/C VHS.** Lois Smith, Christian Slater, Tandy Cronyn, Brooke Tracy, Dina Merrill, Dan Ziskie, Karl Taylor,

Noelle Parker, John Cunningham, J.C. Quinn; **D:** Adam Holender. *NO*

Twisted **1996 (PG-13)** Four people become trapped in a fantasy world where nothing is as it seems. An airline passenger loses his identity, a housewife finds romance, a con man find a new mark, and a hired killer decides to retire—or at least that's what they believe. From the Australian TV series "Twisted Tales." **86m/C VHS.** *AU* Geoffrey Rush, Rachel Ward, Bryan Brown, Kimberly Davies, Jill McKay; **D:** Samantha Lang, Christopher Robbin Collins, Gregor Jordan, Catherine Millar. *PZA*

Twisted Brain 🎬 *Horror High* **1974 (R)** An honor student develops a serum that makes him half man and half beast. Now he can exact revenge on all the jocks and cheerleaders who have humiliated him in the past. Cardi is okay, the rest of the cast is awful. Silly, horrific teen monster epic. **89m/C VHS, Beta.** Pat Cardi, Austin Stoker, Rosie Holotik, John Niland, Joyce Hash, Jeff Alexander, Joe "Mean Joe" Greene; **D:** Larry N. Stouffer. *NO*

Twisted Justice 🎬½ **1989** Set in 2020, Heavener is a cop determined to stop a ruthless killer. Matters become complicated, however, when his gun is taken away. Now he's forced to rely on his cunning to outwit his sadistic opponent. **90m/C VHS.** David Heavener, Erik Estrada, Jim Brown, Shannon Tweed, James Van Patten, Don Stroud, Karen Black, Lori Warren; **D:** David Heavener; **W:** David Heavener. *NO*

Twisted Love 🎬½ **1995 (R)** Wallflower becomes obsessed with the most popular guy in school. He has a motorcycle accident-that-wasno-accident and winds up in her tender care. Sounds like "Misery" to me.**CW:** Violence, sexuality, and some language. **80m/C VHS.** Lisa Dean Ryan, Mark Paul Gosselaar, Soleil Moon Frye; **D:** Eb Lottimer. *NHO*

Twisted Nightmare 🎬 **1987 (R)** The people responsible for a young retarded boy's death are hunted by a strange figure lurking in the shadows. **95m/C Beta.** Rhonda Gray, Cleve Hall, Brad Bartrum, Robert Padilla; **D:** Paul Hunt. *TWE*

Twisted Obsession 🎬🎬 **1990 (R)** A man becomes passionately obsessed with a woman, and it leads to murder. **109m/C VHS, Beta, LV.** Jeff Goldblum, Miranda Richardson, Anemone, Dexter Fletcher, Daniel Ceccaldi, Liza Walker, Jerome Natali, Arielle Dombasle; **D:** Fernando Trueba; **C:** Jose Luis Alcaine; **M:** Antoine Duhamel. *ART*

Twister 🎬🎬 **1989 (PG-13)** An intriguing independent feature about a bizarre midwestern family, its feverish eccentricities and eventual collapse. Awaiting a cult following. **93m/C VHS, Beta, LV.** Dylan McDermott, Crispin Glover, Harry Dean Stanton, Suzy Amis, Jenny Wright, Lindsay Christman, Lois Chiles; **D:** Michael Almereyda; **W:** Michael Almereyda; **C:** Renato Berta; **M:** Hans Zimmer. *ART, VES*

Twister 🎬🎬½ **1996 (PG-13)** Director De Bont's sophomore directorial effort is another non-stop adrenaline drive, but instead of a mad bomber, nature is the bad guy. Hunt leads a collegiate team of storm chasing scientists thourgh Oklahoma in hopes of placing a robotic mechanism inside a tornado which, in turn, will help them predict and prepare for future funnel forces. There's also the matter of Hunt's soon-to-be exhusband Paxton, and a competitor (Elwes) who's in charge of a slick group of rival scientists. There's a lot of things flying around, including trucks, houses, cows and the plausibility of the plot. But a contrived plot didn't keep from making $100 million dollars in its first two weeks of release. Some nice chemistry between Hunt and Paxton, apparently the only people who can still look attractive in high winds and blowing debris.**CW:** Intense depiction of very bad weather. **105m/C VHS, LV, Letterbox, Closed Caption, DVD.** Bill Paxton, Helen Hunt, Cary Elwes, Jami Gertz, Alan Ruck, Lois Smith, Sean Whalen, Gregory Sporleder, Abraham Benrubi, Jake Busey; **D:** Jan De Bont; **W:** Michael Crichton, Anne-Marie Martin; **C:** Jack N. Green; **M:** Mark Mancina. MTV Movie Awards '97: Best Action Sequence; Nomina-

tions: Academy Awards '96: Best Sound, Best Visual Effects; MTV Movie Awards '97: Best Female Performance (Hunt); Golden Raspberry Awards '96: Worst Supporting Actress (Gertz). *WAR*

Twister Kicker 🎬 **1985** When the woman he loves is in jeopardy, an invincible man battles the best of fighters from three continents. Despite all this action, it's pretty ho-hum. **93m/C VHS.** Wang Hoi, Yeung Oi Wa, Po Pei. *NO*

Twitch of the Death Nerve 🎬🎬 *Bay of Blood; Last House on the Left, Part 2; Carnage* **1971 (R)** Four vacationers are relentlessly pursued by a homicidal maniac armed with a sickle, bent on decapitation. Supposedly the inspiration for the "Friday the 13th" series. **87m/C VHS, Beta.** *IT* Claudine Auger, Chris Avran, Isa Miranda, Claudio Volonte, Luigi Pistilli; **D:** Mario Bava. *NO*

Two Assassins in the Dark 🎬 **198?** Martial arts adventure about a pair of kung-fu killers who fight in the dark. **90m/C VHS, Beta.** Wang Tao, Chang Yi, Lung Chun-Eng. *NO*

Two Bits 🎬🎬½ *A Day to Remember* **1996 (PG-13)** Depression-era drama tells the story of a 12-year-old boy and his emotional coming of age. Title refers to a quarter Gennaro (Barone, in his film debut) seeks in order to attend the grand opening of a glamorous, air-conditioned movie palace. A heavily made-up Pacino (looking suspiciously like Marlon Brando in the garden scene of "The Godfather"), co-stars as the boy's grandfather, who leaves him his last quarter. Gramps promises that he can collect later that day, when, he says, he will die. Fine performances all around and some powerful scenes go a long way toward masking the fact that the material is a bit too thin to stretch over an entire feature film.**CW:** Mature themes. **85m/C VHS, LV, Closed Caption.** Al Pacino, Gerlando Barone, Mary Elizabeth Mastrantonio, Joe Grifasi, Joanna Merlin, Andy Romano, Ron McLarty, Donna Mitchell, Patrick Borriello, Mary Lou Rosato, Rosemary DeAngelis; **D:** James Foley; **W:** Joseph Stefano; **C:** Juan Ruiz-Anchia; **M:** Jane Musky; **V:** Alec Baldwin. *TOU*

Two Bits & Pepper 🎬🎬½ **1995 (PG)** Bumbling criminals (both played by Piscopo) still manage to kidnap a a young girl and her friend and it's up to the title characters, a pet horse and a pony, to attempt a daring rescue. **90m/C VHS, Closed Caption.** Joe Piscopo, Lauren Eckstrom, Rachel Crane, Perry Stephens, Kathrin Lautner, Dennis Weaver; **D:** Corey Michael Eubanks; **W:** Corey Michael Eubanks; **C:** Jacques Haitkin; **M:** Louis Febre. *REP*

Two by Forsyth 🎬🎬 **1986** Two short films based on stories by Frederick Forsyth, one dealing with a dying millionaire's clever efforts to prevent his fortune from being inherited by greedy relatives, the other about a mild-mannered stamp dealer who avenges himself on a nasty gossip columnist. **60m/C VHS, Beta.** Dan O'Herlihy, Cyril Cusack, Milo O'Shea, Shirley Anne Field.

2 By 4 🎬🎬 **1998** Johnnie (Smallhorne) is an Irish construction worker employed by his hard-living Uncle Trump (O'Neill) in New York. Though he's got a steady job, good friends, and a loving girlfriend in Maria (Topper), Johnnie's plagued by nightmares of something that happened in his childhood. And his apparent childhood abuse leads him to drugs, drink, and a certain sexual ambiguity as his repressed memories try to force their way to the surface. **90m/C VHS.** Terrence McGoff, Jimmy Smallhorne, Chris O'Neill, Bradley Fitts, Kimberly Topper; **D:** Jimmy Smallhorne; **W:** Terrence McGoff, Fergus Tighe, Jimmy Smallhorne; **C:** Declan Quinn. Sundance Film Festival '98: Best Cinematography. *NYR*

Two Daughters 🎬🎬🎬 *Teen Kanya* **1961** Director Ray wrote the scripts for two stories based on the writings of Nobel Prize winner Rabindranath Tagore. "The Postmaster" covers the relationship between an ambitious young man who befriends his servant without realizing the consequences of his actions. "The Conclusion" finds a solemn young scholar declining to marry the girl arranged to be his intended and instead marrying a high-spirited young woman who doesn't want to give up her freedoms. Bengali with English subtitles. 114m/B VHS. *IN* Chandana Banerjee, Anil Chatterjee, Soumitra Chatterjee; *D:* Satyajit Ray; *W:* Satyajit Ray. COL

Two Days in the Valley ✓✓✓ 1996

(R) Film adds two days with ten characters in one locale and one half dozen separate plots and tries to come up with a dark comedy/thriller and winning debut for Herzfeld. It succeeds, mostly. San Fernando Valley is the backdrop, with a diverse ensemble of disturbed characters thrown together by the murder of a philandering spouse. Disjointed, and some plot threads are left hanging, but there's some fine comic moments and interesting character development, especially Aiello's culinary hitman, Dosmo Pizzo. Theron's Helga adds eye candy. For those too young to remember "Dynasty," you may want to check out the intense cat-fight between Hatcher's Becky Foxx and Helga.*CW:* Violence, sexuality and language. 105m/C VHS, Closed Caption. Danny Aiello, Jeff Daniels, Marsha Mason, Teri Hatcher, Glenne Headly, James Spader, Eric Stoltz, Greg Cruttwell, Peter Horton, Charlize Theron, Keith Carradine, Louise Fletcher, Austin Pendleton, Paul Mazursky, Kathleen Luong; *D:* John Herzfeld; *W:* John Herzfeld; *C:* Oliver Wood; *M:* Anthony Marinelli. Nominations: Golden Raspberry Awards '96: Worst Supporting Actress (Hatcher). HBO

Two Deaths ✓✓ 1994 (R) Sex, brutality,

power, madness, death, revolution—sounds like a Roeg concoction. In 1989 Romania, the Ceaucescu government is under siege and a civil war rages outside. But inside the opulent apartment of cynical Dr. Daniel Pavenic (Gambon) calmness prevails, as three longtime friends join him for their annual reunion dinner. Dinner is served by Pavenic's housekeeper Ana (Braga), who has a strange, disturbing relationship with the possessive doctor that he relates to his friends. His candor leads to similar revelations by his companions. Based on the novel "The Two Deaths of Senora Puccini" by Stephen Dobyns.*CW:* Strong violence, including a graphic abortion scene, nudity/sexuality and related dialogue. 102m/C VHS. *GB* Michael Gambon, Sonia Braga, Patrick Malahide, Nickolas Grace, John Shrapnel, Ion Caramitru; *D:* Nicolas Roeg; *W:* Allan Scott; *C:* Witold Stok; *M:* Hans Zimmer. FXL

Two English Girls ✓✓✓½ Les Deux An-

glaises et le Continent 1972 (R) A pre-WWI French lad, with a possessive mother, loves two English sisters, one an impassioned, reckless artist, the other a repressed spinster. Tenderly delineates the triangle's interrelating love and friendship over seven years. Based on the novel "Les Deux Anglaises et le Continent" by Henri-Pierre Roche. In French with English subtitles. 108m/C VHS, Beta, LV. *FR* Jean-Pierre Leaud, Kika Markham, Stacey Tendeter, Sylvia Marriott, Marie Mansert, Philippe Leotard; *D:* Francois Truffaut; *C:* Nestor Almendros; *M:* Georges Delerue. HMV, FOX

Two Evil Eyes ✓✓ Due Occhi Diabolici 1990

(R) Horror kings Romero and Argento each direct an Edgar Allan Poe tale in this release, hence the title. Barbeau, the scheming younger wife of a millionaire, hypnotizes her husband with the help of her lover in "The Facts in the Case of M. Valdemar." When hubby dies too soon to validate changes made in his will, the lovers decide to freeze him for two weeks in order that death can be recorded at the correct time. In "Black Cat" a crime photographer used to photographing gore adopts a feline friend and starts getting sick on the job. 121m/C VHS, Beta, LV. *IT* Adrienne Barbeau, Ramy Zada, Harvey Keitel, Madeleine Potter, Bingo O'Malley, E.G. Marshall, John Amos, Sally Kirkland, Kim Hunter, Martin Balsam, Tom Atkins; *D:* George A. Romero, Dario Argento; *W:* George A. Romero, Dario Argento, Franco Ferrini; *C:* Giuseppe Maccari, Peter Reniers; *M:* Pino Donaggio. FXV, VTR

Two-Faced Woman ✓✓✓ 1941 Garbo,

in her last film, attempts a ruse when she finds her husband may be interested in an old flame. Pretending to be her twin sister in an attempt to lure Douglas away from the other woman, she's fooled a little herself. Romantic comedy unfortunately miscasts Garbo as an Americanized ski bunny. 90m/B VHS, Beta. Greta Garbo, Melvyn Douglas, Constance Bennett, Roland Young, Ruth Gordon, Robert Sterling, George Cleveland, Frances Carson; *D:* George Cukor; *C:* Joseph Ruttenberg. MGM

The Two Faces of Dr. Jekyll ✓✓½

House of Fright; Jekyll's Inferno 1960 Henry Jekyll's (Massie) experiments lead to the release of his suave alter ego Edward Hyde. When Hyde discovers that Jekyll's long-suffering wife has taken up with his best friend, Hyde pits everyone against each other, while Jekyll struggles to retain control over his insidious other half. 87m/C VHS, Closed Caption. *GB* Paul Massie, Dawn Addams, Christopher Lee, David Kossoff, Francis De Wolff, Oliver Reed, Norma Marla, Terry Quinn; *D:* Terence Fisher; *W:* Wolf Mankowitz; *C:* Jack Asher. COL

The Two Faces of Evil ✓ 1982 A fami-

ly's vacation turns into a night of unbearable terror when they pick up a sinister hitchhiker. 60m/C VHS, Beta. Anna Calder-Marshall, Gary Raymond, Denholm Elliott, Pauline Delany, Philip Latham; *D:* Peter Sasdy, Alan Gibson. ART

Two Fathers' Justice 1985 Two dads,

one tough and one a wimp, seek revenge on the men who killed their kids. Made for television. 100m/C VHS. Robert Conrad, George Hamilton, Brooke Bundy, Catherine Corkill, Whitney Kershaw, Greg Terrell; *D:* Rod Holcomb. MCG

Two Fisted Justice ✓ 1931 A cowboy

protects a town against a daring and deadly Indian attack. 45m/B VHS, Beta. Tom Tyler. VDM

Two-Fisted Justice ✓ 1943 The Range

Busters do their part to maintain law and order in the old West. 55m/B VHS, Beta. John "Dusty" King, David Sharpe, Max Terhune. NOS, DVT

Two-Fisted Law ✓½ 1932 McCoy plays a

rancher who borrows big bucks from the corrupt Oakman, who's actually a land grabber. McCoy then teams up with a posse to bring the evildoer to justice. Early (and small) screen roles for Wayne and Brennan. 58m/B VHS. Tim McCoy, Tully Marshall, Wheeler Oakman, Alice Day, Wallace MacDonald, John Wayne, Walter Brennan; *D:* David Ross Lederman. COL

Two for Texas ✓✓½ 1997 Young buck

Holland (Bairstow) and grizzled adventurer Allison (Kristofferson) manage to escape from a Louisiana chain gang and decide to head to Texas so they can join in the Texas Volunteer Army under Sam Houston (Skerritt). Soon, they're part of a group sent to San Jacinto in order to avenge the massacre at the Alamo. Kind of plodding cable western based on the novel by James Lee Burke. 96m/C VHS. Kris Kristofferson, Scott Bairstow, Tom Skerritt, Peter Coyote, Irene Bedard, Victor Rivers; *D:* Rod Hardy; *W:* Larry Brothers; *C:* David Connell; *M:* Lee Holdridge. TTC

Two for the Road ✓✓✓½ 1967 After

over a decade of marriage, Finney and Hepburn look back and find only fragments of their relationship. Mancini score adds poignancy to the couple's reflections on their stormy life. Touching and well-acted. 112m/C VHS, LV, Letterbox. *GB* Audrey Hepburn, Albert Finney, Eleanor Bron, William Daniels, Claude Dauphin, Nadia Gray, Jacqueline Bisset, Georges Descrieres, Gabrielle Middleton, Judy Cornwell, Irene Hilda, Roger Dann, Libby Morris, Yves Barsac; *D:* Stanley Donen; *W:* Frederic Raphael; *C:* Christopher Challis; *M:* Henry Mancini. Nominations: Academy Awards '67: Best Story & Screenplay. BTV, FUS, MOV

Two for the Seesaw ✓✓✓ 1962 Mitch-

hum stars as a Nebraska attorney who comes to New York and gets involved with MacLaine. Humorous and touching comedy-drama worked better on stage, because the large screen magnified

the talkiness of Gibson's play. Unusual casting of Mitchum as a Midwest lawyer and MacLaine as a New York Jewish bohemian. 119m/B VHS, LV, Letterbox, Closed Caption. Robert Mitchum, Shirley MacLaine, Edmon Ryan, Elisabeth Fraser, Eddie Firestone, Billy Gray, Vic Lundin; *D:* Robert Wise; *W:* Isobel Lennart; *M:* Andre Previn. Nominations: Academy Awards '62: Best Black and White Cinematography, Best Song ("Song fromm Two for the Seesaw (Second Chance)"). MGM

Two Friends ✓✓ 1986 Campion's first fea-

ture, made for Austrailian TV, depicts the severing of the friendship between 15-year-olds Kelly (Bidenko) and Louise (Coles). Separated physically and emotionally as they begin growing up and attending different schools, the film flashes back to moments in their once inseparable friendship. 76m/C VHS, Letterbox. *AU* Kris Bidenko, Emma Coles, Peter Hehir, Kris McQuade; *D:* Jane Campion; *W:* Helen Garner; *C:* Julian Penney; *M:* Martin Armiger. NYF, MIL

Two Girls and a Guy ✓✓✓ 1998 (R)

Graham and Wagner find out that Downey's been two-timing them and they confront him at his apartment. Only don't expect the usual revenge scenario. Yeah, it's talky, but the dialogue (much of it improvised) is great. Downey is at his best, playing an irresistibly charismatic actor backed into a (real and figurative) corner by his lifestyle while Graham and Wagner avoid the wronged-woman cliches. In one of the all-time male fantasies ever, Downey's character still gets to have sex with one of the women even after his lie has been exposed. The MPAA had a little problem with that, since that scene, like most of the rest of the movie, was shot in real time.*CW:* A strong sex scene, strong language and sexual dialogue, and for a violent image. 92m/C VHS. Robert Downey Jr., Heather Graham, Natasha Gregson Wagner, Angel David; *D:* James Toback; *W:* James Toback; *C:* Barry Markowitz. NYR

Two Girls and a Sailor ✓✓✓ 1944

Wartime musical revue loosely structured around a love triangle involving a sailor on leave. Vintage hokum with lots of songs. ♫Paper Doll; The Young Man with a Horn; Concerto for Index Finger; Take it Easy; Ritual Fire Dance; Inka Dinka Doo; My Mother Told Me; A Love Like Ours; In A Moment of Madness. 124m/B VHS, Beta, LV. June Allyson, Gloria De Haven, Van Johnson, Xavier Cugat, Jimmy Durante, Tom Drake, Lena Horne, Harry James, Gracie Allen, Virginia O'Brien, Jose Iturbi, Carlos Ramirez, Donald Meek, Ben Blue; *Cameos:* Buster Keaton; *D:* Richard Thorpe; *C:* Robert L. Surtees. Nominations: Academy Awards '44: Best Original Screenplay. MGM

Two Graves to Kung-Fu ✓ 1982 (R)

Young kung-fu student is framed for murder. When the real murderers kill his teacher, he escapes from prison to seek revenge. 95m/C VHS, Beta. Liu Chia-Yung, Shek Kin, Chen Hung-Lieh. GEM

The Two Great Cavaliers ✓ 1973 A

Ming warrior has a hard time with the Manchurian army, fending it off as he must with only his bare instep, heel, and wrist. 95m/C VHS, Beta. Chen Shing, Mao Ying; *D:* Yeung Ching Chen. UNI

Two Gun Man ✓½ 1931 America's first

singing cowboy, Ken Maynard, performs hair-raising stunts in this old oater. One of the first "talkies!" 60m/B VHS, Beta. Ken Maynard, Lafe McKee, Charles "Blackie" King, Tom London, Lucille Powers; *D:* Phil Rosen. GPV, VCN, DVT

Two-Gun Man from Harlem 1938 Big

city guy travels to the wild West in search of a little truth. 60m/B VHS. Herbert Jeffries, Marguerite Whitten, Mantan Moreland, Matthew "Stymie" Beard; *D:* Richard C. Kahn. NOS, TPV

Two-Gun Troubador ✓ The Lone Trouba-

dor 1937 A masked singing cowboy struggles to uncovers his father's murderer. 59m/B VHS, Beta. Fred Scott, Claire Rochelle, John Merton. NOS, BAR, HEG

200 Motels ✓½ 1971 (R) Rambling, non-

narrative self-indulgent video album by and about Frank Zappa and the Mothers of Invention, as they document a long and especially grueling road tour. For fans only. **99m/C VHS, Beta.** Frank Zappa, Ringo Starr; **D:** Frank Zappa. *MVD, MGM*

Two If by Sea 🎬½ *Stolen Hearts* 1995 (R) Small-time hood Frank (Leary) and his girlfriend Roz (Bullock) hole up in a New England mansion after Frank steals a valuable Matisse painting. Between verbal sparring matches, the two try to mingle with the upper crusty residents with predictable results. Pursuing the pair are the FBI, led by the deluded O'Malley (Kotto), and Frank's bonehead cousin Beano (Robson) and his trio of dim henchmen. Tries to be a caper/romantic comedy but fails to deliver on all fronts. The usually caustic Leary takes some of the edge off of his trademark bitter humor, and the alleged witty repartee is just plain annoying as a result. Nova Scotia turns in a fine performance as New England. *CW:* Language. **96m/C VHS, LV, Closed Caption.** Sandra Bullock, Denis Leary, Stephen Dillane, Yaphet Kotto, Wayne Robson, Jonathan Tucker, Mike Starr, Michael Badalucco, Lenny Clarke, John Friesen; **D:** Bill Bennett; **W:** Denis Leary, Michael Armstrong; **C:** Andrew Lesnie. *WAR*

The Two Jakes 🎬🎬 1990 (R) Ten years have passed and Jake Gittes is still a private investigator in this sequel to 1974's "Chinatown." When a murder occurs while he's digging up dirt on an affair between the wife of a real estate executive and the executive's partner, Jake must return to Chinatown to uncover the killer and face the painful memories buried there. Despite solid dialogue and effective performances, it's unreasonably difficult to follow if you haven't seen "Chinatown." Outstanding photography by Vilmos Zsigmond. **137m/C VHS, Beta, LV, Letterbox, Closed Caption.** Jack Nicholson, Harvey Keitel, Meg Tilly, Madeleine Stowe, Eli Wallach, Ruben Blades, Frederic Forrest, David Keith, Richard Farnsworth, Tracey Walter; **D:** Jack Nicholson; **W:** Robert Towne; **C:** Vilmos Zsigmond; **M:** Van Dyke Parks. *PAR, FCT*

Two Kinds of Love 🎬🎬 1985 Adapted from Peggy Mann's novel "There Are Two Kinds of Terrible," this is the story of a young boy who learns to love his distant, workaholic father after his protective mother suddenly dies. Made for television. **94m/C VHS, Beta, Closed Caption.** Rick Schroder, Lindsay Wagner, Peter Weller; **D:** Jack Bender. *FOX*

Two Lost Worlds woof! 1950 A young hero battles monstrous dinosaurs, pirates, and more in this cheapy when he and his shipmates are shipwrecked on an uncharted island. Don't miss the footage from "Captain Fury," "One Billion B.C.," and "Captain Caution" and Arness long before his Sheriff Dillon fame, and his "big" role in "The Thing." **63m/B VHS, Beta.** James Arness, Laura Elliott, Bill Kennedy; **D:** Norman Dawn. *NO*

Two Men & a Wardrobe 1958 Polanski's project while a student at the Polish Film Institute. Consideration of modern man's lack of privacy and made without dialogue. Two men emerge from the sea carrying nothing but a large piece of furniture. Absurd and funny. **19m/B VHS, Beta. D:** Roman Polanski. *IHF, GVV*

Two Minute Warning 🎬 1976 (R) A sniper plans to take out the president of the United States at an NFL playoff game in this boring, pointless, disaster film that goes on forever. Features all the ready-made characters inherent in the genre, but, until its too late, precious little of the mayhem. To get caught watching the TV version, which features more characters and an additional subplot, would be truly disastrous. **116m/C VHS, LV.** Charlton Heston, John Cassavetes, Martin Balsam, Beau Bridges, Marilyn Hassett, David Janssen, Jack Klugman, Walter Pidgeon, Gena Rowlands; **D:** Larry Peerce; **M:** Charles Fox. Nominations: Academy Awards '76: Best Film Editing. *USH*

The Two Mrs. Carrolls 🎬🎬½ 1947 Bogart is a psycho-killer/artist who paints portraits of his wives as the Angel of Death—and then kills them. The married Bogart falls for Stanwyck, poisons his current wife, and the two marry. After a few years, Bogart falls for Smith and decides to rid himself of Stanwyck in the same manner as his first killing. Stanwyck, however, becomes increasingly suspicious and calls on an old beau for help. Melodrama cast Bogart against type (not always successfully). Filmed in 1945, but was unreleased until 1947. **99m/B VHS.** Humphrey Bogart, Barbara Stanwyck, Alexis Smith, Nigel Bruce, Pat O'Moore, Ann Carter; **D:** Peter Godfrey. *MGM*

Two Moon Junction 🎬½ 1988 (R) A soon-to-be-wed Southern debutante enters into a wild love affair with a rough-edged carnival worker. Poorly acted, wildly directed, with many unintentional laughs. **104m/C VHS, Beta, LV.** Sherilyn Fenn, Richard Tyson, Louise Fletcher, Burl Ives, Kristy McNichol, Millie Perkins, Don Galloway, Herve Villechaize, Dabbs Greer, Jay Hawkins; **D:** Zalman King; **W:** Zalman King; **M:** Jonathan Elias. Golden Raspberry Awards '88: Worst Supporting Actress (McNichol). *COL*

Two Much 🎬½ 1996 (PG-13) Banderas does double duty as a con man pretending to be twins in order to romance two sisters (Griffith and Hannah). Embarrassingly light comedy suffers from a complicated plot (which still manages to leave holes), weak or non-existent characterization, and a general lack of humor. About the only thing it has going for it is Cusack as a wisecracking secretary. It was on the set of this film that Banderas and Griffith started their real-life romance. While that may have helped the boxoffice and gossip columns in Banderas's homeland, the fireworks didn't find their way to the screen. *CW:* Sexual situations and dialogue. **118m/C VHS, LV, Closed Caption.** Melanie Griffith, Antonio Banderas, Daryl Hannah, Joan Cusack, Danny Aiello, Eli Wallach, Vincent Schiavelli; **D:** Fernando Trueba; **W:** Fernando Trueba, David Trueba; **C:** Jose Luis Alcaine; **M:** Michel Camilo. Nominations: Golden Raspberry Awards '96: Worst Actress (Griffith), Worst Supporting Actress (Hannah). *TOU*

Two Mules for Sister Sara 🎬🎬🎬 1970 (PG) American mercenary in 19th century Mexico gets mixed up with a cigar-smoking nun and the two make plans to capture a French garrison. MacLaine and Eastwood are great together. Based on a Boetticher story. **105m/C VHS, Beta.** Clint Eastwood, Shirley MacLaine; **D:** Donald Siegel; **W:** Albert Maltz; **M:** Ennio Morricone. *USH*

Two Nights with Cleopatra 🎬½ *Due Notti Con Cleopatra* 1954 A piece of Italian pizza involving Cleopatra's double (also played by Loren) falling in love with one of the guards. Notable only for the 19-year-old Sophia's brief nudity. **77m/C VHS, Beta.** *IT* Sophia Loren, Ettore Manni, Alberto Sordi, Paul Muller, Alberto Talegalli, Rolf Tasna, Gianni Cavalieri, Fernando Bruno, Riccardo Garrone, Carlo Dale; **D:** Mario Mattoli; **W:** Nino Maccari, Ettore Scola. *VDM*

Two of a Kind 🎬🎬½ 1982 In his television movie debut, Burns plays an elderly man whose mentally handicapped grandson helps him put the starch back in his shirt. Sensitively produced and performed. **102m/C VHS, Beta, Closed Caption.** George Burns, Robby Benson, Cliff Robertson, Barbara Barrie, Frances Lee McCain, Geri Jewell, Ronny Cox; **D:** Roger Young. *FOX*

Two of a Kind 🎬 1983 (PG) Angels make a bet with God—two selfish people will redeem themselves or God can blow up the Earth. Bad acting, awful direction, and the script needs divine intervention. **88m/C VHS, Beta, LV, Closed Caption.** John Travolta, Olivia Newton-John, Charles Durning, Beatrice Straight, Scatman Crothers, Oliver Reed; **D:** John Herzfeld; **C:** Fred W. Koenekamp. *FOX*

The Two of Us 🎬🎬🎬½ *Le Vieil Homme Et L'Enfant; Claude; The Old Man and the Boy* 1968 Young Jewish boy flees Nazi-occupied Paris to live in the country with an irritable, bigoted guardian. Sensitive, eloquent movie about racial prejudice and anti-Semitism. In French with English subtitles. **86m/B VHS.** *FR* Michel Simon, Alain Cohen, Luce Fabiole, Roger Carel, Paul Preboist, Charles Denner; **D:** Claude Berri; **M:** Georges Delerue. *NO*

Two or Three Things I Know About Her 🎬🎬 *Deux ou Trois Choses Que Je Sais d'Elle* 1966 Inspired by a magazine article about housewife-prostitutes, Godard takes on the bourgeoise. Juliette (Vlady) is a wife and mother who lives in the suburbs of Paris and goes into the city once a week to work as a prostitute in order to buy consumer goods. French with subtitles. **95m/C VHS.** *FR* Marina Vlady, Anny Duperey, Roger Montsoret, Jean Narboni, Raoul Levy; **D:** Jean-Luc Godard; **W:** Jean-Luc Godard; **C:** Raoul Coutard. *NYF*

Two Plus One 🎬🎬 1995 Triangular drama about Yuppie relationships, set in Philadelphia. Romantic couple searches for happiness and decides to invite a third person to join their relationship. Newcomer Lewis is the sister of actress Juliette. **85m/C VHS.** William Sage, Deirdre Lewis, Tony Vinto; **D:** Eugene Martian. *SCO*

Two Rode Together 🎬🎬½ 1961 A Texas marshal and an army lieutenant negotiate with the Comanches for the return of captives, but complications ensue. **109m/C VHS, Beta, LV.** James Stewart, Richard Widmark, Shirley Jones, Linda Cristal, Andy Devine, John McIntire; **D:** John Ford. *COL*

The Two Sisters 1937 Goldstein, in her only film role, plays an older sister who sacrifices everything for the younger. The younger thanks her by stealing her fiance. In Yiddish with English subtitles. **70m/B VHS.** Jenney Goldstein, Michael Rosenberg. *ALD*

Two Small Bodies 🎬🎬 1993 Police detective Brann investigates the disappearance of two young children, suspecting their mother Eileen may have murdered them. Two character study set in Eileen's home with both verbally recreating versions of the possible crime. Based on the play by Neal Bell. **85m/C VHS.** Fred Ward, Suzy Amis; **D:** Beth B; **W:** Beth B, Neal Bell. *ORI*

2000 Maniacs 🎬🎬½ 1964 One of cult director Lewis' most enjoyably watchable films. A literal Civil War "ghost town" takes its revenge 100 years after being slaughtered by renegade Union soldiers by luring unwitting "yankee" tourists to their centennial festival. The hapless Northerners are then chopped, crushed, ripped apart etc. while the ghostly rebels party. Quite fun in a cartoonishly gruesome sort of way. Filmed in St. Cloud, FL. **75m/C VHS, Beta.** Thomas Wood, Connie Mason, Jeffrey Allen, Ben Moore, Gary Bakeman, Jerome Eden, Shelby Livingston, Michael Korb, Yvonne Gilbert, Mark Douglas, Linda Cochran, Vincent Santo, Andy Wilson; **D:** Herschell Gordon Lewis; **W:** Herschell Gordon Lewis; **C:** Herschell Gordon Lewis. *SMW*

2001: A Space Odyssey 🎬🎬🎬🎬 1968 Space voyage to Jupiter turns chaotic when a computer, HAL 9000, takes over. Seen by some as a mirror of man's historical use of machinery and by others as a grim vision of the future, the special effects and music are still stunning. Critically acclaimed and well accepted by some, simply confusing to others. Martin Balsam originally recorded the voice of HAL, but was replaced by Rain. From Arthur C. Clarke's novel "The Sentinel." Followed by a sequel "2010: The Year We Make Contact." Laserdisc edition is presented in letterbox format and features a special supplementary section on the making of "2001," a montage of images from the film, production documents, memos and photos. Also included on the disc is a NASA film entitled "Art and Reality," which offers footage from the Voyager I and II flybys of Jupiter. **139m/C VHS, Beta, LV, Letterbox.** *GB* Keir Dullea, Gary Lockwood, William Sylvester, Dan Richter; **D:** Stanley Kubrick; **W:** Arthur C. Clarke, Stanley Kubrick; **C:** Geoffrey Unsworth; **V:** Douglas Raines. Academy Awards '68: Best Visual Effects, National Film Registry '91;; Nominations: Academy Awards '68: Best Art Direction/Set Decoration, Best Director (Kubrick), Best Story & Screenplay. *MGM, CRC, FCT*

2010: The Year We Make Contact ✍✍✍ 1984 (PG)

The film version of Arthur C. Clarke's novel "The Sentinel" continues in this sequel to "2001: A Space Odyssey." Americans and Russians unite to investigate the abandoned starship Discovery's decaying orbit around Jupiter and try to determine why the HAL 9000 computer sabotaged its mission years before, while signs of cosmic change are detected on and around the giant planet. 116m/C VHS, Beta, LV, Letterbox, Closed Caption. Roy Scheider, John Lithgow, Helen Mirren, Bob Balaban, Keir Dullea, Madolyn Smith, Mary Jo Deschanel; D: Peter Hyams; W: Peter Hyams; M: David Shire; V: Douglas Rains. Nominations: Academy Awards '84: Best Art Direction/Set Decoration, Best Costume Design, Best Makeup, Best Sound. MGM

2020 Texas Gladiators woof! 1985 (R)

In the post-nuclear holocaust world, two groups, one good, one evil, battle for supremacy. 91m/C VHS, Beta. IT Harrison Muller, Al Cliver, Daniel Stephen, Peter Hooten, Al Yamanouchi, Sabrina Santi; D: Kevin Mancuso.

2069: A Sex Odyssey ✍½ 1978 (R)

Team of beautiful, sensuous astronauts are sent to Earth to obtain male sperm which they must bring back to Venus. Tongue-in-cheek soft core sci-fi spoof. 73m/C VHS, Beta. Alena Penz, Nina Fredric, Gerti Sneider, Raul Retzer, Catherine Conti, Heidi Hammer, Michael Mein, Herb Heesel; D: George Keil. HHE

Two Tickets to Broadway ✍✍½ 1951

A small-town singer and a crooner arrange a hoax to get themselves on Bob Crosby's television show. Appealing but lightweight. ♪Let the Worry Bird Worry For You; Pagliacci; There's No Tomorrow; Manhattan; Big Chief Hole in the Ground; The Closer You Are; Baby, You'll Never Be Sorry; Pelican Falls High; It Began In Yucatan. 106m/C VHS, Beta. Tony Martin, Janet Leigh, Gloria De Haven, Joi Lansing; D: James V. Kern; M: Leo Robin, Jule Styne; Performed by: Smith & Dale. Nominations: Academy Awards '51: Best Sound. TTC

Two to Tango ✍½ 1988 (R)

A hired assassin goes to Buenos Aires to kill a crime boss, and falls in love with his tango-dancing mistress. Based on the novel by J.P. Feinman. 87m/C VHS, Beta. AR Don Stroud, Adrienne Sachs; D: Hector Olivera. NO

Two-Way Stretch ✍✍½ 1960

Three prison inmates in a progressive jail plan to break out, pull a diamond heist, and break back in, all in the same night. Fast-paced slapstick farce. 84m/B VHS, Beta. GB Peter Sellers, Wilfrid Hyde-White, Liz Fraser, David Lodge; D: Robert Day. NO

Two Weeks in Another Town ✍✍ 1962

Douglas and Robinson are a couple of Hollywood has-beens who set out to make a comeback picture but meet with adversity at every turn. Extremely sappy melodrama is based on Irwin Shaw's trashy novel and represents one of director Minnelli's poorer efforts. Laserdisc features a letterboxed screen and the original movie trailer. 107m/C VHS, LV, Letterbox, Closed Caption. Kirk Douglas, Edward G. Robinson, Cyd Charisse, George Hamilton, Daliah Lavi, Claire Trevor, James Gregory, Rosanna Schiaffino, George Macready, Stefan Schnabel, Vito Scotti, Leslie Uggams; D: Vincente Minnelli; C: Milton Krasner. MGM

Two Weeks to Live ✍½ 1943

The comedy team inherits a railroad line, only to find it's a pile of junk. 60m/B VHS, Beta. Lum & Abner, Franklin Pangborn. NOS, DVT

Two Weeks with Love ✍✍ 1950

Reynolds and family wear funny bathing suits in the Catskills in the early 1900s while the Debster sings songs and blushes into young adulthood. ♪Aba Daba Honeymoon; The Oceana Roll; A Heart That's Free; By the Light of the Silvery Moon; My Hero; Row, Row, Row; That's How I Need You; Beautiful Lady. 92m/C VHS. Debbie Reynolds, Jane Powell, Ricardo Montalban, Louis Calhern, Ann Harding, Phyllis Kirk, Carleton Carpenter, Clinton Sundberg, Gary Gray; D: Roy Rowland. MGM, FCT

Two Women ✍✍✍✍ La Ciociara 1961

A mother and her 13-year-old daughter travel war-torn Italy during WWII and must survive lack of food, crazed monks and brutal soldiers. Tragic, moving, well-directed. Loren received well-deserved Oscar. In Italian with English subtitles or dubbed. 99m/B VHS, Beta. IT Sophia Loren, Raf Vallone, Eleonora Brown, Jean-Paul Belmondo; D: Vittorio De Sica; W: Cesare Zavattini, Vittorio De Sica; M: Armando Trovajoli. Academy Awards '61: Best Actress (Loren); British Academy Awards '61: Best Actress (Loren); Cannes Film Festival '61: Best Actress (Loren); Golden Globe Awards '62: Best Foreign Film; New York Film Critics Awards '61: Best Actress (Loren). COL, BTV

Two Wondrous Tigers ✍ 1979

Awesome Kung-fu gang terrorizes a small town until a local dares to out-chop the bullies. 87m/C VHS, Beta. John Chang; D: Wilson Tong. TWE

The Two Worlds of Jenny Logan ✍✍½ 1979

A woman travels back and forth in time whenever she dons a 19th century dress she finds in her old house. She is also able to fall in love twice, in different centuries. Made for television and adapted from "Second Sight," a novel by David Williams. Stylish and well made. 97m/C VHS, Beta. Lindsay Wagner, Marc Singer, Alan Feinstein, Linda Gray, Constance McCashin, Henry Wilcoxon, Irene Tedrow, Joan Darling, Allen Williams, Pat Corley, Gloria Stuart; D: Frank de Felitta. ART

Two Wrongs Make a Right ✍ 1989

A quiet nightclub owner beats and clubs his way through his tough neighborhood to protect himself and his woman. Low budget actioner with standard plot and cool, atmospheric tone. 85m/C VHS, Beta. Ivan Rogers, Ron Blackstone, Rich Komenich; D: Robert Brown; W: Ivan Rogers. UNI

Two Years Before the Mast ✍✍½ 1946

Charles Stewart (Ladd) is the privileged son of a ship owner who discovers just how difficult a sailor's life in the 1840's can be. Drinking in a Boston waterfront dive, he's shanghaied and pressed into service aboard the S.S. Pilgrim, which is bound for California. Sadistic Captain Thompson (da Silva) brutalizes the men in an effort to set a record time for the voyage. Stewart and the crew eventually mutiny and face trial back in Boston. Based on the novel by Richard Henry Dana. 98m/B VHS, Closed Caption. Alan Ladd, Howard da Silva, Brian Donlevy, William Bendix, Barry Fitzgerald, Albert Dekker, Darryl Hickman, Esther Fernandez; D: John Farrow; W: George Bruce, Seton I. Miller; C: Ernest Laszlo; M: Victor Young. USH

Twogether ✍✍½ 1994 (R)

Struggling artist John (Cassavetes) and environmentalist Allison (Bakke) have this lust thing going on. It leads to a drunken Las Vegas wedding and a quickie divorce but they still don't keep their hands off of each other (or any other body parts) and Allison gets pregnant. They decide to become partners in raising the baby but first they'll have to do some growing up of their own. Also available unrated. 108m/C VHS, Closed Caption. Brenda Bakke, Nick Cassavetes, Jeremy Piven, Jim Beaver; D: Andrew Chiaramonte; W: Andrew Chiaramonte; C: Eugene Shlugleit; M: Nigel Holton. COL

Tycoon ✍✍½ 1947

Wayne goes to Latin America to build a road for an American industrialist. When the industrialist insists on a shorter but more dangerous route, Wayne must satisfy his own sense of honor. Meanwhile, he's found romance with the industrialist's half-Spanish daughter. Long, but well-acted. 129m/C VHS, Beta, LV. John Wayne, Laraine Day, Cedric Hardwicke, Judith Anderson, James Gleason, Anthony Quinn; D: Richard Wallace. CCB, TTC

Typhoon Treasure ✍ 1939

Whilst recovering his sunken treasure, the hero battles bad guys, savage natives and a crocodile, all of whom could probably have made a more sophisticated film. 68m/B VHS. AU Campbell Copelin, Gwen Munro, Joe Valli, Douglas Herald; D: Noel Monkman. NOS, LOO

Tyrant of Lydia Against the Son of Hercules 1963

Hercules' son takes on a wicked king in this startling adventure. ?m/C VHS, Beta. IT Gordon Scott, Massimo Serato. SNC

Tyson ✍✍ 1995

Based on the life of former World Heavyweight Champion, Mike Tyson (White) who rose from the streets of Brownsville to a million dollar lifestyle and a spectacular fall to a rape conviction and a prison term (which are handled in voiceover). Story begins with trainer Cus D'Amato (Scott) finding unpolished and troubled young Tyson and training him for the Junior Olympics. When promoter Don King (Winfield) enters the picture, Tyson's career really takes off. Pulls no punches about Tyson's short fuse and brutal abilities. Based on the book "Fire and Fear: The Inside Story of Mike Tyson" by Jose Torres. 90m/C VHS. Michael Jai White, Paul Winfield, George C. Scott, Malcolm Jamal Warner, Tony LoBianco, James B. Sikking, Clark Gregg, Kristen Wilson, Sheila Wills, Holt McCallany, Lilyan Chauvin, Georg Stanford Brown, Joe Santos, Charles Napier; D: Uli Edel; W: Robert Johnson; M: Stewart Copeland. HBO

U-Boat Prisoner ✍ 1944

Bennett is an American sailor who's captured by a Nazi U-boat. He promptly defeats the crew, leaving the U-boat to the mercy of a U.S. destroyer. Silly, silly, silly. 65m/B VHS. Bruce (Herman Brix) Bennett, John Abbott, John Wood, Kenneth MacDonald, Erik Rolf, John Wengraf; D: Lew (Louis Friedlander) Landers. GPV

U-Turn ✍✍½ Stray Dogs 1997 (R)

Bobby (Penn) is a two-bit gambler on his way to pay off the balance of a debt in Las Vegas (the down payment was two of his fingers) when he is stranded in the town of Superior, Arizona. He becomes mixed up with a married couple (Nolte and Lopez), each of whom want Bobby to kill the other. Adding to the fun in this Mayberry on mescaline are the walking grease pit of a mechanic (Thornton) and a local tough guy named TNT (Phoenix), who thinks Bobby is making a play for his nymphet girlfriend (Danes). Also appearing is the stock issue Oliver Stone wise old Indian who dispenses wisdom, or something like it. The characters meet for the predestined showdown in the desert, with predictable results. Stone has a good time slapping stereotypical noir characters and putting his unique twist on them, although you may not have as much fun watching them. CW: Strong violence, sexuality and language. 125m/C VHS, LV, Closed Caption, DVD. Sean Penn, Jennifer Lopez, Claire Danes, Nick Nolte, Joaquin Rafael (Leaf) Phoenix, Powers Boothe, Billy Bob Thornton, Jon Voight, Abraham Benrubi, Julie Hagerty, Bo Hopkins, Valery Nikolaev, Aida Linares, Laurie Metcalf, Liv Tyler; D: Oliver Stone; W: John Ridley; C: Robert Richardson; M: Ennio Morricone. Nominations: Golden Raspberry Awards '97: Worst Supporting Actor (Voight), Worst Director (Stone). COL

UFO: Target Earth ✍ 1974 (G)

Scientist attempts to fish flying saucer out of lake and costs studio $70,000. 80m/C VHS. Nick Plakias, Cynthia Cline, Phil Erickson; D: Michael de Gaetano. MOV

Uforia ✍✍ 1981

Two rival evangelists meet up with a UFO-infatuated girl. Under her guidance, they wait for UFO encounters they intend to use to milk their revivalist audiences. Sometimes clumsy, but more often fun. 92m/C VHS, Beta. Cindy Williams, Harry Dean Stanton, Fred Ward; D: John Binder; W: John Binder; M: Richard Baskin. USH

Ugetsu ✍✍✍½ Ugetsu Monogatari 1953

The classic film that established Mizoguchi's reputation outside of Japan. Two 16th century Japanese peasants venture from their homes in pursuit of dreams, and encounter little more than their own hapless folly and a bit of the supernatural. A wonderful mix of comedy and action with nifty camera movement. Based on the stories of Akinara Ueda. In Japanese with English subtitles. 96m/B VHS, Beta, LV, 8mm. JP Machiko Kyo, Masayuki Mori, Kinuyo Tanaka, Sakae Ozawa; D: Kenji Mizoguchi. Venice Film Festival '53: Silver Prize; Nominations: Academy Awards '55: Best Costume Design (B & W). HMV, WFV, DVT

The Ugly ⅛⅛½ 1996 Confessed serial killer Simon (Rotondo) has celebrity shrink Karen (Hobbs) evaluate him to determine whether he's cured or has to stand trial for his crimes. Through flashbacks, dream sequences, and fantasies (both Simon's and the doc's), Simon's screwed-up past is revealed: mentally and physically abused by an unstable mother (Ward-Leeland) and picked on by bullies, he commits his first murder at 13. First-time director Reynolds' use of red herrings, alternate points of view, and mixing of perspectives can be hard to follow, but they do ratchet up the suspense. He also doesn't scrimp on the gore, which is highly stylized and effective. **93m/C VHS.** NZ Paolo Rotondo, Rebecca Hobbs, Jennifer Ward-Lealand, Roy Ward, Vanessa Byrnes; **D:** Scott Reynolds; **W:** Scott Reynolds; **C:** Simon Raby; **M:** Victoria Kelly. NYR

The Ugly American ⅛⅛½ 1963 A naive American ambassador to a small, civil-war-torn Asian country fights a miniature Cold War against northern communist influence. Too preachy, and the "Red Menace" aspects are now very dated, but Brando's performance is worth watching. Based on the William J. Lederer novel. **120m/C VHS, Beta.** Marlon Brando, Sandra Church, Eiji Okada, Pat Hingle, Arthur Hill; **D:** George Englund; **W:** Stewart Stern. USH

The Ugly Dachshund ⅛⅛½ 1965 Jones and Pleshette are married dog lovers who raise Dachshunds. When Ruggles convinces them to take a Great Dane puppy, the fun begins! The Great Dane thinks he is a Dachshund because he has been raised with them—just imagine what happens when such a large dog acts as if he is small! Kids will love this wacky Disney film. **93m/C VHS, Beta.** Dean Jones, Suzanne Pleshette, Charlie Ruggles, Kelly Thordsen, Parley Baer; **D:** Norman Tokar; **C:** Edward Colman. DIS, OM

UHF ⅛⅛ 1989 (PG-13) A loser is appointed manager of a bargain-basement UHF television station. He turns it around via bizarre programming ideas. Some fun parodies of TV enhance this minimal story. Developed solely as a vehicle for Yankovic. **97m/C VHS, Beta, LV, Closed Caption.** Weird Al Yankovic, Kevin McCarthy, Victoria Jackson, Michael Richards, David Bowie, Anthony Geary; **D:** Jay Levey; **M:** John Du Prez. ORI

Ulee's Gold ⅛⅛⅛ 1997 (R) Slow-paced, deliberate character study, set in the Florida panhandle. Ulysses "Ulee" Jackson (Fonda) is a widowed, middle-aged Vietnam vet who puts most of his energies into his work as a beekeeper, much to the detriment of his family. Son Jimmy (Wood) is in prison and druggie daughter-in-law Helen (Dunford) has disappeared, leaving the taciturn Ulee to care for his troubled granddaughters, teenaged Casey (Biel) and nine-year-old Penny (Zima). But their ordinary lives change when Helen turns up in Orlando with two violent hoods from Jimmy's past and Ulee must not only rescue her but find the emotional release to make them all a home. Splendidly moving performance from Fonda. **CW:** Language. **111m/C VHS, Closed Caption.** Peter Fonda, Tom Wood, Vanessa Zima, Jessica Biel, Christine Dunford, Patricia Richardson, Steve Flynn, Dewey Weber, J. Kenneth Campbell; **D:** Victor Nunez; **W:** Victor Nunez; **C:** Virgil Marcus Mirano; **M:** Charles Engstrom. Golden Globe Awards '98: Best Actor—Drama (Fonda); New York Film Critics Awards '97: Best Actor (Fonda); Nominations: Academy Awards '97: Best Actor (Fonda); Independent Spirit Awards '98: Best Actor (Fonda), Best Director (Nunez), Best Film, Best Screenplay, Best Supporting Actress (Richardson); Screen Actors Guild Award '97: Best Actor (Fonda). ORI

Ulterior Motives ⅛½ 1992 (R) P.I. Jack Blaylock agrees to protect a pretty reporter from Japanese gangsters. He finds himself caught up in deception and betrayal and uses all his considerable, and violent, skills to make certain he does his job. **CW:** Some strong violence. **90m/C VHS, Closed Caption.** Thomas Ian Griffith, Mary Page Keller,

Joe Yamanaka, Ellen Crawford, Ken Howard, Tyra Ferrell; **D:** James Becket. IMP

Ultimate Desires ⅛⅛ 1991 (R) When a high class hooker is brutally killed, beautiful Scoggins puts on what there is of the victim's clothes in order to solve the mystery. But trouble lies in wait as she actually begins to enjoy her funky new double life. Can she solve the crime before becoming lost in her own hot fantasy world? **CW:** Language, strong violence and drug content, and strong sexuality. **93m/C VHS, Beta, Closed Caption.** Tracy Scoggins, Brion James, Marc Singer, Marc Baur, Marc Bennett, Suzy Joachim, Jason Scott, John Wood; **D:** Lloyd A. Simanol.

The Ultimate Imposter ⅛ 1979 A secret agent acquires voluminous knowledge through a computer brain linkup, but can only retain the knowledge for 72 hours. In that timespan he has to rescue a defecting Russian from hordes of assassins. Made for television. **97m/C VHS, Beta.** Keith Andes, Erin Gray, Joseph Hacker, Macon McCalman; **D:** Paul Stanley. USH

The Ultimate Thrill ⅛½ The Ultimate Chase 1974 (PG) Businessman's paranoia about his wife's affairs leads him to follow her to Colorado on a ski holiday and stalk her lovers. Well-filmed skiing scenes and not much else. **84m/C VHS, Beta.** Britt Ekland, Barry Brown, Michael Blodgett, John Davis Chandler, Eric (Hans Gudegast) Braeden; **D:** Robert Butler. GEM, CNG

The Ultimate Warrior ⅛⅛½ 1975 (R) Yul Brynner must defend the plants and seeds of a pioneer scientist to help replenish the world's food supply in this thriller set in 2012. **92m/C VHS, Beta.** Yul Brynner, Max von Sydow, Joanna Miles, Richard Kelton, Lane Bradbury, William Smith; **D:** Robert Clouse; **W:** Robert Clouse. WAR

Ultra Warrior ⅛½ Welcome to Oblivion 1992 (R) A basic post-apocalyptic adventure tale of a radioactive earth, mutants, and various battles by the good guys to save the planet. **CW:** Violence and sexuality. **80m/C VHS.** Dack Rambo, Meshach Taylor, Clare Beresford. NHO

Ultraviolet ⅛½ 1991 (R) Another warning against playing the good samaritan. Young couple on vacation in Death Valley try to help a stranded stranger only to have him turn on them. **CW:** Language, violence, and sensuality. **80m/C VHS, Closed Caption.** Esai Morales, Stephen Meadows, Patricia Healy; **D:** Mark Griffiths. NHO

Ulysses ⅛⅛½ Ulisse 1955 An Italian made version of the epic poem by Homer, as the warrior returns to his homeland and the ever-faithful Penelope after the Trojan war. Ambitious effort provides for the ultimate mixed review. Douglas is good in the role and his songs along the ten-year way are well visualized. Sometimes sluggish with poor dubbing. Seven writers helped bring Homer to the big screen. **104m/C VHS, Beta.** IT Kirk Douglas, Silvana Mangano, Anthony Quinn, Rossana Podesta; **D:** Mario Camerini. WAR, OM

Ulysses ⅛⅛½ 1967 James Joyce's probably unfilmable novel was given a noble effort in this flawed film covering a day in the life of Leopold Bloom as he wanders through Dublin. Shot in Ireland with a primarily Irish cast. **140m/B VHS, LV, Letterbox.** Milo O'Shea, Maurice Roeves, T.P. McKenna, Martin Dempsey, Sheila O'Sullivan, Barbara Jefford; **D:** Joseph Strick. Nominations: Academy Awards '67: Best Adapted Screenplay. MFV

Ulysses' Gaze ⅛⅛ The Look of Ulysses; To Vlemma Tou Odyssea; The Gaze of Ulysses 1995 Nameless Greek-American filmmaker (Keitel) journeys across the Balkans from Athens to Sarajevo while making a documentary on pioneer filmmakers, the Manakia brothers, who ignored national and ethnic strife in order to record the lives of ordinary people. Keitel has heard that some undeveloped film shot by the brothers has turned up in Sarajevo and he's determined to see it despite the turmoil in Bosnia. Moving and pessimistic depiction of the Balkan conflict seen through a

filmmaker's eyes. English and Greek with subtitles. **173m/C VHS.** GR FR IT Harvey Keitel, Maia Morgenstern, Erland Josephson, Thanassis Vengos, Yorgos Michalokopoulos, Dora Volonaki; **D:** Theo Angelopoulos; **W:** Theo Angelopoulos, Tonino Guerra, Petros Markaris; **C:** Yorgos Arvanitis; **M:** Eleni Karaindrou. Cannes Film Festival '95: Grand Jury Prize. FXL

Ulzana's Raid ⅛⅛⅛ 1972 (R) An aging scout and an idealistic Cavalry lieutenant lock horns on their way to battling a vicious Apache chieftain. A violent, gritty western that enjoyed critical re-evaluation years after its first release. **103m/C VHS, Beta, LV, Closed Caption.** Burt Lancaster, Bruce Davison, Richard Jaeckel, Lloyd Bochner, Jorge Luke; **D:** Robert Aldrich; **C:** Joseph Biroc. USH

Umberto D ⅛⅛⅛ 1955 A government pensioner, living alone with his beloved dog, struggles to keep up a semblance of dignity on his inadequate pension. De Sica considered this his masterpiece. A sincere, tender treatment of the struggles involved with the inevitability of aging. In Italian with English subtitles. Laser edition features letterboxed print. **89m/B VHS, Beta, LV, 8mm, Letterbox.** IT Carlo Battista, Maria Pia Casilio, Lina Gennari; **D:** Vittorio De Sica; **W:** Cesare Zavattini, Vittorio De Sica. New York Film Critics Awards '55: Best Foreign Film; Nominations: Academy Awards '56: Best Story. HMV, HHT, DVT

Umbrellas of Cherbourg ⅛⅛⅛½ Les Parapluies De Cherbourg; Die Regenschirme Von Cherbourg 1964 A bittersweet film operetta with no spoken dialog. Deneuve is the teenaged daughter of a widow who owns an umbrella shop. She and her equally young boyfriend are separated by his military duty in Algeria. Finding she is pregnant, the girl marries a wealthy man, and when her former lover returns, he too marries someone else. But when they meet once again will their love be rekindled? Lovely photography and an evocative score enhance the story. In French with subtitles; also available dubbed in English (not with the same effectiveness). Oscar nominee for cinematography and story. **90m/C VHS, Beta.** FR Catherine Deneuve, Nino Castelnuovo, Anne Vernon, Ellen Farner, Marc Michel, Mireille Perrey, Jean Champion, Alfred Wolff, Dorothee Blanck; **D:** Jacques Demy; **W:** Jacques Demy; **M:** Michel Legrand. Cannes Film Festival '64: Best Film; Nominations: Academy Awards '65: Best Foreign Language Film, Best Song ("I Will Wait for You"), Best Story & Screenplay, Best Original Score. FXL, ART

Un Air de Famille ⅛⅛ 1996 Comedy, adapted from a play, about a dysfunctional family. They're meeting at the family's rundown bar to celebrate the birthday of son Philippe's (Yordanoff) silly wife, Yolande (Frot). The bar is run by his brother Henri (Bacri), whose wife calls to say she's left him, while their tactless mother (Maurier) frets over their sister, Betty (Jaoui), who's 30 and still single. What no one knows is that Betty has been secretly seeing Denis (Darroussin), the bartender, whom everyone thinks is simple but is actually the only one with any clue to the family's hypocrisy. French with subtitles. **107m/C VHS.** FR Jean-Pierre Bacri, Agnes Jaoui, Jean-Pierre Darroussin, Catherine Frot, Claire Maurier, Wladimir Yordanoff; **D:** Cedric Klapisch; **W:** Jean-Pierre Bacri, Agnes Jaoui, Cedric Klapisch; **C:** Benoit Delhomme. Cesar Awards '97: Best Supporting Actor (Darroussin), Best Supporting Actress (Frot), Best Writing; Nominations: Cesar Awards '97: Best Director (Klapisch), Best Film. NYR

Un Chien Andalou ⅛⅛⅛⅛ An Andalusian Dog 1928 Masterful surrealist short features a host of classic sequences, including a razor across an eye, a severed hand lying in the street, ants crawling from a hole in a man's hand, priests, dead horses, and a piano dragged across a room. A classic. Score features both Wagner and tango. **20m/B VHS, Beta.** FR Pierre Batcheff, Simone Marevil, Jaime Miravilles, Luis Bunuel, Salvador Dali; **D:** Luis Bunuel, Salvador Dali; **W:** Luis Bunuel, Salvador Dali. HHT, GVV

Un Coeur en Hiver 🎬🎬½ *A Heart in Winter* **1993** An anti-romance romantic drama where passion is frozen and real emotion is reserved for the inanimate. Serious Stephane (Auteuil) is a master craftsman at repairing violins; his partner Maxime (Dussollier) runs the business side and deals with the musicians, including beautiful violinist Camille (Beart) with whom he has fallen in love. Camille is single-mindedly fixated on her career and she recognizes a kindred spirit in Stephane but their calculated emotional seduction causes problems for all. Can be frustrating since the smooth surface of the characters is rarely cracked. In French with English titles. **100m/C VHS, LV.** *FR* Emmanuelle Beart, Daniel Auteuil, Andre Dussollier, Elisabeth Bourgine, Brigitte Catillon, Maurice Garrel, Miriam Boyer; **D:** Claude Sautet; **W:** Yves Ulmann, Jacques Fieschi, Jerome Tonnerre. Cesar Awards '93: Best Director (Sautet), Best Supporting Actor (Dussollier); Nominations: British Academy Awards '93: Best Foreign Film. *REP*

Un Singe en Hiver 🎬🎬½ *A Monkey in Winter; It's Hot in Hell* **1962** A young wanderer (Belmondo) befriends a crusty old alcoholic (Gabin) who has kept his vow to abstain since his village survived the German bombing of WWII. Moving tale of regret and the passage of time. In French with English subtitles. **105m/B VHS, Beta.** Jean-Paul Belmondo, Jean Gabin, Suzanne Flon, Paul Frankeur; **D:** Henri Verneuil. *BAR*

The Unapproachable 🎬🎬½ **1982** A rendition of the Polish director's two one-act plays concerning a reclusive aging stage star being manipulated by her hangers-on. **92m/C VHS, Beta.** *PL* Leslie Caron, Daniel Webb, Leslie Malton; **D:** Krzysztof Zanussi. *MGM*

The Unbearable Lightness of Being 🎬🎬🎬½ **1988** (R) Tomas (Day Lewis), a young Czech doctor in the late 1960s, leads a sexually and emotionally carefree existence with a number of women, including provocative artist Olin. When he meets the fragile Binoche, he may be falling in love for the first time. On the eve of the 1968 Russian invasion of Czechoslovakia the two flee to Switzerland, but Binoche can't reconcile herself to exile and returns, followed by the reluctant Tomas who has lost his position because of his new-found political idealism. They lead an increasingly simple life, drawn ever closer together. The haunting ending caps off superb performances. Based on the novel by Milan Kundera. **172m/C VHS, Beta, LV, Closed Caption.** Daniel Day-Lewis, Juliette Binoche, Lena Olin, Derek De Lint, Erland Josephson, Pavel Landovsky, Donald Moffat, Daniel Olbrychski, Stellan Skarsgard, Tormek Bork, Bruce Myers, Pavel Slaby, Pascale Kalensky, Jacques Ciron, Anne Lonnberg, Laszlo Szabo, Vladimir Valenta, Clovis Cornillac, Leon Lissek, Consuelo de Haviland; **D:** Philip Kaufman; **W:** Jean-Claude Carriere, Philip Kaufman; **C:** Sven Nykvist; **M:** Mark Adler, Ernie Fosselius, Leos Janacek. British Academy Awards '88: Best Adapted Screenplay; Independent Spirit Awards '89: Best Director (Kaufman), Best Film; National Society of Film Critics Awards '88: Best Cinematography; Nominations: Academy Awards '88: Best Adapted Screenplay, Best Cinematography. *ORI*

The Unbeaten 28 🎬 **198?** A group of kung fu masters is forced to fight for their lives against evil criminals. **90m/C VHS, Beta.** Lisa Chang, Meng Fei, Lung Sikar; **D:** Joseph Kuo. *MPI*

The Unbelievable Truth 🎬🎬½ **1990** (R) Ex-con Robocop-to-be Burke meets armaged-don-obsessed model and sparks fly until bizarre murder occurs. Quirky black comedy shot in less than two weeks. **CW:** Adult situations; language, mild violence, and sexual situations. **100m/C VHS, LV.** Adrienne Shelly, Robert John Burke, Christopher Cooke, Julia Mueller, Julia McNeal, Mark Bailey, Gary Sauer, Kathrine Mayfield; **D:** Hal Hartley; **W:** Hal Hartley; **C:** Michael Spiller; **M:** Jim Coleman. *THV*

The Unborn 🎬½ **1991** (R) An infertile wife gets inseminated at unorthodox clinic. But once pregnant she suspects that her unborn baby is a monstrous being. Tasteless B-movie with an A-performance from Adams; if the rest had been up to her standard this could have been another "Stepford Wives." Instead it cons out with cheap gore. **CW:** Some language, violence and gore, and sensuality. **85m/C VHS, LV.** Brooke Adams, Jeff Hayenga, James Karen, K. Callan, Jane Cameron; **D:** Rodman Flender. *COL*

The Unborn 2 🎬 **1994** (R) Greene's blood-craving baby thinks nothing of feasting off the babysitter until a gun-wielding avenger comes to the rescue. Some notably gross scenes. **CW:** Some language and violence and gore. **84m/C VHS, LV.** Michele Greene, Scott Valentine, Robin Curtis; **D:** Rick Jacobson. *NHO*

The Unbreakable Alibi 🎬🎬 **1983** A wealthy young man asks Tommy and Tuppence Beresford to help him prove that one of two alibis an Australian journalist created is false. Based on the mysteries by Agatha Christie. Made for television. **51m/C VHS, Beta.** *GB* Francesca Annis, James Warwick. *TPV*

Uncaged 🎬 *Angel in Red* **1991** (R) Five beautiful young prostitutes hit Sunset Strip, each of them dreaming of a better life. When a crazy pimp brutally murders one of their friends, they set out to avenge that girl, and her broken dreams. **CW:** Strong sensuality, strong violence, and strong language. **78m/C VHS, LV.** Leslie Bega, Jeffrey Dean Morgan, Pamella O'Pella, Gregory Millar, Henry Brown, Jason Oliver, Elena Sahagun; **D:** William Duprey; **W:** Robert Alden, Joan Freeman, Catherine Cyran. *COL*

The Uncanny woof! **1978** Horror anthology of three tales concerned with feline attempts to control the world. Waste of good cast and cats on silly stories. Not released in the U.S. **85m/C VHS, Beta.** *GB* Peter Cushing, Ray Milland, Samantha Eggar, Donald Pleasence; **D:** Denis Heroux.

Uncensored 🎬½ **1985** This fast-paced comedy special features dozens of hilarious skits and sketches. **60m/C VHS, Beta.** Murray Langston, Cassandra Peterson, John Paragon, Ben Powers. *NO*

Uncertain Glory 🎬🎬 **1944** Errol plays a French thief who's willing to pretend to be a saboteur and die for his country. Based on a story by Joe May and Laszlo Vadnay. **102m/B VHS.** Errol Flynn, Paul Lukas, Jean Sullivan, Lucile Watson, Faye Emerson, James Flavin, Douglass Dumbrille, Dennis Hoey, Sheldon Leonard; **D:** Raoul Walsh; **W:** Laszlo Vadnay, Max Brand. *MGM*

The Unchastened Woman 🎬🎬 **1925** A married couple is torn apart by infidelity despite their impending parenthood, and wife Bara heads overseas to run wild and have the baby. She returns with a foreign flame, whom she dumps when erstwhile husband finds fatherly feelings in his heart. One of Bara's last films. **52m/B VHS, Beta.** Theda Bara, Wyndham Standing, Dale Fuller, John Miljan; **D:** James Young. *GPV, FCT*

Uncivilized 🎬🎬 **1994** Young couple, on a vacation in the mountains, run into a gang of drug runners who don't want their whereabouts revealed. So, the duo have to play a deadly game of hide-and-seek to survive. **90m/C VHS.** Martin Kove, Rick Aiello. *SWI*

Uncle Buck 🎬🎬🎬 **1989** (PG) When Mom and Dad have to go away suddenly, the only babysitter they can find is good ol' Uncle Buck, a lovable lout who spends much of his time smoking cigars, trying to make up with his girlfriend, and enforcing the teenage daughter's chastity. More intelligent than the average slob/teen comedy with a heart, due in large part to Candy's dandy performance. Memorable pancake scene. **100m/C VHS, Beta, LV, DVD.** John Candy, Amy Madigan, Jean Kelly, Macaulay Culkin, Jay Underwood, Gaby Hoffman, Laurie Metcalf, Elaine Bromka, Garrett M. Brown; **D:** John Hughes; **W:** John Hughes; **C:** Ralf Bode; **M:** Ira Newborn. *USH*

Uncle Moses 🎬🎬½ **1932** The clash of old-world values and new-world culture in a story of East European Jewish immigrants transplanted to turn of the century New York's Lower East Side. Patriarch Uncle Moses struggles to keep tradition-al family values as romantic difficulties and labor union struggles intrude. Based on the novel by Sholem Asch. In Yiddish with English subtitles. **87m/B VHS.** Maurice Schwartz, Rubin Goldberg, Judith Abarbanel, Zvee Scooler; **D:** Sidney Goldin, Aubrey Scotto. *ERG, NCJ*

Uncle Sam woof! **1998** (R) The box art is cool but this is basically a video horror. Desert Storm hero Sam Harper (Fralick) returns home—in a coffin. Only he doesn't stay dead and decides to liven up his small town's Fourth of July celebration by dressing up as Uncle Sam and going on a killing spree. **CW:** Violence, language, brief nudity. **91m/C VHS, LV, DVD.** David Fralick, Timothy Bottoms, Robert Forster, Isaac Hayes, Bo Hopkins; **D:** William Lustig. *APX*

Uncle Tom's Cabin 🎬🎬 **1914** Satisfying version of Harriet Beecher Stowe's tale from the view of a founder of the underground railroad. Lucas was the first black actor to garner a lead role. **54m/C VHS, Beta.** Mary Eline, Irving Cummings, Sam Lucas; **D:** William Robert Daly. *GPV, FCT, DVT*

Uncle Tom's Cabin 🎬½ *Onkel Toms Hutte; La Case de L'Oncle Tom; Cento Dollari D'Odio; Cica Tomina Koliba* **1969** (G) Ambitious adaptation of Harriet Beecher Stowe's stirring book about the Southern slavery and the famous underground railroad devised to aid those most determined to reach freedom. The film has the habit of drifting away from the facts. Though set in Kentucky, the picture was filmed in Yugoslavia with an international cast. **120m/C VHS, Beta.** *FR IT YU GE* Herbert Lom, John Kitzmiller, O.W. Fischer, Eleanora Rossi-Drago, Mylene Demongeot, Juliette Greco; **D:** Geza von Radvanyi; **V:** Ella Fitzgerald. *XVC, AFR*

Uncle Tom's Cabin 🎬🎬½ **1987** The first American sound version of this film. Excellent cast and interestingly adapted script are perfect for a message that is still socially relevant today. Based on the novel by Harriet Beecher Stowe. Made for television. **110m/C VHS.** Avery Brooks, Kate Burton, Bruce Dern, Paula Kelly, Phylicia Rashad, Kathryn Walker, Edward Woodward, Frank Converse, George Coe, Albert Hall; **D:** Stan Lathan. *FCT, WOV*

Uncle Was a Vampire 🎬🎬 **1959** Lee stars as Count Dracula in this vampire story. **?m/C VHS.** Christopher Lee, Kay Fisher. *SNC*

Uncommon Valor 🎬🎬½ **1983** (R) After useless appeals to the government for information on his son listed as "missing in action" in Vietnam, Colonel Rhodes takes matters into his own hands. Hackman is solid and believable as always, surrounded with good cast in generally well-paced film. **105m/C VHS, Beta, LV, 8mm, Closed Caption.** Gene Hackman, Fred Ward, Reb Brown, Randall "Tex" Cobb, Robert Stack, Patrick Swayze, Harold Sylvester, Tim Thomerson; **D:** Ted Kotcheff; **C:** Stephen Burum; **M:** James Horner. *PAR*

Unconquered 🎬🎬½ **1947** Silly epic about America finds indentured servant Abby (Goddard), meeting Virginia militia man Christopher Holden (Cooper). He nobly buys her contract and frees her but scurvy trader Martin Garth (da Silva) manages to get Abby working in his saloon. Garth also illegally sells guns to the local Seneca Indian tribe and persuades their chief, Guyasuta (Karloff), to attack the colonists. Cooper has to keep rescuing Goodard throughout the movie, as well as battling da Silva and helping the settlers fight Indians. Based on the novel "The Judas Tree" by Neil H. Swanson. **147m/C VHS, Closed Caption.** Gary Cooper, Paulette Goddard, Howard da Silva, Boris Karloff, Cecil Kellaway, Ward Bond, Katherine DeMille, Henry Wilcoxon, Sir C. Aubrey Smith, Victor Varconi, Virginia Grey, Mike Mazurki, Porter Hall; **D:** Cecil B. DeMille; **W:** Charles Bennett, Jesse Lasky Jr., Frederic M. Frank; **C:** Ray Rennahan; **M:** Victor Young. *USH*

The Undead 🎬🎬 **1957** A prostitute is accidentally sent back to the Middle Ages as the result of a scientific experiment and finds herself condemned to die for witchcraft. Early Corman script filled with convoluted storylines, laughable characters, violence, and heaving bosoms. **75m/B VHS.** Pamela Duncan, Richard Garland, Allison Hayes, Mel Welles, Billy Barty; *D:* Roger Corman. *NOS, MLB, HEG*

Undeclared War *♂♂* **1991 (R)** Suspenseful espionage thriller that takes you behind the scenes of an international terrorist plot, which has been cleverly disguised as a bloody global revolution. Intense action heightened by conflicts between worldwide intelligence networks, the news media and terrorist organizations.*CW:* Strong action violence. **103m/C VHS, LV, Closed Caption.** Vernon Wells, David Hedison, Olivia Hussey, Peter Lapis; *D:* Ringo Lam. *IMP*

Undefeatable *♂½* **1994 (R)** Rothrock is out to avenge the murder of her sister at the hands of a serial killer who, coincidentally, happens to be a martial arts expert. You watch for Cynthia to kick butt for plot anyway.*CW:* Violence, nudity, language. **88m/C VHS.** Cynthia Rothrock, Don Niam, John Miller, Donna Jason; *D:* Godfrey Hall. *FXV*

The Undefeated *♂♂* **1969 (G)** A Confederate and Yankee find they must team up on the Rio Grande. They attempt to build new lives in the Spanish held Mexico territory, but are caught in the battle for Mexican independence. Standard fare made palatable only by Wayne and Hudson. **119m/C VHS, Beta, LV, Closed Caption.** John Wayne, Rock Hudson, Lee Meriwether, Merlin Olsen, Bruce Cabot, Ben Johnson, Jan-Michael Vincent, Harry Carey Jr., Antonio Aguilar, Roman Gabriel; *D:* Andrew V. McLaglen; *C:* William Clothier. *FOX*

Under California Stars *♂♂* *Under California Skies* **1948** Shady gang making a living rounding up wild horses decides they can make more money by capturing Rogers' horse, Trigger. **71m/C VHS, Beta.** Roy Rogers, Andy Devine, Jane Frazee, The Pioneers; *D:* William Witney. *NOS, VYY, DVT*

Under Capricorn *♂♂½* **1949** Bergman is an Irish lass who helped her convict husband Cotten out to 1830s Australia where he makes a fortune. She turns to drink, perhaps because of his neglect, and has her position usurped by a housekeeper with designs on her husband. When Bergman's cousin (Wilding) arrives, Cotten may have cause for his violent jealousy. There's a plot twist involving old family skeletons, but this is definitely lesser Hitchcock. Adapted from the Helen Simpson novel. Remade in 1982. **117m/C VHS, Beta, LV.** GB Ingrid Bergman, Joseph Cotten, Michael Wilding, Margaret Leighton, Jack Watling, Cecil Parker, Denis O'Dea; *D:* Alfred Hitchcock; *C:* Jack Cardiff. *VES*

Under Capricorn *♂♂* **1982** An Australian remake of the 1949 Hitchcock film about family secrets, an unhappy marriage, and violence set in 1830s' Australia. **120m/C VHS, Beta.** AU Lisa Harrow, John Hallam, Peter Cousens, Julia Blake, Catherine Lynch; *D:* Rod Hardy.

Under Colorado Skies *♂½* **1947** Medical student Hale is accused of robbery and escapes the law to clear his name. **65m/C VHS, Closed Caption.** Monte Hale, Adrian Booth, Paul Hurst, Tom London; *D:* R.G. Springsteen; *W:* Louise Rousseau; *C:* Alfred S. Keller. *REP*

Under Fire *♂♂♂½* **1983 (R)** Three foreign correspondents, old friends from the past working together, find themselves in Managua, witnessing the 1979 Nicaraguan revolution. In a job requiring objectivity, but a situation requiring taking sides, they battle with their ethics to do the job right. Fine performances, including Harris as a mercenary. Interesting view of American media and its political necessities. **128m/C VHS, Beta, LV.** Gene Hackman, Nick Nolte, Joanna Cassidy, Ed Harris, Richard Masur, Hamilton Camp, Jean-Louis Trintignant; *D:* Roger Spottiswoode; *W:* Ron Shelton, Clayton Frohman; *M:* Jerry Goldsmith. Nominations: Academy Awards '83: Best Original Score. *VES*

Under Investigation *♂♂½* **1993 (R)** Burned out cop Hamlin is after a crazed killer. His cool lover Pacula turns out to be the prime suspect. Who's deceiving who?*CW:* Murders and sex scenes. **94m/C VHS.** Harry Hamlin, Joanna Pacula, Ed

Lauter, Richard Beymer, Lydie Denier; *D:* Kevin Meyer; *W:* Kevin Meyer. *NLC*

Under Milk Wood *♂♂½* **1973 (PG)** An adaptation of the Dylan Thomas play about the lives of the residents of a village in Wales. Burton and O'Toole are wonderful in this uneven, but sometimes engrossing film. **90m/C VHS, Beta.** GB Richard Burton, Elizabeth Taylor, Peter O'Toole, Glynis Johns, Vivien Merchant; *D:* Andrew Sinclair. *FOX*

Under Montana Skies *♂½* **1930** An early talkie western features music and comedy in abundance, relegating the action to second place. A singing cowboy protects a travelling burlesque show from evildoers. **55m/B VHS, Beta.** Kenneth Harlan, Dorothy Gulliver, Lafe McKee, Ethel Wales, Slim Summerville; *D:* Richard Thorpe. *GPV*

Under Nevada Skies *♂♂½* **1946** Fairly good matinee-era western centers on a missing map to a uranium deposit, climaxing with Rogers heading a posse of Indian allies to the rescue. The Sons of the Pioneers contribute songs. **69m/B VHS.** Roy Rogers, George "Gabby" Hayes, Dale Evans, Douglass Dumbrille, Tristram Coffin, Rudolph Anders, Iron Eyes Cody; *D:* Frank McDonald. *NOS, HEG*

Under Satan's Sun *♂♂♂* *Under the Sun of Satan; Sous le Soleil de Satan* **1987** A rural priest is tortured by what he sees as his sins and failings to his parishioners. He is further tempted from the straight path by a beautiful murderess, a worldly priest, and, perhaps by Satan in disguise. Stylized film is not easily accessible, but Depardieu's performance is worth the effort. Based on the Georges Bernanos book "Diary of a Country Priest." In French with English subtitles. **97m/C VHS.** FR Gerard Depardieu, Sandrine Bonnaire, Yann Dedet, Alain Artur, Maurice Pialat; *D:* Maurice Pialat; *W:* Maurice Pialat. Cannes Film Festival '87: Best Film. *NYF, FCT, CVC*

Under Siege *♂♂* **1992 (R)** The USS Missouri becomes the battleground for good-guy-with-a-secret-past Seagal. He's up against the deranged Jones, as an ex-Special Forces leader, and Busey, a corrupt naval officer looking to steal the battleship's nuclear arsenal. May be predictable (especially the graphic violence) but the action is fast, the villains swaggering, and Seagal efficient at dispatching the enemy. Work for "Die Hard 3" was reportedly scrapped after Warner announced this film because DH's John McClane was supposed to save the passengers of a boat from terrorists. Sound familiar?*CW:* Language, strong violence, and strong sensuality. **100m/C VHS, Beta, LV, 8mm, Letterbox, Closed Caption.** Steven Seagal, Tommy Lee Jones, Gary Busey, Patrick O'Neal, Erika Eleniak; *D:* Andrew Davis; *W:* J.F. Lawton; *M:* Gary Chang. Nominations: Academy Awards '92: Best Sound, Best Sound Effects Editing. *WAR*

Under Siege 2: Dark Territory *♂♂* **1995 (R)** Kicking terrorists' butts and slinging hash have worn out ex-Navy SEAL and gourmet chef Casey Ryback (Seagal), so he takes a little vacation to the Rocky Mountains. By coincidence, the train he boards is command central for psychotic computer expert Dane's (Bogosian) scheme to control the world's deadliest satellite. Pretty familiar territory for Seagal, who's acting technique consists of "look mad and hurt poeple." Bigger budget means bigger, and more frequent, explosions. Bogosian takes over the Jones/Busey role of evil villain-talented actor.*CW:* Strong violence and language. **100m/C VHS, LV, Closed Caption.** Steven Seagal, Eric Bogosian, Katherine Heigl, Morris Chestnut, Everett McGill, Andy Romano, Nick Mancuso, Brenda Bakke; *D:* Geoff Murphy; *W:* Richard Hatem; *C:* Robbie Greenberg; *M:* Basil Poledouris. *WAR*

Under Suspicion *♂♂♂½* **1992 (R)** Christmas 1959 in Brighton finds seedy private eye Tony Aaron and his wife faking adultery cases for those desperate to get around England's strict divorce laws. Sordid tale takes a turn when Tony bursts in to snap incriminating photos and finds both his wife and their client, a famous artist, murdered. Dark who-dunnit has some interesting

twists that could have made it exceptional rather than the conventional melodrama it turned out to be. Neeson is very good as the charmingly sleazy Tony but nobody else stands out, except the unfortunately miscast San Giacomo. Theatrical feature debut for director Moore. **99m/C VHS, LV, Closed Caption.** GB Liam Neeson, Laura San Giacomo, Alphonsia Emmanuel, Kenneth Cranham, Maggie O'Neill, Martin Grace, Stephen Moore; *D:* Simon Moore; *W:* Simon Moore; *M:* Christopher Gunning. *COL*

Under the Biltmore Clock *♂♂* **1985** F. Scott Fitzgerald's story, "Myra Meets His Family," is the basis for this American Playhouse installment for PBS television. It is outwit or be outwitted in this tale of a fortune-hunting '20s flapper who is outsmarted by the man she has set her sights on when he hires actors to play his eccentric "family." **70m/C VHS, Beta, LV, 8mm.** Sean Young, Lenny Von Dohlen, Barnard Hughes; *D:* Neal Miller. *NLC*

Under the Boardwalk *♂½* **1989 (R)** A pair of star-crossed teenage lovers struggle through familial and societal differences in 1980s California. This is, like, bogus, ya know. **102m/C VHS, Beta, LV.** Keith Coogan, Danielle von Zerneck, Richard Joseph Paul, Hunter von Leer, Tracey Walter, Roxana Zal, Dick Miller, Sonny Bono, Corky Carroll; *D:* Fritz Kiersch; *C:* Don Burgess. *VTR*

Under the Cherry Moon *♂½* **1986 (PG-13)** Prince portrays a fictional musician of the 1940s who travels to the French Riviera, seeking love and money. Songs include "Under the Cherry Moon," "Kiss," "Anotherloverholeinyohead," "Sometimes It Snows in April," and "Mountains." A vanity flick down to its being filmed in black and white. **100m/B VHS, Beta, LV, Closed Caption.** Prince, Jerome Benton, Francesca Annis, Kristin Scott Thomas; *D:* Prince; *C:* Michael Ballhaus. Golden Raspberry Awards '86: Worst Picture, Worst Actor (Prince), Worst Supporting Actor (Benton), Worst Director (Prince), Worst Song ("Love or Money"). *MVD, WAR, FCT*

Under the Domim Tree *♂♂½* *Etz Hadomim Tafus* **1995** Sequel to "The Summer of Aviya," set in 1953, finds 15-year-old Aviya (Cohen) living in an Israeli community with other teenagers who were scarred by the Holocaust. As they get to know one another, each must deal with their own tormented memories. Based on a memoir by Almagor, who plays Aviya's institutionalized mother. Hebrew with subtitles. **102m/C VHS.** IS Kaipo Cohen, Julino Mer, Ohad Knoller, Orli Perl, Riki Blich, Gila Almagor; *D:* Eli Cohen; *W:* Gila Almagor, Eyal Sher; *C:* David Gurfinkel; *M:* Benny Nagari. *FXL*

Under the Earth *♂♂♂* *Debajo del Mundo* **1986 (R)** An Argentine-Czech co-production, depicting the plight of a family of Polish Jews forced to live underground for two years to avoid the Nazis. Harrowing and critically well-received. In Spanish with subtitles. **100m/C VHS, Beta, LV.** SP Victor Laplace; *D:* Beda Ocampo Feijoo, Juan Bautista Stagnaro. *SWC*

Under the Gun *♂♂* **1988 (R)** A cop recruits a lawyer to help him find the man who murdered his brother. Action drives this formulaic plot along. **89m/C VHS, LV.** Sam Jones, Vanessa L(ynne) Williams, John Russell, Michael Halsey; *D:* James Sbardellati; *W:* James Sbardellati, Almer John Davis. *IME*

Under the Gun *♂½* **1995 (R)** Debt-ridden club owner Frank Torrance (Norton) is in trouble with everyone he knows. But he can't clear his debts just by quitting the business, so he decides to fight back.*CW:* Strong violence, language and some drug content. **90m/C VHS, LV.** Richard Norton, Kathy Long; *D:* Matthew George. *TRI*

Under the Hula Moon *♂♂½* **1995 (R)** Buzzard (Baldwin) and Betty (Lloyd) Wall are living unhappily in the charmless desert town of Cactus Gulch. Their trailer home is festooned in faux-Hawaiian finery and the duo dream of the day they can actually move to their island paradise. Buzz's invented an ultraprotective sunscreen that may be their ticket out, if his prison-escapee, trigger-happy half-brother Turk (Penn), who's also kidnapped Betty, doesn't get them all killed first. Charming lead performances—very lightweight story.*CW:* Violence, language, some sexuality. **94m/C VHS.** Stephen Baldwin, Emily Lloyd, Christopher Penn, Musetta Vander, Edie McClurg, Pruitt Taylor Vince, Bill Campbell, Carel Struycken, R. Lee Ermey; *D:* Jeff Celentano; *W:* Jeff Celentano; *C:* Phil Parmet. TTC

Under the Rainbow woof! 1981 (PG)
Comic situations encountered by a talent scout and a secret service agent in a hotel filled with Munchkins during filming of "The Wizard of Oz." Features midgets, spies, and a prevailing lack of taste. International intrigue adds to the strange attempt at humor. **97m/C VHS, Beta.** Chevy Chase, Carrie Fisher, Eve Arden, Joseph Maher, Robert Donner, Mako, Pat McCormick, Billy Barty, Zelda Rubinstein; *D:* Steve Rash; *W:* Pat McCormick, Martin Smith, Harry Hurwitz, Fred Bauer, Pat Bradley. WAR

Under the Red Robe 🎬🎬½ 1936 A
French soldier of fortune is trapped into aiding Cardinal Richelieu in his persecution of the Huguenots and winds up falling in love with the sister of his intended victim. Good costume adventure-drama. Sjostrom's last film as a director. **82m/B VHS, Beta.** *GB* Raymond Massey, Conrad Veidt, Annabella, Romney Brent; *D:* Victor Sjostrom; *C:* James Wong Howe. NOS, HHT, WFV

Under the Roofs of Paris 🎬🎬🎬½
Sous les Toits de Paris 1929 An early French sound film about the lives of young Parisian lovers. A gentle, highly acclaimed melodrama. In French with English subtitles. **95m/B VHS, Beta.** *FR* Albert Prejean, Pola Illery, Gaston Modot; *D:* Rene Clair; *C:* Georges Perinal. VYY, NOS, CAB

Under the Volcano 🎬🎬🎬 1984 An alco-holic British ex-consul finds his life further deteriorating during the Mexican Day of the Dead in 1939. His half-brother and ex-wife try to save him from himself, but their affair sends him ever-deeper into his personal hell. Finney's performance is pathetic and haunting. Adapted from the novel by Malcolm Lowry. **112m/C VHS, Beta, LV.** Albert Finney, Jacqueline Bisset, Anthony Andrews, Katy Jurado; *D:* John Huston; *M:* John Beal, Alex North. Los Angeles Film Critics Association Awards '84: Best Actor (Finney); Nominations: Academy Awards '84: Best Actor (Finney), Best Original Score. USH

Under the Yum-Yum Tree 🎬🎬½
1963 When womanizing landlord Hogan's (Lemmon) ex-fiance Irene (Adams) moves out, he doesn't pine. Instead he plots to romance her niece Robin (Lynley) who's just moved into his building. But his romantic shenanigans are thwarted by the presence of fiance David (Jones), who's living platonically with Robin to test their compatibility. Silly sex comedy based on the play by Roman. **110m/C VHS.** Jack Lemmon, Carol Lynley, Dean Jones, Edie Adams, Imogene Coca, Paul Lynde, Robert Lansing, Bill Bixby; *D:* David Swift; *W:* David Swift, Lawrence Roman; *C:* Joseph Biroc; *M:* Frank De Vol. COL

Under Western Stars 🎬 1945 Roy's first starring vehicle. A newly elected congressman goes to Washington and fights battles for his constituents, caught in the middle of the Dust Bowl and drought. **83m/B VHS, Beta.** Roy Rogers, Smiley Burnette; *D:* Jean Yarbrough. NOS, DVT, VCN

The Underachievers 🎬 1988 (R) A night school is the scene for typical libido-oriented gags, but this time instead of teenagers it's adult education providing the plot. Only a few real laughs in this one. **90m/C VHS, Beta.** Barbara Carrera, Edward Albert, Michael Pataki, Vic Tayback, Garrett Morris, Susan Tyrrell; *D:* Jackie Kong. ART, VES

Undercover 🎬½ 1987 (R) Routine cop action film in which an eastern detective finds himself undercover in a southern high school in search of a cop-murdering drug ring. Plagued with cliches. Director Stockwell is appropriately better known for his role as "Cougar" in "Top Gun." **92m/C VHS, Closed Caption.** David Neidorf, Jennifer Jason Leigh, Barry Corbin, David Harris, Kathleen Wilhoite; *D:* John Stockwell; *M:* Bruce Smeaton. WAR

Undercover 🎬½ 1994 (R) Police detective (and hot babe) Cindy Hanen (Massey) gets an undercover assignment to capture a murderer who's targeted an upscale brothel. It's an excuse for interesting undies (or less).*CW:* Sexuality, nudity. **93m/C VHS.** Athena Massey, Tom Tayback, Anthony Guidera, Rena Riffel, Jeffrey Dean Morgan, Meg Foster; *D:* Alexander Gregory Hippolyte; *W:* Lalo Wolf, Oola Bloome. APX

Undercover Blues 🎬🎬½ 1993 (PG-13)
Comedy-thriller starring Turner and Quaid as married spies Jane and Jeff Blue, on parental leave from the espionage biz, who are on vacation with their 11-month-old daughter in New Orleans. But the holiday is interrupted when they're recruited by their boss to stop an old adversary from selling stolen weapons. The leads play cute together and the baby is adorable but this is strictly routine escapism. Stick with "The Thin Man" instead.*CW:* One use of strong language and mock violence. **90m/C VHS, LV, Letterbox, Closed Caption.** Kathleen Turner, Dennis Quaid, Fiona Shaw, Stanley Tucci, Larry Miller, Obba Babatunde, Park Overall, Tom Arnold, Saul Rubinek, Michelle Schuelke; *D:* Herbert Ross; *W:* Ian Abrams; *M:* David Newman. MGM

Undercover Cop 🎬🎬 1994 True story of Sergeant George Aguilar and the high-speed chase that left one dead and the police dealing their revenge on all the offenders. **90m/C VHS.** Danny Trejo, Kevin Anthony Cole; *D:* Martin Greene; *W:* Glenn A. Bruce; *M:* Randall Kent Heddon.

Undercover Man 🎬½ 1936 A Wells Fargo agent goes undercover to expose a crooked sheriff. **57m/B VHS.** Johnny Mack Brown, Suzanne Kaaren, Ted Adams, Lloyd Ingraham, Horace Murphy; *D:* Albert Ray. NOS, DVT, RXM

The Underdog 🎬½ 1943 After the bank forecloses, a farm family must move to the city. The family's young son has only his loyal dog to turn to for friendship, but the gallant animal proves his mettle by rounding up a gang of spies plotting some WWII sabotage. Believe it if you dare. **65m/B VHS, Beta, 8mm.** Barton MacLane, Bobby Larson, Jan Wiley; *D:* William Nigh. VYY

Undergrads 🎬🎬🎬 1985 A bright generational Disney comedy with Carney, estranged from his stick-in-the-mud son, deciding to attend college with his free-thinking grandson. Made for television. **102m/C VHS, Beta.** Art Carney, Chris Makepeace, Jackie Burroughs, Len Birman; *D:* Steven Hilliard Stern. DIS

Underground 🎬🎬🎬 *Once Upon a Time There Was a Country* 1995 Exhausting black comedy, set in Yugoslavia from 1941 to 1992, follows the adventures of Marko (Manojlovic) and his best friend Blacky (Ristovski). They run a black-market operation and lead Communist Party meetings while trying to avoid the Gestapo in WWII Belgrade. Hiding out in a cellar, where refugees have put together a munitions factory, the treacherous Marko manages to convince everyone that the war is still going on—20 years later in fact—until the truth unexpectedly comes out (thanks to a pet monkey). The final section sees Marko unscrupulously dealing arms and drugs amidst the breakup of Yugoslavia in a civil war and the violence on all sides. **192m/C VHS.** *FR GE HU* Miki Manojlovic, Lazar Ristovski, Mirjana Jokovic, Slavko Stimac, Ernst Stotzner, Srdan Todorovic, Mirjana Karanovic; *Cameos:* Emir Kusturica; *D:* Emir Kusturica; *W:* Emir Kusturica, Dusan Kovacevic; *C:* Vilko Filac; *M:* Goran Bregovic. Cannes Film Festival '95: Best Film; Nominations: Independent Spirit Awards '98: Best Foreign Language Film. NYR

The Underground 🎬🎬 1997 (R) A rap artist is gunned down by a gang and Sgt. Brian Donnegan (Fahey) and his partner Scully (Tigar) are on the investigation. But when Scully is killed by the same scum, Donnegan is partnered with a rookie (McFall) and the duo must infiltrate L.A.'s music scene to get their suspects. **92m/C VHS, Closed Caption.** Jeff Fahey, Ken Tigar, Michael McFall. PMH

Underground Aces woof! 1980 (PG) A group of parking lot attendants transforms a sheik into an attendant in order to help him meet the girl of his dreams. A bad "Car Wash" spinoff. **93m/C VHS, Beta.** Dirk Benedict, Melanie Griffith, Frank Gorshin, Jerry Orbach, Robert Hegyes, Audrey Landers; *D:* Robert Butler; *W:* Jim Carabatsos. ART, VES

Underground Rustlers 🎬 1941 The Range Busters are commissioned by the government to stop unscrupulous gold-marketeers. **58m/B VHS, Beta.** Ray Corrigan, Max Terhune, John "Dusty" King; *D:* S. Roy Luby. VDM

Underground Terror 🎬 1988 A gang of murderers, organized by a psychopath, rampages through the New York City subway system. One cop enthusiastically tries to snuff out each one. **91m/C VHS.** Doc Dougherty, Lenny Y. Loftin; *D:* James McCalmont. NO

Underground U.S.A. 🎬 1984 Street hustler picks up a has-been underground movie star at the chic New York new wave disco, The Mudd Club. **85m/C VHS, Beta.** Patti Astor, Eric Mitchell; *D:* Eric Mitchell. NO

The Underneath 🎬🎬🎬 1995 (R) Recovering gambling addict Michael Chambers (Gallagher) returns home after skipping out on his debts and his wife Rachel (sultry newcomer Elliott) several years before. Old passions ignite in more ways than one, and Michael's lust for his ex, now married to a hot-tempered hoodlum, leads him to risk it all for a final big score. Moody and tense study of the complexities of emotion is capped by smart lead performances but style wins out over substance and the finale definitely leaves more questions than answers. Remake of the 1949 film noir classic "Criss Cross," based on Don Tracy's novel of the same name.*CW:* Some violence, language and a discreet sex scene. **99m/C VHS.** Shelley Duvall, Richard Linklater, Dennis Hill, Peter Gallagher, Alison Elliott, William Fichtner, Elisabeth Shue, Adam Trese, Paul Dooley, Joe Don Baker, Anjanette Comer, Harry Goaz, Vincent Gaskins, Tony Perenski, Helen Cates, John Martin, David Jensen, Joseph Chrest; *D:* Steven Soderbergh; *W:* Daniel Fuchs, Sam Lowry; *C:* Elliot Davis; *M:* Cliff Martinez. Nominations: Independent Spirit Awards '96: Best Cinematography. USH

Undersea Kingdom 1936 Adventure beneath the ocean floor. In 12 chapters of 13 minutes each; the first chapter runs 20 minutes. Later re-edited into one film, "Sharad of Atlantis." **226m/B VHS, LV.** Ray Corrigan, Lon Chaney Jr.; *D:* B. Reeves Eason. NOS, SNC, VCN

Understudy: The Graveyard Shift 2 🎬½ 1988 (R) Vampire survives poorly directed cliche-riddled original to be cast as a vampire cast as a vampire in a horror movie within a horrible sequel. **88m/C VHS, Beta, LV.** *CA* Wendy Gazelle, Mark Soper, Silvio Oliviero, Ilse von Glatz, Tim Kelleher; *D:* Gerard Ciccoritti; *C:* Barry Stone. NO

The Undertaker and His Pals 🎬🎬
1967 Undertaker teams up with diner owners in murder scheme to improve mortician's business and expand restaurateurs' menu. Pretty violent stuff, with some good laughs and a campy flare, but not for every one's palate. **70m/C VHS.** Ray Dannis, Brad Fulton, Larrene Ott, Robert Lowery, Sally Frei; *D:* David C. Graham. MTH

The Undertaker's Wedding 🎬🎬 1997 (R) Undertaker fakes the death and burial of a mob boss to stem a local mob war but then makes the big mistake of falling in love with the new "widow." **90m/C VHS, Closed Caption.** Adrien Brody, Jeff Wincott, Kari Wuhrer, Burt Young, Holly Gagnier, Nicholas Pasco; *D:* John Bradshaw; *W:* John Bradshaw; *C:* Edgar Egger. CAF

Undertow 🎬🎬 1995 (R) Drifter Jack Ketchum (Phillips) loses control of his car in a storm and wakes up in the secluded cabin of paranoid Lyle Yates (Dance) and his terrified wife, Willie (Sara). Since the storm's worse, Jack can't leave—too bad for him that Willie's so darn attractive and Lyle's so crazy. Cable thriller.*CW:* Vio-

lence, language and some sexuality. **90m/C VHS, Closed Caption.** Lou Diamond Phillips, Mia Sara, Charles Dance; *D:* Eric Red; *W:* Kathryn Bigelow, Eric Red; *C:* Geza Sinkovics; *M:* John Frizzell. *REP*

Underwater! 🎬🎬 **1955** A team of skin divers faces danger when they try to retrieve treasure from a Spanish galleon. The second film after "The Outlaw" masterminded by Howard Hughes, primarily to show off Russell's figure. **99m/C VHS, Beta, LV.** Jane Russell, Richard Egan, Gilbert Roland, Jayne Mansfield; *D:* John Sturges. *TTC*

Underworld 🎬🎬🎬 **1927** Inspired gangster saga finds bank robber Bull Weed (Bancroft) befriending a genteel bum, known as Rolls Royce (Brook), and taking him into his gang. The bum has brains and soon makes Weed king of the underworld but there's jealousy when Weed's moll Feathers (Brent) falls for Royce. Climactic shootout set a standard for the genre. **85m/B VHS.** George Bancroft, Clive Brook, Evelyn Brent, Larry Semon, Fred Kohler Sr.; *D:* Josef von Sternberg. Academy Awards '28: Best Story. *GPV*

Underworld 🎬🎬 **1996 (R)** Considering the on-screen talent, this crime comedy/thriller is a disappointment. Ex-wiseguy Johnny Crown (Leary) studied psychotherapy in the joint and, when he's released, decides to put his new knowledge to work on bossman Frank Gavilan (Mantegna), who may be behind the hit on Johnny's old man. Contrived dialogue and story but a sleek-looking production. *CW:* Pervasive strong language and violence, and for sexuality. **95m/C VHS, LV, Closed Caption.** Denis Leary, Joe Mantegna, Annabella Sciorra, Larry Bishop, Abe Vigoda, James Tolkan, Robert Costanzo; *D:* Roger Christian; *W:* Larry Bishop; *C:* Steven Bernstein; *M:* Anthony Marinelli. *THV*

Underworld Scandal 🎬🎬 **1947** An editor attempts to break up a ring of basketball game fixers. **?m/C VHS.** Philip Reed, Hillary Brooke. *SNC*

The Underworld Story 🎬🎬½ **1950** Big city journalist at large moves to smalltown New England after losing job for unethical reporting and uncovers scheme to frame innocent man for murder. Solid performances. **90m/B VHS.** Dan Duryea, Herbert Marshall, Gale Storm, Howard da Silva, Michael O'Shea, Mary Anderson, Gar Moore, Melville Cooper, Frieda Inescort, Art Baker, Harry Shannon, Alan Hale Jr., Steve Dunne, Roland Winters; *D:* Cy Endfield. *FOX, FCT*

Underworld, U.S.A. 🎬🎬🎬 **1960** A man infiltrates a tough crime syndicate to avenge his father's murder, which winds up with him caught between the mob and the feds. A well-acted and directed look at the criminal underworld. **99m/B VHS, Beta.** Cliff Robertson, Dolores Dorn, Beatrice Kay, Robert Emhardt, Larry Gates, Paul Dubov; *D:* Samuel Fuller; *W:* Samuel Fuller; *C:* Hal Mohr. *COL*

The Undying Monster 🎬🎬½ *The Hammond Mystery* **1942** Upper crusty Brit is werewolf with insatiable appetite. Familiar story with lots of atmosphere and style. **63m/B VHS.** James Ellison, Heather Angel, John Howard, Bramwell Fletcher, Heather Thatcher, Aubrey Mather, Halliwell Hobbes, Heather Wilde; *D:* John Brahm; *C:* Lucien Ballard. *MOV*

The Unearthing 🎬 **1993 (R)** An unwanted pregnancy seems to find a happy solution when a woman decides to marry the heir to a wealthy estate and pass off her child as his. Only the family has some very strange tastes, including a taste for the blood of the unborn. Based on a Filipino vampire legend (!). **83m/C VHS, LV.** Norman Moses, Tina Ona Paukstelis; *D:* Wyre Martin, Barry Poltermann; *W:* Wyre Martin, Barry Poltermann.

The Unearthly 🎬½ **1957** A mad scientist is trying to achieve immortality through his strange experiments, but all he winds up with is a basement full of mutants. When his two latest about-to-be victims fall in love, the doctor's mutant assistant decides enough is enough and things come to an unpleasant end. Carradine is typecast. Absurd, but fun. **76m/B VHS, Beta.** John Carradine, Tor Johnson, Allison Hayes, Myron Healey; *D:* Brooke L. Peters. *SNC, DVT, MLB*

The Unearthly Stranger 🎬🎬½ **1964** Earth scientist marries woman and decides she's from another planet. Not a nineties style gender drama; seems she's part of an invading alien force, but really does love her earth man. Surprisingly good low-budget sci-fi. **75m/B VHS.** *GB* John Neville, Gabriella Licudi, Philip Stone, Patrick Newell, Jean Marsh, Warren Mitchell; *D:* John Krish. *MOV*

Uneasy Terms 🎬 **1948** Rennie is a detective investigating the murder of one of his own clients. Evidence points to stepchildren and inheritance money but things may not be as they seem. Written for the screen by Peter Cheyney, adapted from his own novel. **91m/B VHS, Beta.** *GB* Michael Rennie, Moira Lister, Faith Brook, Joy Shelton, Patricia Goddard, Barry Jones, Nigel Patrick, Paul Carpenter, Marie Ney, Sydney Tafler, J.H. Roberts, John Robinson; *D:* Vernon Sewell; *W:* Peter Cheyney. *SNC*

An Unexpected Family 🎬🎬½ **1996** **(PG)** Barbara Whitney (Channing) is a Manhattan career woman who is unwillingly thrust into the role of surrogate mom when her irresponsible sister, Ruth (Ebersole), dumps her two children at Barbara's door. Along with her friend Sam (Collins), Barbara and the children slowly make a new family but, after a year, Ruth returns, demanding her children back. Predictable made for cable fare is redeemed by good performances from Channing and Ebersole. **93m/C VHS, Closed Caption.** Stockard Channing, Stephen Collins, Christine Ebersole, Noah Fleiss, Chelsea Russo; *D:* Larry Elikann; *W:* Lee Rose; *C:* Eric Van Haren Noman; *M:* Tom Scott. *USH*

Unexplained Laughter 🎬 **1989** A cynical journalist vacations in Wales with her timid vegetarian friend and stumbles across a mystery in this darkly comic British TV-movie. **85m/C VHS.** *GB* Diana Rigg, Elaine Page, Jon Finch. *FCT, VCO*

Unfaithfully Yours 🎬🎬🎬½ **1948** A conductor suspects his wife is cheating on him and considers his course of action. He imagines punishment scenarios while directing three classical works. Well-acted by all, but particularly by Harrison as the egotistical and jealous husband. Another of Sturges' comedic gems. Remade in 1984. **105m/B VHS, Beta, LV, Closed Caption.** Rex Harrison, Linda Darnell, Kurt Kreuger, Rudy Vallee, Lionel Stander, Edgar Kennedy; *D:* Preston Sturges; *C:* Victor Milner. *FOX*

Unfaithfully Yours 🎬🎬 **1984 (PG)** A symphony conductor suspects his wife of fooling around with a musician; in retaliation, he plots an elaborate scheme to murder her with comic results. No match for the 1948 Preston Sturges film it's based on. **96m/C VHS, Beta, LV, Closed Caption.** Dudley Moore, Nastassia Kinski, Armand Assante, Albert Brooks, Cassie Yates, Richard Libertini, Richard B. Shull; *D:* Howard Zieff; *W:* Valerie Curtin, Barry Levinson, Robert Klane; *M:* Bill Conti. *FOX*

Unfinished Business 🎬🎬½ **1989** A 17 year-old girl leads a troubled adolescent life with her divorced parents. She decides running away will ease her problems—not a smart move. Sequel to "Nobody Waved Goodbye." **88m/C VHS, Beta.** *CA* Isabelle Mejias, Peter Kastner, Leslie Toth, Peter Spence, Chuck Shamata, Julie Biggs; *D:* Don Owen. *JEF*

An Unfinished Piece for a Player Piano 🎬🎬🎬½ **1977** A general's widow invites family and friends to a weekend house party in 1910 Russia. Romantic and familial entanglements begin to intrude in a lyrical adaptation of Chekov's play "Platonov." In Russian with English subtitles. **100m/C VHS, Beta.** *RU* Alexander Kalyagin, Elena Solovei, Antonina Shuranova, Oleg Tabakov, Yuri Bogatyrev, Nikita Mikhalkov; *D:* Nikita Mikhalkov. *FCT, CVC*

Unforgettable 🎬🎬 **1996 (R)** Unfortunately, the film doesn't live up to its title. On-the-edge medical examiner David Krane (Liotta) has barely escaped conviction for his wife's brutal murder. Living under a cloud of suspicion, he turns to university researcher Martha Briggs (Fiorentino, wasted as a nerdy scientist), whose experiments

in memory transference lead David to believe he can uncover the killer. But, like a Chinese puzzle box, one discovery only leads to a further complication. Too many, in fact, for the story to stay focused (and the ending is less than satisfying). *CW:* Strong violence, language and nudity. **116m/C VHS, LV, Closed Caption.** Ray Liotta, Linda Fiorentino, Peter Coyote, Christopher McDonald, Kim Cattrall, David Paymer, Kim Coates, Duncan Fraser, Garwin Sanford; *D:* John Dahl; *W:* Bill Geddie; *C:* Jeffrey Jur; *M:* Christopher Young. *MGM*

An Unforgettable Summer 🎬🎬½ **1994** The elegant Marie-Therese Dumitriu (Scott Thomas) has married Army officer Petre (Bleont) and tried to focus on maintaining a serene life, following the Communist takeover of Romania. When Petre is transferred to an isolated border town, he and his family are caught between what the Army demands and what is just. The local Bulgarian peasants are accused of attrocities against the soldiers and Petre is ordered to execute a group of them as an example—guilty or not. Set in 1925 and based on the short story "La Salade" by Petru Dumitriu. English, French, and Romanian with subtitles. **82m/C VHS.** *RO* Kristin Scott Thomas, Claudiu Bleont, Olga Tudorache, George Constantin; *D:* Lucian Pintilie; *W:* Lucian Pintilie; *C:* Calin Ghibu; *M:* Anton Suteu. *NYF*

The Unforgiven 🎬🎬🎬 **1960** A western family is torn asunder when it is suspected that the eldest daughter is of Indian birth. Film takes place in 1850s' Texas. One of Huston's weakest ventures, but viewed in terms of 1950s' prejudices it has more resonance. Fine acting from all the cast, especially Gish. Watch for the stunning Indian attack scene. **123m/C VHS, Beta, LV, Letterbox.** Burt Lancaster, Audrey Hepburn, Lillian Gish, Audie Murphy, John Saxon, Charles Bickford, Doug McClure, Joseph Wiseman, Albert Salmi; *D:* John Huston. *MGM, BTV*

Unforgiven 🎬🎬🎬½ **1992 (R)** Will Munny (Eastwood) lives a quiet life with his stepchildren on his failing pig farm, but his desperado past catches up with him when the Schofield Kid invites him to a bounty hunt. Munny reluctantly agrees, mistakenly believing that once the killing is through he can take up his peaceful ways again. Enter sadistic sheriff Little Bill Daggett (Hackman), who doesn't want any gunmen messing up his town. Eastwood uses his own status as a screen legend to full advantage as the aging gunman who realizes too late that his past can never be forgotten. Director Eastwood is also in top form with his well-seasoned cast and myth-defying Old West realism. Surprising critical and boxoffice hit. The laserdisc version is available in letterbox format. *CW:* Language, violence, and sexual scene. **131m/C VHS, Beta, LV, Letterbox, Closed Caption, DVD.** Clint Eastwood, Gene Hackman, Morgan Freeman, Richard Harris, Jaimz Woolvett, Saul Rubinek, Frances Fisher, Anna Thomson, David Mucci, Rob Campbell, Anthony James; *D:* Clint Eastwood; *W:* David Peoples; *C:* Jack N. Green; *M:* Lennie Niehaus. Academy Awards '92: Best Director (Eastwood), Best Film Editing, Best Picture, Best Supporting Actor (Hackman); British Academy Awards '92: Best Director (Eastwood), Best Film, Best Supporting Actor (Hackman); Directors Guild of America Awards '92: Best Director (Eastwood); Golden Globe Awards '93: Best Director (Eastwood), Best Supporting Actor (Hackman); Los Angeles Film Critics Association Awards '92: Best Actor (Eastwood), Best Director (Eastwood), Best Film, Best Screenplay, Best Supporting Actor (Hackman); New York Film Critics Awards '92: Best Supporting Actor (Hackman); National Society of Film Critics Awards '92: Best Director (Eastwood), Best Film, Best Screenplay, Best Supporting Actor (Hackman); Nominations: Academy Awards '92: Best Actor (Eastwood), Best Art Direction/Set Decoration, Best Cinematography, Best Original Screenplay, Best Sound. *WAR, MOV, BTV*

The Unholy 🎬½ **1988 (R)** A New Orleans priest battles a demon that's killing innocent parishioners. Confusing and heavy-handed. **100m/C VHS, Beta, LV.** Ben Cross, Hal Holbrook, Trevor Howard, Ned Beatty, William Russ, Jim Carroll; *D:* Camilo Vila; *W:* Philip Yordan; *M:* Roger Bellon. *ART, VES, HHE*

Unholy Four ♂½ *A Stranger Came Home* 1954 An amnesiac returns home after three years to attempt to find out which of his three fishing buddies left him for dead. Confusing at times, but has some suspenseful moments. 80m/B VHS, Beta, LV. *GB* Paulette Goddard, Paul Carpenter, William Sylvester, Patrick Holt, Russell Napier; *D:* Terence Fisher; *W:* Michael Carreras. *NO*

Unholy Rollers ♂ *Leader of the Pack* 1972 (R) Jennings stars as a factory worker who makes it big as a tough, violent roller derby star. Typical "Babes-on-Wheels" film that promises nothing and delivers even less. 88m/C VHS. Claudia Jennings, Louis Quinn, Betty Anne Rees, Roberta Collins, Alan Vint, Candice Roman; *D:* Vernon Zimmerman. *HBO*

The Unholy Three ♂♂♂½ 1925 Ventriloquist Chaney, working with other carnival cohorts, uses his talent to gain entrance to homes which he later robs. Things go awry when two of the gang strike out on their own and the victim is killed. When the wrong man is accused, his girl, one of Chaney's gang, begs Chaney to get him free, which he does by using his vocal talents. Chaney decides being a criminal is just too hard and goes back to his ventriloquism. 70m/B VHS. Lon Chaney Sr., Harry Earles, Victor McLaglen, Mae Busch, Matt Moore, Matthew Betz, William Humphreys; *D:* Tod Browning. *NO*

The Unholy Three ♂♂♂ 1930 Chaney remade his silent hit of 1925 for his first and only talking picture (he died before the film was released). The story is essentially the same. Chaney is a ventriloquist who, with his circus friends, work as scam artists and thieves. When an innocent man is accused of their crimes Chaney tries his ventriloquist tricks to come to his aid, only in this version Chaney is exposed as a fraud and is sent to prison. Rumors that Chaney was a mute had him agreeing to appear in a "talkie" and he actually used five different voices for his various roles. 75m/B VHS, LV. Lon Chaney Sr., Lila Lee, Elliott Nugent, Harry Earles, John Miljan; *D:* Jack Conway. *FCT*

Unholy Wife ♂♂½ 1957 A young woman plans to murder her wealthy husband, but her plan goes awry when she accidentally kills someone else. Muddled and heavy-handed, with Steiger chewing scenery. 94m/C VHS, Beta. Rod Steiger, Diana Dors, Tom Tryon, Marie Windsor, Beulah Bondi; *D:* John Farrow. *HHE*

Unhook the Stars ♂♂½ 1996 (R) Director Cassavetes does mom Rowlands proud (and she him) with the lead role of widowed Mildred, who discovers there's life after the kids leave the nest. At loose ends, Mildred befriends her wild young neighbor Monica (Tomei), who conveniently needs a babysitter for her solemn six-year-old son, J.J. (Lloyd). Monica also tries to get Mildred to loosen up by taking her to a local joint, where French-Canadian trucker Tommy (Depardieu) knows a good woman when he sees one. Mildred makes some tentative steps towards independence and we get to enjoy the stellar Rowlands once again.*CW:* Strong language. 105m/C VHS, LV, Closed Caption. Gena Rowlands, Marisa Tomei, Gerard Depardieu, Moira Kelly, Jake Lloyd, David Sherrill; *D:* Nick Cassavetes; *W:* Helen Caldwell, Nick Cassavetes; *C:* Phedon Papamichael; *M:* Steven Hufsteter. Nominations: Screen Actors Guild Award '96: Best Actress (Rowlands), Best Supporting Actress (Tomei). *TOU*

Unicorn ♂♂ 1983 A small boy hears the legend that if one rubs the horn of a Unicorn his wishes will come true. Mistakenly he buys a one-horned goat and sets out to fulfill his dreams. 29m/C VHS, Beta. *GB* Diana Dors, David Kossoff, Celia Johnson; *D:* Carol Reed. *NLC*

Unidentified Flying Oddball ♂♂½ 1979 (G) An astronaut and his robotic buddy find their spaceship turning into a time machine that throws them back into Arthurian times and at the mercy of Merlin the magician. Futuristic version of Twain's "A Connecticut Yankee at King Arthur's Court." 92m/C VHS, Beta. Dennis Dugan, Jim Dale, Ron

Moody, Kenneth More, Rodney Bewes; *D:* Russ Mayberry. *DIS*

The Uninvited ♂♂♂ 1944 A brother and sister buy a house in England, only to find it is haunted. Doors open and close by themselves, strange scents fill the air, and they hear sobbing during the night. Soon they are visited by a woman with an odd link to the house—her mother is the spirit who haunts the house. Chilling and unforgettable, this is one of the first films to deal seriously with ghosts. 99m/B VHS, LV. Ray Milland, Ruth Hussey, Donald Crisp, Cornelia Otis Skinner, Gail Russell, Alan Napier, Dorothy Stickney; *D:* Lewis Allen; *W:* Dodie Smith; *C:* Charles B(ryant) Lang; *M:* Victor Young. Nominations: Academy Awards '44: Best Black and White Cinematography. *USH*

The Uninvited woof! 1988 A mutant cat goes berserk onboard a luxury yacht, killing the passengers one by one with big, nasty, pointy teeth. 89m/C VHS, Beta, LV. George Kennedy, Alex Cord, Clu Gulager, Toni Hudson, Eric Larson, Shari Shattuck, Austin Stoker; *D:* Greydon Clark. *NO*

Uninvited ♂♂½ 1993 (R) Grady is a mysterious old man who leads eight misfits to the top of a sacred mountain with the promise of finding gold. But the fortune hunters have trespassed in a sacred Indian burial ground and find their nightmares becoming a violent reality.*CW:* Violence and sexuality. ?m/C VHS, LV, Closed Caption. Jack Elam, Christopher Boyer, Erin Noble, Bari Buckner, Jerry Rector, Zane Paolo, Dennis Gibbs, Ted Haler, Eno Brutto; *D:* Michael Derek Bohusz; *W:* Michael Derek Bohusz. *IMP, IME*

Union City ♂♂ 1981 (R) Deborah "Blondie" Harry's husband gets a little edgy when someone steals the milk. Murder ensues, and they're on the run from the law. Intended as a film noir spoof, and not without some good moments. 82m/C VHS, Beta, LV. Deborah Harry, Everett McGill, Dennis Lipscomb, Pat Benatar; *D:* Mark Reichart. *COL*

Union Pacific ♂♂♂ 1939 Full DeMille treatment highlights this saga about the building of America's first transcontinental railroad. Jeff Butler (McCrea) is the construction overseer who must battle saboteurs and Indians (although the U.S. Cavalry does arrive to save the day). He also gets to fall for self-sufficient postmistress Mollie Monahan (Stanwyck). DeMille borrowed the actual golden spike used to drive in the last rail in 1869 for his reenactment of the completion celebration. Based on the book "Trouble Shooters" by Ernest Haycox. 136m/B VHS, Closed Caption. Joel McCrea, Barbara Stanwyck, Robert Preston, Brian Donlevy, Akim Tamiroff, Lynne Overman, Robert Barrat, Anthony Quinn, Stanley Ridges, Henry Kolker, Evelyn Keyes, Regis Toomey; *D:* Cecil B. DeMille; *W:* Walter DeLeon, Jesse Lasky Jr., C. Gardner Sullivan; *C:* Victor Milner. *USH*

Union Station ♂♂ 1950 Holden plays the chief of the railway police for Chicago's Union Station. He learns the station is to be used as a ransom drop in a kidnapping; but for all his security, the main thug gets away with the money, and the hunt is on. Good acting raises this film above the ordinary. 80m/B VHS, Beta. William Holden, Barry Fitzgerald, Nancy Olson, Jan Sterling, Lee Marvin, Allene Roberts, Lyle Bettger; *D:* Rudolph Mate; *C:* Daniel F. Fapp. *BAR*

U.S. Marshals ♂♂ 1998 (PG-13) Jones reprises his Oscar-winning role from "The Fugitive" as the hound dog U.S. Marshal Sam Gerard in this lackluster sequel. Gerard tracks down Sheridan (Snipes) who is framed for a double homicide of two federal agents. Gerard's probing reveals that Sheridan really isn't the average Joe he seems, and the presence of shifty agent Downey, Jr. further confirms Gerard's suspicions of a government cover-up. Jones remains solid in a popular role, supported well by his sidekick Cosmo (Pantolino). The stunts equal if not better its predecessor, yet a poorly developed Sheridan, compounded by Snipes' lack of intensity drag this chase movie down to a slow crawl.*CW:* Some scenes of violence and brief language. 133m/C

VHS. Tommy Lee Jones, Robert Downey Jr., Wesley Snipes, Joe Pantoliano, Kate Nelligan, Irène Jacob, Daniel Roebuck; *D:* Stuart Baird; *W:* John Pogue; *C:* Andrzej Bartkowiak; *M:* Jerry Goldsmith. *WAR*

Universal Soldier ♂♂ 1992 (R) A reporter discovers a secret government project to design perfect robo-soldiers by using the bodies of dead GIs, including tough guys Lundgren and Van Damme who were killed in Vietnam. But the knowledge is going to get her killed until Van Damme has flashbacks of his past (the soldier's memories have supposedly been erased) and agrees to help her. Lundgren doesn't have the same compassion and goes after them both. Big-budget thriller with some good action sequences and a lot of violence.*CW:* Strong language and strong graphic violence. 98m/C VHS, LV, Closed Caption, DVD. Jean-Claude Van Damme, Dolph Lundgren, Ally Walker, Ed O'Ross, Jerry Orbach; *D:* Roland Emmerich. *ART*

The Unkissed Bride ♂ *Mother Goose A Go-Go* 1966 (PG) A young newlywed couple are driven to distraction by the husband's inexplicable fainting spells and his strange obsession with Mother Goose. 82m/C VHS, Beta. Tommy Kirk, Anne Helm, Danica D'Hondt, Henny Youngman; *D:* Jack H. Harris.

The Unknown ♂♂♂½ 1927 Typically morbid Chaney fare has him working as a circus freak while trying to win the heart of his assistant. After drastic romancing he's still rejected by her, so he plots to kill the object of her intentions. Ghoulish as it is, the picture is really top-notch. 60m/B VHS. Lon Chaney Sr., Norman Kerry, Joan Crawford, Nick De Ruiz, Frank Lanning, John St. Polis; *D:* Tod Browning. *FCT*

Unknown Island ♂½ 1948 Scientists travel to a legendary island where dinosaurs supposedly still exist. Bogus dinosaurs and cliche script. 76m/C VHS. Virginia Grey, Philip Reed, Richard Denning, Barton MacLane; *D:* Jack Bernhard. *NOS, MOV, HEG*

Unknown Origin ♂♂ *The Alien Within; Roger Corman Presents: The Alien Within* 1995 (R) Scientific crew is stuck in an underwater installation with a deadly parasite. It's "Aliens" under the sea but a few twists will tweak your interest. Made for cable.*CW:* Violence; nudity; brief language. 75m/C VHS. Roddy McDowall, Melanie Shatner, Alex Hyde-White, Don Stroud; *D:* Scott Levy; *W:* Alex Simon; *M:* Christopher Lennertz. *NHO*

Unknown Powers woof! 1980 (PG) Science and drama are combined to examine ESP and magic. Are they gifts or curses, and how are peoples' lives affected by them? Members of the cast introduce various sections of this totally inept film. 97m/C VHS, Beta. Samantha Eggar, Will Geer, Roscoe Lee Browne; *D:* Don Como. *GEM*

The Unknown Ranger ♂½ 1936 Allen's first cowboy role has him foiling a gang of rustlers. The real highlight turns out to be the battle between his horse and a wild stallion. Eat your heart out, Trigger! 57m/B VHS. Robert Allen, Harry Woods, Martha Tibbetts, Hal Taliaferro, Robert "Buzzy" Henry; *D:* Spencer Gordon Bennet. *GPV*

Unknown World ♂ 1951 A group of scientists tunnel to the center of the Earth to find a refuge from the dangers of the atomic world. Big start winds down fast. Director Terry Morse sometimes credited as Terrell O. Morse. 73m/B VHS, Beta. Bruce Kellogg, Marilyn Nash, Victor Kilian, Jim Bannon; *D:* Terry Morse; *M:* Ernest Gold. *NOS, SNC*

Unlawful Entry ♂♂ 1992 (R) After a break-in, Karen and Michael Carr naturally call the cops. Handsome, polite policeman Pete Davis responds to the call and agrees to help burglar-proof their home. But Pete has some definite quirks—he falls for the beauteous Karen and begins stalking the couple, deciding to get rid of Michael in order to have his wife. A lurid combination of the worst moments of "Internal Affairs" and "Fatal Attraction" undermines this usually talented cast.*CW:* Language, terror and violence, and sexuality. **107m/C VHS, LV, Letterbox, Closed Caption.** Kurt Russell, Ray Liotta, Madeleine Stowe, Roger E. Mosley, Ken Lerner, Deborah Offner, Carmen Argenziano, Andy Romano, Barry W. Blaustein, Dick Miller; *D:* Jonathan Kaplan; *W:* Lewis Colick; *C:* Jamie Anderson; *M:* James Horner. **FXV**

Unlawful Passage 1994 (R) Vacation turns into a nightmare when a man's wife is kidnapped. **?m/C VHS.** Lee Horsley. **YHV**

An Unmarried Woman 🐾🐾🐾 1978 (R) Suddenly divorced her husband of 17 years, a woman deals with change. She enters the singles scene, copes with her daughter's growing sexuality, and encounters a new self-awareness. Mazursky puts real people on screen from start to finish. **124m/C VHS, Beta.** Jill Clayburgh, Alan Bates, Cliff Gorman, Michael Murphy; *D:* Paul Mazursky; *W:* Paul Mazursky; *M:* Bill Conti. Cannes Film Festival '78: Best Actress (Clayburgh); Los Angeles Film Critics Association Awards '78: Best Screenplay; New York Film Critics Awards '78: Best Screenplay; National Society of Film Critics Awards '78: Best Screenplay; Nominations: Academy Awards '78: Best Actress (Clayburgh), Best Original Screenplay, Best Picture. **FOX**

Unmasked Part 25 🐾½ 1988 A second-generation serial killer takes up where dad left off. This one is intended to be a parody of slasher films, but it's still very bloody. **85m/C VHS, Beta.** *GB* Gregory Cox, Fiona Evans, Edward Brayshaw, Debbie Lee London; *D:* Anders Palm.

Unmasking the Idol 🐾 1986 A suave hero with tongue firmly in check battles Ninja warlords. Sequel to "Order of the Black Eagle." **90m/C VHS, Beta.** *GB* Ian Hunter, William T. Hicks, Charles K. Bibby; *D:* Worth Keeter. **CEL**

The Unnamable 🐾 1988 The adaptation of the H.P. Lovecraft story about a particular New England ancestral home haunted by a typically Lovecraftian bloodthirsty demon borne of a woman hundreds of years before. College students, between trysts, investigate the myths about it. Uncut version, unseen in theatres, available only on video good for a few giggles and thrills. **87m/C VHS, Beta, LV.** Charles King, Mark Kinsey Stephenson, Alexandra Durrell, Laura Albert, Eben Ham, Blane Wheatley, Mark Parra, Katrin Alexandre; *D:* Jean-Paul Ouellette; *W:* Jean-Paul Ouellette; *C:* Tom Fraser. **VTR, THV**

The Unnamable 2: The Statement of Randolph Carter 🐾½ *H.P. Lovecraft's The Unnamable Returns; The Unnamable Returns* 1992 (R) Randolph Carter is investigating a series of murders at Miskatonic University. Evidence leads Carter back to a 17th-century warlock who had the misfortune to summon an evil creature known as Alyda. The half-demon, half-woman now wants to permanently return to the mortal plane and every new victim just helps her evil purpose along. Based on a story by H.P. Lovecraft. *CW:* Nudity and horror violence. **104m/C VHS, LV, Closed Caption.** Mark Kinsey Stephenson, John Rhys-Davies, David Warner, Julie Strain, Maria Ford, Charles Klausmeyer; *D:* Jean-Paul Ouellette; *W:* Jean-Paul Ouellette; *C:* Greg Gardiner.

Unnatural 🐾🐾½ 1952 A mad scientist creates a souless child from the genes of a murderer and a prostitute. The child grows up to be the beautiful Neff, who makes a habit of seducing and destroying men. Dark, arresting film from a very popular German story. **90m/B VHS.** Hildegarde Neff, Erich von Stroheim, Karl-Heinz Boehm, Harry Meyen, Harry Helm, Denise Vernac, Julia Koschka; *D:* Arthur Maria Rabenalt. **SNC**

Unnatural Causes 🐾🐾🐾 1986 A dying Vietnam vet believes that his illness is the result of exposure to Agent Orange. With the help of a VA counselor, they lobby for national programs to assist other veterans who have been exposed to the chemical and together bring publicity to the issue. A made-for-television drama that is exceptionally well-acted. **96m/C VHS, Beta, LV.** John Ritter, Patti LaBelle, Alfre Woodard, John Sayles, Sean McCann, John Vargas, Gwen E. Davis; *D:* Lamont Johnson; *W:* John Sayles; *M:* Charles Fox. **NO**

Unnatural Pursuits 🐾🐾 1991 Playwright Simon Gray's black comic look at a British playwright's sojourn from London to L.A., Dallas, and New York and the Broadway debut of his new work. Alcoholic Hamish Partt (Bates), in the throes of a midlife crisis, is plagued by ego, indignities, and hostile actors, audiences, and critics as he tries desperately to work. Made for British TV. **60m/C VHS.** *GB* Alan Bates, Keith Szarabajka, Deborah Rush, John Mahoney, Tom Hickey, Richard Wilson, David Healy, Jack Gilpin, Paul Zimet, Bob Balaban; *W:* Simon Gray. **TVC**

An Unremarkable Life 🐾🐾 1989 (PG) Two aging sisters live symbiotically together, until one views the other's romantic attachment to a charming widower as destructive to her own life. **97m/C VHS, Beta.** Shelley Winters, Patricia Neal, Mako, Rochelle Oliver, Charles S. Dutton, Lily Knight; *D:* Amin Q. Chaudhri. **IME, COL**

Unsane 🐾🐾½ *Tenebrae; Sotto gli Occhi dell'Assassino* 1982 A mystery novelist realizes that a series of bizarre murders strangely resembles the plot of his latest book. Bloody fun from Argento. **91m/C VHS.** *IT* Anthony (Tony) Franciosa, John Saxon, Daria Nicolodi, Giuliano Gemma, Christian Borromeo, Mirella D'Angelo, Veronica Lario, Ania Pieroni, Carola Stagnaro, John Steiner, Lara Wendell; *D:* Dario Argento; *W:* Dario Argento; *C:* Luciano Tovoli.

The Unseen 🐾½ 1980 Three young women from a television station are covering a story in a remote area of California. Before nightfall, two are horribly killed, leaving the third to come face to face with the terror. **91m/C VHS, Beta.** Barbara Bach, Sydney Lassick, Stephen Furst; *D:* Peter Foleg. **NO**

Unsettled Land 🐾🐾 1988 (PG) Young Israeli settlers try to survive the elements and Bedouin attackers in Palestine during the 1920s. **109m/C VHS, Beta, LV, 8mm.** *IS* Kelly McGillis, John Shea, Arnon Zadok, Christine Boisson; *D:* Uri Barbash. **NLC**

The Unsinkable Molly Brown 🐾🐾🐾 1964 A spunky backwoods girl is determined to break into the upper crust of Denver's high society and along the way survives the sinking of the Titanic. This energetic version of the Broadway musical contains many Meredith Willson ("Music Man") songs and lots of hokey, good-natured fun. ♫Colorado Is My Home; Leadville Johnny Brown (Soliloquy); I Ain't Down Yet; Belly Up to the Bar, Boys; He's My Friend; I've Already Started; The Beautiful People of Denver; I May Never Fall in Love with You; Up Where the People Are. **128m/C VHS, Beta, LV, Letterbox.** Debbie Reynolds, Harve Presnell, Ed Begley Sr., Martita Hunt, Hermione Baddeley; *D:* Charles Walters; *C:* Daniel F. Fapp; *M:* Meredith Willson. Nominations: Academy Awards '64: Best Actress (Reynolds), Best Adapted Score, Best Art Direction/Set Decoration (Color), Best Color Cinematography, Best Costume Design (Color), Best Sound. **MGM**

The Unstoppable Man 🐾½ 1959 The son of an American businessman is kidnapped while they are in London. No pushover he, dad develops his own plan to destroy the criminals, eventually pursuing them with a flame thrower. **68m/B VHS, Beta.** *GB* Cameron Mitchell, Marius Goring, Harry H. Corbett, Lois Maxwell, Denis Gilmore; *D:* Terry Bishop. **NOS, SNC**

Unstrung Heroes 🐾🐾½ 1995 (PG) Semi-autobiographical tale of Steven Lidz (Watt), growing up in 1960s California with a mother who is dying of cancer (MacDowell) and a nutty professor-type father (Turturro) who refuses to accept her illness. A desperate Steven goes to live with his two oddball uncles (Richards and Chaykin) who provide understanding and insight for the youngster, as well as a new name, Franz. Moving and quirky without being sappy, Keaton's feature debut avoids what would've been easy stereotypes. Based on the autobiography by Franz Lidz. **93m/C VHS, LV, Closed Caption.** Andie MacDowell, John Turturro, Michael Richards, Maury Chaykin, Nathan Watt, Kendra Krull; *D:* Diane Keaton; *W:* Richard LaGravenese; *C:* Phedon Papamichael; *M:* Thomas Newman. Nominations: Academy Awards '95: Best Original Score. **HPH**

Unsuitable Job for a Woman 🐾🐾½ 1982 Independent Cordelia Gray, following the death of her boss, takes over his detective agency and gets involved with murder. Based on the novel by P.D. James. **94m/C VHS, Beta.** *GB* Pippa Guard, Paul Freeman, Billie Whitelaw; *D:* Christopher Petit. **NO**

The Untamable 🐾🐾 1923 Unusual silent about volatile woman suffering from schizophrenia. **65m/B VHS, Beta.** Gladys Walton, Malcolm McGregor, John St. Polis, Etta Lee; *D:* Herbert Blache. **GPV, FCT**

Untamed Heart 🐾🐾½ 1993 (PG-13) Adam (Slater), the painfully shy busboy with a heart condition, loves Caroline (Tomei), the bubbly waitress, from afar. She doesn't notice him until he saves her from some would-be rapists and their love blooms in the coffee shop where they both work. Tomei and Slater are both strong in the leads and Perez, as Caroline's best buddy Cindy, hurls comic barbs with ease. Charmingly familiar surroundings help set this formulaic romance apart. Filmed on location in Minneapolis. Laserdisc version is in letterbox format. *CW:* Strong language, strong violence, and sensuality. **102m/C VHS, Beta, LV, Letterbox, Closed Caption.** Christian Slater, Marisa Tomei, Rosie Perez, Kyle Secor, Willie Garson; *D:* Tony Bill; *W:* Tom Sierchio; *M:* Cliff Eidelman. MTV Movie Awards '93: Most Desirable Male (Slater), Best Kiss (Christian Slater/Marisa Tomei). **MGM**

Until September 🐾🐾 1984 (R) An American tourist becomes stranded in Paris. She meets and falls in love with a married banker while she is stuck in her hotel. Routine romance. **96m/C VHS, Beta, Closed Caption.** Karen Allen, Thierry Lhermitte, Christopher Cazenove, Johanna Pavlis; *D:* Richard Marquand; *M:* John Barry. **MGM**

Until the End of the World 🐾🐾🐾½ 1991 (R) Convoluted road movie set in 1999 follows the travails of Sam Farber (Hurt) through 15 cities in eight countries on four continents as he is chased by Dommartin, his lover (Neill), a bounty hunter, a private detective, and bank robbers, until all wind up in the Australian outback. And this is only the first half of the movie. For true cinematic satisfaction, don't expect logic—just go with the flow. Visually stunning, unexpectedly humorous, with excellent performances from an international cast. Footage created with high definition (HDTV) video technology is a technological first. The soundtrack features Lou Reed, David Byrne, U2, and others. *CW:* Language and sensuality. **158m/C VHS, Beta, LV, Closed Caption.** William Hurt, Solveig Dommartin, Sam Neill, Max von Sydow, Ruediger Vogler, Ernie Dingo, Jeanne Moreau; *D:* Wim Wenders; *W:* Wim Wenders, Peter Carey; *M:* Graeme Revell. **WAR**

Until They Get Me 🐾½ 1918 Northern Mountie rides horse in silence as he tracks criminal to the edge of the earth. **58m/B VHS, Beta.** Pauline Starke, Joe King. **GPV, FCT**

Until They Sail 🐾🐾½ 1957 Soap opera set in New Zealand during WWII. Plot centers around the lives of four sisters involved in love and murder. Dee's film debut. Based on a story by James Michener. **95m/B VHS, Closed Caption.** Jean Simmons, Joan Fontaine, Paul Newman, Piper Laurie, Charles Drake, Sandra Dee, Wally Cassell, Alan Napier; *D:* Robert Wise; *W:* Robert Anderson. **MGM**

The Untold Story 🐾🐾 *The Untold Story: Human Meat Roast Pork Buns* 1993 New restaurant owner Wong discovers that the previous owner and his family mysteriously disappeared. Then the police detective (Lee) on the case makes a very shocking discovery. Modern cult classic includes footage cut from the original Hong Kong release and its violence is not for the squeamish. Cantonese with subtitles. **95m/C VHS, LV, Letterbox.** *HK* Anthony Wong, Danny Lee; *D:* Herman Yau. **TAI**

The Untouchables 🐾🐾🐾½ 1987 (R) Big-budget, fast-paced, and exciting re-evaluation of the popular TV series about the real-life battle between Treasury officer Eliot Ness and crime boss Al Capone in 1920s' Chicago. History sometimes takes a back seat to Hollywood's imagination in the screenplay, but it doesn't really matter since there are splendid performances by De Niro as Capone and Connery as Ness' mentor to help it look realistic. Costner does a fine job showing the change in Ness from naive idealism to steely conviction. Beautifully filmed with excellent special effects. 119m/C VHS, Beta, LV, 8mm, Letterbox, Closed Caption. Kevin Costner, Sean Connery, Robert De Niro, Andy Garcia, Charles Martin Smith, Billy Drago, Richard Bradford, Jack Kehoe; **D:** Brian DePalma; **W:** David Mamet; **C:** Stephen Burum; **M:** Ennio Morricone. Academy Awards '87: Best Supporting Actor (Connery); Golden Globe Awards '88: Best Supporting Actor (Connery); National Board of Review Awards '87: Best Supporting Actor (Connery); Nominations: Academy Awards '87: Best Art Direction/Set Decoration, Best Costume Design, Best Original Score. PAR, BTV

Unveiled 🎞🎞½ 1994 (R) Stephanie Montgomery's (Zane) friend falls victim to a killer in Marrakesh. So Steph sets out to trap the killer, with the help of government official Peter (Hubley).**CW:** Language, brief nudity, and sexual situations. 103m/C VHS, LV, Closed Caption. Lisa Zane, Whip Hubley, Nicholas Chinlund, Martha Gehman; **D:** William Cole; **W:** Michael Diamond, Roger Kumble; **M:** Christopher Tyng. FXV

Unzipped 🎞🎞🎞 1994 (R) Witty, behind-the-scenes look at whiz-kid fashion designer Isaac Mizrahi as he prepares for the showing of his 1994 collection. Alternately filmed in black-and-white and color in a variety of film stocks, Keeve (Mizrahi's former lover) captures Mizrahi's varying moods, from his creative struggles to his unique sense of humor and gift for mimicry. Highlights include scenes with Mizrahi's doting mother. Fashionphiles will love every minute, and strictly off-the-rack viewers can enjoy the supermodels on parade.**CW:** Some language. 76m/C VHS, LV, Closed Caption. **D:** Douglas Keeve. Sundance Film Festival '95: Audience Award. WAR

Up Against the Wall 🎞🎞 1991 (PG-13) A black kid from the Chicago projects attends school in the affluent suburbs, but there too he must resist temptation, crime and violence. A well-intentioned but didactic cautionary drama, adapted from the book by African-American author/commentator Dr. Jawanza Kunjufu. 103m/C VHS. Marla Gibbs, Stoney Jackson, Catero Colbert, Ron O'Neal, Salli Richardson; **D:** Ron O'Neal. BMG

Up Close and Personal 🎞🎞🎞 1996 (PG-13) Ambitious Reno card dealer Tally Atwater (Pfeiffer) wants to get into broadcasting and finds her chance at a Miami TV station where she's mentored by successful veteran-reporter-turned-producer Warren Justice (Redford). They fall in love but find their careers clashing as Tally climbs the media success ladder. Originally inspired by the tragic life of NBC reporter Jessica Savitch, whose problems with drugs and abusive relationships led to a sad ending, film turned into a star-powered romance with media trappings and another variation of "A Star is Born." It's now "suggested" by Alanna Nash's book "Golden Girl."**CW:** Brief strong language, some sensuality and depictions of violence. 124m/C VHS, LV, Closed Caption. Michelle Pfeiffer, Robert Redford, Kate Nelligan, Stockard Channing, Joe Mantegna, Glenn Plummer, James Rebhorn, Noble Willingham, Scott Bryce, Raymond Cruz, Dedee Pfeiffer, Miguel Sandoval, James Karen; **D:** Jon Avnet; **W:** Joan Didion, John Gregory Dunne; **C:** Karl Walter Lindenlaub; **M:** Thomas Newman. Nominations: Academy Awards '96: Best Song ("Because You Loved Me"); Golden Globe Awards '97: Best Song ("Because You Loved Me"). TOU

Up/Down/Fragile 🎞🎞 Haut Bas Fragile 1995 New Wavish musical following the fortunes of three young women in Paris. Louise (Denicourt) has just emerged from a coma after several years and is living in a tiny apartment though she has inherited the antiques-filled home of an aunt; Ninon (Richard) has fled from her gangster boyfriend and gotten a job as a delivery girl; and the

adopted Ida (Cote) has become obsessed with learning the identities of her biological parents. Their link is Roland (Marcon) who knows all three. The mood's more important than the plot anyway. French with subtitles. 169m/C VHS. FR Marianne Denicourt, Laurence Cote, Nathalie Richard, Andre Marcon, Anna Karina; **D:** Jacques Rivette; **C:** Christophe Pollock; **M:** Francois Breant. CPA

Up from the Depths 🎞½ 1979 (R) Something from beneath the ocean is turning the paradise of Hawaii into a nightmare. Prehistoric fish are returning to the surface with one thing on their minds—lunch. "Jaws" rip-off played for humor. 85m/C VHS, Beta. Sam Bottoms, Suzanne Reed, Virgil Frye; **D:** Charles B. Griffith; **W:** Alfred Sweeney; **M:** James Horner. ART, VES

Up in Arms 🎞🎞 1944 Danny Kaye's first film presents a typical Kaye scenario: he plays a twitching hypochondriac who is drafted into the Army and sneaks his girlfriend aboard the troopship bound for the Pacific. Features an appearance by the Goldwyn Girls. Remake of the film "The Nervous Wreck." ♫Theatre Lobby Number; Now I Know; All Out for Freedom; Tess's Torch Song; Melody in 4-F. 105m/C VHS. Danny Kaye, Dinah Shore, Constance Dowling, Dana Andrews, Margaret Dumont, Goldwyn Girls, Lyle Talbot, Louis Calhern, Charles Halton; **D:** Elliott Nugent; **C:** Ray Rennahan. Nominations: Academy Awards '44: Best Song ("Now I Know"), Scoring of a Musical. HBO

Up in Central Park 🎞🎞½ 1948 Poor adaptation of the hit Broadway musical (the studio removed much of Romberg's score) about Irish immigrant lass Rosie Moore (Durbin), who teams up with New York reporter John Matthews (Haymes) to expose corrupt politician Boss Tweed (Price). Without the songs, the plot is shown to be wafer-thin. ♫When She Walks in the Room; Carousel in the Park; Oh Say Do You See What I See?; Pace, Pace Mio Dio. 88m/B VHS, Closed Caption. Deanna Durbin, Dick Haymes, Vincent Price, Albert Sharpe, Tom Powers, Hobart Cavanaugh, Thurston Hall; **D:** William A. Seiter; **W:** Dorothy Fields, Herbert Fields, Karl Tunberg; **C:** Milton Krasner; **M:** Sigmund Romberg. USH

Up in the Air 🎞🎞 1940 Darro and Moreland have ambitions as radio comedians, and their friend Reynolds wants to be a singer. Their break comes when other performers are murdered on the air. First, though, they must solve the killings. 62m/B VHS. Frankie Darro, Marjorie Reynolds, Mantan Moreland, Gordon Jones, Tristram Coffin, John Holland, Carleton Young; **D:** Howard Bretherton. NOS

Up Periscope 🎞🎞½ 1959 Garner is a demolitions expert unwillingly assigned to a submarine commanded by O'Brien. His mission: to sneak onto a Japanese-held island and steal a top-secret code book. Trouble is, O'Brien may not wait for Garner to complete his mission before taking the sub back underwater. A routine submarine film. 111m/C VHS, LV, Letterbox. James Garner, Edmond O'Brien, Andra Martin, Alan Hale Jr., Carleton Carpenter, Frank Gifford, Richard Bakalayan; **D:** Gordon Douglas. WAR

Up River 🎞 1979 Wealthy land baron rapes and murders the wife of a simple pioneer, who is beaten and whose homestead is burned by the baron as well. The pioneer lives to seek terrible vengeance. 90m/C VHS. Jeff Corey, Morgan Stevens, Debbie AuLuce; **D:** Carl Kitt. NO

Up the Academy 🎞 Mad Magazine's Up the Academy; The Brave Young Men of Weinberg 1980 (R) Four teenaged delinquents are sent to an academy for wayward boys where they encounter a sadistic headmaster and a gay dance instructor. Sometimes inventive, often tasteless fare from "Mad" magazine. 88m/C VHS, Beta. Ron Leibman, Ralph Macchio, Barbara Bach, Tom Poston, Stacey Nelkin, Wendell Brown, Tom Citera; **D:** Robert Downey. WAR

Up the Creek 🎞🎞 1958 Crazy antics abound in this tale of an old British destroyer, a black-market scheme run by the crew, and the new skipper whose hobby is rocket building. Followed by "Further Up the River." 83m/B VHS, Beta. GB David Tomlinson, Wilfrid Hyde-White, Peter Sellers, Vera Day, Michael Goodliffe, Lionel Jeffries; **D:** Val Guest. MON

Up the Creek 🎞½ 1984 (R) Four college losers enter a whitewater raft race to gain some respect for their school. The soundtrack features songs by Heart, Cheap Trick and The Beach Boys. Routine. 95m/C VHS, Beta, LV. Tim Matheson, Jennifer Runyon, Stephen Furst, John Hillerman, James B. Sikking, Julia Montgomery, Jeana Tomasina; **D:** Robert Butler; **M:** William Goldstein. ART, VES

Up the Down Staircase 🎞🎞🎞 1967 A naive, newly trained New York public school teacher is determined to teach the finer points of English literature to a group of poor students. She almost gives up until one student actually begins to learn. Good production and acting. Based on Bel Kaufman's novel. 124m/C VHS. Sandy Dennis, Patrick Bedford, Eileen Heckart, Ruth White, Jean Stapleton, Sorrell Booke; **D:** Robert Mulligan. WAR, OM

Up the Sandbox 🎞🎞 1972 (R) A bored housewife fantasizes about her life in order to avoid facing her mundane existence. Fine acting from Streisand, with real problems of young mothers accurately shown. 98m/C VHS, Beta. Barbra Streisand, David Selby, Jane Hoffman, Barbara Rhoades; **D:** Irvin Kershner; **C:** Gordon Willis; **M:** Billy Goldenberg. WAR

Up to a Certain Point 🎞🎞 Up to a Point; Hasta Cierto Punto 1983 Writer Oscar believes he has a liberal attitude (to go along with Cuban political ideology) but his belief is shaken when he interviews workers on the Havana docks about their notions of machismo. Seems when Oscar falls for a sexy dockworker his ideas of maleness and a woman's place are more traditional than he imagines. Spanish with subtitles. 70m/C VHS. CU Oscar Alvarez, Mirta Ibarra, Omar Valdes, Coralia Veloz, Rogelio Blain, Ana Vina; **D:** Tomas Gutierrez Alea; **W:** Tomas Gutierrez Alea; **M:** Leo Brower. NYF

Up Your Alley 🎞🎞 1989 (R) A female reporter, pursuing a story on homelessness, and a skidrow bum find romance. Langston, who produced and co-wrote the film, is better known as "The Unknown Comic." 90m/C VHS, Beta, LV. Linda Blair, Murray Langston, Ruth Buzzi, Johnny Dark, Bob Zany, Yakov Smirnoff; **D:** Bob Logan. ART

Uphill All the Way 🎞🎞 1985 A couple of card-cheatin' good old boys are pursued by posses and cavalry alike, and end up killing real outlaws. Made for television. 91m/C VHS, Beta. Roy Clark, Mel Tillis, Glen Campbell, Trish Van Devere, Burl Ives, Burt Reynolds; **D:** Frank Q. Dobbs. VTR

Upper Crust 🎞½ 1988 Boring tale of corruption and greed that takes place at the highest levels of American business and government. 95m/C VHS, Beta. Frank Gorshin, Broderick Crawford, Nigel Davenport. NO

The Uprising 🎞🎞🎞 1981 A Nicaraguan drama filmed just months after the 1979 Sandinista revolution, wherein a young guard of Somoza retains his job for the money, while his father is active in the revolutionary forces. In Spanish with English subtitles. 96m/C VHS, Beta. SP **D:** Peter Lilienthal. KIV

Uptown Angel 🎞🎞 1990 (R) A young woman is determined to work her way out of her home on the wrong side of town. Black cast brings new life to old premise. 90m/C VHS. Caron Tate, Cliff McMullen, Gloria Davis Hill, Tracy Hill; **D:** Joy Shannon; **W:** Joy Shannon. XVC

Uptown New York 🎞🎞 1932 A young man pressured by his family marries a rich girl instead of the woman he loves, who in turn marries a man she does not love. Routine melodrama. 81m/B VHS, Beta. Jack Oakie, Shirley Green, Leon Ames, Shirley Grey, George Cooper, Raymond Hatton; **D:** Victor Schertzinger. NOS, FCT, DVT

Uptown Saturday Night 🐾🐾½ 1974 (PG) Two working men attempt to recover a stolen lottery ticket from the black underworld after being ripped off at an illegal gambling place. Good fun, with nice performances from both leads and from Belafonte doing a black "Godfather" parody of Brando. Followed by "Let's Do It Again." 104m/C VHS, Beta. Sidney Poitier, Bill Cosby, Harry Belafonte, Flip Wilson, Richard Pryor, Calvin Lockhart; **D:** Sidney Poitier; **W:** Richard Wesley; **C:** Fred W. Koenekamp. WAR

The Uranium Conspiracy 🐾½ 1978 (PG) A secret agent and a mercenary soldier try to stop a shipment of uranium out of Zaire from falling into enemy hands. It won't be easy. 100m/C VHS, Beta. Fabio Testi, Janet Agren, Assaf Dayan. NO

Uranus 🐾🐾🐾 1991 (R) After WWII a French provincial town has been liberated from Nazi invaders—but not its own suspicions, as citizens try to rebuild knowing some of them collaborated with the enemy. An important subject is heavily talked over in static fashion, with a robust Depardieu either a standout or a ham as the earthy saloon-keeper. Based on a novel by Marcel Ayme, himself accused of pro-Vichy leanings during the era. In French with English subtitles. 100m/C VHS, LV. FR Gerard Depardieu, Michel Blanc, Jean-Pierre Marielle, Philippe Noiret, Gerard Desarthe, Michel Galabru, Fabrice Luchini, Daniel Prevost; **D:** Claude Berri; **W:** Claude Berri; **M:** Jean-Claude Petit. NO

Urban Cowboy 🐾🐾½ 1980 (PG) A young Texas farmer comes to Houston to work in a refinery. After work he hangs out at Gilley's, a roadhouse bar. Here he and his friends, dressed in their cowboy gear, drink, fight, and prove their manhood by riding a mechanical bull. Film made Winger a star, was an up in Travolta's roller coaster career, and began the craze for country western apparel and dance and them there mechanical bulls. Ride 'em, cowboy! 135m/C VHS, Beta, LV. John Travolta, Debra Winger, Scott Glenn, Madolyn Smith, Barry Corbin; **D:** James Bridges; **W:** James Bridges, Aaron Latham; **C:** Reynaldo Villalobos; **M:** Ralph Burns. PAR

Urban Crossfire 🐾🐾½ 1994 (PG-13) Two veteran white Brooklyn detectives investigating gang violence are aided by a young black patrolman whose partner was killed by a gang leader. Solid cast, fast paced action. **CW:** Profanity, brief nudity, and violence, drug abuse. 95m/C VHS, LV. Mario Van Peebles, Ray Sharkey, Peter Boyle, Michael Boatman; **D:** Dick Lowry. NHO

Urban Warriors 🐾 1975 Savage barbarians roam and pillage a post-nuclear war Earth, but one invincible warrior ushers them out. 90m/C VHS, Beta. Karl Landgren, Alex Vitale, Deborah Keith; **D:** Joseph Warren.

Urge to Kill 🐾 1984 (PG) A man returning from a mental hospital after pleading temporary insanity to the murder of his girlfriend returns to her town and tries to uncover the truth, with the help of her younger sister. Made for television. 96m/C VHS, Beta. Karl Malden, Holly Hunter, William Devane, Alex McArthur; **D:** Mike Robe. FOX, VTR

Urotsukidoj 1: Legend of the Overfiend 🐾🐾 The Wandering Kid 1993 (NC-17) Legend has it that the world is made up of Humans, Man-Beasts, and Monster-Demons. Every 3000 years superfiend Chojin is supposed to unite the three into a single Land of Eternity. However, the heroic Amano discovers this land will be a nightmare world and unless he can successfully battle Chojin humanity may not survive. Ultra-violent and sexually explicit. Animated; dubbed into English. 108m/C VHS. JP CPM, MOV

Urotsukidoj 2: Legend of the Demon Womb 🐾🐾 1993 The fiendish Dr. Munhihausen's life work has been to render the dimensional boundaries between the World of Man-Beasts and the World of Monster Demons and to conjure the dreaded Overfiend. Years later, his son seeks to find a way to conquer the Overfiend and his cohorts from Hell and assume its powers for himself. Munhihausen's efforts may

soon be rewarded when his hapless cousin, who accidentally received the demon's blood, begins developing monstrous powers. Animated; dubbed from Japanese. 88m/C VHS. JP CPM, MOV

Ursus in the Valley of the Lions 🐾½ The Mighty Ursus; Ursus 1962 Ursus attempts to rescue his love from druids but is dismayed to find that she has taken up homicide in her free time. 92m/C VHS. IT SP Ed Fury, Luis Prendes, Moira Orfei, Cristina Gajoni, Maria Luisa Merlo; **D:** Carlo Campogalliani. SNC

Urusei Yatsura Movie 1: Only You 198? Lum is a Princess of the Oni, an alien race who have come to repossess Earth. The planet's one chance is for an earthling to beat Lum in the Oni's national sport—tag. When unlucky teenager Ataru Moroboshi is chosen he actually beats Lum. Which means he has to marry her. In Japanese with English subtitles. 100m/C VHS. JP ANI

Urusei Yatsura Movie 2: Beautiful Dreamer 1992 Unlucky teenager Ataru Moroboshi and his classmates at Tomobiki High School find themselves reliving the day before the School Festival over and over again. Funny and dreamlike. In Japanese with English subtitles. 90m/C VHS, LV. JP Oshii Mamoru. CPM, ANI

Urusei Yatsura Movie 3: Remember My Love 1985 A magician family friend of Princess Lum put a curse on her at birth when she wasn't invited to Lum's christening (shades of "Sleeping Beauty")—that Lum would never be happy with her true love. But Ataru is the real victim. When the magician happens upon him in the new amusement park she turns him into a pink hippotamus to spite Lum. In Japanese with English subtitles. 93m/C VHS, LV. JP ANI

Urusei Yatsura Movie 4: Lum the Forever 1986 When a great cherry tree is cut down near while Lum and friends are making a movie she mysteriously loses her horns, and with them her powers. In Japanese with English subtitles. 94m/C VHS, LV. JP ANI, ING

Urusei Yatsura Movie 5: The Final Chapter 19?? Boy meets girl with Japanimation twist. Lum's fiance, Lupa, is introduced and the fate of the Earth is in Ataru's hands. Japanese with English subtitles. 90m/C VHS, LV. JP

Urusei Yatsura Movie 6: Always My Darling 1991 Space princess Lupica abducts Aturu in order to get the greatest love potion in the galaxy. Lum wants him back. In Japanese with English subtitles. 77m/C VHS. JP ANI, ING

Used Cars 🐾🐾🐾 1980 (R) A car dealer is desperate to put his jalopy shop competitors out of business. The owners go to great lengths to stay afloat. Sometimes too obnoxious, but often funny. 113m/C VHS, Beta, LV, 8mm. Kurt Russell, Jack Warden, Deborah Harmon, Gerrit Graham, Joe Flaherty, Michael McKean; **D:** Robert Zemeckis; **W:** Robert Zemeckis. COL

Used People 🐾🐾½ 1992 (PG-13) A study in ethnicity and characterization, three Oscar-winning actresses lead a talented cast playing a Jewish family living in Queens in 1969. When the father dies, Joe (Mastroianni), an old friend with an old torch for the widow, Pearl (MacLaine), shows up at the funeral and manages to charm her into a date for coffee. Pearl's new relationship with her Italian suitor affects each of the somewhat off-balance family members and washes the whole clan with a sense of hope and renewal. Adpated from screenwriter Graff's play "The Grandma Plays" that was based on memories of his grandmother. Director Kidron's American debut. 116m/C VHS, LV, Letterbox, Closed Caption. Shirley MacLaine, Marcello Mastroianni, Kathy Bates, Marcia Gay Harden, Jessica Tandy, Sylvia Sidney, Bob Dishy, Joe Pantoliano, Matthew Branton, Louis Guff, Charles Cioffi, Doris Roberts, Helen Hanft; **D:** Beeban Kidron; **W:** Todd Graff; **M:** Rachel Portman. FXV

Users 🐾🐾 1978 Small-town girl who worked as a prostitute meets a faded film star and becomes involved in the movie business. Ode to decadent Hollywood. Based on the Joyce Haber novel. Made for television. 125m/C VHS, Beta. Jaclyn Smith, Tony Curtis, John Forsythe, Red Buttons, George Hamilton; **D:** Joseph Hardy; **M:** Maurice Jarre.

The Usual Suspects 🐾🐾🐾½ 1995 (R) Twisted noir-thriller about some crooks, a $91 million heist, and mysterious crime lord Keyser Soze. Customs agent Kujan (Palminteri) tries to get a straight story out of small-time con man "Verbal" Kint (Spacey) about a burning tanker in the San Pedro harbor, 27 dead bodies, and the other four temperamental criminals involved: ex-cop-turned thief Keaton (Byrne), explosives expert Hockney (Pollak), and hot-headed partners McManus (Baldwin) and Fenster (Del Toro). Nothing is as it seems, and the ending keeps everyone guessing, right up to the final credits. Terrific performances from all complement the intelligent, humorous script. And yes, the title does come from the famous line in "Casablanca." **CW:** Violence; substantial amount of strong language. 105m/C VHS, LV, Closed Caption, DVD. Kevin Spacey, Gabriel Byrne, Chazz Palminteri, Kevin Pollak, Stephen Baldwin, Benicio Del Toro, Giancarlo Esposito, Pete Postlethwaite, Dan Hedaya, Suzy Amis, Paul Bartel, Peter Greene; **D:** Bryan Singer; **W:** Christopher McQuarrie; **C:** Newton Thomas Sigel; **M:** John Ottman. Academy Awards '95: Best Original Screenplay, Best Supporting Actor (Spacey); British Academy Awards '95: Best Original Screenplay; Independent Spirit Awards '96: Best Screenplay, Best Supporting Actor (Del Toro); National Board of Review Awards '95: Best Supporting Actor (Spacey); New York Film Critics Awards '95: Best Supporting Actor (Spacey); Broadcast Film Critics Association Awards '95: Best Supporting Actor (Spacey); Nominations: British Academy Awards '95: Best Film; Golden Globe Awards '96: Best Supporting Actor (Spacey); Independent Spirit Awards '96: Best Cinematography; Screen Actors Guild Award '95: Best Supporting Actor (Spacey). PGV

Utah 🐾🐾 1945 A musical comedy star who inherits a ranch wishes to sell it to finance one of her shows. She is persuaded not to by Rogers, the ranch foreman. 54m/B VHS, Beta. Roy Rogers, Dale Evans, George "Gabby" Hayes; **D:** John English. NOS, VDM, VCN

Utah Trail 🐾 1938 Lawman Ritter is hired to stop a gang of cattle rustlers. Cheapie oater made for Grand National, which went bankrupt soon after. 57m/B VHS, Beta. Tex Ritter; **D:** Al(bert) Herman. NOS, VCN, DVT

Utamaro and His Five Women 🐾🐾½ Five Women Around Utamaro; Utamaro O Meguru Gonin No Onna 1946 Utamaro is a legendary 19th-century Edo artist who gained inspiration from Tokyo's "floating world," of courtesans, brothels, drinking parties, and violent passions. His gorgeous portraits worship women but he dislikes the complications that flesh-and-blood females bring. Heavily stylized look at the artistic impulse. In Japanese with English subtitles. 89m/B VHS. JP Minnosuke Bando, Kinuyo Tanaka, Kotaro Bando, Hisato Osawa, Tamezo Mochizuki, Hiroko Kawasaki; **D:** Kenji Mizoguchi; **W:** Yoshikata Yoda. NYF, FCT

Utilities 🐾½ Getting Even 1983 (PG) A frustrated social worker enlists the help of his friends in his efforts to impress an attractive policewoman by taking on a large corporate utility. 94m/C VHS, Beta, LV. CA Robert Hays, Brooke Adams, John Marley, Ben Gordon, Helen Burns; **D:** Harvey Hart. ART, VES

Utopia 🐾🐾 Atoll K; Robinson Crusoeland; Escapade 1951 Laurel and Hardy inherit a paradisaical island, but their peace is disturbed when uranium is discovered. Final screen appearance of the team is diminished by poor direction and script. 82m/B VHS, Beta. FR Stan Laurel, Oliver Hardy, Suzy Delair, Max Elloy; **D:** Leo Joannon. CNG, MRV, VYY

Utu 🐾🐾 1983 (R) A Maori tribesman serving with the colonizing British army in 1870 explodes into ritual revenge when his home village is slaughtered. Filmed in New Zealand. 104m/C VHS, Beta, Closed Caption. NZ Anzac Wallace, Kelly Johnson,

Tim Elliot, Bruno Lawrence; **D:** Geoff Murphy; **M:** John Charles. *KIV, FOX*

Utz 🎬🎬½ **1993** The Baron von Utz (Mueller-Stahl) collects both women and priceless porcelain figures. When his friend, art dealer Marius Fischer (Riegert), travels to Prague for a visit he finds that both Utz's housekeeper (Fricker), who has suffered from unrequited love, and the porcelain have disappeared. So Marius teams up with the Baron's old friend Dr. Orlick (Scofield) to find out what's going on. Based on the novel by Bruce Chatwin. **95m/C VHS.** *GB GE IT* Armin Mueller-Stahl, Peter Riegert, Brenda Fricker, Paul Scofield; **D:** George Sluizer. *FRF, BTV, FCT*

V 🎬🎬🎬 **1983** Very creepy sci-fi miniseries that spawned a short-lived TV show. Advanced aliens, known as the Visitors, come to Earth on a seemingly friendly quest. But their human-like appearance is a facade—as is their mission. Fake skin masks a reptilian hide and what they want is complete planetary control. Naturally, some earthlings don't fall for their smooth talk and a resistance movement is born. Followed by miniseries conclusion "V: The Final Battle." **190m/C VHS.** Marc Singer, Jane Badler, Faye Grant, Robert Englund, Michael Durrell, Peter Nelson, Neva Patterson, Andrew Prine, Richard Herd, Rafael Campos; **D:** Kenneth Johnson; **W:** Kenneth Johnson. *WAR, MOV*

V: The Final Battle 🎬🎬½ **1984** It's four-months since the Visitors appeared on earth, proclaiming their false friendship. But a resistance movement knows these reptiles, who hide behind a human appearance, are only interested in harvesting earth's inhabitants as a new food source. Continuation of the TV miniseries "V." **285m/C VHS, Closed Caption.** Marc Singer, Robert Englund, Michael Ironside; **D:** Richard T. Heffron. *WAR*

The Vacillations of Poppy Carew 🎬🎬½ **1994** Free-spirited Poppy is just trying to make funeral arrangements for her father when she becomes involved in a series of unexpected and complicated romances. Based on a novel by Mary Wesley. **109m/C VHS.** *GB* Tara Fitzgerald, Sian Phillips, Charlotte Coleman; **D:** James Cellan Jones. *VTR, CCB*

The Vagabond **1916** The Little Tramp is a pathetic fiddler making a scanty living who rescues a damsel in distress. Silent with musical soundtrack added. **20m/B VHS, Beta.** Charlie Chaplin, Edna Purviance, Eric Campbell, Albert Austin; **D:** Charlie Chaplin. *CAB, GVV, VYY*

Vagabond 🎬🎬🎬½ *Sans Toit Ni Loi* **1985** Bleak, emotionally shattering, powerful and compelling, this film traces the peripatetic life of an amoral and selfish young French woman who has no regard for social rules and tremendous fear of responsibility in her drifting yet inexorable journey into death. Told via flashbacks from the moment when she is found dead, alone, and unaccounted for by the roadside, this film will not leave you unscathed. Written by New Wave director Varda. In French with English subtitles. **105m/C VHS, LV.** *FR* Sandrine Bonnaire, Macha Meril, Stephane Freiss, Elaine Cortadellas, Marthe Jarnias, Yolanda Moreau; **D:** Agnes Varda; **W:** Agnes Varda; **C:** Patrick Blossier. Cesar Awards '86: Best Actress (Bonnaire); Los Angeles Film Critics Association Awards '86: Best Actress (Bonnaire), Best Foreign Film. *HMV, TPV*

Vagabond Lover 🎬🎬½ **1929** The amusing tale of the loves, hopes, and dreams of an aspiring saxophone player. Rudy croons through his megaphone in his movie debut. Appealing, with Dressler sparkling in the role of the wealthy aunt. 🎵 *If You Were the Only Girl in the World; A Little Kiss Each Morning; Heigh Ho Everybody; Piccolo Pete; I Love You; I'll Be Reminded of You; I'm Just a Vagabond Lover.* **66m/B VHS, Beta.** Rudy Vallee, Sally Blane, Marie Dressler; **D:** Marshall Neilan. *VYY, RXM, DVT*

The Vagrant 🎬 **1992 (R)** Run-of-the-mill trooper with a mind game playing dorothot inhabiting the home of a young exec. A series of murders has this wimp yuppie wondering how to get rid of his unwelcome intruder. **CW:** Some violence and some sensuality. **91m/C VHS, Closed Caption.** Bill Paxton, Michael Ironside, Marshall Bell, Stuart Pankin; **D:** Chris Walas. *MGM*

Valdez Is Coming 🎬🎬½ **1971 (PG)** Though not a world-class western, this filmed-in-Spain saga does feature a probing script (based on an Elmore Leonard novel) on the nature of race relations. Fine performance by Lancaster as a Mexican-American who ignites the passions of a town, and ultimately confronts the local land baron. **90m/C VHS, Closed Caption.** Burt Lancaster, Susan Clark, Jon Cypher, Barton Heyman, Richard Jordan, Frank Silvera, Hector Elizondo; **D:** Edwin Sherin; **W:** David Rayfiel. *MGM*

Valentino 🎬🎬 **1977 (R)** Another one of director Russell's flamboyantly excessive screen biographies, this time of silent screen idol Rudolph Valentino (Nureyev). The details hardly matter but the movie is told in flashback from Valentino's funeral to his beginnings as a dance instructor and his eventual success as a screen lover. Nureyev is noticeably stiff in his screen debut but at least he possesses some charisma. **127m/C VHS.** *GB* Rudolf Nureyev, Leslie Caron, Michelle Phillips, Carol Kane, Felicity Kendal, Seymour Cassel, Peter Vaughan, William Hootkins, Huntz Hall, David DeKeyser, Alfred Marks, Anton Diffring; **D:** Ken Russell; **W:** Mardik Martin, Ken Russell, John Byrum. *MGM*

Valentino Returns 🎬🎬 **1988 (R)** A kid in 1955 California buys a pink Cadillac he nicknames "Valentino Returns," thinking it will help him meet girls, as his parents undergo a stormy divorce. Weak script fades fast from fine premise, good start. Nice period feel. **97m/C VHS, Beta, LV.** Frederic Forrest, Veronica Cartwright, Jenny Wright, Barry Tubb; **D:** Peter Hoffman. *THV*

Valley Girl 🎬🎬½ *Bad Boyz* **1983 (R)** Slight but surprisingly likeable teen romantic-comedy inspired by Frank Zappa novelty tune. Title stereotype falls for a leather-jacketed rebel. Really. It may look like a music video, but the story is straight from "Romeo and Juliet" via Southern California. Helped launch Cage's career. Music by Men at Work, Culture Club, and others. **95m/C VHS, Beta, LV.** Nicolas Cage, Deborah Foreman, Colleen Camp, Frederic Forrest; **D:** Martha Coolidge; **W:** Wayne Crawford; **C:** Frederick Elmes. *VES*

The Valley Obscured by the Clouds 🎬🎬 **1972** A group of dropouts and seekers search for the valley of the gods in the wilds of New Guinea, and experience a sexual and spiritual metamorphosis. In French with English subtitles. **106m/C VHS.** *FR* **D:** Barbet Schroeder; **C:** Nestor Almendros; **M:** Pink Floyd. *FCT, WAR, BTV*

The Valley of Decision 🎬🎬🎬 **1945** Entertaining poor-girl-meets-rich-boy story with Peck as a wealthy mill owner who falls in love with beautiful housemaid Garson (the Queen of MGM at the time). Set in 1870 Pittsburgh; based on Marcia Davenport's novel. **111m/B VHS.** Gregory Peck, Greer Garson, Donald Crisp, Lionel Barrymore, Preston Foster, Gladys Cooper, Marsha Hunt, Reginald Owen, Dan Duryea, Jessica Tandy, Barbara Everest; **D:** Tay Garnett; **W:** John Meehan, Sonya Levien; **C:** Joseph Ruttenberg. Nominations: Academy Awards '45: Best Actress (Garson), Best Original Dramatic/Comedy Score. *MGM*

Valley of Fire 🎬🎬 **1951** Autry is the mayor of a boom town that suffers from a lack of women. He decides to import a caravan of brides for the men in town but villains attempt to kidnap the women. **63m/B VHS, Beta.** Gene Autry, Gail Davis, Pat Buttram; **D:** John English. *CCB*

The Valley of Gwangi 🎬🎬🎬 **1969 (G)** One of the best prehistoric-monster-westerns out there. Cowboys discover a lost valley of dinosaurs and try to capture a vicious, carnivorous allosaurus. Bad move, kemosabe! The creatures move via the stop-motion model animation by f/x maestro Ray Harryhausen, here at his finest. **88m/C VHS, Beta, LV.** James Franciscus, Gila Golan, Richard Carlson, Laurence Naismith, Freda Jackson; **D:** James O'Connolly; **W:** William Bast. *WAR*

Valley of Terror 🎬½ **1938** Maynard is framed for cattle rustling. Can he prove his innocence? **59m/B VHS, Beta.** Kermit Maynard, Harley Wood, John Merton, Jack Ingram, Dick Curtis, Roger Williams; **D:** Al(bert) Herman. *NOS, CCB, DVT*

Valley of the Dolls 🎬🎬 **1967 (PG)** Camp/trash classic was rated as a bomb by many critics but is really of the so-bad-it's-good variety. Three beauties, Tate, Duke, and Parkins, dream of Hollywood stardom but fall victim to Hollywood excess, including drug dependency (the "dolls" of the title). There's unhappy love affairs, porno parts, health risks, and hysterics of various kinds—all designed to have you dropping your jaw in disbelief. The bathroom scene between Duke and Hayward involving a wig is not to be missed. Based on the novel by Jacqueline Susann who has a bit part as a reporter. Remade for television as "Jacqueline Susann's Valley of the Dolls" in 1981. **123m/C VHS.** Barbara Parkins, Patty Duke, Sharon Tate, Paul Burke, Tony Scotti, Martin Milner, Susan Hayward, Charles Drake, Lee Grant, Alex Davion, Robert Harris, Robert Viharo, Joey Bishop, George Jessel; **Cameos:** Jacqueline Susann; **D:** Mark Robson; **W:** Dorothy Kingsley, Helen Deutsch; **C:** William H. Daniels; **M:** John Williams. Nominations: Academy Awards '67: Best Adapted Score. *FXV, BTV*

Valley of the Eagles 🎬½ **1951** When his wife and partner take off into the Lapland wilderness with his new invention, a scientist leads the police across the tundra in pursuit. Setting is at least a plus. **83m/B VHS, Beta.** *GB* Jack Warner, Nadia Gray, John McCallum, Martin Boddey, Christopher Lee; **D:** Terence Young; **M:** Nino Rota.

Valley of the Lawless 🎬 **1936** A cowboy rides into trouble aplenty while out searching for treasure. A routine western for Brown fans only. **59m/B VHS, Beta, LV.** Johnny Mack Brown; **D:** Robert North Bradbury; **W:** Robert North Bradbury. *NO*

Valley of the Sun 🎬🎬🎬 **1942** A government agent tracks a crooked Indian liaison to prevent an Indian uprising in Arizona. Ball, well before her "Lucy" days, plays the restaurant owner both men romance. Better than average, with good cast, some laughs, and lots of excitement. **84m/B VHS, Beta.** Lucille Ball, James Craig, Cedric Hardwicke, Dean Jagger, Peter Whitney, Billy Gilbert, Tom Tyler, Antonio Moreno, George Cleveland, Hank Bell; **D:** George Marshall. *TTC*

Valley of Wanted Men 🎬½ **1935** Three cons escape during a jailbreak and one uses his wits and nerve to prove another was framed. **56m/B VHS, Beta, 8mm.** Frankie Darro. *VYY*

Valmont 🎬🎬🎬 **1989 (R)** Another adaptation of the Choderlos de Laclos novel "Les Liaisons Dangereuses." Various members of the French aristocracy in 1782 mercilessly play each other for fools in a complex game of lust and deception. Firth and Bening are at first playfully sensual, then the stakes get too high. They share an interesting bathtub scene. Well-acted, the 1988 Frears version, "Dangerous Liaisons," is edgier. Seeing the two films together makes for interesting comparisons of characters and styles. **137m/C VHS, Beta, LV, Closed Caption.** Colin Firth, Meg Tilly, Annette Bening, Fairuza Balk, Sian Phillips, Jeffrey Jones, Fabia Drake, Henry Thomas, Vincent Schiavelli, T.P. McKenna, Ian McNeice; **D:** Milos Forman; **W:** Jean-Claude Carriere; **M:** Christopher Palmer. Cesar Awards '90: Best Art Direction/Set Decoration, Best Costume Design; Nominations: Academy Awards '89: Best Costume Design. *ORI*

The Vals 🎬½ **1985 (R)** The glibly hip lethargy which is characteristic of four southern California teenaged girls turns to socially conscious resolve when a local orphanage is threatened. Like, for sure. **100m/C VHS, Beta.** Jill Carroll, Elana Stratheros, Gina Calabrese, Michelle Laurita, Chuck Connors, Sonny

Bono, John Carradine, Michael Leon; **D:** James Polakof. **ART, VES**

Vamp 🎬½ 1986 (R) Two college freshmen encounter a slew of weird, semi-vampiric people in a seamy red-light district nightclub. Starts cute but goes kinky. Jones is great as the stripping vampire. **93m/C VHS, Beta, LV, Closed Caption.** Grace Jones, Chris Makepeace, Robert Rusler, Gedde Watanabe, Sandy Baron, Dedee Pfeiffer, Billy Drago, Lisa Lyons; **D:** Richard Wenk; **W:** Richard Wenk; **C:** Elliot Davis; **M:** Jonathan Elias. **VTR**

Vamping 🎬½ 1984 (PG) Struggling musician plans to burglarize a wealthy widow's home. Once inside, he finds himself attracted to his proposed victim. Tedious going. **110m/C VHS, Beta, Closed Caption.** Patrick Duffy, Catherine Hyland, Rod Arrants, Fred A. Keller; **D:** Frederick King Keller. **FOX**

The Vampire 🎬🎬 *Mark of the Vampire* 1957 Pale man with big teeth attempts to swindle a beautiful babe out of fortune. Followed by "The Vampire's Coffin." **95m/B VHS.** MX Abel Salazar, Ariadne Welter, German Robles, Carmen Montejo, Jose Luis Jimenez; **D:** Fernando Mendez. **SNC**

Vampire at Midnight 🎬½ 1988 Fairly stupid homicide detective stalks a rampaging vampire in Los Angeles. Occasional moments of gratuitous sex thrown in for good measure. **93m/C VHS, Beta, Closed Caption.** Jason Williams, Gustav Vintas, Jeanie Moore, Christina Whitaker, Leslie Milne; **D:** Gregory McClatchy. **FOX**

The Vampire Bat 🎬🎬½ 1932 A mad scientist and a vampire bat and its supernatural demands set the stage for murders in a small town. Sets and actors borrowed from Universal Studios in this low-budget flick that looks and plays better than it should. Weird and very exploitative for 1932, now seems dated. **69m/B VHS, Beta.** Lionel Atwill, Fay Wray, Melvyn Douglas, Dwight Frye, Maude Eburne, George E. Stone; **D:** Frank Strayer; **W:** Edward T. Lowe; **C:** Ira Morgan. **VYY, SNC, WFV**

Vampire Circus 🎬🎬½ 1971 (R) A circus appears in an isolated Serbian village in the 19th century but instead of bringing joy and happiness, this circus brings only death, mutilation and misery. It seems all the members are vampires who have the unique ability to transform themselves into animals. They intend to take revenge on the small town, whose inhabitants killed their evil ancestor 100 years previously. Excellent Hammer production. **84m/C LV.** GB Adrienne Corri, Laurence Payne, Thorley Walters, John Moulder-Brown, Lynne Frederick, Elizabeth Seal, Anthony Corlan, Richard Owens, Domini Blythe, David Prowse; **D:** Robert W. Young; **W:** Judson Kinberg; **C:** Moray Grant. **IME**

Vampire Cop 🎬½ 1990 (R) A vampire cop (not to be confused with zombie, maniac, midnight, psycho, future or Robo) teams up with a beautiful reporter to 'collar' a drug kingpin.**CW:** Language, strong violence, and strong sensuality. **89m/C VHS.** Melissa Moore, Ed Cannon, Terence Jenkins. **ATL**

The Vampire Happening 🎬½ 1971 (R) An actress discovers to her chagrin that her ancestors were vampires and so is she. **90m/C VHS, Beta.** GE Ferdinand "Ferdy" Mayne; **D:** Freddie Francis. **NO**

The Vampire Hookers 🎬 *Cemetery Girls; Sensuous Vampires; Night of the Bloodsuckers; Twice Bitten* 1978 (R) Man in makeup recruits bevy of beautiful bloodsuckers to lure warm blooded victims to his castle. High ham performance by Carradine. **82m/C VHS, Beta.** PH John Carradine, Bruce Fairbairn, Trey Wilson, Karen Stride, Lenka Novak, Katie Dolan, Lex Winter; **D:** Cirio H. Santiago. **NO**

Vampire in Brooklyn 🎬 1995 (R) Murphy switches gears to play a Carribean vampire traveling to New York in search of his vampiric lady love—who turns out to be half-vamp-half-cop Bassett. As in "Coming to America," Murphy plays multiple characters, but that's three times the disappointment. Stale humor and cheap horror effects do little to break the zombie curse pla-

guing Murphy's career. Three days into filming, a stunt double for Bassett was killed after doing a routine jump on the set, providing a bad omen Murphy should have heeded.**CW:** Strong language and vampire violence. **103m/C VHS.** Eddie Murphy, Angela Bassett, Kadeem Hardison, Allen Payne, Zakes Mokae, John Witherspoon; **D:** Wes Craven; **W:** Charles Murphy, Christopher Parker, Michael Lucker; **C:** Mark Irwin; **M:** J. Peter Robinson. **PAR**

Vampire Journals 🎬🎬½ 1996 (R) Revenge-minded Zachary (Gunn) vows to destroy Ash (Morris), the ancient vampire who created him centuries before, especially when they both become interested in the same mortal woman, Sofia (Cerre). Shot on location in Transylvania.**CW:** Nudity, sexual situations, violence. **82m/C VHS.** David Gunn, Jonathan Morris, Kirsten Cerre, Starr Andreeff; **D:** Ted Nicolaou. **FLL**

The Vampire Lovers 🎬🎬½ 1970 (R) An angry father goes after a lesbian vampire who has ravished his daughter and other young girls in a peaceful European village. Innovative story was soon used in countless other vampire vehicles. Hammer Studio's first horror film with nudity, another addition to the genre which spread rapidly. Based on the story "Carmilla" by Sheridan Le Fanu. Followed by "Lust for a Vampire." **91m/C VHS, Beta.** GB Ingrid Pitt, Pippa Steele, Madeleine Smith, Peter Cushing, George Cole, Dawn Addams, Kate O'Mara, Ferdinand "Ferdy" Mayne, Douglas Wilmer, Harvey Hall; **D:** Roy Ward Baker; **W:** Tudor Gates; **C:** Moray Grant. **ORI, MLB**

The Vampire People 🎬½ *The Blood Drinkers* 1966 (PG) A dwarf-assisted vampire attempts to save the life of his true love by transplanting her sister's heart. Typical Filipino vampire movie. In color and sepia-tone. **79m/C VHS, Beta.** PH Ronald Remy, Amalia Fuentes, Eddie Fernandez, Eva Montez; **D:** Gerardo (Gerry) De Leon. **SNC**

Vampire Raiders—Ninja Queen WOOF! 1989 The white ninjas versus the black ninjas. The evil black ninjas are plotting to infiltrate the hotel industry. The white ninjas come to the rescue. **90m/C VHS.** Agnes Chan, Chris Petersen; **D:** Bruce Lambert. **TWE**

Vampire Vixens from Venus 🎬 1994 Three hideous drug smuggling aliens transform themselves into bodacious babes on earth so they can get what they came for. Seems their drug fix is derived from the life essence of men and they plan to drain every last drop they can. **90m/C VHS.** Michelle (McClellan) Bauer, Charlie Callas. **SHR**

Vampirella 🎬½ *Roger Corman Presents: Vampirella* 1996 (R) Inhabitants of the planet Drakulon use a synthetic concoction to quench their thirst for blood. When Vampirella's (Soto) stepfather is murdered by rebels, led by Vlad Tepes (Daltrey), she must pursue them to earth to get justice. There she finds two opposing forces—the vampires led by Tepes and a paramilitary group led by Adam Van Helsing (Paul), who's out to cleanse the planet of the interlopers. But it's Vampirella who wants a final confrontation with Tepes (in Las Vegas, no less). Made for cable.**CW:** Violence and some nudity. **90m/C VHS.** Talisa Soto, Roger Daltrey, Richard Joseph Paul, Angus Scrimm, Tom Deters, Cimna Harney, Brian Bloom; **D:** Jim Wynorski. **NO**

The Vampire's Coffin 🎬½ *El Ataud Del Vampiro; El Ataud Del Coffin* 1958 Count Lavud is relieved when faithful servant removes stake implanted in his heart. **86m/B VHS.** MX Abel Salazar, Ariadne Welter, German Robles; **D:** Fernando Mendez. **SNC**

The Vampire's Ghost 🎬 1945 A 400-hundred-year-old vampire/zombie, doomed to walk the earth forever, heads the African underworld. He can't be killed and can even go out during the day if he wears sunglasses. His future's so bright he's just gotta wear shades. **59m/B VHS.** John Abbott, Peggy Stewart; **D:** Lesley Selander. **NOS, DVT, HEG**

Vampire's Kiss 🎬🎬🎬 1988 (R) Cage makes this one worthwhile; his twisted transformation from pretentious post-val dude to psychotic yuppie from hell is inspired. If his demented torment of his secretary (Alonso) doesn't give you the creeps, his scene with the cockroach will. Cage fans will enjoy his facial aerobics; Beals fans will appreciate her extensive sucking scenes (she's the vamp of his dreams). More for psych majors than horror buffs. **103m/C VHS, Beta, LV.** Nicolas Cage, Elizabeth Ashley, Jennifer Beals, Maria Conchita Alonso, Kasi Lemmons, Bob Lujan, David Hyde Pierce; **D:** Robert Bierman; **W:** Joe Minion; **C:** Stefan Czapsky; **M:** Colin Towns. **NO**

Vampyr 🎬🎬🎬🎬 *Vampyr, Ou L'Etrange Aventure de David Gray; Vampyr, Der Traum des David Gray; Not Against the Flesh; Castle of Doom; The Strange Adventure of David Gray; The Vampire* 1931 Dreyer's classic portrays a hazy, dreamlike world full of chilling visions from the point of view of a young man who believes himself surrounded by vampires and who dreams of his own burial in a most disturbing way. Evil lurks around every corner as camera angles, light and shadow sometimes overwhelm plot. A high point in horror films based on a collection of horror stories by Sheridan Le Fanu. In German with English subtitles. **75m/B VHS, Beta.** GE FR Julian West, Sybille Schmitz, Henriette Gerard, Maurice Schutz, Rena Mandel, Jan Hieronimko, Albert Bras; **D:** Carl Theodor Dreyer; **W:** Carl Theodor Dreyer, Christen Jul; **C:** Rudolph Mate; **M:** Wolfgang Zeller. **KIV, NOS, SNC**

The Vampyr 🎬🎬 1992 Uncut version of the BBC musical production about a lustful vampire. Text sets present-day lyrics to the 1827 opera by Heinrich Marschner. Vampire Ripley (Ebrahim) has just been set free in London after having been trapped in an underground tomb for 200 years. Unless he puts the bite on three lovely ladies within three days he will be condemned to eternal damnation. Everyone gets to sing in the nude. Surreally amusing. **115m/C VHS.** GB Omar Ebrahim, Willemijn Van Gent, Fiona O'Neill, Sally-Ann Shepherdson. **FOX**

Vampyres 🎬🎬½ *Vampyres, Daughters of Dracula; Blood Hunger; Satan's Daughters; Daughters of Dracula* 1974 (R) Alluring female vampires coerce unsuspecting motorists to their castle for a good time, which ends in death. Anulka was the centerfold girl in "Playboy"'s May 1973 issue. **90m/C VHS, Beta.** GB Marianne Morris, Anulka, Murray Brown, Brian Deacon, Sally Faulkner, Michael Byrne, Karl Lanchbury, Bessie Love, Elliott Sullivan; **D:** Joseph Jose Ramon Larraz; **W:** Diane Daubeney; **C:** Harry Waxman. **VTR**

The Van 🎬 *Chevy Van* 1977 (R) A recent high school graduate passes on the college scene so he can spend more time picking up girls in his van. A lame sex (and sexist) comedy. **92m/C VHS, Beta.** Stuart Getz, Deborah White, Danny DeVito, Harry Moses, Maurice Barkin; **D:** Sam Grossman. **NO**

The Van 🎬🎬🎬 1995 (R) The last of writer Roddy Doyle's Barrytown trilogy (following "The Commitments" and "The Snapper") is set in 1989-90, in Dublin, where baker Bimbo (O'Kelly) has just lost his job. Tired of sitting around the pub, he takes his redundancy money and buys a filthy, dilapidated fish 'n' chips van, which he decides to run with best friend Larry (Meany), with their families helping out. The months pass quickly and their venture turns out to be a big success but the close quarters puts a strain on the mens' friendship until Bimbo has another idea.**CW:** Strong language. **105m/C VHS, Closed Caption.** GB Donal O'Kelly, Colm Meaney, Ger Ryan, Caroline Rotwell, Neili Conroy, Ruaidhri Conroy; **D:** Stephen Frears; **W:** Roddy Doyle; **C:** Oliver Stapleton; **M:** Eric Clapton, Richard Hartley. **FXV**

Van Gogh 🎬🎬🎬 1992 (R) "One doesn't produce 100 masterpieces in a state of depression—Van Gogh died from having had a glimpse of happiness." This is the way director Pialat sums up his approach to the last 67 days in the life of Vincent Van Gogh. Dutronc is skillful in portraying Van Gogh as a man with no excuses, and even a sense of humor. Not a psychological portrait and offers no answers—it's simply one artist's view of another. In French with English subtitles. **CW:** Nudity and sexuality. **155m/C VHS. FR** Jacques Dutronc, Alexandra London, Gerard Sety, Bernard Le Coq, Corinne Bourdon; **D:** Maurice Pialat; **W:** Maurice Pialat; **M:** Edith Vesperini. Cesar Awards '92: Best Actor (Dutronc). *COL, FCT*

Van Nuys Blvd. 🎬½ **1979 (R)** The popular boulevard is the scene where the cool southern California guys converge for cruising and girl watching, so naturally it's where a country hick comes to test his drag racing skills and check out the action. **93m/C VHS, Beta.** Bill Adler, Cynthia Wood, Dennis Bowen, Melissa Prophet; **D:** William Sachs. *NO*

Vanina Vanini 🎬🎬🎬½ **1961** An acclaimed Rossellini historical drama about the daughter of an Italian aristocrat in 1824 who nurses and falls in love with a wounded patriot hiding in her house. Based on a Stendhal short story. In Italian with English subtitles. **113m/B VHS, Beta. IT** Sandra Milo, Laurent Terzieff; **D:** Roberto Rossellini. *FCT*

The Vanishing 🎬🎬🎬 *Spoorloos* **1988** When his wife suddenly disappears, a young husband finds himself becoming increasingly obsessed with finding her. Three years down the road, his world has become one big, mad nightmare. Then, just as suddenly, the answer confronts him, but the reality of it may be too horrible to face. Well-made dark thriller based on "The Golden Egg" by Tim Krabbe. In French and Dutch with English subtitles. Remade by Sluizer in 1992. **107m/C VHS. NL FR** Barnard Pierre Donnadieu, Johanna Ter Steege, Gene Bervoetc; **D:** George Sluizer. *FXL*

The Vanishing 🎬🎬½ **1993 (R)** Director Sluizer remakes his own 1988 Dutch film "Spoorloos" to lesser effect. Tense thriller about the disappearance of a woman (Bullock) at a highway rest stop. Her boyfriend (Sutherland) becomes obsessed with locating her, searching for some three years as he is haunted by her memory. Unlike the Dutch original, the remake resorts to a clumsy ending designed for feel-good appeal. Based on the novel "The Golden Egg" by Tim Krabbe. **CW:** Language and terror and violence. **110m/C VHS, Closed Caption.** Jeff Bridges, Kiefer Sutherland, Nancy Travis, Sandra Bullock, Park Overall, Lisa Eichhorn, George Hearn, Maggie Linderman, Lynn Hamilton; **D:** George Sluizer; **W:** Todd Graff; **M:** Jerry Goldsmith. *FOX*

Vanishing Act 🎬🎬½ **1988 (PG)** While on his honeymoon, Harry Kenyon reports his wife missing to the local police. Within a short period of time his wife is found, but Harry says the woman is an impostor. This thriller follows Harry's desperate attempt to get to the truth. Made for television. **94m/C VHS, Beta.** Mike Farrell, Margot Kidder, Elliott Gould, Fred Gwynne, Graham Jarvis; **D:** David Greene; **W:** Richard Levinson, William Link. *THV*

Vanishing American 🎬🎬 **1926** The mistreatment of the American Indian is depicted in this sweeping Western epic. Musical score. **114m/B VHS, Beta.** Richard Dix, Noah Beery Sr.; **D:** George B. Seitz. *GPV, VYY*

Vanishing Legion **1931** Western serial with outdoor action and gunplay. Twelve chapters, 13 minutes each. **156m/B VHS, Beta.** Frankie Darro, Harry Carey Sr.; **D:** B. Reeves Eason. *GPV, NOS, VCN*

Vanishing Point 🎬🎬 **1971 (PG)** An ex-racer makes a bet to deliver a souped-up car from Denver to San Francisco in 15 hours. Taking pep pills along the way, he eludes police, meets up with a number of characters, and finally crashes into a roadblock. Rock score helps attract this film's cult following. **98m/C VHS, Beta, LV.** Barry Newman, Cleavon Little, Gilda Texler, Dean Jagger, Paul Koslo, Robert Donner, Severn Darden, Victoria Medlin; **D:** Richard Sarafian; **C:** John A. Alonzo. *FOX*

Vanishing Prairie 🎬🎬🎬 **1954** This documentary examines the wonders of nature that abound in the American prairie. From the "True-Life Adventures" series. **60m/C VHS, Beta. D:** James Nelson Algar. Academy Awards '54: Best Feature Documentary. *DIS*

The Vanishing Westerner 🎬🎬 **1950** A cowboy, falsely accused of murder, works to vindicate himself and uncovers a series of robberies. This one has enough plot twists to take it out of the routine. **60m/B VHS, Beta.** Monte Hale, Arthur Space, Aline Towne, Paul Hurst, Roy Barcroft, Richard Anderson, William Phipps, Rand Brooks; **D:** Philip Ford. *DVT*

Vanishing Wilderness 🎬🎬 **1973 (G)** This documentary looks at the wild animals roaming across North America. **90m/C VHS, Beta. D:** Arthur Dubs. *VTR*

Vanity Fair 🎬🎬 **1932** Loy stars in this tale of a wily and manipulative woman looking for the perfect marriage. This was the 58th film for the 27-year-old Loy, but even she couldn't save it. Of course, none of the three films based on the story by Thackeray have done it justice. **67m/B VHS.** Myrna Loy, Conway Tearle, Barbara Kent, Walter Byron, Anthony Bushell, Billy Bevan, Montagu Love, Mary Forbes; **D:** Chester M. Franklin. *NOS, HEG*

Vanity Fair 🎬🎬½ **1967** BBC TV adaptation of William Makepeace Thackeray's satire on human folly in 19th-century England. Amoral governess (and anti-heroine) Becky Sharp (Hampshire) will stop at nothing to climb the social ladder, aided by a wealthy marriage and her own audacity, which ultimately leads to scandal. **250m/C VHS. GB** Susan Hampshire, Robert Flemyng, Richard Caldicot, Barbara Couper, Roy Marsden, Bryan Marshall; **D:** David Giles. *FCT, TVC*

Vanya on 42nd Street 🎬🎬🎬½ **1994 (PG)** Group of actors in street clothes rehearse a workshop production of Chekhov's play, "Uncle Vanya," in New York's dilapidated New Amsterdam Theater. Theatrical director Gregory first gets his group together in 1989, with Mamet's contemporary adaptation, and they continue to work in private until Malle films their production some four years later before a small, select audience. Shawn, best known for "My Dinner with Andre" portrays Vanya with depth and complexity. The other actors shine as well, often against type, in this complex Russian drama of desperation. **119m/C VHS, LV.** Wallace Shawn, Julianne Moore, Brooke Smith, Larry Pine, George Gaynes, Lynn Cohen, Madhur Jaffrey, Phoebe Brand, Jerry Mayer, Andre Gregory; **D:** Louis Malle; **W:** Andre Gregory, David Mamet; **C:** Declan Quinn; **M:** Joshua Redman. Nominations: Independent Spirit Awards '95: Best Supporting Actor (Pine), Best Supporting Actress (Smith). *COL*

Varan the Unbelievable 🎬 *Daikaiju Baran; The Monster Baran* **1961** A chemical experiment near a small island in the Japanese archipelago disturbs a prehistoric monster beneath the water. The awakened monster spreads terror on the island. Most difficult part of this movie is deciding what the rubber monster model is supposed to represent. **70m/B VHS, Beta. JP** Myron Healey, Tsuruko Kobayashi; **D:** Inoshiro Honda. *NOS, VCI*

Varieties on Parade 🎬 **1952** A vaudeville show on film, featuring an array of second-rate comics and musical personalities. Sad to watch its demise. **55m/B VHS, Beta, LV.** Jackie Coogan, Eddie Garr, Tom Neal, Iris Adrian. *NO*

Variety 🎬🎬🎬🎬 **1925** Simple and tragic tale of a scheming young girl and the two men of whom she takes advantage. The European circus in all its beautiful sadness is the setting. Extraordinary cast and superb cinematography. Silent. **104m/B VHS, Beta. GE** Emil Jannings, Lya de Putti, Warwick Ward, Werner Krauss; **D:** E.A. Dupont. *VYY, NOS, DVT*

Variety 🎬🎬½ **1983** A girl takes a job selling tickets in a Times Square porn theatre. Her initial loathing for the genre gives way to a fascination with its clients, one of whom is a gangster, and

she becomes drawn to the seamy world inside. An independently made feature. **101m/C VHS, Beta.** Sandy McLeod, Will Patton, Richard Davidson; **D:** Bette Gordon.

Variety Lights 🎬🎬🎬½ *Luci Del Varieta; Lights of Variety* **1951** Fellini's first (albeit joint) directorial effort, wherein a young girl runs away with a travelling vaudeville troupe and soon becomes its main attraction as a dancer. Filled with Fellini's now-familiar delight in the bizarre and sawdust/tinsel entertainment. In Italian with English subtitles. **93m/B VHS, Beta. IT** Giulietta Masina, Peppino de Filippo, Carla Del Poggio, Folco Lulli; **D:** Federico Fellini; **W:** Federico Fellini, Tullio Pinelli, Ennio Flaiano, Alberto Lattuada. *HMV, CVC*

Vasectomy: A Delicate Matter woof! *Vasectomy* **1986 (PG-13)** A mother of eight issues a final decree to her husband about their sex life. He must get a vasectomy or there won't be any. As good as it sounds. **92m/C VHS, Beta.** Paul Sorvino, Abe Vigoda, Cassandra Edwards, Lorne Greene, Ina Balin, June Wilkinson, William Marshall; **D:** Robert Burge; **W:** Robert Burge. *WOV*

Vatican Conspiracy 🎬½ **1981** The members of the Vatican's College of Cardinals do everything in their power to discredit a newly appointed radical pontiff. **90m/C VHS, Beta.** Terence Stamp; **D:** Marcello Aliprandi. *NO*

Vault of Horror 🎬🎬½ *Tales from the Crypt II* **1973 (R)** A collection of five terrifying tales based on original stories from the E.C. comic books of the 1950s. Stories include, "Midnight Mess," "Bargain in Death," "This Trick'll Kill You," "The Neat Job," and "Drawn and Quartered." **86m/C VHS, Beta. GB** Terry-Thomas, Curt Jurgens, Glynis Johns, Dawn Addams, Daniel Massey, Tom Baker, Michael Craig, Anna Massey, Denholm Elliott; **D:** Roy Ward Baker; **W:** Milton Subotsky.

Vegas 🎬 **1978** A private detective, with Las Vegas beauties as assistants and pursuers, solves the murder of a teenage runaway girl. Pilot for television series. Scriptwriter Mann went on to do "Miami Vice." **74m/C VHS, Beta.** Robert Urich, June Allyson, Tony Curtis, Will Sampson, Greg Morris; **D:** Richard Lang; **W:** Michael Mann.

Vegas in Space woof! **1994** Four male astronauts take a secret mission to the planet Clitoris, the all-female pleasure plant where men are forbidden to trod. To capture a heinous villainous, they swallow gender-reversal pills in order to infiltrate the resort as show-girls. Typical Troma trash. Boasts an all-transvestite cast. **85m/C VHS.** Doris Fish, Miss X, Ginger Quest, Ramona Fischer, Lori Naslund, Timmy Spence, Silvana Nova, Sandelle Kincaid, Tommy Pace, Arturo Galster, Jennifer Blowdryer, Freida Lay, Tippi; **D:** Phillip R. Ford; **W:** Phillip R. Ford, Doris Fish, Miss X; **C:** Robin Clark; **M:** Ramona Fischer, Timmy Spence. *TTV*

The Vegas Strip Wars 🎬🎬 *Las Vegas Strip War* **1984** Rival casino owners battle it out in the land of lady luck. Unmemorable except for Jones's Don King impersonation and the fact that it was Hudson's last TV movie. **100m/C VHS, Beta.** Rock Hudson, James Earl Jones, Noriyuki "Pat" Morita, Sharon Stone, Robert Costanzo; **D:** George Englund. *ART*

Vegas Vacation 🎬 **1996 (PG)** It may not have come out under the "National Lampoon" banner but you'll recognize both the characters and the situations. The innocent Griswold clan head from their Chicago home to the bright lights and gambling temptations of Las Vegas. Clark (Chase) blows all their money, Ellen (D'Angelo) reveals a hidden passion for Wayne Newton, daughter Audrey (Nichols) decides to become a go-go dancer, and son Rusty (Embry) turns into a high roller who draws the attention of the mob. Oh yeah, dimwit cousin Eddie (Quaid) also tries to supply a few yucks. **98m/C VHS, LV, Closed Caption.** Chevy Chase, Beverly D'Angelo, Randy Quaid, Ethan Embry, Miriam Flynn, Marisol Nichols, Shae D'Lyn, Wallace Shawn, Wayne Newton; **Cameos:** Sid Caesar, Julia Sweeney, Christie Brinkley; **D:** Stephen Kessler; **W:** Elisa Bell; **M:** Joel McNeely. *WAR*

Velnio Nuotaka 🎬🎬½ *The Devil's Bride* **1975** A popular Lithuanian musical based on the play "Baltargio Malunas" by K. Boruta. English subtitles. **78m/C VHS, Beta.** *LI IHF*

Velvet Smooth 🎬 **1976 (R)** A protection agency's sultry boss, Velvet Smooth, gets involved solving the problems of a numbers racket. **89m/C VHS.** Johnnie Hill; *D:* Janace Fink. *NO*

Velvet Touch 🎬🎬🎬 **1948** Well-engineered thriller about an actress who craftily murders her producer. A theatre-loving police detective winds up accusing the wrong woman—sending the overwrought murderess into a moral tailspin. Things don't work out as you may expect. Fine acting. **97m/B VHS, Beta.** Rosalind Russell, Leo Genn, Claire Trevor, Sydney Greenstreet, Leon Ames, Frank McHugh, Walter Kingsford, Dan Tobin, Lex Barker, Nydia Westman; *D:* John Gage; *W:* Leo Rosten. *TTC*

The Velvet Vampire 🎬🎬 *Cemetery Girls; Through the Looking Glass; The Waking Hour* **1971 (R)** Yarnall is a sexy, sun-loving, dune buggy-riding vampiress who seduces a young, sexy, swinging, Southern California couple in her desert home. Lots of atmosphere to go along with the blood and nudity. **82m/C VHS, Beta, LV.** Michael Blodgett, Sherry Miles, Celeste Yarnall, Gene Shane, Jerry Daniels, Sandy Ward, Paul Prokop, Chris Woodley, Robert Tessier; *D:* Stephanie Rothman; *W:* Stephanie Rothman, Maurice Jules, Charles S. Swartz; *C:* Daniel Lacambre.

Vendetta 🎬½ **1985** A woman gets herself arrested and sent to the penitentiary in order to exact revenge there for her sister's death. Acting and pacing make this better than the average sexploitation flick. **89m/C VHS, Beta.** Karen Chase, Sandy Martin, Durga McBroom, Kin Shriner, Eugene Glazer; *D:* Bruce Logan; *M:* David Newman. *ART, VES*

Vendetta for the Saint 🎬 **1968** A feature-length episode of the television series "The Saint," in which Simon Templar pursues a Sicilian mobster on a personal vendetta. **98m/C VHS, Beta.** *GB* Roger Moore; *D:* James O'Connolly. *FOX*

Vengeance 🎬🎬 **1937** A police officer resigns in shame after failing to thwart a holdup. He attempts to redeem himself by working on his own to infiltrate the same gang. **61m/B VHS.** Lyle Talbot, Wendy Barrie, Wally Albright, Marc Lawrence; *D:* Del Lord. *VYY, MOV*

Vengeance 🎬 **1980** Four burglars take hostages after their robbery is bungled, but they won't get away—especially after the hostages die. **92m/C VHS, Beta.** Sally Lockett, Nicholas Jacquez, Bob Elliott; *D:* Bob Blizz. *NO*

Vengeance 🎬 **1986** A low-budget film about rebels fighting off an authoritarian government. **114m/C VHS, Beta.** Jason Miller, Lea Massari; *D:* Antonio Isasi. *TWE*

Vengeance 🎬🎬 *Vengeance: The Story of Tony Cimo* **1989 (R)** A bereaved young man strikes out against the injustice of his parents' murder. His revenge against the killers takes him several steps beyond the law, and he's not so sure it was the right idea. Made for television. **90m/C VHS, LV.** Brad Davis, Roxanne Hart, Brad Dourif, William Conrad; *D:* Marc Daniels. *IME*

Vengeance Is Mine 🎬🎬🎬 **1979** Told in flashbacks, the film focuses on the life of a habitual criminal whose life of deprivation leads to murder. Contains violence and nudity. Based on a true story. In Japanese with English subtitles. **129m/C VHS, LV.** *JP* Ken Ogata; *D:* Shohei Imamura. *FCT*

Vengeance Is Mine woof! **1984 (R)** A demented farmer captures three criminals and tortures them in horrifyingly sadistic ways. Gratuitously grisly. **90m/C VHS, Beta, LV.** Ernest Borgnine, Michael J. Pollard, Hollis McLaren; *D:* John Trent. *VTR, GEM*

Vengeance of the Snowmaid 🎬½ **197?** Some Kung Fu creepies raped her mom. Now nobody can get a sword in edgewise on the Snow Maid as she seeks revenge. **82m/C VHS, Beta.** Mo Ka Kei, Chen Chen. *NO*

Vengeance of the Zombies 🎬½ **1972** A madman seeks revenge by setting an army of walking corpses to stalk the streets of London. **90m/C VHS, Beta.** *SP* Paul Naschy; *D:* Leon Klimovsky. *SNC*

Vengeance Valley 🎬🎬 **1951** Lancaster and Walker are foster brothers with Walker being an envious weasel who always expects Lancaster to get him out of scrapes. Lancaster is even accused of a crime committed by Walker and must work to clear himself. Good cast is let down by uneven direction. **83m/C VHS, Beta.** Burt Lancaster, Joanne Dru, Robert Walker, Sally Forrest, John Ireland, Hugh O'Brian; *D:* Richard Thorpe. *NOS, DVT, CAB*

Venice, Venice 🎬🎬½ **1992 (R)** Alternately earnest and satirical, Jaglom pokes fun at himself and movie-making in a movie about, well, himself and movie-making. Consciously straddling the genre fence, he uses real people and events, but adopts a pseudonym, Dean. In Venice, Italy, young filmmaker Alard decides to make a film about Dean/Jaglom, a plot which creates the effect of two mirrors reflecting each other into infinity. Dean/Jaglom and Alard return to Venice, California, where he conducts auditions for a movie in which he will star and direct. Art imitating life or life imitating art? More importantly, does it really matter? *CW:* Language. **108m/C VHS.** Nelly Alard, Henry Jaglom, Suzanne Bertish, Melissa Leo, Daphna Kastner, David Duchovny, Diane Salinger, Zack Norman, Marshall Barer, John Landis, Pierre Cottrell, Edna Fainaru, Klaus Hellwig; *D:* Henry Jaglom; *W:* Henry Jaglom; *C:* Hanania Baer. *FXL*

Venom woof! **1982 (R)** Deadly black mamba is loose in an elegant townhouse, terrorizing big-name cast. The snake continually terrorizes an evil kidnapper, his accomplices and his kidnapped victim. Participants walk through tired cliches with that far-away look in their eyes—like they wish they were anywhere else. Original director Tobe Hooper was replaced. **92m/C VHS, Beta.** *GB* Sterling Hayden, Klaus Kinski, Sarah Miles, Nicol Williamson, Cornelia Sharpe, Susan George, Michael Gough, Oliver Reed; *D:* Piers Haggard; *W:* Robert B. Carrington; *M:* Michael Kamen. *VES*

Venus Against the Son of Hercules **1962** Our hero must use all his genetically procured musculature in his battle against the lovely but deadly Venus. **?m/C VHS, Beta.** *IT* Roger Brown, Jackie Lane. *SNC*

Venus in Furs 🎬½ *Paroxismus; Puo Una Morta Rivivere Per Amore?; Venus in Peltz* **1970 (R)** Jazz musician working in Rio de Janeiro becomes obsessed with a mysterious woman; she resembles a murder victim whose body he discovered months earlier. Weird mix of horror, sadism, black magic, and soft porn. **90m/C VHS, Beta.** *GB* James Darren, Klaus Kinski, Barbara McNair, Dennis Price, Maria Rohm; *D:* Jess (Jesus) Franco. *REP, TPV*

Venus Rising 🎬🎬 **1995 (R)** In the year 2000, Eve and August manage to escape from the island prison on which they were raised. They discover that the mainland world features emotions that are controlled by drugs and love is only a game on the virtual reality network. Hunted, the fugitives try to fit in and figure out what's real and what's fantasy. Be forewarned—Fairchild's role is very small. *CW:* Violence, sexuality, and some language. **91m/C VHS, Closed Caption.** Audie England, Costas Mandylor, Billy Wirth, Morgan Fairchild; *D:* Leora Barish; *W:* Leora Barish. *COL*

Venus the Ninja 🎬 **198?** A comely female Ninja battles an evil warlord. **90m/C VHS, Beta.** Pearl Cheung, Meng Fei; *D:* Sze Ma Peng. *TWE*

Vera Cruz 🎬🎬½ **1953** Two soldiers of fortune become involved in the Mexican Revolution of 1866, a stolen shipment of gold, divided loyalties, and gun battles. Less than innovative plot is made into an exciting action flick. **94m/C VHS, Beta, LV.** Gary Cooper, Burt Lancaster, Denise Darcel, Cesar Romero, George Macready, Ernest Borgnine, Charles Bronson, Jack Elam; *D:* Robert Aldrich; *C:* Ernest Laszlo. *MGM, FOX, FCT*

Verboten! 🎬🎬½ **1959** In post-war occupied Berlin, an American G.I. falls in love with a German girl. Good direction maintains a steady pace. **93m/B VHS.** James Best, Susan Cummings, Paul Dubov; *D:* Samuel Fuller. *IME*

Verdi 🎬🎬 **1953** The story of the Italian operatic composer and the loves of his life. Dubbed in English. **80m/C VHS.** *IT* Pierre Cressoy. *FCT*

The Verdict 🎬🎬🎬 **1982 (R)** Newman plays an alcoholic failed attorney reduced to ambulance chasing. A friend gives him a supposedly easy malpractice case which turns out to be a last chance at redeeming himself and his career. Adapted from the novel by Barry Reed. One of Newman's finest performances. **122m/C VHS, Beta, LV.** Paul Newman, James Mason, Charlotte Rampling, Jack Warden, Milo O'Shea, Lindsay Crouse; *D:* Sidney Lumet; *W:* David Mamet; *C:* Andrzej Bartkowiak. National Board of Review Awards '82: Best Director (Lumet); Nominations: Academy Awards '82: Best Actor (Newman), Best Adapted Screenplay, Best Director (Lumet), Best Picture, Best Supporting Actor (Mason). *FOX*

Vermont Is for Lovers 🎬½ **1992** Pre-wedding jitters consume stressed-out Manhattanites Marya (Cohn) and George (Thrush) when they travel to bucolic Tunbridge, Vermont to get married on Marya's Aunt Ann's farm. After continuously arguing, they decide to spend the day before the wedding apart and George wanders around the community asking marriage advice from various old-timers. The Yuppie leads aren't terribly compelling and neither is the improvised dialogue. **86m/C VHS.** George Thrush, Marya Cohn, Ann O'Brien; *D:* John O'Brien; *C:* John O'Brien; *M:* Tony Silbert. *FCT, KIV*

Verne Miller 🎬🎬 **1988 (R)** A film of the true story of Verne Miller, Al Capone's hit man. After rescuing a friend from the Feds, Miller is hunted down by both the cops and the mob. **95m/C VHS, Beta, LV.** Scott Glenn, Barbara Stock, Thomas G. Waites, Lucinda Jenney, Sonny Carl Davis; *D:* Rod Hewitt. *NLC*

The Vernonia Incident 🎬½ **1989** Urban guerillas invade a small town, killing the police chief. The townspeople gather up their shotguns and fight back. That's entertainment. **95m/C VHS, Beta.** David Jackson, Shawn Stevens, Floyd Ragner, Ed Justice, Robert Louis Jakson; *D:* Ray Etheridge; *W:* Ray Etheridge. *NO*

Veronico Cruz 🎬🎬½ *La Dueda Interna; The Debt* **1987** Despite its sincerity, Pereira's feature debut offers muddled response to the human waste incurred by the Falklands War. Set in a tiny remote village in the Argentinean mountains, the film's narrative is derived from the growing friendship between a shepherd boy and a teacher from the city. Well-meaning anti-war movie. In Spanish with English subtitles. **96m/C VHS.** *AR GB* Juan Jose Camero, Gonzalo Morales, Rene Olaguivel, Guillermo Delgado; *D:* Miguel Pereira. *CCN, TPV*

Veronika Voss 🎬🎬🎬 *Die Sehns Ucht Der Veronika Voss* **1982 (R)** Highlights the real life of fallen film star Sybille Schmitz who finally took her own life out of despair. Played by Zech, Voss is exploited by her physician to turn over all of her personal belongings for morphine. A lover discovers the corruption and reveals it to the authorities. This causes great upheaval resulting in Voss' suicide. Highly metaphoric and experimental in its treatment of its subject. In German with English subtitles. **105m/C VHS.** *GE* Rosel Zech, Hilmar Thate, Conny Froboess, Anna Marie Duringer, Volker Spengler; *D:* Rainer Werner Fassbinder; *M:* Peer Raben. *FCT*

Vertigo 🎬🎬🎬 **1958 (PG)** Hitchcock's romantic story of obsession, manipulation and fear. Stewart plays a detective forced to retire after his fear of heights causes the death of a fellow policeman and, perhaps, the death of a woman he'd been hired to follow. The appearance of her double (Novak), whom he compulsively transforms into the dead girl's image, leads to a mesmerizing cycle of madness and lies. Features Herrmann's haunting music. 126m/C VHS, LV, Closed Caption, DVD. James Stewart, Kim Novak, Barbara Bel Geddes, Tom Helmore, Ellen Corby, Henry Jones, Raymond Bailey, Lee Patrick; **D:** Alfred Hitchcock; **W:** Sam Taylor; **C:** Robert Burks; **M:** Bernard Herrmann. National Film Registry '89;; Nominations: Academy Awards '58: Best Art Direction/Set Decoration, Best Sound. *USH, TLF*

A Very Brady Christmas 🐾🐾 1988 Many of the original Bradys returned for this yuletide special. After Mike and Carol's vacation plans go awry, they decide to invite the whole bunch home for a family reunion. This was the highest rated television movie in 1989. Spawned yet another unsuccessful "Brady" series sequel. 94m/C VHS, Closed Caption. Florence Henderson, Robert Reed, Ann B. Davis, Maureen McCormick, Eve Plumb, Jennifer Runyon, Barry Williams, Christopher Knight, Michael Lookinland, Jerry Houser, Caryn Richman; **D:** Peter Baldwin. *PAR*

A Very Brady Sequel 🐾🐾½ 1996 (PG-13) They're back! The cast from the surprise hit "The Brady Bunch Movie" returns and Brady mom Carol (Long) is shocked when her presumed dead first husband Roy Martin (Matheson) suddenly appears on their doorstep. The Bradys must travel to Hawaii to attempt to save the family (based on a three-part episode from the original TV series). The stuck-in-the-'70s gang is still too far-out for the '90s, but in Hawaii it's always a sunshine day. Not as good as the first, but still worth a few laughs.**CW:** Sex-related humor and drug content. Watch out for innuendos about Greg and Marcia. 90m/C VHS, Beta, Closed Caption. Shelley Long, Gary Cole, Tim Matheson, Christopher Daniel Barnes, Christine Taylor, Paul Sutera, Jennifer Elise Cox, Henriette Mantel, Olivia Hack, Jesse Lee; **D:** Arlene Sanford; **W:** Harry Elfont, Deborah Kaplan, Stan Zimmerman, James Berg; **C:** Mac Ahlberg; **M:** Guy Moon. Nominations: MTV Movie Awards '97: Best Kiss (Christopher Daniel Barnes/Christine Taylor). *PAR*

A Very British Coup 🐾🐾🐾 199? McAnally plays Harry Perkins, a former steelworker who gets involved in British politics. Although a left-wing radical, the charismatic Perkins is actually elected Prime Minister. However, his radical policies cause the entrenched government officials to conspire to bring him down. And you thought American politics were dirty! Made for British television. 180m/C VHS. **GB** Ray McAnally. *SIG, TVC, FUS*

Very Close Quarters 🐾 1984 Thirty people face many trials and tribulations as they share an apartment in Moscow. Interesting cast is wasted in this mostly unfunny flick. 97m/C VHS, Beta. Shelley Winters, Paul Sorvino, Theodore Bikel, Farley Granger; **D:** Vladmir Rif. *ART, VES*

A Very Curious Girl 🐾🐾½ *La Fiancee du Pirate; Dirty Mary; Pirate's Fiancee* 1969 (R) A peasant girl realizes she is being used by the male population of her village, and decides to charge them for sex, creating havoc. In French with English subtitles. 105m/C VHS, Beta. **FR** Bernadette LaFont, Georges Geret; **D:** Nelly Kaplan. *NO*

The Very Edge 🐾🐾½ 1963 A pregnant woman suffers a miscarriage after being brutally attacked. The repercussions nearly destroy her marriage until her attacker is caught. A disturbing psycho-drama. 90m/B VHS, Beta. **GB** Anne Heywood, Richard Todd, Jeremy Brett, Jack Hedley, Barbara Mullen, Maurice Denham, William Lucas, Gwen Watford, Patrick Magee; **D:** Cyril Frankel; **W:** Elizabeth Jane Howard. *NO*

A Very Natural Thing 🐾🐾 1973 Twenty-six-year-old Jason leaves the priesthood to pursue a gay lifestyle in New York. He becomes a teacher, meets ad exec David, and finds love. Considered to be the first film to explore homosexuality in a realistic manner, made by a gay director, and given national, commercial distribution. 85m/C VHS. Robert Joel, Curt Gareth, Bo White; **D:** Christopher Larkin; **W:** Christopher Larkin, Joseph Coencas. *WBF*

A Very Old Man with Enormous Wings 🐾🐾 *Un Senor Muy Viejo Con Unas Alas Enormes* 1988 An angel, battered during a hurricane, seeks refuge on a tiny Caribbean island. There, two men keep him and charge an increasingly curious world admission to view the creature. A colorful, musical expose of human failings based on a story by Gabriel Garcia Marquez. In Spanish with English subtitles. 90m/C VHS, LV. **SP IT** Daisy Granados, Asdrubal Melendez, Luis Alberto Ramirez, Fernando Birri; **D:** Fernando Birri. *FXL, FCT*

A Very Private Affair 🐾🐾½ *La Vie Privee; Vita Privata* 1962 A movie star finds that she has no privacy from the hordes of fans and paparazzi who flock to her side. The glare of publicity helps to destroy her relationship with a married director, and to fuel her desire for privacy, a desire that ends tragically. An appealing, better-than-average Bardot vehicle, it is nonetheless below-average (early) Malle. In French with English subtitles. 95m/C VHS, Beta. **FR** Marcello Mastroianni, Brigitte Bardot; **D:** Louis Malle. *MGM*

V.I. Warshawski 🐾🐾 1991 (R) The filmmakers seem to think they can slum with the oldest cliches in detective shows just as long as the tough gumshoe is a woman. They're wrong. Turner is terrific as the leggy shamus of the title (from a popular series of books by Sara Paretsky), but the plot is nothing special, featuring stock characters in the killing of a pro athlete and a real-estate deal.**CW:** Language and moments of violence. 89m/C VHS, Beta, LV, Closed Caption. Kathleen Turner, Jay O. Sanders, Angela Goethals, Charles Durning; **D:** Jeff Kanew; **W:** Nick Thiel, David Aaron Cohen; **M:** Randy Edelman. *HPH*

Via Appia 🐾🐾 1992 Fictional documentary about Frank, a German airline steward who brings a film crew with him when travels back to Rio de Janeiro in search of the street hustler who gave him AIDS. Grim guided tour of the city's gay subculture along the "Via Appia," the Rio district where the male prostitutes hang out. Film is firmly unapologetic for its sexual explicitness and lack of moralizing. In German and Portuguese with English subtitles. 90m/C VHS. **GE BR** Peter Senner, Guilherme de Padua, Yves Jansen, Margaridt Schmidt, Luiz Kleber; **D:** Jochen Hick; **W:** Jochen Hick. *MOV, FCT*

Vibes 🐾 1988 (PG) Two screwball psychics are sent on a wild goose chase through the Ecuadorean Andes in search of cosmic power and, of course, fall in love. Flat offering from the usually successful team of writers, Lowell Ganz and Babaloo Mandel ("Splash" and "Night Shift"). Lauper's first starring role (and so far, her last). 99m/C VHS, Beta, Closed Caption. Jeff Goldblum, Cyndi Lauper, Julian Sands, Googy Gress, Peter Falk, Elizabeth Pena; **D:** Ken Kwapis; **W:** Babaloo Mandel, Lowell Ganz; **C:** John Bailey; **M:** James Horner. *COL*

Vibrations 🐾🐾½ 1994 (R) Anamika (Applegate), a dance club manager, befriends TJ (Marshall), a homeless, alcoholic, once-promising musician who lost his hands in a brutal attack. The duo find romance as Anamika encourages TJ to try again.**CW:** Language; some sexuality. 104m/C VHS, LV, Closed Caption. James Marshall, Christina Applegate, Faye Grant, Paige Turco, Bruce Altman, David Burke, Scott Cohen, Shane Butterworth; **D:** Michael Paseornek; **W:** Michael Paseornek; **M:** Bob Christianson. *TOU*

Vice Academy 🐾½ 1988 (R) Two females join the Hollywood vice squad. Allen was a former porn queen. 90m/C VHS, Beta, LV. Linnea Quigley, Ginger Lynn Allen, Karen Russell, Jayne Hamil, Ken Abraham, Stephen Steward, Jeannie Carol; **D:** Rick Sloane.

Vice Academy 2 🐾 1990 (R) Two vice cop babes try to stop a female crime boss from dumping aphrodisiacs in the city's water supply. 90m/C VHS, Beta. Linnea Quigley, Ginger Lynn Allen, Jayne Hamil, Scott Layne, Jay Richardson, Joe Brewer, Marina Benvenga, Teagan Clive; **D:** Rick Sloane.

Vice Academy 3 woof! 1991 (R) The worst of the series, and not just because cult actress Linnea Quigley is absent. Wit, pacing and even sets are nonexistent as the girls battle a toxic villainess called Malathion.**CW:** Nudity. 88m/C VHS, Beta. Ginger Lynn Allen, Elizabeth Kaitan, Julia Parton, Jay Richardson, Johanna Grika, Steve Mateo; **D:** Rick Sloane; **W:** Rick Sloane.

Vice Squad 🐾🐾 1931 Lukas is forced to turn police informer to save his own neck, which almost ruins him. Just when he thinks he's free of the cops they come back threatening the woman he loves unless he plays stoolie again. Rather flat, but the different cop/criminal angle makes for some unusual twists. 80m/B VHS, Beta, LV. Paul Lukas, Kay Francis, Helen Johnson, William B. Davidson, Esther Howard; **D:** John Cromwell; **C:** Charles B(ryant) Lang.

Vice Squad woof! 1982 (R) Violent and twisted killer-pimp goes on a murderous rampage, and a hooker helps a vice squad plainclothesman trap him. Sleazy and disturbing, with little to recommend it. 97m/C VHS, Beta, LV. Wings Hauser, Season Hubley, Gary Swanson, Cheryl "Rainbeaux" Smith; **D:** Gary Sherman; **W:** Robert Vincent O'Neil. *NLC*

Vice Versa 🐾🐾🐾 1988 (PG) Another 80s comedy about a workaholic father and his 11-year-old son who switch bodies, with predictable slapstick results. Reinhold and Savage carry this, appearing to have a great time in spite of overdone story. 97m/C VHS, Beta, LV, Closed Caption. Judge Reinhold, Fred Savage, Swoosie Kurtz, David Proval, Corinne Bohrer, Jane Kaczmarek, William Prince, Gloria Gifford; **D:** Brian Gilbert; **W:** Dick Clement, Ian LaFrenais; **M:** David Shire. *COL*

Vicious 🐾 1988 A bored young woman falls in with people your mother warned you about and soon their high school hi-jinks turn into murder. Graphic violence. 88m/C VHS. Tamblyn Lord, Craig Pearce, Tiffany Dowe; **D:** Karl Zwicky. *NO*

The Vicious Circle 🐾🐾½ *The Circle* 1957 A prominent London physician becomes involved in murder and an international crime ring when he agrees to perform an errand for a friend. Good performances and tight pacing. 84m/B VHS, Beta. **GB** John Mills, Wilfrid Hyde-White, Rene Ray, Lionel Jeffries, Noelle Middleton; **D:** Gerald Thomas. *NO*

Vicious Circles 🐾🐾 1997 (R) Decidedly kinky erotic thriller finds Dylan (Hipp) getting arrested for drug possession in Paris. So his half-sister and lover Andi (Lowery) decides to help raise the money for his release by working as a hooker for mystery man March (Gazzara). As Andi gets more involved in her new lifestyle, she also discovers that March was somehow connected to the death of a tycoon's daughter.**CW:** Aberrant sexual content, language and drug use. 90m/C VHS. Carolyn Lowery, Ben Gazzara, Paul Hipp; **D:** Alexander Whitelaw. *THV*

Victim 🐾🐾🐾½ 1961 A successful married English barrister (Bogarde) with a hidden history of homosexuality is threatened by blackmail after the death of his ex-lover. When the blackmailers, who are responsible for his lover's suicide, are caught, Bogarde decides to prosecute them himself, even though it means revealing his hidden past. One of the first films to deal straightforwardly with homosexuality. Fine performances. 100m/B VHS. **GB** Dirk Bogarde, Sylvia Syms, Dennis Price, Peter McEnery, Nigel Stock, Donald Churchill, Anthony Nicholls, Hilton Edwards, Norman Bird, Derren Nesbitt, Alan McNaughton, Noel Howlett, Charles Lloyd Pack, John Barrie, John Bennett; **D:** Basil Dearden; **W:** John McCormick, Janet Green. *HMV*

Victim of Beauty 🐾🐾 1991 A small-town girl comes to the big city and becomes a successful model. However, she then becomes the victim of a fatal attraction killer as all her would-be suitors get killed off one by one. Made for cable television. 90m/C VHS, Closed Caption. Jennifer Rubin, Sally Kellerman, Stephen Shellan, Peter Outerbridge; **Cameos:** Michael Ironside; **D:** Paul Lynch. *WOV, PMS*

Victim of Desire 🎦½ *1994* **(R)** Mysterious death of an embezzler is investigated, only the investigator falls for the sexy widow and begins to doubt her innocence. Also available in an unrated version. *CW:* Sexuality; violence; some language. 85m/C **VHS.** Shannon Tweed, Julie Strain. *NHO*

Victim of Love 🎦🎦 *1991* **(PG-13)** A therapist doesn't know whom to believe when she finds out she and one of her more neurotic patients are sharing the same boyfriend. Only the patient claims the man murdered his wife to be with his lover. Who will be the next victim? Made for television. 92m/C **VHS, Beta, LV.** Pierce Brosnan, JoBeth Williams, Virginia Madsen, Georgia Brown; *D:* Jerry London.

Victimless Crimes *1990* **(R)** The seemingly victimless crime of robbing art galleries turns deadly when betrayal and murder enter the picture. *CW:* Language and violence. 85m/C **VHS.** Debra Sandlund, Craig Bierko, Larry Brandenburg, Peggy Dunne, Richard Redlin, Cheryl Lynn Bruce; *D:* Peter Hawley. *NO*

Victor/Victoria 🎦🎦🎦 *1982* **(PG)** An unsuccessful actress in Depression-era Paris impersonates a man impersonating a woman and becomes a star. Luscious music and sets. Warren as femme fatale and Preston as Andrews' gay mentor are right on target; Garner is charming as the gangster who falls for the woman he thinks she is. 🎵 You and Me; The Shady Dame from Seville; Le Jazz Hot; Crazy World; Chicago Illinois; Gay Peree. 133m/C **VHS, Beta, LV, Letterbox.** Julie Andrews, James Garner, Robert Preston, Lesley Ann Warren, Alex Karras, John Rhys-Davies; *D:* Blake Edwards; *W:* Blake Edwards; *M:* Henry Mancini. Academy Awards '82: Original Song Score and/or Adaptation; Cesar Awards '83: Best Foreign Film; Golden Globe Awards '83: Best Actress—Musical/Comedy (Andrews); National Board of Review Awards '82: Best Supporting Actor (Preston); Writers Guild of America Awards '82: Best Adapted Screenplay; Nominations: Academy Awards '82: Best Actress (Andrews), Best Adapted Screenplay, Best Art Direction/Set Decoration, Best Costume Design, Best Supporting Actor (Preston), Best Supporting Actress (Warren). *MGM*

Victoria Regina 🎦🎦 *1961* In a succession of vignettes, the life of Queen Victoria is viewed, from her ascension to the throne of England in 1837 through the celebration of her Diamond Jubilee. A presentation from "George Schaefer's Showcase Theatre." Made for television. 76m/C **VHS, Beta.** Julie Harris, James Donald, Felix Aylmer, Pamela Brown, Basil Rathbone; *D:* George Schaefer. *FHS*

Victory 🎦🎦½ *1981* **(PG)** Soccer match between WWII American prisoners of war and a German team is set up so that the players can escape through the sewer tunnels of Paris. Of course they want to finish the game first. Not particularly believable as either a soccer flick (even with Pele and other soccer stars) or a great escape, but watchable. 116m/C **VHS, Beta, Closed Caption.** Sylvester Stallone, Michael Caine, Max von Sydow, Pele, Carole Laure, Bobby Moore, Daniel Massey; *D:* John Huston; *W:* Jeff Maguire, Djordje Milicevic; *M:* Bill Conti. *FOX, WAR*

The Victory 🎦🎦 *1988* **(PG)** In 1967 Montreal, an American college exchange student falls in love with a French-Canadian co-ed. Can love survive their different cultures? 95m/C **VHS, Beta.** Vincent Van Patten, Cloris Leachman, Eddie Albert, Claire Pimpare, Nicholas Campbell, Jack Wetherall, Jacques Godin, Marthe Mercure; *D:* Larry Kent.

The Video Dead woof! *1987* **(R)** Gorefarce in which murderous zombies emerge from a possessed television and wreak havoc. 90m/C **VHS, Beta.** Roxanna Augesen, Rocky Duvall, Michael St. Michaels; *D:* Robert Scott. *NLC*

Video Murders 🎦 *1987* A police detective tracks down a rapist/murderer who tapes all his own crimes. 90m/C **VHS, Beta.** Eric Brown, Virginia Loridans, John Ferita. *TWE*

Video Violence 🎦 *1987* A gory spoof about a video store owner who discovers that his customers have grown bored with the usual Hollywood horror movies and decide to shoot some

flicks of their own. Followed by a sequel. 90m/C **VHS, Beta.** Art Neill, Jackie Neill, William Toddie, Bart Sumner; *D:* Gary P. Cohen. *NO*

Video Violence Part 2...The Exploitation! 🎦 *1987* Two sickos named Howard and Eli run a cable television network where talk show guests are spindled and mutilated. 90m/C **VHS, Beta.** Uke, Bart Sumner, Lee Miller; *D:* Gary P. Cohen. *NO*

Video Wars woof! *1984* Video games explode randomly. A wicked computer whiz is behind it all in a blackmail scheme. 90m/C **VHS.** George Diamond. *BFV*

Videodrome 🎦🎦 *1983* Woods is a cable TV programmer with a secret yen for sex and violence, which he satisfies by watching a pirated TV show. "Videodrome" appears to show actual torture and murder, and also seems to control the thoughts of its viewers—turning them into human VCRs. Cronenberg's usual sick fantasies are definitely love 'em or leave 'em. Special effects by Rick Baker. 87m/C **VHS, Beta, LV.** *CA* James Woods, Deborah Harry, Sonja Smits, Peter Dvorsky; *D:* David Cronenberg; *W:* David Cronenberg; *C:* Mark Irwin; *M:* Howard Shore. Genie Awards '84: Best Director (Cronenberg). *MGM*

Vietnam, Texas 🎦 *1990* **(R)** Vietnam vet leaves his past to become a priest. But he returns to violence when he discovers his Vietnamese daughter is in the hands of Houston's most relentless gangster. 101m/C **VHS, Beta, LV.** Robert Ginty, Haing S. Ngor, Tamlyn Tomita, Tim Thomerson; *D:* Robert Ginty; *W:* C. Courtney Joyner, Tom Badal. *COL*

Vietnam War Story 1 *1988* Three hard-hitting Vietnam War stories on tape. "The Mine," "Home," and "The Pass." Each is an intimate account straight from the men who lived them. Poignant and action-packed. Made for television. 87m/C **VHS, Closed Caption.** Eriq La Salle, Nicholas Cascone, David Harris, Tom Fridley. *NO*

Vietnam War Story 2 *1988* Three short, made-for-television war stories set in Vietnam: "An Old Ghost Walks the Earth," "R & R," and "The Fragging." 90m/C **VHS, Beta, Closed Caption.** Tim Guinee, Tate Donovan, Cynthia Bain, Wesley Snipes, David Niedorf. *NO*

Vietnam War Story 3 *1989* Three episodes of the television series: "Separated," "Dusk to Dawn" and "The Promise." 90m/C **VHS, Beta.** Tom Hodges, Todd Graff, Gregory Cooke, Francois Chau, Stacy Edwards, Laura Harrington, Raymond Cruz. *NO*

A View to a Kill 🎦🎦 *1985* **(PG)** This James Bond mission takes him to the United States, where he must stop the evil Max Zorin from destroying California's Silicon Valley. Feeble and unexciting plot with unscary villain. Duran Duran performs the catchy title tune. Moore's last appearance as 007. 131m/C **VHS, Beta, LV, Letterbox, Closed Caption.** *GB* Roger Moore, Christopher Walken, Tanya Roberts, Grace Jones, Patrick Macnee, Lois Maxwell, Dolph Lundgren, Desmond Llewelyn; *D:* John Glen; *W:* Michael G. Wilson; *M:* John Barry. *FOX, TLF*

Vigil 🎦🎦🎦 *1984* A stark, dreamy parable about a young girl, living on a primitive farm in a remote New Zealand valley, who watches her family collapse after a stranger enters their territory. Visually ravishing and grim; Ward's first American import. Predecessor to "The Navigator." 90m/C **VHS.** *NZ* Penelope Stewart, Bill Kerr, Fiona Kay, Gordon Shields, Frank Whitten; *D:* Vincent Ward; *W:* Vincent Ward. *FXL*

Vigilante woof! *Street Gang 1983* **(R)** Frustrated ex-cop, tired of seeing criminals returned to the street, joins a vigilante squad dedicated to law and order. Often ridiculous and heavy handed. 91m/C **VHS, Beta.** Carol Lynley, Robert Forster, Rutanya Alda; *D:* William Lustig. *ART, VES*

The Vigilantes Are Coming 🎦🎦 *1936* "The Eagle" sets out to avenge his family and upsets a would-be dictator's plot to establish an empire in California. In 12 chapters; the first is 32 minutes, and additional chapters are 18 min-

utes each. 230m/B **VHS, Beta.** Bob Livingston, Kay Hughes, Guinn "Big Boy" Williams, Raymond Hatton, William Farnum; *D:* Mack V. Wright, Ray Taylor. *NOS, VCN, DVT*

Vigilantes of Boom Town 🎦🎦½ *1946* A championship prize fight is the cover for a bank robbery which must be foiled by Red Ryder. 54m/B **VHS, Beta.** Allan "Rocky" Lane, Robert (Bobby) Blake, Peggy Stewart, Martha Wentworth, Roscoe Karns, Roy Barcroft, George Turner, John Dehner; *D:* R.G. Springsteen. *NOS, VCN*

Viking Massacre 🎦🎦½ *Knives of the Avenger; I Coltelli Del Vendicatore 1965* Brutal ax-bearing Vikings ruin the days of hundreds in this primitive story of courage and desperation. John Hold is the pseudonym for director Mario Bava. 90m/C **VHS, Beta.** *IT* Cameron Mitchell; *D:* John Hold. *NO*

The Viking Sagas 🎦 *1995* **(R)** Kjartan (Moeller) is the warrior who must avenge his father's execution, defend his people, and fight for his country's survival against evil oppressors. At least there's a beautiful babe around to offer him some comfort. The Icelandic scenery is the best thing about the movie. *CW:* Brutal and bloody Viking combat; some sexuality. 83m/C **VHS, LV, Closed Caption.** Ralph Moeller, Ingibjorg Stefansdottir, Sven-Ole Thorsen; *D:* Michael Chapman; *W:* Dale Herd, Paul R. Gurian; *M:* George S. Clinton. *NLC*

The Vikings 🎦🎦½ *1958* A Viking king and his son kidnap a Welsh princess and hold her for ransom. Depicts the Vikings' invasion of England. Great location footage of both Norway and Brittany. Basic costume epic with good action scenes. Narrated by Welles. 116m/C **VHS, Beta, LV, Letterbox.** Kirk Douglas, Ernest Borgnine, Janet Leigh, Tony Curtis, James Donald, Alexander Knox; *D:* Richard Fleischer; *W:* Calder Willingham; *C:* Jack Cardiff. *MGM*

Villa Rides 🎦🎦 *1968* A flying gun-runner aids Francisco "Pancho" Villa's revolutionary Mexican campaign. Considering the talent involved, this one is a disappointment. Check out Brynner's hair. 125m/C **VHS, Beta.** Yul Brynner, Robert Mitchum, Charles Bronson, Herbert Lom, Jill Ireland, Robert Towne; *D:* Buzz Kulik; *W:* Robert Towne, Sam Peckinpah; *C:* Jack Hildyard; *M:* Maurice Jarre. *BAR*

A Village Affair 🎦🎦½ *1995* Ward is a young wife and mother, living what appears to be a perfect life in a quiet English village, when she meets a neighbor's daughter (Fox) who's just returned from America. Fox makes her interests clear and soon the two women are having an affair that shatters the peacefulness around them. Based on a novel by Joanna Trollope. 108m/C **VHS.** *GB* Sophie Ward, Kerry Fox, Nathaniel Parker, Claire Bloom, Michael Gough, Barbara Jefford, Jeremy Northam, Rosalie Crutchley; *D:* Moira Armstrong; *W:* Alma Cullen; *C:* John Else. *VTR, VIF*

Village of the Damned 🎦🎦🎦 *1960* A group of unusual children are born in a small English village. They avoid their fathers and other men, except for the one who is their teacher. He discovers they are the vanguard of an alien invasion and leads the counter-attack. Exciting and bone-chilling low-budget thriller. From the novel, "The Midwich Cuckoos," by John Wyndham. The sequel, "The Children of the Damned" (1964) is even better. 78m/B **VHS, Beta, LV.** *GB* George Sanders, Barbara Shelley, Martin Stephens, Laurence Naismith, Michael C. Goetz, Michael Gwynn, John Phillips, Richard Vernon, Jenny Laird, Richard Warner, Thomas Heathcote, Charlotte Mitchell, John Stuart, Bernard Archard; *D:* Wolf Rilla; *W:* Wolf Rilla, Stirling Silliphant, George Harley. *MGM, MLB*

Village of the Damned 🎦½ *1995* **(R)** The quiet town of Midwich, California, has been enveloped by a strange force that seems to have impregnated the local women. The albino children born of this incident have disturbing telepathic powers that they display through their bright orange and red eyes—supposedly precipitating a plot to take control. A pale remake of the 1960 British horror classic, which was based on John Wyndham's novel "The Midwich Cuckoos." Fails to capture the eeriness of it's predecessor and is bogged down with awkward casting, absurd dialogue, and a brood of children with glowing eyes that make them less like a threat and more like Nintendo addicts. **CW:** Some sci-fi terror and violence. **98m/C VHS, LV, Closed Caption.** Christopher Reeve, Kirstie Alley, Linda Kozlowski, Mark Hamill, Meredith Salenger, Michael Pare, Peter Jason, Constance Forslund, Karen Kahn; **D:** John Carpenter; **W:** John Carpenter, David Himmelstein; **C:** Gary B. Kibbe; **M:** John Carpenter, Dave Davies. *USH*

Village of the Giants 🎬 1965 A group of beer-guzzling teenagers become giants after eating a mysterious substance invented by a 12-year-old genius. Fun to pick out all the soon-to-be stars. Totally silly premise with bad special effects and minimal plot follow-through. Based on an H.G. Wells story. **82m/C VHS, Beta.** Ron Howard, Johnny Crawford, Tommy Kirk, Beau Bridges, Freddy Cannon, Beau Brummel; **D:** Bert I. Gordon; **M:** Jack Nitzsche. *NLC, MLB*

The Villain 🎬½ *Cactus Jack* 1979 (PG) An unfunny spoof of "B" westerns that is almost like a live-action "Roadrunner" cartoon. Douglas plays Cactus Jack, a highwayman who keeps trying to kidnap fair damsel Ann-Margret. Hero Schwarzenegger keeps rescuing her. Lynde is amusing as the uptight Indian chief Nervous Elk. **93m/C VHS.** Kirk Douglas, Ann-Margret, Arnold Schwarzenegger, Paul Lynde, Foster Brooks, Ruth Buzzi, Jack Elam, Strother Martin, Robert Tessier, Mel Tillis; **D:** Hal Needham. *COL*

The Villain Still Pursued Her 🎬🎬 1941 A poor hero and rich villain vie for the sweet heroine in this satire of old-fashioned temperance melodrama. Keaton manages to shine as the hero's sidekick. **67m/B VHS, Beta.** Anita Louise, Alan Mowbray, Buster Keaton, Hugh Herbert; **D:** Eddie Cline. *NOS, VYY, DVT*

Vincent & Theo 🎬🎬🎬½ 1990 (PG-13) The story of Impressionist painter Vincent van Gogh, and his brother Theo, a gallery owner who loved his brother's work, yet could not get the public to buy it. Increasing despair and mental illness traps both men, as each struggles to create beauty in a world where it has no value. Altman has created a stunning portrait of "the artist" and his needs. The exquisite cinematography will make you feel as if you stepped into van Gogh's work. **138m/C VHS, Beta, LV.** Tim Roth, Paul Rhys, Johanna Ter Steege, Wladimir Yordanoff; **D:** Robert Altman. *TVC*

Vincent, Francois, Paul and the Others 🎬🎬🎬 *Vincent, Francois, Paul et les Autres* 1976 Three middle-aged Frenchmen rely on their friendships to endure a host of mid-life crises. In French with English subtitles. **113m/C VHS, Beta, LV, Letterbox.** *FR* Yves Montand, Gerard Depardieu, Michel Piccoli, Stephane Audran; **D:** Claude Sautet. *FCT, CVC, TPV*

Vincent: The Life and Death of Vincent van Gogh 🎬🎬🎬 1987 Van Gogh's work and creativity is examined in a documentary manner through his life and his letters. Thoughtful and intriguing production. Narrated by John Hurt as van Gogh. **99m/C VHS, LV.** *AU* **D:** Paul Cox; **W:** Paul Cox; **M:** Norman Kaye; **V:** John Hurt. *FCT, CRY, SIG*

The Vindicator 🎬🎬 *Frankenstein '88* 1985 (R) A scientist killed in a lab accident is transformed into a cyborg who runs amok and murders indiscriminately. A modernized Frankenstein, with interesting special effects and well drawn characters. **92m/C VHS, Beta, Closed Caption.** *CA* Terri Austin, Richard Cox, David McIlwraith, Pam Grier; **D:** Jean-Claude Lord. *FOX*

The Vineyard 🎬 1989 (R) Hapless victims are lured to a Japanese madman's island, where he drinks their blood and maintains a questionable immortality. **95m/C VHS, Beta, LV.** James Hong, Karen Witter, Michael Wong; **D:** James Hong, Bill Rice. *VTR*

Violated 🎬 1953 Pathetic production about New York police attempting to track down a sex-maniac murderer who slays his victims and then gives them a haircut. Unbelievably bad. **78m/B VHS.** Wim Holland, Lili Dawn, Mitchell Kowal, Vicki Carlson, William Martell; **D:** Walter Strate. *SNC*

Violated woof! 1984 A detective endeavors to implicate a local businessman in the rapes of two beautiful women. Exploitative and dreary. **88m/C VHS, Beta.** John Heard, J.C. Quinn, April Daisy White, Samantha Fox; **D:** Richard Cannistraro. *ART, VES*

Violence at Noon 🎬🎬🎬 1966 Highly disturbing film in which two women protect a brutal sex murderer from the law. Living among a quiet community of intellectuals, this conspiracy ends in a shocking finale in Oshima's stylized masterpiece. In Japanese with English subtitles. **99m/B VHS, Closed Caption.** *JP* Saeda Kawaguchi, Akiko Koyama; **D:** Nagisa Oshima. *KIV*

Violent Breed 🎬 1983 A CIA operative is sent on a mission to put a black marketeer out of business. **91m/C VHS, Beta.** *IT* Henry Silva, Harrison Muller, Woody Strode; **D:** Fernando Di Leo. *MGM*

The Violent Men 🎬🎬½ *Rough Company* 1955 Big-time land baron Robinson is trying to push out all other landowners in the valley, including Ford. At first Ford refuses to fight back, but after one of Robinson's henchmen kills one of his hired hands, he starts an all-out war against Robinson to save his land. Stanwyck as Robinson's wife and Keith as his brother are wicked as the two urging him on and having an affair behind his back. Based on the novel "Rough Company" by Donald Hamilton. **95m/C VHS, LV, Letterbox.** Glenn Ford, Barbara Stanwyck, Edward G. Robinson, Dianne Foster, Brian Keith, May Wynn; **D:** Rudolph Mate; **C:** Burnett Guffey. *COL*

Violent Ones woof! 1968 Three men who are suspected of raping a young girl are threatened with lynching by an angry mob of townspeople. Badly acted, poorly directed, uneven and feeble. **96m/C VHS, Beta.** Fernando Lamas, David Carradine; **D:** Fernando Lamas. *REP*

Violent Professionals 🎬½ *La Polizia vuole Giustizia* 1973 Suspended cop runs into resistance inside and outside the force when he infiltrates the mob to get the goods on a crime boss. **100m/C VHS, Beta.** *IT* Richard Conte, Luc Merenda; **D:** Sergio Martino. *NO*

Violent Women 🎬 1959 Five female convicts escape and embark on a bloody journey through the countryside, pursued by the authorities. Shows women can be just as brutal as any man. **61m/C VHS, Beta.** Jennifer Slater, Jo Ann Kelly, Sandy Lyn, Eleanor Blair, Pati Magee; **D:** Barry Mahon. *THV*

The Violent Years woof! *Female* 1956 Spoiled high-school debutantes form a vicious all-girl gang and embark on a spree that includes murder, robbery, and male rape. Justice wins out in the end. Exploitive trash written by Wood, who directed the infamous "Plan 9 from Outer Space." **60m/B VHS, Beta.** Jean Moorehead, Barbara Weeks, Glenn Corbett; **D:** Edward D. Wood Jr., Franz Eichhorn; **W:** Edward D. Wood Jr. *SNC, RHI, NOA*

Violent Zone 🎬 1989 Mercenaries go on a supposed rescue mission in the wilderness. **92m/C VHS.** John Douglas, Chad Hayward, Christopher Weeks; **D:** John Garwood; **W:** David Pritchard, John Bushelman.

Violets Are Blue 🎬🎬½ 1986 (PG-13) Two high-school sweethearts are reunited in their hometown years later and try to rekindle their romance—even though the man is married. **86m/C VHS, Beta, LV, Closed Caption.** Kevin Kline, Sissy Spacek, Bonnie Bedelia, John Kellogg, Augusta Dabney, Jim Standford; **D:** Jack Fisk; **W:** Naomi Foner; **C:** Ralf Bode; **M:** Patrick Williams. *COL*

Violette 🎬🎬🎬 *Violette Noziere* 1978 (R) Fascinating true-life account of a 19-year-old French girl in the 1930s who, bored with her life and wanting to be with her lover, decides to poison her parents so she can receive her inheritance. Her

mother survives but her father dies, and the girl is sent to prison for murder. Extraordinary performance by Huppert and the film is visually stunning. **122m/C VHS.** *FR* Isabelle Huppert, Stephane Audran, Jean Carmet, Jean Francoise, Bernadette LaFont; **D:** Claude Chabrol. Cannes Film Festival '78: Best Actress (Huppert); Cesar Awards '79: Best Supporting Actress (Audran). *NYF*

VIP, My Brother Superman 1990 The Vips are modern-day descendants of superbeings about to become legends in their own times. SuperVip is broad of chest and pure in spirit while his brother MiniVip possesses only limited powers. From the creator of "Allegro Non Troppo" comes this enticing, amusing piece of animation. **90m/C VHS.** **D:** Bruno Bozzetto. *EXP, TPV*

Viper 🎬 1988 A woman battles a cryptic anti-terrorist band to avenge the murder of her husband. **96m/C VHS.** Linda Purl, Chris Robinson, James Tolkan; **D:** Peter Maris.

The V.I.P.'s 🎬🎬🎬 1963 Slick, sophisticated drama set in the V.I.P. lounge of a British airport. Trapped by fog, several of the passengers get acquainted and are forced to face their problems as they spend the night in the airport lounge. Taylor stars as Frances Andros, a wealthy young woman leaving her husband (Burton) for life in the U.S. with her lover, Jourdan. A movie tycoon, an Australian entrepreneur, his secretary, and a duchess are among the other passengers grounded by the fog. Both Rutherford and Smith give excellent performances and it was a tossup as to which actress would be nominated for the Oscar. **119m/C VHS.** *GB* Elizabeth Taylor, Richard Burton, Louis Jourdan, Elsa Martinelli, Maggie Smith, Rod Taylor, Orson Welles, Linda Christian, Dennis Price; **D:** Anthony Asquith; **W:** Terence Rattigan; **C:** Jack Hildyard; **M:** Miklos Rozsa. Academy Awards '63: Best Supporting Actress (Rutherford); Golden Globe Awards '64: Best Supporting Actress (Rutherford); National Board of Review Awards '63: Best Supporting Actress (Rutherford). *MGM*

Virgin Among the Living Dead 🎬 1971 (R) Young woman travels to remote castle when she hears of relative's death. Once there, she finds the residents a tad weird and has bad dreams in which zombies chase her. Bizarre even for Franco, who seems to have been going through a "Pasolini" phase while making this one. **90m/C VHS, Beta.** *SP* Christina von Blanc, Britt Nichols, Howard Vernon, Anne Libert, Rose Kiekens, Paul Muller; **D:** Jess (Jesus) Franco. *NO*

The Virgin and the Gypsy 🎬🎬½ 1970 (R) An English girl brought up in a repressive household in 1920s England falls in love with a gypsy. Based on the novel by D.H. Lawrence. Directorial debut of Miles. **92m/C VHS.** *GB* Joanna Shimkus, Franco Nero, Honor Blackman, Mark Burns; **D:** Christopher Miles; **W:** Alan Plater. *NO*

Virgin High 🎬 1990 (R) Three young men sneak into an all-girls Catholic boarding school with hilarious consequences. Ward (TV's Robin, from "Batman") makes a special appearance in bondage in this sex farce. **90m/C VHS, LV.** Burt Ward, Linnea Quigley, Tracy Dali, Richard Gabai, Catherine McGuiness, Chris Dempsey; **D:** Richard Gabai; **W:** Richard Gabai, Jeff Neal. *COL*

Virgin Machine 🎬🎬 *Jungfrauenmaschine* 1988 Lesbian journalist Dorothy Muller (Blum) is unhappy in her native Hamburg and decides to move to California to pursue her idea of romantic love. English and German with English subtitles. **91m/B VHS.** *GE* Ina Blum, Susie Bright, Shelley Mars, Dominique Gaspar; **D:** Monika Treut; **W:** Monika Treut; **C:** Elfi Mikesch. *FRF*

The Virgin of Nuremberg 🎬½ *Horror Castle; Terror Castle; Castle of Terror; La Vergine di Norimberga* 1965 A young woman enters her new husband's ancestral castle and is stalked by the specter of a legendary sadist. **82m/C VHS, Beta.** *IT* Rossana Podesta, George Riviere, Christopher Lee, Jim Dolen; **D:** Anthony (Antonio Margheriti) Dawson. *MOV*

The Virgin Queen 🎬🎬🎬 1955 Davis stars in this historical drama, which focuses on the stormy relationship between the aging Queen and Sir Walter Raleigh. Collins is the lady-in-waiting who is the secret object of Raleigh's true affections. Previously, Davis played Queen Elizabeth I in "Elizabeth and Essex." Davis holds things together. 92m/C VHS, Beta, Closed Caption. Bette Davis, Richard Todd, Joan Collins, Herbert Marshall, Dan O'Herlihy, Jay Robinson, Romney Brent; D: Henry Koster. Nominations: Academy Awards '55: Best Costume Design (Color). FOX

Virgin Queen of St. Francis High 🎬 1988 (PG) Two high school foes make a bet that one of them can take the "virgin" title away from gorgeous Christensen by summer's end. She has to fight off their advances, but grows to like Straface. 89m/C VHS, Beta, LV. CA Joseph R. Straface, Stacy Christensen, J.T. Wotton; D: Francesco Lucente.

Virgin Sacrifice 🎬 1959 A great white hunter looking for zoo-bound jaguars confronts the virgin-sacrificing, Tiger God-revering natives of Guatemala. 67m/C VHS, Beta, LV. David Dalie, Antonio Gutierrez, Angelica Morales, Fernando Wagner; D: Fernando Wagner. NO

The Virgin Soldiers 🎬🎬½ 1969 (R) A British comedy about greenhorn military recruits stationed in Singapore, innocent of women as well as battle, and their struggles to overcome both situations. A good cast raises this above the usual low-brow sex farce. Based on the novel by Leslie Thomas. Followed by "Stand Up Virgin Soldiers." 96m/C VHS, Beta. GB Hywel Bennett, Nigel Davenport, Lynn Redgrave, Nigel Patrick, Rachel Kempson, Jack Shepherd, Tsai Chin; D: John Dexter; W: John Hopkins. COL

The Virgin Spring 🎬🎬🎬½ Jungfrukallan 1959 Based on a medieval ballad and set in 14th-century Sweden. The rape and murder of a young innocent spurs her father to vengeance and he kills her attackers. Over the girl's dead body, the father questions how God could have let any of it happen, but he comes to find solace and forgiveness. Stunning Bergman compositions. In Swedish with English subtitles; also available in dubbed version. 88m/B VHS, Beta. SW Max von Sydow, Birgitta Valberg, Gunnel Lindblom, Brigitta Pattersson, Axel Duborg; D: Ingmar Bergman; C: Sven Nykvist. Academy Awards '60: Best Foreign Language Film; Golden Globe Awards '61: Best Foreign Film; Nominations: Academy Awards '60: Best Costume Design (B & W). HMV

The Virgin Witch 🎬½ Lesbian Twins 1970 (R) Two beautiful sisters are sent to the British countryside, ostensibly for a modeling job. They soon find themselves in the midst of a witches' coven however, and discover one of them is to be sacrificed. The Michelles were "Playboy" magazine's first sister centerfolds. 89m/C VHS, Beta. GB Anne Michelle, Vicki Michelle, Patricia Haines, Keith Buckley, James Chase, Neil Hallett; D: Ray Austin.

Virginia City 🎬🎬🎬 1940 Action-packed western drama set during the Civil War. Flynn is a Union soldier who escapes from a Confederate prison run by Scott, after learning of a gold shipment being sent by Southern sympathizers to aid the Confederacy. He ends up in Virginia City (where the gold-laden wagon train is to leave from) and falls for a dance-hall girl (Hopkins) who turns out to be a Southern spy working for Scott but who falls for Flynn anyway. Bogart is miscast as a half-breed outlaw who aids Scott but wants the gold for himself. Considered a follow-up to "Dodge City." 121m/C VHS. Errol Flynn, Miriam Hopkins, Randolph Scott, Humphrey Bogart, Frank McHugh, Alan Hale, Guinn "Big Boy" Williams, Douglass Dumbrille, Charles Halton; D: Michael Curtiz; M: Max Steiner. MGM

The Virginia Hill Story 🎬🎬 1976 Fictionalized biography of mobster Bugsy Siegel's girlfriend who, in the mid-'50s, was subpoenaed to appear before the Kefauver investigation on crime in the U.S. As the examining lawyer

presents questions regarding her background and connections with the underworld, we see the story of her life. Made for television. 90m/C VHS, Beta. Dyan Cannon, Harvey Keitel, Robby Benson, Allen (Goorwitz) Garfield, John Vernon; D: Joel Schumacher. NO

The Virginian 🎬🎬½ 1923 The second silent version of Owen Wister's classic western novel, inferior to both the 1914 Cecil B. DeMille silent and the 1929 Victor Fleming talkie. Harlan plays the title role as the cowpoke who leads a posse against cattle rustlers and falls in love with a schoolteacher. 79m/B VHS. Kenneth Harlan, Florence Vidor, Russell Simpson, Pat O'Malley, Raymond Hatton; D: Tom Forman. GPV

The Virginian 🎬🎬🎬 1929 A classic early-talkie western about a ranch-hand defeating the local bad guys. One line of dialogue has become, with modification, a standard western cliche: "If you want to call me that, smile." Based on the novel by Owen Wister. With this starring role, Cooper broke away from the juvenile lovers he had been playing to the laconic, rugged male leads he would be known for. Huston is perfectly cast as the outlaw leader. 95m/B VHS, Beta. Gary Cooper, Walter Huston, Richard Arlen, Chester Conklin, Eugene Pallette; D: Victor Fleming. BAR

The Virginian 🎬🎬½ 1946 Cowboy good guy, known as the Virginian (McCrea), and his best pal Steve (Tufts) both fall for Molly (Britton), the Eastern-bred schoolmarm who's come to their Wyoming town. Steve wants to make some quick money and joins up with leader Trampas' (Donlevy) cattle rustling gang. So the Virginian is forced to choose between friendship and the code of the west and Molly wonders if she can accept the country's harsh ways. Based on Owen Wister's 1902 novel. 87m/C VHS, Closed Caption. Joel McCrea, Sonny Tufts, Barbara Britton, Brian Donlevy, Fay Bainter, Tom Tully, Henry O'Neill, William Frawley; D: Stuart Gilmore; W: Frances Goodrich, Albert Hackett; C: Harry Hallenberger; M: Daniele Amfitheatrof. USH

Viridiana 🎬🎬🎬🎬 1961 Innocent girl, with strong ideas about goodness, visits her worldly uncle's home before she takes her vows as a nun. He has developed a sick obsession for her, but after drugging the girl he finds he cannot violate her purity. He tells her, however, she is no longer chaste so she will not join the church. After her uncle's suicide, Viridiana learns she and his illegitimate son Jorge have inherited her uncle's run-down estate. Viridiana opens the house to all sorts of beggars, who take shameless advantage, while Jorge works slowly to restore the estate and improve the lives of those around him. Considered to be one of Bunuel's masterpieces and a bitter allegory of Spanish idealism versus pragmatism and the state of the world. In Spanish with English subtitles. 90m/B VHS, Beta. SP MX Silvia Pinal, Francesco Rabal, Fernando Rey, Margarita Lozano, Victoria Zinny; D: Luis Bunuel; W: Luis Bunuel. Cannes Film Festival '61: Best Film. NOS, HHT, DVT

Virtual Assassin 🎬🎬 Cyberjack 1995 (R) 21st century sci-fi actioner finds the crooked Zef (James) leading his band of thugs into a research lab to steal a powerful computer virus. Naturally, the janitor (Dudikoff) just happens to be an ex-cop with a score to settle with Zef. Predictable but with decent special effects. CW: Language, violence, brief nudity. 99m/C VHS, LV. CA JP Michael Dudikoff, Brion James, Jon Cuthbert, Suki Kaiser, James Thom; D: Robert Lee; W: Eric Poppen. TTC

Virtual Combat 🎬🎬 1995 (R) Ex-cop Quarry (Wilson) teams up with some cyber-girls to stop a madman who's able to manipulate virtual reality programs into living beings and releases a killer who wants to lead a destructive virtual army. 97m/C VHS. Don "The Dragon" Wilson, Athena Massey, Loren Avedon, Kenneth McLeod, Turhan Bey, Stella Stevens; D: Andrew Stevens. APX

Virtual Desire 🎬½ 1995 (R) Brad Collins is bored with his marriage and finds some excitement via sexual games on the Internet. But someone is taking a very close interest in Brad's virtual amours and when his wife is murdered, Brad becomes the prime suspect. CW: Strong sexuality. 92m/C VHS, LV. Michael Meyer, Julie Strain, Gail Harris. TRI

Virtual Encounters 🎬🎬½ 1996 (R) Top-drawer soft-core fluff follows busy executive Amy (Elizabeth Kaitan), whose birthday present is a session of virtual wish fulfillment at a high-tech fantasyland. The fantasies involve masks, leather, desks, broccoli...well, O.K., the broccoli is an exaggeration. This is sexy and kinky, not sick. The action is slickly staged and well photographed by director Richards. Also available in an unrated version at 84 minutes. CW: Nudity, strong sexual content. 80m/C VHS. Elizabeth Kaitan, Taylore St. Claire, Rob Lee; D: Cybil Richards; C: Cybil Richards. AFE

Virtual Seduction 🎬🎬 1996 (R) Liam's (Fahey) taken a job testing a virtual reality pod that can interpret what the user wants—and Liam wants to see his dead girlfriend Paris (Genzel). Only he spends so much time with the virtual Paris, that his real-life gal Laura (Dolenz) is worried about his health and sanity—too bad project developer Grant (Novak) isn't so concerned. CW: Some strong sexuality, violence and language. 84m/C VHS. Jeff Fahey, Ami Dolenz, Carrie Genzel, Frank Novak, Meshach Taylor; D: Paul Ziller. NHO

Virtue's Revolt 🎬½ 1924 A small-town girl is corrupted by the sleazy world of showbiz. Silent. 51m/B VHS, Beta. Edith Thornton, Crauford Kent. NO

Virtuosity 🎬½ 1995 (R) Ex-cop-with-a-tragic-past Parker Barnes (Washington) is sprung from prison to help capture computer-generated killer Sid 6.7 (Crowe), who escapes from cyberspace and goes on a rampage in 1997 Los Angeles. Seems this virtual reality bad guy has a personality composed of some 200 serial killers and criminal minds so Parker's got his work cut out for him. But criminal-behavior psychologist Madison Carter (Lynch) is around to lend her expert advice. Both the charismatically evil Crowe and the sufferingly noble Washington are wasted in this effects-laden thriller that sacrifices character for flash. CW: Strong futuristic violence, some brutal beatings, some language. 105m/C VHS, Beta, Closed Caption. Denzel Washington, Russell Crowe, Kelly Lynch, Stephen Spinella, William Forsythe, Louise Fletcher, William Fichtner, Costas Mandylor, Kevin J. O'Connor; D: Brett Leonard; W: Eric Bernt; C: Gale Tattersall; M: Christopher Young. PAR

Virus 🎬 Fukkatsu no Hi 1982 (PG) After nuclear war and plague destroy civilization, a small group of people gather in Antarctica and struggle with determination to carry on life. A look at man's genius for self-destruction and his endless hope. 102m/C VHS, Beta. JP George Kennedy, Sonny Chiba, Glenn Ford, Robert Vaughn, Stuart Gillard, Stephanie Faulkner, Ken Ogata, Bo Svenson, Olivia Hussey, Chuck Connors, Edward James Olmos; D: Kinji Fukasaku. VTR

Virus 🎬½ 1996 (PG-13) Secret Service agent Ken Fairchild (Bosworth) finds out that biological-warfare chemicals have been spilt in a national park that's the site for an ecological summit between the president and world leaders. It's up to Fairchild and a park ranger (Pinsent) to battle the minions of the chemical's manufacturer who wants to keep the whole thing quiet. CW: Violence, language. 90m/C VHS. Brian Bosworth, Leah K. Pinsent; D: Allan Goldstein. THV

Virus 1998 (R) Curtis, Sutherland, and Baldwin are members of a tugboat crew whose boat has been wrecked by a typhoon. They take refuge aboard a Russian research ship only to discover the Russian crew has been eliminated by a strange life form. The electricity-based alien considers humanity a virus but has taken to ripping apart humans and using their various parts to build itself a body. Not yet reviewed. CW: Sci-fi violence/gore, and for language. **?m/C VHS.** Jamie Lee Curtis, William Baldwin, Donald Sutherland, Joanna Pacula, Sherman Augustus, Clifford Curtis; **D:** John Bruno. *NYR*

The Vision *♂♂* **1987** Suspenseful British production about televangelists who attempt to control their viewers' minds through worldwide satellite broadcasting. **103m/C VHS, Beta.** *GB* Lee Remick, Dirk Bogarde, Helena Bonham Carter, Eileen Atkins; **D:** Norman Stone. *NO*

Vision Quest *♂♂½* *Crazy for You* **1985 (R)** A high school student wants to win the Washington State wrestling championship and the affections of a beautiful older artist. He gives it his all as he trains for the meet and goes after his "vision-quest." A winning performance by Modine raises this above the usual teen coming-of-age movie. Madonna sings "Crazy for You" in a nightclub. Based on novel by Terry Davis. **107m/C VHS, Beta, LV, Closed Caption.** Matthew Modine, Linda Fiorentino, Ronny Cox, Roberts Blossom, Daphne Zuniga, Charles Hallahan, Michael Schoeffling; **D:** Harold Becker; **W:** Darryl Ponicsan; **Performed by:** Madonna. *WAR*

Visions *♂½* **1990** A man's ability to "see" murders before they happen leads police to suspect him of committing them, and he must clear himself. **90m/C VHS.** Joe Balogh, Alice Villarreal, Tom Taylor, A.R. Newman, J.R. Pella; **D:** Stephen E. Miller. *NO*

Visions of Evil *♂* **1973** A young woman, recently released from a mental institution, is plagued by a series of terrifying visions when she moves into a house where a brutal axe murder took place. **85m/C VHS, Beta.** Lori Sanders, Dean Jagger.

Visions of Light: The Art of Cinematography *♂♂♂* **1993** Excellent documentary on the way films look and how the art of photographing movies can contribute as much, if not more, than cast, director, and script. Scenes from 125 films, from "Birth of a Nation" to "GoodFellas" are shown, with commentary from a number of cinematographers, including Gordon Willis, William A. Fraker, Conrad Hall, Ernest Dickerson, Vilmos Zsigmond, and Michael Chapman, on how they achieved certain effects and their collaborations with the director of the film. **95m/C VHS, LV.** **D:** Arnold Glassman, Todd McCarthy; **W:** Todd McCarthy. New York Film Critics Awards '93: Best Feature Documentary; National Society of Film Critics Awards '93: Best Feature Documentary. *FOX*

Visitants *♂* **1987** Aliens descend irreverently on a small town in the 1950s, with unexpected comedic results. **93m/C VHS, Beta.** Marcus Vaughter, Johanna Grika, Joel Hile, Nicole Rio; **D:** Rick Sloane. *TWE*

Visiting Hours *♂* *The Fright; Get Well Soon* **1982 (R)** Psycho-killer slashes his female victims and photographs his handiwork. Grant is one of his victims who doesn't die, so the killer decides to visit the hospital and finish the job. Fairly graphic and generally unpleasant. **101m/C VHS, Beta.** *CA* Lee Grant, William Shatner, Linda Purl, Michael Ironside; **D:** Jean-Claude Lord; **W:** Brian Taggert; **M:** Jonathan Goldsmith. *FOX*

The Visitor *♂½* **1980 (R)** Affluent handsome doctor and mate conspire with grisly devil worshipers to conceive devil child. **90m/C VHS.** Mel Ferrer, Glenn Ford, Lance Henriksen, John Huston, Shelley Winters, Joanne Nail, Sam Peckinpah; **D:** Giullo Paradisi. *UAV, HHE*

Visitor from the Grave *♂* **1981** When an American heiress and her boyfriend dispose of a dead man's body, his spirit comes back to haunt them. This annoys them. **60m/C VHS, Beta.** Simon MacCorkindale, Kathryn Leigh Scott, Gareth Thomas, Mia Nadasi. *ART*

The Visitors *♂½* **1989 (R)** Ghosts come to stay at a young family's dream house in Sweden. Not exactly a novel treatment or a novel premise. **102m/C VHS, Beta, LV.** *SW* Keith Berkeley, Lena Endre, John Force, John Olsen, Joanna Berg, Brent Landiss, Patrick Ersgard; **D:** Joakim Ersgard. *THV*

The Visitors *♂♂* *Les Visiteurs* **1995 (R)** Time travel comedy features 12th century knight Godefroy (Reno) and his vassal Jacquasse (Clavier) crossing paths with a powerful witch (and evidently pissing her off) since she casts a spell causing Godefroy to accidentally kill his father-in-law. So Godefroy contacts a wizard to give him a time travel potion so he can go back and stop the shooting. Too bad the potion hurls knight and vassal forward into present-day France. French with subtitles. **CW:** Language. **106m/C VHS, LV, Closed Caption.** *FR* Jean Reno, Christian Clavier, Mariann Chazel, Valerie Lemercier, Christian Bujeau; **D:** Jean-Marie Poire; **W:** Christian Clavier, Jean-Marie Poire; **C:** Jean-Yves Le Mener; **M:** Eric Levi. *TOU*

Vital Signs *♂* **1990 (R)** Hackneyed drama about six medical students enduring the tribulations of their profession. **102m/C VHS, Beta, LV, Closed Caption.** Adrian Pasdar, Diane Lane, Jack Gwaltney, Laura San Giacomo, Jane Adams, Tim Ransom, Bradley Whitford, Lisa Jane Persky, William Devane, Norma Aleandro, Jimmy Smits, James Karen, Telma Hopkins; **D:** Marisa Silver; **W:** Jeb Stuart; **M:** Miles Goodman. *FOX*

Viva Knievel *WOOF!* *Seconds to Live* **1977 (PG)** Crooks plan to sabotage Knievel's daredevil jump in Mexico and then smuggle cocaine back into the States in his coffin. Unintentionally campy. **106m/C VHS, Beta.** Evel Knievel, Gene Kelly, Lauren Hutton, Red Buttons, Leslie Nielsen, Cameron Mitchell, Marjoe Gortner, Albert Salmi, Dabney Coleman; **D:** Gordon Douglas; **M:** Charles Bernstein. *WAR*

Viva Las Vegas *♂♂½* *Love in Las Vegas* **1963** Race car driver Elvis needs money to compete against rival Danova in the upcoming Las Vegas Grand Prix. He takes a job in a casino and romances fellow employee Ann-Margret, who turns out to be his rival for the grand prize in the local talent competition. Good pairing between the two leads, and the King does particularly well with the title song. ♫ The Lady Loves Me; Viva Las Vegas; What'd I Say; I Need Somebody to Lean On; Come On, Everybody; Today, Tomorrow and Forever; If You Think I Don't Need You; Appreciation; My Rival. **85m/C VHS, Beta, LV, Letterbox.** Elvis Presley, Ann-Margret, William Demarest, Jack Carter, Cesare Danova, Nicky Blair, Larry Kent; **D:** George Sidney; **C:** Joseph Biroc. *MGM*

Viva Maria! *♂♂½* **1965 (R)** Tongue-in-cheek comedy with Bardot and Moreau as two dancers (both named Maria) in a show traveling through Mexico. The two become incensed by the poverty of the peasants and decide to turn revolutionary (especially after Moreau has an affair with revolutionary leader Hamilton, who promptly gets killed). The two French sex symbols are a fine match. **119m/C VHS.** *FR IT* Jeanne Moreau, Brigitte Bardot, George Hamilton, Paulette Dubost, Claudio Brook; **D:** Louis Malle; **W:** Louis Malle, Jean-Claude Carriere; **M:** Georges Delerue. *MGM*

Viva Max *♂♂½* **1969** A blundering modern-day Mexican general and his men recapture the Alamo, and an equally inept American force, headed by Winters, is sent to rout them out. Mostly works, with some very funny scenes. Ustinov is great. **93m/C VHS.** Peter Ustinov, Jonathan Winters, John Astin, Pamela Tiffin, Keenan Wynn; **D:** Jerry Paris. *REP*

Viva Villa! *♂♂♂* **1934** Exciting action biography of Mexican revolutionary Pancho Villa, well-portrayed by the exuberant Beery. The film follows the early Robin Hood-like exploits of Villa and his men who soon join Walthall and his peasant army in overthrowing the government. But Villa's bandito instincts and ego cause problems and a power struggle ensues. Director Howard Hawks went uncredited for his work on the film, being fired by the studio after an incident while on location in Mexico. **115m/B VHS, LV.** Wallace Beery, Fay Wray, Stuart Erwin, Leo Carrillo, Donald Cook, George E. Stone, Joseph Schildkraut, Henry B. Walthall, Katherine DeMille, David Durand, Frank Puglia; **D:** Jack Conway; **W:** Ben Hecht. Nominations: Academy Awards '34: Best Adapted Screenplay, Best Picture, Best Sound. *MGM, MOV, BTV*

Viva Zapata! *♂♂♂♂* **1952** Chronicles the life of Mexican revolutionary Emiliano Zapata. Brando is powerful as he leads the peasant revolt in the early 1900s, only to be corrupted by power and greed. Quinn well deserved his Best Supporting Actor Oscar for his performance as Zapata's brother. Based on the novel "Zapata the Unconquered" by Edgcumb Pinchon. **112m/B VHS, Beta, LV.** Marlon Brando, Anthony Quinn, Jean Peters, Margo, Arnold Moss, Joseph Wiseman, Mildred Dunnock; **D:** Elia Kazan; **W:** John Steinbeck; **M:** Alex North. Academy Awards '52: Best Supporting Actor (Quinn); British Academy Awards '52: Best Actor (Brando); Cannes Film Festival '52: Best Actor (Brando); Nominations: Academy Awards '52: Best Actor (Brando), Best Art Direction/Set Decoration (B & W), Best Story & Screenplay, Best Original Dramatic/Comedy Score. *FOX, BTV*

Vivacious Lady *♂♂♂* **1938** Romantic comedy about a mild-mannered college professor who marries a chorus girl. Problems arise when he must let his conservative family and his former fiancee in on the marriage news. Good performances. Appealing. **90m/B VHS, Beta.** Ginger Rogers, James Stewart, James Ellison, Beulah Bondi, Charles Coburn, Jack Carson, Franklin Pangborn; **D:** George Stevens. Nominations: Academy Awards '38: Best Cinematography, Best Sound. *CCB*

Vive L'Amour *♂♂* *Aiqing Wansui* **1994** A furnished Taipei luxury apartment is the setting for three characters who make use of the space but have little connection to each other. Guimei is the real estate agent who's trying to sell the apartment and uses it for casual sex, including an encounter with street vendor Zhaorong. The third part of the triangle is young salesman Kangsheng, who's broken into the place to commit suicide but is forestalled by Zhaorong, with whom Kangsheng then becomes sexually intrigued. The trio come and go, mostly alone, so dialogue is at a minimum. Taiwanese with subtitles. **118m/C VHS.** *TW* Yang Guimei, Chen Zhaorong, Li Kangsheng; **D:** Tsai Ming-Liang. *FXL*

Vogues of 1938 *♂♂* *All This and Glamour Too; Vogues* **1937** As a lark, a rich girl takes a job as a fashion model and incurs the displeasure of Baxter, the owner of the chic fashion house where she works. An early Technicolor fashion extravaganza. ♫ That Old Feeling; Lovely One; Turn On the Red Hot Heat (Burn the Blues Away); King of Jam. **110m/C VHS, Beta.** Joan Bennett, Warner Baxter, Helen Vinson, Mischa Auer, Hedda Hopper, Penny Singleton, Alan Mowbray; **D:** Irving Cummings. Nominations: Academy Awards '37: Best Interior Decoration, Best Song ("That Old Feeling"). *NO*

Volcano *♂♂* **1997 (PG-13)** L.A. has already had to deal with earthquakes, mudslides, raging fires, riots and the acting career of Anna Nicole Smith. Now it's completely roasted by millions of gallons of molten lava. This overblown Rescue 911 has Mike Roark (Jones), the standard take-charge guy, trying to avert total destruction while being assisted by the brainy-but-beautiful seismologist Dr. Amy Barnes (Heche). Many tongue-in-cheek jokes about the general state of chaos in L.A. even on the best of days; but aside from these, the dialogue is cheesy beyond belief. The special effects are very impressive, however. Wilshire Blvd. was actually recreated on a 17-acre set (believed to be the biggest ever) in order to meet its fiery doom. **CW:** Intense depiction of urban disaster and related injuries. **120m/C VHS, Closed Caption.** Tommy Lee Jones, Anne Heche, Gaby Hoffman, Don Cheadle, Keith David, John Corbett, Michael Rispoli, John Carroll Lynch, Jacqueline Kim; **D:** Mick Jackson; **W:** Billy Ray, Jerome Armstrong; **C:** Theo van de Sande; **M:** Alan Silvestri. *FXV*

Volcano: Fire on the Mountain *♂½* *Fire on the Mountain* **1997 (PG)** Cheesy TV disaster flick finds geologist Cortese trying to convince both his boss and the residents of Angel Falls, California that a nearby volcano is about to blow. **99m/C VHS.** Dan Cortese, Cynthia Gibb, Brian Kerwin; **D:**

Graeme Campbell; **C:** Tobias Schliessler; **M:** David Michael Frank. *THV*

Volere Volare 🎬🎬½ **1992 (R)** Shy sound engineer Nichetti shares a studio with his brother. The brother employs a bevy of beauties to dub sound effects onto soft-core porn films while Nichetti works on dubbing classic cartoons. He becomes so involved in his work he actually turns into a cartoon figure, which does nothing for his love life. Then he meets Martina, who's strangely attracted to this cartoon figure. Quirky comedy mixes animation and live action with too many gimmicks and not enough heart. In Italian with English subtitles.**CW:** Nudity. **92m/C VHS, LV.** *IT* Maurizio Nichetti, Angela Finocchiaro, Mariella Valentini, Patrizio Roversi, Remo Remotti, Renato Scarpa; **D:** Maurizio Nichetti, Guido Manuli; **W:** Maurizio Nichetti, Guido Manuli. Montreal World Film Festival '92: Best Director (Nichetti). *COL, FCT*

Volpone 🎬🎬🎬 **1939** A classic adaptation of Ben Jonson's famous tale. A greedy merchant pretends he is dying, leaving a fortune behind, in order see what his family will do to become his heir. In French with English subtitles. **95m/B VHS, Beta.** *FR* Harry Baur, Louis Jouvet, Fernand Ledoux; **D:** Maurice Tourneur. *NOS, HHT, HEG*

Volunteers 🎬🎬 **1985 (R)** Ivy League playboy joins the newly formed Peace Corps to escape gambling debts and finds himself on a bridge-building mission in Thailand. Has its comedic moments, especially with Candy. **107m/C VHS, Beta, LV.** Tom Hanks, John Candy, Rita Wilson, Tim Thomerson, Gedde Watanabe, George Plimpton, Ernest Harada; **D:** Nicholas Meyer; **M:** James Horner. *NO*

Von Ryan's Express 🎬🎬🎬 **1965** An American Air Force colonel leads a group of prisoners-of-war in taking control of a freight train in order to make their exciting escape from a WWII P.O.W. camp in Italy. Strong cast. **117m/C VHS, Beta, LV, Letterbox.** Frank Sinatra, Trevor Howard, Brad Dexter, Raffaella Carra, Sergio Fantoni, John Leyton, Vito Scotti, Edward Mulhare, Adolfo Celi, James Brolin, James B. Sikking; **D:** Mark Robson; **W:** Wendell Mayes; **C:** William H. Daniels; **M:** Jerry Goldsmith. *FOX, FCT*

Voodoo 🎬🎬 **1995 (R)** College student Andy (Feldman) must battle a fraternity, lead by an evil voodoo priest, when they decide to make his girlfriend their next human sacrifice.**CW:** Violence/gore; some nudity. **91m/C VHS, LV, Closed Caption.** Corey Feldman, Sarah Douglas, Jack Nance, Joel J. Edwards; **D:** Rene Eram; **W:** Brian DiMuccio, Dino Vindeni; **M:** Keith Bilderbeck. *APX*

Voodoo Black Exorcist 🎬 **1989** Some 3000 years ago, a black prince was buried alive for messin' with another man's woman. Now he's back...and he's mad—real mad. He's prepared to kill just about everyone. Can he be stopped before all in the modern world are dead?? **m/C VHS.** Aldo Sambrel, Tenyeka Stadle, Fernando Sancho. *HHE*

Voodoo Dawn 🎬🎬 **1989 (R)** Two New Yorkers travel to the Deep South to visit a friend who, it turns out, is the latest victim in a series of really gross voodoo murders. A beautiful girl is written into the plot, and the New York guys have an excuse to stay in voodooville, even though bimbolina's southern accent comes and goes for no discernable reason. Filmed near Charleston, South Carolina, and co-written by Russo of "Night of the Living Dead" fame. **83m/C VHS.** Raymond St. Jacques, Theresa Merritt, Gina Gershon, Kirk Baily, Billy "Sly" Williams, J. Grant Albrecht, Tony Todd; **D:** Steven Fierberg; **W:** John Russo, Jeffrey Delman.

Voodoo Woman 🎬 **1957** An innocent girl is lured into the jungle by an evil scientist who is trying to create the perfect woman to commit murders. He turns the girl into an ugly monster in an attempt to get her to obey his telepathic commands. A campy classic that's as bad as it sounds. **77m/B VHS.** Marla English, Tom Conway, Mike Connors, Lance Fuller; **D:** Edward L. Cahn. *COL, PAR*

Vortex 🎬½ **1981** Punk/film noir style in which a female private eye becomes immersed in corporate paranoia and political corruption. **87m/C VHS.** Lydia Lunch, James Russo, Bill Rice, Richard France, Ann Magnuson, Haoui Montaug, Adele Bertei, Bill Landis; **D:** Scott B, Beth B; **W:** Scott B, Beth B; **C:** Steven Fierberg; **M:** Lydia Lunch, Adele Bertei. *ICA*

Voulez-Vous Danser Avec Moi? 🎬🎬 *Come Dance with Me; Do You Want to Dance with Me?* **1959** A young bride endeavors to clear her husband of murder charges and find the real killer. In French with English subtitles. **90m/C VHS, Beta.** *FR* Brigitte Bardot, Henri Vidal; **D:** Michel Boisrond. *BAR*

A Vow to Kill 🎬🎬½ **1994 (PG-13)** Predictable made-for-cable thriller finds the wealthy Phillips marrying the charming Grieco after a whirlwind courtship. Then, on their honeymoon, she accidentally learns that her new husband has contacted her family and is masquerading as a kidnapper—demanding a large ransom for her safe release. But maybe it's not such a masquerade after all.**CW:** Some terror/violence. **91m/C VHS, Beta, Closed Caption.** Julianne Phillips, Richard Grieco, Gordon Pinsent, Tom Cavanagh, Nicole Oliver; **D:** Harry S. Longstreet; **W:** Harry S. Longstreet, Sean Silas. *PAR*

Voyage 🎬½ **1993 (R)** Boring rip-off of "Dead Calm" and other couple-in-peril-from-psycho-on-boat films. Hauer and Allen are having marital problems and decide to sail away from their troubles with new-found friends Roberts and Nielson. Only their guests are sociopaths. Hauer takes a breather from his psycho roles for a turn as the good guy while Roberts could do his patented crazy act in his sleep. Made for cable television. **?m/C VHS.** Rutger Hauer, Karen Allen, Eric Roberts, Connie Nielson; **D:** John MacKenzie. *ITC*

Voyage en Balloon 🎬🎬½ **1959** This is the delightful story of a young boy (played by the star of "The Red Balloon") who stows away on his grandfather's hot air balloon for an adventurous trip across France. **82m/C VHS, Beta.** *FR* Pascal Lamorisse, Andre Gille, Maurice Baquet; **D:** Albert Lamorisse; **W:** Albert Lamorisse. *COL*

Voyage en Douce 🎬🎬 **1981** Helene and Lucie have been friends since childhood. Helene wants to rent a summer house, and Lucie, fed up with her marriage, agrees to join her on a leisurely journey through the south of France. Thoughtful look at friendship among women. French with subtitles. **95m/C VHS.** *FR* Dominique Sanda, Geraldine Chaplin; **D:** Michel DeVille. *NYF*

Voyage in Italy 🎬🎬½ *Viaggio in Italia; Voyage to Italy; The Lonely Woman; Strangers* **1953** Narrative of a marriage finds unhappy English couple Bergman and Sanders travelling by car to Naples. However, various crises manage to reunite them. Critically mauled upon its release, this third collaboration between Bergman and Rossellini, following "Stromboli" and "Europa '51," later became a big hit with New Wave directors. **83m/B VHS.** *IT* Ingrid Bergman, George Sanders; **D:** Roberto Rossellini; **W:** Roberto Rossellini, Vitaliano Brancatti; **C:** Enzo Serafin; **M:** Renzo Rssellini. *ITC*

The Voyage of Tanai 🎬🎬 **1975 (G)** A young Polynesian battles nature's snarls on his quest to save his village. **90m/C VHS, Beta.** **D:** John Latos. *NO*

Voyage of Terror: The Achille Lauro Affair 🎬🎬½ **1990** Recounting of the 1985 Italian cruise-ship hijacking by four Palestinians. Lancaster is the wheelchair-bound Leon Klinghoffer and Saint is wife Marilyn. Shot on the actual ship and route where the tragedy occurred. Originally a made-for-television miniseries. **120m/C VHS, Closed Caption.** Burt Lancaster, Eva Marie Saint, Robert Culp, Brian Bloom, Dominique Sanda, Rebecca Schaeffer, Joseph Nasser, Gabriele Ferzetti, Renzo Montagnani; **D:** Alberto Negrin.

Voyage of the Damned 🎬🎬🎬 **1976 (G)** The story of one of the most tragic incidents of WWII. In 1939, 1,937 German-Jewish refugees fleeing Nazi Germany are bound for Cuba aboard the Hamburg-America liner S.S. St. Louis. They are refused permission to land in Cuba (and everywhere else) and must sail back to Germany and certain death. Based on the novel by Gordon Thomas and Max Morgan-Witts. **134m/C VHS, Beta.** Faye Dunaway, Max von Sydow, Oskar Werner, Malcolm McDowell, Orson Welles, James Mason, Lee Grant, Katharine Ross, Ben Gazzara, Lynne Frederick, Wendy Hiller, Jose Ferrer, Luther Adler, Sam Wanamaker, Denholm Elliott, Nehemiah Persoff, Julie Harris, Maria Schell, Janet Suzman; **D:** Stuart Rosenberg; **C:** Billy Williams; **M:** Lalo Schifrin. Golden Globe Awards '77: Best Supporting Actress (Ross); Nominations: Academy Awards '76: Best Adapted Screenplay, Best Supporting Actress (Grant), Best Original Score. *FOX*

Voyage of the Heart 🎬🎬 **1990** An aging fisherman meets up with a sexy college girl and the passion begins. **88m/C VHS.** Bill Aldrij, Dunja Djordjenic.

Voyage of the Rock Aliens 🎬 **1987** A quasi-satiric space farce about competing alien rock stars. **97m/C VHS.** Pia Zadora, Tom Nolan, Craig Sheffer, Rhema, Ruth Gordon, Michael Berryman, Jermaine Jackson; **D:** James Fargo.

The Voyage of the Yes 🎬🎬 **1972 (PG)** Two teenagers, one white and one black, in a small sailboat hit rough weather and battle the elements while learning about themselves. Average made-for-television movie. **100m/C VHS.** Desi Arnaz Jr., Mike Evans, Beverly Garland, Skip Homeier, Della Reese, Scoey Mitchell; **D:** Lee H. Katzin. *NO*

A Voyage' Round My Father 🎬🎬🎬 **1989** John Mortimer's adaptation of his semi-autobiographical stage play. Olivier is the eccentric, opinionated blind barrister-father and Bates the exasperated son as both try to come to terms with their stormy family relationship. Well-acted and directed. Made for television. **85m/C VHS, Beta.** *GB* Laurence Olivier, Alan Bates, Jane Asher, Elizabeth Sellars; **D:** Alvin Rakoff. *HBO*

Voyage-Suprise 🎬🎬🎬 **1946** A slapstick comedy about a crazy old man who runs a mystery tour from a dilapidated bus as he takes an unknowing mob of tourists on a cross-country escapade through a brothel, a wedding, criminals, police, terrorists and the Haute-Provence. In French with English subtitles. **108m/B VHS, Beta.** *FR* Martine Carol, Sioel; **D:** Pierre Prevert; **C:** Jean Bourgoin. *FCT, FST*

Voyage to Italy 🎬🎬½ **1953** An unhappy couple, on the verge of divorce, inherit a house in Italy and make a trip to see it. In Italy, they dally with other people but realize their attachment to each other demands they attempt to salvage their marriage. Not the best of the Rossellini-Bergman collaborations. Poor editing and directing undermine weak script. Sanders and Bergman do their best. **87m/B VHS, Beta.** Ingrid Bergman, George Sanders; **D:** Roberto Rossellini. *NOS, FCT*

Voyage to the Bottom of the Sea 🎬🎬🎬 **1961** The crew of an atomic submarine must destroy a deadly radiation belt which has set the polar ice cap ablaze. Fun stuff, with good special effects and photography. Later became a television show. **106m/C VHS, Beta, LV, Letterbox, Closed Caption.** Walter Pidgeon, Joan Fontaine, Barbara Eden, Peter Lorre, Robert Sterling, Michael Ansara, Frankie Avalon; **D:** Irwin Allen; **W:** Irwin Allen, Charles Bennett; **C:** Winton C. Hoch. *FOX, FCT*

Voyage to the Planet of Prehistoric Women woof! *Gill Woman; Gill Women of Venus* **1968** Astronauts journey to Venus, where they discover a race of gorgeous, sea-shell clad women led by Van Doren, as well as a few monsters. Incomprehensible but fun. The third film incorporating the Russian "Planeta Burg" footage. Directed (and narrated) by Bogdanovich under the pseudonym Derek Thomas. **78m/C VHS.**

Mamie Van Doren, Mary Mark, Paige Lee; **D:** Peter Bogdanovich. *SNC*

Voyage to the Prehistoric Planet 🎬½ *Voyage to a Prehistoric Planet* **1965** In the year 2020, an expedition to Venus is forced to deal with dinosaurs and other perils. In the making of this movie, Roger Corman edited in special effects and additional footage from a recently acquired Russian film, "Planeta Burg," and his own "Queen of Blood." **80m/C VHS.** Basil Rathbone, Faith Domergue, Marc Shannon, Christopher Brand; **D:** Curtis Harrington. *NOS, SNC*

Voyager 🎬🎬🎬 **1991 (PG-13)** Restless, middle-aged engineer Walter Faber (Shepherd) tells his life story in a series of flashbacks. Twenty years before (the film starts in 1957) he abandons his pregnant girlfriend who promises to get an abortion. He laters hears she married, had a child, and divorced. While sailing to New York from France Walter falls in love with a young student and accompanies her to Greece to visit her mother. Only then does he realize her true identity, leading to a tragic conclusion. Shepherd's is a glum, repressed performance (in keeping with the character) while Delpy personifies youthful sweetness. Based on the novel "Homo Faber" by Max Frisch. **110m/C VHS, LV.** *FR GE* Sam Shepard, Julie Delpy, Barbara Sukowa, Dieter Kirchlechner, Traci Lind, Deborrra-Lee Furness, August Zirner, Thomas Heinze; **D:** Volker Schlondorff; **W:** Volker Schlondorff, Rudy Wurlitzer.

The Voyeur 🎬 **1994** After ten years of marriage, a couple tries to ignite those sexual fires by spending a weekend in Napa Valley and indulging in erotic sexual games. Based on Lonnie Barbach's book "Erotic Edge." **80m/C VHS.** Al Sapienza, Kim Dawson; **D:** Deborah Shames; **W:** Udana Power. *TPV*

Vukovar 🎬🎬🎬 **1994** Vukovar is a Croat town just across the Danube river from Serbia, in the former Yugoslavia, where different ethnic groups had managed to coexist peacefully. When Croatian Anna (Jokovic) marries her childhood sweetheart, the Serbian Toma (Isakovic), however, their celebration is marred by nationalist demonstrations. Soon Anna's pregnant, Toma has been drafted, and the town comes under siege, with Tomas' parents fleeing, Anna's family killed in a bombing, and Ann herself struggling to survive. Film was condemned by the Croatian government as pro-Serbian propaganda though director Draskovic, a Serbian whose parents are Croatian and Bosnian, strove to be nonpartisan. Serbo-Croatian with subtitles. **94m/C VHS.** *YU* Mirjana Jokovic, Boris Isakovic, Monica Romic; **D:** Boro Draskovic; **W:** Boro Draskovic, Maja Draskovic; **C:** Aleksandar Petkovic. *NYF*

Vulcan God of Fire woof! *Vulcan, Son of Jupiter* **1962** Flash is a muscle-bound Vulcan fighting off cheesy monsters in an effort to win the hand of Venus. **76m/C VHS, Beta.** *IT* Rob Flash, Gordon Mitchell, Bella Cortez; **D:** Emmimo Salvi. *TWE*

Vulture 🎬 **1967** In an attempt to carry out a curse on the descendants of the man who killed his forefather, a scientist tries an atomic transmutation experiment and winds up combining himself with a bird. **91m/C VHS, Beta.** Robert Hutton, Akim Tamiroff, Broderick Crawford, Diane Clare, Philip Friend, Patrick Holt, Annette Carell; **D:** Lawrence Huntington. *NO*

Vultures 🎬 **1984** A dying patriarch summons his predatory family to his home in order to straighten out the distribution of inheritance. One by one, they fall victim to a mysterious murderer. **101m/C VHS, Beta.** Yvonne De Carlo, Stuart Whitman, Jim Bailey, Meredith MacRae, Aldo Ray; **D:** Paul Leder.

W 🎬½ *I Want Her Dead* **1974 (PG)** A woman and her husband are terrorized and must find out why. A single letter "W" is found at the scene of the crimes. Notable only as model Twiggy's first film. **95m/C VHS, Beta.** Twiggy, Dirk Benedict, John Vernon, Eugene Roche; **D:** Richard Quine. *ART, VES*

Wackiest Ship in the Army 🎬🎬½ **1961** A completely undisciplined warship crew must smuggle an Australian spy through Japanese waters during WWII. Odd, enjoyable mixture of action and laughs. Became a TV series. In the middle of the war effort, Nelson straps on a guitar and sings "Do You Know What It Means to Miss New Orleans." **99m/C VHS, Beta, LV.** Jack Lemmon, Ricky Nelson, Chips Rafferty, John Lund, Mike Kellin, Patricia Driscoll; **D:** Richard Murphy. *COL*

Wackiest Wagon Train in the West 🎬 **1977 (G)** Hapless wagon master is saddled with a dummy assistant as they guide a party of five characters across the West. Based on the minor TV sitcom "Dusty's Trail." Produced by the same folks who delivered the similarly premised TV series "Gilligan's Island" and "The Brady Bunch." **86m/C VHS, Beta.** Bob Denver, Forrest Tucker, Jeannine Riley.

Wacko woof! **1983 (PG)** Group of nymphettes and tough guys get caught up in a wild Halloween-pumpkin-lawnmower murder. This spoof of the "Halloween" series works too hard for as few laughs as it gets. **84m/C VHS, Beta, LV.** Stella Stevens, George Kennedy, Joe Don Baker, Andrew Dice Clay; **D:** Greydon Clark. *VES*

The Wacky World of Wills & Burke 🎬🎬 **1985** Comedy based on the adventures of Wills and Burke, the two 19th-century explorers who led the first unsuccessful expedition across the outback—the Lewis and Clark of Australia, if you will. In real life they died during the adventure, a less than wacky finale. "Burke and Wills," out the same year, was a serious treatment of the same story. **102m/C VHS, Beta.** *AU* Garry McDonald, Kim Gyngell, Peter Collingwood, Jonathon Hardy, Mark Little; **D:** Bob Weis. *NO*

Wag the Dog 🎬🎬½ **1997 (R)** Based on the book "American Hero" by Larry Beinhart and adapted by Hilary Henkin and David Mamet. Over-the-top Hollywood producer (Hoffman) is hired by White House officials to stage a military attack against the U.S. to divert media attention from accusations that the President fondled a Girl Scout. Show biz insiders say Hoffman's Motss resembles one-time studio head Robert Evans, Washington insiders wonder if it's a documentary. In fact, the entire film is one big insider's joke. Luckily, it's smart enough, and short enough, to avoid becoming tiresome. Look for cameos by Woody Harrelson and Willie Nelson. Filmed in a speedy 29 days on a $15 million budget. **CW:** Language. **96m/C VHS, LV, Closed Caption, Beta.** Dustin Hoffman, Robert De Niro, Anne Heche, Woody Harrelson, Denis Leary, Willie Nelson, Andrea Martin, Suzanne Cryer, John Michael Higgins, Suzy Plakson, Kirsten Dunst, William H. Macy, Michael Belson; **D:** Barry Levinson; **W:** Hilary Henkin, David Mamet; **C:** Robert Richardson; **M:** Mark Knopfler. National Board of Review Awards '97: Best Supporting Actress (Heche); Nominations: Academy Awards '97: Best Actor (Hoffman), Best Adapted Screenplay; Golden Globe Awards '98: Best Actor—Musical/Comedy (Hoffman), Best Film—Musical/Comedy, Best Screenplay; Screen Actors Guild Award '97: Best Actor (Hoffman); Writers Guild of America '97: Best Adapted Screenplay. *NLC*

Wager of Love 🎬 **1990** While vacationing on their annual pleasure cruise, four women bet on their individual power of seduction. They find themselves competing for passion as each woman's erotic adventure unravels in this exciting and sensual tale. **75m/C VHS, Closed Caption.** Steve Landers, Shelly Johnson, Elliot Silverman, Lisa Cook; **D:** Jason Holt. *CEL*

Wages of Fear 🎬🎬🎬🎬 *Le Salaire de la Peur* **1955** American oil company controls a desolate Central American town whose citizens desperately want out—so desperately that four are willing to risk a suicide mission to deliver nitroglycerine to put out a well-fire raging 300 miles away. The company's cynical head has offered $2000 to each man, enough to finance escape from the hell-hole they live in. Complex, multi-dimensional drama concentrates on character development for the first half—crucial to the film's greatness. This is the restored version. Remade by William Friedkin as "Sorcerer" in 1977. Based on a novel by Georges Arnaud. In French with English subtitles. **138m/B VHS, Beta, LV.** *FR* Yves Montand, Charles Vanel, Peter Van Eyck, Vera Clouzot, Folco Lulli, William Tubbs; **D:** Henri-Georges Clouzot; **W:** Henri-Georges Clouzot; **M:** Georges Auric. British Academy Awards '54: Best Film; Cannes Film Festival '53: Best Actor (Vanel), Best Film. *HHT, SNC, VYY*

Wagner: The Complete Epic 🎬🎬 **1985** The unedited version of the epic made-for-television miniseries dramatizing the life of German composer Richard Wagner. The excellent photography does justice to the elaborate production, shot on some 200 different locations. The actors cringe in the presence of the subject's grandeur; Burton, a shell of his former cinematic self, is painful to watch in his last released film. Frankly, this is way too long. **540m/C VHS, Beta.** *GB HU* Richard Burton, Vanessa Redgrave, Ralph Richardson, John Gielgud, Laurence Olivier; **D:** Tony Palmer. *MVD, KUL*

Wagner: The Movie 🎬½ **1985** Slightly half it's original length, the world's biggest biopic is still huge, sweeping, and long. Incoherent and over-acted. Wagner's music is conducted by Sir Georg Solti. Made for television. **300m/C VHS, Beta.** *GB HU* Richard Burton, Vanessa Redgrave, John Gielgud, Franco Nero, Laurence Olivier; **D:** Tony Palmer. *MVD, GLV*

Wagon Master 🎬🎬🎬 **1950** Two cowboys are persuaded to guide a group of Mormons, led by Bond, in their trek across the western frontier. They run into a variety of troubles, including a band of killers who joins the wagon train to escape a posse. Sensitively directed, realistic and worthwhile. Inspired the TV series "Wagon Train." Also available colorized. **85m/B VHS, Beta, LV, Closed Caption.** Ben Johnson, Joanne Dru, Harry Carey Jr., Ward Bond, Jane Darwell, James Arness; **D:** John Ford. *TTC*

Wagon Tracks 🎬🎬½ **1919** Hart searches for the man responsible for his brother's death. **64m/B VHS.** William S. Hart, Jane Novak, Robert McKim, Lloyd Bacon; **D:** Lambert Hillyer. *GPV*

Wagon Trail 🎬🎬½ **1935** The sheriff's son is blackmailed into helping a gang of robbers, with terrible consequences for himself and his father (Carey), who is fired from his job after the son breaks jail. The new sheriff is secretly chief of the outlaw band. Carey rides back into town and eventually virtue triumphs. Good, tense—but not too tense—western. **59m/B VHS, Beta.** Harry Carey Sr.; **D:** Harry Fraser. *VCN*

Wagon Wheels 🎬🎬 *Caravans West* **1934** Recycling was in vogue in '34, when unused footage from "Fighting Caravans" (1931) with Gary Cooper was used to remake the very same plot. The result is biodegradable. Settlers heading to Oregon are ambushed by bad guy Blue, employed by fur traders. Blue sics Injuns on them too, but don't worry, they make it. Adapted from Zane Grey's novel "Fighting Caravans." **54m/B VHS, Beta.** Randolph Scott, Monte Blue, Gail Patrick, Billy Lee; **D:** Charles T. Barton. *NOS, DVT*

Wagons East 🎬 **1994 (PG-13)** Fed up with prairie hardships, pioneers decide to hitch up to a wagon train and head east. Candy (who died during filming) plays the drunken former wagonmaster hired to get them back home, with Lewis (out of his depth) as a neurotic ex-doctor, and McGinley stuck in the role of a gay bookseller that reeks of stereotypical mannerisms. Script is desperate for humor, which it never finds, and it's hard to watch Candy's performance knowing this mess was his last role. **CW:** Off-color humor. **100m/C VHS, LV, Closed Caption.** John Candy, Richard Lewis, Ellen Greene, John C. McGinley, Robert Picardo, William Sanderson, Thomas F. Duffy, Russell Means, Rodney Grant, Michael Horse, Gailard Sartain, Lochlyn Munro, Stuart Proud Eagle Grant; **D:** Peter Markle; **W:** Matthew Carlson, Jerry Abrahamson. *ART*

Wagon's Westward 🎬½ 1940 Good government agent Morris assumes identity of bad twin brother, who's in jail, in order to catch some outlaws. 53m/B VHS. Chester Morris, Buck Jones, Guinn "Big Boy" Williams, Douglas Fowley, George "Gabby" Hayes, Anita Louise, Ona Munson; **D:** Lew (Louis Friedlander) Landers. *GPV*

Waikiki 🎬½ 1980 Two private eyes set out to prove that their friend is not the "cane field murderer" who is terrorizing the Hawaiian island of Oahu. Harmless but pointless TV pilot. 96m/C VHS, Beta. Dack Rambo, Steve Marachuk, Donna Mills, Cal Bellini, Darren McGavin; **D:** Ron Satlof. *ORI*

Waikiki Wedding 🎬🎬🎬 1937 Enjoyable musical about a scheming pineapple promoter (Crosby) who meets the woman of his dreams in a contest he concocted. Contest winner Ross dislikes Hawaii and wants to go home and Crosby must keep her from going...first for business reasons and later, for love. Supporting cast includes Hawaiian Prince Leilani and a pig. Lots of song and dance and Hawaiian sunsets, along with Burns and Raye, the other couple destined for love on the islands, keep the story moving. 🎵Sweet Leilani; Sweet Is the Word for You; In a Little Hula Heaven; Blue Hawaii; Okolehao; Nani Ona Pua. 89m/B VHS, Closed Caption. Bing Crosby, Bob Burns, Martha Raye, Shirley Ross, George Barbier, Leif Erickson, Grady Sutton, Granville Bates, Anthony Quinn; **D:** Frank Tuttle; **W:** Frank Butler, Don Hartman, Walter DeLeon, Francis Martin; **C:** Karl Struss; **M:** Leo Robin, Ralph Rainger. Academy Awards '37: Best Song ("Sweet Leilani"). *USH*

Wait Till Your Mother Gets Home 🎬🎬 1983 "Mr. Mom"-like zaniness abounds as a football coach cares for the kids and does chores while his wife takes her first job in 15 years. Almost too darn cute, but well written. Made for television. 97m/C VHS, Beta. Paul Michael Glaser, Dee Wallace Stone, Peggy McKay, David Doyle, Raymond Buktenica, James Gregory, Joey Lawrence, Lynne Moody; **D:** Bill Persky.

Wait Until Dark 🎬🎬🎬 1967 A photographer unwittingly smuggles a drug-filled doll into New York, and his blind wife, alone in their apartment, is terrorized by murderous crooks in search of it. A compelling thriller based on the Broadway hit by Frederick Knott, who also wrote "Dial M for Murder." The individual actors' performances were universally acclaimed in this spinetingler. 105m/C VHS, Beta, LV. Audrey Hepburn, Alan Arkin, Richard Crenna, Efrem Zimbalist Jr., Jack Weston; **D:** Terence Young; **W:** Robert B. Carrington; **C:** Charles B(ryant) Lang; **M:** Henry Mancini. Nominations: Academy Awards '67: Best Actress (Hepburn). *WAR*

Wait Until Spring, Bandini 🎬🎬½ 1990 (PG-13) A flavorful immigrant tale about a transplanted Italian family weathering the winter in 1925 Colorado, as seen through the eyes of a young son. Alternately funny and moving, with one of Dunaway's scenery-chewing performances as a local temptation for the father. Based on the autobiographical novel by John Fante, co-produced by Francis Ford Coppola. 104m/C VHS, Closed Caption. Joe Mantegna, Faye Dunaway, Burt Young, Ornella Muti, Alex Vincent, Renata Vanni, Michael Bacall, Daniel Wilson; **D:** Dominique Deruddere; **M:** Angelo Badalamenti. *WAR*

Waiting for Guffman 🎬🎬 1996 (R) The eccentric citizens of Blaine, Missouri, plan an original musical ("Red, White, and Blaine") to celebrate the town's 150th anniversary with the aid of former New Yorker and semi-hysteric Corky St. Claire (Guest) as their director. Everyone's very game—and almost completely talentless. The Guffman of the title is the Broadway producer Corky knows and whom he's invited to see their disaster-in-the-making. A little too deliberately quirky for its own good. **CW:** Brief strong language. 84m/C VHS, Closed Caption. Christopher Guest, Eugene Levy, Catherine O'Hara, Parker Posey, Fred Willard, Lewis Arquette, Matt Keeslar; **D:** Christopher Guest; **W:** Christopher Guest, Eugene Levy; **C:** Roberto Schaefer;

M: Michael McKean, Harry Shearer, Christopher Guest. Nominations: Independent Spirit Awards '98: Best Actor (Guest), Best Film, Best Screenplay. *WAR*

Waiting for the Light 🎬🎬½ 1990 (PG) When a woman takes over a small-town diner, she gets the surprise of her life. Seems an angel has made his home there and now the townsfolk are flocking to see him. MacLaine is wonderful and Garr is fetching and likeable. Set during the Cuban missile crisis. Enjoyable, tame comedy. 94m/C VHS, LV, 8mm, Closed Caption. Shirley MacLaine, Teri Garr, Vincent Schiavelli, John Bedford Lloyd; **D:** Christopher Monger; **W:** Christopher Monger. *COL*

Waiting for the Moon 🎬½ 1987 (PG) Hunt as Alice B. Toklas is a relative treat in this ponderous, frustrating biopic about Toklas and Gertrude Stein, her lover. Made for "American Playhouse" on PBS. 88m/C VHS, Beta, Closed Caption. Linda Hunt, Linda Bassett, Andrew McCarthy, Bruce McGill, Jacques Boudet, Bernadette LaFont; **D:** Jill Godmilow. Sundance Film Festival '87: Grand Jury Prize. *FOX*

Waiting to Exhale 🎬🎬🎬 1995 (R) Adaptation of Terry McMillan's novel about four African-American women hoping to reach the point in their love lives when they can relax and stop waiting for the right man. After the string of dogs and users they choose, you want to tell them not to hold their breath. The women are supposed to be close friends, but all of their stories are broken up into vignettes. This erodes the ensemble feeling of the movie, but performances are strong all around. Retaining the book's feel of just-between-friends girl talk, it may be a little harsh for those who are, shall we say, estrogen-challenged. A lush R&B soundtrack is the perfect backdrop for the ladies' soulful yearning for real love. **CW:** Language and some strong sexuality. 120m/C VHS. Whitney Houston, Angela Bassett, Loretta Devine, Lela Rochon, Gregory Hines, Dennis Haysbert, Mykelti Williamson, Michael Beach, Leon, Wendell Pierce, Donald A. Faison, Jeffrey D. Sams, Toyomichi Kurita; **Cameos:** Wesley Snipes; **D:** Forest Whitaker; **W:** Ronald Bass; **M:** Babyface. MTV Movie Awards '96: Best Song ("Sittin' Up in My Room"); Nominations: MTV Movie Awards '96: Breakthrough Performance (Rochon), Best Song ("Exhale (Shoop Shoop)"). *FXV*

Waitress woof! *Soup to Nuts* 1981 (R) Three beautiful girls are waitresses in a crazy restaurant where the chef gets drunk, the kitchen explodes, and the customers riot. Awful premise, worse production. 85m/C VHS, Beta. Jim Harris, Carol Drake, Carol Bever; **D:** Lloyd (Samuel Weil) Kaufman. *NO*

Wake Island 🎬🎬🎬 1942 After Pearl Harbor, a small group of Marines face the onslaught of the Japanese fleet on a small Pacific Island. Although doomed, they hold their ground for 16 days. Exciting, realistic, and moving. The first film to capitalize on early "last stands" of WWII; also among the most popular war movies. Shown to soldiers in training camps with great morale-raising success. 88m/B VHS, Beta. Robert Preston, Brian Donlevy, William Bendix, MacDonald Carey, Albert Dekker, Walter Abel, Rod Cameron, Barbara Britton; **D:** John Farrow. New York Film Critics Awards '42: Best Director (Farrow); Nominations: Academy Awards '42: Best Director (Farrow), Best Original Screenplay, Best Picture, Best Supporting Actor (Bendix). *USH, TLF*

Wake of the Red Witch 🎬🎬½ 1949 Wayne captains the ship of the title and battles shipping tycoon Adler for a fortune in pearls and the love of a beautiful woman (Russell). Wayne shows impressive range in a non-gun-totin' role. 106m/B VHS, Beta. John Wayne, Gail Russell, Gig Young, Luther Adler, Henry Daniell; **D:** Edward Ludwig. *REP*

Walk, Don't Run 🎬🎬½ 1966 Romantic comedy involving a British businessman (Grant) unable to find a hotel room in Tokyo due to the crowds staying for the 1964 summer Olympic Games. He winds up renting a room from an Embassy secretary (Eggar) and then meets and invites Hutton, a member of the U.S. Olympic walking team, also without a place to stay, to share it

with him. Grant then proceeds to play matchmaker, despite the fact that Eggar has a fiance. Grant's last film. Innocuous, unnecessary remake of "The More the Merrier." 114m/C VHS, Beta. Cary Grant, Samantha Eggar, Jim Hutton, Jim Standing, Miiko Taka; **D:** Charles Walters; **M:** Quincy Jones. *COL*

A Walk in the Clouds 🎬🎬½ 1995 (PG-13) Gorgeously photographed, if sappy, romantic fantasy finds WWII vet Paul Sutton (Reeves), returning to his unhappy marriage and salesman job. So when the good-hearted Paul meets beautiful Victoria (Sanchez-Gijon), the pregnant and unmarried daughter of a possessive Napa vineyard owner (Giannini), he's more than happy to help by posing as her husband. Naturally, dad is livid at their "marriage" and Paul falls in love with his sham bride. Quinn gets to do his part as wise family patriarch and yes, there's even a grape harvest (and some grape stomping) to put everyone in the proper romantic mood. Based on the 1942 Italian film "Four Steps in the Clouds." **CW:** Moments of sensuality and war action. 103m/C VHS, Closed Caption. Keanu Reeves, Aitana Sanchez-Gijon, Giancarlo Giannini, Anthony Quinn, Angelica Aragon, Evangelina Elizondo, Freddy Rodriguez, Debra Messing; **D:** Alfonso Arau; **W:** Robert Mark Kamen; **C:** Emmanuel Lubezki; **M:** Leo Brower. Golden Globe Awards '96: Best Score; Nominations: MTV Movie Awards '96: Most Desirable Male (Reeves), Best Kiss (Keanu Reeves/Aitana Sanchez-Gijon). *FXV*

Walk in the Spring Rain 🎬🎬½ 1970 (PG) The bored wife of a college professor follows him to rural Tennessee when he goes on sabbatical, where she meets the married Quinn and the two begin an affair. When Quinn's disturbed son learns of the affair, he attacks the woman, with tragic results. Fine cast should have had better effect on low-key script. 98m/C VHS, Beta. Ingrid Bergman, Anthony Quinn, Fritz Weaver, Katherine Crawford, Tom Fielding, Virginia Gregg; **D:** Guy Green; **W:** Stirling Silliphant; **C:** Charles B(ryant) Lang; **M:** Elmer Bernstein. *NO*

A Walk in the Sun 🎬🎬🎬½ *Salerno Beachhead* 1946 The trials of a group of infantrymen in WWII from the time they land in Italy to the time they capture their objective, a farmhouse occupied by the Germans. Excellent ensemble acting shows well the variety of civilians who make up any fighting force and explores their fears, motivations, and weaknesses. Producer and director Milestone also made "All Quiet on the Western Front" and the Korean War masterpiece "Pork Chop Hill." Released in the final days of the war, almost concurrently with two other WWII films of the first echelon, "The Story of G.I. Joe" and "They Were Expendable." 117m/B VHS, Beta, LV, 8mm. Dana Andrews, Richard Conte, John Ireland, Lloyd Bridges, Sterling Holloway; **D:** Lewis Milestone; **W:** Robert Rossen. *LUM, NOS, DVT*

Walk into Hell 🎬🎬 1957 A mining engineer and his assistant searching for oil meet the primitive natives of New Guinea. Tedious at times and dated, but pleasant enough. 91m/C VHS, Beta. AU Chips Rafferty, Francoise Christophe, Reg Lye; **D:** Lee Robinson. *VYY, NLC*

Walk Like a Man 🎬½ 1987 (PG) In a take-off of Tarzan movies, Mandel plays a man raised by wolves. Comic problems arise when he is found by his mother and the family attempts to civilize him. Juvenile script wastes fine cast. 86m/C VHS, Beta. Howie Mandel, Christopher Lloyd, Cloris Leachman, Colleen Camp, Amy Steel, George DiCenzo; **D:** Melvin Frank. *MGM*

Walk on the Wild Side 🎬🎬 1962 In 1930s New Orleans, a man searches for his long-lost love, finds her working in a whorehouse and fights to save her from the lesbian madame Stanwyck. Melodrama, based only loosely on the Nelson Algren novel and adapted by cult novelist John Fante, with Edmund Morris. Much-troubled on the set, and it shows. 114m/B VHS, Beta. Jane Fonda, Laurence Harvey, Barbara Stanwyck, Capucine, Anne Baxter; **D:** Edward Dmytryk; **M:** Elmer Bernstein.

Nominations: Academy Awards '62: Best Song ("Walk on the Wild Side"). COL

Walk Softly, Stranger 🐾🐾 1950 Two-bit crook is reformed by the love of an innocent peasant girl. If you can stand the cliche masquerading as a plot, the performances are good. **81m/B VHS, Beta.** Alida Valli, Joseph Cotten, Spring Byington, Paul Stewart, Jack Paar, Jeff Donnell, John McIntire; **D:** Robert Stevenson. TTC

Walk the Proud Land 🐾🐾½ 1956 Story of Indian agent John Clum (Murphy), who fights for the rights of the Apache in 1870s Arizona and who convinces their leader Geronimo (Silverheels) to surrender to the authorities. Adapted from the biography "Apache Agent" by Woodworth Clum. **88m/C VHS.** Audie Murphy, Jay Silverheels, Anne Bancroft, Pat Crowley, Charles Drake; **D:** Jesse Hibbs; **W:** Jack Sher, Gil Doud; **C:** Harold Lipstein. USH

Walkabout 🐾🐾🐾½ 1971 (PG) Beautifully told and filmed story (by Roeg in his debut) about a nameless young brother (John, Roeg's six-year-old son) and sister (Agutter), who are abandoned in the Australian outback when their father kills himself. The children wander, with little chance of survival, until a young aborigine (Gumpilil) finds them. He interrupts his own "walkabout," a rite of passage, to teach them to survive, leading to betrayal and tragedy. Based on a novel by James Vance Marshall. **100m/C VHS.** AU Jenny Agutter, Lucien John, David Gumpilil, John Meillon; **D:** Nicolas Roeg; **W:** Edward Bond; **C:** Nicolas Roeg; **M:** John Barry. HMV

Walker 🐾🐾 1987 (R) Slapdash, tongue-in-cheek historical pastiche about the real-life American William Walker (played previously in "Burn!" by Marlon Brando), and how he led a revolution in Nicaragua in 1855 and became its self-declared president. A bitter, revisionist farce never for a moment attempting to be accurate. Matlin's unfortunate, though fortunately brief, follow-up to her Oscar-winning performance. **95m/C VHS, Beta.** Ed Harris, Richard Masur, Peter Boyle, Rene Auberjonois, Marlee Matlin, Miguel Sandoval; **D:** Alex Cox; **W:** Rudy Wurlitzer; **M:** Joe Strummer. USH

Walker: Texas Ranger: Deadly Reunion 🐾🐾½ 1994 Feature-length version of the TV series finds Walker (Norris) trying to protect a senator, with presidential leanings and big enemies, who's been targeted by a killer posing as a cop. In addition to the usual good guys, Walker is assisted by veteran ex-Ranger Laredo (Whitman), who has his own reasons for going after the bad guy. **92m/C VHS, Closed Caption.** Chuck Norris, Clarence Gilyard Jr., Sheree J. Wilson, Noble Willingham, Stuart Whitman, Jonathan Banks. WAR

Walker: Texas Ranger: One Riot, One Ranger 🐾🐾½ 1993 (PG-13) Norris sticks with the action-adventure mode with this tv pilot movie about Cordell Walker, a good guy with a code and some martial arts skills, who teams up with an ex-gridiron star and a female district attorney to go after lawbreakers. This time its bank robbers and three hoods after a teenaged girl. **96m/C VHS, LV, Closed Caption.** Chuck Norris, Sheree J. Wilson, Clarence Gilyard Jr., Gailard Sartain, Floyd "Red Crow" Westerman, James Drury; **D:** Virgil W. Vogel; **W:** Louise McCarn. MOV

Walking and Talking 🐾🐾½ 1996 (R) Low-budget, lighthearted estrogen romp through the lives of two best friends in New York, Amelia (Keener) and Laura (Heche), going through commitment crises. Freshman writer/director Holofcener scores by making a lackluster story imminently watchable. Likable cast of mostly unknowns (Heche was deemed a rising star at a recent Cannes Festival) deliver Holofcener's clever and humorous exchanges. Corrigan's video store clerk and all-around "ugly guy" is a highlight. Brit Bragg brings in a worthy score. **CW:** Sexuality, language and brief drug use. **86m/C VHS, LV, Closed Caption.** Anne Heche, Catherine Keener, Liev Schreiber, Todd Field, Kevin Corrigan, Randall Batinkoff, Joseph Siravo, Vinny Pastore, Lynn Cohen, Andrew

Holofcener; **D:** Nicole Holofcener; **W:** Nicole Holofcener; **C:** Michael Spiller; **M:** Billy Bragg. Nominations: Independent Spirit Awards '97: Best Actress (Keener), Best Supporting Actor (Corrigan). MAX

Walking Back 🐾🐾 1926 Troubled teens go for joyride and bash mirthmobile to smithereens. The body shop agrees to give them a different car, but they find themselves in the middle of a heist at a plant belonging to the father of one of the boys. **53m/B VHS, Beta.** Sue Carol, Richard Walling, Ivan Lebedeff, Robert Edeson, Florence Turner, Arthur Rankin; **D:** Rupert Julian. GPV, FCT

The Walking Dead 🐾🐾 1994 (R) Depicts the Vietnam War from the perspectives of four black and one white Marine assigned to rescue POWs from a North Vietnam camp in 1972. Fairly routine story with stock characters (by-the-book sergeant, family man, naive youngster, cynical hustler) and flashbacks to depict their back home struggles. Cast tries but is defeated by a one-dimensional script. **CW:** Graphic war violence; strong language; brief sexuality. **89m/C VHS.** Joe Morton, Eddie Griffin, Allen Payne, Vonte Sweet, Roger Floyd; **D:** Preston A. Whitmore II; **W:** Preston A. Whitmore II; **C:** John L. Demps Jr.; **M:** Gary Chang. HBO

Walking on Air 1987 Ray Bradbury's story comes to life as a handicapped boy dreams of completing a real space walk. Originally aired on PBS as part of the "Wonderworks" series. **60m/C VHS.** Lynn Redgrave, Jordan Marder, James Treuer, Katheryn Trainor; **D:** Ed Kaplan. HMV, FCT, BTV

Walking Tall 🐾🐾½ 1973 (R) A Tennessee sheriff takes a stand against syndicate-run gambling and his wife is murdered in response. Ultra-violent crime saga wowed the movie going public and spawned several sequels and a TV series. Based on the true story of folk-hero Buford Pusser, admirably rendered by Baker. **126m/C VHS, Beta, LV.** Joe Don Baker, Elizabeth Hartman, Noah Beery Jr., Gene Evans, Rosemary Murphy, Felton Perry; **D:** Phil Karlson; **W:** Mort Briskin. ART

Walking Tall: Part 2 🐾🐾 1975 (PG) Club-wielding Tennessee sheriff Buford Pusser, this time played less memorably by Svenson, attempts to find the man who killed his wife. Even more violent than the original. **109m/C VHS, Beta, LV.** Bo Svenson, Noah Beery Jr., Angel Tompkins, Richard Jaeckel; **D:** Earl Bellamy. ART, VES

Walking Tall: The Final Chapter 🐾½ 1977 (PG) The final months in the life of Tennessee sheriff Buford Pusser and the mystery surrounding his death. It wasn't the final chapter. Still to come: a TV flick and series. **112m/C VHS, Beta, LV.** Bo Svenson, Forrest Tucker, Leif Garrett, Morgan Woodward; **D:** Jack Starrett; **C:** Robert B. Hauser. ART

Walking the Edge 🐾½ 1983 (R) A widow hires a taxi driver to help her seek vengeance against the men who killed her husband and her son. Forster does what he can with the lousy story and script. **94m/C VHS, Beta.** Robert Forster, Nancy Kwan, Joe Spinell, Aarika Wells; **D:** Norbert Meisel; **W:** Curt Allen. ART

Walking Through the Fire 🐾🐾½ 1980 A young woman's real-life struggle with Hodgkin's disease. Her fight for her own and her unborn baby's survival is a stirring testament to the power of faith. Absorbing made-for-television drama. **143m/C VHS, Beta.** Bess Armstrong, Tom Mason, Bonnie Bedelia, Richard Masur, Swoosie Kurtz, J.D. Cannon, June Lockhart; **D:** Robert Day. TLF

Walking Thunder 🐾🐾½ 1994 (PG) The McKay family are stranded in the Rocky Mountains in 1850 when their wagon is destroyed by a grizzly bear. But they're rescued by a mountain man (Read) and a Sioux medicine man (Thin Elk), who introduce young Jacob to a number of adventures. It's wholesome, old-fashioned kid entertainment. **95m/C VHS.** John Denver, James Read, David Tom, Chief Ted Thin Elk. RAT

The Wall 🐾🐾🐾½ Guney's The Wall; Le Mur; Duvar 1983 The last film by Guney, author of "Yol," about orphaned boys in prison in the Turkish capitol of Ankara trying to escape and/or rebel after ceaseless rapings, beatings and injustice. An acclaimed, disturbing film made from Guney's own experience. He died in 1984, three years after escaping from prison. Brutal and horrifying. In Turkish with English subtitles. **117m/C VHS, Beta.** TU Ayse Emel Mesci, Saban, Sisko; **D:** Yilmaz Guney; **W:** Yilmaz Guney. NO

Wall Street 🐾🐾🐾 1987 (R) Stone's energetic, high-minded big business treatise in which naive, neophyte stockbroker Sheen is seduced into insider trading by sleek entrepreneur Douglas, much to his blue-collar father's chagrin. A fast-moving drama of '80s-style materialism with a mesmerizing, award-winning performance by Douglas as greed personified. Expert direction by Stone, who co-wrote the not-very-subtle script. His father, to whom this film is dedicated, was a broker. Look for Stone in a cameo. **126m/C VHS, Beta, LV, Closed Caption.** Michael Douglas, Charlie Sheen, Martin Sheen, Daryl Hannah, Sean Young, James Spader, Hal Holbrook, Terence Stamp, Richard Dysart, John C. McGinley, Saul Rubinek, James Karen, Josh Mostel, Millie Perkins, Cecilia Peck, Grant Shaud, Franklin Cover; **Cameos:** Oliver Stone; **D:** Oliver Stone; **W:** Oliver Stone, Stanley Weiser; **C:** Robert Richardson; **M:** Stewart Copeland. Academy Awards '87: Best Actor (Douglas); Golden Globe Awards '88: Best Actor—Drama (Douglas); National Board of Review Awards '87: Best Actor (Douglas); Golden Raspberry Awards '87: Worst Supporting Actress (Hannah). FOX, BTV

Wall Street Cowboy 🐾 1939 When his land is threatened, a cowboy fights big business in the big city. **54m/B VHS, Beta.** Roy Rogers. NOS, DVT, TIM

Wallaby Jim of the Islands 🐾🐾 1937 The singing captain of a pearl fishing boat must protect his treasure from marauding pirates. Pleasant enough musical adventure. **61m/B VHS.** George Houston, Douglas Walton; **D:** Charles Lamont. NOS, DVT, HEG

The Walloping Kid 🐾½ 1926 A B-western with photography done in Monument Valley. Silent with original organ music. **67m/B VHS, Beta, 8mm.** Kit Carson, Pauline Curley; **D:** Robert J. Horner. VYY

Walls of Glass 🐾🐾½ Flanagan 1985 (R) An aging New York cabby tries to make it as an actor. Effective performances by all override the thin plot. Slow and uneven, but involving. **85m/C VHS, Beta.** Geraldine Page, Philip Bosco, William Hickey, Olympia Dukakis, Brian Bloom, Linda Thorson; **D:** Scott Goldstein.

The Walls of Malapaga 🐾🐾 Au-Dela des Grilles; Le Mura di Malapaga 1949 Frenchman Gabin, who's killed his mistress, stows away aboard a ship to Italy. He arrives in Genoa only to have all his money and papers stolen. Gabin then meets Miranda, a lonely waitress with a young daughter, and the two fall in love. But it's only temporary as the authorities come closing in. French with subtitles. **91m/C VHS.** FR IT Jean Gabin, Isa Miranda, Vera Talchi, Andrea Checchi, Robert Dalban; **D:** Rene Clement; **W:** Jean Aurenche, Pierre Bost; **M:** Roman Vlad. Academy Awards '50: Best Foreign Language Film. FCT

Walpurgis Night 🐾🐾🐾 Valborgmassoafton 1941 Soapy Swedish drama about abortion was racy for its time. Office gal Bergman secretly loves her boss (Hanson). His wife refuses to have children and goes through an abortion. An unscrupulous fellow blackmails her with this knowledge. Bergman bides her time. Stay tuned... Interesting document on the mores of another time. In Swedish with English subtitles. **82m/B VHS, Beta.** SW Lars Hanson, Karin Carlsson, Victor Sjostrom, Ingrid Bergman, Erik Berglund, Sture Lagerwall, Georg Rydeberg, Georg Blickingberg; **D:** Gustaf Edgren. WAC

The Waltons: A Thanksgiving Story 1973 As the Walton family anticipates the Thanksgiving holiday, John-Boy prepares for college entrance exams and Jenny Pendleton's visit. John-Boy suffers a head injury and is faced with a risky operation that may either help him or leave him permanently disabled. A holiday special from the television series. 100m/C VHS. Richard Thomas, Ralph Waite, Michael Learned, Will Geer, Ellen Corby, Judy Norton-Taylor, Kami Cotler, Jon Walmsley, Mary McDonough, Eric Scott, David W. Harper; **D:** Philip Leacock. IGP

The Waltons: The Christmas Carol 🎬🎬 1980 The winter solstice brings no special joy to Walton's mountain; WWII has taken many men, with short wave reports indicating the Nazi terror spreading across Europe. But huddled in the glow of Walton's barn, the children rediscover the true meaning of Christmas. 94m/C VHS, Beta, Closed Caption. Judy Norton-Taylor, Jon Walmsley, Mary McDonough, Eric Scott, Kami Cotler, Joe Conley, Ronnie Clare, Leslie Winston, Peggy Rea; **D:** Lawrence Dobkin. ORI

Waltz Across Texas 🎬🎬½ 1983 Young oil man Jastrow and good-lookin' rock scientist Archer at first don't take to each other, but there's something in the air, and romance blossoms. Jastrow and Archer cowrote and coproduced, and cohabitated as spouses in real-life. 100m/C VHS, Beta. Terry Jastrow, Anne Archer, Mary Kay Place, Richard Farnsworth; **D:** Ernest Day; **C:** Robert Elswit. VES

Waltz King 🎬🎬 1963 Typically hokey Disney biography of the young composer Johann Strauss during his Old Viennese heyday. Fine music, pretty German locations. Well-made family fare. 94m/C VHS, Beta. Kerwin Mathews, Senta Berger, Brian Aherne; **D:** Steve Previn. DIS

Waltz of the Toreadors 🎬🎬🎬 The Amorous General 1962 Retired general Sellers doesn't care for his wealthy, shrewish wife and tries to rekindle a 17-year-old romance with a French woman. It doesn't work out (seems his illegitimate son also has a soft spot for the lady), but the general decides to keep his eyes open for other possibilities. Interestingly cast adaptation of Jean Anouilh's play. Sellers is hilarious, as usual. 105m/C VHS, Beta. GB Peter Sellers, Dany Robin, Margaret Leighton, Cyril Cusack; **D:** John Guillermin. NO

A Waltz Through the Hills 1988 Two orphans head into the Australian outback and experience many adventures en route to the coast where they can set sail for England and their grandparents. Aired on PBS as part of the "Wonderworks" series. 116m/C VHS, Closed Caption. Tina Kemp, Andre Jansen, Ernie Dingo, Dan O'Herlihy; **D:** Frank Arnold. HMV, FCT

Wanda Nevada 🎬½ 1979 (PG) Gambler Fonda wins nubile young Shields in a poker game, so he drags her with him to the Grand Canyon to look for gold. Director/star Fonda sure picked a lemon for his only screen appearance with dad Henry (a grizzled old varmint appearing briefly). Shields is in her usual form—stellar for a shampoo commercial. 105m/C VHS, Closed Caption. Peter Fonda, Brooke Shields, Henry Fonda, Fiona Lewis, Luke Askew, Ted Markland, Severn Darden, Paul Fix; **D:** Peter Fonda. MGM

Wanda, the Sadistic Hypnotist 🎬 1967 A comely vixen hypnotizes an innocent pedestrian, ties him up and whips him to indulge her whims. Despite the "victim's" protests, she unleashes a gang of sexually playful women on him, and he is subjected to a multitude of "tortures." 70m/C VHS. Katharine Shubeck, Janice Sweet, Dick Dangerfield, Daryl Cobinot; **D:** Gregory Corarito. SMW, TPV

The Wanderer 🎬🎬 Le Grand Meaulnes 1967 Two friends fall in love—Frantz with Valentine and his friend Augustin with Frantz's sister, Yvonne. When the two women disappear on Frantz's wedding day, the two men begin a search to find both the women and the reasons for their disappearance. In French with English subtitles. 108m/C

VHS. FR Brigitte Fossey, Jean Blaise, Alain Noury, Juliette Villard; **D:** Jean-Gabriel Albicocco. CVC

Wanderers 🎬🎬🎬½ 1979 (R) Richard Price's acclaimed novel about youth gangs coming of age in the Bronx in 1963. The "Wanderers," named after the Dion song, are a gang of Italian-American teenagers about to graduate high school, who prowl the Bronx with the feeling that something is slipping away from them. Fascinating, funny and touching. Manz is unforgettable as a scrappy gal. A wonderful 60s soundtrack (Dion, the Four Seasons) colors this "coming of age hard way" film. 113m/C VHS, Beta. Ken Wahl, John Friedrich, Karen Allen, Linda Manz; **Cameos:** Richard Price; **D:** Philip Kaufman; **W:** Philip Kaufman; **C:** Michael Chapman. WAR

Wandering Jew 🎬🎬½ 1920 An excellent print of the rare Austrian film version of the classic legend, one of at least three silent versions. A Jew is condemned to wander the earth for eternity. 65m/B VHS, Beta. AT Rudolf Schildkraut, Joseph Schildkraut. GVV

The Wannsee Conference 🎬🎬🎬½ Wannseekonferenz 1984 A startling, important film depicting, in real time, the conference held at the Wannsee on January 20, 1942, during which 14 members of the Nazi hierarchy decided in 85 minutes the means and logistics of effecting the Final Solution. Recreated from the original secretary's notes. Horrifying and chilling. Along with "Shoah," a must-see for understanding the Holocaust and the psychology of genocide. In German with English subtitles. 87m/C VHS, Beta, LV. GE Dietrich Mattausch, Gerd Brockmann, Friedrich Beckhaus; **D:** Heinz Schirk. HMV, GLV, BTV

Wanted: Babysitter woof! 1975 A young student accidentally becomes involved by her roommate in a plot to kidnap the child she is babysitting. Schneider is truly awful; Italian comic Pazzetto is at sea in a bad role as her boyfriend. Also released as "The Babysitter." 90m/C VHS, Beta. Robert Vaughn, Vic Morrow, Maria Schneider, Renato Pozzetto, Nadja Tiller, Carl Mohner, Sydne Rome; **D:** Rene Clement.

Wanted: Dead or Alive 1959 This western series, which ran from 1958-61, launched the career of McQueen who starred as bounty hunter Josh Randall. In this episode, "Reunion for Revenge," Randall must protect the man in his custody from escaped criminals with vengeance on their mind. Also available colorized. Additional episodes available. 22m/B VHS, Beta. Steve McQueen, Wright King, Jane Burns, James Coburn, Cloris Leachman, John Baer, Ralph Meeker; **D:** Thomas Carr, Richard Donner. MOV

Wanted Dead or Alive 🎬½ 1986 (R) Ex-CIA agent Hauer is now a high-tech bounty hunter assigned to bring in an international terrorist. When the terrorist kills Hauer's friend and girlfriend, he forgets the $50,000 bonus for bringing him in alive. Official "sequel" to the Steve McQueen television series with Hauer as the McQueen character's great-grandson. The link is meaningless, and the plot is a thin excuse for much violence and anti-terrorist flag-waving. 104m/C VHS, Beta, LV, Closed Caption. Rutger Hauer, Gene Simmons, Robert Guillaume, William Russ, Jerry Hardin, Mel Harris; **D:** Gary Sherman; **W:** Brian Taggert. VTR

Wanted: The Perfect Guy 🎬🎬½ 1990 Danny and Melanie try to find Mister Right for their divorced Mom (Kahn). An Emmy Award winner about single parents and their children. 45m/C VHS. Madeline Kahn, Melanie Mayron. AIM

The War 🎬🎬½ 1994 (PG-13) Post-Vietnam war drama, set in 1970 Mississippi, centers on a children's battle over a treehouse but becomes a sermon on love, death, family values, pacifism, and the physical and spiritual wounds of war. After helping son Stu (Wood) and daughter Lidia (Randall) build their treehouse, troubled Vietnam vet Stephen Simmons (Costner) tries to coax Stu to make peace with the bullies trying to take it

over. However cliched, director Avnet allows a talented cast of kids to thoughtfully express a child's view of the world but gosh-darn-it the preachy tone can get down-right annoying. 126m/C VHS, LV, Closed Caption. Elijah Wood, Kevin Costner, Lexi Randall, Mare Winningham, Christine Baranski, Bruce A. Young, Gary Basaraba, Raynor Scheine, Nick Searcy; **D:** Jon Avnet; **W:** Kathy McWorter. USH

War & Love 🎬🎬 1984 (PG-13) Two Jewish teenagers in Warsaw are torn apart by WWII and Nazi persecution. After the war they search for each other. Sincere, but not adequately developed, drama based on the book "The Survivors" by film's producer Jack Eisner. 112m/C VHS, Beta. Sebastian Keneas, Kyra Sedgwick; **D:** Moshe Mizrahi. MGM, SWC

War and Peace 🎬🎬½ 1956 Lengthy adaptation of Tolstoy's great (and likewise lengthy) novel about three families caught up in Russia's Napoleonic Wars from 1805 to 1812; filmed in Rome. Bad casting and confused script (by six writers) are somewhat overcome by awesome battle scenes and Hepburn. Remade in 1968. 208m/C VHS, Beta, LV. Audrey Hepburn, Mel Ferrer, Henry Fonda, Anita Ekberg, Vittorio Gassman, John Mills, Oscar Homolka, Herbert Lom, Helmut Dantine; **D:** King Vidor; **M:** Nino Rota. Golden Globe Awards '57: Best Foreign Film; Nominations: Academy Awards '56: Best Color Cinematography, Best Costume Design (Color), Best Director (Vidor). PAR

War and Peace 🎬🎬🎬 1968 The massive Russian production of Leo Tolstoy's masterpiece, adapting the classic tome practically scene by scene. All of the production took place in the Soviet Union. So painstaking that it took more than five years to finish, no other adaptation can touch it. Hugely expensive ($100 million, claimed the Russians), wildly uneven production. Great scenes of battle and aristocratic life. Though this version is far from perfect, one asks: Is it humanly possible to do screen justice to such a novel? In Russian with English subtitles. On four tapes. (Beware the two-part, poorly dubbed version that was also released.) 373m/C VHS, Beta, LV. RU Lyudmila Savelyeva, Sergei Bondarchuk, Vyacheslav Tihonov, Hira Ivanov-Golarko, Irina Gubanova, Antonina Shuranova; **D:** Sergei Bondarchuk; **C:** Jack Cardiff. Academy Awards '68: Best Foreign Language Film; Golden Globe Awards '69: Best Foreign Film; New York Film Critics Awards '68: Best Foreign Film; Nominations: Academy Awards '68: Best Art Direction/Set Decoration. KUL, TVC, TPV

War & Remembrance, Part 1 🎬½ 1988 Tedious sequel to the epic television miniseries "The Winds of War," based on the novel by Herman Wouk. Historical fiction is created around the events of WWII, including Nazi persecution and naval battles in the Pacific. Seven cassette series. Followed by "War and Remembrance: The Final Chapter." 120m/C VHS, Beta. Robert Mitchum, Jane Seymour, Hart Bochner, Victoria Tennant, Barry Bostwick, Polly Bergen, David Dukes, Michael Woods, Sharon Stone, Robert Morley, Sami Frey, Chaim Topol, John Rhys-Davies, Ian McShane, William Schallert, Jeremy Kemp, Steven Berkoff, Robert Hardy, Ralph Bellamy, John Gielgud; **D:** Dan Curtis. MPI, MOV

War & Remembrance, Part 2 🎬½ 1989 The final installments of the excruciatingly boring and long mini-series. Herman Wouk's historical fiction concerning the last years of WWII. Six cassettes, in Hi-Fi stereo. 120m/C VHS, Beta. Robert Mitchum, Jane Seymour, Hart Bochner, Ralph Bellamy, Victoria Tennant, Barry Bostwick, John Gielgud, Polly Bergen, David Dukes, Michael Woods; **D:** Dan Curtis. MPI

War & Remembrance, Part 3 1988 A brief glimmer of hope appears in this volume involving the lovers' reunion in Hawaii and the military power's changing of hands due to command of the Americans following the infamous Midway battle. 120m/C VHS, Beta. Robert Mitchum, Jane Seymour, Hart Bochner, Victoria Tennant, Polly Bergen, David Dukes, Michael Woods; **D:** Dan Curtis. MPI

War & Remembrance, Part 4 1988
The middle part of 1942 sees its way through the American infiltration of Guadacanal, the treacherous stranglehold of Nazi Germany on Europe and other parts of the world, and the defiance toward defeat of the Russian Army. 120m/C VHS, Beta. Robert Mitchum, Jane Seymour, Hart Bochner, Victoria Tennant, Polly Bergen, David Dukes, Michael Woods; *D:* Dan Curtis. *MPI*

War & Remembrance, Part 5 1988 As 1942 draws to a close, Wouk's well-known character, Pug, finds himself heading for a new assignment. North Africa welcomes the Allies in lieu of the Nazis. Stalingrad is mortified by an everstrong Nazi invasion. 120m/C VHS, Beta. Robert Mitchum, Jane Seymour, Hart Bochner, Victoria Tennant, Polly Bergen, David Dukes, Michael Woods; *D:* Dan Curtis. *MPI*

War & Remembrance, Part 6 1988 After leaving his dear cruiser behind, Pug says hello to Russia. The Ally leaders meet with much to discuss. Hitler is getting stronger and shrewder. 120m/C VHS, Beta. Robert Mitchum, Jane Seymour, Hart Bochner, Victoria Tennant, Polly Bergen, David Dukes, Michael Woods; *D:* Dan Curtis. *MPI*

War & Remembrance, Part 7 1988 The Sicilian win by Patton brings about the devestation of Mussolini. Hitler's henchman are getting nervous and tired of battle. Germany succumbs to Allied troops in North Africa. 120m/C VHS, Beta. Robert Mitchum, Jane Seymour, Hart Bochner, Victoria Tennant, Polly Bergen, David Dukes, Michael Woods; *D:* Dan Curtis. *MPI*

War & Remembrance: The Final Chapter, Part 8 1989 The final episodes of Herman Wouk's sweeping saga, following "The Winds of War" and "War and Remembrance," deal with the struggle of a Jewish family in war-torn Europe. Natalie and her son, Louis, are trapped in a ghetto under the reign of a vicious Nazi, who considers a bribe for the sake of the mother and son. On five cassettes. 120m/C VHS, Beta. Robert Mitchum, Jane Seymour, Hart Bochner, Victoria Tennant, Polly Bergen, David Dukes, Michael Woods, Sharon Stone, Robert Morley, Sami Frey, Chaim Topol, John Rhys-Davies, Ian McShane, William Schallert, Jeremy Kemp, Steven Berkoff, Robert Hardy, Ralph Bellamy, John Gielgud; *D:* Dan Curtis. *MPI, MOV*

War & Remembrance: The Final Chapter, Part 9 1989 Both D-Day and an assassination of Hitler are in the works. Natalie and Louis are still in a desperate situation with the tyrannical Nazi endangering them constantly. 120m/C VHS, Beta. Robert Mitchum, Jane Seymour, Hart Bochner, Victoria Tennant, Polly Bergen, David Dukes, Michael Woods; *D:* Dan Curtis. *MPI*

War & Remembrance: The Final Chapter, Part 10 1989 Though Louis becomes gravely ill, Natalie and Aaron are shipped to Auschwitz. Hitler lives in spite of the botched assasination threat, but the allies are closing in rapidly. 120m/C VHS, Beta. Robert Mitchum, Jane Seymour, Hart Bochner, Victoria Tennant, Polly Bergen, David Dukes, Michael Woods; *D:* Dan Curtis. *MPI*

War & Remembrance: The Final Chapter, Part 11 1989 The infamous Battle of the Bulge takes place. Louis is taken away in the Nazi retreat. Natalie and Aaron continue to defy death in Auschwitz. 120m/C VHS, Beta. Robert Mitchum, Jane Seymour, Hart Bochner, Victoria Tennant, Polly Bergen, David Dukes, Michael Woods; *D:* Dan Curtis. *MPI*

War & Remembrance: The Final Chapter, Part 12 1989 The climax culminates into the death of both FDR and Hitler, whose suicide shocked and relieved an entire world. The Nazi reign of terror crumbles, and the allies are victorious. But this series ends on the note of displacement and the effort of rebuilding what has so quickly and deftly been destroyed. 120m/C VHS, Beta. Robert Mitchum, Jane Seymour, Hart Bochner, Victoria Tennant, Polly Bergen, David Dukes, Michael Woods; *D:* Dan Curtis. *MPI*

War Arrow ⅃⅃ 1953 Army Major Howell Brady (Chandler) is sent by Washington to end the Kiowa uprisings in Texas in this cavalry vs. Indians western. Along the way, he tries to win the heart of O'Hara. 79m/C VHS, Closed Caption. Maureen O'Hara, Jeff Chandler, Suzan Ball, John McIntire, Noah Beery Jr., Henry Kleinbach Brandon, Dennis Weaver, Jay Silverheels; *D:* George Sherman; *W:* John Michael Hayes. *USH*

The War at Home ⅃½ 1996 (R) In 1972 Vietnam vet Jeremy Collier (Estevez) has been home in the Dallas suburbs for a year but the war and its effects still linger. Mom Maureen (Bates) is a conservative control freak and dad Bob (Sheen) just can't connect, while teenaged sis Karen (Williams) is going through her own rebellion. The tense situation comes to a bitter head over a Thanksgiving weekend. Based on the 1984 play "Home Front" by James Duff.*CW:* War-related shooting, an intense sequence of violent threat, and for language. 124m/C VHS, LV, Closed Caption. Kathy Bates, Martin Sheen, Emilio Estevez, Kimberly Williams, Carla Gugino, Geoffrey Blake, Corin "Corky" Nemec, Ann Hearn; *D:* Emilio Estevez; *W:* James Duff; *C:* Peter Levy; *M:* Basil Poledouris. *TOU*

War Between the Tates ⅃⅃ 1976 A college professor's affair with a female student is the basis for a tension filled stand-off with his wife. Mediocre made for television adaptation of the Allison Lurie novel, somewhat redeemed by Ashley's performance. 90m/C VHS, Beta. Richard Crenna, Elizabeth Ashley, Granville Van Dusen; *D:* Lee Philips; *M:* John Barry. *TLF*

The War Boy ⅃⅃½ 1985 (R) Difficulties encountered by a young Canadian boy as he grows up in Central Europe during WWII. Not to be compared with "Empire of the Sun" or "Hope and Glory," both of which were released later; successful in its modest ambitions. Beautiful performance from 12-year-old star Hopely. 86m/C VHS. CA Helen Shaver, Kenneth Welsh, Jason Hopely; *D:* Allan Eastman. *HHE*

War Brides ⅃ 198? Civil War brides confront life after the war. Low-budget drama. 100m/C VHS, Beta. Elizabeth Richardson, Sharry Fleet, Sonja Smits. *TWE*

War Bus Commando ⅃ 1989 A fully loaded bus is the only way out when soldiers are caught behind enemy lines in Afghanistan. A case of the spoof comes first: The plot is almost exactly the same as "Stripes"—only this one isn't funny. In Hi-Fi. 90m/C VHS. *IT* Savina Gersak, Mark Gregory, John Vernon; *D:* Frank Valenti. *NO*

War in Space ⅃ 1977 Powerful U.N. Space Bureau Starships and UFOs band together to battle alien invaders among the volcanoes and deserts of Venus. 91m/C VHS, Beta. *JP* Kensaku Marita, Yuko Asano, Ryo Ikebe. *VDA*

War in the Sky ⅃⅃⅃ 1982 Director William Wyler's documentary account of the Army Air Corps in action. Extraordinary footage of the Thunderbolt, the P47 Fighter, and the B17 Bomber. 90m/C VHS, Beta. *D:* William Wyler. *GEM*

The War Lord ⅃⅃⅃ 1965 Set in the 11th century, Heston stars as Chrysagon, a Norman knight and war lord who commands a peasant village. While battling his enemies, he becomes enamored of a peasant girl named Bronwyn (Forsyth), who is unfortunately engaged to someone else. Pulling rank, Chrysagon uses an ancient law that allows noblemen the first night with a bride and the two fall in love. The two vow to never part, but that sets the stage for even more bloody battles. Fine acting and great production values make this a well-adapted version of the play "The Lovers" by Leslie Stevens. 121m/C VHS, Beta, LV, Letterbox. Charlton Heston, Richard Boone, Rosemary Forsyth, Guy Stockwell, Niall MacGinnis, Henry Wilcoxon, James Farentino, Maurice Evans, Michael Conrad; *D:* Franklin J. Schaffner; *W:* John Collier, Millard Kaufman; *C:* Russell Metty. *USH*

War Lover ⅃⅃½ 1962 An American daredevil flying captain and his co-pilot find themselves vying for the affections of a woman during WWII in England. Seeks human frailty beneath surface heroism. McQueen is impressive, no thanks to mediocre script. Excellent aerial photography, and featuring one of only a very few serviceable WWII B-17s then remaining. Based on John Hersey's novel. 105m/B VHS, Beta, LV. *GB* Steve McQueen, Robert Wagner, Shirley Anne Field, Bill Edwards, Gary Cockrell; *D:* Philip Leacock; *W:* Howard Koch. *GKK*

War of the Buttons ⅃⅃½ 1995 (PG) Two sleepy Irish fishing villages provide childish battle grounds for two groups of local lads. The Ballys (Ballydowse village), lead by Fergus (Fitzgerald), and the Carricks (Carrickdowse), with leader Geronimo (Coffey), have an intense rivalry and capture by the other gang leads to the removal of every clothing button for the unfortunate captive. When Fergus becomes a Carrick victim, he organizes a retaliatory strike, and emotions threaten to overwhelm all concerned. Based on the French novel "La Guerre des Boutons" by Louis Pergaud. Filmed on location in West Cork, Ireland. 94m/C VHS. Gregg Fitzgerald, John Coffey, Liam Cunningham, Paul Batt, Eveanna Ryan, Colm Meaney, Johnny Murphy; *D:* John Roberts; *W:* Colin Welland; *C:* Bruno de Keyzer; *M:* Rachel Portman. *WAR*

The War of the Colossal Beast ⅃½ *The Terror Strikes* 1958 This sequel to "The Amazing Colossal Man" finds the 70-foot Colonel Manning even angrier at the attempts to kill him when he was in the first film. So he wreaks more havoc until scolded by his sister into committing suicide for being such a troublemaker. Cheesy special effects but good for a laugh. 68m/B VHS. Dean Parkin, Sally Fraser, Russ Bender, Roger Pace, Charles Stewart; *D:* Bert I. Gordon. *COL*

War of the Gargantuas ⅃ *Furankenshutain No Kaijusanda Tai Gailah; Sanda Tai Gailah; Duel of the Gargantuas* 1970 (G) Tokyo is once again the boxing ring for giant monsters. This time it's a good gargantua (half human, half monster) against a bad gargantua. This is a strange one. 92m/C VHS, LV, Closed Caption. *JP* Russ Tamblyn, Kumi Mizuno, Kipp Hamilton, Yu Fujiki. *PAR*

War of the Robots ⅃ 1978 A dying alien civilization kidnaps two brilliant Earth scientists in the hope that they'll help it survive. 99m/C VHS, Beta, LV. Antonio Sabato Jr., Melissa Long, James R. Stuart. *VCI*

The War of the Roses ⅃⅃⅃ 1989 (R) Acidic black comedy about a well-to-do suburban couple who can't agree on a property settlement in their divorce so they wage unreserved and ever-escalating combat on each other, using their palatial home as a battleground. Expertly and lovingly (if that's the word) directed by DeVito, who plays the lawyer. Turner and Douglas are splendid. Adapted from the novel by Warren Adler. Laserdisc version includes previously deleted scenes and commentary from DeVito. 116m/C VHS, Beta, LV, Letterbox, Closed Caption. Michael Douglas, Kathleen Turner, Danny DeVito, Marianne Saegebrecht, Sean Astin, G.D. Spradlin, Peter Donat, Heather Fairfield, Dan Castellaneta, Danitra Vance, Tony Crane; *D:* Danny DeVito; *W:* Michael Leeson; *C:* Stephen Burum; *M:* David Newman. *FOX, IME*

War of the Wildcats ⅃⅃½ *In Old Oklahoma* 1943 Fast-moving western with Wayne as a tough cowboy battling a powerful land baron. They fight over land, oil and a woman. Unusual because Wayne's character acts on behalf of the Indians to drill and transport oil. 102m/B VHS. John Wayne, Martha Scott, Albert Dekker, George "Gabby" Hayes, Sidney Blackmer; *D:* Albert Rogell. Nominations: Academy Awards '43: Best Sound, Best Original Dramatic/Comedy Score. *REP*

War of the Wizards 🐾½ *The Phoenix* **1981** (PG) Low-budget sci-fi thriller about an alien woman with supernatural powers who comes to take over the Earth. But, lucky for all earthlings, she's challenged by a hero-type just in the nick of time. **90m/C VHS, Beta.** Richard Kiel; *D:* Richard Caan. *NO*

The War of the Worlds 🐾🐾🐾½ **1953** H.G. Wells's classic novel of the invasion of Earth by Martians, updated to 1950s California, with spectacular special effects of destruction caused by the Martian war machines. Pretty scary and tense; based more on Orson Welles's radio broadcast than on the book. Still very popular; hit the top 20 in sales when released on video. Classic thriller later made into a TV series. Produced by George Pal, who brought the world much sci-fi, including "The Time Machine," "Destination Moon," and "When Worlds Collide," and who appears here as a street person. **85m/C VHS, Beta, LV.** Gene Barry, Ann Robinson, Les Tremayne, Lewis Martin, Robert Cornthwaite, Sandro Giglio; *D:* Byron Haskin; *C:* George Barnes. Academy Awards '53: Best Special Effects; Nominations: Academy Awards '53: Best Film Editing, Best Sound. *PAR*

War Party 🐾🐾 **1989** (R) During a 100-year commemoration of an Indian massacre in the Midwest, a murder occurs and a lynch mob chases a pack of young Blackfeet into the mountains before the inevitable showdown. A feeble attempt at portraying the unfair treatment of Native Americans. Un-subtle, Hollywood style, this time in favor of the Indians, and therefore un-serious. Too bad; the premise had potential. **99m/C VHS, Beta, LV, Closed Caption.** Kevin Dillon, Billy Wirth, Tim Sampson, M. Emmet Walsh; *D:* Franc Roddam; *C:* Brian Tufano. *HBO*

The War Room 🐾🐾🐾 **1993** (PG) Eye opening, sometimes disturbing documentary presents a behind the scenes peek at what really goes on during a Presidential campaign. When filming began in June '92 Bill Clinton was an unknown political quantity and advisors George Stephanopoulous and James Carville were masterminding his campaign. The "War Room" refers to the building in Little Rock where they struggled to organize a small army of volunteers into a winning team. Highlights include the Democratic National Convention, the North Carolina leg of Clinton's campaign bus tour, three Presidential debates, and the week leading up to election night. **93m/C VHS, LV, Closed Caption.** *D:* Chris Hegedus, D.A. Pennebaker. National Board of Review Awards '93: Best Feature Documentary; Nominations: Academy Awards '93: Best Feature Documentary. *THV*

The War Wagon 🐾🐾🐾 **1967** The Duke plans revenge on Cabot, the greedy mine owner who stole his gold claim and framed him for murder for which he spent years in prison. He assembles a gang to aid him, including a wise-cracking Indian (Keel) and the man sent by Cabot to kill him (Douglas). Wayne's plan is to steal the gold being shipped in Cabot's armor-plated stagecoach, the "war wagon." Well-written, good performances, lots of action. Based on the book "Badman" by Clair Huffaker. The laserdisc version is available in letterbox format. **101m/C VHS, Beta, LV, Letterbox.** John Wayne, Kirk Douglas, Howard Keel, Robert Walker Jr., Keenan Wynn, Bruce Dern, Bruce Cabot, Joanna Barnes; *D:* Burt Kennedy; *C:* William Clothier. *USH*

Warbirds 🐾🐾 **1988** (R) American pilots are off to quell a revolution in a Middle East country. Too little action fails to support mediocre plot and characters. **88m/C VHS, Beta.** Jim Eldert, Cully Holland, Bill Brinsfield; *D:* Ulli Lommel; *W:* Ulli Lommel. *VTR, THV*

Warbus 🐾🐾 **1985** (R) Marines lead a school bus load of Americans through war-torn Vietnam to safety. Decent action and surprisingly enjoyable characters. Otherwise mediocre. **90m/C VHS, Beta.** Daniel Stephen, Romano Kristoff, Urs Althaus; *D:* Ted Kaplan. *NLC*

WarCat 🐾 *Angel of Vengeance* **1988** The daughter of a green beret fights for her life against a blood-thirsty gang. **78m/C VHS.** Macka Foley, Jannina Poynter, David O'Hara, Carl Erwin; *D:* Ted V. Mikels. *TWE*

Ward Six 🐾🐾 **19??** An insane asylum is the setting for various analogies regarding the perception of reality as defined by societal values. When it is felt that the residing physician is no more sane than his patients, he is placed among them, in Ward Six. Adapted from a story by Anton Chekhov. In Serbian with English subtitles. **93m/C VHS, Beta.** *YU D:* Lucian Pintilie. *FCT*

Wardogs 🐾½ *The Assassination Team* **1987** A man tries to rescue his brother from becoming one of an elite, brainwashed group of ex-Vietnam vets trained by the government as professional assassins. Might not have been quite so bad; promising inversion of many 'Nam cliches wrecked by unnecessary violence and bad acting. **95m/C Beta.** *SW* Tim Earle, Bill Redvers; *D:* Daniel Hubenbecker. *NO*

WarGames 🐾🐾½ **1983** (PG) A young computer whiz, thinking that he's sneaking an advance look at a new line of video games, breaks into the country's NORAD missile-defense system and challenges it to a game of Global Thermonuclear Warfare. The game might just turn out to be the real thing. Slick look at the possibilities of an accidental start to WWIII. Entertaining and engrossing, but with a B-grade ending. **110m/C VHS, Beta, LV, Closed Caption.** Matthew Broderick, Dabney Coleman, John Wood, Ally Sheedy; *D:* John Badham; *W:* Walter F. Parkes, Lawrence Lasker. Nominations: Academy Awards '83: Best Cinematography, Best Original Screenplay, Best Sound. *FOX*

Warhead 🐾½ **1996** (R) Special Forces Ranger Tannen (Zagarino) has to stop a renegade military group, led by his former compatriot Craft (Lara), that have stolen a nuclear warhead and are threatening Washington.*CW:* Strong violence and some language. **97m/C VHS.** Frank Zagarino, Joe Lara, Elizabeth Giordano; *D:* Mark Roper; *W:* Jeff Albert; *C:* Rod Stewart; *M:* Robert O. Ragland. *THV*

Warkill 🐾🐾½ **1965** WWII action set in the jungles of the Philippines. Journalist who idolizes violent, hard-edged colonel, loses his illusions, but gains a more genuine respect for his men. Not-bad war flick. **99m/C VHS, Beta.** George Montgomery, Tom Drake, Eddie Infante; *D:* Ferde Grofe Jr.; *W:* Ferde Grofe Jr.

Warlock 🐾🐾🐾 **1959** Claustrophic, resonant town-bound tale of a marshal (Fonda) and his adoring sidekick (Quinn) who clean up a town which then turns against him. Unusual story, fine performances carry this well beyond the run-of-the-mill cow flick. Fonda re-established himself at the box office as a western star, after "Stage Struck" and "Twelve Angry Men." From the novel by Oakley Hall. Look for "Bones" McCoy from "Star Trek" in a bit part. **122m/C VHS, Beta.** Henry Fonda, Anthony Quinn, Richard Widmark, Dorothy Malone, Wallace Ford, Richard Arlen, Regis Toomey, DeForest Kelley; *D:* Edward Dmytryk; *W:* Robert Alan Aurthur. *VTR, FOX*

Warlock 🐾🐾½ **1991** (R) It's 1691 and the most powerful warlock (Sands) in the New World is only hours away from execution. Luckily, his pal, Satan, whisks him (and witchhunter Grant, by mistake) three hundred years in the future to present-day Los Angeles, where he crash-lands in Singer's house. Surprisingly witty dialogue and neat plot twists outshine occasionally cheesy special effects. **103m/C VHS, Closed Caption.** Richard E. Grant, Julian Sands, Lori Singer, Mary Woronov, Richard Kuss, Kevin O'Brien, Anna Levine, Allan Miller, David Carpenter; *D:* Steve Miner; *W:* David N. Twohy; *C:* David Eggby; *M:* Jerry Goldsmith. *THV*

Warlock Moon 🐾½ **1973** Young woman is lured to a secluded spa and falls prey to a coven of witches. **75m/C VHS, Beta.** *MX* Laurie Walters, Joe Spano, Edna Macafee, Ray Goman, Steve Solinsky, Charles Raino; *D:* Bill Herbert. *UNI*

Warlock: The Armageddon 🐾🐾½ **1993** (R) Sequel finds Sands back again as the sinister Warlock. This time he's out to gather six Druidic rune stones which have the power to summon Satan's emissary (in the wrong hands) or to stop his nefarious activities (in the right ones). A sect in a small California town serves as the keeper of the stones, only their designated champions are two unprepared teenagers. Sands has all the fun, gleefully dispatching his would-be opponents with some good special effects.*CW:* Violence. **93m/C VHS.** Julian Sands, Chris Young, Paula Marshall, Steve Kahan, Charles Hallahan, R.G. Armstrong, Bruce Glover, Zach Galligan, Dawn Ann Billings, Joanna Pacula; *D:* Anthony Hickox; *W:* Kevin Rock, Sam Bernard. *THV*

Warlords 🐾½ **1988** (R) Lone soldier Carradine battles mutant hordes in a post-apocalyptic desert. Amateurish futuristic drivel. **87m/C VHS, Beta, LV.** David Carradine, Sid Haig, Ross Hagen, Fox Harris, Robert Quarry, Victoria Sellers, Brinke Stevens, Dawn Wildsmith; *D:* Fred Olen Ray. *THV*

Warlords from Hell woof! **1987** (R) Two young men motorcycling through Mexico are captured by a bloodthirsty gang and forced to do hard labor in the marijuana fields. We can only hope that they just learn to say no. **76m/C VHS, Beta.** Brad Henson, Jeffrey Rice; *D:* Clark Henderson. *WAR*

Warlords of the 21st Century 🐾½ *Battletruck* **1982** Bandit gang speed around the galaxy in an indestructible battle cruiser. Then the boys are challenged by a space lawman. Gratuitously violent action pic lacking real action. Filmed on planet New Zealand. **91m/C VHS, Beta.** Michael Beck, Annie McEnroe, James Wainwright; *D:* Harley Cokliss; *W:* Harley Cokliss, Irving Austin, John Beech; *C:* Chris Menges.

Warlords 3000 🐾½ **1993** (R) In the future, Earth is a barren wasteland ravaged by raging electrical storms. Deadly cancers are rampant and the few people who have survived take their comfort in a hallucinogenic drug that provides a temporary pleasure and a permanent madness. Drug lords control the planet but one man is out to eliminate the scum and save the future. **92m/C VHS.** Jay Roberts Jr., Denise Marie Duff, Steve Blanchard, Wayne Duvall; *D:* Faruque Ahmed; *W:* Ron Herbst, Faruque Ahmed. *COL*

Warm Nights on a Slow-Moving Train 🐾🐾 **1987** (R) A hot-blooded schoolteacher turns tricks for cash to support her brother on the Sunday-night train to Melbourne, until she meets a stranger who has a deadly masquerade of his own. Interestingly different; much sex, as you can imagine. Australian-made. **90m/C VHS, Beta, LV.** *AU* Wendy Hughes, Colin Friels, Norman Kaye, John Clayton, Peter Whitford; *D:* Bob Ellis; *W:* Bob Ellis, Denny Lawrence. *PAR*

Warm Summer Rain 🐾½ **1989** (R) A young couple meet under unusual circumstances and develop a relationship in a desert cabin as they reflect on their unfulfilled pasts. Lust, self-doubt and longing for something to hold onto draw them together as the days pass. Thoroughly self-indulgent romantic comedy that's oddly self-pitying and poorly directed. **85m/C VHS, Beta, LV.** Kelly Lynch, Barry Tubb; *D:* Joe Gayton. *COL*

The Warning 🐾 **1980** A pair of proverbial honest cops investigate ties between the mob and the police department. Hard to follow. **101m/C VHS, Beta.** *IT* Martin Balsam, Giuliano Gemma, Giancarlo Zanetti; *D:* Damiano Damiani.

Warning from Space 🐾½ *The Mysterious Satellite; The Cosmic Man Appears in Tokyo; Space Men Appear in Tokyo; Unknown Satellite Over Tokyo; Uchujin Tokyo Ni Arawaru* **1956** Aliens visit Earth to warn of impending cosmic doom. When it becomes apparent that the one-eyed starfish look is off-putting, they assume human form. Japanese sci-fi. **87m/B VHS.** *JP* Toyomi Karita, Keizo Kawasaki, Isao Yamagata, Shozo Nanbu, Buntaro Miake, Mieko Nagai, Kiyoko Hirai; *D:* Koji Shima. *NOS, SMW, SNC*

Warning Shadows 🎬🎬🎬 1923 Classic example of interior German Expressionism. Brilliantly portrays a jealous husband's emotions and obsessions through shadows. Innocent events seem to reek of sin. A seldom-seen study of the oft-precarious distinction between love and obsession; directly influenced by the classic "The Cabinet of Dr. Caligari." Silent with German and English titles. 93m/B VHS, Beta, 8mm. *GE* Fritz Kortner; *D:* Arthur Robison. *GPV, FCT, GLV*

Warning Sign 🎬½ 1985 (R) A high-tech thriller in which a small town is terrorized by the accidental release of an experimental virus at a research facility. Shades of "The Andromeda Strain" and "The China Syndrome," though less originality and quality. 99m/C VHS, Beta, Closed Caption. Sam Waterston, Kathleen Quinlan, Yaphet Kotto, Richard Dysart, Rick Rossovich; *D:* Hal Barwood; *W:* Hal Barwood, Matthew Robbins; *C:* Dean Cundey. *FOX*

The Warrior & the Sorceress 🎬½ 1984 (R) Mercenary Carradine offers his services to rival factions fighting for control of a water well in an impoverished desert village located on a planet with two suns. He attempts to aggravate the conflicts between the factions, playing the shifty go-between. The sorceress is topless throughout. "A Fistful of Dollars" goes to outer space. Inoffensive, except that better judgment is expected of Carradine. 81m/C VHS, Beta, LV. David Carradine, Luke Askew, Maria Socas, Harry Townes; *D:* John Broderick; *W:* John Broderick. *ART, VES*

Warrior of Justice 🎬 1996 Karate instructor has one of his students disappear after competing in a secret tournament. He then uncovers a black market ring specializing in selling human organs that's run by a former opponent. 90m/C VHS. Richard Lynch, Jorge Rivero, Nick Hill, Ian Jacklin, Jorgo Ognenovski; *D:* Jorgo Ognenovski, Mike Tristano. *HVF*

Warrior of the Lost World woof! 1984 A warrior must destroy the evil Omega Force who tyrannically rules the world in the distant future, etcetera, etcetera. One-size-fits-all premise; horrible special effects; miserably directed. Only for really hard-core Pleasence fans. 90m/C VHS, Beta. Robert Ginty, Persis Khambatta, Donald Pleasence; *D:* David Worth. *NO*

Warrior Queen 🎬 1987 (R) Long ago in ancient Rome, overly histrionic mayor Pleasence married porn queen with a wandering eye Fox, and much gratuitous sex and erupting volcanoes resulted. Even the score blows. Also available in an "Unrated" version. Brit pop star Fox is billed as Stasia Micula. 69m/C VHS, LV. Sybil Danning, Donald Pleasence, Richard Hill, Josephine Jacqueline Jones, Tally Chanel, Samantha Fox. *ART, VES*

Warrior Spirit 🎬🎬½ 1994 (PG-13) After getting kicked out of their prep school, two boys decide to head for the Yukon and search for gold. *CW:* Adventure violence. 94m/C VHS. Lukas Haas, Jimmy Herman, Allan Musy; *D:* Rene Manzor. *THV*

The Warriors 🎬🎬½ *The Dark Avenger* 1955 Swashbuckling adventure about Prince Edward's valiant rescue of Lady Joan and her children from the clutches of the evil Count De Ville. Flynn looks old and pudgy, but buckles his way gallantly through intrepid adventure. Also the last Flynn to see: fun, but more or less completely derivative and familiar. Filmed in England. 85m/C VHS, Beta. *GB* Errol Flynn, Peter Finch, Joanne Dru, Yvonne Furneaux, Noel Willman, Michael Hordern; *D:* Henry Levin. *FOX, MLB*

The Warriors 🎬🎬½ 1979 (R) Action story about a turf battle between New York City street gangs that rages from Coney Island to the Bronx. Silly plot works because of fine performances and direction, excellent use of action and color, and nonstop pace. Fight scenes are very carefully, even obviously, choreographed. 94m/C VHS, Beta, LV. Michael Beck, James Remar, Deborah Van Valkenburgh, Thomas G. Waites, David Patrick Kelly; *D:* Walter Hill; *W:* Walter Hill. *PAR*

Warriors 🎬🎬 1994 (R) Col. Frank Vail (Busey) is the leader of a top secret government anti-terrorist hit squad, considered so deadly that its members are confined behind the walls of a military prison. But when Vail escapes, it's up to his lethal protege Colin Newl (Pare) to hunt him down. 100m/C VHS, LV, Closed Caption. Gary Busey, Michael Pare; *D:* Shimon Dotan. *REP*

Warriors from Hell 🎬½ 1990 (R) Western forces in a small African country battle rebel fighters who threaten the hapless native villagers. *CW:* Language and violence. 90m/C VHS. Deon Stewardson, Shayne Leith, Adrienne Pierce, Glen Gabela, Hector Manthanda, Ivan Dean, Connie Chume; *D:* Ronnie Isaacs; *W:* Ronnie Isaacs. *COL*

Warriors of the Apocalypse woof! *Searchers of the Voodoo Mountain; Time Raiders* 1985 (R) After a nuclear holocaust, heavily sworded and loin-clothed men search for the secret of eternal life and instead find an Amazon realm in the jungle. A terrible waste of post-apocalyptic scenery. 96m/C VHS, Beta. Michael James, Debrah Moore, Ken Metcalfe, Franco Guerrero; *D:* Bobby Suarez. *ART*

Warriors of the Wasteland woof! *The New Barbarians; I Nuovi Barbari* 1983 (R) It's the year 2019, and the world has been devastated by a nuclear war. The few survivors try to reach a distant land which emits radio signals indicating the presence of human life. They are hindered by attacks from the fierce homosexual Templars, led by a self-proclaimed priest called One. Mindless rip-off of "Road Warrior" and obviously made on the proverbial shoestring budget. Dubbed. 92m/C VHS, Beta. *IT* Fred Williamson, Timothy Brent, Anna Kanakis; *D:* Enzo G. Castellari. *NO*

Warriors of Virtue 🎬🎬½ 1997 (PG) Teenaged Ryan Jefers (Yedidia) is transported to the land of Tao where he learns the five virtues (righteousness, benevolence, integrity, wisdom, and loyalty) from the kangaroo-like Warmblood warriors, who live in harmony with humans. Then he must use his knowledge to fight the evil Komodo (MacFadyen), who wishes to steal the energy from Tao to make himself immortal. Nice message for the kids, with enough action to keep them interested, but the Warmbloods are dorky-looking. 101m/C VHS. Mario Yedidia, Angus McFadyen, Marlee Shelton, Chao-Li Chi; *D:* Ronny Yu; *W:* Michael Vickerman, Hugh Kelley; *C:* Peter Pau; *M:* Don Davis. *MGM*

The Wash 🎬🎬🎬 1988 Quiet domestic drama about a couple who drift apart after 40 years of marriage. Set interestingly among Japanese-Americans in California; treats social and cultural factors with intelligence. Superb cast takes it a notch higher. 94m/C VHS, Beta, LV. Mako, Nobu McCarthy, Sab Shimono; *D:* Michael Toshiyuki Uno; *W:* Philip Kan Kotanda; *C:* Walt Lloyd.

Washington Affair 🎬🎬 1977 (PG) A tale of intrigue in the nation's capital. Sullivan is a businessman who uses women and blackmail to capture government contracts. Selleck is the hapless bureaucrat he preys on. Remake of Stoloff's own "Intimacy" was not released until "Magnum P.I." became a hit. 90m/C VHS, Beta. Tom Selleck, Carol Lynley, Barry Sullivan; *D:* Victor Stoloff.

Washington Mistress 🎬½ 1981 Eminently ordinary made-for-TV grist about Capitol Hill aide Arnaz, politician Jordan, and their affair. Listless performances. 96m/C VHS. Lucie Arnaz, Richard Jordan, Tony Bill; *D:* Peter Levin. *NO*

Washington Square 🎬🎬🎬 1997 (PG) Adaptation of Henry James' novel, which was previously filmed as "The Heiress." Set in 19th-century New York City (filmed in Baltimore), wealthy spinster Catherine Sloper (Leigh), against the will of her overbearing father (Finney), is pursued by a handsome fortune hunter (Chaplin). Director Holland tends to bluntly simplify James' complex undertones, and Leigh's facial ticks can't equal "The Heiress'" Olivia de Havilland's painful plainness; nonetheless, definitely worth seeing. 115m/C VHS, LV, Closed Caption. Jennifer Jason Leigh,

Ben Chaplin, Albert Finney, Maggie Smith, Judith Ivey, Betsy Brantley, Jennifer Garner, Peter Maloney, Robert Stanton; *D:* Agnieszka Holland; *W:* Carol Doyle; *C:* Jerzy Zielinski; *M:* Jan A.P. Kaczmarek. *TOU*

The Wasp Woman 🎬½ 1959 In her quest for eternal beauty, a woman uses a potion made from wasp enzymes. Naturally, she turns into a wasp monster at night. Good fun, courtesy of Corman. 84m/B VHS. Susan Cabot, Fred Eisley, Barboura Morris, Michael Marks, William Roerick, Frank Gerstle, Bruno Ve Sota, Frank Wolff; *D:* Roger Corman; *W:* Leo Gordon; *C:* Harry Neumann. *NOS, RHI, SNC*

Wasp Woman 🎬🎬 1996 (R) Equally campy cable remake of the 1959 flick finds ex-supermodel-turned-cosmetics company exec Janice Starlin (Rubin) discovering that her fading beauty is causing problems both with her company and her love life. So she turns to a mysterious doctor for help and injects herself with his untested serum, an experimental wasp hormone. She's hoping to discover a fountain of youth and is instead transformed into a nasty-tempered giant insect. Cool, disgusting makeup/costuming. *CW:* Monster violence and sexuality. 81m/C VHS. Jennifer Rubin, Daniel J. Travanti, Maria Ford; *D:* Jim Wynorski. *NHO*

Watch It 🎬🎬🎬 1993 (R) Four self-absorbed 20-something guys share a house in Chicago for the summer. They pursue a post-adolescent game, consisting of increasingly complicated practical jokes, where the unsuspecting victim is set up for a "watch it" gag. The rivalry escalates, and turns increasingly unpleasant, when cousins John and Michael vie for the affections of Anne, who's wary of involvement because of male selfishness. A first-rate cast with recognizable situations and emotions. *CW:* Language and sexual scene. 102m/C VHS. Jon Tenney, Peter Gallagher, Suzy Amis, John C. McGinley, Tom Sizemore, Lili Taylor, Cynthia Stevenson, Terri Hawkes, Jordanna Capra; *D:* Tom Flynn; *W:* Tom Flynn; *M:* Stanley Clarke. *PAR*

Watch Me 🎬 1996 (R) Photog Paul (Medford) is inspired by new neighbor babe Elise (Burns) and secretly snaps her through the window. Meanwhile, Elise is peeking in on Paul's would-be gal Samantha (Burton) who's having sex with his best bud Alex (Sherwin). Paul of course wants to get more personally involved with Elise (especially after he finds out about Samantha). Lots of nudity—no heat. *CW:* Erotic content, and for some language. 90m/C VHS. Robert Medford, Kelly Burns, Jennifer Burton, Steven Sherwin; *D:* Lipo Ching; *W:* Beth Salmon; *C:* Andreas Kossak; *M:* Yoav Goren. *TRI*

Watch Me When I Kill 🎬 1981 (R) We'd rather not. A young nightclub dancer stops by a drugstore seconds after the owner was killed. She doesn't see the killer's face, but his rasping voice remains to torment her and the viewer. Dubbed. 95m/C VHS, Beta. *IT* Richard Stewart, Sylvia Kramer, Anthony Bido. *NO*

Watch on the Rhine 🎬🎬🎬½ 1943 Couple involved with the anti-Nazi underground has escaped the country, but is pursued and harassed by Nazi agents. Adapted by Hammett and Hellman from her play. Performed on stage before the U.S. entered the war, it was the first American play and movie to portray the ugliness of fascism as an ideology, as opposed to the more devious evil of its practical side. The Production Code at the time required that a killer always be punished; the murderer (whose screen motives had been noble) refused to film the offending scene, which explains the tacked-on ending. Superb drama from a pair of highly gifted writers and a great cast. Shumlin also directed the play. 114m/B VHS, Beta. Bette Davis, Paul Lukas, Donald Woods, Beulah Bondi, Geraldine Fitzgerald, George Coulouris, Henry Daniell, Helmut Dantine; *D:* Herman Shumlin; *W:* Lillian Hellman, Dashiell Hammett; *C:* Hal Mohr; *M:* Max Steiner. Academy Awards '43: Best Actor (Lukas); Golden Globe Awards '44: Best Actor—Drama (Lukas); New York Film Critics Awards '43: Best Actor (Lukas), Best Film; Nominations: Academy Awards '43: Best Picture, Best Screenplay, Best Supporting Actress (Watson). FOX, MGM, FCT

Watch the Birdie ✓✓½ 1950 It's Skelton three times over as cameraman, father, and grandfather! First, he accidentally films a scam that would send the lovely Miss Dahl filing for bankruptcy. Later a crazy chase scene unfolds, that will have viewers rolling, as Skelton the cameraman nabs the bad guys and turns them over to the cops. Light fun that will charm Skelton fans. **70m/B VHS, Beta.** Red Skelton, Arlene Dahl, Ann Miller, Leon Ames; **D:** Jack Donohue. MGM

Watched ✓✓ 1973 A former U.S. attorney, gone underground, has a nervous breakdown and kills the narcotics agent who has him under surveillance. Self-important, too serious social/political conspiracy drama of the Watergate era. Keach and Yulin are good, but not good enough to save it. **95m/C VHS, Beta.** Stacy Keach, Harris Yulin, Bridgit Polk; **D:** John Parsons. ART, VES

The Watcher in the Woods ✓✓ 1981 (PG) When an American family rents an English country house, the children are haunted by the spirit of a long-missing young girl. A very bland attempt at a ghost story. **83m/C VHS, Beta.** Bette Davis, Carroll Baker, David McCallum, Ian Bannen, Lynn-Holly Johnson; **D:** John Hough; **W:** Brian Clemens. DIS

Watchers ✓✓ 1988 (R) From the suspense novel by Dean R. Koontz, a secret experiment goes wrong, creating half-human monsters. A boy and his extremely intelligent dog are soon pursued. Low-budget, Corman-influenced production is tacky but effective. **99m/C VHS, Beta, LV.** Barbara Williams, Michael Ironside, Corey Haim, Duncan Fraser, Blu Mankuma, Dale Wilson, Colleen Winton; **D:** Jon Hess; **W:** Bill Freed, Damien Lee; **C:** Richard Leiterman; **M:** Joel Goldsmith. ART

Watchers 2 ✓✓ 1990 (R) Sequel to "Watchers" follows the further adventures of a super-intelligent golden retriever who leads a Marine to an animal psychologist and then attempts to warn them both of a mutant killer. The dog says woof, but this movie doesn't quite. Fun for lovers of hounds or horror flicks. **101m/C VHS, Beta, LV.** Marc Singer, Tracy Scoggins; **D:** Thierry Notz; **M:** Rick Conrad. ART

Watchers 3 ✓✓½ 1994 (R) A secret military outpost in the South American jungles is attacked by a carnivorous predator. Ex-military convicts are sent to rescue the remaining survivors and to make certain the government experiment that started the terror never comes to light. **CW:** Language; violence; gore. **95m/C VHS.** Wings Hauser, Gregory Scott Cummins, Daryl Roach, John K. Linton, Lolita Ronalds, Frank Novak; **D:** Jeremy Stanford. NHO

Watchers Reborn ✓✓ 1998 (R) Genetically-engineered mutants stalk the innocent with only a hyper-intelligent golden retreiver (of course!) able to stop them. Based on the novel "Watchers" by Dean R. Koontz. **CW:** Monster-related violence and gore. **83m/C VHS.** Mark Hamill, Lisa Wilcox, Stephen Macht, Lou Rawls, Floyd Levine, Kane Hodder; **D:** John Carl Buechler; **W:** Sean Dash; **M:** Terry Plumeri. NHO

Water ✓ 1985 (PG-13) The resident governor of a Caribbean British colony juggles various predatory interests when a valuable mineral water resource is found. The good cast is wasted in this all-too-silly effort. **89m/C VHS, Beta.** GB Michael Caine, Brenda Vaccaro, Leonard Rossiter, Valerie Perrine, Jimmie Walker; **Cameos:** Eric Clapton, George Harrison, Fred Gwynne, Ringo Starr; **D:** Dick Clement; **W:** Dick Clement, Ian LaFrenais, Bill Persky. PAR

Water Babies ✓✓ Slip Slide Adventures 1979 (G) When a chimney sweep's 12-year-old apprentice is wrongly accused of stealing silver, the boy and his dog fall into a pond and eventually rescue some of the characters they find there. Combination of live-action and animated fairy-tale story set in 19th-century London. Boring, unless you're a young child with equivalent standards. Based on

the book by Charles Kingsley. **93m/C VHS, Beta.** GB James Mason, Billie Whitelaw, David Tomlinson, Paul Luty, Sammantha Coates; **D:** Lionel Jeffries.

The Water Engine ✓✓½ 1992 Charles Lang (Macy) is a luckless machinist struggling to survive in Depression-era Chicago. Lang invents a remarkable engine, that runs on water, and holds the promise of limitless, cheap power. To protect his invention he finds a seedy patent attorney (Mahoney), which leads to the sinister Oberman (Mantegna), a mysterious and powerful figure who wants Lang's invention—at any cost. Based on the play by David Mamet; made for cable TV. **110m/C VHS.** Charles Durning, Patti LuPone, William H. Macy, John Mahoney, Joe Mantegna, Joanna Miles, Mike Nussbaum, Treat Williams, Andrea Marcovicci, Peter Michael Goetz, David Mamet; **D:** Steven Schachter; **W:** David Mamet; **C:** Bryan England. TTC

Water Rustlers ✓½ 1939 Unscrupulous land baron builds a dam on his side of the creek with the intention of drying out the cattle pastures. Heroine Page, whose pop has been rubbed out by varmints, and good guy/lover O'Brien save her property and avenge her father. Second of three Page westerns. **55m/B VHS, Beta.** Dorothy Page, Dave O'Brien; **D:** Samuel Diege. VCN, VDM

The Waterdance ✓✓✓ 1991 (R) Autobiographical film based on the experiences of writer/co-director Jimenez. When writer Joel Garcia (Stoltz) is paralyzed in a hiking accident he finds himself dealing with not only the rehab process itself but his feelings, the feelings of his married lover, and those of his fellow patients. Deals unsentimentally with all the physical adjustments, including the sexual ones. Resolutions may be predictable but the performances rise above any script weaknesses. The title refers to Hill's dream of dancing on water—and the fear of drowning if he stops. **CW:** Language and sensuality. **106m/C VHS, LV, Closed Caption.** Eric Stoltz, Wesley Snipes, William Forsythe, Helen Hunt, Elizabeth Pena, Grace Zabriskie; **D:** Neal Jimenez, Michael Steinberg; **W:** Neal Jimenez; **C:** Mark Plummer; **M:** Michael Convertino. Independent Spirit Awards '93: Best First Feature, Best Screenplay; Sundance Film Festival '92: Best Screenplay, Audience Award. COL, PMS, BTV

Waterfront ✓½ 1939 Dreary dockside melodrama, with drinking and brawling longshoreman Jim (Morgan) avenging his brother's death. Based on the play "Blindspot" by Kenyon Nicholson. **59m/B VHS.** Dennis (Stanley Morner) Morgan, Gloria Dickson, Marie Wilson, Larry Williams, Sheila Bromley, Ward Bond, Frank Faylen; **D:** Terry Morse; **W:** Arthur Ripley, Lee Katz. GPV

Waterfront ✓✓ 1944 Nazis coerce German-Americans into helping them in WWII-era San Francisco. Credulity defying spy doings, but that's okay. Fairly entertaining wartime drama about paranoia on the home front. **68m/B VHS, Beta.** John Carradine, J. Carrol Naish, Terry Frost, Maris Wrixon, Edwin Maxwell; **D:** Steve Sekely. SNC, VCI

Waterfront ✓✓½ 1983 Effective romantic drama set in Melbourne, Australia. Australian workers strike after taking forced pay cuts. As a result, Italian immigrants are hired as scabs to keep the docks going. Despite the tension, an Italian woman and an Australian man fall deeply in love, only to find that they must struggle to keep that love alive. **294m/C VHS, Beta.** AU Jack Thompson, Greta Scacchi, Frank Gallacher, Tony Rickards, Mark Little, Jay Mannering, Ray Barrett, Chris Haywood, Warren Mitchell, Noni Hazlehurst, John Karlsen, Elin Jenkins; **D:** Chris Thomson. PAR

Waterhole #3 ✓✓½ 1967 (PG) Three Confederate army buddies steal a fortune in gold bullion from the Union Army and hide it in a waterhole in the desert. One of the funnier entries in the Western comedy genre. **95m/C VHS.** James Coburn, Carroll O'Connor, Margaret Blye, Claude Akins, Bruce Dern, Joan Blondell, James Whitmore; **D:** William A. Graham; **C:** Robert Burks; **M:** Dave Grusin. PAR

Waterland ✓✓ 1992 (R) Meandering drama about a history teacher who tries to solve a personal crisis by using his class as a sounding board to describe his troubled past in England. Dark secrets abound, including incest, madness, murder, and the terrifying love between the teacher and his childhood bride. Melancholy, overwrought but partially redeemed by the lead performances of Irons and his (real-life and cinematic) wife, Cusack. The film's setting has been unfortunately moved from London to Pittsburgh, destroying story links. Based on the novel by Graham Swift. **CW:** Language and sexuality and an abortion scene. **95m/C VHS, LV, Letterbox.** Jeremy Irons, Ethan Hawke, Sinead Cusack, John Heard, Grant Warnock, Lena Headey, Pete Postlethwaite, Cara Buono; **D:** Stephen Gyllenhaal; **W:** Peter Prince; **C:** Robert Elswit; **M:** Carter Burwell. NLC, COL

Waterloo ✓✓ 1971 (G) Massive chronicle of Napoleon's European conquests and eventual defeat at the hands of Wellington. Filmed on location in Italy and the Ukraine, it bombed due largely to Steiger's bizarre rendition of Napoleon. **122m/C VHS, Closed Caption.** IT RU Rod Steiger, Orson Welles, Virginia McKenna, Michael Wilding, Jack Hawkins, Christopher Plummer, Jack Hawkins, Dan O'Herlihy, Terence Alexander, Rupert Davies, Ivo Garrani, Gianni "John" Garko; **D:** Sergei Bondarchuk; **W:** H.A.L. Craig, Sergei Bondarchuk; **M:** Nino Rota. PAR, FCT, FUS

Waterloo Bridge ✓✓✓ 1940 In London during WWI, a soldier from an aristocratic family and a ballet dancer begin a tragic romance when they meet by chance on the foggy Waterloo Bridge. When he's listed as dead, her despair turns her to prostitution. But then he returns from POW camp, they once again meet by accident on Waterloo Bridge, and their romance resumes. Four-hanky drama with fine performances by Leigh (her first after "Gone with the Wind") and Taylor. **109m/B VHS, Beta, LV, Closed Caption.** Vivien Leigh, Robert Taylor, Lucile Watson, Sir C. Aubrey Smith, Maria Ouspenskaya, Virginia Field; **D:** Mervyn LeRoy; **C:** Joseph Ruttenberg. Nominations: Academy Awards '40: Best Black and White Cinematography, Best Original Score. MGM

Watermelon Man ✓✓ 1970 (R) The tables are turned for a bigoted white guy when he wakes up one morning to discover he has become a black man. Broad comedy with not much place to go is still engaging. Cambridge takes on both roles, appearing in unconvincing white makeup. **97m/C VHS, Beta, LV.** Godfrey Cambridge, Erin Moran, Estelle Parsons, Howard Caine; **D:** Melvin Van Peebles. COL, FCT

The Watermelon Woman ✓✓ 1997 Cheryl (Dunye) is a young, black, lesbian video store clerk who wants to be a documentary filmmaker. She becomes obsessed with a black actress seen in some 1930's black films, who was known only as the "Watermelon Woman." Doing research, Cheryl discovers the woman's name was Fae Richards (Bronson) and that she was a lesbian who had an affair with her white director. While deciding to film a documentary about Fae, Cheryl's personal life begins to parallel Fae's when she briefly falls for white customer, Diana (Turner). **85m/C VHS.** Cheryl Dunye, Valerie Walker, Guinevere Turner, Lisa Marie Bronson; **D:** Cheryl Dunye; **W:** Cheryl Dunye; **C:** Michelle Crenshaw; **M:** Bill Coleman. FRF

Watership Down ✓✓½ 1978 (PG) Wonderfully animated story based on Richard Adams's allegorical novel about how a group of rabbits escape fear and overcome oppression while searching for a new and better home. It's really an adult theme with sufficient violence to the poor wittle wabbits to scare the kiddies. **92m/C VHS, Beta, LV, 8mm.** GB D: Martin Rosen; **W:** Martin Rosen; **V:** Ralph Richardson, Zero Mostel, John Hurt, Denholm Elliott, Harry Andrews, Michael Hordern, Joss Ackland. WAR, TVC

Waterworld 🎬🎬½ **1995 (PG-13)** "The Man From Atlantis" meets "Mad Max." Industry knives sharpened with glee before release, with some insiders calling this luck impaired project "Fishtar" and "Kevin's Gate." With an estimated $150 million budget, the film must look to overseas sales and secondary markets to make any money. Most of said budget seems to have ended up on screen, which makes for a visually striking, and at times daunting, film. Costner, who did just about everything but cater the meals, stars as Mariner, a mutant man-fish who reluctantly helps human survivors search for the mythical Dryland since the polar ice caps melted, flooding the earth. The bad guys are the Smokers, led by the evil Hopper, who can play these roles in his sleep. Entertaining, but not riveting, as the budget and PR hype leads one to expect. The floating set was anchored (not very well, apparently) off the Hawaiian coast and was lost once during a tropical storm. Costner bet the boat on this one and stands to lose more than just money. With rumors of internal production battles, out of control budgets, and his other recent boxoffice disappointments, his star power is in question.**CW:** Some intense scenes of action violence, brief nudity and language. **135m/C VHS, LV, Closed Caption, DVD.** Kevin Costner, Dennis Hopper, Jeanne Tripplehorn, Tina Majorino, Michael Jeter, R.D. Call, Robert Joy; **D:** Kevin Reynolds; **W:** Peter Rader, Marc Norman, David N. Twohy; **C:** Dean Semler; **M:** James Newton Howard. Golden Raspberry Awards '95: Worst Supporting Actor (Hopper); Nominations: Academy Awards '95: Best Sound; Golden Raspberry Awards '95: Worst Picture, Worst Actor (Costner). **USH**

Wavelength 🎬🎬½ **1983 (PG)** A rock star living in the Hollywood Hills with his girlfriend stumbles on an ultra-secret government project involving friendly aliens from outer space recovered from a recent UFO crash site. Fun, enthusiastically unoriginal cheap sci-fi. Soundtrack by Tangerine Dream. **87m/C VHS, Beta, LV.** Robert Carradine, Cherie Currie, Keenan Wynn; **D:** Mike Gray; **W:** Mike Gray; **M:** Tangerine Dream. **VTR**

Wavelength 🎬½ **1996 (R)** Physicist and Oxford professor Paul Higgins (Piven) has a few problems—a wife, Claire (Williams), a girlfriend, Lucy (Walker), Lucy's father who just happens to be the head of the physics department, and a mysterious presence (Attenborough) who's trying to help Paul with his research on nuclear fission. Piven's character is so selfish you'll wonder why either woman wants him and the happy ending feels contrived. **94m/C VHS, Closed Caption. GB** Jeremy Piven, Kelli Williams, Liza Walker, James Villiers, James Faulkner, Richard Attenborough, Byrne Piven, Nicholas Marco, Dominic West; **D:** Benjamin Fry; **W:** Benjamin Fry; **C:** Chris Middleton; **M:** Michael Storey. **PAR**

Wax, or the Discovery of Television Among the Bees 🎬🎬 **1993** Intricate and eccentric fable dealing with alternate realities and perceptions. Jacob Maker (Blair) keeps a hive of very unusual bees, a family legacy passed down from his grandfather. Jacob begins experiencing a eerie communication with his bees and suffering mysterious blackouts, which cause him to perceive the world through blurred bee vision. New Mexico desert setting provides a surreal and desolate landscape. **85m/C VHS.** David Blair, Meg Savlov, Florence Ormezzano, William S. Burroughs; **D:** David Blair; **W:** David Blair; **M:** Beo Morales, Brooks Williams. **FRF**

Waxwork 🎬½ **1988 (R)** A wax museum opens up, and it is soon evident that the dummies are not what they seem. Garbled nonthriller. Available in a 100-minute unrated version. **97m/C VHS, Beta, LV.** Zach Galligan, Deborah Foreman, Michelle Johnson, Dana Ashbrook, Miles O'Keeffe, Patrick Macnee, David Warner, John Rhys-Davies; **D:** Anthony Hickox; **W:** Anthony Hickox; **C:** Gerry Lively; **M:** Roger Bellon. **ART**

Waxwork 2: Lost in Time 🎬🎬½ *Lost in Time* **1991 (R)** A young couple (Galligan and Schnarre) barely escape with their lives when the infamous waxworks museum burns down. A severed hand also gets loose and follows Schnarre home and murders her stepfather, leaving her to take the blame. In order to prove her innocence, the couple must travel through a bizarre time machine. Extraordinary special effects, strange plot twists, and recreations of scenes from past horror movies make this a highly entertaining sequel.**CW:** Language and comic horror violence. **104m/C VHS, Closed Caption.** Zach Galligan, Alexander Godunov, Bruce Campbell, Michael Des Barres, Monika Schnarre, Martin Kemp, Sophie Ward, Marina Sirtis, Juliet Mills, John Ireland, Patrick Macnee, David Carradine, Drew Barrymore; **D:** Anthony Hickox; **W:** Anthony Hickox; **C:** Gerry Lively. **ART**

Waxworks 🎬🎬🎬 **1924** A major achievement in German Expressionism, in which a poet imagines scenarios in a wax museum fairground that involve Jack the Ripper, Ivan the Terrible, and Haroun al-Rashid. Influential and considered ahead of its time. Silent. **63m/B VHS, Beta. GE** William Dieterle, Emil Jannings, Conrad Veidt, Werner Krauss, John Gottowt, Olga Belajeff; **D:** Paul Leni; **W:** Henrik Galeen. **SNC, NOS, ART**

Way Back Home 🎬🎬 *Old Greatheart; Other People's Business* **1932** Man wants to adopt a boy to release him from the clutches of his cruel guardian. Minor role for the then unknown Davis. **81m/B VHS, Beta.** Phillips Lord, Frank Albertson, Bette Davis; **D:** William A. Seiter; **M:** Max Steiner. **TTC, FCT**

Way Down East 🎬🎬🎬 **1920** Melodramatic silent drama of a country girl who is tricked into a fake marriage by a scheming playboy. The famous final scene of Gish adrift on the ice floes is in color. One of Griffith's last critical and popular successes. This tape includes the original Griffith-approved musical score. Remade in 1935 with Henry Fonda. **107m/B VHS, Beta, LV.** Lillian Gish, Richard Barthelmess, Lowell Sherman, Creighton Hale; **D:** D.W. Griffith. **NOS, BAR, VYY**

Way Down South 🎬½ **1939** The orphan son of a plantation owner tries to take over his father's estate, only to find out that the place has been run into the ground by a corrupt lawyer and a cruel slave driver. Black poet Hughes and actor Muse collaborated on the screenplay. German-born director Vorhaus was in his second year in Hollywood, after making his mark in Britain directing talkies. ♫Good Ground; Louisiana; Nobody Know De Trouble I See; Sometimes I Feel Like a Motherless Child; Lord I You Can't Come Send One Angel Down. **62m/B VHS.** Bobby Breen, Alan Mowbray, Ralph Morgan, Clarence Muse, Steffi Duna, Sally Blane, Edwin Maxwell; **D:** Bernard Vorhaus; **W:** Clarence Muse, Langston Hughes. Nominations: Academy Awards '39: Best Score. **NOS**

Way He Was 🎬🎬 **1976 (R)** A satirical re-enactment of the events that led up to the Watergate burglary and the coverup that followed. **87m/C VHS, Beta.** Steve Friedman, Al Lewis, Merrie Lynn Ross, Doodles Weaver. **VCI**

Way of the Black Dragon 🎬 **1981** When slave-trading drug traffickers threaten the moral fiber of our nation, two commandoes join forces to halt their operation. **88m/C VHS, Beta.** Ron Van Cliff, Carter Wang, Charles Bonet; **D:** Chan Wui Ngai. **TWE**

Way of the West 🎬½ **1935** Them durn pesky sheepherders are up to it again! Okay, so the cow/sheep thing is a classic western plot, but here it's offered perfunctorily. **52m/B VHS, Beta.** Wally Wales, William Desmond, Art Mix, Jim Sheridan, Bobby Nelson; **D:** Robert Emmett Tansey. **NOS, DVT, RXM**

The Way Out 🎬🎬 *Dial 999* **1956** Average crime drama starring Nelson as a fugitive accused of killing a bookie. **90m/C VHS. GB** Gene Nelson, Mona Freeman, John Bentley, Michael Goodliffe, Sydney Tafler; **D:** Montgomery Tully. **SNC**

Way Out West 🎬🎬🎬 **1937** The classic twosome journey way out west to deliver the deed to a gold mine to the daughter of their late prospector pal. The obligatory romance is missing, but you'll be laughing so hard you won't notice. One of Stan and Ollie's best. Score includes the song "Trail of the Lonesome Pine." Also included on this tape is a 1932 Todd and Pitts short, "Red Noses." Available colorized. **86m/B VHS, Beta, Closed Caption.** Stan Laurel, Oliver Hardy, Rosina Lawrence, James Finlayson, Sharon Lynne, ZaSu Pitts, Thelma Todd, William Haines; **D:** James W. Horne. Nominations: Academy Awards '37: Best Score. **CCB, MLB, VTR**

The Way We Were 🎬🎬🎬 **1973 (PG)** Big boxoffice hit follows a love story between opposites from the 1930s to the 1950s. Streisand is a Jewish political radical who meets the handsome WASP Redford at college. They're immediately attracted to one another, but it takes years before they act on it and eventually marry. They move to Hollywood where Redford is a screenwriter and left-wing Streisand becomes involved in the Red scare and the blacklist, much to Redford's dismay. Though always in love, their differences are too great to keep them together. An old-fashioned and sweet romance, with much gloss. Hit title song sung by Streisand. Adapted by Arthur Laurents from his novel. ♫The Way We Were. **118m/C VHS, Beta, LV, 8mm, Letterbox.** Barbra Streisand, Robert Redford, Bradford Dillman, Viveca Lindfors, Herb Edelman, Murray Hamilton, Patrick O'Neal, James Woods, Sally Kirkland; **D:** Sydney Pollack; **W:** Arthur Laurents; **C:** Harry Stradling Jr.; **M:** Marvin Hamlisch. Academy Awards '73: Best Song ("The Way We Were"), Best Original Dramatic/Comedy Score; Golden Globe Awards '74: Best Song ("The Way We Were"); Nominations: Academy Awards '73: Best Actress (Streisand), Best Art Direction/Set Decoration, Best Cinematography, Best Costume Design. **COL**

The Way West 🎬½ **1967** A wagon train heads to Oregon. A poor and muddled attempt at recreating the style of a John Ford western. What really galls is that it's based on the Pulitzer-winning novel by A.B. Guthrie, Jr. Boy, is the book better than the movie. Field's first film. **122m/C VHS.** Kirk Douglas, Robert Mitchum, Richard Widmark, Lola Albright, Michael Witney, Stubby Kaye, Sally Field, Jack Elam; **D:** Andrew V. McLaglen; **C:** William Clothier. **MGM**

Wayne Murder Case 🎬🎬🎬 *Strange Adventure* **1938** A fast-moving, cleverly constructed murder mystery. A rich old man dies just as he is about to sign a new will. Though no one was standing near him, a knife is found stuck in his back. **61m/B VHS, Beta.** June Clyde, Regis Toomey, Jason Robards Sr. **SNC, VYY**

Wayne's World 🎬🎬🎬 **1992 (PG-13)** Destined to become one of the top movies of all time—Not! This "Saturday Night Live" skit proved to be so popular that it got its own movie, not unlike the plot, which has slimy producer Lowe take the public access "Wayne's World" into the world of commercial television. The zany duo of Wayne and Garth are as much fun on the big screen as they are on SNL and there are many funny moments, several of which are destined to become comedy classics. A huge boxoffice hit that spawned a sequel. **93m/C VHS, LV.** Mike Myers, Dana Carvey, Rob Lowe, Tia Carrere, Brian Doyle-Murray, Lara Flynn Boyle, Kurt Fuller, Colleen Camp, Donna Dixon, Ed O'Neill; *Cameos:* Alice Cooper, Meat Loaf; **D:** Penelope Spheeris; **W:** Mike Myers, Bonnie Turner, Terry Turner; **M:** J. Peter Robinson. MTV Movie Awards '92: Best On-Screen Duo (Mike Myers/Dana Carvey). **PAR, FCT**

Wayne's World 2 🎬🎬 **1993 (PG-13)** Good-natured rerun of the original has plenty of sophomoric gags, but feels tired. Wayne and Garth are on their own, planning a major concert, Waynestock. "If you book them they will come," Jim Morrison says in a dream. Meanwhile, Wayne's girlfriend (Carrere) is falling for slimeball record promoter Walken. Offers a few brilliantly funny segments. If you liked the "Bohemian Rhapsody" spot in the original, get ready for the Village People number. Heston has a funny cameo, and Walken and Basinger push the limits without going over the top. Feature film debut for director Surjik.**CW:** Ribald humor. **94m/C VHS, Beta, LV, Closed Caption.** Mike Myers, Dana Carvey, Tia Carrere, Christopher Walken, Ralph Brown, Kim Basinger, James

Hong, Chris Farley, Ed O'Neill, Olivia D'Abo, Kevin Pollak, Drew Barrymore; *Cameos:* Charlton Heston, Rip Taylor; *D:* Stephen Surjik; *W:* Mike Myers, Bonnie Turner, Terry Turner; *M:* Carter Burwell. Nominations: MTV Movie Awards '94: Best On-Screen Duo (Mike Myers/Dana Carvey), Best Kiss (Dana Carvey/Kim Basinger). *PAR*

The Wayward Wife 🐾🐾 *La Provinciale* 1952 Young woman, married to a university professor, is blackmailed over her less-than-respectable past. Based on the novel by Alberto Moravia. Italian with subtitles. 92m/B VHS. *IT* Gina Lollobrigida, Gabriele Ferzetti, Franco Interlenghi, Renaldo Baldini; *D:* Mario Soldati. *FCT*

W.C. Fields Comedy Bag 1933 Compilation of three classic Fields shorts: "The Golf Specialist" (1930), "The Dentist" (1932) and "The Fatal Glass of Beer" (1933). 56m/B VHS, Beta. W.C. Fields, Babe Kane, Dorothy Granger, George Chandler. *BAR*

W.C. Fields: Flask of Fields 1930 Three classic Fields shorts: "The Golf Specialist" (1930), in which J. Effington Bellweather finds himself teaching a lovely young lady how to play the game; "The Fatal Glass of Beer" (1933); and "The Dentist" (1932), in which Fields tackles a room filled with patients. 61m/B VHS, Beta, 8mm. W.C. Fields, Babe Kane, Elise Cavanna, Bud Jamison, Rosemary Theby. *VYY*

We All Loved Each Other So Much 🐾🐾🐾½ 1977 Sensitive comedy follows three friends over 30 years, beginning at the end of WWII. All three have loved the same woman, an actress. Homage to friendship and to postwar Italian cinema. Includes a full-scale recreation of the fountain scene in "La Dolce Vita." In Italian with English subtitles. 124m/C VHS, Beta, LV. *IT* Vittorio Gassman, Nino Manfredi, Stefano Satta Flores, Stefania Sandrelli, Marcello Mastroianni, Federico Fellini; *D:* Ettore Scola. *COL*

We Are the Children 🐾🐾 1987 Cynical reporter covering the famine in Ethiopia meets an idealistic nurse who's been living there for years. Romance blossoms among the starving in made-for-TV drama co-produced by Danson. 92m/C VHS, Beta. Ally Sheedy, Ted Danson, Judith Ivey, Zia Mohyeddin; *D:* Robert M. Young.

We Dive at Dawn 🐾🐾🐾 1943 Interesting, tense British submarine drama. The "Sea Tiger" attempts to sink the German battleship "Brandenburg" off Denmark. Good cast. Mills prepared for the role by riding an actual submarine, turning "a pale shade of pea-green" when it crash-dived. 98m/B VHS, Beta. *GB* Eric Portman, John Mills; *D:* Anthony Asquith. *NOS, DVT, VEC*

We of the Never Never 🐾🐾 1982 (G) In turn-of-the-century Australia a city-bred woman marries a cattle rancher and moves from civilized Melbourne to the barren outback of the Northern Territory. Based on the autobiographical story written by Jeannie Gunn, the first white woman to travel in the aboriginal wilderness. She finds herself fighting for her own rights as well as for those of the aborigines in this sincere, well-done film. 136m/C VHS, Beta. *AU* Angela Punch McGregor, Arthur Dignam, Tony Barry; *D:* Igor Auzins. *COL*

We the Living 🐾🐾½ 1942 The torpid long-lost and restored Italian version of Ayn Rand's unique political tome. Deals with a young Soviet woman in revolutionary Petrograd who is slowly ruined by the system and her affair with a romantic counter-revolutionary. Made under the Fascists' nose during WWII. A fascinating dialectic between utopian melodrama and Rand dogma. In Italian with subtitles. 174m/B VHS, Beta, LV. *IT* Alida Valli, Rossano Brazzi, Fosco Giachetti; *D:* Goffredo Alessandrini. *LUM*

We Think the World of You 🐾🐾🐾 1988 (PG) When bisexual Oldman goes to prison, his lover Bates, whose feelings are unresolved and complex, finds friendship with Oldman's dog. Odd, oft-bitter comedy-drama of love and loyalty characterized by excellent acting and respectful,

gentle direction. From the novel by Joseph R. Ackerly. 94m/C VHS, Beta, LV. *GB* Alan Bates, Gary Oldman, Frances Barber, Liz Smith, Max Wall, Kerry Wise; *D:* Colin Gregg. *NLC*

We Will Not Enter the Forest 🐾🐾🐾 1979 Moral dilemmas afflict a group of French Resistance fighters during WWII when they must decide what to do with four German deserters they've captured. In French with subtitles. 88m/C VHS, Beta. *FR* Marie-France Pisier; *D:* Georges Dumoulin. *FCT*

The Weaker Sex 🐾🐾½ 1949 Typical patriotic British weepie finds a British widow and her daughters trying to hold on to hope as D-Day approaches. 89m/B VHS. *GB* Ursula Jeans, Cecil Parker, Joan Hopkins, Derek Bond, Lana Morris; *D:* Roy Ward Baker. *FCT*

Weapons of Death 🐾 1983 Kung Fu expert Lee splatters his enemies all over San Francisco's Chinatown. 90m/C VHS, Beta. Eric Lee, Bob Ramos, Ralph Catellanos. *NO*

Weapons of Mass Distraction 🐾🐾 1997 (R) Two megalomanical multimedia tycoons set out to destroy each other in this black cable comedy. Lionel Powers (Byrne) wants to buy pro football's Tucson Titans and so does his arch-rival Julian Messenger (Kingsley). So there's bribery and blackmail and airing of dirty family laundry all over the place. No heroes here but occasionally some sharp satire. *CW:* Language, sexuality and depiction of a suicide. 105m/C VHS. Gabriel Byrne, Ben Kingsley, Mimi Rogers, Jeffrey Tambor, Illeana Douglas, Paul Mazursky, Kathy Baker, Chris Mulkey, R. Lee Ermey, Caroline Aaron, Jason Lee, Christina Pickles; *D:* Stephen Surjik; *W:* Larry Gelbart; *C:* Alan Kivilo; *M:* Don Davis. *HBO*

Weather in the Streets 🐾½ 1984 (PG) A young woman enters into an ill-fated love affair after spending a few moments with an aristocratic married man. Cliched drama set in England between the two world wars. 108m/C VHS, Beta. Michael York, Joanna Lumley, Lisa Eichhorn, Isabel Dean, Norman Pitt; *M:* Carl Davis. *NO*

Web of Deceit 🐾🐾½ 1990 (PG-13) Defense lawyer Purl returns to her Southern hometown to defend an unjustly accused teenager. She falls in love with the prosecutor, but could he be the killer? Shades of "Jagged Edge." Good, suspenseful made-for-TV movie. 93m/C VHS, Beta, Closed Caption. Linda Purl, James Read, Paul DeSouza, Larry Black, Len Birman, Barbara Rush; *D:* Sandor Stern; *W:* Sandor Stern. *PAR*

Web of Deception 🐾 1971 (R) A jewel thief disappears with five million dollars worth of jewels. When the case turns to murder, a private detective becomes the prime suspect. 90m/C VHS, Beta. *SP* Thomas Hunter, Aelina Nathaniel, Gabriele Tinti, Marilia Branco. *NO*

Web of the Spider 🐾🐾 *Nella Stretta M Orsa Del Ragno; In the Grip of the Spider; Dracula in the Castle of Blood; And Comes the Dawn...But Colored Red* 1970 Kinski as Poe is really the only good thing about this run-of-the-mill horror outing. A man stays the night in a spooky house to prove it's not haunted. Remake of "Castle of Blood." 94m/C VHS. *GE FR IT* Anthony (Tony) Franciosa, Klaus Kinski, Michele Mercier, Peter Carsten, Karin Field; *D:* Anthony (Antonio) Margheriti) Dawson. *SNC*

A Wedding 🐾½ 1978 (PG) The occasion of a wedding leads to complications galore for the relatives and guests on the happy day. Silent film legend Gish's 100th screen role. Miserable, self-indulgent outing for Altman, who went through quite a dry spell after "Nashville." 125m/C VHS, Beta. Mia Farrow, Carol Burnett, Lillian Gish, Lauren Hutton, Viveca Lindfors, Geraldine Chaplin, Paul Dooley, Howard Duff, Dennis Christopher, Peggy Ann Garner, John Considine, Nina Van Pallandt, Dina Merrill, Pat McCormick, Vittorio Gassman, Desi Arnaz Jr.; *D:* Robert Altman; *W:* John Considine, Allan Nicholls, Patricia Resnick, Robert Altman. *FOX*

Wedding Band 🐾🐾 1989 Episodic comedy about a rock 'n' roll band that plays all sorts of weddings. Thin and lame but inoffensive. 95m/C VHS, Beta, LV. William Katt, Joyce Hyser, Tino Insana, Fran Drescher, David Rasche, Joe Flaherty, Tim Kazurinsky, James Belushi; *D:* Daniel Raskov. *COL*

The Wedding Banquet 🐾🐾🐾 *Xiyan; Hsi Yen* 1993 (R) Charming story about a clash of customs and secrets. Naturalized American Wai Tung (Chao, in his debut) lives comfortably with his lover Simon (Lichtenstein) while hiding the fact that he's gay from his Chinese parents. To appease his parents and get his "wife" a green card, he marries for convenience and watches as the deception snowballs. Comedy of errors was shot on a small budget ($750,000) and examines small details with as much care as the larger ones. A fine effort from director Lee that's solidly humorous, but also poignant. In English and Chinese with English subtitles. *CW:* Language. 111m/C VHS, LV, Closed Caption. *TW* Winston Chao, May Chin, Mitchell Lichtenstein, Sihung Lung, Ah-Leh Gua; *D:* Ang Lee; *W:* Ang Lee, Neil Peng, James Schamus. Nominations: Academy Awards '93: Best Foreign Language Film; Golden Globe Awards '94: Best Foreign Film; Independent Spirit Awards '94: Best Actor (Lichtenstein); Best Actress (Chin), Best Director (Lee), Best Film, Best Screenplay, Best Supporting Actress (Gua). *FOX*

Wedding Bell Blues 🐾🐾 1996 (R) Three 30ish single friends/roommates cope with a variety of crises. Pregnant Tanya (Porikova) learns that her boyfriend Tom (Edson) has no intention of marrying her, Micki's (Warner) fiance has just called off their wedding, and Jasmine's (Douglas) conservative parents are upset by their promiscuous daughter's approach to life. Stressed, the women decide to seek their fortunes in Vegas—preferably through some quickie marriages and even quickier divorces. Looks like it was shot on a shoestring budget and the lighting could be better, but the dialogue rings true and the actors do a decent job. Look for Seinfeld's TV mom as Micki's overbearing mother and Jackson as a disgruntled shopper. Reynolds plays herself. *CW:* Sex-related content. 100m/C VHS. Illeana Douglas, Paulina Porizkova, Julie Warner, John Corbett, Jonathan Penner, Richard Edson, Charles Martin Smith, Stephanie Beacham, Carla Gugino, Leo Rossi, John Capodice, Richard Edson, Victoria Jackson, Jeff Seymour; *Cameos:* Debbie Reynolds; *D:* Dana Lustig; *W:* Annette Goliti Gutierrez; *C:* Kent Wakeford; *M:* Paul Christian Gordon, Tal Bergman. *BMG*

The Wedding Gift 🐾🐾🐾 *Wide-Eyed and Legless* 1993 (PG-13) Offbeat charm and humor go a long way to overcome the inherent tragedy in this true story made for British TV. Longtime happily marrieds Diana (Walters) and Deric (Broadbent) Longden are struggling to cope with Diana's mysterious and increasingly debilitating illness, which causes blackouts, pain, and the inability to use her limbs. Diana comes to accept the fact that she's going to die and decides to find her hubby a new wife, aided by Deric's friendship with a blind novelist (Thomas). Terrific performances keep the mawkishness at bay. Based on Deric Longden's books "Diana's Story" and "Lost for Words." 87m/C VHS, LV, Closed Caption. *GB* Julie Walters, Jim Broadbent, Sian Thomas, Thora Hird, Andrew Lancel, Anastasia Mulrooney; *D:* Richard Loncraine; *W:* Jack Rosenthal; *C:* Remi Adefarasin. *MAX*

Wedding in Blood 🐾🐾🐾 1974 (PG) Two French lovers plot to kill their respective spouses, and proceed to do so amid calamity and much table-turning. Sharp social satire and suspenseful mystery. Based on a true story. In French with English subtitles. 98m/C VHS, Beta. *FR IT* Claude Pieplu, Stephane Audran, Michel Piccoli; *D:* Claude Chabrol. *COL*

A Wedding in Galilee 🐾🐾🐾 *Noce In Galilee* 1987 The elder of a Palestinian village is given permission to have a traditional wedding ceremony for his son if Israeli military officers can attend as the guests of honor. As the event approaches, conflicts arise among the villagers, the family, and the Israelis. Long but fascinating treatment of traditional culture in the modern world amidst political tension. In Arabic and Hebrew, with English subtitles. 113m/C VHS, LV. *BE FR* Ali M. El Aleili, Nazih Akleh, Anna Achdian; *D:* Michel Khleifi. *KIV*

Wedding in White 🎬🎬 1972 (R) A rape and out-of-wedlock pregnancy trouble a poor British clan living in Canada during WWII. Sad, glum way to spend an evening. Kane is good in a noncomic role. Her screen father cares more for her honor than he does for her. 103m/C VHS, Beta. *CA* Donald Pleasence, Carol Kane, Leo Phillips; *D:* William Fruet.

The Wedding March 🎬🎬🎬🎬 1928 Von Stroheim's famous silent film about romantic couplings in pre-WWI Vienna. The director also stars as a prince preparing to marry for money, who falls in love with a beautiful, but poor woman. Romance and irony, with a memorable finale. Like many of his other great films, it was taken from him and re-edited. Initially the first of two halves; the second, "The Honeymoon," has been lost. Next to "Greed," his most successful film. 113m/B VHS, Beta. Erich von Stroheim, Fay Wray, ZaSu Pitts, George Fawcett, Maude George, Matthew Betz, George Nicholls, Cesare Gravina; *D:* Erich von Stroheim; *C:* Hal Mohr; *M:* Gaylord Carter. *PAR*

The Wedding Party 🎬½ 1969 Apprehensive groom is overwhelmed by his too-eager bride and her inquisitive relatives at a prenuptial celebration. Hokey, dull, would-be comedy. First screen appearances of both Clayburgh and De Niro (spelled DeNero in the credits). 90m/C VHS, Beta. Jill Clayburgh, Robert De Niro, William Finley; *D:* Brian DePalma, Cynthia Munroe, Wilford Leach; *W:* Brian DePalma. *NO*

Wedding Rehearsal 🎬🎬½ 1932 A young nobleman thwarts his grandmother's plans to marry him off by finding suitors for all the young ladies offered to him until he finally succumbs to the charms of his mother's secretary. Enjoyable, fun comedy. First featured roles for actresses Oberon, Barrie, and Gardner. 84m/B VHS, Beta, LV. Merle Oberon, Roland Young, John Loder, Wendy Barrie, Maurice Evans, Joan Gardner; *D:* Alexander Korda.

The Wedding Singer 🎬🎬½ 1997 (PG-13) Despite almost nonexistent pacing and a script full of holes, "Singer" is an enjoyably goofy look at the mid '80s. Surprisingly toned-down and appealing Sandler is Robbie Hart, wedding singer, ultimate nice guy, and rock-star wannabe, who's jilted at the altar. Waitress Barrymore is engaged to a skirt-chasing stock broker. It's immediately clear that they belong together, and the rest of the movie is spent on them chasing each other through various contrived obstacles, to the obvious ending. Features great cameos by punkrocker Billy Idol, Jon Lovitz (as a rival wedding singer), and Steve Buscemi (excellent as the groom's jealous "dad always liked you best" brother). Musical highlight is Sandler's heartfelt rendition of the J. Geils Band's "Love Stinks." Isn't it a little scary that we're already spoofing the '80s? *CW:* Sex-related material and language. 96m/C VHS, LV, DVD. Adam Sandler, Drew Barrymore, Christine Taylor, Alan Covert, Matthew Glave, Ellen A. Dow, Angela Featherstone, Alexis Arquette, Christina Pickles, Jon Lovitz, Steve Buscemi, Kevin Nealon; *Cameos:* Billy Idol; *D:* Frank Coraci; *W:* Tim Herlihy; *C:* Tim Suhrstedt; *M:* Teddy Castellucci. MTV Movie Awards '98: Best Kiss (Adam Sandler/Drew Barrymore); Nominations: MTV Movie Awards '98: Best On-Screen Duo (Adam Sandler/Drew Barrymore), Best Comedic Performance (Sandler). *NLC*

Wee Willie Winkie 🎬🎬🎬 1937 (PG) A precocious little girl is taken in by a British regiment in India. Sugar-coated. If you're a cinematic diabetic, be warned. If you're a Temple fan, you've probably already seen it. If not, you're in for a treat. Inspired by the Rudyard Kipling story. 99m/B VHS, Beta, Closed Caption. Shirley Temple, Victor McLaglen, Sir C. Aubrey Smith, June Lang, Michael Whalen, Cesar Romero, Constance Collier; *D:* John Ford; *C:*

Arthur C. Miller. Nominations: Academy Awards '37: Best Interior Decoration. *FOX*

Weeds 🎬🎬🎬 1987 (R) A highly fictionalized account of the career of Rick Cluchey, who, as a lifer in San Quentin federal prison, wrote a play. He was eventually paroled and went on to form a theatre group made up of ex-cons. Original and often enjoyable with a tight ensemble performance. Filmed on location at Stateville Correctional Center in Illinois, with inmates serving as extras. 115m/C VHS, Beta, LV. Nick Nolte, Rita Taggart, William Forsythe, Lane Smith, Joe Mantegna, Ernie Hudson, John Toles-Bey, Mark Rolston, Anne Ramsey, Charlie Rich; *D:* John Hancock; *W:* John Hancock, Dorothy Tristan; *M:* Angelo Badalamenti. *HBO*

Week-End In Havana 🎬🎬½ 1941 Set in pre-revolution Cuba, this frothy musical finds salesgirl Faye on a long-awaited cruise when her ship gets stranded in Havana. She's escorted around town by shipping-official Payne and catches the eye of gambler-lothario Romero, who has a jealous girlfriend in Miranda. Fun fluff. ♫Romance and Rhumba; Tropical Magic; The Nango; A Weekend in Havana; When I Love, I Love; Maria Inez; Rebola a Bola. 80m/C VHS. Alice Faye, John Payne, Cesar Romero, Carmen Miranda, Cobina Wright Jr., George Barbier, Sheldon Leonard, Billy Gilbert; *D:* Walter Lang; *W:* Karl Tunberg; *M:* Alfred Newman. *FXV*

Weekend 🎬🎬🎬 1967 A Parisian couple embark on a drive to the country. On the way they witness and are involved in horrifying highway wrecks. Leaving the road they find a different, equally grotesque kind of carnage. Godard's brilliant, surreal, hyper-paranoiac view of modern life was greatly influenced by the fact that his mother was killed in an auto accident in 1954 (he himself suffered a serious motorcycle mishap in 1975). In French with English subtitles. 105m/C VHS. *FR IT* Mireille Darc, Jean Yanne, Jean-Pierre Kalfon, Valerie Lagrange, Jean-Pierre Leaud, Yves Beneyton; *D:* Jean-Luc Godard; *W:* Jean-Luc Godard; *M:* Antoine Duhamel. *NYF, FCT*

Weekend at Bernie's 🎬🎬½ *Hot and Cold* 1989 (PG-13) Two computer nerds discover embezzlement at their workplace after being invited to their boss's beach house for a weekend party. They find their host murdered. They endeavor to keep up appearances by (you guessed it) dressing and strategically posing the corpse during the party. Kiser as the dead man is memorable, and the two losers gamely keep the silliness flowing. Lots of fun. 101m/C VHS, VHS, Beta. Andrew McCarthy, Jonathan Silverman, Catherine Mary Stewart, Terry Kiser, Don Calfa, Louis Giambalvo; *D:* Ted Kotcheff; *W:* Robert Klane; *M:* Andy Summers. *ART*

Weekend at Bernie's 2 🎬½ 1993 (PG) Unlikely but routine sequel to the original's cavorting cadaver slapstick, except now McCarthy and Silverman are frantically hunting for Bernie's (Kiser) cash stash, a quest that takes them and poor dead Bernie to the Caribbean. See Bernie get stuffed in a suitcase, see Bernie hang glide, see Bernie tango, see Bernie attract the opposite sex. Thin script with one-joke premise done to death but fun for those in the mood for the postmortem antics of a comedic stiff. Plenty of well-executed gags involving the well-preserved corpse (particularly one that's been dead for two films now) should lure back fans of the 1989 original. 89m/C VHS, LV, Closed Caption. Andrew McCarthy, Jonathan Silverman, Terry Kiser, Steve James, Troy Beyer, Barry Bostwick; *D:* Robert Klane; *W:* Robert Klane; *M:* Peter Wolf. *COL*

Weekend at the Waldorf 🎬🎬🎬 1945 Glossy, americanized remake of "Grand Hotel" set at the famous Park Avenue hotel, the Waldorf-Astoria, in New York City. Turner and Rogers star in the roles originated by Joan Crawford and Greta Garbo. Johnson and Pidgeon play their love interests. Combining drawing room comedy with slapstick and a touch of romance proved to be a hit, as this film was one of the top grossers of

1945 and was just what war-weary moviegoers wanted to see. Based on the play "Grand Hotel" by Vicki Baum. 130m/B VHS. Ginger Rogers, Walter Pidgeon, Van Johnson, Lana Turner, Robert Benchley, Edward Arnold, Leon Ames, Warner Anderson, Phyllis Thaxter, Keenan Wynn, Porter Hall, Samuel S. Hinds; *D:* Robert Z. Leonard; *W:* Samuel Spewack, Bella Spewack, Guy Bolton. *MGM*

A Weekend in the Country 🎬🎬½ 1996 (R) Ensemble comedy finds a varied group of couples and would-be couples traveling to California's wine country for a weekend of relaxation at a bed and breakfast inn. Nothing quite works out as planned but Cupid's arrow does strike. Made for cable movie filmed on location in Temecula, CA. *CW:* Some language. 94m/C VHS, Closed Caption. Rita Rudner, Faith Ford, Christine Lahti, Jack Lemmon, Richard Lewis, Dudley Moore, Betty White, Dan Cortese, Jennifer Elise Cox; *D:* Martin Bergman; *W:* Rita Rudner, Martin Bergman; *M:* Patrick Williams. *HMK*

Weekend of Shadows 🎬🎬🎬 1977 Confident, moralistic murder drama about a posse after an innocent immigrant they believe has killed a woman. Police sergeant Roberts is interested only in his reputation, not in justice. Posse member Waters begins to sympathize with the hunted man and defends his innocence. Intelligent, well-conceived, and professionally directed. 94m/C VHS, Beta. John Waters, Melissa Jaffer, Graeme Blundell, Wyn Roberts, Barbara West, Graham Rouse; *D:* Tom Jeffrey.

Weekend Pass 🎬 1984 (R) Moronic rookie sailors who have just completed basic training are out on a weekend pass, determined to forget everything they have learned. They find this surprisingly easy to do. 92m/C VHS, Beta, LV. D.W. Brown, Peter Ellenstein, Phil Hartman, Patrick Hauser, Chip McAllister; *D:* Lawrence Bassoff; *W:* Lawrence Bassoff; *C:* Bryan England. *ART, VES*

Weekend War 🎬🎬½ 1988 (PG-13) A group of National Guardsmen are sent to the Honduras for their annual tour of duty. But when a guerilla war between Honduras and Nicaragua breaks out, the Guardsmen are forced to fight for their lives. The "Bridge on the River Kwai" finale features the dilemma over a bridge linking the two countries. Made for television. *CW:* War violence. 96m/C VHS. Daniel Stern, Stephen Collins, Charles Haid, Evan Mirand, Michael Beach, Scott Paulin, James Tolkan; *D:* Steven Hilliard Stern; *M:* Brad Fiedel. *COL*

Weekend Warriors 🎬½ 1986 (R) Young film-studio employees evade the draft in 1961 by enlisting for National Guard weekend duty. Grade "C" dumb comedy from professional celebrity and first-time director Convy. 88m/C VHS, Beta. Chris Lemmon, Lloyd Bridges, Daniel Greene, Tom Villard, Vic Tayback; *D:* Bert Convy; *W:* Bruce Belland; *M:* Perry Botkin. *ART*

Weekend with the Babysitter woof! *Weekend Babysitter* 1970 (R) Sordid teen drama about a weekend babysitter who goes to a film director's house and babysits everyone but the kids, running into a heroin-smuggling ring along the way. Casting-couch story with a twist. 93m/C VHS, Beta. Susan Roman, George E. Carey, James Almanzar, Luanne Roberts; *D:* Don Henderson.

Weep No More My Lady 🎬🎬 1993 (PG-13) Suspense-filled whodunit about a wealthy businessman who comes between two sisters and a sibling rivalry that turns into a deadly game of murder. Based on the best-selling book by Mary Higgins Clark. 92m/C VHS, Closed Caption. Daniel J. Travanti, Shelley Winters, Kristin Scott Thomas. *REP*

Weird Science 🎬🎬 1985 (PG-13) Hall is appealing, and Hughes can write dialogue for teens with the best of them. However, many of the jokes are in poor taste, and the movie seems to go on forever. Hall and his nerdy cohort Mitchell-Smith use a very special kind of software to create the ideal woman who wreaks zany havoc in their lives from the outset. 94m/C VHS, Beta, LV,

Closed Caption. Kelly Le Brock, Anthony Michael Hall, Ilan Mitchell-Smith, Robert Downey Jr., Bill Paxton; **D:** John Hughes; **W:** John Hughes; **C:** Matthew F. Leonetti; **M:** Ira Newborn. *USH*

Weird Woman/Frozen Ghost 1944 In 1944's "Weird Woman" professor Chaney and his South Seas bride suffer the wrath of a jealous woman. In 1945's "The Frozen Ghost" hypnotist Chaney is ruined when a volunteer dies on stage. He relaxes at a friend's (who happens to own a wax museum) where he comes under a diabolical plot to drive him mad. Based on radio's "The Inner Sanctum Mysteries." 125m/B VHS. Lon Chaney Jr., Evelyn Ankers, Ralph Morgan, Lois Collier, Douglass Dumbrille, Elena Verdugo, Anne Gwynne, Milburn Stone, Martin Kosleck; **D:** Harold Young, Reginald LeBorg; **W:** Brenda Weisberg, Bernard Schubert, Lucille Ward. *USH*

Weird World of LSD 🐾½ 1967 Cheap exploitation film featuring the evil effects of LSD. ?m/C VHS. Terry Tessem, Ann Lindsay, Yolanda Morino. *SNC, TPV*

The Weirdo 🐾 1989 "The Jerk" meets Freddie Krueger. This film is absolutely wretched, even by horror movie standards. 86m/C VHS, Beta. Steve Burlington, Jessica Straus; **D:** Andy Milligan. *NO*

Welcome Back Mr. Fox 1983 An award-winning science fiction short wherein an obnoxious movie producer cheats death by being cryogenically frozen, and then wakes up years later no wiser for the experience. Suitably, he receives his comeuppance. 21m/C VHS, Beta. E.D. Phillips, Gustav Vintas; **D:** Walter W. Pitt III. *NO*

Welcome Home 🐾🐾 1989 (R) A missing-in-action Vietnam vet (Kristofferson) leaves his wife and children in Cambodia to return to America more than 15 years after he was reported dead. He finds his first wife remarried and discovers a teenaged son he unknowingly fathered. This plotless, sporadically moving film was Schaffner's last. Made for cable television. 92m/C VHS, Beta, LV. Kris Kristofferson, JoBeth Williams, Sam Waterston, Brian Keith, Trey Wilson, Thomas Wilson Brown; **D:** Franklin J. Schaffner; **C:** Fred W. Koenekamp; **M:** Henry Mancini. *VES, ART*

Welcome Home, Roxy Carmichael 🐾🐾 1990 (PG-13) Ryder, as a young misfit, is the bright spot in this deadpan, would-be satire. Hollywood star Roxy Charmichael returns to her small Ohio hometown and begins fantasizing that she is really her mother. It is obvious why this deadpan, hard-to-follow movie was a boxoffice flop. 98m/C VHS, Beta, LV, 8mm, Closed Caption. Winona Ryder, Jeff Daniels, Laila Robins, Dinah Manoff, Ava Fabian, Robbie Kiger, Sachi Parker; **D:** Jim Abrahams; **C:** Paul Elliott. *PAR*

Welcome Stranger 🐾🐾½ 1947 New doctor's ideas clash with the old doctor's ways in a small town until the younger saves the live of the elder. Crosby and Fitzgerald star as the two clashing medics in this reunion of the cast of "Going My Way." He wins the heart of the town and the heart of local teacher Caulfield in the meantime. Sheekman's script calls for Marx Brothers'-like comedy and director Nugent appears in a cameo as another doctor. 107m/B VHS, Closed Caption. Bing Crosby, Barry Fitzgerald, Joan Caulfield, Wanda Hendrix, Frank Faylen, Elizabeth Patterson, Robert Shayne, Don Beddoe, Percy Kilbride, Larry Young; **Cameos:** Elliott Nugent; **D:** Elliott Nugent; **W:** Arthur Sheekman; **C:** Lionel Lindon; **M:** Johnny Burke, James Van Heusen. *USH*

Welcome to Blood City 🐾½ 1977 An anonymous totalitarian organization kidnaps a man and transports him electronically into a fantasy western town where the person who murders the most people becomes the town's "kill master." Amateurish and low-budget. 96m/C VHS, Beta. Jack Palance, Keir Dullea, Samantha Eggar, Barry Morse. *ART*

Welcome to 18 🐾 1987 (PG-13) Three girls, just out of high school, take summer jobs at a dude ranch, work a local casino, flirt, tease and get in trouble. The movie isn't funny in the least,

and is filled with utter nonsense. Hargitay is the daughter of actress Jayne Mansfield. 91m/C VHS, Beta. Courtney Thorne-Smith, Mariska Hargitay, Jo Ann Willette, Christine Kaufmann; **D:** Terry Carr. *ART*

Welcome to L.A. 🐾🐾🐾 1977 (R) Rudolph's ambitious directorial debut focuses on the sexual escapades of a group of Southern Californians. Based on the music suite "City of the One Night Stands" by Baskin, which also (unfortunately) serves as the soundtrack. Rudolph improved greatly after this initial effort. 106m/C VHS, Beta, Closed Caption. Sissy Spacek, Sally Kellerman, Keith Carradine, Geraldine Chaplin, Lauren Hutton, Viveca Lindfors, Harvey Keitel, John Considine; **D:** Alan Rudolph; **W:** Alan Rudolph; **M:** Richard Baskin. *FOX*

Welcome to Sarajevo 🐾🐾🐾½ 1997 (R) Fresh, unusual take on the siege of Sarajevo in 1992. A group of news correspondents, including British reporter Michael Henderson (Dillane), find themselves in the middle of the siege, and become disillusioned when the conflict is largely ignored by the rest of the world. Film sheds perspective when a particularly bloody massacre takes a backseat to the marital troubles of the royal family. Henderson becomes personally involved when his daily coverage of an orphanage sparks him to become a hero to the orphaned Emily (Sarajevan actress Nusevic). Intermingling actual news footage, Winterbottom shows the violence on a personal level. Solid supporting characters include Harrelson as the wonderfully egotistic American celeb journalist. Strong emotional content is tempered by the smart and savvy gallows humor, which keeps melodrama miles away. Loosely based on a true story by ITN reporter, Michael Nicholson.**CW:** Brutal images/war atrocities and language. 102m/C VHS, LV, Letterbox, Closed Caption. Stephen Dillane, Woody Harrelson, Marisa Tomei, Kerry Fox, Emily Lloyd, Emira Nusevic, Juliet Aubrey, Zoran Janjic, Goran Visnjic, James Nesbitt, Igor Dzambazov, Gordana Gadzic, Drazen Sivak, Vesna Orel; **D:** Michael Winterbottom; **W:** Frank Cottrell Boyce; **C:** Daf Hobson; **M:** Adrian Johnston. *TOU*

Welcome to Spring Break 🐾½ 1988 (R) College co-eds are stalked by a killer on the beaches of Florida. 92m/C VHS, Beta, LV. John Saxon, Michael Parks. *NO*

Welcome to the Dollhouse 🐾🐾½ 1995 (R) Eleven-year-old, glasses-wearing Dawn Wiener (Matarazzo) is the middle child of a middle-class family in an average New Jersey town. It's her first year in junior high and Dawn's bewildered—by school, by family, by life in general, and where she fits in. Puberty sucks.**CW:** Language. 87m/C VHS, LV, Closed Caption. Heather Matarazzo, Brendan Sexton III, Daria Kalinina, Matthew Faber, Angela Pietropinto, Eric Mabius; **D:** Todd Solondz; **W:** Todd Solondz; **C:** Randy Drummond; **M:** Jill Wisoff. Independent Spirit Awards '97: Debut Performance (Matarazzo); Sundance Film Festival '96: Grand Jury Prize; Nominations: Independent Spirit Awards '97: Best Director (Solondz), Best Film, Best Supporting Actor (Faber), Debut Performance (Sexton). *COL*

The Well 🐾🐾🐾 1951 A young black girl disappears and a white man (Morgan) is accused of kidnapping her. When it is discovered that the girl is trapped in a deep well, Morgan's expertise is needed to help free her. 85m/B VHS, Beta. Richard Rober, Harry (Henry) Morgan, Barry Kelley, Christine Larson; **D:** Leo Popkin, Russel Rouse; **C:** Ernest Laszlo. Nominations: Academy Awards '51: Best Film Editing, Best Story & Screenplay. *VCI*

The Well 🐾🐾 1997 Repression, isolation, and tragedy set in barren rural Australia. Drab, middleaged Hester (Rabe) hires spirited teenager Katherine (Otto) to help out on her bleak farm. Hester soon becomes emotional dependent on Katherine, who eventually convinces her to sell the property so they can travel to Europe. (Yes, "The Servant" will come to mind.) But a car accident (caused by Katherine) claims the life of a mystery man and Hester decides to hide the body in an unused well. Then they discover all their

money has been stolen, probably by their dead friend, and just who's going down the well to retrieve it? Based on a novel by Elizabeth Jolley. 101m/C VHS. **AU** Pamela Rabe, Miranda Otto, Paul Chubb; **D:** Samantha Lang; **W:** Laura Jones; **C:** Mandy Walker; **M:** Stephen Rae. Australian Film Institute '97: Best Actress (Rabe), Best Adapted Screenplay, Best Art Direction/Set Decoration; Nominations: Australian Film Institute '97: Best Actress (Otto), Best Cinematography, Best Costume Design, Best Director (Lang), Best Film, Best Film Editing, Best Sound, Best Score. *NYR*

Well-Digger's Daughter 🐾🐾🐾 *La Fille Du Puisatier* 1946 As her lover goes off to war, a well-digger's daughter discovers that she is pregnant causing both sets of parents to feud over who's to blame. This is the first film made in France after the end of WWII and marks the return of the French film industry. In French with English subtitles. 142m/B VHS, Beta. **FR** Raimu, Josette Day, Fernandel, Charpin; **D:** Marcel Pagnol. *NOS, DVT, HEG*

Wend Kuuni 🐾🐾 *God's Gift* 1982 A fable for modern times set in Burkina Faso before the coming of Islam or Christianity. A mute, memoryless child is found by a peddler and adopted by the peddler's village. One day the boy finds a body hanging from a tree. Shocked, he recovers his speech and tells the story of his tragic past, when he and his mother were cast out of their own village. When his mother dies, the boy is bereft of family and tradition. Without these ties to his history he loses both speech and memory. In More with English subtitles. 70m/C VHS. **D:** Gaston Kabore. *KIV*

We're Back! A Dinosaur's Story 🐾🐾½ 1993 (G) Animated adventures of a pack of revived dinosaurs who return to their old stomping grounds—which are now modern-day New York City. Smart-mouth human boy Louie and his girlfriend Cecilia take the dinos under their wing (so to speak), wise them up to modern life, and try to prevent their capture by the evil Professor Screweyes. Slow-moving with some violence. Adapted from the book by Hudson Talbott. 78m/C VHS, LV. **D:** Dick Zondag, Ralph Zondag, Phil Nibbelink, Simon Wells; **W:** John Patrick Shanley; **V:** John Goodman, Felicity Kendal, Walter Cronkite, Joey Shea, Jay Leno, Julia Child, Kenneth Mars, Martin Short, Rhea Perlman, Rene LeVant, Blaze Berdahl, Charles Fleischer, Yeardley Smith. *USH*

We're in the Legion Now 🐾½ 1937 Denny and Barnett star as a couple of American gangsters who join the French Foreign Legion to escape rival hoods from back home. 56m/B VHS, Beta, 8mm. Reginald Denny, Vince Barnett, Esther Ralston. *VYY*

We're in the Navy Now 1927 The famed comedy duo is back again with another armed forces farce. A mild successor to "Behind the Front." 60m/B VHS, Beta. Wallace Beery, Raymond Hatton. *GPV, FCT*

We're No Angels 🐾🐾½ 1955 Three escapees from Devil's Island hide out with the family of a kindly French storekeeper. One of Bogart's few comedies. From the French stage play of the same name. Claustrophobic and talky. Later remade with De Niro and Penn. 103m/C VHS. Humphrey Bogart, Aldo Ray, Joan Bennett, Peter Ustinov, Basil Rathbone, Leo G. Carroll; **D:** Michael Curtiz; **C:** Loyal Griggs. *PAR*

We're No Angels 🐾🐾½ 1989 (R) Two escaped cons disguise themselves as priests and get in the appropriate series of jams. De Niro and Penn play off each other well, turning in fine comic performances. Distantly related to the 1955 film of the same name and the David Mamet play. 110m/C VHS, Beta, Closed Caption. Robert De Niro, Sean Penn, Demi Moore, Hoyt Axton, Bruno Kirby, James Russo, John C. Reilly, Ray McAnally, Wallace Shawn; **D:** Neil Jordan; **W:** David Mamet; **C:** Philippe Rousselot; **M:** George Fenton. *PAR*

We're Not Dressing 🎞🎞🎞 1934 Loose musical adaptation of J.M. Barrie's "The Admirable Crichton" with the butler transformed into singing sailor Crosby. Fabulously wealthy heiress Lombard invites her pals for a South Seas yachting adventure. Only the ship gets wrecked and everyone winds up on a small island where the practical Crosby whips everyone into shape (and romances Lombard). Burns and Allen supply additional comedy as a pair of botanists who just happen to be studying the local fauna. 🎵Good Night Lovely Little Lady; I'll Sing About the Birds and the Bees; It's Just a New Spanish Custom; Let's Play House; Love Thy Neighbor; May I?; Once in a Blue Moon; She Reminds Me of You. **74m/B VHS, LV, Closed Caption.** Bing Crosby, Carole Lombard, George Burns, Gracie Allen, Ethel Merman, Leon Errol, Ray Milland; **D:** Norman Taurog; **W:** Horace Jackson, Francis Martin; **M:** Harry Revel, Mack Gordon. *USH*

We're Not Married 🎞🎞🎞 1952 Five couples learn that they are not legally married when a judge realizes his license expired before he performed the ceremonies. The story revolves around this quintet of couples who now must cope with whether or not they really do want to be married. Although the episodes vary in quality, the Allen-Rogers sequence is excellent. Overall, the cast performs well in this lightweight comedy. **85m/B VHS, Closed Caption.** Ginger Rogers, Fred Allen, Victor Moore, Marilyn Monroe, Paul Douglas, David Wayne, Eve Arden, Louis Calhern, Zsa Zsa Gabor, James Gleason, Jane Darwell, Eddie Bracken, Mitzi Gaynor; **D:** Edmund Goulding; **W:** Nunnally Johnson, Dwight Taylor. *FXV*

We're Talkin' Serious Money 🎞🎞½ 1992 (PG-13) Sal and Charlie are a couple of loser scam-artists always after the elusive big score. They borrow $10,000 from the mob for another get-rich-quick scheme and wind up over their heads with both the mob and the FBI out to get them. **92m/C VHS, LV.** Dennis Farina, Leo Rossi, Fran Drescher, John Lamotta; **D:** James Lemmo; **W:** Leo Rossi, James Lemmo; **M:** Scott Grusin. *COL*

Werewolf 🎞 1995 (R) A remote desert town is stricken by an ancient curse that turns its occupants into werewolves at the full moon. This doesn't help the tourism industry.**CW:** Sex scene. **99m/C VHS, LV.** George Rivero, Fred Cavalli, Adrianna Miles, Richard Lynch, Joe Estevez, R.C. Bates, Heidi Bjorn, Randall Oliver, Nena Belini, Tony Zarindast; **D:** Tony Zarindast; **W:** Tony Zarindast; **C:** Robert Hayes, Dan Gilman. *APX*

Werewolf in a Girl's Dormitory 🎞 *Lycanthropus; The Ghoul in School* 1961 Girls' school headmaster undergoes dental transformation at night. Atrocious dubbing, with equally atrocious theme song "The Ghoul in School." **82m/B VHS.** *IT* Barbara Lass, Carl Schell, Curt Lowens, Maurice Marsac; **D:** Richard Benson. *SMW, SNC*

Werewolf of London 🎞🎞½ 1935 A scientist searching for a rare Tibetan flower is attacked by a werewolf. He scoffs at the legend, but once he's back in London, he goes on a murderous rampage every time the moon is full. Dated but worth watching as the first werewolf movie made. **75m/B VHS.** Henry Hull, Warner Oland, Valerie Hobson, Lester Matthews, Spring Byington, Lawrence Grant, Zeffie Tilbury; **D:** Stuart Walker; **W:** Robert Harris, John Colton; **C:** Charles Stumar. *USH*

Werewolf of Washington 🎞🎞 1973 (PG) Stockwell is a White House press secretary with a problem—he turns into a werewolf. And bites the President, among others. Sub-plot involves a short mad scientist who operates a secret monster-making lab in a White House bathroom. Occasionally engaging horror spoof and political satire made during Watergate era. **90m/C VHS, Beta.** Dean Stockwell, Biff McGuire, Clifton James, Jane House, Beeson Carroll, Michael Dunn; **D:** Milton Moses Ginsberg; **W:** Milton Moses Ginsberg; **C:** Bob Baldwin. *NO*

The Werewolf vs. the Vampire Woman 🎞½ *Shadow of the Werewolf; Blood Moon; Night of Walpurgis; La Noche de Walpurgis* 1970 (R) Hirsute Spanish wolfman teams with two female students in search of witch's tomb. One is possessed by the witch, and eponymous title results. **82m/C VHS.** *SP GE* Paul Naschy, Gaby Fuchs, Barbara Capell, Patty Shepard, Valerie Samarine, Julio Pena, Andres Resino; **D:** Leon Klimovsky. *SNC, HEG*

Werewolves on Wheels *woof!* 1971 (R) A group of bikers are turned into werewolves due to a Satanic spell. A serious attempt at a biker/werewolf movie, however, too violent and grim, not at all funny, and painful to sit through. McGuire had a hit with "Eve of Destruction." **85m/C VHS, Beta.** Stephen Oliver, Severn Darden, Donna Anderson, Duece Barry, Billy Gray, Barry McGuire; **D:** Michel Levesque. *UNI*

Wes Craven Presents Mind Ripper 🎞🎞 *Mind Ripper* 1995 (R) A top secret government experiment, intended to produce a superhuman, goes wrong and traps the scientists in a remote desert outpost with their deadly, pissed-off creation.**CW:** Sci-fi gore; some language. **90m/C VHS.** Lance Henriksen, John Diehl, Natasha Gregson Wagner, Dan Blom, Claire Stansfield; **D:** Joe Gayton; **W:** Jonathan Craven, Phil Mittleman; **C:** Fernando Arguelles; **M:** J. Peter Robinson. *AVE*

Wes Craven's New Nightmare 🎞🎞🎞 1994 (R) Seems the six previous conjurings of Freddy's tortured but fictional soul have inadvertently created a real supernatural force bent on tormenting the lives of retired scream queen Langenkamp, her son (Hughes), writer-director Craven, and surprisingly mild alter-ego Englund. Craven's solution is to write a script that reunites series principals for a final showdown with the slashmaster in Hell. Clever and original in a genre known for neither trait, this movie-in-a-movie-about-a-movie is equal parts playful gimmick and inspired terror that will give even the most seasoned Kruegerphile the heebie-jeebies.**CW:** explicit horror, violence, and gore; language 112m/C VHS, LV, Closed Caption. Robert Englund, Heather Langenkamp, Miko Hughes, David Newsom, Tracy Middendorf, Fran Bennett, John Saxon, Wes Craven, Robert Shaye, Sara Risher, Marianne Maddalena; **D:** Wes Craven; **W:** Wes Craven; **C:** Mark Irwin; **M:** J. Peter Robinson. Nominations: Independent Spirit Awards '95: Best Film. *NLC*

West-Bound Limited 🎞🎞½ 1923 A romantic adventurer rescues a girl from certain death as a train is about to hit her, and the two fall in love. Lucky for him, she happens to be the boss' daughter. This film is a good example of classic silent melodrama with music score. **70m/B VHS, Beta.** John Harron, Ella Hall, Claire McDowell. *VYY*

West of Nevada 🎞🎞 1936 A rare film, featuring the Lieutenant Governor of Nevada (and Clara Bow's husband) in a fast-moving adventure about a band of Indians who must protect their gold from thieves. Bell is the good guy who aids the Indians. **59m/B VHS, Beta.** Rex Bell, Joan Barclay, Al "Fuzzy" St. John, Steve Clark. *GVV*

West of Pinto Basin 🎞🎞 1940 The Range Busters are riding around checking the territory for badmen in this tale of the old west. The music score includes "That Little Prairie Gal of Mine," "Rhythm of the Saddle," and "Ridin' the Trail Tonight." **60m/B VHS, Beta.** Ray Corrigan, Max Terhune, John "Dusty" King, Jack Perrin. *NOS, DVT*

West of the Divide 🎞🎞½ 1934 A young cowboy (Wayne) impersonates an outlaw in order to hunt down his father's killer and find his missing younger brother. He saves a proud rancher and his feisty daughter along the way. A remake of "Partners of the Trail," and a solid early Wayne oater. **53m/B VHS, Beta.** John Wayne, George "Gabby" Hayes, Lloyd Whitlock, Yakima Canutt; **D:** Robert North Bradbury. *COL, REP, NOS*

West of the Law 🎞🎞 1942 A group of ranchers turn to lawmen for protection from a band of outlaws. Part of the Rough Riders series. **60m/B VHS, Beta.** Buck Jones, Tim McCoy, Raymond Hatton; **D:** Howard Bretherton. *NOS, VCN, DVT*

West of the Pecos 🎞🎞½ 1945 Rill (Hale) is a society gal on her way to the family ranch in Texas. She's disguised as a boy for safety, which turns out to be a smart idea when outlaws attack the stagecoach. Fortunately, Pecos Smith (Mitchum) is also around to lend a hand. Based on the novel by Zane Grey; first filmed in 1935. **66m/B VHS.** Robert Mitchum, Barbara Hale, Richard Martin, Thurston Hall, Rita (Paula) Corday, Russell Hopton, Harry Woods; **D:** Edward Killy; **C:** Russell Metty. *GPV*

West of Zanzibar 🎞🎞½ 1928 Chaney plays an ivory trader, ruling a jungle kingdom, who lives for revenge on the man who left him a cripple. He decides to ruin the man's daughter and turn her into a prostitute but his plan backfires. Chaney and director Browning offer a steamy atmosphere amidst a number of script flaws. **63m/B VHS, LV.** Lon Chaney Sr., Lionel Barrymore, Warner Baxter, Mary Nolan; **D:** Tod Browning. *FCT*

The West Point Story 🎞🎞½ *Fine and Dandy* 1950 Cagney stars as an on-the-skids Broadway director offered a job staging a show at West Point. Seems cadet MacRae has written a musical and his uncle happens to be a producer. Cagney, with girlfriend Mayo, finds all the rules and regulations getting the better of his temper, so much so that he's told unless he can conform to academy standards the show won't go on! Day is the showgirl MacRae falls for. Cagney's energy and charm carry the too-long film but it's not one of his better musical efforts. 🎵Ten Thousand Sheep; You Love Me; By the Kissing Rock; Long Before I Knew You; Brooklyn; It Could Only Happen in Brooklyn; Military Polka. **107m/B VHS.** James Cagney, Virginia Mayo, Gordon MacRae, Doris Day, Roland Winters, Gene Nelson, Alan Hale Jr., Wilton Graff, Jerome Cowan; **D:** Roy Del Ruth; **W:** John Monks Jr., Charles Hoffman, Irving Wallace; **M:** Sammy Cahn, Jule Styne. Nominations: Academy Awards '50: Scoring of a Musical. *WAR, MVD*

West Side Story 🎞🎞🎞½ 1961 Gang rivalry and ethnic tension on New York's West Side erupts in a ground-breaking musical. Loosely based on Shakespeare's "Romeo and Juliet," the story follows the Jets and the Sharks as they fight for their turf while Tony and Maria fight for love. Features frenetic and brilliant choreography by co-director Robbins, who also directed the original Broadway show, and a high-caliber score by Bernstein and Sondheim. Wood's voice was dubbed by Marni Nixon and Jimmy Bryant dubbed Beymer's. The laserdisc version includes the complete storyboards, production sketches, re-issue trailer, and an interview with Wise in a letterbox format with digital stereo surround sound. 🎵Prologue; Jet Song; Something's Coming; Dance at the Gym; Maria; America; Tonight; One Hand, One Heart; Gee, Officer Krupke. **151m/C VHS, Beta, LV, Letterbox, Closed Caption.** Natalie Wood, Richard Beymer, Russ Tamblyn, Rita Moreno, George Chakiris, Simon Oakland, Ned Glass; **D:** Robert Wise, Jerome Robbins; **W:** Ernest Lehman; **C:** Daniel F. Fapp; **M:** Leonard Bernstein, Stephen Sondheim. Academy Awards '61: Best Art Direction/Set Decoration (Color), Best Color Cinematography, Best Costume Design (Color), Best Director (Wise), Best Film Editing, Best Picture, Best Sound, Best Supporting Actor (Chakiris), Best Supporting Actress (Moreno), Scoring of a Musical; Directors Guild of America Awards '61: Best Director (Wise), Best Director (Robbins); Golden Globe Awards '62: Best Film—Musical/Comedy, Best Supporting Actor (Chakiris), Best Supporting Actress (Moreno), National Film Registry '97'; New York Film Critics Awards '61: Best Film; Nominations: Academy Awards '61: Best Adapted Screenplay. *MGM, OM*

West to Glory 🎞½ 1947 Glory isn't necessarily exciting, as the hero helps a Mexican rancher save his gold and jewels from evildoers in this slow-paced oater. **61m/B VHS.** Eddie Dean, Roscoe

Ates, Dolores Castle, Gregg Barton, Alex Montoya, Harry Vejar; *D:* Ray Taylor. *NOS*

Western 🐺🐺 1996 Spaniard Paco (Lopez), a traveling rep for a shoe manufacturer in France, picks up hitchhiking Russian emigre Nino (Bourdo) and soon finds himself minus car, shoe samples, and luggage. He's rescued by local beauty Marinette (Vitali) and, since he's been fired, decides to hang around the town where she lives. But when Paco spots Nino again, he promptly beats him up, sending the Russian to the hospital. Oddly, this serves as a bond for the two men and they decide to do a little traveling through Brittany together, with Paco trying to teach the naive Nino how to pick up pretty girls. Funny, if extended, French road trip. French with subtitles. **136m/C VHS.** *FR* Sergei Lopez, Sacha Bourdo, Elisabeth Vitali, Marie Matheron, Basile Siekoua; *D:* Manuel Poirier; *W:* Jean-Francois Goyet, Manuel Poirier; *C:* Nara Keo Kosal; *M:* Bernardo Sandoval. Cannes Film Festival '97: Special Jury Prize. *NYR*

Western Double Feature 1 1938 In "Utah" (1945, 55 minutes), Rogers foils a land swindle and helps a lady ranch owner; in "Man from Music Mountain" (1938, 60 minutes), Autry foils a worthless gold mining stock swindle. **115m/B VHS, Beta.** Roy Rogers, Dale Evans, George "Gabby" Hayes, Gene Autry, Smiley Burnette; *D:* Joseph Kane. *HHT*

Western Double Feature 1: Wild Bill & Sunset Carson 194? Double feature: in "Calling Wild Bill Elliott" (1943), Wild Bill comes to the aid of homesteaders; in "Santa Fe Saddlemates" (1945), Carson breaks up a diamond smuggling ring. **120m/B VHS, Beta.** Wild Bill Elliott, Sunset Carson; *D:* Spencer Gordon Bennet.

Western Double Feature 2 1933 Wayne and Hayes are teamed together in two hour-long B-westerns: "Star Packer" (1934) and "West of the Divide" (1933). **120m/B VHS, Beta.** John Wayne, George "Gabby" Hayes; *D:* Robert North Bradbury. *HHT*

Western Double Feature 2: Wayne & Hale *Nightriders; Home on the Range* 198? Double feature; in "Night Riders" (1939), Wayne battles injustice; in "Home on the Range" (1946, color), Hale protects a wild animal refuge. **120m/B VHS, Beta.** John Wayne, Monte Hale; *D:* George Sherman.

Western Double Feature 3 1936 Two Wayne westerns are on this tape: "Helltown" (1938, 59 minutes), in which Wayne catches a cattle rustler; and "Winds of the Wasteland" (1936, 54 minutes), where he plays an out-of-work Pony Express rider. **113m/B VHS, Beta.** John Wayne, Johnny Mack Brown, Marsha Hunt, Phyllis Fraser; *D:* Charles T. Barton, Mack V. Wright. *HHT*

Western Double Feature 3: Rogers & Allen 1950 Double feature. In "Twilight in the Sierras" (1950), Rogers catches a gang of crooks; in "Under Mexicali Stars" (1950), Allen is a cowboy who uncovers a counterfeiting ring. **134m/C VHS, Beta.** Roy Rogers, Dale Evans, Rex Allen; *D:* William Witney.

Western Double Feature 4 1937 Rogers plays a dual role in a case of mistaken identity in "Billy the Kid Returns" (1938, 56 minutes); in "Round Up Time in Texas" (1937, 56 minutes), Autry is framed on a charge of diamond smuggling. **112m/B VHS, Beta.** Roy Rogers, Gene Autry, Smiley Burnette; *D:* Joseph Kane. *HHT*

Western Double Feature 4: Rogers & Evans *Don't Fence Me In; Sheriff of Wichita* 194? In "Don't Fence Me In" (1945), Rogers helps out a woman reporter; in "Sheriff of Wichita" (1948), a frontier investigator solves a crime. **120m/B VHS, Beta.** Roy Rogers, Dale Evans, George "Gabby" Hayes, Allan "Rocky" Lane.

Western Double Feature 5 1935 Wayne stars in both halves of this double feature: in "Desert Trail" (1935, 54 minutes), he plays a rodeo star; in "Man from Utah" (1934, 55 minutes), he brings a gang of murderers to justice.

109m/B VHS, Beta. John Wayne, Polly Ann Young; *D:* Robert North Bradbury. *HHT*

Western Double Feature 5: Rogers & Autry 1937 "The Big Show" (1937) features songs, action, and horses; in "Home in Oklahoma" (1946), Roger tracks down a murderer. **108m/B VHS, Beta.** Gene Autry, Roy Rogers, Smiley Burnette; *D:* Mack V. Wright, William Witney.

Western Double Feature 6: Rogers & Trigger *Trigger, Jr.; Gangs of Sonora* 1950 "Trigger Jr." (1950) is the story of Trigger's colt; "Gangs of Sonora" (1941, black and white) deals with a fight to save a small frontier newspaper. **120m/C VHS, Beta.** Roy Rogers, Dale Evans, Bob Livingston, Bob Steele; *D:* William Witney.

Western Double Feature 7: Wild Bill & Crabbe *Phantom of the Plains; Prairie Rustlers* 1945 "Phantom of the Plains" deals with a plan to save a woman from a gigolo; "Prairie Rustlers" tells of the problems of a man who is the identical double of Billy the Kid. **120m/B VHS, Beta.** Wild Bill Elliott, Buster Crabbe.

Western Double Feature 8: Hale & Carradine 194? In "Silver Spurs" (1943), ranchers wanting to get the right-of-way through oil land run into an ambitious resort owner; in "Out California Way" (1946), Hale is a young cowboy looking for work in Hollywood. **121m/B VHS, Beta.** Roy Rogers, Monte Hale, John Carradine.

Western Double Feature 9: LaRue & Beery 194? In "Cheyenne Takes Over" (1947), LaRue battles outlaws; in "Tulsa Kid" (1940), a young man must face a gunfighter. **120m/B VHS, Beta.** Lash LaRue, Donald (Don "Red") Barry, Noah Beery Sr.

Western Double Feature 10: Roy, Dale, & Trigger 198? In "Bells of Coronado" (1950), Rogers must solve a murder and uranium ore theft; in "King of the Cowboys" (1943, black and white), Roy investigates a band of saboteurs. **120m/C VHS, Beta.** Roy Rogers, Dale Evans; *D:* William Witney.

Western Double Feature 11 1950 Roy and Trigger act as modern day Robin Hoods to end crooked dealing in the West; Roy hides behind a smile and a song to nab a deputy and a ranch owner. **121m/B VHS, Beta.** Roy Rogers, Penny Edwards, Gordon Jones, George "Gabby" Hayes.

Western Double Feature 12 1944 Red Ryder learns of a plot to scare ranchers into selling out before an oil strike is discovered; the Three Musketeers are sent to the Caribbean as U.S. envoys to sell Army horses. **108m/B VHS, Beta.** Bob Livingston, Wild Bill Elliott, Duncan Renaldo, Robert (Bobby) Blake.

Western Double Feature 13 194? Red Ryder foils outlaws trying to swindle the Duchess' stage line in a small frontier town in "Wagon Wheels Westward" (1945). "Rocky Mountain Rangers" (1940), features the Three Mesquiteers pursuing the deadly Barton Gang. **108m/B VHS, Beta.** Red Ryder, Bob Livingston, Robert (Bobby) Blake.

Western Double Feature 14 1952 Outlaws, good guys, and romance on the old frontier. Amateur Robin Hoods steal back money wrongfully taken. **123m/B VHS, Beta.** Tim Holt, Jack Holt, Nan Leslie, Noreen Nash.

Western Double Feature 15 1950 Rogers breaks up a cattle rustling ring; the good guys try to bring law and order to a vast Wyoming territory plagued by a crooked political boss. **122m/B VHS, Beta.** Roy Rogers, Penny Edwards, Donald (Don "Red") Barry, Lynn Merrick.

Western Double Feature 16 1946 Autry is sent to quell a revolution in Mexico; Rogers's horse Lady and Hayes's horse Golden Sovereign are the focal points of the second part of this double feature. **108m/B VHS, Beta.** Gene Autry, Smiley Burnette, Roy Rogers, George "Gabby" Hayes.

Western Double Feature 17 194? Rogers stars in "The Golden Stallion" (1949). Roy battles diamond smugglers who use wild horses to transport the goods. "The Cherokee Flash" (1945), starring Carson, deals with a respectable citizen's outlaw past catching up to him. **121m/C VHS, Beta.** Roy Rogers, Sunset Carson; *D:* William Witney.

Western Double Feature 18 194? A Rogers double feature: in "Eyes of Texas" (1948), a westerner turns his ranch into a camp for war-orphaned boys; in "Helldorado" (1946), Roy travels to Las Vegas. **108m/B VHS, Beta.** Roy Rogers, Andy Devine, Dale Evans; *D:* William Witney.

Western Double Feature 19 1945 Rogers helps a young woman foil a plot by crooks to swindle her inheritance. Roy appears in his first starring role (1938) and fights an outlaw gang. **108m/B VHS, Beta.** Roy Rogers, Dale Evans, Pat Brady.

Western Double Feature 21 194? Roy battles crooks in "Susanna Pass" (1949). In "Sheriff of Las Vegas" (1944), Red must find the murderer of Judge Blackwell. **121m/C VHS, Beta.** Roy Rogers, Red Ryder, Dale Evans, Robert (Bobby) Blake; *D:* William Witney.

Western Double Feature 22 194? A Rogers double feature: "Under California Stars" (1948), Roy rounds up a gang of wild horse rustlers; "San Fernando Valley" (1944), Roy brings law and order to the valley. **108m/B VHS, Beta.** Roy Rogers; *D:* William Witney.

Western Double Feature 24 194? In "Cowboy and the Senorita" (1944), Roy solves the mystery of a missing girl. "Colorado Serenade" (1946) is a musical western in Cinecolor starring Dean. **122m/C VHS, Beta.** Roy Rogers, Dale Evans, Eddie Dean.

Western Frontier 🐺🐺 1935 Ordinary cowpoke Maynard is called on to lead the fight against a band of outlaws led by the Indian-raised sister he never knew he had. Action-packed, fast, and fun. Maynard's first outing for Columbia. **56m/B VHS, Beta.** Ken Maynard, Lucille Browne, Nora Lane, Robert "Buzzy" Henry, Frank Yaconelli; *D:* Al(bert) Herman. *NOS, DVT*

Western Gold 1937 Western set during the Civil War in which the character played by Smith Ballew is sent west to stop thieves who are stealing gold from the Union. **57m/C VHS.** Smith Ballew, Heather Angel, Leroy Mason, Howard Hickman, Ben Alexander, Frank McGlynn, Otis Harlan, Tom London, Bud Osborne; *D:* Howard Bretherton. *GPV*

Western Justice 🐺🐺 1935 Good Guy Steele brings western-style justice to a lawless town. Ordinary oater with horses, etc., and a few chuckles on the side. **56m/B VHS, Beta.** Bob Steele; *D:* Robert North Bradbury. *VTR, NOS*

Western Mail 🐺🐺 1942 Yet another western in which the hero goes undercover so he can bring the bad guys to justice. Yaconelli plays a guitar tune, accompanied by his monkey. **54m/B VHS.** Tom George Duryea Keene, Frank Yaconelli, Leroy Mason, Jean Trent, Fred Kohler Jr.; *D:* Robert Emmett Tansey. *NOS, DVT, HEG*

Western Pacific Agent 🐺🐺 1951 A Western Pacific agent chases an outlaw who has committed robbery and murder. The agent falls in love with the victim's sister and, of course, prevails. Rather violent. **62m/B VHS, Beta, LV.** Kent Taylor, Sheila Ryan, Mickey Knox, Robert Lowery; *D:* Sam Newfield. *NO*

Western Trails 🐺 1938 Forgettable western about the clean-up of a Wild West town terrorized by outlaws. Thin script, bad acting, and a little singin' and funnin' around. **59m/B VHS, Beta.** Bob Baker, Marjorie Reynolds, Robert Burns; *D:* George Waggner. *NOS, DVT, HEG*

Western Union 🐺🐺🐺½ 1941 A lavish, vintage epic romantically detailing the political machinations, Indian warfare, and frontier adventure that accompanied the construction of the Western Union telegraph line from Omaha, Nebraska, to Salt Lake City, Utah, during the Civil War. A thoroughly entertaining film in rich Technicolor. This was Lang's second western, following his personal favorite, "The Return of Frank James." Writer Carson utilized the title, but not the storyline, of a Zane Grey book. The German Lang showed himself a master of the most American of genres, yet made only one more western, "Rancho Notorious" (1952), another masterpiece. **94m/C VHS, Beta, Closed Caption.** Randolph Scott, Robert Young, Dean Jagger, Slim Summerville, Virginia Gilmore, John Carradine, Chill Wills, Barton MacLane, Minor Watson, Charles Middleton, Irving Bacon; **D:** Fritz Lang. *FOX, MLB*

The Westerner ♂♂♂½ 1940 A sly, soft-spoken drifter champions Texas border homesteaders in a land war with the legendary Judge Roy Bean. "The Law West of the Pecos" sentences drifter Cooper to hang, but Cooper breaks out of jail. He falls for damsel Davenport and stays in the area, advocating the rights of homesteaders to Brennan. Brennan's Bean is unforgettable and steals the show from Cooper. Film debuts of actors Tucker and Andrews. Amazing cinematography; Brennan's Oscar was his third, making him the first performer to pull a hat trick. **100m/B VHS, Beta, LV.** Gary Cooper, Walter Brennan, Doris Davenport, Dana Andrews, Forrest Tucker, Charles Halton; **D:** William Wyler; **C:** Gregg Toland. Academy Awards '40: Best Supporting Actor (Brennan); Nominations: Academy Awards '40: Best Interior Decoration, Best Story. *HBO, BTV*

Westfront 1918 ♂♂♂ 1930 A dogmatic anti-war film by the German master (his first talkie), about German and French soldiers on the fields of WWI, dying together without victory. Stunning in its portrayal of war's futility, with excellent photography that achieves a palpable realism. In German with English subtitles. **90m/B VHS, Beta.** *GE* Gustav Diesl, Fritz Kampers, Claus Clausen, Hans Joachim Moebis; **D:** G.W. Pabst. *GLV, NLC*

Westward Ho ♂½ 1935 Wayne is determined to bring to justice his parents' slayer. Haven't we seen this one before? Seems the bad guys have corrupted his brother. Wayne's group of vigilantes is called "The Singing Riders," so naturally he sings—or is made to appear to. He looks and sounds ridiculous. **55m/B VHS.** John Wayne, Sheila Mannors; **D:** Robert North Bradbury. *REP, VCN, NOS*

Westward Ho, the Wagons! ♂½ 1956 The promised land lies in the west, but to get there these pioneers must pass unfriendly savages, thieves, villains, and scoundrels galore. Suitable for family viewing, but why bother? Well, the cast does include four Mouseketeers. **94m/B VHS, Beta.** Fess Parker, Kathleen Crowley, Jeff York, Sebastian Cabot, George Reeves; **D:** William Beaudine; **M:** George Bruns. *DIS*

Westward the Women ♂♂♂ 1951 Taylor is Buck Wyatt, a scout hired to wagon-train 150 mail-order brides from Chicago to California. When his lustful hired hands turn out to be all hands, Taylor and the ladies must fight off attacking Indians on their own. Notable film allowing women to be as tough as men is not your typical western. Based on the Frank Capra story. **116m/C VHS, Closed Caption.** Robert Taylor, Denise Darcel, Hope Emerson, John McIntire, Beverly Dennis, Lenore Lonergan, Marilyn Erskine, Julie Bishop, Renata Vanni, Frankie Darro, George Chandler; **D:** William A. Wellman; **W:** Charles Schnee; **C:** William Mellor; **M:** Jeff Alexander. *MGM*

Westworld ♂♂♂ 1973 (PG) Crichton wrote and directed this story of an adult vacation resort of the future which offers the opportunity to live in various fantasy worlds serviced by lifelike robots. Brolin and Benjamin are businessmen who choose a western fantasy world. When an electrical malfunction occurs, the robots begin to go berserk. Brynner is perfect as a western gunslinging robot whose skills are all too real. **90m/C VHS, Beta, LV, Letterbox.** Yul Brynner, Richard Benjamin, James Bro-

lin, Dick Van Patten, Majel Barrett; **D:** Michael Crichton; **W:** Michael Crichton. *MGM*

Wet and Wild Summer woof! 1992 (R) Topless beach resort is the playground for stud lifeguards and sexy resort owners. **95m/C VHS, LV.** Christopher Atkins, Elliott Gould, Julian McMahon, Rebecca Cross; **D:** Maurice Murphy. *THV*

Wet Gold ♂ 1984 A beautiful young woman and three men journey to retrieve a sunken treasure. Nice scenery. Proves that it is possible to make "The Treasure of the Sierra Madre" without making a classic. John Huston, where are you? Made for television. **90m/C VHS, Beta.** Brooke Shields, Brian Kerwin, Burgess Meredith, Tom Byrd; **D:** Dick Lowry. *NO*

Wetherby ♂♂♂ 1985 (R) Playwright David Hare's first directorial effort, which he also wrote, about a Yorkshire schoolteacher whose life is shattered when a young, brooding stranger comes uninvited to a dinner party, and then shoots himself in her living room. Compelling but oh, so dark. Richardson, who plays a young Redgrave, is actually Redgrave's daughter. **97m/C VHS, Beta, Closed Caption.** *GB* Vanessa Redgrave, Ian Holm, Judi Dench, Joely Richardson, Tim McInnery, Suzanna Hamilton; **D:** David Hare; **W:** David Hare; **M:** Nick Bicat. Berlin International Film Festival '85: Golden Berlin Bear; National Society of Film Critics Awards '85: Best Actress (Redgrave). *MGM*

Whale for the Killing ♂♂½ 1981 An ecologist stranded in a remote Alaskan fishing village battles to save a beached humpback whale from a malicious Russian fisherman. Platitudinous and self-congratulatory, if well-meaning. Made for television from a book by Farley Mowat. **145m/C VHS, Beta, Closed Caption.** Richard Widmark, Peter Strauss, Dee Wallace Stone, Bruce McGill, Kathryn Walker; **D:** Richard T. Heffron; **M:** Basil Poledouris. *FOX*

Whale Music ♂♂ 1994 Off-beat saga of a burned-out rock star and the runaway who invades his life. Desmond Howl (Chaykin) has retreated to a tumbledown estate in the Pacific Northwest, tired of the music grind, and wanting to devote himself to his masterwork—a symphony for whales. Runaway Claire (Preston) provides a surprisingly welcome presence in contrast to Howl's other visitors—ex-wife Fay (Dale), who wants him to sell the estate, rapacious recording exec Kenneth (Welsh), and Howl's brother, singer Daniel (Gross), who happens to be dead and haunting his sibling. Haphazard direction helps dissipate powerful lead performances. Adapted from the novel by Paul Quarrington. **100m/C VHS.** *CA* Maury Chaykin, Cyndy Preston, Jennifer Dale, Kenneth Welsh, Paul Gross; **D:** Richard J. Lewis; **W:** Paul Quarrington, Richard J. Lewis; **C:** Vic Sarin; **M:** George Blondheim. Genie Awards '94: Best Actor (Chaykin), Best Song ("Claire"), Best Sound; Nominations: Genie Awards '94: Best Director (Lewis), Best Film. *NYR*

Whale of a Tale ♂ 1976 (G) A young boy trains a killer whale to appear in the big show in the main tank at "Marineland." **90m/C VHS, Beta.** William Shatner, Marty Allen, Abby Dalton, Andy Devine, Nancy O'Conner; **D:** Ewing Miles Brown. *VCI*

The Whales of August ♂♂♂½ 1987 Based on the David Berry play, the story of two elderly sisters—one caring, the other cantankerous, blind, and possibly senile—who decide during a summer in Maine whether or not they should give up their ancestral house and enter a nursing home. Gish and Davis are exquisite to watch, and the all-star supporting cast is superb—especially Price as a suave Russian. Lovingly directed by Anderson in his first US outing. **91m/C VHS, Beta, LV, 8mm.** Lillian Gish, Bette Davis, Vincent Price, Ann Sothern, Mary Steenburgen, Harry Carey Jr., Tisha Sterling, Margaret Ladd; **D:** Lindsay Anderson; **W:** David Berry. National Board of Review Awards '87: Best Actress (Gish); Nominations: Academy Awards '87: Best Supporting Actress (Sothern). *NLC*

The Wharf Rat ♂♂ 1995 (R) Waterfront con man Petey Martin (Phillips) teams up with journalist Dexter Ireland (Ticotin) to avenge the murder of his policeman brother by a group of corrupt cops lead by the crazy Doc (Reinhold). Made for cable. **CW:** Violence and language. **88m/C VHS, Closed Caption.** Lou Diamond Phillips, Rachel Ticotin, Judge Reinhold, Rita Moreno, Scott Cohen; **D:** Jimmy Huston; **W:** Jimmy Huston; **C:** Levie Isaacks; **M:** Mervyn Warren. *PAR*

What a Carve-Up! ♂♂ No Place Like Homicide 1962 A group of relatives gather in an old, spooky mansion to hear the reading of a will. Tries too hard. Remake of "The Ghoul." **87m/B VHS.** *GB* Kenneth Connor, Sidney James, Shirley Eaton, Donald Pleasence, Dennis Price, Michael Gough; **D:** Pat Jackson. *SNC*

What a Way to Die ♂½ 1970 (R) An evil assassin plots dispatching with a difference. **87m/C VHS, Beta.** William Berger, Anthony Baker, Helga Anders, Georgia Moll; **D:** Helmut Foernbacher. *NO*

What a Woman! ♂♂½ La Fortuna di Essere Donna; Lucky to Be a Woman 1956 Shop girl Antonietta (Loren) becomes a star thanks to a sensational photo of her taken by a paparazzo (Mastroianni) that appears on the cover of a popular magazine. With the aid of a talent agent (Boyer), Antonietta becomes a famous fashion model. Only our photographer gets jealous when she ignores him for the debonair agent. **95m/B VHS.** *IT* Sophia Loren, Marcello Mastroianni, Charles Boyer, Elisa Cegan, Nino Besozzi; **D:** Alessandro Blasetti; **W:** Ennio Flaiano, Suso Cecchi D'Amico, Alessandro Continenza; **C:** Otello Martelli. *HTV*

What About Bob? ♂♂♂ 1991 (PG) Bob, a ridiculously neurotic patient, follows his psychiatrist on vacation, turning his life upside down. The psychiatrist's family find Bob entertaining and endearing. Murray is at his comedic best; Dreyfuss's overly excitable characterization occasionally wears thin. **99m/C VHS, Beta, LV.** Richard Dreyfuss, Bill Murray, Julie Hagerty, Charlie Korsmo, Tom Aldredge, Roger Bowen, Fran Brill, Kathryn Erbe, Doris Belack, Susan Willis; **D:** Frank Oz; **W:** Tom Schulman, Alvin Sargent; **C:** Michael Ballhaus; **M:** Miles Goodman. *TOU*

What Comes Around ♂♂ 1985 (PG) A good-ole-boy drama about a doped-up country singer who is kidnapped by his brother for his own good. The singer's evil manager sends his stooges out to find him. Might have been funny, but isn't. But is it meant to be? Good Reed songs; mildly interesting plot. **92m/C VHS, Beta, LV, Closed Caption.** Jerry Reed, Bo Hopkins, Arte Johnson, Barry Corbin; **D:** Jerry Reed. *NLC*

What Did You Do in the War, Daddy? ♂½ 1966 Unfunny comedy set in WWII about a group of weary American soldiers trying to get a small town in Sicily to surrender. Things don't go smoothly thanks to a combination soccer game/wine festival, not to mention the Germans deciding to attack. Director Edwards comedic verve deserted him. **119m/C VHS.** Dick Shawn, James Coburn, Sergio Fantoni, Giovanna Ralli, Aldo Ray, Harry (Henry) Morgan, Carroll O'Connor, Jay Novello, Vito Scotti; **D:** Blake Edwards; **W:** William Peter Blatty, Blake Edwards; **M:** Henry Mancini. *MGM*

What Do You Say to a Naked Lady? ♂♂½ 1970 Funt takes his Candid Camera to the streets to find out how people react when confronted by nude members of the opposite sex. Sporadically hilarious. **92m/C VHS, Beta.** **D:** Allen Funt. *FOX*

What Ever Happened To... ♂♂½ 1993 Sisters play sisters as the Redgraves (in their first film together) tackle this remake of "What Ever Happened to Baby Jane?" in all its demented glory. Former actress Blanche (Vanessa) and former child star "Baby Jane" (Lynn) are living in a decaying mansion, which Blanche, confined to a wheelchair, is talking about selling. "Baby" snaps (not that she was ever very stable) and proceeds to torment her sis (more than usual). **94m/C VHS.** Vanessa Redgrave, Lynn Redgrave,

Bruce A. Young, Amy Steel, John Scott Clough, John Glover; **D:** David Greene; **W:** Brian Taggert. *FCT*

What Ever Happened to Baby Jane? 🐾🐾½ 1962
Davis and Crawford portray aging sisters and former child stars living together in a decaying mansion. When the demented Jane (Davis) learns of her now-crippled sister's (Crawford) plan to institutionalize her, she tortures the wheelchair-bound sis. Davis plays her part to the hilt, unafraid of Aldrich's unsympathetic camera, and the viciousness of her character. She received her tenth Oscar nomination for the role. **132m/B VHS, Beta, LV, Letterbox, Closed Caption.** Bette Davis, Joan Crawford, Victor Buono, Anna Lee, B.D. Merrill, Maidie Norman; **D:** Robert Aldrich; **W:** Lukas Heller; **C:** Ernest Haller. Nominations: Academy Awards '62: Best Actress (Davis), Best Black and White Cinematography, Best Costume Design (B & W), Best Sound, Best Supporting Actor (Buono). *WAR*

What Happened to Rosa? 🐾🐾🐾
1921 This early Goldwyn release, a whimsical Cinderella story, casts Normand as an endearing shop girl duped by a gypsy's bogus predictions. Believing herself to be the reincarnation of a Castillian noblewoman she dons a fancy gown, attends a fancy shipboard ball and captures the heart of the fancy doctor of her dreams. But fearing his rejection of her true identity she slips away during the chaos of a brawl, leading the good doctor to believe that she is dead. A comedy of errors unfolds before they meet again and live happily ever after. No doubt it jerked a few tears in its day. **42m/B VHS.** Mabel Normand, Hugh Thompson, Doris Pawn, Tully Marshall, Eugenie Besserer, Buster Trow; **D:** Victor Schertzinger. *NOS, FHV*

What Happened Was... 🐾🐾 1994 (R)
Two-character study about a weirdly nightmarish first date. Law secretary Jackie (Sillas) has been eyeing bookish paralegal Michael (Noonan) and finally invites him for dinner at her loft. The two struggle to relax and make small talk that turns into some unexpected soul baring. Emotionally distant Michael is unexpectedly hostile about his job and claims to be writing an expose of their law firm while overly friendly Jackie is writing a children's book, which turns out to be jarringly violent and apparently autobiographical. Provides an idiosyncratic, if limited, appeal thanks to a compelling performance by Sillas.**CW:** Some language; verbal description of child abuse. **92m/C VHS.** Tom Noonan, Karen Sillas; **D:** Tom Noonan; **W:** Tom Noonan; **C:** Joe DeSalvo; **M:** Lodovico Sorret. Sundance Film Festival '94: Best Screenplay, Grand Jury Prize; Nominations: Independent Spirit Awards '95: Best Actress (Sillas). *HMK*

What Have I Done to Deserve This? 🐾🐾🐾
Que He Hecho Yo Para Merecer Esto! 1985 A savage parody on Spanish mores, about a speed-addicted housewife who ends up selling her son and killing her husband with a ham bone. Black, black comedy, perverse and funny as only Almodovar can be. In Spanish with subtitles. Nudity and profanity. **100m/C VHS, Beta, LV.** Carmen Maura, Chus Lampreave; **D:** Pedro Almodovar; **W:** Pedro Almodovar. *CCN, TPV*

What! No Beer? 🐾🐾 1933
Two dim-bulb friends decide to put their money into a defunct brewery hoping for the end of Prohibition. They start up operations too soon and wind up attracting the unwelcome attentions of gangster bootleggers and the cops. Mediocre comedy and Keaton's last starring role as his own problems with alcohol affected his work. **66m/B VHS.** Buster Keaton, Jimmy Durante, Phyllis Barry, Roscoe Ates, John Miljan, Henry Armetta, Edward Brophy; **D:** Edward Sedgwick. *MGM*

What Price Glory? 🐾🐾🐾 1952
Remake of the 1926 silent classic about a pair of comradely rivals for the affections of women in WWI France. Strange to have Ford directing an offbeat comedy, but it works: masterful direction, good acting. Demarest broke both legs in a motorcycle accident during shooting. **111m/C VHS, Beta.** James Cagney, Dan Dailey, Corinne Calvet, William Demarest,

James Gleason, Robert Wagner, Max Casey Adams Showalter, Craig Hill, Marisa Pavan; **D:** John Ford. *FOX, FCT*

What Price Hollywood? 🐾🐾🐾 1932
Aspiring young starlet decides to crash film world by using an alcoholic director as her stepping stone. Bennett is lovely; Sherman is superb as an aging, dissolute man who watches his potential slip away. From a story by Adela Rogers St. Johns. Remade three times as "A Star is Born." **88m/B VHS, Beta, LV.** Constance Bennett, Lowell Sherman, Neil Hamilton; **D:** George Cukor; **C:** Charles Rosher; **M:** Max Steiner. Nominations: Academy Awards '32: Best Story. *CCB, TTC, FCT*

What the Moon Saw 🐾🐾½ 1990
When a young boy is confronted by a less than friendly theatre owner, he uses favorite scenes from "Sinbad" to deal with the aggressor. **86m/C VHS, Closed Caption.** Pat Evison; **D:** Pino Amenta. *FHE, BTV*

What the Peeper Saw 🐾🐾
Night Hair Child; Child of the Night 1972 The wife of a wealthy author finds her comfortable life turning into a terrifying nightmare when her young stepson starts acting funny. Juicy and terrifying. **97m/C VHS, Beta.** Britt Ekland, Mark Lester, Hardy Kruger, Lilli Palmer. *VCI*

What Waits Below 🐾½ 1983 (PG)
A scientific expedition encounters a lost race living in caves in South America. Good cast, bad acting, and lousy script. Might have been much better. **88m/C VHS, Beta.** Timothy Bottoms, Robert Powell, Lisa Blount; **D:** Don Sharp. *ART*

Whatever Happened to Aunt Alice? 🐾🐾🐾 1969 (PG)
After murdering her husband to inherit his estate, a poor, eccentric widow develops an awful habit: she hires maids, only to murder them and steal their savings. The only evidence is a growing number of trees by the drive. Sleuth Ruth Gordon (of "Harold and Maude" fame, acting here just as odd) takes the job in hopes of solving the mystery. Thoroughly amusing. **101m/C VHS, Beta.** Geraldine Page, Ruth Gordon, Rosemary Forsyth, Robert Fuller, Mildred Dunnock; **D:** Lee H. Katzin; **C:** Joseph Biroc. *FOX, MLB*

Whatever Happened to Susan Jane? 🐾½ 1984
A bored housewife searches for an off-beat college friend, and enters into the seamy, strange world of San Francisco's lunatic fringe. Music by Tuxedo Moon, Indoor Life and other punk groups. **90m/C VHS, Beta.** *NO*

What's Eating Gilbert Grape 🐾🐾🐾
Gilbert Grape 1993 (PG-13) Offbeat is mildly descriptive. Depp stars as Gilbert Grape, the titular head of a very dysfunctional family living in a big house in a small Iowa town. His Momma (Cates) weighs more than 500 pounds and hasn't left the house in seven years, he has two squabbling teenage sisters, and 17-year-old brother Arnie (DiCaprio) is mentally retarded and requires constant supervision. What's a good-hearted grocery clerk to do? Well, when free-spirited Becky (Lewis) is momentarily marooned in town, Gilbert may have found a true soulmate. Performances, especially DiCaprio's, save this from the oddball/cute factor although this flick would have benefitted from streamlining, particularly the scenes involving Depp and bad-haircut Lewis. Based on the novel by Hedges. **118m/C VHS, Beta, LV, Closed Caption.** Johnny Depp, Leonardo DiCaprio, Juliette Lewis, Mary Steenburgen, Darlene Cates, Laura Harrington, Mary Kate Schellhardt, Kevin Tighe, John C. Reilly, Crispin Glover, Penelope Branning; **D:** Lasse Hallstrom; **W:** Peter Hedges; **M:** Alan Parker, Bjorn Isfalt. National Board of Review Awards '93: Best Supporting Actor (DiCaprio); Nominations: Academy Awards '93: Best Supporting Actor (DiCaprio); Golden Globe Awards '94: Best Supporting Actor (DiCaprio).*PAR*

What's Good for the Goose 🐾🐾½
1969 Stuffy, married financial institution executive's lifestyle receives a major overhaul when he attends a banking conference and meets a beautiful and free-spirited young woman whom he takes as a lover. Unfortunately, he perpetually finds her in bed with other men, and then his wife gets in on the act, too. Classic British humor.

104m/C VHS. *GB* Norman Wisdom, Sally Geeson, Sarah Atkinson, Sally Bazely; **D:** Menahem Golan; **W:** Norman Wisdom, Menahem Golan; **M:** Reg Tilsley. *NMD*

What's Love Got to Do with It? 🐾🐾½ 1993 (R)
Energetic biopic of powerhouse songstress Tina Turner. Short sequences cover her early life before moving into her abusive relationship with Ike and solo comeback success. Bassett may not look like Tina, but her exceptionally strong performance leaves no question as to who she's supposed to be, even during on-stage Tina sequences. Some credibility is lost when Turner is shown in the final concert sequence—Gibson would have been wise to let Bassett finish what she started. Fishburne is a sympathetic but still chilling Ike, rising to the challenge of showing both Ike's initial charm and longtime cruelty. Based on "I, Tina" by Turner and Kurt Loder.**CW:** Strong language, domestic violence and drug use, and some sexuality. **118m/C VHS, LV, Closed Caption.** Angela Bassett, Laurence "Larry" Fishburne, Vanessa Bell Calloway, Jenifer Lewis, Phyllis Stickney, Khandi Alexander, Pamela Tyson, Penny Johnson, Rae'ven Kelly, Robert Miranda, Chi; **D:** Brian Gibson; **W:** Kate Lanier; **C:** Jamie Anderson; **M:** Stanley Clarke. Golden Globe Awards '94: Best Actress—Musical/Comedy (Bassett); Blockbuster Entertainment Awards '95: Female Newcomer, Video (Bassett); Nominations: Academy Awards '93: Best Actor (Fishburne), Best Actress (Bassett); MTV Movie Awards '94: Best Female Performance (Bassett). *TOU*

What's New Pussycat? 🐾🐾🐾
Quoi De Neuf, Pussycat? 1965 A young engaged man, reluctant to give up the girls who love him, seeks the aid of a married psychiatrist who turns out to have problems of his own. Allen's first feature as both actor and screenwriter. Oscar-nominated title song sung by Tom Jones. **108m/C VHS, Beta, LV, Letterbox.** Peter Sellers, Peter O'Toole, Romy Schneider, Paula Prentiss, Woody Allen, Ursula Andress, Capucine; **D:** Clive Donner; **W:** Woody Allen; **M:** Burt Bacharach, Hal David. Nominations: Academy Awards '65: Best Song ("What's New Pussycat?"). *FOX, FCT*

What's the Matter with Helen? 🐾🐾½ 1971 (PG)
Two women, the mothers of murderous sons, move to Hollywood to escape their past and start a new life. They open a school for talented children, and seem to be adjusting to their new lives until strange things start happening. It is soon revealed that one of the mothers is a psychotic killer, and the other becomes part of an eerie finale. A fine starring vehicle for two aging actresses. Great score. **101m/C VHS.** Debbie Reynolds, Shelley Winters, Dennis Weaver, Agnes Moorehead, Michael MacLiammoir; **D:** Curtis Harrington. Nominations: Academy Awards '71: Best Costume Design. *MGM*

What's Up, Doc? 🐾🐾🐾 1972 (G)
A shy musicologist from Iowa (Ryan) travels to San Francisco with his fiance (Kahn) for a convention. He meets the eccentric Streisand at his hotel and becomes involved in a chase to recover four identical flight bags containing top secret documents, a wealthy woman's jewels, the professor's musical rocks, and Streisand's clothing. Bogdanovich's homage to the screwball comedies of the '30s. Kahn's feature film debut. **94m/C VHS, Beta.** Barbra Streisand, Ryan O'Neal, Kenneth Mars, Austin Pendleton, Randy Quaid, Madeline Kahn; **D:** Peter Bogdanovich; **W:** David Newman, Buck Henry, Robert Benton; **M:** Artie Butler. Writers Guild of America '72: Best Original Screenplay. *WAR*

What's Up Front 🐾½
The Fall Guy; A Fourth for Marriage 1963 Occasionally funny '60s gag-fest about an ogle-eyed bra salesman who decides to sell door-to-door in order to save a failing brassiere company. Filmed in "Girl-O-Rama" by the young Vilmos Zsigmond. Dated and weird, with camp value. No nudity. Costumes were done by Frederick's of Hollywood. **90m/C VHS, Beta.** Tommy Holden, Marilyn Manning, Carolyn Walker, William Watters; **D:** Bob Wehling. *RHI*

What's Up, Tiger Lily? 🐕🐕🐕 1966
This legitimate Japanese spy movie—"Kagi No Kag" (Key of Keys), a 1964 Bond imitation—was re-edited by Woody Allen, who added a new dialogue track, with hysterical results. Characters Terri and Suki Yaki are involved in an international plot to secure egg salad recipe; Allen's brand of Hollywood parody and clever wit sustain the joke. Music by the Lovin' Spoonful, who make a brief appearance. 90m/C VHS, Beta, LV. JP Woody Allen, Tatsuya Mihashi, Mie Hama, Akiko Wakabayashi; D: Woody Allen, Senkichi Taniguhi; M: Jack Lewis. VES

Wheel of Fortune 🐕🐕 A Man Betrayed; Citadel of Crime 1941 A shrewd small-town lawyer, working on a case in the big city, is forced to expose his girlfriend's father as a crooked politician. Strange to see the Duke here in the lead, but what the hey. Not great, but interesting. 83m/B VHS. John Wayne, Frances Dee, Edward Ellis, Ward Bond, Wallace Ford; D: John H. Auer. REP

The Wheeler Dealers 🐕🐕🐕 Separate Beds 1963 Garner plays a supposedly penniless investor (actually a Texas millionaire) who comes to New York stock analyst Remick for investment advice. Her shyster boss (Backus) tells her to sell the aw-shucks cowboy worthless stock which turns out to be worth a fortune. Zany spoof of Wall Street ethics. 100m/C VHS. James Garner, Lee Remick, Jim Backus, Phil Harris, Shelley Berman, Chill Wills, John Astin, Louis Nye; D: Arthur Hiller. MGM

Wheels of Fire 🐕 Vindicator 1984 (R) The earth is a wasteland controlled by sadistic highway hoodlums. When they kidnap the hero's sister, he fights back in a flame-throwing car. Horrible "Road Warrior" rip-off. 81m/C VHS, Beta, LV. Gary Watkins, Lynda Wiesmeier; D: Cirio H. Santiago. ART, VES

Wheels of Terror 🐕 1990 (R) Possessed black car stalks children in isolated village. Bus driver Cassidy gets behind the wheel of V-8 super-charged school bus to initiate most interminable chase scene in screen history. 86m/C VHS, Beta. Joanna Cassidy, Marcie Leeds, Carlos Cervantes, Arlen Dean Snyder; D: Christopher Cain; M: Jay Gruska. PAR

When a Man Loves a Woman 🐕🐕½ To Have and to Hold; Significant Other 1994 (R) Time to get suspicious when song titles become film titles. Alice Green (Ryan) is the mother in a perfect little family, with a loving husband (Garcia), two little girls, and a satisfying career. She's also a closet alcoholic. Less about her alcoholism than the effect on her family and her hubby in particular, shown as a '90s sort of guy who allows Alice to keep her secret. Ryan's detox treatments and struggle back to sobriety are fertile ground for psycho-babble and 12-step cliches, but solid performances save this picture from drying out. CW: Language. 126m/C VHS, LV, Closed Caption. Meg Ryan, Andy Garcia, Lauren Tom, Philip S. Hoffman, Tina Majorino, Mae Whitman, Ellen Burstyn, Eugene Roche, Latanya Richardson; D: Luis Mandoki; W: Ronald Bass, Al Franken; M: Zbigniew Preisner. Blockbuster Entertainment Awards '95: Drama Actress, Video (Ryan); Nominations: MTV Movie Awards '95: Best Female Performance (Ryan), Most Desirable Male (Garcia); Screen Actors Guild Award '94: Best Actress (Ryan). TOU

When a Man Rides Alone 🐕🐕 1933 Tyler relieves trains of their gold shipments in order to reimburse swindled investors. Lovely Lacey frowns on his initiative, so he kidnaps her to keep her quiet. The two fall in love, and the man who rides alone works beside his beloved. 60m/B VHS. Tom Tyler, Adele Lacey, Alan Bridge, Robert Burns, Frank Ball, Alma Chester, Bud Osborne; D: J.P. McGowan. NOS, GPV

When a Man Sees Red 🐕½ 1934 Jones is a ranch foreman whose new boss is Campbell (she inherited the property). The two argue constantly but then come to realize all the fighting is just hiding true love. 60m/B VHS. Buck Jones, Peggy Campbell, Dorothy Revier, Syd Saylor, Leroy

Mason, Charles French, Robert F. (Bob) Kortman; D: Alan James. GPV

When a Stranger Calls 🐕½ 1979 (R) Babysitter is terrorized by threatening phone calls and soon realizes that the calls are coming from within the house. Story was expanded from director Walton's short film "The Sitter." Distasteful and unlikely, though the first half or so is tight and terrifying. 97m/C VHS, Beta, LV. Carol Kane, Charles Durning, Colleen Dewhurst, Rachel Roberts, Rutanya Alda, Carmen Argenziano, Kirsten Larkin, Ron O'Neal, Tony Beckley; D: Fred Walton; W: Fred Walton, Steve Feke; C: Don Peterman. COL

When a Stranger Calls Back 🐕🐕½ 1993 (R) Sequel to "When a Stranger Calls" finds college student Julia Jenz (Schoelen) still trying to put her life together five years after a terrifying ordeal with a stalker. She turns to her advisor Jill (Kane), who went through a similar fate, but once Jill becomes involved she again becomes the pawn of a psychopath. It's up to retired detective John Clifford (Durning), who saved Jill before, to do his heroics once again. Scary opening sequence but suspense peters out toward the end. Made for cable television. 94m/C VHS, LV, Closed Caption. Carol Kane, Charles Durning, Jill Schoelen, Gene Lythgow, Karen Austin; D: Fred Walton; W: Fred Walton. USH

When a Woman Ascends the Stairs 🐕🐕 Onna Ga Kaidan O Agaru Toki 1960 A young widow with an elderly mother and a useless brother supports them all by working as a Ginza bar hostess. As she approaches the perilous professional age of 30, Keiko must decide whether to open her own bar or marry once again. In Japanese with English subtitles. 110m/B VHS. JP Hideko Takamine, Tatsuya Nakadai, Masayuki Mori; D: Mikio Naruse. WAC

When Angels Fly 🐕 1982 In this emotional tale of love and murder, a young woman sets out to find the exact circumstances surrounding the mysterious death of her sister. 96m/C VHS, Beta. Jennifer Dale, Robin Ward. UNI, MOV

When Comedy was King 1959 A compilation of the greatest silent screen comedians, including Keaton, Chaplin, Langdon, and Turpin. 81m/C VHS, Beta, LV. Buster Keaton, Charlie Chaplin, Harry Langdon, Ben Turpin; D: Robert Youngson. NO

When Danger Follows You Home 🐕🐕½ 1997 (PG-13) Ann Werden (Williams), a psychologist at a county mental health facility, becomes interested in the case of a disturbed patient who calls himself Gogel, a computer genius with an FBI file. When Gogel mysteriously dies in Anne's home, she finds herself accused of manslaughter—and then her son is kidnapped. Anne's got a lot to figure out if she wants her life to go back to normal. CW: Some violence. 92m/C VHS, Closed Caption. JoBeth Williams, William Russ, Michael Manasseri, Vanessa King, Susan Hogan, Duncan Fraser, Nicolas Surovy; D: David Peckinpah. USH

When Dinosaurs Ruled the Earth 🐕🐕 1970 (G) When "One Million Years B.C." ruled the boxoffice the Brits cranked out a few more lively prehistoric fantasies. A sexy cavegirl, exiled because of her blond hair, acquires a cave-beau and a dinosaur guardian. Stop-motion animation from Jim Danforth, story by J.G. Ballard. Under the name Angela Dorian, Vetri was Playmate of the Year in 1968 (A.D.). 96m/C VHS, Beta, LV. GB Victoria Vetri, Robin Hawdon, Patrick Allen, Drewe Henley, Sean Caffrey, Magda Konopka, Imogen Hassall, Patrick Holt, Jan Rossini; D: Val Guest; W: Val Guest. WAR, FCT, MLB

When Every Day was the Fourth of July 🐕🐕½ 1978 A nine-year-old girl asks her father, a lawyer, to defend a mute handyman accused of murder, knowing this will bring on him the contempt of the community. Well handled, but see "To Kill a Mockingbird" first. Based on producer/director Curtis's childhood. Sequel: "The Long Days of Summer." Made for television.

100m/C VHS, Beta. Katy Kurtzman, Dean Jones, Louise Sorel, Harris Yulin, Chris Petersen, Geoffrey Lewis, Scott Brady, Henry Wilcoxon, Michael Pataki; D: Dan Curtis. ART

When Father was Away on Business 🐕🐕🐕½ 1985 (R) Set in 1950s Yugoslavia. A family must take care of itself when the father is sent to jail for philandering with a woman desired by a Communist Party offical. The moving story of the family's day-to-day survival is seen largely through the eyes of the father's six-year-old son, who believes dad is "away on business." In Yugoslavian with English subtitles. 144m/C VHS. YU Moreno D'E Bartolli, Miki Manojlovic, Mirjana Karanovic; D: Emir Kusturica. Cannes Film Festival '85: Best Film; Nominations: Academy Awards '85: Best Foreign Language Film. FXL

When Gangland Strikes 🐕🐕 1956 A country lawyer, blackmailed by the mob, tries to protect his family without caving in. Unexceptional remake of "Main Street Lawyer." 70m/B VHS. Raymond Greenleaf, Marjie Millar, Anthony Caruso, Jack Perrin, John Hudson; D: R.G. Springsteen; M: Van Alexander. REP

When Harry Met Sally... 🐕🐕🐕 1989 (R) Romantic comedy follows the long relationship between two adults who try throughout the changes in their lives (and their mates) to remain platonic friends—and what happens when they don't. Wry and enjoyable script is enhanced by wonderful performances. Another directorial direct hit for "Meathead" Reiner, and a tour de force of comic screenwriting for Ephron, with improvisational help from Crystal. Great songs by Sinatra sound-alike Connick. 96m/C VHS, Beta, LV, 8mm, Letterbox, Closed Caption. Billy Crystal, Meg Ryan, Carrie Fisher, Bruno Kirby, Steven Ford, Lisa Jane Persky, Michelle Nicastro, Harley Jane Kozak; D: Rob Reiner; W: Nora Ephron; M: Harry Connick Jr., Marc Shaiman. British Academy Awards '89: Best Original Screenplay; Nominations: Academy Awards '89: Best Original Screenplay. NLC

When Hell Broke Loose 🐕½ 1958 Routine WWII actioner about a small-time crook (Bronson) who joins the Army, changes his ways because of the love of a good woman, and gets a chance to be a hero when he stumbles upon a Nazi assassination plot against General Eisenhower. 78m/B VHS. Charles Bronson, Violet Rensing, Richard Jaeckel, Arvid Nelson, Robert Easton; D: Kenneth Crane; W: Oscar Brodney. PAR

When Hell Was in Session 🐕🐕🐕 1982 In more than seven years as a prisoner of the Viet Cong, Holbrook is subjected to torture, starvation, and psychological warfare to break his will. Based on the true story of Navy Commander Jeremiah Denton. Painful and violent. Made for TV. 98m/C VHS, Beta. Hal Holbrook, Eva Marie Saint, Ronny Cox; D: Paul Krasny. TLF

When He's Not a Stranger 🐕🐕🐕 1989 Date rape is the subject of this made-for-television drama. Lyn is a college freshman who goes to a campus party hosted by the football team. When Ron, the star quarterback, invites Lyn to his dorm room, the situation gets out of hand. Only Lyn calls it rape and Ron calls her a liar. Intense performances are a highlight of this well-done story. 100m/C VHS. Annabeth Gish, John Terlesky, Kevin Dillon, Paul Dooley, Kim Meyers; D: John Gray. TRI

When I Close My Eyes 🐕🐕 Ko Zaprem Oci 1993 First independent film from Slovenia is a thriller in which rural postal employee Ana uses one crime to cover another. When a motorcyclist robs the post office while Ana is working, she uses his crime to steal some money for herself. But then Ana becomes obsessed with the thief and decides to track him down. Slovenian with subtitles. 94m/C VHS. Petra Govc, Mario Selih, Mira Sardo; D: Franci Slak; W: Franci Slak, Silvan Furlan; C: Sven Pepeonik. NYF

When Knights were Bold 🎬🎬½ **1936**
An English nobleman living in India inherits a castle in his native land. Returning home, he is knocked unconscious by a falling suit of armor while trying to impress a young lady and dreams himself back to medieval days. Enjoyable comedy about that ubiquitous British class hierarchy. **55m/B VHS, Beta.** Fay Wray, Jack Buchanan, Martita Hunt; *C:* Frederick A. (Freddie) Young. *VYY*

When Ladies Meet 🎬🎬½ *Strange Skirts* **1941** Entertaining story of a love quadrangle that features several of MGM's top stars of the '40s. In this remake of the 1933 film, Crawford plays a novelist and an early proponent of the women's liberation movement. She falls in love with her publisher (Marshall), who just happens to be married to Garson. Meanwhile, Taylor, who is in love with Crawford, attempts to show her that he is a more suitable match for her than Marshall, but Crawford has yet to catch on. The lengthy dialogue on women's rights is badly dated, but the real-life rivalry between Crawford and Garson adds a certain bite to their witty exchanges. **105m/B VHS, Closed Caption.** Joan Crawford, Robert Taylor, Greer Garson, Herbert Marshall, Spring Byington; *D:* Robert Z. Leonard; *W:* Anita Loos, S.K. Lauren. Nominations: Academy Awards '41: Best Interior Decoration. *MGM*

When Lightning Strikes woof! **1934**
Lightning the Wonder Dog prevents the owner of a rival lumber company from stealing his master's land. He gets to use his talents of running, swimming, barking, and smoking cigars. Proves that real woofers were made way back when, even though in 1934 they didn't feature scantily clad babes. Part of Video Yesteryear's Golden Turkey series. **51m/B VHS, Beta.** Francis X. Bushman. *VYY*

When Nature Calls woof! **1985 (R)** A city family "gets back to nature" in this collection of mostly ineffective gags and poor satirical ideas. Probably your first and last chance to see Liddy and Mays on screen together. **76m/C VHS, Beta, LV.** Davie Orange, Barbara Marineau, Nicky Beim, Tina Marie Staiano, Willie Mays, G. Gordon Liddy; *D:* Charles Kaufman.

When Night Is Falling 🎬🎬🎬 **1995 (R)** Camille (Bussieres) is a professor of mythology at a Calvinist college in Toronto and engaged to theologian Martin (Czerny). Vaguely unsatisfied, Camille meets Petra (Crawford), a trapeze artist in a traveling circus, gets drawn into her world, falls in love, and must decide what she wants from her life. Lots of yearning, romance, and fantasy. Lesbian lovemaking scenes caused a ratings problem (the MPAA originally deemed them worthy of NC-17). *CW:* Strong sexuality and some language. **96m/C VHS.** *CA* Pascale Bussieres, Rachael Crawford, Henry Czerny, David Fox, Don McKellar, Tracy Wright; *D:* Patricia Rozema; *W:* Patricia Rozema; *C:* Douglas Koch; *M:* Lesley Barber. *EVE*

When Pigs Fly 🎬🎬 **1993** A story with two ghosts, a rocking chair, and a lonely, struggling musician. Lilly (Faithful) and young Ruthie (Bella) are the ghosts, who both happen to have died in the same rocking chair a century apart. The chair is now in the possession of down-and-out jazz musician Marty (Molina), who doesn't know how to react to his unworldly visitors. Whimsical but not cloying. **94m/C VHS.** Marianne Faithfull, Alfred Molina, Seymour Cassel, Rachael Bella; *D:* Sara Driver; *W:* Ray Dobbins; *C:* Robby Muller; *M:* Joe Strummer. *PEG*

When Saturday Comes 🎬🎬½ **1995**
Feel-good working-class drama follows Sheffield-born Jimmy Muir (Bean), whose life revolves around a job in a brewery, the local pub, chasing girls, and playing football (soccer) on the weekends. He gets involved with co-worker Annie (Lloyd), whose Uncle Ken (Postlethwaite) coaches the local semi-pro team and who offers Jimmy a chance to play. His success leads to a trial with the pros, Sheffield United, which Jimmy blows by getting drunk. After losing his job, his girl, and having his brother die in an accident,

Jimmy struggles to pull himself together, and maybe get a second chance. **97m/C VHS.** *GB* Sean Bean, Emily Lloyd, Pete Postlethwaite, John McEnery, Ann Bell, Craig Kelly; *D:* Maria Giese; *W:* Maria Giese; *C:* Gerry Fisher; *M:* Anne Dudley. *WHA*

When Taekwondo Strikes 🎬 **1983 (R)** One brave Taekwondo master leads the Korean freedom fighters against the occupying army of WWII Japan. **95m/C VHS, Beta.** Jhoon Rhee, Ann Winton, Angela Mao, Huang Ing Sik; *D:* Raymond Chow.

When the Bough Breaks 🎬🎬 **1986** A psychologist helps the police with the case of a murder-suicide witnessed by a child. He finds one sick society at work in this unkinder, ungentler TV thriller, based on the novel by Jonathan Kellerman. Danson co-produced. **100m/C VHS.** Ted Danson, Richard Masur, Rachel Ticotin, David Huddleston, James Noble, Kim Miyori, Merritt Butrick; *D:* Waris Hussein. *WOV*

When the Bough Breaks 🎬🎬 **1993 (R)** A Texas police chief (Sheen) discovers seven severed hands and turns to a forensic expert (Walker) for help. But then the specialist discovers a psychic link that leads to a mentally disturbed child and the serial killer. *CW:* Violence; mature themes; language. **103m/C VHS, Closed Caption.** Ally Walker, Martin Sheen, Ron Perlman; *D:* Michael Cohn; *W:* Michael Cohn; *C:* Michael Bonvillain. *TTC*

When the Bullet Hits the Bone 🎬 **1996 (R)** Particularly nasty vigilante flick as EMS doc Jack Davies (Wincott) decides to get even while trying to help drug-addicted hooker Lisa (Johnson) get away from her vicious pimp. *CW:* Strong action violence and language. **82m/C VHS.** Jeff Wincott, Michelle Johnson, Doug O'Keefe, Richard Fitzpatrick; *D:* Damian Lee; *W:* Damian Lee. *NHO*

When the Cat's Away 🎬🎬🎬 *Chacun Cherche Son Chat* **1996 (R)** Touching Gallic frolic finds introverted Parisian make-up artist face-to-face with adventure while searching for her lost cat. Chloe (Clavel) eventually comes out of her shell, as the search for little Gris-Gris brings her into contact with a wide variety of characters, some lonely, like herself, played by real people and real cats. Best non-actor kudos to Renee Le Calm as Madame Renee, the kooky neighborhood cat lady, with her network of cat fanciers acting as the reconnaissance party for the runaway feline. Director Klapisch's comedy also tackles weightier topics along the way, including lonliness, homelessness, racism, and the moderization of a city steeped with history. Stylishly spare with adept photography, seems almost semi-documentary. *CW:* Brief strong sex scene and some language. **91m/C VHS.** *FR* Garance Clavel, Zinedine Soualem, Olivier Py, Renee Le Calm; *D:* Cedric Klapisch; *W:* Cedric Klapisch; *C:* Benoit Delhomme. *COL*

When the Clouds Roll By 🎬🎬🎬 **1919** Psycho-satire pits demented doctor against Fairbanks in experiment to make him suicidal basket case. Fairbanks seems to contract ferocious nightmares, passionate superstitions, a spurning lover, and a warrant for his arrest, none of which suppresses his penchant for acrobatics. **77m/B VHS, Beta.** Douglas Fairbanks Sr., Herbert Grimwood, Kathleen Clifford, Frank Campeau, Ralph Lewis, Daisy Robinson, Albert MacQuarrie; *D:* Victor Fleming. *GPV, FCT*

When the Dark Man Calls 🎬🎬½
1995 (R) Shock ending and a strong lead performance by Van Ark enhance this cable TV mystery. Call-in radio shrink Julianne Kaiser (Van Ark) is stalked by ex-con Parmenter (Lewis). Twenty-five years ago he testified that he murdered her parents although the bitter man's always proclaimed his innocence. Now Kaiser is having grisly flashbacks to her childhood but can she figure out the truth before Parmenter kills her? Based on a novel by Stuart M. Kaminsky. *CW:* Violence and terror. **89m/C VHS, Closed Caption.** Joan Van Ark, Geoffrey Lewis, Chris Sarandon, James Read, Frances Hyland,

Janet-Laine Green; *D:* Nathaniel Gutman; *W:* Pablo F. Fenjves. *PAR*

When the Greeks 🎬🎬 *Ton Kero Ton Hellinon* **1981** At the turn of the century, a rich young landowner is kidnapped by a group of nationalist bandits who demand a hefty ransom. But soon the young man realizes he's seeing his true Greek heritage for the first time and begins to identify with his captors. Greek with subtitles. **100m/C VHS.** *GR* Alexis Damianos, Kostas Arzoglou, George Sampanis, Stavros Mermighis; *D:* Lakis Papasthis; *W:* Lakis Papasthis; *M:* George Papadakis. *FCT*

When the Legends Die 🎬🎬🎬 **1972**
(PG) A Ute Indian strives to preserve his heritage in an often harsh modern world. Recorded in hi-fi. **105m/C VHS, Beta.** Richard Widmark, Frederic Forrest; *D:* Stuart Millar. *FOX*

When the Line Goes Through 🎬
1971 A drifter arrives in a small West Virginia town and changes the lives of two pretty sisters. **90m/C VHS, Beta.** Martin Sheen, Davey Davidson, Beverly Washburn. *NO*

When the North Wind Blows 🎬🎬
1974 (G) An old, lone trapper hunts for and later befriends the majestic snow tiger of Siberia in the Alaskan wilderness. A good family film. **113m/C VHS, Beta.** Henry Kleinbach Brandon, Herbert Nelson, Dan Haggerty; *D:* Stewart Raffill. *VCI*

When the Party's Over 🎬🎬½ **1991 (R)** Twenty-somethings share a southern California house and a hip—but ultimately empty—lifestyle. **114m/C VHS.** Rae Dawn Chong, Fisher Stevens, Elizabeth Berridge, Sandra Bullock, Brian McNamara, Kris Kramm; *D:* Matthew Irmas. *ART*

When the Screaming Stops 🎬 **1973**
(R) A hunter is hired to find out who has been cutting the hearts out of young women who reside in a small village near the Rhine River. Turns out it's a she-monster who rules a kingdom beneath the river. Bad effects; gory gore; outlandish plot. All the ingredients, in other words, of a classic dog. **86m/C VHS, Beta.** *SP* Tony Kendall, Helga Line, Sylvia Tortosa; *D:* Armando de Ossorio. *ART*

When the Time Comes 🎬🎬 **1991**
(PG-13) A woman dying of cancer wants to take her own life, but when her husband refuses, she seeks the help of a male friend. Excellent acting doesn't provide the needed depth. Less a disease-of-the-week TV movie, more of an ethical-dilemma-of-the-week, and just as trivial. **94m/C VHS, Closed Caption.** Bonnie Bedelia, Brad Davis, Terry O'Quinn, Karen Austin, Donald Moffat, Wendy Schaal; *D:* John Erman; *M:* Marvin Hamlisch. *REP*

When the West Was Young 🎬½
Wild Horse Mesa **1932** An outdoor adventure about rounding up horses in the Old West. Based on a novel by Zane Grey. **58m/B VHS, Beta.** Randolph Scott, Sally Blane, Guinn "Big Boy" Williams; *D:* Henry Hathaway. *NOS, DVT, VYY*

When the Whales Came 🎬🎬½ **1989**
(PG) A conservationist fable about two children and a grizzled old codger living on a remote British isle during WWI. They try to avert disaster as mysterious narwhal whales descend on the island. Moralistic and uninvolving; poorly acted; slumber-inducing. Adapted from the novel by Morpugo. **100m/C VHS, Beta, LV, Closed Caption.** *GB* Paul Scofield, Helen Mirren, David Threlfall, David Suchet, Jeremy Kemp, Max Rennie, Helen Pearce, Barbara Jefford; *D:* Clive Rees; *W:* Michael Morpugo; *M:* Christopher Gunning, Ruth Rennie. *FOX*

When the Wind Blows 🎬🎬🎬 **1986** An animated feature about a retired British couple when their peaceful and naive—life in the country is destroyed by nuclear war. Poignant, sad, and thought-provoking, and just a little scary. Features the voices of Ashcroft and Mills; Roger Waters, David Bowie, Squeeze, Genesis, Hugh Cornell, and Paul Hardcastle all contribute to the soundtrack. Based on the novel by Raymond Briggs. **80m/C VHS, Beta, LV, Closed Caption.** *GB D:* Jimmy T. Murakami; *V:* Peggy Ashcroft, John Mills. *ART*

When Thief Meets Thief 🎬½ 1937 A cat burglar finds his world turned upside down when he begins to fall in love with one of his victims. Not much happening except a few nice stunts by Fairbanks. 85m/B VHS, Beta. *GB* Douglas Fairbanks Jr., Valerie Hobson, Alan Hale, Jack Melford, Leo Genn, Ian Fleming; *D:* Raoul Walsh. NOS, SNC

When Time Expires 🎬🎬 1997 (PG-13) Extraterrestrial scientist from the future time travels to present-day earth to stop the planet's destruction by evil forces.*CW:* Some violence and sensuality. 93m/C VHS, Closed Caption. Richard Grieco, Cynthia Geary, Mark Hamill, Tim Thomerson, Chad Everett; *D:* David Bourla; *W:* David Bourla; *C:* Dean Lent. EVE

When Time Ran Out 🎬 1980 (PG) A volcano erupts on a remote Polynesian island covered with expensive hotels and tourists with no way to escape. Contains scenes not seen in the theatrically released print of the film. A very good cast is wasted in this compilation of disaster film cliches. 144m/C VHS, Beta. Paul Newman, Jacqueline Bisset, William Holden, Ernest Borgnine, Edward Albert, Barbara Carrera, Valentina Cortese, Burgess Meredith, Noriyuki "Pat" Morita, Red Buttons; *D:* James Goldstone; *W:* Stirling Silliphant; *C:* Fred W. Koenekamp; *M:* Lalo Schifrin. Nominations: Academy Awards '80: Best Costume Design. WAR

When We Were Kings 1996 (PG) Chronicles the 1974 heavyweight championship fight, held in Zaire, between underdog Muhammad Ali and George Foreman. Gast uses original footage of the prefight hype as well as current interviews from George Plimpton and Norman Mailer (who covered the fight at the time) and Spike Lee. 94m/C VHS, LV. *D:* Leon Gast. Academy Awards '96: Best Feature Documentary; Broadcast Film Critics Association Awards '96: Best Feature Documentary. PGV

When Wolves Cry 🎬½ *The Christmas Tree* 1969 (G) Tearjerker about an estranged father and young son reunited on a Corsican vacation. Their newfound joy sours when the lad is diagnosed with a fatal illness. Hardly one of Holden's best films. 108m/C VHS, Beta. William Holden, Virna Lisi, Brook Fuller, Andre Bourvil; *D:* Terence Young. GEM, VCI

When Women Had Tails 🎬½ *Quando De Donne Avevando La Coda* 1970 (R) A primitive comedy about prehistoric man's discovery of sex. And boy, did they ever discover it. Harmless (more or less), though not exactly cerebral. Followed by "When Women Lost Their Tails." 99m/C VHS, Beta. *IT* Senta Berger, Frank Wolff; *D:* Pasquale Festa Campanile; *M:* Ennio Morricone. SNC

When Women Lost Their Tails 🎬 1975 (R) Ostensible sequel to "When Women Had Tails" about prehistoric cavemen and their sexual habits. 94m/C VHS, Beta. *IT* Senta Berger; *D:* Pasquale Festa Campanile; *M:* Ennio Morricone. NO

When Worlds Collide 🎬🎬½ 1951 (G) Another planet is found to be rushing inevitably towards earth, but a select group of people attempt to escape in a spaceship; others try to maneuver their way on board. Oscar-quality special effects and plot make up for cheesy acting and bad writing. 81m/C VHS, Beta, LV. Richard Derr, Barbara Rush, Larry Keating, Peter Hanson; *D:* Rudolph Mate; *C:* William Howard Greene. Academy Awards '51: Best Special Effects; Nominations: Academy Awards '51: Best Color Cinematography.PAR

When Your Lover Leaves 🎬 1983 Alleged comedy about a woman, dumped by her married boyfriend, who gets involved in a short-lived relationship with a neighbor. When that also doesn't work out, she decides she must first do something to please herself. Here endeth the lesson. Produced by Fonzie and Richie of "Happy Days." Made for television. 100m/C VHS. Valerie Perrine, Betty Thomas, David Ackroyd, Ed O'Neill, Dwight Schultz, Shannon Wilcox; *D:* Jeff Bleckner; *M:* Randy Edelman. VTR

When's Your Birthday? 🎬🎬½ 1937 Brown stars in this comedy about a prize-fighter who is working his way through astrology school with his fighting skills. The stars, in turn, tell him when to fight. Lame zaniness (what other kind is there?) meant as a vehicle for Brown, though Kennedy is funnier. The opening sequence, an animated cartoon showing the influence of the moon over the planets, was filmed in Technicolor. 77m/B VHS, Beta. Joe E. Brown, Marian Marsh, Edgar Kennedy; *D:* Harry Beaumont. NOS, VYY, JEF

Where 🎬🎬 1994 Young man living in Budapest begins a psycho-sexual relationship with a young woman that explores the nature of domination and submission. After moving to Los Angeles, he subjects himself to the whims of a student. In English and Hungarian with subtitles. ?m/C VHS. HU *D:* Gabor Zabo. WAC

Where Angels Fear to Tread 🎬🎬🎬 1991 (PG) Another turn-of-the-century tale of the English in Italy from the pen of E.M. Forster. Widowed, 40ish Lilia (Mirren) is urged by her stuffy in-laws to spend some time in Italy. Much to everyone's dismay she impulsively marries a 21-year-old Italian—with disastrous consequences. Based on Forster's first novel, the characters are more stereotypical and the story less defined than his later works and the movies made from them. Impressive performances and beautiful settings make up for a somewhat lackluster direction that isn't up to the standards set by the team of Merchant Ivory, responsible for the Forster films "A Room with a View" and "Howard's End." 112m/C VHS, LV, Closed Caption. *GB* Rupert Graves, Helena Bonham Carter, Judy Davis, Helen Mirren, Giovanni Guidelli, Barbara Jefford, Thomas Wheatley, Sophie Kullman; *D:* Charles Sturridge; *M:* Rachel Portman. NLC

Where Angels Go, Trouble Follows 🎬🎬½ 1968 Follow-up to "The Trouble with Angels," with Russell reprising her role as the wise Mother Superior challenged by her mischief loving students. Younger, modern nun Stevens tries to convince Russell to update her old-fashioned ways and persuades her to take the convent students on a bus trip to a California peace rally. A very young Saint James is one of the convent's irrepressible troublemakers. Very dated but still mildly amusing. 94m/C VHS, Closed Caption. Rosalind Russell, Stella Stevens, Binnie Barnes, Mary Wickes, Susan St. James, Dolores Sutton, Alice Rawlings; *Cameos:* Milton Berle, Arthur Godfrey, Van Johnson, Robert Taylor; *D:* James Neilson; *W:* Blanche Hanalis. COL

Where Are the Children? 🎬½ 1985 (R) Based on Mary Higgins Clark's bestseller. A woman who was cleared of murdering the children from her first marriage remarries. Then the children from her second marriage are kidnapped. Sustains suspense completely, until it falls apart. 92m/C VHS, Beta, Closed Caption. Jill Clayburgh, Max Gail, Barnard Hughes, Clifton James, Harley Cross, Elisabeth Harnois, Elizabeth Wilson, Frederic Forrest; *D:* Bruce Malmuth. COL

Where Eagles Dare 🎬🎬🎬 1968 (PG) During WWII, a small group of Allied commandos must rescue an American general held by the Nazis in a castle in the Bavarian Alps. Relentless plot twists and action keep you breathless. Well-made suspense/adventure. Alistair MacLean adapted his original screenplay into a successful novel. 158m/C VHS, Beta, LV, Letterbox. Clint Eastwood, Richard Burton, Mary Ure, Michael Hordern, Anton Diffring, Ingrid Pitt, Patrick Wymark, Robert Beatty; *D:* Brian G. Hutton. MGM, TLF

Where East Is East 🎬🎬½ 1929 In Indochina a badly scarred trapper (Chaney) lives with his daughter (Velez) and sells wild animals to circuses. Velez falls in love with a circus owner's son but finds out her own mother, seeking revenge on her ex-husband, trying to seduce the young man. A gorilla figures in the plot as well. Chaney's makeup, which contributed to his "Man of a Thousand Faces" nickname, highlights a contrived movie. 140m/B VHS. Lon Chaney Sr., Lupe Velez, Estelle Taylor, Lloyd Hughes. FCT

Where Have All the People Gone? 🎬 1974 Solar explosion turns most of Earth's inhabitants to dust while the Anders family vacations in a cave. The family tries to return home amid the devastation. Bad timing, bad acting, bad script. Made for television. 74m/C VHS, Beta. Peter Graves, Kathleen Quinlan, Michael-James Wixted, George O'Hanlon Jr., Verna Bloom; *D:* John Llewellyn Moxey. ORI

Where Is My Child? 🎬🎬½ 1937 Immigration to the New World brings only misfortune and betrayal in this tale of Jews in Eastern Europe between 1911 and 1937, as many experience the loss of family ties and religion. In Yiddish with English subtitles. 92m/B VHS. Celia Adler, Anna Lillian, Morris Strassberg; *D:* Abraham Leff, Harry Lynn. NCJ

Where Is My Friend's House? 🎬🎬 *Where is the Friend's Home?; Khaneh-Je Doost Kojast?* 1987 At the village school, Mohamed is told by his teacher that he'll be expelled if he doesn't do his homework in the required exercise book. But that evening schoolmate Ahmed realizes he's taken Mohamed's book by mistake so he sets off to find his friend's house in a neighboring village. However, Ahmed gets lost and none of the adults he meets will help him. Farsi with subtitles. Followed by "Life and Nothing More..." and "Through the Olive Trees." 90m/C VHS. Babek Ahmed Poor, Ahmed Ahmed Poor, Kheda Barech Defai; *D:* Abbas Kiarostami; *W:* Abbas Kiarostami; *C:* Farhad Saba. FCT

Where Love Has Gone 🎬🎬½ 1964 A soaper about a teenage daughter who kills her nympho mother's current boyfriend. Her divorced parents end up dragging the ordeal out in a murder trial/custody battle and a lot of family skeletons come out of their closets. Davis is the manipulative grand dame grandmother. Based on the novel by Harold Robbins. 114m/C VHS, Closed Caption. Bette Davis, Susan Hayward, Joey Heatherton, Jane Greer, George Macready; *D:* Edward Dmytryk; *W:* John Michael Hayes. Nominations: Academy Awards '64: Best Song ("Where Love Has Gone").PAR, FCT

Where Sleeping Dogs Lie 🎬🎬 1991 (R) A struggling writer moves into an abandoned California home five years after a wealthy family was murdered there. While doing research for his novel on their brutal killings, he revives their ghosts as well as the very real presence of their killer.*CW:* Language. 92m/C VHS, Closed Caption. Dylan McDermott, Tom Sizemore, Sharon Stone; *D:* Charles Finch. COL

Where the Boys Are 🎬🎬½ 1960 Four college girls go to Fort Lauderdale to have fun and meet boys during their Easter vacation. Features the film debuts of Francis, who had a hit single with the film's title song, and Prentiss. Head and shoulders above the ludicrous '84 remake. 99m/C VHS, Beta, LV, Letterbox. George Hamilton, Jim Hutton, Yvette Mimieux, Connie Francis, Paula Prentiss, Dolores Hart; *D:* Henry Levin. MGM

Where the Boys Are '84 WOOF! 1984 (R) Horrible remake of the 1960 comedy still features girls searching for boys during spring break in Fort Lauderdale. Telling about its era: charm gives way to prurience. 95m/C VHS, Beta, Closed Caption. Lisa Hartman Black, Wendy Schaal, Lorna Luft, Lynn-Holly Johnson; *D:* Hy Averback; *W:* Jeff Burkhart. Golden Raspberry Awards '84: Worst Supporting Actress (Johnson). FOX

Where the Buffalo Roam 🎬½ 1980 (R) Early starring role for Murray as the legendary "gonzo" journalist Hunter S. Thompson. Meandering satire based on Thompson's books "Fear and Loathing in Las Vegas" and "Fear and Loathing on the Campaign Trail '72." Either confusing or offensively sloppy, depending on whether you've read Thompson. Music by Neil Young, thank goodness, or this might be a woof. 98m/C VHS, Beta. Bill Murray, Peter Boyle, Susan Kellerman; *D:* Art Linson; *M:* Neil Young. USH

Where the Bullets Fly ✓✓ 1966 Fast-paced Bond spoof. A British spy takes on the intelligence forces of several governments in his search for a new fuel elixir. Fun, if not scintillating. 88m/C VHS. *GB* Tom Adams, Dawn Addams, Michael Ripper, Tim Barrett; **D:** John Gilling. *FOX*

Where the Day Takes You ✓✓½ 1992 (R) Runaways on Hollywood Boulevard are depicted in an unfortunately heavy-handed drama. King (Mulroney) is the slightly older leader of a group of street kids who tries to discourage his friends from getting involved in the violence and drugs they see all around them. He falls in love with new runaway Heather (Boyle) but their love is blighted by the relentless bleakness of their lives. Among the other members of King's "family" are Astin, as a young druggie in thrall to his older dealer (MacLachlan) and Getty, as a young hustler drawn to violence. The story's predictability undercuts some convincing acting. **CW:** Language and violence and drug use. 105m/C VHS, LV, **Letterbox, Closed Caption.** Dermot Mulroney, Lara Flynn Boyle, Balthazar Getty, Sean Astin, James LeGros, Ricki Lake, Kyle MacLachlan, Rob Knepper, Peter Dobson, Stephen Tobolowsky, Will Smith, Adam Baldwin, Christian Slater, Nancy McKeon, Alyssa Milano, David Arquette, Leo Rossi, Rachel Ticotin; **D:** Marc Rocco; **W:** Michael Hitchcock, Kurt Voss, Marc Rocco; **M:** Mark Morgan; **V:** Laura San Giacomo. *COL*

Where the Eagle Flies ✓✓ *Pickup on 101* 1972 (PG) Ersatz '60s rock 'n' roll road movie shuffles together free spirited college coed, hobo with heart of gold, and rock and roller who's making a lane change out of the fast track. 93m/C VHS. Jack Albertson, Lesley Ann Warren, Martin Sheen, Michael Ontkean; **D:** John Florea. *NO*

Where the Green Ants Dream ✓✓½ *Wo Die Grunen Ameisen Traumen* 1984 A mining excavation in the Outback is halted by Aborigines who declare ownership of the sacred place where the mythical green ants are buried. A minor entry in the Herzog vision of modern-versus-primal civilization. Too obvious and somehow unsure of itself artistically. 99m/C VHS. *GE* Bruce Spence, Wandjuk Marika, Roy Marika, Ray Barrett, Norman Kaye, Colleen Clifford; **D:** Werner Herzog. *XVC*

Where the Heart Is ✓✓ 1990 (R) Wealthy dad Coleman kicks his spoiled kids out on the streets to teach them the value of money. Meant as farce with a message. Flops in a big way; one senses it should have been much better. 111m/C VHS, LV, **Closed Caption.** Dabney Coleman, Uma Thurman, Joanna Cassidy, Suzy Amis, Crispin Glover, Christopher Plummer; **D:** John Boorman; **W:** John Boorman, Telsche Boorman. National Society of Film Critics Awards '90: Best Cinematography. *TOU*

Where the Hot Wind Blows ✓✓ *La Legge; La Loi; The Law* 1959 The sexual scene in Sicily is sadly not succinctly summarized in this so-so cinematic soap. Cross-generational and cross-class couplings are constant. Think of it as "The Last Picture Show" in a similarly sorry setting, except boring. 120m/C VHS, Beta. *FR IT* Gina Lollobrigida, Marcello Mastroianni, Yves Montand, Melina Mercouri, Paolo Stoppa; **D:** Jules Dassin; **W:** Jules Dassin. *VYY, NOS, FCT*

Where the Lilies Bloom ✓✓✓ 1974 (G) The touching story of four backwoods children who are left orphans when their father dies. They don't report his death to authorities, because they are afraid the family will be separated and sent to an orphanage. Stanton is great as the crusty landlord the children gradually accept as a friend. Based on the book by Vera and Bill Cleaver. 96m/C VHS. Julie Gholson, Jan Smithers, Matthew Burrill, Helen Harmon, Harry Dean Stanton, Rance Howard, Sudie Bond, Tom Spratley, Helen Bragdon, Alice Beardsley; **D:** William A. Graham. *MGM*

Where the North Begins ✓ 1947 A Mountie ransacks the Canadian countryside in search of crime. 41m/B VHS, Beta, LV. Russell Hayden, Jennifer Holt. *NO*

Where the Red Fern Grows ✓✓½ 1974 (G) A young boy in Dust Bowl-era Oklahoma learns maturity from his love and responsibility for two Redbone hounds. Well produced, but tends to be hokey; good family fare. Followed by a sequel nearly 20 years later. 97m/C VHS, Beta. James Whitmore, Beverly Garland, Jack Ging, Lonny Chapman, Stewart Peterson; **D:** Norman Tokar; **C:** Dean Cundey. *FHE, VES, HHE*

Where the Red Fern Grows: Part 2 ✓✓½ 1992 (G) Sequel to one of the most popular family movies of all time starring Brimley as Grandpa Coleman. Set deep in the Louisiana woods, this magical coming of age tale will touch the hearts of young and old viewers alike. 105m/C VHS, Closed Caption. Wilford Brimley, Doug McKeon, Lisa Whelchel, Chad McQueen; **D:** Jim McCullough. *VCI*

Where the River Runs Black ✓✓ 1986 (PG) An orphaned Indian child is raised in the Brazilian jungles by river dolphins. He is eventually befriended by a kindly priest who brings him into the modern world of violence and corruption. Slow pace is okay until the boy arrives at the orphanage, at which point the dolphin premise sadly falls by the wayside. 96m/C VHS, Beta, **Closed Caption.** Charles Durning, Peter Horton, Ajay Naidu, Conchata Ferrell, Alessandro Rabelo, Castulo Guerra; **D:** Christopher Cain; **C:** Juan Ruiz-Anchia; **M:** James Horner. *FOX*

Where the Rivers Flow North ✓✓½ 1994 (PG-13) Vermont logger Noel Lord (Torn) has lived on the land all his life and doesn't want to sell out to the power company. His blunt-talking Indian housekeeper/lover Bangor (Cardinal) knows it's best to take the money and move on. Set in 1927 and adapted from the novella by Howard Frank Mosher. Flat storytelling with a good performance by Cardinal. **CW:** One sexual reference. 104m/C VHS. Rip Torn, Tantoo Cardinal, Bill Raymond, Mark Margolis, John Griesemer, Amy Wright, Dennis Mientka, Jusef Bulos; **Cameos:** Michael J. Fox, Treat Williams; **D:** Jay Craven; **W:** Jay Craven, Don Bredos. *APX*

Where the Sky Begins 1984 From the director of "Black Orpheus," this is a seven-part recreated history of turn-of-the-century aviation. 420m/C VHS, Beta. *FR* **D:** Marcel Camus. *VCD*

Where the Spirit Lives ✓✓½ 1989 (PG) Native children kidnapped by Canadian government are forced to live in dreadful boarding schools where they are abused emotionally and physically. St. John is a new arrival who refuses to put up with it and tries to escape. Engrossing and moving. 97m/C VHS. *CA* Michelle St. John; **D:** Bruce Pittman. *BTV, HHE, UWA*

Where There's Life ✓✓½ 1947 Wisecracking Hope is a New York DJ about to be married to Marshe when he discovers he's the heir to the kingdom of Borovia (whose last king was assassinated). Hasso works her feminine wiles as the general who's guarding Hope when the assassins come after him. Oh, and Marshe and her cop brother Bendix are tracking him down to go through with the wedding ceremony. Frantic antics. 75m/B VHS. Bob Hope, Signe Hasso, William Bendix, Vera Marshe, George Coulouris, George Zucco, Dennis Hoey, John Alexander; **D:** Sidney Lanfield; **W:** Melville Shavelson, Allen Boretz. *USH*

Where Time Began ✓✓ 1977 (G) The discovery of a strange manuscript of a scientist's journey to the center of the earth leads to the decision to recreate the dangerous mission. Based on Jules Verne's classic novel "Journey to the Center of the Earth," but not anywhere near as fun or stirring. 87m/C VHS, Beta. Kenneth More, Pep Munne, Jack Taylor; **D:** J. Piquer Simon.

Where Trails Divide ✓½ 1937 Keene is a U.S. Marshal who poses as a lawyer to bring a gang of thieves to justice. Lacks action. 54m/B VHS. Tom George Duryea Keene, Eleanor Stewart, Warner Richmond, David Sharpe, Charles French, Hal Price, Bud Osborne; **D:** Robert North Bradbury. *GPV*

Where Trails End ✓✓ 1942 Novel sci-fi western set during WWII with just about everything, including phosphorescent-clothed good guys, Nazis, scoundrels, literate horses, and Gallic sidekicks. Interestingly different. 54m/B VHS, Beta. Tom George Duryea Keene, Joan Curtis, Charles "Blackie" King; **D:** Robert Emmett Tansey. *VDM, VYY*

Where Truth Lies ✓✓ 1996 (R) After a severe breakdown, troubled psychiatrist Ian Lazarre (Savage) is sent to a clinic run by the sinister Dr. Renquist (McDowell). Lazarre's given an experimental drug that causes him to have visions of executed serial killer Jonas Keller (Forrest) and also to develop ESP. The plot doesn't make much sense in any case. 92m/C VHS. John Savage, Kim Cattrall, Malcolm McDowell, Sam Jones, Eric Pierpont, Candice Daly, Dennis Forrest; **D:** William H. Molina; **W:** Ted Perkins; **C:** William H. Molina; **M:** David Wurst, Eric Wurst. *PAR*

Where Were You When the Lights Went Out? ✓½ 1968 (PG) A complicated, unsuccessful farce about a retiring Broadway actress, her jealous, possibly philandering husband, her greedy agent, an embezzler, and a citywide blackout. Film was actually not based on the 1965 New York City blackout but on a French play, "Monsieur Masure" by Claude Magnier, which was written nine years before. 94m/C VHS. Doris Day, Patrick O'Neal, Robert Morse, Terry-Thomas, Lola Albright, Steve Allen, Jim Backus, Ben Blue, Pat Paulsen; **D:** Hy Averback. *MGM, MOV*

Where's Piccone ✓✓✓ 1984 A woman attempts, with the assistance of a two-bit hustler, to locate her missing husband, only to discover that he has led a double life in the Neapolitan underworld. Giannini as the sleazy hubby is perfectly cast. On-target social and political satire. In Italian with English subtitles. 110m/C VHS, Beta. *IT* Giancarlo Giannini, Lina Sastri, Aldo Giuffre, Clelia Rondinelli; **D:** Nanni Loy. *FCT, WBF, TPV*

Where's Poppa? ✓✓✓ *Going Ape* 1970 A Jewish lawyer's senile mother constantly ruins his love life, and he considers various means of getting rid of her, including dressing up as an ape to scare her to death. Filled with outlandish and often tasteless humor, befitting its reign as a black comedy cult classic. Adapted by Robert Klane from his novel. 84m/C VHS, Beta, **Closed Caption.** George Segal, Ruth Gordon, Ron Leibman, Vincent Gardenia, Rob Reiner, Trish Van Devere; **D:** Carl Reiner; **C:** Jack Priestley. *FOX*

Where's the Money, Noreen? ✓✓½ 1995 (PG-13) Noreen's (Phillips) out on parole and trailed by the police who believe she knows the whereabouts of the $3 million she helped to steal 12 years before. Made for cable. **CW:** Scene of sensuality and some violence. 93m/C VHS, Beta, **Closed Caption.** Julianne Phillips, A. Martinez, Nigel Bennett, Colm Feore; **D:** Artie Mandelberg; **W:** Carla Jean Wagner; **C:** Brenton Spencer; **M:** Richard Bellis. *PAR*

Where's Willie? ✓✓ 1977 (G) Willie is a very bright boy; perhaps a little too bright. When he reveals his latest invention to the folks in his small town, everyone is out to get him. 91m/C VHS, Beta. Guy Madison, Henry Darrow, Kate Woodville, Marc Gilpin; **D:** John Florea. *NO*

Which Way Home ✓✓ 1990 A Red Cross nurse attempts to flee Cambodia with four young orphans. An Australian smuggler befriends and helps her. Way too long and wandering, though like many a TV movie, it means well. 141m/C VHS, Beta, **Closed Caption.** Cybill Shepherd, John Waters, Peta Toppano, John Ewart, Ruben Santiago-Hudson, Marc Gray; **D:** Carl Schultz; **W:** Michael Laurence. *TTC*

Which Way Is Up? ✓✓½ 1977 (R) Pryor plays three roles in this story of an orange picker who accidentally becomes a union hero. He leaves his wife and family at home while he seeks work in Los Angeles. There he finds himself a new woman, starts a new family, and sells out to the capitalists. American version of the Italian comedy "The Seduction of Mimi" tries with mixed success for laughs. Pryor as a dirty old man is the high point. **94m/C VHS, Beta.** Richard Pryor, Lonette McKee, Margaret Avery, Morgan Woodward, Marilyn Coleman; **D:** Michael A. Schultz; **W:** Carl Gottlieb; **C:** John A. Alonzo. *USH*

Which Way to the Front? 🎬½ 1970
(G) Assorted Army rejects form a guerilla band and wage their own small-scale war during WWII. **96m/C VHS, Beta.** Jerry Lewis, Jan Murray, George L. Baxt, Steve Franken; **D:** Jerry Lewis; **W:** Dee Caruso. *WAR*

Whiffs 🎬 1975 (PG)
A gullible man plays guinea pig in an Army experiment on germ warfare which leaves him with the intellect of a chimpanzee. Naturally, he then devises a plan to use the volatile gas in a chain of bank robberies. The title is appropriate—this movie is a stinker. **91m/C VHS, Beta.** Elliott Gould, Eddie Albert, Harry Guardino, Godfrey Cambridge, Jennifer O'Neill, Alan Manson; **D:** Ted Post; **W:** Malcolm Marmorstein. Nominations: Academy Awards '75: Best Song ("Now That We're in Love").

While I Live 🎬½ 1947
Woman meets female pianist with uncanny resemblance to sister who's been dead 25 years and rethinks her position on reincarnation. **85m/B VHS, Beta.** *GB* Tom Walls, Clifford Evans, Carole Raye, Patricia Burke, Sonia Dresdel, John Warwick; **D:** John Harlow; **C:** Frederick A. (Freddie) Young. *SNC*

While the City Sleeps 🎬🎬🎬 1956
Three newspaper reporters vie to crack the case of a sex murderer known as "The Lipstick Killer" with the editorship of their paper the prize. Good thriller-plus with the emphasis on the reporters' ruthless methods of gaining information rather than on the killer's motivations. Lang's last big success. Based on "The Bloody Spur" by Charles Einstein. **100m/B VHS, Beta, LV.** Dana Andrews, Rhonda Fleming, George Sanders, Howard Duff, Thomas Mitchell, Ida Lupino, Vincent Price, Mae Marsh; **D:** Fritz Lang; **C:** Ernest Laszlo. *VCI*

While You Were Sleeping 🎬🎬🎬
1995 (PG) Feel-good romantic comedy finds lonely Lucy Moderatz (Bullock) collecting tokens for the Chicago train system and admiring Yuppie lawyer Peter Callaghan (Gallagher) as he commutes to and fro. Fate conspires to throw them together when Lucy rescues Peter after a mugging. Trouble is, he's not conscious so Lucy goes to the hospital with him, where she's mistaken for his fiancee. She continues the charade and is warmly welcomed by the Callaghan family, with the exception of Peter's brother, Jack (Pullman), who smells a rat even as he falls under the token collector's spell. Meanwhile, Peter remains in a coma, allowing Jack and Lucy to supply romantic comedy. Gallagher brings a serenity to his role as the unconscious Peter, while Bullock and Pullman take the predictable plot and deliver performances that earn them another notch on the climb to stardom. **103m/C VHS, LV, Closed Caption.** Sandra Bullock, Bill Pullman, Peter Gallagher, Jack Warden, Peter Boyle, Glynis Johns, Micole Mercurio, Jason Bernard, Michael Rispoli, Ally Walker, Monica Keena; **D:** Jon Turteltaub; **W:** Fred Lebow, Daniel G. Sullivan; **C:** Phedon Papamichael; **M:** Randy Edelman. Blockbuster Entertainment Awards '96: Comedy Actress, Video (Bullock), Comedy Actress, Theatrical (Bullock); Nominations: Golden Globe Awards '96: Best Actress—Musical/Comedy (Bullock); MTV Movie Awards '96: Best Female Performance (Bullock), Most Desirable Female (Bullock). *TOU*

Whirlwind Horseman 🎬 1938
Substandard horse opera. Maynard's search for a gold prospector friend leads him to a rancher and his pretty daughter. He beats up some bad guys, etcetera. **60m/B VHS, Beta.** Ken Maynard, Joan Barclay, Bill Griffith; **D:** Robert F. "Bob" Hill. *NOS, DVT, VCN*

Whiskey Galore 🎬🎬🎬½ Tight Little Island
1948 During WWII, a whiskey-less Scottish island gets a lift when a ship, carrying 50,000 cases of spirits, wrecks off the coast. A full-scale rescue operation and the evasion of both local and British government authorities ensue. The classic Ealing studio comedy is based on the actual wreck of a cargo ship off the Isle of Eriskay in 1941. **81m/B**

VHS, Beta. *GB* Basil Radford, Joan Greenwood, Gordon Jackson, James Robertson Justice; **D:** Alexander MacKendrick. *HMV*

Whiskey Mountain 🎬 1977 (PG)
Two couples go on a treasure hunt to Whiskey Mountain but instead find terror. **95m/C VHS, Beta.** Christopher George, Preston Pierce, Linda Borgeson, Roberta Collins, Robert Leslie; **D:** William Grefe. *BFV*

A Whisper to a Scream 🎬🎬 1988 (R)
An actress, in researching a film part, takes a job at a telephone sex service, creating different personas as she talks to keep herself interested. Soon, women resembling the personas are being murdered. Great premise fails to deliver fully, though there is some suspense. **96m/C VHS, Beta, LV.** *CA* Nadia Capone, Yaphet Kotto, Lawrence Bayne, Silvio Oliviero; **D:** Robert Bergman; **W:** Robert Bergman, Gerard Ciccoritti. *NO*

The Whispering 🎬🎬 1994 (R)
Scary little low-budget tale about an insurance investigator who's checking out several suicides and meets up with the Grim Reaper (who just happens to be female). **CW:** Sexuality, language and violence/gore. **88m/C VHS.** Leif Garrett, Leslie Danon, Tom Patton, Maxwell Rutherford, Mette Holt; **D:** Gregory Gieras; **W:** Leslie Danon. *APX*

Whispering City 🎬🎬🎬 1947
A female reporter receives an inside tip incriminating a prominent attorney in a murder committed several years earlier. She tries to get the evidence she needs before she becomes his latest victim. Highly suspenseful, thanks to competent scripting and directing. **89m/B VHS, Beta.** *CA* Helmut Dantine, Mary Anderson, Paul Lukas; **D:** Fedor Ozep. *NOS, SNC*

Whispering Shadow 1933
Serial starring the master criminal known as the "faceless whisperer." Twelve chapters, 13 minutes each. **156m/B VHS, Beta.** Bela Lugosi, Robert Warwick; **D:** Al(bert) Herman, Colbert Clark. *NOS, SNC, VCN*

Whispers 🎬🎬 1989 (R)
Psycho Le Clerc repeatedly bothers writer Tennant even though she seems to have killed him. This dismays police guy Sarandon. Based on the novel by Dean R. Koontz. **96m/C VHS, LV.** Victoria Tennant, Chris Sarandon, Jean LeClerc; **D:** Douglas Jackson; **W:** Anita Doohan, Don Carmody. *ART*

Whispers in the Dark 🎬🎬 1992 (R)
A psychiatrist counsels two odd patients—one is an ex-con turned painter with a violent streak, the other is a woman who reveals her kinky sexual experiences with a mystery man. Things get interesting when the doctor finds out her new lover is her patient's mystery man, and the patient turns up murdered. Confusing thriller seems forced but the experienced cast is worth watching. **CW:** Language, strong violence, and strong sexuality. **103m/C VHS, Beta, LV, Letterbox, Closed Caption.** Annabella Sciorra, Jamey Sheridan, Anthony LaPaglia, Jill Clayburgh, John Leguizamo, Deborah Kara Unger, Alan Alda, Anthony Heald; **D:** Christopher Crowe; **W:** Christopher Crowe; **C:** Michael Chapman; **M:** Thomas Newman. *PAR, PMS*

Whispers of White 🎬½ 1993 (R)
Bridgetown's mayor has been trying for years to put a stop to the drug dealing going on in his fair community. Finally, his new Chief of Police decides to deploy a special task force to clean-up the streets—using whatever methods are necessary (and they're all violent). **98m/C VHS.** Nicholette Goulet, Anthony De Sardo, Tony Craig, April Bransome, Ron Gorton Sr.; **D:** Ron Gorton Sr.; **W:** Ron Gorton Sr.

The Whistle Blower 🎬🎬🎬 1987
A young government worker in England with a high-security position mysteriously dies. His father, a former intelligence agent, begins investigating his son's death and discovers sinister Soviet-related conspiracies. A lucid, complex British espionage thriller. Adapted from the John Hale novel by Julian Bond. **98m/C VHS, Beta, LV, Closed Caption.** *GB* Michael Caine, Nigel Havers, John Gielgud, James Fox, Felicity Dean, Gordon Jackson, Barry Foster, David Langton; **D:** Simon Langton; **W:** Julian Bond; **M:** John Scott. *NLC*

Whistle Down the Wind 🎬🎬🎬½ 1962
Three children of strict religious upbringing find a murderer hiding in their family's barn and believe him to be Jesus Christ. A well done and hardly grim or dull allegory of childhood innocence based on a novel by Mills's mother, Mary Hayley Bell. For a film relying heavily on child characters, it's important to portray childhood well and realistically. That is done here, as in "To Kill a Mockingbird." Mills is perfect. The film is Forbes's directorial debut and Richard Attenborough's second production. **98m/B VHS, Beta.** *GB* Hayley Mills, Bernard Lee, Alan Bates; **D:** Bryan Forbes; **M:** Malcolm Arnold. *NLC*

Whistle Stop 🎬🎬 1946
A small-town girl divides her attentions between low-life gambler Raft, and villainous nightclub owner McLaglen, who plans a robbery-murder to get rid of any rivals. A forgettable gangster drama. **85m/B VHS, Beta.** George Raft, Ava Gardner, Victor McLaglen; **D:** Leonide Moguy; **W:** Philip Yordan. *NOS, DVT, FCT*

Whistlin' Dan 🎬🎬 1932
Yet another lead cowpoke sets out to avenge the murder of a close relative. Maynard whistles while he walks (and rides) woodenly through this one. **60m/B VHS, Beta.** Ken Maynard, Joyzelle Joyner, Lew Meehan, Georges Renevant, Dan Terry, Harlan E. Knight, Bud McClure, Hank Bell, Iron Eyes Cody, Frank Ellis; **D:** Phil Rosen. *NOS, VCI, GPV*

Whistling Bullets 🎬🎬½ 1936
Action galore in the story of an undercover Texas Ranger infiltrating a gang of thieves. The low budget doesn't detract from an exciting script and tight direction. **58m/B VHS, Beta.** Kermit Maynard, Jack Ingram; **D:** John English. *NOS, DVT, RXM*

Whistling in Brooklyn 🎬🎬½ 1943
Skelton again plays radio crime-solver Wally Benton in this third and last entry following "Whistling in the Dark" and "Whistling in Dixie." A cop-killer and the Brooklyn Dodgers baseball team figure in the mystery, which finds Skelton a suspect in the crimes. **87m/B VHS.** Red Skelton, Ann Rutherford, Jean Rogers, Rags Ragland, Ray Collins, Henry O'Neill, William Frawley, Sam Levene; **D:** Sylvan Simon; **M:** George Bassman. *MGM*

Whistling in Dixie 🎬🎬½ 1942
The second appearance of Skelton as radio sleuth Wally "The Fox" Benton (following "Whistling in the Dark") finds him traveling to Georgia with girlfriend Carol (Rutherford). She's worried about an ex-sorority sister who knows the secret of a hidden Civil War treasure. When Wally gets involved, humorous trouble follows. Followed by "Whistling in Brooklyn." **73m/B VHS, Beta.** Red Skelton, Ann Rutherford, George Bancroft, Guy Kibbee, Diana Lewis, Peter Whitney, Rags Ragland; **D:** Sylvan Simon; **W:** Nat Perrin. *MGM, FCT*

Whistling in the Dark 🎬🎬🎬 1941
Skelton plays Wally Benton, a radio sleuth nicknamed "The Fox," in the first of a three-film series. Veidt (an always excellent villain) is the leader of a phony religious cult, after the money of one of his followers. He decides to kidnap Skelton and have him come up with a plan for the perfect murder but of course there are all sorts of comic complications. Skelton's first starring role is a clever comic mystery and a remake of the 1933 film. Followed by "Whistling in Dixie" and "Whistling in Brooklyn." **78m/B VHS.** Red Skelton, Ann Rutherford, Conrad Veidt, Virginia Grey, Rags Ragland, Eve Arden, Don Douglas, Don Costello, Paul Stanton, William Tannen, Reed Hadley; **D:** Sylvan Simon. *MGM*

Whitcomb's War 🎬½ 1987
Small town becomes a battleground among a host of comic characters who are unaware who really is in charge. **67m/C VHS.** Patrick Pankhurst, Leon Charles, Bill Morey, Robert Denison, Garnett Smith; **D:** Russell S. Doughten Jr. *RDF*

The White Balloon 🎬🎬🎬½ Badkonake
Sefid 1995 Beautifully told story from the viewpoint of determined seven-year-old Tehranian Razieh (Mohammadkhani), who wants to properly celebrate the Islamic New Year by buying a particular-

ly plump goldfish (a symbol of harmony) from the pet shop. She manages to beg the money from her mother and sets off but, distracted by the street sights, Reziah loses the banknote, which falls into a street grate. Various characters seek to help her out but it's Reziah's resourceful brother Ali (Kafili) who gets a balloon seller to finally retrieve the money. Farsi with subtitles. **85m/C VHS.** Aida Mohammadkhani, Mohsen Kalifi, Fereshteh Sadr Ofrani, Anna Bourkowska, Mohammad Shahani, Mohammad Bahktiari; *D:* Jafar Panahi; *W:* Abbas Kiarostami; *C:* Farzad Jowdat. New York Film Critics Awards '96: Best Foreign Film. *HMK*

The White Buffalo 🎬🎬 *Hunt to Kill* **1977 (PG)** A strange, semi-surreal western parable about the last days of Wild Bill Hickok (Bronson) and his obsession with a mythical white buffalo that represents his fear of mortality. Something of a "Moby Dick" theme set in the Wild West. Clumsy but intriguing. **97m/C VHS, Beta.** Charles Bronson, Jack Warden, Will Sampson, Kim Novak, Clint Walker, Stuart Whitman, John Carradine, Slim Pickens, Cara Williams, Douglas Fowley; *D:* J. Lee Thompson; *M:* John Barry. *MGM*

White Cargo 🎬🎬½ **1942** Lamarr holds the corny story together with one of her best-known roles as sultry native girl Tondelayo. Pidgeon is a cynical African rubber planter who advises new assistant Carlson against Lamarr's sarong-clad charms. But hormones speak louder than warnings and Pidgeon has to take some strong action to save Carlson from this femme fatale. Based on the novel "Hell's Playground" by Ida Vera Simonton and adapted for both stage and screen by Gordon. **90m/B VHS.** Hedy Lamarr, Walter Pidgeon, Richard Carlson, Frank Morgan, Reginald Owen, Bramwell Fletcher, Henry O'Neill, Clyde Cook, Richard Ainley; *D:* Richard Thorpe; *W:* Leon Gordon; *M:* Bronislau Kaper. *MGM*

White Cargo 🎬1½ **1996** Detective Joe Hargatay is investigating a series of fashion model murders that lead him to Chinatown gangsters, corrupt cops, and the crazy world of model agencies. **92m/C VHS.** David Bradley, Shannon Tweed, Lydie Denier, Tommy (Tiny) Lister, David Groh; *D:* Daniel Reardon. *TCE*

White Christmas 🎬🎬🎬 **1954** Two ex-army buddies become a popular comedy team and play at a financially unstable Vermont inn at Christmas for charity's sake. Many swell Irving Berlin songs rendered with zest. Paramount's first Vista Vision film. Presented in widescreen on laserdisc. ♫The Best Things Happen While You're Dancing; Love, You Didn't Do Right By Me; Choreography; Count Your Blessings Instead of Sheep; What Can You Do With a General; Mandy; The Minstrel Show; Sisters; Heat Wave. **120m/C VHS, Beta, LV, 8mm, Letterbox, Closed Caption.** Bing Crosby, Danny Kaye, Rosemary Clooney, Vera-Ellen, Dean Jagger; *D:* Michael Curtiz; *W:* Norman Panama; *C:* Loyal Griggs. Nominations: Academy Awards '54: Best Song ("Count Your Blessings Instead of Sheep"). *PAR, FUS*

The White Cliffs of Dover 🎬🎬🎬 **1944** Prime example of a successful 40s "women's weepie." American Dunne goes to England in 1914, falls in love, and marries the British Marshal. He joins the WWI troops and is killed, without knowing he had a son. Dunne raises the boy in England as a new threat looms with the rise of Hitler. Now grown, he goes off to do his duty and she joins the Red Cross, where she sees him again among the wounded, another victim of the ravages of war. Dunne is fine in her noble, sacrificing role. McDowall is the young son with Taylor (with whom he'd already worked in "Lassie Come Home") as a childhood friend. Based on the poem by Alice Duer Miller. Bring the hankies. **126m/B VHS.** Irene Dunne, Alan Marshal, Frank Morgan, Peter Lawford, Gladys Cooper, May Whitty, Sir C. Aubrey Smith, Roddy McDowall, Van Johnson, Elizabeth Taylor, June Lockhart, John Warburton, Jill Esmond, Norma Varden, Tom Drake, Arthur Shields; *D:* Clarence Brown. Nominations: Academy Awards '44: Best Black and White Cinematography. *MGM, MOV*

White Comanche 🎬1½ **1967** Half-breed twins battle themselves and each other to a rugged climax. **90m/C VHS, Beta.** William Shatner, Joseph Cotten, Perla Cristal, Rossana Yanni; *D:* Gilbert Kay. *NOS, VCI, VTR*

The White Dawn 🎬🎬½ **1975 (PG)** Three whalers are stranded in the Arctic in the 1890s and are taken in by an Eskimo vilage. They teach the villagers about booze, gambling, and other modern amenities. Resentment grows until a clash ensues. All three leads are excellent, especially Oates. Much of the dialogue is in an Eskimo language, subtitled in English, as in "Dances with Wolves." **110m/C VHS, Beta, LV.** Warren Oates, Timothy Bottoms, Louis Gossett Jr., Simonie Kopapik, Joanasie Salomonie; *D:* Philip Kaufman; *C:* Michael Chapman; *M:* Henry Mancini. *PAR*

White Dwarf 🎬1½ **1995** Confusing sci-fi adventure finds edgy Manhattan internist Driscoll Rampart (McDonough) serving his residency on Rusta, a war-torn planet located in a white-dwarf star system. The planet is divided into two hemispheres, one in perpetual darkness and the other in constant light. Rampart learns the ropes from mystical doc Akada (Winfield), who's also involved in a peace accord between Rusta's warring leaders. Visually striking but overly ambiguous—probably because it was intended as the pilot for a weekly series. **91m/C VHS, Closed Caption.** Paul Winfield, Neal McDonough, CCH Pounder, Ele Keats, Michael McGrady, Katy Boyer; *D:* Peter Markle; *W:* Bruce Wagner; *M:* Stewart Copeland. *CAF*

White Eagle 🎬🎬 **1932** A white man who believes himself to be an Indian gets a job as a Pony Express rider and gets mixed up with horse rustlers. When he finds out who he really is, he is free to marry the white woman he's had his eye on. Interesting plot twist caused by the narrow-mindedness of the Hays Office. **64m/B VHS.** Buck Jones, Barbara Weeks, Robert Ellis, Jason Robards Sr., Robert Elliott, Jim Thorpe, Ward Bond; *D:* Lambert Hillyer. *DVT, HEG*

White Fang 🎬🎬🎬 **1991 (PG)** Boy befriends canine with big teeth and both struggle to survive in third celluloid rendition of Alaska during the Gold Rush. Beautiful cinematography. Fun for the entire family based on Jack London's book. Followed by "White Fang 2: The Myth of the White Wolf." **109m/C VHS, LV, Closed Caption.** Klaus Maria Brandauer, Ethan Hawke, Seymour Cassel, James Remar, Susan Hogan; *D:* Randal Kleiser; *W:* Jeanne Rosenberg, Nick Thiel, David Fallon; *C:* Tony Pierce-Roberts; *M:* Basil Poledouris. *TOU, DIS, TVC*

White Fang 2: The Myth of the White Wolf 🎬🎬 **1994 (PG)** White boy and his wolf-dog lead starving Native American tribe to caribou during the Alaskan Gold Rush. Simplistic story with obvious heroes and villains, yes, but this is also wholesome (and politically correct) family fare compliments of Disney. Focuses less on the wolf, a flaw, and more on Bairstow and his love interest Craig, a Haida Indian princess, while exploring Native American mythology and dreams in sequences that tend to loose the action cold. Still, kids will love it, and there are plenty of puppies to achieve required awwww factor. Beautiful scenery filmed on location in Colorado and British Columbia. **106m/C VHS, LV, Closed Caption.** Scott Bairstow, Alfred Molina, Geoffrey Lewis, Charmaine Craig, Victoria Racimo, Paul Coeur, Anthony Michael Ruivivar, Al Harrington; *Cameos:* Ethan Hawke; *D:* Ken Olin; *W:* David Fallon; *M:* John Debney. *TOU*

White Fang and the Hunter 🎬🎬 **1985 (G)** The adventures of a boy and his dog who survive an attack from wild wolves and then help to solve a murder mystery. Loosely based on the novel by Jack London. **87m/C VHS, Beta.** Pedro Sanchez, Robert Wood; *D:* Alfonso Brescia. *VTR, HHE*

White Fire 🎬🎬 *Three Steps to the Gallows* **1953** Brady, in search of his lost brother, gets involved in a smuggling ring. Seems the brother is falsely accused of murder and about to hang. Brady and

bar singer Castle solve the case. Good photography; bad script. **82m/C VHS, Beta.** *GB* Scott Brady, Mary Castle, Ferdinand "Ferdy" Mayne; *D:* John Gilling. *NOS, SNC, VYY*

White Fire 🎬 **1983** Two jewel thieves will stop at nothing to own White Fire, a two hundred-carat diamond. **90m/C VHS, Beta.** Robert Ginty, Fred Williamson. *TWE*

White Fury **1990** Couples on a campout are victimized by sleazy hoodlums during a snowstorm. **89m/C VHS.** Deke Anderson, Sean Holton, Douglas Hartier, Christine Shinn, Chastity Hammons; *D:* David A. Prior.

White Ghost 🎬 **1988 (R)** An Intelligence Officer who disappeared in the jungles of Asia 18 years ago is ready to come back to the United States, but not everyone wants to see him again. **90m/C VHS, Beta.** William Katt, Rosalind Chao, Martin Hewitt, Wayne Crawford, Reb Brown; *D:* B.J. Davis. *TWE*

White Gold 🎬🎬🎬 **1928** Shepherd's son weds Mexican woman and his disgruntled father contrives apparent rendezvous between the wife and a ranch-hand, who's found dead in her bedroom. Seems no one believes the wife's story. Unprecedented, dark, silent drama. **73m/B VHS, Beta.** Jetta Goudal, Kenneth Thomson, George Bancroft, George Nicholls Jr., Clyde Cook; *D:* William K. Howard. *GPV*

White Gorilla woof! **1947** A great white hunter sets out to kill a gigantic white gorilla that is terrorizing the black natives. Imperialist trash. On any informed person's list of all-time worst movies, but not everyone wants to see him again. **62m/B VHS, Beta, LV.** Ray Corrigan, Lorraine Miller. *NO*

White Heat 🎬🎬🎬½ **1949** A classic gangster film with one of Cagney's best roles as a psychopathic robber/killer with a mother complex. The famous finale—perhaps Cagney's best-known scene—has Cagney trapped on top of a burning oil tank shouting "Made it, Ma! Top of the world!" before the tank explodes. Cagney's character is allegedly based on Arthur "Doc" Barker and his "Ma," and his portrayal is breathtaking. Also available colorized. **114m/B VHS, Beta, LV, Closed Caption.** James Cagney, Virginia Mayo, Edmond O'Brien, Margaret Wycherly, Steve Cochran; *D:* Raoul Walsh; *M:* Max Steiner. Nominations: Academy Awards '49: Best Story. *MGM, FOX*

White Hot 🎬1½ **1988 (R)** A young businessman loses his prestigious Wall Street job, and in order to live the good life, he resorts to selling drugs. Benson stars and directs. **95m/C VHS, Beta, LV.** Robby Benson, Tawny Kitaen, Danny Aiello, Sally Kirkland, Judy Tenuta; *D:* Robby Benson.

White Hot: The Mysterious Murder of Thelma Todd 🎬🎬 **1991** Thelma Todd was a Hollywood starlet found dead under strange circumstances in 1935. Buffs have sought a solution to the maybe-murder ever since; this treatment (based on the book "Hot Toddy" by Andy Edmunds) leaves too many loose ends for purists and isn't sufficiently gripping for the uninitiated. **95m/C VHS.** Loni Anderson, Robert Davi, Paul Dooley, Lawrence Pressman; *D:* Paul Wendkos. *NO*

White Hunter, Black Heart 🎬🎬🎬 **1990 (PG)** Eastwood casts himself against type as Hustonesque director who is more interested in hunting large tusked creatures than shooting the film he came to Africa to produce. Based on Peter Viertel's 1953 account of his experiences working on James Agee's script for Huston's "African Queen." Eastwood's Huston impression is a highlight, though the story occasionally wanders off with the elephants. **112m/C VHS, Beta, LV, 8mm, Closed Caption.** Clint Eastwood, Marisa Berenson, George Dzundza, Jeff Fahey, Timothy Spall, Charlotte Cornwell, Mel Martin, Alun Armstrong, Richard Vanstone; *D:* Clint Eastwood; *W:* Peter Viertel, James Bridges, Burt Kennedy; *C:* Jack N. Green; *M:* Lennie Niehaus. *MGM, FCT, WAR*

White Huntress ✁½ *Golden Ivory* 1957 Two brothers venturing into the jungle encounter a beautiful young woman, the daughter of a settlement leader. Meanwhile, a killer is on the loose. 60m/C VHS, Beta. *GB* Robert Urquhart, John Bentley, Susan Stephen; *D:* George Breakston. *SNC*

The White Legion ✁½ 1936 Workers and engineers push their way through steaming jungles and reeking swamps while building the Panama Canal. Many fall victim to yellow fever. Physician Keith does some medical sleuthing and saves the day. Plodding, predictable drama. 81m/B VHS, Beta. Ian Keith, Tala Birell, Snub Pollard; *D:* Karl Brown. *VYY*

White Lie ✁✁½ 1991 (PG-13) Len Madison, Jr. (Hines), a press secretary for the mayor of New York, receives an old photo of a lynched black man who he learns is his father, hung for raping a white woman. Madison returns to his Southern hometown to find out the truth behind his father's death, assisted by a white doctor (O'Toole) whose mother was a rape victim. They fall in love, adding to an already complicated situation, and incur the wrath of locals who are trying to keep the truth hidden. Based on the novel "Louisiana Black" by Samuel Charters. 93m/C VHS, Closed Caption. Gregory Hines, Annette O'Toole, Bill Nunn; *D:* Bill Condon. *USH*

White Light ✁✁ 1990 (R) "Flatliners" with a flatfoot; after a near-death experience a cop returns with memories of a beautiful woman. He tries to find out who she is/was in plodding fashion. The voyage to the afterlife is represented by a jog through a storm sewer.*CW:* Language, violence, and sensuality. 96m/C VHS, LV. Martin Kove, Allison Hossack, Martha Henry, Heidi von Palleske, James Purcell, Bruce Boa; *D:* Al Waxman.

White Lightning ✁✁½ *McKlusky* 1973 (PG) Good ol' boy Reynolds plays a moonshiner going after the crooked sheriff who murdered his brother. Good stunt-driving chases enliven the formula. The inferior sequel is "Gator." 101m/C VHS, Beta. Burt Reynolds, Ned Beatty, Bo Hopkins, Jennifer Billingsley, Louise Latham; *D:* Joseph Sargent; *W:* William W. Norton Sr.; *M:* Charles Bernstein. *MGM*

White Line Fever ✁✁½ 1975 (PG) A young trucker's search for a happy life with his childhood sweetheart is complicated by a corrupt group in control of the long-haul trucking business. Well-done action film of good triumphing over evil. 89m/C VHS, Beta, LV. Jan-Michael Vincent, Kay Lenz, Slim Pickens, L.Q. Jones, John David Garfield; *D:* Jonathan Kaplan; *W:* Jonathan Kaplan, Ken Friedman; *C:* Fred W. Koenekamp. *COL*

White Mama ✁✁✁ 1980 A poor widow (Davis, in a splendid role) takes in a street-wise black kid (Harden) in return for protection from the neighborhood's dangers, and they discover friendship. Poignant drama, capably directed by Cooper, featuring sterling performances all around Made-for-TV drama at its best. 96m/C VHS, Beta. Bette Davis, Ernest Harden, Eileen Heckart, Virginia Capers, Lurene Tuttle, Anne Ramsey; *D:* Jackie Cooper. *ART*

White Mane ✁✁✁ 1952 The poignant, poetic story of a proud and fierce white stallion that continually eludes attempts by ranchers to capture it. In French with English subtitles. 38m/B VHS, Beta, LV. Alain Emery, Frank Silvera; *D:* Albert Lamorisse. Cannes Film Festival '52: Best Film. *NLC, HMV*

White Man's Burden ✁✁ 1995 (R) In a world where blacks have all the wealth and power, and whites comprise the struggling underclasses, Caucasian factory worker Louis Pinnock (John Travolta) is fired by his bigoted black CEO (Belafonte) due to a misunderstanding. Driven by poverty-level financial strain, Louis kidnaps his wealthy boss to show him how the other half lives. Gimmicky premise is full of reversed stereotypes, such as black cops beating a white guy, and skinheads taking over as inner-city gangsters. Treads too lightly, and rehashes too many familiar sto-

ries, to make any real impact. Travolta had to be talked into this role by "Pulp Fiction" producer Lawrence Bender.*CW:* Strong language, some violence. 89m/C VHS, Closed Caption. John Travolta, Harry Belafonte, Kelly Lynch, Margaret Avery, Tom Bower, Carrie Snodgress, Sheryl Lee Ralph; *D:* Desmond Nakano; *W:* Desmond Nakano; *C:* Willy Kurant; *M:* Howard Shore. *HBO*

White Men Can't Jump ✁✁ 1992 (R) Sometimes they can't act either. Small-time con man Harrelson stands around looking like a big nerd until someone dares him to play basketball and he proves to be more adept than he looks. After he beats Snipes, they become friends and start hustling together. Harrelson lays to rest the rumor that he can't act; here, he proves it. Fast-paced, obscenity-laced dialogue does not cover up for the fact that the story hovers between dull and dismal, redeemed only by the surreal "Jeopardy" game show sequence and the convincing b-ball action. Snipes manages to rise above the material as well as the rim, while Perez, as wooden Woody's spitfire Hispanic girlfriend, is appropriately energetic.*CW:* Language and sensuality. 115m/C VHS. Wesley Snipes, Woody Harrelson, Rosie Perez, Tyra Ferrell, Cylk Cozart, Kadeem Hardison, Ernest Harden, John Jones; *D:* Ron Shelton; *W:* Ron Shelton; *C:* Russell Boyd. *FXV*

White Mile ✁✁½ 1994 (R) Abusive L.A. advertising exec Dan Cutler (Alda) invites his top execs and important clients on a white-water rafting expedition along the Chilko River in the Canadian Rockies (filmed at Northern California's Russian River). But competition and arrogance causes the deaths of several participants and the widow of one sues the agency for damages. Alda excels in arrogant, self-serving nastiness. Fact-based TV movie based on court transcripts.*CW:* Language. 97m/C VHS, LV. Alan Alda, Peter Gallagher, Robert Loggia, Fionnula Flanagan, Dakin Matthews, Bruce Altman, Robert Picardo, Max Wright, Jack Gilpin, Ken Jenkins; *D:* Robert Butler; *W:* Michael Butler. *HBO*

White Mischief ✁✁✁ 1988 (R) An alternately ghastly and hilarious indictment of the English upper class between the World Wars, and the decadence the British colonists perpetrated in Kenya, which came to world attention with the murder of the philandering Earl of Errol in 1941. Exquisitely directed and photographed. Acclaimed and grandly acted, especially by Scacchi; Howard's last appearance. 108m/C VHS, Beta, LV, 8mm. Greta Scacchi, Charles Dance, Joss Ackland, Sarah Miles, John Hurt, Hugh Grant, Geraldine Chaplin, Trevor Howard, Murray Head, Susan Fleetwood, Alan Dobie, Jacqueline Pearce; *D:* Michael Radford; *W:* Michael Radford; *C:* Roger Deakins; *M:* George Fenton. *NLC*

White Nights ✁✁✁ 1957 Based on a love story by Dostoyevski. A young woman pines for the return of her sailor while a mild-mannered clerk is smitten by her. Both of their romantic fantasies are explored the dance-hall cadence is mixed with dreamy, fantastic flashbacks. In Italian with English subtitles. Equally good Soviet version made in 1959. 107m/C VHS. *IT* Maria Schell, Jean Marais, Marcello Mastroianni; *D:* Luchino Visconti; *M:* Nino Rota. *FCT*

White Nights ✁✁½ 1985 (PG-13) A Russian ballet dancer who defected to the U.S. (Baryshnikov) is a passenger on a jet that crashes in the Soviet Union. With the aid of a disillusioned expatriate tap dancer (Hines), he plots to escape again. The excellent dance sequences elevate the rather lame story. ♫ Say You, Say Me. 135m/C VHS, Beta, LV, Letterbox, Closed Caption. Mikhail Baryshnikov, Gregory Hines, Isabella Rossellini, Helen Mirren, Jerzy Skolimowski, Geraldine Page; *D:* Taylor Hackford; *C:* David Watkin; *M:* Michel Colombier. Academy Awards '85: Best Song ("Say You, Say Me"); Golden Globe Awards '86: Best Song ("Say You, Say Me"); Nominations: Academy Awards '85: Best Song ("Separate Lives (Love Theme from White Nights)"). *COL, MOV*

White of the Eye ✁✁✁ 1988 (R) A murdering lunatic is on the loose in Arizona, and an innocent man must find him to acquit himself of the murders. A tense, effective thriller; dazzling technique reveals the experimental films of the 1960s. 111m/C VHS, Beta, Closed Caption. David Keith, Cathy Moriarty, Art Evans, Alan Rosenberg, Michael Greene, Alberta Watson, Marc Hayashi; *D:* Donald Cammell; *W:* China Cammell, Donald Cammell; *M:* Nick Mason, Rick Fenn, George Fenton. *PAR*

The White Orchid ✁✁ 1954 Romantic triangle ventures into the wilds of Mexico in search of Toltec ruins. Exceptional sets. 81m/C VHS, Beta. William Lundigan, Peggy Castle, Armando Silvestre, Rosenda Monteros; *D:* Reginald LeBorg. *SNC, DVT, HEG*

White Palace ✁✁½ 1990 (R) Successful widowed Jewish lawyer Spader is attracted to older, less educated hamburger waitress Sarandon, and ethnic/cultural strife ensues, as does hot sex. Adapted from the Glenn Savan novel, it starts out with promise but fizzles toward the end. 103m/C VHS, LV, Closed Caption. Susan Sarandon, James Spader, Jason Alexander, Eileen Brennan, Griffin Dunne, Kathy Bates, Steven Hill, Rachel Levin, Corey Parker, Spiros Focas, Renee Taylor, Kim Myers; *D:* Luis Mandoki; *W:* Alvin Sargent, Ted Tally; *C:* Lajos Koltai; *M:* George Fenton. *USH, FCT, CCB*

White Phantom: Enemy of Darkness ✁ 1987 Ninja warriors in modern day society battling against other evil ninjas. 89m/C VHS, Beta. Page Leong, Jay Roberts Jr., Bo Svenson; *D:* Dusty Nelson; *W:* David Hamilton, Chris Gallagher. *THV*

White Pongo woof! 1945 A policeman goes undercover with a group of British biologists to capture a mythic white gorilla believed to be the missing link. A camp jungle classic with silly, cheap special effects. 73m/B VHS, Beta. Richard Fraser, Maris Wrixon, Lionel Royce; *D:* Sam Newfield. *SNC, NOS, HHT*

The White Rose ✁✁✁ 1923 An aspiring minister travels to see the world he intends to save, and winds up falling from grace. Complicated menage a trois is finally sorted out at the end. Silent. 120m/B VHS, Beta. Mae Marsh, Carol Dempster, Ivor Novello, Neil Hamilton, Lucille LaVerne; *D:* D.W. Griffith. *GPV*

The White Rose ✁✁✁ 1983 The true story of a group of dissident students in Munich in 1942, who put their lives in danger by distributing leaflets telling the truth of what was going on in the concentration camps. Hans Scholl was an Army officer who discovered the truth and told the others. In the end, most of the students were captured by the Gestapo and executed. "The White Rose" was the name of the group, but none survived to tell where the name came from. Verhoeven's film telling is engrossing and compelling, with excellent acting from the young cast. In German with English subtitles. 108m/C VHS, Beta. *GE* Lena Stolze, Wulf Kessler, Oliver Siebert, Ulrich Tucker; *D:* Michael Verhoeven. *MGM, GLV, SWC*

White Sands ✁✁½ 1992 (R) When a dead man's body is found at a remote Indian reservation clutching a gun and a briefcase filled with $500,000, the local sheriff (Dafoe) takes his identity to see where the money leads. Using a phone number found on a piece of paper in the dead man's stomach, the sheriff follows clues until he finds himself mixed up with a rich woman (Mastrantonio) who sells black market weapons and uses the money to support "worthy" causes, and an FBI man (Jackson) who uses him as bait to lure a CIA turncoat/arms dealer (Rourke). Sound confusing? It is, and despite the strong cast and vivid scenery of the southwest United States, this film just doesn't cut it.*CW:* Language, violence, and sensual scene. 101m/C VHS, Beta, LV, Closed Caption. Willem Dafoe, Mary Elizabeth Mastrantonio, Mickey Rourke, Mimi Rogers, Samuel L. Jackson, M. Emmet Walsh, James Rebhorn, Maura Tierney, Beth Grant, Miguel Sandoval, John Lafayette; *Cameos:* Fred Dalton Thompson, John P. Ryan; **D:** Roger Donaldson; **W:** Daniel Pyne; **C:** Peter Menzies Jr.; **M:** Patrick O'Hearn. *WAR, FCT*

The White Shadow, Vol. 1 1978
After an injury curtails his career with the Chicago Bulls, Ken Reeves (Howard) becomes the basketball coach at Carver High School in Los Angeles, an inner-city school with a team of wisecracking players. The pilot episode finds Reeves trying to adjust to his new life and help his students. **60m/C VHS.** Ken Howard, Ed Bernard, Kevin Hooks, Byron Stewart, Thomas Carter, Timothy Van Patten, Ira Angustain, Joan Pringle, Eric Kilpatrick, Nathan Cook, Ken Michelman. *MOV, MTM*

White Shadows in the South Seas ♂♂½ 1929
Alcohol, drugs, and prostitution take their toll on the native population of Tahiti in this early talkie. Blue plays a western doctor who marries the daughter of a native chief. However, he finds greed for the island's pearl treasures drawing other unscrupulous westerners to destroy the unspoiled paradise. **88m/B VHS.** Monte Blue, Robert Anderson, Raquel Torres; **D:** Woodbridge S. Van Dyke; **C:** Clyde De Vinna. Academy Awards '29: Best Cinematography: *FCT*

The White Sheik ♂♂♂ *Lo Sceicco Bianco* 1952
Fellini's first solo effort. A newly wed bride meets her idol from the comic pages (made with photos, not cartoons; called fumetti) and runs off with him. She soon finds he's as ordinary as her husband. Brilliant satire in charming garb. Remade as "The World's Greatest Lover." Woody Allen's "The Purple Rose of Cairo" is in a similar spirit. **86m/B VHS.** *IT* Alberto Sordi, Giulietta Masina, Brunella Bova, Leopoldo Trieste; **D:** Federico Fellini; **W:** Federico Fellini, Tullio Pinelli, Ennio Flaiano; **M:** Nino Rota. *HMV, VDM, AUD*

The White Sin ♂♂ 1924
An innocent country girl hires on as maid of a rich woman and is seduced and abandoned by the woman's profligate son, but everything turns out all right by the end of the third handkerchief. Silent with original organ music. **93m/B VHS, Beta, 8mm.** Madge Bellamy, John Bowers, Billy Bevan; **D:** William A. Seiter. *VYY*

The White Sister ♂♂♂½ 1923
Gish is an Italian aristocrat driven from her home by a conniving sister. When her true love (Colman) is reported killed she decides to become a nun and enters a convent. When her lover does return he tricks her into leaving the convent but before he can persuade her to renounce her vows Vesuvius erupts and he goes off to warn the villagers, dying for his efforts. Gish then re-dedicates herself to her faith. Colman's first leading role, which made him a romantic star. Filmed on location in Italy. **108m/B VHS, Beta.** Lillian Gish, Ronald Colman, Gail Kane, J. Barney Sherry, Charles Lane; **D:** Henry King. *DVT, HEG*

White Slave ♂ *Amazonia: The Catherine Miles Story* 1986 (R)
An Englishwoman is captured by bloodthirsty cannibals and, rather than being eaten, is tormented and made a slave. **90m/C VHS, Beta.** Elvire Avoray, Will Gonzales, Andrew Louis Coppola; **D:** Roy Garrett. *NO*

White Squall ♂♂½ 1996 (PG-13)
Based on the 1960 true story of 13 young men who become students at Ocean Academy, a year-long adventure spent aboard the brigantine Albatross. Bridges plays the ship's captain and surrogate dad. The boys agonize over their various crises, making the first half of the movie into a veritable "Dead Poets Yachting Society." However, a sudden storm overtakes the ship in the Caribbean and several crew members are killed. There's a shift to a "Caine Mutiny" type trial in which Bridges must prove the tragedy was not his fault while the survivors rally to his defense. Director Scott excels at showing the fury of nature in the prolonged storm scene, but takes his time getting there. **CW:** Some sexuality and a traumatic shipwreck. **128m/C VHS, LV, Letterbox, Closed Caption.** Jeff Bridges, Scott Wolf, Caroline Goodall, Balthazar Getty, John Savage, Jeremy Sisto, Jason Marsden, David Selby,

Zeljko Ivanek, Ryan Phillippe, David Lascher, Eric Michael Cole, Julio Mechoso, Ethan Embry; **D:** Ridley Scott; **W:** Todd Robinson; **C:** Hugh Johnson; **M:** Jeff Rona. *TOU*

White Tiger ♂♂½ 1923
Three crooks pull off a major heist and hide out in a mountain cabin where their mistrust of each other grows. **81m/C VHS.** Priscilla Dean, Matt Moore, Raymond Griffith, Wallace Beery; **D:** Tod Browning. *GPV, FCT*

White Tiger ♂½ 1995 (R)
DEA agent Mike Ryan (Daniels) decides to take the law into his own fists when his partner Grogan (Craven) is murdered by Chinese gang/drug leader Victor Chow (Tagawa). **CW:** Non-stop violence and language, and for sexuality and drug content. **93m/C VHS, Closed Caption.** Gary Daniels, Matt Craven, Cary-Hiroyuki Tagawa, Julia Nickson-Soul; **D:** Richard Martin; **W:** Gordon Melbourne; **C:** Gregory Middleton; **M:** Graeme Coleman. *HMK*

The White Tower ♂♂♂ 1950
Five men and a woman set out to scale the infamous White Tower in the Alps. Each person's true nature is revealed as he or she scales the peak, which has defied all previous attempts. Slightly overwrought, but exciting. Filmed in Technicolor on location in the Swiss Alps. **98m/C VHS, Beta.** Glenn Ford, Claude Rains, Cedric Hardwicke, Oscar Homolka, Lloyd Bridges; **D:** Ted Tetzlaff; **W:** Paul Jarrico. *HHT, TTC*

White Water Summer ♂½ *Rites of Summer* 1987 (PG)
A group of young adventurers trek into the Sierras, and find themselves struggling against nature and each other to survive. Bacon is the rugged outdoorsman (yeah, sure) who shows them what's what. Chances are it was never at a theatre near you, and with good reason. **90m/C VHS, Beta, LV.** Kevin Bacon, Sean Astin, Jonathan Ward, Matt Adler; **D:** Jeff Bleckner; **M:** Michael Boddicker. *COL*

White Wolves 2: Legend of the Wild ♂♂½ 1994 (PG)
Troubled teens are on a school assignment involving a conservation foundation's rescue of a pair of young wolves. They must overcome lots of obstacles, including the fact that they can't stand each other. Average teens-in-the-woods adventure. **95m/C VHS.** Corin "Corky" Nemec, Justin Whalin, Jeremy London, Elizabeth Berkley, Ernie Reyes Jr., Ele Keats; **D:** Terence H. Winkless; **C:** John Aronson. *NHO*

White Wolves 3: Cry of the White Wolf ♂♂½ 1998 (PG)
A plane crash strands three teens in the wilderness where they must depend on themselves, and the mystical white wolf, for survival. **82m/C VHS.** Rodney Grant, Mercedes McNab, Robin Clarke, Tracy Brooks Swope, Mick Cain, Margaret Howell; **D:** Victoria Muspratt. *NHO*

The White Zombie ♂♂♂ 1932
Lugosi followed his success in "Dracula" with the title role in this low-budget horror classic about the leader of a band of zombies who wants to steal a beautiful young woman from her new husband. Set in Haiti; the first zombie movie. Rich and dark, though ludicrous. Based on the novel "The Magic Island" by William Seabrook. **73m/B VHS, Beta.** Bela Lugosi, Madge Bellamy, John Harron, Joseph Cawthorn, Robert Frazer, Brandon Hurst, George Burr Macannan, John Peters, Dan Crimmins, Clarence Muse; **D:** Victor Halperin; **W:** Garnett Weston; **C:** Arthur Martinelli; **M:** Xavier Cugat. *VYY, NOS, CAB*

WhiteForce ♂ 1988 (R)
A secret agent tracks an enemy. His government tracks him. He runs around with a big machine gun and a couple of hand grenades. He fires the gun and throws the grenades. **90m/C Beta.** Sam Jones, Kimberly Pistone; **D:** Eddie Romero. *NO*

Whitewater Sam ♂♂½ 1978 (G)
Whitewater Sam and his Siberian Husky, Sybar, embark on an exciting trip through the uncharted wilds of the Great Northwest. The likeable, intelligent hound steals the show. Good family adventure. **87m/C VHS, Beta.** Keith Larsen; **D:** Keith Larsen; **W:** Keith Larsen. *MON*

Who Am I This Time? ♂♂♂ 1982
Two shy people can express their love for each other only through their roles in a local theatre production of "A Streetcar Named Desire." Good cast responds well to competent direction from Demme; poignant, touching, and memorable. Based on a story by Kurt Vonnegut, Jr. Made for television. **60m/C VHS, Beta, LV.** Susan Sarandon, Christopher Walken, Robert Ridgely; **D:** Jonathan Demme. *MON, BTV*

Who Done It? ♂♂ 1942
Average Abbott and Costello comedy about two would-be radio mystery writers, working as soda-jerks, who play detective after the radio station's president is murdered. **77m/B VHS, Beta.** Bud Abbott, Lou Costello, William Gargan, Patric Knowles, Louise Allbritton, Don Porter, Jerome Cowan, William Bendix, Mary Wickes; **D:** Erle C. Kenton. *USH*

Who Done It? ♂♂½ 1956
Film debut of the rakish Hill as ice-rink sweeper, Hugo Dill. When Dill comes into some money and a dog, he launches a private investigating firm. A woman enters the picture and Hugo discovers his sleuthing has gotten him in over his head. Lots of typical gags and car chases. **79m/B VHS, Closed Caption.** *GB* Benny Hill, Belinda Lee, David Kossoff, Ernest Thesiger; **D:** Basil Dearden. *REP*

Who Framed Roger Rabbit ♂♂♂½ 1988 (PG)
Technically marvelous, cinematically hilarious, eye-popping combination of cartoon and live action create a Hollywood of the 1940s where cartoon characters are real and a repressed minority working in films. A 'toon-hating detective is hired to uncover the unfaithful wife of 2-D star Roger, and instead uncovers a conspiracy to wipe out all 'toons. Special appearances by many cartoon characters from the past. Coproduced by Touchstone (Disney) and Amblin (Spielberg). Adapted from "Who Censored Roger Rabbit?" by Gary K. Wold. **104m/C VHS, Beta, LV, Letterbox.** Bob Hoskins, Christopher Lloyd, Joanna Cassidy, Alan Tilvern, Stubby Kaye; **D:** Robert Zemeckis; **W:** Jeffrey Price, Peter S. Seaman; **C:** Dean Cundey; **M:** Alan Silvestri; **V:** Charles Fleischer, Mae Questel, Kathleen Turner, Amy Irving, Mel Blanc, June Foray, Frank Sinatra. Academy Awards '88: Best Film Editing, Best Visual Effects; Nominations: Academy Awards '88: Best Art Direction/Set Decoration, Best Cinematography, Best Sound. *TOU*

Who Has Seen the Wind? ♂♂ 1977
Two boys grow up in Saskatchewan during the Depression. So-so family viewing drama. Ferrer as a bootlegger steals the otherwise small-paced show. **102m/C VHS, Beta, Closed Caption.** Jose Ferrer, Brian Painchaud, Charmion King, Helen Shaver.

Who Is Killing the Great Chefs of Europe? ♂♂♂ *Too Many Chefs; Someone is Killing the Great Chefs of Europe* 1978 (PG)
A fast-paced, lightly handled black comedy. When a gourmand, well-played by Morley, learns he must lose weight to live, a number of Europe's best chefs are murdered according to their cooking specialty. A witty, crisp, international mystery based on Ivan and Nan Lyon's novel. **112m/C VHS, Closed Caption.** George Segal, Jacqueline Bisset, Robert Morley, Jean-Pierre Cassel, Philippe Noiret, Jean Rochefort, Joss Ackland, Nigel Havers; **D:** Ted Kotcheff; **M:** Henry Mancini. Los Angeles Film Critics Association Awards '78: Best Supporting Actor (Morley). *WAR*

Who Is the Black Dahlia? ♂♂♂ 1975
In L.A. in 1947, a detective tries to find out who murdered a star-struck 22-year-old woman nicknamed "The Black Dahlia" (Arnaz). Based on a famous unsolved murder case which was later the basis for "True Confessions." Made for TV. **96m/C VHS, Beta.** Efrem Zimbalist Jr., Lucie Arnaz, Ronny Cox, MacDonald Carey, Linden Chiles; **D:** Joseph Pevney; **W:** Robert W. Lenski. *WOV*

Who Killed Baby Azaria? ♂♂ 1983
Parents are arrested for infanticide after they claim their baby was stolen by a wild dog while vacationing on a supposedly haunted Australian mountain, or was it an aboriginal spirit that absconded with the tyke? Less compelling than the

American remake, "A Cry in the Dark." Made for Australian TV. **96m/C VHS, Beta.** AU Elaine Hudson, John Hamblin, Peter Carroll; **D:** Judy Rymer.

Who Killed Doc Robbin? *Sinister House; Curley and His Gang in the Haunted Mansion* 1948 A group of youngsters try to clear their friend, Dan, the town handyman, when the sinister Dr. Robbin is murdered. The follow-up to "The Adventures of Curley and His Gang"; intended as part of a Roach kid-comedy series in the manner of "Our Gang." Fast pace and lots of slapstick give a first impression of spirited juvenile hijinks, but not much is genuinely funny. And the names of the two black kids—"Dis" and "Dat"—aren't funny either. **50m/C VHS, Beta.** Larry Olsen, Don Castle, Bernard Carr, Virginia Grey. *SNC, NOS, HHT*

Who Killed Mary What's 'Er Name? *&&* *Death of a Hooker* 1971 (PG) A diabetic ex-fighter tracks a prostitute's killer through Greenwich Village. Illogical, incredible and disjointed attempt at comedy/mystery. Odd, unsatisfying ending, with the boxer going into a coma. Good supporting cast. **90m/C VHS, Beta.** Red Buttons, Sylvia Miles, Conrad Bain, Ron Carey, David Doyle, Sam Waterston; **D:** Ernie Pintoff. *GEM*

Who Shot Pat? *&&½* *Who Shot Patakango?* 1992 (R) Funny, nostalgic, coming of age story set in '50s Brooklyn. Knight stars as Bic Bickham, the leader of a clean-living "gang" of seniors at a Brooklyn vocational school. Memorable vintage soundtrack features hits by legendary artists Chuck Berry and Bo Diddly. **CW:** Language. **102m/C VHS, Closed Caption.** David Knight, Sandra Bullock, Kevin Otto, Aaron Ingram, Brad Randall; **D:** Robert Brooks; **W:** Halle Brooks, Robert Brooks. *WAR*

Who Slew Auntie Roo? *&&½* *Whoever Slew Auntie Roo?; Gingerbread House* 1971 (PG) An updated twist on the Hansel and Gretel fairy tale. Features Winters as an odd, reclusive widow mistaken for the fairy tale's children-eating witch by one of the orphans at her annual Christmas party—with dire consequences. **90m/C VHS, Beta.** Shelley Winters, Ralph Richardson, Mark Lester, Lionel Jeffries, Hugh Griffith; **D:** Curtis Harrington; **W:** Robert Blees. *VES*

Whodunit *&* 1982 (R) The bad horror flicks always seem to have (usually young) characters murdered one at a time, often on a remote island. This loser is no exception. **82m/C VHS, Beta.** Rick Bean, Gary Phillips; **D:** Bill Naud; **W:** Anthony Shaffer. *ART, VES*

The Whole Shootin' Match *&&&* 1979 Two 30-something Texas nobodies chase the American Dream via a sure-fire invention called the Kitchen Wizard, after failing in the small-animal biz and polyurethane. Offbeat, low-budget independent feature shot interestingly in sepia tones. Sympathetic and human. **108m/C VHS.** Matthew L. Perry, Sonny Carl Davis, Doris Hargrave; **D:** Eagle Pennell. *NO*

The Whole Town's Talking *&&&* 1935 Meek clerk Arthur Jones (Robinson) usually leads an uneventful life, until the police arrest him, thinking he's escaped mobster Killer Mannion (Robinson again). Arthur manages to prove his identity and is issued an ID card to settle the confusion, but the mix-up has hit the papers and when Mannion finds out about his double, he steals the card and kidnaps Arthur's Aunt Agatha (Ellsler) and coworker Wilhelmina (Arthur) to ensure his cooperation. Mannion goes on a crime spree and Arthur must figure a way out of his double trouble. Based on a novel by William R. Burnett. **95m/B VHS.** Edward G. Robinson, Jean Arthur, Arthur Hohl, Wallace Ford, Arthur Byron, Donald Meek, Paul Harvey, Effie Ellsler; **D:** John Ford; **W:** Jo Swerling, Robert Riskin; **C:** Joseph August. *COL*

The Whole Wide World *&&&* 1996 (PG) Adaptation of Novalyne Price Ellis' memoirs about her friendship with "Conan the Barbarian" pulp writer Robert E. Howard. In 1933, proper young Cross Plains, Texas schoolteacher (and aspiring writer) Price (Zellweger) arranges an in-

troduction to local eccentric Howard (D'Onofrio), who lives with his overprotective, dying mother (Wedgeworth) and respected doctor father (Presnell) while churning out his bloody tales. Howard has few, if any, social skills but his unpredictability appeals to the sensible Price and the two have a turbulent emotional relationship that never blooms into a full romance. Howard committed suicide in 1936 at the age of 30. **111m/C VHS, LV, Closed Caption.** Renee Zellweger, Vincent D'Onofrio, Ann Wedgeworth, Harve Presnell, Helen Cates, Benjamin Mouton, Michael Corbett, Marion Eaten, Leslie Berger, Chris Shearer, Sandy Walper, Dell Aldrich, Libby Villari, Antonia Bogdanovich, Elizabeth D'Onofrio, Stephen Marshall; **D:** Dan Ireland; **W:** Michael Scott Myers, Novalyne Price Ellis; **C:** Claudio Rocha; **M:** Hans Zimmer, Harry Gregson-Williams. Nominations: Independent Spirit Awards '97: Best Actress (Zellweger). *COL*

Who'll Save Our Children? *&&&* 1982 Two children are abandoned and left on the doorstep of a middle-aged, childless couple. Years later the natural parents, now reformed, attempt to reclaim their children. Well cast and topical. Made for TV. **96m/C VHS, Beta.** Shirley Jones, Len Cariou, Conchata Ferrell, Frances Sternhagen, Cassie Yates, David Hayward; **D:** George Schaefer. *TLF*

Who'll Stop the Rain? *&&&½* *Dog Soldiers* 1978 (R) A temperamental Vietnam vet (Nolte) is enlisted in a smuggling scheme to transport a large amount of heroin into California. An excellent blend of drama, comedy, action, suspense, and tragedy. Based on Robert Stone's novel "Dog Soldiers." Outstanding period soundtrack by Creedence Clearwater Revival, including title song. Violent and compelling tale of late-'60s disillusionment. **126m/C VHS, Beta, LV.** Nick Nolte, Tuesday Weld, Michael Moriarty, Anthony Zerbe, Richard Masur, Ray Sharkey, David Opatoshu, Charles Haid, Gail Strickland; **D:** Karel Reisz; **W:** Judith Rascoe. *MGM*

Wholly Moses! *woof!* 1980 (PG) Set in biblical times, this alleged comedy concerns a phony religious prophet who begins to believe that his mission is to lead the chosen. Horrible ripoff of "Life of Brian," released the previous year. What a cast—what a waste! **125m/C VHS, Beta, LV.** Dudley Moore, Laraine Newman, James Coco, Paul Sand, Dom DeLuise, Jack Gilford, John Houseman, Madeline Kahn, Richard Pryor, John Ritter; **D:** Gary Weis. *COL*

Whoopee! *&&* 1930 Cantor stars in his first sound picture as a rich hypochondriac sent out west for his health, where he encounters rugged cowboys and Indians. Filmed in two-color Technicolor and based on Ziegfeld's 1928 Broadway production with the same cast. Dances supervised by Busby Berkeley. ♫ The Song of the Setting Sun; Mission Number; Makin' Whoopee; A Girlfriend of a Boyfriend of Mine; My Baby Just Cares for Me; I'll Still Belong to You; Stetson. **93m/C VHS.** Eddie Cantor, Ethel Shutta, Paul Gregory, Eleanor Hunt, Betty Grable; **D:** Thornton Freeland. Nominations: Academy Awards '31: Best Interior Decoration. *HBO*

The Whoopee Boys *&* 1986 (R) A New York lowlife in Palm Beach tries to reform himself by saving a school for needy children so his rich girlfriend will marry him. Full of unfunny jokes and very bad taste, with no redeeming qualities whatever. **89m/C VHS, Beta, LV.** Michael O'Keefe, Paul Rodriguez; **D:** John Byrum; **W:** Jeff Buhai; **C:** Ralf Bode; **M:** Jack Nitzsche. *PAR*

Whoops Apocalypse *&&½* 1983 Satiric account of events leading up to WWIII. Invasion in South America leads British prime minister to suggest nuclear retaliation. Uneven, lacking in the Strangelovian element, but funny in spots. Based on the British TV television series and scripted by series writers Marshall and Renwick. **137m/C VHS, Beta.** GB John Cleese, John Barron, Richard Griffiths, Peter Jones, Bruce Montague, Barry Morse, Rik Mayall, Ian Richardson, Alexei Sayle, Herbert Lom, Joanne Pearce; **D:** Tom Bussmann; **W:** Andrew Marshall, David Renwick. *NO*

Whoops Apocalypse *&&* 1988 (R) America's first female president Swit, recently ensconced after the untimely death of the ex-circus clown previous president, is forced to contend with hotheaded superpowers who want to kick off WWIII with a bang. Uneven black comedic satire of holocaust genre. Based on the BBC TV series. **93m/C VHS, Beta.** Loretta Swit, Peter Cook, Michael Richards. *MGM*

Whore *&&* *If You Can't Say It, Just See It* 1991 (R) Ken Russell's gritty night in the life of cynical prostitute Theresa Russell is strong medicine, a powerful antidote to sappy Hollywood films that glorify streetwalking. Also available in the 92-minute original uncut version, an 85-minute NC-17 version, and an alternate R-Rated version. **CW:** Strong sexual dialogue, some violence, and strong sexual situations. **80m/C VHS, Closed Caption.** Theresa Russell, Antonio Vargas; **D:** Ken Russell; **W:** Ken Russell, Deborah Dalton. *THV*

Whore 2 *&½* *Bad Girls* 1994 (R) Jack is a middle-aged writer who moves into Hell's Kitchen in order to do research for a book about prostitutes. Then Jack gets involved with two of the girls—the tough, jealous Lori and childlike Mary Lou. **CW:** Strong sexuality and language; violence; drug use. **85m/C VHS, LV.** Amos Kollek, Marla Sucharetza, Mari Nelson; **D:** Amos Kollek; **W:** Amos Kollek. *THV*

Who's Afraid of Virginia Woolf? *&&&&* 1966 Nichols debuts as a director in this biting Edward Albee play. A teacher and his wife (Segal and Dennis) are invited to the home of a burned-out professor and his foul-mouthed, bitter, yet seductive wife (Burton and Taylor). The guests get more than dinner, as the evening deteriorates into brutal verbal battles between the hosts. Taylor and Dennis won Oscars; Burton's Oscar-nominated portrait of the tortured husband is magnificent. Richard and Liz's best film together. **127m/B VHS, Beta, LV, Letterbox.** Richard Burton, Elizabeth Taylor, George Segal, Sandy Dennis; **D:** Mike Nichols; **W:** Ernest Lehman; **M:** Alex North. Academy Awards '66: Best Actress (Taylor), Best Art Direction/Set Decoration (B & W), Best Black and White Cinematography, Best Costume Design (B & W), Best Supporting Actress (Dennis); British Academy Awards '66: Best Actor (Burton), Best Actress (Taylor), Best Film; National Board of Review Awards '66: Best Actress (Taylor); New York Film Critics Awards '66: Best Actress (Taylor); Nominations: Academy Awards '66: Best Actor (Burton), Best Adapted Screenplay, Best Director (Nichols), Best Film Editing, Best Picture, Best Sound, Best Supporting Actor (Segal), Best Original Score. *WAR, BTV*

Who's Got the Action? *&½* 1963 Martin and Turner are a husband and wife divided by his love of playing the ponies. In order to keep his gambling under control Turner schemes to become his new bookie. But when Martin suddenly goes on a winning streak, the new bookie is in trouble with her former competition, who just happen to be the Mob. Strained, flat comedy with Turner especially miscast. **93m/C VHS.** Lana Turner, Dean Martin, Walter Matthau, Eddie Albert, Nita Talbot, Margo, Paul Ford, John McGiver, Jack Albertson; **D:** Daniel Mann; **W:** Jack Rose. *PAR*

Who's Harry Crumb? *&½* 1989 (PG-13) Bumbling detective Candy can't even investigate a routine kidnapping! His incompetence is catching: the viewer can't detect a single genuinely funny moment. Candy is the only likeable thing in this all-around bad, mindless farce. **95m/C VHS, Beta, LV, Closed Caption.** John Candy, Jeffrey Jones, Annie Potts, Tim Thomerson, Barry Corbin, Shawnee Smith, Valri Bromfield, Renee Coleman, Joe Flaherty, Lyle Alzado, James Belushi, Stephen Young; **D:** Paul Flaherty; **W:** Robert Conte; **M:** Michel Colombier. *COL*

Who's Minding the Mint? *&&&* 1967 A money checker at the U.S. Mint must replace $50,000 he accidentally destroyed. He enlists a retired money printer and an inept gang to infiltrate the mint and replace the lost cash, with predictable chaos resulting. Non-stop zaniness in this wonderful comedy that never got its due

when released. Thieves who befriend Hutton include Denver of "Gilligan's Island" and Farr, later of "M*A*S*H." **97m/C VHS, Beta.** Jim Hutton, Dorothy Provine, Milton Berle, Joey Bishop, Bob Denver, Walter Brennan, Jamie Farr; *D:* Howard Morris; *C:* Joseph Biroc. *GKK*

Who's That Girl? ♂ 1987 (PG) A flighty, wrongly convicted parolee kidnaps her uptight lawyer and they have wacky adventures as she goes in search of the crumb that landed her in the pokey. Plenty of Madonna tunes, if that's what you like; they briefly keep you from wondering why you're not laughing. Kind of a remake (a bad one) of "Bringing Up Baby" (1938). **94m/C VHS, Beta, LV, 8mm, Closed Caption.** Madonna, Griffin Dunne, John Mills, Haviland Morris; *D:* James Foley; *C:* Jan De Bont. Golden Raspberry Awards '87: Worst Actress (Madonna). *WAR*

Who's That Knocking at My Door? ♂♂♂ *J.R.; I Call First* 1968 Interesting debut for Scorsese, in which he exercises many of the themes and techniques that he polished for later films. An autobiographical drama about an Italian-American youth growing up in New York City, focusing on street life, Catholicism and adolescent bonding. Begun as a student film called "I Call First"; later developed into a feature. Keitel's film debut. **90m/B VHS, Beta.** Harvey Keitel, Zena Bethune; *D:* Martin Scorsese. *FCT, WAR*

Who's the Man? ♂♂ 1993 (R) Two clowning companions who work in a barbershop in Harlem get recruited onto the police force to investigate a murder. Doctor Dre and Ed Lover (themselves) make use of their hip-hop music connections and full-throttle slapstick humor to enliven the search. Salt of "Salt 'n' Pepa," is the female lead and Ice-T plays a gangster. First-time director Demme works his star duo for both foolish and vulgar humor. Filming done mostly on location in Harlem. Includes a lengthy list of cameo appearances by several hip-hop performers. For fans; based on a story by Dre, Lover, and Seth Greenland. **124m/C VHS, Closed Caption.** Ed Lover, Cheryl "Salt" James, Ice-T, Jim Moody, Colin Quinn, Kim Chan, Rozwill Young, Badja Djola, Richard Bright, Denis Leary, Andre B. Blake, Bill Bellamy; *D:* Ted Demme; *W:* Seth Greenland; *M:* Michael Wolff. *NLC, IME, COL*

Who's Who ♂♂ 1978 In a satire on climbing the British social ladder, workers in a London brokerage firm struggle with class issues and find the higher you climb, the more you find greed, pettiness, and stupidity. Made for British television. **75m/C VHS.** *GB* Bridget Kane, Simon Chandler, Adam Norton, Philip Davis, Joolia Cappleman; *D:* Mike Leigh; *W:* Mike Leigh. *WBF, BTV, FCT*

Whose Child Am I? ♂ 1975 (R) A woman so desperately wants a child of her own that she doesn't mind who the father is. Ludicrous and vulgar. **90m/C VHS.** Kate O'Mara, Paul Freeman, Edward Judd, Felicity Devonshire; *D:* Lawrence Britten. *ATL*

Whose Life Is It Anyway? ♂♂ 1/2 1981 (R) Black humor abounds. Sculptor Dreyfuss is paralyzed from the neck down in an auto accident. What follows is his struggle to persuade the hospital authorities to let him die. Excellent cast headed impressively by Dreyfuss; Lahti as his doctor and hospital head Cassavetes also are superb. From Brian Clark's successful Broadway play. **118m/C VHS, Beta.** Richard Dreyfuss, John Cassavetes, Christine Lahti, Bob Balaban, Kenneth McMillan, Kaki Hunter, Thomas Carter; *D:* John Badham; *W:* Reginald Rose, Brian Clark. *MGM*

Why Change Your Wife? ♂♂ 1/2 1920 A rare, recently re-discovered silent comedy. Swanson and Meighan play married couple Beth and Robert who find themselves drifting apart after ten years of marriage. Robert becomes involved with someone else and Beth demands a divorce. After Robert remarries, Beth decides she wants him back and the real fun begins as she tries every trick in the book to regain her ex-husband. Piano scored. **100m/B VHS, Beta.** Gloria Swan-

son, Thomas Meighan, Bebe Daniels; *D:* Cecil B. DeMille. *GPV*

Why Does Herr R. Run Amok? ♂♂ *Warum Läuft Herr R Amok?* 1969 Notorious Fassbinder black comedy about a middle-class man, unable to cope with the increasing problems of modern life, who suddenly murders his family. The characters are called by the actors' names to heighten the sense of reality. Film is based on a case history. In German with English subtitles. **88m/C VHS.** *GE* Kurt Raab, Lilith Ungerer, Amadeus Fengler, Hanna Schygulla, Franz Maron; *D:* Rainer Werner Fassbinder, Michael Fengler; *W:* Rainer Werner Fassbinder, Michael Fengler. *NYF, FCT, ING*

Why Has Bodhi-Darma Left for the East ♂♂ 1989 Set in a remote monastery in the Korean mountains, film follows an old master, close to death, who must lead his disciples in their search for spiritual freedom. The film's title is a Zen koan—an unanswerable riddle that serves as an aid on the path to enlightenment. Korean with subtitles. **135m/C VHS.** *D:* Bae Young-kyun; *W:* Bae Young-kyun; *C:* Bae Young-kyun. *MIL*

Why Me? ♂♂ 1990 (R) Two jewel thieves unknowingly steal an enormously valuable ruby ring and are in over their heads trying to evade the cops and everyone else. In the same vein as the much-funnier "Nuns on the Run," this caper is done in by bad acting and too much ill-conceived slapstick. Adapted by Donald E. Westlake from his own novel. **96m/C VHS, LV, Closed Caption.** Christopher Lambert, Christopher Lloyd, Kim Greist, J.T. Walsh, Michael J. Pollard, Tony Plana, John Hancock, Lawrence Tierney; *D:* Gene Quintano; *W:* Donald E. Westlake. *COL*

Why Shoot the Teacher ♂♂♂ 1979 A young teacher sent to a one-room schoolhouse in a small prairie town in Saskatchewan during the Depression gets a cold reception on the cold prairie. One of the more popular films at the Canadian box office. Cort was Harold in "Harold and Maude." Based on the novel by Max Braithwaite. **101m/C VHS, Beta.** *CA* Bud Cort, Samantha Eggar, Chris Wiggins; *D:* Silvio Narizzano; *W:* James DeFelice.

The Wicked ♂ *Outback Vampires* 1989 Though packaged as serious horror, this is a cheap, tacky spoof with folks stranded at the country residence of a vampire family. Sole point of interest: these Transylvanian cliches take place in the Australian outback. Kids might actually like this (gore isn't severe), if they can surmount the thick Down Under accents. **87m/C VHS.** Brett Cumo, Richard Morgan, Angela Kennedy, Maggie Blinco, John Doyle; *D:* Colin Eggleston.

Wicked City ♂♂ 1992 Humans are uneasily coexisting with Reptoids (creatures that can assume human shape) in this sci-fi tale based on a Japanese comic strip. Then Hong Kong police discover a plot by the Reptoids to destroy mankind and rule the world (what else is new). Nifty special effects. Available dubbed or in Cantonese with subtitles. **88m/C VHS.** *HK* Jacky Cheung, Leon Lai, Michelle Li; *D:* Peter Mak. *FXL*

The Wicked Lady ♂♂ 1945 Posh but lame costume drama about a bored 17th century noblewoman who takes to highway robbery to spice up her life. Credulity-stretcher extraordinaire. Based on "The Life and Death of Wicked Lady Skelton" by Magdalen King-Hall. Mason is cheeky as a fellow highwayman. Remade in 1983 with Faye Dunaway. **103m/B VHS, Beta.** *GB* James Mason, Margaret Lockwood, Patricia Roc, Michael Rennie, Felix Aylmer, Enid Stamp-Taylor, Griffith Jones; *D:* Leslie Arliss. *NO*

The Wicked Lady ♂ 1/2 1983 (R) Remake of the 1945 costumer about a 17th-century noblewoman trying her hand at highway robbery. More noted for its low-cut costumes and racy humor than any talent involved. **99m/C VHS, Beta.** *GB* Faye Dunaway, John Gielgud, Denholm Elliott, Alan Bates, Glynis Barber, Oliver Tobias, Prunella Scales; *D:* Michael Winner; *W:* Michael Winner; *C:* Jack Cardiff; *M:* Tony Banks. *MGM*

Wicked Stepmother ♂ 1989 (PG-13) A family discovers that an aged stepmother is actually a witch. Davis walked off the film shortly before she died, and was replaced by Carrera. Davis's move was wise; the result is dismal, and would have been had she stayed. As it is the viewer wonders: How come the stepmother isn't Davis anymore? Davis's unfortunate last role. **90m/C VHS, Beta.** Bette Davis, Barbara Carrera, Colleen Camp, Lionel Stander, David Rasche, Tom Bosley, Seymour Cassel, Evelyn Keyes, Richard Moll, Laurene Landon; *D:* Larry Cohen; *W:* Larry Cohen; *C:* Bryan England; *M:* Robert Folk. *MGM*

The Wicker Man ♂♂♂ 1/2 1975 The disappearance of a young girl leads a devoutly religious Scottish policeman to an island whose denizens practice bizarre pagan sexual rituals. An example of occult horror that achieves its mounting terror without gratuitous gore. The first original screenplay by playwright Shaffer. Beware shortened versions that may still lurk out there; the 103-minute restored director's cut is definitive. **103m/C VHS, Beta.** Edward Woodward, Christopher Lee, Britt Ekland, Diane Cilento, Ingrid Pitt, Lindsay Kemp, Irene Sunters, Walter Carr, Geraldine Cowper, Lesley Mackie; *D:* Robin Hardy; *W:* Anthony Shaffer. *REP*

Wide Awake ♂♂ 1/2 1997 (PG) After the death of his beloved grandfather (Loggia), a young Catholic school boy (Cross) begins a mission to find God in order to find out if his grandpa is O.K. He asks difficult questions of his parents (Leary and Delaney) and teachers, including O'Donnell as a sports obsessed nun who compares Jesus and his disciples to a baseball team. He explores Judaism, Islam and Buddhism as well as Christianity. Finally he has an encounter with an angel that restores his faith. While Cross comes across well, the fellow youngsters in the movie have a stagy stiffness to their lines and expressions that lend the movie a hokey feel. **88m/C VHS.** Joseph Cross, Dana Delany, Rosie O'Donnell, Denis Leary, Robert Loggia, Dan Lauria, Timothy Reifsnyder, Camryn Manheim; *D:* M. Night Shyamalan; *W:* M. Night Shyamalan; *C:* Adam Holender; *M:* Edmund Choi. *NYR*

Wide Open Faces ♂♂ 1938 Every crook in town is looking for some missing stolen loot. Soda jerk Brown outwits them all in his own inimitable way. The story may be predictable, but Brown's physical humor keeps things interesting. **67m/B VHS.** Joe E. Brown, Jane Wyman, Alison Skipworth, Alan Baxter, Lucien Littlefield, Sidney Toler, Berton Churchill, Barbara Pepper, Stanley Fields, Horace Murphy; *D:* Kurt Neumann; *C:* Paul Vogel. *NOS*

Wide Sargasso Sea ♂♂ 1992 (NC-17) Jamaica in the 1840s is a seething, mysterious paradise—a former British slave colony with a mix of powerful voodoo culture, beauty, and eroticism providing a very potent brew, a perfect setting for this soaper. Based on the novel by Jean Rhys, which is something of a prequel to Charlotte Bronte's "Jane Eyre." Properly English Edward Rochester meets and marries the tragic Antoinette—the same mad wife locked in the attic in the Bronte novel. Explicit nudity and sex earn the NC-17, but the film is tragic without being sensationalized. Also available in an edited R-rated and unrated versions. *CW:* Strong sexuality. **98m/C VHS, LV, Closed Caption.** *AU* Karina Lombard, Nathaniel Parker, Rachel Ward, Michael York, Martine Beswick, Claudia Robinson, Rowena King, Huw Christie Williams; *D:* John Duigan; *W:* Jan Sharp, Carole Angier, John Duigan; *C:* Geoff Burton; *M:* Stewart Copeland. *NLC, IME, BTV*

The Widow ♂♂ 1976 A story about a woman slowly learning to deal with her own grief, her children's traumas and monetary worries after the death of her husband. Straightforward, passable made for TV domestic drama based on Lynn Caine's best-selling novel. **99m/C VHS, Beta.** Michael Learned, Farley Granger, Bradford Dillman, Robert Lansing; *D:* J. Lee Thompson. *TLF*

Widow Couderc 🐾🐾🐾 1974 A provincial widow unknowingly includes an escaped murderer among her liaisons. Based on a novel by Georges Simenon. In French with English subtitles. 92m/C VHS, Beta. **FR** Simone Signoret, Alain Delon; **D:** Pierre Granier-Deferre. *FCT*

Widow's Kiss 🐾🐾 1994 (R) Sean Sager (Astin) is suspicious when his wealthy dad Justin (Davison) dies in the arms of sexy, widowed Vivian (D'Angelo). So he hires detective Eddie Costello (Haysbert), who learns that the widow has left a number of dead husbands behind. But Sean's in desperate trouble when he discovers Vivian gets dad's fortune if Sean should die. Rather dull cable drama wastes its talented cast. *CW:* Some strong sexuality, language and some violence. 103m/C VHS. MacKenzie Astin, Beverly D'Angelo, Bruce Davison, Dennis Haysbert, Michael Woolson, Barbara Rush, Anna Maria Horsford, Michael Des Barres; **D:** Peter Foldy; **W:** Peter Foldy, Mark Donnelly; **C:** Doyle Smith; **M:** Robert Sprayberry. *HBO*

Widow's Nest 🐾🐾 1977 Three widowed sisters live in a bizarre fantasy world when they lock themselves in a dingy mansion in Cuba of the 1930s. Filmed in Spain. 90m/C VHS, Beta. Patricia Neal, Susan Oliver, Lila Kedrova, Valentina Cortese; **D:** Tony Navarro. *NO*

Widow's Peak 🐾🐾½ 1994 (PG) 1920s Irish community is run by a dictatorship of well-to-do widows with Mrs. Doyle-Counihan (Plowright) at the helm. Troubles begin for the town non-widow (Farrow) upon the arrival of recently widowed Broome (Richardson), who attracts Dunbar, the nitwit son of Plowright. Entertaining performances (Farrow shows that success is possible after the Wood-man) and beautiful scenery help boost a script that seems torn between whimsical comedy and dark drama. 98m/C VHS, LV. Mia Farrow, Joan Plowright, Natasha Richardson, Adrian Dunbar, Jim Broadbent, John Kavanagh, Gerard McSorley, Anne Kent, Rynagh O'Grady, Michael James Ford, Garrett Keogh; **D:** John Irvin; **W:** Hugh Leonard; **M:** Carl Davis. *NLC*

The Wife 🐾🐾 1995 (R) The routine of married psychotherapists Jack (Noonan) and Rita (Hagerty), who live in an isolated Vermont farmhouse, is disrupted by the unexpected (and unwelcome) appearance of Jack's patient Cosmo (Shawn), who's in crisis, and his wife Arlie (Young). Everyone's got secrets and marital dilemmas that come spilling out over too much wine. A variation on "Who's Afraid of Virginia Woolf?" *CW:* Language, some nudity. 101m/C VHS, Letterbox. Tom Noonan, Julie Hagerty, Karen Young, Wallace Shawn; **D:** Tom Noonan; **W:** Tom Noonan; **C:** Joe DeSalvo; **M:** Lodovico Sorret. *FXL*

Wife Versus Secretary 🐾🐾🐾½ 1936 Excellent acting against type creates a near-perfect picture of romantic relationships. Harlow and Gable play a secretary and her boss who have a wonderful professional relationship, but Loy worries something else is afoot. Could have been a heavy-handed soap opera, but the witty dialogue and Brown's fine pacing make it much more. Stewart later claimed that he purposely messed up his romantic scenes with Harlow in order to spend more time in her arms. 89m/B VHS. Clark Gable, Jean Harlow, Myrna Loy, May Robson, Hobart Cavanaugh, James Stewart, George Barbier, Gilbert Emery; **D:** Clarence Brown. *MGM*

Wifemistress 🐾🐾½ Mogliamante; Lover, Wife 1979 (R) In the early 1900s, an invalid wife resents her neglectful husband. When he goes into hiding because of a murder he didn't commit, she begins to drift into a world of sexual fantasies. Fine performances. Italian dialogue with English subtitles. 101m/C VHS, Beta. **IT** Marcello Mastroianni, Laura Antonelli; **D:** Marco Vicario. *COL*

Wigstock: The Movie 🐾🐾½ 1995 (R) Documentary of the eponymous annual Labor Day event in Manhattan, billed as the Super Bowl of drag. Shils intercuts stage numbers with interviews from a variety of the talented, witty festival performers, such as Lypsinka, Mistress Formika, and RuPaul. One of the best numbers is performed by the Duelling Bankheads (as in Tallulah) singing "Born to Be Wild." Like the event itself, documentary is more a celebration than a probing, psychological look at drag. Won't appeal to everyone, but a lot of fun for those who can appreciate high hair and high fashion. *CW:* Sex-related material and language. 92m/C VHS. **D:** Barry Shils. *HMK*

The Wilby Conspiracy 🐾🐾🐾 1975 (PG) A political activist and an Englishman on the wrong side of the law team up to escape the clutches of a prejudiced cop in apartheid Africa. The focus of the film is on the chase, not the political uprising taking place around it. Well-done chase film with fine performances throughout. 101m/C VHS, Closed Caption. Sidney Poitier, Michael Caine, Nicol Williamson, Prunella Gee, Persis Khambatta, Saeed Jaffrey, Rutger Hauer, Helmut Dantine; **D:** Ralph Nelson; **W:** Rod Amateau. *MGM, FCT*

The Wild Aces 🐾½ 1985 A relentless action flick with real documentary footage of the aerial war above Vietnam. 58m/C VHS, Beta. *BMV, FGF*

Wild America 🐾🐾🐾 1997 (G) Warner Bros. invades Disney's well-marked territory of family-friendly real-life adventure with this bio of famed nature documentarians Mark, Marty, and Marshall Stouffer. Pic focuses on the origins of the boys' fascination with animals, which started when their parents gave them a used 16mm camera to mess around with. After getting some footage of backyard wildlife, they're hooked, and hit the road to find more dangerous (and endangered) beasts to shoot (in the good way). As you would expect, the scenery and camera work are splendid, and any expected wild animal gore and violence has been toned way down. There's plenty to hold the interest of adults as well as children, with a big assist going to the clever script. Title is taken from Marty Stouffer's long-running PBS nature series. 105m/C VHS, Closed Caption, DVD. Jonathan Taylor Thomas, Devon Sawa, Scott Bairstow, Jamey Sheridan, Frances Fisher; **D:** William Dear; **W:** David Michael Wieger; **C:** David Burr; **M:** Joel McNeely. *WAR*

The Wild and the Free 🐾🐾 1980 Light-hearted comedy about research chimps. The lab-raised bunch become the instruments for radioactive experimenting. Scheming scientists return the chimps to their home to save them from their demise. Made for TV. 100m/C VHS, Beta. Granville Van Dusen, Linda Gray, Bill Gribble; **D:** James Hill. *ART*

Wild & Wooly 🐾½ 1978 In 1903, a tough cowgirl and her friends must prevent the assassination of the President. Made for television. 120m/C VHS, Beta. Chris DeLisle, Susan Bigelow, Elyssa Davalos, Jessica Walter, Doug McClure, David Doyle, Ross Martin, Vic Morrow, Charles Seibert, Sherry Bain, Paul Burke; **D:** Philip Leacock; **M:** Charles Bernstein.

The Wild Angels 🐾🐾½ 1966 (PG) Excessively violent film but B-movie classic about an outlaw biker gang and the local townspeople. Typical Corman fodder was one of AIP's most successful productions. 124m/C VHS. Peter Fonda, Nancy Sinatra, Bruce Dern, Diane Ladd, Michael J. Pollard, Gayle Hunnicutt; **D:** Roger Corman; **W:** Charles B. Griffith; Peter Bogdanovich. *ORI*

Wild at Heart 🐾🐾🐾½ 1990 (R) Dern and Cage are on the lam, going across country to escape her mother, his parole officer, and life. Humorous and frightening, sensual and evocative as only Lynch can be. Sweet love story of Sailor and Lula is juxtaposed with the violent and bizarre, obsessive brand of love of the people they encounter. Unmistakable Wizard of Oz imagery sprinkled throughout, as are some scenes of graphic violence. Ladd is unnerving as Dern's onscreen mother (she also has the role off-screen). 125m/C VHS, Beta, LV, Letterbox, Closed Caption. Nicolas Cage, Laura Dern, Diane Ladd, Willem Dafoe, Isabella Rossellini, Harry Dean Stanton, Crispin Glover, Grace Zabriskie, J.E. Freeman, Freddie Jones, Sherilyn Fenn, Sheryl Lee; **D:** David Lynch; **W:** David Lynch; **C:** Frederick Elmes; **M:** Angelo Badalamenti. Cannes Film Festival '90: Best Film; Independent Spirit Awards '91: Best Cinematography; Nominations: Academy Awards '90: Best Supporting Actress (Ladd). *CCB, IME, FCT*

The Wild Beasts woof! Savage Beasts 1985 Children and animals clash violently after drinking water tainted with PCP. Disgusting premise; unredeemably violent. 92m/C VHS, Beta. John Aldrich, Lorraine De Selle; **D:** Franco Prosperi. *ART*

Wild Bill 🐾🐾½ 1995 (R) Realistic, un-heroic portrait of Wild Bill Hickok (Bridges), seen mostly in flashback. From trapper and lawman to his last days in Deadwood, South Dakota, focus is on the events haunting the glaucoma-stricken, opium-addicted legend in his later years, such as twice deserting his true love (Lane). Action packed first 20 minutes mellows along with the aging Hickok and the rest gets a bit talky for a Western, albeit an arty one. Bridges's Hickok is brilliant, but Barkin is given a somewhat tedious Calamity Jane. Based on the novel "Deadwood" by Pete Dexter and the play "Fathers and Sons" by Thomas Babe. *CW:* Western violence; sex scene. 97m/C VHS, LV, Closed Caption. Jeff Bridges, Ellen Barkin, John Hurt, Diane Lane, Keith Carradine, Christina Applegate, Bruce Dern, James Gammon, David Arquette, Marjoe Gortner; **D:** Walter Hill; **W:** Walter Hill; **C:** Lloyd Ahern; **M:** Van Dyke Parks. *MGM*

The Wild Bunch 🐾🐾🐾🐾 1969 (R) Acclaimed western about a group of aging outlaws on their final rampage, realizing time is passing them by. Highly influential in dialogue, editing style, and lyrical slow-motion photography of violence; Peckinpah's main claim to posterity. Holden and Ryan create especially memorable characters. Arguably the greatest western and one of the greatest American films of all times. Beware of shortened versions; after a pre-release showing to the East Coast critics, producer Feldman cut key scenes without Peckinpah's knowledge or consent. 145m/C VHS, Beta, LV, DVD. William Holden, Ernest Borgnine, Robert Ryan, Warren Oates, Strother Martin, L.Q. Jones, Albert Dekker, Bo Hopkins, Edmond O'Brien, Ben Johnson, Jaime Sanchez, Emilio Fernandez, Dub Taylor; **D:** Sam Peckinpah; **W:** Walon Green, Sam Peckinpah; **C:** Lucien Ballard. National Society of Film Critics Awards '69: Best Cinematography; Nominations: Academy Awards '69: Best Story & Screenplay, Best Original Score. *WAR*

Wild Cactus 🐾🐾 1992 (R) Philip and Alexandria Marcus decide to take a romantic vacation at a desert resort where they meet up with a homicidal ex-con and his seductive girlfriend. The two couples find themselves entangled in some violent and kinky games. An unrated version is also available. *CW:* Language, strong violence, and strong language. 92m/C VHS, Closed Caption. David Naughton, India Allen, Gary Hudson, Michelle Moffett, Kathy Shower, Robert Z'Dar, Paul Gleason, Anna Karin, David Wells; **D:** Jag Mundhra; **W:** Carl Austin. *IMP*

The Wild Child 🐾🐾🐾½ L'Enfant Sauvage 1970 (G) The brilliant film based on the journal of a 19th century physician who attempts to educate and civilize a young boy who has been found living in the wilderness, without any comprehension of human life. Tenderly told coming of age tale, with surprising sensitivity for its subject. In French with English subtitles. 85m/B VHS. **FR D:** Francois Truffaut; **W:** Jean Gruault; **C:** Nestor Almendros; **M:** Antoine Duhamel. National Board of Review Awards '70: Best Director (Truffaut); National Society of Film Critics Awards '70: Best Cinematography. *MGM, FCT*

Wild Country 🐾½ 1947 Tame western. A U.S. Marshal races to stop the bad guy from killing the late sheriff's daughter and snatching her ranch. 57m/B VHS. Eddie Dean, Roscoe Ates, Peggy Wynn, Douglas Fowley, I. Stanford Jolley, William "Bill" Fawcett; **D:** Ray Taylor. *NOS, HEG*

The Wild Country 🎬🎬½ *The Newcomers* 1971 (G) Children's fare detailing the trials and tribulations of a Pittsburgh family moving into an inhospitable Wyoming ranch in the 1880s. Based on the novel "Little Britches" by Ralph Moody. 92m/C VHS, Beta. Steve Forrest, Ron Howard, Clint Howard, Rance Howard; *D:* Robert Totten; *M:* Robert F. Brunner. *DIS*

The Wild Duck 🎬½ 1984 (PG) A father discovers that his beloved daughter is illegitimate and turns against her. To regain his love, she plans to sacrifice her most prized possession. Irons overacts; Ullmann almost disappears into the woodwork. Child star Jones is insufferable, and the whole family squeaks with "literary" pomposity. A horrid adaptation of the classic Ibsen play. 96m/C VHS, Beta. *AU* Jeremy Irons, Liv Ullmann, Lucinda Jones, Arthur Dignam; *D:* Henri Safran. *ART, VES*

Wild Engine/Mistaken Orders 🎬🎬 1923 The early screen daredevil Holmes stars in two railroad-and-betrayal epics. 48m/B VHS, Beta. Helen Holmes, Jack Hoxie, Hoot Gibson. *CCB*

Wild Frontier 🎬🎬½ 1948 A rugged old lawman and his sons team up to rid a town of outlaws. Lane, playing a character with his own name for first time, takes over from his murdered father and roots out the evildoer (Holt). Decent, enjoyable, good-guys-win western. 59m/B VHS, Beta. Allan "Rocky" Lane, Jack Holt. *DVT*

Wild Geese 🎬🎬 1978 (R) The adventure begins when a veteran band of mercenaries land deep inside Africa to rescue the imprisoned leader of an emerging African nation, in the interest of protecting British commercial interest. Their mission meets an unexpected turn when they are betrayed by their financial backers. Too much training in the early part; too long; too much dialogue. Where's the action? 132m/C VHS, Beta, LV. *GB* Richard Burton, Roger Moore, Richard Harris, Hardy Kruger, Stewart Granger, Frank Finlay, Jeff Corey; *D:* Andrew V. McLaglen; *W:* Reginald Rose. *FOX*

Wild Geese 2 🎬½ 1985 (R) Lame sequel to the flamed and overlong "Wild Geese," which depended on its name stars. More of the same, this time sans Burton, Harris and Moore. Sure, it's got Olivier, but it still stinks. 124m/C VHS, Beta. *GB* Laurence Olivier, Edward Fox, Scott Glenn, Barbara Carrera, Robert Webber; *D:* Peter Hunt; *W:* Reginald Rose. *MGM*

Wild Guitar woof! 1962 A swinging youth cycles into Hollywood and, improbably, becomes an instant teenidol. Considered a top contender for "Worst Picture of All Time" honors. 92m/B VHS, Beta. Arch Hall Jr.; *D:* Ray Dennis Steckler. *RHI*

Wild Gypsies 🎬 1969 A band of gypsies seek revenge against a renegade member who returned to rape and pillage. Without merit except for the good photography of Steven Burum, who has become respected doing cinematographically intriguing films like "Rumblefish." 85m/C VHS, Beta, LV. Todd Grange, Gayle Clark, Laurel Welcome.

Wild Hearts Can't Be Broken 🎬🎬🎬 1991 (G) Depicts the true-life story of Sonora Webster, a small town Georgia girl who runs away from a foster home to join a carnival in the early 1930s, hoping to become a stunt rider. She becomes a horse-diver (a Depression-era sideshow phenomena) and is blinded in a diving accident, but returns to find romance and ride again. Storyline has little screen tension, but it doesn't detract from this fresh family film with a feisty heroine, a sweet romance, and horses. Nice U.S. screen debut for British actress Anwar. 89m/C VHS, Beta, Closed Caption. Gabrielle Anwar, Cliff Robertson, Dylan Kussman, Michael Schoeffling, Kathleen York, Frank Renzulli; *D:* Steve Miner; *W:* Oley Sassone; *M:* Mason Daring. *DIS*

Wild Horse 🎬½ *Silver Devil* 1931 Gibson is the lead (in his favorite talking role), but his magnificent mount Mut commands most of the attention. Interesting historically as an example of stars' (Gibson's in this case) difficulty adjusting to

talking pictures. 68m/B VHS, Beta. Hoot Gibson, Stepin Fetchit, Edmund Cobb, Alberta Vaughn; *D:* Richard Thorpe, Sidney Algier. *NOS, GPV, VYY*

Wild Horse Canyon 🎬🎬 1925 Yakima Canutt, the man credited with creating the profession of stunt man, stars in this tale about a lady rancher who requires saving from her evil foreman. The climactic stampede scene gives Yakima a chance to demonstrate a high dive off a cliff and a somersault onto his horse. Silent, with musical score. 68m/B VHS, Beta. Yakima Canutt, Edward Cecil, Helene Rosson, Jay Talbet. *NOS, GPV, VYY*

Wild Horse Canyon 🎬½ 1939 One of those westerns designed to run as half of a double-feature, this one's shorter than most, but hardly notable. The hero goes after a rustler who shot his brother. 57m/B VHS. Jack Randall, Dorothy Short, Frank Yaconelli, Dennis Moore, Warner Richmond, Charles "Blackie" King, Sherry Tansey; *D:* Robert F. "Bob" Hill. *NOS, GPV*

Wild Horse Hank 🎬🎬 1979 A young woman risks everything to save a herd of wild mustangs from being slaughtered for use as dog food. Creena is good; otherwise, it's sentimental family fare. Based on the novel "The Wild Horse Killers" by Mel Ellis. 94m/C VHS, Beta. *CA* Linda Blair, Richard Crenna, Michael Wincott, Al Waxman; *D:* Eric Till. *ART, VES*

Wild Horse Phantom 🎬🎬 1944 A Wild West banker plans to fake a robbery in a diabolical deception to part honest ranchers from their lands. Surely this man's not a member of the F.D.I.C. Okay sagebrush saga. 56m/B VHS, Beta. Buster Crabbe, Al "Fuzzy" St. John, Charles "Blackie" King, John Merton, Lane Chandler, Edward Cassidy, Bud Osborne; *D:* Sam Newfield. *GPV*

Wild Horse Rodeo 🎬½ 1937 When a gunman appears at a rodeo, trouble starts. Part of "The Three Mesquiteers" series. Ordinary action-packed western, the good guys win. Actor Dick Weston, who sings, later gained fame as singing cowboy Roy Rogers. 53m/B VHS, Beta. Ray Corrigan. *NOS, DVT*

Wild Horses 🎬🎬 1982 A man attempts to make a living by capturing and selling wild horses. Adventure fans will love this film which deals with the common theme of man against nature. 88m/C VHS, Beta. *NZ* Keith Aberdein, John Bach, Robyn Gibbes; *D:* Derek Morton. *VES*

Wild Horses 🎬🎬 1984 Ex-rodeo champ Rogers is hankering to escape his dull life. He joins a roundup of wild horses and with Dawber's help exposes a bureaucrat's scheme for them. Rogers is likable and sings, but the supporting cast carries this one. Made for TV. 90m/C VHS, Beta. Kenny Rogers, Pam Dawber, Ben Johnson, Richard Masur, David Andrews, Karen Carlson; *D:* Dick Lowry. *NO*

Wild Horses 🎬🎬 *Caballos Salvajes* 1995 Elderly Jose (Alterio) resorts to bank robbery to recover his $15,000 nest egg. Young employee Pedro (Sbarablia) gives him $500,000 and offers to be the old man's hostage. The unlikely duo hit the road for Patagonia and send the press messages detailing the money's suspects origins and their own good intentions. Spanish with subtitles. 122m/C VHS, Letterbox. *AR* Hector Alterio, Leonardo Sbaraglia, Cecilia Dopazo; *D:* Marcelo Pineyro; *W:* Marcelo Pineyro, Aida Bortnik; *C:* Alfredo Mayo; *M:* Andres Calamaro. *NYF*

Wild in the Country 🎬🎬½ 1961 Backwoods delinquent Presley is aided in his literary aspirations by woman psychiatrist Lange. Okay, so that's fairly novel. Strange plot lines but in general Elvis is going to college and reading and writing and singing and playing his guitar. Meanwhile Weld wanders around seductively to provide that hint of Tennessee Williams ambience as interpreted by Odet but hey, who cares? Interesting if convoluted Elvis dramatic turn. 🎵Wild in the Country; In My Way; I Slipped, I Stumbled, I Fell; Lonely Man. 114m/C VHS, Beta. Elvis Presley, Hope Lange, Tuesday Weld, Millie Perkins, John Ireland, Gary

Lockwood, Alan Napier; *D:* Philip Dunne; *W:* Clifford Odets; *C:* William Mellor. *FOX, MVD*

Wild in the Streets 🎬🎬½ 1968 Satire set in the future, where a malcontent rock star becomes president after the voting age is lowered to 14. Adults over 30 are imprisoned and fed a daily dose of LSD. The president gets his comeuppance when challenged by even younger youths. Very groovy, very political in its own way, very funny. 97m/C VHS, Beta, LV. Shelley Winters, Christopher Jones, Hal Holbrook, Richard Pryor, Diane Varsi, Millie Perkins, Ed Begley Sr.; *D:* Barry Shear; *M:* Les Baxter. Nominations: Academy Awards '68: Best Film Editing. *HBO*

The Wild Life 🎬 1984 (R) A recent high school graduate takes on a wild and crazy wrestler as his roommate in a swinging singles apartment complex. The same writer and producer as "Fast Times at Ridgemont High" but lacks that film's commercial success. Just as adolescent, though. 96m/C VHS, Beta, LV, Closed Caption. Christopher Penn, Randy Quaid, Rick Moranis, Hart Bochner, Eric Stoltz, Jenny Wright, Lea Thompson, Sherilyn Fenn, Lee Ving, Ashley St. John, Francesca "Kitten" Natividad; *D:* Art Linson; *W:* Cameron Crowe. *USH*

Wild Man 🎬 1989 A Las Vegas gambling magnate with supernatural powers decides to avenge the murder of his friend and sets out on an adventure to find the killer. Crummy acting in yet another "ex-agent called back for one more mission" yarn. 106m/C VHS, Beta. Ginger Lynn Allen, Michelle (McClellan) Bauer, Don Scribner, Kathleen Middleton; *D:* Fred J. Lincoln. *CEL*

Wild Mustang 🎬🎬½ 1935 Sheriff's son (Gordon) joins some outlaws to help father (Carey) spring a trap. The plan is sidetracked, and Gordon is captured and nearly branded by the baddies. Don't worry, though; everything turns out all right. Good western. 62m/B VHS, Beta. Harry Carey Sr., Del Gordon; *D:* Harry Fraser. *NOS, VCN, DVT*

The Wild One 🎬🎬🎬½ 1954 The original biker flick: two motorcycle gangs descend upon a quiet midwestern town and each other. Brando is the leader of one, struggling against social prejudices and his own gang's lawlessness to find love and a normal life. The classic tribute to 1950s rebelliousness. Based vaguely on a real incident in California. Quaint after nearly 40 years, but still the touchstone for much that has come since, and still a central role in Brando's now-long career. Brando himself believes it failed to explore Motivations for youth gangs and violence, only depicting them. Banked in Britain until 1967. 79m/B VHS, Beta, LV, Closed Caption. Marlon Brando, Lee Marvin, Mary Murphy, Robert Keith, Jerry Paris, Alvy Moore, Jay C. Flippen; *D:* Laslo Benedek; *C:* Hal Mohr. *COL*

Wild Ones on Wheels woof! *Drivers to Hell* 1962 A gang of teenage hot-rod punks meet an ex-con in the Mojave desert who is searching for the half-a-million bucks he buried there years earlier. Before they find out where the money is, they kill him. In an attempt to find the stash, they kidnap the dead con's wife, hoping she'll sing like a bird. Plenty of unintended laughter. 92m/B VHS, Beta. Francine York, Edmund Tontini, Robert Blair; *D:* Rudolph Cusumano. *SNC*

Wild Orchid 🎬 1990 (R) One of the most controversial theatrical releases of 1990. Rourke is a mystery millionaire involved with two beautiful women in lovely Rio de Janeiro. Bisset is strange as an international real estate developer with unusual sexual mores. Very explicit sex scenes, but otherwise mostly boring and unbelievable. Rourke allegedly took his method-acting technique to the limit in the last love scene with Otis. Available in an unrated version as well. From the producers of "9 1/2 Weeks." Followed by an unrelated sequel. 107m/C VHS, Beta, LV, Closed Caption. Mickey Rourke, Jacqueline Bisset, Carre Otis, Assumpta Serna, Bruce Greenwood; *D:* Zalman King; *W:* Zalman King. *COL, FCT*

Wild Orchid 2: Two Shades of Blue woof! 1992 (R) Blue's jazz-musician, heroin addict dad dies after a bad fix and she's sold into prostitution, until she runs away to find her true love and live a "normal" life. Effort from soft-core expert King has nothing to do with the first "Wild Orchid" and is almost laughably bad. Siemaszko is whiny, the plot is unbelievable, and the dialogue is unintentionally funny. Yes, you get sex, lots of it, but rather than passionate, it merely looks staged. Also available in an unrated version at 111 minutes. **CW:** Language, drug content, and strong sensuality. 105m/C VHS, Closed Caption. Nina Siemaszko, Wendy Hughes, Brent Fraser, Robert Davi, Tom Skerritt, Joe Dallesandro, Christopher McDonald, Liane Curtis; **D:** Zalman King; **W:** Zalman King. COL

Wild Orchids 🎬🎬½ 1928 A husband suspects his wife of infidelity while they take a business cruise to Java. One of Garbo's earliest silent films. Garbo is lushly surrounded with great scenery, costumes and sets, making the best of her as she makes the best of a cheery tale. 119m/B VHS, Beta. Greta Garbo, Lewis Stone, Nils Asther; **D:** Sidney Franklin; **C:** William H. Daniels. MGM, FCT

The Wild Pair 🎬½ Hollow Point; Devil's Odds 1987 (R) Two cops track down a cocaine smuggling ring and uncover a private army planning to conquer the United States. Lloyd Bridges is memorable as a rabid right-winger, and the wild pairing of Bubba and Beau inspires head-scatching. Otherwise, what we have here is a typical action pic, complete with car chases. Beau Bridges' inauspicious feature directing debut. 89m/C VHS, Beta, LV. Beau Bridges, Bubba Smith, Lloyd Bridges, Gary Lockwood, Raymond St. Jacques; **D:** Beau Bridges; **M:** John Debney. VTR

Wild Palms 🎬🎬 1993 In 2007 Los Angeles, Harry (Belushi) takes a job at a TV station that offers virtual reality programming to viewers, only this isn't benign technology. Delany is stuck in a thankless role as his wife, Cattrall is his former lover, but Dickinson has the most fun as Harry's power-mad mother-in-law who's also a sadistic co-conspirator of a nasty senator (Loggia). Lesson in weird style over substance really doesn't make much sense, but unlike "Twin Peaks" (to which this TV miniseries was heavily compared) it at least has an ending. Executive producer Stone has a cameo which concerns the JFK conspiracy. Based on the comic strip by Wagner. In two parts. 300m/C VHS, Closed Caption. James Belushi, Robert Loggia, Dana Delany, Kim Cattrall, Angie Dickinson, Ernie Hudson, Bebe Neuwirth, Nick Mancuso, Charles Hallahan, Robert Morse, David Warner, Ben Savage, Bob Gunton, Brad Dourif, Charles Rocket; **Cameos:** Oliver Stone; **D:** Phil Joanou, Kathryn Bigelow, Keith Gordon, Pete Hewitt; **W:** Bruce Wagner; **C:** Phedon Papamichael; **M:** Ryuichi Sakamoto. FCT

Wild Party 🎬🎬½ 1974 (R) It's 1929, a year of much frivolity in Hollywood. Drinking, dancing, maneuvering and almost every sort of romance are the rule of the night at silent film comic Jolly Grimm's sumptuous, star-studded party that climaxes with, among other things, a murder. Well performed but somehow hollow; ambitious Ivory effort unfortunately falls short. Based on Joseph Moncure March's poem, and loosely on the Fatty Arbuckle scandal. 90m/C VHS, Beta. Raquel Welch, James Coco, Perry King, David Dukes, Royal Dano, Tiffany Bolling; **D:** James Ivory; **C:** Walter Lassally.

Wild Pony 🎬 1983 A young boy spurns his new stepfather, preferring to live with his pony instead. Reversal of the evil-stepmother-and-girl-loves-horse theme. 87m/C VHS, Beta. Marilyn Lightstone, Art Hindle, Josh Byrne; **D:** Kevin Sullivan; **M:** Hagood Hardy. FHE, VES, ART

Wild Rapture 🎬 1950 The hunting and dissecting of an elephant and gorilla, a look at a tribe that practices lip-splitting, and other gruesome events abound in this shock-fest. Banned for 18 years. 68m/B VHS, Beta. NOS, HEG

Wild Rebels 🎬 1971 (R) A two-faced member of a ruthless motorcycle gang informs the police of the gang's plans to rob a bank. Lots of bullet-flying action. Dumb, ordinary biker flick; star Pastrano was a former boxing champ in real life. 90m/C VHS, Beta. Steve Alaimo, Willie Pastrano, John Vella, Bobbie Byers; **D:** William Grefe.

Wild Reeds 🎬🎬🎬 Les Roseaux Sauvages 1994 Emotional coming of age tale set in 1962 (at the end of the French war in Algeria) and focusing on three classmates at a French boarding school. Sensitive Francois (Morel) is just coming to the realization that he likes boys, particularly working-class Serge (Rideau) who's attracted to Francois's confidante Maite (Bouchez). The provocateur is Algerian-born Henri (Gorny), a bitter political militant who enjoys his battles with classmates and teachers alike. Politics and youthful passions are forced into crises. French historical/political context may prove a barrier. French with subtitles. 110m/C VHS. **FR** Gael Morel, Stephane Rideau, Elodie Bouchez, Frederic Gorny, Michele Moretti; **D:** Andre Techine; **W:** Gilles Taurand, Olivier Massart, Andre Techine; **C:** Jeanne Lapoirie. Cesar Awards '95: Best Director (Techine), Best Film, Best Writing; Los Angeles Film Critics Association Awards '95: Best Foreign Film; National Society of Film Critics Awards '95: Best Foreign Film. FXL

The Wild Ride 🎬🎬 1960 Nicholson, in an early starring role, portrays a rebellious punk of the Beat generation who hotrods his way into trouble and tragedy. He kidnaps now-straight ex-buddy Bean's squeeze (Carter); kills a few cops; then is killed. Interesting only if you're interested in Nicholson. 59m/B VHS, Beta. Jack Nicholson, Georgianna Carter, Robert Bean; **D:** Harvey Berman. SNC, NOS, VYY

Wild Riders woof! Angels for Kicks 1971 (R) Two ruthless, amoral bikers molest, kidnap, rape, and beat two beautiful, naive young society ladies. Despicable story, with deplorable acting, but the ending, in which a husband slays a biker with a cello, surely is unique. 91m/C VHS, Beta. Alex Rocco, Elizabeth Knowles, Sherry Bain, Arell Blanton; **D:** Richard Kanter.

Wild Rovers 🎬🎬 1971 (PG) An aging cowboy and his younger colleague turn to bank robbing and are pursued by a posse in a wacky comedy-adventure from director Edwards. Uneven script and too much referential baggage (faint shades of "Butch Cassidy") doom this valiant effort, with the two stars hanging right in there all the way. 138m/C VHS, Beta, LV, Letterbox. William Holden, Ryan O'Neal, Karl Malden, Lynn Carlin, Tom Skerritt, Joe Don Baker, Rachel Roberts, Moses Gunn; **D:** Blake Edwards; **W:** Blake Edwards; **M:** Jerry Goldsmith. MGM

Wild Side 🎬🎬 1995 (R) Bank employee Alex (Heche) moonlights as a hooker and gets caught in a federal sting operation. Forced to inform on one of her clients, Bruno (Walken), who's involved in a money-laundering scheme, Alex complicates matters by falling in love with Bruno's mistress, Victoria (Chen). The unrated version is 96 minutes. Original director Cammell (who retained his screenwriter's credit) removed his name from the film after disagreeing with cuts made by the production company. **CW:** Strong sexuality, language, and violence, including a rape. 90m/C VHS, Closed Caption. Anne Heche, Christopher Walken, Joan Chen, Steven Bauer; **D:** Franklyn Brauner; **W:** Donald Cammell, China Cammell. EVE

Wild Strawberries 🎬🎬🎬🎬 Smultron-Stallet 1957 Bergman's landmark film of fantasy, dreams and nightmares. An aging professor, on the road to accept an award, must come to terms with his anxieties and guilt. Brilliant performance by Sjostrom, Sweden's first film director and star. Excellent use of flashbacks and film editing. An intellectual and emotional masterpiece. In Swedish with English subtitles. 90m/B VHS, Beta, LV, 8mm. **SW** Victor Sjostrom, Bibi Andersson, Max von Sydow, Ingrid Thulin, Gunnar Bjornstrand, Folke Sundquist, Bjorn Bjelvenstam; **D:** Ingmar Bergman; **W:** Ingmar Bergman. Golden Globe Awards '60: Best Foreign Film; Nomina-

tions: Academy Awards '59: Best Story & Screenplay. VYY, HMV, FOX

Wild Style 🎬🎬 1983 Zoro, a mild-mannered Bronx teenager, spends his evenings spray-painting subway cars. Intended as a depiction of urban street life, including graffiti, break-dancing and rap music. Mildly interesting social comment, but unconvincing as cinema. Too "realistic," with too little vision. 82m/C VHS, Beta. Lee George Quinones, Fredrick Braithwaite, Dondi White; **D:** Charlie Ahearn; **M:** Fred Brathwaite. FCT

Wild Thing 🎬½ 1987 (PG-13) A modern variation on the Wild Child/Tarzan myth, as a feral kid stalks a crime-ridden ghetto. Sayles, a usually imaginative writer and director, really takes a dive here. And of course, the Troggs' overplayed title hit is abused as the theme. 92m/C VHS, Beta, LV. Kathleen Quinlan, Rob Knepper, Robert Davi, Betty Buckley, Maury Chaykin; **D:** Max Reid, Ken Cameron; **W:** John Sayles; **M:** George S. Clinton, Guy Moon. NO

Wild Things 🎬🎬 1998 (R) Titillating pulp friction can't decide between modern noir and swampy spoof. Miami guidance counselor and high school heartthrob fodder Sam Lombardo (Dillon) lectures on sex crimes and gets accused of rape by two school girls: snotty rich Kelly (Richards) and trailer trash Suzie (Campbell). The seemingly upright investigator (Bacon) tries to figure out who's telling the truth. Murray pops up doing his best Bill Murray, but his hilarious presence doesn't play next to the oh-so-serious Dillon and gang. Even more out of place is Wagner's wooden cameo as Kelly's father. Speaking of wooden, the normally fine Russell is reduced to similar stereotype as Kelly's vampy, conniving mother. Endless exercise in audience manipulation has plot twists and turns relentlessly continue through the credits for no apparent reason. **CW:** Strong sexuality, nudity, language and some violence. 108m/C VHS. Matt Dillon, Neve Campbell, Kevin Bacon, Denise Richards, Theresa Russell, Daphne Rubin-Vega, Bill Murray, Robert Wagner, Carrie Snodgress, Jeffery Perry, Marc Macaulay; **D:** John McNaughton; **W:** Steven Peters; **C:** Jeffrey L. Kimball; **M:** George S. Clinton. NYR

Wild Times 🎬🎬 1979 Too long but pleasant rendition of the life of High Candill, early Wild West showman. Based on the novel by Brian Garfield. Made for TV, originally in two parts. 200m/C VHS, Beta. Sam Elliott, Trish Stewart, Ben Johnson, Dennis Hopper, Pat Hingle; **D:** Richard Compton.

Wild Weed 🎬 The Devil's Weed; She Shoulda Said No; Marijuana the Devil's Weed 1949 Funny smelling cigarettes ruin the lives of all who inhale. Viewers' advice: just say no. Leed's actual drug bust with Robert Mitchum got her the lead. 70m/B VHS. Lila Leeds, Alan Baxter, Lyle Talbot, Jack Elam, David Gorcey; **D:** Sam Newfield. SNC, AOV, TPV

Wild West 🎬🎬 Prairie Outlaws 1946 The hero and loyal companions (with names like Skinny, Stormy, and Soapy) tackle desperadoes trying to stop telegraph line construction. More mild than wild, it was later trimmed and released under its alternate title, but here you're getting the original. 73m/C VHS. Eddie Dean, Roscoe Ates, Lash LaRue, Robert "Buzzy" Henry, Sarah Padden, Louise Currie, Warner Richmond, Chief Yowlachie, Bud Osborne; **D:** Robert Emmett Tansey. NOS, HEG

Wild West 1987 A compilation of scenes from dozens of western films. 90m/C VHS, Beta. John Wayne, Clint Eastwood, Steve McQueen, Charles Bronson. NO

Wild West 🎬🎬 1993 Three Pakistani brothers, living in London, decide to form an American-style country and western band they call the Honky Tonk Cowboys and dream of making it big in Nashville. A little romance, lots of energy, but too many gags leave the film unfocused. 83m/C VHS. **GB** Naveen Andrews, Sarita Choudhury, Ronny Jhutti, Ravi Kapoor; **D:** David Attwood; **W:** Harwant Bains. THV

Wild Wheels woof! 1975 (PG) A group of dune-buggy enthusiasts seek revenge against a gang of motorcyclists who have ravaged a small California beach town. 81m/C VHS, Beta. Casey Kasem, Dovie Beams, Terry Stafford, Robert Dix. *GEM*

Wild, Wild Planet 🎬½ 1965 Alien beings from a distant planet are miniaturizing Earth's leaders in a bid to destroy our planet, and a dubbed, wooden hero comes to the rescue. A rarely seen Italian SF entry, great fun for genre fans. A must for "robot girls in skin tight leather outfits" completists. 93m/C VHS, Beta. *IT* Tony Russell, Lisa Gastoni, Massimo Serato, Franco Nero; *D:* Anthony (Antonio Margheriti) Dawson. *SMW*

Wild, Wild West Revisited 🎬🎬½ 1979 A feature-length reprise of the tongue-in-cheek western series. Irreverent and fun, in the spirit of its admirable predecessor-though it's probably just as well the proposed new series didn't see fruition. Made for television. 95m/C VHS, Beta. Robert Conrad, Ross Martin, Harry (Henry) Morgan, Rene Auberjonois; *D:* Burt Kennedy. *FOX*

Wild, Wild World of Jayne Mansfield 🎬🎬 1968 The life and times of Mansfield are explored in this unique documentary, which was unfinished at the time of her death. Jayne takes the viewer on a worldwide examination of sexual mores, from prostitution, nudist colonies, and the racy strip clubs of Europe, to the transvestite and topless bars of America. Perverse (but did you expect otherwise?), footage of her fatal car crash was included. 89m/C VHS, Beta. Jayne Mansfield. *VDM, DVT, TPV*

Wild Women 🎬 1953 Extremely hilarious schlocker about a safari of white men captured by a savage tribe of jungle women. Total camp. ?m/C VHS. Lewis Wilson, Frances Dubay, Dana Wilson. *SNC, HEG*

Wild Women 🎬½ 1970 Five female convicts are released during the Texas/Mexico dispute to help smuggle arms to American forces. Innocuous western, original in a made-for-TV kind of way. 90m/C VHS, Beta. Hugh O'Brian, Anne Francis, Marilyn Maxwell, Marie Windsor; *D:* Don Taylor. *FOX*

Wild Women of Wongo 🎬½ 1959 The denizens of a primitive isle, essentially beautiful women and ugly men, meet the natives of a neighboring island, handsome men and ugly women. Not quite bad enough to be true camp fun, but stupidly silly in a low-budget way. 73m/C VHS, Beta. Pat Crowley, Ed Fury, Adrienne Bourbeau, Jean Hawkshaw, Johnny Walsh; *D:* James L. Wolcott. *DVT, HEG*

The Wild World of Batwoman 🎬🎬 *She Was a Hippy Vampire* 1966 A campy cult film in which Batwoman and a bevy of Bat Girls are pitted against an evil doctor in order to find the prototype of an atomic hearing aid/nuclear bomb. 70m/C VHS, Beta. Katherine Victor, George Andre, Steve Brodie, Lloyd Nelson; *D:* Jerry Warren. *RHI, SNC, DVT*

Wild Zone 🎬 1989 (R) An American ex-soldier combats mercenaries in Africa in order to rescue his kidnapped father. 100m/C VHS, Beta, LV. Edward Albert, Philip Brown, Carla Herd; *D:* Percival Rubens. *COL*

Wildcard 🎬½ 1992 (PG-13) When a veteran pilot is killed in a helicopter crash, a friend suspects foul play. He calls in Preacher, a special forces veteran, to investigate and what he discovers is murder, greed, and corruption. 86m/C VHS, LV. Powers Boothe, Cindy Pickett, Rene Auberjonois, Terry O'Quinn, M. Emmet Walsh, John Lacy; *D:* Mel Damski; *W:* Scobie Richardson. *USH*

Wildcat 🎬🎬 1942 Crabbe, famous as the serials' Flash Gordon, is a villain in this petrochemical adventure. The hero overextends his credit when he buys an oil well and must produce a gusher or else. 73m/B VHS. Richard Arlen, Arline Judge, Buster Crabbe, William Frawley, Arthur Hunnicutt, Elisha Cook Jr., Billy Benedict; *D:* Frank McDonald. *NOS*

Wildcats 🎬🎬 1986 (R) A naive female physed teacher (Hawn) is saddled with the job of coach for a completely undisciplined, inner city, high school football team. Formulaic, connect-the-dots comedy; moderately funny, and of course Hawn triumphs in adversity, but at nearly two hours a very long sitcom episode. 106m/C VHS, Beta, LV, Closed Caption. Goldie Hawn, James Keach, Swoosie Kurtz, Bruce McGill, M. Emmet Walsh, Woody Harrelson, Wesley Snipes, Tab Thacker; *D:* Michael Ritchie; *M:* James Newton Howard. *WAR*

Wilde 🎬🎬 1997 (R) The witty Wilde is making something of a resurgence in film, plays, and books. The Irish author/playwright (portrayed by look-alike Fry) is enjoying the London limelight and his family life with wife Constance (Ehle) and their two sons, while privately acknowledging his attraction to men. Unfortunately, this leads Oscar into a mad passion for sulky, neurotic pretty boy Bosie Douglas (Law), whose aristocratic father, the Marquess of Queensbury (Wilkinson), wants moral revenge on Wilde. His affair with Bosie leads to a celebrated trial for Oscar and a tragic outcome. Adapted from the biography by Richard Ellman. *CW:* Strong sexuality and language. 115m/C VHS. *GB* Stephen Fry, Jude Law, Vanessa Redgrave, Jennifer Ehle, Michael Sheen, Zoe Wanamaker, Tom Wilkinson, Gemma Jones, Judy Parfitt; *D:* Brian Gilbert; *C:* Martin Fuhrer; *M:* Debbie Wiseman. Nominations: British Academy Awards '97: Best Supporting Actress (Ehle), Best Supporting Actress (Wanamaker). *NYR*

Wilder Napalm 🎬½ 1993 (PG-13) Lame comedy about two at-odds brothers, the woman they both love, and their dangerous pyrokinetic abilities. Wilder (Howard) and Wallace (Quaid) Foudroyant have been feuding for years—and not just over the fact that Wallace is in love with Wilder's wife Vida (Winger). Wallace wants to use their family "gift" to become rich and famous but Wilder doesn't want them to exploit their fiery powers. They finally decide on an incendiary showdown to settle the score once and for all. Good actors lost in witless characters and a incoherent plot. 109m/C VHS, LV, Letterbox, Closed Caption. Dennis Quaid, Arliss Howard, Debra Winger, M. Emmet Walsh, Jim Varney, Mimi Lieber, Marvin J. McIntyre; *D:* Glenn Gordon Caron; *W:* Vince Gilligan; *M:* Michael Kamen. *COL*

Wildest Dreams 🎬½ *Bikini Genie* 1990 (R) Released from its bottle by a lovely nebbish, a genie puts a love spell on one beautiful girl after another in order to find him the right one, resulting in a bevy of women clamoring for our hero's attention. 84m/C VHS, Beta, LV. James Davies, Heidi Paine, Deborah Blaisdell, Ruth Collins, Jane Hamilton, Jill Johnson; *D:* Chuck Vincent. *ART, VES*

Wildfire 🎬½ 1945 Two horse traders come to the aid of ranchers beset by horse thieves. Early color outing for Steele. Harmless, ordinary oater. 60m/C VHS, Beta, LV. Bob Steele, Sterling Holloway, John Miljan, William Farnum, Eddie Dean, Sarah Padden, Frank Ellis; *D:* Robert Emmett Tansey. *NOS, VDM, HEG*

Wildfire 🎬🎬 1988 (PG) As teenagers, Frank and Kay run away to get married but Frank is sent to prison for robbing a bank and Kay winds up making a new life for herself. Released from prison after eight years, Frank discovers Kay is married with two children and doesn't want anything further to do with him. But when Frank violates his parole, Kay discovers she can't leave him again and the two go on the run together. 98m/C VHS, LV, Closed Caption. Steven Bauer, Linda Fiorentino, Will Patton, Marshall Bell; *D:* Zalman King; *W:* Zalman King; *C:* Bill Butler; *M:* Maurice Jarre. *USH*

Wildflower 🎬🎬🎬 1991 Set in the Depression-era South, Alice is a 17 year-old partially deaf girl who also suffers from epilepsy. Her stepfather believes she's possessed and confines her to a shed. Growing up ignorant and abused Alice is befriended by a neighboring brother and sister who decide to rescue her. A three-hankie family picture with moving performances and inspirational themes. Based on the novel "Alice" by Sara

Flanigan. Made for cable television. 94m/C VHS, Closed Caption. Patricia Arquette, Beau Bridges, Susan Blakely, William McNamara, Reese Witherspoon, Collin Wilcox Paxton; *D:* Diane Keaton. *WOV*

Wilding 🎬½ 1990 A pair of cops are on the trail of a gang of kids who go "wilding," which involves sprees of killing, raping and looting. Exploitive fare based on horrible, recent events in New York. The filmmakers skirt controversy by making the criminals rich suburban kids. 92m/C VHS, Beta. Wings Hauser, Joey Travolta, Karen Russell, Steven Cooke; *D:* Eric Louzil.

Wildrose 🎬🎬🎬 1985 Eichhorn is memorable as a recent divorcee who must assert herself among her otherwise all-male co-workers in a Minnesota strip mine. She finds a new love, and tries to put her life back together. Filmed on location. 96m/C VHS, Beta. Lisa Eichhorn, Tom Bower, James Cada; *D:* John Hanson; *W:* John Hanson, Eugene Corr. *ART*

Will: G. Gordon Liddy 🎬🎬½ 1982 The life of the Watergate conspirator, based on his autobiography. Made for TV. Producer/star Conrad reportedly objected strongly to cuts from the original three-hour length, apparently with cause: the first half is superficial pap. The portrayal of Liddy's time in prison, though, is fascinating, and Conrad is excellent. 100m/C VHS. Robert Conrad, Kathy Cannon, Gary Bayer, Peter Ratray, James Rebhorn, Red West, Maurice Woods, Danny Lloyd; *D:* Robert Liebmann. *ART*

Will Penny 🎬🎬🎬½ 1967 Just back from a cattle drive, a range-wandering loner looks for work in the wrong place and offends a family of outlaws who come after him. His escape from them leads to another kind of trap—one set by a love-hungry woman (Hackett, in a strong performance). Heston considers this film his personal best, and he's probably right. Superbly directed western, with excellent cinematography and professional, realistic portrayals, flopped in theatres, moviegoers preferring simultaneous Heston outing "Planet of the Apes." 109m/C VHS, Beta, LV, Closed Caption. Charlton Heston, Joan Hackett, Donald Pleasence, Lee Majors, Bruce Dern, Anthony Zerbe, Ben Johnson, Clifton James; *D:* Tom Gries; *C:* Lucien Ballard; *M:* Elmer Bernstein. *PAR*

Will Success Spoil Rock Hunter? 🎬🎬½ 1957 Dated advertising satire finds ad man Hunter (Randall) hoping to get the key to the executive washroom but he may instead find himself on the unemployment line unless he can convince the profitable Stay-Put lipstick account not to change agencies. One day Rock see movie star Rita Marlowe (Mansfield), and her kissable lips, on TV and tries to convince her to endorse the product but she'll only agree if he'll pose as her new boyfriend to make ex-beau Bobo (Mansfield's real-life hubby Hargitay) jealous. Naturally, the lipstick ads take off bigtime but success does indeed spoil Rock (at least temporarily). Very slightly based on the play by George Axelrod. 94m/C VHS. Tony Randall, Jayne Mansfield, Betsy Drake, Mickey Hargitay, John Williams, Henry Jones, Joan Blondell; *Cameos:* Groucho Marx; *D:* Frank Tashlin; *W:* Frank Tashlin; *C:* Joe MacDonald; *M:* Cyril Mockridge. *FXV*

Willa 🎬🎬 1979 Raffin, a hash-joint waitress with two kids and one in the pipeline, is deserted by her husband and determines to get ahead by becoming a trucker. Okay made-for-TV drama. 95m/C VHS, Beta. Cloris Leachman, Deborah Raffin, Clu Gulager, John Amos, Diane Ladd; *D:* Claudio Guzman, Joan Darling; *M:* John Barry.

Willard 🎬🎬 1971 (PG) Willard is a lonely, psychotic youngster who trains a group of rats, his only friends, to attack his enemies. Not as disgusting as it might have been (rated PG), but pretty weird and not redeemed by any sense of style or humor. Popular at the boxoffice; followed by inferior "Ben." Based on by Stephen Gilbert's novel "Ratman's Notebooks." 95m/C VHS, Beta, LV.

Bruce Davison, Ernest Borgnine, Elsa Lanchester, Sondra Locke, Michael Dante, J. Pat O'Malley; **D:** Daniel Mann; **W:** Gilbert Ralston; **C:** Robert B. Hauser; **M:** Alex North. *PAR*

William Faulkner's Old Man 🐾🐾½
Old Man 1997 **(PG)** TV adaptation of a part of Faulkner's 1939 novel "The Wild Palms" that is set in the '20s. The "Old Man" in question is the mighty Mississippi, which has flooded leaving a pregnant Tripplehorn, abandoned by her husband, stranded and about to give birth. But prison-farm inmate Howard is sent by the warden to row to her rescue, becoming a surrogate father when the baby is born, and traveling the river to New Orleans to get mother and child to safety. 98m/C VHS. Jeanne Tripplehorn, Arliss Howard, Leo Burmester; **D:** John Kent Harrison; **W:** Horton Foote. *HMK*

William Shakespeare's Romeo and Juliet 🐾🐾🐾
Romeo and Juliet 1996 **(PG-13)** Bright, loud update of Shakespeare's tragedy of feuding families and first love. Contemporary fantasy setting, Verona Beach, and attitude (the Montagues and the Capulets are business rivals), with the 16th-century Elizabethan language intact, although Luhrmann's said to have cut half the text. Hot-blooded Romeo (DiCaprio) takes one look at angelic Juliet (Danes) and falls immediately in love/lust. This doesn't please Juliet's family, including quick-tempered cousin Tybalt (Leguizamo) who goes after Romeo with far-reaching consequences. DiCaprio's remarkable and the young duo look wonderful together. A big hit with the teens. Filmed in Mexico City.**CW:** Scenes of contemporary violence and some sensuality. 120m/C VHS, LV, **Closed Caption.** Leonardo DiCaprio, Claire Danes, John Leguizamo, Paul Sorvino, Brian Dennehy, Diane Venora, Pete Postlethwaite, Paul Rudd, Harold Perrineau Jr., Jesse Bradford, Miriam Margolyes, Vondie Curtis-Hall, Christina Pickles, M. Emmet Walsh; **D:** Baz Luhrmann; **W:** Baz Luhrmann, Craig Pearce; **C:** Donald McAlpine; **M:** Nellee Hooper. British Academy Awards '97: Best Adapted Screenplay, Best Art Direction/Set Decoration, Best Director (Luhrmann), Best Score; MTV Movie Awards '97: Best Female Performance (Danes); Nominations: Academy Awards '96: Best Art Direction/Set Decoration; British Academy Awards '97: Best Cinematography, Best Film Editing, Best Sound; MTV Movie Awards '97: Best Film, Best Male Performance (DiCaprio), Best On-Screen Duo (Leonardo DiCaprio/Clare Danes), Best Song ("#1 Crush"), Best Kiss (Leonardo DiCaprio/Claire Danes). *FXV*

Willie & Phil 🐾🐾½
1980 **(R)** At the start of the '70s, two buddies (Ontkean and Sharkey) fall for the same girl (Kidder). They become a threesome and are entangled in each other's lives for the rest of the decade. Insightful comedy-drama. 111m/C VHS, LV. Michael Ontkean, Margot Kidder, Ray Sharkey, Jan Miner, Julie Bovasso, Natalie Wood, Laurence "Larry" Fishburne, Louis Guss, Kaki Hunter, Kristine DeBell; **D:** Paul Mazursky; **W:** Paul Mazursky; **C:** Sven Nykvist; **M:** Claude Bolling. *FOX*

The Willies 🐾🐾
1990 **(PG-13)** Three youngsters gross each other out with juvenile tales of horror and scariness while camping out in the backyard. Pointless but not without a few yuks (in both senses of the term). 120m/C VHS, LV. James Karen, Sean Astin, Kathleen Freeman, Jeremy Miller; **D:** Brian Peck.

Willow 🐾🐾½
1988 **(PG)** Blockbuster fantasy epic combines the story of Moses with "Snow White," dwarves and all. Willow is the little Nelwyn who finds the lost baby Daikini and is assigned the task of returning her safely to her people. Willow discovers that the girl is actually a sacred infant who is destined to overthrow the evil queen Bavmorda and rule the land. As you might expect from executive producer George Lucas, there is much action and plenty of clever, high-quality special effects. But the "Star Wars"-esque story (by Lucas) is strangely predictable, and a bit too action-packed. Not really for children. 118m/C VHS, Beta, LV, 8mm, **Closed Caption.** Warwick Davis, Val Kilmer, Jean Marsh, Joanne Whalley, Billy Barty, Pat Roach, Ruth Greenfield, Patricia Hayes, Gavan O'Herlihy, Kevin Pollak; **D:** Ron Howard; **W:** Bob Dolman; **M:** James Horner. *COL*

Willy Wonka & the Chocolate Factory 🐾🐾🐾½
1971 **(G)** When the last of five coveted "golden tickets" falls into the hands of sweet but very poor Charlie, he and his Grandpa Joe get a tour of the most wonderfully strange chocolate factory in the world. The owner is the most curious hermit ever to hit the big screen. He leads the five young "winners" on a thrilling and often dangerous tour of his fabulous factory. Adapted from Roald Dahl's "Charlie and the Chocolate Factory." Without a doubt one of the best "kid's" movies ever made; a family classic worth watching again and again. ♫Willy Wonka, the Candy Man; Cheer Up, Charlie; I've Got a Golden Ticket; Oompa-Loompa-Doompa-Dee-Doo; Pure Imagination. 100m/C VHS, Beta, LV, **Closed Caption.** Gene Wilder, Jack Albertson, Denise Nickerson, Peter Ostrum, Roy Kinnear, Aubrey Woods, Michael Bollner, Ursula Reit, Leonard Stone, Dodo Denney; **D:** Mel Stuart; **M:** Leslie Bricusse. Nominations: Academy Awards '71: Original Song Score and/or Adaptation. *WAR, HMV*

Wilma 🐾🐾
1977 Based on the true story of Wilma Rudolph, a young black woman who overcame childhood illness to win three gold medals at the 1960 Olympics. Plodding made-for-TV biography suffers from sub-par script and acting. 100m/C VHS, Beta. Joe Seneca, Cicely Tyson, Shirley Jo Finney; **D:** Bud Greenspan; **M:** Irwin Bazelon. *COL, FCT*

Wilson 🐾🐾🐾
1944 Biography of Woodrow Wilson from his days as the head of Princeton University, to the governorship of New York, and as U.S. President during WWI. After the war, Wilson conceives of the League of Nations but is unable to sell it to a U.S. still bent on isolationism. This lavish film won critical plaudits but was a major money-loser. 154m/C VHS. Alexander Knox, Charles Coburn, Geraldine Fitzgerald, Thomas Mitchell, Ruth Nelson, Cedric Hardwicke, Vincent Price, William Eythe, Mary Anderson, Sidney Blackmer, Stanley Ridges, Eddie Foy Jr., Charles Halton; **D:** Henry King; **W:** Lamar Trotti; **C:** Leon Shamroy; **M:** Alfred Newman. Academy Awards '44: Best Color Cinematography, Best Film Editing, Best Interior Decoration, Best Original Screenplay, Best Sound; Golden Globe Awards '45: Best Actor—Drama (Knox); Nominations: Academy Awards '44: Best Actor (Knox), Best Director (King), Best Picture, Best Original Dramatic/Comedy Score. *MOV, BTV*

Wimps 🐾
1987 **(R)** A collegiate wimp is subjected to a brutal fraternity initiation, but eventually gets the girl. Cheap ripoff of Cyrano de Bergerac, turned into a teen sex flick. 94m/C VHS, Beta. Louie Bonanno, Jim Abele, Deborah Blaisdell; **D:** Chuck Vincent. *ART*

Win, Place, or Steal 🐾½
The Big Payoff; Three For the Money; Just Another Day at the Races 1972 **(PG)** Lame comedy set at the racetrack about three grown men and their adolescent schemes to win big. Better you should scratch. 88m/C VHS, Beta. McLean Stevenson, Alex Karras, Dean Stockwell; **D:** Richard Bailey. *ART, VES*

Winchester '73 🐾🐾🐾½
1950 Superb acting and photography characterize this classic, landmark western. Simple plot—cowboy Stewart pursues his stolen state-of-the-art rifle as it changes hands—speeds along and carries the viewer with it, ending with an engrossing and unforgettable shoot-out. Almost singlehandedly breathed new life into the whole genre. Laser videodisc version contains a special narration track provided by Stewart. Mann's and Stewart's first teaming. 82m/C VHS, Beta, LV. James Stewart, Shelley Winters, Stephen McNally, Dan Duryea, Millard Mitchell, John McIntire, Will Geer, Jay C. Flippen, Rock Hudson, Tony Curtis, Charles Drake; **D:** Anthony Mann; **C:** William H. Daniels. *USH*

The Wind 🐾🐾🐾🐾
1928 One of the last great silents still stands as a magnificent entertainment. Gish, in possibly her best role, is an innocent Easterner who finds herself married to a rough cowpoke and raped by a married man in a bleak frontier town. Director Sjostrom has a splendid feel for landscape, and the drama—climaxing

with a tumultuous desert storm—is intense yet fully believable. Based on the novel by Dorothy Scarborough. 74m/B VHS, Beta. Lillian Gish, Lars Hanson, Montagu Love, Dorothy Cumming, Edward Earle, William Orlamond; **D:** Victor Sjostrom; **W:** Frances Marion. National Film Registry '93. *MGM*

The Wind 🐾
1987 Foster is terrorized by Hauser while attempting to write her next thriller in Greece. Let's hope her book is more exciting than this movie. Shot on location in Greece. 92m/C VHS, Beta. Meg Foster, Wings Hauser, Steve Railsback, David McCallum, Robert Morley; **D:** Nico Mastorakis. *ART*

Wind 🐾🐾½
1992 **(PG-13)** Sailor Will Parker (Modine) chooses the opportunity to be on the America's Cup team over girlfriend Grey and then has the dubious honor of making a technical error that causes their loss. Undaunted, he locates Grey and her new engineer boyfriend (Skarsgard) and convinces them to design the ultimate boat for the next set of races. ESPN carried extensive coverage of the America's Cup races for the first time in the summer of '92 and viewers discovered that a little goes a long way. The same holds true for "Wind" which has stunning race footage, but little else. The script lacks substance and was written as filming progressed, and it shows.**CW:** Some sensuality. 123m/C VHS, LV, 8mm, Letterbox, **Closed Caption.** Matthew Modine, Jennifer Grey, Cliff Robertson, Jack Thompson, Stellan Skarsgard, Rebecca Miller, Ned Vaughn; **D:** Carroll Ballard; **W:** Rudy Wurlitzer, Mac Gudgeon; **C:** John Toll; **M:** Basil Poledouris. *COL*

The Wind and the Lion 🐾🐾🐾
1975 **(PG)** In turn-of-the-century Morocco, a sheik (Connery) kidnaps a feisty American woman (Bergen) and her children and holds her as a political hostage. President Teddy Roosevelt (Keith) sends in the Marines to free the captives, who are eventually released by their captor. Directed with venue and style by Milius. Highly entertaining, if heavily fictionalized. Based very loosely on a historical incident. 120m/C VHS, Beta, LV, Letterbox. Sean Connery, Candice Bergen, Brian Keith, John Huston, Geoffrey Lewis; **D:** John Milius; **W:** John Milius; **C:** Billy Williams; **M:** Jerry Goldsmith. Nominations: Academy Awards '75: Best Sound, Best Original Score. *MGM*

The Wind in the Willows 🐾🐾
1996 **(PG)** Kenneth Grahame's 1908 children's book gets the Monty Python treatment. Set in Edwardian England, but with a definitely modern slant, Jones' adaptation removes much of the gentle whimsy and replaces it with Pythonesque skits. Mole (Coogan) wakes up one day to find his home being bulldozed by the industrialist weasels who have purchased the property from the motorcar-infatuated Mr. Toad (Jones). Toad keeps selling more land to buy more cars as the weasels take over the area and Toad is sent to jail for reckless driving. Mole, along with friends Rat (Idle) and Badger (Williamson) must help him escape and reclaim his land. Grahame's early 20th century fable railing against modern industrialism's encroachment on the countryside becomes a satire on 90's consumerism and corporate greed. Mighty heady stuff for a kid's movie. 88m/C VHS. *GB* Terry Jones, Steve Coogan, Eric Idle, Anthony Sher, Nicol Williamson, John Cleese, Stephen Fry, Bernard Hill, Michael Palin, Nigel Planer, Julia Sawalha, Victoria Wood, Richard James; **D:** Terry Jones; **W:** Terry Jones; **C:** David Tattersall; **M:** John Du Prez, Terry Jones. *NYR*

A Wind Named Amnesia 1993
A strange amnesia wind sweeps away all of mankind's knowledge and human civilization vanishes. Then a mysterious young man is miraculously re-educated and searches for those who destroyed man's memories. In Japanese with English subtitles. 80m/C VHS. *JP* **D:** Kazuo Yamazaki; **W:** Hideyuki Kikuchi. *CPM*

The Wind That Walks 1985
Two girls trek into the New Jersey wilds after an unknown animal called by the Indians "the wind that walks." 30m/C Beta. *NJN*

Windjammer ⰔⰔ **1937** Western star O'Brien took a break from the lone prairie to make this seafaring rescue drama. He is a deputy state's attorney who signs up for a yacht race in order to serve a subpoena. Bad guys arrive on the scene, and the initially moody yacht denizens rely on our trusty hero to save them. Decent adventure. **75m/B VHS.** George O'Brien, Constance Worth; **D:** Sam Newfield. *NOS, DVT, HEG*

Windmills of the Gods ⰔⰔ½ *Sidney Sheldon's Windmills of the Gods* **1988** Glamor, romance, intrigue, and politics all mixed together in eastern Europe. Smith is named ambassador to Romania, finds the suave Wagner in residence, and becomes the target of assassins. Based on the novel by Sidney Sheldon. Made for television. **95m/C VHS.** Jaclyn Smith, Robert Wagner, Franco Nero, Christopher Cazenove, David Ackroyd, Jean-Pierre Aumont, Ruby Dee, Jeffrey DeMunn, Michael Moriarty, Ian McKellen, Susan Tyrrell; **D:** Lee Philips; **W:** John Gay; **M:** Perry Botkin. *ART*

Windom's Way ⰔⰔⰔ **1957** Finch, in a strong role in this intriguing political drama, is an idealistic doctor in a remote village in Malaysia. He juggles a failing marriage and a budding romance, then finds himself caught in a local labor dispute. He works for a peaceful solution, but is captured by an insurgent army. Disillusioned, he plans to leave the country, but his wife persuades him to stay and tend the wounded. Based on a novel by James Ramsey Ullman. **90m/B VHS, Beta.** *GB* Peter Finch, Mary Ure; **D:** Ronald Neame. *NO*

The Window ⰔⰔⰔ½ **1949** A little boy (Disney star Driscoll, intriguingly cast by director, Tetzlaff) has a reputation for telling lies, so no one believes him when he says he witnessed a murder...except the killers. Almost unbearably tense, claustrophobic thriller about the helplessness of childhood. Tetzlaff clearly learned more than a thing or two from the master, Hitchcock, for whom he photographed "Notorious." Based on the novella "The Boy Who Cried Murder" by Cornell Woolrich. Driscoll was awarded a special miniature Oscar as Outstanding Juvenile for his performance. **73m/B VHS, Beta, LV.** Bobby Driscoll, Barbara Hale, Arthur Kennedy, Ruth Roman; **D:** Ted Tetzlaff. Nominations: Academy Awards '49: Best Film Editing.

Window Shopping ⰔⰔ½ **1986** Multiple, confusing romances occur at the "Toison d' Or" shopping mall in Paris. A modern, French homage to the classic Hollywood musical. In French with English subtitles. **96m/C VHS.** *FR* Delphine Seyrig, Charles Denner, Fanny Cottencon, Miriam Boyer, Lio, Pascale Salkin, Jean-Francois Balmer; **D:** Chantal Akerman; **W:** Chantal Akerman. *WAC, FCT*

Window to Paris ⰔⰔ **1995 (PG-13)** East and West meet unexpectedly when a poor music teacher (Dontsov) rents a room in St. Petersburg with a secret window that opens onto a Paris rooftop. Loony adventures ensue as Dontsov and his friends escape their dreary existence to exploit the bounties of Western capitalism in this sharp satire of Russian social ills. Relentless humor based on cross-cultural stereotypes wears thin (the Russians are cantankerous drunks; the Parisians, self-important snobs), but it keeps a sunny cast upon what could have been a scathing commentary. Russian and French with subtitles. **CW:** Contains momentary nudity. **92m/C VHS, LV.** *RU* FR Serguej Dontsov, Agnes Soral, Viktor Michailov, Nina Oussatova; **D:** Yuri Mamin; **W:** Arkadi Tigai, Yuri Mamin; **M:** Aleksei Zalivalov, Yuri Mamin. *COL*

Windows Ⱄ **1980 (R)** A lonely lesbian (Ashley) becomes obsessed with her quiet neighbor (Shire) and concocts a plot to get close to her. Director Willis is known for his unbeatable cinematography, most notably for Woody Allen in "Manhattan." His debut in the chair is a miserable, offensive flop. **93m/C VHS.** Talia Shire, Joe Cortese, Elizabeth Ashley, Kay Medford, Linda Gillin; **D:** Gordon Willis; **C:** Gordon Willis; **M:** Ennio Morricone. *NO*

Windrider Ⱄ½ **1986** Simple love story made in Australia. A wind surfer and a rock star become lovers. Self-indulgent overwrought garbage with rare moments of promise. **83m/C VHS.** *AU* Tom Burlinson, Nicole Kidman, Charles Tingwell, Jill Perryman, Simon Chilvers; **D:** Vincent Monton. *MGM*

Windrunner ⰔⰔ½ **1994 (PG)** Angry at his football-star dad and rejected by the local high school team, Greg Cima (Wiles) finds an unlikely ally in the spirit of Native American Olympic hero Jim Thorpe (Means). Seems Thorpe needs some aid to return to the spirit world and, by coaching Cima, he'll also get the help he needs. Believable performances and an exploration of the power of Native American mysticism help the unlikely premise along. **110m/C VHS.** Russell Means, Jason Wiles, Amanda Peterson, Margot Kidder, Jake Busey, Max Casella, Bruce Weitz; **D:** William Clark; **W:** Mitch Davis; **M:** Arthur Kempel. *AVE*

The Winds of Jarrah Ⱄ½ **1983** English woman runs from broken heart to Australia to become nanny for misogynist, and Harlequin code prevails. Based on a Harlequin romance novel. **78m/C VHS, Beta.** *AU* Terence Donovan, Susan Lyons; **D:** Mark Egerton; **M:** Bruce Smeaton. *NO*

The Winds of Kitty Hawk ⰔⰔ **1978** Visually interesting but talky account of the Wright brothers attempt to beat their rival Glenn Curtiss and his backer, phone man Alexander Graham Bell. Rule of thumb: Fast-forward through the parts when they are on the ground, or see Stacy Keach's public-TV version instead. **96m/C VHS, Beta.** Michael Moriarty, David Huffman, Kathryn Walker, Eugene Roche, John Randolph, Scott Hylands; **D:** E.W. Swackhamer; **M:** Charles Bernstein.

Winds of the Wasteland ⰔⰔ½ **1936** Would-be Pony Express contractors, Wayne and Chandler, race rivals to land government work. Competent western that put Wayne on the Hollywood map. **54m/B VHS.** John Wayne, Phyllis Fraser, Lane Chandler, Yakima Canutt; **D:** Mack V. Wright. *REP, NOS, VCN*

The Winds of War ⰔⰔ **1983** On seven tapes, the excruciatingly long and dull television mini-series based on Herman Wouk's bestseller about WWII. The book was much better; Mitchum appears to be fighting sleep unsuccessfully for much of the show. Two follow-ups were produced: "War and Remembrance" and "War and Remembrance: The Final Chapter." **900m/C VHS, Beta, Closed Caption.** Robert Mitchum, Ali MacGraw, Ralph Bellamy, Polly Bergen, Jan-Michael Vincent, David Dukes, John Houseman, Victoria Tennant, Peter Graves, Chaim Topol, Ben Murphy, Jeremy Kemp, Anton Diffring, Lawrence Pressman, Andrew Duggan, Barbara Steele; **D:** Dan Curtis. *PAR, MOV*

Windwalker ⰔⰔⰔ **1981** Howard, the only cast member who is not a Native American, is an aged chief who shares the memories of his life with his grandchildren. Filmed in the Crow and Cheyenne Indian languages and subtitled in English throughout. A beautifully photographed, intelligent independent project. **108m/C VHS, Beta.** Trevor Howard, James Remar, Dusty Iron Wing McCrea; **D:** Keith Merrill. *FOX*

Windy City ⰔⰔ **1984 (R)** A group of seven childhood friends must come to terms with the harsh realities of their failed ambitions when they meet for a weekend in Chicago. Told from the point of view of one of the group, recounting the sorts of memories we all prefer to forget. Typical and overwrought '80s yuppie reunion/regret drama. Aren't these people too young to be unhappy? **103m/C VHS, Beta, LV, Closed Caption.** John Shea, Kate Capshaw, Josh Mostel, Jeffrey DeMunn, Lewis J. Stadlen, James Sutorius; **D:** Armyan Bernstein; **W:** Armyan Bernstein; **M:** Jack Nitzsche. *FOX*

A Wing and a Prayer ⰔⰔⰔ **1944** Better-than-average WWII Air Force action flick. Battles rage throughout the Pacific theater and the men aboard the aircraft carrier struggle to do their part to save the world for freedom. Fine cast receives Hathaway's excellent unsentimental direction. **97m/B VHS.** Don Ameche, Dana Andrews, William Eythe, Charles Bickford, Cedric Hardwicke, Kevin O'Shea, Richard Jaeckel, Harry (Henry) Morgan; **D:** Henry Hathaway. Nominations: Academy Awards '44: Best Original Screenplay. *FOX*

Wing Chun ⰔⰔ **1994** Wing Chun (Yeoh) battles horse stealing bandits and the male chauvinists around her that don't think a woman can be strong and independent (as well as a fighting expert). Chinese with subtitles or dubbed. **93m/C VHS, LV.** *HK* Michelle Yeoh, Donnie Yan, Waise Lee; **D:** Yuen Woo Ping. *TAI*

Wings ⰔⰔ½ **1927** The silent classic about friends, Rogers and Arlen, their adventures in the Air Corps during WWI, and their rivalry for the hand of a woman. Contains actual footage of combat flying from the Great War. Won the very first Best Picture Oscar. Too-thin plot hangs on (barely) to the stirring, intrepid dogfight scenes. **139m/B VHS, Beta, LV.** Clara Bow, Charles "Buddy" Rogers, Richard Arlen, Gary Cooper; **D:** William A. Wellman. Academy Awards '27: Best Picture, National Film Registry '97. *BTV, PAR*

Wings of Danger Ⱄ *Dead on Course* **1952** A pilot tries to save his friend from blackmailing gold smugglers. **72m/B VHS, Beta, LV.** *GB* Zachary Scott, Kay Kendall, Robert Beatty, Naomi Chance; **M:** Malcolm Arnold. *MLB, RXM*

Wings of Desire ⰔⰔⰔ½ *Der Himmel Uber Berlin* **1988 (PG-13)** An ethereal, haunting modern fable about one of many angels observing human life in and above the broken existence of Berlin, and how he begins to long to experience life as humans do. A moving, unequivocable masterpiece, with as many beautiful things to say about spiritual need as about the schizophrenic emptiness of contemporary Germany; Wenders' magnum opus. In German with English subtitles, and with black-and-white sequences. **130m/C VHS, Beta, LV.** *GE* Bruno Ganz, Peter Falk, Solveig Dommartin, Otto Sander, Curt Bois; **D:** Wim Wenders; **W:** Wim Wenders, Peter Handke; **C:** Henri Alekan; **M:** Jurgen Knieper. Independent Spirit Awards '89: Best Foreign Film; Los Angeles Film Critics Association Awards '88: Best Cinematography, Best Foreign Film; New York Film Critics Awards '88: Best Cinematography; National Society of Film Critics Awards '88: Best Cinematography. *ORI, GLV, MOV*

Wings of Eagles ⰔⰔ½ **1957** Hollywood biography of Frank 'Spig' Wead, a famous WWI aviation pioneer turned screenwriter. Veers wildly from comedy to stolid drama, though Bond's lampoon of Ford as "John Dodge" is justly famous. **110m/C VHS, Beta.** John Wayne, Ward Bond, Maureen O'Hara, Dan Dailey, Edmund Lowe, Ken Curtis, Kenneth Tobey, Sig Rumann, Veda Ann Borg; **D:** John Ford; **C:** Paul Vogel. *MGM*

Wings of Fame ⰔⰔ½ **1993 (R)** Comic afterlife fantasy skewering celebrity status. Recently departed celebs check into a posh hotel, but as their fame on earth declines so do their afterlife accomodations, until they reach the state of oblivion. The latest hotel arrivals are a renowned, arrogant actor (O'Toole) and the frustrated writer (Firth) whose claim to fame has come from murdering him. **109m/C VHS, Beta, Closed Caption.** Peter O'Toole, Colin Firth; **D:** Otakar Votocek; **W:** Herman Koch, Otakar Votocek. *PAR*

The Wings of the Dove ⰔⰔⰔ½ **1997 (R)** Beautifully acted and filmed romance "inspired by" Henry James's 1902 novel. Updated to 1910, this triangular tale focuses on well-bred-but-penniless Kate Croy (Bonham Carter), who's been taken in by her imperious Aunt Maude (Rampling) with the expectation that she marry well. And this doesn't mean Kate's present beau, poor journalist Milton Densher (Roache). But when Kate meets gentle American heiress Millie Theale (Elliott), learns she's dying, and that she's also intrigued by Merton, the wheels begin to turn. A trip to Venice sets Kate's plan in motion but leads to unexpected developments for all concerned. **CW:** Sexuality, nudity. **101m/C VHS, LV,**

Closed Caption. *GB* Helena Bonham Carter, Linus Roache, Alison Elliott, Elizabeth McGovern, Charlotte Rampling, Alex Jennings, Michael Gambon; *D:* Iain Softley; *W:* Hossein Amini, *C:* Eduardo Serra; *M:* Gabriel Yared. British Academy Awards '97: Best Cinematography, Best Makeup; Los Angeles Film Critics Association Awards '97: Best Actress (Bonham Carter); National Board of Review Awards '97: Best Actress (Bonham Carter); Broadcast Film Critics Association Awards '97: Best Actress (Bonham Carter); Nominations: Academy Awards '97: Best Actress (Bonham Carter), Best Adapted Screenplay, Best Cinematography, Best Costume Design; British Academy Awards '97: Best Actress (Bonham Carter), Best Adapted Screenplay, Best Costume Design; Golden Globe Awards '98: Best Actress (Bonham Carter); Screen Actors Guild Award '97: Best Actress (Bonham Carter), Best Supporting Actress (Elliott); Writers Guild of America '97: Best Adapted Screenplay. *TOU*

Wings of the Morning 🐾🐾½ 1937 Maria (Annabella), a descendant of Spanish gypsies, comes to Ireland with her grandmother (Vanbrugh) who's entering a horse in the Epsom Downs Derby. Maria disguises herself as a boy so she can ride in the race but is discovered by Canadian horse-trainer Kerry (Fonda), who promptly falls in love with her. Legendary tenor John McCormack sings several songs. The first British movie to be filmed in Technicolor. **89m/C VHS.** *GB* Annabella, Henry Fonda, Edward Underdown, Irene Vanbrugh, Leslie Banks, Stewart Rome; *D:* Harold Schuster; *W:* Tom Geraghty; *C:* Jack Cardiff, Henry Imus, Ray Rennahan; *M:* Arthur Benjamin. *KIV*

Wings Over the Pacific 🐾½ 1943 Love and his daughter Cooper are living quietly on a Pacific island when a pair of pilots, American Norris and the Nazi Guttman, crash-land after a dogfight. The island is strategic because of its oil supply but Norris manages to prevent the Nazis from taking control and wins Cooper's love in the process. Veteran actor Love died shortly before the film's release. **60m/B VHS.** Montagu Love, Inez Cooper, Edward Norris, Henry Guttman, Robert Armstrong, Ernie Adams; *D:* Phil Rosen; *W:* George Wallace Sayre. *GPV*

The Winner 🐾🐾 1996 (R) Philip (D'Onofrio) is on a winning streak at the Vegas Pair-A-Dice casino and the target of estranged brother Wolf (Madsen), temperamental lounge singer Louise (DeMornay), and various other con artists and thugs, all of whom want to separate him from his winnings. Lots of good actors but this Vegas story is nothing new. Based on the play "A Darker Purpose" by Riss. *CW:* Strong language, along with some violence and sexuality. **90m/C VHS.** Vincent D'Onofrio, Michael Madsen, Rebecca DeMornay, Delroy Lindo, Frank Whaley, Billy Bob Thornton, Richard Edson; *D:* Alex Cox; *W:* Wendy Riss; *C:* Denis Maloney; *M:* Daniel Licht. *ART*

A Winner Never Quits 🐾🐾½ 1986 (PG) A true story based on the life of 1940s baseball player Pete Gray. As a boy Gray lost his right arm above the elbow in an accident. He's determined to prove himself as a baseball player and during WWII is given a tryout, although his teammates consider him a sideshow freak. A Memphis sportswriter takes an interest in Pete's career and Gray's success on the field leads to a career with the St. Louis Browns. Along the way he becomes the inspiration to a young fan, who's also lost an arm. Made for television. **96m/C VHS.** Keith Carradine, Mare Winningham, Huckleberry Fox, Dennis Weaver, Dana Delany, G.W. Bailey, Charles Hallahan, Fionnula Flanagan, Jack Kehoe; *D:* Mel Damski; *W:* Burt Prelutsky. *COL*

Winner Takes All 🐾🐾 1986 (R) A young college student during the Vietnam War comes to grips with maturity and growing pains. **94m/C VHS, Beta, Closed Caption.** *GB* Jason Connery, Diane Cilento.

Winners of the West 1940 A landowner schemes to prevent a railroad from running through his property. The railroad's chief engineer leads the good guys in an attempt to prevent sabotage. A fun serial in 13 chapters, full of shooting, blown-up bridges, locomotives afire, etc., and, of course, the requisite damsel in distress. **250m/B**

VHS. Anne Nagel, Dick Foran, James Craig, Harry Woods; *D:* Ray Taylor, Ford Beebe. *GPV, VCN, NOS*

Winners Take All 🐾🐾 1987 (PG-13) A handful of friends compete in Supercross races. Spirited but thoroughly cliche sports flick. **103m/C VHS, Beta, LV, Closed Caption.** Don Michael Paul, Kathleen York, Robert Krantz; *D:* Fritz Kiersch. *NLC*

Winning 🐾🐾🐾 1969 (PG) A race car driver (Newman) will let nothing, including his new wife (Woodward), keep him from winning the Indianapolis 500. Newman does his own driving. Thomas' film debut. **123m/C VHS, Beta, LV, Letterbox.** Paul Newman, Joanne Woodward, Robert Wagner, Richard Thomas, Clu Gulager; *D:* James Goldstone; *M:* Dave Grusin. *USH*

Winning of the West 🐾🐾 1953 Yodelin' ranger Autry vows to protect a crusading publisher from unscrupulous crooks, including his own dog-gone brothers. The brothers see the light, and the two corral the varmints. Autry tunes include "Cowboy Blues," "Cowpoke Poking Along," and "Find Me My 45." **57m/B VHS, Beta.** Gene Autry, Smiley Burnette, Gail Davis, Richard Crane; *D:* George Archainbaud. *CCB*

The Winning Team 🐾🐾½ 1952 Reagan stars in this biography of baseball legend Grover Cleveland Alexander and Day plays his dedicated wife. Some controversial issues were glossed over in the film, such as Alexander's real-life drinking problem and the fact that he had epilepsy. Although this was one of Reagan's favorite roles, he was upset by the studio's avoidance of all-too-human problems. Nonetheless, it's an entertaining enough movie about a very talented ballplayer. **98m/B VHS, LV, Closed Caption.** Doris Day, Ronald Reagan, Frank Lovejoy, Eve Miller, James Millican, Russ Tamblyn; *D:* Lewis Seiler. *WAR*

The Winslow Boy 🐾🐾🐾½ 1948 A cadet at the Royal Naval College is wrongly accused of theft and expelled. Donat as the boy's lawyer leads a splendid cast. Despite consequences for his family, the boy's father (Hardwicke) sues the government and fights his son's battle, as the case makes the papers and he approaches bankruptcy. Plot would seem far-fetched if it weren't based on fact. Absorbing. Based on a play by Rattigan, who co-wrote the script. **112m/B VHS, Beta.** *GB* Robert Donat, Cedric Hardwicke, Margaret Leighton, Frank Lawton, Kathleen Harrison, Basil Radford; *D:* Anthony Asquith; *W:* Terence Rattigan; *C:* Frederick A. (Freddie) Young. *HEG*

Winter Flight 🐾🐾 1984 A small, gentle British drama about an RAF recruit and a barmaid who quickly become lovers, and then are confronted with her pregnancy. **105m/C VHS, Beta.** *GB* Reece Dinsdale, Nicola Cowper, Gary Olsen; *D:* Roy Battersby. *MGM*

The Winter Guest 🐾🐾🐾 1997 (R) Rickman's directorial debut looks at the lives of eight people living in a remote and icy Scottish village, focusing on the fictional relationship between real-life mother and daughter Law and Thompson. Introspective and somewhat stagey, but fine performances and excellent use of the desolate landscape make this a worthwhile debut effort. Based on the play by Sharman Macdonald, which she and Rickman adapted for the screen. *CW:* Language and brief sensuality. **106m/C VHS, LV, Closed Caption.** *GB* Emma Thompson, Phyllida Law, Sheila Reid, Sandra Voe, Gary Hollywood, Arlene Cockburn, Douglas Murphy, Sean Biggerstaff; *D:* Alan Rickman; *W:* Alan Rickman, Sharman MacDonald; *C:* Seamus McGarvey; *M:* Michael Kamen. *NLC*

Winter Kills 🐾🐾🐾 1979 (R) Distinctive political black comedy suffers a hilariously paranoid version of American public life. Bridges, the younger brother of a U.S. president assassinated 15 years earlier, uncovers the plot. Huston is delightful as Bridges' horny old father. Uneven, but well worth seeing; flopped at the boxoffice, but was re-released in 1983. Taylor was not billed. **97m/C VHS, Beta, LV.** Jeff Bridges, John Huston, Anthony Perkins, Richard Boone, Sterling Hayden, Eli Wallach, Ralph

Meeker, Belinda Bauer, Dorothy Malone, Toshiro Mifune, Elizabeth Taylor, Donald Moffat, Tisa Farrow, Brad Dexter, Joe Spinell; *D:* William Richert; *M:* Maurice Jarre. *COL*

The Winter Light 🐾🐾🐾½ *Nattvardsgaesterna* 1962 The second film in Bergman's famous trilogy on the silence of God, preceded by "Through a Glass Darkly" and followed by "The Silence." Bleak and disturbing view of a tortured priest who searches for the faith and guidance he is unable to give his congregation. Hard to swallow for neophyte Bergmanites, but challenging, deeply serious and rewarding for those accustomed to the Swede's angst. Polished and personal. In Swedish with English subtitles. **80m/B VHS, Beta, LV.** *SW* Gunnar Bjornstrand, Ingrid Thulin, Max von Sydow; *D:* Ingmar Bergman; *W:* Ingmar Bergman; *C:* Sven Nykvist. *NLC*

Winter Meeting 🐾🐾 1948 Overwrought drama with Bette Davis starring as a spinster poetess who falls in love with a war hero who wants to be a priest. Very talky script, of interest only as the sole romantic lead for James Davis, whose claim to fame was westerns and the TV series "Dallas." **104m/B VHS, Closed Caption.** Bette Davis, Janis Paige, James Davis, John Hoyt, Florence Bates, Walter Baldwin, Ransom Sherman; *D:* Bretaigne Windust; *M:* Max Steiner. *MGM*

The Winter of Our Dreams 🐾🐾½ 1982 Down Under slice of seamy life as a heroin-addicted prostitute becomes involved with an unhappy bookshop owner. Davis shines in otherwise slow and confusing drama. **89m/C VHS, Beta.** *AU* Judy Davis, Bryan Brown, Cathy Downes, Baz Luhrmann, Peter Mochrie, Mervyn Drak, Margie McCrae, Marcie Deane-Johns; *D:* John Duigan. Australian Film Institute '81: Best Actress (Davis). *ART*

Winter People 🐾🐾½ 1989 (PG-13) A clockmaking widower and a woman living alone with her illegitimate son experience tough times together with feuding families in a Depression-era Appalachian community. Silly, rehashed premise doesn't deter McGillis, who gamely gives a fine performance. Based on the novel by John Ehle. **109m/C VHS, Beta, LV, 8mm, Closed Caption.** Kurt Russell, Kelly McGillis, Lloyd Bridges, Mitchell Ryan, Jeffrey Meek, Eileen Ryan, Amelia Burnette; *D:* Ted Kotcheff; *W:* Carol Sobieski; *M:* John Scott. *NLC*

Winterbeast 🐾 1992 Winter resort community dwellers begin mysteriously disappearing until somebody remembers that the resort was built over a sacred Indian burial ground. Sgt. Bill Whitman, the valiant park ranger and his Barney Fife-like assistant Stillman, question the town's wise old sage, Sheldon, who's sitting on a secret that could threaten the entire community. **77m/C VHS.** Tim R. Morgan, Mike Magri. *TEM, MOV*

Winterset 🐾🐾 1936 A son seeks to clear his father's name of a falsely accused crime 15 years after his electrocution. Powerful at the time, though time has lessened its impact. Loosely based on the trial of Sacco and Vanzetti and adapted from Maxwell Anderson's Broadway play, with stars in the same roles. Meredith's film debut. **85m/B VHS, Beta.** Burgess Meredith, Margo, John Carradine; *D:* Alfred Santell. Nominations: Academy Awards '36: Best Interior Decoration, Best Score. *MON, HHT, CAB*

Wintertime 🐾½ 1943 Forgettable and mindless Henie musical. Plot revolves around Henie travelling in Canada with her wealthy uncle, and saving an old, run-down hotel. An appearance by Woody Herman and his Orchestra give the film a much-needed boost. Based on a story by Arthur Kober. **82m/B VHS.** Sonja Henie, Jack Oakie, Cesar Romero, Carole Landis, S.Z. Sakall, Cornel Wilde, Woody Herman; *D:* John Brahm; *W:* E. Edwin Moran, Jack Jevne, Lynn Starling. *FXV*

Wired 🐾 1989 (R) A justly lambasted, unintentionally hilarious biography of comic genius and overdose victim John Belushi, very loosely based on Bob Woodward's bestselling muckraking book. The chronicle of addiction and tragedy is tried here as a weird sort of comedy; was it meant as a tribute to its off-kilter subject? If so, it misses by a mile. And, we're sorry, but Chiklis doesn't cut it as Belushi—who would?! **112m/C VHS, Beta, LV.** Michael Chiklis, Ray Sharkey, Patti D'Arbanville, J.T. Walsh, Gary Groomes, Lucinda Jenney, Alex Rocco, Jere Burns, Billy Preston; **D:** Larry Peerce; **M:** Basil Poledouris. *ART*

Wired to Kill woof! 1986 (R) In a futuristic world, two teenagers seek justice for their parents' murder by building a remote-controlled erector set programmed for revenge. Laughably porous plot drops any pretence of credibility. Dizzyingly bad. **96m/C VHS, Beta.** Merritt Butrick, Emily Longstreth, Devin Hoelscher, Frank Collison; **D:** Francis Schaeffer. *ART*

Wisdom ⅟₂ 1987 (R) Unemployed young guy (Estevez) becomes a bank robber with Robin Hood aspirations, coming to the aid of American farmers by destroying mortgage records. Estevez became the youngest person to star in, write, and direct a major motion picture. And, my goodness, it shows. **109m/C VHS, Beta, LV, Closed Caption.** Emilio Estevez, Demi Moore, Tom Skerritt, Veronica Cartwright; **D:** Emilio Estevez; **M:** Danny Elfman. *WAR*

Wise Blood 🎬🎬🎬 1979 (PG) Gothic drama about a drifter who searches for sin and becomes a preacher for a new religion, The Church Without Christ. Excellent cast in achingly realistic portrayal of ersatz religion, southern style. Many laughs are more painful than funny. Superb, very dark comedy from Huston. Adapted from the Flannery O'Connor novel. **106m/C VHS, Beta.** Brad Dourif, John Huston, Ned Beatty, Amy Wright, Harry Dean Stanton; **D:** John Huston; **M:** Alex North. *USH*

Wise Guys 🎬⅟₂ 1986 (R) Two small-time hoods decide to rip off the mob. When their boss figures out their plan he decides to set them up instead. Lame black comedy that has too few moments. **100m/C VHS, Beta, Closed Caption.** Joe Piscopo, Danny DeVito, Ray Sharkey, Captain Lou Albano, Dan Hedaya, Julie Bovasso, Patti LuPone; **D:** Brian DePalma; **M:** Ira Newborn. *FOX, FCT*

Wisecracks 🎬🎬🎬 1993 Women comics perform and talk about their work in this documentary directed by Gail Singer. The comics featured have, in some cases, little more in common than their work, but all share interesting perspectives on what they do. Interesting mix of performance clips and interviews sometimes includes banal comments about the nature of comedy, but is more often insightful, especially remarks by seasoned vet Phyllis Diller. Although there exists here the potential for an angry feminist diatribe on gender-based humor, the focus is more towards talented women who are just plain funny. **93m/C VHS; Performed by:** Whoopi Goldberg, Paula Poundstone, Ellen DeGeneres, Kim Wayans, Pam Stone, Joy Behar, Maxine Lapidus, Phyllis Diller, Jenny Jones. *MNC*

Wish Me Luck 🎬⅟₂ 1995 A babe genie (Avalon) has a dilemma—unless she can make a man of a geek college student (Gesner) in 48 hours, she'll become the property of an evil sorcerer for a thousand years. She gets three equally bodacious college cheerleaders to help her out. Also available in an edited version that cuts six minutes worth of fleshy fantasies. **91m/C VHS.** Avalon Anders, Zen Gesner; **D:** Philip Jones. *SDE*

Wish Upon a Star 🎬🎬⅟₂ 1996 (PG) Battling teenage sisters Alexia (Heigl) and Haley (Harris) wind up switching identities when bookish Haley wishes on a falling star to be popular Alexia. Naturally, this confuses everyone but the sisters get to see how their other sibling feels. **90m/C VHS.** Katherine Heigl, Danielle Harris. *WAR*

Wish You Were Here 🎬🎬🎬 1987 Poignant yet funny slice of British postwar life roughly based on the childhood memoirs of famous madame, Cynthia Payne. A troubled and freedom-loving teenager expresses her rebellion in sexual experimentation. Mum is dead and Dad just doesn't understand, so what's a girl to do, but get

the boys excited? Lloyd, in her first film, plays the main character with exceptional strength and feistiness. Payne's later life was dramatized in the Leland-scripted "Personal Services." **92m/C VHS, Beta, LV.** *GB* Emily Lloyd, Tom Bell, Clare Clifford, Barbara Durkin, Geoffrey Hutchings, Charlotte Barker, Chloe Leland, Trudy Cavanagh, Jesse Birdsall, Geoffrey Durham, Pat Heywood; **D:** David Leland; **W:** David Leland; **M:** Stanley Myers. British Academy Awards '87: Best Original Screenplay; National Society of Film Critics Awards '87: Best Actress (Lloyd). *TVC*

Wishful Thinking 🎬🎬 1992 A lovelorn screenwriter rescues a peculiar man from mysterious assassins and receives a magical writing pad for his efforts. It seems that whatever Michael writes on the paper will come true, so he decides to write himself into the life of the luscious Diane. **94m/C VHS.** Murray Langston, Michelle Johnson, Ruth Buzzi, Billy Barty, Johnny Dark, Ray "Boom Boom" Mancini, Vic Dunlop, Kip Addotta; **D:** Murray Langston.

The Wishing Ring 🎬🎬🎬 1914 Light and charming romance, beautifully filmed by Tourneur, based on Owen Davis' play. The son of an earl in Old England is expelled from college and told by his father he must earn half a crown on his own before the family will take him back. With the help of a minister's daughter, he sets things right. **50m/B VHS, Beta.** Vivian Martin, Alec B. Francis, Chester Barnett, Simeon Wiltsie, Walter Morton; **D:** Maurice Tourneur; **W:** Maurice Tourneur. *GPV*

The Wishmaker 1985 A young man squanders the three wishes granted to him for helping a strange old woman and her timid daughter. **54m/C VHS, Beta.** *GEM*

Wishman 🎬🎬⅟₂ 1993 Hollywood hustler Basie Banks (Le Mat) meets Hitch (Lewis), a two million-year-old genie whose magic bottle has been stolen. In exchange for Banks' help in recovering his home, Hitch agrees to help Banks get the girl of his dreams. **89m/C VHS.** Paul LeMat, Geoffrey Lewis, Paul Gleason, Quin Kessler, Nancy Parsons, Gailard Sartain, Brion James; **D:** Mike Marvin; **W:** Mike Marvin. *MNC*

Wishmaster 🎬 *Wes Craven Presents Wishmaster* 1997 (R) An evil genie grants wishes to those who stumble upon him, but he also gets his kicks by destroying the lives of those naive enough to play along. Anemic horror tale that's as thin on plot as it is on scares. Standard-issue exploding chest cavities and flying heads can't easily erase the boredom. Make-up artist turned director Kurtzman should have wished for some directorial skills, because he hasn't got a clue. Don't be misled by Wes Craven's name, his association with this dud is meant to lure the least discriminating of horror fans.**CW:** Horror violence and gore, and for language. **90m/C VHS, Closed Caption.** Tammy Lauren, Andrew Divoff, Robert Englund, Chris Lemmon, Theodore (Ted) Raimi, John Byner, Jenny O'Hara; **Cameos:** Tony Todd, Kane Hodder; **D:** Robert Kurtzman; **W:** Peter Atkins; **C:** Jacques Haitkin; **M:** Harry Manfredini. *ART*

The Wistful Widow of Wagon Gap 🎬🎬 *The Wistful Widow* 1947 Lou, a traveling salesman, accidentally kills a man, and according to the law of the west he has to take care of the dead man's widow and children—all seven of them. Because the family is so unsavory, Lou knows that no other man will kill him, so he allows himself to be appointed sheriff and clears the town of lowlifes. Usual Abbott & Costello fare is highlighted with their zany antics. **78m/B VHS.** Bud Abbott, Lou Costello, Marjorie Main, George Cleveland, Gordon Jones, William Ching, Peter Thompson, Glenn Strange, Olin Howlin; **D:** Charles T. Barton. *USH*

The Witch 🎬⅟₂ *La Strega in Amore; Aura* 1966 Historian hired by family to assemble the late father's works falls in love with beautiful daughter. Seems she's no angel. **103m/B VHS.** *IT* Rosanna Schiaffino, Richard Johnson, Sarah Ferrati, Gian Marie Volonte, Margherita Guzzinati; **D:** Damiano Damiani. *SNC*

Witch Hunt 🎬🎬⅟₂ 1994 (R) Mock fantasy/mystery set in 1953 Hollywood. Private eye H. Phillip Lovecraft (Hopper) is hired by actress Kim Hudson (Miller) to shadow her philandering studio hubby Gottlieb (Rosenberg), who dies in an untimely fashion. The kicker is that witchcraft is commonplace, with the studio hiring witches and warlocks to cast spells. Also, a blowhard senator (Bogosian) is heading a McCarthy-like campaign to ban magic and Lovecraft fears his sorceress friend (Ralph) is going to be the scapegoat for Gottlieb's murder. Great special effects; fuzzy plot.**CW:** Some strong language; scene of nudity. **101m/C VHS.** Dennis Hopper, Penelope Ann Miller, Eric Bogosian, Sheryl Lee Ralph, Julian Sands, Alan Rosenberg, Valerie Mahaffey, Debi Mazar; **D:** Paul Schrader; **W:** Joseph Dougherty; **M:** Angelo Badalamenti. *HBO*

Witch Who Came from the Sea 🎬⅟₂ 1976 (R) Witch terrorizes all the ships at sea, but doesn't exactly haunt the viewer. **98m/C VHS, Beta.** Millie Perkins, Lonny Chapman, Vanessa Brown, Peggy Feury, Rick Jason; **D:** Matt Cimber. *UNI*

A Witch Without a Broom 🎬⅟₂ *Una Bruja Sin Escoba* 1968 Shoestring time travel fantasy. When an American professor catches the eye of a 15th century apprentice witch, the trip begins. Since the witch is only learning the ropes, they end up visiting a number of periods other than their own before the professor gets home. **78m/C VHS.** *SP* Jeffrey Hunter, Maria Perschy, Perla Cristal, Gustavo Rojo; **D:** Joe Lacy. *NO*

Witchboard 🎬🎬⅟₂ 1987 (R) During a college party, a group of friends bring out the Ouija board and play with it for laughs. One of the girls discovers she can use the board to communicate with a small boy who died years before. In her effort to talk with him she unwittingly releases the evil spirit of an ax murderer who haunts and murders members of the group. An entertaining, relatively inoffensive member of its genre that displays some attention to characterization and plot. **98m/C VHS, Beta, LV.** Todd Allen, Tawny Kitaen, Stephen Nichols, Kathleen Wilhoite, Burke Byrnes, Rose Marie, James W. Quinn, Judy Tatum, Gloria Hayes, J.P. Luebsen, Susan Nickerson; **D:** Kevin S. Tenney; **W:** Kevin S. Tenney; **C:** Roy Wagner; **M:** Dennis Michael Tenney. *NO*

Witchboard 2: The Devil's Doorway 🎬🎬⅟₂ 1993 (R) There seem to be a lot of doorways to hell because someone is always finding a new one (and making a movie about it). This time it's the innocent Paige Benedict (Dolenz), who moves into an artist's loft and finds an old Ouija board in a closet. Through the board, Paige is contacted by a former tenant who claims to be a murder victim. Soon her fellow tenants are dying in violent and mysterious ways and Paige's dreams are haunted by evil. What hath she wrought—and can she get it back in the closet where it belongs. **98m/C VHS, LV, Closed Caption.** Ami Dolenz, Laraine Newman, Timothy Gibbs, John Gatins, Julie Michaels, Marvin Kaplan; **D:** Kevin S. Tenney; **W:** Kevin S. Tenney; **C:** David Lewis; **M:** Dennis Michael Tenney. *REP*

Witchboard 3: The Possession 🎬🎬⅟₂ 1995 (R) A Ouija board opens the gates to hell (yet again or we wouldn't have a movie) and the board's spirit steals Brian's soul and takes control of his body—much to the bewilderment of his girlfriend Julie.**CW:** Strong sexuality and violence; language. **93m/C VHS, Closed Caption.** David Nerman, Locky Lambert, Cedric Smith, Donna Sarrasin; **D:** Peter Svatek; **W:** Kevin S. Tenney, Jon Ezrine; **C:** Barry Gravelle. *REP*

Witchcraft woof! 1988 (R) A young mother meets a couple killed three centuries ago for performing witchcraft. They want her baby, of course, to be the son of the devil. "Rosemary's Baby" ripoff, that is thoroughly predictable. **90m/C VHS, Beta, LV.** Anat "Topol" Barzilai, Gary Sloan, Lee Kisman, Deborah Scott; **D:** Robert Spera. *VSE*

Witchcraft 2: The Temptress *

1990 (R) A sensuous woman seduces an innocent young man into the rituals of witchcraft and the occult. Sequel to "Witchcraft" does not succeed where original failed, but does have a fair share of sex and violence. **88m/C VHS, Beta, LV.** Charles Solomon, Mia Ruiz, Delia Sheppard; **D:** Mark Woods. *VSE*

Witchcraft 3: The Kiss of Death *

1990 (R) Once a master of the occult, William Spanner now seeks only to live a normal life. His plans are changed, however, when a sensual creature from Hell is sent to seduce him. More sex and violence, with an emphasis on sex. The best of the "Witchcraft" trio, for those trying to plan a festive evening. **CW:** Language, violence, and strong sensuality. **85m/C VHS.** Charles Solomon, Lisa Toothman, William L. Baker, Lena Hall; **D:** R.L. Tillmanns. *VSE*

Witchcraft 4: Virgin Heart *

1992 (R) Supernatural horror continues as attorney Will Spanner sinks even deeper into his enemy's satanic trap in this shocking sequel to the popular series. His only hope is to use his own black magic powers and to enlist the help of a seductive stripper (Penthouse Pet Strain). **CW:** Language, horror violence, and sexuality. **92m/C VHS, LV, Closed Caption.** Charles Solomon, Julie Strain, Clive Pearson, Jason O'Gulihar, Lisa Jay Harrington, Barbara Dow; **D:** James Merendino. *VSE*

Witchcraft 5: Dance with the Devil *

1992 (R) This undistinguished horror series continues with several unsuccessful people finding the unpleasant loopholes in their satanic contracts. A demon named Cain is behind all the trouble. The horror special effects are cheap but there are several soft-core sex scenes (pointless to the plot) which provide a minimal interest. An unrated version is also available. **CW:** Language, violence, and strong sexuality. **94m/C VHS.** Marklen Kennedy, Carolyn Taye-Loren, Nicole Sassaman, Aysha Hauer, David Huffman; **D:** Talun Hsu. *VSE*

Witchcraft 6: The Devil's Mistress *

1994 (R) Police detectives Lutz and Garner's new case involves young women turning up naked and dead. Turns out satanic disciple Savanti is expected to impress the boss with a virgin sacrifice before an impending eclipse. But since virgins are scarce, he's having a real tough time. Practically no gore but lots of skin, along with hit-or-miss humor. **86m/C VHS.** Kurt Alan, John E. Holiday, Bryan Nutter, Jerry Spicer, Shannon Lead; **D:** Julie Davis; **W:** Julie Davis. *VSE*

Witchcraft 7: Judgement Hour *

1995 (R) Modern-day warlock must sacrifice his earthly existence to kill an evil vampire. **CW:** Strong sexuality and language. **91m/C VHS.** David Byrnes, April Breneman, Alisa Christensen, John Cragen, Loren Schmalle; **D:** Michael Paul Girard; **W:** Peter Fleming; **C:** Denis Maloney; **M:** Miriam Cutler. *APX*

Witchcraft 8: Salem's Ghost **

Salem's Ghost **1995 (R)** Warlock Simon Winfrough (Van Landingham) was burned at the stake in 1692 but if you could keep a dead satanist in his grave there'd be no movie. So when Simon's spirit is accidentally awakened by the Dunaways (Grober and Korf) in their Salem home, they seek the help of exorcist McArthur (Overmyer). **CW:** Some language; horror violence; strong sensuality. **90m/C VHS.** Lee Grober, Kim Kopf, Tom Overmyer, Jack Van Landingham, David Weills, Anthoni Stuart; **D:** Joseph John Barmettler Jr.; **W:** Joseph John Barmettler Jr.; **C:** Denis Maloney. *APX*

Witchcraft 9: Bitter Flesh *

1996 (R) Yet another sequel to the endless erotic horror series finds the LAPD investigating a series of murders. They get a tip from a strange call girl who claims to be chanelling the spirit of a warlock, who's about to open the gates to hell. **CW:** Strong sexual content, and for language and some violence. **90m/C VHS.** Landon Hall, David Byrnes, Stephanie Beaton, Mikul Robins; **D:** Michael Paul Girard; **W:** Stephen J. Downing; **C:** Jeff Gateman; **M:** Michael Paul Girard. *VSE*

Witchcraft through the Ages ***

Haxan **1922** The demonic Swedish masterpiece in which witches and victims suffer against various historical backgrounds. Nightmarish and profane, especially the appearance of the Devil as played under much make-up by Christiansen himself. Silent. **74m/B VHS, Beta.** *SW* Maren Pedersen, Clara Pontoppidan, Oscar Stribolt, Benjamin Christiansen, Tora Teje, Elith Pio, Karen Winther, Emmy Schonfeld, John Andersen; **D:** Benjamin Christiansen; **C:** Johan Ankerstjerne. *MPI, GPV, WFV*

Witchery *

Witchcraft **1988** A photographer and his girlfriend vacation at a New England hotel where they discover a horrifying, satanic secret. One by one (as always, in this kind of bad flick, in the interest of "suspense"), people are killed off. Seems it's a witch, bent on revenge. Forget room service and bar the door. **96m/C VHS, Beta.** David Hasselhoff, Linda Blair, Catherine Hickland, Hildegarde Knef, Leslie Cumming, Bob Champagne, Richard Farnsworth, Michael Manches; **D:** Fabrizio Laurenti, Martin Newlin. *THV*

The Witches ***½

1990 (PG) Nine-year-old boy on vacation finds himself in the midst of a witch convention, and grand high witch Huston plans to turn all children into furry little creatures. The boy, with the help of his good witch grandmother, attempts to prevent the mass transmutation of children into mice. Top-notch fantasy probably too spooky for the training wheel set. Wonderful special effects; the final project of executive producer Jim Henson. Based on Roald Dahl's story. **92m/C VHS, Beta, LV, 8mm, Closed Caption.** Anjelica Huston, Mai Zetterling, Jasen Fisher, Rowan Atkinson, Charlie Potter, Bill Paterson, Brenda Blethyn, Jane Horrocks; **D:** Nicolas Roeg; **W:** Allan Scott; **M:** Stanley Myers. Los Angeles Film Critics Association Awards '90: Best Actress (Huston); National Society of Film Critics Awards '90: Best Actress (Huston). *WAR, FCT, ORI*

Witches' Brew **

1979 (PG) Three young women try to use their undeveloped skills in witchcraft and black magic to help Garr's husband get a prestigious position at a university, with calamitous results. Oft-funny spoof is silly and oft-predictable. Turner's role is small as an older, experienced witch. **98m/C VHS, Beta.** Teri Garr, Richard Benjamin, Lana Turner, Kathryn Leigh Scott; **D:** Richard Shorr, Herbert L. Strock.

Witches' Mountain *

1971 A troubled couple is captured by a coven of witches in the Pyrenees. Dull and pointless. **98m/C VHS, Beta.** *MX* Patty Shepard, John Caffari, Monica Randall; **D:** Raul Artigot. *UNI, HEG*

The Witches of Eastwick **½

1987 (R) "Mad Max" director Miller meets Hollywood in this unrestrained, vomit-filled treatment of John Updike's novel about three lonely small-town New England women and their sexual liberation. A strange, rich, overweight and balding, but nonetheless charming man knows their deepest desires and makes them come true with decadent excess. Raunchy fun, with Nicholson over-acting wildly as the Mephisto. Miller lends a bombastic violent edge to the effort, sometimes at the expense of the story. Filmed on location in Cohasset, Massachusetts. **118m/C VHS, Beta, LV, 8mm, Closed Caption.** Jack Nicholson, Cher, Susan Sarandon, Michelle Pfeiffer, Veronica Cartwright, Richard Jenkins, Keith Joakum, Carel Struycken; **D:** George Miller; **W:** Michael Cristofer; **C:** Vilmos Zsigmond; **M:** John Williams. Los Angeles Film Critics Association Awards '87: Best Actor (Nicholson); New York Film Critics Awards '87: Best Actor (Nicholson); Nominations: Academy Awards '87: Best Sound, Best Original Score. *WAR*

Witchfire *

1986 (R) After their pyschiatrist dies in an automobile accident, three maniacal women escape from an asylum and hide out in the woods. Winters then holds seances to contact the dead doctor, but instead captures a young, very much alive hunter. For dedicated fans of Winters. **92m/C VHS, Beta.** Shelley Winters, Gary Swanson, David Mendenhall, Corinne Chateau; **D:** Vincent J. Privitera; **W:** Vincent J. Privitera. *ART*

The Witching woof! *Necromancy* 1972

Poorly made story of man's continuing quest for supernatural power. Welles slums as the high priest out to get victim Franklin. **90m/C VHS, Beta.** Orson Welles, Pamela Franklin, Michael Ontkean, Lee Purcell, Lisa James, Harvey Jason, Terry Quinn; **D:** Bert I. Gordon; **W:** Bert I. Gordon, Gail March; **C:** Winton C. Hoch. *NO*

The Witching of Ben Wagner **½

1995 (G) Strange occurrences have Ben believing his friend Regina and her grandmother may be witches. But, if so, they're friendly ones as they help Ben adjust to a new home and neighborhood. **96m/C VHS, Closed Caption.** Justin Gocke, Harriet Hall, Sam Bottoms; **D:** Paul Annett. *AVE*

Witching Time *½

1984 Elvira presents this film, in which a young composer is visited by a horny 17th-century witch while his wife is away from home. When the wife returns, both women fight to possess him. **60m/C VHS, Beta.** Jon Finch, Prunella Gee, Patricia Quinn, Ian McCulloch; **D:** Don Leaver. *ART*

The Witchmaker *

Legend of Witch Hollow; Witchkill **1969** Remote, crocodile-infested bayou in Louisiana is the scene of witchcraft and the occult as young girls are murdered in order for a group of witches to become youthful again. **101m/C VHS, Beta.** John Lodge, Alvy Moore, Thordis Brandt, Anthony Eisley, Shelby Grant, Robyn Millan; **D:** William O. Brown; **W:** William O. Brown. *NO*

The Witch's Mirror **

1960 A sorceress plots to destroy the murderer of her goddaughter. The murderer, a surgeon, begins a project to restore the disfigured face and hands of his burned second wife, and he doesn't care how he gets the materials. For true fans of good bad horror flicks. Badly dubbed (which adds to the charm); dark (of course); and offbeat (naturally). **75m/B VHS, Beta.** *MX* Rosita Arenas, Armando Calvo, Isabela Corona, Dina De Marco; **D:** Chano Urueto. *SNC, HHT*

WitchTrap *

1989 (R) Lame sequel to "Witchboard." A mansion's new owner hires psychics to exorcise the disturbed ghost of his predecessor. **87m/C VHS, Beta, LV.** James W. Quinn, Kathleen Bailey, Linnea Quigley; **D:** Kevin S. Tenney. *IME*

With Honors **½

1994 (PG-13) Pesci is a bum who finds desperate Harvard student Fraser's Honors thesis, and, like any quick-witted bum with a yen for literature, holds it for ransom. Desperate to salvage his future gold card, Fraser and his roommates agree to fix Joe's homeless state. Self-involved students learn something about love and life while Madonna drones in the background. Fraser is believable as the ambitious student about to endure Pesci's enlightenment. Pesci is Pesci, doing his best to overcome numerous script difficulties. **100m/C VHS, LV.** Joe Pesci, Brendan Fraser, Moira Kelly, Patrick Dempsey, Josh Hamilton, Gore Vidal; **D:** Alek Keshishian; **W:** William Mastrosimone; **M:** Patrick Leonard. Nominations: Golden Globe Awards '95: Best Song ("I'll Remember"); MTV Movie Awards '95: Best Song ("I'll Remember"). *WAR*

With Kit Carson Over the Great Divide **½

1925 A large-scale silent western about a doctor's family gone asunder and then reunited during the Fremont expeditions out of St. Louis in the 1840s. Snow's final screen appearance. Recently refound. Fun cinematic history (in two senses of the phrase). Beautiful landscape. **72m/B VHS, Beta, 8mm.** Roy Stewart, Henry B. Walthall, Marguerite Snow, Sheldon Lewis, Earl Metcalfe; **D:** Frank S. Mattison. *VYY*

With Six You Get Eggroll **

A Man in Mommy's Bed **1968 (G)** A widow with three sons and a widower with a daughter elope and then must deal with the antagonism of their children and even their dogs. Brady Bunch-esque family comedy means well, but doesn't cut it. Hershey's debut. Jamie Farr, William Christopher, and Vic Tayback have small parts. To date, Day's last big-screen appearance. **95m/C VHS, Beta.** Doris Day, Brian Keith, Pat Carroll, Alice Ghostley, Vic Tayback, Jamie

Farr, William Christopher, Barbara Hershey; **D:** Howard Morris; **C:** Harry Stradling Jr. *FOX*

Within the Rock ♂♂ 1996 (R) Space crew must shift a wandering moon before it collides with earth but beyond that problem they've got an alien predator that's escaped. **CW:** Some sci-fi violence and gore. 91m/C VHS. Xander Berkeley, Bradford Tatum, Brian Krause, Caroline Barclay, Calvin Levels, Earl Boen, Dale Dye; **D:** Gary J. Tunnicliffe. *APX*

Withnail and I ♂♂♂½ 1987 (R) A biting and original black comedy about a pair of unemployed, nearly starving English actors during the late 1960s. They decide to retreat to a country house owned by Withnail's uncle, for a vacation and are beset by comic misadventures, particularly when the uncle, who is gay, starts to hit on his nephew's friend. Robinson, who scripted "The Killing Fields," makes his successful directorial debut, in addition to drafting the screenplay from his own novel. Co-produced by George Harrison and Richard Starkey (Ringo Starr). 108m/C VHS, Beta, LV. *GB* Richard E. Grant, Paul McGann, Richard Griffiths, Ralph Brown, Michael Elphick; **D:** Bruce Robinson; **W:** Bruce Robinson; **M:** David Dundas. *FCT*

Without a Clue ♂♂½ 1988 (PG) Spoof of the Sherlock Holmes legend, in which Holmes is actually portrayed by a bumbling, skirt-chasing actor, and Watson is the sole crime-solving mastermind, hiring the actor to impersonate the character made famous by the doctor's published exploits. The leads have some fun and so do we; but laughs are widely spaced. 107m/C VHS, Beta, LV, Closed Caption. *GB* Michael Caine, Ben Kingsley, Jeffrey Jones, Lysette Anthony, Paul Freeman, Nigel Davenport, Peter Cook, Pat Keen; **D:** Thom Eberhardt; **W:** Gary Murphy, Larry Strawther; **M:** Henry Mancini. *ORI*

Without a Trace ♂♂ 1983 (PG) One morning, a six-year-old boy is sent off to school by his loving mother, never to return. The story of the mother's relentless search for her son. Cardboard characters, wildly unrealistic ending that is different from the real-life incident on which it's based. Scripted by Gutcheon from her book "Still Missing." Jaffe's directorial debut. 119m/C VHS, Beta. Kate Nelligan, Judd Hirsch, Stockard Channing, David Dukes; **D:** Stanley R. Jaffe; **C:** John Bailey; **M:** Jack Nitzsche. *FOX*

Without Anesthesia ♂♂ *Rough Treatment; Bez Znieczulenia* 1978 Journalist Jerzy returns from a trip abroad to discover his wife has left him for an obnoxious young writer. Against advice, Jerzy fights the divorce and searches for an explanation. Meanwhile, he has mysteriously fallen out of political favor and finds his career falling apart as well. Polish with English subtitles. 111m/C VHS. *PL* Zbigniew Zapasiewicz, Ewa Dalkowska, Krystyna Janda, Andrzej Seweryn; **D:** Andrzej Wajda; **W:** Agnieszka Holland, Andrzej Wajda. *NYF*

Without Evidence ♂♂ 1996 When Oregon correctional director Michael Francke (Garrett) is visiting younger brother Kevin (Plank) in Florida, he mentions his suspicions about an operation within his department involving drugs in prison. Then the next phone call Kevin gets is that Michael's been murdered. When he heads to Oregon, Kevin seems to be getting the official runaround and becomes increasingly suspicious about a coverup. A tension-building true story that remains unsolved. 132m/C VHS. Scott Plank, Anna Gunn, Andrew Prine, Angelina Jolie, Paul Perri, Alan Nause, Ernie Garrett; **D:** Gill Dennis; **W:** Gill Dennis, Phil Stanford; **C:** Victor Nunez; **M:** Franco Piersanti. *NYR*

Without Honors ♂♂ 1932 A man seeks to restore the reputation of his dead brother, accused of murder and theft. He joins the Texas Rangers and brings the real criminals to justice. Excellent location shooting lifts ordinary early western. 62m/B VHS, Beta, LV. Harry Carey Sr., Mae Busch, Gibson Gowland, George "Gabby" Hayes; **D:** William Nigh. *NO*

Without Limits ♂♂♂ Pre 1997 (PG-13) Second biopic about '70s long-distance runner Steve Prefontaine (after 1996's "Prefontaine") focuses mainly on Prefontaine's (Crudup) relationship with his University of Oregon coach Bill Bowerman (Sutherland), who later was a co-founder of Nike. Also explores the heartbreak of the 1972 Olympics. Crudup does a fine job exploring the runner's playful arrogance, fearlessness, and iconoclasm (especially when dealing with the corrupt AAU). Sutherland, playing a three-dimensional character for the first time in a while, gives a fine performance. Kenny Moore, a close friend and fellow '72 Olympian, wrote the script with director Towne, with the full cooperation of Bowerman and Prefontaine's girlfriend. **CW:** Brief sexual material and brief strong language. 117m/C VHS. Billy Crudup, Donald Sutherland, Monica Potter, Jeremy Sisto, Matthew Lillard, Billy Burke, Dean Norris, Gabriel Olds, Judith Ivey; **D:** Robert Towne; **W:** Robert Towne, Kenny Moore; **C:** Conrad Hall; **M:** Randy Miller. *NYR*

Without Love ♂♂½ 1945 Tracy is a scientist, Hepburn, a woman with an empty basement for his laboratory. Since the neighbors would be scandalized by the idea of unmarried people living together, however platonically, they decide to get married, although each has sworn off romance. Snappy dialogue, expertly rendered by the Tracy/Hepburn team. Terrific supporting cast keeps this minimally plotted outing afloat. Adapted from the play of the same name by Philip Barry. 113m/B VHS, Beta. Spencer Tracy, Katharine Hepburn, Lucille Ball, Keenan Wynn, Carl Esmond, Patricia Morison, Felix Bressart; **D:** Harold Bucquet; **W:** Donald Ogden Stewart; **C:** Karl Freund. *MGM*

Without Love ♂♂ 1980 Ambitious young journalist experiences resentment from her peers because of her aggressive methods, and they decide to teach her a lesson by drawing her into a situation destined for disaster. In Polish with English subtitles. 104m/C VHS. *PL* **D:** Barbara Sass. *FCT*

Without Mercy ♂½ 1995 (R) Marine platoon is shafted by the government when they're left to die while on a U.N. peacekeeping mission in Africa. POW survivor John Carter (Zagarino) then winds up in Asia and gets set up by ex-soldier and general bad guy Larsen (Kove), who he must constantly battle in order to survive. **CW:** Strong violence, and for some sexuality and language. 88m/C VHS, LV, Closed Caption. Frank Zagarino, Martin Kove, Ayu Azhari, Frans Tumbuan; **D:** Robert Anthony; **W:** Robert Anthony; **C:** Gerry Lively. *ART*

Without Reservations ♂♂½ 1946 Hollywood-bound novelist Colbert encounters Marine flyer Wayne and his pal (DeFore) aboard a train. She decides he would be perfect for her newest movie. They both dislike her famous book and don't realize they're traveling with the renowned author. Misadventures and misunderstandings abound as this trio make their way to Tinseltown. Of course, Colbert and Wayne fall in love. Boxoffice success with a tired script and too few real laughs. The Duke is interesting but miscast. Based on the novel "Thanks, God, I'll Take It From Here" by Jane Allen. 101m/B VHS, Beta, LV. Claudette Colbert, John Wayne, Don DeFore, Phil Brown, Frank Puglia; *Cameos:* Louella Parsons, Cary Grant, Jack Benny; **D:** Mervyn LeRoy; **C:** Milton Krasner. *VCI, VCN, TTC*

Without Warning ♂♂½ *The Story Without A Name* 1952 Inexperienced director and actors pull out a minor success in this fairly ordinary murder mystery, about a serial killer of beautiful blondes. 75m/C VHS. *FR* Maurice Ronet, Adam Williams, Gloria Franklin, Edward Binns; **D:** Arnold Laven. *NO*

Without Warning: The James Brady Story ♂♂♂ 1991 (R) White House Press Secretary Brady took a bullet in the brain during the 1981 shooting of President Reagan, and made a slow, grueling recovery. This fine made for cable TV film spares none of it, concentrating on the stricken man and his family, and

opting out of disease-of-the-week cliches (though the pic's politics won't please the gun-adorers). Based on Mollie Dickinson's biography "Thumbs Up." **CW:** Language. 120m/C VHS. Beau Bridges, Joan Allen, David Strathairn, Christopher Bell, Gary Grubbs, Bryan Clark, Steve Flynn, Christine Healy, Susan Brown; **D:** Michael Toshiyuki Uno; **W:** Robert Bolt. *HBO*

Witness ♂♂♂½ 1985 (R) A young Amish boy traveling from his father's funeral witnesses a murder in a Philadelphia bus station. The investigating detective (Ford, in one of his best roles) soon discovers the killing is part of a conspiracy involving corruption in his department. He follows the child and his young widowed mother to their home in the country. A thriller with a difference, about the encounter of alien worlds, with a poignant love story. McGillis, in her first major role, is luminous as the Amish mother, while Ford is believable as both a cop and a sensitive man. An artfully crafted drama, richly focusing on the often misunderstood Amish lifestyle. 112m/C VHS, Beta, LV, 8mm, Closed Caption. Harrison Ford, Kelly McGillis, Alexander Godunov, Lukas Haas, Josef Sommer, Danny Glover, Patti LuPone; **D:** Peter Weir; **C:** John Seale; **M:** Maurice Jarre. Academy Awards '85: Best Film Editing, Best Original Screenplay; Writers Guild of America '85: Best Original Screenplay; Nominations: Academy Awards '85: Best Actor (Ford), Best Art Direction/Set Decoration, Best Cinematography, Best Director (Weir), Best Picture, Best Original Score.*PAR, HMV*

Witness for the
Prosecution ♂♂♂½ 1957 An unemployed man is accused of murdering a wealthy widow whom he befriended. Ailing defense attorney Laughton can't resist taking an intriguing murder case, and a straitforward court case becomes increasingly complicated in this energetic adaptation of an Agatha Christie story and stage play. Outstanding performances by Laughton, with excellent support by real life wife, Lanchester, as his patient nurse. Power, as the alleged killer, and Dietrich as a tragic woman are top-notch (see if you can detect Dietrich in an unbilled second role). 116m/B VHS, Beta, LV, Letterbox. Charles Laughton, Tyrone Power, Marlene Dietrich, Elsa Lanchester, John Williams, Henry Daniell, Una O'Connor; **D:** Billy Wilder; **W:** Harry Kurnitz, Billy Wilder. Golden Globe Awards '58: Best Supporting Actress (Lanchester); Nominations: Academy Awards '57: Best Actor (Laughton), Best Director (Wilder), Best Film Editing, Best Picture, Best Sound, Best Supporting Actress (Lanchester). *MGM, FOX, MLB*

Witness to the Execution ♂♂ 1994 (PG-13) It's 1999 and Tycom Entertainment, a pay-per-view network, is looking for some hot entertainment. Top exec Jessica (Young) decides to televise the electric chair execution of convicted criminal Dennis Casterline (Daly). But Casterline claims to be innocent and as the execution date nears Jessica is unsettled by new evidence that may supports his claim. The cutthroat TV execs provide amusement but this TV movie fare quickly becomes muddled. **CW:** Thematic elements and violence. 92m/C VHS. Sean Young, Timothy Daly, Len Cariou, George Newbern; **D:** Tommy Lee Wallace; **W:** Thomas Baum. *THV*

Wittgenstein ♂♂ 1993 Complicated, experimental portrait of Viennese-born philosopher Ludwig Wittgenstein (Johnson), executed as a series of blackout sketches (that feature a green Martian dwarf and such friends as Bertrand Russell and Ottoline Morrell). Assumes a familiarity with the eccentric Wittgenstein's ideas but does manage to convey some emotion and wit. 75m/C VHS. *GB* Karl Johnson, Michael Gough, Tilda Swinton, John Quentin, Nabil Shaban; **D:** Derek Jarman; **W:** Derek Jarman, Terry Eagleton, Ken Butler. *KIV*

Wives Under Suspicion ♂♂½ 1938 While prosecuting a man who murdered his wife out of jealousy, a district attorney finds his own home life filled with similar tension. Director Whale's unnecessary remake of his own earlier film, "The Kiss Before the Mirror." He is best known for "Frankenstein." 75m/B VHS, Beta. Warren William, Gail

Patrick, Constance Moore, William Lundigan; **D:** James Whale. *NOS, DVT, HEG*

The Wiz ✍✍ 1978 (G) Black version of the long-time favorite "The Wizard of Oz," based on the Broadway musical. Ross plays a Harlem schoolteacher who is whisked away to a fantasy version of New York City in a search for her identity. Some good character performances and musical numbers, but generally an overblown and garish effort with Ross too old for her role. Pryor is poorly cast, but Jackson is memorable as the Scarecrow. High-budget ($24 million) production with a ton of name stars, lost $11 million, and cooled studios on black films. Horne's number as the good witch is the best reason to sit through this one. ♫The Feeling That We Have; Can I Go On Not Knowing; Glinda's Theme; He's the Wizard; Soon as I Get Home; You Can't Win; Ease on Down the Road; What Would I Do If I Could Feel?; Slide Some Oil to Me. 133m/C **VHS, Beta, LV, Letterbox.** Diana Ross, Michael Jackson, Nipsey Russell, Ted Ross, Mabel King, Thelma Carpenter, Richard Pryor, Lena Horne; **D:** Sidney Lumet; **W:** Joel Schumacher; **C:** Oswald Morris; **M:** Quincy Jones. Nominations: Academy Awards '78: Best Art Direction/Set Decoration, Best Cinematography, Best Costume Design, Original Song Score and/or Adaptation. *USH, FCT*

The Wizard ✍1/2 1989 (PG) Facing the dissolution of his dysfunctional family, a youngster decides to take his autistic, video game-playing little brother across the country to a national video competition. Way too much plot in pretentious, blatantly commercial feature-length Nintendo ad, featuring the kid from "The Wonder Years." For teen video addicts only. 99m/C **VHS, Beta, LV, Closed Caption.** Fred Savage, Beau Bridges, Christian Slater, Luke Edwards, Jenny Lewis; **D:** Todd Holland; **W:** David Chisholm. *USH*

The Wizard of Gore ✍ 1970 (R) The prototypical Lewis splatter party, about a magician whose on-stage mutilations turn out to be messily real. High camp and barrels of bright movie blood. 96m/C **VHS, Beta.** Ray Sager, Judy Cler, Wayne Ratay, Jim Rau, Don Alexander, Monika Blackwell, Corinne Kirkin; **D:** Herschell Gordon Lewis; **W:** Allen Kahn; **C:** Alex Ameri, Daniel Krogh. *SMW*

The Wizard of Loneliness ✍✍1/2 1988 (PG-13) A disturbed young boy goes to live with his grandparents during WWII, and slowly discovers family secrets centering on his aunt. Excellent performances barely save an aimless plot with an overdone denouement. Based on the novel by John Nichols. 110m/C **VHS, Beta, LV, Closed Caption.** Lukas Haas, Lea Thompson, John Randolph, Lance Guest, Anne Pitoniak, Jeremiah Warner, Dylan Baker; **D:** Jenny Bowen; **W:** Nancy Larson; **C:** Richard Bowen; **M:** Michel Colombier. *NO*

The Wizard of Oz ✍✍1/2 1925 An early silent version of the L. Frank Baum fantasy, with notable plot departures from the book and later 1939 adaptation, starring long-forgotten comedian Semon as the Scarecrow, supported by a pre-Laurel Hardy as the Tin Woodman. With music score. 93m/B **VHS, Beta, 8mm.** Larry Semon, Dorothy Dwan, Bryant Washburn, Charles Murray, Oliver Hardy, Josef Swickard, Virginia Pearson; **D:** Larry Semon. *NOS, VYY, MLB*

The Wizard of Oz ✍✍✍✍ 1939 From the book by L. Frank Baum. Fantasy about a Kansas farm girl (Garland, in her immortal role) who rides a tornado to a brightly colored world over the rainbow, full of talking scarecrows, munchkins and a wizard who bears a strange resemblance to a Kansas fortune-teller. She must outwit the Wicked Witch if she is ever to go home. Delightful performances from Lahr, Bolger, and Hamilton; King Vidor is uncredited as co-director. Director Fleming originally wanted Deanna Durbin or Shirley Temple for the role of Dorothy, but settled for Garland who made the song "Over the Rainbow" her own. She received a special Academy Award for her performance. For the 50th anniversary of its release, "The Wizard of Oz" was restored and

includes rare film clips of Bolger's "Scarecrow Dance" and the cut "Jitterbug" number, and shots by Buddy Ebsen as the Tin Man before he became ill and left the production. Laserdisc edition includes digital sound, commentary by film historian Ronald Haver, and test footage, trailers and stills, as well as Jerry Maren talking about his experiences as a Munchkin. Yet another special release of the film, "The Ultimate Oz," contains a documentary on the making of the film, a reproduction of the original script, still photos, and liner notes. ♫Munchkinland; Ding Dong the Witch is Dead; Follow the Yellow Brick Road; If I Only Had a Brain/a Heart/the Nerve; If I Were the King of the Forest; The Merry Old Land of Oz; Threatening Witch; Into the Forest of the Wild Beast; The City Gates are Open. 101m/C **VHS, Beta, LV, Closed Caption, DVD.** Judy Garland, Margaret Hamilton, Ray Bolger, Jack Haley, Bert Lahr, Frank Morgan, Charley Grapewin, Clara Blandick, Mitchell Lewis, Billie Burke; **D:** Victor Fleming; **W:** Noel Langley; **M:** Herbert Stothart. Academy Awards '39: Best Song ("Over the Rainbow"), Best Original Score, National Film Registry '89;. Nominations: Academy Awards '39: Best Color Cinematography, Best Interior Decoration, Best Picture, Best Special Effects. *MGM, TLF, RDG*

The Wizard of Speed and Time ✍✍1/2 1988 (PG) A special-effects wizard gets the break of his life when he's hired by a movie studio, but there's more to this particular studio than he realizes. Jittlov, a real special-effects expert, plays himself in this personally financed production. Although brimming with inside jokes and references, this self-indulgence succeeds with its enthusiasm and ambition, despite being rather obviously self-produced. Unique special effects make it memorable. 95m/C **VHS, LV, Closed Caption.** Mike Jittlov, Richard Kaye, Page Moore, David Conrad, Steve Brodie, John Massari, Frank Laloggia, Philip Michael Thomas, Angelique Pettyjohn, Arnetia Walker, Paulette Breen; **D:** Mike Jittlov; **W:** Mike Jittlov, Richard Kaye, Deven Chierighino; **C:** Russell Carpenter; **M:** John Massari.

Wizards ✍✍1/2 1977 (PG) A good, bumbling sorcerer battles for the sake of a magic kingdom and its princess against his evil brother who uses Nazi propaganda films to inspire his army of mutants. Profane, crude, & typically Bakshian fantasy with great graphics. Animated. 81m/C **VHS, Beta, LV, Closed Caption. D:** Ralph Bakshi; **W:** Ralph Bakshi; **M:** Andrew Belling; **V:** Bob Holt, Jesse Wells, Richard Romanus, David Proval. *FOX*

Wizards of the Demon Sword ✍ 1994 (R) Group of warriors battle over a sword with the power to control the world.**CW:** Some nudity and violence. 90m/C **VHS.** Lawrence Tierney, Michael Berryman, Russ Tamblyn, Lyle Waggoner, Blake Bahner, Heidi Paine, Dan Speaker, Jay Richardson, Dawn Wildsmith; **D:** Fred Olen Ray; **W:** Dan Golden, Ernest Farino. *TTV*

Wizards of the Lost Kingdom ✍1/2 1985 (PG) A boy magician, aided by various ogres and swordster Svenson battles an all-powerful wizard for control of his kingdom. Family fare a bit too clean and harmless. 76m/C **VHS, Beta.** Bo Svenson, Vidal Peterson, Thom Christopher; **D:** Hector Olivera.

Wizards of the Lost Kingdom 2 ✍ 1989 (PG) A boy wizard is charged with vanquishing the evil tyrants from three kingdoms. Barely a sequel; no plot continuation or cast from earlier kiddie sword epic. 80m/C **VHS, Beta.** David Carradine, Bobby Jacoby, Lana Clarkson, Mel Welles, Susan Lee Hoffman, Sid Haig; **D:** Charles B. Griffith.

WKRP in Cincinnati, Vol. 1 1978 In the pilot episode for the TV sitcom, WKRP is a failing radio station with the cautious Arthur Carlson as the station manager (the station is owned by his mother). Andy Travis is hired as the new program director to turn things around and promptly turns WKRP towards rock and roll. Other regulars included newsman Les Nesman, sales manager Herb Tarlek, DJs Dr. Johnny Fever and Venus Flytrap, as well as ever-efficient secretary Jennifer Marlowe. 50m/C **VHS.** Gary Sandy, Gordon

Jump, Loni Anderson, Richard Sanders, Frank Bonner, Jan Smithers, Howard Hesseman, Tim Reid *MTM*

Wolf ✍ 1986 To everyone's lasting regret, an ex-Vietnam POW strives to rescue an American ambassador kidnapped by Central American rebels. 95m/C **VHS, Beta.** J. Antonio Carreon, Ron Marchini; **D:** Charlie Ordonez. *TWE*

Wolf ✍✍1/2 1994 (R) Harrison's original script is massaged by Nichols into an upscale new age men's movement horror spectacle lacking a suitable climax. Stressed out Manhattan book editor Will Randall (Nicholson) car hits a wolf on a country road and he's bitten when he tries to help the animal. Normally a wishy-washy guy, he notices some distinctly hairy changes to both his body and personality, leading him to make some drastic changes at work by knocking off his firm's greedy honchos and taking over. Talk about being ruthless in business. Boss' daughter Pfeiffer takes a shine to Randall's new animal magnetism, but is just visual candy. Walks a fine line between black comedy, camp, romance, and horror, though Jack baying at the moon seems sort of campy.**CW:** Language and werewolf attacks. 125m/C **VHS, Beta, LV, 8mm, Closed Caption.** Jack Nicholson, Michelle Pfeiffer, James Spader, Kate Nelligan, Christopher Plummer, Richard Jenkins, Om Puri, Eileen Atkins, David Hyde Pierce, Ron Rifkin, Prunella Scales; **D:** Mike Nichols; **W:** Wesley Strick, Jim Harrison; **C:** Giuseppe Rotunno; **M:** Ennio Morricone. *COL*

The Wolf at the Door ✍✍1/2 1987 (R) A well-appointed, sincere biography of impressionist Paul Gauguin in the middle period of life, during his transition from the petty demands of his Parisian life to the freedom of Tahiti. Not definitive or compelling, but serves the purpose of a biography—arousing interest in the subject's life and art. 90m/C **VHS, Beta, Closed Caption.** *DK FR* Donald Sutherland, Jean Yanne, Sofie Graboel, Ghita Norby, Max von Sydow, Merete Voldstedlund, Fanny Bastien, Valerie Morea; **D:** Henning Carlsen; **W:** Christopher Hampton; **M:** Roger Bourland. *FOX*

Wolf Blood ✍✍1/2 1925 When Dick (Chesebro) is hurt in an accident, Dr. Horton uses wolf's blood for a transfusion. Soon there are unexplained deaths and Dick fears he's becoming a man-beast. Early precursor to the wolfman films. 68m/B **VHS.** George Chesebro, Marguerite Clayton, Ray Hanford, Roy Watson, Milburn Morante; **D:** George Chesebro, George Mitchell. *GPV*

Wolf Call ✍1/2 1939 Carroll plays the son of a miner who travels with his devoted hound to see his father's old mine and start it working again. Gangsters and a beautiful Indian maiden get in his way. Master and pooch both find romance, and both sing. From the Jack London novel. 62m/B **VHS, Beta, 8mm.** John Carroll, Movita, Wheeler Oakman, Peter George Lynn; **D:** George Waggner. *VYY, FCT*

Wolf Dog ✍ 1933 A boy and his dog. Outdoor action and adventure. Twelve chapters, 13 minutes each. 156m/B **VHS, Beta.** Frankie Darro, Patricia "Boots" Mallory; **D:** Harry Fraser, Colbert Clark. *SNC, VCN, MLB*

Wolf Lake ✍1/2 1979 WWII veteran, whose son was killed in Vietnam, and a Vietnam army deserter clash with tragic consequences during their stay at a Canadian hunting lodge. Steiger gives it a go, but overwrought revenge pic resists quality upgrade. 90m/C **VHS, Beta.** Rod Steiger, David Hoffman, Robin Mattson, Jerry Hardin, Paul Mantu; **D:** Burt Kennedy.

The Wolf Man ✍✍✍1/2 1941 Fun, absorbing classic horror with Chaney as a man bitten by werewolf Lugosi. His dad thinks he's gone nuts, his screaming gal pal just doesn't understand, and plants on the Universal lot have no roots. Ouspenskaya's finest hour as the prophetic gypsy woman. Ow-oooo! Chilling and thrilling. 70m/B **VHS, Beta, LV.** Lon Chaney Jr., Claude Rains, Maria Ouspenskaya, Ralph Bellamy, Bela Lugosi, Warren William, Patric Knowles, Evelyn Ankers; **D:** George Waggner; **W:** Curt Siodmak; **C:** Joseph Valentine. *USH*

Wolf Trap 🐾🐾 1957 Trapped indeed—small town veterinarian is suffocating in a marriage to an older, domineering and needy wife. The two adopt an orphaned teenager, which turns out to be a big mistake as the unhappy husband gradually falls in love with the girl. Czech with subtitles. **95m/C VHS.** *CZ D:* Jiri Weiss. *FCT*

Wolfen 🐾🐾🐾 1981 (R) Surrealistic menace darkens this original and underrated tale of super-intelligent wolf creatures terrorizing New York City. Police detective Finney tries to track down the beasts before they kill again. Notable special effects in this thriller, which covers environmental and Native American concerns while maintaining the tension. Feature film debuts of Hines and Venora. Based on the novel by Whitley Strieber. Available in widescreen on laserdisc. **115m/C VHS, Beta, LV, Letterbox.** Albert Finney, Gregory Hines, Tom Noonan, Diane Venora, Edward James Olmos, Dick O'Neill, Dehl Berti, Peter Michael Goetz, Sam Gray, Ralph Bell; *D:* Michael Wadleigh; *W:* Michael Wadleigh, David Eyre; *C:* Gerry Fisher; *M:* James Horner. *WAR*

Wolfheart's Revenge 1925 An honest cowboy, helped by Wolfheart the Wonder Dog, steps in when a sheep rancher is murdered. Silent film with original organ score. **64m/B VHS, Beta, 8mm.** Guinn "Big Boy" Williams. *VYY, GPV*

The Wolfman 🐾 1982 In 1910, a young man learns that his family is heir to the curse of the Werewolf. Same old stuff. **91m/C VHS, Beta.** Earl Owensby, Kristina Reynolds; *D:* Worth Keeter. *NO*

The Wolves 🐾🐾🐾 1982 Gosha shows the world of the yakuza (gangster) during the 1920s. Reminiscent of the samurai, the movie combines ancient Japanese culture with the rapidly changing world of 20th Century Japan. In Japanese with English subtitles. **131m/C VHS, LV, Letterbox.** *JP* Tatsuya Nakadai; *D:* Hideo Gosha. *NO*

The Wolves 🐾🐾 1995 (PG-13) Blackie (Dalton) and his sister Barbara (Hocking) have inherit some land in the Alaskan wilderness that evil businessman King (Harmstorf) wants to use as a toxic waste dump. But when Blackie befriends native guide Chilkoot (Cardinal) and rescues an injured wolf, he decides to fight King and his henchmen.*CW:* Violence. **87m/C VHS.** Darren Dalton, Kristen Hocking, Raimund Harmstorf, Ben Cardinal, John Furey; *D:* Steve Carver; *W:* Steven Peters, Art Bernd; *C:* Eugene Shugleit. *THV*

A Woman and a Woman 🐾🐾 1980 Covers a ten-year period in the friendship of Barbara and Irena and how it survives their professional and personal conflicts. In Polish with English subtitles. **99m/C VHS.** *PL* Halina Labonarska, Anna Romantowska; *D:* Richard Bugajski. *FCT*

A Woman at Her Window 🐾🐾½ *Une Femme a sa Fentre* 1977 Aristocratic, jaded Margot (Schneider), the wife of dissolute nobleman Rico (Orsini), is pursued by capitalistic businessman Raoul (Noiret). But Margot herself is taken by idealistic Michel (Lanoux), a communist evading the secret police in 1936 Greece, and has a daughter from their brief and ultimately tragic union. Years later, Margot's now-grown daughter returns to Greece to learn more about her parents. Adapted from the novel by Pierre Drieu La Rochelle. French with subtitles. **110m/C VHS.** *FR* Romy Schneider, Philippe Noiret, Victor Lanoux, Umberto Orsini, Delia Boccardo, Gastone Moschin, Carl Mohner; *D:* Pierre Granier-Deferre; *W:* Pierre Granier-Deferre, Jorge Semprun. *FCT, CVC*

A Woman at War 🐾🐾½ 1994 (PG-13) True-story of a young woman's heroic fight against the Nazis. Nineteen-year-old Helene Moskiewicz (Plimpton) has had her parents arrested by the Gestapo in occupied Brussels, Belgium. She joins the resistance and falls for Franz Boehler (Stoltz), a young businessman who is not above lining his pockets with Nazi profits. When persecution of the Jews intensifies, Helene risks infiltrating Gestapo headquarters in order to save lives.*CW:* Some acts of violence. **115m/C VHS,**

Closed Caption. Martha Plimpton, Eric Stoltz; *D:* Edward Bennett; *W:* Edward Bennett. *REP*

A Woman Called Golda 🐾🐾🐾 1982 Political drama following the life and career of Golda Meir, the Israeli Prime Minister and one of the most powerful political figures of the 20th century. Davis portrays the young Golda, Bergman taking over as she ages. Superior made-for-television bio-epic. **192m/C VHS, Beta.** Ingrid Bergman, Leonard Nimoy, Anne Jackson, Ned Beatty, Robert Loggia, Judy Davis; *D:* Alan Gibson; *W:* Steven Gethers, Howard Gast. *PAR*

A Woman Called Moses 🐾🐾½ 1978 The story of Harriet Ross Tubman, who bought her freedom from slavery, founded the underground railroad, and helped lead hundreds of slaves to freedom before the Civil War. Wonderful performance by Tyson but the made-for-television film is bogged down by a so-so script. Based on the novel by Marcy Heldish. **200m/C VHS.** Cicely Tyson, Dick Anthony Williams, Will Geer, Robert Hooks, Hari Rhodes, James Wainwright; *D:* Paul Wendkos; *W:* Lonnie Elder III. *XVC, FCT, CCP*

Woman Condemned 🐾½ 1933 A reporter tries to clear a woman's name of murder. **58m/B VHS, Beta, LV.** Mischa Auer, Lola Lane, Claudia Dell, Richard Hemingway. *NO*

Woman Hater 🐾🐾 1949 Delightful farce about the belief in the single life. Confirmed bachelor plays games with a single woman. They eventually disregard their solitary ways in favor of romance. **101m/B VHS.** Stewart Granger, Edwige Feuillere, Ronald Squire, Mary Jerrold; *D:* Terence Young. *HMK*

The Woman He Loved 🐾🐾½ 1988 The infamous romance of Edward VIII, who gave up the throne of England for American divorcee, Wallis Warfield Simpson. Seymour and Andrews are fine in their roles but the made-for-television drama is slow-going. **100m/C VHS.** Anthony Andrews, Jane Seymour, Olivia de Havilland, Lucy Gutteridge, Julie Harris, Robert Hardy, Phyllis Calvert; *D:* Charles Jarrott. *VTR*

A Woman, Her Men and Her Futon 🐾🐾 1992 (R) A beautiful woman tries to find her identity by having a number of lovers but none can satisfy her every need.*CW:* Language and strong sexuality. **90m/C VHS, Closed Caption.** Jennifer Rubin, Lance Edwards, Grant Show, Michael Ceveris, Delaune Michel, Robert Lipton; *D:* Mussef Sibay; *W:* Mussef Sibay; *M:* Joel Goldsmith. *REP*

Woman Hunt woof! *The Highest Bidder* 1972 (R) Men kidnap women, then hunt them in the jungle for fun. So deeply offensive, we would give it negative bones if we could. "Hee Haw" bimbo Todd plays a sadistic lesbian. **81m/C VHS, Beta.** John Ashley, Lisa Todd, Eddie Garcia, Laurie Rose; *D:* Eddie Romero. *NLC*

The Woman Hunter 🐾½ 1972 A wealthy woman recovering from a traffic accident in Mexico believes someone is after her for her jewels and possibly her life. Eden dressed well, if nothing else; suspense builds ploddingly to a "Yeah, sure" climax. Made for television. **73m/C VHS, Beta.** Barbara Eden, Robert Vaughn, Stuart Whitman, Sydney Chaplin, Larry Storch, Enrique Lucero; *D:* Bernard L. Kowalski. *NO*

Woman in Black 🐾🐾½ 1989 Chilling ghost story set in 1925 and adapted from the novel by Susan Hill. Soliciter Arthur Kidd is sent to a remote house to settle the estate of a client. He's haunted by the mysterious figure of a woman in black, who according to the locals, has put a curse on the village. Arthur's driven close to the edge of sanity by the ghostly figure and the tragedy that haunts the past. Made for television. **100m/C VHS.** *GB* Adrian Rawlins; *D:* Herbert Wise. *VCO, FCT, TVC*

Woman in Brown 🐾🐾½ *The Vicious Circle; The Circle* 1948 It's Hungary, 1882, and five Jewish men are on trial for the murder of a man who actually committed suicide. Despite the prejudice and hatred from the locals, their lawyer believes

in and fights for their innocence. **77m/B VHS, Beta.** Conrad Nagel, Fritz Kortner, Reinhold Schunzel, Philip Van Zandt, Eddie LeRoy, Edwin Maxwell; *D:* W. Lee Wilder. *SNC*

A Woman in Flames 🐾🐾🐾 *Die Flambierte Frau* 1984 (R) A bored middle-class housewife leaves her overbearing husband and becomes a high-priced prostitute. She has a passionless affair with an aging bisexual gigolo. Dark and dreary tale of human relationships and the role of sex in people's lives. Interesting but depressing. **106m/C VHS, Beta.** *GE* Gudrun Landgrebe, Robert Van Ackeren, Matthieu Carriere, Gabriele Lafari, Hanns Zischler; *D:* Robert Van Ackeren. *GLV*

The Woman in Green 🐾🐾 *Sherlock Holmes and the Woman in Green* 1945 Murder victims are found with missing index fingers, and it's up to Holmes and Watson to try to solve this apparently motiveless crime. Available colorized. **68m/B VHS, LV, Closed Caption.** Basil Rathbone, Nigel Bruce, Hillary Brooke, Henry Daniell, Paul Cavanagh, Frederick Worlock, Mary Gordon, Billy Bevan; *D:* Roy William Neill. *SNC, REP, VYY*

Woman in Grey 🐾🐾 1919 A man and a woman battle with wits when they attempt to locate and unravel the Army Code while staying one step ahead of J. Haviland Hunter, a suave villain after the same fortune. Silent. **205m/B VHS, Beta.** Arline Pretty, Henry Sell. *NOS, CCB, MLB*

The Woman in Question 🐾🐾½ *Five Angles on Murder* 1950 When carnival fortune teller Astra (Kent) is murdered, Police Inspector Lodge (MacRae) finds that all her acquaintances have differing views about her character, making his investigation even more difficult. **82m/B VHS.** *GB* Jean Kent, Dirk Bogarde, Susan Shaw, Duncan MacRae, John McCallum, Hermione Baddeley, Charles Victor, Lana Morris, Vida Hope, Joe Linnane, Duncan Lament, Bobbie Scroggins, Anthony Dawson, John Boxer, Julian D'Albie, Josephine Middleton, Everley Gregg, Albert Chevalier, Richard Pearson; *D:* Anthony Asquith; *W:* John Cresswell; *C:* Desmond Dickinson; *M:* John Wooldridge. *HMV*

The Woman in Red 🐾🐾½ 1984 (PG-13) Executive Wilder's life unravels when he falls hard for stunning Le Brock. Inferior Hollywood-ized remake of the ebullient "Pardon Mon Affaire." Somehow the French seem to do the sexual force thing with more verve, but this one has its moments, and Wilder is likeable. Music by Stevie Wonder. ("I Just Called to Say I Love You; Don't Drive Drunk; It's More Than You; It's You; Love Light in Flight; Moments Aren't Moments; Weakness; Woman in Red. **87m/C VHS, Beta, LV.** Gene Wilder, Charles Grodin, Kelly Le Brock, Gilda Radner, Judith Ivey, Joseph Bologna; *D:* Gene Wilder; *W:* Gene Wilder; *M:* John Morris. Academy Awards '84: Best Song ("I Just Called to Say I Love You"); Golden Globe Awards '85: Best Song ("I Just Called to Say I Love You"). *ART, VES*

Woman in the Dunes 🐾🐾🐾🐾 *Suna No Onna; Woman of the Dunes* 1964 Splendid, resonant allegorical drama. A scientist studying insects in the Japanese sand dunes finds himself trapped with a woman in a hut at the bottom of a pit. Superbly directed and photographed (by Hiroshi Segawa). Scripted by Kobo Abe from his acclaimed novel. In Japanese with English subtitles. **123m/B VHS.** *JP* Eiji Okada, Kyoko Kishida, Koji Mitsui, Hiroko Ito, Sen Yano; *D:* Hiroshi Teshigahara; *M:* Toru Takemitsu. Cannes Film Festival '64: Grand Jury Prize; Nominations: Academy Awards '65: Best Director (Teshigahara), Best Foreign Language Film. *CVC, NYF, VDM*

Woman in the Moon 🐾🐾½ *By Rocket to the Moon; Girl in the Moon* 1929 Assorted people embark on a trip to the moon and discover water, and an atmosphere, as well as gold. Lang's last silent outing is nothing next to "Metropolis," with a rather lame plot (greedy trip bashers seek gold), but interesting as a vision of the future. Lang's predictions about space travel often hit the mark. Silent with music. **115m/B VHS, Beta.** *GE* Klaus Pohl, Willy Fritsch, Gustav von Wagenheim, Gerda Maurus; *D:* Fritz Lang. *VYY, IHF, LSV*

Woman in the Shadows 🎬🎬 1934 A ex-con retreats to the woods for serenity and peace, but is assaulted by mysterious women, jealous lovers, and gun-slinging drunks, until he explodes. A man can only take so much. From a Dashiell Hammett story. 70m/B VHS, Beta. Fay Wray, Ralph Bellamy, Melvyn Douglas, Roscoe Ates, Joe King. *VYY*

Woman in the Window 🎬🎬🎬 1944 Psycho-melodrama finds staid college professor Richard Wanley straying off the straight and narrow into a world of trouble—thanks to beautiful model Alice (Bennett). She invites him over but when her jealous boyfriend Claude (Loft) arrives unexpectedly, he attacks them both and Richard kills Claude in self-defense. Thinking no one will believe them, and afraid of scandal, the inept duo bury the body in the woods. Too bad Richard's best friend Frank (Massey) is the D.A. and there's a blackmailer around. Or is there? Surprise ending. Based on the novel "Once Off Guard" by J.H. Wallis. 99m/B VHS, Closed Caption. Edward G. Robinson, Joan Bennett, Raymond Massey, Arthur Loft, Dan Duryea, Edmund Breon, Dorothy Peterson, Robert (Bobby) Blake; *D:* Fritz Lang; *W:* Nunnally Johnson; *C:* Milton Krasner; *M:* Arthur Lange. Nominations: Academy Awards '45: Best Original Dramatic/Comedy Score. *MGM*

The Woman in White 🎬🎬½ 1997 The happy hours half-sisters, outgoing Marian (Fitzgerald) and shy Laura (Waddell), spend with their eccentric Uncle Fairlie (Richardson) soon turn sinister when Laura is married off to the seemingly charming Sir Percival Glyde (Wilby). Sir Percival quickly appears to be conspiring with the suspicious Count Fosco (Callow) to take control of Laura's money. When Marian visits her sister, she's alarmed by Laura's decline and equally unnerved by the mysterious woman in white, Anne (Vidler), who seems to know Glyde and tries to warn the sisters of impending danger. Based on the novel by Wilkie Collins, who also wrote "The Moonstone." ?m/C VHS. *GB* Tara Fitzgerald, Justine Waddell, James Wilby, Simon Callow, Ian Richardson, Andrew Lincoln, Susan Vidler, John Standing, Corin Redgrave; *D:* Tim Fywell; *W:* David Pirie; *M:* David Ferguson. *VTR*

The Woman Inside 🎬½ 1983 (R) Low-budget gender-bender depicts the troubled life of a Vietnam veteran who decides on a sex-change operation to satisfy his inner yearnings. Blondell's unfortunate last role as his/her aunt. Cheesy like Limburger; almost too weird and boring even for camp buffs. 94m/C VHS, Beta. *CA* Gloria Manon, Dave Clark, Joan Blondell; *D:* Joseph Van Winkle. *NO*

A Woman Is a Woman 🎬🎬🎬 *Une Femme Est Une Femme; La Donna E Donna* 1960 Godard's affectionate sendup of Hollywood musicals is a hilarious comedy about a nightclub dancer (Karina) who desperately wants a baby. When boyfriend Belmondo balks, she asks his best friend Brialy. Much ado is had, with the three leads all splendid. Godard's first film shot in color and cinemascope, with great music. In French with English subtitles. 88m/C VHS. *FR* Jean-Claude Brialy, Jean-Paul Belmondo, Anna Karina, Marie DuBois; *D:* Jean-Luc Godard; *M:* Michel Legrand. *INT*

A Woman Named Jackie 🎬🎬½ 1991 (PG) Three-part TV miniseries covering the life of Jacqueline Bouvier Kennedy Onassis. Downey offers a pretty picture as the enigmatic and beleaguered heroine but this version is simplistic at best. Based on the book by C. David Heymann. On three cassettes. 246m/C VHS, LV. Roma Downey, Stephen Collins, William Devane, Joss Ackland, Rosemary Murphy, Wendy Hughes, Josef Sommer; *D:* Larry Peerce; *W:* Roger O. Hirson. *NHO, IME*

The Woman Next Door 🎬🎬🎬 *La Femme d'a Cote* 1981 (R) One of Truffaut's last films before his sudden death in 1984. The domestic drama involves a suburban husband who resumes an affair with a tempestuous now-married woman after she moves next door, with domestic complications all around. An insightful, humanistic paean to passion and fidelity by the great artist, though one of his lesser works. Supported by strong outings from the two leads. In French with English subtitles. 106m/C VHS, Beta, LV. *FR* Gerard Depardieu, Fanny Ardant, Michele Baumgartner, Veronique Silver, Roger Van Hool; *D:* Francois Truffaut; *W:* Suzanne Schiffman; *M:* Georges Delerue. *HMV, FOX*

A Woman Obsessed 🎬 1988 (R) Pathetic, over-cooked drama about a woman obsessed with her long-lost son. "Ruth Raymond" is really porn-flick vet Georgina Spelvin. Soon-to-be camp classic takes itself with utter seriousness. 105m/C VHS, VHS, Beta. Ruth Raymond, Gregory Patrick, Troy Donahue, Linda Blair; *D:* Chuck Vincent.

A Woman of Affairs 🎬🎬 1928 Garbo, who can't have the guy she really loves (Gilbert), marries scoundrel. When she finds out husband's true profession, he kills himself and Gilbert comes back. In order to preclude happy ending, she decides the affair wasn't meant to be and expires. Tragically. Silent. 90m/B VHS. Greta Garbo, John Gilbert, Lewis Stone, Johnny Mack Brown, Douglas Fairbanks Jr., Hobart Bosworth, Dorothy Sebastian; *D:* Clarence Brown. *MGM, FCT*

Woman of Desire 🎬 1993 (R) Christina Ford (Derek) is a femme fatale who is yachting with rich boyfriend Ted when there is a terrible storm. Christina, Ted, and yacht captain Jack are washed overboard and Jack is found washed ashore with no memory. When Christina turns up she claims Jack killed Ted. So Jack gets a lawyer, Walter J. Hill (played by the redoubtable Mitchum) but is he wily enough to discredit the deceitful Christina? Bo's body is once again on display. Also available in an unrated version. 97m/C VHS, LV, Closed Caption. Bo Derek, Jeff Fahey, Steven Bauer, Robert Mitchum. *THV*

A Woman of Distinction 🎬🎬🎬 1950 Slapstick comedy with potential to be ordinary is taken over the top by a good, vivacious cast. Russell, the stuffy Dean of a women's college, is driven to distraction by a reporter linking her romantically to Milland, a visiting professor. 85m/C VHS, Beta, LV. Ray Milland, Rosalind Russell, Edmund Gwenn, Francis Lederer; *Cameos:* Lucille Ball; *D:* Edward Buzzell. *COL*

Woman of Paris/Sunnyside 🎬🎬🎬½ 1923 This double feature highlights the talents of Charlie Chaplin. "A Woman of Paris" is the tragic story of a French country girl who winds up a kept woman. Chaplin's only dramatic directional outing; he makes only a cameo appearance. Straightforward but hip story of sex and society. In "Sunnyside," an example of high Chaplin highjinks, the comic plays a hotel handyman who can't win. 111m/B VHS, Beta. Adolphe Menjou, Edna Purviance, Carl Miller, Lydia Knott; *Cameos:* Charlie Chaplin; *D:* Charlie Chaplin. *FOX*

A Woman of Rome 🎬🎬 *La Romana* 1956 Standard Italian star vehicle, with Lollobrigida portraying a successful prostitute in Rome who decides to change her life. Dubbed. 93m/B VHS, Beta. *IT* Gina Lollobrigida, Daniel Gelin, Franco Fabrizi, Raymond Pellegrin; *D:* Luigi Zampa. *NOS, FCT*

A Woman of Substance, Episode 1: Nest of Vipers 🎬🎬½ 1984 The woman of the title, Emma Harte, rises from poverty to wealth and power through self-discipline. First episode of three. Made-for-TV saga with our heroine working as a servant for the snooty Fairley family. 100m/C VHS, Beta. Jenny Seagrove, Barry Bostwick, Deborah Kerr; *D:* Don Sharp. *ART*

A Woman of Substance, Episode 2: The Secret Is Revealed 🎬🎬½ 1984 Emma Harte struggles to rise from a life of poverty to wealth and social acceptance. Second miniseries episode has Emma fighting to get by in the big city. Fun TV drama. 100m/C VHS, Beta. Jenny Seagrove, Barry Bostwick, Deborah Kerr; *D:* Don Sharp. *ART*

A Woman of Substance, Episode 3: Fighting for the Dream 🎬🎬½ 1984 Third installment is pretty good romantic TV saga. Rags-to-riches Emma finds love and happiness—at last! 100m/C VHS, Beta. Jenny Seagrove, Barry Bostwick, Deborah Kerr; *D:* Don Sharp. *ART*

The Woman of the Town 🎬🎬½ 1944 Frontier marshal and newspaperman Bat Masterson is portrayed convincingly by Dekker as a very human hero who seeks justice when the woman he loves, a dance hall girl who works in the town for social causes, is killed by an unscrupulous rancher. Fictionalized but realistic western shows "heroes" as good, ordinary people. 90m/B VHS, Beta. Claire Trevor, Albert Dekker, Barry Sullivan, Henry Hull, Porter Hall, Percy Kilbride; *D:* George Archainbaud; *M:* Miklos Rozsa. Nominations: Academy Awards '44: Best Original Dramatic/Comedy Score. *NOS, HEG, FCT*

Woman of the Year 🎬🎬🎬 1942 First classic Tracy/Hepburn pairing concerns the rocky marriage of a renowned political columnist and a lowly sportswriter. Baseball scene with Hepburn at her first game is delightful. Hilarious, rich entertainment that tries to answer the question "What really matters in life?" Tracy and Hepburn began a close friendship that paralleled their quarter-century celluloid partnership. Hepburn shepherded Kamin and Lardner's Oscar-winning script past studio chief Louis B. Mayer, wearing four-inch heels to press her demands. Mayer caved in, Tracy was freed from making "The Yearling," and the rest is history. 114m/B VHS, Beta, LV. Spencer Tracy, Katharine Hepburn, Fay Bainter, Dan Tobin, Reginald Owen, Roscoe Karns, William Bendix, Minor Watson; *D:* George Stevens; *W:* Ring Lardner Jr., Michael Kanin; *C:* Joseph Ruttenberg; *M:* Franz Waxman. Academy Awards '42: Best Original Screenplay; Nominations: Academy Awards '42: Best Actress (Hepburn). *MGM*

A Woman Rebels 🎬🎬½ 1936 A young Victorian woman challenges Victorian society by fighting for women's rights. Excellent performance from Hepburn lifts what might have been a forgettable drama. Screen debut of Van Heflin. Based on Netta Syrett's "Portrait of a Rebel." 88m/B VHS, Beta. Katharine Hepburn, Herbert Marshall, Elizabeth Allan, Donald Crisp, Van Heflin; *D:* Mark Sandrich. *CCB*

Woman Times Seven 🎬🎬½ *Sept Fois Femme; Sette Volte Donna* 1967 (PG) Italian sexual comedy: seven sketches, each starring MacLaine with a different leading man. Stellar cast and good director should have delivered more, but what they have provided has its comedic moments. 99m/C VHS, Beta. *IT FR* Shirley MacLaine, Peter Sellers, Rossano Brazzi, Vittorio Gassman, Lex Barker, Elsa Martinelli, Robert Morley, Alan Arkin, Michael Caine, Patrick Wymark, Anita Ekberg, Philippe Noiret; *D:* Vittorio De Sica. *COL, NLC*

A Woman Under the Influence 🎬🎬🎬 1974 (R) Strong performances highlight this overlong drama about a family's disintegration. Rowlands is the lonely, middle-aged housewife who's having a breakdown and Falk is her blue-collar husband who can't handle what's going on. 147m/C VHS, Beta, Closed Caption. Gena Rowlands, Peter Falk, Matthew Cassel, Matthew Laborteaux, Christina Grisanti; *D:* John Cassavetes; *W:* John Cassavetes. Golden Globe Awards '75: Best Actress—Drama (Rowlands); National Board of Review Awards '74: Best Actress (Rowlands), National Film Registry '90;; Nominations: Academy Awards '74: Best Actress (Rowlands), Best Director (Cassavetes). *TOU, FCT*

Woman Undone 🎬🎬½ *Joshua Tree* 1995 (R) Husband Allen Hansen (Quaid) and wife Terri (McDonnell) are involved in a car crash on a lonely stretch of desert highway. He dies, she's thrown clear, but an autopsy reveals he was actually shot in the head before the accident. Then attorney Ross Bishop (Elliott) gets involved and in a California courtroom Terri must prove that her unhappy marriage wasn't ended by murder. *CW:* Strong sexuality, language and some domestic abuse. 91m/C VHS, LV, Closed Caption. Mary McDonnell, Randy Quaid, Sam Elliott, Benjamin Bratt; **D:** Evelyn Purcell; **W:** William Mickelberry; **C:** Toyomichi Kurita; **M:** Daniel Licht. *REP*

The Woman Who Came Back ✓✓ **1945** A young woman who believes she suffers from a witch's curse returns to her small hometown with unhappy results. Good cast; bad script. Indifference inducing. **69m/B VHS, Beta.** Nancy Kelly, Otto Kruger, John Loder, Ruth Ford, Jeanne Gail; **D:** Walter Colmes. *COL*

The Woman Who Loved Elvis ✓½ **1993 (PG-13)** TV movie about an obsessive fan who converts her home into an Elvis shrine. **CW:** Some sexuality. **?m/C VHS.** Roseanne, Tom Arnold, Cynthia Gibb, Sally Kirkland, Danielle Harris, Joe Guzaldo; **D:** Bill Bixby. *THV*

The Woman Who Willed a Miracle ✓✓ **1983** Made-for-television drama has a devoted mother encouraging her mentally retarded son to pursue his interest in the piano. **72m/C VHS, Beta.** Cloris Leachman, James Noble; **D:** Sharron Miller. *NO*

Woman With a Past ✓✓½ **1992 (PG-13)** Reed gets out of an abusive marriage only to have her ex kidnap their kids. Since the law's no help she hires a bounty hunter to find them—committing armed robbery to pay the fees. Caught and imprisoned, Reed escapes, changes her identity, remarries, and even is reunited with her sons. Then she's suddenly arrested when her fugitive status comes to light 10 years later. Based on a true story; made for TV melodrama. **CW:** Thematic elements and scenes of abusive behavior. **95m/C VHS.** Pamela Reed, Dwight Schultz, Paul Le-Mat, Carrie Snodgress, Richard Lineback; **D:** Mimi Leder. *NHO*

A Woman Without Love ✓✓✓ **1951** A rarely seen film from Bunuel's Mexican period based on a classic Guy de Maupassant tale about a forbidden romance. Family tragedy results later when the husband "misbequeaths" his fortune. Minor but fascinating bug-the-bourgeoisie Bunuel. In Spanish with English subtitles. **91m/C VHS, Beta.** *MX* Rosario Granados, Julio Villareal, Tito Junco; **D:** Luis Bunuel. *XVC*

A Woman's Face ✓✓✓ *En Kvinnas Ansikte* **1938** An unpleasant, bitter woman with a hideous scar on her face blackmails illicit lovers as a form of revenge for a happiness she doesn't know. She even plots to murder a child for his inheritance. But after plastic surgery, she becomes a nicer person and doubts her plan. Lean, tight suspense with a bang-up finale. In Swedish with English subtitles. Remade in Hollywood in 1941. **100m/B VHS, Beta.** *SW* Ingrid Bergman, Anders Henrikson, Karin Carlsson, Georg Rydeberg, Goran Bernhard, Tore Svennberg; **D:** Gustaf Molander. *WAC*

A Woman's Face ✓✓✓ **1941** A physically and emotionally scarred woman becomes part of a blackmail ring. Plastic surgery restores her looks and her attitude. Begins with a murder trial and told in flashbacks; tight, suspenseful remake of the 1938 Swedish Ingrid Bergman vehicle. Climax will knock you out of your chair. **107m/B VHS, Beta.** Joan Crawford, Conrad Veidt, Melvyn Douglas, Osa Massen, Reginald Owen, Albert Basserman, Marjorie Main, Donald Meek, Charles Quigley, Henry Daniell, George Zucco, Robert Warwick; **D:** George Cukor. *MGM*

A Woman's Guide to Adultery ✓✓½ **1993** Four female friends, living and working in London, find their lives turned upside down by their passions for unavailable men. Political advisor Jo (Donohoe) is involved with married politician Martin (McElhinney) while art tutor Jennifer (Gillies) wants her student David (Morrissey), despite his having a live-in girlfriend. Ad execs Helen (Lacey) and Michael (Dunbar) find their marriage in tatters when Helen admits to an affair with their boss and photographer Rose (Russell) breaks her own rule about adultery by getting involved with married university instructor Paul (Bean). Based on the novel by

Carol Clewlow. Made for TV. **145m/C VHS.** *GB* Theresa Russell, Amanda Donohoe, Sean Bean, Adrian Dunbar, Ingrid Lacey, Fiona Gillies, Neil Morrissey, Danny Webb, Ian McElhinney, Julie Peasgood, Caroline Lee-Johnson; **D:** David Hayman; **W:** Frank Cottrell Boyce; **C:** Graham Frake; **M:** Daemion Barry. *VCO*

A Woman's Secret ✓✓ **1949** O'Hara admits to murder she didn't commit. Why? It's as indiscernible as why the plot should be muddled by flashbacks. RKO lost big bucks on this one. **85m/B VHS, Beta.** Maureen O'Hara, Melvyn Douglas, Gloria Grahame, Bill Williams, Victor Jory, Jay C. Flippen; **D:** Nicholas Ray; **W:** Herman J. Mankiewicz. *TTC, FCT*

A Woman's Tale ✓✓✓ **1992 (PG-13)** The superlative performance of Florence highlights this look at aging and death. Martha, 78, has been diagnosed with terminal lung cancer. She is looked after by a much-younger nurse and in turn looks after the older friends who share her apartment house. This gentle story quietly depicts the feisty, joyous Martha's last days and the simple pleasures she derives from her remaining time. Florence herself died from cancer not long after completing the film. **94m/C VHS, LV, Closed Caption.** *AU* Sheila Florence, Gosia Dobrowolska, Norman Kaye, Chris Haywood, Myrtle Woods, Ernest Gray, Monica Maughan, Bruce Myles, Alex Menglet; **D:** Paul Cox; **W:** Paul Cox. Australian Film Institute '91: Best Actress (Florence). *ORI, BTV*

A Woman's World ✓✓✓ **1954** Slick, sophisticated look at big business in the '50s, with Webb as the boss who chooses his next general manager based on the suitability of the executive's wives. Beautiful costumes, witty dialogue, and good acting make this worthwhile viewing. Plus, film offers a nostalgic look at New York in the '50s, with several shots of Fifth Avenue, Macy's, Park Avenue, and the long-gone Stork Club. Based on a story by Mona Williams. **94m/C VHS.** Clifton Webb, June Allyson, Van Heflin, Lauren Bacall, Fred MacMurray, Arlene Dahl, Cornel Wilde, Elliott Reid, Margalo Gillmore, Alan Reed, David Hoffman, George Melford; **D:** Jean Negulesco; **W:** Claude Binyon, Richard Sale, Mary Loos, Howard Lindsay, Russel Crouse. *FXV*

Wombling Free ✓✓ **1977** An English girl makes friends with a race of tiny, litter-hating furry creatures called Wombles. The creatures are visible only to the little girl because she is the only one who believes. Together they try to clean up a dirty world. British society is less cutting-edge about social roles, etc. than our enlightened one; be prepared for retrograde characterizations. Fun scene with Kelly/Astaire-style dance number. **86m/C VHS, Beta, Closed Caption.** *GB* Bonnie Langford, David Tomlinson; **D:** Lionel Jeffries; **M:** George Bassman. *COL*

The Women ✓✓✓½ **1939** A brilliant adaptation of the Clare Boothe Luce stage comedy about a group of women who destroy their best friends' reputations at various social gatherings. Crawford's portrayal of the nasty husband-stealer is classic, and the fashion-show scene in Technicolor is one not to miss. Hilarious bitchiness all around. Remade semi-musically as "The Opposite Sex." Another in that long list of stellar 1939 pics. **133m/B VHS, Beta, LV.** Norma Shearer, Joan Crawford, Rosalind Russell, Joan Fontaine, Mary Boland, Lucile Watson, Margaret Dumont, Paulette Goddard, Ruth Hussey, Marjorie Main; **D:** George Cukor; **W:** Anita Loos; **C:** Joseph Ruttenberg. *MGM*

Women & Men: In Love There Are No Rules ✓✓½ **1991 (R)** Made for cable extravaganza chronicling the relationships of three couples, each adapted from the short story of a renowned author. Irwin Shaw's "Return to Kansas City" tells of a young boxer who is prematurely pushed into a match by his ambitious wife. In Carson McCullers' "A Domestic Dilemma," a marriage begins to crumble thanks to an alcoholic wife. Finally, Henry Miller's "Mara" has an aging man and a young Parisian prostitute spending a revealing evening together. **CW:** Some language. **90m/C VHS, LV, Closed Caption.** Matt Dillon, Kyra Sedgwick, Ray Liotta, Andie MacDowell, Scott Glenn, Juliette

Binoche, Jerry Stiller; **D:** Kristi Zea, Walter Bernstein, Mike Figgis. *HBO*

Women & Men: Stories of Seduction ✓✓½ **1990** Three famous short stories are brought to the screen in this made-for-TV collection. Mary McCarthy's "The Man in the Brooks Brothers Shirt," Dorothy Parker's "Dusk Before Fireworks," and Hemingway's "Hills Like White Elephants" between them cover every aspect of male-female relationships. Since there are three casts and three directors, there is little to join the stories in style, calling attention to some flaws in pacing and acting ability; still, worth watching. **90m/C VHS, LV, Closed Caption.** James Woods, Melanie Griffith, Peter Weller, Elizabeth McGovern, Beau Bridges, Molly Ringwald; **D:** Ken Russell, Tony Richardson, Frederic Raphael. *HBO, FCT*

Women from the Lake of Scented Souls ✓✓ **1994** Mournful film, set in a rural Chinese village, focuses on matriarchal businesswoman Xiang (Gaowa), who runs the local sesame oil making factory that has just attracted the attention of Japanese investors. Seems the water of the nearby lotus-covered lake, scene of local tragedies, is Xiang's special ingredient. With her new-found wealth, Xiang is able to purchase a very reluctant bride, Huanhuan (Yujuan), for her mentally retarded son—a disaster in the making. Rich detail and nuanced performances; Chinese with subtitles. **105m/C VHS.** *CH* Siqin Gaowa, Wu Yujuan, Lei Luosheng, Chen Baoguo; **D:** Xie Fei; **W:** Xie Fei; **C:** Bao Xianran; **M:** Wang Liping. *AVI*

Women in Cell Block 7 woof! *Diario Segreto Di Un Carcere Femminele* **1977 (R)** Exploitative skinfest about women in prison suffering abuse from their jailers and each other. Seems that one of the prisoners knows the location of massive heroin stash. Badly dubbed. **100m/C VHS, Beta.** *IT* Anita Strindberg, Eve Czemeys, Olga Bisera, Jane Avril, Valeria Fabrizi, Jenny Tamburi; **D:** Rino Di Silvestro. *NO*

Women in Fury woof! **1984** A woman is sentenced to imprisonment in a mostly lesbian Brazilian jail, and subsequently leads a breakout. **94m/C VHS, Beta.** *BR* Suzanne Carvalno, Gloria Cristal, Zeni Pereira, Leonardo Jose. *ART*

Women in Love ✓✓✓ **1970 (R)** Drama of two steamy affairs, based on D.H. Lawrence's classic novel. Deservedly Oscar-winning performance by Jackson; controversial nude wrestling scene with Bates and Reed is hard to forget. Plot is dumped on in favor of atmosphere. Followed nearly two decades later (1989) by a "prequel": "The Rainbow," also from Lawrence, also directed by Russell and starring Jackson. **129m/C VHS, Beta, LV.** *GB* Glenda Jackson, Jennie Linden, Alan Bates, Oliver Reed, Michael Gough, Eleanor Bron; **D:** Ken Russell; **C:** Billy Williams; **M:** Georges Delerue. Academy Awards '70: Best Actress (Jackson); Golden Globe Awards '71: Best Foreign Film; National Board of Review Awards '70: Best Actress (Jackson); New York Film Critics Awards '70: Best Actress (Jackson); National Society of Film Critics Awards '70: Best Actress (Jackson); Nominations: Academy Awards '70: Best Adapted Screenplay, Best Cinematography, Best Director (Russell). *MGM, FOX, BTV*

Women in Prison ✓✓ *Women without Names* **1949** A pseudo-documentary style expose of the hardships endured by women in Italian detention camps following WWII. Controversial for its examination of such themes as human rights, abortion, lesbianism, and sexuality. English, French, Italian, with English subtitles. **94m/C VHS.** *IT* Simone Simon; **D:** Geza Radvanyi; **W:** Geza Radvanyi. *FCT*

The Women of Brewster Place ✓✓✓ **1989** Seven black women living in a tenement fight to gain control of their lives. (Men in general don't come out too well.) Excellent, complex script gives each actress in a fine ensemble headed by Winfrey in her TV dramatic debut) time in the limelight. Pilot for the series "Brewster Place." Based on the novel by Gloria Naylor. Winfrey was executive producer. **180m/C VHS, Beta.** Oprah Winfrey, Mary Alice, Olivia Cole, Robin

Givens, Moses Gunn, Jackee, Paula Kelly, Lonette McKee, Paul Winfield, Cicely Tyson; *D:* Donna Deitch; *W:* Karen Hall; *M:* David Shire. *ITC, MRG, FCT*

Women of the Prehistoric Planet woof!
1966 On a strange planet, the members of a space rescue mission face deadly perils. Typical bad sci-fi of its era, with horrid special effects, including "giant" lizards. Get this: there's one woman, and she's not of the planet in question. See if you can last long enough to catch the amazing plot twist at the end. 87m/C VHS. Wendell Corey, Irene Tsu, Robert Ito, Stuart Margolin, Lyle Waggoner, Adam Roarke, Merry Anders; *D:* Arthur C. Pierce. *EEL*

Women of Valor 🎞½
1986 During WWII, a band of American nurses stationed in the Philippines are captured by the Japanese and struggle to survive in a brutal POW camp. TV feature was made 40 years too late, adding up to a surreal experience. 95m/C VHS, Beta. Susan Sarandon, Kristy McNichol, Alberta Watson, Valerie Mahaffey, Suzanne Lederer, Pat Bishop, Terry O'Quinn, Neva Patterson; *D:* Buzz Kulik; *M:* Georges Delerue. *VTR*

The Women on the Roof 🎞🎞
Kvinnorna pa Taket Naive Linnea (Ooms) rents an attic apartment in Stockholm, just before the start of WWI. Her neighbor is Anna (Bergstrom), an artist working on a tableaux that soon involves Linnea, as the women become friends and then lovers. The reappearance of Anna's former boyfriend Willy (Skarskard) leads to a menage a trois until an accident compels Anna to reveal secrets that alter their lives. Swedish with subtitles. 86m/C VHS. *SW* Helena Bergstrom, Amanda Ooms, Stellan Skarsgard; *D:* Carl-Gustaf Nykvist; *W:* Carl-Gustaf Nykvist, Lasse Summanen; *C:* Jorgen Persson, Ulf Brantas. *HTV*

Women on the Verge of a Nervous Breakdown 🎞🎞🎞½
Mujeres al Borde de un Ataque de Nervios 1988 (R) Surreal and hilarious romp through the lives of film dubber Maura, her ex-lover, his crazed ex-mistress, his new lover, his son, and his son's girlfriend. There's also Maura's friend Barranco, who inadvertently lent her apartment to Shiite terrorists and now believes the police are after her as an accomplice in an airline hijacking. They meet in a comedy of errors, missed phone calls, and rental notices, while discovering the truth and necessity of love. Fast-paced and full of black humor, with loaded gazpacho serving as a key element. Introduced Almodovar to American audiences. In Spanish with English subtitles. 88m/C VHS, Beta, LV, Letterbox. *SP* Carmen Maura, Fernando Guillen, Julieta Serrano, Maria Barranco, Rossy de Palma, Antonio Banderas; *D:* Pedro Almodovar; *W:* Pedro Almodovar; *C:* Jose Luis Alcaine; *M:* Bernardo Bonazzi. New York Film Critics Awards '88: Best Foreign Film; Nominations: Academy Awards '88: Best Foreign Language Film. *ORI*

Women Unchained woof!
197? (R) Five women escape from a maximum security prison and make a run for the Mexican border, shunning civilized behavior along the way. Much less-than-honorable entry in desperate women genre. 82m/C VHS, Beta. Carolyn Judd, Teri Guzman, Darlene Mattingly, Angel Colbert, Bonita Kalem; *D:* Kent Osborne; *W:* Kent Osborne. *GEM*

Women's Club 🎞½
1987 (R) Table-turning sex comedy about a wealthy matron who patronizes a talented (?) young movie writer, but really wants—you know what. She begins lending his services to friends—and does he ever get worn out! This excuse may be intended to be uproarious, but it's hard to tell. And all that sex gets very perfunctory after awhile. 89m/C VHS, Beta. Michael Pare, Maud Adams, Eddie Velez; *D:* Sandra Weintraub; *M:* Paul Antonelli. *ART, VES*

Women's Prison Escape 🎞½
Cell Block Girls 19?? Four tough broads blow the pen and are forced to high-tail it through the Everglades. They can't decide which is worse, the snakes and 'gators, or the corrupt and sleazy life they left behind. Only cinematic pairing of Rooney

and Lurch. 90m/C VHS. Ted Cassidy, Chris Robinson, Mickey Rooney; *D:* Chris Robinson. *QVD*

Women's Prison Massacre woof!
1985 Four male convicts temporarily detained at a woman's prison (why?) violently take hostages and generally make trouble for the authorities and the women. Horribly dubbed. 89m/C VHS, Beta. *IT* Laura Gemser, Lorraine De Selle, Francoise Perrot, Ursula Flores, Gabriele Truti; *D:* Gilbert Roussel. *ART, VES*

Wonder Man 🎞🎞½
1945 When a brash nightclub entertainer (Kaye) is killed by gangsters, his mild-mannered twin brother (Kaye) takes his place to smoke out the killers. One of Kaye's better early films. The film debuts of Vera-Ellen and Cochran. Look for Mrs. Howell of "Gilligan's Island." ♫So In Love; Bali Boogie; Ortchi Chornya; Opera Number. 98m/C VHS. Danny Kaye, Virginia Mayo, Vera-Ellen, Steve Cochran, S.Z. Sakall, Otto Kruger; *D:* H. Bruce Humberstone; *C:* Victor Milner. Academy Awards '45: Best Special Effects; Nominations: Academy Awards '45: Best Song ("So in Love"), Best Sound, Scoring of a Musical. *HBO*

The Wonderful, Horrible Life of Leni Riefenstahl
1993 Documentary portrait of Hitler's favorite filmmaker. At 91, Riefenstahl tells of her start as an actress, her first directorial effort "The Blue Light" (1932), and the two infamous propaganda films, "Triumph of the Will" (1935) and "Olympia" (1938), which still provoke. She discusses her relationship with Hitler and Joseph Goebbels and the accusations that have continued to haunt her life. Still active, Riefenstahl's current work documents the Nuba tribes of Africa and underwater filming of rare aquatic life in the Seychelles Islands. German with English subtitles. 180m/C VHS. *GE D:* Ray Muller. *KIV*

The Wonderful Ice Cream Suit 🎞½
1998 (PG) Slapstick hokum based on Bradbury's 1957 story "The Magic White Suit." Cash-poor barrio sharpster Gomez (Mantegna) would like to buy a flashy white suit he sees in a shop window and manages to convince four more men of roughly the same size to pony up some money and have shares in the suit. Each take a turn wearing the garment and find their various dreams coming true. 77m/C VHS. Joe Mantegna, Esai Morales, Edward James Olmos, Clifton Gonzalez Gonzalez, Gregory Sierra, Liz Torres, Sid Caesar, Howard Morris, Lisa Vidal, Mike Moroff; *D:* Stuart Gordon; *W:* Ray Bradbury; *C:* Max Ahlberg. *TOU*

The Wonderful World of the Brothers Grimm 🎞🎞½
1962 Big-budget fantasy based very loosely on the Grimm Brothers' lives and three of their stories: "The Dancing Princesses," "The Cobbler and the Elves," and "The Singing Bone." Good, fun Puppetoon scenes, but leaves much else to be desired. A megawatt cast and the ubiquitous hand of producer-director Pal are not enough to cover the flaws. The biographical parts are hokey, and the tales used are the wrong ones. Disappointing but historically interesting. The second-ever story film done in Cinerama. ♫The Theme From the Wonderful World of the Brothers Grimm; Gypsy Rhapsody; Christmas Land; Ah-Oom; Above the Stars; Dee-Are-A-Gee-O-En (Dragon). 134m/C VHS, Beta, LV, Letterbox. Laurence Harvey, Karl-Heinz Boehm, Claire Bloom, Buddy Hackett, Terry-Thomas, Russ Tamblyn, Yvette Mimieux, Oscar Homolka, Walter Slezak, Beulah Bondi, Martita Hunt, Otto Kruger, Barbara Eden, Jim Backus, Arnold Stang; *D:* Henry Levin, George Pal; *W:* William Roberts; *C:* Paul Vogel. Academy Awards '62: Best Costume Design (Color); Nominations: Academy Awards '62: Best Adapted Score, Best Art Direction/Set Decoration (Color), Best Color Cinematography. *MGM*

Wonderland 🎞🎞🎞
The Fruit Machine 1988 Campy thriller follows two young gay boys in England, inadvertent witnesses to a murder, who find themselves on the run. Fast paced, dreamy atmosphere makes up for the sometimes confusing plot. Often overlooked British import. 103m/C VHS, LV. *GB* Emile Charles, Tony Forsyth, Robert Steph-

ens, Clare Higgins, Bruce Payne, Robbie Coltrane; *D:* Philip Saville; *W:* Frank Clarke; *M:* Hans Zimmer. *VTR, VEU*

Wonderland Cove 🎞
1975 Seafaring adventurer adopts five orphan children and embarks on journeys to exotic locales. 78m/C Beta. Clu Gulager, Sean Marshall, Randi Kiger, Lori Walsh; *D:* Jerry Thorpe.

The Wonders of Aladdin 🎞½
Les Mille Et Une Nuits; Le Meraviglie Di Aladino 1961 Slapstick comedy based on the ancient rubbed-lamp-and-genie chestnut. Kids'll love it; adults will yawn. 93m/C VHS, Beta. *IT FR* Donald O'Connor, Vittorio De Sica; *D:* Henry Levin, Mario Bava. *NLC*

Wonderwall: The Movie 🎞½
1969 Bizarre characters trip over themselves in love while groovy music plays in background. 82m/C VHS, Beta. *GB* Jack MacGowran, Jane Birkin, Irene Handl; *D:* Joe Massot; *M:* George Harrison, Eric Clapton, Ravi Shankar. *FCT, MVD*

Wonsan Operation 🎞
1978 U.N. soldiers plunge into the muddy depths of enemy territory in search of secret information that would end the Korean War. Dubbed. 100m/C VHS, Beta. Lew Montania, Frederick Hill; *D:* Terrence Sul. *VDA*

Woo 🎞🎞
1997 (R) Knock-out party girl Darlene "Woo" Bates (Pinkett Smith) agrees to a blind date with nice-guy law student Tim (Davidson) on the advice of her cross-dressing psychic. Tim wants to do the right thing and be honorable, but Woo seduces, endangers, and humiliates him at every turn. When Tim finally stands up for himself, she has a change of heart and appreciates his better qualities. Somewhat mean-spirited comedy trods familiar urban cliches and blind-date disaster territory, but Pinkett Smith's turn could be a star-maker. *CW:* Sexual content and language. 80m/C VHS. Jada Pinkett Smith, Tommy Davidson, Duane Martin, Dave Chappelle, L.L. Cool J., Paula Jai Parker, Darrell Heath, Pam Grier, Isaac Hayes; *D:* Daisy von Scherler Mayer; *W:* David Johnson; *C:* Jean Lepine; *M:* Michel Colombier. *NYR*

Woodchipper Massacre woof!
1989 Aunt Tess is frozen in the freezer, waiting to be turned into whatever the fleshy equivalent of woodchips is by her three unloving relations, and her totally evil son has just broken out of prison looking to retrieve his inheritance. You think you have problems? You'll have one less if you leave this one on the shelf. 90m/C VHS, Beta. Jon McBride, Patricia McBride; *D:* Jon McBride. *DMP*

The Wooden Gun 🎞🎞½
1979 Conflicts arise between two teenage factions in 1950s Tel Aviv: native Israelis, and the children of Jews arrived from Europe since WWII. In Hebrew with English subtitles. 91m/C VHS, Beta. *IS D:* Han Moshenson. *ERG, FCT*

Wooden Horse 🎞🎞🎞
1950 Lean thriller of British POWs escaping a Nazi camp through a tunnel beneath their exercise horse. Based on a true incident in 1943 and on "The Tunnel Escape" by Eric Williams; set the tone for all British prison-camp movies to follow: stiff upper lip and all that, and adolescent-style trickery reminiscent of English boarding schools. 98m/C VHS, Beta. Anthony Steel, Leo Genn, David Tomlinson, Bryan Forbes, Peter Finch; *D:* Jack Lee. *NO*

The Wooden Man's Bride 🎞🎞
1994 The inhabitants of this austere 1920s, northwest Chinese community live in stone fortresses, fearful of being attacked by roving armed bandits. Which is what happens to the bridal party of Young Mistress (Lan), who's kidnapped by bandit leader Tang (Mingjun). She's released unharmed when her servant Kui (Shih) impresses Tang with his bravery but her bridegroom has been killed in a freak accident and formidable Madame Liu (Yumei), who runs the fortress, forces her to marry a wooden likeness of the deceased. Despairing Young Mistress begins an affair with Kui, which can only end badly. Mandarin with subtitles. 114m/C VHS. *CH* Wang Lan, Chang Shih, Wang Yu-mei, Kao Mingjun; *D:* Huang Jianxin; *W:* Yang Zhengguang; *C:* Zhang Xiaoguang; *M:* Zhang Dalong. *HMK*

Woodstock 🎬🎬🎬🎬 **1970 (R)** Step into the way-back machine and return to the times of luv, peace, and understanding. Powerful chronicle of the great 1969 Woodstock rock concert celebrates the music and lifestyle of the late '60s. More than 400,000 spectators withstood lack of privacy, bathrooms, parking, and food while wallowing in the mud for four days to catch classic performances by a number of popular performers and groups. Martin Scorsese helped edit the documentary, trail-blazing in its use of split-screen montage. A director's cut is available at 225 minutes. **180m/C VHS, Beta, LV, Letterbox, Closed Caption.** *D:* Michael Wadleigh. Academy Awards '70: Best Feature Documentary, National Film Registry '96;; Nominations: Academy Awards '70: Best Film Editing, Best Sound. *MVD, WAR*

Woodstock '94 **1994** The 25th anniversary of the original festival was celebrated with a three-day music explosion (complete with mud). Includes backstage footage and interviews with some of the 30 acts, including Aerosmith, Peter Gabriel, Blind Melon, Metallica, and the Red Hot Chili Peppers. **165m/C VHS.** *PGV, MVD*

Woof! 🎬🎬½ **1990** Follows the misadventures of a boy who metamorphosed into a dog. **82m/C VHS, Closed Caption.** *D:* David Cobham. *FHE, UND, BTV*

The Word 🎬🎬🎬 **1978** Intriguing premise has an archeologist finding a perviously unknown text purporting to be written by the younger brother of Jesus. If authentic and publicized, it would wreak theological havoc. Janssen is off to Italy to check up; he finds murder and skullduggery. Well-acted, interesting story. **300m/C VHS, Beta, LV.** David Janssen, James Whitmore, Florinda Bolkan, Eddie Albert, Geraldine Chaplin, Hurd Hatfield, John Huston, Kate Mulgrew, Janice Rule, Nicol Williamson; *D:* Richard Lang; *M:* Alex North.

Words and Music 🎬🎬½ **1948** Plot based on the careers of Rodgers and Hart is little more than a peg on which to hang lots of classic songs, sung by a parade of MGM stars. Also includes Kelly's dance recreation of "Slaughter on Tenth Avenue." Good advice: if no one's singing or dancing, fast forward. **122m/C VHS, Beta.** Mickey Rooney, Tom Drake, Judy Garland, Gene Kelly, Lena Horne, Mel Torme, Cyd Charisse, Marshall Thompson, Janet Leigh, Betty Garrett, June Allyson, Perry Como, Vera-Ellen, Ann Sothern; *D:* Norman Taurog; *M:* Richard Rodgers, Lorenz Hart. *MGM*

Words by Heart **1984** An African American family in turn of the century Missouri faces issues of discrimination and prejudice. Twelve-year-old Lena wins a speech contest and begins to question her place in the community and her aspirations for a better life. Based on a book by Ouida Sebestyen. Aired by PBS as part of the "Wonderworks" family movie series. **116m/C VHS, Closed Caption.** Charlotte Rae, Robert Hooks, Alfre Woodard; *D:* Robert Thompson. *FCT, HMV*

Work/Police 🎬🎬🎬½ **1916** Two Chaplin two-reelers. In "Work (The Paper Hanger)" (1915), a family hires Charlie and cohorts Armstrong and Purviance to re-paper a house. Little did they know! In "Police" (1916), Charlie plays an ex-con released into the cruel world. Unremittingly hilarious. Silent with music score. **54m/B VHS, Beta.** Charlie Chaplin, Billy Armstrong, Charles Insley, Marta Golden, Edna Purviance; *D:* Charlie Chaplin. *VYY*

Workin' for Peanuts **1985** A young man who sells beer at a baseball stadium falls in love with the stadium owner's daughter. **52m/C VHS, Beta, Closed Caption.** Carl Marotte, Jessica Steer. *NO*

Working Girl 🎬🎬🎬 **1988 (R)** Romantic comedy set in the Big Apple has secretary Griffith working her way to the top in spite of her manipulative boss (Weaver in a powerful parody). Griffith gets her chance to shine when Weaver breaks a leg. She meets Ford for business that turns to romance. A 1980s Cinderella story that's sexy, funny, and sharply written and directed. Nice work by Ford, but this is definitely Griffith's movie. And

keep an eye on gal pal Cusack. 🎵Let the River Run. **115m/C VHS, Beta, LV, Closed Caption.** Melanie Griffith, Harrison Ford, Sigourney Weaver, Joan Cusack, Alec Baldwin, Philip Bosco, Ricki Lake, Nora Dunn, Olympia Dukakis, Oliver Platt, James Lally, Kevin Spacey, Robert Easton; *D:* Mike Nichols; *W:* Kevin Wade; *C:* Michael Ballhaus; *M:* Carly Simon, Rob Mounsey. Academy Awards '88: Best Song ("Let the River Run"); Golden Globe Awards '89: Best Actress—Musical/Comedy (Griffith), Best Film—Musical/Comedy, Best Song ("Let the River Run"), Best Supporting Actress (Weaver); Nominations: Academy Awards '88: Best Actress (Griffith), Best Director (Nichols), Best Picture, Best Supporting Actress (Cusack, Weaver). *FOX*

Working Girls 🎬 **1975 (R)** Three girls who share an apartment in Los Angeles are willing to do anything for money. And they do. For lack of anything else to recommend, watch for the striptease by Peterson, better known as Elvira on TV. **80m/C VHS, Beta.** Sarah Kennedy, Laurie Rose, Mark Thomas, Cassandra Peterson; *D:* Stephanie Rothman. *VCI*

Working Girls 🎬🎬🎬 **1987** An acclaimed, controversial look by independent filmmaker Borden into lives of modern brothel prostitutes over the period of one day. The sex is realistically candid and perfunctory; the docudrama centers on a prostitute who has a Yale graduate and aspiring photographer living with a female lover. Compelling, touching, and lasting, with sexually candid language and scenery. **93m/C VHS, Beta.** Amanda Goodwin, Louise Smith, Ellen McElduff, Maurisia Zach, Janne Peters, Helen Nicholas; *D:* Lizzie Borden; *W:* Lizzie Borden, Sandra Kay; *M:* David Van Tiegham. *COL, NLC, HHE*

Working Winnie/Oh So Simple **1922** Two rare, second-echelon short silent comedies. **61m/B VHS, Beta, 8mm.** Ethlyn Gibson, Bobby Ray. *VYY*

The World According to Garp 🎬🎬🎬 **1982 (R)** Comedy turns to tragedy in this relatively faithful version of John Irving's popular (and highly symbolic) novel, adapted by Steve Tesich. Chronicles the life of T.S. Garp, a struggling everyman beset by the destructive forces of modern society. Nevertheless, Garp maintains his optimism even as his life unravels around him. At the core of the film is a subplot involving a group of extreme feminists inspired in part by Garp's mother, the author of "A Sexual Suspect." Close and Lithgow (as a giant transsexual) are spectacular, while Williams is low-key and tender as the beleaguered Garp. Ultimately pointless, perhaps, but effectively and intelligently so. **136m/C VHS, Beta, LV, Closed Caption.** Robin Williams, Mary Beth Hurt, John Lithgow, Glenn Close, Hume Cronyn, Jessica Tandy, Swoosie Kurtz, Amanda Plummer, Warren Berlinger, Brandon Maggart; *Cameos:* George Roy Hill; *D:* George Roy Hill; *W:* Steve Tesich; *M:* David Shire. Los Angeles Film Critics Association Awards '82: Best Supporting Actor (Lithgow), Best Supporting Actress (Close); National Board of Review Awards '82: Best Supporting Actress (Close); New York Film Critics Awards '82: Best Supporting Actor (Lithgow); Nominations: Academy Awards '82: Best Supporting Actor (Lithgow), Best Supporting Actress (Close). *WAR*

The World Accuses 🎬½ **1935** A woman takes a job in a nursery, unaware that one child is her own, put up for adoption after her wealthy husband died. Then, her ex-lover shows up in her attic after escaping from prison and takes her hostage. Whew! Everything works out, except that the viewer is left confused and incredulous. **62m/B VHS.** Vivian Tobin, Dickie Moore, Russell Hopton, Cora Sue Collins, Mary Carr; *D:* Charles Lamont. *NOS, DVT*

World and Time Enough 🎬½ **1995** Sculptor Mark's (Guidry) father compulsively designed Gothic cathedrals and after his death Mark decides to build his own version in a field belonging to a sympathetic cleric. Meanwhile, his equally eccentric lover, garbage-collector Joey (Giles), goes on a search for his birth parents. Lots of symbols, not much sense. **90m/C VHS.** Matt Guidry, Gregory G. Giles, Kraig Swartz, Peter Macon; *D:* Eric Mueller; *W:* Eric Mueller; *C:* Kyle Bergersen; *M:* Eugene Huddleston. *FCT*

A World Apart 🎬🎬🎬½ **1988 (PG)** Cinematographer Menges' first directoral effort is a blistering, insightful drama told from the point of view of a 13-year-old white girl living in South Africa, oblivious to apartheid until her crusading journalist mother is arrested under the 90-Day Detention Act, under which she might remain in prison permanently. Political morality tale is also a look at the family-vs-cause choices activists must make. Heavily lauded, with good reason; the autobiographical script is based on Slovo's parents, persecuted South African journalists Joe Slovo and Ruth First. **114m/C VHS, Beta, LV, Closed Caption.** *GB* Barbara Hershey, Jodhi May, Linda Mvusi, David Suchet, Jeroen Krabbe, Paul Freeman, Tim Roth; *D:* Chris Menges; *W:* Shawn Slovo; *C:* Peter Biziou; *M:* Hans Zimmer. British Academy Awards '88: Best Original Screenplay; Cannes Film Festival '88: Best Actress (Hershey), Best Actress (May, Mvusi), Grand Jury Prize; New York Film Critics Awards '88: Best Director (Menges).

The World Gone Mad 🎬🎬½ *The Public Be Hanged; Public Be Damned* **1933** During Prohibition, a tough reporter discovers the district attorney is the intended victim of a murder plot involving crooked Wall Street types. Full circle: this interesting drama of white-collar crime is again topical, though dialogue heavy and desultory. **70m/B VHS, Beta.** Pat O'Brien, Louis Calhern, J. Carrol Naish; *D:* Christy Cabanne. *NOS, CAB, DVT*

World Gone Wild 🎬½ **1988 (R)** Action yarn about a post-apocalyptic world of the future where an evil cult leader brainwashes his disciples. Together they battle a small band of eccentrics for the world's last water source. Stale rehash (with ineffective satiric elements) of the Mad Max genre, served with Ant for campy appeal. **95m/C VHS, Beta, LV.** Bruce Dern, Michael Pare, Adam Ant, Catherine Mary Stewart, Rick Podell; *D:* Lee H. Katzin; *C:* Don Burgess. *VTR*

The World in His Arms 🎬🎬½ **1952** Action and romance, circa 1850. Seal hunter Jonathan Clark (Peck) and his crew are in San Francisco when he meets beautiful Countess Marina Selanova (Blyth), who's fleeing an arranged marriage and is anxious to join her Uncle (Rumann), who happens to be the Governor General of Alaska (which is under Russian control). The twosome fall quickly in love but Marina's kidnapped by her would-be fiance, Prince Semyon (Esmond), who takes off for Alaska and Clark must go to rescue his love. Based on the book by Rex Beach. **104m/C VHS, Beta.** Gregory Peck, Ann Blyth, Anthony Quinn, Carl Esmond, Sig Rumann, John McIntire, Hans Conried, Andrea King; *D:* Raoul Walsh; *W:* Borden Chase; *C:* Russell Metty; *M:* Frank Skinner. *USH*

The World Is Full of Married Men woof! **1980 (R)** A philandering ad exec gets involved with a reckless model, inspiring his fed-up wife also to look for extramarital sex. Promiscuously raunchy melodrama was written by the queen of sleaze, Jackie Collins, based on her novel. **106m/C VHS, Beta.** *GB* Anthony (Tony) Franciosa, Carroll Baker, Sherrie Croon, Gareth Hunt, Paul Nicholas; *D:* Robert W. Young; *W:* Jackie Collins. *FOX*

The World of Abbott & Costello **1964** Compilation of the duo's most famous routines from their 18 films, including the frog in the soup sketch from "The Wistful Widow of Wagon Gap," the cobra skit from "Abbott & Costello Meet the Mummy," and their legendary baseball routine "Who's on First?" from "The Naughty Nineties." **75m/B VHS, Closed Caption.** Bud Abbott, Lou Costello. *USH*

The World of Apu 🎬🎬🎬🎬 *Apu Sansat; Apur Sansar* **1959** Finale of director Ray's acclaimed Apu trilogy (following "Pather Panchali" and "Aparajito"). Aspiring writer Apu drops out of the university for want of money and takes up with an old chum. An odd circumstance leads him to marry his friend's cousin, whom he comes to love. She dies in childbirth (though her baby boy lives); Apu is deeply distraught, destroys the novel he was working on, and becomes a wanderer. His friend finds him five years later and helps him begin again with his young son. Wonderfully human, hopeful story told by a world-class director. From the novel "Aparajito" by B. Bandopadhaya. In Bengali with English subtitles. **103m/B VHS, Beta. IN** Soumitra Chatterjee, Sharmila Tagore, Alok Charkravarty, Swapan Makerji; *D:* Satyajit Ray; *W:* Satyajit Ray; *M:* Ravi Shankar. *HHT, VYY, DVT*

The World of Henry Orient 🎬🎬🎬½
1964 Charming, eccentric comedy about two 15-year-old girls who, madly in love with an egotistical concert pianist, pursue him all around New York City. Sellers is hilarious, Walker and Spaeth are adorable as his teen groupies; Bosley and Lansbury are great as Walker's indulgent parents. For anyone who has ever been uncontrollably infatuated. Screenplay by the father/daughter team, Nora and Nunnally Johnson, based on Nora Johnson's novel. **106m/C VHS, Beta, LV, Letterbox, Closed Caption.** Peter Sellers, Tippy Walker, Merrie Spaeth, Tom Bosley, Angela Lansbury, Paula Prentiss, Phyllis Thaxter, Bibi Osterwald; *D:* George Roy Hill; *W:* Nunnally Johnson, Nora Johnson; *C:* Boris Kaufman; *M:* Elmer Bernstein. *MGM, FCT*

A World of Strangers 🎬🎬🎬
1962 A harsh look at apartheid through the eyes of an Englishman who has traveled to South Africa to manage a publishing house. Filmed in strict secrecy in Johannesburg due to the film's aggressive condemnation of the practice. Based on a novel by Nadine Gordimer. **89m/B VHS. DK** Ivan Jackson, Zakes Mokae; *D:* Henning Carlsen. *CVC*

The World of Suzie Wong 🎬🎬
1960 Asian prostitute Kwan plays cat-and-mouse with American painter Holden. She lies to him about her profession, her family, and herself. His association with her ruins relationships in his life. Why, then, does he not get a clue? Good question, not answered by this soap opera that would be a serious drama. Offensively sanitized picture of the world of prostitution in an Asian metropolis. On the other hand, it's all nicely shot, much of it on location in Hong Kong. Based on Paul Osborn's play which was taken from Richard Mason's novel. **129m/C VHS, Beta, LV.** *GB* William Holden, Nancy Kwan, Sylvia Syms, Michael Wilding, Laurence Naismith, Jacqueline "Jackie" Chan; *D:* Richard Quine; *C:* Geoffrey Unsworth. *PAR*

World of the Depraved 🎬
1967 Tango (Storm) runs an exercise club for young lovelies that are systematically being stalked by the mysterious full moon sex killer. Enter police detectives Riley and Hamilton (Decker, Reed), joking types who peep on their charges through keyholes, etc. When the plot finally gets around to the issue of the killer, the point of the movie has already been made clear. Silly, trivial, sophomoric humor lacking a trace of sincerity. Volume 6 of Frank Henenlotter's Sexy Shockers series. **73m/C VHS.** Tempest Storm, Johnnie Decker, Larry Reed; *D:* Herbert Jeffries; *W:* Herbert Jeffries. *SMW*

The World Owes Me a Living 🎬🎬
1947 Melodrama about pilot Farrar losing his memory in a plane crash and Campbell trying to spark his recollection of the past. **91m/B VHS.** *GB* David Farrar, Judy Campbell, Jack Livesey, John Laurie; *D:* Vernon Sewell; *W:* Vernon Sewell. *LOO*

World War II: When Lions Roared 🎬🎬½
1994 The "Lions" are Franklin Delano Roosevelt, Winston Churchill, and Joseph Stalin. The three Allied leaders formed an uneasy alliance to crush Hitler and Mussolini, all against much internal treachery. Uses lots of WWII newsreel footage. Made for television; on two cassettes. **186m/C VHS.** John Lithgow, Bob Hoskins, Michael Caine, Ed Begley Jr., Jan Tiska; *D:* Joseph Sargent; *W:* David W. Rintels; *C:* John A. Alonzo. *MPI*

World War III 🎬🎬½
1986 How's that for a title? A Russian plot is afoot to seize and destroy the Alaskan pipeline. When the plot is discovered, negotiation is needed to prevent world war. Exec-

utive branch showdown ensues between U.S. prez Hudson and Soviet chief Keith. Director Boris Sagal was killed on location, whereupon Greene took over, and shooting was moved indoors with dramatic tension lost in the transition. Made for TV. **186m/C VHS, Beta, Closed Caption.** Brian Keith, David Soul, Rock Hudson, Cathy Lee Crosby, Katherine Helmond, Robert Prosky, James Hampton, Richard Yniguez, Herbert Jefferson Jr.; *D:* David Greene; *W:* Robert L. Joseph. *FOX*

The Worldly Madonna 🎬🎬½ 1922
Young plays two roles as Janet, a convent novitiate, and her cabaret dancer sister, Lucy. Lucy thinks she's killed a man and Janet agrees to change places with her. **47m/B VHS.** Clara Kimball Young, Richard Tucker, George Hackathorne, William P. Carleton, Jean De Limur, William Marion, Milla Davenport; *D:* Harry Garson. *GPV, FCT*

The World's Greatest Athlete 🎬🎬
1973 (G) Lame Disney comedy about a Tarzan-like jungle-man (Vincent) recruited by an unsuccessful American college coach (Amos) and his bumbling assistant (Conway). Fun special effects, weak script add up to mediocre family fare. Cameo by Howard Cosell as—who else?—himself. **89m/C VHS, Beta.** Jan-Michael Vincent, Tim Conway, John Amos, Roscoe Lee Browne, Dayle Haddon; *Cameos:* Howard Cosell; *D:* Robert Scheerer; *W:* Dee Caruso; *M:* Marvin Hamlisch. *DIS, OM*

World's Greatest Lover 🎬🎬½ 1977
(PG) Milwaukee baker Rudi Valentine, played oft-hilariously by Wilder, tries to make it big in 1920s Hollywood. He has a screen test as a Hollywood movie sheik, but his wife (Kane) leaves him for the real McCoy. Episodic and uneven, it's alternately uproarious, touching and downright raunchy. **89m/C VHS, LV.** Gene Wilder, Carol Kane, Dom DeLuise, Fritz Feld, Carl Ballantine, Michael Huddleston, Matt Collins, Ronny Graham; *D:* Gene Wilder; *W:* Gene Wilder. *FOX*

The World's Oldest Living Bridesmaid 🎬🎬½ 1992
Hokey romantic comedy about a successful woman attorney who just can't find Mr. Right. Brenda feels even worse when she attends yet another friend's wedding. However, when she hires a younger, male secretary (former model Wimmer) the romantic sparks fly. An appealing and attractive cast helps this made-for-television fare. **100m/C VHS.** Donna Mills, Brian Wimmer, Beverly Garland, Winston Reckert, Art Hindle, Laura Press; *D:* Joseph L. Scanlan.

The Worm Eaters woof! 1977 (PG)
Mean developers want to take over a reclusive worm farmer's land. He unleashes his livestock on them. The bad guys turn into—eeck!—"worm people." A truck runs over our hero nearly 75 minutes too late to save the viewer. **75m/C VHS, Beta.** Herb Robins, Barry Hostetler, Lindsay Armstrong Black; *D:* Herb Robins; *W:* Herb Robins. *INC*

The Worst of Hollywood: Vol. 1
1990 Two really bad movies for your viewing displeasure. "Maniac" is a mad-scientist fest and "Protect Your Daughter" warns of the perils of the Flapper era. **115m/B VHS, Beta.** Bill Woods, Horace Carpenter, Phyllis Diller; *D:* Dwain Esper. *INC*

The Worst of Hollywood: Vol. 2
1990 A von Stroheim-fest of mediocrity. In "Fugitive Road" Erich plays an Austrian officer of the First World War. "The Crime of Dr. Crespi" has him portray a mad scientist. **131m/B VHS, Beta.** Erich von Stroheim, Dwight Frye; *D:* Erich von Stroheim. *INC*

The Worst of Hollywood: Vol. 3
1990 Two more awful, exploitive docudramas. "Nation Aflame" features many silent screen stars who teach the virtues of living in racial harmony. "Probation" boasts the first screen appearance of Grable, as a promiscuous woman who ends up in prison. **140m/B VHS, Beta.** Betty Grable. *INC*

The Worst Witch 🎬🎬½ 1986 (G)
Fantasy about a school for young witches where the educational lessons never go quite as planned. Adapted from the children's book "The Worst

Witch" by Jill Murphy. **70m/C VHS, Beta, LV.** Diana Rigg, Charlotte Rae, Tim Curry, Fairuza Balk; *D:* Robert M. Young. *IME*

Worth Winning 🎬🎬½ 1989 (PG-13)
A notoriously eligible Philadelphia bachelor takes a bet to become engaged to three women within three months, and finds himself in hot water. A critically dead-in-the-water chucklefest. **103m/C VHS, Beta, LV, Closed Caption.** Mark Harmon, Lesley Ann Warren, Madeleine Stowe, Maria Holvoe, Mark Blum, Andrea Martin, Alan Blumenfeld, Brad Hall, Tony Longo; *D:* Will MacKenzie; *W:* Sara Parriott, Josann McGibbon. *FOX*

The Would-Be Gentleman 🎬🎬½ 1958
The Comedie Francaise troupe performs Moliere's famous farce-comedy. Valuable as a record of the famous troupe on stage. When they're long gone, our grandkids can enjoy this. We can too (if we can't afford the trip to France), though it's less a film than a filming of a play. In French with English subtitles. **93m/C VHS, Beta.** *FR* Louis Seigner, Jean Meyer, Jean Piat. *DVT*

Woyzeck 🎬🎬🎬 1978
Chilling portrayal of a man plunging into insanity. Mired in the ranks of the German Army, Woyzeck is harassed by his superiors and tortured in scientific experiments, gradually devolving into homicidal maniac. Based on Georg Buchner play. In German with English subtitles. **82m/C VHS.** *GE* Klaus Kinski, Eva Mattes, Wolfgang Reichmann, Josef Bierbichler; *D:* Werner Herzog; *W:* Werner Herzog. *NYF*

WR: Mysteries of the Organism 🎬🎬🎬 1971
Makavejev's breakthrough film, a surreal, essayist exploration of the conflict/union between sexuality and politics—namely, Wilheim Reich and Stalin. A raunchy, bitterly satiric non-narrative that established the rule-breaking Yugoslav internationally. In Serbian with English subtitles. **84m/C VHS, Beta.** Milena Dravic, Jagoda Kaloper, Tuli Kupferberg, Jackie Curtis; *D:* Dusan Makavejev; *W:* Dusan Makavejev. *FCT*

The Wraith 🎬½ 1987 (PG-13)
Drag-racing Arizona teens find themselves challenged by a mysterious, otherworldly stranger. Hot cars; cool music; little else to recommend it. Lousy script; ludicrous excuse for a premise. Most of the stars herein are related to somebody famous. **92m/C VHS, Beta, LV.** Charlie Sheen, Nick Cassavetes, Sherilyn Fenn, Randy Quaid, Matthew Barry, Clint Howard, Griffin O'Neal; *D:* Mike Marvin; *W:* Mike Marvin. *ART*

Wrangler 🎬🎬½ 1988
When an Australian rancher dies his daughter tries to hang on to the family ranch from a ruthless creditor. She also has to deal with the attentions of two men—one a businessman and the other a cattleman, both equally dashing and handsome. Beautiful scenery of the Australian Outback as well as romance and adventure. **93m/C VHS, LV, Letterbox.** Jeff Fahey, Tushka Bergen, Steven Vidler, Richard Moir, Shane Briant, Drew Forsythe, Cornelia Frances, Sandy Gore, Frederick Parslow; *D:* Ian Barry; *W:* John Sexton; *M:* Mario Millo. *NO*

The Wreck of the Mary Deare 🎬🎬½ 1959
Slow-moving adventure drama focusing on the wreck of the freighter called the Mary Deare. Heston plays a ship salvager who comes upon a seemingly empty ship one night and Cooper is the only crew member on board. Special effects are the main attraction in this interesting sea drama. Film originally was to be directed by Hitchcock, but he turned down the offer to do "North by Northwest." **105m/C VHS, LV, Letterbox, Closed Caption.** *GB* Gary Cooper, Charlton Heston, Michael Redgrave, Emlyn Williams, Cecil Parker, Alexander Knox, Virginia McKenna, Richard Harris; *D:* Michael Anderson Sr. *MGM*

The Wrestler 🎬 1973
All-star wrestling, which is fictional anyway, gets said treatment in the appropriate way. Honest promoter (yeah, sure) bumps heads with bad-guy crooks who want in on the action. Made-for-TV opportunity for Asner to slum. **103m/C VHS, Beta.** Ed Asner, Elaine Giftos, Verne Gagne, Harold Sakata.

Wrestling Ernest Hemingway ⊘⊘
1993 (PG-13) A shy barber and a rollicking sea captain, both 75 and retired, form an unlikely companionship in a Florida retirement mecca. Duvall is the persnickety introvert who quietly follows routine and Harris is the would-be ladies' man whose endless tall tales include having tangled with Papa Hemingway in his youth. They share walks in the park, little league baseball from the bleachers, and coffee klatches that reveal the emptiness of their lives. Director Haines' focus on the principals' emotional baggage considerably dampens the proceedings. Depression in the elderly may be a topic that is not quite ready to come out of Hollywood's closet.**CW:** Language. 123m/C VHS, LV, Closed Caption. Robert Duvall, Richard Harris, Piper Laurie, Shirley MacLaine, Sandra Bullock; **D:** Randa Haines; **W:** Steve Conrad; **C:** Lajos Koltai; **M:** Michael Convertino. WAR

Wrestling Women vs. the Aztec Ape woof! *Doctor of Doom* 1962 An unclassifiable epic wherein female wrestlers battle a mad doctor and his Aztec robot gorilla. Dubbed badly, of course. Much anticipated follow-up to "Wrestling Women vs. the Aztec Mummy." 75m/C VHS, Beta. **MX** Elizabeth Campbell, Lorena Velasquez, Armando Silvestre, Roberto Canedo; **D:** Rene Cardona Sr. RHI, HHT, SNC

Wrestling Women vs. the Aztec Mummy woof! *Las Luchadoras Contra La Momia; Rock and Roll Wrestling Women Vs. the Aztec Mummy* 1959 Women, broad of shoulder, wrestle an ancient Aztec wrestler who comes to life. Furnished with a new rock soundtrack. 88m/C VHS, Beta. **MX** Lorena Velasquez, Armando Silvestre; **D:** Rene Cardona Sr. SNC, RHI, HHT

Write to Kill ⊘½ 1991 (R) A young mystery writer seeks revenge when his brother is murdered by a ring of counterfeiters.**CW:** Language, violence, and sensuality. 120m/C VHS, LV. Scott Valentine, Chris Mulkey, Joan Severance, G.W. Bailey, Ray Wise; **D:** Ruben Preuss. COL

Writer's Block ⊘⊘ 1991 (R) Fairchild is a successful thriller writer whose latest books feature a serial killer. She decides to kill the character off and is soon stalked by a psycho who is using her plots for some copy-cat killings. Tepid made for cable television movie with San Diego locations the only highlight. 90m/C VHS, Beta, Closed Caption. Morgan Fairchild, Joe Regalbuto, Michael Praed, Cheryl Anderson, Mary Ann Pascal, Douglas Rowe, Ned Bellamy; **D:** Charles Correll; **W:** Elisa Bell. PAR

Written on the Wind ⊘⊘⊘½ 1956 Sirk's frenzied, melodrama-as-high-art dissection of both the American Dream and American movies follows a Texas oil family's self-destruction through wealth, greed and unbridled lust. Exaggerated depiction of and comment on American ambition and pretension, adapted from Robert Wilder's novel. 99m/C VHS, Beta. Lauren Bacall, Rock Hudson, Dorothy Malone, Robert Stack, Robert Keith, Grant Williams, Edward Platt, Harry Shannon; **D:** Douglas Sirk; **W:** George Zuckerman; **C:** Russell Metty. Academy Awards '56: Best Supporting Actress (Malone); Nominations: Academy Awards '56: Best Song ("Written on the Wind"), Best Supporting Actor (Stack). USH, BTV

The Wrong Arm of the Law ⊘⊘⊘
1963 Loopy gangster yarn about a trio of Aussie gangsters who arrive in London and upset the local crime balance when they dress up as cops and confiscate loot from apprehended robbers. General confusion erupts among the police, the local crooks, and the imposters. Riotous and hilarious, with Sellers leading a host of familiar faces. 94m/B VHS, Beta. **GB** Peter Sellers, Lionel Jeffries, Nanette Newman, Bernard Cribbins, Dennis Price; **D:** Cliff Owen; **M:** Richard Rodney Bennett. MON

The Wrong Box ⊘⊘⊘ 1966 Two elderly Victorian brothers try to kill each other so that one of them may collect the large inheritance left to them. Based on a Robert Louis Stevenson novel. Well-cast black comedy replete with sight gags, many of which flop. 105m/C VHS, Beta. **GB** Peter Sellers, Dudley Moore, Peter Cook, Michael Caine, Ralph Richardson, John Mills; **D:** Bryan Forbes; **W:** Larry Gelbart; **M:** John Barry. COL

The Wrong Guys ⊘ 1988 (PG) Five giants of stand-up comedy star as a group of men who reunite their old boy scout pack and go camping. A crazed convict mistakes them for FBI agents. It's supposed to get zany after that, but succeeds only in being clumsy and embarassing. 86m/C VHS, Beta, LV, Closed Caption. Richard Lewis, Richard Belzer, Louie Anderson, Tim Thomerson, Franklin Ajaye, John Goodman, Ernie Hudson, Timothy Van Patten; **D:** Danny Bilson; **W:** Danny Bilson, Paul DeMeo. VTR

Wrong Is Right ⊘⊘ *The Man With The Deadly Lens* 1982 (R) A black action comedy about international terrorism, news reporting and the CIA. Connery is terrific, as usual, as a TV reporter in a head-scratching attempt at satire of our TV-influenced society. 117m/C VHS, Beta, LV. Sean Connery, Katharine Ross, Robert Conrad, George Grizzard, Henry Silva, G.D. Spradlin, John Saxon, Leslie Nielsen, Robert Webber, Rosalind Cash, Hardy Kruger, Dean Stockwell, Ron Moody, Jennifer Jason Leigh; **D:** Richard Brooks; **W:** Richard Brooks; **C:** Fred W. Koenekamp. COL

The Wrong Man ⊘⊘⊘½ 1956 Nightclub musician Fonda is falsely accused of a robbery and his life is destroyed. Taken almost entirely from the real-life case of mild-mannered bass player "Manny" Balestrero; probes his anguish at being wrongly accused; and showcases Miles (later to appear in "Psycho") and her character's agony. Harrowing, especially following more lighthearted Hitchcock fare such as "The Trouble with Harry." Part of the "A Night at the Movies" series, this tape simulates a 1956 movie evening with a color Bugs Bunny cartoon, "A Star Is Bored," a newsreel and coming attractions for "Toward the Unknown." 126m/B VHS, Beta, LV, Closed Caption. Henry Fonda, Vera Miles, Anthony Quayle, Nehemiah Persoff; **D:** Alfred Hitchcock; **C:** Robert Burks. WAR, MLB

The Wrong Man ⊘⊘½ 1993 (R) American sailor Alex Walker (Anderson) is framed for the murder of a Mexican smuggler. He eludes the police and winds up hitching a ride from wacko couple Phillip (Lithgow) and Missy Mills (Arquette). Missy does topless table dancing and is very interested in their fugitive passenger. Alex may be better off with the police. Made for cable television.**CW:** Nudity. 98m/C VHS, LV, Closed Caption. Kevin Anderson, John Lithgow, Rosanna Arquette, Robert Harper; **D:** Jim McBride; **C:** Alfonso Beato. REP

The Wrong Move ⊘⊘½ 1978 A loose adaptation of Goethe's "Sorrows of Young Werther" by screenwriter Peter Handke. Justly acclaimed and engrossing, though slow. Kinski's first film. A young poet, searching for life's meaning, wanders aimlessly through Germany. In German with English subtitles. 103m/C VHS, Beta. **GE** Nastassia Kinski, Hanna Schygulla, Ruediger Vogler, Hans-Christian Blech; **D:** Wim Wenders. FCT, GLV, TPV

The Wrong Road ⊘½ 1937 A young couple embark on a robbery spree, and subsequently end up in prison. On their release, they search for the loot they had previously hidden, but find the man who was holding it for them has died. Will they ever recover their ill-gotten stash? 62m/B VHS, Beta. Richard Cromwell, Helen Mack, Lionel Atwill, Horace McMahon, Russ Powell, Billy Bevan, Marjorie Main, Rex Evans; **D:** James Cruze. SNC

The Wrong Woman ⊘⊘½ 1995 (PG-13) When Melanie Brooke's (McKeon) boss is murdered, she's framed to take by rap by the company's sleazy comptroller (Field). Melanie begins a desperate hunt for the real culprit with the killer and the cops both after her.**CW:** Scenes of violence. 90m/C VHS, Closed Caption. Nancy McKeon, Chelsea Field. REP

Wrongfully Accused 1998 (PG-13) Yet another Nielsen spoof, "The Fugitive" (along with several other movies)is the target this time around. He's violinist Ryan Jack Harrison who has a tryst with a socialite (Le Brock) and then gets convicted of her husband's (York) murder. Harrison escapes, determined to find the actual killer—the one-armed, one-legged, and one-eyed man—while being hunted by marshal Fergus Falls (Crenna). Not yet reviewed.**CW:** Sex-related humor and language. ?m/C VHS. Leslie Nielsen, Richard Crenna, Kelly Le Brock, Michael York; **D:** Pat Proft; **W:** Pat Proft. NYR

Wuthering Heights ⊘⊘⊘⊘ 1939 The first screen adaptation of Emily Bronte's romantic novel about the doomed love between Heathcliff and Cathy on the Yorkshire moors. Dynamically captures the madness and ferocity of the classic novel, remaining possibly the greatest romance ever filmed. Excellent performances from Wyler's sure direction, particularly Olivier's, which made him a star, and Oberon in her finest hour as the exquisite but selfish Cathy. Remade twice, in 1953 (by Luis Bunuel) and in 1970. 104m/B VHS, Beta, LV. Laurence Olivier, Merle Oberon, David Niven, Geraldine Fitzgerald, Flora Robson, Donald Crisp, Cecil Kellaway, Leo G. Carroll, Miles Mander, Hugh Williams; **D:** William Wyler; **W:** Ben Hecht, Charles MacArthur; **C:** Gregg Toland; **M:** Alfred Newman. Academy Awards '39: Best Black and White Cinematography; New York Film Critics Awards '39: Best Film; Nominations: Academy Awards '39: Best Actor (Olivier), Best Director (Wyler), Best Interior Decoration, Best Picture, Best Screenplay, Best Supporting Actress (Fitzgerald), Best Original Score.HBO, HMV

Wuthering Heights ⊘⊘½ *Abismos de Pasion* 1953 Bunuel tackles the Bronte classic during his Mexican period, and comes up with a film containing little passion, but much of the customary Bunuel manic cynicism. The 1939 version is far superior, but fans of Bunuel will probably enjoy this one. Loosely adapted; in Spanish with English subtitles. Remade in another English-language version in 1970. 90m/B VHS, Beta. **MX** Irasema Dilian, Jorge Mistral, Lilia Prado, Ernesto Alonso; **D:** Luis Bunuel. XVC

Wuthering Heights ⊘⊘½ 1970 (G) The third screening of the classic Emily Bronte romance about two doomed lovers. Fuest's version features excellent photography, and Calder-Marshall's and Dalton's performances are effective, but fail even to approach the intensity and pathos of the 1939 film original (or of the book). Filmed on location in Yorkshire, England. 105m/C VHS, Beta. **GB** Anna Calder-Marshall, Timothy Dalton, Harry Andrews, Pamela Brown, Judy Cornwell, James Cossins, Rosalie Crutchley, Hilary Dwyer, Hugh Griffith, Ian Ogilvy; **D:** Robert Fuest. CNG, KAR, TVC

Wyatt Earp ⊘⊘½ 1994 (PG-13) Revisionist epic suffers from bad timing as it follows "Tombstone" in telling the story of tarnished badge Earp (Costner), his brothers, and tubercular friend Doc Holliday (Quaid). Costner is barely believable as a 20-something lad, but fares better as he ages. Forty pounds lighter and likely delusional from lack of food, Quaid is unrecognizable but terrific, hacking his way to supporting Oscar mention. 'Course, Val Kilmer got there first. Huge cast finds screen time precious, even though film is some 40 minutes too long, due to prolonged intro to early Wyatt life. Originally envisioned as a TV miniseries till sheriff Costner took a hankering to bring tall tale to the big screen. Filmed on location in Sante Fe, New Mexico. For the full Earp effect, see it with "Tombstone" and relive the legend.**CW:** Some language, strong gunfights, and some sensuality. 191m/C VHS, LV, Letterbox, Closed Caption. Kevin Costner, Dennis Quaid, Gene Hackman, Jeff Fahey, Mark Harmon, Michael Madsen, Catherine O'Hara, Bill Pullman, Isabella Rossellini, Tom Sizemore, JoBeth Williams, Mare Winningham, Betty Buckley, Adam Baldwin, Rex Linn, Todd Allen, David Andrews, Linden Ashby, Annabeth Gish, Joanna Going, Martin Kove, Tea Leoni, James Caviezel, Karen Grassle; **D:** Lawrence Kasdan; **W:**

Dan Gordon, Lawrence Kasdan; **C:** Owen Roizman; **M:** James Newton Howard. Golden Raspberry Awards '94: Worst Remake/Sequel, Worst Actor (Costner). Nominations: Academy Awards '94: Best Cinematography; Golden Raspberry Awards '94: Worst Picture. *WAR*

Wyatt Earp: Return to Tombstone 🎬🎬½ 1994
O'Brian, who starred in TV's "The Life and Legend of Wyatt Earp" from 1955 to 1961, returns to Tombstone in 1914. Colorized clips from the series are used for flashbacks. Filmed on location in Tombstone, Arizona. **94m/C VHS, LV.** Hugh O'Brian, Bruce Boxleitner, Paul Brinegar, Harry Carey Jr., Bo Hopkins, Martin Kove, Don Meredith, Alex Hyde-White, Jay Underwood. *ORI*

Wyoming Outlaw 🎬🎬 1939
Based on an actual incident, the story revolves around a small-town man who kills an outlaw. Barry, in the role that made him a western star, is forced into crime after a corrupt politician extorts money from him in exchange for a job. Lincoln, the screen's first Tarzan, appears in a supporting role. **62m/B VHS.** John Wayne, Ray Corrigan, Raymond Hatton, Donald (Don "Red") Barry, Adele Pearce, Leroy Mason, Charles Middleton, Elmo Lincoln, Jack Ingram, Yakima Canutt, Curly Dresden; **D:** George Sherman. *NOS, MLB*

The X-Files Movie 1998 (PG-13)
The TV series' fifth-season cliffhanger continues in the big screen adaptation, which is also supposed to have a plot clear enough so viewers unfamiliar with the series can still figure out what's going on. Creator Chris Carter has kept the plot strictly under wraps but it involves the show's "mythology" episodes, dealing with the Cigarette-Smoking Man and his fellow conspirators, the alleged abduction of Mulder's sister, colonizing aliens, and related paranormal perplexities. As if that wasn't enough, there's supposed to be a hint of romance between Mulder and Scully as well. **CW:** Some intense violence and gore. **?m/C VHS.** David Duchovny, Gillian Anderson, Martin Landau, Mitch Pileggi, William B. Davis, John Neville, Blythe Danner, Glenne Headly, Terry O'Quinn, Armin Mueller-Stahl, Lucas Black; **D:** Rob Bowman; **W:** Chris Carter, Frank Spotnitz; **C:** John Bartley; **M:** Mark Snow. *NYR*

The X-Files: Pilot Episode/Deep Throat 1993
By-the-book FBI agent Dana Scully (Anderson) is first paired with maverick Fox Mulder (Duchovny), who's devoted to the study of unexplained phenomena and works only on cases outside the mainstream. In the pilot episode they investigate the mysterious deaths of Oregon high school students. "Deep Throat" finds Mulder investigating the disappearance of a test pilot—the sixth at the same air force base. Mulder's given encouragement and information from a government contact known only by his code name. Additional episodes available. **90m/C VHS, Closed Caption.** David Duchovny, Gillian Anderson, Charles Cioffi, Cliff DeYoung, Zachary Ansley, Jerry Hardin; **D:** Robert Mandel, Daniel Sackheim; **W:** Chris Carter. *FXV, MOV*

X from Outer Space 🎬 1967 (PG)
A space voyage to Mars brings back a giant rampaging creature. Badly dubbed. **85m/C VHS, Beta.** *JP* Eiji Okada, Peggy Neal, Toshiya Wazaki, Itoko Harada, Shinichi Yanagisawa, Franz Gruber, Keisuke Sonoi, Mike Daning, Torahiko Hamada; **D:** Nazui Nihonmatsu. *ORI*

X Marks the Spot 🎬🎬 1942
When a police sergeant is killed, his detective son investigates his murder. He's drawn into a crime ring which smuggles rubber (a scarce commodity during WWII). Quick pacing enlivens standard cliches. **55m/B VHS, Beta.** Damian O'Flynn, Helen Parrish, Dick Purcell, Jack LaRue, Neil Hamilton, Robert E. Homans, Anne Jeffreys, Dick Wessel, Vince Barnett; **D:** George Sherman. *SNC*

X: The Man with X-Ray Eyes 🎬🎬🎬
The Man With the X-Ray Eyes; X 1963 First-rate Corman has Milland gain power to see through solid materials. Predates Little Caesars campaign. **79m/C VHS, Beta, LV.** Ray Milland, Diana Van Der Vlis, Harold J. Stone, John Hoyt, Don Rickles, Dick Miller, Jonathan

---

Haze; **D:** Roger Corman; **W:** Ray Russell, Robert Dillon; **C:** Floyd Crosby; **M:** Les Baxter. *WAR*

X, Y & Zee 🎬½ *Zee & Co* 1972 (R)
A brassy, harsh version of the menage a trois theme, wherein the vicious wife (Taylor) of a philanderer (Caine) decides to avenge herself by seducing his mistress. An embarrassment for everyone involved. **110m/C VHS, Beta.** Michael Caine, Elizabeth Taylor, Susannah York, Margaret Leighton; **D:** Brian G. Hutton; **W:** Edna O'Brien; **C:** Billy Williams. *COL*

Xanadu woof! 1980 (PG)
Dorky star-vehicle remake (of 1947's "Down to Earth") eminently of its era, which is now better forgotten. Newton-John is a muse who descends to Earth to help two friends open a roller disco. In the process she proves that as an actor, she's a singer. Kelly attempts to soft shoe some grace into the proceedings, though he seems mystified as anyone as to why he's in the movie. Don Bluth adds an animated sequence. ♫I'm Alive; The Fall; Don't Walk Away; All Over the World; Xanadu; Magic; Suddenly; Dancing; Suspended in Time. **96m/C VHS, Beta, LV.** Olivia Newton-John, Michael Beck, Gene Kelly, Sandahl Bergman; **D:** Robert Greenwald; **W:** Richard Danus. Golden Raspberry Awards '80: Worst Director (Greenwald). *USH*

Xica 🎬🎬🎬 1976
A diamond rush in 18th century Brazil transformed that country's interior into a place of undreamed wealth and excess. Black slave Xica uses her sexual allure to rise out of poverty and capture the attentions of Joao, the governor of the diamond-mining town. She gleefully wields her increasing wealth and power, becoming the unofficial Empress of Brazil. Reportedly based on a real-life character. In Portuguese with English subtitles. **109m/C VHS.** *BR* Zeze Motta, Walmor Chagas, Altair Lima, Jose Wilker, Marcus Vinicius, Elke Maravilha; **D:** Carlos Diegues; **W:** Joao Felicio. *NYF, BTV, FCT*

Xtro woof! 1983 (R)
An Englishman, abducted by aliens three years before, returns to his family with a deadly, transforming disease. Slime-bucket splatter flick notable for the scene where a woman gives birth to a full-grown man, and various sex slashings. **80m/C VHS, Beta, LV.** *GB* Philip Sayer, Bernice Stegers, Danny Brainin, Simon Nash, Maryam D'Abo, David Cardy, Anna Wing, Peter Mandell, Robert Fyfe; **D:** Harry Bromley Davenport; **W:** Robert Smith, Iain Cassie; **C:** John Metcalfe. *NLC*

Xtro 2: The Second Encounter 🎬🎬 1991 (R)
Research facility conducts an experiment to transfer people to a parallel dimension. Out of the three researchers sent to the other side, only one returns, unconscious. Turns out that he is playing host to a biohazardous creature brought over from the other dimension who escapes into the air shafts and threatens to kill everyone in the building. One more problem: if the creature isn't killed, the computer system will fill the building with radiation. Sound familiar? It should, because this is a low-budget remake of "Alien." Good photography, adequate acting, but Vincent just isn't credible as a brilliant scientist. A sequel to "Xtro" in name only. **CW:** Language and sci-fi/horror violence. **92m/C VHS, LV.** *CA* Jan-Michael Vincent, Paul Koslo, Tara Buckman, Jano Frandsen, Nicholas Lea, W.F. Wadden, Rolf Reynolds, Nic Amoroso, Tracy Westerholm; **D:** Harry Bromley Davenport. *NLC*

Xtro 3: Watch the Skies 🎬🎬 1995 (R)
Military unit arrives at a remote island where the government has covered up a UFO landing. However, the island is now inhabited by a pissed-off alien whose mate has been killed. **CW:** Sci-fi violence and gore, strong language. **90m/C VHS, LV.** Sal Landi, Jim Hanks, Robert Culp, Andrew Divoff, Karen Moncrieff; **D:** Harry Bromley Davenport. *TRI*

The Yakuza 🎬🎬½ *Brotherhood of the Yakuza* 1975 (R)
An ex G.I. (Mitchum) returns to Japan to help an old army buddy find his kidnapped daughter. He learns the daughter has been kidnapped by the Japanese version of the Mafia (the Yakuza) and he must call on old acquaintances to help

---

free her. A westernized oriental gangster drama with a nice blend of buddy moments action ancient ritual, and modern Japanese locations. **112m/C VHS, Beta, LV, Letterbox.** Robert Mitchum, Richard Jordan, Ken Takakura, Brian Keith, Herb Edelman; **D:** Sydney Pollack; **W:** Paul Schrader, Leonard Schrader, Robert Towne; **M:** Dave Grusin. *WAR*

Yanco 🎬🎬 1964
A young Mexican boy makes visits to an island where he plays his homemade violin. Unfortunately, no one can understand or tolerate his love for music, save for an elderly violinist, who gives him lessons on an instrument known as "Yanco." No dialogue. Not exactly riveting, but sensitively played. **95m/B VHS, Beta.** *MX* Ricardo Ancona, Jesus Medina, Maria Bustamante. *WFV, DVT*

A Yank in Australia 🎬🎬 1943
Australian farce/war mystery/romance/documentary tells the story of two WWII newspaper reporters whose ship gets torpedoed, stranding them in the Australian outback, where they manage to foil a Japanese invasion. **56m/B VHS, Beta, 8mm.** *AU* VYY

Yank in Libya 🎬½ 1942
No, not the American bombing raid of Khadafy, rather a low-budget WWII adventure pitting an American man and an English girl against Libyan Arabs and Nazis. **65m/B VHS, Beta.** Walter Woolf King, Joan Woodbury, H.B. Warner, Parkyakarkus. *VCI*

A Yank in the R.A.F. 🎬🎬½ 1941
Power's enthusiastic performance as a brash American pilot boosts this dated WWII adventure. He and his British allies seem more concerned over who gets showgirl Betty Grable than in the Nazis, but climactic air attacks retain excitement. Produced by Darryl F. Zanuck to drum up American support for embattled Britain and France. **98m/B VHS, Beta.** Tyrone Power, Betty Grable, John Sutton, Reginald Gardiner; **D:** Henry King. *FOX, FCT*

Yankee Clipper 🎬🎬½ 1927
Deceit, treachery, and romance are combined in this depiction of a fierce race from China to New England between the American ship Yankee Clipper, and the English ship Lord of the Isles. Silent. **68m/B VHS, Beta.** William Boyd, Elinor Fair, Frank "Junior" Coghlan, John Miljan, Walter Long; **D:** Rupert Julian. *GPV, VYY, CCB*

Yankee Doodle Dandy 🎬🎬🎬🎬 1942
Nostalgic view of the Golden Era of show business and the man who made it glitter—George M. Cohan. His early days, triumphs, songs, musicals and romances are brought to life by the inexhaustible Cagney in a rare and wonderful song-and-dance performance. Told in flashback, covering the Irishman's struggling days as a young song writer and performer to his salad days as the toast of Broadway. Cagney, never more charismatic, dances up a storm, reportedly inventing most of the steps on the spot. ♫Give My Regards to Broadway; Yankee Doodle Dandy; You're a Grand Old Flag; Over There; I Was Born in Virginia; Off the Record; You're a Wonderful Girl; Blue Skies, Grey Skies; Oh You Wonderful Girl. **126m/B VHS, Beta, LV, Closed Caption.** James Cagney, Joan Leslie, Walter Huston, Richard Whorf, Irene Manning, Rosemary DeCamp, Jeanne Cagney, S.Z. Sakall, Walter Catlett, Frances Langford, Eddie Foy Jr., George Tobias, Michael Curtiz; **D:** Michael Curtiz; **W:** Robert Buckner; **C:** James Wong Howe. Academy Awards '42: Best Actor (Cagney), Best Sound, Scoring of a Musical, National Film Registry '93;, New York Film Critics Awards '42: Best Actor (Cagney); Nominations: Academy Awards '42: Best Director (Curtiz), Best Film Editing, Best Picture, Best Story, Best Supporting Actor (Huston). *MGM, FOX, FCT*

Yankee Doodle in Berlin 🎬🎬½ 1919
A spoof of WWI dramas, with the hero dressing up as a woman and seducing the Kaiser into giving up his war plans. Typical Sennett slapstick with a music and effects score added to the silent film. **60m/B VHS, Beta.** Ford Sterling, Ben Turpin, Marie Prevost, Bothwell Browne. *GPV, CCB*

Yankee Zulu 🐾🐾 1995 (PG) A young black boy, Zulu, and a young white boy, Rhino, begin a friendship in their South African homeland that is torn apart by apartheid. Twenty-five years later, they are reunited by chance and forced into race-reversal roles that lead to a number of comedic disasters and a renewal of their boyhood friendship. 89m/C VHS, **Closed Caption.** *SA* Leon Schuster, John Matshikiza, Wilson Dunster, Terri Treas; *D:* Gray Hofmeyr; *W:* Leon Schuster, Gray Hofmeyr. *COL*

Yanks 🐾🐾 1979 An epic-scale but uneventful drama depicts the legions of American soldiers billeted in England during WWII, and their impact—mostly sexual—on the staid Britons. No big story, no big deal, despite a meticulous recreation of the era. 139m/C VHS, LV, **Closed Caption.** Richard Gere, Vanessa Redgrave, William Devane, Lisa Eichhorn, Rachel Roberts, Chick Vennera, Arlen Dean Snyder, Annie Ross; *D:* John Schlesinger; *W:* Colin Welland, Walter Bernstein; *M:* Richard Rodney Bennett. British Academy Awards '79: Best Supporting Actress (Roberts); National Board of Review Awards '79: Best Director (Schlesinger). *USH*

A Year in Provence 🐾🐾 1989 Retired London executive Peter Mayle and his wife Annie decide to leave England to live in the south of France. They buy a 200-year-old farmhouse and experience all the trials and amusements of forging a new life in a different country, complete with different language and customs. They hoped for tranquility and what they got were eccentric neighbors, endless renovations, lots of company, and a taste for good food and drink. Based on Mayle's autobiographical novels "A Year in Provence" and "Tonjours Provence" and filmed on location. Made for British television. On four cassettes, each depicting one season of the year. 360m/C VHS. *GB* John Thaw, Lindsay Duncan, Bernard Spiegel, Jean-Pierre Delage, Maryse Kuster, Louis Lyonnet; *D:* David Tucker; *W:* Michael Sadler. *AEH, SIG, BTV*

The Year My Voice Broke 🐾🐾🐾 1987 (PG-13) Above-average adolescent drama: a girl breaks a boy's heart by getting pregnant by a tougher, older boy, then leaves town. Blues-inducing, explicit, and not pleasant, but good acting from newcomers carries the day. Followed by "Flirting." 103m/C VHS, Beta, LV. *AU* Noah Taylor, Leone Carmen, Ben Mendelsohn, Graeme Blundell, Lynette Curran, Malcolm Robertson, Judi Farr; *D:* John Duigan; *W:* John Duigan; *C:* Geoff Burton; *M:* Christine Woodruff. Australian Film Institute '87: Best Film. *ART*

The Year of Living Dangerously 🐾🐾🐾½ 1982 (PG) Political thriller features Gibson as an Australian journalist covering a political story in Indonesia, circa 1965. During the coup against President Sukarno, he becomes involved with a British attache (Weaver) at the height of the bloody fighting and rioting in Jakarta. Hunt is excellent as male photographer Billy Swan, central to the action as the moral center. Rumored to be based on the activities of CNN's Peter Arnett, although the original source is a novel by C.J. Koch, who reportedly collaborated/battled with Weir on the screenplay. Fascinating, suspenseful film, set up brilliantly by Weir. Shot on location in the Philippines (then moved to Sydney after cast and crew were threatened). First Australian movie financed by a U.S. studio. 114m/C VHS, Beta, LV, Letterbox, **Closed Caption.** *AU* Mel Gibson, Sigourney Weaver, Linda Hunt, Michael Murphy; *D:* Peter Weir; *W:* Peter Weir, David Williamson; *C:* Russell Boyd; *M:* Maurice Jarre. Academy Awards '83: Best Supporting Actress (Hunt); Los Angeles Film Critics Association Awards '83: Best Supporting Actress (Hunt); National Board of Review Awards '83: Best Supporting Actress (Hunt); New York Film Critics Awards '83: Best Supporting Actress (Hunt). *MGM, BTV*

Year of the Comet 🐾🐾 1992 (PG-13) Amusing adventure/romantic comedy throws straightlaced Maggie (Miller) together with carefree Oliver (Daly) in a quest for a rare bottle of wine. Fine wine is Maggie's passion, and snagging this particular bottle will boost her status in the family business. Oliver is a pretzels and beer

kind of guy, but his boss wants this bottle and will pay a lot to get it. Wants to be another "Romancing the Stone," but plot and characters are too thin. Nice chemistry between Miller and Daly sort of saves this one despite a disappointing script. Beautiful location shots of Scotland. 135m/C VHS, LV, **Closed Caption.** Penelope Ann Miller, Timothy Daly, Louis Jourdan, Art Malik, Ian Richardson, Ian McNeice, Timothy Bentinck, Julia McCarthy, Jacques Mathou; *D:* Peter Yates; *W:* William Goldman; *M:* Hummie Mann. *NLC*

Year of the Dragon 🐾🐾½ 1985 (R) Polish police Captain Stanley White of the NYPD vows to neutralize the crime lords running New York's Chinatown. Brilliant cinematography, well-done action scenes with maximum violence, a racist hero you don't want to root for, murky script, and semi-effective direction are the highlights of this tour through the black market's underbelly and hierarchy. Based on Robert Daley's novel. 136m/C VHS, LV, **Closed Caption.** Mickey Rourke, John Lone, Ariane, Leonard Termo, Raymond J. Barry; *D:* Michael Cimino; *W:* Oliver Stone, Michael Cimino. *MGM*

Year of the Gun 🐾🐾½ 1991 (R) McCarthy is an American journalist in Rome who begins a novel based on the political instability around him, using the names of real people in his first draft. Soon, ambitious photojournalist Stone wants to collaborate with him, and the Red Brigade terrorist group wants to "remove" anyone associated with the book. Although failing on occasion to balance the thin line it establishes between reality and perception, "Gun" aspires to powerful drama, offering a realistic look at the lives and priorities of political terrorists. Love scenes between Stone and McCarthy are torrid. 111m/C VHS, LV, 8mm. Andrew McCarthy, Sharon Stone, Valeria Golino, John Pankow, Mattia Sbragia, George Murcell; *D:* John Frankenheimer; *W:* David Ambrose, Jay Presson Allen; *M:* Bill Conti. *COL*

Year of the Horse 🐾🐾 1997 (R) Jarmusch's documentary on the nearly 30-year rock phenomenon of Neil Young & Crazy Horse. Looking as gritty as some of Horse's riffs sound, pic intercuts footage of the band's performances in '76, '86, and the latest '96 European and U.S. tours shot on Super-8, High Fi-8 video, and 16 mm. Jarmusch wisely lets songs run full-length with complete performances intact, though lesser fans of the band may not be as thrilled about that. Falls short in capturing the spirit and essence of the band and their drive to stay together after all these years, but does show some cool behind-the-scenes moments that make it worthwhile to rock fans. *CW:* Language and drug content. 107m/C VHS. *D:* Jim Jarmusch. *NYR*

Year of the Quiet Sun 🐾🐾🐾½ 1984 (PG) A poignant, acclaimed love story about a Polish widow and an American soldier who find each other in the war-torn landscape of 1946 Europe. Beautifully rendered, with a confident sense of time and place, making this much more than a simple love story. In Polish with English subtitles. 106m/C VHS, Beta, LV. *PL GE* Scott Wilson, Maja Komorowska; *D:* Krzysztof Zanussi. Venice Film Festival '84: Best Film. *BAR, WAR*

The Yearling 🐾🐾🐾½ 1946 This family classic is a tear-jerking adaptation of the Marjorie Kinnan Rawlings novel about a young boy's love for a yearling fawn during the post civil-war era. His father's encouragement and his mother's bitterness play against the story of unqualified love amid poverty and the boy's coming of age. Wonderful footage of Florida. Jarman was awarded a special Oscar as outstanding child actor. 128m/C VHS, Beta, LV. Gregory Peck, Jane Wyman, Claude Jarman Jr., Chill Wills, Henry Travers, Jeff York, Forrest Tucker, June Lockhart, Margaret Wycherly; *D:* Clarence Brown; *C:* Charles Rosher. Academy Awards '46: Best Color Cinematography, Best Interior Decoration; Golden Globe Awards '47: Best Actor—Drama (Peck); Nominations: Academy Awards '46: Best Actor (Peck), Best Actress (Wyman), Best Director (Brown), Best Film Editing, Best Picture. *KUI, MGM, TLF*

The Yearling 🐾🐾½ 1994 TV remake of the classic Marjorie Kinnan Rawlings novel about a boy and his orphaned fawn. The Baxters are struggling in '30s Florida: Pa Penny (Strauss) is a hardscrabble farmer and severe Ma Ora (Smart) has lost three of her four children. Surviving son, 12-year-old Jody (Horneff), gets more than his share of life's hard lessons—with even his adored pet causing problems. On the cloying side, the 1946 big-screen version is still the one to watch. Filmed in South Carolina. 98m/C VHS. Peter Strauss, Jean Smart, Wil Horneff, Brad Greenquist, Jarred Blanchard, Philip S. Hoffman, Nancy Moore Atchison; *D:* Rod Hardy; *W:* Joe Wiesenfeld; *M:* Lee Holdridge. *CAF*

The Yellow Cab Man 🐾🐾½ 1950 Skelton plays a cab driver who is also an inventor of safety gadgets. When he invents unbreakable elastic glass he finds various crooks after him for the formula. Skelton's wacky inventions are amusing and the movie culminates in a breakneck chase through a home show exposition. 85m/B VHS. Red Skelton, Gloria De Haven, Walter Slezak, Edward Arnold, James Gleason, Jay C. Flippen, Paul Harvey; *D:* Jack Donohue. *MGM*

Yellow Cargo 🐾🐾 1936 Ingenious "B" movie about a pair of undercover agents who blow the lid off a smuggling scam. It seems that the smugglers have been masquerading as a movie crew, and use disguised Chinese "extras" to transport their goods. The agents pose as actors to infiltrate the gang. 70m/B VHS, Beta. Conrad Nagel, Eleanor Hunt, Vince Barnett, Jack LaRue, Claudia Dell; *D:* Crane Wilbur; *W:* Crane Wilbur. *SNC, DVT*

Yellow Dust 🐾½ 1936 Dull story of a gold miner (Dix) who hits a big strike but before he can make good on it he's accused of a series of stagecoach robberies. So he goes undercover to clear his name. Based on the play "Mother Lode" by Dan Totheroh and George O'Neil. 68m/B VHS. Richard Dix, Leila Hyams, Andy Clyde, Onslow Stevens, Moroni Olsen, Jessie Ralph; *D:* Wallace Fox. *GPV*

Yellow Earth 🐾🐾½ 1989 In 1939 a soldier arrives in a small Chinese village to research folk songs. He becomes involved in the lives of a local peasant family, including a 14-year-old girl who wishes to escape from a pre-arranged marriage. Mixture of poetry, dance, music, and drama set against the barren landscape of the title. In Mandarin Chinese with English subtitles. 89m/C VHS. *CH* Xue Bai, Wang Xueqi, Tan Tuo, Liu Qiang; *D:* Chen Kaige; *W:* Zhang Ziliang. *FXL, FCT, BTV*

Yellow Hair & the Fortress of Gold 🐾½ *Yellow Hair and the Pecos Kid* 1984 (R) Princess who's part Indian and her sidekick fight bad guys and seek gold. Well-meaning, self-conscious parody. 102m/C VHS, Beta. *SP* Laurene Landon, Ken Robertson; *D:* Matt Cimber; *W:* Matt Cimber. *ART*

The Yellow Rose of Texas 🐾🐾 1944 Rogers works as an undercover insurance agent (he's singing on a river boat) to clear the name of an old man falsely accused of a stagecoach robbery. The usual melodious Rogers lead. 55m/B VHS, Beta. Roy Rogers, Dale Evans, Grant Withers, Harry Shannon; *D:* Joseph Kane. *NOS, VCN, CAB*

Yellow Submarine 🐾🐾🐾½ 1968 (G) The acclaimed animated fantasy based on a plethora of mid-career Beatles songs, sees the Fab Four battle the Blue Meanies for the sake of Sgt. Pepper, the Nowhere Man, Strawberry Fields, and Pepperland. The first full-length British animated feature in 14 years features a host of talented cartoonists. Fascinating LSD-esque animation and imagery. Speaking voices provided by John Clive (John), Geoff Hughes (Paul), Peter Batten (George), and Paul Angelis (Ringo). The Beatles themselves do appear in a short scene at the end of the film. Martin fills in as music director, and Segal of "Love Story" fame co-scripts. ♪Yellow Submarine; All You Need is Love; Hey, Bulldog; When I'm Sixty Four; Nowhere Man; Lucy in the Sky With Diamonds; Sgt. Pepper's Lonely Hearts Club Band; A Day in the Life; All Together Now.

87m/C VHS, Beta, LV. *GB* **D:** George Duning, Dick Emery; **W:** Erich Segal; **M:** George Martin. *MVD, MGM*

Yellowbeard 🐾🐾 1982 (PG) An alleged comedy with a great cast who wander about with little direction. Follows the efforts of an infamous pirate (Chapman) to locate a buried treasure using the map tattooed on the back of his son's head. Final role for Feldman, who died during production. 97m/C VHS, Beta, LV. **D:** Graham Chapman, Peter Boyle, Richard "Cheech" Marin, Thomas Chong, Peter Cook, Marty Feldman, Martin Hewitt, Michael Hordern, Eric Idle, Madeline Kahn, James Mason, John Cleese, Susannah York, David Bowie; **D:** Mel Damski; **W:** Graham Chapman, Peter Cook, Bernard McKenna. *VES*

Yellowneck 🐾🐾 1955 A handful of Confederate Army soldiers desert, hoping to cross the Florida Everglades and eventually reach Cuba. The swamp takes its toll, however, and one by one the men fall by the wayside. A sole survivor reaches the coast. Will the escape boat be waiting for him? 83m/C VHS. Lin McCarthy, Stephen Courtleigh, Berry Kroeger, Harold Gordon, Bill Mason; **D:** R. John Hugh. *FCT*

Yellowstone 🐾🐾 1936 An ex-con is murdered at Yellowstone National Park, at the site of a hidden cache of money, of which assorted folks are in search. Uncomplicated, well-meaning mystery. 65m/B VHS, Beta, 8mm. Andy Devine, Ralph Morgan, Judith Barrett; **D:** Arthur Lubin. *NOS, DVT, VYY*

Yentl 🐾🐾½ 1983 (PG) The famous Barbra adaptation of Isaac Bashevis Singer's story set in 1900s Eastern Europe about a Jewish girl who masquerades as a boy in order to study the Talmud, and who becomes enmeshed in romantic miscues. Lushly photographed, with a repetitive score that nevertheless won an Oscar. Singer was reportedly appalled by the results of Streisand's hyper-controlled project. ♫A Piece of Sky; No Matter What Happens; This Is One of Those Moments; Tomorrow Night; Where Is It Written; No Wonder; The Way He Makes Me Feel; Papa, Can You Hear Me; Will Someone Ever Look at Me That Way?. 134m/C VHS, Beta, LV, Closed Caption. Barbra Streisand, Mandy Patinkin, Amy Irving, Nehemiah Persoff, Steven Hill, Allan Corduner, Ruth Goring, David DeKeyser, Bernard Spear; **D:** Barbra Streisand; **C:** David Watkin; **M:** Michel Legrand, Alan Bergman, Marilyn Bergman. Academy Awards '83: Original Song Score and/or Adaptation; Golden Globe Awards '84: Best Director (Streisand), Best Film—Musical/Comedy; Nominations: Academy Awards '83: Best Art Direction/Set Decoration, Best Song ("Papa, Can You Hear Me?", "The Way He Makes Me Feel"), Best Supporting Actress (Irving). *MGM, IME*

Yes, Giorgio 🐾🐾 1982 (PG) Opera singer Pavarotti in his big-screen debut. He has an advantage over other non-actors trapped in similar situations (e.g., Hulk Hogan): He can sing (but of course, not wrestle). Lame plot (famous opera star falls for lady doctor) is the merest excuse for the maestro to belt out "If We Were in Love," "I Left My Heart in San Francisco," and arias by Verdi, Donizetti, and Puccini. 111m/C VHS, Beta, LV. Luciano Pavarotti, Kathryn Harrold, Eddie Albert, James Hong; **D:** Franklin J. Schaffner; **W:** Norman Steinberg; **M:** John Williams. Nominations: Academy Awards '82: Best Song ("If We Were in Love").*MGM*

Yes, Sir, Mr. Bones 🐾½ 1951 Entertaining but dated musical about a boy who wanders into a rest home and inspires the old folks there to reminisce about their days as riverboat minstrels. ♫I Want to Be a Minstrel Man; Stay Out of the Kitchen; Is Your Rent Paid Up in Heaven?; Flying Saucers; Memphis Bill; Southland. 60m/B VHS, Beta. Pete Daily, Jimmy O'Brien, Sally Anglim, Cotton Watts, Chick Watts, Chet Davis, F.E. Miller, Scatman Crothers; **D:** Ron Ormond; **W:** Ron Ormond. *FCT*

The Yesterday Machine woof! 1963 Camp sci-fi: A mad doctor tries to bring back Hitler. Don't worry, though: the good guys win. Predictable, dumb drivel. 85m/B VHS, Beta. Tim Holt, James Britton, Jack Herman; **D:** Russ Marker. *SNC, VCD*

Yesterday, Today and Tomorrow 🐾🐾🐾½ Ieri, Oggi E Domani; She Out What She Asked For 1964 Trilogy of comic sexual vignettes featuring Loren and her many charms. She plays a black marketeer, a wealthy matron, and a prostitute. Funny, and still rather racy. Loren at her best, in all senses; includes her famous striptease for Mastroianni. 119m/C VHS. *IT FR* Sophia Loren, Marcello Mastroianni, Tony Pica, Giovanni Ridolfi; **D:** Vittorio De Sica. Academy Awards '64: Best Foreign Language Film; British Academy Awards '64: Best Actor (Mastroianni). *JEF, HHE*

Yesterday's Hero 🐾½ 1979 A fading soccer star finds his career and love-life on the upswing. Poor production with equally lame pop music score. 95m/C VHS, Beta. *GB* Ian McShane, Suzanne Somers, Adam Faith, Paul Nicholas, Glynis Barber, Sandy Ratcliff; **D:** Neil Leifer; **W:** Jackie Collins. *HHE*

Yesterday's Target 🐾🐾 1996 (R) Paul (Baldwin), Jessica (Haiduk), and Carter (Carter) all possess special psychic powers in their future society, which is on the verge of destruction. They're sent back in time to rescue a young boy who may hold the key to saving their world but a glitch leaves them with collective amnesia and ruthless hunter Holden (McDowell) on their trail. 80m/C VHS, Closed Caption. Daniel Baldwin, Stacy Haiduk, T.K. Carter, LeVar Burton, Malcolm McDowell, Trevor Goddard; **D:** Barry Samson. *REP*

Yidl Mitn Fidl 🐾🐾 Yiddle with a Fiddle; Castle in the Sky 1936 Disguised as a man, a young woman travels about the countryside with a group of musicians, revealing her female identity only after falling for a man. One of Picon's finest roles and Green's biggest successes. Vaudevillian fare in Yiddish with English subtitles. ♫Yiddle With His Fiddle; Arye With His Bass. 92m/B VHS, Beta. *PL* Molly Picon, Simche Fostel, Max Bozyk, Leon Liebgold; **D:** Joseph Green. *ERG, DVT, TPV*

Yin & Yang of Mr. Go 🐾 1971 (R) A CIA operative must retrieve the stolen plans of an awesome weapons system. Set in Hong Kong, features a strong cast in a tangled tale of no particular merit. Unworthy spoof of Oriental intrigue flicks. 89m/C VHS, Beta. Jeff Bridges, James Mason, Broderick Crawford, Burgess Meredith; **D:** Burgess Meredith; **W:** Burgess Meredith. *NO*

Yodelin' Kid From Pine Ridge 🐾½ The Hero of Pine Ridge 1937 Autry tries to stop a war between cattlemen and woodsmen in Georgia. Standard horse opera notable for its location. 59m/B VHS, Beta. Gene Autry, Smiley Burnette, Betty Bronson, Charles Middleton, Art Mix; **D:** Joseph Kane. *NOS, VCN, DVT*

Yog, Monster from Space 🐾 The Space Amoeba 1971 (G) When a spaceship crashes somewhere near Japan, the aliens in it create monsters out of ordinary critters in order to destroy all the cities. A promoter gets a gleam in his eye and sees the potential for a vacation spot featuring the viscious creatures. Standard Japanese monster flick with the usual out-of-synch dub machine. Dubbed. 105m/C VHS, Beta. *JP* Akira Kubo, Yoshio Tsuchiya; **D:** Inoshiro Honda. *SNC*

Yojimbo 🐾🐾🐾🐾 1961 Two clans vying for political power bid on the services of a samurai (Mifune) who comes to town. The samurai sells his services to both parties, with devastating results for all. In Japanese with English subtitles or dubbed. Re-made by Sergio Leone as the western "A Fist Full of Dollars." 110m/B VHS, Beta, LV, 8mm, Letterbox. *JP* Toshiro Mifune, Eijiro Tono, Suuzu Yamda, Seizaburo Kawazu, Isuzu Yamada; **D:** Akira Kurosawa; **W:** Hideo Oguni, Shinobu Hashimoto, Akira Kurosawa; **M:** Masaru Sato. Nominations: Academy Awards '61: Best Costume Design (B & W). *VYY, HHT, NOS*

Yol 🐾🐾🐾½ 1982 (PG) Five Turkish prisoners are granted temporary leave to visit their families. An acclaimed, heartfelt film, written by Guney while he himself was in prison. A potent protest against totalitarianism. In Turkish with English subtitles. 126m/C VHS, Beta. *TU* Tarik Akan, Serif Sezer;

D: Serif Goren; **W:** Yilmaz Guney; **M:** Sebastian Argol. Cannes Film Festival '82: Best Film. *COL, AUD*

Yolanda and the Thief 🐾🐾½ 1945 A charming, forgotten effort from the Arthur Freed unit about a con man who convinces a virginal South American heiress that he is her guardian angel. Songs include a lengthy Dali-esque ballet built around "Will You Marry Me?" ♫This is the Day for Love; Angel; Yolanda; Coffee Time; Will You Marry Me. 109m/C VHS, Beta. Fred Astaire, Lucille Bremer, Leon Ames, Mildred Natwick; **D:** Vincente Minnelli; **C:** Charles Rosher; **M:** Arthur Freed, Harry Warren. *MGM*

Yongkari Monster of the Deep 🐾 Dai Koesu Yongkari; Monster Yongkari; Great Monster Yongkari 1967 (PG) A giant burrowing creature is causing earthquakes and generally ruining scores of Japanese models. Dubbed. 79m/C VHS, Beta. Oh Young Il, Nam Chung-Im; **D:** Kim Ki-dak. *ORI*

Yor, the Hunter from the Future 🐾 Il Mondo Di Yor; The World of Yor 1983 (PG) Lost in a time warp where the past and the future mysteriously collide, Yor sets out on a search for his real identity, with his only clue a golden medallion around his neck. 88m/C VHS, Beta, LV. *IT* Reb Brown, Corinne Clery, John Steiner; **D:** Anthony (Antonio Margheriti) Dawson; **W:** Anthony (Antonio Margheriti) Dawson, Robert Bailey. *COL*

You and Me 🐾🐾½ 1938 Joe Dennis (Raft) is an ex-con now employed at the same department store as Helen (Sidney). They fall in love and marry without Helen admitting she's on parole herself and the rules forbid her to wed. When Joe realizes his marriage is illegal (and his wife's a liar), he picks up with his old gang and plans a robbery but Helen intervenes before any damage is done, except to Joe's ego. The duo finally manage to work out their problems and later get married for real. Schizophrenic film is an uneasy mixture of comedy, pathos, romance, crime, and even some songs by Lang's associate Kurt Weill. 90m/B VHS. George Raft, Sylvia Sidney, Harry Carey Sr., Robert Cummings, Barton MacLane, Warren Hymer, Roscoe Karns, George E. Stone; **D:** Fritz Lang; **W:** Virginia Van Upp; **C:** Charles Lang Jr.; **M:** Boris Morros. *USH*

You Can't Cheat an Honest Man 🐾🐾🐾 1939 The owner of a misfit circus suffers a variety of headaches including the wisecracks of Charlie McCarthy. Contains Field's classic ping-pong battle and some of his other best work. 79m/B VHS, Beta. W.C. Fields, Edgar Bergen, Constance Moore, Eddie Anderson, Mary Forbes, Thurston Hall; **D:** George Marshall; **C:** Milton Krasner. *BAR*

You Can't Fool Your Wife 🐾🐾 1940 Ball in two roles gives zip to this otherwise ordinary marital comedy. Previously blah hubby has a fling; previously blah better half wins him back with glamour. 69m/C VHS, Beta. Lucille Ball, James Ellison, Robert Coote, Emma Dunn, Nita Naldi; **D:** Ray McCarey. *TTC*

You Can't Hurry Love 🐾 1988 (R) A jilted-at-the-altar Ohio bachelor moves to Los Angeles and flounders in the city's fast-moving fast lane. A dull film with Fonda, daughter of "Easy Rider" Peter, playing a minor role. 92m/C VHS, Beta, LV. David Leisure, Scott McGinnis, Sally Kellerman, Kristy McNichol, Charles Grodin, Anthony Geary, Bridget Fonda, David Packer, Frank Bonner; **D:** Richard Martini; **C:** Peter Collister. *ART, VES*

You Can't Take It with You 🐾🐾🐾½ 1938 The Capra version of the Kaufman-Hart play about an eccentric New York family and their nonconformist houseguests. Alice Sycamore (Arthur), the stable family member of an offbeat clan of free spirits, falls for Tony Kirby (Stewart), the down-to-earth son of a snooty, wealthy and not always quite honest family. Amidst the confusion over this love affair, the two families rediscover the simple joys of life. 127m/B VHS, Beta, LV, Closed Caption. James Stewart, Jean Arthur, Lionel Barrymore, Spring Byington, Edward Arnold, Mischa Auer, Donald Meek, Samuel S. Hinds, Ann Miller, H.B. Warner, Halliwell Hobbes, Dub Taylor, Mary Forbes, Eddie Anderson, Harry

Davenport, Lillian Yarbo; *D:* Frank Capra; *W:* Robert Riskin. Academy Awards '38: Best Director (Capra), Best Picture; Nominations: Academy Awards '38: Best Cinematography, Best Film Editing, Best Screenplay, Best Sound, Best Supporting Actress (Byington). *COL, BTV*

You Can't Take It with You 🎬🎬🎬

1984 Taped performance of the Kaufman and Hart comedy about the strange pastimes of the Sycamore family who must behave themselves to impress their daughter's boyfriend's stuffy family. **116m/C VHS, Beta, LV.** Colleen Dewhurst, James Coco, Jason Robards Jr., Elizabeth Wilson, George Rose; *D:* Ellis Raab. *COL, VES, ART*

You Gotta Stay Happy 🎬🎬½ 1948

Heiress Dee Dee Dillwood (Fontaine) marries the man (Parker) her family approves of and realizes her mistake on their wedding night honeymoon in New York. Distraught, she manages to hide out in the room of failing airplane cargo company owner Marvin Payne (Stewart). He takes her with him on a California-bound cargo flight that winds up crashlanding in a field. By this time Dee Dee and Marvin are in love but then he finds out the truth about his would-be fiancee. **101m/B VHS, Closed Caption.** James Stewart, Joan Fontaine, Eddie Albert, Willard Parker, Roland Young, Halliwell Hobbes, Stanley Prager, Mary Forbes, Percy Kilbride, William "Billy" Bakewell; *D:* H.C. Potter; *W:* Karl Tunberg; *C:* Russell Metty; *M:* Daniele Amfitheatrof. *USH*

You Light Up My Life woof! 1977 (PG)

Sappy sentimental story of a young singer trying to break into the music business. Debbie Boone's version of the title song was a radio smash, the constant playing of which drove many people over the edge. 🎵You Light Up My Life. **91m/C VHS, Beta.** Didi Conn, Michael Zaslow, Melanie Mayron; *D:* Joseph Brooks; *W:* Joseph Brooks; *M:* Joseph Brooks. Academy Awards '77: Best Song ("You Light Up My Life"); Golden Globe Awards '78: Best Song ("You Light Up My Life"). *COL*

You Must Remember This 199? When

Uncle Buddy (Guillaume) receives a mysterious trunk, Ella's curiosity gets the best of her. She opens the trunk to discover a number of old movies made by W.B. Jackson—Uncle Buddy. Ella takes the films to a movie archive to find out about her uncle's past as an independent black filmmaker. After researching the history of black cinema, Ella convinces her uncle to be proud of his contribution to the film world. Includes a viewers' guide. Part of the "Wonderworks" series. **110m/C VHS.** Robert Guillaume, Tim Reid, Daphne Maxwell Reid, Vonetta McGee. *HMV, BTV, FCT*

You Only Live Once 🎬🎬½ 1937 Ex-

con Fonda wants to mend his ways and tries to cross into Canada with his girlfriend in tow. Impressively scripted, but a glum and dated Depression-era tale. **86m/B VHS, Beta.** Henry Fonda, Sylvia Sidney, Ward Bond, William Gargan, Barton MacLane, Margaret Hamilton, Jean Dixon, Warren Hymer, Chic Sale, Guinn "Big Boy" Williams, Jerome Cowan, John Wray, Jonathan Hale, Ben Hall, Jean Stoddard, Wade Boteler, Henry Taylor, Walter DePalma; *D:* Fritz Lang. *NO*

You Only Live Twice 🎬🎬½ 1967 (PG)

007 travels to Japan to take on arch-nemesis Blofeld, who has been capturing Russian and American spacecraft in an attempt to start WWIII. Great location photography; theme sung by Nancy Sinatra. Implausible plot, however, is a handicap, even though this is Bond. **125m/C VHS, Beta, LV, Letterbox.** *GB* Sean Connery, Mie Hama, Akiko Wakabayashi, Tetsuro Tamba, Karin Dor, Charles Gray, Donald Pleasence, Tsai Chin, Bernard Lee, Lois Maxwell, Desmond Llewelyn; *D:* Lewis Gilbert; *C:* Frederick A. (Freddie) Young; *M:* John Barry. *MGM, TLF*

You So Crazy 🎬½ Martin Lawrence You So

Crazy **1994** Scandalous star of television show "Martin" and host of HBO's "Def Comedy Jam" follows in the footsteps of raunchy humorists Richard Pryor and Eddie Murphy. Threatened with an NC-17 rating, Lawrence refused to edit and Miramax, the original distributor, dropped it. It was picked up by Samuel Goldwyn, who released

the original version, uncut and unrated. Filmed live at the Brooklyn Academy of Music, Lawrence displays too little of his considerable talent, and too much vulgarity and poor taste. **85m/C VHS.** Martin Lawrence; *D:* Thomas Schlamme; *C:* Arthur Albert. *HBO*

You Talkin' to Me? 🎬 1987 (R) Fledg-

ling actor who idolizes De Niro moves to the West Coast for his big break. He fails, so he dyes his hair blond and digs the California lifestyle. Embarrassingly bad. **97m/C VHS, Beta.** Chris Winkler, Jim Youngs, Faith Ford; *D:* Charles Winkler; *W:* Charles Winkler. *MGM*

You Were Never Lovelier 🎬🎬🎬½

1942 Charming tale of a father who creates a phony Romeo to try to interest his daughter in marriage. Astaire appears and woos Hayworth in the flesh. The dancing, of course, is superb, and Hayworth is stunning. 🎵Dearly Beloved; I'm Old Fashioned; Shorty George; Wedding in the Spring; You Were Never Lovelier. **98m/B VHS, Beta, LV.** Fred Astaire, Rita Hayworth, Leslie Brooks, Xavier Cugat, Adolphe Menjou, Larry Parks; *D:* William A. Seiter; *M:* Jerome Kern, Johnny Mercer. Nominations: Academy Awards '42: Best Song ("Dearly Beloved"), Best Sound, Scoring of a Musical. *COL*

You'll Find Out 🎬🎬 1940 A comic mix of

music and mystery as Kay Kyser and his Band, along with a debutante in distress, are terrorized by Lugosi, Karloff, and Lorre. 🎵The Bad Humor; I'd Know You Anywhere; You've Got Me This Way; Like the Fella Once Said; I've Got a One-Track Mind; Don't Think it Ain't Been Charming. **97m/B VHS, Beta.** Peter Lorre, Kay Kyser, Boris Karloff, Bela Lugosi, Dennis O'Keefe, Helen Parrish; *D:* David Butler. Nominations: Academy Awards '40: Best Song ("I'd Know You Anywhere"). *HHT, MLB*

You'll Never Get Rich 🎬🎬🎬 1941 A

Broadway dance director is drafted into the Army, where his romantic troubles cause him to wind up in the guardhouse more than once. He of course gets the girl. Exquisitely funny. 🎵Since I Kissed My Baby Goodbye; The A-stairable Rag; Shootin' the Works for Uncle Sam; Wedding Cake Walk; Dream Dancing; Boogie Barcarolle; So Near and Yet So Far. **88m/B VHS, Beta, LV.** Fred Astaire, Rita Hayworth, Robert Benchley; *D:* Sidney Lanfield. Nominations: Academy Awards '41: Best Song ("Since I Kissed My Baby Goodbye"), Scoring of a Musical. *COL*

The Young Americans 🎬🎬 1993 (R)

Tough New York cop John Harris (Keitel) is sent to London to aid the police with their investigations into a series of killings related to a drug smuggling operation working out of the club scene. Harris wants to tie everything to the sleazeball gangster Carl Frazer (Mortensen) that he's been trailing. Slick formula with hard-working cast. Debut for 25-year-old director Cannon. **108m/C VHS, LV.** *GB* Harvey Keitel, Viggo Mortensen, Iain Glen, John Wood, Keith Allen, Craig Kelly, Thandie Newton, Terence Rigby; *D:* Danny Cannon; *W:* Danny Cannon, David Hilton; *M:* David Arnold. *ART*

Young & Free 🎬½ 1978 Following the

death of his parents, a young man must learn to face the perils of an unchartered wilderness alone. Ultimately he must choose between returning to civilization, or remain with his beloved wife and life in the wild. **87m/C VHS, Beta.** Erik Larsen; *D:* Keith Larsen. *MON*

Young and Innocent 🎬🎬🎬 The Girl Was

Young **1937** Somewhat uneven thriller about a police constable's daughter who helps a fugitive prove he didn't strangle a film star. **80m/B VHS, Beta, LV.** *GB* Derrick DeMarney, Nova Pilbeam, Percy Marmont, Edward Rigby, Mary Clare, John Longden, George Curzon, Basil Radford, Pamela Carme, George Merritt, J.H. Roberts, Jerry Verno, H.F. Maltby, John Miller, Beatrice Varley, Syd Crossley, Frank Atkinson, Torin Thatcher; *D:* Alfred Hitchcock; *W:* Charles Bennett, Alma Reville, Gerald Savory, Antony Armstrong, Edwin Greenwood. *SNC, NOS, VDM*

The Young and the Guilty 🎬🎬 1958

Two star-crossed teenagers are frustrated in their romance when their parents find one of their love letters and hit the ceiling. Told not to see each other again, the two take to sneaking around, which adds an edge to their relationship. Moving performances by the two young leads. **65m/B VHS.** Phyllis Calvert, Andrew Ray, Edward Chapman, Janet Munro, Campbell Singer; *D:* Peter Cotes. *NOS*

Young & Willing 🎬🎬½ 1942 A group of

struggling actors gets hold of a terrific play and tries various schemes to get it produced. Based on the Broadway Play "Out of the Frying Pan" by Francis Swann. Unexceptional but enjoyable comedy. **83m/B VHS, Beta.** William Holden, Susan Hayward, Eddie Bracken, Robert Benchley, Martha O'Driscoll, Barbara Britton; *D:* Edward H. Griffith; *W:* Virginia Van Upp. *NO*

Young Aphrodites 🎬🎬½ Mikres Aphrodi-

tes **1963** Two young teenagers of a primitive Greek tribe discover sexuality. An acclaimed film retelling the myth of Daphnis and Chloe. Narrated in English. **87m/B VHS, Beta.** *GR D:* Nikos Koundouros. Berlin International Film Festival '63: Best Director (Koundouros). *NLC*

Young at Heart 🎬🎬½ 1954 Fanny

Hurst's lighthearted tale of a cynical hard-luck musician who finds happiness when he falls for a small town girl. A remake of the 1938 "Four Daughters." 🎵Young at Heart; Someone to Watch Over Me; One for My Baby; Hold Me in Your Arms; Ready, Willing and Able; Till My Love Comes Back to Me; There's a Rising Moon For Every Falling Star; You, My Love. **117m/C VHS.** Frank Sinatra, Doris Day, Gig Young, Ethel Barrymore, Dorothy Malone, Robert Keith, Elisabeth Fraser, Alan Hale Jr.; *D:* Gordon Douglas; *W:* Julius J. Epstein, Liam O'Brien. *REP*

Young Bess 🎬🎬🎬½ 1953 Simmons and

real-life husband Granger star in this splashy costume drama about 16th century England's young Queen. Features outstanding performances by Simmons as Elizabeth I and Laughton (repeating his most famous role) as Henry VIII. Based on the novel by Margaret Irwin. **112m/C VHS.** Jean Simmons, Stewart Granger, Deborah Kerr, Charles Laughton, Kay Walsh, Guy Rolfe, Kathleen Byron, Cecil Kellaway, Rex Thompson; *D:* George Sidney; *W:* Jan Lustig, Arthur Wimperis; *C:* Charles Rosher; *M:* Miklos Rozsa. Nominations: Academy Awards '53: Best Art Direction/Set Decoration (Color), Best Costume Design (Color). *MGM*

Young Bill Hickok 🎬🎬 1940 A Rogers

vehicle in the form of a very fictionalized biography of the famous gunfighter. **54m/B VHS, Beta.** Roy Rogers, George "Gabby" Hayes. *NOS, DVT, TIM*

Young Blood 🎬🎬 1933 A cowboy robs

from the rich to help the poor. He's also interested in a foreign actress having trouble bonding with the townfolk. Lots of old fashioned western violence. **61m/B VHS, Beta.** Bob Steele, Charles "Blackie" King, Helen Foster; *D:* Phil Rosen. *NOS, DVT*

The Young Bruce Lee 19?? Bruce

learns and uses the deadly skills that made him famous while only knee-high to a grasshopper. **90m/C VHS, Beta.** Han Kwok Choi. *MGI*

Young Buffalo Bill 🎬🎬 1940 Buffalo Bill

battles the Spanish land-grant patrons. **54m/B VHS, Beta.** Roy Rogers, George "Gabby" Hayes, Pauline Moore; *D:* Joseph Kane. *NOS, DVT*

Young Caruso 🎬🎬 1951 Dramatic biogra-

phy of legendary tenor Enrico Caruso, following his life from childhood poverty in Naples to the beginning of his rise to fame. Dubbed in English. **78m/B VHS, Beta.** Gina Lollobrigida, Ermanno Randi, Mario del Monaco. *VYY, NOS, MVD*

Young Catherine 🎬🎬🎬 1991 Made-for-

TV account of Russia's strongest female ruler, the girl who would be Catherine the Great. Star-studded cast and excellent production values. Script and strong cast make Ormond look like a lightweight. Filmed in Leningrad. Also available in 186-minute version. **150m/C VHS, Beta, Closed**

Caption. Vanessa Redgrave, Christopher Plummer, Marthe Keller, Franco Nero, Julia Ormond, Maximilian Schell, Reece Dinsdale, Mark Frankel; **D:** Michael Anderson Sr.; **W:** Chris Bryant. *TTC*

Young Charlie Chaplin ♂♂ 1988 A
British-made TV biography of the legendary silent screen comic. 160m/C VHS, Beta. Ian McShane, Twiggy; **M:** Rachel Portman. *NO*

A Young Connecticut Yankee in King Arthur's Court ♂ 1995 A mo-
dern-day teenager timetravels back to the court of King Arthur and Camelot. Based on the book by Mark Twain. 93m/C VHS. Michael York, Theresa Russell, Nick Mancuso, Philippe Ross, Jack Langedijk, Polly Shannon, Paul Hopkins; **D:** Ralph L. Thomas; **W:** Ralph L. Thomas, Frank Encarnacao; **C:** John Berrie; **M:** Alan Reeves. *CAF*

Young Doctors in Love ♂♂ 1982 (R)
Spoof of medical soap operas features a chaotic scenario at City Hospital, where the young men and women on the staff have better things to do than attend to their patients. Good cast keeps this one alive, though many laughs are forced. Includes cameos by real soap star, including then-General Hospital star Moore. 95m/C VHS, Beta, LV. Dabney Coleman, Sean Young, Michael McKean, Harry Dean Stanton, Hector Elizondo, Patrick Macnee, Pamela Reed; *Cameos:* Demi Moore, Janine Turner; **D:** Garry Marshall; **W:** Michael Elias, Rich Eustis; **M:** Maurice Jarre. *PAR, VES*

Young Dragon ♂½ 1977 (R) The Young
Dragon's girlfriend is kidnapped by the underworld society, and he sets out to rescue her single-handedly. 90m/C VHS. Yang Sze, Lo Lai, Yuen Man Chi, Wong Ching, Nora Miao. *SUN*

Young Einstein ♂♂ 1989 (PG) A goofy, ir-
reverent Australian farce starring, directed, co-scripted and co-produced by Serious, depicting Einstein as a young Outback clod who splits beer atoms and invents rock and roll. Winner of several Aussie awards. Fun for the kids. 91m/C VHS, Beta, LV, Closed Caption. *AU* Yahoo Serious, Odile Le Clezio, John Howard, Pee Wee Wilson, Su Cruickshank; **D:** Yahoo Serious; **W:** Yahoo Serious; **M:** Martin Armiger. *WAR*

Young Frankenstein ♂♂♂♂ 1974 (PG)
Young Dr. Frankenstein (Wilder), a brain surgeon, inherits the family castle back in Transylvania. He's skittish about the family business, but when he learns his grandfather's secrets, he becomes obsessed with making his own monster. Wilder and monster Boyle make a memorable song-and-dance team to Irving Berlin's "Puttin' on the Ritz," and Hackman's cameo as a blind man is inspired. Garr ("What knockers!" "Oh, sank you!") is adorable as a fraulein, and Leachman ("He's vass my—boyfriend!") is wonderfully scary. Wilder saves the creature with a switcheroo, in which the doctor ends up with a certain monster-sized body part. Hilarious parody. 108m/B VHS, Beta, LV, Closed Caption. Peter Boyle, Gene Wilder, Marty Feldman, Madeline Kahn, Cloris Leachman, Teri Garr, Kenneth Mars, Richard Haydn, Gene Hackman; **D:** Mel Brooks; **W:** Mel Brooks, Gene Wilder; **C:** Gerald Hirschfeld; **M:** John Morris. Nominations: Academy Awards '74: Best Adapted Screenplay, Best Sound. *FOX, HMV*

The Young Graduates ♂ 1971 (PG)
Hormonally imbalanced teens come of age in spite of meandering plot. Features "Breaking Away" star Christopher in big screen debut. 99m/C VHS. Patricia Wymer, Steven Stewart, Gary Rist, Bruce Kirby, Jennifer Ritt, Dennis Christopher; **D:** Robert Anderson.

Young Guns ♂♂½ 1988 (R) A sophomoric
Wild Bunch look-alike that ends up resembling a western version of the Bowery Boys. Provides a portrait of Billy the Kid and his gang as they move from prairie trash to demi-legends. Features several fine performances by a popular group of today's young stars. 107m/C VHS, Beta, LV, Closed Caption. Emilio Estevez, Kiefer Sutherland, Lou Diamond Phillips, Charlie Sheen, Casey Siemaszko, Dermot Mulroney, Terence Stamp, Terry O'Quinn, Jack Palance, Brian Keith, Patrick Wayne, Sharon Thomas; **D:** Christopher Cain;

W: John Fusco; **M:** Anthony Marinelli, Brian Backus, Brian Banks. *ART, VFS*

Young Guns 2 ♂♂ 1990 (PG-13) Brat
Pack vehicle neo-Western sequel about Billy the Kid (Estevez) and his gang. This time they're making a run for the border with the law on their trail. 105m/C VHS, LV, Letterbox, Closed Caption. Emilio Estevez, Kiefer Sutherland, Lou Diamond Phillips, Christian Slater, William L. Petersen, Alan Ruck, R.D. Call, James Coburn, Balthazar Getty, Jack Kehoe, Rob Knepper, Jenny Wright, Tracey Walter, Ginger Lynn Allen, Jon Bon Jovi; **D:** Geoff Murphy; **W:** John Fusco; **M:** Alan Silvestri. Golden Globe Awards '91: Best Song ("Blaze of Glory"); Nominations: Academy Awards '90: Best Song ("Blaze of Glory"). *BTV, CCB*

Young Hercules ♂♂½ 1997 (PG-13) Sev-
enteen-year-old Herc (Bohen) is a confused teen, torn between his mortal and immortal sides. So concerned mom Alcmene sends the kid to Cherion's academy where Herc can learn to be a warrior and where he'll meet friends and rivals Iolus (O'Gorman), Prince Jason (Conrad), and the beautiful Yvenna (Stewart). Oh yes, war god Ares (Smith) also shows up, trying to prevent half-brother Herc and his friends from obtaining the golden fleece for Jason's dying father. **CW:** Continuous adventure violence and peril. 93m/C VHS, Closed Caption. Ian Bohen, Dean O'Gorman, Johna Stewart, Chris Conrad, Kevin Smith; **D:** T.J. Scott; **W:** Robert Tapert, Andrew Dettmann, Daniel Truly. *USH*

The Young in Heart ♂♂♂ 1938 A
lonely, old woman allows a family of con-artists into her life for companionship. Impressed by her sweet nature, the parasitic brood reforms. The cute comedy was a real crowd-pleaser in its day, especially after the bittersweet ending was replaced with a happier variety. Based on the novel "The Gay Banditti" by I.A.R. Wylie. 90m/C VHS. Janet Gaynor, Douglas Fairbanks Jr., Paulette Goddard, Roland Young, Billie Burke, Minnie Dupree, Richard Carlson, Charles Halton; **D:** Richard Wallace; **W:** Charles Bennett, Paul Osborn. Nominations: Academy Awards '38: Best Cinematography, Best Original Score. *NO*

Young Ivanhoe ♂♂½ 1995 Ivanhoe
learns how to be a warrior, with some help from Robin Hood and the Black Knight, inspiring others to follow him into battle to save their land from seizure by the Norman invaders. 96m/C VHS. Stacy Keach, Nick Mancuso, Margot Kidder, Kris Holdenried, Rachel Blanchard, Matthew Daniels; **D:** Ralph L. Thomas; **W:** Ralph L. Thomas, Frank Encarnacao; **C:** John Berrie; **M:** Alan Reeves. *CAF*

Young Lady Chatterly 2 ♂½ 1985 A
poor sequel to the popular MacBride film, with only the name of the Lawrence classic. Chatterly inherits the family mansion and fools around with the servants and any one else who comes along. Unrated version with 13 minutes of deleted footage is also available. 87m/C VHS, Beta, LV. Sybil Danning, Adam West, Harlee MacBride; **D:** Alan Roberts. *ART*

The Young Land ♂½ 1959 Less-than-in-
spiring western does feature a good performance by Hopper as malcontent bully Hatfield Carnes. Carnes kills a respected Mexican in a barroom gunfight in 1848 California and sheriff Jim Ellison (Wayne) is quick to call territorial judge Isham (O'Herlihy) to ensure a fair trial—with the rest of the Spanish-speaking town looking on in skepticism. Based on the story "Frontier Frenzy" by John Reese. 88m/C VHS. Dennis Hopper, Patrick Wayne, Dan O'Herlihy, Yvonne Craig, Ken Curtis, Pedro Gonzalez-Gonzalez; **D:** Ted Tetzlaff; **W:** Norman S. Hall; **C:** Winton C. Hoch, Henry Sharp; **M:** Dimitri Tiomkin. Nominations: Academy Awards '59: Best Song ("Strange Are the Ways of Love"). *HTV*

The Young Lions ♂♂♂ 1958 A cynical
WWII epic following the experiences of a young American officer and a disillusioned Nazi in the war's last days. Martin does fine in his first dramatic role. As the Nazi, Brando sensitively considers the belief that Hitler would save Germany. A realistic anti-war film. 167m/B VHS, Beta, LV, Letterbox. Marlon Brando, Montgomery Clift, Dean Martin,

Hope Lange, Barbara Rush, Lee Van Cleef, Maximilian Schell, Dr Edward Dmytryk, W: Edward Anhalt. Nominations: Academy Awards '58: Best Black and White Cinematography, Best Sound, Best Original Dramatic/Comedy Score. *FOX*

Young Love, First Love ♂½ 1979 A
made-for-television movie about a young woman who must decide whether to have sex with her boyfriend. Sound familiar? Pretty blah, earnest story, though well cast. 100m/C VHS, Beta. Valerie Bertinelli, Leslie Ackerman, Timothy Hutton, Arlen Dean Snyder, Fionnula Flanagan; **D:** Steven Hilliard Stern. *ART*

Young Love—Lemon Popsicle 7 ♂
1987 (R) Three hunks stalk the beaches in search of babes. 91m/C VHS, Beta. Yftach Katzur, Zachi Noy, Jonathan Segall, Sonja Martin; **D:** Walter Bennett. *WAR*

Young Man with a Horn ♂♂♂ 1950
Dorothy Baker's novel, which was loosely based on the life of jazz immortal Bix Beiderbecke, was even more loosely adapted for this film, featuring Kirk as an angst-ridden trumpeter who can't seem to hit that mystical "high note." ♫The Very Thought of You; I May be Wrong; The Man I Love; Too Marvelous for Words; With a Song in My Heart; Pretty Baby; I Only Have Eyes for You; Limehouse Blues; Melancholy Rhapsody. 112m/B VHS, Beta, LV. Kirk Douglas, Doris Day, Lauren Bacall, Hoagy Carmichael; **D:** Michael Curtiz. *WAR*

Young Master ♂♂ 1980 Chan, searching
for his missing brother, is mistaken for a fugitive and has to save himself from bounty hunters and police. Oh, and get the real bad guys so he can clear his name. Chinese with subtitles or dubbed. 90m/C VHS, LV. *HK* Jackie Chan; **D:** Jackie Chan. *TAI*

Young Mr. Lincoln ♂♂♂½ 1939 A
classy Hollywood biography of Lincoln in his younger years from log-cabin country boy to idealistic Springfield lawyer. A splendid drama, and one endlessly explicated as an American masterpiece by the French auteur critics in "Cahiers du Cinema." 100m/B VHS, Beta, LV, Closed Caption. Henry Fonda, Alice Brady, Marjorie Weaver, Arleen Whelan, Eddie Collins, Ward Bond, Donald Meek, Richard Cromwell, Eddie Quillan, Charles Halton; **D:** John Ford; **W:** Lamar Trotti. Nominations: Academy Awards '39: Best Story. *FOX*

The Young Nurses ♂♂ Nightingale 1973
(R) The fourth entry in the Roger Corman produced "nurses" series. Three sexy nurses uncover a drug ring run from their hospital, headed by none other than director Fuller. Also present is Moreland, in his last role. Preceded by "The Student Nurses," "Private Duty Nurses," "Night Call Nurses," followed by "Candy Stripe Nurses." Also on video as "Young L.A. Nurses 3." 77m/C VHS, Beta. Jean Manson, Ashley Porter, Angela Gibbs, Zack Taylor, Dick Miller, Jack LaRue, William Joyce, Sally Kirkland, Allan Arbus, Mary Doyle, Don Keefer, Nan Martin, Mantan Moreland, Samuel Fuller; **D:** Clinton Kimbrough. *NLC*

Young Nurses in Love ♂ 1989 (R)
Low-budget sex farce in which a foreign spy poses as a nurse to steal sperm from a sperm bank donated by world leaders, celebrities and geniuses. 82m/C VHS, Beta, LV. Jeanne Marie, Alan Fisher, Barbra Robb, James Davies; **D:** Chuck Vincent. *ART, VES*

The Young One ♂♂½ La Joven; Island of
Shame 1961 Traver (Hamilton) is a black jazz musician who escapes from his southern town when he's wrongly accused of raping a white woman. He hides out on a small island which is used as a private hunting ground for rich sportsmen, overseen by Miller (Scott), the game keeper. Hamilton gets work as the new handyman and becomes close to the young Evalyn (Meersman). When Miller rapes Evalyn, it's Traver who's once again accused until things can be put right. Racist elements are heavy-handed; one of Bunuel's lesser efforts. Based on the story "Travelin' Man" by Peter Matthiessen. 94m/B VHS. *MX* Bernie Hamilton, Zachary Scott, Kay Meersman, Claudio Brook, Graham

Denton; **D:** Luis Bunuel; **W:** Hugo Butler, Luis Bunuel. *CVC, FCT*

The Young Ones 1988 Three episodes from the hilarious, offbeat British television sitcom about four violently eccentric college roommates. Episodes included are "Oil," "Boring," and "Flood." **96m/C VHS, Beta.** *GB* Rik Mayall, Ade Edmondson, Nigel Planer, Christopher Ryan, Alexei Sayle; **D:** Geoffrey Posner. *FOX*

Young People ♫♫½ 1940 (G) Temple's 12 in this lesser vehicle and almost-adolescence doesn't serve her well with this tired plot. She's an orphan adopted by showbiz team Oakie and Greenwood who've decided to retire to rural life. They even get to put on a show to prove to the small-minded small-towners what a swell trio they are. Temple's last film for 20th-Century Fox does include nostalgic clips from earlier Shirley hits, including "Stand Up and Cheer" and "Curly Top," to explain her character's background. ♫Tra-La-La; Fifth Avenue; I Wouldn't Take a Million; The Mason-Dixon Line; Young People. **78m/C VHS, Closed Caption.** Shirley Temple, Jack Oakie, Charlotte Greenwood, Arleen Whelan, George Montgomery, Kathleen Howard; **D:** Allan Dwan; **W:** Edwin Blum, Don Ettlinger. *FXV*

The Young Philadelphians ♫♫♫
The City Jungle 1959 Ambitious young lawyer Newman works hard at making an impression on the snobbish Philadelphia upper crust. As he schemes and scrambles, he woos debutante Rush and defends buddy Vaughn on a murder charge. Long, but worth it. Part of the "A Night at the Movies" series, this package simulates a 1959 movie evening with a Bugs Bunny cartoon, "People Are Bunny," a newsreel and coming attractions for "The Nun's Story" and "The Hanging Tree." **136m/B VHS, Beta.** Paul Newman, Barbara Rush, Alexis Smith, Billie Burke, Brian Keith, John Williams, Otto Kruger, Robert Vaughn; **D:** Vincent Sherman; **C:** Harry Stradling; **M:** Ernest Gold. Nominations: Academy Awards '59: Best Black and White Cinematography, Best Costume Design (B & W), Best Supporting Actor (Vaughn). *WAR*

The Young Poisoner's Handbook ♫♫♫ 1994 (R) Based on the true story of London teenager Graham (O'Conor), who's obsessed with chemistry and at odds with his stepmother. So, he poisons her chocolates and she dies. Sent to Broadmoor prison for the criminally insane, Graham comes under the care of Dr. Ziegler (Sher), who, eight years later, recommends Graham for parole. Now working in a photographic lab, Graham decides to experiment with doctoring his co-workers tea—which results in eight more deaths before Graham is caught. Locked up again, Graham spends his time writing a poisoner's handbook for Dr. Ziegler. Be warned that the sufferings of the poisoned victims are gruesome. **CW:** Murders by poisoning, language and some nude photos. **99m/C VHS, Closed Caption.** *GB* Hugh O'Conor, Anthony Sher, Ruth Sheen, Charlotte Coleman, Roger Lloyd Pack, Paul Stacey, Samantha Edmonds, Charlie Creed-Miles; **D:** Benjamin Ross; **W:** Benjamin Ross, Jeff Rawle; **C:** Hubert Taczanowski; **M:** Robert Lane, Frank Strobel. *CAF*

Young Sherlock Holmes ♫♫ 1985 **(PG-13)** Holmes and Watson meet as schoolboys. They work together on their first case, solving a series of bizarre murders gripping London. Watch through the credits for an interesting plot twist. Promising "what if" sleuth tale crashes and burns, becoming a typical high-tech Spielberg film. Second half bears too strong a resemblance to "Indiana Jones and the Temple of Doom." **109m/C VHS, Beta, LV, 8mm, Closed Caption.** Nicholas Rowe, Alan Cox, Sophie Ward, Freddie Jones, Michael Hordern; **D:** Barry Levinson; **W:** Chris Columbus; **M:** Bruce Broughton. *PAR*

Young Tiger ♫♫ 1980 (R) First a 90-minute movie never before seen in the U.S. featuring an expert in martial arts who is accused of murder. Next is a 12-minute documentary featuring Jackie Chan, kung-fu sensation, demonstrating his skills. What an evening. **102m/C VHS, Beta.** Jackie Chan. *GEM*

Young Tom Edison ♫♫½ 1940 Two teenaged years in the life of Thomas Alva Edison, as he drives his family crazy with his endless experiments on his way to becoming the famed inventor. Rooney manages to be enthusiastic without being overwhelming. Followed by "Edison the Man," with Spencer Tracy in the adult role. **82m/B VHS, Beta.** Mickey Rooney, Fay Bainter, George Bancroft, Virginia Weidler, Eugene Pallette, Victor Kilian, Bobby Jordan, Lloyd Corrigan; **D:** Norman Taurog; **W:** Dore Schary, Bradbury Foote, Hugo Butler. *MGM, FCT, BTV*

Young Warlord ♫♫ 1975 Arthur roams western England in 500 AD, leading a band of guerrilla cavalrymen. When the Saxons invade, Arthur unites the tribe, holds off the attack and becomes king. **97m/C VHS, Beta.** Oliver Tobias, Michael Gothard, Jack Watson, Brian Blessed; **D:** Peter Sasdy. *NO*

Young Warriors ♫½ 1983 (R) Frat boys turn vigilante to avenge a street gang murder. Weird mix of teen sex comedy, insufferable self-righteous preachiness, and violence. **104m/C VHS, Beta.** Ernest Borgnine, James Van Patten, Richard Roundtree, Lynda Day George, Dick Shawn; **D:** Lawrence Foldes; **W:** Lawrence Foldes, Richard Matheson, Russell W. Colgin; **C:** Mac Ahlberg. *MGM*

Young Winston ♫♫♫ 1972 (PG) Based on Sir Winston Churchill's autobiography "My Early Life: A Roving Commission." Follows him through his school days, journalistic career in Africa, early military career, and his election to Parliament at the age of 26. Ward is tremendous as the prime minister-to-be. **145m/C VHS, Beta.** *GB* Simon Ward, Robert Shaw, Anne Bancroft, John Mills, Jack Hawkins, Ian Holm, Anthony Hopkins, Patrick Magee, Edward Woodward, Jane Seymour; **D:** Richard Attenborough. Golden Globe Awards '73: Best Foreign Film; Nominations: Academy Awards '72: Best Art Direction/Set Decoration, Best Costume Design, Best Story & Screenplay. *COL, TVC*

Youngblood ♫♫ 1986 (R) An underdog beats the seemingly insurmountable odds and becomes a hockey champion. Some enjoyable hockey scenes although the success storyline is predictable. **111m/C VHS, Beta, LV.** Rob Lowe, Patrick Swayze, Cynthia Gibb, Ed Lauter, George Finn, Fionnula Flanagan, Keanu Reeves; **D:** Peter Markle. *MGM*

Younger & Younger ♫♫½ 1994 (R) Jonathan Younger (Sutherland) is forced to run the family storage business after his long-suffering wife Penny (Davidovich) dies. The business starts to fail, even after Jonathan's son (Fraser) arrives to help out, and the widower begins having visions of the woman he mistreated. And each time he sees her she looks younger and more beautiful than ever. **97m/C VHS, LV, Closed Caption.** Donald Sutherland, Brendan Fraser, Lolita Davidovich, Sally Kellerman, Julie Delpy, Linda Hunt; **D:** Percy Adlon; **W:** Percy Adlon, Felix Adlon; **C:** Bernd Heinl; **M:** Hans Zimmer. *PAR*

Your Place or Mine ♫½ 1983 Self-indulgent made-for-television yuppie pap about middle-aged singles trying to find the right mate. **100m/C VHS, Beta.** Bonnie Franklin, Robert Klein, Peter Bonerz, Tyne Daly, Penny Fuller; **D:** Robert Day; **M:** Gerald Alters. *ART*

Your Ticket Is No Longer Valid ♫ 1984 (R) Prurient excuse for a serious drama. Impotent failed businessman has disturbing erotic dreams about his girlfriend. Adapted from a novel by Romain Gary. **96m/C VHS, Beta.** *CA* Richard Harris, George Peppard, Jeanne Moreau; **D:** George Kaczender. *VES*

Your Turn Darling ♫♫ *A Toi De Faire; Mignonne* 1963 French espionage thriller with Constantine once again playing Lemmy Caution, a U.S. secret agent involved with a gang of spies. **93m/C VHS.** *FR* Eddie Constantine, Gaia Germani, Elga Andersen; **D:** Bernard Borderie. *SNC*

You're a Big Boy Now ♫♫♫ 1966 Kastner, a virginal young man working in the New York Public Library, is told by his father to move out of his house and grow up. On his own, he soon becomes involved with man-hating actress

Hartman and a discotheque dancer. A wild and weird comedy. Coppola's commercial directorial debut. **96m/C VHS, Beta.** Elizabeth Hartman, Geraldine Page, Peter Kastner, Julie Harris, Rip Torn, Michael Dunn, Tony Bill, Karen Black; **D:** Francis Ford Coppola; **W:** Francis Ford Coppola. Nominations: Academy Awards '66: Best Supporting Actress (Page). *WAR*

You're a Good Man, Charlie Brown 1987 A filmed version of Charles Schulz's Broadway musical, based on his famous characters. **60m/C VHS, Beta.** *BAR, KAR*

You're in Love, Charlie Brown 1967 The animated Peanuts gang in a new adventure about Charlie Brown and the proverbial little red-haired girl. **30m/C VHS, Beta.** *BAR*

You're Jinxed, Friend, You've Met Sacramento ♫♫ 1970 The tongue-in-cheek adventures of a cool-headed cowboy as he passes from town to colorful town. Great title, too. **99m/C VHS, Beta.** Ty Hardin, Christian Hay, Jenny Atkins; **D:** George Cristallini. *UNI*

Yours, Mine & Ours ♫♫½ 1968 Bigger, better, big screen version of "The Brady Bunch." It's the story of a lovely lady (Ball) with eight kids who marries a a widower (Fonda) who has ten. Imagine the zany shenanigans! Family comedy manages to be both wholesome and funny. Based on a true story. **114m/C VHS, Beta, LV, Closed Caption.** Lucille Ball, Henry Fonda, Van Johnson, Tim Matheson, Tom Bosley, Tracy Nelson; **D:** Melville Shavelson; **W:** Melville Shavelson. *MGM*

Youth Aflame woof! *Hoodlum Girls* 1959 Trash film that tells the tale of two sisters—one good, one bad. Poor dialogue and weak performances do, however, make for some great camp. Based on a story by Helen Kiedy. **61m/B VHS.** Joy Reese, Warren Burr, Kay Morley, Michael Owen, Rod Rogers; **D:** Elmer Clifton; **W:** Elmer Clifton. *SNC*

Youth on Parole ♫½ 1937 Same old story: Boy gets paroled. Girl gets paroled. Parolee meets parolette and romance blossoms as they beat a further rap. **60m/B VHS.** Marian Marsh, Gordon Oliver. *LOO, VYY*

You've Got to Have Heart ♫ 1977 (R) A young bridegroom's life gets complicated after he does not sexually satisfy his bride on their wedding night. **98m/C VHS, Beta.** Carroll Baker, Edwige French.

You've Ruined Me, Eddie ♫ 1958 A spoiled rich girl gets knocked up and her boyfriend will never know peace again. Meanwhile, their once quiet town is outraged. **m/B VHS.** *SMW, TPV*

Yukon Flight ♫♫ 1940 A Renfrew of the Mounties adventure. The hero finds illegal gold mining operations and murder in the Yukon. **57m/B VHS, Beta.** James Newill, Dave O'Brien. *NOS, VCN*

The Yum-Yum Girls ♫½ 1978 (R) Pair of innocent girls arrive in New York City to pursue their dreams. Gives an inside looks at the fashion industry. Not as funny or as cute as it wants to be. **89m/C VHS, Beta.** Judy Landers, Tanya Roberts, Barbara Tully, Michelle Daw; **D:** Barry Rosen. *USH*

Yuma 1970 An old-style made-for-television Western about a sheriff (Walker) who rides into town, cleans it up, and saves his own reputation from a plot to discredit him. Dull in places, but action-packed ending saves the day. **73m/C VHS, Beta.** Clint Walker, Barry Sullivan, Edgar Buchanan; **D:** Ted Post; **M:** George Duning. *VTR*

Yuri Nosenko, KGB ♫♫½ 1986 Fact-based account of a KGB defector and the CIA agent who must determine if he's on the up-and-up. Made for British television. **85m/C VHS.** *GB* Tommy Lee Jones, Oleg Rudnik, Josef Sommer, Ed Lauter, George Morfogen, Stephen D. Newman; **D:** Mick Jackson. *CNG*

Z ♫♫♫♫ 1969 The assassination of a Greek nationalist in the 1960s and its aftermath are portrayed by the notorious political director as a gripping detective thriller. Excellent performances, adequate cinematic techniques, and important politics in this highly acclaimed film. **128m/C VHS, Beta, LV.** *FR* Yves Montand, Jean-Louis Trintignant, Irene Papas, Charles Denner, Georges Geret, Jacques Perrin, Francois Perier, Marcel Bozzuffi; *D:* Constantin Costa-Gavras; *W:* Constantin Costa-Gavras. Academy Awards '69: Best Film Editing, Best Foreign Language Film; Cannes Film Festival '69: Special Jury Prize, Best Actor (Trintignant); Golden Globe Awards '70: Best Foreign Film; New York Film Critics Awards '69: Best Director (Costa-Gavras), Best Film; National Society of Film Critics Awards '69: Best Film; Nominations: Academy Awards '69: Best Adapted Screenplay, Best Director (Costa-Gavras), Best Picture; Cannes Film Festival '69: Best Film. *FXL*

Zabriskie Point 🦴🦴🦴 1970 (R) Antonioni's first U.S. feature. A desultory, surreal examination of the American way of life. Worthy but difficult. Climaxes with a stylized orgy in Death Valley. **112m/C VHS, Beta, LV.** Mark Frechette, Daria Halprin, Paul Fix, Rod Taylor, Harrison Ford, G.D. Spradlin; *D:* Michelangelo Antonioni; *W:* Michelangelo Antonioni, Sam Shepard, Fred Gardner, Tonino Guerra, Clare Peploe. *MGM, MLB*

Zachariah 🦴🦴½ 1970 (PG) A semi-spoof '60s rock western, wherein two gunfighters given to pursuing wealth-laden bands of outlaws separate and experience quixotic journeys through the cliched landscape. Scripted by members of The Firesign Theater and featuring appearances by Country Joe and The Fish, The New York Rock Ensemble, and The James Gang. **93m/C VHS, Beta.** Don Johnson, John Rubinstein, Pat Quinn, Dick Van Patten; *D:* George Englund. *FOX*

Zafarinas 🦴🦴 *Moriras en Chafarinas* 1994 (R) Zafarinas is an ancient walled city on the island of Melilla that houses a military barracks. Two suspicious deaths force Commander Contreras (Ladoire) to release zealous corporal Jaime (Sanz) and Corporal Cidraque (Albala) from the stockades to investigate. Then there's a third death and things just aren't what they seem. Spanish with subtitles. *CW:* Language and some violence. **85m/C VHS.** *SP* Jorge Sanz, Javier Albala, Oscar Ladoire, Maria Barranco; *D:* Pedro Olea; *W:* Pedro Olea, Fernando Lalana; *C:* Paco Femenia. *RVN, TPV*

Zalmen or the Madness of God 🦴🦴½ 1975 Elie Wiesel's mystical story about a rabbi's struggle against religious persecution in post-Stalin Russia. **120m/C VHS, Beta.** Joseph Wiseman. *WNE*

Zandalee woof! 1991 (R) The sexual adventures of a bored sexy young woman who has a fling with her husband's friend. Bad script, graphic sex. Also available in an unrated version. *CW:* Sexual dialogue and language and strong sensuality. **100m/C VHS, LV, Closed Caption.** Nicolas Cage, Judge Reinhold, Erika Anderson, Viveca Lindfors, Aaron Neville, Joe Pantoliano, Ian Abercrombie, Marisa Tomei, Zach Galligan; *D:* Sam Pillsbury; *W:* Mari Kornhauser. *ART*

Zandy's Bride 🦴½ 1974 (PG) Basic story about a rancher who sents for a mail-order bride. She's shocked by his ill-treatment of her and stands up to his bullying, thus winning his respect and love. Beautiful scenery, courtesy of Big Sur, California, but predictable all-around and essentially a waste of an experienced cast. Based on the novel "The Stranger" by Lillian Bos Ross. **97m/C VHS.** Gene Hackman, Liv Ullmann, Eileen Heckart, Harry Dean Stanton, Joe Santos, Sam Bottoms, Susan Tyrrell, Frank Cady; *D:* Jan Troell; *W:* Marc Norman; *C:* Jordan Cronenweth; *M:* Michael Franks. *WAR*

The Zany Adventures of Robin Hood 🦴 1984 Hackneyed spoof of the Robin Hood legend. Medieval man robs from the rich to help the poor. Not nearly as funny as. Mel Brooks' TV series that spoofed "Robin Hood." **95m/C VHS, Beta.** George Segal, Morgan Fairchild, Roddy McDowall, Roy Kinnear, Janet Suzman, Tom Baker; *D:* Ray Austin.

Zapped! 🦴 1982 (R) Teen genius discovers he possesses telekinetic powers. He does the natural thing, using his talent to remove clothing from nearby females. A teen boy's dream come true. **98m/C VHS, Beta, LV.** Scott Baio, Willie Aames,

Robert Mandan, Felice Schachter, Scatman Crothers, Roger Bowen, Marya Small, Greg Bradford, Hilary Beane, Sue Ane Langdon, Heather Thomas, Merritt Butrick, LaWanda Page, Rosalind Katon; *D:* Robert J. Rosenthal; *M:* Charles Fox. *NLC*

Zapped Again 🦴 1989 (R) The lame-brained sequel to 1982's "Zapped" about a high schooler who has telekinetic powers and lust on his mind. **93m/C VHS, Beta, LV, 8mm.** Todd Eric Andrews, Kelli Williams, Reed Rudy, Linda Blair, Karen Black, Lyle Alzado; *D:* Doug Campbell. *COL*

Zardoz 🦴🦴 1973 A surreal parable of the far future, when Earth society is broken into strict classes: a society of intellectuals, a society of savages, and an elite unit of killers who keep the order. Connery is the man who destroys the old order of things. Visually interesting but pretentious. **105m/C VHS, Beta, LV, Letterbox.** Sean Connery, Charlotte Rampling, John Alderson, Sara Kestelman; *D:* John Boorman; *W:* John Boorman. *FOX*

Zarkorr! The Invader 🦴 1996 (PG) Aliens studying earth decide humans need a challenge (like we don't have enough problems of our own) so they send a 185-foot tall, laser-eyed monster to crush (American) cities and cause general terror in the population. And who's our hero? A postal worker—aided by a five-inch tall alien girl. Low-budget spoof has its moments, but eventually wears thin. **80m/C VHS, LV.** Rhys Pugh, Deprise Grossman, Mark Hamilton, Charles Schneider, Eileen Wesson; *D:* Aaron Osborne; *W:* Benjamin Carr; *C:* Joe C. Maxwell; *M:* Richard Band. *AFE*

Zatoichi: Master Ichi and a Chest of Gold 🦴🦴 1964 A violent thriller about a blind gambler and former samurai who tries to clear his name after being framed for a gold robbery. Adapted from a novel by Kazuo Miyagawa. In Japanese with English subtitles. **83m/C VHS.** *JP* Shintaro Katsu; *D:* Kazuo Ikehiro. *FCT*

Zatoichi: The Blind Swordsman and the Chess Expert 🦴🦴 1965 Zatoichi, the blind gambler and former samurai, befriends a master chess player and gets involved with Japanese gangsters. In Japanese with English subtitles. **87m/C VHS.** *JP* Shintaro Katsu; *D:* Kenji Misumi. *FCT*

Zatoichi: The Blind Swordsman and the Fugitives 🦴🦴 1968 This time Zatoichi, the blind masseur and master swordsman, is pitted against a band of outlaws. When the local bandits brutalize the countryside Zatoichi steps in to defend the weak and faces a showdown with outlaw leader Genpachiro. In Japanese with English subtitles. **82m/C VHS.** *JP* Shintaro Katsu, Yumiko Nogawa, Kayo Mikimoto, Kyosuke Machida; *D:* Kimiyoshi Yasuda. *FCT*

Zatoichi: The Blind Swordsman's Vengeance 🦴🦴 1966 Zatoichi defends a dying man against a group of gangsters who have taken over an isolated village. In Japanese with English subtitles. **83m/C VHS.** *JP* Shintaro Katsu, Shigeru Amachi, Kei Sato, Mayumi Ogawa; *D:* Tokuzo Tanaka. *FCT*

Zatoichi: The Life and Opinion of Masseur Ichi 🦴🦴 1962 The first film in the action series about the Zen-like blind masseur, gambler, and swordsman. Zatoichi is drawn into a revenge match between two ruthless gangs. When one gang tries to hire him the other hires a savage killer. This sets in motion a war between the yakuza gangs and mercenary samurai. In Japanese with English subtitles. **96m/C VHS.** *JP* Shintaro Katsu, Masayo Mari, Ryuzo Shimada, Gen Mitamura, Shigeru Amachi; *D:* Kenji Misumi. *FCT*

Zatoichi vs. Yojimbo 🦴🦴🦴½ *Zatoichi Meets Yojimbo; Zato Ichi To Yojimbo* 1970 The legendary blind warrior-samurai, Zatoichi, wants to retire, but his village is being held captive by outlaws. He is forced to fight Yojimbo, the crude wandering samurai without a master, and the sparks really fly! This was a comic send-up of Akira Kurosawa's "Yojimbo" with Mifune recreating his role

here and playing it for laughs. Subtitled. **90m/C VHS.** *JP* Toshiro Mifune, Shintaro Katsu, Osamu Takizawa; *D:* Kihachi Okamoto. *VDA*

Zatoichi: Zatoichi's Flashing Sword 🦴🦴 1964 Blind swordsman Zatoichi gets caught up in a feud between two competing yakuza bosses. When Zatoichi declares his allegience to Tsumugi, the unhappy Yasu tries to get his revenge. In Japanese with English subtitles. **82m/C VHS.** *JP* Shintaro Katsu, Mayumi Nagisa, Naoko Kubo, Ryutaro Gami, Yutaka Nakamura; *D:* Kazuo Ikehiro. *FCT*

Zazie dans le Metro 🦴🦴🦴½ *Zazie in the Underground; Zazie in the Subway* 1961 One of Malle's early movies, this is one of the best of the French New Wave comedies. A young girl, wise beyond her years, visits her drag queen uncle in Paris. She wants to ride the subway, but the ensuing hilarious adventures keep her from her goal. In French with English subtitles. **92m/C VHS.** *FR* Catherine Demonget, Philippe Noiret, Carla Marlier; *W:* Louis Malle. *NYF*

Zebra Force 🦴 1976 (R) Group of army veterans embark on a personal battle against organized crime, using their military training with deadly precision. Non-distinguished substandard action-adventure. **81m/C VHS, Beta.** Mike Lane, Richard X. Slattery, Rockne Tarkington, Glenn Wilder, Anthony Caruso; *D:* Joe Tornatore.

Zebra in the Kitchen 🦴🦴½ 1965 A 12-year-old boy living in a small town is upset when he sees the run-down condition of the local zoo. So he decides to set all the animals free, which causes pandemonium in the town. Pleasant family fare. **92m/C VHS.** Jay North, Martin Milner, Andy Devine, Joyce Meadows, Jim Davis; *D:* Ivan Tors. *MGM, BTV*

Zebrahead 🦴🦴🦴 1992 (R) Zack and Nikki are two high schoolers in love—which would be okay except Zack's white and Nikki's black. Writer/director Drazan's expressive debut features one of last appearances by Sharkey as Zack's dad. Outstanding performances by the young and largely unknown cast, particularly Rapaport and Wright, and a great musical score enrich the action. Filmed on location in Detroit, with plenty of authentic Motown scenery to chew on, including Cody High School and a shootout at the eastside Skateland. Developed with assistance by the Sundance Institute. *CW:* Strong langauge. **102m/C VHS, LV, 8mm, Closed Caption.** Michael Rapaport, N'Bushe Wright, Ray Sharkey, DeShonn Castle, Ron Johnson, Marsha Florence, Paul Butler, Abdul Hassan Sharif, Dan Ziskie, Candy Ann Brown, Helen Shaver, Luke Reilly, Martin Priest, Kevin Corrigan; *D:* Tony Drazan; *W:* Tony Drazan; *C:* Maryse Alberti; *M:* Taj Mahal. Sundance Film Festival '92: Filmmakers Trophy. *COL*

A Zed & Two Noughts 🦴🦴🦴 1988 A serio-comic essay by the acclaimed British filmmaker. Twin zoologists, after their wives are killed in an accident, explore their notions of death by, among other things, filming the decay of animal bodies absconded from the zoo. Heavily textured and experimental; Greenaway's second feature film. **115m/C VHS, Beta.** *GB* Eric Deacon, Brian Deacon, Joss Ackland, Andrea Ferreol, Frances Barber; *D:* Peter Greenaway; *W:* Peter Greenaway; *C:* Sacha Vierny; *M:* Michael Nyman. *TPV*

Zelig 🦴🦴🦴½ 1983 (PG) Documentary spoof stars Allen as Leonard Zelig, the famous "Chameleon Man" of the 1920s, whose personality was so vague he would assume the characteristics of those with whom he came into contact, and who had a habit of showing up among celebrities and at historic events. Filmed in black-and-white; intersperses bits of newsreal and photographs with live action. Allen-style clever filmmaking at its best. **79m/B VHS, Beta, LV, 8mm.** Woody Allen, Mia Farrow, Susan Sontag, Saul Bellow, Irving Howe; *D:* Woody Allen; *W:* Woody Allen; *C:* Gordon Willis. New York Film Critics Awards '83: Best Cinematography; Nominations: Academy Awards '83: Best Cinematography, Best Costume Design. *WAR*

Zelly & Me 🎬🎬🎬 *Phoebe* 1988 (PG) A strange little drama about a young orphan living with her maniacally possessive grandmother, who forces the child into her own interior life through humiliation and isolation from anyone she cares for. Well-acted and interesting film that suffers from an overly introspective plot and confusing gaps in the narrative. Look for director Lynch on the other side of the camera. 87m/C VHS, Beta, LV, **Closed Caption.** Isabella Rossellini, Alexandra Johnes, David Lynch, Glynis Johns, Kaiulani Lee, Joe Morton; *D:* Tina Rathborne; *W:* Tina Rathborne; *C:* Mikael Salomon; *M:* Pino Donaggio. COL

Zentropa 🎬🎬 1992 (R) Clever cinematic allusions and visuals aside, this is essentially a conventional thriller. German-American pacifist Leopold travels to Germany in 1945 to help in the postwar rebuilding. He finds work as a sleeping-car conductor for a giant railway system called Zentropa and finds himself romancing the mysterious Katharina, who draws the hapless Leopold into an intrigue involving Nazi sympathizers. Director von Trier uses the voice of Von Sydow as an omniscient narrator to address the audience and move the story along. Filmed primarily in black-and-white with bursts of color denoting dramatic moments. In English and German with English subtitles.*CW:* Violent scenes. 112m/C VHS, Beta, LV, **Closed Caption.** GE Jean-Marc Barr, Barbara Sukowa, Udo Kier, Eddie Constantine; *D:* Lars von Trier; *W:* Niels Vorsel, Lars von Trier. TOU

Zeppelin 🎬🎬½ 1971 (G) During WWI, the British enlist the aid of York as a double agent. His mission is to steal Germany's plans for a super-dirigible. Accompanying the Germans on the craft's maiden voyage, York discovers they are actually on a mission to steal British treasures. Although the script is poor, the battle scenes and the blimp itself are very impressive. 102m/C VHS, Beta, LV, **Closed Caption.** GB Michael York, Elke Sommer, Peter Carsten, Marius Goring, Anton Diffring, Andrew Keir, Rupert Davies, Alexandra Stewart; *D:* Etienne Perier. WAR, FCT

Zeram 🎬🎬 1991 Zeram is a giant renegade space alien lured to earth by a female bounty hunter. How does she expect to capture it? Why with a warp machine, space bazooka, electric shield, and a computer named Bob, of course. Dubbed. 92m/C VHS. JP Yuko Moriyama, Yukihiro Hotaru, Kunihiko Ida; *D:* Keita Amemiya; *W:* Hajime Matsumoto. FXL, FCT

Zero 1984 WWII story about the building of the zero fighter that was used to devastating effect in the invasion of Pearl Harbor. 128m/C VHS, Beta. Yuzo Kayama, Tetsuro Tamba; *D:* Toshio Masuda. NO

Zero Boys WOOF! 1986 (R) Teenage survivalists in the Californian wilderness are stalked by a murderous lunatic. Exploitative and mean-spirited. 89m/C VHS, Beta. Daniel Hirsch, Kelli Maroney, Nicole Rio, Joe Phelan; *D:* Nico Mastorakis. ART

Zero Degrees Kelvin 🎬🎬½ *Zero Kelvin; Kjaerlighetens Kjotere* 1995 Brrrr! Get the ice scraper ready, because you may have to clear off your TV screen in this chilly tale of trappers in 1920s Greenland. Henrik Larsen (Eidsvold), a poet living in Oslo, decides to join the band of trappers after his girlfriend Gertrude (Martens) spurns his marriage proposal. On his arrival in the stark and frozen landscape, he is forced to share a cabin with the stoic, silent Holm (Sundquist) and the lewd, violent Randbaek (Skarsgard). Randbaek holds the newcomer and his city-boy ways in disdain, creating an air of tension and menace that inevitably results in a clash between the two. Instead of dwelling on the action aspect, director Moland uses the minimalist landscape to echo the psychological battles the men must face with the frigid terrain and between themselves. Norwegian with subtitles. 113m/C VHS. NO Garb B. Eidsvold, Stellan Skarsgard, Bjorn Sundquist, Camilla Martens; *D:* Hans Petter Moland; *W:* Hans Petter Moland, Lars Bill Lundheim; *C:* Philip Ogaard; *M:* Terje Rypdal. KIV

Zero Effect 🎬🎬½ 1997 (R) A cross between Howard Hughes and Sherlock Holmes, brilliant, eccentric detective Daryl Zero (Pullman), who, along with his harried helper Steve Arlo (Stiller), takes on the case of a blackmailed timber tycoon (O'Neal) in this comedic whodunit. The normally reclusive sleuth bites the bullet and agrees to trek to Oregon to personally investigate the particularly intriguing case, which also involves an attractive paramedic (Dickens). Pullman pulls off another quirky leading man performance with flair. Stiller is stellar as the exasperated assistant. Fresh idea and hip humor mark this debut for 22-year-old writer/director Kasdan, son of director Lawrence Kasdan.*CW:* Language. 150m/C VHS. Bill Pullman, Ben Stiller, Ryan O'Neal, Kim Dickens, Angela Featherstone; *D:* Jake Kasdan; *W:* Jake Kasdan; *C:* Bill Pope. WAR

Zero for Conduct 🎬🎬🎬🎬 *Zero de Conduit* 1933 Vigo's classic French fantasy about an outrageous rebellion of schoolboys against bureaucratic adults. More of a visual poem than a drama, it inspired Lindsay Anderson's "If...." One of only four films created by Vigo before his early death. Banned across Europe at release. In French with English subtitles. 49m/B VHS, Beta. FR Jean Daste, Robert Le Flon, Louis Lef'evre, Constantin Kelber, Gerard de Bedarieux; *D:* Jean Vigo; *W:* Jean Vigo; *C:* Boris Kaufman. VYY, NOS, HHT

Zero for Conduct/Taris/A Propos de Nice 1991 Three short films by the famed Jean Vigo. "Zero for Conduct" is a fascinating and fluid surrealist film about rebellion in a boy's prep school. "Taris" consists of underwater footage of the swimmer Jean Taris, and "A Propos de Nice" is a documentary that focuses on the great economic schism of the rich and the poor in the popular French vacation spot, Nice. 75m/B VHS. FR *D:* Jean Renoir. NO

Zero Patience 🎬🎬 1994 Yes, it's an audacious film musical about AIDS myths and ghosts and Victorian explorers—among other things. Infamous Patient Zero (Fauteux) is the Canadian flight attendant reputed to have carried the virus to North America. Ghostly Zero pleads for someone to tell his story and his cause is taken up by Victorian explorer Sir Richard Francis Burton (Robinson), who happens to have achieved eternal life after an encounter with the Fountain of Youth, and who is also preparing an exhibit on contagious diseases. Sharp mix of politics, humor, and fantasy. 100m/C VHS. CA John Robinson, Normand Fauteux, Dianne Heatherington, Ricardo Keens-Douglas; *D:* John Greyson; *W:* John Greyson; *M:* Glenn Schellenberg. CCN

Zero Population Growth 🎬½ *Z.P.G.* 1972 In the 21st century the government has decreed that no babies may be born for a 30-year span in order to control the population. But Chaplin and Reed secretly have a child and when they are discovered are sent to be executed. Can they escape? Maudlin and simplistic. 95m/C VHS. Oliver Reed, Geraldine Chaplin, Diane Cilento, Don Gordon; *D:* Michael Campus; *W:* Frank de Felitta, Max Ehrlich. PAR

Zero to Sixty 🎬 1978 (PG) Newly divorced man finds his car has been repossessed for non-payment. Seeking out the manager of the finance company, he gets a job as a repo man with a sassy 16-year-old girl as his assistant. Repartee develops, stuff happens, and the movie ends. 96m/C VHS, Beta. Darren McGavin, Sylvia Miles, Denise Nickerson, Joan Collins; *D:* Don Weis; *M:* John Beal.

Zero Tolerance 🎬🎬½ 1993 (R) FBI agent Jeff Douglas (Patrick) is assigned to travel to Mexico and pick up a drug-runner who works for the White Hand cartel, whose latest product is liquid heroin. When they are ambushed Douglas is forced to carry a shipment of drugs across the border—the lives of his wife and child hang in the balance. But after the dirty deed is done, Douglas finds his family has been murdered anyway. So he sets out to execute the cartel druglords.*CW:*

Language and violence and drug-related scenes. 92m/C VHS, LV, **Closed Caption.** Robert Patrick, Miles O'Keeffe, Mick Fleetwood, Titus Welliver, Jeffrey Anderson-Gunter, Gustav Nintas, Michael Gregory, Maurice Lamont; *D:* Joseph Merhi; *W:* Jacobsen Hart. PMH, WEA

Zertigo Diamond Caper 🎬 1982 Utilizing his heightened senses, a blind boy solves a diamond caper and proves his mother's innocence. 50m/C VHS, Beta. Adam Rich, David Groh, Jane Elliot. GEM

Zeus and Roxanne 🎬🎬 1996 (PG) Hey, I know! Let's combine "Flipper" and "Benji" with "The Parent Trap!" You know, for the kids! Marine biologist and single mom Mary Beth (Quinlan) meets her unconventional (and conveniently widowed) new neighbor Terry (Guttenberg) and his dog Zeus. Cuteness ensues. Mary Beth's daughters and Terry's young son go about getting the two adults together. Meanwhile, Zeus and Roxanne, Mary Beth's dolphin, strike up a unique friendship of their own. Showing up to provide drama is evil guy Claude (Vosloo), who is vying for the same grant as Mary Beth. Unlikely animal couple steals the show, and the story would have benefitted from focusing on the entertaining bond between those two and less on the human romance. Not much appeal for anyone over the age of nine. 98m/C VHS, **Closed Caption, DVD.** Kathleen Quinlan, Steve Guttenberg, Arnold Vosloo, Miko Hughes, Dawn McMillan, Majandra Delfino, Jennifer Howell; *D:* George Miller; *W:* Tom Benedek; *C:* David Connell; *M:* Bruce Rowland. HBO

Ziegfeld Follies 🎬🎬½ 1946 A lavish revue of musical numbers and comedy sketches featuring many MGM stars of the WWII era. Highlights include Astaire and Kelly's only duet and a Astaire-Bremer ballet number. ♫Bring on Those Wonderful Men; Bring on Those Beautiful Girls; The Drinking Song; La Traviata; This Heart is Mine; Love; When Television Comes; There's Beauty Everywhere; The Babbitt and the Bromide. 115m/C VHS, Beta, LV. Fred Astaire, Judy Garland, Gene Kelly, Red Skelton, Fanny Brice, William Powell, Jimmy Durante, Edward Arnold, Lucille Bremer, Hume Cronyn, Victor Moore, Lena Horne, Lucille Ball, Esther Williams; *D:* Vincente Minnelli; *C:* Charles Rosher. MGM, MLB

Ziegfeld Girl 🎬🎬🎬 1941 Three star-struck girls are chosen for the Ziegfeld follies and move on to success and heartbreak. Lavish costumes and production numbers in the MGM style. ♫You Stepped Out of a Dream; I'm Always Chasing Rainbows; Minnie from Trinidad; Mr. Gallagher & Mr. Shean; You Never Looked So Beautiful. 131m/B VHS, Beta, LV. James Stewart, Judy Garland, Hedy Lamarr, Lana Turner, Tony Martin, Jackie Cooper, Ian Hunter, Charles Winninger, Al Shean, Edward Everett Horton, Philip Dorn, Paul Kelly, Eve Arden, Dan Dailey, Fay Holden, Felix Bressart, Mae Busch, Reed Hadley; *D:* Robert Z. Leonard. MGM

Zipperface 🎬 1992 A Palm Beach serial killer is making mincemeat of the local prostitutes. In order to capture the scum, the prerequisite beautiful police detective goes undercover only to find herself the killer's biggest thrill. 90m/C VHS, LV. Dona Adams, David Clover, John Dagnen; *D:* Mansour Pourmand.

Zis Boom Bah 🎬½ 1942 Musical-comedy star buys a cafe for her college son. He and his friends transform the place into a restaurant-theatre with predictable results. ♫Annabella; It Makes No Difference When You're In the Army; Put Your Trust in the Moon; Zis Boom Bah; Good News Tomorrow; I've Learned to Smile Again. 61m/B VHS, Beta. Peter Lind Hayes, Mary Healy, Grace Hayes, Huntz Hall, Benny Rubin. NOS, HEG, DVT

The Zodiac Killer 🎬½ 1971 (R) Based on a true story, this tells the violent tale of the San Francisco murders that occurred in the late 1960s. Doesn't have the suspense it should. 87m/C VHS, Beta. Tom Pittman, Hal Reed, Bob Jones, Ray Lynch; *D:* Tom Hanson.

Zoltan...Hound of Dracula 🐾½ *Dracula's Dog* 1978 The vampire and his bloodthirsty dog go to Los Angeles to find the last of Count Dracula's living descendants. Campy and just original enough to make it almost worth watching. 85m/C VHS, Beta. Michael Pataki, Reggie Nalder, Jose Ferrer, Jan Shutan, Libbie Chase, John Levin; **D:** Albert Band; **W:** Frank Ray Perilli; **M:** Andrew Belling. REP, VCI, FCT

Zombie 🐾 *Zombie Flesh-Eaters; Island of the Living Dead; Zombi 2* 1980 Italian-made white-men-in-the-Caribbean-with-flesh-eating-zombies cheapie. 91m/C VHS, Beta, LV. IT Tisa Farrow, Ian McCulloch, Richard Johnson, Al Cliver, Auretta Gay, Olga Karlatos, Stefania D'Amario, Ugo Bologna, Monica Zanchi; **D:** Lucio Fulci; **W:** Elisa Briganti; **C:** Sergio Salvati. VTR

Zombie and the Ghost Train 🐾🐾 *Zombie ja Kummitusjuna* 1991 Absurdist punk comedy about the vicissitudes of a down-and-out bass player. Finnish with subtitles. 88m/C VHS. FI **D:** Mika Kaurismaki; **W:** Mika Kaurismaki; **C:** Olli Varja; **M:** Mauri Sumen. FRF

The Zombie Army 🐾 1993 Tough drill sergeant tries to whip a bunch of raw female recruits to muster for a special mission. Toward that end, the government has conveniently bought a defunct lunatic asylum as a training ground. Only problem is that a few of the former inmates have been left behind and are able to menace the troops with their penchant for psychotic weirdness. 80m/C VHS. Eileen Saddow. TEM, MOV

Zombie High 🐾 *The School That Ate My Brain* 1987 (R) Students at a secluded academy are being lobotomized by the school president. Mindless, in two senses of the word. 91m/C VHS, Beta. Virginia Madsen, Richard Cox, Kay E. Kuter, James Wilder, Sherilyn Fenn, Paul Williams, Scott Coffey; **D:** Ron Link. VTR

Zombie Island Massacre 🐾 1984 (R) In this trying film, tourists travel to see a voodoo ritual, and then are systematically butchered by the rite-inspired zombies. Featuring former congressional wife and "Playboy" magazine model Jenrette. 89m/C VHS, Beta. Rita Jenrette, David Broadnax; **D:** John N. Carter. TTV

Zombie Lake 🐾 *El Lago de los Muertos Vivientes; The Lake of the Living Dead* 1980 Killed in an ambush by villagers during WWII, a group of Nazi soldiers turned zombies reside in the town's lake, preying on unsuspecting swimmers, especially dog paddling nude young women. Laughable FX, almost bad enough to be good. From the team that produced "Oasis of the Zombies." 90m/C VHS. FR SP Howard Vernon, Pierre Escourrou, Anouchka, Anthony Mayans, Nadine Pascale, Jean Rollin; **D:** J.A. Laser, Jean Rollin; **W:** A. L. Mariaux, Julian Esteban. VCI

Zombie Nightmare woof! 1986 (R) A murdered teenager is revived by a voodoo queen and slaughters his punk-teen assailants. Cheap and stupid just about sums this one up. Music by Motorhead, Death Mask, Girlschool, and Thor. 89m/C VHS, Beta. Adam West, Jon Mikl Thor, Tia Carrere, Frank Dietz, Linda Singer, Mandn E. Turbride, Hamibh McEwen; **D:** John Bravman.

Zombies of Moratau woof! 1957 A diver and his girlfriend seek to retrieve an undersea treasure of diamonds protected by zombies. So boring you'll want to die. 70m/B VHS, Beta. Gregg Palmer, Allison Hayes, Jeff Clark, Autumn Russel, Joel Ashley; **D:** Edward L. Cahn. COL, MLB

Zombies of the Stratosphere *Satan's Satellites* 1952 A serial in 12 chapters in which a cosmic policeman fights Zombies attempting to blow the Earth out of orbit. Also available in a 93-minute, colorized version. 152m/B VHS, Beta, LV. Judd Holdren, Aline Towne, Leonard Nimoy, John Crawford, Ray Boyle; **D:** Fred Brannon. REP, VCN, MLB

Zombies on Broadway 🐾🐾½ *Loonies On Broadway* 1944 Two press agents travel to the Caribbean in search of new talent, but find Lugosi performing experiments on people and turning them into sequel material. RKO hoped this would

be equally successful follow-up to "I Walked with a Zombie." 68m/B VHS, LV. Wally Brown, Alan Carney, Bela Lugosi, Anne Jeffreys, Sheldon Leonard, Frank Jenks, Russell Hopton, Joseph Vitale, Ian Wolfe, Louis Jean Heydt, Darby Jones, Sir Lancelot; **D:** Gordon Douglas. TTC, FCT, IME

Zombiethon 🐾½ 1986 A campy compilation of clips from cheapo zombie films, such as "Space Zombies," "Zombie Lake," and "The Invisible Dead." 90m/C VHS, Beta. Dominique Singleton, Janelle Lewis, Tracy Burton. NO

Zone of the Dead 🐾 1978 A mortician is using his morgue for other than embalming—and it isn't pretty! 81m/C VHS, Beta. John Ericson, Ivor Francis, Charles Aidman, Bernard Fox. NO

Zone Troopers 🐾½ 1984 (PG) Five American G.I.'s in WWII-ravaged Europe stumble upon a wrecked alien spacecraft and enlist the extraterrestrial's help in fending off the Nazis. 86m/C VHS, Beta. Timothy Van Patten, Tim Thomerson, Art LaFleur, Biff Manard; **D:** Danny Bilson; **W:** Danny Bilson, Paul DeMeo; **C:** Mac Ahlberg; **M:** Richard Band. ART

Zontar, the Thing from Venus 🐾 1966 Scientist is taken over by alien batlike thing from Venus, and attempts to take over the Earth. A parody of itself. 68m/C VHS. John Agar, Anthony Huston, Susan Bjorman, Pat Delaney, Warren Hammack; **D:** Larry Buchanan; **W:** Larry Buchanan; **C:** John Alcott. SNC, VDM

The Zoo Gang 🐾½ 1985 (PG-13) A group of teens want to open a nightclub. Will they bring their dream to fruition, or will the mean rival gang foil their plans? 96m/C VHS, Beta. Jackie Earle Haley, Tiffany Helm, Ben Vereen, Jason Gedrick, Eric Gurry; **D:** John Watson, Pen Densham; **W:** John Watson, Pen Densham; **M:** Patrick Gleeson. VTR

Zooman 🐾🐾🐾 1995 (R) Hard-hitting message on violence and responsibility. Gang member Zooman (Kain) spots members of a rival gang in a Brooklyn neighborhood, whips out his gun, and begins firing. When the shooting stops, a little girl sitting on her stoop is dead—what's even worse for her estranged parents is the fact that obvious witnesses refuse to identify the gunman for fear of their own safety. So father Reuben (Gossett Jr.) puts up a sign about their plight, attracting lots of media attention, and neighborhood hostility. Based on Fuller's 1978 play "Zooman and the Sign." Made for cable TV. **CW:** Strong language; some violent content. 95m/C VHS, Closed Caption. Louis Gossett Jr., Charles S. Dutton, Khalil Kain, Cynthia Martells, CCH Pounder, Vondie Curtis-Hall, Hill Harper; **D:** Leon Ichaso; **W:** Charles Fuller. REP

Zoot Suit 🐾🐾🐾 1981 (R) Based on Luis Valdez' play, this murder mystery/musical is rooted in the historical Sleepy Lagoon murder in the 1940s. Valdez plays a Mexican-American accused of the crime. His friends (and defense lawyers) rally around him to fight this travesty of justice. Lots o'music and dancing. 104m/C VHS, LV. Edward James Olmos, Daniel Valdez, Tyne Daly, Charles Aidman, John Anderson; **D:** Luis Valdez; **W:** Luis Valdez. USH, FCT

Zora Is My Name! 🐾🐾½ 1990 The funny, moving story of Zora Neal Hurston, a Black writer known for her stories and folklore of the rural South of the '30s and '40s. From PBS's American Playhouse. 90m/C VHS, LV. Ruby Dee, Louis Gossett Jr. PBS, KAR, FCT

Zorba the Greek 🐾🐾🐾½ *Zormba* 1964 A young British writer (Bates) comes to Crete to find himself by working his father's mine. He meets Zorba, an itinerant Greek laborer (Quinn), and they take lodgings together with an aging courtesan, who Zorba soon romances. The writer, on the other hand, is attracted to a lovely young widow. When she responds to him, the townsmen jealously attack her. Zorba teaches the young man the necessary response to life and its tragedies. Based on a novel by Nikos Kazantzakis. Masterpiece performance from Quinn. Beautifully photographed, somewhat overlong. Film later

written for stage production. 142m/B VHS, Beta, LV. Anthony Quinn, Alan Bates, Irene Papas, Lila Kedrova, D: Mihaal Oacuoyannis, C: Walter Lassally. Academy Awards '64: Best Art Direction/Set Decoration (B & W), Best Black and White Cinematography, Best Supporting Actress (Kedrova); National Board of Review Awards '64: Best Actor (Quinn); Nominations: Academy Awards '64: Best Actor (Quinn), Best Adapted Screenplay, Best Director (Cacoyannis), Best Picture. BTV, FUS

Zorro Rides Again 1937 Zorro risks his life to outwit gangsters endeavoring to secure ancestor's property. In 12 chapters; the first runs 30 minutes, the rest 17. 217m/B VHS, Beta. John Carroll, Helen Christian, Noah Beery Sr., Duncan Renaldo; **D:** William Witney, John English. NOS, VCN, VDM

Zorro, the Gay Blade 🐾🐾½ 1981 (PG) Tongue-in-cheek sword play with Hamilton portraying the swashbuckling crusader and his long-lost brother, Bunny Wigglesworth, in this spoof of the Zorro legend. The fashion-conscious hero looks his best in plum. Leibman is fun to watch. 96m/C VHS, Beta, Closed Caption. George Hamilton, Lauren Hutton, Brenda Vaccaro, Ron Leibman; **D:** Peter Medak; **W:** Greg Alt; **C:** John A. Alonzo. FOX

Zorro's Black Whip 1944 A young girl dons the mask of her murdered brother (Zorro) to fight outlaws in the old West. Serial in 12 episodes. 182m/B VHS, LV. George Lewis, Linda Stirling, Lucien Littlefield, Francis McDonald, Tom London; **D:** Spencer Gordon Bennet; **W:** Wallace Grissell. NOS, GPV, REP

Zorro's Fighting Legion 1939 Zorro forms a legion to help the president of Mexico fight a band of outlaws endeavoring to steal gold shipments. A serial in 12 chapters. 215m/B VHS, LV. Reed Hadley, Sheila Darcy; **D:** William Witney, John English. NOS, VCN, VDM

Zotz! 🐾🐾 1962 The holder of a magic coin can will people dead by uttering "zotz"; spies pursue the mild-mannered professor who possesses the talisman. Adapted from a Walter Karig novel. Typical William Castle fare; his gimic in the theatrical release of the movie was to distribute plastic "zotz" coins to the theatre patrons. 87m/B VHS, Beta. Tom Poston, Julia Meade, Jim Backus, Fred Clark, Cecil Kellaway; **D:** Ray Russell; **W:** Ray Russell. COL

Zou Zou 🐾🐾½ 1934 Lavish backstage musical/drama of a laundress who fills in for the leading lady on opening night and becomes a hit. Baker's talking picture debut. In French with English subtitles. 92m/B VHS, LV. FR Josephine Baker, Jean Gabin; **D:** Marc Allegret. MVD, KIV, AUD

Zu: Warriors of the Magic Mountain 🐾🐾 1983 The forces of evil are plotting to take over the world and a warrior endures the perils of the Zu Mountains in order to find the Twin Swords, the only weapons capable of defeating the demons. Cantonese with subtitles or dubbed. 98m/C VHS, Letterbox. HK Adam Cheng, Yuen Biao, Bridget Lin, Sammo Hung; **D:** Tsui Hark. TAI, FCT

Zulu 🐾🐾½ 1964 In 1879, a small group of British soldiers try to defend their African outpost from attack by thousands of Zulu warriors. Amazingly, the British win. Dated colonial epic based on an actual incident; battle scenes are magnificent. Prequel "Zulu Dawn" (1979) depicts British mishandling of the situation that led to the battle. 139m/C VHS, Beta, LV, Letterbox, Closed Caption. Michael Caine, Jack Hawkins, Stanley Baker, Nigel Green; **D:** Cy Endfield; **M:** John Barry. NLC

Zulu Dawn 🐾🐾🐾 1979 (PG) An historical epic about British troops fighting the Zulus at Ulandi in 1878. Shows the increasing tensions between the British colonial government and the Zulus. Stunning landscapes unfortunately don't translate to the small screen. Good but unoriginal colonial-style battle drama. 117m/C VHS, Beta, LV. Burt Lancaster, Peter O'Toole, Denholm Elliott, Nigel Davenport, John Mills, Simon Ward, Bob Hoskins, Freddie Jones; **D:** Douglas Hickox; **M:** Elmer Bernstein. TWE

Zvenigora 🎬🎬🎬🎬 **1928** Dovzhenko's first major film, and a lyrical revelation in the face of Soviet formality: a passionate, funny fantasy tableaux of 1,000 years of Ukrainian history, encompassing wild folk myths, poetic drama, propaganda and social satire. Silent. **73m/B VHS, Beta.** *RU* Mikola Nademsy, Alexander Podorozhny, Semyon Svashenko; *D:* Alexander Dovzhenko. *FCT*

Category List

The **Category Index** contains genre, sub-genre, thematic, or significant scene classifications, ranging from the very general terms (comedy, drama) to the fairly particular (phone terror, killer cars, exploding fish tanks). The terms are defined (more or less) below. We've done our best to provide serious subject references while also including fun categories and lists to make your video viewing experience a little more enjoyable. No one list is all-inclusive. We are continuously reclassifying, adding, and subtracting movies. Many of the categories in this list are new, and therefore represent only a beginning. We're also trying to pare down some of the bigger categories, like **Romance**, by creating more focused subject categories, such as **Lovers on the Lam** or **Romantic Triangles**. *VideoHound* invites readers to participate in this pastime by sending in suggestions for new categories and adding movies to existing ones. **An asterisk (*) denotes a new category for this edition.**

ABBA-ca-da-bra: Australian films pay homage to the kitschy '70s pop icons, reviving "Dancing Queen" and "Waterloo"

Action-Adventure: Adrenaline testers for those weary of the conventions of plot-think Stallone, think Snipes, and quit thinking

Adoption & Orphans: Cute kids lacking permanent authority figures, ranging from *Annie* to *Wild Hearts Can't Be Broken*

Adventure Drama: Action with more attention to dramatic content-*Apocalypse Now* to *Robin Hood, Prince of Thieves*

Advertising: Corporate shenanigans at the agency-*How to Get Ahead in Advertising* to *The Horse in the Gray Flannel Suit*

Africa: Banana Republic franchise; *Out of Africa* to *Zulu Dawn*

African America: Dominant African American themes

AIDS: Someone usually dies; *An Early Frost* to *Longtime Companion*

Air Disasters: Contraptions up in the sky, but not for long

Airborne: Contraptions up in the sky

Alien Beings-Benign: Friendly space visitors, including *Howard the Duck* and little buddy *E.T.*

Alcatraz: Prison island off San Francisco, aka *The Rock*

Alien Babes: Women who possess otherworldly beauty (and appetites)

Alien Beings-Vicious: Not-so-friendly space visitors, notably the multi-jawed *Alien* continually harassing Sigourney Weaver

Aliens Are People, Too: Space visitors pretend to be human, or just take over the bodies—*Invasion of the Body Snatchers* kinda stuff

American South: Theatrics amid much brow mopping and drawling; *A Streetcar Named Desire* rattling down *Flamingo Road*

America's Heartland: Generally heartwarming small-town sagas

*The Amish: Butter churns, barn raisings, buggies, and (usually) bothersome outsiders

Amnesia: Phone call for *Anastasia*

Amusement Parks: Cotton candy, ferris wheels, Coney Island, *Godzilla on Monster Island*, *Rollercoaster*

Angels: Benevolent winged visitors from above: *Wings of Desire*

Animated Musicals: Boys, girls, dogs, ducks, birds, mice, and monkeys croon; many of Disney vintage, including *Aladdin* and *Sleeping Beauty*

Animation & Cartoons: Antics of Daffy, Donald, Bugs, Mickey, Chip, Dale, Tom, Jerry, Fred, Wilma, Charlie, and the rest of the gang

Anthology: More than one story to a cassette

Anti-Heroes: From *Billy Jack* to *Dirty Harry* to *Thelma & Louise*

Anti-War War Movies: Recognizes that war really is hell-from *All Quiet on the Western Front* to *Glory* to *M*A*S*H*

Apartheid: Afrikaans term for racial segregation in South Africa

Art & Artists: They paint, pause, and propagate with equal passion

Asia: *China White, Red Dust, Sand Pebbles*

Asian America: Asian experience in the US-*The Joy Luck Club, Come See the Paradise*

Assassinations: Lincoln, *JFK, La Femme Nikita, Times of Harvey Milk*, and more

*Astronauts: Houston, we have a problem.

At the Drive-In: Scenes in which people watch movies...at the drive-in.

At the Movies: The movie within a movie or movies about watching the movies, from *The Purple Rose of Cairo* to *Last Action Hero* to *Matinee*

*At the Video Store: Scenes from a video store, *Clerks, Remote Control*

Avant-garde: Ahead of its time or completely bewildering to most in the audience

Babysitting: Supervision of small-fry pranksters not your own; *Uncle Buck* to *The Hand that Rocks the Cradle*

Bad Dads: Daddy-Os with unpredictable mean streak:*The Shining, Kiss Daddy Goodbye*

Bad Hair Days: Oddly coiffed characters

Ballet: On your toes-*The Turning Point*

Ballooning: Up, up and away, or *Around the World in 80 Days*

Baltimore: Take a look at the Maryland city, hometown of director Barry Levinson and favorite digs of John Waters

Bar & Grill: Most, if not all, of the action takes place in a drinking establishment.

Baseball: Action on the diamond, ranging from *Bull Durham* to *A League of Their Own* to *Rookie of the Year*

Basketball: Roundball thrillers, including the memorable *The Fish that Saved Pittsburgh* and *White Men Can't Jump*

Bathroom Scenes: Encompassing bathtubs, hottubs, showers, sinks and toilets, including *Psycho, Fatal Attraction* and that poor fellow in *Jurassic Park*

Beach Blanket Bingo: Annette, Frankie, sand, surf, bikinis

Beach Driving: Enjoy the feel of sand between your treads

*Bears: Most of 'em are looking for more than just pic-i-nic baskets

Beatniks: Jazz beards, bongos, poetry that doesn't rhyme, berets

Beauty Pageants: From the heartless to the hilarious, beauty is a big business-*Smile* girls!

Behind the Scenes: Peek behind show business curtain, from *A Chorus Line* to *Truth or Dare*

Berlin: City in Germany divided after WWII, now it's one big happy city again

Bicycling: Two wheels, no motor, much leg action and sweating

Big Battles: Big-budget (or at least illusion of such) clash of large, opposing military forces, from *Cromwell* to *Ran*

Big Budget Stinkers: Millions spent for no apparent reason

Big Daddies: Usually troublesome, with Freudian overtones

Big Digs: Anthropology and archaeology, from Indiana Jones to various mummy on-the-loose stories

Big Ideas: Philosophy, ideology and other semi-mental pursuits somehow translated to film

Big Rigs: *Smokey and the Bandit* speed down *Thieves' Highway* in a *Convoy*

Bigfoot/Yeti: Large, hairy, seldom-seen beast with really big feet

Bikers: Usually with a mean streak and traveling in leather-clad packs

Birds: Beaks, feathers, talons, bird #%!; *The Birds*, *Beaks: The Movie*, *Howard the Duck*

Bisexuality: Going both ways-*Basic Instinct*, *Three of Hearts*

Black Comedy: Funny in a biting or despairing sort of way, from *The Addams Family* to *The Hospital*

Black Gold: Oil, that is; aka *Oklahoma Crude*

Blackmail: I'm gonna tell, unless... *The Last Seduction*, *Letter to My Killer*

Blaxploitation: '70s remakes of horror classics with black casts: *Blacula*, *Blackenstein*, *Dr. Black, Mr. Hyde*

Blindness: Can't see or sight impaired; *Afraid of the Dark*

Bloody Mayhem: Expanded scenes of arterial explosions, including *Blood Bride*, *Blood Cult*, *Blood Diner*, *Blood Feast*, *Blood Lake*, *Blood Legacy*, *Blood Mania*, and *Bloodbath in Psycho Town*

Bloody Messages: Cryptic warnings to the living written in the blood of the poor slob who was just killed—*Redrum*

Bodyguards: Costner looks after Whitney's personal business

Books: As a major plot device: *La Lectrice* to *Crossing Delancey*

Boom!: Really big explosions, bombs, and other noisy or fiery messes popular in big budget action flicks

Boomer Reunions: thirtysomethings gather and reminisce: *The Big Chill*

Boston: Beantown, where everybody knows your name.

Bounty Hunters: Bring 'em back dead or alive—for a price

Bowling: Heavy round ball is thrown down waxed alley toward club-like pins; all fall down

Boxing: Yo, Adrian!

Bringing Up Baby: *Look Who's Talking* to *Raising Arizona*, plus infants with that little something different-*Alien 3*, *Enemy Mine*, *Basket Case 3: The Progeny*

Buddies: Butch and Sundance, Bill and Ted, Rubin and Ed, *Thelma and Louise*

Buddy Cops: Couple of police hanging together, usually practicing limited repartee at a donut shop; *Lethal Weapon*, *Tango and Cash*

*Buried Alive: I'm not quite dead, yet! Hello, Mr. grave digger person, hello!

Buses: Large truck-like passenger vehicles-*Speed*, *The Big Bus*, *The Trip to Bountiful*

Cabbies: Where to, Mac?

Calcutta: Big, overpopulated city in India

Camelot (New): The exploits of JFK, Jackie, and various relatives and hangers-on

Camelot (Old): The exploits of King Arthur and his *Knights of the Round Table*

Campus Capers: What really goes on at college-*Assault of the Party Nerds*

Canada: Renfrew of the Mounties plus lots of wilderness and the occasional hockey puck

Canine Cops: He's a cop, he's got a badge, he's a dog-*K-9*, *Turner & Hooch*

Cannibalism: People who eat people are the luckiest people; *Alive*, *Rabid Grannies*, *Cannibal Women in the Avocado Jungle of Death*, *The Cook, the Thief, His Wife & Her Lover*

Capitol Capers: Hollywood versions of hijinks in Washington, D.C.-*Dave*, *Mr. Smith Goes to Washington*, *All the President's Men*

Carnivals & Circuses: Big top, little top, domes: *Shakes the Clown* to *Rollercoaster*, plus *Big Top Pee Wee*, *State Fair*, and metaphoric circuses: *Brewster McCloud*, *La Strada*

Cats: Lesser vertebrate nonetheless much beloved by Hollywood

Cave People: From the most primitive (*The Clan of the Cave Bear*) to the fairly modernized (*The Flintstones*)

Central America: Mostly Latin warfare, with at least three sides to every conflict

Chases: Who are those guys? Someone's after someone else, usually at high-speed with transportation ranging from horses to autos to bikes to trains to trucks

Cheerleaders: Give me an A! *The Positively True Adventures of the Alleged Texas Cheerleader-Murdering Mom* meets *Revenge of the Cheerleaders*

Chicago: City in Illinois, right at the bottom of Lake Michigan

Child Abuse: Not very funny at all-*Mommie Dearest*, *Fallen Angel*

Childhood Visions: Stories dominated by the kid point of view, or by an adult flashbacking to childhood; *Au Revoir Les Enfants*, *Home Alone*

China: *The Last Emperor* to *Red Sorghum* to *The World of Suzie Wong*

Christmas: Reindeer, Santa, children make appearance amid much sentimentality

Cinderella Stories: Gal down on her luck meets fairy godmother (or father) and finds true love-*Pretty Woman*, *Flashdance*, *Cinderella*

Civil Rights: Fighting for equality-*The Autobiography of Miss Jane Pittman*, *Mississippi Burning*

Civil War: The Yankees against the Confederates; aka *The Blue and the Gray*

Classic Horror: Boris Karloff, Vincent Price, piercing screams

Cloning Around: Makin' copies—of people or animals. *Multiplicity* to *Jurassic Park*

Clowns: Big red noses, huge feet, painted smiles frighten many

Cockroaches: Creepy crawlies signifying the work of the supernatural, or a lack of housekeeping skills

Cold Spots: Set in a frostbitten locale with lots of shivering; *Ice Station Zebra*, *Never Cry Wolf*, *Quest for Fire*

Comedy: Yuk fests not listed in other comedy categories-*Fletch*, *I Wanna Hold Your Hand*, *Tampopo*

Comedy Anthologies: More than one yuk fest on a cassette

Comedy Drama: Drama with a comedic touch or comedy underwired with drama-*Avalon*, *The Big Chill*, *Fried Green Tomatoes*, *One Flew Over the Cuckoo's Nest*, *Tootsie*

Comedy Mystery: Wacky whodunits like *Murder by Death*, *Clue*

Comedy Sci-Fi: Laughs in space! *Spaceballs*

Comic Adventure: Adventurous romps liberally laced with humor: *Romancing the Stone* to *Bird on a Wire* to *Crocodile Dundee*

Coming of Age: Hard-fought adolescent battle for adulthood, led by *American Graffiti*, *The Apprenticeship of Duddy Kravitz*, *The Karate Kid*

Computers: Bits and bytes play major role

*Concentration/Internment Camps: Nazis used them for their "final solution" while the U.S. used them to imprison Japanese-Americans

Concert Films: Rock or comedy concerts-from *Woodstock* to *Divine Madness* to *Eddie Murphy: Raw*

Contemporary Musicals: Thematically modern and made during last 20 years; *All That Jazz*

Contemporary Noir: Dark and moody or tributes to dark and moody that pay homage to the original Film Noir genre-*Blue Velvet*, *9 Weeks*, *sex, lies, and videotape*, *Wild Orchid*

Cops: Police and pseudo-police work, including *Action Jackson*, *Blue Steel*, *The Choirboys*, *RoboCop*, *Lethal Weapon*, *National Lampoon's Loaded Weapon 1*

Corporate Shenanigans: Big Business runs amuck-*Barbarians at the Gate*, *Wall Street*

Credits Chaos!: Don't rewind yet, 'cuz it's not over till it's over

Creepy Houses: Scary dwellings-*Amityville Horror* 1 through 33

Crime & Criminals: Bad guys and gals, including *Avenging Disco Godfather*, *The Grifters*, *In Cold Blood*

*Crime Drama: Gangster family dysfunction, heists gone awry, packin' pathos with your piece. *The Godfather*, *Goodfellas*, *Reservoir Dogs*.

Crime Sprees: Bad guy, gal or couple goes on a crime binge and other tales of obsessional criminal activity, including *Bonnie & Clyde*, *The Boys Next Door*

Crimes of Passion: Love, sex, and death

Crop Dusters: Down on the farm: *Bitter Harvest*, *Pelle the Conqueror*, *Jean de Florette*, *The River*

Cult Items: Recognized for that something different by a relatively small group (at least initially) of boomer-type people: *Basket Case*, *Blood Simple*, *Harold and Maude*, *Mad Max*, and the greatest cult of them all-*The Rocky Horror Picture Show*

Cult Items-New: Revered by a relatively large group of Generation X-type people: *Bill & Ted's Excellent Adventure*, *Grease*, *Sixteen Candles*, *The Sure Thing*

*Culture Clash: Hilarity ensues (or sometimes not) as people from vastly different backgrounds try to interact. *Deliverance*, *Witness*, *George of the Jungle*

Cults: Something like a gang but more intense and usually governed by a state of mind similar to irrationality-*Helter Skelter*

Cyberpunk: Dark, moody, futuristic flicks-*Blade Runner*, *Freejack*, *Tank Girl*

Dads: Fathers play a major role

Dance Fever: Whole lotta foot-tapping going on, including *An American in Paris*, *Daddy Long Legs*, and *Dirty Dancing*

Dates from Hell: Fun evening for two singles turns into a nightmare for one of them-*Bye Bye Love*, *Singles*, *Something Wild*

A Day In The Life: All the action takes place within a 24-hour period

*Deadly Implants: Where is that ticking coming from?

Deafness: Can't hear or hearing impaired; *Bridge to Silence*, *The Miracle Worker*

Death & The Afterlife: Could be ghosts, could be voices from the beyond, could be any number of post-dead things-*Beetlejuice*, *Carnival of Souls*, *Flatliners*, *Poltergeist*, *Weekend at Bernie's*

Death Row: Waitin' for a call from the Governor; *Dead Man Walking*, *Angels with Dirty Faces*

Dedicated Teachers: From *The Dead Poet's Society* to *The Blackboard Jungle* to *The Miracle Worker*

Deep Blue: The sea around us, including *ffolkes* and *Splash*

Demons & Wizards: Swords, sorcery and wrinkled old men with wands-*The Alchemist*, *The Hobbit*, *The Sword & the Sorcerer*

Dental Mayhem: Tooth-pickin' uproars; *Marathon Man*, *The Dentist*

Desert War/Foreign Legion: Big battles among the dunes

Deserts: Endless beach minus the water-*Ishtar*, *Lawrence of Arabia*

Detective Spoofs: Putting together clues in humorous fashion-*The Adventures of Sherlock Holmes' Smarter Brother*, *The Naked Gun*

Detectives: Clue happy but often grizzled and cynical-*The Drowning Pool*, *V.I. Warshawski*

Devils: Some may meet on *Judgment Day*

Devil's Island: French Island prison in the South Atlantic

Dinosaurs: *Jurassic Park* and other less animated thundering lizards

Disaster Flicks: Natural and man-made, including 47 *Airport* sequels

Disco Musicals: '70s tackiness reigns supreme, from *Saturday Night Fever* to *Xanadu*

Disease of the Week: Bulimia, anorexia, polio, cancer, and so on

Disorganized Crime: Stupid crime, including *Amos and Andrew*, *Dog Day Afternoon*, *Home Alone*, *Quick Change*

Divorce: Breaking up is hard to do; *Accidental Tourist*, *Heartburn*, *Kramer vs. Kramer*

Doctors & Nurses: Men and women in scrubs concerned about health of complete strangers for profit, often to the dismay of the patient-*Autopsy, Candy Stripe Nurses, Dead Ringers*

Docudrama: *The Thin Blue Line* between documentaries and drama

Documentary: Real life manipulated on film-*A Brief History of Time, The Last Waltz, Paris Is Burning, Roger and Me*

*Dogs In Peril: Manipulative plot device, usually in disaster flicks, where things blow up just as Fido high-tails it out of there.

Down Under: Australian, New Zealand settings-*The Rescuers Down Under, Gallipoli, The Man from Snowy River, The Thorn Birds*

Dragons: Legendary medieval lizards, usually with fiery dispositions; *Dragonheart, Pete's Dragon*

Drama: Conflict, tension, climax, resolution

Dream Girls: Product of male mid-life crisis; *Battling Amazons, Cycle Vixens, The Doll Squad, The Woman in Red*

Earthquakes: Common occurrence in California

*Eat Me: Characters end up as food. *Jurassic Park, Soylent Green, Alive*

Eco-Vengeance!: Nature wreaks havoc on man-watch out for *Alligators, Frogs* and *Piranhas*

Edibles: Something's cooking-*Babette's Feast, Like Water for Chocolate*

Elephants: Pachyderms play a BIG part in the plot—*Dumbo, Larger Than Life*

Elevators: Sometimes the oddest things happen in them...

Emerging Viruses: Deadly virus spreads like wildfire as frantic medical personnel search for a cure; think ebola

The Empire State Building: Used to be the tallest building in NYC, still the most famous

Erotic Thrillers: Hot sex and murder, including *Basic Instinct, Body of Evidence*

*Escaped Cons: They busted outta the joint, now they're makin' a run for it. *Con Air, We're No Angels, Papillon, Fled*

Ethics & Morals: Examination of values (or lack of)-*Crimes & Misdemeanors, Judgment at Nuremberg*

Etiquette: Usually comedy of manners: *Educating Rita, My Fair Lady* **Evil Doctors:** Don't go to these guys for a checkup-*Malice, Dead Ringers,* and *Doctor X*

*Executing Justice: Bad guys come back from being executed to cause more trouble. *Fallen, Shocker*

Exploding Fish Tanks: Aquariums go crash, fish go splash

Exploitation: Rigged to take advantage of viewer, including historic treats like *Reefer Madness* and more recent ventures such as *Sleazemania*

Explorers: Going boldly where no man or woman has regularly gone before

Extraordinary Pairings: Jesse James meets Frankenstein's Daughter

Eyeballs!: Unnerving scenes involving pupils, irises, lids, and occasionally, lashes

Fairs & Expositions: Short term amusement parks: *State Fair*

Family Ties: Blood runs deep-*Back to the Future, Five Easy Pieces, The Godfather, Homeward Bound, Lorenzo's Oil, The Mosquito Coast, Rocket Gibraltar*

Fantasy: Tales of the imagination, including *Alice and her looking glass, E.T., Ladyhawke, My Stepmother Is an Alien*

Fast Cars: *Eat My Dust;* racing in the street or on the track; *The Last American Hero*

Feds: Men and women of the Bureau, the Agency, or any national police organization with an acronym and a dress code

Female Bonding: Women get together, usually to the men's dismay; *Waiting to Exhale*

Femme Fatale: She done him and him and him wrong

Fencing: En garde, dude

Film & Film History: *America at the Movies;* includes movies important to film history

Film Noir: Dark and moody or tributes to dark and moody—*Farewell, My Lovely, The Postman Always Ring Twice, The Third Man, Who Framed Roger Rabbit?*

Film Stars: Movies or bios about cinema celebs, real or make-believe-Bogie, Chaplin, Sinatra

Filmmaking: The making of a film within a film: *The Player*

Firemen: *Backdraft, Fahrenheit 451,* and other tales of brave people with hoses

Fires: *Frankenstein, Quest for Fire, Pyrates*

Flashback: Why I remember like it was yesterday. It all started when...*The Usual Suspects, Casablanca*

Flatulence: Embarrassing gaseous emissions

Floods: Water, water everywhere

*Florida: Beaches, retirement communities, swamps, Spring Training, Disney World.

Flower Children: The sixties are still alive at *Alice's Restaurant*—reflect on *The Big Chill, The Doors,* and *Woodstock;* we all live in a *Yellow Submarine*

Folklore & Mythology: Age-old adult tales covering Atlantis, little people, Hercules, Ulysses

Football: Everything from terrorist attacks on the Superbowl (*Black Sunday*) to prison competition (*The Longest Yard*) plus *Diner*

Foreign Intrigue: Overseas mystery, with emphasis on accent and location

Frame-ups: Someone's set up to take the rap: *My Cousin Vinny* to *Consenting Adults*

France: From *Dirty Rotten Scoundrels* to *The Moderns* to *Gigi* to *The Last Metro* to *Killer Tomatoes Eat France*

Front Page: *Citizen Kane, All the President's Men, The Philadelphia Story,* and other journalistic stories

Fugitives: Running from the law; *Breathless, Nowhere to Hide, Posse*

Funerals: The final good-bye-*Four Weddings and a Funeral, Gardens of Stone, The Big Chill*

Gambling: Aces and Eights, *The Color of Money, Eight Men Out, Honeymoon in Vegas*

Game Shows: *The Running Man* and *Queen for a Day*

Gangs: Criminally enterprising teens and adults running in packs: *State of Grace, Miller's Crossing, Public Enemy, The Wanderers*

Gays: Gay themes-*Kiss of the Spider Woman, The Hunger*

Gender Bending: *The Crying Game, La Cage aux Folles, Her Life as a Man* and other instances of boys becoming girls and vice versa

Generation X: Slacking in the '90s-*Reality Bites, Singles*

Genetics: Fooling with the double helix-*The Fly*

Genies: *Aladdin* finds magic lamp filled with compressed Robin Williams

Genre Spoofs: Wacky takes on serious films, starting with the granddaddy of them all: *Airplane!*

Germany: *The Blue Angel, Wings of Desire*

Ghosts, Ghouls, & Goblins: *Ghostbusters, Topper, Poltergeist*

Giants: *The Amazing Colossal Man* visits *Village of the Giants*

Gifted Children: Kids show amazing talents that astound adults, from *Rookie of the Year* to *Little Man Tate*

Gigolos: Men try the oldest profession in the world, working around biological limitations

Go Fish: Casting a line in the river that runs through it; *Man of Aran, A Fish Called Wanda, Captains Courageous*

Going Native: Outsiders try to blend in; *Dances with Wolves, The Swiss Family Robinson*

*Going Postal: Neither rain, snow, sleet, nor dead of night....Hello, Newman

Golf: Slow boring game best experienced on screen ("Be the ball, Danny")

Good Earth: Ecology, environment, nature, sod

Grand Hotel: Checkout time is noon; *Blame It on the Bellboy*

Great Britain: Thwarted royals (*Charles & Diana: A Palace Divided, Edward and Mrs. Simpson*), kings (*King Ralph*), queens (*The Naked Civil Servant*), class distinctions (*The Ruling Class*), vanished empires (*Cromwell, A Man for All Seasons*), criminals (*The Krays, The Long Good Friday*) plus multiple stiff upper lips, the Brontes, and Dickens

Great Death Scenes: Signing off with style or elaboration; *Buffy the Vampire Killer, Bonnie and Clyde, Breaker Morant*

Great Depression: The era, not the state of mind-*Bound for Glory, Of Mice and Men, The Grapes of Wrath, Rambling Rose*

Great Escapes: Seizing the day for freedom-*The Big Doll House, Escape from Alcatraz, Papillon*

Growing Older: *On Golden Pond, *batteries not included, Cocoon, Driving Miss Daisy, The Shootist, The Wild Bunch*

Guys in Kilts: Celtic hunks like *Rob Roy* in plaid skirts

Gymnastics: Human pretzels like *Nadia*

Hackers: Computer whiz kids cause havoc—or just change their grades

*Halloween: *Trick or Treat!*

Happy Hookers: Prostitution with a rosy glow; *The Happy Hooker Goes to Hollywood* and meets *Pretty Woman*

Hard Knock Life: Poverty and bad luck; *City of Joy, The Match Factory Girl*

*Harlem: Part of New York City you don't see in the tourism brochures

Hearts!: Unnerving scenes involving human hearts, generally seen by the audience and almost always still pumping

Hawaii: The 50th state, fun in the sun, if the volcanoes are behaving.

Heaven Sent: Visits or returns from the place where good souls and all dogs go-*Field of Dreams* to *Made in Heaven* to *Oh God!*

Heists: The big lift

Hell High School: Place where adolescents gather against their will; also known as *Rock 'n' Roll High School*

The Help: Female: Maids, nannies, governesses, cooks, housekeepers

The Help: Male: Butlers, chauffeurs, manservants, valets

*Hide the Dead Guy: What to do with those pesky bodies after the killing's done?

High School Reunions: Adults gather to impress other adults they didn't like as adolescents

Hispanic America: Dominant Hispanic American themes (*Salsa, Mi Vida Loca*)

Historical Drama: Usually at least loosely based on a real incident or personality

Hit Men: Boys and girls armed with silencers; *Prizzi's Honor, Romeo is Bleeding*

Hockey: *Slap Shot* and other icy tales of passing the puck

Holidays: Easter, Thanksgiving, New Year's, Halloween, but generally not Christmas

Holocaust: *Playing for Time, Schindler's List*

Home Alone: Kids find themselves without adult supervision-*Adventures in Babysitting* to *Young Sherlock Holmes*

The Homefront: U.S./Canada: The war at home during WWII—looking for spies, rationing, waiting for word about "the boys."

The Homefront: England: Air raids, stiff upper lips, they were a lot closer to the action, and were just as worried about their sons and husbands.

Homeless: Street people with no homes

Horrible Holidays: Holidays with a ghoulish twist-*Bloody New Year, Halloween, My Bloody Valentine, Silent Night, Bloody Night*

Horror: Modern cut 'em up scare theater

Horror Anthologies: More than one scarefest on a cassette

Horror Comedy: Tongue-in-bloody cheek-*The Fearless Vampire Killers, Piranha, Sorority Babes in the Slimeball Bowl-A-Rama*

Horses: Can you say *Black Beauty?*

Hospitals & Medicine: Dysfunctional institutional health care-*Article 99*, *The Hospital*, *One Flew Over the Cuckoo's Nest*, *Young Doctors in Love*

Hostage!: People held against their will for bargaining purposes

Houston: That big city in Texas where J.R. didn't live, but Roger Clemens did.

Hunted!: Humans tracking humans for trophy purposes

Hunting: Where's dat wascally wabbit? *Caddyshack*, *The Bear*, *White Hunter*, *Black Heart*

Hurling: What goes down sometimes comes back up-*The Exorcist*, *Parenthood*

I Love Detroit: The Motor City, home of Motown, lots of cars, and-VideoHound

Identity: Who am I? Who are you? Who are we? Why do you ask so many questions?

Immigration: Melting pot stories-*Avalon*, *Far and Away*, *Living on Tokyo Time*

*Impending Retirement: Gold watch, a party, some tearful goodbyes...but there's always those darn loose ends to tie up first

Incest: Implied or actual relationships among family members-*The Grifters*, *Spanking the Monkey*

India: On the road to *Bombay*

Interviews: When asked questions, people talk

Inventors & Inventions: Those wacky folks and their newfangled machines; *Chitty Chitty Bang Bang*

Invisibility: Now you see 'em, now you don't

Interracial Affairs: Couple from different racial backgrounds cause trauma for family and friends -*Mississippi Masala*, *Jungle Fever*

Ireland: Aye, make that a pint for take away; *The Field*, *Cal*, *The Playboys*

Islam: Religious themes

Island Fare: Thin, isolated stretch of land surrounded by water notorious for encouraging natural appetites in men and women

Israel: *Cast a Giant Shadow*, *Exodus*

Italy: Passion, vino, lust, vino, Sophia Loren

It's a Conspiracy, Man!: Just because you're paranoid doesn't mean they're not out to get you

Japan: *Land of the Rising Sun*, *Godzilla*, *Hiroshima, Mon Amour*

Japanimation: Animated cartoons from Japan with cult following

Judaism: *Fiddler on the Roof* meets *Funny Girl*

Jungle Stories: Tarzan, tribes, trees, treasure, temperature, temptresses, tigers

Justice Prevails?: The verdict's in, but is it fair? *And Justice for All*, *In the Name of the Father*, *Presumed Innocent*

*Karaoke: This Japanese import usually runs best on alcohol

Kidnapped!: Held for ransom or just for the heck of it-*A Perfect World*, *Raising Arizona*

Killer Apes: *King Kong* lives on *The Planet of the Apes*

Killer Appliances: Defrosted refrigerator goes on killing binge

Killer Beasts: Cloned dinosaurs run amuck in backyard, destroying patio

Killer Brains: Literally has a mind of its own, i.e., *The Brain That Wouldn't Die*

Killer Bugs: Giant and/or miserably mean spiders, ants, bees, worms, flies, slugs, tarantulas, wasps, and other creepy things

Killer Cars: You should have changed *Christine*'s oil

Killer Dogs: Fido takes a walk on the wild side-*Cujo*, baby

Killer Dreams: More like nightmares on elm street

Killer Kats: Kitties with a killer instinct

Killer Pigs: Evil swine

Killer Plants: Too much fertilizer produces killer tomatoes (stewed)

Killer Rodents: Nasty mice, rats, bats, and shrews

Killer Toys: Demented play things develop homicidal urges; why hello, Chucky

Kindness of Strangers: Baffling altruistic behavior

King of Beasts (Dogs): Need we say more?

Korean War: *M*A*S*H* and friends

L.A.: Smoggy city in California also known as Los Angeles or the City of Angels; includes Hollywood & Beverly Hills

Labor & Unions: *Hoffa* and other working stiffs

Late Bloomin' Love: Better late than not blooming at all

Law & Lawyers: Tom Cruise joins *The Firm* and other realistic legal adventures

Leprechauns: The wee mischievious people of Irish lore who carry around pots o' gold

Lesbians: Lesbian themes-*Lianna*, *Bar Girls*

Libraries & Librarians: Important things happen where you can't talk—sometimes people even read!

Life Imitates Art: (Kids, don't try this at home. They did.)

Lifeguards: Rescuers of the swimming-challenged

London: City in merry old England, home to many generations of the most famous royals

Loner Cops: *Dirty Harry* Syndrome

Lost Worlds: From *Brigadoon* to *The People That Time Forgot*

Lottery Winners: Ordinary schmoes get rich quick. Be careful what you wish for...

Lovable Loonies: Crazy, but not Norman Bates crazy; *Crazy People*, *Benny & Joon*

Lovers on the Lam: Couple commit crimes and find themselves on the run-*Badlands*, *Natural Born Killers*, *True Romance*

Macho Men: Ah-nuld, The Duke, Van Damme, Stallone, Burt, Clint, Norris, Seagal, and many more cases of excessive testosterone

Mad Scientists: *The Brain That Wouldn't Die* spends an evening with *Frankenhooker*

Magic: Hocus pocus, often with evil intent

Magic Carpet Rides: *Aladdin* joins *Sinbad the Sailor* for *The Golden Voyage of Sinbad*

Marriage: Wedding bells, honeymoons, affairs, divorce, and growing old together, as well as the occasional unfortunate marital union with a blood-sucking vampire or knife-wielding satanist

Martial Arts: Fists of Aluminum Foil; much head-kicking, rib-crunching, chop-socky action

Martyred Pop Icons: For us, they gave their all; Buddy Holly, Elvis, Marilyn, James Dean, *Stardust Memories*

Mass Media: From *Network* to *Broadcast News* to *My Favorite Year*

May-December Romance: Older people meet younger people and the romantic sparks fly; *Harold and Maude* visit *Atlantic City*.

The Meaning of Life: The search for the elusive answer-*My Life*, *The Remains of the Day*, *Shadowlands*

Medieval Romps: Dirty peasants, deodorized and glorified kings and queens, splendid knights in shining armor, and one for all and all for one

Meltdown: Or how I learned to stop worrying and love the bomb; also bad wiring at local nuclear plants

Men: What is man? Is he neither fish nor fowl? Or perhaps linoleum?

Men in Prison: Working on a chain gang; what we have here is a failure to communicate

Mental Retardation: *Bill*, *Charly*, *Dominick*, *Lenny*, *Raymond* (definitely)

Metamorphosis: Ch-ch-ch-changes-From *The Fly* to *Wolf*

Meteors, Asteroids & Comets: Chunks of stuff wizzing through space, sometimes they land and cause problems

Mexico: *South of Sante Fe* and *Against All Odds*

Miami: Extremely warm coastal city in southern Florida

Middle East: Desert fare and camel close-ups ranging from *Ishtar* to *Lawrence of Arabia* to *The Jewel of the Nile*

Military: Air Force: Flyboys fight America's aerial battles

Military: Army: GIs, Grunts, Dogfaces

Military Comedy: Marching to a different drummer, including *Stripes*, *M*A*S*H* and *No Time for Sergeants*

Military: Foreign: Armed forces of other nations are the focus

Military: Marines: Jarheads. The first ones in and the last ones out.

Military: Navy: Fighting on the high seas and in the air

Miners & Mining: Helmets with the little flashlights are nifty; *Matewan* and *McCabe & Mrs. Miller*

Minnesota: Northern state that makes Michigan seem like the tropics. Home of theTwin cities and Prince, eh?

Missing Persons: People who disappear for a variety of reasons, sometimes because other people have taken them away

Missionaries: On a mission from God to save native populations

Misspelled Titles: Not proper Anglish

Mistaken Identity: You mean to say you're not the King of France?

*Model Behavior: Fashion and models are the center of attention—but isn't that the point? *Looker*, *Gia*, *Unzipped*, *Ready to Wear*

Modern Cowboys: Fun-lovin' rascals adept at riding horses through busy city streets or with a yen to experience mid-life crisis by doing a rodeo

Moms: Maternal figures have a prominent role

Monkeyshines: Critters from the jungle, sometimes cute and fluffy, often wreaking havoc-*Congo*, *Monkey Trouble*, *Outbreak*

Monster Moms: Loving on the outside, evil on the inside—*Mommie Dearest*, *Serial Mom*

Monsters, General: Not killer beasts, bugs, plants, appliances, aliens, toys, giants, vampires, werewolves, or politicians

Montreal: Cosmopolitan city of francophones currently in Canada

Moscow: City in Russia (the country formerly known as USSR)

Motor Vehicle Dept.: *Chitty Chitty Bang Bang* at the *Car Wash*, plus *Tucker*, *Herbie*, and the *Repo Man*

Mountaineering: *Cliffhangers*

Movie & TV Trailers: Snippets of stuff

Mummies: Dead guys with leather-like skin, often wrapped in sheets

Murderous Children: *Children of the Corn* hang out on the outskirts of the *Village of the Damned*...isn't that near the 7-Eleven of Doom?

Music: *Amadeus* meets *The Fabulous Baker Boys* and *The Commitments* by way of *Mo' Better Blues* at *The Cotton Club*

Musical Comedy: Laughter, singing, and dancing

Musical Drama: Singing and dancing, less laughter, more tension

Musical Fantasy: Singing and dancing in a figment of someone's imagination

Musicals: High-energy singing and dancing, often for no particular reason

Musician Biopics: Real-life musicians get the Hollywood treatment

Mutiny: Gang of disgruntled sailors takes over the ship

Mystery & Suspense: Edge-of-the-couch thrillers and whodunits

Nannies & Governesses: Musically-inclined women raise kids for rich people too busy to do it themselves

Nashville: Tennessee city that country music and Robert Altman made famous

Nashville Narratives: *Honkytonk Man* elopes with the *Coal Miner's Daughter*

Native America: Dancing with the wolves on *Pow Wow Highway*

Nazis & Other Paramilitary Slugs: *The Boys from Brazil* and *The Dirty Dozen* plus SS she-wolf *Ilsa* and modern David Duke adaptations

Negative Utopia: Things seemed so perfect until...

New Black Cinema: Spike is *Godfather*

New York, New York: It's a hell of a town...

New Orleans: City in Louisiana that boasts the Mardi Gras and cajun cookin'

New Year's Eve: Stay up late, count down with Dick Clark, drink too much, greet the New Year feeling like...

Niagara Falls: Little upstate New York border town where honeymooners and barrel riders gather. Oh yeah, they have some water thing there, too...

Nifty '50s: *Grease, La Bamba, The Man in the Moon, Peggy Sue Got Married, School Ties* and 60 more from the Eisenhower era

Nightclubs: *Casablanca*, of course

No-Exit Motel: Sleazy motels with extremely lenient late-checkout policies

Not-So-True Identity: People pass themselves off as something else; *Soul Man, Gentleman's Agreement*

Nuns & Priests: Collars and habits; *Agnes of God, The Cardinal, Going My Way, Nuns on the Run, Sister Act*

Nuns With Guns: Sister Mary Margaret has traded up from the ol' yardstick. Better practice that penmanship.

Nursploitation!: *Night Call Nurses* offer *Tender Loving Care* in *The Hospital of Terror*

Obsessive Love: You like me. You really, really, *really* like me.

Occult: Witches, warlocks, devil worshippers, spell makers, spell breakers, haunted houses, and so on

Office Surprise: Office supplies used as weapons

Oldest Profession: It's not accounting

The Olympics: *Chariots of Fire* and other tales of athletic discipline

On the Rocks: Alcoholism, alcohol, barflies, moonshining, Prohibition-*Arthur, Days of Wine and Roses, Papa's Delicate Condition, My Favorite Year*

Only the Lonely: 50 ways to play solitaire-*The Cemetery Club, The Heart Is a Lonely Hunter, Sleepless in Seattle*

Opera: Shouting in a melodic way while in costume

Order in the Court: Courtroom tales, including *The Accused, And Justice for All, A Few Good Men, Witness for the Prosecution*

Organized Crime: Gangsters with Franklin Planners

Otherwise Engaged: Couple buys ring, sets date, and gets ready to march down the aisle, sometimes with a new fiancee-*Moonstruck, Only You, Sleepless in Seattle*

Outtakes & Bloopers: Inadvertent laugh riots

Overlooked Gems: No box office to speak of, but worth a rent

Pacific Islands: Hawaii, Tahiti, Philippines, etc.

Paperboys: Kids who toss papers everywhere but your front porch

Parades & Festivals: *Animal House* and *Ferris Bueller's Day Off*

Parallel Universes: There's a whole other world out there-*Cool World, Who Framed Roger Rabbit?*

Parenthood: Moms, dads, substitutes-*Dutch, Ma Barker's Killer Brood, Father of the Bride, Three Men and a Baby, Yours, Mine, and Ours, Raising Arizona*

Paris: Ze city in France with rude occupants and ze Eiffel Tower

Party Hell: *Psycho Girls* have fun at a sleepover until *Monsters Crash the Pajama Party* and it becomes *The Slumber Party Massacre*

Patriotism & Paranoia: Run the flag up the pole and salute it-Rambo, Patton, Norris, etc.

Peace: *Friendly Persuasion, Gandhi*

Period Piece: Costume epics or evocative of a certain time and place-*Bugsy, Cleopatra, Doctor Zhivago, The French Lieutenant's Woman, Swing Kids*

Persian Gulf War: Smart bombs away

*Philadelphia: Famous Pennsylvania city that's home to *Rocky*, the Liberty Bell, cheesesteaks, and Bobby Higginson

Phobias!: Eeeeeeeeeeeeeeeek!

Phone Sex: Is it really the next best thing to being there?

Phone Terror: *Don't Answer the Phone*

Physical Problems: *My Left Foot, Coming Home, The Elephant Man, The Other Side of the Mountain, Untamed Heart, The Waterdance*

Pigs: Loveable swine-*Gordy, Babe the Gallant Pig*

Pill Poppin': Life with a drugstore cowboy; consumption of drugs, mostly illegal or in extra-large dosages

Pirates: Avast, ye scurvy dogs! *Captain Blood* drops in on *Treasure Island*

Pittsburgh: City in western Pennsylvania, home of sports teams fond of the colors black and yellow.

Poetry: Not exactly a booming category, but think of *Poetic Justice*

Poisons: *Arsenic and Old Lace* and *D.O.A.*

Political Conspiracy: *All the President's Men* present a *Clear and Present Danger* to the Constitution

Politics: *Bob Roberts, Mandela, Whoops Apocalypse*

Pool: *The Hustler*

Pornography: *Hardcore, Body Double*

Post Apocalypse: No more convenience stores

Postwar: After effects of war, generally WWI or WWII but sometimes the Civil War, the War of 1812, the Revolutionary War, and the Ohio Automobile Dealers War

POW/MIA: Captured by the enemy

Pregnant Men: Ahh-nuld fails the *Rabbit Test*

Pregnant Pauses: Humorous takes on pregnancy and birth-*Nine Months, She's Having a Baby*

Presidency: Mr. Lincoln, *JFK*, LBJ, FDR, and, of course, *Dave*

Price of Fame: What goes up...

Production Problems: When bad things happen to good (*The Crow*) and bad (*Vampire in Brooklyn*) movies

*Prom: A night you'll always remember...which isn't necessarily a good thing. Right, *Carrie*?

Propaganda: Deliberately stretching the truth in order to persuade

Protests: Hell no, we won't go (to bad movies)! Make popcorn, not war!

Psycho-Thriller: It's all in your mind-*Bad Influence, House of Games, The Silence of the Lambs*

Psychotics/Sociopaths: *Killer Inside Me, Reservoir Dogs, The Stepfather*

Puppets: Usually with strings, but also muppets

Pure Ego Vehicles: Big stars doing their big star thing—*Hudson Hawk, Harlem Nights, Yes, Giorgio*

*Rabbits: *Harvey* has a *Fatal Attraction* for the *Nasty Rabbit*

Race Against Time: Tick, tock, tick, tock-*China Syndrome, Lorenzo's Oil*

Radio: Over the airwaves-*Choose Me, The Fisher King, Radio Days, Sleepless in Seattle*

Rags to Riches: Grit, determination, and hustling (or just pure dumb luck) lead to fortune-*Trading Places, Working Girls*

Rape: Victims and often their revenge

Rebel With a Cause: Bucking the establishment for a reason

Rebel Without a Cause: Bucking the establishment just because it's the establishment

The Red Cross: Organization that helps those in need of blood, disaster relief, and war relief; also monitors treatment of POWs

Red Scare: Cold War and Communism-*The Commies Are Coming, The Commies Are Coming, Reds*

Religion: *Witness, The Last Temptation of Christ*

Religious Epics: Charlton Heston parts the Red Sea-religion on a really big scale

Renegade Body Parts: Hands, fingers, eyes, brains with a life of their own

Repressed Men: Often British (*see* Anthony Hopkins or Hugh Grant), always with plenty of stiffness in upper lip and little elsewhere

Rescue Missions: I'll save you-*The Searcher, Free Willy*

Rescue Missions Involving Time Travel: I'll save you in another dimension-*Back to the Future*

The Resistance: WWII rebels with an anti-Nazi cause

Revenge: A key motivating factor-*Cape Fear, Death Wish, Hamlet*

Revolutionary War: Fought over tea

*Reincarnation: Death is just a temporary transition period—make sure you don't fall down the evolutionary ladder

Rio: As in de Janeiro—that swingin' South American party town.

Road Trip: Escapism courtesy of two- and four-wheel vehicles-*Easy Rider, Coupe de Ville, Pee Wee's Big Adventure, Wild at Heart*

Roaring '20s: Flappers, prohibition, bobbed hair

Robots/Androids: Mechanical but fascinating; *Blade Runner* and *The Terminator*

Rock Stars on Film: But can they act? Prince (Symbol), Sting, Elvis, Lennon, The Monkees, Whitney, and so on

Rodeos: Rope tricks with steers

Role Reversal: Vice versa; empathy test-*Freaky Friday, My Fair Lady, Switch, Soul Man*

Roll Over Beethoven: Plot revolves around the music-meister, or he makes an appearance-*Bill & Ted's Excellent Adventure, Immortal Beloved*

Romantic Adventures: Love among the chases and explosions-*The African Queen, Romancing the Stone*

Romantic Comedy: Falling in love has its hilarious moments-*French Kiss, Crossing Delancey, Modern Romance, Much Ado About Nothing*

Romantic Drama: Love thing leads to tension and anxiety-*Cyrano de Bergerac, Far and Away, Sommersby, Tender Mercies*

Romantic Triangles: Three where there's only room for two-*The Age of Innocence, Casablanca, Three of Hearts*

*Rome—Ancient Emperors ran the show, feeding Christians to the lions, using V for U, having orgies, and throwing up on purpose...those were the days!

*Rome—Modern: Capital city of Italy. The Pope has a little place there

Roommates from Hell: Sometimes they won't do the dishes, sometimes they're homicidal-*Single White Female*

Royalty: Emperors, kings, queens, princes, princesses, crowns, scepters

Royalty, British: Emperors, kings, queens, etc in Merry Olde England

Royalty, Russian: Emperors, czars, and czarinas who ran things in Moscow till those mean old Bolsheviks showed up

Running: Jogging, panting, collapsing

Russia: Back in what used to be the USSR

Sail Away: Vessels on the water-*Mutiny on the Bounty, Erik the Viking, Mister Roberts*

Saints: *Bernadette, Saint Joan, A Time for Miracles*

Salespeople: Have I got a deal for you...

Salvation Army: Paramilitary charity with Santa Clauses on every corner

San Francisco: Set in the Northern California city known for hills and sourdough bread

Sanity Check: Inmates running the asylum; also deviant mental states

Satanism: *Speak of the Devil*

Satire & Parody: Biting social commentary or genre spoofs, including *Being There, Airplane!, Down and Out in Beverly Hills, I'm Gonna Git You Sucka, Monty Python's The Meaning of Life, The Player*

Savants: Half-minded geniuses; *Rain Man, Forrest Gump*

Scams, Stings & Cons: The hustle-*The Billionaire Boys Club, The Color of Money, A Fish Called Wanda, The Grifters, The Sting*

Scared 'Chuteless: Jumping out of airplanes without the proper equipment. Good candidates for a bad case of cement poisoning

School Daze: Education, school, and teachers, generally grammar school days-*Lean on Me, Dead Poet's Society, To Sir, with Love, Teachers*

Sci Fi: Imagination fueled by science and a vision of the future

Science & Scientists: *Altered States, Darkman, Them, They, Son of Flubber, The Story of Louis Pasteur*

Scotland: Lush hills, thick brogues, kilts, bagpipes, and *Whiskey Galore*

Screwball Comedy: Snappy repartee between a man and a woman dealing with an impossibly silly situation

Scuba: Wet suits, including *The Abyss, Navy SEALS*

Sculptors: Artists who like to work with clay, rock, hammers, and chisels

Sea Critter Attack: Monsters from the deep (and not so deep) surface and surprise-*Jaws, Orca, Moby Dick*

Sea Disasters: We've sprung a leak-*The Poseidon Adventure*

Seattle: Showcases the city in Washington state where it rains a lot; the home of grunge rock

Serial Killers: They just won't stop-*Henry: Portrait of a Serial Killer, The Rosary Murders*

Serials: Segmented adventures; Heyday was in the 1930s-*The Adventures of Red Ryder, The Little Rascals, Flash Gordon*

Sex & Sexuality: Focus is on lust, for better or worse-*Alfie, Barbarella, Emmanuelle, Looking for Mr. Goodbar, Rambling Rose, She's Gotta Have It*

Sex on the Beach: Flashing the fish and getting sand in the darndest places; the most famous couple was in *From Here to Eternity* and *Airplane!* lost no time making fun of them

Sexploitation: Softcore epics usually lacking in plot but not skin-*The Erotic Adventures of Pinocchio*

Sexual Abuse: Victims and their stories-*Twin Peaks, Fire Walk with Me*

Sexual Harassment: When I say no, I mean it

Shipwrecked: Stranded on an island when your boat sinks

Showbiz Comedies: Laughter behind the scenes in Hollywood or on Broadway

Showbiz Dramas: Tension behind the scenes in Hollywood or on Broadway

Showbiz Musicals: Singing and dancing behind the scenes in Hollywood or on Broadway

Showbiz Thrillers: Screaming behind the scenes in Hollywood or on Broadway

Shrinks: Psychiatry or equivalent, including *The Prince of Tides, One Flew Over the Cuckoo's Nest*

Shutterbugs: Photographers and their pictures-*The Public Eye, The Eyes of Laura Mars, Peeping Tom*

Silent Films: No small talk/no big talk/no talk talk

Silent Horror/Fantasy Classics: Silent screams, expressions of terror

Single Parents: Divorced or widowed, they're doing the work of two—and they're back in the dating scene, usually assisted by match-making kids

Singles: Not always swinging but still solidly single-*About Last Night, Singles, When Harry Met Sally*

Skateboarding: Teens on wheels-*Gleaming the Cube*

Skating: Roller and ice, including *The Cutting Edge, Xanadu*

Skiing: Slap on a couple of waxed boards and off you go-*Downhill Racer, Swinging Ski Girls*

Skinheads: Nazi wannabes wreak havok and cause trouble

Skydiving: Jumping from a plane with a polyester slip

Slapstick Comedy: Humor of the physical sort, including Abbott and Costello, the Marx Brothers, sports comedies, Ernest, Pink Panther, Home Alone, the Three Stooges

Slavery: *Roots, Spartacus*

Slice of Life: Charming small stories of life the way it might be-*The Bicycle Thief, Fried Green Tomatoes, Marty*

Snakes: Slithering creatures who frighten many-*Raiders of the Lost Ark*

Soccer: Known as football outside of the USA-*Victory, Ladybugs*

South America: Right below North America-*Aguirre, the Wrath of God, The Mission*

Southern Belles: Southern gals ooze charm-*Blaze, Driving Miss Daisy, Steel Magnolias*

Space Operas: Going where no spam has gone before-*Alien, Star Trek, 2001: A Space Odyssey, Apollo 13*

Spaghetti Western: Clint with a squint, *A Fistful of Dollars, My Name is Nobody, Once Upon a Time in the West*

Spain: *Siesta*

Speculation: In search of...

Spies & Espionage: Trench coats, dark glasses, Bond, *North by Northwest*

Sports Comedies: Humorous athletic tales, generally not based on a true story

Sports Dramas: Intense athletic tales, often based on a true story

Spousal Abuse: *The Burning Bed, What's Love Got to Do With It?*

Stagestruck: Stories of the theatre; *Broadway Melody* sung at the *Stage Door* by *The Dolly Sisters*

Stalked: No, I do not want to switch to MCI

Star Gazing: Not Hollywood stars, astrology/astronomy type stars

Stepparents: New spouse hiding either alien origins or sociopathic tendencies greets existing clan

Stewardesses: *Three Guys Named Mike* go to *Stewardess School* and meet *Blazing Stewardesses*

Stolen from Asia: American remakes of Asian classics— usually Kurosawa's; *Seven Samurai* becomes *The Magnificent Seven*

Stolen from Europe: American remakes of European fare; *A Walk in the Clouds, The Vanishing, Scent of a Woman*

Stolen From France: Hollywood goes to its favorite remake well; *Diabolique, Cousins, Nine Months, Three Men and a Baby*

Storytelling: *Amazing Stories, Grim Prairie Tales*

Strained Suburbia: Neighborhood is not what it seems-*Dennis the Menace, Neighbors, Edward Scissorhands*

Strippers: Take it off, take it all off

Struggling Musicians: Talented, but still reaching for the top

Stupid Is...: Stupidity on purpose-*Billy Madison, Dumb and Dumber*; or dumbness as a plot device-*Being There, Forrest Gump*

Submarines: Deep sea diving; *Das Boot, Up Periscope, Run Silent, Run Deep, Hunt for Red October*

Subways: A train for shorter trips-*Speed, The Taking of Pelham One Two Three*

Suicide: Premature ends-*The Big Chill, Scent of a Woman, Romeo and Juliet*

Summer Camp: Where children go to misbehave, including *Meatballs* and *Sleepaway Camp*

Super Heroes: Men and women of extraordinary strength and abilities wearing silly- looking costumes

Supernatural Comedies: *Beetlejuice* marries *She-Devil* and they take *The Ghost Train* to their *Haunted Honeymoon*

Supernatural Cop Thrillers: *Angel Heart, Maniac Cop, Wolfen*

Supernatural Horror: Forces from beyond terrorize those who are here

Supernatural Martial Arts: Kung fu *From Beyond the Grave*

Supernatural Westerns: Forces from beyond terrorize cowboys in the Old West

Surfing: Awesome wave, dude! *Mad Wax, The Surf Movie, Surf Nazis Must Die, Endless Summer*

Survival: *Alive, The Bridge over the River Kwai, Testament*

Suspended Animation: Frozen in time-*Coma, Late for Dinner*

Swashbucklers: Crossed swords and rope swinging, including *Robin Hood*, Zorro, various Musketeers, *Captain Blood, The Three Amigos*

Swimming: Ranging from *Gremlins* to *Jaws* to *The Swimmer* to *Cocoon*

Swingers: *Bob & Carol & Ted & Alice* try *Group Marriage* and Carol and Alice become *Swinging Wives*

*Swingin' '70s: Disco, bad clothes, cool cars, sexual freedom, the Me Generation

Sword & Sandal: *See* Arnold Schwarzenegger's early career

Tattoos: *The Illustrated Man* visits *Cape Fear* to do battle with *Cyber Bandits*

Team Efforts: Working together pays off-*Hoosiers, Memphis Belle, Renaissance Man*

Tearjerkers: Crying fests-*Love Story, Steel Magnolias, Old Yeller*

Technology-Rampant: Machines that wreak havoc-*Metropolis, Death Ray 2000, Blade Runner*

Teen Angst: Adolescent anxieties, including *Baby It's You* and almost everything produced or directed by John Hughes

Tennis: Anyone?

Terminal Confusion: Luggage gets mixed up at the airport, bus station, etc. Trouble usually follows

Terror in Tall Buildings: From *Die Hard* to *Speed* to *The Towering Inferno*

Terrorism: Love affairs with hidden bombs

Thanksgiving: Huge dinner, football, familial angst, turkey coma, Christmas shopping may now commence

*This Is My Life: Autobiographies starring the subject-Muhammed Ali in *The Greatest*, Audie Murphy goes *To Hell and Back*

This Is Your Life: Biography and autobiography, including *The Babe Ruth Story, Amazing Howard Hughes, Amadeus, Catherine the Great, Great Balls of Fire, Raging Bull, What's Love Got to Do With It?*

3-D Flicks: Bring your special glasses

Thumbs Up: Hitchin' a ride-*Even Cowgirls Get the Blues, The Hitcher*

Time Travel: Fast forward or reverse with Bill and Ted, *Dr. Who, Back to the Future*, and *Peggy Sue Got Married*

Time Warped: You wake up in an era not your own; *Austin Powers*, the Bradys and the Cleavers coping with the '90s

Titanic: The unsinkable ship that hit an iceberg its first time out...and sunk. It was in all the papers

Tokyo: Crowded city in Japan terrorized by Godzilla

Torn in Two (or More): *Sybil* and *Dr. Jekyll and Mr. Hyde* are *Raising Cain* leading *Separate Lives* on the *Edge of Sanity*

*Toronto: Big city in Canada where they don't make you speak French. Home of Skydome and the Hockey Hall of Fame

Torrid Love Scenes: Steamy and/or sticky-*Angel Heart, Bull Durham, From Here to Eternity, Risky Business, The Unbearable Lightness of Being*

Toys: *Babes in Toyland, The Toy, Toys*

Tragedy: The fate of humankind, magnified-*King Lear, Madame Bovary, Tess, The World According to Garp*

Trains: Rhythm of the clickity clack-*Romance on the Orient Express, Throw Momma from the Train, Running Scared, The Silver Streak*

Trapped with a Killer!: And there's no escape-*Dead Calm, Misery, The Shining*

Treasure Hunt: Looking for hidden riches-*Klondike Fever, Treasure of Sierra Madre, Romancing the Stone*

Trees & Forests: Can't see one for the other, that wilderness paradox-includes *Mr. Sycamore* and *The Wizard of Oz*

True Crime: Based on fact, including *The Boston Strangler, The Executioner's Song, Helter Skelter*

True Stories: Approximations of real-life events often significantly fictionalized for the screen, including *All The President's Men, Chariots of Fire, Cry Freedom, Heart Like a Wheel, The Killing Fields, Silkwood*

TV Movies: First shown on broadcast, cable, or foreign television (BBC, etc.)-*Adam, Autobiography of Miss Jane Pittman, Barbarians at the Gate, I Claudius, Longtime Companion, The Day After*

TV Pilot Movies: Some became series; some did not

TV Series: Collections, anthologies, and individual episodes of memorable shows-*I Love Lucy, Star Trek, The Fugitive*

Twins: *Double Trouble, Double Vision, Mirror Images*

Twister!: The big wind not caused by Mexican food that picks up heavy things (houses, cows, trucks) and deposits them elsewhere

Unexplained Phenomena: No apparent reason for an event

Up All Night: Movie takes place mostly after the sun goes down and *Before Sunrise*

Urban Drama: *American Me* to *Boyz N the Hood* to *Grand Canyon* to *Zebrahead*

The USO: Entertained the troops through two world wars and a variety of police actions—with Bob Hope usually leading the way

Vacations: From *City Slickers* to *Deliverance* to *Fraternity Vacation*

Vampire Babes: Blood sucking dames-*The Brides of Dracula*

Vampire Spoof: Comedic blood suckers, including *Buffy, Andy Warhol's Dracula, Dracula Sucks*

Vampires: More serious vein of blood sucking varmint, including *Dracula* in his many manifestations

Variety: Little bit of everything

Venice: Italian city of gondolas

Veterans: Retired fighting men (and women)-*Alamo Bay* to *Who'll Stop the Rain*

Vietnam War: *Platoon, Hamburger Hill, Apocalypse Now, Good Morning, Vietnam*

Vigilantes: Individuals take the law into their own hands-*Death Wish, The Outlaw Josie Wales*

***Virtual Reality:** High-tech video game that seems real...to computer geeks

Viva Las Vegas!: Celebrating America's tackiest city-*Honeymoon in Vegas, Sister Act*

Volcanoes: Mountain blowing off steam, including *Joe Versus the Volcano*

Volleyball: *Side Out* used to be the only one till we remembered the barechested boys from *Top Gun*

Voodoo: From *Angel Heart* to *How to Stuff a Wild Bikini* to *Weekend at Bernie's 2*

Waitresses: *Alice Doesn't Live Here Anymore*, she went to *Atlantic City* to get some *Mystic Pizza*

War Between the Sexes: Men and women battle for supremacy-*It Happened One Night, The King and I, He Said, She Said, Romancing the Stone, When Harry Met Sally, The War of the Roses, Thelma & Louise*

War, General: Generally any conflict that defies other classification-*The Alamo, Gunga Din, The Last of the Mohicans*

Wedding Bells: Memorable weddings; *Father of the Bride, Four Weddings and a Funeral, Sixteen Candles, The Wedding*

Wedding Hell: Horror-filled or anxiety-ridden weddings; *The Blood Spattered Bride, The Brides Wore Blood, The Graduate, Wedding Banquet*

Werewolves: Full moon wonders, like *Wolf*

Western Comedy: Gags and horses-*Ballad of Cable Hogue, Blazing Saddles, Rancho Deluxe, Support Your Local Sheriff*

Westerns: Cowboys, cowgirls, horses and jingle jangling spurs on the frontier

Westrogens: The Old West through women's eyes

***Whales:** Really big sea-faring mammals. It's best to just stay out of their way...Just ask *Pinoccio*

Whitewater Rafting: Wild ride down a raging river, often in the company of a psycho

Wild Kingdom: Animals on their own and interacting with confused humans, including *The Bear, Dumbo, Born Free, Free Willy, Never Cry Wolf*

Wilderness: More trees than a forest, plus wild critters-*The Life and Times of Grizzly Adams*

Witchcraft: From *Hocus Pocus* to *Three Sovereigns for Sarah* to *The Wizard of Oz*

Women: Impressive women, less than impressive women, and issues concerning women-*Crimes of the Heart, My Brilliant Career, Passion Fish, Working Girls*

Women Cops: Female officers of the law

Women in Prison: The things that go on in the big doll house

Women in War: Nurses, WACs, WAVES, USO performers, sometimes prisoners—they also served...

Wonder Women: *Attack of the 50-Foot Woman, Ripley, La Femme Nikita, Supergirl*

World War I: The First Big One, including *African Queen, Gallipoli, Grand Illusion*

World War II: The Last Big One, including *A Bridge Too Far, Guadalcanal Diary, The Guns of Navarone, Hope and Glory, Memphis Belle, Tora! Tora! Tora!*

Wrestling: Choreographed sport involving men and women-*No Holds Barred, All the Marbles, Wrestling Women vs. the Aztec Ape*

Writers: Tortured souls who put pen to paper when they're not putting bottle to lips. Does not include the ink-stained wretches of the journalistic trade

***The Wrong Man:** ...has been accused or convicted. *The Fugitive* is in a *Frenzy* because *Jack's Back*.

Wrong Side of the Tracks: Often involves relationship with someone on the right side-*Cannery Row, The Flamingo Kid, Pretty in Pink, White Palace*

You Lose, You Die: Sports goes nuts-only the winner survives; *Arena, Rollerball, Tron*

Yuppie Nightmares: Young adults find best-laid plans for attaining wealth and privilege going astray-*Baby Boom, Desperately Seeking Susan, The Mighty Ducks, Pacific Heights, Something Wild, Wall Street*

Zombie Soldiers: Recently undead in the army-*They Saved Hitler's Brain*

Zombies: Recently undead everywhere-*I Walked with a Zombie, Night of the Living Dead*

Category Index

The **Category Index** includes subject terms ranging from straight genre descriptions (Drama, Comedy, etc.) to more off-the-wall themes (Nuns with Guns, Eyeballs!). These terms can help you identify unifying themes (Baseball, Heists), settings (Miami, Nifty '50s), events (The Great Depression, World War II), occupations (Clowns, Cops, Doctors & Nurses), or suddenly animate objects (Killer Appliances, Killer Cars). Category definitions and cross-references precede the index; category terms are listed alphabetically. **A tipped triangle indicates a video rated three bones or higher**.

ABBA-ca-da-bra

The Adventures of Priscilla, Queen of the Desert▸
Muriel's Wedding▸

Abortion

The Choice
Choices
Citizen Ruth
Critical Choices
Daddy's Gone A-Hunting▸
Eye of God▸
Family Life
If These Walls Could Talk
Listen to Me
Maria's Child
Panic in Needle Park▸
A Private Matter▸
Rain Without Thunder
Roe vs. Wade▸
Rude
Silent Victim
The Story of Women▸
Walpurgis Night▸

Action Adventure

see also Adventure Drama; Boom!; Comic Adventure; Disaster Flicks; Macho Men; Martial Arts; Romantic Adventures; Swashbucklers

The Abductors
Above and Beyond▸
Above the Law
The Abyss▸
Aces: Iron Eagle 3
Across the Great Divide
Act of Vengeance
Action in Arabia
Action Jackson
Action U.S.A.
Adventure of the Action Hunters

The Adventurers
Adventures of Captain Fabian
The Adventures of Captain Marvel
Adventures of Don Juan▸
The Adventures of Ford Fairlane
The Adventures of Frank and Jesse James
The Adventures of Huckleberry Finn
The Adventures of Marco Polo
Adventures of Red Ryder
The Adventures of Rex & Rinty
The Adventures of Rin Tin Tin
Adventures of Smilin' Jack
The Adventures of Tartu
The Adventures of Tarzan
The Adventures of the Masked Phantom
The Adventures of Tom Sawyer
After the Fall of Saigon
Against All Flags▸
Ain't No Way Back
Alamut Ambush
Ali Baba and the 40 Thieves▸
Alice to Nowhere
Alien Private Eye
All the Brothers Were Valiant
The Amateur
The Amazing Spider-Man
The Amazing Transparent Man
Amazon Jail
Amazon Warrior
Amazons
American Autobahn
American Born
American Commandos
American Cop
American Eagle
American Justice
American Ninja 3: Blood Hunt
American Streetfighter 2: The Full Impact
American Yakuza
Americano
The Amsterdam Kill
Anaconda

And Then You Die▸
Android
Angel 3: The Final Chapter
Angel of Death
Angel of Destruction
Angel Unchained
Angel's Brigade
Angels Die Hard
Angels from Hell
Angels One Five
Angels' Wild Women
The Annihilators
Antarctica
Appointment in Honduras
Archer: The Fugitive from the Empire
Ark of the Sun God
Armed for Action
Armed Response
Army of One
Around the World Under the Sea
Aroused
Arrest Bulldog Drummond
Ashanti, Land of No Mercy
Assassin
The Assassination Game
Assassins
Assault on a Queen
Assault on Agathon
Assault with a Deadly Weapon
Assignment Skybolt
At Gunpoint
At Sword's Point
Atlantis, the Lost Continent
Atom Man vs. Superman
Ator the Fighting Eagle
Attack Force Z
The Avenger
The Avengers
Avenging Force
Baby Cart 4: Heart of a Parent...Heart of a Child
Back in Action
Back in Business
Back to Back
Back to Bataan
Background to Danger▸

Bad Attitude
Bad Blood
Bad Boys
Bad Guys
Badge 373
Bagdad
Bail Out
Baja
Ballbuster
Ballistic
Band of the Hand
The Banker
Banzai Runner
Barb Wire
Barbarian Queen
Barbarian Queen 2: The Empress Strikes Back
The Barbarians
The Barbary Coast
Bare Knuckles
Bat 21
Batman
Batman▸
Batman and Robin
Batman Forever▸
Batman Returns
Battle of Neretva
Battle of the Commandos
Battle of Valiant
Baywatch the Movie: Forbidden Paradise
The Beast
Beasts
Bedford Incident
Behind Enemy Lines
Behind the Mask
Bells of Coronado
The Belstone Fox
Beretta's Island
Berlin Tunnel 21
Best Revenge
A Better Tomorrow
A Better Tomorrow, Part 2
A Better Tommorow, Part 3
Beyond Fear
Beyond Forgiveness
Beyond Justice

Beyond the Call of Duty
Beyond the Carribean
Beyond the Law
Big Bad John
The Big Bust Out
Big Chase
The Big Doll House
The Big Hit▸
The Big House▸
Big Jim McLain
Big Steal▸
The Big Sweat
The Big Wheel
Billy the Kid in Texas
Bimini Code
Birds of Prey
Black Brigade
Black Caesar
The Black Cobra
Black Cobra 2
Black Cobra 3: The Manila Connection
The Black Coin
The Black Devils of Kali
Black Dog
Black Eliminator
Black Force
Black Force 2
Black Gestapo
Black Magic
Black Market Rustlers
Black Oak Conspiracy
Black Out
The Black Pirate▸
The Black Raven
Black Scorpion 2: Ground Zero
Black Shampoo
The Black Six
Black Snow
The Black Stallion▸
The Black Stallion Returns
Black Sunday
The Black Swan▸
Black Terrorist
Black Water Gold
The Black Widow
Blackbeard the Pirate

Category Index

1017

Action

Action

If Looks Could Kill
Illegal Entry: Formula for Fear
The Immortals
In Deadly Heat
In God's Hands
In Gold We Trust
In Hot Pursuit
In Search of the Castaways♪
In Your Face
Incident at Deception Ridge
The Incredible Hulk
The Incredible Hulk Returns
The Incredible Journey
Indio
Indio 2: The Revolt
Inside Edge
Inside Information
The Inside Man
Inside Out
Instant Justice
Interceptor
Interpol Connection
The Invaders
Invaders from Mars
Invasion Force
Invasion U.S.A.
Invincible Barbarian
Invincible Gladiators
The Invincible Six
The Invisible Monster
Iron Angel
The Iron Crown
Iron Eagle
Iron Eagle 2
Iron Eagle 4
Iron Horsemen
Iron Thunder
Ironheart
Ironmaster
The Island
The Island at the Top of the World
Island of the Lost
Istanbul
Jacare
Jack Higgins' On Dangerous Ground
Jack the Giant Killer♪
Jackie Chan's First Strike♪
Jail Bait
Jailbait
Jailbreakin'
Jakarta
Jaws of Death
Jericho
Jericho Fever
Jessi's Girls
The Jesus Trip
Jet Attack/Paratroop Command
Jive Turkey
Johnny Handsome♪
Johnny Shiloh
Jornada de Muerte
Journey
Journey of Honor
Journey to the Lost City
Judge & Jury
Judge Dredd
Judgment Night
Jungle Assault
The Jungle Book
Jungle Bride
Jungle Drums of Africa
Jungle Heat
Jungle Hell
Jungle Inferno
Jungle Master
Jungle Raiders
Jungle Siren
Jungle Warriors
Jungleground
Junior G-Men
Junior G-Men of the Air
The Junkman
K-9000
Kagemusha♪
Karate Warriors
Keep Talking Baby
Kelly of the Secret Service

Kelly's Heroes
Kentucky Blue Streak
The Key to Rebecca
Kickboxer the Champion
Kicks
Kid and the Killers
Kidnapped
The Kill
Kill Alex Kill
Kill Factor
Kill Line
Kill or Be Killed
Kill Slade
Killcrazy
Killer Commandos
Killer Force
Killers
The Killer's Edge
Killing at Hell's Gate
The Killing Device
The Killing Edge
The Killing Game
Killing in the Sun
The Killing Man
Killing Streets
The Killing Zone
Killzone
Kilma, Queen of the Amazons
Kim♪
Kim
Kindergarten Ninja
King Arthur, the Young Warlord
King Boxers
King Dinosaur
King Kong
King Kong Lives
King Kong vs. Godzilla
King of the Congo
King of the Damned
King of the Forest Rangers
King of the Kongo
King of the Mountain
King of the Rocketmen
King Solomon's Mines♪
King's Ransom
The King's Thief
Kinjite: Forbidden Subjects
Knightriders
Knock Off
Knock Outs
Koroshi
Kounterfeit
Kowloon Assignment
L.A. Bounty
L.A. Gangs Rising
L.A. Heat
L.A. Vice
L.A. Wars
Lady of the Lake
Lady Street Fighter
Lady Terminator
Lafayette Escadrille
Land of the Pharaohs
Laser Mission
Laserblast
The Last Boy Scout
The Last Contract
The Last Flight of Noah's Ark
Last Flight to Hell
The Last Hit
The Last Hour
Last Man Standing
Last Mercenary
The Last of the Mohicans♪
The Last of the Redmen
Last Plane Out
The Last Reunion
The Last Samurai
The Last Valley
The Last Warrior
Last Witness
Laughing at Danger
Law of the Jungle
Law of the Sea
Law of the Wild
The Lawless Land
Le Mans♪
The Leatherneck
The Left Hand of God♪

The Legend of Gator Face
The Legend of Hillbilly John
Legend of the Lost
Legend of the Lost Tomb
Legend of the Northwest
Legends of the North
Legion of Iron
Legion of Missing Men
Let 'Em Have It
Lethal Games
Lethal Tender
Lethal Weapon♪
Lethal Weapon 2♪
Lethal Weapon 3
Lethal Weapon 4
Lethal Woman
Let's Get Harry
Liberty & Bash
License to Kill
The Lifetaker
Light at the Edge of the World
The Light in the Forest
Lightblast
Lightning Bolt
Lion Man
The Lion of Africa
The Lion's Share
Little Bigfoot
Little Laura & Big John
Little Marines
Little Ninjas
Little Treasure
The Littlest Horse Thieves
The Littlest Viking
Live and Let Die
Live Wire
Live Wire: Human Timebomb
The Lives of a Bengal Lancer♪
The Living Daylights♪
The Lone Runner
Long John Silver
The Long Kiss Goodnight
The Long Ships
Loophole
Lords of Magick
The Lost City
Lost City of the Jungle
The Lost Command
The Lost Continent
The Lost Empire
The Lost Idol/Shock Troop
The Lost Patrol♪
Lost Squadron
The Lost Tribe
The Lost World
Love and Bullets
The Loves of Hercules
The Lucifer Complex
Mad Dog
Mad Max♪
Mad Max: Beyond Thunderdome
Mad Wax: The Surf Movie
Madman
The Magic Stone
The Magic Sword
The Magic Voyage of Sinbad
Magnum Force
Mainline Run
Malaya
Malibu Express
Malone
Mama's Dirty Girls
A Man, a Woman and a Killer
Man from Cairo
Man from Deep River
The Man from U.N.C.L.E.
The Man in the Iron Mask♪
The Man Inside
Man on a String
The Man Who Would Be King♪
Managua
Manfish
Manhunt
Manhunt in the African Jungle
Mankillers
Marauder
March or Die
Mark of the Beast

Mark of Zorro♪
The Mark of Zorro♪
Marked for Death
Marked for Murder
Marked Man
Marked Money
Marshal Law
Martial Law
Martial Law 2: Undercover
Mask of Death
Mask of the Dragon
The Masked Marvel
Massive Retaliation
Master Blaster
Master Key
Master Ninja
Master of Dragonard Hill
Masterminds
Max Is Missing
Maximum Breakout
Maximum Force
Maximum Risk
Maya
McBain♪
McQ
Mean Frank and Crazy Tony
Mean Guns
Mean Johnny Barrows
Mean Machine
The Mechanic
Melvin Purvis: G-Man
Men of Sherwood Forest
Men of the Fighting Lady♪
Men of War
Menace on the Mountain
The Mercenaries
Mercenary
Mercenary Fighters
Merchants of War
Mercury Rising
Mercy
Merlin
Merrill's Marauders
Messalina vs. the Son of Hercules
The Messenger
Metro
Miami Beach Cops
Miami Cops
Miami Hustle
Miami Vendetta
Midnight Ride
Midnight Warrior
Midnite Spares
Mighty Jungle
Mind Trap
Mines of Kilimanjaro
Ministry of Vengeance
Missing in Action
Missing in Action 2: The Beginning
Missing Link
Mission Batangas
Mission Corbari
Mission: Impossible♪
Mission in Morocco
Mission Manila
Mission to Kill
Mr. Majestyk
Mister Mean
Mistress of the Apes
Mob War
Model by Day
Mole Men against the Son of Hercules
Molly and Gina
The Mollycoddle
Money to Burn
The Mongols
Mooncussers
Moonfleet
Moonraker
Moonshine County Express
Morgan the Pirate
Mortal Kombat 1: The Movie
Mortal Kombat 2: Annihilation
Most Wanted
Mother Lode
Motor Psycho

Mountain Charlie
Mountains of the Moon♪
Moving Target
Murder on Flight 502
Murder One
Mutiny
Mutiny on the Bounty♪
Mutiny on the Bounty
My Family Treasure
My New Partner
Mysterious Island of Beautiful Women
Mystery Island
Mystery of the Million Dollar Hockey Puck
Mystery Squadron
Nabonga
Nails
The Naked and the Dead
The Naked Angels
The Naked Prey♪
Naked Warriors
Namu, the Killer Whale
Napoleon
Napoleon and Samantha♪
Nasty Hero
Nate and Hayes
Navajo Blues
The Navigator♪
Navy SEALS
The Negotiator
Neptune Factor
Neutron and the Black Mask
Neutron vs. the Amazing Dr. Caronte
Neutron vs. the Death Robots
Neutron vs. the Maniac
Never Let Me Go
Never Pick Up a Stranger
Never Say Die
Never Say Never Again
Never So Few
Never Too Young to Die
The New Adventures of Tarzan
Next of Kin
Nick Knight
Nick of Time
Night Ambush
Night Children
Night Flight from Moscow
Night of the Fox
Night of the Juggler
Night of the Running Man
Night of the Sharks
The Night Patrol
Night Siege Project: Shadowchaser 2
Night Vision
Nightforce
Nightmare at Noon
Nikki, the Wild Dog of the North
9 1/2 Ninjas
1990: The Bronx Warriors
Ninja 3: The Domination
Ninja Connection
Ninja, the Violent Sorcerer
No Contest
No Dead Heroes
No Escape
No Escape, No Return
No Holds Barred
No Man's Land
No Mercy
No Safe Haven
No Way Back
Nomad Riders
North Star
Northeast of Seoul
Northville Cemetery Massacre
Nowhere to Run
Nukie
Number 1 of the Secret Service
A Nymphoid Barbarian in Dinosaur Hell
Nyoka and the Tigermen
Octopussy
The Odyssey of the Pacific
Off Limits
O.H.M.S.

Old Ironsides⤴
Omoo Omoo, the Shark God
On Deadly Ground
On Her Majesty's Secret
   Service⤴
On the Run
Once a Hero
Once a Thief⤴
One Down, Two to Go!
One-Eyed Soldiers
One Man Out
One Man's Justice
One Million Years B.C.
One Step to Hell
One Way Out
Operation C.I.A.
Operation Condor
Operation: Delta Force
Operation Intercept
Orca
Ordeal in the Arctic
Order of the Black Eagle
Order of the Eagle
Order to Kill
Organized Crime & Triad Bureau
The Original Flash Gordon
   Collection
Original Gangstas
Orphans of the North
Osa
The Other Side of the Law
Out of Control
The Outfit
The Outlaw Bikers—Gang Wars
Outpost in Morocco
Overkill
Overthrow
Overture
Pacific Inferno
Panther Squad
Paper Tiger
Paradise Canyon
The Pathfinder
Pattern for Plunder
Pay or Die
Payback
Peacemaker
Pentathlon
Perfect Crime
Perfect Lies
Perfect Target
The Perfect Weapon
The Perils of Pauline
Perils of the Darkest Jungle
The Persuaders
Phantom Express
The Phantom Flyer
Phantom of the Air
Phoenix
P.I. Private Investigations
Picasso Trigger
Pink Cadillac
The Pink Jungle
Pirate Ship
Pirate Warrior
Pirates of the Coast
Pirates of the Seven Seas
Platoon the Warriors
Platypus Cove
Pocahontas: The Legend
Point Break
Point of Impact
The Polar Bear King
Police Story
The Port of Missing Girls
The P.O.W. Escape
Powder Keg
Pray for Death
Prayer of the Rollerboys
The President's Plane Is Missing
President's Target
Presumed Guilty
Prettykill
Prey for the Hunter
Primary Target
Prime Risk
Prince Valiant
Prison Planet
Prisoner of Zenda⤴

Prisoner of Zenda
Private Life of Don Juan
Private Road: No Trespassing
Private War
Private Wars
The Professional
Professionals
Project A: Part 2
Project: Eliminator
Project: Shadowchaser
Protector
Provoked
Psychopath
Public Enemies
Pucker Up and Bark Like a Dog
Punch the Clock
The Punisher
Pure Danger
Python Wolf
Queen of Diamonds
Queen of the Amazons
Queen of the Jungle
Queen of the Road
The Quest
Quest for Fire⤴
Quest of the Delta Knights
Quick
Quiet Cool
Quiet Fire
Quiet Thunder
Quo Vadis
The Racers
Radar Patrol vs. Spy King
Radar Secret Service
The Rage
Rage of Honor
Rage to Kill
Raiders of Atlantis
Raiders of Ghost City
Raiders of the Sun
Rainbow Drive
The Rainbow Gang
Raising Heroes
Rambo: First Blood, Part 2
Rambo 3
Ransom Money
Ranson's Folly
Rapa Nui
The Rape of the Sabines
Rapid Fire
Raven
Ravenhawk
Raw Deal
Raw Justice
The Razor: Sword of Justice
Real Bullets
The Real McCoy
Reason to Die
Rebel Storm
Recoil
Red Ball Express
Red Dawn
Red Dust⤴
The Red Fury
Red Heat
Red Line
Red Scorpion
Red Scorpion 2
Red Signals
Red Snow
Red Tent⤴
Relentless 2: Dead On
Rent-A-Cop
Repo Jake
Rescue Force
Retrievers
Retroactive
Return Fire
The Return of Casey Jones
Return of Chandu
The Return of Eliot Ness
The Return of Grey Wolf
Return of Superfly
Return of the Dragon
Return of the Man from
   U.N.C.L.E.
Return of the Tiger
Return to Africa
Return to Fantasy Island

Return to Macon County
Return to Savage Beach
Return to the Lost World
Revenge of the Barbarians
Revenge of the Ninja
The Revenger
Revolt of the Barbarians
Revolver
Ricco
The Riddle of the Sands
Riding High
Ring of Steel
Rip-Off
The Rip Off
Rip Roarin' Buckaroo
Ripper Man
River of Death
River of Diamonds
River of Evil
Road House
Road Kill USA
The Road Killers
The Road Warrior⤴
Roadkill
Robbers of the Sacred Mountain
Robby
Robin Hood⤴
Robin Hood...The Legend:
   Herne's Son
Robin Hood...The Legend:
   Robin Hood and the Sorcerer
Robin Hood...The Legend: The
   Swords of Wayland
Robin Hood...The Legend: The
   Time of the Wolf
Robinson Crusoe
Robinson Crusoe & the Tiger
Robinson Crusoe of Clipper
   Island
Robinson Crusoe of Mystery
   Island
RoboCop 2
RoboCop 3
The Rock⤴
Rock House
The Rocketeer⤴
Rocketship X-M
Rogue Lion
Rogue Male
Roller Blade Warriors: Taken By
   Force
Rollercoaster
Rolling Vengeance
The Rookie
Rosebud
R.O.T.O.R.
Rough Cut
Rough Riders
Roughnecks
The Rousters
Royal Warriors
Royce
Ruckus
Rudyard Kipling's the Second
   Jungle Book: Mowgli and
   Baloo
Rulers of the City
Rumble in the Streets
Run
Run, Angel, Run!
Run, Rebecca, Run
Runaway
The Runaway Barge
Runaway Nightmare
Running Blind
Running Cool
Running Hot
The Running Man
Running Scared
Rush
Rush Hour
The Russian Terminator
The Rutanga Tapes
Safari 3000
Saga of the Vagabond
Sahara⤴
Sahara
Saigon Commandos
Saints and Sinners

Salty
Salvador⤴
Samar
Samson Against the Sheik
Samurai 1: Musashi Miyamoto⤴
Samurai 2: Duel at Ichijoji
   Temple⤴
Samurai 3: Duel at Ganryu
   Island⤴
Samurai Rebellion⤴
Sands of Sacrifice
Sanjuro⤴
S.A.S. San Salvador
The Satan Killer
Satan's Sadists
Savage!
Savage Beach
Savage Dawn
Savage Drums
Savage Fury
The Savage Girl
Savage Instinct
Savage Island
The Scarlet & the Black
Scorpion Spring
Sea Devils
Sea Hound
Sea of Sand
Sea Prince and the Fire Child
The Sea Wolf⤴
The Sea Wolf
Search and Destroy
Second Chance
Secret Agent Super Dragon
The Secret Code
Secret Mission
The Secret of El Zorro
Secret of the Ice Cave
Sgt. Kabukiman N.Y.P.D.
Serial Bomber
Serpent Island
Sesame Street Presents: Follow
   That Bird
Set It Off
Seven Blows of the Dragon
Seven Magnificent Gladiators
Seven Sinners⤴
The Seven-Ups
The Seventh Coin
The Seventh Voyage of Sinbad⤴
Sex, Love and Cold Hard Cash
Shadow Man
Shadow of Chikara
Shadow of the Eagle
Shadow of the Wolf
Shadowhunter
Shaft in Africa
Shaft's Big Score
Shakedown
Shaker Run
Shamus
Shaolin Ex-Monk
Shaolin Vengence
Shark Hunter
Shark River
Sharks' Treasure
Sharky's Machine
Sharpe's Battle
Sharpe's Company
Sharpe's Eagle
Sharpe's Enemy
Sharpe's Gold
Sharpe's Honour
Sharpe's Justice
Sharpe's Legend
Sharpe's Mission
Sharpe's Regiment
Sharpe's Revenge
Sharpe's Rifles
Sharpe's Siege
Sharpe's Sword
Sharpe's Waterloo
S*H*E
She Devils in Chains
Sheba, Baby
Sheena
The Sheik⤴
Shelter
Shep Comes Home

Ships in the Night
Shipwrecked
Shogun's Ninja
Shoot
Shoot the Sun Down
Showdown at the Equator
Sidekicks
Sidewinder One
The Sign of Zorro
Silent Hunter
Silent Trigger
Silk 2
Silk Degrees
Sinbad and the Eye of the Tiger
Sinbad of the Seven Seas
Sinbad, the Sailor⤴
633 Squadron
Sixteen Fathoms Deep
The Skateboard Kid
Skeleton Coast
Ski Bum
Ski Troop Attack
Skull: A Night of Terror
Skull & Crown
Sky Hei$t
Sky High
Sky Pirates
Skyscraper
Slate, Wyn & Me
Slaughter
Slaughter's Big Ripoff
Slave of the Cannibal God
Sloane
Slow Burn
Smokey & the Hotwire Gang
Smuggler's Cove
SnakeEater
SnakeEater 2: The Drug Buster
SnakeEater 3: His Law
The Soldier
Soldier Boyz
Soldier's Fortune
Solo
Solo Voyage: The Revenge
Son of Captain Blood
Son of Fury⤴
Son of Kong
The Son of Monte Cristo
Son of Samson
Son of Sinbad
Son of Zorro
S.O.S. Coast Guard
Sourdough
South Beach
South of Pago Pago
South Seas Massacre
Southern Comfort⤴
Space Mutiny
Space Raiders
Space Riders
Spacehunter: Adventures in the
   Forbidden Zone
The Spanish Main
Spartacus⤴
Spawn
Special Investigator
Speed 2: Cruise Control
Speeding Up Time
Speedtrap
Spiderman: The Deadly Dust
Spiders⤴
The Spirit of Youth
Spitfire
The Spoilers
Spy
Spy in Black⤴
Spy Smasher
Spy Smasher Returns
The Spy Who Loved Me
Stalking Danger
Stamp Day for Superman
Stand and Deliver
Standoff
Star Quest
Starbird and Sweet William
Starchaser: The Legend of Orin
Starflight One
Stargate
Starship Troopers⤴

Action

Adolescence

Adoption & Orphans

Adventure

Advertising

see also Front Page; Mass Media

Hyper-Sapien: People from
   Another Star
Intruders
It Came from Outer Space •
Josh Kirby...Time Warrior:
   Chapter 5, Journey to the
   Magic Cavern
Labyrinth♪
The Last Starfighter
Mac and Me
Man Facing Southeast♪
The Man from Atlantis
The Man Who Fell to Earth♪
Martians Go Home!
Masters of Venus
Men in Black♪
Missile to the Moon
Moon Pilot
Morons from Outer Space
Munchie
My Stepmother Is an Alien
My Uncle: The Alien
Mysterious Two
Nukie
Official Denial
Pajama Party
Pet Shop
The Phantom Planet
Project: Genesis
Purple People Eater
Real Men
Repo Man♪
Return of the Jedi♪
Search for the Gods
Simon
Spaced Invaders
Star Knight
Star Trek 3: The Search for
   Spock
Star Trek 4: The Voyage Home♪
Star Trek: First Contact♪
Star Wars♪
Stardust Memories
Starlight
Starman♪
Starship Invasions
Suburban Commando
Super Mario Bros.
Supergirl
Superman: The Movie♪
Superman 2♪
Superman 3
Superman 4: The Quest for
   Peace
Teenage Mutant Ninja Turtles 2:
   The Secret of the Ooze
The Terronauts
The 27 Day
The Twilight Zone
UFO: Target Earth
Vegas in Space
Voyage of the Rock Aliens
War of the Robots
Warning from Space
Wavelength
When Time Expires
Zarkorr! The Invader

Alien Beings—
Vicious

see also *Alien Beings—*
   Benign; Space Operas
The Adventures of Buckaroo
   Banzai Across the Eighth
   Dimension♪
Alien♪
Alien 3
The Alien Agenda: Out of the
   Darkness
Alien Contamination
Alien Dead
The Alien Factor
Alien Massacre
Alien Nation: Dark Horizon
Alien Predators
Alien Prey
Alien: Resurrection♪

Alien Seed
Alien Space Avenger
Alien Terminator
Alienator
Aliens♪
Aliens Are Coming
The Alpha Incident
The Ambushers
The Angry Red Planet
The Arrival
The Astounding She-Monster
The Astro-Zombies
Atomic Submarine
Backlash: Oblivion 2
Bad Channels
Bad Taste
Battle Beyond the Stars
Battle of the Worlds
Battlestar Galactica
Bio Hazard
The Blob
The Blob♪
Bloodsuckers from Outer Space
Blue Flame
Blue Monkey
Body Snatchers
The Borrower
The Brain
The Brain Eaters
The Brain from Planet Arous
Breeders
Cat Women of the Moon
Class of Nuke 'Em High 3: The
   Good, the Bad and the
   Subhumanoid
The Cosmic Monsters
Creature
Creeping Terror
The Cremators
Critters
Critters 2: The Main Course
Critters 3
Critters 4
Crossworlds
The Curse
D-Day on Mars
The Dark
Dark Breed
Dark Star♪
Dark Universe
Day the World Ended
Day Time Ended
Dead Space
Dead Weekend
Deceit
Deep Red
Deep Space
Destroy All Monsters
Destroy All Planets
Devil Girl from Mars
Dr. Alien
Doctor Who
Doctor Who: An Unearthly Child
Doctor Who and the Daleks
Dollman
Dracula vs. Frankenstein
Earth vs. the Flying Saucers
Eat and Run
The Empire Strikes Back♪
Encounter at Raven's Gate
End of the World
Escape from Galaxy Three
Escapes
Evils of the Night
The Eye Creatures
Eyes Behind the Stars
The Fear Chamber
The Fifth Element
First Man into Space
Flight to Mars
Forbidden World
Forbidden Zone: Alien
   Abduction
Frankenstein Meets the Space
   Monster
From Beyond♪
Galaxy Invader
Galaxy of Terror
Gamera vs. Guiron

Gamera vs. Zigra
Ghidrah the Three Headed
   Monster
The Giant Claw
The Giant Spider Invasion
God Told Me To
Godzilla vs. King Ghidora
Godzilla vs. the Cosmic Monster
Grand Tour: Disaster in Time
The Green Slime
Gremlins♪
Gremlins 2: The New Batch♪
The Guyver
Guyver 2: Dark Hero
Hands of Steel
The Hidden♪
The Hidden 2
The High Crusade
High Desert Kill
Horror of the Blood Monsters
Horror Planet
The Human Duplicators
Hybrid
I Come in Peace
I Married a Monster from Outer
   Space
Independence Day♪
Invader
The Invaders
Invaders from Mars
Invasion
Invasion Earth: The Aliens Are
   Here!
Invasion of the Animal People
Invasion of the Bee Girls♪
Invasion of the Body Snatchers♪
Invasion of the Body Stealers
Invasion of the Girl Snatchers
Invasion of the Saucer Men
Invasion of the Space Preachers
Invisible Adversaries
Invisible Invaders
Island of the Burning Doomed
It Came from Outer Space♪
It Came from Outer Space 2
It Conquered the World
It! The Terror from Beyond
   Space
J-Men Forever!♪
Killer Klowns from Outer Space
Killers from Space
Killings at Outpost Zeta
Kronos
Laboratory
Leviathan
Lifeform
Liquid Sky♪
Lords of the Deep
Lost in Space
Mars Attacks!
Mars Needs Women
The Martian Chronicles: Part 3
Masters of Venus
Men in Black♪
Metallica
Midnight Movie Massacre
Mindwarp
Mission Mars
Mom and Dad Save the World
Monolith
The Monolith Monsters
Monster
Monster a Go-Go!
Monster High
Moontrap
Munchies
The Mysterians
Night Beast
Night Caller from Outer Space
Night of the Blood Beast
Night of the Creeps
No Survivors, Please
Not of This Earth
Oblivion
The Outer Limits: Galaxy Being
The Outer Limits: Sandkings♪
The P.A.C.K.
Peacemaker
Pet Shop

Phantom from Space
The Phantom Planet
The Pink Chiquitas
Plan 9 from Outer Space
Plan 10 from Outer Space
Planet of Blood
Planets Against Us
Predator
Predator 2
The Puppet Masters
Quatermass 2♪
Quatermass and the Pit
The Quatermass Experiment♪
Radar Men from the Moon
Reactor
Remote Control
The Return
Return of the Aliens: The Deadly
   Spawn
Return of the Jedi♪
Revenge of the Teenage Vixens
   from Outer Space
Robot Monster
Rock 'n' Roll Nightmare
Scared to Death
Sci-Fighters
The Silencers
The Sinister Invasion
Slapstick of Another Kind
Son of Blob
Space Jam
Species
Species 2
Specimen
Split
Split Second
Star Crystal
Star Hunter
Star Trek: The Motion Picture
Star Trek 3: The Search for
   Spock
Star Trek: First Contact♪
Star Trek: The Cage
Star Wars♪
Stargate
Starship Invasions
Stephen King's The Langoliers
Stephen King's The
   Tommyknockers
Strange Invaders
The Stranger from Venus
Super Mario Bros.
Superman 2♪
A Taste for Flesh and Blood
Teen Alien
Teenagers from Outer Space
Terror of Mechagodzilla
They
They Came from Beyond Space
They Live
The Thing♪
The Thing
This Island Earth
Time Runner
Time Walker
Tripods: The White Mountains
20 Million Miles to Earth
The Twilight Zone
The Unearthly Stranger
Unknown Origin
V♪
V: The Final Battle
Vampire Vixens from Venus
Village of the Damned♪
Village of the Damned
Virus
War in Space
War of the Wizards
The War of the Worlds♪
When Time Expires
Wicked City
Wild, Wild Planet
Within the Rock
Women of the Prehistoric Planet
X from Outer Space
Xtro
Xtro 2: The Second Encounter
Xtro 3: Watch the Skies
Zarkorr! The Invader

Zeram
Zombies of the Stratosphere
Zontar, the Thing from Venus

Aliens Are People,
Too

see also *Alien Beings—*
   Benign; Alien Beings—
      Vicious

Alien♪
Alien 3
Alien: Resurrection♪
Aliens♪
The Arrival
Body Snatchers
The Hidden♪
The Hidden 2
The Invader
The Invaders
Invaders from Mars
Invasion of the Body Snatchers♪
Mars Attacks!
Men in Black♪
My Stepmother Is an Alien
Not Like Us
Planet of the Vampires
The Puppet Masters
Species 2
Star Portal
Starlight
Starman♪
The Thing♪
The Thing
V♪
V: The Final Battle
The X-Files Movie

American Indians

see *Native America*

American South

see also *Miami; Nashville*
   Narratives; New Orleans;
      Southern Belles

Ain't No Way Back
Alligator Alley
Andersonville♪
Angel Baby
Angel City
Angel Heart
The Apostle♪
As Summers Die
The Autobiography of Miss Jane
   Pittman♪
Baby Doll♪
Bad Georgia Road
The Ballad of the Sad Cafe
Bastard out of Carolina
The Beguiled♪
Belizaire the Cajun
Between Heaven and Hell♪
Beulah Land
The Big Easy♪
Black Like Me
Blind Vengeance
Boxcar Bertha
Bucktown
Camilla
Cape Fear♪
Cat on a Hot Tin Roof♪
Cat on a Hot Tin Roof
The Chamber
Chiefs
Christy
Cold Sassy Tree♪
The Color Purple♪
Cries of Silence
Crossroads
Dancer, Texas - Pop. 81♪
Dead Right
The Delta
Delta Heat
Dixiana
Driving Miss Daisy♪

Evil Clutch
Evil Dead
Evil Dead 2: Dead by Dawn
Evil Ed
Evil Laugh
The Evil Within
Evils of the Night
The Executioner
Exquisite Corpses
The Eye Creatures
Eyes of a Stranger
The Fan
Fatal Games
Fatal Pulse
The Fear
The Fiend
Fiend Without a Face
Final Exam
The Final Terror
First Blood
The First Power
Flesh and Blood
Flesh and Blood Show
Forbidden World
Forced Entry
The Forest
Forever Evil
Frankenstein '80
Freddy's Dead: The Final
 Nightmare
The Freeway Maniac
Friday the 13th
Friday the 13th, Part 2
Friday the 13th, Part 3
Friday the 13th, Part 4: The
 Final Chapter
Friday the 13th, Part 5: A New
 Beginning
Friday the 13th, Part 6: Jason
 Lives
Friday the 13th, Part 7: The New
 Blood
Friday the 13th, Part 8: Jason
 Takes Manhattan
Frightmare
From Dusk Till Dawn
Frozen Terror
The Funhouse
Gates of Hell
The Ghastly Ones
Ghoulies
Girly
Goblin
The Godfather, Part 3♪
The Gore-Gore Girls
Gore-Met Zombie Chef From
 Hell
Graduation Day
The Granny
The Graveyard
Greedy Terror
Grim Reaper
Grotesque
Gruesome Twosome
Hack O'Lantern
Halloween♪
Halloween 2: The Nightmare
 Isn't Over!
Halloween 3: Season of the
 Witch
Halloween 4: The Return of
 Michael Myers
Halloween 5: The Revenge of
 Michael Myers
Halloween 6: The Curse of
 Michael Myers
Hamburger Hill
Hard-Boiled
He Knows You're Alone
Headless Eyes
Heartstopper
Hellcats
Hellmaster
Hello Mary Lou: Prom Night 2
Hellraiser 3: Hell on Earth
Helter Skelter
Helter Skelter Murders
Henry: Portrait of a Serial Killer
 2: Mask of Sanity

The Hidden♪
The Hidden 2
Hide and Go Shriek
The Hitcher
Hollywood Chainsaw Hookers
The Hollywood Strangler Meets
 the Skid Row Slasher
The Horror Show
Hospital Massacre
Hospital of Terror
The House by the Cemetery
House of Death
House of Psychotic Women
House of Whipcord
House on the Edge of the Park
The House on Tombstone Hill
The House that Bled to Death
The Howling♪
Howling 2: Your Sister Is a
 Werewolf
Howling 4: The Original
 Nightmare
Howling 5: The Rebirth
Howling 6: The Freaks
Humanoids from the Deep
Humongous
I Come in Peace
I Drink Your Blood
I Eat Your Skin
I, Madman
I Spit on Your Grave
Ice Cream Man
Icebox Murders
Illtown
The Initiation
Innocent Blood
Interview with the Vampire
Intruder
Invasion of the Blood Farmers
Island of Blood
Jason Goes to Hell: The Final
 Friday
Junior
Keep My Grave Open
Kid
Killcrazy
The Killer♪
The Killer Elite
Killer Workout
The Killing Game
L.A. Gangs Rising
The Last Don
The Last Gasp
The Last Horror Film
Last House on the Left
Last Man Standing
The Lawnmower Man
Leatherface: The Texas
 Chainsaw Massacre 3
The Legend of Blood Castle
Leprechaun
Leprechaun 2
Listen
Looker
Love Butcher
Lunatic
The Mad Butcher
The Mad Executioners
Madhouse
Madman
The Majorettes
The Mangler
Maniac
Maniac Cop 2
Maniac Cop 3: Badge of Silence
Maniac Warriors
Mardi Gras Massacre
Marked for Death
Martin♪
Masque of the Red Death
The Meateater
Meet the Feebles
Midnight
Monster
Monty Python and the Holy
 Grail♪
Motel Hell
The Movie House Massacre
Murder-in-Law

Mutator
The Mutilator
My Bloody Valentine
Nail Gun Massacre
Naked Massacre
Neon Maniacs
Never Pick Up a Stranger
New York Ripper
Next of Kin
The Night Brings Charlie
Night of a Thousand Cats
Night of Bloody Horror
Night of the Bloody Apes
Night of the Bloody Transplant
Night of the Demons
Night of the Demons 2
Night of the Demons 3
Night of the Living Dead♪
Night of the Living Dead
Night of the Scarecrow
Night of the Strangler
Night of the Zombies
Night Ripper
Night School
Night Screams
Night Warning
Nightmare
A Nightmare on Elm Street
A Nightmare on Elm Street 2:
 Freddy's Revenge
A Nightmare on Elm Street 3:
 Dream Warriors
A Nightmare on Elm Street 4:
 Dream Master
A Nightmare on Elm Street 5:
 Dream Child
Nightstalker
Noon Sunday
Offerings
The Offspring
Out Cold
Out of the Body
The Outing
Overexposed
Phantom of the Mall: Eric's
 Revenge
Pieces
Platoon Leader
Play Dead
Popcorn
Possession
Predator
Predator 2
The Prey
Prime Evil
Prom Night
Prom Night 3: The Last Kiss
Prom Night 4: Deliver Us from
 Evil
Psycho 3
Psycho from Texas
Psychopath
Pumpkinhead
Pumpkinhead 2: Blood Wings
Puppet Master
Puppet Master 2
Puppet Master 3: Toulon's
 Revenge
Puppet Master 4
Puppet Master 5: The Final
 Chapter
The Pyx♪
Queen Margot♪
Quiet Fire
Rabid Grannies
Rambo 3
Ran♪
The Rats Are Coming! The
 Werewolves Are Here!
Re-Animator♪
Redneck Zombies
Rest in Pieces
Return of the Aliens: The Deadly
 Spawn
Return of the Family Man
Return to Horror High
Revenge
The Ripper
Road Games

RoboCop♪
RoboCop 2
Rocktober Blood
Ruby
The Rue Morgue Massacres
S.A.S. San Salvador
Savage!
Sawbones
Scalpel
Scanners
Scanners 2: The New Order
Scanners 3: The Takeover
Scanners: The Showdown
Scream♪
Scream 2♪
Scream, Baby, Scream
Scream Bloody Murder
Scream of the Demon Lover
Screamers
The Screaming Dead
Seven Doors of Death
The Severed Arm
Shadowzone
Shakma
She Came on the Bus
Shock! Shock! Shock!
Shocker
Shrieker
The Silence of the Lambs♪
Silent Night, Deadly Night
Silent Night, Deadly Night 2
Silent Night, Deadly Night 3:
 Better Watch Out!
Silent Night, Deadly Night 4:
 Initiation
Silent Rage
Silk
Skinner
The Slasher
Slaughter High
Slaughter Hotel
Slaughterhouse
The Slayer
The Slayer/The Scalps
Sleepaway Camp
Sleepaway Camp 2: Unhappy
 Campers
Sleepaway Camp 3: Teenage
 Wasteland
The Slumber Party Massacre
Slumber Party Massacre 2
Snow Kill
Society
Sometimes They Come
 Back...Again
Sorority House Massacre
Sorority House Massacre 2:
 Nighty Nightmare
Spare Parts
Species 2
Splatter University
Split Second
Stagefright
Star Time
Steps from Hell
Stone Cold
Strait-Jacket
The Strangler
Stripped to Kill II: Live Girls
Stuff Stephanie in the Incinerator
Swamp of the Lost Monster
Tales from the Crypt Presents
 Bordello of Blood
TC 2000
Terminal Choice
Terror at Tenkiller
Terror on Tour
Terror Train
The Texas Chainsaw Massacre
Texas Chainsaw Massacre 2
The Texas Chainsaw Massacre
 4: The Next Generation
They're Playing with Fire
Things
Thirst
This World, Then the Fireworks
Three on a Meathook
The Thrill Killers
The Toolbox Murders

Top of the Heap
Torment
Torture Chamber of Baron Blood
Torture Train
The Tower of London
Town that Dreaded Sundown
The Toxic Avenger
The Toxic Avenger, Part 2
Twin Peaks: Fire Walk with Me
Twisted Brain
Twitch of the Death Nerve
The Two Faces of Evil
2000 Maniacs
Uncle Sam
Underground Terror
Unmasked Part 25
The Unnamable
Unsane
The Unseen
Vengeance Is Mine
Vicious
The Video Dead
Video Violence
Video Violence Part 2...The
 Exploitation!
The Vineyard
Violent Women
Visiting Hours
The Visitor
Voodoo Black Exorcist
Walking Tall
Walking Tall: Part 2
Waxwork
Waxwork 2: Lost in Time
Welcome to Blood City
Welcome to Spring Break
Wes Craven's New Nightmare♪
When the Screaming Stops
The Wicked
The Wild Bunch♪
Witchboard
The Wizard of Gore
Woodchipper Massacre
Xtro
Zero Boys
Zombie
Zombie Island Massacre
Zone of the Dead

Bloody Messages

see also Bloody Mayhem

Die Hard♪
Fatal Vision
Harold and Maude♪
Helter Skelter
The Jagged Edge
Seven♪
The Shining
Stephen King's The Night Flier
The Untouchables♪

Boating

see Sail Away

Bodyguards

Absolute Power
Assassination
Black Belt
Blackjack
The Bodyguard
The Chase
Fatal Beauty
Fatal Past
First Kid
Genuine Risk
Get Shorty♪
Guarding Tess
Half a Loaf of Kung Fu
Heat
In the Line of Fire♪
La Scorta♪
Man on Fire
Mr. Nanny
My Bodyguard♪
Night Eyes 4: Fatal Passion

Buddies

The Wild Life
Wild Rovers
Windy City
Winners Take All
Withnail and I♪
Wrestling Ernest Hemingway
The Wrong Guys
The Wrong Road
The Yakuza
Yankee Zulu
Young Guns 2
Young Hercules
You're in Love, Charlie Brown
Zorba the Greek♪

Buddy Cops

see also Canine Cops;
Cops; Women Cops

Another 48 Hrs.
Another Stakeout
Arizona Heat
Bad Boys
Car 54, Where Are You?
City Heat
Collision Course
Cop Land♪
Exit to Eden
48 Hrs.♪
Gang Related
The Glimmer Man
The Hard Way♪
Internal Affairs
La Chevre♪
Lethal Weapon♪
Lethal Weapon 2♪
Lethal Weapon 3
Lethal Weapon 4
Liberty & Bash
Men in Black♪
Metro
Money Train
Mulholland Falls
National Lampoon's Loaded
    Weapon 1
Night Children
Nighthawks
The Presidio
Red Heat
Renegades
The Rookie
Shakedown
Shoot to Kill♪
Speed♪
Stakeout
Tango and Cash

Buried Alive

Buried Alive
Buried Alive 2
The Fall of the House of Usher
The Fall of the House of Usher♪
The Fall of the House of Usher
The House of Usher
La Chute de la Maison Usher♪
The Oblong Box
Premature Burial

Buses

The Adventures of Priscilla,
    Queen of the Desert♪
All God's Children
Beavis and Butt-Head Do
    America
The Big Bus
Bull Durham♪
Bus Stop♪
Dirty Harry♪
Forrest Gump♪
The Fugitive♪
The Gauntlet
Get On the Bus♪
Heart and Souls
Incident at Deception Ridge
Lady on the Bus
The Laughing Policeman

A League of Their Own♪
Long Journey Back
Love Field
Magical Mystery Tour
A Man of No Importance♪
Mexican Bus Ride
National Lampoon's Senior Trip
Pardon My Sarong
Planes, Trains & Automobiles
Ride
The Runaway Bus
Speed♪
Spice World: The Movie
The Sweet Hereafter♪
The Trip to Bountiful♪
Wheels of Terror
Where Angels Go, Trouble
    Follows

Cabbies

The Bishop's Wife♪
Blood & Donuts
Conspiracy Theory♪
Crossing Delancey♪
Daylight
D.C. Cab
Escape from New York
Fall
The Fifth Element
Look Who's Talking♪
Night on Earth♪
Pulp Fiction♪
The Right Connections
Scrooged
She's the One
Taxi Blues♪
Taxi Driver♪
The Taxi Mystery
The Yellow Cab Man

Calcutta

see also India

The Adversary
Baraka♪
City of Joy
Days and Nights in the Forest
The Quest

Camelot (New)

see also Assassinations;
Presidency

Jacqueline Bouvier Kennedy
JFK♪
The JFK Conspiracy
JFK: Reckless Youth
Kennedy
Prince Jack
PT 109
Robert Kennedy and His Times
Ruby

Camelot (Old)

see also Medieval Romps;
Swashbucklers

Camelot
A Connecticut Yankee♪
A Connecticut Yankee in King
    Arthur's Court
Excalibur♪
First Knight
A Kid in King Arthur's Court
Kids of the Round Table
King Arthur, the Young Warlord
Knights of the Round Table
Merlin♪
Merlin and the Sword
Monty Python and the Holy
    Grail♪
Prince Valiant
Quest for Camelot
The Sword in the Stone♪
Sword of Lancelot
Sword of the Valiant

A Young Connecticut Yankee in
    King Arthur's Court

Campus Capers

see also Hell High School;
School Daze

Accident
The Affairs of Dobie Gillis
All-American Murder
American Tiger
Animal Behavior
Assault of the Party Nerds
Attack of the Killer Refrigerator
Baby Love
Bachelor of Hearts
Back to School
Beware
Beyond Dream's Door
Black Christmas
Black Tower
Blood Cult
Blood Sisters
Blue Chips
Breeders
Bride of Killer Nerd
The Campus Corpse
Campus Knights
Campus Man
Carnal Knowledge♪
The Cheerleaders
Cheers for Miss Bishop
A Chump at Oxford
Circle of Friends
College♪
College Swing
Computer Beach Party
The Computer Wore Tennis
    Shoes
The Cousins♪
Dead Man on Campus
Deadly Lessons
Deadly Obsession
Deadly Possession
Death Screams
Didn't You Hear?
Doctor in the House♪
Dorm That Dripped Blood
Ernest Rides Again
Escapade in Florence
Father Was a Fullback
Final Exam
First Affair
First Love
First Time
Foreign Student
Francis Goes to West Point
Fraternity Vacation
The Freshman♪
The Freshman
Fright Night 2
Getting Away With Murder
Getting In
Ghoulies 3: Ghoulies Go to
    College
Girl Crazy♪
Girls Night Out
The Gladiator♪
Glory Daze
Good News
Good Will Hunting
Gotcha!
Gross Anatomy
Gross Misconduct
Hamburger...The Motion Picture
Harmon of Michigan
Harrad Experiment
Harrad Summer
HauntedWeen
The Heart of Dixie
Hell Night
Higher Education
Higher Learning
Horse Feathers♪
H.O.T.S.
The House on Sorority Row
House Party 2: The Pajama Jam
How I Got into College
I Don't Buy Kisses Anymore

The Initiation
Initiation of Sarah
I.Q.
Is There Life Out There?
Jock Petersen
Kicking and Screaming♪
The Kid with the 200 I.Q.
A Killer in Every Corner
Killer Party
Knock Outs
Lady Killer
Let's Go Collegiate
Life 101
Little Sister
A Little Stiff
Love and Other Catastrophes
Lover's Knot
Lucky Jim
Malice
A Matter of Degrees
Mazes and Monsters
Midnight Madness
The Mirror Has Two Faces
The Misadventures of Merlin
    Jones
Monkey's Uncle
Monster on the Campus
Mortuary Academy
Mugsy's Girls
Murder on the Campus
My Lucky Star
My Sex Life...Or How I Got Into
    an Argument
The Naked Witch
National Lampoon's Animal
    House♪
Navy Blue and Gold
Necessary Roughness
A Night in the Life of Jimmy
    Reardon
Night of the Creeps
Nightwish
The Nutty Professor♪
An Occasional Hell
Odd Jobs
Oleanna
The Paper Chase♪
Parallel Lives
Party Animal
P.C.U.
Pieces
Pigskin Parade
Pledge Night
Preppies
The Program
A Reason to Believe
Return Engagement
Revenge of the Nerds
Revenge of the Nerds 2: Nerds
    in Paradise
Revenge of the Nerds 3: The
    Next Generation
Ring of Terror
Roommate
Roommates
Rosalie
R.P.M.* (*Revolutions Per
    Minute)
Rudy
Rush Week
Scent of a Woman♪
School Daze♪
School Spirit
Scream 2♪
The Seniors
Sensation
Senseless
Shallow Grave
Silent Madness
Silent Scream
The Sixth Man
Sky High
Slipping into Darkness
A Small Circle of Friends
Sniper♪
Sorority Babes in the Slimeball
    Bowl-A-Rama
Sorority Girl
Sorority House Massacre

Sorority House Massacre 2:
    Nighty Nightmare
Sorority House Party
Soul Man
South Beach Academy
Spellbound
The Spirit of West Point
Splatter University
Splitz
Spring Break
Stitches
The Student Affair
The Sure Thing♪
Surviving Desire♪
Sweet Young Thing
Tag: The Assassination Game
Talking Walls
Tall Lie
Tall Story
Teen Wolf Too
Three in the Attic
Three in the Cellar
Threesome
Toga Party
Undergrads♪
Unforgettable
The Unnamable
The Unnamable 2: The
    Statement of Randolph Carter
Up the Creek
The Victory
Voodoo
War Between the Tates
Wavelength
When He's Not a Stranger♪
The Wild Life
Wish Me Luck
Witchboard
Witches' Brew
With Honors
Zis Boom Bah

Canada

see also Cold Spots;
Hockey

Abducted
The Adjuster
The Agency
American Boyfriends
The Amityville Curse
And Then You Die♪
Angel Square
Angela
Anne of Avonlea♪
Anne of Green Gables♪
The Apprenticeship of Duddy
    Kravitz♪
Atlantic City♪
The Bay Boy
Beautiful Dreamers
The Big Crimewave
Big Meat Eater
Big Red
Black Christmas
Black Robe♪
Blades of Courage
Blood Clan
Blood of the Hunter
Blood Relations
The Bloody Brood
Boy in Blue
The Boys Club
The Boys of St. Vincent♪
Breaking All the Rules
The Brood
Buffalo Jump♪
Bullies
Busted Up
By Design
By Way of the Stars
Bye Bye Blues
Cafe Romeo
Camilla
Canada's Sweetheart: The Saga
    of Hal C. Banks
Canadian Bacon
Candy Mountain
The Cariboo Trail

Childhood

Big Bully
Big Fella
Black Beauty🞂
The Black Stallion🞂
Blank Check
Bogus
The Borrowers
Boys Will Be Boys
Brighton Beach Memoirs
Broken Harvest
But Where Is Daniel Wax?
Cameron's Closet
Camp Nowhere
Captain January
Careful, He Might Hear You🞂
Casey's Shadow
Casper🞂
The Cat
Celia: Child Of Terror
The Cellar
Chapter in Her Life
Child in the Night
The Children Are Watching Us🞂
Children of Divorce
Child's Play
China, My Sorrow
Chocolat🞂
The Christmas Box
A Christmas Reunion
A Christmas Story
Chronicle of a Boy Alone
Cinema Paradiso🞂
The Client
Clifford
Clubhouse Detectives
Cria🞂
Crooklyn🞂
Curly Sue
D.A.R.Y.L.
David Copperfield🞂
Days of Heaven🞂
Demons in the Garden🞂
Dennis the Menace
Dennis the Menace Strikes
   Again
Desert Bloom🞂
Deutschland im Jahre Null🞂
The Diary of Anne Frank🞂
Digger
Diva🞂
Don't Tell Mom the Babysitter's
   Dead
D3: The Mighty Ducks
The Education of Little Tree🞂
The Elementary School
Ellen Foster
Emma's Shadow🞂
Empire of the Sun🞂
Escapade🞂
E.T.: The Extra-Terrestrial🞂
Eternity and a Day
Eve's Bayou🞂
Fairytale: A True Story
The Fallen Idol🞂
Fanny and Alexander🞂
Far Away and Long Ago
Father🞂
The Flame Trees of Thika🞂
Flight of the Grey Wolf
Flight of the Innocent
Fly Away Home🞂
For a Lost Soldier
Forbidden Games🞂
Fresh
Girl from Hunan🞂
A Girl of the Limberlost
The Golden Seal
The Goonies
Grazuole
The Green House
Grizzly Mountain
Harriet the Spy
Heavyweights
Heidi
Heidi🞂
Heidi
Heidi🞂
Home Alone🞂
Home Alone 2: Lost in New York

Home for Christmas
Home of Angels
Homecoming
Honey, I Shrunk the Kids
Hook
Hope
Hope and Glory🞂
House Arrest
How Green Was My Valley🞂
Hue and Cry🞂
The Indian in the Cupboard
Into the West🞂
Invaders from Mars
Jack
Jack Be Nimble
Jacquot🞂
James and the Giant Peach🞂
Joey
John and Julie
Josh and S.A.M.
Journey for Margaret🞂
Kazaam🞂
The Kid from Left Field
The Kid with the Broken Halo
Kids of the Round Table
King of the Hill🞂
The Kitchen Toto🞂
Kolya🞂
The Lady in White🞂
Lassie's Great Adventure
Last Action Hero
The Last Winter
Lawnmower Man 2: Beyond
   Cyberspace
Lazarillo🞂
Le Grand Chemin🞂
Leave It to Beaver
Leolo🞂
Les Violons du Bal
Lies My Father Told Me🞂
Little Big League
Little Buddha
Little Fugitive🞂
Little Lord Fauntleroy
Little Man Tate🞂
The Little Princess🞂
A Little Princess🞂
The Little Rascals
The Littlest Horse Thieves
Look Who's Talking
Look Who's Talking, Too
Lord of the Flies
Lord of the Flies
Lost in Yonkers🞂
Louisiana Story🞂
Love Film
Ma Vie en Rose🞂
Madeline
Magic in Mirror: Fowl Play
Magic in the Water
Magic of Lassie
Man of the House
Matilda🞂
The Member of the Wedding
Merlin of the Crystal Cave
The Miracle of Marcelino
The Mirror🞂
Ms. Bear
Misty
Mommie Dearest
Mosby's Marauders
My Childhood🞂
My Friend Flicka🞂
My Life As a Dog🞂
My Mother's Castle🞂
My Name Is Ivan🞂
National Velvet🞂
The Neon Bible🞂
New York Stories🞂
The Night of the Shooting
   Stars🞂
North
Nothing Personal🞂
Now and Then
Old Swimmin' Hole
Oliver!🞂
Oliver Twist
An Orphan Boy of Vienna

Orphans🞂
Other Voices, Other Rooms
Our Gang
The Pagemaster
Paradise🞂
The Parent Trap
Parents🞂
Paulie
Peck's Bad Boy
Pelle the Conqueror🞂
The Pillow Book
Pixote🞂
Pollyanna🞂
Poltergeist🞂
Poltergeist 2: The Other Side
Poltergeist: The Legacy
Ponette
A Poor Little Rich Girl🞂
The Poor Little Rich Girl
Powder
Psycho 4: The Beginning
The Quest
The Quiet Room
Radio Flyer
The Rag Nymph
The Railway Children🞂
Real Genius🞂
The Red Balloon🞂
The Red Pony🞂
The Reflecting Skin
Return from Witch Mountain
Richie Rich
The Right Connections
Rock-a-Doodle
Roll of Thunder, Hear My Cry
Running Free
Salaam Bombay!🞂
Savage Sam
Searching for Bobby Fischer🞂
The Secret Garden🞂
The Secret Garden
The Secret Garden🞂
The Secret Garden
Sidekicks
The Silence of Neto
The Silences of the Palace🞂
The Skateboard Kid 2
Slappy and the Stinkers
Sling Blade🞂
The Slingshot🞂
Small Change🞂
Sounds of Silence
Spirit of the Beehive🞂
Square Shoulders
Star Kid🞂
Stealing Home
Stephen King's It
Sudden Terror
Sudie & Simpson🞂
The Summer of Aviya🞂
A Summer to Remember🞂
Sunday Daughters🞂
Sunday's Children🞂
Taps
Three Wishes
The Tin Drum🞂
Tito and Me🞂
To Kill a Mockingbird🞂
Toothless
Toto le Heros🞂
Toy Story🞂
Trading Mom
Train to Hollywood🞂
Treasure Island🞂
Turf Boy
12 Monkeys🞂
An Unexpected Family
Unicorn
Wait Until Spring, Bandini
Walkabout🞂
Walking Thunder
The War
The War Boy
Welcome to Sarajevo🞂
Welcome to the Dollhouse
What the Moon Saw
When Father was Away on
   Business🞂
Where's Willie?

Whistle Down the Wind🞂
White Fang🞂
Wide Awake
The Wild Country
Willy Wonka & the Chocolate
   Factory🞂
The Witching of Ben Wagner
The Wizard of Loneliness
Wombling Free
A World Apart🞂
The Yearling
Yes, Sir, Mr. Bones
Zazie dans le Metro🞂
Zero for Conduct🞂
Zeus and Roxanne

Children

   see Animated Musicals;
   Animation & Cartoons;
   Childhood Visions;
   Storytelling

China

   see also Asia

Adventures of Smilin' Jack
The Amazing Panda Adventure
Battle of China
Bethune
Beyond the Next Mountain
The Bitter Tea of General Yen🞂
The Blue Kite🞂
Blush
China
China Cry
China, My Sorrow
Chinese Box
Crows and Sparrows🞂
The Day the Sun Turned Cold🞂
Deadly Target
Dragon Seed
Empire of the Sun🞂
Ermo
Farewell My Concubine🞂
Fight to the Death
The General Died at Dawn🞂
Girl from Hunan🞂
The Good Earth🞂
A Great Wall🞂
The Horse Thief🞂
The Inn of the Sixth Happiness🞂
Iron & Silk
The Joy Luck Club🞂
Ju Dou🞂
Kashmiri Run
The Keys of the Kingdom🞂
The Killer🞂
Knock Off
Lai Shi: China's Last Eunuch
The Last Emperor🞂
The Leatherneck
M. Butterfly
The Mountain Road
Mulan
Princess Yang Kwei Fei🞂
Raise the Red Lantern🞂
Red Corner
Red Firecracker, Green
   Firecracker
Red Sorghum🞂
The Reincarnation of Golden
   Lotus🞂
The Sand Pebbles🞂
Shadows of the Orient
Shadows Over Shanghai
Shanghai Express🞂
Shanghai Triad🞂
The Silk Road
Soldier of Fortune
Song of Exile
The Story of Qiu Ju🞂
The Story of Xinghua
Tai-Pan
Temptation of a Monk
Temptress Moon
To Live🞂

Women from the Lake of
   Scented Souls
The Wooden Man's Bride
The World of Suzie Wong

Christmas

   see also Holidays; Horrible
                Holidays

ABC Stage 67: Truman Capote's
   A Christmas Memory
All I Want for Christmas
An American Christmas Carol
Babes in Toyland
Batman Returns
Benji's Very Own Christmas
   Story
Bernard and the Genie
The Best Christmas Pageant
   Ever
The Bishop's Wife🞂
Black Christmas
Bloodbeat
Breathing Room
A Charlie Brown Christmas
Child's Christmas in Wales
The Christmas Box
A Christmas Carol
A Christmas Carol
A Christmas Carol🞂
The Christmas Coal Mine
   Miracle
Christmas Comes to Willow
   Creek
Christmas in Connecticut🞂
Christmas in Connecticut
Christmas in July🞂
The Christmas Kid
Christmas Lilies of the Field
A Christmas Reunion
A Christmas Story🞂
The Christmas That Almost
   Wasn't
A Christmas to Remember
The Christmas Wife
A Christmas Without Snow
Die Hard🞂
Diner🞂
Don't Open Till Christmas
Dorm That Dripped Blood
A Dream for Christmas🞂
Elves
Ernest Saves Christmas
Funny Farm
The Gathering
The Gathering: Part 2
George Balanchine's The
   Nutcracker
The Gift of Love
Gremlins🞂
Here Comes Santa Claus
Hobo's Christmas
Holiday Affair
Holiday Inn🞂
Home Alone🞂
Home Alone 2: Lost in New York
Home Alone 3
Home for Christmas
Home of Angels
Homecoming: A Christmas Story
A House Without a Christmas
   Tree
How the Grinch Stole
   Christmas🞂
It Came Upon a Midnight Clear
It's a Bundyful Life
It's a Wonderful Life🞂
Jingle All the Way
The Kid Who Loved Christmas
Kramer vs. Kramer🞂
Lady on a Train🞂
The Lemon Drop Kid
Lethal Weapon🞂
Lily in Winter
The Lion in Winter🞂
The Little Drummer Girl🞂
The Little Match Girl
Little Rascals Christmas Special
Little Women🞂

The Long Kiss Goodnight
Ma Saison Preferee✸
The Man in the Santa Claus Suit
The Man Upstairs
March of the Wooden Soldiers✸
A Matter of Principle
Merry Christmas, Mr.
   Lawrence✸
Mickey's Christmas Carol✸
A Midnight Clear✸
A Midwinter's Tale
Miracle Down Under
Miracle in the Wilderness
Miracle on 34th Street✸
Miracle on 34th Street
Mrs. Santa Claus
Mr. Corbett's Ghost
Mixed Nuts
The Muppet Christmas Carol
My Uncle: The Alien
The Mystery of Edwin Drood
National Lampoon's Christmas
   Vacation
Nativity
The Night of the Hunter✸
The Night They Saved
   Christmas
The Nightmare Before
   Christmas✸
The Nutcracker Prince
Nutcracker: The Motion Picture
One Magic Christmas
Prancer
The Preacher's Wife
The Railway Children✸
Reckless
The Ref✸
Remember the Night✸
Riot
The Robe
Roots: The Gift
Rudolph & Frosty's Christmas in
   July
Rudolph the Red-Nosed
   Reindeer
Santa Claus
Santa Claus Conquers the
   Martians
Santa Claus Is Coming to Town
Santa Claus: The Movie
The Santa Clause
Santa with Muscles
Scrooge
Scrooge
Scrooged
Silent Night, Deadly Night
Silent Night, Deadly Night 2
Silent Night, Deadly Night 3:
   Better Watch Out!
Silent Night, Deadly Night 5: The
   Toymaker
Silent Night, Lonely Night
Sleepless in Seattle
A Smoky Mountain Christmas
The Sum of Us✸
Susan Slept Here
A Tale of Winter
Terror in Toyland
Thirteenth Day of Christmas
Three Godfathers✸
A Time to Remember
To All a Goodnight
To Grandmother's House We
   Go
Trading Places
Trail of Robin Hood
Trapped In Paradise
Turbulence
Untamed Heart
A Very Brady Christmas
The Waltons: The Christmas
   Carol
While You Were Sleeping✸
White Christmas✸
Who Slew Auntie Roo?

CIA

*see Feds; Spies &
   Espionage*

Cinderella Stories

Angus
Arthur
B.A.P.'s
Boogie Nights✸
Born Yesterday✸
Born Yesterday
Celestial Clockwork
Cinderella
Cinderella
Ever After: A Cinderella Story
Evita
First Love
Flashdance
Hero
The Little Mermaid✸
Milk Money
The Mirror Has Two Faces
Mrs. Winterbourne
My Fair Lady✸
Once Around
Pretty Woman✸
Pygmalion✸
Splash
A Star Is Born✸
Stroke of Midnight
Up Close and Personal✸
Working Girl✸
The World of Suzie Wong

Circuses

*see Carnivals & Circuses;
   Clowns*

Cities

see Urban Drama

City Lights

*see Baltimore; Berlin;
   Boston; Calcutta; Capitol
   Capers; Chicago; I Love
   Detroit; L.A.; London;
   Miami; Moscow; New
   Orleans; New York, New
   York; Paris; San
   Francisco; Seattle; Tokyo;
   Urban Drama; Venice;
   Viva Las Vegas!*

Civil Rights

see also Apartheid; Slavery
An African Dream
And the Children Shall Lead
As Summers Die
The Autobiography of Miss Jane
   Pittman✸
Bucktown
The Bus Is Coming
The Color Purple✸
The Conversation✸
Crisis at Central High✸
Driving Miss Daisy✸
A Dry White Season✸
Dutchman✸
The Ernest Green Story
Final Comedown
For Us, the Living
Freedom Road
The Fringe Dwellers
Game for Vultures
Gang in Blue
George Wallace
Get On the Bus✸
Ghosts of Mississippi
Half Slave, Half Free

Hank Aaron: Chasing the
   Dream✸
Hawmns!
The Heart of Dixie
Hidden Agenda
Home of the Brave✸
King✸
The Kitchen Toto✸
Long Shadows
The Long Walk Home✸
Malcolm X: Make It Plain
The McMasters
Mississippi Burning✸
Mr. & Mrs. Loving✸
A Nation Aflame
Panther
The Red Fury
The Ring
Rosewood✸
A Soldier's Story✸
The Two of Us✸
We of the Never Never✸

Civil War

*see also American South;
   Southern Belles*
Abraham Lincoln
Alvarez Kelly
Andersonville✸
The Andersonville Trial✸
Bad Company✸
Band of Angels
The Beguiled✸
The Birth of a Nation✸
Blood at Sundown
Bloody Trail
The Blue and the Gray
The Bushwackers
Cavalry
Cavalry Charge
Charlotte Forten's Mission:
   Experiment in Freedom✸
Civil War Diary
The Civil War, Episode 1: The
   Cause—1861✸
The Civil War, Episode 2: A Very
   Bloody Affair—1862✸
The Civil War, Episode 3:
   Forever Free—1862✸
The Civil War, Episode 4: Simply
   Murder—1863✸
The Civil War, Episode 5: The
   Universe of Battle—1863✸
The Civil War, Episode 6: Valley
   of the Shadow of Death—
   1864✸
The Civil War, Episode 7: Most
   Hallowed Ground—1864✸
The Civil War, Episode 8: War Is
   All Hell—1865✸
The Civil War, Episode 9: The
   Better Angels of Our
   Nature—1865✸
Class of '61
Colorado
Copper Canyon
Dark Command✸
Drums in the Deep South
Escape from Fort Bravo
Finger on the Trigger
The Fool Killer
Friendly Persuasion✸
Frontier Pony Express
Frontier Scout
The General✸
General Spanky
Gettysburg✸
The Ghost Brigade
Glory✸
Gone with the Wind✸
The Good, the Bad and the
   Ugly✸
Gore Vidal's Lincoln
Great Day in the Morning
The Great Locomotive Chase
Hangman's Knot
Hellbenders
The Horse Soldiers

How the West Was Won✸
Ironclads
It Happened In New Orleans
Johnny Shiloh
Kansas Pacific
Last Stand at Saber River
Little Women✸
Little Women
Little Women✸
The Littlest Rebel
Louisiana
Love Me Tender
Love's Savage Fury
Macho Callahan
The McMasters
Menace on the Mountain
Mosby's Marauders
Mysterious Island✸
No Drums, No Bugles
North and South Book 1✸
North and South Book 2✸
Of Human Hearts
The Old Maid✸
Oldest Confederate Widow Tells
   All✸
The Ordeal of Dr. Mudd✸
Pharoah's Army
The Private History of a
   Campaign That Failed
Raiders of Ghost City
Raintree County
Rebel Love
Rebel Vixens
The Red Badge of Courage✸
The Rose and the Jackal
Run of the Arrow
The Sacketts
Shadow of Chikara
The Shadow Riders
Shenandoah✸
Sommersby
South of St. Louis
A Southern Yankee
The Supernaturals
Tramplers
True Women
The Undefeated
Virginia City✸
War Brides
Way Down South
Western Gold
Yellowneck

Classic Horror

*see also Horror; Horror
   Anthologies*
The Abominable Dr. Phibes✸
And Now the Screaming Starts
The Ape
The Ape Man
The Appointment
Asylum
Asylum of Satan
Atom Age Vampire
Attack of the Beast Creatures
Attack of the Mayan Mummy
Attack of the Swamp Creature
Avenging Conscience
The Awakening
Barn of the Naked Dead
The Bat✸
The Bat
The Bat People
The Beast from Haunted Cave
Bedlam✸
Before I Hang✸
The Birds✸
The Black Cat✸
The Black Room✸
Black Sabbath✸
The Black Scorpion
Black Sunday✸
Black Werewolf
Blood and Roses
Blood Beast Terror
Blood Island
Blood of Dracula
Blood of Dracula's Castle

Blood of the Vampire
The Bloodsuckers
Bluebeard
The Body Snatcher✸
The Bride
The Bride of Frankenstein✸
Bride of the Gorilla
Bride of the Monster
Bring Me the Vampire
The Brute Man
Burn Witch, Burn!✸
The Cabinet of Dr. Caligari✸
Carnival of Souls✸
Castle of Blood
Castle of Evil
Castle of the Living Dead
Cat Girl
Cat in the Cage
Cat People✸
Cat People
Cauldron of Blood
Cave of the Living Dead
Chamber of Horrors
The Changeling
Circus of Fear
Condemned to Live
The Conqueror Worm✸
Corridors of Blood
Count Dracula
Count Yorga, Vampire
The Crawling Eye
Creature from the Black
   Lagoon✸
Creature of Destruction
Creature of the Walking Dead
The Creature Walks Among Us
Creature with the Blue Hand
The Creeper
The Creeping Flesh
Creeping Terror
Creepshow
Creepshow 2
The Crime of Dr. Crespi
Crimes at the Dark House✸
Crimes of Dr. Mabuse✸
The Crimes of Stephen Hawke
The Crimson Cult
Crucible of Horror
Cry of the Banshee
Cry of the Werewolf
Crypt of the Living Dead
The Curse of Frankenstein✸
Curse of the Devil
Curse of the Swamp Creature
Cyclops
Dance of the Damned
Daughters of Darkness✸
Dementia 13
Demon Barber of Fleet Street
Demons of the Mind
The Devil Bat
The Devil Bat's Daughter
Devil Doll✸
Devil Kiss
Dr. Death, Seeker of Souls
Dr. Jekyll and Mr. Hyde✸
Dr. Jekyll and Mr. Hyde
Doctor X
Dolly Dearest
Dorian Gray
Dracula✸
Dracula
Dracula A.D. 1972
Dracula/Garden of Eden
Dracula (Spanish Version)
Dracula vs. Frankenstein
Dracula's Daughter✸
Dracula's Great Love
Dracula's Last Rites
Dracula's Widow
The Evil of Frankenstein
The Exorcist✸
Eye of the Demon
Eyes of Fire
Eyes of the Panther
The Fall of the House of Usher
The Fall of the House of Usher✸
The Fall of the House of Usher
Fangs of the Living Dead

Steelyard Blues
Stepmonster
The Stick-Up
The Sting 2
Stingray
Stop! or My Mom Will Shoot
Stop That Cab
Stuntwoman
Suburban Commando
Suffering Bastards
The Suitors
Summer Night
Summer Night with Greek
    Profile, Almond Eyes & Scent
    of Basil
Sunburn
Super Fuzz
Super Soul Brother
Surf Nazis Must Die
Surf Ninjas
Survivors
Swashbuckler
The Tall Blond Man with One
    Black Shoe⁄
Tall, Tan and Terrific
A Taxing Woman's Return⁄
Teenage Mutant Ninja Turtles:
    The Movie
Teenage Mutant Ninja Turtles 2:
    The Secret of the Ooze
Teenage Mutant Ninja Turtles 3
Terminal Exposure
That Man from Rio
That Sinking Feeling⁄
They Met in Bombay
The Thief Who Came to Dinner
Think Big
This Time I'll Make You Rich
Those Daring Young Men in
    Their Jaunty Jalopies
Those Fantastic Flying Fools
Those Magnificent Men in Their
    Flying Machines⁄
Three Amigos
Three Fugitives
Three Kinds of Heat
The Three Musketeers⁄
3 Ninjas
3 Ninjas Kick Back
3 Ninjas Knuckle Up
Thunder and Lightning
Thunder in the Pines
Title Shot
Toga Party
Tom and Huck⁄
Too Hot to Handle⁄
Top Dog
Topkapi⁄
Tough Guys
Treasure of the Moon Goddess
Trenchcoat
TripleCross
Trouble in Store
The Trouble with Spies
True Lies
12 Plus 1⁄
Twins
Under the Hula Moon
Under the Rainbow
Up the Creek
Uphill All the Way
Uptown Saturday Night
Van Nuys Blvd.
Vice Academy
Vice Academy 2
Vice Academy 3
Viva Maria!
Wackiest Ship in the Army
We're No Angels
When the Clouds Roll By⁄
Who Killed Mary What's 'Er
    Name?
The Wild and the Free
Wishman
World Gone Wild
Wrong Is Right
Year of the Comet
The Yum-Yum Girls

Coming of Age

see also Teen Angst

A la Mode
A Nos Amours⁄
The Abe Lincoln of Ninth
    Avenue
Across the Great Divide
The Affairs of Annabel
Ah, Wilderness!⁄
Alan & Naomi
All Fall Down
All Over Me⁄
All the Right Moves
All Things Fair
Aloha Summer
Alpine Fire
Amarcord⁄
American Boyfriends
American Graffiti⁄
An American Summer
Among the Cinders
... And the Earth Did Not
    Swallow Him
Angela⁄
Angelo My Love⁄
Anne of Green Gables⁄
Anthony Adverse
Aparajito⁄
The Apprenticeship of Duddy
    Kravitz⁄
Au Revoir Les Enfants⁄
An Awfully Big Adventure
Babe⁄
Baby It's You⁄
Back Door to Heaven⁄
Battling Bunyon
Beautiful Thing⁄
Big⁄
The Big Bet
The Big Red One⁄
Billy Bathgate
Billyboy
The Birch Interval
Blue Fin
Blue Jeans
The Blue Kite⁄
The Blue Lagoon
Blue River
Blue Velvet⁄
Boss' Son⁄
The Boys in Company C
Boys Life
Breaking Away⁄
Breaking Home Ties
Brighton Beach Memoirs
A Bronx Tale⁄
The Buddha of Suburbia⁄
Buddy's Song
By Way of the Stars
Calendar Girl
Can You Feel Me Dancing?
Can't Buy Me Love
Carnal Knowledge⁄
The Chicken Chronicles
China, My Sorrow
Christy
The Cinder Path
Circle of Friends
City Boy⁄
Civil War Diary
Class
Class of '44
The Claw
Closely Watched Trains⁄
Clowning Around 2
Cocktail
Cold Sassy Tree⁄
Come and See⁄
Courage Mountain
Courtship⁄
Crazy Moon
Cria⁄
The Crossing
Crossing the Bridge
A Cry in the Wild⁄
Cry of Battle
Culpepper Cattle Co.

Dakota
Damien: Omen 2
Dancer, Texas Pop. 81⁄
David Holzman's Diary⁄
Dead Beat
Dead Poets Society⁄
December
The Deer Hunter⁄
Desert Bloom⁄
The Devil's Playground⁄
Diner⁄
Dirty Dancing⁄
Dogfight⁄
Dragstrip Girl
D3: The Mighty Ducks
Dutch Girls
The Dwelling Place
Eat Drink Man Woman⁄
The Education of Little Tree⁄
Edward Scissorhands⁄
Ellen Foster
Emanon
Ernesto
Experience Preferred... But Not
    Essential
The Eyes of Youth
Eyes Right!
Family Prayers
Fandango
Fast Times at Ridgemont High⁄
Father⁄
Feelin' Screwy
Fellini Satyricon⁄
Fiesta
The Fire in the Stone
First Affair
First Love
The First Time
The Flamingo Kid⁄
For a Lost Soldier
For Love Alone
Forever
Forever Young
The 400 Blows⁄
Foxes
Freedom Is Paradise⁄
Freud Leaving Home
Friends Forever⁄
A Friendship in Vienna
Frogs!
Gas Food Lodging⁄
A Generation⁄
The Getting of Wisdom
Gidget
A Girl of the Limberlost
The Glass Virgin
Go Tell It On the Mountain
Going All the Way
The Gold & Glory
Goodbye Columbus⁄
Goodbye, Miss 4th of July
Goodbye, My Lady
The Graduate⁄
The Grass Harp
The Great Outdoors
The Great Santini⁄
Gregory's Girl⁄
Grown Ups
Hairspray⁄
Hangin' with the Homeboys⁄
Happy Birthday, Gemini
Hard Choices⁄
Heathers⁄
Heaven Help Us
A Hero Ain't Nothin' But a
    Sandwich
Higher Education
Hole in the Sky
Holy Matrimony
Homeboy
Homework
The Horse⁄
The Horsemen
Hot Moves
The Hour of the Star⁄
How I Learned to Love Women
Huck and the King of Hearts
The Human Comedy⁄
Hurricane Streets

I Don't Want to Talk About It
I Know Why the Caged Bird
    Sings⁄
I Love You, I Love You Not
I Vitelloni⁄
If Looks Could Kill
Il Sorpasso
In Praise of Older Women
In the Custody of Strangers⁄
Indian Paint
The Inheritors
Inventing the Abbotts
The Islander
Jacob Have I Loved
Jerry Maguire⁄
Joey
Johnny Be Good
Jory
The Journey of Natty Gann⁄
Junior High School
The Karate Kid⁄
The Karate Kid: Part 2
The Karate Kid: Part 3
Kicking and Screaming⁄
King of the Gypsies
King of the Hill⁄
Kings Row⁄
Kipperbang
The Kitchen Toto⁄
La Boum
La Symphonie Pastorale⁄
Labyrinth⁄
The Last Prostitute
Late Summer Blues
The Lawrenceville Stories
Le Grand Chemin⁄
Le Sexe des Etoiles
The Learning Tree
Les Mistons⁄
L'Homme Blesse⁄
Life 101
The Lion King⁄
Little Ballerina
A Little Romance⁄
Little Women⁄
Little Women
The Littlest Viking
The Long Day Closes⁄
The Lords of Flatbush
Lost Legacy: A Girl Called Hatter
    Fox
Love Film
Lucas⁄
Maid to Order
The Man from Snowy River
The Man in the Moon⁄
A Man of Passion
The Man Without a Face
The Mango Tree
Martha and I⁄
Matinee
Mean Streets⁄
The Member of the Wedding⁄
The Member of the Wedding
Men of Ireland
Metropolitan⁄
Mickey
A Midnight Clear⁄
Milk Money
Mirrors
Mischief
Monika
More American Graffiti
Mosby's Marauders
Murmur of the Heart⁄
My American Cousin⁄
My Apprenticeship⁄
My Bodyguard⁄
My Brilliant Career⁄
My Girl
My Girl 2
My Life As a Dog⁄
My Tutor
My Universities⁄
Mystic Pizza⁄
Next Stop, Greenwich Village⁄
Nicholas Nickleby⁄
A Night in the Life of Jimmy
    Reardon

1969⁄
No Regrets for Our Youth ⁄
No Secrets
No Time for Sergeants⁄
Norman Loves Rose
The Nostradamus Kid
Now and Then
Odd Birds
Oddballs
Ode to Billy Joe
Oh, What a Night
Old Enough
One on One
Only the Brave
Oranges Are Not the Only Fruit
The Other Side of Sunday
Other Voices, Other Rooms
Out of the Blue⁄
The Outsiders
Over the Edge⁄
Over the Summer
The Pallbearer
Palm Beach
Palookaville⁄
The Paper Chase⁄
Paradise
The Passing of Evil
Pather Panchali⁄
Pauline at the Beach⁄
P.C.U.
Peck's Bad Boy
Peppermint Soda⁄
Peter Lundy and the Medicine
    Hat Stallion
A Place in the World⁄
Platoon⁄
Portrait of a Lady
Portrait of a Lady⁄
The Power of One
The Prodigal
Promised Land⁄
Quadrophenia⁄
Racing with the Moon⁄
Rambling Rose⁄
Ramparts of Clay⁄
The Rascals
The Razor's Edge⁄
The Razor's Edge
The Red Fury
Red Kiss⁄
Red Nights
The Reivers⁄
Reunion⁄
Risky Business⁄
The River⁄
A River Runs Through It⁄
A Room with a View⁄
Rudyard Kipling's The Jungle
    Book
Rumble Fish⁄
The Run of the Country⁄
St. Elmo's Fire
Samurai 1: Musashi Miyamoto⁄
The Sandlot⁄
Sands of Iwo Jima⁄
Sarafina!⁄
Savage Is Loose
Scent of a Woman⁄
The Scent of Green Papaya⁄
Season of Change
A Secret Space
Secrets
A Separate Peace
Seven Minutes in Heaven
Shaking the Tree
Sharma & Beyond
She's Out of Control
Shipwrecked
Shout
Showgirls
Side Show
The Silence of Neto
The Silences of the Palace⁄
Sixteen
The Slingshot⁄
Small Faces⁄
Smooth Talk⁄
Snow: The Movie
Soldier of Orange⁄

Some Kind of Wonderful
Sons of Steel
Sounder↗
Sous Sol
Spanking the Monkey↗
Spy of Napoleon
Square Dance
Stacking
Star Wars↗
Starlight Hotel
The Stripper
Stuckey's Last Stand
Studs Lonigan
Summer Affair
Summer Fantasy
Summer Holiday
Summer Interlude↗
Summer of '42↗
Summer Vacation: 1999
Sunnyside
Sweet 15
Swing Kids
The Sword in the Stone↗
Teenage Mutant Ninja Turtles 2:
    The Secret of the Ooze
Telling Lies in America
Tex
That Brennan Girl
That Naughty Girl
That Night
That Was Then...This Is Now
There Goes My Baby
36 Fillete↗
This Boy's Life↗
Those Glory, Glory Days
Thunder Alley
A Tiger's Tale
Time of the Gypsies↗
Time Stands Still↗
A Time to Remember
Toby Tyler↗
Tomboy & the Champ
Tonio Kroger
Top Gun
Totally F***ed Up
A Tree Grows in Brooklyn↗
Twenty-One
Twist & Shout↗
Two Bits
Two Daughters↗
Unstrung Heroes
Vision Quest
Walking and Talking
Wanderers↗
What's Eating Gilbert Grape↗
Where the Red Fern Grows:
    Part 2
Who Has Seen the Wind?
Who Shot Pat?
Who's That Knocking at My
    Door?↗
Why Shoot the Teacher↗
Wide Awake
Wild America↗
The Wild Child↗
Wild Reeds↗
Winner Takes All
The Wishing Ring↗
With Honors
The Year My Voice Broke↗
The Yearling↗
The Yearling
The Young and the Guilty
The Young Graduates
Young Guns 2
Young Love, First Love
Young Sherlock Holmes
Young Tom Edison
Youngblood
You're a Big Boy Now↗
Zapped!

Computers

*see also Robots &
Androids; Technology-
Rampant*

The Computer Wore Tennis
Shoes

Cyberstalker
Dangerous Game
Demon Seed↗
Desk Set↗
The Double O Kid
Electric Dreams
Evilspeak
Fair Game
Hackers
Hard Drive
Homewrecker
The Honeymoon Machine
Hostile Intent
The Human Factor
Interface
Johnny Mnemonic
Jumpin' Jack Flash
Jurassic Park↗
The Lawnmower Man
Lawnmower Man 2: Beyond
    Cyberspace
Mission: Impossible↗
The Net
Pi
Playing Dangerous
Prime Risk
The Scorpio Factor
Superman 3
Tin Man
Twilight Man
Virtual Assassin
Virtual Desire
WarGames

Concentration/
Internment Camps

*see also Nazis & Other
Paramilitary Slugs; POW/
MIA*

Bent
The Boxer and Death↗
Come See the Paradise↗
Forced March
The Hiding Place
Holocaust↗
I Love You, I Love You Not
The Last Butterfly
Life is Beautiful
Merry Christmas, Mr.
    Lawrence↗
One Day in the Life of Ivan
    Denisovich↗
Paradise Road
Playing for Time↗
Schindler's List↗
Seven Beauties↗
Sophie's Choice↗
A Town Like Alice
Triumph of the Spirit↗

Concert Films

*see also Rock Stars on
Film*

Benny Hill's Crazy World
The Best of Abbott & Costello
    Live
The Best of the Kids in the Hall
Clark & McCullough
Eddie Murphy: Raw
Gimme Shelter
Hollywood Goes to War
Jo Jo Dancer, Your Life Is
    Calling
John Cleese on How to Irritate
    People
The Last Waltz
Lenny↗
Mr. Mike's Mondo Video
Monster in a Box↗
Monterey Pop↗
Monty Python Live at the
    Hollywood Bowl
National Lampoon's Class of '86
Punchline
Scrambled Feet

Search for Signs of Intelligent
    Life in the Universe↗
The Secret Policeman's Other
    Ball↗
Secret Policeman's Private Parts
A Session with the Committee
Sex, Drugs, Rock & Roll: Eric
    Bogosian
Spalding Gray: Terrors of
    Pleasure
Steve Martin Live
Stop Making Sense↗
Wisecracks↗
Woodstock↗
Year of the Horse
You Can't Take It with You↗
You So Crazy

Contemporary
Musicals

see also Musicals

Absolute Beginners
All That Jazz↗
The Apple
Blame It on the Night
Body Beat
Breakin'↗
Breakin' 2: Electric Boogaloo
Breakin' Through
Breaking Glass
A Chorus Line
Fame↗
The Josephine Baker Story↗
One from the Heart

Contemporary Noir

see also Film Noir

After Dark, My Sweet↗
After Hours↗
Against All Odds
Albino Alligator
The American Friend↗
Angel Dust
Angel Heart
Barocco
Betty Blue↗
The Big Easy↗
Blade Runner↗
Blood Simple↗
Blue Velvet↗
Bodies, Rest & Motion
Bodily Harm
Body Double↗
Body Heat↗
Bring Me the Head of Alfredo
    Garcia
Bulletproof Heart↗
Cafe Society
Cape Fear↗
Chinatown↗
Choose Me↗
City of Industry
The Crude Oasis
Cutter's Way
Dance with a Stranger↗
Dark City
Deceiver
Devil in a Blue Dress↗
D.O.A.
Dogwatch
Dressed to Kill
The Driver
Experiment in Terror↗
Eyes of Laura Mars
Fatal Attraction↗
52 Pick-Up
First Degree
The Girl in a Swing
Goodbye, Lover
The Grifters↗
Guncrazy
Hammett
Hard Eight↗
The Horseplayer
The Hot Spot
Husbands and Lovers

The Hustle
Kill Me Again
The Kill-Off
Killing Zoe
Kiss of Death
L.A. Confidential↗
The Last Seduction↗
Le Samourai↗
Live Flesh↗
The Locusts
The Long Goodbye↗
Love Walked In
The Manchurian Candidate↗
Manhunter↗
Marlowe
Mirage
Mulholland Falls
The Music of Chance
Narrow Margin
Night Moves↗
9 1/2 Weeks
No Way Out↗
One False Move↗
Palmetto
Performance↗
Promised Land↗
The Public Eye↗
Pulp Fiction↗
Purple Noon↗
Red Rock West↗
Reservoir Dogs↗
The Rich Man's Wife
River of Grass
Romeo Is Bleeding
sex, lies and videotape↗
Shattered
The Silence of the Lambs↗
Something Wild
The Spanish Prisoner↗
Stormy Monday
Taxi Driver↗
Tequila Sunrise
Things to Do In Denver When
    You're Dead↗
This World, Then the Fireworks
To Live & Die in L.A.↗
Track 29
Trouble in Mind↗
True Believer
True Confessions↗
Twilight↗
Twin Peaks
Two Days in the Valley↗
The Two Jakes
U-Turn
The Underneath↗
Union City
The Usual Suspects↗
Who'll Stop the Rain?↗
Wild at Heart↗
Wild Orchid
Wild Orchid 2: Two Shades of
    Blue
Wild Things

Cooking

see Edibles

Cops

*see also Buddy Cops;
Canine Cops; Detectives;
Future Cops; Loner Cops;
Women Cops*

Above Suspicion
Abraxas: Guardian of the
    Universe
Across 110th Street
Action Jackson
Adrenalin: Fear the Rush
The Adventures of a Gnome
    Named Gnorm
Alien Nation
Alone in the Neon Jungle
American Cop
American Justice
The Amsterdam Kill

Animal Instincts
Arizona Heat
Armed and Dangerous
Assault on Precinct 13↗
At Gunpoint
Back in Action
Back in Business
Backstreet Justice
Bad Boys
B.A.D. Cats
Bad Lieutenant↗
Badge of the Assassin
Badge 373
Ballbuster
Ballistic
Band of the Hand
Bang
Before Morning
Belfast Assassin
Bellamy
Beretta's Island
Best Kept Secrets
Best Seller↗
Beverly Hills Cop↗
Beverly Hills Cop 2
Beverly Hills Cop 3
Beyond Forgiveness
Beyond the Law
Big Chase
Big Combo↗
The Big Easy↗
The Big Heat↗
Big Score
The Big Slice
Black Day Blue Night
Black Dragon
Black Eliminator
The Black Marble↗
Black Rain
Blackmail↗
Blackout
Blade
Blade Boxer
Blind Faith
Blink
Blood for Blood
Blood on the Badge
Bloodfist 7: Manhunt
Bloodhounds
Bloody Avenger
Blown Away
Blue Desert
Blue Flame
The Blue Knight
The Blue Lamp↗
Blue Steel
Blue Thunder
Blues Brothers 2000
Bodily Harm
Bophal↗
The Boston Strangler
Brainscan
Brannigan
Brass
Breach of Trust
Breaking Point
Broken Badge↗
Bulletproof
Bullets or Ballots↗
Bunco
Busting
Cafe Society
Car 54, Where Are You?
Caroline at Midnight
The Carpathian Eagle
Carpool
A Case of Deadly Force↗
Champion Operation
The Chase
Chiefs
China Moon
Chinatown Connection
The Chinatown Murders: Man
    Against the Mob
Choice of Weapons
The Choirboys
Chungking Express↗
City Hall↗
City Heat

Crime

Crime Drama

Crime Sprees

Zontar, the Thing from Venus

Cult Items Now

see also Cult Items

The Adventures of Baron
  Munchausen↗
Airplane!↗
Better Off Dead
Bill & Ted's Excellent Adventure
The Blues Brothers↗
The Brady Bunch Movie↗
The Breakfast Club↗
Caddyshack
Fast Times at Ridgemont High↗
Ferris Bueller's Day Off↗
A Fish Called Wanda↗
Grease↗
Heathers↗
I Shot Andy Warhol↗
Joe's Apartment
Mystery Science Theater 3000:
  The Movie
National Lampoon's Animal
  House↗
Pretty in Pink
Real Genius↗
St. Elmo's Fire
Saturday Night Fever
Sixteen Candles↗
The Sure Thing↗
This Is Spinal Tap↗
The Untold Story
Wayne's World↗

Cults

see also Occult; Satanism

Bad Dreams
The Believers
Beware! Children at Play
Blinded by the Light
Blood Clan
Bloodbath
Burial of the Rats
Children of the Corn 2: The Final
  Sacrifice
Cobra Woman
Cult of the Cobra
The Dark Secret of Harvest
  Home
Deadly Blessing
Death of an Angel
The Deceivers
Divided by Hate
Fatal Passion
Force: Five
Forever Evil
The Guyana Tragedy: The Story
  of Jim Jones
Helter Skelter
Helter Skelter Murders
The House on Todville Road
In the Line of Duty: Ambush in
  Waco
The Lightning Incident
Lord of Illusions
The Mephisto Waltz↗
Mind, Body & Soul
Next One
The Night God Screamed
Night of the Death Cult
Putney Swope↗
The Pyx↗
Raging Angels
The Reincarnate
Rest in Pieces
Revenge
Sabaka
Safe↗
Servants of Twilight
Shock 'Em Dead
Shocking Asia
The Snake Hunter Strangler
The Snake People
The Spellbinder
Split Image↗
Steps from Hell

Suicide Cult
Thou Shalt Not Kill...Except
Ticket to Heaven↗
Treasure of the Four Crowns
Withnail and I↗

Culture Clash

At Play in the Fields of the Lord↗
The Beverly Hillbillies
Black Robe↗
The Brother from Another
  Planet↗
Brothers in Trouble
Cabaret↗
City of Joy
Coneheads
Conrack↗
Dead Heart↗
Deliverance↗
The Emerald Forest↗
Encino Man
The Europeans↗
For Richer or Poorer
George of the Jungle↗
Gorillas in the Mist↗
Greystoke: The Legend of
  Tarzan, Lord of the Apes
Heat and Dust↗
Lawrence of Arabia↗
Leningrad Cowboys Go America
The Mission↗
Mississippi Masala↗
Mister Johnson↗
Moonlighting↗
Moscow on the Hudson↗
A Passage to India↗
Quigley Down Under
Rush Hour
The Sheltering Sky↗
Shogun↗
Someone Else's America↗
Splash
Starman↗
Swept from the Sea
Thunderheart↗
Witness↗
Zorba the Greek↗

Cyberpunk

Arcade
Blade Runner↗
The Crow 2: City of Angels
Cyborg
Cyborg 2
Cyborg Cop
Cyborg Soldier
Demolition Man
Escape from L.A.
Escape from New York
The Fifth Element
Freejack
Ghost in the Shell
Hackers
Johnny Mnemonic
The Lawnmower Man
Lawnmower Man 2: Beyond
  Cyberspace
Mad Max↗
Mad Max: Beyond
  Thunderdome
Megaville
Nemesis
Overdrawn at the Memory Bank
The Road Warrior↗
RoboCop↗
RoboCop 2
RoboCop 3
Tank Girl
TekWar
The Terminator↗
Terminator 2: Judgment Day↗
Tetsuo 2: Body Hammer
Tetsuo: The Iron Man
Total Recall↗
Tron

Universal Soldier
Virtual Combat
Virtuosity

Dads

**see also Bad Dads; Moms;
  Monster Moms; Parenthood**

Address Unknown
The Adventures of Pinocchio
The Brady Bunch Movie↗
Broken English
Bye Bye, Love
Carpool
Dad
Eat Drink Man Woman↗
Eden Valley
Father of the Bride↗
Father's Day
The Favorite Son↗
Fear
Getting Even with Dad
Ghost Dad
A Goofy Movie
Honey, We Shrunk Ourselves
House Arrest
Imaginary Crimes↗
In His Father's Shoes
In the Gloaming↗
Indiana Jones and the Last
  Crusade↗
Invisible Dad
Jingle All the Way
Jungle 2 Jungle
Kolya↗
Liar Liar
Life with Father↗
Like Father, Like Son
Lone Star↗
Magic in the Water
Memories of Me
Mr. Mom↗
Mom and Dad Save the World
My Father Is Coming
My Father the Hero
My Stepmother Is an Alien
National Lampoon's Christmas
  Vacation
National Lampoon's Dad's Week
  Off
National Lampoon's European
  Vacation
National Lampoon's Vacation↗
Nick of Time
Parenthood↗
Raising Arizona↗
The Run of the Country↗
The Shepherd of the Hills↗
She's the One
A Simple Wish
Sleepless in Seattle↗
So I Married an Axe Murderer
The Stupids
The Sum of Us↗
Superdad
Three Men and a Baby↗
Three Men and a Cradle↗
Three Men and a Little Lady
A Time to Kill↗
To Gillian on Her 37th Birthday
A Very Brady Sequel
Wait Till Your Mother Gets
  Home
The War at Home

Dance Fever

**see also Ballet; Disco
  Musicals**

Alive and Kicking
All That Jazz↗
An American in Paris↗
Anchors Aweigh↗
April In Paris
Babes in Arms
The Bacchantes
The Band Wagon↗
The Barefoot Contessa↗

The Barkleys of Broadway↗
Beat Street
The Belle of New York
Bert Rigby, You're a Fool
The Best of the Kenny Everett
  Video Show
Billy Rose's Jumbo↗
Black Orpheus↗
Blood Wedding↗
Body Moves
Body Rock
Boogie Nights↗
Born to Dance
Breakin'
Breakin' 2: Electric Boogaloo
Breakin' Through
Broadway Melody of 1940
Cabin in the Sky↗
Can-Can
Captain January
Carefree↗
Carmen↗
Charleston↗
A Chorus Line
Chu Chu & the Philly Flash
Cover Girl↗
Curdled
Daddy Long Legs↗
Dames↗
Dance or Die
Dance With Me
Dancing Lady
Danzon↗
Deadly Dancer
Delightfully Dangerous
Delivery Boys
Dirty Dancing↗
The Discovery Program
Doll Face
The Eighties
El Amor Brujo↗
Everybody's Dancin'
Everyone Says I Love You↗
Faith
Fame↗
Fass Black
Fast Forward
Faster Pussycat! Kill! Kill!
Femmes de Paris
Flashdance
Flower Drum Song
Flying Down to Rio
Follies Girl
Follow the Fleet↗
Footlight Parade↗
Footloose
The Forbidden Dance
42nd Street↗
French Can-Can↗
The Gay Divorcee↗
Ginger & Fred↗
Girl in Gold Boots
Girls Just Want to Have Fun
Give a Girl a Break
The Glass Slipper
Gold Diggers of 1933↗
Gold Diggers of 1935↗
Gotta Dance, Gotta Sing
Grease↗
Grease 2
The Harvey Girls↗
Heavenly Bodies
Hit the Deck
Holiday in Havana
Idiot's Delight↗
The In Crowd
Isadora↗
It Started in Naples↗
Kiss Me Kate↗
Lambada
Last Dance
The Last Dance
Le Bal↗
Legs
Les Girls
Let's Dance
Liquid Dreams
Little Ballerina
Mad Youth

Manhattan Merengue!
Mantis in Lace
Meet Me in Las Vegas
Michael
Midnight Dancer
Minsky's Follies
Music in My Heart
Neurotic Cabaret
No Time for Romance
Nutcracker: The Motion Picture
Orgy of the Dead
Out to Sea
Paris Is Burning↗
Party Girl↗
Pennies From Heaven↗
Pilot
The Pirate↗
Portrait of a Showgirl
Portrait of a Stripper
Queen of the Stardust
  Ballroom↗
Risky Business↗
Roberta↗
Romance in Manhattan
Rooftops
Roseland↗
Salome, Where She Danced
Salsa
Saturday Night Fever
Scent of a Woman↗
Second Chorus
Seven Brides for Seven
  Brothers↗
Shag: The Movie↗
Shall We Dance↗
Shall We Dance?↗
Showgirls
Silk Stockings↗
Singin' in the Rain↗
Slashdance
So This Is Paris↗
Spirit of '76
Staying Alive
Stepping Out↗
The Story of Vernon and Irene
  Castle↗
Strictly Ballroom↗
Stripped to Kill II: Live Girls
Summer Stock↗
Sunset Strip
Sweet Charity↗
Swing Kids
Swing Time↗
Take Me Out to the Ball Game
Tango
Tango Bar
The Tango Lesson
Tap
Taxi Dancers
Teen Wolf
Thank God It's Friday
That's Dancing!
That's Entertainment, Part 2
That's Entertainment, Part 3
They Shoot Horses, Don't
  They?↗
Those Lips, Those Eyes
Top Hat↗
The Turning Point
Urban Cowboy
What's the Matter with Helen?
Words and Music
Yankee Doodle Dandy↗
You Were Never Lovelier↗
You'll Never Get Rich↗
Ziegfeld Follies
Ziegfeld Girl↗
Zou Zou

Dates From Hell

see also Singles

After Hours↗
Blind Date
Bye Bye, Love
Ed's Next Move
Harold and Maude↗
Night of the Creeps
Reality Bites

Detectives

Detroit
see I Love Detroit

Devils
Beauty and the Devil

The Craft
Dark Angel: The Ascent
The Devil & Max Devlin
The Devils♪
The Devil's Advocate
Faust♪
Gates of Hell 2: Dead
    Awakening
God, Man and Devil
Guardian of the Abyss
Haunted Symphony
Hell's Belles
High Strung
Highway to Hell
Judgment Day
Legend
Les Visiteurs du Soir♪
Magic Hunter
The Mangler
Mr. Frost
Mother Joan of the Angels♪
Needful Things
The Prophecy
Second Time Lucky
The Sorrows of Satan♪
Stephen King's The Stand
Tales from the Hood
The Witches of Eastwick

Devil's Island

see also Great Escapes;
Men in Prison

Papillon♪
Passage to Marseilles♪
We're No Angels

Dinosaurs

see also Killer Beasts

Adventures in Dinosaur City
At the Earth's Core
Baby ... Secret of the Lost
    Legend
Barney's Great Adventure
Carnosaur
Carnosaur 2
Carnosaur 3: Primal Species
Caveman
Clifford
The Crater Lake Monster
Dennis the Menace: Dinosaur
    Hunter
Dinosaur Island
Dinosaur Valley Girls
Dinosaurus!
Ganjasaurus Rex
Josh Kirby...Time Warrior:
    Chapter 1, Planet of the Dino-
    Knights
Jurassic Park♪
King Dinosaur
The Land Before Time♪
The Land Before Time 2: The
    Great Valley Adventure
The Land Before Time 3: The
    Time of the Great Giving
The Land Before Time 4:
    Journey Through the Mists
The Land Before Time 5: The
    Mysterious Island
The Land that Time Forgot
The Land Unknown
The Lost Continent
The Lost World
The Lost World: Jurassic Park 2
Massacre in Dinosaur Valley
My Science Project
A Nymphoid Barbarian in
    Dinosaur Hell
One Million B.C.
One Million Years B.C.
One of Our Dinosaurs Is Missing
The People That Time Forgot
Planet of Dinosaurs
Prehysteria
Prehysteria 2
Prehysteria 3

Pterodactyl Woman from
    Beverly Hills
Return to the Lost World
Sound of Horror
Super Mario Bros.
Tammy and the T-Rex
Teenage Caveman
Theodore Rex
Toy Story♪
Two Lost Worlds
Unknown Island
The Valley of Gwangi♪
We're Back! A Dinosaur's Story
When Dinosaurs Ruled the
    Earth

Disaster Flicks

see also Action Adventure;
Air Disasters; Meltdown;
Sea Disasters

Accident
After the Shock
Airport♪
Airport '75
Airport '77
Alive
Armageddon
Assignment Outer Space
Asteroid
Avalanche
Avalanche Express
Beyond the Poseidon Adventure
The Big Bus
The Cassandra Crossing
The China Syndrome♪
City on Fire
The Concorde: Airport '79
The Crash of Flight 401
Dante's Peak
Daylight
Dead Ahead: The Exxon Valdez
    Disaster♪
Deep Impact
The Doomsday Flight
Earthquake
Final Warning
Fire
Fire and Rain
Firestorm
Firestorm: 72 Hours in Oakland
Flood!
Flood: A River's Rampage
Gray Lady Down
Hard Rain
The Hindenburg
The Hurricane♪
Hurricane
In Old Chicago
Independence Day♪
Last Days of Pompeii
The Last Voyage
The Last Woman on Earth
The Lost Missile
Meteor
A Night to Remember♪
Planet on the Prowl
The Poseidon Adventure
The Rains Came
Raise the Titanic
Red Alert
St. Helen's, Killer Volcano
Snowblind
Snowbound
S.O.S. Titanic
Space: 1999—Alien Attack♪
The Survivalist
Survivor
Tailspin: Behind the Korean
    Airline Tragedy
Terror on the 40th Floor
Tidal Wave
Titanic♪
The Towering Inferno
Tragedy of Flight 103: The
    Inside Story♪
Twister
Two Minute Warning

Volcano
Volcano: Fire on the Mountain
When Time Ran Out
White Squall

Disco Musicals

see also Musicals

Can't Stop the Music
Car Wash
KISS Meets the Phantom of the
    Park
Pirate Movie
The Rocky Horror Picture
    Show♪
Saturday Night Fever
Thank God It's Friday
The Wiz
Xanadu

Disease of the Week

see also AIDS; Emerging
Viruses

The Affair♪
The Ann Jillian Story
Bang the Drum Slowly
Beaches♪
The Best Little Girl in the World♪
Between Two Women
Bobby Deerfield
The Boy in the Plastic Bubble
Brian's Song♪
Camille♪
The Carrier
The Cassandra Crossing
Champions
Checking Out
Children of the Corn 4: The
    Gathering
Chinese Box
C.H.U.D.
Cleo from 5 to 7♪
Contagious
Cries and Whispers♪
Crystal Heart
The Curse
Damien: The Leper Priest
Daybreak
Dead Man Walking
Dead Space
Dick Barton, Special Agent
The Doctor
A Dream of Kings♪
Duet for One
Dying Young
An Early Frost♪
East of Kilimanjaro
The End♪
Eric♪
The First Deadly Sin
First Do No Harm
Fourth Wish
Gaby: A True Story♪
Germicide
Glory Enough for All: The
    Discovery of Insulin
Go Now♪
Griffin and Phoenix: A Love
    Story
Incredible Melting Man
Interrupted Melody♪
Intimate Contact♪
Isle of the Dead
Jack
Jericho Fever
John Grisham's The Rainmaker
Killer on Board
L.A. Bad
The Last Best Year
Last Breath
The Last Man on Earth
Lightning Over Water
Lorenzo's Oil♪
Love Affair: The Eleanor & Lou
    Gehrig Story♪
Love Story♪
Mad Death

Marvin's Room
A Matter of WHO
Millou to Go
Miss Evers' Boys
A Mother's Prayer
My Father's House
My Life
Nasty Rabbit
Niagara, Niagara
On Her Majesty's Secret
    Service♪
Panic in Echo Park
Parting Glances♪
Philadelphia♪
Pilgrim, Farewell
The Plague
The Plague Dogs
The Pride of the Yankees♪
Princes in Exile
Project: Alien
Promises in the Dark
The Proud Ones
Quarantine
Question of Faith
A Quiet Duel
Rabid
Rasputin: Dark Servant of
    Destiny♪
Reborn
Right of Way
The Road to Galveston
The Road to Wellville
The Shadow Box♪
Shadowlands♪
A Shining Season♪
Silence Like Glass
The Silver Streak
Six Weeks
Stigma
Sunchaser
Terms of Endearment♪
Terror Creatures from the Grave
A Time to Live
Walking Through the Fire
The Wedding Gift♪
When the Time Comes
When Wolves Cry
The White Legion
Xtro

Disorganized Crime

see also Crime &
Criminals; Organized Crime

Ace Crawford, Private Eye
Airheads
Albino Alligator
Amos and Andrew
The Apple Dumpling Gang
The Apple Dumpling Gang
    Rides Again
Armed and Dangerous
Baby on Board
Baby's Day Out
Bottle Rocket
Cop and a Half
Crackers
Disorganized Crime
Dr. Otto & the Riddle of the
    Gloom Beam
8 Heads in a Duffel Bag
Ernest Goes to Jail
Fargo♪
Finders Keepers
A Fine Mess
Get Shorty♪
Glitch!
Gravesend
Gridlock'd♪
The Gun in Betty Lou's Handbag
Happy New Year
Headless Body in Topless Bar
Her Alibi
Herbie Goes Bananas
Home Alone♪
Home Alone 2: Lost in New York
I Wonder Who's Killing Her
    Now?
Inside the Law

The Italian Job
The Jerky Boys
Keys to Tulsa
Kicked in the Head
Killing Zoe
The League of Gentlemen♪
Leather Jackets
Lunch Wagon
Mad Dog and Glory♪
A Man, a Woman, and a Bank
Man of the House
Menage♪
Mexican Hayride
Milo Milo
Miss Grant Takes Richmond
Mixed Nuts
Mutant on the Bounty
The Night They Robbed Big
    Bertha's
Ocean's 11
Once Upon a Crime
101 Dalmatians
Oscar
Out on a Limb
Palookaville♪
Pouvoir Intime
Quick Change
Ransom Money
Reservoir Dogs♪
Round Trip to Heaven
Ruthless People♪
St. Benny the Dip
See No Evil, Hear No Evil
Shake Hands with Murder
The Shot
Silver Bears
Sister Act
Sitting Ducks♪
Stop! My Mom Will Shoot
Stop That Cab
Suicide Kings
The Super
Super Soul Brother
Survivors
Tall, Tan and Terrific
The Thief Who Came to Dinner
Things to Do In Denver When
    You're Dead♪
Three Kinds of Heat
Thrilled to Death
Too Many Crooks
Trapped In Paradise
Truth or Consequences, N.M.
Two If by Sea
We're Talkin' Serious Money
The Wrong Arm of the Law♪
The Young in Heart♪

Divorce

see also Marriage; Singles

The Accidental Tourist♪
All I Want for Christmas
Alpha Beta
The Awful Truth♪
Between Friends
A Bill of Divorcement
Breaking Up
Breaking Up Is Hard to Do
Bye Bye, Love
California Suite♪
Can She Bake a Cherry Pie?
Cheaper to Keep Her
Children of Divorce
Clara's Heart
Cold Heat
A Conspiracy of Love
Cross My Heart
Desert Hearts♪
Divorce American Style
Divorce His, Divorce Hers
Divorce—Italian Style♪
The Divorcee
Early Frost
Edie & Pen
Escapade♪
E.T.: The Extra-Terrestrial♪
Every Other Weekend♪
The Ex

Drama

Drama

Drama

Long Read Home
The Long Voyage Home↗
The Long Walk Home↗
A Long Way Home
The Long Weekend
The Longest Day↗
Longtime Companion↗
Look Back in Anger
Look Back in Anger
Look Back in Anger↗
The Lookalike
Looking for Miracles
Looking for Mr. Goodbar
The Looking Glass War
Lord Jim↗
Lord of the Flies↗
Lord of the Flies
The Lords of Discipline
The Lords of Flatbush
Lorenzo's Oil↗
Lorna Doone
Los Olvidados↗
The Losers
Losing Chase
Losing Isaiah↗
Lost Angels
Lost Boundaries
Lost Highway
The Lost Honor of Katharina
    Blum↗
Lost Horizon↗
Lost in the Barrens
The Lost Language of Cranes↗
Lost Legacy: A Girl Called Hatter
    Fox
Lost Moment
The Lost One
The Lost Weekend↗
The Lost World
Lotna
Lotto Land
The Lotus Eaters
Love↗
Love and a .45
Love Child
Love Field
Love Film
Love for Lydia
Love Leads the Way
The Love Machine
Love Matters
Love on the Dole↗
Love Strange Love
Love Under Pressure
Love Your Mama
Loved
Loveless
Lovely ... But Deadly
The Loves of Edgar Allen Poe
Lovey: A Circle of Children 2
The Lower Depths↗
Loyalties
Loyola, the Soldier Saint
Lucy and Desi: Before the
    Laughter
Lumiere
Luna Park
Lush Life
Lust for Freedom
Lust for Life↗
Luzia
M. Butterfly
Ma Barker's Killer Brood
Ma Saison Preferee↗
Maborosi↗
Mac↗
MacArthur
MacArthur's Children↗
Machine Gun Kelly
Machine to Kill Bad People
The Mack
Macon County Line
Macumba Love
Mad About Music↗
Mad City
Mad Death
Mad Dog Morgan
The Mad Whirl
Mad Youth

Madame Bovary↗
Madame Curie↗
Madame Rosa↗
Madame X
M.A.D.D.: Mothers Against
    Drunk Driving
Made in Argentina
Mademoiselle
Mademoiselle Fifi
The Madness of King George↗
Madonna: Innocence Lost
The Madwoman of Chaillot
Mae West
Maedchen in Uniform↗
Magdalene
Magee and the Lady
The Magic Bubble
The Magic Flute↗
Magic of Lassie
The Magic of the Golden Bear:
    Goldy 3
The Magician↗
The Magnificent Ambersons↗
The Magnificent Yankee↗
Mahogany
Maids of Wilko
Maitresse
Major Barbara↗
Make Me an Offer
Make-Up
Making Love
The Makioka Sisters↗
Malarek
Malcolm X↗
Malibu High
Malicious
Malou
Malta Story
Mamma Roma↗
A Man Called Adam
A Man Called Peter↗
A Man Escaped↗
Man Facing Southeast↗
Man Friday
The Man in the Glass Booth↗
The Man in the Gray Flannel
    Suit
Man in the Wilderness
A Man in Uniform
The Man Inside
A Man Like Eva↗
Man of a Thousand Faces↗
Man of Flowers
Man of Iron↗
Man of Marble↗
A Man of No Importance↗
A Man of Passion
Man of Violence
Man on the Run
The Man Outside
The Man Who Broke 1,000
    Chains
The Man Who Captured
    Eichmann
The Man Who Cried
The Man Who Laughs↗
The Man Who Never Was↗
Man with a Cross
The Man with the Golden Arm↗
The Man Without a Face
Man, Woman & Child
Mandinga
Mandingo
Mandy↗
The Mango Tree
Manhattan Melodrama↗
Manhunter
Maniac
The Manions of America
Manipulator
Manny & Lo↗
Manon of the Spring↗
Mansfield Park
Marat/Sade↗
Marbella
Marciano
Marianne and Juliane↗
Maria's Day↗
Maria's Lovers

Maricela
Marie↗
Marilyn: The Untold Story↗
Marine Raiders
The Mark of the Hawk↗
Mark Twain and Me
Marked Woman↗
Marquis de Sade
A Married Man
Married People, Single Sex
Married People, Single Sex 2:
    For Better or Worse
Married Too Young
A Married Woman↗
Martin Chuzzlewit
Martin's Day
Marvin & Tige
Mary and Joseph: A Story of
    Faith
Mary, My Dearest
Mary White
Masculine Feminine↗
Mask↗
The Mask of Dijon
Mass Appeal
Massacre at Central High
Massacre in Rome
Masseuse
Master Harold and the Boys↗
Master of the House↗
Master Race
Mata Hari↗
The Match Factory Girl↗
Matewan↗
A Matter of Dignity
A Matter of Honor
A Matter of Life and Death
A Matter of Principle
Maurice↗
Max
Max and Helen
Maximum Security
Maybe I'll Be Home in the Spring
Mayflower Madam
Mayhem
McKenzie Break↗
McVicar
Me & Veronica
Mean Dog Blues
Medea
The Mediterranean in Flames
Medium Cool↗
Meet Dr. Christian
Meet John Doe↗
Meet Sexton Blake
Meetings with Remarkable Men
Melanie
Melanie Darrow
Melody for Three
The Member of the Wedding↗
The Member of the Wedding
Memorial Day
Memories of a Marriage↗
Memories of Underdevelopment
Memory of Us
Memphis
The Men↗
Men Are Not Gods
Men in Love
Men of Boys Town
Men of Ireland
Men of Two Worlds
The Men Who Tread on the
    Tiger's Tail
The Men's Club
Mephisto↗
The Merchant of Four Seasons↗
The Merchant of Venice↗
Mercy Mission
The Mermaids of Tiburon
Merry Christmas, Mr.
    Lawrence↗
Mesmerized
The Messenger of the Blessed
    Virgin
The Messiah↗
Messidor
Mickey
Mickey One

Mid-Channel
Mid Knight Rider
The Midas Touch
The Middleman
A Midnight Clear↗
Midnight Cop
Midnight Cowboy↗
Midnight Dancer
Midnight Dancers
Midnight Express↗
Midnight in the Garden of Good
    and Evil
The Mighty Pawns
The Migrants
Mikey & Nicky
Miles from Home
Miles to Go before I Sleep
Millions
Mina Tannenbaum
Mindwalk: A Film for Passionate
    Thinkers↗
Mine Own Executioner↗
A Minor Miracle
The Miracle↗
The Miracle
Miracle at Moreaux
Miracle Down Under
Miracle in Harlem
Miracle in Rome
Miracle Kid
Miracle of Our Lady of Fatima
The Miracle of the Bells
Miracle of the Heart: A Boys
    Town Story
The Miracle of the White
    Stallions
Miracle on Ice
Miracle on 34th Street↗
The Miracle Woman
The Miracle Worker↗
Mirele Efros
The Mirror↗
The Misfits↗
Mishima: A Life in Four
    Chapters↗
Miss A & Miss M
Miss All-American Beauty
Ms. Bear
Miss Mary
Miss Melody Jones
Miss Rose White↗
Missing↗
Mission of the Shark
Mission to Glory
Mississippi Burning↗
Missouri Traveler↗
Mrs. Brown↗
Mrs. Dalloway
Mrs. Miniver↗
Mrs. Parker and the Vicious
    Circle
Mrs. Parkington
Mrs. R's Daughter
Mr. Ace
Mr. & Mrs. Bridge↗
Mr. Arkadin↗
Mr. Corbett's Ghost
Mr. Emmanuel
Mister Halpren & Mister Johnson
Mr. Inside, Mr. Outside
Mister Johnson↗
Mr. Klein↗
Mr. Smith Goes to Washington↗
Mistral's Daughter
Mistress↗
Mistress Pamela
Mistrial
Misunderstood
Mo' Better Blues
The Moderns↗
Modigliani
Mohammed: Messenger of God
Molly Maguires
Mommie Dearest
Mon Amie Max
Mon Oncle Antoine↗
Mona Lisa↗
Money to Burn
A Mongolian Tale

Monika
Monkey Grip↗
Monsieur Beaucaire
Monsieur Vincent↗
Monsignor
Monsignor Quixote
Monte Carlo
Monte Carlo Nights
A Month in the Country↗
The Moon and Sixpence↗
Moon in the Gutter
Moonlight and Valentino
Moonlighting↗
Moonrise
Moonshine Highway
Moonshine Mountain
Morals for Women
More
Morituri↗
Morning Glory
Mortal Danger
The Mortal Storm↗
Mortal Thoughts
Moscow Does Not Believe in
    Tears↗
Moscow Parade
Moses
The Mosquito Coast
Most Wanted
Mother↗
Mother & Daughter: A Loving
    War
Mother and Son
Mother Doesn't Always Know
    Best
Mother Joan of the Angels↗
Mother Kusters Goes to
    Heaven↗
Mother Night↗
Mother of Kings
Mother Teresa: In the Name of
    God's Poor
A Mother's Prayer
Motorcycle Gang
Mouchette↗
Moulin Rouge↗
The Mountain
The Mountain Road
A Movie Star's Daughter
Movie Stuntmen
Moving Out
Moving Violation
Mozart: A Childhood Chronicle↗
The Mozart Story
Murder Elite
Murder for Sale
Murder in Coweta County
Murder In the First
Murder in the Old Red Barn
The Murder of Mary Phagan↗
Murder on Lenox Avenue
Murder on the Bayou↗
Murder Ordained
Murderers Are Among Us
Muriel↗
Murph the Surf
Murphy's War
Murrow
Music Box
The Music of Chance
The Music Teacher
Mussolini & I
The Muthers
Mutiny in the Big House
Mutual Respect
My Apprenticeship↗
My Boy
My Boys Are Good Boys
My Brilliant Career↗
My Childhood↗
My Family↗
My Father, My Rival
My Father's Glory↗
My Father's House
My First Wife
My Girl Tisa
My Left Foot↗
My Life

Drama

Vision Quest
Vital Signs
Vortex
Voyage en Douce
Voyage in Italy
Voyage of Terror: The Achille
  Lauro Affair
Voyage of the Damned✒
A Voyage' Round My Father✒
Voyage to Italy
The Voyeur
Vukovar✒
Wager of Love
Wages of Fear✒
Wagner: The Complete Epic
Wagner: The Movie
Waiting for the Moon
Waiting to Exhale✒
Walkabout✒
The Walking Dead
Walking on Air
Walking Tall
Walking Tall: Part 2
Walking Tall: The Final Chapter
Walking the Edge
Walking Through the Fire
The Wall✒
Wall Street✒
The Waltons: The Christmas
  Carol
Wanda, the Sadistic Hypnotist
Wanderers✒
Wandering Jew
Wanted: The Perfect Guy
The War
War & Remembrance, Part 1
War & Remembrance, Part 2
War & Remembrance, Part 3
War & Remembrance, Part 4
War & Remembrance, Part 5
War & Remembrance, Part 6
War & Remembrance, Part 7
War & Remembrance: The Final
  Chapter, Part 8
War & Remembrance: The Final
  Chapter, Part 9
War & Remembrance: The Final
  Chapter, Part 10
War & Remembrance: The Final
  Chapter, Part 11
War & Remembrance: The Final
  Chapter, Part 12
The War at Home
War Between the Tates
War Brides
War of the Buttons
Ward Six
WarGames
The Warning
Warning Shadows✒
The Wash✒
Washington Affair
Washington Square✒
Watch on the Rhine✒
The Water Engine
The Waterdance✒
Waterfront
Waterland
Way Back Home
The Wayward Wife
We Are the Children
We of the Never Never✒
We Will Not Enter the Forest✒
The Wedding Gift✒
A Wedding in Galilee✒
Wedding in White
Wee Willie Winkie✒
Weeds✒
Weekend✒
Weekend of Shadows✒
Welcome to L.A.
Welcome to Sarajevo✒
The Well
Well-Digger's Daughter✒
Wend Kuuni
Westfront 1918✒
Wetherby✒
Whale for the Killing
Whale Music

Whale of a Tale
The Whales of August✒
The Wharf Rat
What Comes Around
What Happened Was...
What Price Glory?✒
What Price Hollywood?✒
What the Moon Saw
What's Eating Gilbert Grape✒
When a Man Loves a Woman
When a Woman Ascends the
  Stairs
When Danger Follows You
  Home
When Every Day was the Fourth
  of July
When Father was Away on
  Business✒
When Gangland Strikes
When Hell Was in Session✒
When He's Not a Stranger✒
When the Greeks
When the Line Goes Through
When the Party's Over
When the Whales Came
When Wolves Cry
Where
Where Angels Fear to Tread✒
Where Have All the People
  Gone?
Where Is My Child?
Where Is My Friend's House?✒
Where Love Has Gone
Where the Day Takes You
Where the Eagle Flies
Where the Green Ants Dream
Where the Hot Wind Blows
Where the Lilies Bloom✒
Where the Red Fern Grows:
  Part 2
Where the Rivers Flow North
While the City Sleeps✒
Whistle Down the Wind✒
The White Balloon✒
White Heat✒
White Hunter, Black Heart✒
The White Legion
White Lie
White Mama✒
White Mane✒
White Man's Burden
White Mile
White Nights
White Shadows in the South
  Seas
The White Sin
White Tiger
Who Shot Pat?
The Whole Wide World✒
Who'll Save Our Children?✒
Who'll Stop the Rain?✒
Whore
Whore 2
Who's Afraid of Virginia Woolf?✒
Who's That Knocking at My
  Door?✒
Whose Child Am I?
Why Has Bodhi-Darma Left for
  the East
Why Shoot the Teacher✒
The Wicked Lady
The Widow
Wifemistress
The Wilby Conspiracy✒
The Wild Child✒
The Wild Duck
Wild Engine/Mistaken Orders
Wild Guitar
Wild Horse Hank
Wild in the Country
The Wild One✒
Wild Ones on Wheels
Wild Orchid
Wild Orchid 2: Two Shades of
  Blue
Wild Orchids
Wild Party
Wild Pony
Wild Reeds✒

The Wild Ride
Wild Strawberries✒
Wild Style
Wild Wheels
Wildcat
Wilde
Wildflower✒
Wildrose✒
Will: G. Gordon Liddy
Willa
William Faulkner's Old Man
Wilma
Wilson✒
Windom's Way✒
Windows
Windrunner
The Winds of War
Windwalker✒
Windy City
The Winner
A Winner Never Quits
Winner Takes All
The Winslow Boy✒
The Winter Guest✒
The Winter Light✒
The Winter of Our Dreams
Winterset
Without Anesthesia
Without Evidence
Without Love
Without Warning: The James
  Brady Story✒
Witness✒
Witness to the Execution
Wittgenstein
Wives Under Suspicion
The Wizard of Loneliness
Wolf Lake
Wolf Trap
The Wolves✒
A Woman and a Woman
A Woman, Her Men and Her
  Futon
Woman in Brown
A Woman in Flames✒
Woman in the Dunes✒
Woman in the Shadows
The Woman Inside
A Woman Named Jackie
A Woman Obsessed
A Woman of Rome
A Woman Rebels
A Woman Under the Influence✒
The Woman Who Willed a
  Miracle
Woman With a Past
A Woman's Secret
A Woman's Tale✒
A Woman's World✒
Women & Men: In Love There
  Are No Rules
Women & Men: Stories of
  Seduction
Women from the Lake of
  Scented Souls
Women in Cell Block 7
Women in Love✒
The Women of Brewster Place✒
Women of Valor
Women Unchained
Wonsan Operation
The Wooden Gun
The Wooden Man's Bride
Words by Heart
Workin' for Peanuts
Working Girls
A World Apart✒
The World Gone Mad
The World of Apu✒
A World of Strangers✒
World War II: When Lions
  Roared
The Worldly Madonna
Woyzeck✒
The Wrestler
Wrestling Ernest Hemingway
The Wrong Move
The Wrong Road

X Marks the Spot
Xica✒
Yanco
A Yank in the R.A.F.
Year of the Dragon
Year of the Gun
The Yearling
Yellow Cargo
Yellow Earth
Yol✒
You Must Remember This
You Only Live Once
Young Aphrodites
Young Charlie Chaplin
The Young Graduates
The Young in Heart✒
The Young Lions✒
Young Love, First Love
The Young Nurses
The Young One
The Young Philadelphians✒
Young Tom Edison
Young Winston✒
Your Ticket Is No Longer Valid
Youth Aflame
You've Ruined Me, Eddie
Yuri Nosenko, KGB
Zabriskie Point✒
Zalmen or the Madness of God
Zandalee
Zelly & Me✒
Zero Degrees Kelvin
The Zoo Gang
Zooman✒
Zora Is My Name!
Zorba the Greek✒
Zvenigora✒

Dream Girls

see also Beauty Pageants

A la Mode
Alien Women
American Graffiti✒
Angus
Barb Wire
The Barbarians
Baywatch the Movie: Forbidden
  Paradise
Beauties of the Night
Beautiful Girls
Beauty School
Beverly Hills Knockouts
Bikini Bistro
The Bikini Car Wash Company
The Bikini Car Wash Company 2
Bikini Drive-In
Bikini Island
Bikini Summer
Bikini Summer 3: South Beach
  Heat
Blondes Have More Guns
Bluebeard
Bolero
Burial of the Rats
Calendar Girl Murders
California Girls
Cannonball Run
Cannonball Run 2
Can't Buy Me Love
Cheerleader Camp
The Chosen One: Legend of the
  Raven
City of Women
Cover Me
Creatures the World Forgot
Cupid
Cycle Vixens
Daddy-O
Day of the Warrior
Deadly Weapons
Def Jam's How to Be a Player
Desperate Cargo
Desperate Moves
Devil Girl from Mars
The Devil's Hand
Diamonds Are Forever✒
Dinosaur Valley Girls

Divine Nymph
Do or Die
Dr. Alien
Dr. Goldfoot and the Bikini
  Machine
Dr. No✒
The Doll
The Doll Squad
The Dolls
Domino
Downhill Willie
Dracula: Dead and Loving It
Dream Trap
Dreaming of Rita
Dumb & Dumber
Emmanuelle
Emmanuelle 4
Emmanuelle & Joanna
Emmanuelle in the Country
Emmanuelle on Taboo Island
Emmanuelle, the Joys of a
  Woman
Emmanuelle, the Queen
Emmanuelle's Daughter
Enchanted Island
Evil Toons
Exotica✒
Fair Game
Fate
Femme Fontaine: Killer Babe for
  the C.I.A.
Fire Maidens from Outer Space
Fireballs
Forbidden Planet✒
Forbidden Zone: Alien
  Abduction
Gamera vs. Guiron
Gator Bait
Ghosts Can't Do It
Girl Shy✒
Gold of the Amazon Women
Goldeneye✒
The Grace Kelly Story
Great Bikini Off-Road Adventure
Guns
Hard Hunted
Helen of Troy
Hell's Belles
Hercules and the Princess of
  Troy
Hired to Kill
Hollywood Boulevard 2
Hollywood or Bust
How I Learned to Love Women
How to Succeed with Girls
I, A Woman
I Married a Centerfold
I Posed for Playboy
It Takes a Thief
Jokes My Folks Never Told Me
Junk Mail
Kiss and Kill
La Collectionneuse
Last Dance
Les Girls
Les Mistons
The Lion of Thebes✒
The Loves of Hercules
Malibu Hot Summer
A Man with a Maid
Masseuse
The Mermaids of Tiburon
Mirror Images
Mirror Images 2
Mirror Mirror 3: The Voyeur
Missile to the Moon
Mysterious Island of Beautiful
  Women
Mystery Date
Naked Souls
Naked Warriors
National Lampoon's Vacation✒
Never Say Never Again
Nine Ages of Nakedness
A Nymphoid Barbarian in
  Dinosaur Hell
Oxford Blues
Panther Squad
Party Incorporated

Category Index

Family

Seven Alone
Seven Beauties⏴
7 Faces of Dr. Lao⏴
Severance
Sex and the Single Parent
Shadow of a Doubt⏴
The Shadow Riders
Shadows⏴
Shameless
The Shanghai Gesture
Shark River
Shattered⏴
The Sheep Has Five Legs
The Shell Seekers
Shenandoah⏴
The Shepherd of the Hills⏴
Sherman's March: An
 Improbable Search for Love
She's So Lovely
She's the One
Shiloh⏴
Shine⏴
The Shining Hour
Shoot the Moon
Shy People⏴
Siberiade⏴
The Sibling
Sibling Rivalry
The Sicilian Connection
Sidewalks of New York
The Silence⏴
Silence
The Silence of Neto
The Silences of the Palace⏴
Silent Rebellion
Silent Tongue
Silent Witness
The Silver Stallion: King of the
 Wild Brumbies
Simple Justice
Simple Men⏴
The Sin of Madelon Claudet⏴
Since You Went Away⏴
A Sinful Life
Sinners
Sins of the Mind
Sioux City
The Sister-in-Law
Sister My Sister
The Sisters⏴
Sisters⏴
Sisters of the Gion
Sisters, Or the Balance of
 Happiness
Six in Paris
Sixteen Candles⏴
The Sixth Man
'68
Skag⏴
Skeletons
Skin Game
Skylark
Slaughter of the Innocents
The Sleazy Uncle
Slightly Scarlet
The Slingshot⏴
Small Sacrifices
Smilin' Through⏴
Smoke
Smoke Signals
The Snapper⏴
Snowbound
Snowy River, the MacGregor
 Saga: The Race
Sofie
The Solitary Man
Some Mother's Son⏴
Something in the Wind
Something to Talk About
Sometimes a Great Notion⏴
Sometimes They Come
 Back...Again
Son-in-Law
Son of Flubber
Son of Frankenstein⏴
Son of Fury⏴
The Son of the Shark
Song of the Exile
Song of the Islands

Sons
Sons of Katie Elder⏴
Sons of Steel
Sorceress
Sorrento Beach
Sorrows of Gin
Soul Food
The Sound of Music⏴
Sous Sol
South Central
South of Hell Mountain
South Riding
The Southerner⏴
Souvenir
The Spanish Gardener⏴
Spanking the Monkey⏴
Special Olympics
Spectre
Spencer's Mountain
Spider Baby
Spirit Rider⏴
Spitfire
Splendor
Split Decisions
Split Image
Splitting Heirs
Sprague
Star Maps
Star Spangled Rhythm⏴
State Fair⏴
State Fair
State of Grace⏴
Steal Big, Steal Little
Stealing Beauty
Stella
Stella Dallas⏴
The Stepfather⏴
Stepfather 2: Make Room for
 Daddy
Stepfather 3: Father's Day
Stepmonster
Stepsisters
Still Not Quite Human
The Stolen Children⏴
The Stone Boy⏴
Stop! or My Mom Will Shoot
The Storm Within⏴
The Story of Boys & Girls⏴
The Story of Esther Costello
The Story of Jacob & Joseph⏴
Storyville
The Strange Door
Strange Interlude⏴
Strange Interlude
Strange Shadows in an Empty
 Room
The Stranger
Strangers in the City
Strangers: The Story of a Mother
 and Daughter⏴
Strapless
Street Girls
Street Hero
Street Hitz
Street Justice
A Streetcar Named Desire⏴
Striking Distance
Striptease
Struggle
Stuck on You
The Stupids
The Subject Was Roses⏴
The Substance of Fire
The Substitute Wife
Suddenly, Last Summer⏴
Suffering Bastards
Sugar Cane Alley⏴
Sugar Hill
The Sum of Us⏴
Summer Holiday
Summer Magic
The Summer of Aviya
Summer of Fear
Summer Snow
Summer Wishes, Winter Dreams
A Sunday in the Country⏴
Sunday's Children⏴
The Sundowners⏴
Sure Fire

Susan and God⏴
Susana⏴
Suture
Suzanne
Swedenhielms
The Sweeper
The Sweet Hereafter⏴
Sweet Nothing⏴
Sweet Smell of Success⏴
Sweetie⏴
The Swiss Family Robinson⏴
Switched at Birth
Sylvester
Table Settings
The Tale of Ruby Rose⏴
A Tale of Winter
Tales from Avonlea, Vol. 1: The
 Journey Begins
Tank
Tatie Danielle⏴
Tears in the Rain
Teenage Exorcist
The Tempest⏴
Temptress Moon
Ten Days Wonder
The Tenant of Wildfell Hall
Teorema
Termini Station
Terms of Endearment⏴
Terranova
Testament⏴
Tevye
Tex
Texas Jack
Texas Lightning
Thank You & Good Night
That Eye, the Sky
That Was Then...This Is Now
There's No Business Like Show
 Business⏴
They Watch
Things in Their Season
The Third Sex
Third Walker⏴
This Boy's Life⏴
This Happy Breed⏴
This Is My Life
This Property Is Condemned⏴
A Thousand Acres
A Thousand Clowns⏴
Threads⏴
Three Brothers⏴
Three Daring Daughters
The Three Lives of Karen
The Three Lives of Thomasina⏴
Three Men and a Cradle⏴
3 Ninjas
3 Ninjas Kick Back
The Three Sisters
Three Smart Girls⏴
Three Violent People
The Three Weird Sisters
Three Wishes
Three's Trouble
Thrillkill
Through a Glass Darkly⏴
Thursday's Child
The Ticket
Ticket to Heaven⏴
The Tie that Binds
Tiger Warsaw
Till Marriage Do Us Part
Till There was You
Time Flies When You're Alive
Time Indefinite
A Time of Destiny
Time Stands Still⏴
A Time to Live
A Time to Live and a Time to Die
Time Without Pity
Timemaster
'Tis a Pity She's a Whore
Titanic⏴
Tito and Me⏴
To All My Friends on Shore⏴
To Dance with the White Dog⏴
To Die For 2: Son of Darkness
To Gillian on Her 37th Birthday

To Grandmother's House We
 Go
To Live⏴
To Paris with Love
To Sleep with Anger⏴
Toby McTeague
Tokyo Story⏴
Toll of the Desert
Tollbooth
Tommy Boy
Toughlove
Toys
Toys in the Attic
Track 29
The Tracker
Trade Secrets
Trading Mom
Traenen in Florenz
Traffic Jam
The Trail of the Lonesome Pine⏴
Trained to Kill
Tramp at the Door
Trapped In Paradise
Traps
Traveller⏴
Travels with My Aunt
Treacherous Crossing
Treasure of the Sierra Madre⏴
The Tree of Wooden Clogs⏴
The Trip to Bountiful⏴
Trois Couleurs: Blanc⏴
Trois Couleurs: Bleu⏴
Tromeo & Juliet
Troublemakers
True Blood
True Confessions⏴
True Love⏴
True West⏴
True Women
Trusting Beatrice
The Turning
The Tuttles of Tahiti⏴
Twelfth Night
29th Street
Twice in a Lifetime⏴
The Twilight of the Golds
Twister
Two Bits
2 By 4
Two Kinds of Love
Two Much
The Two Sisters
Two Small Bodies
The Ugly Dachshund
Ulee's Gold⏴
Un Air de Famille
Uncle Buck⏴
Uncle Moses
Uncommon Valor
Under the Boardwalk
Under the Hula Moon
Under the Volcano⏴
Undergrads⏴
Uneasy Terms
An Unexpected Family
The Unforgiven⏴
Unhook the Stars
An Unremarkable Life
Unstrung Heroes
Until They Sail
Up/Down/Fragile
Up the Sandbox
The Uprising⏴
Used People
The Vacillations of Poppy Carew
Vegas Vacation
Vengeance
Vengeance Valley
A Very Brady Christmas
A Very Brady Sequel
Vigil⏴
Vincent & Theo⏴
Violette⏴
Viridiana⏴
Voyage en Balloon
A Voyage' Round My Father⏴
Voyage to Italy
Voyager⏴
Vultures

Wagon Tracks
Wait Till Your Mother Gets
 Home
A Walk in the Clouds
Walk in the Spring Rain
Walkabout⏴
Walking Thunder
The Waltons: A Thanksgiving
 Story
The Waltons: The Christmas
 Carol
The War
War & Remembrance, Part 1
War & Remembrance, Part 2
War & Remembrance: The Final
 Chapter, Part 8
War & Remembrance: The Final
 Chapter, Part 9
The War at Home
Waterfront
The Wedding Banquet⏴
Wedding Bell Blues
Wedding in White
Weep No More My Lady
Welcome Home
Welcome to the Dollhouse
Whale Music
The Whales of August⏴
What About Bob?⏴
What Ever Happened To...
What Ever Happened to Baby
 Jane?⏴
What the Peeper Saw
What's Eating Gilbert Grape⏴
When a Man Loves a Woman
When Nature Calls
When Saturday Comes
When Wolves Cry
Where East Is East
Where Have All the People
 Gone?
Where Love Has Gone
Where the Heart Is
Where the Lilies Bloom⏴
Where's Poppa?⏴
While You Were Sleeping⏴
The White Balloon⏴
The White Cliffs of Dover⏴
White Mane⏴
Why Does Herr R. Run Amok?
Wicked Stepmother
Wide Awake
Widow's Kiss
Wild America⏴
Wild at Heart⏴
The Wild Country
The Wild Duck
Wild Pony
Wild West
Wild Zone
Wilder Napalm
Wildflower⏴
William Shakespeare's Romeo
 and Juliet⏴
The Winds of War
The Wings of the Dove⏴
The Winner
The Winter Guest⏴
Winter Kills⏴
Winter People
Winterset
Wish Upon a Star
The Wistful Widow of Wagon
 Gap
With Six You Get Eggroll
Without Evidence
The Wizard
The Wizard of Loneliness
The Wolves
The Woman in White
A Woman Under the Influence⏴
Women on the Verge of a
 Nervous Breakdown⏴
Woodchipper Massacre
The World Accuses
World and Time Enough
A World Apart⏴
The World of Apu⏴
The Worldly Madonna

Farming

Fast Cars

Feds

Frame-Ups

Man Outside
The Manhunt
The Mighty Quinn
Mr. Wise Guy
Most Wanted
Moving Target
Murder♪
Murphy's Law
My Cousin Vinny♪
My Fellow Americans
Nasty Hero
Nightmare in Badham County
Nightwatch
No Escape, No Return
North by Northwest♪
Now and Forever
The Obsessed
Off the Wall
Palmetto
Phantom Lady♪
Powder Burn
Presumed Innocent♪
Prime Suspect
Prison Break
Red Corner
The Rich Man's Wife
Rubdown
The Shadow Conspiracy
Shakes the Clown
Shelter
The Sphinx
Stir Crazy
Sunset Heat
Suspended Alibi
Tank
TekWar
Today I Hang
U.S. Marshals
Voulez-Vous Danser Avec Moi?
White Fire
Wild Things
The Wrong Man
The Wrong Woman

France

see also **Paris**

A la Mode
The Accompanist
The Advocate♪
The Ambassador's Daughter
An American in Paris♪
An American Werewolf in Paris
And Soon the Darkness
Arch of Triumph♪
Arch of Triumph
Bedtime Story
Big Fella
Bluebeard's Eighth Wife
Borsalino♪
Breathless♪
Buffet Froid♪
Can-Can
Cannes Man
Captain Scarlett
Carnival in Flanders♪
Carve Her Name with Pride
Catherine & Co.
Cesar♪
Charade♪
Chasing Butterflies
Cloud Waltzing
Danton♪
Desiree
Diane
Dirty Rotten Scoundrels♪
Dr. Petiot
The Dreamed Life of Angels
Dubarry
The Duellists♪
Dupont Lajoie
The Elusive Corporal♪
Ever After: A Cinderella Story
Fanfan la Tulipe♪
The Fatal Image
The Foreman Went to France
Forget Paris
Frantic♪
French Connection 2♪

French Intrigue
French Kiss
The French Lesson
French Postcards
The French Woman
Gentlemen Prefer Blondes♪
Gigi♪
Harvest♪
Hate♪
Heart of a Nation♪
Hellraiser 4: Bloodline
The Horseman on the Roof
How to Steal a Million♪
Is Paris Burning?♪
Jefferson in Paris
Joan of Paris♪
Killer Tomatoes Eat France
Killing Zoe
Kings Go Forth
La Ceremonie♪
La Collectionneuse
La Marseillaise♪
La Passante♪
La Silence de la Mer♪
La Vie de Boheme♪
The Lacemaker♪
Ladies Man
Lafayette Escadrille
The Last Metro♪
Last Tango in Paris♪
The Last Time I Saw Paris
The Last Train
Le Bal♪
Le Complot♪
Le Corbeau♪
Le Gendarme de Saint-Tropez
Le Joli Mai
Le Million♪
Les Grandes Manoeuvres♪
Les Miserables♪
The Life of Emile Zola♪
The Longest Day♪
Lovely to Look At♪
Loves & Times of Scaramouche
Ma and Pa Kettle on Vacation
Madame Bovary♪
Mademoiselle Fifi
The Man in the Iron Mask♪
The Man in the Iron Mask
The Man in the Iron Mask♪
Man on the Eiffel Tower♪
Maniac
Manon
Marie Antoinette
Marius♪
Maximum Risk
May Fools♪
Me and the Colonel
Mr. Klein♪
The Moderns♪
Monkeys, Go Home!
Monsieur Beaucaire
Monsieur Verdoux♪
The Moonraker
Moulin Rouge♪
The Mountain
My Father's Glory♪
Napoleon♪
Napoleon
A New Kind of Love
The Night and the Moment
The Old Lady Who Walked in
  the Sea
O.S.S.♪
Paths of Glory♪
Piaf
Prisoner of Honor♪
The Private Affairs of Bel Ami♪
The Proprietor
Quality Street
Quatorze Juliet
Queen Margot♪
Ready to Wear
The Red Inn
Reign of Terror
Reunion in France
Ridicule♪
Round Midnight♪
The Rules of the Game♪

Saint Joan
The Scarlet Pimpernel♪
Silk Stockings♪
Sister My Sister
Spy of Napoleon
Suite 16
Surviving Picasso
A Tale of Two Cities♪
A Tale of Two Cities
A Tale of Winter
Theatre of Death
This Land Is Mine♪
Those Magnificent Men in Their
  Flying Machines♪
To Catch a Thief♪
Total Eclipse
Tropic of Cancer♪
True Colors
Uncertain Glory
Until September
Uranus♪
Valmont♪
Waterloo
Western
What Price Glory?♪
Window to Paris
A Year in Provence♪

Friendship

see **Buddies**

Front Page

see also **Mass Media;**
Shutterbugs

Absence of Malice
Act of Passion: The Lost Honor
  of Kathryn Beck
Action in Arabia
The Adventures of Nellie Bly
Alice in the Cities♪
All the President's Men♪
American Autobahn
AngKor: Cambodia Express
Another Time, Another Place
Anzio
The Average Woman
The Barcelona Kill
The Beniker Gang
Between the Lines♪
The Big Hurt
Big News
Big Town
Big Town After Dark
Blessed Event♪
Boca
Boeing Boeing
Brenda Starr
Broadway Melody of 1936♪
Bulldog Edition
A Bunny's Tale
Call Northside 777♪
Caroline at Midnight
Chinese Box
Circumstantial Evidence
Citizen Kane♪
City in Fear♪
Cobb♪
Concrete Beat
Continental Divide
Cover Story
Criminal Act
Cry Freedom
Cut and Run
Dark Secrets
Dark Side of Genius
Dead Air
Dead Connection
Deadline
Deadly Exposure
Deep Impact
Defense of the Realm♪
The Devil's Commandment
Diamond Trail
Diary of a Serial Killer
The Disappearance of Garcia
  Lorca

Double Cross
Double Edge
Double Exposure
Down Came a Blackbird
Everything Happens at Night♪
Eyes Behind the Stars
Eyes of a Stranger
A Face in the Fog
Far East
Fast Money
Father Hood
Fatherland
Fever Pitch
Final Extra
Finnegan Begin Again
Fit for a King
A Flash of Green
Fletch
Fletch Lives
The Forbidden Quest
Foreign Correspondent♪
Francis Covers the Big Town
Freeze Frame
The Front Page♪
The Front Page
Fun
Gentleman's Agreement♪
The Ghost and Mr. Chicken
The Great Muppet Caper♪
Grown Ups
Headline Woman
Heads
Heat Wave♪
Her Life as a Man
Hero♪
His Girl Friday♪
Hit the Ice
Hour of Decision
The Hudsucker Proxy♪
Hue and Cry♪
Hustling♪
I Cover the Waterfront
I Love Trouble
The Image
In and Out
An Inconvenient Woman
The Infiltrator
The Innocent Sleep
Invasion of Privacy
Istanbul
Johnny Come Lately
Journey for Margaret♪
Just One of the Guys
Keeper of the City
Keeper of the Flame
Kid from Not-So-Big
Kill Slade
The Killing Beach
The Killing Device
The Killing Fields♪
Killing Stone
L.A. Confidential♪
La Dolce Vita♪
Lana in Love
The Last Word
Late Extra
Let 'er Go Gallegher
Lethal Charm
Libeled Lady♪
Lip Service♪
L'Odeur des Fauves
Lonelyhearts
Love Is a Many-Splendored
  Thing
The Love Machine
Malarek
The Man Inside
Man of Iron♪
Mean Season
Meet John Doe♪
Midnight Edition
Midnight in the Garden of Good
  and Evil
Midnight Warrior
Mrs. Parker and the Vicious
  Circle
Mr. Nice Guy
Money Talks
Murder on the Campus

Murrow
Mystic Circle Murder
Natas ... The Reflection
News at Eleven
Newsfront♪
Newsies
Night Hunter
The Night Stalker
The Night Strangler
The Nightmare Years
Nina Takes a Lover
No Time to Die
Not for Publication
Nothing Sacred♪
Novel Desires
November Conspiracy
The Odessa File
One Fine Day
One Man Out
The Other Woman
The Outlaws Is Coming!
The Paper♪
Paper Lion
Paralyzed
The Payoff
The Pelican Brief
Perfect
The Philadelphia Story♪
Platinum Blonde♪
The Ploughman's Lunch♪
Primary Motive
Private Investigations
Profile
Qui Etes Vous, Mr. Sorge?
Reckless Disregard
Reed: Insurgent Mexico
Resurrection of Zachary
  Wheeler
Revenge of the Radioactive
  Reporter
Riding on Air
Roman Holiday♪
Roxie Hart
The Rumor Mill
Safari 3000
Salome, Where She Danced
Salvador♪
Savage Capitalism
Scandal
Scream 2♪
The Secrets of Wu Sin
Seeds of Doubt
Sex and the Single Girl
Sex Through a Window
The Shadow Conspiracy
Shock Corridor♪
Short Fuse
Shriek in the Night
Shy People♪
The Sixth Man
Skeletons
Somewhere I'll Find You♪
Soul Patrol
Special Bulletin♪
Speed Reporter
Spice World: The Movie
Star Reporter
Stavisky♪
Stay Tuned for Murder
Stephen King's The Night Flier
Straight Talk
The Strange Love of Molly
  Louvain
Stranger on the Third Floor♪
Street Smart
Sucker Money
Superman: The Movie♪
Sweet Rosie O'Grady
Sweet Smell of Success♪
Switching Channels
Tainted Blood
Tarnished Angels♪
Teacher's Pet♪
That Certain Age
That Lucky Touch
They All Kissed the Bride
They Got Me Covered
The Thirteenth Man
Thirteenth Reunion

Gangs

Gays

Horror

Pin...
Pinocchio's Revenge
Piranha
The Pit
Plague of the Zombies
Play Dead
Playroom
Pledge Night
Plutonium Baby
Point of Terror
Popcorn
Possession
Possession: Until Death Do You Part
The Power
Premature Burial
The Prey
Primal Rage
Prime Evil
Prince of Darkness
Prison
Project: Nightmare
Project Vampire
Prom Night
Prom Night 3: The Last Kiss
Prom Night 4: Deliver Us from Evil
Prophecy
The Prophecy 2: Ashtown
The Prowler
The Psychic
Psychic Killer
Psycho 4: The Beginning
Psycho Cop
Psycho Cop 2
Psycho from Texas
Psychopath
Pumpkinhead 2: Blood Wings
Puppet Master
Puppet Master 2
Puppet Master 3: Toulon's Revenge
Puppet Master 4
Puppet Master 5: The Final Chapter
The Pyx⬥
Rabid
Race with the Devil
Raging Angels
Rana: The Legend of Shadow Lake
Rape
Rasputin the Mad Monk
The Rats Are Coming! The Werewolves Are Here!
Rattled
Rattlers
The Raven⬥
Razorback
Red Blooded American Girl
The Redeemer
The Reincarnate
The Rejuvenator
Relative Fear
The Reptile
Rest in Pieces
The Resurrected
Retribution
The Return of Count Yorga
Return of Dracula
Return of the Ape Man
Return of the Evil Dead
Return of the Family Man
Return to Boggy Creek
Return to Horror High
Return to Salem's Lot
Revenge
Revenge in the House of Usher
Revenge of Doctor X
The Revenge of Frankenstein
Revenge of the Dead
Revenge of the Living Zombies
Revenge of the Radioactive Reporter
Revenge of the Zombies
Ring of Terror
The Ripper
The Robot vs. the Aztec Mummy
Rock 'n' Roll Nightmare

Rocktober Blood
Rodan
Rogue
Rosemary's Baby⬥
Ruby
The Rue Morgue Massacres
Rumpelstiltskin
Run, Stranger, Run
The Runestone
Rush Week
Sabaka
The Sadist
The Saga of the Draculas
Salem's Lot
Samson in the Wax Museum
Samson vs. the Vampire Women
Satan in High Heels
The Satanic Rites of Dracula
Satanik
Satan's Black Wedding
Satan's Cheerleaders
Satan's Princess
Satan's School for Girls
Satan's Touch
Satanwar
Saturday Night Shockers
The Savage Bees
Savage Intruder
Savage Weekend
Savages
Sawbones
Scalpel
Scanner Cop 2: Volkin's Revenge
Scanners
Scanners 2: The New Order
Scanners 3: The Takeover
Scanners: The Showdown
Scared Stiff
Scared to Death
The Scars of Dracula
Schizo
Schizoid
Science Crazed
Scorpion with Two Tails
The Scorpion's Tail
Scream⬥
Scream 2⬥
Scream, Baby, Scream
Scream Blacula Scream
Scream Dream
Scream of Fear⬥
Scream of the Demon Lover
Screamers
The Screaming Dead
The Screaming Skull
Screams of a Winter Night
Screamtime
Season of the Witch
Seducers
See No Evil⬥
Seedpeople
Seeds of Evil
Seizure
The Sender
The Sentinel
The Serpent and the Rainbow
Serpent's Lair
Servants of Twilight
The 7 Brothers Meet Dracula
Seven Deaths in the Cat's Eye
Seven Doors of Death
The Seventh Victim⬥
The Severed Arm
Severed Ties
Sex Is Crazy
Shadow Creature
Shadow of Chinatown
Shadows Run Black
ShadowZone: The Undead Express
Shakma
The Shaman
The She-Beast
She Came on the Bus
She Demons
She-Freak
The Shining

Shock 'Em Dead
Shock! Shock! Shock!
Shock Waves
Shocker
Shriek of the Mutilated
Shrieker
The Sibling
Silent Madness
Silent Night, Bloody Night
Silent Night, Deadly Night
Silent Night, Deadly Night 2
Silent Night, Deadly Night 3: Better Watch Out!
Silent Night, Deadly Night 4: Initiation
Silent Night, Deadly Night 5: The Toymaker
Silent Scream
Silver Bullet
The Sinister Invasion
Sinner's Blood
The Sins of Dorian Gray
Sinthia: The Devil's Doll
Sisters⬥
Sisters of Satan
Skinned Alive
Skinner
The Skull
Skullduggery
Slashdance
Slaughter High
Slaughter Hotel
The Slaughter of the Vampires
Slaughterhouse
Slaughterhouse Rock
The Slayer
The Slayer/The Scalps
Sleazemania III: The Good, the Bad & the Sleazy
Sledgehammer
Sleep of Death
Sleepaway Camp
Sleepaway Camp 2: Unhappy Campers
Sleepaway Camp 3: Teenage Wasteland
Sleepwalkers
Slime City
The Slime People
Slithis
Slugs
The Slumber Party Massacre
Slumber Party Massacre 2
Slumber Party Massacre 3
The Snake Hunter Strangler
The Snake People
The Snake Woman
Snowbeast
Society
Sole Survivor
Something Weird
Sometimes They Come Back
Sometimes They Come Back...Again
Son of Blob
Sorority House Massacre
Sorority House Massacre 2: Nighty Nightmare
Sound of Horror
Sounds of Silence
Spasms
The Spawning
Species 2
Spectre
The Spectre of Edgar Allen Poe
The Speed Lovers
The Spell
The Spellbinder
Spellcaster
Spiritism
Spirits
Spirits of the Dead⬥
Splatter University
Spontaneous Combustion
Spookies
Squirm
Sssssss
Stage Fright
Stagefright

Stanley
Stay Awake
Stephen King's Golden Years
Stephen King's It
Stephen King's The Night Flier
Stephen King's The Stand
Stephen King's The Tommyknockers
Steps from Hell
Stepsisters
Stones of Death
Strait-Jacket
Strange Behavior
Strange Case of Dr. Jekyll & Mr. Hyde
The Strange Door
Strange World of Coffin Joe
The Strangeness
Strangers
Strays
Stuff Stephanie in the Incinerator
Subspecies
Sugar Cookies
Suicide Cult
Summer of Fear
Sundown
Superstition
The Surgeon
Survivor
Suspiria⬥
Swamp of the Lost Monster
The Swarm
Sweet 16
Tainted Image
Tales from the Crypt
Tales from the Gimli Hospital
Tales of Terror
Tales That Witness Madness
Tarantulas: The Deadly Cargo
Taste the Blood of Dracula
Teenage Gang Debs
Teenage Strangler
Teenage Zombies
The Tell-Tale Heart
The Tempter
Tentacles
The Terror
Terror at Red Wolf Inn
Terror at Tenkiller
Terror at the Opera
Terror Beach
Terror Eyes
Terror in the Haunted House
Terror in the Swamp
Terror in the Wax Museum
Terror in Toyland
Terror on Tour
Terror Out of the Sky
Terror Train
Terrorgram
Testament of Dr. Mabuse
Theatre of Death
They Bite
They Came from Within
They Saved Hitler's Brain
Things
Things 2
Thirst
The Thirsty Dead
The 13th Floor
Thirteenth Reunion
The Thousand Eyes of Dr. Mabuse
301, 302
Three on a Meathook
Time of the Apes
The Tingler⬥
To All a Goodnight
To Die For
To Die For 2: Son of Darkness
To Sleep with a Vampire
To the Devil, a Daughter
Tomb
Tomb of Ligeia⬥

Tomb of the Undead
Tomb of Torture
Tombs of the Blind Dead
Tomcat: Dangerous Desires
The Toolbox Murders
Tormented
Torso
Torture Chamber of Baron Blood
The Torture Chamber of Dr. Sadism
Torture Dungeon
Torture Train
The Touch of Satan
Tower of Evil
Tower of Screaming Virgins
Track of the Moonbeast
Track of the Vampire
Transmutations
Trap Them & Kill Them
Trapped Alive
Trick or Treat
Trick or Treats
Trilogy of Terror
Trilogy of Terror 2
Troll
Troll 2
Truth or Dare?
Twice Dead
Twice-Told Tales⬥
Twilight People
Twilight Zone: The Movie
Twins of Evil
Twinsanity
Twisted
Twisted Brain
Twisted Nightmare
Twitch of the Death Nerve
Two Evil Eyes
The Two Faces of Dr. Jekyll
The Two Faces of Evil
2000 Maniacs
The Ugly
The Unborn
The Unborn 2
The Uncanny
Uncle Sam
Uncle Was a Vampire
The Undead
Understudy: The Graveyard Shift 2
The Unearthing
The Unearthly
The Unholy
The Uninvited⬥
The Uninvited
Unmasked Part 25
The Unnamable
The Unnamable 2: The Statement of Randolph Carter
The Unseen
The Untold Story
Vampire at Midnight
Vampire Circus
Vampire Cop
The Vampire Hookers
Vampire Journals
The Vampire Lovers
Vampyres
Varan the Unbelievable
Vault of Horror
The Velvet Vampire
Vengeance Is Mine
Vengeance of the Zombies
Venom
Venus in Furs
The Video Dead
Video Violence
Video Violence Part 2...The Exploitation!
Videodrome
Village of the Damned
The Vindicator
The Vineyard
Virgin Among the Living Dead
The Virgin of Nuremberg
The Virgin Witch
Virus
Visions of Evil
The Visitor

Category Index

1102

Riding High
Rolling Home
The Rounders
Run for the Roses
Running Wild
Saddle Buster
Saratoga
Shooting Fish
Silver Stallion
The Silver Stallion: King of the
   Wild Brumbies
Something to Talk About
Speedy⋆
The Story of Seabiscuit
Sundown Saunders
Sylvester
Tennessee Stallion
Texas to Bataan
Thoroughbreds Don't Cry
Three Men on a Horse⋆
Turf Boy
Two Bits & Pepper
The Undefeated
Western Double Feature 16
When the West Was Young
White Mane⋆
Wild Hearts Can't Be Broken⋆
Wild Horse Hank
Wild Horses
Wild Pony
Win, Place, or Steal
Winds of the Wasteland
Wings of the Morning

Hospitals & Medicine

   see also Disease of the
      Week; Doctors & Nurses;
      Emerging Viruses; Sanity
      Check; Shrinks

Article 99
B.O.R.N.
Britannia Hospital
Carry On Nurse
A Child Is Waiting⋆
China Beach
City of Joy
The Clonus Horror
Coma⋆
Come to the Stable⋆
Critical Care
Critical Condition
Dead Ringers⋆
Desperate Measures
Disorderlies
Disorderly Orderly
Doctor at Large
Dr. Kildare's Strange Case
Doctors' Wives
East of Kilimanjaro
The Egyptian
ER
Extreme Measures
For Roseanna
Frankenstein General Hospital
The Fugitive⋆
Green for Danger
Gross Anatomy
Halloween 2: The Nightmare
   Isn't Over!
Hard-Boiled
The Hasty Heart
Horror Hospital
The Hospital⋆
Hospital Massacre
Hospital of Terror
In for Treatment⋆
In Love and War
The Interns
Invasion
Junior
The Kingdom
Lifespan
Like Father, Like Son
Miss Evers' Boys
Naked Is Better
Nine Months
Nurse

One Flew Over the Cuckoo's
   Nest⋆
The Red Squirrel
State of Emergency
A Stolen Face
The Surgeon
Tales from the Gimli Hospital
Tender Loving Care
Threshold
12 Monkeys⋆
The Ugly
Vital Signs
Welcome Stranger
Where Truth Lies
While You Were Sleeping⋆
Whose Life Is It Anyway?⋆
Young Doctors in Love

Hostage!

   see also Kidnapped!;
      Missing Persons

Against the Wall⋆
Air Force One⋆
Airheads
Albino Alligator
Amos and Andrew
Autumn Born
Black Cobra 2
Black Fox: Good Men and Bad
Blackout
Blast
Blood of the Hunter
Body Count
The Boys Club
Cadillac Man
Carpool
Codename: Vengeance
Cold Sweat
Cul de Sac⋆
Days of Hell
Dead Ahead
Dead Silence
Deadly Outbreak
Death and the Maiden⋆
Death Stalk
Demolition High
Die Hard⋆
Die Hard 2: Die Harder⋆
Distortions
Dog Day Afternoon⋆
Door to Door Maniac
Escape from New York
Face the Evil
Fall Time
Fatal Mission
Field of Fire
Firestorm
48 Hours to Live
Headless Body in Topless Bar
The Heist
Hostage Train
Hostages⋆
Housewife
Human Bomb
Iron Eagle
The Jesus Trip
Johnny 100 Pesos
King of Comedy⋆
The Last Samurai
The Legend of Wolf Mountain
Lethal Tender
Live! From Death Row
Mad City
Masterminds
Midnight Fear
Mr. Reliable: A True Story
Mistrial
The Negotiator
Nick of Time
No Contest
Nothing to Lose
One Way Out
Open Fire
Operation Thunderbolt
A Perfect World
A Prayer in the Dark
Provoked
Quake

Quick Change
The Ref⋆
Rock All Night
Rush Hour
The Seventh Floor
Sex and the Other Man
S.F.W.
The Shot
Skyscraper
Snatched
Space Marines
Spaghetti House
Speed 2: Cruise Control
Split Second
Stand Off
A Stranger Is Watching
Stranglehold
Stripteaser
Sudden Death
Suddenly⋆
Sweet Hostage
The Taking of Pelham One Two
   Three⋆
Terror Stalks the Class Reunion
Three Ninjas: High Noon at
   Mega Mountain
The Trap
Truth or Consequences, N.M.
12 Monkeys⋆
Vengeance

Housekeepers

   see The Help: Female

Houston

Apollo 13⋆
The Bad News Bears in
   Breaking Training
Brewster McCloud⋆
Dance With Me
The Evening Star
Full Fathom Five
Jason's Lyric
Last Night at the Alamo⋆
Night Game
Reality Bites
The Swarm
Terms of Endearment⋆
Urban Cowboy
Vietnam, Texas

Hunted!

   see also Survival

Arctic Blue
Beyond Fear
Beyond Rangoon
Bigfoot: The Unforgettable
   Encounter
Bounty Hunter 2002
The Cursed Mountain Mystery
Cyborg 2
Damned River
Deadly Game
Death Hunt
Decoy
Deliverance⋆
Desperate Prey
Diary of a Hitman
Dominion
Ex-Cop
Eyes of the Beholder
Fair Game
Final Round
5 Dark Souls
Fortress
Freejack
Fugitive X
The Ghost of Fletcher Ridge
The Good Guys and the Bad
   Guys
Hard Target
The Hunted
Hunter's Blood
Illegal Entry: Formula for Fear
Incident at Deception Ridge

Jungleground
Killing at Hell's Gate
Ladykillers
The Last of the Dogmen
Last Witness
Little Bigfoot
Maximum Risk
Midnight Murders
The Most Dangerous Game⋆
The Naked Prey⋆
Nemesis 2: Nebula
Nightmare at Bittercreek
Overkill
The Pest
Prey for the Hunter
Project Shadowchaser 3000
Rumble in the Streets
Shadowhunter
Shoot to Kill⋆
Solo
Southern Comfort⋆
Star Hunter
Survival Quest
Surviving the Game
Trial and Error
Uncivilized
Warriors
Yesterday's Target

Hunting

   see also Go Fish

The Amazing Panda Adventure
The Bear⋆
The Belstone Fox
The Bridge to Nowhere
Caddyshack⋆
Dan Candy's Law
Deadly Prey
First Blood
Forest of Little Bear
Frostbiter: Wrath of the Wendigo
The Ghost and the Darkness
Git!
Harry Black and the Tiger
The Hunt⋆
The Last Hunt
The Last Safari
Mogambo⋆
Night of the Grizzly
Shoot
Shooting
Those Calloways
To Catch a Yeti
White Hunter, Black Heart⋆

Hurling

Ace Ventura: When Nature Calls
Anaconda
Blood Simple⋆
Car Wash
The Crying Game⋆
The Cutting Edge
Dogfight⋆
Eating Raoul⋆
The Exorcist⋆
Fear and Loathing in Las Vegas
52 Pick-Up
Heathers⋆
Jaws⋆
Kingpin
Monty Python's The Meaning of
   Life⋆
My Giant
National Lampoon's Animal
   House⋆
Parenthood⋆
Poltergeist 2: The Other Side
The Sandlot⋆
Sirens
Stand By Me⋆
This Is Spinal Tap⋆
The Verdict⋆
The Witches of Eastwick

I Love Detroit

   see also Fast Cars; Motor
      Vehicle Dept.

Aspen Extreme
Beverly Hills Cop
Beverly Hills Cop 2
Beverly Hills Cop 3
Bird on a Wire
Chameleon Street⋆
Collision Course
Coupe de Ville
Crimewave
Crossing the Bridge
Detroit 9000
The Dollmaker
Gridlock'd⋆
Grosse Pointe Blank⋆
Hoffa⋆
Indian Summer
The Last Word
Let's Kill All the Lawyers
Mirrors
Mr. Mom⋆
One in a Million: The Ron
   LeFlore Story
Paper Lion
Presumed Innocent⋆
Private Parts
Renaissance Man
RoboCop⋆
RoboCop 2
RoboCop 3
RoboCop the Series: The Future
   of Law Enforcement
Roger & Me⋆
The Rosary Murders
Scarecrow
Tiger Town
True Romance
Tucker: The Man and His
   Dream⋆
Zebrahead⋆

Identity

   see also Amnesia; Role
      Reversal

Babyfever
Boys
Brainwaves
The Broken Chain
Changes
The Crimes of Stephen Hawke
Dark City
The Dark Half
Dark Passage
Diabolically Yours
Dr. Heckyl and Mr. Hype
Don Juan DeMarco
Dumbo⋆
The Effect of Gamma Rays on
   Man-in-the-Moon Marigolds⋆
Face/Off⋆
Far Out Man
Floating Life
Get On the Bus⋆
The Great Gabbo
High Country
Higher Learning
Joe Versus the Volcano
Leon the Pig Farmer
Ma Vie en Rose⋆
Marnie⋆
Maximum Risk
Middle Age Crazy
Midnight⋆
The Mirror Has Two Faces
Montenegro⋆
Mother Night⋆
Moving Out
My Brilliant Career⋆
My Dinner with Andre⋆
Nevil Shute's The Far Country
Next Year If All Goes Well
The Nutty Professor⋆
Old Boyfriends
Orlando⋆
Other Voices, Other Rooms

Partner♪
Pocketful of Miracles♪
Point of No Return
The Promise
Rebel Without a Cause♪
Return of the Secaucus 7♪
Ruby in Paradise♪
Secrets and Lies
Sorrows of Gin
The Stranger
Torment
Touki Bouki
Vincent, Francois, Paul and the Others♪
The Woman in Question
Woof!
The Wrong Move
Zelig♪

Immigration

An American Tail
Arizona
Avalon♪
Blood Red
Borderline
Bread and Chocolate♪
Brothers in Trouble
Buck Privates Come Home♪
Bye-Bye
Combination Platter
Coming to America♪
The Cowboy Way
Does This Mean We're Married?
Drachenfutter♪
Driving Me Crazy
El Super♪
The Emigrants♪
Enemies, a Love Story♪
Far and Away
Floating Life
Green Card
Heaven Before I Die
Hester Street♪
I Can't Sleep
I Cover the Waterfront
The Immigrant♪
The Italian
Journey of Hope♪
A King in New York
La Promesse
Letters from Alou
Living on Tokyo Time
Manhattan Merengue!
The Manions of America
Maricela
Miami Rhapsody
Midnight Auto Supply
Monkey Business♪
Moscow on the Hudson♪
My Girl Tisa
My Sweet Victim
The New Land♪
Nueba Yol
O Quatrilho
Pelle the Conqueror♪
Sky High
Skyline♪
Someone Else's America♪
Wait Until Spring, Bandini
Where Is My Child?

Impending Retirement

Lethal Weapon♪
Love to Kill
Major League 3: Back to the Minors
The Mask of Zorro
Seven♪
Sonatine♪
Suicide Ride

Incest

see also **Family Ties**

Against the Wind

Andy Warhol's Frankenstein
Angels and Insects♪
The Cement Garden
The Grifters♪
The House of Yes
Innocent Lies
My Sister, My Love
Natural Born Killers
Spanking the Monkey♪
The Sweet Hereafter♪
This World, Then the Fireworks
'Tis a Pity She's a Whore
U-Turn
Vicious Circles
Waterland

India

see also **Calcutta**

The Adversary
Aparajito
Autobiography of a Princess
Bandit Queen
Bhowani Junction
The Big City
The Black Devils of Kali
Black Narcissus♪
Charulata
City of Joy
Conduct Unbecoming
The Courtesans of Bombay♪
The Deceivers
Distant Thunder♪
Drums
Ele, My Friend
The Far Pavilions
Fire
Flame Over India♪
Gandhi♪
Gunga Din♪
Heat and Dust♪
The Home and the World♪
Hullabaloo Over Georgie & Bonnie's Pictures
In Custody
Jalsaghar
The Jewel in the Crown
Journey to the Lost City
Jungle Hell
Kama Sutra: A Tale of Love
Kim♪
Kim
The Lives of a Bengal Lancer♪
The Mahabharata
The Man Who Would Be King♪
Masala
Maya
The Middleman
Mother Teresa: In the Name of God's Poor
Mountbatten: The Last Viceroy
Octopussy
A Passage to India♪
Pather Panchali♪
The Rains Came
The Razor's Edge
The River♪
Rudyard Kipling's The Jungle Book
Sabaka
Shakespeare Wallah♪
Spices♪
Staying On
Two Daughters♪
Wee Willie Winkie♪
The World of Apu♪

Interracial Affairs

Bleeding Hearts
The Bodyguard
Bulworth
Cafe au Lait♪
Chinese Box
Come See the Paradise♪
Corrina, Corrina
Driving Miss Daisy♪
A Fight for Jenny

Guess Who's Coming to Dinner♪
Jungle Fever♪
The Liberation of L.B. Jones
Love Field
Machine Gun Blues
Made in America
Miami Rhapsody
Mississippi Masala
Mr. & Mrs. Loving♪
Norman, Is That You?
A Patch of Blue
Pocahontas♪
The Story of a Three Day Pass
Taxi Blues♪
The Watermelon Woman
The Wedding Banquet♪
Zebrahead♪

Interviews

see also **This is Your Life**

Bugs Bunny Superstar
Chuck Berry: Hail! Hail! Rock 'n' Roll
The Compleat Beatles
Cult People
Hearts of Darkness: A Filmmaker's Apocalypse♪
Hedda Hopper's Hollywood
The JFK Conspiracy
La Salamandre
Roger & Me♪
Stripper
The Thin Blue Line♪
When Harry Met Sally...♪
When We Were Kings
Wisecracks♪
The Wonderful, Horrible Life of Leni Riefenstahl

Inventors & Inventions

see also **Mad Scientists; Science & Scientists**

Chairman of the Board
Chitty Chitty Bang Bang
C.H.O.M.P.S.
The Demi-Paradise♪
Edison the Man
The Great Moment
Hidden Enemy
Homer Comes Home
Homewrecker
Honey, I Blew Up the Kid
Honey, I Shrunk the Kids
Honey, We Shrunk Ourselves
Invisible Mom
The Machine
The Man in the White Suit♪
The Man Who Fell to Earth♪
The Mosquito Coast
Mystery Plane
Not Quite Human
Not Quite Human 2
The Nut
Roaring Speedboats
Rogue's Gallery
So This Is Washington
The Sound and the Silence
The Spanish Prisoner♪
Spitfire♪
Still Not Quite Human
The Story of Alexander Graham Bell♪
Theremin: An Electronic Odyssey♪
Time Chasers
Under the Hula Moon
The Water Engine
Where's Willie?
The Whole Shootin' Match♪
The Yellow Cab Man
Young Tom Edison

Invisibility

Abbott and Costello Meet the Invisible Man
The Amazing Transparent Man
Clash of the Titans
The Dancing Princesses
Dick Tracy vs. Crime Inc.
Doctor Faustus
Dr. Orloff's Invisible Horror
Golden Voyage of Sinbad
Invisible Agent
The Invisible Avenger
Invisible Dad
The Invisible Dead
The Invisible Dr. Mabuse♪
Invisible Invaders
The Invisible Kid
The Invisible Man♪
The Invisible Man Returns♪
The Invisible Maniac
The Invisible Man's Revenge
Invisible Mom
The Invisible Monster
The Invisible Strangler
The Invisible Terror
Invisible: The Chronicles of Benjamin Knight
The Invisible Woman♪
Leapin' Leprechauns
Mad Monster Party
The Man Who Wasn't There
Memoirs of an Invisible Man
Mr. Superinvisible
My Magic Dog
The New Invisible Man
Now You See Him, Now You Don't
Panama Menace
The Phantom Creeps
Phantom from Space
Phantom 2040 Movie: The Ghost Who Walks
Return of Chandu
Riding with Death
Sound of Horror

Ireland

see also **Great Britain**

Belfast Assassin
Beloved Enemy♪
Blown Away
The Boxer
The Break
Broken Harvest
The Brylcreem Boys
Cal♪
Captain Boycott
Children in the Crossfire
Circle of Deceit
Circle of Friends
The Commitments♪
The Crying Game♪
Danny Boy♪
Darby O'Gill & the Little People♪
The Dawning
The Dead♪
December Bride
The Devil's Own♪
Far and Away
The Field♪
The Fighting Prince of Donegal
Fools of Fortune
Four Days in July
Frankie Starlight
The General♪
Hear My Song♪
Hennessy
I See a Dark Stranger♪
In the Name of the Father♪
The Informer
The Informer♪
Into the West♪
Irish Cinderella
James Joyce: A Portrait of the Artist as a Young Man
Johnny Nobody
Lamb

Leprechaun
The Lonely Passion of Judith Hearne♪
Man of Aran♪
A Man of No Importance♪
The Manions of America
The Matchmaker
Men of Ireland
Michael Collins♪
Moondance
My Left Foot♪
Nothing Personal♪
Odd Man Out♪
Oh, Mr. Porter
The Playboys♪
Poltergeist: The Legacy
Prayer for the Dying
The Purple Taxi
Quiet Day In Belfast♪
The Quiet Man♪
Rawhead Rex
The Real Charlotte
River of Unrest
The Run of the Country♪
Ryan's Daughter
Scarlett
The Secret of Roan Inish♪
Shake Hands with the Devil♪
The Snapper♪
Some Mother's Son♪
Song o' My Heart♪
Spectre
Spellbreaker: Secret of the Leprechauns
Taffin
Trojan Eddie♪
Ulysses
The Van♪
War of the Buttons
Widow's Peak
Wings of the Morning

Islam

see also **Middle East**

Hamsin♪
Malcolm X: Make It Plain
Mohammed: Messenger of God
The Suitors

Island Fare

see also **Pacific Islands; Sex on the Beach**

The Adventures of Sadie
All the Brothers Were Valiant
Atlantis, the Lost Continent
Bare Essentials
Baywatch: The Movie: Forbidden Paradise
Bikini Island
Bird of Paradise
Blacksnake!
The Blue Lagoon
Body Trouble
The Bounty
Cabin Boy
Captain Ron
The Castaway Cowboy
Chandu on the Magic Island
Club Paradise
Conqueror & the Empress
The Cover Girl Murders
Crusoe
Cutthroat Island
Cyber Bandits
Deadly Currents
Dinosaur Island
Dungeon of Harrow
Echoes of Paradise
Emmanuelle on Taboo Island
Escape from Atlantis
Exit to Eden
Father Goose
Flipper♪
F.P. 1
Gilligan's Island: Meet the Crew
Hawk of the Wilderness

Macho

American Ninja
American Ninja 2: The Confrontation
American Ninja 4: The Annihilation
Assassins
Atlas
Atom Man vs. Superman
The Avenger
Backdraft
Bad Boys🗡
Bail Out
Bail Out at 43,000
The Barbarians
Beastmaster 3: The Eye of Braxus
Black Cobra 2
The Black Pirate🗡
Bloodsport 3
Blue Blazes Rawden
Body Armor
Bootleg
Brannigan
A Bridge Too Far
Brutal Glory
Buck Rogers in the 25th Century
Bulletproof
Cannonball Run
Cannonball Run 2
Captain America
Chasers
Chino
The Cobra
Codename: Terminate
Colossus and the Amazon Queen
Combat Killers
Con Air🗡
Conan the Barbarian🗡.
Conan the Destroyer
Conquest of Mycene
Convoy
Cool Hand Luke🗡
Coriolanus, Man without a Country
Cyborg Cop
Cyborg Soldier
Daylight
Dead Man Walking
Deadly Spygames
Deathstalker 4: Match of Titans
Delta Force 3: The Killing Game
D.I.
Diamonds Are Forever🗡
Dick Tracy🗡
Dick Tracy, Detective
Dick Tracy, Detective/The Corpse Vanishes
Dick Tracy Meets Gruesome
Dick Tracy Returns
Dick Tracy: The Original Serial, Vol. 1🗡
Dick Tracy: The Original Serial, Vol. 2🗡
Dick Tracy vs. Crime Inc.
Dick Tracy vs. Cueball
Dick Tracy's Dilemma
The Dirty Dozen🗡
The Dirty Dozen: The Deadly Mission
The Dirty Dozen: The Fatal Mission
The Dirty Dozen: The Next Mission
Dirty Harry🗡
Dr. No🗡
The Dogs of War
The Dolls
Donnie Brasco🗡
Double Impact
Double Revenge
Dragon Fury 2
Duel of Champions
Dune Warriors
Eastern Condors
Excessive Force
Fast Gun
Fatal Combat
Fearless Tiger

A Few Good Men🗡
Firestorm
Firewalker
First Blood
First Knight
Fist
Fist of Glory
Fist of the North Star
A Fistful of Dollars🗡
For Your Eyes Only🗡
Force of One
Forced Vengeance
Fury on Wheels
Futurekick
Gator
Giant🗡
The Giant of Marathon
The Giant of Metropolis
The Giants of Thessaly
The Gladiator🗡
Gladiator of Rome
Gladiators 7
The Glimmer Man
Goliath Against the Giants
Goliath and the Dragon
Gone with the Wind🗡
The Green Hornet
Greystoke: The Legend of Tarzan, Lord of the Apes
Guns
Hangfire
Hard Knox
Hard Promises
Hard to Kill
Hawkeye
Heat🗡
Hell in the Pacific🗡
Hellfighters
Hercules
Hercules 2
Hercules Against the Moon Men
Hercules and the Princess of Troy
Hercules in New York
Hercules the Legendary Journeys, Vol. 1: And the Amazon Women
Hercules the Legendary Journeys, Vol. 2: The Lost Kingdom
Hercules the Legendary Journeys, Vol. 3: The Circle of Fire
Hercules the Legendary Journeys, Vol. 4: In the Underworld
Hero of Rome
Heroes Three
Highlander: The Final Dimension
Hired to Kill
The Hitman
Hooper
The Horsemen
Hot Shots! Part Deux🗡
The Hustle
I Come in Peace
Infra-Man
The Invaders
Invasion U.S.A.
The Iron Crown
Jingle All the Way
Judex
Judge & Jury
Kill and Kill Again
The Killing Zone
Kindergarten Cop
Kinjite: Forbidden Subjects
K2: The Ultimate High
Kull the Conqueror
Last Action Hero
Last Flight to Hell
The Last Samurai
The Last Warrior
Legend of the Lone Ranger
Lethal Tender
License to Kill🗡
The Lion of Thebes🗡
The Long Ships
Machoman

Maciste in Hell
Mad Wax: The Surf Movie
The Magnificent Matador
The Magnificent Seven🗡
Magnum Force
The Mambo Kings🗡
A Man Called Rage
The Man with the Golden Gun
The Masked Marvel
Master Blaster
McBain🗡
Mean Guns
Medusa Against the Son of Hercules
Men of War
Mercenary
Messalina vs. the Son of Hercules
Messenger of Death
Missing in Action
Missing in Action 2: The Beginning
Mr. Majestyk
Mobsters
Mole Men against the Son of Hercules
Murphy's Law
Neutron and the Black Mask
Neutron vs. the Amazing Dr. Caronte
Neutron vs. the Death Robots
Neutron vs. the Maniac
Never Say Die
Never Say Never Again
No Holds Barred
No Way Back
Nomad Riders
The Odyssey
One Down, Two to Go!
One-Eyed Jacks🗡
One Man Jury
Operation: Delta Force
Out for Justice
Park Avenue Logger
Partners
Party Animal
Paternity
Patton🗡
Police Story
Prison Planet
Project A: Part 2
Ragin' Cajun
Raging Bull🗡
Rambo: First Blood, Part 2
Rambo 3
Ransom🗡
Raw Deal
Raw Justice
Red Scorpion 2
Return to Savage Beach
Revolt of the Barbarians
The Road Warrior🗡
Robin Hood🗡
Rocky🗡
Rocky 2
Rocky 3
Rocky 4
Rocky 5
Roland the Mighty
Rollercoaster
The Rookie
Rough Riders
The Runaway Barge
Samson Against the Sheik
Samson and His Mighty Challenge
Samson and the 7 Miracles of the World
Sands of Iwo Jima🗡
Savage
The Searchers🗡
Seven
Seven Magnificent Gladiators
The Seventh Voyage of Sinbad🗡
The Shadow
Shaft🗡
Shaft's Big Score
Sharpe's Battle
Sharpe's Company

Sharpe's Eagle
Sharpe's Enemy
Sharpe's Gold
Sharpe's Honour
Sharpe's Justice
Sharpe's Legend
Sharpe's Mission
Sharpe's Regiment
Sharpe's Revenge
Sharpe's Rifles
Sharpe's Siege
Sharpe's Sword
Sharpe's Waterloo
Shootfighter 2: Kill or Be Killed!
Silent Action
Sinbad of the Seven Seas
Sirocco
Soldier's Fortune
Son of Sinbad
Sorcerer
Spawn🗡
Speed🗡
Spy Smasher Returns
Stagecoach🗡
Steel
Steel Cowboy
Stone Cold
Stormquest
Street Fighter
Street Law
Street Soldiers
A Streetcar Named Desire🗡
Suburban Commando
Superargo
Superman: The Movie🗡
Superman 2🗡
Superman 3
Superman 4: The Quest for Peace
Superman & the Mole Men
Swamp Fire
Swashbuckler
The Swordsman
Tango and Cash
Tarzan and the Green Goddess
Tarzan, the Ape Man🗡
Tarzan, the Ape Man
Tarzan's Revenge
Ten to Midnight
Terror of Rome Against the Son of Hercules
Terror of the Steppes
Test Pilot🗡
Thief🗡
Thieves of Fortune
The 13th Mission
Thor and the Amazon Women
Thunder Warrior 3
Thunderball
Tiger Joe
Too Late the Hero🗡
Tor
Total Recall🗡
Tough Guy
Triumph of the Son of Hercules
Two Mules for Sister Sara🗡
Tyrant of Lydia Against the Son of Hercules
Under Siege
Under Siege 2: Dark Territory
Venus Against the Son of Hercules
The Viking Sagas
Virus
Viva Villa!🗡
Vulcan God of Fire
Warlords 3000
Where Eagles Dare🗡
White Lightning
Wild Bill
The Wild Bunch🗡
Windjammer

The Ape Man
Atom Age Vampire
Attack of the 60-Foot Centerfold
Attack of the Swamp Creature
Before I Hang🗡
Bela Lugosi Meets a Brooklyn Gorilla
Beverly Hills Bodysnatchers
Bloodbath at the House of Death
Bloodlust
Body Armor
The Body Shop
Bowery Boys Meet the Monsters
The Brain that Wouldn't Die
Brenda Starr
Bride of Re-Animator
Bride of the Monster
Captain America
Captive Wild Woman
The Cars That Ate Paris🗡
Castle of Evil
Castle of the Creeping Flesh
The City of Lost Children🗡
The Cobweb
The Corpse Vanishes
Creator
Creature of the Walking Dead
The Creeper
The Creeping Flesh
The Creeps
The Crime of Dr. Crespi
Crimes of Dr. Mabuse🗡
The Curse of the Aztec Mummy
Cyborg Cop
Darkman🗡
Darkman 2: The Return of Durant
Darkman 3: Die Darkman Die
The Dead Next Door
Dead Pit
Dead Sleep
Death Warmed Up
Deep Red
Devil Doll🗡
Dr. Black, Mr. Hyde
Doctor Blood's Coffin
Doctor Butcher M.D.
Dr. Caligari
Dr. Cyclops
Dr. Death, Seeker of Souls
Dr. Frankenstein's Castle of Freaks
Dr. Goldfoot and the Bikini Machine
Dr. Jekyll and Mr. Hyde🗡
Dr. Jekyll and Mr. Hyde
Dr. Jekyll and Sister Hyde
Dr. Jekyll and the Wolfman
Dr. Jekyll's Dungeon of Death
Dr. No🗡
Dr. Orloff's Monster
Doctor X
Donovan's Brain🗡
The Double O Kid
Embryo
Evil Town
The Fear Chamber
The Flesh Eaters
Frankenhooker
Frankenstein🗡
Frankenstein
Frankenstein and the Monster from Hell
Frankenstein '80
Frankenstein General Hospital
Frankenstein Must Be Destroyed
Frankenstein Unbound🗡
Frankenstein's Daughter
Freaked
The Freakmaker
Geisha Girl
The Giant Spider Invasion
Girl in His Pocket
The Head
Hellmaster
Hideous Sun Demon
House of Frankenstein
Hyena of London
The Immortalizer

Mad Scientists

see also Inventors & Inventions; Science & Scientists

Alien Terminator

Marriage

Fourth Story⬧
French Twist
Frieda
From the Terrace
Fulfillment
Full of Life
Fun with Dick and Jane
Gaslight⬧
A Gathering of Eagles
A Gentle Woman
George Washington
George Washington: The
  Forging of a Nation
Gertrud⬧
Get Out Your Handkerchiefs⬧
Getting Up and Going Home
The Ghost and the Guest
Giant⬧
The Gift of Love
Girl from Hunan⬧
Goin' to Town
The Good Wife
Gore Vidal's Lincoln
Grace of My Heart
Grand Isle
Grand Theft Auto
The Grass Is Greener
Greed⬧
The Greek Tycoon
Grievous Bodily Harm
Group Marriage
Grown Ups
Grumpier Old Men
The Guardsman⬧
Guess Who's Coming to
  Dinner⬧
Guest Wife
A Guide for the Married Man⬧
A Guide for the Married Woman
The Hairdresser's Husband
Halfmoon
Hamsun
A Handful of Dust⬧
Hard Promises
Harriet Craig⬧
The Hawk
Head Above Water
The Heartbreak Kid⬧
Heartburn
Heaven's Prisoners
Helas pour Moi
Hell-Ship Morgan
Here We Go Again!
High Heels
High Society⬧
Highway Patrolman
Hindsight
Homecoming⬧
Honeymoon
Honeymoon Academy
Hope Floats
The Horrible Dr. Hichcock
Hostage for a Day
Hot Spell
Hotel Room
The Householder
How to Break Up a Happy
  Divorce
How to Commit Marriage
How to Make an American Quilt
How to Marry a Millionaire
How to Murder Your Wife⬧
The Howards of Virginia
Hurry, Charlie, Hurry
Husbands and Lovers
Husbands and Wives⬧
Hush
I Do! I Do!
I Dood It
I Like It Like That⬧
I Love My...Wife
I Love You Again⬧
I Love You ... Goodbye
I Love You Rosa
I Love You to Death
I Married a Vampire
I Married a Woman
I Only Want You to Love Me
I Was a Male War Bride⬧

I Will, I Will for Now
I Wonder Who's Killing Her
  Now?
Il Bell'Antonio
Il Grido
Illicit
Illusions
I'm on My Way/The Non-Stop
  Kid
Immortal Bachelor
The Imported Bridegroom
In Celebration⬧
In Name Only
Indecent Proposal
Infinity
The Innocent⬧
Intersection
Intimate Story
Intimate Strangers
Intruso
The Invasion of Carol Enders⬧
The Invisible Ghost
It Started with a Kiss
It Takes Two
Java Head⬧
Jenny
The Jeweller's Shop
Josepha⬧
Ju Dou⬧
Jubal
Jubilee Trail
Jude⬧
Jude the Obscure
Juliet of the Spirits⬧
Just Like Weather⬧
The Keeper
Keeper of the Flame
The Kettles on Old MacDonald's
  Farm
The Kill-Off
Killing Heat
A Kind of Loving⬧
Kiss and Be Killed
Kuni Lemel in Tel Aviv
La Bete Humaine⬧
La Chienne⬧
La Vengeance d'une Femme
La Vie Continue
Lady Chatterley's Lover
Lady Godiva
Lady L
Lady Windermere's Fan
Last Breath
The Last Dance
The Last Days of Chez Nous
The Last Married Couple in
  America
L'Atalante⬧
Late Spring⬧
Laurel & Hardy: Be Big
Le Beau Mariage⬧
Le Bonheur
Le Bonheur Est Dans le Pre
Le Chat⬧
Lea
L'Enfer⬧
Leo Tolstoy's Anna Karenina
Lesson in Love
Let's Get Married
A Letter to Three Wives⬧
Lianna
The Liars
Liar's Moon
Lie Down with Lions
Life of Oharu⬧
Like It Never Was Before
Linda
Listen, Darling
A Little Sex
Lonely Wives
The Long Haul
The Long, Long Trailer
Losing Chase
Lost Highway
Lost Honeymoon
The Lotus Eaters
Loulou⬧
Love, Cheat & Steal
Love from a Stranger

Love Matters
Love Walked In
The Lovers⬧
Lovers and Other Strangers⬧
Loving Couples
Lucy and Desi: Before the
  Laughter
Lust and Revenge
Ma Saison Preferee⬧
Maborosi⬧
Madame Bovary
Madame Butterfly
Made for Each Other⬧
Made in Heaven
Making Love
The Makioka Sisters⬧
Man from Nowhere
Man of the House
The Man Who Cried
Manhattan Murder Mystery⬧
Mannequin
Maria Chapdelaine⬧
The Marriage Circle⬧
Marriage Is Alive and Well
Marriage Italian Style⬧
The Marriage of Maria Braun⬧
Married?
Married People, Single Sex 2:
  For Better or Worse
Married to It
Married Too Young
A Married Woman⬧
The Marrying Kind
Martha and I⬧
Marty⬧
Mary, Queen of Scots
Matrimaniac
Max, Mon Amour
McLintock!⬧
The Member of the Wedding
Memories of a Marriage⬧
Memory of Us
Men...⬧
The Merry Widow
Mexican Spitfire at Sea
Miami Rhapsody
Microwave Massacre
Mid-Channel
Midnight⬧
Midnight Crossing
Mighty Aphrodite
The Millionairess
Miracle of Morgan's Creek⬧
The Mirror Has Two Faces
Misbehaving Husbands
Mrs. Dalloway
Mr. & Mrs. Loving⬧
Mr. & Mrs. Smith⬧
Mr. Love
Mr. Mom⬧
Mr. Skeffington⬧
Mr. Sycamore
Mr. Wonderful
Mistress⬧
Modern Love
The Money Pit
Montana
Moon over Harlem
The Moon's Our Home
Mouth to Mouth
Multiplicity
Murder at 45 R.P.M.
Murder Czech Style
Murder So Sweet
Murders in the Zoo
Muriel's Wedding
The Music Lovers
My Dear Secretary
My First Wife
My Little Chickadee⬧
My Michael⬧
My New Gun
My Other Husband
My Sweet Victim
Naked Jungle
The New Age
Niagara
Nightkill
Nina Takes a Lover

Normal Life
Not Tonight Darling
The Notorious Lady
Nouvelle Vague
Now and Forever
Nudo di Donna⬧
Nurse Marjorie
O Quatrilho
Odd Obsession
O'Hara's Wife
The O.J. Simpson Story
Oldest Confederate Widow Tells
  All⬧
On Approval⬧
On Golden Pond⬧
On Her Majesty's Secret
  Service⬧
On Valentine's Day
One Good Turn
One Night in the Tropics
One of My Wives Is Missing
One Trick Pony
Only with Married Men
Orchestra Wives⬧
Overnight Sensation
The Paint Job
Paint Your Wagon
The Painted Veil
Pajama Tops
The Palm Beach Story⬧
Paper Marriage
A Paper Wedding⬧
Paradise⬧
Pardon Mon Affaire⬧
Pardon Mon Affaire, Too!
Paris, France
Passion in Paradise
A Passion to Kill
Pedale Douce
Peggy Sue Got Married
The Penitent
Pennies From Heaven⬧
Perfect Alibi
The Perfect Bride
Perfect Crime
The Perfect Marriage
A Perfect Murder
Period of Adjustment⬧
Persuasion
Pete 'n' Tillie
Pete Townshend: White City
Petulia
Phaedra
Phffft!
The Philadelphia Story⬧
The Piano⬧
Picture Bride
A Piece of Pleasure⬧
Pipe Dreams
Platinum Blonde⬧
Playing Dead
Portrait of a Lady⬧
Portrait of Teresa⬧
The Postman Always Rings
  Twice⬧
The Postman Always Rings
  Twice
Praying Mantis
Prelude to a Kiss
Primary Colors
The Primitive Lover
Prisoner of Second Avenue
Prisoners of Inertia
Private Life
Private Lives⬧
Promises! Promises!
Provincial Actors
Prowler
The Pumpkin Eater⬧
The Purchase Price
Pushing Hands
Quartet⬧
Queen Bee
Queen Margot⬧
Question of Faith
Race for Life
Rachel and the Stranger⬧
Raging Bull⬧
Raise the Red Lantern⬧

Rape and Marriage: The Rideout
  Case
Rebecca⬧
Reckless⬧
The Rector's Wife
Red Rock West⬧
Revenge of the Stepford Wives
Reversal of Fortune⬧
Rich and Famous
Rich and Strange
The Rich Man's Wife
Rider from Tucson
Riptide⬧
Risky Business
Rocky 2
Romantic Englishwoman⬧
The Roof
Rose of Washington Square
Roseanne: An Unauthorized
  Biography
A Royal Scandal
Runaways
Ryan's Daughter
Safe Passage
Santa Fe
Sarah's Child
Satan's Black Wedding
Saturday Night and Sunday
  Morning⬧
Savage Attraction
Say Yes!
Scar of Shame
Scarlet Dawn
Scenes from a Mall
Scenes from a Marriage⬧
Scorchers
Score
Season of Fear
Second Chance
Secret Beyond the Door
Secrets of Women⬧
Seems Like Old Times
Send Me No Flowers⬧
Separate Vacations
Separate Ways
Seven Chances⬧
Seven Days Ashore/Hurry,
  Charlie, Hurry
The Seven Year Itch⬧
The Seventeenth Bride
Sex and the Single Girl
Sexpot
Sexual Malice
Shadowlands⬧
The Shakiest Gun in the West
The Shame⬧
Shattered
She and He
She-Devil
She Waits
She's Having a Baby
She's So Lovely
She's the One
Shoot the Moon
Shooting Elizabeth
Sibling Rivalry
Silent Tongue
Silent Victim
Sin Takes a Holiday
The Singing Blacksmith
The Single Standard
The Sisters⬧
Sketch Artist
Skinner's Dress Suit
The Slugger's Wife
Smash Palace
Smash-Up: The Story of a
  Woman⬧
Smoking/No Smoking
Smouldering Fires
Snoopy's Getting Married,
  Charlie Brown
Snow White: A Tale of Terror
So This Is Paris⬧
Sofie
The Soft Skin⬧
Something to Talk About
Soul Food
Sound of Murder

Night Hunter
Night Master
Night of the Kickfighters
Night of the Warrior
9 1/2 Ninjas
Nine Deaths of the Ninja
Ninja 3: The Domination
Ninja Academy
Ninja: American Warrior
Ninja Brothers of Blood
Ninja Champion
Ninja Checkmate
Ninja Commandments
Ninja Condors
Ninja Connection
Ninja Death Squad
Ninja Demon's Massacre
Ninja Destroyer
Ninja Dragon
Ninja Exterminators
Ninja Fantasy
Ninja Hunt
Ninja Massacre
Ninja Masters of Death
Ninja Mission
Ninja Nightmare
Ninja of the Magnificence
Ninja Operation: Licensed to
    Terminate
Ninja Phantom Heroes
The Ninja Pirates
Ninja Powerforce
Ninja Showdown
Ninja Squad
Ninja Strike Force
Ninja Supremo
Ninja Swords of Death
Ninja the Battalion
Ninja the Protector
Ninja, the Violent Sorcerer
Ninja Turf
Ninja Vengeance
Ninja vs. Ninja
Ninja vs. the Shaolin
Ninja's Extreme Weapons
No Retreat, No Surrender
No Retreat, No Surrender 2
No Retreat, No Surrender 3:
    Blood Brothers
The Noble Ninja
Octagon
Of Cooks and Kung-Fu
Omega Cop
One Down, Two to Go!
One-Eyed Swordsman
One Man Army
Only the Strong
Open Fire
Operation Condor
Operation Golden Phoenix
Operation Orient
Out for Blood
Out for Justice
Overkill
The Perfect Weapon
Phoenix the Ninja
The Power of the Ninjitsu
The Power Within
Pray for Death
Prodigal Boxer: The Kick of
    Death
The Prodigal Son
Professional Killers 1
Protector
Pursuit
Pushed to the Limit
Queen Boxer
The Quest
Rage and Honor
Rage and Honor 2: Hostile
    Takeover
Rage of Honor
Rage of Wind
Ragin' Cajun
Rapid Fire
Raw Force
Raw Target
Real Bruce Lee
Red Sun Rising

Redemption: Kickboxer 5
Remo Williams: The Adventure
    Begins
Renegade Monk
Renegade Ninja
Retrievers
Return of the Chinese Boxer
Return of the Dragon
Return of the Scorpion
Return of the Street Fighter
Return of the Tiger
Revenge of the Ninja
Ring of Fire
Ring of Fire 2: Blood and Steel
Ring of Fire 3: Lion Strike
Ring of Steel
Riot
Rivals of the Silver Fox
Roller Blade
Rumble in the Bronx
Sakura Killers
Sanshiro Sugata⚬
Scorpion
Seven Blows of the Dragon
The 7 Brothers Meet Dracula
Shadow Killers
Shao Lin Popeye
Shaolin Ex-Monk
Shaolin Executioner
Shaolin Kung Fu Mystagogue
Shaolin Temple Strikes Back
Shaolin Traitor
Shaolin Vengence
Shinobi Ninja
Shogun's Ninja
Shootfighter 2: Kill or Be Killed!
Shootfighter: Fight to the Death
Showdown
Showdown at the Equator
Showdown in Little Tokyo
Sidekicks
Silent Assassins
Silent Rage
Sister Street Fighter
Slaughter in San Francisco
Sleepy Eyes of Death: The
    Chinese Jade
Sloane
Snake in the Eagle's Shadow 2
Snuff-Bottle Connection
Space Ninja: Sword of the
    Space Ark
Steel Fisted Dragon
Stickfighter
Sting of the Dragon Masters
Story of the Dragon
The Stranger and the Gunfighter
Stranglehold
The Street Fighter
The Street Fighter's Last
    Revenge
Street Hunter
Street Soldiers
Super Ninjas
Supercop
Surf Ninjas
Survival Game
Survival of a Dragon
Sword of Doom⚬
Sword of Fury II
Sword of Honor
Swords of Death
Tai Chi 2
Talons of the Eagle
Tattoo Connection
Teenage Mutant Ninja Turtles:
    The Movie
Teenage Mutant Ninja Turtles 2:
    The Secret of the Ooze
Ten Brothers of Shao-lin
They Call Me Bruce?
They Still Call Me Bruce
The Three Avengers
3 Ninjas
Three Ninjas: High Noon at
    Mega Mountain
3 Ninjas Kick Back
3 Ninjas Knuckle Up
Thundering Ninja

Tiger Claws
Tiger Heart
Tigershark
Timecop
TNT Jackson
To Be the Best
To the Death
Tongs: An American Nightmare
Top Dog
Tough Guy
Trancers 3: Deth Lives
Triple Impact
The True Game of Death
24 Hours to Midnight
Twister Kicker
Two Assassins in the Dark
Two Graves to Kung-Fu
The Two Great Cavaliers
Two Wondrous Tigers
The Unbeaten 28
Undefeatable
Unmasking the Idol
Vampire Raiders—Ninja Queen
Vengeance of the Snowmaid
Venus the Ninja
Warrior of Justice
Way of the Black Dragon
Weapons of Death
When Taekwondo Strikes
White Phantom: Enemy of
    Darkness
White Tiger
Wing Chun
Without Mercy
The Young Bruce Lee
Young Dragon
Young Master
Young Tiger
Zatoichi: Master Ichi and a
    Chest of Gold
Zatoichi: The Blind Swordsman
    and the Chess Expert
Zatoichi: The Blind Swordsman's
    Vengeance
Zatoichi vs. Yojimbo⚬

Martyred Pop Icons

see also *Rock Stars on
    Film*

Basquiat⚬
Beatlemania! The Movie
Blue Hawaii
Bob Dylan: Don't Look Back⚬
The Buddy Holly Story⚬
Bus Stop⚬
Clambake
The Doors
The Doors: Soft Parade, a
    Retrospective
Elvis and Me
Elvis: The Movie
Forever James Dean
Fun in Acapulco
I Shot Andy Warhol⚬
James Dean Story
John & Yoko: A Love Story
King Creole
Kissin' Cousins
La Bamba⚬
Lenny⚬
Live a Little, Love a Little
Love Me Tender
Marilyn: The Untold Story⚬
Norma Jean and Marilyn
Paradise, Hawaiian Style
The Real Buddy Holly Story
Rebel Without a Cause⚬
The Rose⚬
Roustabout
Sgt. Pepper's Lonely Hearts
    Club Band
The Seven Year Itch⚬
Speedway
Spinout
Stardust Memories
Stay Away, Joe
This Is Elvis
Train to Hollywood⚬

The Trouble with Girls (and How
    To Get Into It)⚬

Mass Media

see also *Front Page; Radio*
America
And Nothing But the Truth
At Home with the Webbers
Behind the Rising Sun
Bigfoot: The Unforgettable
    Encounter
Blankman
Broadcast News⚬
A Case of Libel
Chill Factor
The China Syndrome⚬
Crimetime
A Cry in the Dark⚬
Dead Men Don't Die
Death Watch⚬
Demonstone
E. Nick: A Legend in His Own
    Mind
Eternity
Exiled to Shanghai
Eyewitness
A Face in the Crowd⚬
France/Tour/Detour/Deux/
    Enfants⚬
The Gladiators
The Groove Tube
Groundhog Day⚬
Hero⚬
Hollywood Scandals and
    Tragedies
I Was a Teenage TV Terrorist
The Image
In and Out⚬
Indictment: The McMartin Trial⚬
International House
King of the Airwaves
The Late Shift
Lipstick Camera
Live! From Death Row
Livin' Large
The Lost Honor of Katharina
    Blum⚬
Love and a .45
Loving You
Mad City
Max Headroom, the Original
    Story
Medium Cool⚬
Meet Wally Sparks
Mr. Reliable: A True Story
My Favorite Year⚬
National Lampoon's Attack of
    the 5 Ft. 2 Women
Natural Born Killers⚬
Network⚬
News at Eleven
Nothing Sacred⚬
The Passenger⚬
Pray TV
Primary Colors
Prime Suspect
Prime Time Murder
Private Parts
Quiz Show⚬
Ratings Game
Ready to Wear
Riders of the Storm
Scrooged
The Second Civil War
The Seduction
Sex Through a Window
S.F.W.
Six Fois Deux/Sur et Sous la
    Communication⚬
Soft and Hard
The Story of Esther Costello
The Stuff
Superstar: The Life and Times of
    Andy Warhol⚬
Switching Channels
Tabloid!
The Thrill of It All!
To Die For⚬

Tomorrow Never Dies
The Truman Show⚬
Tunnelvision
UHF
Up Close and Personal⚬
Videodrome
Wayne's World⚬
Weapons of Mass Distraction
Welcome to Sarajevo⚬
Wild Horses
Witness to the Execution
Zelig⚬

May-December Romance

see also *Coming of Age;
    Growing Older; Romantic
    Adventures; Romantic
    Comedy; Romantic Drama*
All That Heaven Allows⚬
Atlantic City⚬
Cass Timberlane
The Color of Evening
Goodbye Again
The Graduate⚬
Harold and Maude⚬
Live Bait
Love in the Afternoon
Nelly et Monsieur Arnaud⚬
The Pallbearer
Reckless⚬
Roman Spring of Mrs. Stone⚬
Sabrina⚬
Six Days, Seven Nights
That Obscure Object of Desire⚬
Tim
Trojan Eddie⚬

The Meaning of Life

The Apostle⚬
At Home with the Webbers
Badlands⚬
Being Human
The Blood of Others
Breathing Lessons⚬
The Castle⚬
The Collector⚬
The Designated Mourner
End of the Road
Field of Dreams⚬
The French Lieutenant's
    Woman⚬
Full Body Massage
Funny Face⚬
Galaxies Are Colliding
Gospa
Heaven Can Wait⚬
Here Comes Mr. Jordan⚬
Joey Breaker⚬
Julian Po
Land and Freedom⚬
Life Upside Down
Love and Death⚬
Monty Python's The Meaning of
    Life⚬
My Life
My Own Private Idaho⚬
The Razor's Edge⚬
The Razor's Edge
The Remains of the Day⚬
Shadowlands⚬
The Sheltering Sky⚬
The Trial
Why Has Bodhi-Darma Left for
    the East
Wings of Desire⚬
Zabriskie Point⚬

Medieval Romps

see also *Camelot (Old);
    Historical Drama; Period
    Piece; Swashbucklers*
The Adventures of Robin Hood⚬
Army of Darkness⚬

Some Mother's Son�later
Soul Vengeance
Space Rage
Stir Crazy
Taking Care of Business
Tank
Terminal Island
Terror of the Bloodhunters
Terror on Alcatraz
There was a Crooked Man
They Never Come Back
They Went That-a-Way & That-
　a-Way
Tomb of the Undead
Torture Ship
Triumph of the Spirit⋪
Truth or Die
Two-Way Stretch
Ulee's Gold⋪
Weeds⋪
William Faulkner's Old Man
Without Evidence
Women's Prison Massacre
Yol⋪

Mental Retardation
see also Physical Problems;
Savants

Bill⋪
Bill: On His Own⋪
Charly⋪
A Child Is Waiting⋪
A Dangerous Woman
Dark Night of the Scarecrow
A Day in the Death of Joe Egg⋪
Dominick & Eugene⋪
The Eighth Day
Family Pictures⋪
Heart of Dragon
Homer and Eddie
Larry
L'Enfant d'Eau
The Locusts
Lovey: A Circle of Children 2
Malcolm
Of Mice and Men⋪
Rain Man⋪
The Rain People⋪
Shooting Fish
Sling Blade⋪
Slipping into Darkness
Some Folks Call It a Sling
　Blade⋪
Square Dance
Sweetie⋪
Tim
Two of a Kind
What's Eating Gilbert Grape⋪
The Wizard
The Woman Who Willed a
　Miracle

Metamorphosis
see also Genetics;
Werewolves

An American Werewolf in
　London⋪
Boogie Nights⋪
Cat People⋪
Cat People
The Company of Wolves⋪
The Curse of the Werewolf
The Fly⋪
The Fly⋪
The Fly 2
The Howling⋪
I Was a Teenage Werewolf
The Lair of the White Worm⋪
Naked Lunch⋪
The Nutty Professor⋪
Silver Bullet
Species
Stephen King's Thinner
Vampire in Brooklyn
Wasp Woman
When the Cat's Away⋪

Wolfen⋪
The Wolfman
Woof!

Meteors, Asteroids, and Comets
see also Alien Beings—
Vicious; Disaster Flicks;
Space Operas

Alien Dead
Armageddon
The Blob
The Blob⋪
Creepshow
The Day It Came to Earth
Day of the Triffids⋪
Deep Impact
Die, Monster, Die!
The Invisible Ray
Lifeforce
Meteor
The Meteor Man
Meteor Monster
The Monolith Monsters
Night of the Comet
The Phantom Creeps
The Pink Chiquitas
Return of the Aliens: The Deadly
　Spawn
Stalker⋪
Trapped in Space

Mexico
see also Central America

Across the Bridge
Against All Odds
The Black Scorpion
The Border⋪
Borderline
Breakout
A Bullet for the General
Bullfighter & the Lady
Bullfighters
Captain from Castile⋪
The Cisco Kid
Commando Squad
Crazy from the Heart⋪
Danzon⋪
Desperado⋪
Django
8 Heads in a Duffel Bag
El Mariachi⋪
Escape from Cell Block 3
The Falcon in Mexico
Five Giants from Texas
Found Alive
From Dusk Till Dawn
Fun in Acapulco
Highway Patrolman
His Kind of Woman⋪
Holiday in Mexico
A Home of Our Own
In 'n Out
Interval
Juarez
Kid from Spain
Like Water for Chocolate⋪
Los Olvidados⋪
Love Has Many Faces
The Magnificent Seven⋪
The Mask of Zorro
The Masked Rider
Mexican Hayride
The Night of the Iguana⋪
Octaman
Old Gringo
On the Line
Out to Sea
The Pearl⋪
The Professionals⋪
The Proud Ones
Pure Luck
Que Viva Mexico⋪
Reed: Insurgent Mexico⋪
Rough Magic
The Scout

Shoot the Living, Pray for the
　Dead
Sonny and Jed
South of Santa Fe
Survival Run
Three Amigos
The Torch
Touch of Evil⋪
Treasure of the Sierra Madre⋪
Two Mules for Sister Sara⋪
Valdez Is Coming
Vera Cruz
Villa Rides
Viva Villa!⋪
Viva Zapata!⋪
Warlords from Hell
The White Orchid
Wild Rovers

Miami
see also American South

Ace Ventura: Pet Detective
Band of the Hand
The Birdcage⋪
Blood & Wine
Curdled
Elmore Leonard's Gold Coast
Fair Game
Fires Within
Get Shorty⋪
Illtown
Miami Beach Cops
Miami Blues
Miami Cops
Miami Horror
Miami Hustle
Miami Rhapsody
Miami Supercops
Miami Vendetta
Miami Vice
Miami Vice 2: The Prodigal Son
Off and Running
The Perez Family
The Pest
Pronto
Ride
Scarface⋪
Two Much
Wild Things

Middle East
see also Desert War/
Foreign Legion; Deserts;
Genies; Islam; Israel;
Persian Gulf War;
Terrorism

Abbott and Costello Meet the
　Mummy
Ali Baba and the Forty Thieves
Ali Baba and the 40 Thieves⋪
The Ambassador
The Arab Conspiracy
Arabian Nights
The Assignment
Bagdad
Bloodstone
A Casualty of War
Chain of Command
Cleopatra
Counterforce
The Crusades
Cup Final
Eagles Attack at Dawn
The Egyptian
Fictitious Marriage
Five Graves to Cairo⋪
Flame of Araby
The Flight of the Phoenix⋪
The Glory Boys
The Great Armored Car Swindle
The Guns and the Fury
Halfmoon
Hamsin⋪
Hanna K.
Harum Scarum
Held Hostage

Honeybaby
Hostages⋪
Ilsa, Harem Keeper of the Oil
　Sheiks
The Invincible Six
Iran: Days of Crisis
Iron Eagle
Iron Eagle 2
Ishtar
The Jewel of the Nile
Joseph
Khartoum
Killing Streets
King Richard and the Crusaders
Lawrence of Arabia⋪
Legend of the Lost Tomb
Life and Nothing More ...
The Lighthorsemen⋪
The Lone Runner
A Matter of WHO
Mercenary
Moses
Not Without My Daughter
On Wings of Eagles
Paradise
Raiders of the Lost Ark⋪
Rescue Force
The Road to Morocco⋪
The Robe
Rosebud
Sadat
The Sheik⋪
The Silences of the Palace⋪
Sirocco
Son of Ali Baba
The Spy Who Loved Me
The Taste of the Cherry
Three Days in Beirut
Through the Olive Trees⋪
Torn Apart
Trident Force
Unveiled
Warbirds
A Wedding in Galilee⋪
The White Balloon⋪

Military: Air Force
see also Airborne

Afterburn⋪
Air Force⋪
Battle Hymn
Call to Glory
Hot Shots!⋪
Hot Shots! Part Deux
McHale's Navy Joins the Air
　Force
Memphis Belle⋪
Sergeant Matlovich vs. the U.S.
　Air Force
Strategic Air Command
War Lover

Military: Army

Battle of the Bulge
Battle of the Commandos
The Big Red One⋪
Buffalo Soldiers⋪
Call Out the Marines
Casualties of War⋪
Combat!
Combat Killers
Courage Under Fire⋪
The Court Martial of Billy
　Mitchell⋪
The Court Martial of Jackie
　Robinson⋪
Dead Men Can't Dance
The Dirty Dozen⋪
The Dirty Dozen: The Deadly
　Mission
The Dirty Dozen: The Fatal
　Mission
The Dirty Dozen: The Next
　Mission
Ernest in the Army
Francis Joins the WACs

G.I. Blues
Godzilla
The Green Berets
In Pursuit of Honor
In the Army Now
Independence Day⋪
The Major and the Minor⋪
M*A*S*H⋪
M*A*S*H: Goodbye, Farewell &
　Amen⋪
A Midnight Clear⋪
Never Wave at a WAC
1941
Operation Dumbo Drop
Patton⋪
The Peacemaker
The Perfect Furlough
Platoon⋪
Platoon Leader
Private Benjamin
Regeneration
Saving Private Ryan
A Soldier's Story⋪
Starship Troopers⋪
Steel
The Story of a Three Day Pass
Stripes
Tomahawk
Wackiest Ship in the Army

Military Comedy
see also Comedy; War,
General

Abbott and Costello in the
　Foreign Legion
Abroad with Two Yanks
Article 99
As You Were
At War with the Army
The Baby and the Battleship
Basic Training
Best Defense
Best Foot Forward
Biloxi Blues
Black and White in Color⋪
The Captain from Koepenick
Caught in the Draft⋪
Chesty Anderson USN
Clipped Wings
Combat Academy
Don't Go Near the Water
Down Periscope
Ensign Pulver
Ernest in the Army⋪
The Flying Deuces⋪
Follow That Camel
Follow the Leader
Francis Goes to West Point
Francis in the Navy
Francis Joins the WACs
Getting Wasted
G.I. Blues
G.I. Jane
Going Under
Here Come the Marines
Hillbilly Blitzkrieg
Hot Shots!⋪
Hot Shots! Part Deux
In the Army Now
Jumping Jacks
Le Gendarme de Saint-Tropez
Leave It to the Marines
Major Payne
A Man Called Sarge
M*A*S*H⋪
M*A*S*H: Goodbye, Farewell &
　Amen⋪
McHale's Navy
McHale's Navy Joins the Air
　Force
Miracle of Morgan's Creek⋪
Mr. Walkie Talkie
The Mouse That Roared⋪
Never Wave at a WAC
1941
No Time for Sergeants⋪
The Odd Squad
Off Limits

The Beautiful Blonde from Bashful Bend
Being There
Betrayed
The Big Lebowski
Big Mouth
Billy the Kid Returns
Bittersweet Love
Black Glove
Blackjack
Blame It on the Bellboy
Blind Justice
Blondie Knows Best
Body Snatchers
Borderline
Boy's Reformatory
Brighton Strangler
Broadway Limited
Broken Melody
Bullets or Ballots
Bullseye!
Bundle of Joy
Buona Sera, Mrs. Campbell
Bushwhacked
Butler's Dilemma
Camp Cucamonga: How I Spent My Summer Vacation
The Capture
Caroline?
Carry On Admiral
A Case of Deadly Force
CB4: The Movie
Center of the Web
The Challengers
Chameleon Street
Charade
Charley's Aunt
The Chase
Colonel Chabert
Convicted
Convicts at Large
Cornbread, Earl & Me
A Couch in New York
The Couch Trip
Counterblast
Court Jester
Dave
Deadwood
Deconstructing Sarah
The Desert Song
Don Juan DeMarco
Don't Tell Her It's Me
Double Play
Double Take
Double Vision
El Mariachi
Ernest Goes to Jail
Erotic Touch of Hot Skin
Evergreen
Every Man's Law
Execution of Raymond Graham
F/X 2: The Deadly Art of Illusion
Family Reunion
Fargo Express
Fatal Exposure
Father
Feet First
Fighting Parson
Five Graves to Cairo
Gangway
The Gay Divorcee
Generale Della Rovere
Gentleman Bandit
Get That Man
The Glass Bottom Boat
Good Neighbor Sam
The Great Dictator
Grosse Fatigue
The Gun in Betty Lou's Handbag
Gunfire
Gunsmoke Trail
Hell on Frisco Bay
Her Life as a Man
Hero
High & Low
High Lonesome
Highway 13
His Brother's Ghost
His Wife's Lover

Hittin' the Trail
Hollywood Chaos
Hometown Boy Makes Good
Honolulu
A House in the Hills
Houseguest
I Love You
I Want to Live!
I Will, I Will for Now
If Looks Could Kill
The Imposter
In Person
In Society
The Inspector General
Instant Kung-Fu Man
Invasion of the Body Snatchers
It Started with Eve
It Takes Two
It! The Terror from Beyond Space
Jade
Johnny Handsome
Johnny Stecchino
Junk Mail
Kansas City Confidential
Keaton's Cop
Kid from Spain
Killer Dill
The Killing Time
A Kiss Before Dying
Lady Killer
Landslide
The Last Contract
The Last Winter
Laughing at Danger
Laurel & Hardy: The Hoose-Gow
Law of the Underworld
Le Bonheur Est Dans le Pre
Life Is a Long Quiet River
Lisa
The Little Drummer Girl
Little Sister
The Lookalike
Lost Highway
Love at Large
Lucky Cisco Kid
Mad About Music
Made in America
Maid's Night Out
The Man in the Raincoat
The Man on the Box
Man on the Run
The Man Who Knew Too Little
The Man with One Red Shoe
Manhandled
The Mark of Zorro
McHale's Navy Joins the Air Force
Meet the Deedles
Meet the Mob
Mexican Spitfire/Smartest Girl in Town
Miami Hustle
The Misadventures of Mr. Wilt
Mississippi Mermaid
Mistaken Identity
Mr. Klein
Monsignor Quixote
The Monster
Monte Carlo Nights
My Geisha
My Man Godfrey
My Outlaw Brother
My Twentieth Century
Mystery Date
Naked Tango
Naughty Marietta
Never a Dull Moment
Next of Kin
Nick and Jane
The Night We Never Met
Nightfall
Nobody's Perfect
North by Northwest
The Nutt House
The Obsessed
Obsession
One Body Too Many
Only You

Opportunity Knocks
Oscar
Out of Bounds
Out on a Limb
Palmy Days
Paper Mask
Pardon My Sarong
The Passenger
Phantom Fiend
Phantom Killer
Picture Perfect
Pier 23
The Player
The Pope Must Diet
Prelude to a Kiss
The Princess Comes Across
Private Life of Don Juan
The Private Secretary
Profile
Purple Noon
Ranson's Folly
Rattler Kid
Red Firecracker, Green Firecracker
The Red Half-Breed
Red Heat
Red Rock West
The Reluctant Agent
The Reluctant Astronaut
Return of Jesse James
The Return of Martin Guerre
Return of the Tall Blond Man With One Black Shoe
River Beat
Romance on the High Seas
Running Hot
Ruyblas
St. Benny the Dip
The Santa Clause
Santa with Muscles
The Scar
Scream of Fear
Seconds
The Secret of My Success
A Self-Made Hero
The 7th Commandment
She Must Be Seeing Things
The Sinister Invasion
Sister Act
Sister Act 2: Back in the Habit
Six Gun Gospel
Six of a Kind
Small Kill
Smokey and the Bandit, Part 3
Social Error
Soldat Duroc...Ca Va Etre Ta Fete!
Someone at the Door
Something in the Wind
Splitting Heirs
Stolen Identity
A Stolen Life
Straight Talk
The Stupids
The Suitors
Sunday
Supergrass
Support Your Local Gunfighter
Suture
Switched at Birth
Tattle Tale
10 Rillington Place
The Tenth Man
Texas Carnival
Texas Cyclone
They Knew What They Wanted
The Thin Blue Line
Things Change
The 39 Steps
Tombstone Terror
Top Hat
Toto le Heros
True Identity
The Truth About Cats and Dogs
Twelfth Night
Two Much
The Unholy Three
The Well

We're No Angels
West of the Pecos
While You Were Sleeping
White Eagle
White of the Eye
Who's Harry Crumb?
Wings of the Morning
Withnail and I
The Worldly Madonna
The Wrong Guys
Young Master
Zertigo Diamond Caper

Model Citizens

Blackjack
Cover Girl
Cover Girl Models
The Cover Girl Murders
Covergirl
Daniella by Night
Darling
Designing Woman
Eyes of Laura Mars
Fall
Funny Face
Gia
In and Out
Intimate Deception
Looker
Mahogany
Model Behavior
Model by Day
Nothing Underneath
Obsession: A Taste for Fear
The Pink Jungle
Portfolio
Ready to Wear
Slaves of New York
So Fine
Tight Spot
Unzipped
What a Woman!
What's New Pussycat?
When the Cat's Away

Modern Cowboys

see also Western Comedy; Westerns

Another Pair of Aces: Three of a Kind
Barbarosa
Bronco Billy
City Slickers
City Slickers 2: The Legend of Curly's Gold
Coogan's Bluff
The Cowboy Way
Dudes
8 Seconds
The Electric Horseman
Fool for Love
The Last of the Dogmen
Lonely Are the Brave
My Heroes Have Always Been Cowboys
Rhinestone
Ruby Jean and Joe
Samurai Cowboy
Sweet Creek County War
Toy Story
True West
Wild Horses

Moms

see also Bad Dads; Dads; Monster Moms; Parenthood

Amazing Grace
Aurora
Baby Boom
Bastard out of Carolina
Bogus
The Brady Bunch Movie
Children of the Revolution
The Daytrippers
Dead Ahead

Every Other Weekend
First Do No Harm
Freaky Friday
House Arrest
I Remember Mama
Irt the Gloaming
The Incredible Shrinking Woman
Invisible Mom
Little Women
Made in America
Manny & Lo
Mermaids
Mrs. Winterbourne
Mom and Dad Save the World
Mother
A Mother's Prayer
Nightmare
On My Own
Only the Lonely
Our Sons
Postcards from the Edge
The River Wild
Rockabye
Rumpelstiltskin
She-Devil
She's Having a Baby
So I Married an Axe Murderer
Some Mother's Son
Spanking the Monkey
Stop! or My Mom Will Shoot
Striptease
Throw Momma from the Train
To Each His Own
To See Paris and Die
Trading Mom
Troop Beverly Hills
A Very Brady Sequel
The War at Home
The Winter Guest

Monkeyshines

see also Jungle Stories; Wild Kingdom

Born to Be Wild
Buddy
Congo
Dunston Checks In
Ed
George of the Jungle
King Kong
King Kong
Monkey Shines
Monkey Trouble
Outbreak

Monster Moms

see also Bad Dads; Dads; Moms; Parenthood

The Anniversary
The Baby
Bad Boy Bubby
Bellissima
Beyond the Door
Big Bad Mama
Big Bad Mama 2
Carrie
Dead Alive
Deadly Advice
Die! Die! My Darling!
Ed and His Dead Mother
Flesh Eating Mothers
Gorgo
The Grifters
Gypsy
Hush
Invaders from Mars
The Locusts
Ma Barker's Killer Brood
Mad Youth
The Manchurian Candidate
Mom
Mommie Dearest
Mommy
Mommy 2: Mommy's Day
Mother
Mother's Boys

Mystery

Mystery

Rude Awakening
Rule #3
Run If You Can
Runaways
Russian Roulette
Saboteur✏
The Saint
The Saint in London
The Saint in New York
The Saint Strikes Back
The Saint Strikes Back: Criminal Court
The Saint Takes Over
The Saint's Double Trouble
The Saint's Vacation/The Narrow Margin
The Salamander
The Salzburg Connection
Sanctuary of Fear
Sanders of the River✏
Sapphire✏
Savage Hearts
Savages
Save Me
Scalp Merchant
Scam
Scandal Man
Scandalous
Scared to Death/Dick Tracy's Dilemma
Scarlet Claw✏
The Scarlet Clue
Scarlet Street✏
Scavengers
Scene of the Crime
Scene of the Crime
Scenes from a Murder
Schemes
Schnelles Geld
Scissors
Scorned
Scorpio
The Scorpio Factor
Scotland Yard Inspector
Scream
Scream Bloody Murder
Scream for Help
Screamer
The Sculptress
Sea of Love✏
Seance on a Wet Afternoon✏
Season of Fear
The Second Woman
The Secret Adversary
Secret Agent 00
Secret of the Black Trunk
The Secret Passion of Robert Clayton
The Set Up
Seven Doors to Death
Seven Hours to Judgment
The Seven-Per-Cent Solution✏
The Seventh Sign
Sexpot
Sexton Blake and the Hooded Terror
Sexual Intent
Sexual Malice
Sexual Response
Shades of Fear
The Shadow
The Shadow Conspiracy
Shadow Dancing✏
The Shadow Man
Shadow of a Doubt✏
Shadow of a Scream
Shadow of the Thin Man✏
Shadow Play
The Shadow Strikes
Shadows on the Stairs
Shaft✏
Shallow Grave
The Shanghai Cobra
Shattered
Shattered Image
Shattered Silence
She Waits
Sherlock Holmes and the Deadly Necklace

Sherlock Holmes and the Incident at Victoria Falls
Sherlock Holmes and the Secret Weapon✏
Sherlock Holmes Faces Death✏
Sherlock Holmes in Washington
Sherlock Holmes: The Master Blackmailer
Sherlock Holmes: The Sign of Four
Sherlock Holmes: The Silver Blaze
Sherlock Holmes: The Voice of Terror
She's Dressed to Kill
Shock!
Shoot to Kill
A Shot in the Dark
The Shout✏
A Show of Force
Show Them No Mercy✏
Shriek in the Night
Side Show
Sidney Sheldon's Bloodline
The Sign of Four
The Silencer
Silent Assassins
Silent Fall
Silent Killers
The Silent Mr. Sherlock Holmes
Silent Motive
The Silent Partner✏
The Silent Passenger
Silhouette
Sins of Desire
Sins of the Night
Sioux City
The Sister-in-Law
Sister, Sister
Sisters of Death
Skeletons
Sketch Artist
Sketch Artist 2: Hands That See
Sketches of a Strangler
Sky Liner
Slamdance
The Slasher
Slaughter of the Innocents
Slayground
Sleeping Car to Trieste
Sleepwalk
Sleuth✏
Slightly Honorable
Slightly Scarlet
Slipping into Darkness
Sliver
Slow Burn
Small Kill
Smart-Aleck Kill
Smile, Jenny, You're Dead
Smilla's Sense of Snow
Smooth Talker
Snatched
Sneakers
Snow Kill
Snowblind
Soft Deceit
Sois Belle et Tais-Toi
Soldier of the Night
Somebody Has to Shoot the Picture✏
Someone Behind the Door
Someone to Watch Over Me✏
Song of the Thin Man
Sound of Murder
Spaceways
The Spaniard's Curse
Spare Parts
Special Police
The Specialist
The Speckled Band✏
Spectre of the Rose
Spellbound✏
Spenser: Ceremony
Spenser: Pale Kings & Princes
The Sphinx
Sphinx
The Spider and the Fly
Spider Woman✏

Spiders✏
The Spider's Stratagem✏
Sprague
Sputnik
Spy Story
The Spy Who Came in from the Cold✏
The Spy Within
S*P*Y*S
The Squeaker
The Squeeze
Stacey
Stage Fright✏
Stamp of a Killer
Star of Midnight
Star Time
State Department File 649
State of Things✏
Station
Stay Tuned for Murder
The Stepmother
The Stepsister
Stick
Still Life
Still of the Night
A Stolen Face
Stolen Painting
Stone Cold Dead
Stormy Monday
The Strange Affair of Uncle Harry
Strange Confession
The Strange Countess
Strange Shadows in an Empty Room
Strange Tales/Ray Bradbury Theatre
The Stranger✏
A Stranger Among Us
Stranger in the House
Stranger in Town
A Stranger Is Watching
Stranger on the Third Floor✏
The Stranger Within
Strangers
Strangers on a Train✏
The Strangler
Strangler of Blackmoor Castle
Strangler of the Swamp
Stray Dog✏
Strike Force
Stripped to Kill
Stripped to Kill II: Live Girls
A Study in Scarlet
A Study in Terror✏
The Substitute
Subterfuge
Sucker Money
Sudden Fear✏
Sudden Terror
Suddenly✏
Summer Heat
Summer's Children
Sunstroke
Surrogate
Suspect
Suspicion✏
Suspicion
Svengali
Swamp Thing
Sweet Murder
Swiss Conspiracy
Tag: The Assassination Game
Tagget
Tainted Blood
Take Two
Taking the Heat
Tale of a Vampire
Tales from the Darkside
Tales of the Unexpected
The Tall Blond Man with One Black Shoe✏
Tangiers
Tangled Destinies
Target
The Tattered Web
The Taxi Mystery
The Teacher
Telefon

Temptation
Ten Days Wonder
Ten Little Indians
10 Rillington Place✏
Tequila Sunrise
Tereza✏
Terminal Choice
Terminal Entry
The Terror
Terror at London Bridge
Terror by Night
Terror by Night/Meeting at Midnight
Terror Stalks the Class Reunion
Terror Street
Terrorists
There Goes Kelly
They Call Me Mr. Tibbs!
They Meet Again
They Only Kill Their Masters
They Watch
They Won't Believe Me✏
They're Playing with Fire
Thief
Thief✏
Thief of Hearts
The Thin Man✏
The Thin Man Goes Home
Third Degree Burn
The Third Key
The Third Man✏
Third Solution
13th Guest
The Thirteenth Man
The Thirty-Nine Steps
The 39 Steps✏
This Is a Hijack
This Lightning Always Strikes Twice
This Man Must Die✏
This Sweet Sickness
Threat
Three by Hitchcock
Three Cases of Murder✏
Three Days of the Condor✏
Thrilled to Death
Thrillkill
Through Naked Eyes
Thundersquad
Tiara Tahiti
The Ticket
Ticket of Leave Man
Tiger Bay✏
Tightrope✏
Till Death Do Us Part
Till There was You
Time for Revenge
Time Is Running Out
A Time to Die
Time Without Pity
Times to Come✏
To Catch a King
To Catch a Thief✏
To Kill a Clown
To Kill a Stranger
The Todd Killings
Tomorrow at Seven
Tony Rome
Too Scared to Scream
Topaz✏
Torment
Torn Curtain
Total Exposure
Touch Me Not
Touch of Evil✏
Tough Assignment
Tough Guys Don't Dance
Tourist Trap
Town that Dreaded Sundown
Traces of Red
Track 29
Trade Secrets
The Train Killer
The Trap
Trapped
Trauma
Treacherous Crossing
Trespasses
Trial and Error

Trial by Jury
The Triumph of Sherlock Holmes
Tropical Heat
The Trouble with Harry✏
True Believer
True Crime
True Lies
Twenty Dollar Star
Twilight✏
Twilight Man
Twin Peaks
Twin Sisters
Twisted Obsession
Two by Forsyth
Two Fathers' Justice
The Two Jakes
Two Minute Warning
Ultimate Desires
The Ultimate Imposter
The Ultimate Thrill
Ultraviolet
The Unbreakable Alibi
Under Capricorn
Under Investigation
Under Suspicion
Undercover
Uneasy Terms
Unholy Four
Unholy Wife
Union City
Union Station
Unsane
Unsuitable Job for a Woman
Unveiled
Up in the Air
Urge to Kill
The Usual Suspects✏
Utz
The Vagrant
Vamping
The Vanishing✏
The Vanishing
Vanishing Act
Vatican Conspiracy
Vegas
Velvet Touch✏
Vertigo✏
The Very Edge
Vicious
The Vicious Circle
Victim of Beauty
Victim of Desire
Victim of Love
Video Murders
Violette✏
The Vision
Visions
Visiting Hours
Voulez-Vous Danser Avec Moi?
A Vow to Kill
Vultures
W
Waikiki
Wanted: Babysitter
Warm Nights on a Slow-Moving Train
Warning Sign
Watched
The Way Out
Wayne Murder Case✏
Weep No More My Lady
Whatever Happened to Aunt Alice?✏
When a Stranger Calls
When a Stranger Calls Back
When Angels Fly
When I Close My Eyes
When the Bough Breaks
Where Are the Children?
Where Sleeping Dogs Lie
Where's the Money, Noreen?
A Whisper to a Scream
Whispering City✏
Whispering Shadow
Whispers in the Dark
The Whistle Blower✏
White Fire

Negative Utopia

New Black Cinema

New Orleans

New Year's Eve

New York, New York

Oceans

see Deep Blue; Go Fish;
Mutiny; Scuba; Sea Critter
Attack; Shipwrecked;
Submarines

Oedipal Allegories

see also Family Ties;
Incest

Office Surprise

Oil

see Black Gold

Oldest Profession

see also Gigolos; Happy
Hookers; Women in Prison

Oldest

High Stakes
Highway Patrolman
Hindsight
Hollywood Chainsaw Hookers
Hollywood Vice Sqaud
Honky Tonk Girl
Hotel Room
The Hustle
Hustler Squad
Hustler White
Hustling⟋
I Want to Live!⟋
Impulse
Irma La Douce
Jack's Back⟋
Jade
Jamon, Jamon
John Carpenter's Vampires
Johns
Just a Gigolo
Justine
Keetje Tippel
Killing Zoe
Kinjite: Forbidden Subjects
Kiss the Night
Kitty and the Bagman
Klute⟋
La Chienne⟋
L.A. Confidential⟋
L.A. Crackdown
L.A. Crackdown 2
Ladies of the Lotus
Lady in Waiting
Lady of the Evening
Lady of the House
The Last Prostitute
The Last Temptation of Christ⟋
Leaving Las Vegas⟋
Les Miserables⟋
Life of Oharu⟋
A Life of Sin
Little Ladies of the Night
Lola Montes⟋
Love by Appointment
Love Strange Love
The Mack
Madame Rosa⟋
Magdalene
Malibu High
Mamma Roma⟋
Man of Flowers
The Man Who Knew Too Little
Manon
Marriage Italian Style⟋
Mayflower Madam
McCabe & Mrs. Miller⟋
Miami Blues
Mid Knight Rider
Midnight Auto Supply
Midnight Cop
Midnight Cowboy⟋
Midnight Dancers
Miss Sadie Thompson⟋
The Missionary
Moll Flanders
Mon Homme
Mona Lisa⟋
Murderlust
Murphy's Law
My Life to Live⟋
My Mother's Secret Life
My Own Private Idaho⟋
My Pleasure Is My Business
Naked Kiss
Naked Tango
Nana
Nana
Never on Sunday⟋
New York's Finest
Night Friend
Night of the Generals⟋
Night Shift
Night Slasher
The Night They Robbed Big
   Bertha's
Nightmare in Badham County
Nights of Cabiria⟋
Nightwatch
No One Cries Forever

No Prince for My Cinderella
The Nun
Nuts⟋
Off Limits
Oldest Profession
Olivia
One Night Only
Out of the Dark
Padre Nuestro
Pandora's Box⟋
Panic in Needle Park⟋
Party Girls
The Passing of Evil
Pennies From Heaven⟋
Personal Services
Pigalle
The Players Club⟋
Poker Alice
Postcards from America
Pretty Baby⟋
Pretty Woman⟋
Prettykill
Prime Cut
Prime Suspect 3⟋
The Pyx⟋
Queen Kelly⟋
Quick, Let's Get Married
Rain
Raw Justice
Reason to Die
Red Kimono
The Ripper
Risky Business⟋
Room 43
Roots of Evil
Saint Jack⟋
Sandakan No. 8⟋
Sansho the Bailiff⟋
Scarred
Schnelles Geld
Scorchers
Secret Games
Secrets of a Married Man
Sessions
Sex, Love and Cold Hard Cash
Shadow of Angels
Sharky's Machine
The Silencer
Single Room Furnished
Sisters of Gion⟋
Sketches of a Strangler
Skin Art
Spenser: Ceremony
SS Girls
S.S. Love Camp No. 27
Star Maps
Stone Cold Dead
Storyville
Street Girls
Street of Forgotten Women
Street of Shame⟋
Street Smart
Streetwalkin'
The Substitute Wife
The Sun's Burial⟋
Sweet Charity⟋
Sweet Revenge
Sweet Sweetback's Baadasssss
   Song⟋
Sweet Trash
The Sword and the Cross
Talons of the Eagle
Taxi Driver⟋
They Were So Young
Things
Things to Do In Denver When
   You're Dead⟋
Thousand Pieces of Gold⟋
Tightrope⟋
The Toilers and the Wayfarers
Tokyo Decadence
Too Young to Die
Trading Places
Traffic in Souls⟋
Train Station Pickups
Tricks
Tricks of the Trade
Truck Stop Women
Twenty Dollar Star

No Prince for My Cinderella
Twin Peaks: Fire Walk with Me
Twin Sisters
Two or Three Things I Know
   About Her
Ultimate Desires
Uncaged
Utamaro and His Five Women
The Vampire Hookers
Via Appia
Vice Squad
Vicious Circles
Walk on the Wild Side
Warm Nights on a Slow-Moving
   Train
Warrior Queen
Waterloo Bridge⟋
Whore
Whore 2
Wild Bill
Wild Orchid 2: Two Shades of
   Blue
Wild Side
The Winter of Our Dreams
A Woman in Flames⟋
A Woman of Rome
Working Girls
Working Girls⟋
The World of Suzie Wong

The Olympics
see also Sports Dramas
Alex
American Anthem
Best of the Best
Blades of Courage
Blast
Breaking the Surface: The Greg
   Louganis Story
Chariots of Fire⟋
Cool Runnings
Crossbar
The Cutting Edge
The First Olympics: Athens 1896
Going for the Gold: The Bill
   Johnson Story
International Velvet
The Jesse Owens Story
Life Is a Circus, Charlie Brown/
   You're the Greatest, Charlie
   Brown
A Million to One
Miracle on Ice
Pentathlon
Personal Best⟋
Prefontaine
Run for the Dream: The Gail
   Devers Story
Running Brave
Special Olympics
Sword of Gideon
Tokyo Olympiad
21 Hours at Munich⟋
Walk, Don't Run
Wilma
Without Limits⟋

On the Rocks
see also Pill Poppin'
Arthur⟋
Arthur 2: On the Rocks
Barfly⟋
Betty
The Big Hangover
The Big Lebowski⟋
Black Angel⟋
Blue Heaven
Break of Hearts
Casino⟋
The Chamber
Clean and Sober⟋
Cocktail
Come Back, Little Sheba⟋
Country Girl
Country Girl
Country Life
The Crossing Guard⟋

A Cry for Love
Dance of Life
Dancer, Texas - Pop. 81⟋
Danger in the Skies
Dangerous
Days of Wine and Roses
Days of Wine and Roses⟋
Desert Bloom⟋
The Devil at 4 O'Clock
The Devil Thumbs a Ride⟋
The Devil Thumbs a Ride/
   Having Wonderful Crime
Dona Flor and Her Two
   Husbands⟋
Drunken Angel⟋
Drunks
Educating Rita⟋
8 Heads in a Duffel Bag
El Dorado⟋
The Electric Horseman
The Entertainer⟋
Fat City⟋
The Fire Within⟋
Fish Hawk
The Flaming Teen-Age
Flesh and Bone⟋
Frances⟋
A Free Soul
Georgia⟋
Gervaise⟋
The Great Man Votes⟋
The Green Man⟋
Heaven's Prisoners
Honkytonk Man
Hot Summer in Barefoot County
I Live with Me Dad
I'll Cry Tomorrow⟋
The Informer⟋
Ironweed
Izzy & Moe
Jack and Sarah
Jack the Bear
Kill Cruise
The Last American Hero⟋
Last Time Out
Le Beau Serge⟋
Leaving Las Vegas⟋
License to Kill
Living Proof: The Hank Williams
   Jr. Story
Long Day's Journey into Night⟋
Long Day's Journey into Night
Long Day's Journey Into Night⟋
The Lost Weekend⟋
M.A.D.D.: Mothers Against
   Drunk Driving
Marvin & Tige
Mean Dog Blues
Mrs. Parker and the Vicious
   Circle
The Morning After
My Favorite Year⟋
My Name is Joe
Once Were Warriors⟋
One Too Many
Only When I Laugh⟋
Papa's Delicate Condition⟋
Police Court
Reuben, Reuben⟋
The Robe
Scent of a Woman⟋
The Secret Rapture
Shakes the Clown
She's So Lovely
The Sin of Harold Diddlebock
The Singing Blacksmith
Skin Deep
Sling Blade⟋
Smash-Up: The Story of a
   Woman⟋
A Star Is Born⟋
A Star Is Born
Straight Up
Stranded
Strange Brew
Struggle
Stuart Saves His Family
Tales of Ordinary Madness
Ten Nights in a Bar Room

Ten Nights in a Bar-Room
The Tenant of Wildfell Hall
Termini Station
Tree's Lounge
TwentyFourSeven
Under Capricorn
Under the Volcano⟋
Unnatural Pursuits
The Verdict⟋
Wagons East
What Price Hollywood?⟋
When a Man Loves a Woman
Whiskey Galore⟋
White Lightning
Willa
The Winning Team

Only the Lonely
Abducted
The Abduction of Kari Swenson
All That Heaven Allows⟋
An Autumn Afternoon⟋
The Ballad of Little Jo
Bed of Roses
Betrayal
Birdman of Alcatraz⟋
The Body Shop
Breakfast in Paris
The Browning Version⟋
The Cemetery Club
Choose Me⟋
A Chorus of Disapproval
A Christmas Without Snow
Citizen Kane⟋
Cotter
Cowboys Don't Cry
Cyrano de Bergerac⟋
Cyrano de Bergerac
Cyrano de Bergerac⟋
A Day in the Country⟋
Desperately Seeking Susan
Didn't You Hear?
Dirty Dishes⟋
Distant Thunder
Docks of New York⟋
Doin' Time on Planet Earth
The Doll
A Doll's House
A Doll's House⟋
Eat Drink Man Woman⟋
The Eclipse⟋
El Super⟋
An Empty Bed⟋
The Enchanted Cottage
Escapade in Japan
E.T.: The Extra-Terrestrial⟋
Every Man for Himself & God
   Against All⟋
Eye of the Needle
Fiances
The Final Alliance
Fire
Full Moon in Blue Water
Full Moon in Paris
The Game of Love
The Gun in Betty Lou's Handbag
Harold and Maude⟋
The Heart Is a Lonely Hunter⟋
Heavy⟋
Hell Hounds of Alaska
High Country
Hiroshima, Mon Amour⟋
The Hunchback of Notre Dame⟋
The Hunchback of Notre Dame
Husband Hunting
Husbands and Wives⟋
I Don't Give a Damn
I Sent a Letter to My Love⟋
In the White City⟋
Inside Out
Kaspar Hauser
La Petite Sirene
La Vie Continue
Lana in Love
The Last Best Year
The Last Horror Film
Les Bons Debarras
Les Voleurs⟋

Organized

Period

The Rose and the Jackal
Rosewood
Roxie Hart
Ruyblas
Saga of the Vagabond
The St. Valentine's Day
  Massacre
Salome
Samurai Rebellion
Samurai Reincarnation
San Francisco
The Sandlot
Sansho the Bailiff
The Saragossa Manuscript
Sarah, Plain and Tall
Saratoga Trunk
Savage Messiah
The Scarlet Letter
Scarlett
The Scent of Green Papaya
School for Scandal
School Ties
Sea Devils
The Sea Hawk
Season of Change
The Secret Garden
The Secret Garden
Secrets
The Seekers
Sense & Sensibility
Sense and Sensibility
Senso
Sergeant Rutledge
The Sexual Life of the Belgians
Shadow on the Sun
Shadowlands
Shag: The Movie
Shake Hands with the Devil
Shanghai Triad
Sharpe's Battle
Sharpe's Company
Sharpe's Eagle
Sharpe's Enemy
Sharpe's Gold
Sharpe's Honour
Sharpe's Justice
Sharpe's Legend
Sharpe's Mission
Sharpe's Regiment
Sharpe's Revenge
Sharpe's Rifles
Sharpe's Siege
Sharpe's Sword
Sharpe's Waterloo
Sherlock Holmes: The Master
  Blackmailer
Shogun
The Shooting Party
Shopworn Angel
Show Boat
The Sign of Four
Silas Marner
Sirens
Sister Dora
Sister My Sister
Skin Game
Skylark
The Slingshot
Smart-Aleck Kill
Snowy River, the MacGregor
  Saga: The Race
Sofie
Something for Everyone
Sommersby
Son of Fury
Song Without End
Sorceress
Souls at Sea
The Sound and the Silence
Splendor in the Grass
Spring Symphony
Squanto: A Warrior's Tale
Star!
The Star Maker
Stars and Stripes Forever
The Stars Fell on Henrietta
The Stationmaster's Wife
The Stick-Up

The Story of Alexander Graham
  Bell
The Strange Woman
Strawberry and Chocolate
The Substitute Wife
Sudie & Simpson
Sugartime
The Summer of Ben Tyler
A Summer Story
Sunday's Children
Surviving Picasso
Swept from the Sea
Swing Kids
Swing Shift
Swoon
Swords of Death
Tai-Pan
A Tale of Two Cities
A Tale of Two Cities
A Tale of Two Cities
Tales from Avonlea, Vol. 1: The
  Journey Begins
Tales from the Gimli Hospital
Tamango
Taras Bulba
Tchaikovsky
Temptation of a Monk
The Tenant of Wildfell Hall
Terranova
Tess
The Texans
That Forsyte Woman
That Night
That Thing You Do!
That'll Be the Day
They Came to Cordura
They Shoot Horses, Don't
  They?
Thieves Like Us
Three Comrades
The Three Musketeers
Throne of Blood
The Tigress
A Time to Live and a Time to Die
Tito and Me
Tom and Huck
Tom & Viv
Tom Jones
Tom Sawyer
Torrents of Spring
Total Eclipse
Tous les Matins du Monde
Trading Hearts
Trahir
Traps
Tune in Tomorrow
20,000 Leagues Under the Sea
Twenty-Four Eyes
Two Bits
The Two Jakes
Two Nights with Cleopatra
Two Years Before the Mast
Under Capricorn
Under the Biltmore Clock
Under the Volcano
An Unfinished Piece for a Player
  Piano
An Unforgettable Summer
Used People
Utamaro and His Five Women
Valentino
Valentino Returns
The Valley of Decision
Valmont
Van Gogh
Vanity Fair
Victoria Regina
The Viking Sagas
The Vikings
The Virgin Queen
Viva Villa!
The War
War and Peace
The Warriors
Washington Square
The Water Engine
We of the Never Never
The Wedding Singer
Wend Kuuni

What's the Matter with Helen?
When the Greeks
Where Angels Fear to Tread
Where the Rivers Flow North
White Hot: The Mysterious
  Murder of Thelma Todd
The Wicked Lady
Wide Sargasso Sea
Wild Bill
Wild Hearts Can't Be Broken
Wild Party
Wild Reeds
Wilde
William Faulkner's Old Man
The Wind in the Willows
The Wings of the Dove
A Winner Never Quits
Witch Hunt
The Wolves
A Woman at Her Window
Woman in Black
The Woman in White
A Woman Rebels
Women in Love
The Women on the Roof
The Wooden Man's Bride
The World in His Arms
Wrangler
Xica
The Yearling
Yellow Earth
Yentl
Young Bess
Young Sherlock Holmes

Persian Gulf War

see also Desert War/
Foreign Legion

Courage Under Fire
The Heroes of Desert Storm
The Human Shield

Philadelphia

Birdy
Blow Out
Downtown
The Garbage-Picking, Field
  Goal-Kicking Philadelphia
  Phenomenon
Happy Birthday, Gemini
I Don't Buy Kisses Anymore
Kitty Foyle
Mannequin
Mannequin 2: On the Move
Marnie
Money for Nothing
My Little Girl
Nasty Habits
Philadelphia
The Philadelphia Story
Rocky
Rocky 2
Rocky 3
Rocky 4
Rocky 5
Stonewall
Trading Places
12 Monkeys
Two Bits
Two Plus One
Up Close and Personal
The Watermelon Woman
Winter Kills
Witness
The Young Philadelphians

Philanthropy

see Kindness of Strangers

Phobias!

Arachnophobia
Blackjack
Body Double
Copycat

High Anxiety
Home Remedy
Inside Out
Pontiac Moon
Vertigo

Phone Sex

see also Sex & Sexuality;
Sexploitation

Denise Calls Up
Girl 6
Listen
Mouth to Mouth
1-900
Short Cuts
The Truth About Cats and
  Dogs
Walking and Talking
A Whisper to a Scream

Phone Terror

Are You Lonesome Tonight
Black Sabbath
Call Me
Dead Connection
Dial Help
Don't Answer the Phone
The Jerky Boys
Lady Beware
Lisa
Listen
Midnight Lace
The Night Caller
976-EVIL
976-EVIL 2: The Astral Factor
Party Line
Scream
Scream 2
Smooth Talker
Sorry, Wrong Number
Sorry, Wrong Number
Telefon
When a Stranger Calls
When a Stranger Calls Back

Photography

see Shutterbugs

Physical Problems

see also Blindness;
Deafness; Mental
Retardation; Savants

Acorn People
The Affair
An Affair to Remember
Amy
Autumn Sonata
The Big Lebowski
Big Street
Born on the Fourth of July
Breaking the Waves
A Brief History of Time
Broken Strings
The Brute Man
Catherine Cookson's The
  Wingless Bird
Chained for Life
Chinese Roulette
Choices
Coming Home
Cries of Silence
The Crippled Masters
Crossbar
A Day in the Death of Joe Egg
Eden
El Cochecito
The Elephant Man
Endgame
Even Cowgirls Get the Blues
Fireworks
Frankie Starlight
George Wallace
The Glass Menagerie

Go Now
Good Luck
Gray's Anatomy
A Gun, A Car, A Blonde
Hearing Voices
Hugo Pool
The Hunchback
The Hunchback of Notre Dame
The Hunchback of Notre Dame
The Hunchback of Notre Dame
I Don't Want to Talk About It
Inside Moves
It's Good to Be Alive
Joni
Knife in the Head
Lea
Lewis and Clark and George
Lightning Jack
Long Journey Back
Looking for Richard
Love Affair
Love Affair
Mac and Me
The Man with the Golden Arm
The Man Without a Face
Mask
The Men
The Miracle Worker
Mrs. Munck
Monkey Shines
Mute Witness
My Left Foot
Next Victim
Niagara, Niagara
Night Monster
Of Human Bondage
Off the Mark
One-Eyed Swordsman
The Other Side of the Mountain
The Other Side of the Mountain,
  Part 2
Paperback Romance
Passion Fish
The Penalty
The People vs. Larry Flynt
The Phantom of the Opera
The Pit
Powder
Ratboy
Reach for the Sky
Rear Window
Regarding Henry
Revolver
Richard III
Ride a Wild Pony
The River
Roxanne
Rumble in the Bronx
Scent of a Woman
The Secret
Seizure: The Story of Kathy
  Morris
The Seventh Veil
Silence
Silence Like Glass
Silver Bullet
Skag
The Sky Pilot
The Small Back Room
Sound of Love
Special Olympics
The Spiral Staircase
Spiral Staircase
Steel
The Steel Claw
Stella Maris
The Story of Esther Costello
The Stratton Story
Suite 16
Talk to Me
The Terry Fox Story
A Test of Love
Things to Do In Denver When
  You're Dead
To All My Friends on Shore
Untamed Heart
Vibrations
Walking on Air
The Waterdance

Psychotics

Fast Gun
Fatal Attraction⬧
Fear
Fear City
The Fear Inside
The Fiance
The Fool Killer
Force of Evil
From Dusk Till Dawn
Gallowglass⬧
The Gingerbread Man
Girl in Black Stockings
The Glimmer Man
Guardian Angel
Guilty as Sin
Headless Body in Topless Bar
Heat⬧
Helter Skelter
Helter Skelter Murders
Homage
Homer and Eddie
Honeymoon
The Hostage
Hot Potato
Hot Touch
House of Terror
The Housekeeper
Hush
Hush Little Baby, Don't You Cry
I Know What You Did Last
   Summer⬧
In the Line of Fire⬧
In the Mouth of Madness
Invasion of Privacy
The Invisible Terror
Kalifornia
Keys to Tulsa
Killer Inside Me
Killing Obsession
Killing Zoe
Killzone
Kiss the Girls
Lightning Bolt
The Lightship
The Little Girl Who Lives Down
   the Lane
Live Wire
Lunatic
The Machine
The Mad Bomber
The Mad Executioners
Mademoiselle
A Man in Uniform
Maniac Warriors
Maternal Instincts
Meet the Deedles
Metro
Midnight 2: Sex, Death, and
   Videotape
Midnight Edition
Midnight Fear
Midnight Ride
Misbegotten
Mommie Dearest
Mondo Balardo
Most Wanted
Mother's Boys
Moving Targets
Murder Elite
Murderlust
The Naked Flame
Naked Massacre
Natural Enemy
The Neighbor
Office Killer
One Good Turn
Pacific Heights⬧
The Paperboy
Past Midnight
Perfect Family
Perfect Victims
Play Nice
Playgirl Killer
Poison Ivy
Pretty Poison⬧
Prime Time Murder
Psycho⬧
Psycho 2
Psycho 3

Psycho 4: The Beginning
Psycho Girls
Psychos in Love
Quake
The Rage
Rampage
Relentless
Repulsion⬧
Reservoir Dogs⬧
Retroactive
The Rich Man's Wife
Ricochet⬧
The River Wild
The Road Killers
Roadkill
The Sadist
Sarah's Child
Savage Abduction
Scream⬧
Scream 2⬧
The Sea Wolf⬧
The Secretary
The Seduction
Seven Hours to Judgment
The Seventh Floor
The Shining
The Silencer
Single White Female
The Sister-in-Law
Skinner
Small Kill
Speed⬧
Speed 2: Cruise Control
Stalked
Starved
The Stepfather⬧
Stepfather 2: Make Room for
   Daddy
Stepfather 3: Father's Day
Still Life
Stripped to Kill
Stripteaser
Sweet Hostage
Tainted Blood
The Taking of Beverly Hills
Tall, Dark and Deadly
Ted & Venus
The Temp
The Tenant⬧
Tetsuo: The Iron Man
A Thin Line Between Love and
   Hate
Thirteenth Day of Christmas
Three the Hard Way
Through the Eyes of a Killer
To Die For⬧
Truth or Consequences, N.M.
Turbulence
Twin Peaks: Fire Walk with Me
The Two Mrs. Carrolls
U-Turn
Ultraviolet
Unlawful Entry
The Vanishing
Vice Squad
Violence at Noon⬧
Voyage
What Ever Happened to Baby
   Jane?⬧
When a Stranger Calls Back
Whispers
White Heat⬧
Writer's Block
The Young Poisoner's
   Handbook⬧
Zero Degrees Kelvin
The Zombie Army

Puppets

see also Killer Toys; Toys
The Adventures of Pinocchio
Alice in Wonderland
Curse of the Puppet Master
The Dark Crystal⬧
Devil Doll
The Great Gabbo
The Great Rupert⬧
Lili⬧

Magic
Meet the Feebles
Pinocchio⬧
Puppet Master
Puppet Master 2
Puppet Master 4
Puppet Master 5: The Final
   Chapter
A Rat's Tale
The Sound of Music⬧

Pure Ego Vehicles

*see also Big Budget
Stinkers; Macho Men;
Rock Stars on Film*
The Adventures of Ford Fairlane
Air America
Assault of the Rebel Girls
The Big One
Charade
Conan the Destroyer
The Dead Pool
Fire Down Below
Gummo
Harlem Nights
Hello, Dolly!
Hudson Hawk
I Got the Hook-Up
The Jazz Singer
Last Action Hero
Le Repos du Guerrier
Marie Antoinette
Modern Love
On Deadly Ground
Private Parts
Purple Rain
Rambo 3
Richard Petty Story
Running Out of Luck
The Scarlet Letter
Sidekicks
SnakeEater
Sophia Loren: Her Own Story
Staying Alive
Sweet Country Road
Tarzan, the Ape Man
Thank Your Lucky Stars⬧
A Thin Line Between Love and
   Hate
To Hell and Back
Torch Song
200 Motels
Under the Cherry Moon
Vampire in Brooklyn
Waterworld
What Comes Around
Wildcats
The Wizard of Speed and Time
Yes, Giorgio

Queens

see Royalty

Rabbits

Alice⬧
Alice in Wonderland⬧
Alice's Adventures in
   Wonderland
The Bugs Bunny/Road Runner
   Movie
Bugs Bunny Superstar
Fatal Attraction⬧
Harvey⬧
Mona Lisa⬧
Monty Python and the Holy
   Grail⬧
Nasty Rabbit
Roger & Me⬧
Space Jam
Watership Down
Who Framed Roger Rabbit⬧

Race Against Time

Acceptable Risks

Alien Space Avenger
The Andromeda Strain
Apollo 13⬧
Balto
Bitter Harvest⬧
Blown Away
The Borrowers
Broken Arrow
Chain Reaction
The China Syndrome⬧
Coma⬧
The Corporation
Daylight
D.O.A.⬧
D.O.A.
Escape from L.A.
Fail-Safe⬧
Free Willy 2: The Adventure
   Home
Free Willy 3: The Rescue
Germicide
Grand Tour: Disaster in Time
Hell Commandos
In Pursuit of Honor
Independence Day⬧
Jet Over the Atlantic
Killer on Board
Last Dance
Last Flight Out: A True Story
Lorenzo's Oil⬧
Nick of Time
Octopussy
Once Upon a Forest
Outbreak⬧
Panic in Echo Park
Panic in the Streets⬧
The Peacemaker
Prisoner in the Middle
Pursuit⬧
A Rat's Tale
Robot in the Family
The Silver Streak
Somebody Has to Shoot the
   Picture⬧
Sudden Death
The Taking of Beverly Hills
Things to Do In Denver When
   You're Dead⬧
Time Is Running Out
Time Lock
Time Without Pity
Twister
WarGames

Radio

see also Mass Media
Airheads
Bad Channels
Breakfast in Hollywood
Bye Bye, Love
Carefree⬧
Choose Me⬧
Citizens Band⬧
City in Panic
Comfort and Joy⬧
The Couch Trip
Danger on the Air
Dead Air
Dirty Mind of Young Sally
The Fisher King⬧
FM
Freeway
Girls Night Out
Good Morning, Vietnam⬧
The Great American Broadcast⬧
The Hucksters
The Jackpot
The Key Man
Laser Moon
Look Who's Laughing
Love Serenade
The Man Who Came to Dinner⬧
Midnight Confessions
My Dream Is Yours
The Next Voice You Hear
The Night Caller
Night Rhythms
No Trace

Old Barn Dance
On the Air Live with Captain
   Midnight
Once Upon a Honeymoon
Open House
People Are Funny
People's Choice
The Phantom Broadcast
Play Misty for Me⬧
Pot O' Gold
Power 98
Private Parts
Psycho 4: The Beginning
Pump Up the Volume
Rachel River
Radio Days⬧
Radioland Murders
Rebecca of Sunnybrook Farm
Rude
Sexual Response
Sleepless in Seattle⬧
Straight Talk
Strike Up the Band
Talk Radio⬧
Telling Lies in America
There Goes Kelly
The Truth About Cats and
   Dogs⬧
Tune in Tomorrow
Up in the Air
Whistling in Brooklyn
Who Done It?
WKRP in Cincinnati, Vol. 1

Rags to Riches

*see also Price of Fame;
Wrong Side of the Tracks*
The Abe Lincoln of Ninth
   Avenue
Aladdin⬧
All the King's Men⬧
The Amorous Adventures of Moll
   Flanders
Annie
B.A.P.'s
Better Late Than Never
The Beverly Hillbillies
Blank Check
Body Slam
Boogie Nights⬧
Breaking Glass
Brewster's Millions
The Buddy Holly Story⬧
Callie and Son
Can You Hear the Laughter?
   The Story of Freddie Prinze
Christmas in July⬧
Citizen Kane⬧
Coal Miner's Daughter⬧
Covergirl
Craig's Wife⬧
Daddy Long Legs⬧
Dangerous When Wet
Darling⬧
Dodsworth⬧
Dreamer
Drifting Souls
Emperor Jones
Evita
Fifth Avenue Girl
Footlight Parade⬧
For Richer, For Poorer
Forever Amber
Give a Girl a Break
Great Expectations
The Great Rupert⬧
Hero⬧
Honeyboy
The Hudsucker Proxy⬧
I Love Melvin
It Could Happen to You
Jailhouse Rock⬧
The Jerk
Jimmy Hollywood
Joseph Andrews
Kept Husbands
A Kid for Two Farthings
Kipps⬧

West Side Story⬧
The Wild Angels
The Wild One⬧
The Wild Ride

Red Cross

China Beach⬧
One Against the Wind⬧
The White Cliffs of Dover⬧

Red Scare

see also Russia/USSR

Arsenal⬧
Baltic Deputy⬧
The Bamboo Saucer
Battle Beneath the Earth
Chapayev⬧
China Cry
China, My Sorrow
Coming Out of the Ice⬧
Comment Ca Va?
The Commies Are Coming, the
  Commies Are Coming
Commissar⬧
Comrade X
Conspirator
Death of a Bureaucrat⬧
Earth⬧
Eminent Domain
Fellow Traveler⬧
Golden Gate
The Great Armored Car Swindle
Guilty by Suspicion
Guilty of Treason
Hands Up⬧
Hawthorne of the USA
Indochine⬧
The Inner Circle⬧
The Interrogation⬧
Invasion U.S.A.
Jet Pilot
Little World of Don Camillo⬧
Man of Iron⬧
Man of Marble⬧
The Manchurian Candidate⬧
Mandela⬧
Matinee
Mother Kusters Goes to
  Heaven⬧
Mother of Kings
Never Let Me Go
Nicholas and Alexandra
Night Crossing
Night Flight from Moscow
The Oak
Oh, Bloody Life!
Open Doors⬧
Red Dawn
The Red Menace
Red Nightmare
Reds⬧
Requiem for Dominic⬧
Revolution! A Red Comedy⬧
The She-Beast
Sideburns
Strike⬧
The Theme⬧
Thoughts Are Free⬧
Tito and Me⬧
Tobor the Great
Trahir⬧
The Ugly American
Uranus⬧
When Father was Away on
  Business⬧

Reincarnation

*see also Death & the
  Afterlife*

Angel on My Shoulder⬧
Angel on My Shoulder
Audrey Rose
Chances Are⬧
Cleo/Leo
Creature of Destruction

Dead Again⬧
Devi⬧
Fluke
Heart and Souls
Heaven Can Wait⬧
Here Comes Mr. Jordan⬧
I Married a Witch⬧
Little Buddha
Oh, Heavenly Dog!
On a Clear Day You Can See
  Forever
The Reincarnation of Peter
  Proud
The Search for Bridey Murphy
Switch⬧

Religion

*see also Buddhism; Islam;
  Judaism; Missionaries;
  Nuns & Priests; Religious
  Epics; Saints*

Abduction of St. Anne
Absolution
The Addiction
Androcles and the Lion
Angel Baby
Angela
Anna
The Apostle⬧
Augustine of Hippo⬧
The Avenging Angel
Before the Rain⬧
Bernadette
The Big Squeeze
The Birch Interval
Blood of Jesus
Body and Soul
Breaking the Waves⬧
Brides of Christ
Brigham Young: Frontiersman
Broken Vows
Brother Cadfael
Brother Cadfael 2
Brother Sun, Sister Moon
Brothers in Arms
Caligari's Cure⬧
Camila⬧
Catholics⬧
Chariots of Fire⬧
Children of Fury
The Church⬧
Citizen Ruth
Come to the Stable⬧
Commandments
The Confessional
Conquest of Space
Contact
The Convent
Cosmic Slop
The Courageous Mr. Penn
Cracker: The Big Crunch
Crimes of Passion⬧
Critical Choices
The Crucible⬧
A Cry from the Mountain
Day of Judgment
Day of Triumph
Dead Man Walking⬧
Def by Temptation
Devi⬧
The Devil at 4 O'Clock
The Disappearance of Aimee⬧
Divided by Hate
Dr. Syn
Dr. Syn, Alias the Scarecrow
A Dream for Christmas⬧
El Cid⬧
El: This Strange Passion⬧
Emanon
Enjo
Entertaining Angels: The
  Dorothy Day Story
Extramuros
Eye of God⬧
The Favor, the Watch, & the
  Very Big Fish
The Fiend

Final Judgement
The Flowers of St. Francis⬧
A Fool and His Money
Francesco
Friendly Persuasion⬧
From a Far Country: Pope John
  Paul II
The Garden
The Gaucho⬧
The Ghoul
Glory! Glory!⬧
Go Down Death
The Godfather, Part 3⬧
God's Gun
Gospa
Greaser's Palace
The Greatest Story Ever Told
Green Pastures⬧
The Guyana Tragedy: The Story
  of Jim Jones
Hail Mary
Hallelujah!⬧
Harvest of Fire
Hazel's People
Heavens Above⬧
Helas pour Moi
Hellfire
Holy Matrimony
The Hoodlum Priest⬧
Household Saints⬧
The Hunchback
I, the Worst of All
I'd Climb the Highest Mountain⬧
In the Line of Duty: Ambush in
  Waco
Inherit the Wind⬧
The Inquiry
Invasion of the Space Preachers
Iron Horsemen
Jerusalem
Jesus
Jesus Christ, Superstar⬧
Jesus of Nazareth
Jesus of Nazareth⬧
The Jesus Trip
The Jew
Joan of Arc
Joni
The Judas Project: The Ultimate
  Encounter
Klondike Annie
La Chartreuse de Parme
Lamb
The Last Temptation of Christ⬧
Laughing Sinners
Leap of Faith
Leaves from Satan's Book
The Light of Faith
Lilies
Little Buddha
Little Church Around the Corner
The Littlest Angel
Love and Faith⬧
Lust and Revenge
Luther
Major Barbara⬧
A Man Called Peter⬧
Marjoe
Martin Luther
Mary, Queen of Scots
The Messenger of the Blessed
  Virgin
The Milky Way⬧
The Miracle⬧
Miracle in Rome
The Miracle of Marcelino
Miracle of Our Lady of Fatima
The Miracle Woman
Mohammed: Messenger of God
Monsieur Vincent⬧
Monsignor Quixote
Monty Python's Life of Brian⬧
A Mormon Maid
Mother Joan of the Angels⬧
Mother Teresa: In the Name of
  God's Poor
The Neon Bible
The Next Voice You Hear
The Night of the Iguana⬧

Nostalghia
One Man's Way
Oranges Are Not the Only Fruit
Ordet⬧
The Other Side of Sunday
Padre Nuestro
Pass the Ammo
The Passion of Darkly Noon
The Passion of Joan of Arc⬧
The Passover Plot
The Penitent
Peter and Paul
Pi
Pray TV
A Prayer in the Dark
Preacherman
The Preacher's Wife
Priest
Prisoner of Rio
The Private Secretary
The Prodigal Planet
Promised a Miracle
Queen Margot⬧
Quo Vadis⬧
Quo Vadis
Rain
The Rapture
The Rector's Wife
Red Planet Mars
Resurrection⬧
Return to Paradise
The Robe
RoGoPaG
Romero
Sacrilege
St. Benny the Dip
Saint Joan
Salome
Salvation!
Sanctuary of Fear
The Scarlet Letter⬧
Sebastiane⬧
Shadowlands⬧
Shiokari Pass
The Sky Pilot
The Song of Bernadette⬧
Susan and God⬧
Tales from the Crypt Presents
  Bordello of Blood
That Eye, the Sky
This Stuff'll Kill Ya!
Through a Glass Darkly⬧
Touch
Tournament
Trapped by the Mormons
The Vision
When Night Is Falling⬧
Where Angels Go, Trouble
  Follows
Whistle Down the Wind⬧
Whistling in the Dark⬧
Whitcomb's War
The White Rose⬧
Wholly Moses!
Why Has Bodhi-Darma Left for
  the East
Wide Awake
The Winter Light⬧
Wise Blood⬧
Witness⬧
The Word
The Worldly Madonna

Religious Epics

see also Religion

Abraham
The Agony and the Ecstasy
...And God Spoke
Barabbas
Ben-Hur⬧
The Bible
The Bible...In the Beginning⬧
Cleopatra
David
David and Bathsheba⬧
Demetrius and the Gladiators
The Egyptian
El Cid⬧

From the Manger to the Cross
The Gospel According to St.
  Matthew⬧
In the Name of the Pope-King⬧
Jacob
Jesus of Nazareth
Joseph
Judith of Bethulia⬧
A Man for All Seasons⬧
Moses
The Prodigal
The Robe
Samson and Delilah
The Sign of the Cross
Sodom and Gomorrah
The Song of Bernadette⬧
The Story of David⬧
The Story of Jacob & Joseph⬧
The Story of Ruth
The Sword and the Cross
The Ten Commandments
The Ten Commandments⬧

Renegade Body Parts

*see also Horror; Killer
  Brains*

The Addams Family
Addams Family Values
And Now the Screaming Starts
The Beast with Five Fingers
Blood of Ghastly Horror
Body Parts
The Brain that Wouldn't Die
The Crawling Eye
The Crawling Hand
Demonoid, Messenger of Death
Doctor Butcher M.D.
8 Heads in a Duffel Bag
Evil Dead 2: Dead by Dawn
Gravesend
The Hand
Hands of a Stranger
The Hands of Orlac
How to Get Ahead in
  Advertising⬧
The Kingdom
Mad Love⬧
The Man with Two Brains⬧
Mindkiller
Severed Ties
Virus
Waxwork 2: Lost in Time

Repressed Men

see also Men

The Age of Innocence⬧
Bitter Moon
Bleak Moments
The Bodyguard
Box of Moonlight
Creation of Adam
The Eighth Day
El
Falling Down
The Game⬧
In and Out⬧
Like It Never Was Before
Love & Death on Long Island
Maurice⬧
The Preacher's Wife
The Remains of the Day⬧
Shadowlands⬧
Sirens
Zero Degrees Kelvin

Rescue Missions

*see also Rescue Missions
  Involving Time Travel*

Alaska
Alone in the Woods
The Amazing Panda Adventure
Any Place But Home
Apollo 13⬧
Balto
Behind Enemy Lines

Revolutionary War

Rio

Road Trip

see also Bikers; Chases; Fast Cars; Motor Vehicle Dept.

Role Reversal

see also Gender Bending;
Identity
Age Isn't Everything
All of Me
Anastasia⬧
Anastasia: The Mystery of Anna
Angel
Angel on My Shoulder⬧
Angel on My Shoulder
Babe⬧
Bad Manners
The Bank Dick⬧
Before Morning
Belfast Assassin
Big⬧
Biggles
Billy Madison
Blood of Dracula
Bloodlink
The Captain from Koepenick
Captive Heart⬧
Cheech and Chong's The
    Corsican Brothers
Christmas in Connecticut⬧
Cinderfella
Clambake
Class Act
Cleo/Leo
Coming to America⬧
Condorman
The Couch Trip
Courage⬧
Dating the Enemy
Dave⬧
The Deputy Drummer
Desperately Seeking Susan
Devil's Canyon
Dr. Black, Mr. Hyde
Doctor Detroit
Doctor Dolittle
Dr. Heckyl and Mr. Hype
Dr. Jekyll and Mr. Hyde⬧
Dr. Jekyll and Mr. Hyde
Doctors and Nurses
Down and Out in Beverly Hills
Dream a Little Dream
A Dream of Passion
18 Again!
Extremities
The $5.20 an Hour Dream
For Ladies Only
48 Hrs.⬧
Freaky Friday
The Gladiator⬧
The Grand Duchess and the
    Waiter⬧
The Great Gabbo
Greystoke: The Legend of
    Tarzan, Lord of the Apes
Guest Wife
Gunfire
Heart Like a Wheel
Her Life as a Man
Hero⬧
Hiding Out
Identity Crisis
The Incredible Mr. Limpet
Iron Maze
Jekyll and Hyde
Johnny Guitar⬧
Junior
Just One of the Guys
Kagemusha⬧
Kim⬧
Kings and Desperate Men
La Femme Nikita⬧
La Ronde⬧
The Lady Vanishes⬧
The Lady Vanishes
Ladybugs
Law and Order
Liana, Jungle Goddess
Like Father, Like Son
Liquid Sky⬧
Lonely Wives
Maid to Order
Male and Female⬧

The Man Who Haunted Himself
The Man Who Wagged His Tail
Man with Two Heads
Mrs. Winterbourne
Monkey Business⬧
Moon over Parador
My Blue Heaven
My Fair Lady⬧
Naked Souls
Now, Voyager⬧
Opportunity Knocks
Overboard
Panamint's Bad Man
Paris When It Sizzles
People's Choice
Performance⬧
Persona⬧
Pocketful of Miracles⬧
Point of No Return
Posse⬧
The Prince and the Pauper⬧
The Prince and the Pauper
Prisoner of Zenda⬧
Prisoner of Zenda
Psycho⬧
Quicksilver
Rabbit Test
The Raggedy Rawney
Raid on Rommel
Red Lion
Red Rock Outlaw
Rendez-Moi Ma Peau
Rider of the Law
The Road to Yesterday
Roman Holiday⬧
Satanik
Savages
Scalpel
The Scarlet Pimpernel⬧
September Affair
The Shaggy D.A.
The Shaggy Dog
Showdown in Little Tokyo
Silent Night, Deadly Night
Slapstick of Another Kind
A Slightly Pregnant Man
Small Town Boy
Something Special
Sommersby
Song of Texas
A Stolen Face
Stoogemania
Straight Talk
Summer Night with Greek
    Profile, Almond Eyes & Scent
    of Basil
Super Soul Brother
Sweet Revenge
Switch⬧
Sylvia Scarlett
Taking Care of Business
A Tale of Two Cities⬧
The Tango Lesson
That's My Baby!
Tomboy
Tootsie⬧
Trading Places
Triple Echo
The Two Faces of Dr. Jekyll
Ultimate Desires
Vice Versa⬧
Victor/Victoria⬧
Wait Till Your Mother Gets
    Home
Watermelon Man
White Man's Burden
White Sands
Wish Upon a Star
Wonder Man
Yankee Zulu
Yentl
Yidl Mitn Fidl

Roll Over Beethoven

see also Musician Biopics
Beethoven Lives Upstairs
Beethoven's Nephew
Bill & Ted's Excellent Adventure

Immortal Beloved

Romance

see Late Bloomin' Love;
    Lovers on the Lam;
    Romantic Adventures;
    Romantic Comedy;
    Romantic Drama; Romantic
    Triangles

Romantic
Adventures

The African Queen⬧
Arabian Nights
The Avengers
Baby ... Secret of the Lost
    Legend
Bagdad
Captain from Castile⬧
Destiny Turns on the Radio
Ever After: A Cinderella Story
Fanfan la Tulipe⬧
Flame of Araby
Gun Crazy⬧
Guncrazy
Gypsy Angels
The Jewel of the Nile
Joe Versus the Volcano
The Last of the Mohicans⬧
Lie Down with Lions
The Mask of Zorro
Mogambo⬧
Oscar and Lucinda
Pocahontas⬧
The Proposition
Red Dust⬧
Romancing the Stone⬧
Rough Magic
Six Days, Seven Nights
Son of Ali Baba
A Thousand and One Nights

Romantic Comedy

Abdulla the Great
About Last Night...⬧
Acqua e Sapone
Adam's Rib⬧
Addicted to Love
The Admiral Was a Lady
Adorable Julia
The Adventures of Sadie
Aggie Appleby, Maker of Men
Alfredo, Alfredo
All Night Long⬧
All Tied Up
The Allnighter
All's Fair
...Almost
Almost an Angel
Almost Pregnant
Almost You
The Ambassador's Daughter
American Dreamer
American Friends
American Matchmaker
The American President⬧
Amore!
The Amorous Adventures of Moll
    Flanders
And You Thought Your Parents
    Were Weird!
Animal Behavior
Anna Christie
Anna Karenina⬧
Annabel Takes a Tour/Maid's
    Night Out
Annie Hall⬧
Another Chance
Another Thin Man
The Apartment⬧
April Fools
Are Parents People?
Arthur⬧
Arthur 2: On the Rocks

As Good As It Gets⬧
Ask Any Girl
Avanti!
Baby Boom
Babycakes
Bachelor Apartment
Bachelor Bait
Bachelor in Paradise
Bachelor Party
Back to the Beach
Bahama Passage
Baja Oklahoma
Ball of Fire⬧
The Balloonatic/One Week
Bar Girls
Bare Essentials
Barefoot in the Park⬧
Barnaby and Me
The Bashful Bachelor
Battling Butler
Beachcomber⬧
The Beautician and the Beast
Bed & Breakfast
Belle Epoque⬧
Bells Are Ringing⬧
Benny & Joon
Best Legs in the 8th Grade
Betsy's Wedding
Beyond Tomorrow
Birds & the Bees
Blame It on Rio
Blind Date
Blonde Crazy
Blue Country
Bluebeard's Eighth Wife
Bobo
Bombshell⬧
Boom Town
Boomerang
Born Yesterday⬧
Born Yesterday
Boyfriends
Boyfriends & Girlfriends
Breakfast at Tiffany's⬧
Breaking Up
Breath of Scandal
Breathing Room
The Bride Came C.O.D.
Bull Durham⬧
But Not for Me
The Butcher's Wife
Butterflies
Bye Bye Baby
Cactus Flower
Cafe au Lait⬧
Cafe Romeo
California Casanova
California Suite⬧
Came a Hot Friday
The Cameraman⬧
Can She Bake a Cherry Pie?
Can't Buy Me Love
Can't Hardly Wait
Captain's Paradise⬧
Car Trouble
Career Opportunities
Cartier Affair
Casanova
Casanova Brown
Casanova '70
The Cemetery Club
Chances Are⬧
A Change of Seasons
Changing Habits
Charley's Aunt
Chasing Amy
The Cheerful Fraud
Chilly Scenes of Winter
Christmas in Connecticut⬧
Christmas in Connecticut
Class of '44
The Clock⬧
Closely Watched Trains⬧
Clueless⬧
Cold Feet
Come Blow Your Horn⬧
Come September
Comeback Kid
Coming to America⬧

Continental Divide
Cool Blue
A Touch in New York
A Countess from Hong Kong
Court Jester⬧
The Cowboy and the Lady
Crazy in Love
Crazy Moon
Creator
Crocodile Dundee⬧
Cross My Heart
Crossing Delancey⬧
Curly Sue
Dance With Me
The Dark Side of the Heart
Date with an Angel
Dating the Enemy
Dear Brigitte
Dear Detective
Decameron Nights
Defending Your Life⬧
The Demi-Paradise⬧
Designing Woman⬧
Desk Set⬧
Desperate Moves
Desperately Seeking Susan
The Devil & Miss Jones⬧
Diary of a Seducer
Different Story
Dirty Rotten Scoundrels⬧
The Divorce of Lady X
Doc Hollywood
Doctor in Distress
Dr. Jack/For Heaven's Sake
Does This Mean We're Married?
Dollar
Dona Flor and Her Two
    Husbands⬧
Dona Herlinda & Her Son
Don't Do It
Don't Hang Up
Don't Tell Her It's Me
Dream Date
Dream for an Insomniac
Dream Trap
Dreaming of Rita
Dreams Come True
East and West⬧
Edie & Pen
Ed's Next Move
Electric Dreams
Elsa, Elsa
The Englishman Who Went Up a
    Hill But Came Down a
    Mountain⬧
Eversmile New Jersey
Every Girl Should Be Married
Every Which Way But Loose
Face the Music
The Facts of Life
Fall
The Farmer's Daughter⬧
The Farmer's Other Daughter
Fate
Father Goose
The Favor
Feelin' Screwy
Feet First
Fifth Avenue Girl
A Fine Romance
First Time
Flirt
Foolin' Around
Fools Rush In
For Better or Worse
For Heaven's Sake⬧
For Love of Ivy
For Love or Money
For Roseanna
For the Love of Mary
Forget Paris
A Forgotten Tune for the Flute⬧
Forty Carats
Four Weddings and a Funeral⬧
Framed
Frankie and Johnny⬧
French Exit
French Kiss
The French Lesson

Romantic

The Caine Mutiny Court Martial↗
Captain Caution
Captain Horatio Hornblower↗
Captain Ron
Captains Courageous↗
Captains Courageous
Captain's Paradise↗
The Captain's Table
Carry On Admiral
Carry On Cruising
China Seas
Christopher Columbus
The Coast Patrol
Convoy
A Countess from Hong Kong
The Crew
Crimson Tide↗
Cruise into Terror
Damn the Defiant↗
Dangerous Charter
Dangerous Passage
Dark Tide
Das Boot↗
Day of the Assassin
The Day Will Dawn↗
Dead Ahead: The Exxon Valdez
    Disaster↗
Dead Calm↗
Dead Reckoning
Dead Tides
Deadly Voyage
Death Cruise
Death Ship
Death Tide
The Deep
Deep Rising
Destroyer↗
Die Hard: With a Vengeance
Disney's Storybook Classics
Dixie Jamboree
Doctor at Sea
Don Winslow of the Coast Guard
The Dove
Down Periscope
Down to the Sea in Ships
Ensign Pulver
Erik, the Viking
Escape from Atlantis
The Evil Below
Far from Home: The Adventures
    of Yellow Dog
Feet First
Ferry to Hong Kong
The Fighting Sullivans↗
The Final Countdown↗
Flat Top
Flight of the Intruder
Flipper↗
Francis in the Navy
Friday the 13th, Part 8: Jason
    Takes Manhattan
Gangway
Geheimeke WB1
Ghost Ship
The Gift Horse
A Girl in Every Port
Give Me a Sailor
Going Overboard
Going Under
Golden Rendezvous
Goliath Awaits
Gone Fishin'
Gray Lady Down
The Great Lover
Gun Cargo
The Hairy Ape
Haunted Harbor
The Haunted Sea
Hawaii Calls
He Is My Brother
Hell-Ship Morgan
History Is Made at Night↗
Horror of the Zombies
The Hunt for Red October↗
I Conquer the Sea
In Which We Serve↗
The Incredible Mr. Limpet
The Incredible Petrified World
Ironclads

Isle of Forgotten Sins
JAG
Jaws↗
Jaws 2
The Jewel of the Nile
John Paul Jones
Juggernaut↗
Kill Cruise
Killer on Board
King Kelly of the U.S.A.
Knife in the Water↗
The Last of Sheila
The Last Voyage
Law of the Sea
Le Crabe Tambour↗
The Legend of Sea Wolf
The Legend of the Sea Wolf
Lifeboat↗
Light at the Edge of the World
The Lightship
Live and Let Die
Loch Ness
Long John Silver
The Long Ships
The Long Voyage Home↗
Lord Jim↗
Love Affair↗
The Magic Stone
A Majority of One
Manfish
McHale's Navy
The Mermaids of Tiburon
Mister Roberts↗
Monkey Business↗
Moon in Scorpio
Moran of the Lady Letty
Muppet Treasure Island
Murder on the High Seas
Mutiny
The Mutiny of the Elsinore
Mutiny on the Bounty
Mutiny on the Bounty
Mystery Liner
The Mystery of the Mary Celeste
The Navigator↗
The Navy Comes Through
New Moon
A Night to Remember↗
The Odyssey
Old Ironsides↗
One Crazy Summer
Operation Petticoat↗
Out to Sea
Oxford Blues
Passenger↗
Pirate Ship
The Port of Missing Girls
The Poseidon Adventure
The Princess Comes Across↗
PT 109
Pueblo Affair↗
Pursuit of the Graf Spee
Rainbow Warrior
Reaching for the Moon
Reap the Wild Wind
Rich and Strange
Roaring Speedboats
Romancing the Stone↗
Run Silent, Run Deep↗
The Sand Pebbles↗
Save the Lady
Sea Chase
Sea Devils
Sea Racketeers
The Sea Wolf↗
The Sea Wolf
Shades of Fear
Sharks' Treasure
She Shall Have Music
Ship Ahoy
Ship of Fools↗
Ships in the Night
Shout at the Devil
Sinbad, the Sailor↗
Sink the Bismarck↗
Souls at Sea
South Seas Massacre
Speed 2: Cruise Control
Steamboat Bill, Jr.↗

Submarine Seahawk
Swashbuckler
Tamango
Task Force
Temptation
Tentacles of the North
They Were Expendable↗
Three Daring Daughters
Thunder in Paradise
Till There was You
Titanic↗
Titanic
Titanic↗
To Gillian on Her 37th Birthday
To Have & Have Not↗
Today We Live
Torpedo Run
Transatlantic Merry-Go-Round
Treacherous Crossing
The Treasure of Jamaica Reef
Two Years Before the Mast
U-Boat Prisoner
Under Siege
The Unsinkable Molly Brown↗
Up the Creek
Virus
Voyage
Voyage of Terror: The Achille
    Lauro Affair
Voyage of the Damned↗
Wake of the Red Witch
Waterworld
We're Not Dressing↗
White Squall
Wild Orchids
Wind
Windjammer
Windrider
Witch Who Came from the Sea
Woman of Desire
Wonderland Cove
The World in His Arms
The Wreck of the Mary Deare
Yankee Clipper

Saints

***see also* Religion**

Augustine of Hippo↗
Bernadette
Brother Sun, Sister Moon
The Flowers of St. Francis↗
Francesco
Joan of Arc
The Messenger of the Blessed
    Virgin
Miracle in Rome
Miracle of Our Lady of Fatima
The Passion of Joan of Arc↗
The Proprietor
Saint Joan
Sebastiane↗
The Song of Bernadette↗
Therese↗
A Time for Miracles

Salespeople

***see also* Corporate
Shenanigans**

Adventures in Babysitting
The Bible and Gun Club
Cadillac Man
Death of a Salesman↗
The Fan
Glengarry Glen Ross↗
Jingle All the Way
Miss Rose White↗
The Music Man↗
Pennies From Heaven↗
The Rainmaker↗
Tin Men
Trojan Eddie↗

The Salvation Army

Guys and Dolls↗
Major Barbara↗

San Francisco

see also Earthquakes

After the Block
All Dogs Go to Heaven 2
Armistead Maupin's Tales of the
    City
Barbary Coast↗
The Barbary Coast
Beyond the Door
Big Trouble in Little China
Cardiac Arrest
Chan Is Missing↗
The Chinatown Kid
Clowning Around 2
Copycat
The Dead Pool
Desperate Measures
Desperate Moves
Dim Sum: A Little Bit of Heart↗
Dirty Harry↗
Dr. Jekyll's Dungeon of Death
Doctor Who
Dogfight↗
Dogwatch
Dream with the Fishes
Dying to Remember
The Enforcer
An Eye for an Eye
The Fan
Fanci's Persuasion
Final Analysis
Fisherman's Wharf
Flame of the Barbary Coast
Flower Drum Song
Fools
48 Hrs.↗
Foul Play↗
Freebie & the Bean
The Frisco Kid
George of the Jungle↗
Golden Gate
Ground Zero
Hello, Frisco, Hello
Homeward Bound 2: Lost in San
    Francisco
I Remember Mama↗
Invasion of the Body Snatchers↗
It Came from Beneath the Sea↗
Key to the City
Kicks
Kuffs
Lady from Louisiana
Lady of the House
The Laughing Policeman
Lightblast
Magnum Force
Metro
Monster in the Closet
Mysterious Mr. Wong
Nightmare in Blood
Nina Takes a Lover
Nine Months
Pacific Heights↗
Poltergeist: The Legacy
The Presidio
The Rock↗
The Saint Strikes Back
Salome, Where She Danced
San Francisco↗
Serial↗
The Shock
The Single Standard
The Sisters↗
A Smile Like Yours
Stealing Heaven
Sudden Impact
Time After Time↗
Times of Harvey Milk
Weapons of Death
Whatever Happened to Susan
    Jane?
What's Up, Doc?↗
Wild West
The Zodiac Killer

Sanity Check

see also Doctors & Nurses;
    Hospitals & Medicine;
    Shrinks

Aguirre, the Wrath of God↗
Alone in the Dark
American Eagle
Amos
An Angel at My Table↗
Anguish
Another Time, Another Place
Appointment with Fear
Arsenic and Old Lace↗
Asylum
Asylum of Satan
Bad Dreams
Beauty on the Beach
Bedlam↗
Behind Locked Doors
The Bell Jar
Beyond Therapy
A Blade in the Dark
Blood Frenzy
Blood Salvage
Blood Song
Bloody Wednesday
Body Chemistry
Boxing Helena
The Boys Next Door
Brain Dead↗
Buried Alive
Camille Claudel↗
Captain Newman, M.D.
The Carpenter
Cat in the Cage
Cause for Alarm
Chattahoochee
Clockwise
Coast to Coast
The Cobweb
The Collector↗
Committed
Conspiracy Theory↗
The Couch Trip
The Cracker Factory
Crazed
Crazy Fat Ethel II
Crazy People
Crime and Punishment↗
The Crime of Dr. Crespi
Criminally Insane
Crow Hollow
Cry Wolf
Cutting Class
Dark Obsession
Dark Places
Dark Sanity
Dark Waters
Darkroom
A Day at the Races↗
Dead Man Out↗
Dead of Night↗
Dead Pit
Deadly Innocence
Deadly Intruder
Deadly Strangers
The Deadly Trap
Death Kiss
Death Nurse
Dementia 13
A Demon in My View
Demons of the Mind
Deranged
Despair↗
Desperate Living
Deutschland im Jahre Null↗
Devi↗
The Devil Bat
The Devil Bat's Daughter
Devil Doll↗
The Devil in Silk
Devil in the Flesh
Devil Times Five
Devil Wears White
The Devil's Advocate
Diary of a Mad Housewife↗
Diary of a Madman
Diary of a Young Comic

Future Force
Future Hunters
Future Zone
Futurekick
Futureworld
Galactic Gigolo
Galaxis
Galaxy Invader
Galaxy of Terror
Game of Survival
Gamera, the Invincible
Gamera vs. Barugon
Gamera vs. Gaos
Gamera vs. Guiron
Gamera vs. Zigra
The Gamma People
Gappa the Trifibian Monster
Gattaca↗
Geisha Girl
Generations: Mind Control-From
   the Future
Ghidrah the Three Headed
   Monster
Ghost in the Shell
Ghost Patrol
The Giant Claw
The Giant Gila Monster
The Giant Spider Invasion
The Gladiators
Glen and Randa
Godzilla
Godzilla, King of the Monsters
Godzilla 1985
Godzilla on Monster Island
Godzilla Raids Again
Godzilla vs. Biollante
Godzilla vs. King Ghidora
Godzilla vs. Megalon
Godzilla vs. Monster Zero
Godzilla vs. Mothra
Godzilla vs. the Cosmic Monster
Godzilla vs. the Sea Monster
Godzilla vs. the Smog Monster
Godzilla's Revenge
Gorath
Gorgo
Grand Tour: Disaster in Time
The Green Slime
The Groundstar Conspiracy↗
GUY: Awakening of the Devil
The Guyver
Guyver 2: Dark Hero
H-Man
Habitat
Half Human
The Handmaid's Tale
Hands of Steel
Hangar 18
Hardware
Heartbeeps
Heatseeker
Heavy Metal↗
The Hidden↗
The Hidden 2
Hide and Seek
Hideous Sun Demon
The High Crusade
High Desert Kill
Highlander 2: The Quickening
The Hitchhiker's Guide to the
   Galaxy
Hollywood Boulevard 2
Hologram Man
Homewrecker
Horror Planet
Horrors of the Red Planet
Howard the Duck
The Human Duplicators
The Human Vapor
Humanoid Defender
Hybrid
Hyper-Sapien: People from
   Another Star
Hyper Space
I Come in Peace
I Married a Monster from Outer
   Space
Iceman↗
Idaho Transfer

The Illustrated Man↗
In the Aftermath: Angels Never
   Sleep
In the Cold of the Night
Incredible Melting Man
The Incredible Petrified World
The Incredible Shrinking Man↗
Independence Day↗
Infra-Man
Innerspace
Interzone
Intruder Within
Intruders
Invader↗
The Invader
The Invaders
Invaders from Mars
Invasion
Invasion Earth: The Aliens Are
   Here!
Invasion of the Animal People
Invasion of the Bee Girls↗
Invasion of the Body Snatchers↗
Invasion of the Body Stealers
Invasion of the Girl Snatchers
Invasion of the Space Preachers
Invisible Adversaries
The Invisible Boy
Invisible Invaders
The Invisible Man Returns↗
The Invisible Terror
Invisible: The Chronicles of
   Benjamin Knight
Island of Terror↗
Island of the Burning Doomed
Island of the Lost
It Came from Beneath the Sea↗
It Came from Outer Space↗
It Came from Outer Space 2
It Conquered the World
It! The Terror from Beyond
   Space
Josh Kirby...Time Warrior:
   Chapter 6, Last Battle for the
   Universe
Journey Beneath the Desert
Journey to the Center of the
   Earth↗
Journey to the Center of the
   Earth
Journey to the Center of Time
Journey to the Far Side of the
   Sun↗
Killers from Space
The Killing Edge
Killings at Outpost Zeta
King Dinosaur
King Kong vs. Godzilla
The Kirlian Witness
Knights
Kronos
Krull
Kurt Vonnegut's Harrison
   Bergeron
Laboratory
The Land that Time Forgot
The Land Unknown
Laserblast
Last Chase
Last Exit to Earth
The Last Starfighter
Last War
The Last Woman on Earth
Lathe of Heaven
The Lawless Land
The Lawnmower Man
Lawnmower Man 2: Beyond
   Cyberspace
Legion
Leprechaun 4: In Space
Leviathan
Lifeforce
Lifeform
Lifepod
Light Years
Liquid Sky↗
The Living Dead
Lobster Man from Mars
Lock 'n' Load

Logan's Run
Lolita 2000
Looker
Lords of the Deep
The Lost Empire
Lost in Space
The Lost Missile
Lost Planet Airmen
The Love Factor
The Lucifer Complex
Making Mr. Right
A Man Called Rage
The Man from Atlantis
The Man Who Fell to Earth↗
Mandroid
Manhunt of Mystery Island
Maniac Warriors
The Manster
Marooned
Mars
Mars Attacks!
Mars Needs Women
The Martian Chronicles: Part 1
The Martian Chronicles: Part 2
The Martian Chronicles: Part 3
Masters of Venus
Meet the Hollowheads
Megaforce
Megaville
Mesa of Lost Women
Metallica
Metalstorm: The Destruction of
   Jared Syn
Metamorphosis
Meteor Monster
Metropolis↗
Midnight Movie Massacre
Millenium
Mimic
Mind Snatchers
Mind Trap
Mind Warp
Mindwarp
Misfits of Science
Missile to the Moon
Mission Galactica: The Cylon
   Attack
Mission Mars
Mission Stardust
Mistress of the World
The Mole People
Monkey Boy
Monolith
The Monolith Monsters
Monster a Go-Go!
Monster from Green Hell
Monster from the Ocean Floor
The Monster Maker
The Monster of Piedras Blancas
Monster on the Campus
The Monster That Challenged
   the World
Moon 44
Moon Pilot
Moonbase
Moontrap
Mortal Challenge
Mosiac Project
Mosquito
Mothra↗
Murder by Moonlight
Murder in Space
Mutant Hunt
Mutant Species
Mutator
The Mysterians
Mysterious Island↗
Mysterious Two
Mystery Science Theater 3000:
   The Movie
Naked Souls
Navy vs. the Night Monsters
Nemesis
Nemesis 2: Nebula
Nemesis 3: Time Lapse
Neon City
The Nest
Neutron and the Black Mask

Neutron vs. the Amazing Dr.
   Caronte
Neutron vs. the Death Robots
New Crime City: Los Angeles
   2020
New Eden
The New Gladiators
The New Invisible Man
Next One
Night Beast
Night Caller from Outer Space
Night of the Blood Beast
Nightfall
Nightflyers
984: Prisoner of the Future
1984↗
No Survivors, Please
Norman's Awesome Experience
Not Like Us
Not of This Earth
Nude on the Moon
Oblivion
Octaman
Official Denial
Omega Doom
Omega Man
On the Comet↗
One Million B.C.
The Original Fabulous
   Adventures of Baron
   Munchausen
The Original Flash Gordon
   Collection
The Outer Limits: Galaxy Being
The Outer Limits: Sandkings↗
Outland
The P.A.C.K.
Parasite
Past Perfect
Peacemaker
The People
The People That Time Forgot
People Who Own the Dark
The Phantom Empire
Phantom from Space
The Phantom from 10,000
   Leagues
The Phantom Planet
Phase 4
Phenomenal and the Treasure
   of Tutankamen
The Philadelphia Experiment
Philadelphia Experiment 2
Phoenix
Phoenix the Warrior
Plan 9 from Outer Space
Plan 10 from Outer Space
Planet Burg
Planet Earth
Planet of Blood
Planet of Dinosaurs
Planet of the Apes↗
Planet of the Vampires
Planet on the Prowl
Planets Against Us
Plughead Rewired: Circuitry
   Man 2
The Postman
The Power Within
Precious Find
Predator
Predator 2
Prehistoric Women
Primal Impulse
Primal Scream
Prisoners of the Lost Universe
The Professor
Programmed to Kill
Project A-ko
Project: Alien
Project: Genesis
Project Metalbeast: DNA
   Overload
Project Moon Base
Project Shadowchaser 3000
Proteus
Prototype↗
Prototype X29A
PSI Factor

The Psychotronic Man
Pulse
The Puma Man
The Puppet Masters
The Purple Monster Strikes
Purple People Eater
Quarantine
Quatermass 2↗
Quatermass and the Pit
Quatermass Conclusion
The Quatermass Experiment↗
Queen of Outer Space
Quest for Love
The Quiet Earth↗
Quintet
Radar Men from the Moon
Radioactive Dreams
Raiders of Atlantis
Rats
Ravager
Reactor
Rebel Storm
Red Planet Mars
Redline
Remote Control
Replikator: Cloned to Kill
Resistance
Resurrection of Zachary
   Wheeler
The Return
Return from Witch Mountain
Return of Chandu
The Return of Swamp Thing
Return of the Aliens: The Deadly
   Spawn
Return of the Fly
Return of the Jedi↗
Return to Frogtown
Revenge of the Teenage Vixens
   from Outer Space
Riding with Death
Robinson Crusoe on Mars
Robo-Chic
RoboCop the Series: The Future
   of Law Enforcement
Roboman
Robot Holocaust
Robot Jox
Robot Monster
Robot Wars
Rock & Roll Cowboys
Rocket Attack U.S.A.
Rocketship
Rocketship X-M
Rocky Jones, Space Ranger
Rocky Jones, Space Ranger:
   Renegade Satellite
Roller Blade
Roller Blade Warriors: Taken By
   Force
Rollerball
R.O.T.O.R.
Runaway
Running Against Time
Running Delilah
The Running Man
Rush
Saturn 3
Savage
Scanner Cop
Scanner Cop 2: Volkin's
   Revenge
Sci-Fighters
Scream and Scream Again
Screamers
The Sea Serpent
Search and Destroy
The Secret of the Golden Eagle
The Secret of the Telegian
The Sender
The Sex Machine
Shadow Warriors
Shadowzone
She
The Silencers
Silent Running↗
The Sisterhood
Skeeter
Sky Pirates

Science & Scientists

Scotland

Sex on the Beach

see also Island Fare

Sexploitation

see also Erotic Thrillers;
     Exploitation

Sexploitation

Champagne for Breakfast
Cheering Section
The Cheerleaders
Cheerleaders' Wild Weekend
Cherry Hill High
Chesty Anderson USN
Class Reunion
Cleo/Leo
Corruption
The Curious Dr. Humpp
Dandelions
Deadly Embrace
Def Jam's How to Be a Player
Delinquent School Girls
Devil's Wedding Night
Dinosaur Island
Dirty Mind of Young Sally
Domino
Dracula Sucks
Ecstasy
Emily
Emmanuelle
Emmanuelle 4
Emmanuelle 5
Emmanuelle 6
Emmanuelle & Joanna
Emmanuelle in the Country
Emmanuelle on Taboo Island
Emmanuelle, the Joys of a
   Woman
Erotic Escape
Erotic Touch of Hot Skin
Fanny Hill: Memoirs of a Woman
   of Pleasure
Fantasies
Feelin' Up
Firehouse
The First Nudie Musical
Flesh Gordon
Flesh Gordon 2: Flesh Gordon
   Meets the Cosmic
   Cheerleaders
Fleshpot on 42nd Street
Forever Emmanuelle
The French Woman
Ghosts Can't Do It
Gimme an F
Ginger
The Girl, the Body and the Pill
Goodbye Emmanuelle
Great Bikini Off-Road Adventure
The Happy Hooker
The Happy Hooker Goes to
   Washington
Hard to Die
Hardbodies
Help Wanted Female
Hollywood Boulevard 2
Hollywood High
Hollywood High, Part 2
Hollywood Hot Tubs
Hollywood Hot Tubs 2:
   Educating Crystal
Homework
Honkytonk Nights
Hot Moves
Hot T-Shirts
H.O.T.S.
How to Make a Doll
Ilsa, She-Wolf of the SS
Ilsa, the Tigress of Siberia
Ilsa, the Wicked Warden
Inferno in Paradise
Inhibition
Inn of Temptation
Invasion of the Girl Snatchers
The Invisible Maniac
Joy of Sex
Kandyland
Knock Outs
Lady Godiva Rides
Last Dance
Liana, Jungle Goddess
Liquid Dreams
Little Miss Innocence
Love Desperados
The Love Factor
Love Notes
Lust for Freedom

Mistress Pamela
Modern Girls
Mondo Balardo
My Pleasure Is My Business
My Therapist
Mysterious Jane
Naked Killer
The Naked Sword of Zorro
Naked Venus
Nature's Playmates
Naughty Knights
Night Call Nurses
The Night Evelyn Came Out of
   the Grave
The Night Porter
Nine Ages of Nakedness
Nude on the Moon
Nurse on Call
Orgy of the Dead
Pagan Island
Paranoia
Party Favors
Party Plane
Perfect Timing
The Perils of Gwendoline
The Perverse Countess
Please Don't Eat My Mother
Prehistoric Bimbos in
   Armageddon City
Preppies
The Prime Time
Private Duty Nurses
Private Passions
Profile for Murder
Rebel Vixens
Red Shoe Diaries 2: Double
   Dare
Return to the Blue Lagoon
Revenge of the Cheerleaders
Revenge of the Virgins
Sacrilege
Saturday Night Sleazies, Vol. 1
Screen Test
Sea of Dreams
The Seducers
Sensual Partners
The Sensuous Teenager
Sex Adventures of the Three
   Musketeers
Sex and Buttered Popcorn
Sex and Zen
Sex Is Crazy
Sex Through a Window
Shanty Tramp
She Came on the Bus
She Devils in Chains
Slammer Girls
Slumber Party Massacre 3
Snapshot
Snowballing
Sorority Babes in the Slimeball
   Bowl-A-Rama
Sorority House Party
Spaced Out
The Speed Lovers
S.S. Love Camp No. 27
The Story of O, Part 2
Strange World of Coffin Joe
The Student Nurses
The Student Teachers
Submission
Suburban Roulette
Sugar Cookies
Superchick
Supervixens
Sweater Girls
Sweet Georgia
Sweet Young Thing
The Swinging Cheerleaders
Swinging Wives
Takin' It All Off
Tarzana, the Wild Girl
Tender Loving Care
Test Tube Teens from the Year
   2000
Texas Layover
Thinkin' Big
Tokyo Decadence
Tomcat: Dangerous Desires

Train Station Pickups
Truck Stop
Truck Stop Women
2069: A Sex Odyssey
Ultimate Desires
The Vampire Hookers
Venus in Furs
Vice Academy
Vice Academy 2
Vice Academy 3
Wanda, the Sadistic Hypnotist
Wild Orchid 2: Two Shades of
   Blue
Witchcraft 2: The Temptress
Witchcraft 3: The Kiss of Death
Witchcraft 5: Dance with the
   Devil
World of the Depraved
The Young Nurses
The Zombie Army

Sexual Abuse

   see also Rape; Spousal
      Abuse

The Accused
The Bed You Sleep In
Boxing Helena
The Boys of St. Vincent✍
The Devils✍
Fall from Innocence
Fortune and Men's Eyes
Heart of the Stag
Ilsa, Harem Keeper of the Oil
   Sheiks
Loved
Mesmerized
The Night Porter
Priest
Prime Suspect: The Lost Child✍
Romper Stomper
Twin Peaks: Fire Walk with Me

Sexual Harrassment

Brilliant Lies
Disclosure
Foxfire
G.I. Jane
Improper Conduct
Oleanna

Ships

   see Deep Blue; Mutiny;
   Sail Away; Shipwrecked;
   Submarines

Shipwrecked

   see also Sea Disasters

Adventures of Eliza Fraser
Benji the Hunted
The Black Pirate✍
The Black Stallion✍
Blue Fin
The Blue Lagoon
Cabeza de Vaca✍
Dungeon of Harrow
Eye of the Needle
Far from Home: The Adventures
   of Yellow Dog
Greystoke: The Legend of
   Tarzan, Lord of the Apes
Hawk of the Wilderness
He Is My Brother
Humongous
The Island of Dr. Moreau
Island of Lost Souls✍
Island of the Lost
Jungle Bride
Kilma, Queen of the Amazons
The Legend of the Sea Wolf
Light at the Edge of the World
Male and Female✍
The Most Dangerous Game✍
Mutiny on the Bounty✍

Mutiny on the Bounty✍
My Favorite Wife✍
Pardon My Sarong
Princess Caraboo
Project: Genesis
Revenge of Doctor X
Rich and Strange
Robby
Robinson Crusoe
Robinson Crusoe & the Tiger
Sea Gypsies
The Sea Wolf✍
The Sea Wolf
She Gods of Shark Reef
Shipwreck Island
Shogun✍
Summer Affair
Swept Away...✍
Swept from the Sea
The Swiss Family Robinson✍
Trader Tom of the China Seas
20,000 Leagues Under the Sea✍
Two Lost Worlds

Showbiz Comedies

The Big Broadcast of 1938
The Big Picture
Blazing Saddles
Bloodhounds of Broadway
Boardinghouse Blues
The Boy Friend✍
Broadway Melody
Broadway Melody of 1936✍
Broadway Melody of 1938
Broadway Melody of 1940
Bullets Over Broadway✍
Cannes Man
Cats Don't Dance
The Comic
The Dark Backward
The Day the Women Got Even
Delirious
Dog Pound Shuffle✍
Ella Cinders
The Errand Boy
Everybody Sing
Extra Girl
Forever Female✍
Free and Easy
Funny Bones✍
George White's Scandals
Get Shorty✍
Good Times
Grave Secrets
Gypsy✍
Gypsy
The Hard Way✍
Hear My Song✍
Here Comes Cookie
Hollywood Boulevard 2
Hollywood Chaos
Hollywood in Trouble
Hollywood Party
Hollywood Shuffle
Hooper
I'll Do Anything
It's a Date
It's a Great Feeling
Joey Breaker
Lady Killer✍
Let's Make Love
Life with Mikey
Main Street to Broadway
Merton of the Movies
A Midwinter's Tale
Mr. Saturday Night
Movies Money Murder
The Muppet Movie✍
The Muppets Take Manhattan✍
My Dream Is Yours
My Favorite Year✍
Nancy Goes to Rio
The Night They Raided
   Minsky's✍
Nudity Required
Panama Hattie
Panic Button
The Party✍

Pick a Star
Postcards from the Edge✍
The Prince and the Showgirl
The Producers✍
Ratings Game
The Real Blonde
Rubberface
Salut l'Artiste✍
Second Fiddle
The Shot
Silent Movie
Soapdish✍
S.O.B.
Star Spangled Rhythm✍
Swingers✍
Tapeheads
There's No Business Like Show
   Business✍
Tune in Tomorrow
Wag the Dog
Waiting for Guffman
Who Framed Roger Rabbit✍
The Wizard of Speed and Time
World's Greatest Lover
Young & Willing
Young People

Showbiz Dramas

Actors and Sin
All About Eve✍
American Blue Note
The Ann Jillian Story
Anna✍
The Barefoot Contessa✍
The Big Knife✍
Blast-Off Girls
The Bodyguard
Boogie Nights✍
Cassie
A Chorus Line
The Comic
Concrete Angels
Dangerous
Day for Night✍
The Day of the Locust✍
Doll Face
The Dresser✍
Ernie Kovacs: Between the
   Laughter
Fame✍
For the Boys
Frances✍
From the Journals of Jean
   Seberg
Funny Girl✍
Funny Lady
The Girl Said No
Grace of My Heart
Happily Ever After
Hard Part Begins
Hollywood Dreams
Hollywood Heartbreak
Hollywood Mystery
The Jacksons: An American
   Dream
King of Comedy✍
La Dolce Vita✍
The Last Metro✍
Last Summer In the Hamptons✍
The Last Tycoon✍
Lenny✍
The Lonely Lady
Lucy and Desi: Before the
   Laughter
Madonna: Innocence Lost
A Man Called Adam
Max
Mickey One
Mommie Dearest
Network✍
Once in Paris...
Payday
The Player✍
Postcards from the Edge✍
Pure Country
Rainbow Over Broadway
Sam's Son
Second Coming of Suzanne

Silent

The White Rose➤
The White Sin
The White Sister➤
White Tiger
Why Change Your Wife?
Wild Horse Canyon
Wild Orchids
The Wind➤
Wings
The Wishing Ring➤
Witchcraft through the Ages➤
With Kit Carson Over the Great
   Divide
The Wizard of Oz
Wolf Blood
Wolfheart's Revenge
Woman in Grey
Woman in the Moon
A Woman of Affairs
Woman of Paris/Sunnyside➤
Work/Police➤
Working Winnie/Oh So Simple
The Worldly Madonna
Yankee Clipper
Yankee Doodle in Berlin
Zvenigora➤

Silent Horror/ Fantasy Classics
see also Silent Films

Aelita: Queen of Mars
The Cabinet of Dr. Caligari➤
Dante's Inferno
Dr. Jekyll and Mr. Hyde➤
The Golem➤
The Hunchback of Notre Dame➤
La Chute de la Maison Usher➤
Les Vampires
Metropolis➤
The Monster➤
Nosferatu➤
The Penalty
The Phantom of the Opera➤
The Thief of Baghdad➤
20,000 Leagues Under the Sea➤
Vampyr➤
The Wizard of Oz

Single Parents
see also Bringing Up Baby; Parenthood

Baby Boom
Bogus
Bye Bye, Love
Kramer vs. Kramer➤
One Fine Day
The Players Club➤
Sleepless in Seattle➤
Zeus and Roxanne

Singles
see also Dates From Hell

About Last Night...➤
Beautiful Girls
Before Sunrise
Boys' Night Out➤
Breakfast at Tiffany's➤
Bye Bye, Love
Crossing Delancey➤
Ed's Next Move
Everyone Says I Love You➤
Everything Relative
Forget Paris
He Said, She Said
Kicking and Screaming➤
Metropolitan➤
Mr. Wonderful
Mr. Wrong
Mystic Pizza
The Opposite Sex and How to
   Live With Them
Pillow Talk➤
Reality Bites
St. Elmo's Fire

Singles➤
Sleepless in Seattle➤
Sliding Doors
That Touch of Mink
The Thing Called Love
Trial and Error
Wedding Bell Blues
When Harry Met Sally...➤
When the Cat's Away➤
The Wild Life

Sixties
see Flower Children

Skateboarding

Gleaming the Cube
Gummo
Skateboard
The Skateboard Kid 2

Skating
see also Hockey

Airborne
Blades of Courage
Breaking the Ice
The Cutting Edge
Derby➤
Everything Happens at Night➤
Frolics on Ice
Hans Brinker
Happy Landing
Ice Castles
Ice Pawn
Iceland
My Lucky Star
One in a Million➤
Roller Boogie
Schizo
Sun Valley Serenade
Unholy Rollers
Wintertime
Xanadu

Skiing

Aspen Extreme
Avalanche
Better Off Dead
Club Med
Downhill Racer
Downhill Willie
Dumb & Dumber
Fire and Ice
Fire, Ice and Dynamite
For Your Eyes Only➤
Going for the Gold: The Bill
   Johnson Story
Hot Dog...The Movie!
Iced
Lost and Found
The Man Who Skied Down
   Everest
On Her Majesty's Secret
   Service➤
One Last Run
The Other Side of the Mountain
The Other Side of the Mountain,
   Part 2
Red Snow
Reno and the Doc
Ski Bum
Ski Patrol
Ski School
Ski School 2
Ski Troop Attack
Skier's Dream
Snow: The Movie
Snowball Express
Snowballin'
Snowballing
Snowblind
Striker's Mountain
Tales from the Snow Zone

Skinheads
see also Nazis & Other Paramilitary Slugs

All American Werewolf in Paris
Cracker: To Be a Somebody
The Infiltrator
Luna Park
Meantime
Red Scorpion 2
Romper Stomper
Skin
Surf Nazis Must Die
The Turning

Skydiving

Drop Zone
Fandango
Honeymoon in Vegas
Point Break
Terminal Velocity

Slapstick Comedy
see also Comedy; Screwball Comedy

Abbott and Costello Go to Mars
Abbott and Costello in
   Hollywood
Abbott and Costello in the
   Foreign Legion
Abbott and Costello Meet
   Captain Kidd
Abbott and Costello Meet Dr.
   Jekyll and Mr. Hyde
Abbott and Costello Meet
   Frankenstein➤
Abbott and Costello Meet the
   Invisible Man➤
Abbott and Costello Meet the
   Keystone Kops
Abbott and Costello Meet the
   Killer, Boris Karloff
Abbott and Costello Meet the
   Mummy
Abroad with Two Yanks
Ace Crawford, Private Eye
Ace Ventura: Pet Detective
Ace Ventura: When Nature Calls
The Adventurer
The Adventures of Buckaroo
   Banzai Across the Eighth
   Dimension➤
Africa Screams
After the Fox
Air Raid Wardens
All Night Long/Smile Please
All of Me
All Over Town
Alvin Purple
Alvin Rides Again
American Aristocracy
American Pluck
Amos and Andrew
Animal Crackers➤
Any Which Way You Can
Armed and Dangerous
Around the World in 80 Ways
Around the World in a Daze
Assault and Matrimony
At the Circus
At War with the Army
Baby's Day Out
The Bad News Bears➤
The Bad News Bears Go to
   Japan
The Bad News Bears in
   Breaking Training
Bakery/Grocery Clerk
The Bank Dick➤
The Barber Shop➤
The Barefoot Executive
The Battle of the Sexes➤
Bean➤
Bedtime for Bonzo
Beethoven
Beethoven's 2nd

The Bellboy
Bellhop/The Noon Whistle
Beverly Hills Ninja
Big Mouth
Big Store
Block-heads➤
Bohemian Girl➤
Bonnie Scotland
Bowery Boys Meet the Monsters
Boy, Did I Get a Wrong Number!
Boys Will Be Boys
Brain Donors
Buck Privates
Buck Privates Come Home➤
Bullfighters
Buster Keaton Rides Again/The
   Railrodder
The Caddy
Caddyshack➤
Caddyshack 2
Candleshoe
Cannonball/Dizzy Heights and
   Daring Hearts
Carry On at Your Convenience
Carry On Behind
Carry On Camping
Carry On Cruising
Carry On Doctor➤
Carry On Emmanuelle
Carry On England
Carry On Henry VIII
Carry On Nurse
Carry On 'Round the Bend
Casanova's Big Night
The Case of the Mukkinese
   Battle Horn
The Champion/His New Job➤
Charlie Chaplin: The Early
   Years, Vol. 1
Charlie Chaplin: The Early
   Years, Vol. 2
Charlie Chaplin: The Early
   Years, Vol. 3
Charlie Chaplin: The Early
   Years, Vol. 4
Cheech and Chong: Still
   Smokin'
Cheech and Chong: Things Are
   Tough All Over
Cheech and Chong's Next
   Movie
Cheech and Chong's The
   Corsican Brothers
Cheech and Chong's Up in
   Smoke
Christmas in July➤
A Chump at Oxford
Cinderfella
Cockeyed Cavaliers
College➤
Comin' Round the Mountain
Cord & Dischords/Naughty
   Nurse
Count/Adventurer
Cracking Up
The Cure
Dance with Me, Henry
A Day at the Races➤
The Delicate Delinquent
The Dentist➤
Detective School Dropouts
Disorderly Orderly
Don't Raise the Bridge, Lower
   the River
Don't Shove/Two Gun Gussie
Doughboys
Dragons Forever
Duck Soup➤
Dumb & Dumber
Ernest Goes to Africa
Ernest Goes to Camp
Ernest Goes to Jail
Ernest Goes to School
Ernest Rides Again
Ernest Scared Stupid
The Errand Boy
Family Jewels
The Fatal Glass of Beer
The Feud

Finders Keepers
A Fine Mess
Flim-Flam Man
Flubber
The Flying Deuces➤
Folks!
Follow That Camel
For Auld Lang Syne: The Marx
   Brothers
Francis Covers the Big Town
Francis Goes to the Races
Francis Goes to West Point
Francis in the Haunted House
Francis in the Navy
Francis Joins the WACs
Francis the Talking Mule➤
Free and Easy
The Fuller Brush Girl
The Fuller Brush Man
Funny Farm
George Washington Slept Here➤
Get Smart, Again!
The Ghost and Mr. Chicken
Ghost in the Noonday Sun
Ghost on the Loose
Gilligan's Island: Meet the Crew
A Girl in Every Port
The Gods Must Be Crazy➤
The Gods Must Be Crazy 2
Going Bananas
The Gorilla
Great Guns
The Great Lover
The Great Race
A Guide for the Married Man➤
Gus
Half-Shot at Sunrise
Hands Up
Hardly Working
A Hash House Fraud/The
   Sultan's Wife
Have Rocket Will Travel
Here Come the Co-Eds
Hold That Ghost➤
Hollywood or Bust
Home Alone➤
Home Alone 2: Lost in New York
Home Alone 3
The Horn Blows at Midnight➤
Horse Feathers➤
Hot Lead & Cold Feet
I Hate Blondes
In Society
Ishtar
It's a Mad, Mad, Mad, Mad
   World
Jack & the Beanstalk
The Jerk
Jingle All the Way
Jour de Fete➤
Julia Misbehaves➤
Jumping Jacks
Kentucky Kernels
The Kettles in the Ozarks
The Kettles on Old MacDonald's
   Farm
The Klutz
The Last Remake of Beau Geste
Laughfest
Laurel & Hardy and the Family
Laurel & Hardy: Another Fine
   Mess
Laurel & Hardy: At Work
Laurel & Hardy: Be Big
Laurel & Hardy: Below Zero
Laurel & Hardy: Berth Marks
Laurel & Hardy: Blotto
Laurel & Hardy: Brats
Laurel & Hardy: Chickens Come
   Home
Laurel & Hardy Comedy
   Classics, Vol. 7
Laurel & Hardy: Hog Wild
Laurel & Hardy: Laughing Gravy
Laurel & Hardy: Men O'War
Laurel & Hardy: Night Owls
Laurel & Hardy On the Lam
Laurel & Hardy: Perfect Day
Laurel & Hardy Spooktacular

Slavery

Slice of Life

One Third of a Nation
Our Town✦
Our Town
Our Vines Have Tender
  Grapes✦
The Out-of-Towners✦
Over the Brooklyn Bridge
Papa's Delicate Condition✦
The Paper Chase✦
The Patriots✦
Pete 'n' Tillie
Pharmacist
Phenomenon
The Playboys✦
The Pope of Greenwich Village
Priest
Prisoner of Second Avenue
Queens Logic
The Quiet Room
Rachel River
Raggedy Man✦
Raging Bull✦
Rainy Day
Rambling Rose✦
Real Life✦
Return of the Secaucus 7✦
Return to Mayberry
Reuben, Reuben✦
Rhythm Thief
Riff Raff✦
A River Runs Through It✦
The Road to Life
Room at the Top✦
Roommates
Rosalie Goes Shopping✦
Ruby in Paradise✦
The Rules of the Game✦
Same Time, Next Year✦
Saturday Night and Sunday
  Morning✦
The Search for One-Eyed Jimmy
Short Cuts✦
A Single Girl
Sinners
Sinners in Paradise
Sisters of the Gion
The Smallest Show on Earth✦
Smithereens
Smoke
Some Came Running✦
The Southerner✦
The Star Maker
State Fair✦
State Fair
Steamboat Bill, Jr.✦
Steel Magnolias✦
Stranger than Paradise✦
Strong Medicine
Stroszek✦
Sugarbaby✦
The Sun Shines Bright
Tex
That Sinking Feeling✦
The Time of Your Life✦
Tin Men
To Kill a Mockingbird✦
Toni✦
Tonio Kroger
A Touch of Class✦
The Tree of Wooden Clogs✦
Tree's Lounge
Trouble in the Glen
True Love✦
Twenty Bucks✦
29th Street
Twice in a Lifetime✦
Twist & Shout✦
Two Days in the Valley✦
The Two Sisters
Unhook the Stars
Urban Cowboy
Used People
Waiting for Guffman
Walls of Glass
Wanderers✦
Watch It✦
A Wedding
When the Party's Over
The White Balloon✦

The Whole Shootin' Match✦
Who's That Knocking at My
  Door?✦
Why Shoot the Teacher?✦
Wild Style
Wish You Were Here✦
Women from the Lake of
  Scented Souls
Zombie and the Ghost Train
Zorba the Greek✦

Snakes

see also *Wild Kingdom*
Anaconda
Black Cobra
Copperhead
The Craft
Curse 2: The Bite
Fer-De-Lance
Green Snake
Halfmoon
Indiana Jones and the Last
  Crusade✦
Indiana Jones and the Temple of
  Doom✦
Jennifer
Journey to the Lost City
Lewis and Clark and George
Natural Born Killers
Raiders of the Lost Ark✦
Rattled
Rattlers
The Reptile
The Road Warrior✦
Silver Stallion
The Snake People
Spasms
Sssssss
Stanley
Women's Prison Escape

Soccer

The Big Green
The Club✦
Cracker: To Be a Somebody
Cup Final
The Final Goal
Go Now✦
The Goalie's Anxiety at the
  Penalty Kick✦
Gregory's Girl✦
The Hero
Hot Shot
Hothead
Ladybugs
Long Shot
Those Glory, Glory Days
Victory
When Saturday Comes
Yesterday's Hero

South America

see also *Central America*
Aguirre, the Wrath of God✦
Amazon
The Americano
Americano
Apartment Zero✦
At Play in the Fields of the Lord✦
Bananas✦
Black Orpheus✦
Boca
Burden of Dreams✦
The Burning Season✦
Bye Bye Brazil
Catch the Heat
Clear and Present Danger
The Colombian Connection
The Dark Side of the Heart✦
Death and the Maiden✦
Death in the Garden
Diplomatic Immunity
800 Leagues Down the Amazon
El Muerto
The Emerald Forest✦

Evita
Fitzcarraldo✦
Five Came Back
Four Days in September
The Fugitive✦
Funny, Dirty Little War
Fury
Green Fire
Green Mansions
Happy Together
The Hour of the Star✦
The House of the Spirits
I Don't Want to Talk About It
It's All True
Johnny 100 Pesos
Last Flight to Hell
The Last Movie
Latin Lovers
Let's Get Harry
Little Mother
Managua
Max Is Missing
Mighty Jungle
Miracles
Miss Mary
Missing✦
The Mission✦
Monster
Moon over Parador
The Muthers
Naked Jungle✦
Naked Tango
Nancy Goes to Rio
Night Gallery✦
Nostromo
O Quatrilho
Of Love and Shadows
One Man Out
Only Angels Have Wings✦
Overkill
The Pink Jungle
A Place in the World✦
The Plague
Quilombo
Rodrigo D.: No Future
Romancing the Stone✦
A Shadow You Soon Will Be
Shoot to Kill
Simon Bolivar
The Story of Fausta
Sweet Country
Terranova
Terror in the Jungle
The Three Caballeros
To Kill a Stranger
Wild Orchid
Xica✦
You Were Never Lovelier✦

Southern Belles

see also *American South;*
  Nashville Narratives
Blaze
Cat on a Hot Tin Roof✦
Cat on a Hot Tin Roof
Crimes of the Heart✦
Dear Dead Delilah
Driving Miss Daisy✦
The Glass Menagerie✦
Gone with the Wind✦
Hush, Hush, Sweet Charlotte✦
Jezebel✦
Miss Firecracker✦
Nashville✦
North and South Book 1✦
North and South Book 2✦
Other Voices, Other Rooms
Queen Bee
Rich in Love
Scarlett
Scorchers
Steel Magnolias✦
A Streetcar Named Desire✦
The Trip to Bountiful✦

Space Operas

see also *Alien Beings—*
  Benign; Alien Beings
    Vicious
Alien✦
The Apocalypse
Apollo 13✦
Assignment Outer Space
Battle Beyond the Stars
Battle Beyond the Sun
Battlestar Galactica
The Black Hole
Buck Rogers Conquers the
  Universe
Capricorn One✦
Cat Women of the Moon
Conquest of Space
Contact
Countdown
Creature
Dark Breed
Dark Side of the Moon
Dark Star✦
The Day the Sky Exploded
Destination Moon
Destination Moonbase Alpha
Destination Saturn
Doctor Who and the Daleks
Escape from Planet Earth
Event Horizon
Explorers
Fire Maidens from Outer Space
First Encounter
First Men in the Moon
First Spaceship on Venus✦
Flight to Mars
Forbidden Planet✦
From the Earth to the Moon
Galaxy of Terror
Gattaca✦
The Green Slime
Hangar 18
Have Rocket Will Travel
Heavens Above✦
Hellraiser 4: Bloodline
Horror Planet
Horrors of the Red Planet
Independence Day✦
Journey to the Far Side of the
  Sun✦
Killings at Outpost Zeta
Laser Mission
The Last Starfighter
Lifepod
Lost in Space
Marooned
Megaforce
Mission Galactica: The Cylon
  Attack
Mission Mars
Mom and Dad Save the World
Moon 44
Moonraker
Moontrap
Murder in Space
Mutant on the Bounty
Mystery Science Theater 3000:
  The Movie
Nude on the Moon
Outland
Planet Burg
Planet of Dinosaurs
Planet of the Apes✦
Planet of the Vampires
Precious Find
Project Moon Base
PSI Factor
The Reluctant Astronaut
Return of the Jedi✦
Return to Earth
The Right Stuff✦
Robinson Crusoe on Mars
RocketMan
Rocketship X-M
Silent Running✦
Solar Crisis
Solaris
Space Mutiny

Space Rage
Space Raiders
Spaceballs
Star Crash
Star Slammer
Star Trek: The Motion Picture
Star Trek 2: The Wrath of Khan✦
Star Trek 3: The Search for
  Spock
Star Trek 4: The Voyage Home✦
Star Trek 5: The Final Frontier
Star Trek 6: The Undiscovered
  Country
Star Trek: First Contact✦
Star Trek Generations✦
Star Trek the Next Generation:
  Encounter at Farpoint
Star Wars✦
Starship
Tales from a Parallel Universe:
  Eating Pattern
Tales from a Parallel Universe:
  Giga Shadow
The Terranauts
Three Stooges in Orbit
Transformations
Trapped in Space
2001: A Space Odyssey✦
2010: The Year We Make
  Contact✦
Vegas in Space
Voyage to the Planet of
  Prehistoric Women
Voyage to the Prehistoric Planet
Walking on Air
Warlords of the 21st Century
Woman in the Moon
Women of the Prehistoric Planet

Spaghetti Western

see also *Western Comedy;*
    Westerns
Ace High
Beyond the Law
Boot Hill
Bullet for Sandoval
Chino
A Fistful of Dollars✦
A Fistful of Dynamite✦
Five Giants from Texas
For a Few Dollars More
The Good, the Bad and the
  Ugly✦
The Grand Duel
Gun Fight at Red Sands
Hang 'Em High
Hellbenders
A Minute to Pray, a Second to
  Die
My Name Is Nobody
Once Upon a Time in the West✦
Rough Justice
The Ruthless Four
Spaghetti Western
Straight to Hell
The Stranger and the Gunfighter
Stranger in Paso Bravo
Take a Hard Ride
Tramplers
Trinity Is Still My Name
You're Jinxed, Friend, You've
  Met Sacramento

Spain

Against the Wind
Ay, Carmela!✦
Barcelona✦
The Barcelona Kill
Behold a Pale Horse
Belle Epoque✦
Blood and Sand✦
Caper of the Golden Bulls
The Castilian
Desire✦
The Disappearance of Garcia
  Lorca

Spain

Extramuros
Fiesta
For Whom the Bell Tolls⋗
I'm the One You're Looking For
Land and Freedom⋗
Lazarillo
Letters from Alou
Live Flesh⋗
Marbella
The Naked Maja
Pandora and the Flying
  Dutchman
The Pride and the Passion
Sand and Blood
Siesta
The Spanish Gardener⋗
Surprise Attack
The Sword of El Cid
A Touch of Class⋗

Speculation

Sasquatch

Spies & Espionage

see also Feds; Foreign
  Intrigue; Terrorism
Above Suspicion⋗
Access Code
Across the Pacific⋗
Action in Arabia
Adventures in Spying
The Adventures of Tartu
Against the Wind
Agent on Ice
Air Raid Wardens
Alamut Ambush
Alfred Hitchcock's Aventure
  Malgache
Alfred Hitchcock's Bon Voyage
Alien Women
All Through the Night⋗
The Amateur
Arabesque
Armored Command
Artists and Models
As If It Were Raining
Assassin
The Assassination Game
The Assassination Run
The Atomic Kid
Attack of the Robots
Austin Powers: International
  Man of Mystery⋗
Avalanche Express
The Avengers
Background to Danger⋗
Bad Company
Bear Island
Beaumarchais the Scoundrel
Behind Enemy Lines
The Berlin Conspiracy
Berlin Express⋗
Betrayed⋗
Big Deadly Game
Big Jim McLain
The Big Lift
Black Box Affair
Black Brigade
The Black Dragons
Black Eagle
The Black Windmill
Blue Ice
Boris and Natasha: The Movie
The Bourne Identity⋗
British Intelligence
Bulldog Drummond at Bay
Bulldog Drummond Escapes
Bullet to Beijing
Bulletproof
Cairo
Call Me Bwana
Call Out the Marines
Canadian Mounties vs. Atomic
  Invaders
Caravan to Vaccares
Carve Her Name with Pride

Casablanca⋗
Casino Royale
A Casualty of War
Charge of the Model T's
Chu Chu & the Philly Flash
Clear and Present Danger
Clipped Wings
Cloak and Dagger
Cloak & Dagger
Code Name Alpha
Code Name: Chaos
Code Name: Dancer
Code Name: Diamond Head
Code Name: Emerald
Codename: Foxfire
Codename: Icarus
Codename Kyril
Codename: Wildgeese
Cold War Killers
Company Business
Comrades in Arms
Condorman
Conspirator
Counterblast
The Counterfeit Traitor⋗
Cowboy Commandos
Criminals Within
Dandy in Aspic
Danger Man
Daniel
Daniella by Night
Dark Journey⋗
Darling Lili
Dawn Express
The Day and the Hour
The Day of the Dolphin
The Day of the Jackal⋗
The Day Will Dawn⋗
Dead Aim
Deadly Currents
The Deadly Game
Deadly Recruits
Deadly Rivals
Deadly Spygames
The Deadly Trap
Death Ray 2000
Death Rides the Range
Deathcheaters
Defense Play
Delta Force Commando 2
Desperate Cargo
Diamonds Are Forever⋗
Diplomatic Courier⋗
Dishonored
Dr. No⋗
The Doll Squad
Don't Drink the Water
Don't Raise the Bridge, Lower
  the River
Doomsday Gun
Double Agents
Double Deal
The Double O Kid
Down Among the Z Men
Duck Soup⋗
The Dunera Boys⋗
Edge of Darkness⋗
Edge of Darkness
The Eiger Sanction
Embassy
Emissary
The Endless Game
Enforcer from Death Row
The English Patient⋗
An Englishman Abroad⋗
Enigma
Erik
Escape from Fort Bravo
Escape from the KGB
The Executioner
The Experts
Eye of the Needle
Eyewitness
The Falcon and the Snowman⋗
The Falcon's Brother
Fall from Grace
The Fallen Sparrow⋗
False Faces

The Fantastic World of D.C.
  Collins
Federal Agent
Final Assignment
The Final Option
Fire Over England⋗
Firefall
Firefox
Firehead
First Yank into Tokyo
Five Fingers⋗
Five for Hell
Five Graves to Cairo⋗
Flight from Vienna
Flight to Nowhere
Flying Blind
For Your Eyes Only⋗
Foreign Correspondent⋗
The Foreigner
The Formula
The Fourth Protocol⋗
Francis Gary Powers: The True
  Story of the U-2 Spy
French Intrigue
From Russia with Love⋗
Funeral in Berlin⋗
The General Died at Dawn⋗
A Generation⋗
Get Smart, Again!
Girl Hunters
Girls Are for Loving
The Glass Bottom Boat
Golden Earrings
Goldeneye⋗
Goldfinger⋗
Gotcha!
The Great Armored Car Swindle
Green Inferno
The Groundstar Conspiracy⋗
Gunpowder
Hanky Panky
Happy Anniversary 007: 25
  Years of James Bond
Hard Ticket to Hawaii
Harriet the Spy
The Heat of the Day
Heroes in Hell
Heroes Stand Alone
Hidden Enemy
Hillbillies in a Haunted House
The Holcroft Covenant
Holt of the Secret Service
Honeybaby
Honeymoon Academy
Hopscotch⋗
Hostage
The Hot Line
Hotel Reserve⋗
Hour of the Assassin
The House on Carroll Street
The House on Garibaldi Street
House on 92nd Street⋗
The Human Factor
The Hunt for Red October⋗
Hunter
I Dood It
I See a Dark Stranger⋗
I Stand Condemned
The Ice Runner
Ice Station Zebra
If Looks Could Kill
The Impossible Spy⋗
The In-Laws⋗
In the Secret State
The Innocent
The Inside Man
Inside the Lines
Internecine Project
Intrigue
Invisible Agent
The Ipcress File⋗
Ishtar
It Means That to Me
J-Men Forever!⋗
Jackie Chan's First Strike⋗
Jakarta
Jet Pilot
The Jigsaw Man
Joan of Paris⋗

Journey into Fear⋗
Journey into Fear
Jumpin' Jack Flash
Jungle Drums of Africa
Keep Talking Baby
The KGB: The Secret War
Kill Castro
Kill Factor
Kim⋗
Kim
Koroshi
La Cage aux Folles 2
Ladies Man
Laser Mission
Last Embrace⋗
Le Magnifique
License to Kill
License to Kill⋗
Lie Down with Lions
Lightning Bolt
Lipstick Camera
Lisbon
The Little Drummer Girl⋗
Live and Let Die
The Living Daylights⋗
The Looking Glass War
Loaded Guns
The Lost One
Lost Diamond
Love on the Run
M. Butterfly
Ma and Pa Kettle on Vacation
Mackintosh Man
Madame Sin
Malone
Man from Headquarters
The Man from U.N.C.L.E.
The Man on the Box
The Man Outside
The Man Who Knew Too Little
The Man Who Never Was⋗
The Man Who Wasn't There
The Man with One Red Shoe
The Man with the Golden Gun
Marie Galante⋗
Maroc 7
Mata Hari⋗
Mata Hari
The Mediterranean in Flames
The Mercenaries
Midnight in Saint Petersburg
Mind Trap
Mindfield
Ministry of Fear⋗
Mission Impossible
Mission: Impossible⋗
Mission Phantom
Mission to Venice
Mr. Superinvisible
The Monocle
Monte Carlo
Moonraker
Morituri⋗
Mother Night⋗
Murder for Sale
Murder on the Midnight Express
Murderers' Row
My Favorite Blonde⋗
My Favorite Brunette
My Name Is Ivan⋗
The Mysterious Lady
Mystery Plane
Nasty Rabbit
Never Say Never Again
Never Too Young to Die
Night Flight from Moscow
A Night in Casablanca⋗
Night Train to Munich⋗
Ninja Champion
No Dead Heroes
No Way Out⋗
North by Northwest⋗
Notorious⋗
The Nude Bomb
Number 1 of the Secret Service
Octopussy
The Odessa File
Old Mother Riley's Ghosts

On Her Majesty's Secret
  Service⋗
On the Edge
Once Upon a Honeymoon
One Armed Executioner
One of Our Dinosaurs Is Missing
Operation C.I.A.
Operation Crossbow⋗
O.S.S.⋗
The Osterman Weekend
Overture
The Package
Panama Hattie
Panama Menace
Panama Patrol
Paper Tiger
Paradisio
Pascali's Island⋗
Patriot Games⋗
The Peking Blond
A Perfect Spy
Permission To Kill
The Persuaders
Philby, Burgess and MacLean:
  Spy Scandal of the Century
Phoenix Team
Picasso Trigger
Pickup on South Street⋗
President's Mistress
Prime Risk
The Prize⋗
Protocol
Provocateur
Pueblo Affair⋗
A Question of Attribution
Qui Etes Vous, Mr. Sorge?
The Quiller Memorandum⋗
Ravishing Idiot
Rebel Love
Reilly: Ace of Spies⋗
Retrievers
Return of the Man from
  U.N.C.L.E.
Return to Savage Beach
Rio Rita
Robinson Crusoe of Mystery
  Island
Roboman
Robot Pilot
Running Blind
Running Delilah
Running Scared
The Russia House
Russian Roulette
The Rutanga Tapes
Sabotage⋗
Saboteur⋗
The Saint
The Saint's Vacation/The
  Narrow Margin
Samurai
S.A.S. San Salvador
Scorpio
Sea Devils
Sebastian
Second Best Secret Agent in the
  Whole Wide World
The Secret Agent⋗
Secret Agent
The Secret Agent
Secret Agent 00
The Secret Agent Club
Secret Agent 00-Soul
Secret Agent Super Dragon
Secret Mission
Secret Weapon
Secret Weapons
Sell Out
Shack Out on 101⋗
Shadows Over Shanghai
The Shakiest Gun in the West
S*H*E
Shining Through
Ship Ahoy
A Show of Force
Sky High
Sky Liner
Sneakers
Snuff-Bottle Connection

Supernatural

Initiation of Sarah
Inquisition
Invasion of the Blood Farmers
Invasion of the Zombies
Invitation to Hell
It's Alive!
Jaws of Satan
J.D.'s Revenge
Jennifer
Judgment Day
Kill and Go Hide
Kill, Baby, Kill♪
The Kiss
Kiss Daddy Goodbye
Kwaidan♪
Land of the Minotaur
The Last Gasp
The Last Man on Earth
The Legacy
The Legend of Hell House♪
Let's Scare Jessica to Death
Lisa and the Devil
The Living Head
Lord of Illusions
The Loves of Irina
Lurkers
Lust for a Vampire
The Man and the Monster
Manhattan Baby
Maniac
The Manitou
Manos, the Hands of Fate
Mardi Gras for the Devil
Mardi Gras Massacre
Mark of the Devil
Mark of the Devil 2
Mary, Mary, Bloody Mary
Maxim Xul
The Medusa Touch
The Mephisto Waltz♪
Meridian: Kiss of the Beast
Messiah of Evil
Midnight
Midnight Cabaret
Midnight's Child
Mirror, Mirror
Mirror of Death
The Monster Demolisher
The Mummy's Revenge
Near Dark♪
Necromancer: Satan's Servant
Necropolis
Neon Maniacs
The Nesting
Netherworld
The Night Evelyn Came Out of
   the Grave
Night Life
Night Nurse
Night of Horror
Night of the Death Cult
Night of the Demons
Night of the Demons 2
Night of the Ghouls
Night of the Sorcerers
The Night Stalker
The Night Strangler
Night Vision
Night Visitor
Nightmare Castle
Nightmare in Blood
Nightmare Sisters
Nightmare Weekend
Nightstalker
Nightwish
Nomads
Nothing But the Night
The Occultist
Of Unknown Origin
The Offspring
The Omen
Omen 4: The Awakening
The Oracle
Orgy of the Dead
Orgy of the Vampires
The Other♪
Other Hell
Out of the Body
The Outing

Patrick
Pet Sematary
Pet Sematary 2
Phantasm
Phantasm II
Phantom of the Ritz
Phantoms
Poltergeist♪
Poltergeist 2: The Other Side
Poltergeist 3
Poltergeist: The Legacy
The Possessed
The Possession of Joel Delaney
The Premonition
The Prophecy
The Psychic
Psychomania
Pumpkinhead
Rawhead Rex
The Relic
Revolt of the Zombies
Sarah's Child
Seduced by Evil
The Sleeping Car
Sleepstalker: The Sandman's
   Last Rites
Sorceress
Specters
Stephen King's Thinner
Supernatural
The Supernaturals
Terror Creatures from the Grave
They Watch
13 Ghosts
The Turn of the Screw
The Visitors
Witchcraft 4: Virgin Heart
The Wraith

Supernatural Martial Arts

Baby Cart at the River Styx
Baby Cart to Hades
The Crow
Hellbound
The Heroic Trio
Ninja, the Violent Sorcerer
Remo Williams: The Adventure
   Begins
Sgt. Kabukiman N.Y.P.D.
The 7 Brothers Meet Dracula
Vampire Raiders—Ninja Queen
Zu: Warriors of the Magic
   Mountain

Supernatural Westerns

Back to the Future, Part 3♪
Billy the Kid Versus Dracula
The Devil's Mistress
Ghostriders
Grim Prairie Tales
Into the Badlands
Jesse James Meets
   Frankenstein's Daughter
John Carpenter's Vampires
Mad at the Moon
Sundown
Timerider

Surfing

see also Beach Blanket Bingo
Aloha Summer
Beach Blanket Bingo♪
Beach Party
Big Wednesday
Bikini Beach
Blackrock
California Dreaming
Chairman of the Board
Computer Beach Party
The Endless Summer♪
The Endless Summer 2♪

Escape from L.A.
Follow Me
Gidget
How to Stuff a Wild Bikini
In God's Hands
Lauderdale
Mad Wax: The Surf Movie
Meet the Deedles
Muscle Beach Party
North Shore
Point Break
Puberty Blues
Red Surf
Ride the Wild Surf
South Beach Academy
Summer City
Surf Nazis Must Die
Surf Party
Surf 2

Survival

see also Hunted!; Negative
Utopia; Post Apocalypse
Abandon Ship
Adrift
Adventure Island
Adventures of Eliza Fraser
The Alaska Wilderness
   Adventure
Alive
Alive: 20 Years Later
Alpine Fire
And I Alone Survived
Antarctica
Arctic Blue
Attack of the Beast Creatures
The Aviator
Back from Eternity
Bat 21
Black Rain♪
Born Killer
Born Wild
The Bridge on the River Kwai♪
Buffalo Rider
A Bullet Is Waiting
Cage 2: The Arena of Death
Caged in Paradiso
Captain January
A Captive in the Land
Challenge To Be Free
Cheyenne Warrior
Clearcut
Cliffhanger♪
Clown
Cold River
Cool Hand Luke♪
Courage Under Fire♪
Damned River
Das Boot♪
The Dawson Patrol
The Day After♪
Daylight
Dead Calm♪
Deadly Harvest
Deadly Prey
Death Hunt
Def-Con 4
Deliverance♪
Delos Adventure
Delusion
Desperate Target
The Devil at 4 O'Clock
Diamonds of the Night♪
The Dive
Dust Devil
Earthling
Edge of Honor
Empire of the Sun♪
Endangered
Endgame
Enemy Mine
Enemy Territory
Erendira
Eric♪
Escape from Hell
Escapist
Far from Home: The Adventures
   of Yellow Dog

Fearless♪
Fight for Your Life
Firehawk
Five Came Back
Flight from Glory
Flight from Singapore
Flight of the Eagle
The Flight of the Phoenix♪
The Forbidden Quest
Fortress
Found Alive
Gas-s-s-s!
The Ghost of Fletcher Ridge
Grave of the Fireflies♪
He Is My Brother
Heaven and Earth
Heaven Knows, Mr. Allison♪
Heck's Way Home
Heroes for Sale♪
High Ice
High Noon♪
Hunter's Blood
The Incredible Journey
The Interrogation♪
The Island♪
The Island at the Top of the
   World
Island of the Blue Dolphins
Island of the Lost
Jeremiah Johnson♪
Jungle Inferno
Just Before Dawn
Kameradschaft♪
Killing at Hell's Gate
The Killing Fields♪
King Rat♪
The Land that Time Forgot
The Last Chance♪
Last Exit to Brooklyn♪
The Last Flight of Noah's Ark
Le Dernier Combat♪
Legend of Alfred Packer
The Legend of Wolf Mountain
L'Enfant d'Eau
The Leopard Son
The Life and Death of Colonel
   Blimp♪
Lifeboat♪
Lily Was Here
Little Dorrit, Film 1: Nobody's
   Fault♪
Little Dorrit, Film 2: Little Dorrit's
   Story♪
Lord of the Flies♪
Lord of the Flies
Lost
Love on the Dole♪
Male and Female♪
Man in the Wilderness
Manon
Melody
Merry Christmas, Mr.
   Lawrence♪
Mr. Robinson Crusoe
The Mosquito Coast
The Most Dangerous Game♪
My Side of the Mountain
Mysterious Island♪
The Naked Prey♪
Nightmare at Bittercreek
Nightmare at Noon
Objective, Burma!♪
On the Beach♪
Once Before I Die
Ordeal in the Arctic
Osa
Out of Control
Packin' It In
Pagan Island
Panic in the Year Zero!
Paradise
Perfect Witness
Phone Call from a Stranger
Pioneer Woman
The Poseidon Adventure
Proteus
Quest for Fire♪
Ravager
The Return of Grey Wolf

Return of the Jedi♪
The Revolt of Job♪
Robby
Robinson Crusoe
Sahara♪
Savage Hunger
Savage Is Loose
Sea Gypsies
The Sea Shall Not Have Them
Seven Days in May♪
Shadow of the Wolf
She'll Be Wearing Pink Pajamas
Shipwreck Island
Silence
Silence of the North
Six Days, Seven Nights
Skyline♪
Sniper
Snowbound
S.O.S. Pacific
Sourdough
Stagecoach♪
Standoff
Starbird and Sweet William
Storm and Sorrow
Survival of Spaceship Earth
Survival Quest
Survival Run
The Survivalist
Sweet Sweetback's Baadasssss
   Song♪
The Swiss Family Robinson♪
The Terror
Testament♪
Thief♪
Three Came Home♪
The Ticket
Titanic
Trouble in Paradise
Tundra
Unsettled Land
Voyage
The Voyage of the Yes
Vukovar♪
Wagon Master♪
Walkabout♪
Walking Thunder
Warriors of the Apocalypse
Waterworld
The White Dawn
White Fang and the Hunter
White Water Summer
White Wolves 3: Cry of the
   White Wolf
Wild America♪
Zarkorr! The Invader

Suspended Animation

Alien 3
Aliens♪
Austin Powers: International
   Man of Mystery♪
Buck Rogers in the 25th Century
Chances Are♪
Coma♪
Dragon Fury 2
Encino Man
Forever Young
Late for Dinner

Suspense

see Mystery & Suspense

Swashbucklers

see also Action Adventure; Fencing; Medieval Romps

Abbott and Costello Meet Captain Kidd
Adventures of Captain Fabian
Adventures of Don Juan➤
The Adventures of Robin Hood➤
Against All Flags
Ali Baba and the Forty Thieves
Ali Baba and the 40 Thieves➤
Anthony Adverse
Arabian Nights
At Sword's Point
The Black Pirate➤
The Black Swan➤
Blackbeard the Pirate
Blackbeard's Ghost
Bluebeard
The Bold Caballero
The Buccaneer
Captain Blood➤
Captain Horatio Hornblower➤
Captain Kidd
Captain Kronos: Vampire Hunter➤
Captain Ron
Cartouche
The Challenge
Cheech and Chong's The Corsican Brothers
China Seas➤
Conqueror & the Empress
Corsair
The Corsican Brothers
The Count of Monte Cristo
The Count of Monte Cristo➤
The Count of Monte Cristo
Court Jester➤
Crimson Pirate➤
Cutthroat Island
Dancing Pirate
Dr. Syn
Dr. Syn, Alias the Scarecrow
Don Juan DeMarco
Don Q., Son of Zorro
The Elusive Pimpernel
Executioner of Venice
Fanfan la Tulipe➤
Fearless Tiger
The Fencing Master
The Fifth Musketeer
The Fighting Prince of Donegal
First Knight
The Flame & the Arrow➤
The Four Musketeers➤
Ghost in the Noonday Sun
Gun Cargo
Gypsy
Hawk of the Wilderness
Hell Ship Mutiny
Highlander: The Gathering
His Majesty O'Keefe
Hook
The Iron Mask
The Island
Island Trader
The King's Thief
Kojiro➤
The Lady and the Highwayman
The Lamb
The Lives of a Bengal Lancer➤
Long John Silver
Magic Island
The Man in the Iron Mask➤
The Man in the Iron Mask
The Man in the Iron Mask➤
Marauder
Mark of Zorro➤
The Mark of Zorro➤
The Mask of Zorro
The Master of Ballantrae
Master of Dragonard Hill
Monty Python's The Meaning of Life➤
Mooncussers
Moonfleet

Moran of the Lady Letty
Morgan the Pirate
Muppet Treasure Island
My Favorite Year➤
My Wicked, Wicked Ways
The Naked Sword of Zorro
Nate and Hayes
Naughty Marietta
New Moon
The Ninja Pirates
Old Ironsides➤
The Phantom
The Pirate➤
Pirate Movie
Pirate Warrior
Pirates
The Pirates of Penzance
Pirates of the Coast
Pirates of the Seven Seas
The Princess and the Pirate➤
The Princess Bride➤
Prisoner of Zenda➤
Prisoner of Zenda
Project A: Part 2
Quest of the Delta Knights
The Return of the Musketeers
Ring of the Musketeers
Robin Hood➤
Romola
Royal Flash➤
Scaramouche➤
The Scarlet Pimpernel➤
The Sea Hawk➤
Sea Hound
The Secret of El Zorro
Shipwrecked
The Sign of Zorro
Sinbad and the Eye of the Tiger
Sinbad, the Sailor➤
Smuggler's Cove
Son of Ali Baba
Son of Captain Blood
Son of Fury➤
The Son of Monte Cristo
Son of Zorro
South of Pago Pago
South Seas Massacre
The Spanish Main
The Story of Robin Hood & His Merrie Men➤
Swashbuckler
The Swiss Family Robinson➤
Sword & the Sorcerer
Sword of Sherwood Forest
The Swordsman
Tharus Son of Attila
Three Amigos
The Three Musketeers
The Three Musketeers
The Three Musketeers
The Three Musketeers
The Three Musketeers
Tiger of the Seven Seas
Treasure Island➤
Treasure Island
Treasure of the Golden Condor
Treasure of the Moon Goddess
Two Lost Worlds
Under the Red Robe
Wallaby Jim of the Islands
The Warriors
The Wicked Lady
Yellowbeard
Zorro, the Gay Blade

Swimming

see also Deep Blue; Go Fish; Island Fare; Lifeguards; Pacific Islands; Sea Critter Attack

Alex
Barracuda
Bathing Beauty
The Bridges at Toko-Ri➤
Cocoon➤
Dangerous When Wet
Dawn!

Easy to Love
Gremlins➤
Jaws➤
The Man from Atlantis
Million Dollar Mermaid
Neptune's Daughter
Off the Mark
Splash
Swim Team
The Swimmer➤
Thrill of a Romance

Swingers

Barfly➤
Bob & Carol & Ted & Alice
A Change of Seasons
Group Marriage
Invasion of the Bee Girls➤
Looking for Mr. Goodbar
9 1/2 Weeks
The Party➤
The Swap
The Swinging Cheerleaders
Swinging Wives

Swingin' '70s

Boogie Nights➤
Dazed and Confused➤
Donnie Brasco➤
Drugstore Cowboy➤
Fear and Loathing in Las Vegas
54
Gia
The Ice Storm➤
Nothing Personal➤
Prefontaine
Spirit of '76
Without Limits➤

Sword & Sandal

Ali Baba and the Forty Thieves
Ali Baba and the 40 Thieves➤
Alone Against Rome
Arabian Nights
The Avenger
Colossus and the Amazon Queen
Colossus of the Arena
Coriolanus, Man without a Country
Fabiola➤
Fire Monsters Against the Son of Hercules
Giants of Rome
Gladiator of Rome
Gladiators 7
Goliath Against the Giants
Goliath and the Barbarians
Goliath and the Dragon
Goliath and the Sins of Babylon
Gor
Hercules
Hercules Against the Moon Men
Hercules and the Captive Women
Hercules and the Princess of Troy
Hercules in the Haunted World
Hercules, Prisoner of Evil
Hercules Unchained
Hero of Rome
The Invincible Gladiator
The Last Days of Pompeii
Revenge of the Barbarians
Revolt of the Barbarians
Roland the Mighty
Samson
Samson Against the Sheik
Samson and His Mighty Challenge
Samson and the 7 Miracles of the World
Sins of Rome
Son of Ali Baba

Sons of Hercules in the Land of Darkness
Sword of Venus
Terror of the Steppes
Thor and the Amazon Women

Tattoos

Blue Tiger
Cape Fear➤
The Crow 2: City of Angels
Cyber Bandits
Down Periscope
Escape from L.A.
Foxfire
The Illustrated Man➤
Lust in the Dust➤
The Night of the Hunter➤
Son-in-Law
Tattoo
Teresa's Tattoo
Waterworld
The Yakuza

Team Efforts

The Alamo➤
The Bad News Bears Go to Japan
The Bad News Bears in Breaking Training
Breaking Away➤
The Club➤
Coach
Codename: Foxfire
Codename: Wildgeese
Crossfire
The Cutting Edge
The Dirty Dozen➤
The Dirty Dozen: The Deadly Mission
The Dirty Dozen: The Fatal Mission
The Dirty Dozen: The Next Mission
Dirty Hands
The Doll Squad
D2: The Mighty Ducks
D3: The Mighty Ducks
Eddie
Finger on the Trigger
Force Five
Force 10 from Navarone
The Guns of Navarone➤
Hoosiers➤
Kill and Kill Again
Ladybugs
Let's Get Harry
The Losers
The Magnificent Seven➤
Major League 3: Back to the Minors
Memphis Belle➤
The Mighty Ducks
Miracle on Ice
Necessary Roughness
Race the Sun
Renaissance Man
Seven Magnificent Gladiators
Seven Samurai➤
Silverado➤
The Sixth Man
Soldier Boyz
Space Jam
Steel
Sunset Park
That Thing You Do!➤
Three the Hard Way
Twister
Uncommon Valor
The Untouchables➤
Victory
White Squall
Wild Geese
Wild Geese 2
Wind

Tearjerkers

Acorn People
An Affair to Remember
After the Promise
All Dogs Go to Heaven
All Fall Down
All Mine to Give
Another Time, Another Place
Baby Face
Back Street
Balboa
Ballad in Blue
Bang the Drum Slowly
Bang the Drum Slowly➤
Beaches
Big Bluff
Bittersweet Love
Black Eyes
Blind Spot
Blood of Jesus
Blossoms in the Dust
Bonjour Tristesse➤
Bouquet of Barbed Wire
Breaking the Rules
Brian's Song➤
The Cabin in the Cotton
Camille
Carrie➤
Carry On Cruising
Cast the First Stone
The Champ➤
The Champ
Chantilly Lace
The Cheat➤
Chinatown After Dark
Choices
Christmas Comes to Willow Creek
City That Never Sleeps
City Without Men
Claudia
Coquette
The Country Kid➤
The Courtney Affair
Craig's Wife➤
Crawlspace
Curly Sue
Dance Fools Dance➤
Dead Wrong
Death Be Not Proud➤
Dedee d'Anvers
Delinquent Parents
A Different Kind of Love
A Dog of Flanders
Dog Pound Shuffle➤
An Early Frost➤
Easy Virtue
The Eddy Duchin Story
Eric➤
Escape Me Never
The Evening Star
Fine Things
Fire Down Below
Flamingo Road➤
The Forbidden City
Fortune's Fool
Found Alive
Fourth Wish
Fulfillment
Gangs, Inc.
The Garden of Allah➤
The Gathering
The Gathering: Part 2
Ghost➤
Girl from Chicago
The Girl Who Had Everything
Goodbye, Mr. Chips➤
Goodbye, My Lady
Great Day
The Greatest Question
Griffin and Phoenix: A Love Story
Harlow
Hearts of Humanity
Heaven and Earth
Heaven's a Drag
Hell-Ship Morgan
Her Silent Sacrifice

Tearjerkers

High Gear
A Home of Our Own
Honky Tonk↗
Hot Spell
Human Desire
Human Hearts
I Conquer the Sea
I Sent a Letter to My Love↗
Ice Castles
If Ever I See You Again
In This Our Life
Inside Daisy Clover
Intermezzo↗
Jack the Bear
Johnny Belinda
Johnny Belinda
Johnny Eager↗
Journey for Margaret↗
Keep Punching
The Kid with the Broken Halo
La Bete Humaine↗
La Chienne↗
Lady Caroline Lamb
The Lady Without Camelias
The Last Best Year
Le Jour Se Leve↗
Legends of the Fall
Leopard in the Snow
Leper
Letter from an Unknown
    Woman↗
The Little Match Girl
The Little Princess
A Little Princess
Look Who's Talking Now
Love Affair↗
Love Affair
Love Affair: The Eleanor & Lou
    Gehrig Story↗
Love Butcher
The Love Flower
Love Has Many Faces
Love in the Present Tense
Love Songs
Love Story↗
Lovers of Their Time
Loving
Lure of the Sila
Madame Butterfly
Madame X
Magnificent Obsession
Man of Evil
The Manxman
Marvin's Room
Matters of the Heart
Mayerling
Mildred Pierce↗
Miles to Go
Millie
Mimi
The Miniver Story
Miss Julie
Mrs. Silly
Mr. Holland's Opus↗
Mr. Skeffington↗
Mistress
Moment in Time
Moon over Harlem
A Mormon Maid
Mother and Son
Murder on Lenox Avenue
The Nest
The Night Cry
Night Life in Reno
Nomads of the North
Now, Voyager↗
Old Yeller↗
Only Angels Have Wings↗
An Orphan Boy of Vienna
The Other Side of the Mountain
The Other Side of the Mountain,
    Part 2
Our Sons
Our Time
Paradise Road
The Passing of the Third Floor
    Back
Pattes Blanches
Peg O' My Heart

Penny Serenade↗
A Place in the Sun↗
The Pride of the Yankees↗
The Promise
Question of Faith
A Question of Guilt
Quicksand
The Racket
Rage of Angels
The Rains Came
Random Harvest↗
Rebecca of Sunnybrook Farm
Red Kimono
Remolina de Pasiones
Rikisha-Man↗
The Road to Ruin
Romola
Scar of Shame
Secrets of a Married Man
Seizure: The Story of Kathy
    Morris
Sex
Shadowlands↗
She Goes to War
A Shining Season↗
The Shock
Shopworn Angel↗
Silent Night, Lonely Night
The Sin of Madelon Claudet↗
Since You Went Away↗
Six Weeks
Smilin' Through↗
Sommersby
Sooner or Later
Sparrows↗
Steel Magnolias↗
Stella
Stella Dallas↗
Stella Maris↗
Stolen Hours
The Story of Esther Costello
Strangers: The Story of a Mother
    and Daughter↗
Stromboli
Struggle
Suds
Summer and Smoke
A Summer Place
Sunny
Sunny Skies
Susan Lenox: Her Fall and Rise
Tango
Tell Me That You Love Me
Tender Comrade
Terms of Endearment↗
Test Tube Babies
That Certain Woman
They Drive by Night↗
Things in Their Season
This Boy's Life↗
Three Secrets
Thursday's Child
Tiefland
A Time to Live
To Gillian on Her 37th Birthday
Tomorrow's Children
The Tong Man
Torch Song
Toute Une Nuit↗
Traffic in Souls↗
Trapped by the Mormons
Under the Roofs of Paris↗
The Underdog
The Unholy Three↗
Untamed Heart
Uptown New York
Walk on the Wild Side
Walpurgis Night↗
Waterfront
Waterloo Bridge↗
Way Down East↗
The Weaker Sex
Welcome Home
West-Bound Limited
West of Zanzibar
When Wolves Cry
Where East Is East
Where the Red Fern Grows
The White Cliffs of Dover↗

The White Rose↗
Wide Sargasso Sea
Winter Meeting
Without a Trace
A Woman of Affairs
The World Accuses
The World Is Full of Married Men
The World Owes Me a Living
Written on the Wind↗
X, Y & Zee
The Yearling↗

Technology-Rampant

*see also Computers; Killer
Appliances; Robots &
Androids*

A Nous la Liberte↗
The Android Affair
Armageddon: The Final
    Challenge
Assassin
Attack of the Killer Refrigerator
Attack of the Robots
Baby Girl Scott
Back to the Future↗
Batman Forever↗
Best Defense
The Bionic Woman
Black Cobra 3: The Manila
    Connection
The Black Hole
Blade Runner↗
Blades
Bloodlust
Brainscan
Bullet to Beijing
Chandu the Magician
Charly
Chopping Mall
Circuitry Man
Colossus: The Forbin Project↗
The Companion
Computer Beach Party
Computer Wizard
The Corporation
Crash and Burn
The Creation of the Humanoids
Cyber Bandits
Cyber-Tracker 2
Death Ray 2000
Defense Play
Demon Seed↗
Denise Calls Up
Detonator 2: Night Watch
Diamonds Are Forever↗
Digital Man
Dr. Goldfoot and the Bikini
    Machine
Downdraft
Dungeonmaster
Duplicates
Electric Dreams
The Eliminators
Eve of Destruction
Evolver
Fail-Safe↗
Fair Game
Family Viewing↗
The Fifth Element
Final Mission
The Final Programme
The Fly↗
The Fly↗
The Fly 2
Future Cop
Futureworld
Geheimakte WB1
Ghost in the Machine
Goldeneye↗
Hackers
Hide and Seek
Hologram Man
Hostile Intent
Improper Channels
Interface
Johnny Mnemonic

A Joke of Destiny, Lying in Wait
    Around the Corner Like a
    Bandit
Judge Dredd
A King in New York
Lawnmower Man 2: Beyond
    Cyberspace
The Lift
Live Wire: Human Timebomb
Lost in Space
Lost Legacy: A Girl Called Hatter
    Fox
Maximum Overdrive
Metropolis↗
Microwave Massacre
Modern Times↗
Mon Oncle↗
Moonraker
The Mosaic Project
Mosiac Project
The Munsters' Revenge
Murder by Phone
Murder by Television
Mutant Hunt
Mutant Species
The Net
New Crime City: Los Angeles
    2020
Night of the Kickfighters
Nightflyers
One Deadly Owner
Out of Order
Panique↗
The Philadelphia Experiment
Plughead Rewired: Circuitry
    Man 2
The Power Within
Project: Eliminator
Project: Shadowchaser
The Quiet Earth↗
Rage
Ravager
Redline
Remote
Replikator: Cloned to Kill
RoboCop↗
RoboCop 2
RoboCop 3
RoboCop the Series: The Future
    of Law Enforcement
Robot Holocaust
Robot Jox
Rock & Roll Cowboys
R.O.T.O.R.
Runaway
Screamers
Search and Destroy
The Seventh Floor
Shadowzone
Shaker Run
Shocker
Short Circuit
Short Circuit 2
Small Soldiers
Sneakers
Solo
Space: 1999
Speaking Parts↗
Speed 2: Cruise Control
The Spy Who Loved Me
Stay Tuned
Steel and Lace
Strange New World
Terminal Choice
Terminal Entry
Terminal Impact
The Terminal Man
The Terminator↗
Terrorvision
Things to Come↗
Thrillkill
Touki Bouki
Tron
12:01
Twisted
2001: A Space Odyssey↗
The Ultimate Imposter
The Unborn
Under Siege 2: Dark Territory

The Vindicator
Virtuosity
WarGames
Warning Sign
Weird Science
Westworld↗
Wild Palms
The Wind in the Willows
Wired to Kill
Wrestling Women vs. the Aztec
    Ape
Zardoz

Teen Angst

*see also Coming of Age;
Hell High School*

Above the Rim
Abuse
Across the Tracks
Address Unknown
Adventures in Dinosaur City
Age Isn't Everything
Ah, Wilderness!↗
Airborne
Alex
All Over Me↗
All Things Fair
American Graffiti↗
An American Summer
Amor Bandido
Andy Hardy Gets Spring Fever
Andy Hardy Meets Debutante
Andy Hardy's Double Life
Andy Hardy's Private Secretary
Angel
Angels with Dirty Faces↗
Angus
Annie O
Anything for Love
Art for Teachers of Children
Autumn Moon
Baby It's You↗
The Baby-Sitters Club
The Bachelor and the Bobby-
    Soxer↗
Backstreet Dreams
Bad Boys↗
Bad Ronald↗
The Basketball Diaries
Battle of the Bullies
The Bay Boy
Beach Blanket Bingo↗
Beach House
Beach Party
The Beat
Beautiful Thing↗
Before and After
The Beniker Gang
Berserker
The Best Little Girl in the World↗
Better Off Dead
Beverly Hills 90210
Beverly Hills 90210: The
    Graduation
Beyond Innocence
The Big Bet
Big Bully
Big Girls Don't Cry...They Get
    Even
Big Town
Bikini Beach
Bill & Ted's Excellent Adventure
Blackboard Jungle↗
Bleeding Hearts
Blood of Dracula
BMX Bandits
Body Snatchers
Book of Love
Born Innocent
Born to Be Wild
Boston Kickout
A Boy Called Hate
Boys
The Boys Club
Boys Life
Boy's Reformatory
Boyz N the Hood↗
The Brady Bunch Movie↗

Television

Tennis

Terminal Confusion

Terror in Tall Buildings

Terrorism

Malcolm X♦
Malcolm X: Make It Plain
A Man Called Peter♦
Man of a Thousand Faces♦
Mandela♦
Marciano
Marco
Marie♦
Marie Antoinette
Marilyn: The Untold Story♦
Marjoe
Martin Luther
Mary of Scotland♦
Mary White
A Matter of Life and Death
McVicar
Melody Master
Michael Collins♦
The Miracle Worker♦
Mishima: A Life in Four
   Chapters♦
Mrs. Parker and the Vicious
   Circle
Mo' Better Blues
Modigliani
Mommie Dearest
Monsieur Vincent♦
Mother Teresa: In the Name of
   God's Poor
Moulin Rouge♦
Mozart: A Childhood Chronicle♦
The Mozart Story
Murderers Among Us: The
   Simon Wiesenthal Story♦
Murrow
The Music Lovers
Mussolini & I
My Apprenticeship♦
My Childhood♦
My Father's Glory♦
My Left Foot♦
My Universities♦
My Wicked, Wicked Ways
Nadia
The Naked Civil Servant♦
The Naked Maja
Nancy Astor
Napoleon♦
Napoleon
Ned Kelly
Nerolio
Nicholas and Alexandra
Nico Icon♦
Night and Day
Nijinsky
Nixon♦
Norma Jean and Marilyn
Nostradamus
Nurse Edith Cavell♦
Onassis
One in a Million: The Ron
   LeFlore Story
One Man's Way
The Outlaw
Padre Padrone♦
Pancho Barnes
Pancho Villa
Papa's Delicate Condition♦
Patton♦
Patty Hearst
Paul Robeson
The People vs. Larry Flynt♦
Perfumed Nightmare♦
The Perils of Pauline
Personal Services
Peter and Paul
Peter the Great♦
Piaf
Pistol: The Birth of a Legend
Poor Little Rich Girl: The
   Barbara Hutton Story
Pope John Paul II
Portrait of a Rebel: Margaret
   Sanger
Postcards from America
Prefontaine
Prick Up Your Ears♦
Pride of St. Louis
The Pride of the Yankees♦

Priest of Love
Prince Jack
Private Parts
PT 109
The Queen of Mean
Queenie
Raging Bull♦
Rainbow
Rasputin♦
Rasputin: Dark Servant of
   Destiny♦
Rasputin the Mad Monk
The Raven
A Real American Hero
The Real Buddy Holly Story
Rebound: The Legend of Earl
   "The Goat" Manigault
Reilly: Ace of Spies♦
Rembrandt♦
Rembrandt—1669
Return to Earth
Rhapsody in Blue♦
Rhodes
Richard Petty Story
Riel
Ring of Bright Water♦
The Rise and Fall of Legs
   Diamond
The Rise of Louis XIV♦
Rita Hayworth: The Love
   Goddess
Robert Kennedy and His Times
Rodeo Girl
Romero
Rosa Luxemburg
Roseanne: An Unauthorized
   Biography
Rosie: The Rosemary Clooney
   Story
Ruby
Run for the Dream: The Gail
   Devers Story
Rush♦
Sadat
Saint-Ex: The Story of the
   Storyteller
Sakharov♦
Samaritan: The Mitch Snyder
   Story♦
Savage Messiah♦
Schindler's List♦
Sebastiane♦
The Secret Diary of Sigmund
   Freud
Secret Honor♦
Selena
A Sense of Freedom♦
The Seven Little Foys♦
Seven Years in Tibet
The Sexual Life of the Belgians
Shadow on the Sun
Shadowlands♦
Shine♦
The Sicilian
Sid & Nancy
Silent Victory: The Kitty O'Neil
   Story♦
Simon Bolivar
Sinatra
Sister Kenny♦
Six Wives of Henry VIII♦
Soldier in Love
Somebody Up There Likes Me♦
Song of Norway
A Song to Remember♦
Song Without End
Sophia Loren: Her Own Story
The Sound and the Silence
The Spectre of Edgar Allen Poe
Spirit of St. Louis♦
Spitfire♦
Spring Symphony
Spymaker: The Secret Life of
   Ian Fleming
Squizzy Taylor
Stalin
Star!
Stars and Stripes Forever♦
Stevie

Story of Adele H.♦
The Story of Alexander Graham
   Bell♦
The Story of Dr. Wassell
The Story of Louis Pasteur♦
The Story of Vernon and Irene
   Castle♦
The Stratton Story♦
Striker's Mountain
Sugartime
Sunday's Children♦
Sunrise at Campobello♦
Surviving Picasso
Swann
Sweet Dreams
Sweet Love, Bitter
Sylvia
Taxi zum Klo♦
Tchaikovsky
Teamster Boss: The Jackie
   Presser Story♦
The Ten Commandments♦
The Testament of Orpheus♦
That Hamilton Woman♦
Theremin: An Electronic
   Odyssey♦
Therese♦
32 Short Films about Glenn
   Gould♦
This Boy's Life♦
This Is Elvis
Three Came Home♦
Three Little Words
Till the Clouds Roll By
Till the Clouds Roll By/A Star Is
   Born♦
A Time for Miracles
To Hell and Back
To Kill a Priest
To Race the Wind
Tom & Viv♦
Tom Horn
Total Eclipse
The Trials of Oscar Wilde♦
Truman
Tyson
Up Close and Personal♦
Valentino
Van Gogh
Veronika Voss♦
Victoria Regina
Vincent & Theo♦
Vincent: The Life and Death of
   Vincent van Gogh♦
The Virgin Queen♦
The Virginia Hill Story
Viva Villa!♦
Viva Zapata!♦
A Voyage' Round My Father♦
Wagner: The Complete Epic
Wagner: The Movie
Wait Until Spring, Bandini
Waiting for the Moon♦
Walk the Proud Land
Waltz King
Weeds♦
What's Love Got to Do with It?
White Hunter, Black Heart♦
Who's That Knocking at My
   Door?♦
Wild America♦
Wild Bill
Wild Hearts Can't Be Broken♦
Wild, Wild World of Jayne
   Mansfield
Wilde
Will: G. Gordon Liddy
Wilma
Wilson♦
The Winds of Kitty Hawk
Wings of Eagles
A Winner Never Quits
The Winning Team
Wired
Without Limits♦
Without Warning: The James
   Brady Story♦
Wittgenstein
The Wolf at the Door

A Woman Called Golda♦
A Woman Called Moses
The Woman He Loved
A Woman Named Jackie
The Wonderful, Horrible Life of
   Leni Riefenstahl
The Wonderful World of the
   Brothers Grimm
Words and Music
Wyatt Earp
Yankee Doodle Dandy♦
Young Bill Hickok
Young Buffalo Bill
Young Caruso
Young Charlie Chaplin♦
Young Einstein
Young Mr. Lincoln♦
Young Tom Edison
Young Winston♦
Zora Is My Name!

3-D Flicks

Amityville 3: The Demon
Andy Warhol's Frankenstein
Cat Women of the Moon
Creature from the Black
   Lagoon♦
The Creature Walks Among Us
Devil's Canyon
Dogs of Hell
Dynasty
Flesh and Blood Show
The French Line
Friday the 13th, Part 3
Gun Fury
House of Wax♦
It Came from Outer Space♦
Jaws 3
Kiss Me Kate♦
The Man Who Wasn't There
The Mask
Miss Sadie Thompson♦
Paradisio
Parasite
Revenge of the Creature
Robot Monster
Spacehunter: Adventures in the
   Forbidden Zone
Starchaser: The Legend of Orin
The Stranger Wore a Gun

Thrillers

*see Erotic Thrillers;
   Mystery & Suspense;
   Psycho-Thriller*

The Assignment
The Break
Casualties
Caught Up
Cold Around the Heart
Disturbing Behavior
Double Take
Face Down
The Game♦
Heaven's Burning
Homegrown
The Innocent Sleep
The Jackal
Killing Time
The November Men
Provocateur
The Real Thing
The Ripper
Seeds of Doubt
Shades of Black
Snake Eyes
The Spanish Prisoner♦
Starved
Sweet Evil

Thumbs Up

Alligator Eyes
Blood Simple♦
Diary of a Teenage Hitchhiker
Even Cowgirls Get the Blues
The Hitcher
The Hitchhiker
Hitchhiker 2
Hitchhiker 3
Hitchhiker 4
Hitchhikers
The Hitchhiker's Guide to the
   Galaxy
Josh and S.A.M.
Kalifornia
Larger Than Life
Melvin and Howard♦
My Own Private Idaho♦
The Sure Thing♦
Thelma & Louise♦

Time Travel

*see also Rescue Missions
   Involving Time Travel*

Adventures in Dinosaur City
The Alien Agenda: Out of the
   Darkness
Amazing Mr. Blunden
A.P.E.X.
Army of Darkness♦
The Arrival
Back to the Future♦
Back to the Future, Part 2
Back to the Future, Part 3♦
Battle for the Planet of the Apes
Beastmaster 2: Through the
   Portal of Time
Being Human
Beneath the Planet of the Apes
Beyond the Time Barrier
Biggles
Bill & Ted's Bogus Journey
Bill & Ted's Excellent Adventure
Blue Flame
The Blue Yonder
Brother Future
Buck Rogers in the 25th Century
A Connecticut Yankee♦
A Connecticut Yankee in King
   Arthur's Court
Conquest of the Planet of the
   Apes
Day Time Ended
Dinosaur Valley Girls
Doctor Mordrid: Master of the
   Unknown
Doctor Who
Doctor Who: An Unearthly Child
Doctor Who and the Daleks
The Eliminators
Escape from the Planet of the
   Apes♦
Escapes
The Final Countdown♦
Frankenstein Unbound♦
Freejack
Future Zone
Galaxis
Godzilla vs. King Ghidora
Grand Tour: Disaster in Time
Grizzly Mountain
Hercules in New York
Highlander 2: The Quickening
Highlander: The Final Dimension
Hocus Pocus
Idaho Transfer
In His Father's Shoes
The Indian in the Cupboard
The Jetsons Meet the
   Flintstones
Josh Kirby...Time Warrior:
   Chapter 1, Planet of the Dino-
   Knights
Josh Kirby...Time Warrior:
   Chapter 2, The Human Pets

Tragedy

A Very Private Affair
The Virgin Spring↗
Voyager↗
The Walls of Malapaga
The Wedding Gift↗
Where Angels Fear to Tread↗
The White Cliffs of Dover↗
White Mile
The White Sister↗
William Shakespeare's Romeo and Juliet↗
A Woman at Her Window
The Woman Next Door↗
The Wooden Man's Bride
The World According to Garp↗

Trains

see also Subways

Across the Bridge
Alberto Express
Avalanche Express
Before Sunrise
Berlin Express↗
Blood and Steel
Boxcar Bertha
The Brain
Breakheart Pass
Broken Arrow
Bullet to Beijing
Cafe Express
The Cassandra Crossing
Chattanooga Choo Choo
Closely Watched Trains↗
Color of a Brisk and Leaping Day
Courage Under Fire↗
Dakota
Danger Lights
Death Train
The Denver & Rio Grande
Detonator
The Dirty Dozen: The Fatal Mission
End of the Line
Express to Terror
Finders Keepers
Flame Over India↗
The Flying Scotsman
From Russia with Love↗
The Fugitive↗
The General↗
The Ghost and the Darkness
The Ghost Train
The Glory Trail
Go Kill and Come Back
Great K & A Train Robbery
The Great Locomotive Chase
The Great Train Robbery↗
The Grey Fox↗
Grit of the Girl Telegrapher/In the Switch Tower
The Harvey Girls↗
Horror Express
Hostage Train
Hot Lead & Cold Feet
The Illusion Travels by Streetcar
Indiscretion of an American Wife
Inner Sanctum
Interrupted Journey
Jesse James at Bay
The Journey of Natty Gann↗
La Bete Humaine↗
The Lady Eve↗
Lady on a Train↗
The Lady Vanishes↗
The Lady Vanishes
The Major and the Minor↗
Malcolm
Man Who Loved Cat Dancing
Man Without a Star↗
Midnight Limited
The Millionaire's Express
Mrs. Winterbourne
Mouvements du Desir
Murder on the Midnight Express
Murder on the Orient Express↗
My Twentieth Century↗

Mystery Mountain
Narrow Margin
The Newton Boys
Night Train to Munich↗
Night Train to Terror
Night Train to Venice
No. 17↗
The Odyssey of the Pacific
Oh, Mr. Porter
Once Upon a Time in the West↗
Panic on the 5:22
Paris Express
The Peacemaker
Phantom Express
Plunder Road
Prison Train
Railrodder↗
Red Signals
The Return of Casey Jones
Rhythm on the Range
The Road Home
The Road to Yesterday
Robbery
Romance on the Orient Express
Runaway Train↗
Running Scared
The Saint's Vacation/The Narrow Margin
Saratoga Trunk
Shanghai Express↗
The Silver Streak
Silver Streak↗
The Sleeping Car
Sleeping Car to Trieste
Some Like It Hot↗
Strangers on a Train↗
Subway
Switchback
A Tale of Winter
Terror Train
Three for Bedroom C
3:10 to Yuma↗
Throw Momma from the Train↗
Thunder Over Texas
Torture Train
Tough Guys
Tracks
Trading Places
The Trail of the Lonesome Pine↗
The Train↗
The Train Killer
Train Robbers
Train to Tombstone
Two Weeks to Live
Under Siege 2: Dark Territory
Union Pacific↗
Von Ryan's Express↗
Warm Nights on a Slow-Moving Train
Wild Engine/Mistaken Orders
Without Reservations
Zentropa

Transvestites & Transsexuals

see Gender Bending

Trapped with a Killer!

see also Psychotics/ Sociopaths

Adrift
Air Force One↗
Alien Terminator
Blind Witness
Blink
Blood at Sundown
Blood Bride
Clue
Con Air↗
Copycat
Dead Calm↗
Deadbolt
Extremities
Eye of the Needle

Eyes of the Beholder
Fatal Attraction↗
Headless Body in Topless Bar
Hider in the House
Kalifornia
Kiss the Girls
Lifepod
The Maddening
Manhunter↗
Misery↗
Mute Witness
Narrow Margin
Pacific Heights↗
The Penthouse
The Shining
The Silence of the Lambs↗
Slaughter of the Innocents
Ten Little Indians
The Terror
Terror Train
Through the Eyes of a Killer
The Tie that Binds
Tracks of a Killer↗
Turbulence
Undertow
Unveiled
Virus
Voyage
Wait Until Dark↗
What's the Matter with Helen?
When a Stranger Calls
When a Stranger Calls Back

Treasure Hunt

Abbott and Costello Meet the Mummy
Adventure of the Action Hunters
The Adventurers
All the Brothers Were Valiant
Big Mouth
Blue Jeans and Dynamite
Cabo Blanco
Call of the Wild
City Slickers 2: The Legend of Curly's Gold
Comin' Round the Mountain
Curse of the Crystal Eye
Cutthroat Island
Enemy Gold
Ernest Rides Again
Finger on the Trigger
Girls in Prison
Gold Diggers: The Secret of Bear Mountain
The Goonies
The Grave
Greedy
Green Fire
The Haunted Sea
Hear No Evil
Hunters of the Golden Cobra
Inside Out
The Jewel of the Nile
Kelly's Heroes
Klondike Fever
Kull the Conqueror
Legends of the North
Les Aventuriers
Lewis and Clark and George
Lust in the Dust↗
Max Is Missing
The Mermaids of Tiburon
Missing Pieces
Muppet Treasure Island
My Family Treasure
One-Eyed Soldiers
Operation Condor
Operation Golden Phoenix
Pattern for Plunder
The Phantom of the Range
The Pink Jungle
Romancing the Stone↗
Rudyard Kipling's The Jungle Book
The Secret of the Golden Eagle
Secret of the Ice Cave
Shadow of Chikara
Tarzan's Secret Treasure

Terror on Alcatraz
That Man from Rio
There Goes the Neighborhood
Thieves of Fortune
Tom and Huck
Treasure Island↗
Treasure Island
The Treasure of Jamaica Reef
The Treasure of Matecumbe
The Treasure of the Amazon
Treasure of the Four Crowns
Treasure of the Golden Condor
Treasure of the Sierra Madre↗
Treasure of the Yankee Zephyr
The Treasure Seekers
Trespass
Uninvited
Warrior Spirit
Whistling in Dixie
The Wrong Road

Trees & Forests

see also Good Earth; Wilderness

Big Trees↗
The Burning Season↗
Crosscut
Dr. Tarr's Torture Dungeon
Equinox↗
Evil Dead
Fatal Passion
Ferngully: The Last Rain Forest
5 Dark Souls
Forest Warrior
Himatsuri
Hole in the Sky
The Ice Flood
King of the Forest Rangers
Lassie: Adventures of Neeka
Les Grandes Gueules
Lunatic
The Many Adventures of Winnie the Pooh
Mr. Sycamore
The Night Brings Charlie
The Passion of Darkly Noon
Poltergeist 2: The Other Side
Redwood Curtain
Redwood Forest Trail
Return of the Jedi↗
Surfacing
Vertigo↗
The Watcher in the Woods
Where the Rivers Flow North
The Wizard of Oz↗

True Crime

see also Crime & Criminals; This is Your Life; True Stories

At Close Range↗
Ballad of Gregorio Cortez↗
Beyond Reasonable Doubt
Billionaire Boys Club
Black Oak Conspiracy
Black Panther
Blackrock
Blanche Fury
Bluebeard↗
Boomerang↗
The Boston Strangler
Chicago Joe & the Showgirl
Citizen X↗
Compulsion↗
Crime of the Century
Danger of Love
Deadly Voyage
Death Scream
The Deliberate Stranger↗
Dick Turpin
Dillinger
Dr. Petiot
Double-Crossed
Echoes in the Darkness
The Elegant Criminal
The Executioner's Song

The Falcon and the Snowman↗
Final Appeal
The General↗
Getting Gotti
Gotti
Great Gold Swindle
The Great St. Louis Bank Robbery
Headless Body in Topless Bar
Helter Skelter
Helter Skelter Murders
The Hillside Strangler
Honor Thy Father and Mother: The True Story of the Menendez Brothers
I Can't Sleep
In Cold Blood
Johnny 100 Pesos
Killer: A Journal of Murder
L'Appat
Mad Dog Morgan
The Man from the Pru
The Man in the Attic
McVicar
Midnight in the Garden of Good and Evil
Mrs. Soffel
Money Movers
Murder in Coweta County
Murder in New Hampshire: The Pamela Smart Story
Murder in Texas↗
Murder So Sweet
Murph the Surf
The Newton Boys
Normal Life
Nowhere to Run
The O.J. Simpson Story
The Onion Field↗
Our Mother's Murder
Path to Paradise
The People vs. Jean Harris↗
Perfect Crime
The Preppie Murder
Prince of the City↗
The Pursuit of D.B. Cooper
Rainbow Warrior
Rampage
Rule #3
Sister My Sister
Squizzy Taylor
Stalking Laura
Stand Off
Swoon↗
Till Murder Do Us Part
Too Young to Die
Triple Cross↗
Undercover Cop
The Untouchables↗
Verne Miller
Without Evidence
The Zodiac Killer

True Stories

see also This is Your Life; True Crime

The Abduction of Kari Swenson
Above and Beyond↗
The Accused↗
Act of Vengeance
Adam↗
The Adventures of Nellie Bly
After the Promise
After the Shock
Afterburn↗
Against the Wall↗
Al Capone↗
The Alamo↗
Alamo Bay
Alive
All Mine to Give
All the President's Men↗
Alvarez Kelly
The Ambush Murders
Amelia Earhart: The Final Flight
An American Story
The Amityville Horror
Amor Bandido

Category Index

1188

TV Pilot Movies

Camilla
Cancel My Reservation
Captain Ron
Casual Sex?
City Slickers
Claire's Knee⋆
Cold Fever
Come September
The Comfort of Strangers⋆
Crackerjack
Dangerous Prey
Dead Cold
Deadly Intruder
Death Stalk
Death Weekend
Deliverance⋆
Demon Lust
Devil Wears White
Dirty Dancing⋆
Don't Drink the Water
8 Heads in a Duffel Bag
Enchanted April
Far from Home
A Far Off Place
The Fatal Image
A Fatal Inversion
Frantic
Fraternity Vacation
Gidget Goes Hawaiian
Gidget Goes to Rome
Grotesque
Harry and the Hendersons
Head Above Water
The Hills Have Eyes
Home Alone⋆
Home Alone 2: Lost in New York
Hot Pursuit
The Inkwell
Judgment Day
Killing at Hell's Gate
La Collectionneuse
Last Summer in the Hamptons⋆
Lena's Holiday
Lie Down with Dogs
Like It Never Was Before
Little Bigfoot
The Long, Long Trailer
Love! Valour! Compassion!
The Lunatic
Magic in the Water
Magic Kid
The Man Who Knew Too Much⋆
The Man Who Knew Too Much
Mr. Hobbs Takes a Vacation⋆
Mr. Hulot's Holiday⋆
A Month by the Lake
My Father the Hero
My Grandpa Is a Vampire
National Lampoon's Christmas
    Vacation
National Lampoon's Dad's Week
    Off
National Lampoon's European
    Vacation
National Lampoon's Vacation⋆
Nightmare at Bittercreek
Ollie Hopnoodle's Haven of Bliss
The Out-of-Towners⋆
Overkill
Pauline at the Beach⋆
Poor White Trash 2
Ring of Fire 3: Lion Strike
The River Wild
Russian Roulette
Six Days, Seven Nights
The Slayer/The Scalps
Spellbreaker: Secret of the
    Leprechauns
Spring Break
Stealing Beauty
The Sucker
Summer Fling
Summer Rental
Swallows and Amazons
A Tale of Winter
Target
Terror at Red Wolf Inn
Terror at Tenkiller
Tracks of a Killer

Twitch of the Death Nerve
The Two Faces of Evil
Two If by Sea
Uncivilized
Unlawful Passage
Vegas Vacation
Week-End In Havana
Weekend at Bernie's
A Weekend in the Country
Welcome to Spring Break
Where the Boys Are '84
The Wild Life
Witchery

Vampire Babes

see also Up All Night;
Vampires

The Addiction
The Brides of Dracula
Buffy the Vampire Slayer⋆
Captain Kronos: Vampire
    Hunter⋆
The Craving
Crypt of the Living Dead
Daughters of Darkness⋆
Demon Queen
Dracula's Daughter⋆
Fangs of the Living Dead
The Fearless Vampire Killers⋆
Fright Night
From Dusk Till Dawn
The Girl with the Hungry Eyes
Habit
Interview with the Vampire
John Carpenter's Vampires
Karmina
The Kiss
Lemora, Lady Dracula
Lust for a Vampire
Mary, Mary, Bloody Mary
The Midnight Hour
Nadja⋆
Night of the Sorcerers
Night Shade
Nightlife
Once Bitten
Samson vs. the Vampire
    Women
Saturday the 14th Strikes Back
Stephen King's The Night Flier
Tales from the Crypt Presents
    Bordello of Blood
Twins of Evil
Vamp
The Vampire Lovers
Vampyres
The Velvet Vampire

Vampire Spoof

see also Horror Comedy;
Vampires

Andy Warhol's Dracula⋆
Beverly Hills Vamp
Buffy the Vampire Slayer⋆
Dracula & Son
Dracula Blows His Cool
Dracula: Dead and Loving It
Dracula Sucks
Dracula: Up in Harlem
Dracula vs. Frankenstein
The Fearless Vampire Killers⋆
Gore-Met Zombie Chef From
    Hell
I Married a Vampire
Karmina
Love at First Bite
The Malibu Beach Vampires
My Best Friend Is a Vampire
My Grandpa Is a Vampire
Near Dark⋆
Once Bitten
A Polish Vampire in Burbank
Rockula
Teen Vamp
Vamp
The Vampire Happening

Vampires

see also Up All Night;
Vampires Dul vu; Vampire
Spoof

The Addiction
Alien Massacre
The Bat People
Beast of Morocco
Billy the Kid Versus Dracula
The Black Room
Black Sabbath⋆
Black Vampire
Blacula
Blade
Blood & Donuts
Blood and Roses
Blood Freak
Blood of Dracula's Castle
Blood of the Vampire
The Blood Spattered Bride
Blood Thirst
Blood Ties
Bloodlust: Subspecies 3
Bloodstone: Subspecies 2
The Bloodsuckers
Bloodsuckers from Outer Space
The Bloody Vampire
Body Snatcher from Hell
Bram Stoker's Dracula
The Brides of Dracula
Bring Me the Vampire
Buffy the Vampire Slayer⋆
Captain Kronos: Vampire
    Hunter⋆
Carmilla
Cave of the Living Dead
Children of the Night
Condemned to Live
Count Dracula
Count Yorga, Vampire
The Craving
Crypt of the Living Dead
Curse of the Undead
Dance of the Damned
Dark Shadows
Dark Shadows: Episode 1
Daughter of Darkness
Daughters of Darkness⋆
Dead Men Walk
Demon Queen
The Devil Bat
The Devil Bat's Daughter
Devil's Wedding Night
Dr. Terror's House of Horrors
Dracula⋆
Dracula
Dracula A.D. 1972
Dracula: Dead and Loving It
Dracula/Garden of Eden
Dracula Has Risen from the
    Grave
Dracula Rising
Dracula (Spanish Version)
Dracula vs. Frankenstein
Dracula's Daughter⋆
Dracula's Great Love
Dracula's Last Rites
Dracula's Widow
Elvira, Mistress of the Dark
Embrace of the Vampire
Evil's Commandment
Evils of the Night
Fangs of the Living Dead
Fright Night
Fright Night 2
From Dusk Till Dawn
Genie of Darkness
Ghost Stories: Graveyard
    Thriller
Grave of the Vampire
Graveyard Shift
Habit
Heartstopper
The Horror of Dracula⋆
Horror of the Blood Monsters
House of Dark Shadows
House of Dracula

House of Frankenstein
The House that Dripped Blood
Howling 6: The Freaks
The Hunger
I Like Bats
Innocent Blood
Interview with the Vampire
Invasion of the Vampires
Isle of the Dead
John Carpenter's Vampires
Karmina
Kiss of the Vampire
The Last Man on Earth
Lemora, Lady Dracula
Les Vampires
Let's Scare Jessica to Death
Lifeforce
The Lost Boys
The Lost Platoon
The Loves of Irina
Lust for a Vampire
Mark of the Vampire⋆
Martin⋆
Mary, Mary, Bloody Mary
The Midnight Hour
Midnight Kiss
Midnight Movie Massacre
The Monster Club
The Monster Demolisher
The Monster Squad
My Grandpa Is a Vampire
My Son, the Vampire
Nadja⋆
Near Dark⋆
Nick Knight
Night Hunter
Night of Dark Shadows
Night of the Sorcerers
The Night Stalker
Nightlife
Nightmare in Blood
Ninja, the Violent Sorcerer
Nocturna
Nosferatu⋆
Not of This Earth
Once Bitten
Orgy of the Vampires
Pale Blood
Planet of Blood
Planet of the Vampires
Project Vampire
Rabid
Red Blooded American Girl
The Reflecting Skin
The Return of Count Yorga
Return of the Vampire
Return to Salem's Lot
The Saga of the Draculas
Salem's Lot
Samson vs. the Vampire
    Women
The Satanic Rites of Dracula
The Scars of Dracula
Scream Blacula Scream
The 7 Brothers Meet Dracula
ShadowZone: The Undead
    Express
The Slaughter of the Vampires
Sleepwalkers
Son of Dracula⋆
Stephen King's The Night Flier
Subspecies
Sundown
Tale of a Vampire
Tales from the Crypt Presents
    Bordello of Blood
Taste the Blood of Dracula
Theatre of Death
Thirst
The Thirsty Dead
To Die For
To Die For 2: Son of Darkness
To Sleep with a Vampire
Track of the Vampire
Transylvania Twist
Twins of Evil
Uncle Was a Vampire
Understudy: The Graveyard
    Shift 2

The Unearthing
Vamp
The Vampire
Vampire at Midnight
The Vampire Bat
Vampire Circus
Vampire Cop
The Vampire Happening
The Vampire Hookers
Vampire in Brooklyn
Vampire Journals
The Vampire Lovers
The Vampire People
Vampirella
The Vampire's Coffin
The Vampire's Ghost
Vampire's Kiss⋆
Vampyr⋆
The Vampyr
Vampyres
The Velvet Vampire
The Werewolf vs. the Vampire
    Woman
The Wicked
Witchcraft 7: Judgement Hour
Zoltan...Hound of Dracula

Variety

Follow the Boys⋆
Give a Girl a Break
Heller in Pink Tights
Here Comes Cookie
Hollywood Goes to War
If You Don't Stop It...You'll Go
    Blind
In the Money
International House
Minsky's Follies
Mr. Mike's Mondo Video
Parade⋆
The Pee Wee Herman Show
Pee Wee's Playhouse Festival
    of Fun
Sleazemania
Strictly G.I.
That's Dancing!
That's Singing: The Best of
    Broadway
Varieties on Parade
Ziegfeld Follies

Venice

see also Italy

Blame It on the Bellboy
The Children
The Comfort of Strangers⋆
Dangerous Beauty⋆
Death in Venice⋆
Don't Look Now⋆
Everyone Says I Love You⋆
Indiana Jones and the Last
    Crusade⋆
A Little Romance⋆
Night Train to Venice
Only You
Othello⋆
Panic Button
Summertime⋆
Venice, Venice
Walk, Don't Run
The Wings of the Dove⋆

Veterans

see also Postwar

Air Force One⋆
Alamo Bay
American Eagle
Americana
Anatomy of Terror
Angels from Hell
The Annihilators
Article 99
Ashes and Embers
Backfire
Bad Company⋆

Westerns

The Outlaw
Outlaw Country
The Outlaw Deputy
Outlaw Express
Outlaw Fury
Outlaw Gang
The Outlaw Josey Wales⏵
Outlaw Justice
Outlaw of the Plains
Outlaw Roundup
Outlaw Rule
The Outlaw Tamer
Outlaw Trail
Outlaw Women
Outlaws of Sonora
Outlaws of the Desert
Outlaws of the Range
Outlaw's Paradise
Overland Mail
Overland Stage Raiders⏵
The Ox-Bow Incident⏵
Painted Desert
The Painted Stallion
Pair of Aces
Pale Rider⏵
Pals of the Range
Pals of the Saddle
Panamint's Bad Man
Pancho Villa
Pancho Villa Returns
Pardon My Gun
Paroled to Die
Partners of the Trail
Passion
Pat Garrett & Billy the Kid⏵
Pecos Kid
Peter Lundy and the Medicine
    Hat Stallion
The Phantom Bullet
The Phantom Empire
Phantom Gold
The Phantom of the Range
Phantom of the West
Phantom Patrol
Phantom Rancher
Phantom Ranger
The Phantom Rider
Phantom Thunderbolt
Pinto Canyon
Pinto Rustlers
Pioneer Marshal
Pioneer Woman
The Pioneers
Pistoleros Asesinos
A Place Called Glory
The Plainsman
The Pocatello Kid
The Pony Express
Pony Express Rider⏵
Pony Post
Posse⏵
Powdersmoke Range
The Prairie King
Prairie Moon
Prairie Pals
The Prairie Pirate
Prescott Kid
The Professionals⏵
The Proud and the Damned
Proud Men
Proud Rebel⏵
Public Cowboy No. 1
Purple Vigilantes
Pursued⏵
The Quick and the Dead
Quigley Down Under
Racketeers of the Range
Rage at Dawn
Raiders of Red Gap
Raiders of Sunset Pass
Raiders of the Border
Rainbow Ranch
Rainbow's End
Ramrod
The Ramrodder
Rancho Notorious⏵
Randy Rides Alone

Range Busters
Range Feud
The Range Feud/Two Fisted
    Law
Range Law
Range Renegades
Range Rider
Range Riders
Rangeland Empire
Rangeland Racket
Ranger and the Lady
Ranger's Roundup
The Rangers Step In
Rangers Take Over
The Rare Breed
Rattler Kid
Rawhide
Rawhide⏵
Rawhide Romance
A Reason to Live, a Reason to
    Die
Red Desert
Red Garters
Red Headed Stranger
Red River⏵
Red River Valley
Red Rock Outlaw
The Red Rope
Red Sun
The Redhead from Wyoming
Redwood Forest Trail
Renegade Girl
Renegade Ranger/Scarlet River
Renegade Trail
Renfrew of the Royal Mounted
Renfrew on the Great White
    Trail
The Restless Breed
The Return of a Man Called
    Horse
Return of Draw Egan
Return of Frank James⏵
Return of Jesse James
The Return of Josey Wales
Return of the Bad Men
Return of the Lash
Return of the Seven
Return of Wildfire
Return to Lonesome Dove
Return to Snowy River⏵
Revenge of the Virgins
The Revenge Rider
Ride 'Em Cowgirl
Ride Him, Cowboy⏵
Ride in the Whirlwind
Ride Lonesome
Ride, Ranger, Ride
Ride the High Country⏵
Ride the Man Down
Ride the Wind
Ride to Glory
Rider from Tucson
Rider of the Law
Riders of Death Valley
Riders of Destiny
Riders of Pasco Basin
Riders of the Desert
Riders of the Purple Sage
Riders of the Range
Riders of the Range/Storm Over
    Wyoming
Riders of the Rockies
Riders of the Timberline
Riders of the West
Riders of the Whistling Pines
Riders of the Whistling Skull
Ridin' Down the Canyon
Ridin' on a Rainbow
Ridin' the California Trail
Ridin' the Lone Trail
Ridin' the Trail
Ridin' Thru
The Riding Avenger
Riding On
Riding Speed
Riding the Sunset Trail⏵
The Riding Tornado
Rim of the Canyon
Rimfire

Rin Tin Tin, Hero of the West
Rio Bravo⏵
Rio Conchos⏵
Rio Diablo
Rio Grande⏵
Rio Grande Raiders
Rio Lobo
Rio Rattler
River of No Return
Road Agent
The Roamin' Cowboy
Roamin' Wild
Roarin' Lead
Roaring Guns
Roaring Ranch
Roaring Six Guns
Robbery Under Arms
Robin Hood of Texas
Robin Hood of the Pecos
Rock River Renegades
Rockwell: A Legend of the Wild
    West
Rocky Mountain Rangers
Rodeo Girl
Rogue of the Range
Rogue of the Rio Grande
Roll Along Cowboy
Roll on Texas Moon
Roll, Wagons, Roll
Rollin' Plains
Romance on the Range
Rooster Cogburn
Rootin' Tootin' Rhythm
Rose of Rio Grande
Rough Night in Jericho
Rough Riders of Cheyenne
Rough Riders' Roundup
Rough Ridin' Rhythm
Rough Riding Rangers
Round-Up Time in Texas
Rounding Up the Law
Run of the Arrow
Running Wild
Rustler's Hideout
Rustlers of Red Dog
Rustler's Paradise
Rustler's Roundup
Rustler's Valley
The Sacketts
Sacred Ground
Saddle Buster
Saddle Mountain Round-Up
Saga of Death Valley
Sagebrush Law
Sagebrush Trail⏵
Salute to the "King of the
    Cowboys," Roy Rogers
San Antonio
San Fernando Valley
Sandflow
Santa Fe
Santa Fe Bound
Santa Fe Marshal
Santa Fe Stampede
Santa Fe Trail
Santa Fe Uprising
Santee
Sartana's Here...Trade Your
    Pistol for a Coffin
Savage Journey
Savage Land
Savage Wilderness
Scalps
The Searchers⏵
Sergeant Rutledge⏵
Seven Cities of Gold
Seventh Cavalry
The Shadow Riders
Shadows of Death
Shalako
Shane⏵
She Wore a Yellow Ribbon⏵
Sheriff of Tombstone
Shine on, Harvest Moon
Shoot the Living, Pray for the
    Dead
Shoot the Sun Down
The Shooting
The Shootist⏵

Shotgun
The Showdown
Showdown
Showdown at Boot Hill
Showdown at Williams Creek
Silent Code
Silent Tongue
Silent Valley
Silver Bandit
The Silver Bullet
Silver City Bonanza
Silver City Kid
Silver Lode
Silver Queen
Silver River
Silver Spurs
Silver Stallion
Silver Star
Silverado⏵
Sing, Cowboy, Sing
Singing Buckaroo
Singing Cowboys, Vol. 2
The Singing Cowgirl
The Singing Cowboy
Siringo
Six Gun Gospel
Six Gun Rhythm
Six Shootin' Sheriff
Sky Bandits
Sky High
Slaughter Trail
Smoke in the Wind
Smokey Smith
Sodbusters
Soldier Blue
The Sombrero Kid
Somewhere in Sonora
Son of a Gun
Son of God's Country
Son of the Morning Star⏵
Song of Arizona
Song of Nevada
Song of Old Wyoming
Song of Texas
Song of the Gringo
Song of the Trail
Songs and Bullets
Sonora Stagecoach
Sons of Katie Elder⏵
Sons of the Pioneers
South of Monterey
South of St. Louis
South of Santa Fe
South of the Border
South of the Rio Grande
Southward Ho!
Spirit of the West
Springfield Rifle
Springtime in the Rockies
Springtime in the Sierras
Spurs
Square Dance Jubilee
Stage to Mesa City
Stagecoach⏵
Stagecoach
Stagecoach to Denver
The Stalking Moon
Standing Tall
The Star Packer
Station West⏵
Stone of Silver Creek
Storm over Wyoming
Storm Rider
Stormy Trails
Straight Shootin'
The Stranger from Pecos
The Stranger Wore a Gun
Stranger's Gold
Strawberry Roan
Sudden Death
Sundance and the Kid
Sundown Fury
Sundown Kid
Sundown Riders
Sundown Saunders
Sunrise Trail
Sunset
Sunset in El Dorado
Sunset on the Desert
Sunset Range

Sunset Serenade
Sunset Trail
Suddenin Pass
Sweet Georgia
Swifty
Talion
Tall in the Saddle
The Tall Men
The Tall T
Tall Tale: The Unbelievable
    Adventures of Pecos Bill
Taste of Death
Telegraph Trail
Tell Them Willie Boy Is Here⏵
Ten Wanted Men
Tennessee's Partner
Tension at Table Rock
Terror in a Texas Town
Terror of Tiny Town
Terror Trail
Test of Donald Norton
Tex Rides with the Boy Scouts
The Texans
Texas
Texas Bad Man
Texas Buddies
Texas Cyclone
Texas Gunfighter
Texas Guns
Texas Jack
Texas John Slaughter:
    Geronimo's Revenge
Texas John Slaughter:
    Stampede at Bitter Creek
Texas Justice
Texas Kid
Texas Lady
Texas Legionnaires
Texas Masquerade
Texas Pioneers
The Texas Rangers
The Texas Rangers Ride Again
Texas Terror
Texas to Bataan
Texas Trouble
Texas Wildcats
The Texican
They Died with Their Boots On⏵
Thousand Pieces of Gold⏵
Three Bullets for a Long Gun
Three Desperate Men
Three Faces West
Three in the Saddle
3:10 to Yuma⏵
Three Texas Steers
Three Violent People
Three Word Brand
The Throwback
Thunder in God's Country
Thunder in the Desert
Thunder Mountain
Thunder Over Texas
Thunder Pass
Thunder River Feud
Thunder Trail
Thundering Gunslingers
Thundering Trail
The Tin Star⏵
The Tioga Kid
To the Last Man
Today We Kill, Tomorrow We
    Die
Toll Gate
Toll of the Desert
Tom Horn
Tom Mix Compilation 1
Tom Mix Compilation 2
Tomahawk
Tombstone⏵
Tombstone Canyon
Tombstone Terror
Tonto Basin Outlaws
The Tonto Kid
The Topeka Terror
The Tracker
The Trackers
Trail Beyond
Trail Drive
Trail of Robin Hood

Wrestling

Writers

Zombies

Kibbles and Series List

The **Kibbles** and **Series** indexes have been combined into one index. This is where you'll find info on where your favorite movies came from—literary, theatrical, cartoon, and television adaptations to name a few, as well as the behind the scenes talents that make movies possible, such as producers and special effects wizards. Another important feature of this index is the quality check it provides with categories like **Woofs!**, **4 Bones**, and **Top Grossing Films** by year. This index also provides information on recurring characters like James Bond, Zorro, or Mike Hammer, as well as notable screen partnerships. Some examples include Abbott & Costello, Hope & Crosby, and De Niro & Scorsese. **A tipped triangle denotes a three-bone or higher rating** The categories are as follows, with an asterisk (*) denoting a new category:

Adapted from:
a Book
a Cartoon
a Fairy Tale
a Game
a Play or Musical
a Poem
a Song
a Story
an Article
an Opera
Comics
Memoirs or Diaries
Television
the Radio

Alien and Rip-Offs
Amy Fisher
Andy Hardy
B/W & Color Combos
Basic Instinct and Rip-Offs
BBC TV Productions
Beach Party
Billy the Kid
Blondie

Books to Film:
Louisa May Alcott
Eric Ambler
Kingsley Amis
Hans Christian Andersen
Maya Angelou
Isaac Asimov
Jane Austen
*Russell Banks
Clive Barker
J.M. Barrie
*Thomas Berger
Ambrose Bierce
Maeve Binchy
Robert Bloch
Judy Blume
Ray Bradbury
Barbara Taylor Bradford

*The Brontes
Pearl S. Buck
Frances Hodgson Burnett
Edgar Rice Burroughs
William Burroughs
James M. Cain
Truman Capote
Barbara Cartland
Willa Cather
Raymond Chandler
Paddy Chayefsky
John Cheever
Anton Chechov
Agatha Christie
Tom Clancy
Mary Higgins Clark
Arthur C. Clarke
James Clavell
Jackie Collins
Richard Condon
Joseph Conrad
Pat Conroy
Robin Cook
Catherine Cookson
James Fenimore Cooper
Stephen Crane
Michael Crichton
Clive Cussler
Roald Dahl
Miguel de Cervantes
Guy de Maupassant
Daniel Defoe
*Len Deighton
Phillip K. Dick
Charles Dickens
E.L. Doctorow
Sir Arthur Conan Doyle
Daphne Du Maurier
Alexandre Dumas
*Lois Duncan
Dominick Dunne
George Eliot
Bret Easton Ellis

Howard Fast
Edna Ferber
Henry Fielding
F. Scott Fitzgerald
Gustov Flaubert
Ian Fleming
Ken Follett
E.M. Forster
Frederick Forsyth
Rumer Godden
Nikolai Gogol
William Goldman
David Goodis
Elizabeth Goudge
Kenneth Grahame
Graham Greene
Zane Grey
John Grisham
H. Rider Haggard
Arthur Hailey
Alex Haley
Dashiell Hammett
Thomas Hardy
Harlequin Romances
Jim Harrison
Nathaniel Hawthorne
Ernest Hemingway
O. Henry
Patricia Highsmith
James Hilton
S.E. Hinton
Victor Hugo
Fanny Hurst
John Irving
Washington Irving
Susan Isaacs
Rona Jaffe
John Jakes
Henry James
James Jones
James Joyce
Franz Kafka
Stephen King

Rudyard Kipling
Dean R. Koontz
Judith Krantz
Louis L'Amour
D.H. Lawrence
John Le Carre
Harper Lee
Elmore Leonard
Sinclair Lewis
*Ira Levin
Astrid Lindgren
Jack London
H.P. Lovecraft
Robert Ludlum
Peter Maas
Alistair MacLean
Norman Mailer
*Richard Matheson
W. Somerset Maugham
Colleen McCullough
Ian McEwan
*Terry McMillan
Larry McMurtry
Herman Melville
James Michener
L.M. Montgomery
Vladimir Nabokov
Joyce Carol Oates
*John O'Hara
Marcel Pagnol
Nicholas Pileggi
Edgar Allan Poe
Katherine Ann Porter
Mario Puzo
Ruth Rendell
Anne Rice
Harold Robbins
Sir Walter Scott
Sidney Sheldon
Mary Shelley
Danielle Steel
John Steinbeck
Stendahl

Robert Louis Stevenson
Bram Stoker
Harriet Beecher Stowe
Jacqueline Susann
Jonathan Swift
Paul Theroux
Jim Thompson
James Thurber
J.R.R. Tolkien
Leo Tolstoy
Scott Turow
Mark Twain
John Updike
Leon Uris
Jules Verne
Kurt Vonnegut
Alice Walker
Edgar Wallace
Joseph Wambaugh
Evelyn Waugh
H.G. Wells
Edith Wharton
William Wharton
Oscar Wilde
Thornton Wilder
Virginia Woolf
Cornell Woolrich
Herman Wouk

The Bowery Boys
*Buffalo Bill Cody
Bulldog Drummond
Carry On
Charlie Brown and the
    Peanuts Gang
Charlie Chan
Classics
Corman's Mama

Director/Star Teams:
*Boetticher & Scott
*Capra & Stewart
Carpenter & Russell
*Donner & Gibson

Kibbles and Series Index

Recurrent characters, cinematic collaborations, various adaptations, and important behind-the-scenes personnel information is the focus of the **Kibbles and Series Index**. These categories are listed alphabetically. **A tipped triangle indicates a video rated three bones or higher.**

Adapted

Adapted

Adapted

Adventures of Red Ryder
Adventures of Smilin' Jack
The Amazing Spider-Man
Arcadia of My Youth
Barbarella
The Belles of St. Trinian's ✐
Big Zapper
Blondie
Blondie Has Trouble
Blondie Hits the Jackpot
Blondie in Society
Blondie Knows Best
Blondie Takes a Vacation
Blondie's Blessed Event
Casper ✐
Cool World
Crimewave
Dennis the Menace
Dennis the Menace: Dinosaur
   Hunter
Dennis the Menace Strikes
   Again
Dick Tracy
Dick Tracy vs. Cueball
Dick Tracy's Dilemma
Dr. Strange
Edward Scissorhands ✐
Elvira, Mistress of the Dark
Fatty Finn
The Fighting Redhead
The Flash
The Flash 2: Revenge of the
   Trickster
Flash Gordon
Flesh Gordon 2: Flesh
   Gordon Meets the Cosmic
   Cheerleaders
The Flintstones
Friday Foster
Frostbiter: Wrath of the
   Wendigo
George of the Jungle ✐
The Great St. Trinian's Train
   Robbery
The Guyver
Guyver 2: Dark Hero
Heavy Metal ✐
Hillbilly Blitzkrieg
Howard the Duck
It's a Great Life
Jane & the Lost City
Kowloon Assignment
Li'l Abner
Little Nemo: Adventures in
   Slumberland
Little Orphan Annie
The Mask ✐
Maybe ... Maybe Not
Mighty Morphin Power
   Rangers: The Movie
Mr. Magoo
Pee Wee's Big Adventure ✐
The Perils of Gwendoline
Petit Con
Phantom 2040 Movie: The
   Ghost Who Walks
The Pink Panther ✐
The Pink Panther Strikes
   Again ✐
Prince Valiant
The Pure Hell of St. Trinian's
Reg'lar Fellers
The Return of Swamp Thing
Richie Rich
The Sad Sack
Supergirl
Superman 2 ✐
Tank Girl
Teenage Mutant Ninja
   Turtles: The Movie
Teenage Mutant Ninja Turtles
   2: The Secret of the Ooze

Teenage Mutant Ninja Turtles
   3
Timecop
Tom and Jerry: The Movie
Turbo: A Power Rangers
   Movie
The Villain
Wicked City
Wild Palms
The Wild World of Batwoman

Adapted from a Fairy Tale

The Adventures of Pinocchio
Aladdin
Aladdin ✐
Aladdin and His Wonderful
   Lamp
Alice in Wonderland
Alice's Adventures in
   Wonderland
Beanstalk
Beauty and the Beast ✐
Beauty and the Beast
Beauty and the Beast ✐
The Blue Light ✐
The Boy Who Left Home to
   Find Out About the
   Shivers
Butterfly Ball
Cannon Movie Tales: Red
   Riding Hood
Cannon Movie Tales:
   Sleeping Beauty
Cannon Movie Tales: The
   Emperor's New Clothes
Casey at the Bat
Cinderella ✐
Cinderella
Cinderella 2000
Cinderfella
The Company of Wolves ✐
The Dancing Princesses
Deadtime Stories
Donkey Skin ✐
Dos Cruces en Danger Pass ✐
The Emperor's New Clothes
Ever After: A Cinderella Story
Fairy Tales
Freeway
Frog
Fun & Fancy Free ✐
George Balanchine's The
   Nutcracker
The Glass Slipper
Goldilocks & the Three Bears
Green Snake
Hans Christian Andersen
Hansel and Gretel
Happily Ever After
A Hungarian Fairy Tale ✐
Irish Cinderella
Jack & the Beanstalk
La Petite Sirene
Les Visiteurs du Soir ✐
The Little Match Girl
The Little Mermaid
The Little Mermaid ✐
Little Red Riding Hood
The Magic Fountain
The Magic Sword
Magical Wonderland
March of the Wooden
   Soldiers ✐
Mother Goose Rock 'n'
   Rhyme
The NeverEnding Story ✐
The NeverEnding Story 3:
   Escape from Fantasia
The Nightingale
The Nutcracker Prince

Nutcracker: The Motion
   Picture
Once Upon a Brothers Grimm
Peter Pan ✐
The Pied Piper of Hamelin
Pin...
Pinocchio ✐
Pinocchio
Pinocchio's Revenge
Pinocchio's Storybook
   Adventures
The Princess and the Pea
The Princess and the
   Swineherd
The Princess Bride ✐
Princess Cinderella
The Princess Who Never
   Laughed
Puss 'n Boots
Rapunzel
Red Riding Hood
Rip van Winkle
Rumpelstiltskin
The Scalawag Bunch
Sleeping Beauty ✐
Sleeping Beauty
The Snow Queen
Snow White
Snow White: A Tale of Terror
Snow White and the Seven
   Dwarfs
Snow White and the Three
   Stooges
The Swan
The Swan Princess
The Tale of the Frog Prince ✐
The Three Little Pigs
Thumbelina
The Tin Soldier
Tom Thumb ✐
Who Slew Auntie Roo?
The Wishmaker
The Witches ✐
The Wonderful World of the
   Brothers Grimm
The Wonders of Aladdin

Adapted from a Game

Clue
Double Dragon
Mortal Kombat 1: The Movie
Mortal Kombat 2: Annihilation
Street Fighter
Super Mario Bros.
Tag: The Assassination
   Game

Adapted from a Play or Musical

Abe Lincoln in Illinois ✐
The Adventures of Robin
   Hood ✐
Aelita: Queen of Mars
Age Old Friends ✐
Agnes of God
Ah, Wilderness! ✐
Alfie ✐
Alice
All My Sons ✐
Amadeus ✐
American Buffalo
Anastasia
Animal Crackers ✐
The Animal Kingdom ✐
Anna Christie ✐
Anna Christie
Annie
The Anniversary
Another Country
Any Wednesday

Arsenic and Old Lace ✐
As Is
As You Desire Me ✐
August
The Avenger
The Awful Truth ✐
Babes in Arms
Babes in Toyland
Baby Doll ✐
Baby, the Rain Must Fall
The Bacchantes
The Bad Seed
The Balcony ✐
The Ballad of the Sad Cafe
Bar Girls
Barefoot in the Park ✐
Beatlemania! The Movie
Beau Brummel
Beau Brummel ✐
Beautiful Thing ✐
Becket ✐
Becky Sharp
Being at Home with Claude
Bells Are Ringing ✐
Bent
Best Foot Forward
The Best Little Whorehouse in
   Texas
The Best Man ✐
Betrayal
Beyond Therapy
The Big Knife ✐
Big News
Billie
Biloxi Blues
The Birth of a Nation ✐
Bitter Sweet
Black Limelight
Black Lizard
Black Orpheus ✐
Blessed Event ✐
Blithe Spirit ✐
Blood Wedding ✐
Bluebeard's Eighth Wife ✐
Bodies, Rest & Motion
Bophal ✐
Born Yesterday ✐
Born Yesterday
Boy Meets Girl ✐
The Boys in the Band ✐
The Boys Next Door
Breaking the Code
Breaking Up
Breath of Scandal
The Brig ✐
Brigadoon ✐
Brighton Beach Memoirs ✐
Brilliant Lies
Broadway Bound
Broken Glass
A Bronx Tale ✐
A Brother's Kiss
The Browning Version ✐
The Browning Version
Bus Stop ✐
Butterflies Are Free ✐
Bye, Bye, Birdie ✐
Cabaret ✐
Cactus Flower
Caesar and Cleopatra
California Suite ✐
Can-Can
Casablanca ✐
Casanova Brown
Cast a Dark Shadow ✐
Casual Sex?
The Cat and the Canary
Cat on a Hot Tin Roof ✐
Cat on a Hot Tin Roof
Cavalcade ✐
Cease Fire
Ceiling Zero ✐
The Chalk Garden ✐

Chapter Two
Charm of La Boheme
The Chase
The Cheap Detective ✐
Children of a Lesser God ✐
The Children's Hour
Chimes at Midnight ✐
China
The Chocolate Soldier
A Chorus Line
A Chorus of Disapproval
Circle of Love
Clarence Darrow ✐
Clarence, the Cross-eyed
   Lion ✐
Clash by Night ✐
The Climax
Cold Comfort
Columbo: Prescription Murder
Come Back, Little Sheba ✐
Come Back to the Five &
   Dime Jimmy Dean, Jimmy
   Dean ✐
Come Blow Your Horn ✐
Command Decision
Conduct Unbecoming
The Connection
Cool Mikado
Coquette
The Corn Is Green ✐
Cosi ✐
The Count of the Old Town
Country Girl ✐
County Fair
Craig's Wife ✐
Crimes of the Heart
The Crucible ✐
Curse of the Starving Class
Cyrano de Bergerac
Cyrano de Bergerac ✐
Da
Daddy's Dyin'...Who's Got the
   Will?
Damn Yankees ✐
A Day in the Death of Joe
   Egg ✐
Day of Wrath ✐
Daybreak
Dead End ✐
Dead Heart ✐
Death and the Maiden ✐
Death of a Salesman ✐
Deathtrap
The Desert Song
The Designated Mourner
Desire Under the Elms
Desk Set ✐
Desperate Hours ✐
Detective Story ✐
Devil Girl from Mars
The Devils ✐
The Devil's Brother
The Devil's Disciple ✐
Dial "M" for Murder ✐
Diary of a Hitman
The Dining Room
Dinner at Eight ✐
Disraeli ✐
The Divorce of Lady X
The Doctor and the Devils
Doctor X
Doll Face
A Doll's House
A Doll's House ✐
Don't Drink the Water
Double Wedding ✐
Dracula ✐
The Dresser ✐
Driving Miss Daisy ✐
Drunks
DuBarry Was a Lady
Duet for One
Dumb Waiter

Books

Classics

Disney

Breakin' Through
Candleshoe
The Castaway Cowboy
The Cat from Outer Space
Charley and the Angel
Charlie, the Lonesome
    Cougar
Cheetah
Child of Glass
The Computer Wore Tennis
    Shoes
Condorman
Darby O'Gill & the Little
    People♪
Davy Crockett and the River
    Pirates
Davy Crockett, King of the
    Wild Frontier♪
The Devil & Max Devlin
Dr. Syn, Alias the Scarecrow
D3: The Mighty Ducks
Emil and the Detectives
Escapade in Florence
Escape to Witch Mountain♪
A Far Off Place
The Fighting Prince of
    Donegal
Flight of the Grey Wolf
Flight of the Navigator
Flubber
Freaky Friday
Fun & Fancy Free♪
The Girl Who Spelled
    Freedom♪
The Gnome-Mobile
Gone Are the Days
A Goofy Movie
The Great Locomotive Chase
Greyfriars Bobby
Gus
Heavyweights
Herbie Goes Bananas
Herbie Goes to Monte Carlo
Herbie Rides Again
Homeward Bound: The
    Incredible Journey♪
Honey, I Blew Up the Kid
Honey, I Shrunk the Kids
Honey, We Shrunk Ourselves
The Horse in the Gray Flannel
    Suit
The Horse Without a Head
Horsemasters
Hot Lead & Cold Feet
The Hunchback of Notre
    Dame♪
In Search of the Castaways♪
The Incredible Journey
Iron Will
The Island at the Top of the
    World
Johnny Shiloh
Johnny Tremain & the Sons of
    Liberty
The Journey of Natty Gann♪
Justin Morgan Had a Horse
King of the Grizzlies
The Last Flight of Noah's Ark
Lt. Robin Crusoe, U.S.N.
The Light in the Forest
The Littlest Horse Thieves
The Littlest Outlaw
Lots of Luck
The Love Bug
Love Leads the Way
Mary Poppins♪
Menace on the Mountain
Mickey's Christmas Carol♪
Million Dollar Duck
Miracle Down Under
The Miracle of the White
    Stallions

The Misadventures of Merlin
    Jones
Monkeys, Go Home!
Monkey's Uncle
Moon Pilot
The Moon-Spinners
Mooncussers
Mosby's Marauders
My Dog, the Thief
Napoleon and Samantha♪
Never a Dull Moment
Newsies
Night Crossing
Nikki, the Wild Dog of the
    North
The Nine Lives of Elfego Baca
No Deposit, No Return
The North Avenue Irregulars
Now You See Him, Now You
    Don't
Old Yeller♪
The One and Only, Genuine,
    Original Family Band♪
101 Dalmatians
One Little Indian
One Magic Christmas
One of Our Dinosaurs Is
    Missing
The Parent Trap
Pete's Dragon
Pocahontas
Pollyanna♪
Return from Witch Mountain
Return to Oz
Ride a Wild Pony♪
Rob Roy—The Highland
    Rogue
The Rocketeer♪
Sammy, the Way-Out Seal
Savage Sam
Scandalous John
The Secret of El Zorro
The Shaggy D.A.
The Shaggy Dog
The Sign of Zorro
Smith!
Smoke
Snowball Express
So Dear to My Heart♪
Son of Flubber
The Story of Robin Hood &
    His Merrie Men♪
Summer Magic
Superdad
The Swiss Family Robinson♪
The Sword & the Rose
Tall Tale: The Unbelievable
    Adventures of Pecos Bill
Ten Who Dared
That Darn Cat
Third Man on the Mountain
Those Calloways
The Three Lives of
    Thomasina♪
3 Ninjas
3 Ninjas Kick Back
A Tiger Walks
Toby Tyler♪
Tom and Huck♪
Tonka
Toothless
Toy Story♪
Treasure Island♪
The Treasure of Matecumbe
20,000 Leagues Under the
    Sea♪
The Ugly Dachshund
Undergrads♪
Unidentified Flying Oddball
Waltz King
The Watcher in the Woods
Westward Ho, the Wagons!
White Fang♪

White Fang 2: The Myth of the
    White Wolf
The Wild Country
Wild Hearts Can't Be Broken♪
The World's Greatest Athlete

Doc Holliday

Cheyenne Autumn
Gunfight at the O.K. Corral♪
Hour of the Gun
My Darling Clementine♪
The Outlaw
Tombstone♪
Wyatt Earp

Dr. Christian

Courageous Dr. Christian
Dr. Christian Meets the
    Women
Meet Dr. Christian
Melody for Three
Remedy for Riches
They Meet Again

Dr. Mabuse

Das Testament des Dr.
    Mabuse♪
Dr. Mabuse, Parts 1 & 2♪
Dr. Mabuse vs. Scotland Yard
The Invisible Dr. Mabuse♪
The Return of Dr. Mabuse
The Thousand Eyes of Dr.
    Mabuse

Dr. Seuss

The 5000 Fingers of Dr. T.♪
How the Grinch Stole
    Christmas♪

Dracula

Abbott and Costello Meet
    Frankenstein♪
The Best of the Two Ronnies
Blood of Dracula
Blood of Dracula's Castle
Bram Stoker's Dracula♪
The Brides of Dracula
Count Dracula
Count Dracula's Great Love
The Creeps
Dracula♪
Dracula
Dracula A.D. 1972
Dracula & Son
Dracula: Dead and Loving It
Dracula/Garden of Eden
Dracula Has Risen from the
    Grave
Dracula, Prince of Darkness
Dracula Rising
Dracula (Spanish Version)
Dracula Sucks
Dracula: Up in Harlem
Dracula vs. Frankenstein
Dracula's Daughter♪
Dracula's Great Love
Dracula's Last Rites
Dracula's Widow
The Horror of Dracula♪
House of Dracula
House of Frankenstein
Hysterical
Love at First Bite
Mad Monster Party
The Monster Squad
Nocturna
Return of Dracula
Return of the Vampire
The Satanic Rites of Dracula

The Scars of Dracula
The Screaming Dead
Son of Dracula♪
Taste the Blood of Dracula
To Die For
Transylvania 6-5000
Vampire Circus
Waxwork
Zoltan...Hound of Dracula

Elvisfilm

Blue Hawaii
Change of Habit
Charro!
Clambake
Double Trouble
Easy Come, Easy Go
Elvis and Me
Elvis in Hollywood♪
Elvis: The Movie
Flaming Star♪
Follow That Dream
Frankie and Johnny
Fun in Acapulco
G.I. Blues
Girl Happy
Girls! Girls! Girls!
Harum Scarum
Heartbreak Hotel
Honeymoon in Vegas
It Happened at the World's
    Fair
Jailhouse Rock♪
Kid Galahad
King Creole
Kissin' Cousins
Live a Little, Love a Little
Love Me Tender
Loving You
Paradise, Hawaiian Style
Rock-a-Doodle
Roustabout
Speedway
Spinout
Stay Away, Joe
This Is Elvis
Tickle Me
Top Secret!♪
The Trouble with Girls (and
    How To Get Into It)♪
True Romance
Viva Las Vegas
Wild in the Country
The Woman Who Loved Elvis

"E.T." & Rip-Offs

E.T.: The Extra-Terrestrial♪
Mac and Me
Magic in the Water

Faerie Tale Theatre

Aladdin and His Wonderful
    Lamp
Beauty and the Beast
The Boy Who Left Home to
    Find Out About the
    Shivers
Cinderella
The Dancing Princesses
The Emperor's New Clothes
Goldilocks & the Three Bears
Hansel and Gretel
Jack & the Beanstalk
The Little Mermaid
Little Red Riding Hood
The Nightingale
The Pied Piper of Hamelin
Pinocchio
The Princess and the Pea
The Princess Who Never
    Laughed

Puss 'n Boots
Rapunzel
Rip van Winkle
Rumpelstiltskin
Sleeping Beauty
The Snow Queen
Snow White and the Seven
    Dwarfs
The Tale of the Frog Prince♪
The Three Little Pigs
Thumbelina

The Falcon

The Amityville Curse
The Devil's Cargo
The Falcon in Hollywood
The Falcon in Mexico
The Falcon Takes Over/
    Strange Bargain
The Falcon's Adventure/
    Armored Car Robbery
The Falcon's Brother

Family Viewing

The Absent-Minded
    Professor♪
Adventures in Dinosaur City
Adventures in Spying
The Adventures of Bullwhip
    Griffin
The Adventures of
    Huckleberry Finn
The Adventures of Mark
    Twain♪
The Adventures of Pinocchio
African Journey
Aladdin♪
Aladdin and His Wonderful
    Lamp
Alaska
All Dogs Go to Heaven 2
Almost Partners
The Amazing Dobermans
The Amazing Panda
    Adventure
An American Tail
An American Tail: Fievel
    Goes West
Amy
Anastasia
And the Children Shall Lead
And You Thought Your
    Parents Were Weird!
Andre
Angels in the Outfield
Anne of Avonlea♪
Anne of Green Gables♪
The Apple Dumpling Gang
The Apple Dumpling Gang
    Rides Again
The Aristocats♪
Ava's Magical Adventure
Babar: The Movie
Babe♪
Babes in Toyland
Baby's Day Out
Back to Hannibal: The Return
    of Tom Sawyer and
    Huckleberry Finn
The Ballad of Paul Bunyan
Bambi♪
The Barefoot Executive
Barney's Great Adventure
Batman♪
Batman Forever♪
Be My Valentine, Charlie
    Brown
Beauty and the Beast♪
Beethoven
Beethoven's 2nd
Behave Yourself!

A League of Their Own
Lethal Weapon 3
Patriot Games
Sister Act
Under Siege
Unforgiven
Wayne's World
White Men Can't Jump

Top Grossing Films of 1993
Aladdin
Cliffhanger
A Few Good Men
The Firm
Free Willy
The Fugitive
In the Line of Fire
Indecent Proposal
Jurassic Park
Sleepless in Seattle

Top Grossing Films of 1994
Ace Ventura: Pet Detective
Clear and Present Danger
The Client
The Flintstones
Forrest Gump
The Lion King
The Mask
Maverick
Speed
True Lies

Top Grossing Films of 1995
Ace Ventura: When Nature Calls
Apollo 13
Batman Forever
Casper
Die Hard: With a Vengeance
Goldeneye
Jumanji
Pocahontas
Seven
Toy Story

Top Grossing Films of 1996
The Birdcage
Broken Arrow
The Cable Guy
Courage Under Fire
Eraser
The First Wives Club
The Hunchback of Notre Dame
Independence Day
Jack
Jerry Maguire
Mission: Impossible
The Nutty Professor
101 Dalmatians
Phenomenon
Ransom
The Rock
Space Jam
Star Trek: First Contact
A Time to Kill
Twister

Top Grossing Films of 1997
Air Force One
Batman and Robin
Con Air
Conspiracy Theory

Contact
Face/Off
Flubber
George of the Jungle
Hercules
I Know What You Did Last Summer
Jerry Maguire
Liar Liar
The Lost World: Jurassic Park 2
Men in Black
My Best Friend's Wedding
Scream
Scream 2
Star Wars
Titanic
Tomorrow Never Dies

The Trail Blazers
Arizona Whirlwind
Death Valley Rangers
The Law Rides Again
Outlaw Trail

Trash
The Adventurers
The Alien Factor
Alien Massacre
Alien Prey
All the Lovin' Kinfolk
The Allnighter
Alone in the T-Shirt Zone
Amazon Women on the Moon
America
American Tickler
Andy Warhol's Bad
Andy Warhol's Dracula
Andy Warhol's Frankenstein
Angel of H.E.A.T.
Assassin of Youth
Assault of the Killer Bimbos
The Astounding She-Monster
The Astro-Zombies
Attack of the Beast Creatures
Attack of the Giant Leeches
Attack of the Killer Tomatoes
Bad Girls Go to Hell
Barn of the Naked Dead
The Beast of Yucca Flats
The Beast that Killed Women
The Beautiful, the Bloody and the Bare
Bela Lugosi Meets a Brooklyn Gorilla
The Bellboy and the Playgirls
Best Buns on the Beach
Beverly Hills Bodysnatchers
Beverly Hills Knockouts
The Big Gag
Bikini Drive-In
The Bitch
Black Venus
Blazing Stewardesses
Blood Freak
Blood of Ghastly Horror
Bloodlust
Bloodsucking Freaks
Bloodsucking Nazi Zombies
Body of Evidence
Bottoms Up
Brain of Blood
Candy Tangerine Man
The Carpetbaggers
The Castle of Fu Manchu
Cheerleader Camp
Cocaine Fiends
The Commies Are Coming, the Commies Are Coming
The Conqueror
The Corpse Grinders

Corruption
The Crater Lake Monster
Creature of Destruction
Creeping Terror
Crypt of the Living Dead
Curse of the Blue Lights
Curse of the Living Dead
Cyborg
Cycle Vixens
Dead Aim
The Dead Next Door
Delinquent School Girls
Demons
Desperate Living
Desperate Teenage Lovedolls
Detour to Danger
Dolemite
Dolemite 2: Human Tornado
Dracula vs. Frankenstein
Drop Dead Fred
Drum
Drums O'Voodoo
Dungeon of Harrow
Eegah!
Escape from Planet Earth
Fat Guy Goes Nutzoid
Female Trouble
The Fifth Floor
Film House Fever
Five Minutes to Love
Flesh and Blood Show
Frankenstein '80
Frankenstein Meets the Space Monster
Frostbiter: Wrath of the Wendigo
Fun Down There
Galactic Gigolo
Ghoul School
Glen or Glenda: Confessions of Ed Wood
Gore-Met Zombie Chef From Hell
Gun Cargo
Heartstopper
Hitchhikers
Hold Me, Thrill Me, Kiss Me
Hollywood After Dark
Hollywood Chainsaw Hookers
The Hollywood Strangler Meets the Skid Row Slasher
Honkytonk Nights
Horror of Party Beach
The House of Usher
I Spit on Your Grave
I Was a Zombie for the FBI
Ilsa, Harem Keeper of the Oil Sheiks
Ilsa, She-Wolf of the SS
Ilsa, the Tigress of Siberia
Impulse
In the Cold of the Night
Incredibly Strange Creatures Who Stopped Living and Became Mixed-Up Zombies
Infra-Man
Invasion of the Bee Girls
Island of Lost Girls
It's Not the Size That Counts
Jail Bait
Jungle Master
Killer Tomatoes Eat France
Killer Tomatoes Strike Back
Lady Godiva Rides
The Last Season
The Lonely Lady
Lost, Lonely, and Vicious
A Man Called Rage
Man with Two Heads
Manos, the Hands of Fate
Master Blaster

Microwave Massacre
Midnight 2: Sex, Death, and Videotape
Mind Trap
Mondo Balardo
Mondo Trasho
Motel Hell
Multiple Maniacs
The Naked Flame
A Night in Heaven
Night of the Cobra Woman
Night of the Demon
Night of the Ghouls
Nightmare
A Nymphoid Barbarian in Dinosaur Hell
On the Edge: The Survival of Dana
Once Is Not Enough
One Down, Two to Go!
One More Saturday Night
Orgy of the Dead
Out of the Body
The Outcast
Pagan Island
The Perverse Countess
Phantasm
Pink Flamingos
Plan 9 from Outer Space
Please Don't Eat My Mother
Pot, Parents, and Police
The Power
The Psychic
Queen of Outer Space
Rabid Grannies
Rat Pfink a Boo-Boo
The Rats Are Coming! The Werewolves Are Here!
Reform School Girl
Return of the Family Man
Return of the Killer Tomatoes!
Return to the Blue Lagoon
Revenge of the Virgins
Robot Monster
Rush
Satan in High Heels
Satan's Cheerleaders
Saturday the 14th Strikes Back
Savage Intruder
Screen Test
Sgt. Kabukiman N.Y.P.D.
She Demons
She-Devils on Wheels
The Sinister Invasion
The Sinister Urge
Slaves in Bondage
Sleazemania III: The Good, the Bad & the Sleazy
Some Call It Loving
Sorority Girl
Space Monster
The Speed Lovers
Streetfight
Sweet Georgia
Sweet Trash
Tarzan, the Ape Man
Teenage Gang Debs
Teenage Mother
Teenage Strangler
Teenagers from Outer Space
Terror in the Jungle
Texas Layover
They Saved Hitler's Brain
Tomboy
Torture Dungeon
Train Station Pickups
The Trial of Billy Jack
Troma's War
Unholy Rollers
Valley of the Dolls
Vampire Vixens from Venus
Vegas in Space

Violated
The Violent Years
White Pongo
Wild Ones on Wheels
Wild Women of Wongo
Winterbeast
World of the Depraved
Youth Aflame
You've Ruined Me, Eddie
The Zombie Army

Troma Films
Beware! Children at Play
Blades
Blondes Have More Guns
Bloodsucking Freaks
Bugged!
Cannibal! The Musical
Chopper Chicks in Zombietown
The Chosen One: Legend of the Raven
Class of Nuke 'Em High
Class of Nuke 'Em High 2: Subhumanoid Meltdown
Class of Nuke 'Em High 3: The Good, the Bad and the Subhumanoid
Combat Shock
Cry Uncle
Deadly Daphne's Revenge
Evil Clutch
Fat Guy Goes Nutzoid
Ferocious Female Freedom Fighters
Frostbiter: Wrath of the Wendigo
Girls School Screamers
I Married a Vampire
I Was a Teenage TV Terrorist
Malibu Hot Summer
Monster in the Closet
A Nymphoid Barbarian in Dinosaur Hell
Preacherman
Rabid Grannies
Redneck Zombies
Sgt. Kabukiman N.Y.P.D.
Splatter University
Squeeze Play
Stuck on You
Student Confidential
Surf Nazis Must Die
The Toxic Avenger
The Toxic Avenger, Part 2
The Toxic Avenger, Part 3: The Last Temptation of Toxie
Troma's War
Tromeo & Juliet
Vegas in Space
Wizards of the Demon Sword
Zombie Island Massacre

Universal Studios' Classic Horror
Abbott and Costello Meet Dr. Jekyll and Mr. Hyde
Abbott and Costello Meet Frankenstein
Abbott and Costello Meet the Killer, Boris Karloff
The Black Cat
The Bride of Frankenstein
Creature from the Black Lagoon
The Creature Walks Among Us
Dracula
Dracula (Spanish Version)
Dracula's Daughter

Awards Index

The **Awards Index** lists films honored (or dishonored, in some cases) by over 20 national and international award bodies, representing over 100 categories of recognition. This information can also be found in the reviews, following the credits. Nominations have been added, increasing the usefulness (and size) of this index. **Only features available on video and reviewed in the main section are listed in this index; movies not yet released on video are not covered here.** As award-winning and nominated films find their way to video, they will be added to the review section and covered in this index. **The award winners are listed first and have a star preceding them.** The awards covered include:

Academy Awards
Australia Film Institute
British Academy of Film and Television Arts
Broadcast Film Critics Awards
Cannes Film Festival
Cesar Awards (French)
Directors Guild of America
Genie Awards (Canadian)
Golden Globe
Golden Raspberries

Independent Spirit Awards
Los Angeles Film Critics Association Awards
Montreal Film Festival
MTV Movie Awards
National Board of Review Awards
National Film Registry
National Society of Film Critics Awards
New York Film Critics Awards
Screen Actors Guild Awards
Sundance Film Festival
Toronto-City Awards
Writers Guild of America

ACADEMY AWARDS

ACTOR

1928
★ Emil Jannings/*Last Command*
Charlie Chaplin/*The Circus*

1930
★ George Arliss/*Disraeli*
Wallace Beery/*The Big House*
Ronald Colman/*Bulldog Drummond*

1931
★ Lionel Barrymore/*A Free Soul*
Richard Dix/*Cimarron*
Adolphe Menjou/*The Front Page*

1932
★ Wallace Beery/*The Champ*
★ Fredric March/*Dr. Jekyll and Mr. Hyde*
Alfred Lunt/*The Guardsman*

1933
★ Charles Laughton/*The Private Life of Henry VIII*
Paul Muni/*I Am a Fugitive from a Chain Gang*

1934
★ Clark Gable/*It Happened One Night*

William Powell/*The Thin Man*

1935
★ Victor McLaglen/*The Informer*
Clark Gable/*Mutiny on the Bounty*
Charles Laughton/*Mutiny on the Bounty*
Franchot Tone/*Mutiny on the Bounty*

1936
★ Paul Muni/*The Story of Louis Pasteur*
Gary Cooper/*Mr. Deeds Goes to Town*
Walter Huston/*Dodsworth*
William Powell/*My Man Godfrey*
Spencer Tracy/*San Francisco*

1937
★ Spencer Tracy/*Captains Courageous*
Charles Boyer/*Conquest*
Fredric March/*A Star Is Born*
Paul Muni/*The Life of Emile Zola*

1938
★ Spencer Tracy/*Boys Town*
Charles Boyer/*Algiers*
James Cagney/*Angels with Dirty Faces*
Robert Donat/*The Citadel*
Leslie Howard/*Pygmalion*

1939
★ Robert Donat/*Goodbye, Mr. Chips*
Clark Gable/*Gone with the Wind*
Laurence Olivier/*Wuthering Heights*
Mickey Rooney/*Babes in Arms*
James Stewart/*Mr. Smith Goes to Washington*

1940
★ James Stewart/*The Philadelphia Story*
Charlie Chaplin/*The Great Dictator*
Henry Fonda/*The Grapes of Wrath*
Raymond Massey/*Abe Lincoln in Illinois*
Laurence Olivier/*Rebecca*

1941
★ Gary Cooper/*Sergeant York*
Cary Grant/*Penny Serenade*
Walter Huston/*The Devil & Daniel Webster*
Robert Montgomery/*Here Comes Mr. Jordan*
Orson Welles/*Citizen Kane*

1942
★ James Cagney/*Yankee Doodle Dandy*
Ronald Colman/*Random Harvest*
Gary Cooper/*The Pride of the Yankees*

Walter Pidgeon/*Mrs. Miniver*

1943
★ Paul Lukas/*Watch on the Rhine*
Humphrey Bogart/*Casablanca*
Gary Cooper/*For Whom the Bell Tolls*
Walter Pidgeon/*Madame Curie*
Mickey Rooney/*The Human Comedy*

1944
★ Bing Crosby/*Going My Way*
Charles Boyer/*Gaslight*
Barry Fitzgerald/*Going My Way*
Cary Grant/*None But the Lonely Heart*
Alexander Knox/*Wilson*

1945
★ Ray Milland/*The Lost Weekend*
Bing Crosby/*The Bells of St. Mary's*
Gene Kelly/*Anchors Aweigh*
Gregory Peck/*The Keys of the Kingdom*
Cornel Wilde/*A Song to Remember*

1946
★ Fredric March/*The Best Years of Our Lives*
Laurence Olivier/*Henry V*
Larry Parks/*The Jolson Story*

Gregory Peck/*The Yearling*
James Stewart/*It's a Wonderful Life*

1947
★ Ronald Colman/*A Double Life*
John Garfield/*Body and Soul*
Gregory Peck/*Gentleman's Agreement*
William Powell/*Life with Father*

1948
★ Laurence Olivier/*Hamlet*
Lew Ayres/*Johnny Belinda*
Montgomery Clift/*The Search*

1949
★ Broderick Crawford/*All the King's Men*
Kirk Douglas/*Champion*
Gregory Peck/*Twelve O'Clock High*
John Wayne/*Sands of Iwo Jima*

1950
★ Jose Ferrer/*Cyrano de Bergerac*
Louis Calhern/*The Magnificent Yankee*
William Holden/*Sunset Boulevard*
James Stewart/*Harvey*
Spencer Tracy/*Father of the Bride*

Awards Index

1247

1990
- ★ Jeremy Irons/*Reversal of Fortune*
- Kevin Costner/*Dances with Wolves*
- Robert De Niro/*Awakenings*
- Gerard Depardieu/*Cyrano de Bergerac*
- Richard Harris/*The Field*

1991
- ★ Anthony Hopkins/*The Silence of the Lambs*
- Warren Beatty/*Bugsy*
- Robert De Niro/*Cape Fear*
- Nick Nolte/*The Prince of Tides*
- Robin Williams/*The Fisher King*

1992
- ★ Al Pacino/*Scent of a Woman*
- Robert Downey, Jr./*Chaplin*
- Clint Eastwood/*Unforgiven*
- Stephen Rea/*The Crying Game*
- Denzel Washington/*Malcolm X*

1993
- ★ Tom Hanks/*Philadelphia*
- Daniel Day-Lewis/*In the Name of the Father*
- Laurence "Larry" Fishburne/*What's Love Got to Do with It?*
- Anthony Hopkins/*The Remains of the Day*
- Liam Neeson/*Schindler's List*

1994
- ★ Tom Hanks/*Forrest Gump*
- Morgan Freeman/*The Shawshank Redemption*
- Nigel Hawthorne/*The Madness of King George*
- Paul Newman/*Nobody's Fool*
- John Travolta/*Pulp Fiction*

1995
- ★ Nicolas Cage/*Leaving Las Vegas*
- Richard Dreyfuss/*Mr. Holland's Opus*
- Anthony Hopkins/*Nixon*
- Sean Penn/*Dead Man Walking*
- Massimo Troisi/*The Postman*

1996
- ★ Geoffrey Rush/*Shine*
- Tom Cruise/*Jerry Maguire*
- Ralph Fiennes/*The English Patient*
- Woody Harrelson/*The People vs. Larry Flynt*
- Billy Bob Thornton/*Sling Blade*

1997
- ★ Jack Nicholson/*As Good As It Gets*
- Matt Damon/*Good Will Hunting*
- Robert Duvall/*The Apostle*
- Peter Fonda/*Ulee's Gold*
- Dustin Hoffman/*Wag the Dog*

ACTOR—SUPPORTING

1936
- ★ Walter Brennan/*Come and Get It*
- Mischa Auer/*My Man Godfrey*
- Stuart Erwin/*Pigskin Parade*
- Basil Rathbone/*Romeo and Juliet*
- Akim Tamiroff/*The General Died at Dawn*

1937
- ★ Joseph Schildkraut/*The Life of Emile Zola*
- Ralph Bellamy/*The Awful Truth*
- Thomas Mitchell/*The Hurricane*
- H.B. Warner/*Lost Horizon*
- Roland Young/*Topper*

1938
- John Garfield/*Four Daughters*
- Gene Lockhart/*Algiers*
- Robert Morley/*Marie Antoinette*

1939
- ★ Thomas Mitchell/*Stagecoach*
- Brian Aherne/*Juarez*
- Harry Carey, Sr./*Mr. Smith Goes to Washington*
- Brian Donlevy/*Beau Geste*
- Claude Rains/*Mr. Smith Goes to Washington*

1940
- ★ Walter Brennan/*The Westerner*
- Albert Basserman/*Foreign Correspondent*
- William Gargan/*They Knew What They Wanted*
- Jack Oakie/*The Great Dictator*
- James Stephenson/*The Letter*

1941
- ★ Donald Crisp/*How Green Was My Valley*
- Walter Brennan/*Sergeant York*
- Charles Coburn/*The Devil & Miss Jones*
- James Gleason/*Here Comes Mr. Jordan*
- Sydney Greenstreet/*The Maltese Falcon*

1942
- ★ Van Heflin/*Johnny Eager*

- William Bendix/*Wake Island*
- Walter Huston/*Yankee Doodle Dandy*
- Frank Morgan/*Tortilla Flat*
- Henry Travers/*Mrs. Miniver*

1943
- ★ Charles Coburn/*The More the Merrier*
- Charles Bickford/*The Song of Bernadette*
- J. Carrol Naish/*Sahara*
- Claude Rains/*Casablanca*
- Akim Tamiroff/*For Whom the Bell Tolls*

1944
- ★ Barry Fitzgerald/*Going My Way*
- Hume Cronyn/*The Seventh Cross*
- Claude Rains/*Mr. Skeffington*
- Clifton Webb/*Laura*
- Monty Woolley/*Since You Went Away*

1945
- ★ James Dunn/*A Tree Grows in Brooklyn*
- Michael Chekhov/*Spellbound*
- John Dall/*The Corn Is Green*

1946
- ★ Harold Russell/*The Best Years of Our Lives*
- William Demarest/*The Jolson Story*
- Claude Rains/*Notorious*
- Clifton Webb/*The Razor's Edge*

1947
- ★ Edmund Gwenn/*Miracle on 34th Street*
- Charles Bickford/*The Farmer's Daughter*
- Robert Ryan/*Crossfire*
- Richard Widmark/*Kiss of Death*

1948
- ★ Walter Huston/*Treasure of the Sierra Madre*
- Charles Bickford/*Johnny Belinda*
- Jose Ferrer/*Joan of Arc*
- Oscar Homolka/*I Remember Mama*

1949
- ★ Dean Jagger/*Twelve O'Clock High*
- John Ireland/*All the King's Men*
- Arthur Kennedy/*Champion*
- Ralph Richardson/*The Heiress*
- James Whitmore/*Battleground*

1950
- ★ George Sanders/*All About Eve*
- Jeff Chandler/*Broken Arrow*

- Sam Jaffe/*The Asphalt Jungle*
- Erich von Stroheim/*Sunset Boulevard*

1951
- ★ Karl Malden/*A Streetcar Named Desire*
- Leo Genn/*Quo Vadis*
- Peter Ustinov/*Quo Vadis*

1952
- ★ Anthony Quinn/*Viva Zapata!*
- Arthur Hunnicutt/*The Big Sky*
- Victor McLaglen/*The Quiet Man*
- Jack Palance/*Sudden Fear*

1953
- ★ Frank Sinatra/*From Here to Eternity*
- Eddie Albert/*Roman Holiday*
- Jack Palance/*Shane*
- Robert Strauss/*Stalag 17*
- Brandon de Wilde/*Shane*

1954
- ★ Edmond O'Brien/*The Barefoot Contessa*
- Lee J. Cobb/*On the Waterfront*
- Karl Malden/*On the Waterfront*
- Rod Steiger/*On the Waterfront*
- Tom Tully/*The Caine Mutiny*

1955
- ★ Jack Lemmon/*Mister Roberts*
- Joe Mantell/*Marty*
- Sal Mineo/*Rebel Without a Cause*
- Arthur O'Connell/*Picnic*

1956
- ★ Anthony Quinn/*Lust for Life*
- Don Murray/*Bus Stop*
- Anthony Perkins/*Friendly Persuasion*
- Robert Stack/*Written on the Wind*

1957
- ★ Red Buttons/*Sayonara*
- Sessue Hayakawa/*The Bridge on the River Kwai*
- Arthur Kennedy/*Peyton Place*
- Russ Tamblyn/*Peyton Place*

1958
- ★ Burl Ives/*The Big Country*
- Theodore Bikel/*The Defiant Ones*
- Lee J. Cobb/*The Brothers Karamazov*
- Arthur Kennedy/*Some Came Running*
- Gig Young/*Teacher's Pet*

1959
- ★ Hugh Griffith/*Ben-Hur*
- Arthur O'Connell/*Anatomy of a Murder*

- George C. Scott/*Anatomy of a Murder*
- Robert Vaughn/*The Young Philadelphians*
- Ed Wynn/*The Diary of Anne Frank*

1960
- ★ Peter Ustinov/*Spartacus*
- Jack Kruschen/*The Apartment*
- Sal Mineo/*Exodus*
- Chill Wills/*The Alamo*

1961
- ★ George Chakiris/*West Side Story*
- Montgomery Clift/*Judgment at Nuremberg*
- Peter Falk/*Pocketful of Miracles*
- Jackie Gleason/*The Hustler*
- George C. Scott/*The Hustler*

1962
- ★ Ed Begley, Sr./*Sweet Bird of Youth*
- Victor Buono/*What Ever Happened to Baby Jane?*
- Telly Savalas/*Birdman of Alcatraz*
- Omar Sharif/*Lawrence of Arabia*
- Terence Stamp/*Billy Budd*

1963
- ★ Melvyn Douglas/*Hud*
- Bobby Darin/*Captain Newman, M.D.*
- Hugh Griffith/*Tom Jones*
- John Huston/*The Cardinal*

1964
- ★ Peter Ustinov/*Topkapi*
- John Gielgud/*Becket*
- Stanley Holloway/*My Fair Lady*
- Edmond O'Brien/*Seven Days in May*
- Lee Tracy/*The Best Man*

1965
- ★ Martin Balsam/*A Thousand Clowns*
- Ian Bannen/*The Flight of the Phoenix*
- Tom Courtenay/*Doctor Zhivago*
- Michael Dunn/*Ship of Fools*
- Frank Finlay/*Othello*

1966
- ★ Walter Matthau/*The Fortune Cookie*
- Mako/*The Sand Pebbles*
- James Mason/*Georgy Girl*
- George Segal/*Who's Afraid of Virginia Woolf?*
- Robert Shaw/*A Man for All Seasons*

1967
- ★ George Kennedy/*Cool Hand Luke*
- John Cassavetes/*The Dirty Dozen*

ACTOR—SUPPORTING
_cont.

Gene Hackman/Bonnie & Clyde
Cecil Kellaway/Guess Who's Coming to Dinner
Michael J. Pollard/Bonnie & Clyde

1968
★ Jack Albertson/The Subject Was Roses
Seymour Cassel/Faces
Daniel Massey/Star!
Jack Wild/Oliver!
Gene Wilder/The Producers

1969
★ Gig Young/They Shoot Horses, Don't They?
Rupert Crosse/The Reivers
Elliott Gould/Bob & Carol & Ted & Alice
Jack Nicholson/Easy Rider
Anthony Quayle/Anne of the Thousand Days

1970
★ John Mills/Ryan's Daughter
Richard Castellano/Lovers and Other Strangers
Chief Dan George/Little Big Man
Gene Hackman/I Never Sang For My Father
John Marley/Love Story

1971
★ Ben Johnson/The Last Picture Show
Jeff Bridges/The Last Picture Show
Leonard Frey/Fiddler on the Roof
Richard Jaeckel/Sometimes a Great Notion
Roy Scheider/The French Connection

1972
★ Joel Grey/Cabaret
Eddie Albert/The Heartbreak Kid
James Caan/The Godfather
Robert Duvall/The Godfather
Al Pacino/The Godfather

1973
★ John Houseman/The Paper Chase
Vincent Gardenia/Bang the Drum Slowly
Jack Gilford/Save the Tiger
Jason Miller/The Exorcist
Randy Quaid/The Last Detail

1974
★ Robert De Niro/The Godfather, Part 2
Fred Astaire/The Towering Inferno
Jeff Bridges/Thunderbolt & Lightfoot
Michael V. Gazzo/The Godfather, Part 2
Lee Strasberg/The Godfather, Part 2

1975
★ George Burns/The Sunshine Boys
Brad Dourif/One Flew Over the Cuckoo's Nest
Burgess Meredith/The Day of the Locust
Chris Sarandon/Dog Day Afternoon
Jack Warden/Shampoo

1976
★ Jason Robards, Jr./All the President's Men
Ned Beatty/Network
Burgess Meredith/Rocky
Laurence Olivier/Marathon Man
Burt Young/Rocky

1977
★ Jason Robards, Jr./Julia
Mikhail Baryshnikov/The Turning Point
Peter Firth/Equus
Alec Guinness/Star Wars
Maximilian Schell/Julia

1978
★ Christopher Walken/The Deer Hunter
Bruce Dern/Coming Home
Richard Farnsworth/Comes a Horseman
John Hurt/Midnight Express
Jack Warden/Heaven Can Wait

1979
★ Melvyn Douglas/Being There
Robert Duvall/Apocalypse Now
Frederic Forrest/The Rose
Justin Henry/Kramer vs. Kramer
Mickey Rooney/The Black Stallion

1980
★ Timothy Hutton/Ordinary People
Judd Hirsch/Ordinary People
Michael O'Keefe/The Great Santini
Joe Pesci/Raging Bull
Jason Robards, Jr./Melvin and Howard

1981
★ John Gielgud/Arthur
James Coco/Only When I Laugh
Ian Holm/Chariots of Fire
Jack Nicholson/Reds

Howard E. Rollins, Jr./Ragtime

1982
★ Louis Gossett, Jr./An Officer and a Gentleman
Charles Durning/The Best Little Whorehouse in Texas
John Lithgow/The World According to Garp
James Mason/The Verdict
Robert Preston/Victor/Victoria

1983
★ Jack Nicholson/Terms of Endearment
Charles Durning/To Be or Not to Be
John Lithgow/Terms of Endearment
Sam Shepard/The Right Stuff
Rip Torn/Cross Creek

1984
★ Haing S. Ngor/The Killing Fields
Adolph Caesar/A Soldier's Story
John Malkovich/Places in the Heart
Noriyuki "Pat" Morita/The Karate Kid
Ralph Richardson/Greystoke: The Legend of Tarzan, Lord of the Apes

1985
★ Don Ameche/Cocoon
Klaus Maria Brandauer/Out of Africa
William Hickey/Prizzi's Honor
Robert Loggia/The Jagged Edge
Eric Roberts/Runaway Train

1986
★ Michael Caine/Hannah and Her Sisters
Tom Berenger/Platoon
Willem Dafoe/Platoon
Denholm Elliott/A Room with a View
Dennis Hopper/Hoosiers

1987
★ Sean Connery/The Untouchables
Albert Brooks/Broadcast News
Morgan Freeman/Street Smart
Vincent Gardenia/Moonstruck
Denzel Washington/Cry Freedom

1988
★ Kevin Kline/A Fish Called Wanda
Alec Guinness/Little Dorrit, Film 1: Nobody's Fault
Martin Landau/Tucker: The Man and His Dream
River Phoenix/Running on Empty

Dean Stockwell/Married to the Mob

1989
★ Denzel Washington/Glory
Danny Aiello/Do the Right Thing
Dan Aykroyd/Driving Miss Daisy
Marlon Brando/A Dry White Season
Martin Landau/Crimes & Misdemeanors

1990
★ Joe Pesci/Goodfellas
Bruce Davison/Longtime Companion
Andy Garcia/The Godfather, Part 3
Graham Greene/Dances with Wolves
Al Pacino/Dick Tracy

1991
★ Jack Palance/City Slickers
Tommy Lee Jones/JFK
Harvey Keitel/Bugsy
Ben Kingsley/Bugsy
Michael Lerner/Barton Fink

1992
★ Gene Hackman/Unforgiven
Jaye Davidson/The Crying Game
Jack Nicholson/A Few Good Men
Al Pacino/Glengarry Glen Ross
David Paymer/Mr. Saturday Night

1993
★ Tommy Lee Jones/The Fugitive
Leonardo DiCaprio/What's Eating Gilbert Grape
Ralph Fiennes/Schindler's List
John Malkovich/In the Line of Fire
Pete Postlethwaite/In the Name of the Father

1994
★ Martin Landau/Ed Wood
Samuel L. Jackson/Pulp Fiction
Chazz Palminteri/Bullets Over Broadway
Paul Scofield/Quiz Show
Gary Sinise/Forrest Gump

1995
★ Kevin Spacey/The Usual Suspects
James Cromwell/Babe
Ed Harris/Apollo 13
Brad Pitt/12 Monkeys
Tim Roth/Rob Roy

1996
★ Cuba Gooding, Jr./Jerry Maguire
William H. Macy/Fargo
Armin Mueller-Stahl/Shine

Edward Norton/Primal Fear
James Woods/Ghosts of Mississippi

1997
★ Robin Williams/Good Will Hunting
As Good As It Gets
Robert Forster/Jackie Brown
Anthony Hopkins/Amistad
Burt Reynolds/Boogie Nights

ACTRESS

1928
★ Janet Gaynor/Sunrise
Gloria Swanson/Sadie Thompson

1929
★ Mary Pickford/Coquette
Bessie Love/Broadway Melody

1930
★ Norma Shearer/The Divorcee
Greta Garbo/Anna Christie
Greta Garbo/Romance

1931
★ Marie Dressler/Min & Bill
Marlene Dietrich/Morocco
Irene Dunne/Cimarron
Norma Shearer/A Free Soul

1932
★ Helen Hayes/The Sin of Madelon Claudet
Lynn Fontanne/The Guardsman

1933
★ Katharine Hepburn/Morning Glory
May Robson/Lady for a Day
Diana Wynyard/Cavalcade

1934
★ Claudette Colbert/It Happened One Night
Grace Moore/One Night of Love
Norma Shearer/The Barretts of Wimpole Street

1935
★ Bette Davis/Dangerous
Katharine Hepburn/Alice Adams
Miriam Hopkins/Becky Sharp

1936
★ Luise Rainer/The Great Ziegfeld
Irene Dunne/Theodora Goes Wild
Carole Lombard/My Man Godfrey
Norma Shearer/Romeo and Juliet

ACTRESS ,cont.

1976

★ **Faye Dunaway/**Network
Marie-Christine Barrault/Cousin, Cousine
Talia Shire/Rocky
Sissy Spacek/Carrie
Liv Ullmann/Face to Face

1977

★ **Diane Keaton/**Annie Hall
Anne Bancroft/The Turning Point
Jane Fonda/Julia
Shirley MacLaine/The Turning Point
Marsha Mason/The Goodbye Girl

1978

★ **Jane Fonda/**Coming Home
Ingrid Bergman/Autumn Sonata
Ellen Burstyn/Same Time, Next Year
Jill Clayburgh/An Unmarried Woman
Geraldine Page/Interiors

1979

★ **Sally Field/**Norma Rae
Jill Clayburgh/Starting Over
Jane Fonda/The China Syndrome
Marsha Mason/Chapter Two
Bette Midler/The Rose

1980

★ **Sissy Spacek/**Coal Miner's Daughter
Ellen Burstyn/Resurrection
Goldie Hawn/Private Benjamin
Mary Tyler Moore/Ordinary People
Gena Rowlands/Gloria

1981

★ **Katharine Hepburn/**On Golden Pond
Diane Keaton/Reds
Marsha Mason/Only When I Laugh
Susan Sarandon/Atlantic City
Meryl Streep/The French Lieutenant's Woman

1982

★ **Meryl Streep/**Sophie's Choice
Julie Andrews/Victor/Victoria
Jessica Lange/Frances
Sissy Spacek/Missing
Debra Winger/An Officer and a Gentleman

1983

★ **Shirley MacLaine/**Terms of Endearment
Jane Alexander/Testament
Meryl Streep/Silkwood
Julie Walters/Educating Rita

Debra Winger/Terms of Endearment

1984

★ **Sally Field/**Places in the Heart
Judy Davis/A Passage to India
Jessica Lange/Country
Vanessa Redgrave/The Bostonians
Sissy Spacek/The River

1985

★ **Geraldine Page/**The Trip to Bountiful
Anne Bancroft/Agnes of God
Whoopi Goldberg/The Color Purple
Jessica Lange/Sweet Dreams
Meryl Streep/Out of Africa

1986

★ **Marlee Matlin/**Children of a Lesser God
Jane Fonda/The Morning After
Sissy Spacek/Crimes of the Heart
Kathleen Turner/Peggy Sue Got Married
Sigourney Weaver/Aliens

1987

★ **Cher/**Moonstruck
Glenn Close/Fatal Attraction
Holly Hunter/Broadcast News
Sally Kirkland/Anna
Meryl Streep/Ironweed

1988

★ **Jodie Foster/**The Accused
Glenn Close/Dangerous Liaisons
Melanie Griffith/Working Girl
Meryl Streep/A Cry in the Dark
Sigourney Weaver/Gorillas in the Mist

1989

★ **Jessica Tandy/**Driving Miss Daisy
Isabelle Adjani/Camille Claudel
Pauline Collins/Shirley Valentine
Jessica Lange/Music Box
Michelle Pfeiffer/The Fabulous Baker Boys

1990

★ **Kathy Bates/**Misery
Anjelica Huston/The Grifters
Julia Roberts/Pretty Woman
Meryl Streep/Postcards from the Edge
Joanne Woodward/Mr. & Mrs. Bridge

1991

★ **Jodie Foster/**The Silence of the Lambs
Geena Davis/Thelma & Louise

Laura Dern/Rambling Rose
Bette Midler/For the Boys
Susan Sarandon/Thelma & Louise

1992

★ **Emma Thompson/**Howard's End
Catherine Deneuve/Indochine
Mary McDonnell/Passion Fish
Michelle Pfeiffer/Love Field
Susan Sarandon/Lorenzo's Oil

1993

★ **Holly Hunter/**The Piano
Angela Bassett/What's Love Got to Do with It?
Stockard Channing/Six Degrees of Separation
Emma Thompson/The Remains of the Day
Debra Winger/Shadowlands

1994

★ **Jessica Lange/**Blue Sky
Jodie Foster/Nell
Miranda Richardson/Tom & Viv
Winona Ryder/Little Women
Susan Sarandon/The Client

1995

★ **Susan Sarandon/**Dead Man Walking
Elisabeth Shue/Leaving Las Vegas
Sharon Stone/Casino
Meryl Streep/The Bridges of Madison County
Emma Thompson/Sense and Sensibility

1996

★ **Frances McDormand/**Fargo
Brenda Blethyn/Secrets and Lies
Diane Keaton/Marvin's Room
Kristin Scott Thomas/The English Patient
Emily Watson/Breaking the Waves

1997

★ **Helen Hunt/**As Good As It Gets
Helena Bonham Carter/The Wings of the Dove
Julie Christie/Afterglow
Judi Dench/Mrs. Brown
Kate Winslet/Titanic

ACTRESS— SUPPORTING

1936

★ **Gale Sondergaard/**Anthony Adverse
Beulah Bondi/The Gorgeous Hussy
Alice Brady/My Man Godfrey
Bonita Granville/These Three

Maria Ouspenskaya/Dodsworth

1937

★ **Alice Brady/**In Old Chicago
Andrea Leeds/Stage Door
Anne Shirley/Stella Dallas
Claire Trevor/Dead End

1938

★ **Fay Bainter/**Jezebel
Beulah Bondi/Of Human Hearts
Spring Byington/You Can't Take It with You
Milza Korjus/The Great Waltz

1939

★ **Hattie McDaniel/**Gone with the Wind
Geraldine Fitzgerald/Wuthering Heights
Edna May Oliver/Drums Along the Mohawk
Maria Ouspenskaya/Love Affair
Olivia de Havilland/Gone with the Wind

1940

★ **Jane Darwell/**The Grapes of Wrath
Judith Anderson/Rebecca
Ruth Hussey/The Philadelphia Story
Barbara O'Neil/All This and Heaven Too
Marjorie Rambeau/Primrose Path

1941

★ **Mary Astor/**The Great Lie
Sara Allgood/How Green Was My Valley
Patricia Collinge/The Little Foxes
Teresa Wright/The Little Foxes
Margaret Wycherly/Sergeant York

1942

★ **Teresa Wright/**Mrs. Miniver
Gladys Cooper/Now, Voyager
Agnes Moorehead/The Magnificent Ambersons
Susan Peters/Random Harvest
May Whitty/Mrs. Miniver

1943

★ **Katina Paxinou/**For Whom the Bell Tolls
Gladys Cooper/The Song of Bernadette
Paulette Goddard/So Proudly We Hail
Anne Revere/The Song of Bernadette
Lucile Watson/Watch on the Rhine

1944

★ **Ethel Barrymore/**None But the Lonely Heart

Jennifer Jones/Since You Went Away
Angela Lansbury/Gaslight
Aline MacMahon/Dragon Seed
Agnes Moorehead/Mrs. Parkington

1945

★ **Anne Revere/**National Velvet
Eve Arden/Mildred Pierce
Ann Blyth/Mildred Pierce
Angela Lansbury/Picture of Dorian Gray
Joan Lorring/The Corn Is Green

1946

★ **Anne Baxter/**The Razor's Edge
Ethel Barrymore/The Spiral Staircase
Lillian Gish/Duel in the Sun
Flora Robson/Saratoga Trunk
Gale Sondergaard/Anna and the King of Siam

1947

★ **Celeste Holm/**Gentleman's Agreement
Ethel Barrymore/The Paradine Case
Gloria Grahame/Crossfire
Marjorie Main/Egg and I
Anne Revere/Gentleman's Agreement

1948

★ **Claire Trevor/**Key Largo
Barbara Bel Geddes/I Remember Mama
Ellen Corby/I Remember Mama
Agnes Moorehead/Johnny Belinda
Jean Simmons/Hamlet

1949

★ **Mercedes McCambridge/**All the King's Men
Ethel Barrymore/Pinky
Celeste Holm/Come to the Stable
Elsa Lanchester/Come to the Stable
Ethel Waters/Pinky

1950

★ **Josephine Hull/**Harvey
Celeste Holm/All About Eve
Nancy Olson/Sunset Boulevard
Thelma Ritter/All About Eve

1951

★ **Kim Hunter/**A Streetcar Named Desire
Lee Grant/Detective Story

1952

★ **Gloria Grahame/**The Bad and the Beautiful
Jean Hagen/Singin' in the Rain
Colette Marchand/Moulin Rouge

Terry Moore/*Come Back, Little Sheba*

1953
★ **Donna Reed/***From Here to Eternity*
Grace Kelly/*Mogambo*
Marjorie Rambeau/*Torch Song*
Thelma Ritter/*Pickup on South Street*

1954
★ **Eva Marie Saint/***On the Waterfront*
Nina Foch/*Executive Suite*
Katy Jurado/*Broken Lance*

1955
★ **Jo Van Fleet/***East of Eden*
Betsy Blair/*Marty*
Peggy Lee/*Pete Kelly's Blues*
Marisa Pavan/*The Rose Tattoo*
Natalie Wood/*Rebel Without a Cause*

1956
★ **Dorothy Malone/***Written on the Wind*
Mildred Dunnock/*Baby Doll*
Eileen Heckart/*The Bad Seed*
Mercedes McCambridge/*Giant*
Patty McCormack/*The Bad Seed*

1957
★ **Miyoshi Umeki/***Sayonara*
Elsa Lanchester/*Witness for the Prosecution*
Hope Lange/*Peyton Place*
Diane Varsi/*Peyton Place*

1958
★ **Wendy Hiller/***Separate Tables*
Peggy Cass/*Auntie Mame*
Martha Hyer/*Some Came Running*
Maureen Stapleton/*Lonelyhearts*
Cara Williams/*The Defiant Ones*

1959
★ **Shelley Winters/***The Diary of Anne Frank*
Hermione Baddeley/*Room at the Top*
Susan Kohner/*Imitation of Life*
Juanita Moore/*Imitation of Life*
Thelma Ritter/*Pillow Talk*

1960
★ **Shirley Jones/***Elmer Gantry*
Glynis Johns/*The Sundowners*
Janet Leigh/*Psycho*

1961
★ **Rita Moreno/***West Side Story*

Fay Bainter/*The Children's Hour*
Judy Garland/*Judgment at Nuremberg*
Lotte Lenya/*Roman Spring of Mrs. Stone*
Una Merkel/*Summer and Smoke*

1962
★ **Patty Duke/***The Miracle Worker*
Mary Badham/*To Kill a Mockingbird*
Shirley Knight/*Sweet Bird of Youth*
Angela Lansbury/*The Manchurian Candidate*
Thelma Ritter/*Birdman of Alcatraz*

1963
★ **Margaret Rutherford/***The V.I.P.'s*
Diane Cilento/*Tom Jones*
Edith Evans/*Tom Jones*
Joyce Redman/*Tom Jones*
Lilia Skala/*Lilies of the Field*

1964
★ **Lila Kedrova/***Zorba the Greek*
Gladys Cooper/*My Fair Lady*
Edith Evans/*The Chalk Garden*
Grayson Hall/*The Night of the Iguana*
Agnes Moorehead/*Hush, Hush, Sweet Charlotte*

1965
★ **Shelley Winters/***A Patch of Blue*
Ruth Gordon/*Inside Daisy Clover*
Joyce Redman/*Othello*
Maggie Smith/*Othello*
Peggy Wood/*The Sound of Music*

1966
★ **Sandy Dennis/***Who's Afraid of Virginia Woolf?*
Wendy Hiller/*A Man for All Seasons*
Jocelyn Lagarde/*Hawaii*
Vivien Merchant/*Alfie*
Geraldine Page/*You're a Big Boy Now*

1967
★ **Estelle Parsons/***Bonnie & Clyde*
Carol Channing/*Thoroughly Modern Millie*
Mildred Natwick/*Barefoot in the Park*
Beah Richards/*Guess Who's Coming to Dinner*
Katharine Ross/*The Graduate*

1968
★ **Ruth Gordon/***Rosemary's Baby*
Lynn Carlin/*Faces*
Sondra Locke/*The Heart Is a Lonely Hunter*
Kay Medford/*Funny Girl*

Estelle Parsons/*Rachel, Rachel*

1969
★ **Goldie Hawn/***Cactus Flower*
Cathy Burns/*Last Summer*
Dyan Cannon/*Bob & Carol & Ted & Alice*
Sylvia Miles/*Midnight Cowboy*
Susannah York/*They Shoot Horses, Don't They?*

1970
★ **Helen Hayes/***Airport*
Karen Black/*Five Easy Pieces*
Sally Kellerman/*M*A*S*H*
Maureen Stapleton/*Airport*

1971
★ **Cloris Leachman/***The Last Picture Show*
Ann-Margret/*Carnal Knowledge*
Ellen Burstyn/*The Last Picture Show*
Margaret Leighton/*The Go-Between*

1972
★ **Eileen Heckart/***Butterflies Are Free*
Jeannie Berlin/*The Heartbreak Kid*
Geraldine Page/*Pete 'n' Tillie*
Susan Tyrrell/*Fat City*
Shelley Winters/*The Poseidon Adventure*

1973
★ **Tatum O'Neal/***Paper Moon*
Linda Blair/*The Exorcist*
Candy Clark/*American Graffiti*
Madeline Kahn/*Paper Moon*
Sylvia Sidney/*Summer Wishes, Winter Dreams*

1974
★ **Ingrid Bergman/***Murder on the Orient Express*
Valentina Cortese/*Day for Night*
Madeline Kahn/*Blazing Saddles*
Diane Ladd/*Alice Doesn't Live Here Anymore*
Talia Shire/*The Godfather, Part 2*

1975
★ **Lee Grant/***Shampoo*
Ronee Blakley/*Nashville*
Sylvia Miles/*Farewell, My Lovely*
Lily Tomlin/*Nashville*
Brenda Vaccaro/*Once Is Not Enough*

1976
★ **Beatrice Straight/***Network*
Jane Alexander/*All the President's Men*
Jodie Foster/*Taxi Driver*

Lee Grant/*Voyage of the Damned*
Piper Laurie/*Carrie*

1977
★ **Vanessa Redgrave/***Julia*
Leslie Browne/*The Turning Point*
Quinn Cummings/*The Goodbye Girl*
Melinda Dillon/*Close Encounters of the Third Kind*
Tuesday Weld/*Looking for Mr. Goodbar*

1978
★ **Maggie Smith/***California Suite*
Dyan Cannon/*Heaven Can Wait*
Penelope Milford/*Coming Home*
Maureen Stapleton/*Interiors*
Meryl Streep/*The Deer Hunter*

1979
★ **Meryl Streep/***Kramer vs. Kramer*
Jane Alexander/*Kramer vs. Kramer*
Barbara Barrie/*Breaking Away*
Candice Bergen/*Starting Over*
Mariel Hemingway/*Manhattan*

1980
★ **Mary Steenburgen/***Melvin and Howard*
Eileen Brennan/*Private Benjamin*
Eva LeGallienne/*Resurrection*
Cathy Moriarty/*Raging Bull*
Diana Scarwid/*Inside Moves*

1981
★ **Maureen Stapleton/***Reds*
Melinda Dillon/*Absence of Malice*
Jane Fonda/*On Golden Pond*
Joan Hackett/*Only When I Laugh*
Elizabeth McGovern/*Ragtime*

1982
★ **Jessica Lange/***Tootsie*
Glenn Close/*The World According to Garp*
Teri Garr/*Tootsie*
Kim Stanley/*Frances*
Lesley Ann Warren/*Victor/Victoria*

1983
★ **Linda Hunt/***The Year of Living Dangerously*
Cher/*Silkwood*
Glenn Close/*The Big Chill*
Amy Irving/*Yentl*
Alfre Woodard/*Cross Creek*

1984
★ **Peggy Ashcroft/***A Passage to India*
Glenn Close/*The Natural*
Lindsay Crouse/*Places in the Heart*
Christine Lahti/*Swing Shift*
Geraldine Page/*The Pope of Greenwich Village*

1985
★ **Anjelica Huston/***Prizzi's Honor*
Margaret Avery/*The Color Purple*
Amy Madigan/*Twice in a Lifetime*
Meg Tilly/*Agnes of God*
Oprah Winfrey/*The Color Purple*

1986
★ **Dianne Wiest/***Hannah and Her Sisters*
Tess Harper/*Crimes of the Heart*
Piper Laurie/*Children of a Lesser God*
Mary Elizabeth Mastrantonio/*The Color of Money*
Maggie Smith/*A Room with a View*

1987
★ **Olympia Dukakis/***Moonstruck*
Norma Aleandro/*Gaby: A True Story*
Anne Archer/*Fatal Attraction*
Anne Ramsey/*Throw Momma from the Train*
Ann Sothern/*The Whales of August*

1988
★ **Geena Davis/***The Accidental Tourist*
Joan Cusack/*Working Girl*
Frances McDormand/*Mississippi Burning*
Michelle Pfeiffer/*Dangerous Liaisons*
Sigourney Weaver/*Working Girl*

1989
★ **Brenda Fricker/***My Left Foot*
Anjelica Huston/*Enemies, a Love Story*
Lena Olin/*Enemies, a Love Story*
Julia Roberts/*Steel Magnolias*
Dianne Wiest/*Parenthood*

1990
★ **Whoopi Goldberg/***Ghost*
Annette Bening/*The Grifters*
Lorraine Bracco/*Goodfellas*
Diane Ladd/*Wild at Heart*
Mary McDonnell/*Dances with Wolves*

The Longest Day
Period of Adjustment

1963
8 1/2
Hud
Love with the Proper
   Stranger

1964
★ Zorba the Greek
The Americanization of
   Emily
Hush, Hush, Sweet
   Charlotte
The Night of the Iguana
Seven Days in May

1965
★ Ship of Fools
King Rat
A Patch of Blue
The Slender Thread
The Spy Who Came in
   from the Cold

1966
★ Who's Afraid of Virginia
   Woolf?
The Fortune Cookie
The Gospel According to
   St. Matthew
Is Paris Burning?

ART DIRECTION (COLOR)

1947
★ Black Narcissus
Life with Father

1948
★ The Red Shoes
Joan of Arc

1949
★ Little Women
Adventures of Don Juan

1950
★ Samson and Delilah
Destination Moon

1951
★ An American in Paris
David and Bathsheba
Quo Vadis
The Tales of Hoffmann

1952
★ Moulin Rouge
Hans Christian Andersen
The Merry Widow
The Quiet Man
The Snows of Kilimanjaro

1953
★ The Robe
Knights of the Round
   Table
Lili
Young Bess

1954
★ 20,000 Leagues Under the
   Sea
Brigadoon
Desiree
Red Garters
A Star Is Born

1955
★ Picnic

Daddy Long Legs
Guys and Dolls
Love Is a Many-
   Splendored Thing
To Catch a Thief

1956
★ The King and I
Around the World in 80
   Days
Giant
Lust for Life
The Ten Commandments

1959
★ Ben-Hur
Journey to the Center of
   the Earth
North by Northwest
Pillow Talk

1960
★ Spartacus
Cimarron
It Started in Naples
Sunrise at Campobello

1961
★ West Side Story
Breakfast at Tiffany's
El Cid
Flower Drum Song
Summer and Smoke

1962
★ Lawrence of Arabia
The Music Man
Mutiny on the Bounty
That Touch of Mink
The Wonderful World of
   the Brothers Grimm

1963
★ Cleopatra
The Cardinal
Come Blow Your Horn
How the West Was Won
Tom Jones

1964
★ My Fair Lady
Becket
Mary Poppins
The Unsinkable Molly
   Brown

1965
★ Doctor Zhivago
The Agony and the
   Ecstasy
The Greatest Story Ever
   Told
Inside Daisy Clover
The Sound of Music

1966
★ Fantastic Voyage
Gambit
Juliet of the Spirits
The Oscar
The Sand Pebbles

CINEMATOGRAPHY

1928
★ Sunrise
My Best Girl
Sadie Thompson
The Tempest

1929
★ White Shadows in the
   South Seas

Our Dancing Daughters

1930
★ All Quiet on the Western
   Front
Anna Christie
Hell's Angels

1931
★ Tabu: A Story of the South
   Seas
Cimarron
Morocco
Svengali

1932
★ Shanghai Express
Arrowsmith
Dr. Jekyll and Mr. Hyde

1933
★ A Farewell to Arms
The Sign of the Cross

1934
★ Cleopatra

1935
★ A Midsummer Night's
   Dream
Barbary Coast
The Crusades
Les Miserables

1936
★ Anthony Adverse
The General Died at Dawn
The Gorgeous Hussy

1937
★ The Good Earth
Dead End

1938
★ The Great Waltz
Algiers
Jezebel
Mad About Music
Vivacious Lady
You Can't Take It with You
The Young in Heart

1957
★ The Bridge on the River
   Kwai
An Affair to Remember
Funny Face
Peyton Place
Sayonara

1967
★ Bonnie & Clyde
Camelot
Doctor Dolittle
The Graduate
In Cold Blood

1968
★ Romeo and Juliet
Funny Girl
Ice Station Zebra
Oliver!
Star!

1969
★ Butch Cassidy and the
   Sundance Kid
Anne of the Thousand
   Days
Bob & Carol & Ted & Alice
Hello, Dolly!
Marooned

1970
★ Ryan's Daughter
Airport
Patton
Tora! Tora! Tora!
Women in Love

1971
★ Fiddler on the Roof
The French Connection
The Last Picture Show
Nicholas and Alexandra
Summer of '42

1972
★ Cabaret
Butterflies Are Free
The Poseidon Adventure
1776
Travels with My Aunt

1973
★ Cries and Whispers
The Exorcist
Jonathan Livingston
   Seagull
The Sting
The Way We Were

1974
★ The Towering Inferno
Chinatown
Earthquake
Lenny
Murder on the Orient
   Express

1975
★ Barry Lyndon
The Day of the Locust
Funny Lady
The Hindenburg
One Flew Over the
   Cuckoo's Nest

1976
★ Bound for Glory
King Kong
Logan's Run
Network
A Star Is Born

1977
★ Close Encounters of the
   Third Kind
Islands in the Stream
Julia
Looking for Mr. Goodbar
The Turning Point

1978
★ Days of Heaven
The Deer Hunter
Heaven Can Wait
Same Time, Next Year
The Wiz

1979
★ Apocalypse Now
All That Jazz
The Black Hole
Kramer vs. Kramer
1941

1980
★ Tess
The Blue Lagoon
Coal Miner's Daughter
The Formula
Raging Bull

1981
★ Reds
Excalibur
On Golden Pond
Ragtime
Raiders of the Lost Ark

1982
★ Gandhi
Das Boot
E.T.: The Extra-Terrestrial
Sophie's Choice
Tootsie

1983
★ Fanny and Alexander
Flashdance
The Right Stuff
WarGames
Zelig

1984
★ The Killing Fields
Amadeus
The Natural
A Passage to India
The River

1985
★ Out of Africa
The Color Purple
Murphy's Romance
Ran
Witness

1986
★ The Mission
Peggy Sue Got Married
Platoon
A Room with a View
Star Trek 4: The Voyage
   Home

1987
★ The Last Emperor
Broadcast News
Empire of the Sun
Hope and Glory
Matewan

1988
★ Mississippi Burning
Rain Man
Tequila Sunrise
The Unbearable Lightness
   of Being
Who Framed Roger
   Rabbit

1989
★ Glory
The Abyss
Blaze
Born on the Fourth of July
The Fabulous Baker Boys

1990
★ Dances with Wolves
Avalon
Dick Tracy
The Godfather, Part 3
Henry & June

1991
★ JFK
Bugsy
The Prince of Tides
Terminator 2: Judgment
   Day
Thelma & Louise

CINEMATOGRAPHY
cont.

1992
★ A River Runs Through It
  Hoffa
  Howard's End
  The Lover
  Unforgiven

1993
★ Schindler's List
  Farewell My Concubine
  The Fugitive
  The Piano
  Searching for Bobby
    Fischer

1994
★ Legends of the Fall
  Forrest Gump
  The Shawshank
    Redemption
  Trois Couleurs: Rouge
  Wyatt Earp

1995
★ Braveheart
  Batman Forever
  A Little Princess
  Sense and Sensibility
  Shanghai Triad

1996
★ The English Patient
  Evita
  Fargo
  Fly Away Home
  Michael Collins

1997
★ Titanic
  Amistad
  Kundun
  L.A. Confidential
  The Wings of the Dove

CINEMATOGRAPHY (B & W)

1939
★ Wuthering Heights
  First Love
  Gunga Din
  Intermezzo
  Juarez
  Only Angels Have Wings
  The Rains Came
  Stagecoach

1940
★ Rebecca
  Abe Lincoln in Illinois
  All This and Heaven Too
  Boom Town
  Foreign Correspondent
  The Letter
  The Long Voyage Home
  Waterloo Bridge

1941
★ How Green Was My Valley
  The Chocolate Soldier
  Citizen Kane
  Dr. Jekyll and Mr. Hyde
  Here Comes Mr. Jordan
  Sergeant York
  Sun Valley Serenade
  Sundown
  That Hamilton Woman

1942
★ Mrs. Miniver
  Kings Row
  The Magnificent
    Ambersons
  The Pride of the Yankees
  Talk of the Town

1943
★ The Song of Bernadette
  Air Force
  Casablanca
  Five Graves to Cairo
  The Human Comedy
  Madame Curie
  The North Star
  Sahara
  So Proudly We Hail

1944
★ Laura
  Double Indemnity
  Dragon Seed
  Gaslight
  Going My Way
  Lifeboat
  Since You Went Away
  Thirty Seconds Over
    Tokyo
  The Uninvited
  The White Cliffs of Dover

1945
★ Picture of Dorian Gray
  The Keys of the Kingdom
  The Lost Weekend
  Mildred Pierce
  Spellbound

1946
★ Anna and the King of Siam

1947
★ Great Expectations
  The Ghost and Mrs. Muir
  Green Dolphin Street

1948
★ The Naked City
  I Remember Mama
  Johnny Belinda
  Portrait of Jennie

1949
★ Battleground
  Champion
  Come to the Stable
  The Heiress

1950
★ The Third Man
  All About Eve
  The Asphalt Jungle
  Sunset Boulevard

1951
★ A Place in the Sun
  Strangers on a Train
  A Streetcar Named Desire

1952
★ The Bad and the Beautiful
  The Big Sky
  Sudden Fear

1953
★ From Here to Eternity
  Julius Caesar
  Martin Luther
  Roman Holiday

1954
★ On the Waterfront
  Country Girl
  Executive Suite
  Sabrina

1955
★ The Rose Tattoo
  Blackboard Jungle
  I'll Cry Tomorrow
  Marty
  Queen Bee

1956
★ Somebody Up There Likes
    Me
  Baby Doll
  The Bad Seed
  The Harder They Fall

1958
★ The Defiant Ones
  Desire Under the Elms
  I Want to Live!
  Separate Tables
  The Young Lions

1959
★ The Diary of Anne Frank
  Anatomy of a Murder
  Career
  The Gazebo
  Some Like It Hot
  The Young Philadelphians

1960
  The Apartment
  The Facts of Life
  Inherit the Wind
  Psycho

1961
★ The Hustler
  The Absent-Minded
    Professor
  The Children's Hour
  Judgment at Nuremberg
  One, Two, Three

1962
★ The Longest Day
  Birdman of Alcatraz
  To Kill a Mockingbird
  Two for the Seesaw
  What Ever Happened to
    Baby Jane?

1963
★ Hud
  The Balcony
  Lilies of the Field
  Love with the Proper
    Stranger

1964
★ Zorba the Greek
  The Americanization of
    Emily
  Hush, Hush, Sweet
    Charlotte
  The Night of the Iguana

1965
★ Ship of Fools
  In Harm's Way
  King Rat
  Morituri
  A Patch of Blue

1966
★ Who's Afraid of Virginia
    Woolf?

  The Fortune Cookie
  Georgy Girl
  Is Paris Burning?
  Seconds

CINEMATOGRAPHY (COLOR)

1939
★ Gone with the Wind
  Drums Along the Mohawk
  The Four Feathers
  The Private Lives of
    Elizabeth & Essex
  The Wizard of Oz

1940
★ The Thief of Bagdad
  Bitter Sweet
  The Blue Bird
  Down Argentine Way
  Northwest Passage

1941
★ Blood and Sand
  Billy the Kid
  Blossoms in the Dust
  Dive Bomber
  Louisiana Purchase

1942
★ The Black Swan
  Arabian Nights
  Captains of the Clouds
  The Jungle Book
  Reap the Wild Wind
  To the Shores of Tripoli

1943
★ The Phantom of the Opera
  For Whom the Bell Tolls
  Heaven Can Wait
  Hello, Frisco, Hello
  Lassie, Come Home
  Thousands Cheer

1944
★ Wilson
  Cover Girl
  Meet Me in St. Louis

1945
★ Leave Her to Heaven
  Anchors Aweigh
  National Velvet
  A Song to Remember
  The Spanish Main

1946
★ The Yearling
  The Jolson Story

1947
★ Black Narcissus
  Life with Father

1948
★ Joan of Arc
  The Loves of Carmen
  The Three Musketeers

1949
★ She Wore a Yellow Ribbon
  The Barkleys of Broadway
  Jolson Sings Again
  Little Women

1950
★ King Solomon's Mines
  Broken Arrow
  The Flame & the Arrow
  Samson and Delilah

1951
★ An American in Paris
  David and Bathsheba
  Quo Vadis
  Show Boat
  When Worlds Collide

1952
★ The Quiet Man
  Hans Christian Andersen
  Ivanhoe
  Million Dollar Mermaid
  The Snows of Kilimanjaro

1953
★ Shane
  All the Brothers Were
    Valiant
  Beneath the 12-Mile Reef
  Lili
  The Robe

1954
★ Three Coins in the
    Fountain
  The Egyptian
  Rear Window
  Seven Brides for Seven
    Brothers
  The Silver Chalice

1955
★ To Catch a Thief
  Guys and Dolls
  Love Is a Many-
    Splendored Thing
  A Man Called Peter
  Oklahoma!

1956
★ Around the World in 80
    Days
  The Eddy Duchin Story
  The King and I
  The Ten Commandments
  War and Peace

1958
★ Gigi
  Auntie Mame
  Cat on a Hot Tin Roof
  South Pacific

1959
★ Ben-Hur
  The Five Pennies
  The Nun's Story

1960
★ Spartacus
  The Alamo
  Butterfield 8
  Exodus

1961
★ West Side Story
  Fanny
  Flower Drum Song
  One-Eyed Jacks

1962
★ Lawrence of Arabia
  Gypsy
  Hatari!
  Mutiny on the Bounty
  The Wonderful World of
    the Brothers Grimm

1963
★ Cleopatra
  The Cardinal
  How the West Was Won

Irma La Douce
It's a Mad, Mad, Mad, Mad
World

1964
★ My Fair Lady
Becket
Cheyenne Autumn
Mary Poppins
The Unsinkable Molly
Brown

1965
★ Doctor Zhivago
The Agony and the
Ecstasy
The Great Race
The Greatest Story Ever
Told
The Sound of Music

1966
★ A Man for All Seasons
Fantastic Voyage
Hawaii
The Professionals
The Sand Pebbles

COSTUME DESIGN

1957
★ Les Girls
An Affair to Remember
Funny Face
Pal Joey
Raintree County

1958
★ Gigi
Bell, Book and Candle
The Buccaneer
Some Came Running

1967
★ Camelot
Bonnie & Clyde
The Happiest Millionaire
The Taming of the Shrew
Thoroughly Modern Millie

1968
★ Romeo and Juliet
The Lion in Winter
Oliver!
Planet of the Apes
Star!

1969
★ Anne of the Thousand
Days
Hello, Dolly!
Sweet Charity
They Shoot Horses, Don't
They?

1970
★ Cromwell
Airport
Darling Lili
Scrooge

1971
★ Nicholas and Alexandra
Bedknobs and
Broomsticks
Death in Venice
Mary, Queen of Scots
What's the Matter with
Helen?

1972
★ Travels with My Aunt
The Godfather

Lady Sings the Blues
The Poseidon Adventure
Young Winston

1973
★ The Sting
Cries and Whispers
Tom Sawyer
The Way We Were

1974
★ The Great Gatsby
Chinatown
Daisy Miller
The Godfather, Part 2
Murder on the Orient
Express

1975
★ Barry Lyndon
The Four Musketeers
Funny Lady
The Magic Flute
The Man Who Would Be
King

1976
Bound for Glory
The Incredible Sarah
The Passover Plot
The Seven-Per-Cent
Solution

1977
★ Star Wars
Airport '77
Julia
A Little Night Music
The Other Side of
Midnight

1978
★ Death on the Nile
Days of Heaven
The Swarm
The Wiz

1979
★ All That Jazz
Agatha
Butch and Sundance: The
Early Days
The Europeans
La Cage aux Folles

1980
★ Tess
The Elephant Man
My Brilliant Career
Somewhere in Time
When Time Ran Out

1981
★ Chariots of Fire
The French Lieutenant's
Woman
Pennies From Heaven
Ragtime
Reds

1982
★ Gandhi
Sophie's Choice
Tron
Victor/Victoria

1983
★ Fanny and Alexander
Cross Creek
Heart Like a Wheel
The Return of Martin
Guerre
Zelig

1984
★ Amadeus
The Bostonians
A Passage to India
Places in the Heart
2010: The Year We Make
Contact

1985
★ Ran
The Color Purple
The Journey of Natty
Gann
Out of Africa
Prizzi's Honor

1986
★ A Room with a View
The Mission
Otello
Peggy Sue Got Married
Pirates

1987
★ The Last Emperor
The Dead
Empire of the Sun
Maurice
The Untouchables

1988
★ Dangerous Liaisons
Coming to America
A Handful of Dust
Sunset
Tucker: The Man and His
Dream

1989
★ Henry V
The Adventures of Baron
Munchausen
Driving Miss Daisy
Harlem Nights
Valmont

1990
★ Cyrano de Bergerac
Avalon
Dances with Wolves
Dick Tracy
Hamlet

1991
★ Bugsy
The Addams Family
Barton Fink
Hook
Madame Bovary

1992
★ Bram Stoker's Dracula
Enchanted April
Howard's End
Malcolm X
Toys

1993
★ The Age of Innocence
Orlando
The Piano
The Remains of the Day
Schindler's List

1994
★ The Adventures of
Priscilla, Queen of the
Desert
Bullets Over Broadway
Little Women
Maverick
Queen Margot

1995
★ Restoration
Braveheart
Richard III
Sense and Sensibility
12 Monkeys

1996
★ The English Patient
Angels and Insects
Emma
Hamlet
Portrait of a Lady

1997
★ Titanic
Amistad
Kundun
Oscar and Lucinda
The Wings of the Dove

COSTUME DESIGN (B & W)

1948
★ Hamlet

1949
★ The Heiress

1950
★ All About Eve
Born Yesterday
The Magnificent Yankee

1951
★ A Place in the Sun
A Streetcar Named Desire

1952
★ The Bad and the Beautiful
Affair in Trinidad
Carrie
Sudden Fear

1953
★ Roman Holiday
From Here to Eternity

1954
★ Sabrina
The Earrings of Madame
De...
Executive Suite
Indiscretion of an
American Wife
It Should Happen to You

1955
★ I'll Cry Tomorrow
The Pickwick Papers
Queen Bee
The Rose Tattoo
Ugetsu

1956
★ Solid Gold Cadillac
Seven Samurai

1959
★ Some Like It Hot
Career
The Diary of Anne Frank
The Young Philadelphians

1960
★ The Facts of Life
Never on Sunday
The Rise and Fall of Legs
Diamond
Seven Thieves
The Virgin Spring

1961
★ La Dolce Vita
The Children's Hour
Judgment at Nuremberg
Yojimbo

1962
Days of Wine and Roses
The Man Who Shot Liberty
Valance
The Miracle Worker
Phaedra
What Ever Happened to
Baby Jane?

1963
★ 8 1/2
Love with the Proper
Stranger
The Stripper
Toys in the Attic

1964
★ The Night of the Iguana
Hush, Hush, Sweet
Charlotte
Kisses for My President

1965
★ Darling
Morituri
Ship of Fools
The Slender Thread

1966
★ Who's Afraid of Virginia
Woolf?
The Gospel According to
St. Matthew
Morgan!

COSTUME DESIGN (COLOR)

1948
★ Joan of Arc

1949
★ Adventures of Don Juan

1950
★ Samson and Delilah
That Forsyte Woman

1951
★ An American in Paris
David and Bathsheba
The Great Caruso
Quo Vadis
The Tales of Hoffmann

1952
★ Moulin Rouge
The Greatest Show on
Earth
Hans Christian Andersen
The Merry Widow

1953
★ The Robe
The Band Wagon
How to Marry a Millionaire
Young Bess

1954
★ Gate of Hell
Brigadoon
Desiree
A Star Is Born
There's No Business Like
Show Business

DIRECTOR ⌐cont.

Gus Van Sant/*Good Will Hunting*

FILM

1927
★ Wings

1928
Last Command

1929
★ Broadway Melody

1930
★ All Quiet on the Western
   Front
The Big House
Disraeli
The Divorcee

1931
★ Cimarron
The Front Page
Trader Horn

1932
★ Grand Hotel
Arrowsmith
The Champ
Shanghai Express

1933
★ Cavalcade
A Farewell to Arms
42nd Street
I Am a Fugitive from a
   Chain Gang
Lady for a Day
Little Women
The Private Life of Henry
   VIII
She Done Him Wrong
Smilin' Through

1934
★ It Happened One Night
The Barretts of Wimpole
   Street
Cleopatra
Flirtation Walk
The Gay Divorcee
One Night of Love
The Thin Man
Viva Villa!

1935
★ Mutiny on the Bounty
Alice Adams
Broadway Melody of 1936
Captain Blood
David Copperfield
The Informer
Les Miserables
The Lives of a Bengal
   Lancer
A Midsummer Night's
   Dream
Naughty Marietta
Ruggles of Red Gap
Top Hat

1936
★ The Great Ziegfeld
Anthony Adverse
Dodsworth
Libeled Lady
Mr. Deeds Goes to Town
Romeo and Juliet

San Francisco
The Story of Louis Pasteur
A Tale of Two Cities
Three Smart Girls

1937
★ The Life of Emile Zola
The Awful Truth
Captains Courageous
Dead End
The Good Earth
In Old Chicago
Lost Horizon
100 Men and a Girl
Stage Door
A Star Is Born

1938
★ You Can't Take It with You
The Adventures of Robin
   Hood
Alexander's Ragtime Band
Boys Town
The Citadel
Four Daughters
Grand Illusion
Jezebel
Pygmalion
Test Pilot

1939
★ Gone with the Wind
Dark Victory
Goodbye, Mr. Chips
Love Affair
Mr. Smith Goes to
   Washington
Ninotchka
Of Mice and Men
Stagecoach
The Wizard of Oz
Wuthering Heights

1940
★ Rebecca
All This and Heaven Too
Foreign Correspondent
The Grapes of Wrath
The Great Dictator
Kitty Foyle
The Letter
The Long Voyage Home
Our Town
The Philadelphia Story

1941
★ How Green Was My Valley
Blossoms in the Dust
Citizen Kane
Here Comes Mr. Jordan
The Little Foxes
The Maltese Falcon
Sergeant York
Suspicion

1942
★ Mrs. Miniver
Kings Row
The Magnificent
   Ambersons
The Pride of the Yankees
Random Harvest
Talk of the Town
Wake Island
Yankee Doodle Dandy

1943
★ Casablanca
For Whom the Bell Tolls
Heaven Can Wait
The Human Comedy
In Which We Serve
Madame Curie

The More the Merrier
The Ox-Bow Incident
The Song of Bernadette
Watch on the Rhine

1944
★ Going My Way
Double Indemnity
Gaslight
Since You Went Away
Wilson

1945
★ The Lost Weekend
Anchors Aweigh
The Bells of St. Mary's
Mildred Pierce
Spellbound

1946
★ The Best Years of Our
   Lives
Henry V
It's a Wonderful Life
The Razor's Edge
The Yearling

1947
★ Gentleman's Agreement
The Bishop's Wife
Crossfire
Great Expectations
Miracle on 34th Street

1948
★ Hamlet
Johnny Belinda
The Red Shoes
The Snake Pit
Treasure of the Sierra
   Madre

1949
★ All the King's Men
Battleground
The Heiress
A Letter to Three Wives
Twelve O'Clock High

1950
★ All About Eve
Born Yesterday
Father of the Bride
King Solomon's Mines
Sunset Boulevard

1951
★ An American in Paris
A Place in the Sun
Quo Vadis
A Streetcar Named Desire

1952
★ The Greatest Show on
   Earth
High Noon
Ivanhoe
Moulin Rouge
The Quiet Man

1953
★ From Here to Eternity
Julius Caesar
The Robe
Roman Holiday
Shane

1954
★ On the Waterfront
The Caine Mutiny
Country Girl
Seven Brides for Seven
   Brothers

Three Coins in the
   Fountain

1955
★ Marty
Love Is a Many-
   Splendored Thing
Mister Roberts
Picnic
The Rose Tattoo

1956
★ Around the World in 80
   Days
Friendly Persuasion
Giant
The King and I
The Ten Commandments

1957
★ The Bridge on the River
   Kwai
Peyton Place
Sayonara
Twelve Angry Men
Witness for the
   Prosecution

1958
★ Gigi
Auntie Mame
Cat on a Hot Tin Roof
The Defiant Ones
Separate Tables

1959
★ Ben-Hur
Anatomy of a Murder
The Diary of Anne Frank
The Nun's Story
Room at the Top

1960
★ The Apartment
The Alamo
Elmer Gantry
The Sundowners

1961
★ West Side Story
Fanny
The Guns of Navarone
The Hustler
Judgment at Nuremberg

1962
★ Lawrence of Arabia
The Longest Day
The Music Man
Mutiny on the Bounty
To Kill a Mockingbird

1963
★ Tom Jones
Cleopatra
How the West Was Won
Lilies of the Field

1964
★ My Fair Lady
Becket
Dr. Strangelove, or: How I
   Learned to Stop
   Worrying and Love the
   Bomb
Mary Poppins
Zorba the Greek

1965
★ The Sound of Music
Darling
Doctor Zhivago
Ship of Fools

A Thousand Clowns

1966
★ A Man for All Seasons
Alfie
The Russians Are
   Coming, the Russians
   Are Coming
The Sand Pebbles
Who's Afraid of Virginia
   Woolf?

1967
★ In the Heat of the Night
Bonnie & Clyde
Doctor Dolittle
The Graduate
Guess Who's Coming to
   Dinner

1968
★ Oliver!
Funny Girl
The Lion in Winter
Rachel, Rachel
Romeo and Juliet

1969
★ Midnight Cowboy
Anne of the Thousand
   Days
Butch Cassidy and the
   Sundance Kid
Hello, Dolly!
Z

1970
★ Patton
Airport
Five Easy Pieces
Love Story
M*A*S*H

1971
★ The French Connection
A Clockwork Orange
Fiddler on the Roof
The Last Picture Show
Nicholas and Alexandra

1972
★ The Godfather
Cabaret
Deliverance
The Emigrants
Sounder

1973
★ The Sting
American Graffiti
Cries and Whispers
The Exorcist
A Touch of Class

1974
★ The Godfather, Part 2
Chinatown
The Conversation
Lenny
The Towering Inferno

1975
★ One Flew Over the
   Cuckoo's Nest
Barry Lyndon
Dog Day Afternoon
Jaws
Nashville

1976
★ Rocky
All the President's Men
Bound for Glory

Network
Taxi Driver

1977
★ Annie Hall
  The Goodbye Girl
  Julia
  Star Wars
  The Turning Point

1978
★ The Deer Hunter
  Coming Home
  Heaven Can Wait
  Midnight Express
  An Unmarried Woman

1979
★ Kramer vs. Kramer
  All That Jazz
  Apocalypse Now
  Breaking Away
  Norma Rae

1980
★ Ordinary People
  Coal Miner's Daughter
  The Elephant Man
  Raging Bull
  Tess

1981
★ Chariots of Fire
  Atlantic City
  On Golden Pond
  Raiders of the Lost Ark
  Reds

1982
★ Gandhi
  E.T.: The Extra-Terrestrial
  Missing
  Tootsie
  The Verdict

1983
★ Terms of Endearment
  The Big Chill
  The Dresser
  The Right Stuff
  Tender Mercies

1984
★ Amadeus
  The Killing Fields
  A Passage to India
  Places in the Heart
  A Soldier's Story

1985
★ Out of Africa
  The Color Purple
  Kiss of the Spider Woman
  Prizzi's Honor
  Witness

1986
★ Platoon
  Children of a Lesser God
  Hannah and Her Sisters
  The Mission
  A Room with a View

1987
★ The Last Emperor
  Broadcast News
  Fatal Attraction
  Hope and Glory
  Moonstruck

1988
★ Rain Man
  The Accidental Tourist

Dangerous Liaisons
Mississippi Burning
Working Girl

1989
★ Driving Miss Daisy
  Born on the Fourth of July
  Dead Poets Society
  Field of Dreams
  My Left Foot

1990
★ Dances with Wolves
  Awakenings
  Ghost
  The Godfather, Part 3
  Goodfellas

1991
★ The Silence of the Lambs
  Beauty and the Beast
  Bugsy
  JFK
  The Prince of Tides

1992
★ Unforgiven
  The Crying Game
  A Few Good Men
  Howard's End
  Scent of a Woman

1993
★ Schindler's List
  The Fugitive
  In the Name of the Father
  The Piano
  The Remains of the Day

1994
★ Forrest Gump
  Four Weddings and a
    Funeral
  Pulp Fiction
  Quiz Show
  The Shawshank
    Redemption

1995
★ Braveheart
  Apollo 13
  Babe
  The Postman
  Sense and Sensibility

1996
★ The English Patient
  Fargo
  Jerry Maguire
  Secrets and Lies
  Shine

1997
★ Titanic
  As Good As It Gets
  The Full Monty
  Good Will Hunting
  L.A. Confidential

FEATURE DOCUMENTARY

1942
★ Prelude to War

1954
★ Vanishing Prairie

1961
★ The Sky Above, the Mud
    Below

1970
★ Woodstock

1971
★ The Hellstrom Chronicle

1972
★ Marjoe

1975
★ The Man Who Skied Down
    Everest

1976
★ Harlan County, U.S.A.

1977
  The Children of Theatre
    Street

1983
★ Times of Harvey Milk

1988
  Let's Get Lost

1989
★ Common Threads: Stories
    from the Quilt

1993
  The War Room

1996
★ When We Were Kings

FILM EDITING

1934
  Cleopatra
  One Night of Love

1935
★ A Midsummer Night's
    Dream
  David Copperfield
  The Informer
  Les Miserables
  The Lives of a Bengal
    Lancer
  Mutiny on the Bounty

1936
★ Anthony Adverse
  Come and Get It
  The Great Ziegfeld
  Lloyds of London
  A Tale of Two Cities
  Theodora Goes Wild

1937
★ Lost Horizon
  The Awful Truth
  Captains Courageous
  The Good Earth
  100 Men and a Girl

1938
★ The Adventures of Robin
    Hood
  Alexander's Ragtime Band
  The Great Waltz
  Test Pilot
  You Can't Take It with You

1939
★ Gone with the Wind
  Goodbye, Mr. Chips
  Mr. Smith Goes to
    Washington
  The Rains Came
  Stagecoach

1940
  The Grapes of Wrath
  The Letter
  The Long Voyage Home
  Rebecca

1941
★ Sergeant York
  Citizen Kane
  Dr. Jekyll and Mr. Hyde
  How Green Was My
    Valley
  The Little Foxes

1942
★ The Pride of the Yankees
  Mrs. Miniver
  Talk of the Town
  Yankee Doodle Dandy

1943
★ Air Force
  Casablanca
  Five Graves to Cairo
  For Whom the Bell Tolls
  The Song of Bernadette

1944
★ Wilson
  Going My Way
  None But the Lonely Heart
  Since You Went Away

1945
★ National Velvet
  The Bells of St. Mary's
  The Lost Weekend
  Objective, Burma!
  A Song to Remember

1946
★ The Best Years of Our
    Lives
  It's a Wonderful Life
  The Jolson Story
  The Killers
  The Yearling

1947
★ Body and Soul
  The Bishop's Wife
  Gentleman's Agreement
  Green Dolphin Street
  Odd Man Out

1948
★ The Naked City
  Joan of Arc
  Johnny Belinda
  Red River
  The Red Shoes

1949
★ Champion
  All the King's Men
  Battleground
  Sands of Iwo Jima
  The Window

1950
★ King Solomon's Mines
  Sunset Boulevard
  The Third Man

1951
★ A Place in the Sun
  An American in Paris
  Quo Vadis
  The Well

1952
★ High Noon

Come Back, Little Sheba
Flat Top
The Greatest Show on
  Earth
Moulin Rouge

1953
★ From Here to Eternity
  The Moon Is Blue
  Roman Holiday
  The War of the Worlds

1954
★ On the Waterfront
  The Caine Mutiny
  Seven Brides for Seven
    Brothers
  20,000 Leagues Under the
    Sea

1955
★ Picnic
  Blackboard Jungle
  The Bridges at Toko-Ri
  Oklahoma!
  The Rose Tattoo

1956
★ Around the World in 80
    Days
  The Brave One
  Giant
  Somebody Up There Likes
    Me
  The Ten Commandments

1957
★ The Bridge on the River
    Kwai
  Gunfight at the O.K. Corral
  Pal Joey
  Sayonara
  Witness for the
    Prosecution

1958
★ Gigi
  Auntie Mame
  Cowboy
  The Defiant Ones
  I Want to Live!

1959
★ Ben-Hur
  Anatomy of a Murder
  North by Northwest
  The Nun's Story
  On the Beach

1960
★ The Apartment
  The Alamo
  Inherit the Wind
  Spartacus

1961
★ West Side Story
  Fanny
  The Guns of Navarone
  Judgment at Nuremberg
  The Parent Trap

1962
★ Lawrence of Arabia
  The Longest Day
  The Manchurian
    Candidate
  The Music Man
  Mutiny on the Bounty

1963
★ How the West Was Won
  The Cardinal

FILM EDITING
⌐cont.

Cleopatra
The Great Escape
It's a Mad, Mad, Mad, Mad
World

1964
★ Mary Poppins
Becket
Father Goose
Hush, Hush, Sweet
Charlotte
My Fair Lady

1965
★ The Sound of Music
Cat Ballou
Doctor Zhivago
The Flight of the Phoenix
The Great Race

1966
★ Grand Prix
Fantastic Voyage
The Russians Are
Coming, the Russians
Are Coming
The Sand Pebbles
Who's Afraid of Virginia
Woolf?

1967
★ In the Heat of the Night
The Dirty Dozen
Doctor Dolittle
Guess Who's Coming to
Dinner

1968
★ Bullitt
Funny Girl
The Odd Couple
Oliver!
Wild in the Streets

1969
★ Z
Hello, Dolly!
Midnight Cowboy
They Shoot Horses, Don't
They?

1970
★ Patton
Airport
M*A*S*H
Tora! Tora! Tora!
Woodstock

1971
★ The French Connection
The Andromeda Strain
A Clockwork Orange
Kotch
Summer of '42

1972
★ Cabaret
Deliverance
The Godfather
The Hot Rock
The Poseidon Adventure

1973
★ The Sting
American Graffiti
The Day of the Jackal
The Exorcist

Jonathan Livingston
Seagull

1974
★ The Towering Inferno
Blazing Saddles
Chinatown
Earthquake
The Longest Yard

1975
★ Jaws
Dog Day Afternoon
The Man Who Would Be
King
One Flew Over the
Cuckoo's Nest
Three Days of the Condor

1976
★ Rocky
All the President's Men
Bound for Glory
Network
Two Minute Warning

1977
★ Star Wars
Close Encounters of the
Third Kind
Julia
Smokey and the Bandit
The Turning Point

1978
★ The Deer Hunter
The Boys from Brazil
Coming Home
Midnight Express
Superman: The Movie

1979
★ All That Jazz
Apocalypse Now
The Black Stallion
Kramer vs. Kramer
The Rose

1980
★ Raging Bull
Coal Miner's Daughter
The Competition
The Elephant Man
Fame

1981
★ Raiders of the Lost Ark
Chariots of Fire
The French Lieutenant's
Woman
On Golden Pond
Reds

1982
★ Gandhi
Das Boot
E.T.: The Extra-Terrestrial
An Officer and a
Gentleman
Tootsie

1983
★ The Right Stuff
Blue Thunder
Flashdance
Silkwood
Terms of Endearment

1984
★ The Killing Fields
Amadeus
The Cotton Club
A Passage to India

Romancing the Stone

1985
★ Witness
A Chorus Line
Out of Africa
Prizzi's Honor
Runaway Train

1986
★ Platoon
Aliens
Hannah and Her Sisters
The Mission
Top Gun

1987
★ The Last Emperor
Broadcast News
Empire of the Sun
Fatal Attraction
RoboCop

1988
★ Who Framed Roger Rabbit
Die Hard
Gorillas in the Mist
Mississippi Burning
Rain Man

1989
★ Born on the Fourth of July
The Bear
Driving Miss Daisy
The Fabulous Baker Boys
Glory

1990
★ Dances with Wolves
Ghost
The Godfather, Part 3
Goodfellas
The Hunt for Red October

1991
★ JFK
The Commitments
The Silence of the Lambs
Terminator 2: Judgment
Day
Thelma & Louise

1992
★ Unforgiven
Basic Instinct
The Crying Game
A Few Good Men
The Player

1993
★ Schindler's List
The Fugitive
In the Line of Fire
In the Name of the Father
The Piano

1994
★ Forrest Gump
Hoop Dreams
Pulp Fiction
The Shawshank
Redemption
Speed

1995
★ Apollo 13
Babe
Braveheart
Crimson Tide
Seven

1996
★ The English Patient

Evita
Fargo
Jerry Maguire
Shine

1997
★ Titanic
Air Force One
As Good As It Gets
Good Will Hunting
L.A. Confidential

MAKEUP

1981
★ An American Werewolf in
London
Heartbeeps

1982
★ Quest for Fire
Gandhi

1984
★ Amadeus
Greystoke: The Legend of
Tarzan, Lord of the
Apes
2010: The Year We Make
Contact

1985
★ Mask
The Color Purple
Remo Williams: The
Adventure Begins

1986
★ The Fly
The Clan of the Cave Bear
Legend

1987
★ Harry and the Hendersons
Happy New Year

1988
★ Beetlejuice

1989
★ Driving Miss Daisy
The Adventures of Baron
Munchausen
Dad

1990
★ Dick Tracy
Cyrano de Bergerac
Edward Scissorhands

1991
★ Terminator 2: Judgment
Day
Hook
Star Trek 6: The
Undiscovered Country

1992
★ Bram Stoker's Dracula
Batman Returns
Hoffa

1993
★ Mrs. Doubtfire
Philadelphia
Schindler's List

1994
★ Ed Wood
Forrest Gump
Mary Shelley's
Frankenstein

1995
★ Braveheart
My Family
Roommates

1996
★ The Nutty Professor
Ghosts of Mississippi
Star Trek: First Contact

1997
★ Men in Black
Mrs. Brown
Titanic

ADAPTED SCORE

1962
★ The Music Man
Billy Rose's Jumbo
Gypsy
The Wonderful World of
the Brothers Grimm

1963
★ Irma La Douce
Bye, Bye, Birdie
A New Kind of Love
Sundays & Cybele
The Sword in the Stone

1964
★ My Fair Lady
A Hard Day's Night
Robin and the 7 Hoods
The Unsinkable Molly
Brown

1965
★ The Sound of Music
Cat Ballou
A Thousand Clowns

1966
★ A Funny Thing Happened
on the Way to the
Forum
The Gospel According to
St. Matthew
Return of the Seven
The Singing Nun

1967
★ Camelot
Guess Who's Coming to
Dinner
Valley of the Dolls

1968
★ Oliver!
Star!

ORIGINAL DRAMATIC/
COMEDY SCORE

1941
★ The Devil & Daniel
Webster
Ball of Fire
Cheers for Miss Bishop
Citizen Kane
Dr. Jekyll and Mr. Hyde
How Green Was My
Valley
King of the Zombies
The Little Foxes
Lydia
Sergeant York
So Ends Our Night
Sundown
Suspicion
Tanks a Million

SCORING OF A MUSICAL *cont.*

1946
- ★ The Jolson Story
- Blue Skies
- The Harvey Girls
- Night and Day

1948
- ★ Easter Parade
- Emperor Waltz
- The Pirate
- Romance on the High Seas

1949
- ★ On the Town
- Jolson Sings Again
- Look for the Silver Lining

1950
- Cinderella
- Three Little Words
- The West Point Story

1951
- ★ An American in Paris
- Alice in Wonderland
- The Great Caruso
- Show Boat

1952
- Hans Christian Andersen
- The Medium
- Singin' in the Rain

1953
- The Band Wagon
- Calamity Jane
- The 5000 Fingers of Dr. T
- Kiss Me Kate

1954
- ★ Seven Brides for Seven Brothers
- Carmen Jones
- The Glenn Miller Story
- A Star Is Born
- There's No Business Like Show Business

1955
- ★ Oklahoma!
- Daddy Long Legs
- Guys and Dolls
- It's Always Fair Weather
- Love Me or Leave Me

1956
- ★ The King and I
- The Eddy Duchin Story
- High Society
- Meet Me in Las Vegas

1958
- ★ Gigi
- Damn Yankees
- South Pacific

1959
- The Five Pennies
- Li'l Abner
- Sleeping Beauty

1960
- ★ Song Without End
- Bells Are Ringing
- Can-Can
- Let's Make Love

1961
- ★ West Side Story
- Babes in Toyland
- Flower Drum Song
- Paris Blues

1968
- Finian's Rainbow
- Funny Girl

1969
- ★ Hello, Dolly!
- Goodbye, Mr. Chips
- Paint Your Wagon
- Sweet Charity
- They Shoot Horses, Don't They?

ORIGINAL SCORE

1938
- ★ The Adventures of Robin Hood
- Breaking the Ice
- The Cowboy and the Lady
- Marie Antoinette
- The Young in Heart

1939
- ★ The Wizard of Oz
- Dark Victory
- Eternally Yours
- Golden Boy
- Gone with the Wind
- Gulliver's Travels
- The Man in the Iron Mask
- Nurse Edith Cavell
- Of Mice and Men
- The Rains Came
- Wuthering Heights

1940
- ★ Pinocchio
- Arizona
- Dark Command
- The Grapes of Wrath
- The Great Dictator
- The Howards of Virginia
- The Letter
- The Long Voyage Home
- The Mark of Zorro
- My Favorite Wife
- One Million B.C.
- Rebecca
- The Thief of Bagdad
- Waterloo Bridge

1962
- ★ Lawrence of Arabia
- Mutiny on the Bounty
- Taras Bulba
- To Kill a Mockingbird

1963
- ★ Tom Jones
- Cleopatra
- 55 Days at Peking
- How the West Was Won
- It's a Mad, Mad, Mad, Mad World

1964
- ★ Mary Poppins
- Becket
- The Fall of the Roman Empire
- Hush, Hush, Sweet Charlotte
- Mary Poppins
- The Pink Panther

1965
- ★ Doctor Zhivago
- The Agony and the Ecstasy
- The Greatest Story Ever Told
- A Patch of Blue
- Umbrellas of Cherbourg

1966
- ★ Born Free
- The Bible
- Cool Hand Luke
- Hawaii
- The Sand Pebbles
- Who's Afraid of Virginia Woolf?

1967
- ★ Thoroughly Modern Millie
- Doctor Dolittle
- Far from the Madding Crowd
- In Cold Blood
- Thoroughly Modern Millie

1968
- ★ The Lion in Winter
- Planet of the Apes
- The Shoes of the Fisherman
- The Thomas Crown Affair

1969
- ★ Butch Cassidy and the Sundance Kid
- Anne of the Thousand Days
- The Reivers
- The Wild Bunch

1970
- ★ Love Story
- Airport
- Cromwell
- Patton

1975
- ★ Jaws
- Bite the Bullet
- One Flew Over the Cuckoo's Nest
- The Wind and the Lion

1976
- ★ The Omen
- Bugsy Malone
- Obsession
- The Outlaw Josey Wales
- Taxi Driver
- Voyage of the Damned

1977
- ★ Star Wars
- Close Encounters of the Third Kind
- Julia
- Mohammed: Messenger of God
- The Spy Who Loved Me

1978
- ★ Midnight Express
- The Boys from Brazil
- Days of Heaven
- Heaven Can Wait
- Superman: The Movie

1979
- ★ A Little Romance
- The Amityville Horror
- The Champ

- Star Trek: The Motion Picture
- 10

1980
- ★ Fame
- Altered States
- The Elephant Man
- The Empire Strikes Back
- Tess

1981
- ★ Chariots of Fire
- Dragonslayer
- On Golden Pond
- Ragtime
- Raiders of the Lost Ark

1982
- ★ E.T.: The Extra-Terrestrial
- Gandhi
- An Officer and a Gentleman
- Poltergeist
- Sophie's Choice

1983
- ★ The Right Stuff
- Cross Creek
- Return of the Jedi
- Terms of Endearment
- Under Fire

1984
- ★ A Passage to India
- Indiana Jones and the Temple of Doom
- The Natural
- The River
- Under the Volcano

1985
- ★ Out of Africa
- Agnes of God
- The Color Purple
- Silverado
- Witness

1986
- ★ Round Midnight
- Aliens
- Hoosiers
- The Mission
- Star Trek 4: The Voyage Home

1987
- ★ The Last Emperor
- Cry Freedom
- Empire of the Sun
- The Untouchables
- The Witches of Eastwick

1988
- ★ The Milagro Beanfield War
- The Accidental Tourist
- Dangerous Liaisons
- Gorillas in the Mist
- Rain Man

1989
- ★ The Little Mermaid
- Born on the Fourth of July
- The Fabulous Baker Boys
- Field of Dreams
- Indiana Jones and the Last Crusade

1990
- ★ Dances with Wolves
- Avalon
- Ghost
- Havana

- Home Alone

1991
- ★ Beauty and the Beast
- Bugsy
- The Fisher King
- JFK
- The Prince of Tides

1992
- ★ Aladdin
- Basic Instinct
- Chaplin
- Howard's End
- A River Runs Through It

1993
- ★ Schindler's List
- The Age of Innocence
- The Firm
- The Fugitive
- The Remains of the Day

1994
- ★ The Lion King
- Forrest Gump
- Interview with the Vampire
- Little Women
- The Shawshank Redemption

1995
- ★ Pocahontas
- The American President
- Sabrina
- Toy Story
- Unstrung Heroes

1996
- ★ Emma
- The First Wives Club
- The Hunchback of Notre Dame
- James and the Giant Peach
- The Preacher's Wife

1997
- ★ Titanic
- Amistad
- Good Will Hunting
- Kundun
- L.A. Confidential

SONG

1934
- ★ "The Continental"/The Gay Divorcee
- "Carioca"/Flying Down to Rio

1935
- ★ "Lullaby of Broadway"/Gold Diggers of 1935
- "Cheek to Cheek"/Top Hat
- "Lovely to Look At"/Roberta

1936
- ★ "The Way You Look Tonight"/Swing Time
- "A Melody from the Sky"/The Trail of the Lonesome Pine
- "Did I Remember"/Suzy
- "I've Got You Under My Skin"/Born to Dance
- "My Own"/That Certain Age

1937
★ "Sweet Leilani"/Waikiki Wedding
"That Old Feeling"/ Vogues of 1938
"They Can't Take That Away From Me"/Shall We Dance

1938
★ "Thanks for the Memories"/The Big Broadcast of 1938
"Always and Always"/ Mannequin
"Change Partners and Dance with Me"/ Carefree
"Now It Can Be Told"/ Alexander's Ragtime Band
"The Cowboy and the Lady"/The Cowboy and the Lady

1939
★ "Over the Rainbow"/The Wizard of Oz
"Faithful Forever"/ Gulliver's Travels
"I Poured My Heart Into Song"/Second Fiddle
"Wishing"/Love Affair

1940
★ "When You Wish Upon a Star"/Pinocchio
"Down Argentine Way"/ Down Argentine Way
"I'd Know You Anywhere"/You'll Find Out
"It's a Blue World"/Music in My Heart
"Love of My Life"/ Second Chorus
"Only Forever"/Rhythm on the River
"Our Love Affair"/Strike Up the Band

1941
★ "The Last Time I Saw Paris"/Lady Be Good
"Baby Mine"/Dumbo
"Be Honest With Me"/ Ridin' on a Rainbow
"Boogie Woogie Bugle Boy of Company B"/ Buck Privates
"Chattanooga Choo Choo"/Sun Valley Serenade
"Since I Kissed My Baby Goodbye"/You'll Never Get Rich

1942
★ "White Christmas"/ Holiday Inn
"Dearly Beloved"/You Were Never Lovelier
"How About You?"/ Babes on Broadway
"I've Got a Gal in Kalamazoo"/Orchestra Wives
"Love Is a Song"/Bambi

1943
★ "You'll Never Know"/ Hello, Frisco, Hello

"Happiness Is a Thing Called Joe"/Cabin in the Sky
"My Shining Hour"/The Sky's the Limit
"That Old Black Magic"/ Star Spangled Rhythm
"They're Either Too Young or Too Old"/ Thank Your Lucky Stars
"We Mustn't Say Goodbye"/Stage Door Canteen

1944
★ "Swinging on a Star"/ Going My Way
"I Couldn't Sleep A Wink Last Night"/Higher and Higher
"I'll Walk Alone"/Follow the Boys
"Long Ago and Far Away"/Cover Girl
"Now I Know"/Up in Arms
"Sweet Dreams Sweetheart"/Hollywood Canteen
"The Trolley Song"/Meet Me in St. Louis

1945
★ "It Might as Well Be Spring"/State Fair
"Accentuate the Positive"/Here Come the Waves
"Anywhere"/Tonight and Every Night
"Aren't You Glad You're You"/The Bells of St. Mary's
"I Fall in Love Too Easily"/Anchors Aweigh
"More and More"/Can't Help Singing
"So in Love"/Wonder Man
"Some Sunday Morning"/San Antonio

1946
★ "On the Atchison, Topeka and Santa Fe"/ The Harvey Girls
"I Can't Begin to Tell You"/The Dolly Sisters
"You Keep Coming Back Like a Song"/Blue Skies

1947
"I Wish I Didn't Love You So"/The Perils of Pauline
"Pass That Peace Pipe"/ Good News

1948
★ "Buttons and Bows"/The Paleface
"It's Magic"/Romance on the High Seas

1949
★ "Baby It's Cold Outside"/Neptune's Daughter
"It's a Great Feeling"/It's a Great Feeling

"Lavender Blue"/So Dear to My Heart
"Through a Long and Sleepless Night"/ Come to the Stable

1950
★ "Be My Love"/The Toast of New Orleans
"Bibbidy-Bobbidi-Boo"/ Cinderella

1951
★ "In the Cool, Cool, Cool of the Evening"/Here Comes the Groom
"Too Late Now"/Royal Wedding
"Wonder Why"/Rich, Young and Pretty

1952
★ "High Noon (Do Not Forsake Me, Oh My Darlin')"/High Noon
"Am I in Love"/Son of Paleface
"Because You're Mine"/ Because You're Mine
"Thumbelina"/Hans Christian Andersen
"Zing a Little Zong"/Just for You

1953
★ "Secret Love"/Calamity Jane
"My Flaming Heart"/ Small Town Girl
"Sadie Thompson's Song (Blue Pacific Blues)"/Miss Sadie Thompson
"That's Amore"/The Caddy
"The Moon is Blue"/The Moon Is Blue

1954
★ "Three Coins in the Fountain"/Three Coins in the Fountain
"Count Your Blessings Instead of Sheep"/ White Christmas
"Hold My Hand"/Susan Slept Here
"The Man That Got Away"/A Star Is Born

1955
★ "Love Is a Many-Splendored Thing"/ Love Is a Many-Splendored Thing
"(Love Is) The Tender Trap"/The Tender Trap
"I'll Never Stop Loving You"/Love Me or Leave Me
"Something's Gotta Give"/Daddy Long Legs

1956
★ "Que Sera, Sera"/The Man Who Knew Too Much
"Friendly Persuasion (Thee I Love)"/Friendly Persuasion
"True Love"/High Society
"Written on the Wind"/ Written on the Wind

1957
★ "An Affair to Remember"/An Affair to Remember
"Tammy"/Tammy and the Bachelor

1958
★ "Gigi"/Gigi
"A Very Precious Love"/ Marjorie Morningstar
"Almost in Your Arms (Love Song from Houseboat)"/ Houseboat
"To Love and Be Loved"/Some Came Running

1959
★ "High Hopes"/A Hole in the Head
"Strange Are the Ways of Love"/The Young Land
"The Best of Everything"/The Best of Everything
"The Five Pennies"/The Five Pennies
"The Hanging Tree"/The Hanging Tree

1960
★ "Never on Sunday"/ Never on Sunday
"The Facts of Life"/The Facts of Life
"The Green Leaves of Summer"/The Alamo

1961
★ "Moon River"/Breakfast at Tiffany's
"Bachelor in Paradise"/ Bachelor in Paradise
"Love Theme (The Falcon and the Dove)"/El Cid
"Pocketful of Miracles"/ Pocketful of Miracles

1962
★ "Days of Wine and Roses"/Days of Wine and Roses
"Love Song (Follow Me)"/Mutiny on the Bounty
"Song fromm Two for the Seesaw (Second Chance)"/Two for the Seesaw
"Walk on the Wild Side"/ Walk on the Wild Side

1963
★ "Call Me Irresponsible"/ Papa's Delicate Condition
"Charade"/Charade
"It's a Mad, Mad, Mad World"/It's a Mad, Mad, Mad, Mad World
"More"/Mondo Cane
"So Little Time"/55 Days at Peking

1964
★ "Chim Chim Cher-ee"/ Mary Poppins

"Hush, Hush, Sweet Charlotte"/Hush, Hush, Sweet Charlotte
"My Kind of Town"/ Robin and the 7 Hoods
"Where Love Has Gone"/Where Love Has Gone

1965
★ "The Shadow of Your Smile"/The Sandpiper
"I Will Wait for You"/ Umbrellas of Cherbourg
"The Ballad of Cat Ballou"/Cat Ballou
"The Sweetheart Tree"/ The Great Race
"What's New Pussycat?"/What's New Pussycat?

1966
★ "Born Free"/Born Free
"Alfie"/Alfie
"Georgy Girl"/Georgy Girl
"My Wishing Doll"/ Hawaii

1967
★ "Talk to the Animals"/ Doctor Dolittle
"The Bare Necessities"/ The Jungle Book
"The Look of Love"/ Casino Royale
"Thoroughly Modern Millie"/Thoroughly Modern Millie

1968
★ "The Windmills of Your Mind"/The Thomas Crown Affair
"Chitty Chitty Bang Bang"/Chitty Chitty Bang Bang
"For Love of Ivy"/For Love of Ivy
"Funny Girl"/Funny Girl
"Star!"/Star!

1969
★ "Raindrops Keep Fallin' on My Head"/Butch Cassidy and the Sundance Kid
"Come Saturday Morning"/The Sterile Cuckoo
"Jean"/The Prime of Miss Jean Brodie
"True Grit"/True Grit
"What Are You Doing the Rest of Your Life?"/The Happy Ending

1970
★ "For All We Know"/ Lovers and Other Strangers
"Thank You Very Much"/ Scrooge
"Till Love Touches Your Life"/Madron
"Whistling Away the Dark"/Darling Lili

1971
★ "Theme from Shaft"/ Shaft

SONG *cont.*

1941

★ Citizen Kane
The Devil & Miss Jones
Sergeant York

1942

★ Woman of the Year
One of Our Aircraft Is
Missing
The Road to Morocco
Wake Island

1943

Air Force
In Which We Serve
The North Star
So Proudly We Hail

1944

★ Wilson
Hail the Conquering Hero
Miracle of Morgan's Creek
Two Girls and a Sailor
A Wing and a Prayer

1945

Dillinger

1946

★ The Seventh Veil
The Blue Dahlia
Children of Paradise
Notorious
The Road to Utopia
To Each His Own

1947

★ The Bachelor and the
Bobby-Soxer
Body and Soul
A Double Life
Monsieur Verdoux
Shoeshine

1956

★ The Red Balloon
La Strada
The Ladykillers

1974

★ Chinatown
Alice Doesn't Live Here
Anymore
The Conversation
Day for Night
Harry and Tonto

1975

★ Dog Day Afternoon
Amarcord
And Now My Love
Lies My Father Told Me
Shampoo

1976

★ Network
Cousin, Cousine
The Front
Rocky
Seven Beauties

1977

★ Annie Hall
The Goodbye Girl
The Late Show
Star Wars
The Turning Point

1978

★ Coming Home
Autumn Sonata
The Deer Hunter

Interiors
An Unmarried Woman

1979

★ Breaking Away
All That Jazz
And Justice for All
The China Syndrome
Manhattan

1980

★ Melvin and Howard
Brubaker
Fame
Mon Oncle D'Amerique
Private Benjamin

1981

★ Chariots of Fire
Absence of Malice
Arthur
Atlantic City
Reds

1982

★ Gandhi
Diner
E.T.: The Extra-Terrestrial
An Officer and a
Gentleman
Tootsie

1983

★ Tender Mercies
The Big Chill
Fanny and Alexander
Silkwood
WarGames

1984

★ Places in the Heart
Beverly Hills Cop
Broadway Danny Rose
El Norte
Splash

1985

★ Witness
Back to the Future
Brazil
The Official Story
The Purple Rose of Cairo

1986

★ Hannah and Her Sisters
Crocodile Dundee
My Beautiful Laundrette
Platoon
Salvador

1987

★ Moonstruck
Au Revoir Les Enfants
Broadcast News
Hope and Glory
Radio Days

1988

★ Rain Man
Big
Bull Durham
A Fish Called Wanda
Running on Empty

1989

★ Dead Poets Society
Crimes & Misdemeanors
Do the Right Thing
sex, lies and videotape
When Harry Met Sally...

1990

★ Ghost

Alice
Avalon
Green Card
Metropolitan

1991

★ Thelma & Louise
Boyz N the Hood
Bugsy
The Fisher King
Grand Canyon

1992

★ The Crying Game
Husbands and Wives
Lorenzo's Oil
Passion Fish
Unforgiven

1993

★ The Piano
Dave
In the Line of Fire
Philadelphia
Sleepless in Seattle

1994

★ Pulp Fiction
Bullets Over Broadway
Four Weddings and a
Funeral
Heavenly Creatures
Trois Couleurs: Rouge

1995

★ The Usual Suspects
Braveheart
Mighty Aphrodite
Nixon
Toy Story

1996

★ Fargo
Jerry Maguire
Lone Star
Secrets and Lies
Shine

1997

★ Good Will Hunting
As Good As It Gets
Boogie Nights
Deconstructing Harry
The Full Monty

SCREENPLAY

1935

★ The Informer
The Lives of a Bengal
Lancer
Mutiny on the Bounty

1936

After the Thin Man
Dodsworth
Mr. Deeds Goes to Town
My Man Godfrey

1937

★ The Life of Emile Zola
The Awful Truth
Captains Courageous
Stage Door

1938

★ Pygmalion
The Citadel
Four Daughters
You Can't Take It with You

1939

★ Gone with the Wind

Goodbye, Mr. Chips
Wuthering Heights

1940

★ The Philadelphia Story
The Grapes of Wrath
Kitty Foyle
The Long Voyage Home
Rebecca

1941

★ Here Comes Mr. Jordan
How Green Was My
Valley
The Little Foxes
The Maltese Falcon

1942

★ Mrs. Miniver
The Forty-Ninth Parallel
The Pride of the Yankees
Random Harvest
Talk of the Town

1943

★ Casablanca
The More the Merrier
The Song of Bernadette
Watch on the Rhine

1944

★ Going My Way
Double Indemnity
Gaslight
Laura
Meet Me in St. Louis

1945

★ The Lost Weekend
Mildred Pierce
A Tree Grows in Brooklyn

1946

★ The Best Years of Our
Lives
Anna and the King of Siam
Brief Encounter
The Killers
Open City

1947

★ Miracle on 34th Street
Boomerang
Crossfire
Gentleman's Agreement
Great Expectations

1948

★ Treasure of the Sierra
Madre
Johnny Belinda
The Search
The Snake Pit

1949

★ A Letter to Three Wives
All the King's Men
The Bicycle Thief
Champion
The Fallen Idol

1950

★ All About Eve
The Asphalt Jungle
Born Yesterday
Broken Arrow
Father of the Bride

1951

★ A Place in the Sun
The African Queen
Detective Story
La Ronde

A Streetcar Named Desire

1952

★ The Bad and the Beautiful
Five Fingers
High Noon
The Man in the White Suit
The Quiet Man

1953

★ From Here to Eternity
Cruel Sea
Lili
Roman Holiday
Shane
Titanic

1954

★ Country Girl
The Caine Mutiny
Rear Window
Sabrina
Seven Brides for Seven
Brothers

1955

★ Marty
Bad Day at Black Rock
Blackboard Jungle
East of Eden
Interrupted Melody
Love Me or Leave Me

STORY

1928

★ Underworld
Last Command

1931

Public Enemy

1932

★ The Champ
What Price Hollywood?

1933

The Prizefighter and the
Lady
Rasputin and the Empress

1934

★ Manhattan Melodrama
Hide-Out

1935

Broadway Melody of 1936

1936

★ The Story of Louis Pasteur
Fury
The Great Ziegfeld
San Francisco
Three Smart Girls

1937

★ A Star Is Born
In Old Chicago
100 Men and a Girl

1938

★ Boys Town
Alexander's Ragtime Band
Angels with Dirty Faces
Mad About Music
Test Pilot

1939

★ Mr. Smith Goes to
Washington
Bachelor Mother
Love Affair
Ninotchka

1990
★ Journey of Hope

1991
★ Mediterranee

1992
★ Indochine

1993
★ Belle Epoque

1994
★ Burnt by the Sun

1995
★ Antonia's Line

1996
★ Kolya
★ Ridicule
A Chef in Love
Ridicule

1997
★ Character

AUSTRALIAN FILM INSTITUTE

ACTOR

1974
★ Jack Thompson/Sunday Too Far Away

1975
★ John Meillon/Fourth Wish

1976
★ Simon Burke/The Devil's Playground
★ Nick Tate/The Devil's Playground

1978
★ Bill Hunter/Newsfront

1979
★ Mel Gibson/Tim

1980
★ Jack Thompson/Breaker Morant

1981
★ Mel Gibson/Gallipoli

1983
★ Norman Kaye/Man of Flowers

1984
★ John Hargreaves/My First Wife

1986
★ Colin Friels/Malcolm

1987
★ Leo McKern/Travelling North

1989
★ Sam Neill/A Cry in the Dark

1990
★ Max von Sydow/Father

1991
★ Hugo Weaving/Proof

1992
★ Russell Crowe/Romper Stomper

1993
★ Harvey Keitel/The Piano

1994
★ Nicholas Hope/Bad Boy Bubby
Terence Stamp/The Adventures of Priscilla, Queen of the Desert
Hugo Weaving/The Adventures of Priscilla, Queen of the Desert

1995
★ John Lynch/Angel Baby

1996
★ Geoffrey Rush/Shine
John Brumpton/Life
Noah Taylor/Shine
Aden Young/River Street

1997
★ Richard Roxburgh/Doing Time for Patsy Cline
Michael Caton/The Castle
Matt Day/Kiss or Kill
Jeremy Sims/Idiot Box

ACTOR—SUPPORTING

1991
★ Russell Crowe/Proof

1992
★ Barry Otto/Strictly Ballroom
Bill Hunter/The Last Days of Chez Nous

1994
Bill Hunter/Muriel's Wedding
John Polson/The Sum of Us

1995
★ Ray Barrett/Sorrento Beach

1996
★ Armin Mueller-Stahl/Shine
Ray Barrett/Brilliant Lies
Robert Morgan/Life
Barry Otto/Cosi

1997
★ Andrew S. Gilbert/Kiss or Kill
Chris Haywood/Kiss or Kill
Simon Lyndon/Blackrock
Charles Tingwell/The Castle

ACTRESS

1977
★ Pat Bishop/Don's Party

1980
★ Tracey Mann/Hard Knocks

1981
★ Judy Davis/The Winter of Our Dreams

1982
★ Noni Hazlehurst/Monkey Grip

1983
★ Wendy Hughes/Careful, He Might Hear You

1985
★ Noni Hazlehurst/Fran

1986
★ Judy Davis/Kangaroo

1987
★ Judy Davis/High Tide

1989
★ Meryl Streep/A Cry in the Dark

1990
★ Julia Blake/Father

1991
★ Sheila Florence/A Woman's Tale

1992
★ Lisa Harrow/The Last Days of Chez Nous

1993
★ Holly Hunter/The Piano

1994
★ Toni Collette/Muriel's Wedding

1995
★ Jacqueline McKenzie/Angel Baby
Caroline Gillmer/Sorrento Beach
Caroline Goodall/Sorrento Beach
Lisa Harrow/That Eye, the Sky

1996
★ Judy Davis/Children of the Revolution
Gia Carides/Brilliant Lies
Claudia Karvan/Dating the Enemy
Frances O'Connor/Love and Other Catastrophes

1997
★ Pamela Rabe/The Well
Frances O'Connor/Kiss or Kill
Frances O'Connor/Thank God He Met Lizzie
Miranda Otto/The Well

ACTRESS—SUPPORTING

1992
★ Pat Thomsen/Strictly Ballroom

1994
★ Rachel Griffiths/Muriel's Wedding
Jeanie Drynan/Muriel's Wedding

Deborah Kennedy/The Sum of Us

1995
★ Toni Collette/Lilian's Story
★ Amanda Douge/That Eye, the Sky

1996
★ Toni Collette/Cosi
Zoe Carides/Brilliant Lies
Alice Garner/Love and Other Catastrophes
Annete Shun-Wah/Floating Life

1997
★ Cate Blanchett/Thank God He Met Lizzie
Annie Byron/Doing Time for Patsy Cline
Sophie Lee/The Castle
Rebecca Smart/Blackrock

ART DIRECTION

1996
★ Children of the Revolution

1997
★ The Well
Doing Time for Patsy Cline
Idiot Box
Thank God He Met Lizzie

CINEMATOGRAPHY

1988
★ The Navigator

1992
★ Black Robe

1993
★ The Piano

1994
The Adventures of Priscilla, Queen of the Desert
Bad Boy Bubby

1995
★ Angel Baby

1996
★ Shine

1997
★ Doing Time for Patsy Cline
Blackrock
Kiss or Kill
The Well

COSTUME DESIGN

1992
★ Strictly Ballroom

1993
★ The Piano

1994
★ The Adventures of Priscilla, Queen of the Desert

1996
★ Children of the Revolution

1997
★ Doing Time for Patsy Cline

Kiss or Kill
Thank God He Met Lizzie
The Well

DIRECTOR

1988
★ Vincent Ward/The Navigator

1991
★ Jocelyn Moorhouse/Proof

1992
★ Baz Luhrmann/Strictly Ballroom
Gillian Armstrong/The Last Days of Chez Nous

1993
★ Jane Campion/The Piano

1994
★ Rolf de Heer/Bad Boy Bubby
Stephan Elliott/The Adventures of Priscilla, Queen of the Desert
P.J. Hogan/Muriel's Wedding

1995
★ Michael Rymer/Angel Baby
Richard Franklin/Sorrento Beach
John Ruane/That Eye, the Sky

1996
★ Scott Hicks/Shine
Paul Cox/Lust and Revenge
Peter Duncan/Children of the Revolution
Clara Law/Floating Life

1997
★ Bill Bennett/Kiss or Kill
David Caesar/Idiot Box
Chris Kennedy/Doing Time for Patsy Cline
Samantha Lang/The Well

FILM

1974
★ Sunday Too Far Away

1976
★ The Devil's Playground

1978
★ Newsfront

1979
★ My Brilliant Career

1980
★ Breaker Morant

1981
★ Gallipoli

1982
★ Lonely Hearts

1983
★ Careful, He Might Hear You

FILM ⟋cont.

1984
- ★ *A Test of Love*

1985
- ★ *Bliss*

1986
- ★ *Malcolm*

1987
- ★ *The Year My Voice Broke*

1988
- ★ *The Navigator*

1989
- ★ *A Cry in the Dark*

1990
- ★ *Flirting*

1991
- ★ *Proof*

1992
- ★ *Strictly Ballroom*
  The Last Days of Chez Nous

1993
- ★ *The Piano*

1994
- ★ *Muriel's Wedding*
  The Adventures of Priscilla, Queen of the Desert
  Bad Boy Bubby
  The Sum of Us

1995
- ★ *Angel Baby*
  Sorrento Beach
  That Eye, the Sky

1996
- ★ *Shine*
  Children of the Revolution
  Life
  Love and Other Catastrophes
  Mr. Reliable: A True Story

1997
- ★ *Kiss or Kill*
  Blackrock
  Doing Time for Patsy Cline
  The Well

FILM EDITING

1991
- ★ *Proof*

1992
- ★ *Strictly Ballroom*

1993
- ★ *The Piano*

1994
- ★ *Bad Boy Bubby*

1995
- ★ *Angel Baby*

1996
- ★ *Shine*

1997
- ★ *Kiss or Kill*
  Idiot Box
  Thank God He Met Lizzie
  The Well

SCORE

1992
- ★ *Romper Stomper*

1993
- ★ *The Piano*

1996
- ★ *Shine*

1997
- ★ *Doing Time for Patsy Cline*
  Idiot Box
  Road to Nhill
  The Well

SOUND

1992
- ★ *Romper Stomper*

1993
- ★ *The Piano*

1994
- ★ *Muriel's Wedding*

1996
- ★ *Shine*

1997
- ★ *Kiss or Kill*
  Doing Time for Patsy Cline
  Idiot Box
  The Well

ADAPTED SCREENPLAY

1994
- ★ *The Sum of Us*

1995
- ★ *Sorrento Beach*

1996
- ★ *Cosi*

1997
- ★ *The Well*
  Blackrock

ORIGINAL SCREENPLAY

1994
- ★ *Bad Boy Bubby*
  The Adventures of Priscilla, Queen of the Desert
  Muriel's Wedding

1995
- ★ *Angel Baby*

1996
- ★ *Shine*

1997
- ★ *The Castle*
  Doing Time for Patsy Cline
  Kiss or Kill
  Road to Nhill

SCREENPLAY

1991
- ★ *Proof*

1992
- ★ *Strictly Ballroom*

1993
- ★ *The Piano*

FILM—FOREIGN LANGUAGE

1992
- ★ *Truly, Madly, Deeply*

1993
- ★ *The Crying Game*

1994
- ★ *Four Weddings and a Funeral*

1995
- ★ *Once Were Warriors*
  Heavenly Creatures
  Priest
  Pulp Fiction

1996
- ★ *Fargo*
  Burnt by the Sun
  Dead Man Walking
  Trainspotting

1997
- ★ *Secrets and Lies*

BRITISH ACADEMY OF FILM AND TELEVISION ARTS

ACTOR

1952
- ★ **Marlon Brando/***Viva Zapata!*

1953
- ★ **Marlon Brando/***Julius Caesar*
- ★ **John Gielgud/***Julius Caesar*

1954
- ★ **Marlon Brando/***On the Waterfront*
- ★ **Kenneth More/***Doctor in the House*

1955
- ★ **Ernest Borgnine/***Marty*
- ★ **Laurence Olivier/***Richard III*

1956
- ★ **Francois Perier/***Gervaise*

1957
- ★ **Henry Fonda/***Twelve Angry Men*
- ★ **Alec Guinness/***The Bridge on the River Kwai*

1958
- ★ **Trevor Howard/***The Key*

- ★ **Sidney Poitier/***The Defiant Ones*

1959
- ★ **Jack Lemmon/***Some Like It Hot*
- ★ **Peter Sellers/***I'm All Right Jack*

1960
- ★ **Jack Lemmon/***The Apartment*

1961
- ★ **Peter Finch/***No Love for Johnnie*
- ★ **Paul Newman/***The Hustler*

1962
- ★ **Burt Lancaster/***Birdman of Alcatraz*
- ★ **Peter O'Toole/***Lawrence of Arabia*

1963
- ★ **Dirk Bogarde/***The Servant*
- ★ **Marcello Mastroianni/***Divorce—Italian Style*

1964
- ★ **Richard Attenborough/***Seance on a Wet Afternoon*
- ★ **Marcello Mastroianni/***Yesterday, Today and Tomorrow*

1965
- ★ **Dirk Bogarde/***Darling*
- ★ **Lee Marvin/***Cat Ballou*

1966
- ★ **Richard Burton/***Who's Afraid of Virginia Woolf?*
- ★ **Rod Steiger/***The Pawnbroker*

1967
- ★ **Paul Scofield/***A Man for All Seasons*
- ★ **Rod Steiger/***In the Heat of the Night*

1968
- ★ **Spencer Tracy/***Guess Who's Coming to Dinner*

1969
- ★ **Dustin Hoffman/***Midnight Cowboy*

1970
- ★ **Robert Redford/***Butch Cassidy and the Sundance Kid*

1971
- ★ **Peter Finch/***Sunday, Bloody Sunday*

1972
- ★ **Gene Hackman/***The French Connection*

1973
- ★ **Walter Matthau/***Pete 'n' Tillie*

1974
- ★ **Jack Nicholson/***Chinatown*

- ★ **Jack Nicholson/***The Last Detail*

1975
- ★ **Al Pacino/***Dog Day Afternoon*

1976
- ★ **Jack Nicholson/***One Flew Over the Cuckoo's Nest*

1977
- ★ **Peter Finch/***Network*

1978
- ★ **Richard Dreyfuss/***The Goodbye Girl*

1979
- ★ **Jack Lemmon/***The China Syndrome*

1980
- ★ **John Hurt/***The Elephant Man*

1981
- ★ **Burt Lancaster/***Atlantic City*

1982
- ★ **Ben Kingsley/***Gandhi*

1983
- ★ **Michael Caine/***Educating Rita*
- ★ **Dustin Hoffman/***Tootsie*

1984
- ★ **Haing S. Ngor/***The Killing Fields*

1985
- ★ **William Hurt/***Kiss of the Spider Woman*

1986
- ★ **Bob Hoskins/***Mona Lisa*

1987
- ★ **Sean Connery/***The Name of the Rose*

1988
- ★ **John Cleese/***A Fish Called Wanda*

1989
- ★ **Daniel Day-Lewis/***My Left Foot*

1990
- ★ **Philippe Noiret/***Cinema Paradiso*

1991
- ★ **Anthony Hopkins/***The Silence of the Lambs*

1992
- ★ **Robert Downey, Jr./***Chaplin*

1993
- ★ **Anthony Hopkins/***The Remains of the Day*
  Daniel Day-Lewis/*In the Name of the Father*

1994
- ★ **Hugh Grant/***Four Weddings and a Funeral*

ACTRESS— SUPPORTING
cont.

1977

★ **Jenny Agutter**/*Equus*

1978

★ **Geraldine Page**/*Interiors*
★ **Vanessa Redgrave**/*Julia*

1979

★ **Rachel Roberts**/*Yanks*

1982

★ **Rohini Hattangady**/*Gandhi*
★ **Maureen Stapleton**/*Reds*

1983

★ **Jamie Lee Curtis**/*Trading Places*

1984

★ **Liz Smith**/*A Private Function*

1985

★ **Rosanna Arquette**/*Desperately Seeking Susan*

1986

★ **Judi Dench**/*A Room with a View*

1987

★ **Susan Wooldridge**/*Hope and Glory*

1988

★ **Judi Dench**/*A Handful of Dust*

1989

★ **Michelle Pfeiffer**/*Dangerous Liaisons*

1990

★ **Whoopi Goldberg**/*Ghost*

1991

★ **Kate Nelligan**/*Frankie and Johnny*

1992

★ **Miranda Richardson**/*Damage*

1993

★ **Miriam Margolyes**/*The Age of Innocence*
Holly Hunter/*The Firm*
Maggie Smith/*The Secret Garden*

1994

★ **Kristin Scott Thomas**/*Four Weddings and a Funeral*
Winona Ryder/*The Age of Innocence*

1995

★ **Kate Winslet**/*Sense and Sensibility*
Joan Allen/*Nixon*
Mira Sorvino/*Mighty Aphrodite*

Elizabeth Spriggs/*Sense and Sensibility*

1996

★ **Juliette Binoche**/*The English Patient*
Lauren Bacall/*The Mirror Has Two Faces*
Marianne Jean-Baptiste/*Secrets and Lies*
Lynn Redgrave/*Shine*

1997

★ **Sigourney Weaver**/*The Ice Storm*
Jennifer Ehle/*Wilde*
Lesley Sharp/*The Full Monty*
Zoe Wanamaker/*Wilde*

ART DIRECTION

1997

★ **William Shakespeare's Romeo and Juliet**

CINEMATOGRAPHY

1995

★ *Braveheart*
Apollo 13
The Madness of King George
Sense and Sensibility

1996

★ *The English Patient*

1997

★ *The Wings of the Dove*
L.A. Confidential
Titanic
William Shakespeare's Romeo and Juliet

COSTUME DESIGN

1997

★ *Mrs. Brown*
L.A. Confidential
Titanic
The Wings of the Dove

DIRECTOR

1955

★ **Laurence Olivier**/*Richard III*

1968

★ **Mike Nichols**/*The Graduate*

1969

★ **John Schlesinger**/*Midnight Cowboy*

1970

★ **George Roy Hill**/*Butch Cassidy and the Sundance Kid*

1971

★ **John Schlesinger**/*Sunday, Bloody Sunday*

1972

★ **Bob Fosse**/*Cabaret*

1973

★ **Francois Truffaut**/*Day for Night*

1974

★ **Roman Polanski**/*Chinatown*

1975

★ **Stanley Kubrick**/*Barry Lyndon*

1976

★ **Milos Forman**/*One Flew Over the Cuckoo's Nest*

1977

★ **Woody Allen**/*Annie Hall*

1978

★ **Alan Parker**/*Midnight Express*

1979

★ **Francis Ford Coppola**/*Apocalypse Now*

1980

★ **Akira Kurosawa**/*Kagemusha*

1981

★ **Louis Malle**/*Atlantic City*

1982

★ **Richard Attenborough**/*Gandhi*

1983

★ **Bill Forsyth**/*Local Hero*

1984

★ **Wim Wenders**/*Paris, Texas*

1986

★ **Woody Allen**/*Hannah and Her Sisters*

1987

★ **Oliver Stone**/*Platoon*

1988

★ **Louis Malle**/*Au Revoir Les Enfants*

1989

★ **Kenneth Branagh**/*Henry V*

1990

★ **Martin Scorsese**/*Goodfellas*

1991

★ **Alan Parker**/*The Commitments*

1992

★ **Clint Eastwood**/*Unforgiven*

1993

★ **Steven Spielberg**/*Schindler's List*

1994

★ **Mike Newell**/*Four Weddings and a Funeral*
Richard Attenborough/*Shadowlands*
Jane Campion/*The Piano*
James Ivory/*The Remains of the Day*

1995

★ **Michael Radford**/*The Postman*
Mel Gibson/*Braveheart*
Nicholas Hytner/*The Madness of King George*
Ang Lee/*Sense and Sensibility*

1996

★ **Joel Coen**/*Fargo*
Scott Hicks/*Shine*
Mike Leigh/*Secrets and Lies*
Anthony Minghella/*The English Patient*

1997

★ **Baz Luhrmann**/*William Shakespeare's Romeo and Juliet*
James Cameron/*Titanic*
Peter Cattaneo/*The Full Monty*
Curtis Hanson/*L.A. Confidential*

FILM

1947

★ *The Best Years of Our Lives*
★ *Odd Man Out*

1948

★ *The Fallen Idol*
★ *Hamlet*

1949

★ *The Bicycle Thief*
★ *The Third Man*

1950

★ *All About Eve*
★ *The Blue Lamp*

1951

★ *La Ronde*
★ *The Lavender Hill Mob*

1953

★ *Forbidden Games*
★ *Genevieve*

1954

★ *Hobson's Choice*
★ *Wages of Fear*

1955

★ *Richard III*

1956

★ *Gervaise*
★ *Reach for the Sky*

1957

★ *The Bridge on the River Kwai*

1958

★ *Room at the Top*

1959

★ *Ben-Hur*
★ *Sapphire*

1960

★ *The Apartment*
★ *Saturday Night and Sunday Morning*

1961

★ *Ballad of a Soldier*
★ *The Hustler*
★ *A Taste of Honey*

1962

★ *Lawrence of Arabia*

1963

★ *Tom Jones*

1964

★ *Dr. Strangelove, or: How I Learned to Stop Worrying and Love the Bomb*

1965

★ *The Ipcress File*
★ *My Fair Lady*

1966

★ *The Spy Who Came in from the Cold*
★ *Who's Afraid of Virginia Woolf?*

1967

★ *A Man for All Seasons*

1968

★ *The Graduate*

1969

★ *Midnight Cowboy*

1970

★ *Butch Cassidy and the Sundance Kid*

1971

★ *Sunday, Bloody Sunday*

1972

★ *Cabaret*

1973

★ *Day for Night*

1975

★ *Alice Doesn't Live Here Anymore*

1976

★ *One Flew Over the Cuckoo's Nest*

1977

★ *Annie Hall*

1978

★ *Julia*

1979

★ *Manhattan*

1980

★ *The Elephant Man*

1981

★ *Chariots of Fire*

1982

★ *Gandhi*

1983

★ *Educating Rita*

1984

★ *The Killing Fields*

**BROADCAST
FILM CRITICS
ASSOCIATION
AWARDS**

ACTOR

ACTOR—SUPPORTING

1993
- ★ *32 Short Films about Glenn Gould*

1994
- ★ *Exotica*

1995
- ★ *Magic in the Water*

1996
- ★ *Crash*
  Le Polygraphe
  Lilies

1997
- ★ *The Sweet Hereafter*

COSTUME DESIGN

1992
- ★ *Leolo*

1993
- ★ *Shadow of the Wolf*

1994
- ★ *Exotica*

1995
- ★ *Margaret's Museum*

1996
- ★ *Lilies*
  Blood & Donuts
  Kids in the Hall: Brain Candy
  Swann

1997
- ★ *Karmina*

DIRECTOR

1980
- ★ **Bob (Benjamin) Clark/** *Murder by Decree*

1981
- ★ **Francis Mankiewicz/** *Les Bons Debarras*

1983
- ★ **Phillip Borsos/** *The Grey Fox*

1984
- ★ **Bob (Benjamin) Clark/** *A Christmas Story*
- ★ **David Cronenberg/** *Videodrome*

1986
- ★ **Sandy Wilson/** *My American Cousin*

1987
- ★ **Denys Arcand/** *The Decline of the American Empire*

1988
- ★ **Jean-Claude Lauzon/** *Night Zoo*

1989
- ★ **David Cronenberg/** *Dead Ringers*

1990
- ★ **Denys Arcand/** *Jesus of Montreal*

1991
- ★ **Bruce Beresford/** *Black Robe*

1992
- ★ **David Cronenberg/** *Naked Lunch*

1993
- ★ **Francois Girard/** *32 Short Films about Glenn Gould*

1994
- ★ **Atom Egoyan/** *Exotica*
  Richard J. Lewis/ *Whale Music*
  Lea Pool/ *Mouvements du Desir*
  Mina Shum/ *Double Happiness*

1995
- ★ **Robert Lepage/** *The Confessional*

1996
- ★ **David Cronenberg/** *Crash*
  John Fawcett/ *The Boys Club*
  John Greyson/ *Lilies*
  Robert Lepage/ *Le Polygraphe*
  Bruce McDonald/ *Hard Core Logo*

1997
- ★ **Atom Egoyan/** *The Sweet Hereafter*
  Thom Fitzgerald/ *The Hanging Garden*
  Gabriel Pelletier/ *Karmina*
  Lynne Stopkewich/ *Kissed*

FILM

1980
- ★ *The Changeling*

1981
- ★ *Les Bons Debarras*

1982
- ★ *Ticket to Heaven*

1983
- ★ *The Grey Fox*

1984
- ★ *The Terry Fox Story*

1985
- ★ *The Bay Boy*

1986
- ★ *My American Cousin*

1987
- ★ *The Decline of the American Empire*

1988
- ★ *Night Zoo*

1989
- ★ *Dead Ringers*

1990
- ★ *Jesus of Montreal*

1991
- ★ *Black Robe*

1992
- ★ *Naked Lunch*

1993
- ★ *32 Short Films about Glenn Gould*

1994
- ★ *Exotica*
  Double Happiness
  King of the Airwaves
  Mon Amie Max
  Whale Music

1995
- ★ *The Confessional*

1996
- ★ *Lilies*
  Crash
  Hard Core Logo
  Le Polygraphe
  Long Day's Journey Into Night

1997
- ★ *The Sweet Hereafter*
  The Hanging Garden
  Karmina
  Kissed

FILM EDITING

1992
- ★ *Leolo*

1993
- ★ *32 Short Films about Glenn Gould*

1994
- ★ *Double Happiness*

1995
- ★ *Dance Me Outside*

1996
- ★ *Crash*
  The Boys Club
  Hard Core Logo
  Lilies
  Long Day's Journey Into Night

1997
- ★ *The Sweet Hereafter*

SCORE

1992
- ★ *Being at Home with Claude*

1993
- ★ *Cadillac Girls*

1994
- ★ *Exotica*

1995
- ★ *Margaret's Museum*

1996
- ★ *Curtis's Charm*
  Lilies
  Screamers
  Swann

1997
- ★ *The Sweet Hereafter*

SONG

1994
- ★ *"Claire"/Whale Music*

1996
- ★ *"Swamp Baby, Who the Hell Do You Think You Are?"/Hard Core Logo*
  "Some Days It's Dark"/ Kids in the Hall: Brain Candy

SOUND

1992
- ★ *Naked Lunch*

1993
- ★ *Le Sexe des Etoiles*
- ★ *The Lotus Eaters*

1994
- ★ *Whale Music*

1995
- ★ *Magic in the Water*

1996
- ★ *Lilies*
  Crash
  Hard Core Logo
  Kids in the Hall: Brain Candy
  Le Polygraphe

1997
- ★ *The Sweet Hereafter*

ADAPTED SCREENPLAY

1992
- ★ *Naked Lunch*

1994
- ★ *Love and Human Remains*

1995
- ★ *Margaret's Museum*

1996
- ★ *Crash*
  Curtis's Charm
  Hard Core Logo
  Le Polygraphe
  Lilies

ORIGINAL SCREENPLAY

1992
- ★ *Leolo*

1993
- ★ *The Lotus Eaters*

1994
- ★ *Exotica*

1996
- ★ *Sous Sol*
  Blood & Donuts
  The Boys Club

SCREENPLAY

1997
- ★ *The Hanging Garden*

Karmina
Kissed
The Sweet Hereafter

CANNES

ACTOR

1946
- ★ **Ray Milland/** *The Lost Weekend*

1949
- ★ **Edward G. Robinson/** *House of Strangers*

1951
- ★ **Michael Redgrave/** *The Browning Version*

1952
- ★ **Marlon Brando/** *Viva Zapata!*

1953
- ★ **Charles Vanel/** *Wages of Fear*

1955
- ★ **Spencer Tracy/** *Bad Day at Black Rock*

1958
- ★ **Paul Newman/** *The Long, Hot Summer*

1961
- ★ **Anthony Perkins/** *Goodbye Again*

1962
- ★ **Murray Melvin/** *A Taste of Honey*

1963
- ★ **Richard Harris/** *This Sporting Life*

1964
- ★ **Saro Urzi/** *Seduced and Abandoned*

1965
- ★ **Terence Stamp/** *The Collector*

1966
- ★ **Per Oscarsson/** *Hunger*

1969
- ★ **Jean-Louis Trintignant/** *Z*

1971
- ★ **Riccardo Cucciolla/** *Sacco & Vanzetti*

1973
- ★ **Giancarlo Giannini/** *Love and Anarchy*

1974
- ★ **Jack Nicholson/** *The Last Detail*

1977
- ★ **Fernando Rey/** *Elisa, Vida Mia*

1978
- ★ **Jon Voight/** *Coming Home*

ACTOR ⟋cont.

1979
★ Jack Lemmon/*The China Syndrome*

1981
★ Ugo Tognazzi/*The Tragedy of a Ridiculous Man*

1982
★ Jack Lemmon/*Missing*

1984
★ Alfredo Landa/*The Holy Innocents*
★ Francesco Rabal/*The Holy Innocents*

1985
★ William Hurt/*Kiss of the Spider Woman*

1986
★ Michel Blanc/*Menage*
★ Bob Hoskins/*Mona Lisa*

1987
★ Marcello Mastroianni/*Dark Eyes*

1988
★ Forest Whitaker/*Bird*

1989
★ James Spader/*sex, lies and videotape*

1990
★ Gerard Depardieu/*Cyrano de Bergerac*

1991
★ John Turturro/*Barton Fink*

1992
★ Tim Robbins/*The Player*

1993
★ David Thewlis/*Naked*

1994
★ Ge You/*To Live*

1995
★ Jonathan Pryce/*Carrington*

1996
★ Daniel Auteuil/*The Eighth Day*
★ Pascal Duquenne/*The Eighth Day*

1997
★ Sean Penn/*She's So Lovely*

1998
★ Peter Mullan/*My Name is Joe*

ACTRESS

1946
★ Michele Morgan/*La Symphonie Pastorale*

1951
★ Bette Davis/*All About Eve*

1952
★ Lee Grant/*Detective Story*

1953
★ Shirley Booth/*Come Back, Little Sheba*

1956
★ Susan Hayward/*I'll Cry Tomorrow*

1957
★ Giulietta Masina/*Nights of Cabiria*

1958
★ Bibi Andersson/*Brink of Life*
★ Eva Dahlbeck/*Brink of Life*
★ Ingrid Thulin/*Brink of Life*

1959
★ Simone Signoret/*Room at the Top*

1960
★ Melina Mercouri/*Never on Sunday*

1961
★ Sophia Loren/*Two Women*

1962
★ Katharine Hepburn/*Long Day's Journey into Night*
★ Rita Tushingham/*A Taste of Honey*

1965
★ Samantha Eggar/*The Collector*

1966
★ Vanessa Redgrave/*Morgan!*

1967
★ Pia Degermark/*Elvira Madigan*

1969
★ Vanessa Redgrave/*Isadora*

1971
★ Kitty Winn/*Panic in Needle Park*

1973
★ Joanne Woodward/*The Effect of Gamma Rays on Man-in-the-Moon Marigolds*

1974
★ Marie-Jose Nat/*Les Violons du Bal*

1975
★ Valerie Perrine/*Lenny*

1976
★ Dominique Sanda/*The Inheritance*

1978
★ Jill Clayburgh/*An Unmarried Woman*
★ Isabelle Huppert/*Violette*

1979
★ Sally Field/*Norma Rae*

1981
★ Isabelle Adjani/*Quartet*

1982
★ Jadwiga Jankowska Cieslak/*Another Way*

1984
★ Helen Mirren/*Cal*

1985
★ Norma Aleandro/*The Official Story*
★ Cher/*Mask*

1986
★ Barbara Sukowa/*Rosa Luxemburg*

1987
★ Barbara Hershey/*Shy People*

1988
★ Barbara Hershey/*A World Apart*
★ Jodhi May/*A World Apart*
★ Linda Mvusi/*A World Apart*

1989
★ Meryl Streep/*A Cry in the Dark*

1991
★ Irene Jacob/*The Double Life of Veronique*

1992
★ Pernilla August/*The Best Intentions*

1993
★ Holly Hunter/*The Piano*

1994
★ Virna Lisi/*Queen Margot*

1995
★ Helen Mirren/*The Madness of King George*

1996
★ Brenda Blethyn/*Secrets and Lies*

1997
★ Kathy Burke/*Nil by Mouth*

1998
★ Elodie Bouchez/*The Dreamed Life of Angels*
★ Natacha Regnier/*The Dreamed Life of Angels*

DIRECTOR

1951
★ Luis Bunuel/*Los Olvidados*

1952
★ Christian-Jaque/*Fanfan la Tulipe*

1955
★ Jules Dassin/*Rififi*

1957
★ Robert Bresson/*A Man Escaped*

1958
★ Ingmar Bergman/*Brink of Life*

1959
★ Francois Truffaut/*The 400 Blows*

1969
★ Vojtech Jasny/*All My Good Countrymen*

1976
★ Ettore Scola/*Down & Dirty*

1978
★ Nagisa Oshima/*The Empire of Passion*

1979
★ Terrence Malick/*Days of Heaven*

1982
★ Werner Herzog/*Fitzcarraldo*

1983
★ Robert Bresson/*L'Argent*

1984
★ Bertrand Tavernier/*A Sunday in the Country*

1985
★ Andre Techine/*Rendez-vous*

1986
★ Martin Scorsese/*After Hours*

1989
★ Emir Kusturica/*Time of the Gypsies*

1990
★ Pavel Lounguine/*Taxi Blues*

1991
★ Joel Coen/*Barton Fink*

1992
★ Robert Altman/*The Player*

1993
★ Mike Leigh/*Naked*

1994
★ Nanni Moretti/*Caro Diario*

1995
★ Mathieu Kassovitz/*Hate*

1996
★ Joel Coen/*Fargo*

1997
★ Wong Kar-Wai/*Happy Together*

1998
★ John Boorman/*The General*

FILM

1946
★ *The Lost Weekend*

1949
★ *The Third Man*

1951
★ *Los Olvidados*
★ *Miracle in Milan*
★ *Miss Julie*

1952
★ *Othello*
★ *White Mane*

1953
★ *Wages of Fear*

1954
★ *Gate of Hell*

1957
★ *Friendly Persuasion*

1958
★ *The Cranes Are Flying*

1959
★ *Black Orpheus*

1960
★ *La Dolce Vita*

1961
★ *Viridiana*

1964
★ *Umbrellas of Cherbourg*

1966
★ *A Man and a Woman*

1967
★ *Blow-Up*
★ *Dutchman*

1969
★ *If...*
Z

1970
★ *M*A*S*H*

1971
★ *The Go-Between*

1973
★ *Scarecrow*

1974
★ *The Conversation*

1976
★ *Taxi Driver*

1977
★ *Padre Padrone*

1978
★ *The Tree of Wooden Clogs*

1979
- ★ Apocalypse Now
- ★ The Tin Drum

1980
- ★ All That Jazz
- ★ Kagemusha

1981
- ★ Man of Iron

1982
- ★ Missing
- ★ Yol

1983
- ★ The Ballad of Narayama

1984
- ★ Paris, Texas

1985
- ★ Dance with a Stranger
- ★ When Father was Away on Business

1986
- ★ The Mission

1987
- ★ Under Satan's Sun

1988
- ★ Pelle the Conqueror

1989
- ★ sex, lies and videotape

1990
- ★ Overseas: Three Women with Man Trouble
- ★ Wild at Heart

1991
- ★ Barton Fink

1992
- ★ The Best Intentions
- ★ My New Gun

1993
- ★ Farewell My Concubine
- ★ The Piano

1994
- ★ Pulp Fiction

1995
- ★ Underground

1996
- ★ Secrets and Lies

1997
- ★ The Eel
- ★ The Taste of the Cherry

1998
- ★ Eternity and a Day

GRAND JURY PRIZE

1951
- ★ All About Eve

1957
- ★ Kanal
- ★ The Seventh Seal

1958
- ★ Mon Oncle

1961
- ★ Mother Joan of the Angels

1964
- ★ Woman in the Dunes

1965
- ★ Kwaidan

1967
- ★ Accident
- ★ Alfie

1971
- ★ Johnny Got His Gun

1972
- ★ Solaris

1976
- ★ Cria

1978
- ★ The Shout

1979
- ★ Siberiade

1980
- ★ Mon Oncle D'Amerique

1982
- ★ The Night of the Shooting Stars

1983
- ★ Monty Python's The Meaning of Life

1985
- ★ Birdy

1987
- ★ Repentance

1988
- ★ A World Apart

1989
- ★ Cinema Paradiso
- ★ Too Beautiful for You

1990
- ★ Tilai

1991
- ★ La Belle Noiseuse

1992
- ★ The Stolen Children

1993
- ★ Faraway, So Close!

1994
- ★ Burnt by the Sun
- ★ To Live

1995
- ★ Ulysses' Gaze

1996
- ★ Breaking the Waves

1997
- ★ The Sweet Hereafter

1998
- ★ Life is Beautiful

SPECIAL JURY PRIZE

1960
- ★ L'Avventura

1969
- ★ Z

1970
- ★ The Strawberry Statement

1972
- ★ Slaughterhouse Five

1985
- ★ Colonel Redl

1986
- ★ Therese

1989
- ★ Jesus of Montreal

1990
- ★ Hidden Agenda

1993
- ★ Raining Stones

1994
- ★ Queen Margot

1995
- ★ Carrington

1996
- ★ Crash

1997
- ★ Western

CESAR

ACTOR

1978
- ★ Jean Rochefort/Le Crabe Tambour

1979
- ★ Michel Serrault/La Cage aux Folles

1981
- ★ Gerard Depardieu/The Last Metro

1983
- ★ Philippe Leotard/La Balance

1984
- ★ Coluche/Tchao Pantin

1986
- ★ Christopher Lambert/Subway
  Jean-Hugues Anglade/Betty Blue

1987
- ★ Daniel Auteuil/Jean de Florette

1988
- ★ Richard Bohringer/Le Grand Chemin

1990
- ★ Philippe Noiret/Life and Nothing But

1991
- ★ Gerard Depardieu/Cyrano de Bergerac

1992
- ★ Jacques Dutronc/Van Gogh

1994
- ★ Pierre Arditti/Smoking/No Smoking
  Daniel Auteuil/The Separation
  Gerard Depardieu/Colonel Chabert
  Jean Reno/The Professional
  Jean-Louis Trintignant/Trois Couleurs: Rouge

1995
- ★ Gerard Lanvin/The Favorite Son

1996
- ★ Michel Serrault/Nelly et Monsieur Arnaud
  Vincent Cassel/Hate
  Alain Chabat/French Twist
  Jean-Louis Trintignant/Fiesta

1997
- ★ Philippe Torreton/Captain Conan
  Daniel Auteuil/The Eighth Day
  Charles Berling/Ridicule
  Patrick Timsit/Pedale Douce

1998
- ★ Andre Dussollier/Same Old Song

ACTOR—SUPPORTING

1977
- ★ Claude Brasseur/Pardon Mon Affaire

1978
- ★ Jacques Dufilho/Le Crabe Tambour

1979
- ★ Jacques Villeret/Robert et Robert

1980
- ★ Jean Bouise/Hothead

1983
- Jean-Hugues Anglade/L'Homme Blesse

1984
- ★ Richard Anconina/Tchao Pantin

1986
- ★ Michel Boujenah/Three Men and a Cradle
  Jean-Hugues Anglade/Subway

1989
- ★ Patrick Chesnais/La Lectrice

1991
- ★ Jacques Weber/Cyrano de Bergerac

1993
- ★ Andre Dussollier/Un Coeur en Hiver

1995
- ★ Jean-Hugues Anglade/Queen Margot
- ★ Eddy Mitchell/Le Bonheur Est Dans le Pre

1996
- Jean-Hugues Anglade/Nelly et Monsieur Arnaud
  Jean-Pierre Cassel/La Ceremonie
  Ticky Holgado/French Twist
  Michael Lonsdale/Nelly et Monsieur Arnaud

1997
- ★ Jean-Pierre Darroussin/Un Air de Famille

1998
- ★ Jean-Pierre Bacri/Same Old Song

ACTRESS

1978
- ★ Simone Signoret/Madame Rosa

1979
- Romy Schneider/A Simple Story

1981
- ★ Catherine Deneuve/The Last Metro

1982
- ★ Isabelle Adjani/Possession

1983
- ★ Nathalie Baye/La Balance

1984
- ★ Isabelle Adjani/One Deadly Summer

1985
- ★ Sabine Azema/A Sunday in the Country

1986
- ★ Sandrine Bonnaire/Vagabond

1988
- ★ Anemone/Le Grand Chemin

1989
- ★ Isabelle Adjani/Camille Claudel

1990
- ★ Carole Bouquet/Too Beautiful for You

1991
- ★ Anne Parillaud/La Femme Nikita

ACTRESS ~cont.

1993
★ Catherine Deneuve/*Indochine*

1994
★ Juliette Binoche/*Trois Couleurs: Bleu*
Isabelle Huppert/*The Separation*
Irene Jacob/*Trois Couleurs: Rouge*

1995
★ Isabelle Adjani/*Queen Margot*
Anemone/*Pas Tres Catholique*
Sabine Azema/*Le Bonheur Est Dans le Pre*

1996
★ Isabelle Huppert/*La Ceremonie*
Emmanuelle Beart/*Nelly et Monsieur Arnaud*
Juliette Binoche/*The Horseman on the Roof*
Sandrine Bonnaire/*La Ceremonie*

1997
★ Fanny Ardant/*Pedale Douce*
Catherine Deneuve/*Les Voleurs*

1998
★ Ariane Ascaride/*Marius and Jeannette*

ACTRESS— SUPPORTING

1976
★ Marie-France Pisier/*Cousin, Cousine*

1979
★ Stephane Audran/*Violette*

1984
★ Suzanne Flon/*One Deadly Summer*

1987
★ Emmanuelle Beart/*Jean de Florette*

1989
★ Helene Vincent/*Life Is a Long Quiet River*

1991
★ Dominique Blanc/*May Fools*

1992
★ Anne Brochet/*Tous les Matins du Monde*

1993
★ Dominique Blanc/*Indochine*

1995
★ Clothilde Courau/*Elisa*
★ Virna Lisi/*Queen Margot*

Dominique Blanc/*Queen Margot*
Carmen Maura/*Le Bonheur Est Dans le Pre*

1996
★ Annie Girardot/*Les Miserables*
Jacqueline Bisset/*La Ceremonie*
Claire Nadeau/*Nelly et Monsieur Arnaud*

1997
★ Catherine Frot/*Un Air de Famille*

1998
★ Agnes Jaoul/*Same Old Song*

ART DIRECTION

1978
★ *Providence*

1981
★ *The Last Metro*

1984
★ *Moon in the Gutter*

1985
★ *Swann in Love*

1986
★ *Subway*

1987
★ *Pirates*

1988
★ *Au Revoir Les Enfants*

1989
★ *Camille Claudel*

1990
★ *Valmont*

1991
★ *Cyrano de Bergerac*

1992
★ *Delicatessen*

1993
★ *Indochine*

1994
★ *Smoking/No Smoking*

1995
★ *Farinelli*

1996
★ *The City of Lost Children*
The Horseman on the Roof

1997
★ *Microcosmos*

1998
★ *The Fifth Element*

CINEMATOGRAPHY

1978
★ *Le Crabe Tambour*

1980
★ *Tess*

1981
★ *The Last Metro*

1982
★ *Diva*

1983
★ *La Truite*

1984
★ *Tchao Pantin*

1985
★ *A Sunday in the Country*

1987
★ *Therese*

1988
★ *Au Revoir Les Enfants*

1989
★ *Camille Claudel*

1991
★ *Cyrano de Bergerac*

1992
★ *Tous les Matins du Monde*

1993
★ *Indochine*

1994
★ *Germinal*

1995
★ *Queen Margot*

1996
★ *The Horseman on the Roof*
The City of Lost Children
Hate

1997
★ *Microcosmos*

1998
★ *The Fifth Element*

COSTUME DESIGN

1985
★ *Swann in Love*

1987
★ *Pirates*

1988
★ *Beatrice*

1989
★ *Camille Claudel*

1990
★ *Valmont*

1991
★ *Cyrano de Bergerac*

1994
★ *Germinal*

1995
★ *Queen Margot*

1996
The City of Lost Children

The Horseman on the Roof

DIRECTOR

1978
★ Alain Resnais/*Providence*

1980
★ Roman Polanski/*Tess*

1981
★ Francois Truffaut/*The Last Metro*

1983
★ Andrzej Wajda/*Danton*

1984
★ Ettore Scola/*Le Bal*

1986
★ Michel DeVille/*Peril*

1987
★ Alain Cavalier/*Therese*

1988
★ Louis Malle/*Au Revoir Les Enfants*

1990
★ Bertrand Blier/*Too Beautiful for You*

1991
★ Jean-Paul Rappeneau/*Cyrano de Bergerac*

1992
★ Alain Corneau/*Tous les Matins du Monde*

1993
★ Claude Sautet/*Un Coeur en Hiver*

1994
★ Alain Resnais/*Smoking/No Smoking*
Luc Besson/*The Professional*
Krzysztof Kieslowski/*Trois Couleurs: Rouge*

1995
★ Andre Techine/*Wild Reeds*
Etienne Chatiliez/*Le Bonheur Est Dans le Pre*
Patrice Chereau/*Queen Margot*
Nicole Garcia/*The Favorite Son*

1996
★ Claude Sautet/*Nelly et Monsieur Arnaud*
Josiane Balasko/*French Twist*
Claude Chabrol/*La Ceremonie*
Mathieu Kassovitz/*Hate*
Jean-Paul Rappeneau/*The Horseman on the Roof*

1997
★ Patrice Leconte/*Ridicule*
★ Bertrand Tavernier/*Captain Conan*

Cedric Klapisch/*Un Air de Famille*
Andre Techine/*Les Voleurs*

1998
★ Luc Besson/*The Fifth Element*

FILM

1977
★ *Mr. Klein*

1978
★ *Providence*

1980
★ *Tess*

1981
★ *The Last Metro*

1983
★ *La Balance*

1984
★ *Le Bal*

1986
★ *Three Men and a Cradle*

1987
★ *Therese*

1988
★ *Au Revoir Les Enfants*

1989
★ *Camille Claudel*

1990
★ *Too Beautiful for You*

1991
★ *Cyrano de Bergerac*

1992
★ *Tous les Matins du Monde*

1993
★ *Les Nuits Fauves*

1994
★ *Smoking/No Smoking*
The Professional
Trois Couleurs: Rouge

1995
★ *Wild Reeds*
The Favorite Son
Le Bonheur Est Dans le Pre
Queen Margot

1996
★ *Hate*
French Twist
The Horseman on the Roof
La Ceremonie
Nelly et Monsieur Arnaud

1997
★ *Captain Conan*
★ *Ridicule*
Les Voleurs
Microcosmos
Pedale Douce
Un Air de Famille

1998
★ *Same Old Song*

FILM EDITING

1994
★ Trois Couleurs: Bleu

1996
★ Hate
  The Horseman on the Roof
  Nelly et Monsieur Arnaud

1997
★ Microcosmos

1998
★ Same Old Song

SCORE

1977
★ The Judge and the Assassin

1978
★ Providence

1979
★ Get Out Your Handkerchiefs

1980
★ Love on the Run

1981
★ The Last Metro

1982
★ Diva

1983
★ The Return of Martin Guerre

1984
★ Le Bal

1988
★ Field of Honor

1989
★ The Big Blue

1990
★ Life and Nothing But

1991
★ Cyrano de Bergerac

1992
★ Tous les Matins du Monde

1993
★ The Lover

1994
★ Trois Couleurs: Rouge

1995
★ Elisa

1996
  The City of Lost Children
  The Horseman on the Roof
  Nelly et Monsieur Arnaud

1997
★ Microcosmos

SOUND

1977
★ Mado

1978
★ Providence

1979
★ L'Etat Sauvage

1981
★ The Last Metro

1982
★ Diva

1983
★ La Passante

1984
★ Tchao Pantin

1986
★ Subway

1988
★ Au Revoir Les Enfants

1989
★ The Big Blue

1990
★ Monsieur Hire

1991
★ Cyrano de Bergerac

1993
★ Indochine

1994
★ Trois Couleurs: Bleu

1995
★ Farinelli

1996
★ The Horseman on the Roof
  Hate
  Nelly et Monsieur Arnaud

1997
★ Microcosmos

1998
★ Same Old Song

WRITING

1977
★ The Judge and the Assassin

1978
★ Providence

1980
★ Buffet Froid

1981
★ The Last Metro

1983
★ The Return of Martin Guerre

1984
★ L'Homme Blesse
★ One Deadly Summer

1985
★ A Sunday in the Country

1986
★ Three Men and a Cradle

1987
★ Therese

1988
★ Au Revoir Les Enfants

1989
★ Life Is a Long Quiet River

1990
★ Too Beautiful for You

1991
★ La Discrete

1992
★ Delicatessen

1994
★ Smoking/No Smoking

1995
★ Wild Reeds
  Le Bonheur Est Dans le Pre

1996
★ French Twist
  Hate
  La Ceremonie
  Nelly et Monsieur Arnaud

1997
★ Un Air de Famille

1998
★ Same Old Song

FILM—FOREIGN LANGUAGE

1980
★ Manhattan

1981
★ Kagemusha

1982
★ The Elephant Man

1983
★ Victor/Victoria

1984
★ Fanny and Alexander

1985
★ Amadeus

1986
★ The Purple Rose of Cairo

1987
★ The Name of the Rose

1988
★ The Last Emperor

1989
★ Bagdad Cafe

1990
★ Dangerous Liaisons

1991
★ Dead Poets Society
★ Toto le Heros

1993
★ High Heels

1996
★ Land and Freedom

1997
★ Breaking the Waves
  Fargo
  The Postman
  Secrets and Lies

1998
★ Brassed Off

DIRECTORS GUILD OF AMERICA

DIRECTOR

1948
★ Joseph L. Mankiewicz/A Letter to Three Wives

1949
★ Carol Reed/The Third Man

1950
★ Joseph L. Mankiewicz/All About Eve

1951
★ George Stevens/A Place in the Sun

1952
★ John Ford/The Quiet Man

1953
★ Fred Zinnemann/From Here to Eternity

1954
★ Elia Kazan/On the Waterfront
★ Billy Wilder/Sabrina

1955
★ Delbert Mann/Marty

1956
★ George Stevens/Giant

1957
★ David Lean/The Bridge on the River Kwai

1958
★ Vincente Minnelli/Gigi

1959
★ William Wyler/Ben-Hur

1960
★ Billy Wilder/The Apartment

1961
★ Jerome Robbins/West Side Story
★ Robert Wise/West Side Story

1962
★ David Lean/Lawrence of Arabia

1963
★ Tony Richardson/Tom Jones

1964
★ George Cukor/My Fair Lady

1965
★ Robert Wise/The Sound of Music

1966
★ Fred Zinnemann/A Man for All Seasons

1967
★ Mike Nichols/The Graduate

1968
★ Anthony Harvey/The Lion in Winter

1969
★ John Schlesinger/Midnight Cowboy

1970
★ Charles Jarrott/Anne of the Thousand Days
★ Franklin J. Schaffner/Patton

1971
★ William Friedkin/The French Connection

1972
★ Francis Ford Coppola/The Godfather

1973
★ George Roy Hill/The Sting

1974
★ Francis Ford Coppola/The Godfather, Part 2

1975
★ Milos Forman/One Flew Over the Cuckoo's Nest

1976
★ John G. Avildsen/Rocky

1977
★ Woody Allen/Annie Hall

1978
★ Michael Cimino/The Deer Hunter

1979
★ Robert Benton/Kramer vs. Kramer

1980
★ Robert Redford/Ordinary People

1981
★ Warren Beatty/Reds

1982
★ Richard Attenborough/Gandhi

1983
★ James L. Brooks/Terms of Endearment

1984
★ Milos Forman/Amadeus

DIRECTOR ~cont.

1985
★ Steven Spielberg/The Color Purple

1986
★ Oliver Stone/Platoon

1987
★ Bernardo Bertolucci/The Last Emperor

1988
★ Barry Levinson/Rain Man

1989
★ Oliver Stone/Born on the Fourth of July

1990
★ Kevin Costner/Dances with Wolves

1991
★ Jonathan Demme/The Silence of the Lambs

1992
★ Clint Eastwood/ Unforgiven

1993
★ Steven Spielberg/ Schindler's List
Jane Campion/The Piano
Andrew Davis/The Fugitive
James Ivory/The Remains of the Day
Martin Scorsese/The Age of Innocence

1994
★ Robert Zemeckis/Forrest Gump
Frank Darabont/The Shawshank Redemption
Mike Newell/Four Weddings and a Funeral
Robert Redford/Quiz Show
Quentin Tarantino/Pulp Fiction

1995
★ Ron Howard/Apollo 13
Mike Figgis/Leaving Las Vegas
Mel Gibson/Braveheart
Ang Lee/Sense and Sensibility
Michael Radford/The Postman

1996
★ Anthony Minghella/The English Patient
Joel Coen/Fargo
Cameron Crowe/Jerry Maguire
Scott Hicks/Shine
Mike Leigh/Secrets and Lies

1997
★ James Cameron/Titanic
James L. Brooks/As Good As It Gets
Curtis Hanson/L.A. Confidential

Steven Spielberg/ Amistad
Gus Van Sant/Good Will Hunting

FEATURE DOCUMENTARY

1992
★ Joe Berlinger/Brother's Keeper
★ Bruce Sinofsky/Brother's Keeper

1995
★ Steve James/Hoop Dreams
★ Terry Zwigoff/Crumb

1996
★ Al Pacino/Looking for Richard

GOLDEN GLOBE AWARDS
ACTOR—DRAMA

1944
★ Paul Lukas/Watch on the Rhine

1945
★ Alexander Knox/Wilson

1946
★ Ray Milland/The Lost Weekend

1947
★ Gregory Peck/The Yearling

1948
★ Ronald Colman/A Double Life

1949
★ Laurence Olivier/Hamlet

1950
★ Broderick Crawford/All the King's Men

1951
★ Jose Ferrer/Cyrano de Bergerac

1953
★ Gary Cooper/High Noon

1955
★ Marlon Brando/On the Waterfront

1956
★ Ernest Borgnine/Marty

1957
★ Kirk Douglas/Lust for Life

1958
★ Alec Guinness/The Bridge on the River Kwai

1959
★ David Niven/Separate Tables

1960
★ Anthony (Tony) Franciosa/Career

1961
★ Burt Lancaster/Elmer Gantry

1962
★ Maximilian Schell/ Judgment at Nuremberg

1963
★ Gregory Peck/To Kill a Mockingbird

1964
★ Sidney Poitier/Lilies of the Field

1965
★ Peter O'Toole/Becket

1966
★ Omar Sharif/Doctor Zhivago

1967
★ Paul Scofield/A Man for All Seasons

1968
★ Rod Steiger/In the Heat of the Night

1969
★ Peter O'Toole/The Lion in Winter

1970
★ John Wayne/True Grit

1971
★ George C. Scott/Patton

1972
★ Gene Hackman/The French Connection

1973
★ Marlon Brando/The Godfather

1974
★ Al Pacino/Serpico

1975
★ Jack Nicholson/ Chinatown

1976
★ Jack Nicholson/One Flew Over the Cuckoo's Nest

1977
★ Peter Finch/Network

1978
★ Richard Burton/Equus

1979
★ Jon Voight/Coming Home

1980
★ Dustin Hoffman/Kramer vs. Kramer

1981
★ Robert De Niro/Raging Bull

1982
★ Henry Fonda/On Golden Pond

1983
★ Robert Duvall/Tender Mercies
★ Ben Kingsley/Gandhi

1984
★ Tom Courtenay/The Dresser

1985
★ F. Murray Abraham/ Amadeus

1986
★ Jon Voight/Runaway Train

1987
★ Bob Hoskins/Mona Lisa

1988
★ Michael Douglas/Wall Street

1989
★ Dustin Hoffman/Rain Man

1990
★ Tom Cruise/Born on the Fourth of July

1991
★ Jeremy Irons/Reversal of Fortune

1992
★ Nick Nolte/The Prince of Tides

1993
★ Al Pacino/Scent of a Woman

1994
★ Tom Hanks/Philadelphia
Daniel Day-Lewis/In the Name of the Father
Harrison Ford/The Fugitive
Anthony Hopkins/The Remains of the Day
Liam Neeson/Schindler's List

1995
★ Tom Hanks/Forrest Gump
Richard Dreyfuss/Mr. Holland's Opus
Morgan Freeman/The Shawshank Redemption
Paul Newman/Nobody's Fool
Brad Pitt/Legends of the Fall
John Travolta/Pulp Fiction

1996
★ Nicolas Cage/Leaving Las Vegas
Anthony Hopkins/Nixon
Ian McKellen/Richard III
Sean Penn/Dead Man Walking

1997
★ Geoffrey Rush/Shine

Ralph Fiennes/The English Patient
Mel Gibson/Ransom
Woody Harrelson/The People vs. Larry Flynt
Liam Neeson/Michael Collins

1998
★ Peter Fonda/Ulee's Gold
Matt Damon/Good Will Hunting
Daniel Day-Lewis/The Boxer
Leonardo DiCaprio/ Titanic
Djimon Hounsou/ Amistad

ACTOR—MUSICAL/ COMEDY

1951
★ Fred Astaire/Three Little Words

1953
★ Donald O'Connor/Singin' in the Rain

1954
★ David Niven/The Moon Is Blue

1955
★ James Mason/A Star Is Born

1956
★ Tom Ewell/The Seven Year Itch

1957
★ Cantinflas/Around the World in 80 Days

1958
★ Frank Sinatra/Pal Joey

1960
★ Jack Lemmon/Some Like It Hot

1961
★ Jack Lemmon/The Apartment

1962
★ Glenn Ford/Pocketful of Miracles

1963
★ Marcello Mastroianni/ Divorce—Italian Style

1965
★ Rex Harrison/My Fair Lady

1966
★ Lee Marvin/Cat Ballou

1967
★ Alan Arkin/The Russians Are Coming, Russians Are Coming

1968
★ Richard Harris/Camelot

1969
★ Ron Moody/Oliver!

1970
★ Peter O'Toole/Goodbye, Mr. Chips

1971
★ Albert Finney/Scrooge

1972
★ Chaim Topol/Fiddler on the Roof

1974
★ George Segal/A Touch of Class

1975
★ Art Carney/Harry and Tonto

1976
★ Walter Matthau/The Sunshine Boys

1977
★ Kris Kristofferson/A Star Is Born

1978
★ Richard Dreyfuss/The Goodbye Girl

1979
★ Warren Beatty/Heaven Can Wait

1980
★ Peter Sellers/Being There

1981
★ Ray Sharkey/Idolmaker

1982
★ Dudley Moore/Arthur

1983
★ Dustin Hoffman/Tootsie

1984
★ Michael Caine/Educating Rita

1985
★ Dudley Moore/Micki & Maude

1986
★ Jack Nicholson/Prizzi's Honor

1987
★ Paul Hogan/Crocodile Dundee

1988
★ Robin Williams/Good Morning, Vietnam

1989
★ Tom Hanks/Big

1990
★ Morgan Freeman/Driving Miss Daisy

1991
★ Gerard Depardieu/Green Card

1992
★ Robin Williams/The Fisher King

1993
★ Tim Robbins/The Player

1994
★ Robin Williams/Mrs. Doubtfire
Johnny Depp/Benny & Joon
Tom Hanks/Sleepless in Seattle
Kevin Kline/Dave
Colm Meaney/The Snapper

1995
★ Hugh Grant/Four Weddings and a Funeral
Jim Carrey/The Mask
Johnny Depp/Ed Wood
Arnold Schwarzenegger/Junior
Terence Stamp/The Adventures of Priscilla, Queen of the Desert

1996
★ John Travolta/Get Shorty
Michael Douglas/The American President
Harrison Ford/Sabrina
Steve Martin/Father of the Bride Part II
Patrick Swayze/To Wong Foo, Thanks for Everything, Julie Newmar

1997
★ Tom Cruise/Jerry Maguire
Antonio Banderas/Evita
Kevin Costner/Tin Cup
Tom Cruise/Jerry Maguire
Nathan Lane/The Birdcage
Eddie Murphy/The Nutty Professor

1998
★ Jack Nicholson/As Good As It Gets
Jim Carrey/Liar Liar
Dustin Hoffman/Wag the Dog
Samuel L. Jackson/Jackie Brown
Kevin Kline/In and Out

ACTOR—SUPPORTING

1945
★ Barry Fitzgerald/Going My Way

1947
★ Clifton Webb/The Razor's Edge

1948
★ Edmund Gwenn/Miracle on 34th Street

1949
★ Walter Huston/Treasure of the Sierra Madre

1950
★ James Whitmore/Battleground

1952
★ Peter Ustinov/Quo Vadis

1954
★ Frank Sinatra/From Here to Eternity

1955
★ Edmond O'Brien/The Barefoot Contessa

1957
★ Earl Holliman/The Rainmaker

1958
★ Red Buttons/Sayonara

1959
★ Burl Ives/The Big Country

1960
★ Stephen Boyd/Ben-Hur

1961
★ Sal Mineo/Exodus

1962
★ George Chakiris/West Side Story

1963
★ Omar Sharif/Lawrence of Arabia

1964
★ John Huston/The Cardinal

1965
★ Edmond O'Brien/Seven Days in May

1966
★ Oskar Werner/The Spy Who Came in from the Cold

1967
★ Richard Attenborough/The Sand Pebbles

1968
★ David Attenborough/Doctor Dolittle

1970
★ Gig Young/They Shoot Horses, Don't They?

1971
★ John Mills/Ryan's Daughter

1972
★ Ben Johnson/The Last Picture Show

1973
★ Joel Grey/Cabaret

1974
★ John Houseman/The Paper Chase

1975
★ Fred Astaire/The Towering Inferno

1976
★ Richard Benjamin/The Sunshine Boys

1977
★ Laurence Olivier/Marathon Man

1978
★ Peter Firth/Equus

1979
★ John Hurt/Midnight Express

1980
★ Melvyn Douglas/Being There
★ Robert Duvall/Apocalypse Now

1981
★ Timothy Hutton/Ordinary People

1982
★ John Gielgud/Arthur

1983
★ Louis Gossett, Jr./An Officer and a Gentleman

1984
★ Jack Nicholson/Terms of Endearment

1985
★ Haing S. Ngor/The Killing Fields

1986
★ Klaus Maria Brandauer/Out of Africa

1987
★ Tom Berenger/Platoon

1988
★ Sean Connery/The Untouchables

1989
★ Martin Landau/Tucker: The Man and His Dream

1990
★ Denzel Washington/Glory
Joe Pesci/Goodfellas

1991
★ Bruce Davison/Longtime Companion

1992
★ Jack Palance/City Slickers

1993
★ Gene Hackman/Unforgiven

1994
★ Tommy Lee Jones/The Fugitive
Leonardo DiCaprio/What's Eating Gilbert Grape
Ralph Fiennes/Schindler's List
John Malkovich/In the Line of Fire
Sean Penn/Carlito's Way

1995
★ Martin Landau/Ed Wood

Kevin Bacon/The River Wild
Samuel L. Jackson/Pulp Fiction
Gary Sinise/Forrest Gump
John Turturro/Quiz Show

1996
★ Brad Pitt/12 Monkeys
Ed Harris/Apollo 13
John Leguizamo/To Wong Foo, Thanks for Everything, Julie Newmar
Tim Roth/Rob Roy
Kevin Spacey/The Usual Suspects

1997
★ Edward Norton/Primal Fear
Cuba Gooding, Jr./Jerry Maguire
Samuel L. Jackson/A Time to Kill
Paul Scofield/The Crucible
James Woods/Ghosts of Mississippi

1998
★ Burt Reynolds/Boogie Nights
Rupert Everett/My Best Friend's Wedding
Anthony Hopkins/Amistad
Burt Reynolds/Boogie Nights
Jon Voight/John Grisham's The Rainmaker
Robin Williams/Good Will Hunting

ACTRESS—DRAMA

1944
★ Jennifer Jones/The Song of Bernadette

1945
★ Ingrid Bergman/Gaslight

1946
★ Ingrid Bergman/The Bells of St. Mary's

1947
★ Rosalind Russell/Sister Kenny

1949
★ Jane Wyman/Johnny Belinda

1950
★ Olivia de Havilland/The Heiress

1951
★ Gloria Swanson/Sunset Boulevard

1953
★ Shirley Booth/Come Back, Little Sheba

1954
★ Audrey Hepburn/Roman Holiday

ACTRESS—DRAMA
cont.

1955
★ Grace Kelly/*Country Girl*

1956
★ Anna Magnani/*The Rose Tattoo*

1957
★ Ingrid Bergman/*Anastasia*

1958
★ Joanne Woodward/*The Three Faces of Eve*

1959
★ Susan Hayward/*I Want to Live!*

1960
★ Elizabeth Taylor/*Suddenly, Last Summer*

1961
★ Greer Garson/*Sunrise at Campobello*

1962
★ Geraldine Page/*Summer and Smoke*

1963
★ Geraldine Page/*Sweet Bird of Youth*

1966
★ Samantha Eggar/*The Collector*

1967
★ Anouk Aimee/*A Man and a Woman*

1969
★ Joanne Woodward/*Rachel, Rachel*

1970
★ Genevieve Bujold/*Anne of the Thousand Days*

1971
★ Ali MacGraw/*Love Story*

1972
★ Jane Fonda/*Klute*

1974
★ Marsha Mason/*Cinderella Liberty*

1975
★ Gena Rowlands/*A Woman Under the Influence*

1976
★ Louise Fletcher/*One Flew Over the Cuckoo's Nest*

1977
★ Faye Dunaway/*Network*

1978
★ Jane Fonda/*Julia*

1979
★ Jane Fonda/*Coming Home*

1980
★ Sally Field/*Norma Rae*

1981
★ Mary Tyler Moore/*Ordinary People*

1982
★ Meryl Streep/*The French Lieutenant's Woman*

1983
★ Meryl Streep/*Sophie's Choice*

1984
★ Shirley MacLaine/*Terms of Endearment*

1985
★ Sally Field/*Places in the Heart*

1986
★ Whoopi Goldberg/*The Color Purple*

1987
★ Marlee Matlin/*Children of a Lesser God*

1988
★ Sally Kirkland/*Anna*
★ Sigourney Weaver/*Gorillas in the Mist*

1989
★ Jodie Foster/*The Accused*
★ Shirley MacLaine/*Madame Sousatzka*

1990
★ Michelle Pfeiffer/*The Fabulous Baker Boys*

1991
★ Kathy Bates/*Misery*

1992
★ Jodie Foster/*The Silence of the Lambs*

1993
★ Emma Thompson/*Howard's End*

1994
★ Holly Hunter/*The Piano*
Juliette Binoche/*Trois Couleurs: Bleu*
Michelle Pfeiffer/*The Age of Innocence*
Emma Thompson/*The Remains of the Day*
Debra Winger/*A Dangerous Woman*

1995
★ Jessica Lange/*Blue Sky*
Jodie Foster/*Nell*
Jennifer Jason Leigh/*Mrs. Parker and the Vicious Circle*
Miranda Richardson/*Tom & Viv*
Meryl Streep/*The River Wild*

1996
★ Sharon Stone/*Casino*
Susan Sarandon/*Dead Man Walking*
Elisabeth Shue/*Leaving Las Vegas*
Meryl Streep/*The Bridges of Madison County*
Emma Thompson/*Sense and Sensibility*

1997
★ Brenda Blethyn/*Secrets and Lies*
Courtney Love/*The People vs. Larry Flynt*
Kristin Scott Thomas/*The English Patient*
Meryl Streep/*Marvin's Room*
Emily Watson/*Breaking the Waves*

1998
★ Judi Dench/*Mrs. Brown*
Helena Bonham Carter/*The Wings of the Dove*
Jodie Foster/*Contact*
Jessica Lange/*A Thousand Acres*
Kate Winslet/*Titanic*

ACTRESS—MUSICAL/ COMEDY

1951
★ Judy Holliday/*Born Yesterday*

1955
★ Judy Garland/*A Star Is Born*

1956
★ Jean Simmons/*Guys and Dolls*

1957
★ Deborah Kerr/*The King and I*

1958
★ Kay Kendall/*Les Girls*

1959
★ Rosalind Russell/*Auntie Mame*

1960
★ Marilyn Monroe/*Some Like It Hot*

1961
★ Shirley MacLaine/*The Apartment*

1963
★ Rosalind Russell/*Gypsy*

1964
★ Shirley MacLaine/*Irma La Douce*

1965
★ Julie Andrews/*Mary Poppins*

1966
★ Julie Andrews/*The Sound of Music*

1967
★ Lynn Redgrave/*Georgy Girl*

1968
★ Anne Bancroft/*The Graduate*

1969
★ Barbra Streisand/*Funny Girl*

1971
★ Carrie Snodgress/*Diary of a Mad Housewife*

1972
★ Twiggy/*The Boy Friend*

1973
★ Liza Minnelli/*Cabaret*

1974
★ Glenda Jackson/*A Touch of Class*

1975
★ Raquel Welch/*The Three Musketeers*

1976
★ Ann-Margret/*Tommy*

1977
★ Barbra Streisand/*A Star Is Born*

1978
★ Diane Keaton/*Annie Hall*
★ Marsha Mason/*The Goodbye Girl*

1979
★ Ellen Burstyn/*Same Time, Next Year*
★ Maggie Smith/*California Suite*

1980
★ Bette Midler/*The Rose*

1981
★ Sissy Spacek/*Coal Miner's Daughter*

1982
★ Bernadette Peters/*Pennies From Heaven*

1983
★ Julie Andrews/*Victor/ Victoria*

1984
★ Julie Walters/*Educating Rita*

1985
★ Kathleen Turner/*Romancing the Stone*

1986
★ Kathleen Turner/*Prizzi's Honor*

1987
★ Sissy Spacek/*Crimes of the Heart*

1988
★ Cher/*Moonstruck*

1989
★ Melanie Griffith/*Working Girl*

1990
★ Jessica Tandy/*Driving Miss Daisy*

1991
★ Julia Roberts/*Pretty Woman*
Andie MacDowell/*Green Card*

1992
★ Bette Midler/*For the Boys*

1993
★ Miranda Richardson/*Enchanted April*

1994
★ Angela Bassett/*What's Love Got to Do with It?*
Stockard Channing/*Six Degrees of Separation*
Anjelica Huston/*Addams Family Values*
Diane Keaton/*Manhattan Murder Mystery*
Meg Ryan/*Sleepless in Seattle*

1995
★ Jamie Lee Curtis/*True Lies*
Geena Davis/*Speechless*
Andie MacDowell/*Four Weddings and a Funeral*
Shirley MacLaine/*Guarding Tess*
Emma Thompson/*Junior*

1996
★ Nicole Kidman/*To Die For*
Annette Bening/*The American President*
Sandra Bullock/*While You Were Sleeping*
Toni Collette/*Muriel's Wedding*
Vanessa Redgrave/*A Month by the Lake*

1997
★ Madonna/*Evita*
Glenn Close/*101 Dalmatians*
Frances McDormand/*Fargo*
Debbie Reynolds/*Mother*
Barbra Streisand/*The Mirror Has Two Faces*

1998
★ Helen Hunt/*As Good As It Gets*
Joey Lauren Adams/*Chasing Amy*
Pam Grier/*Jackie Brown*
Jennifer Lopez/*Selena*
Julia Roberts/*My Best Friend's Wedding*

ACTRESS— SUPPORTING

1945
★ Agnes Moorehead/*Mrs. Parkington*

BEST FILM— DRAMA cont.

1995
★ Forrest Gump
Legends of the Fall
Nell
Pulp Fiction
Quiz Show

1996
★ Sense and Sensibility
Apollo 13
Braveheart
The Bridges of Madison
County
Leaving Las Vegas

1997
★ The English Patient
Breaking the Waves
The People vs. Larry Flynt
Secrets and Lies
Shine

1998
★ Titanic
Amistad
The Boxer
Good Will Hunting
L.A. Confidential

BEST FILM—MUSICAL/ COMEDY

1952
★ An American in Paris

1955
★ Carmen Jones

1956
★ Guys and Dolls

1957
★ The King and I

1958
★ Les Girls

1959
★ Gigi

1960
★ Some Like It Hot

1961
★ The Apartment
★ Song Without End

1962
★ West Side Story

1963
★ The Music Man
★ That Touch of Mink

1964
★ Tom Jones

1965
★ My Fair Lady

1966
★ The Sound of Music

1967
★ The Russians Are Coming,
the Russians Are
Coming

1968
★ The Graduate

1969
★ Oliver!

1971
★ M*A*S*H

1972
★ Fiddler on the Roof

1973
★ Cabaret

1974
★ American Graffiti

1975
★ The Longest Yard

1976
★ The Sunshine Boys

1977
★ A Star Is Born

1978
★ The Goodbye Girl

1979
★ Heaven Can Wait

1980
★ Breaking Away

1981
★ Coal Miner's Daughter

1982
★ Arthur

1983
★ Tootsie

1984
★ Yentl

1985
★ Romancing the Stone

1986
★ Prizzi's Honor

1987
★ Hannah and Her Sisters

1988
★ Hope and Glory

1989
★ Working Girl

1990
★ Driving Miss Daisy

1991
★ Green Card

1992
★ Beauty and the Beast

1993
★ The Player

1994
★ Mrs. Doubtfire
Dave
Much Ado about Nothing
Sleepless in Seattle
Strictly Ballroom

1995
★ The Lion King
The Adventures of
Priscilla, Queen of the
Desert
Ed Wood
Four Weddings and a
Funeral
Ready to Wear

1996
★ Babe
The American President
Get Shorty
Sabrina
Toy Story

1997
★ Evita
The Birdcage
Everyone Says I Love You
Fargo
Jerry Maguire

1998
★ As Good As It Gets
The Full Monty
Men in Black
My Best Friend's Wedding
Wag the Dog

DIRECTOR

1944
★ Henry King/The Song of
Bernadette

1945
★ Leo McCarey/Going My
Way

1946
★ Billy Wilder/The Lost
Weekend

1947
★ Frank Capra/It's a
Wonderful Life

1948
★ Elia Kazan/Gentleman's
Agreement

1949
★ John Huston/Treasure of
the Sierra Madre

1950
★ Robert Rossen/All the
King's Men

1951
★ Billy Wilder/Sunset
Boulevard

1953
★ Cecil B. DeMille/The
Greatest Show on Earth

1954
Fred Zinnemann/From
Here to Eternity

1955
★ Elia Kazan/On the
Waterfront

1956
★ Joshua Logan/Picnic

1957
★ Elia Kazan/Baby Doll

1958
★ David Lean/The Bridge on
the River Kwai

1959
★ Vincente Minnelli/Gigi

1960
★ William Wyler/Ben-Hur

1962
★ Stanley Kramer/
Judgment at Nuremberg

1963
★ David Lean/Lawrence of
Arabia

1965
★ George Cukor/My Fair
Lady

1966
★ David Lean/Doctor
Zhivago

1967
★ Fred Zinnemann/A Man
for All Seasons

1968
★ Mike Nichols/The
Graduate

1969
★ Paul Newman/Rachel,
Rachel

1970
★ Charles Jarrott/Anne of
the Thousand Days

1971
★ Arthur Hiller/Love Story

1972
★ William Friedkin/The
French Connection

1973
★ Francis Ford Coppola/
The Godfather

1974
★ William Friedkin/The
Exorcist

1975
★ Roman Polanski/
Chinatown

1976
★ Milos Forman/One Flew
Over the Cuckoo's Nest

1977
★ Sidney Lumet/Network

1978
★ Herbert Ross/The Turning
Point

1979
★ Michael Cimino/The Deer
Hunter

1980
★ Francis Ford Coppola/
Apocalypse Now

1981
★ Robert Redford/Ordinary
People

1982
★ Warren Beatty/Reds

1983
★ Richard Attenborough/
Gandhi

1984
★ Barbra Streisand/Yentl

1985
★ Milos Forman/Amadeus

1986
★ John Huston/Prizzi's
Honor

1987
★ Oliver Stone/Platoon

1988
★ Bernardo Bertolucci/The
Last Emperor

1989
★ Clint Eastwood/Bird

1990
★ Oliver Stone/Born on the
Fourth of July
Martin Scorsese/
Goodfellas

1991
★ Kevin Costner/Dances
with Wolves

1992
★ Oliver Stone/JFK

1993
★ Clint Eastwood/
Unforgiven

1994
★ Steven Spielberg/
Schindler's List
Jane Campion/The Piano
Andrew Davis/The
Fugitive
James Ivory/The
Remains of the Day
Martin Scorsese/The Age
of Innocence

1995
★ Robert Zemeckis/Forrest
Gump
Robert Redford/Quiz
Show
Oliver Stone/Natural Born
Killers
Quentin Tarantino/Pulp
Fiction
Edward Zwick/Legends
of the Fall

1996
★ Mel Gibson/Braveheart
Mike Figgis/Leaving Las
Vegas
Ron Howard/Apollo 13
Ang Lee/Sense and
Sensibility
Rob Reiner/The American
President
Martin Scorsese/Casino

1997
- ★ **Milos Forman**/*The People vs. Larry Flynt*
- **Joel Coen**/*Fargo*
- **Scott Hicks**/*Shine*
- **Anthony Minghella**/*The English Patient*
- **Alan Parker**/*Evita*

1998
- ★ **James Cameron**/*Titanic*
- **James L. Brooks**/*As Good As It Gets*
- **Curtis Hanson**/*L.A. Confidential*
- **Jim Sheridan**/*The Boxer*
- **Steven Spielberg**/*Amistad*

SCORE

1948
- ★ *Life with Father*

1949
- ★ *The Red Shoes*

1950
- ★ *The Inspector General*

1951
- ★ *Sunset Boulevard*

1952
- ★ *September Affair*

1953
- ★ *High Noon*

1960
- ★ *On the Beach*

1961
- ★ *The Alamo*

1962
- ★ *The Guns of Navarone*

1963
- ★ *To Kill a Mockingbird*

1965
- ★ *The Fall of the Roman Empire*

1966
- ★ *Doctor Zhivago*

1967
- ★ *Hawaii*

1968
- ★ *Camelot*

1969
- ★ *The Shoes of the Fisherman*

1970
- ★ *Butch Cassidy and the Sundance Kid*

1971
- ★ *Love Story*

1972
- ★ *Shaft*

1973
- ★ *The Godfather*

1974
- ★ *Jonathan Livingston Seagull*

1975
- ★ *The Little Prince*

1976
- ★ *Jaws*

1977
- ★ *A Star Is Born*

1978
- ★ *Star Wars*

1979
- ★ *Midnight Express*

1980
- ★ *Apocalypse Now*

1981
- ★ *The Stunt Man*

1983
- ★ *E.T.: The Extra-Terrestrial*

1984
- ★ *Flashdance*

1985
- ★ *A Passage to India*

1986
- ★ *Out of Africa*

1987
- ★ *The Mission*

1988
- ★ *The Last Emperor*

1989
- ★ *Gorillas in the Mist*

1990
- ★ *The Little Mermaid*

1991
- ★ *The Sheltering Sky*

1993
- ★ *Aladdin*

1994
- ★ *Heaven and Earth*
- *The Nightmare Before Christmas*
- *The Piano*
- *Schindler's List*
- *Trois Couleurs: Bleu*

1995
- ★ *The Lion King*
- *Forrest Gump*
- *Interview with the Vampire*
- *Legends of the Fall*
- *Nell*

1996
- ★ *A Walk in the Clouds*
- *Braveheart*
- *Don Juan DeMarco*
- *Pocahontas*
- *Sense and Sensibility*

1997
- ★ *The English Patient*
- *The Hunchback of Notre Dame*
- *Michael Collins*

The Mirror Has Two Faces
Shine

1998
- ★ *Titanic*
- *Gattaca*
- *Kundun*
- *L.A. Confidential*
- *Seven Years in Tibet*

SONG

1965
- ★ "Circus World"/*Circus World*

1968
- ★ "If Ever I Should Leave You"/*Camelot*

1969
- ★ "The Windmills of Your Mind"/*The Thomas Crown Affair*

1970
- ★ "Jean"/*The Prime of Miss Jean Brodie*

1971
- ★ "Whistling Away the Dark"/*Darling Lili*

1972
- ★ "Life Is What You Make It"/*Kotch*

1973
- ★ "Ben"/*Ben*

1974
- ★ "The Way We Were"/*The Way We Were*

1975
- ★ "I Feel Love"/*Benji*

1976
- ★ "I'm Easy"/*Nashville*

1977
- ★ "Evergreen"/*A Star Is Born*

1978
- ★ "You Light Up My Life"/*You Light Up My Life*

1980
- ★ "The Rose"/*The Rose*

1981
- ★ "Fame"/*Fame*

1982
- ★ "Arthur's Theme"/*Arthur*

1983
- ★ "Up Where We Belong"/*An Officer and a Gentleman*

1984
- ★ "Flashdance...What a Feeling"/*Flashdance*

1985
- ★ "I Just Called to Say I Love You"/*The Woman in Red*

1986
- ★ "Say You, Say Me"/*White Nights*

1987
- ★ "Take My Breath Away"/*Top Gun*

1988
- ★ "(I've Had) the Time of My Life"/*Dirty Dancing*

1989
- ★ "Let the River Run"/*Working Girl*

1990
- ★ "Under the Sea"/*The Little Mermaid*

1991
- ★ "Blaze of Glory"/*Young Guns 2*

1993
- ★ "A Whole New World"/*Aladdin*

1994
- ★ "Streets of Philadelphia"/*Philadelphia*
- "(You Made Me) Thief of Your Heart"/*In the Name of the Father*
- "Again"/*Poetic Justice*
- "Stay"/*Faraway, So Close!*
- "The Day I Fall in Love"/*Beethoven's 2nd*

1995
- ★ "Can You Feel the Love Tonight?"/*The Lion King*
- "Circle of Life"/*The Lion King*
- "Far Longer than Forever"/*The Swan Princess*
- "I'll Remember"/*With Honors*
- "Look What Love Has Done"/*Junior*
- "The Color of the Night"/*Color of Night*

1996
- ★ "Colors of the Wind"/*Pocahontas*
- "Have You Ever Really Loved a Woman?"/*Don Juan DeMarco*
- "Hold Me, Thrill Me, Kiss Me, Kill Me"/*Batman Forever*
- "Moonlight"/*Sabrina*
- "You Got a Friend in Me"/*Toy Story*

1997
- ★ "You Must Love Me"/*Evita*
- "Because You Loved Me"/*Up Close and Personal*
- "For the First Time"/*One Fine Day*
- "I've Finally Found Someone"/*The Mirror Has Two Faces*

"That Thing You Do!"/*That Thing You Do!*

1998
- ★ "My Heart Will Go On"/*Titanic*
- "Go the Distance"/*Hercules*
- "Journey to the Past"/*Anastasia*
- "Once Upon a December"/*Anastasia*
- "Tomorrow Never Dies"/*Tomorrow Never Dies*

SCREENPLAY

1948
- ★ *Miracle on 34th Street*

1949
- ★ *The Search*

1950
- ★ *Battleground*

1951
- ★ *All About Eve*

1953
- ★ *Five Fingers*

1954
- ★ *Lili*

1955
- ★ *Sabrina*

1966
- ★ *Doctor Zhivago*

1967
- ★ *A Man for All Seasons*

1968
- ★ *In the Heat of the Night*

1969
- ★ *Charly*

1970
- ★ *Anne of the Thousand Days*

1971
- ★ *Love Story*

1972
- ★ *The Hospital*

1973
- ★ *The Godfather*

1974
- ★ *The Exorcist*

1975
- ★ *Chinatown*

1976
- ★ *One Flew Over the Cuckoo's Nest*

1977
- ★ *Network*

1978
- ★ *The Goodbye Girl*

1979
- ★ *Midnight Express*

SCREENPLAY
~cont.

1980
★ Kramer vs. Kramer

1981
★ The Ninth Configuration

1982
★ On Golden Pond

1983
★ Gandhi

1984
★ Terms of Endearment

1985
★ Amadeus

1986
★ The Purple Rose of Cairo

1987
★ The Mission

1988
★ The Last Emperor

1989
★ Running on Empty

1990
★ Born on the Fourth of July
  Goodfellas

1991
★ Dances with Wolves

1993
★ Scent of a Woman

1994
★ Schindler's List
  Philadelphia
  The Piano
  The Remains of the Day
  Short Cuts

1995
★ Pulp Fiction
  Forrest Gump
  Four Weddings and a
   Funeral
  Mr. Holland's Opus
  Quiz Show
  The Shawshank
   Redemption

1996
★ Sense and Sensibility
  The American President
  Braveheart
  Dead Man Walking
  Get Shorty

1997
★ The People vs. Larry Flynt
  The English Patient
  Fargo
  Lone Star
  Shine

1998
★ Good Will Hunting
  As Good As It Gets
  L.A. Confidential
  Titanic
  Wag the Dog

FILM—FOREIGN LANGUAGE

1950
★ The Bicycle Thief

1955
★ Genevieve

1956
★ Ordet

1957
★ Richard III
★ War and Peace

1959
★ A Night to Remember

1960
★ Black Orpheus
★ Odd Obsession
★ Wild Strawberries

1961
★ The Virgin Spring

1962
★ Two Women

1963
★ Divorce—Italian Style

1964
★ Tom Jones

1965
★ Marriage Italian Style
★ Sallah

1966
★ Darling

1967
★ Alfie
★ A Man and a Woman

1969
★ Romeo and Juliet
★ War and Peace

1970
★ Z

1971
★ Rider on the Rain
★ Women in Love

1972
★ Sunday, Bloody Sunday

1973
★ Young Winston

1974
★ The Pedestrian

1975
★ Scenes from a Marriage

1976
★ Lies My Father Told Me

1977
★ Face to Face

1978
★ A Special Day

1979
★ Autumn Sonata

1980
★ La Cage aux Folles

1981
★ Tess

1982
★ Chariots of Fire

1983
★ Gandhi

1984
★ Fanny and Alexander

1985
★ A Passage to India

1986
★ The Official Story

1987
★ The Assault

1988
★ My Life As a Dog

1989
★ Pelle the Conqueror

1990
★ Cinema Paradiso

1991
★ Cyrano de Bergerac

1992
★ Europa, Europa

1993
★ Indochine

1994
★ Farewell My Concubine
  Flight of the Innocent
  Trois Couleurs: Bleu
  The Wedding Banquet

1995
★ Farinelli
  Eat Drink Man Woman
  Queen Margot
  To Live
  Trois Couleurs: Rouge

1996
★ Les Miserables
  Brother of Sleep
  French Twist
  Shanghai Triad

1997
★ Kolya
  The Eighth Day
  Luna e L'Altra
  Prisoner of the Mountains
  Ridicule

1998
★ Ma Vie en Rose
  Artemisia
  Lea

INDEPENDENT SPIRIT AWARDS
ACTOR

1986
★ M. Emmet Walsh/Blood
  Simple

1987
★ James Woods/Salvador

1988
★ Dennis Quaid/The Big
  Easy

1989
★ Edward James Olmos/
  Stand and Deliver

1990
★ Matt Dillon/Drugstore
  Cowboy

1991
★ Danny Glover/To Sleep
  with Anger

1992
★ River Phoenix/My Own
  Private Idaho

1993
★ Harvey Keitel/Bad
  Lieutenant

1994
★ Jeff Bridges/American
  Heart
  Vincent D'Onofrio/
   Household Saints
  Mitchell Lichtenstein/
   The Wedding Banquet
  Matthew Modine/Equinox
  Tyrin Turner/Menace II
   Society

1995
★ Samuel L. Jackson/Pulp
  Fiction
  Sihung Lung/Eat Drink
   Man Woman
  William H. Macy/Oleanna
  Campbell Scott/Mrs.
   Parker and the Vicious
   Circle
  Jon Seda/I Like It Like
   That

1996
★ Sean Penn/Dead Man
  Walking
  Nicolas Cage/Leaving
   Las Vegas
  Tim Roth/Little Odessa
  Jimmy Smits/My Family
  Kevin Spacey/Swimming
   with Sharks

1997
★ William H. Macy/Fargo
  Chris Cooper/Lone Star
  Christopher Penn/The
   Funeral

1998
★ Robert Duvall/The
  Apostle
  Peter Fonda/Ulee's Gold
  Christopher Guest/
   Waiting for Guffman
  Philip Baker Hall/Hard
   Eight
  John Turturro/Box of
   Moonlight

ACTOR—SUPPORTING

1988
★ Morgan Freeman/Street
  Smart

1989
★ Lou Diamond Phillips/
  Stand and Deliver

1990
★ Max Perlich/Drugstore
  Cowboy

1991
★ Bruce Davison/Longtime
  Companion

1992
★ David Strathairn/City of
  Hope

1993
★ Steve Buscemi/Reservoir
  Dogs

1994
★ Christopher Lloyd/
  Twenty Bucks
  David Chung/
   Combination Platter
  Tate Donovan/Inside
   Monkey Zetterland
  Todd Field/Ruby in
   Paradise
  Edward Furlong/
   American Heart

1995
★ Chazz Palminteri/Bullets
  Over Broadway
  Giancarlo Esposito/
   Fresh
  Larry Pine/Vanya on 42nd
   Street
  Eric Stoltz/Pulp Fiction
  Nicholas Turturro/
   Federal Hill

1996
★ Benicio Del Toro/The
  Usual Suspects
  James LeGros/Living in
   Oblivion
  David Morse/The
   Crossing Guard
  Max Perlich/Georgia
  Harold Perrineau, Jr./
   Smoke

1997
★ Benicio Del Toro/
  Basquiat
★ Jason Lee/Chasing Amy
  Kevin Corrigan/Walking
   and Talking
  Matthew Faber/Welcome
   to the Dollhouse
  Gary Farmer/Dead Man
  Richard Jenkins/Flirting
   with Disaster

1998
  Efrain Figueroa/Star
  Maps
  Samuel L. Jackson/Hard
   Eight
  Ajay Naidu/subUrbia
  Roy Scheider/The Myth
   of Fingerprints

ACTRESS

1986
★ Geraldine Page/The Trip
  to Bountiful

1987
- ★ Isabella Rossellini/*Blue Velvet*

1988
- ★ Sally Kirkland/*Anna*

1989
- ★ Jodie Foster/*Five Corners*

1990
- ★ Andie MacDowell/*sex, lies and videotape*

1991
- ★ Anjelica Huston/*The Grifters*

1992
- ★ Judy Davis/*Impromptu*

1993
- ★ Fairuza Balk/*Gas Food Lodging*

1994
- ★ Ashley Judd/*Ruby in Paradise*
  Suzy Amis/*The Ballad of Little Jo*
  May Chin/*The Wedding Banquet*
  Ariyan Johnson/*Just Another Girl on the I.R.T.*
  Emma Thompson/*Much Ado about Nothing*

1995
- ★ Linda Fiorentino/*The Last Seduction*
  Jennifer Jason Leigh/*Mrs. Parker and the Vicious Circle*
  Karen Sillas/*What Happened Was...*
  Lauren Velez/*I Like It Like That*
  Chien-Lien Wu/*Eat Drink Man Woman*

1996
- ★ Elisabeth Shue/*Leaving Las Vegas*
  Jennifer Jason Leigh/*Georgia*
  Elina Lowensohn/*Nadja*
  Julianne Moore/*Safe*
  Lili Taylor/*The Addiction*

1997
- ★ Frances McDormand/*Fargo*
  Maria Conchita Alonso/*Caught*
  Scarlett Johansson/*Manny & Lo*
  Catherine Keener/*Walking and Talking*
  Renee Zellweger/*The Whole Wide World*

1998
- ★ Julie Christie/*Afterglow*
  Stacy Edwards/*In the Company of Men*
  Alison Folland/*All Over Me*
  Lisa Harrow/*Sunday*
  Robin Wright Penn/*Loved*

ACTRESS— SUPPORTING

1988
- ★ Anjelica Huston/*The Dead*

1989
- ★ Rosana De Soto/*Stand and Deliver*

1990
- ★ Laura San Giacomo/*sex, lies and videotape*

1991
- ★ Sheryl Lee Ralph/*To Sleep with Anger*

1992
- ★ Diane Ladd/*Rambling Rose*

1993
- ★ Alfre Woodard/*Passion Fish*

1994
- ★ Lili Taylor/*Household Saints*
  Lara Flynn Boyle/*Equinox*
  Ah-Leh Gua/*The Wedding Banquet*
  Lucinda Jenney/*American Heart*
  Julianne Moore/*Short Cuts*

1995
- ★ Dianne Wiest/*Bullets Over Broadway*
  V.S. Brodie/*Go Fish*
  Carla Gallo/*Spanking the Monkey*
  Kelly Lynch/*Forbidden Choices*
  Brooke Smith/*Vanya on 42nd Street*

1996
- ★ Mare Winningham/*Georgia*
  Jennifer Lopez/*My Family*
  Vanessa Redgrave/*Little Odessa*
  Chloe Sevigny/*Kids*
  Celia Weston/*Dead Man Walking*

1997
- ★ Elizabeth Pena/*Lone Star*
  Mary Kay Place/*Manny & Lo*
  Queen Latifah/*Set It Off*
  Lili Taylor/*Girls Town*
  Lily Tomlin/*Flirting with Disaster*

1998
- ★ Debbi Morgan/*Eve's Bayou*
  Farrah Fawcett/*The Apostle*
  Amy Madigan/*Loved*
  Miranda Richardson/*The Apostle*
  Patricia Richardson/*Ulee's Gold*

CINEMATOGRAPHY

1986
- ★ Trouble in Mind

1987
- ★ Platoon

1988
- ★ Matewan

1989
- ★ The Unbearable Lightness of Being

1990
- ★ Drugstore Cowboy

1991
- ★ Wild at Heart

1992
- ★ Kafka

1993
- ★ Night on Earth

1994
- ★ Menace II Society
  American Heart
  Chain of Desire
  Equinox
  Ruby in Paradise

1995
- ★ Barcelona
  Eat Drink Man Woman
  Forbidden Choices
  I Like It Like That
  Suture

1996
- ★ Leaving Las Vegas
  Little Odessa
  Nadja
  The Underneath
  The Usual Suspects

1997
- ★ Fargo
  Bound
  Color of a Brisk and Leaping Day
  Dead Man
  The Funeral

1998
- ★ Kama Sutra: A Tale of Love
  The Bible and Gun Club
  Habit
  Hard Eight
  Sunday

DIRECTOR

1986
- ★ Joel Coen/*Blood Simple*
- ★ Martin Scorsese/*After Hours*

1987
- ★ Oliver Stone/*Platoon*

1988
- ★ John Huston/*The Dead*

1989
- ★ Ramon Menendez/*Stand and Deliver*

1990
- ★ Steven Soderbergh/*sex, lies and videotape*

1991
- ★ Charles Burnett/*To Sleep with Anger*

1992
- ★ Martha Coolidge/*Rambling Rose*

1993
- ★ Carl Franklin/*One False Move*

1994
- ★ Robert Altman/*Short Cuts*
  Ang Lee/*The Wedding Banquet*
  Victor Nunez/*Ruby in Paradise*
  Robert Rodriguez/*El Mariachi*
  John Turturro/*Mac*

1995
- ★ Quentin Tarantino/*Pulp Fiction*
  John Dahl/*Red Rock West*
  Ang Lee/*Eat Drink Man Woman*
  Roman Polanski/*Death and the Maiden*
  Alan Rudolph/*Mrs. Parker and the Vicious Circle*

1996
- ★ Mike Figgis/*Leaving Las Vegas*
  Michael Almereyda/*Nadja*
  Ulu Grosbard/*Georgia*
  Todd Haynes/*Safe*
  John Sayles/*The Secret of Roan Inish*

1997
- ★ Joel Coen/*Fargo*
  Abel Ferrara/*The Funeral*
  David O. Russell/*Flirting with Disaster*
  Todd Solondz/*Welcome to the Dollhouse*
  Robert M. Young/*Caught*

1998
- ★ Robert Duvall/*The Apostle*
  Larry Fessenden/*Habit*
  Victor Nunez/*Ulee's Gold*
  Paul Schrader/*Touch*
  Wim Wenders/*The End of Violence*

FILM

1986
- ★ After Hours

1987
- ★ Platoon

1988
- ★ River's Edge

1989
- ★ Stand and Deliver

1990
- ★ sex, lies and videotape

1991
- ★ The Grifters

1992
- ★ Rambling Rose

1993
- ★ The Player

1994
- ★ Short Cuts
  Equinox
  Much Ado about Nothing
  Ruby in Paradise
  The Wedding Banquet

1995
- ★ Pulp Fiction
  Bullets Over Broadway
  Eat Drink Man Woman
  Mrs. Parker and the Vicious Circle
  Wes Craven's New Nightmare

1996
- ★ Leaving Las Vegas
  The Addiction
  Living in Oblivion
  Safe
  The Secret of Roan Inish

1997
- ★ Fargo
  Dead Man
  The Funeral
  Lone Star
  Welcome to the Dollhouse

1998
- ★ The Apostle
  Chasing Amy
  Loved
  Ulee's Gold
  Waiting for Guffman

FIRST FEATURE

1987
- ★ She's Gotta Have It

1988
- ★ Dirty Dancing

1989
- ★ Mystic Pizza

1990
- ★ Heathers

1991
- ★ Metropolitan

1992
- ★ Straight Out of Brooklyn

1993
- ★ The Waterdance

1994
- ★ El Mariachi
  American Heart
  Combination Platter
  Mac
  Menace II Society

1995
- ★ Spanking the Monkey
  Clean, Shaven

FIRST FEATURE
cont.

Clerks
I Like It Like That
Suture

1996
★ The Brothers McMullen
Kids
Little Odessa
Picture Bride
River of Grass

1997
★ Sling Blade
Big Night
I Shot Andy Warhol
Manny & Lo
Tree's Lounge
Tony Shalhoub/*Big Night*
Stanley Tucci/*Big Night*

1998
★ Eve's Bayou
The Bible and Gun Club
Hard Eight
In the Company of Men
Star Maps

SCREENPLAY

1986
★ The Trip to Bountiful

1987
★ Platoon

1988
★ River's Edge

1989
★ Stand and Deliver

1990
★ Drugstore Cowboy

1991
★ To Sleep with Anger

1992
★ My Own Private Idaho

1993
★ The Waterdance

1994
★ Short Cuts
Combination Platter
Household Saints
Ruby in Paradise
The Wedding Banquet

1995
★ Pulp Fiction
Bullets Over Broadway
Eat Drink Man Woman
Mrs. Parker and the
    Vicious Circle
Red Rock West

1996
★ The Usual Suspects
Leaving Las Vegas
Living in Oblivion
Safe
The Secret of Roan Inish

1997
★ Chasing Amy
★ Fargo

Dead Man
Flirting with Disaster
The Funeral
Lone Star

1998
The Apostle
Touch
Ulee's Gold
Waiting for Guffman

DEBUT
PERFORMANCE

1995
★ Sean Nelson/*Fresh*
Jeff Anderson/*Clerks*
Jeremy Davies/*Spanking
    the Monkey*
Alicia Witt/*Fun*
Renee Zellweger/*Love
    and a .45*

1996
★ Justin Pierce/*Kids*
Jason Andrews/*Rhythm
    Thief*
Lisa Bowman/*River of
    Grass*
Gabriel Casseus/*New
    Jersey Drive*
Rose McGowan/*The
    Doom Generation*

1997
★ Heather Matarazzo/
    *Welcome to the
    Dollhouse*
Jena Malone/*Bastard out
    of Carolina*
Brendan Sexton, III/
    *Welcome to the
    Dollhouse*
Arie Verveen/*Caught*
Jeffrey Wright/*Basquiat*

1998
★ Aaron Eckhart/*In the
    Company of Men*
Tyron Burton/*Squeeze*
Eddie Cutanda/*Squeeze*
Phuong Duong/*Squeeze*
Lysa Flores/*Star Maps*
Darling Narita/*Bang*
Douglas Spain/*Star Maps*

FILM—FOREIGN
LANGUAGE

1986
★ Kiss of the Spider Woman

1987
★ A Room with a View

1988
★ My Life As a Dog

1989
★ Wings of Desire

1990
★ My Left Foot

1992
★ An Angel at My Table

1993
★ The Crying Game

1994
★ The Piano
Like Water for Chocolate

Naked
Orlando
The Story of Qui Ju

1995
★ Trois Couleurs: Rouge
The Blue Kite
The Boys of St. Vincent
Ladybird, Ladybird
32 Short Films about
    Glenn Gould

1996
★ Before the Rain
The City of Lost Children
Exotica
I Am Cuba
Through the Olive Trees

1997
Breaking the Waves
Chungking Express
Lamerica
Secrets and Lies
Trainspotting

1998
★ The Sweet Hereafter
Happy Together
Mouth to Mouth
Nenette and Boni
Underground

LOS ANGELES
FILM CRITICS
ASSOCIATION
AWARDS
ACTOR

1976
★ Robert De Niro/*Taxi
    Driver*

1977
★ Richard Dreyfuss/*The
    Goodbye Girl*

1978
★ Jon Voight/*Coming Home*

1979
★ Dustin Hoffman/*Kramer
    vs. Kramer*

1980
★ Robert De Niro/*Raging
    Bull*

1981
★ Burt Lancaster/*Atlantic
    City*

1982
★ Ben Kingsley/*Gandhi*

1983
★ Robert Duvall/*Tender
    Mercies*

1984
★ Albert Finney/*Under the
    Volcano*
F. Murray Abraham/
    Amadeus

1985
★ William Hurt/*Kiss of the
    Spider Woman*

1986
★ Bob Hoskins/*Mona Lisa*

1987
★ Steve Martin/*Roxanne*
★ Jack Nicholson/*Ironweed*
★ Jack Nicholson/*The
    Witches of Eastwick*

1988
★ Tom Hanks/*Big*
★ Tom Hanks/*Punchline*

1989
★ Daniel Day-Lewis/*My Left
    Foot*

1990
★ Jeremy Irons/*Reversal of
    Fortune*

1991
★ Nick Nolte/*The Prince of
    Tides*

1992
★ Clint Eastwood/
    Unforgiven

1993
★ Anthony Hopkins/*The
    Remains of the Day*
★ Anthony Hopkins/
    Shadowlands

1994
★ John Travolta/*Pulp
    Fiction*

1995
★ Nicolas Cage/*Leaving Las
    Vegas*

1996
★ Geoffrey Rush/*Shine*

1997
★ Robert Duvall/*The
    Apostle*

ACTOR—SUPPORTING

1977
★ Jason Robards, Jr./*Julia*

1978
★ Robert Morley/*Who Is
    Killing the Great Chefs
    of Europe?*

1979
★ Melvyn Douglas/*Being
    There*
★ Melvyn Douglas/*The
    Seduction of Joe Tynan*

1980
★ Timothy Hutton/*Ordinary
    People*

1981
★ John Gielgud/*Arthur*

1982
★ John Lithgow/*The World
    According to Garp*

1983
★ Jack Nicholson/*Terms of
    Endearment*

1984
★ Adolph Caesar/*A
    Soldier's Story*

1985
★ John Gielgud/*Plenty*
★ John Gielgud/*The
    Shooting Party*

1986
★ Dennis Hopper/*Blue
    Velvet*
★ Dennis Hopper/*Hoosiers*

1987
★ Morgan Freeman/*Street
    Smart*

1988
★ Alec Guinness/*Little
    Dorrit, Film 1: Nobody's
    Fault*
★ Alec Guinness/*Little
    Dorrit, Film 2: Little
    Dorrit's Story*

1989
★ Danny Aiello/*Do the Right
    Thing*

1990
★ Joe Pesci/*Goodfellas*

1991
★ Michael Lerner/*Barton
    Fink*

1992
★ Gene Hackman/
    Unforgiven

1993
★ Tommy Lee Jones/*The
    Fugitive*

1994
★ Martin Landau/*Ed Wood*

1995
★ Don Cheadle/*Devil in a
    Blue Dress*

1996
★ Edward Norton/*Everyone
    Says I Love You*
★ Edward Norton/*The
    People vs. Larry Flynt*
★ Edward Norton/*Primal
    Fear*

1997
★ Burt Reynolds/*Boogie
    Nights*

ACTRESS

1976
★ Liv Ullmann/*Face to Face*

1978
★ Jane Fonda/*Coming
    Home*

1979
★ Sally Field/*Norma Rae*

1980
★ Sissy Spacek/*Coal
    Miner's Daughter*

Chris Farley/*Beverly Hills Ninja*
Janeane Garofalo/*The Truth About Cats and Dogs*
Eddie Murphy/*The Nutty Professor*
Robin Williams/*The Birdcage*

1998

★ Jim Carrey/*Liar Liar*
Rupert Everett/*My Best Friend's Wedding*
Mike Myers/*Austin Powers: International Man of Mystery*
Adam Sandler/*The Wedding Singer*
Will Smith/*Men in Black*

FILM

1992

★ *Terminator 2: Judgment Day*

1993

★ *A Few Good Men*

1994

★ *Menace II Society*
The Fugitive
Jurassic Park
Philadelphia
Schindler's List

1995

★ *Pulp Fiction*
The Crow
Forrest Gump
Interview with the Vampire
Speed

1996

★ *Seven*
Apollo 13
Braveheart
Clueless
Dangerous Minds

1997

★ *Scream*
Independence Day
Jerry Maguire
The Rock
William Shakespeare's Romeo and Juliet

1998

★ *Titanic*
Austin Powers: International Man of Mystery
Face/Off
Good Will Hunting
Men in Black

KISS

1992

★ Macaulay Culkin/Anna Chlumsky/*My Girl*

1993

★ Christian Slater/Marisa Tomei/*Untamed Heart*

1994

★ Demi Moore/Woody Harrelson/*Indecent Proposal*

Christian Slater/Patricia Arquette/*True Romance*
Dana Carvey/Kim Basinger/*Wayne's World 2*
Ethan Hawke/Winona Ryder/*Reality Bites*
Jason James Richter/*Willy/Free Willy*

1995

★ Jim Carrey/Lauren Holly/*Dumb & Dumber*
Arnold Schwarzenegger/Jamie Lee Curtis/*True Lies*
Ethan Hawke/Julie Delpy/*Before Sunrise*
Keanu Reeves/Sandra Bullock/*Speed*
Woody Harrelson/Juliette Lewis/*Natural Born Killers*

1996

★ Natasha Henstridge/Anthony Guidera/*Species*
Antonio Banderas/Salma Hayek/*Desperado*
Jim Carrey/Sophie Okonedo/*Ace Ventura: When Nature Calls*
Keanu Reeves/Aitana Sanchez-Gijon/*A Walk in the Clouds*
Winona Ryder/Dermot Mulroney/*How to Make an American Quilt*

1997

★ Vivica A. Fox/Will Smith/*Independence Day*
Christopher Daniel Barnes/Christine Taylor/*A Very Brady Sequel*
Jennifer Tilly/Gina Gershon/*Bound*
John Travolta/Kyra Sedgwick/*Phenomenon*
Leonardo DiCaprio/Claire Danes/*William Shakespeare's Romeo and Juliet*

1998

★ Adam Sandler/Drew Barrymore/*The Wedding Singer*
Joey Lauren Adams/Carmen Llywelyn/*Chasing Amy*
Kate Winslet/Leonardo DiCaprio/*Titanic*
Kevin Kline/Tom Selleck/*In and Out*
Matt Damon/Minnie Driver/*Good Will Hunting*

MOST DESIRABLE FEMALE

1992

★ Linda Hamilton/*Terminator 2: Judgment Day*

1993

★ Sharon Stone/*Basic Instinct*

1994

★ Janet Jackson/*Poetic Justice*
Kim Basinger/*The Getaway*
Demi Moore/*Indecent Proposal*
Sharon Stone/*Sliver*

1995

★ Sandra Bullock/*Speed*
Halle Berry/*The Flintstones*
Cameron Diaz/*The Mask*
Demi Moore/*Disclosure*
Sharon Stone/*The Specialist*

1996

★ Alicia Silverstone/*Clueless*
Sandra Bullock/*While You Were Sleeping*
Nicole Kidman/*To Die For*
Michelle Pfeiffer/*Dangerous Minds*

MOST DESIRABLE MALE

1992

★ Keanu Reeves/*Point Break*

1993

★ Christian Slater/*Untamed Heart*

1994

★ William Baldwin/*Sliver*
Tom Cruise/*The Firm*
Val Kilmer/*Tombstone*
Jean-Claude Van Damme/*Hard Target*
Denzel Washington/*The Pelican Brief*

1995

★ Brad Pitt/*Interview with the Vampire*
Tom Cruise/*Interview with the Vampire*
Andy Garcia/*When a Man Loves a Woman*
Keanu Reeves/*Speed*
Christian Slater/*Interview with the Vampire*

1996

★ Brad Pitt/*Seven*
Antonio Banderas/*Desperado*
Mel Gibson/*Braveheart*
Val Kilmer/*Batman Forever*
Keanu Reeves/*A Walk in the Clouds*

ON-SCREEN DUO

1992

★ Mike Myers/Dana Carvey/*Wayne's World*

1993

★ Mel Gibson/Danny Glover/*Lethal Weapon 3*

1994

★ Harrison Ford/Tommy Lee Jones/*The Fugitive*
Johnny Depp/Mary Stuart Masterson/*Benny & Joon*
Mike Myers/Dana Carvey/*Wayne's World 2*
Tom Hanks/Denzel Washington/*Philadelphia*
Tom Hanks/Meg Ryan/*Sleepless in Seattle*

1995

★ Keanu Reeves/Sandra Bullock/*Speed*
Jim Carrey/Jeff Daniels/*Dumb & Dumber*
John Travolta/Samuel L. Jackson/*Pulp Fiction*
Tom Cruise/Brad Pitt/*Interview with the Vampire*
Woody Harrelson/Juliette Lewis/*Natural Born Killers*

1996

★ Chris Farley/David Spade/*Tommy Boy*
Brad Pitt/Morgan Freeman/*Seven*
Chris Tucker/Ice Cube/*Friday*
Martin Lawrence/Will Smith/*Bad Boys*
Tom Hanks/Tim Allen/*Toy Story*

1997

★ Sean Connery/Nicolas Cage/*The Rock*
Beavis/Butt-head/*Beavis and Butt-Head Do America*
Leonardo DiCaprio/Clare Danes/*William Shakespeare's Romeo and Juliet*
Peter Stormare/Steve Buscemi/*Fargo*
Robin Williams/Nathan Lane/*The Birdcage*

1998

★ John Travolta/Nicolas Cage/*Face/Off*
Adam Sandler/Drew Barrymore/*The Wedding Singer*
Kate Winslet/Leonardo DiCaprio/*Titanic*
Matt Damon/Ben Affleck/*Good Will Hunting*
Tommy Lee Jones/Will Smith/*Men in Black*

SONG

1992

★ "(Everything I Do) I Do for You"/*Robin Hood: Prince of Thieves*

1993

★ "I Will Always Love You"/*The Bodyguard*

1994

★ "Will You Be There"/*Free Willy*
"All for Love"/*The Three Musketeers*
"I Can't Help Falling in Love"/*Sliver*
"I'm Gonna Be 500 Miles"/*Benny & Joon*
"Streets of Philadelphia"/*Philadelphia*
"When I Fall in Love"/*Sleepless in Seattle*

1995

★ "Big Empty"/*The Crow*
"Can You Feel the Love Tonight"/*The Lion King*
"Girl, You'll Be A Woman Soon"/*Pulp Fiction*
"I'll Remember"/*With Honors*
"Regulate"/*Above the Rim*

1996

★ "Sittin' Up in My Room"/*Waiting to Exhale*
"Exhale (Shoop Shoop)"/*Waiting to Exhale*
"Gangsta's Paradise"/*Dangerous Minds*
"Hold Me, Thrill Me, Kiss Me, Kill Me"/*Batman Forever*
"I Believe I Can Fly"/*Space Jam*
"Kiss from a Rose"/*Batman Forever*

1997

★ "Machinehead"/*Fear*
"#1 Crush"/*William Shakespeare's Romeo and Juliet*
"Change the World"/*Phenomenon*
"Don't Cry for Me Argentina"/*Evita*

1998

★ "Men in Black"/*Men in Black*
"A Song for Mama"/*Soul Food*
"Deadweight"/*A Life Less Ordinary*
"Mouth"/*An American Werewolf in Paris*
"My Heart Will Go On"/*Titanic*

NEW FILMMAKER

1992

★ John Singleton/*Boyz N the Hood*

1993

★ Carl Franklin/*One False Move*

1994

★ Steven Zaillian/*Searching for Bobby Fischer*

NEW FILMMAKER
~cont.

1995
* ★ Steve James/*Hoop Dreams*

1996
* ★ Wes Anderson/*Bottle Rocket*

1997
* ★ Doug Liman/*Swingers*

VILLAIN

1992
* ★ Rebecca DeMornay/*The Hand that Rocks the Cradle*

1993
* ★ Jennifer Jason Leigh/*Single White Female*

1994
* ★ Alicia Silverstone/*The Crush*
* T-Rex/*Jurassic Park*
* Macaulay Culkin/*The Good Son*
* John Maikovich/*In the Line of Fire*
* Wesley Snipes/*Demolition Man*

1995
* ★ Dennis Hopper/*Speed*
* Tom Cruise/*Interview with the Vampire*
* Jeremy Irons/*The Lion King*
* Tommy Lee Jones/*Blown Away*
* Demi Moore/*Disclosure*

1996
* ★ Kevin Spacey/*Seven*
* Jim Carrey/*Batman Forever*
* Tommy Lee Jones/*Batman Forever*
* Joe Pesci/*Casino*
* John Travolta/*Broken Arrow*

1997
* ★ Jim Carrey/*The Cable Guy*
* Robert De Niro/*The Fan*
* Edward Norton/*Primal Fear*
* Kiefer Sutherland/*A Time to Kill*
* Mark Wahlberg/*Fear*

1998
* ★ Mike Myers/*Austin Powers: International Man of Mystery*
* John Travolta/Nicolas Cage/*Face/Off*
* Gary Oldman/*Air Force One*
* Al Pacino/*The Devil's Advocate*
* Billy Zane/*Titanic*

BEST DANCE SEQUENCE

1995
* ★ John Travolta/Uma Thurman/*Pulp Fiction*
* Arnold Schwarzenegger/Tia Carrere/*True Lies*
* Jim Carrey/Cameron Diaz/*The Mask*
* The Brady Kids/*The Brady Bunch Movie*

1998
* ★ Mike Myers/Londoners/*Austin Powers: International Man of Mystery*
* Cameron Diaz/Ewan McGregor/*A Life Less Ordinary*
* Cast/*The Full Monty*
* Lisa Kudrow/Mira Sorvino/Alan Cumming/*Romy and Michele's High School Reunion*
* Mark Wahlberg/cast/*Boogie Nights*

BEST MALE PERFORMANCE

1992
* ★ Arnold Schwarzenegger/*Terminator 2: Judgment Day*

1993
* ★ Denzel Washington/*Malcolm X*

1994
* ★ Tom Hanks/*Philadelphia*
* Tom Cruise/*The Firm*
* Harrison Ford/*The Fugitive*
* Val Kilmer/*Tombstone*
* Robin Williams/*Mrs. Doubtfire*

1995
* ★ Brad Pitt/*Interview with the Vampire*
* Tom Hanks/*Forrest Gump*
* Brandon Lee/*The Crow*
* Keanu Reeves/*Speed*
* John Travolta/*Pulp Fiction*

1996
* ★ Jim Carrey/*Ace Ventura: When Nature Calls*
* Mel Gibson/*Braveheart*
* Tom Hanks/*Apollo 13*
* Brad Pitt/*12 Monkeys*
* Denzel Washington/*Crimson Tide*

1997
* ★ Tom Cruise/*Jerry Maguire*
* Leonardo DiCaprio/*William Shakespeare's Romeo and Juliet*
* Eddie Murphy/*The Nutty Professor*
* Will Smith/*Independence Day*
* John Travolta/*Phenomenon*

1998
* ★ Leonardo DiCaprio/*Titanic*
* Nicolas Cage/*Face/Off*
* Matt Damon/*Good Will Hunting*
* Samuel L. Jackson/*Jackie Brown*
* John Travolta/*Face/Off*

BEST FEMALE PERFORMANCE

1992
* ★ Linda Hamilton/*Terminator 2: Judgment Day*

1993
* ★ Sharon Stone/*Basic Instinct*

1994
* ★ Janet Jackson/*Poetic Justice*
* Angela Bassett/*What's Love Got to Do with It?*
* Demi Moore/*Indecent Proposal*
* Julia Roberts/*The Pelican Brief*
* Meg Ryan/*Sleepless in Seattle*

1995
* ★ Sandra Bullock/*Speed*
* Jamie Lee Curtis/*True Lies*
* Jodie Foster/*Nell*
* Meg Ryan/*When a Man Loves a Woman*
* Uma Thurman/*Pulp Fiction*

1996
* ★ Alicia Silverstone/*Clueless*
* Sandra Bullock/*While You Were Sleeping*
* Michelle Pfeiffer/*Dangerous Minds*
* Susan Sarandon/*Dead Man Walking*
* Sharon Stone/*Casino*

1997
* ★ Claire Danes/*William Shakespeare's Romeo and Juliet*
* Sandra Bullock/*A Time to Kill*
* Neve Campbell/*Scream*
* Helen Hunt/*Twister*
* Madonna/*Evita*

1998
* ★ Neve Campbell/*Scream 2*
* Vivica A. Fox/*Soul Food*
* Helen Hunt/*As Good As It Gets*
* Julia Roberts/*My Best Friend's Wedding*
* Kate Winslet/*Titanic*

FIGHT

1996
* ★ Adam Sandler/Bob Barker/*Happy Gilmore*

1997
* ★ Fairuza Balk/Robin Tunney/*The Craft*
* Jackie Chan/A ladder/*Jackie Chan's First Strike*
* Jim Brown/A Martian/*Mars Attacks!*
* Jim Carrey/Matthew Broderick/*The Cable Guy*
* Pamela Lee/A Guy/*Barb Wire*

1998
* ★ Will Smith/alien/*Men in Black*
* Demi Moore/Viggo Mortensen/*G.I. Jane*
* Harrison Ford/Gary Oldman/*Air Force One*
* Michelle Yeoh/bad guys/*Tomorrow Never Dies*
* Milla Jovovich/aliens/*The Fifth Element*

NATIONAL BOARD OF REVIEW AWARDS

ACTOR

1945
* ★ Ray Milland/*The Lost Weekend*

1946
* ★ Laurence Olivier/*Henry V*

1948
* ★ Walter Huston/*Treasure of the Sierra Madre*

1949
* ★ Ralph Richardson/*The Fallen Idol*
* ★ Ralph Richardson/*The Heiress*

1953
* ★ James Mason/*Julius Caesar*

1955
* ★ Ernest Borgnine/*Marty*

1957
* ★ Alec Guinness/*The Bridge on the River Kwai*

1958
* ★ Spencer Tracy/*Last Hurrah*

1960
* ★ Robert Mitchum/*Home from the Hill*
* ★ Robert Mitchum/*The Sundowners*

1961
* ★ Albert Finney/*Saturday Night and Sunday Morning*

1963
* ★ Rex Harrison/*Cleopatra*

1964
* ★ Anthony Quinn/*Zorba the Greek*

1965
* ★ Lee Marvin/*Cat Ballou*
* ★ Lee Marvin/*Ship of Fools*

1966
* ★ Paul Scofield/*A Man for All Seasons*

1967
* ★ Peter Finch/*Far from the Madding Crowd*

1968
* ★ Cliff Robertson/*Charly*

1969
* ★ Peter O'Toole/*Goodbye, Mr. Chips*

1970
* ★ George C. Scott/*Patton*

1971
* ★ Gene Hackman/*The French Connection*

1972
* ★ Peter O'Toole/*Man of La Mancha*
* ★ Peter O'Toole/*The Ruling Class*

1973
* ★ Al Pacino/*Serpico*

1974
* ★ Gene Hackman/*The Conversation*

1975
* ★ Jack Nicholson/*One Flew Over the Cuckoo's Nest*

1976
* ★ David Carradine/*Bound for Glory*

1977
* ★ John Travolta/*Saturday Night Fever*

1978
* ★ Laurence Olivier/*The Boys from Brazil*

1979
* ★ Peter Sellers/*Being There*

1980
* ★ Robert De Niro/*Raging Bull*

1981
* ★ Henry Fonda/*On Golden Pond*

1982
* ★ Ben Kingsley/*Gandhi*

1983
* ★ Tom Conti/*Merry Christmas, Mr. Lawrence*
* ★ Tom Conti/*Reuben, Reuben*

1984
- ★ Victor Banerjee/*A Passage to India*

1985
- ★ William Hurt/*Kiss of the Spider Woman*
- ★ Raul Julia/*Kiss of the Spider Woman*

1986
- ★ Paul Newman/*The Color of Money*

1987
- ★ Michael Douglas/*Wall Street*

1988
- ★ Gene Hackman/*Mississippi Burning*

1989
- ★ Morgan Freeman/*Driving Miss Daisy*

1990
- ★ Robert De Niro/*Awakenings*
- ★ Robin Williams/*Awakenings*

1991
- ★ Warren Beatty/*Bugsy*

1992
- ★ Jack Lemmon/*Glengarry Glen Ross*

1993
- ★ Anthony Hopkins/*The Remains of the Day*
- ★ Anthony Hopkins/*Shadowlands*

1994
- ★ Tom Hanks/*Forrest Gump*

1995
- ★ Nicolas Cage/*Leaving Las Vegas*

1996
- ★ Tom Cruise/*Jerry Maguire*

1997
- ★ Jack Nicholson/*As Good As It Gets*

ACTOR—SUPPORTING

1954
- ★ John Williams/*Sabrina*

1957
- ★ Sessue Hayakawa/*The Bridge on the River Kwai*

1958
- ★ Albert Salmi/*The Bravados*

1961
- ★ Jackie Gleason/*The Hustler*

1962
- ★ Burgess Meredith/*Advise and Consent*
- ★ Jason Robards, Jr./*Long Day's Journey into Night*

1963
- ★ Melvyn Douglas/*Hud*

1964
- ★ Martin Balsam/*The Carpetbaggers*

1965
- ★ Harry Andrews/*The Agony and the Ecstasy*

1966
- ★ Robert Shaw/*A Man for All Seasons*

1967
- ★ Paul Ford/*The Comedians*

1968
- ★ Leo McKern/*The Shoes of the Fisherman*

1969
- ★ Philippe Noiret/*Topaz*

1970
- ★ Frank Langella/*Diary of a Mad Housewife*

1971
- ★ Ben Johnson/*The Last Picture Show*

1972
- ★ Joel Grey/*Cabaret*
- ★ Al Pacino/*The Godfather*

1973
- ★ John Houseman/*The Paper Chase*

1975
- ★ Charles Durning/*Dog Day Afternoon*

1976
- ★ Jason Robards, Jr./*All the President's Men*

1977
- ★ Tom Skerritt/*The Turning Point*

1978
- ★ Richard Farnsworth/*Comes a Horseman*

1979
- ★ Paul Dooley/*Breaking Away*

1980
- ★ Joe Pesci/*Raging Bull*

1981
- ★ Jack Nicholson/*Reds*

1982
- ★ Robert Preston/*Victor/Victoria*

1983
- ★ Jack Nicholson/*Terms of Endearment*

1984
- ★ John Malkovich/*Places in the Heart*

1985
- ★ Klaus Maria Brandauer/*Out of Africa*

1986
- ★ Daniel Day-Lewis/*My Beautiful Laundrette*
- ★ Daniel Day-Lewis/*A Room with a View*

1987
- ★ Sean Connery/*The Untouchables*

1988
- ★ River Phoenix/*Running on Empty*

1989
- ★ Alan Alda/*Crimes & Misdemeanors*

1990
- ★ Joe Pesci/*Goodfellas*

1991
- ★ Anthony Hopkins/*The Silence of the Lambs*

1992
- ★ Jack Nicholson/*A Few Good Men*

1993
- ★ Leonardo DiCaprio/*What's Eating Gilbert Grape*

1994
- ★ Gary Sinise/*Forrest Gump*

1995
- ★ Kevin Spacey/*Seven*
- ★ Kevin Spacey/*The Usual Suspects*

1996
- ★ Edward Norton/*Everyone Says I Love You*
- ★ Edward Norton/*The People vs. Larry Flynt*
- ★ Edward Norton/*Primal Fear*

1997
- ★ Greg Kinnear/*As Good As It Gets*

ACTRESS

1953
- ★ Jean Simmons/*The Robe*

1954
- ★ Grace Kelly/*Country Girl*

1958
- ★ Ingrid Bergman/*The Inn of the Sixth Happiness*

1960
- ★ Greer Garson/*Sunrise at Campobello*

1961
- ★ Geraldine Page/*Summer and Smoke*

1962
- ★ Anne Bancroft/*The Miracle Worker*

1963
- ★ Patricia Neal/*Hud*

1964
- ★ Kim Stanley/*Seance on a Wet Afternoon*

1965
- ★ Julie Christie/*Darling*
- ★ Julie Christie/*Doctor Zhivago*

1966
- ★ Elizabeth Taylor/*Who's Afraid of Virginia Woolf?*

1968
- ★ Liv Ullmann/*Hour of the Wolf*

1970
- ★ Glenda Jackson/*Women in Love*

1971
- ★ Irene Papas/*Trojan Women*

1972
- ★ Cicely Tyson/*Sounder*

1973
- ★ Liv Ullmann/*The New Land*

1974
- ★ Gena Rowlands/*A Woman Under the Influence*

1975
- ★ Isabelle Adjani/*Story of Adele H.*

1976
- ★ Liv Ullmann/*Face to Face*

1977
- ★ Anne Bancroft/*The Turning Point*

1978
- ★ Ingrid Bergman/*Autumn Sonata*

1979
- ★ Sally Field/*Norma Rae*

1980
- ★ Sissy Spacek/*Coal Miner's Daughter*

1982
- ★ Meryl Streep/*Sophie's Choice*

1983
- ★ Shirley MacLaine/*Terms of Endearment*

1984
- ★ Peggy Ashcroft/*A Passage to India*

1985
- ★ Whoopi Goldberg/*The Color Purple*

1986
- ★ Kathleen Turner/*Peggy Sue Got Married*

1987
- ★ Lillian Gish/*The Whales of August*

- ★ Holly Hunter/*Broadcast News*

1988
- ★ Jodie Foster/*The Accused*

1989
- ★ Michelle Pfeiffer/*The Fabulous Baker Boys*

1990
- ★ Mia Farrow/*Alice*

1991
- ★ Geena Davis/*Thelma & Louise*
- ★ Susan Sarandon/*Thelma & Louise*

1992
- ★ Emma Thompson/*Howard's End*

1993
- ★ Holly Hunter/*The Piano*

1994
- ★ Miranda Richardson/*Tom & Viv*

1995
- ★ Emma Thompson/*Carrington*
- ★ Emma Thompson/*Sense and Sensibility*

1996
- ★ Frances McDormand/*Fargo*

1997
- ★ Helena Bonham Carter/*The Wings of the Dove*

ACTRESS—SUPPORTING

1958
- ★ Kay Walsh/*The Horse's Mouth*

1959
- ★ Edith Evans/*The Nun's Story*

1960
- ★ Shirley Jones/*Elmer Gantry*

1961
- ★ Ruby Dee/*A Raisin in the Sun*

1962
- ★ Angela Lansbury/*The Manchurian Candidate*

1963
- ★ Margaret Rutherford/*The V.I.P.'s*

1964
- ★ Edith Evans/*The Chalk Garden*

1965
- ★ Joan Blondell/*The Cincinnati Kid*

1966
- ★ Vivien Merchant/*Alfie*

ACTRESS— SUPPORTING ‚cont.

1969
★ Pamela Franklin/*The Prime of Miss Jean Brodie*

1970
★ Karen Black/*Five Easy Pieces*

1971
★ Cloris Leachman/*The Last Picture Show*

1972
★ Marisa Berenson/*Cabaret*

1973
★ Sylvia Sidney/*Summer Wishes, Winter Dreams*

1974
★ Valerie Perrine/*Lenny*

1975
★ Ronee Blakley/*Nashville*

1976
★ Talia Shire/*Rocky*

1977
★ Diane Keaton/*Annie Hall*

1978
★ Angela Lansbury/*Death on the Nile*

1979
★ Meryl Streep/*Kramer vs. Kramer*
★ Meryl Streep/*The Seduction of Joe Tynan*

1980
★ Eva LeGallienne/*Resurrection*

1982
★ Glenn Close/*The World According to Garp*

1983
★ Linda Hunt/*The Year of Living Dangerously*

1984
★ Sabine Azema/*A Sunday in the Country*

1985
★ Rosanna Arquette/*Desperately Seeking Susan*

1986
★ Dianne Wiest/*Hannah and Her Sisters*

1987
★ Olympia Dukakis/*Moonstruck*

1988
★ Frances McDormand/*Mississippi Burning*

1989
★ Mary Stuart Masterson/*Immediate Family*

1990
★ Winona Ryder/*Mermaids*

1991
★ Kate Nelligan/*Frankie and Johnny*

1992
★ Judy Davis/*Husbands and Wives*

1993
★ Winona Ryder/*The Age of Innocence*

1994
★ Rosemary Harris/*Tom & Viv*

1995
★ Mira Sorvino/*Mighty Aphrodite*

1996
★ Juliette Binoche/*The English Patient*
★ Kristin Scott Thomas/*The English Patient*

1997
★ Anne Heche/*Donnie Brasco*
★ Anne Heche/*Wag the Dog*

DIRECTOR

1943
★ William A. Wellman/*The Ox-Bow Incident*

1945
★ Jean Renoir/*The Southerner*

1946
★ William Wyler/*The Best Years of Our Lives*

1948
★ Federico Fellini/*Paisan*

1949
★ Vittorio De Sica/*The Bicycle Thief*

1950
★ John Huston/*The Asphalt Jungle*

1951
★ Akira Kurosawa/*Rashomon*

1953
★ George Stevens/*Shane*

1954
★ Renato Castellani/*Romeo and Juliet*

1955
★ William Wyler/*Desperate Hours*

1956
★ John Huston/*Moby Dick*

1957
★ David Lean/*The Bridge on the River Kwai*

1958
★ John Ford/*Last Hurrah*

1959
★ Fred Zinnemann/*The Nun's Story*

1962
★ David Lean/*Lawrence of Arabia*

1963
★ Tony Richardson/*Tom Jones*

1965
★ John Schlesinger/*Darling*

1966
★ Fred Zinnemann/*A Man for All Seasons*

1967
★ Richard Brooks/*In Cold Blood*

1968
★ Franco Zeffirelli/*Romeo and Juliet*

1969
★ Alfred Hitchcock/*Topaz*

1970
★ Francois Truffaut/*The Wild Child*

1971
★ Ken Russell/*The Devils*

1972
★ Bob Fosse/*Cabaret*

1973
★ Ingmar Bergman/*Cries and Whispers*

1974
★ Francis Ford Coppola/*The Conversation*

1975
★ Robert Altman/*Nashville*
★ Stanley Kubrick/*Barry Lyndon*

1976
★ Alan J. Pakula/*All the President's Men*

1977
★ Luis Bunuel/*That Obscure Object of Desire*

1978
★ Ingmar Bergman/*Autumn Sonata*

1979
★ John Schlesinger/*Yanks*

1980
★ Robert Redford/*Ordinary People*

1981
★ Warren Beatty/*Reds*

1982
★ Sidney Lumet/*The Verdict*

1983
★ James L. Brooks/*Terms of Endearment*

1984
★ David Lean/*A Passage to India*

1985
★ Akira Kurosawa/*Ran*

1986
★ Woody Allen/*Hannah and Her Sisters*

1987
★ Steven Spielberg/*Empire of the Sun*

1988
★ Alan Parker/*Mississippi Burning*

1989
★ Kenneth Branagh/*Henry V*

1990
★ Kevin Costner/*Dances with Wolves*

1991
★ Jonathan Demme/*The Silence of the Lambs*

1992
★ James Ivory/*Howard's End*

1993
★ Martin Scorsese/*The Age of Innocence*

1994
★ Quentin Tarantino/*Pulp Fiction*

1995
★ Ang Lee/*Sense and Sensibility*

1996
★ Joel Coen/*Fargo*

1997
★ Curtis Hanson/*L.A. Confidential*

FILM

1991
★ *The Silence of the Lambs*

1992
★ *Howard's End*

1993
★ *Schindler's List*

1994
★ *Forrest Gump*
★ *Pulp Fiction*

1995
★ *Sense and Sensibility*

1996
★ *Shine*

1997
★ *L.A. Confidential*

FEATURE DOCUMENTARY

1991
★ *Hearts of Darkness: A Filmmaker's Apocalypse*

1992
★ *Brother's Keeper*

1993
★ *The War Room*

1994
★ *Hoop Dreams*

1997
★ *Fast, Cheap & Out of Control*

FILM—FOREIGN LANGUAGE

1991
★ *Europa, Europa*

1992
★ *Indochine*

1993
★ *Farewell My Concubine*

1994
★ *Eat Drink Man Woman*

1997
★ *Shall We Dance?*

NATIONAL FILM REGISTRY

1989
★ *The Best Years of Our Lives*
★ *Casablanca*
★ *Citizen Kane*
★ *The Crowd*
★ *Dr. Strangelove, or: How I Learned to Stop Worrying and Love the Bomb*
★ *The General*
★ *Gone with the Wind*
★ *The Grapes of Wrath*
★ *High Noon*
★ *Intolerance*
★ *The Learning Tree*
★ *The Maltese Falcon*
★ *Mr. Smith Goes to Washington*
★ *Modern Times*
★ *On the Waterfront*
★ *The Searchers*
★ *Singin' in the Rain*
★ *Snow White and the Seven Dwarfs*
★ *Some Like It Hot*
★ *Star Wars*
★ *Sunrise*
★ *Sunset Boulevard*
★ *Vertigo*
★ *The Wizard of Oz*

1990
★ *All About Eve*
★ *All Quiet on the Western Front*
★ *Bringing Up Baby*

★ Dodsworth
★ Duck Soup
★ Fantasia
★ The Freshman
★ The Godfather
★ The Great Train Robbery
  Cinema Begins
★ Harlan County, U.S.A.
★ How Green Was My Valley
★ It's a Wonderful Life
★ Ninotchka
★ Raging Bull
★ Rebel Without a Cause
★ Red River
★ Sullivan's Travels
★ Top Hat
★ Treasure of the Sierra
  Madre
★ A Woman Under the
  Influence

1991

★ Blood of Jesus
★ Chinatown
★ City Lights
★ David Holzman's Diary
★ Frankenstein
★ Gigi
★ Greed
★ I Am a Fugitive from a
  Chain Gang
★ The Italian
★ King Kong
★ Lawrence of Arabia
★ The Magnificent
  Ambersons
★ My Darling Clementine
★ Out of the Past
★ A Place in the Sun
★ A Poor Little Rich Girl
★ Prisoner of Zenda
★ Shadow of a Doubt
★ Tevye
★ 2001: A Space Odyssey

1992

★ Adam's Rib
★ Annie Hall
★ The Bank Dick
★ The Big Parade
★ The Birth of a Nation
★ Bonnie & Clyde
★ Carmen Jones
★ Detour
★ Dog Star Man
★ Double Indemnity
★ Footlight Parade
★ The Gold Rush
★ Letter from an Unknown
  Woman
★ Morocco
★ Nashville
★ The Night of the Hunter
★ Paths of Glory
★ Psycho
★ Ride the High Country
★ Salt of the Earth

1993

★ An American in Paris
★ Badlands
★ The Black Pirate
★ Blade Runner
★ Cat People
★ The Cheat
★ The Godfather, Part 2
★ His Girl Friday
★ It Happened One Night
★ Lassie, Come Home
★ A Night at the Opera
★ Nothing But a Man
★ One Flew Over the
  Cuckoo's Nest

★ Shadows
★ Shane
★ Sweet Smell of Success
★ Touch of Evil
★ The Wind
★ Yankee Doodle Dandy

1994

★ The African Queen
★ The Apartment
★ The Cool World
★ E.T.: The Extra-Terrestrial
★ Force of Evil
★ Freaks
★ Hell's Hinges
★ Invasion of the Body
  Snatchers
★ The Lady Eve
★ Louisiana Story
★ The Manchurian
  Candidate
★ Marty
★ Meet Me in St. Louis
★ Midnight Cowboy
★ Pinocchio
★ Safety Last
★ Scarface
★ Tabu: A Story of the South
  Seas
★ Taxi Driver

1995

★ The Adventures of Robin
  Hood
★ All That Heaven Allows
★ American Graffiti
★ The Band Wagon
★ Cabaret
★ Chan Is Missing
★ The Conversation
★ The Day the Earth Stood
  Still
★ El Norte
★ The Four Horsemen of the
  Apocalypse
★ Fury
★ The Hospital
★ The Last of the Mohicans
★ North by Northwest
★ The Philadelphia Story
★ Stagecoach
★ To Kill a Mockingbird

1996

★ The Awful Truth
★ Broken Blossoms
★ The Deer Hunter
★ Destry Rides Again
★ The Graduate
★ The Heiress
★ The Jazz Singer
★ M*A*S*H
★ Mildred Pierce
★ The Outlaw Josey Wales
★ The Producers
★ The Road to Morocco
★ She Done Him Wrong
★ Shock Corridor
★ Show Boat
★ The Thief of Baghdad
★ To Be or Not to Be
★ Woodstock

1997

★ Ben-Hur
★ The Big Sleep
★ The Bridge on the River
  Kwai
★ The Great Dictator
★ Harold and Maude
★ How the West Was Won
★ The Hustler

★ Knute Rockne: All
  American
★ Little Fugitive
★ Mean Streets
★ The Naked Spur
★ Rear Window
★ Return of the Secaucus 7
★ The Thin Man
★ West Side Story
★ Wings

NATIONAL SOCIETY OF FILM CRITICS AWARDS

ACTOR

1966

★ Michael Caine/Alfie

1967

★ Rod Steiger/In the Heat of
  the Night

1968

★ Per Oscarsson/Hunger

1969

★ Jon Voight/Midnight
  Cowboy

1970

★ George C. Scott/Patton

1971

★ Peter Finch/Sunday,
  Bloody Sunday

1972

★ Al Pacino/The Godfather

1973

★ Marlon Brando/Last
  Tango in Paris

1974

★ Jack Nicholson/
  Chinatown
★ Jack Nicholson/The Last
  Detail

1975

★ Jack Nicholson/One Flew
  Over the Cuckoo's Nest

1976

★ Robert De Niro/Taxi
  Driver

1977

★ Art Carney/The Late
  Show

1978

★ Gary Busey/The Buddy
  Holly Story

1979

★ Dustin Hoffman/Kramer
  vs. Kramer

1980

★ Peter O'Toole/The Stunt
  Man

1981

★ Burt Lancaster/Atlantic
  City

1982

★ Dustin Hoffman/Tootsie

1983

★ Gerard Depardieu/The
  Return of Martin Guerre

1984

★ Steve Martin/All of Me

1985

★ Jack Nicholson/Prizzi's
  Honor

1986

★ Bob Hoskins/Mona Lisa

1987

★ Steve Martin/Roxanne

1988

★ Michael Keaton/
  Beetlejuice
★ Michael Keaton/Clean
  and Sober

1989

★ Daniel Day-Lewis/My Left
  Foot

1990

★ Robert De Niro/
  Awakenings
★ Jeremy Irons/Reversal of
  Fortune

1991

★ River Phoenix/My Own
  Private Idaho

1992

★ Stephen Rea/The Crying
  Game

1993

★ David Thewlis/Naked

1994

★ Paul Newman/Nobody's
  Fool

1995

★ Nicolas Cage/Leaving Las
  Vegas

1996

★ Eddie Murphy/The Nutty
  Professor

1997

★ Robert Duvall/The
  Apostle

ACTOR—SUPPORTING

1967

★ Gene Hackman/Bonnie &
  Clyde

1968

★ Seymour Cassel/Faces

1969

★ Jack Nicholson/Easy
  Rider

1970

★ Chief Dan George/Little
  Big Man

1972

★ Eddie Albert/The
  Heartbreak Kid
★ Joel Grey/Cabaret

1973

★ Robert De Niro/Mean
  Streets

1975

★ Henry Gibson/Nashville

1976

★ Jason Robards, Jr./All
  the President's Men

1977

★ Edward Fox/A Bridge Too
  Far

1978

★ Richard Farnsworth/
  Comes a Horseman

1979

★ Frederic Forrest/
  Apocalypse Now
★ Frederic Forrest/The
  Rose

1980

★ Joe Pesci/Raging Bull

1981

★ Robert Preston/S.O.B.

1982

★ Mickey Rourke/Diner

1983

★ Jack Nicholson/Terms of
  Endearment

1984

★ John Malkovich/Places in
  the Heart

1985

★ John Gielgud/Plenty
★ John Gielgud/The
  Shooting Party

1986

★ Dennis Hopper/Blue
  Velvet

1987

★ Morgan Freeman/Street
  Smart

1988

★ Dean Stockwell/Married
  to the Mob

1989

★ Beau Bridges/The
  Fabulous Baker Boys

1990

★ Bruce Davison/Longtime
  Companion

1991

★ Harvey Keitel/Mortal
  Thoughts
★ Harvey Keitel/Thelma &
  Louise

1992

★ Gene Hackman/
  Unforgiven

ACTOR— SUPPORTING _cont._

1993
★ Ralph Fiennes/ _Schindler's List_

1994
★ Martin Landau/ _Ed Wood_

1995
★ Don Cheadle/ _Devil in a Blue Dress_

1996
★ Martin Donovan/ _Portrait of a Lady_
★ Tony Shalhoub/ _Big Night_

1997
★ Burt Reynolds/ _Boogie Nights_

ACTRESS

1967
★ Bibi Andersson/ _Persona_

1968
★ Liv Ullmann/ _The Shame_

1969
★ Vanessa Redgrave/ _Isadora_

1970
★ Glenda Jackson/ _Women in Love_

1971
★ Jane Fonda/ _Klute_

1972
★ Cicely Tyson/ _Sounder_

1973
★ Liv Ullmann/ _The New Land_

1974
★ Liv Ullmann/ _Scenes from a Marriage_

1975
★ Isabelle Adjani/ _Story of Adele H._

1976
★ Sissy Spacek/ _Carrie_

1977
★ Diane Keaton/ _Annie Hall_

1978
★ Ingrid Bergman/ _Autumn Sonata_

1979
★ Sally Field/ _Norma Rae_

1980
★ Sissy Spacek/ _Coal Miner's Daughter_

1981
★ Marilia Pera/ _Pixote_

1982
★ Meryl Streep/ _Sophie's Choice_

1983
★ Debra Winger/ _Terms of Endearment_

1984
★ Vanessa Redgrave/ _The Bostonians_

1985
★ Vanessa Redgrave/ _Wetherby_

1986
★ Chloe Webb/ _Sid & Nancy_

1987
★ Emily Lloyd/ _Wish You Were Here_

1988
★ Judy Davis/ _High Tide_

1989
★ Michelle Pfeiffer/ _The Fabulous Baker Boys_

1990
★ Anjelica Huston/ _The Grifters_
★ Anjelica Huston/ _The Witches_

1991
★ Alison Steadman/ _Life Is Sweet_

1992
★ Emma Thompson/ _Howard's End_

1993
★ Holly Hunter/ _The Piano_

1994
★ Jennifer Jason Leigh/ _Mrs. Parker and the Vicious Circle_

1995
★ Elisabeth Shue/ _Leaving Las Vegas_

1996
★ Emily Watson/ _Breaking the Waves_

1997
★ Julie Christie/ _Afterglow_

ACTRESS— SUPPORTING

1969
★ Sian Phillips/ _Goodbye, Mr. Chips_

1970
★ Lois Smith/ _Five Easy Pieces_

1971
★ Ellen Burstyn/ _The Last Picture Show_

1972
★ Jeannie Berlin/ _The Heartbreak Kid_

1973
★ Valentina Cortese/ _Day for Night_

1974
★ Bibi Andersson/ _Scenes from a Marriage_

1975
★ Lily Tomlin/ _Nashville_

1976
★ Jodie Foster/ _Taxi Driver_

1977
★ Ann Wedgeworth/ _Citizens Band_

1978
★ Meryl Streep/ _The Deer Hunter_

1979
★ Meryl Streep/ _Kramer vs. Kramer_
★ Meryl Streep/ _Manhattan_
★ Meryl Streep/ _The Seduction of Joe Tynan_

1980
★ Mary Steenburgen/ _Melvin and Howard_

1981
★ Maureen Stapleton/ _Reds_

1982
★ Jessica Lange/ _Tootsie_

1983
★ Sandra Bernhard/ _King of Comedy_

1984
★ Melanie Griffith/ _Body Double_

1985
★ Anjelica Huston/ _Prizzi's Honor_

1986
★ Dianne Wiest/ _Hannah and Her Sisters_

1987
★ Kathy Baker/ _Street Smart_

1988
★ Mercedes Ruehl/ _Married to the Mob_

1989
★ Anjelica Huston/ _Enemies, a Love Story_

1990
★ Annette Bening/ _The Grifters_

1991
★ Jane Horrocks/ _Life Is Sweet_

1992
★ Judy Davis/ _Husbands and Wives_

1993
★ Madeleine Stowe/ _Short Cuts_

1994
★ Dianne Wiest/ _Bullets Over Broadway_

1995
★ Joan Allen/ _Nixon_

1996
★ Barbara Hershey/ _Portrait of a Lady_

1997
★ Julianne Moore/ _Boogie Nights_

CINEMATOGRAPHY

1967
★ _In the Heat of the Night_

1968
★ _Bullitt_

1969
★ _The Wild Bunch_

1970
★ _My Night at Maud's_
★ _The Wild Child_

1971
★ Vittorio Storaro/ _The Conformist_

1972
★ _Cries and Whispers_

1973
★ _The Long Goodbye_

1974
★ _The Parallax View_
  The Godfather, Part 2

1975
★ _Barry Lyndon_

1976
★ _Bound for Glory_

1977
★ _Aguirre, the Wrath of God_

1978
★ _Days of Heaven_

1979
★ _Being There_
★ _The Black Stallion_

1980
★ _Raging Bull_

1981
★ _Pennies From Heaven_

1982
★ _Diva_

1983
★ _Never Cry Wolf_

1984
★ _Comfort and Joy_
★ _The Killing Fields_

1985
★ _Ran_

1986
★ _Blue Velvet_

1987
★ _Hope and Glory_

1988
★ _Wings of Desire_

1989
★ _The Fabulous Baker Boys_

1990
★ _Where the Heart Is_

1991
★ _Barton Fink_

1992
★ _Raise the Red Lantern_

1993
★ _Schindler's List_

1994
★ _Ed Wood_

1995
★ _Devil in a Blue Dress_

1996
★ _Breaking the Waves_
★ _Dead Man_

1997
★ _Kundun_

DIRECTOR

1966
★ Michelangelo Antonioni/ _Blow-Up_

1967
★ Ingmar Bergman/ _Persona_

1968
★ Ingmar Bergman/ _Hour of the Wolf_
★ Ingmar Bergman/ _The Shame_

1969
★ Francois Truffaut/ _Stolen Kisses_

1970
★ Ingmar Bergman/ _The Passion of Anna_

1971
★ Bernardo Bertolucci/ _The Conformist_

1972
★ Luis Bunuel/ _The Discreet Charm of the Bourgeoisie_

1973
★ Francois Truffaut/ _Day for Night_

1974
★ Francis Ford Coppola/ _The Conversation_
★ Francis Ford Coppola/ _The Godfather, Part 2_

1975
★ Robert Altman/ _Nashville_

1976
★ Martin Scorsese/ _Taxi Driver_

★ Elizabeth Taylor/*Who's Afraid of Virginia Woolf?*

1968

★ Joanne Woodward/*Rachel, Rachel*

1969

★ Jane Fonda/*They Shoot Horses, Don't They?*

1970

★ Glenda Jackson/*Women in Love*

1971

★ Jane Fonda/*Klute*

1972

★ Liv Ullmann/*Cries and Whispers*

★ Liv Ullmann/*The Emigrants*

1973

★ Joanne Woodward/*Summer Wishes, Winter Dreams*

1974

★ Liv Ullmann/*Scenes from a Marriage*

1975

★ Isabelle Adjani/*Story of Adele H.*

1976

★ Liv Ullmann/*Face to Face*

1977

★ Diane Keaton/*Annie Hall*

1978

★ Ingrid Bergman/*Autumn Sonata*

1979

★ Sally Field/*Norma Rae*

1980

★ Sissy Spacek/*Coal Miner's Daughter*

1982

★ Meryl Streep/*Sophie's Choice*

1983

★ Shirley MacLaine/*Terms of Endearment*

1984

★ Peggy Ashcroft/*A Passage to India*

1985

★ Norma Aleandro/*The Official Story*

1986

★ Sissy Spacek/*Crimes of the Heart*

1987

★ Holly Hunter/*Broadcast News*

1988

★ Meryl Streep/*A Cry in the Dark*

1989

★ Michelle Pfeiffer/*The Fabulous Baker Boys*

1990

★ Joanne Woodward/*Mr. & Mrs. Bridge*

1991

★ Jodie Foster/*The Silence of the Lambs*

1992

★ Emma Thompson/*Howard's End*

1993

★ Holly Hunter/*The Piano*

1994

★ Linda Fiorentino/*The Last Seduction*

1995

★ Jennifer Jason Leigh/*Georgia*

1996

★ Emily Watson/*Breaking the Waves*

1997

★ Julie Christie/*Afterglow*

ACTRESS— SUPPORTING

1969

★ Dyan Cannon/*Bob & Carol & Ted & Alice*

1970

★ Karen Black/*Five Easy Pieces*

1971

★ Ellen Burstyn/*The Last Picture Show*

1972

★ Jeannie Berlin/*The Heartbreak Kid*

1973

★ Valentina Cortese/*Day for Night*

1974

★ Valerie Perrine/*Lenny*

1975

★ Lily Tomlin/*Nashville*

1976

★ Talia Shire/*Rocky*

1978

★ Mona Washbourne/*Stevie*

1979

★ Meryl Streep/*Kramer vs. Kramer*

★ Meryl Streep/*Manhattan*

★ Meryl Streep/*The Seduction of Joe Tynan*

1980

★ Mary Steenburgen/*Melvin and Howard*

1982

★ Jessica Lange/*Tootsie*

1983

★ Linda Hunt/*The Year of Living Dangerously*

1984

★ Christine Lahti/*Swing Shift*

1985

★ Anjelica Huston/*Prizzi's Honor*

1986

★ Dianne Wiest/*Hannah and Her Sisters*

1987

★ Vanessa Redgrave/*Prick Up Your Ears*

1988

★ Diane Venora/*Bird*

1989

★ Jennifer Jason Leigh/*Last Exit to Brooklyn*

★ Lena Olin/*Enemies, a Love Story*

1990

★ Jennifer Jason Leigh/*Miami Blues*

1991

★ Judy Davis/*Barton Fink*

★ Judy Davis/*Naked Lunch*

1992

★ Miranda Richardson/*The Crying Game*

1993

★ Gong Li/*Farewell My Concubine*

1994

★ Dianne Wiest/*Bullets Over Broadway*

1995

★ Mira Sorvino/*Mighty Aphrodite*

1996

★ Courtney Love/*The People vs. Larry Flynt*

1997

★ Joan Cusack/*In and Out*

CINEMATOGRAPHY

1980

★ *Tess*

1981

★ *Chariots of Fire*

1982

★ *Sophie's Choice*

1983

★ *Zelig*

1984

★ *The Killing Fields*

1985

★ *Out of Africa*

1986

★ *A Room with a View*

1987

★ *The Last Emperor*

1988

★ *Wings of Desire*

1989

★ *Do the Right Thing*

1990

★ *The Sheltering Sky*

1991

★ *Barton Fink*

1992

★ *The Player*

1993

★ *Schindler's List*

1994

★ *Ed Wood*

1996

★ *Breaking the Waves*

★ *Dead Man*

1997

★ *Kundun*

DIRECTOR

1935

★ John Ford/*The Informer*

1937

★ Gregory La Cava/*Stage Door*

1938

★ Alfred Hitchcock/*The Lady Vanishes*

1939

★ John Ford/*Stagecoach*

1940

★ John Ford/*The Grapes of Wrath*

★ John Ford/*The Long Voyage Home*

1941

★ John Ford/*How Green Was My Valley*

1942

★ John Farrow/*Wake Island*

1943

★ George Stevens/*The More the Merrier*

1944

★ Leo McCarey/*Going My Way*

1945

★ Billy Wilder/*The Lost Weekend*

1946

★ William Wyler/*The Best Years of Our Lives*

1947

★ Elia Kazan/*Gentleman's Agreement*

1948

★ John Huston/*Treasure of the Sierra Madre*

1949

★ Carol Reed/*The Fallen Idol*

1950

★ Joseph L. Mankiewicz/*All About Eve*

1951

★ Elia Kazan/*A Streetcar Named Desire*

1952

★ Fred Zinnemann/*High Noon*

1953

★ Fred Zinnemann/*From Here to Eternity*

1954

★ Elia Kazan/*On the Waterfront*

1955

★ David Lean/*Summertime*

1956

★ John Huston/*Moby Dick*

1957

★ David Lean/*The Bridge on the River Kwai*

1958

★ Stanley Kramer/*The Defiant Ones*

1959

★ Fred Zinnemann/*The Nun's Story*

1960

★ Billy Wilder/*The Apartment*

1961

★ Robert Rossen/*The Hustler*

1963

★ Tony Richardson/*Tom Jones*

1964

★ Stanley Kubrick/*Dr. Strangelove, or: How I Learned to Stop Worrying and Love the Bomb*

1965

★ John Schlesinger/*Darling*

1966

★ Fred Zinnemann/*A Man for All Seasons*

1967

★ Mike Nichols/*The Graduate*

★ Mike Nichols/*In the Heat of the Night*

1968

★ Paul Newman/*Rachel, Rachel*

DIRECTOR ⏵cont.

1969
★ Constantin Costa-Gavras/Z

1970
★ Bob Rafelson/Five Easy Pieces

1971
★ Stanley Kubrick/A Clockwork Orange

1972
★ Ingmar Bergman/Cries and Whispers

1973
★ Francois Truffaut/Day for Night

1974
★ Federico Fellini/Amarcord

1975
★ Robert Altman/Nashville

1976
★ Alan J. Pakula/All the President's Men

1977
★ Woody Allen/Annie Hall

1978
★ Terrence Malick/Days of Heaven

1979
★ Woody Allen/Manhattan

1980
★ Jonathan Demme/Melvin and Howard

1981
★ Sidney Lumet/Prince of the City

1982
★ Sydney Pollack/Tootsie

1983
★ Ingmar Bergman/Fanny and Alexander

1984
★ David Lean/A Passage to India

1985
★ John Huston/Prizzi's Honor

1986
★ Woody Allen/Hannah and Her Sisters

1987
★ James L. Brooks/ Broadcast News

1988
★ Chris Menges/A World Apart

1989
★ Paul Mazursky/Enemies, a Love Story

1990
★ Martin Scorsese/ Goodfellas
★ Whit Stillman/ Metropolitan

1991
★ Jonathan Demme/The Silence of the Lambs

1992
★ Robert Altman/The Player

1993
★ Jane Campion/The Piano

1994
★ Quentin Tarantino/Pulp Fiction

1995
★ Ang Lee/Sense and Sensibility

1996
★ Lars von Trier/Breaking the Waves

1997
★ Curtis Hanson/L.A. Confidential

FILM

1935
★ The Informer

1936
★ Mr. Deeds Goes to Town

1937
★ The Life of Emile Zola

1938
★ The Citadel

1939
★ Wuthering Heights

1940
★ The Grapes of Wrath

1941
★ Citizen Kane

1942
★ In Which We Serve

1943
★ Watch on the Rhine

1944
★ Going My Way

1945
★ The Lost Weekend

1946
★ The Best Years of Our Lives

1947
★ Gentleman's Agreement

1948
★ Treasure of the Sierra Madre

1949
★ All the King's Men

1950
★ All About Eve

1951
★ A Streetcar Named Desire

1952
★ High Noon

1953
★ From Here to Eternity

1954
★ On the Waterfront

1955
★ Marty

1956
★ Around the World in 80 Days

1957
★ The Bridge on the River Kwai

1958
★ The Defiant Ones

1959
★ Ben-Hur

1960
★ The Apartment

1961
★ West Side Story

1963
★ Tom Jones

1964
★ My Fair Lady

1965
★ Darling

1966
★ A Man for All Seasons

1967
★ In the Heat of the Night

1968
★ The Lion in Winter

1969
★ Z

1970
★ Five Easy Pieces

1971
★ A Clockwork Orange

1972
★ Cries and Whispers

1973
★ Day for Night

1974
★ Amarcord

1975
★ Nashville

1976
★ All the President's Men

1977
★ Annie Hall

1978
★ The Deer Hunter

1979
★ Kramer vs. Kramer

1980
★ Ordinary People

1981
★ Reds

1982
★ Gandhi

1983
★ Terms of Endearment

1984
★ A Passage to India

1985
★ Prizzi's Honor

1986
★ Hannah and Her Sisters

1987
★ Broadcast News

1988
★ The Accidental Tourist

1989
★ My Left Foot

1990
★ Goodfellas

1991
★ The Silence of the Lambs

1992
★ The Player

1993
★ Schindler's List

1994
★ Quiz Show

1995
★ Leaving Las Vegas

1996
★ Fargo

1997
★ L.A. Confidential

FEATURE DOCUMENTARY

1992
★ Brother's Keeper

1993
★ Visions of Light: The Art of Cinematography

1994
★ Hoop Dreams

1997
★ Fast, Cheap & Out of Control

SCREENPLAY

1956
★ Around the World in 80 Days

1958
★ The Defiant Ones

1959
★ Anatomy of a Murder

1960
★ The Apartment

1961
★ Judgment at Nuremberg

1963
★ Hud

1964
★ The Servant

1966
★ A Man for All Seasons

1967
★ Bonnie & Clyde

1968
★ Pretty Poison

1969
★ Bob & Carol & Ted & Alice

1970
★ My Night at Maud's

1971
★ The Last Picture Show
★ Sunday, Bloody Sunday

1972
★ Cries and Whispers

1973
★ American Graffiti

1974
★ Scenes from a Marriage

1975
★ Story of Adele H.

1976
★ Network

1977
★ Annie Hall

1978
★ An Unmarried Woman

1979
★ Breaking Away

1980
★ Melvin and Howard

1981
★ Atlantic City

1982
★ Tootsie

1983
★ Local Hero

1984
★ Places in the Heart

1985
★ The Purple Rose of Cairo

1986
★ My Beautiful Laundrette

1987
★ *Broadcast News*

1988
★ *Bull Durham*

1989
★ *Drugstore Cowboy*

1990
★ *Mr. & Mrs. Bridge*

1991
★ *Naked Lunch*

1992
★ *The Crying Game*

1993
★ *The Piano*

1994
★ *Pulp Fiction*

1996
★ *Mother*

1997
★ *L.A. Confidential*

FILM—FOREIGN LANGUAGE

1936
★ *Carnival in Flanders*

1937
★ *Mayerling*

1938
★ *Grand Illusion*

1939
★ *Harvest*

1940
★ *The Baker's Wife*

1946
★ *Open City*

1948
★ *Paisan*

1949
★ *The Bicycle Thief*

1951
★ *Miracle in Milan*

1952
★ *Forbidden Games*

1955
★ *Diabolique*
★ *Umberto D*

1956
★ *La Strada*

1957
★ *Gervaise*

1958
★ *Mon Oncle*

1959
★ *The 400 Blows*

1960
★ *Hiroshima, Mon Amour*

1961
★ *La Dolce Vita*

1963
★ *8 1/2*

1964
★ *That Man from Rio*

1965
★ *Juliet of the Spirits*

1966
★ *The Shop on Main Street*

1968
★ *War and Peace*

1978
★ *Bread and Chocolate*

1979
★ *The Tree of Wooden Clogs*

1980
★ *Mon Oncle D'Amerique*

1981
★ *Pixote*

1982
★ *Time Stands Still*

1983
★ *Fanny and Alexander*

1984
★ *A Sunday in the Country*

1985
★ *Ran*

1986
★ *The Decline of the American Empire*

1987
★ *My Life As a Dog*

1988
★ *Women on the Verge of a Nervous Breakdown*

1989
★ *The Story of Women*

1990
★ *The Nasty Girl*

1991
★ *Europa, Europa*

1992
★ *Raise the Red Lantern*

1993
★ *Farewell My Concubine*

1994
★ *Trois Couleurs: Rouge*

1996
★ *The White Balloon*

1997
★ *Ponette*

SCREEN ACTORS GUILD AWARDS
ACTOR

1994
★ **Tom Hanks**/*Forrest Gump*
Morgan Freeman/*The Shawshank Redemption*
Paul Newman/*Nobody's Fool*
Tim Robbins/*The Shawshank Redemption*
John Travolta/*Pulp Fiction*

1995
★ **Nicolas Cage**/*Leaving Las Vegas*
Anthony Hopkins/*Nixon*
James Earl Jones/*Cry, the Beloved Country*
Sean Penn/*Dead Man Walking*
Massimo Troisi/*The Postman*

1996
★ **Geoffrey Rush**/*Shine*
Tom Cruise/*Jerry Maguire*
Ralph Fiennes/*The English Patient*
Woody Harrelson/*The People vs. Larry Flynt*
Billy Bob Thornton/*Sling Blade*

1997
★ **Jack Nicholson**/*As Good As It Gets*
Matt Damon/*Good Will Hunting*
Robert Duvall/*The Apostle*
Peter Fonda/*Ulee's Gold*
Dustin Hoffman/*Wag the Dog*

ACTOR—SUPPORTING

1994
★ **Martin Landau**/*Ed Wood*
Gary Sinise/*Forrest Gump*

1995
★ **Ed Harris**/*Apollo 13*
Kevin Bacon/*Murder In the First*
Kenneth Branagh/*Othello*
Don Cheadle/*Devil in a Blue Dress*
Kevin Spacey/*The Usual Suspects*

1996
★ **Cuba Gooding, Jr.**/*Jerry Maguire*
Hank Azaria/*The Birdcage*
Nathan Lane/*The Birdcage*
William H. Macy/*Fargo*
Noah Taylor/*Shine*

1997
★ **Robin Williams**/*Good Will Hunting*

Billy Connolly/*Mrs. Brown*
Anthony Hopkins/*Amistad*
Greg Kinnear/*As Good As It Gets*
Burt Reynolds/*Boogie Nights*

ACTRESS

1994
★ **Jodie Foster**/*Nell*
Jessica Lange/*Blue Sky*
Meg Ryan/*When a Man Loves a Woman*
Susan Sarandon/*The Client*
Meryl Streep/*The River Wild*

1995
★ **Susan Sarandon**/*Dead Man Walking*
Joan Allen/*Nixon*
Elisabeth Shue/*Leaving Las Vegas*
Meryl Streep/*The Bridges of Madison County*
Emma Thompson/*Sense and Sensibility*

1996
★ **Frances McDormand**/*Fargo*
Brenda Blethyn/*Secrets and Lies*
Diane Keaton/*Marvin's Room*
Gena Rowlands/*Unhook the Stars*
Kristin Scott Thomas/*The English Patient*

1997
★ **Helen Hunt**/*As Good As It Gets*
Helena Bonham Carter/*The Wings of the Dove*
Judi Dench/*Mrs. Brown*
Pam Grier/*Jackie Brown*
Kate Winslet/*Titanic*
Robin Wright Penn/*She's So Lovely*

ACTRESS—SUPPORTING

1994
★ **Dianne Wiest**/*Bullets Over Broadway*
Sally Field/*Forrest Gump*
Robin Wright Penn/*Forrest Gump*

1995
★ **Kate Winslet**/*Sense and Sensibility*
Stockard Channing/*Smoke*
Anjelica Huston/*The Crossing Guard*
Mira Sorvino/*Mighty Aphrodite*
Mare Winningham/*Georgia*

1996
★ **Lauren Bacall**/*The Mirror Has Two Faces*
Juliette Binoche/*The English Patient*

Marisa Tomei/*Unhook the Stars*
Gwen Verdon/*Marvin's Room*
Renee Zellweger/*Jerry Maguire*

1997
★ **Kim Basinger**/*L.A. Confidential*
★ **Gloria Stuart**/*Titanic*
Minnie Driver/*Good Will Hunting*
Alison Elliott/*The Wings of the Dove*
Julianne Moore/*Boogie Nights*

CAST

1995
★ *Apollo 13*
Get Shorty
How to Make an American Quilt
Nixon
Sense and Sensibility

1996
★ *The Birdcage*
The English Patient
Marvin's Room
Shine
Sling Blade

1997
★ *The Full Monty*
Boogie Nights
Good Will Hunting
L.A. Confidential
Titanic

SUNDANCE FILM FESTIVAL
CINEMATOGRAPHY

1990
★ *House Party*

1991
★ *Daughters of the Dust*

1992
★ *Swoon*

1994
★ *Suture*

1995
★ *Angela*
★ *Crumb*

1996
★ *Color of a Brisk and Leaping Day*

1997
★ *Hurricane Streets*

1998
★ *2 By 4*

DIRECTOR

1997
★ **Morgan J. Freeman**/*Hurricane Streets*

1998
★ **Darren Aronofsky**/*Pi*

SCREENPLAY

1991
★ Hangin' with the Homeboys
★ Trust

1992
★ The Waterdance

1993
★ Combination Platter

1994
★ What Happened Was...

1995
★ Living in Oblivion

1996
★ Big Night

1997
★ Sunday

1998
★ High Art

AUDIENCE AWARD

1989
★ sex, lies and videotape

1990
★ Longtime Companion

1991
★ Pastime

1992
★ Brother's Keeper
★ The Waterdance

1993
★ El Mariachi

1994
★ Hoop Dreams
★ Spanking the Monkey

1995
★ Picture Bride
★ Unzipped

1996
★ The Spitfire Grill

1997
★ Hurricane Streets
★ Love Jones

1998
★ Smoke Signals

FILMMAKERS TROPHY

1989
★ Powwow Highway

1992
★ A Brief History of Time
★ Zebrahead

1993
★ Fly by Night

1994
★ Clerks
★ Fresh

1995
★ Angela

1996
★ Girls Town

1997
★ In the Company of Men

1998
★ Smoke Signals

GRAND JURY PRIZE

1978
★ Girlfriends

1981
★ Gal Young 'Un
★ Heartland

1982
★ Street Music

1984
★ Old Enough

1985
★ Blood Simple

1986
★ Smooth Talk

1987
★ The Trouble with Dick
★ Waiting for the Moon

1988
★ Heat and Sunlight

1989
★ True Love

1990
★ Chameleon Street

1991
★ Paris Is Burning
★ Poison

1992
★ In the Soup

1993
★ Public Access
★ Ruby in Paradise

1994
★ What Happened Was...

1995
★ The Brothers McMullen
★ Crumb

1996
★ Welcome to the Dollhouse

1997
★ Sunday

1998
★ Slam

SPECIAL JURY PRIZE

1987
★ River's Edge

1990
★ To Sleep with Anger

1991
★ Straight Out of Brooklyn

1992
★ The Hours and Times

1993
★ Just Another Girl on the I.R.T.

1994
★ Fresh

1995
★ Heavy
★ Rhythm Thief

TORONTO-CITY AWARD

CANADIAN FEATURE FILM

1985
★ Canada's Sweetheart: The Saga of Hal C. Banks

1986
★ The Decline of the American Empire

1987
★ Family Viewing

1988
★ Outside Chance of Maximillian Glick

1989
★ Roadkill

1990
★ H

1991
★ The Adjuster

1994
★ Exotica

1995
★ Live Bait

1996
★ Long Day's Journey Into Night

1997
★ The Hanging Garden
★ The Sweet Hereafter

WRITERS GUILD OF AMERICA

ADAPTED SCREENPLAY

1968
★ Goodbye Columbus

1969
★ Butch Cassidy and the Sundance Kid
★ Midnight Cowboy

1970
★ I Never Sang For My Father
★ M*A*S*H

1971
★ The French Connection
★ Kotch

1972
★ Cabaret
★ The Godfather

1973
★ Paper Moon
★ Serpico

1974
★ The Apprenticeship of Duddy Kravitz
★ The Godfather, Part 2

1975
★ One Flew Over the Cuckoo's Nest
★ The Sunshine Boys

1976
★ All the President's Men
★ The Pink Panther Strikes Again

1977
★ Julia
★ Oh, God!

1978
★ Heaven Can Wait
★ Midnight Express

1979
★ Being There
★ Kramer vs. Kramer

1980
★ Airplane!
★ Ordinary People

1981
★ On Golden Pond
★ Rich and Famous

1982
★ Missing
★ Victor/Victoria

1983
★ Reuben, Reuben
★ Terms of Endearment

1984
★ The Killing Fields

1985
★ Prizzi's Honor

1986
★ A Room with a View

1987
★ Roxanne

1988
★ Dangerous Liaisons

1989
★ Driving Miss Daisy

1990
★ Dances with Wolves

1991
★ The Silence of the Lambs

1992
★ The Player

1993
★ Schindler's List
The Fugitive
In the Name of the Father
The Joy Luck Club
The Remains of the Day

1994
★ Forrest Gump
Little Women
The Madness of King George
Quiz Show
The Shawshank Redemption

1995
★ Sense and Sensibility
Apollo 13
Babe
Get Shorty
Leaving Las Vegas

1996
★ Sling Blade
The Birdcage
Emma
The English Patient
Trainspotting

1997
★ L.A. Confidential
Donnie Brasco
The Ice Storm
Wag the Dog
The Wings of the Dove

ORIGINAL SCREENPLAY

1967
★ Bonnie & Clyde

1968
★ The Producers

1969
★ Bob & Carol & Ted & Alice

1970
★ The Out-of-Towners
★ Patton

1971
★ The Hospital
★ Sunday, Bloody Sunday

1972
★ The Candidate
★ What's Up, Doc?

1973
★ Save the Tiger
★ A Touch of Class

1974
★ Blazing Saddles
★ Chinatown

1975
★ Dog Day Afternoon
★ Shampoo

1976
★ The Bad News Bears
★ Network

1977
★ Annie Hall
★ The Turning Point

1978
★ Coming Home
★ Movie, Movie

1979
★ Breaking Away

★ The China Syndrome

1980
★ Melvin and Howard
★ Private Benjamin

1981
★ Arthur
★ Reds

1982
★ E.T.: The Extra-Terrestrial
★ Tootsie

1983
★ The Big Chill
★ Tender Mercies

1984
★ Broadway Danny Rose

1985
★ Witness

1986
★ Hannah and Her Sisters

1987
★ Moonstruck

1988
★ Bull Durham

1989
★ Crimes & Misdemeanors

1990
★ Avalon

1991
★ Thelma & Louise

1992
★ The Crying Game

1993
★ The Piano
Dave
In the Line of Fire
Philadelphia
Sleepless in Seattle

1994
★ Four Weddings and a
Funeral
The Adventures of
Priscilla, Queen of the
Desert
Bullets Over Broadway
Ed Wood
Heavenly Creatures

1995
★ Braveheart
The American President
Clueless
Mighty Aphrodite
Muriel's Wedding

1996
★ Fargo
Jerry Maguire
Lone Star
Secrets and Lies
Shine

1997
★ As Good As It Gets
Boogie Nights
The Full Monty
Good Will Hunting
Titanic

GOLDEN RASPBERRY AWARDS
WORST PICTURE

1980
★ Can't Stop the Music

1981
★ Mommie Dearest

1983
★ The Lonely Lady

1984
★ Bolero

1985
★ Rambo: First Blood, Part 2

1986
★ Howard the Duck
★ Under the Cherry Moon

1987
★ Leonard Part 6

1988
★ Cocktail

1989
★ Star Trek 5: The Final
Frontier

1990
★ The Adventures of Ford
Fairlane
★ Ghosts Can't Do It

1991
★ Hudson Hawk

1992
★ Shining Through

1993
★ Indecent Proposal

1994
★ Color of Night
North
On Deadly Ground
The Specialist
Wyatt Earp

1995
★ Showgirls
Congo
It's Pat: The Movie
Waterworld

1996
★ Striptease
Barb Wire
Ed
The Island of Dr. Moreau
The Stupids

1997
★ The Postman
Anaconda
Batman and Robin
Fire Down Below
Speed 2: Cruise Control

WORST REMAKE/
SEQUEL

1994
★ Wyatt Earp

The Flintstones

1995
★ The Scarlet Letter

1997
★ Speed 2: Cruise Control
Batman and Robin
Home Alone 3
The Lost World: Jurassic
Park 2
McHale's Navy

WORST ACTOR

1980
★ Neil Diamond/The Jazz
Singer

1981
★ Klinton Spilsbury/Legend
of the Lone Ranger

1983
★ Christopher Atkins/A
Night in Heaven

1984
★ Sylvester Stallone/
Rhinestone

1985
★ Sylvester Stallone/
Rambo: First Blood,
Part 2
★ Sylvester Stallone/Rocky
4

1986
★ Prince/Under the Cherry
Moon

1987
★ Bill Cosby/Leonard Part 6

1988
★ Sylvester Stallone/
Rambo 3

1989
★ William Shatner/Star Trek
5: The Final Frontier

1990
★ Andrew Dice Clay/The
Adventures of Ford
Fairlane

1991
★ Kevin Costner/Robin
Hood: Prince of Thieves

1992
★ Sylvester Stallone/Stop!
or My Mom Will Shoot

1993
★ Burt Reynolds/Cop and a
Half

1994
★ Kevin Costner/Wyatt
Earp
Macaulay Culkin/Getting
Even with Dad
Macaulay Culkin/The
Pagemaster
Macaulay Culkin/Richie
Rich
Bruce Willis/Color of
Night
Bruce Willis/North

1995
★ Pauly Shore/Jury Duty
Kevin Costner/
Waterworld
Kyle MacLachlan/
Showgirls
Sylvester Stallone/
Assassins
Sylvester Stallone/Judge
Dredd

1996
★ Tom Arnold/Big Bully
★ Tom Arnold/Carpool
★ Tom Arnold/The Stupids
★ Pauly Shore/Bio-Dome
Keanu Reeves/Chain
Reaction
Adam Sandler/Bulletproof
Adam Sandler/Happy
Gilmore
Sylvester Stallone/
Daylight

1997
★ Kevin Costner/The
Postman
Val Kilmer/The Saint
Shaquille O'Neal/Steel
Steven Seagal/Fire Down
Below
Jon Voight/Anaconda

WORST ACTRESS

1980
★ Brooke Shields/The Blue
Lagoon

1981
★ Bo Derek/Tarzan, the Ape
Man
★ Faye Dunaway/Mommie
Dearest

1982
★ Pia Zadora/Butterfly

1983
★ Pia Zadora/The Lonely
Lady

1984
★ Bo Derek/Bolero

1985
★ Linda Blair/Night Patrol
★ Linda Blair/Savage Island
★ Linda Blair/Savage
Streets

1986
★ Madonna/Shanghai
Surprise

1987
★ Madonna/Who's That
Girl?
★ Liza Minnelli/Arthur 2: On
the Rocks

1988
★ Liza Minnelli/Rent-A-Cop

1990
★ Bo Derek/Ghosts Can't Do
It

1991
★ Sean Young/A Kiss
Before Dying

1992
★ Melanie Griffith/Shining
Through
★ Melanie Griffith/A
Stranger Among Us

1993
★ Madonna/Body of
Evidence

1994
★ Sharon Stone/Intersection
★ Sharon Stone/The
Specialist
Uma Thurman/Even
Cowgirls Get the Blues

1995
★ Elizabeth Berkley/
Showgirls

1996
★ Demi Moore/Striptease
Whoopi Goldberg/Bogus
Whoopi Goldberg/Eddie
Whoopi Goldberg/
Theodore Rex
Melanie Griffith/Two
Much
Demi Moore/The Juror
Julia Roberts/Mary Reilly

1997
★ Demi Moore/G.I. Jane
Sandra Bullock/Speed 2:
Cruise Control
Fran Drescher/The
Beautician and the
Beast
Lauren Holly/A Smile Like
Yours
Lauren Holly/Turbulence
Alicia Silverstone/Excess
Baggage

WORST SUPPORTING
ACTOR

1980
★ John Adams/Gloria
★ Laurence Olivier/The
Jazz Singer

1981
★ Steve Forrest/Mommie
Dearest

1982
★ Ed McMahon/Butterfly

1983
★ Jim Nabors/Stroker Ace

1985
★ Rob Lowe/St. Elmo's Fire

1986
★ Jerome Benton/Under the
Cherry Moon

1987
★ David Mendenhall/Over
the Top

1988
★ Dan Aykroyd/Caddyshack
2

1989
★ Christopher Atkins/Listen
to Me

1985

★ **Brigitte Nielsen/***Red Sonja*
★ **Brigitte Nielsen/***Rocky 4*

1987

★ **David Mendenhall/***Over the Top*

1990

★ **Sofia Coppola/***The Godfather, Part 3*

1991

★ **Vanilla Ice/***Cool As Ice*

1992

★ **Pauly Shore/***Encino Man*

1993

★ **Janet Jackson/***Poetic Justice*

1994

★ **Anna Nicole Smith/***Naked Gun 33 1/3: The Final Insult*

1995

★ **Elizabeth Berkley/***Showgirls*
  David Caruso/*Kiss of Death*
  Cindy Crawford/*Fair Game*
  Julia Sweeney/*It's Pat: The Movie*

1996

★ **Pamela Anderson/***Barb Wire*
  Ellen DeGeneres/*Mr. Wrong*

1997

★ **Dennis Rodman/***Double Team*
  Tori Spelling/*The House of Yes*
  Howard Stern/*Private Parts*
  Chris Tucker/*The Fifth Element*
  Chris Tucker/*Money Talks*

The **Foreign Film Index** classifies movies by the country of record in which they were produced. Since a film may be financed or produced in more than one country, some videos will appear with more than one country of origin. The codes appear in the review, immediately following the color/black and white designation before the credits. In this index, movies are listed alphabetically by country. **A tipped triangle indicates a video rated three bones or higher**.

Key to Country Origination Tags

AL Algerian	**CZ** Czech	**IA** Iranian	**PL** Polish
AR Argentinian	**DK** Danish	**IR** Irish	**PT** Portuguese
AU Australian	**NL** Dutch	**IS** Israeli	**RO** Romanian
AT Austrian	**PH** Filipino	**IT** Italian	**RU** Russian
BE Belgian	**FI** Finnish	**JP** Japanese	**SA** South African
BR Brazilian	**FR** French	**KO** Korean	**SP** Spanish
GB British	**GE** German	**LI** Lithuanian	**SW** Swedish
CA Canadian	**GR** Greek	**MA** Macedonian	**SI** Swiss
CN Cantonese	**HK** Hong Kong	**MX** Mexican	**TW** Taiwanese
CH Chinese	**HU** Hungarian	**NZ** New Zealand	**TU** Turkish
CL Colombian	**IC** Icelandic	**NI** Nicaraguan	**VZ** Venezuelan
CU Cuban	**IN** Indian	**NO** Norwegian	**VT** Vietnamese
		PV Peruvian	**YU** Yugoslavian

Algerian

The Battle of Algiers▸

Argentinean

Camila▸
Chronicle of a Boy Alone
The Curious Dr. Humpp
The Dark Side of the Heart
The Devil's Possessed
The Enchanted Forest
Eversmile New Jersey
Far Away and Long Ago
Fridays of Eternity
Funny, Dirty Little War
I Don't Want to Talk About It
Killing Grandpa
La Boca del Lobo
Made in Argentina
Man Facing Southeast▸
Miss Mary
The Official Story▸
A Place in the World▸
A Shadow You Soon Will Be
The Stranger▸
Tango Bar
Time for Revenge
Times to Come▸
Two to Tango
Veronico Cruz
Wild Horses

Australian

ABC's of Love & Sex,
   Australia Style
The Adventures of Priscilla,
   Queen of the Desert▸
Air Hawk
Alex

Alice to Nowhere
Alison's Birthday
All the Rivers Run
...Almost
Alvin Purple
Alvin Rides Again
American Roulette
Angel Baby▸
Anzacs: The War Down
   Under▸
Archer's Adventure
Around the World in 80 Ways
Attack Force Z
Babe▸
Back of Beyond
Backlash
Bad Boy Bubby
Barnaby and Me
Barry McKenzie Holds His
   Own
Between Wars
The Big Hurt
Black Robe
Blackrock
Blackwater Trail
Bliss▸
Blood Money
Bloodmoon
Blue Fin
Body Melt
Boulevard of Broken Dreams
Breaker Morant▸
Breakfast in Paris
Brilliant Lies
Burke & Wills
Cactus
Caddie
Camel Boy
Careful, He Might Hear You▸
Carry Me Back
The Cars That Ate Paris▸
The Castle
Celia: Child Of Terror

Children of the Revolution
The City's Edge
Clowning Around
Clowning Around 2
The Club▸
The Coca-Cola Kid▸
Color Me Dead
Contagion
Cosi▸
Country Life
Crocodile Dundee▸
The Crossing
A Cry in the Dark▸
The Custodian
Dangerous Summer
Dark Age
Dark Forces
Dating the Enemy
Dead Calm▸
Dead Easy
Dead End Drive-In
Dead Heart▸
Deadly Possession
Death in Brunswick
Death of a Soldier
Demonstrator
Desperate Prey
The Devil's Playground▸
Dingo
Dogs in Space
Doing Time for Patsy Cline▸
Don's Party▸
The Dunera Boys▸
Dusty
Earthling
East and West▸
Echo Park
Echoes of Paradise
The Efficiency Expert
The Empty Beach
Endplay
Escape 2000
Eureka Stockade

The Everlasting Secret Family
Fair Game
Fantasy Man
Fast Talking
Father
Fatty Finn
The Fire in the Stone
Fists of Blood
Flirting▸
Floating Life
For Love Alone
Fortress
Forty Thousand Horsemen
Fran
Frenchman's Farm
The Fringe Dwellers
Gallagher's Travels
Gallipoli▸
Georgia
The Getting of Wisdom
The Good Wife
Grendel, Grendel, Grendel
Gross Misconduct
Ground Zero▸
Hard Knocks
Heatwave▸
Heaven Tonight
Heaven's Burning
High Rolling in a Hot Corvette
High Tide▸
The Highest Honor
Hotel de Love
Howling 3: The Marsupials
I Live with Me Dad
Idiot Box
In Search of Anna
An Indecent Obsession
Inn of the Damned
Innocent Prey
The Irishman
Joey
Kangaroo▸
The Killing Beach

Killing of Angel Street
Kiss or Kill
Kitty and the Bagman
The Last Bastion
The Last Days of Chez Nous
The Last Wave▸
Life
The Lighthorsemen▸
Lilian's Story
Little Boy Lost
Lonely Hearts▸
Long John Silver
The Long Weekend
Love and Other Catastrophes
Love Serenade
Lust and Revenge
Mad Dog Morgan
Mad Max: Beyond
   Thunderdome
Magee and the Lady
Malcolm
The Man from Snowy River
Man of Flowers
The Mango Tree
Mesmerized
Midnight Dancer
Miracle Down Under
Mr. Reliable: A True Story
Money Movers
Monkey Grip▸
Moving Targets
Muriel's Wedding▸
My Brilliant Career▸
My First Wife
The Naked Country
Napoleon
Nevil Shute's The Far Country
Newsfront▸
Next of Kin
No Room to Run
Norman Loves Rose
Now and Forever
The Odd Angry Shot

Australian

One Crazy Night
Only the Brave
Overlanders⬧
Palm Beach
Panic Station
Paperback Romance
Patrick
Phar Lap
The Piano⬧
Picnic at Hanging Rock⬧
Plumber
Poor Girl, a Ghost Story
Prince and the Great Race
Prisoner Cell Block H
Prisoners of the Sun⬧
Proof⬧
Puberty Blues
Puzzle
Queen of the Road
The Quest
The Quiet Room
Quigley Down Under
Razorback
Rebel
Reckless Kelly
Return of Captain Invincible
Return to Snowy River⬧
Ride a Wild Pony⬧
The Right Hand Man
Rikky and Pete
River Street
Road Games
Road to Nhill
Romper Stomper
Run, Rebecca, Run
Sara Dane
Savage Attraction
Second Time Lucky
Shame
Shine⬧
Silver City
The Silver Stallion: King of the
   Wild Brumbies
Sirens
Sky Pirates
Smuggler's Cove
Snowy River, the MacGregor
   Saga: The Race
Sorrento Beach
Squizzy Taylor
Starstruck
Strangers
Stranglehold
Strictly Ballroom⬧
The Sum of Us⬧
Summer City
Sunday Too Far Away⬧
Survivor
Sweet Talker
Sweetie⬧
The Tale of Ruby Rose⬧
Talk
Tearaway
A Test of Love
Thank God He Met Lizzie
That Eye, the Sky
Three's Trouble
Thundering Forest
Tim
Touch & Go
A Town Like Alice
Traps
Travelling North
Treasure of the Yankee
   Zephyr
Tunnel Vision
Twisted
Two Friends
Typhoon Treasure
Under Capricorn
Vincent: The Life and Death
   of Vincent van Gogh⬧

The Wacky World of Wills &
   Burke
Walk into Hell
Walkabout⬧
Warm Nights on a Slow-
   Moving Train
Waterfront
We of the Never Never⬧
The Well
Who Killed Baby Azaria?
Wide Sargasso Sea
The Wild Duck
Windrider
The Winds of Jarrah
The Winter of Our Dreams
A Woman's Tale⬧
A Yank in Australia
The Year My Voice Broke⬧
The Year of Living
   Dangerously⬧
Young Einstein

Austrian

The Hands of Orlac
Heidi⬧
Time Troopers
Wandering Jew

Belgian

Between Heaven and Earth
A Couch in New York
Daens
Daughters of Darkness⬧
The Devil's Nightmare
Dust⬧
The Eighth Day
Farinelli
La Promesse
Les Rendez-vous D'Anna
Ma Vie en Rose⬧
Man Bites Dog
Mascara
The Music Teacher
Night and Day⬧
One Sings, the Other Doesn't
The Passion of Darkly Noon
Rabid Grannies
The Sexual Life of the
   Belgians
Suite 16
Toute Une Nuit⬧
A Wedding in Galilee⬧

Brazilian

Amor Bandido
Antonio Das Mortes
At Midnight, I'll Take Your
   Soul
Awakenings of the Beast
Black God & White Devil
Black Orpheus⬧
Bye Bye Brazil
The Dolphin
Dona Flor and Her Two
   Husbands⬧
Earth Entranced
Four Days in September
Gabriela
Hallucinations of a Deranged
   Mind
Happily Ever After
The Hour of the Star⬧
How Tasty Was My Little
   Frenchman
I Love You
Killer Fish
Kiss of the Spider Woman⬧

Lady on the Bus
Luzia
O Quatrilho
Opera do Malandro
Pixote⬧
Quilombo
Savage Capitalism
The Story of Fausta
Strange World of Coffin Joe
Subway to the Stars
Via Appia
Women in Fury
Xica⬧

British

Abandon Ship
Abdulla the Great
Abigail's Party
The Abominable Dr. Phibes⬧
Above Us the Waves⬧
Absolute Beginners
Absolutely Fabulous: The
   Last Shout
Absolution
Accident
Accused
Across the Bridge
Action for Slander
The Adventurers
Adventures of a Private Eye
Adventures of a Taxi Driver
The Adventures of Sadie
The Adventures of Sherlock
   Holmes: Hound of the
   Baskervilles
The Adventures of Tartu
The Advocate⬧
The Affair
An Affair in Mind
The Affair of the Pink Pearl
Afraid of the Dark
The African Queen⬧
After Darkness
After Julius
After Pilkington
After the Fox
Afterward
Agatha Christie's Miss Marple
Agatha Christie's The Pale
   Horse
Alamut Ambush
Alfie⬧
Alias John Preston
Alice⬧
Alice's Adventures in
   Wonderland
Alien Women
Alive and Kicking
All Creatures Great and
   Small⬧
American Friends
American Roulette
And Nothing But the Truth
And Now for Something
   Completely Different⬧
And Now the Screaming
   Starts
And Soon the Darkness
Angel with the Trumpet
Angels and Insects⬧
Anna Karenina
The Anniversary
Another Country
Another Time, Another Place
Another Time, Another Place⬧
Antonia and Jane⬧
Apartment Zero⬧
Appointment with Crime
Aria
Armistead Maupin's Tales of
   the City

The Arsenal Stadium Mystery
As You Like It
The Asphyx⬧
The Assassination Bureau⬧
Assassination of Trotsky
The Assassination Run
Assault
Assault on Agathon
Asylum
At the Earth's Core
The Atomic Man
August
The Awakening
An Awfully Big Adventure
The Baby and the Battleship
Baby Love
Bachelor of Hearts
Backbeat⬧
Bad Behavior
Ballad in Blue
The Ballad of the Sad Cafe
Ballet Shoes
Bananas Boat
Band of Gold⬧
Bandit Queen
Battle Beneath the Earth
Battle Hell
The Battle of the Sexes⬧
The Bawdy Adventures of
   Tom Jones
Beachcomber⬧
Bean⬧
Beast in the Cellar
Beast of Morocco
Beat Girl
Beautiful Thing⬧
Bedazzled⬧
Before the Rain⬧
The Belles of St. Trinian's⬧
Bellman and True
The Belly of an Architect⬧
Benny Hill's Crazy World
Bent
Bernard and the Genie
Best Enemies
The Best of Cracker
   Mysteries⬧
The Best of Lovejoy Mysteries
The Best of the Two Ronnies
Betrayal
Bewitched
Bhaji on the Beach
Big Fella
The Big Man: Crossing the
   Line⬧
Big Zapper
Biggles
Billy Budd⬧
Billy Liar⬧
The Bitch
Bitter Sweet
Black Beauty
The Black Cat
Black Eyes
Black Limelight
Black Narcissus⬧
The Black Velvet Gown
Black Werewolf
Blackmail⬧
Blackout
Blake's Seven
Blanche Fury
Bleak House
Bleak Moments
The Bliss of Mrs. Blossom⬧
Blithe Spirit⬧
Blockhouse
Blonde Blackmailer
Blood Beast Terror
Blood Island
Blood of the Vampire
The Blood on Satan's Claw⬧

Bloodbath at the House of
   Death
The Bloodsuckers
Blow-Up⬧
Blue
Blue Blood
The Blue Lamp⬧
Blue Money
Blue Murder at St. Trinian's⬧
Bobo
Body & Soul⬧
The Body in the Library
The Body Vanished
Bonnie Prince Charlie
The Borrowers⬧
The Borrowers
Boston Kickout
The Boxer
The Boy Friend⬧
Boyfriends
The Brain
Bramwell
Brassed Off
Brazil⬧
Breaking Glass
Breaking the Code
The Bretts
The Brides of Dracula
Brideshead Revisited⬧
The Bridge on the River
   Kwai⬧
A Bridge Too Far
Brief Encounter⬧
Bright Smiler
Brighton Rock⬧
Brimstone & Treacle⬧
Britannia Hospital
Broken Melody
Brother Cadfael
Brother Cadfael 2
Brothers in Law
Brothers in Trouble
The Browning Version⬧
The Brylcreem Boys
The Buccaneers⬧
The Buddha of Suburbia⬧
Buddy's Song
Bugsy Malone
Bulldog Drummond at Bay
Bulldog Jack⬧
Bullet to Beijing
Bullshot
Burn Witch, Burn!⬧
Burning Secret
Buster
Butler's Dilemma
Butterflies
Butterfly Ball
Butterfly Kiss
Caesar and Cleopatra
Call Him Mr. Shatter
Calling Paul Temple
Candles at Nine
A Canterbury Tale⬧
Captain Boycott
Captain Horatio Hornblower
Captain Kronos: Vampire
   Hunter⬧
Captain's Paradise⬧
The Captain's Table
Captive Heart⬧
Captives
Car Trouble
Caravaggio⬧
Carlton Browne of the F.O.
Carrington
Carrington, V.C.⬧
Carry On Admiral
Carry On at Your
   Convenience
Carry On Behind
Carry On Camping
Carry On Cleo

Monty Python's Flying Circus
Monty Python's Life of Brian
Monty Python's The Meaning
   of Life
The Moon Stallion
Moondance
Moonlight Sonata
Moonlighting
The Moonraker
Moonraker
Morgan!
Morons from Outer Space
The Moth
Mountbatten: The Last
   Viceroy
The Mouse That Roared
Much Ado about Nothing
The Mummy
The Muppet Movie
Murder
Murder at the Baskervilles
Murder by Moonlight
Murder in the Footlights
Murder in the Old Red Barn
A Murder Is Announced
Murder of a Moderate Man
Murder on the Campus
Murder on the Orient
   Express
Murders at Lynch Cross
Murphy's War
The Music Lovers
Mute Witness
My Friend Walter
My Name is Joe
My Son, the Vampire
Mysterious Island
The Mystery of Edwin Drood
Naked
The Naked Edge
The Naked Truth
Nancy Astor
The Nanny
Nasty Habits
Ned Kelly
Negatives
Never Let Go
Never Too Late to Mend
Next Victim
Nice Girl Like Me
Nicholas Nickleby
Night Ambush
Night and the City
The Night and the Moment
Night Beat
Night Birds
Night Caller from Outer Space
The Night Has Eyes
Night of the Laughing Dead
Night Train to Munich
The Night Visitor
Night Watch
The Nightcomers
Nighthawks
Nightmare
Nightscare
Nil by Mouth
Nine Days a Queen
1984
99 Women
No Comebacks
No Highway in the Sky
No Love for Johnnie
No Surrender
No Trace
Norman Conquest
The Norman Conquests, Part
   1: Table Manners
The Norman Conquests, Part
   2: Living Together
The Norman Conquests, Part
   3: Round and Round the
   Garden

Northanger Abbey
Nothing But the Night
Nothing Personal
Number 1 of the Secret
   Service
No. 17
Nuts in May
O Lucky Man!
The Oblong Box
The Obsessed
The October Man
Octopussy
The Odd Job
Odd Man Out
The Odessa File
Of Human Bondage
The Offence
Office Romances
Oh, Alfie
Oh, Mr. Porter
O.H.M.S.
The Old Curiosity Shop
Old Mother Riley's Ghosts
Old Spanish Custom
Oliver!
Oliver Twist
Oliver Twist
On Approval
On Her Majesty's Secret
   Service
On the Fiddle
One Day in the Life of Ivan
   Denisovich
One-Eyed Soldiers
One Million Years B.C.
One of Our Aircraft Is
   Missing
One Wish Too Many
Only Two Can Play
Open All Hours
Oranges Are Not the Only
   Fruit
Order of the Black Eagle
Orlando
Out of Season
Out of the Shadows
Overture
Paid to Kill
Paper Marriage
Paper Mask
Paper Tiger
Paperhouse
Paranoiac
Party! Party!
Pascali's Island
A Passage to India
The Passing of the Third Floor
   Back
The Passion of Darkly Noon
Passport to Pimlico
Pattern for Plunder
Paul and Michelle
The People That Time Forgot
A Perfect Spy
Performance
Permission To Kill
Personal Services
The Persuaders
Persuasion
Persuasion
Peter's Friends
Phantom Fiend
The Phantom Light
The Phantom of the Opera
Philby, Burgess and
   MacLean: Spy Scandal of
   the Century
The Pickwick Papers
Pictures
Piece of Cake
The Pillow Book
Pimpernel Smith
Pink Floyd: The Wall

The Pink Panther
The Pink Panther Strikes
   Again
Pink String and Sealing Wax
Plague of the Zombies
Playing Away
A Pocketful of Rye
Poldark
Poldark 2
The Pope Must Diet
Porridge
Portrait of a Lady
Portrait of a Lady
Postmark for Danger
Postmark for Danger/
   Quicksand
Power
Power Play
Prick Up Your Ears
Pride and Prejudice
Pride and Prejudice
Priest
Priest of Love
The Prime of Miss Jean
   Brodie
Prime Suspect
Prime Suspect 2
Prime Suspect 3
Prime Suspect 5: Errors of
   Judgment
Prime Suspect: Inner Circles
Prime Suspect: The Lost
   Child
Prime Suspect: The Scent of
   Darkness
The Prince and the Pauper
Prince Valiant
The Princess and the Goblin
The Prisoner
The Prisoner: Arrival
A Private Function
Private Life of Don Juan
The Private Life of Henry VIII
The Private Life of Sherlock
   Holmes
The Private Secretary
Privates on Parade
Promise Her Anything
The Promoter
Proteus
Providence
Psychomania
Psychopath
Pulp
The Pumpkin Eater
Puppet on a Chain
The Pure Hell of St. Trinian's
Pursuit of the Graf Spee
Pygmalion
Quadrophenia
Quartet
Quatermass 2
Quatermass and the Pit
Quatermass Conclusion
The Quatermass Experiment
Queen of Hearts
The Queen of Spades
Quest for Love
A Question of Attribution
Race for Life
The Rag Nymph
The Railway Children
The Rainbow
Raining Stones
Rasputin the Mad Monk
Rattle of a Simple Man
Reach for the Sky
The Real Charlotte
Rebecca
Reckless
The Rector's Wife
The Red Shoes
Redneck

Regeneration
Reilly: Ace of Spies
The Remains of the Day
Rembrandt
Rentadick
The Reptile
Repulsion
The Return of the Borrowers
The Return of the Musketeers
Return of the Soldier
Reunion
Revenge
The Revenge of Frankenstein
Revolution
Rhodes
Rich and Strange
Richard III
Richard's Things
The Riddle of the Sands
Riff Raff
The Ring
Ring of Bright Water
Ripping Yarns
Rita, Sue & Bob Too
Roadhouse Girl
Robbery
Robbery Under Arms
Robin and Marian
Robin Hood: The Movie
Robin Hood...The Legend:
   Herne's Son
Robin Hood...The Legend:
   Robin Hood and the
   Sorcerer
Robin Hood...The Legend:
   The Swords of Wayland
Robin Hood...The Legend:
   The Time of the Wolf
Roboman
The Rocking Horse Winner
Rogue Male
Rogue's Yarn
Romance with a Double
   Bass
Romantic Englishwoman
Romeo and Juliet
Room at the Top
Room to Let
A Room with a View
Rough Magic
Royal Flash
A Royal Scandal
The Ruling Class
Rumpole of the Bailey
Rumpole of the Bailey:
   Rumpole's Return
The Runaway Bus
Running Blind
Ryan's Daughter
Saigon: Year of the Cat
Sailing Along
The Sailor Who Fell from
   Grace with the Sea
The Saint
Saint-Ex: The Story of the
   Storyteller
Salaam Bombay!
The Salamander
Sammy & Rosie Get Laid
Sanders of the River
Sapphire
The Satanic Rites of Dracula
Saturday Night and Sunday
   Morning
Saturn 3
Savage Messiah
Say Hello to Yesterday
Scandal
The Scarlet Pimpernel
The Scars of Dracula
Schizo
School for Scandal
Scotland Yard Inspector

Scott of the Antarctic
Scream and Scream Again
Scream of Fear
Scrooge
Scrooge
Scrubbers
The Sculptress
Scum
Sea Devils
Sea of Sand
Sea Wolves
Seance on a Wet Afternoon
Seaside Swingers
Sebastian
Second Best
Second Best Secret Agent in
   the Whole Wide World
Second Chance
The Secret Adversary
The Secret Agent
The Secret Agent
The Secret Four
The Secret Garden
Secret Mission
The Secret of the Loch
Secret Places
The Secret Policeman's Other
   Ball
Secret Policeman's Private
   Parts
The Secret Rapture
Secrets
Secrets and Lies
The Sender
Sense & Sensibility
Sense and Sensibility
A Sense of Freedom
The Servant
The 7 Brothers Meet Dracula
The Seventh Veil
Sexton Blake and the Hooded
   Terror
Shades of Fear
Shadey
The Shadow
The Shadow Man
Shadowlands
Shaka Zulu
Shallow Grave
Shameless
Sharpe's Battle
Sharpe's Company
Sharpe's Eagle
Sharpe's Enemy
Sharpe's Gold
Sharpe's Honour
Sharpe's Justice
Sharpe's Legend
Sharpe's Mission
Sharpe's Regiment
Sharpe's Revenge
Sharpe's Rifles
Sharpe's Siege
Sharpe's Sword
Sharpe's Waterloo
Shattered
She Shall Have Music
The Shell Seekers
Sherlock Holmes and the
   Incident at Victoria Falls
Sherlock Holmes: The Master
   Blackmailer
Shirley Valentine
Shooting Fish
The Shooting Party
Shopping
A Shot in the Dark
The Shout
Shout at the Devil
Sidewalks of London
The Sign of Four
Silas Marner
The Silent Enemy

British

Filipino

Caged Fury
Circle of Fear
The Deadly and the Beautiful
Devil Woman
Horror of the Blood Monsters
Mad Doctor of Blood Island
Midnight Dancers
Night of the Cobra Woman
Once Before I Die
Perfumed Nightmare⬆
Raw Force
Stickfighter
Stryker
Terror Is a Man
The Thirsty Dead
Turumba⬆
Twilight People
The Vampire Hookers
The Vampire People

Finnish

Ariel⬆
The Day the Earth Froze
Leningrad Cowboys Go
  America
The Match Factory Girl⬆
Zombie and the Ghost Train

French

A la Mode
A Nos Amours⬆
A Nous la Liberte⬆
The Accompanist
Act of Aggression
Adorable Julia
Afraid of the Dark
After the Fall of New York
Akermania, Vol. 1⬆
Alberto Express
Ali Baba and the 40 Thieves⬆
Alice in Wonderland
Alphaville⬆
The American Friend⬆
And God Created Woman
And Hope to Die
And Now My Love
Andy Warhol's Dracula⬆
Andy Warhol's Frankenstein
Angele⬆
Another Man, Another
  Chance
Artemisia
As If It Were Raining
Assassination of Trotsky
The Associate
Atlantic City⬆
Attack of the Robots
Au Revoir Les Enfants⬆
Augustin
The Avenger
Babar: The Movie
Babette's Feast
Back to the Wall
The Baker's Wife⬆
Band of Outsiders
Bandits
Barbarella
Barjo
Barocco
Basileus Quartet
The Battle of Austerlitz
The Battle of El Alamein
Baxter
The Bear⬆
Beatrice⬆
Beau Pere⬆
Beaumarchais the Scoundrel
Beauties of the Night
Beauty and the Beast⬆

Beauty and the Devil
Beethoven
Beethoven's Nephew
Before the Rain⬆
Belle Americaine
Belle de Jour⬆
Bernadette
The Best Way
Betty
Betty Blue⬆
Between Heaven and Earth
The Big Grab
Bilitis
Bizarre Bizarre⬆
Black and White in Color⬆
Black Orpheus⬆
Black Tights
Blood and Black Lace
Blood and Roses
The Blood of Others
Bloodsucking Nazi Zombies
Blue Country
Blue Jeans
Bluebeard
Bob le Flambeur⬆
Bonjour Tristesse⬆
Borsalino⬆
Boudu Saved from Drowning⬆
Boy Meets Girl⬆
Boyfriends & Girlfriends
The Brain
Breaking the Waves⬆
Breathless⬆
The Bride Is Much Too
  Beautiful
The Bride Wore Black⬆
Buffet Froid⬆
Burnt by the Sun⬆
By the Blood of Others⬆
Bye-Bye
Cafe au Lait⬆
Caged Women
Camille Claudel⬆
Candy Mountain
Captain Blackjack
Captain Conan
Carnival in Flanders⬆
Carrington
Cartouche⬆
Casque d'Or⬆
Castle of Blood
Castle of the Living Dead
Cat and Mouse⬆
The Cat o' Nine Tails
Catch Me a Spy
Catherine & Co.
Cathy's Curse
Celestial Clockwork
The Cement Garden
Cesar⬆
Cesar & Rosalie⬆
Charles et Lucie⬆
Charlie Bravo
Chasing Butterflies
A Chef in Love
Children of Paradise⬆
Chinese Box
Chloe in the Afternoon⬆
Choice of Arms
Christ Stopped at Eboli⬆
Circle of Love
Circonstances Attenuantes
Circus Angel⬆
City of Joy
The City of Lost Children⬆
Claire's Knee⬆
Cleo from 5 to 7⬆
The Clockmaker⬆
Cobra
A Coeur Joie
Cold Sweat
Colonel Chabert⬆
Comment Ca Va?

The Confessional
Confidentially Yours⬆
The Conformist⬆
Conquest of Mycene
Conseil de Famille
Contempt⬆
The Convent
Conversation Piece⬆
A Couch in New York
Coup de Grace
Coup de Torchon⬆
Cousin, Cousine⬆
The Cousins⬆
Crainquebille⬆
Crazy for Love
The Crazy Ray⬆
The Crime of Monsieur
  Lange⬆
Cross My Heart
The Crucible⬆
The Cry of the Owl
Cyrano de Bergerac⬆
Daddy Nostalgia⬆
Daens
Damage⬆
Dangerous Liaisons
Daniella by Night
Danton⬆
Daughters of Darkness⬆
The Day and the Hour
Day for Night⬆
A Day in the Country⬆
The Day the Sky Exploded
The Daydreamer
De Mayerling a Sarajevo
Deadly Sting
The Deadly Trap
Dear Detective
Death in the Garden
Death Watch⬆
The Decameron⬆
Delicatessen⬆
Delusions of Grandeur⬆
The Demons
Devil in the Flesh⬆
The Devil, Probably
The Devil's Commandment
The Diabolical Dr. Z
Diabolically Yours
Diabolique⬆
Diary of a Chambermaid⬆
Diary of a Country Priest⬆
Diary of a Seducer
Dingo
Dirty Dishes⬆
Dirty Hands
The Discreet Charm of the
  Bourgeoisie⬆
Diva⬆
Dr. Bethune⬆
Dr. Petiot
Dog Day
Donkey Skin⬆
Dos Cruces en Danger Pass⬆
Double Agents
Double Identity
The Double Life of Veronique
Dracula & Son
The Dreamed Life of Angels
Dressmaker
Duke of the Derby
Dupont Lajoie
Dust⬆
The Eagle Has Two Heads⬆
The Earrings of Madame
  De...⬆
Edith & Marcel
The Eighth Day
The Eighties
The Elegant Criminal
Elena and Her Men⬆
Elisa
Elsa, Elsa

Emmanuelle
Emmanuelle 4
Emmanuelle 5
Emmanuelle & Joanna
Emmanuelle in the Country
Emmanuelle on Taboo Island
Emmanuelle, the Joys of a
  Woman
Empty Canvas
End of Desire
Enigma
Entr'acte
Entre-Nous⬆
Erendira
Erotic Escape
Et La Tenoresse?...Bordel!
Eternal Return
Eternity and a Day
Every Other Weekend⬆
The Eyes, the Mouth
Fahrenheit 451⬆
Fanfan la Tulipe⬆
Fanny
Fantastic Planet⬆
Farinelli
Fatal Fix
The Favor, the Watch, & the
  Very Big Fish
The Favorite Son⬆
Fellini's Roma
Femmes de Paris
Fernandel the Dressmaker
Field of Honor
Fiesta
The Fire Within⬆
First Name: Carmen⬆
The Flower of My Secret⬆
Forbidden Fruit⬆
Forbidden Games⬆
Fort Saganne
Four Adventures of Reinette
  and Mirabelle⬆
Four Bags Full
The 400 Blows⬆
France/Tour/Detour/Deux/
  Enfants⬆
Frantic⬆
Franz
French Can-Can⬆
The French Detective⬆
The French Touch
French Twist
The French Way
Fresh
From Hell to Victory
Full Moon in Paris⬆
The Game Is Over
A Gentle Woman
Germinal⬆
Gervaise⬆
Get Out Your Handkerchiefs⬆
The Gift
Girl in His Pocket
A Girl on Her Own
Godson⬆
Going Places⬆
The Golden Coach⬆
Goliath and the Dragon
Grain of Sand⬆
Grand Illusion⬆
The Great War
The Green House
The Green Room⬆
Grisbi
Grosse Fatigue⬆
Hail Mary
The Hairdresser's Husband⬆
The Hands of Orlac
Hanna K.
Happy New Year⬆
Harem
Harvest⬆
Hate⬆

Head of the Family
Head Over Heels⬆
Heart of a Nation⬆
Heat of Desire
Helas pour Moi
Her and She and Him
Hercules Against the Moon
  Men
Here and Elsewhere
High Heels
Hiroshima, Mon Amour⬆
The Holes
Holiday Hotel
Honor Among Thieves
The Horror Chamber of Dr.
  Faustus⬆
The Horse of Pride
The Horseman on the Roof
Hothead
Howling 2: Your Sister Is a
  Werewolf
The Hunchback of Notre
  Dame
I Can't Sleep
I Killed Rasputin
I Love All of You
I Love You, I Love You Not
I Sent a Letter to My Love⬆
Icy Breasts⬆
In the Realm of the Senses⬆
Indochine⬆
The Infernal Trio
Innocent Lies
The Invaders
Investigation
Invitation au Voyage
Irma Vep
Is Paris Burning?⬆
Istanbul
It Happened in the Park
It Means That to Me
Italian Straw Hat
J'Accuse⬆
Jacko & Lise
Jacquot
Jailbird's Vacation
Je Tu Il Elle
Jean de Florette⬆
Jenny Lamour
Jesus of Montreal⬆
Josepha⬆
Jour de Fete⬆
Journey Beneath the Desert
Journey to the Lost City
The Joy of Knowledge
Judex
The Judge and the Assassin⬆
Jules and Jim⬆
Jupiter's Thigh
Just Another Pretty Face
Kapo⬆
The Killing Game
The King of Hearts⬆
King of the Airwaves
The Klutz
L.627⬆
La Balance⬆
La Belle Noiseuse⬆
La Bete Humaine⬆
La Boum
La Cage aux Folles⬆
La Cage aux Folles 2
La Cage aux Folles 3: The
  Wedding
La Ceremonie⬆
La Chartreuse de Parme
La Chevre⬆
La Chienne⬆
La Chute de la Maison
  Usher⬆
La Collectionneuse
La Discrete⬆
La Femme Nikita⬆

La Grande Bouffe
La Grande Vadrouille
La Lectrice
La Marseillaise
La Merveilleuse Visite
La Nuit de Varennes
La Passante
La Petite Sirene
La Promesse
La Ronde
La Rupture
La Silence de la Mer
La Symphonie Pastorale
La Truite
La Vengeance d'une Femme
The Lacemaker
The Ladies of the Bois de Bologne
Lady Chatterley's Lover
Lady L
L'Age D'Or
L'Amour en Herbe
Lancelot of the Lake
Landscape in the Mist
L'Anne Sainte
L'Annee des Meduses
L'Appat
L'Argent
The Last Metro
Last Tango in Paris
The Last Train
The Last Winters
Last Year at Marienbad
L'Atalante
Le Bal
Le Beau Mariage
Le Beau Serge
Le Bonheur
Le Bonheur Est Dans le Pre
Le Boucher
Le Cas du Dr. Laurent
Le Cavaleur
Le Chat
Le Complot
Le Corbeau
Le Crabe Tambour
Le Dernier Combat
Le Doulos
Le Gendarme de Saint-Tropez
Le Gentleman D'Epsom
Le Grand Chemin
Le Joli Mai
Le Jour Se Leve
Le Jupon Rouge
Le Magnifique
Le Million
Le Petit Amour
Le Plaisir
Le Repos du Guerrier
Le Samourai
Le Schpountz
Le Secret
Le Sex Shop
L'Ecole Buisoniere
L'Eleve
L'Enfer
Leon Morin, Priest
Leonor
Les Assassins de L'Ordre
Les Aventuriers
Les Biches
Les Bonnes Femmes
Les Carabiniers
Les Comperes
Les Enfants Terrible
Les Grandes Gueules
Les Grandes Manoeuvres
Les Miserables
Les Mistons
Les Nuits Fauves
Les Rendez-vous D'Anna
Les Vampires

Les Violons du Bal
Les Visiteurs du Soir
Les Voleurs
L'Etat Sauvage
Letters from My Windmill
Letters to an Unknown Lover
L'Homme Blesse
License to Kill
L'Idiot
Life and Nothing But
Life Is a Long Quiet River
Life Upside Down
Liliom
Little Indian, Big City
The Little Thief
Little World of Don Camillo
Live Flesh
L'Odeur des Fauves
Lola
Lola Montes
Loulou
Love After Love
Love and the Frenchwoman
A Love in Germany
Love on the Run
Love Play
Love Songs
Love Without Pity
The Lover
The Lovers
Lovers Like Us
The Loves of Hercules
The Lower Depths
Lucky Luciano
Lumiere
Ma Saison Preferee
Ma Vie en Rose
Madame Bovary
Madame Butterfly
Madame Rosa
Mademoiselle
The Mahabharata
Maids of Wilko
Make Room for Tomorrow
Mama Dracula
Mama, There's a Man in Your Bed
A Man and a Woman
A Man and a Woman: 20 Years Later
Man from Nowhere
A Man in Love
The Man in the Raincoat
Man in the Silk Hat
Man on Fire
The Man Who Loved Women
Manon of the Spring
Maria Chapdelaine
Maria Chapdelaine
Marius
Marius and Jeannette
Marquis
A Married Woman
Marry Me, Marry Me
Martin Luther
Masculine Feminine
Mauvaise Graine
Max, Mon Amour
May Fools
Mayerling
Melodie en Sous-Sol
Menage
Microcosmos
The Milky Way
Mill of the Stone Women
Mina Tannenbaum
Minnesota Clay
Mississippi Mermaid
Mr. Hulot's Holiday
Mr. Klein
Mr. Peek-A-Boo
Modigliani

Mon Amie Max
Mon Homme
Mon Oncle
Mon Oncle D'Amerique
The Mongols
The Monocle
Monsieur Hire
Monsieur Vincent
Moon in the Gutter
Morgan the Pirate
Mouchette
Murder at 45 R.P.M.
Muriel
Murmur of the Heart
My Best Friend's Girl
My Father's Glory
My Life and Times with Antonin Artaud
My Life to Live
My Mother's Castle
My New Partner
My Night at Maud's
My Other Husband
My Sex Life...Or How I Got Into an Argument
The Mystery of Alexina
Nais
The Name of the Rose
Nana
Napoleon
Napoleon
Nelly et Monsieur Arnaud
Nenette and Boni
Next Summer
Next Year If All Goes Well
Night and Day
The Night and the Moment
Night Flight from Moscow
1900
No Fear, No Die
No Problem
Noir et Blanc
Nostradamus
Nous N'Irons Plus au Bois
Nouvelle Vague
Numero Deux
The Nun
The Old Lady Who Walked in the Sea
Oldest Profession
Olivier, Olivier
One Deadly Summer
One Sings, the Other Doesn't
One Wild Moment
One Woman or Two
The Outside Man
Overseas: Three Women with Man Trouble
Pain in the A—
Panique
Pantaloons
Parade
Pardon Mon Affaire
Pardon Mon Affaire, Too!
Paris Belongs to Us
Paris, Texas
Pas Tres Catholique
The Passion of Joan of Arc
Passion of Love
Pattes Blanches
Paul and Michelle
Pauline at the Beach
Pedale Douce
The Peking Blond
Pepe Le Moko
Peppermint Soda
Peril
The Perils of Gwendoline
The Perverse Countess
Petit Con
Phaedra
Phantom of Liberty
Pickpocket

Picnic on the Grass
Pierrot le Fou
Pigalle
The Pillow Book
The Plague
Planets Against Us
Playtime
Poil de Carotte
Police
Ponette
Possession
Pouvoir Intime
Princess Academy
Princess Tam Tam
Prix de Beaute
Prize of Peril
The Professional
A Propos de Nice
The Proud Ones
A Pure Formality
Purple Noon
The Purple Taxi
Quartet
Quatorze Juliet
Queen Margot
Quest for Fire
Qui Etes Vous, Mr. Sorge?
Ramparts of Clay
Ran
Rape of Love
The Rape of the Sabines
The Rascals
Ravishing Idiot
The Red and the Black
The Red Balloon
Red Balloon/Occurrence at Owl Creek Bridge
The Red Inn
Red Kiss
Red Sun
Rendez-Moi Ma Peau
Rendez-vous
Rendezvous in Paris
The Respectful Prostitute
The Return of Dr. Mabuse
The Return of Martin Guerre
The Return of the Musketeers
Return of the Tall Blond Man With One Black Shoe
Reunion
Ricco
Rider on the Rain
Ridicule
Rififi
The Rise of Louis XIV
The River
Road to Salina
Roads to the South
Robert et Robert
Rough Magic
Round Midnight
Ruyblas
The Sacrifice
Salut l'Artiste
Same Old Song
Samson and the 7 Miracles of the World
Sand and Blood
Sans Soleil
Scene of the Crime
Scoumoune
Secret Agent Super Dragon
A Self-Made Hero
The Separation
Seven Deadly Sins
Shanghai Triad
The Sheep Has Five Legs
Sheer Madness
Shoot the Piano Player
The Silences of the Palace
A Simple Story
Sincerely Charlotte
A Single Girl

Six Fois Deux/Sur et Sous la Communication
Six in Paris
The Slap
Small Change
Smiling Madame Beudet/The Seashell and the Clergyman
Smoking/No Smoking
Soft and Hard
The Soft Skin
Sois Belle et Tais-Toi
Soldat Duroc...Ca Va Etre Ta Fete!
Someone Else's America
Son of Samson
The Son of the Shark
The Sorrow and the Pity
Soviet Spy
Special Police
Spirits of the Dead
Spoiled Children
Sputnik
State of Siege
Stay As You Are
Stealing Beauty
Stolen Kisses
The Storm Within
Stormy Waters
The Story of a Cheat
The Story of a Love Story
Story of Adele H.
The Story of Women
Subway
The Sucker
Sugar Cane Alley
Summer
A Sunday in the Country
Sundays & Cybele
Swann in Love
Swashbuckler
Sweet Ecstasy
Swimming Pool
Sylvia and the Phantom
Sympathy for the Devil
A Tale of Springtime
A Tale of Winter
The Tall Blond Man with One Black Shoe
Tamango
Tartuffe
Tatie Danielle
Tchao Pantin
Ten Days Wonder
The Tenant
Terror of Rome Against the Son of Hercules
Tess
The Testament of Dr. Cordelier
The Testament of Orpheus
That Man from Rio
That Naughty Girl
There Goes Barder
Therese
The Things of Life
36 Fillete
This Man Must Die
This Special Friendship
This Sweet Sickness
The 317th Platoon
Three Lives and Only One Death
Three Men and a Cradle
Tiger of the Seven Seas
Time Out for Love
Toni
Too Beautiful for You
Too Pretty to Be Honest
Too Shy to Try
Topaze
Toto le Heros
Tournament

French

Tous les Matins du Monde
Toute Une Nuit
Traffic
Trahir
The Trial
Tricheurs
Triple Cross
Tristana
Trois Couleurs: Blanc
Trois Couleurs: Bleu
Trois Couleurs: Rouge
12 Plus 1
Twist
Two English Girls
The Two of Us
Two or Three Things I Know About Her
Ulysses' Gaze
Umbrellas of Cherbourg
Un Air de Famille
Un Chien Andalou
Un Coeur en Hiver
Uncle Tom's Cabin
Under Satan's Sun
Under the Roofs of Paris
Underground
Up/Down/Fragile
Uranus
Utopia
Vagabond
The Valley Obscured by the Clouds
Vampyr
Van Gogh
The Vanishing
A Very Curious Girl
A Very Private Affair
Vincent, Francois, Paul and the Others
Violette
The Visitors
Viva Maria!
Volpone
Voulez-Vous Danser Avec Moi?
Voyage en Balloon
Voyage en Douce
Voyage-Suprise
Voyager
Wages of Fear
The Walls of Malapaga
The Wanderer
We Will Not Enter the Forest
Web of the Spider
Wedding in Blood
A Wedding in Galilee
Weekend
Well-Digger's Daughter
Western
When the Cat's Away
Where the Hot Wind Blows
Where the Sky Begins
Widow Couderc
The Wild Child
Wild Reeds
Window Shopping
Window to Paris
Without Warning
The Wolf at the Door
A Woman at Her Window
A Woman Is a Woman
The Woman Next Door
Woman Times Seven
The Wonders of Aladdin
The Would-Be Gentleman
Yesterday, Today and Tomorrow
Your Turn Darling
Z
Zazie dans le Metro
Zero for Conduct
Zero for Conduct/Taris/A Propos de Nice

Zombie Lake
Zou Zou

German

Aguirre, the Wrath of God
Ali: Fear Eats the Soul
The American Friend
The American Soldier
Among the Cinders
Andy Warhol's Frankenstein
Angry Harvest
Anita, Dances of Vice
The Avenger
Backstairs
Bagdad Cafe
Baron Munchausen
Battleforce
The Berlin Affair
Berlin Alexanderplatz
Beware of a Holy Whore
Beyond Silence
The Bitter Tears of Petra von Kant
The Black Abbot
Black Beauty
A Black Veil for Lisa
Blood and Black Lace
Bloody Moon
The Blue Angel
The Blue Hour
The Blue Light
The Blum Affair
Boarding School
The Brain
The Bridge
Brother of Sleep
The Cabinet of Dr. Caligari
The Captain from Koepenick
The Castle
The Castle of Fu Manchu
The Cat o' Nine Tails
The Catamount Killing
Cave of the Living Dead
Celeste
The Cement Garden
Cesare Borgia
Charm of La Boheme
The Children
Chinese Boxes
Chinese Roulette
Christiane F.
Circus of Fear
Club Extinction
Code Name Alpha
Codename: Wildgeese
Colonel Redl
Commandos
The Conformist
Congress Dances
The Cop & the Girl
A Couch in New York
Count Dracula
Coup de Grace
Creature with the Blue Hand
Crimes of Dr. Mabuse
Curse of the Yellow Snake
The Damned
Dandelions
Das Boot
Das Testament des Dr. Mabuse
Daughter of Death
Daughters of Darkness
David
Dead Eyes of London
Deadline
Deadly Game
Death Watch
The Decameron
Deep End
Despair

Deutschland im Jahre Null
The Devil in Silk
Diary of a Lost Girl
Die Grosse Freiheit Nr. 7
Dr. Mabuse, Parts 1 & 2
Dr. Mabuse vs. Scotland Yard
Door with the Seven Locks
Dorian Gray
Drachenfutter
Dracula vs. Frankenstein
Eclipse
Effi Briest
Erendira
Europa, Europa
Every Man for Himself & God Against All
Fabulous Adventures of Baron Munchausen
Faraway, So Close!
Faust
Fight for Gold
First Love
First Spaceship on Venus
Fitzcarraldo
Flatfoot
Flirt
For Your Love Only
Forger of London
Forget Mozart
Fortune's Fool
Fox and His Friends
F.P. 1
F.P. 1 Doesn't Answer
Frankenstein '80
Frozen Alive
Full Hearts & Empty Pockets
Geheimakte WB1
Germany in Autumn
The Goalie's Anxiety at the Penalty Kick
Gods of the Plague
The Golem
Halfmoon
Hanussen
The Head
Heart of Glass
Heidi
Heimat 1
Heimat 2
The High Crusade
Homecoming
Horrors of Spider Island
The House of 1000 Dolls
I Love You, I Love You Not
I Only Want You to Love Me
In a Year of 13 Moons
The Indian Scarf
The Inheritors
Inn on the River
The Innocent
Invisible Adversaries
The Invisible Dr. Mabuse
Jack the Ripper
Journey to the Lost City
Joyless Street
Jud Suess
The Jumper
Jungle Warriors
Just a Gigolo
Kameradschaft
Kamikaze '89
Kaspar Hauser
King, Queen, Knave
Kings of the Road—In the Course of Time
Knife in the Head
Kolberg
Kriemhilde's Revenge
La Passante
The Lacemaker
Land and Freedom
The Last Five Days
The Last Laugh

The Last Tomahawk
Lea
Les Miserables
Les Rendez-vous D'Anna
Let It Rock
Lethal Obsession
Liebelei
Lisbon Story
The Lost Honor of Katharina Blum
The Lost One
A Love in Germany
Ludwig
M
The Mad Executioners
Maedchen in Uniform
Malou
The Man Inside
A Man Like Eva
Marianne and Juliane
Mark of the Devil
Mark of the Devil 2
The Marriage of Maria Braun
Martha and I
Master Touch
Maybe ... Maybe Not
Me and Him
Men...
Menschenfrauen
Metropolis
Mission Stardust
Mr. Superinvisible
The Monster of London City
Moon 44
Mother Kusters Goes to Heaven
Mozart: A Childhood Chronicle
Murderers Are Among Us
My Father Is Coming
The Mysterious Magician
Naked in the Night
The Name of the Rose
The Nasty Girl
Nelly et Monsieur Arnaud
Nico Icon
Night Flight from Moscow
1900
99 Women
No Survivors, Please
Nosferatu
The Odessa File
Oldest Profession
One Arabian Night
The Oppermann Family
An Orphan Boy of Vienna
Othello
Out of Order
Pandora's Box
Paris, Texas
Passion
The Passion of Darkly Noon
The Pedestrian
The Phantom of Soho
Possession
The Practice of Love
The Princess and the Swineherd
The Promise
Q Ships
Querelle
A Rat's Tale
Requiem for Dominic
The Return of Dr. Mabuse
Reunion
The Revolt of Job
Roboman
Rosa Luxemburg
Rosalie Goes Shopping
Sacred Mountain/White Flame
Salmonberries
Satan's Brew

Savage Attraction
The Scarlet Letter
Schnelles Geld
Schtonk
The Scorpion Woman
The Second Awakening of Christa Klages
Secret Agent Super Dragon
Secret of the Black Trunk
Secrets of a Soul
The Seducers
Seduction: The Cruel Woman
The Serpent's Egg
Shadow of Angels
Shattered
Sheer Madness
Sherlock Holmes and the Deadly Necklace
Shocking Asia
Siegfried
Signs of Life
Singing the Blues in Red
Sisters, Or the Balance of Happiness
Slavers
Smilla's Sense of Snow
Someone Else's America
Spiders
Spies
Spring Symphony
The Squeaker
Stalingrad
State of Things
The Stationmaster's Wife
The Strange Countess
Stranger than Paradise
Strangler of Blackmoor Castle
The Street
Stroszek
Student of Prague
A Study in Terror
Sugarbaby
The Surgeon
Swann in Love
Swiss Conspiracy
Symphony in the Mountains
Tales of Erotica
Taxi zum Klo
Teenage Wolfpack
They Were So Young
'38: Vienna Before the Fall
The Thousand Eyes of Dr. Mabuse
The Three Penny Opera
Tiefland
The Tin Drum
Tonio Kroger
The Torture Chamber of Dr. Sadism
Tower of Screaming Virgins
Traenen in Florenz
Triumph of the Will
Tromba, the Tiger Man
Uncle Tom's Cabin
Underground
Utz
The Vampire Happening
Vampyr
Variety
Veronika Voss
Via Appia
Virgin Machine
Voyager
The Wannsee Conference
Warning Shadows
Waxworks
Web of the Spider
The Werewolf vs. the Vampire Woman
Westfront 1918
Where the Green Ants Dream
The White Rose

Italian

Japanese

Urusei Yatsura Movie 2: Beautiful Dreamer
Urusei Yatsura Movie 3: Remember My Love
Urusei Yatsura Movie 4: Lum the Forever
Urusei Yatsura Movie 5: The Final Chapter
Urusei Yatsura Movie 6: Always My Darling
Utamaro and His Five Women
Varan the Unbelievable
Vengeance Is Mine✒
Violence at Noon✒
Virtual Assassin
Virus
War in Space
War of the Gargantuas
Warning from Space
What's Up, Tiger Lily?✒
When a Woman Ascends the Stairs
A Wind Named Amnesia
The Wolves✒
Woman in the Dunes✒
X from Outer Space
Yog, Monster from Space
Yojimbo✒
Zatoichi: Master Ichi and a Chest of Gold
Zatoichi: The Blind Swordsman and the Chess Expert
Zatoichi: The Blind Swordsman and the Fugitives
Zatoichi: The Blind Swordsman's Vengeance
Zatoichi: The Life and Opinion of Masseur Ichi
Zatoichi vs. Yojimbo✒
Zatoichi: Zatoichi's Flashing Sword
Zeram

Korean

Crocodile
301, 302
Why Has Bodhi-Darma Left for the East

Lithuanian

Adomas Nori Buti Zmogumi
Velnio Nuotaka

Luxembourg

Jack Higgins' On Dangerous Ground

Macedonian

Before the Rain✒

Mexican

Arizona
Attack of the Mayan Mummy
Black Pit of Dr. M
The Bloody Vampire
The Brainiac
Bring Me the Vampire
Cabeza de Vaca✒
Children of Sanchez
Conquest
Creature of the Walking Dead

The Criminal Life of Archibaldo de la Cruz✒
Cronos
Crossfire
The Curse of the Aztec Mummy
The Curse of the Crying Woman
Curse of the Devil
Curse of the Stone Hand
Dance of Death
Death in the Garden
Dona Herlinda & Her Son
El
El Bruto
El Mariachi✒
Erendira
The Exterminating Angel✒
Face of the Screaming Werewolf
The Fear Chamber
Fearmaker
Fever Mounts at El Pao
Flor Silvestre
Foxtrot
Genie of Darkness
The Great Madcap
Guns for Dollars
Highway Patrolman
The Illusion Travels by Streetcar✒
Invasion of the Vampires
Invasion of the Zombies
Jungle Warriors
Like Water for Chocolate✒
The Living Coffin
The Living Head
Los Olvidados✒
The Man and the Monster
Maria Candelaria
Mary, My Dearest
Mexican Bus Ride
The Monster Demolisher
Nazarin✒
Neutron and the Black Mask
Neutron vs. the Amazing Dr. Caronte
Neutron vs. the Death Robots
Neutron vs. the Maniac
The New Invisible Man
Night of a Thousand Cats
Night of the Bloody Apes
Pancho Villa Returns
The Pearl✒
Reed: Insurgent Mexico
The Robot vs. the Aztec Mummy
Samson in the Wax Museum
Samson vs. the Vampire Women
Santa Claus
Santa Sangre✒
Savage!
The Sinister Invasion
Sisters of Satan
The Snake People
Spiritism
Susana✒
Swamp of the Lost Monster
Target Eagle
Tintorera...Tiger Shark
The Torch
Torero
The Treasure of the Amazon
Triumphs of a Man Called Horse
The Vampire
The Vampire's Coffin
Viridiana✒
Warlock Moon
Witches' Mountain
The Witch's Mirror
A Woman Without Love✒

Wrestling Women vs. the Aztec Ape
Wrestling Women vs. the Aztec Mummy
Wuthering Heights
Yanco
The Young One

New Zealand

Absent Without Leave
Among the Cinders
An Angel at My Table✒
Bad Blood
Bad Taste✒
Beyond Reasonable Doubt
The Bridge to Nowhere
Broken English
Came a Hot Friday
Crush
Dangerous Orphans
Dark of the Night
Dead Alive
Desperate Remedies
Forgotten Silver
Goodbye Pork Pie
Heart of the Stag
Heavenly Creatures✒
Hot Target
Iris
Jack Be Nimble
Loaded
Meet the Feebles
Mesmerized
Nate and Hayes
The Navigator✒
Never Say Die
Nutcase
Once Were Warriors✒
The Quiet Earth✒
Second Time Lucky
Shaker Run
The Silent One
Sleeping Dogs
Smash Palace
Starlight Hotel
Sylvia
Tearaway
Treasure of the Yankee Zephyr
The Ugly
Utu✒
Vigil✒
Wild Horses

Nicaraguan

Alsino and the Condor✒

Norwegian

Edvard Munch
Hamsun
Junk Mail
One Day in the Life of Ivan Denisovich✒
The Other Side of Sunday
Pathfinder✒
Shipwrecked
Zero Degrees Kelvin

Peruvian

Alias, La Gringa

Polish

Ashes and Diamonds✒
Baritone

A Brivele der Mamen✒
Camera Buff
Colonel Wolodyjowski
The Conductor
Danton✒
Deja Vu
The Deluge
Der Purimshpiler
The Double Life of Veronique
The Dybbuk✒
Enigma Secret
Family Life
Fever✒
First Spaceship on Venus✒
Foul Play
From a Far Country: Pope John Paul II
A Generation✒
Greta✒
Hands Up✒
Hero of the Year
Illumination
In an Old Manor House
In Desert and Wilderness
Innocent Sorcerers
The Interrogation✒
Kanal✒
Karate Polish Style
Knife in the Water✒
Korczak✒
Land of Promise
Leper
Lotna
Maids of Wilko
Mamele
Man of Iron✒
Man of Marble✒
Moonlighting✒
Mother Joan of the Angels✒
Mother of Kings
Nights and Days
No End
Paper Marriage
Passenger✒
Pharaoh
Provincial Actors
The Saragossa Manuscript
The Silent Touch
The Singing Blacksmith
The Structure of Crystals
Train to Hollywood
Trois Couleurs: Blanc✒
Trois Couleurs: Rouge✒
The Unapproachable
Without Anesthesia
Without Love
A Woman and a Woman
Year of the Quiet Sun✒
Yidl Mitn Fidl

Portuguese

Black Orpheus✒
The Convent
The Demons
In the White City✒
The Jew
Life Is Beautiful
Return of the Evil Dead
Tombs of the Blind Dead

Romanian

The Oak
Trahir✒
An Unforgettable Summer

Russian

Adomas Nori Buti Zmogumi

Aelita: Queen of Mars
Alexander Nevsky✒
The Amphibian Man
Andrei Rublev✒
Arsenal✒
Ashik Kerib✒
Autumn Marathon
Ballad of a Soldier✒
Baltic Deputy✒
The Battleship Potemkin✒
Bed and Sofa✒
Burglar✒
Burnt by the Sun✒
Chapayev✒
The Children of Theatre Street
The Cigarette Girl of Mosselprom
Close to Eden
The Color of Pomegranates✒
Come and See✒
Commissar✒
The Cranes Are Flying✒
Creation of Adam
Crime and Punishment
The Day the Earth Froze
Dersu Uzala✒
Don Quixote✒
Earth✒
The Errors of Youth
A Forgotten Tune for the Flute✒
Freedom Is Paradise✒
Freeze-Die-Come to Life✒
Fury Is a Woman✒
The General Line✒
The Girl with the Hat Box
Guerilla Brigade
Happiness
I Am Cuba
The Inspector General
Ivan the Terrible, Part 1✒
Ivan the Terrible, Part 2✒
Jazzman✒
Kindergarten✒
Kino Pravda/Enthusiasm
The Lady with the Dog✒
The Legend of Suram Fortress
Little Vera✒
Luna Park
The Magic Voyage of Sinbad
The Man with a Movie Camera✒
The Mirror✒
Moscow Does Not Believe in Tears✒
Moscow Parade
Mother✒
My Apprenticeship✒
My Childhood✒
My Name Is Ivan✒
My Universities✒
No Greater Love
Oblomov✒
Orphans✒
The Overcoat✒
The Patriots✒
Peter the First: Part 1
Peter the First: Part 2
Planet Burg
Prisoner of the Mountains✒
Private Life
Que Viva Mexico✒
Rasputin✒
Repentance✒
The Road to Life
Shadows of Forgotten Ancestors✒
The Shooting Party
Siberiade✒
Sideburns
A Slave of Love✒

Venezuelan

Shoot to Kill

Vietnamese

Cyclo
The Scent of Green Papaya⬦

Yugoslavian

The Battle of Austerlitz
Battle of Neretva
Battleforce
Cave of the Living Dead
Hey, Babu Riba
Innocence Unprotected
Kapo⬦
The Love Affair, or The Case
    of the Missing Switchboard
    Operator⬦
Man Is Not a Bird
One-Eyed Soldiers
Operation Cross Eagles
Romance of a Horsethief
The She-Beast
Son of Samson
Stealing Heaven
Sweet Movie
Time of the Gypsies⬦
Tito and Me⬦
Track of the Vampire
Uncle Tom's Cabin
Vukovar⬦
Ward Six
When Father was Away on
    Business⬦

The **Cast Index** provides a complete videography for cast members with more than one appearance on video. The listings for the actor names follow an alphabetical sort by last name (although the names appear in a first name last name format). The videographies are listed chronologically, from most recent film to earliest appearance, making it easier to trace the development of your favorite actor's career. When a cast member appears in more than one film in the same year, these movies are listed alphabetically within the year.

Beverly Aadland
Assault of the Rebel Girls '59
Raiders of Sunset Pass '43

Lee Aaker
Courage of Rin Tin Tin '83
Rin Tin Tin, Hero of the West '55
Hondo '53
The Atomic City '52

Angela Aames
Basic Training '86
Bachelor Party '84
The Lost Empire '83

Willie Aames
Cut and Run '85
Paradise '82
Zapped! '82
Scavenger Hunt '79
Frankenstein '73

Caroline Aaron
Primary Colors '98
Deconstructing Harry '97
Weapons of Mass Distraction '97
House Arrest '96
A Modern Affair '94
Alice '90
Edward Scissorhands '90
Crimes & Misdemeanors '89
Heartburn '86

Judith Abarbanel
American Matchmaker '40
The Cantor's Son '37
Uncle Moses '32

Bruce Abbott
Melanie Darrow '97
The Prophecy 2: Ashtown '97
The Demolitionist '95
Dillinger '91
Bride of Re-Animator '89
Trapped '89
Bad Dreams '88
Interzone '88
Summer Heat '87
Re-Animator '84

Bud Abbott
The World of Abbott & Costello '64

Dance with Me, Henry '56
Abbott and Costello Meet the Mummy '55
Abbott and Costello Meet the Keystone Kops '54
The Best of Abbott & Costello Live '54
Hollywood Goes to War '54
Abbott and Costello Go to Mars '53
Abbott and Costello Meet Captain Kidd '52
Abbott and Costello Meet Dr. Jekyll and Mr. Hyde '52
Jack & the Beanstalk '52
Lost in Alaska '52
Abbott and Costello Meet the Invisible Man '51
Comin' Round the Mountain '51
Abbott and Costello in the Foreign Legion '50
Abbott and Costello Meet the Killer, Boris Karloff '49
Africa Screams '49
Abbott and Costello Meet Frankenstein '48
Mexican Hayride '48
The Noose Hangs High '48
Buck Privates Come Home '47
The Wistful Widow of Wagon Gap '47
Little Giant '46
The Time of Their Lives '46
Abbott and Costello in Hollywood '45
Here Come the Co-Eds '45
The Naughty Nineties '45
In Society '44
Lost in a Harem '44
Hit the Ice '43
Pardon My Sarong '42
Ride 'Em Cowboy '42
Rio Rita '42
Who Done It? '42
Buck Privates '41
Hold That Ghost '41
In the Navy '41
Keep 'Em Flying '41
One Night in the Tropics '40

Diahnne Abbott
Jo Jo Dancer, Your Life Is Calling '86
Love Streams '84
King of Comedy '82
New York, New York '77

John Abbott
The Merry Widow '52
Adventure Island '47
Anna and the King of Siam '46
Deception '46
Humoresque '46
Pursuit to Algiers '45
The Vampire's Ghost '45
Cry of the Werewolf '44
The Falcon in Hollywood '44
U-Boat Prisoner '44

Philip Abbott
The Fantastic World of D.C. Collins '84
Hangar 18 '80
The Invisible Boy '57

Kareem Abdul-Jabbar
Slam Dunk Ernest '95
Purple People Eater '88
Chuck Berry: Hail! Hail! Rock 'n' Roll '87
Fletch '85
Airplane! '80
The Fish that Saved Pittsburgh '79
Game of Death '79

Alfred Abel
Metropolis '26
Dr. Mabuse, Parts 1 & 2 '22

Walter Abel
Grace Quigley '84
Silent Night, Bloody Night '73
Quick, Let's Get Married '71
Mirage '65
Raintree County '57
The Indian Fighter '55
Prudential Family Playhouse '50
Curley '47
Fabulous Joe '47
Kid from Brooklyn '46
13 Rue Madeleine '46

Mr. Skeffington '44
So Proudly We Hail '43
Holiday Inn '42
Wake Island '42
Law of the Underworld '38
Fury '36
The Three Musketeers '35

Jim Abele
Student Affairs '88
Wimps '87

Tim Abell
Death and Desire '97
Hybrid '97
Night Shade '97
Sexual Roulette '96
Masseuse '95
Over the Wire '95

Ian Abercrombie
Rattled '96
Test Tube Teens from the Year 2000 '93
Army of Darkness '92
Zandalee '91
Curse 4: The Ultimate Sacrifice '90
Puppet Master 3: Toulon's Revenge '90
Catacombs '89
Kicks '85

Keith Aberdein
Smash Palace '82
Wild Horses '82

Abigail
Breaking Loose '90
Adventures of Eliza Fraser '76

F. Murray Abraham
Baby Face Nelson '97
Mimic '97
Larry McMurtry's Dead Man's Walk '96
Looking for Richard '96
Children of the Revolution '95
Dillinger and Capone '95
Mighty Aphrodite '95
Surviving the Game '94
By the Sword '93
Last Action Hero '93
Nostradamus '93

Sweet Killing '93
Mobsters '91
Beyond the Stars '89
An Innocent Man '89
Intimate Power '89
Slipstream '89
Third Solution '89
The Name of the Rose '86
Amadeus '84
Scarface '83
Madman '79
The Big Fix '78
All the President's Men '76
The Ritz '76
The Sunshine Boys '75
Prisoner of Second Avenue '74
Serpico '73
They Might Be Giants '71

Ken Abraham
Marked for Murder '89
Deadly Embrace '88
Vice Academy '88
Creepozoids '87

Michele Abrams
Buffy the Vampire Slayer '92
Cool World '92

Victoria Abril
French Twist '95
Jimmy Hollywood '94
Kika '93
Intruso '93
High Heels '91
Lovers: A True Story '90
Tie Me Up! Tie Me Down! '90
Baton Rouge '88
Max, Mon Amour '86
After Darkness '85
L'Addition '85
Padre Nuestro '85
Moon in the Gutter '83
On the Line '83

James Acheson
The Garden of Redemption '97
Kazaam '96
Body Language '92

Sharon Acker
Happy Birthday to Me '81
Off Your Rocker '80
The Hanged Man '74

- Race the Sun '96
- To Die For '95

John Agar
- Body Bags '93
- Fear '90
- Miracle Mile '89
- King Kong '76
- Hell Raiders '68
- Curse of the Swamp Creature '66
- Johnny Reno '66
- Zontar, the Thing from Venus '66
- Cavalry Command '63
- Invisible Invaders '59
- Jet Attack/Paratroop Command '58
- The Brain from Planet Arous '57
- The Daughter of Dr. Jekyll '57
- Flesh and the Spur '57
- The Mole People '56
- Revenge of the Creature '55
- Tarantula '55
- Along the Great Divide '51
- Sands of Iwo Jima '49
- She Wore a Yellow Ribbon '49
- Fort Apache '48

Tetchie Agbayani
- Deathfight '93
- Rikky and Pete '88
- Gymkata '85
- The Dolls '83

Carlos Agosti
- The Bloody Vampire '62
- Invasion of the Vampires '61

Pierre Agostino
- Las Vegas Serial Killer '86
- The Hollywood Strangler Meets the Skid Row Slasher '79

Janet Agren
- Night of the Sharks '89
- Magdalene '88
- Aladdin '86
- Hands of Steel '86
- Gates of Hell '83
- Panic '83
- Emerald Jungle '80
- Perfect Crime '78
- The Uranium Conspiracy '78

Kris Aguilar
- Fist of Steel '93
- Bloodfist '89

Jenny Agutter
- The Buccaneers '95
- Child's Play 2 '90
- Darkman '90
- Dark Tower '87
- Secret Places '85
- Silas Marner '85
- An American Werewolf in London '81
- Amy '81
- Survivor '80
- Dominique Is Dead '79
- The Riddle of the Sands '79
- Sweet William '79
- Gunfire '78
- The Eagle Has Landed '77
- Equus '77
- The Man in the Iron Mask '77
- Logan's Run '76
- Walkabout '70
- The Railway Children '70
- Star! '68

Brian Aherne
- Sword of Lancelot '63
- Waltz King '63
- The Best of Everything '59
- The Swan '56
- A Bullet Is Waiting '54
- Prince Valiant '54
- I Confess '53
- Titanic '53
- Forever and a Day '43
- A Night to Remember '42
- Smilin' Through '41
- The Lady in Question '40
- Beloved Enemy '36
- I Live My Life '35
- Sylvia Scarlett '35

Bjorje Ahistedt
- Sunday's Children '94
- Emma's Shadow '88

Philip Ahn
- Paradise, Hawaiian Style '66
- Shock Corridor '63
- Battle Hymn '57
- His Majesty O'Keefe '60
- Impact '49
- Back to Bataan '45
- Betrayal from the East '44
- China Sky '44
- The Story of Dr. Wassell '44
- China '43
- Hawaii Calls '38
- The General Died at Dawn '36

Charles Aidman
- Prime Suspect '82
- Zoot Suit '81
- House of the Dead '80
- Zone of the Dead '78
- The Barbary Coast '74
- The Invasion of Carol Enders '74
- Picture of Dorian Gray '74
- Adam at 6 a.m. '70
- Menace on the Mountain '70
- Countdown '68
- Hour of the Gun '67

Danny Aiello
- The Last Don '97
- Mojave Moon '96
- Two Days in the Valley '96
- Two Much '96
- City Hall '95
- The Road Home '95
- Power of Attorney '94
- The Professional '94
- Ready to Wear '94
- The Cemetery Club '93
- Me and the Kid '93
- The Pickle '93
- Ruby '92
- The Closer '91
- Hudson Hawk '91
- Mistress '91
- Once Around '91
- 29th Street '91
- Jacob's Ladder '90
- The Lost Idol/Shock Troop '80s
- Do the Right Thing '89
- Harlem Nights '89
- The January Man '89
- The Preppie Murder '89
- Third Solution '89
- White Hot '88
- Alone in the Neon Jungle '87
- Man on Fire '87
- Moonstruck '87
- The Pick-Up Artist '87
- Radio Days '87
- Key Exchange '85
- Protector '85
- The Purple Rose of Cairo '85
- The Stuff '85
- Old Enough '84
- Once Upon a Time in America '84
- Chu Chu & the Philly Flash '81
- Fort Apache, the Bronx '81
- Hide in Plain Sight '80
- Question of Honor '80
- Defiance '79
- Bloodbrothers '78
- Fingers '78
- The Front '76
- Hooch '76
- The Godfather, Part 2 '74
- Bang the Drum Slowly '73
- Deathmask '69

Rick Aiello
- Hollywood Confidential '97
- Endangered '94
- Uncivilized '94
- The Closer '91
- 29th Street '91

Anouk Aimee
- Ready to Wear '94
- Dr. Bethune '90
- A Man and a Woman: 20 Years Later '86
- Success Is the Best Revenge '84
- The Tragedy of a Ridiculous Man '81
- Justine '69
- A Man and a Woman '66
- 8 1/2 '63
- Sodom and Gomorrah '62
- Lola '61
- La Dolce Vita '60
- Modigliani '58
- Paris Express '53
- The Golden Salamander '51

Richard Ainley
- I Dood It '43
- White Cargo '42

Holly Aird
- Intimate Relations '95
- Over Indulgence '87
- The Flame Trees of Thika '81

Maria Aitken
- Grave Indiscretions '96
- A Fish Called Wanda '88

Michael Aitkens
- Moving Targets '87
- The Highest Honor '84

Franklin Ajaye
- The Wrong Guys '88
- Fraternity Vacation '85
- The Jazz Singer '80
- Convoy '78
- Car Wash '76

Chantal Akerman
- Akermania, Vol. 1 '92
- Je Tu Il Elle '74

Andra Akers
- Desert Hearts '86
- E. Nick: A Legend in His Own Mind '84

Karen Akers
- Heartburn '86
- The Purple Rose of Cairo '85

Claude Akins
- The Gambler Returns: The Luck of the Draw '93
- Falling from Grace '92
- The Curse '87
- Manhunt for Claude Dallas '86
- Monster in the Closet '86
- Pecos Bill '86
- The Concrete Cowboys '79
- Killer on Board '77
- Tarantulas: The Deadly Cargo '77
- The Big Push '75
- Eric '75
- Battle for the Planet of the Apes '73
- The Death Squad '73
- A Man Called Sledge '71
- The Night Stalker '71
- The Devil's Brigade '68
- Waterhole #3 '67
- Return of the Seven '66
- The Killers '64
- Merrill's Marauders '62
- Comanche Station '60
- Rio Bravo '59
- The Kettles on Old MacDonald's Farm '57
- Sea Chase '55
- The Caine Mutiny '54
- From Here to Eternity '53

Marc Alaimo
- The Fence '94
- Quicksand: No Escape '91
- Arena '89
- Tango and Cash '89
- Archer: The Fugitive from the Empire '81

Steve Alaimo
- Alligator Alley '72
- Wild Rebels '71
- The Hooked Generation '69

Craig Alan
- Endangered '94
- Sex Crimes '92

Nelly Alard
- Venice, Venice '92
- Eating '90

Joe Alaskey
- Bank Robber '93
- Lucky Stiff '88

Maria Alba
- Chandu on the Magic Island '34
- Return of Chandu '34
- Mr. Robinson Crusoe '32

Captain Lou Albano
- Body Slam '87
- Wise Guys '86

Josh Albee
- The Runaways '75
- The Adventures of Tom Sawyer '73

Kevin Alber
- Alien Terminator '95
- Burial of the Rats '95
- The Showgirl Murders '95

Anna Maria Alberghetti
- Cinderfella '60
- The Last Command '55
- Here Comes the Groom '51
- The Medium '51

Luis Alberni
- Harvest Melody '43
- The Great Man Votes '38
- Hats Off '37
- Dancing Pirate '36
- Goodbye Love '34
- One Night of Love '34
- Man from Monterey '33
- The Sphinx '33
- The Big Stampede '32

Hans Albers
- Die Grosse Freiheit Nr. 7 '45
- Baron Munchausen '43
- F.P. 1 Doesn't Answer '33
- The Blue Angel '30

Eddie Albert
- The Big Picture '89
- Out of Sight, Out of Her Mind '89
- The Victory '88
- Turnaround '87
- Brenda Starr '86
- Dress Gray '86
- Head Office '86
- Stitches '85
- Burning Rage '84
- Dreamscape '84
- The Act '82
- Yes, Giorgio '82
- Goliath Awaits '81
- Peter and Paul '81
- Take This Job & Shove It '81
- Beulah Land '80
- Foolin' Around '80
- How to Beat the High Cost of Living '80
- The Concorde: Airport '79 '79
- The Birch Interval '78
- The Crash of Flight 401 '78
- The Word '78
- Moving Violation '76
- Devil's Rain '75
- Escape to Witch Mountain '75
- Whiffs '75
- The Longest Yard '74
- McQ '74
- Fireball Forward '72
- The Heartbreak Kid '72
- Captain Newman, M.D. '63
- The Miracle of the White Stallions '63
- Who's Got the Action? '63
- The Longest Day '62
- Beloved Infidel '59
- The Teahouse of the August Moon '56
- I'll Cry Tomorrow '55
- Oklahoma! '55
- Roman Holiday '53
- Actors and Sin '52
- Carrie '52
- The Fuller Brush Girl '50
- You Gotta Stay Happy '48
- Smash-Up: The Story of a Woman '47
- The Perfect Marriage '46
- Bombardier '43

Edward Albert
- The Man in the Iron Mask '97
- The Secret Agent Club '96
- Space Marines '96
- Guarding Tess '94
- Hard Drive '94
- Red Sun Rising '94
- Sorceress '94
- Broken Trust '93
- The Ice Runner '93
- Sexual Malice '93
- Shootfighter: Fight to the Death '93
- Body Language '92
- Exiled in America '90
- Accidents '89
- Mind Games '89
- Wild Zone '89
- Fist Fighter '88
- The Heist '88
- The Rescue '88
- The Underachievers '88
- Distortions '87
- Terminal Entry '87
- Getting Even '86
- Ellie '84
- Time to Die '83
- Butterfly '82
- House Where Evil Dwells '82
- Galaxy of Terror '81
- The Squeeze '80
- When Time Ran Out '80
- Silent Victory: The Kitty O'Neil Story '79
- The Greek Tycoon '78
- The Rip Off '78
- The Domino Principle '77
- The Purple Taxi '77
- Death Cruise '74
- Forty Carats '73
- Butterflies Are Free '72
- The Fool Killer '65

Laura Albert
- Blood Games '90
- Dr. Caligari '89
- Death by Dialogue '88
- The Unnamable '88

Guido Alberti
- Ten Days Wonder '72
- Casanova '70 '65

Frank Albertson
- Psycho '60
- Nightfall '56
- Killer Dill '47
- It's a Wonderful Life '46
- Louisiana Purchase '41
- Man Made Monster '41
- Room Service '38
- Navy Blue and Gold '37
- Fury '36
- Ah, Wilderness! '35
- Hollywood Mystery '34
- Rainbow Over Broadway '33
- Way Back Home '32
- Big Business Girl '31

Jack Albertson
- Charlie and the Great Balloon Chase '82
- Dead and Buried '81
- Marriage Is Alive and Well '80
- The Poseidon Adventure '72
- Where the Eagle Flies '72
- Willy Wonka & the Chocolate Factory '71
- Changes '69
- Justine '69
- The Subject Was Roses '68
- Flim-Flam Man '67
- How to Murder Your Wife '64
- Kissin' Cousins '64
- The Patsy '64
- Roustabout '64
- Who's Got the Action? '63
- Days of Wine and Roses '62
- Period of Adjustment '62
- Lover Come Back '61
- Miracle on 34th Street '47

Dan Albright
- I Know What You Did Last Summer '97
- To Dance with the White Dog '93

Hardie Albright
- Mom & Dad '47
- The Jade Mask '45
- Sunset in El Dorado '45
- Champagne for Breakfast '35
- Sing Sing Nights '35
- The Scarlet Letter '34
- The Purchase Price '32

Lola Albright
- The Impossible Years '68
- Where Were You When the Lights Went Out? '68

Kenny Rogers as the Gambler '80
The Groundstar Conspiracy '72
Pocket Money '72

Ann Bell
When Saturday Comes '95
Champions '84
The Statue '71

Christopher Bell
Skylark '93
Sarah, Plain and Tall '91
Without Warning: The James Brady Story '91

Dan Bell
The Shot '96
Terror Eyes '87

Darryl M. Bell
Mr. Write '92
School Daze '88

Edward Bell
Image of Passion '86
The Premonition '75

E.E. Bell
Grizzly Mountain '97
800 Leagues Down the Amazon '93

Hank Bell
Valley of the Sun '42
Border Vengeance '35
The Fiddlin' Buckaroo '33
Beyond the Rockies '32
The Big Stampede '32
South of Santa Fe '32
Whistlin' Dan '32

James Bell
Tribute to a Bad Man '56
A Lawless Street '55
Teenage Crime Wave '55
The Leopard Man '43
My Friend Flicka '43

Jeanne Bell
Fass Black '77
The Muthers '76
TNT Jackson '75
Policewomen '73

Marie Bell
Phedre '68
Hotel Paradiso '66
Sandra of a Thousand Delights '65

Marshall Bell
Starship Troopers '97
Too Fast, Too Young '96
Payback '94
The Vagrant '92
The Heroes of Desert Storm '91
Air America '90
Leather Jackets '90
Total Recall '90
Johnny Be Good '88
Tucker: The Man and His Dream '88
Twins '88
Wildfire '88
No Way Out '87
A Nightmare on Elm Street 2: Freddy's Revenge '85

Rex Bell
Law of the Sea '38
Stormy Trails '36
West of Nevada '36
The Tonto Kid '35
Diamond Trail '33
Fighting Texans '33
Rainbow Ranch '33
Broadway to Cheyenne '32
Battling with Buffalo Bill '31

Tobin Bell
Serial Killer '95
New Eden '94
The Firm '93
Ruby '92
False Identity '90

Tom Bell
Swept from the Sea '97
Feast of July '95
The Cinder Path '94
Prime Suspect 3 '93
Prime Suspect '92
Let Him Have It '91
Prospero's Books '91

The Krays '90
Wish You Were Here '87
Royal Flash '75
Dressed for Death '74
Quest for Love '71
Ballad in Blue '66

Vanessa Bell
Memphis '91
Coming to America '88

Rachael Bella
Household Saints '93
When Pigs Fly '93

Bill Bellamy
Def Jam's How to Be a Player '97
Love Jones '96
Who's the Man? '93

Diana Bellamy
Amelia Earhart: The Final Flight '94
The Nest '88

Madge Bellamy
Northwest Trail '46
The Ivory Handled Gun '35
Law for Tombstone '35
Stone of Silver Creek '35
The White Zombie '32
The White Sin '24
Soul of the Beast '23
Lorna Doone '22

Ned Bellamy
Carnosaur '93
Writer's Block '91

Ralph Bellamy
Pretty Woman '90
War & Remembrance, Part 2 '89
War & Remembrance: The Final Chapter, Part 8 '89
The Good Mother '88
War & Remembrance, Part 1 '88
Disorderlies '87
Fourth Wise Man '85
Love Leads the Way '84
Trading Places '83
The Winds of War '83
Oh, God! '77
The Boy in the Plastic Bubble '76
Nightmare in Badham County '76
Return to Earth '76
Murder on Flight 502 '75
Search for the Gods '75
Missiles of October '74
Cancel My Reservation '72
Doctors' Wives '70
Rosemary's Baby '68
The Professionals '66
Sunrise at Campobello '60
The Defender '57
The Court Martial of Billy Mitchell '55
Delightfully Dangerous '45
Guest in the House '45
Lady on a Train '45
The Ghost of Frankenstein '42
Dive Bomber '41
Footsteps in the Dark '41
The Wolf Man '41
Brother Orchid '40
Dance, Girl, Dance '40
His Girl Friday '40
Boy Meets Girl '38
Carefree '38
The Awful Truth '37
Healer '36
Hands Across the Table '35
Spitfire '34
Woman in the Shadows '34
Ace of Aces '33

Clara Bellar
David '97
Rendezvous in Paris '95

Harry Bellaver
The Lemon Drop Kid '51
No Way Out '50
House on 92nd Street '45

Annie Belle
House on the Edge of the Park '84
Forever Emmanuelle '82
Naked Paradise '78

Kathleen Beller
Time Trackers '88
Cloud Waltzing '87
Surfacing '84
Sword & the Sorcerer '82
Touched '82
Fort Apache, the Bronx '81
The Manions of America '81
No Place to Hide '81
Mother & Daughter: A Loving War '80
Promises in the Dark '79
Are You in the House Alone? '78
The Betsy '78
Mary White '77
The Godfather, Part 2 '74

Agostina Belli
The Chosen '77
The Sex Machine '76

Cynthia Belliveau
The Dark '94
The Spider and the Fly '94
The Dream Team '89
A New Life '88

Gina Bellman
David '97
Silent Trigger '97
Leon the Pig Farmer '93

Sara Bellomo
Bikini Drive-In '94
Beach Babes from Beyond Infinity '93

Gil Bellows
Snow White: A Tale of Terror '97
The Substance of Fire '96
Black Day Blue Night '95
Miami Rhapsody '95
Silver Strand '95
Love and a .45 '94
The Shawshank Redemption '94

Pamela Bellwood
Double Standard '88
Cellar Dweller '87
Cocaine: One Man's Seduction '83
Hangar 18 '80
Deadman's Curve '78

Jean-Paul Belmondo
Les Miserables '95
Swashbuckler '84
Stuntwoman '81
Le Magnifique '76
Scoumoune '74
Stavisky '74
High Heels '72
Borsalino '70
The Brain '69
Mississippi Mermaid '69
Casino Royale '67
Is Paris Burning? '66
Pierrot le Fou '65
That Man from Rio '64
Cartouche '62
Un Singe en Hiver '62
Le Doulos '61
Leon Morin, Priest '61
Two Women '61
Love and the Frenchwoman '60
A Woman Is a Woman '60
Breathless '59
Sois Belle et Tais-Toi '58

Robert Beltran
Managua '97
Star Trek Voyager: Caretaker '95
Bugsy '91
The Chase '91
Kiss Me a Killer '91
To Die Standing '91
El Diablo '91
Scenes from the Class Struggle in Beverly Hills '89
Gaby: A True Story '87
Latino '85
Night of the Comet '84
Eating Raoul '82

Mark Beltzman
Billy Madison '94
Mo' Money '92

James Belushi
Living in Peril '97
Retroactive '97

Gang Related '96
Jingle All the Way '96
Race the Sun '96
Destiny Turns on the Radio '95
Parallel Lives '94
Separate Lives '94
Royce '93
Wild Palms '93
Once Upon a Crime '92
Traces of Red '92
Curly Sue '91
Diary of a Hitman '91
Only the Lonely '91
The Palermo Connection '91
The Masters of Menace '90
Mr. Destiny '90
Taking Care of Business '90
Homer and Eddie '89
K-9 '89
Wedding Band '89
Who's Harry Crumb? '89
Red Heat '88
The Principal '87
Real Men '87
About Last Night... '86
Jumpin' Jack Flash '86
Little Shop of Horrors '86
Salvador '86
Birthday Boy '86
The Man with One Red Shoe '85
Best Legs in the 8th Grade '84
Trading Places '83
Thief '81
The Fury '78
Mutant Video '76

John Belushi
Continental Divide '81
Neighbors '81
The Blues Brothers '80
1941 '79
Old Boyfriends '79
All You Need Is Cash '78
Goin' South '78
National Lampoon's Animal House '78

Richard Belzer
Get On the Bus '96
Girl 6 '96
Not of This Earth '96
The Invaders '95
The Puppet Masters '94
Mad Dog and Glory '93
The Flash 2: Revenge of the Trickster '91
Off and Running '90
The Big Picture '89
Fletch Lives '89
Freeway '88
The Wrong Guys '88
America '86
Flicks '85
Night Shift '82
Fame '80
The Groove Tube '72

Paul Ben-Victor
Maximum Risk '96
Metro '96
Houseguest '94

Brian Benben
Radioland Murders '94
I Come in Peace '90
Mortal Sins '90
Clean and Sober '88
Gangster Wars '81

Robert Benchley
The Road to Utopia '46
It's in the Bag '45
The Stork Club '45
Weekend at the Waldorf '45
The Sky's the Limit '42
I Married a Witch '42
The Major and the Minor '42
Young & Willing '42
Nice Girl? '41
You'll Never Get Rich '41
Foreign Correspondent '40
China Seas '35

Russ Bender
Navy vs. the Night Monsters '66
Anatomy of a Psycho '61
Suicide Battalion/Hell Squad '58
The War of the Colossal Beast '58
The Amazing Colossal Man '57

It Conquered the World '56

Michael C. Bendetti
Amanda and the Alien '95
Netherworld '90

William Bendix
For Love or Money '63
Johnny Nobody '61
Deep Six '58
Crashout '55
Dangerous Mission '54
Blackbeard the Pirate '52
A Girl in Every Port '52
Macao '52
Detective Story '51
Big Steal '49
A Connecticut Yankee in King Arthur's Court '49
Babe Ruth Story '48
The Time of Your Life '48
Where There's Life '47
The Blue Dahlia '46
Dark Corner '46
Two Years Before the Mast '46
It's in the Bag '45
Abroad with Two Yanks '44
The Hairy Ape '44
Lifeboat '44
China '43
Guadalcanal Diary '43
The Glass Key '42
Star Spangled Rhythm '42
Wake Island '42
Who Done It? '42
Woman of the Year '42

Leonor Benedetto
A Place in the World '92
Condemned to Hell '80s

Billy Benedict
Bride of the Monster '56
Ghost Chasers '51
Master Minds '49
Spook Busters '48
Bowery Buckaroos '47
Hard-Boiled Mahoney '47
Follow the Leader '44
Wildcat '42

Brooks Benedict
The Dropkick '27
Ranson's Folly '26
The Freshman '25

Dirk Benedict
Alaska '96
November Conspiracy '96
Official Denial '93
Shadow Force '92
Blue Tornado '90
Body Slam '87
Ruckus '81
Follow That Car '80
Underground Aces '80
Mission Galactica: The Cylon Attack '79
Scavenger Hunt '79
Battlestar Galactica '78
Cruise into Terror '78
W '74
Ssssssss '73
Georgia, Georgia '72

Paul Benedict
Attack of the 50 Ft. Woman '93
The Addams Family '91
The Freshman '90
Babycakes '89
Cocktail '88
The Chair '87
Desperate Moves '86
Mandingo '75

Richard Benedict
Beginning of the End '57
Breakdown '53
Omoo Omoo, the Shark God '49
O.S.S. '46

Yves Beneyton
Letters to an Unknown Lover '84
The Lacemaker '77
Weekend '67

John Benfield
Prime Suspect: Inner Circles '95
Prime Suspect: The Scent of Darkness '95
Prime Suspect: The Lost Child '94

Raoul Billerey
The Little Thief '89
Le Grand Chemin '87

Dawn Ann Billings
Warlock: The Armageddon '93
Trancers 3: Deth Lives '92

Earl Billings
One False Move '91
Stakeout '87

Barbara Billingsley
Leave It to Beaver '97
Back to the Beach '87
Eye of the Demon '87

Jennifer Billingsley
Hollywood Man '76
The Thirsty Dead '74
White Lightning '73
Chrome Hearts '70
Lady in a Cage '64

Peter Billingsley
Arcade '93
Beverly Hills Brats '89
Russkies '87
Dirt Bike Kid '86
The Hoboken Chicken
   Emergency '84
A Christmas Story '83
Death Valley '81

Sybilla Binder
The Golden Salamander '51
Blanche Fury '48
Counterblast '48

Herman Bing
Bitter Sweet '40
Bluebeard's Eighth Wife '38
Every Day's a Holiday '38
The Great Waltz '38
Maytime '37
Tango '36
That Girl from Paris '36
Crimson Romance '34
The Merry Widow '34
The Guardsman '31

Barbara Bingham
Beyond Darkness '92
Soldier's Fortune '91
Friday the 13th, Part 8: Jason
   Takes Manhattan '89

Geoffrey Binney
Raw Force '81
Hot Potato '76

Edward Binns
Return to Eden '89
Danger in the Skies '79
Oliver's Story '78
Night Moves '75
Hunter '73
The Americanization of Emily '64
A Public Affair '62
Compulsion '59
Curse of the Undead '59
Twelve Angry Men '57
Beyond a Reasonable Doubt '56
Without Warning '52

Juliette Binoche
The English Patient '96
A Couch in New York '95
The Horseman on the Roof '95
Trois Couleurs: Bleu '93
Damage '92
Emily Bronte's Wuthering
   Heights '92
Women & Men: In Love There
   Are No Rules '91
The Unbearable Lightness of
   Being '88
Hail Mary '85
Rendez-vous '85

Thelma Biral
Fridays of Eternity '81
El Muerto '75

Maurice Biraud
The Last Train '74
The Big Grab '63

Paul Birch
Queen of Outer Space '58
Apache Woman '55
Day the World Ended '55

Thora Birch
Alaska '96

Now and Then '95
Clear and Present Danger '94
Monkey Trouble '94
Hocus Pocus '93
Patriot Games '92
All I Want for Christmas '91
Paradise '91

Billie Bird
Dennis the Menace '93
The End of Innocence '90
Home Alone '90
Ernest Saves Christmas '88

Norman Bird
Hands of the Ripper '71
Burn Witch, Burn! '62
Victim '61

Jesse Birdsall
Nightscare '93
Getting It Right '89
Wish You Were Here '87

Tala Birell
The Purple Heart '44
The White Legion '36
Crime and Punishment '35

Jane Birkin
French Intrigue
Same Old Song '97
Daddy Nostalgia '90
La Belle Noiseuse '90
Beethoven's Nephew '88
Le Petit Amour '87
Dust '85
Evil under the Sun '82
Make Room for Tomorrow '81
Death on the Nile '78
Catherine & Co. '76
Seven Deaths in the Cat's Eye
   '72
Too Pretty to Be Honest '72
Romance of a Horsethief '71
Swimming Pool '70
Wonderwall: The Movie '69
Blow-Up '66

Len Birman
Web of Deceit '90
Undergrads '85
Captain America '79
Captain America 2: Death Too
   Soon '79
Lies My Father Told Me '75

Matt Birman
Family of Cops 2: Breach of
   Faith '97
Back in Action '94

Serafina Birman
Ivan the Terrible, Part 2 '46
Ivan the Terrible, Part 1 '44
The Girl with the Hat Box '27

David Birney
Nightfall '88
Prettykill '87
The Five of Me '81
Mom, the Wolfman and Me '80
Oh, God! Book 2 '80
Choice of Weapons '76
Caravan to Vaccares '74
Murder or Mercy '74
Only with Married Men '74

Reed Birney
Crimewave '85
Four Friends '81

Debbie Bishop
Sid & Nancy '86
Scrubbers '82

Ed Bishop
Saturn 3 '80
S.O.S. Titanic '79
Brass Target '78
The Devil's Web '74
Journey to the Far Side of the
   Sun '69

Jennifer Bishop
House of Terror '87
Jaws of Death '76
Jessi's Girls '75
Impulse '74
Horror of the Blood Monsters '70
The Female Bunch '69

Joey Bishop
Betsy's Wedding '90
Delta Force '86

Valley of the Dolls '67
Who's Minding the Mint? '67
Texas Across the River '66
Deep Six '58
The Naked and the Dead '58

Julie Bishop
Westward the Women '51
The Last of the Redmen '47
Rhapsody in Blue '45
Action in the North Atlantic '43
Northern Pursuit '43

Kelly Bishop
Private Parts '96
Miami Rhapsody '95
Queens Logic '91
Dirty Dancing '87

Larry Bishop
Trigger Happy '96
Underworld '96
Soul Hustler '76
How Come Nobody's On Our
   Side? '73
Angel Unchained '70
The Savage Seven '68

Pat Bishop
Women of Valor '86
Don's Party '76

Wes Bishop
Dixie Dynamite '76
Chrome and Hot Leather '71

William Bishop
Breakdown '53
The Redhead from Wyoming '53
Harriet Craig '50

Steve Bisley
Fast Talking '78
The Highest Honor '84
Chain Reaction '80
Mad Max '80

Whit Bissell
Spencer's Mountain '63
The Time Machine '60
No Name On the Bullet '59
Teenage Frankenstein '58
I Was a Teenage Werewolf '57
Invasion of the Body Snatchers
   '56
Shack Out on 101 '55
Creature from the Black Lagoon
   '54
Devil's Canyon '53
Boots Malone '52
The Lost Continent '51
He Walked by Night '48
Raw Deal '48

Jacqueline Bisset
Dangerous Beauty '98
La Ceremonie '95
Crime Broker '94
The Maid '90
Wild Orchid '90
Scenes from the Class Struggle
   in Beverly Hills '89
High Season '88
Choices '86
Anna Karenina '85
Forbidden '85
Under the Volcano '84
Class '83
Rich and Famous '81
When Time Ran Out '80
Together? '79
The Greek Tycoon '78
Who Is Killing the Great Chefs of
   Europe? '78
The Deep '77
Le Magnifique '76
St. Ives '76
Spiral Staircase '75
Murder on the Orient Express
   '74
Day for Night '73
The Thief Who Came to Dinner
   '73
Life & Times of Judge Roy Bean
   '72
The Mephisto Waltz '71
Secrets '71
Airport '70
The Passing of Evil '70
The First Time '69
Bullitt '68
The Detective '68

Casino Royale '67
Two for the Road '67
Cul de Sac '66

Josie Bissett
Baby Monitor: Sound of Fear '97
Mikey '92
All-American Murder '91
Book of Love '91

Chhabi Biswas
Devi '60
Jalsaghar '58

Bill Bixby
Death of the Incredible Hulk '90
The Trial of the Incredible Hulk
   '89
The Incredible Hulk Returns '88
The Incredible Hulk '77
Kentucky Fried Movie '77
Fantasy Island '76
Rich Man, Poor Man '76
The Apple Dumpling Gang '75
The Barbary Coast '74
Speedway '68
Clambake '67
Under the Yum-Yum Tree '63

Denise Bixler
The Assassination Game '92
Evil Dead 2: Dead by Dawn '87

Dragan Bjelogric
Pretty Village, Pretty Flame '96
Hey, Babu Riba '88

Anita Bjork
Secrets of Women '52
Miss Julie '50

Halvar Bjork
Autumn Sonata '78
The New Land '73

Anna Bjorn
Sword & the Sorcerer '82
More American Graffiti '79

Gunnar Bjornstrand
Autumn Sonata '78
Face to Face '76
The Rite '69
The Shame '68
Persona '66
The Winter Light '62
Through a Glass Darkly '61
The Magician '58
Wild Strawberries '57
The Seventh Seal '56
Dreams '55
Smiles of a Summer Night '55
Lesson in Love '54

Jack Black
The Jackal '97
The Cable Guy '96
The NeverEnding Story 3:
   Escape from Fantasia '94

Karen Black
Cries of Silence '97
Invisible Dad '97
Children of the Corn 4: The
   Gathering '96
Crimetime '96
Movies Money Murder '96
Plan 10 from Outer Space '95
Bound and Gagged: A Love
   Story '93
Auntie Lee's Meat Pies '92
Caged Fear '92
Children of the Night '92
The Double O Kid '92
Final Judgement '92
Hitz '92
Rubin & Ed '92
Evil Spirits '91
Haunting Fear '91
Quiet Fire '91
The Children '90
Club Fed '90
The Killer's Edge '90
Mirror, Mirror '90
Night Angel '90
Overexposed '90
Love Under Pressure '80s
Homer and Eddie '89
Twisted Justice '89
Zapped Again '89
Dixie Lanes '88
The Heist '88
The Invisible Kid '88

Out of the Dark '88
Eternal Evil '87
Hostage '87
It's Alive 3: Island of the Alive
   '87
Invaders from Mars '86
Cut and Run '85
The Hitchhiker '85
Martin's Day '85
Bad Manners '84
Killing Heat '84
The Little Mermaid '84
Savage Dawn '84
Can She Bake a Cherry Pie? '83
Come Back to the Five & Dime
   Jimmy Dean, Jimmy Dean '82
Separate Ways '82
Chanel Solitaire '81
Miss Right '81
The Last Word '80
The Squeeze '80
Killer Fish '79
Mr. Horn '79
Capricorn One '78
In Praise of Older Women '78
The Rip Off '78
Burnt Offerings '76
Family Plot '76
Airport '75 '75
Crime & Passion '75
The Day of the Locust '75
Nashville '75
Trilogy of Terror '75
The Great Gatsby '74
Law and Disorder '74
Little Laura & Big John '73
The Pyx '73
Portnoy's Complaint '72
Born to Win '71
A Gunfight '71
Five Easy Pieces '70
Easy Rider '69
You're a Big Boy Now '66
The Prime Time '60

Lucas Black
The X-Files Movie '98
Ghosts of Mississippi '96
Sling Blade '96

Maurice Black
Sixteen Fathoms Deep '34
Marked Money '28

Ryan Black
Dance Me Outside '95
Geronimo '93

Shane Black
As Good As It Gets '97
Predator '87

Richard Blackburn
Sugartime '95
Eating Raoul '82
Lemora, Lady Dracula '73

Honor Blackman
The First Olympics: Athens 1896
   '84
The Cat and the Canary '79
To the Devil, a Daughter '76
Fright '71
The Virgin and the Gypsy '70
Lola '81
Shalako '68
Goldfinger '64
Jason and the Argonauts '63
A Matter of WHO '62
A Night to Remember '58
Suspended Alibi '56
Glass Tomb '55
Green Grow the Rushes '51
Conspirator '49

Joan Blackman
Macon County Line '74
Daring Game '68
Blue Hawaii '62
Kid Galahad '62
Career '59
Good Day for a Hanging '58

Sidney Blackmer
Rosemary's Baby '68
How to Murder Your Wife '64
Tammy and the Bachelor '57
Beyond a Reasonable Doubt '56
High Society '56
People Will Talk '51
Buffalo Bill '44

Brandauer ⟋cont.

Streets of Gold '86
Out of Africa '85
Quo Vadis '85
Colonel Redl '84
Kindergarten '84
Never Say Never Again '83
Mephisto '81
The Salzburg Connection '72

Larry Brandenburg
Major League 3: Back to the
　Minors '98
Mo' Money '92
Victimless Crimes '90

Walter Brandi
Terror Creatures from the Grave
　'66
The Bloody Pit of Horror '65
The Slaughter of the Vampires
　'62

Jonathan Brandis
Sidekicks '93
Ladybugs '92
NeverEnding Story 2: The Next
　Chapter '91
Stephen King's It '90
Stepfather 2: Make Room for
　Daddy '89

Jocelyn Brando
A Question of Love '78
Nightfall '89
Ten Wanted Men '54
The Big Heat '53

Luisina Brando
I Don't Want to Talk About It '94
Miss Mary '86
The Lion's Share '79

Marlon Brando
The Island of Dr. Moreau '96
Don Juan DeMarco '94
Christopher Columbus: The
　Discovery '92
The Freshman '90
A Dry White Season '89
The Godfather 1902-1959: The
　Complete Epic '81
The Formula '80
Apocalypse Now '79
Superman: The Movie '78
Missouri Breaks '76
Last Tango in Paris '73
The Godfather '72
The Nightcomers '72
Burn! '70
The Night of the Following Day
　'69
A Countess from Hong Kong '67
Reflections in a Golden Eye '67
The Appaloosa '66
The Chase '66
Morituri '65
Bedtime Story '63
The Ugly American '63
Mutiny on the Bounty '62
One-Eyed Jacks '61
The Fugitive Kind '60
The Young Lions '58
Sayonara '57
The Teahouse of the August
　Moon '56
Guys and Dolls '55
Desiree '54
On the Waterfront '54
The Wild One '54
Julius Caesar '53
Viva Zapata! '52
A Streetcar Named Desire '51
The Men '50

Rikki Brando
The Bikini Car Wash Company 2
　'92
Buford's Beach Bunnies '92

Clark Brandon
Fast Food '89
My Tutor '82

David Brandon
Beyond Darkness '89
Good Morning, Babylon '87
Stagefright '87

Henry Kleinbach Brandon
Assault on Precinct 13 '76
When the North Wind Blows '74
The Land Unknown '57
The Searchers '56
War Arrow '53
Drums of Fu Manchu '40
The Garden of Allah '36
March of the Wooden Soldiers
　'34

Michael Brandon
The Disappearance of Kevin
　Johnson '95
Rich and Famous '81
A Change of Seasons '80
Promises in the Dark '79
Red Alert '77
James Dean '76
Lovers and Other Strangers '70

Luis Brandoni
A Shadow You Soon Will Be '94
Made in Argentina '86

Carlo Brandt
Ridicule '96
Indochine '92

Carolyn Brandt
The Hollywood Strangler Meets
　the Skid Row Slasher '79
Rat Pfink a Boo-Boo '66
The Thrill Killers '65
Incredibly Strange Creatures
　Who Stopped Living and
　Became Mixed-Up Zombies
　'63

Betsy Brantley
Schizopolis '97
Washington Square '97
Little Lord Fauntleroy '95
Final Appeal '93
Havana '90
I Come in Peace '90
Dreams Lost, Dreams Found '87
The Fourth Protocol '87
Another Country '84
Five Days One Summer '82

Albert Bras
Vampyr '31
Napoleon '27

Nicoletta Braschi
Life is Beautiful '97
The Monster '96
Johnny Stecchino '92
Mystery Train '89
Down by Law '86

Keefe Brasselle
Skirts Ahoy! '52
Streets of Sin '49

Claude Brasseur
Josepha '82
Lobster for Breakfast '82
La Boum '81
A Simple Story '79
L'Etat Sauvage '78
Pardon Mon Affaire, Too! '77
Pardon Mon Affaire '76
Act of Aggression '73
Band of Outsiders '64
The Elusive Corporal '62

Pierre Brasseur
Carthage in Flames '60
Il Bell'Antonio '60
The Horror Chamber of Dr.
　Faustus '59
Children of Paradise '44

Benjamin Bratt
Woman Undone '95
The River Wild '94
Texas '94
Blood In ... Blood Out: Bound by
　Honor '93
Demolition Man '93
Bright Angel '91
One Good Cop '91

Andre Braugher
City of Angels '98
Get On the Bus '96
Primal Fear '96
The Tuskegee Airmen '95
Striking Distance '93
Class of '61 '92

The Court Martial of Jackie
　Robinson '90
Somebody Has to Shoot the
　Picture '90
Glory '89

Pinkas Braun
Samson and Delilah '96
Praying Mantis '83
The Man Outside '68
Mission Stardust '68

Asher Brauner
Living to Die '91
American Eagle '90
Merchants of War '90
Treasure of the Moon Goddess
　'88
B.A.D. Cats '80
Boss' Son '78
Switchblade Sisters '75

Bart Braverman
Hollywood Hot Tubs 2:
　Educating Crystal '89
Alligator '80
The Great Texas Dynamite
　Chase '76

Jay Brazeau
Kissed '96
Slam Dunk Ernest '95

Rossano Brazzi
Third Solution '89
Fear City '85
Formula for a Murder '85
The Far Pavilions '84
Final Justice '84
The Final Conflict '81
A Time for Miracles '80
Dr. Frankenstein's Castle of
　Freaks '74
Mr. Kingstreet's War '71
The Adventurers '70
The Italian Job '69
One Step to Hell '68
Bobo '67
Woman Times Seven '67
The Christmas That Almost
　Wasn't '66
Rome Adventure '62
South Pacific '58
Legend of the Lost '57
The Story of Esther Costello '57
Summertime '55
The Barefoot Contessa '54
Three Coins in the Fountain '54
We the Living '42

Sebastian Breaks
The Big Switch '70
The Heroes of Telemark '65

Peter Breck
Decoy '95
Highway 61 '91
Benji '74
The Crawling Hand '63
Shock Corridor '63
The Beatniks '60

Larry Breeding
A Matter of Life and Death '81
Street Music '81

Bobby Breen
Escape to Paradise '39
Fisherman's Wharf '39
Way Down South '39
Breaking the Ice '38
Hawaii Calls '38
Make a Wish '37
It Happened in New Orleans '36
Let's Sing Again '36

Patrick Breen
Fallen Angels 2 '93
For Love or Money '93
Passed Away '92
Nobody's Perfect '90

Paulette Breen
The Wizard of Speed and Time
　'88
The Clonus Horror '79

Tracy Bregman
The Concrete Jungle '82
Happy Birthday to Me '81

Jana Brejchova
Loves of a Blonde '65

Fabulous Adventures of Baron
　Munchausen '61
The Original Fabulous
　Adventures of Baron
　Munchausen '61

Jacques Brel
Pain in the A— '77
Franz '72
Les Assassins de L'Ordre '71

Lucille Bremer
Behind Locked Doors '48
Human Gorilla '48
Till the Clouds Roll By '46
Till the Clouds Roll By/A Star Is
　Born '46
Ziegfeld Follies '46
Yolanda and the Thief '45
Meet Me in St. Louis '44

Ewen Bremmer
Trainspotting '95
Naked '93

El Brendel
The Beautiful Blonde from
　Bashful Bend '49
I'm from Arkansas '44
Happy Landing '38
Big Trail '30

Brid Brennan
Trojan Eddie '96
Cracker: Brotherly Love '95
Saint-Ex: The Story of the
　Storyteller '95
Four Days in July '85

Eileen Brennan
Changing Habits '96
If These Walls Could Talk '96
Reckless '95
Murder So Sweet '93
I Don't Buy Kisses Anymore '92
Texasville '90
White Palace '90
Stella '89
The New Adventures of Pippi
　Longstocking '88
Rented Lips '88
Sticky Fingers '88
Blood Vows: The Story of a
　Mafia Wife '87
Babes in Toyland '86
Clue '85
Fourth Wise Man '85
The Funny Farm '82
Pandemonium '82
Private Benjamin '80
My Old Man '79
The Cheap Detective '78
FM '78
The Death of Richie '76
Great Smokey Roadblock '76
Murder by Death '76
My Father's House '75
Daisy Miller '74
Scarecrow '73
The Sting '73
Playmates '72
The Last Picture Show '71
Divorce American Style '67

Michael Brennan
Fright '71
No Trace '50

Walter Brennan
Smoke in the Wind '75
Home for the Holidays '72
Support Your Local Sheriff '69
The One and Only, Genuine,
　Original Family Band '68
The Gnome-Mobile '67
Who's Minding the Mint? '67
The Oscar '66
Those Calloways '65
How the West Was Won '63
Rio Bravo '59
Tammy and the Bachelor '57
Glory '56
Goodbye, My Lady '56
At Gunpoint '55
Far Country '55
Bad Day at Black Rock '54
Along the Great Divide '51
Best of the Badmen '50
The Showdown '50
Ticket to Tomahawk '50
The Green Promise '49

Task Force '49
Blood on the Moon '48
Red River '48
My Darling Clementine '46
A Stolen Life '46
Dakota '45
The Princess and the Pirate '44
To Have & Have Not '44
The North Star '43
Hangmen Also Die '42
The Pride of the Yankees '42
Meet John Doe '41
Nice Girl? '41
Sergeant York '41
Northwest Passage '40
The Westerner '40
Stanley and Livingstone '39
The Story of Vernon and Irene
　Castle '39
They Shall Have Music '39
The Adventures of Tom Sawyer
　'38
The Cowboy and the Lady '38
The Texans '38
Come and Get It '36
Fury '36
The Moon's Our Home '36
Prescott Kid '36
These Three '36
Barbary Coast '35
The Invisible Man '33
Man of Action '33
Phantom of the Air '33
Texas Cyclone '32
Two-Fisted Law '32
The Range Feud/Two Fisted
　Law '31

Amy Brenneman
Daylight '96
Fear '96
Casper '95
Heat '95

Dori Brenner
Infinity '96
Silent Victim '92
For the Boys '91
Baby Boom '87
Sex and the Single Parent '82
Altered States '80
Summer Wishes, Winter Dreams
　'73

Evelyn Brent
The Payoff '43
The Seventh Victim '43
Holt of the Secret Service '42
Robot Pilot '41
Daughter of the Tong '39
Panama Lady '39
Law West of Tombstone '38
The President's Mystery '36
Song of the Trail '36
The Silver Horde '30
Last Command '28
Underworld '27
Love 'Em and Leave 'Em '26
Trapped by the Mormons '22

George Brent
Born Again '78
FBI Girl '52
Man Bait '52
Montana Belle '52
Out of the Blue '47
The Spiral Staircase '46
Tomorrow Is Forever '46
Experiment Perilous '45
In This Our Life '42
Silver Queen '42
The Great Lie '41
The Fighting 69th '40
Dark Victory '39
The Old Maid '39
The Rains Came '39
Jezebel '38
In Person '35
The Painted Veil '34
Baby Face '33
Female '33
42nd Street '33
The Purchase Price '32
They Call It Sin '32
Lightning Warrior '31

Linda Brent
Death Valley Rangers '44
Below the Border '42

Avery Brooks
The Big Hit '98
Spenser: Pale Kings & Princes '94
The Ernest Green Story '93
Spenser: Ceremony '93
Star Trek Deep Space Nine: Emissary '93
Roots: The Gift '88
Uncle Tom's Cabin '87
Half Slave, Half Free '85

Clarence Brooks
Bronze Buckaroo '39
Harlem Rides the Range '39

Conrad Brooks
Bikini Drive-In '94
Plan 9 from Outer Space '56

David Brooks
Magic in the Mirror: Fowl Play '96
Scream for Help '86

Elisabeth Brooks
The Forgotten One '89
The Howling '81

Foster Brooks
Oddballs '84
Cracking Up '83
The Villain '79
Super Seal '77

Geraldine Brooks
Johnny Tiger '66
The Green Glove '52
Challenge to Lassie '49
Reckless Moment '49
Cry Wolf '47
The Possessed '47

Hildy Brooks
Forbidden Love '82
The Chosen '81

Jean Brooks
Boss of Big Town '43
The Leopard Man '43
The Seventh Victim '43
Boot Hill Bandits '42

Joel Brooks
The Man Who Captured Eichmann '96
Indecent Proposal '93
Are You Lonesome Tonight '92

Leslie Brooks
The Cobra Strikes '48
Romance on the High Seas '48
The Scar '48
Tonight and Every Night '45
City Without Men '43
You Were Never Lovelier '42

Louise Brooks
Overland Stage Raiders '38
Prix de Beaute '30
Diary of a Lost Girl '29
Pandora's Box '28
It's the Old Army Game '26
Love 'Em and Leave 'Em '26

Mel Brooks
Dracula: Dead and Loving It '95
Robin Hood: Men in Tights '93
Life Stinks '91
Spaceballs '87
To Be or Not to Be '83
History of the World: Part 1 '81
High Anxiety '77
Silent Movie '76
Blazing Saddles '74
Twelve Chairs '70
Putney Swope '69

Phyllis Brooks
Dangerous Passage '44
Silver Spurs '43
The Shanghai Gesture '42
Slightly Honorable '40
Little Miss Broadway '38
Rebecca of Sunnybrook Farm '38
In Old Chicago '37

Rand Brooks
Comanche Station '60
The Vanishing Westerner '50
Ladies of the Chorus '49
Hopalong Cassidy: Borrowed Trouble '48

Hopalong Cassidy: Dangerous Venture '48
Hopalong Cassidy: False Paradise '48
Hopalong Cassidy: Silent Conflict '48
Hopalong Cassidy: Sinister Journey '48
Hopalong Cassidy: The Dead Don't Dream '48
Hopalong Cassidy: Hoppy's Holiday '47
Hopalong Cassidy: The Marauders '47
Hopalong Cassidy: Unexpected Guest '47
Hopalong Cassidy: The Devil's Playground '46
The Sombrero Kid '42
Gone with the Wind '39

Randi Brooks
Colors '88
Cop '88
Hamburger...The Motion Picture '86
Tightrope '84
Forbidden Love '82

Randy Brooks
Black Snow '93
Reservoir Dogs '92

Ray Brooks
Office Romances '86
House of Whipcord '75
Tiffany Jones '75
Flesh and Blood Show '73
Daleks—Invasion Earth 2150 A.D. '66
The Knack '65

Richard Brooks
The Crow 2: City of Angels '96
The Substitute '96
Chameleon '95
Machine Gun Blues '95
Memphis '91
To Sleep with Anger '90
84 Charlie Mopic '89
Shocker '89
Shakedown '88
Short Fuse '88
The Hidden '87

Edward Brophy
Last Hurrah '58
Roaring City '51
Renegade Girl '46
Swing Parade of 1946 '46
Cover Girl '44
The Thin Man Goes Home '44
Destroyer '43
Dance, Girl, Dance '40
The Invisible Woman '40
Great Guy '36
Kelly the Second '36
Mad Love '35
Show Them No Mercy '35
Evelyn Prentice '34
Hide-Out '34
What! No Beer? '33
The Champ '32
Speak Easily '32
Doughboys '30
The Cameraman '28

Kevin Brophy
Delos Adventure '86
The Seduction '82
Time Walker '82
Hell Night '81

Pierce Brosnan
Dante's Peak '97
Tomorrow Never Dies '97
Mars Attacks! '96
The Mirror Has Two Faces '96
Detonator 2: Night Watch '95
Goldeneye '95
Don't Talk to Strangers '94
Love Affair '94
The Broken Chain '93
Detonator '93
Entangled '93
Mrs. Doubtfire '93
The Lawnmower Man '92
Live Wire '92
Mister Johnson '91
Murder 101 '91
Victim of Love '91

Around the World in 80 Days '89
The Heist '89
The Deceivers '88
Noble House '88
Taffin '88
The Fourth Protocol '87
Nomads '86
Remington Steele, Vol. 1: License to Steele '82
The Carpathian Eagle '81
The Manions of America '81
The Long Good Friday '80
The Mirror Crack'd '80

Collette Brosset
Belle Americaine '61
Femmes de Paris '53

Dr. Joyce Brothers
The Lonely Guy '84
Desperate Lives '82
Embryo '76

Liliane Brousse
Maniac '63
Paranoiac '62

Amelda Brown
Little Dorrit, Film 1: Nobody's Fault '88
Little Dorrit, Film 2: Little Dorrit's Story '88

Barbara Brown
My Sister Eileen '55
Ma and Pa Kettle on Vacation '53
Home Town Story '51
Ma and Pa Kettle Back on the Farm '51
Ma and Pa Kettle Go to Town '50
Hollywood Canteen '44
The Fighting Sullivans '42

Barry Brown
He Who Walks Alone '78
The Disappearance of Aimee '76
The Ultimate Thrill '74
Bad Company '72

Bille Brown
Oscar and Lucinda '97
Fierce Creatures '96

Blair Brown
The Day My Parents Ran Away '93
Passed Away '92
Strapless '90
Stealing Home '88
Hands of a Stranger '87
The Bad Seed '85
A Flash of Green '85
Kennedy '83
Continental Divide '81
Altered States '80
One Trick Pony '80
And I Alone Survived '78
The Choirboys '77

Bobby Brown
A Thin Line Between Love and Hate '96
Mother Goose Rock 'n' Rhyme '90

Bryan Brown
Dead Heart '96
Twisted '96
Full Body Massage '95
The Last Hit '93
Blame It on the Bellboy '92
Devlin '92
Dead in the Water '91
F/X 2: The Deadly Art of Illusion '91
Prisoners of the Sun '91
Sweet Talker '91
Cocktail '88
Gorillas in the Mist '88
F/X '86
The Good Wife '86
Tai-Pan '86
The Empty Beach '85
Far East '85
Rebel '85
A Town Like Alice '85
Give My Regards to Broad Street '84
Kim '84
Parker '84

The Thorn Birds '83
The Winter of Our Dreams '82
Blood Money '80
Breaker Morant '80
Palm Beach '79
The Irishman '78
Money Movers '78
Newsfront '78

Charles D. Brown
Follow Me Quietly '49
Merton of the Movies '47
Brother Orchid '40
Old Swimmin' Hole '40
Shopworn Angel '38
Dance of Life '29

Clancy Brown
Flubber '97
Starship Troopers '97
Female Perversions '96
Donor Unknown '95
The Shawshank Redemption '94
Last Light '93
Past Midnight '92
Pet Sematary 2 '92
Ambition '91
Cast a Deadly Spell '91
Love, Lies and Murder '91
Blue Steel '90
Season of Fear '89
Shoot to Kill '88
Highlander '86
The Bride '85
Bad Boys '83

David G. Brown
Chasing Dreams '81
Deadly Harvest '72

D.W. Brown
Mischief '85
Weekend Pass '84

Dwier Brown
Deconstructing Sarah '94
Lily in Winter '94
The Cutting Edge '92
Galaxies Are Colliding '92
Mom and Dad Save the World '92
The Guardian '90
Field of Dreams '89

Eric Brown
Video Murders '87
They're Playing with Fire '84
Private Lessons '81

Gary Brown
Invasion of the Space Preachers '90
The Glory Boys '84

Gaye Brown
Mata Hari '85
Masque of the Red Death '65

Georg Stanford Brown
Tyson '95
Ava's Magical Adventure '94
Murder without Motive '92
House Party 2: The Pajama Jam '91
Alone in the Neon Jungle '87
North and South Book 1 '85
The Jesse Owens Story '84
The Kid with the Broken Halo '82
The Night the City Screamed '80
Roots: The Next Generation '79
Colossus: The Forbin Project '70
Dayton's Devils '68

Georgia Brown
Victim of Love '91
Love at Stake '87
Actor: The Paul Muni Story '78
Tales That Witness Madness '73
Nothing But the Night '72
Long Ago Tomorrow '71
The Fixer '68

Henry Brown
Uncaged '91
Stepfather 2: Make Room for Daddy '89
The Man in the Glass Booth '75

James Brown
Doctor Detroit '83
The Blues Brothers '80

James Brown
Courage of Rin Tin Tin '83
Adios Amigo '75
Targets '68
Rin Tin Tin, Hero of the West '55
Objective, Burma! '45

Jim Brown
He Got Game '98
Mars Attacks! '96
Original Gangstas '96
The Divine Enforcer '91
Crack House '89
L.A. Vice '89
Twisted Justice '89
I'm Gonna Git You Sucka '88
L.A. Heat '88
The Running Man '87
Pacific Inferno '85
One Down, Two to Go! '82
Fingers '78
Kid Vengeance '75
Take a Hard Ride '75
Three the Hard Way '74
Slaughter's Big Ripoff '73
Slaughter '72
El Condor '70
The Passing of Evil '70
100 Rifles '69
Riot '69
Dark of the Sun '68
Ice Station Zebra '68
The Dirty Dozen '67
Rio Conchos '64

Joe E. Brown
The Comedy of Terrors '64
It's a Mad, Mad, Mad, Mad World '63
Some Like It Hot '59
Around the World in 80 Days '56
Show Boat '51
The Tender Years '47
Pin-Up Girl '44
The Gladiator '38
Wide Open Faces '38
Fit for a King '37
Riding on Air '37
When's Your Birthday? '37
Earthworm Tractors '36
A Midsummer Night's Dream '35
Lottery Bride '30

Johnny Mack Brown
Apache Uprising '66
Border Bandits '46
Gentleman from Texas '46
The Stranger from Pecos '45
Lawmen '44
Partners of the Trail '44
Raiders of the Border '44
Range Law '44
Ghost Rider '43
Six Gun Gospel '43
Texas Kid '43
Ride 'Em Cowboy '42
Boss of Bullion City '41
Bury Me Not on the Lone Prairie '41
Man from Montana '41
The Masked Rider '41
Pony Post '40
Riders of Pasco Basin '40
Oregon Trail '39
Fire Alarm '38
Flaming Frontiers '38
Boothill Brigade '37
The Gambling Terror '37
Guns in the Dark '37
A Lawman Is Born '37
Crooked Trail '36
Desert Phantom '36
Rogue of the Range '36
Undercover Man '36
Valley of the Lawless '36
Western Double Feature 3 '36
Between Men '35
Branded a Coward '35
Courageous Avenger '35
Every Man's Law '35
Rustlers of Red Dog '35
Belle of the Nineties '34
Female '33
Fighting with Kit Carson '33
Coquette '29
The Single Standard '29
Annapolis '28
Our Dancing Daughters '28

Brown ✕cont.

A Woman of Affairs '28

Juanita Brown
Black Starlet '74
Caged Heat '74

Judy Brown
The Manhandlers '73
The Big Doll House '71

Julie Brown
Clueless '95
Fist of the North Star '95
Out There '95
National Lampoon's Attack of the 5 Ft. 2 Women '94
Nervous Ticks '93
The Opposite Sex and How to Live With Them '93
Raining Stones '93
Shakes the Clown '92
Spirit of '76 '91
Earth Girls Are Easy '89
Bloody Birthday '80

Lou Brown
Death Games '82
Alison's Birthday '79
The Irishman '78

Murray Brown
Vampyres '74
Dracula '73

Pamela Brown
Dracula '73
Wuthering Heights '70
Secret Ceremony '69
Cleopatra '63
Victoria Regina '61
Lust for Life '56
Alice in Wonderland '50
I Know Where I'm Going '45
One of Our Aircraft Is Missing '41

Paul Brown
Butterfly Kiss '94
Anne of Green Gables '85
Morons from Outer Space '85
Transmutations '85

Peter Brown
The Aurora Encounter '85
The Concrete Jungle '82
Act of Vengeance '74
Eagles Attack at Dawn '74
Memory of Us '74
Slashed Dreams '74
Chrome and Hot Leather '71
Hard Frame '70
Ride the Wild Surf '64
A Tiger Walks '64
Merrill's Marauders '62
Red Nightmare '62
Darby's Rangers '58
The Commies Are Coming, the Commies Are Coming '57

Phil Brown
Tropic of Cancer '70
Operation Cross Eagles '69
The Hidden Room '49
Without Reservations '46

Philip Brown
Wild Zone '89
Eye of the Needle '81
Special Olympics '78

Ralph Brown
Ivanhoe '97
Wayne's World 2 '93
Alien 3 '92
The Crying Game '92
Impromptu '90
Buster '88
Withnail and I '87

Reb Brown
Last Flight to Hell
Cage 2: The Arena of Death '94
The Firing Line '91
Street Hunter '90
The Cage '89
Mercenary Fighters '88
Space Mutiny '88
White Ghost '88
Strike Commando '87
Death of a Soldier '85

Howling 2: Your Sister Is a Werewolf '85
Uncommon Valor '83
Yor, the Hunter from the Future '83
Captain America '79
Captain America 2: Death Too Soon '79

Ritza Brown
The McGuffin '85
Ator the Fighting Eagle '83

Robert Brown
The Living Daylights '87
Pilgrim, Farewell '82
One Million Years B.C. '66
Tower of London '62
Shake Hands with the Devil '59

Roger Brown
Tall Tale: The Unbelievable Adventures of Pecos Bill '95
Don't Cry, It's Only Thunder '82
Paper Lion '68
Venus Against the Son of Hercules '62

Ron Brown
The Legend of Black Thunder Mountain '79
Charlie, the Lonesome Cougar '67

Sara Suzanne Brown
Killer Looks '94
Secret Games 2: The Escort '93
Test Tube Teens from the Year 2000 '93

Stephen Brown
Beyond Darkness '92
Metamorphosis '90

Thomas Wilson Brown
Skeletons '96
Diggstown '92
Honey, I Shrunk the Kids '89
Welcome Home '89

Tim Brown
Pacific Inferno '85
Code Name: Zebra '84
A Place Called Today '72

Timothy Brown
The Dynamite Brothers '74
Girls Are for Loving '73
Sweet Sugar '72

Tom Brown
The Choppers '61
Operation Haylift '50
Ringside '49
Buck Privates Come Home '47
Adventures of Smilin' Jack '43
The Payoff '43
In Old Chicago '37
Maytime '37
Navy Blue and Gold '37
I'd Give My Life '36
Anne of Green Gables '34

Vanessa Brown
Witch Who Came from the Sea '76
The Fighter '52
Three Husbands '50
The Ghost and Mrs. Muir '47

W. Earl Brown
Scream '96
Dead Air '94
Excessive Force '93

Wally Brown
Girl Rush '44
Zombies on Broadway '44

Woody Brown
Animal Instincts 2 '94
Dominion '94
Secret Games 3 '94
Alligator 2: The Mutation '90
The Rain Killer '90
The Accused '88

Charles A. Browne
Federal Agent '36
Tailspin Tommy '34

Coral Browne
Dreamchild '85
American Dreamer '84

An Englishman Abroad '83
Eleanor: First Lady of the World '82
Theatre of Blood '73
The Ruling Class '72
The Killing of Sister George '69
Auntie Mame '58
The Courtney Affair '47

Leslie Browne
Dancers '87
Nijinsky '80
The Turning Point '77

Lucille Browne
Cheyenne Rides Again '38
Texas Terror '35
Western Frontier '35
Brand of Hate '34
Law of the Wild '34
The Devil's Brother '33
Mystery Squadron '33

Roscoe Lee Browne
Dear God '96
Last Summer In the Hamptons '96
Forest Warrior '95
The Pompatus of Love '95
Naked in New York '93
The Mambo Kings '92
Moon 44 '90
For Us, the Living '88
Legal Eagles '86
Haunting of Harrington House '82
Nothing Personal '80
Unknown Powers '80
King '78
Twilight's Last Gleaming '77
Logan's Run '76
Superfly T.N.T. '73
The World's Greatest Athlete '73
The Cowboys '72
The Liberation of L.B. Jones '70
Black Like Me '64
The Connection '61

Suzanne Browne
The Bikini Car Wash Company 2 '92
The Bikini Car Wash Company '90

Ricou Browning
Flipper's New Adventure '64
The Creature Walks Among Us '56
Creature from the Black Lagoon '54

Brenda Bruce
Splitting Heirs '93
Antonia and Jane '91
December Bride '91
Back Home '90
The Tenth Man '88
That'll Be the Day '73
Nightmare '63
Peeping Tom '60

Cheryl Lynn Bruce
Daughters of the Dust '91
Victimless Crimes '90
Music Box '89

Colin Bruce
Chicago Joe & the Showgirl '90
Crusoe '89
Gotham '88

David Bruce
Jungle Hell '55
Pier 23 '51
Can't Help Singing '45
Lady on a Train '45
Salome, Where She Danced '45
Calling Dr. Death/Strange Confession '43
The Mad Ghoul '43
The Sea Wolf '41

Kate Bruce
Struggle '31
The Idol Dancer '20
Judith of Bethulia '14

Lenny Bruce
Dynamite Chicken '70
Dance Hall Racket '58

Nigel Bruce
Limelight '52
Julia Misbehaves '48

The Two Mrs. Carrolls '47
Dressed to Kill '46
Terror by Night '46
Terror by Night/Meeting at Midnight '46
The Corn Is Green '45
House of Fear '45
Pursuit to Algiers '45
Son of Lassie '45
The Woman in Green '45
The Pearl of Death '44
Scarlet Claw '44
Spider Woman '44
Lassie, Come Home '43
Sherlock Holmes Faces Death '43
Sherlock Holmes in Washington '43
Journey for Margaret '42
Roxie Hart '42
Sherlock Holmes and the Secret Weapon '42
Sherlock Holmes: The Voice of Terror '42
The Chocolate Soldier '41
Suspicion '41
The Blue Bird '40
Rebecca '40
Susan and God '40
The Adventures of Sherlock Holmes '39
The Hound of the Baskervilles '39
The Rains Came '39
The Last of Mrs. Cheyney '37
Thunder in the City '37
The Charge of the Light Brigade '36
The Trail of the Lonesome Pine '36
Becky Sharp '35
She '35
The Scarlet Pimpernel '34
Stand Up and Cheer '34
Treasure Island '34

Virginia Bruce
Strangers When We Meet '60
State Department File 649 '49
Action in Arabia '44
Pardon My Sarong '42
The Invisible Woman '40
Let Freedom Ring '39
Born to Dance '36
The Great Ziegfeld '36
Let 'Em Have It '35
Jane Eyre '34

Patrick Bruel
Sabrina '95
Secret Obsession '88
Bandits '86

Eddie Brugman
Broken Mirrors '85
Keetje Tippel '75

Beau Brummel
Three Bullets for a Long Gun '73
Village of the Giants '65

Bo Brundin
Headless Eyes '83
Shoot the Sun Down '81
Russian Roulette '75

Valeria Bruni-Tedeschi
Mon Homme '96
Nenette and Boni '96

Fernando Bruno
Time Out for Love '61
Two Nights with Cleopatra '54

Philip Bruns
The Opposite Sex and How to Live With Them '93
Dead Men Don't Die '91
Return of the Living Dead 2 '88
The Stunt Man '80

Eric Bruskotter
Major League 3: Back to the Minors '98
Starship Troopers '97
Major League 2 '94

Dora Bryan
Screamtime '83
Hands of the Ripper '71

The Great St. Trinian's Train Robbery '66
A Taste of Honey '61
Small Hotel '57
My Son, the Vampire '52
No Trace '50
The Fallen Idol '49

Jane Bryan
Each Dawn I Die '39
The Old Maid '39
The Sisters '38
Kid Galahad '37
Marked Woman '37

Zachery Ty Bryan
First Kid '96
Magic Island '95
Bigfoot: The Unforgettable Encounter '94

Joyce Bryant
East Side Kids '40
Across the Plains '39

Lee Bryant
Alien Nation: Dark Horizon '94
Half Slave, Half Free '85

Michael Bryant
Hamlet '96
Sakharov '84
Girly '70
Goodbye, Mr. Chips '69

Nana Bryant
The Private War of Major Benson '55
Harvey '50
Ladies of the Chorus '49
Eyes of Texas '48
Inner Sanctum '48
Big Town '47
The Possessed '47
Give Me a Sailor '38
Sinners in Paradise '38

Pamela Bryant
Tigershark '87
Lunch Wagon '81

Virginia Bryant
The Barbarians '87
Demons 2 '87

William Bryant
Mountain Family Robinson '79
Corvette Summer '78

Claudia Bryar
Psycho 2 '83
Green Eyes '76

Scott Bryce
Up Close and Personal '96
Stalking Laura '93

Andrew Bryniarski
Cyborg 3: The Recycler '95
The Program '93
Batman Returns '92

Yul Brynner
Death Rage '77
Futureworld '76
The Ultimate Warrior '75
Night Flight from Moscow '73
Westworld '73
Fuzz '72
Catlow '71
Light at the Edge of the World '71
Romance of a Horsethief '71
Battle of Neretva '69
The Madwoman of Chaillot '69
The Magic Christian '69
Villa Rides '67
Triple Cross '67
Cast a Giant Shadow '66
The Poppy Is Also a Flower '66
Return of the Seven '66
Morituri '65
Invitation to a Gunfighter '64
Taras Bulba '62
The Magnificent Seven '60
Solomon and Sheba '59
The Testament of Orpheus '59
The Brothers Karamazov '58
The Buccaneer '58
Anastasia '56
The King and I '56
The Ten Commandments '56
Port of New York '49

Burnette *cont.*

Ridin' on a Rainbow '41
South of the Border '39
Billy the Kid Returns '38
Hollywood Stadium Mystery '38
The Man from Music Mountain '38
Oh Susannah '38
Old Barn Dance '38
Prairie Moon '38
Rootin' Tootin' Rhythm '38
Western Double Feature 1 '38
Big Show '37
Boots & Saddles '37
Dick Tracy '37
Dick Tracy: The Original Serial, Vol. 1 '37
Dick Tracy: The Original Serial, Vol. 2 '37
Git Along Little Dogies '37
Round-Up Time in Texas '37
Springtime in the Rockies '37
Western Double Feature 4 '37
Western Double Feature 5: Rogers & Autry '37
Yodelin' Kid From Pine Ridge '37
Old Corral '36
Red River Valley '36
Ride, Ranger, Ride '36
The Adventures of Rex & Rinty '35
Harmony Lane '35
Melody Trail '35
The Phantom Empire '35
Dude Ranger '34
In Old Santa Fe '34
Mystery Mountain '34

Bob Burns
Waikiki Wedding '37
Rhythm on the Range '36

Carol Burns
Bad Blood '87
Dusty '85
Prisoner Cell Block H '80

Edmund Burns
Sea Devils '31
Sunny Side Up '28
Made for Love '26

Edward Burns
No Looking Back '98
Saving Private Ryan '98
She's the One '96
The Brothers McMullen '94

George Burns
Radioland Murders '94
18 Again! '88
Oh, God! You Devil '84
Two of a Kind '82
Oh, God! Book 2 '80
Going in Style '79
Sgt. Pepper's Lonely Hearts Club Band '78
Oh, God! '77
The Sunshine Boys '75
The Burns and Allen Show '50
Honolulu '39
College Swing '38
A Damsel in Distress '37
Here Comes Cookie '35
Love in Bloom '34
Six of a Kind '34
We're Not Dressing '34
International House '33

Jennifer Burns
Josh Kirby...Time Warrior: Chapter 5, Journey to the Magic Cavern '96
Josh Kirby...Time Warrior: Chapter 6, Last Battle for the Universe '96
Josh Kirby...Time Warrior: Chapter 1, Planet of the Dino-Knights '95
Josh Kirby...Time Warrior: Chapter 2, The Human Pets '95
Josh Kirby...Time Warrior: Chapter 3, Trapped on Toyworld '95

Josh Kirby...Time Warrior: Chapter 4, Eggs from 70 Million B.C. '95
Haunted Symphony '94
The Liar's Club '93

Jere Burns
Santa Fe '97
Greedy '94
The Gambler Returns: The Luck of the Draw '93
Wired '89

Marilyn Burns
Future Kill '85
Kiss Daddy Goodbye '81
Eaten Alive '76
Helter Skelter '76
The Texas Chainsaw Massacre '74

Marion Burns
Dawn Rider/Frontier Horizon '39
Dawn Rider '35
Paradise Canyon '35

Mark Burns
Bullseye! '90
House of the Living Dead '73
Death in Venice '71
The Virgin and the Gypsy '70
The Charge of the Light Brigade '68

Michael Burns
Santee '73
Thumb Tripping '72
That Cold Day in the Park '69

Robert Burns
Confessions of a Serial Killer '87
Terror in the Jungle '68

Robert Burns
Western Trails '38
Gun Law '33
When a Man Rides Alone '33
South of Santa Fe '32

Raymond Burr
Delirious '91
Showdown at Williams Creek '91
The Defense Never Rests '90
Perry Mason: The Case of the Lost Love '87
Godzilla 1985 '85
Perry Mason Returns '85
Airplane 2: The Sequel '82
Peter and Paul '81
The Curse of King Tut's Tomb '80
The Night the City Screamed '80
Out of the Blue '80
The Return '80
Love's Savage Fury '79
Centennial '78
Tomorrow Never Comes '77
Crime of Passion '57
Godzilla, King of the Monsters '56
Great Day in the Morning '56
A Man Alone '55
They Were So Young '55
Casanova's Big Night '54
Party Girls for Sale '54
Passion '54
Rear Window '54
Thunder Pass '54
FBI Girl '52
Horizons West '52
Meet Danny Wilson '52
Bride of the Gorilla '51
His Kind of Woman '51
A Place in the Sun '51
Borderline '50
Key to the City '50
Love Happy '50
Adventures of Don Juan '49
Black Magic '49
Pitfall '48
Raw Deal '48
Station West '48
Desperate '47

Robert Burr
Netherworld '90
The Possession of Joel Delaney '72

Jackie Burroughs
Careful '94

Tales from Avonlea, Vol. 1: The Journey Begins '90
Final Notice '89
John and the Missus '87
The Housekeeper '86
Anne of Green Gables '85
Undergrads '85
125 Rooms of Comfort '83

William S. Burroughs
Wax, or the Discovery of Television Among the Bees '93
Bloodhounds of Broadway '89
Drugstore Cowboy '89

Darren E. Burrows
Class of 1999 '90
Cry-Baby '90

Saffron Burrows
Lovelife '97
The Matchmaker '97
Hotel de Love '96
Circle of Friends '94

Ellen Burstyn
Deceiver '97
The Baby-Sitters Club '95
The Color of Evening '95
Follow the River '95
How to Make an American Quilt '95
Roommates '95
The Spitfire Grill '95
Getting Gotti '94
Getting Out '94
Primal Secrets '94
When a Man Loves a Woman '94
The Cemetery Club '93
Grand Isle '92
Dying Young '91
Hanna's War '88
Act of Vengeance '86
Something in Common '86
Into Thin Air '85
Twice in a Lifetime '85
The Ambassador '84
The People vs. Jean Harris '81
Silence of the North '81
Resurrection '80
A Dream of Passion '78
Same Time, Next Year '78
Providence '77
Alice Doesn't Live Here Anymore '74
Harry and Tonto '74
Thursday's Game '74
The Exorcist '73
The King of Marvin Gardens '72
The Last Picture Show '71
Alex in Wonderland '70
Tropic of Cancer '70

Benny Burt
Hawaiian Buckaroo '38
Sea Racketeers '37

Harry Burton
Devices and Desires '91
Fortunes of War '87

Jennifer Burton
Death and Desire '97
Watch Me '92
Truck Stop Women '74

Julian Burton
Masque of the Red Death '65
A Bucket of Blood '59

Kate Burton
Ellen Foster '97
August '95
Love Matters '93
Uncle Tom's Cabin '87
Big Trouble in Little China '86

LeVar Burton
Star Trek: First Contact '96
Yesterday's Target '96
Parallel Lives '94
Star Trek Generations '94
Star Trek the Next Generation, the Final Episode: All Good Things... '94
Firestorm: 72 Hours in Oakland '93
Roots: The Gift '88

Star Trek the Next Generation: Encounter at Farpoint '87
The Midnight Hour '86
The Supernaturals '86
And the Children Shall Lead '85
The Jesse Owens Story '84
Acorn People '82
Grambling's White Tiger '81
The Guyana Tragedy: The Story of Jim Jones '80
The Hunter '80
One in a Million: The Ron LeFlore Story '78
Billy: Portrait of a Street Kid '77
Roots '77

Norman Burton
Bloodsport '88
Bad Guys '86
Crimes of Passion '84
Mausoleum '83
Fade to Black '80
The Terminal Man '74
Save the Tiger '73
Diamonds Are Forever '71
Jud '71
Simon, King of the Witches '71
Attack of the Mayan Mummy '63
Fright '56

Richard Burton
Wagner: The Complete Epic '85
Wagner: The Movie '85
1984 '84
Absolution '81
Circle of Two '80
Lovespell '79
Breakthrough '78
The Medusa Touch '78
Wild Geese '78
Equus '77
The Exorcist 2: The Heretic '77
The Gathering Storm '74
The Klansman '74
Massacre in Rome '73
Under Milk Wood '73
Assassination of Trotsky '72
Bluebeard '72
Divorce His, Divorce Hers '72
Hammersmith Is Out '72
Raid on Rommel '71
Anne of the Thousand Days '69
Doctor Faustus '68
Where Eagles Dare '68
The Comedians '67
The Taming of the Shrew '67
Who's Afraid of Virginia Woolf? '66
The Sandpiper '65
The Spy Who Came in from the Cold '65
Becket '64
The Night of the Iguana '64
Cleopatra '63
The Tempest '63
The V.I.P.'s '63
The Longest Day '62
The Bramble Bush '60
Ice Palace '60
Look Back in Anger '58
Alexander the Great '55
The Desert Rats '53
The Robe '53
Green Grow the Rushes '51
The Last Days of Dolwyn '49

Robert Burton
Trilogy of Terror '75
A Reason to Live, a Reason to Die '73
The Slime People '63
Invasion of the Animal People '62
The Gallant Hours '60
Compulsion '59
Teenage Frankenstein '58
The Tall T '57
A Man Called Peter '55
Above and Beyond '53
All the Brothers Were Valiant '53
The Girl Who Had Everything '53

Tony Burton
Flipping '96
Mission of Justice '92
House Party 2: The Pajama Jam '91
Armed and Dangerous '86

Oceans of Fire '86
The Shining '80
Blackjack '78
Assault on Precinct 13 '76

Wendell Burton
East of Eden '80
Fortune and Men's Eyes '71
The Sterile Cuckoo '69

Sean Bury
Paul and Michelle '74
Friends '71
If... '69

Steve Buscemi
Armageddon '98
The Big Lebowski '97
Con Air '97
The Wedding Singer '97
Escape from L.A. '96
Fargo '96
The Search for One-Eyed Jimmy '96
Tree's Lounge '96
Desperado '95
Kansas City '95
Things to Do In Denver When You're Dead '95
Airheads '94
Floundering '94
Living in Oblivion '94
Pulp Fiction '94
Somebody to Love '94
Ed and His Dead Mother '93
The Hudsucker Proxy '93
The Last Outlaw '93
Twenty Bucks '93
Crisscross '92
In the Soup '92
Reservoir Dogs '92
Trusting Beatrice '92
Barton Fink '91
Billy Bathgate '91
King of New York '90
Tales from the Darkside: The Movie '90
Mystery Train '89
New York Stories '89
Heart '87
Parting Glances '86

Mae Busch
The Mad Monster '42
Ziegfeld Girl '41
Laurel & Hardy Comedy Classics, Vol. 7 '30s
Marie Antoinette '38
Bohemian Girl '36
Laurel & Hardy Comedy Classics, Vol. 6 '35
Laurel & Hardy Comedy Classics, Vol. 3 '34
Sucker Money '34
Laurel & Hardy Comedy Classics, Vol. 1 '33
Sons of the Desert '33
Doctor X '32
Without Honors '32
Defenders of the Law '31
The Unholy Three '25
Foolish Wives '22

Gary Busey
Fear and Loathing in Las Vegas '98
Diary of a Serial Killer '97
The Real Thing '97
Rough Riders '97
Steel Sharks '97
Black Sheep '96
Lethal Tender '96
Lost Highway '96
The Rage '96
Carried Away '95
Man with a Gun '95
Breaking Point '94
Drop Zone '94
Surviving the Game '94
Warriors '94
Fallen Angels 1 '93
The Firm '93
Rookie of the Year '93
Canvas: The Fine Art of Crime '92
Chrome Soldiers '92
South Beach '92
Under Siege '92

The World Gone Mad '33
Night After Night '32
They Call It Sin '32
Blonde Crazy '31
The Blot '21
Too Wise Wives '21

Alice Calhoun
Tentacles of the North '26
The Man on the Box '25

Monica Calhoun
The Players Club '98
Bagdad Cafe '88

Rory Calhoun
Pure Country '92
Roller Blade Warriors: Taken By
    Force '90
Bad Jim '90
Hell Comes to Frogtown '88
Avenging Angel '85
Angel '84
Mission to Glory '80
Motel Hell '80
Flatbed Annie and Sweetiepie:
    Lady Truckers '79
The Rebels '79
Midnight Auto Supply '78
Operation Cross Eagles '69
Dayton's Devils '68
Emerald of Artama '67
Apache Uprising '66
Finger on the Trigger '65
Hard Drivin' '60
Treasure of Pancho Villa '55
A Bullet Is Waiting '54
River of No Return '54
I'd Climb the Highest Mountain
    '51
Ticket to Tomahawk '50
Adventure Island '47
The Red House '47

Joseph Cali
The Lonely Lady '83
The Competition '80

Brandon Call
For the Boys '91
The Adventures of Ford Fairlane
    '90
Blind Fury '90

R.D. Call
Last Man Standing '96
Waterworld '95
Other People's Money '91
Stephen King's Golden Years
    '91
Young Guns 2 '90

James Callahan
Blood for Blood '95
Prison for Children '93
Outlaw Blues '77
Lady Sings the Blues '72
Tropic of Cancer '70

K. Callan
Saved by the Light '97
Frankie and Johnny '91
The Unborn '91
A Touch of Class '73

Michael Callan
Leprechaun 3 '95
Freeway '88
Donner Pass: The Road to
    Survival '84
Double Exposure '82
The Cat and the Canary '79
Lepke '75
Photographer '75
Frasier the Sensuous Lion '73
Cat Ballou '65
Bon Voyage! '62
The Interns '62
Gidget Goes Hawaiian '61
Mysterious Island '61

Rebecca Callard
The Return of the Borrowers '96
The Borrowers '93

Charlie Callas
Vampire Vixens from Venus '94
Big Mouth '67

Joseph Calleia
The Light in the Forest '58
Touch of Evil '58
The Littlest Outlaw '54
The Caddy '53

Branded '50
The Noose Hangs High '48
Deadline at Dawn '46
Gilda '46
The Glass Key '42
The Jungle Book '42
The Monster and the Girl '41
Sundown '41
My Little Chickadee '40
Five Came Back '39
Golden Boy '39
Algiers '38
Marie Antoinette '38
After the Thin Man '36
Riff Raff '35

Dayton Callie
Executive Target '97
The Last Days of Frankie the Fly
    '96

Simon Callow
The Woman in White '97
Ace Ventura: When Nature Calls
    '95
Four Weddings and a Funeral
    '94
Street Fighter '94
The Crucifer of Blood '91
Mr. & Mrs. Bridge '90
The Good Father '87
Maurice '87
A Room with a View '86
Amadeus '84

Cab Calloway
The Blues Brothers '80
The Littlest Angel '69
The Cincinnati Kid '65
Sensations of 1945 '44
Stormy Weather '43
Manhattan Merry-Go-Round '37
Hi-De-Ho '35
International House '33

Kirk Calloway
Cinderella Liberty '73
Summertree '71

Vanessa Bell
Calloway
Daylight '96
America's Dream '95
Crimson Tide '95
What's Love Got to Do with It?
    '93

Michael Caloz
Little Men '98
Screamers '96

Donald Calthrop
The Phantom Light '35
Scrooge '35
No. 17 '32
Blackmail '29

Bill Calvert
Body Waves '92
C.H.U.D. 2: Bud the Chud '89
Terror Squad '87

Phyllis Calvert
The Woman He Loved '88
Indiscreet '58
The Young and the Guilty '58
Mandy '53
Man of Evil '48
The Magic Bow '47
Men of Two Worlds '46
The Man in Grey '45
Kipps '41

Corinne Calvet
Dr. Heckyl and Mr. Hype '80
Too Hot to Handle '76
Apache Uprising '66
Far Country '55
What Price Glory? '52

Henry Calvin
The Sign of Zorro '60
Toby Tyler '59

John Calvin
Dragonworld '94
The Magic Bubble '93
Primary Target '89
Ghostwarrior '86
California Dreaming '79

Armando Calvo
Satanik '69
The Witch's Mirror '60

Pablito Calvo
The Man Who Wagged His Tail
    '57
The Miracle of Marcelino '55

Godfrey Cambridge
Friday Foster '75
Whiffs '75
Son of Blob '72
Cotton Comes to Harlem '70
Watermelon Man '70
The President's Analyst '67
Gone Are the Days '63
Purlie Victorious '63

Juan Jose Camero
Veronico Cruz '87
El Muerto '75
Far Away and Long Ago '74

Candace Cameron
Frankenstein Sings...The Movie
    '95
Sharon's Secret '95

Dean Cameron
Ski School 2 '94
Sleep with Me '94
Miracle Beach '92
Ski School '91
Rockula '90
Bad Dreams '88
Summer School '87

Jane Cameron
The Unborn '91
Pair of Aces '90

Kirk Cameron
Listen to Me '89
Like Father, Like Son '87
The Best of Times '86

Rod Cameron
Midnight Auto Supply '78
Psychic Killer '75
Evel Knievel '72
The Last Movie '71
The Electronic Monster '57
Manhunt in the African Jungle
    '54
Ride the Man Down '53
Jungle '52
Salome, Where She Danced '45
G-Men vs. the Black Dragon '43
Wake Island '42
The Monster and the Girl '41

Jesse Cameron-
Glickenhaus
Timemaster '95
Slaughter of the Innocents '93

Terry Camillieri
Bill & Ted's Excellent Adventure
    '89
The Cars That Ate Paris '74

Colleen Camp
She Devils in Chains
Speed 2: Cruise Control '97
Die Hard: With a Vengeance '95
Greedy '94
The Magic Bubble '93
Sliver '93
Wayne's World '92
Backfield in Motion '91
Wicked Stepmother '89
Track 29 '88
Illegally Yours '87
Police Academy 4: Citizens on
    Patrol '87
Walk Like a Man '87
Screwball Academy '86
Clue '85
D.A.R.Y.L. '85
Doin' Time '85
Police Academy 2: Their First
    Assignment '85
Rosebud Beach Hotel '85
Joy of Sex '84
Smokey and the Bandit, Part 3
    '83
Valley Girl '83
The Seduction '82
They All Laughed '81
Cloud Dancer '80
Deadly Games '80
Apocalypse Now '79
Game of Death '79
Lady of the House '78
Midnight Auto Supply '78

Seducers '77
Smile '75
The Last Porno Flick '74
The Swinging Cheerleaders '74
Cat in the Cage '68

Hamilton Camp
Almost Heroes '97
Attack of the 50 Ft. Woman '93
Arena '89
Casey at the Bat '85
Lots of Luck '85
Rosebud Beach Hotel '85
Meatballs 2 '84
Under Fire '83
Eating Raoul '82

Frank Campanella
Blood Red '88
Chesty Anderson USN '76

Joseph Campanella
The Glass Cage '96
Magic Kid '92
No Retreat, No Surrender 3:
    Blood Brothers '91
Original Intent '91
Body Chemistry '90
Club Fed '90
Last Call '90
Down the Drain '89
Steele Justice '87
Comic Book Kids '82
Plutonium Incident '82
Hangar 18 '80
Meteor '79
Return to Fantasy Island '77
Sky Hei$t '75
Terror on the 40th Floor '74
Ben '72
Murder Once Removed '71
The President's Plane Is Missing
    '71
The Fugitive: The Final Episode
    '67
The St. Valentine's Day
    Massacre '67

Beatrice Campbell
The Master of Ballantrae '53
Last Holiday '50

Bill Campbell
Rudyard Kipling's the Second
    Jungle Book: Mowgli and
    Baloo '97
The Brylcreem Boys '96
Lover's Knot '96
Out There '95
Under the Hula Moon '95
Armistead Maupin's Tales of the
    City '93
The Night We Never Met '93
Bram Stoker's Dracula '92
The Rocketeer '91
Crime Story: The Complete
    Saga '86

Bruce Campbell
McHale's Navy '97
Escape from L.A. '96
Tornado! '96
The Hudsucker Proxy '93
Army of Darkness '92
Lunatics: A Love Story '92
Mindwarp '91
Sundown '91
Waxwork 2: Lost in Time '91
Maniac Cop 2 '90
Moontrap '89
Maniac Cop '88
Evil Dead 2: Dead by Dawn '87
Crimewave '85
Evil Dead '83
Going Back '83

Cheryl Campbell
The Mill on the Floss '97
The Shooting Party '85
Greystoke: The Legend of
    Tarzan, Lord of the Apes '84
Chariots of Fire '81
McVicar '80
Lillie '79

Christian Campbell
Born to Run '93
City Boy '93

David James
Campbell
Killer Workout '86
Killzone '85

Eric Campbell
Triple Trouble/Easy Street '18
Charlie Chaplin: The Early
    Years, Vol. 1 '17
Charlie Chaplin: The Early
    Years, Vol. 2 '17
Count/Adventurer '17
The Cure '17
Charlie Chaplin: The Early
    Years, Vol. 3 '16
Charlie Chaplin: The Early
    Years, Vol. 4 '16
The Fireman '16
The Vagabond '16
The Floorwalker/By the Sea '15

Glen Campbell
Uphill All the Way '85
True Grit '69

Judy Campbell
Dust to Dust '85
Cry of the Penguins '71
Bonnie Prince Charlie '48
The World Owes Me a Living '47
Convoy '40

Julia Campbell
Diary of a Serial Killer '97
Romy and Michele's High
    School Reunion '97
Lone Justice '93
Livin' Large '91
Opportunity Knocks '90

Kate Campbell
Monte Carlo Nights '34
Ghost Valley '32

Ken Campbell
Down Periscope '96
Smart Money '88
Letter to Brezhnev '86
Joshua Then and Now '85

Louise Campbell
Bulldog Drummond's Peril '38
Bulldog Drummond's Revenge/
    Bulldog Drummond's Peril '38
Bulldog Drummond Comes Back
    '37
Bulldog Drummond's Revenge
    '37

Naomi Campbell
Girl 6 '96
Invasion of Privacy '96
Miami Rhapsody '95
Cool As Ice '91

Nell Campbell
Great Expectations '97
Lisztomania '75

Neve Campbell
54 '98
Wild Things '98
Scream 2 '97
The Canterville Ghost '96
The Craft '96
Scream '96
Northern Passage '95
The Dark '94

Nicholas Campbell
The Boys Club '96
Guitarman '95
No Contest '94
Naked Lunch '91
The Big Slice '90
The Victory '88
Rampage '87
Going Home '86
Certain Fury '85
Knights of the City '85
July Group '70s
Fast Company '78

Peggy Campbell
Big Calibre '35
Stone of Silver Creek '35
When a Man Sees Red '34

Rob Campbell
Hostile Waters '97
The Crucible '96
Lone Justice 2 '93
Unforgiven '92

Dantine cont.

Mrs. Miniver '42
The Navy Comes Through '42
To Be or Not to Be '42

Ray Danton
Apache Blood '75
The Centerfold Girls '74
Secret Agent Super Dragon '66
Conqueror & the Empress '64
The Longest Day '62
The Rise and Fall of Legs
   Diamond '60
A Majority of One '56
I'll Cry Tomorrow '55

Tony Danza
The Garbage-Picking, Field
   Goal-Kicking Philadelphia
   Phenomenon '98
Love to Kill '97
North Shore Fish '97
Twelve Angry Men '97
Illtown '96
Angels in the Outfield '94
She's Out of Control '89
Truth or Die '86
Single Bars, Single Women '84
Going Ape! '81

Maia Danzinger
The Ice Storm '97
Last Exit to Brooklyn '90
Dr. Heckyl and Mr. Hype '80

Ho Chung Dao
Bruce Li in New Guinea '80
Bruce Li the Invincible '80
Invincible '80

Sun Dao-Lin
The Go-Masters '82
Crows and Sparrows '49

**Ingeborga
Dapkounaite**
Seven Years in Tibet '97
Jack Higgins' On Dangerous
   Ground '95
Burnt by the Sun '94

Patti D'Arbanville
The Fan '96
Blind Spot '93
Deadly Conspiracy '91
Snow Kill '90
Wired '89
Call Me '88
Fresh Horses '88
The Boys Next Door '85
Real Genius '85
Modern Problems '81
The Fifth Floor '80
Hog Wild '80
Time After Time '79
Big Wednesday '78
Bilitis '77
Flesh '68

Patrika Darbo
Fast Money '96
Leaving Normal '92
Daddy's Dyin'...Who's Got the
   Will? '90

Kim Darby
Halloween 6: The Curse of
   Michael Myers '95
Teen Wolf Too '87
Better Off Dead '85
Embassy '85
The Capture of Grizzly Adams
   '82
Enola Gay: The Men, the
   Mission, the Atomic Bomb '80
Flatbed Annie and Sweetiepie:
   Lady Truckers '79
The One and Only '78
Rich Man, Poor Man '76
Don't Be Afraid of the Dark '73
The Streets of San Francisco '72
The Grissom Gang '71
The People '71
The Strawberry Statement '70
Generation '69
True Grit '69

Mireille Darc
Intruder '77

Icy Breasts '75
Return of the Tall Blond Man
   With One Black Shoe '74
The Tall Blond Man with One
   Black Shoe '72
The Peking Blond '68
Weekend '67

Denise Darcel
Vera Cruz '53
Westward the Women '51
Thunder in the Pines '49

Alexander D'Arcy
Dead Pigeon on Beethoven
   Street '72
Blood of Dracula's Castle '69
Fanny Hill: Memoirs of a Woman
   of Pleasure '64
Horrors of Spider Island '59
Soldier of Fortune '55
The Awful Truth '37
Prisoner of Zenda '37

Jake D'Arcy
Gregory's Girl '80
A Sense of Freedom '78

Roy D'Arcy
Legion of Missing Men '37
Revolt of the Zombies '36

Sheila Darcy
Tumbledown Ranch in Arizona
   '41
Irish Luck '39
Zorro's Fighting Legion '39

Severn Darden
Once Upon a Midnight Scary '90
Back to School '86
Real Genius '85
Saturday the 14th '81
Wanda Nevada '79
The Disappearance of Aimee '76
Jackson County Jail '76
Battle for the Planet of the Apes
   '73
The Day of the Dolphin '73
The Legend of Hillbilly John '73
Conquest of the Planet of the
   Apes '72
Playmates '72
Hired Hand '71
Vanishing Point '71
Werewolves on Wheels '71
The President's Analyst '67
Dead Heat on a Merry-Go-
   Round '66

Florence Darel
A la Mode '94
The Stolen Children '92
A Tale of Springtime '92

Bobby Darin
Run, Stranger, Run '73
The Happy Ending '69
Captain Newman, M.D. '63
Hell Is for Heroes '62
Pressure Point '62
State Fair '62
Come September '61

Johnny Dark
Wishful Thinking '96
Up Your Alley '89
Rip-Off '77

Joan Darling
Sunnyside '79
The Two Worlds of Jenny Logan
   '79

Linda Darlow
The Amy Fisher Story '93
Immediate Family '89

Gerard Darmon
Obsession: A Taste for Fear '89
Betty Blue '86
Diva '82

Linda Darnell
Dakota Incident '56
Second Chance '53
Blackbeard the Pirate '52
Island of Desire '52
No Way Out '50
A Letter to Three Wives '49
Unfaithfully Yours '48
Forever Amber '47
Anna and the King of Siam '46
My Darling Clementine '46

Buffalo Bill '44
City Without Men '43
The Loves of Edgar Allen Poe
   '42
Blood and Sand '41
Brigham Young: Frontiersman
   '40
The Mark of Zorro '40

Steve Darrell
The Adventures of Frank and
   Jesse James '48
Lightning Raiders '45

James Darren
Boss' Son '78
Venus in Furs '70
Gidget Goes to Rome '63
Diamond Head '62
Gidget Goes Hawaiian '61
The Guns of Navarone '61
All the Young Men '60
The Gene Krupa Story '59
Gidget '59
Gunman's Walk '58

Danielle Darrieux
A Chef in Love '96
Scene of the Crime '87
L'Anne Sainte '78
Le Cavaleur '78
Murder at 45 R.P.M. '65
Bluebeard '63
The Red and the Black '57
Alexander the Great '55
Lady Chatterley's Lover '55
The Earrings of Madame De...
   '54
Five Fingers '52
Le Plaisir '52
La Ronde '51
Rich, Young and Pretty '51
Ruyblas '38
The Rage of Paris '38
Mayerling '36
Mauvaise Graine '33

Frankie Darro
Westward the Women '51
Riding High '50
Let's Go Collegiate '41
The Gang's All Here '40
Up in the Air '40
Boy's Reformatory '39
Irish Luck '39
Tough Kid '39
Anything for a Thrill '37
Devil Diamond '37
Tough to Handle '37
Black Gold '36
The Phantom Empire '35
Valley of Wanted Men '35
Broadway Bill '34
Burn 'Em Up Barnes '34
Wolf Dog '33
Devil Horse '32
Lightning Warrior '31
Vanishing Legion '31

**Jean-Pierre
Darroussin**
Marius and Jeannette '97
Un Air de Famille '96

Henry Darrow
The Last of the Finest '90
L.A. Bounty '89
In Dangerous Company '88
Death Blow '87
Computer Wizard '77
Where's Willie? '77

John Darrow
Monte Carlo Nights '34
The Lady Refuses '31
Ten Nights in a Bar-Room '31
Hell's Angels '30

Oliver Darrow
Bad Girls from Mars '90
Spirits '90
The Channeler '89

Paul Darrow
Guardian of the Abyss '82
Blake's Seven '78

Tony Darrow
Me and the Mob '94
Goodfellas '90

Lili Darvas
Love '71

24 Hours in a Woman's Life '61
Meet Me in Las Vegas '56

Bella Darvi
The Racers '55
The Egyptian '54

Jane Darwell
Last Hurrah '58
Girls in Prison '56
The Bigamist '53
We're Not Married '52
The Lemon Drop Kid '51
Redwood Forest Trail '50
Three Husbands '50
Wagon Master '50
Three Godfathers '48
The Red Stallion '47
I Live in Grosvenor Square '46
The Great Gildersleeve '43
The Ox-Bow Incident '43
Tender Comrade '43
All Through the Night '42
The Loves of Edgar Allen Poe
   '42
The Devil & Daniel Webster '41
Brigham Young: Frontiersman
   '40
The Grapes of Wrath '40
Gone with the Wind '39
Jesse James '39
The Rains Came '39
Little Miss Broadway '38
Captain January '36
Craig's Wife '36
The Poor Little Rich Girl '36
Curly Top '35
One Night of Love '34
Finishing School '33

Stacey Dash
Cold Around the Heart '97
Hoodlum '96
Clueless '95
Illegal in Blue '95
Black Water '94
Renaissance Man '94
Mo' Money '92
Moving '88

Jules Dassin
Never on Sunday '60
Rififi '54

Jean Daste
The Green Room '78
Grand Illusion '37
The Crime of Monsieur Lange
   '36
L'Atalante '34
Zero for Conduct '33
Boudu Saved from Drowning '32

Alex Datcher
The Expert '95
Body Bags '93
Passenger 57 '92
Rage and Honor '92

Kristin Datillo
Child of Darkness, Child of Light
   '91
Pyrates '91
Mirror, Mirror '90

James Daughton
Girlfriend from Hell '89
Blind Date '84
Swim Team '79
Malibu Beach '78

Claude Dauphin
Les Miserables '78
Madame Rosa '77
Rosebud '75
The Madwoman of Chaillot '69
Two for the Road '67
Is Paris Burning? '66
Lady L '65
Tiara Tahiti '62
April In Paris '52
Casque d'Or '52
Le Plaisir '52

Elyssa Davalos
A House in the Hills '93
Jericho Fever '93
Wild & Wooly '78

Richard Davalos
Something Wicked This Way
   Comes '83
Blood Legacy '73

Cool Hand Luke '67
Sea Chase '55
East of Eden '54

Harry Davenport
December 7th: The Movie '91
Riding High '50
That Forsyte Woman '50
Tell It to the Judge '49
For the Love of Mary '48
Three Daring Daughters '48
The Bachelor and the Bobby-
   Soxer '47
The Farmer's Daughter '47
Courage of Lassie '46
The Enchanted Forest '45
Jack London '44
Meet Me in St. Louis '44
The Thin Man Goes Home '44
The Ox-Bow Incident '43
Son of Fury '42
Kings Row '41
That Uncertain Feeling '41
All This and Heaven Too '40
Foreign Correspondent '40
Lucky Partners '40
Gone with the Wind '39
The Hunchback of Notre Dame
   '39
The Story of Alexander Graham
   Bell '39
The Cowboy and the Lady '38
Marie Antoinette '38
You Can't Take It with You '38
Fit for a King '37

Mary Davenport
Home Movies '79
Sisters '73

Nigel Davenport
Death by Prescription '80s
Upper Crust '88
Without a Clue '88
Mountbatten: The Last Viceroy
   '86
A Christmas Carol '84
Greystoke: The Legend of
   Tarzan, Lord of the Apes '84
Chariots of Fire '81
Nighthawks '81
Cry of the Innocent '80
The Ordeal of Dr. Mudd '80
Soul Patrol '80
Zulu Dawn '79
The Island of Dr. Moreau '77
Phase 4 '74
Picture of Dorian Gray '74
Dracula '73
Living Free '72
The Last Valley '71
Mary, Queen of Scots '71
The Virgin Soldiers '69
Sebastian '68
A Man for All Seasons '66
Ladies Who Do '63
Peeping Tom '60

Robert Davi
An Occasional Hell '96
Body Count '95
The Dangerous '95
The Dogfighters '95
Showgirls '95
Blind Justice '94
Cops and Robbersons '94
No Contest '94
Maniac Cop 3: Badge of Silence
   '93
Mardi Gras for the Devil '93
The November Men '93
Quick '93
Son of the Pink Panther '93
Center of the Web '92
Christopher Columbus: The
   Discovery '92
Wild Orchid 2: Two Shades of
   Blue '92
Illicit Behavior '91
The Taking of Beverly Hills '91
White Hot: The Mysterious
   Murder of Thelma Todd '91
Amazon '90
Legal Tender '90
Maniac Cop 2 '90
Peacemaker '90
Predator 2 '90
License to Kill '89
Die Hard '88

Woo '97
Escape from L.A. '96
Mars Attacks! '96
Original Gangstas '00
Serial Killer '95
Bill & Ted's Bogus Journey '91
Class of 1999 '90
The Package '89
Above the Law '88
On the Edge '86
Badge of the Assassin '85
Stand Alone '85
The Vindicator '85
Something Wicked This Way
  Comes '83
Tough Enough '83
Fort Apache, the Bronx '81
Greased Lightning '77
Drum '76
Bucktown '75
Friday Foster '75
Sheba, Baby '75
Foxy Brown '74
Coffy '73
Naked Warriors '73
Scream Blacula Scream '73
The Big Bird Cage '72
Twilight People '72
The Big Doll House '71

Roosevelt Grier
Sophisticated Gents '81
The Seekers '79
The Glove '78
The Big Push '75
The Treasure of Jamaica Reef
  '74

Jonathan Gries
Casualties '97
Kill Me Again '89
Pucker Up and Bark Like a Dog
  '89
Fright Night 2 '88
Real Genius '85
Joy Sticks '83
Swap Meet '79

Joe Grifasi
One Fine Day '96
Sunday '96
Two Bits '96
Money Train '95
Heavy '94
Benny & Joon '93
Household Saints '93
City of Hope '91
The Feud '90
Presumed Innocent '90
Chances Are '89
Perfect Witness '89
Ironweed '87
Matewan '87
F/X '86
Bad Medicine '85
Still of the Night '82
Gentleman Bandit '81
On the Yard '79

Simone Griffeth
The Patriot '86
Hot Target '85
Delusion '84
Death Race 2000 '75
Sixteen '72

Ethel Griffies
The Birds '63
The Mystery of Edwin Drood '35

Josephine Griffin
The Spanish Gardener '57
Postmark for Danger '56
The Man Who Never Was '55

Lorie Griffin
Aloha Summer '88
Cheerleader Camp '88

Rhonda Griffin
The Creeps '97
Hideous '97

Robert Griffin
Monster from Green Hell '58
Crime of Passion '57
I Was a Teenage Werewolf '57

Tony Griffin
Robin Hood: Men in Tights '93
Evil Laugh '86

Andy Griffith
Spy Hard '96
Return to Mayberry '85
Hustler's Rhapsody '85
Fatal Vision '84
Murder in Coweta County '83
Murder in Texas '81
From Here to Eternity '79
Centennial '78
Hearts of the West '75
Savages '75
Pray for the Wildcats '74
Andy Griffith Show '60
No Time for Sergeants '58
A Face in the Crowd '57

Anthony Griffith
Panther '95
Tales from the Hood '95

Corine Griffith
Dracula/Garden of Eden '28
The Garden of Eden '28

Eva Griffith
Ride a Wild Pony '75
The Turn of the Screw '74

Gordon Griffith
Outlaws of the Range '36
Little Annie Rooney '25

Hugh Griffith
The Big Scam '79
Legend of the Werewolf '75
The Passover Plot '75
Craze '74
Luther '73
Diary of Forbidden Dreams '73
The Final Programme '73
Doctor Phibes Rises Again '72
The Abominable Dr. Phibes '71
The Canterbury Tales '71
Who Slew Auntie Roo? '71
Cry of the Banshee '70
Start the Revolution Without Me
  '70
Wuthering Heights '70
The Fixer '68
Oliver! '68
Oh Dad, Poor Dad (Momma's
  Hung You in the Closet & I'm
  Feeling So Sad) '67
How to Steal a Million '66
Tom Jones '63
The Counterfeit Traitor '62
Mutiny on the Bounty '62
Exodus '60
Ben-Hur '59
Lucky Jim '58
The Sleeping Tiger '54
Kind Hearts and Coronets '49
The Last Days of Dolwyn '49

James Griffith
The Legend of Sleepy Hollow
  '79
The Amazing Transparent Man
  '60
Bullwhip '58
Tribute to a Bad Man '56

Kenneth Griffith
The Englishman Who Went Up a
  Hill But Came Down a
  Mountain '95
Four Weddings and a Funeral
  '94
The Final Option '82
Night of the Laughing Dead '75
Revenge '71
The Assassination Bureau '69
Koroshi '67
The Frightened City '61
Circus of Horrors '60
Tiger Bay '59
Lucky Jim '58
A Night to Remember '58

Melanie Griffith
Two Much '96
Buffalo Girls '95
Mulholland Falls '95
Now and Then '95
Milk Money '94
Nobody's Fool '94
Born Yesterday '93
Shining Through '92
A Stranger Among Us '92
Paradise '91
The Bonfire of the Vanities '90

In the Spirit '90
Pacific Heights '90
Women & Men: Stories of
  Seduction '90
Cherry 2000 '88
The Milagro Beanfield War '88
Stormy Monday '88
Working Girl '88
Something Wild '86
Fear City '85
Body Double '84
She's in the Army Now '81
Underground Aces '80
Steel Cowboy '78
Joyride '77
One on One '77
The Drowning Pool '75
Night Moves '75
Smile '75
Harrad Experiment '73

Raymond Griffith
All Quiet on the Western Front
  '30
Hands Up '26
The Night Club '25
Paths to Paradise '25
White Tiger '23

Thomas Ian Griffith
John Carpenter's Vampires '97
Kull the Conqueror '97
Behind Enemy Lines '96
Hollow Point '95
Beyond Forgiveness '94
Crackerjack '94
Excessive Force '93
Ulterior Motives '92
The Karate Kid: Part 3 '89

Tom Griffith
Hawk and Castile
Night Beast '83
The Alien Factor '78

Tracy Griffith
Skeeter '93
All Tied Up '92
The Finest Hour '91
Fast Food '89
The First Power '89
Sleepaway Camp 3: Teenage
  Wasteland '89
The Good Mother '88

Linda Griffiths
Reno and the Doc '84
Lianna '83
Overdrawn at the Memory Bank
  '83

Rachel Griffiths
My Best Friend's Wedding '97
Jude '96
Children of the Revolution '95
Cosi '95
Muriel's Wedding '94

Richard Griffiths
Guarding Tess '94
Blame It on the Bellboy '92
Naked Gun 2 1/2: The Smell of
  Fear '91
Withnail and I '87
Shanghai Surprise '86
Whoops Apocalypse '83

Jeff Griggs
Breaking Point '94
Eden 5 '93
Eden 3 '93
Eden 4 '93
Eden '92

Johanna Grika
Vice Academy 3 '91
Visitants '87

Frank Grimes
Catherine Cookson's The
  Wingless Bird '97
The Dive '89
Crystalstone '88

Gary Grimes
Cahill: United States Marshal '73
Class of '44 '73
Culpepper Cattle Co. '72
Summer of '42 '71

Scott Grimes
Frogs! '90s
Night Life '90
Frog '89

Critters 2: The Main Course '88
Critters '86
It Came Upon a Midnight Clear
  '84

Tammy Grimes
High Art '98
A Modern Affair '94
Backstreet Justice '93
Mr. North '88
America '86
No Big Deal '83
The Runner Stumbles '79

Herbert Grimwood
Romola '25
When the Clouds Roll By '19

Anouk Grinberg
Mon Homme '96
A Self-Made Hero '95

Nikolai Grinko
Stalker '79
Andrei Rublev '66

Stephen Grives
Flambards
Horror Planet '80

George Grizzard
Scarlett '94
Iran: Days of Crisis '91
Caroline? '90
False Witness '89
The Deliberate Stranger '86
Embassy '85
Bachelor Party '84
Oldest Living Graduate '82
Wrong Is Right '82
Attica '80
Seems Like Old Times '80
Comes a Horseman '78
The Stranger Within '74
Pueblo Affair '73
Advise and Consent '62
From the Terrace '60

Larry Groce
Paradise Park '90s
Heroes of the Heart '94

Charles Grodin
My Summer Story '94
Beethoven's 2nd '93
Dave '93
Heart and Souls '93
So I Married an Axe Murderer
  '93
Beethoven '92
Clifford '92
Taking Care of Business '90
Midnight Run '88
You Can't Hurry Love '88
The Couch Trip '87
Ishtar '87
Grown Ups '86
Last Resort '86
Movers and Shakers '85
The Lonely Guy '84
The Woman in Red '84
The Great Muppet Caper '81
The Incredible Shrinking Woman
  '81
It's My Turn '80
Seems Like Old Times '80
Real Life '79
Sunburn '79
The Grass Is Always Greener
  Over the Septic Tank '78
Heaven Can Wait '78
Just Me & You '78
King Kong '76
The Meanest Men in the West
  '76
11 Harrowhouse '74
The Heartbreak Kid '72
Catch-22 '70
Rosemary's Baby '68
Sex and the College Girl '64

Kathryn Grody
Hombres Armados '97
The Lemon Sisters '90
Quick Change '90
Parents '89

David Groh
Last Exit to Earth '96
White Cargo '96
Illegal in Blue '95
Broken Vows '87

Hot Shot '86
Zertigo Diamond Caper '82
A Hero Ain't Nothin' But a
  Sandwich '78

Ake Gronberg
Sawdust & Tinsel '53
Monika '52

Herbert Gronemeyer
Spring Symphony '86
Das Boot '81

Sam Groom
Deadly Eyes '82
Deadly Games '80
Run for the Roses '78
Beyond the Bermuda Triangle
  '75
Betrayal '74
The Baby Maker '70

Arye Gross
Mother Night '96
Hexed '93
The Opposite Sex and How to
  Live With Them '93
Boris and Natasha: The Movie
  '92
A Midnight Clear '92
Shaking the Tree '92
For the Boys '91
Coupe de Ville '90
A Matter of Degrees '90
The Experts '89
Tequila Sunrise '88
The Couch Trip '87
House 2: The Second Story '87
Soul Man '86

Edan Gross
Best of the Best 2 '93
And You Thought Your Parents
  Were Weird! '91

Mary Gross
The Santa Clause '94
There Goes the Neighborhood
  '92
Best of Eddie Murphy '89
Troop Beverly Hills '89
Big Business '88
Casual Sex? '88
Feds '88
Baby Boom '87
The Couch Trip '87
Club Paradise '86

Michael Gross
Snowbound '97
Kounterfeit '96
Sometimes They Come
  Back...Again '96
Tremors 2: Aftershocks '96
In the Heat of Passion 2:
  Unfaithful '94
Firestorm: 72 Hours in Oakland
  '93
Alan & Naomi '92
Cool As Ice '91
Midnight Murders '91
A Connecticut Yankee in King
  Arthur's Court '89
Tremors '89
Big Business '88
In the Line of Duty: The FBI
  Murders '88
Summer Fantasy '84

Paul Gross
Whale Music '94
Armistead Maupin's Tales of the
  City '93
Aspen Extreme '93
Northern Extremes '93
Buffalo Jump '90
Cold Comfort '90

Brigitte Grothum
Inn on the River '62
The Strange Countess '61

Deborah Grover
Mania '80s
The Christmas Wife '88

Robin Groves
Silver Bullet '85
The Nesting '80

Robert Grubb
Mad Max: Beyond
  Thunderdome '85
Remember Me '85

Uta Hagen
Reversal of Fortune '90
The Boys from Brazil '78
The Other '72

Julie Hagerty
Boys Will Be Boys '97
U-Turn '97
The Wife '95
Noises Off '92
What About Bob? '91
Reversal of Fortune '90
Bloodhounds of Broadway '89
Rude Awakening '89
Necessary Parties '88
Beyond Therapy '86
Bad Medicine '85
Goodbye, New York '85
Lost in America '85
Airplane 2: The Sequel '82
A Midsummer Night's Sex
    Comedy '82
Airplane! '80
The Day the Women Got Even
    '80

Dan Haggerty
Grizzly Mountain '97
Abducted 2: The Reunion '94
Cheyenne Warrior '94
Ice Pawn '92
Deadly Diamonds '91
Mind Trap '91
Soldier's Fortune '91
The Inheritor '90
Repo Jake '90
Spirit of the Eagle '90
Chance '89
The Channeler '89
The Chilling '89
Elves '89
Night Wars '88
Abducted '86
Angels Die Hard '84
The Capture of Grizzly Adams
    '82
California Gold Rush '81
King of the Mountain '81
Desperate Women '78
Terror Out of the Sky '78
Blood Brothers '78
The Adventures of Frontier
    Fremont '75
Life & Times of Grizzly Adams
    '74
When the North Wind Blows '74
The Shrieking '73
Starbird and Sweet William '73
Bury Me an Angel '71
The Tender Warrior '71

Kenichi Hagiwara
Traffic Jam '91
Kagemusha '80

Michael Hagiwara
Josh Kirby...Time Warrior:
    Chapter 5, Journey to the
    Magic Cavern '96
Prehysteria 2 '94

Marvin Hagler
Indio 2: The Revolt '92
Indio '90

Larry Hagman
Primary Colors '98
Nixon '95
S.O.B. '81
President's Mistress '78
The Eagle Has Landed '77
Intimate Strangers '77
The Big Bus '76
Mother, Jugs and Speed '76
Harry and Tonto '74
Hurricane '74
Antonio '73
Deadly Encounter '72
No Place to Run '72
Son of Blob '72
Three in the Cellar '70
The Group '66
In Harm's Way '65
Ensign Pulver '64
Fail-Safe '64

Archie Hahn
Glory Years '87
Meatballs 2 '84
Protocol '84

Eric Hahn
Pray TV '80
Fist of Glory '95
Crossfire '89

Gisela Hahn
Big Boss '77
Mr. Scarface '77

Jess Hahn
Mama Dracula '80
Mean Frank and Crazy Tony '75
The Grand Duel '73
The Night of the Following Day
    '69
Triple Cross '67
Secret Agent Super Dragon '66

Jessica Hahn
Bikini Summer 2 '92
Thunder & Mud '89

Mang Hai
Buddha Assassinator '82
Hell's Wind Staff '82

Charles Haid
Broken Trust '95
Cooperstown '93
The Fire Next Time '93
The Chinatown Murders: Man
    Against the Mob '92
Freeze Frame '92
Storyville '92
In the Line of Duty: A Cop for the
    Killing '90
Night Breed '90
Fire and Rain '89
Cop '88
The Great Escape 2: The Untold
    Story '88
The Rescue '88
Weekend War '88
Children in the Crossfire '84
Hill Street Blues, Vol. 1: Hill
    Street Station '81
Twirl '81
Altered States '80
Deathmoon '78
Oliver's Story '78
Who'll Stop the Rain? '78
The Choirboys '77

Ion Haiduc
Bloodlust: Subspecies 3 '93
Bloodstone: Subspecies 2 '92

Stacy Haiduk
Yesterday's Target '96
Luther the Geek '90
Steel and Lace '90

Sid Haig
The Forbidden Dance '90
Wizards of the Lost Kingdom 2
    '89
Warlords '88
Commando Squad '87
Aftermath '85
Busting '74
The Deadly and the Beautiful '73
The Big Bird Cage '72
The Big Doll House '71
Chrome Hearts '70
Track of the Vampire '66
Spider Baby '64

Kenneth Haigh
The Bitch '78
Cleopatra '63
Teenage Bad Girl '59

Louisa Haigh
Shipwrecked '90
Murderers Among Us: The
    Simon Wiesenthal Story '89

Marian Hailey
Jenny '70
Lovers and Other Strangers '70

Corey Haim
Snowboard Academy '96
Demolition High '95
Life 101 '95
Dream a Little Dream 2 '94
Fast Getaway 2 '94
National Lampoon's Last Resort
    '94
Anything for Love '93
Blown Away '93
Just One of the Girls '93
The Double O Kid '92

Oh, What a Night '92
Dream Machine '91
Fast Getaway '91
Prayer of the Rollerboys '91
Dream a Little Dream '89
License to Drive '88
Watchers '88
The Lost Boys '87
Lucas '86
Murphy's Romance '85
Secret Admirer '85
Silver Bullet '85
A Time to Live '85
First Born '84

Patricia Haines
The Virgin Witch '70
Night Caller from Outer Space
    '66

Richard Haines
An African Dream '90
Alien from L.A. '87

William Haines
The Girl Said No '37
Way Out West '37
Show People '28
Little Annie Rooney '25

Khrystyne Haje
Cyborg 3: The Recycler '95
Scanner Cop 2: Volkin's
    Revenge '94
Scanners: The Showdown '94

Haji
Faster Pussycat! Kill! Kill! '66
Motor Psycho '65

Alan Hale
Stars in My Crown '50
Adventures of Don Juan '49
The Inspector General '49
My Girl Tisa '48
South of St. Louis '48
Pursued '47
The Man I Love '46
Night and Day '46
The Adventures of Mark Twain
    '44
Action in the North Atlantic '43
Destination Tokyo '43
Thank Your Lucky Stars '43
This Is the Army '43
Captains of the Clouds '42
Desperate Journey '42
Gentleman Jim '42
Footsteps in the Dark '41
Strawberry Blonde '41
The Fighting 69th '40
Santa Fe Trail '40
The Sea Hawk '40
They Drive by Night '40
Virginia City '40
Dodge City '39
The Man in the Iron Mask '39
The Private Lives of Elizabeth &
    Essex '39
The Adventures of Marco Polo
    '38
The Adventures of Robin Hood
    '38
Algiers '38
Listen, Darling '38
The Prince and the Pauper '37
Stella Dallas '37
Thin Ice '37
When Thief Meets Thief '37
Our Relations '36
The Crusades '35
Last Days of Pompeii '35
Great Expectations '34
It Happened One Night '34
Little Minister '34
The Lost Patrol '34
Of Human Bondage '34
The Scarlet Letter '34
The Sin of Madelon Claudet '31
Susan Lenox: Her Fall and Rise
    '31
The Leatherneck '28
Power '28
Dick Turpin '25
The Covered Wagon '23
Robin Hood '22
The Trap '22
The Four Horsemen of the
    Apocalypse '21

Alan Hale, Jr.
Hambone & Hillie '84
Johnny Dangerously '84
The Fifth Musketeer '79
The North Avenue Irregulars '79
The Giant Spider Invasion '75
There was a Crooked Man '70
Gilligan's Island: Meet the Crew
    '64
The Crawling Hand '63
Hard Drivin' '60
Up Periscope '59
Battle Hymn '57
Casey Jones and Fury (Brave
    Stallion) '57
All Mine to Give '56
The Indian Fighter '55
Young at Heart '54
Big Trees '52
At Sword's Point '51
Home Town Story '51
The Underworld Story '50
The West Point Story '50
It Happens Every Spring '49
Rim of the Canyon '49
The Spirit of West Point '47
To the Shores of Tripoli '42

Barbara Hale
The Defense Never Rests '90
Perry Mason: The Case of the
    Lost Love '87
Perry Mason Returns '85
Flight of the Grey Wolf '76
The Giant Spider Invasion '75
Buckskin '68
The Oklahoman '56
Seventh Cavalry '56
A Lion Is in the Streets '53
Last of the Comanches '52
The Jackpot '50
The Clay Pigeon '49
Jolson Sings Again '49
The Window '49
The Boy with the Green Hair '48
First Yank into Tokyo '45
West of the Pecos '45
The Falcon in Hollywood '44
Going to Town '44

Binnie Hale
Love from a Stranger '37
The Phantom Light '35

Creighton Hale
Shop Angel '32
The Cat and the Canary '27
The Marriage Circle '24
Broken Hearts of Broadway '23
The Idol Dancer '20
Way Down East '20

Georgia Hale
The Gold Rush '25
Gold Rush/Payday '25

Georgina Hale
Castaway '87
Mahler '74
The Boy Friend '71
The Devils '71

Jean Hale
In Like Flint '67
The St. Valentine's Day
    Massacre '67
Psychomania '63

Jonathan Hale
The Judge '49
Call Northside 777 '48
Silver River '48
Blondie Knows Best '46
Hollywood Canteen '44
It's a Great Life '43
Blondie's Blessed Event '42
Hangmen Also Die '42
Blondie in Society '41
Blondie Has Trouble '40
The Saint Takes Over '40
The Saint's Double Trouble '40
The Saint Strikes Back '39
The Story of Alexander Graham
    Bell '39
Blondie '38
Bringing Up Baby '38
Exiled to Shanghai '37
Saratoga '37
You Only Live Once '37

Louise Closser Hale
Today We Live '33
Shanghai Express '32
Devotion '31
Platinum Blonde '31

Monte Hale
Western Double Feature 2:
    Wayne & Hale '80s
Missourians '50
Trail of Robin Hood '50
The Vanishing Westerner '50
Western Double Feature 8: Hale
    & Carradine '40s
Outcasts of the Trail '49
Pioneer Marshal '49
Son of God's Country '48
Under Colorado Skies '47

Sonnie Hale
It's Love Again '36
Evergreen '34

Brian Haley
McHale's Navy '97
That Darn Cat '96
Baby's Day Out '94

Jack Haley
People Are Funny '46
George White's Scandals '45
Treasure of Fear '45
Higher and Higher '44
One Body Too Many '44
Take It Big '44
Moon over Miami '41
The Wizard of Oz '39
Alexander's Ragtime Band '38
Rebecca of Sunnybrook Farm
    '38
Pick a Star '37
Pigskin Parade '36
The Poor Little Rich Girl '36

Jackie Earle Haley
Maniac Cop 3: Badge of Silence
    '93
Dollman '90
The Zoo Gang '85
Losin' It '82
Breaking Away '79
The Bad News Bears Go to
    Japan '78
The Bad News Bears in
    Breaking Training '77
Damnation Alley '77
The Bad News Bears '76

H.B. Halicki
Deadline Auto Theft '83
The Junkman '82
Gone in 60 Seconds '74

Albert Hall
Get On the Bus '96
Devil in a Blue Dress '95
Major Payne '95
Malcolm X '92
Hearts of Darkness: A
    Filmmaker's Apocalypse '91
Separate But Equal '91
Betrayed '88
Uncle Tom's Cabin '87
The Long, Hot Summer '86
Apocalypse Now '79

Anthony Michael Hall
Exit in Red '97
The Death Artist '95
The Grave '95
Hail Caesar '94
Me and the Mob '94
Texas '94
The Adventures of a Gnome
    Named Gnorm '93
Six Degrees of Separation '93
Into the Sun '92
Edward Scissorhands '90
Johnny Be Good '88
Out of Bounds '86
The Breakfast Club '85
Weird Science '85
Sixteen Candles '84
National Lampoon's Vacation
    '83
Six Pack '82

Arch Hall, Jr.
Deadwood '65
Nasty Rabbit '64
The Sadist '63

Hill ✎cont.

Puppet Master 5: The Final
   Chapter '94
Puppet Master 4 '93

Wendy Hiller
Anne of Avonlea '87
The Lonely Passion of Judith
   Hearne '87
Mountbatten: The Last Viceroy
   '86
Making Love '82
The Curse of King Tut's Tomb
   '80
The Elephant Man '80
The Cat and the Canary '79
Voyage of the Damned '76
Murder on the Orient Express
   '74
David Copperfield '70
A Man for All Seasons '66
Toys in the Attic '63
Separate Tables '58
Something of Value '57
I Know Where I'm Going '45
Major Barbara '41
Pygmalion '38

John Hillerman
Hands of a Murderer '90
Around the World in 80 Days '89
Assault and Matrimony '87
Little Gloria...Happy at Last '84
Up the Creek '84
History of the World: Part 1 '81
Magnum P.I.: Don't Eat the
   Snow in Hawaii '80
Marathon '80
Betrayal '78
Audrey Rose '77
Blazing Saddles '74
Chinatown '74
The Outside Man '73
Paper Moon '73
The Thief Who Came to Dinner
   '73
The Last Picture Show '71
Lawman '71

Verna Hillie
House of Mystery '34
Trail Beyond '34
Man of the Forest '33

Candace Hilligoss
Curse of the Living Corpse '64
Carnival of Souls '62

Beverly Hills
Knights & Emeralds '87
Brides of the Beast '68

Gillian Hills
Demons of the Mind '72
Beat Girl '60

Daisy Hilton
Chained for Life '51
Saturday Night Shockers '50
Freaks '32

George Hilton
Dead for a Dollar '70s
Day of the Maniac '77
Guns for Dollars '73
The Next Victim '71
The Scorpion's Tail '71
Blade of the Ripper '70
Bullet for Sandoval '70
The Ruthless Four '70
Sartana's Here...Trade Your
   Pistol for a Coffin '70
The Battle of El Alamein '68
Any Gun Can Play '67

Violet Hilton
Chained for Life '51
Freaks '32

Madeline Hinde
The Fiend '71
The Bloodsuckers '70

Art Hindle
The World's Oldest Living
   Bridesmaid '92
Dixie Lanes '88
Into the Fire '88
Surrogate '88
The Gunfighters '87

J. Edgar Hoover '87
Say Yes! '86
Raw Courage '84
The Man Who Wasn't There '83
Wild Pony '83
Desperate Lives '82
Octagon '80
The Brood '79
The Power Within '79
Invasion of the Body Snatchers
   '78

Earl Hindman
The Ballad of the Sad Cafe '91
Murder in Coweta County '83
The Taking of Pelham One Two
   Three '74

Ciaran Hinds
Ivanhoe '97
Jane Eyre '97
Oscar and Lucinda '97
Some Mother's Son '96
The Affair '95
Mary Reilly '95
Persuasion '95
A Dark Adapted Eye '93
Hostages '93
The Man Who Cried '93
Prime Suspect 3 '93
December Bride '91

Cindy Hinds
Deadline '82
The Brood '79

Samuel S. Hinds
It's a Wonderful Life '46
Scarlet Street '45
The Strange Affair of Uncle
   Harry '45
Weekend at the Waldorf '45
Son of Dracula '43
Pardon My Sarong '42
Ride 'Em Cowboy '42
Blossoms in the Dust '41
Man Made Monster '41
It's a Date '40
Destry Rides Again '39
Devil's Party '38
Test Pilot '38
You Can't Take It with You '38
Navy Blue and Gold '37
Rhythm on the Range '36
The Raven '35
Deluge '33
Gabriel Over the White House
   '33

Gregory Hines
Subway Stories '97
The Cherokee Kid '96
Good Luck '96
The Preacher's Wife '96
Trigger Happy '96
A Stranger in Town '95
Waiting to Exhale '95
Bleeding Hearts '94
Dead Air '94
Renaissance Man '94
T Bone N Weasel '92
A Rage in Harlem '91
White Lie '91
Eve of Destruction '90
Tap '89
Off Limits '87
Running Scared '86
White Nights '85
The Cotton Club '84
Puss 'n Boots '84
Deal of the Century '83
Eubie! '82
History of the World: Part 1 '81
Wolfen '81

Johnny Hines
The Speed Spook '24
A Girl's Folly '17
Tillie Wakes Up '17

Robert Hines
Devices and Desires '91
Hellraiser '87

Pat Hingle
Batman and Robin '97
A Thousand Acres '97
Larger Than Life '96
Batman Forever '95
Truman '95
Lightning Jack '94

The Quick and the Dead '94
Batman Returns '92
Citizen Cohn '92
The Habitation of Dragons '91
The Grifters '90
Batman '89
LBJ: The Early Years '88
Baby Boom '87
The Private History of a
   Campaign That Failed '87
In 'n Out '86
Manhunt for Claude Dallas '86
Maximum Overdrive '86
Brewster's Millions '85
Broken Badge '85
The Falcon and the Snowman
   '85
Lady from Yesterday '85
Going Berserk '83
Running Brave '83
Sudden Impact '83
The Act '82
Of Mice and Men '81
Elvis: The Movie '79
Norma Rae '79
Running Scared '79
Wild Times '79
The Gauntlet '77
Tarantulas: The Deadly Cargo
   '77
Hazel's People '75
Running Wild '73
Bloody Mama '70
Hang 'Em High '67
Invitation to a Gunfighter '64
The Ugly American '63
The Strange One '57

Darby Hinton
Malibu Express '85
The Treasure of Jamaica Reef
   '74
Firecracker '71

Bill Hinzman
Revenge of the Living Zombies
   '88
The Majorettes '87

Paul Hipp
Midnight in the Garden of Good
   and Evil '97
Vicious Circles '97
The Funeral '96
Bad Channels '92

Akihiko Hirata
Godzilla vs. the Cosmic Monster
   '74
The Secret of the Telegian '61
H-Man '59

Thora Hird
The Wedding Gift '93
Consuming Passions '88
The Nightcomers '72
Rattle of a Simple Man '64
A Kind of Loving '62
The Entertainer '60
Dangerous Youth '58
Conspirator '49

Daniel Hirsch
Lady Avenger '89
Zero Boys '86
Sky High '84

Judd Hirsch
Independence Day '96
The Great Escape 2: The Untold
   Story '88
Running on Empty '88
Brotherly Love '85
Teachers '84
The Goodbye People '83
Without a Trace '83
Marriage Is Alive and Well '80
Ordinary People '80
King of the Gypsies '78
Sooner or Later '78
Legend of Valentino '75
Fury on Wheels '71

Robert Hirsch
The Hunchback of Notre Dame
   '57
Mademoiselle Striptease '57

Alice Hirson
Blind Date '87
Miss All-American Beauty '82

Christianne Hirt
Firestorm '97
For the Moment '94
Blades of Courage '88

Patricia Hitchcock
Psycho '60
Strangers on a Train '51

Judith Hoag
Acting on Impulse '93
Switched at Birth '91
Fine Things '90
A Matter of Degrees '90
Teenage Mutant Ninja Turtles:
   The Movie '90

Doug Hobart
The Death Curse of Tartu '66
The Professor '58

Rose Hobart
Cass Timberlane '47
The Farmer's Daughter '47
Conflict '45
The Mad Ghoul '43
Susan and God '40
Dr. Jekyll and Mr. Hyde '32
East of Borneo '31

Halliwell Hobbes
You Gotta Stay Happy '48
Casanova Brown '44
Gaslight '44
Sherlock Holmes Faces Death
   '43
Journey for Margaret '42
Son of Fury '42
The Undying Monster '42
You Can't Take It with You '38
Dr. Jekyll and Mr. Hyde '32

Peter Hobbs
In the Mood '87
Next One '84

Mara Hobel
Mommie Dearest '81
Sorrows of Gin '79

Valerie Hobson
The Promoter '52
Interrupted Journey '49
Kind Hearts and Coronets '49
The Rocking Horse Winner '49
Train of Events '49
Blanche Fury '48
Great Expectations '46
The Adventures of Tartu '43
Clouds Over Europe '39
Spy in Black '39
Drums '38
When Thief Meets Thief '37
The Bride of Frankenstein '35
The Mystery of Edwin Drood '35
Werewolf of London '35

Kristen Hocking
The Wolves '95
Bitter Vengeance '94

Kane Hodder
Watchers Reborn '98
Pumpkinhead 2: Blood Wings
   '94
Jason Goes to Hell: The Final
   Friday '93
Friday the 13th, Part 8: Jason
   Takes Manhattan '89
Friday the 13th, Part 7: The New
   Blood '88

Douglas Hodge
Middlemarch '93
A Fatal Inversion '92
Dark Obsession '90
Salome's Last Dance '88

Kate Hodge
Desire '95
The Hidden 2 '94
Rapid Fire '92
Love Kills '91
Leatherface: The Texas
   Chainsaw Massacre 3 '89

Patricia Hodge
The Moonstone '97
The Leading Man '96
The Heat of the Day '91
Spymaker: The Secret Life of
   Ian Fleming '90
The Shell Seekers '89
Diamond's Edge '88

Sunset '88
Dust to Dust '85
Betrayal '83

Eddie Hodges
Live a Little, Love a Little '68
Summer Magic '63
The Adventures of Huckleberry
   Finn '60
A Hole in the Head '59

Tom Hodges
The Baby Doll Murders '92
Vietnam War Story 3 '89

Earle Hodgins
The Topeka Terror '45
Colt Comrades '43
Hoppy Serves a Writ '43
The Bashful Bachelor '42
Inside the Law '42
Boss of Bullion City '41
Santa Fe Marshal '40
Heroes of the Alamo '37
A Lawman Is Born '36
Aces and Eights '36
Law for Tombstone '35

John Hodiak
Dragonfly Squadron '54
Ambush at Tomahawk Gap '53
Conquest of Cochise '53
Across the Wide Missouri '51
The Miniver Story '50
Battleground '49
Malaya '49
Command Decision '48
Homecoming '48
Love from a Stranger '47
The Harvey Girls '46
Lifeboat '44

Paul Hoerbiger
The Third Man '49
The Mozart Story '48

Dennis Hoey
David and Bathsheba '51
Golden Earrings '47
Where There's Life '47
Anna and the King of Siam '46
Roll on Texas Moon '46
House of Fear '45
A Thousand and One Nights '45
The Pearl of Death '44
Spider Woman '44
Uncertain Glory '44
Sherlock Holmes and the Secret
   Weapon '42
Son of Fury '42
Power '34

Abbie Hoffman
Born on the Fourth of July '89
Heavy Petting '89

Basil Hoffman
The Ice Runner '93
The Double O Kid '92
Communion '89
Lambada '89
Love at First Bite '79

David Hoffman
Children in the Crossfire '84
Wolf Lake '79
A Woman's World '54

Dustin Hoffman
Mad City '97
Sphere '97
Wag the Dog '97
Sleepers '96
American Buffalo '95
Outbreak '94
Hero '92
Billy Bathgate '91
Hook '91
Dick Tracy '90
Family Business '89
Rain Man '88
Ishtar '87
Death of a Salesman '86
Tootsie '82
Agatha '79
Kramer vs. Kramer '79
Straight Time '78
All the President's Men '76
Marathon Man '76
Lenny '74
Papillon '73
Alfredo, Alfredo '72

Western Mail '42
Where Trails End '42
The Driftin' Kid '41
Dynamite Canyon '41
Riding the Sunset Trail '41
Renegade Ranger/Scarlet River '38
God's Country and the Man '37
Where Trails Divide '37
Desert Gold '36
Drift Fence '36
The Glory Trail '36
Hong Kong Nights '35
Our Daily Bread '34
Cheyenne Kid '33
Beyond the Rockies '32
Come On Danger! '32
Ghost Valley '32
Saddle Buster '32
Pardon My Gun '30
Marked Money '28

Catherine Keener
Out of Sight '98
The Real Blonde '97
Box of Moonlight '97
The Destiny of Marty Fine '96
If These Walls Could Talk '96
Walking and Talking '96
Living in Oblivion '94
Johnny Suede '92
Survival Quest '89

Matt Keeslar
The Last Days of Disco '98
Sour Grapes '98
The Deli '97
Mr. Magoo '97
Waiting for Guffman '96
The Run of the Country '95
The Stupids '95
Safe Passage '94

Jack Kehler
Lost Highway '96
My Fellow Americans '96
The Shot '96
The Invaders '95
Blindsided '93
Casualties of Love: The "Long Island Lolita" Story '93
Bloodstone '88

Jack Kehoe
Falling Down '93
Servants of Twilight '91
Young Guns 2 '90
The Untouchables '87
A Winner Never Quits '86
On the Nickel '80
The Fish that Saved Pittsburgh '79
Law and Disorder '74
Serpico '73

Andrew Keir
Rob Roy '95
Dragonworld '94
Absolution '81
The Thirty-Nine Steps '79
Zeppelin '71
The Night Visitor '70
Daleks—Invasion Earth 2150 A.D. '66
Dracula, Prince of Darkness '66
The Fighting Prince of Donegal '66
Lord Jim '65
Cleopatra '63
Suspended Alibi '56

Harvey Keitel
Cop Land '97
Fairytale: A True Story '97
City of Industry '96
Head Above Water '96
Blue in the Face '95
Clockers '95
From Dusk Till Dawn '95
Smoke '95
Ulysses' Gaze '95
Imaginary Crimes '94
Monkey Trouble '94
Pulp Fiction '94
Somebody to Love '94
Dangerous Game '93
The Piano '93
Point of No Return '93
Rising Sun '93
The Young Americans '93

Bad Lieutenant '92
Reservoir Dogs '92
Sister Act '92
Bugsy '91
Mortal Thoughts '91
Thelma & Louise '91
Two Evil Eyes '90
The Two Jakes '90
The January Man '89
Blindside '88
The Last Temptation of Christ '88
The Inquiry '87
The Pick-Up Artist '87
The Men's Club '86
Off Beat '86
Camorra: The Naples Connection '85
Star Knight '85
Corrupt '84
Falling in Love '84
Exposed '83
The Border '82
La Nuit de Varennes '82
Death Watch '80
Saturn 3 '80
Eagle's Wing '79
Blue Collar '78
Fingers '78
The Duellists '77
Welcome to L.A. '77
Buffalo Bill & the Indians '76
Mother, Jugs and Speed '76
Taxi Driver '76
The Virginia Hill Story '76
Shining Star '75
Alice Doesn't Live Here Anymore '74
Mean Streets '73
Who's That Knocking at My Door? '68

Brian Keith
Rough Riders '97
Entertaining Angels: The Dorothy Day Story '96
National Lampoon's Favorite Deadly Sins '95
Picture Windows '95
The Gambler Returns: The Luck of the Draw '93
Escape '90
Bull of the West '89
Welcome Home '89
Young Guns '88
The Alamo: Thirteen Days to Glory '87
Death Before Dishonor '87
World War III '86
Charlie Chan and the Curse of the Dragon Queen '81
Sharky's Machine '81
The Mountain Men '80
The Chisholms '79
Meteor '79
The Seekers '79
Centennial '78
Hooper '78
Joe Panther '76
The Loneliest Runner '76
The Longest Drive '76
The Wind and the Lion '75
The Yakuza '75
Scandalous John '71
McKenzie Break '70
Suppose They Gave a War and Nobody Came? '70
With Six You Get Eggroll '68
Reflections in a Golden Eye '67
Nevada Smith '66
The Rare Breed '66
The Russians Are Coming, the Russians Are Coming '66
The Hallelujah Trail '65
Those Calloways '65
A Tiger Walks '64
The Fugitive: Premiere Episode '63
Johnny Shiloh '63
Savage Sam '63
Moon Pilot '62
Deadly Companions '61
The Parent Trap '61
Ten Who Dared '60
The Young Philadelphians '59
Dino '57
Nightfall '56

Run of the Arrow '56
Tight Spot '55
The Violent Men '55
Arrowhead '53

David Keith
Invasion of Privacy '96
Judge & Jury '96
Born Wild '95
Deadly Sins '95
Gold Diggers: The Secret of Bear Mountain '95
Major League 2 '94
Temptation '94
Texas '94
Till the End of the Night '94
Raw Justice '93
Caged Fear '92
Desperate Motives '92
Liar's Edge '92
Off and Running '90
The Two Jakes '90
The Further Adventures of Tennessee Buck '88
Heartbreak Hotel '88
White of the Eye '88
The Curse '87
Gulag '85
Firestarter '84
Independence Day '83
The Lords of Discipline '83
An Officer and a Gentleman '82
Back Roads '81
Take This Job & Shove It '81
Brubaker '80
The Great Santini '80
The Rose '79

Donald Keith
Outlaw Justice '32
Branded Men '31
Bare Knees '28
Dancing Mothers '26
Free to Love '25
My Lady of Whims '25

Ian Keith
It Came from Beneath the Sea '55
Dick Tracy's Dilemma '47
Scared to Death/Dick Tracy's Dilemma '47
Song of Old Wyoming '45
The Chinese Cat '44
Corregidor '43
Man from Thunder River '43
The Payoff '43
Mary of Scotland '36
The White Legion '36
The Crusades '35
The Three Musketeers '35
Queen Christina '33
The Sign of the Cross '33
Manhandled '24

Penelope Keith
The Norman Conquests, Part 1: Table Manners '80
The Norman Conquests, Part 2: Living Together '80
The Norman Conquests, Part 3: Round and Round the Garden '80
Madhouse Mansion '74

Robert Keith
Cimarron '60
Men in War '57
My Man Godfrey '57
Between Heaven and Hell '56
Written on the Wind '56
Love Me or Leave Me '55
Drum Beat '54
The Wild One '54
Young at Heart '54
Battle Circus '53
Devil's Canyon '53
Small Town Girl '53
Here Comes the Groom '51
I Want You '51
Boomerang '47

Rosalind Keith
Bad Boy '39
Theodora Goes Wild '36

Sheila Keith
House of the Long Shadows '82
The Comeback '77
The Confessional '75
Frightmare '74

Robert Kellard
Gentleman from Dixie '41
Drums of Fu Manchu '40

Cecil Kellaway
Quick, Let's Get Married '71
Getting Straight '70
Guess Who's Coming to Dinner '67
Spinout '66
Hush, Hush, Sweet Charlotte '65
The Cardinal '63
Zotz! '62
Interrupted Melody '55
The Prodigal '55
The Beast from 20,000 Fathoms '53
Young Bess '53
Francis Goes to the Races '51
Harvey '50
Kim '50
Portrait of Jennie '48
Unconquered '47
Monsieur Beaucaire '46
The Postman Always Rings Twice '46
Love Letters '45
I Married a Witch '42
Birth of the Blues '41
Brother Orchid '40
The House of the Seven Gables '40
The Letter '40
The Mummy's Hand '40
Gunga Din '39
Wuthering Heights '39
Maid's Night Out '38

Tina Kellegher
Scarlett '94
The Snapper '93

Hiram Keller
Countryman '83
Lifespan '75
Ciao Federico! Fellini Directs Satyricon '69
Fellini Satyricon '69

Marthe Keller
Mon Amie Max '94
Young Catherine '91
The Nightmare Years '89
Dark Eyes '87
Red Kiss '85
The Amateur '82
The Formula '80
Black Sunday '77
Bobby Deerfield '77
Marathon Man '76
And Now My Love '74

Mary Page Keller
Any Place But Home '97
The Colony '95
Ulterior Motives '92
Scared Stiff '87

Barbara Kellerman
The Chronicles of Narnia '89
Quatermass Conclusion '79

Sally Kellerman
The Student Affair '97
Mirror, Mirror 2: Raven Dance '94
Ready to Wear '94
Younger & Younger '94
Boris and Natasha: The Movie '92
Victim of Beauty '91
Doppelganger: The Evil Within '90
All's Fair '89
Secret of the Ice Cave '89
You Can't Hurry Love '88
Meatballs 3 '87
Someone to Love '87
Three for the Road '87
Back to School '86
The KGB: The Secret War '86
That's Life! '86
Moving Violations '85
Secret Weapons '85
Dempsey '83
Dirkham Detective Agency '83
September Gun '83
Fatal Attraction '80
Foxes '80
Loving Couples '80

Serial '80
A Little Romance '79
Centennial '78
It Rained All Night the Day I Left '78
Magee and the Lady '78
Welcome to L.A. '77
The Big Bus '76
Rafferty & the Gold Dust Twins '75
Slither '73
Last of the Red Hot Lovers '72
A Reflection of Fear '72
Brewster McCloud '70
M*A*S*H '70
April Fools '69
The Boston Strangler '68
Hands of a Stranger '62
Reform School Girl '57

Susan Kellerman
Elvira, Mistress of the Dark '88
Oh, Heavenly Dog! '80
Where the Buffalo Roam '80

Barry Kelley
Jack the Giant Killer '62
Carrie '52
Francis Goes to the Races '51
The Well '51
The Asphalt Jungle '50
Ma and Pa Kettle '49
Too Late for Tears '49

DeForest Kelley
Star Trek 6: The Undiscovered Country '91
Bull of the West '89
Star Trek 5: The Final Frontier '89
Star Trek 4: The Voyage Home '86
Star Trek 3: The Search for Spock '84
Star Trek 2: The Wrath of Khan '82
Star Trek: The Motion Picture '80
Star Trek Bloopers '69
Apache Uprising '66
Warlock '59
The Law and Jake Wade '58
Gunfight at the O.K. Corral '57
The Man in the Gray Flannel Suit '56
Illegal '55
Fear in the Night '47

Kimberly Kelley
Midnight Tease 2 '95
Hard Bounty '94

Sheila Kelley
Santa Fe '97
One Fine Day '96
Deconstructing Sarah '94
The Secretary '94
Passion Fish '92
Singles '92
Pure Luck '91
Soapdish '91
Mortal Passions '90
Breaking In '89

Mike Kellin
Sleepaway Camp '83
On the Yard '79
Girlfriends '78
Next Stop, Greenwich Village '76
Freebie & the Bean '74
The Last Porno Flick '74
Riot '67
The Boston Strangler '68
The Incident '67
Invitation to a Gunfighter '64
Hell Is for Heroes '62
The Great Impostor '61
Wackiest Ship in the Army '61
The Mountain Road '60
Lonelyhearts '58
At War with the Army '50

Catherine Kellner
Rosewood '96
Six Degrees of Separation '93

John Kellogg
Jacob Have I Loved '88
Violets Are Blue '86
The Enforcer '51

The Pocatello Kid '31
Range Law '31
Two Gun Man '31
Oklahoma Cyclone '30

Charmion King
Anne of Green Gables '85
Who Has Seen the Wind? '77

Damu King
Blackjack '78
Black Godfather '74
Black Starlet '74

Dave King
Revolution '85
The Long Good Friday '80
Naughty Knights '71

Erik King
Joey Breaker '93
Casualties of War '89

Joe King
Alexander's Ragtime Band '38
Woman in the Shadows '34
Shifting Sands '18
Until They Get Me '18

John "Dusty" King
Haunted Ranch '43
Two-Fisted Justice '43
Arizona Stagecoach '42
Boot Hill Bandits '42
Law of the Jungle '42
Rock River Renegades '42
Texas to Bataan '42
Thunder River Feud '42
Trail Riders '42
Fugitive Valley '41
Kid's Last Ride '41
Saddle Mountain Round-Up '41
Tonto Basin Outlaws '41
Trail of the Silver Spurs '41
Tumbledown Ranch in Arizona '41
Underground Rustlers '41
Half a Soldier '40
Midnight Limited '40
Trailing Double Trouble '40
West of Pinto Basin '40
Ace Drummond '36

Kenneth King
Jade '95
Polyester '81

Leslie King
Cotton Candy '82
Gas Pump Girls '79

Mabel King
Dead Men Don't Die '91
The Wiz '78
Black Vampire '73

Meegan King
Money to Burn '83
Sweater Girls '78

Morgana King
A Time to Remember '90
The Godfather, Part 2 '74
The Godfather '72

Perry King
A Cry in the Night '93
Jericho Fever '93
Switch '91
Danielle Steel's Kaleidoscope '90
The Prize Pulitzer '89
Disaster at Silo 7 '88
The Hasty Heart '86
Killing Hour '84
Class of 1984 '82
Search and Destroy '81
City in Fear '80
The Cracker Factory '79
Love's Savage Fury '79
Different Story '78
Andy Warhol's Bad '77
The Choirboys '77
Lipstick '76
Mandingo '75
The Lords of Flatbush '74
Wild Party '74
The Possession of Joel Delaney '72
Slaughterhouse Five '72

Regina King
Jerry Maguire '96

A Thin Line Between Love and Hate '96
Friday '95
Higher Learning '94
Poetic Justice '93

Rowena King
To Play the King '93
Wide Sargasso Sea '92

Stephen King
Stephen King's Golden Years '91
Pet Sematary '89
Creepshow 2 '87
Maximum Overdrive '86
Creepshow '82

Tony King
The Last Hunter '80
Sparkle '76
Report to the Commissioner '74
Gordon's War '73

Walter Woolf King
Smart Alecks '42
Today I Hang '42
Yank in Libya '42
Swiss Miss '38
A Night at the Opera '35

Wright King
Invasion of the Bee Girls '73
Dangerous Charter '62
Wanted: Dead or Alive '59

Yolanda King
Ghosts of Mississippi '96
America's Dream '95

Zalman King
Galaxy of Terror '81
Blue Sunshine '78
The Passover Plot '75
Ski Bum '75
Deadly Fieldtrip '74
Smile, Jenny, You're Dead '74
Some Call It Loving '73

King John III
Psycho from Texas '83
Black Bikers from Hell '70
The Outlaw Bikers—Gang Wars '70

Walter Kingsford
Velvet Touch '48
My Favorite Blonde '42
The Man in the Iron Mask '39
It Could Happen to You '37
The Invisible Ray '36
The Story of Louis Pasteur '36

Ben Kingsley
The Assignment '97
Weapons of Mass Distraction '97
Moses '96
Twelfth Night '96
Joseph '95
Species '95
Death and the Maiden '94
Dave '93
Schindler's List '93
Searching for Bobby Fischer '93
Sneakers '92
Bugsy '91
The Children '90
The Fifth Monkey '90
Murderers Among Us: The Simon Wiesenthal Story '89
Slipstream '89
Pascali's Island '88
Without a Clue '88
Maurice '87
Turtle Diary '86
Harem '85
Silas Marner '85
Betrayal '83
Gandhi '82
Hard Labour '73

Danitza Kingsley
Jack's Back '93
South of Reno '87
Amazons '86

Susan Kingsley
The Dollmaker '84
Old Enough '84

Alex Kingston
Moll Flanders '96
Carrington '95

The Infiltrator '95

Natalie Kingston
His Private Secretary '33
Tarzan the Tiger '29
Baby Face Harry Langdon '26
His First Flame '26
All Night Long/Smile Please '24

Sam Kinison
It's a Bundyful Life '92
Back to School '86

Amelia Kinkade
Night of the Demons 3 '97
Night of the Demons 2 '94

Kathleen Kinmont
Stormswept '95
Texas Payback '95
C.I.A. 2: Target Alexa '94
Final Round '93
C.I.A.: Code Name Alexa '92
Sweet Justice '92
Night of the Warrior '91
The Art of Dying '90
Roller Blade Warriors: Taken By Force '90
Bride of Re-Animator '89
SnakeEater 2: The Drug Buster '89
Halloween 4: The Return of Michael Myers '88
Phoenix the Warrior '88
Rush Week '88
Fraternity Vacation '85
Hardbodies '84
Final Impact '91

Greg Kinnear
As Good As It Gets '97
Dear God '96
A Smile Like Yours '96
Sabrina '95

Roy Kinnear
The Return of the Musketeers '89
A Man for All Seasons '88
Pirates '86
The Zany Adventures of Robin Hood '84
Hawk the Slayer '81
The Adventures of Sherlock Holmes' Smarter Brother '78
Herbie Goes to Monte Carlo '77
The Hound of the Baskervilles '77
The Four Musketeers '75
Ripping Yarns '75
Juggernaut '74
Melody '71
Willy Wonka & the Chocolate Factory '71
Taste the Blood of Dracula '70

Terry Kinney
Critical Choices '97
George Wallace '97
Fly Away Home '96
Sleepers '96
Devil in a Blue Dress '95
The Good Old Boys '95
Body Snatchers '93
The Firm '93
JFK: Reckless Youth '93
Talent for the Game '91
Murder Ordained '87

Leonid Kinskey
Can't Help Singing '45
I Married an Angel '42
Lady for a Night '42
Somewhere I'll Find You '42
Broadway Limited '41
Down Argentine Way '40
Everything Happens at Night '39
The Great Waltz '38
Les Miserables '35
Duck Soup '33

Klaus Kinski
Rough Justice '87
Timestalkers '87
Crawlspace '86
Gangster's Law '86
Creature '85
His Name was King '85
Star Knight '85
Codename: Wildgeese '84
The Little Drummer Girl '84

The Secret Diary of Sigmund Freud '84
Beauty and the Beast '83
Android '82
Burden of Dreams '82
Fitzcarraldo '82
The Soldier '82
Venom '82
Buddy Buddy '81
Schizoid '80
The French Woman '79
Woyzeck '78
Liberators '77
Night of the Assassin '77
Operation Thunderbolt '77
Jack the Ripper '76
Lifespan '75
Primal Impulse '74
Shoot the Living, Pray for the Dead '73
Aguirre, the Wrath of God '72
Count Dracula '71
Slaughter Hotel '71
Creature with the Blue Hand '70
Double Face '70
The Ruthless Four '70
Venus in Furs '70
Web of the Spider '70
And God Said to Cain '60s
Twice a Judas '60s
A Bullet for the General '68
Deadly Sanctuary '68
Psychopath '68
Circus of Fear '67
Fistful of Death '67
Five for Hell '67
Five Golden Dragons '67
Heroes in Hell '67
Target for Killing '66
Doctor Zhivago '65
Fighting Fists of Shanghai Joe '65
For a Few Dollars More '65
The Squeaker '65
The Indian Scarf '63
Door with the Seven Locks '62
Inn on the River '62
Dead Eyes of London '61
The Avenger '60
A Time to Love & a Time to Die '58

Nastassia Kinski
Bella Mafia '97
One Night Stand '97
Father's Day '96
Crackerjack '94
Terminal Velocity '94
Faraway, So Close! '93
Torrents of Spring '90
Magdalene '88
Spring Symphony '86
Harem '85
Revolution '85
The Hotel New Hampshire '84
Maria's Lovers '84
Unfaithfully Yours '84
Boarding School '83
Exposed '83
Moon in the Gutter '83
Paris, Texas '83
Cat People '82
One from the Heart '82
Tess '80
For Your Love Only '79
Stay As You Are '78
The Wrong Move '78
To the Devil, a Daughter '76

Bruce Kirby
Rave Review '95
Getting Up and Going Home '92
Throw Momma from the Train '87
Armed and Dangerous '86
Fyre '78
Cinderella Liberty '73
The Young Graduates '71

Bruno Kirby
Donnie Brasco '96
Sleepers '96
The Basketball Diaries '94
Fallen Angels 2 '93
Golden Gate '93
City Slickers '91
The Freshman '90
Bert Rigby, You're a Fool '89

We're No Angels '89
When Harry Met Sally... '89
Nitti: The Enforcer '88
Good Morning, Vietnam '87
Tin Men '87
Flesh and Blood '85
Birdy '84
This Is Spinal Tap '84
Kiss My Grits '82
The Godfather 1902-1959: The Complete Epic '81
Modern Romance '81
Borderline '80
Between the Lines '77
The Godfather, Part 2 '74
Harrad Experiment '73

Jay Kirby
Sundown Riders '48
Border Patrol '43
Colt Comrades '43
Hoppy Serves a Writ '43
Leather Burners '43
Lost Canyon '43

Michael Kirby
Shadows and Fog '92
Swoon '91
Another Woman '88
The Girl in Blue '74

Joe Kirk
Impact '49
The Noose Hangs High '48
The Naughty Nineties '45
Smart Alecks '42

Phyllis Kirk
The Sad Sack '57
Back from Eternity '56
River Beat '54
House of Wax '53
Three Guys Named Mike '51
A Life of Her Own '50
Our Very Own '50
Two Weeks with Love '50

Tommy Kirk
Blood of Ghastly Horror '72
It's Alive! '68
Mars Needs Women '66
The Unkissed Bride '66
Monkey's Uncle '65
Village of the Giants '65
Pajama Party '64
The Misadventures of Merlin Jones '63
Savage Sam '63
Son of Flubber '63
Bon Voyage! '62
Escapade in Florence '62
Moon Pilot '62
The Absent-Minded Professor '61
Babes in Toyland '61
Horsemasters '61
The Swiss Family Robinson '60
The Shaggy Dog '59
Old Yeller '57

Donald Kirke
A Night for Crime '42
Oh Susannah '38
Country Gentlemen '36

Sally Kirkland
Amnesia '96
Excess Baggage '96
Cheatin' Hearts '93
Eye of the Stranger '93
Gunmen '93
The Woman Who Loved Elvis '93
Double Jeopardy '92
Double Threat '92
Forever: A Ghost of a Love Story '92
Hit the Dutchman '92
Primary Motive '92
Prime Time Murder '92
In the Heat of Passion '91
JFK '91
Bullseye! '90
Heat Wave '90
Revenge '90
Two Evil Eyes '90
Best of the Best '89
Cold Feet '89
High Stakes '89
Paint It Black '89
White Hot '88

Western Pacific Agent '51

Terence Knox
The Invaders '95
The Spy Within '94
Murder So Sweet '93
Children of the Corn 2: The Final
  Sacrifice '92
Forever: A Ghost of a Love
  Story '92
Snow Kill '90
Hard Rain—The Tet 1968 '89
Tripwire '89
City Killer '87
Distortions '87
The Mighty Pawns '87
Murder Ordained '87
Tour of Duty '87
Humanoid Defender '85
Rebel Love '85
Circle of Power '83

Peggy Knudsen
Istanbul '57
Copper Canyon '50
The Big Sleep '46
Humoresque '46
Never Say Goodbye '46
A Stolen Life '46

Gustav Knuth
Heidi '65
Tromba, the Tiger Man '52

Keiju Kobayashi
Godzilla 1985 '85
Tidal Wave '75

Jeff Kober
Elmore Leonard's Gold Coast
  '97
The Big Fall '96
Demolition High '95
One Man's Justice '95
Automatic '94
Tank Girl '94
Lone Justice '93
The Baby Doll Murders '92
Keep the Change '92
The First Power '89
Alien Nation '88
China Beach '88
Lucky Stiff '88
Out of Bounds '86

Marianne Koch
A Place Called Glory '66
A Fistful of Dollars '64
Frozen Alive '64
The Monster of London City '64

Walter Koenig
Star Trek Generations '94
Star Trek 6: The Undiscovered
  Country '91
Moontrap '89
Star Trek 5: The Final Frontier
  '89
Star Trek 4: The Voyage Home
  '86
Star Trek 3: The Search for
  Spock '84
Star Trek 2: The Wrath of Khan
  '82
Star Trek: The Motion Picture
  '80
Star Trek Bloopers '69

Michiyo Kogure
Street of Shame '56
Shin Heike Monogatari '55
A Geisha '53

Fred Kohler, Sr.
The Texas Rangers '36
Honor of the Range '34
Deluge '33
The Fiddlin' Buckaroo '33
Texas Bad Man '32
Fighting Caravans '31
Underworld '27
Riders of the Purple Sage '25
Anna Christie '23

Fred Kohler, Jr.
Daniel Boone: Trail Blazer '56
Calling Wild Bill Elliott '43
Western Mail '42
Pigskin Parade '36
Pecos Kid '35
Toll of the Desert '35
The Man from Hell '34

Lee Kohlmar
Death from a Distance '36
Love in Bloom '35

Susan Kohner
The Gene Krupa Story '59
Imitation of Life '59
Dino '57

Hiroshi Koizumi
Dagora, the Space Monster '65
Godzilla vs. Mothra '64
Attack of the Mushroom People
  '63

Clarence Kolb
Impact '49
Caught in the Draft '41
His Girl Friday '40
Honolulu '39
Give Me a Sailor '38

Henry Kolker
Union Pacific '39
The Cowboy and the Lady '38
Charlie Chan in Paris '35
Mad Love '35
The Mystery Man '35
The Ghost Walks '34
Baby Face '33
Rasputin and the Empress '33
Coquette '29

Amos Kollek
Whore 2 '94
Double Edge '92
Goodbye, New York '85

Tetsu Komai
The Princess Comes Across '36
Hong Kong Nights '35

Hosei Komatsu
A Taxing Woman's Return '88
Double Suicide '69

Rich Komenich
Henry: Portrait of a Serial Killer
  2: Mask of Sanity '96
Two Wrongs Make a Right '89

Liliana Komorowska
The Assignment '97
Martial Outlaw '93
Scanners 3: The Takeover '92

Maja Komorowska
Year of the Quiet Sun '84
Maids of Wilko '79
Family Life '71

Queen Kong
Slashdance '89
Deathstalker 2: Duel of the
  Titans '87

Magda Konopka
When Dinosaurs Ruled the
  Earth '70
Satanik '69

Phyllis Konstam
Skin Game '31
Murder '30

Guich Koock
Picasso Trigger '89
Square Dance '87
American Ninja '85
Seven '79

Milos Kopecky
Fabulous Adventures of Baron
  Munchausen '61
The Original Fabulous
  Adventures of Baron
  Munchausen '61

Bernie Kopell
Get Smart, Again! '89
Combat Academy '86
The Love Boat '70s
The Loved One '65

Kim Kopf
Stormswept '95
Witchcraft 8: Salem's Ghost '95

Karen Kopins
Lady in Waiting '94
Archie: Return to Riverdale '90
Jake Speed '86
Creator '85
Once Bitten '85

Arnold Korff
Doughboys '30

The Haunted Castle '21

Jon Korkes
Syngenor '90
Jaws of Satan '81
The Day of the Dolphin '73
Little Murders '71

Harvey Korman
Jingle All the Way '96
Dracula: Dead and Loving It '95
Based on an Untrue Story '93
Betrayal of the Dove '92
Munchies '87
Film House Fever '86
The Longshot '86
Gone Are the Days '84
Curse of the Pink Panther '83
History of the World: Part 1 '81
Herbie Goes Bananas '80
Americathon '79
Bud and Lou '78
High Anxiety '77
Blazing Saddles '74
Huckleberry Finn '74
April Fools '69

Mary Kornman
Our Gang Comedy Festival 2 '89
Our Gang Comedy Festival '88
Swing It, Professor '37
The Adventurous Knights '35
Desert Trail '35
Queen of the Jungle '35
Our Gang '26
The Return of Our Gang '25

Charlie Korsmo
Can't Hardly Wait '98
The Doctor '91
Hook '91
What About Bob? '91
Dick Tracy '90
Heat Wave '90
Men Don't Leave '89

**Robert F. (Bob)
Kortman**
Guns of the Law '44
Fugitive Valley '41
Hopalong Cassidy: Renegade
  Trail '39
Law of the Texan '38
The Rangers Step In '37
Sandflow '37
Robinson Crusoe of Clipper
  Island '36
The Crimson Trail '35
Feud of the West '35
When a Man Sees Red '34
The Fiddlin' Buckaroo '33
Phantom Thunderbolt '33
Rainbow Ranch '33
Terror Trail '33
Island of Lost Souls '32
The Lone Defender '32

Fritz Kortner
Woman in Brown '48
Pandora's Box '28
The Hands of Orlac '25
Warning Shadows '23
Backstairs '21

Charles Korvin
Ship of Fools '65
Berlin Express '48

Sylva Koscina
Lisa and the Devil '75
The Slasher '74
Hornet's Nest '70
Deadly Sanctuary '68
The Secret War of Harry Frigg
  '68
Juliet of the Spirits '65
Hercules Unchained '59
Hercules '58

Martin Kosleck
The Flesh Eaters '64
House of Horrors '46
Pursuit to Algiers '45
The Mummy's Curse '44
Weird Woman/Frozen Ghost '44
All Through the Night '42
Foreign Correspondent '40

Paul Koslo
Downdraft '96
Judge & Jury '96
Chained Heat 2 '92

Project: Shadowchaser '92
Xtro 2: The Second Encounter
  '91
Robot Jox '90
A Night in the Life of Jimmy
  Reardon '88
The Annihilators '85
Roots: The Next Generation '79
Maniac '77
Rooster Cogburn '75
Joe Kidd '72
Omega Man '71
Vanishing Point '71

David Kossoff
Unicorn '83
The Two Faces of Dr. Jekyll '60
The Mouse That Roared '59
Who Done It? '56
Svengali '55

Kane Kosugi
Journey of Honor '91
Pray for Death '85
Revenge of the Ninja '83

Sho Kosugi
Journey of Honor '91
Blind Fury '90
Kingfisher the Killer '80s
Phoenix the Ninja '80s
Aloha Summer '88
Black Eagle '88
Rage of Honor '87
Nine Deaths of the Ninja '85
Pray for Death '85
Ninja 3: The Domination '84
Revenge of the Ninja '83
Enter the Ninja '81
Master Ninja '72
Shaolin Temple Strikes Back '72

Elias Koteas
Fallen '97
Gattaca '97
Crash '95
The Prophecy '95
Sugartime '95
Camilla '94
Exotica '94
Power of Attorney '94
Chain of Desire '93
Cyborg 2 '93
Teenage Mutant Ninja Turtles 3
  '93
The Adjuster '91
Almost an Angel '90
Desperate Hours '90
Look Who's Talking, Too '90
Teenage Mutant Ninja Turtles:
  The Movie '90
Friends, Lovers & Lunatics '89
Malarek '88
Blood Red '88
Full Moon in Blue Water '88
Tucker: The Man and His Dream
  '88
Some Kind of Wonderful '87

Oded Kotler
Hanna K. '83
My Michael '75

Yaphet Kotto
Out of Sync '95
Two If by Sea '95
Dead Badge '94
The Puppet Masters '94
Almost Blue '93
Extreme Justice '93
In Self Defense '93
Chrome Soldiers '92
Freddy's Dead: The Final
  Nightmare '91
Hangfire '91
After the Shock '90
Jigsaw Murders '89
Ministry of Vengeance '89
Tripwire '89
Midnight Run '88
A Whisper to a Scream '88
Prettykill '87
The Running Man '87
Terminal Entry '87
Eye of the Tiger '86
Harem '86
Badge of the Assassin '85
The Park Is Mine '85
Warning Sign '85
The Star Chamber '83

Fighting Back '82
Brubaker '80
Rage '80
Alien '79
Blue Collar '78
Monkey Hustle '77
Raid on Entebbe '77
Drum '76
Friday Foster '75
Sharks' Treasure '75
Report to the Commissioner '74
Truck Turner '74
Live and Let Die '73
Across 110th Street '72
Housewife '72
Man & Boy '71
Five Card Stud '68
The Thomas Crown Affair '68
Nothing But a Man '64

Hubert Kounde
Hate '95
Cafe au Lait '94

Nancy Kovack
Frankie and Johnny '65
The Outlaws Is Coming! '65
Diary of a Madman '63
Jason and the Argonauts '63

Ernie Kovacs
North to Alaska '60
Strangers When We Meet '60
Bell, Book and Candle '58
Best of Ernie Kovacs '56

Geza Kovacs
Return to the Lost World '93
Baby on Board '92

Martin Kove
Baby Face Nelson '97
Grizzly Mountain '97
Judge & Jury '96
Mercenary '96
Final Equinox '95
Without Mercy '95
Death Match '94
Endangered '94
Uncivilized '94
Wyatt Earp '94
Wyatt Earp: Return to
  Tombstone '94
Future Shock '93
The Outfit '93
President's Target '93
Shootfighter: Fight to the Death
  '93
To Be the Best '93
Firehawk '92
Project: Shadowchaser '92
White Light '90
The Karate Kid: Part 3 '89
Steele Justice '87
The Karate Kid: Part 2 '86
Rambo: First Blood, Part 2 '85
The Karate Kid '84
Seven '79
Last House on the Left '72

Harley Jane Kozak
Dark Planet '97
Titanic '96
The Android Affair '95
Magic in the Water '95
The Amy Fisher Story '93
The Favor '92
All I Want for Christmas '91
Necessary Roughness '91
The Taking of Beverly Hills '91
Arachnophobia '90
Side Out '90
Parenthood '89
When Harry Met Sally... '89

Linda Kozlowski
Village of the Damned '95
Backstreet Justice '93
The Neighbor '93
Almost an Angel '90
Crocodile Dundee 2 '88
Pass the Ammo '88
Target: Favorite Son '87
Crocodile Dundee '86

Jeroen Krabbe
Dangerous Beauty '98
The Odyssey '97
The Disappearance of Garcia
  Lorca '97
Farinelli '94

MacLane ✎cont.

The Half-Breed '51
Let's Dance '50
Silver River '48
Treasure of the Sierra Madre '48
Unknown Island '48
The Spanish Main '45
Treasure of Fear '45
Cry of the Werewolf '44
The Mummy's Ghost '44
Nabonga '44
Bombardier '43
Marine Raiders '43
Song of Texas '43
The Underdog '43
All Through the Night '42
Big Street '42
Dr. Jekyll and Mr. Hyde '41
The Maltese Falcon '41
Western Union '41
Melody Ranch '40
Mutiny in the Big House '39
Bullets or Ballots '38
Prison Break '38
You and Me '38
The Prince and the Pauper '37
You Only Live Once '37
Black Fury '35
The Case of the Lucky Legs '35
Ceiling Zero '35
"G" Men '35
Man of the Forest '33
To the Last Man '33

Mary MacLaren
A Lawman Is Born '37
The New Frontier '35

Gavin MacLeod
Scruples '80
The Love Boat '70s
Only with Married Men '74
Kelly's Heroes '70
The Party '68
The Sand Pebbles '66
McHale's Navy Joins the Air
    Force '65
McHale's Navy '64
Compulsion '59

Michael MacLiammoir
What's the Matter with Helen?
    '71
Othello '52

Ellie MacLure
Air Hawk '84
Heat of the Flame '82
Alvin Purple '73

Aline MacMahon
I Could Go on Singing '63
The Man from Laramie '55
The Flame & the Arrow '50
The Search '48
Dragon Seed '44
The Lady Is Willing '42
Back Door to Heaven '39
Ah, Wilderness! '35
I Live My Life '35
Gold Diggers of 1933 '33
Heroes for Sale '33

Fred MacMurray
The Swarm '78
Beyond the Bermuda Triangle
    '75
Charley and the Angel '73
The Happiest Millionaire '67
Follow Me, Boys! '66
Kisses for My President '64
Son of Flubber '63
Bon Voyage! '62
The Absent-Minded Professor
    '61
The Apartment '60
The Shaggy Dog '59
Good Day for a Hanging '58
At Gunpoint '55
The Caine Mutiny '54
A Woman's World '54
Borderline '50
Never a Dull Moment '50
Father Was a Fullback '49
The Miracle of the Bells '48
Egg and I '47

Singapore '47
Double Indemnity '44
Above Suspicion '43
The Lady Is Willing '42
Dive Bomber '41
Remember the Night '40
My Love For Yours '39
Swing High, Swing Low '37
The Princess Comes Across '36
The Texas Rangers '36
The Trail of the Lonesome Pine
    '36
Alice Adams '35
Hands Across the Table '35

Robert MacNaughton
I Am the Cheese '83
E.T.: The Extra-Terrestrial '82

Patrick Macnee
Thunder in Paradise 2 '94
The Gambler Returns: The Luck
    of the Draw '91
The Hound of London '93
Thunder in Paradise '93
Sherlock Holmes and the
    Incident at Victoria Falls '91
Waxwork 2: Lost in Time '91
Chill Factor '90
Around the World in 80 Days '89
Cult People '89
Lobster Man from Mars '89
Masque of the Red Death '89
Sorry, Wrong Number '89
Transformations '88
Waxwork '88
Shadey '87
Down Under '86
A View to a Kill '85
This Is Spinal Tap '84
Return of the Man from
    U.N.C.L.E. '83
Rehearsal for Murder '82
Young Doctors in Love '82
The Howling '81
Sea Wolves '81
Spaceship '81
Sweet 16 '81
Battlestar Galactica '78
Dead of Night '77
King Solomon's Treasure '76
The Bloodsuckers '70
Les Girls '57
A Christmas Carol '51
The Elusive Pimpernel '50

Peter MacNeill
The Hanging Garden '97
Crash '95

Peter MacNicol
Bean '97
Dracula: Dead and Loving It '95
Roswell: The U.F.O. Cover-Up
    '94
Addams Family Values '93
Hard Promises '92
Housesitter '92
American Blue Note '89
Ghostbusters 2 '89
Heat '87
Sophie's Choice '82
The Boy Who Left Home to Find
    Out About the Shivers '81
Dragonslayer '81

Elle Macpherson
Batman and Robin '97
The Edge '97
Jane Eyre '96
The Mirror Has Two Faces '96
If Lucy Fell '95
Sirens '94
Alice '90

George MacQuarrie
The Idol Dancer '20
The Love Flower '20

Gordon MacRae
Danger in the Skies '79
Carousel '56
Oklahoma! '55
By the Light of the Silvery Moon
    '53
The Desert Song '53
On Moonlight Bay '51
Tea for Two '50
The West Point Story '50
Look for the Silver Lining '49

Heather MacRae
Secrets of Three Hungry Wives
    '78
Bang the Drum Slowly '73
The Connection '73

Meredith MacRae
Husbands, Wives, Money, and
    Murder '86
Vultures '84
Sketches of a Strangler '78
Bikini Beach '64

Michael MacRae
Masterminds '96
Madhouse '87
Isle of Secret Passion '85
Dear Detective '78
Great Ride '78
Greedy Terror '78

George Macready
The Return of Count Yorga '71
Tora! Tora! Tora! '70
Night Gallery '69
The Great Race '65
The Human Duplicators '64
Where Love Has Gone '64
Taras Bulba '62
Two Weeks in Another Town '62
Paths of Glory '57
I Beheld His Glory '53
Julius Caesar '53
The Stranger Wore a Gun '53
Vera Cruz '53
The Green Glove '52
Detective Story '51
The Nevadan '50
The Doolins of Oklahoma '49
Knock on Any Door '49
The Big Clock '48
Black Arrow '48
Coroner Creek '48
Down to Earth '47
Gilda '46
The Seventh Cross '44

Bill Macy
Murder In the First '95
Me, Myself & I '92
The Doctor '91
Sibling Rivalry '90
Bad Medicine '85
Casey at the Bat '85
Movers and Shakers '85
My Favorite Year '82
Serial '80
Diary of a Young Comic '79
The Jerk '79
The Late Show '77
Oh! Calcutta! '72

William H. Macy
Air Force One '97
Boogie Nights '97
Wag the Dog '97
Down Periscope '96
Fargo '96
Ghosts of Mississippi '96
Andersonville '95
Mr. Holland's Opus '95
Being Human '94
Children of Fury '94
Dead on Sight '94
ER '94
Oleanna '94
Benny & Joon '93
Searching for Bobby Fischer '93
Twenty Bucks '93
A Private Matter '92
The Water Engine '92
Homicide '91

Ciaran Madden
Ivanhoe '97
Fortunes of War '87
A Married Man '84
Black Werewolf '75

John Madden
Little Giants '94
P.K. and the Kid '85

Peter Madden
Kiss of the Vampire '62
The Loneliness of the Long
    Distance Runner '62

Victor Maddern
I'm All Right Jack '59
Blood of the Vampire '58

Abandon Ship '57

Amy Madigan
Loved '97
Female Perversions '96
Riders of the Purple Sage '96
The Dark Half '91
Field of Dreams '89
Roe vs. Wade '89
Uncle Buck '89
Prince of Pennsylvania '88
Nowhere to Hide '87
Alamo Bay '85
Twice in a Lifetime '85
Places in the Heart '84
Streets of Fire '84
Love Letters '83
The Ambush Murders '82
Love Child '82

James Madio
The Basketball Diaries '94
Hero '92

Guy Madison
Computer Wizard '77
Where's Willie? '77
Hell Commandos '69
Special Forces '68
Bang Bang Kid '67
Superargo '67
Five Giants from Texas '66
The Snake Hunter Strangler '66
Cold Steel for Tortuga '65
Place in Hell '65
Apaches Last Battle '64
Conqueror & the Empress '64
Executioner of Venice '63
Jet Over the Atlantic '59
Bullwhip '58
Savage Wilderness '55
Drums in the Deep South '51
Till the End of Time '46
Since You Went Away '44

Noel Madison
Footsteps in the Dark '41
Sailing Along '38
Gangway '37
The House of Secrets '37
A Nation Aflame '37
Cocaine Fiends '36

Rock Madison
Creature of the Walking Dead
    '60
Man Beast '55

Philip Madoc
A Mind to Kill '95
Space: 1999—Alien Attack '79

Ruth Madoc
Agatha Christie's The Pale
    Horse '96
Hi-Di-Hi '88

Madonna
Evita '96
Girl 6 '96
Blue in the Face '95
Four Rooms '95
Dangerous Game '93
Body of Evidence '92
A League of Their Own '92
Shadows and Fog '92
Truth or Dare '91
Dick Tracy '90
Bloodhounds of Broadway '89
Who's That Girl? '87
Shanghai Surprise '86
Desperately Seeking Susan '85
Certain Sacrifice '80

Michael Madsen
The Sender '98
Species 2 '98
Diary of a Serial Killer '97
Executive Target '97
Love to Kill '97
Donnie Brasco '96
The Last Days of Frankie the Fly
    '96
Red Line '96
The Winner '96
Free Willy 2: The Adventure
    Home '95
Man with a Gun '95
Mulholland Falls '95
Species '95
Dead Connection '94
Season of Change '94

Wyatt Earp '94
Almost Blue '93
Free Willy '93
The Getaway '93
A House in the Hills '93
Money for Nothing '93
Beyond the Law '92
Fatal Instinct '92
Inside Edge '92
Reservoir Dogs '92
Straight Talk '92
Trouble Bound '92
The Doors '91
Thelma & Louise '91
The End of Innocence '90
Kill Me Again '89
Shadows in the Storm '88
The Natural '84
Racing with the Moon '84

Virginia Madsen
John Grisham's The Rainmaker
    '97
Ghosts of Mississippi '96
Just Your Luck '96
The Prophecy '95
Bitter Vengeance '94
Blue Tiger '94
Caroline at Midnight '93
Linda '93
Becoming Colette '92
Candyman '92
Highlander 2: The Quickening
    '91
Love Kills '91
Victim of Love '91
The Hot Spot '90
Ironclads '90
The Heart of Dixie '89
Third Degree Burn '89
Gotham '88
Hot to Trot! '88
Mr. North '88
Long Gone '87
Slamdance '87
Zombie High '87
Fire with Fire '86
Modern Girls '86
Creator '85
The Hearst and Davies Affair '85
Dune '84
Electric Dreams '84

Roma Maffia
Kiss the Girls '97
The Heidi Chronicles '95
Nick of Time '95
Disclosure '94

Macha Magal
S.S. Experiment Camp 2 '86
SS Girls '78

Cass Magda
Blade Boxer '97
Hawk's Vengeance '96

Patrick Magee
The Monster Club '85
The Black Cat '81
Chariots of Fire '81
Rough Cut '80
Sleep of Death '79
Telefon '77
Barry Lyndon '75
A Killer in Every Corner '74
Luther '74
And Now the Screaming Starts
    '73
The Final Programme '73
Asylum '72
Demons of the Mind '72
Young Winston '72
A Clockwork Orange '71
The Fiend '71
King Lear '71
Trojan Women '71
Cromwell '70
Anzio '68
Marat/Sade '66
Portrait in Terror '66
Die, Monster, Die! '65
Masque of the Red Death '65
Masque of the Red Death/
    Premature Burial '65
The Skull '65
Seance on a Wet Afternoon '64
Dementia 13 '63
The Very Edge '63

Malone *cont.*

The Last Voyage '60
Warlock '59
Man of a Thousand Faces '57
Tarnished Angels '57
Sincerely Yours '56
Tension at Table Rock '56
Written on the Wind '56
Artists and Models '55
At Gunpoint '55
Battle Cry '55
The Fast and the Furious '54
Young at Heart '54
Scared Stiff '53
Torpedo Alley '53
The Bushwackers '52
The Nevadan '50
South of St. Louis '48
The Big Sleep '46
Night and Day '46

Jena Malone
Contact '97
Ellen Foster '97
Hope '97
Bastard out of Carolina '96
Hidden in America '96

Mollie Malone
Battling Bunyon '24
Straight Shootin' '17

Patrick Malone
Grand Canyon '91
Rock 'n' Roll High School
   Forever '91

Michael Maloney
Hamlet '96
A Midwinter's Tale '95
Othello '95
Truly, Madly, Deeply '91
Henry V '89
Sharma & Beyond '84

Peter Maloney
Washington Square '97
Robot in the Family '94

H.F. Maltby
Pygmalion '38
Young and Innocent '37

Leonard Maltin
Forgotten Silver '96
Gremlins 2: The New Batch '90

Robert Mammone
Heaven's Burning '97
The Crossing '92

Biff Manard
Trancers 2: The Return of Jack
   Deth '90
Zone Troopers '84

Ray "Boom Boom" Mancini
The Search for One-Eyed Jimmy
   '96
Wishful Thinking '92
Timebomb '91
Backstreet Dreams '90
The Dirty Dozen: The Fatal
   Mission '88
Oceans of Fire '86

Nick Mancuso
Misbegotten '98
Past Perfect '98
Marquis de Sade '97
The Ex '96
The Invader '96
Provocateur '96
Under Siege 2: Dark Territory
   '95
A Young Connecticut Yankee in
   King Arthur's Court '95
Young Ivanhoe '95
Flinch '94
Suspicious Agenda '94
The Takeover '94
Wild Palms '93
Lies Before Kisses '92
Rapid Fire '92
Fatal Exposure '91
Lena's Holiday '90
Double Identity '89
Death of an Angel '86
Half a Lifetime '86

Embassy '85
Blame It on the Night '84
Heartbreakers '84
Maria Chapdelaine '84
Tell Me That You Love Me '84
Legend of Walks Far Woman '82
Mother Lode '82
Ticket to Heaven '81
Death Ship '80
The House on Garibaldi Street
   '79
Nightwing '79

Robert Mandan
National Lampoon's Last Resort
   '94
Perry Mason: The Case of the
   Lost Love '87
In Love with an Older Woman
   '82
Zapped! '82
Return of the Rebels '81
The Best of Soap: Jessica's
   Wonderful Life '70s
The Best of Soap: Who Killed
   Peter? '77

Howie Mandel
Kurt Vonnegut's Harrison
   Bergeron '95
Mother Goose Rock 'n' Rhyme
   '90
Little Monsters '89
Walk Like a Man '87
A Fine Mess '86
The Princess Who Never
   Laughed '84
Gas '81

Miles Mander
Brighton Strangler '45
The Brighton Strangler/Before
   Dawn '45
Picture of Dorian Gray '45
Murder, My Sweet '44
The Pearl of Death '44
Scarlet Claw '44
Five Graves to Cairo '43
Guadalcanal Diary '43
Return of the Vampire '43
Shadows on the Stairs '41
Primrose Path '40
The Little Princess '39
Stanley and Livingstone '39
The Three Musketeers '39
Wuthering Heights '39
The Tower of London '39
Mad Miss Manton '38
Don Quixote '35
The Three Musketeers '35
The Private Life of Henry VIII '33
Murder '30

Barbara Mandrell
Burning Rage '84
The Concrete Cowboys '79

Costas Mandylor
Shelter '98
Double Take '97
Stand-Ins '97
Last Exit to Earth '96
Crosscut '95
Delta of Venus '95
Fist of the North Star '95
Portraits of a Killer '95
Venus Rising '95
Virtuosity '95
Almost Dead '94
Fatal Past '94
The Doors '91
Mobsters '91
Soapdish '91
Triumph of the Spirit '89

Larry Manetti
The Corporation '96
Body Chemistry 4: Full Exposure
   '95
Exit '95
C.I.A. 2: Target Alexa '94
The Take '90
Magnum P.I.: Don't Eat the
   Snow in Hawaii '80

Nino Manfredi
Alberto Express '92
In the Name of the Pope-King
   '85
Cafe Express '83
Nudo di Donna '83

Spaghetti House '82
We All Loved Each Other So
   Much '77
Down & Dirty '76
Bread and Chocolate '74
Head of the Family '71

Silvana Mangano
Dark Eyes '87
Dune '84
Conversation Piece '75
Ludwig '72
Death in Venice '71
The Decameron '70
Teorema '68
Oedipus Rex '67
Barabbas '62
The Great War '59
Mambo '55
Ulysses '55
The Gold of Naples '54
Anna '51
Bitter Rice '49
Lure of the Sila '49

Karin Mani
Avenging Angel '85
Alley Cat '84

Cindy Manion
The Toxic Avenger '86
Preppies '84

Dudley Manlove
The Creation of the Humanoids
   '62
Plan 9 from Outer Space '56

Byron Mann
Red Corner '97
Street Fighter '94

Hank Mann
City Lights '31
Spite Marriage '29

Leonard Mann
Corrupt '84
Night School '81

Leslie Mann
George of the Jungle '97
The Cable Guy '96
Last Man Standing '96
She's the One '96

Terrence Mann
True Women '97
Mrs. Santa Claus '96
Critters 4 '91
The Ten Million Dollar Getaway
   '91
Critters 2: The Main Course '88
Critters '86
A Chorus Line '85

Tracey Mann
Fast Talking '86
Hard Knocks '80

David Manners
The Mystery of Edwin Drood '35
The Black Cat '34
The Death Kiss '33
A Bill of Divorcement '32
The Mummy '32
They Call It Sin '32
Three Broadway Girls '32
Dracula '31
The Miracle Woman '31

Lucie Mannheim
Hotel Reserve '44
High Command '37
The 39 Steps '35

Ettore Manni
City of Women '81
Street People '76
The Battle of El Alamein '68
Heroes in Hell '67
Mademoiselle '66
Giants of Rome '63
Hercules and the Captive
   Women '63
The Battle of Austerlitz '60
Angel in a Taxi '59
Two Nights with Cleopatra '54

Vic Manni
Trapped In Paradise '94
29th Street '91

Marilyn Manning
The Sadist '63

What's Up Front '63
Eegah! '62

Sheila Mannors
Desert Phantom '36
Kelly of the Secret Service '36
Prescott Kid '36
Lawless Range '35
Westward Ho '35

Dinah Manoff
Welcome Home, Roxy
   Carmichael '90
Bloodhounds of Broadway '89
Backfire '88
Child's Play '88
Table Settings '84
I Ought to Be in Pictures '82
For Ladies Only '81
Ordinary People '80
The Possessed '77

Miki Manojlovic
Artemisia '97
Someone Else's America '96
Underground '95
Every Other Weekend '91
When Father was Away on
   Business '85

Jayne Mansfield
Single Room Furnished '68
Wild, Wild World of Jayne
   Mansfield '68
Las Vegas Hillbillys '66
Dog Eat Dog '64
Promises! Promises! '63
Panic Button '62
The Loves of Hercules '60
It Takes a Thief '59
Will Success Spoil Rock Hunter?
   '57
The Female Jungle '56
The Girl Can't Help It '56
Hell on Frisco Bay '55
Illegal '55
Pete Kelly's Blues '55
Underwater! '55

Sally Mansfield
Rocky Jones, Space Ranger '54
Rocky Jones, Space Ranger:
   Renegade Satellite '54

Leonor Manso
Made in Argentina '86
House of Shadows '83
Far Away and Long Ago '74

Alan Manson
Whiffs '75
Let's Scare Jessica to Death '71

Paul Mantee
Lurking Fear '94
The Manitou '78
Robinson Crusoe on Mars '64

Joe Mantegna
The Wonderful Ice Cream Suit
   '98
A Call to Remember '97
Face Down '97
The Last Don '97
Albino Alligator '96
Stephen King's Thinner '96
Underworld '96
Up Close and Personal '96
Above Suspicion '95
Captain Nuke and the Bomber
   Boys '95
An Eye for an Eye '95
For Better or Worse '95
Forget Paris '95
National Lampoon's Favorite
   Deadly Sins '95
Airheads '94
Baby's Day Out '94
State of Emergency '94
Fallen Angels 2 '93
Searching for Bobby Fischer '93
Body of Evidence '92
The Comrades of Summer '92
The Water Engine '92
Bugsy '91
Family Prayers '91
Homicide '91
Queens Logic '91
Alice '90
The Godfather, Part 3 '90
Wait Until Spring, Bandini '90
Things Change '88

House of Games '87
Suspect '87
Weeds '87
Critical Condition '86
The Money Pit '86
Off Beat '86
Three Amigos '86
Compromising Positions '85
Second Thoughts '83
Elvis: The Movie '79

Henrietta Mantel
A Very Brady Sequel '96
The Brady Bunch Movie '95

Michael Mantell
Sins of the Mind '97
Dead Funny '94
The Night We Never Met '93
City of Hope '91
Eight Men Out '88

Randolph Mantooth
Terror at London Bridge '85
The Seekers '79

Leslie Manville
Secrets and Lies '95
High Hopes '88
High Season '88
Dance with a Stranger '85
Grown Ups '80

Linda Manz
Gummo '97
The Snow Queen '83
Out of the Blue '80
Orphan Train '79
Wanderers '79
Days of Heaven '78

Angela Mao
The Association '80s
When Taekwondo Strikes '83
Return of the Tiger '78
Sting of the Dragon Masters '74

Adele Mara
Night Time in Nevada '48
Robin Hood of Texas '47
The Inner Circle '46
Bells of Rosarita '45
Twilight on the Rio Grande '41

Mary Mara
Bound '96
Love Potion #9 '92
Mr. Saturday Night '92

Steve Marachuk
Hot Target '85
Piranha 2: The Spawning '82
The Spawning '82
Waikiki '80

Jean Marais
Stealing Beauty '96
Dos Cruces en Danger Pass '71
Donkey Skin '70
The Rape of the Sabines '61
The Battle of Austerlitz '60
The Testament of Orpheus '59
Girl in His Pocket '57
White Nights '57
Elena and Her Men '56
Orpheus '49
The Eagle Has Two Heads '48
Ruyblas '48
The Storm Within '48
Beauty and the Beast '46
Eternal Return '43

Cindy Maranne
Provoked '89
Slashdance '89

Dominique Marcas
La Vie de Boheme '93
Dr. Petiot '90

Marcel Marceau
Silent Movie '76
Barbarella '68

Sophie Marceau
Leo Tolstoy's Anna Karenina '96
Braveheart '95
Police '85
Fort Saganne '84
La Boum '81

Fredric March
Hombre '67
Seven Days in May '64
Inherit the Wind '60

The Seventh Voyage of Sinbad '58

Thom Mathews
Heatseeker '95
Bloodmatch '91
Midnight Cabaret '90
Down Twisted '89
Return of the Living Dead 2 '88
Alien from L.A. '87
Friday the 13th, Part 6: Jason Lives '86

Marion Mathie
Dracula Has Risen from the Grave '68
Lolita '62

Samantha Mathis
The American President '95
Broken Arrow '95
How to Make an American Quilt '95
Jack and Sarah '95
Little Women '94
The Music of Chance '93
Super Mario Bros. '93
The Thing Called Love '93
This Is My Life '92
Pump Up the Volume '90

Jacques Mathou
Ridicule '96
The Hairdresser's Husband '92
Year of the Comet '92
Betty Blue '86

Marlee Matlin
Dead Silence '96
It's My Party '95
Hear No Evil '93
The Linguini Incident '92
Bridge to Silence '89
Walker '87
Children of a Lesser God '86

Daniel Matmor
Buffalo Heart: The Pain of Death '96
The Mangler '94

John Matshikiza
Yankee Zulu '95
Dust Devil '93
Mandela '87
Dust '85

Eiko Matsuda
Sweet Evil '95
In the Realm of the Senses '76

Yusaku Matsuda
Black Rain '89
The Family Game '83
Murder in the Doll House '79

Eva Mattes
The Promise '94
A Man Like Eva '83
Celeste '81
David '79
In a Year of 13 Moons '78
Woyzeck '78
Stroszek '77
The Bitter Tears of Petra von Kant '72

Pam Matteson
Prehysteria 3 '95
Punchline '88

Walter Matthau
Neil Simon's The Odd Couple 2 '98
Out to Sea '97
I'm Not Rappaport '96
The Grass Harp '95
Grumpier Old Men '95
I.Q. '94
Dennis the Menace '93
Grumpy Old Men '93
JFK '91
The Incident '89
The Couch Trip '87
Pirates '86
Movers and Shakers '85
Survivors '83
I Ought to Be in Pictures '82
Buddy Buddy '81
First Monday in October '81
Hopscotch '80
Little Miss Marker '80
California Suite '78
Casey's Shadow '78

House Calls '78
The Bad News Bears '76
The Sunshine Boys '75
Earthquake '74
The Front Page '74
The Laughing Policeman '74
The Taking of Pelham One Two Three '74
Charley Varrick '73
Pete 'n' Tillie '72
Kotch '71
A New Leaf '71
Plaza Suite '71
Cactus Flower '69
Hello, Dolly! '69
The Odd Couple '68
Secret Life of an American Wife '68
A Guide for the Married Man '67
The Fortune Cookie '66
Mirage '66
Ensign Pulver '64
Fail-Safe '64
Charade '63
Who's Got the Action? '63
Lonely Are the Brave '62
Strangers When We Meet '60
King Creole '58
A Face in the Crowd '57
The Indian Fighter '55
The Kentuckian '55
Atomic Attack '50

A.E. Matthews
Carry On Admiral '57
Made in Heaven '52
The Iron Duke '34

Al Matthews
American Roulette '88
The Sender '82

Brian Matthews
Red Nights '87
The Burning '82

Dakin Matthews
Bean '97
Rough Riders '97
White Mile '94
The Temp '93
In a Stranger's Hand '92
Revolver '92
Child's Play 3 '91
My Brother's Wife '89
Naked Lie '89
Permanent Record '88
Nuts '87

Francis Matthews
The McGuffin '85
Dracula, Prince of Darkness '66
Rasputin the Mad Monk '66
Murder Ahoy '64
The Hellfire Club '61
Corridors of Blood '58
The Revenge of Frankenstein '58
Small Hotel '57
Bhowani Junction '56

Fritz Matthews
Born Killer '89
Hell on the Battleground '88
Deadly Prey '87

Jessie Matthews
The Hound of the Baskervilles '77
Candles at Nine '44
Forever and a Day '43
Sailing Along '38
Gangway '37
It's Love Again '36
Evergreen '34

Lester Matthews
King Richard and the Crusaders '54
The Invisible Man's Revenge '44
The Raven '35
Werewolf of London '35

Liesl Matthews
Air Force One '97
A Little Princess '95

Robin Mattson
In Between '92
Take Two '87
Captain America '79
Hot Rod '79

Wolf Lake '79
Return to Macon County '75
Candy Stripe Nurses '74
Bonnie's Kids '73
Namu, the Killer Whale '66

Victor Mature
Samson and Delilah '84
After the Fox '66
The Long Haul '57
Savage Wilderness '55
Betrayed '54
Dangerous Mission '54
Demetrius and the Gladiators '54
The Egyptian '54
The Robe '53
Androcles and the Lion '52
The Las Vegas Story '52
Million Dollar Mermaid '52
Samson and Delilah '50
Easy Living '49
Kiss of Death '47
My Darling Clementine '46
Footlight Serenade '42
Seven Days' Leave '42
The Shanghai Gesture '42
Song of the Islands '42
I Wake Up Screaming '41
Captain Caution '40
No, No Nanette '40
One Million B.C. '40

John Matuszak
Down the Drain '89
Ghost Writer '89
One Man Force '89
The Goonies '85
Ice Pirates '84
Caveman '81
North Dallas Forty '79
Semi-Tough '77

Johanna Matz
The Life and Loves of Mozart '59
They Were So Young '55
Party Girls for Sale '54

Joan Maude
The Temptress '49
Power '34

Monica Maughan
A Woman's Tale '92
Cactus '86
Prisoner Cell Block H '80

Sarah Maur-Thorp
River of Death '90
Edge of Sanity '89
Ten Little Indians '89

Carmen Maura
Le Bonheur Est Dans le Pre '95
Between Heaven and Earth '93
Ay, Carmela! '90
Baton Rouge '88
Women on the Verge of a Nervous Breakdown '88
Law of Desire '86
Matador '86
Extramuros '85
What Have I Done to Deserve This? '85
Dark Habits '84
Pepi, Luci, Bom and Other Girls on the Heap '80

Joshua Maurer
Taken Away '89
Tour of Duty '87

Nicole Maurey
Day of the Triffids '63
The Jayhawkers '59
Me and the Colonel '58
Rogue's Yarn '56

Claire Maurier
Un Air de Famille '96
La Cage aux Folles '78
Sweet Ecstasy '62
The 400 Blows '59
Back to the Wall '56

Gerda Maurus
Woman in the Moon '29
Spies '28

Edwin Maxwell
Woman in Brown '48
Swamp Fire '46
Waterfront '44
Behind Prison Walls '43

Way Down South '39
Mystery Liner '34
Night of Terror '33
The Taming of the Shrew '29

Frank Maxwell
The Haunted Palace '63
Shame '61
Lonelyhearts '58

John Maxwell
Prowler '51
Boss of Big Town '43
The Payoff '43
Honky Tonk '41

Larry Maxwell
Public Access '93
Poison '91

Lois Maxwell
Eternal Evil '87
A View to a Kill '85
For Your Eyes Only '81
Moonraker '79
The Spy Who Loved Me '77
The Man with the Golden Gun '74
Live and Let Die '73
Diamonds Are Forever '71
On Her Majesty's Secret Service '69
You Only Live Twice '67
Thunderball '65
Goldfinger '64
From Russia with Love '63
The Haunting '63
Dr. No '62
Lolita '62
The Unstoppable Man '59
Time Without Pity '57

Marilyn Maxwell
Wild Women '70
Arizona Bushwackers '67
Off Limits '53
The Lemon Drop Kid '51
Key to the City '50
Champion '49
Summer Holiday '48
The Show-Off '46
Lost in a Harem '44

Paul Maxwell
Cloud Waltzing '87
Going Home '86

Roberta Maxwell
The Postman '97
Dead Man Walking '95
Philadelphia '93
Psycho 3 '86
Lois Gibbs and the Love Canal '82
The Changeling '80

Deborah May
Caged Fear '92
Johnny Be Good '88
Rage of Angels '83

Donald May
Bogie: The Last Hero '80
Kisses for My President '64

Elaine May
In the Spirit '90
California Suite '78
A New Leaf '71
Enter Laughing '67
Luv '67

Jack May
Night Slasher '84
He Kills Night After Night After Night '70

Jodhi May
Sister My Sister '94
The Last of the Mohicans '92
Eminent Domain '91
Max and Helen '90
A World Apart '88

Mathilda May
The Jackal '97
Prince Brat and the Whipping Boy '95
Becoming Colette '92
The Cry of the Owl '92
Naked Tango '91
Lifeforce '85
Letters to an Unknown Lover '84

Rik Mayall
Drop Dead Fred '91
Little Noises '91
The Young Ones '88
Whoops Apocalypse '83
Eye of the Needle '81

Anthony Mayans
Heat of the Flame '82
Zombie Lake '80
Sex Is Crazy '79

Eddie Mayehoff
How to Murder Your Wife '64
Artists and Models '55
The Stooge '51

Chip Mayer
Liar Liar '96
Survivor '87
Our Family Business '81

Ray Mayer
Swing It, Sailor! '37
Special Investigator '36

Peter Mayhew
Return of the Jedi '83
The Empire Strikes Back '80

John Maynard
Biohazard: The Alien Force '95
Dark Universe '93

Ken Maynard
Arizona Whirlwind '44
Death Valley Rangers '44
Harmony Trail '44
The Law Rides Again '43
Death Rides the Range '40
Lightning Strikes West '40
Flaming Lead '39
Phantom Rancher '39
Six Shootin' Sheriff '38
Whirlwind Horseman '38
Boots of Destiny '37
Desert Guns/Six-Shootin' Sheriff '36
Tombstone Canyon '35
Trail Drive '35
Western Frontier '35
Honor of the Range '34
In Old Santa Fe '34
Mystery Mountain '34
Drum Taps '33
The Fiddlin' Buckaroo '33
The Lone Avenger '33
Phantom Thunderbolt '33
Strawberry Roan '33
Between Fighting Men '32
Come On Tarzan '32
Dynamite Ranch '32
False Faces '32
Fargo Express '32
Hell Fire Austin '32
Sunset Trail '32
Texas Gunfighter '32
Whistlin' Dan '32
Arizona Terror '31
Branded Men '31
The Pocatello Kid '31
Range Law '31
Two Gun Man '31
Fightin' Ranch '30
The Fighting Legion '30
Fighting Thru '30
Mountain Justice '30
$50,000 Reward '25

Kermit Maynard
The Black Lash '52
Trail of Robin Hood '50
Ambush Trail '46
'Neath Canadian Skies '46
Gangster's Den '45
The Stranger from Pecos '45
Devil Riders '44
Frontier Outlaws '44
Texas Kid '43
Along the Sundown Trail '42
Arizona Stagecoach '42
The Mysterious Rider '42
Prairie Pals '42
Billy the Kid '41
Bury Me Not on the Lone Prairie '41
Man from Montana '41
Pony Post '40
Riders of Pasco Basin '40
The Showdown '40
Valley of Terror '38

Harold Pruett
The Perfect Daughter '96
Precious Find '96
Spellcaster '91
Summer Camp Nightmare '86

Jonathan Pryce
David '97
Regeneration '97
Tomorrow Never Dies '97
Evita '96
Carrington '95
The Age of Innocence '93
Barbarians at the Gate '93
A Business Affair '93
Deadly Advice '93
Shades of Fear '93
Shopping '93
Thicker Than Water '93
Glengarry Glen Ross '92
The Adventures of Baron
 Munchausen '89
The Man from the Pru '89
The Rachel Papers '89
Consuming Passions '88
Man on Fire '87
Haunted Honeymoon '86
Jumpin' Jack Flash '86
Brazil '85
The Doctor and the Devils '85
Loophole '83
The Ploughman's Lunch '83
Praying Mantis '83
Something Wicked This Way
 Comes '83
Breaking Glass '80

Nicholas Pryor
Hail Caesar '94
Hoffa '92
Pacific Heights '90
Brain Dead '89
Nightbreaker '89
Morgan Stewart's Coming Home
 '87
The Falcon and the Snowman
 '85
Into Thin Air '85
Risky Business '83
East of Eden '80
The $5.20 an Hour Dream '80
Last Song '80
The Fish that Saved Pittsburgh
 '79
Damien: Omen 2 '78
Gumball Rally '76
The Life and Assassination of
 the Kingfish '76
Night Terror '76
Force Five '75
The Happy Hooker '75
Smile '75

Richard Pryor
Lost Highway '96
Another You '91
Harlem Nights '89
See No Evil, Hear No Evil '89
Moving '88
Critical Condition '86
Jo Jo Dancer, Your Life Is
 Calling '86
Brewster's Millions '85
Superman 3 '83
Some Kind of Hero '82
The Toy '82
Bustin' Loose '81
Stir Crazy '80
Wholly Moses! '80
Blue Collar '78
California Suite '78
The Wiz '78
Greased Lightning '77
Which Way Is Up? '77
Bingo Long Traveling All-Stars &
 Motor Kings '76
Car Wash '76
Silver Streak '76
Adios Amigo '75
Uptown Saturday Night '74
Hit! '73
The Mack '73
Some Call It Loving '73
Lady Sings the Blues '72
Dynamite Chicken '70
Black Brigade '69
Wild in the Streets '68

Roger Pryor
Identity Unknown '45
Kid Sister '45
Meet the Mob '42
Panama Menace '41
The Man They Could Not Hang
 '39
Headline Woman '35
Belle of the Nineties '34
Lady by Choice '34

Wojciech Pszoniak
Angry Harvest '85
Danton '82
Land of Promise '74

Tito Puente
The Mambo Kings '92
Radio Days '87

Robert Pugh
A Mind to Murder '96
Priest '94
Thicker Than Water '93
Danger UXB '81

Willard Pugh
Puppet Master 5: The Final
 Chapter '94
CB4: The Movie '93
Ambition '91
A Rage in Harlem '91
Native Son '86
The Color Purple '85

Frank Puglia
20 Million Miles to Earth '57
The Black Hand '50
Bagdad '49
Without Reservations '46
Ali Baba and the Forty Thieves
 '43
Billy the Kid '41
The Fatal Hour '40
Bulldog Drummond's Revenge
 '37
Viva Villa! '34
Romola '25

Aldo Puglisi
Marriage Italian Style '64
Seduced and Abandoned '64

Bill Pullman
The End of Violence '97
Zero Effect '97
Independence Day '96
Lost Highway '96
Mistrial '96
Casper '95
Mr. Wrong '95
While You Were Sleeping '95
The Last Seduction '94
Wyatt Earp '94
Malice '93
Nervous Ticks '93
Sleepless in Seattle '93
Sommersby '93
Crazy in Love '92
The Favor '92
A League of Their Own '92
Newsies '92
Singles '92
Bright Angel '91
Going Under '91
Liebestraum '91
Sibling Rivalry '90
Brain Dead '89
Cold Feet '89
The Accidental Tourist '88
Rocket Gibraltar '88
The Serpent and the Rainbow
 '87
Spaceballs '87
Ruthless People '86

Lilo (Liselotte)
Pulver
The Nun '66
A Global Affair '63
A Time to Love & a Time to Die
 '58

Dick Purcell
Captain America '44
Timber Queen '44
Phantom Killer '42
X Marks the Spot '42
King of the Zombies '41
The Abe Lincoln of Ninth
 Avenue '39

Heroes in Blue '39
Irish Luck '39
Tough Kid '39

James Purcell
Playroom '90
White Light '90

Lee Purcell
Movies Money Murder '96
Long Road Home '91
The Incredible Hulk Returns '88
To Heal a Nation '88
Jailbait: Betrayed By Innocence
 '86
Space Rage '86
Eddie Macon's Run '83
Homework '82
Killing at Hell's Gate '81
Kenny Rogers as the Gambler
 '80
Stir Crazy '80
Big Wednesday '78
Summer of Fear '78
The Amazing Howard Hughes
 '77
Mr. Majestyk '74
The Witching '72
Adam at 6 a.m. '70

Noel Purcell
Mutiny on the Bounty '62
Lust for Life '56
Land of Fury '55
Encore '52
Captain Boycott '47

Reginald Purdell
Brighton Rock '47
Candles at Nine '44
Clouds Over Europe '39
The Old Curiosity Shop '35

Edmund Purdom
After the Fall of New York '85
Don't Open Till Christmas '84
Ator the Fighting Eagle '83
Big Boss '77
Mr. Scarface '77
Dr. Frankenstein's Castle of
 Freaks '74
Rulers of the City '71
Nefertiti, Queen of the Nile '64
Herod the Great '60
The King's Thief '55
The Prodigal '55
Athena '54
The Egyptian '54
The Student Prince '54

Carolyn Purdy-
Gordon
Dolls '87
From Beyond '86
Re-Animator '84

James Purefoy
The Tide of Life '96
Feast of July '95

Om Puri
The Ghost and the Darkness '96
Brothers in Trouble '95
In Custody '94
Wolf '94
City of Joy '92

Linda Purl
Incident at Deception Ridge '94
Natural Causes '94
Accidental Meeting '93
In Self Defense '93
Body Language '92
Spies, Lies and Naked Thighs
 '91
Web of Deceit '90
Viper '88
Outrage! '86
Visiting Hours '82
The Adventures of Nellie Bly '81
High Country '81
The Manions of America '81
The Night the City Screamed '80
The Flame Is Love '79
Last Cry for Help '79
Little Ladies of the Night '77
Eleanor & Franklin '76
Crazy Mama '76

Edna Purviance
The Chaplin Revue '58
Woman of Paris/Sunnyside '23

The Kid '21
The Kid/Idle Class '21
Rink/Immigrant '10s
Three Charlies and One
 Phoney! '18
Triple Trouble/Easy Street '18
Charlie Chaplin: The Early
 Years, Vol. 1 '17
Charlie Chaplin: The Early
 Years, Vol. 2 '17
Count/Adventurer '17
The Cure '17
Burlesque of Carmen '16
Charlie Chaplin: The Early
 Years, Vol. 3 '16
Charlie Chaplin: The Early
 Years, Vol. 4 '16
The Fireman '16
The Vagabond '16
Work/Police '16
The Champion/His New Job '15
Charlie Chaplin: Night at the
 Show '15
Charlie Chaplin...Our Hero! '15
The Floorwalker/By the Sea '15
His Prehistoric Past/The Bank
 '15
Tramp & a Woman '15

Alexandra Purvis
Ronnie and Julie '97
Poltergeist: The Legacy '96

John Putch
Alone in the Woods '95
Fallen Angels 2 '93
Curfew '88
Impure Thoughts '86
Jaws 3 '83

Hy Pyke
Halloween Night '90
Lemora, Lady Dracula '73

Denver Pyle
Legend of the Northwest '78
Blood Brothers '77
Mountain Man '77
Hawmps! '76
The Adventures of Frontier
 Fremont '75
Life & Times of Grizzly Adams
 '74
Murder or Mercy '74
The Legend of Hillbilly John '73
Bonnie & Clyde '67
The Rounders '65
Geronimo '62
Naked Hills '56
Seventh Cavalry '56
Hills of Utah '51
Oklahoma Annie '51
Dynamite Pass '50
Rim of the Canyon '49
Too Late for Tears '49

John Pyper-Ferguson
For Richer or Poorer '97
Hard Core Logo '96
Space Marines '96
Killer Image '92
Showdown at Williams Creek '91

John Quade
And You Thought Your Parents
 Were Weird! '91
The Tracker '88
Tigershark '87
Fury to Freedom: The Life Story
 of Raul Ries '85
Dirkham Detective Agency '83
Peter Lundy and the Medicine
 Hat Stallion '77
Night Terror '76

Stephen Quadros
Auntie Lee's Meat Pies '92
C.I.A.: Code Name Alexa '92
Shock 'Em Dead '90

Dennis Quaid
The Parent Trap '98
Switchback '97
Dragonheart '96
Gang Related '96
Something to Talk About '95
Wyatt Earp '94
Flesh and Bone '93
Undercover Blues '93
Wilder Napalm '93
Come See the Paradise '90

Postcards from the Edge '90
Great Balls of Fire '89
D.O.A. '88
Everybody's All American '88
The Big Easy '87
Innerspace '87
Suspect '87
Enemy Mine '85
Dreamscape '84
Bill: On His Own '83
Jaws 3 '83
The Right Stuff '83
Tough Enough '83
Johnny Belinda '82
All Night Long '81
Bill '81
Caveman '81
The Night the Lights Went Out in
 Georgia '81
Gorp '80
The Long Riders '80
Breaking Away '79
The Seniors '78
September 30, 1955 '77

Randy Quaid
Hard Rain '97
Get On the Bus '96
Independence Day '96
Kingpin '96
Last Dance '96
Moonshine Highway '96
Vegas Vacation '96
Larry McMurtry's Streets of
 Laredo '95
Legends of the North '95
Woman Undone '95
Bye Bye, Love '94
Curse of the Starving Class '94
Next Door '94
The Paper '94
Frankenstein '93
Freaked '93
Days of Thunder '90
Martians Go Home! '90
Quick Change '90
Texasville '90
Bloodhounds of Broadway '89
National Lampoon's Christmas
 Vacation '89
Out Cold '89
Parents '89
Caddyshack 2 '88
Dead Solid Perfect '88
LBJ: The Early Years '88
Moving '88
No Man's Land '87
Sweet Country '87
The Wraith '87
Fool for Love '86
The Slugger's Wife '85
A Streetcar Named Desire '84
The Wild Life '84
National Lampoon's Vacation
 '83
Inside the Third Reich '82
Heartbeeps '81
Of Mice and Men '81
Foxes '80
The Guyana Tragedy: The Story
 of Jim Jones '80
The Long Riders '80
To Race the Wind '80
The Last Ride of the Dalton
 Gang '79
Midnight Express '78
The Choirboys '77
Three Warriors '77
Bound for Glory '76
Missouri Breaks '76
Breakout '75
The Apprenticeship of Duddy
 Kravitz '74
The Last Detail '73
Paper Moon '73
What's Up, Doc? '72
The Last Picture Show '71

John Qualen
I'll Take Sweden '65
A Patch of Blue '65
Those Calloways '65
Cheyenne Autumn '64
7 Faces of Dr. Lao '63
The Man Who Shot Liberty
 Valance '62
Terror in the Haunted House '58
The Searchers '56

Meet Wally Sparks '97
The Stepsister '97
Showgirls '95
Star Quest '94
Heart Condition '90
Mistress 8?
L.A. Law '86
Always '85

Victoria Racimo
White Fang 2: The Myth of the White Wolf
Ernest Goes to Camp '87
Roanoak '86
Prophecy '79
Green Eyes '76
Search for the Gods '75
G.I. Executioner '71

Basil Radford
Passport to Pimlico '49
Whiskey Galore '48
The Winslow Boy '48
Captive Heart '47
Dead of Night '45
Night Train to Munich '40
The Lady Vanishes '38
Young and Innocent '37

Natalie Radford
The Android Affair '95
Tomcat: Dangerous Desires '93

Ken Radley
Mr. Reliable: A True Story '95
Sniper '92

Gilda Radner
Haunted Honeymoon '86
Movers and Shakers '85
The Woman in Red '84
Hanky Panky '82
First Family '80
Mr. Mike's Mondo Video '79
All You Need Is Cash '78

Jerzy Radziwilowicz
No End '84
Man of Iron '81
Man of Marble '78

Cassidy Rae
National Lampoon's Favorite Deadly Sins '95
Evolver '94

Charlotte Rae
Thunder in Paradise '93
The Worst Witch '86
Words by Heart '84
The Triangle Factory Fire Scandal '79
Sidewinder One '77
Queen of the Stardust Ballroom '75
Bananas '71
The Hot Rock '70
Jenny '70

Chips Rafferty
Skullduggery '70
Double Trouble '67
Wackiest Ship in the Army '61
The Sundowners '60
Walk into Hell '57
The Desert Rats '53
Eureka Stockade '49
Overlanders '46
Forty Thousand Horsemen '41

Frances Rafferty
Curley '47
Money Madness '47
Abbott and Costello in Hollywood '45
Mrs. Parkington '44

Deborah Raffin
Morning Glory '93
Scanners 2: The New Order '91
Night of the Fox '90
Noble House '88
Claudia '85
Death Wish 3 '85
Jungle Heat '84
Killing at Hell's Gate '81
For the Love of It '80
Touched by Love '80
Willa '79
Hanging on a Star '78
How to Pick Up Girls '78
Snowblind '78
Maniac '77

God Told Me To '76
Nightmare in Badham County '76
The Sentinel '76
Once Is Not Enough '75
The Dove '74
Forty Carats '73

George Raft
Sextette '78
Casino Royale '67
Five Golden Dragons '67
Jet Over the Atlantic '59
Some Like It Hot '59
The Best of Abbott & Costello Live '54
Man from Cairo '54
I'll Get You '53
Loan Shark '52
Outpost in Morocco '49
Mr. Ace '46
Nocturne '46
Whistle Stop '46
Johnny Angel '45
Follow the Boys '44
Background to Danger '43
House Across the Bay '40
They Drive by Night '40
Each Dawn I Die '39
Spawn of the North '38
You and Me '38
Souls at Sea '37
Night After Night '32
Palmy Days '31
Scarface '31

Rags Ragland
The Canterville Ghost '44
DuBarry Was a Lady '43
Whistling in Brooklyn '43
Panama Hattie '42
Whistling in Dixie '42
Whistling in the Dark '41

William Ragsdale
National Lampoon's Favorite Deadly Sins '95
Mannequin 2: On the Move '91
Fright Night 2 '88
Fright Night '85

Umberto Raho
Aladdin '86
The Night Evelyn Came Out of the Grave '71
Satanik '69

Steve Railsback
Stranger in the House '97
Barb Wire '96
Calendar Girl '93
Final Mission '93
Nukie '93
Private Wars '93
Save Me '93
Forever: A Ghost of a Love Story '92
Quake '92
Sunstroke '92
Scissors '91
Alligator 2: The Mutation '90
Assassin '89
The Forgotten '89
Deadly Intent '88
Blue Monkey '87
Distortions '87
Scenes from the Goldmine '87
The Survivalist '87
The Wind '87
Armed and Dangerous '86
Lifeforce '85
Torchlight '85
The Golden Seal '83
Trick or Treats '82
Escape 2000 '81
Deadly Games '80
The Stunt Man '80
From Here to Eternity '79
Angela '77
Helter Skelter '76

Sam Raimi
Indian Summer '93
Innocent Blood '92
Maniac Cop '88
Thou Shalt Not Kill...Except '87

Theodore (Ted) Raimi
Wishmaster '97

The Shot '96
Clear and Present Danger '94
Skinner '93
Army of Darkness '92
The Finishing Touch '92
Lunatics: A Love Story '92
Shocker '89
Evil Dead 2: Dead by Dawn '87
Thou Shalt Not Kill...Except '87

Raimu
Well-Digger's Daughter '46
Heart of a Nation '43
Cesar '36
The Baker's Wife '33
Fanny '32
Marius '31

Jack Raine
The Ghoul '34
Night Birds '31

Luise Rainer
Tiefland '44
The Great Waltz '38
The Good Earth '37
The Great Ziegfeld '36

Christina Raines
North Shore '87
Quo Vadis '85
Nightmares '83
Silver Dream Racer '83
Touched by Love '80
Centennial '78
The Duellists '77
The Sentinel '76
Nashville '75
Russian Roulette '75
The Shrieking '73
Stacey '73

Ella Raines
Ride the Man Down '53
Impact '49
The Senator was Indiscreet '47
The Strange Affair of Uncle Harry '45
Hail the Conquering Hero '44
Phantom Lady '44
Tall in the Saddle '44

Ford Rainey
Bed & Breakfast '90
The Cellar '90
Strangers: The Story of a Mother and Daughter '79
Mountain Man '77
Babe! '75
Strange New World '75
Sixteen '72
My Sweet Charlie '70

Claude Rains
The Greatest Story Ever Told '65
Lawrence of Arabia '62
Battle of the Worlds '61
The Pied Piper of Hamelin '57
Lisbon '56
Paris Express '53
The White Tower '50
Angel on My Shoulder '46
Caesar and Cleopatra '46
Deception '46
Notorious '46
Mr. Skeffington '44
Passage to Marseilles '44
Forever and a Day '43
The Phantom of the Opera '43
Casablanca '42
Now, Voyager '42
Here Comes Mr. Jordan '41
Kings Row '41
The Wolf Man '41
The Sea Hawk '40
Juarez '39
Mr. Smith Goes to Washington '39
They Made Me a Criminal '39
The Adventures of Robin Hood '38
Four Daughters '38
The Prince and the Pauper '37
They Won't Forget '37
Anthony Adverse '36
The Mystery of Edwin Drood '35
The Evil Mind '34
The Invisible Man '33

Tommy Rall
Dancers '87
My Sister Eileen '55
Seven Brides for Seven Brothers '51
Kiss Me Kate '53

Giovanna Ralli
Sex with a Smile '76
Caper of the Golden Bulls '67
What Did You Do in the War, Daddy? '66

Jessie Ralph
They Met in Bombay '41
The Bank Dick '40
The Blue Bird '40
Drums Along the Mohawk '39
Double Wedding '37
The Last of Mrs. Cheyney '37
After the Thin Man '36
Little Lord Fauntleroy '36
San Francisco '36
Yellow Dust '36
I Live My Life '35
Les Miserables '35
Evelyn Prentice '34
One Night of Love '34

Sheryl Lee Ralph
Bogus '96
White Man's Burden '95
Witch Hunt '94
Sister Act 2: Back in the Habit '93
The Distinguished Gentleman '92
Mistress '91
To Sleep with Anger '90
The Mighty Quinn '89
Codename: Foxfire '85

Esther Ralston
Tin Pan Alley '40
Shadows of the Orient '37
We're in the Legion Now '37
To the Last Man '33
Lonely Wives '31
Old Ironsides '26
$50,000 Reward '25
Lucky Devil '25
Oliver Twist '22

Jobyna Ralston
The Kid Brother '27
Dr. Jack/For Heaven's Sake '26
For Heaven's Sake '26
The Freshman '25
Girl Shy '24

Vera Ralston
Jubilee Trail '54
Hoodlum Empire '52
The Fighting Kentuckian '49
Dakota '45

Cecil Ramage
Kind Hearts and Coronets '49
King of the Damned '36

Enrique Rambal
The Man and the Monster '65
The Exterminating Angel '62

Marjorie Rambeau
Man of a Thousand Faces '57
A Man Called Peter '55
Forever Female '53
Torch Song '53
Primrose Path '40
Santa Fe Marshal '40
The Rains Came '39
Laughing Sinners '31
Min & Bill '30

Dack Rambo
Ultra Warrior '92
River of Diamonds '90
The Spring '89
Waikiki '80
Hit Lady '74

Henry Ramer
The Big Slice '90
Hockey Night '84
Reno and the Doc '84
Starship Invasions '77
My Pleasure Is My Business '74

Carlos Ramirez
Anchors Aweigh '45
Bathing Beauty '44
Two Girls and a Sailor '44

Frank Ramirez
Miracle in Rome '88
Smith! '69

Harold Ramis
Love Affair '94
The Best of John Candy on SCTV '80s
Ghostbusters 2 '89
Stealing Home '88
Baby Boom '87
Ghostbusters '84
Stripes '81

Rudy Ramos
The Spy Within '94
Blindsided '93
Colors '88
Open House '86
Quicksilver '86

Charlotte Rampling
The Wings of the Dove '97
Invasion of Privacy '96
D.O.A. '88
Angel Heart '87
Mascara '87
Max, Mon Amour '86
The Verdict '82
Stardust Memories '80
Orca '77
The Purple Taxi '77
Foxtrot '76
Farewell, My Lovely '75
Sardinia Kidnapped '75
Ski Bum '75
Caravan to Vaccares '74
The Night Porter '74
'Tis a Pity She's a Whore '73
Zardoz '73
Asylum '72
The Damned '69
Georgy Girl '66

Anne Elizabeth Ramsey
The Final Cut '96
A League of Their Own '92

Bruce Ramsay
Dead Beat '94
Killing Zoe '94
The New Age '94
Alive '93

Remak Ramsay
Addicted to Love '96
Mr. & Mrs. Bridge '90
The Dining Room '86

Anne Ramsey
Perfect Alibi '94
The River Pirates '94
Meet the Hollowheads '89
Another Chance '88
Dr. Hackenstein '88
Throw Momma from the Train '87
Weeds '87
Deadly Friend '86
The Goonies '85
A Small Killing '81
Marilyn: The Untold Story '80
White Mama '80
The Black Marble '79
Goin' South '78
The Boy in the Plastic Bubble '76

Bruce Ramsey
Curdled '95
Hellraiser 4: Bloodline '95

Logan Ramsey
Dr. Hackenstein '88
Say Yes! '86
Conspiracy of Terror '75
Confessions of Tom Harris '72
Fury on Wheels '71
The Hoodlum Priest '61

Lois Ramsey
Road to Nhill '97
River Street '95

Marion Ramsey
Police Academy 6: City Under Siege '89
Police Academy 5: Assignment Miami Beach
Police Academy 3: Back in Training '86

Rowe *cont.*

A Pleasure Doing Business '79
Goodbye, Norma Jean '75
Hitchhikers '72

Nevan Rowe
Nutcase '83
Sleeping Dogs '82

Nicholas Rowe
Sharpe's Enemy '94
The Lawrenceville Stories '80s
Young Sherlock Holmes '85

Victoria Rowell
Barb Wire '96
Dumb & Dumber '94
The Distinguished Gentleman '92

Steve Rowland
Naked Youth '59
Gun Glory '57

Gena Rowlands
Hope Floats '98
Paulie '98
She's So Lovely '97
Unhook the Stars '96
The Neon Bible '95
Something to Talk About '95
Parallel Lives '94
Crazy in Love '92
Night on Earth '91
Once Around '91
Montana '90
Another Woman '88
Light of Day '87
An Early Frost '85
Love Streams '84
Rapunzel '82
The Tempest '82
Gloria '80
Strangers: The Story of a Mother and Daughter '79
Brink's Job '78
A Question of Love '78
Opening Night '77
Two Minute Warning '76
A Woman Under the Influence '74
Faces '68
Tony Rome '67
A Child Is Waiting '63
Lonely Are the Brave '62

Polly Rowles
Power '86
Springtime in the Rockies '37

Richard Roxburgh
Doing Time for Patsy Cline '97
Oscar and Lucinda '97
Thank God He Met Lizzie '97
Children of the Revolution '95
Talk '95

Lionel Royce
White Pongo '45
My Favorite Blonde '42
Panama Menace '41
The Road to Zanzibar '41

Roselyn Royce
Retrievers '82
Malibu Hot Summer '74

Virginia Roye
Pace That Kills '28
The Road to Ruin '28

Selena Royle
Robot Monster '53
The Big Hangover '50
My Dream Is Yours '49
A Date with Judy '48
Moonrise '48
Summer Holiday '48
Cass Timberlane '47
Courage of Lassie '46
The Harvey Girls '46
Mrs. Parkington '44
The Fighting Sullivans '42

William Royle
Mr. Wong in Chinatown '39
Mutiny in the Big House '39
The Rains Came '39

Gregory Rozakis
Five Corners '88

Abduction '75

Alma Rubens
She Goes to War '29
Mystery of the Leaping Fish/ Chess Fever '25
The Americano '17

Jan Rubes
Flood: A River's Rampage '97
The Birds 2: Land's End '94
D2: The Mighty Ducks '94
By Way of the Stars '92
Class Action '91
Deceived '91
The Amityville Curse '90
Descending Angel '90
Blind Fear '89
Courage Mountain '89
The Kiss '88
Blood Relations '88
Dead of Winter '87
Charlie Grant's War '80

Benny Rubin
The Tender Trap '55
Torch Song '53
The Noose Hangs High '48
The Bashful Bachelor '42
Mr. Wise Guy '42
Zis Boom Bah '42
Sunny '41
Sunny Skies '30

Jennifer Rubin
Kisses in the Dark '97
Loved '97
Little Witches '96
Screamers '96
Wasp Woman '96
Saints and Sinners '94
Deceptions 2: Edge of Deception '94
Playmaker '94
Red Scorpion 2 '94
Stranger by Night '94
Bitter Harvest '93
The Crush '93
The Fear Inside '92
A Woman, Her Men and Her Futon '92
Delusion '91
Victim of Beauty '91
Bad Dreams '88
Blueberry Hill '88
Permanent Record '88
A Nightmare on Elm Street 3: Dream Warriors '87

Saul Rubinek
Past Perfect '98
Blackjack '98
The Android Affair '95
Hiroshima '95
Nixon '95
Open Season '95
Synapse '95
Getting Even with Dad '94
I Love Trouble '94
And the Band Played On '93
The Quarrel '93
True Romance '93
Undercover Blues '93
Man Trouble '92
Unforgiven '92
The Bonfire of the Vanities '90
Obsessed '88
Outside Chance of Maximillian Glick '88
Wall Street '87
Half a Lifetime '86
Against All Odds '84
Soup for One '82
Young Doctors in Love '82
The Agency '81
Ticket to Heaven '81
Death Ship '80
Highpoint '80

Giulia Rubini
Stranger in Paso Bravo '73
Adios, Hombre '67
Journey Beneath the Desert '61

Sergio Rubini
A Pure Formality '94
Intervista '87

John Rubinstein
Mercy '96
Norma Jean and Marilyn '95

RoboCop the Series: The Future of Law Enforcement '94
Another Stakeout '93
Shadow on the Sun '88
Someone to Watch Over Me '87
Happily Ever After '82
Killjoy '81
She's Dressed to Kill '79
Defiant '70
Getting Straight '70
Zachariah '70
The Trouble with Girls (and How To Get Into It) '69

Zelda Rubinstein
Little Witches '96
Acting on Impulse '93
Teen Witch '89
Anguish '88
Poltergeist 3 '88
Poltergeist 2: The Other Side '86
Sixteen Candles '84
Poltergeist '82
Under the Rainbow '81

Alan Ruck
Twister '96
Speed '94
Star Trek Generations '94
Young Guns 2 '90
Three Fugitives '89
Three for the Road '87
Ferris Bueller's Day Off '86
Hard Knox '83

Paul Rudd
The Object of My Affection '98
The Locusts '97
Overnight Delivery '96
William Shakespeare's Romeo and Juliet '96
Clueless '95
Beulah Land '80
Last Song '80
Johnny We Hardly Knew Ye '77

Michael Rudder
Buying Time '89
Blindside '88

John Ruddock
Martin Luther '53
The Fallen Idol '49

Herbert Rudley
Beloved Infidel '59
The Jayhawkers '59
Artists and Models '55
The Scar '48
Rhapsody in Blue '45
The Seventh Cross '44
Abe Lincoln in Illinois '40

Rita Rudner
A Weekend in the Country '96
Peter's Friends '92

Joshua Rudoy
Flatliners '90
Harry and the Hendersons '87

Reed Rudy
Zapped Again '89
Free Ride '86

Mercedes Ruehl
Gia '98
North Shore Fish '97
Subway Stories '97
For Roseanna '96
Indictment: The McMartin Trial '95
Last Action Hero '93
Lost in Yonkers '93
Another You '91
The Fisher King '91
Crazy People '90
Slaves of New York '89
Big '88
Married to the Mob '88
Leader of the Band '87
Radio Days '87
84 Charing Cross Road '86
Heartburn '86

Heinz Ruehmann
Ship of Fools '65
The Captain from Koepenick '56

Leonora Ruffo
Hercules in the Haunted World '64
Goliath and the Dragon '61

Rufus
Les Miserables '95
Erendira '83
Jonah Who Will Be 25 in the Year 2000 '76

Charlie Ruggles
Follow Me, Boys! '66
The Ugly Dachshund '65
Papa's Delicate Condition '63
Son of Flubber '63
All in a Night's Work '61
The Parent Trap '61
Look for the Silver Lining '49
The Lovable Cheat '49
Ramrod '47
The Perfect Marriage '46
A Stolen Life '46
The Invisible Woman '40
Balalaika '39
Breaking the Ice '38
Bringing Up Baby '38
Ruggles of Red Gap '35
Goodbye Love '34
Six of a Kind '34
Murders in the Zoo '33
Melody Cruise '32

Vyto Ruginis
The Devil's Advocate '97
A Thousand Acres '97
Clean Slate '94
The Last Gasp '94
Descending Angel '90

Barbara Ruick
Carousel '56
The Affairs of Dobie Gillis '53

Anthony Michael Ruivivar
Starship Troopers '97
Race the Sun '96
White Fang 2: The Myth of the White Wolf '94

Janice Rule
American Flyers '85
L.A. Bad '85
Missing '82
The Word '78
Gumshoe '72
Doctors' Wives '70
The Swimmer '68
The Ambushers '67
Alvarez Kelly '66
The Chase '66
Invitation to a Gunfighter '64
Battle Shock '56

Sig Rumann
The Errand Boy '61
Wings of Eagles '57
Houdini '53
Ma and Pa Kettle on Vacation '53
Stalag 17 '53
The World in His Arms '52
Emperor Waltz '48
The Dolly Sisters '46
A Night in Casablanca '46
House of Frankenstein '44
Sweet Rosie O'Grady '43
To Be or Not to Be '42
Love Crazy '41
That Uncertain Feeling '41
Bitter Sweet '40
Comrade X '40
Ninotchka '39
Only Angels Have Wings '39
The Great Waltz '38
A Day at the Races '37
Nothing Sacred '37
On the Avenue '37
Thin Ice '37
The Bold Caballero '36
The Princess Comes Across '36
A Night at the Opera '35
Marie Galante '34

Run DMC
The Show '95
Tougher than Leather '88

Jenny Runacre
Hussy '80
The Passenger '75
The Final Programme '73
The Creeping Flesh '72
The Canterbury Tales '71

Joseph Runningfox
Lakota Woman: Siege at Wounded Knee '94
Geronimo '93
The Avenging '92

Jennifer Runyon
Carnosaur '93
A Man Called Sarge '90
18 Again! '88
The In Crowd '88
A Very Brady Christmas '88
Blue De Ville '86
The Falcon and the Snowman '85
Up the Creek '84
To All a Goodnight '80

Ying Ruocheng
Little Buddha '93
The Last Emperor '87

RuPaul
The Brady Bunch Movie '95
A Mother's Prayer '95

Al Ruscio
The Garbage-Picking, Field Goal-Kicking Philadelphia Phenomenon '98
The Cage '89
Romero '89
Deadly Force '83

Elizabeth Ruscio
Death Benefit '96
Glory Daze '96
The Positively True Adventures of the Alleged Texas Cheerleader-Murdering Mom '93
Hider in the House '90

Barbara Rush
Widow's Kiss '94
Web of Deceit '90
The Seekers '79
Portrait of Grandpa Doc '77
Superdad '73
Moon of the Wolf '72
Hombre '67
Robin and the 7 Hoods '64
Come Blow Your Horn '63
The Bramble Bush '60
Strangers When We Meet '60
The Young Philadelphians '59
Harry Black and the Tiger '58
The Young Lions '58
Magnificent Obsession '54
It Came from Outer Space '53
First Legion '51
When Worlds Collide '51

Deborah Rush
In and Out '97
Reckless '95
Unnatural Pursuits '91
Family Business '89
Parents '89
The Purple Rose of Cairo '85

Geoffrey Rush
Les Miserables '97
Twisted '96
Children of the Revolution '95
Shine '95

Claire Rushbrook
Spice World: The Movie '97
Secrets and Lies '95

Jared Rushton
Pet Sematary 2 '92
A Cry in the Wild '90
Honey, I Shrunk the Kids '89
Big '88
The Lady in White '88

Joseph Ruskin
The Criminal Mind '93
Cyber-Tracker '93
Firepower '93
Prizzi's Honor '85
Captain America '79
The Gypsy Warriors '78

Robert Rusler
The Assassination Game '92
Final Embrace '92
Sometimes They Come Back '91
The Game of Love '90
Shag: The Movie '89
Thrashin' '86

Vamp '86
A Nightmare on Elm Street 2:
   Freddy's Revenge '85

Tim Russ
Star Trek Voyager: Caretaker
   '95
Bitter Vengeance '94
Night Eyes 2 '91

William Russ
When Danger Follows You
   Home '97
Aspen Extreme '93
Traces of Red '92
Crazy from the Heart '91
Pastime '91
Disorganized Crime '89
The Unholy '88
Dead of Winter '87
The Long, Hot Summer '86
Wanted Dead or Alive '86
Beer '85
The Right Stuff '83

Andy Russell
Copacabana '47
The Stork Club '45

Betsy Russell
Amore! '93
Delta Heat '92
The Prize Pulitzer '89
Trapper County War '89
Cheerleader Camp '88
Avenging Angel '85
Out of Control '85
Tomboy '85
Private School '83

Bing Russell
Elvis: The Movie '79
Billy the Kid Versus Dracula '66
Stakeout '62
Good Day for a Hanging '58
Suicide Battalion/Hell Squad '58

Clive Russell
Oscar and Lucinda '97
Cracker: Brotherly Love '95
Margaret's Museum '95

Elizabeth Russell
Curse of the Cat People '44
Cat People '42
The Corpse Vanishes '42
Meet the Mob '42

Gail Russell
Great Dan Patch '49
Wake of the Red Witch '49
Moonrise '48
Angel and the Badman '47
The Uninvited '44

Jane Russell
Darker than Amber '70
Born Losers '67
Johnny Reno '66
The Tall Men '55
Underwater! '55
The French Line '54
Gentlemen Prefer Blondes '53
The Road to Bali '53
The Las Vegas Story '52
Macao '52
Montana Belle '52
Son of Paleface '52
Double Dynamite '51
His Kind of Woman '51
The Paleface '48
The Outlaw '43

John Russell
Under the Gun '88
Pale Rider '85
Runaways '84
The Changeling '80
Smoke in the Wind '75
Blood Legacy '73
Noon Sunday '71
Buckskin '68
Hostile Guns '67
Apache Uprising '66
Rio Bravo '59
Jubilee Trail '54
The Sun Shines Bright '53
Hoodlum Empire '52
Man in the Saddle '51
Oklahoma Annie '51
Forever Amber '47
The Blue Bird '40

Karen Russell
Dead Certain '92
Lethal Games '90
Shock 'Em Dead '90
Wilding '90
Easy Wheels '89
Vice Academy '88

Ken Russell
Tales of Erotica '93
The Russia House '90

Kimberly Russell
The O.J. Simpson Story '94
Hangin' with the Homeboys '91

Kurt Russell
Breakdown '96
Escape from L.A. '96
Executive Decision '96
Stargate '94
Tombstone '93
Captain Ron '92
Unlawful Entry '92
Backdraft '91
Tango and Cash '89
Winter People '89
Tequila Sunrise '88
Overboard '87
The Best of Times '86
Big Trouble in Little China '86
Mean Season '85
Swing Shift '84
Silkwood '83
Amber Waves '82
The Thing '82
Escape from New York '81
Used Cars '80
Elvis: The Movie '79
The Christmas Coal Mine
   Miracle '77
The Captive: The Longest Drive
   2 '76
The Longest Drive '76
Search for the Gods '75
Sniper '75
Charley and the Angel '73
Superdad '73
Now You See Him, Now You
   Don't '72
The Barefoot Executive '71
The Computer Wore Tennis
   Shoes '69
The Horse in the Gray Flannel
   Suit '68
The One and Only, Genuine,
   Original Family Band '68
The Adventures of Bullwhip
   Griffin '66
Follow Me, Boys! '66
Mosby's Marauders '66
Guns of Diablo '64
It Happened at the World's Fair
   '63

Monte Russell
Lily in Winter '94
Laurel Avenue '93

Nipsey Russell
Car 54, Where Are You? '94
The Wiz '78
Car 54, Where Are You? '61

Reb Russell
Outlaw Rule '36
Arizona Badman '35
Border Vengeance '35
The Man from Hell '34

Robert Russell
Bedazzled '68
The Conqueror Worm '68

Rosalind Russell
Where Angels Go, Trouble
   Follows '68
Oh Dad, Poor Dad (Momma's
   Hung You in the Closet & I'm
   Feeling So Sad) '67
The Trouble with Angels '66
Gypsy '62
Hollywood Bloopers '50s
Auntie Mame '58
A Majority of One '56
Picnic '55
Never Wave at a WAC '52
A Woman of Distinction '50
Tell It to the Judge '49
Velvet Touch '48
Sister Kenny '46

They Met in Bombay '41
His Girl Friday '40
The Women '39
The Citadel '38
Craig's Wife '36
China Seas '35
Forsaking All Others '35
Reckless '35
Evelyn Prentice '34

Theresa Russell
Wild Things '98
Grave Indiscretions '96
The Proposition '96
Public Enemies '96
Trade Off '95
A Young Connecticut Yankee in
   King Arthur's Court '95
Being Human '94
The Spy Within '94
Thicker Than Water '93
A Woman's Guide to Adultery
   '93
Cold Heaven '92
Kafka '91
Whore '91
Impulse '90
Physical Evidence '89
Aria '88
Track 29 '88
Black Widow '87
Insignificance '85
The Razor's Edge '84
Eureka! '81
Straight Time '78
The Last Tycoon '76

Tony Russell
The Hard Ride '71
Wild, Wild Planet '65

James Russo
Love to Kill '97
No Way Home '97
The Postman '97
The Real Thing '97
American Strays '96
Donnie Brasco '96
Condition Red '95
Panther '95
The Set Up '95
Bad Girls '94
The Secretary '94
Dangerous Game '93
Dario Argento's Trauma '93
Cold Heaven '92
Illicit Behavior '91
Intimate Stranger '91
A Kiss Before Dying '91
My Own Private Idaho '91
We're No Angels '89
Blue Iguana '88
Freeway '88
China Girl '87
Extremities '86
Beverly Hills Cop '84
Fast Times at Ridgemont High
   '82
Vortex '81

Michael Russo
Pure Danger '96
Demonic Toys '90
Nitti: The Enforcer '88

Rene Russo
Lethal Weapon 4 '98
Buddy '97
Ransom '96
Tin Cup '96
Get Shorty '95
Outbreak '94
In the Line of Fire '93
Freejack '92
Lethal Weapon 3 '92
One Good Cop '91
Mr. Destiny '90
Major League '89

Leon Russom
The Big Lebowski '97
A Private Matter '92
Long Road Home '91
Silver Bullet '85

Richard Rust
Double Revenge '89
The Great Gundown '75
The Student Nurses '70
The Naked Angels '69
Comanche Station '60

Legend of Tom Dooley '59

Babe Ruth
The Pride of the Yankees '42
Heading Home '24

Mary Ruth
Gentleman from Dixie '41
Riot Squad '41

Ann Rutherford
They Only Kill Their Masters '72
Operation Haylift '50
Adventures of Don Juan '49
The Secret Life of Walter Mitty
   '47
Whistling in Brooklyn '43
Andy Hardy's Double Life '42
Orchestra Wives '42
Whistling in Dixie '42
Life Begins for Andy Hardy '41
Whistling in the Dark '41
Andy Hardy Meets Debutante
   '40
Pride and Prejudice '40
Andy Hardy Gets Spring Fever
   '39
Gone with the Wind '39
A Christmas Carol '38
Love Finds Andy Hardy '38
Of Human Hearts '38
Doughnuts & Society '36
Fighting Marines '36
The Lawless Nineties '36
Melody Trail '35
Ghost City '32

Margaret Rutherford
To See Such Fun '81
Chimes at Midnight '67
A Countess from Hong Kong '67
Murder Most Foul '65
Murder Ahoy '64
Murder at the Gallop '63
The V.I.P.'s '63
Murder She Said '62
The Smallest Show on Earth '57
The Runaway Bus '54
Curtain Up '53
Innocents in Paris '53
Trouble in Store '53
Importance of Being Earnest '52
The Happiest Days of Your Life
   '50
Passport to Pimlico '49
Blithe Spirit '45
The Demi-Paradise '43

Susan Ruttan
Funny About Love '90
A Perfect Little Murder '90
Sweet 15 '90
Chances Are '89
Fire and Rain '89
Bad Dreams '88
Eye of the Demon '87
L.A. Law '86
Bad Manners '84

Barbara Rutting
The Squeaker '65
The Phantom of Soho '64
River of Evil '64

Sif Ruud
Like It Never Was Before '95
Face to Face '76

Wolf Ruvinskis
Neutron vs. the Death Robots
   '62
Neutron vs. the Maniac '62
Neutron and the Black Mask '61
Neutron vs. the Amazing Dr.
   Caronte '61

Basil Ruysdael
Davy Crockett, King of the Wild
   Frontier '55
Carrie '52
People Will Talk '51
Broken Arrow '50
High Lonesome '50

Anne Ryan
All the Lovin' Kinfolk '89
Three O'Clock High '87

Eddie Ryan
Breakfast in Hollywood '46
The Fighting Sullivans '42

Eileen Ryan
The Crossing Guard '94

Benny & Joon '93
Winter People '89
At Close Range '86

Fran Ryan
Future OG
Chances Are '89
Gunsmoke: Return to Dodge '87
Quiet Cool '86
Pale Rider '85
Eyes of Fire '84
Private School '83
Johnny Belinda '82

Ger Ryan
Moll Flanders '96
The Van '95

Irene Ryan
The Beverly Hillbillies '62
Heading for Heaven '47

James Ryan
Redemption: Kickboxer 5 '95
The Last Samurai '90
Pursuit '90
Rage to Kill '88
Space Mutiny '88
Go for the Gold '84
Kill and Kill Again '81
Kill or Be Killed '80

John P. Ryan
Bound '96
American Cyborg: Steel Warrior
   '94
C.I.A. 2: Target Alexa '94
Hoffa '92
Star Time '92
Delta Force 3: The Killing Game
   '91
Class of 1999 '90
Delta Force 2: Operation
   Stranglehold '90
Eternity '90
Best of the Best '89
Paramedics '88
Rent-A-Cop '88
Death Wish 4: The Crackdown
   '87
Three O'Clock High '87
Avenging Force '86
City of Shadows '86
Runaway Train '85
Breathless '83
The Right Stuff '83
The Postman Always Rings
   Twice '81
It's Alive 2: It Lives Again '78
Death Scream '75
It's Alive '74
Cops and Robbers '73
Shamus '73

Kathleen Ryan
Try and Get Me '50
Captain Boycott '47
Odd Man Out '47

Lisa Dean Ryan
Twisted Love '95
Hostile Intentions '94

Meg Ryan
City of Angels '98
Addicted to Love '96
Courage Under Fire '96
French Kiss '95
I.Q. '94
Restoration '94
When a Man Loves a Woman
   '94
Flesh and Bone '93
Sleepless in Seattle '93
Prelude to a Kiss '92
The Doors '91
Joe Versus the Volcano '90
When Harry Met Sally... '89
D.O.A. '88
The Presidio '88
Promised Land '88
Innerspace '87
Armed and Dangerous '86
Top Gun '86
Amityville 3: The Demon '83
Rich and Famous '81

Mitchell Ryan
Grosse Pointe Blank '97
The Devil's Own '96
Liar Liar '96

Howard St. John
Strange Bedfellows '65
Strait-Jacket '64
Lover Come Back '61
Li'l Abner '59
I Died a Thousand Times '55
Illegal '55
The Tender Trap '55

Jill St. John
Out There '95
Around the World in 80 Days '89
The Act '82
The Concrete Jungle '82
Diamonds Are Forever '71
Eight on the Lam '67
Tony Rome '67
The Oscar '66
Come Blow Your Horn '63
Roman Spring of Mrs. Stone '61

Michelle St. John
Smoke Signals '98
Geronimo '93
Spirit Rider '93
Where the Spirit Lives '89

John St. Polis
Rocky Mountain Rangers '40
Phantom Ranger '38
Death from a Distance '36
Terror Trail '33
Coquette '29
Party Girls '29
The Unknown '27
The Untamable '23

Lucile Saint-Simon
The Hands of Orlac '60
Les Bonnes Femmes '60

Marin Sais
The Fighting Redhead '50
Lightning Raiders '45
Frontier Outlaws '44

Frankie Sakai
Master Mind '73
Last War '68
Mothra '62

S.Z. Sakall
The Student Prince '54
Small Town Girl '53
Lullaby of Broadway '51
Tea for Two '50
In the Good Old Summertime '49
Look for the Silver Lining '49
My Dream Is Yours '49
Romance on the High Seas '48
The Dolly Sisters '45
Never Say Goodbye '46
Christmas in Connecticut '45
San Antonio '45
Wonder Man '45
Hollywood Canteen '44
Wintertime '43
Casablanca '42
Yankee Doodle Dandy '42
Ball of Fire '41
The Devil & Miss Jones '41
It's a Date '40

Sumiko Sakamota
The Ballad of Narayama '83
The Pornographers '66

Ryuichi Sakamoto
The Last Emperor '87
Merry Christmas, Mr. Lawrence '83

Amy Sakasitz
Mad Love '95
Dennis the Menace '93
A Home of Our Own '93

Harold Sakata
Black Eliminator '70s
Goin' Coconuts '78
Kill Factor '78
Jaws of Death '76
Impulse '74
The Wrestler '73
Goldfinger '64

Gene Saks
Deconstructing Harry '97
I.Q. '94
Nobody's Fool '94
A Fine Romance '92
The One and Only '78

Prisoner of Second Avenue '74
A Thousand Clowns '65

Renato Sala
Full Metal Ninja '89
Ninja of the Magnificence '89

Abel Salazar
The Man and the Monster '65
The Brainiac '61
The Curse of the Crying Woman '61
The Living Head '59
The Vampire's Coffin '58
The Vampire '57

Theresa Saldana
Angel Town '89
Double Revenge '89
The Night Before '88
The Evil That Men Do '84
Raging Bull '80
Defiance '79
I Wanna Hold Your Hand '78

Chic Sale
You Only Live Once '37
The Fighting Westerner '35
Treasure Island '34

Kario Salem
Savage '96
Killing Zoe '94
1492: Conquest of Paradise '92
Triumph of the Spirit '89
Centennial '78

Pamela Salem
After Darkness '85
Salome '85
Never Say Never Again '83

Meredith Salenger
Village of the Damned '95
Dead Beat '94
Edge of Honor '91
Dream a Little Dream '89
The Kiss '88
A Night in the Life of Jimmy Reardon '88
The Journey of Natty Gann '85

John Salew
Kind Hearts and Coronets '49
Beware of Pity '46

Diane Salinger
Last Summer In the Hamptons '96
One Night Stand '95
The Scarlet Letter '95
The Magic Bubble '93
Venice, Venice '92
The Butcher's Wife '91
The Morning After '86
Creature '85
Pee Wee's Big Adventure '85

Matt Salinger
Babyfever '94
Fortunes of War '94
Firehawk '92
Captain America '89
Options '88
Manhunt for Claude Dallas '86
Power '86

Pascale Salkin
Akermania, Vol. 1 '92
Window Shopping '86
The Eighties '83

John Salley
Eddie '96
Bad Boys '95

Peter Sallis
Taste the Blood of Dracula '70
The Curse of the Werewolf '61

Albert Salmi
Breaking In '89
Gore Vidal's Billy the Kid '89
Jesse '88
Born American '86
Hard to Hold '84
The Guns and the Fury '83
Love Child '82
St. Helen's, Killer Volcano '82
Superstition '82
Sweet Creek County War '82
Dragonslayer '81
Kill Castro '80
The Mercenaries '80
Steel '80

Black Oak Conspiracy '77
Empire of the Ants '77
Moonshine County Express '77
Viva Knievel '77
The Meanest Men in the West '70
Lawman '71
Menace on the Mountain '70
The Ambushers '67
Hour of the Gun '67
The Unforgiven '60
The Bravados '58
Bang the Drum Slowly '56

Colin Salmon
Tomorrow Never Dies '97
Captives '94
Prime Suspect 2 '93

Frank S. Salsedo
Magic in the Water '95
Creepshow 2 '87

Jennifer Salt
Out of the Darkness '85
Sisters '73
Play It Again, Sam '72
Hi, Mom! '70

Renato Salvatori
La Cicada '83
State of Siege '73
Burn! '70
The Organizer '64
RoGoPaG '62
Rocco and His Brothers '60

Aldo Sambrel
Hot Blood '89
Voodoo Black Exorcist '89
Navajo Joe '67
The Texican '66

Udo Samel
Kaspar Hauser '93
Knife in the Head '78

Emma Samms
Humanoids from the Deep '96
Star Quest '94
Delirious '91
Illusions '91
The Shrimp on the Barbie '90
A Connecticut Yankee in King Arthur's Court '89
The Lady and the Highwayman '89
Goliath Awaits '81

Robert Sampson
The Arrival '90
Dark Side of the Moon '90
Netherworld '90
Robot Jox '90
Re-Animator '84
Gates of Hell '80
The Grass Is Always Greener Over the Septic Tank '78
Ethan '71

Will Sampson
Poltergeist 2: The Other Side '86
Roanoak '86
Insignificance '85
Fish Hawk '79
From Here to Eternity '79
Standing Tall '78
Vegas '78
The Hunted Lady '77
Orca '77
The White Buffalo '77
Buffalo Bill & the Indians '76
One Flew Over the Cuckoo's Nest '75

Jeffrey D. Sams
Hope '97
Soul Food '97
Waiting to Exhale '95
Fly by Night '93

Joanne Samuel
Gallagher's Travels '87
Queen of the Road '84
Mad Max '80
Alison's Birthday '79

Laura San Giacomo
Suicide Kings '97
The Apocalypse '96
The Right to Remain Silent '95
Nina Takes a Lover '95
Stephen King's The Stand '94
Stuart Saves His Family '94

Under Suspicion '92
Once Around '91
Pretty Woman '90
Quigley Down Under '90
Vital Signs '90
sex, lies and videotape '89
Miles from Home '88

Olga San Juan
The Beautiful Blonde from Bashful Bend '49
One Touch of Venus '48
Blue Skies '46

Henry Sanada
Royal Warriors '86
Shogun's Ninja '83

Jaime Sanchez
The Wild Bunch '69
The Pawnbroker '65

Pedro Sanchez
Night and the City '92
White Fang and the Hunter '85
Any Gun Can Play '67

Aitana Sanchez-Gijon
Love Walked In '97
Mouth to Mouth '95
A Walk in the Clouds '95

Fernando Sancho
Voodoo Black Exorcist '89
Blood at Sundown '88
Return of the Evil Dead '75

Jose Sancho
Live Flesh '97
Ay, Carmela! '90

Paul Sand
Frozen Assets '92
Getting Up and Going Home '92
Teen Wolf Too '87
The Last Fling '86
Can't Stop the Music '80
Second Coming of Suzanne '80
Wholly Moses! '80
The Legend of Sleepy Hollow '79
Great Bank Hoax '78
Once Upon a Brothers Grimm '77

Dominique Sanda
Joseph '95
I, the Worst of All '90
Voyage of Terror: The Achille Lauro Affair '90
Cabo Blanco '81
Voyage en Douce '81
Damnation Alley '77
The Inheritance '76
1900 '76
Steppenwolf '74
Mackintosh Man '73
The Story of a Love Story '73
The Conformist '71
The Garden of the Finzi-Continis '71
First Love '70
A Gentle Woman '69

Walter Sande
I'll Take Sweden '65
Rim of the Canyon '49
The Red House '47
Nocturne '46
Don Winslow of the Navy '43

Otto Sander
The Promise '94
Faraway, So Close! '93
Wings of Desire '88
Rosa Luxemburg '86

John Sanderford
Leprechaun '93
The Alchemist '81

Dirk Sanders
Pierrot le Fou '65
Black Tights '60

George Sanders
Psychomania '73
Doomwatch '72
Endless Night '71
Invasion of the Body Stealers '69
One Step to Hell '68
Good Times '67
The Quiller Memorandum '66

The Amorous Adventures of Moll Flanders '65
A Shot in the Dark '64
In Search of the Castaways '62
The Last Voyage '60
Village of the Damned '60
Solomon and Sheba '59
From the Earth to the Moon '58
Outcasts of the City '58
Death of a Scoundrel '56
While the City Sleeps '56
Jupiter's Darling '55
The King's Thief '55
Moonfleet '55
King Richard and the Crusaders '54
Voyage in Italy '53
Voyage to Italy '53
Ivanhoe '52
Captain Blackjack '51
All About Eve '50
Samson and Delilah '50
The Falcon Takes Over/Strange Bargain '49
Forever Amber '47
The Ghost and Mrs. Muir '47
The Private Affairs of Bel Ami '47
The Saint Strikes Back: Criminal Court '46
The Strange Woman '46
Picture of Dorian Gray '45
The Strange Affair of Uncle Harry '45
Action in Arabia '44
The Moon and Sixpence '43
This Land Is Mine '43
The Black Swan '42
The Falcon's Brother '42
Son of Fury '42
Tales of Manhattan '42
The Son of Monte Cristo '41
Sundown '41
Bitter Sweet '40
Foreign Correspondent '40
The House of the Seven Gables '40
Rebecca '40
The Saint Takes Over '40
The Saint's Double Trouble '40
Allegheny Uprising '39
Mr. Moto's Last Warning '39
Nurse Edith Cavell '39
The Saint in London '39
The Saint Strikes Back '39
Lloyds of London '36

Henry Sanders
Deadly Sunday '82
Boss' Son '78

Hugh Sanders
The Fighter '52
Pride of St. Louis '52
The Magnificent Yankee '50

Jay O. Sanders
Neil Simon's The Odd Couple 2 '98
For Richer or Poorer '97
Kiss the Girls '97
The Matchmaker '97
Daylight '96
The Big Green '95
Three Wishes '95
Angels in the Outfield '94
Down Came a Blackbird '94
Hostages '93
My Boyfriend's Back '93
JFK '91
Meeting Venus '91
V.I. Warshawski '91
Mr. Destiny '90

Richard Sanders
Forbidden Choices '94
Neon City '91
WKRP in Cincinnati, Vol. 1 '78

Martyn Sanderson
An Angel at My Table '89
Beyond Reasonable Doubt '80
Solo '77

William Sanderson
George Wallace '97
Last Man Standing '96
Lone Justice 3: Showdown at Plum Creek '96
Andersonville '95

River of Death '90
That's Adequate '90
Blue Jeans and Dynamite '80s
Brutal Glory '89
Buried Alive '89
C.H.U.D. 2: Bud the Chud '89
Eminent '00
Skeleton Coast '89
Transylvania Twist '89
Captive Rage '88
Hitchhiker 4 '87
Nightstick '87
Prince of Bel Air '87
Black Moon Rising '86
Delta Force '86
Hour of the Assassin '86
Murrow '86
The Last Bastion '84
Return of the Man from U.N.C.L.E. '83
Superman 3 '83
Inside the Third Reich '82
Virus '82
S.O.B. '81
Battle Beyond the Stars '80
City in Fear '80
Hangar 18 '80
Kill Castro '80
The Mercenaries '80
Question of Honor '80
The Rebels '79
Brass Target '78
Centennial '78
The Lucifer Complex '78
Starship Invasions '77
Wanted: Babysitter '75
The Towering Inferno '74
The Woman Hunter '72
The Shaming '71
The Statue '71
Julius Caesar '70
The Bridge at Remagen '69
Bullitt '68
The Man from U.N.C.L.E. '64
The Magnificent Seven '60
The Young Philadelphians '59
Good Day for a Hanging '58
Teenage Caveman '58

Vince Vaughn
The Locusts '97
The Lost World: Jurassic Park 2 '97
Swingers '96

Ron Vawter
King of the Hill '93
Philadelphia '93
Swoon '91
Internal Affairs '90
sex, lies and videotape '89
Sudden Death '77

Yul Vazquez
Fresh '94
Fly by Night '93

Bruno Ve Sota
The Choppers '61
Creature of the Walking Dead '60
Attack of the Giant Leeches '59
The Wasp Woman '59
The Gunslinger '56
Daughter of Horror '55

Isela Vega
Barbarosa '82
Bordello '79
Drum '76
Joshua '76
Bring Me the Head of Alfredo Garcia '74
The Fear Chamber '68

Conrad Veidt
Above Suspicion '43
All Through the Night '42
Casablanca '42
Whistling in the Dark '41
A Woman's Face '41
The Thief of Bagdad '40
Spy in Black '39
Dark Journey '37
King of the Damned '36
The Passing of the Third Floor Back '36
Under the Red Robe '36
Power '34
F.P. 1 '33

Congress Dances '31
The Beloved Rogue '27
The Man Who Laughs '27
The Hands of Orlac '25
Waxworks '24
Cesare Borgia '23
The Cabinet of Dr. Caligari '19

Reginald Vel Johnson
The Great American Sex Scandal '94
Posse '93
Die Hard 2: Die Harder '90
Die Hard '88

Lorena Velasquez
Wrestling Women vs. the Aztec Ape '62
Samson vs. the Vampire Women '61
Wrestling Women vs. the Aztec Mummy '59

Eddie Velez
Bitter Vengeance '94
Romero '89
Rooftops '89
Split Decisions '88
Women's Club '87
Doin' Time '85

Lupe Velez
Mexican Spitfire at Sea '42
Playmates '41
Mexican Spitfire/Smartest Girl in Town '40
Mad About Money '37
Hollywood Party '34
Palooka '34
Hell Harbor '30
Where East Is East '29
Stand and Deliver '28
The Gaucho '27

Evelyn Venable
Mrs. Wiggs of the Cabbage Patch '42
Lucky Cisco Kid '40
The Frontiersmen '38
Hollywood Stadium Mystery '38
Alice Adams '35
Harmony Lane '35
The Little Colonel '35

Amy Veness
Madeleine '50
Man of Evil '48
This Happy Breed '47

Chick Vennera
Alone in the Woods '95
Body Chemistry 4: Full Exposure '95
Double Threat '92
The Terror Within 2 '91
Last Rites '88
The Milagro Beanfield War '88
Kidnapped '87
Yanks '79
Thank God It's Friday '78

Diane Venora
The Jackal '97
The Substitute '96
Surviving Picasso '96
William Shakespeare's Romeo and Juliet '96
Heat '95
Three Wishes '95
Bird '88
Ironweed '87
F/X '86
Terminal Choice '85
The Cotton Club '84
Wolfen '81

Wanda Ventham
Out of the Shadows '90s
Captain Kronos: Vampire Hunter '74
Blood Beast Terror '67

John Ventimiglia
The Funeral '96
Girls Town '95
Angela '94

Clyde Ventura
Gator Bait '73
Bury Me an Angel '71

Jesse Ventura
Ricochet '91

Abraxas: Guardian of the Universe '90
Boxcar Blues '90
Repossessed '90
Thunderground '89
Predator '87
The Running Man '87

Lino Ventura
Sword of Gideon '86
The Medusa Touch '78
Les Aventuriers '77
Pain in the A— '77
The Slap '76
The French Detective '75
Happy New Year '74
Jailbird's Vacation '74
Les Grandes Gueules '65
The Three Penny Opera '62
Mistress of the World '59
Modigliani '58
Grisbi '53

Richard Venture
Red Corner '97
Truman '95
Scent of a Woman '92
Street Hawk '84
Missing '82
The Effect of Gamma Rays on Man-in-the-Moon Marigolds '73

Massimo Venturiello
My Wonderful Life '90
Rorret '87

Billy Vera
The Doors '91
Finish Line '89

Victoria Vera
A Man of Passion '90s
Monster Dog '82

Vera-Ellen
White Christmas '54
The Belle of New York '52
Happy Go Lovely '51
Love Happy '50
Three Little Words '50
On the Town '49
Words and Music '48
Wonder Man '45

Gwen Verdon
In Cold Blood '96
Marvin's Room '96
Oldest Confederate Widow Tells All '95
Alice '90
Cocoon: The Return '88
Nadine '87
Cocoon '85
The Cotton Club '84
Legs '83
Damn Yankees '58

Maribel Verdu
Belle Epoque '92
Lovers: A True Story '90

Elena Verdugo
Boss' Son '78
Cyrano de Bergerac '50
The Big Sombrero '49
Little Giant '46
House of Frankenstein '44
Weird Woman/Frozen Ghost '44
The Moon and Sixpence '43

Ben Vereen
Intruders '92
The Kid Who Loved Christmas '90
Mother Goose Rock 'n' Rhyme '90
Buy & Cell '89
The Zoo Gang '85
Breakin' Through '84
The Jesse Owens Story '84
Puss 'n Boots '84
Pippin '81
All That Jazz '79
Roots '77
Funny Lady '75
Gas-s-s-s! '70

Tom Verica
The Assassination File '96
Breach of Conduct '94
800 Leagues Down the Amazon '93

Die Hard 2: Die Harder '90

Bernard Verley
Helas pour Moi '94
Pas Tres Catholique '93
Phantom of Liberty '74
Chloe in the Afternoon '72
The Milky Way '68

Harold Vermilyea
Emperor Waltz '48
Sorry, Wrong Number '48

Denise Vernac
Unnatural '52
The Mask of Dijon '46

Karen Verne
The Seventh Cross '44
All Through the Night '42
Sherlock Holmes and the Secret Weapon '42
Kings Row '41

Guy Verney
Martin Luther '53
Fame Is the Spur '47
This Happy Breed '47

Pierre Vernier
Betty '92
Mama, There's a Man in Your Bed '89

Jerry Verno
The Belles of St. Trinian's '53
Sidewalks of London '38
Non-Stop New York '37
Young and Innocent '37
The 39 Steps '35

Anne Vernon
Therese & Isabelle '67
Umbrellas of Cherbourg '64

Bobby Vernon
Teddy at the Throttle/Speeding Along '17
Teddy at the Throttle '16
A Hash House Fraud/The Sultan's Wife '15

Howard Vernon
Revenge in the House of Usher '82
Zombie Lake '80
The Demons '74
The Perverse Countess '73
Dr. Orloff's Invisible Horror '72
The Screaming Dead '72
Virgin Among the Living Dead '71
The Invisible Dead '70
Castle of the Creeping Flesh '68
Triple Cross '67
The Diabolical Dr. Z '65
The Awful Dr. Orloff '62
La Silence de la Mer '47

John Vernon
Malicious '95
Hostage for a Day '94
Sodbusters '94
Bail Out '90
Mob Story '90
Terminal Exposure '89
War Bus Commando '89
Deadly Stranger '88
Dixie Lanes '88
I'm Gonna Git You Sucka '88
Killer Klowns from Outer Space '88
Blue Monkey '87
Ernest Goes to Camp '87
Nightstick '87
Doin' Time '85
Fraternity Vacation '85
The Blood of Others '84
Jungle Warriors '84
Chained Heat '83
Curtains '83
Savage Streets '83
Herbie Goes Bananas '80
National Lampoon's Animal House '78
Angela '77
Golden Rendezvous '77
Journey '77
A Special Day '77
The Outlaw Josey Wales '76
The Virginia Hill Story '76
Brannigan '75
The Barbary Coast '74

The Black Windmill '74
W '74
Charley Varrick '73
Hunter '73
Dirty Harry '71
Justine '69
Tell Them Willie Boy Is Here '69

Kate Vernon
Flood: A River's Rampage '97
Downdraft '96
Bloodknot '95
Probable Cause '95
The Sister-in-Law '95
Dangerous Touch '94
Soft Deceit '94
Malcolm X '92
Mob Story '90
Hostile Takeover '88
The Last of Philip Banter '87
Alphabet City '84
Roadhouse 66 '84

Richard Vernon
The Return of the Borrowers '96
The Human Factor '79
The Duchess of Duke Street '78
The Satanic Rites of Dracula '73
A Hard Day's Night '64
Village of the Damned '60

Wally Vernon
Square Dance Jubilee '51
Gunfire '50
Broadway Serenade '39
Happy Landing '38

Christine Veronica
Party Incorporated '89
Love Notes '88

Cec Verrell
Three of Hearts '93
Mad at the Moon '92
Eye of the Eagle '87
Silk '86

Odile Versois
Le Crabe Tambour '77
Cartouche '62
To Paris with Love '55

Veruschka
The Bride '85
Blow-Up '66

Charlotte Very
Trois Couleurs: Bleu '93
A Tale of Winter '92

Tricia Vessey
Bean '97
Standoff '97

Victoria Vetri
Invasion of the Bee Girls '73
Group Marriage '72
When Dinosaurs Ruled the Earth '70

Karin Viard
The Separation '94
Delicatessen '92

Martha Vickers
Big Bluff '55
The Big Sleep '46
The Man I Love '46

Yvette Vickers
Evil Spirits '91
Beach Party '63
Attack of the Giant Leeches '59

John Vickery
Deconstructing Sarah '94
Rapid Fire '92

Charles Victor
Motor Patrol '50
The Woman in Question '50
San Demetrio, London '47
Seven Days' Leave '42

Henry Victor
Sherlock Holmes and the Secret Weapon '42
King of the Zombies '41
Freaks '32
The Mummy '32
The Beloved Rogue '27

Katherine Victor
The Wild World of Batwoman '66
House of the Black Death '65
Curse of the Stone Hand '64

Roommate '84

Barbara Wilkin
Six in Paris '68
The Flesh Eaters '64

June Wilkinson
Vasectomy: A Delicate Matter '86
Sno-Line '85
Frankenstein's Great Aunt Tillie '83
The Florida Connection '74
The Bellboy and the Playgirls '62
Macumba Love '60

Tom Wilkinson
Rush Hour '98
Oscar and Lucinda '97
Wilde '97
The Full Monty '96
The Ghost and the Darkness '96
Smilla's Sense of Snow '96
Martin Chuzzlewit '94
Priest '94
Prime Suspect '92
Paper Mask '91
Sylvia '86

Lee Wilkof
Private Parts '96
Chattahoochee '89

Fred Willard
Waiting for Guffman '96
Prehysteria 3 '95
Sodbusters '94
High Strung '91
Portrait of a White Marriage '88
Roxanne '87
The History of White People in America '85
Lots of Luck '85
Moving Violations '85
How to Beat the High Cost of Living '80
Americathon '79
Salem's Lot '79
Chesty Anderson USN '76

Warren William
Black Tower '50
The Private Affairs of Bel Ami '47
Fear '46
Strange Illusion '45
The Wolf Man '41
Arizona '40
The Man in the Iron Mask '39
Wives Under Suspicion '38
The Firefly '37
Madame X '37
Go West, Young Man '36
Satan Met a Lady '36
The Case of the Lucky Legs '35
Cleopatra '34
Employees' Entrance '33
Gold Diggers of 1933 '33
Lady for a Day '33
Skyscraper Souls '32
Three on a Match '32

Adam Williams
North by Northwest '59
The Badlanders '58
Fear Strikes Out '57
Without Warning '52
Queen for a Day '51

Allen Williams
Scorpion '86
The Two Worlds of Jenny Logan '79

Barbara Williams
Krippendorf's Tribe '98
Family of Cops 2: Breach of Faith '97
Inventing the Abbotts '97
Family of Cops '95
Digger '94
Spenser: Pale Kings & Princes '94
Spenser: Ceremony '93
Indecency '92
Oh, What a Night '92
City of Hope '91
Peter Gunn '89
Watchers '88
Tiger Warsaw '87
Jo Jo Dancer, Your Life Is Calling '86

Tell Me That You Love Me '84
Thief of Hearts '84

Barry Williams
A Very Brady Christmas '88
The Brady Bunch '69

Bill Williams
Flight of the Grey Wolf '76
The Giant Spider Invasion '75
Buckskin '68
Storm Rider '57
Torpedo Alley '53
Son of Paleface '52
Adventures of Kit Carson '51
Cavalry Charge '51
The Cariboo Trail '50
Operation Haylift '50
The Clay Pigeon '49
The Stratton Story '49
A Woman's Secret '49
Deadline at Dawn '46
Till the End of Time '46

Billy Dee Williams
Giant Steps
Mask of Death '97
Steel Sharks '97
Moving Target '96
Dangerous Passion '95
Triplecross '95
Alien Intruder '93
Percy & Thunder '93
The Jacksons: An American Dream '92
Driving Me Crazy '91
Batman '89
Secret Agent 00-Soul '89
Deadly Illusion '87
Number One with a Bullet '87
Courage '86
Oceans of Fire '86
Fear City '85
Shooting Stars '85
Christmas Lilies of the Field '84
The Imposter '84
Marvin & Tige '84
Chiefs '83
From "Star Wars" to "Jedi": The Making of a Saga '83
Return of the Jedi '83
Nighthawks '81
Children of Divorce '80
The Empire Strikes Back '80
The Hostage Tower '80
Bingo Long Traveling All-Stars & Motor Kings '76
Mahogany '75
Hit! '73
Final Comedown '72
The Glass House '72
Lady Sings the Blues '72
Brian's Song '71
The Out-of-Towners '70
Black Brigade '69

Billy "Sly" Williams
Mission of Justice '92
Voodoo Dawn '89

Cara Williams
The White Buffalo '77
Never Steal Anything Small '59
The Defiant Ones '58
Meet Me in Las Vegas '56
Boomerang '47

Caroline Williams
Leprechaun 3 '95
Stepfather 2: Make Room for Daddy '89
Texas Chainsaw Massacre 2 '86

Charles Williams
Born to Be Wild '38
Hollywood Stadium Mystery '38

Chuck Williams
Dark Rider '91
Soultaker '90

Cindy Williams
Meet Wally Sparks '97
Bingo '91
Big Man on Campus '89
Rude Awakening '89
Tricks of the Trade '88
Spaceship '81
Uforia '81
More American Graffiti '79
The First Nudie Musical '75
The Conversation '74

The Migrants '74
American Graffiti '73
The Killing Kind '73
Travels with My Aunt '72
Gas-s-s-s! '70

Clara Williams
Hell's Hinges '16
The Italian '15

Clarence Williams, III
George Wallace '97
Half-Baked '97
Hoodlum '96
Rebound: The Legend of Earl "The Goat" Manigault '96
The Road to Galveston '96
Sprung '96
The Immortals '95
The Silencers '95
Tales from the Hood '95
Against the Wall '94
Sugar Hill '94
Dangerous Relations '93
Deep Cover '92
My Heroes Have Always Been Cowboys '91
Maniac Cop 2 '90
The House of Dies Drear '88
I'm Gonna Git You Sucka '88
The Last Innocent Man '87
Perfect Victims '87
Tough Guys Don't Dance '87
52 Pick-Up '86
Purple Rain '84
The Mod Squad '68

Cynda Williams
Caught Up '98
Gang in Blue '96
Spirit Lost '96
Condition Red '95
Machine Gun Blues '95
The Sweeper '95
The Tie that Binds '95
Armistead Maupin's Tales of the City '93
The Ghost Brigade '93
Tales of Erotica '93
One False Move '91
Mo' Better Blues '90

Dick Anthony Williams
The Players Club '98
Edward Scissorhands '90
Mo' Better Blues '90
Tap '89
For Us, the Living '88
Keeping On '81
Sophisticated Gents '81
The Night the City Screamed '80
An Almost Perfect Affair '79
A Woman Called Moses '78

D.J. Williams
The Courageous Mr. Penn '41
The Crimes of Stephen Hawke '36
Murder in the Old Red Barn '36

Edy Williams
Bad Girls from Mars '90
Rented Lips '88
Mankillers '87
Hellhole '85
Bad Manners '84
Hollywood Hot Tubs '84
Beyond the Valley of the Dolls '70
Secret Life of an American Wife '68

Emlyn Williams
Deadly Game '82
The Wreck of the Mary Deare '59
The Last Days of Dolwyn '49
This England '42
The Stars Look Down '39
The Citadel '38
The Iron Duke '34

Esther Williams
That's Entertainment '74
Jupiter's Darling '55
Dangerous When Wet '53
Easy to Love '53
Million Dollar Mermaid '52

Skirts Ahoy! '52
Texas Carnival '51
The Duchess of Idaho '50
Pagan Love Song '50
Neptune's Daughter '49
Take Me Out to the Ball Game '49
On an Island with You '48
Ziegfeld Follies '46
Thrill of a Romance '45
Bathing Beauty '44
A Guy Named Joe '44
Andy Hardy's Double Life '42

Grant Williams
Brain of Blood '71
Escape from Planet Earth '67
The Leech Woman '59
The Incredible Shrinking Man '57
The Monolith Monsters '57
Written on the Wind '56

Guinn "Big Boy" Williams
Hidden Guns '56
Springfield Rifle '52
Nevada '44
The Desperadoes '43
Hands Across the Border '43
Lure of the Islands '42
Mr. Wise Guy '42
Billy the Kid '41
The Fighting 69th '40
Virginia City '40
Wagon's Westward '40
Bad Lands '39
Dangerous Holiday '37
Feud of the Trail '37
You Only Live Once '37
Gun Play '36
Kelly the Second '36
The Vigilantes Are Coming '36
Danger Trails '35
Powdersmoke Range '35
Heritage of the Desert '33
Mystery Squadron '33
The Phantom Broadcast '33
When the West Was Young '32
The Phantom '31
Burning Daylight '28
Wolfheart's Revenge '25
Rounding Up the Law '22

Guy Williams
Captain Sinbad '63
The Prince and the Pauper '62
The Sign of Zorro '60
I Was a Teenage Werewolf '57
The Secret of El Zorro '57
Savage Wilderness '55

Hal Williams
Don't Look Back: The Story of Leroy "Satchel" Paige '81
On the Nickel '80

Harland Williams
Half-Baked '97
RocketMan '97
Down Periscope '96
Dumb & Dumber '94

Heathcote Williams
The Odyssey '97
The Tango Lesson '97
Cold Light of Day '95
Orlando '92

Hugh Williams
Khartoum '66
Elizabeth of Ladymead '48
A Girl in a Million '46
The Day Will Come '42
Secret Mission '42
One of Our Aircraft Is Missing '41
The Human Monster '39
Inspector Hornleigh '39
Wuthering Heights '39
Bitter Sweet '33

Ian Patrick Williams
Bad Channels '92
Bloodmoon '90
Dolls '87

Jason Williams
Danger Zone 3: Steel Horse War '90
Danger Zone 2 '89

Vampire at Midnight '88
Danger Zone '87
Cheerleaders' Wild Weekend '85
Copkillers '77
Flesh Gordon '72

Jim Williams
Ex-Cop '93
Living to Die '91
The Newlydeads '87
Island of Blood '86
The Executioner '78

JoBeth Williams
When Danger Follows You Home '97
Jungle 2 Jungle '96
Ruby Jean and Joe '96
Parallel Lives '94
Wyatt Earp '94
Chantilly Lace '93
Final Appeal '93
Sex, Love and Cold Hard Cash '93
Me, Myself & I '92
Stop! or My Mom Will Shoot '92
Dutch '91
Switch '91
Victim of Love '91
Child in the Night '90
Welcome Home '89
Memories of Me '88
Murder Ordained '87
Desert Bloom '86
Poltergeist 2: The Other Side '86
American Dreamer '84
Teachers '84
Adam '83
The Big Chill '83
The Day After '83
Endangered Species '82
Poltergeist '82
The Dogs of War '81
Stir Crazy '80
Kramer vs. Kramer '79

John Williams
The Secret War of Harry Frigg '68
Double Trouble '67
Dear Brigitte '65
24 Hours in a Woman's Life '61
The Young Philadelphians '59
Island in the Sun '57
Witness for the Prosecution '57
D-Day, the Sixth of June '56
To Catch a Thief '55
Dial "M" for Murder '54
Sabrina '54

Kelli Williams
Snowbound '97
Wavelength '96
Lifepod '93
There Goes My Baby '92
Till Murder Do Us Part '92
Zapped Again '89

Kenneth Williams
Carry On Emmanuelle '78
Carry On Behind '75
Carry On 'Round the Bend '72
Carry On at Your Convenience '71
Carry On Camping '71
Carry On Henry VIII '71
Carry On Doctor '68
Follow That Camel '67
Carry On Cowboy '66
Carry On Screaming '66
Carry On Cleo '65
Carry On Cruising '62

Kimberly Williams
The War at Home '96
Father of the Bride Part II '95
Coldblooded '94
Indian Summer '93
Father of the Bride '91

Malinda Williams
High School High '96
A Thin Line Between Love and Hate '96
Laurel Avenue '93

Mark Williams
The Borrowers '97
101 Dalmatians '96
Kill Line '91

Cast Index

Zerbe *cont.*

Omega Man '71
The Liberation of L.B. Jones '70
They Call Me Mr. Tibbs! '70
Cool Hand Luke '67
Will Penny '67

Catherine Zeta-Jones

The Mask of Zorro '98
The Phantom '96
Titanic '96
The Cinder Path '94
The Return of the Native '94
Splitting Heirs '93
Christopher Columbus: The
    Discovery '92

Mai Zetterling

Hidden Agenda '90
The Witches '90
Only Two Can Play '62
Pattern for Plunder '62
Truth About Women '58
Abandon Ship '57
Frieda '47
Night Is My Future '47

Monica Zetterlund

The New Land '73
The Emigrants '72

Sonja Ziemann

A Matter of WHO '62
Made in Heaven '52

Ian Ziering

The Corporation '96
No Way Back '96
The Fighter '95
Beverly Hills 90210: The
    Graduation '93
Beverly Hills 90210 '90

Madeline Zima

Mr. Nanny '93
The Hand that Rocks the Cradle
    '92

Efrem Zimbalist, Jr.

The Avenging '92
Hot Shots! '91
Shooting Stars '85
Scruples '80
The Gathering: Part 2 '79
Family Upside Down '78
Terror Out of the Sky '78
Airport '75 '75
Who Is the Black Dahlia? '75
Wait Until Dark '67
By Love Possessed '61
Deep Six '58
Band of Angels '57
House of Strangers '49

Stephanie Zimbalist

Dead Ahead '96
The Great Elephant Escape '95
Jericho Fever '93
The Story Lady '93
Caroline? '90
The Killing Mind '90
Personals '90
Love on the Run '85
Remington Steele, Vol. 1:
    License to Steele '82
Tomorrow's Child '82
The Awakening '80
The Babysitter '80
The Triangle Factory Fire
    Scandal '79
Centennial '78
Forever '78
Long Journey Back '78
Magic of Lassie '78
The Gathering '77

Victoria Zinny

Beyond the Door 3 '91
Viridiana '61

William Zipp

Future Force '89
Jungle Assault '89
Death Chase '87
Mankillers '87

August Zirner

The Promise '94
Voyager '91

Hanns Zischler

The Cement Garden '93
Francesco '93
Club Extinction '89
A Woman in Flames '84
Les Rendez-vous D'Anna '78
Kings of the Road—In the
    Course of Time '76

Dan Ziskie

Dangerous Passion '95
Zebrahead '92
Twisted '86

Adrian Zmed

Improper Conduct '94
Eyewitness to Murder '93
The Other Woman '92
Bachelor Party '84
The Final Terror '83
Grease 2 '82
For the Love of It '80

Michael Zorek

Hot Moves '84
Private School '83

Louis Zorich

Commandments '96
Cheap Shots '91
City of Hope '91
Death of a Salesman '86
Newman's Law '74

Vera Zorina

Follow the Boys '44
Louisiana Purchase '41
The Goldwyn Follies '38

Zouzou

S*P*Y*S '74
Chloe in the Afternoon '72

Rod Zuanic

Fast Talking '86
Mad Max: Beyond
    Thunderdome '85

George Zucco

David and Bathsheba '51
Madame Bovary '49
The Pirate '48
The Devil Thumbs a Ride/
    Having Wonderful Crime '47
Scared to Death/Dick Tracy's
    Dilemma '47
Where There's Life '47
Scared to Death '46
Fog Island '45
Having Wonderful Crime '45
House of Frankenstein '44
The Mummy's Ghost '44
Return of the Ape Man '44
The Seventh Cross '44
The Black Raven '43
Dead Men Walk '43
The Mad Ghoul '43
Sherlock Holmes in Washington
    '43
The Black Swan '42
The Mad Monster '42
The Mummy's Tomb '42
My Favorite Blonde '42
The Monster and the Girl '41
A Woman's Face '41
The Mummy's Hand '40
The Adventures of Sherlock
    Holmes '39
The Hunchback of Notre Dame
    '39
Arrest Bulldog Drummond '38
Bulldog Drummond in Africa/
    Arrest Bulldog Drummond '38
Marie Antoinette '38
Three Comrades '38
The Bride Wore Red '37
The Firefly '37
Saratoga '37
Souls at Sea '37

Alex Zuckerman

Freaked '93
Me and the Kid '93

Daphne Zuniga

Stand-Ins '97
Charlie's Ghost: The Secret of
    Coronado '94
800 Leagues Down the Amazon
    '93
Prey of the Chameleon '91
Eyes of the Panther '90

The Fly 2 '89
Gross Anatomy '89
Staying Together '89
Last Rites '88
Spaceballs '87
Modern Girls '86
Quarterback Princess '85
The Sure Thing '85
Vision Quest '85
The Initiation '84

Jose Zuniga

Con Air '97
Hurricane Streets '96
Ransom '96
Crooklyn '94

Dianik Zurakowska

Orgy of the Vampires '73
The Hanging Woman '72
Cauldron of Blood '67

Jahi JJ Zuri

Omega Doom '96
Nemesis 2: Nebula '94

Yoshitaka Zushi

Akira Kurosawa's Dreams '90
Dodes 'ka-den '70

Brad Zutaut

Knock Outs '92
Nudity Required '90
Hardbodies 2 '86

Noam Zylberman

Love and Hate: A Marriage
    Made in Hell '90
Outside Chance of Maximillian
    Glick '88

Elsa Zylberstein

Farinelli '94
Mina Tannenbaum '93

The **Director Index** provides a complete videography for any director with a video credit. The listings for the director names follow an alphabetical sort by last name (although the names appear in a first name last name format). The videographies are listed chronologically, from most recent film to directorial debut. If a director helmed more than one film in the same year, these movies are listed alphabetically within the year. Use this index in conjunction with the **Cast** (immediately preceding this index), **Writer**, and **Cinematographer** indexes (immediately following) to see where some of today's hottest directors got their starts.

Paul Aaron
In Love and War '91
Imperial Navy '80s
Maxie '85
Deadly Force '83
Force of One '79
The Miracle Worker '79
Different Story '78

Dodo Abashidze
Ashik Kerib '88

Charles Abbott
The Adventures of the Masked Phantom '38

George Abbott
Damn Yankees '58
The Pajama Game '57
Too Many Girls '40

Alan Abel
Is There Sex After Death? '71

Jeanne Abel
Is There Sex After Death? '71

Lewis Abernathy
House 4: Home Deadly Home '91

Derwin Abrahams
Northwest Trail '46
Border Vigilantes '41

Jim Abrahams
Jane Austen's Mafia! '98
First Do No Harm '97
Hot Shots! Part Deux '93
Hot Shots! '91
Welcome Home, Roxy Carmichael '90
Big Business '88
Ruthless People '86
Top Secret! '84
Police Squad! Help Wanted! '82
Airplane! '80

Ivan Abramson
East and West '24

Tengiz Abuladze
Repentance '87

Jon Acevski
Freddie the Frog '92

Jovan Acin
Hey, Babu Riba '88

Robert Ackerman
Safe Passage '94

Rodney Ackland
Thursday's Child '43

David Acomba
Night Life '90

Catlin Adams
Sticky Fingers '88

Daniel Adams
Primary Motive '92
A Fool and His Money '88

Doug Adams
Blackout '88

Al Adamson
Cinderella 2000 '78
Hospital of Terror '78
Kill Factor '78
Black Samurai '77
Blazing Stewardesses '75
Jessi's Girls '75
Texas Layover '75
The Dynamite Brothers '74
I Spit on Your Corpse '74
Angels' Wild Women '72
Blood of Ghastly Horror '72
Brain of Blood '71
Dracula vs. Frankenstein '71
Horror of the Blood Monsters '70
Blood of Dracula's Castle '69
The Female Bunch '69
Gun Riders '69
Satan's Sadists '69

Victor Adamson
Boss Cowboy '35
Rawhide Romance '34
Fighting Cowboy '33

Gilbert Adler
Tales from the Crypt Presents Bordello of Blood '96

Joseph Adler
Scream, Baby, Scream '69
Sex and the College Girl '64

Lou Adler
Cheech and Chong's Up in Smoke '79

Percy Adlon
Younger & Younger '94
Salmonberries '91
Rosalie Goes Shopping '89
Bagdad Cafe '88
Sugarbaby '85
The Last Five Days '82
Celeste '81

Ed Adlum
Invasion of the Blood Farmers '72

Edvin Adolphson
The Count of the Old Town '34

Gabriel Aghion
Pedale Douce '96

Frank Agrama
Dawn of the Mummy '82

Joseph Louis Agraz
Treasure of the Moon Goddess '88

Javier Aguirre
The Rue Morgue Massacres '73
Dracula's Great Love '72

Agust Agustsson
Maya '82

Charlie Ahearn
Wild Style '83

Mac Ahlberg
Gangsters '79
I, A Woman '66

Faruque Ahmed
Warlords 3000 '93

John Ainsworth
Pattern for Plunder '62

Chantal Akerman
A Couch in New York '95
Akermania, Vol. 1 '92
Night and Day '91
Window Shopping '86
The Eighties '83
Toute Une Nuit '82
Les Rendez-vous D'Anna '78

News from Home '76
Je Tu Il Elle '74

Moustapha Akkad
Lion of the Desert '81
Mohammed: Messenger of God '77

Jordan Alan
Terminal Bliss '91

Benito Alazraki
Invasion of the Zombies '61
Spiritism '61

Rafael Morena Alba
Exorcism's Daughter '74

Jean-Gabriel Albicocco
The Wanderer '67

Hans Albin
No Survivors, Please '63

Carlton J. Albright
Luther the Geek '90

Feliz Alcala
Fire Down Below '97

Alan Alda
Betsy's Wedding '90
A New Life '88
Sweet Liberty '86
The Four Seasons '81

Thomas Alderman
The Severed Arm '73

Will Aldis
Stealing Home '88

Adell Aldrich
The Kid from Left Field '79

Robert Aldrich
...All the Marbles '81
The Frisco Kid '79
The Choirboys '77
Twilight's Last Gleaming '77
The Hustle '75
The Longest Yard '74
Ulzana's Raid '72
The Grissom Gang '71
Too Late the Hero '70
The Killing of Sister George '69
The Dirty Dozen '67

The Flight of the Phoenix '65
Hush, Hush, Sweet Charlotte '65
Four for Texas '63
Sodom and Gomorrah '62
What Ever Happened to Baby Jane? '62
Autumn Leaves '56
The Big Knife '55
Kiss Me Deadly '55
Apache '54
Vera Cruz '53

Goffredo Alessandrini
We the Living '42

Ottavio Alessi
The Seducers '70

Bill Alexander
Tartuffe '90

Jason Alexander
For Better or Worse '95

Tom Alexander
The Dark Dealer '95

Grigori Alexandrov
Que Viva Mexico '32
Ten Days That Shook the World '27

James Nelson Algar
Vanishing Prairie '54
The Adventures of Ichabod and Mr. Toad '49
The Legend of Sleepy Hollow '49

Sidney Algier
Wild Horse '31

Dan Algrant
Naked in New York '93

Marcello Aliprandi
Vatican Conspiracy '81

Howard Alk
Janis: A Film '74

Don Allan
Jungleground '95

Marc Allegret
Sois Belle et Tais-Toi '58
Mademoiselle Striptease '57

Richard Baskin
Sing '89

Jules Bass
Flight of Dragons '82
The Last Unicorn '82
The Return of the King '80
The Hobbit '78
The Ballad of Paul Bunyan '72
Santa Claus Is Coming to Town '70
Mad Monster Party '68

Kim Bass
Ballistic '94

Saul Bass
Phase 4 '74

Lawrence Bassoff
Hunk '87
Weekend Pass '84

William Bast
James Dean '76

Michal Bat-Adam
Boy Takes Girl '83

Alexei Batalov
The Overcoat '59

Joy Batchelor
Animal Farm '55

Kent Bateman
Headless Eyes '83

Bradley Battersby
Blue Desert '91

Roy Battersby
Cracker: Brotherly Love '95
Mr. Love '86
Winter Flight '84

Giacomo Battiato
Blood Ties '87
Hearts & Armour '83

Murray Battle
Stand Off '93

L. Frank Baum
His Majesty, the Scarecrow of Oz/The Magic Cloak of Oz '14
Patchwork Girl of Oz '14

Lewis Baumander
Future Fear '97

Noah Baumbach
Kicking and Screaming '95

Lamberto Bava
Demons 2 '87
Demons '86
Blastfighter '85
Devilfish '84
A Blade in the Dark '83
Frozen Terror '80

Mario Bava
Beyond the Door 2 '79
Lisa and the Devil '75
Torture Chamber of Baron Blood '72
Twitch of the Death Nerve '71
Hatchet for the Honeymoon '70
Danger: Diabolik '68
Kill, Baby, Kill '66
Planet of the Vampires '65
Black Sabbath '64
Blood and Black Lace '64
Hercules in the Haunted World '64
The Invaders '63
The Wonders of Aladdin '61
Black Sunday '60

Craig R. Baxley
Twilight Man '96
The Avenging Angel '95
Deconstructing Sarah '94
Deep Red '94
Stone Cold '91
I Come in Peace '90
Action Jackson '88

John Baxter
Love on the Dole '41
Old Mother Riley's Ghosts '41

Michael Bay
Armageddon '98
The Rock '96
Bad Boys '95

Rolf Bayer
Pacific Inferno '85

Stephen Bayly
Diamond's Edge '88
Coming Up Roses '87

Camillo Bazzoni
Black Lemons '80s

David Beaird
Scorchers '92
It Takes Two '88
Pass the Ammo '88
My Chauffeur '86
Party Animal '83
Octavia '82

Rick Beairsto
Close to Home '86

Chris Bearde
Hysterical '83

Alan Beattie
Stand Alone '85
Delusion '84

Warren Beatty
Bulworth '98
Dick Tracy '90
Reds '81

William Beaudine
Billy the Kid Versus Dracula '66
Jesse James Meets Frankenstein's Daughter '65
Lassie's Great Adventure '62
Ten Who Dared '60
Westward Ho, the Wagons! '56
Bela Lugosi Meets a Brooklyn Gorilla '52
Here Come the Marines '52
Ghost Chasers '51
Blues Busters '50
Smugglers' Cove '48
Spook Busters '48
Bowery Buckaroos '47
Hard-Boiled Mahoney '47
Infamous Crimes '47
Mom & Dad '47
Follow the Leader '44
The Ape Man '43
Ghost on the Loose '43
Here Comes Kelly '43
Spotlight Scandals '43
Miracle Kid '42
The Panther's Claw '42
Phantom Killer '42
Turf Boy '42
Misbehaving Husbands '41
Robot Pilot '41
Sparrows '26
Little Annie Rooney '25
The Country Kid '23

Gabrielle Beaumont
Beastmaster 3: The Eye of Braxus '95
Carmilla '89
He's My Girl '87
Gone Are the Days '84
Death of a Centerfold '81
The Godsend '79

Harry Beaumont
The Show-Off '46
When's Your Birthday? '37
Dance Fools Dance '31
Laughing Sinners '31
Broadway Melody '29
Our Dancing Daughters '28
Beau Brummel '24

Gorman Bechard
Cemetery High '89
Galactic Gigolo '87
Psychos in Love '87

George Beck
Behave Yourself! '52

Martin Beck
Last Game '80
Challenge '74

Reginald Beck
The Long Dark Hall '51

Harold Becker
Mercury Rising '98
City Hall '95
Malice '93
Sea of Love '89
The Boost '88

Vision Quest '85
Taps '81
The Black Marble '79
The Onion Field '79

Jacques Becker
Modigliani '58
Ali Baba and the 40 Thieves '54
Grisbi '53
Casque d'Or '52

Jean Becker
Elisa '94
One Deadly Summer '83

Josh Becker
Lunatics: A Love Story '92
Thou Shalt Not Kill...Except '87

Terry Becker
The Thirsty Dead '74

Vernon Becker
A Man with a Maid '73

James Becket
Natural Causes '94
Ulterior Motives '92

Ron Beckstrom
Sarah's Child '96

James Gavin Bedford
Red Shoe Diaries 8: Night of Abandon '97

Terry Bedford
Slayground '84

Ford Beebe
My Dog Shep '46
The Invisible Man's Revenge '44
Don Winslow of the Coast Guard '43
Don Winslow of the Navy '43
Night Monster '42
The Masked Rider '41
Riders of Death Valley '41
Winners of the West '40
Buck Rogers Conquers the Universe '39
Destination Saturn '39
Oregon Trail '39
The Phantom Creeps '39
Flash Gordon: Mars Attacks the World '38
Red Barry '38
Radio Patrol '37
Tim Tyler's Luck '37
Ace Drummond '36
The Man from Gun Town '36
The Adventures of Rex & Rinty '35
Laughing at Life '33
The Last of the Mohicans '32
Shadow of the Eagle '32

Greg Beeman
Bushwhacked '95
Mom and Dad Save the World '92
License to Drive '88

Tom Beeman
The Legend of Black Thunder Mountain '79

Charles Beeson
Agatha Christie's The Pale Horse '96

Jean-Jacques Beineix
Betty Blue '86
Moon in the Gutter '83
Diva '82

Jean-Pierre Bekolo
Quartier Mozart '92

Arnold Belgard
East of Kilimanjaro '57

A. Dean Bell
Backfire! '94

Alan Bell
The Hitchhiker's Guide to the Galaxy '81
Ripping Yarns '75

Dan Bell
The Shot '96

Jeffrey Bell
Radio Inside '94

Martin Bell
Hidden in America '96
American Heart '92

Streetwise '84

Earl Bellamy
Magic on Love Island '80
Desperate Women '78
Speedtrap '78
Fire '77
Sidewinder One '77
Flood! '76
Against a Crooked Sky '75
Seven Alone '75
Walking Tall: Part 2 '75
The Trackers '71
Justice of the West '61

Donald P. Bellisario
JAG '95
Last Rites '88

Marco Bellocchio
Devil in the Flesh '87
Henry IV '85
The Eyes, the Mouth '83

Yannick Bellon
Rape of Love '79

Vera Belmont
Red Kiss '85

Jerry Belson
Surrender '87
Jekyll & Hyde...Together Again '82

Remy Belvaux
Man Bites Dog '91

Maria-Luisa Bemberg
I Don't Want to Talk About It '94
I, the Worst of All '90
Miss Mary '86
Camila '84

Jacob Ben-Ami
Green Fields '37

Don Bendell
The Instructor '83

Jack Bender
Lone Justice 3: Showdown at Plum Creek '96
Lone Justice 2 '93
Child's Play 3 '91
My Brother's Wife '89
Side By Side '88
Tricks of the Trade '88
The Midnight Hour '86
Letting Go '85
Two Kinds of Love '85
Shattered Vows '84
In Love with an Older Woman '82

Joel Bender
Midnight Kiss '93
Rich Girl '91
The Immortalizer '89
Gas Pump Girls '79

Laslo Benedek
Assault on Agathon '75
The Night Visitor '70
Daring Game '68
Namu, the Killer Whale '66
The Wild One '54
Port of New York '49

Terry Benedict
Painted Hero '95

Roberto Benigni
Life is Beautiful '97
The Monster '96
Johnny Stecchino '92

Richard Benjamin
Mrs. Winterbourne '96
Milk Money '94
Made in America '93
Mermaids '90
Downtown '89
Little Nikita '88
My Stepmother Is an Alien '88
The Money Pit '86
City Heat '84
Racing with the Moon '84
My Favorite Year '82

Richard Benner
Happy Birthday, Gemini '80
Outrageous! '77

Rick Bennet
Balance of Power '96

Spencer Gordon Bennet
Atomic Submarine '59
Submarine Seahawk '59
King of the Congo '52
Atom Man vs. Superman '50
Pirates of the High Seas '50
Western Double Feature 1: Wild Bill & Sunset Carson '40s
Superman: The Serial, Vol. 1 '48
The Black Widow '47
D-Day on Mars '45
Manhunt of Mystery Island '45
The Purple Monster Strikes '45
Perils of the Darkest Jungle '44
Zorro's Black Whip '44
Calling Wild Bill Elliott '43
The Masked Marvel '43
The Secret Code '42
Arizona Bound '41
Gunman from Bodie '41
Across the Plains '39
The Rangers Step In '37
The Unknown Ranger '36
Get That Man '35
The Fighting Rookie '34
Last Frontier '32
Midnight Warning '32
Marked Money '28

Bill Bennett
Kiss or Kill '97
Two If by Sea '95
Backlash '86

Compton Bennett
The Gift Horse '52
King Solomon's Mines '50
That Forsyte Woman '50
The Seventh Veil '46

Edward Bennett
A Woman at War '94

Gary Bennett
Rain Without Thunder '93

Richard Bennett
Harper Valley P.T.A. '78

Rodney Bennett
Monsignor Quixote '91
Sense & Sensibility '85

Wallace C. Bennett
George! '70

Walter Bennett
Young Love—Lemon Popsicle 7 '87

Patricia Benoit
Subway Stories '97

Leon Benson
Flipper's New Adventure '64

Richard Benson
Werewolf in a Girl's Dormitory '61
The Day the Sky Exploded '57

Robby Benson
Modern Love '90
White Hot '88

Steve Benson
Endgame '85

Anna Benson Gyles
Swann '96

Thomas Bentley
Murder at the Baskervilles '37
The Old Curiosity Shop '35

Robert Benton
Twilight '98
Nobody's Fool '94
Billy Bathgate '91
Nadine '87
Places in the Heart '84
Still of the Night '82
Kramer vs. Kramer '79
The Late Show '77
Bad Company '72

Yakov Bentsvi
Legion of Iron '90

Obie Benz
Heavy Petting '89

Luc Beraud
Heat of Desire '84

Ratings Game '84

Tom Dewier
Death by Dialogue '88

Patrick Dewolf
Innocent Lies '95

Peter Dews
The Taming of the Shrew '81

John Dexter
I Want What I Want '72
The Virgin Soldiers '69

Maury Dexter
Hell's Belles '69
Surf Party '64

Bernard Deyries
Here Come the Littles: The
Movie '85

Robert Dhery
Belle Americaine '61

Fernando Di Leo
Violent Breed '83
Mr. Scarface '77
Kidnap Syndicate '76
Loaded Guns '75
Manhunt '73
Slaughter Hotel '71

Mario Di Leo
The Final Alliance '89

Rino Di Silvestro
Women in Cell Block 7 '77

Lucian S. Diamonde
Forbidden Zone: Alien
Abduction '96

Jose Diaz Morales
Loyola, the Soldier Saint '52

Tom DiCillo
The Real Blonde '97
Box of Moonlight '96
Living in Oblivion '94
Johnny Suede '92

Nigel Dick
Dead Connection '94
Deadly Intent '88
Private Investigations '87

Ernest R. Dickerson
Blind Faith '98
Bulletproof '96
Surviving the Game '94
Tales from the Crypt Presents
Demon Knight '94
Juice '92

Thorold Dickinson
Hill 24 Doesn't Answer '55
The Queen of Spades '49
Men of Two Worlds '46
Gaslight '40
The Arsenal Stadium Mystery
'39
High Command '37

Lance Dickson
Hollywood Heartbreak '89

Marc Didden
Istanbul '85

Samuel Diege
Ride 'Em Cowgirl '41
The Singing Cowgirl '39
Water Rustlers '39
King of the Sierras '38

Carlos Diegues
Subway to the Stars '87
Quilombo '84
Bye Bye Brazil '79
Xica '76

Baruch Dienar
They Were Ten '61

Alan Dienstag
The Moneytree '93

William Dieterle
Quick, Let's Get Married '71
Mistress of the World '59
Omar Khayyam '57
Elephant Walk '54
Salome '53
Boots Malone '52
September Affair '50
The Accused '48
Portrait of Jennie '48
Love Letters '45

The Devil & Daniel Webster '41
The Hunchback of Notre Dame
'39
Juarez '39
The Life of Emile Zola '37
Satan Met a Lady '36
The Story of Louis Pasteur '36
A Midsummer Night's Dream '35
Fashions of 1934 '34
Female '33
Scarlet Dawn '32

Helmut Dietl
Schtonk '92

Eric Dignam
Loved '97
Denial: The Dark Side of
Passion '91

Richard Dilello
Riot in the Streets '96

John Francis Dillon
Millie '31
Suds '20

Steve DiMarco
Back in Action '94

Dennis Dimster
Mikey '92

Mark Dindal
Cats Don't Dance '97

Pece Dingo
Midnight Cabaret '90

John Dingwall
The Custodian '94

Michael Dinner
Hot to Trot! '88
Off Beat '86
Heaven Help Us '85

Carlo DiPalma
Blonde in Black Leather '77

Mark Dippe
Spawn '97

John Dirlam
Fatal Instinct '93

Mark DiSalle
The Perfect Weapon '91
Kickboxer '89

Ivan Dixon
Percy & Thunder '93
The Spook Who Sat By the Door
'73

Ken Dixon
Slave Girls from Beyond Infinity
'87

Will Dixon
Guitarman '95

Edward Dmytryk
He Is My Brother '75
The Human Factor '75
Bluebeard '72
Anzio '68
Shalako '68
Alvarez Kelly '66
Mirage '66
The Carpetbaggers '64
Where Love Has Gone '64
Walk on the Wild Side '62
Warlock '59
The Young Lions '58
Raintree County '57
The Mountain '56
The Left Hand of God '55
Soldier of Fortune '55
Broken Lance '54
The Caine Mutiny '54
Mutiny '52
The Hidden Room '49
Crossfire '47
Till the End of Time '46
Back to Bataan '45
Cornered '45
Murder, My Sweet '44
Behind the Rising Sun '43
Captive Wild Woman '43
Hitler's Children '43
Seven Miles from Alcatraz/Flight
from Glory '43
Tender Comrade '43
Her First Romance '40
Trail of the Hawk '37

Tony B. Dobb
Blue Tornado '90

Frank Q. Dobbs
Uphill All the Way '85

Lawrence Dobkin
The Waltons: The Christmas
Carol '80
Sixteen '72

Kevin J. Dobson
Gold Diggers: The Secret of
Bear Mountain '95
Miracle in the Wilderness '91
Squizzy Taylor '84
Demolition '77
Image of Death '77
The Mango Tree '77

James Dodson
Quest of the Delta Knights '93
Deadly Rivals '92

Donald M. Dohler
Deadly Neighbor '91
Fiend '83
Night Beast '83
The Alien Factor '78

Jacques Doillon
Ponette '95
La Vengeance d'une Femme '89

Lou Doillon
La Puritaine '88

Martin Dolman
American Tiger '89
Hands of Steel '86
After the Fall of New York '85

Jerzy Domaradzki
Lilian's Story '95

Roger Donaldson
Dante's Peak '97
Species '95
The Getaway '93
White Sands '92
Cadillac Man '90
Cocktail '88
No Way Out '87
Marie '85
The Bounty '84
Nutcase '83
Sleeping Dogs '82
Smash Palace '82

Vincent J. Donehue
Peter Pan '76
Sunrise at Campobello '60
Lonelyhearts '58

Stanley Donen
Blame It on Rio '84
Saturn 3 '80
Movie, Movie '78
The Little Prince '74
Bedazzled '68
Two for the Road '67
Arabesque '66
Charade '63
The Grass Is Greener '61
Damn Yankees '58
Indiscreet '58
Funny Face '57
The Pajama Game '57
It's Always Fair Weather '55
Deep in My Heart '54
Seven Brides for Seven Brothers
'54
Give a Girl a Break '53
Love Is Lovelier Than Ever '52
Singin' in the Rain '52
Royal Wedding '51
On the Town '49

Walter Doniger
Mad Bull '77

Dennis Donnelly
The Toolbox Murders '78

Thomas Michael Donnelly
The Garden of Redemption '97

Tom Donnelly
Blindsided '93
Quicksilver '86

Clive Donner
Charlemagne '95
Stealing Heaven '88
Babes in Toyland '86

Merlin and the Sword '85
A Christmas Carol '84
To Catch a King '84
Oliver Twist '82
The Scarlet Pimpernel '82
Charlie Chan and the Curse of
the Dragon Queen '81
The Nude Bomb '80
The Thief of Baghdad '78
Rogue Male '76
Luv '67
What's New Pussycat? '65

Richard Donner
Lethal Weapon 4 '98
Conspiracy Theory '97
Assassins '95
Maverick '94
Lethal Weapon 3 '92
Radio Flyer '92
Lethal Weapon 2 '89
Tales from the Crypt '89
Scrooged '88
Lethal Weapon '87
The Goonies '85
Ladyhawke '85
The Toy '82
Inside Moves '80
Superman: The Movie '78
The Omen '76
Lola '69
Wanted: Dead or Alive '59

Mary Agnes Donoghue
Paradise '91

Jack Donohue
Assault on a Queen '66
Babes in Toyland '61
Lucky Me '54
Watch the Birdie '50
The Yellow Cab Man '50

Jim Donovan
Provocateur '96

Martin Donovan
The Substitute '93
Death Dreams '92
Mad at the Moon '92
Apartment Zero '88

Paul Donovan
Tales from a Parallel Universe: I
Worship His Shadow '97
Northern Extremes '93
George's Island '91
Norman's Awesome Experience
'88
Def-Con 4 '85

Tom Donovan
Lovespell '79

Mark Donskoi
My Universities '40
My Apprenticeship '39
My Childhood '38

Lee Doo-yong
Silent Assassins '88

Thomas Doran
Spookies '85

Jacques Dorfman
Shadow of the Wolf '92

Robert Dornhelm
The Break '97
Requiem for Dominic '91
Cold Feet '89
Echo Park '86
The Children of Theatre Street
'77

Doris Dorrie
Me and Him '89
Men... '85

Nelson Pereira dos Santos
How Tasty Was My Little
Frenchman '71

Shimon Dotan
Sworn Enemies '96
Warriors '94
The Finest Hour '91

Jean Douchet
Six in Paris '68

Russell S. Doughten, Jr.
Whitcomb's War '87
The Hostage '67

Gordon Douglas
Viva Knievel '77
Slaughter's Big Ripoff '73
Skullduggery '70
They Call Me Mr. Tibbs! '70
The Detective '68
Lady in Cement '68
Chuka '67
In Like Flint '67
Tony Rome '67
Harlow '65
Rio Conchos '64
Robin and the 7 Hoods '64
Call Me Bwana '63
Follow That Dream '61
Up Periscope '59
Sincerely Yours '56
The McConnell Story '55
Them! '54
Young at Heart '54
Great Missouri Raid '51
Kiss Tomorrow Goodbye '50
The Nevadan '50
Only the Valiant '50
The Doolins of Oklahoma '49
Black Arrow '48
If You Knew Susie '48
Dick Tracy vs. Cueball '46
First Yank into Tokyo '45
The Falcon in Hollywood '44
Girl Rush '44
Zombies on Broadway '44
The Great Gildersleeve '43
Broadway Limited '41
Saps at Sea '40

Kirk Douglas
Posse '75

Neil Douglas
Sinner's Blood '70

Peter Douglas
A Tiger's Tale '87

Lorenzo Doumani
Storybook '95
Amore! '93
Mad About You '90

Alexander Dovzhenko
Earth '30
Arsenal '29
Zvenigora '28

Kathleen Dowdey
Blue Heaven '84

Kevin Dowling
Mojave Moon '96
The Sum of Us '94

Robert Downey
Hugo Pool '97
Too Much Sun '90
Rented Lips '88
America '86
Up the Academy '80
Greaser's Palace '72
Putney Swope '69

Michael Drach
Les Violons du Bal '74

Mircea Dragan
Oil '78

Bert L. Dragin
Twice Dead '88
Summer Camp Nightmare '86

Srdjan Dragojevic
Pretty Village, Pretty Flame '96

Stan Dragoti
Necessary Roughness '91
She's Out of Control '89
The Man with One Red Shoe '85
Mr. Mom '83
Love at First Bite '79

Jim Drake
Based on an Untrue Story '93
Speed Zone '88
Police Academy 4: Citizens on
Patrol '87
Mr. Bill's Real Life Adventures
'86

Leonardo Favio
Chronicle of a Boy Alone '64

John Fawcett
The Boys Club '96

Neill Fearnley
Black Ice '92

Linda Feferman
Seven Minutes in Heaven '86

Xie Fei
A Mongolian Tale '94
Women from the Lake of
  Scented Souls '94
Girl from Hunan '86

Beda Ocampo Feijoo
Under the Earth '86

Felix Feist
Donovan's Brain '53
Big Trees '52
Guilty of Treason '50
Threat '49
The Devil Thumbs a Ride '47
The Devil Thumbs a Ride/
  Having Wonderful Crime '47
George White's Scandals '45
Deluge '33

Dennis Feldman
Real Men '87

Gene Feldman
Danny '79

John Feldman
Dead Funny '94
Alligator Eyes '90

John Harmon Feldman
Lovelife '97

Marty Feldman
The Last Remake of Beau Geste
  '77

Federico Fellini
Intervista '87
Ginger & Fred '86
And the Ship Sails On '83
City of Women '81
Orchestra Rehearsal '78
Amarcord '73
Fellini's Roma '72
The Clowns '71
Fellini Satyricon '69
Spirits of the Dead '68
Juliet of the Spirits '65
8 1/2 '63
Boccaccio '70 '62
La Dolce Vita '60
Nights of Cabiria '57
The Swindle '55
La Strada '54
I Vitelloni '53
Love in the City '53
The White Sheik '52
Variety Lights '51

Georg Fenady
Arnold '73
Terror in the Wax Museum '73

Huang Feng
Sting of the Dragon Masters '74

Michael Fengler
Why Does Herr R. Run Amok?
  '69

Philip Fently
The Baron '88

Claude Feraldo
Trade Secrets '90s

Rene Feret
The Mystery of Alexina '86

Larry Ferguson
Gunfighter's Moon '96
Beyond the Law '92

Michael Ferguson
The Glory Boys '84

Norman Ferguson
The Three Caballeros '45

Guy Ferland
Telling Lies in America '96
The Babysitter '95

Emilio Fernandez
Flor Silvestre '58

The Torch '50
The Pearl '48
Maria Candelaria '46

Pablo Fero
Me, Myself & I '92

Dean Ferrandini
Overkill '96

Abel Ferrara
Subway Stories '97
The Funeral '96
The Addiction '95
Body Snatchers '93
Dangerous Game '93
Bad Lieutenant '92
Cat Chaser '90
King of New York '90
China Girl '87
The Gladiator '86
Fear City '85
Ms. 45 '81
Driller Killer '74

Romano Ferrara
Planets Against Us '61

Jeff Ferrell
Revenge of the Teenage Vixens
  from Outer Space '86

Jose Ferrer
State Fair '62
Return to Peyton Place '61

Mel Ferrer
Green Mansions '59

Marco Ferreri
Tales of Ordinary Madness '83
La Grande Bouffe '73
L'Udienza '71
El Cochecito '60

Robert A. Ferretti
Fear '88

Frank Ferrin
Sabaka '55

Stan Ferris
Tulips '81

George Ferron
The Scalawag Bunch '75

Giorgio Ferroni
The Bacchantes '63
Conquest of Mycene '63
Mill of the Stone Women '60

Larry Fessenden
Habit '97

Louis Feuillade
Les Vampires '15

Jacques Feyder
Knight Without Armour '37
Carnival in Flanders '35
The Kiss '29
Crainquebille '23

Leonard Fields
King Kelly of the U.S.A. '34

Michael Fields
Bright Angel '91
Noon Wine '84

Steven Fierberg
Voodoo Dawn '89

Douglas Fifthian
Touch Me Not '74

Mike Figgis
One Night Stand '97
Leaving Las Vegas '95
The Browning Version '94
Mr. Jones '93
Liebestraum '91
Women & Men: In Love There
  Are No Rules '91
Internal Affairs '90
Stormy Monday '88

Ivan Fila
Lea '96

Charles Finch
Circle of Passion '97
Where Sleeping Dogs Lie '91
Priceless Beauty '90

Nigel Finch
Stonewall '95
The Lost Language of Cranes
  '92

David Fincher
The Game '97
Seven '95
Alien 3 '92

Michael Findlay
Shriek of the Mutilated '74

Roberta Findlay
Lurkers '88
Prime Evil '88
Blood Sisters '86
The Oracle '85

John P. Finegan
Girls School Screamers '86

Janace Fink
Velvet Smooth '76

Kenneth Fink
Tricks '97
Tall, Dark and Deadly '95
Stephen King's Golden Years
  '91

Michael Fink
Black Force '75

Ken Finkleman
Head Office '86
Airplane 2: The Sequel '82

Joe Finley
Barbarian Queen 2: The
  Empress Strikes Back '89

Edward Finney
King of the Stallions '42
Riot Squad '41
Silver Stallion '41

Rex Firlin
The Death of Adolf Hitler '84

Sam Firstenberg
Operation: Delta Force '97
Cyborg Soldier '94
Blood Warriors '93
American Samurai '92
Delta Force 3: The Killing Game
  '91
One More Chance '90
Riverbend '89
American Ninja 2: The
  Confrontation '87
My African Adventure '87
Avenging Force '86
American Ninja '85
Breakin' 2: Electric Boogaloo '84
Ninja 3: The Domination '84
Revenge of the Ninja '83

Michael Firth
Sylvia '86
Heart of the Stag '84

Michael Fischa
Delta Heat '92
Crack House '89
My Mom's a Werewolf '89
Death Spa '87

Max Fischer
Entangled '93
Killing 'Em Softly '85

Deirdre Fishel
Risk '94

David Fisher
Toy Soldiers '84
Liar's Moon '82

Jack Fisher
Torn Apart '89

Mary Ann Fisher
Lords of the Deep '89

Terence Fisher
Frankenstein and the Monster
  from Hell '74
Frankenstein Must Be Destroyed
  '69
Island of the Burning Doomed
  '67
Dracula, Prince of Darkness '66
Island of Terror '66
The Gorgon '64
The Phantom of the Opera '62
Sherlock Holmes and the Deadly
  Necklace '62
The Curse of the Werewolf '61
The Brides of Dracula '60
Sword of Sherwood Forest '60
The Two Faces of Dr. Jekyll '60

The Hound of the Baskervilles
  '59
The Mummy '59
The Horror of Dracula '58
The Revenge of Frankenstein
  '58
The Curse of Frankenstein '57
Race for Life '55
Robin Hood: The Movie '55
Blackout '54
Unholy Four '54
Four Sided Triangle '53
Spaceways '53
Three Stops to Murder '53
Man Bait '52
A Stolen Face '52

Tom Fisher
Cannibal Campout '88

Bill Fishman
Car 54, Where Are You? '94
Tapeheads '89

Jack Fisk
Final Verdict '91
Daddy's Dyin'...Who's Got the
  Will? '90
Violets Are Blue '86
Raggedy Man '81

Christopher Fitchett
Fair Game '82
Blood Money '80

Jon FitzGerald
Apart from Hugh '94

Thom Fitzgerald
The Hanging Garden '97

George Fitzmaurice
The Last of Mrs. Cheyney '37
Suzy '36
As You Desire Me '32
Mata Hari '32
Raffles '30
Son of the Sheik '26

James A. Fitzpatrick
Lady of the Lake '28

Robert S. Fiveson
The Clonus Horror '79

Paul Flaherty
Clifford '94
Who's Harry Crumb? '89
18 Again! '88

Robert Flaherty
Louisiana Story '48
Elephant Boy '37
Man of Aran '34
Tabu: A Story of the South Seas
  '31
Moana, a Romance of the
  Golden Age '26

Freddie Fleck
The Magnificent Ambersons '42

Gary Fleder
Kiss the Girls '97
Things to Do In Denver When
  You're Dead '95
The Companion '94

Dave Fleischer
Hoppity Goes to Town '41
Gulliver's Travels '39

Max Fleischer
Max Fleischer's Documentary
  Features '23

Richard Fleischer
Million Dollar Mystery '87
Red Sonja '85
Conan the Destroyer '84
Amityville 3: The Demon '83
Tough Enough '83
The Jazz Singer '80
Ashanti, Land of No Mercy '79
The Prince and the Pauper '78
The Incredible Sarah '76
Mandingo '75
Mr. Majestyk '74
The Don Is Dead '73
Soylent Green '73
The New Centurions '72
See No Evil '71
10 Rillington Place '71
Tora! Tora! Tora! '70
The Boston Strangler '68
Doctor Dolittle '67

Fantastic Voyage '66
Barabbas '62
Compulsion '59
The Vikings '58
Between Heaven and Hell '56
20,000 Leagues Under the Sea
  '54
The Narrow Margin '52
Armored Car Robbery '50
The Clay Pigeon '49
Follow Me Quietly '49
Trapped '49

Andrew Fleming
The Craft '96
Threesome '94
Bad Dreams '88

Edward Fleming
Topsy Turvy '84

Erik Fleming
Cyber Bandits '94

Victor Fleming
Joan of Arc '48
Adventure '45
A Guy Named Joe '44
Tortilla Flat '42
Dr. Jekyll and Mr. Hyde '41
Gone with the Wind '39
The Wizard of Oz '39
Test Pilot '38
Captains Courageous '37
The Farmer Takes a Wife '35
Reckless '35
Treasure Island '34
Bombshell '33
Red Dust '32
The Virginian '29
Hula '28
Mantrap '26
The Mollycoddle '20
When the Clouds Roll By '19

Gordon Flemyng
Cloud Waltzing '87
Philby, Burgess and MacLean:
  Spy Scandal of the Century
  '84
Daleks—Invasion Earth 2150
  A.D. '66
Doctor Who and the Daleks '65

Rodman Flender
Leprechaun 2 '94
In the Heat of Passion '91
The Unborn '91

Mandie Fletcher
Deadly Advice '93

Clive Fleury
Tunnel Vision '95
Fatal Past '94

Theodore J. Flicker
Soggy Bottom U.S.A. '84
Playmates '72
Three in the Cellar '70
The President's Analyst '67

James T. Flocker
Ground Zero '88
Ghosts That Still Walk '77
The Secret of Navajo Cave '76

John Florea
Hot Child in the City '87
Computer Wizard '77
Where's Willie? '77
The Invisible Strangler '76
Where the Eagle Flies '72
Island of the Lost '68

Isaac Florentine
The Fighter '95
Desert Kickboxer '92

Robert Florey
Outpost in Morocco '49
The Beast with Five Fingers '46
Ex-Lady '33
Murders in the Rue Morgue '32
The Cocoanuts '29

Aldo Florio
Five Giants from Texas '66

Calvin Floyd
Sleep of Death '79

Drago Floyd
Troll 2 '92

Cheers for Miss Bishop '41
Seven Sinners '40
Slightly Honorable '40
Eternally Yours '39
Joy of Living '38
Stand-In '37
China Seas '35
The Flying Fool '29

Tony Garnett
Deep in the Heart '83

Lila Garrett
Terraces '77

Otis Garrett
Danger on the Air '38

Roy Garrett
White Slave '86
Eyes Behind the Stars '72

Mick Garris
Stephen King's The Stand '94
Sleepwalkers '92
Psycho 4: The Beginning '90
Critters 2: The Main Course '88

Andrew Garroni
Body of Influence '93

Harry Garson
The Worldly Madonna '22
Mid-Channel '20

John Garwood
Violent Zone '89

Jerome Gary
Traxx '87
Stripper '86

Louis Gasnier
Murder on the Yukon '40
Reefer Madness '38
Topaze '33
Kismet '20

Mark Gasper
An Empty Bed '90

Leon Gast
When We Were Kings '96

Mae Gaston
Seven Keys to Baldpate '17

Nils Gaup
North Star '96
Shipwrecked '90
Pathfinder '87

Roberto Gavaldon
The Littlest Outlaw '54

Eleanor Gaver
Slipping into Darkness '88

Victor Gaviria
Rodrigo D.: No Future '91

Joe Gayton
Wes Craven Presents Mind Ripper '95
Warm Summer Rain '89

Armand Gazarian
Prison Planet '92
Game of Survival '89

Gyula Gazdag
Stand Off '89
A Hungarian Fairy Tale '87

Glenn Gebhard
Desert Steel '94
One Last Run '89

Dieter Geissler
Deadly Game '83

Bruce Geller
The Savage Bees '76

Augusto Genina
Prix de Beaute '30
Cyrano de Bergerac '25

Arnaldo Genoino
Herod the Great '60

John Gentil
Battle of Valiant '63

Giacomo Gentilomo
Hercules Against the Moon Men '64

George W. George
James Dean Story '57

Jim George
Rover Dangerfield '91

Matthew George
Under the Gun '95

Peter George
Surf Nazis Must Die '87

Tony Gerber
Some Mother's Son '96

Maurice Geraghty
Sword of Monte Cristo '51

Fred Gerber
Rent-A-Kid '95

Haile Gerima
Ashes and Embers '82
Bush Mama '76

Marion Gering
Thunder in the City '37

Pietro Germi
Alfredo, Alfredo '72
Seduced and Abandoned '64
Divorce—Italian Style '62
Four Ways Out '57

Chris Gerolmo
Citizen X '95

Clyde Geronimi
101 Dalmatians '61
Sleeping Beauty '59
Alice in Wonderland '51
The Adventures of Ichabod and Mr. Toad '49
The Legend of Sleepy Hollow '49

Peter Gerretsen
Night Friend '87

Michael G. Gerrick
Stephen King's Golden Years '91

Theodore Gershuny
Silent Night, Bloody Night '73

Nicolas Gessner
Black Water '94
Quicker Than the Eye '88
It Rained All Night the Day I Left '78
The Little Girl Who Lives Down the Lane '76
Someone Behind the Door '71
12 Plus 1 '70
The Peking Blond '68

Steven Gethers
The Hillside Strangler '89
Jenny's War '85
Jacqueline Bouvier Kennedy '81
Damien: The Leper Priest '80
Billy: Portrait of a Street Kid '77

Francis Giacobetti
Emmanuelle 4 '84
Emmanuelle, the Joys of a Woman '76

David Giancola
Time Chasers '95

Alfredo Gianelli
Mother Doesn't Always Know Best '60s

Duncan Gibbins
A Case for Murder '93
Eve of Destruction '90
Fire with Fire '86

Pamela Gibbons
Midnight Dancer '87

Rodney Gibbons
Little Men '98
Stranger in the House '97
The Neighbor '93

Gwyneth Gibby
Marquis de Sade '97

Alan Gibson
The Charmer '89
Martin's Day '85
Silent Scream '84
The Two Faces of Evil '82
A Woman Called Golda '82
The Satanic Rites of Dracula '73
Dracula A.D. 1972 '72
Twinsanity '70

Brian Gibson
The Juror '96
What's Love Got to Do with It? '93

The Josephine Baker Story '90
Murderers Among Us: The Simon Wiesenthal Story '89
Poltergeist 2: The Other Side '86
Breaking Glass '80

Mel Gibson
Braveheart '95
The Man Without a Face '93

Robert Gibson
Snow: The Movie '83

Tom Gibson
Singing Buckaroo '37

Gregory Gieras
The Whispering '94

Maria Giese
When Saturday Comes '95

Brian Gilbert
Wilde '95
Tom & Viv '94
Not Without My Daughter '90
Vice Versa '88
The French Lesson '86
Sharma & Beyond '84

Lewis Gilbert
Haunted '95
Stepping Out '91
Shirley Valentine '89
Not Quite Paradise '86
Educating Rita '83
Moonraker '79
The Spy Who Loved Me '77
Paul and Michelle '74
Friends '71
The Adventurers '70
You Only Live Twice '67
Alfie '66
Damn the Defiant '62
Sink the Bismarck '60
Ferry to Hong Kong '59
A Cry from the Streets '57
Reach for the Sky '56
Cast a Dark Shadow '55
The Sea Shall Not Have Them '55
Tough Guy '53

David Giler
Black Bird '75

David Giles
A Murder Is Announced '87
Mansfield Park '85
Vanity Fair '67

Tom Giles
Journey Through Rosebud '72

Joseph Gilford
Max '79

Mark Gilhuis
Bloody Wednesday '87

Jack Gill
Body Armor '97

Tony Jiti Gill
Murder-in-Law '97

Stuart Gillard
RocketMan '97
Poltergeist: The Legacy '96
The Outer Limits: Sandkings '95
Teenage Mutant Ninja Turtles 3 '93
A Man Called Sarge '90
Paradise '82

Jeff Gillen
Deranged '74

Jim Gillespie
I Know What You Did Last Summer '97

Terry Gilliam
Fear and Loathing in Las Vegas '98
12 Monkeys '95
The Fisher King '91
The Adventures of Baron Munchausen '89
Brazil '85
Time Bandits '81
Jabberwocky '77
Monty Python and the Holy Grail '75

Sidney Gilliat
Endless Night '71

The Great St. Trinian's Train Robbery '66
Only Two Can Play '62
Green for Danger '47

John Gilling
Night Caller from Outer Space '66
Plague of the Zombies '66
The Reptile '66
Where the Bullets Fly '66
Mania '60
It Takes a Thief '59
The Gamma People '56
The Gilded Cage '54
White Fire '53
My Son, the Vampire '52
No Trace '50

Stuart Gilmore
The Half-Breed '51
Hot Lead '51
The Virginian '46

Frank D. Gilroy
The Gig '85
Once in Paris... '79
From Noon Till Three '76
Desperate Characters '71

Milton Moses Ginsberg
Werewolf of Washington '73

Brad F. Ginter
Flesh Feast '69

Robert Ginty
Vietnam, Texas '90
Bounty Hunters '89

Christian Gion
Here Comes Santa Claus '84

Jose Giovanni
Boomerang '76
Gypsy '75

Marita Giovanni
Bar Girls '95

Buddy Giovinazzo
No Way Home '97
Combat Shock '84

Bob Giraldi
Hiding Out '87
Club Med '83

Franco Giraldi
A Minute to Pray, a Second to Die '67

Andre Girard
Qui Etes Vous, Mr. Sorge? '61

Bernard Girard
Little Moon & Jud McGraw '78
Mind Snatchers '72
Hard Frame '70
A Name for Evil '70
Dead Heat on a Merry-Go-Round '66

Francois Girard
32 Short Films about Glenn Gould '93

Michael Paul Girard
Witchcraft 9: Bitter Flesh '96
Witchcraft 7: Judgement Hour '95

Bernard Giraudeau
Gone with the West '72

William Girdler
The Manitou '78
Day of the Animals '77
Grizzly '76
Sheba, Baby '75
Asylum of Satan '72
Three on a Meathook '72

Francois Girod
The Elegant Criminal '92
L'Etat Sauvage '78
The Infernal Trio '74

Marcel Gisler
The Blue Hour '91

Wyndham Gittens
Tim Tyler's Luck '37

Paul Michael Glaser
Kazaam '96
The Air Up There '94
The Cutting Edge '92

The Running Man '87
Band of the Hand '86
The Amazons '84

Arnold Glassman
Visions of Light: The Art of Cinematography '93

Leslie Linka Glatter
The Proposition '97
Now and Then '95
State of Emergency '94
Into the Homeland '87

Richard Glatzer
Grief '94

Michie Gleason
Summer Heat '87

John Glen
Aces: Iron Eagle 3 '92
Christopher Columbus: The Discovery '92
License to Kill '89
The Living Daylights '87
A View to a Kill '85
Octopussy '83
For Your Eyes Only '81

John Glenister
After Julius '78

Bert Glennon
South of Santa Fe '32
Paradise Island '30

Peter Glenville
The Comedians '67
Hotel Paradiso '66
Becket '64
Summer and Smoke '61
Me and the Colonel '58
The Prisoner '55

James Glickenhaus
Timemaster '95
Slaughter of the Innocents '93
McBain '91
Shakedown '88
Protector '85
The Soldier '82
Exterminator '80

Paul Glickler
Running Scared '79
The Cheerleaders '72

Arne Glimcher
Just Cause '94
The Mambo Kings '92

Greg Glionna
Meet the Parents '91

Wolfgang Gluck
'38: Vienna Before the Fall '88

Don Glut
Dinosaur Valley Girls '96

Tom Gniazdowski
Death Collector '89

Constantine S. Gochis
The Redeemer '76

Jean-Luc Godard
Helas pour Moi '94
Nouvelle Vague '90
Aria '88
King Lear '87
Hail Mary '85
Soft and Hard '85
First Name: Carmen '83
Scenario du Film Passion '82
Here and Elsewhere '70s
France/Tour/Detour/Deux/ Enfants '78
Comment Ca Va? '76
Six Fois Deux/Sur et Sous la Communication '76
Numero Deux '75
Sympathy for the Devil '70
Six in Paris '68
Oldest Profession '67
Weekend '67
Masculine Feminine '66
Two or Three Things I Know About Her '66
Alphaville '65
The Joy of Knowledge '65
A Married Woman '65
Pierrot le Fou '65
Band of Outsiders '64

The Triumph of Sherlock Holmes '35

Alfred Hitchcock
Family Plot '76
Frenzy '72
Topaz '69
Torn Curtain '66
Marnie '64
The Birds '63
Psycho '60
North by Northwest '59
Vertigo '58
The Man Who Knew Too Much '56
The Wrong Man '56
To Catch a Thief '55
The Trouble with Harry '55
Dial "M" for Murder '54
Rear Window '54
I Confess '53
Strangers on a Train '51
Stage Fright '50
Under Capricorn '49
Rope '48
The Paradine Case '47
Notorious '46
Spellbound '45
Alfred Hitchcock's Aventure Malgache '44
Alfred Hitchcock's Bon Voyage '44
Lifeboat '44
Shadow of a Doubt '43
Saboteur '42
Mr. & Mrs. Smith '41
Suspicion '41
Foreign Correspondent '40
Rebecca '40
Jamaica Inn '39
The Lady Vanishes '38
Young and Innocent '37
Sabotage '36
The Secret Agent '36
The 39 Steps '35
The Man Who Knew Too Much '34
No. 17 '32
Rich and Strange '32
Skin Game '31
Juno and the Paycock '30
Murder '30
Blackmail '29
The Manxman '29
Champagne '28
The Farmer's Wife '28
Three by Hitchcock '28
Easy Virtue '27
The Ring '27
The Lodger '26

Carl K. Hittleman
Kentucky Rifle '55

Rupert Hitzig
Backstreet Dreams '90
Night Visitor '89

Jack B. Hively
California Gold Rush '81
The Adventures of Huckleberry Finn '78
Starbird and Sweet William '73
Lassie: Adventures of Neeka '68

Jack Hively
Four Jacks and a Jill '41
The Saint Takes Over '40
The Saint's Double Trouble '40

A.J. Hixon
Little Marines '90

Godfrey Ho
Lethal Panther '90
Ninja Champion '80s
Hands of Death '88
The Dragon's Showdown '83
Ninja Destroyer '70s

Yim Ho
The Day the Sun Turned Cold '94

Fredric Hobbs
Alabama's Ghost '72

Lyndall Hobbs
Back to the Beach '87

Gregory Hoblit
Fallen '97
Primal Fear '96

Class of '61 '92
Roe vs. Wade '89
L.A. Law '86

Victoria Hochberg
Sweet 15 '90
Jacob Have I Loved '88

Roberta Hodes
A Secret Space '88

Mike Hodges
Black Rainbow '91
Florida Straits '87
Prayer for the Dying '87
Morons from Outer Space '85
Missing Pieces '83
Flash Gordon '80
The Terminal Man '74
Pulp '72

Jeno Hodl
Triplecross '95
American Kickboxer 2: To the Death '93
Deadly Obsession '88

Mark Hoeger
The Little Match Girl '84

Jeremy Hoenack
The Dark Ride '84

Arthur Hoerl
Drums O'Voodoo '34

Michael Hoey
Navy vs. the Night Monsters '66

Ernest Hofbauer
Code Name Alpha '67

Herman Hoffman
The Invisible Boy '57
It's a Dog's Life '55

Jerzy Hoffman
Leper '76
The Deluge '73
Colonel Wolodyjowski '69

John Hoffman
Strange Confession '45
Calling Dr. Death/Strange Confession '43

Julian Hoffman
The Bloody Brood '59

Michael Hoffman
One Fine Day '96
Restoration '94
Soapdish '91
Promised Land '88
Some Girls '88

Peter Hoffman
Valentino Returns '88

Tamar Simon Hoffs
The Allnighter '87

Gray Hofmeyr
Yankee Zulu '95
Dirty Games '93
The Light in the Jungle '91

Jack Hofsiss
Cat on a Hot Tin Roof '84
Family Secrets '84
I'm Dancing as Fast as I Can '82

David Hogan
Most Wanted '97
Barb Wire '96

James Hogan
The Mad Ghoul '43
The Texas Rangers Ride Again '40
Bulldog Drummond's Bride '39
Bulldog Drummond's Secret Police '39
Arrest Bulldog Drummond '38
Bulldog Drummond's Peril '38
The Texans '38
Bulldog Drummond Escapes '37
Arizona Mahoney '36
The Broken Mask '28

P.J. Hogan
My Best Friend's Wedding '97
Muriel's Wedding '94

Michael Hohensee
Mad Wax: The Surf Movie '90

Rod Holcomb
Convict Cowboy '95
Dead to Rights '93

Royce '93
Chains of Gold '92
China Beach '88
Blind Justice '86
Chase '85
Stark '85
Two Fathers' Justice '85
Cartier Affair '84
The Red Light Sting '84
Captain America '79

John Hold
Viking Massacre '65

Anton Holden
Aroused '66

Lansing C. Holden
She '35

William Hole, Jr.
The Devil's Hand '61

Adam Holender
Twisted '86

Agnieszka Holland
Washington Square '97
Total Eclipse '95
The Secret Garden '93
Olivier, Olivier '92
Europa, Europa '91
To Kill a Priest '89
Angry Harvest '85
Fever '81
Provincial Actors '79

Steve Holland
How I Got into College '89
One Crazy Summer '86
Better Off Dead '85

Todd Holland
Krippendorf's Tribe '98
The Wizard '89

Tom Holland
Stephen King's Thinner '96
Stephen King's The Langoliers '95
The Temp '93
Child's Play '88
Fatal Beauty '87
Fright Night '85

Eli Hollander
Out '88

Allan Holleb
School Spirit '85
Candy Stripe Nurses '74

Doug Holloway
Fast Money '83

Graham Holloway
Chasing the Deer '94

Ben Holmes
Maid's Night Out '38
The Saint in New York '38

Fred Holmes
Harley '90
Dakota '88

Nicole Holofcener
Walking and Talking '96

Jason Holt
Swindle '92
Wager of Love '90

Seth Holt
The Nanny '65
Scream of Fear '61

Allen Holubar
Heart of Humanity '18

Roger Holzberg
Midnight Crossing '87

Allan Holzman
Intimate Stranger '91
Programmed to Kill '86
Grunt! The Wrestling Movie '85
Out of Control '85
Forbidden World '82

Edward Holzman
Body Strokes '95
Seduce Me: Pamela Principle 2 '94

Lau Shing Hon
To Live and Die in Hong Kong '89

Inoshiro Honda
Yog, Monster from Space '71

Godzilla's Revenge '69
Destroy All Monsters '68
Godzilla vs. Monster Zero '68
Dagora, the Space Monster '65
Ghidrah the Three Headed Monster '65
Godzilla vs. Mothra '64
Gorath '64
Attack of the Mushroom People '63
Mothra '62
Varan the Unbelievable '61
H-Man '59
Half Human '58
The Mysterians '58
Rodan '56

Elliot Hong
They Call Me Bruce? '82
Kill the Golden Goose '79

James Hong
The Vineyard '89
Girls Next Door '79

Ron Honthaner
The House on Skull Mountain '74

Randall Hood
Die Sister, Die! '74

Harry Hook
The Last of His Tribe '92
Lord of the Flies '90
The Kitchen Toto '87

Ted Hooker
Crucible of Terror '72

Kevin Hooks
Black Dog '98
Fled '96
Murder without Motive '92
Passenger 57 '92
Strictly Business '91
Roots: The Gift '88

Lance Hool
Steel Dawn '87
Missing in Action 2: The Beginning '85

Tobe Hooper
The Mangler '94
Body Bags '93
I'm Dangerous Tonight '90
Spontaneous Combustion '89
Invaders from Mars '86
Texas Chainsaw Massacre 2 '86
Lifeforce '85
Poltergeist '82
The Funhouse '81
Salem's Lot '79
Eaten Alive '77
The Texas Chainsaw Massacre '74

Claudia Hoover
Double Exposure '93

Harry Hope
Swift Justice '88

Margot Hope
Femme Fontaine: Killer Babe for the C.I.A. '95

Anthony Hopkins
August '95

Arthur Hopkins
His Double Life '33

Billy Hopkins
I Love You, I Love You Not '97

John Hopkins
Torment '85

Stephen Hopkins
Lost in Space '98
The Ghost and the Darkness '96
Blown Away '94
Judgment Night '93
Dangerous Game '90
Predator 2 '90
A Nightmare on Elm Street 5: Dream Child '89

Dennis Hopper
Chasers '95
The Hot Spot '90
Backtrack '89
Colors '88
Out of the Blue '80
The Last Movie '71

Easy Rider '69

E. Mason Hopper
Hong Kong Nights '35
Held for Murder '32
Shop Angel '32
Square Shoulders '29

Jerry Hopper
Madron '70
The Private War of Major Benson '55
Pony Express '53
The Atomic City '52

Russell Hopton
Black Gold '36
Song of the Trail '36

Richard Horian
Student Confidential '87

Andrew Horn
Doomed Love '83

Leonard Horn
Hunter '73

Jeffrey Hornaday
Shout '91

James W. Horne
Holt of the Secret Service '42
Green Archer '40
All Over Town '37
Way Out West '37
Bohemian Girl '36
Bonnie Scotland '35
College '27
Laughing at Danger '24

Harry Horner
New Faces of 1952 '54
Beware, My Lovely '52
Red Planet Mars '52

Robert J. Horner
The Walloping Kid '26

Peter Horton
The Cure '95
Amazon Women on the Moon '87

Bob Hoskins
The Raggedy Rawney '90

Dan Hoskins
Chopper Chicks in Zombietown '91

Robert Hossein
I Killed Rasputin '67

Joy Houck, Jr.
The St. Tammany Miracle '94
Creature from Black Lake '76
Night of the Strangler '73
Mind Warp '72

John Hough
Duel of Hearts '92
The Dying Truth '91
The Lady and the Highwayman '89
American Gothic '88
Howling 4: The Original Nightmare '88
Biggles '85
The Black Arrow '84
Triumphs of a Man Called Horse '83
Incubus '82
The Watcher in the Woods '81
Brass Target '78
Return from Witch Mountain '78
Escape to Witch Mountain '75
Dirty Mary Crazy Larry '74
The Legend of Hell House '73
Treasure Island '72
Twins of Evil '71
Sudden Terror '70

Bobby Houston
Caged Fear '92
Trust Me '89
Bad Manners '84

Clyde Houston
Foxstyle '73

Robert Houston
Shogun Assassin '80

Tony Houston
Outlaw Riders '72

Ellen Hovde
Trumps '83

Peter Kelly
The Dawson Patrol '78
Ron Kelly
King of the Grizzlies '69
Rory Kelly
Sleep with Me '94
Jack Kemp
Miracle in Harlem '48
Ralph Kemplen
The Spaniard's Curse '58
David Kendall
Luggage of the Gods '87
James Kennaway
Tunes of Glory/Horse's Mouth
'60
Arthur Kennedy
Assault with a Deadly Weapon
'82
Burt Kennedy
Suburban Commando '91
Dynamite and Gold '88
The Trouble with Spies '87
More Wild, Wild West '80
The Concrete Cowboys '79
Wild, Wild West Revisited '79
Wolf Lake '79
Killer Inside Me '76
All the Kind Strangers '74
Train Robbers '73
Hannie Caulder '72
Ride to Glory '71
Support Your Local Gunfighter
'71
The Good Guys and the Bad
Guys '69
Support Your Local Sheriff '69
The War Wagon '67
Return of the Seven '66
The Rounders '65
Chris Kennedy
Doing Time for Patsy Cline '97
Ken Kennedy
Grizzly Adams: The Legend
Continues '90
Mission to Glory '80
Iron Angel '64
Leon Isaac Kennedy
Knights of the City '85
Lou Kennedy
Breathing Fire '91
Michael Kennedy
The Heist '97
Robin of Locksley '95
Hard Evidence '94
Red Scorpion 2 '94
The Swordsman '92
Talons of the Eagle '92
One Man Out '89
Caribe '87
Tom Kennedy
Time Walker '82
Larry Kent
The Victory '88
Chris Kentis
Grind '96
Eric Kenton
Fight for the Title '57
Erle C. Kenton
House of Dracula '45
House of Frankenstein '44
The Ghost of Frankenstein '42
Pardon My Sarong '42
Who Done It? '42
Melody for Three '41
They Meet Again '41
Remedy for Riches '40
Escape to Paradise '39
Island of Lost Souls '32
Bare Knees '28
Roeland Kerbosch
For a Lost Soldier '93
Patrick Kerby
Ex-Cop '93
James V. Kern
The Second Woman '51
Two Tickets to Broadway '51
Never Say Goodbye '46

Russell Kern
Spittin' Image '83
Sarah Kernochan
Marjoe '72
Lodge Kerrigan
Clean, Shaven '93
Irvin Kershner
RoboCop 2 '90
Traveling Man '89
Never Say Never Again '83
The Empire Strikes Back '80
Eyes of Laura Mars '78
Raid on Entebbe '77
The Return of a Man Called
Horse '76
S*P*Y*S '74
Up the Sandbox '72
Flim-Flam Man '67
A Fine Madness '66
The Hoodlum Priest '61
Emmanuel Kervyn
Rabid Grannies '89
Harry Kerwin
Barracuda '78
God's Bloody Acre '75
Cheering Section '73
Mike Kesey
Killing for Love '95
Alek Keshishian
With Honors '94
Truth or Dare '91
Bruce Kessler
Cruise into Terror '78
Deathmoon '78
Simon, King of the Witches '71
Angels from Hell '68
Stephen Kessler
Vegas Vacation '96
Kliff Keuhl
Murder Rap '87
Michael Keusch
Huck and the King of Hearts '93
Just One of the Girls '93
Samurai Cowboy '93
Lena's Holiday '90
Riffat A. Khan
Feelin' Screwy '90
Michel Khleifi
A Wedding in Galilee '87
Kim Ki-dak
Yongkari Monster of the Deep
'67
Abbas Kiarostami
The Taste of the Cherry '96
Through the Olive Trees '94
Life and Nothing More ... '92
Where Is My Friend's House?
'87
Beeban Kidron
Swept from the Sea '97
To Wong Foo, Thanks for
Everything, Julie Newmar '95
Shades of Fear '93
Used People '92
Antonia and Jane '91
Oranges Are Not the Only Fruit
'89
Fritz Kiersch
The Stranger '95
Shattered Image '93
Into the Sun '92
Under the Boardwalk '89
Gor '88
Winners Take All '87
Tuff Turf '85
Children of the Corn '84
Krzysztof Kieslowski
Trois Couleurs: Blanc '94
Trois Couleurs: Rouge '94
Trois Couleurs: Bleu '93
The Double Life of Veronique
'91
No End '84
Camera Buff '79
Gerard Kikoine
Buried Alive '89
Edge of Sanity '89
Dragonard '88

Jon Killough
Skinned Alive '89
Edward Killy
Don Amigo/Stage to Chino '40s
West of the Pecos '45
Nevada '44
Richard H. Kim
Kill Line '91
Clinton Kimbrough
The Young Nurses '73
Bruce Kimmel
Spaceship '81
Anthony Kimmins
Captain's Paradise '53
Bonnie Prince Charlie '48
Mine Own Executioner '47
John Kincade
Back to Back '90
Terminal Entry '87
Tim Kincaid
The Occultist '89
Maximum Thrust '88
She's Back '88
Mutant Hunt '87
Necropolis '87
Robot Holocaust '87
Bad Girls Dormitory '84
Allan King
By Way of the Stars '92
Allan Winton King
Silence of the North '81
Allen King
Termini Station '89
Burton King
The Adorable Cheat '28
The Man from Beyond '22
George King
The Case of the Frightened
Lady '39
Crimes at the Dark House '39
The Face at the Window '39
Sexton Blake and the Hooded
Terror '38
The Crimes of Stephen Hawke
'36
Demon Barber of Fleet Street
'36
Henry King
Beloved Infidel '59
The Bravados '58
Carousel '56
Love Is a Many-Splendored
Thing '55
The Snows of Kilimanjaro '52
David and Bathsheba '51
I'd Climb the Highest Mountain
'51
The Gunfighter '50
Twelve O'Clock High '49
Captain from Castile '47
Wilson '44
The Song of Bernadette '43
The Black Swan '42
A Yank in the R.A.F. '41
Jesse James '39
Stanley and Livingstone '39
Alexander's Ragtime Band '38
In Old Chicago '37
Lloyds of London '36
Marie Galante '34
Hell Harbor '30
She Goes to War '29
Romola '25
The White Sister '23
Tol'able David '21
Louis King
Dangerous Mission '54
Sabre Jet '53
Bulldog Drummond Comes Back
'37
Bulldog Drummond's Revenge
'37
Special Investigator '36
Drifting Souls '32
Border Law '31
The Fighting Sheriff '31
Rick King
A Passion to Kill '94
Quick '93
Kickboxer 3: The Art of War '92

Prayer of the Rollerboys '91
Forced March '90
The Killing Time '87
Hot Shot '86
Hard Choices '84
Robert Lee King
Boys Life '94
Stephen King
Maximum Overdrive '86
Zalman King
In God's Hands '98
Delta of Venus '95
Red Shoe Diaries 3: Another
Woman's Lipstick '93
Red Shoe Diaries 4: Auto
Erotica '93
Red Shoe Diaries '92
Red Shoe Diaries 2: Double
Dare '92
Wild Orchid 2: Two Shades of
Blue '92
Wild Orchid '90
Two Moon Junction '88
Wildfire '88
Alan Kingsberg
Almost Partners '87
Jack Kinney
1001 Arabian Nights '59
The Legend of Sleepy Hollow
'49
Keisuke Kinoshita
Twenty-Four Eyes '54
Teinosuke Kinugasa
Gate of Hell '54
Alex Kirby
The Chronicles of Narnia '89
John Mason Kirby
Savage Weekend '80
Robert Kirk
Destroyer '88
David Kirkland
The Tomboy '24
John Kirkland
Curse of the Headless
Horseman '72
Klaus Kirschner
Mozart: A Childhood Chronicle
'76
John Kirsh
Jesus '79
Ephraim Kishon
Sallah '63
**Takeshi "Beat"
Kitano**
Fireworks '97
Sonatine '96
Lek Kitiparaporn
AngKor: Cambodia Express '81
Martin Kitrosser
Daddy's Girl '96
The Fiance '96
Carl Kitt
Up River '79
Robert J. Kizer
Death Ring '93
Hell Comes to Frogtown '88
Godzilla 1985 '85
Alf Kjellin
The Girls of Huntington House
'73
The McMasters '70
Robert Klane
Weekend at Bernie's 2 '93
Thank God It's Friday '78
Cedric Klapisch
Un Air de Famille '96
When the Cat's Away '96
Damian Klaus
Futurekick '91
Dennis Klein
One More Saturday Night '86
Randal Kleiser
It's My Party '95
Honey, I Blew Up the Kid '92
White Fang '91

Getting It Right '89
Big Top Pee Wee '88
Flight of the Navigator '86
Grandview U.S.A. '84
Summer Lovers '82
The Blue Lagoon '80
Grease '78
The Gathering '77
The Boy in the Plastic Bubble
'76
Walter Klenhard
The Haunting of Seacliff Inn '94
Richard Kletter
The Android Affair '95
Dangerous Indiscretion '94
Max Kleven
Bail Out '90
Deadly Stranger '88
Ruckus '81
Roland Klick
Let It Rock '86
Elem Klimov
Come and See '85
Rasputin '85
Leon Klimovsky
The Devil's Possessed '74
Orgy of the Vampires '73
The Saga of the Draculas '72
Vengeance of the Zombies '72
Dr. Jekyll and the Wolfman '71
The Werewolf vs. the Vampire
Woman '71
Ben Kline
Lightning Warrior '31
Herbert Kline
The Fighter '52
Tony Klinger
Butterfly Ball '76
Werner Klinger
Secret of the Black Trunk '62
Elmar Klos
The Shop on Main Street '65
Death Is Called Engelchen '63
Andre Klotzel
Savage Capitalism '93
Steven Kloves
Flesh and Bone '93
The Fabulous Baker Boys '89
Alexander Kluge
Germany in Autumn '78
Pavel Klushantsev
Planet Burg '62
Castleton Knight
The Flying Scotsman '29
Robert Knights
Double Vision '92
The Dawning '88
A Dedicated Man '86
Ebony Tower '86
Lovers of Their Time '85
Edwin H. Knopf
The Light of Western Stars '30
Bernard Knowles
Frozen Alive '64
Murder on Approval '56
Norman Conquest '53
The Magic Bow '47
Werner Knox
Scalps '83
Philip Ko
Platoon the Warriors '88
Masaki Kobayashi
Samurai Rebellion '67
Kwaidan '64
The Human Condition: A
Soldier's Prayer '61
The Human Condition: Road to
Eternity '59
The Human Condition: No
Greater Love '58
Howard W. Koch
Badge 373 '73
Born Reckless '59
Girl in Black Stockings '57
Philip Koch
Pink Nights '87

David Koepp
The Trigger Effect '96

Manfred Kohler
Target for Killing '66

Pancho Kohner
Mr. Sycamore '74

Marja Kok
In for Treatment '82

Ana Kokkinos
Only the Brave '94

Winrich Kolbe
Star Trek Voyager: Caretaker '95
Star Trek the Next Generation, the Final Episode: All Good Things... '94

Amos Kollek
Whore 2 '94
Double Edge '92
High Stakes '89
Forever, Lulu '87
Goodbye, New York '85

Xavier Koller
Squanto: A Warrior's Tale '94
Journey of Hope '90

James Komack
Porky's Revenge '85

Sergei Komarov
A Kiss for Mary Pickford '27

Andrei Konchalovsky
The Odyssey '97
The Inner Circle '91
Homer and Eddie '89
Tango and Cash '89
Shy People '87
Duet for One '86
Runaway Train '85
Maria's Lovers '84
Siberiade '79

Jackie Kong
The Underachievers '88
Blood Diner '87
Night Patrol '85
The Being '83

Joseph Kong
Thundering Ninja '80s
Clones of Bruce Lee '80

Barbara Kopple
Fallen Champ: The Untold Story of Mike Tyson '93
Keeping On '81
Harlan County, U.S.A. '76

Alexander Korda
That Hamilton Woman '41
Rembrandt '36
Private Life of Don Juan '34
The Private Life of Henry VIII '33
Wedding Rehearsal '32
Marius '31

Zoltan Korda
Cry, the Beloved Country '51
Sahara '43
The Jungle Book '42
The Four Feathers '39
Drums '38
Elephant Boy '37
Sanders of the River '35
If I Were Rich '33

Hirokazu Kore-eda
Maborosi '95

Harmony Korine
Gummo '97

John Korty
Redwood Curtain '95
Getting Out '94
They Watch '93
Eye on the Sparrow '91
Long Road Home '91
Cast the First Stone '89
Baby Girl Scott '87
Deadly Business '86
The Ewok Adventure '84
The Haunting Passion '83
A Christmas Without Snow '80
Forever '78
Oliver's Story '78
The Autobiography of Miss Jane Pittman '74
Class of '63 '73

Silence '73
The People '71

Waldemar Korzenioswsky
The Chair '87

Grigori Kosintsev
Don Quixote '57

Peter Kosminsky
Emily Bronte's Wuthering Heights '92

Henry Koster
The Singing Nun '66
Dear Brigitte '65
Mr. Hobbs Takes a Vacation '62
Flower Drum Song '61
The Story of Ruth '60
The Naked Maja '59
My Man Godfrey '57
D-Day, the Sixth of June '56
A Man Called Peter '55
The Virgin Queen '55
Desiree '54
The Robe '53
Stars and Stripes Forever '52
No Highway in the Sky '51
Harvey '50
Come to the Stable '49
The Inspector General '49
The Bishop's Wife '47
It Started with Eve '41
First Love '39
Three Smart Girls Grow Up '39
The Rage of Paris '38
100 Men and a Girl '37
Three Smart Girls '36

Tom Kotani
The Bushido Blade '80

Ted Kotcheff
Family of Cops '95
Red Shoe Diaries 5: Weekend Pass '95
Hidden Assassin '94
Red Shoe Diaries 3: Another Woman's Lipstick '93
Folks! '92
Weekend at Bernie's '89
Winter People '89
Switching Channels '88
Joshua Then and Now '85
Uncommon Valor '83
First Blood '82
Split Image '82
North Dallas Forty '79
Who Is Killing the Great Chefs of Europe? '78
Fun with Dick and Jane '77
The Apprenticeship of Duddy Kravitz '74
Billy Two Hats '74
Tiara Tahiti '62

Jerzy Kotkowski
In an Old Manor House '84

Jim Kouf
Gang Related '96
Disorganized Crime '89
Miracles '86

Nikos Koundouros
Young Aphrodites '63

Steven Kovacks
'68 '87

Andras Kovacs
Cold Days '66

Paul Koval
Blue Movies '88

Bernard L. Kowalski
Nashville Beat '89
B.A.D. Cats '80
Marciano '79
Nativity '78
Ssssssss '73
The Woman Hunter '72
Macho Callahan '70
Stiletto '69
Attack of the Giant Leeches '59
Night of the Blood Beast '58

Soeren Kragh-Jacobsen
Emma's Shadow '88

Frank Kramer
God's Gun '75
This Time I'll Make You Rich '75
Five for Hell '67

Jerry Kramer
Modern Girls '86

Remi Kramer
High Velocity '76

Stanley Kramer
The Runner Stumbles '79
The Domino Principle '77
Oklahoma Crude '73
Bless the Beasts and Children '71
R.P.M.* (*Revolutions Per Minute) '70
Guess Who's Coming to Dinner '67
Ship of Fools '65
It's a Mad, Mad, Mad, Mad World '63
Judgment at Nuremberg '61
Inherit the Wind '60
On the Beach '59
The Defiant Ones '58
The Pride and the Passion '57
Not as a Stranger '55

Norman Krasna
The Ambassador's Daughter '56
The Big Hangover '50

Paul Krasny
Drug Wars 2: The Cocaine Cartel '92
Back to Hannibal: The Return of Tom Sawyer and Huckleberry Finn '90
When Hell Was in Session '82
Centennial '78
Joe Panther '76
Christina '74

Lee Kresel
Alakazam the Great! '61

Harold F. Kress
The Painted Hills '51

John Krish
Man Who Had Power Over Women '70
The Unearthly Stranger '64

Srinivas Krishna
Masala '91

Suri Krishnamma
A Man of No Importance '94

Allen Kroeker
Showdown at Williams Creek '91
Age Old Friends '89
Heaven on Earth '89
Tramp at the Door '87

Bill Krohn
It's All True '93

Jon Kroll
Amanda and the Alien '95

Frank Krom
To Play or To Die '91

Jeremy Joe Kronsberg
Going Ape! '81

Steve Kroschel
Running Free '94

Bill Kroyer
Ferngully: The Last Rain Forest '92

Lisa Krueger
Manny & Lo '96

Michael Krueger
Mindkiller '87
Night Vision '87

Stanley Kubrick
Full Metal Jacket '87
The Shining '80
Barry Lyndon '75
A Clockwork Orange '71
2001: A Space Odyssey '68
Dr. Strangelove, or: How I Learned to Stop Worrying and Love the Bomb '64
Lolita '62
Spartacus '60

Paths of Glory '57
The Killing '56
Killer's Kiss '55

Andrew J. Kuehn
Flush '81

Steven Kuether
Demons of Ludlow '75

Lev Kuleshov
The Extraordinary Adventures of Mr. West in the Land of the Bolsheviks '24

Lev Kulijanov
Crime and Punishment '70

Buzz Kulik
Around the World in 80 Days '89
Women of Valor '86
Rage of Angels '83
The Hunter '80
From Here to Eternity '79
The Lindbergh Kidnapping Case '76
Babe! '75
Bad Ronald '74
Pioneer Woman '73
Shamus '73
Brian's Song '71
Riot '69
Sergeant Ryker '68
Villa Rides '68

Edward Kull
Tarzan and the Green Goddess '38
The New Adventures of Tarzan '35

Victor Kulle
Illusions '91

Kei Kumai
Love and Faith '78
Sandakan No. 8 '74

Harry Kumel
Daughters of Darkness '71

Joseph Kuo
Dragon's Claw '80s
The Unbeaten 28 '80s
Born Invincible '76
Shaolin Temple Strikes Back '72

Koreyoshi Kurahara
Hiroshima '95
Antarctica '84

Hanif Kureishi
London Kills Me '91

Akira Kurosawa
Rhapsody in August '91
Akira Kurosawa's Dreams '90
Ran '85
Kagemusha '80
Dersu Uzala '75
Dodes 'ka-den '70
Red Beard '65
High & Low '62
Sanjuro '62
Yojimbo '61
The Bad Sleep Well '60
The Hidden Fortress '58
The Lower Depths '57
Throne of Blood '57
I Live in Fear '55
Seven Samurai '54
Ikiru '52
The Idiot '51
Rashomon '51
Scandal '50
A Quiet Duel '49
Stray Dog '49
Drunken Angel '48
No Regrets for Our Youth '46
The Men Who Tread on the Tiger's Tail '45
Sanshiro Sugata '43

Mitsuo Kurotsuchi
Traffic Jam '91

Robert Kurtzman
Wishmaster '97
The Demolitionist '95

Diane Kurys
Love After Love '94
A Man in Love '87
Entre-Nous '83
Peppermint Soda '77

Donald Kushner
First & Ten '85

Emir Kusturica
Underground '95
Arizona Dream '91
Time of the Gypsies '90
When Father was Away on Business '85

Ken Kwapis
The Beautician and the Beast '97
Dunston Checks In '95
He Said, She Said '91
Vibes '88
Sesame Street Presents: Follow That Bird '85
The Beniker Gang '83

Richard Kwietniowski
Love & Death on Long Island '97

Jeff Kwitny
Beyond the Door 3 '91
Iced '88

William Kyriakis
Dark Odyssey '57

Paul Kyriazi
Omega Cop '90
Crazed Cop '88
Death Machines '76

Bruce La Bruce
Hustler White '96

Gregory La Cava
Primrose Path '40
Fifth Avenue Girl '39
Stage Door '37
My Man Godfrey '36
Gabriel Over the White House '33
Big News '29
His First Command '29
Feel My Pulse '28
Running Wild '27

Steven La Rocque
Samantha '92

Eriq La Salle
Rebound: The Legend of Earl "The Goat" Manigault '96

Richard LaBrie
Good Luck '96

Jeanne Labrune
Sand and Blood '87

Neil LaBute
In the Company of Men '96

Harry Lachman
Castle in the Desert '42
The Loves of Edgar Allen Poe '42
Charlie Chan in Rio '41
Murder over New York '40
Our Relations '36
Baby, Take a Bow '34

Georges Lacombe
Seven Deadly Sins '53

Joe Lacy
A Witch Without a Broom '68

Diane Ladd
Mrs. Munck '95

Aldo Lado
Paralyzed '70s

Edward Laemmle
Texas Bad Man '32

John Lafia
Man's Best Friend '93
Child's Play 2 '90
Blue Iguana '88

Jean LaFleur
Mystery of the Million Dollar Hockey Puck '80s
Ilsa, the Tigress of Siberia '79

Ron Lagomarsino
Dinner at Eight '89

Craig Lahiff
Heaven's Burning '97
Ebbtide '94
Strangers '90
Deadly Possession '88

Delbert Mann
Lily in Winter '94
Ironclads '90
The Last Days of Patton '86
Love Leads the Way '84
The Member of the Wedding '83
Night Crossing '81
All Quiet on the Western Front '79
Home to Stay '79
Torn Between Two Lovers '79
The Birch Interval '78
Breaking Up '78
Francis Gary Powers: The True Story of the U-2 Spy '76
No Place to Run '72
She Waits '71
David Copperfield '70
The Pink Jungle '68
Heidi '67
A Gathering of Eagles '63
That Touch of Mink '62
Lover Come Back '61
Desire Under the Elms '58
Separate Tables '58
Marty '55

Edward Mann
Hooch '76
Cauldron of Blood '67
Hallucination '67

Farhad Mann
Lawnmower Man 2: Beyond Cyberspace '95
Return to Two Moon Junction '93

Michael Mann
Heat '95
The Last of the Mohicans '92
Manhunter '86
The Keep '83
Thief '81
The Jericho Mile '79

Kim Manners
K-9000 '89

Michelle Manning
Blue City '86

Peter Manoogian
Seedpeople '92
Demonic Toys '90
Arena '89
Enemy Territory '87
The Eliminators '86
Dungeonmaster '83

Mark Manos
Josh Kirby...Time Warrior: Chapter 4, Eggs from 70 Million B.C. '95
Liquid Dreams '92

Manoussos Manoussakis
The Enchantress '85

Duncan Mansfield
Sweetheart of the Navy '37

Scott Mansfield
Deadly Games '80

Joe Mantello
Love! Valour! Compassion! '96

Guido Manuli
Volere Volare '92

Ray Manzarek
The Doors: Soft Parade, a Retrospective '69

Rene Manzor
Red Shoe Diaries 8: Night of Abandon '97
Warrior Spirit '94

Robert Marcarelli
I Don't Buy Kisses Anymore '92
Original Intent '91

Terry Marcel
Jane & the Lost City '87
Prisoners of the Lost Universe '84
Hawk the Slayer '81

Siro Marcellini
Gangster's Law '86

Alex March
Master Mind '73

Firehouse '72
Paper Lion '68

Rafael Romero Marchent
Garringo '69

David Marconi
The Harvest '92

G.D. Marcum
Gates of Hell 2: Dead Awakening '96

Adam Marcus
Jason Goes to Hell: The Final Friday '93

James Marcus
Double Cross '92

Mitch Marcus
A Boy Called Hate '95

Paul Marcus
Prime Suspect: The Scent of Darkness '95

Philip Marcus
Terror on Alcatraz '86

Andreas Marfori
Desperate Crimes '93
Evil Clutch '89

Stuart Margolin
How the West was Fun '95
Medicine River '94
Paramedics '88
The Glitter Dome '84
A Shining Season '79

Jeff Margolis
Oscar's Greatest Moments: 1971-1991 '92

Edwin L. Marin
The Cariboo Trail '50
Abilene Town '46
Mr. Ace '46
Nocturne '46
Johnny Angel '45
Show Business '44
Tall in the Saddle '44
Invisible Agent '42
Miss Annie Rooney '42
A Christmas Carol '38
Everybody Sing '38
Listen, Darling '38
I'd Give My Life '36
The Death Kiss '33
A Study in Scarlet '33

Richard "Cheech" Marin
Born in East L.A. '87

Lex Marinos
An Indecent Obsession '85
Remember Me '85

Peter Maris
Diplomatic Immunity '91
Hangfire '91
True Blood '89
Viper '88
Terror Squad '87
Land of Doom '84
Delirium '77

Chris Marker
Sans Soleil '82
Le Joli Mai '62

Russ Marker
The Yesterday Machine '63

Anthony Markes
Bikini Island '91
Last Dance '95

David Markey
1991: The Year Punk Broke '92
Desperate Teenage Lovedolls '84

Monte Markham
Neon City '91
Defense Play '88

Kelly Markin
Tiger Claws '91

Gabriel Markiw
Mob Story '90

Jancarlo Markiw
Mob Story '90

Fletcher Markle
The Incredible Journey '63
Jigsaw '49

Peter Markle
The Last Days of Frankie the Fly '96
White Dwarf '95
Wagons East '94
Through the Eyes of a Killer '92
El Diablo '90
Nightbreaker '89
Bat 21 '88
Youngblood '86
Hot Dog...The Movie! '83
The Personals '83

Goran Markovic
Tito and Me '92

Murray Markowitz
Left for Dead '78

Robert Markowitz
David '97
The Tuskegee Airmen '95
Afterburn '92
Love, Lies and Murder '91
Decoration Day '90
Too Young to Die '90
Kojak: The Belarus File '85
My Mother's Secret Life '84
Pray TV '82
A Long Way Home '81

Arthur Marks
Monkey Hustle '77
J.D.'s Revenge '76
Bucktown '75
Friday Foster '75
Bonnie's Kids '73
Detroit 9000 '73
Togetherness '70

Ross Kagen Marks
The Twilight of the Golds '97
Homage '95

Morley Markson
Off Your Rocker '80

Brad Marlowe
At Home with the Webbers '94

Malcolm Marmorstein
Dead Men Don't Die '91

Richard Marquand
Hearts of Fire '87
The Jagged Edge '85
Until September '84
Return of the Jedi '83
Eye of the Needle '81
The Legacy '79

Jacques Marquette
Meteor Monster '57

Leon Marr
Dancing in the Dark '86

Roberto Marrtero
Thirty-Six Hours of Hell '77

David Marsh
Stormswept '95
Lords of Magick '88

Ray Marsh
The Last Porno Flick '74

Philip Marshak
Cataclysm '81
Dracula Sucks '79

Frank Marshall
Congo '95
Alive '93
Arachnophobia '90

Garry Marshall
Dear God '96
Exit to Eden '94
Frankie and Johnny '91
Pretty Woman '90
Beaches '88
Overboard '87
Nothing in Common '86
The Flamingo Kid '84
Young Doctors in Love '82

George Marshall
Eight on the Lam '67
Boy, Did I Get a Wrong Number! '66
How the West Was Won '63

Papa's Delicate Condition '63
The Gazebo '59
It Started with a Kiss '59
The Mating Game '59
The Sad Sack '57
Red Garters '54
Houdini '53
Off Limits '53
Scared Stiff '53
Fancy Pants '50
Never a Dull Moment '50
My Friend Irma '49
The Perils of Pauline '47
The Blue Dahlia '46
Monsieur Beaucaire '46
Star Spangled Rhythm '42
Valley of the Sun '42
Pot O' Gold '41
Texas '41
The Ghost Breakers '40
Destry Rides Again '39
You Can't Cheat an Honest Man '39
The Goldwyn Follies '38
Show Them No Mercy '35
Pack Up Your Troubles '32

Penny Marshall
The Preacher's Wife '96
Renaissance Man '94
A League of Their Own '92
Awakenings '90
Big '88
Jumpin' Jack Flash '86

Tonie Marshall
Pas Tres Catholique '93

William Marshall
The Phantom Planet '61
Adventures of Captain Fabian '51

Eugene Martian
Two Plus One '95

Charles Martin
One Man Jury '78
Death of a Scoundrel '56
My Dear Secretary '49

Darnell Martin
I Like It Like That '94

D'Urville Martin
Fass Black '77
Dolemite '75

Eugenio Martin
Pancho Villa '72
It Happened at Nightmare Inn '70

Frank Martin
Elvis in Hollywood '93
Doctor Butcher M.D. '80

Gene Martin
Bad Man's River '72
Horror Express '72

James Aviles Martin
Flesh Eating Mothers '89

Lionel C. Martin
Def Jam's How to Be a Player '97

Michael Martin
I Got the Hook-Up '98

Richard Martin
White Tiger '95
Elizabeth R '72

Steven M. Martin
Theremin: An Electronic Odyssey '95

Vince Martin
The Cursed Mountain Mystery '93

Wyre Martin
The Unearthing '93

Chuck Martinez
Nice Girls Don't Explode '87

Rene Martinez, Jr.
The Guy from Harlem '77

Gilberto Martinez Solares
Face of the Screaming Werewolf '59

Richard Martini
Cannes Man '96
Limit Up '89
You Can't Hurry Love '88

Raymond Martino
Skyscraper '95
To the Limit '95
DaVinci's War '92
American Born '89

Sergio Martino
Casablanca Express '89
The Opponent '89
The Great Alligator '81
Screamers '80
Slave of the Cannibal God '79
Day of the Maniac '77
The Cheaters '76
Sex with a Smile '76
Torso '73
Violent Professionals '73
The Next Victim '71
The Scorpion's Tail '71
Blade of the Ripper '70

Leslie Martinson
Return to Africa '89
The Fantastic World of D.C. Collins '84
The Kid with the 200 I.Q. '83
The Kid with the Broken Halo '82
Batman '66
PT 109 '63
Hot Rod Girl '56
The Atomic Kid '54

Andrew Marton
Africa Texas Style '67
Around the World Under the Sea '65
Clarence, the Cross-eyed Lion '65
Green Fire '55
Gypsy Colt '54
Men of the Fighting Lady '54

Mike Marvin
Wishman '93
The Wraith '87
Hamburger...The Motion Picture '86

Joseph Mascelli
The Atomic Brain '64

Francesco Maselli
Time of Indifference '64
Love in the City '53

Giuseppe Masini
Journey Beneath the Desert '61

Herbert Mason
Lady in Distress '39

Noel Mason Smith
Fighting Pilot '35
The Night Patrol '26

Francesco Massaro
Private Affairs '89

Ivana Massetti
Domino '88

Joe Massot
Space Riders '83
Wonderwall: The Movie '69

Quentin Masters
Dangerous Summer '82
The Stud '78
Thumb Tripping '72

Peter Masterson
Lily Dale '96
Arctic Blue '93
Night Game '89
Blood Red '88
Full Moon in Blue Water '88
The Trip to Bountiful '85

Nico Mastorakis
Hired to Kill '91
Ninja Academy '90
In the Cold of the Night '89
Terminal Exposure '89
Glitch! '88
Nightmare at Noon '87
The Wind '87
Zero Boys '86
Blind Date '84
Next One '84
Sky High '84

Camillo Mastrocinque
Full Hearts & Empty Pockets '63

Armand Mastroianni
Cameron's Closet '89
Double Revenge '89
Distortions '87
The Supernaturals '86
Killing Hour '84
He Knows You're Alone '80

Toshio Masuda
Zero '84
Last Days of Planet Earth '74
Tora! Tora! Tora! '70

Orestes Matacena
Tainted '88

Eddy Matalon
Sweet Killing '93
Blackout '78
Cathy's Curse '77

Vivian Matalon
Private Contentment '83

Rudolph Mate
For the First Time '59
Deep Six '58
Three Violent People '57
The Violent Men '55
Second Chance '53
The Green Glove '52
When Worlds Collide '51
Branded '50
Union Station '50
The Dark Past '49
D.O.A. '49

Tim Matheson
Buried Alive 2 '97
Tails You Live, Heads You're Dead '95
Breach of Conduct '94

Sean Mathias
Bent '97

Daniel Matmor
Buffalo Heart: The Pain of Death '96

Shue Matsubayashi
Last War '68
I Bombed Pearl Harbor '60

Bruno Mattei
Seven Magnificent Gladiators '84
Night of the Zombies '83

Marius Mattei
Moving Target '89

Charles Matthau
The Grass Harp '95
Doin' Time on Planet Earth '88

Paul Matthews
Breeders '97
Grim '95

Burny Mattinson
The Great Mouse Detective '86

Frank S. Mattison
With Kit Carson Over the Great Divide '25

Sally Mattison
Slumber Party Massacre 3 '90

Mario Mattoli
Two Nights with Cleopatra '54

Arne Mattson
The Girl '86
The Doll '62

Norman Maurer
The Outlaws Is Coming! '65
Around the World in a Daze '63

Robert Mauri
Invincible Gladiators '64
The Slaughter of the Vampires '62

Rich Mauro
Nick and Jane '96

Garth Maxwell
Jack Be Nimble '94

John Maxwell
The Man I Love '46

Paul Maxwell
Superargo '67

Peter Maxwell
Platypus Cove '86
The Highest Honor '84
Run, Rebecca, Run '81
Touch & Go '80
Plunge Into Darkness '77

Ronald F. Maxwell
Gettysburg '93
Kidco '83
The Night the Lights Went Out in Georgia '81
Little Darlings '80

Bradford May
Asteroid '97
Darkman 3: Die Darkman Die '95
Madonna: Innocence Lost '95
Darkman 2: The Return of Durant '94
Marilyn & Bobby: Her Final Affair '94
Lethal Lolita—Amy Fisher: My Story '92
Mortal Sins '92

Elaine May
Ishtar '87
Mikey & Nicky '76
The Heartbreak Kid '72
A New Leaf '71

Joe May
The House of the Seven Gables '40
The Invisible Man Returns '40
Homecoming '28

Paul May
Dr. Mabuse vs. Scotland Yard '64

Russ Mayberry
Challenge of a Lifetime '85
A Matter of Life and Death '81
The $5.20 an Hour Dream '80
Marriage Is Alive and Well '80
The Rebels '79
Unidentified Flying Oddball '74
Fer-De-Lance '74
Probe '72
The Jesus Trip '71

Daisy von Scherler Mayer
Madeline '98
Woo '97
Party Girl '94

Gerald Mayer
The Man Inside '76

Paul Mayersberg
The Last Samurai '90
Nightfall '88
Captive '87

Les Mayfield
Flubber '97
Miracle on 34th Street '94
Encino Man '92

Tony Maylam
Split Second '92
The Burning '82
The Sins of Dorian Gray '82
The Riddle of the Sands '79

Ken Maynard
Honor of the Range '34
The Fiddlin' Buckaroo '33
Strawberry Roan '33

Archie Mayo
Angel on My Shoulder '46
A Night in Casablanca '46
Crash Dive '43
Orchestra Wives '42
The Great American Broadcast '41
House Across the Bay '40
They Shall Have Music '39
The Adventures of Marco Polo '38
Petrified Forest '36
The Case of the Lucky Legs '35
Night After Night '32
Illicit '31
Svengali '31

Melanie Mayron
The Baby-Sitters Club '95

David Maysles
Gimme Shelter '70

Michael Mazo
Crackerjack '94
Time Runner '92
Possession: Until Death Do You Part '90

Paul Mazursky
Faithful '95
The Pickle '93
Scenes from a Mall '91
Enemies, a Love Story '89
Moon over Parador '88
Down and Out in Beverly Hills '86
Moscow on the Hudson '84
The Tempest '82
Willie & Phil '80
An Unmarried Woman '78
Next Stop, Greenwich Village '76
Harry and Tonto '74
Blume in Love '73
Alex in Wonderland '70
Bob & Carol & Ted & Alice '69

Joseph Mazzuca
Sisters of Death '76

Paolo Mazzucato
Moonbase '97

Don McBrearty
Race to Freedom: The Story of the Underground Railroad '94
Child's Christmas in Wales '88
American Nightmare '81

Jim McBride
Pronto '97
The Wrong Man '93
Blood Ties '92
Great Balls of Fire '89
The Big Easy '87
Breathless '83
Hot Times '74
Glen and Randa '71
David Holzman's Diary '67

Jon McBride
Woodchipper Massacre '89
Cannibal Campout '88

Gene McCabe
Follow Me '69

Robert McCahon
Running Wild '73

Howard McCain
Shadow of a Scream '97
No Dessert Dad, 'Til You Mow the Lawn '94

Rod McCall
Lewis and Clark and George '97
Cheatin' Hearts '93

James McCalmont
Escape from Safehaven '88
Underground Terror '88

Tim McCann
Desolation Angels '95

Leo McCarey
An Affair to Remember '57
Good Sam '48
The Bells of St. Mary's '45
Going My Way '44
Once Upon a Honeymoon '42
Love Affair '39
The Awful Truth '37
Milky Way '36
Ruggles of Red Gap '35
Belle of the Nineties '34
Six of a Kind '34
Duck Soup '33
Kid from Spain '32
Indiscreet '31

Ray McCarey
You Can't Fool Your Wife '40
Devil's Party '38
The Mystery Man '35

John P. McCarthy
Song of the Gringo '36
The Return of Casey Jones '34
Fighting Champ '33
The Forty-Niners '32

Cavalier of the West '31
Mother and Son '31
Sunrise Trail '31
Oklahoma Cyclone '30

Michael McCarthy
Operation Amsterdam '60
Crow Hollow '52

Peter McCarthy
Floundering '94

Todd McCarthy
Visions of Light: The Art of Cinematography '93

John McCauley
Rattlers '76

Michael McClary
Annie O '95

Gregory McClatchy
Vampire at Midnight '88

Mick McCleery
The Alien Agenda: Out of the Darkness '96

David McClendon
G. Whilliker! '93

Arn McConnell
Shock! Shock! Shock! '87

Bret McCormick
Time Tracers '97
Rumble in the Streets '96
Blood on the Badge '92
Tabloid! '88

George McCowan
Return to Fantasy Island '77
Murder on Flight 502 '75
Frogs '72
Savage Run '70

Peter McCubbin
Home for Christmas '90

Jim McCullough
Where the Red Fern Grows: Part 2 '92
Mountaintop Motel Massacre '86
The Aurora Encounter '85
Charge of the Model T's '76

Bruce McDonald
Hard Core Logo '96
Dance Me Outside '95
Highway 61 '91
Roadkill '89

Frank McDonald
Thunder Pass '54
Apache Chief '50
The Big Sombrero '49
My Pal Trigger '46
Song of Arizona '46
Under Nevada Skies '46
Bells of Rosarita '45
Sunset in El Dorado '45
Treasure of Fear '45
Gambler's Choice '44
One Body Too Many '44
Take It Big '44
Timber Queen '44
Wildcat '42
Twilight on the Rio Grande '41

Michael James McDonald
The Death Artist '95
The Crazysitter '94

Peter McDonald
Rambo 3 '88

Rodney McDonald
Steel Sharks '97
Scorned 2 '96
Night Eyes 4: Fatal Passion '95
Night Eyes 2 '91

Donald McDougall
Chinese Web '78

Ross McElwee
Time Indefinite '93
Sherman's March: An Improbable Search for Love '86

Bernard McEveety, Sr.
The Broadway Drifter '27

Bernard McEveety
Roughnecks '80
Centennial '78
The Bears & I '74
One Little Indian '73
Napoleon and Samantha '72
The Brotherhood of Satan '71

Vincent McEveety
Gunsmoke: Return to Dodge '87
Amy '81
Herbie Goes Bananas '80
The Apple Dumpling Gang Rides Again '79
Herbie Goes to Monte Carlo '77
Gus '76
The Treasure of Matecumbe '76
The Castaway Cowboy '74
Charley and the Angel '73
Superdad '73
Million Dollar Duck '71
Menace on the Mountain '70
Smoke '70
Firecreek '68

Bruce McFarlane
Kill Slade '89

William F. McGaha
Iron Horsemen '71
The Speed Lovers '68

William McGann
American Empire '42
In Old California '42
Dr. Christian Meets the Women '40

Darren McGavin
Run, Stranger, Run '73

Scott McGehee
Suture '93

Robert McGinley
Shredder Orpheus '89

Scott McGinnis
The Last Gasp '94
Caroline at Midnight '93

Dorrell McGowan
The Showdown '50

J.P. McGowan
Rough Ridin' Rhythm '37
Deadwood Pass '33
Drum Taps '33
Lone Bandit '33
The Outlaw Tamer '33
When a Man Rides Alone '33
Hurricane Express '32
Mark of the Spur '32
Near the Rainbow's End '30
Below the Deadline '29
Red Signals '27
Road Agent '26
Blood and Steel '25

Robert McGowan
Old Swimmin' Hole '40
Frontier Justice '35

Stuart E. McGowan
The Billion Dollar Hobo '78
The Showdown '50

Tom McGowan
Savage Journey '83
Cataclysm '81

Douglas McGrath
Emma '96

Joseph McGrath
Great McGonagall '75
Digby, the Biggest Dog in the World '73
The Magic Christian '69
The Bliss of Mrs. Blossom '68
30 Is a Dangerous Age, Cynthia '68
Casino Royale '67

Sean McGregor
Devil Times Five '74
Gentle Savage '73

Thomas McGuane
92 in the Shade '76

Don McGuire
The Delicate Delinquent '56

Doug McHenry
Jason's Lyric '94

O'Herlihy *cont.*

The Flame Is Love '79
Peter Lundy and the Medicine Hat Stallion '77
Smith! '69
The One and Only, Genuine, Original Family Band '68
The Fighting Prince of Donegal '66
Mosby's Marauders '66

Don Ohlmeyer
The Heroes of Desert Storm '91

Kazuki Ohmori
Godzilla vs. Biollante '89

Tom O'Horgan
Futz '69

Kihachi Okamoto
Zatoichi vs. Yojimbo '70
Red Lion '69
Sword of Doom '67

Steven Okazaki
Living on Tokyo Time '87

Kazuyoshi Okuyama
The Mystery of Rampo '94

Sidney Olcott
The Claw '27
Ranson's Folly '26
Monsieur Beaucaire '24
From the Manger to the Cross '15

Gary Oldman
Nil by Mouth '96

Enrico Oldoini
Bye Bye Baby '88

Pedro Olea
Zafarinas '94
The Fencing Master '92

Ronan O'Leary
Riders to the Sea '88

Joel Oliansky
The Competition '80

Ken Olin
In Pursuit of Honor '95
White Fang 2: The Myth of the White Wolf '94

David Oliver
Cave Girl '85

Richard Oliver
A Girl to Kill For '90

Robert Oliver
Dr. Frankenstein's Castle of Freaks '74

Ron Oliver
Tales from a Parallel Universe: Super Nova '97
Liar's Edge '92
Prom Night 3: The Last Kiss '89

Ruby L. Oliver
Love Your Mama '89

Hector Olivera
A Shadow You Soon Will Be '94
Play Murder for Me '91
Two to Tango '88
Cocaine Wars '86
Barbarian Queen '85
Wizards of the Lost Kingdom '85
Funny, Dirty Little War '83
Fridays of Eternity '81
El Muerto '75

Laurence Olivier
The Prince and the Showgirl '57
Richard III '55
Hamlet '48
Henry V '44

Marty Ollstein
Dangerous Love '87

Ermanno Olmi
The Tree of Wooden Clogs '78
Fiances '63

Edward James Olmos
American Me '92

William Olsen
Return to Eden '89
Getting It On '83

David O'Malley
Easy Wheels '89
Kid Colter '85
Mountain Man '77

Carlo Ombra
Dracula Blows His Cool '82

Kazuki Omori
Godzilla vs. King Ghidora '91

Ron O'Neal
Up Against the Wall '91
Superfly T.N.T. '73

Douglas F. Oneans
Sno-Line '85

Lawrence O'Neil
Breast Men '97

Robert Vincent O'Neil
Avenging Angel '85
Angel '84
Paco '75
The Deadly and the Beautiful '73
Blood Mania '70

Marcel Ophuls
The Sorrow and the Pity '71

Max Ophuls
Lola Montes '55
The Earrings of Madame De... '54
Le Plaisir '52
La Ronde '51
Caught '49
Reckless Moment '49
Letter from an Unknown Woman '48
De Mayerling a Sarajevo '40
La Signora di Tutti '34
Liebelei '32

Peer J. Oppenheimer
Terror in Paradise '90

Charlie Ordonez
Forgotten Warrior '86
Wolf '86

Wyott Ordung
Monster from the Ocean Floor '54

Mario Orfini
Fair Game '89

Valery Orgorodnikov
Burglar '87

Ruth Orkin
Little Fugitive '53

Dominic Orlando
Knights of the City '85

Susan Orlikoff-Simon
Image of Passion '86

Stuart Orme
Ivanhoe '97
The Sculptress '97
The Puppet Masters '94
Hands of a Murderer '90
The Heist '89

James Ormerod
Frankenstein '82
Next Victim '74

Ron Ormond
The Girl from Tobacco Row '66
The Black Lash '52
Mesa of Lost Women '52
King of the Bullwhip '51
Yes, Sir, Mr. Bones '51

Peter Ormrod
Eat the Peach '86

Alan Ormsby
Deranged '74

Bruce Ornstein
Jack and His Friends '92

Gary Orona
Stripshow '96
Great Bikini Off-Road Adventure '94
The Bikini Car Wash Company 2 '92

James Orr
Man of the House '95
Mr. Destiny '90
Breaking All the Rules '85

Valentino Orsini
Smugglers '75

Kenny Ortega
Hocus Pocus '93
Newsies '92

Aaron Osborne
Zarkorr! The Invader '96

Kent Osborne
Women Unchained '70s

Mamoru Oshii
Ghost in the Shell '95

Nagisa Oshima
Max, Mon Amour '86
Merry Christmas, Mr. Lawrence '83
In the Realm of Passion '80
The Empire of Passion '76
In the Realm of the Senses '76
Violence at Noon '66
The Cruel Story of Youth '60
The Sun's Burial '60

Cliff Osmond
The Penitent '88

Jaime Osorio Gomez
Confessing to Laura '90

Sam O'Steen
The Best Little Girl in the World '81
Sparkle '76
Brand New Life '72

Suzanne Osten
The Mozart Brothers '86

Thaddeus O'Sullivan
Nothing Personal '95
December Bride '91

Gerd Oswald
Crime of Passion '57
Paris Holiday '57

Richard Oswald
The Lovable Cheat '49
My Song Goes Round the World '34
Cesare Borgia '23

Dominique Othenin-Girard
Beyond Desire '94
Private Lessons, Another Story '94
Omen 4: The Awakening '91
Night Angel '90
Halloween 5: The Revenge of Michael Myers '89
After Darkness '85

Katsuhiro Otomo
Akira '89

Matteo Ottaviano
Single Room Furnished '68

Henry Otto
Dante's Inferno '24

Filippo Ottoni
Detective School Dropouts '85

Lar Henrik Ottoson
Gorilla '56

Idrissa Ouedraogo
Tilai '90

Jean-Paul Ouellette
The Unnamable 2: The Statement of Randolph Carter '92
Chinatown Connection '90
The Unnamable '88

Gerard Oury
Delusions of Grandeur '76
The Brain '69
La Grande Vadrouille '66
The Sucker '65

Cliff Owen
The Bawdy Adventures of Tom Jones '76
The Wrong Arm of the Law '63

Don Owen
Unfinished Business '89

Richard Owens
Killer Likes Candy '78

Earl Owensby
Manhunter '83

Jan Oxenberg
Thank You & Good Night '91

Frank Oz
In and Out '97
The Indian in the Cupboard '95
Housesitter '92
What About Bob? '91
Dirty Rotten Scoundrels '88
Little Shop of Horrors '86
The Muppets Take Manhattan '84
The Dark Crystal '82

Sakae Ozawa
The Street Fighter's Last Revenge '79
The Street Fighter '75

Fedor Ozep
Whispering City '47

Ali Ozgenturk
The Horse '82

Yasujiro Ozu
An Autumn Afternoon '62
Drifting Weeds '59
Equinox Flower '58
Tokyo Story '53
Early Summer '51
Late Spring '49
Record of a Tenement Gentleman '47

G. W. Pabst
Don Quixote '35
Kameradschaft '31
The Threepenny Opera '31
Westfront 1918 '30
Diary of a Lost Girl '29
Pandora's Box '28
Joyless Street '25
Secrets of a Soul '25

Al Pacino
Looking for Richard '96

Frank Packard
In Your Face '77

Calvin Jackson Padget
The Battle of El Alamein '68
Secret Agent Super Dragon '66

Anthony Page
Human Bomb '97
Middlemarch '93
Final Warning '90
The Nightmare Years '89
Scandal in a Small Town '88
Heartbreak House '86
Monte Carlo '86
Forbidden '85
Bill: On His Own '83
The Grace Kelly Story '83
Johnny Belinda '82
Absolution '81
Bill '81
The Lady Vanishes '79
I Never Promised You a Rose Garden '77
F. Scott Fitzgerald in Hollywood '76
Missiles of October '74
Alpha Beta '73
Pueblo Affair '73

Teddy Page
Blood Debts '83

Marcel Pagliero
The Respectful Prostitute '52

Marcel Pagnol
Letters from My Windmill '54
Topaze '51
Well-Digger's Daughter '46
Le Schpountz '38
Harvest '37
Cesar '36
Angele '34
The Baker's Wife '33

John Paizs
The Big Crimewave '86

Alan J. Pakula
The Devil's Own '96
The Pelican Brief '93
Consenting Adults '92

Presumed Innocent '90
See You in the Morning '89
Orphans '87
Dream Lover '85
Sophie's Choice '82
Rollover '81
Starting Over '79
Comes a Horseman '78
All the President's Men '76
The Parallax View '74
Klute '71
The Sterile Cuckoo '69

George Pal
7 Faces of Dr. Lao '63
The Wonderful World of the Brothers Grimm '62
Atlantis, the Lost Continent '61
The Time Machine '60
Tom Thumb '58

Laszlo Pal
Journey to Spirit Island '92

Tom Palazzolo
Caligari's Cure '82

Euzhan Palcy
A Dry White Season '89
Sugar Cane Alley '83

Larry Pall
Off Your Rocker '80

Jean Marie Pallardy
Truck Stop

Rospo Pallenberg
Cutting Class '89

Anders Palm
Dead Certain '92
Murder on Line One '90
Unmasked Part 25 '88

Thomas Palmer, Jr.
Forever: A Ghost of a Love Story '92

Tony Palmer
The Children '90
Wagner: The Complete Epic '85
Wagner: The Movie '85

Conrad Palmisano
Busted Up '86
Space Rage '86

Bruce Paltrow
A Little Sex '82

Herve Palud
Little Indian, Big City '95

Rick Pamplin
Provoked '89

George Pan-Andreas
Crime Killer '85

Jafar Panahi
The White Balloon '95

Norman Panama
Barnaby and Me '77
I Will, I Will for Now '76
How to Commit Marriage '69
The Road to Hong Kong '62
The Trap '59
Court Jester '56
Above and Beyond '53

Gleb Panfilov
The Theme '79

Domenico Paolella
Pirates of the Coast '61

Deno Paoli
The Legend of Frank Woods '77

Phedon Papamichael
Dark Side of Genius '94
Sketch Artist '92

Michael Papas
The Lifetaker '89

Lakis Papastathis
When the Greeks '81

Giullo Paradisi
Spaghetti House '82
The Visitor '80

Roger Paradiso
Kisses in the Dark '97

Sergei Paradjanov
Ashik Kerib '88
The Legend of Suram Fortress '85

Michael Raeburn
Jit '94
Killing Heat '84
Laserblast '78

Bob Rafelson
Blood & Wine '96
Picture Windows '95
Tales of Erotica '93
Man Trouble '92
Mountains of the Moon '90
Black Widow '87
The Postman Always Rings
Twice '81
Stay Hungry '76
The King of Marvin Gardens '72
Five Easy Pieces '70
Head '68

Piccio Raffanini
Obsession: A Taste for Fear '89

Kevin Rafferty
The Atomic Cafe '82

Stewart Raffill
Tammy and the T-Rex '94
Mannequin 2: On the Move '91
Mac and Me '88
Ice Pirates '84
The Philadelphia Experiment '84
Sea Gypsies '78
Across the Great Divide '76
The Adventures of the
Wilderness Family '76
High Risk '76
When the North Wind Blows '74
The Tender Warrior '71

Alan Rafkin
How to Frame a Figg '71
The Shakiest Gun in the West
'68
The Ghost and Mr. Chicken '66

Ubaldo Ragona
The Last Man on Earth '64

Ed Ragozzini
Sasquatch '76

Ken Raich
Hollywood Hot Tubs 2:
Educating Crystal '89

Steve Railsback
The Spy Within '94

Sam Raimi
The Quick and the Dead '94
Army of Darkness '92
Darkman '90
Evil Dead 2: Dead by Dawn '87
Crimewave '85
Evil Dead '83

Paul Raimondi
Crosscut '95

Yvonne Rainer
The Man Who Envied Women
'85

Frank Rainone
Me and the Mob '94

Alvin Rakoff
A Voyage' Round My Father '89
The First Olympics: Athens 1896
'84
Mister Halpren & Mister Johnson
'83
Dirty Tricks '81
Death Ship '80
City on Fire '78
King Solomon's Treasure '76
Say Hello to Yesterday '71
Room 43 '58

Alexander Ramati
The Assisi Underground '84

Victor Rambaldi
Decoy '95

Vittoria Rambaldi
Primal Rage '90

Harold Ramis
Multiplicity '96
Stuart Saves His Family '94
Groundhog Day '93
Club Paradise '86
National Lampoon's Vacation
'83
Caddyshack '80

Patrick Rand
Mom '89

Addison Randall
The Killing Zone '90
Chance '89
East L.A. Warriors '89

Tony Randel
Rattled '96
Fist of the North Star '95
One Good Turn '95
Ticks '93
Amityville 1992: It's About Time
'92
Children of the Night '92
Hellbound: Hellraiser 2 '88

Arthur Rankin, Jr.
Flight of Dragons '82
The Return of the King '80
The Hobbit '78
The Ballad of Paul Bunyan '72
Santa Claus Is Coming to Town
'70

Lazlo Ranody
Nobody's Daughter '76

Mort Ransen
Margaret's Museum '95

Whitney Ransick
Hand Gun '93

Krishna Rao
Crossworlds '96

Frederic Raphael
Women & Men: Stories of
Seduction '90

Joel Rapp
The Battle of Blood Island '60

Mark Rappaport
From the Journals of Jean
Seberg '95
Rock Hudson's Home Movies
'92

**Jean-Paul
Rappeneau**
The Horseman on the Roof '95
Cyrano de Bergerac '90
Swashbuckler '84
Lovers Like Us '75

Irving Rapper
Born Again '78
Joseph & His Brethren '60
Marjorie Morningstar '58
The Brave One '56
Forever Female '53
Deception '46
The Corn Is Green '45
Rhapsody in Blue '45
The Adventures of Mark Twain
'44
Now, Voyager '42

Steve Rash
Eddie '96
Son-in-Law '93
Queens Logic '91
Can't Buy Me Love '87
Rich Hall's Vanishing America
'86
Under the Rainbow '81
The Buddy Holly Story '78

Jay Raskin
I Married a Vampire '87

Daniel Raskov
A Kiss Goodnight '94
The Masters of Menace '90
Wedding Band '89

Lars Rasmussen
The Littlest Viking '94

Tina Rathborne
Zelly & Me '88

Brett Ratner
Rush Hour '98
Money Talks '97

Gregory Ratoff
Abdulla the Great '56
Black Magic '49
The Heat's On '43
The Corsican Brothers '42
Footlight Serenade '42
Adam Had Four Sons '41
Intermezzo '39

Rose of Washington Square '39

Jans Rautenbach
No One Cries Forever '85

Max Raven
The Abomination '88

Ousama Rawi
The Housekeeper '86

John Rawlins
Shark River '53
Dick Tracy Meets Gruesome '47
Dick Tracy's Dilemma '47
Arabian Nights '42
Sherlock Holmes: The Voice of
Terror '42

Albert Ray
Undercover Man '36
Dancing Man '33
Shriek in the Night '33
13th Guest '32

Bernard B. Ray
Movie Stuntmen '53
Buffalo Bill Rides Again '47
House of Errors '42
Broken Strings '40
Roamin' Wild '36
Speed Reporter '36
Texas Jack '35
The Silver Bullet '34

Fred Olen Ray
Invisible Dad '97
Night Shade '97
Fugitive Rage '96
Invisible Mom '96
Attack of the 60-Foot Centerfold
'95
Bikini Drive-In '94
Inner Sanctum 2 '94
Wizards of the Demon Sword
'94
Dinosaur Island '93
Mind Twister '93
Possessed by the Night '93
Haunting Fear '91
Inner Sanctum '91
Bad Girls from Mars '90
Evil Toons '90
Mob Boss '90
Spirits '90
Alienator '89
Beverly Hills Vamp '88
Hollywood Chainsaw Hookers
'88
Terminal Force '88
Warlords '88
Commando Squad '87
Cyclone '87
Deep Space '87
Phantom Empire '87
Star Slammer '87
Armed Response '86
Tomb '86
Bio Hazard '85
Alien Dead '79

Nicholas Ray
55 Days at Peking '63
The King of Kings '61
Party Girl '58
Rebel Without a Cause '55
Johnny Guitar '53
The Lusty Men '52
Flying Leathernecks '51
On Dangerous Ground '51
Born to Be Bad '50
In a Lonely Place '50
Knock on Any Door '49
They Live by Night '49
A Woman's Secret '49

Satyajit Ray
The Stranger '92
The Home and the World '84
The Middleman '76
Distant Thunder '73
The Adversary '71
Days and Nights in the Forest
'70
Charulata '64
The Big City '63
Two Daughters '61
Devi '60
The World of Apu '59
Aparajito '58
Jalsaghar '58
Pather Panchali '54

**Herman C.
Raymaker**
The Night Cry '26

Jack Raymond
The Speckled Band '31

Tom Raymonth
Battle of the Eagles '81

Spiro Razatos
Class of 1999 2: The Substitute
'93
Fast Getaway '91

Daniel Reardon
White Cargo '96

Bill Rebane
The Capture of Bigfoot '79
The Alpha Incident '76
The Giant Spider Invasion '75

Ito Rebane
They '77

Robert Rector
Don't Change My World '83

Eric Red
Bad Moon '96
Undertow '95
Body Parts '91
Cohen and Tate '88

Robert Redford
The Horse Whisperer '97
Quiz Show '94
A River Runs Through It '92
The Milagro Beanfield War '88
Ordinary People '80

Carol Reed
Unicorn '83
Oliver! '68
The Agony and the Ecstasy '65
The Key '58
Trapeze '56
The Fallen Idol '49
The Third Man '49
Odd Man Out '47
Immortal Battalion '44
Kipps '41
Night Train to Munich '40
The Stars Look Down '39

James Reed
Mission Phantom '79

Jerry Reed
What Comes Around '85

Joel M. Reed
Night of the Zombies '81
Bloodsucking Freaks '75
G.I. Executioner '71

Luther Reed
Dixiana '30

Roland D. Reed
The House of Secrets '37
Red Lights Ahead '36

Theodore Reed
The Nut '21

William Reed
Scorpion '86

Clive Rees
When the Whales Came '89
Blockhouse '73

Jerry Rees
The Marrying Man '91

Christopher Reeve
In the Gloaming '97

Geoffrey Reeve
Souvenir '88
Caravan to Vaccares '74
Puppet on a Chain '72

Matt Reeves
The Pallbearer '95
Future Shock '93

Michael Reeves
The Conqueror Worm '68
The She-Beast '65

Thomas G. Reeves
Angry Joe Bass '76

Patrick Regan
Kiss Daddy Goodbye '81

Godfrey Reggio
Powaqqatsi: Life in
Transformation '88
Koyaanisqatsi '83

Francisco Regueiro
Padre Nuestro '85

Kelly Reichardt
River of Grass '94

Mark Reichart
Union City '81

Alastair Reid
Nostromo '96
Armistead Maupin's Tales of the
City '93
Teamster Boss: The Jackie
Presser Story '92
Traffik '90
Shattered '72
Baby Love '69

**Dorothy Davenport
Reid**
Sucker Money '34
Linda '29

Max Reid
Wild Thing '87

Tim Reid
Once Upon a Time ... When We
Were Colored '95
The Little Mermaid '78

William Reilly
Men of Respect '91

Carl Reiner
That Old Feeling '96
Fatal Instinct '93
Sibling Rivalry '90
Bert Rigby, You're a Fool '89
Summer School '87
Summer Rental '85
All of Me '84
The Man with Two Brains '83
Dead Men Don't Wear Plaid '82
The Jerk '79
The One and Only '78
Oh, God! '77
Where's Poppa? '70
The Comic '69
Enter Laughing '67

Jeff Reiner
Serpent's Lair '95
Trouble Bound '92
Blood & Concrete: A Love Story
'90

Lucas Reiner
Spirit of '76 '91

Rob Reiner
Ghosts of Mississippi '96
The American President '95
North '94
A Few Good Men '92
Misery '90
When Harry Met Sally... '89
The Princess Bride '87
Stand By Me '86
The Sure Thing '85
This Is Spinal Tap '84

Gottfried Reinhardt
Betrayed '54

John Reinhardt
Open Secret '48

Max Reinhardt
A Midsummer Night's Dream '35

Deborah Reinisch
Caught in the Act '93

Harald Reinl
Fight for Gold '86
Hell Hounds of Alaska '73
The Torture Chamber of Dr.
Sadism '69
The Invisible Dr. Mabuse '62
Forger of London '61
The Return of Dr. Mabuse '61

Irving Reis
Three Husbands '50
The Falcon Takes Over/Strange
Bargain '49
All My Sons '48
The Bachelor and the Bobby-
Soxer '47

Max Dugan Returns '83
I Ought to Be in Pictures '82
Pennies From Heaven '81
Nijinsky '80
California Suite '78
The Goodbye Girl '77
The Turning Point '77
The Seven-Per-Cent Solution '76
Funny Lady '75
The Sunshine Boys '75
The Last of Sheila '73
Play It Again, Sam '72
The Owl and the Pussycat '70
Goodbye, Mr. Chips '69
Goodbye Love '34

Nat Ross
April Fool '26

Neil Rossati
Tides of War '90

Roberto Rossellini
The Messiah '75
Augustine of Hippo '72
Blaise Pascal '71
The Rise of Louis XIV '66
RoGoPaG '62
Vanina Vanini '61
Era Notte a Roma '60
Generale Della Rovere '60
Seven Deadly Sins '53
Voyage in Italy '53
Voyage to Italy '53
Europa '51 '52
The Flowers of St. Francis '50
Stromboli '50
Amore '48
Machine to Kill Bad People '48
The Miracle '48
Deutschland im Jahre Null '47
Paisan '46
Open City '45
Man with a Cross '43

Robert Rossen
Lilith '64
The Hustler '61
They Came to Cordura '59
Island in the Sun '57
Alexander the Great '55
Mambo '55
All the King's Men '49
Body and Soul '47

Franco Rossi
Quo Vadis '85

Arthur Rosson
Boots of Destiny '37
Hidden Gold '33
The Concentratin' Kid '30
Trailing Trouble '30
The Last Outlaw '27

Kaspar Rostrup
Memories of a Marriage '90

Bobby Roth
Keeper of the City '92
The Game of Love '90
The Man Inside '90
Rainbow Drive '90
Dead Solid Perfect '88
Baja Oklahoma '87
Heartbreakers '84
Circle of Power '83
Boss' Son '78

Cy Roth
Fire Maidens from Outer Space '56

Joe Roth
Coupe de Ville '90
Revenge of the Nerds 2: Nerds in Paradise '87
Streets of Gold '86

Lynn Roth
Changing Habits '96

Phillip J. Roth
A.P.E.X. '94
Digital Man '94
Prototype X29A '92
Red Snow '91

Stephanie Rothman
Working Girls '75
Terminal Island '73
Group Marriage '72
The Velvet Vampire '71

The Student Nurses '70
Track of the Vampire '66

William Rotsler
Mantis in Lace '68

Brigitte Rouan
Overseas: Three Women with Man Trouble '90

Jean Rouch
Six in Paris '68
Jaguar '56

Jacques Rouffio
La Passante '83

Raymond Rouleau
The Crucible '57

Russel Rouse
Caper of the Golden Bulls '67
The Oscar '66
Fastest Gun Alive '56
The Thief '52
The Well '51

Gilbert Roussel
Women's Prison Massacre '85

George Rowe
Fatal Mission '89

Peter Rowe
Personal Exemptions '88
Take Two '87
Lost '86

Tom Rowe
Get Rita '75

Richard A. Rowland
Burning Daylight '28

Roy Rowland
Girl Hunters '63
The Seven Hills of Rome '58
Gun Glory '57
Meet Me in Las Vegas '56
Hit the Deck '55
The 5000 Fingers of Dr. T '53
Bugles in the Afternoon '52
Two Weeks with Love '50
Our Vines Have Tender Grapes '45

William Rowland
Flight to Nowhere '46
Follies Girl '43

Christopher Rowley
Soul Patrol '80

Jean-Claude Roy
Deadly Sting '82

Fanchon Royer
Bell Ringer of Antigua '46

Patricia Rozema
When Night Is Falling '95
I've Heard the Mermaids Singing '87

Janosz Rozsa
Sunday Daughters '80

John Ruane
That Eye, the Sky '94
Death in Brunswick '90

Michael Rubbo
The Peanut Butter Solution '85

Andy Ruben
Streets '90

J. Walter Ruben
Java Head '35
Riff Raff '35
Ace of Aces '33

Joseph Ruben
Money Train '95
The Good Son '93
Sleeping with the Enemy '91
True Believer '89
The Stepfather '87
Dreamscape '84
Gorp '80
Joyride '77
Pom Pom Girls '76

Nik Rubenfeld
Alien Private Eye '87

Percival Rubens
Sweet Murder '90
Wild Zone '89
Survival Zone '84
Mr. Kingstreet's War '71

Harold Rubie
Island Trader '71

Howard Rubie
Scalp Merchant '77

Bruce Joel Rubin
My Life '93

Joseph Rubin
The Sister-in-Law '74

Rick Rubin
Tougher than Leather '88

Sergio Rubini
The Station '92

John Rubino
Lotto Land '95

B.A. Rudnick
Expose '97

Alan Rudolph
Afterglow '97
Mrs. Parker and the Vicious Circle '94
Equinox '93
Mortal Thoughts '91
Love at Large '89
The Moderns '88
Made in Heaven '87
Trouble in Mind '86
Choose Me '84
Songwriter '84
Endangered Species '82
Roadie '80
Welcome to L.A. '77
Barn of the Naked Dead '73
Premonition '71

Louis Rudolph
Double Standard '88

Wesley Ruggles
Somewhere I'll Find You '42
Arizona '40
I'm No Angel '33
No Man of Her Own '32
Cimarron '31

Raul Ruiz
Three Lives and Only One Death '96
On Top of the Whale '82
The Hypothesis of the Stolen Painting '78

Craig T. Rumar
Instant Justice '86

Robert Rundle
The Divine Enforcer '91

Katja Rupe
Germany in Autumn '78

Richard Rush
Color of Night '94
The Stunt Man '80
Freebie & the Bean '74
Getting Straight '70
Psych-Out '68
The Savage Seven '68
Hell's Angels on Wheels '67

Chuck Russell
Eraser '96
The Mask '94
The Blob '88
A Nightmare on Elm Street 3: Dream Warriors '87

David O. Russell
Flirting with Disaster '95
Spanking the Monkey '94

Jay Russell
End of the Line '88

Ken Russell
Tales of Erotica '93
Lady Chatterley '92
Prisoner of Honor '91
Whore '91
Women & Men: Stories of Seduction '90
The Rainbow '89
Aria '88
The Lair of the White Worm '88
Salome's Last Dance '88
Gothic '87
Crimes of Passion '84
Altered States '80
Valentino '77
Lisztomania '75

Tommy '75
Mahler '74
Savage Messiah '72
The Boy Friend '71
The Devils '71
The Music Lovers '71
Women in Love '70
Dante's Inferno: Life of Dante Gabriel Rossetti '69

Ray Russell
Zotz! '62

William D. Russell
Best of the Badmen '50
The Green Promise '49

Aaron Russo
Rude Awakening '89

John Russo
Midnight 2: Sex, Death, and Videotape '93
Midnight '81

Mario Russo
The Naked Maja '59

Marti Rustam
Evils of the Night '85

Mark Rutland
Prime Suspect '88

Todd Rutt
Shock! Shock! Shock! '87

Frank Ryan
Can't Help Singing '45
Call Out the Marines '42

Terence Ryan
The Brylcreem Boys '96

Edgar Ryazanov
A Forgotten Tune for the Flute '88
Private Life '82

Mark Rydell
Crime of the Century '96
Intersection '93
For the Boys '91
The River '84
On Golden Pond '81
The Rose '79
Harry & Walter Go to New York '76
Cinderella Liberty '73
The Cowboys '72
The Reivers '69

Renny Rye
Lipstick On Your Collar '94

Stellan Rye
Student of Prague '13

John Ryman
Galaxies Are Colliding '92

Judy Rymer
Who Killed Baby Azaria? '83

Michael Rymer
Angel Baby '95

Paul Sabella
All Dogs Go to Heaven 2 '95

Ira Sachs
The Delta '97

William Sachs
The Last Hour '91
Galaxina '80
Van Nuys Blvd. '79
Incredible Melting Man '77
South of Hell Mountain '70

Daniel Sackheim
The X-Files: Pilot Episode/Deep Throat '93

Alan Sacks
Dubeat-E-O '84

James Sadwith
Sinatra '92
Bluffing It '87

Eddie Saeta
Dr. Death, Seeker of Souls '73

Henri Safran
The Wild Duck '84
Norman Loves Rose '82

Boris Sagal
Masada '81
Angela '77
The Runaway Barge '75

Omega Man '71
Night Gallery '69
Girl Happy '65
Guns of Diablo '64

Leontine Sagan
Maedchen in Uniform '31

Malcolm St. Clair
Bullfighters '45
The Bashful Bachelor '42
The Grand Duchess and the Waiter '26

Christopher St. John
Top of the Heap '72

Gene Saks
Brighton Beach Memoirs '86
Mame '74
Last of the Red Hot Lovers '72
Cactus Flower '69
The Odd Couple '68
Barefoot in the Park '67

Henry Sala
Nightmare Weekend '86

Richard Sale
Abandon Ship '57
Let's Make It Legal '51
Ticket to Tomahawk '50

Leander Sales
Don't Let Your Meat Loaf '95

Sidney Salkow
The Last Man on Earth '64
Twice-Told Tales '63
City Without Men '43

David Salle
Search and Destroy '94

Mikael Salomon
Hard Rain '97
A Far Off Place '93

Victor Salva
Powder '95
Nature of the Beast '94
Clown House '88

Jaime Salvador
Boom in the Moon '46

Gabriele Salvatores
Mediterraneo '91

Emmimo Salvi
Vulcan God of Fire '62

Calogero Salvo
Terranova '91

Hal Salwen
Denise Calls Up '95

Glen Salzman
Rubberface '81

Salvatore Samperi
Ernesto '79
Submission '77
Malicious '74

Keith Samples
A Smile Like Yours '96

Edwards Sampson
The Fast and the Furious '54

Coke Sams
Ernest Goes to School '94

Barry Samson
Hard Way Out: Bloodfist 8 '96
Yesterday's Target '96
The Ice Runner '93
Ice Pawn '92

Stuart Samuels
Visions of Light: The Art of Cinematography '93

Fang Mui San
The Amsterdam Connection '70s

Denis Sanders
Invasion of the Bee Girls '73
One Man's Way '63

Ake Sandgren
The Slingshot '93

Jay Sandrich
For Richer, For Poorer '92
Seems Like Old Times '80

Mark Sandrich
Here Come the Waves '45
So Proudly We Hail '43
Holiday Inn '42

Suzanne Schiffman
Sorceress '88

Lawrence Schiller
Double Jeopardy '92
Double Exposure: The Story of
    Margaret Bourke-White '89
The Executioner's Song '82
Marilyn: The Untold Story '80

Vittorio Schiraldi
Fangs '75

Heinz Schirk
The Wannsee Conference '84

Piero Schivazappa
The Frightened Woman '71

Eric L. Schlagman
Punch the Clock '90

Frieder Schlaich
Halfmoon '95

Thomas Schlamme
Kingfish: A Story of Huey P.
    Long '95
You So Crazy '94
So I Married an Axe Murderer
    '93
Crazy from the Heart '91
Miss Firecracker '89
Spalding Gray: Terrors of
    Pleasure '88

George Schlatter
Norman, Is That You? '76

John Schlesinger
An Eye for an Eye '95
Cold Comfort Farm '94
The Innocent '93
A Question of Attribution '91
Pacific Heights '90
Madame Sousatzka '88
The Believers '87
The Falcon and the Snowman
    '85
An Englishman Abroad '83
Separate Tables '83
Honky Tonk Freeway '81
Yanks '79
Marathon Man '76
The Day of the Locust '75
Sunday, Bloody Sunday '71
Midnight Cowboy '69
Far from the Madding Crowd '67
Darling '65
Billy Liar '63
A Kind of Loving '62

Volker Schlondorff
Palmetto '98
Murder on the Bayou '91
Voyager '91
The Handmaid's Tale '90
Death of a Salesman '86
Swann in Love '84
The Tin Drum '79
Coup de Grace '78
Germany in Autumn '78
The Lost Honor of Katharina
    Blum '75
An Occurrence at Owl Creek
    Bridge/Coup de Grace '62

**Jay Schlossberg-
Cohen**
Night Train to Terror '84

Daniel Schmid
Shadow of Angels '76

Rick Schmidt
A Man, a Woman and a Killer

Thomas J. Schmidt
Girls on the Road '73

David Schmoeller
The Arrival '90
Curse 4: The Ultimate Sacrifice
    '90
Netherworld '90
Catacombs '89
Puppet Master '89
Crawlspace '86
The Seduction '82
Tourist Trap '79

Julian Schnabel
Basquiat '96

Paul Schneider
Daniel and the Towers '90s

Honor Thy Father and Mother:
    The True Story of the
    Menendez Brothers '94
Babycakes '89
Something Special '86

**Robert Allen
Schnitzer**
Kandyland '87
The Premonition '75

**Ernest B.
Schoedsack**
Mighty Joe Young '49
Dr. Cyclops '40
Last Days of Pompeii '35
King Kong '33
Son of Kong '33
The Most Dangerous Game '32
Chang: A Drama of the
    Wilderness '27

**Pierre
Schoendoerffer**
Le Crabe Tambour '77
The 317th Platoon '65

Jan Scholtz
Emissary '92

Skip Schoolnik
Hide and Go Shriek '87

Renen Schorr
Late Summer Blues '87

Dale Schott
The Care Bears Movie 2: A New
    Generation '86

Leonard Schrader
Naked Tango '91

Paul Schrader
Touch '96
Witch Hunt '94
Light Sleeper '92
The Comfort of Strangers '91
Patty Hearst '88
Light of Day '87
Mishima: A Life in Four Chapters
    '85
Cat People '82
American Gigolo '79
Hardcore '79
Blue Collar '78

Myrl A. Schreibman
Liberty & Bash '90
Angel of H.E.A.T. '82

William Schreiner
A Sinful Life '89

John F. Schreyer
Naked Youth '59

Barbet Schroeder
Desperate Measures '98
Before and After '95
Kiss of Death '94
Single White Female '92
Reversal of Fortune '90
Barfly '87
Tricheurs '84
Maitresse '77
The Valley Obscured by the
    Clouds '72
More '69

Frank C. Schroeder
Pistol: The Birth of a Legend '90

Michael Schroeder
The Glass Cage '96
Cover Me '95
Cyborg 3: The Recycler '95
Mortuary Academy '91
Relentless 2: Dead On '91
Damned River '89
Out of the Dark '88

Peter Schubert
Germany in Autumn '78

Tom Schulman
8 Heads in a Duffel Bag '96

Patrick Schulmann
Et La Tenoresse?...Bordell '84
Rendez-Moi Ma Peau '81

Carl Schultz
Deadly Currents '93
Which Way Home '90
The Seventh Sign '88

Travelling North '87
Careful, He Might Hear You '84
Blue Fin '78

Michael A. Schultz
The Great American Sex
    Scandal '94
Livin' Large '91
For Us, the Living '88
Disorderlies '87
Timestalkers '87
Krush Groove '85
The Last Dragon '85
Three Days in Beirut '83
Carbon Copy '81
Scavenger Hunt '79
Sgt. Pepper's Lonely Hearts
    Club Band '78
Greased Lightning '77
Which Way Is Up? '77
Car Wash '76
Cooley High '75
Honeybaby '74

Bob Schulz
Robbers of the Sacred Mountain
    '83

Douglas Schulze
Hellmaster '92

Joel Schumacher
Batman and Robin '97
A Time to Kill '96
Batman Forever '95
The Client '94
Falling Down '93
Dying Young '91
Flatliners '90
Cousins '89
The Lost Boys '87
St. Elmo's Fire '85
D.C. Cab '84
The Incredible Shrinking Woman
    '81
The Virginia Hill Story '76

Phillip Schuman
Jailbird Rock '88

Reinhold Schunzel
Balalaika '39
Fortune's Fool '21

Harold Schuster
Black Beauty/Courage of Black
    Beauty '57
Courage of Black Beauty '57
The Finger Man '55
Kid Monk Baroni '52
So Dear to My Heart '49
The Tender Years '47
Breakfast in Hollywood '46
Marine Raiders '43
My Friend Flicka '43
Dinner at the Ritz '37
Wings of the Morning '37

Jan Schutte
Drachenfutter '87

Douglas Schwartz
Baywatch the Movie: Forbidden
    Paradise '95
Thunder in Paradise 2 '94
Thunder in Paradise '93
Peacekillers '71

Maurice Schwartz
Tevye '39

Stefan Schwartz
Shooting Fish '98

**Arnold
Schwarzenegger**
Christmas in Connecticut '92
Tales from the Crypt, Vol. 3 '90

Ettore Scola
The Family '87
Macaroni '85
La Nuit de Varennes '82
Le Bal '82
Passion of Love '82
A Special Day '77
We All Loved Each Other So
    Much '77
Down & Dirty '76

Martin Scorsese
Italianamerican/The Big Shave
Kundun '97
Casino '95

The Age of Innocence '93
Cape Fear '91
Goodfellas '90
New York Stories '89
The Last Temptation of Christ
    '88
The Color of Money '86
After Hours '85
King of Comedy '82
Raging Bull '80
The Last Waltz '78
New York, New York '77
Taxi Driver '76
Alice Doesn't Live Here
    Anymore '74
Mean Streets '73
Boxcar Bertha '72
Who's That Knocking at My
    Door? '68

Campbell Scott
Big Night '95

Cynthia Scott
Strangers in Good Company '91

Darin Scott
Caught Up '98

George C. Scott
Descending Angel '90
Don't Look Back: The Story of
    Leroy "Satchel" Paige '81
Savage Is Loose '74
Rage '72
The Andersonville Trial '70

James Scott
Strike It Rich '90

Michael Scott
Heck's Way Home '95
Sharon's Secret '95
Dangerous Heart '93
Ladykiller '92

Oz Scott
Bustin' Loose '81

Peter Graham Scott
Subterfuge '68

Ridley Scott
G.I. Jane '97
White Squall '96
1492: Conquest of Paradise '92
Thelma & Louise '91
Black Rain '89
Someone to Watch Over Me '87
Legend '86
Blade Runner '82
Alien '79
The Duellists '77

Robert Scott
The Video Dead '87

T.J. Scott
Young Hercules '97
TC 2000 '93

Tony Scott
The Fan '96
Crimson Tide '95
True Romance '93
The Last Boy Scout '91
Days of Thunder '90
Revenge '90
Beverly Hills Cop 2 '87
Top Gun '86
The Hunger '83

Aubrey Scotto
Uncle Moses '32

George Scribner
Oliver & Company '88

Sandra Seacat
In the Spirit '90

Steven Seagal
On Deadly Ground '94

James Seale
Asylum '97

John Seale
Till There was You '91

Francis Searle
Profile '54
Someone at the Door '50
Things Happen at Night '48
A Girl in a Million '46

Fred F. Sears
The Giant Claw '57

Earth vs. the Flying Saucers '56
Teenage Crime Wave '55
Ambush at Tomahawk Gap '53
Bonanza Town '51

Victor Sears
Ninja the Battalion '90
Ninja's Extreme Weapons '90

George Seaton
Showdown '73
Airport '70
The Counterfeit Traitor '62
Teacher's Pet '58
Country Girl '54
The Big Lift '50
Miracle on 34th Street '47

Beverly Sebastian
Running Cool '93
The American Angels: Baptism
    of Blood '89
Gator Bait 2: Cajun Justice '88
Delta Fox '77
Gator Bait '73

Ferd Sebastian
Running Cool '93
The American Angels: Baptism
    of Blood '89
Gator Bait 2: Cajun Justice '88
Rocktober Blood '85
On the Air Live with Captain
    Midnight '79
Delta Fox '77
Flash & Firecat '75
Gator Bait '73
Hitchhikers '72

Gregg Sebelious
The Day the Earth Froze '59

David Secter
Feelin' Up '76

Mike Sedan
Lap Dancing '95
Married People, Single Sex 2:
    For Better or Worse '94
Night Fire '94
Married People, Single Sex '93

Edward Sedgwick
Ma and Pa Kettle Back On the
    Farm '51
A Southern Yankee '48
Air Raid Wardens '43
The Gladiator '38
Fit for a King '37
Pick a Star '37
Riding on Air '37
What! No Beer? '33
Speak Easily '32
Parlor, Bedroom and Bath '31
Doughboys '30
Free and Easy '30
Spite Marriage '29
The Cameraman '28

Jakov Sedlar
Gospa '94

John Sedwick
Dark Shadows '67

Paul Seed
The Affair '95
To Play the King '93
Dead Ahead: The Exxon Valdez
    Disaster '92

Charles Seeling
Rounding Up the Law '22

Steven Seemayer
Miami Vendetta '87

Alex Segal
The Story of David '76

Peter Segal
My Fellow Americans '96
Tommy Boy '95
Naked Gun 33 1/3: The Final
    Insult '94

Stu Segall
Illegal in Blue '95
Drive-In Massacre '74

Peter Sehr
Kaspar Hauser '93

**Arthur Allan
Seidelman**
The Summer of Ben Tyler '96
Harvest of Fire '95

Till *cont.*

Buffalo Jump '90
Bridge to Terabithia '85
A Case of Libel '83
If You Could See What I Hear '82
Improper Channels '82
An American Christmas Carol '79
Mary and Joseph: A Story of Faith '79
Wild Horse Hank '79
Bethune '77
Hot Millions '68

George Tillman, Jr.
Soul Food '97

R.L. Tillmanns
Witchcraft 3: The Kiss of Death '90

Bruce W. Timm
Batman: Mask of the Phantasm '93

James Tinling
Tales of Robin Hood '52

Robert Tinnell
Frankenstein and Me '96
Kids of the Round Table '96

George Tirl
Pay Off '89

Douglas Tirola
A Reason to Believe '95

Stacy Title
The Last Supper '96

Moufida Tlatli
The Silences of the Palace '94

Johnny To
The Heroic Trio '93

James Toback
Two Girls and a Guy '98
The Pick-Up Artist '87
Exposed '83
Fingers '78

Marice Tobias
Pulsebeat '85

Ricardo Tognazzi
La Scorta '94

Norman Tokar
Candleshoe '78
The Cat from Outer Space '78
No Deposit, No Return '76
The Apple Dumpling Gang '75
Where the Red Fern Grows '74
Snowball Express '72
The Boatniks '70
The Horse in the Gray Flannel Suit '68
The Happiest Millionaire '67
Follow Me, Boys! '66
Those Calloways '65
The Ugly Dachshund '65
A Tiger Walks '64
Savage Sam '63
Big Red '62
Sammy, the Way-Out Seal '62

Sergio Toledo
One Man's War '90

Michael Tolkin
The New Age '94
The Rapture '91

Stephen Tolkin
Daybreak '93
Stephen King's Golden Years '91

Stanley Tong
Mr. Magoo '97
Jackie Chan's First Strike '96
Rumble in the Bronx '96
Supercop '92

Wilson Tong
Two Wondrous Tigers '79

Tom Topor
Judgment '90

Ralph Toporoff
American Blue Note '89

Burt Topper
Soul Hustler '76
The Hard Ride '71
The Strangler '64
Tank Commando '59
Hell Squad '58
Suicide Battalion/Hell Squad '58

Rip Torn
The Telephone '87

Giuseppe Tornatore
The Star Maker '95
A Pure Formality '94
Everybody's Fine '90
Cinema Paradiso '88

Joe Tornatore
Curse of the Crystal Eye '93
Grotesque '87
Code Name: Zebra '84
Zebra Force '76

Robert Torrance
Mutant on the Bounty '89

Fina Torres
Celestial Clockwork '94
Oriane '85

Gabe Torres
December '91

Miguel Contreras Torres
Pancho Villa Returns '50

Cinzia Torrini
Hotel Colonial '88

Ivan Tors
Zebra in the Kitchen '65

Peter Tors
Looking for Trouble '96

Bruce Toscano
The Jar '84

Robert Totten
Dark Before Dawn '89
The Sacketts '79
Pony Express Rider '76
The Red Pony '76
Huckleberry Finn '75
The Wild Country '71

Mikhail Toumanichulli
Solo Voyage: The Revenge '86

Jacques Tourneur
The Comedy of Terrors '64
The Giant of Marathon '60
Curse of the Demon '57
Great Day in the Morning '56
Nightfall '56
Appointment in Honduras '53
The Flame & the Arrow '50
Stars in My Crown '50
Easy Living '49
Berlin Express '48
Out of the Past '47
Canyon Passage '46
Experiment Perilous '45
Days of Glory '43
I Walked with a Zombie '43
The Leopard Man '43
Cat People '42

Maurice Tourneur
Volpone '39
Lorna Doone '22
The Last of the Mohicans '20
Pride of the Clan '18
A Girl's Folly '17
A Poor Little Rich Girl '17
Trilby '17
The Wishing Ring '14

Robert Towne
Without Limits '97
Tequila Sunrise '88
Personal Best '82

Bud Townsend
Coach '78
Terror at Red Wolf Inn '72
Nightmare in Wax '69

Patrice Townsend
Beach Girls '82

Robert Townsend
B.A.P.'s '97
The Meteor Man '93

The Five Heartbeats '91
Eddie Murphy: Raw '87
Hollywood Shuffle '87

Wendy Toye
Three Cases of Murder '55

Ian Toynton
The Maid '90

Shiro Toyoda
Snow Country '57
Mistress '53

Benno Trachtmann
The Jumper '85

Jean-Claude Tramont
As Summers Die '86
All Night Long '81

Alfred Travers
Dual Alibi '47

Bill Travers
Christian the Lion '76

Joey Travolta
Navajo Blues '97
Hard Vice '94

Stephen Traxler
Slithis '78

Peter S. Traynor
Seducers '77

Brian Trenchard-Smith
Escape Clause '96
Leprechaun 4: In Space '96
Leprechaun 3 '95
Night of the Demons 2 '94
Official Denial '93
The Siege of Firebase Gloria '89
Day of the Panther '88
Out of the Body '88
Fists of Blood '87
Dead End Drive-In '86
The Quest '86
BMX Bandits '83
Day of the Assassin '81
Escape 2000 '81
Deathcheaters '76

John Trent
Vengeance Is Mine '84
Best Revenge '83
Middle Age Crazy '80
Crossbar '79
Find the Lady '75
The Bushbaby '70

Georg Tressler
Teenage Wolfpack '57

Blair Treu
The Paper Brigade '96

Monika Treut
Erotique '94
My Father Is Coming '91
Seduction: The Cruel Woman '89
Virgin Machine '88

Dale Trevillion
One Man Force '89
Las Vegas Weekend '85

Gus Trikonis
The Rumor Mill '86
Love on the Run '85
Jungle Heat '84
Dempsey '83
First Affair '83
Miss All-American Beauty '82
Take This Job & Shove It '81
Twirl '81
Touched by Love '80
She's Dressed to Kill '79
The Evil '78
Moonshine County Express '77
Nashville Girl '76

Nadine Trintignant
Next Summer '84

Mike Tristano
Warrior of Justice '96

Victor Trivas
The Head '59

Bryan Trizers
PSI Factor '80

Rose Troche
Go Fish '94

Jan Troell
Hamsun '96
Flight of the Eagle '82
Hurricane '79
Zandy's Bride '74
The New Land '73
The Emigrants '72

Tzipi Trope
Tell Me That You Love Me '84

Gary Trousdale
The Hunchback of Notre Dame '96
Beauty and the Beast '91

Gary A. Troy
Computer Beach Party '88

Fernando Trueba
Two Much '96
Belle Epoque '92
Twisted Obsession '90

Francois Truffaut
Confidentially Yours '83
The Woman Next Door '81
The Last Metro '80
The Green Room '78
Love on the Run '78
The Man Who Loved Women '77
Small Change '76
Story of Adele H. '75
Day for Night '73
Two English Girls '72
The Wild Child '70
Mississippi Mermaid '69
The Bride Wore Black '68
Stolen Kisses '68
Fahrenheit 451 '66
The Soft Skin '64
Jules and Jim '62
Shoot the Piano Player '62
The 400 Blows '59
Les Mistons '57

Michael Truman
Koroshi '66

Dalton Trumbo
Johnny Got His Gun '71

Douglas Trumbull
Brainstorm '83
Silent Running '71

Glenn Tryon
Beauty for the Asking '39
Law West of Tombstone '38
Small Town Boy '37

Manolis Tsafos
Rip-Off '77

Chan Tsi-liang
Lai Shi: China's Last Eunuch '88

Shinya Tsukamoto
Tetsuo 2: Body Hammer '97
Tetsuo: The Iron Man '92

Slava Tsukerman
Liquid Sky '83

Stanley Tucci
Big Night '95

Michael Tuchner
Rainbow Warrior '94
Firestorm: 72 Hours in Oakland '93
The Misadventures of Mr. Wilt '90
Mistress '87
Trapped in Silence '86
Amos '85
Not My Kid '85
Adam '83
Trenchcoat '83
The Hunchback of Notre Dame '82
The Summer of My German Soldier '78
The Old Curiosity Shop '75

Anand Tucker
Saint-Ex: The Story of the Storyteller '95

David Tucker
Bramwell '95
A Year in Provence '89

George Tucker
Traffic in Souls '13

James Tucker
Steps from Hell '92
Lunatic '91

Phil Tucker
Dance Hall Racket '58
Robot Monster '53

Roger Tucker
Deadly Recruits '86

Richard Tuggle
Out of Bounds '86
Tightrope '84

Montgomery Tully
Battle Beneath the Earth '68
The Terrornauts '67
Dead Lucky '60
The House in Marsh Road '60
Strange Awakening '58
The Electronic Monster '57
The Key Man '57
The Way Out '56
Glass Tomb '55
Paid to Kill '54

Ching Siu Tung
The Executioners '93
The Heroic Trio '93

Sandy Tung
Across the Tracks '89

Gary J. Tunnicliffe
Within the Rock '96

Saul J. Turell
The Love Goddesses '65

Sophia Turkiewicz
Silver City '84

Rosemarie Turko
Scarred '84
Dungeonmaster '83

Zygmund Turkow
The Jolly Paupers '38

Lawrence Turman
Second Thoughts '83

Ann Turner
Celia: Child Of Terror '89

Chester Turner
Black Devil Doll from Hell '84

Clive Turner
The Howling: New Moon Rising '95

Paul Turner
Hedd Wyn '92

Robert Turner
Digger '94

Jon Turteltaub
Phenomenon '96
While You Were Sleeping '95
Cool Runnings '93
3 Ninjas '92
Driving Me Crazy '91

John Turturro
Mac '93

Frank Tuttle
Hell on Frisco Bay '55
This Gun for Hire '42
Waikiki Wedding '37
Roman Scandals '33
Love 'Em and Leave 'Em '26
Lucky Devil '25

Derek Twist
Green Grow the Rushes '51

David N. Twohy
The Arrival '96
Grand Tour: Disaster in Time '92

Tomu Uchida
Swords of Death '71

Seiichiro Uchikawa
One-Eyed Swordsman '63

Liv Ullmann
Sofie '92

Juanma Bajo Ulloa
Butterfly Wings '91

Edgar G. Ulmer
Journey Beneath the Desert '61

The Amazing Transparent Man '60
Beyond the Time Barrier '60
Naked Venus '58
The Daughter of Dr. Jekyll '57
St. Benny the Dip '51
Club Havana '46
Detour '46
The Strange Woman '46
Strange Illusion '45
Bluebeard '44
Girls in Chains '43
Isle of Forgotten Sins '43
Jive Junction '43
American Matchmaker '40
The Light Ahead '39
Moon over Harlem '39
The Singing Blacksmith '38
The Black Cat '34
Thunder Over Texas '34

Ron Underwood
Speechless '94
Heart and Souls '93
City Slickers '91
Tremors '89

Lawrence Unger
Novel Desires '92

Michael Toshiyuki Uno
The Road to Galveston '96
Blind Spot '93
Without Warning: The James Brady Story '91
The Wash '88

Jeff Ureles
Cheap Shots '91

Frank Urson
The Night Club '25

Chano Urueto
The Witch's Mirror '60
The Living Head '59

Peter Ustinov
Hammersmith Is Out '72
Lady L '65
Billy Budd '62

Jamie Uys
The Gods Must Be Crazy 2 '89
The Gods Must Be Crazy '84
Dingaka '65

Jack Vacek
Rock House '92

Roger Vadim
And God Created Woman '88
Game of Seduction '82
Beauty and the Beast '83
Night Games '80
Barbarella '68
Spirits of the Dead '68
The Game Is Over '66
Circle of Love '64
Le Repos du Guerrier '62
Blood and Roses '61
Dangerous Liaisons '60
And God Created Woman '57

Steve Vagnino
A Pleasure Doing Business '79

Ladislao Vajda
The Man Who Wagged His Tail '57
The Miracle of Marcelino '55

Luis Valdez
The Cisco Kid '94
La Bamba '87
Zoot Suit '81

Frank Valenti
Delta Force Commando 2 '90
War Bus Commando '89

Jon Valentine
Night of the Living Babes '87

Jean Valere
Time Out for Love '61

Tonino Valerii
My Name Is Nobody '74
A Reason to Live, a Reason to Die '73

Jean-Marc Vallee
Los Locos Posse '97

Nick Vallelonga
In the Kingdom of the Blind the Man with One Eye Is King '94
A Brilliant Disguise '93

Robert Van Ackeren
A Woman in Flames '84

Jean-Claude Van Damme
The Quest '96

Rudolf Van Den Berg
Cold Light of Day '95

Mike van Diem
Character '97

Jaco Van Dormael
The Eighth Day '95
Toto le Heros '91

Bruce Van Dusen
Cold Feet '84

Woodbridge S. Van Dyke
Cairo '42
I Married an Angel '42
Journey for Margaret '42
Shadow of the Thin Man '41
Bitter Sweet '40
I Love You Again '40
Andy Hardy Gets Spring Fever '39
Another Thin Man '39
Marie Antoinette '38
Rosalie '38
Sweethearts '38
Personal Property '37
After the Thin Man '36
Love on the Run '36
Rose Marie '36
San Francisco '36
Forsaking All Others '35
I Live My Life '35
Naughty Marietta '35
Hide-Out '34
Manhattan Melodrama '34
The Thin Man '34
Penthouse '33
The Prizefighter and the Lady '33
Tarzan, the Ape Man '32
Trader Horn '31
White Shadows in the South Seas '29

Theo van Gogh
1-900 '94

Ruud Van Hemert
Army Brats '84

Buddy Van Horn
Pink Cadillac '89
The Dead Pool '88
Any Which Way You Can '80

Hugo Van Lawick
The Leopard Son '96

Mario Van Peebles
Gang in Blue '96
Panther '95
Posse '93
New Jack City '91

Melvin Van Peebles
Gang in Blue '96
Tales of Erotica '93
Identity Crisis '90
Sweet Sweetback's Baadasssss Song '71
Watermelon Man '70
The Story of a Three Day Pass '68

Gus Van Sant
Good Will Hunting '97
To Die For '95
Even Cowgirls Get the Blues '94
My Own Private Idaho '91
Drugstore Cowboy '89

Sterling Van Wagenen
Alan & Naomi '92

Joseph Van Winkle
The Woman Inside '83

Eric Van Zuylen
In for Treatment '82

Florestano Vancini
That Long Night in '43 '60

William Vanderkloot
Dead Aim '87

Norman Thaddeus Vane
Taxi Dancers '93
Midnight '89
Club Life '86
The Black Room '82
Frightmare '81

Carlo Vanzina
Millions '91
My Wonderful Life '90
Dagger Eyes '80s
The Gamble '88
Nothing Underneath '85

Agnes Varda
Jacquot '91
Le Petit Amour '87
Vagabond '85
One Sings, the Other Doesn't '77
Le Bonheur '65
Cleo from 5 to 7 '61

Mike Vardy
The Final Cut '95

Marcel Varnel
Oh, Mr. Porter '37
Chandu the Magician '32

Henri Vart
Secret Obsession '88

Gregory Vasiliev
Chapayev '34

Sergei Vasiliev
Chapayev '34

Joseph B. Vasquez
Manhattan Merenquel '95
Street Hitz '92
Hangin' with the Homeboys '91
The Bronx War '90

Bruno Ve Sota
The Brain Eaters '58
The Female Jungle '56

Francis Veber
Out on a Limb '92
Three Fugitives '89
Les Comperes '83
La Chevre '81

Pastor Vega
Portrait of Teresa '79

Carlos Velo
Torero '56

Danny Vendramini
Desperate Prey '94

Louis Venosta
Kisses in the Dark '97

Itsvan Ventilla
Nicole '72

Gore Verbinski
Mouse Hunt '97

Ben Verbong
Lily Was Here '89

Carlo Verdone
Acqua e Sapone '83

Pat Verducci
True Crime '95

Enrique Vergara
The Snake People '68

Jan Verheyen
The Little Death '95

Michael Verhoeven
The Nasty Girl '90
Killing Cars '85
The White Rose '83

Paul Verhoeven
Starship Troopers '97
Showgirls '95
Basic Instinct '92
Total Recall '90
RoboCop '87
Flesh and Blood '85
Spetters '80
The 4th Man '79
Soldier of Orange '78

Keetje Tippel '75
Turkish Delights '73
The Eternal Waltz '54

Henri Verneuil
Night Flight from Moscow '73
The Big Grab '63
Melodie en Sous-Sol '63
Un Singe en Hiver '62
Just Another Pretty Face '58
The Sheep Has Five Legs '54
Forbidden Fruit '52

Henry Vernon
Danger Zone '87

Richard Vernon
The Shadow Man '53

Stephen Verona
Talking Walls '85
Pipe Dreams '76
The Lords of Flatbush '74

Todd Verow
Frisk '95

Wim Verstappen
Fatal Error '83

Dziga Vertov
Kino Pravda/Enthusiasm '31
The Man with a Movie Camera '29

Robert Veze
Bikini Summer '91

Michael Vianey
Special Police '85

Marco Vicario
Wifemistress '79
The Sensual Man '74

Lindsey C. Vickers
The Appointment '82

Edward Victor
Alley Cat '84

Alberto Vidaurri
Stormy Nights '97

Steven Vidler
Blackrock '97

Charles Vidor
Song Without End '60
The Swan '56
Love Me or Leave Me '55
Rhapsody '54
Hans Christian Andersen '52
The Loves of Carmen '48
Gilda '46
A Song to Remember '45
Cover Girl '44
The Desperadoes '43
The Tuttles of Tahiti '42
The Lady in Question '40

King Vidor
Solomon and Sheba '59
War and Peace '56
Man Without a Star '55
Ruby Gentry '52
Beyond the Forest '49
The Fountainhead '49
Duel in the Sun '46
Comrade X '40
Northwest Passage '40
The Citadel '38
Stella Dallas '37
The Texas Rangers '36
Our Daily Bread '34
Bird of Paradise '32
The Champ '32
Street Scene '31
Hallelujah! '29
The Crowd '28
Show People '28
The Big Parade '25
Peg O' My Heart '22
The Sky Pilot '21
The Jack Knife Man '20

Berthold Viertel
The Passing of the Third Floor Back '36
Rhodes '36

Emilio Vieyra
The Curious Dr. Humpp '70

Daniel Vigne
One Woman or Two '85
The Return of Martin Guerre '83

Robert G. Vignola
The Scarlet Letter '34

Jean Vigo
L'Atalante '34
Zero for Conduct '33
A Propos de Nice '29

Camilo Vila
Options '88
The Unholy '88

Felix Vilars
Devil Woman '76

Ray Villalobos
Hollywood Confidential '97

Reynaldo Villalobos
Conagher '91

Agustin Villaronga
In a Glass Cage '86

Joseph Vilsmaier
Brother of Sleep '95
Stalingrad '94

Christian Vincent
The Separation '94
La Discrete '90

Chuck Vincent
Enrapture '90
Wildest Dreams '90
Bedroom Eyes 2 '89
Cleo/Leo '89
Party Incorporated '89
Young Nurses in Love '89
Sexpot '88
Student Affairs '88
Thrilled to Death '88
A Woman Obsessed '88
Deranged '87
New York's Finest '87
Sensations '87
Slammer Girls '87
Wimps '87
If Looks Could Kill '86
Hollywood Hot Tubs '84
C.O.D. '83
Preppies '82
Hot T-Shirts '79
A Matter of Love '78
American Tickler '76

Harry Vincent
She Came on the Bus '69

Jerry Vint
Another Chance '88

Will Vinton
The Adventures of Mark Twain '85

Albert T. Viola
Preacherman '83
Cry of the Penguins '71

Joe Viola
Hot Box '72
Angels Hard as They Come '71

Clement Virgo
Rude '96

Luchino Visconti
The Innocent '76
Conversation Piece '75
Ludwig '72
Death in Venice '71
The Damned '69
Sandra of a Thousand Delights '65
Boccaccio '70 '62
Rocco and His Brothers '60
White Nights '57
Senso '54
Bellissima '51
La Terra Trema '48
Ossessione '42

Tony Vitale
Kiss Me, Guido '97

Laszlo Vitezy
Red Earth

Joseph Vittorie
The Criminal Mind '93

Piero Vivarelli
Satanik '69

Virgil W. Vogel
Walker: Texas Ranger: One Riot, One Ranger '93

The **Writer Index** provides a videography for any writer with a video credit. The listings for the writer names follow an alphabetical sort by last name (although the names appear in a first name last name format). The videographies are listed chronologically, from most recent film to their first. If a writer wrote (or script doctored) more than one film in the same year, these movies are listed alphabetically within the year. Used in conjunction with the **Cast** index, this index will let you find actors and actresses who wrote themselves juicy parts (with varying degrees of success). Directors also tend to show up here, either before their directorial ambitions surfaced, or after they'd gained enough clout to get one of their scripts to the screen.

Dough Aarniokoski
Puppet Master 4 '93

Paul Aaron
Laurel Avenue '93
Octagon '80

Paul Abbott
Reckless '97

Scott Abbott
Breach of Conduct '94

Lewis Abernathy
Deepstar Six '89

Anthony Able
Project: Alien '89

Jim Abrahams
Hot Shots! Part Deux '93
Hot Shots! '91
The Naked Gun: From the Files of Police Squad '88
Top Secret! '84
Police Squad! Help Wanted! '82
Airplane! '80
Kentucky Fried Movie '77

Jerry Abrahamson
Wagons East '94

Jack Abramoff
Red Scorpion '89

Robert Abramoff
Red Scorpion '89

Celia Abrams
Easy Wheels '89

Ian Abrams
Undercover Blues '93

Jeffrey Abrams
Gone Fishin' '97
Forever Young '92
Regarding Henry '91
Taking Care of Business '90

Tom Abrams
The Desperate Trail '94

Jon Acevski
Freddie the Frog '92

Jovan Acin
Hey, Babu Riba '88

Rodney Ackland
Thursday's Child '43
The Forty-Ninth Parallel '41

Allen Actor
Dungeonmaster '83
Terror at Red Wolf Inn '72

Alfred Adam
Belle Americaine '61

Catlin Adams
Sticky Fingers '88

Daniel Adams
Primary Motive '92
A Fool and His Money '88

Gerald Drayson Adams
Duel at Silver Creek '52
Flame of Araby '51

Mikhaila Max Adams
Excess Baggage '96

Richard DeLong Adams
Our Mother's Murder '97

Ewart Adamson
Circumstantial Evidence '35

Richard Adcock
Hyper-Sapien: People from Another Star '86

Alan J. Adler
Metalstorm: The Destruction of Jared Syn '83
The Concrete Jungle '82
Parasite '82
The Alchemist '81

Gilbert Adler
Tales from the Crypt Presents Bordello of Blood '96
Children of the Corn 2: The Final Sacrifice '92

Eleonore Adlon
Rosalie Goes Shopping '89
Bagdad Cafe '88

Felix Adlon
Younger & Younger '94
Salmonberries '91

Percy Adlon
Younger & Younger '94
Salmonberries '91
Rosalie Goes Shopping '89
Bagdad Cafe '88
Sugarbaby '85
Celeste '81

Nelly Adnil
Silent Victim '92

Gilles Adrien
The City of Lost Children '95
Delicatessen '92

Ben Affleck
Good Will Hunting '97

James Agee
The Night of the Hunter '55
The African Queen '51

Gabriel Aghion
Pedale Douce '96

Faruque Ahmed
Warlords 3000 '93

Kamal Ahmed
The Jerky Boys '95

Chantal Akerman
A Couch in New York '95
Night and Day '91
Window Shopping '86
The Eighties '83
Les Rendez-vous D'Anna '78
News from Home '76

Andra Akers
Toute Une Nuit '82

William M. Akers
Ernest Rides Again '93

Norman Aladjem
Firewalker '86

Jordan Alan
Terminal Bliss '91

Jeff Albert
Warhead '96
Danger Zone '95
Live Wire: Human Timebomb '95
Terminal Impact '95
Never Say Die '94

Marvin H. Albert
Rough Night in Jericho '67

Luis Alcoriza
Death in the Garden '56
El '52

Alan Alda
Betsy's Wedding '90
A New Life '88
Sweet Liberty '86
The Four Seasons '81
The Seduction of Joe Tynan '79

Robert Alden
Uncaged '91
Streetwalkin' '85

Steve Alden
Fall Time '94

Phillip Alderton
The Expendables '89

Will Aldis
Clifford '92
Stealing Home '88
The Couch Trip '87
Back to School '86

David Alexander
Dead Ahead '96

Kurt Alexander
De Mayerling a Sarajevo '40

Ronald Alexander
Billie '65

Scott Alexander
The People vs. Larry Flynt '96
That Darn Cat '96
Ed Wood '94
Problem Child 2 '91
Problem Child '90

Scott Lawrence Alexander
Spaced Invaders '90

Danielle Alexandra
G.I. Jane '97

Michel Alexandre
L.627 '92

Sherman Alexie
Smoke Signals '98

Richard Alfieri
Harvest of Fire '95
A Friendship in Vienna '88
Echoes '83
Children of Rage '75

Dan Algrant
Naked in New York '93

Arif Aliev
Prisoner of the Mountains '96

Ranald Allan
The Crossing '92

Ted Allan
Dr. Bethune '90
Love Streams '84
Falling in Love Again '80
Lies My Father Told Me '75

Pat Allee
Bums '93

Chris Allen
The Last Remake of Beau Geste '77

Corey Allen
Avalanche '78

Curt Allen
Alligator 2: The Mutation '90
Blind Vengeance '90
Bloodstone '88
Hollywood Harry '86
Walking the Edge '83

Irwin Allen
Five Weeks in a Balloon '62
Voyage to the Bottom of the Sea '61

Janis Allen
The Double Negative '80
Meatballs '79

Jay Presson Allen
Year of the Gun '91
Deathtrap '82
Prince of the City '81
Just Tell Me What You Want '80
Funny Lady '75
Forty Carats '73
Cabaret '72
Travels with My Aunt '72

Carlo Liconti
Goodnight, Michelangelo '89

Alice Liddle
Permanent Record '88

Jeff Lieberman
Blue Sunshine '78
Squirm '76

Robert Liebmann
The Blue Angel '30

Jimmy Lifton
Phoenix '95
Mirror, Mirror 2: Raven Dance '94

Walter Lima, Jr.
The Dolphin '87

Kevin J. Lindenmuth
The Alien Agenda: Out of the Darkness '96

Howard Lindsay
A Woman's World '54

Michael Lindsay-Hogg
The Object of Beauty '91

Jonnie Lindsell
I Don't Buy Kisses Anymore '92

Jon Lindstrom
Dreaming of Rita '94

Graham Linehan
The Matchmaker '97

Eugene Ling
Lost Boundaries '49

Caroline Link
Beyond Silence '96

William Link
Vanishing Act '88
Rollercoaster '77
The Execution of Private Slovik '74
Columbo: Prescription Murder '67

Richard Linklater
Before Sunrise '94
Dazed and Confused '93
Slacker '91

Eugene Lipinski
Perfectly Normal '91

William R. Lipman
The Texas Rangers Ride Again '40

Jeremy Lipp
The P.O.W. Escape '86

Ken Lipper
City Hall '95

W.P. Lipscomb
Beware of Pity '46
Pygmalion '38
A Tale of Two Cities '36
Les Miserables '35

Shelley List
And Baby Makes Six '79

Stephen Lister
Monolith '93

Robert Littell
The Amateur '82

Ezra Litwack
The Butcher's Wife '91

William Lively
Range Renegades '48

Alan Llwyd
Hedd Wyn '92

Robert Locash
BASEketball '98
High School High '96
Naked Gun 33 1/3: The Final Insult '94
CB4: The Movie '93

Gene Lockhart
Forever and a Day '43

Walter Lockwood
Battling for Baby '92

Leo Loeb
Abbott and Costello Meet Dr. Jekyll and Mr. Hyde '52

Norman Loftis
Small Time '91

Christopher Lofton
True Women '97

Bob Logan
Repossessed '90

Helen Logan
Hello, Frisco, Hello '43
Iceland '42
Lucky Cisco Kid '40
Tin Pan Alley '40

John Logan
Tornado! '96

Joshua Logan
Mister Roberts '55

Tom Logan
Dream Trap '90

Christopher Logue
Crusoe '89
Savage Messiah '72

J. Anthony Loma
A Man of Passion '90s

Ulli Lommel
Warbirds '88
Strangers in Paradise '86
Devonsville Terror '83
Brainwaves '82

Richard Loncraine
Richard III '95

Robby London
Happily Ever After '93

Alexandra Long
Thank God He Met Lizzie '97

Joan Long
Caddie '76

Nathan Long
The Sender '98
Guyver 2: Dark Hero '94

Harry S. Longstreet
A Vow to Kill '94
Sex, Love and Cold Hard Cash '93

Stephen Longstreet
Silver River '48

Anita Loos
I Married an Angel '42
They Met in Bombay '41
When Ladies Meet '41
Susan and God '40
The Women '39
Saratoga '37
San Francisco '36
The Girl from Missouri '34
Hold Your Man '33
Struggle '31
His Picture in the Papers '16

Mary Loos
A Woman's World '54

Temistocles Lopez
Chain of Desire '93

Robert Lord
Heroes for Sale '33
The Purchase Price '32
Big Business Girl '31

Dean Lorey
Major Payne '95
Jason Goes to Hell: The Final Friday '93
My Boyfriend's Back '93

Ray Loriga
Live Flesh '97

James Lorinz
Me and the Mob '94

Eb Lottimer
Love Matters '93

Patrick Loubert
125 Rooms of Comfort '83

David Loucka
Eddie '96
The Dream Team '89

David Loughery
Money Train '95
Tom and Huck '95
The Three Musketeers '93
Passenger 57 '92

Pavel Lounguine
Luna Park '91
Taxi Blues '90

Michael James Love
Gaby: A True Story '87

Josephine Lovett
Our Modern Maidens '29

Robert Lovy
Plughead Rewired: Circuitry Man 2 '94

Steven Lovy
Plughead Rewired: Circuitry Man 2 '94
Circuitry Man '90

Edward T. Lowe
House of Dracula '45
House of Frankenstein '44
Tangled Destinies '32
The Vampire Bat '32

Sherman Lowe
Bury Me Not on the Lone Prairie '41
The Masked Rider '41
Pony Post '40

Richard Lowenstein
Dogs in Space '87

Sam Lowry
The Underneath '95

Nanni Loy
Head of the Family '71

Jean-Bernard Luc
Monsieur Vincent '47

Craig Lucas
Reckless '95
Longtime Companion '90

George Lucas
Return of the Jedi '83
Raiders of the Lost Ark '81
Star Wars '77
American Graffiti '73
THX 1138 '71

William Luce
Lucy and Desi: Before the Laughter '91

Michael Lucker
Vampire in Brooklyn '95

Graham Ludlow
Jack London's The Call of the Wild '97

William Ludwig
Gun Glory '57
Interrupted Melody '55
Oklahoma! '55
Athena '54
The Merry Widow '52
The Sun Comes Up '49
The Hills of Home '48

Kurt Luedtke
Out of Africa '85
Absence of Malice '81

Baz Luhrmann
William Shakespeare's Romeo and Juliet '96
Strictly Ballroom '92

Steve Lukanic
For Richer or Poorer '97

Eric Luke
Still Not Quite Human '92
Explorers '85

Sidney Lumet
Night Falls on Manhattan '96
Q & A '90
Prince of the City '81

Vernon Lumley
Forbidden Zone: Alien Abduction '96

Bigas Luna
Jamon, Jamon '93
Anguish '88

Zoe Tamerlaine Lund
Bad Lieutenant '92

Lars Bill Lundheim
Zero Degrees Kelvin '95

Semyon Lunghin
Rasputin '85

Ida Lupino
Private Hell 36 '54
Streets of Sin '49

Evan Lurie
Hologram Man '95

Arnost Lustig
Diamonds of the Night '64

Jan Lustig
Young Bess '53
Homecoming '48

John Lutz
The Ex '96

Leslie Lyles
Me & Veronica '93

Brad Lynch
Mr. Frost '89

David Lynch
Lost Highway '96
Twin Peaks: Fire Walk with Me '92
Wild at Heart '90
Blue Velvet '86
Dune '84
The Elephant Man '80
Eraserhead '78

Jennifer Lynch
Boxing Helena '93

Martin Lynch
Prayer for the Dying '87

Thomas W. Lynch
The Pathfinder '97

Barre Lyndon
To Please a Lady '50
House on 92nd Street '45

Jonathan Lynn
Nuns on the Run '90
Clue '85

Judd B. Lynn
Shootfighter: Fight to the Death '93

Fibe Ma
Mr. Nice Guy '98
Rumble in the Bronx '96
Supercop '92

John Maass
Curdled '95

Elise MacAdam
Office Killer '97

Charles MacArthur
Wuthering Heights '39
Twentieth Century '34
Rasputin and the Empress '33

Nino Maccari
Two Nights with Cleopatra '54

Ruggero Maccari
The Family '87
A Special Day '77

Kurt MacCarley
Sexual Intent '94

Colin MacDonald
Sharpe's Honour '94

Mike MacDonald
Beauty School '93

Philip MacDonald
The Body Snatcher '45

Sharman MacDonald
The Winter Guest '97

Ranald MacDougall
Queen Bee '55
June Bride '48
Mildred Pierce '45
Objective, Burma! '45

Roger MacDougall
The Mouse That Roared '59

Billy Mackinnon
Small Faces '95

Gilles Mackinnon
Small Faces '95

Patricia MacLachlan
Journey '95
Skylark '93

Bernard MacLaverty
Hostages '93
Lamb '85

Cal '84

Alison Maclean
Crush '93

Stephen MacLean
Around the World in 80 Ways '86

Matt MacManus
Flight of the Navigator '86

Angus MacPhail
Dead of Night '45

Don MacPherson
The Avengers '98
The Big Man: Crossing the Line '91
Absolute Beginners '86

Malcolm MacRury
The Man Without a Face '93

Guy Maddin
Careful '94

Brent Maddock
Tremors 2: Aftershocks '96
Heart and Souls '93
Ghost Dad '90
Tremors '89
Short Circuit 2 '88
*batteries not included '87
Short Circuit '86

Ben Maddow
The Asphalt Jungle '50

Diana Maddox
The Changeling '80

Larry Maddox
Raw Target '95

Robert Madero
All Tied Up '92
Mausoleum '83

David Madsen
Copycat '95

Doug Magee
Beyond the Call '96
Cold Light of Day '95
Somebody Has to Shoot the Picture '90

Maria Maggenti
The Incredibly True Adventure of Two Girls in Love '95

Mark Magidson
Baraka '93

Jymn Magon
A Goofy Movie '94

Gerard Maguire
Gross Misconduct '93

Jeff Maguire
In the Line of Fire '93
Victory '81

Redge Mahaffey
Life 101 '95
Quest of the Delta Knights '93
Deadly Rivals '92

John Lee Mahin
Heaven Knows, Mr. Allison '57
Johnny Eager '42
Dr. Jekyll and Mr. Hyde '41
Love on the Run '36

Anthony Mahon
The Premonition '75

Clelle Mahon
Pagan Island '60

Richard Maibaum
License to Kill '89
The Living Daylights '87
S*H*E '79
Thunderball '65
The Great Gatsby '49
O.S.S. '46

F.X. Maier
Switchblade Sisters '75

Norman Mailer
King Lear '87
Tough Guys Don't Dance '87

Stewart Main
Desperate Remedies '93

Daniel Mainwaring
Invasion of the Body Snatchers '56

Anton Giulio Majano
Atom Age Vampire '61

Dusan Makavejev
Montenegro '81
Sweet Movie '75
WR: Mysteries of the Organism '71
Innocence Unprotected '68
The Love Affair, or The Case of the Missing Switchboard Operator '67
Man Is Not a Bird '65

Anne Makepeace
Thousand Pieces of Gold '91

Curzio Malaparte
The Forbidden Christ '50

Gloria Maley
Horror Planet '80

Nick Maley
Horror Planet '80

Terrence Malick
Days of Heaven '78
Badlands '74
Pocket Money '72

Gregory S. Malins
...And God Spoke '94

Louis Malle
May Fools '90
Au Revoir Les Enfants '87
Murmur of the Heart '71
Viva Maria! '65
The Fire Within '64
Zazie dans le Metro '61
The Lovers '59

Miles Malleson
Nine Days a Queen '36
Lorna Doone '34
Night Birds '31

James Mallon
Mystery Science Theater 3000: The Movie '96

Mark Malone
Bulletproof Heart '95
Signs of Life '89
Dead of Winter '87

Albert Maltz
Two Mules for Sister Sara '70
The Robe '53
Broken Arrow '50
Cloak and Dagger '46
This Gun for Hire '42

David Mamet
The Edge '97
The Spanish Prisoner '97
Wag the Dog '97
American Buffalo '95
Oleanna '94
Vanya on 42nd Street '94
A Life in the Theater '93
Glengarry Glen Ross '92
Hoffa '92
The Water Engine '92
Homicide '91
We're No Angels '89
Things Change '88
House of Games '87
The Untouchables '87
The Verdict '82
The Postman Always Rings Twice '81

Yuri Mamin
Window to Paris '95

Chan Man-keung
Summer Snow '94

Milcho Manchevski
Before the Rain '94

Don Mancini
Child's Play 3 '91
Child's Play 2 '90
Child's Play '88

Babaloo Mandel
Father's Day '96
Multiplicity '96
Forget Paris '95
City Slickers 2: The Legend of Curly's Gold '94
Greedy '94
A League of Their Own '92
Mr. Saturday Night '92

City Slickers '91
Parenthood '89
Vibes '88
Gung Ho '85
Spies Like Us '85
Splash '84
Night Shift '82

Cynthia Mandelberg
The Grace Kelly Story '83

Dharan Mandrayar
Ele, My Friend '93

Neil Mandt
Hijacking Hollywood '97

Nino Manfredi
Bread and Chocolate '74

James Mangold
Cop Land '97
Heavy '94
Oliver & Company '88

Herman J. Mankiewicz
Pride of St. Louis '52
A Woman's Secret '49
Citizen Kane '41
Dinner at Eight '33

Joseph L. Mankiewicz
The Honey Pot '67
Cleopatra '63
Guys and Dolls '55
The Barefoot Contessa '54
Julius Caesar '53
People Will Talk '51
All About Eve '50
No Way Out '50
A Letter to Three Wives '49
The Keys of the Kingdom '44
Forsaking All Others '35
I Live My Life '35
Diplomaniacs '33

Tom Mankiewicz
Dragnet '87
Ladyhawke '85
The Eagle Has Landed '77
The Cassandra Crossing '76
Mother, Jugs and Speed '76
The Man with the Golden Gun '74
Live and Let Die '73
Diamonds Are Forever '71

Wolf Mankowitz
The Day the Earth Caught Fire '61
The Two Faces of Dr. Jekyll '60

Abby Mann
Indictment: The McMartin Trial '95
Murderers Among Us: The Simon Wiesenthal Story '89
King '78
Report to the Commissioner '74
The Detective '68
Ship of Fools '65
A Child Is Waiting '63
Judgment at Nuremberg '61

Edward Mann
Cauldron of Blood '67

Edward Andrew Mann
Seizure '74

Farhad Mann
Lawnmower Man 2: Beyond Cyberspace '95

Michael Mann
Heat '95
The Last of the Mohicans '92
Manhunter '86
The Keep '83
Thief '81
Vegas '78

Myra Mann
Indictment: The McMartin Trial '95

Stanley Mann
Firestarter '84
Eye of the Needle '81
The Mouse That Roared '59

K. Mannah
Bloodmatch '91

Albert Mannheimer
Three Daring Daughters '48

Bruce Manning
First Love '39
Three Smart Girls Grow Up '39
Mad About Music '38
That Certain Age '38

Mark Manos
Liquid Dreams '92

Jean Manse
Forbidden Fruit '52

Michael Mansfield
The Bridge '59

Guido Manuli
Volere Volare '92

Susan Manus
If These Walls Could Talk '96

Xiao Mao
The Blue Kite '93

Scott Marcano
Bio-Dome '96

Robert Marcarelli
Original Intent '91

Gail March
The Witching '72

Joseph Moncure March
Hell's Angels '30

David Marconi
The Harvest '92

Lawrence B. Marcus
The Stunt Man '80
Justine '69
Petulia '68

Mitch Marcus
A Boy Called Hate '95

Andreas Marfori
Evil Clutch '89

Herbert Margolis
The Kettles on Old MacDonald's Farm '57
Francis in the Haunted House '56
Ma and Pa Kettle '49

A. L. Mariaux
Bloodsucking Nazi Zombies '82
Zombie Lake '80

Theresa Marie
Head Above Water '96

Richard "Cheech" Marin
Cheech and Chong's The Corsican Brothers '84
Cheech and Chong: Still Smokin' '83
Cheech and Chong: Things Are Tough All Over '82
Cheech and Chong's Nice Dreams '81
Cheech and Chong's Next Movie '80
Cheech and Chong's Up in Smoke '79

Frances Marion
Dinner at Eight '33
The Champ '32
The Big House '30
The Wind '28
Tillie Wakes Up '17

Diane Markey
Picture Bride '94

Petros Markaris
Ulysses' Gaze '95

Chris Marker
Sans Soleil '82

Gene Markey
On the Avenue '37
Female '33

David Markov
Raging Angels '95

Goran Markovic
Tito and Me '92

Mitch Markowitz
Crazy People '90

Good Morning, Vietnam '87

Dennis Marks
Tom and Jerry: The Movie '93

Leo Marks
Peeping Tom '60

Megan Marks
The Sister-in-Law '95

Ben Markson
Lady Killer '33

George Markstein
The Odessa File '74

Brian Marlow
Supernatural '33

Andrew Marlowe
Air Force One '97

Brad Marlowe
At Home with the Webbers '94

Malia Scotch Marmo
Once Around '91

Malcolm Marmorstein
Konrad '90s
Dead Men Don't Die '91
Return from Witch Mountain '78
Pete's Dragon '77
Mary, Mary, Bloody Mary '76
Whiffs '75
S*P*Y*S '74

Gabriel Garcia Marquez
Letters from the Park '88
Miracle in Rome '88
Mary, My Dearest '83

Leon Marr
Dancing in the Dark '86

Michel Marriott
New Jersey Drive '95

David Marsh
Stormswept '95

Terence Marsh
Haunted Honeymoon '86

Andrew Marshall
Whoops Apocalypse '83

Neil Marshall
Killing Time '97

Roger Marshall
And Now the Screaming Starts '73

Tonie Marshall
Pas Tres Catholique '93

D.M. Marshman, Jr.
Sunset Boulevard '50

William Martell
Crash Dive '96
Hard Evidence '94

Al Martin
Money Madness '47
Blondie Knows Best '46
The Invisible Ghost '41
Kelly of the Secret Service '36
Prison Shadows '36

Anne-Marie Martin
Twister '96

Charles Martin
My Dear Secretary '49

Claude Martin
Blood and Roses '61

Darnell Martin
I Like It Like That '94

Francis Martin
One Night in the Tropics '40
The Big Broadcast of 1938 '38
Waikiki Wedding '37
The Princess Comes Across '36
Rhythm on the Range '36
Strike Me Pink '36
We're Not Dressing '34

Helen Martin
The Lady Confesses '45
The Invisible Ghost '41

Mardik Martin
Raging Bull '80
New York, New York '77
Valentino '77

Mean Streets '73

Robert Martin
Basket Case 3: The Progeny '92

Steve Martin
A Simple Twist of Fate '94
L.A. Story '91
Roxanne '87
Three Amigos '86
The Man with Two Brains '83
Dead Men Don't Wear Plaid '82
The Jerk '79

Steven M. Martin
Theremin: An Electronic Odyssey '94

Troy Kennedy Martin
Hostile Waters '97

William E. Martin
Harry and the Hendersons '87

Wyre Martin
The Unearthing '93

Yves Andre Martin
Hidden Assassin '94

Denny Martin Flinn
Star Trek 6: The Undiscovered Country '91

Raymond Martino
To the Limit '95
DaVinci's War '92
American Born '89
Angels of the City '89

Sergio Martino
The Great Alligator '81
Torso '73

Mike Marvin
Wishman '93
The Wraith '87

Arthur Marx
Cancel My Reservation '72
Eight on the Lam '67
I'll Take Sweden '65
A Global Affair '63

R.J. Marx
Double Obsession '93
Master of Dragonard Hill '89
Dead Man Walking '88
Dragonard '88
Gor '88
Outlaw of Gor '87
Platoon Leader '87
C.O.D. '83

David Masiel
Crosscut '95

Judi Ann Mason
Sister Act 2: Back in the Habit '93

Lesley Mason
Man from Monterey '33

Sarah Y. Mason
Golden Boy '39
Little Women '33

Scott Mason
Ride Him, Cowboy '32

Olivier Massart
Wild Reeds '94

Icel Dobell Massey
Magic in the Water '95

Master P
I Got the Hook-Up '98

Quentin Masters
PSI Factor '80

Nico Mastorakis
Hired to Kill '91
Bloodstone '88
Glitch! '88
Blind Date '84
Blood Tide '82

William Mastrosimone
The Burning Season '94
With Honors '94
Sinatra '92
The Beast '88
Extremities '86

Fred Mata
Santa with Muscles '96

Orestes Matacena
Bitter Sugar '96
Eddy Matalon
Sweet Killing '93
Diego Matamoros
Murdered Innocence '94
Berkely Mather
The Long Ships '64
John C. Mather
Devil Girl from Mars '54
Chris Matheson
Mr. Wrong '95
A Goofy Movie '94
Bill & Ted's Bogus Journey '91
Bill & Ted's Excellent Adventure '89
Richard Matheson
Trilogy of Terror 2 '96
Loose Cannons '90
Jaws 3 '83
Young Warriors '83
Somewhere in Time '80
Trilogy of Terror '75
Dracula '73
Dying Room Only '73
The Legend of Hell House '73
The Night Strangler '72
Duel '71
The Night Stalker '71
Die! Die! My Darling! '65
The Comedy of Terrors '64
The Raven '63
Burn Witch, Burn! '62
Tales of Terror '62
Master of the World '61
The Pit and the Pendulum '61
The Twilight Zone '61
The Fall of the House of Usher '60
The Incredible Shrinking Man '57
Richard Christian Matheson
Three O'Clock High '87
Melissa Mathison
Kundun '97
The Indian in the Cupboard '95
The Escape Artist '82
E.T.: The Extra-Terrestrial '82
The Black Stallion '79
Daniel Matmor
Buffalo Heart: The Pain of Death '96
Francisca Matos
A Million to Juan '94
Hajime Matsumoto
Zeram '91
Takashi Matsuoka
Pale Blood '92
Paul Matthews
The Proposition '96
Grim '95
Tom Matthews
Mad City '97
Burny Mattinson
The Fox and the Hound '81
John Mattson
Free Willy 3: The Rescue '97
Free Willy 2: The Adventure Home '95
Milk Money '94
Nat Mauldin
The Preacher's Wife '96
Ned Mauldin
Renaissance Man '94
J. Stephen Maunder
Talons of the Eagle '92
Armistead Maupin
The Celluloid Closet '95
Michael Maurer
Red Hot '95
Robert Mauri
The Slaughter of the Vampires '62
Rich Mauro
Nick and Jane '96

Garth Maxwell
Jack Be Nimble '94
Richard Maxwell
Shadow of China '01
The Serpent and the Rainbow '87
The Challenge '82
Ronald F. Maxwell
Gettysburg '93
Elaine May
Primary Colors '98
The Birdcage '95
Ishtar '87
Heaven Can Wait '78
Mikey & Nicky '76
A New Leaf '71
Toshiro Mayazumi
Enjo '58
Bernard Maybeck
The Cover Girl Murders '93
Carl Mayer
Shattered '21
The Cabinet of Dr. Caligari '19
Daisy von Scherler Mayer
Party Girl '94
Edwin Justus Mayer
They Met in Bombay '41
Desire '36
Lise Mayer
Suite 16 '94
Wendell Mayes
Monsignor '82
Love and Bullets '79
Go Tell the Spartans '78
Bank Shot '74
Death Wish '74
The Poseidon Adventure '72
Hotel '67
In Harm's Way '65
Von Ryan's Express '65
Advise and Consent '62
Anatomy of a Murder '59
The Hanging Tree '59
The Hunters '58
Spirit of St. Louis '57
Melanie Mayron
Sticky Fingers '88
Craig Mazin
Senseless '98
RocketMan '97
Dan Mazur
Night of the Scarecrow '95
Steve Mazur
Liar Liar '96
The Little Rascals '94
Paul Mazursky
The Pickle '93
Scenes from a Mall '91
Enemies, a Love Story '89
Moon over Parador '88
Down and Out in Beverly Hills '86
Moscow on the Hudson '84
The Tempest '82
Willie & Phil '80
An Unmarried Woman '78
Next Stop, Greenwich Village '76
Harry and Tonto '74
Blume in Love '73
Alex in Wonderland '70
Bob & Carol & Ted & Alice '69
I Love You, Alice B. Toklas! '68
Kevin Mcarthy
Moving Target '96
Jim McBride
Great Balls of Fire '89
Breathless '83
Hot Times '74
Glen and Randa '71
David Holzman's Diary '67
Robert McCahon
Running Wild '73
Rod McCall
Lewis and Clark and George '97

Tim McCanlies
Dennis the Menace Strikes Again '98
Tim McCann
Desolation Angels '95
Leo McCarey
An Affair to Remember '57
Going My Way '44
My Favorite Wife '40
Love Affair '39
Louise McCarn
Walker: Texas Ranger: One Riot, One Ranger '93
John P. McCarthy
Beyond the Rockies '32
Peter McCarthy
Car 54, Where Are You? '94
Floundering '94
Todd McCarthy
Visions of Light: The Art of Cinematography '93
Nick McCarty
Merlin '92
John McClain
Cairo '42
Albert McCleery
The Lady Is Willing '42
Mick McCleery
The Alien Agenda: Out of the Darkness '97
Jonas McCord
Class of '61 '92
Mark McCorkle
Aladdin and the King of Thieves '96
John McCormick
Living on Tokyo Time '87
Victim '61
Pat McCormick
Under the Rainbow '81
Randall McCormick
Speed 2: Cruise Control '97
Horace McCoy
The Texas Rangers Ride Again '40
The Trail of the Lonesome Pine '36
Bruce McCulloch
Kids in the Hall: Brain Candy '96
Jim McCullough, Jr.
The St. Tammany Miracle '94
Philomena McDonagh
Far from the Madding Crowd '97
Bruce McDonald
Dance Me Outside '95
John McDonald
By the Sword '93
Kevin McDonald
Kids in the Hall: Brain Candy '96
Michael James McDonald
The Death Artist '95
Revenge of the Red Baron '93
Kevin McDonough
I Was a Teenage TV Terrorist '87
Michael McDowell
Stephen King's Thinner '96
Tales from the Darkside: The Movie '90
Beetlejuice '88
Maureen McElheron
The Tune '92
Alan B. McElroy
Spawn '97
Todd McFarlane's Spawn '97
Rapid Fire '92
Halloween 4: The Return of Michael Myers '88
Ross McElwee
Time Indefinite '93

Sherman's March: An Improbable Search for Love '86
Donald McEnery
Hercules '97
J.P. McEvoy
Love in Bloom '35
Ian McEwan
The Good Son '93
The Innocent '93
William F. McGaha
The Speed Lovers '68
Michael McGann
Leapin' Leprechauns '95
Mark Thomas McGee
Sins of Desire '92
Bad Girls from Mars '90
Rex McGee
Pure Country '92
Scott McGehee
Suture '93
Kathleen McGhee-Anderson
Sunset Park '96
Josann McGibbon
The Favor '92
Three Men and a Little Lady '90
Worth Winning '89
Sean McGinley
Scorned 2 '96
Sexual Roulette '96
Jim McGlynn
Traveller '96
Terrence McGoff
2 By 4 '98
Jimmy McGovern
Go Now '98
Cracker: Brotherly Love '95
Cracker: Men Should Weep '94
Cracker: The Big Crunch '94
Cracker: To Be a Somebody '94
Priest '94
The Best of Cracker Mysteries '93
Dorrell McGowan
The Showdown '50
Stuart E. McGowan
The Showdown '50
Douglas McGrath
Emma '96
Bullets Over Broadway '94
Born Yesterday '93
Patrick McGrath
Grave Indiscretions '96
John McGreevey
Captains Courageous '95
Consenting Adult '85
Night Crossing '81
Hot Rod Girl '56
Thomas McGuane
Cold Feet '89
Tom Horn '80
Missouri Breaks '76
92 in the Shade '76
Rancho Deluxe '75
Don McGuire
Tootsie '82
Suppose They Gave a War and Nobody Came? '70
The Delicate Delinquent '56
Meet Danny Wilson '52
William Anthony McGuire
The Great Ziegfeld '36
Kid from Spain '32
Jay McInerney
Gia '98
Hotel Room '93
Douglas Lloyd McIntosh
Disaster at Silo 7 '88
Chris McIntyre
Backstreet Justice '93

Dennis McIntyre
State of Grace '90
Jim McKay
Girls Town '96
Malcolm McKay
Maria's Child '93
Steven McKay
Darkman 2: The Return of Durant '94
Diggstown '92
Michael McKean
The Return of Spinal Tap '92
The Big Picture '89
Don McKellar
Dance Me Outside '95
32 Short Films about Glenn Gould '93
Highway 61 '91
Roadkill '89
Ian McKellen
Richard III '95
Bernard McKenna
Yellowbeard '83
Vince McKewin
Fly Away Home '96
Josh McKinney
Suicide Kings '97
Mark McKinney
Kids in the Hall: Brain Candy '96
Duncan McLachlan
Born Wild '95
The Double O Kid '92
John McLaughlin
The Last Good Time '94
Sheila McLaughlin
She Must Be Seeing Things '87
Steve McLean
Postcards from America '95
Victor McLeod
Boss of Bullion City '41
Bury Me Not on the Lone Prairie '41
The Masked Rider '41
Tom McLoughlin
Friday the 13th, Part 6: Jason Lives '86
Robert McMullen
Hell's Belles '69
Larry McMurtry
Larry McMurtry's Dead Man's Walk '96
Larry McMurtry's Streets of Laredo '95
Falling from Grace '92
Memphis '91
Montana '90
The Last Picture Show '71
Terrance McNally
Love! Valour! Compassion! '96
Frankie and Johnny '91
Earth Girls Are Easy '89
Sean McNamara
Three Ninjas: High Noon at Mega Mountain '97
John McNaughton
Henry: Portrait of a Serial Killer '90
Scott McPherson
Marvin's Room '96
Christopher McQuarrie
The Usual Suspects '95
Public Access '93
James McTernan
Small Kill '93
John McTiernan
Nomads '86
Kathy McWorter
The War '94
Bruce Mead
Appointment with Fear '85
Nick Mead
Bank Robber '93

Herb Meadow
The Redhead from Wyoming '53
Shane Meadows
TwentyFourSeven '97
John Meagher
Fantasy Man '84
Irene Mecchi
Hercules '97
The Lion King '94
Russell Medcroft
Angel '37
Julio Medem
The Red Squirrel '93
Mark Medoff
Santa Fe '97
Homage '95
City of Joy '92
Clara's Heart '88
Apology '86
Children of a Lesser God '86
Off Beat '86
Good Guys Wear Black '78
Cary Medoway
The Heavenly Kid '85
John Meehan
Three Daring Daughters '48
The Valley of Decision '45
Madame X '37
Thomas Meehan
Spaceballs '87
One Magic Christmas '85
Annie '82
Leslie Megahey
The Advocate '93
Francis Megahy
The Disappearance of Kevin
    Johnson '95
Robert T. Megginson
F/X '86
Myron Meise
It's All True '93
Gordon Melbourne
Bulletproof Heart '95
White Tiger '95
Ib Melchior
Robinson Crusoe on Mars '64
James Melkonian
The Jerky Boys '95
Kay Mellor
Jane Eyre '97
Band of Gold '95
Greg Mellott
Jackie Chan's First Strike '96
Shootfighter 2: Kill or Be Killed!
    '96
Lewis Meltzer
Autumn Leaves '56
Shark River '53
Comanche Territory '50
Jean-Pierre Melville
Le Samourai '67
Les Enfants Terrible '50
La Silence de la Mer '47
Ivan Menchell
The Cemetery Club '93
Aaron Mendelsohn
Air Bud '97
George Menduluk
Stone Cold Dead '80
Ramon Menendez
Money for Nothing '93
Stand and Deliver '88
Robin Menken
Teen Witch '89
Nina Menkes
Queen of Diamonds '91
Tina "Tigr" Mennett
Kamikaze Hearts '91
Gian-Carlo Menotti
The Medium '51
Jiri Menzel
Larks on a String '68
Closely Watched Trains '66

David Mercer
Morgan! '66
Tony Merchant
Different for Girls '96
Anne Meredith
Bastard out of Carolina '96
Losing Chase '96
Burgess Meredith
Yin & Yang of Mr. Go '71
Sean Meredith
Texas '94
James Merendino
Hard Drive '94
Terrified '94
Joseph Merhi
Last Man Standing '95
Angels of the City '89
Agnes Merlet
Artemisia '97
The Son of the Shark '93
William Mernit
Private Lessons, Another Story
    '94
Lawrence Merrick
Black Bikers from Hell '70
Monte Merrick
Oliver Twist '97
8 Seconds '94
Mr. Baseball '92
Memphis Belle '90
Staying Together '89
Norman Merrill
The Taking of Flight 847: The Uli
    Derickson Story '88
Roger Merton
Down the Wyoming Trail '39
Marta Meszaros
Adoption '75
Stephen Metcalfe
Roommates '95
Cousins '89
Jacknife '89
Florida Straits '87
Tim Metcalfe
Killer: A Journal of Murder '95
Kalifornia '93
Iron Maze '91
Fright Night 2 '88
Million Dollar Mystery '87
Three for the Road '87
Revenge of the Nerds '84
Radley Metzger
The Cat and the Canary '79
The Alley Cats '65
Andrew Meyer
Night of the Cobra Woman '72
Kevin Meyer
A Smile Like Yours '96
Under Investigation '93
Invasion of Privacy '92
Marlane X. Meyer
Better Off Dead '94
Michael Meyer
Stormy Nights '97
Nicholas Meyer
Sommersby '93
Company Business '91
Star Trek 6: The Undiscovered
    Country '91
Star Trek 4: The Voyage Home
    '86
Time After Time '79
The Seven-Per-Cent Solution
    '76
Invasion of the Bee Girls '73
Russ Meyer
Supervixens '75
Faster Pussycat! Kill! Kill! '66
Turi Meyer
Chairman of the Board '97
Leprechaun 2 '94
Nancy Meyers
The Parent Trap '98
Father of the Bride '91
Baby Boom '87
Irreconcilable Differences '84

Protocol '84
Private Benjamin '80
Patrick Meyers
K2: The Ultimate High '92
Menno Meyjes
Foreign Student '94
Lorne Michaels
Three Amigos '86
Boleslaw Michalek
A Love in Germany '84
Danton '82
Michael Michaud
King of the Airwaves '94
Roger Michell
The Buddha of Suburbia '92
Dave Michener
The Great Mouse Detective '86
The Fox and the Hound '81
William Mickelberry
Black Dog '98
Woman Undone '95
Lizzie Mickery
The Ice House '97
Anne-Marie Mieville
First Name: Carmen '83
Numero Deux '75
Radu Mihaileanu
Trahir '93
Gordan Mihic
Someone Else's America '96
Ted V. Mikels
Blood Orgy of the She-Devils '74
The Corpse Grinders '71
The Astro-Zombies '67
Elfi Mikesch
Seduction: The Cruel Woman
    '89
Nikita Mikhalkov
Burnt by the Sun '94
Bernard Miles
The Guinea Pig '48
Jean-Louis Milesi
Marius and Jeannette '97
Lewis Milestone
Arch of Triumph '48
Djordje Milicevic
Iron Will '93
Toby McTeague '87
Runaway Train '85
Victory '81
Frank Military
Blind Faith '98
Buffalo Soldiers '97
John Milius
Rough Riders '97
Clear and Present Danger '94
Geronimo: An American Legend
    '93
Farewell to the King '89
Red Dawn '84
Conan the Barbarian '82
Apocalypse Now '79
Big Wednesday '78
The Wind and the Lion '75
Dillinger '73
Magnum Force '73
Evel Knievel '72
Jeremiah Johnson '72
Life & Times of Judge Roy Bean
    '72
Ronald Millar
Never Let Me Go '53
The Miniver Story '50
Oscar Millard
The Conqueror '56
No Highway in the Sky '51
Come to the Stable '49
Annie Miller
The Little Thief '89
Arthur Miller
The Crucible '96
Everybody Wins '90
The Misfits '61
Bruce Miller
The Assassination File '96

Chris Miller
Multiplicity '96
Claude Miller
The Accompanist '93
The Little Thief '89
This Sweet Sickness '77
The Best Way '76
David Keith Miller
The Glass Cage '96
F.E. Miller
Harlem Rides the Range '39
Frank Miller
RoboCop 3 '91
Geof Miller
Deepstar Six '89
George Miller
Babe '95
Lorenzo's Oil '92
Mad Max: Beyond
    Thunderdome '85
The Road Warrior '82
Mad Max '80
Gregory Miller
Conflict of Interest '93
Harvey Miller
Getting Away With Murder '96
Bad Medicine '85
Cannonball Run 2 '84
Protocol '84
Jekyll & Hyde...Together Again
    '82
Private Benjamin '80
James Mitchell Miller
The Pathfinder '94
Jennifer Miller
Family Pictures '93
The Dark Secret of Harvest
    Home '78
**Michael Alexander
Miller**
Dream Man '94
Rebecca Miller
Angela '94
Seton I. Miller
Istanbul '57
Singapore '47
Two Years Before the Mast '46
Ministry of Fear '44
The Black Swan '42
Here Comes Mr. Jordan '41
The Adventures of Robin Hood
    '38
Kid Galahad '37
The Eagle and the Hawk '33
Murders in the Zoo '33
Victor Miller
Friday the 13th '80
Winston Miller
Cavalry Charge '51
Bertram Millhauser
The Invisible Man's Revenge '44
The Texans '38
Andy Milligan
Man with Two Heads '72
The Rats Are Coming! The
    Werewolves Are Here! '72
Bill Milling
Body Trouble '92
Hugh Mills
Blanche Fury '48
Personal Property '37
Sherry Mills
The Adventures of Pinocchio '96
Paula Milne
Hollow Reed '95
Mad Love '95
H.A. Milton
Piranha 2: The Spawning '82
Boyan Milushev
Bird of Prey '95
Daniel Minahan
I Shot Andy Warhol '96
Michael Miner
Deadly Weapon '88
RoboCop '87

Anthony Minghella
The English Patient '96
Truly, Madly, Deeply '91
Joe Minion
Motorama '91
Vampire's Kiss '88
Julia and Julia '87
Susan Minot
Stealing Beauty '96
Sam Mintz
Here Comes Cookie '35
Brad Mirman
Truth or Consequences, N.M.
    '97
Knight Moves '93
Body of Evidence '92
Dan Mirvish
omaha (the movie) '95
Josef Mischel
Isle of the Dead '45
Yukio Mishima
Black Lizard '68
C. Gaby Mitchell
Fallen Angels 2 '93
Duke Mitchell
The Executioner '78
Gene Mitchell
Flipping '96
The Takeover '94
Julian Mitchell
August '95
Another Country '84
Elizabeth R '72
Keith Mitchell
Eddie '96
Melissa Mitchell
Temptress '95
Steve Mitchell
Chopping Mall '86
Robert Mitchum
Thunder Road '58
Robert Mittenthal
Hail Caesar '94
Frederic Mitterrand
Madame Butterfly '95
Phil Mittleman
Wes Craven Presents Mind
    Ripper '95
Hayao Miyazaki
My Neighbor Totoro '93
Wilson Mizner
Heroes for Sale '33
Kenji Mizoguchi
Sisters of the Gion '36
Moshe Mizrahi
Every Time We Say Goodbye
    '86
La Vie Continue '82
I Sent a Letter to My Love '81
I Love You Rosa '72
Peter Modos
A Happy New Year! '79
David Moessinger
Daddy-O '59
John Moffitt
Rhythm on the Range '36
Clifford Mohr
Lady Dragon 2 '93
Hans Petter Moland
Zero Degrees Kelvin '95
Rafael Moleon
Baton Rouge '88
Edouard Molinaro
Beaumarchais the Scoundrel '96
Pain in the A— '77
Ferenc Molnar
Tales of Manhattan '42
Paul Monash
George Wallace '97
Kingfish: A Story of Huey P.
    Long '95
Stalin '92
Salem's Lot '79

Edward Tang
Mr. Nice Guy '98
Rumble in the Bronx '96
Supercop '92
Operation Condor '91
Project A: Part 2 '87

Senkichi Taniguhi
A Quiet Duel '49

William Tannen
Inside Edge '92

Alain Tanner
Messidor '77
Jonah Who Will Be 25 in the Year 2000 '76
La Salamandre '71

Robert Emmett Tansey
The Driftin' Kid '41
Dynamite Canyon '41

Robert Tapert
Young Hercules '97

Daniel Taplitz
Commandments '96
Black Magic '92

Daniel Taradash
The Other Side of Midnight '77
Doctors' Wives '70
Hawaii '66
Morituri '65
Bell, Book and Candle '58
Picnic '55
Desiree '54
From Here to Eternity '53
Don't Bother to Knock '52
Rancho Notorious '52
Knock on Any Door '49
Golden Boy '39

Quentin Tarantino
Jackie Brown '97
Four Rooms '95
From Dusk Till Dawn '95
Pulp Fiction '94
True Romance '93
Reservoir Dogs '92

Sooni Taraporevala
Mississippi Masala '92
Salaam Bombay! '88

Andrei Tarkovsky
Nostalghia '83
Andrei Rublev '66

Erik Tarloff
Car 54, Where Are You? '94

Frank Tarloff
A Guide for the Married Man '67
Father Goose '64

Jack Tarpon
Dangerous Indiscretion '94

Bela Tarr
Almanac of Fall

Frank Tashlin
Cinderfella '60
Will Success Spoil Rock Hunter? '57
Artists and Models '55
The Lemon Drop Kid '51
The Fuller Brush Girl '50

Robert Tasker
Doctor X '32

Jacques Tati
Parade '74

Anna Maria Tato
The Night and the Moment '94

John Tatoulis
The Silver Stallion: King of the Wild Brumbies '93

Frank Taubes
The Mask '61

Gilles Taurand
Les Voleurs '96
Wild Reeds '94

Catherine Tavel
Night Fire '94
Married People, Single Sex '93

Bertrand Tavernier
Captain Conan '96
L'Appat '94
L.627 '92
Life and Nothing But '89
Round Midnight '86
A Sunday in the Country '84
Coup de Torchon '81
Death Watch '80
Spoiled Children '77
The Judge and the Assassin '75

Paolo Taviani
Fiorile '93
Good Morning, Babylon '87
Kaos '85
The Night of the Shooting Stars '82
Padre Padrone '77
Allonsanfan '73
St. Michael Had a Rooster '72

Vittorio Taviani
Fiorile '93
Good Morning, Babylon '87
Kaos '85
The Night of the Shooting Stars '82
Padre Padrone '77
Allonsanfan '73
St. Michael Had a Rooster '72

Vincent Tavier
Man Bites Dog '91

David Taylor
DROP Squad '94

Donald Taylor
The Hands of Orlac '60

Doug Taylor
The Carpenter '89

Dwight Taylor
We're Not Married '52
Rhythm on the River '40
Top Hat '35
Today We Live '33

Eric Taylor
The Phantom of the Opera '43
Son of Dracula '43
Black Friday '40

Finn Taylor
Dream with the Fishes '97
Pontiac Moon '94

Greg Taylor
The Christmas Box '95

Jim Taylor
Citizen Ruth '96

Lili Taylor
Girls Town '95

Philip John Taylor
Lust in the Dust '85

Renee Taylor
Love Is All There Is '96
Lovers and Other Strangers '70

Roderick Taylor
The Star Chamber '83

Sam Taylor
Vertigo '58
The Freshman '25
Girl Shy '24

Steve Taylor
Sorority House Party '92

Theodore Taylor
Showdown '73

Pierre Tchernia
Belle Americaine '61

Andre Techine
Les Voleurs '96
Wild Reeds '94
Ma Saison Preferee '93
Barocco '76

Dave Tedder
Shock 'Em Dead '90

Maurizio Tedesco
Specters '87

Miguel Tejada-Flores
Screamers '96
Tails You Live, Heads You're Dead '95
Almost Dead '94
Fright Night 2 '88

William Templeton
The Fallen Idol '49

Daisuke Tengan
The Eel '96

Victoria Tennant
Edie & Pen '95

Kevin S. Tenney
Pinocchio's Revenge '96
Witchboard 3: The Possession '95
Witchboard 2: The Devil's Doorway '93
Peacemaker '90
Witchboard '87

Gay Partington Terry
The Toxic Avenger, Part 2 '89
The Toxic Avenger, Part 3: The Last Temptation of Toxie '89

Steve Tesich
American Flyers '85
Eleni '85
The World According to Garp '82
Eyewitness '81
Four Friends '81
Breaking Away '79

Graham Tetley
Dark of the Night '85

Herbert Tevos
Mesa of Lost Women '52

Joan Tewkesbury
Cold Sassy Tree '89
A Night in Heaven '83
Nashville '75
Thieves Like Us '74

David Thacker
Broken Glass '96

Sylvia Thalberg
Now and Forever '34

Kirk R. Thatcher
Muppet Treasure Island '96

Meg Thayer
Hidden Assassin '94

Paul Theroux
Chinese Box '97

Jacques Thery
To Each His Own '46

Harvey Thew
The Trail of the Lonesome Pine '36
Supernatural '33
Illicit '31

Jack Thibeau
Off Limits '88

Nick Thiel
The Associate '96
V.I. Warshawski '91
White Fang '91
Fire Birds '90
Shipwrecked '90
The Experts '89

Robert Thoeren
Singapore '47
Mrs. Parkington '44

Robert Thom
Death Race 2000 '75

Michael Thoma
The Set Up '49

Anna Thomas
My Family '94
A Time of Destiny '88
El Norte '83
End of August '82

Antony Thomas
Rhodes '97

Dave Thomas
Strange Brew '83

Dylan Thomas
The Three Weird Sisters '48

Jerry Thomas
The Fighting Redhead '50

Jim Thomas
Executive Decision '96
Predator 2 '90
The Rescue '88
Predator '87

John Thomas
Executive Decision '96
Predator 2 '90
The Rescue '88
Predator '87

Michael Thomas
Backbeat '94
Deception '92
Scandal '89
Burke & Wills '85
Ladyhawke '85
The Hunger '83

Muffy Mead Thomas
Sarah's Child '96

Ralph Thomas
The Doors '91

Ralph L. Thomas
A Young Connecticut Yankee in King Arthur's Court '95
Young Ivanhoe '95

Ross Thomas
Bad Company '94

Theodore Thomas
Frank and Ollie '95

Camille Thomasson
The Disappearance of Christina '93

Caroline Thompson
Buddy '97
Black Beauty '94
The Nightmare Before Christmas '93
The Secret Garden '93
The Addams Family '91
Edward Scissorhands '90

Carolyn Thompson
Homeward Bound: The Incredible Journey '93

Daniele Thompson
Queen Margot '94

Donald G. Thompson
The Evil '78

Donald W. Thompson
Sidekicks '93

Emma Thompson
Sense and Sensibility '95

Ernest Thompson
Sweet Hearts Dance '88
On Golden Pond '81

Keene Thompson
Love in Bloom '35
Palmy Days '31

Larry Thompson
The Addams Family '91

Peggy Thompson
The Lotus Eaters '93

Rob Thompson
The Cowboy Way '94
Ratboy '86
Hearts of the West '75

Ron Stacker Thompson
America's Dream '95

Scott Thompson
Kids in the Hall: Brain Candy '96

Selma Thomson
Taken Away '89

Billy Bob Thornton
Don't Look Back '96
A Family Thing '96
Sling Blade '96
Some Folks Call It a Sling Blade '94
One False Move '91

Ralph Thornton
Blood of Dracula '57
I Was a Teenage Werewolf '57

Roderick Thorp
Rainbow Drive '90

George Tibbles
How to Frame a Figg '71

Leo Tichat
Night Train to Venice '93

Ernest Tidyman
Stark '85
Shaft's Big Score '72

Robert Tiffe
Sword of Honor '94

Arkadi Tigai
Window to Paris '95

Fergus Tighe
2 By 4 '98

George Tillman, Jr.
Soul Food '97

Alison Tilson
Road to Nhill '97

Patrick Timsit
Pedale Douce '96

Douglas Tirola
A Reason to Believe '95

Moufida Tlatli
The Silences of the Palace '94

James Toback
Two Girls and a Guy '98
Bugsy '91
The Pick-Up Artist '87
Exposed '83
Fingers '78
The Gambler '74

Stephen Tobolowsky
True Stories '86

Angela Todd
Subway Stories '97

Peter Tolan
My Fellow Americans '96

George Toles
Careful '94

John Toles-Bey
A Rage in Harlem '91

Jonathan Tolins
The Twilight of the Golds '97

Michael Tolkin
Deep Impact '98
The Burning Season '94
The New Age '94
Deep Cover '92
The Player '92
The Rapture '91
Gleaming the Cube '89

Stephen Tolkin
Daybreak '93
Captain America '89

Motofumi Tomikawa
The Eel '96

Elliot Tong
Jackie Chan's First Strike '96

Stanley Tong
Jackie Chan's First Strike '96

Jerome Tonnerre
Un Coeur en Hiver '93

Rhet Topham
976-EVIL '88
Trick or Treat '86

Tom Topor
Judgment '90
The Accused '88
Nuts '87

Burt Topper
The Hard Ride '71
Tank Commando '59
Suicide Battalion/Hell Squad '58

Tracy Torme
Fire in the Sky '93
The Spellbinder '88

Giuseppe Tornatore
The Star Maker '95
A Pure Formality '94
Everybody's Fine '90
Cinema Paradiso '88

Antonio Toro
Amityville: A New Generation '93
Amityville 1992: It's About Time '92

Peter Torokvei
Guarding Tess '94
Hostage for a Day '94
Caddyshack 2 '88
Armed and Dangerous '86
Back to School '86
Real Genius '85

Fina Torres
Celestial Clockwork '94
Gabe Torres
December '91
Joan Torres
Blacula '72
Miguel Contreras Torres
Pancho Villa Returns '50
Peter Tors
Looking for Trouble '96
Wellyn Totman
Fighting Champ '33
Robert Totten
Death of a Gunfighter '69
Maurice Tourneur
The Wishing Ring '14
Robert Towne
Without Limits '98
Mission: Impossible '96
Love Affair '94
The Firm '93
Days of Thunder '90
The Two Jakes '90
Tequila Sunrise '88
Personal Best '82
Shampoo '75
The Yakuza '75
Chinatown '74
The Last Detail '73
Villa Rides '68
Tomb of Ligeia '64
The Last Woman on Earth '61
Jack Townley
All Over Town '37
Leo Townsend
Beach Blanket Bingo '65
How to Stuff a Wild Bikini '65
Bikini Beach '64
It Started with Eve '41
Robert Townsend
The Meteor Man '93
The Five Heartbeats '91
Hollywood Shuffle '87
Sher Townsend
Beach Blanket Bingo '65
Mark Trafficante
The Halfback of Notre Dame '96
Nick Tramontane
Jackie Chan's First Strike '96
Joey Travolta
To the Limit '95
Hard Vice '94
Stephen Traxler
Slithis '78
Monika Treut
Erotique '94
My Father Is Coming '91
Seduction: The Cruel Woman '89
Virgin Machine '88
Dale Trevillion
Beyond Desire '94
One Man Force '89
Las Vegas Weekend '85
Dorothy Tristan
Weeds '87
Victor Trivas
The Head '59
Rose Troche
Go Fish '94
Jan Troell
The New Land '73
The Emigrants '72
Massimo Troisi
The Postman '94
Roberto Troni
Boston Kickout '95
Joseph Tropiano
Big Night '95
Guy Trosper
Darby's Rangers '58
The Stratton Story '49

Lamar Trotti
I'd Climb the Highest Mountain '51
Cheaper by the Dozen '50
Captain from Castile '47
Wilson '44
Immortal Sergeant '43
The Ox-Bow Incident '43
Brigham Young: Frontiersman '40
The Story of Alexander Graham Bell '39
Young Mr. Lincoln '39
Alexander's Ragtime Band '38
In Old Chicago '37
George Trow
The Proprietor '96
David Trueba
Two Much '96
Fernando Trueba
Two Much '96
Francois Truffaut
The Man Who Loved Women '77
Small Change '76
Day for Night '73
Mississippi Mermaid '69
Shoot the Piano Player '62
The 400 Blows '59
Daniel Truly
Young Hercules '97
Dalton Trumbo
The Horsemen '70
The Fixer '68
Hawaii '66
Exodus '60
Spartacus '60
The Brave One '56
Roman Holiday '53
Gun Crazy '49
Our Vines Have Tender Grapes '45
A Guy Named Joe '44
Thirty Seconds Over Tokyo '44
Alan R. Trustman
The Arab Conspiracy '76
Hit! '73
Lady Ice '73
They Call Me Mr. Tibbs! '70
Bullitt '68
The Thomas Crown Affair '68
Glenn Tryon
Small Town Boy '37
Tom Tryon
The Other '72
Dean Tschetter
Bloodsucking Pharoahs of Pittsburgh '90
Shinya Tsukamoto
Tetsuo 2: Body Hammer '97
Tetsuo: The Iron Man '92
Stanley Tucci
Big Night '95
Fred Tuch
The Speed Lovers '68
James Tucker
Steps from Hell '92
Lunatic '91
Larry Tucker
Alex in Wonderland '70
Bob & Carol & Ted & Alice '69
Harry Tugend
Birth of the Blues '41
Caught in the Draft '41
Second Fiddle '39
My Lucky Star '38
Pigskin Parade '36
Jim Tully
The Raven '35
Karl Tunberg
Ben-Hur '59
Beau Brummel '54
Up in Central Park '48
You Gotta Stay Happy '48
Week-End in Havana '41
Sandy Tung
Across the Tracks '89

Rosemarie Turko
Scarred '84
Ann Turner
The Killing Beach '92
Barbara Turner
Georgia '95
Bonnie Turner
The Brady Bunch Movie '95
Tommy Boy '95
Coneheads '93
Wayne's World 2 '93
Wayne's World '92
Clive Turner
The Howling: New Moon Rising '95
Dennis Turner
Poor Little Rich Girl: The Barbara Hutton Story '87
Guinevere Turner
Go Fish '94
Terry Turner
The Brady Bunch Movie '95
Tommy Boy '95
Coneheads '93
Wayne's World 2 '93
Wayne's World '92
Catherine Turney
Cry Wolf '47
The Man I Love '46
Saul Turteltaub
For Roseanna '96
John Turturro
Mac '93
Derek Twist
Non-Stop New York '37
John Twist
Band of Angels '57
Helen of Troy '55
King Richard and the Crusaders '54
Pittsburgh '42
David N. Twohy
G.I. Jane '97
The Arrival '96
Waterworld '95
Terminal Velocity '94
The Fugitive '93
Grand Tour: Disaster in Time '92
Warlock '91
Critters 2: The Main Course '88
Jonathan Tydor
The Hard Truth '94
Ashley Tyler
America's Dream '95
Evan Tylor
Stag '97
Steve Tymon
Hindsight '97
Mirror Mirror 3: The Voyeur '96
Dark Secrets '95
Kenneth Tynan
Macbeth '71
Nona Tyson
The Hot Spot '90
Bob Tzudiker
Anastasia '97
Jane Ubell
Precious Find '96
Yale Udoff
Eve of Destruction '90
Alfred Uhry
Rich in Love '93
Driving Miss Daisy '89
Mystic Pizza '88
Daniel Ullman
Good Day for a Hanging '58
Elwood Ullman
Ma and Pa Kettle at Waikiki '55
The Stooge '51
Liv Ullmann
Sofie '92
Yves Ulmann
Un Coeur en Hiver '93

Edgar G. Ulmer
The Black Cat '34
Gladys Unger
The Mystery of Edwin Drood '35
Great Expectations '34
Matt Unger
Bikini Bistro '94
Margaret Unsworth
Othello '65
Tara Untiedt
Provoked '89
Rocco Urbisci
Jo Jo Dancer, Your Life Is Calling '86
Jeff Ureles
Cheap Shots '91
Leon Uris
Gunfight at the O.K. Corral '57
Anatoli Usov
The Inner Circle '91
Peter Ustinov
Hot Millions '68
Lady L '65
Billy Budd '62
Immortal Battalion '44
Pierre Uytterhoeven
Bandits '86
Jack Vacek
Rock House '92
Roger Vadim
Blood and Roses '61
Dangerous Liaisons '60
And God Created Woman '57
Laszlo Vadnay
Uncertain Glory '44
Roger Vailand
Blood and Roses '61
Ladislao Vajda
The Miracle of Marcelino '55
Emilio Diaz Valcarcel
A Life of Sin '92
Luis Valdez
The Cisco Kid '94
La Bamba '87
Zoot Suit '81
Val Valentine
The Belles of St. Trinian's '53
Nick Vallelonga
In the Kingdom of the Blind the Man with One Eye Is King '94
A Brilliant Disguise '93
Thanassis Valtinos
Landscape in the Mist '88
Edgar van Cossart
Baby Monitor: Sound of Fear '97
Jean-Claude Van Damme
Double Impact '91
Lionheart '90
Kickboxer '89
Anne Van De Putte
To Play or To Die '91
Sytze Van Der Laan
Lily Was Here '89
Keith Van Der Wat
Three Bullets for a Long Gun '73
Mike van Diem
Character '97
Jaco Van Dormael
The Eighth Day '95
Toto le Heros '91
Dale Van Every
Souls at Sea '37
Murders in the Rue Morgue '32
Trader Horn '31
Ad van Kempen
1-900 '94
Vincent Van Patten
The Break '95
Mario Van Peebles
Los Locos Posse '97

Melvin Van Peebles
Panther '95
Tales of Erotica '93
Sophisticated Gents '81
Greased Lightning '77
Sweet Sweetback's Baadasssss Song '71
The Story of a Three Day Pass '68
Gus Van Sant
Even Cowgirls Get the Blues '94
My Own Private Idaho '91
Drugstore Cowboy '89
Virginia Van Upp
Young & Willing '42
You and Me '38
Leigh Vance
The Frightened City '61
Chris Vander Stappen
Ma Vie en Rose '97
Norman Thaddeus Vane
Taxi Dancers '93
Rolfe E. Vanlo
The Informer '29
Agnes Varda
Jacquot '91
Vagabond '85
One Sings, the Other Doesn't '77
Le Bonheur '65
Cleo from 5 to 7 '61
Michael Varhol
The Big Picture '89
Pee Wee's Big Adventure '85
The Last Word '80
John Varley
Millenium '89
Joe Vasquez
Riot in the Streets '96
Joseph B. Vasquez
Manhattan Merengue! '95
Hangin' with the Homeboys '91
Francis Veber
My Father the Hero '93
Three Fugitives '89
Les Comperes '83
Partners '82
La Cage aux Folles 2 '81
Hothead '82
La Cage aux Folles '78
Pain in the A— '77
Le Magnifique '76
Return of the Tall Blond Man With One Black Shoe '74
The Tall Blond Man with One Black Shoe '72
Anthony Veiller
Moulin Rouge '52
Red Planet Mars '52
The Killers '46
Carlos Velo
Torero '56
Danny Vendramini
Desperate Prey '94
Louis Venosta
Kisses in the Dark '97
Michael Ventura
Echo Park '86
Roadie '80
Ben Verbong
Lily Was Here '89
Luis Enrique Vergara
The Fear Chamber '68
Mark Verheiden
Timecop '94
Michael Verhoeven
The Nasty Girl '90
Paul Verhoeven
Flesh and Blood '85
Soldier of Orange '78
Cynthia Verlaine
The Substitute '93

Robert M. Young
Triumph of the Spirit '89
Ballad of Gregorio Cortez '83

Terence Young
Mayerling '68
On Approval '44

Waldemar Young
Desire '36
The Crusades '35
The Lives of a Bengal Lancer '35
The Sign of the Cross '33
Island of Lost Souls '32

Bae Young-kyun
Why Has Bodhi-Darma Left for the East '89

Jerry Younkins
The Demon Lover '77

Galen Yuen
Riot in the Streets '96

Lang Yun
Ermo '94

Brian Yuzna
H.P. Lovecraft's Necronomicon: Book of the Dead '93
From Beyond '86

Bruce Zabel
Mortal Kombat 2: Annihilation '97
Official Denial '93

Steve Zacharias
Eddie '96
Revenge of the Nerds 4: Nerds in Love '94

Steven Zaillian
Clear and Present Danger '94
Jack the Bear '93
Schindler's List '93
Searching for Bobby Fischer '93
Awakenings '90
The Falcon and the Snowman '85

Nancy Zala
Round Numbers '91

Alex Zamm
Chairman of the Board '97

Krzysztof Zanussi
Illumination '73
Family Life '71
The Structure of Crystals '69

Barnardino Zapponi
Deep Red: Hatchet Murders '75

Mier Zarchi
I Spit on Your Grave '77

Tony Zarindast
Werewolf '95

Yolande Zauberman
Ivan and Abraham '94

Cesare Zavattini
The Garden of the Finzi-Continis '71
Two Women '61
Umberto D '55
Bellissima '51
Miracle in Milan '51
The Bicycle Thief '48
Shoeshine '47
The Children Are Watching Us '44

Edward Zebrowski
Trois Couleurs: Bleu '93
The Structure of Crystals '69

Franco Zeffirelli
Jane Eyre '96
Hamlet '90
The Taming of the Shrew '67

Paul Zehrer
Blessing '94

Alfred Zeisler
Enemy of Women '44

Susan Zelouf
Curse 2: The Bite '88

Yuri Zeltser
Playmaker '94
Midnight Edition '93

Robert Zemeckis
Trespass '92
Back to the Future, Part 3 '90
Back to the Future, Part 2 '89
Back to the Future '85
Used Cars '80
1941 '79
I Wanna Hold Your Hand '78

Michael Zettler
Sweet Lorraine '87

Ni Zhen
Blush '95

Yang Zhengguang
The Wooden Man's Bride '94

Shan Yuan Zhu
China, My Sorrow '89

Claude Zidi
My New Partner '84

Ulrich Zieger
Faraway, So Close! '93

Scott Ziehl
Red Line '96
Money to Burn '94

Zhang Ziliang
Yellow Earth '89

Paul Ziller
Caged Heat 3000 '95

Julian Zimet
Horror Express '72
Pancho Villa '72
Circus World '64

Maurice Zimm
Good Day for a Hanging '58

Harv Zimmel
Snow Kill '90
Shoot to Kill '88

Paul Zimmerman
A Modern Affair '94

Stan Zimmerman
A Very Brady Sequel '96

Vernon Zimmerman
Fade to Black '80

Stephen Zito
Diana: Her True Story '93
Full Exposure: The Sex Tape Scandals '89

Lee David Zlotoff
The Spitfire Grill '95

Erick Zonca
The Dreamed Life of Angels '98

David Zucker
BASEketball '98
High School High '96
Naked Gun 33 1/3: The Final Insult '94
Naked Gun 2 1/2: The Smell of Fear '91
The Naked Gun: From the Files of Police Squad '88
Top Secret! '84
Police Squad! Help Wanted! '82
Airplane! '80
Kentucky Fried Movie '77

Jerry Zucker
The Naked Gun: From the Files of Police Squad '88
Top Secret! '84
Police Squad! Help Wanted! '82
Airplane! '80
Kentucky Fried Movie '77

George Zuckerman
Tarnished Angels '57
Written on the Wind '56

Carl Zuckmayer
The Blue Angel '30

Wojciech Zukrowski
Lotna '64

Marcos Zurinaga
The Disappearance of Garcia Lorca '96

Valerio Zurlini
The Girl with a Suitcase '60

Alan Zweibel
North '94
Dragnet '87

Edward Zwick
Special Bulletin '83

Cinematographer Index

T he **Cinematographer Index** provides a videography for any cinematographer, or Director of Photography, as they are also known, with a video credit. The listings for the cinematographer names follow an alphabetical sort by last name (although the names appear in a first name last name format). The videographies are listed chronologically, from oldest film to the most recent. If a cinematographer lensed more than one film in the same year, these movies are listed alphabetically within the year. Many of today's top directors started as cinematographers, the people responsible for the "look" of a movie.

Miguel Abal
Killing Grandpa '91
Barry Abrams
Friday the 13th '80
Thomas Ackerman
George of the Jungle '97
Jumanji '95
Baby's Day Out '94
Dennis the Menace '93
National Lampoon's Christmas
 Vacation '89
Beetlejuice '88
Back to School '86
Girls Just Want to Have Fun '85
Frankenweenie '84
Roadhouse 66 '84
Foxfire Light '82
Barry Ackroyd
My Name is Joe '98
Land and Freedom '95
Ladybird, Ladybird '93
Raining Stones '93
Remi Adefarasin
Sliding Doors '97
Hollow Reed '95
Captives '94
Bitter Harvest '93
The Wedding Gift '93
The Lost Language of Cranes
 '92
Truly, Madly, Deeply '91
Matthew Aeberhard
The Leopard Son '96
Javier Aguirresarobe
Fiesta '95
Outrage '93
Lloyd Ahern
Last Man Standing '96
Turbulence '96
Wild Bill '95
Geronimo: An American Legend
 '93
Trespass '92
Mac Ahlberg
Good Burger '97
The Second Civil War '97
The Late Shift '96

A Very Brady Sequel '96
The Brady Bunch Movie '95
Beverly Hills Cop 3 '94
My Boyfriend's Back '93
Innocent Blood '92
Oscar '91
Robot Jox '90
The Horror Show '89
Prison '88
House 2: The Second Story '87
From Beyond '86
Ghostwarrior '86
House '86
Ghoulies '84
Prime Risk '84
Re-Animator '84
Zone Troopers '84
Chained Heat '83
Metalstorm: The Destruction of
 Jared Syn '83
Young Warriors '83
My Tutor '82
Parasite '82
The Seduction '82
Hell Night '81
Nocturna '79
I, A Woman '66
Max Ahlberg
The Wonderful Ice Cream Suit
 '98
Pierre Aim
Hate '95
Cafe au Lait '94
Robert Alazraki
Another 9 1/2 Weeks '96
My Father's Glory '91
The Old Lady Who Walked in
 the Sea '91
Conseil de Famille '86
Love Songs '85
Romano Albani
Troll '86
Creepers '85
Arthur Albert
Beverly Hills Ninja '96
Happy Gilmore '96
One Night Stand '95
You So Crazy '94
By the Sword '93

Surf Ninjas '93
Passed Away '92
Heart Condition '90
Miss Firecracker '89
The Principal '87
The Squeeze '87
Streets of Gold '86
The Boys Next Door '85
Odd Jobs '85
Night of the Comet '84
Maryse Alberti
I Love You, I Love You Not '97
Stag '97
Tales of Erotica '93
Zebrahead '92
Poison '91
Jose Luis Alcaine
Two Much '96
Ay, Carmela! '90
Tie Me Up! Tie Me Down! '90
Twisted Obsession '90
Women on the Verge of a
 Nervous Breakdown '88
Rustler's Rhapsody '85
Demons in the Garden '82
John Alcott
Beastmaster '82
The Shining '80
Terror Train '80
A Clockwork Orange '71
Zontar, the Thing from Venus
 '66
Henri Alekan
Wings of Desire '88
Mayerling '68
Forbidden Fruit '52
Nestor Almendros
Billy Bathgate '91
New York Stories '89
Nadine '87
Heartburn '86
Places in the Heart '84
Confidentially Yours '83
Pauline at the Beach '83
Sophie's Choice '82
Still of the Night '82
The Blue Lagoon '80
The Last Metro '80
Kramer vs. Kramer '79

Days of Heaven '78
Goin' South '78
The Green Room '78
Love on the Run '78
Madame Rosa '77
The Man Who Loved Women
 '77
Maitresse '76
Story of Adele H. '75
Cockfighter '74
Chloe in the Afternoon '72
Two English Girls '72
The Valley Obscured by the
 Clouds '72
Claire's Knee '71
The Wild Child '70
More '69
My Night at Maud's '69
Six in Paris '68
La Collectionneuse '67
Alan Almond
Brothers in Trouble '95
Loaded '94
John A. Alonzo
The Grass Harp '95
Star Trek Generations '94
World War II: When Lions
 Roared '94
The Meteor Man '93
Clifford '92
Cool World '92
Housesitter '92
The Guardian '90
Internal Affairs '90
Navy SEALS '90
Physical Evidence '89
Steel Magnolias '89
Roots: The Gift '88
Overboard '87
Real Men '87
Jo Jo Dancer, Your Life Is
 Calling '86
Nothing in Common '86
The Hit '85
Out of Control '85
No Small Affair '84
Runaway '84
Blue Thunder '83
Cross Creek '83
Scarface '83

Back Roads '81
Zorro, the Gay Blade '81
Tom Horn '80
Norma Rae '79
Casey's Shadow '78
The Cheap Detective '78
Beyond Reason '77
Black Sunday '77
Which Way Is Up? '77
The Bad News Bears '76
I Will, I Will for Now '76
Farewell, My Lovely '75
Once Is Not Enough '75
Chinatown '74
Conrack '74
Lady Sings the Blues '72
Pete 'n' Tillie '72
Sounder '72
Harold and Maude '71
Vanishing Point '71
Bloody Mama '70
Herbert S. Alpert
The Mask '61
John Alton
Elmer Gantry '60
The Brothers Karamazov '58
Designing Woman '57
The Catered Affair '56
Tea and Sympathy '56
The Teahouse of the August
 Moon '56
Big Combo '55
Battle Circus '53
An American in Paris '51
Father of the Bride '50
Reign of Terror '49
He Walked by Night '48
Raw Deal '48
T-Men '47
Courageous Dr. Christian '40
Alex Ameri
The Wizard of Gore '70
Juan Amoros
Mouth to Mouth '95
Sons of Trinity '95
Jamie Anderson
Neil Simon's The Odd Couple 2
 '98
Grosse Pointe Blank '97

1737 Cinematographer Index

Butler ✗cont.

One Flew Over the Cuckoo's
  Nest '75
The Conversation '74
The Execution of Private Slovik
  '74
The Return of Count Yorga '71
The Rain People '69

David L. Butler
Simon, King of the Witches '71

Michael C. Butler
Jaws 2 '78

Frank Byers
Ride '98
Shiloh '97
Trigger Happy '96

Lamberto Caimi
Fiances '63

Thomas Callaway
Caught Up '98
Night of the Scarecrow '95
Cartel '90
Steel and Lace '90
Action U.S.A. '89
Lady Avenger '89
Assault of the Killer Bimbos '88
Slave Girls from Beyond Infinity
  '87
Slumber Party Massacre 2 '87

Antonio Calvache
I Got the Hook-Up '98

Maurizio Calvesi
Nerolio '96
Acla's Descent into Floristella
  '87

Paul Cameron
The Last Supper '96

John Campbell
Rough Magic '95
Even Cowgirls Get the Blues '94
My Own Private Idaho '91

Yves Cape
Ma Vie en Rose '97

Brian Capener
Smoke Signals '98

Robert Caramico
Eaten Alive '76
Lemora, Lady Dracula '73

Jack Cardiff
Million Dollar Mystery '87
Tai-Pan '86
Cat's Eye '85
Rambo: First Blood, Part 2 '85
Conan the Destroyer '84
The Far Pavilions '84
Scandalous '84
The Wicked Lady '83
The Dogs of War '81
Ghost Story '81
The Awakening '80
Avalanche Express '79
The Fifth Musketeer '79
A Man, a Woman, and a Bank
  '79
Death on the Nile '78
The Prince and the Pauper '78
Ride a Wild Pony '75
War and Peace '68
Fanny '61
The Vikings '58
Legend of the Lost '57
The Prince and the Showgirl '57
The Brave One '56
The Barefoot Contessa '54
The Master of Ballantrae '53
The African Queen '51
Pandora and the Flying
  Dutchman '51
Under Capricorn '49
The Red Shoes '48
Black Narcissus '47
Stairway to Heaven '46
Wings of the Morning '37
Last Days of Pompeii '35

Michael Cardone
Black Day Blue Night '95

James Carman
Hustler White '96

Russell Carpenter
Money Talks '97
Titanic '97
The Indian in the Cupboard '95
True Lies '94
Hard Target '93
The Lawnmower Man '92
Pet Sematary 2 '92
Solar Crisis '92
The Perfect Weapon '91
Death Warrant '90
Cameron's Closet '89
Critters 2: The Main Course '88
The Lady in White '88
The Wizard of Speed and Time
  '88
Sole Survivor '84

Ellis W. Carter
Diary of a Madman '63
Curse of the Undead '59
The Incredible Shrinking Man
  '57

James L. Carter
Gunfighter's Moon '96
Ruby Jean and Joe '96
Convict Cowboy '95
Destiny Turns on the Radio '95
The Last Ride '94
One False Move '91
Back to Back '90
Playroom '90
Spaced Invaders '90
Leatherface: The Texas
  Chainsaw Massacre 3 '89
Deadly Weapon '88
In Dangerous Company '88
Terminal Entry '87
Paradise Motel '84
Home Movies '79

Henri Cartier-Bresson
A Day in the Country '46

Alan Caso
George Wallace '97
Ed '96
The Good Old Boys '95
Stepfather 3: Father's Day '92
84 Charlie Mopic '89

David Castillo
Manhattan Merengue! '95

Francois Catonne
My Life and Times with Antonin
  Artaud '93
Indochine '92

Alan Caudillo
The Shot '96

Bernard Cavile
Marius and Jeannette '97

Sarah Cawley
Mercy '96
A Reason to Believe '95

Eric Cayla
Karmina '96

Christopher Challis
S.O.S. Titanic '79
The Little Prince '74
Mary, Queen of Scots '71
Two for the Road '67
The Long Ships '64

Caroline Champetier
A Single Girl '96
Helas pour Moi '94

Tom Chaney
Mosquito '95
Frostbiter: Wrath of the Wendigo
  '94

Gu Changwei
The Gingerbread Man '97
Farewell My Concubine '93
Ju Dou '90
Life on a String '90
Red Sorghum '87

Michael Chapman
Six Days, Seven Nights '98
Primal Fear '96
Space Jam '96
The Fugitive '93

Rising Sun '93
Whispers in the Dark '92
Doc Hollywood '91
Kindergarten Cop '90
Quick Change '90
Ghostbusters 2 '89
Gotham '88
Scrooged '88
Shoot to Kill '88
The Lost Boys '87
The Man with Two Brains '83
Dead Men Don't Wear Plaid '82
Personal Best '82
Raging Bull '80
Hardcore '79
Wanderers '79
Fingers '78
Invasion of the Body Snatchers
  '78
The Last Waltz '78
The Arab Conspiracy '76
The Front '76
Taxi Driver '76
The White Dawn '75
The Last Detail '73

Ron Chapman
Shock 'Em Dead '90

Dominique Chapuis
Mina Tannenbaum '93
Pas Tres Catholique '93
The Little Thief '89
Sugar Cane Alley '83

Rodney Charters
Blind Faith '98
Kull the Conqueror '97
Frame by Frame '95
Sleepwalkers '92
Psycho 4: The Beginning '90

Chuy Chavez
Star Maps '97

Claudio Chea
Bitter Sugar '96

Enrique Chediak
Hurricane Streets '96

Michael G. Chin
Chan Is Missing '82

Steven Chivers
Dust Devil '93

Alain Choquart
Captain Conan '96

Josep Civit
A House in the Hills '93

Richard Clabaugh
Phantoms '97
Children of the Corn 4: The
  Gathering '96
No Way Back '96
The Prophecy '95

Barbara Claman
Beastmaster 3: The Eye of
  Braxus '95

Robin Clark
Vegas in Space '94

Tony Clark
The Quiet Room '96

Charles Clarke
Captain from Castile '47

Ghislan Cloquet
Four Friends '81
I Sent a Letter to My Love '81
Tess '80
Love and Death '75
Donkey Skin '70
A Gentle Woman '69
Marry Me, Marry Me '69
Mouchette '67
Mickey One '65
The Fire Within '64
Belle Americaine '61
Girl in His Pocket '57

William Clothier
Train Robbers '73
Big Jake '71
The Cheyenne Social Club '70
Chisum '70
Rio Lobo '70
The Undefeated '69
Bandolero! '68
The Devil's Brigade '68

Firecreek '68
Hellfighters '68
The War Wagon '67
The Way West '67
The Rare Breed '66
Shenandoah '65
Cheyenne Autumn '64
Donovan's Reef '63
McLintock! '63
The Man Who Shot Liberty
  Valance '62
Merrill's Marauders '62
The Comancheros '61
Deadly Companions '61
The Alamo '60
The Horse Soldiers '59
Darby's Rangers '58
Lafayette Escadrille '58
Blood Alley '55
Sea Chase '55
Phantom from Space '53

Hugo Colace
The Dark Side of the Heart '92

Terence Cole
Bullet to Beijing '95

Andy Collins
Brassed Off '96

Peter Collister
The Replacement Killers '98
The Beautician and the Beast
  '97
Dunston Checks In '95
Higher Learning '94
Poetic Justice '93
Livin' Large '91
Problem Child '90
All's Fair '89
Limit Up '89
Halloween 4: The Return of
  Michael Myers '88
Pulse '88
You Can't Hurry Love '88
Can't Buy Me Love '87
He's My Girl '87
Eye of the Tiger '86
Getting Even '86
The KGB: The Secret War '86
The Supernaturals '86
Avenging Angel '85
Odd Jobs '85

Edward Colman
The Love Bug '68
Blackbeard's Ghost '67
The Gnome-Mobile '67
The Happiest Millionaire '67
The Adventures of Bullwhip
  Griffin '66
Monkey's Uncle '65
That Darn Cat '65
Those Calloways '65
The Ugly Dachshund '65
Mary Poppins '64
The Misadventures of Merlin
  Jones '63
Savage Sam '63
Son of Flubber '63
Big Red '62
The Absent-Minded Professor
  '61
Babes in Toyland '61
The Shaggy Dog '59

Christopher Condon
Evil Spawn '87

David Connell
Moby Dick '98
Two for Texas '97
Stephen King's The Night Flier
  '96
Zeus and Roxanne '96
Buffalo Girls '95
Silver Strand '95
The Ascent '94
Fifty/Fifty '93
Gross Misconduct '93
Heaven Tonight '93
Over the Hill '92
NeverEnding Story 2: The Next
  Chapter '91
Les Patterson Saves the World
  '90
Slate, Wyn & Me '87
The Aviator '85
All the Rivers Run '84

Richard Conners
Just Another Girl on the I.R.T.
  '93

Jack Conroy
Homeward Bound 2: Lost in San
  Francisco '96
Broken Harvest '94
The Hunted '94
The Playboys '92
Silent Tongue '92

Steven Consentino
The Show '95

James A. Contner
Monkey Shines '88
Jaws 3 '83

Fabio Conversi
Pedale Douce '96
Love After Love '94

Denys Coop
And Now the Screaming Starts
  '73
Asylum '72
King and Country '64

Wilkie Cooper
Maniac '63
Sea of Sand '58
Abandon Ship '57
Captain Boycott '47

John Coquillon
The Changeling '80
Cry of the Banshee '70
Scream and Scream Again '70
The Oblong Box '69
The Conqueror Worm '68

Gilles Corbeil
Balance of Power '96

Ericson Core
Exit in Red '97
187 '97
The Show '95

Don A. Coscarelli
Phantasm '79

Paul Cotteret
Mauvaise Graine '33

Michael Coulter
My Giant '98
Fairytale: A True Story '97
The Neon Bible '95
Sense and Sensibility '95
Being Human '94
Four Weddings and a Funeral
  '94
Foreign Affairs '93
The Long Day Closes '92
Monster in a Box '92
Dark Obsession '90
Breaking In '89
The Dressmaker '89
The Good Father '87
The Gospel According to Vic '87
Housekeeping '87
No Surrender '86
Gregory's Girl '80
That Sinking Feeling '79

Curt Courant
De Mayerling a Sarajevo '40

Raoul Coutard
Dr. Bethune '90
Dangerous Moves '84
First Name: Carmen '83
Le Crabe Tambour '77
The Bride Wore Black '68
Two or Three Things I Know
  About Her '66

Jack Cox
The Magic Bow '47

Michelle Crenshaw
The Watermelon Woman '97

Mik Cribben
Beware! Children at Play '95

Jordan Cronenweth
Final Analysis '92
State of Grace '90
Gardens of Stone '87
Just Between Friends '86
Peggy Sue Got Married '86
Stop Making Sense '84
Best Friends '82
Blade Runner '82

Shotgun '55

Nicolette Freeman
Road to Nhill '97

Henry Freulich
Good Day for a Hanging '58
Bonanza Town '51

Karl Freund
Key Largo '48
South of St. Louis '48
Without Love '45
A Guy Named Joe '43
The Seventh Cross '44
DuBarry Was a Lady '43
Tortilla Flat '42
The Chocolate Soldier '41
Pride and Prejudice '40
Balalaika '39
Rose of Washington Square '39
Letter of Introduction '38
Conquest '37
The Good Earth '37
Murders in the Rue Morgue '32
Dracula '31
Metropolis '26
The Golem '20

John Friberg
Alice Sweet Alice '76

Ron Fricke
Baraka '93

Martin Fuhrer
Wilde '97

Tak Fujimoto
A Thousand Acres '97
That Thing You Do! '96
Devil in a Blue Dress '95
Grumpier Old Men '95
Philadelphia '93
Night and the City '92
The Silence of the Lambs '91
Cocoon: The Return '88
Married to the Mob '88
Ferris Bueller's Day Off '86
Pretty in Pink '86
Something Wild '86
Swing Shift '84

Rodrigo Garcia
Gia '98
Four Rooms '95
Indictment: The McMartin Trial '95

Ron Garcia
The Great White Hype '96

Greg Gardiner
Homegrown '97
Suture '93
The Unnamable 2: The Statement of Randolph Carter '92

Mike Garfath
Lamb '85

Lee Garmes
A Big Hand for the Little Lady '66
D-Day, the Sixth of June '56
Desperate Hours '55
Land of the Pharaohs '55
Actors and Sin '52
The Lusty Men '52
Detective Story '51
Our Very Own '50
Caught '49
The Paradine Case '47
The Secret Life of Walter Mitty '47
Guest in the House '45
Love Letters '45
Footlight Serenade '42
The Jungle Book '42
Lydia '41
Angels Over Broadway '40
Dreaming Lips '37
Smilin' Through '33
Shanghai Express '32
Strange Interlude '32
Dishonored '31
Scarface '31
Disraeli '30
Morocco '30

Paul Garnett
Charley's Aunt '25

Andres Garreton
Intimate Relations '95

Miguel Garzon
Highway Patrolman '91

Dave Gasperik
Bang '91

Jeff Gateman
Witchcraft 9: Bitter Flesh '96

Gaetano Antonio "Tony" Gaudio
The Red Pony '49
I've Always Loved You '46
A Song to Remember '45
Days of Glory '43
The Great Lie '41
High Sierra '41
The Man Who Came to Dinner '41
Brother Orchid '40
The Fighting 69th '40
The Letter '40
Juarez '39
The Old Maid '39
Dawn Patrol '38
Kid Galahad '37
The Life of Emile Zola '37
Anthony Adverse '36
The Story of Louis Pasteur '36
The Mask of Fu Manchu '32
Little Caesar '30
The Gaucho '27
The Notorious Lady '27
Kismet '20

Eric Gautier
Irma Vep '96
My Sex Life...Or How I Got Into an Argument '96
The Favorite Son '94

David Geddes
The Colony '95
Incident at Deception Ridge '94

Lu Gengxin
Ermo '94

Henry W. Gerrard
The Most Dangerous Game '32

Merritt B. Gerstad
Strike Me Pink '36
Freaks '32

Maury Gertsman
Invisible Invaders '59
Red Ball Express '52
Singapore '47

Michael Gfelner
Santa with Muscles '96

Calin Ghibu
An Unforgettable Summer '94

Rodney Gibbons
Natural Enemy '96
Screamers '96
My Bloody Valentine '81

Gerald Gibbs
Devil Doll '64

Paul Gibson
The Refrigerator '91

Sue Gibson
Mrs. Dalloway '97

Peter Gilbert
Prefontaine '96
Hoop Dreams '94

Pierre Gill
Los Locos Posse '97

Dan Gilman
Werewolf '95

Paul Gilpin
Tarzan and the Lost City '98
Dangerous Ground '96
Cry, the Beloved Country '95

Aldo Giordani
Atom Age Vampire '61

Basco Giurato
A Pure Formality '94

Irving Glassberg
Tarnished Angels '57
Duel at Silver Creek '52
The Lawless Breed '52
The Strange Door '51

Pierre William Glenn
Small Change '76

Bert Glennon
House of Wax '53
The Red House '47
Lloyds of London '36

James Glennon
Citizen Ruth '96
Lifeform '96
Mojave Moon '96
Mrs. Munck '95
In the Deep Woods '91

Paul Glickman
God Told Me To '76
Tracks '76
Dracula vs. Frankenstein '71

Richard C. Glouner
The Dunwich Horror '70

Agnes Godard
The Dreamed Life of Angels '98
Nenette and Boni '96
I Can't Sleep '93

Angel Goded
Mary, My Dearest '83

Stephen Goldblatt
Batman and Robin '97
Striptease '96
Batman Forever '95
The Pelican Brief '93
The Hunger '83

Eric Goldstein
Naked Souls '95

Carlos Gonzalez
Original Gangstas '96
Mutant Species '95

Frederic Goodich
The Student Affair '97

Gerald R. Goozie
Hostile Intent '97
Electra '95
Specimen '95

Mark J. Gordon
Fall Time '94

Melinda Sue Gordon
The Destiny of Marty Fine '96

Michael Gornick
Day of the Dead '85
Creepshow '82
Dawn of the Dead '78
Martin '77

Arthur Grant
Demons of the Mind '72
Dynasty of Fear '72
Taste the Blood of Dracula '70
Frankenstein Must Be Destroyed '69
Dracula Has Risen from the Grave '68
Plague of the Zombies '66
The Reptile '66
Paranoiac '62
The Phantom of the Opera '62
The Curse of the Werewolf '61
John and Julie '55

Moray Grant
Vampire Circus '71
The Horror of Frankenstein '70
The Vampire Lovers '70

Barry Gravelle
Witchboard 3: The Possession '95

Gary Graver
The Corporation '96
Friend of the Family 2 '96
Scorned 2 '96
Sexual Roulette '96
Femme Fontaine: Killer Babe for the C.I.A. '95
Midnight Tease 2 '95
Night Eyes 4: Fatal Passion '95
Dracula vs. Frankenstein '71

Mark W. Gray
Back to Back '96

Richard Greatrex
Mrs. Brown '97

Guy Green
I Am a Camera '55

Captain Horatio Hornblower '51
Madeleine '50
Blanche Fury '48
Oliver Twist '48
Great Expectations '48
Immortal Battalion '44

Jack N. Green
Absolute Power '97
Midnight in the Garden of Good and Evil '97
Speed 2: Cruise Control '97
Traveller '96
Twister '96
The Amazing Panda Adventure '95
The Bridges of Madison County '95
The Net '95
Bad Company '94
A Perfect World '93
Rookie of the Year '93
Unforgiven '92
Deceived '91
White Hunter, Black Heart '90
Bird '88
Heartbreak Ridge '86

Adam Greenberg
Rush Hour '98
Sphere '97
Eraser '96
First Knight '95
Near Dark '87
Once Bitten '85

Robbie Greenberg
Fools Rush In '97
Sunset Park '96
Under Siege 2: Dark Territory '95
Free Willy '93
All I Want for Christmas '91
Far North '88
The Milagro Beanfield War '88
Creator '85
Sweet Dreams '85

William Howard Greene
When Worlds Collide '51
The Big Cat '49
Can't Help Singing '45
Salome, Where She Danced '45
The Climax '44
Cobra Woman '44
Ali Baba and the Forty Thieves '43
The Phantom of the Opera '43
The Shepherd of the Hills '41
Nothing Sacred '37
A Star Is Born '37
The Garden of Allah '36
The Trail of the Lonesome Pine '36

Jack Greenhalgh
Money Madness '47
Dead Men Walk '43

George Greenough
Blackrock '97

David Gribble
The Quest '96

Garett Griffin
Lover's Knot '96
Space Marines '96

Loyal Griggs
The Greatest Story Ever Told '65
In Harm's Way '65
The Slender Thread '65
Papa's Delicate Condition '63
Girls! Girls! Girls! '62
G.I. Blues '60
The Buccaneer '58
Hot Spell '58
The Sad Sack '57
Three Violent People '57
The Tin Star '57
The Ten Commandments '56
The Bridges at Toko-Ri '55
We're No Angels '55
Elephant Walk '54
White Christmas '54
Shane '53
Cavalry Charge '51

Francis Grumman
Gang Boys '97

Alexander Grusynski
The Craft '96
Maximum Risk '96
Angus '95
I Like It Like That '94
Tremors '89
Bad Dreams '88

Enrique Guerner
The Miracle of Marcelino '55

Burnett Guffey
The Great White Hope '70
The Learning Tree '69
Bonnie & Clyde '67
How to Succeed in Business without Really Trying '67
King Rat '65
Birdman of Alcatraz '62
Kid Galahad '62
Gidget '59
Me and the Colonel '58
The Strange One '57
The Harder They Fall '56
Tight Spot '55
The Violent Men '55
Human Desire '54
From Here to Eternity '53
Sirocco '51
In a Lonely Place '50
All the King's Men '49
Knock on Any Door '49
Reckless Moment '49

David Gurfinkel
Under the Domim Tree '95

Manfred Guthe
Poltergeist: The Legacy '96
The Stupids '95

Carl Guthrie
House on Haunted Hill '58
Lady Godiva '55
Francis Covers the Big Town '53
Francis Goes to West Point '52

Ron Hagen
Talk '95

Marcus Hahn
The Demolitionist '95

Rob Hahn
In and Out '97

Jacques Haitkin
Wishmaster '97
The Big Squeeze '96
Fist of the North Star '95
One Good Turn '95
Two Bits & Pepper '95
Evolver '94
Silence of the Hams '93
Shocker '89
To Die For '89
A Nightmare on Elm Street 2: Freddy's Revenge '85
A Nightmare on Elm Street '84
House Where Evil Dwells '82
Galaxy of Terror '81

Chuck Hall
Alice Sweet Alice '76

Conrad Hall
Without Limits '97
Searching for Bobby Fischer '93
Tequila Sunrise '88
Black Widow '87
Incubus '82
Marathon Man '76
The Day of the Locust '75
Smile '75
Electra Glide in Blue '73
Fat City '72
Butch Cassidy and the Sundance Kid '69
The Happy Ending '69
Hell in the Pacific '69
Tell Them Willie Boy Is Here '69
Cool Hand Luke '67
Divorce American Style '67
In Cold Blood '67
Harper '66
The Professionals '66
Morituri '65

Harry Hallenberger
The Virginian '46

Lassally ⟨cont.⟩

Run, Stranger, Run '73
Savages '72
Something for Everyone '70
Zorba the Greek '64
Tom Jones '63
The Loneliness of the Long
  Distance Runner '62
A Taste of Honey '61

Andrew Laszlo
Poltergeist 2: The Other Side '86
The Funhouse '81
The Owl and the Pussycat '70

Ernest Laszlo
Logan's Run '76
Showdown '73
Airport '70
Daddy's Gone A-Hunting '69
Star! '68
Luv '67
Fantastic Voyage '66
Ship of Fools '65
Baby, the Rain Must Fall '64
Four for Texas '63
It's a Mad, Mad, Mad, Mad
  World '63
Judgment at Nuremberg '61
Inherit the Wind '60
While the City Sleeps '56
The Big Knife '55
The Kentuckian '55
Kiss Me Deadly '55
Apache '54
Naked Jungle '54
The Moon Is Blue '53
Stalag 17 '53
Vera Cruz '53
The Well '51
D.O.A. '49
Impact '49
The Road to Rio '47
Two Years Before the Mast '46

Philip Lathrop
Deadly Friend '86
The Monster of Piedras Blancas
  '57

Paul Laufer
Frankie Starlight '95

Dan Laustsen
Nightwatch '96

Charles Lawton, Jr.
Comanche Station '60
Cowboy '58
Gunman's Walk '58

Vernon Layton
The Englishman Who Went Up a
  Hill But Came Down a
  Mountain '95

Robert Le Febvre
Casque d'Or '52

Jean-Yves Le Mener
The Visitors '95

Marcel Le Picard
The Invisible Ghost '41

Robert Leacock
Looking for Richard '96

John Leatherbarrow
The Thief and the Cobbler '96

Sam Leavitt
The Man in the Glass Booth '75
Star Spangled Girl '71
The Passing of Evil '70
Desperados '69
Guess Who's Coming to Dinner
  '67
Major Dundee '65
Advise and Consent '62
Diamond Head '62
Cape Fear '61
Seven Thieves '60
Anatomy of a Murder '59
Pork Chop Hill '59
The Defiant Ones '58
The Court Martial of Billy
  Mitchell '55
The Man with the Golden Arm
  '55
Carmen Jones '54

A Star Is Born '54
The Thief '52

Pavel Lebeshev
Prisoner of the Mountains '96

Robert Lechterman
The Deli '97

Philip Lee
Galaxies Are Colliding '92

Robert Lefebvre
Her and She and Him '69

Jacques Lefrancois
Robert et Robert '78

Richard Leiterman
Watchers '88

Claude Lelouch
Les Miserables '95

James Lemmo
Maniac Cop 2 '90

Piotr Lenar
A Rat's Tale '98

Andrew Lennie
Doing Time for Patsy Cline '97

Denis Lenoir
The Secret Agent '96
Carrington '95
The Separation '94
Dingo '92

Dean Lent
When Time Expires '97
Acting on Impulse '93
Gas Food Lodging '92

Miklos Lente
Happy Birthday to Me '81

John R. Leonetti
Spy Hard '96
The Mask '94

Matthew F. Leonetti
Species 2 '98
Mortal Kombat 2: Annihilation
  '97
Fled '96
Star Trek: First Contact '96
Strange Days '95
Dead Again '91
Weird Science '85
Poltergeist '82

Jean Lepine
Woo '97
Beyond the Call '96
The Player '92

Andrew Lesnie
Babe '95
Two If by Sea '95
Temptation of a Monk '94

Pierre Letarte
Dangerous Minds '95
Sugartime '95
The Boys of St. Vincent '93

Richard Letterman
The Ex '96

Charles Levey
The Search for One-Eyed Jimmy
  '96

Moshe Levin
Hard Justice '95

Peter Levy
Lost in Space '98
The War at Home '96
Broken Arrow '95
Cutthroat Island '95
A Nightmare on Elm Street 5:
  Dream Child '89

David Lewis
Chairman of the Board '97
The Proposition '96
The Set Up '95
Witchboard 2: The Devil's
  Doorway '93
The Hills Have Eyes, Part 2 '84

**Herschell Gordon
Lewis**
Color Me Blood Red '64
2000 Maniacs '64
Blood Feast '63

Denis Lewiston
The Canterville Ghost '96

Nightmare '91
The House on Straw Hill '76

Pierre Lhomme
Mon Homme '96

Matthew Libatique
Pi '98

Charlie Lieberman
Henry: Portrait of a Serial Killer
  '90

Stephen Lighthill
The Crying Child '96
Evil Has a Face '96
Open Season '95

Doug Liman
Swingers '96

Jong Lin
Eat Drink Man Woman '94
Pushing Hands '92

Edward Linden
King Kong '33

Lionel Linden
O.S.S. '46

**Karl Walter
Lindenlaub**
The Jackal '97
Red Corner '97
Independence Day '96
Up Close and Personal '96
The Last of the Dogmen '95
Rob Roy '95

John Lindley
Michael '96
Money Train '95
I Love Trouble '94
The Good Son '93
Sneakers '92
Father of the Bride '91
Field of Dreams '89
The Serpent and the Rainbow
  '87
The Stepfather '87

Lionel Lindon
Generation '69
Pendulum '69
Dead Heat on a Merry-Go-
  Round '66
Grand Prix '66
The Trouble with Angels '66
McHale's Navy Joins the Air
  Force '65
All Fall Down '62
The Manchurian Candidate '62
Alias Jesse James '59
I Want to Live! '58
Lonely Man '57
Around the World in 80 Days '56
Conquest of Space '55
A Man Alone '55
Casanova's Big Night '54
Destination Moon '50
Only the Valiant '50
My Favorite Brunette '47
Welcome Stranger '47
The Blue Dahlia '46
Monsieur Beaucaire '46
The Road to Utopia '46
Going My Way '44

Robert Lindsay
Maniac '80

Philip Linzey
Bloodknot '95

Jerzy Lipman
Lotna '64

Harold Lipstein
No Name On the Bullet '59
Walk the Proud Land '56
The Private War of Major
  Benson '55

Gerry Lively
The Brylcreem Boys '96
DNA '97
Children of the Corn 3: Urban
  Harvest '95
Friday '95
Hellraiser 4: Bloodline '95
Without Mercy '95
H.P. Lovecraft's Necronomicon:
  Book of the Dead '93
Hellraiser 3: Hell on Earth '92

Waxwork 2: Lost in Time '91
Waxwork '88

Walt Lloyd
Feeling Minnesota '96
Private Parts '96
Empire Records '95
Frank and Jesse '94
Short Cuts '93
Kafka '91
To Sleep with Anger '90
Down Twisted '89
sex, lies and videotape '89
The Wash '88
Dangerously Close '86

Bryan Loftus
The Company of Wolves '85

Dietrich Lohmann
Deep Impact '98
The Peacemaker '97
The Machine '94
A Couch in New York '95

Raoul Lomas
Children of the Corn '84

Chris Lombardi
Theremin: An Electronic
  Odyssey '95

Gordon C. Lonsdale
The Last Don '97

Pierre Lorraine
Little Indian, Big City '95

Emmanuel Lubezki
Great Expectations '97
The Birdcage '95
A Little Princess '95
A Walk in the Clouds '95
Twenty Bucks '93

William Lubtchansky
Every Other Weekend '91

Yang Lun
Red Firecracker, Green
  Firecracker '93

Bernard Lutic
Colonel Chabert '94

Chester Lyons
Mad Love '35

Jingle Ma
Mr. Magoo '97
Jackie Chan's First Strike '96
Rumble in the Bronx '96

Syd Macartney
Transmutations '85

Julio Macat
Home Alone 3 '97
My Fellow Americans '96
The Nutty Professor '96
Moonlight and Valentino '95

Giuseppe Maccari
Two Evil Eyes '90

Joe MacDonald
Will Success Spoil Rock Hunter?
  '57

Thierry Machado
Microcosmos '96

Laurent Machuel
Three Lives and Only One
  Death '96
Diary of a Seducer '95

Jack MacKenzie
Return of Dracula '58
Isle of the Dead '45

John Mackey
Crucible of Horror '69

Kenneth Macmillan
Almost Heroes '97
Inventing the Abbotts '97
Mr. & Mrs. Loving '96

Glen MacPherson
Regeneration '97
Doctor Who '96
Captains Courageous '95
First Degree '95

Yonezo Maeda
Minbo—Or the Gentle Art of
  Japanese Extortion '92

Paul Maibaum
Tornado! '96

Waxwork 2: Lost in Time '91
Waxwork '88

Down, Out and Dangerous '95
Stephen King's The Langoliers
  '95

David Makin
Kids in the Hall: Brain Candy '96

Michael Maley
Farmer & Chase '96

Denis Maloney
Body Count '97
The Winner '96
Baja '95
Witchcraft 7: Judgement Hour
  '95
Witchcraft 8: Salem's Ghost '95
Natural Causes '94

Joseph Mangine
Alligator 2: The Mutation '90

Tom Mangravite
The Hunger '83

Teodoro Maniaci
Clean, Shaven '95

Isidore Mankofsky
The Heidi Chronicles '95
Second Coming of Suzanne '80

Hong Manley
Tales of Erotica '93

Bahram Manocheri
Bleak Moments '71

Mauro Marchetti
Cemetery Man '95

Alain Marcoen
La Promesse '96

William Margulies
How to Frame a Figg '71
The Love God? '70
The Ghost and Mr. Chicken '66
McHale's Navy '64

Francis Marin
The Texican '66

Barry Markowitz
Two Girls and a Guy '98
The Apostle '97
Sling Blade '96

Jack Marquette
A Bucket of Blood '59

Jacques Marquette
Creature from the Haunted Sea
  '60

Jack Marta
Earth vs. the Spider '58

Otello Martelli
What a Woman! '56
Anna '51

Arthur Martinelli
Supernatural '33
The White Zombie '32

Nino Martinetti
Lust and Revenge '95

Miriana Marusic
The Castle '97

Joseph Mascelli
Incredibly Strange Creatures
  Who Stopped Living and
  Became Mixed-Up Zombies
  '63

Mario Masini
Padre Padrone '77
St. Michael Had a Rooster '72

Steve Mason
Buddy '97
That Old Feeling '96

Rudolph Mate
Cover Girl '44
Vampyr '31

James Mathers
The Forgotten One '89

John Mathieson
Twin Town '97
Bye-Bye '96
Pigalle '95

Christian Matras
Fanfan la Tulipe '51
L'Idiot '46

The **Composer Index** provides a videography for any composer, arranger, lyricist, or band that has provided an original music score for a film now on video. The listings for the composer names follow an alphabetical sort by last name (although the names appear in a first name last name format). The videographies are listed chronologically, from most recent film to the first. If a composer provided music for more than one film in the same year, these movies are listed alphabetically within the year.

Michael Abene
Goodbye, New York '85
Barron Abramovitch
Profile for Murder '96
Tracks of a Killer '95
Hard Evidence '94
AC/DC
Maximum Overdrive '86
Jack Ackerman
Faces '68
Barry Adamson
Gas Food Lodging '92
Delusion '91
Richard Addinsell
A Christmas Carol '51
Blithe Spirit '45
Gaslight '40
South Riding '37
John Addison
The Phantom of the Opera '90
Something in Common '86
Code Name: Emerald '85
Grace Quigley '84
Eleanor: First Lady of the
    World '82
Love's Savage Fury '79
The Bastard '78
A Bridge Too Far '77
Joseph Andrews '77
The Seven-Per-Cent Solution
    '76
Swashbuckler '76
Ride a Wild Pony '75
Luther '74
Sleuth '72
Cry of the Penguins '71
Start the Revolution Without
    Me '70
The Charge of the Light
    Brigade '68
The Honey Pot '67
A Fine Madness '66

Torn Curtain '66
The Amorous Adventures of
    Moll Flanders '65
The Loved One '65
Guns at Batasi '64
Tom Jones '63
The Loneliness of the Long
    Distance Runner '62
A Taste of Honey '61
The Entertainer '60
Carlton Browne of the F.O.
    '59
Look Back in Anger '58
Lucky Jim '58
Reach for the Sky '56
Larry Adler
King and Country '64
Great Chase '63
A Cry from the Streets '57
Genevieve '53
Mark Adler
Decoy '95
Slam Dunk Ernest '95
Eat a Bowl of Tea '89
The Unbearable Lightness of
    Being '88
Heat and Sunlight '87
Yashushi Akutagawa
An Actor's Revenge '63
Robert Alcivar
Blind Witness '89
Naked Lie '89
Hysterical '83
One from the Heart '82
Olly Olly Oxen Free '78
Butterflies Are Free '72
Jeff Alexander
Gun Glory '57
Westward the Women '51
Van Alexander
Strait-Jacket '64
Platinum High School '60

Girls' Town '59
Jaguar '56
When Gangland Strikes '56
The Atomic Kid '54
Eric Allaman
Down Twisted '89
Angel 3: The Final Chapter
    '88
The Battleship Potemkin '25
Cameron Allan
Jericho Fever '93
JFK: Reckless Youth '93
The Good Wife '86
Midnite Spares '85
Billy Allen
The Acid Eaters '67
Dave Allen
The Harvest '92
Eric Allen
Bleak Moments '71
Peter Allen
Crackerjack '94
Woody Allen
Sleeper '73
Byron Allred
Don't Answer the Phone '80
Gerald Alters
Your Place or Mine '83
John Altman
The Garden of Redemption
    '97
The Matchmaker '97
A Royal Scandal '96
Bhaji on the Beach '94
Funny Bones '94
Bad Behavior '92
Hear My Song '91
Ed Alton
My Demon Lover '87
Minette Alton
Devlin '92

Children of Divorce '80
Dave Alvin
Border Radio '88
William Alwyn
Madeleine '50
Captain Boycott '47
Daniele Amfitheatrof
The Last Hunt '56
You Gotta Stay Happy '48
Singapore '47
O.S.S. '46
The Virginian '46
David Amram
The Arrangement '69
The Manchurian Candidate
    '62
Splendor in the Grass '61
Anastasia
Before the Rain '94
Laurie Anderson
Monster in a Box '92
Swimming to Cambodia '87
Something Wild '86
Pete Anderson
Chasers '94
Pascal Andreacchio
Le Bonheur Est Dans le Pre
    '95
Dwight Andrews
The Piano Lesson '94
Gerard Anfosso
Blue Country '77
Cousin, Cousine '76
**Antonio Ramirez
Angel**
The Awful Dr. Orloff '62
Scott Angley
Clerks '94
George Antheil
Actors and Sin '52

Paul Antonelli
China O'Brien '88
Out of the Dark '88
Princess Academy '87
Women's Club '87
Avenging Angel '85
Louis Applebaum
Lost Boundaries '49
Philip Appleby
Nothing Personal '95
Maria's Child '93
Shimon Arama
Bigfoot: The Unforgettable
    Encounter '94
Sebastian Argol
Yol '82
Eddie Arkin
Pretty Smart '87
Hardbodies 2 '86
Modern Girls '86
Harold Arlen
Last Summer In the
    Hamptons '96
Gay Purr-ee '62
Cabin in the Sky '43
Strike Me Pink '36
Martin Armiger
Thank God He Met Lizzie '97
The Crossing '92
Sweetie '89
Young Einstein '89
Two Friends '86
Michael Armstrong
Silent Night, Deadly Night 2
    '87
David Arnold
Godzilla '98
A Life Less Ordinary '97
Tomorrow Never Dies '97
Independence Day '96
The Last of the Dogmen '95

The Black Hole '79
Game of Death '79
Hanover Street '79
Moonraker '79
Willa '79
The Betsy '78
Star Crash '78
The Deep '77
First Love '77
The Gathering '77
The White Buffalo '77
Eleanor & Franklin '76
King Kong '76
Robin and Marian '76
War Between the Tates '76
The Day of the Locust '75
Love Among the Ruins '75
Shampoo '75
The Man with the Golden Gun '74
The Tamarind Seed '74
A Doll's House '73
Alice's Adventures in Wonderland '72
Diamonds Are Forever '71
The Last Valley '71
Mary, Queen of Scots '71
Murphy's War '71
They Might Be Giants '71
Walkabout '71
Monte Walsh '70
Midnight Cowboy '69
On Her Majesty's Secret Service '69
The Lion in Winter '68
Petulia '68
Dutchman '67
You Only Live Twice '67
Born Free '66
The Chase '66
The Quiller Memorandum '66
The Wrong Box '66
The Ipcress File '65
King Rat '65
The Knack '65
Thunderball '65
Goldfinger '64
Seance on a Wet Afternoon '64
Zulu '64
From Russia with Love '63
Dr. No '62
Beat Girl '60
Never Let Go '60

Lionel Bart
Black Beauty '71

Steve Bartek
Meet the Deedles '98
Romy and Michele's High School Reunion '97
Cabin Boy '94
Coldblooded '94
Guilty as Charged '92
Past Midnight '92

Dee Barton
Thunderbolt & Lightfoot '74
High Plains Drifter '73
Play Misty for Me '71

Richard Baskin
Uforia '81
Honeysuckle Rose '80
Welcome to L.A. '77
Buffalo Bill & the Indians '76
Nashville '75

Kevin Bassinson
Beanstalk '94
Cyborg '89

George Bassman
Wombling Free '77
Ride the High Country '62
The Joe Louis Story '53

The Postman Always Rings Twice '46
Abbott and Costello in Hollywood '45
The Clock '45
The Canterville Ghost '44
Best Foot Forward '43
Cabin in the Sky '43
Whistling in Brooklyn '43
For Me and My Gal '42
Panama Hattie '42
Babes on Broadway '41
Big Store '41
Lady Be Good '41
Go West '40
Too Many Girls '40
Babes in Arms '39
Everybody Sing '38
A Damsel in Distress '37
A Day at the Races '37

Les Baxter
The Beast Within '82
Born Again '78
Switchblade Sisters '75
Devil & Leroy Basset '73
Frogs '72
Torture Chamber of Baron Blood '72
The Big Doll House '71
Cry of the Banshee '70
The Dunwich Horror '70
Hell's Belles '69
Terror in the Jungle '68
Wild in the Streets '68
Dr. Goldfoot and the Bikini Machine '66
Beach Blanket Bingo '65
How to Stuff a Wild Bikini '65
Bikini Beach '64
Black Sabbath '64
The Comedy of Terrors '64
Muscle Beach Party '64
Pajama Party '64
Battle Beyond the Sun '63
Beach Party '63
The Invaders '63
The Raven '63
X: The Man with X-Ray Eyes '63
Panic in the Year Zero! '62
Samson and the 7 Miracles of the World '62
Tales of Terror '62
Alakazam the Great! '61
Goliath and the Dragon '61
Master of the World '61
The Pit and the Pendulum '61
Black Sunday '60
The Fall of the House of Usher '60
Goliath and the Barbarians '60
The Bride & the Beast '58
Lone Ranger and the Lost City of Gold '58
Girl in Black Stockings '57
The Invisible Boy '57
The Key Man '57
Storm Rider '57
Battle Shock '56
Monika '52

Irwin Bazelon
Wilma '77

David Beal
The Take '90

Jeff Beal
Love Is All There Is '96
Power 98 '96
The Fence '94
Ring of Steel '94
Cheap Shots '91

John Beal

The Offspring '87
Killer Party '86
The Stone Boy '84
Under the Volcano '84
Lookin' to Get Out '82
The Funhouse '81
The Man with Bogart's Face '80
Defiance '79
Zero to Sixty '78

Michael Bearden
DROP Squad '94

The Beatles
Let It Be '70

Christophe Beck
Past Perfect '98
Hostile Intent '97
Crossworlds '96

Jeff Beck
Blue Chips '94

Joe Beck
Goodbye, Norma Jean '75

Frank Becker
American Kickboxer 1 '91
Terminal Bliss '91

Danny Beckerman
Fortress '85

Hal Beckett
Power of Attorney '94

Stephen Bedell
Jersey Girl '92

Michael Been
Light Sleeper '92

Daniel Bell
Fanny and Alexander '83

David Bell
Larry McMurtry's Dead Man's Walk '96
There Goes the Neighborhood '92
Memphis '91
Final Justice '84
Killing at Hell's Gate '81

Thom Bell
The Fish that Saved Pittsburgh '79

Wayne Bell
Last Night at the Alamo '83
Eaten Alive '76
The Texas Chainsaw Massacre '74

Andrew Belling
Starchaser: The Legend of Orin '85
The Deerslayer '78
Zoltan...Hound of Dracula '78
Wizards '77
End of the World '76
The Killing Kind '73

Richard Bellis
How the West was Fun '95
Where's the Money, Noreen? '95
The Spider and the Fly '94
Blind Man's Bluff '91
Double-Crossed '91
Stephen King's It '90
Fallen Angel '81
Breaking Up Is Hard to Do '79
A Shining Season '79

Roger Bellon
The Last Don '97
The Unholy '88
Waxwork '88
Princess Academy '87

Marco Beltrami
Mimic '97
Scream 2 '97
Scream '96

Vassal Benford
Class Act '91
House Party 2: The Pajama Jam '91

Arthur Benjamin
Wings of the Morning '37

James Bennett
Poison '91
Swoon '91

Richard Rodney Bennett
Swann '96
Four Weddings and a Funeral '94
Enchanted April '92
The Attic: The Hiding of Anne Frank '88
Poor Little Rich Girl: The Barbara Hutton Story '87
Ebony Tower '86
Return of the Soldier '82
Yanks '79
Brink's Job '78
Equus '77
Permission To Kill '75
Murder on the Orient Express '74
Lady Caroline Lamb '73
Nicholas and Alexandra '71
Secret Ceremony '69
Far from the Madding Crowd '67
The Nanny '65
Billy Liar '63
Heavens Above '63
The Wrong Arm of the Law '63
Only Two Can Play '62
The Mark '61
The Devil's Disciple '59
Indiscreet '58

David Benoit
The Stars Fell on Henrietta '94
Captive Hearts '87

Jean-Marie Benoit
King of the Airwaves '94

Robby Benson
Die Laughing '80

David Bergeaud
Prince Valiant '97
Donor Unknown '95
Twice Dead '88

Cary Berger
Suture '93

Alan Bergman
Yentl '83

Marilyn Bergman
Yentl '83

Tal Bergman
Wedding Bell Blues '96

Michael Berkeley
Twenty-One '91

Irving Berlin
Le Bal '82
Easter Parade '48
Second Fiddle '39
Alexander's Ragtime Band '38
Carefree '38
On the Avenue '37
Follow the Fleet '36
Top Hat '35
The Cocoanuts '29
Hallelujah! '29

James Bernard
Frankenstein and the Monster from Hell '74

The 7 Brothers Meet Dracula '73
The Scars of Dracula '70
Taste the Blood of Dracula '70
Dracula Has Risen from the Grave '68
Torture Garden '67
Dracula, Prince of Darkness '66
Plague of the Zombies '66
The Gorgon '64
Kiss of the Vampire '62
The Hound of the Baskervilles '59
The Horror of Dracula '58
Across the Bridge '57
The Curse of Frankenstein '57
Quatermass 2 '57
The Quatermass Experiment '56

Marie Bernard
Strangers in Good Company '91

Charles Bernstein
Miss Evers' Boys '97
Rumpelstiltskin '96
Excessive Force '93
Final Appeal '93
The Sea Wolf '93
Payoff '91
Caroline? '90
Ivory Hunters '90
Too Young to Die '90
The Allnighter '87
Dudes '87
The Man Who Broke 1,000 Chains '87
April Fool's Day '86
Deadly Friend '86
The Last Fling '86
The Long, Hot Summer '86
The Rumor Mill '86
Chase '85
Secret Weapons '85
A Nightmare on Elm Street '84
Cujo '83
The Entity '83
Independence Day '83
Sadat '83
Bogie: The Last Hero '80
Coast to Coast '80
Foolin' Around '80
The Hunter '80
Scruples '80
The House on Garibaldi Street '79
Love at First Bite '79
Are You in the House Alone? '78
Steel Cowboy '78
Wild & Wooly '78
The Winds of Kitty Hawk '78
Outlaw Blues '77
Viva Knievel '77
Gator '76
Nightmare in Badham County '76
A Small Town in Texas '76
Mr. Majestyk '74
Invasion of the Bee Girls '73
Pigs '73
The Shrieking '73
White Lightning '73

Elmer Bernstein
Twilight '98
Buddy '97
John Grisham's The Rainmaker '97
Bulletproof '96
Hoodlum '96

Bernstein cont.

Devil in a Blue Dress '95
Frankie Starlight '95
Roommates '95
Canadian Bacon '94
Search and Destroy '94
The Age of Innocence '93
The Cemetery Club '93
Fallen Angels 1 '93
The Good Son '93
Lost in Yonkers '93
Mad Dog and Glory '93
The Babe '92
Cape Fear '91
Oscar '91
A Rage in Harlem '91
Rambling Rose '91
The Grifters '90
My Left Foot '89
Slipstream '89
Da '88
Funny Farm '88
The Good Mother '88
A Night in the Life of Jimmy Reardon '88
Amazing Grace & Chuck '87
Leonard Part 6 '87
Hamburger...The Motion Picture '86
Legal Eagles '86
Three Amigos '86
The Black Cauldron '85
Gulag '85
Spies Like Us '85
Bolero '84
The Ewok Adventure '84
Ghostbusters '84
Class '83
Prince Jack '83
Spacehunter: Adventures in the Forbidden Zone '83
Trading Places '83
Airplane 2: The Sequel '82
Five Days One Summer '82
An American Werewolf in London '81
The Chosen '81
Going Ape! '81
Heavy Metal '81
Honky Tonk Freeway '81
Stripes '81
Airplane! '80
The Great Santini '80
The Guyana Tragedy: The Story of Jim Jones '80
Saturn 3 '80
The Chisholms '79
Meatballs '79
Zulu Dawn '79
Bloodbrothers '78
Little Women '78
National Lampoon's Animal House '78
Slap Shot '77
From Noon Till Three '76
The Incredible Sarah '76
The Shootist '76
The Old Curiosity Shop '75
McQ '74
Report to the Commissioner '74
The Trial of Billy Jack '74
Cahill: United States Marshal '73
Amazing Mr. Blunden '72
Big Jake '71
See No Evil '71
Doctors' Wives '70
The Liberation of L.B. Jones '70

Walk in the Spring Rain '70
The Bridge at Remagen '69
Guns of the Magnificent Seven '69
True Grit '69
I Love You, Alice B. Toklas! '68
The Scalphunters '68
Thoroughly Modern Millie '67
Will Penny '67
Cast a Giant Shadow '66
Hawaii '66
Return of the Seven '66
The Hallelujah Trail '65
Sons of Katie Elder '65
Baby, the Rain Must Fall '64
The Carpetbaggers '64
The World of Henry Orient '64
The Great Escape '63
Hud '63
Love with the Proper Stranger '63
Birdman of Alcatraz '62
To Kill a Mockingbird '62
Walk on the Wild Side '62
By Love Possessed '61
The Comancheros '61
Summer and Smoke '61
From the Terrace '60
The Magnificent Seven '60
The Rat Race '60
The Buccaneer '58
Desire Under the Elms '58
God's Little Acre '58
Kings Go Forth '58
Some Came Running '58
Fear Strikes Out '57
Men in War '57
Sweet Smell of Success '57
The Tin Star '57
The Ten Commandments '56
It's a Dog's Life '55
The Man with the Golden Arm '55
Make Haste to Live '54
Silent Raiders '54
Cat Women of the Moon '53
Robot Monster '53
Boots Malone '52
Never Wave at a WAC '52
Sudden Fear '52

Leonard Bernstein

On the Town '91
West Side Story '61
On the Waterfront '54

Peter Bernstein

Rough Riders '97
Fifty/Fifty '93
Nightbreaker '89
Remote Control '88
The Alamo: Thirteen Days to Glory '87
Morgan Stewart's Coming Home '87
Miracles '86
Broken Badge '85
The Ewoks: Battle for Endor '85
Kicks '85
My Science Project '85
Bolero '84
The Ewok Adventure '84
Summer Fantasy '84
Surf 2 '84
Club Med '83
Hot Dog...The Movie! '83
National Lampoon's Class Reunion '82
Silent Rage '82

Adele Bertei

Vortex '81

Peter Best

Doing Time for Patsy Cline '97
Country Life '95
Muriel's Wedding '94
Crocodile Dundee 2 '88
High Tide '87
Crocodile Dundee '86

Harry Betts

Cheech and Chong's Nice Dreams '81
Big Mouth '67

Amin Bhatia

Once a Thief '96
Just One of the Girls '93
Black Ice '92
Iron Eagle 2 '88
Storm '87

Nick Bicat

The Passion of Darkly Noon '95
The Hawk '93
The Reflecting Skin '91
Strapless '90
Stealing Heaven '88
Wetherby '85
To Catch a King '84
Oliver Twist '82
The Scarlet Pimpernel '82

Arnold Bieber

Smoke '93
Small Time '91

Keith Bilderbeck

Voodoo '95

Jean-Marie Billy

La Promesse '96

Rene Marc Bini

Grosse Fatigue '94

Jeff Bird

Niagara, Niagara '97

Nathan Birnbaum

Chain of Desire '93

Edgar Bischoff

La Silence de la Mer '47

Johnny Bishop

The Gods Must Be Crazy '84

Karen Black

Can She Bake a Cherry Pie? '83

Stanley Black

Maniac '63
The Battle of the Sexes '60
Jack the Ripper '60
Mania '60
The Crawling Eye '58

Wendy Blackstone

Love Walked In '97
New Jersey Drive '95
Tales of Erotica '93
Only You '92
Eddie Macon's Run '83

Ruben Blades

Q & A '90
The Story of Fausta '88

Howard Blake

A Month in the Country '87
Amityville 3: The Demon '83
The Lords of Discipline '83
Amityville 2: The Possession '82
Flash Gordon '80
The Riddle of the Sands '79
S.O.S. Titanic '79
The Odd Job '78

Ronee Blakley

Lightning Over Water '80

Terence Blanchard

Gia '98
Gia '98
Eve's Bayou '97

Get On the Bus '96
Til There Was You '96
Clockers '95
Assault at West Point: The Court-Martial of Johnson Whittaker '94
Crooklyn '94
The Inkwell '94
Sugar Hill '94
Trial by Jury '94
Malcolm X '92
Jungle Fever '91

Ralph Blane

Athena '54

Larry Blank

Taxi Dancers '93

Arthur Bliss

Abandon Ship '57

George Blondheim

The Halfback of Notre Dame '96
Man with a Gun '95
Red Scorpion 2 '94
Whale Music '94
Gate 2 '92
Bye Bye Blues '89

John Joe Bob Briggs Bloom

Nobody's Fool '94

Kath Bloom

A Little Stiff '91

William Bloom

The Search for One-Eyed Jimmy '96

Frankie Blue

Out There '95

Chris Boardman

Tales from the Crypt Presents Bordello of Blood '96
Prime Target '91
The Color Purple '85

Richard Anthony Boast

Sworn Enemies '96

Jerry Bock

A Stranger Among Us '92

Roland Bocquet

La Balance '82

Michael Boddicker

Freejack '92
F/X 2: The Deadly Art of Illusion '91
The Adventures of Milo & Otis '89
White Water Summer '87
The Adventures of Buckaroo Banzai Across the Eighth Dimension '84
Get Crazy '83

Todd Boekelheide

Digger '94
Nina Takes a Lover '94
Exposure '91
Hearts of Darkness: A Filmmaker's Apocalypse '91
The Blood of Heroes '89
Dear America: Letters Home from Vietnam '88
Dim Sum: A Little Bit of Heart '85

Ed Bogas

Bon Voyage, Charlie Brown '80
A Christmas Without Snow '80
Race for Your Life, Charlie Brown '77
Heavy Traffic '73

Fritz the Cat '72

Geir Bohren

The Other Side of Sunday '96

William Bolcom

Hester Street '75

Martin D. Bolin

Forced to Kill '93

Bill Boll

The Low Life '95
Some Folks Call It a Sling Blade '94

Paul Boll

Roadracers '94

Claude Bolling

The Bay Boy '85
The Awakening '80
Willie & Phil '80
California Suite '78
Silver Bears '78
Le Magnifique '76
The Passenger '75
Catch Me a Spy '71
Borsalino '70
The Day and the Hour '63
The Hands of Orlac '60

Jay Bolton

Stormy Nights '97

Bernardo Bonazzi

Mouth to Mouth '95
All Tied Up '92
Don Juan, My Love '90
Women on the Verge of a Nervous Breakdown '88
Matador '86

Luis Bonfa

Black Orpheus '58

Marc Bonilla

Caught Up '98
Hollywood Confidential '97
National Lampoon's Dad's Week Off '97

Bono

In the Name of the Father '93

Sonny Bono

Good Times '67

Ruud Bos

1-900 '94

John Boshoff

The Gods Must Be Crazy '84

Rick Boston

The Harvest '92

Simon Boswell

The Android Affair '95
Hackers '95
Jack and Sarah '95
Second Best '94
Shallow Grave '94
Dust Devil '93
Love Matters '93
The Turn of the Screw '92
Hardware '90
Santa Sangre '90
Dangerous Obsession '88
Demons 2 '87
Creepers '85

Perry Botkin

Windmills of the Gods '88
Weekend Warriors '86
Silent Night, Deadly Night '84
Tarzan, the Ape Man '81
Goin' South '78
Lady Ice '73
They Only Kill Their Masters '72
Bless the Beasts and Children '71
R.P.M.* (*Revolutions Per Minute) '70

Chris Botti

Hamlisch *cont.*

Open Season '95
Frankie and Johnny '91
When the Time Comes '91
The Experts '89
The January Man '89
Little Nikita '88
Three Men and a Baby '87
A Chorus Line '85
D.A.R.Y.L. '85
A Streetcar Named Desire '84
Romantic Comedy '83
I Ought to Be in Pictures '82
Sophie's Choice '82
The Devil & Max Devlin '81
Pennies From Heaven '81
Ordinary People '80
Seems Like Old Times '80
Ice Castles '79
Starting Over '79
Same Time, Next Year '78
The Spy Who Loved Me '77
Prisoner of Second Avenue '74
Save the Tiger '73
The Sting '73
The Way We Were '73
The World's Greatest Athlete '73
Fat City '72
Bananas '71
Kotch '71
April Fools '69
Take the Money and Run '69
The Swimmer '68

Jan Hammer
Beastmaster 3: The Eye of Braxus '95
A Modern Affair '94
I Come in Peace '90
K-9000 '89

Oscar Hammerstein
Cinderella '97
The Sound of Music '65
Cinderella '64
Flower Drum Song '61
South Pacific '58
Carousel '56
The King and I '56
Oklahoma! '55
Show Boat '51
State Fair '45
Lady Be Good '41
Show Boat '36
Sweet Adeline '35

Richard Hampton
Othello '65

Herbie Hancock
Livin' Large '91
Harlem Nights '89
Action Jackson '88
Colors '88
The George McKenna Story '86
Jo Jo Dancer, Your Life Is Calling '86
Round Midnight '86
A Soldier's Story '84
Death Wish '74
The Spook Who Sat By the Door '73
Blow-Up '66

Jonathan Hannah
Beauty School '93

Erik Hansen
The Deadly Secret '94

E.Y. Harburg
Can't Help Singing '45
Cabin in the Sky '43

John Wesley Harding
The Paint Job '93

Hagood Hardy
Anne of Avonlea '87
Anne of Green Gables '85
Wild Pony '83
Forbidden Love '82
Mazes and Monsters '82
Dirty Tricks '81
An American Christmas Carol '79
Anatomy of a Seduction '79
Home to Stay '79
Klondike Fever '79

John E.R. Hardy
Hedd Wyn '92

John Harle
Butterfly Kiss '94

Leigh Harline
Strange Bedfellows '65
The Facts of Life '60
Savage Wilderness '55
I Want You '51
It Happens Every Spring '49
Snow White and the Seven Dwarfs '37

Craig Harnath
The Castle '97

Udi Harpaz
Hollywood Shuffle '87

Johnny Harris
Ravenhawk '95
Man in the Wilderness '71

Max Harris
Dreamchild '85

George Harrison
Shanghai Surprise '86
Wonderwall: The Movie '69

Michael Allen Harrison
Claire of the Moon '92

Deborah Harry
Rock & Rule '83
Polyester '81

Lorenz Hart
Pal Joey '57
Words and Music '48
I Married an Angel '42
Too Many Girls '40
Babes in Arms '39
Evergreen '34
The Merry Widow '34
Hallelujah, I'm a Bum '33

Mickey Hart
Gang Related '96

Hal Hartley
Simple Men '92

Richard Hartley
The Designated Mourner '97
A Thousand Acres '97

Richard Hartley
The Brylcreem Boys '96

Richard Hartley
Playing God '96
Stealing Beauty '96
Rough Magic '95
The Van '95
An Awfully Big Adventure '94
Princess Caraboo '94
The Rector's Wife '94
The Secret Rapture '93
The Good Father '87
Dance with a Stranger '85

Robert Hartshorne
Boston Kickout '95

Richard Harvey
Jane Eyre '97
Paper Mask '91

Jo Hasaishi
Sonatine '96

Jimmie Haskell
The Dogfighters '95

Greg Hawkes
Anna '87

Roy Hay
Pterodactyl Woman from Beverly Hills '97
Precious Find '96

Fumio Hayasaka
Sansho the Bailiff '54
Seven Samurai '54
Scandal '50

Isaac Hayes
Truck Turner '74

Reed Hays
My Life's in Turnaround '94

Randall Kent Heddon
Undercover Cop '94

Neal Hefti
Sex and the Single Girl '64

Bob Held
Federal Hill '94

Jimi Hendrix
Skier's Dream '88

Nona Hendryx
Gospa '94

Ben Heneghan
The Proposition '96

Jerry Herman
Mrs. Santa Claus '96
Hello, Dolly! '69

Marc Herouet
Night and Day '91

Bernard Herrmann
Cape Fear '91
Psycho 4: The Beginning '90
Obsession '76
Taxi Driver '76
It's Alive '74
Sisters '73
The Bride Wore Black '68
Mysterious Island '61
Psycho '60
North by Northwest '59
The Three Worlds of Gulliver '59
The Seventh Voyage of Sinbad '58
Vertigo '58
The Trouble with Harry '55
Five Fingers '52
The Day the Earth Stood Still '51
On Dangerous Ground '51
The Ghost and Mrs. Muir '47
Anna and the King of Siam '46
Jane Eyre '44
The Magnificent Ambersons '42
Citizen Kane '41
The Devil & Daniel Webster '41

Boo Hewerdine
TwentyFourSeven '97

Werner R. Heymann
They All Kissed the Bride '42

Tom Hiel
Dark Side of Genius '94

John Hill
Tar '97
The Pompatus of Love '95

Marc Hillman
Baxter '89

Graydon Hillock

Midnight Witness '93

Hilmar Orn Hilmarsson
Cold Fever '95
Children of Nature '91

Rupert Hine
Better Off Dead '85

Wilbert Hirsch
An American Werewolf in Paris '97
Mute Witness '95

David Hirschfelder
Sliding Doors '98
Dating the Enemy '95
Shine '95
Tunnel Vision '95

Joel Hirschhorn
Rescue Me '93

David Hirshfelder
Strictly Ballroom '92

Joe Hisaishi
Fireworks '97

Jimmy Hodges
Hindsight '97

Brian Hodgson
The Legend of Hell House '73

Joachim Holbek
Junk Mail '97
Nightwatch '96
Breaking the Waves '95
The Kingdom '95

Mark Holden
Ava's Magical Adventure '94
Beyond Desire '94

Lee Holdridge
The Twilight of the Golds '97
Two for Texas '97
Gunfighter's Moon '96
Holiday Affair '96
Soul of the Game '96
Buffalo Girls '95
Harvest of Fire '95
Prince Brat and the Whipping Boy '94
The Tuskegee Airmen '95
Texas '94
The Yearling '94
Heidi '93
Back to Hannibal: The Return of Tom Sawyer and Huckleberry Finn '90
Old Gringo '89
American Pop '81

Deborah Holland
Out There '95
Circuitry Man '90

Friedrich Hollander
Here Comes Mr. Jordan '41
Remember the Night '40
Angel '37
Desire '36
The Blue Angel '30

Rupert Holmes
No Small Affair '84

Nigel Holton
Cries of Silence '97
Naked Souls '95
Twogether '94
Carnosaur '93
Bloodfist 3: Forced to Fight '92
South of Reno '87

Toshiyuki Honda
Minbo—Or the Gentle Art of Japanese Extortion '92

Arthur Honegger
Harvest '37
Crime and Punishment '35

Nellee Hooper
William Shakespeare's Romeo and Juliet '96

Tobe Hooper
Texas Chainsaw Massacre 2 '86

Anthony Hopkins
August '95

Kenyon Hopkins
The Strange One '57

James Horner
Deep Impact '98
Titanic '97
Courage Under Fire '96
The Devil's Own '96
Ransom '96
To Gillian on Her 37th Birthday '96
Apollo 13 '95
Balto '95
Braveheart '95
Casper '95
Jade '95
Jumanji '95
The Spitfire Grill '95
Legends of the Fall '94
The Pagemaster '94
Bopha! '93
A Far Off Place '93
Jack the Bear '93
The Man Without a Face '93
The Pelican Brief '93
Searching for Bobby Fischer '93
Swing Kids '93
Patriot Games '92
Sneakers '92
Thunderheart '92
Unlawful Entry '92
An American Tail: Fievel Goes West '91
Class Action '91
My Heroes Have Always Been Cowboys '91
Once Around '91
The Rocketeer '91
Another 48 Hrs. '90
I Love You to Death '90
Dad '89
Field of Dreams '89
Glory '89
Honey, I Shrunk the Kids '89
In Country '89
Cocoon: The Return '88
The Land Before Time '88
Red Heat '88
Vibes '88
Willow '88
*batteries not included '87
Project X '87
Aliens '86
An American Tail '86
The Name of the Rose '86
Off Beat '86
Where the River Runs Black '86
Cocoon '85
Commando '85
Heaven Help Us '85
The Journey of Natty Gann '85
P.K. and the Kid '85
Volunteers '85
Star Trek 3: The Search for Spock '84
The Stone Boy '84
Between Friends '83
Brainstorm '83
Gorky Park '83
Krull '83

Marvin ⌐cont.

3 Ninjas '92
J. Mascis
Gas Food Lodging '92
Herve Masini
Pedale Douce '96
Harvey W. Mason
Deadly Outbreak '96
Only the Strong '93
Nick Mason
White of the Eye '88
Roger Mason
Joey '98
Crime Broker '94
Ted Mason
Robot in the Family '94
John Massari
Redemption: Kickboxer 5 '95
The Big Sweat '90
Killer Klowns from Outer
Space '88
The Wizard of Speed and
Time '88
Greg Mathieson
American Flyers '85
Muir Mathieson
This Happy Breed '47
Peter Matz
Stepping Out '91
Torch Song Trilogy '88
Lust in the Dust '85
Brian May
Dr. Giggles '92
Bloodmoon '90
Cloak & Dagger '84
Stage Fright '83
Treasure of the Yankee
Zephyr '83
The Road Warrior '82
Escape 2000 '81
Killing of Angel Street '81
Road Games '81
Mad Max '80
Survivor '80
Patrick '78
Daniel May
Chopper Chicks in
Zombietown '91
Curtis Mayfield
Return of Superfly '90
Piece of the Action '77
Sparkle '76
Superfly '72
Doug Maynard
Patti Rocks '88
Lyle Mays
The Falcon and the Snowman
'85
Toshiro Mayuzumi
The Bible '66
Jim McBride
Great Balls of Fire '89
John McCallum
Grizzly Mountain '97
Little Heroes '91
Dennis McCarthy
Breast Men '97
McHale's Navy '97
Star Trek Generations '94
John McCarthy
Soul Survivor '95
Paris, France '94
Paul McCartney
Le Bal '82
John McCulloch
Careful '94

Garry McDonald
Official Denial '93
John McEuen
The Good Old Boys '95
David McHugh
Changing Habits '96
The Hidden 2 '94
Tales of Erotica '93
Daddy's Dyin'...Who's Got the
Will? '90
The Dream Team '89
Mr. North '88
Mystic Pizza '88
Michael McKean
Waiting for Guffman '96
Mark McKenzie
The Disappearance of Garcia
Lorca '96
Dr. Jekyll and Ms. Hyde '95
Frank and Jesse '94
My Family '94
Rod McKuen
A Boy Named Charlie Brown
'70
Murray McNabb
Once Were Warriors '94
**Robert F.
McNaughton**
Henry: Portrait of a Serial
Killer 2: Mask of Sanity '96
Joel McNeely
Buffalo Soldiers '97
Wild America '97
Flipper '96
Vegas Vacation '96
Gold Diggers: The Secret of
Bear Mountain '95
Radioland Murders '94
Squanto: A Warrior's Tale '94
Terminal Velocity '94
Iron Will '93
Supercop '92
Andy McNeill
Project: Genesis '93
Abigail Mead
Full Metal Jacket '87
Meat Loaf
Car Trouble '86
Medusa
Switchblade Sisters '75
Peter Melnick
Lily Dale '96
Indictment: The McMartin
Trial '95
L.A. Story '91
Wendy Melvoin
Soul Food '97
Felix Mendelssohn
The Bedroom Window '87
Alan Menken
Hercules '97
The Hunchback of Notre
Dame '96
Pocahontas '95
Life with Mikey '93
Aladdin '92
Newsies '92
Beauty and the Beast '91
The Little Mermaid '89
Little Shop of Horrors '86
Johnny Mercer
Last Summer In the
Hamptons '96
Darling Lili '70
Days of Wine and Roses '62
Li'l Abner '59
Dangerous When Wet '53
The Harvey Girls '46
You Were Never Lovelier '42

Wim Mertens
Fiesta '95
Pat Metheny
The Falcon and the Snowman
'85
Michel Michelet
Impact '49
Cynthia Millar
The Run of the Country '95
Three Wishes '95
Marcus Miller
The Sixth Man '97
The Great White Hype '96
Above the Rim '94
House Party '90
Siesta '87
Randy Miller
Without Limits '97
Darkman 3: Die Darkman Die
'95
Darkman 2: The Return of
Durant '94
And You Thought Your
Parents Were Weird! '91
Black Magic Woman '91
Mario Millo
Wrangler '88
The Lighthorsemen '87
Sidney Mills
Fly by Night '93
Chen Ming-Chang
Maborosi '95
Charles Mingus
Shadows '60
Ben Mink
Even Cowgirls Get the Blues
'94
Jon Mirsalis
Grit of the Girl Telegrapher/In
the Switch Tower '15
Paul Misraki
Les Bonnes Femmes '60
Death in the Garden '56
Richard G. Mitchell
The Tenant of Wildfell Hall '96
Bob Mithoff
Sgt. Kabukiman N.Y.P.D. '94
Seedpeople '92
Vic Mizzy
How to Frame a Figg '71
The Love God? '70
The Reluctant Astronaut '67
The Ghost and Mr. Chicken
'66
Cyril Mockridge
Will Success Spoil Rock
Hunter? '57
Solid Gold Cadillac '56
Cheaper by the Dozen '50
Come to the Stable '49
I Was a Male War Bride '49
Miracle on 34th Street '47
The Ox-Bow Incident '43
Mark Moffatt
Back of Beyond '95
High Tide '87
Charlie Mole
Othello '95
Francis Monkman
The Long Good Friday '80
Hugo Montenegro
Charro! '69
Osvaldo Montes
A Shadow You Soon Will Be
'94
The Dark Side of the Heart
'92
Guy Moon

A Very Brady Sequel '96
The Brady Bunch Movie '95
Diving In '90
Sorority Babes in the
Slimeball Bowl-A-Rama '87
Wild Thing '87
Dudley Moore
Six Weeks '82
The Hound of the Baskervilles
'77
Bedazzled '68
30 Is a Dangerous Age,
Cynthia '68
Peter S. Moore
Chameleon Street '89
Thurston Moore
Heavy '94
Beo Morales
Wax, or the Discovery of
Television Among the Bees
'93
Patrick Moraz
The Stepfather '87
La Salamandre '71
Larry Morey
Snow White and the Seven
Dwarfs '37
Mark Morgan
Where the Day Takes You '92
Giorgio Moroder
The NeverEnding Story '84
Cat People '82
Midnight Express '78
Ennio Morricone
Bulworth '98
U-Turn '97
Nostromo '96
The Star Maker '95
Disclosure '94
La Scorta '94
Love Affair '94
The Night and the Moment '94
A Pure Formality '94
Wolf '94
The Bachelor '93
In the Line of Fire '93
Beyond Justice '92
City of Joy '92
The Big Man: Crossing the
Line '91
Bugsy '91
Husbands and Lovers '91
A Time to Die '91
Everybody's Fine '90
State of Grace '90
Tie Me Up! Tie Me Down! '90
Casualties of War '89
The Endless Game '89
Fat Man and Little Boy '89
Time to Kill '89
Cinema Paradiso '88
Frantic '88
Python Wolf '88
A Time of Destiny '88
Rampage '87
The Untouchables '87
La Cage aux Folles 3: The
Wedding '86
The Mission '86
Stalking Danger '86
Hundra '85
Red Sonja '85
Corrupt '84
Once Upon a Time in America
'84
Fatal Error '83
Sahara '83
The Scarlet & the Black '83
Time to Die '83
Butterfly '82
Nana '82

The Thing '82
Treasure of the Four Crowns
'82
La Cage aux Folles 2 '81
Lovers and Liars '81
So Fine '81
The Tragedy of a Ridiculous
Man '81
The Island '80
Windows '80
Cold Eyes of Fear '70s
Almost Human '79
Sidney Sheldon's Bloodline
'79
Autopsy '78
Days of Heaven '78
La Cage aux Folles '78
The Chosen '77
The Exorcist 2: The Heretic
'77
Orca '77
The Desert of the Tartars '76
The Inheritance '76
Moses '76
The Human Factor '75
Leonor '75
Salo, or the 120 Days of
Sodom '75
When Women Lost Their
Tails '74
Arabian Nights '74
La Grande Bourgeoise '74
Le Secret '74
Master Touch '74
My Name Is Nobody '74
The Tempter '74
Allonsanfan '73
Massacre in Rome '73
Night Flight from Moscow '73
Sonny and Jed '73
'Tis a Pity She's a Whore '73
Bluebeard '72
A Fistful of Dynamite '72
The Cat o' Nine Tails '71
Dirty Heroes '71
Divine Nymph '71
Sacco & Vanzetti '71
The Bird with the Crystal
Plumage '70
Burn! '70
The Decameron '70
Two Mules for Sister Sara '70
When Women Had Tails '70
Red Tent '69
Danger: Diabolik '68
Once Upon a Time in the
West '68
Partner '68
Teorema '68
The Good, the Bad and the
Ugly '67
The Hawks & the Sparrows
'67
Hellbenders '67
Navajo Joe '67
Secret Agent 00 '67
The Battle of Algiers '66
Before the Revolution '65
For a Few Dollars More '65
Nightmare Castle '65
A Fistful of Dollars '64
Gun Fight at Red Sands '63
John Morris
Ellen Foster '97
Scarlett '94
Carolina Skeletons '92
Dirty Dancing '87
Ironweed '87
Spaceballs '87
Clue '85
The Doctor and the Devils '85
The Woman in Red '84

Formats Index
Digital

T he **Digital Formats Index** lists videos that are available in formats that take advantage of the new digital technologies. The oldest and most well-known, Laserdisc, often provides bonuses such as extra footage, interviews with cast members, or the original theater trailer. CD-I enjoyed a brief stint as "the next big thing" and serves mainly as a historical bridge to the newest format, DVD (Digital Video Disc). DVDs are the size of regular audio CDs, but hold twice the amount of information as Laserdisc. This index contains comprehensive lists of movies for all three formats.

Cyborg Soldier
Cyclone
Cyrano de Bergerac
Da
Dad
Daddy Long Legs
Daddy's Boys
Daddy's Dyin'...Who's Got the Will?
Daddy's Girl
Daffy Duck's Movie: Fantastic Island
Daffy Duck's Quackbusters
The Dagger of Kamui
Dakota
Damage
Dames
Damien: Omen 2
Damn the Defiant
Damn Yankees
A Damsel in Distress
Dance, Girl, Dance
Dance Macabre
Dance Me Outside
Dance of the Damned
Dance with a Stranger
Dance with Death
Dancers
Dances with Wolves
Dandy in Aspic
Danger Zone
Dangerous
The Dangerous
Dangerous Game
Dangerous Ground
Dangerous Heart
Dangerous Liaisons
Dangerous Life
Dangerous Minds
Dangerous Moves
A Dangerous Place
Dangerous Pursuit
Dangerous Touch
Dangerous When Wet
A Dangerous Woman
Dante's Peak
Danton
Darby O'Gill & the Little People
The Dark
Dark Age
The Dark Backward
Dark Before Dawn
Dark City
The Dark Crystal
Dark Habits
Dark Passage
Dark Planet
Dark Side of the Moon
Dark Star
Dark Tide
Dark Tower
Dark Victory
Dark Waters
The Dark Wind
Darkest Africa
Darkman
Darkman 2: The Return of Durant
Darkman 3: Die Darkman Die
Darling
D.A.R.Y.L.
Das Boot
Date with an Angel
A Date with Judy
Dave
David and Bathsheba
David and Lisa
David Copperfield
David Holzman's Diary
Davy Crockett and the River Pirates
Dawn of the Dead
The Dawning
The Day After
A Day at the Races
The Day My Parents Ran Away
Day of Atonement
Day of the Dead
The Day of the Dolphin
The Day of the Jackal
The Day of the Locust
Day of the Triffids
The Day the Earth Stood Still
Day Time Ended
Daylight
Days of Heaven
Days of Thunder

Days of Wine and Roses
Dazed and Confused
D.C. Cab
The Dead
Dead Again
Dead Aim
Dead Air
Dead Alive
Dead Bang
Dead Calm
Dead Center
Dead Cold
Dead End
Dead Funny
Dead Heat
Dead Man
Dead Man Out
Dead Man Walking
Dead Man's Revenge
Dead Men Can't Dance
Dead Men Don't Wear Plaid
Dead of Night
Dead of Winter
Dead On
Dead Poets Society
The Dead Pool
Dead Presidents
Dead Reckoning
Dead Ringers
Dead Space
Dead Tides
Dead Zone
Deadbolt
Deadfall
Deadline
Deadlock
Deadly Bet
Deadly Companions
Deadly Daphne's Revenge
Deadly Dreams
Deadly Friend
Deadly Illusion
Deadly Outbreak
Deadly Possession
Deadly Rivals
The Deadly Trackers
Deadtime Stories
Deal of the Century
Dealers
Death and the Maiden
Death Becomes Her
Death Before Dishonor
Death Dreams
Death Hunt
Death Machine
Death of a Salesman
Death of a Scoundrel
Death of an Angel
Death on the Nile
Death Ring
Death Warrant
Death Watch
Death Wish
Death Wish 2
Death Wish 3
Death Wish 4: The Crackdown
Death Wish 5: The Face of Death
Deathrow Gameshow
Deathstalker
Deathstalker 2: Duel of the Titans
Deathstalker 3
The Decameron
The Deceivers
December
Deception
Deceptions
Decline of Western Civilization 1
Decoration Day
Decoy
The Deep
Deep Cover
Deep Red
Deepstar Six
The Deer Hunter
Def by Temptation
Def Jam's How to Be a Player
Defending Your Life
Defense of the Realm
Defenseless
Deja Vu
The Delicate Delinquent
Delicatessen
Delirious
Deliverance
Delta Force

Delta Force 2: Operation Stranglehold
Delta Force 3: The Killing Game
Delta of Venus
Delusion
Do or Die
Demetrius and the Gladiators
Demolition Man
The Demolitionist
Demon City Shinjuku
A Demon in My View
Demon Possessed
Demon Seed
Demon Wind
Demonic Toys
Demons
Demons 2
Demonstone
Denial: The Dark Side of Passion
Denise Calls Up
Dennis the Menace
Dennis the Menace: Dinosaur Hunter
Descending Angel
Desert Bloom
The Desert Fox
Desert Hearts
Desert Kickboxer
Desert Phantom
Designing Woman
Desire and Hell at Sunset Motel
Desire Under the Elms
Desiree
Desk Set
Desperado
Desperate Hours
Desperate Measures
Desperate Motives
Desperately Seeking Susan
Destination Moon
Destroyer
Destry Rides Again
The Detective
Detonator 2: Night Watch
Detour
The Devil & Daniel Webster
The Devil at 4 O'Clock
Devil in a Blue Dress
Devil in the Flesh
Devil Monster
The Devil's Advocate
The Devil's Commandment
Devil's Rain
Devlin
Diabolique
Dial "M" for Murder
Diamond Head
Diamond Run
The Diamond Trap
Diamonds Are Forever
Diane
Diary of a Chambermaid
Diary of a Hitman
Diary of a Lost Girl
Diary of a Serial Killer
The Diary of Anne Frank
Dick Tracy
Dick Tracy Returns
Dick Tracy vs. Crime Inc.
Die Hard
Die Hard 2: Die Harder
Die Hard: With a Vengeance
Die, Monster, Die!
Diggstown
Dillinger
Dillinger and Capone
Dim Sum: A Little Bit of Heart
Diner
Dinner at Eight
Diplomaniacs
Diplomatic Immunity
Direct Hit
Dirt Bike Kid
Dirty Dancing
The Dirty Dozen
Dirty Harry
Dirty Mary Crazy Larry
Dirty Rotten Scoundrels
The Disappearance of Christina
Disclosure
The Discreet Charm of the Bourgeoisie
Disorderlies
Disorderly Orderly
Disorganized Crime
Distant Thunder
Distant Voices, Still Lives

The Distinguished Gentleman
Disturbed
Diva
The Dive
The Divorce of Lady X
Do or Die
Do the Right Thing
D.O.A.
Doc Hollywood
The Doctor
Dr. Alien
Dr. Caligari
Dr. Cyclops
Doctor Detroit
Doctor Dolittle
Dr. Giggles
Dr. Jekyll and Mr. Hyde
Dr. No
Dr. Strangelove, or: How I Learned to Stop Worrying and Love the Bomb
Doctor X
Doctor Zhivago
Dodge City
Dodsworth
Does This Mean We're Married?
Dog Day Afternoon
Dogfight
The Dogfighters
The Dogs of War
Doll Face
Dollar
Dollars
Dollman
The Dolls
A Doll's House
Dolly Dearest
Dolores Claiborne
Dominick & Eugene
Domino
Don Juan
Don Juan DeMarco
Don Juan, My Love
Don Q., Son of Zorro
Dona Flor and Her Two Husbands
Dona Herlinda & Her Son
Donnie Brasco
Donovan's Brain
Donovan's Reef
Don't Be a Menace to South Central While Drinking Your Juice in the Hood
Don't Look Now
Don't Mess with My Sister!
Don't Talk to Strangers
Don't Tell Her It's Me
Don't Tell Mom the Babysitter's Dead
The Doors
The Doors: Soft Parade, a Retrospective
Doppelganger: The Evil Within
Double-Crossed
Double Dragon
Double Exposure
Double Exposure: The Story of Margaret Bourke-White
Double Happiness
Double Impact
Double Indemnity
Double Jeopardy
The Double Life of Veronique
Double Take
Double Team
Double Trouble
Down Among the Z Men
Down and Out in Beverly Hills
Down Argentine Way
Down Came a Blackbird
Down the Drain
Down to Earth
Downhill Racer
Downtown
Dracula
Dracula Blows His Cool
Dracula: Dead and Loving It
Dragnet
Dragon: The Bruce Lee Story
Dragonheart
Dragonslayer
Dream a Little Dream
Dream Lover
Dream Machine
Dream Man
The Dream Team
Dreams

Dreamscape
Dressed to Kill
The Dresser
Dressmaker
The Drifter
Drifting Weeds
Drive
Drive-In Massacre
Driving Force
Driving Me Crazy
Driving Miss Daisy
Drop Dead Fred
DROP Squad
Drowning by Numbers
Drugstore Cowboy
Drums
Drums Along the Mohawk
A Dry White Season
D2: The Mighty Ducks
The Duchess and the Dirtwater Fox
Duck Soup
DuckTales the Movie: Treasure of the Lost Lamp
Dudes
Duel of Hearts
The Duellists
Dumb & Dumber
Dumbo
Dune
Dune Warriors
The Dunera Boys
Dungeonmaster
Dunston Checks In
Dynamite and Gold
The Eagle
Early Frost
An Early Frost
Earth Girls Are Easy
Earth vs. the Flying Saucers
Earthquake
East of Eden
Easter Parade
Easy Living
Easy Money
Easy Rider
Easy Wheels
Eat a Bowl of Tea
Eat Drink Man Woman
Eating
Echo Park
Echoes of Paradise
Ed
Ed and His Dead Mother
Ed Wood
Eddie
Eddie and the Cruisers
Eddie and the Cruisers 2: Eddie Lives!
Eddie Macon's Run
Eddie Murphy: Raw
The Eddy Duchin Story
Edge of Sanity
Educating Rita
Edward Scissorhands
Edward II
Egg
Egg and I
The Egyptian
The Eiger Sanction
8 1/2
Eight Men Out
8 Million Ways to Die
8 Seconds
18 Again!
The Eighth Day
84 Charing Cross Road
84 Charlie Mopic
Eijanaika
El Amor Brujo
El Cid
El Dorado
El Mariachi
Electra Glide in Blue
Electric Dreams
The Electric Horseman
Elena and Her Men
Eleni
Elephant Boy
The Elephant Man
Elmer Gantry
The Elusive Corporal
Elvira Madigan
Elvira, Mistress of the Dark
Elvis in Hollywood
Embrace of the Vampire
The Emerald Forest

Home

The Magic Christian
The Magic Flute
Magic Kid
Magic Kid 2
The Magic Voyage
Magical Mystery Tour
The Magician
The Magnificent Ambersons
The Magnificent Seven
Magnum Force
The Mahabharata
Mahogany
The Maid
Maid to Order
Major League
Major League 2
Major Payne
Making Mr. Right
The Makioka Sisters
Malarek
Malcolm
Malcolm X
Malice
Malicious
Mallrats
Malone
The Maltese Falcon
Mama, There's a Man in Your Bed
The Mambo Kings
Mame
Man Bait
A Man Called Horse
A Man Called Sarge
Man Facing Southeast
A Man for All Seasons
Man from Cairo
The Man from Snowy River
Man from Utah
A Man in Love
The Man in the Gray Flannel Suit
The Man Inside
Man of a Thousand Faces
Man of Flowers
Man of La Mancha
A Man of No Importance
Man of the House
Man on Fire
Man Outside
Man Trouble
The Man Who Came to Dinner
The Man Who Could Work Miracles
The Man Who Fell to Earth
The Man Who Knew Too Much
The Man Who Loved Women
The Man Who Shot Liberty Valance
The Man Who Would Be King
The Man with the Golden Gun
The Man with Two Brains
The Man Without a Face
The Manchurian Candidate
Mandingo
The Mangler
Manhattan
Manhattan Melodrama
Manhattan Murder Mystery
The Manhattan Project
Manhunt
Manhunt in the African Jungle
Manhunt of Mystery Island
Manhunter
Maniac Cop 2
The Manitou
Mannequin
Mannequin 2: On the Move
Manny & Lo
Manon of the Spring
Man's Best Friend
Marat/Sade
Marathon Man
March of the Wooden Soldiers
Marie Antoinette
Marius
Mark of Zorro
Marked for Death
Marked for Murder
Marked Man
Marked Woman
Marnie
Marooned
Married to It
Married to the Mob
The Marrying Man
Mars Attacks!

Martial Law 2: Undercover
Martial Outlaw
Martians Go Home!
Martin
Marty
Marvin's Room
The Marx Brothers in a Nutshell
Mary of Scotland
Mary Poppins
Mary Reilly
Mary Shelley's Frankenstein
M*A*S*H
M*A*S*H: Goodbye, Farewell & Amen
The Mask
Mask
Mask of Death
Mask of the Dragon
Masks of Death
Masque of the Red Death
Masque of the Red Death/ Premature Burial
Masquerade
Mass Appeal
Massive Retaliation
The Master of Ballantrae
The Masters of Menace
Masters of the Universe
Matador
The Matchmaker
Matewan
Matilda
Matinee
Maurice
Mausoleum
Maverick
Max Dugan Returns
Max Headroom, the Original Story
Maxie
Maximum Force
Maximum Overdrive
Maximum Risk
Maximum Security
May Fools
May Wine
Maybe ... Maybe Not
Mayerling
Maytime
McCabe & Mrs. Miller
The McConnell Story
McHale's Navy
McLintock!
McQ
McVicar
Me and Him
Me and the Kid
Mean Season
Mean Streets
Meatballs
Meatballs 2
The Mechanic
Mediterraneo
Meet John Doe
Meet Me in Las Vegas
Meet Me in St. Louis
Meet the Hollowheads
Meeting Venus
Mein Kampf: Hitler's Rise and Fall
Melvin and Howard
Memoirs of an Invisible Man
Memorial Valley Massacre
Memories of Me
Memphis
Memphis Belle
Men Are Not Gods
Men at Work
Men Don't Leave
Men in Black
Men of Respect
Men of War
Menace II Society
The Men's Club
Mercenary Fighters
Meridian: Kiss of the Beast
Mermaids
The Merry Widow
Messenger of Death
Metalstorm: The Destruction of Jared Syn
Meteor
The Meteor Man
Metro
Metropolis
Metropolitan
MGM: When the Lion Roars

Miami Blues
Miami Rhapsody
Miami Vice
Miami Vice 2: The Prodigal Son
Michael
Mickey One
Mickey's Christmas Carol
Micki & Maude
Midnight
Midnight Blue
Midnight Cabaret
A Midnight Clear
Midnight Confessions
Midnight Cop
Midnight Cowboy
Midnight Crossing
Midnight Express
Midnight Run
Midnight Tease
Midway
A Midwinter's Tale
Mighty Aphrodite
The Mighty Ducks
Mighty Joe Young
The Mighty Quinn
The Milagro Beanfield War
Mildred Pierce
Miles from Home
Milky Way
The Milky Way
Millenium
Miller's Crossing
Million Dollar Haul
Million Dollar Mystery
The Millionaire's Express
Mimic
Mindfield
Mindwarp
Ministry of Vengeance
Minnesota Clay
A Minor Miracle
The Miracle
Miracle Beach
Miracle in Milan
Miracle in Rome
Miracle in the Wilderness
Miracle Mile
Miracle of Our Lady of Fatima
Miracle on 34th Street
Miracles
The Mirror Crack'd
The Mirror Has Two Faces
Mirror, Mirror
Mirror, Mirror 2: Raven Dance
Mischief
Misery
The Misfits
Miss Firecracker
Ms. 45
Miss Right
Miss Sadie Thompson
Missing
Missing in Action
Missing in Action 2: The Beginning
The Mission
Mission Batangas
Mission Galactica: The Cylon Attack
Mission Manila
Mission of Justice
Mississippi Burning
Mississippi Masala
Mississippi Mermaid
Mrs. Brown
Mrs. Doubtfire
Mrs. Miniver
Mrs. Parker and the Vicious Circle
Mrs. Soffel
Mrs. Winterbourne
Mr. Ace
Mr. & Mrs. Bridge
Mr. & Mrs. Loving
Mr. & Mrs. Smith
Mr. Arkadin
Mr. Baseball
Mr. Blandings Builds His Dream House
Mr. Deeds Goes to Town
Mr. Destiny
Mr. Holland's Opus
Mr. Hulot's Holiday
Mr. Jones
Mr. Lucky
Mr. Magoo
Mr. Mom

Mr. North
Mr. Robinson Crusoe
Mr. Saturday Night
Mr. Skeffington
Mr. Smith Goes to Washington
Mr. Walkie Talkie
Mr. Wonderful
Mr. Write
Mr. Wrong
Mistress
Mixed Nuts
Mo' Better Blues
Mo' Money
Mob Story
Mobsters
Moby Dick
Model by Day
Modern Girls
Modern Romance
Modern Times
The Moderns
Moll Flanders
Mom
Mom and Dad Save the World
Mommie Dearest
Mon Oncle
Mona Lisa
Money for Nothing
The Money Pit
Money Talks
Money to Burn
Money Train
Monkey Business
Monkey Shines
Monkey Trouble
Monolith
Monsieur Hire
Monsieur Verdoux
The Monster Club
Monster High
Monster in a Box
The Monster Squad
Monterey Pop
A Month by the Lake
A Month in the Country
Monty Python and the Holy Grail
Monty Python Live at the Hollywood Bowl
Monty Python's Flying Circus
Monty Python's Life of Brian
Monty Python's Parrot Sketch Not Included
Monty Python's The Meaning of Life
Moon 44
The Moon Is Blue
Moon over Parador
Moonbase
Moonfleet
Moonlight and Valentino
Moonlighting
Moonraker
Moonrise
Moonstruck
Moontrap
More American Graffiti
More! Police Squad
The More the Merrier
Morgan!
Morgan Stewart's Coming Home
Morgan the Pirate
The Morning After
Morning Glory
Morocco
Mortal Danger
Mortal Kombat 2: Annihilation
Mortal Sins
Mortal Thoughts
Mortuary Academy
Moscow Does Not Believe in Tears
Moscow on the Hudson
The Mosquito Coast
Most Wanted
Motel Hell
Mother
Mother's Boys
Motor Patrol
Moulin Rouge
The Mountain Men
Mountains of the Moon
Moving
Moving Target
Moving Violation
Moving Violations
Mozart: A Childhood Chronicle
Much Ado about Nothing

Mulholland Falls
Multiplicity
The Mummy
The Muppet Movie
The Muppets Take Manhattan
Murder at 1600
Murder by Death
Murder by Numbers
Murder in Mind
Murder In the First
Murder, My Sweet
Murder on the Bayou
Murder on the Orient Express
Murder One
Murder Story
Murderous Vision
Muriel's Wedding
Murmur of the Heart
Murphy's Fault
Murphy's Law
Murphy's Romance
Muscle Beach Party
Music Box
The Music Lovers
The Music Man
The Music of Chance
The Music Teacher
Mutant
Mutant Species
Mute Witness
The Mutilator
Mutiny on the Bounty
My American Cousin
My Beautiful Laundrette
My Best Friend's Wedding
My Best Girl
My Bloody Valentine
My Blue Heaven
My Boyfriend's Back
My Chauffeur
My Darling Clementine
My Demon Lover
My Dinner with Andre
My Dog Shep
My Fair Lady
My Family
My Father the Hero
My Favorite Brunette
My Favorite Wife
My Favorite Year
My Fellow Americans
My Friend Irma
My Girl
My Girl 2
My Heroes Have Always Been Cowboys
My Left Foot
My Life
My Life As a Dog
My Little Chickadee
My Little Girl
My Mom's a Werewolf
My Name Is Ivan
My Neighbor Totoro
My New Gun
My New Partner
My Night at Maud's
My Own Private Idaho
My Samurai
My Science Project
My Stepmother Is an Alien
My Summer Story
My Tutor
My Wonderful Life
Mysterious Island
Mystery of the Wax Museum
Mystery Science Theater 3000: The Movie
Mystery Train
Mystic Pizza
Nadine
Nails
Naked
The Naked Gun: From the Files of Police Squad
Naked Gun 33 1/3: The Final Insult
Naked Gun 2 1/2: The Smell of Fear
Naked in New York
Naked Jungle
Naked Kiss
The Naked Prey
The Name of the Rose
Napoleon
Narrow Margin
Nashville

ACE—Ace Video
ADL—Anti-Defamation League of B'nai B'rith
AEH—A & E Home Video
AFE—Amazing Fantasy Entertainment
AFR—Afro-Am Distributing Co.
AHV—Avid Home Video
AIM—AIMS Multimedia
ALD—Alden Films
AMB—Ambrose Video Publishing, Inc.
ANI—AnimEigo Inc. (R)
AOV—Admit One Video
APP—Applause Theatre and Cinema
APX—A-PIX Entertainment Inc.
ART—Artisan Entertainment
ATL—Atlas Entertainment Corp.
ATM—Atomic Pictures
ATS—Acorn Media Publishing
ATV—Atlantic Video
AUD—Audio-Forum
AVA—Avalanche Entertainment
AVE—WarnerVision
AVI—Arrow Video, Inc./Arrow Entertainment
AWA—Award Films International
BAR—Barr Films
BBE—Blockbuster Entertainment Corp.
BFA—Phoenix/Coronet/BFA Films and Video (R)
BFV—Best Film & Video Corp. (W)
BIJ—Bijou Video
BMG—BMG
BMV—Bennett Marine Video
BPG—Bridgestone Multimedia
BST—ETD
BSV—Bosko Video
BTV—Baker & Taylor Video
BUL—Bullfrog Films, Inc.
BWE—BWE (Bonneville Worldwide Entertainment) Video

CAB—Cable Films & Video
CAF—Cabin Fever Entertainment
CAL—California Newsreel
CAT—Creative Arts Television Archive
CCB—Critics' Choice Video, Inc.
CCC—Cyclops Communications Corp.
CCN—Cinevista
CCP—Cambridge Educational (R)
CDV—Television International
CEL—Celebrity Home Entertainment (W)
CFV—Carousel Film & Video
CHF—Churchill Media
CHI—Center for Humanities, Inc.
CIC—Cinema International Canada
CIG—The Cinema Guild
CIN—Cinematrix Releasing
CMB—Columbia House Video Library
CMR—Camera Three Productions, Inc.
CNG—Congress Entertainment, Inc. (R)
CNM—Cinemacabre Video
COL—Columbia Tristar Home Video (W)
CPA—Cinema Parallel
CPM—Central Park Media/U.S. Manga Corps
CRC—Criterion Collection
CRV—Crown Video
CRY—Crystal Productions
CTC—Coast to Coast Video
CTH—Corinth Video
CTL—Capitol Entertainment and Home Video (W)
CVC—Connoisseur Meridian Films
DAP—Dead Alive Productions
DIS—Walt Disney Home Video
DMP—Ariztical Entertainment

DVT—Discount Video Tapes, Inc./Hollywood's Attic (W)
EAG—Eagle Entertainment
ECU—EcuFilm
EEL—Englewood Entertainment LLC
EII—El Independent Cinema
ELE—Electric Productions
ELV—Electric Video
EMI—EMI Video
EPC—Epic Records
ERG—Ergo Media Inc. (R)
EVE—Evergreen Entertainment
EXP—Expanded Entertainment
FAF—Fast Forward
FCT—Facets Multimedia, Inc.
FEI—FM Entertainment, Inc.
FFC—Family Films/Concordia
FFM—Flower Films (R)
FGF—Military/Combat Stock Footage Library
FHE—Family Home Entertainment
FHS—Films for the Humanities & Sciences
FHV—Foothill Video
FLL—Filmakers Library, Inc.
FLL—Full Moon Pictures
FMT—Format International
FOX—CBS/Fox Video
FRA—Video France
FRF—First Run Features
FRG—Fright Video
FRV—First Run Video
FST—Festival Films (R)
FUS—Fusion Video
FXL—Fox/Lorber Home Video
FXV—Twentieth Century Fox Home Entertainment
GEM—Video Gems
GFV—Vision Video/Gateway Films
GKK—Goodtimes Entertainment
GLV—German Language Video Center
GPV—Grapevine Video

GRE—Greycat Films (W)
GRG—Gorgon Video
GVV—Glenn Video Vistas, Ltd. (R)
HBO—HBO Home Video (W)
HCV—Henwood Cinema Video (R)
HEG—Horizon Entertainment
HHE—Hollywood Home Entertainment
HHT—Hollywood Home Theatre
HMK—Hallmark Home Entertainment
HMV—Home Vision Cinema
HPH—Hollywood Pictures Home Video
HSE—High/Scope Educational Research Foundation
HTV—Hen's Tooth Video (W)
HVF—Home Video Films
HVL—Home Video Library
IBT—International Book and Tape Supply
ICA—First Run/Icarus Films
IGP—Ignatius Press
IHF—International Historic Films, Inc.
IME—Image Entertainment
IMP—Imperial Entertainment Corp.
INC—Increase/SilverMine Video (W)
ING—Ingram Entertainment Inc. (W)
INT—Interama, Inc. (R)
IPI—Intrepid Productions Inc.
ITC—ITC
IUF—Pentrex (R)
IVY—Ivy Film/Video
JAF—James #Agee Film Project
JEF—JEF Films, Inc.
JFK—Just for Kids Home Video (W)
JTC—J2 Communications
KAR—Karol Video (R)
KBE—K-Beech Video, Inc.
KEP—Keep the Faith Inc.

KID—Kid Vision
KIT—Kit Parker Video
KIV—Kino on Video (W)
KUI—Knowledge Unlimited, Inc.
KUL—Kultur Video (W)
LBD—VLM Entertainment
LEO—Leo Films (W)
LME—Lucerne Media (R)
LOO—Loonic Video
LRP—Light Rain Productions
LSV—LSVideo, Inc.
LTY—Lightyear Entertainment
LUM—Lumivision Corp.
MAD—Madera Cinevideo
MAS—Mastervision, Inc. (R)
MAX—Miramax Pictures Home Video
MCG—Management Company Entertainment Group (MCEG), Inc.
MET—Metromedia Entertainment
MFI—Firm Direct
MFV—Mystic Fire Video (R)
MGH—McGraw Hill Book Company
MGI—Monarich Group, Inc.
MGM—MGM Home Entertainment
MIL—Milestone Film & Video
MLB—Mike #LeBell's Video (R)
MLT—Music for Little People
MNC—Monarch Home Video
MON—Monterey Home Video (W)
MOR—Morris Video
MOV—Movies Unlimited (R)
MPI—MPI Home Video
MRC—Xenon Entertainment (W)
MRV—Moore Video
MTH—MTI Home Video (W)
MTM—MTM Home Video
MTP—Maryland Public Television
MTX—MNTEX Entertainment, Inc.

MVC—Moviecraft, Inc.
MVD—Music Video Distributors
MWF—Monday/Wednesday/
Friday Video
NCJ—National Center for
Jewish Film
NEW—New Video Group
NFB—National Film Board of
Canada
NHO—New Horizons Home
Video
NJN—New Jersey Network
NLC—New Line Home Video
NMD—Neville Meyer
Distribution (NMD)
NOS—Nostalgia Family Video
NYF—New Yorker Video
NYR—Not Yet Released
ORI—Orion Home Video
ORP—Orphan Entertainment
PAR—Paramount Home Video
PAU—Paulist Productions
PBC—Princeton Book Co.
Publishers
PBS—PBS Home Video
PEG—Peachtree Entertainment
Group, Inc.
PEN—Pentrex Video
PGV—Polygram Video (PV)
PHO—Phoenix Distributors
PIC—Videos.com, Inc.
PMH—PM Entertainment
Group, Inc.
PMR—Premiere Home Video
PMS—Professional Media
Service Corp.
PPI—Planet Pictures, Inc.
PRD—Peter Pan Industries, Inc.
(PPI) (W)
PRE—Prestige Video
PRG—Paragon Home Video
PRV—Prime Video
PSV—Powersports Millennium
PTB—Proud to Be...A Black
Video Collection
PYR—Pyramid Film & Video
PZA—Plaza Entertainment
QHV—Questar Video, Inc.
QVD—Quality Video
RAP—RAP Entertainment Inc.
RAT—Rated Gee!
RDF—Russ #Doughten Films,
Inc.
RDG—Reader's Digest Home
Video
REA—Real Entertainment
REP—Republic Pictures Home
Video
RHI—Rhino Home Video
RHP—Rhapsody Films, Inc.
RHV—Television
Representatives, Inc. (W)
RMF—RM Films International,
Inc. (R)
ROC—Rocket Pictures
RVN—Raven International
RXM—Rex #Miller
SCH—Schoolmasters Video (R)
SCO—Scorpio International,
Ltd.
SCP—Screen Pix Home Video
SDE—Stardance Entertainment
SGE—Arnsell Entertainment
SHE—Showcase Entertainment
SHO—Shokus Video
SHR—Shanachie Entertainment
SHV—Strand Home Video
SIG—Signals
SIM—Simitar Entertainment
SLI—Silver Lake International
SMV—Sony Music Video
Enterprises
SMW—Something Weird Video
SNC—Sinister Cinema
SPC—Spectrum Films, Inc.
STE—Sterling Home
Entertainment
STP—Streamline Pictures
STS—Stagestep

STV—Studio Video Productions
SUN—Sun Video (W)
SVE—Society for Visual
Education, Inc. (SVE)
SWC—Simon Wiesenthal
Center
SWI—ScreenWorks Inc.
TAI—Tai Seng Video Marketing
TCE—Third Coast
Entertainment
TEM—Tempe Video
THA—3M Audio Visual Division
THV—Trimark Home Video
TIM—Timeless Video Inc.
TLF—Time-Life Video and
Television
TOU—Buena Vista Home Video
TPI—Thomson Productions, Inc.
TPV—Tapeworm Video
Distributors
TRI—Triboro Entertainment
Group
TRO—Troma Inc. (W)
TSR—Three Star Releasing
TTC—Turner Home
Entertainment Company
TTV—Troma Team Video
TVC—The Video Catalog
TWE—Trans-World
Entertainment
TWV—Time Warner Viewer's
Edge
UAV—UAV Corporation
UND—Uni Distribution/June
Morishita
UNI—Unicorn Video, Inc.
UNT—Unity Productions
UPI—Universal Productions
International/Gaming Tapes,
Inc.
USH—Universal Studios Home
Video
UWA—University of Washington
Educational Media Collection
VAI—Video Artists International,
Inc.
VAN—Vantage
Communications, Inc.
VBL—Video Bible Library, Inc.
VCD—Video City Productions/
Distributing
VCI—VCI Home Video
VCN—Video Connection
VCO—Video Collectibles
VDA—Video Action (W)
VDC—Vidcrest
VDM—Video Dimensions (W)
VEC—Valencia Entertainment
Corp.
VES—Vestron Video
VHE—VCII Home
Entertainment, Inc.
VIC—Victory Multimedia
VIF—The VideoFinders
Collection
VIP—VIP Video
VNG—Vanguard International
Cinema, Inc.
VRS—Video Resources
VSE—Vista Street
Entertainment (W)
VSM—Video Search of Miami
VTR—Anchor Bay
VYY—Video Yesteryear
WAC—World Artists Home
Video
WAR—Warner Home Video,
Inc.
WAX—Waxworks/Videoworks,
Inc.
WBF—Water Bearer Films
WEA—Warner/Elektra/Atlantic
(WEA) Corporation
WFV—Western Media Systems
WGB—WGBH/Boston
WHA—Wham! USA
WLA—Western L.A. Film
Productions, Inc.
WLF—Wolfe Video

WME—Warren #Miller
Entertainment
WMI—Wellspring Media, Inc.
WNE—WNET/Thirteen Non-
Broadcast
WOM—Wombat Film and Video
WOV—Worldvision Home
Video, Inc.
WRV—Warner Reprise Video
(R)
WSH—Wishing Well Distributing
WST—White Star
WVE—World Video Enterprises,
Inc.
XVC—Xenon
YHV—York Home Video
YOC—Yankee-Oriole Co. (W)
ZGI—Zeitgeist Films Ltd.

Distributor Guide

The **Distributor Guide** provides full contact information, including address, phone, fax and toll-free numbers, for over 340 distributors. The distributors are listed alphabetically within Wholesale or Retail sections. Some distributors sell to both markets, or have not stated which market they serve. These distributors will appear alphabetically at the beginning of this guide. Each video in the main section has at least one and as many as three distributor codes located at the end of the entry. The key to these codes, preceding this guide, will lead you to the appropriate distributor. Those reviews with the code **OM** are on moratorium, meaning that they were distributed at one time, but aren't currently. Since it was once available, an On Moratorium title may show up at your local video store. If the distributor for a movie is not known, the code **NO** will follow the review. New theatrical releases that haven't made it to video at press time have the designation **NYR** (not yet released). These are titles that we expect will be released on video before our next edition. **Warning!** From year to year, a small minority of distributors move without telling anyone, or just plain go out of business. **Warning! Warning!** Studio distributors do not sell to the general public, they generally act as wholesalers, selling only to retail outlets. Many video stores provide an ordering service. If your local video store doesn't have a title you want, you can ask them to order it for you.

A & E HOME VIDEO *(AEH)*
235 E. 45th St.
New York, NY 10017

A-PIX ENTERTAINMENT INC. *(APX)*
200 Madison Ave., 24th Fl.
New York, NY 10016
206-284-4700
800-245-6472
Fax: 206-286-4433

ACE VIDEO *(ACE)*
19749 Dearborn St.
Chatsworth, CA 91311

ACORN MEDIA PUBLISHING *(ATS)*
7910 Woodmont Ave., Ste. 350
Bethesda, MD 20814
301-907-0030
800-999-0212
Fax: 301-907-9049
Email: acorn1@ix.netcom.com

ADMIT ONE VIDEO *(AOV)*
PO Box 66, Sta. O
Toronto, ON, Canada M4A 2M8
416-463-5714
Fax: 416-463-5714

AFRO-AM DISTRIBUTING CO. *(AFR)*
1909 W. 95th St.
Chicago, IL 60643-1105
773-235-4504

JAMES AGEE FILM PROJECT *(JAF)*
316 1/2 E. Main St.
Johnson City, TN 37601
615-926-8637
800-352-5111
Fax: 615-971-2921

AIMS MULTIMEDIA *(AIM)*
9710 DeSoto Ave.
Chatsworth, CA 91311-4409

818-773-4300
800-367-2467
Fax: 818-341-6700
Email:
infa@aims.multimedia.com

ALDEN FILMS *(ALD)*
PO Box 449
Clarksburg, NJ 08510
732-462-3522
Fax: 732-294-0330

AMAZING FANTASY ENTERTAINMENT *(AFE)*
1645 N. Vine St.
Hollywood, CA 90028
213-468-0599

AMBROSE VIDEO PUBLISHING, INC. *(AMB)*
28 W. 44th St.
New York, NY 10036
212-768-7373
800-526-4663
Fax: 212-768-9292
Email: ambrose.com

AMSELL ENTERTAINMENT *(SGE)*
12001 Ventura Pl., 4th Fl., Ste. 404
Studio City, CA 91604
818-766-8500
Fax: 818-766-7873

ANCHOR BAY *(VTR)*
500 Kirts Blvd.
Troy, MI 48084
248-362-4400
800-786-8777
Fax: 248-362-4454

ANTI-DEFAMATION LEAGUE OF B'NAI B'RITH *(ADL)*
Audio-Visual Dept.
823 United Nations Plaza
New York, NY 10017
212-490-2525
Fax: 212-867-0779

APPLAUSE THEATRE AND CINEMA *(APP)*
211 W. 71st St.
New York, NY 10023
212-496-7511
Fax: 212-721-2856

ARIZTICAL ENTERTAINMENT *(DMP)*
405 E. Wetmore, Ste. 117-516
Tucson, AZ 85705
800-356-4386

ARROW VIDEO, INC./ARROW ENTERTAINMENT *(AVI)*
135 W. 50th St., Ste. 1925
New York, NY 10020
212-258-2200
Fax: 212-245-1252

ARTISAN ENTERTAINMENT *(ART)*
15400 Sherman Way
PO Box 10124
Van Nuys, CA 91410-0124
818-988-5060
800-677-0789
Fax: 818-778-3259

ATLANTIC VIDEO *(ATV)*
1290 Avenue of the Americas
New York, NY 10104
212-707-2000

ATLAS ENTERTAINMENT CORP. *(ATL)*
1 Jocama Blvd., Ste. 2E
Old Bridge, NJ 08857
732-591-1155
Fax: 732-591-0660

ATOMIC PICTURES *(ATM)*
PO Box 15824
North Hollywood, CA 91615-5824

AUDIO-FORUM *(AUD)*
96 Broad St.
Guilford, CT 06437

203-453-9794
800-243-1234
Fax: 203-453-9774
Email:
74537.550@compuserve.com

AVALANCHE ENTERTAINMENT *(AVA)*
578 Post Rd. E., No. 712
Westport, CT 06880
203-454-2298
Fax: 203-454-2398

AVID HOME VIDEO *(AHV)*
c/o Live Home Video
15400 Sherman Way
PO Box 10124
Van Nuys, CA 91406
818-908-0303
800-423-7455

AWARD FILMS INTERNATIONAL *(AWA)*
PO Box 93399
Hollywood, CA 90093
800-634-2242

BAKER & TAYLOR VIDEO *(BTV)*
700 N. Austin
Niles, IL 60714
800-775-2800

BARR FILMS *(BAR)*
12801 Schabarum
Irwindale, CA 91706

BENNETT MARINE VIDEO *(BMV)*
8436 W. 3rd St., Ste. 740
Los Angeles, CA 90048
213-951-7570
800-733-8862

BIJOU VIDEO *(BIJ)*
1349 N. Wells
Chicago, IL 60610
312-943-5397
800-932-7111
Fax: 312-337-1270

BLOCKBUSTER ENTERTAINMENT CORP. *(BBE)*
12655 N. Central Expwy., Ste. 600
Dallas, TX 75243
214-866-2200
800-733-1939
Fax: 214-866-2250

BMG *(BMG)*
1540 Broadway, 2yth Fl.
New York, NY 10036
216-543-6466

BOSKO VIDEO *(BSV)*
3802 E. Cudahy Ave.
Cudahy, WI 53110-1234

BRIDGESTONE MULTIMEDIA *(BPG)*
300 N. McKemy Ave.
Chandler, AZ 85226
800-523-0988
Fax: 602-940-8924

BUENA VISTA HOME VIDEO *(TOU)*
PO Box 908
Lakewood, CA 90714-0908
310-233-3120

BULLFROG FILMS, INC. *(BUL)*
PO Box 149
Oley, PA 19547
610-779-8226
800-543-3764
Fax: 610-370-1978
Email: bullfrog@igc.org
   HomePage: http://
   bullfrogfilms.com

BWE (BONNEVILLE WORLDWIDE ENTERTAINMENT) VIDEO *(BWE)*
55 North 300 West, No. 315
Salt Lake City, UT 84110-1160

801-575-3680
800-654-1686

**CABIN FEVER
ENTERTAINMENT** *(CAF)*
100 W. Putnam Ave.
Greenwich, CT 06830
203-863-5200
Fax: 203-863-5258

**CABLE FILMS &
VIDEO** *(CAB)*
PO Box 7171, Country Club Sta.
Kansas City, MO 64113
913-362-2804
800-514-2804
Fax: 913-341-7365
Email:
catchwave@sprintmail.com

**CALIFORNIA
NEWSREEL** *(CAL)*
149 9th St., Ste. 420
San Francisco, CA 94103
415-621-6196
Fax: 415-621-6522
Email:
newsreel@ix.netcom.com

**CAMERA THREE
PRODUCTIONS, INC.** *(CMR)*
PO Box 739
Kent, CT 06757
860-868-1771
Fax: 860-868-9999
Email: catarchive@aol.com

**CAROUSEL FILM &
VIDEO** *(CFV)*
260 5th Ave., Rm. 905
New York, NY 10001
212-683-1660
800-683-1660
Fax: 212-683-1662
Email: carousel@pipeline.com

CBS/FOX VIDEO *(FOX)*
PO Box 900
Beverly Hills, CA 90213
562-373-4800
(888)223-4FOX
Fax: 562-373-4803

**CENTER FOR HUMANITIES,
INC.** *(CHI)*
Box 1000
Mount Kisco, NY 10549
914-666-4100
800-431-1242
Fax: 914-666-5319
Email: gavideo@aol.com

**CENTRAL PARK MEDIA/U.S.
MANGA CORPS** *(CPM)*
250 W. 57th St., Ste. 317
New York, NY 10107
212-977-7456
800-833-7456
Fax: 212-977-8709
HomePage: http://
www.centralparkmedia.com

CHURCHILL MEDIA *(CHF)*
6667 N. Northwestern Hwy.
Chicago, IL 60631
773-775-9550
800-334-7830
Fax: 773-775-5091

THE CINEMA GUILD *(CIG)*
1697 Broadway, Ste. 506
New York, NY 10019
212-246-5522
800-723-5522
Fax: 212-246-5525
Email: thecinema@aol.com
HomePage: http://
www.cinemaguild.com/
cinemaguild

**CINEMA INTERNATIONAL
CANADA** *(CIC)*
8275 Mayrand
Montreal, PQ, Canada H4P 2C8

514-336-9696
Fax: 514-336-9696

CINEMA PARALLEL *(CPA)*
601 River Rd.
Fykesville, MD 21784
800-860-8896
Fax: 410-442-1768

**CINEMACABRE
VIDEO** *(CNM)*
PO Box 10005
Baltimore, MD 21285-0005

**CINEMATRIX
RELEASING** *(CIN)*
22647 Ventura Blvd., Ste. 352
Woodland Hills, CA 91364
818-887-1942

CINEVISTA *(CCN)*
560 W. 43rd, No. 8J
New York, NY 10036
212-947-4373
800-341-CINE
Fax: 212-947-0644

**COAST TO COAST
VIDEO** *(CTC)*
39 W. 19th St., 2nd Fl.
New York, NY 10011
212-727-0390
800-221-3420

**COLUMBIA HOUSE VIDEO
LIBRARY** *(CMB)*
PO Box 1112
Terre Haute, IN 47811
812-262-2001
800-538-7766

**CONNOISSEUR MERIDIAN
FILMS** *(CVC)*
1575 Westwood Blvd., Ste. 205
Los Angeles, CA 90024
310-231-1350
800-529-2300
Fax: 310-231-1359
HomePage: http://
www.meridianvideo.com

CORINTH VIDEO *(CTH)*
34 Gansevoort St.
New York, NY 10014
212-463-0305
800-221-4720
Fax: 212-929-0010

**CREATIVE ARTS TELEVISION
ARCHIVE** *(CAT)*
PO Box 739
Kent, CT 06757
860-868-1771
Fax: 860-868-9999
Email: catarchive@aol.com

**CRITERION
COLLECTION** *(CRC)*
c/o The Voyager Co.
578 Broadway
New York, NY 10012
212-431-5199
800-446-2001
HomePage: http://
www.criterionco.com

**CRITICS' CHOICE VIDEO,
INC.** *(CCB)*
PO Box 749
Itasca, IL 60143
630-775-3300
800-367-7765
Fax: 630-775-3340

CROWN VIDEO *(CRV)*
225 Park Ave., S.
New York, NY 10003

**CRYSTAL
PRODUCTIONS** *(CRY)*
1812 Johns Dr.
Box 2159
Glenview, IL 60025

847-657-8144
800-255-8629
Fax: 847-657-8149
HomePage: http://
www.crystalproductions.com

**CYCLOPS COMMUNICATIONS
CORP.** *(CCC)*
44 Gibson Ave.
Toronto, ON, Canada M5R 1T5
416-926-8981
416-926-9878
Fax: 416-926-9878

**DEAD ALIVE
PRODUCTIONS** *(DAP)*
111 W. Main St.
Mesa, AZ 85201

**RUSS DOUGHTEN FILMS,
INC.** *(RDF)*
5907 Meredith Dr.
Des Moines, IA 50322
515-278-4737
800-247-3456
Fax: 515-278-4738
Email: rdfilms_
msi@dsmnet.com

**EAGLE
ENTERTAINMENT** *(EAG)*
3800 S. Ocean Dr., Ste. 206
Hollywood, FL 33019
954-455-8445
800-923-2453
Email: eaglegame@aol.com

ECUFILM *(ECU)*
810 12th Ave. S.
Nashville, TN 37203
800-251-4091

**EI INDEPENDENT
CINEMA** *(EII)*
68 Forest St.
Montclair, NJ 07042
201-509-1616
Fax: 201-746-6464
Email: eicinema@aol.com

**ELECTRIC
PRODUCTIONS** *(ELE)*
10010 Canoga Ave., No. B-8
Chatsworth, CA 91311-6734

ELECTRIC VIDEO *(ELV)*
PO Box 784
Tiffin, OH 44883
419-447-0110

EMI VIDEO *(EMI)*
1290 Avenue of the Americas,
42nd Fl.
New York, NY 10104
212-492-1200

**ENGLEWOOD
ENTERTAINMENT
LLC** *(EEL)*
10917 Winner Rd.
Independence, MO 64052
816-252-4288
(888)573-5490
Fax: 816-836-3400
Email: moss@kenet.com
HomePage: http://
www.englewd.com

EPIC RECORDS *(EPC)*
550 Madison Ave.
New York, NY 10022-3297
212-833-7442
Fax: 212-833-5719

ETD *(BST)*
13950 Senlac Dr., Ste. 300
Farmers Branch, TX 75234
972-406-0866
800-541-1008

**EVERGREEN
ENTERTAINMENT** *(EVE)*
6100 Wilshire Blvd., Ste. 1400
Los Angeles, CA 90048

**EXPANDED
ENTERTAINMENT** *(EXP)*
28024 Dorothy Dr.

Agoura Hills, CA 91301-2635
818-991-2884
800-996-TOON
Fax: 818-991-3773

**FACETS MULTIMEDIA,
INC.** *(FCT)*
1517 W. Fullerton Ave.
Chicago, IL 60614
773-281-9075
800-331-6197
Fax: 773-929-5437

**FAMILY FILMS/
CONCORDIA** *(FFC)*
3558 S. Jefferson Ave.
St. Louis, MO 63118-3968
314-268-1000
800-325-3040
Fax: 314-268-1329

**FAMILY HOME
ENTERTAINMENT** *(FHE)*
c/o Live Home Video
15400 Sherman Way
PO Box 10124
Van Nuys, CA 91410-0124
818-908-0303
800-677-0789
Fax: 818-778-3259

**FILMAKERS LIBRARY,
INC.** *(FLL)*
124 E. 40th
New York, NY 10016
212-808-4980
800-555-9815
Fax: 212-808-4983
Email: info@filmakers.com
HomePage: http://
www.filmakers.com

**FILMS FOR THE HUMANITIES
& SCIENCES** *(FHS)*
PO Box 2053
Princeton, NJ 08543-2053
609-275-1400
800-257-5126
Fax: 609-275-3767

FIRM DIRECT *(MFI)*
PO Box 5716
Columbia, SC 29250
803-988-1028
800-THE-FIRM
Fax: 803-988-1023
HomePage: http://
www.firmdirect.com

**FIRST RUN
FEATURES** *(FRF)*
153 Waverly Pl.
New York, NY 10014
212-243-0600
800-229-8575
Fax: 212-989-7649

**FIRST RUN/ICARUS
FILMS** *(ICA)*
153 Waverly Pl.
New York, NY 10014
212-727-1711
800-876-1710
Fax: 212-989-7649
Email: frif@echonyc.com

FIRST RUN VIDEO *(FRV)*
622 N. Alpine Dr.
Beverly Hills, CA 90210-3304

**FM ENTERTAINMENT,
INC.** *(FEI)*
1100 S. Robertson Blvd.
Los Angeles, CA 90035
310-777-7501
Fax: 310-777-8301

FOOTHILL VIDEO *(FHV)*
PO Box 547
Tujunga, CA 91043

Fax: 818-353-7242

**FORMAT
INTERNATIONAL** *(FMT)*
2421 E. Washington St.
Indianapolis, IN 46201-4123

**FOX/LORBER HOME
VIDEO** *(FXL)*
419 Park Ave. S., 20th Fl.
New York, NY 10016
212-686-6777
Fax: 212-685-2625

FRIGHT VIDEO *(FRG)*
PO Box 277
North Billerica, MA 01862

**FULL MOON
PICTURES** *(FLL)*
1645 N. Vine St.
Hollywood, CA 90028
213-468-0599

FUSION VIDEO *(FUS)*
100 Fusion Way
Country Club Hills, IL 60478
708-799-2073
Fax: 708-799-8375
HomePage: http://www.fusion-
intl.com

**GERMAN LANGUAGE VIDEO
CENTER** *(GLV)*
7625 Pendleton Pike
Indianapolis, IN 46226-5298
317-547-1257
800-252-1957
Fax: 317-547-1263
HomePage: http://
www.germanvideo.com

**GOODTIMES
ENTERTAINMENT** *(GKK)*
16 E. 40th St., 8th Fl.
New York, NY 10016-0113
212-951-3000
Fax: 212-213-9319
Email: order@gtent.com
HomePage: http://
www.goodtimes.com

GORGON VIDEO *(GRG)*
10750 W. 161st
Orland Park, IL 60462
708-873-3131
800-367-3845
Fax: 708-873-3135

GRAPEVINE VIDEO *(GPV)*
PO Box 46161
Phoenix, AZ 85063
602-973-3661
Fax: 602-973-2973
HomePage: http://
www.grapevinevideo.com

**HALLMARK HOME
ENTERTAINMENT** *(HMK)*
6100 Wilshire Blvd., Ste. 1400
Los Angeles, CA 90048
213-634-3000
Fax: 213-549-3760

**HIGH/SCOPE EDUCATIONAL
RESEARCH
FOUNDATION** *(HSE)*
600 N. River St.
Ypsilanti, MI 48198-2898
313-485-2000
800-40-PRESS
Fax: 313-485-0704

**HOLLYWOOD HOME
ENTERTAINMENT** *(HHE)*
6165 Crooked Creek Rd., Ste. B
Norcross, GA 30092-3105

**HOLLYWOOD HOME
THEATRE** *(HHT)*
9830 Charlieville Blvd.
Beverly Hills, CA 90212
310-203-9868

**HOLLYWOOD PICTURES
HOME VIDEO** *(HPH)*
Fairmont Bldg. 526

500 S. Buena Vista St.
Burbank, CA 91505-9842

HOME VIDEO FILMS *(HVF)*
3213 Florida, No. 200
Kenner, LA 70065
504-464-6671

**HOME VIDEO
LIBRARY** *(HVL)*
Better Homes & Gardens Books
PO Box 10670
Des Moines, IA 50336
800-678-2665
Fax: 515-237-4765

**HOME VISION
CINEMA** *(HMV)*
5547 N. Ravenswood Ave.
Chicago, IL 60640-1199
773-878-2600
800-826-3456
Fax: 773-878-8406
HomePage: http://
www.homevision.com

**HORIZON
ENTERTAINMENT** *(HEG)*
45030 Trevor Ave.
Lancaster, CA 93534
805-940-1040
800-323-2061
Fax: 805-940-8511

IGNATIUS PRESS *(IGP)*
33 Oakland Ave.
Harrison, NY 10528-9974
914-835-4216
Fax: 914-835-8406

**IMAGE
ENTERTAINMENT** *(IME)*
9333 Oso Ave.
Chatsworth, CA 91311
818-407-9100
800-473-3475
Fax: 818-407-9111

**IMPERIAL ENTERTAINMENT
CORP.** *(IMP)*
11846 Ventura Blvd., Ste. 300
Studio City, CA 91604
818-762-0005
Fax: 818-762-0006

**INTERNATIONAL BOOK AND
TAPE SUPPLY** *(IBT)*
PO Box 5153
Long Island City, NY 11105
218-721-4246

**INTERNATIONAL HISTORIC
FILMS, INC.** *(IHF)*
PO Box 29035
Chicago, IL 60629
773-927-2900
Fax: 773-927-9211
HomePage: http://
www.IHFfilm.com

**INTREPID PRODUCTIONS
INC.** *(IPI)*
203 - 2130 W. 3rd Ave.
Vancouver, BC, Canada V6K
1L1
604-737-0530

ITC *(ITC)*
13515 Dulles Technology Dr.
Herndon, VA 22071-3416
703-713-3335
800-638-3757
Fax: 703-713-0065

IVY FILM/VIDEO *(IVY)*
PO Box 18376
Asheville, NC 28814
704-285-9995
800-669-4057
Fax: 704-285-9997
Email: cryspic@aol.com

JEF FILMS, INC. *(JEF)*
Film House
143 Hickory Hill Cir.
Osterville, MA 02655-1322

508-428-7198
(888)JEF-FILM
Fax: 508-428-7198
Email: finchleyrd@aol.com

**J2
COMMUNICATIONS** *(JTC)*
10850 Wilshire Blvd., Ste. 1000
Los Angeles, CA 90024
310-474-5252
800-521-8273
Fax: 310-474-1219

**K-BEECH VIDEO,
INC.** *(KBE)*
9158 Eton Ave.
Chatsworth, CA 91311
818-772-4201
800-255-5923
Fax: 818-772-4245
Email: midmailcamidvid.com
HomePage: http://
www.midvid.com

**KEEP THE FAITH
INC.** *(KEP)*
PO Box 10544
10 Audrey Pl.
Fairfield, NJ 07004
201-244-1990
Fax: 201-244-1990

KID VISION *(KID)*
75 Rockefeller Plaza
New York, NY 10019
212-275-2900
800-3KID-VID
Fax: 212-765-0899

KIT PARKER VIDEO *(KIT)*
c/o Central Park Media
250 W. 57th St., Ste. 317
New York, NY 10107
212-977-7456
Fax: 212-977-8709

**KNOWLEDGE UNLIMITED,
INC.** *(KUI)*
Box 52
Madison, WI 53701-0052
608-836-6660
800-356-2303
Fax: 608-831-1570
Email: ku-mail@ku.com
HomePage: http://
www.ku.com

**LIGHT RAIN
PRODUCTIONS** *(LRP)*
1927 NW Kearney
Portland, OR 97209
503-224-4080
Fax: 503-224-4180

**LIGHTYEAR
ENTERTAINMENT** *(LTY)*
350 5th Ave., Ste. 5101
New York, NY 10118
212-563-4610
800-229-7867
Fax: 212-563-1932
Email:
lightworks@lightworksav.com
HomePage: http://
lightworksav.com

LOONIC VIDEO *(LOO)*
2022 Taraval St., Ste. 6427
San Francisco, CA 94116
510-526-5681

LSVIDEO, INC. *(LSV)*
PO Box 415
Carmel, IN 46032

LUMIVISION CORP. *(LUM)*
877 Federal Blvd.
Denver, CO 80204-3212
303-446-0400
800-776-LUMI
Fax: 303-446-0101

MADERA CINEVIDEO *(MAD)*
311 S. Pine, Ste. 102
Madera, CA 93637

209-661-6000
800-828-8118
Fax: 209-674-3650

**MANAGEMENT COMPANY
ENTERTAINMENT GROUP
(MCEG), INC.** *(MCG)*
1888 Century Park, E., Ste.
1777
Los Angeles, CA 90067-1721
310-282-0871
Fax: 310-282-8303

**MARYLAND PUBLIC
TELEVISION** *(MTP)*
11767 Owings Mills Blvd.
Owings Mills, MD 21117-1499
410-356-5600
800-873-6154
Fax: 410-581-0980

**MCGRAW HILL BOOK
COMPANY** *(MGH)*
Continuing Education Program
4401 Connecticut NW
Lower Level
Washington, DC 20008
202-244-1600
Fax: 202-244-2047

**METROMEDIA
ENTERTAINMENT** *(MET)*
1888 Century Park E., Ste. 700
Los Angeles, CA 90067
310-282-0550
Fax: 310-201-0798

**MGM HOME
ENTERTAINMENT** *(MGM)*
2500 Broadway
Santa Monica, CA 90404-6061
310-449-3000
Fax: 310-449-3100

**MILESTONE FILM &
VIDEO** *(MIL)*
275 W. 96th St., Ste 28C
New York, NY 10025
212-865-7449
Fax: 212-222-8952
Email: milesfilm@aol.com

**MILITARY/COMBAT STOCK
FOOTAGE LIBRARY** *(FGF)*
PO Box 399
Union Washington
Union, WA 98592
206-898-8080
Fax: 206-898-8081

**WARREN MILLER
ENTERTAINMENT** *(WME)*
2540 Frontier Ave., Ste. 104
Boulder, CO 80301
303-442-3430
800-523-7117
Fax: 303-442-3402
Email: robd@wmfilms.com

REX MILLER *(RXM)*
Rte. 1, Box 457-D
East Prairie, MO 63845
314-649-5048

**MIRAMAX PICTURES HOME
VIDEO** *(MAX)*
500 S. Buena Vista St.
Burbank, CA 91521
800-413-5566

**MNTEX ENTERTAINMENT,
INC.** *(MTX)*
500 Kirts Blvd.
Troy, MI 48084-5225
248-362-4400
800-786-8777

**MONARCH HOME
VIDEO** *(MNC)*
2 Ingram Blvd.
La Vergne, TN 37086-7006
615-287-4632
Fax: 615-287-4992
HomePage: http://
www.monarchvideo.com

**MONARICH GROUP,
INC.** *(MGI)*
2550 Corporate Pl., Ste. C103
Monterey Park, CA 91754
213-268-2288
800-700-8998
Fax: 213-268-2233

**MONDAY/WEDNESDAY/
FRIDAY VIDEO** *(MWF)*
123 Scribner Ave.
Staten Island, NY 10301
718-447-1347

MOORE VIDEO *(MRV)*
PO Box 5703
Richmond, VA 23220-0703
804-745-9785
Fax: 804-745-9785

MORRIS VIDEO *(MOR)*
PO Box 1768
Costa Mesa, CA 92628
310-533-4800
800-843-3606
Fax: 714-424-5170

MOVIECRAFT, INC. *(MVC)*
PO Box 438
Orland Park, IL 60462
708-460-9082
Fax: 708-460-9099
Email: larryu@moviecraft.com
HomePage: http://
www.moviecraft.com

MPI HOME VIDEO *(MPI)*
16101 S. 108th Ave.
Orland Park, IL 60462
708-460-0555
Fax: 708-873-3177

MTM HOME VIDEO *(MTM)*
2200 Carolina Place
Fort Mill, SC 29715
803-548-7300
Fax: 803-548-3335

**MUSIC FOR LITTLE
PEOPLE** *(MLT)*
Box 1460
Redway, CA 95560
707-923-3991
800-346-4445
Fax: 707-923-3241

**MUSIC VIDEO
DISTRIBUTORS** *(MVD)*
O'Neill Industrial Center
1210 Standbridge St.
Norristown, PA 19401
610-272-7771
800-888-0486
Fax: 610-272-6074

**NATIONAL CENTER FOR
JEWISH FILM** *(NCJ)*
Brandeis University
Lown Bldg. 102
Waltham, MA 02254-9110
617-899-7044
Fax: 617-736-2070
Email:
ncjf@logos.cc.branders.eu

**NATIONAL FILM BOARD OF
CANADA** *(NFB)*
1251 Avenue of the Americas,
16th Fl.
New York, NY 10020-1173
212-596-1770
800-542-2164
Fax: 212-596-1779

**NEVILLE MEYER
DISTRIBUTION
(NMD)** *(NMD)*
65 High Ridge Road, Ste. 304
Stamford, CT 06905
203-968-8905
Fax: 203-968-2953

**NEW HORIZONS HOME
VIDEO** *(NHO)*
2951 Flowers Rd., S., Ste. 237
Atlanta, GA 30341

404-458-3488
800-854-3323
Fax: 404-458-2679

**NEW JERSEY
NETWORK** *(NJN)*
CN-777
Trenton, NJ 08625-0777
609-777-5000
800-792-8645
Fax: 609-633-2920

**NEW LINE HOME
VIDEO** *(NLC)*
116 N. Robertson Blvd.
Los Angeles, CA 90048
310-967-6670
Fax: 310-854-0602

NEW VIDEO GROUP *(NEW)*
126 5th Ave., 15th Fl.
New York, NY 10011
212-206-8600
800-420-2626
Fax: 212-206-9001

NEW YORKER VIDEO *(NYF)*
16 W. 61st St., 11th Fl.
New York, NY 10023
212-247-6110
800-447-0196
Fax: 212-307-7855

**NOSTALGIA FAMILY
VIDEO** *(NOS)*
PO Box 606
Baker City, OR 97814
503-523-9034
800-784-8362
Fax: 503-523-7115

ORION HOME VIDEO *(ORI)*
MGM
2500 Broadway
Santa Monica, CA 90404-6061
310-449-3000
Fax: 310-449-3100

**ORPHAN
ENTERTAINMENT** *(ORP)*
6902 Sunset Blvd.
Hollywood, CA 90028
213-962-6280

**PARAGON HOME
VIDEO** *(PRG)*
2115 6th Ave.
Seattle, WA 98121
206-441-4500
800-874-9044

**PARAMOUNT HOME
VIDEO** *(PAR)*
Bluhdorn Bldg.
5555 Melrose Ave.
Los Angeles, CA 90038
213-956-3952

**PAULIST
PRODUCTIONS** *(PAU)*
PO Box 1057
Pacific Palisades, CA 90272
310-454-0688
800-624-8613
Fax: 310-459-6549
Email: paulistpro.aol.com

PBS HOME VIDEO *(PBS)*
Catalog Fulfillment Center
PO Box 4030
Santa Monica, CA 90411
800-531-4727
800-645-4PBS

**PEACHTREE
ENTERTAINMENT GROUP,
INC.** *(PEG)*
6669-L Industrial Blvd.
Atlanta, GA 30092
770-449-4268
Fax: 770-449-9739

PENTREX VIDEO *(PEN)*
PO Box 94911
Pasadena, CA 91107

818-793-3400
800-950-9333
Fax: 818-793-3797

**PHOENIX
DISTRIBUTORS** *(PHO)*
405 E. Wetmore Rd., No. 117-516
Tucson, AZ
520-888-5421
800-356-4386

**PLANET PICTURES,
INC.** *(PPI)*
PO Box 1151, Old Chelsea Sta.
New York, NY 10011
212-779-0660
Fax: 212-779-9129

**PLAZA
ENTERTAINMENT** *(PZA)*
304 N. Edinburgh
Los Angeles, CA 90048

**PM ENTERTAINMENT GROUP,
INC.** *(PMH)*
9450 Chivers Ave.
Sun Valley, CA 91352
818-504-6332
800-934-2111
Fax: 818-504-6380

**POLYGRAM VIDEO
(PV)** *(PGV)*
825 8th Ave.
New York, NY 10019
212-333-8000
800-825-7781
Fax: 212-603-7960

**POWERSPORTS
MILLENNIUM** *(PSV)*
18226 Ventura Blvd., Ste. 102
Tarzana, CA 91356-4229
818-708-9995
Fax: 818-708-0598
Email: intl@ps-mill.com
HomePage: http://www.ps-mill.com

**PREMIERE HOME
VIDEO** *(PMR)*
755 N. Highland
Hollywood, CA 90038
213-934-8903
Fax: 213-934-8910

PRESTIGE VIDEO *(PRE)*
4501 Van Nuys Blvd., Ste. 215
Sherman Oaks, CA 91403
818-503-0280
Fax: 818-503-8289
HomePage: http://www.fanta-c.com

PRIME VIDEO *(PRV)*
19749 Dearborn St.
Chatsworth, CA 91311-6510

**PRINCETON BOOK CO.
PUBLISHERS** *(PBC)*
PO Box 831
Hightstown, NJ 08520
609-426-0602
800-220-7149
Fax: 609-426-1344

**PROFESSIONAL MEDIA
SERVICE CORP.** *(PMS)*
19122 S. Vermont Ave.
Gardena, CA 90248
310-532-9024
800-223-7672
Fax: 800-253-8853
Email: promedia@class.org

**PROUD TO BE...A BLACK
VIDEO COLLECTION** *(PTB)*
1235-E East Blvd., Ste. 209
Charlotte, NC 28203
704-523-2227

**PYRAMID FILM &
VIDEO** *(PYR)*
PO Box 1048
Santa Monica, CA 90406-1048

310-828-7577
800-421-2304
Fax: 310-453-9083
Email: info@pyramedia.com
HomePage: http://www.pyramidmedia.com

QUALITY VIDEO *(QVD)*
7399 Bush Lake Rd.
Minneapolis, MN 55439-2027
612-893-0903
800-486-5347
Fax: 612-893-1585
Email: email@qualitydino.com
HomePage: http://www.qualitydino.com

**QUESTAR VIDEO,
INC.** *(QHV)*
680 N. Lakeshore Dr., Ste. 900
Chicago, IL 60611
312-266-9400
800-544-8422
Fax: 312-266-9523

**RAP ENTERTAINMENT
INC.** *(RAP)*
100-707 15th Ave. SW
Calgary, AB, Canada T2R 0R8
403-244-7000
800-565-7777
Fax: 403-245-0511

RATED GEE! *(RAT)*
6132 South 380 West
Murray, UT 84107
801-288-0391
Fax: 801-288-0499

**RAVEN
INTERNATIONAL** *(RVN)*
859 Hollywood Way, Ste. 273
Burbank, CA 91505
818-508-4785

**READER'S DIGEST HOME
VIDEO** *(RDG)*
Reader's Digest Rd.
Pleasantville, NY 10570
800-234-9000

**REAL
ENTERTAINMENT** *(REA)*
2225 Colorado Ave.
Santa Monica, CA 90404
310-449-5315
Fax: 310-449-0025

**REPUBLIC PICTURES HOME
VIDEO** *(REP)*
5700 Wilshire Blvd., Ste. 525
North
Los Angeles, CA 90036-3659
213-965-6900
Fax: 213-965-6963

**RHAPSODY FILMS,
INC.** *(RHP)*
46-2 Becket Hill Rd.
Lyme, CT 06371
860-434-3610
Fax: 860-434-6201

RHINO HOME VIDEO *(RHI)*
10635 Santa Monica Blvd., 2nd Fl.
Los Angeles, CA 90025-4900
310-828-1980
800-843-3670
Fax: 310-453-5529

ROCKET PICTURES *(ROC)*
9536 Wilshire Blvd., Ste. 410
Beverly Hills, CA 90212
310-247-7600

**SCORPIO INTERNATIONAL,
LTD.** *(SCO)*
3375 N. Belt Line Rd., 364
Irving, TX 75062
214-570-7266
Fax: 214-570-7341

**SCREEN PIX HOME
VIDEO** *(SCP)*
1219 1/2 W. El Segundo Blvd.

Gardena, CA 90247-1521
213-242-8880
800-906-4749
Fax: 213-756-1207
Email: spix1@loop.net
HomePage: http://www.screenpix.com

SCREENWORKS INC. *(SWI)*
8019 1/2 Melrose Ave., Ste. 6
Los Angeles, CA 90046
213-782-3865
Fax: 213-782-3868

**SHANACHIE
ENTERTAINMENT** *(SHR)*
13 Laight St.
New York, NY 10013
212-334-0284
Fax: 212-334-5207
Email:
shanach@shaven.ios.com

SHOKUS VIDEO *(SHO)*
PO Box 3125
Chatsworth, CA 91313
818-704-0400
Fax: 818-701-0560

**SHOWCASE
ENTERTAINMENT** *(SHE)*
Warner Center
21800 Oxnard St., Ste. 150
Woodland Hills, CA 91387
818-715-7005

SIGNALS *(SIG)*
7000 Westgate Dr.
St. Paul, MN 55114
612-659-3700
800-669-5225
Fax: 612-659-0083
Email: kyle@rivertrade.com

**SILVER LAKE
INTERNATIONAL** *(SLI)*
18840 Ventura Blvd., Ste. 210
Tarzana, CA 91356
818-757-0007
Fax: 818-757-0038

**SIMITAR
ENTERTAINMENT** *(SIM)*
3850 Annapolis Ln., Ste. 140
Plymouth, MN 55447
612-559-6660
800-486-TAPE
Fax: 612-559-0210

**SIMON WIESENTHAL
CENTER** *(SWC)*
9760 W. Pico Blvd.
Los Angeles, CA 90035-4792
310-553-9036
Fax: 310-553-8007

SINISTER CINEMA *(SNC)*
PO Box 4369
Medford, OR 97501-0168
541-773-6860
Fax: 541-779-8650

**SOCIETY FOR VISUAL
EDUCATION, INC.
(SVE)** *(SVE)*
6677 N. NW Hwy.
Chicago, IL 60631
312-775-9550
800-829-1900
Fax: 312-775-5091
HomePage: http://www.svemedia.com

**SOMETHING WEIRD
VIDEO** *(SMW)*
PO Box 33664
Seattle, WA 98133
206-361-3759
Fax: 206-364-7526

**SONY MUSIC VIDEO
ENTERPRISES** *(SMV)*
550 Madison Ave.
New York, NY 10022
212-833-8000

**SPECTRUM FILMS,
INC.** *(SPC)*
Box 801
Carlsbad, CA 92018
619-434-6191

STAGESTEP *(STS)*
2000 Hamilton St., Ste. C200
Philadelphia, PA 19130
215-636-9000
800-877-3342
Fax: 215-829-0508
Email: stagestep@juno.com

**STARDANCE
ENTERTAINMENT** *(SDE)*
11101 Washington Blvd., Ste.
101
Culver, CA 90232
800-959-8985
Fax: 310-559-8987

**STERLING HOME
ENTERTAINMENT** *(STE)*
11846 Ventura Blvd., 3rd Fl.
Studio City, CA 91604
818-762-0005
Fax: 818-762-0006

**STRAND HOME
VIDEO** *(SHV)*
225 Santa Monica Blvd., Ste.
810
Santa Monica, CA 90401
310-395-5002

**STREAMLINE
PICTURES** *(STP)*
2908 Nebraska Avenue
Santa Monica, CA 90404-4109
310-998-0070
800-846-1453
Fax: 310-998-1145
HomePage: http://www.insv.com/streamline

**STUDIO VIDEO
PRODUCTIONS** *(STV)*
793 Foothills Blvd., Ste. A
San Luis Obispo, CA 93405
805-543-0707
800-541-1843
Fax: 805-549-0352

**TAI SENG VIDEO
MARKETING** *(TAI)*
170 S. Spruce Ave., Ste. 200
San Francisco, CA 94080
415-871-8118
800-888-3836
Fax: 415-871-2392
Email: webstaff@taiseng.com
HomePage: http://www.taiseng.com

**TAPEWORM VIDEO
DISTRIBUTORS** *(TPV)*
27833 Hopkins Ave., Unit 6
Valencia, CA 91355
805-257-4904
Fax: 805-257-4820
Email:
tapewo01@interserv.com
HomePage: http://www.tapeworm.com

**TELEVISION
INTERNATIONAL** *(CDV)*
c/o Jason Films
2825 Wilcrest, Ste. 407
Houston, TX 77042
713-266-3097
Fax: 713-266-3148

TEMPE VIDEO *(TEM)*
Box 6573
Akron, OH 44312
216-628-1950
Fax: 216-628-4316

**THIRD COAST
ENTERTAINMENT** *(TCE)*
12750 Ventura Blvd., Ste. 102
Studio City, CA 91604
818-769-9986

**THOMSON PRODUCTIONS,
INC.** *(TPI)*
PO Box 1225
Orem, UT 84059
801-226-0155
Fax: 801-226-0166

**THREE STAR
RELEASING** *(TSR)*
15745 Stagg St.
Van Nuys, CA 91406

**3M AUDIO VISUAL
DIVISION** *(THA)*
6801 Riverplace Blvd.
Austin, TX 78726-9000
800-328-1371

**TIME-LIFE VIDEO AND
TELEVISION** *(TLF)*
1450 E. Parham Rd.
Richmond, VA 23280
804-266-6330
800-621-7026

**TIME WARNER VIEWER'S
EDGE** *(TWV)*
PO Box 85098
Richmond, VA 23285-5098
800-947-3928
Fax: 203-699-9586

TIMELESS VIDEO INC. *(TIM)*
9943 Canoga Ave., Ste. B2
Chatsworth, CA 91311
818-773-0284
800-478-6734
Fax: 818-773-0176

**TRANS-WORLD
ENTERTAINMENT** *(TWE)*
8899 Beverly Blvd., 8th Fl.
Los Angeles, CA 90048-2412

**TRIBORO ENTERTAINMENT
GROUP** *(TRI)*
12 W. 27th St., 15th Fl.
New York, NY 10001
212-686-6116
Fax: 212-686-6178

**TRIMARK HOME
VIDEO** *(THV)*
2644 30th St.
Santa Monica, CA 90405-3009
310-314-2000
Fax: 310-392-0252

TROMA TEAM VIDEO *(TTV)*
1501 Broadway, Ste. 2605
New York, NY 10036
212-997-0595
Fax: 212-997-0968

**TURNER HOME
ENTERTAINMENT
COMPANY** *(TTC)*
Box 105366
Atlanta, GA 35366
404-827-3066
800-523-0823
Fax: 404-827-3266

**TWENTIETH CENTURY FOX
HOME
ENTERTAINMENT** *(FXV)*
PO Box 900
Beverly Hills, CA 90213
310-369-3900
(888)223-4FOX
Fax: 310-369-5811

UAV CORPORATION *(UAV)*
PO Box 5497
Fort Mill, SC 29715
803-548-7300
800-486-6782
Fax: 803-548-3335

**UNI DISTRIBUTION/JUNE
MORISHITA** *(UND)*
10 Universal City Plaza, Ste.
400
Universal City, CA 91608
818-777-4400
Fax: 818-866-0306

UNICORN VIDEO, INC. *(UNI)*
9025 Eton Ave., Ste. D.
Canoga Park, CA 91304
818-407-1333
800-528-4336
Fax: 818-407-8246

UNITY PRODUCTIONS *(UNT)*
4007 Willowwood Ln.
Aberdeen, SD 57401-9544

UNIVERSAL PRODUCTIONS INTERNATIONAL/GAMING TAPES, INC. *(UPI)*
4415 W. Forest Home Ave.
Milwaukee, WI 53219
414-321-0874
800-522-2107
Fax: 414-321-1917

UNIVERSAL STUDIOS HOME VIDEO *(USH)*
100 Universal City Plz.
Universal City, CA 91608-9955
818-777-1000
Fax: 818-866-1483

UNIVERSITY OF WASHINGTON EDUCATIONAL MEDIA COLLECTION *(UWA)*
Kane Hall
Box 353090
Seattle, WA 98195
206-543-9909
Fax: 206-685-7892

VALENCIA ENTERTAINMENT CORP. *(VEC)*
45030 Trevor Ave.
Lancaster, CA 93534-2648
805-940-1040
800-323-2061
Fax: 805-940-8511

VANGUARD INTERNATIONAL CINEMA, INC. *(VNG)*
15061 Springdale St., Ste. 109
Huntington Beach, CA 92649
714-901-9020
Fax: 714-901-9070

VANTAGE COMMUNICATIONS, INC. *(VAN)*
PO Box 546-G
Nyack, NY 10960
914-268-0715
800-872-0068
Fax: 914-268-3429

VCI HOME VIDEO *(VCI)*
11333 E. 60th Pl.
Tulsa, OK 74146
918-254-6337
800-331-4077
Fax: 918-254-6117
Email: vcihomevideo@mail.webter.com

VCII HOME ENTERTAINMENT, INC. *(VHE)*
13418 Wyandotte St.
North Hollywood, CA 91605
818-764-1777
800-350-1931
Fax: 818-764-0231

VESTRON VIDEO *(VES)*
c/o Live Home Video
15400 Sherman Way
PO Box 10124
Van Nuys, CA 91410-0124
818-988-0303
800-367-7765
Fax: 818-778-3194
Email: cust_serv@live-entertainment.com

VICTORY MULTIMEDIA *(VIC)*
222 N. Sepulveda Blvd., Ste. 1306
El Segundo, CA 90245

310-416-9140
Fax: 310-416-9839

VIDCREST *(VDC)*
PO Box 69642
Los Angeles, CA 90069
213-650-7310
Fax: 213-654-4810

VIDEO ARTISTS INTERNATIONAL, INC. *(VAI)*
158 Linwood Plaza, Ste. 301
Fort Lee, NJ 07024
201-944-0099
800-477-7146
Fax: 201-947-8850

VIDEO BIBLE LIBRARY, INC. *(VBL)*
Box 17515
Portland, OR 97217
360-892-7707
Fax: 360-254-8318

THE VIDEO CATALOG *(TVC)*
7000 Westgate Dr.
St. Paul, MN 55114
612-659-3700
800-733-6656
Fax: 612-659-0083
Email: kyle@rivertrade.com

VIDEO CITY PRODUCTIONS/ DISTRIBUTING *(VCD)*
4266 Broadway
Oakland, CA 94611
510-428-0202
Fax: 510-654-7802

VIDEO COLLECTIBLES *(VCO)*
1500 Clinton St.
Buffalo, NY 14206-9911
800-268-3891
Fax: 800-269-8877
Email: info@collectablesdirect.com
HomePage: http://www.collectablesdirect.com

VIDEO CONNECTION *(VCN)*
3123 W. Sylvania Ave.
Toledo, OH 43613
419-472-7727
800-365-0449
Fax: 419-472-2655

VIDEO FRANCE *(FRA)*
4822 St. Elmo Ave.
Bethesda, MD 20814
301-654-2224
Fax: 301-229-0621
Email: france@wizard.net
HomePage: http://www.francevision.com

VIDEO GEMS *(GEM)*
12228 Venice Blvd., No. 504
Los Angeles, CA 90066

VIDEO RESOURCES *(VRS)*
220 W. 71st St.
New York, NY 10023
212-724-7055
800-442-7055
Fax: 212-595-0189

VIDEO SEARCH OF MIAMI *(VSM)*
PO Box 161917
Miami, FL 33116
305-279-9773
Fax: 305-598-2665

VIDEO YESTERYEAR *(VYY)*
Box C
Sandy Hook, CT 06482
800-243-0987
Fax: 203-797-0819
Email: video@yesteryear.com

THE VIDEOFINDERS COLLECTION *(VIF)*
National Fulfillment Center
425 E. Colorado St.

Glendale, CA 91205
800-799-1199
Fax: 818-637-5276

VIDEOS.COM, INC. *(PIC)*
202 S. Pearl St., Ste. 4
Charlotte, MI 48813
517-541-1630
800-670-9282
Fax: 517-541-1631
Email: steve@videos.com
HomePage: http://www.videos.com

VIP VIDEO *(VIP)*
c/o JEF Films
Film House
143 Hickory Hill Circle
Osterville, MA 02655-1322
508-428-7198
Fax: 508-428-7198

VISION VIDEO/GATEWAY FILMS *(GFV)*
2030 Wentz Church Rd.
Box 540
Worcester, PA 19490-0540
610-584-1893
800-523-0226
Fax: 610-584-4610
Email: visionvideo@aol.com

VLM ENTERTAINMENT *(LBD)*
3200 Doolittle Dr.
Northbrook, IL 60062
847-564-8820
800-950-0255
Fax: 800-564-8656

WALT DISNEY HOME VIDEO *(DIS)*
500 S. Buena Vista St.
Burbank, CA 91521
818-562-3560

WARNER/ELEKTRA/ ATLANTIC (WEA) CORPORATION *(WEA)*
9451 LBJ Fwy., Ste. 107
Dallas, TX 75243
214-234-6200
Fax: 214-699-9343

WARNER HOME VIDEO, INC. *(WAR)*
4000 Warner Blvd.
Burbank, CA 91522
818-954-6000

WARNERVISION *(AVE)*
A Time Warner Company
75 Rockefeller Plz.
New York, NY 10019
212-275-2900
800-95-WARNER
Fax: 212-765-0899

WATER BEARER FILMS *(WBF)*
48 W. 21st St., No. 301
New York, NY 10010
212-242-8686
800-551-8304
Fax: 212-242-4560
Email: WBFVideo@aol.com
HomePage: http://www.wbf.com

WAXWORKS/VIDEOWORKS, INC. *(WAX)*
325 E. 3rd St.
Owensboro, KY 42303
502-926-0008
800-825-8558
Fax: 502-685-0563

WELLSPRING MEDIA, INC. *(WMI)*
65 Bleecker St.
New York, NY 10012
800-538-5856
Fax: 212-475-1790

WESTERN L.A. FILM PRODUCTIONS, INC. *(WLA)*
7425 Clinton St.
Los Angeles, CA 90036-5703

WESTERN MEDIA SYSTEMS *(WFV)*
30941 W. Agoura Rd., Ste. 302
Westlake Village, CA 91361
818-889-7350
Fax: 818-889-7350

WGBH/BOSTON *(WGB)*
PO Box 2284
South Burlington, VT 05407-2284
800-255-9424
Fax: 802-864-9846

WHAM! USA *(WHA)*
200 N. Robertson Blvd.
Beverly Hills, CA 90211
310-275-9380
Fax: 310-275-9301

WHITE STAR *(WST)*
195 Hwy. 36
West Long Branch, NJ 07764
908-229-2343
800-458-5887
Fax: 908-229-0066

WISHING WELL DISTRIBUTING *(WSH)*
PO Box 1008
Silver Lake, WI 53170
414-889-8501
800-888-9355
Fax: 414-889-8591

WNET/THIRTEEN NON-BROADCAST *(WNE)*
356 W. 58th St.
New York, NY 10019
212-560-2000
Fax: 212-582-3297

WOLFE VIDEO *(WLF)*
PO Box 64
New Almaden, CA 95042
408-268-6782
800-438-9653
Fax: 408-268-9449
Email: maria@wolfevideo.com
HomePage: http://www.wolfevideo.com

WOMBAT FILM AND VIDEO *(WOM)*
1560 Sherman Ave., Ste. 100
Evanston, IL 60201
708-328-6700
800-323-9084
Fax: 708-328-6706

WORLD ARTISTS HOME VIDEO *(WAC)*
5150 Wilshire Blvd., Ste. 506
Los Angeles, CA 90036
213-933-7057
800-821-1205
Fax: 213-933-2356
Email: world@worldarfists.com
HomePage: http://www.worldartist.com/world

WORLD VIDEO ENTERPRISES, INC. *(WVE)*
150 Executive Park Blvd., No. 1600
San Francisco, CA 94134-3303
415-468-6218
Fax: 415-468-1381

WORLDVISION HOME VIDEO, INC. *(WOV)*
1700 Broadway
New York, NY 10019-5905
212-261-2700
Fax: 212-261-2950

XENON *(XVC)*
211 Arizona Ave.
Santa Monica, CA 90401

YORK HOME VIDEO *(YHV)*
4733 Lankershim Blvd.
North Hollywood, CA 91602
310-278-1034
800-84-MOVIE
Fax: 818-505-8290

ZEITGEIST FILMS LTD. *(ZGI)*
247 Centre St., 2nd Fl.
New York, NY 10013
212-274-1989
Fax: 212-274-1644
Email: mail@zeitgeistfilm.com

RETAIL

ANIMEIGO INC. *(ANI)*
PO Box 989
Wilmington, NC 28402-0989
910-251-1850
800-242-6463
Fax: 910-763-2376
HomePage: http://www.aminmeigo.com

CAMBRIDGE EDUCATIONAL *(CCP)*
PO Box 2153
Charleston, WV 25328-2153
304-744-9323
800-468-4227
Fax: 304-744-9351
HomePage: http://www.cambridgeol.com/cambridge

CONGRESS ENTERTAINMENT, INC. *(CNG)*
PO Box 845
Tannersville, PA 18372-0845
717-620-2333
800-847-8273
Fax: 717-620-9313
Email: karolyn28@acx.com

ERGO MEDIA INC. *(ERG)*
668 American Legion Dr.
PO Box 2037
Teaneck, NJ 07666
201-692-0404
800-695-3746
Fax: 201-692-0663
Email: ergo@intec.com
HomePage: http://www.jewishvideo.com

FESTIVAL FILMS *(FST)*
6115 Chestnut Ter.
Excelsior, MN 55331-8107
612-470-2172
800-798-6083
Fax: 612-470-2172
Email: fesfilms@aol.com
HomePage: http://members.aol.com/festfilms/

FLOWER FILMS *(FFM)*
10341 San Pablo Ave.
El Cerrito, CA 94530
510-525-0942
800-572-7618
Fax: 510-525-1204
Email: blankfilm@aol.com
HomePage: http://www.lesblank.com

GLENN VIDEO VISTAS, LTD. *(GVV)*
6924 Canby Ave., Ste. 103
Reseda, CA 91335
818-881-8110
Fax: 818-981-5506
Email: mglass@worldnet.att.net

HENWOOD CINEMA VIDEO *(HCV)*
PO Box 376
Jamison, PA 18929-0376
215-552-8584
Fax: 215-788-7186
Email: Cinema376@aol.com

RETARIL *cont.*

INTERAMA, INC. *(INT)*
301 W. 53rd St., Ste. 19E
New York, NY 10019
212-977-4830
Fax: 212-581-6582
Email: InteramaNY@aol.com

KAROL VIDEO *(KAR)*
PO Box 7600
350 N. Pennsylvania Ave.
Wilkes Barre, PA 18773
717-822-8899
Fax: 717-822-8226
Email: karolm@epix.net

**MIKE LEBELL'S
VIDEO** *(MLB)*
75 Freemont Pl.
Los Angeles, CA 90005
213-938-3333
Fax: 213-938-3334
Email: mlvideo@aol.com

LUCERNE MEDIA *(LME)*
37 Ground Pine Rd.
Morris Plains, NJ 07950
201-538-1401
800-341-2293
Fax: 201-538-0855
Email:
lucernemedia@worldnet.att.net

MASTERVISION, INC. *(MAS)*
969 Park Ave.
New York, NY 10028
212-879-0448
HomePage: http://
www.masterv.com

MOVIES UNLIMITED *(MOV)*
3015 Darnell Rd.
Philadelphia, PA 19154
215-637-4444
800-466-8437
Fax: 215-637-2350
Email:
movies@moviesunlimited.com
HomePage: http://
www.moviesunlimited.com

MYSTIC FIRE VIDEO *(MFV)*
524 Broadway, Ste. 604
New York, NY 10012
212-941-0999
800-292-9001
Fax: 212-941-1443
HomePage: http://
www.mysticfire.com

PENTREX *(IUF)*
PO Box 94911
Pasadena, CA 91109-4911
818-793-3400
800-950-9333
Fax: 818-793-3797
Email: pentrex@aol.com
HomePage: http://
www.pentrex.com

**PHOENIX/CORONET/BFA
FILMS AND VIDEO** *(BFA)*
2349 Chaffee Dr.
St. Louis, MO 63146
314-569-0211
800-777-8100
Fax: 314-569-2834
Email:
BFAEduc@worldnet.att.net
Phoenix
films@worldnet.att.net

**RM FILMS INTERNATIONAL,
INC.** *(RMF)*
PO Box 3748
Los Angeles, CA 90078
213-466-7791
Fax: 213-461-4152
HomePage: http://
www.rmfilms.com

**SCHOOLMASTERS
VIDEO** *(SCH)*
745 State Circle
PO Box 1941
Ann Arbor, MI 48106
313-761-5175
800-521-2832
Fax: 313-761-8711
Email: kidvideis@aol.com
HomePage: http://
www.schoolmasters.com

**WARNER REPRISE
VIDEO** *(WRV)*
3300 Warner Blvd.
Burbank, CA 91505-4694
818-846-9090
Fax: 818-953-3329

WHOLESALE

**BEST FILM & VIDEO
CORP.** *(BFV)*
108 New South Rd.
PO Box 9025
Hicksville, NY 11802-9025
516-931-6969
800-527-2189
Fax: 516-931-5959

**CAPITOL ENTERTAINMENT
AND HOME VIDEO** *(CTL)*
6205 Adelaide Dr.
Betthesda, MD 20817
301-564-9700
Fax: 301-564-0797
Email: capent@capitolent.com
HomePage: http://
www.capitolent.com

**CELEBRITY HOME
ENTERTAINMENT** *(CEL)*
22025 Ventura Blvd., Ste. 200
Woodland Hills, CA 91364
818-595-0666
Fax: 818-716-0168

**COLUMBIA TRISTAR HOME
VIDEO** *(COL)*
Sony Pictures Plz.
10202 W. Washington Blvd.
Culver City, CA 90232
310-280-5418
Fax: 310-280-2485
HomePage: http://
www.spe.sony.com

**DISCOUNT VIDEO TAPES,
INC./HOLLYWOOD'S
ATTIC** *(DVT)*
PO Box 7122
Burbank, CA 91510
818-843-3366
Fax: 818-843-3821
HomePage: http://
www.discountvideotapes.com

GREYCAT FILMS *(GRE)*
3829 Delaware Ln.
Las Vegas, NV 89109
702-737-0670
Fax: 702-734-3628
Email: greycat@aol.com

HBO HOME VIDEO *(HBO)*
1100 6th Ave.
New York, NY 10036
212-512-7400
Fax: 212-512-7498
HomePage: http://
www.hbohomevideo.com

HEN'S TOOTH VIDEO *(HTV)*
2805 E. State Blvd.
Fort Wayne, IN 46805
219-471-4332
Fax: 219-471-4449

**INCREASE/SILVERMINE
VIDEO** *(INC)*
6860 Canby Ave., Ste. 118
Reseda, CA 91335

818-342-2880
800-233-2880
Fax: 818-342-4029
Email: quksil@aol.com

**INGRAM ENTERTAINMENT
INC.** *(ING)*
2 Ingram Blvd.
La Vergne, TN 37086-7006
615-287-4000
800-621-1333
HomePage: http://
www.ingramentertainment.com

**JUST FOR KIDS HOME
VIDEO** *(JFK)*
22025 Ventura Blvd., Ste. 200
PO Box 4112
Woodland Hills, CA 91365-0549
818-595-0666
Fax: 818-716-0168

KINO ON VIDEO *(KIV)*
333 W. 39th St., Ste. 503
New York, NY 10018
212-629-6880
800-562-3330
Fax: 212-714-0871
Email: kinoint@infunnse.com
HomePage: http://
www.kino.com

KULTUR VIDEO *(KUL)*
195 Hwy. No. 36
West Long Branch, NJ 07764
908-229-2343
800-458-5887
Fax: 908-229-0066
Email: kultur@monmouth.com
HomePage: http://
www.monmouth.com/kultur

LEO FILMS *(LEO)*
1509 N. Hoover, Ste. 1/2
Los Angeles, CA 90027
213-666-7140
Fax: 213-666-7414
Email: LUSTGAR@IDT.NET
HomePage: http://movies-
online.com

**MONTEREY HOME
VIDEO** *(MON)*
566 St. Charles Dr.
Thousand Oaks, CA 91360-
3901
805-494-7199
800-424-2593
Fax: 805-494-6061

MTI HOME VIDEO *(MTH)*
14216 SW 136th St.
Miami, FL 33186
305-255-8684
800-821-7461
Fax: 305-233-6943
Email: mti@mtivideo.com
HomePage: http://
www.mtivideo.com

**PETER PAN INDUSTRIES,
INC. (PPI)** *(PRD)*
88 St. Francis St.
Newark, NJ 07105
201-344-4214
Fax: 201-344-0465
Email: PPIGROUP@aol.com
HomePage: http://
www.peterpan.com

SUN VIDEO *(SUN)*
15 Donnybrook
Demarest, NJ 07627
201-784-0662
Fax: 201-784-0665
Email:
hs@methodsworkshop.com

**TELEVISION
REPRESENTATIVES,
INC.** *(RHV)*
9911 W. Pico Blvd.
Suite PH-E
Los Angeles, CA 90035

310-552-2660
Fax: 310-552-9039

TROMA INC. *(TRO)*
733 9th Ave.
New York, NY 10019
212-757-4555
800-83-TROMA
Fax: 212-399-9885
HomePage: http://
www.troma.com/home

VIDEO ACTION *(VDA)*
708 W. 1st St.
Los Angeles, CA 90012
213-687-8262
800-422-2241
Fax: 213-687-8425

VIDEO DIMENSIONS *(VDM)*
322 8th Ave., No. 1701
New York, NY 10001
212-929-6135
Fax: 212-929-6135
Email: video@cultvideo.com
HomePage: http://
www.cultvideo.com/
video.html

**VISTA STREET
ENTERTAINMENT** *(VSE)*
9831 W. Pico Blvd., Ste. 4
Los Angeles, CA 90035
310-556-3074
Fax: 310-556-8815

**XENON
ENTERTAINMENT** *(MRC)*
1440 9th St.
Santa Monica, CA 90401
310-451-5510
800-829-1913
Fax: 310-395-4058
HomePage: http://
www.xenonentertainment.com

**YANKEE-ORIOLE
CO.** *(YOC)*
398 Ogden Ave.
Jersey City, NJ 07307-1115
201-656-4348
Fax: 201-656-4348

Web Site Guide

The Internet has become an important resource for movie information, appreciation, and (especially) obsession. For your web surfing enjoyment, we have compiled a comprehensive list of many of the top entertainment websites that will expand your knowledge of either a particular movie, actor, director, or Hollywood studio. If you're looking for information on how to make your own film, there are sites for that, too. The guide is divided into six categories: actors and actresses (ranges from Cher to Elijah Wood); cult movie resources; directors; film magazines; film studios; filmmaker resources; film reviews; general entertainment; individual movies; and video outlets. The sites are listed alphabetically within each category, and each site includes name and URL address information. Actors, directors, and movies may have more than one URL, as they are likely to have more than one site devoted to them. These sites have no description because the name of the website is self-explanatory. The general information websites briefly describe what you can expect to find. Just as you can spend hours flipping through *Videohound*, you can spend hours cruising the web with the sites listed below since a majority of these homepages can link you to other sites on the web.

ACTORS AND ACTRESSES

Ben Affleck
http://www.worldsite.net/~stef/ben.html
http://www.ghgcorp.com/vision/benaffleck/

Tim Allen
http://www.timallenrrr.com/

Gillian Anderson
http://gaws.ao.net/

Jennifer Aniston
http://www.public.iastate.edu/~royal/jenny.html

Fred Astaire
http://members.aol.com/AstaireFan/

Kevin Bacon (The Oracle of)
http://www.cs.virginia.edu/~bct7m/bacon.html

Alec Baldwin
http://sailor.saturn.simplenet.com/alec.html

Stephen Baldwin
http://www.li.net/~yesnet/Opening_Page/Opening_page.htm

Antonio Banderas
http://www.sju.edu/~delvalle/antonio.html

Drew Barrymore
http://www.wfu.edu/~david/drew/

Angela Bassett
http://members.tripod.com/~bholness/angela.html

Halle Berry
http://www.contrib.andrew.cmu.edu/~jack/halle.html

Humphrey Bogart
http://www.cmgww.com/stars/bogart/bogart.html

Kenneth Branagh
http://sfbox.vt.edu:10021/T/tpower/ken.html

Matthew Broderick
http://www.ccn.cs.dal.ca/~ag249http://matt.html

Pierce Brosnan
http://www.mcs.net/~klast/www/brosnan.html

Sandra Bullock
http://www.dancopublishing.com/sandra.htm

Nicholas Cage
http://members.aol.com/ToniGrrl/cage/main.htm

Bruce Campbell
http://spage.com/bruce/

Neve Campbell
http://conceptdesign.simplenet.com/model/neve/

Jim Carrey
http://www.inforamp.net/~petroff/

Cher
http://www.inch.com/~harbur/cher/index.html

Jackie Chan
http://www.pitt.edu/~oren/jackie/jackie.html
http://www.lava.net/~headrush/jc.html

Jean Claude Van Damme
http://www.anaheim.quik.com/tseo/van.htm

George Clooney
http://copper.ucs.indiana.edu/~mtsai/george_clooney.html

Sean Connery
http://www.wsu.edu:8080/~dock/

Kevin Costner
http://www.geocities.com/Hollywood/7555/

Peter Coyote
http://www.petercoyote.com/

Courtney Cox
http://www.azstarnet.com/~polska/cox/ccox.html

Russell Crowe
http://www.csh.rit.edu/~halle/russell.html

Tom Cruise
http://www.thezone.pair.com/cruise/

Maucaulay Culkin
http://www.axe.net./culkin/

Jamie Lee Curtis
http://www.geocities.com/Hollywood/Hills/5752/index.htm

John Cusack
http://www.unm.edu/~matts/John_Cusack.html

Matt Damon
http://www.goodmattdamon.com/

Claire Danes
http://www2.ucsc.edu/people/ddiego/danes/

Geena Davis
http://www.mv.com/users/dld/geena/

Judy Davis
http://elycion.geology.ualberta.ca/~tpreston/judy.html

Daniel Day Lewis
http://www.well.com/user/dkscully/index.htm

James Dean
http://www.americanlegends.com/jamesdean

Rebecca DeMornay
http://web-star.com/rebecca/rebecca.html

Robert DeNiro
http://www.cs.bc.edu/~kawashim/deniro.html

Johnny Depp
http://mastrangelo.polito.it/jonydepp/index.htm
http://www.wigout.com/depp/johnny.html

Cameron Diaz
http://www.cs.uit.no/~haakonb/diaz.html

Leonardo DiCaprio
http://meadow.greenwing.com/leo/

Anti-Leonardo DiCaprio
http://members.tripod.com/~keyser_fan/leosucks.html

Matt Dillion
http://www.angelfire.com/wa/saintfw/index.html

Divine
http://www.chipandtodd.com/chip/divpdoll.html

Michael Douglas
http://www.texas./net/users/mikedoug/

Robert Downey, Jr.
http://www.bserv.com/users/lesliv.htm

Minnie Driver
http://www.bowdish.com/Minnie/minnie.html

Robert Duvall
http://www.geocities.com/Hollywood/9067/duvall.html

Clint Eastwood
http://www.powernet.net/~cal/eastwood.html

Rupert Everett
http://www.plumpton.demon.co.uk/index.htm

Chris Farley
http://pantheon.cis.yale.edu/~odonnell/farley/farley.html

Ralph Fiennes
http://student.www.uchicago.edu/users/cceccare/fiennes.html

Harrison Ford
http://www.smartlink.net/~deej7/ford.html

Jodie Foster
http://www.tcp.com/~mary/foster.html

Vivica A. Fox
http://www.gmi.edu/~maju6406/fox/viv.html

Brendan Fraser
http://www3.mb.sympatico.ca/~tanners/bfmoment.htm

Andy Garcia
http://www.geocities.com/Hollywood/Hills/2620/index.html

Richard Gere
http://www.pair.com/marilynn/gere.htm

Gina Gershon
http://members.aol.com/carebear98/gina_gershon/index.html

Mel Gibson
http://ourworld.compuserve.com/homepages/melward/gibson.htm
http://www.geocities.com/Hollywood/7505/

Whoopi Goldberg
http://www.tu-berlin.de/~gruhlke/forum/whoopi/index.html

Bruce Greenwood
http://greenwood.simplenet.com/

Pam Grier
http://www.sirius.com/~adeemer/blaxploitation/foxybrown/
http://www.inetworld.net/garrick/pamgrier.htm
http://www.dancentury.com/pam_grier/

Gene Hackman
http://www.pair.com/marilynn/hackman.htm

Tom Hanks
http://www.wsu.edu:8080/~jtwillia/hanks.html

Ed Harris
http://www.wenet.net/~mhoopes/edharris.html

Teri Hatcher
http://www.escape.ca/~hazlitt/teri/thind.htm

Rutger Hauer
http://205.158.7.34/people/hauer/

Salma Hayek
http://www.algae.net/al/salmate.html

Anne Heche
http://www.wiltschko.org/heche/heche.htm

Dustin Hoffman
http://www.sky.net/~emily/dustin.html

Sir Anthony Hopkins
http://www.mit.edu:8001/people/douglas/sirtony.html

Helen Hunt
http://www.helenhuntfan.com/

Ice Cube
http://www.icecube.com/

Jeremy Irons
http://webrum.uni-mannheim.de/bwl/kranich/irons/index.shtml

Samuel L. Jackson
http://member.aol.com/gifhack/sam.html

Ashley Judd
http://absolute.simplenet.com/celebs/ashley/index2.html

Michael Keaton
http://www.geocities.com/Broadway/Stage/7162/mkeatona.html

Nicole Kidman
http://www-personal.umich.edu/~rkmead/kidman.html

Val Kilmer
http://www.eskimo.com/~kilmer

Kevin Kline
http://people.delphi.com/dramafan/kevinkline.html

Jude Law
http://www.geocities.com/Wellesley/5890/jude.html

Denis Leary
http://home.interstat.net/~tomveil/DLHP.html

Brandon Lee
http://europa.cs.mun.ca/~loreilly/brandon.htm

Bruce Lee
http://www.infi.net/~danaj/bruce.html

Tea Leoni
http://home.interstat.net/~tomveil/DLHP.html

Juliette Lewis
http://www.solace.mh.se/~alpha/jlwp/jl.htm

Ray Liotta
http://members.aol.com/ecrilley/Ray_Liotta/ray.html

Jennifer Lopez
http://members.xoom.com/goh/index.htm

Michael Madsen
http://members.aol.com/madsen1fan/pp22.htm

John Malkovich
http://members.tripod.com/~AngelBell/index1.html

Steve Martin
http://qlink.queensu.ca/~4kgd/steve/

Marcello Mastroianni
http://www.dolcevita.com

Matthew McConaughey
http://www.geocities.com/Hollywood/Studio/6318/matt1.html

Ewan McGregor
http://www2.ucsc.edu/people/alyjoe/ewan/

Mike Meyers
http://www.geocities.com/Hollywood/Boulevard/2377/miketown.html

Bette Milder
http://www.interactive8.com/bette/

Marilyn Monroe
http://www.ionet.net/~jellenc/marilyn.html

Demi Moore
http://www.diskriter.com/demi/

Julianne Moore
http://opus74.pair.com/moore/index.html

Bill Murray
http://www-personal.engin.umich.edu/~rnw/blllmurray/index.html

Sam Neill
http://kevin.net/~erika/sn.html

Jack Nicholson
http://pegasus.cc.ucf.edu/~cmf80227/jack.html
http://home2.swipnet.se/~w-29085/

Gary Oldman
http://www.csh.rit.edu/~halle/oldman.html
http://home.worldonline.nl/~giso/oldman.htm

Al Pacino
http://pubweb.acns.nwu.edu/~apoorman/pacino.html

Gwyneth Paltrow
http://members.aol.com/fbut40/gwyneth.html

Bill Paxton
http://qlink.queensu.ca/~3bjw6/

Michelle Pfeiffer
http://www.geocities.com/Paris/1032/pfeiffer.html

Brad Pitt
http://www.geocities.com/Hollywood/Hills/4932/Brad_Pitt.html

Parker Posey
http://thicksauce.com/parkerposey/

The Rat Pack
http://www.primenet.com/~drbmbay/

Keanu Reeves
http://www.empirenet.com/~rdaeley/skc/

Denise Richards
http://www.tgi.net/syzygy/denise/

Alan Rickman
http://www.fred.net/karina/rickman.html

Julia Roberts
http://studentweb.tulane.edu/~sbuckle/

Tim Robbins
http://www.bobohead.com/tim/

Chris Rock
http://www.mit.edu/people/jawhite/chris.html

Isabella Rossellini
http://204.140.242.11/FEMMES/ISABELLA/isabella1.shtml

Tim Roth
http://weber.u.washington.edu/~jenhwolf/

Rene Russo
http://www.flash.net/~vault/rene.htm

Meg Ryan
http://web.cs.ualberta.ca/~davidw/MegRyan/meg.cgi

Winona Ryder
http://www.duc.auburn.edu/~harshec/WWW/Winona.html

Adam Sandler
http://www.geocities.com/Hollywood/8075/

Susan Sarandon
http://zen.sunderland.ac.uk/~aa1gha/susan.html

Tom Savini
http://www.savini.com/

Alicia Silverstone
http://homegrohn.com/alicia/

Will Smith
http://www.willsmith.net/

Kevin Spacey
http://www.duke.edu/~jlg1/kevin-spacey.html

David Spade
http://members.aol.com/CarlySpade/index.html

Jimmy Stewart
http://www.jimmy.org
http://www.jimmy.org/films/tph.html

Lili Taylor
http://www.lilitaylor.com/

Charlize Theron
http://www.cryptic.org/theron/

Uma Thurman
http://users.why.net/cfish/uma/uma.html
http://www.duke.edu/~xl2/uma/index.html

Marisa Tomei
http://www.vuse.vanderbilt.edu/~burketrd/tomei.htm

John Travolta
http://www.auburn.edu/~proppka/travolta.htm

Skeet Ulrich
http://www.tfn.net/~sm123/skeet.html

Casper Van Dien
http://members.tripod.com/~malluvian/main.htm

Vince Vaughn
http://www.vincev.com/

Christopher Walken
http://www.ior.com/~cmohney/walken/walken.html

Denzel Washington
http://209.132.70.117/bk/denzel.htm

John Wayne
http://www.napanet.net~donc/

Sigourney Weaver
http://www.pt.hk-r.se/student/di94vno/ripley.html

Bruce Willis
http://www.accsyst.com/writers/bruno.htm

Michael Wincott
http://bud.indirect.com/www/lynna/win.html

Kate Winslet
http://www2.cibola.net/~michaela/kate
http://www.abbagirl.com/kate.html

Elijah Wood
http://www.elijahwood.com/

Chow Yun-Fat
http://studentweb.tulane.edu/~jgoldin/chow.html
http://www.markgor-dl.com/

Billy Zane
http://www.bluedevil.com/bz/

Renee Zellweger
http://members.aol.com/tygre14/zellweger/zellweger.html

CULT MOVIE RESOURCES

AnimEigo
http://www.animeigo.com
Gives extensive history on this rapidly growing Japanese export of animation.

Anime Resources and Info
http://www.best.com:80/~gaxiola/Anime/
Informs users of upcoming anime features and background information on the genre itself.

B.O.S.C.H.
http://huizen.dds.nl/~penquin/index_frame.html
Offers reviews of some off-beat, cheaply made films.

Black Comedies
http://www.losman.com/black.htm
Spotlights those films that humorously poke fun at other peoples' pain and misery.

The Cult Movie Den
http://www.geocities.com/Hollywood/Boulevard/4802/
Provides valuable information on past, present, and future cult movies.

The Cult Shop
http://lasarto.cnde.iastate.edu/Movies/CultShop
Gives the latest information on your favorite cult movie stars like Bruce Campbell and Steve Buscemi. Also offers links to other movie sites.

The Gamera Home Page
http://tswww.cc.emory.edu/~kgowen/gamera.html
A home page devoted to that Japanese superstar turtle, Gamera. Showcases, in depth, all nine of his films from Gamera *to* Gamera vs. Legion.

Hong Kong Movies Home Page
http://egret0.stanford.edu/hk/index.html
An interest in Hong Kong films has significantly increased due to the sudden rise of Jackie Chan and action director John Woo. This comprehensive site offers much information on the Hong Kong film industry. Includes an update of new Hong Kong films, filmographies, interviews, reviews, and a searchable database on Hong Kong actors and actresses.

Mad Prof. Mike's Headbanger Movie Reviews
http://www.dnai.com/~ochobbit/topten.html
Witness the lunatic rantings of Professor Headbanger as he raves about such scholock classics as Teenagers from Outer Space *and* This Island Earth.

Manga Video
http://www.manga.com/
A spin-off of anime, video retailer offering comic books, soundtracks, and fan club information.

Mondo Hell
http://www.losman.com/fod.htm
If you're itching for production information on the Faces of Death video series, then look no further.

Mr. Data's SF Cult TV and Movie Site
http://www.trekman.demon.co.uk/
Includes updates and even an episode guide to the top sci-fi television shows as well as the latest information on upcoming films.

No Place for a Woman: The Family in Film Noir
http://www.obs.net:80/Noir/

Reports on the implications that film noir has had on society. The author, John Blaser, pinpoints the role that women and family have in this genre. Subtopics include,"Pro-family Messages in Film Noir" and "Women's Anti-Family Function in Film Noir."

Professor Neon's TV and Movie Mania
http://www.vortex.com/ProfNeon.html
Covers a gamut of information on film, television, radio and cable industry. When it comes to films, the Professor leans more to sci-fi, cult and weird stuff.

Reel Talk
http://www.reellife.com/PFE/index.html
Allows you to talk amongst yourselves about recent or past cult film releases.

Shock Cinema
http://members.aol.com/shockcin/main.html
On-line version of magazine catering to those fans of bizarre and unconventional cinema.

The Vampyre's Haven
http://www.wam.umd.edu/~mcarter/
A listing of most, not all, vampire films made, including the most obscure ones like Bloedverwatnen *(from the Netherlands) and* Wanda Does Transylvania.

DIRECTORS

Woody Allen
http://www.idt.unit.no/~torp/woody

Pedro Almodovar
http://www.csd.abdn.ac.uk/~eugenio/almodovar.html

Allison Anders
http://home.earthlink.net/~kristinm/aahome.html

Kenneth Anger
http://152.175.1.205/CIAnger.html
http://orpheus.ucsd.edu/av/FVL/catalog/directors/kenneth_anger.html

Roger Avary
http://www.avary.com/

Clive Barker
http://www.webcom.com/tby/cbarker.html

Ingmar Bergman
http://www.eskimo.com/~masonw/Bergman/

Bernardo Bardolucci
http://ctashiro.annenberg.edu/bb.html

Luc Besson
http://www.halcyon.com/theboss/luc/main.htm

Mel Brooks
http://userwww.service.emory.edu/~mgros/brooks/Index.html

Tim Burton
http://www.xs4all.nl/~danhf/burton/title.html
http://home.acadia.net/userpages/joel/timburton/

James Cameron
http://www.soton.ac.uk/~pdc194/cameron/

Frank Capra
http://www.geocities.com/Hollywood/Set/7321/capra1.html

John Carpenter
http://www.pkbaseline.com/screen/strange/people/carpenter/

Jean Cocteau
http://www-scf.usc.edu/~pkon/Cocteau.html

Joel and Ethan Coen
http://www.geocities.com/Hollywood/7042/index.html

Francis Ford Coppola
http://www.lehigh.edu/~mtl2/coppola.html

Wes Craven
http://www.lehigh.edu/~mtl2/coppola.html

David Cronenberg
http://www.kgbmedia.com/wsv/cronen.html

Atom Egoyan
http://www2.cruzio.com/~akreyche/atom.html

Federico Fellini
http://members.aol.com/gerrym22/intro.htm

David Fincher
http://members.aol.com/gerrym22/intro.htm

Terry Gilliam
http://members.aol.com/morgands1/closeup/indices/gillindx.htm
http://www.pythonline.com/plugs/gilliam/index.htm

Jean Luc Godard
http://www.geocities.com/Hollywood/3781/godard.html

Werner Herzog
http://sol.uvic.ca/german/439/herzog.html

Alfred Hitchcock
http://www.qumulus.nl/hitchcock/
http://www.primenet.com/~mwc/

John Hughes
http://www.riverblue.com/hughes/

Krzysztof Kieslowski
http://www.netwiz.net/~rdef/kieslowski.htm

Stanley Kubrick
http://pages.prodigy.com/kubrick/

Akira Kurosawa
http://www.voyagerco.com/movies/directors/kurosawa/

Spike Lee
http://www.voyagerco.com/movies/directors/spike/

David Lynch
http://www.mikedunn.com/lynch.html

Oscar Micheux
http://www.datapub.com/webb/KnowPlace/oscar/gregpr.html

Roman Polanski
http://www.cafeinternet.co.uk/polanski/index.html

Sam Raimi
http://www.pathcom.com/~nooger/raimi/raimi.html

Rob Reiner
http://www.geocities.com/Hollywood/Lot/3827/

Robert Rodriguez
http://members.aol.com/wirerecon/intro.htm
http://www.godamongdirectors.com/rodriguez/index.shtml

John Sayles
http://www-scf.usc.edu/~rskelley/

Martin Scorsese
http://www.afionline.org/Scorsese

Kevin Smith
http://www2.liglobal.com/kevinsmith/

Steven Spielberg
http://www.geocities.com/Hollywood/7839/
http://www.ele.puc-rio.br/~guy/tribute/main.htm

Oliver Stone
http://www.geocities.com/Hollywood/2682

Quentin Tarantino
http://www.GANet.Net/~pg0/quentin/greatbig.htm
http://osiris.sunderland.ac.uk/~ca5sli/home.htm
http://www.xs4all.nl/~mrblond/
http://www.blarg.net/~kbilly/
http://www.calweb.com/~gerrit01/qtshrine/
http://www.tarantino.com/top.shtml

Francios Truffault
http://iihm.imag.fr/truffaut/ (in French)

Gus Van Sant
http://www.geocities.com/Hollywood/Boulevard/3809/

John Waters
http://www.hotwired.com/retina.95/29/waters/index.html
http://www.reed.edu/~mfagan/dreamland.html
http://blackrock.sametz.com/dreamland/
http://www.northcoast.com/~shojo/Waters/

Peter Weir
http://www10.pair.com/crazydv/weir/

Orson Welles
http://www.geocities.com/Hollywood/Academy/7955/orsonwds.html

Wim Wenders
http://www.geocities.com/Hollywood/3294/wenders.html
http://www.greenteam.it/wenders/default.htm

John Woo
http://www.voyagerco.com/movies/directors/woo/

Ed Wood
http://hem2.passagen.se/mwrang/edwood.htm

FILM FESTIVALS

AFI Los Angeles International Film Festival (USA)
http://www.afionline.org/afihomes/aaa.home.html
Features attractions from this huge film festival held every October. Also lists synposes of the films featured.

Berlin Film Festivals
http://www.b.shuttle.de/forum-ifb/
Lists production information on all the films featured in this festival.

California Sun International Animation Film Festival
http://www.csun.edu/~jpr45052/anifest.html
An organization on the California State University campus hosts this annual event showcasing strange techniques in animation.

Cannes Film Festival
http://www.filmscouts.com
Official site gives you a rundown of all the films running in the competition and an icon called "guest book" so that you can go starchasing in cyberspace.

Chicago International Film Festival
http://www.chicago.ddbn.com/filmfest/menu.html
Answers questions in the area of awards, entries, juries and transportation.

Chicago Lesbian and Gay International Film Festival
http://videos.com/outspoken/gllist.htm
Offers a rundown of films featured in this alternative film festival.

Denver International Film Festival
http://www2.csn.net/DenverFilm/
Besides information on the entries, this site offers insight into the Denver Film Society, supporters, new media and workshops.

London Film Festival
http://www.ibmpcug.co.uk/lff.html
Lists the star attendees and has a program diary which records all the relevant action at this film festival.

Montreal World Film Festival
http://www.ffm-montreal.org/home-f.htm
Offers a rundown of the festival in both English and French.

Santa Clarita International Film Festival
http://www.smartlink.net/~director/scviff
Acknowledges the only film festival in Santa Clarita, California specializing in family films.

Seattle International Film Festival
http://www.seattlefilm.com/
Enables you to look at some photo stills from the festival, read audio speeches and check out some internet broadcasts.

Sundance Film Festival
http://www.sundancefilm.com
Official site may not be as exciting as actually rubbing elbows among the hot talent but it does come close. Sections include a daily report, listings of films competing and a guide for getting around. Also has an archive for past festivals.

Toronto International Film Festival
http://www.bell.ca/toronto/filmfest/
Includes cine-bytes and a feature to browse the poster gallery and check out the paparazzi.

Venice Film Festival
http://www.portve.interbusiness.it/wetvenice/biennale/binfoe.html
Includes information on the film festival, as well as news on other cultural activities happening in Venice.

FILM MAGAZINES

Box Office
http://www.boxoff.com
One of the first trade publications to go online, reporting the latest on current films and films in production.

CinemaSpace
http://cinemaspace.berkeley.edu/
Journal dedicated to all aspects of cinema and new media. Covers such areas as film theory, criticism, multimedia lectures and the film program at UC Berkeley.

Film Threat
http://www.filmthreat.com
The irreverrent film magazine may be out of circulation, but this site is the next best thing.

FilmMaker
http://found.cs.nyu.edu/CAT/affiliates/filmmaker/filmmaker.html
Quarterly publication that showcases independent film and filmmakers.

The Hollywood Reporter
http://www.hollywoodreporter.com/
Provides the latest scoop on all major studio happenings.

Millennium Film Journal
http://www.sva.edu/MFJ/
Published articles about independent, experimental, and avant-garde cinema, video, and, more recently, works that use the newer technologies. Also has an archive for past issues.

Premiere
http://www.premieremag.com/
On-line version of the leading entertainment magazine with various segments including a chat circle called schmoozing and a trivia game.

Time Out
http://www.timeout.co.uk./
Provides a rundown of many cultural and art events happening around the world.

FILM STUDIOS

A-Pix Entertainment
http://www.panix.com/~1weston/virtual_combat.shtml
Showcases its most recent releases to home video with plot synopsis, cast information and production tidbits.

Fine Line Features
http://www.flf.com/
The leading studio of independent films presents information on upcoming releases and offers enlightenment to budding filmmakers.

Gramercy Pictures
http://spider.media.philips.com/polygram/PolyGram.html

---

http://www.reelife.com
A division of Polygram, where you can jump to various sites dealing with their movies and music.

October Films
http://www.octoberfilms.com
A bevy of recently released independent films are covered here.

MCA/Universal Cyberwalk
http://www.mca.com
Take a stroll through MCA's family tree of entertainment companies which includes Universal Studios, MCA Home Video, MCA Records and Spencer's Gifts. Links you to coming attractions and to a screening room with current video releases.

MGM Lion's Den
http://www.mgmua.com/
Home of the revamped ShowGirls site, also has coverage on the huge distributor's large slate of theatrical releases. Divided into MGM's niches, such as MGM television and home video.

The Miramax Cafe
http://www.miramax.com/
Walk into a smorgasbord of Miramax delectables. Includes chances to win a trip to premieres and Miramax clothing. Click on their week's specials and get a glimpse into their upcoming and current releases.

MPI Home Video
http://www.mpimedia.com
Answers questions on availibility for MPI video releases.

New Line Cinema
http://www.newline.com
Displays their current and upcoming releases.

Paramount Pictures
http://www.paramount.com
Click on any icon from the movies shown and receive information on production and cast.

Republic Pictures
http://www.republic-pictures.com
Includes countless bits of information on this golden oldie studio, with synopses, reviews, and director information. Also lists its entire film library.

Sony Classics
http://www.spe.sony.com/Pictures/SonyClassics
Focuses on Sony's independent releases and offers links to other sites.

Sony Pictures Entertainment
http://www.spe.sony.com/Pictures/SonyMovies/index.html
Sony (which includes Columbia and TriStar) gives you the latest on their crop of films. Along with film and studio information, you can enter their contests to win movie t-shirts or trips to a Hollywood premiere.

Trimark Pictures
http://www.trimarkpictures.com/
Takes you behind the scenes of their latest releases and gives you a glimpse of future films.

Troma
http://www.troma.com/home
With its #1 citizen Toxie welcoming you, indulge in the finest camp cinema that Troma brought to new heights, or lows. Features information on such classics as Toxic Avenger, Class of Nuke'em High and their latest, Sgt. Kabukiman NYPD.

Twentieth Century Fox Home Entertainment
http://www.tcfhe.com
Promotes the studio's library of films which includes such mega hits as the Star Wars and Die Hard trilogies on video. Divided into a time line enabling you to browse through their collection, beginning with the 1920's and continuing right on to the present.

United International Pictures
http://www.uip.com/
Comes in a variety of languages and has materials on their films which can be downloaded.

Walt Disney Studios
http://www.disney.com
Divided into nine categories where you can find the latest on Disney books, home video, movies, music, shopping, software, television, theater and theme parks.

Warner Brothers
http://www.movies.warnerbros.com/
Get the latest on WB's films, tv programs, music, merchandise, DC comics and kid's programming.

FILMMAKER RESOURCES

American Film Institute
http://www.afionline.org/
The American Film Institute created this site to further its cause of finding talent that will prolong the life of art and film. The site reveals the various courses, studies facilities and grants that this non-profit organziation offers.

American Film Marketing Asssn.(AFMA)
http://www.afma.com
Set up for those who exclusively license, distribute and produce independent films.

Assn. of Independent Video and Filmmakers (AIVF)
http://www.virtualfilm.com/aivf/
Resource that offers information on festivals and self distribution.

Cyber Film School
http://www.cyberfilmschool.com/
Want to become the next Quentin or Spike, but can't afford film school? Try this informative and entertaining venue that teaches the tricks of the trade in areas such as screenwriting, cinematography and producing.

Film Finances
http://www.primenet.com/~ffi/ffihome.html
Check out this site provided by the world leader of financial supplements to film, television and CD-ROM productions if you're looking for financing for a film project.

Filmmakers Foundations (FF)
http://www.filmfound.org
A base for information, training and networking for the novice filmmaker.

Independent Film and Video Makers Internet Resource Guide
http://www.echonyc.com/~mvidal/Indi-Film+Video.html
Questions on funding and film festivals are answered and changes in film and video production are documented on this site.

Mandy's Film and Television Production Directory
http://www.mandy.com/
An international geographical listing of film technicans, facilities and producers. Helpful site for anyone looking for a film crew.

Screenwriter's Online
http://www.screenwriter.com/insider/news.html
Welcomes novice screenwriters to interact with those who are in the business.

Screenwriter's Resources Pages
http://www.teleport.com/~cdeemer/Screenwriters.html
A screenwriter's one-stop resource site. Learn about the format and structure of scripts, how to market your script, network among your peers, receive tips from the pros and become informed of the latest events and seminars.

FILM REVIEWS

Critics Roost
http://moviereviews.com/coc-roost.html

The home of a circle of film critics with their individual slant on film. Women's Lip, The Movie Avenger, The Movie Assassin and J-Man offer their personal perspective on film.

Doug Y's Movie Reviews
http://www.bway.net/~dougy/movies.html
This snappy reviewer includes such categories as Òlf I Were Rex Reed I Would Say.Ó

Film.com
http://www.film.com/film/
Bringing a casual spin on film criticism from self-made critics around the country. Also has a calendar noting upcoming film releases.

The Man Who Viewed Too Much
description:A New York screenwriting student with a soft touch for the art house fluff and mediocre gems, like Joe Versus the Volcano.

Mandel & Patrick's Movie Corner!
http://www.fyi.net/~andre/mand&pat.htm
Two teenaged boys, using a star system, review current releases as well as video releases.

The Movie Mom's Guide to Movies and Videos for Families
http://pages.prodigy.com/VA/rcpj55a/moviemom.html
Created by movie critic and mother, Nell Minow, who gives critiques and advice on how to get children to watch movies that aren't doused in violence.

The Movie Pit
http://www.geocities.com/Athens/9200/index.htm
Offers film reviews of cheesy movies such as Ice-T's and Rutger Hauer's Surviving the Game and Cat from Outer Space.

Movie Reviews by Ellis: The Art and Craft of Cultural Context
http://movie.infocom.net/
Film critic Joan Ellis puts her acerbic and astute observations on the Internet as she examines the cultural innuendoes in current film.

Movie Reviews by Matt and Kenny
http://www.winternet.com/~nudnik/reviews/
Gives skeletal reviews of films but offers a link to information regarding Lucasfilm's THX sound system.

Movie Review Query Engine
http://www.cinema.pgh.pa.us/movie/reviews
Allows you to search on any movie and find all available reviews appearing in the Usernet group rec.arts.movies. reviews.

Mr. Cranky Rates the Movies
http://internet-plaza.net/zone/mrcranky/
The joke here is that this guy doesn't like any movie, hence Cranky. His rating scale is based on bombs and his followers (code names Lizard, and Philm Pham, just to name a few) are as nutty as his reviews.

Out Magazine Movie Reviews
http://www.out.com/out/entertainment/movies.html
On-line version of the gay magazine that includes movie reviews and commentary on gay and lesbian cinema.

Reviews in Rhyme
http://www.datasync.com/~booda/rir/movies.html
Unique, if not juvenile, way of reviewing films that involves poetry done by ÒMs. Dana's 7th Grade English Class.Ó Samples for Speed: ÒDon't go below fifty/The flying bus looks nifty.Ó

Roger Ebert
http://www.suntimes.com/ebert
Newspapers, books, television, now the web. Offers his newspaper film reviews, with an archive that goes back to 1985.

Skew
http://www.ot.com/skew/
Targeted for the teenage crowd, includes adolescent criticisms on films and popular culture.

Teen Movie Critic
http://www.dreamagic.com/roger/teencritic.html
Seventeen year old movie buff from Minnesota offers his thoughts on current theatrical releases. Also has a link to a listing of many video rental stores around America.

The Third Thumb
http://www.ganesa.com/ganesa/~pat/movies/movrev2.html
Gives brief film reviews and has a searchable database.

The Tripper's Multimedia Movie Reviews
http://www.execpc.com/~tripper/movies.html
Offers film clips, music samples and audio clips.

Uncle Bill's Shack O'Movies
http://www.tmsonline.com/movies/
Funny guide takes on such movies as Bound and includes animation (courtesy of Java) to help get his point across.

VideoHound
http://www.videohound.com
Our home page. Includes reviews of current and highlighted video releases, as well as information on other VIP titles.

Women Studies Film Reviews
http://www.inform.umd.edu:8080/EdRes/Topic/womensStudies/Film-Reviews/
Movie reviews with a feminist angle written by Florida radio personality Linda Lopez McAlister and film scholar Cynthia Fuchs.

GENERAL ENTERTAINMENT

Absolut
http://www.absolutvodka.com
Devoted to the annual animation festival that the vodka maker sponsors.

Academy of Motion Picture Arts and Sciences
http://www.oscars.org/ampas/
Site proves that the AMPAS does more than just hand out gold statuettes every year. This homepage reveals this organization's dedication to spreading the love of film around the world. Includes information on AMPAS's various fellowships, educational and historical activities.

The alt.sex.movies Page
http://www.xmission.com/~legalize/asm/asm.html
Includes miscellanous facts on famous porn stars and essays on pornography and censorship.

American Memory
http://lcweb2.loc.gov/papr/mpixhome.html
Collection of historical film stock that can be downloaded from the Library of Congress. Time frame is from 1897 to 1916 and includes such archival footage as President William McKinley's funeral and "actuality films" showing panoramic views of old San Francisco policemen and firemen in action.

Beatrice's Web Guide
http://www.bguide.com
Female based site that links you to the Barbra Striesand museum.

Belles of the Nineties
http://www.netlink.co.uk/user/michael/belle.html
French contemporary actresses (Emmanuelle Beart and Isabelle Huppert to name a few) are showcased with photos, vital statistics and sound clips.

Big Bad Barbarian
http://pages.ripco.com:8080/~bbb/movies.html
There are many popular scripts on the Internet, such as ,Star Wars and Alien, and the barabarian can lead you to them.

The Black Film Center/Archive
http://www.indiana.edu/~bfca/index.html
An academic reference devoted to sharing resources on black cinema.

Black Rebel
http://www.blackrebel.com

Created by the screenwriter of Eraser, Tony Puryear, who sets his site from the rest by offering ÒfunkierÓ viewpoints on film, with added information on music.

Blockbuster Entertainment
http://pwr.com/blockbuster/
Explores all the goodies the chain has to offer from their many stores and the latest contests or sweepstakes going on.

The Cabinet of Dr. Casey
http://www.cat.pdx.edu/~caseyh/horror/index.html
Immense site that includes interviews from artists and actors in horror films and graphics from famous horror movies. Links you to other horror sites such as "The Ooga Booga Page" and "The Page That Dripped Blood".

CelebSite
http://www.celebsite.com
Spinoff of the very popular Mr. Showbiz site that centers on bio, daily news and links on more than 500 celebrities.

Cine Fantom
http://www.sunsite.cs.msu.su/wwwart/cine/
Exposes Russian experimental films and videos.

Cinemafan
http://www.cinemafan.com
Sells the latest video releases and offers film reviews way in advance of films' release.

Cinemedia
http://www.gu.edu.au/gwis/cinemedia/CineMedia.cinema.html
An index which allows you to begin your own search for other entertainment web sites.

Coming Attractions
http://corona.bc.ca/films/
Get the latest information on future movies in production.

Crazy Movie Credits
http://www.cis.ohio-state.edu/hypertext/faq/usenet/movies/crazy-credits/faq.html
If you think that a movie ends when the credits roll, then you're wrong, at least for some movies. This site showcases the end credits of quirky movies that go out of their way to leave the best for last.

Cybersleaze
http://metaverse.com/vibe/sleaze/index.html
Created by former MTV veejay Adam Curry, this site dishes out the dirt on the celebrities, but in a playful way.

Cyber Sightings
http://www.cyberpages.com/cybersightings
Create your own rumors for others to read and perhaps spread. Stumble onto this site, you may very well be convinced that Babe the pig actually can talk but the government is trying to cover it up.

The Darkside of the Web
http://www.cascade.net/darkweb.html
Specializes in shedding light on the bizarre and creepy.

Dermatology in the Cinema
http://www.itsa.ucsf.edu/~vcr/Dermcin.html
Proof that anything can go on the Web. Exposes how skin afflictions are handled in films. Broken down in three categories: ÒRepresentation of Evil;Ó ÒActors with Skin Findings;Ó and Realistic and Sympathetic Portrayals.Ó Informative and healthy.

Dinner and Movie
http://www.dinnerandamovie.com
Helps moviegoers to not only locate their nearest theater but the restaurants surrounding their choice of theater.

Drew's Scripts-o-Rama
http://www.script-o-rama.com
Provides links to pages where transcripts or manuscripts of movie, television, and anime scripts can be found.

The Drudge Report
http://www.lainet.com/~drudge

If you get past the political reports and the weather forecasts that smother this site, you can find some interesting gossip from an anonomous insider from Hollywood.

E! Online
http://www.eonline.com/Hot/Oscar
A fun site to visit come Oscar time. Involves games at the expense of stars not nominated to partake in the festivites.

e drive Entertainment
http://www.edrive.com/
Similar to Mr. Showbiz, it covers the latest news and film releases.

Each Movie
http://www.eachmovie.com
Recommends films you would like based on ratings you have given five similar films. Call it the SAT approach to video viewing.

The Electronic Urban Report
http://www.EURweb.com/
Supports the positive images of African Americans in film and offers the latest celebrity news on the top black stars.

Entertainment Asylum
http://www.asylum.com/hw/index.html
Another news and infotainment site with a trivia game you can play online anonymously with someone else.

The Envelope Please
http://garbo.virtualize.com/
The official site for the Oscars which provides eye catching graphics, an expansive Oscar trivia game and information on production of the award show. Noteworthy feature involves video clips from nominated films which can be downloaded.

Film and Video Resources
http://http2.sils.umich.edu/Public/fvl/film.html
Created by the folks at the University of Michigan School of Information and Library Studies, this site leads you to many of the textual resources available that deal with film and video. Organized according to reviews, filmographies, discussions and other databases.

Film Forum
http://www.filmforum.com/
Showcases the latest releases in New York's leading independent movie house. Offers premiere information on independent features and reportory programming.

Film 100
http://www.film100.com
Ranks Hollywood's top visionaries in filmmaking and film business. Such visionaries include a wide range like John Cassavetes and actor Joseph Cotton.

Filmzone
http://www.Filmzone.com/
Offers information on independent films, including long lost gems and interviews with filmmakers and actors suchs as the Coen Brothers and Jackie Chan. Also gives visitors the current trends in mulitplexes.

Foresight New Media
http://www.foresight.co.uk/ents/
European company that makes web site pages has its own site that can link you to other movie sites.

The Gigaplex
http://www.gigaplex.com/
This site has information divided into 15 plexes that include film, tv, music, theater, books, photos, art, golf, yoga, food, sex, love , travel, puzzles and top ten listings from every spectrum of popular culture.

Girls on Film
http://www.girlsonfilm.com
Four girls talk about pop culture and films.

The GRAFICS Server
http://grafics.histart.umontreal.ca/default-eng.html
Sponsored by a French-Canadian research group that specalizes in the early cinema of Quebec. Much of the information is in

French, but you can dowload many documents and articles on this province's early cinema.

Hollywood Online
http://www.hollywood.com
Packaged like a row of slot machines in Vegas, try your luck at movie trailers, movie trivia, movie chat, vote on the latest contest or check out some real estate in California.

Hollywood Sign
http://www.rfx.com/hollywood/
Shows snapshots of the famous Hollywood sign from various angles.

IndieFilms
http://www.indiefilms.com
An easy, inexpensive way to distribute any feature, short or documentary film you made. Allows independent filmmakers to make contact with potential investors and distributors.

The Internet Entertainment Network
http://www.hollywoodnetwork.com/dealmaking/index.html
Enables you to become a member of the Screenwriters, Producers or Writers Network. Divided into such sites as dealmaking, box office, in- production and script sales.

The Internet Movie Database
http://www.msstate.edu/Movies
The mother of all entertainment databases. Users can frequently update the information and submit their own film reviews. With thousands of movies stored in its database, you can search by title, actor, director, country and even by character name.

The Internet Movie Institute
http://www.dkdigital.com/Netties/
Involves information on movies and awards.

Jam!Movies
http://www.canoe.ca/JamMovies/home.html
A Canadian version of Mr. Showbiz with entertainment news and information.

James Bond
http://www.mcs.net/~klast/www/bond.html
With the arrival and success of Goldeneye, the phenomenon of Bond has invaded cyberspace with his own homepage. Includes a rundown of all Bond villains and their famous lines, and trivia on every Bond film ever made.

Kino on Video
http://www.kino.com/
Kino International showcases a breadth of films from world cinema.

Kinema Club
Includes reviews of Japanese films and dedicated to the exposure of contemporay Japanese films.

Kyle Reece's Theater Guide
http://www.moviewarehouse.com/upcoming.html
Includes a rundown of current movie ideas being considered for future production.

The Left-Wing Film Guide
http://ccme-mac4.bsd.uchicago.edu/DSADocs/Films.html
Helpful guide for any social and political group planning their next movie themed rally. Pick any movie from any of their categories that include feminism, race relations and anti-authoritian struggles.

Library of Congress Archive
http://lcweb2.loc.gov/papr/mpixhome.html
Allows you to download historical film images from the early 1900's.

Local Movie Listings
http://www.actwin.com/movies/other.html
Includes movie theater showtimes from Canada, England and South Africa as well as American cities.

Lucy Lipps
http://www.lucylipps.com/
Includes a Kiss & Tell section which brings you the latest scoop on celebrities and the buzz around Tinseltown.

Martin's Film Noir Page
http://www.pitt.edu/~lewison/Noir/index.html
Extensive site on the popular genre of film.

Movies.com
http://www.movies.com/
Displays the latest films and allows celebrities to welcome visitors onto the site.

The Movie Cliches List
http://www.like.it/vertigo/cliches.html
A vast list of common stereotypes and instances that stifle logic found in film. Divided into over fifty topics including bodily functions, minorities, teenagers and wood. A growing site since people can submit their own materials.

Moviefinder.com
http://www.moviefinder.com/
Presented by E!Online, it's an all in one site that enables you to find, buy or rent a movie. Includes among other things, search engine, archive of film reviews, and listings for local theaters.

MovieLink
http://www.movielink.com/?TP:National
On-line movie guide with listings of local movie theaters in the 22 most populated cities in the country. Features include a section for users to cast their votes for "The American Moviegoer Awards" and a place called the "cafe" for users to chit chat.

Movie Mania
http://www.clicked.com/moviemania/
Find out what's new and what's hot on the video scene. Also keeps you informed of the latest free software available on the Web.

MovieNet
http://www.movienet.com/
A consulting firm used by Hollywood execs seeking information on the latest film projects in production, up and coming directors, acting talent and news on the acquistions of remakes.

The Movie Posters Archive
http://anubis.science.unitn.it/services/movies/index.html
An on-line vault of old movie posters from the sci-fi, horror, animation and classic genres.

Movie Poster Web Page
http://www.musicman.com/mp/mp.html
No, you're not seeing double. This one is a catalog of movie posters available for sale. Includes foreign films.

Movie Snapshot
http://www.moviesnapshot.com/
Reviews, photographs, celebrity interviews, biographies, games and awards.

The Movie Sound Page
http://www.moviesounds.com.html
Download various sound bites from famous flicks and link to other sites.

Movie Recommendation System
http://www.labs.bt.com/innovate/multimed/morse/morse.htm
Your votes count with this site that enables you to rate movies you have seen and based on your rating, will recommend movies you might like. This is not a game, but a service.

Movies at MSN
http://207.68.142.34/movies.movies
Companion piece to Microsoft's Cinemania CD-ROM.

MovieWEB
http://movieweb.com/movie/movie.html
Groups all film studios in to one site and offers production information and still photos of their new releases. Also offers the latest box office statistics.

Mr. Showbiz
http://www.mrshowbiz.com/showbiz/
Bundles the latest entertainment gossip and news with movie and music reviews. Includes an in-depth volume of knowledge on the history of the Academy Awards.

The Muse
http://www.hyperlink.com/muse
Dedicated to the Greek mythology figure who spawned the arts. Among its links for books, music, theater and dance, includes one for cinema where it will showcase such directors as Roman Polanski and Martin Scorsese.

The Obituary Page
http://catless.ncl.ac.uk/Obituary/movies.html
A listing of the latest celebrity deaths in Hollywood.

On Video
http://www.onvideo.org/
Provides extensive calendar dates for upcoming video releases, also offers reviews of the top twenty rentals.

OscarNet
http://www.dkdigital.com/Netties/
Encourages visitors to vote for nominees and for alternative nominations called the "Netty Awards". Visitors can vote for the" Golden Raspberry Awards "for the year's worst performances.

Our Secret Century: Revelations from The Prelinger Archive
http://gopher.well.sf.ca.us:70/11/Art/Experimental.Film.and.Video/secret.
century
Contains footage and information on films from The Prelinger Archives which is a collection of instititutional films made from Ô30's to the early Ô60's. Some of these clips can be seen on The Late Show with David Letterman.

Pathfinder
http://www.pathfinder.com
Created by Time Warner, site links to their magazines that check the pulse of popular culture such as People, Vibe, Groove and Entertainment Weekly.

The Phantasmagoria Graveyard Web Page
http://libstaff.lib.lehigh.edu
Audio website that features the theme music from such horror films as Halloween and The Shining.

Planet Earth
http://www.demon.co.uk/elpasso/planet-earth/index.htm
If you're looking for film and tv memorablilia from such popular movies and series as Alien orSpace 1999, this is the place to order such merchandise. An on-line catalog for costumes, model kits, back issues of specialized magazines and trading cards. You can even post any items you might want to sell.

Popcornq
http://www.popcornq.com
Dedicated to showcasing films dealing with gays and lesbians.

Reel Talk
http://www.reellife.com/PFE/index.html
If you're a movie buff, then join the crowd as you talk amongst yourselves about the latest releases.

Science Fiction Contiuum
http://www.webcreations.com/sjvideo/
A guide to a diverse collection of sci-fi and horror films as well as animation, television and UFO documentaries on video and laser disc.

ScreenSite
http://www.sa.ua.edu/Screesite/
Primarily wants to encourage the teaching and researching of film and television.

Silent Movies
http://www.cs.monash.edu.au/~pringle/silent/
Information on silent films. Includes a listing for many silent film screening and bios on many of the era's top stars such as Charlie Chaplin, Buster Keaton and Lillian Gish.

The Top 25
http://movieweb.com/movie/top25.html
Anxious to see if a certain movie has broken any box office records during its opening week? This site provides the box office ranking of all current releases. Updated every Thursday.

U.C. Berkeley Film Studies Science Fiction Page
http://remarque.berkeley.edu:8001/~xcohen/Resources/localres.html
For avid SciFi film buffs, site has separate pages for such classics as Blade Runner, Star Trek, Alien, Star Wars *and other genre related sites.*

UFO Diaries
http://www.ufo-diaries.com
Learn about new sci-fi releases from Republic Pictures.

Wiretap Archive
http://wiretap.spies.com:70/11/Library/Media/Film
Very straightforward and diverse listing of special interest movies. Categories include: films with rape scenes, film noir listing, railway movies, Japanese monster guide, naval related movies and vampires in movies.

INDIVIDUAL MOVIE SITES

A Perfect Murder
http://www.aperfectmurder.com/

Ace Ventura: When Nature Calls
http://movieweb.com/movie/acevent2/index.html

ACME Animal House Page
http://www.bestware.net/spreng/animal/index.html

Airplane
http://www.d.umn.edu/~elindsko/Airplane/airplane.html

ALIEN Saga
http://found.cs.nyu.edu/michael/alien/

Alien Resurrection
http://www.alien4.com/index2.html

Almost Heroes
http://www.almostheroes.com

Apocalypse Now
http://www.luhsd.k12.ca.us/~nc670597/apocnow.html

Apollo 13
http://www.mca.com/universal_pictures/apollo13/index.html

The Apostle
http://www.octoberfilms.com/apostle/index.html

Armageddon
http://www.armageddon.com

As Good As It Gets
http://www.spe.sony.com/movies/asgoodasitgets/

Austin Powers
http://www.austinpowers.com/

The Avengers
http://www.the-avengers.com

Barney:The Movie
http://www.barneyonline.com/

Batman and Robin
http://www.batman-robin.com/
http://home.revealed.net/riddler/batrob.htm

The Big Lebowski
http://www.lebowski.com/

Black Dog
http://blackdogthemovie.com

Blade
http://www.blademovie.com

Blade Runner
http://kzsu.stanford.edu/uwi/br/off-world.html

Blues Brothers 2000
http://www.blues-brothers-2000.com/

Braveheart
http://www.aloha.net/~brvhrt/index.html

Brazil
http://www.cis.ohio-state.edu/hypertext/faq/usenet/movies/brazil-faq.html

Bulworth
http://www.bulworth.com

The Cable Guy
http://www.thecableguy.com

Can't Hardly Wait
http://ww.spe.sony.com/movies/canhardlywait/index.html

The Chinese Box
http://www.chinesebox.com

A Christmas Story
http://www.easttexas.com/pdlg/c-story/

City of Angels
http://www.city-of-angels.com/

The Crow: City of Angels
http://www.thecrow.com/

Death Race 2000
http://www.mcn.net/~netrencher/dr2k.html

Deep Impact
http://www.deep-impact.com

Desperado/El Mariachi
http://cinemascape.comtecmedia.com/chris/desperado.html

Dr. Dolittle
http://www.drdolittle.com

Eraserhead
http://users.aol.com/RayWolf1/eraser.htm

The Evil Dead
http://www.daze.com/exit13/evil/

Fast Times at Ridgemont High
http://wizvax.net/tuegger/fast-times.html

Fear and Loathing in Las Vegas
http://www.fear-and-loathing.com

The Fifth Element
http://www.cinema1.com/movies97/fifthelement/us.html

From Dusk Till Dawn
http://www.hooked.net/users/cpatubo/fdtd.html

George of the Jungle
movieweb.com/movie/georgejungle/index.html

Get Shorty
http://www.uip.com/getshorty/

Ghostbusters
http://www.nwdc.com/~vostok/ghostbusters.html

The Godfather Trilogy
http://www.exit109.com/~jgeoff/godfathr.html

Godzilla (1998)
http://www.godzilla.com

Gone With the Wind
http://users.aol.com/axlrose75/gone.htm
http://www.franklymydear.com/

Groundhog Day
http://powered.zoo.cs.yale.edu:8000/~miller/hog/groundhog.html

Halloween
http://www.wavenet.com/~gbernard/

He Got Game
http://www.movies.com/hegotgame/index.html

Head Above Water
http://bluedevil.com/bz/haw.htm

Highlander
http://www.highlander-official.com/

Hoop Dreams
http://www.flf.com/hoop/index.htm

The Horse Whisperer
http://www.movies.com/horsewhisperer/index.html

Indiana Jones
http://www.smartlink.net/~deej7/indiana_jones.html

Independence Day
http://www.id4.com/

Jaws
http://www.winternet.com/~tandj04/jaws.html

The Jerk
http://www.hirons.com/~lburgess/jerk.html

John Carpenter's The Thing
http://www.powerup.com.au/~vampire/thing/t-sboard.htm

Jurassic Park
http://uslink.net/~warrior/

L.A. Confidential
http://www.newregency.com/laconfidential/

Les Miserables
http://www.spe.sony.com/movies/lesmierables/

Lost in Space
http://www.dangerwillrobinson.com

The Lost World: Jurassic Park
http://www.powerup.com.au/~stott/LWindex.html
http://wwwo.lost-world.com/
http://nac.net/~users/splat/lw/

Love!Valour!Compassion!
http://www.flf.com/lvc/index.html

Man in the Iron Mask
http://www.ironmask.com/

Men In Black
http://www.meninblack.com/

Mercury Rising
http://www.mercury-rising.com/

Mission Impossible
http://www.missionimpossible.com.

Monty Python's Holy Grail
http://bucket.ualr.edu/holygrail

Mortal Kombat
http://www.newline.com/nlc_releases/nlc_releases.html
http://www.nclpub.com/Relsched/mortal.html
http://www.mortalkombat.com/newsite/index.html

Mulan
http://www.mulan.com

My Best Friend's Wedding
http://www.spe.sony.com/Pictures/SonyMovies/movies/Bestfriend/intro.html

The Negotiator
http://www.newregency.com

Object of My Affection
http://www.filmzone.com/foxmovies.theobjectofmyaffection/

Paulie
http://www.freezone.com/paulie/paulie.html

Players Club
http://www.playersclub.net/

Phantasm
http://www.phantasm.com/

The Pillow Book
http://www.pillowbook.com/

Plan 9 From Outer Space
http://www.eng2.uconn.edu/~jstrip/plan9/

Primary Colors
http://www.primary-colors.com/

Psycho
http://www.geocities.com/Hollywood/1645/index.html

Quest for Camelot
http://www.quest4camelot.com/

Reservoir Dogs
http://www.foresight.co.uk/ents/dogs/

Return of the Texas Chainsaw Massacre
http://chainsaw.crimson.com/rtcm/

Rob Roy
http://www.mgmua.com/robroy/index.html

Rocky Horror Picture Show
http://www-scf.usc.edu/~proulx/RHPS.html
http://www.insv.com/rhps/

Romeo and Juliet
http://www.foxinteractive.com/products/rj.html

Scarface
http://pubweb.acns.nwu.edu/~apoorman/scarface.html

Seven
http://www.filmzone.com/seven

Shaft
http://users.aol.com/PizarroD/shaft.html
http://www.rapidcity.com

Shall We Dance
http://www.cinema1.com/movies97/shallwedance/us.html

The Shining
http://pubweb.acns.nwu.edu/~mdk899/overlook.html

Silence of the Lambs
http://www.pitt.edu/~elkst2/silence.html

Six Days, Seven Nights
http://www.movies.com/6d7n/index.html

Something About Mary
http://www.aboutmary.com

Sound of Music
http://www.perfect.com/som/

Species 2
http://www.mgm.com/speciesII/

Speed 2
http://www.speed2-cruisecontrol.com/site/index_new.htm

Star Trek (Trek Reviews Archive)
http://www.mcs.net/~forbes/trek-reviews/

Star Trek: First Contact
http://www.first-contact.com

Suicide Kings
http://www.suicidekings.com

Sunday
http://www.sundancechannel.com/festival97.webcast/s-19438675097.html

Superfly
http://student-www.uchicago.edu/users/bra9/fly.html

The Sweet Hereafter
http://www.flf.com/sweet/

Tarzan and the Lost City
http://www.tarzan-lostcity.com/

Taxi Driver
http://pilot.msu.edu/user/svoboda/taxi_driver/

Terminator (1 &2)
http://www.maths.tcd.ie/pub/films/terminator/

Tetsuo II: Body Hammer
http://wwwwp.com/69031/home/html
movienet.culnet.fi/mondonet/movies/tesuo.htm (not in english)

That Thing You Do
http://www/thatthingyoudo.com/

This Is Spinal Tap
http://www.spinaltap.com/

Titanic
http://bluedevil.com/bz/tita.htm
http://www.titancimovie.com/
http://www.geocities.com/Hollywood/9251/titanic.html

Trial and Error
http://www.trialanderror.com/

Toy Story
http://www.disney.com/ToyStory/?GL=H

Truck Turner
http://www.castle.net/~dcentury/truck.html

The Truman Show
http://www.truman-show.com/

2001: A Space Odyssey
http://www.lehigh.edu/~pj12/films/2001.html

U.S. Marshals
http://www.usmarshals.com/

The Usual Suspects
http://www.spectra.net/~funkman/spacey/usual/usual/html

The Van
http://www.filmscouts.com/films/van.html

Volcano
http://www.volcano.com/

Wild Things
http://www.sonypictures.com/movies/wildthings/

The X-Files: Fight the Future
http://www.fightthe future.com/

VIDEO OUTLETS

Adventures in Video
http://www.tds.net/aiv/htm
Offers a wide assortment of video titles from self-help to study aides.

Art and Trash Video
http://www.io.org/~imp/athome.htm
An outlet of over 7,500 titles in the art and trash genre that are hard to find.

Best Video
http://www.bestvideo.com
With over 24,000 titles, you can search their inventory via various topics and subject categories. Also includes brief monthly reviews of current releases.

Big Lizard Video
http://www.well.com/user/bigliz/
Order through the mail the most obscure and bizarre films ever made.

Blockbuster
http://pwr.com/blockbuster/
Find video releases, movie merchandise, movie reviews and news here. Ordering is only done through e-mail.

Carpel Video
http://www.peakcom.com/carpel/
If you're only interested in purchasing blank and recycled video tapes, then you've hit the jackpot with this site.

Cinemafan's Movie Warehouse
http://www.moviewarehouse.com
Distributes over 30,000 movie titles, including DVD, laserdisc, VHS and DVD player machines.

CINEVISTA Video
http://www.gayweb.com/112/112home.html
Deals mainly in the distribution of independent gay films and videos.

Family Home Video
http://www.iea.com/~fhv/
On-line ordering service for over 25,000 titles that are also linked to the Internet Movie Database.

Flicks on Disc
http://www.teleport.com/~gilbert/flicks/public_html/index.html
Exclusive to the laser disc market with an expansive list of titles and news of upcoming releases.

HBO Home Video Online
http://hbohomevideo.com/
Along with information of their productions released on video, this site includes sounds, video clips, and celebrity photos.

Ken Crane's Laser Disc Super Store
http://www.kencranes.com/laserdiscs/
Largest retailer of laser discs that can be ordered either through the mail or on-line.

Moovies Online
http://www.bnt.com/moovies/index.html
National video chain based in South Carolina that doesn't merely advertise its products but provides an entertaining and informative tidbits on movies.

The Movie Show Video
http://www.movieshow.com/
Three-store chain in Dallas advertises its entire stock and gives links to other sites.

Movies Unlimited
http://www.moviesunlimited.com
The world's largest video retailer breaks down its huge selection into some interesting sections, such as Fast Forward, which includes information on upcoming releases; Let's Go to the Lobby, has the latest news from Hollywood; and the Studio Tour, which links you to other related sites.

On Reel.com
http://www.reel.com
Video distributor based out of Berkely, California that categorizes films under uncanny subcategories. Hmmm, that sounds familiar. Holds over 85,000 titles.

Picture Palace
http://www.ids.net/picpal/index.html
Enormous on-line catalog that has a comprehensive and searchable database for its 36,000+ titles. Also has special features including a magazine rack and a place for international cinema.

Rocket Video
http://www.rocketvideo.com/
"A virtual video store" that carries over 12,000 VHS titles and 500 laser discs. Has features which include "staff picks" and "coming soon".

World Artists Home Video
http://www.worldartists.com/world
Get up-to-date information on upcoming releases from this underground outlet.